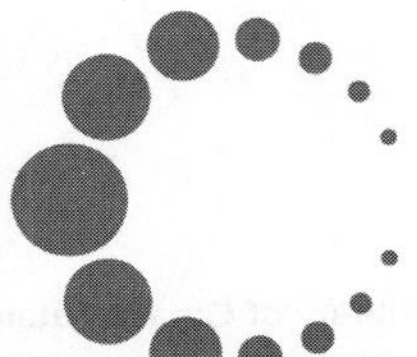

Collins Gage *Canadian Intermediate* Dictionary

Australia Canada Mexico Singapore Spain United Kingdom United States

Previous edition published under the title Gage Canadian Intermediate Dictionary, copyright © 1998

Printed and bound in Canada
1 2 3 4 09 08 07 06 05

0-17-628492-3 school distribution by
Nelson, a division of Thomson Canada Limited
1120 Birchmount Road, Toronto, Ontario, M1K 5G4
www.nelson.com

0-17-629402-3 trade distribution by
HarperCollins Canada
2 Bloor Street East,
Toronto, ON M4W 1A8
www.harpercollins.ca

Collins Gage Canadian reference resources combine the strengths of the Collins and Gage reference lines. They contain the most accurate and up-to-date information, prepared in consultation with Canadian educators for Canadian students.

Collins is one of the world's leading reference publishers. The **Collins Word Web** contains 125 million words of Canadian English and grows at over 1.5 million words per month.

Gage represents a 40-year tradition of Canadian dictionary making. Today, Gage is the reference division of **Thomson Nelson**, Canada's foremost educational publisher.

Page Design: Artplus Ltd.

Database and Imaging: Total Graphics

National Library of Canada Cataloguing in Publication Data

Collins Gage Canadian intermediate dictionary
Previous ed. published under title: Gage Canadian Intermediate Dictionary
ISBN 0-7715-2006-9

English language—Canada—Dictionaries. 2. English language—Dictionaries.
3. Canadianisms (English)—Dictionaries.
I. Title. II. Title: Gage Canadian intermediate dictionary.

PE3237.D68 2005 423 C2005-902133-0

Contents

Collins Gage Canadian Intermediate Dictionary

Reviewers and Consultants (previous editions)

Robert M. Bilan, Head of English,
Oak Park H.S., Winnipeg, Manitoba

Dr. Calvin Brown
Department of Business Computing
University of Winnipeg, Manitoba

Michael Budd
Languages Program Consultant
Essex County Board of Education, Ontario

Johan Cassano, Consultant
York Region District School Board, Ontario

Carol E. Chandler,
Former Curriculum Supervisor
Halifax District School Board, Nova Scotia

Jane Crosbie, Former Consultant
Durham Board of Education, Ontario

Richard Davies, English Teacher
Edmonton Public School Board, Alberta

Dr. Leland Donald
Department of Anthropology
University of Victoria, British Columbia

Professor Libby Garshowitz
Department of Near Eastern Studies
University of Toronto, Ontario

Wanda Gibbons, Language Arts Teacher
Magrath Junior/Senior High School
Magrath, Alberta

Stephen Hurley
Language Arts Teacher
Cardinal Newman Catholic School
Dufferin-Peel CDSB, Ontario

Thayyib Ibrahim
Islamic Society of North America

Pauline Johansen, Vice Principal
Richmond School District # 38, British Columbia

Glen Kirkland, Consultant
Edmonton Catholic School Board, Alberta

Nathalie Lachance
Métis National Council

Frank McCormick, Resource Teacher
Vancouver School District #39, British Columbia

Sister Dorothy Moore, Acting Director
Mi'kmaq Services Division
Nova Scotia Department of Education and Culture

Looee Okalik
Inuit Tapirisat of Canada

Dr. David Pentland
Department of Anthropology
University of Manitoba

Mary Ellen Perley-Waugh, Language Arts Teacher
Laurier Heights School, Edmonton, Alberta

Wendy Phillips, Head of English
Palmer Secondary School,
Richmond, British Columbia

Dom Saliani, Curriculum Leader
Calgary Board of Education, Alberta

Ed Swain
Métis National Council

Linda Szeto, Policy Writer
Nova Scotia Department of Education and Culture

Dixon Taylor, Co-ordinator
Field Services and Aboriginal Education Team
B.C. Ministry of Education, Skills and Training

I.A. Thompson
Department of National Defence
North York, Ontario

Dr. Margaret Thompson
Department of Genetics
Hospital for Sick Children, Toronto, Ontario

Dr. Joan Townsend
Department of Anthropology
University of Manitoba

Original *Intermediate Dictionary* Authors

W.S. Avis, R.J. Gregg, M.W. Scargill, R. Courtney

Additional Reviewers and Consultants (present edition)

Sandra Clarke
Professor of Linguistics
Memorial University of Newfoundland

Barbara P. Harris
Department of Linguistics, University of Victoria
British Columbia

Stacey Austinson, First Nations Education Consultant
New Westminster, British Columbia

Denise L. Clark, English Teacher
Vancouver Technical Secondary, British Columbia

Aron Hoff, History/Geography Teacher
Toronto District School Board, Ontario

Peter Irniq
Commissioner of Nunavut

Toni Kovach, Later Literacy Years Consultant
Hamilton Wentworth Catholic DSB, Ontario

Joanna Quassa, Coordinator
Department of Culture, Language, Elders, and Youth
Iqaluit, Nunavut

Robert Riel, Vice Principal
Niji Mahkwa School, Manitoba

Jacqueline Semchuk, Consultant
Saskatoon Public School Division, Saskatchewan

Gina Tousignant, Department Head of English
Dufferin Peel Roman Catholic DSB, Ontario

Harry Wagner, Director, Curriculum Support
Parkland School Division No. 70, Alberta

Subject Area Consultants

Elizabeth Matlock
Mathematics Literacy Consultant
Waterloo Catholic District School Board, Ontario

Pat Redhead
Supervisor (retired), Social Studies
Edmonton Public Schools, Alberta

Tim Hendrie
Teacher, Language Arts
School District # 79, British Columbia

Maurice DiGiuseppe
Teacher, Science
Toronto Catholic District School Board, Ontario

Byron Stevenson
Information Technology Leader
Toronto District School Board, Ontario

Editorial and Production

Director of Publishing
Beverley Buxton

General Manager, Literacy, Reference, and International
Kevin Martindale

Director of Publishing, Literacy and Reference
Joe Banel

Publisher, Reference
David Friend

Senior Program Manager, Reference
Ann Downar

Executive Managing Editor, Development
Darleen Rotozinski

Executive Managing Editor, Production
Nicola Balfour

Lexicographers
Fraser Sutherland
Debbie Sawczak

Consulting Editor
T.K. Pratt
Professor Emeritus of English,
University of Prince Edward Island

Contributing Editors
Nancy Christoffer
Chelsea Donaldson
Patrick Gallagher
Geraldine Kikuta
Anthony Luengo
Lisa Peterson
Tom Shields

Copy Editor/Proofreader
Sandy Manley

Dictionary Skills Activities
Ron Benson

Production Coordinator
Kathrine Pummell

Creative Director
Angela Cluer

Cover Design
Peter Papayanakis

Printer
Transcontinental Printing Inc.

Canadian English: What's It All Abowt?

T.K. Pratt *Professor Emeritus of English, University of Prince Edward Island*

Courtesy Peter Plant

This cartoon reveals two key things about Canadian English. First, it has its very own accent. Second, Canadian English is similar to—but not identical with—American English. When Canadians say the word *about*, Americans hear something like *aboot* or (as in the cartoon) *abowt.* But when Americans say this word, Canadians hear something like *abaat.* This difference in accents is subtle, but real enough that people on both sides of the border can joke about it.

If you look at the cartoon again, you'll see another difference between Canadians and Americans: we use *kilometres*, Americans don't. This raises another point about Canadian English; we have many words of our own. Some come from French, like *portage* and *tuque*, while others, like *caribou*, *parka*, and *Canada* itself, are from Native languages. Still other words are part of the dialects of our different regions: *outport* (Newfoundland); *shadfly* (Maritimes), *poutine* (Quebec), *hydro* (Ontario), *correction line* (Prairies), *skookum* (British Columbia), and *chimo* (north). In this dictionary you'll find all of these Canadian words and more.

You'll also find help with Canadian English spelling. Depending on what part of the country you live in, you may have been taught *colour* or *color*, *centre* or *center*. The first spelling in each case is the British, while the second is American. Canadians use both. We prefer the British way of spelling *axe*, *catalogue*, *cheque*, *defence*, and *plough*, yet we would never use the British spelling of *gaol* for *jail*, or *kerb* for *curb*.

This blending of British and American English is a natural result of history. Many of the first English speakers in Canada were Americans who fled the Revolution of 1776–83 because they wanted to remain loyal to the British Empire. A second, larger wave of Americans came after the Revolution, looking for land. These two waves laid down the base of Canadian English, in spelling, accent, and words. Then new waves of settlers from the British Isles washed over this base, establishing our national dialect as a unique mix of features.

With immigrants now arriving from all over the world, Canadian English is still changing. So we have *pizza*, *dim sum*, and *samosas* to put beside Canadian-made *butter tarts*, *matrimonial cakes*, and *Nanaimo bars*. Whatever the menu, Canadian English exists and flourishes. And we'll always have the famous Canadian weather—*Alberta clippers*, *black ice*, *chinooks*, *freeze-up*—to talk on and on *abowt!*

English: It's Always, Like, Changing

Sali Tagliamonte *Associate Professor, Department of Linguistics, University of Toronto*

Imagine you overhear one person say, "That's like so random!" and another person say, "That's very unsystematic!" Which person is almost certainly younger and which older? Which one is using "proper" English and which one is using slang? Probably you feel you could guess the right answer to both of those questions. But there's another question that's more interesting: why do the young person and the older person sound so different in the first place?

Let's consider three basic facts about language:
1. Language is always changing.
2. No one can stop language change—not teachers, not parents, not the prime minister.
3. Age has a huge impact on how a person uses language.

In our culture, young people usually try to set themselves apart from the older generation—through clothing and appearance, preferences in music, and particularly through language. That's because language is a very important symbol of social solidarity. As teens come into contact with a wider circle of friends, they are exposed to a range of new language uses. When these new uses spread among more and more teens, new expressions enter English, and sometimes they even influence English grammar. In other words, it's often young people who are the driving force behind language change. Girls are far more likely to use new features of language than boys are, which means that girls are the primary transmitters of new usages.

One of the most interesting changes occurring in English right now is the evolution of the word *like.* As you know, a single word can have many different meanings and functions. *Like* is no exception. Some uses of *like* are considered completely normal, such as "I *like* pizza," "There's nothing *like* pizza," or "I feel *like* pizza." But young people are using *like* in other ways that are sweeping through the language. Here are a few examples:
a) "My mom's *like*, 'Here's your pizza,' and I'm *like*, 'Thanks!'"
b) "Pizza is *like* awesome."
c) "Pizza is *like* my favorite."

The first kind of *like* is used instead of *said* to introduce words that someone else spoke. Young Canadians (especially girls) choose *like* over *said* and other similar words nearly two-thirds of the time. People over 40 hardly ever do. We linguists wonder what will happen as teens get older. Will they keep using *like* this way? Will the boys catch up to the girls? Will the older generation start using this *like* too?

In data I've recently collected, I've found that Canadians between 9 and 19 use *like* a lot. About 4 percent of a young person's average conversation consists of the word *like.* Although that might not sound dramatic, it means that *like* shows up more often than any other word, even *the*, *a*, and *um*! Older people use *like* far less often—about .05 percent of the time. People think that teens use *like* whenever they don't know what to say next, and they're sure this trend is new and bad. Even 60 years ago grammarians were complaining that people were using *like* too much, so it's not exactly a new trend. More importantly, young people are also pushing the boundaries of where *like* can be used, e.g., not just before a noun or adjective, but also before a verb, as in "I just *like* ate the whole pizza," and "I'm *like* eating it all up." These uses follow a definite pattern and suggest that *like* is beginning to take on new roles in the grammar. Which roles will stay and which disappear? We still don't know for sure. Just remember that today's slang often becomes tomorrow's "proper" English. *Keep your ears like open!*

About This Dictionary

The *Collins Gage Canadian Intermediate Dictionary* has a proud history. It was first published over 40 years ago and was called *Dictionary of Canadian English: The Intermediate Dictionary*. It was the first large dictionary that accurately and thoroughly reflected the way Canadians spoke and wrote English. Since 1964, the *Canadian Intermediate* has been continually updated with new words, examples, illustrations, and other features to make sure that students have the best and most useful information at their fingertips.

Like all good dictionaries, the *Canadian Intermediate* gives you a lot of information about how words are spelled, what they mean, and how they are pronounced. You might be surprised, however, to discover how much else you can find out in these pages, and what features are there to help you. You can learn about this dictionary by reading what's below and by looking closely at the "Parts of a Dictionary Entry" page located on the inside front and inside back covers. If you want some more information and some practice, on pages 18–31 there are several activities that will help you get the most out of this dictionary.

Entry Words, Guide Words, and Canadianisms

dejected 338 **deliverance**

de·ject·ed (di jek′tid) *adj* discouraged and sad. <Latin *deicere* to cast down, from *de-* down + *-iecere* to throw> **de·ject′ed·ly** *adv.* **de·jec′tion** *n.*

🍁 **deke** (dēk) *Informal n* especially in hockey, a movement, such as a fake shot, intended to draw a defending player out of position.
v **deked, dek·ing 1** make such a movement. **2** (*often with* ***out***) draw a defending player out of position in this way. <*decoy*>

operation, a delicate situation. **6** showing tact and good taste: *How can I put this in a more delicate way?* <Latin *delicatus* pampered> **del′i·cate·ly** *adv.*

del·i·ca·tes·sen (del′ə kə tes′ən) *n* **1** a store that sells prepared foods, such as cooked meats, smoked fish, cheese, and salads. **2** such foods. <German *Delikatesse* fine food, from French *délicatesse* delicate>

de·li·cious (di lish′əs) *adj* very pleasing or delightful, especially to taste or smell: *delicious apples, a delicious excitement.* <Old French, from Latin *deliciae* delight, pleasure> **de·li′cious·ly** *adv.* **de·li′cious·ness** *n.*

del·i·cate (del′ə kit) *adj* **1** light, fine, or subtle: *a delicate fragrance.* **2** finely fashioned or textured: *delicate woodcarving, delicate silk.* **3** easily broken, hurt, or made ill: *delicate china. He has a delicate constitution and is often sick.* **4** responding to very slight changes: *delicate instruments.* **5** requiring skill or tact: *a delicate heart*

a speech, to [illegible] *a good day* [illegible] *delivered a swift kick to his knee.* **4** set free or rescue: *She was delivered from a life of homelessness.* **5** hand over or give up: *to deliver a fort to the enemy.* <Old French, from Latin *de-* away + *liberare* to free> **de·liv′er·er** *n.*

de·liv·er·ance (di liv′ə rəns) *n* the act of setting free.

Entry words are the main words in the dictionary. They are printed in bold at the beginning of each entry.

Two **guide words** appear at the top of each entry-word page. The word on the left of the page number indicates the first entry word on the page (*dejected*). The word on the right indicates the last entry word (*deliverance*). All the entry words between the two guide words are listed in alphabetical order.

Canadianisms are words that originate in Canada, are used here in a unique way, or are used here more often than in other English-speaking countries. They are marked with a maple leaf icon, as in the word *deke* on the previous page.

Syllables

When an entry word consists of more than one syllable, the syllables are separated by dots.

> **min·i·ser·ies** (min′i sē′rēz) *n* a TV program, especially a drama, in a series of episodes, but not lasting an entire season.

See page 25 for an activity on how to identify syllables and use them to help you spell and add variety to your writing.

Pronunciations

After most entry words, you'll find the **pronunciation** of the word in brackets.

> **nav·i·ga·tor** (nav′ə gā′tər) *n* **1** a person who is qualified to navigate: *The captain took on a special navigator to guide the ship through the dangerous waters. He served as a navigator in the air force.* **2** a person who sails the seas as an explorer: *a story of one of the early navigators.*

The pronunciation has special letters that tell you how to say the word. There are two ways to find out how to interpret the special letters. At the bottom of each right-hand page you'll find a pronunciation key that shows you how to say many of these letters. For example, it tells you that if you see the letter ā, you pronounce it like a in *cake.* You'll find a much more detailed chart of English sounds on pages 16–17.

The pronunciation also contains **stress marks** that tell you which syllables to emphasize. The word *navigator* has two stress marks: a primary stress after the first syllable nav′ and a secondary stress after the third syllable gā′. The primary stress tells you to emphasize that syllable more than the other three; the secondary stress tells you to emphasize that syllable almost as much. If you say *navigator* out loud, you'll hear those stresses.

See page 26 for an activity on how to pronounce a word.

Variants

Variants are slightly different spellings of a word—*colour* and *color,* for example. For these words, you'll find the full entry at the spelling that is preferred by most Canadians. The entry will also show you the variant spelling(s).

col·our or **col·or** (kul′ər) *n* **1** the effect of light waves of different lengths striking the retina of the eye: *Some people are not able to tell the difference between the colour red and the colour green.*

If the variant spelling isn't very common in Canada, you'll find it near the end of the entry.

me·tre[2] (mē′tər) *n* the SI unit for measuring length, equal to 100 centimetres. *Symbol* **m** Also, **meter**. <French, from Greek *metron* measure>

If you look up the less common variant (e.g., *center*), you will find a cross-reference to the main entry, where you will find lots of information about the word.

cen·ter (sen′tər) CENTRE.

There are variants for different pronunciations, too.

as·phalt (as′folt) *or* (ash′folt) BITUMEN.

Parts of Speech

The **part of speech** of an entry word appears as an abbreviation right after its pronunciation. In the following example, *adj* tells you that *delicious* is an adjective.

de·li·cious (di lish′əs) *adj* very pleasing or delightful, especially to taste or smell: *delicious apples, a delicious excitement.* <Old French, from Latin *deliciae* delight, pleasure> **de·li′cious·ly** *adv.* **de·li′cious·ness** *n.*

Other parts of speech and their abbreviations are *n* (noun), *v* (verb), *adv* (adverb), *pron* (pronoun), *prep* (preposition), *conj* (conjunction), and *interj* (interjection).

When the word can function as more than one part of speech, the different abbreviations appear at the beginning of the definition or definitions for each part of speech.

dis·re·gard (dis′ri gärd′) *v* pay no attention to: *Disregard that last e-mail I sent you.*
n **1** lack of attention: *His disregard for the critics gave him more freedom in writing.* **2** lack of proper respect: *You can't treat people's property with such blatant disregard.*

See page 27 for an activity on how to identify parts of speech.

Meanings and Example Sentences

Some words have one meaning only.

min·now (min′ō) *n* a very small freshwater fish, often used as live bait. <Old English *myne*>

Other words have more than one meaning. If a word has multiple meanings, the dictionary provides a different number and definition for each one, with the most common meaning given first. Notice also how the entry for *happy* (see below) provides examples in italics to reinforce the different meanings. Most entry words include example phrases and sentences to help you pin down the meanings.

hap·py (hap′ē) *adj* **hap·pi·er, hap·pi·est** **1** feeling or showing pleasure and joy: *a happy smile.* **2** fortunate: *By a happy chance, I found the lost money.* **3** clever and fitting: *a happy choice of words.* <Middle English, from *hap* luck> **hap′pi·ly** *adv.* **hap′pi·ness** *n.*

Notice how the numbering begins again for each part of speech:

nib·ble (nib′əl) *v* **nib·bled, nib·bling** **1** eat away with quick, small bites, as a rabbit or a mouse does. **2** bite gently or lightly: *A fish nibbled at the bait.*
n **1** an act of nibbling: *We've been fishing all morning and haven't had a nibble.* **2** a small piece, especially of food: *I just want a nibble of the cake.* <probably German or Dutch> **nib′bler** *n.*
nibble at, *Informal* be interested in: *I'm nibbling at the idea of learning to dance.*

If a special form of an entry word has its own meaning, then the special form is printed in bold and its meaning follows.

mar·i·time (mar′ə tīm′) *or* (mer′ə tīm′) *adj* **1** on or near the sea: *a maritime city.* **2** living near the sea: *maritime peoples.* **3** to do with shipping and sailing: *maritime law.* **4** **Maritime** to do with the Maritime Provinces. <Latin *mare* sea>

See page 22 for an activity on how to find the meaning of a word.

Homographs

Homographs are words that have the same spelling but different meanings. English has lots of homographs; *bear* meaning "carry" and *bear* meaning "a large heavily-built mammal" are two. Homographs are listed as separate entry words. Each homograph has a superscript number beside it; *bear*[1], *bear*[2]. The following example shows four homographs in a row:

till[1] (til) *conj, prep* until. <Old English *til*>

till[2] (til) *v* prepare and cultivate land for crops. <Old English *tilian*> **till′a·ble** *adj.*

till[3] (til) *n* a cash register or drawer for money in a store, bank, bar, or restaurant: *The till is under the counter.* <Old English *-tyllan*>

till[4] (til) *n* boulder clay or other sediment deposited by melting glaciers or ice sheets. Compare OUTWASH. <origin uncertain>

Inflected Forms and Derivatives

The different forms of a noun, pronoun, verb, adjective, or adverb are called its **inflected forms**. Most inflected forms follow a standard pattern; for example, to form the plural of dog, you add –*s* to the end to make *dogs*. Inflected forms that are unusual in some way appear right after the abbreviation for part of speech. Here are some examples:

fly[1] (flī) *n, pl* **flies** **1** a housefly. **2** an insect that has two wings. Mosquitoes are flies. **3** a flying insect, such as a butterfly.

sing (sing) *v* **sang, sung, sing·ing** **1** make musical sounds with the voice, especially words with a set melody: *She sings background on this CD.*

much (much) *adj* **more, most** in a great quantity, amount, or degree: *much money, much time.*

well[1] (wel) *adv* **bet·ter, best** **1** in a good, appropriate, profitable, or satisfactory way: *The job was well done. Is everything going well at school?*

A **derivative** is a word formed by adding a prefix or, more often, a suffix to another word. Some of the most common suffixes are *–able, –er, –ful, –ish, –less, –like, –ly, –ment, –ness.* At the end of an entry, you will find a list of any important derivatives.

tire·less (tīr′lis) *adj* with or showing great effort or energy: *a tireless worker.* **tire′less·ly** *adv.* **tire′less·ness** *n.*

See page 23 for an activity on how to use root words to find other words.

Idioms

An **idiom** is a phrase or expression whose meaning cannot be understood from the meanings of its individual words. The expression *as the crow flies* is an example of an idiom. To find the definition of *as the crow flies*, you have to look up the word *crow*, which is the main word in the idiom. Any idioms with the word *crow* in them are shown at the end of the entry.

crow[2] (krō) *n* a large, glossy black bird that makes a harsh cry or caw. <Old English *crawe*>
as the crow flies, in a straight line: *The town is about 10 km away as the crow flies, but about 15 km by road.*
eat crow, *Informal* be forced to admit that you have been wrong.

See page 29 for an activity on how to find the meaning of an idiomatic expression.

Restrictive Labels

Notice that the idiom *eat crow* has the word *Informal* beside it. This is called a **restrictive label** and tells you something special about a word, a meaning of a word, or an idiom. The dictionary uses three kinds of restrictive labels: usage, regional, and subject.

A **usage label** gives you information about when you should use or avoid using a word. For example, the *Informal* label tells you it's best to use the word only when you're writing or speaking in informal situations (like when you're talking with friends). Other usage labels include *Slang, Formal, Poetic, Trademark*, etc.

Regional labels identify words that are used almost exclusively in a certain geographical area, which might be a particular country or an area within Canada.

round·a·bout (round′ə bout′) *adj* indirect: *a roundabout route. I heard about it in a roundabout way.*
n UK a merry-go-round.

🍁 **bar·a·chois** (ba′ rə shwo′) *Atlantic Provinces n* a shallow coastal pond created behind a sandbar that has formed near a beach. <Cdn French>

Subject labels tell you that a word has a technical or special meaning associated with a specific area of study. *Medicine, Grammar,* and *Economics* are all examples of subject labels.

double bar *Music n* a vertical double line on a staff, marking the end of a movement or of an entire piece of music.

Cross-References

A **cross-reference** is like a signpost that directs you to another entry with information related to the one you are reading. Cross-references always appear in SMALL CAPITAL LETTERS.

an·aes·the·sia (an′əs thē′zhə) ANESTHESIA.

my·o·pi·a (mī ō′pē ə) *n* near-sightedness. Compare HYPEROPIA. See VISION for picture. <Latin, from Greek *myein* shut + *ops* eye> **my·op′ic** (mī op′ik) *adj.*

Etymologies

An **etymology** explains the history of a word. It shows earlier forms of the word, including some of the languages through which it developed.

dime (dīm) *n* a ten-cent coin of Canada or the US. <Old French, from Latin *decem* ten>

Some entries include an etymology feature box, which contains detailed background information on a word.

hock·ey (hok′ē) *n* **1** a game played on ice by two teams of six players on skates and carrying hooked sticks with which they try to shoot a black rubber disc, the puck, into the opposing team's goal. **2** a version of this game played on a different surface, such as field hockey, floor hockey, or road hockey.

ETYMOLOGY

Hockey is thought to come from Old French *hoquet,* meaning "shepherd's crook," since hockey sticks resembled shepherds' crooks.

See page 30 for an activity on how to learn about where words come from.

Feature Boxes

Scattered throughout the dictionary you'll find many **feature boxes** that provide interesting facts about words. There are four kinds: etymology (such as the one about hockey above), grammar and usage, confusables, and synonyms.

af·fect[2] (ə fekt′) *v* **1** pretend to have or feel: *to affect an Irish accent. He affected ignorance, but in fact he knew all about it.* **2** assume or put on for effect: *She affects a certain carelessness in dress.* <French, from Latin *affectare* pretend to have>

CONFUSABLES

Affect means "influence": *Rain will affect our plans.*

Effect means "result": *That's not the effect I wanted.*

Notice that **affect** is a verb, and **effect** is usually a noun.

Visuals

Many of the entry words in the dictionary include **visuals** to illustrate what the definitions say, as well as to add information that's useful and interesting. Some visuals require only an image with labels to provide information.

Other visuals include captions with details that go beyond the definition.

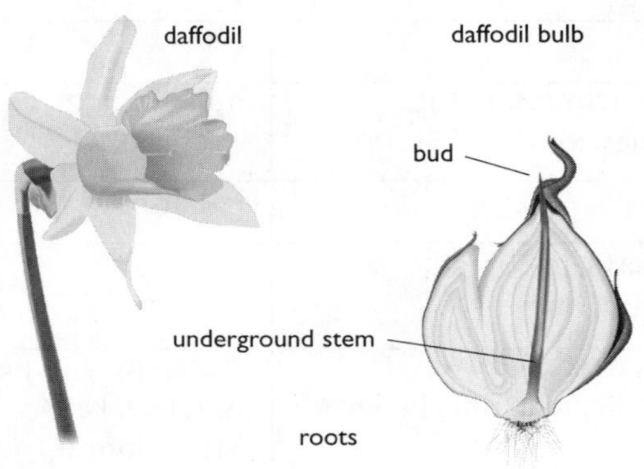

In spite of its ferocious name, the **dragonfly** cannot bite or sting. In fact, it spends a great part of its life not even flying. The eggs are usually laid on water, and the larvae stay in water for as long as several years. Eventually, this insect leaves the water as the adult dragonfly.

daf·fo·dil (daf′ə dil′) *n* a plant that grows from a bulb and has a flower with a trumpet-shaped corona growing out from the centre of its petals. <Latin, from Greek *asphodelos*>

drag·on·fly (drag′ən flī′) *n, pl* **drag·on·flies** a large insect with a long, slender body and two pairs of very thin wings. Dragonflies eat flies, mosquitoes, and other insects.

See page 31 for an activity on how to get information from dictionary visuals.

Sound	Beginnings of words	Middles of words	Ends of words
a	**a**nd, **au**nt	h**a**t, pl**ai**d, h**a**lf, l**au**gh	—
ā	**a**ge, **ai**d, **eigh**t	f**a**ce, f**ai**l, str**aigh**t, p**ay**ment, g**au**ge, br**ea**k, v**ei**n, n**eigh**bour	s**ay**, w**eigh**, bouqu**et**, th**ey**, caf**é**, matin**ée**
à	**ar**t	b**ar**n, baz**aar**, h**ear**t	hurr**ah**
b	**b**ad	ta**b**le, ra**bb**it	ru**b**, e**bb**
ch	**ch**ild	cappu**cc**ino, ri**ch**ness, na**t**ure, wa**tch**ing, ques**ti**on	mu**ch**, ca**tch**
d	**d**o	la**d**y, la**dd**er	re**d**, us**ed**
e	**a**ny, **ae**rial, **ai**r, **e**nd	m**a**ny, s**ai**d, s**ay**s, l**e**t, br**ea**d, l**eo**pard, fr**ie**nd, b**u**ry	—
ē	**e**qual, **ea**t, **ei**ther	m**e**tre, t**ea**m, n**ee**d, rec**ei**ve, p**eo**ple, k**ey**hole, mach**i**ne, bel**ie**ve	alg**ae**, qu**ay**, acn**e**, fl**ea**, b**ee**, k**ey**, Mét**is**, loon**ie**, pit**y**
f	**f**at, **ph**one	a**f**ter, co**ff**ee, o**f**ten, lau**gh**ter, go**ph**er	roo**f**, sni**ff**, cou**gh**, hal**f**, epita**ph**
g	**g**o, **gh**ost, **gu**ess	a**g**o, gi**gg**le, catalo**gu**es	ba**g**, e**gg**, ro**gue**
h	**h**elp, **wh**o	a**h**ead	—
i	**e**namel, **i**n	mess**a**ge, b**ee**n, p**i**n, s**ie**ve, w**o**men, b**u**sy, b**ui**ld, h**y**mn	—
ī	**ai**sle, **aye**, **ei**ther, **eye**, **i**ce, **is**land	h**eigh**t, l**i**ne, al**ig**n, m**igh**t, b**uy**ing, t**y**pe	**aye**, **eye**, l**ie**, h**igh**, b**uy**, sk**y**, d**ye**
j	**g**em, **j**am	e**d**ucate, ba**dg**er, sol**di**er, a**dj**ust, tra**g**ic, exa**gg**erate, en**j**oy	bri**dge**, ra**ge**, ha**jj**
k	**c**oat, **ch**emistry, **k**ind, **q**uick, **qu**ay	re**c**ord, a**cc**ount, e**ch**o, lu**ck**y, a**cq**uire, loo**k**ing, li**qu**or, e**x**tra	ba**ck**, see**k**, wal**k**, tu**que**
l	**l**and, **ll**ama	on**l**y, fo**ll**ow	coa**l**, fi**ll**
m	**m**e	co**m**ing, cli**mb**ing, su**mm**er	cal**m**, hu**m**, co**mb**, sole**mn**
n	**gn**aw, **kn**ife, **n**ut	mi**n**er, ma**nn**er	si**gn**, ma**n**, i**nn**
ng	—	i**n**k, fi**n**ger, si**ng**er	ba**ng**, to**ngue**
o	**a**ll, **al**mond, **au**thor, **aw**ful, **en**core, **ho**nest, **o**dd, **ough**t	w**a**tch, p**al**m, t**au**t, t**augh**t, s**aw**ed, h**o**t, b**ough**t	Ottaw**a**, p**aw**

Sound	Beginnings of words	Middles of words	Ends of words
ō	**o**pen, **oa**th, **ow**n	Ge**o**rge, s**ew**n, h**o**me, b**oa**t, f**ol**k, br**oo**ch, s**ou**l, fl**ow**n	chat**eau**, s**ew**, potat**o**, t**oe**, th**ough**, bl**ow**
ȯ	**o**rder, **oa**r	b**o**rn, b**oa**rd, fl**oo**r, m**ou**rn	—
oi	**oi**l, **oy**ster	b**oi**l, b**oy**hood	b**oy**
ou	**hou**r, **ou**t, **ow**l	b**ou**nd, dr**ough**t, h**ow**l	pl**ough**, n**ow**
p	**p**en	pa**p**er, su**pp**er	u**p**
r	**r**un, **rh**ythm	pa**r**ent, hu**rr**y	bea**r**, bu**rr**
s	**c**ent, **ps**ychology, **s**ay, **sc**ience, **sw**ord	de**c**ent, loo**s**en, mu**sc**le, ma**ss**ive, an**sw**er, e**x**tra	ni**ce**, marvello**us**, mi**ss**, la**x**
sh	**ch**auffeur, **s**ure, **sh**irt	o**c**ean, ma**ch**ine, spe**ci**al, un**s**ure, con**sc**ience, nau**se**ous, ten**si**on, i**ss**ue, mi**ss**ion, na**ti**on	ca**che**, wi**sh**
t	**pt**armigan, **t**ell, **Th**omas	dou**bt**ful, la**t**er, la**tt**er	dou**bt**, crash**ed**, bi**t**, mi**tt**
th	**th**in	too**th**ache	ba**th**
ᴛʜ	**th**en	mo**th**er	smoo**th**, ba**the**
u	**o**ven, **u**p	c**o**me, d**oe**s, fl**oo**d, tr**ou**ble, c**u**p	—
ü	**oo**ze	n**eu**tral, m**o**ve, f**oo**d, gr**ou**p, r**u**le, fr**ui**t	thr**ew**, sh**oe**, carib**ou**, thr**ough**, bl**ue**
u̇	—	w**o**lf, g**oo**d, sh**ou**ld, f**u**ll	—
yü	**Eu**rope, **u**se, **you**, **Yu**kon	b**eau**ty, f**eu**d, d**u**ty	qu**eue**, f**ew**, c**ue**, **you**
v	**v**ery	o**v**er	o**f**, lo**ve**
w	**w**ill, **wh**eat, **o**ne	ch**oi**r, q**u**ick, t**w**in	—
y	**y**oung	opin**i**on, can**y**on	—
z	**x**ylophone	rai**s**in, sci**ss**ors, e**x**act, la**z**y, da**zz**le	ha**s**, ma**ze**, bu**zz**
zh	—	mea**s**ure, divi**si**on	mira**ge**
ə	**a**lone, **e**ssential, **o**blige, **u**pon	spaghetti, fount**ai**n, mom**e**nt, penc**i**l, bott**le**, criticis**m**, butt**o**n, cauti**ou**s, circ**u**s	sof**a**
ər	**ear**ly, **ur**ge	sal**ar**y, t**er**m, l**ear**n, f**ir**st, w**or**d, j**our**ney, t**ur**n, s**yr**up	li**ar**, det**er**, st**ir**, act**or**, f**ur**, b**urr**, meas**ure**

HOW TO Get to Know This Dictionary

Before you start to read a book or magazine, it's always a good idea to flip through the pages to see what it's about. You should do the same thing with this dictionary, or any other reference resource you need to use. You'll find that a dictionary has some of the same features as other books, as well as many other useful features that are its own.

For practice...

As you look for the features listed below in this dictionary, record those you find and those you don't. As well, list up to five additional features you find that are not in the list. Think about the purpose served by each of the features. Make jot notes to help you to remember.

1. Title
2. Author(s)
3. Illustrators and photographers
4. Publisher
5. Publication date
6. ISBN (International Standard Book Number)
7. Table of contents
8. Chapters
9. Exercises
10. Index
11. Glossary
12. Headings
13. Subheadings
14. Captions
15. Visuals (for example, tables, charts, graphs, diagrams, photographs)
16. A variety of print styles and sizes
17. Page numbers
18. Appendix

Try This!

Using a book you're currently reading and the items above, make a list of the features you find and compare it with your dictionary list. Can you explain why some of the features are the same and why some are different?

Use Alphabetical Order to Look Up a Word

When you need to find a word in a dictionary, alphabetical order can help. That's because all the words in a dictionary are arranged in the order of the letters of the alphabet (*a, b, c, d,* etc.). You'll find words starting with the letter *A* near the beginning of the dictionary, those with the letter *Z* near the end, and those with the letter *M* in the middle.

Here's How

Say you want to look up the word *antarctic.* The first letter of the word is *a,* so you would start by flipping to the *A* pages. The second letter is *n,* so next you would skim through *A* looking for words starting with *an.* If you found yourself at the entry word *antagonize,* at the end of page 77, you would not have gone far enough — *g,* the fifth letter in *antagonize,* comes before *r,* the fifth letter in *antarctic.* Flip to the next page to see if *antarctic* is there. (It is, on page 78).

For Practice...

a b c d e f g h i j k l m n o p q r s t u v w x y z

Using the alphabet string above for reference, copy the words below into your notebook in alphabetical order.

ratio	formula	quadrant	square
digit	cylinder	quarter	rectangle
subset	polygon	positive	concave

Try This!

Open to the first page of a book you've recently been reading at school. Make a list of every fifth word in the book to a maximum of 20 words. In a list next to the first one, write the 20 words in alphabetical order.

Over a two-week period, note all the situations in which you see alphabetical order used to organize information. For example, your notes could include telephone directory listings and your teacher's class list for recording information such as test results. At the end of the two weeks, compare your notes with those of others in the class to see how many situations you were able to find.

HOW TO Use the Guide Words

Two guide words appear at the top of each entry-word page in the dictionary. The word on the left indicates the first entry word on the page. The word on the right indicates the last entry word. All the entry words between the two guide words are in alphabetical order.

Here's How

Let's say you're looking for the entry word *alpine.* How can you use guide words to help you find this word?

Start by going to the *A* pages in the dictionary. Flip forward until you reach a page that has an *alp-* word (or another that is very close in spelling) as a guide word. At page 64, *alpaca* is the second guide word. Since *alpa-* comes before *alpi-*, you should then move forward a page. On page 65 you will see *alpha* and *alternate* as the guide words. Since *alpi-* comes between *alph-* and *alte-*, this is the page on which you'll find *alpine.*

For Practice...

The guide words at the top of the dictionary page are *upset* and *upward.* In your notebook, write the words from the following list that you would expect to find on that page.

1. upside	2. urge	3. upsurge	4. uptight
5. upstage	6. upstream	7. used	8. upwind

Check your answers by looking up the dictionary page with *upset* and *upward* as guide words.

Try This!

From a recent piece of your completed writing, choose a one-syllable word, a two-syllable word, and a three-syllable word. List these words in your notebook.

Begin with the one-syllable word. Search for the two guide words that head the page on which you would expect to find the word (but don't look at the entry words on that page). Write these guide words beside the word in your notebook. Now check to see if you selected the correct page. Do the same for the two- and three-syllable words you've listed.

HOW TO Find a Word You Think You Can't Spell

Sometimes when you're writing you want to use a word but you're not sure you can spell it correctly. When you look it up in the dictionary, it's not there, which tells you that you really don't know how to spell it. Don't give up—your dictionary can still help.

Here's How

Start by saying the word aloud and then writing it down the way you think it's spelled. Now look up the word. Sometimes your spelling will be correct. Sometimes it's almost correct and you'll find the word nearby on the same page. If you've written *impordent* because that's the way you pronounce it, you'll probably find the correct spelling (*important*) very quickly.

Sometimes that's not enough. *Inormus* reflects a correct pronunciation but is not a correct spelling. How do you get that word right? Begin by identifying the part or parts of it that might be misspelled—the beginning (*in-*), the middle (*-or-*), or the end (*-mus*). Then turn to the chart on pages 16-17, "Common Spellings of English Sounds."

The chart tells you the short i sound in *in-* can be spelled as either *in-* or *en-*. *Inormus* isn't under *in-*, so look up words beginning with *en-* followed by the *o* sound that you hear in *for*. The chart shows that *o* like *for* in the middle of a word is spelled as *o*, *oa*, *oo*, or *ou*. The word you're looking for might be *enormus*, *enoarmus*, *enoormus*, or *enourmus*. A scan of the page with *eno-* words will quickly tell you that the correct spelling is *enormous*. Now you can also correct the end part (*-mus*) in your original misspelling.

For Practice...

Write each of the misspelled words below in your notebook. Use the dictionary, including the Common Spellings of English Sounds chart (pages 16–17), to help you find the correct spelling of each one. Write the correct spelling beside each misspelling.

1. fosphorus 2. gewulry 3. wairwithall 4. embew 5. sissers

Try This!

Over two weeks, create a list of difficult-to-spell words. At the end of the two weeks, share your list with your classmates and work together to come up with correct spellings. Check these spellings in your dictionary.

HOW TO Find the Meaning of a Word

A dictionary provides meanings for words you don't know or are unsure about.

Here's How

The meaning of an entry word follows immediately after its pronunciation. It is presented as one or more phrases or as single words.

er·rand (er′ənd) *n* a small job that involves a short journey: *He rakes leaves and does other errands for his parents.*

In many cases, a definition is accompanied by an example phrase or sentence that helps to show what the word means: *He rakes leaves and does other errands for his parents.*

If a word has more than one meaning, the dictionary provides a different number for each one, with the most common meaning given first. If you look up the word *tragedy*, for example, you'll see that it has two meanings ("an event causing great suffering" and "a play").

If the dictionary offers more than one meaning of a word, work your way through the numbered definitions until you come to the one that makes sense for what you're reading or want to say. Remember to use the examples to help you choose the right meaning.

For Practice ...

Read each sentence and write down the underlined word in your notebook. Look up the word and read the definitions and any examples. Select the most appropriate meaning and record the number in your notebook.

1. She told me her plan in <u>confidence</u>.
2. He suddenly <u>burst</u> into tears.
3. They heard the <u>fabulous</u> voice of the singer very clearly.
4. It was a <u>bitter</u> February night.
5. They promised to <u>gear</u> the program to our needs.

Try This!

Open the book you're currently reading to any page. Randomly put your finger on a word. Write down the word. Repeat this process until you have a total of ten words. Select the five words that you think will the easiest for you to mime their definitions. Working with a small group of classmates, take turns miming your five words.

HOW TO Use Root Words to Find Other Words

A root word is a word that has no suffixes or prefixes; it stands on its own. F*ree* is the root word of *freedom*, and *safe* of *safely*. If the word you're looking for is not an entry word, knowing its root word can help you track it down.

Here's How

If you look up *safely* in this dictionary, you won't find it as an entry word. What should you do? First, look again at the word and identify its root. The root word of *safely* is *safe* (*safely* with the suffix *–ly* removed). When you look up *safe*, you'll find *safely* in bold face at the end of the definitions for the entry word, identified as an adverb.

n a strong, fireproof box or place that can be locked, used for keeping valuable things safe. <Old French, from Latin *salvus*> **safe′ly** *adv.* **safe′ness** *n.*

If you were tempted to spell it with an extra *e* in the suffix (*safeley*), as it is often misspelled, you will now be able to use the correct spelling instead.

For Practice...

Put each of the following root words in a circle in your notebook. Create as many words as you can by adding prefixes, suffixes, or both. Here's an example.

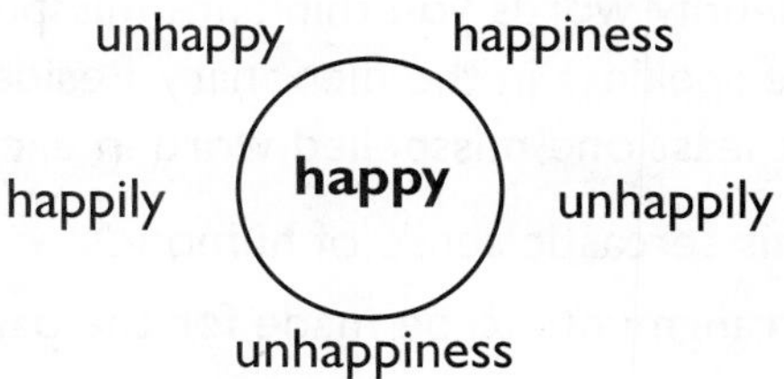

1. correct 2. sad 3. electric 4. manage 5. apply

Look up each root word to see if there are other words to add to your list.

Try This!

Using magazines and newspapers, cut out a variety of root words, prefixes, and suffixes from the various titles, headlines, and advertisements. Create a visually appealing montage that shows different possibilities for combining root words with suffixes and prefixes.

HOW TO Find and Fix Spelling Errors

If your written work will be read by others, use conventional spelling so the reader understands you. A dictionary is one of the best tools you can use to check your spelling.

Here's How

How do you know if you've misspelled a word? If you hesitate a moment before you write a word, there's a good chance you're not sure how to spell it. Another way to spot possible misspellings is to reread your work slowly, watching for words that just seem to look wrong.

When you find a word that you think you may have spelled incorrectly, underline it. Use the first two or three letters of the word to help you locate it in your dictionary.

If you can't find the word, and if you think the spelling difficulty might be in the first few letters, then consider other possible spellings. For example, although you might think the word begins with the letter *f*, perhaps it begins with *ph* (for example, is it *phoenix* or *fenix*?). For more help, see How to Find a Word You Think You Can't Spell on page 21.

Once you've located an entry word, read its definition(s) to confirm you've found what you want. Compare the dictionary spelling with yours and make any necessary corrections.

For Practice...

In the sentences below, identify words you think are misspelled and write them in your notebook. Check the spellings in the dictionary. Beside each word, write the correct spelling. There's at least one misspelled word in each sentence.

1. She finally got tired of his sercastic sense of humour.
2. There were numerus arrangments to be made for the party.
3. Plants use photosinthesus to store the sun's energy.
4. The lawyer exagerated the significence of the other side's arguments.

Try This!

Before you write a final draft, look through your rough draft for words you may have misspelled. Underline them, look them up, and correct them if necessary. Keep an updated list of words you've corrected to use as your own quick spell check.

HOW TO Identify Syllables and Use Them to Help You Spell

Dividing a word into syllables can help you to spell it correctly.

Here's How

A syllable is "a word or part of a word spoken as a unit." The word *see* has one syllable, *software* has two (*soft•ware*), and *syllable* itself has three (*syl•la•ble*). How many syllables can you hear in the word *capability*? How do you figure that out with or without a dictionary?

The word *capability* has five syllables. Where do you think one syllable ends and the next begins? Write the word, separating the syllables with a dot between each one. What you've just done is one way of identifying and recording syllables. You've said the word aloud and then written down its syllables. Try it next time you're trying to spell a hard word.

To make sure you're correct about the syllables in a word (and its spelling), you should also check your dictionary. All the entry words in the dictionary are written in bold and divided into syllables. Here's what *capability* looks like.

ca·pa·bil·i·ty

Is that the same as what you wrote? If not, how and why is yours different?

For Practice...

Say each of the following words aloud, noting the number of syllables you hear. Copy the words into your notebook, using dots to divide them into syllables.

1. begun 2. envy 3. interior 4. providing 5. sprinkle 6. tangerine

Look up each word to see if you were right.

Try This!

Hold a short "syllable chat" with a classmate by dividing your words into syllables as you say them. It•makes•for•a•strange•sound•ing•in•ter•ac•tion•but•gives•you•a•won•der•ful•op•por•tu•ni•ty•to•prac•tise•di•vi•ding•words•in•to•syl•la•bles.

HOW TO Check a Pronunciation

Most people use a dictionary to help them with their reading or writing. This dictionary can also help you with your speaking by telling you how to pronounce a word.

Here's How

The pronunciation of a word is provided in parentheses right after the entry word:

bak·er (bā′kər)

The pronunciation has special letters that tell you how to say the word. At the bottom of each right-hand page you'll find a pronunciation key that shows you how to say many of these letters. For example, it tells you that if you see the letter ā, you pronounce it like *a* in *cake.*

a bat	e bed	i bid	o pot	u cup	th **thin**
ā cake	ē me	ī bite	ō go	ū rude	ᴛʜ **then**
ä bar	ə about	ər over	ô for	ü put	zh measure

The symbol ə, called the schwa, indicates an in-between vowel sound. The schwa sounds like the *a* in *above*, the *e* in *token*, the *i* in *council*, the *o* in *actor*, and the *u* in *treasure.*

For Practice...

Copy the following words into your notebook. Using the abbreviated pronunciation key, mark the vowels in the word to indicate the pronunciation of each of the words. (Ignore any unpronounced vowels at the end of a word such as the e in *costume*.)

1. around 2. costume 3. easy 4. fan 5. inside

6. opening 7. play 8. pull 9. pin 10. ride

When you've finished, check your pronunciation marks by looking up each of the words.

Try This!

Here are some words that cause pronunciation problems for many people. With a partner, take turns saying the first word aloud. Together, talk about the part(s) of the word that, if mispronounced, could lead to a misspelling. Do the same for all the other words and check the pronunciations in the dictionary.

veterinarian Antarctic nuclear February hors d'oeuvre leisure

Add five words to this list that you find tricky to pronounce.

HOW TO Identify Parts of Speech

Words have different functions. Some name a person or thing (*car*), others express an action (*raced*). Yet others help describe (*red*). Altogether, there are eight different functions for words, called the parts of speech. A dictionary tells you what part of speech a word is so you know how to use it.

Here's How

This dictionary identifies the eight parts of speech with the labels in italics shown below:

noun *n*	adjective *adj*	pronoun *pron*	conjunction *conj*
verb *v*	adverb *adv*	preposition *prep*	interjection *interj*

In a word that functions as only one part of speech, the label appears immediately after the pronunciation. When it functions as more than one part of speech, there is a label before each set of definitions. The word *lob* is both a noun and a verb:

lob (lob) *n* **1** a tennis ball hit high to the back of the opponent's court. **2** a slow, underarm throw.

v **lobbed, lob·bing 1** hit a tennis ball high to the back of an opponent's court. **2** throw with a slow, underarm movement. <probably German>

For Practice...

Read the following paragraph.

The new student looked around the classroom. Several of the students huddled around the teacher as she carefully explained the test scores to them. Another group gathered to talk about the co-operative project they were doing, while others read, wrote, talked, and laughed. "Wow!" he thought. "Just as my friends told me." It was a busy and happy classroom. He was glad he had transferred to this school and didn't feel worried anymore.

In your notebook, make a list of the underlined words. Beside each one, write the part of speech you think it is. Check your responses in the dictionary.

Try This!

Open a book, magazine, or newspaper to any page. Beginning at the top of the page, make a list by writing down every tenth word for a total of ten. Beside each word, write down the part of speech you think it is. Look up each of the words in your dictionary to confirm the part of speech. Can any of these ten words function as more than one part of speech? If so, write a sentence in which it functions as a different part of speech.

HOW TO Find Other Ways of Saying Something

Do you ever find that, after rereading something you've written, you want to replace some of the words in your draft? Maybe you've used the same word too often, or maybe you think the words you've chosen won't grab your readers' attention. Perhaps the word just doesn't feel right. A dictionary, with its plentiful stock of words, can help you find a replacement.

Here's How

Imagine that you've included the following sentence in a writing draft: *It was a terrible day.*

When you reread the sentence, you may decide that the word *terrible* won't tell your readers how bad a day it was. As well, you realize that you've used the word once before in an earlier sentence in the draft. What do you do?

Start by looking up the entry word *terrible* and read the four definitions offered there. Do any of them contain a word or words that might work better than *terrible* in your sentence ("extremely bad" perhaps)? Then look at the accompanying synonyms features box, which provides you with possible alternatives (*terrifying, harrowing, disturbing*). From all these options, select the word that you think will best convey how bad that day really was.

For Practice...

Read the sentence below, focusing on the underlined words.

The pirates <u>perceived</u> a city on the horizon with walls that kept it <u>safe</u>.

Look up *perceive* and read all the information provided in the definitions and, if there is one, in the features box. Think about what word(s) you could use to replace *perceived*. Follow the same steps for *safe*, and then rewrite the sentence.

Try This!

Read a recent draft of your writing aloud to yourself or to a partner. Listen for any words you think you might want to replace, underlining each of one. After checking your dictionary, create an "Other Ways to Say It" chart by writing each original sentence (with the underlined word) on chart paper, followed by a revised version. Post the chart and encourage others to provide their own revised versions of the original sentences.

Find the Meaning of an Idiomatic Expression

The following sentence contains an expression called an idiom: *My friend tried to catch my eye*. An idiom is a phrase that has a special meaning. "Catch my eye" doesn't literally mean that someone's eye fell out and a friend tried to catch it. It's just a colourful way of saying "get my attention." If you encounter an odd phrase that you think might be an idiom, you can use this dictionary to check what it means.

Here's How

First, identify the key words in the phrase. In the case of "catch my eye," the key words are *catch* and *eye*. Look up the word *catch*, moving past the definitions to the list of expressions at the end. You'll see such idioms as "catch as catch can" and "catch in the act," but not "catch my eye." But when you look up *eye*, you'll see that "catch your eye," is just one of many idioms that use the word *eye*. There's a definition of each one, and in most cases, an example to show how it's used.

an eye for an eye, punishment or revenge that matches the offence.
be all eyes, watch eagerly and attentively: *We were all eyes as he unwrapped the box.*
catch your eye, attract your attention: *An ad in the paper caught my eye.*

For Practice...

Each of the following sentences contains an idiom (underlined). In your dictionary, write down the literal meaning of each idiom (what the words actually say). Now write down your definition of its actual meaning. Identify the key words to find the idiom in the dictionary. Compare your meaning with the dictionary definition.

1. Her jokes had me in stitches.
2. As he was telling me the details, I was all ears.
3. You don't have to bite my head off about the mistake.
4. Their behaviour was driving their mother up the wall.
5. He couldn't believe it and said she was pulling his leg.

Try This!

Over the next two weeks, list some of the idioms you notice in your reading and conversations. At the end of the two weeks, get together with a partner, share your lists, and look up the meanings for any idioms you don't understand. Choose a favourite and make a poster on which you print the expression and illustrate its literal meaning.

HOW TO Find Out Where a Word Came From

The etymology of a word explains its history. (The word *etymology* comes originally from two ancient Greek words: *etymon*, meaning "original form of a word," and *logos*, meaning "reason.") Knowing where a word came from can help you guess the meaning of similar but unfamiliar words.

Here's How

A word's etymology appears at the end of the definitions inside a pair of angle brackets <>.

trans·form (tran sfôrm′) *v* make a thorough or dramatic change in the form, appearance, or character of, or undergo such a change: *The blizzard transformed the bushes into glittering mounds of snow.* <Latin *trans-* across + *forma* form> **trans′for·ma′tion** *n.*

The Latin word *trans* also appears in common English words such as *transport* and *transfer*, and carries the idea of crossing or movement. Knowing what *trans* means can help you guess the meaning of a less common word such as *intransigence.* Since the prefix *in-* means "not," you might guess that *intransigence* has something to do with "not moving across." And if you look the word up, you'll see that this guess is close to the actual meaning: "unwillingness to agree."

There are also special etymology feature boxes throughout the dictionary containing interesting stories about words. For example, why would a shepherd make a good hockey player? Look up *hockey* to find out.

For Practice...

Write down the following five words in a vertical list, leaving enough space between each to write a short sentence or two.

1. algebra 2. script 3. sinister 4. typhoon 5. ballot

Look up the words. Beside each word on your list, write down the language it originally came from and something interesting you learned from reading the etymology.

Try This!

Do a personal brainstorm and write down five to ten words related to a favourite subject or interest. Select two of the words. Using these words as your base, invent two new words that sound as though they could be authentic and relate to the area. Invent an etymology for each of the two words and share them with a classmate.

Get Information from Dictionary Visuals

Many of the words in this dictionary are accompanied by visuals. You can use these visuals to enrich your understanding of different words and concepts.

Here's How

What kinds of information can you get from a dictionary visual?

1. Start by looking at the image itself. It often provides details that aren't present in the definition or that would be very difficult to explain in words. Many visuals show more than one thing so you can make comparisons, or illustrate a complex process.
2. Look at the labels if there are any. They point out important or interesting features.
3. Read the caption if there is one. The captions always provide information that goes beyond what is offered in the definition.

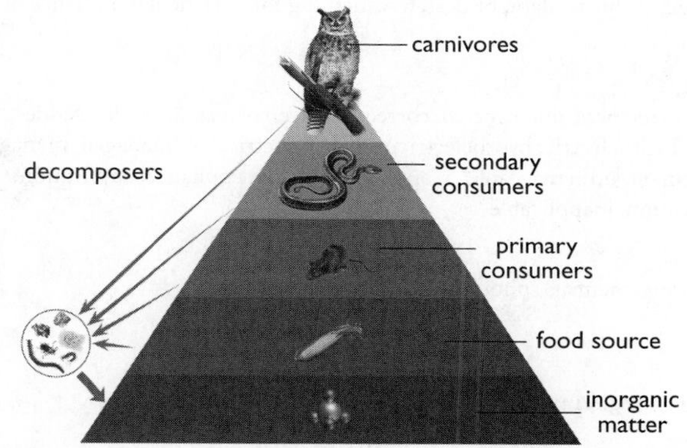

Insects, bacteria, and fungi are **decomposers** that feed on dead materials, breaking down the decaying matter. They then return the nutrients to the soil for plants to use again. Decomposers occupy several positions in the food chain.

For Practice...

Find the visual for the entry word *longitude.*

1. Do lines of longitude run north-south or east-west?
2. How would you describe *equator* in degrees latitude?
3. What is the purpose of intersecting lines of longitude and latitude?

Try This!

Choose one of the following items that you have in your classroom: computer, clock, desk, globe, pen. Pretend that you're preparing a visual (complete with labels and a caption) to accompany the entry word in a dictionary. Look up your word and read the definition. Make a quick sketch and then add labels and a caption that extend the definition. Finally, create a copy suitable for publication.

HOW TO Use the Dictionary: Answers

How to Get to Know This Dictionary
The features found in this dictionary are
1. Title; **4.** Publisher; **5.** Publication date; **6.** ISBN; **7.** Table of contents; **9.** Exercises; **14.** Captions; **15.** Visuals; **16.** A variety of print styles and sizes; **17.** Page numbers; **18.** Appendix

Five additional features might include: index tabs; introduction; cross-references; information boxes; pronunciation key; pronunciations; syllabification dots.

How to Use Alphabetical Order to Look Up a Word
concave, cylinder, digit, formula, polygon, positive, quadrant, quarter, ratio, rectangle, square, subset,

How to Use the Guide Words
The following words would be found on the page with the guide words upset and upward:
1. upside; **3.** upsurge; **4.** uptight; **5.** upstage; **6.** upstream

How to Find a Word You Think You Can't Spell
1. phosphorous or phosphorus; **2.** jewellery or jewelry; **3.** wherewithal; **4.** imbue; **5.** scissors

How to Find the Meaning of a Word
1. sense 4, "an understanding that a piece of information is private"; **2.** verb sense "do something suddenly or violently"; **3.** sense 1, "wonderful or excellent"; **4.** sense 4, "very cold"; **5.** verb sense 2, "adjust, adapt, or design something for a particular audience or purpose"

How to Use Root Words to Find Other Words
1. correction, correctly, correctness, incorrect, incorrectly, incorrectness, uncorrected, correcting, overcorrect; **2.** sadder, saddest, sadly, sadness; **3.** electricity, electrical, electrically, electrician, hydroelectric, hydroelectricity, hydroelectrical; **4.** managed, managing, manager, management, manageable, mismanage, mismanagement, unmanageable; **5.** applied, applying, appliance, application, applicator; applicant; applicable, misapply, reapply, misapplication, inapplicable

How to Find and Fix Spelling Errors
1. sercastic/sarcastic; **2.** numerus/numerous, arrangments/arrangements; **3.** photosinthesus/photosynthesis;
4. exagerated/exaggerated, significence/significance

How to Identify Syllables and Use Them to Help You Spell
1. be•gun; **2.** en•vy; **3.** in•te•ri•or; **4.** pro•vid•ing; **5.** sprin•kle; **6.** tan•ge•rine

How to Check a Pronunciation
1. āble; **2.** costūme; **3.** ēsē; **4.** fan; **5.** insīde; **6.** ōpəning; **7.** plāy; **8.** pŭll; **9.** pin; **10.** rīde

How to Identify Parts of Speech
looked, verb; classroom, noun; around, preposition; carefully, adverb; co-operative, adjective; Wow, interjection; glad, adjective; to, preposition; and, conjunction; anymore, adverb

How to Find Other Ways of Saying Something
Answers will vary, e.g., *The pirates became aware of a city on the horizon, with walls that kept it protected.*

How to Find the Meaning of an Idiom
1. literal meaning, "sewn up with thread; actual meaning, "laughing uncontrollably"; **2.** literal meaning, "completely covered with ears"; actual meaning, "listening eagerly"; **3.** literal meaning, "remove with the teeth"; actual meaning, "be sharply angry with"; **4.** literal meaning, "transporting up a vertical surface"; actual meaning, "making irritated or angry"; **5.** literal meaning, "applying force to a lower limb"; actual meaning, "fool or play a trick on"

How to Find Out Where a Word Came From
1. algebra, Arabic; this mathematics word comes from a medical term originally; **2.** script, Latin; all words with *script* have a meaning connected with writing; **3.** sinister, Latin; the Romans thought that the left-hand side was unlucky; **4.** typhoon, Greek and Cantonese; this word for a strong wind can be traced back to two different languages; **5.** ballot, Italian; in the Middle Ages, people in Venice used to vote using small black and white balls

How to Get Information from Dictionary Visuals
1. north-south; **2.** 0° latitude; **3.** The intersecting lines of longitude and latitude are used to locate and describe specific places.

Aa

a or **A** (ā) *n, pl* **a's** or **A's** **1** the first letter of the English alphabet, or any speech sound represented by it. **2** the first thing in a list or series: *from Point A to Point B.* **3** *Music* the sixth tone in the scale of C major, or a key based on a scale with A as its keynote. **4** a rating indicating the highest quality: *grade A eggs. She got an A on the exam.*
from A to Z, completely: *I learned the subject from A to Z.*

a (ə), (a), *or* (ā) *indefinite article* **1** a word used before a singular noun when the person or thing it refers to is not specific: *There's a man at the door. I need a new coat.* **2** for each or in each: *The caramels are 80 cents a bag. We go there twice a year.* **3** making up one specified unit: *I bought a loaf of bread.* **4** belonging to a class of people or things: *She is a lawyer.* <Old English>

a–[1] *prefix* **1** in a particular place, state, or manner: *abed, aloud, asleep, abuzz.* **2** *Poetic* (*spelled with a hyphen*) in the act or process of: *a-fishing, a-ringing.* <Middle English>

a–[2] *prefix* not or without: *atypical, atonal.*

a–[3] *prefix* to or toward, a form of AD-: *aside, ashore.*

a are(s), a unit of area.

A **1** ampere(s). **2** answer. **3** one of the four main blood groups. The others are B, AB, and O. **4** **Å** angstrom.

A–1 *Informal adj* first-rate; first-class; excellent.

aard·vark (ȧrd′vȧrk) *n* a burrowing mammal of Africa, with a long, flexible snout, and a very long, sticky tongue with which it catches the ants and termites it eats. <Afrikaans, from Dutch *aarde* earth + *vark* pig>

ab–[1] *prefix* away, from, or off: *abnormal, abduct.* <Latin>

ab–[2] *prefix* to or toward; a form of AD- occurring before *b*: *abbreviate.*

AB a human blood type containing the A antigen and the B antigen.

a·back (ə bak′) *adv* **taken aback** surprised and not knowing how to react: *We were taken aback by his strange behaviour.* <Old English *on bæc*>

ab·a·cus (ab′ə kəs) *n, pl* **ab·a·cus·es** or **ab·a·ci** (ab′ə sī′) *or* (ab′ə sē′) a calculating instrument consisting of a frame containing rows of beads or counters that slide back and forth in grooves or on wires. <Latin, from Greek *abacos* board covered with sand (for doing calculations)>

ab·a·lo·ne (ab′ə lō′nē) *n* an edible mollusk of warm seas that has a single, flat, ear-shaped shell with a row of holes along one side and a mother-of-pearl lining. <American Spanish *abulón*>

a·ban·don (ə ban′dən) *v* **1** give up entirely: *to abandon an idea.* **2** leave without intending to return to: *He would never abandon his children.*
n complete freedom from restraint: *She threw back her head and laughed with abandon.* <Old French *abandoner* hand over to another, from Latin *ad-* to + *bandon* control> **a·ban′doned** *adj.* **a·ban′don·ment** *n.*
abandon yourself to, yield completely to a feeling or impulse: *She abandoned herself to grief.*

a·base (ə bās′) *v* **a·based, a·bas·ing** make lower in status or character: *A man who betrays his country abases himself.* <Old French *abaissier*, from Latin *bassus* low>
a·base′ment *n.*

a·bashed (ə basht′) *v* be made to feel embarrassed and confused: *She was a little abashed when the teacher pointed out her mistakes.* <Old French *esbair* to gape>

a·bate (ə bāt′) *v* **a·bat·ed, a·bat·ing** lessen in force or intensity: *The storm has abated.* <Old French *abatre* beat down, from Latin *ad-* to + *battere* to beat>
a·bate′ment *n.*

ab·at·toir (ab′ə twȧr′) *or* (ab′ə twȧr′) *n* a slaughterhouse. <French>

ab·bess (ab′is) *n* the woman in charge of the nuns living in an abbey. <Old French, from Latin *abbas* father + Greek *-issa* (feminine suffix)>

ab·bey (ab′ē) *n* **1** a place where monks or nuns live under the direction of an abbot or abbess. **2** the community of monks or nuns living there. **3** a church or residence that was once an abbey or part of one: *Westminster Abbey.* <Old French, from Latin *abbas* father>

ab·bot (ab′ət) *n* the man in charge of monks living in an abbey. <Latin *abbas* father>

ab·bre·vi·ate (ə brē′vē āt′) *v* **ab·bre·vi·at·ed, ab·bre·vi·at·ing** **1** shorten a word or phrase by letting a part stand for the whole: *We can abbreviate "Saskatchewan" to "Sask."* **2** shorten anything. <Latin *ad-* to + *brevis* short>

ab·bre·vi·a·tion (ə brē′vē ā′shən) *n* a shortened form of a word or phrase standing for the whole, such as *Alta.* for *Alberta* or *MP* for *Member of Parliament.*

CONFUSABLES

An **abbreviation** shortens a word: *pop.* means *population.*

An **acronym** is a word formed from the first letters of two or more words: *ROM* stands for **r**ead-**o**nly **m**emory.

An **initialism** pronounces the first letters of a phrase as letters: *ATM* stands for **a**utomated **t**eller **m**achine.

ABC's *pl n* **1** *Informal* the alphabet: *Some children know their ABC's before kindergarten.* **2** the first or most basic elements of anything: *I can teach you the ABC's of karate.*

ab·di·cate (ab′də kāt′) *v* **ab·di·cat·ed, ab·di·cat·ing** **1** give up the throne while king or queen. **2** abandon or give up a position or duty: *When parents abdicate their responsibilities, children suffer.* <Latin *ab-* away + *dicare* proclaim> **ab′di·ca′tion** *n.* **ab′di·ca′tor** *n.*

ab·do·men (ab′də mən) *n* **1** the part of the body containing the stomach, intestines, liver, spleen, and pancreas in humans and vertebrate animals. **2** the back segment of the body of an insect, spider, or crustacean. <Latin> **ab·dom′i·nal** (ab dom′ə nəl) *adj.*

a bat	e bed	i bid	o pot	u cup	th thin
ā cake	ē me	ī bite	ō go	ū rude	ᴛʜ then
ȧ bar	ə about	ər over	ȯ for	u̇ put	zh measure

ab·duct (ab dukt′) *v* take someone away by force or trickery. <Latin *ab-* away + *ducere* to lead>
ab·duc′tion *n.* **ab·duc′tor** *n.*

🍁 **A·beg·weit** (ȧ′bəg wīt′) *n* Prince Edward Island. <Mi'kmaw = cradle of the waves>

Ab·e·na·ki (ab′ə nȧ′kē) *n, pl* **Ab·e·na·ki** or **Ab·e·na·kis** **1** a member of a First Nations or Native American people living mainly in S Québec and the state of Maine. **2** their Algonquian language.
adj to do with these people or their language. Also called **Waban-Aki**.

ab·er·ra·tion (ab′ə rā′shən) *n* a departure from what is usual or expected. <Latin *ab-* away + *errare* wander> **ab·er′rant** (a ber′ənt) *adj.*

a·bet (ə bet′) *v* **a·bet·ted, a·bet·ting** encourage or help, especially in doing something wrong: *He did the stealing, but she abetted him by distracting the storekeeper.* <Old French *abeter* arouse, from *ad-* to + *beter* urge on> **a·bet′ment** *n.* **a·bet′tor** or **a·bet′ter** *n.*

a·bey·ance (ə bā′əns) *n* a state of temporary inactivity: *We will hold this question in abeyance until we have more detailed information.* <Old French *abeiance* expectation, from Latin *ad-* toward + *batare* gape, reach>

ab·hor (ab hȯr′) *v* **ab·horred, ab·hor·ring** feel disgust or hatred for: *Some people abhor snakes.* <Latin *ab-* from + *horrere* shudder> **ab·hor′rence** *n.*

ab·hor·rent (ab hȯ′rənt) *adj* causing disgust and hate. **ab·hor′rent·ly** *adv.*

a·bide (ə bīd′) *v* **a·bode** or **a·bid·ed, a·bid·ing** **1** (*usually negative*) be able to tolerate something or someone: *I cannot abide liars.* **2** *Poetic or Archaic* endure: *a peace that will abide forever.* <Old English *abidan* stay on> **a·bid′ing** *adj.* **a·bid′ing·ly** *adv.*
abide by, a accept and follow: *to abide by the rules.* **b** remain faithful to: *You must abide by your promise.*

a·bil·i·ty (ə bil′ə tē) *n, pl* **a·bil·i·ties** **1** the power to do a specific thing: *He has lost his ability to remember things.* **2** skill or talent: *musical ability, great ability as a hockey player.* <Old French *ablete*, from Latin *habilis* able>

a·bi·o·gen·e·sis (ā′bī′ō jen′ə sis) *Biology n* the spontaneous production of life from nonliving matter. <Greek *a-* not + *bio-* life + *genesis* creation>

a·bi·o·sis (ā′bī ō′sis) *Biology n* the absence of life. <Greek *a-* not + *biosis* way of living> **a′bi·ot′ic** (ā′bī o′tik) *adj.*

ab·ject (ab′jekt) *adj* **1** extremely bad or miserable: *abject poverty.* **2** to a great degree: *abject fear.* **3** with no pride or dignity: *abject submission.* <Latin *ab-* away + *jacere* to throw> **ab·ject′ly** *adv.*

ab·jure (ab jūr′) *v* **ab·jured, ab·jur·ing** **1** solemnly swear to give up: *He has abjured his evil ways.* **2** avoid or give up: *to abjure alcohol.* <Latin *ab-* away + *jurare* swear> **ab′ju·ra′tion** *n.*

a·blaze (ə blāz′) *adv, adj* on fire or brightly lit: *Lightning set the forest ablaze* (*adv*). *The room was ablaze with lights* (*adj*).

a·ble (ā′bəl) *adj* **a·bler, a·blest** **1** with the power, skill, means, or opportunity to do something: *Are you able to swim? We were not able to attend the wedding.* **2** showing skill or talent: *an able student, an able speech.* <Old French *hable*, from Latin *habere* to handle> **a′bly** *adv.*

–able *suffix* **1** with a specified quality: *lovable.* **2** providing, likely to produce, or subject to: *profitable, debatable, taxable.* <French, from Latin *-abilis*>

a·ble–bod·ied (ā′bəl bod′ēd) *adj* strong and healthy.

a·ble·ism (ā′bə liz′əm) *n* unfair discrimination on the basis of physical or mental disability. **a′ble·ist** *adj, n.*

ab·lu·tion (ə blū′shən) *n* an act of washing oneself, especially when performed as a ritual or ceremony. <Latin *ablutio*, from *ab-* away + *luere* to wash>

ab·ne·gate (ab′nə gāt′) *v* **ab·ne·gat·ed, ab·ne·gat·ing** give up or reject something, especially a right, claim, or privilege: *They abnegated their claim to their mother's property.* <Latin *ab-* off, away + *negare* deny> **ab′ne·ga′tion** *n.*

ab·nor·mal (ab nȯr′məl) *adj* **1** very different from what is normal: *The drug produces an abnormal dilation of the pupil of the eye.* **2** to do with what is abnormal: *abnormal psychology.* **ab′nor·mal′i·ty** *n.* **ab·nor′mal·ly** *adv.*

a·board (ə bȯrd′) *adv, prep* **1** on or onto a ship, train, bus, aircraft, or other vehicle: *All passengers should now be aboard* (*adv*). *They went aboard the ship* (*prep*). **2** *Informal* as part of a group or undertaking: *The company has brought several new staff aboard* (*adv*).
all aboard, a call for passengers to enter a train or other vehicle about to start.

ABO blood group system *n* a way of classifying human blood types based on whether or not antigen A and/or antigen B are present in the red blood cells. In type O, neither are present.

a·bode (ə bōd′) *Poetic n* home.
v a past tense and a past participle of ABIDE.

🍁 **a·boi·teau** (ab′ə tō′) *Nova Scotia, New Brunswick n, pl* **a·boi·teaus** or **a·boi·teaux** **1** a sluice gate in a dike on the Bay of Fundy. **2** the dike itself. Also, **aboideau**. <Cdn French>

a·bol·ish (ə bol′ish) *v* do away with a law or custom completely: *to abolish slavery.* <Old French *abolir*, from Latin *abolere* destroy>

ab·o·li·tion (ab′ə lish′ən) *n* the act of abolishing a system or practice, such as slavery or capital punishment: *the abolition of nuclear weapons.* **ab′o·li′tion·ist** *n.*

ab·o·ma·sum (ab′ə mā′səm) *n* the fourth stomach of cows and other animals that chew the cud. <Latin>

a·bom·i·na·ble (ə bom′ə nə bəl) *adj* disgusting or detestable: *abominable taste in music, abominable cruelty.* <French, from Latin *abominari* see (something) as an evil omen> **a·bom′i·na·ble·ness** *n.* **a·bom′i·na·bly** *adv.*

Abominable Snowman *n* a humanlike monster supposed to live in the Himalayas. Also called **Yeti**.

a·bom·i·nate (ə bom′ə nāt′) *v* **a·bom·i·nat·ed, a·bom·i·nat·ing** detest or be disgusted by.

a·bom·i·na·tion (ə bom′ə nā′shən) *n* something disgusting or detestable: *Untidiness is an abomination to him.*

ab·o·rig·i·nal (ab′ə rij′ə nəl) *adj* **1** having existed in a region from earliest times: *the aboriginal population, aboriginal plants.* **2** **Aboriginal** **a** to do with the earliest inhabitants of a region. **b** 🍁 to do with the First Nations, Métis, or Inuit: *Aboriginal peoples, Aboriginal rights.* <Latin *ab origine* from the beginning>

ab·o·rig·i·ne (ab′ə rij′ə nē) *n* **1** a member of the earliest known population of a region. **2 Aborigine** a member of a dark-skinned people who are the first known inhabitants of Australia. <Latin *ab origine* from the beginning>

a·bort (ə bôrt′) *v* **1** bring or come to an end prematurely: *to abort a space flight. The download aborted because the file was too big.* **2** end the life and development of a fetus. **3** give birth before the fetus has developed enough to live outside the uterus. <Latin *ab-* wrongly + *oriri* be born>

a·bor·tion (ə bôr′shən) *n* **1** the deliberate ending of a pregnancy by causing the fetus to be expelled before it has developed enough to survive outside the uterus. **2** MISCARRIAGE (def. 1).

a·bor·tion·ist (ə bôr′shə nist) *n* a doctor or other person who performs abortions.

a·bor·tive (ə bôr′tiv) *adj* unsuccessful: *The prisoner made several abortive attempts to escape.* **a·bor′tive·ly** *adv.*

a·bound (ə bound′) *v* be plentiful: *Reasons abound why we should not do this.* <Old French, from Latin *abundare* overflow>

abound in (or **with**), have in large numbers or amounts: *Canada abounds in natural resources. The ocean abounds with fish.*

a·bout (ə bout′) *prep* **1** concerning or on the subject of: *a novel about life on the Prairies.* **2** in connection with: *There's something strange about you today.* **3** doing: *to be about your business.* **4** defined or motivated by: *This organization is not about power; it is about justice.*

adv **1** nearly or approximately: *I've about finished my work. There are about 20 of us.* **2** around: *She climbed the hill and looked about.* **3** active: *By six he was already up and about.* **4** in the opposite direction: *Face about!* <Old English *onbutan* on the outside of>

about to, going or ready to: *The plane is about to take off.*

how about, an expression used to suggest or ask something: *How about a game of checkers?*

a·bout–face (ə bout′ fās′) *for n,* (ə bout′ fās′) *for v. n* a turning in the opposite direction: *On hearing her name called, she made an about-face and hurried back to the house. At the first hint of opposition, the policy committee did an about-face.*

v **a·bout-faced, a·bout-fac·ing** turn in the opposite direction.

a·bove (ə buv′) *adv, adj* **1** in a higher place or at a higher level: *We gazed at the stars above* (*adj*). **2** earlier in a book, article, etc.: *the method discussed above* (*adv*). **3** above zero on a scale of temperature: *It was ten above on New Year's Day* (*adj*).

prep **1** at a higher location or level: *A hawk flew above the trees. A captain is above a sergeant.* **2** more than: *If the price is above $50, forget it.* **3** too high in dignity or character for: *He is above cheating.* <Old English *abufan*>

above reproach, blameless: *Her conduct has always been above reproach.*

a·boveboard (ə buv′bôrd′) *adj, adv* fair and honest: *Is the deal aboveboard. to win aboveboard* (*adv*).

a·bove–men·tioned (ə buv′ men′shənd) *adj* previously referred to in a text: *The above-mentioned party was the first of many happy occasions.*

ab·ra·ca·dab·ra (ab′rə kə dab′rə) *n* a word supposed to have magic power. <Latin>

a·brade (ə brād′) *v* **a·brad·ed, a·brad·ing** wear away by rubbing or scraping off: *The rock was abraded over the years by wind and rain. A bad fall had abraded the skin on his knee.* <Latin *ab-* off + *radere* scrape> **ab·ra′sion** *n.*

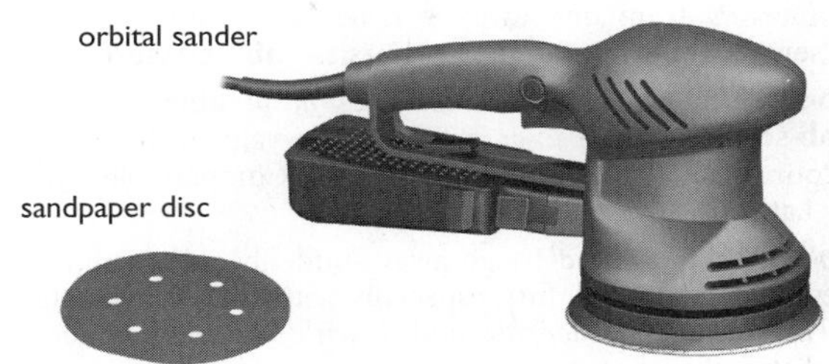

Coarse sandpaper is very **abrasive** and makes a smooth surface rougher (e.g., for painting). Fine sandpaper is not very abrasive and makes a rough surface smooth and polished.

a·bra·sive (ə brā′siv) *adj* **1** wearing or likely to wear away by rubbing: *Most ordinary cleansers are too abrasive to use on silver.* **2** irritating and likely to offend: *an abrasive personality.*

n a substance used for grinding, smoothing, or polishing, such as sandpaper.

a·breast (ə brest′) *adv* side by side: *The soldiers marched three abreast.*

abreast of, keeping up or current with: *Read the newspapers to keep abreast of world events.*

a·bridge (ə brij′) *v* **a·bridged, a·bridg·ing** **1** shorten a text: *An abridged version of a novel is never as good as the original.* **2** make less or take away from: *The rights of citizens must not be abridged without cause.* <Old French *abrégier*, from Latin *abbreviare*> **a·bridg′ment** or **a·bridge′ment** *n.*

a·broad (ə brod′) *adv* **1** outside one's country, especially overseas: *to travel abroad.* **2** moving around; in circulation: *They travelled by night because fewer enemy patrols were abroad then. There's a rumour abroad that you're transferring to another school.*

n foreign countries: *They have just returned from abroad.*

ab·ro·gate (ab′rə gāt′) *v* **ab·ro·gat·ed, ab·ro·gat·ing** cancel a law, right, or formal agreement: *to abrogate citizens' rights by refusing to hold an election.* <Latin *abrogatus* repealed, from *ab-* away + *rogare* propose (a law)> **ab′ro·ga·ble** *adj.* **ab′ro·ga′tion** *n.*

a bat	e bed	i bid	o pot	u cup	th **thin**
ā cake	ē me	ī bite	ō go	ū rude	TH **then**
ȧ bar	ə about	ər over	ȯ for	ů put	zh measure

a·brupt (ə brupt′) *adj* **1** sudden and unexpected: *An emergency brought our visit to an abrupt end.* **2** very steep: *an abrupt slope.* **3** short or blunt in manner: *I'm sorry; my answer was too abrupt.* <Latin *ab-* off + *rumpere* break> **a·brupt′ly** *adv.* **a·brupt′ness** *n.*

abs (abz) *Informal pl n* in full, **abdominals** the abdominal muscles.

ABS antilock braking system.

ab·scess (ab′ses) *n* a collection of pus in the tissues of some part of the body, caused by infection. <Latin *abscessus*, from *abs-* away + *cedere* go. The pus will be "sent away" when the abscess bursts.> **ab′scessed** *adj.*

ab·scis·sa (ab sis′ə) *Mathematics n, pl* **ab·scis·sas** or **ab·scis·sae** (ab sis′ē) *or* (ab sis′ī) the x-value or horizontal coordinate in a system of coordinates. Compare ORDINATE. <Latin *linea abscissa* line cut off>

ab·scond (ab skond′) *v* go away suddenly and secretly to escape justice or a duty, especially with something stolen: *The dishonest teller absconded with the bank's money.* <Latin *abs-* away + *condere* store>

ab·sence (ab′səns) *n* **1** the fact, occasion, or period of being away: *His absence was due to illness. She returned after an absence of six months.* **2** non-existence in a certain place or time: *Darkness is the absence of light.*

ab·sent (ab′sənt) *for adj,* (ab sent′) *for v or prep. adj* **1** not present: *Three students are absent today.* **2** not existing: *Trees are almost completely absent in some parts of the Prairies.* **3** absent-minded: *She said "Yes" in an absent way and kept on reading.*
v (*with a reflexive pronoun*) stay away: *to absent oneself from school.*
prep Law or Formal without: *Absent proper documentation, immigrants will be detained.* <Latin *ab-* away + *esse* to be> **ab′sent·ly** *adv.*

ab·sen·tee (ab′sən tē′) *n* a person who is away.

🍁 **absentee ballot** *n* **1** a system allowing voters who are away from home to vote in an election. **2** all the votes cast in this way.

ab·sen·tee·ism (ab′sən tē′iz əm) *n* the practice or condition of being away: *measures to reduce absenteeism in the workplace. Absenteeism was high during flu season.*

ab·sent–mind·ed (ab′sənt mīn′did) *adj* not aware of what is going on because one is thinking of other things: *I was so absent-minded that I put my books in the fridge instead of in my backpack.* **ab′sent-mind′ed·ly** *adv.* **ab′sent-mind′ed·ness** *n.*

ab·so·lute (ab′sə lūt′) *or* (ab′sə lūt′) *adj* **1** complete and unqualified: *absolute silence, an absolute idiot.* **2** unrestricted by a constitution or system of laws: *an absolute ruler.* **3** certain; positive: *absolute proof.* **4** not dependent on a particular person's perception: *an absolute truth, absolute reality.* **5** not compared with or relative to anything else: *absolute velocity, absolute humidity.*
n an idea, standard, value, etc. that is independent of or not influenced by any other. <Latin *absolutus*, from *ab-* from + *solvere* loosen> **ab′so·lute′ness** *n.*

absolute location *Geography n* the description of location using a grid system such as longitude and latitude or number plus letter, or an address such as a postal address, postal code, or telephone area code.

ab·so·lute·ly (ab′sə lūt′lē) *or* (ab′sə lū′tlē) *adv* **1** completely or utterly: *This can opener is absolutely useless. He is absolutely the finest fellow I know.* **2** *Informal* an emphatic "yes": *"Are you going to the game?" "Absolutely!"*

GRAMMAR AND USAGE

In speech, **absolutely** is often used to show enthusiasm: *That's absolutely the best pizza I've ever had!* In formal writing, use **absolutely** in its original sense of "completely": *I am absolutely sure the test is tomorrow.*

absolute monarchy *n* a monarchy with no limitations on the power or authority of the ruler. Compare CONSTITUTIONAL MONARCHY.

absolute pitch *Music n* the ability to recognize and reproduce any note.

absolute value *Mathematics n* the value of a real number regardless of its positive or negative sign. The absolute value of –5 or +5 is 5.

absolute zero *n* the lowest temperature possible according to scientific theory, equal to about –273°C, or zero on the KELVIN scale.

ab·so·lu·tion (ab′sə lū′shən) *n* a formal release from guilt or punishment, especially forgiveness for a sin. <See ABSOLVE.>

ab·so·lut·ism (ab′sə lū′ tiz əm) *n* **1** a belief in absolute principles, and that no compromises are possible. **2** a system of government in which the power of the ruler is not restricted. **ab′so·lut′ist** *n, adj.*

ab·solve (ab zolv′) *v* **ab·solved, ab·solv·ing** declare a person free from guilt, blame, sin, or duty: *The principal absolved the student of any wrongdoing.* <Latin *ab-* from + *solvere* loosen>

ab·sorb (ab zôrb′) *v* **1** take in or soak up: *A sponge absorbs water. Black objects absorb most of the light that falls on them, reflecting very little.* **2** take in and make a part of itself: *The bloodstream absorbs digested food.* **3** understand and process mentally: *I cannot absorb so much information at once.* **4** take up all the attention of: *That puzzle has absorbed her for hours.* <Latin *ab-* from + *sorbere* suck in> **ab·sorbed′** *adj.* **ab·sorp′tion** *n.*

ab·sorb·ent (ab zôr′bənt) *adj* able to soak up much liquid: *These paper towels are very absorbent.* **ab·sorb′en·cy** *n.*

ab·sorb·ing (ab zôr′bing) *adj* extremely interesting: *The book was so absorbing I could hardly put it down.*

ab·stain (ab stān′) *v* **1** decide not to use or do something: *Athletes usually abstain from smoking.* **2** decline to vote: *She abstained because she disliked both candidates.* <French *abstenir*, from Latin *abs-* off + *tenere* hold>

ab·stain·er (ab stā′nər) *n* a person who abstains, especially from alcoholic drinks.

ab·ste·mi·ous (ab stē′mē əs) *adj* restrained or moderate in eating and drinking. <Latin *abs-* off + *temetum* strong liquor> **ab·ste′mi·ous·ly** *adv.* **ab·ste′mi·ous·ness** *n.*

ab·sten·tion (ab sten′shən) *n* the fact of not voting: *There were five votes in favour, four against, and three abstentions.*

ab·sti·nence (ab′stə nəns) *n* the act of giving up or refraining: *One sure way of avoiding pregnancy is complete abstinence from sexual activity.*

ab·stract (ab′strakt) *for adj or n,* (ab strakt′) *for v.*
adj **1** existing in thought or as an idea, and not to do with any physical thing: *A lump of sugar is a concrete object; the quality of sweetness is abstract. "Honesty" is an abstract noun; "honey" is not.* **2** representing ideas or feelings that have little or no resemblance to physical things: *an abstract painting.* **3** hard to understand: *Nuclear physics is too abstract for beginners.*
n a short summary of a text.
v **1** think of a quality apart from any object or real thing with that quality: *It is hard to abstract beauty from beautiful things.* **2** take away or remove: *to abstract gold from ore.* <Latin *abstractus,* from *abs-* away + *trahere* draw> **ab·stract′ly** *adv.* **ab·stract′ness** *n.*
in the abstract, in theory rather than in practice: *In the abstract we approve of healthy eating, and yet we don't always eat the recommended foods.*

ab·stract·ed (ab strak′tid) *adj* not aware of what is happening because one is thinking of other things.

abstract expressionism *n* a US artistic movement that arose in the 1950s and emphasized the artist's spontaneous emotions expressed through abstract images and the physical action involved in painting.

ab·strac·tion (ab strak′shən) *n* **1** an idea or quality rather than a physical object: *Bravery and length are abstractions.* **2** the state of being not aware of what is happening because one is thinking of other things.

ab·struse (ab strūs′) *adj* hard to understand. <Latin *abstrusus* hidden, from *abs-* away + *trudere* conceal> **ab·struse′ly** *adv.* **ab·struse′ness** *n.*

ab·surd (ab zərd′) *or* (ab sərd′) *adj* so unreasonable or bizarre that it seems ridiculous. <Latin *absurdus* senseless> **ab·surd′i·ty** *n.* **ab·surd′ly** *adv.* **ab·surd′ness** *n.*

ab·surd·ism (ab zərd′iz əm) *or* (ab sərd′iz əm) *n* the belief that the universe has no purpose or meaning, or the artistic movement that expresses this belief.
ab·surd′ist *n, adj.*

a·bun·dant (ə bun′dənt) *adj* very plentiful: *There are abundant oil reserves in Alberta.* <Old French, from Latin *ab-* off + *undare* flow> **a·bun′dance** *n.* **a·bun′dant·ly** *adv.*

a·buse (ə byūz′) *for v,* (ə byūs′) *for n.* *v* **a·bused, a·bus·ing** **1** make bad or wrong use of: *to abuse your authority.* **2** treat badly or cruelly: *The cat had been abused by its former owner.* **3** use harsh and insulting language to: *The angry captain abused the crew at the top of his voice.*
n **1** a wrong or bad use: *the abuse of a privilege.* **2** bad or cruel treatment: *child abuse.* **3** harsh and insulting language: *She hurled a torrent of abuse at us.* **4** a bad practice or custom: *the abuses of evil dictators.* <Old French *abuser,* from Latin *abuti* misuse> **a·bus′er** *n.* **a·bu′sive** (ə byū′siv) *adj.*

a·but (ə but′) *v* **a·but·ted, a·but·ting** (*with **on** or **against***) be next to or have a common boundary: *The sidewalk abuts on the street. The street abuts against the railway.* <Old French *abouter* to border on>

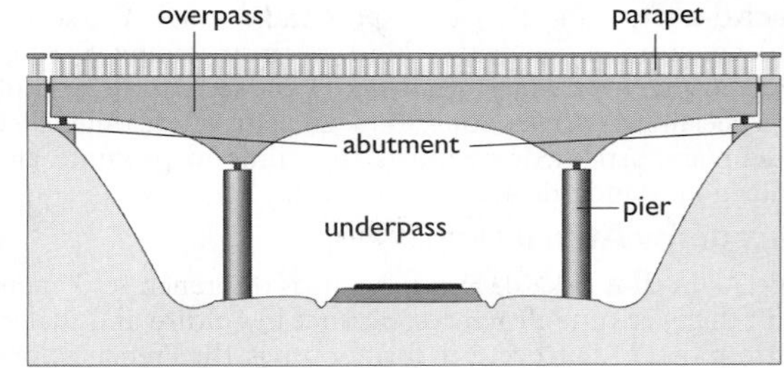

Bridges are specially designed to resist the force of gravity; however, the structure of a bridge generates other forces that also must be resisted.
The **abutments** anchor the bridge to the ground and keep the ends from moving sideways.

a·but·ment (ə but′mənt) *n* a vertical support for an arch or bridge.

a·buzz (ə buz′) *adj* full of humming sounds, such as a room full of excited activity or conversation: *The room was abuzz with preparations for the banquet.*

a·bys·mal (ə biz′məl) *adj* very bad: *Your work has been abysmal this term.* <See ABYSS.> **a·bys′mal·ly** *adv.*

a·byss (ə bis′) *n* **1** a very deep or seemingly bottomless crack in the earth. **2** anything bad that seems endless or measureless: *the abyss of despair.* <Latin, from Greek *a-* without + *byssos* bottom>

a·byss·al zone (ə bis′əl) *Ecology n* the deep part of the ocean, below about 2000 m.

A/C or **a/c** **1** account. **2** air conditioning.

AC or **A.C.** **1** alternating current. **2** air conditioning.

a·ca·cia (ə kā′shə) *n* a tree or shrub with tiny flowers in fluffy round clusters, and fernlike leaves. <Latin, from Greek *akakia*>

ac·a·de·mi·a (ak′ə dē′mē ə) *n* the community of university teachers, scholars, and researchers, together with the places in which they work. <Greek *Akademeia,* the place where Plato taught>

ac·a·dem·ic (ak′ə dem′ik) *adj* **1** to do with schools, colleges, and universities, or the studies that go on there. **2** concerned with the arts and sciences studied for their own sake rather than as commercial, technical, or professional training. **3** theoretical and with no practical significance: *an academic discussion.*
n **1** a scholar or scholarly person. **2** **academics** *pl* academic courses or studies. **ac′a·dem′i·cal·ly** *adv.*

academic freedom *n* the freedom, especially at the college or university level, to teach, discuss, or research without interference from authorities.

academic year *n* the period of the year during which students attend school, college, or university, usually from September until May or June.

a bat	e bed	i bid	o pot	u cup	th **thin**
ā cake	ē me	ī bite	ō go	ū rude	ᴛʜ **then**
à bar	ə about	ər over	ò for	ů put	zh measure

a·cad·e·my (ə kad′ə mē) *n, pl* **a·cad·e·mies** 1 a school devoted to a particular kind of instruction: *a dance academy, a military academy.* 2 a secondary school, especially a private one. 3 a society of distinguished scholars, artists, or scientists that aims to promote and keep up standards in a specific field.

Academy Award OSCAR.

🍁 **A·ca·di·a** (ə kā′dē ə) *n* 1 the areas of French settlement in the Maritime Provinces, distinct in culture and dialect from that of Québec. 2 in former times, the French colony comprising the Maritime Provinces and adjacent parts of Québec and Maine. <French *Acadie*> **A·ca′di·an** *adj, n.*

a·can·thus (ə kan′thəs) *n* a herb or shrub with large, often spiny leaves and spikes of purple or white flowers. <Latin, from Greek *ake* thorn>

a cap·pel·la (ȧ′ kə pel′ə) *Music adj, adv* sung without instrumental accompaniment. <Italian = in the manner of chapel (music)>

ac·cede (ak sēd′) *v* **ac·ced·ed, ac·ced·ing** 1 (*with* ***to***) give in or agree: *to accede to a proposal.* 2 assume an office, title, or position: *When the king died, his eldest daughter acceded to the throne.* 3 become a party to an agreement, or become a member of an organization: *Our government acceded to the treaty.* <Latin *ad-* to + *cedere* yield> **ac·ces′sion** *n.*

ac·cel·er·an·do (ak sel′ə ran′dō) *or* (a chel′ə ran′dō) *Music adv, adj* gradually speeding up. <Italian>

ac·cel·er·ate (ak sel′ə rāt′) *v* **ac·cel·er·at·ed, ac·cel·er·at·ing** 1 go or cause to go faster: *The train accelerated suddenly. Good food and rest will accelerate your recovery.* 2 go or cause to go faster through an academic program: *She is younger than her classmates because she accelerated.* 3 *Physics* change the velocity of a moving object. <Latin *ad-* to + *celer* swift> **ac·cel′er·a′tion** *n.*

ac·cel·er·a·tor (ak sel′ə rā′tər) *n* 1 a device for increasing the speed of a machine, especially the pedal in a motor vehicle that controls the flow of fuel to the engine. 2 *Chemistry* a substance that speeds up a reaction. 3 *Physics* an apparatus for accelerating electrically charged atomic particles or nuclei to very high speeds.

ac·cent (ak′sent) *for n,* (ak′sent) *or* (ak sent′) *for v.*
n 1 a distinctive manner of pronunciation typical of a certain group of speakers: *an Italian accent.* 2 in some languages, a mark over a vowel, indicating how it is to be pronounced. In French, the name *Québec* is written with an accent on the first *e.* 3 force or stress placed on a given syllable in speaking, or a mark (′) showing this: *In "yesterday," the main accent is on the first syllable.* 4 *Poetry* regular emphasis on certain syllables that creates a rhythm. 5 special attention given to something: *In this writing exercise, the accent is on style.* 6 an object providing contrast in a colour scheme: *a yellow room with dark green accents.* 7 *Music* emphasis on a certain note or chord, or the mark (>) placed over the note to indicate this. 8 **accents** *pl Poetic* a tone of voice: *She spoke to her baby in tender accents.*
v 1 pronounce or mark a syllable with an accent. 2 emphasize: *Throughout her speech she accented the gravity of the situation.* <Latin *ad-* to + *canere* to sing>

ac·cen·tu·ate (ak sen′chū āt′) *v* **ac·cen·tu·at·ed, ac·cen·tu·at·ing** 1 emphasize: *Her black hair accentuated the whiteness of her skin.* 2 place stress on a certain syllable in pronunciation. **ac·cen′tu·a′tion** *n.*

ac·cept (ak sept′) *v* 1 take something offered or given: *to accept a gift.* 2 agree to: *to accept a proposal.* 3 tolerate: *We can't accept such rude behaviour.* 4 welcome and approve of a person: *He was soon accepted by his new classmates.* 5 regard as normal or inevitable: *a generally accepted practice.* <Latin *ad-* to + *capere* take> **ac·cept′ance** *n.* **ac·cept′ed** *adj.*

CONFUSABLES

Accept is a verb that means "receive":
Will you accept my apology?

Except is a preposition meaning "other than":
Everyone except me had an umbrella.

ac·cept·a·ble (ak sep′tə bəl) *adj* 1 meeting some standard: *Flowers are an acceptable gift for a sick person.* 2 good enough but not outstanding: *an acceptable performance.* 3 able to be tolerated or allowed: *Driving while drunk is simply not acceptable.* **ac·cept′a·bly** *adv.*

ac·cess (ak′ses) *n* 1 the right or ability to approach, enter, or use: *All students have access to the library. A ramp gives all people access to the theatre.* 2 a means or process of approaching or entering: *A ladder was the only access to the attic. Access to the cottage was hampered by poor roads.*
v 1 retrieve or obtain data: *You can access the information only if you have the password.* 2 approach or reach: *The cottage can only be accessed by boat.* <Latin *accedere* to approach>

ac·ces·si·ble (ak ses′ə bəl) *adj* 1 able to be entered, reached, or obtained. *The building is accessible on weekdays only.* 2 easy to get at or reach: *Accessible controls are designed for people with disabilities.* 3 easily understood and appreciated: *His pictures sell well because they are accessible.* **ac·ces′si·bil′i·ty** *n.*
accessible to, capable of being reached or influenced by: *An open-minded person is accessible to rational argument.*

ac·ces·sion (ak sesh′ən) *n* 1 the act or fact of acquiring rank or power, especially that of a monarch or head of government: *The prince's accession to the throne was welcomed by the people.* 2 a new item added to a collection, such as a book or work of art: *The current exhibit includes several of the gallery's new accessions.* 3 an increase or addition: *an accession of forty students.*

ac·ces·sor·ize (ak ses′ə rīz′) *v* **ac·ces·sor·ized, ac·ces·sor·iz·ing** provide accessories for.

ac·ces·so·ry (ak ses′ə rē) *n, pl* **ac·ces·so·ries** 1 something added that is useful or decorative but not essential: *mirrors, baskets, and other bike accessories. A black scarf and purse would be great accessories for that coat.* 2 *Law* a person who helps another commit a crime without taking part in it: *A person who hides a criminal is an accessory after the fact.*
adj acting as an accessory.

🍁 **access road** *n* 1 a road built to permit entry to a place that is otherwise hard to reach. 2 a road leading onto an expressway.

ac·ci·dent (ak′sə dənt) *n* **1** something harmful or undesirable that happens by chance: *a car accident. She had an accident with her coffee and stained her shirt.* **2** anything that happens without being planned or known about in advance: *Their meeting was an accident.* <Old French, from Latin *accidentis*, from *ad-* to + *cadere* fall>

ac·ci·den·tal (ak′sə den′təl) *adj* **1** happening by chance: *an accidental injury, an accidental discovery.* **2** not essential: *Songs are essential to a musical, but accidental to comedies.*
n Music a sign used to show a change of pitch and placed before a note. **ac′ci·den′tal·ly** *adv.*

ac·ci·dent–prone (ak′sə dənt prōn′) *adj* tending to have accidents.

ac·claim (ə klām′) *v* **1** express public approval: *Critics enthusiatically acclaimed the books of Monica Hughes.* **2** announce or declare with approval: *The newspapers acclaimed the firefighter a hero.* **3** 🍁 elect to an office without opposition: *The voters acclaimed her mayor.*
n a public show of approval: *The actor was received with great acclaim.* <Latin *ad-* to + *clamare* cry out>

ac·cla·ma·tion (ak′lə mā′shən) *n* cheers, applause, or other public show of approval.
by acclamation, 🍁 without opposition in an election: *Since he was the sole candidate, he was elected by acclamation.*

ac·cli·ma·tize (ə klī′mə tīz′) *v* **ac·cli·ma·tized, ac·cli·ma·tiz·ing** make or become accustomed to a new climate or environment: *It took him a long while to acclimatize himself to the high altitude. They soon became acclimatized to city life.* <French *acclimater*> **ac·cli′ma·ti·za′tion** *n.*

ac·co·lade (ak′ə lād′) *or* (ak′ə läd′) *n* **1** (*often plural*) an expression of praise or approval. **2** a tap on the shoulder with the flat side of a sword to mark the bestowal of knighthood on a person. <Provençal *acolada* an embrace about the neck, from Latin *ad-* to + *collum* neck>

ac·com·mo·date (ə kom′ə dāt′) *v* **ac·com·mo·dat·ed, ac·com·mo·dat·ing** **1** have room for: *This big bedroom will accommodate two beds.* **2** help out: *He wanted change for a dollar, but I could not accommodate him.* **3** furnish with lodging and sometimes food: *Can you accommodate a party of five for two weeks?* **4** adjust or adapt: *The eye accommodates itself to darkness.* **5** reconcile or make allowance for: *Surely we can accommodate our differences.* <Latin *ad-* to + *commodus* fitting>

ac·com·mo·dat·ing (ə kom′ə dā′ting) *adj* willing to help or make adjustments: *The woman was accommodating enough to lend me a dollar.* **ac·com′mo·dat′ing·ly** *adv.*

ac·com·mo·da·tion (ə kom′ə dā′shən) *n*
1 accommodations *pl* lodging and sometimes food: *The hotel has accommodations for one hundred guests.* **2** a convenient arrangement or compromise: *Some accommodation will be necessary on your part if our sharing a room is going to work.*

ac·com·pa·ny (ə kum′pə nē) *v* **ac·com·pa·nied, ac·com·pa·ny·ing** **1** go somewhere as a companion: *We're going for a walk; feel free to accompany us.* **2** be or happen in connection with: *Fire is accompanied by heat.* **3** play or sing along with the main performer or performers: *I will accompany the choir on the piano.* <French *accompagner*> **ac·com′pa·ni·ment** *n.* **ac·com′pa·nist** *n.*

ac·com·plice (ə kom′plis) *n* a person who helps another in committing a crime or other wrong deed: *Without an accomplice, the thief could not have got into the house so easily.*

ETYMOLOGY

Most words beginning with *acc-* are related to the Latin prefix *ad-*, which means "to." **Accomplice** is an exception.

In English, *accomplice* started out as *complice*, borrowed directly from French: *The thief must have had a complice.* Listeners mistakenly thought *a* and *complice* were one word, and *accomplice* was born.

ac·com·plish (ə kom′plish) *v* **1** succeed in completing: *Did you accomplish your purpose?* **2** get the work done: *He can accomplish more in a day than any other boy in his class.*

ac·com·plished (ə kom′plisht) *adj* **1** highly skilled: *an accomplished surgeon, an accomplished liar.* **2** well educated and with good social skills: *Their very accomplished daughter entertained us.*

ac·com·plish·ment (ə kom′plish mənt) *n* **1** something that has been achieved successfully: *A perfect test score is quite an accomplishment.* **2** a skill or ability: *A girl of many accomplishments, she was skilled in swimming, writing, and playing hockey.*

ac·cord (ə kôrd′) *v* **1** grant or give: *He was accorded special privileges because of his rank.* **2** (*with* **with**) agree or be in harmony: *Her account of the incident accords with yours.*
n **1** agreement or harmony: *The various groups are now in accord on the issue.* **2** a formal agreement between nations: *to sign an accord.* <Old French *acorder* bring together, from Latin *ad-* to + *cordis* heart>
according to, a in agreement with: *He acted according to the rules.* **b** based on: *Sort these according to size.* **c** as stated by or in: *According to this book, a tiger is really a big cat.*
of your (or **its**) **own accord,** by yourself: *He goes to bed of his own accord now. The door suddenly slammed of its own accord.*
with one accord, all agreeing: *At the winning goal we cheered with one accord.*

ac·cord·ance (ə kôr′dəns) *n* the act of according or granting: *the accordance of certain rights.*
in accordance with, following or complying with: *The inspection was carried out in accordance with government regulations.*

a bat	e bed	i bid	o pot	u cup	th **thin**
ā cake	ē me	ī bite	ō go	ū rude	TH **then**
ä bar	ə about	ər over	ô for	ů put	zh measure

ac·cord·ing·ly (ə kôr′ding lē) *adv* therefore or consequently: *These are the rules; act accordingly or leave. She said she felt sick; accordingly, we sent her home.*

ac·cor·di·on (ə kôr′dē ən) *n* a portable musical wind instrument played by squeezing a bellows with one hand, while pressing keys and buttons with the other. <German *Akkordion,* from Italian *accordare* to tune> **ac·cor′di·on·ist** *n.*

ac·cost (ə kost′) *v* stop a person in order to ask a question, beg for money, etc.: *A ragged beggar accosted him, asking for money.* <French *accoster,* from Latin *accostare* put side by side>

ac·count (ə kount′) *n* **1** a report, story, or explanation: *The newspaper published an account of the trial. She could give no satisfactory account of her absence.* **2** an arrangement with a bank for saving or managing money, or the amount of money in this arrangement: *Mom says that her bank account is very low right now.* **3** an arrangement with a company for buying goods or services on credit or a client in such an arrangement: *Their firm has an account with that advertising agency. That company is one of our biggest accounts.* **4** usually, **accounts** *pl* an ongoing record of money received and spent: *to keep careful accounts.*

v Archaic or Poetic think of as; consider: *The old king was accounted wise.* <Old French *acont,* from Latin *accomptare* count up>

account for, a explain: *Can you account for your strange behaviour?* **b** be the reason for: *Late frosts accounted for the poor fruit crop.* **c** tell what has happened to: *The treasurer has to account for all funds received.*

call (or **bring**) **someone to account,** ask someone to explain or defend his or her actions.

of little (or **no**) **account,** not important or not worth much: *Her opinion is of little account around here.*

on account, as part payment: *If you accept five dollars on account, I can pay the rest next week.*

on account of, because of: *The game was put off on account of rain.*

on no account, under no circumstances.

take into account or **take account of,** make allowance for: *When planning a holiday, you have to take travelling time into account.*

turn to (**your own**) **account,** make profitable use of: *We turned the bad weather to account by learning how to wax our skis properly.*

ac·count·a·ble (ə koun′tə bəl) *adj* **1** required to give an account if asked: *We are each accountable for our own actions.* **2** explainable: *His bad temper is easily accountable; he's had a toothache all day.* **ac·count′a·bil′i·ty** *n.* **ac·count′a·bly** *adv.*

ac·count·ant (ə koun′tənt) *n* a trained professional who keeps or inspects business accounts. **ac·count′an·cy** *n.*

ac·count·ing (ə koun′ting) *n* the work of systematically recording, analyzing, and reporting on data related to business transactions. Also, **accountancy**.

ac·cou·tre (ə kū′tər) *Archaic v* **ac·cou·tred, ac·cou·tring** equip or outfit: *Knights were accoutred in armour.* <French *accoutrer*>

ac·cou·tre·ments (ə kū′trə mənts) *pln* items that help to create an overall effect, such as equipment or uniforms: *A robe and a wand were among the wizard's accoutrements.*

ac·cred·it (ə kred′it) *v* **1** recognize as coming up to an official standard: *a private school accredited by the Ministry of Education.* **2** give a person credit for: *The invention of the telephone is accredited to Alexander Graham Bell.* **3** provide with credentials: *An ambassador is accredited as the representative of his own country in a foreign land.* <French *accréditer*> **ac·cred′i·ta′tion** *n.* **ac·cred′it·ed** *adj.*

ac·cre·tion (ə krē′shən) *n* **1** growth by expansion or accumulation: *the accretion of political power.* **2** the part added. <Latin *ad-* to + *crescere* grow>

ac·crue (ə krū′) *v* **ac·crued, ac·cru·ing** be a result (of): *Knowledge accrues from study. Interest accrues on a savings account.* <Old French *acreue,* from Latin *accrescere* become larger> **ac·cru′al** *n.*

ac·cul·tur·ate (ə kul′chə rāt′) *v* (*often passive*) learn or adopt the culture of a people: *New immigrants acculturate to Canadian society at different rates. You become acculturated faster if you know the language.* <Latin *ac-* to + *culture*> **ac·cul′tu·ra′tion** *n.*

ac·cu·mu·late (ə kyū′myə lāt′) *v* **ac·cu·mu·lat·ed, ac·cu·mu·lat·ing** collect or pile up little by little: *She had accumulated enough money to retire comfortably. Dirty laundry accumulates quickly in this house.* <Latin *ad-* up + *cumulus* heap> **ac·cu′mu·la′tion** *n.*

ac·cu·rate (ak′yə rit) *adj* **1** containing or making no errors: *an accurate report, accurate calculations.* **2** exact and precise. <Latin *ad-* to + *cura* care> **ac′cu·ra·cy** *n.* **ac′cu·rate·ly** *adv.*

ac·curs·ed (ə kər′sid) *or* (ə kərst′) *Poetic adj* **1** damnable or detestable. **2** under a curse. Also, **accurst**.

ac·cuse (ə kyūz′) *v* **ac·cused, ac·cus·ing** claim that someone has done wrong: *She accused her brother of listening at her door.* <Old French, from Latin *ad-* to + *causa* cause> **ac′cu·sa′tion** *n.* **ac·cu′sa·to′ry** *adj.* **ac·cus′er** *n.*

ac·cused (ə kyūzd′) *Law n* **the accused** the person or persons appearing in court on a charge.

ac·cus·tom (ə kus′təm) *v* **1** make someone or something used to: *I must accustom myself to working harder.* **2** (*with* **to**) become familiar with: *She was accustomed to getting up early.* <Old French *acostumer,* from Latin *ad-* to + *consuescere* accustom>

ace (ās) *n* **1** a playing card, domino, or side of a die with one spot. **2** an expert or highly skilled person: *He is an ace at basketball.* **3** a combat pilot who has shot down a large number of enemy planes. **4** *Tennis, Badminton, etc.* a point won by a single stroke.

adj very skilled: *an ace swimmer.*

v **aced, ac·ing 1** *Informal* achieve a high mark, especially in an exam: *He aced all his courses this term.* **2** win or defeat decisively: *The Jays aced the Yankees.* <Old French, from Latin *as* smallest unit>

ace up your sleeve or **ace in the hole,** *Informal* an advantage that is kept hidden until needed.

within an ace of, almost to the point of: *She came within an ace of breaking her neck.*

a·cer·bic (ə sər′bik) *adj* sharp and forthright as a comment or style: *an acerbic remark, an acerbic reviewer.* <French, from Latin *acerbus* sour-tasting> **a·cer′bi·cal·ly** *adv.* **a·cer′bi·ty** *n.*

ac·e·tate (as′ə tāt′) *n* **1** in full, **cellulose acetate** a compound produced by the action of acetic acid and sulphuric acid on cellulose. **2** something made from this substance, such as a fabric, photographic film, or a transparency for use with an overhead projector.

a·ce·tic acid (ə sē′tik) *n* a sour, colourless acid that gives vinegar its distinctive taste.

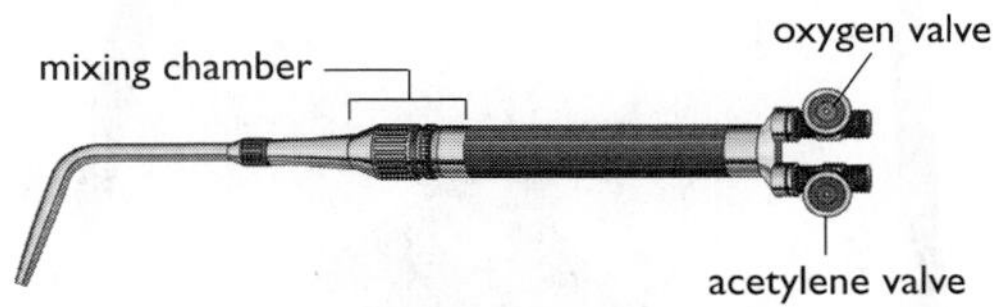

a·cet·y·lene (ə set′ə lēn′) *n* a colourless, poisonous gas that burns with a bright light and very hot flame and is combusted with oxygen in an **acetylene torch** to cut and weld metals.

a·ce·tyl·sal·i·cyl·ic acid (ə sē′təl sal′ə sil′ik) ASPIRIN.

ache (āk) *v* **ached, ach·ing 1** feel continuous physical or emotional pain: *My back aches. Our hearts ached for the orphaned children.* **2** feel a great desire for: *I am aching to see you again.*
n (*often in compounds*) a dull, steady pain: *a stomach ache, a headache.* <Old English *acan*> **ach′ing** *adj.* **ach′ing·ly** *adv.*

a·chene (ā kēn′) *Botany n* a small, dry, hard fruit consisting of one seed with a thin outer covering that does not burst open when ripe. <Latin *achaenium*, from Greek *a-* not + *chainen* gape (because it ripens without bursting)>

a·chieve (ə chēv′) *v* **a·chieved, a·chiev·ing 1** do, get done, or accomplish: *You can't achieve much in a day under these conditions.* **2** earn, reach, or get through effort: *to achieve a goal, to achieve the desired result. Both girls achieved distinction in math.* <Old French *a chief* (come) to a head> **a·chiev′a·ble** *adj.* **a·chieve′ment** *n.* **a·chiev′er** *n.*

A·chil·les heel (ə kil′ēz) *n* a weak point or place: *If they threaten to cut his computer time, he'll do what they want; that's his Achilles heel.* <*Achilles*, hero in Greek myth who could be wounded only in the heel>

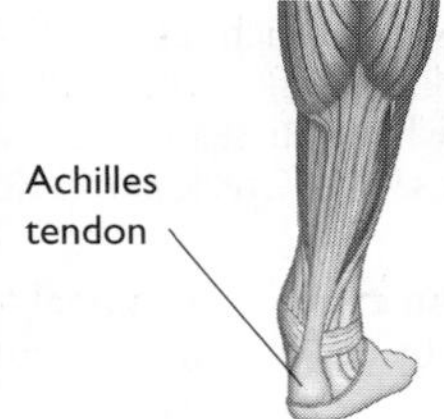

Your **Achilles tendon** allows you to point your foot downward and stand on your toes. It is the largest tendon in the body, and can absorb a great deal of force.

Achilles tendon *n* the strong tendon joining the heel bone to the muscles of the calf: *The Achilles tendon helps to move the ankle joint.* <See ACHILLES HEEL.>

ach·ro·mat·ic (ak′rə mat′ik) *adj* refracting white light without breaking it up into the colours of the spectrum. <Greek *a-* without + *chroma* colour>
ach′ro·mat′i·cal·ly *adv.*

ac·id (as′id) *n* **1** *Chemistry* a compound that yields hydrogen ions when dissolved in water and usually reacts with a base to form a salt. Compare ALKALI, ANTACID. **2** a harsh, bitter or biting quality: *He spoke in a tone full of acid.* **3** acid rock.
adj **1** to do with an acid: *an acid solution.* **2** sour or sharp. **3** biting or bitter in manner or temper: *an acid comment.* <Latin *acidus* sour> **a·cid′ic** *adj.* **ac′id·ly** *adv.*

a·cid·i·fy (ə sid′ə fī′) *v* **a·cid·i·fied, a·cid·i·fy·ing** change into an acid or increase the acid content. **a·cid′i·fi·ca′tion** *n.*

ac·i·dim·e·ter (as′ə dim′ə tər) *n* an instrument that measures the acidity of a substance.

a·cid·i·ty (ə sid′ə tē) *n* an acidic quality or condition: *the acidity of vinegar, the acidity of certain soils.*

🍁 **acid precipitation** *n* rain or snow polluted by acids that form in the atmosphere from industrial waste. Also called **acid rain**. <*acid rain* was coined by Canadian scientist R. Beamish in 1969>

acid rock *n* a style of rock music dating from the late 1960s, known for its harsh and distorted electronic sounds and its association with hallucinogenic drugs. <from a slang name for the hallucogenic drug lysergic *acid* dyethylamide (LSD)>

acid test *n* a test that reveals the true character or worth of something. <from a former test for gold that used nitric acid>

ac·knowl·edge (ak nol′ij) *v* **ac·knowl·edged, ac·knowl·edg·ing 1** admit: *I acknowledge that I have certain faults.* **2** recognize that a person or thing has a certain status: *The boys acknowledged him to be the best player on the team. Other nations refused to acknowledge the government set up by the rebel forces.* **3** express appreciation for or to: *The contributions of various experts are acknowledged in the introduction.* **4** say or show that one has received or noticed something: *She didn't even acknowledge my letter. He acknowledged her greeting with a nod of his head.* <Old English *on-* + *cnawan* know> **ac·knowl′edg·ment** or **ac·knowl′edge·ment** *n.*

ac·me (ak′mē) *n* the highest point: *the acme of his career.* <Greek *akme*>

ac·ne (ak′nē) *n* a skin condition characterized by red pimples, especially on the face. <Latin, from misspelling of Greek *akme* point>

ac·o·lyte (ak′ə līt′) *n* **1** a follower or assistant. **2** a person who helps a priest in certain religious ceremonies. <Old French *acolyt*, from Greek *akolouthos* follower>

a·corn (ā′kôrn) *n* the nut of an oak tree. <Old English *æcern*>

a bat	e bed	i bid	o pot	u cup	th **thin**
ā cake	ē me	ī bite	ō go	ū rude	TH **then**
ä bar	ə about	ər over	ô for	ů put	zh measure

acorn squash *n* a dark green winter squash shaped like an acorn.

a·cous·tic (ə kū′stik) *adj* **1** not using or needing electronic amplification in a musical instrument: *an acoustic guitar.* **2** designed either to reflect or to absorb sound so as to enhance hearing: *acoustic tile for soundproofing. An acoustic baffle has been installed in the concert hall.* **3** to do with ACOUSTICS (def. 2): *acoustic energy, an acoustic stimulus.* **4** activated or detonated by sound waves: *an acoustic mine.* <French *acoustique,* from Greek *akouein* hear> **a·cous′ti·cal·ly** *adv.*

a·cous·tics (ə kū′stiks) *n* **1** (*with plural verb*) the qualities of a room or building that determine how well sounds can be heard in it: *We enjoy singing in the auditorium because the acoustics are so good.* **2** (*with singular verb*) the scientific study of sound: *Acoustics is often concerned with the effects of noise on people.*

ac·quaint (ə kwānt′) *v* make familiar with or aware of something: *They gave us a tour to acquaint us with the neighbourhood. Let me acquaint you with the facts.* <Old French *acointier,* from Latin *ad-* to + *cognoscere* come to know>
be acquainted with, know personally: *He is acquainted with my mother.*

ac·quaint·ance (ə kwān′təns) *n* **1** a person one knows, but who is not a close friend. **2** personal knowledge or experience of a subject: *I have some acquaintance with woodworking.* **ac·quaint′ance·ship** *n.*
make the acquaintance of, get to know: *I made her acquaintance at art camp three years ago.*

acquaintance rape *n* rape by a person whom the victim knows.

ac·qui·esce (ak′wē es′) *v* **ac·qui·esced, ac·qui·esc·ing** accept, agree, or participate in something by not speaking out against it: *We acquiesced in their plan because we could not think of a better one.* <French, from Latin *ad-* to + *quiescere* to agree> **ac′qui·es′cence** *n.*
ac′qui·es′cent *adj.*

ac·quire (ə kwīr′) *v* **ac·quired, ac·quir·ing** get as one's own, either by effort or by receiving: *to acquire a skill. He had acquired a car by the time he was 18.* <Old French *acquerre,* from Latin *ad-* to + *quaerere* seek>

Acquired Immune Deficiency Syndrome AIDS.

ac·qui·si·tion (ak′wə zish′ən) *n* **1** the act or process of acquiring: *Language acquisition starts from earliest infancy.* **2** something acquired: *She showed us her latest acquisition: a motorcycle.*

ac·quis·i·tive (ə kwiz′ə tiv) *adj* fond of getting or acquiring things. **ac·quis′i·tive·ly** *adv.*
ac·quis′i·tive·ness *n.*

ac·quit (ə kwit′) *v* **ac·quit·ted, ac·quit·ting** declare a person not guilty of an offence. <Old French *acquitter,* from Latin *ad-* + *quitare* set free> **ac·quit′tal** *n.*
acquit yourself, do in a specific way: *The soldiers acquitted themselves well in battle.*

a·cre (ā′kər) *n* a nonmetric unit of area equal to about 4000 m^2, used for measuring land. <Old English *æcer* field>

a·cre·age (ā′kə rij) *n* **1** the number of acres: *What is the acreage of the farm?* **2** land or a piece of land measured in acres: *We have most of our acreage in barley this year. She bought a small acreage north of town.*

ac·rid (ak′rid) *adj* **1** with a sharp, bitter, or stinging taste or smell: *acrid fumes.* **2** angry and bitter: *an acrid comment.* <Latin *acris* acid, sharp> **a·crid′i·ty** *n.* **ac′rid·ly** *adv.*

ac·ri·mo·ny (ak′rə mō′nē) *n* bitterness or hostility. <Latin *acris* acid> **ac′ri·mo′ni·ous** *adj.*

Acro is one of the three competitive disciplines in freestyle skiing. (The other two are *aerials* and *moguls.*)

In acro, competitors perform a choreographed routine to music, on a smooth, even slope. Skiers must link their various spins and somersaults using steps, and all must be done in harmony with the music.

ac·ro (ak′ro) *Skiing n* in full, **acrobatic** one of the disciplines in **freestyle skiing**. Formerly called **ballet**.

ac·ro·bat (ak′rə bat′) *n* a person who entertains by performing gymnastic feats, such as on a trapeze or tightrope. <French *acrobate,* from Greek *akron* tip(toe) + *bainen* walk>

ac·ro·bat·ics (ak′rə bat′iks) *n* **1** (*with singular verb*) gymnastic feats, such as swinging on a trapeze or walking on a tightrope. *Acrobatics is my hobby.* **2** (*with plural verb*) manoeuvres that are skilful and complex: *Mental acrobatics are needed to win this game.* **ac′ro·bat′ic** *adj.*

ac·ro·nym (ak′rə nim′) *n* a word formed from the first letters or syllables of other words, such as *UNESCO* (United Nations Educational, Scientific, and Cultural Organization) or WYSIWYG (what you see is what you get). See ABBREVIATION for confusable.<Greek *akron* tip + *onyma* name>

ac·ro·pho·bi·a (ak′rə fō′bē ə) *n* an extreme, irrational fear of high places. <Greek *akron* tip (summit) + *phobia*> **ac′ro·pho′bic** *adj, n.*

a·crop·o·lis (ə krop′ə lis) *n* **1** the fortified hill in the centre of an ancient Greek city that was its religious centre as well as its fortress. **2 the Acropolis** the fortified hill of Athens. <Greek *akron* tip (summit) + *polis* city>

a·cross (ə kros′) *prep* **1** from one side to the other of: *a bridge across a river. She drew a line across the page.* **2** on the other side of: *Europe is across the sea.* **3** on top of and at an angle to: *He laid the boards down one across the other.*
adv **1** from one side to the other: *What is the distance across?* **2** on the other side: *They live across from us.*
across country, through fields and wooded areas: *We followed the road at first, and then struck out across country.*

across–the–board (ə′kros′ ᴛʜə bȯrd′) *adj* affecting all members of a group: *across-the-board salary increases.*

a·cros·tic (ə′kros′tik) *n* a composition in verse or an arrangement of words in which the first, last, or certain other letters in each line, taken in order, spell a word or phrase.
adj to do with such an arrangement: *an acrostic poem.* <Greek *akron* end + *stichos* line of verse>

a·cryl·ic (ə kril′ik) *n* **1** in full, **acrylic resin** a tough, transparent plastic. **2** a paint with a base of acrylic resin. **3** a painting done with such paints: *We bought one of her acrylics.* **4** in full, **acrylic fibre** a strong, lightweight textile fibre made from an acrylic acid.
adj to do with acrylic resin or acrylic fibre. <*acrolein* a liquid used in making acrylic resin>

act (akt) *n* **1** something done: *Stopping to help her was an act of kindness.* **2** the process of doing: *He was caught in the act of stealing.* **3** a main division of a play or opera: *Most modern plays have three acts.* **4** one of several performances on a program: *Your act follows the juggler's.* **5** pretended behaviour, especially to impress or attract attention: *He's not sick; that's just an act.* **6** a law or decree.
v **1** do something: *The firefighters acted promptly and saved the burning house.* **2** behave in a specific way: *Stop acting like a fool.* **3** (*with* ***on***) have an effect: *Yeast acts on dough and makes it rise.* **4** perform in a play, movie, TV show, or other entertainment: *Kiefer Sutherland acts the part of the hero.* **5** behave insincerely, as if playing a role: *You can stop acting; I see right through you. She acted an excitement she did not feel.* **6** (*with* ***as***) serve: *The foam acts as insulation.* <Old French *acte*, from Latin *agere* do>
act for, take the place of: *While the principal was gone, the assistant principal acted for her.*
act on, follow or obey: *I'll act on your suggestion.*
act out, represent in actions or gestures: *Charades is a game where people act out titles or sayings.*
act up, a behave badly: *He was acting up in order to get attention.* **b** be troublesome: *The knee I hurt last summer is acting up again.*
clean up your act, *Informal* improve your behaviour.
get into the act, *Informal* get involved or participate: *At first only a few towns tried recycling, but then we all got into the act.*
get your act together, *Informal* get organized: *If you'd get your act together sooner, you wouldn't have to rush every project.*

act·ing (ak′ting) *adj* temporarily taking another's place and doing his or her duties: *While the principal was sick, one of the teachers became the acting principal.*
n the art or profession of performing in movies, plays, or other entertainments: *She has taken up acting.*

ac·tin·ide series (ak′tə nīd′) *n* a group of elements, including uranium and plutonium, that are naturally radioactive. <See ACTINISM.>

ac·tin·ism (ak′tə niz′əm) *n* a property in light that causes chemical changes. <Greek *aktinos* ray> **ac·tin′ic** *adj.*

ac·tin·i·um (ak tin′ē əm) *n* a radioactive element resembling radium, found in pitchblende after uranium has been extracted. *Symbol* **Ac** <See ACTINISM.>

ac·tion (ak′shən) *n* **1** the process of doing something: *The firefighters' quick action saved the building.* **2 actions** *pl* **a** behaviour: *You will be judged by your actions.* **b** body movements intended to represent ideas or words: *Do you know the actions to that song?* **3** *Informal* exciting or important activities: *Let's go where the action is.* **4** the moving parts of a machine, or the way a thing moves or works: *the action of a pendulum. The action of a watch fits into a very small space.* **5** the effect of one thing on another: *the action of wind on a ship's sails.* **6** armed combat: *Her grandfather was wounded in action.* **7** the events forming a story or plot: *Most of the action takes place in Montréal.* **8** a lawsuit. <Old French, from Latin *agere* do>
in action, doing characteristic work: *You should see this teacher in action.*
man (or **woman** or **person**) **of action,** someone who behaves with energy or initiative.
out of action, not working: *The front yard looks untidy because the lawn mower is out of action.*
plan of action, a plan for actively doing something: *I have two tests this week, so I need a plan of action.*
take action, a begin to act: *The government took action to prevent an epidemic.* **b** start a lawsuit.

ac·tion·a·ble (ak′shə nə bəl) *adj* giving grounds for a lawsuit.

action plan *n* a detailed description of the steps required to achieve a certain goal or solve a certain problem: *If we want to have a School Fair, we need an action plan.*

ac·ti·vate (ak′tə vāt′) *v* **ac·ti·vat·ed, ac·ti·vat·ing 1** put into use or operation: *to activate someone's file. When leaving, key in your code to activate the security system.* **2** *Physics* make radioactive. **3** *Chemistry* speed up a reaction in. **4** purify sewage by treating it with air and bacteria. **ac′ti·va′tion** *n.*

activated carbon *n* carbon whose surface attracts and retains molecules of other substances, used to purify gases and liquids and to recover solvents.

ac·tive (ak′tiv) *adj* **1** acting or capable of acting: *an active volcano.* **2** lively or busy: *an active stock market, an active child.* **3** taking initiative: *He took an active part in organizing the drama club.* **4** in current use: *an active file. Is the computer program active?* **5** *Grammar* to do with the verb form that shows the subject of a verb is performing the action. In *My brother broke the window*, the verb *broke* is in the **active voice**. In *The window was broken by my brother*, the verb *was broken* is in the **passive voice**. Compare PASSIVE. <Old French *actif*, from Latin *agere* do> **ac′tive·ly** *adv.*

a bat	e bed	i bid	o pot	u cup	th thin
ā cake	ē me	ī bite	ō go	ū rude	ᴛʜ then
ȧ bar	ə about	ər over	ȯ for	u̇ put	zh measure

ac·tiv·ism (ak′tə viz′əm) *n* direct action or confrontation in promoting one's views or aims on a social or political issue. **ac′tiv·ist** *n.*

ac·tiv·i·ty (ak tiv′ə tē) *n, pl* **ac·tiv·i·ties** **1** doing things or being busy: *physical activity, mental activity.* **2** a particular action: *the activities of enemy spies.* **3** something planned for people to do or take part in: *The program includes activities for the kids.*

SYNONYMS

Activity is a neutral word that suggests movement: *There was activity at the campground.*

Bustle indicates energetic, noisy movement: *He loved the bustle of the city.*

Commotion implies excited movement: *The movie star's arrival caused a commotion in the crowd.*

act of God *n* (*usually in the context of insurance*) a natural disaster or other event that could not be prevented or foreseen by humans.

Act of Union *n* an act passed by the British Parliament in 1840, uniting Upper and Lower Canada.

ac·tor (ak′tər) *n* **1** a person who acts in plays, movies, or on TV or radio. **2** a person who does something.
bad actor, *Informal* a person, animal, or thing that is always misbehaving.

✱ **ACTRA Award** (ak′trə) *n* an award presented annually by the Association of Canadian Television and Radio Artists, recognizing excellence in work done for TV and radio.

ac·tress (ak′tris) *n* a female actor.

ac·tu·al (ak′chū əl) *adj* **1** existing as a fact: *What she told us was not a dream but an actual happening.* **2** existing now: *the actual state of affairs.* <Old French, from Latin *actus* a doing> **ac′tu·al′i·ty** *n.*

ac·tu·al·ize (ak′chū ə līz′) *v* **ac·tu·al·ized, ac·tu·al·iz·ing** represent something realistically. **ac′tu·al·i·za′tion** *n.*

ac·tu·al·ly (ak′chū ə lē), (ak′chə lē), *or* (ak′shə lē) *adv* in fact: *Are you actually going to the party or just thinking of going?*

ac·tu·ar·y (ak′chū er′ē) *n, pl* **ac·tu·ar·ies** a person who uses statistical information to calculate risks, rates, and premiums for insurance companies. <Latin *actuarius* a person who keeps accounts, from *agere* to do> **ac′tu·ar′i·al** *adj.*

ac·tu·ate (ak′chū āt′) *v* **ac·tu·at·ed, ac·tu·at·ing** **1** motivate: *She was actuated by love for her mother.* **2** put into action: *The pump is actuated by a belt driven by electricity.* <Latin *actuare*, from *actus* action>

a·cu·i·ty (ə kyū′ə tē) *n* sharpness; keenness; acuteness: *mental acuity.* <Latin *acuere* sharpen, from *acus* needle>

a·cu·men (ak′yə mən) *n* sharpness and quickness in seeing and understanding what needs to be done. <Latin *acuere* sharpen>

ac·u·pres·sure (ak′yə presh′ər) *n* a treatment of applying pressure to particular points on the body. Compare ACUPUNCTURE. <blend of *acupuncture* + *pressure*>

ac·u·punc·ture (ak′yə pungk′chər) *n* a method of relieving pain and treating disease by inserting needles into the body at specific points. <Latin *acu-* with a needle + *puncture*>

a·cute (ə kyūt′) *adj* **1** keen, sharp, or highly perceptive: *an acute sense of smell, acute powers of observation.* **2** intense and severe: *an acute shortage of water, acute pain.* **3** of a disease, brief and severe; reaching a crisis within a short time. <Latin *acutus*, from *acuere* sharpen> **a·cute′ly** *adv.* **a·cute′ness** *n.*

acute accent *n* a mark [′] placed over a vowel to show pronunciation.

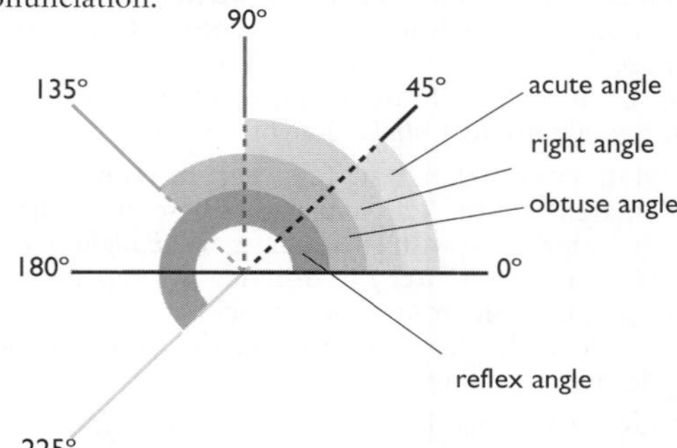

acute angle *Mathematics n* an angle less than 90°.

ad (ad) *Informal n* advertisement.

ad– *prefix* to; toward: *admit, adapt.* <Latin>

AD an abbreviation, placed before dates, of the Latin words *anno Domini*, meaning "in the year of Our Lord," that is, after the birth of Christ: *The Roman empire fell in* AD *410.* Compare CE.

ad·age (ad′ij) *n* a wise saying or proverb: *Remember the old adage, "Haste makes waste."* <French, from Latin *adagium*>

a·da·gio (ə dä′jō) *Music adv, adj* at a slow tempo.
n a passage or composition with a slow tempo, or the tempo itself. <Italian *ad agio* at ease>

ad·a·mant (ad′ə mənt) *adj* firm; unshakeable: *an adamant refusal. She was adamant that we were to stay until everything was finished.* <Old French *adamaunt* the hardest stone, from Greek *a-* not + *daman* conquer> **ad′a·man′tine** (ad′ə man′tēn) *adj.*

Adam's apple (ad′əmz) *n* the lump in the front of the throat, formed by the thyroid cartilage. <from a story of the forbidden apple sticking in the throat of the Biblical character Adam>

a·dapt (ə dapt′) *v* **1** change so as to fit in with certain conditions: *Good writers adapt their language to the age and interests of their readers. The cactus is adapted to the desert environment. She has adapted well to the new school.* **2** modify or alter something for a different use: *to adapt a barn for use as a garage. Her novel has been adapted as a movie.* <Latin *ad-* to + *aptare* fit> **a·dap′tive** *adj.*

a·dapt·a·ble (ə dap′tə bəl) *adj* changing easily or willingly to fit different conditions or requirements: *If you want to work here you have to be adaptable.* **a·dapt′a·bil′i·ty** *n.*

ad·ap·ta·tion (ad′ap tā′shən) *n* **1** something made by adapting another thing: *This movie is an adaptation of a* *novel.* **2** *Biology* a change in the structure, form, or habits of an organism to fit different conditions: *Wings are adaptations of the upper limbs for flight.* **3** the act or process of adapting.

a·dapt·er (ə dap′tər) *n* a device used to adapt one thing to another, such as to fit together parts that do not match, or change the function of a machine: *We will need an adapter to fit this nozzle onto the larger hose. Get an adapter for your computer before you use this scanner.* Also, **adaptor**.

add (ad) *v* **1** put one thing with another or others: *Add another stone to the pile. Add 8 and 2 and you have 10.* **2** build onto an existing structure: *They're adding onto their house.* **3** say further: *She said goodbye, adding that she had enjoyed her visit.* <Latin *ad-* to + *dare* put> **add′er** *n.*
add in, include in a total.
add to, increase: *The fine weather added to our pleasure.*
add up, a come or bring to a total: *Can you add up these figures for me? They add up to 973.* **b** make sense: *His story doesn't add up.*
add up to, *Informal* amount to: *Despite much publicity and a huge budget, the movie didn't add up to much.*

ADD *n* in full, **attention deficit disorder** a disorder that makes it difficult for a person to concentrate or sit still, usually most evident in childhood. Also, **ADHD, attention deficit hyperactivity disorder**.

ad·dend (ad′end) *Mathematics n* a number or quantity to be added to another. <See ADDENDUM.>

ad·den·dum (ə den′dəm) *n, pl* **ad·den·da** (ə den′də) a thing added or to be added, especially to something written: *a brief addendum to a report.* <Latin = thing to be added>

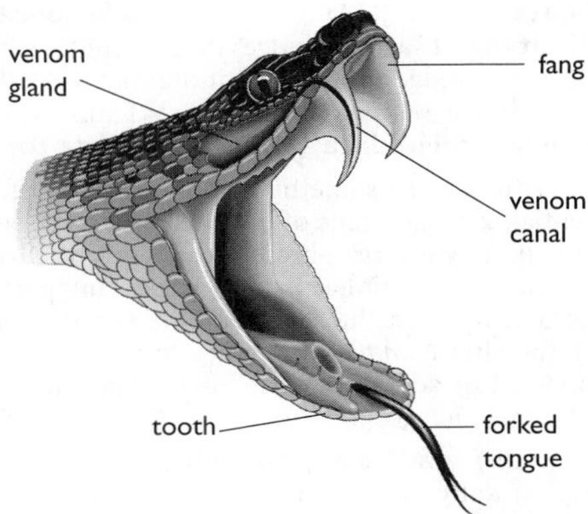

A snake bite by an **adder** puts venom into the blood system, and this interferes with the functioning of the blood and major organs. While painful, the adder's venom is not as deadly as that of other poisonous snakes, such as some kinds of rattlesnakes.

ad·der (ad′ər) *n* **1** a small poisonous snake of Europe and northern Asia that has a black zigzag band along its back. **2** a similar or related snake, such as the puff adder. <Old English *næder*>

ad·dict (ad′ikt) *for n,* (ə dikt′) *for v. n* a person who is dependent on a habit or substance, and cannot quit without feeling bad: *a drug addict, an Internet addict.*
v cause to become dependent on a habit: *This computer game has addicted half the adolescent population.* <Latin *addictus* given over, from *ad-* to + *dicere* agree> **ad·dict′ed** *adj.* **ad·dic′tion** *n.*

ad·dic·tive (ə dik′tiv) *adj* tending to cause addiction: *Nicotine is addictive.* **ad·dic′tive·ness** *n.*

ad·di·tion (ə dish′ən) *n* **1** the act or process of adding: *It's a matter of simple addition: 2 + 3 = 5.* **2** a thing or person added or to be added: *to build an addition to a house. You are the newest addition to our group.*
in addition (to), besides; as well (as): *In addition to her nursing job, she works as a tutor. We have firewood; in addition, we need some kindling.*

ad·di·tion·al (ə dish′ə nəl) *adj* added or extra: *We bought an additional loaf of bread.* **ad·di′tion·al·ly** *adv.*

ad·di·tive (ad′ə tiv) *n* a substance added in small amounts to produce a desirable colour, enhance efficiency, or act as a preservative: *food additives, additives in gasoline.*

additive inverse *Mathematics n* the number which, when added to a given number, will make a total of zero. The additive inverse of 3 is –3. Compare MULTIPLICATIVE INVERSE.

additive theory *Physics n* in full, **additive colour theory** the explanation that colours of light are formed by adding together other colours of light. Adding together the three primary colours of light (red, blue, and green) makes white light. Compare SUBTRACTIVE THEORY. See also PRIMARY COLOUR.

ad·dle (ad′əl) *v* **ad·dled, ad·dling** muddle or confuse: *The wine has addled her.* <Middle English *addle* rotten>

add–on (ad′on′) *n* an extra part or component, often added as an accessory: *The modem is an add-on.*
adj to do with such a part.

ad·dress (ə dres′); *also, for n 1-3,* (ad′res) *n* **1** the place at which a person or group may be found or reached: *Send it to her business address.* **2** the writing on an envelope or package showing where it is to be sent: *The address on this letter is incomplete.* **3** *Computers* a code label representing the exact location of a piece of data stored in memory. **4** speech or writing directed to someone: *the valedictory address at a graduation.*
v **1** speak directly to someone: *I'm addressing these remarks to all of you. He addressed the nation on the subject of the economy.* **2** use titles or other forms in speaking or writing to: *How do you address a mayor?* **3** write on a letter, e-mail message, etc. the information showing where it is to be sent. **4** deal with: *to address the problem at hand.* **5** (*used reflexively*) apply or direct one's energy: *She addressed herself to the task of doing her homework.* <Old French, from Latin *ad-* to + *directare* direct>
of no fixed address, with no permanent residence.

ad·dress·ee (ə dres ē′) *or* (ad′res ē′) *n* the person to whom something is addressed.

a bat	e bed	i bid	o pot	u cup	th **thin**
ā cake	ē me	ī bite	ō go	ū rude	ᴛʜ **then**
ä bar	ə about	ər over	ô for	ů put	zh measure

ad·duce (ə dyūs′) *or* (ə dūs′) *v* **ad·duced, ad·duc·ing** give as a reason, proof, or example: *The author has adduced some statistical data in support of her argument.* <Latin *ad-* to + *ducere* lead>

ad·e·nine (ad′ə nēn′) *or* (ad′ə nin) *n* one of the five nitrogen-containing molecules that form part of DNA and RNA and that encode genetic characteristics.

ad·e·noids (ad′noidz′) *pln* normal glandular tissue in the upper throat behind the nose that usually shrinks and disappears in childhood, but may swell and hinder breathing and speaking. <Greek *aden* gland>

ad·ept (ə dept′) *for adj,* (ad′ept) *or* (ə dept′) *for n. adj* highly skilled: *He's very adept at cooking.*
n an expert: *He is an adept when it comes to crosswords.* <Latin *adeptus,* from *adipisci* reach (a certain level)> **a·dept′ly** *adv.* **a·dept′ness** *n.*

ad·e·quate (ad′ə kwit) *adj* as much or as good as needed: *an adequate supply of food. He is not adequate for the job.* <Latin *adaequare* be equal> **ad′e·qua·cy** *n.* **ad′e·quate·ly** *adv.*

ad·han (ə dän′) *Islam n* the call to prayer, uttered by a muezzin, immediately before each of the five daily prayers. <Arabic>

ADHD See ADD.

ad·here (ad hēr′) *v* **ad·hered, ad·her·ing 1** stick or remain attached: *Mud adheres to shoes.* **2** be or remain committed: *to adhere to a belief. He adhered to his plan in spite of opposition.* <Latin *ad-* to + *haerere* to stick> **ad·her′ence** *n.*

ad·her·ent (ad hē′rənt) *n* a faithful supporter or follower: *a general meeting of members and adherents.*

ad·he·sion (ad hē′zhən) *n* **1** the act or fact of being stuck together. **2** *Physics* attraction between the molecules of different substances. Compare COHESION (def. 2).

ad·he·sive (ad hē′siv) *adj* causing things to stick together: *adhesive tape.*
n a substance, such as glue or rubber cement, used to stick things together. <Latin *ad-* to + *haerere* stick>

ad hoc (ad′ hok′) *adj, adv* for a specific purpose only: *an ad hoc committee (adj). If you don't establish a policy, you have to decide each case ad hoc (adv).* <Latin = for this>

ad hom·i·nem (ad′ hom′ə nem′) *adj, adv* attacking a person's character rather than replying to his or her arguments. Example: *You're just saying that because you're jealous.* <Latin = to the man>

a·dieu (ə dyū′) *Poetic interj, n, pl* **a·dieus** or **a·dieux** (ə dyūz′) goodbye. <Old French *à Dieu* to God>

ad in·fi·ni·tum (ad′ in′fə nī′təm) *adv* without end. <Latin>

ad·i·pose (ad′ə pōs′) *adj* used for the storage of fat in body tissues: *adipose tissue.* <Latin *adeps* fat>

ad·ja·cent (ə jā′sənt) *adj* next to or adjoining: *The house adjacent to ours has been sold.* <Latin *ad-* near + *jacere* lie> **ad·ja′cen·cy** *n.* **ad·ja′cent·ly** *adv.*

adjacent angles *Mathematics n* two angles with the same vertex and sharing a line for one of their sides.

ad·jec·tive (aj′ik tiv) *n* a word, such as *green, strong, sad,* or *important,* that limits or adds to the meaning of a noun. <Old French *adjectif,* from Latin *adjicere* add to> **ad′jec·ti′val** (aj′ik tī′vəl) *adj.* **ad′jec·ti′val·ly** *adv.*

GRAMMAR AND USAGE

Adjectives are describing words that can tell about size (*huge, tiny*), shape (*triangular, round*), colour (*red, turquoise*), and many other characteristics.

Avoid vague, overused adjectives such as *neat, good, nice,* and *bad.* For example, you might replace *nice* with *attractive, charming, elegant, friendly, thoughtful, pleasant, helpful,* or *comfortable.*

A thesaurus can help you find more specific or colourful adjectives.

ad·join (ə join′) *v* be next to or joined with: *Canada adjoins the United States. These two countries adjoin.* <Old French *ajoindre,* from Latin *ad-* to + *jungere* join> **ad·join′ing** *adj.*

ad·journ (ə jərn′) *v* **1** end a meeting, discussion, law court session, or game, often with the intention of resuming it later: *The meeting was adjourned at 10 p.m. We adjourned for lunch.* **2** move to another place for a while: *After supper, we adjourned to the living room.* <Old French *a jorn* (move) to a certain day, from Latin *diurnus* daily> **ad·journ′ment** *n.*

ad·ju·di·cate (ə jū′də kāt′) *v* **ad·ju·di·cat·ed, ad·ju·di·cat·ing 1** act as judge in a dispute between others. **2** act as judge in a competition: *She was asked to adjudicate at the skating competition.* <Latin *ad-* to + *judicare* judge> **ad·ju′di·ca′tion** *n.* **ad·ju′di·ca′tor** *n.*

ad·junct (aj′ungkt) *n* **1** something added that is useful but not essential. **2** an assistant of a more important person. **3** *Grammar* a word or phrase, typically an adverbial phrase, that is an optional or less important part of a sentence. Example: In the sentence *I spotted the book on the shelf,* the phrase *on the shelf* is an adjunct.
adj connected or added to something. <Latin *adjunctus,* from *ad-* + to + *jungere* to join>

ad·jure (ə jūr′) *v* **ad·jured, ad·jur·ing** urge or request someone earnestly or solemnly to do something: *I adjure you to speak the truth.* <Latin *ad-* to + *jurare* swear> **ad′ju·ra′tion** *n.*

ad·just (ə just′) *v* **1** set or alter something so that it achieves the correct fit, appearance, or result: *to adjust a seat to the correct height for a child.* **2** set machinery or controls to work as required: *to adjust a clock to the correct time. She adjusted the brakes on her bicycle.* **3** adapt: *He soon adjusted to his new job. Let your eyes adjust to the dim light.* **4** decide the amount of a settlement of some kind: *to adjust an insurance claim.* <Old French *ajuster,* from Latin ad- to + *justus* right> **ad·just′a·ble** *adj.* **ad·just′er** *n.* **ad·just′ment** *n.*

ad·ju·tant (aj′ə tənt) *n* **1** *Military* an officer who assists a commanding officer. **2** a helper or assistant. <Latin *ad-* to + *juvare* assist>

ad lib (ad′lib′) *adj, adv* spoken or performed without preparation: *Was the speech ad lib (adj) ? an ad-lib speech (adj). He made the speech ad lib (adv).*
n something spoken or performed in this way: *His speech was full of ad libs.*
v **ad lib, ad libbed, ad lib·bing** speak or perform in public without any preparation: *She had ad libbed some of her lines in the play.* <Latin *ad libitum* at pleasure>

ad·min (ad min′) *Informal n, adj* administration; administrative.

ad·min·is·ter (ad min′ə stər) *v* **1** manage the workings of a business, government department, or organization: *A board administers the schools in an area. In former times, the head servant would administer a household.* **2** give or apply: *to administer medicine, to administer justice.* **3** cause someone to undergo: *to administer an oath, to administer an exam.* <Old French, from Latin *ad-* to + *minister* servant, i.e., civil servant>

ad·min·is·tra·tion (ad min′ə strā′shən) *n* **1** the work of managing the workings of a business or organization. **2** the group of officials doing this: *The university administration has improved enrolment procedures. She was part of the Trudeau administration.* **3** *especially US* the period during which a certain government is in power: *This policy was in force throughout the Kennedy administration.* **4** the act of giving out or applying: *the administration of aid to refugees, the administration of justice.* **ad·min′i·stra′tive** *adj.*

ad·min·is·tra·tor (ad min′ə strā′tər) *n* a person who manages or helps to manage a business or institution.

ad·mi·ra·ble (ad′mə rə bəl) *adj* commanding respect and approval. **ad′mi·ra·bly** *adv.*

ad·mi·ral (ad′mə rəl) *n* **1** the commander of a naval fleet or squadron. **2** 🍁 *Newfoundland* in former times, the leader of a fishing fleet. **3** a butterfly that has dark wings with red and white markings. <Old French, from Arabic *amir* commander>

ad·mi·ral·ty (ad′mə rəl tē) *n, pl* **ad·mi·ral·ties** a law, court, or other authority dealing with matters related to the sea and ships.

ad·mi·ra·tion (ad′mə rā′shən) *n* **1** the feeling of wonder, pleasure, and approval. **2** a person who or thing that is admired: *Her strength was the admiration of all her friends.*

ad·mire (ad mīr′) *v* **ad·mired, ad·mir·ing** **1** think of or speak about with wonder, approval, and pleasure: *to admire a hero, to admire a beautiful view. I overheard them admiring the paintings.* **2** like and esteem very much, often romantically. <Latin *ad-* at + *mirari* wonder>
ad·mir′er *n.* **ad·mir′ing·ly** *adv.*

ad·mis·si·ble (ad mis′ə bəl) *adj* allowed, or recognized as valid: *That is hardly an admissible excuse. Abbreviations are not admissible in Scrabble.* **ad·mis′si·bil′i·ty** *n.* **ad·mis′si·bly** *adv.*

ad·mis·sion (ad mish′ən) *n* **1** the right to enter: *This password gives you admission to the castle.* **2** a price paid for the right to enter, especially to enter a public event or show: *We skipped the fall fair; the admission was too expensive.* **3** the act or fact of admitting: *an admission of guilt, the admission of immigrants into a country.* <See ADMIT.>

ad·mit (ad mit′) *v* **ad·mit·ted, ad·mit·ting** **1** say that something damaging or embarrassing is true: *I admit my mistake.* **2** accept as valid: *to admit evidence in a court of law.* **3** allow to enter; let in: *Windows admit light and air to the room. This ticket admits one person to the show.* <Latin *ad-* to + *mittere* allow to go>
admit of, be capable of: *His answer admits of no reply.*

ad·mit·tance (ad mit′əns) *n* permission to enter: *The sign on the door says "No Admittance."*

ad·mit·ted·ly (ad mit′id lē) *adv* indicating that something cannot be denied: *Admittedly, I was wrong.*

ad·mix·ture (ad miks′chər) *n* the act or product of mixing, especially the mixture of a minor ingredient with something else. <Latin *ad-* to + *mixture*>

ad·mon·ish (ad mon′ish) *v* **1** warn or criticize firmly, with a view to helping the person improve: *The teacher admonished her for her carelessness.* **2** urge strongly: *The officer admonished us not to drive too fast.* <Old French, from Latin *ad-* to + *monere* warn> **ad′mo·ni′tion** *n.* **ad·mon′i·to′ry** *adj.*

SYNONYMS

Admonish suggests that the speaker has some authority, and it is most often used in formal situations: *The judge admonished the lawyer for delaying the trial.*

Criticize means "find fault with": *She criticized her friend's bad temper.*

Warn is a more neutral word: *The children were warned to stay close to home.*

ad nauseam (ad noz′ē əm) *adv* to a disgusting or sickening extent: *We could argue about this ad nauseam; let's not.* <Latin = to sickness>

a·do (ə dū′) *n* fuss or trouble: *The family made much ado about the party.* <Middle English *at do* to do>
without further ado, without wasting any more time.

a·do·be (ə dō′bē) *n* especially in the southwestern US and Mexico, a building material made from clay mixed with straw or grass and dried in the sun. <Spanish, from Arabic *al-tub* brick>

ad·o·les·cent (ad′ə les′ənt) *n* a person in the stage between childhood and maturity.
adj to do with this stage: *an adolescent boy, adolescent behaviour.* <Old French, from Latin *ad-* to + *alescere* grow up> **ad′o·les′cence** *n.*

a·dopt (ə dopt′) *v* **1** legally take a child of other parents to bring up as one's own. **2** take or use as one's own: *to adopt a new technique, to adopt someone's idea.* **3** accept formally: *to adopt a policy.* <French, from Latin *ad-* to + *optare* choose> **a·dop′tion** *n.*

a·dop·tive (ə dop′tiv) *adj* related by adoption: *She was very happy with her adoptive parents.*

a bat	e bed	i bid	o pot	u cup	th thin
ā cake	ē me	ī bite	ō go	ū rude	TH then
à bar	ə about	ər over	ò for	ů put	zh measure

a·dor·a·ble (ə dȯ′rə bəl) *Informal adj* delightful and charming. **a·dor′a·bly** *adv.*

a·dore (ə dȯr′) *v* **a·dored, a·dor·ing 1** deeply love and respect. **2** *Informal* like very much. **3** worship. <Old French, from Latin *ad-* to + *orare* pray> **ad′o·ra′tion** *n.* **a·dor′ing·ly** *adv.*

a·dorn (ə dȯrn′) *v* **1** add beauty or distinction to. **2** put ornaments on; decorate. <Old French, from Latin *ad-* to + *ornare* fit out> **a·dorn′ment** *n.*

a·dre·nal (ə drē′nəl) *adj* to do with two ductless glands, the **adrenal glands**, one on top of each kidney, producing adrenalin and other hormones. <Latin *ad-* to + *renal*>

a·dren·a·lin (ə dren′ə lin) *n* **1** a hormone produced by the adrenal glands to help the body cope with sudden stress or danger. **2** *Informal* the state of excitement associated with the production of this hormone: *It was pure adrenalin that kept me going.*

a·drift (ə drift′) *adv, adj* **1** drifting: *We set the little boat adrift on the pond* (*adv*). **2** without guidance or security: *She was adrift in a strange city* (*adj*).

a·droit (ə droit′) *adj* **1** expert in the use of the hands. **2** clever, resourceful, or skilled: *A good teacher is adroit at asking questions.* <French *à droit* properly>
a·droit′ly *adv.* **a·droit′ness** *n.*

ad·sorb (ad zȯrb′) *or* (ad sȯrb′) *Chemistry v* cause a gas, liquid, or dissolved substance to stick to a surface in a thin layer of molecules. <blend of Latin *ad-* to + *absorb*> **ad·sor′bent** *adj.* **ad·sorp′tion** *n.*

ad·u·late (aj′ə lāt′) *v* **ad·u·lat·ed, ad·u·lat·ing** praise too much. <Latin *adulari*> **ad′u·la′tion** *n.*
ad′u·la·to′ry *adj.*

a·dult (ə dult′) *or* (ad′ult) *adj* **1** of full size, grown-up, or mature. **2** of or for adults: *adult tastes.* **3** appealing to sexual interests: *adult videos.*
n **1** a fully grown person, animal, or plant. **2** a person who has reached an age of maturity as defined by law: *In some provinces, a person is an adult at 18.* <Latin *adultus*, from *adolescere* grow up> **a·dult′hood** *n.* **a·dult′ness** *n.*

a·dul·ter·ate (ə dul′tə rāt′) *v* **a·dul·ter·at·ed, a·dul·ter·at·ing** add inferior or impure materials to: *to adulterate milk with water.* <Latin *adulterare* to corrupt> **a·dul′ter·a′tion** *n.*

a·dul·ter·y (ə dul′tə rē) *n, pl* **a·dul·ter·ies** willing sexual intercourse between a married person and someone who is not his or her spouse: *to commit adultery.* <See ADULTERATE.> **a·dul′ter·er** *n.* **a·dul′ter·ess** *n.* **a·dul′ter·ous** *adj.*

ad·vance (ad vans′) *v* **ad·vanced, ad·vanc·ing 1** move forward: *The troops advanced. He advanced his pawn two squares.* **2** make progress: *to advance in knowledge, to advance the cause of peace.* **3** put forward as a suggestion: *to advance an opinion.* **4** make earlier: *Tuesday's meeting has been advanced to Monday.* **5** give ahead of time: *See if your mother will advance you some money on next week's allowance.* **6** lend money: *to advance a loan.*
n **1** the act, process, or amount of advancing: *The parade's advance was very slow. Great advances have been made in medicine.* **2** money or goods given before they are due or as a loan: *The publisher gave her an advance on royalties for her book.* **3 advances** *pl* actions or words meant to start up a romantic relationship or to make a proposal: *She refused his advances.*
adj **1** going ahead: *the advance guard.* **2** done or given ahead of time: *We'll give you advance notice of any price increases.* <Old French, from Latin *ab-* from + *ante* before>
in advance, a (*with* ***of***) before; ahead of. **b** ahead of time: *He paid his rent in advance.*

ad·vanced (ad vanst′) *adj* **1** ahead of most others in progress or development: *an advanced class, advanced theories in physics.* **2** far along in life: *He lived to the advanced age of ninety years.*

ad·vance·ment (ad vans′mənt) *n* **1** the act or fact of moving something forward: *the advancement of knowledge through books.* **2** promotion or progress in one's career: *There is good opportunity for advancement in this job.*

🍁 **advance poll** *n* **1** in a general election, an arrangement allowing people to vote on an earlier date if they expect to be absent from their riding on election day. **2** the votes cast in this way, or their total number.

ad·van·tage (ad van′tij) *n* **1** a favourable condition or circumstance: *Good health is always a great advantage.* **2** a better or superior position: *Her height gave her an unfair advantage over the rest of us.* **3** *Tennis* the first point scored after deuce, indicating that the player will win the game if he or she wins the next point.
v **ad·van·taged, ad·van·tag·ing** help or benefit. <Old French *avantage* being ahead, from Latin *ab-* from + *-ante* before>
take advantage of, a make good use of for yourself: *I'm taking advantage of my illness to catch up on my reading.* **b** use unfairly: *Don't take advantage of him by always asking for help.*
to advantage, with good effect: *Jewellery shows to advantage on a dark background.*
to your advantage, to your benefit or help: *It will be to your advantage to get an extra music credit.*

ad·van·ta·geous (ad′vən tā′jəs) *adj* favourable, helpful, or profitable: *The delay turned out to be advantageous; we had more time to plan.* **ad′van·ta′geous·ly** *adv.* **ad′van·ta′geous·ness** *n.*

ad·vent (ad′vent) **1** the arrival of a notable person, thing, or event: *The advent of spring was a time for festivals in ancient days.* **2 Advent** *Christianity* **a** the birth of Christ. **b** the first season of the church year, including the four Sundays before Christmas. <Latin *adventus*, from *advenire* arrive>

ad·ven·ti·tious (ad′ven tish′əs) *adj* accidentally and not as an essential part: *The romantic life of the author gives his book an adventitious interest.* <See ADVENT.>
ad′ven·ti′tious·ly *adv.* **ad′ven·ti′tious·ness** *n.*

ad·ven·ture (ad ven′chər) *n* **1** an undertaking or activity that involves unknown risks and danger: *She has had many adventures in her career as a detective.* **2** the quality of seeking or enjoying such activity: *You have no spirit of adventure!* **3** any unusual or exciting experience: *It was an adventure to be entirely on his own in a strange city.*
v **ad·ven·tured, ad·ven·tur·ing** engage in daring or exciting activities: *a summer of adventuring in Yukon*

Territory. <Old French, from Latin *advenire* happen to> **ad·ven′ture·some** *adj.* **ad·ven′tur·ous** *adj.*

ad·ven·tur·er (ad ven′chə rər) *n* a person who seeks or has adventures, or who makes a living by unusual or crafty methods rather than by regular work.

ad·verb (ad′vərb) *n* a word, such as *quickly, now, skilfully,* or *very,* that limits or adds to the meaning of a verb, or that is used to qualify adjectives and other adverbs. In *He writes well, She is unusually pretty,* and *I run quite fast,* the adverbs are *well, unusually,* and *quite.* An **adverbial phrase** usually begins with a preposition and indicates place (*in the house*), time (*in September*), or manner (*in a funny way*). <Latin *ad-* to + *verbum* verb>
ad·ver′bi·al *adj.* **ad·ver′bi·al·ly** *adv.*

GRAMMAR AND USAGE

Adverbs are describing words that usually tell how (*slowly, happily*), when (*early, daily*), where (*on, there*), or in what manner (*brightly, softly*).

Avoid overused adverbs such as *really, very,* and *pretty* (as in *pretty quiet*).

A stronger adverb can improve a sentence: *After scoring the winning goal, she grinned ~~happily~~ delightedly.*

ad·ver·sar·y (ad′vər ser′ē) *n, pl* **ad·ver·sar·ies** an enemy or opponent. <See ADVERSE.> **ad′ver·sar′i·al** *adj.*

ad·verse (ad vərs′) *or* (ad′vərs) *adj* **1** unfavourable or harmful: *adverse criticism. Dirt and disease have an adverse effect on the health of children.* **2** acting in a contrary direction: *Adverse winds hindered the ship.* <Old French, from Latin *ad-* toward + *vertere* to turn>
ad·verse′ly *adv.* **ad·verse′ness** *n.*

ad·ver·si·ty (ad vər′sə tē) *n, pl* **ad·ver·si·ties** hardship, trouble, or misfortune.

ad·ver·tise (ad′vər tīz′) *v* **ad·ver·tised, ad·ver·tis·ing** **1** give public notice, especially in the media, of an event, opportunity, new product, etc.: *to advertise a new product on TV, to distribute flyers advertising a sales event. It pays to advertise.* **2** (*with* ***for***) try to find by giving public notice: *to advertise for a job.* **3** make generally known: *You don't have to advertise all our family squabbles!* <Old French, from Latin *advertere* turn attention toward>
ad′ver·tis′er *n.*

ad·ver·tise·ment (ad′vər tīz′mənt) *or* (ad vər′tis mənt) *n* a public notice or announcement, especially one promoting a product or service for sale: *The store has an advertisement in today's paper.*

ad·ver·tis·ing (ad′vər tī′zing) *n* **1** the business of preparing, publishing, or circulating advertisements. **2** advertisements as a group: *There are pages and pages of advertising in this paper.*

ad·vice (ad vīs′) *n* an opinion offered to someone about what should be done: *Take the doctor's advice.* <Old French *avis,* from Latin *mi est visum* (*videre* = see) it seems to me>

ad·vis·a·ble (ad vī′zə bəl) *adj* recommended as wise or sensible: *It is not advisable to travel while you are sick.* **ad·vis′a·bil′i·ty** *n.* **ad·vis′a·bly** *adv.*

ad·vise (ad vīz′) *v* **ad·vised, ad·vis·ing** **1** tell someone what he or she should do: *I advised her to take the bus instead. The city council advises the mayor on matters of policy.* **2** recommend as a course of action: *He advises caution. Do as they advise.* **3** (*often with* ***of***) give notice or inform: *Did you advise them that we were leaving? We were advised of the exam schedule.* **ad·vis′er** or **ad·vi′sor** *n.*

ad·vis·ed·ly (ad vī′zid lē) *adv* after due consideration: *I use the term "lying" advisedly; a lie is exactly what it was.*

ad·vise·ment (ad vī′zmənt) *n* (*with* ***under***) careful consideration: *The lawyer took our case under advisement and promised an answer in two weeks.*

ad·vi·so·ry (ad vī′zə rē) *adj* giving or containing advice: *an advisory letter. The drama coach had an advisory role in making the movie.*
n, pl **ad·vi·so·ries** **1** a memo or other statement containing advice or notice of something: *We received a government advisory on the matter.* **2** a bulletin, especially about impending weather: *a snow advisory.*

ad·vo·ca·cy (ad′və kə sē) *n* the act of publicly supporting or defending something: *advocacy for the poor. The premier's advocacy of the tax cut guaranteed she would be re-elected.*

ad·vo·cate (ad′və kāt′) *for v,* (ad′və kit) *for n.*
v **ad·vo·cat·ed, ad·vo·cat·ing** recommend publicly: *He advocates increased funding for education.*
n **1** a person who publicly promotes a cause or policy: *She is an advocate of the four-day workweek.* **2** a lawyer. <Old French, from Latin *ad-* to + *vocare* call as a witness>

The **adze** on an ice axe allows a mountain climber to cut steps in the ice. Other useful parts of the ice axe are the *pick,* which is dug into the ice to assist in climbing, or to stop a fall, and the *spike,* used for stability and balance where the footing is not secure.

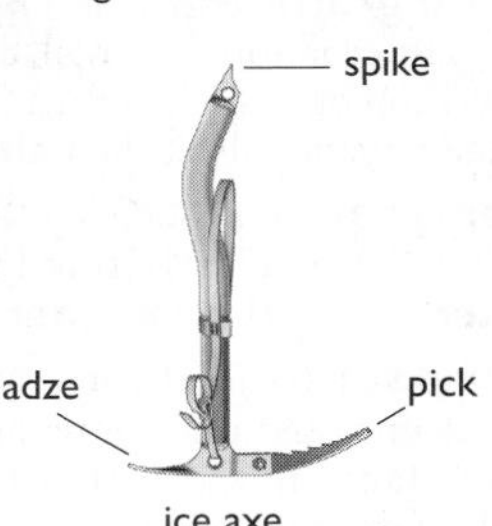

adze (adz) *n* **1** a wood-shaping tool like an axe but with a curved blade whose cutting edge is set across the end of the handle. **2** the flat cutting edge of an ice axe. <Old English *adesa*>

a bat	e bed	i bid	o pot	u cup	th thin
ā cake	ē me	ī bite	ō go	ū rude	TH then
ȧ bar	ə about	ər over	ȯ for	u̇ put	zh measure

ae·gis (ē′jis) *n* official protection or sponsorship: *under the aegis of the Children's Aid. He sought the aegis of the ambassador.* <Latin, from Greek *aigis* shield of Zeus>

ae·on (ē′on) EON.

aer·ate (er′āt) *v* **aer·at·ed, aer·at·ing** put air into a substance. <Latin, from Greek *aer* air> **aer·a′tion** *n.* **aer′a·tor** *n.*

ae·rie (ē′ri) EYRIE.

aer·i·al (er′ē əl) *n* **1** a radio or TV antenna. **2** *Skiing, Snowboarding, etc.* an acrobatic move done in the air.
adj **1** to do with the use of aircraft: *aerial bombardment, aerial photography.* **2** *Botany* growing in the air instead of in soil or water: *aerial ferns.* **3** existing or done in the air: *birds performing an aerial ballet.* <Latin, from Greek *aer* air> **aer′i·al·ly** *adv.*

aer·i·al·ist (er′ē əl ist) *n* an acrobat who performs on a high wire or trapeze.

aerial ladder *n* a long, extendible ladder often used on fire engines.

aero– *combining form* **1** air: *aerodynamics.* **2** aircraft or aviation: *aeronautics.* **3** gas: *aerosol.* <Greek *aer* air>

aer·obe (er′ōb) *n* a micro-organism that uses oxygen to break down food into energy. Compare ANAEROBE. <Greek *aer* air + *bios* life>

aer·o·bic (er ō′bik) *adj* **1** living and growing only where there is oxygen: *Some bacteria are aerobic.* **2** improving blood circulation and the body's use of oxygen by means of vigorous physical exercise.
n **aerobics** *pl* exercises designed to make people breathe more efficiently and improve blood circulation.

aer·o·dy·nam·ic (er′ō dī nam′ik) *adj* sleek and with flowing lines so as to minimize resistance from the air: *Racing cars have an aerodynamic design.*
n **aerodynamics** (*with singular verb*) the branch of physics that studies the forces exerted by gases in motion, especially with the forces acting on an aircraft as it moves through the air.

aer·o·gram (er′ə gram′) *n* a pre-stamped letter form used for international airmail, consisting of a sheet of paper for writing on, which is then folded, sealed, and addressed on the outside. Also called **air letter**.

aer·o·nau·tics (er′ə not′iks) *n* (*with singular verb*) the study or practice of travel through the air.
aer′o·nau′ti·cal *adj.* **aer′o·nau′ti·cal·ly** *adv.*

aer·o·sol (er′ə sol′) *n* a suspension of fine particles in a gas, enclosed under pressure. An **aerosol can** contains a substance mixed with a liquified gas that acts to propel the substance out of the can.

aer·o·space (er′ō spās′) *n* **1** the earth's atmosphere and space beyond it, considered as a continuous region or field. **2** the science and technology that studies aviation and space travel.

ae·ther (ē′thər) ETHER.

aes·thet·ic (es thet′ik) *adj* **1** to do with beauty and what is beautiful: *aesthetic principles, an aesthetic arrangement of furnishings in a room.* **2** sensitive to beauty: *She is the aesthetic one in the family.*
n **aesthetics** (*with singular verb*) the branch of philosophy that studies the principles of beauty. Also, **esthetic**. <Greek *aisthesthai* appreciate>
aes·thet′i·cal·ly *adv.*

aes·the·ti·cian (es′thə tish′ən) *n* **1** a beautician. **2** an expert in aesthetics.

AF or **A.F.** audio frequency.

a·far (ə fär′) *adv, n* far or far away: *to travel afar* (*adv*), *to see from afar* (*n*).

af·fa·ble (af′ə bəl) *adj* easy to talk to. <Old French, from Latin *ad-* to + *fari* speak> **af′fa·bil′i·ty** *n.* **af′fa·bly** *adv.*

af·fair (ə fer′) *n* **1** something done or to be done: *That's my affair.* **2** an action, event, or procedure: *The party was a dull affair. This machine is a complicated affair.* **3** a sexual relationship between two people not married to each other, especially one that lasts only a short while. **4 affairs** *pl* matters of interest or concern, especially business, commercial, or public matters: *affairs of state. He settled his affairs before leaving on his world trip.* <Old French *à faire* to do, from Latin *facere* do>

af·fect[1] (ə fekt′) *for v,* (əf′ekt′) *for n.*
v **1** have an effect on or influence: *The shortage of rain last year affected crops.* **2** stir the emotions of: *She wiped away tears, greatly affected by his story.*
n Psychology a feeling or emotion. <Old French, from Latin *afficere* act on>

af·fect[2] (ə fekt′) *v* **1** pretend to have or feel: *to affect an Irish accent. He affected ignorance, but in fact he knew all about it.* **2** assume or put on for effect: *She affects a certain carelessness in dress.* <French, from Latin *affectare* pretend to have>

CONFUSABLES

Affect means "influence": *Rain will affect our plans.*

Effect means "result": *That's not the effect I wanted.*

Notice that **affect** is a verb, and **effect** is usually a noun.

af·fect·ed[1] (ə fek′tid) *adj* **1** influenced or involved: *I don't care about the schedule change; my classes are not affected.* **2** moved emotionally: *He was much affected by your passionate speech.*

af·fect·ed[2] (ə fek′tid) *adj* in an unnatural, artificial, or pretentious way: *His affected manner changed as soon as the guests had gone. I don't like her; she's so affected.* **af·fect′ed·ly** *adv.*

af·fec·tion (ə fek′shən) *n* fondness or liking.

af·fec·tion·ate (ə fek′shə nit) *adj* feeling fondness, liking, or tenderness: *an affectionate greeting. My sister is very affectionate and likes to be hugged.* **af·fec′tion·ate·ly** *adv.*

af·fi·ance (ə fī′əns) *Poetic v* **af·fi·anced, af·fi·anc·ing** (*usually passive*) promise to marry: *The princess was affianced to an earl.* <Old French, from Latin *ad-* to + *fides* trust>

af·fi·da·vit (af′ə dā′vit) *Law n* a statement written down and sworn to be true: *An affidavit is usually made before a judge or notary public.* <Latin = she or he has stated on oath>

af·fil·i·ate (ə fil′ē āt′) *for v*, (ə fil′ē it) *for n.* *v* **af·fil·i·at·ed, af·fil·i·at·ing** officially attach or connect to an organization: *This relief organization is not affiliated with any church.*
n a person or organization officially attached to something: *We are boycotting that company and all its affiliates.* <Latin *affiliatus* adopted as a son, from *ad-* toward + *filius* son> **af·fil′i·a′tion** *n.*

af·fin·i·ty (ə fin′ə tē) *n, pl* **af·fin·i·ties** **1** a natural attraction or liking: *an affinity for exotic foods. Those two have a strong affinity for each other.* **2** a close relationship or connection, such as between ideas or languages. **3** *Chemistry* an attraction or force between certain particles or substances that makes them form chemical compounds. <Old French, from Latin *affinis* related>

af·firm (ə fərm′) *v* **1** declare to be true: *The prisoner affirmed his innocence.* **2** declare solemnly, as an alternative to taking an oath and with the same legal force. **3** confirm: *The higher court affirmed the lower court's decision.* <Old French, from Latin *affirmare* assert> **af′fir·ma′tion** (af′ər mā′shən) *n.*

af·firm·a·tive (ə fər′mə tiv) *adj* **1** stating that something is so: *His answer was affirmative.* **2** encouraging and supportive: *Thank you for your very affirmative letter about my work.*
n **1** a word or statement that gives assent or indicates agreement. **2 the affirmative** the side arguing in favour of a question being debated. **af·firm′a·tive·ly** *adv.*
in the affirmative, saying yes: *a reply in the affirmative.*

affirmative action *n* a policy of deliberately hiring or accepting for membership more people from groups that have tended to be discriminated against.

af·fix (ə fiks′) *for v*, (af′iks) *for n.* *v* **1** firmly attach one thing to or on another; stick: *Affix the stamp to the envelope.* **2** add a part: *Adverbs are often formed by affixing –ly to the end of an adjective.* **3** add as a stamp or other official mark: *to affix your signature to a document, to affix a government seal on a certificate.* **4** assign blame: *Don't try to affix blame for the collision; it couldn't be helped.*
n **1** *Grammar* a prefix or suffix. **2** something attached. <Old French, from Latin *affixare* fix to>

af·flict (ə flikt′) *v* cause pain to or distress: *to be afflicted with financial troubles.* <Latin *afflictus*, from *ad-* to + *fligere* to strike> **af·flic′tion** *n.*

af·flu·ent (af′lū ənt) *adj* wealthy. <Old French, from Latin *affluere* flow toward> **af′flu·ence** *n.* **af′flu·ent·ly** *adv.*

af·ford (ə fȯrd′) *v* **1** (*with* **can**, **could**, *etc.*) do or spare, especially without money difficulties or risk: *He can't afford a bike. Can you afford the time? I can't afford to take that chance.* **2** provide or supply: *Some trees afford resin. Reading affords pleasure.* <Old English *geforthian* to promote>

af·ford·a·ble (ə fȯr′də bəl) *adj* low priced or reasonably priced: *affordable housing.* **af·ford′a·bly** *adv.*

af·front (ə frunt′) *v* insult or offend: *He affronted us by shouting at us.*
n an insulting action or remark: *To be called such names is an affront.* <Old French, from Latin *ad frontem* to the face>

af·ghan (af′gan) a small blanket or large shawl, knitted or crocheted. <*Afghanistan*, where it was first made>

Af·ghan·i·stan (af gan′ə stan′) *n* a country in southwest Asia. See the APPENDIX. **Af·ghan′i** or **Af′ghan** *adj, n.*

a·fi·cio·na·do (ə fish′ə nä′dō) *n* a person who is enthusiastic about something: *an aficionado of Asian cuisine.* <Spanish *aficioner* become fond of>

a·field (ə fēld′) *adv* at a distance: *The oil companies drilled far afield.*

> **ETYMOLOGY**
>
> The prefix **a–** means "in a particular place, state, or manner." In Old English, people created new adjectives and adverbs by adding *a-* to other words. They added *a-* to *fresh* to make *afresh*, to *glow* to make *aglow*, and to *skew* to make *askew*. Many of these words have become a permanent part of Modern English. Try to spot the ones on this page that fit this pattern.

a·fire (ə fīr′) *adv, adj* on fire: *They set the house afire* (*adv*). *The students were afire with enthusiasm* (*adv*).

AFK e-mail initialism for *a*way *f*rom *k*eyboard.

a·flame (ə flām′) *adv, adj* flaming or on fire: *He set the barbecue aflame* (*adv*). *She was aflame with curiosity* (*adj*).

a·float (ə flōt′) *adv, adj* floating: *We set the toy boat afloat on the pond* (*adv*). *A rumour was afloat that our favourite teacher was retiring* (*adj*).

a·flutt·er (ə flut′ər) *adv* fluttering: *The excitement set his pigeons aflutter.*
adj in a flutter: *The people were aflutter with expectation.*

🍁 **AFN** Assembly of First Nations.

a·foot (ə fu̇t′) *adv, adj* **1** walking: *Did you travel all that way afoot* (*adv*)? **2** going on or in progress: *Preparations for dinner were afoot in the kitchen* (*adj*).

a·fore·men·tioned (ə fȯr′men′shənd) *adj* spoken or written of earlier.

a·fore·said (ə fȯr′sed′) *adj* spoken or written of earlier.

a·fore·thought (ə fȯr′thot′) *Archaic adj* premeditated.
malice aforethought deliberately planned.

a·foul (ə foul′) *adv* in conflict or difficulty with: *to run afoul of regulations.*

a·fraid (ə frād′) *adj* **1** feeling fear: *Are you afraid of the dark?* **2** (*to express polite regret*) sorry: *I'm afraid we won't be able to visit after all.* <Old French *afrayer* upset>

A–frame (ā′frām′) *n* a style of building whose roof slopes steeply, almost reaching the ground on both sides, so as to form triangular or A-shaped end walls.

a·fresh (ə fresh′) *adv* once more: *to start afresh.*

Af·ri·ca (af′rə kə) *n* the continent south of the Mediterranean Sea, bordered by the Atlantic Ocean to the west and the Indian Ocean to the east. <Latin>

a bat	e bed	i bid	o pot	u cup	th thin
ā cake	ē me	ī bite	ō go	ū rude	ᴛʜ then
ä bar	ə about	ər over	ȯ for	u̇ put	zh measure

Af·ri·can (af′rə kən) *adj* **1** to do with Africa or its inhabitants. **2** with ancestors from Africa.
n **1** a native or inhabitant of Africa. **2** a person with ancestors who came from Africa. An **African-Canadian** is a Canadian of African descent or with some African ancestors.

African violet *n* a small tropical perennial plant with fuzzy leaves and purple, pink, or white flowers, often grown as a houseplant.

Af·ri·kaans (af′rə kȧns′) *n* one of the official languages of South Africa. See the APPENDIX.
adj to do with Afrikaans or Afrikaners.

Af·ri·ka·ner (af′rə kȧ′nər) *n* a white native or inhabitant of the Republic of South Africa, especially one of Dutch descent.

af·ro or **Af·ro** (af′rō) *n* a hairstyle that consists of a mass of tight curls, such as the natural hair of many black people, clipped and given a rounded shape.

Afro– *combining form* African: *an Afro-American art form, an Afro-Asian conference.*

aft (aft) *adv, adj* at or to the back of a ship or tail of an aircraft: *Take this container aft* (*adv*). *She had the aft cabin* (*adj*). <Old English *æftan* from behind>

af·ter (af′tər) *prep* **1** next to or behind in position: *The soldiers marched in line one after another.* **2** later in time than: *after supper, the day after today.* **3** in pursuit of: *The dog ran after the rabbit. What are you after?* **4** about or concerning: *Your aunt asked after you.* **5** considering what has happened: *After what she did, who could like her?* **6** in spite of: *After all his suffering, he is still cheerful.* **7** imitating: *a fable after the manner of Aesop.* **8** with the same or related name as: *named after her cousin.*
adv **1** behind: *to follow after.* **2** later: *three hours after.*
conj later than the time that: *After he goes, we can eat.*
adj later: *In after years he regretted the mistakes made in his youth.* <Old English *æfter* further back, later>
after all, a in spite of everything that has happened or been said: *We changed our minds and decided to go after all.* **b** taking everything into account: *She's only a child, after all, so you have to expect childish behaviour. After all, does it really matter?*

af·ter·birth (af′tər bərth′) *n* the placenta and membranes expelled from the uterus after childbirth.

af·ter·burn·er (af′tər bər′nər) *n* in a jet aircraft, an auxiliary engine in which additional fuel is sprayed into the burning exhaust gases to increase thrust.

af·ter–ef·fect (af′tər i fekt′) *n* a result or effect that follows some time later or that lingers on.

af·ter·glow (af′tər glō′) *n* **1** the glow after something bright has gone, such as the glow in the sky after sunset. **2** the good feeling that lingers after a pleasant event.

af·ter·growth (af′tər grōth′) *n* a second growth or stage of growth of vegetation, especially after the first has been destroyed, as by a forest fire or logging.

af·ter·im·age (af′tər im′ij) *n* a visual sensation that persists or returns after the actual object that caused it is removed from sight: *Wherever I looked, I saw an afterimage of the candle flame I had been staring at.*

af·ter·life (af′tər līf′) *n* life or existence after death.

af·ter·math (af′tər math′) *n* a result or consequence, especially a bad one: *The aftermath of war is hunger and disease.* <*after* + Old English *maeth* a mowing>

af·ter·noon (af′tər nūn′) *n* the part of the day between noon and evening: *They arrived in the afternoon.*
adj to do with the afternoon: *an afternoon visit.*

af·ter·shave (af′tər shāv′) *n* an antiseptic and astringent liquid, usually fragrant, for applying to the face after shaving.

af·ter·shock (af′tər shok′) *n* **1** a smaller earthquake felt shortly after the main one. **2** an additional effect felt following a disaster, upset, or upheaval.

af·ter·taste (af′tər tāst′) *n* **1** a taste that remains in the mouth after eating or drinking something. **2** the feeling, usually unpleasant, that lingers after some experience.

af·ter·thought (af′tər thot′) *n* **1** a later thought or further explanation. **2** something added later and not properly integrated into the whole.

af·ter·wards (af′tər wərdz) *adv* later. Also, **afterward**.

af·ter·world (af′tər wərld′) *n* according to some belief systems, a world after death.

a·gain (ə gen′) *or* (ə gān′) *adv* **1** once more: *to try again.* **2** in addition: *The pay was good, and we made half as much again in tips.* <Old English *ongean*>
again and again, many times.
then again, on the other hand or on second thought: *We could drive; then again, it's a lovely day for a walk.*

a·gainst (ə genst′) *or* (ə gānst′) *prep* **1** in an opposite direction to: *sailing against the wind.* **2** in opposition to: *He spoke against the suggestion.* **3** so as to be touching or supported by: *leaning against the wall.* **4** in contrast to: *The mountains showed dark against the sky.* **5** in defence from or preparation for: *A fire is a protection against cold. Squirrels store up nuts against the winter.* **6** as a deduction from: *The charges were entered against the total.* <Old English *ongean* again>
up against it, *Informal* under pressure and with few or no options.

a·gape (ə gāp′) *adj* **1** gaping; with the mouth wide open in wonder or surprise: *She stood agape at the sight.* **2** wide open: *The doors were agape.* <*gape*>

a·gar (ā′gȧr), (ȧ′gər), *or* (ag′ər) *n* a substance similar to gelatin that contains **agar-agar**, extracted from seaweed and used as a thickener in foods. <Malay>

ag·ate (ag′it) *n* **1** a type of quartz with coloured stripes or clouded colours, often polished for use as a gemstone. **2** a playing marble resembling an agate. <French *agathe*, from Greek *achates*> **ag′ate·like′** *adj.*

a·ga·ve (ə gā′vē) *n* a tropical American plant with thick, spiny-edged leaves and a single tall flowering stalk. <Latin, from Greek *agauos* noble, perhaps because of the plant's height>

age (āj) *n* **1** the length of time a person has lived or a thing has existed: *He died at the age of 80.* **2** a period in life: *middle age.* **3** the latter part of life: *the wisdom of age.* **4** a period in history: *the Ice Age, the space age.* **5** *Informal* (*often plural*) a long time: *I haven't seen you for ages.*
v **aged, ag·ing** or **age·ing** **1** grow old: *He is aging rapidly.*

2 cause to seem or feel old: *Fear and worry have aged her.* **3** improve by allowing to mature: *to age wine.* <Old French, from Latin *aevum* era>

of age, old enough to have full legal rights and responsibilities.

–age *suffix* **1** the act of: *breakage.* **2** the cost of: *postage.* **3** the condition or rank of: *peerage.* **4** the home of: *orphanage.* **5** a collection or mass of: *baggage.* <Old French, from Greek>

a·ged (ā′jid) *for 1,* (ājd) *for 2, 3. adj* **1** having lived a long time: *He looks after his aged parents.* **2** of the age of: *a girl aged six.* **3** made more flavourful by keeping for a time: *aged cheese.*

age·ism (āj′iz əm) *n* prejudice based on a person's age, especially against the elderly. **age′ist** *n, adj.*

age·less (āj′lis) *adj* never growing or seeming to grow old or dated: *the ageless quality of good literature.*

a·gen·cy (ā′jən sē) *n, pl* **a·gen·cies** **1** a business firm that has the authority to act for another: *An agency rented my father's house for him.* **2** the offices of such a business: *We walked down to the agency together.* **3** an organization, often governmental, serving the public in some way. **4** action producing an effect; means: *Snow is drifted by the agency of the wind.* <See AGENT.>

a·gen·da (ə jen′də) *n* **1** a list or plan of things to be done: *What's the agenda for this meeting? Daycare funding is part of this government's agenda.* **2** a book for keeping track of assignments or appointments each day: *An agenda is issued to each student in September.* **3** a motive or objective: *You can never take him at face value; he always has an agenda.* <Latin *agendum,* from *agere* do>

a·gent (ā′jənt) *n* **1** a person or company that has the authority to act for another: *a travel agent, a real estate agent.* **2** a person who manages the activities of a writer, actor, musician, or other entertainer. **3** any person who or thing that produces an effect: *an agent of social change. Insects are agents of plant pollination.* **4** a person who obtains information for a government, often in secret: *an intelligence agent.* **5** BOT. <Latin *agentis,* from *agere* do>

✱ **agent general** *n, pl* **agents general** or **agent generals** a representative in a foreign city of a Canadian province.

agent pro·vo·ca·teur (pro vo ka tūr′) *n* a person who incites others to do something that will get them into trouble. <French>

age of consent *n* the age at which a person is legally able to give consent independently, such as to have sexual intercourse or to receive medical treatment.

age–old (āj′ ōld′) *adj* having existed for a long time: *the age-old question of the origin of the universe.*

ag·glu·ti·nate (ə glū′tə nāt′) *v* stick or be stuck together to form a mass, especially blood cells. The substance in blood that causes it to form clots is called **agglutinin.** <Latin *ad-* to + *-glutinis* glue>

ag·gran·dize (ə gran′dīz) *v* **ag·gran·dized, ag·gran·diz·ing** increase in power, wealth, or prestige: *to aggrandize oneself at the expense of others.* <French, from Latin *grandis* large>
ag·gran′dize·ment (ə gran′diz mənt) *n.*

ag·gra·vate (ag′rə vāt′) *v* **ag·gra·vat·ed, ag·gra·vat·ing** **1** make worse or more severe: *His bad temper was aggravated by his headache.* **2** *Informal* annoy, irritate, or provoke: *I was aggravated by her constant whining.* <Latin *ad-* to + *gravis* heavy (as a burden)> **ag′gra·vat′ing** *adj.* **ag′gra·vat′ing·ly** *adv.*

ag·gra·va·tion (ag′rə vā′shən) *n* **1** the act or fact of aggravating, or the condition of being aggravated: *We must try to avoid an aggravation of the crisis. The delay only added to her aggravation.* **2** something that aggravates or irritates.

ag·gre·gate (ag′rə git) *for adj or n,* (ag′rə gāt′) *for v.*
adj **1** combined into one mass or total: *The aggregate value of all the gifts was $1000.* **2** *Botany* composed of many parts or units. **3** *Geology* composed of rock fragments. **4** *Economics* indicating the total supply or demand for goods and services in an economy at one point in time.
n **1** something made by combining or joining elements: *The report was an aggregate of the viewpoints of the committee members.* **2** the total amount. **3** material such as broken stone, sand, or gravel used to make concrete.
v **ag·gre·gat·ed, ag·gre·gat·ing** form a total or mass. <Latin *ad-* to + *gregis* a flock i.e., a group> **ag′gre·gate′ly** *adv.*
in the aggregate, together or as a whole.

ag·gres·sion (ə gresh′ən) *n* **1** the act of attacking another, especially without provocation: *an aggression against a person's rights. In 1914, Germany was guilty of aggression against Belgium.* **2** the habit or tendency of attacking others: *When there is overcrowding, there is an increase in aggression.* **ag·gres′sor** *n.*

ag·gres·sive (ə gres′iv) *adj* **1** attacking or tending to attack: *Animals become aggressive when afraid.* **2** forceful or vigorous: *an aggressive advertising campaign, an aggressive treatment for cancer.* <Latin *ad-* toward + *gradi* to step> **ag·gres′sive·ly** *adv.* **ag·gres′sive·ness** *n.*

ag·grieved (ə grēvd′) *adj* **1** unjustly treated, or complaining of being unjustly treated. **2** upset or troubled by grief: *aggrieved by news of his death.* <Old French, from Latin. See AGGRAVATE.>

a·ghast (ə gast′) *adj* filled with surprise, outrage, or horror: *I was aghast at what vandals had done to our car.* <Old English *gæstan* frighten>

ag·ile (aj′īl) *or* (aj′əl) *adj* **1** moving quickly and easily: *agile gymnasts.* **2** able to think quickly: *an agile mind.* <Old French, from Latin *agilis* (form of *agere* do)>
ag′ile·ly *adv.* **a·gil′i·ty** *n.*

ag·i·tate (aj′ə tāt′) *v* **ag·i·tat·ed, ag·i·tat·ing** **1** make anxious or uneasy: *She was very agitated by the news of her sister's accident.* **2** move or shake: *A breeze agitated the leaves on the trees.* **3** keep arguing about an issue to raise awareness and provoke action: *We have been agitating for less homework, but the teachers ignore us.* <Latin *agitare* move around> **ag′i·tat′ed·ly** *adv.* **ag′i·ta′tion** *n.*

a bat	e bed	i bid	o pot	u cup	th **thin**
ā cake	ē me	ī bite	ō go	ū rude	ᴛʜ **then**
â bar	ə about	ər over	ô for	ů put	zh measure

ag·i·ta·to (aj′ə tä′tō) *Music adv, adj* in a style that conveys restlessness or agitation.

ag·i·ta·tor (aj′ə tā′tər) *n* **1** a person who tries to make people discontented with things as they are. **2** a device for shaking or stirring: *The agitator in the washing machine has stuck.*

a·glow (ə glō′) *adv, adj* glowing: *The cold turned her pale face aglow* (*adv*). *The baby's cheeks were aglow with health* (*adj*).

✱ **ag·lu** (ag′lū) *n* a breathing hole in ice, made by seals. Also, **agloo.** <Inuktitut>

ag·nos·tic (ag nos′tik) *n* a person who believes that nothing can be known with certainty about the existence of God.
adj of or being an agnostic. <Greek *a-* not + *gnostos* to be known> **ag·nos′ti·cism′** *n.*

a·go (ə gō′) *adv* in the past: *I met her two years ago. The first Europeans came to Canada long ago.* <Old English *agan* gone by>

a·gog (ə gog′) *adj* eager or amazed: *We were all agog when he stood up to speak.* <Old French *en* in + *gogue* fun>

ag·o·nize (ag′ə nīz′) *v* **ag·o·nized, ag·o·niz·ing** feel mental anguish: *He agonized over the decision to sell the family farm.* <French, from Greek *agonizesthai* struggle (to win a prize)>

ag·o·niz·ing (ag′ə nī′zing) *adj* causing great anguish or inner struggle: *an agonizing choice.* **ag′o·niz′ing·ly** *adv.*

ag·o·ny (ag′ə nē) *n, pl* **ag·o·nies** great pain or suffering: *the agony of losing a child. She had wrenched her back and was in agony.* <Old French, from Greek *agon* struggle>

ag·o·ra·pho·bi·a (ag′rə fō′bē ə) *or* (ə gó′rə fō′bē ə) *n* abnormal fear of public places or open spaces. <Greek *agora* marketplace + *phobia*> **ag′o·ra·phobe′** *n.* **ag′o·ra·pho′bic** *adj.*

a·gou·ti (ə gū′tē) *n* a tropical American rodent resembling a guinea pig but with longer legs. <Spanish *aguti,* from Tupi (a language of S America) *akuti*>

a·grar·i·an (ə grer′ē ən) *adj* **1** to do with land, its use in farming, or its distribution and ownership: *agrarian disputes between landlords and tenants, agrarian reform.* **2** agricultural. <Latin *ager* field>

a·gree (ə grē′) *v* **a·greed, a·gree·ing 1** have or express the same opinion: *I agree with you. The two of us usually agree on important issues.* **2** (*with* ***with***) approve of: *I don't agree with the way he was treated.* **3** be consistent or in harmony: *The two versions agree in every detail.* **4** consent (to): *She agreed to the proposal.* **5** (*often with* ***on***) come to an understanding or arrangement: *We have agreed on a time and place for the party. They agreed to meet again at a later date.* **6** admit or concede: *I have to agree that I acted thoughtlessly.* **7** *Grammar* have the same number, case, gender, or person: *A verb must agree with its subject.* <Old French, from Latin *ad-* to + *gratus* pleasing>
agree with, have a good effect on: *Eggs do not agree with me; they make me sick.*

a·gree·a·ble (ə grē′ə bəl) *adj* **1** pleasant: *agreeable manners.* **2** ready to agree: *agreeable to a suggestion.* **3** in agreement; suitable (to): *music agreeable to the occasion.* **a·gree′a·ble·ness** *n.* **a·gree′a·bly** *adv.*

a·greed (ə grēd′) *adj* arranged by common consent: *at the agreed signal.*

a·gree·ment (ə grē′mənt) *n* **1** the fact of agreeing: *There was a lack of agreement on some issues.* **2** an arrangement or understanding arrived at between individuals, groups, or nations: *We came up with an agreement about who will do what. Both nations signed the agreement.*

ag·ri·busi·ness (ag′rə biz′nis) *n* all the businesses and industries involved in the large-scale production, processing, and marketing of agricultural products.

ag·ri·cul·ture (ag′rə kul′chər) *n* the science or practice of farming, including the cultivation of crops and rearing of livestock. <Latin *ager* field + *cultura* cultivation> **ag′ri·cul′tur·al** *adj.* **ag′ri·cul′tur·al·ist** *n.*

✱ **ag·ri–food** (ag′rə fūd′) *adj* to do with the raising and marketing of crops and livestock for food. <*agri*(*culture*) + *food*>

a·gron·o·my (ə gron′ə mē) *n* the science of soil management and the selection, production, and rotation of crops. <Greek *agros* field + *nomos* arrangement> **ag·ron′o·mist** *n.*

a·ground (ə ground′) *adv, adj* on or onto the shore, or the bottom in shallow water: *The ship ran aground and stuck in the sand* (*adv*). *The vessel is still aground* (*adj*).
run aground, encounter difficulties that stop progress.

a·gue (ā′gyū) *n* **1** malaria or some other fever that involves chills and sweating. **2** a fit of shivering or fever. <Old French, from Latin *acuta* (*febris*) severe (fever)>

ah (ȧ) *interj* an exclamation expressing such emotions as regret, pity, admiration, discovery, or relief.

a·ha (ȧ hȧ′) *interj* an exclamation of triumph, discovery, or surprise.

a·head (ə hed′) *adv* **1** in front of or before other people or things: *The guide walked ahead of the group.* **2** forward or onward: *The building project is moving ahead.* **3** in advance: *You should call ahead to confirm your flight.* **4** into a leading position in a game: *The Maple Leafs shot ahead 3 to 1.*
adj further along than others: *Some students are ahead in reading.*
ahead of, a in front of or further along than: *We saw a traffic jam ahead of us. She is ahead of me in math.* **b** before: *You should be ready a day or two ahead of the actual wedding date.*
ahead of time, a in advance: *to prepare things ahead of time.* **b** early: *We arrived ten minutes ahead of time.*
get ahead, succeed: *One needs a good education to get ahead today.*

a·hem (ə hem′) *interj* used to attract attention, gain time, or express disapproval. <imitative>

a·him·sa (ə him′sə) *n* among Hindus, Buddhists, and Jains, the principle of respecting all living things and avoiding violence toward them. <Sanskrit *a* without + *himsa* violence>

a·his·tor·i·cal (ā′hi stó′rə kəl) not confined to any time, or not located in time. **a′his·tor′i·cal·ly** *adv.*

–aholic *combining form* one who is obsessed by or addicted to something: *workaholic.* <(*alc*)*oholic*>

a·hoy (ə hoiʹ) *interj* a call used by sailors to attract the attention of people at a distance. <Dutch *hoei* sailboat>

A·hu·ra Maz·da (ə hūrʹə mȧzʹdə) *Zoroastrianism n* the supreme creator and force for good. <Avestan (the oldest Indo-European language) = wise deity>

AI **1** artificial intelligence. **2** artificial insemination.

aid (ād) *v* **1** give help and support to: *Many organizations aid flood victims.* **2** promote or encourage something: *Some people say that eating carrots aids good vision.*
n **1** help or support: *When my arm was broken, I could not get dressed without aid.* **2** assistance given formally by a government or private organization to nations, refugees, or groups of people in need: *The government recently approved two million dollars in international aid.* **3** a person who or thing that helps: *He used pictures and other visual aids to teach the lesson.* <Old French, from Latin *ad-* to + *juvare* help>
in aid of, for or toward the support of: *Proceeds are in aid of cancer research.*

aide (ād) *n* **1** in full, **aide-de-camp** a military officer who acts as assistant and secretary to a superior officer. **2** an assistant to an important person, especially an officeholder or political leader: *She is one of the Prime Minister's aides.* <French>

AIDS (ādz) *n* in full, **Acquired Immune Deficiency Syndrome** a disease of the immune system, caused by a virus transmitted through body fluids, which makes the sufferer susceptible to other diseases from which he or she can die.

AIDS–re·lat·ed complex (ādzʹri lāʹtid) *n* a combination of symptoms, such as weight loss, enlarged lymph nodes, and susceptibility to infections, that often precedes AIDS.

Aikido is unusual among the martial arts because it emphasizes techniques for self-defence that keep the attacker from being seriously hurt.

ai·ki·do (ī kēʹdō) *or* (īʹkēʹdōʹ) *n* a Japanese martial art that uses locks, holds, throws, and leverage against an opponent. <Japanese *ai* together + *ki* spirit + *do* way>

ail (āl) *Poetic or Humorous v* cause someone trouble in mind or body: *What ails you?* <Old English *eglan*>

ai·lan·thus (ā lanʹthəs) *n* a tall tree or shrub with large leaves and clusters of small, greenish flowers. <Latin, from Amboinese (a language of SE Asia) *ailanto* tree of heaven>

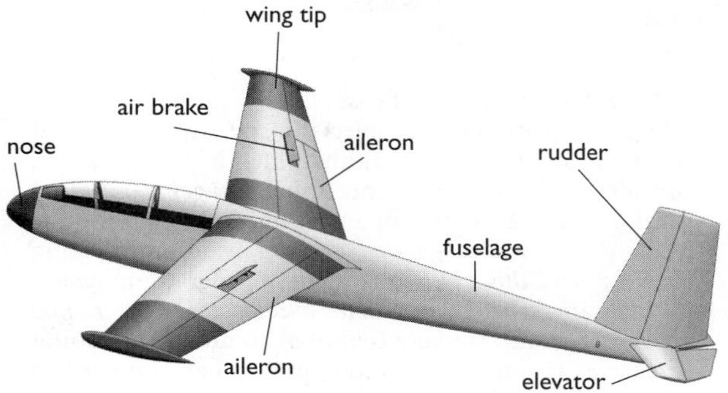

Ailerons control the *roll* of an aircraft, which is the up-and-down motion of the wing tips. The elevators control *pitch*, the up-and-down movement of the nose. The rudder controls *yaw*, the side-to-side movement of the nose.

The ailerons on a glider are fairly close to the fuselage. In a powered aircraft, they would be nearer the wing tips.

ai·ler·on (āʹlə ronʹ) *n* a small, movable section of an aircraft wing, for rolling and banking during flight. <French, from Latin *ala* wing>

ail·ing (āʹling) *adj* **1** ill, especially chronically: *his ailing mother.* **2** failing as a business.

ail·ment (ālʹmənt) *n* an illness, especially a minor one.

aim (ām) *v* **1** point or direct something in order to hit a target: *I didn't aim at the window, but I did break it. That snowball was aimed at my head!* **2** direct efforts or words to influence a particular person or produce a certain result: *The coach's remarks were aimed at the girls who had not played fair. We are aiming toward greater family involvement in education.* **3** *Informal* intend; try: *I aim to go. He aims to be helpful.*
n **1** the act or skill of pointing or directing something at a target: *My aim was so poor that I missed completely.* **2** the direction aimed in. **3** a purpose or goal: *Her aim was to get over eighty percent in every subject.* <Old French *aesmer*, from Latin *aestimare* estimate (direction)>
take aim (at), direct a weapon, words, or action at an opponent or victim: *The newspaper editorial took aim at the new tax policy.*

aim·less (āmʹlis) *adj* with no goal or purpose: *aimless wanderings, an aimless life.* **aimʹless·ly** *adv.* **aimʹless·ness** *n.*

a bat	e bed	i bid	o pot	u cup	th thin
ā cake	ē me	ī bite	ō go	ū rude	ᴛʜ then
ȧ bar	ə about	ər over	ȯ for	ů put	zh measure

ain't (ānt) *Slang contraction* **1** am not; are not; is not. **2** have not; has not.

GRAMMAR AND USAGE

Although **ain't** has existed in English for a long time, it is considered slang, and its use is avoided in formal situations.

air (er) *n* **1 a** the mixture of gases that surrounds the earth, filling the space between objects in the atmosphere and required for plant and animal life. **b** this mixture, considered as necessary for breathing: *I'm going outside to get a little air.* **2** the free or unconfined space over one's head: *Birds fly through the air.* **3** transportation using aircraft: *Send this parcel by air.* **4** the general impression given by anything: *He had an air of importance.* **5** *Informal* air conditioning: *We have central air.* **6 airs** *pl* unnatural or affected manners put on to impress others: *I am fed up with his snobby airs.* **7** a melody.
v **1** expose to fresh air: *to air a room.* **2** make known or mention publicly: *to air your opinion.* **3** broadcast or be broadcast on radio or TV: *The new program will air next week.*
adj **1** operated by air, or carrying or supplying air: *air ducts, air brakes.* **2** to do with transportation by aircraft: *air cargo.* <Latin, from Greek *aer* air> **air′ing** *n.*
by air, on an aircraft: *travel by air.*
clear the air, get rid of uncertainty, tension, or awkwardness by open discussion.
in the air, noticeable all around: *Wild rumours were in the air.*
into thin air, unexpectedly and without leaving a trace: *It just disappeared into thin air.*
on (off) the air, (not) broadcasting or (not) being broadcast: *This station is on the air until 2 a.m. That show has been off the air for years.*
out of thin air, unexpectedly and without explanation: *Her accusation came out of thin air.*
take the air, go outside.
up in the air, *Informal* uncertain: *Our vacation plans are still up in the air.*
walking on air, very happy.

air ambulance *n* an aircraft used as an ambulance.

air·bag (er′bag′) *n* in a motor vehicle, a large plastic bag that inflates in a collision, helping to protect occupants from injury.

air ball *Informal n* a shot in basketball that misses not only the net but the rim and backboard.

air base *n* a headquarters and airfield for the operation of military aircraft.

air bladder *n* an air-filled sac in some plants and animals.

air·borne (er′bôrn′) *adj* **1** carried through the air: *airborne seeds.* **2** transported by aircraft: *airborne troops.* **3** in the air after takeoff: *After another delay, we were finally airborne.*

air brake *n* a brake that is operated with the use of compressed air.

air·brush (er′brush′) *n* a device using compressed air to apply a fine spray of paint or colour onto a surface.
v apply paint or colour with an airbrush, in order to remove blemishes or unwanted details, especially in a photo.

air·bus (er′bus′) *n* a small passenger aircraft flying frequently over a regular route, usually between cities in the same country. <*Airbus,* a trademark>

🍁 **Air Command** *n* the official name for the Canadian air force, formerly called the Royal Canadian Air Force.

air con·di·tion·ing (er′kən dish′ə ning) *n* the treatment of air in buildings, rooms, and other enclosed spaces to regulate temperature and humidity. **air′-con·di′tion** *v.* **air′-con·di′tioned** *adj.* **air′ con·dit′ion·er** *n.*

air–cool (er′ kūl′) *v* remove heat from by blowing cool air in or on: *an air-cooled engine.*

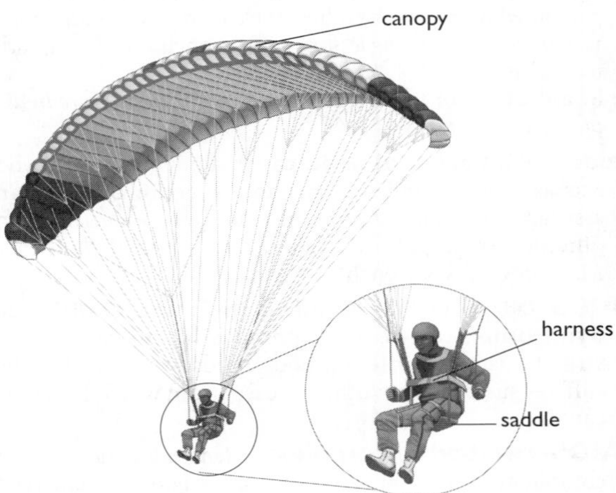

A paraglider is an **aircraft** consisting of a parachute-like canopy that can soar on air currents. Unlike a hang-glider, it does not have a rigid frame.

air·craft (er′kraft′) *n, pl* **air·craft** a vehicle or device for travelling through the air. Aircraft may use machine power, such as a helicopter or airplane, or travel by buoyancy, such as a balloon or a paraglider.

aircraft carrier *n* a warship with a large, flat deck designed as a base for airplanes.

air cushion *n* **1** an inflatable rubber cushion or pad. **2** the layer of compressed air that supports a hovercraft.

air·drop (er′drop′) *n* an act of dropping supplies, troops, or equipment from aircraft. **air′drop** *v.*

air–dry (er′drī′) *v* **air-dried, air-dry·ing** dry or let dry on its own without the aid of heated air.

air·fare (er′fer′) *n* the money paid to travel on an airplane. *Airfare alone would cost you over $1000.*

air·field (er′fēld′) *n* the landing field of an airport.

air·flow (er′flō′) *n* the flow of air, especially the air currents around a moving object such as an airplane.

air·foil (er′foil′) *n* any part of an aircraft's surface that is used to help lift or control it. Ailerons, wings, propellers, rotor blades, and so on are airfoils.

air force *n* usually, **Air Force** the branch of the armed forces that uses aircraft.

air freight *n* **1** the service of transporting cargo by aircraft. **2** the cargo itself. **air′freight** *v.*

air gun *n* a gun that works by compressed air, such as a BB gun.

air hole *n* a hole that allows air to pass through, especially one in the ice covering a body of water, used by aquatic mammals for breathing.

air lane *n* a regular route used by aircraft.

air·less (er′lis) *adj* without a breeze or fresh air.

air letter AEROGRAM.

air·lift (er′lift′) *n* **1** the use of aircraft to transport passengers and freight, typically to a place when land approaches are closed: *an airlift to the flooded city.* **2** something transported by such a system.
v transport by such a system.

air·line (er′līn′) *n* a company operating a system of transportation using aircraft: *Does this airline fly to Iqaluit?*

air·lin·er (er′lī′nər) *n* a large passenger airplane operated by an airline.

air·lock (er′lok′) *n* an airtight compartment between two places with different levels of pressure, in which the air pressure can gradually be adjusted to allow passage from one to the other.

air·mail (er′māl′) *n* **1** mail sent by aircraft. **2** a system of sending mail by aircraft. **air′mail′** *v.*

air mass *Meteorology n* a part of the atmosphere with more or less the same temperature, humidity, and pressure at any given level, moving horizontally over great distances without changing: *a cold air mass.*

air mattress *n* an inflatable rubber mattress used for relaxing on the water.

air mile *n* **1** nautical mile. **2 Air Miles** *Trademark* a rewards program offering free air travel and other free or discounted items or services to customers of sponsoring businesses.

These are the forces that act on an **airplane** in flight.

Elevators, *ailerons*, and the *rudder* are movable surfaces that the pilot adjusts to take advantage of these forces and change the airplane's direction.

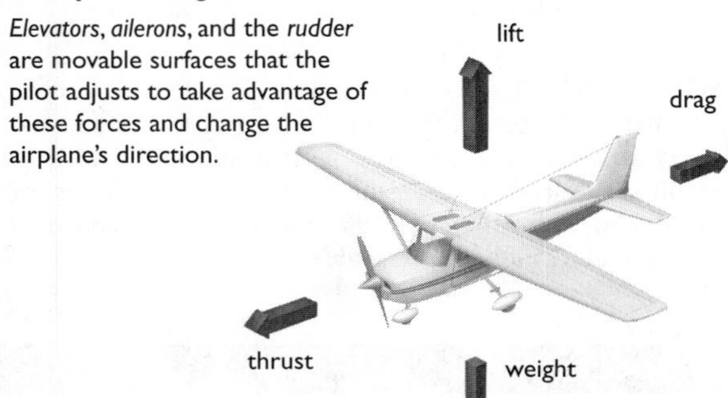

air·plane (er′plān′) *n* a powered, heavier-than-air aircraft, supported in flight by the action of the air flowing past or thrusting upward on its fixed wings.

air plant *n* a plant that grows on other plants and draws nourishment from the air and rain.

air·play (er′plā′) *n* the airing of broadcast material over radio or TV: *That song got a lot of airplay last year.*

air pocket *n* a downward air current formed by a region of low pressure, causing a sudden, short drop in the altitude of an aircraft.

air·port (er′pôrt′) *n* a place where aircraft regularly come to load or unload passengers or freight.

air pressure *n* **1** the force exerted by air confined in a closed space. **2** the force exerted by the atmosphere on surfaces at any given location.

air pump *n* an apparatus for forcing air in or drawing air out of something.

air quality index *n* a numerical value assigned to the air at a certain place and time, representing the degree of pollution.

air rage *n* assault or verbal abuse by an airplane passenger.

air raid *n* an attack in which bombs are dropped by aircraft.

air rifle *n* a rifle that works by compressed air and shoots pellets.

air rights *n* the right to use the space above a building, road, or property: *The developer has bought air rights over the freight yards in order to build a huge office block above the tracks.*

air sac *n* an air-filled space or baglike structure in a plant or animal.

air·ship (er′ship′) *n* a motorized aircraft that is kept aloft by a lighter-than-air gas filling its hull.

air·sick (er′sik′) *adj* sick from the motion experienced when travelling by air. **air′sick′ness** *n.*

air·space (er′spās′) *n* **1** the area of the atmosphere immediately above the earth: *Skyscrapers jutted into the city's airspace.* **2** space in the air with defined limits, such as that controlled by an airport or belonging to a country: *Fighter jets began patrolling American airspace.*

air·speed (er′spēd′) *n* the speed of an aircraft measured in relation to the air through which it moves.

air·stream (er′strēm′) *n* the stream of air created around a moving object such as an aircraft or car.

air strike *n* an attack by missiles or aircraft.

air·strip (er′strip′) *n* a paved or cleared area for airplanes to land and take off.

air·tight (er′tīt′) *adj* **1** so tight that no air or gas can get in or out. **2** with no weak points open to attack: *The lawyer said our case was airtight.*

air·time (er′tīm′) *n* **1** the time when a certain radio or TV program begins to broadcast: *a few minutes to airtime.* **2** an amount of broadcasting time: *The advertising program cost $75 000 in airtime.*

a bat	e bed	i bid	o pot	u cup	th **thin**
ā cake	ē me	ī bite	ō go	ū rude	ᴛʜ **then**
à bar	ə about	ər over	ô for	ů put	zh measure

air–to–air (er′ tū er′) *adj* from one flying aircraft to another: *air-to-air refuelling.*

air–to–ground (er′ tū ground′) *adj* from a flying aircraft to the land surface: *air-to-ground communication.*

air–to–surface (er′ tū sər′fis) *adj* from a flying aircraft to the surface of the sea or other body of water: *air-to-surface missile.*

air traffic controller *n* a person who controls aircraft in an airport, directing pilots to land, take off, taxi, etc. **air traffic control** *n.*

air·waves (er′wāvz′) *pln* the radio frequencies on which radio and TV signals are transmitted.

air·way (er′wā′) *n* **1** a route for aircraft. **2** a passage by which air reaches the lungs. **3** any passage through which air can move.

air·wor·thy (er′wər′ᴛʜē) *adj* **air·wor·thi·er, air·wor·thi·est** fit or safe for flying. **air′wor′thi·ness** *n.*

air·y (er′ē) *adj* **air·i·er, air·i·est** **1** spacious, well-lit, and open to currents of air: *an airy room.* **2** merry or happy: *airy laughter.* **3** appearing not concerned or serious about something important: *her airy dismissal of our proposal.* **4** light, delicate, and insubstantial: *an airy presence.* **air′i·ly** *adv.* **air′i·ness** *n.*

air·y–fair·y (er′ē fer′ē) *Informal adj* impractical or foolishly idealistic: *Sounds like an airy-fairy plan to me.*

aisle (īl) *n* a passageway, such as between rows of seats in room, or between shelves of goods in a supermarket. <Old French, from Latin *ala* wing>

a·jar (ə jär′) *adj* slightly open: *The door was ajar.* <Old English *cierran* turn (i.e., swing open>

a.k.a. also known as.

a·kim·bo (ə kim′bō) *adj* with the hands on the hips and the elbows bent outward: *standing with arms akimbo.* <Middle English *in kenebowe*>

a·kin (ə kin′) *adj* similar: *That statement was akin to a lie. The friends are akin in their love of sports.* <*of kin*>

Ak·we·sas·ne (ak′wə säs′nē) KAHNEWAKE.

–al *suffix* **1** to do with: *ornamental.* **2** the act of: *burial.* <Latin *-alis*>

à la or **a la** (ä′ lä) *prep* in the manner or style of: *a rousing speech à la Pierre Trudeau.* <French, from *à la mode*>

al·a·bas·ter (al′ə bas′tər) *n* a smooth, white, translucent mineral, a variety of gypsum. <Old French, from Greek *alabastros*>

à la carte (a′lə kärt′) *adj, adv* according to the menu, on which each dish is priced separately. Compare TABLE D'HÔTE. <French = according to the bill of fare>

a·lack (ə lak′) *Archaic or Poetic interj* used to express sorrow or regret.

a·lac·ri·ty (ə lak′rə tē) *n* lively and cheerful willingness: *He performed his tasks with alacrity.* <Latin *alacer* brisk>

à la mode or **a la mode** (al′ə mōd′) *or* (ä′lə mōd′) *adj, adv* **1** served with ice cream: *apple pie à la mode (adj).* **2** according to fashion: *dressed à la mode (adv).* <French = in the fashion>

a·larm (ə lärm′) *n* **1** sudden, intense fear or fright. **2** a warning of approaching danger: *The sentry sounded an alarm.* **3** a device or mechanism that gives such a warning or that makes a noise to wake a person up: *The smoke alarm needs new batteries. This clock has an alarm; set it for 7:30.* **4** the sound made by such a device.
v fill with sudden, intense fear; frighten: *She alarmed me by saying that she had a high fever. I was alarmed when she still wasn't home by nightfall.* <Old French, from Italian *all'arme!* to arms> **a·larm′ing** *adj.* **a·larm′ing·ly** *adv.*

alarm clock *n* a clock that can be set to ring or make a noise at a desired time, especially to wake people up.

a·larm·ist (ə lär′mist) *n* a person who is easily alarmed, or who alarms others needlessly or on slight grounds. **a·larm′ism** *n.*

a·las (ə las′) *Poetic interj* used to express sorrow, grief, regret, pity, or dread. <Old French, from Latin *lassus* weary>

Al·ask·an brown bear (ə las′kən) KODIAK BEAR.

al·ba·core (al′bə kôr′) *n, pl* **al·ba·cores** or (*especially collectively*) **al·ba·core** a long-finned, edible fish related to the tuna, found in the Atlantic. <Portuguese, from Arabic *al-bakur*>

Al·ba·ni·a (al bā′nē ə) *n* a country in southeast Europe. See the APPENDIX. **Al·ba′ni·an** *adj, n.*

An **albatross is** known for its ability to remain in flight for days and even weeks in search of food. This seabird can fly all the way around the world on one of these journeys, sometimes in as little as six weeks.

al·ba·tross (al′bə tros′) *n* **1** a large, web-footed seabird, related to the petrel, that can fly long distances and has very long wings. **2** a source of frustration, difficulty, or guilt, especially as a result of one's own actions or mistakes: *This car has become my albatross; I bought it cheap and it's nothing but trouble.*

ETYMOLOGY

The second sense of **albatross**, "a source of frustration, difficulty, or guilt," comes from a famous poem called *The Rime of the Ancient Mariner* by Samuel Taylor Coleridge. In the poem, a sailor brings bad luck on his voyage when he kills an albatross.

al·be·it (ol bē′it) *conj* although or even though: *They have a house of their own, albeit a small one.* <Middle English *al be it* though it be>

Al·ber·ta (al bər′tə) *n* a western Canadian province, between British Columbia and Saskatchewan. Alberta is one of the PRAIRIE PROVINCES. *Abbrev.* **Alta.**;
postal symbol **AB**; URL **www.gov.ab.ca**
adj to do with Alberta: *Alberta beef.* **Al·ber′tan** *n.*

✱ **Alberta clipper** *n* a winter storm that blows quickly into eastern Canada and northeastern US from Alberta.

Al·ber·to·saur (al bər′tə sȯr′) *n* a large, swift, meat-eating dinosaur that lived in North America about seventy million years ago.

al·bi·no (al bī′nō) *n* a person or animal who is born without normal pigment and therefore has a pale, milky skin, very light or white hair, and pink eyes. <Portuguese, from Latin *albus* white> **al′bi·nism′** (al′bə niz′əm) *n.*

al·bum (al′bəm) *n* **1** a book with blank pages for holding photographs, postage stamps, or autographs. **2** such a book when it contains these items: *We made an album of our trip.* **3** a musical recording of several songs on a CD, cassette, or vinyl disc. *He has every album ever made by the Tragically Hip.* <Latin = white>

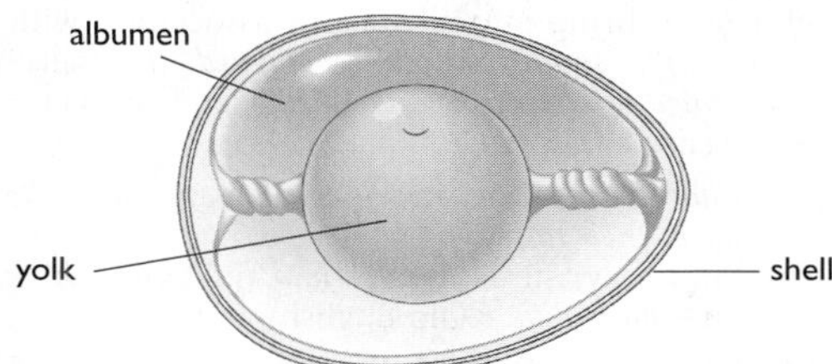

The embryo of an animal develops inside an egg. Although the yolk is the embryo chick's main food source, **albumen** contains water, protein, and nutrients that also contribute to its growth.

al·bu·men (al byū′mən) *or* (al′ byə mən) *n* egg white, consisting mostly of albumin dissolved in water. <Latin *albus* white>

al·bu·min (al byū′mən) *n* the protein in egg white, milk, and blood serum that is soluble in water and can be thickened by heat. <French, from Latin *albus* white>

al·che·my (al′kə mē) *n* **1** an early form of chemistry in medieval times that, among other aims, searched for a way to turn cheap metals into gold. **2** a seemingly magic power or process for changing one thing into another. <Old French *alkemie*, from Greek *chymatos* something poured out>

al·co·hol (al′kə hol′) *n* **1** a colourless, flammable liquid that is fermented from sugar, acts as a drug, and is a part of wine, beer, and other fermented or distilled drinks. **2** any of a group of similar organic compounds. **Wood alcohol** (**methyl alcohol**) is very poisonous. <Arabic *al-kuhl* kohl. The powder kohl is refined by a process of heating and condensing. This process was extended to include liquids, hence distillation.>

al·co·hol·ic (al′kə hol′ik) *adj* **1** to do with alcohol: *alcoholic drinks, an alcoholic addiction.* **2** addicted to alcohol: *his alcoholic mother.*
n a person affected by alcoholism.

al·co·hol·ism (al′kə hol iz′əm) *n* a disease whose chief symptom is the inability to control one's consumption of alcoholic drinks.

al·cove (al′kōv) *n* a space or small room opening off another room: *We have our breakfast in an alcove off the kitchen.* <French, from Arabic *al-kubba* arched room>

al·der (ol′dər) *n* a tree or shrub related to the birches, usually growing in cool, wet parts of the northern hemisphere. <Old English *alor*>

al·der·man (ol′dər mən) *n, pl* **al·der·men** (ol′dər mən) a member of the council of a city or town. The invented terms **alderwoman** and **alderperson** are rarely used; most municipalities have adopted the gender-neutral term **councillor** instead. <Old English *ald* old + *mann* man> **al′der′man′ic** *adj.*

ale (āl) *n* a type of beer made from malt and hops. <Old Engliah *alu*>

a·lert (ə lərt′) *adj* able to think clearly and react quickly: *In order to drive you must be alert.*
n **1** an announcement or signal warning of danger. **2** the time during which this warning is in effect.
v warn of an attack or other danger: *As the storm approached, police tried to alert motorists through radio announcements.* <French, from Italian *all' erta* on the watch> **a·lert′ly** *adv.* **a·lert′ness** *n.*
alert to, noticing immediately: *alert to every sound.*
on the alert, ready at any instant for what is coming.

ale·wife (āl′wīf′) *n, pl* **ale·wives** a food fish of the herring family found in the sea and in the fresh waters of eastern N America. Also called **gaspereau** (gas′pə rō′).

al·ex·an·drine (al′ig zan′drin) *n* a line of poetry with six iambic feet, with a pause (caesura) after the third foot. Example: *He seeks′ out might′y charms′, to trou′ble sleep′y minds′.*
adj to do with this metre. <French *alexandrin*, after Alexander the Great, the subject of a poem in this metre>

al·fal·fa (al fal′fə) *n* a plant grown as food for livestock, with deep roots and cloverlike leaves. <Arabic *al-fasfasah* green fodder>

al·gae (al′jē) *or* (al′jī) *pln, sing* **al·ga** (al′gə) a group of plantlike water organisms that can make their own food and that have chlorophyl but not true stems, roots, or leaves. <Latin = seaweed>

GRAMMAR AND USAGE

Although **algae** is a plural noun, it is sometimes used with a singular verb in informal contexts: *The algae is making it hard to see down into the aquarium.*

a bat	e bed	i bid	o pot	u cup	th **thin**
ā cake	ē me	ī bite	ō go	ū rude	ᴛʜ **then**
ä bar	ə about	ər over	ȯ for	u̇ put	zh measure

al·ge·bra (al′jə brə) *n* a branch of mathematics in which letters or other symbols are used to represent numbers and quantities in expressions and equations.
al′ge·bra′ic (al′jə brā′ik) *adj.* **al′ge·bra′ic·al′ly** *adv.*

ETYMOLOGY

Algebra comes from the Arabic word *al-jabr*, which means "the science of reuniting": *al* (the) + *jabr* (reuniting). However, the Arabs did not invent algebra. It was developed in India around 500 CE, and the Arabs learned about it when they invaded India several hundred years later.

Al·ge·ri·a (al jē′rē ə) *n* a country in N Africa. See the APPENDIX. **Al·ge′ri·an** *n, adj.*

al·gi·cide (al′jə sīd′) *n* a substance that kills algae. <*algae* + *-cide*>

Al·gon·qui·an (al gong′kē ən) *or* (al gong′kwē ən) *n* **1** a group of N American Aboriginal languages, including Abenaki, Blackfoot, Cree, Maliseet, Mi'kmaw, Ojibwa, and Ottawa. **2** a member of any of the peoples that speak these languages.
adj to do with any of these languages or the peoples that speak them.

Al·gon·quin (al gong′kwin) *n, pl* **Al·gon·quin** a member of a First Nations people living in eastern Ontario and Québec.
adj to do with these people. Also, **Algonkin**.

al·go·rithm (al′gə riᴛʜ′əm) *n* a special procedure or set of rules for solving problems of a certain kind, especially by a computer. <*al-Khowarizmi*, 9c mathematician>

a·li·as[1] (ā′lē əs) *n, pl* **a·li·as·es** an assumed name: *The spy's real name was Carla, but she went by the alias of Charlotte.*
adv otherwise named: *The gang leader is Carson, alias Streetman.* <Latin = at another time>

a·li·as[2] (ā′lē əs) *Computers n, pl* **a·li·as·es** **1** a name, usually short and easy to remember or type, that is translated into another name or string, usually long and difficult to remember or type. **2** one of several different names with the same Internet address. <*al*gor*i*thmic *as*sembly language>

al·i·bi (al′ə bī′) *n* **1** a defence that a person accused of an offence was somewhere else when the offence was committed: *Do you have an alibi?* **2** an excuse.

ETYMOLOGY

Alibi is Latin for "somewhere else." Formerly, Latin was the language of law, and lawyers used Latin words and phrases while arguing cases in court. Over time, *alibi* became an English noun: *The accused could not have stolen the money; she was admitted to hospital the day before the theft, and therefore she has an alibi.*

al·ien (ā′lē ən) *n* **1** a being supposed to be from another planet. **2** a person who is not a citizen of the country in which he or she is living. **3** an outsider or stranger.
adj **1** strange, disturbing, or distasteful: *alien ideas.* **2** foreign: *alien customs.* <Old French, from Latin *alienus*, from *alius* other> **al′ien·ness** *n.*
alien to, quite different from: *Unkindness is alien to her nature.*

al·ien·ate (ā′lē ə nāt′) *or* (āl′yə nāt′) *v* **al·ien·at·ed, al·ien·at·ing** **1** cause to become unsympathetic or hostile: *alienate someone's affections. Her insensitivity alienated all her friends.* **2** cause a person to feel as if he or she does not belong: *alienated youth.* **al′ien·a′tion** *n.*

a·light[1] (ə līt′) *v* **a·light·ed, a·light·ing** **1** get down from or get off something: *to alight from a horse.* **2** come down from the air and settle: *The bird alighted on our window sill.* <Old English *alihten*, from light (referring to taking one's weight off something)>
alight on, happen to find: *I alighted on the perfect present for my sister.*

a·light[2] (ə līt′) *adv, adj* on fire or lit up: *He set the candles alight* (*adv*). *Her face was alight with joy* (*adj*). <Old English *aliht* shining>

a·lign (ə līn′) *v* **1** bring into a straight line: *to align the wheels of a car.* **2** bring into alliance or association with others: *The three small companies aligned themselves against their huge competitor.* <French *aligner*, from Latin *ad-* on + *linea* line> **a·lign′ment** *n.*

a·like (ə līk′) *adj* identical or similar to one another: *The sisters are alike in their tastes.*
adv in the same way; similarly: *He and his father think alike. Share and share alike.* <Old English *gelic*>

al·i·men·ta·ry (al′ə men′tə rē) *adj* to do with food and nutrition: *alimentary requirements.* <Latin *alimentum*, from *alere* nourish>

alimentary canal *n* the passage in the body through which food passes from mouth to anus in the process of being digested.

al·i·mo·ny (al′ə mō′nē) *n* money paid by a person for the support of his or her spouse after a separation or divorce. <Latin *alimonia* support, from *alere* nourish>

al·i·phat·ic (al′ə fat′ik) *Chemistry adj* to do with a group of organic compounds whose carbon atoms form open chains rather than rings. <Greek *aleiphar* fat>

al·i·quot (al′ə kwət) *Mathematics adj* able to divide a number without leaving a remainder: *Two is an aliquot part of twelve.* <Latin, from *alios* some + *quot* how many>

a·lit·er·ate (ā′lit′ə rit) *adj* able to read, but not willing to.
n a person who is aliterate. **a′lit′er·a·cy** *n.*

a·live (ə līv′) *adj* **1** living: *The cat was injured but still alive.* **2** in continued activity or operation: *Keep the principles of liberty alive.* **3** energetic or lively. <Old English *on life*>
a·live′ness *n.*
alive to, alert or sensitive to: *Are you alive to what is going on?*
alive with, full or swarming with: *The streets were alive with people.*
look alive! *Informal* hurry up! be quick!

al·ka·li (al′kə lī′) *Chemistry n, pl* **al·ka·lis** or **al·ka·lies** a base or hydroxide that is soluble in water, neutralizes acids and forms salts with them, and turns red litmus paper blue: *Some desert soils contain much alkali.* Compare ACID. <Old French, from Arabic *al-qali* ashes of the plant saltwort (which grows in alkaline soil)>

alkali flat *n* an arid area in which the natural water in ponds and marshes evaporates, leaving large deposits of alkali.

al·ka·line (al′kə līn′) *or* (al′kə lin) *adj* to do with an alkali: *alkaline soil.* Compare ACIDIC. **al′ka·lin′i·ty** (al′kə lin′ə tē) *n.*

alkaline–earth metals *pl n* the metallic elements beryllium, magnesium, calcium, strontium, barium, and radium.

al·ka·lize (al′kə līz′) *Chemistry v* **al·ka·lized, al·ka·liz·ing** make alkaline.

al·ka·loid (al′kə loid′) *n* a substance that contains nitrogen and is found in or obtained from plants, including cocaine, strychnine, morphine, and quinine.

al·kyd (al′kid) *n* a synthetic resin used especially for paints and other finishes.
adj to do with a resin of this kind: *Alkyd paint is oil-based, unlike latex paint.* <blend of *alkyl* (an organic compound) and *acid*>

all (ol) *adj* **1** the whole of: *all Europe.* **2** every one of: *all dogs.* **3** the greatest possible: *with all haste.* **4** (*with a negative*) any: *He denies all connection with the crime.*
pron **1** the whole number or amount: *all of the cake. All of us are going.* **2** everything: *All is well.*
n all that one has: *to give your all. You are my all.*
adv **1** wholly or entirely: *all clean. The cake is all gone.* **2** each or apiece: *The score was even at forty all.* **3** only: *She is all talk and no action.* <Old English *eall*>
all at once, suddenly.
all but, almost or nearly: *He was all but dead from fatigue, but he struggled on.*
all in, *Informal* very tired.
all in all, taking everything into consideration: *All in all, it was an exciting election.*
all of, (*used with a quantity; often ironic*) no less than: *It cost me all of $10 just for bus fare. His "feature article" was all of two paragraphs long.*
all over, a everywhere in, or in all parts of: *I am itchy all over. She has travelled all over the world.* **b** completely finished or ended: *That ugly business is all over now, thank goodness.*
all that ——, (*with an adjective or adverb and usually negative*) not very: *I wasn't all that eager to go along.*
all the more, even more: *You'll be all the more surprised when you hear this.*
as all get-out, *Informal* to an extreme degree: *By then we were hungry as all get-out.*
at all, at any time, in any way, or to any extent: *Did you talk to him at all? She did no work at all.*
for all (that), in spite of (that): *He's a slob and a teaser, but very nice for all that. For all she's a great writer, I haven't much respect for her.*
go all out, *Informal* use all one's resources, without limiting oneself: *They decided to go all out and hire a band for the dance.*
in all, counting all: *sixty people in all.*

Al·lah (al′ə); *Arabic* (à lä′) *Islam n* the one Supreme Being. <Arabic>

al·lay (ə lā′) *v* **al·layed, al·lay·ing** relieve or quiet: *to allay someone's fears.* <Old English *alecgan* lay aside>

all–Ca·na·di·an (ol′kə nā′dē ən) *adj* **1** typically Canadian: *an all-Canadian girl.* **2** made up entirely of Canadians or Canadian elements: *an all-Canadian hockey team.* **3** situated entirely within Canada: *an all-Canadian route.*

🍁 **all–dressed** (ol′drest′) *Informal adj* with all the standard toppings or flavours: *all-dressed potato chips, an all-dressed hot dog.*

al·le·ga·tion (al′ə gā′shən) *n* a claim or accusation without proof that someone has done something wrong or illegal: *She denied the allegations.*

al·lege (ə lej′) *v* **al·leged, al·leg·ing** assert without proof: *This man alleges that his watch was stolen.* <Old French *alegier,* from Latin *allegare* charge (*legis* law)>

SYNONYMS

Allege is usually used in legal situations: *The witness alleged that the driver was speeding.*

Assert means "express a belief forcefully": *He still asserts that the other driver was at fault.*

Claim is somewhat less aggressive: *She claims that she left her purse on the table and now it's gone.*

al·leged (ə lejd′) *adj* asserted or spoken of, but not proven or known to be true: *The alleged theft did not really happen.* **al·leg′ed·ly** (ə lej′i dlē) *adv.*

al·le·giance (ə lē′jəns) *n* loyalty or faithfulness to something or someone: *to swear allegiance to the queen. We owe allegiance to our friends.* <Old French *liege* liege>

al·le·go·ry (al′ə gô′rē) *n, pl* **al·le·go·ries** a story told to explain or teach something, in which each element in the story can be matched with some real person who or thing that it represents. <Old French, from Greek *allos* other + *-agoria* speaking> **al′le·gor′i·cal** *adj.* **al′le·gor′i·cal·ly** *adv.*

al·le·gret·to *Music adv, adj* fairly fast. <Italian, diminutive form of *allegro*>

al·le·gro (ə leg′rō) *or* (ə lā′grō) *Music adv, adj* fast and lively.

al·lele (ə lēl′) *Genetics n* one of two or more alternative forms of genes that have the same position on each of a pair of chromosomes. <short for *allelomorph,* from Greek *allel-* one another + *morphe* form>

al·le·lu·ia (al′ə lü′yə) *n* an exclamation or song of praise to God. Also, **hallelujah**. <Latin, from Hebrew *hallelujah* praise the Lord>

Al·len key (al′ən) *n* a type of screwdriver without a handle, consisting of a small, L-shaped, hexagonal metal bar whose end fits into the hexagonal hole in the head of a screw. Also called **Allen wrench**. <named after the manufacturer>

a bat	e bed	i bid	o pot	u cup	th **thin**
ā cake	ē me	ī bite	ō go	ū rude	TH **then**
à bar	ə about	ər over	ô for	ù put	zh measure

al·ler·gen (al′ər jən) *n* a substance causing an allergic reaction. **al′ler·gen′ic** *adj.*

al·ler·gic (ə lėr′jik) *adj* **1** with an allergy: *He is allergic to eggs and breaks out in a rash if he eats them.* **2** of or caused by an allergy: *Hay fever is an allergic reaction.* **3** *Informal* with a strong dislike: *I'm allergic to washing dishes.*

al·ler·gist (al′ər jist) *n* a doctor specializing in the diagnosis and treatment of allergies.

al·ler·gy (al′ər jē) *n, pl* **al·ler·gies** **1** an unusual sensitiveness to a particular substance: *Her allergy to mangoes prevented her from eating the dessert.* **2** *Informal* strong dislike. <Latin *allergos,* from Greek *allos* different + *ergon* action>

al·le·vi·ate (ə lē′vē āt′) *v* **al·le·vi·at·ed, al·le·vi·at·ing** make easier to tolerate: *to alleviate pain, to alleviate a shortage by sending aid.* <Latin *alleviare* make lighter, from *ad-* up + *levare* raise> **al·le′vi·a′tion** *n.*

SYNONYMS

Alleviate, which means "make something better," often has a medical context: *This lotion alleviates itchiness.*

Abate usually refers to a decrease in force or intensity: *The waves will get smaller when the wind abates.*

Ease can replace either alleviate or abate: *Apply this cream to ease the pain. The rain eased and the sun came out.*

al·ley[1] (al′ē) *n* **1** a lane or narrow back street between or behind buildings. **2** a building fitted with long narrow lanes for the game of bowling. <Old French *alee,* from Latin *ambulare* walk>

al·ley[2] (al′ē) *n* **1** a large white or coloured glass marble used to shoot at the other marbles in a game. **2** **alleys** *pl* (*with singular verb*) a game played with such marbles. <perhaps *alabaster*>

alley cat *n* a stray cat of mixed breed that lives in back streets.

al·ley·way (al′ē wā′) *n* **1** ALLEY[1]. **2** a narrow passageway: *A covered alleyway joins the two buildings.*

al·li·ance (ə lī′əns) *n* **1** a formal bond for nations, groups, or people that agree to help each other, or those sharing such a bond. **2** 🍁 **the Alliance** in full, **the Canadian Alliance** a federal political party in Canada formed in 2000 from some supporters of the Progressive Conservative Party and members of the Reform Party of Canada. In 2003, it merged with the Progressive Conservative party to form the Conservative Party of Canada.

al·lied (ə līd′); *for def. 3, usually* (al′īd) *adj* **1** belonging to an alliance: *allied nations.* **2** associated or related: *Reading and listening are allied activities.* **3** **Allied** to do with the Allies: *the Allied forces.*

Al·lies (al′īz) *pln* **1** the countries that fought against Germany and Austria-Hungary in World War I. **2** the countries that fought against Germany, Italy, and Japan in World War II. Compare AXIS.

An American **alligator** has a rounder snout than an American crocodile.

A cayman has a much narrower snout than either an alligator or a crocodile.

al·li·ga·tor (al′ə gā′tər) *n* a reptile closely related to the crocodile, with a long, thick body and tail, four short legs, powerful jaws with sharp teeth, and eyes and nostrils set on top of the skull. One type of alligator is found in the southern US, the other in China <Spanish *el legarto* the lizard, from Latin *lacerta* lizard>

alligator clip *n* a long, toothed clip used in electrical work.

all–im·por·tant (ol′im pôr′tənt) *adj* essential or extremely important: *When going camping, don't forget the all-important roll of toilet paper.*

all–in·clu·sive (ol′ in klū′siv) *adj* including everything, especially services, goods, tips, and taxes: *The resort has an all-inclusive rate of $750 a week.*

al·lit·er·ate (ə lit′ə rāt′) *v* **al·lit·er·at·ed, al·lit·er·at·ing** have the same first consonant sound of words, such as *slowly sinking sun.* **al·lit′er·a′tion** *n.* **al·lit′er·a·tive** *adj.*

al·lo·cate (al′ə kāt′) *v* **al·lo·cat·ed, al·lo·cat·ing** assign or distribute: *to allocate resources to where they are most needed. The government allocates millions of dollars to education.* <Latin *allocare,* from *ad-* to + *locus* place> **al′lo·ca′tion** *n.*

al·lo·path (al′ə path′) *n* a doctor who uses allopathy.

al·lop·a·thy (ə lop′ə thē) *n* a method of treating a disease by using remedies to produce effects opposite to those caused by the disease. Compare HOMEOPATHY. <Greek *allo-* different + *patheia* suffering>

al·lo·phone (al′ə fōn′) *n* **1** one of the slightly different forms of a speech sound. The *t* in top and the *t* in stop are allophones of the sound *t.* **2** 🍁 *especially Québec* an immigrant whose first language is neither English nor French. <Greek *allo-* different + *-phone*>

al·lot (ə lot′) *v* **al·lot·ted, al·lot·ting** **1** divide and distribute in parts or shares: *The profits have been allotted among the owners of the company.* **2** give as a share: *For the environmental cleanup day, our group was allotted a section of the park.* <Old French *aloter* divide into lots> **al·lot′ment** *n.*

al·lo·trope (al′ə trōp′) *Chemistry n* a form of the same element, with different physical and chemical properties even though composed of the same kind of atoms. <Greek *allo-* different + *tropos* manner>
al′lo·trop′ic *adj.* **al′lo·trop′y** *n.*

all–out (ol′out′) *adj* involving all one's resources or carried to the fullest extent: *an all-out effort, all-out war.*

all·o·ver (ol′ō′vər) *adj* to do with a pattern that is repeated over the whole surface.

al·low (ə lou′) *v* **1** let or permit to happen: *He allowed us to leave early. This software allows you to keep track of your accounts. Smoking is not allowed on the bus.* **2** let someone have: *His parents allow him $10 a week as spending money.* **3** recognize as valid: *to allow a claim, to allow evidence.* **4** add to make up for something: *It takes about an hour, but you ought to allow ten minutes for possible delays.* <Old French *alouer* approve, from Latin *allaudare* to praise. There is another French word *alouer* allocate, from Latin *allocare* to place. By the time *alouer* was adopted into English, both French meanings were combined into one word.> **al·low′a·ble** *adj.* **al·low′a·bly** *adv.*
allow for, take into consideration: *She purposely made the dress large to allow for shrinking.*
allow of, be capable of: *That question allows of no reply.*

al·low·ance (ə lou′əns) *n* **1** an amount allowed to someone, especially, an amount of spending money given regularly: *My weekly allowance is $10.* **2** the amount added or subtracted to make up for something: *The dealer gave us an allowance of $4 000 on our old car; so we got a $20 000 car for $16 000.* **3** the act or fact of allowing: *allowance of a claim.*
make allowance(s) for, a take into consideration: *to make allowance for the weather.* **b** excuse in view of circumstances: *We must make allowances for him; he's new.*

al·loy (al′oi) *for n,* (ə loi′) *for v. n* **1** a metal made by mixing one metal with another, or with some other substance, in order to make something that is harder, lighter, or stronger. **2** an inferior metal mixed in with a more valuable one: *This is not pure gold; there is some alloy in it.*
v **1** blend into an alloy: *to alloy copper and zinc.* **2** make worse by mixing with something bad; debase: *happiness alloyed by recurring doubts.* <Old French, from Latin *ad-* to + *ligare* bind>

all–pow·er·ful (ol′pou′ər fəl) *adj* able to do anything.

all–pur·pose (ol′pər′pəs) *adj* able to be used for many different things: *all-purpose flour.*

all right *adj* **1** (*not before the noun*) reasonably good: *Her work was not excellent, but it was all right.* **2 a** not sick, hurt, or damaged: *Are you all right?* **b** *Informal* able to cope or be content: *Are you all right with that?*
adv **1** reasonably well: *The engine seems to be working all right.* **2** (*as an intensifier*) certainly: *He's clever, all right!*
interj giving assent: *"Will you help me?" "All right."*

all–round (ol′round′) *adj* useful or skilled in several different ways.

all·spice (ol′spīs′) *n* a spice, made from the dried berries of a Caribbean tree, that has a flavour similar to cinnamon, nutmeg, and cloves.

all–star (ol′stär′) *adj* made up of the best players or performers: *an all-star team, an all-star cast.*
n one of these players or performers.

all–ter·rain vehicle (ol′tə rān′) *n* a small open motor vehicle that can be used on rough ground. *Abbrev.* **ATV**

all–time (ol′tīm′) *adj* setting a record: *Interest rates are at an all-time low.*

al·lude (ə lūd′) *v* **al·lud·ed, al·lud·ing** (*with* ***to***) refer to indirectly: *Don't ask him about the science test; don't even allude to it.* See ELUDE for confusable. <Latin *ad-* toward + *ludere* to play>

al·lure (ə lūr′) *v* **al·lured, al·lur·ing** tempt or attract strongly: *Circus life allured him with its action and excitement.*
n irresistible attraction: *the allure of the sea.* <Old French *alurer*, from Latin *ad-* to + *luere* lure> **al·lure′ment** *n.* **al·lur′ing** *adj.* **al·lur′ing·ly** *adv.*

al·lu·sion (ə lū′zhən) *n* an indirect or passing reference, usually understandable only to people familiar with the reference in question: *The third book in the trilogy has many allusions to the other two books, so you should read those first.*

CONFUSABLES

An **allusion** means "a subtle remark": *The teacher's comment was an allusion to our last field trip.*

An **illusion** means "an incorrect idea or impression": *He was under the illusion that the door was locked.*

al·lu·vi·al (ə lū′vē əl) *adj* consisting of or formed by sand or mud that has been left by flowing water: *an alluvial deposit at the mouth of a river.* <Latin *ad-* toward + *luere* wash> **al·lu·vi·um** *n.*

alluvial fan *n* a gently sloped, fan-shaped deposit of mud or sand, resulting from a gradual decrease in the speed of a river or stream.

all–weath·er (ol′ weᴛʜ′ər) *adj* designed to be usable or practical in all kinds of weather: *an all-weather coat.*

al·ly (ə lī′) *for v,* (al′ī) *for n. v* **al·lied, al·ly·ing** unite or associate for mutual help and support: *France has allied itself with Britain in two world wars.*
n, pl **al·lies** **1** a person or nation united with another for mutual help and support: *The US is our ally.* See also ALLIES. **2** a helper or supporter. <Old French, from Latin *ad-* to + *ligare* bind>

al·ma ma·ter (al′mə mä′tər) *or* (al′mə mā′tər) *n* the school, college, or university from which a person has graduated. <Latin = nourishing mother, referring to education as a generous gift>

a bat	e bed	i bid	o pot	u cup	th thin
ā cake	ē me	ī bite	ō go	ū rude	ᴛʜ then
ä bar	ə about	ər over	ȯ for	u̇ put	zh measure

al·ma·nac (ol′mə nak′) *or* (al′mə nak′) *n* an annual book containing statistical information and tables, useful facts, important dates and, sometimes, predictions about the weather for the coming year. <Latin, from Arabic *al-manakh*>

al·might·y (ol mī′tē) *adj* **1** with supreme power. **2** *Informal* huge or very great: *He made such an almighty fuss that we had to leave.*
n **the Almighty** God. **al·might′i·ly** *adv.*

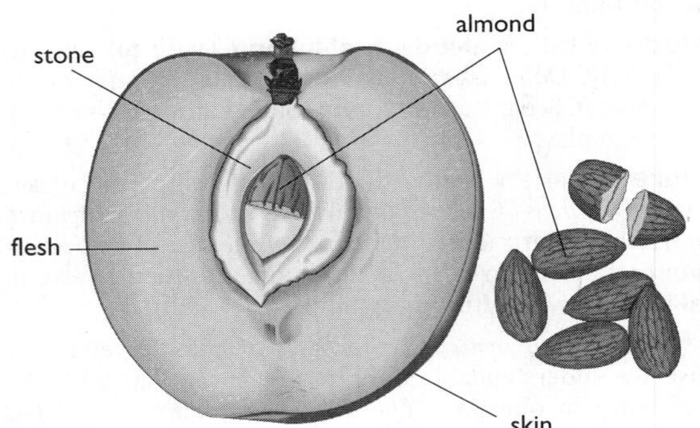

al·mond (ol′mənd), (om′ənd), *or* (am′ənd) *n* the nut of a peachlike fruit that grows on a tree of the rose family. <Old French *almande*, from Greek *amygdale*>

al·most (ol′mōst) *adv* nearly or not quite: *almost 20. I almost hit him.* <Old English *al* all + *mast* most>

alms (omz) *or* (olmz) *pln* money or gifts to help the poor. <Old English *ælmysse*>

alms·giv·ing (omz′giv′ing) *or* (olmz′giv′ing) *n, adj* giving help or gifts to the poor. **alms′giv′er** *n.*

al·ni·co (al′ni kō′) *or* (al nē′kō) *n* an alloy containing aluminum and other metals. <*al*(*uminum*) + *ni*(*ckel*) + *co*(*balt*)>

al·oe (al′ō) *n, pl* **al·oes** **1** a tropical plant of the lily family, with a long spike of flowers and thick, narrow leaves. The **aloe vera** is used in cosmetics and shampoos. **2** **aloes** (*with singular verb*) a laxative made from the juice of the leaves of some aloes. <Old English>

a·loft (ə loft′) *adv* up in the air or in a high place, such as on the mast of a ship: *The sailor climbed aloft to untangle some ropes.* <Old Norse *a* in + *lopt* air>

a·lone (ə lōn′) *adj* (*never precedes a noun*) **1** with no others around: *Are you alone?* **2** without help: *One person alone can do this work.* **3** lonely: *He felt very alone without his friends.* **4** without anything else: *Meat alone is not a good diet.*
adv **1** without help: *She finished the job alone.* **2** with no others around: *The house stood alone on the hill.* <Middle English *al one* all one> **a·lone′ness** *n.*
leave alone, stop or refrain from disturbing or interfering.
leave well enough alone, refrain from interfering or making unnecessary changes.
let alone, a not to mention: *It would have been a hot day for summer, let alone early spring.* **b** leave alone.

a·long (ə long′) *prep* from one end of something to the other: *Flowers were planted along the path. We walked along the street.*
adv **1** further or onward: *Move along. Pass the word along.* **2** carried by or accompanying someone: *Bring your swimsuit along. Sing along with me.* **3** *Informal* there; together with others: *I'll be along in a minute.* <Old English *andlang*>
all along, from the beginning: *He was here all along.*
along the way, a on the route to somewhere: *We stopped twice along the way.* **b** in the process of doing something: *I did it for fun, but I also learned a lot along the way.*
along with, together with: *Have juice along with the food.*
come along, a come with someone. **b** make progress: *He's coming along well in math.*
get along, a manage with at least some success: *We'll get along without her.* **b** live or work in harmony: *He and I don't get along.* **c** leave: *I'll have to be getting along now.*
go along with, agree with or consent to: *to go along with someone's suggestion.*

a·long·side (ə long′sīd′) *for adv,* (ə long′sīd′) *for prep. adv* at or to the side of a person or thing: *to anchor alongside. I stood on the dock while she brought the boat alongside.*
prep (*occasionally with* ***of***) at or to the side of: *The boat was alongside the wharf.*

a·loof (ə lūf′) *adv* off at a distance or apart: *One girl stood aloof from all the others.*
adj withdrawn: *She seems aloof, but she is really just shy.* <16c English *aloof* away to the windward> **a·loof′ly** *adv.* **a·loof′ness** *n.*

a·loud (ə loud′) *adv* loud enough to be heard: *She read the story aloud to the others.*

alp (alp) *n* a high mountain. Compare ALPS.

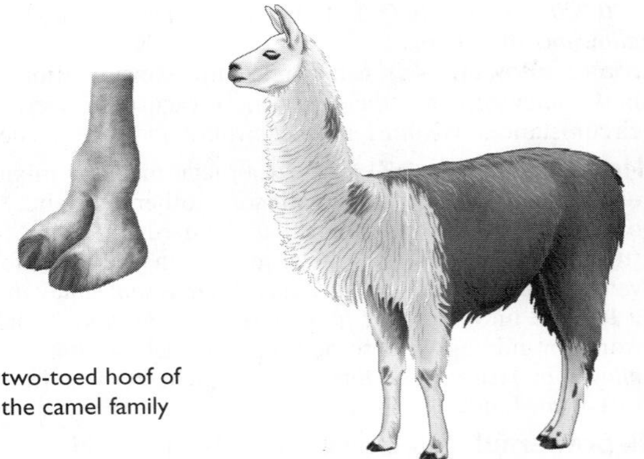

There are four wool-bearing animals native to South America: the **alpaca**, the llama, the guanaco, and the vicuna. Their hoofs resemble those of a camel and, like the camel, they are known for their habit of spitting when angry.

al·pac·a (al pak′ə) *n* a grazing animal of the S American mountains, related to the llama, with long, soft, silky wool that is made into cloth. <Spanish, from Aymara (a language of S America) *allpaca*>

al·pha (al′fə) *n* the first in a series; the beginning of anything.
adj Computers to do with the first version of something, to which changes and improvements are expected before release: *an alpha test.* <first letter of Greek alphabet>

al·pha·bet (al′fə bet′) *n* a set of letters or characters representing sounds, used in writing a language. <*alpha* + *beta* first two letters of the Greek alphabet>

al·pha·bet·i·cal (al′fə bet′ə kəl) *adj* **1** following the order of the alphabet: *an alphabetical listing.* **2** usually, **alphabetic** belonging to the alphabet: *You can enter only alphabetic characters; the program will not recognize numerals.* **al′pha·bet′i·cal·ly** *adv.*

al·pha·bet·ize (al′fə bə tīz′) *v* **al·pha·bet·ized, al·pha·bet·iz·ing** arrange in alphabetical order.

alphabet soup *n* soup containing pieces of pasta in the shape of letters of the alphabet.

alpha decay *Physics n* a radioactive disintegration process in which an alpha particle is released from the atom's nucleus, decreasing the atomic number by two.

al·pha·nu·mer·ic (al′fə nyū mer′ik) *or* (al′fə nū mer′ik) *adj* consisting of both letters and numerals: *Canada has an alphanumeric postal code system.*

alpha particle *Physics n* a positively charged particle made of two protons and two neutrons, released in the disintegration of radium and similar substances. A stream of such particles is called an **alpha ray**.

Today's competitive **alpine** skiers can go as fast as 150 km/h. However, speed isn't limited to modern skiing. In the mid 1800s, miners in California used crude wooden skis, known as longboards, to race straight down rugged mountainsides at speeds of up to 140 km/h.

al·pine (al′pīn) *adj* **1 a** to do with mountains or a mountainous habitat: *alpine meadows, alpine flowers.* **b** to do with downhill skiing as opposed to cross-country. **2 Alpine** to do with the Alps.

alpine fir *n* a fir tree found especially in the mountainous regions of western N America, with a narrow, tapering, crown and curved needles.

Alps (alps) *pln* a range of mountains in southern Europe.

al·read·y (ol red′ē) *adv* **1** by or before this time: *You are half an hour late already. I'm not hungry; I already ate.* **2** so soon: *Must you go already?* **3** *Informal* (*at the end of a sentence*) an expression of impatience: *Enough complaining already!* <*all* + *ready*>

CONFUSABLES

Already refers to a time before now: *She's already done her English homework.*

All ready means "prepared" or "completely ready": *I'm all ready for my vacation.*

Although in speech these can sound the same, it is important to distinguish them in writing.

ALS *n* in full, **amyotrophic lateral sclerosis** a disease characterized by the deterioration of nerve cells, resulting in loss of muscle control. Also called **Lou Gehrig's disease**.

Al·sa·tian (al sā′shən) *adj* of Alsace, a region in northeast France, or its people.
n GERMAN SHEPHERD.

al·so (ol′sō) *adv* in addition, besides, or too: *That dress is pretty; it is also a bargain.* <Old English *alswa*>

al·so–ran (ol′sō ran′) *n* a loser in a contest or race, especially by a large margin.

al·tar (ol′tər) *n* a table or stand in a church or other place of worship, used for certain ceremonies or to hold sacred items. <Old English, from Latin *altus* high>

al·ter (ol′tər) *v* **1** make changes in: *Don't alter my report.* **2** change the design or size of a garment: *I had to have the dress altered to fit.* **3** become different: *Since her trip to Europe, her whole outlook has altered.* <Old French, from Latin *alter* other> **al′ter·a·ble** *adj.* **al′ter·a′tion** *n.*

al·ter·ca·tion (ol′tər kā′ shən) *n* an angry dispute or quarrel. <Latin *altercari* to wrangle>

alter ego *n* **1** a very different side of one's nature. **2** a very intimate friend. <Latin = other self>

al·ter·nate (ol′tər nāt′) *for v,* (ol′tər nit) *or* (ol tər′nit) *for n or adj. v* **al·ter·nat·ed, al·ter·nat·ing 1** (*sometimes with* ***with***) occur, do, or arrange by turns, first one and then the other: *A's and B's alternate in ABABABA. The two of us alternate in doing the dishes. Try to alternate work with play.* **2** reverse direction at regular intervals in an electric current: *AC is an abbreviation for alternating current.*
adj **1** every other: *We have science on alternate days.* **2** alternative: *If that doesn't work, I have an alternate method.* **3** placed or happening by turns, first one and then the other: *A checkerboard has alternate black and white squares.*
n **1** a player who relieves another during a game: *We had ten alternates on our hockey team.* **2** a substitute or backup. <Latin *alter* other> **al′ter·nate·ly** *adv.*

a bat	e bed	i bid	o pot	u cup	th **thin**
ā cake	ē me	ī bite	ō go	ū rude	ᴛʜ **then**
à bar	ə about	ər over	ȯ for	ů put	zh measure

alternate angles *Mathematics pln* two angles at opposite ends and on opposite sides of a transversal (a line that crosses) cutting two other lines.

alternating current *n* an electric current in which the electricity flows first in one direction and then in the other at regular intervals, reversing many times per second. *Abbrev.* **AC** or **A.C.** Compare DIRECT CURRENT.

al·ter·na·tion (ol′tər nā′shən) *n* the act of alternating: *an alternation of red and white stripes in the American flag.*

al·ter·na·tive (ol tər′nə tiv) *adj* consisting of or offering another choice: *There is an alternative menu for vegetarians. There are several alternative ways to do this.*
n **1** the possibility of choosing something else: *We have the alternative of going to a play or to a movie.* **2** one of the things to be chosen: *He chose the first alternative and had pie for dessert.* **3** an option different from the one in question: *The alternative was chocolate cake.* <French, from Latin *alternare* interchange> **al·ter′na·tive·ly** *adv.*

GRAMMAR AND USAGE

Alternative comes from Latin *alter*, meaning "the second of two." However, it is commonly used to mean "one of several possibilities."

alternative medicine *n* medical therapies, such as herbal remedies, naturopathy, and acupuncture, that are not usually taught in medical school.

alternative school *n* a publicly funded school whose curriculum, teaching method, or student body is different from most other schools.

al·ter·na·tor (ol′tər nā′tər) *n* a generator for producing an alternating electric current, such as for the engine of a motor vehicle.

al·though (ol ŦHō′) *conj* even if or in spite of the fact that: *Although it was still raining, they went on the hike.* <Middle English *al thogh*>

al·tim·e·ter (al tim′ə tər) *or* (al′tə mē′tər) *n* an instrument for measuring altitude: *Altimeters are used in aircraft to indicate height above the earth's surface.*

al·ti·tude (al′tə tyūd′) *or* (al′tə tūd′) *n* **1** height above some level, especially sea level: *The airplane is flying at an altitude of 3000 m. The altitude of Calgary is 1079 m.* **2** a high place: *At these altitudes, snow never melts.* **3** *Astronomy* the angular distance of a star, planet, or other celestial body above the horizon. <Latin *altus* high>

altitude sickness *n* a condition caused by a shortage of oxygen due to thinness of the air at high altitudes that causes exhaustion, nausea, and shortness of breath.

al·to (ol′tō) *or* (al′tō) *n, pl* **al·tos** **1** in full, **contralto** the lowest female singing voice, or a singer with such a range. **2** an instrument with a range lower than SOPRANO or TREBLE, in a family of musical instruments.
adj to do with an alto. <Italian, from Latin *contra-* counter to + *alto* high>

alto clef *Music n* the C CLEF that assigns middle C to the third (the middle) line of the staff. Compare BASS CLEF, TENOR CLEF, TREBLE CLEF.

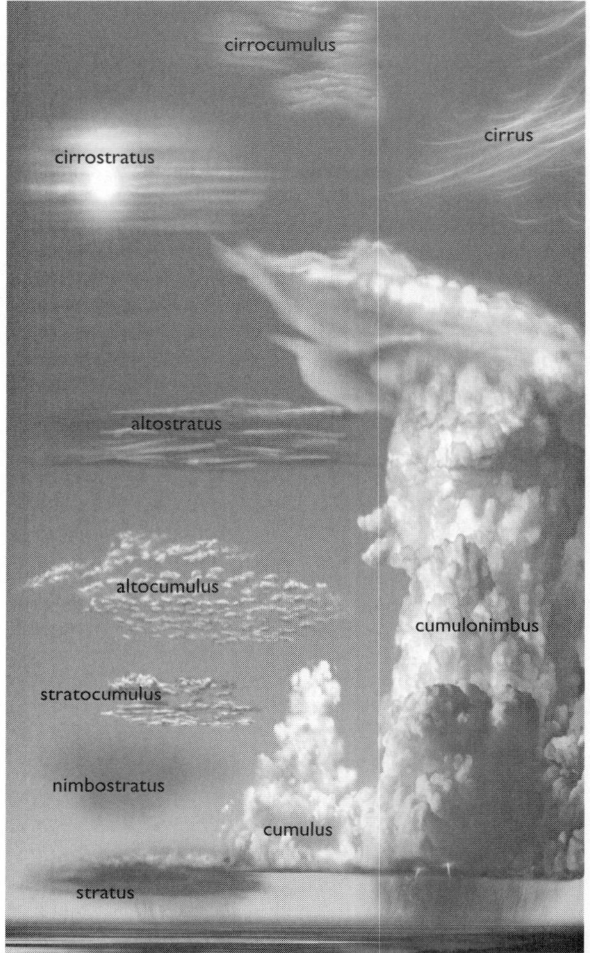

al·to·cu·mu·lus (al′tō kyūm′yə ləs) *or* (ol′tō kyūm′yə ləs) *n, pl* **al·to·cu·mu·li** (-lī′) *or* (-lē′) a fleecy cloud formation with rounded heaps of white or greyish cloud, often partly shaded, at heights of 2 to 7 km. *Abbrev.* **Ac** <Latin *alto* high + *cumulus* heap>

al·to·geth·er (ol′tə geŦH′ər) *adv* **1** all included: *Altogether there were ten books.* **2** completely: *The house was altogether destroyed by fire.* **3** considering everything: *Altogether, I'm sorry I went.* <Old English *all togaedere*>

CONFUSABLES

Altogether means "entirely" or "totally": *It was altogether a beautiful sunset.*

All together means "together in a group": *We were all together waiting for the bus.*

al·to·stra·tus (al′tō strat′əs) *or* (ol′tō strat′əs) *n, pl* **al·to·stra·ti** (-strat′ī) *or* (-strat′ē) a bluish grey, sheetlike cloud formation not sharply defined at the base, occurring at heights of 2 to 7 km. *Abbrev.* **As** <Latin *alto* high + *stratus* spreading out>

al·tru·ism (ol′trū iz′əm) *or* (al′trū iz′əm) *n* concern for the interests and welfare of others. <French *altruisme*, from Latin *alter* other> **al′tru·ist** *n.* **al′tru·is′tic** *adj.*

al·um (al′əm) *n* a colourless crystalline metallic salt, used in dyeing, tanning, and baking powder. <Old French, from Latin *alumen*>

a·lu·mi·na (ə lū′mə nə) *n* aluminum oxide, a white solid that is part of many rocks.

a·lu·min·ize (ə lū′mə nīz′) *v* **a·lu·min·ized, a·lu·min·iz·ing** coat or treat with aluminum.

a·lu·mi·num (ə lū′mə nəm) *n* a silver-white, light, easily worked metallic element that occurs in nature only in combination. *Symbol* **Al** <Latin *aluminis* alum>

a·lum·na (ə lum′nə) *n, pl* **a·lum·nae** (ə lum′nē) *or* (ə lum′nī) a female graduate or former student of a school, college, or university. <Latin, feminine of *alumnus*>

a·lum·nus (ə lum′nəs) *n, pl* **a·lum·ni** (ə lum′nī) a male graduate or former student of a school, college, or university. <Latin = foster child, from *alere* nourish. See ALMA MATER.>

al·ways (ol′wēz) *or* (ol′wāz) *adv* **1** every time or in every case: *Night always follows day.* **2** all the time: *She is always cheerful.* **3** for all time to come: *I'll love you always.* <*all* + *way*>

a·lys·sum (ə lis′əm) *n* a garden plant of the mustard family with greyish leaves and fragrant flowers. <Latin, from Greek *a-* not + *lyssa* rabies, referring to its use as a remedy>

Alz·hei·mer's disease (olts′ hī′mərz) *n* a disease that causes the brain cells to degenerate, leading eventually to severe mental impairment and death. <A. *Alzheimer,* 20c physician>

am (am) first person singular, present tense of BE. <Old English *eom*>

a.m. or **A.M.** (*with a particular time*) after midnight and before noon: *The store opens at 9:30 a.m.*

ETYMOLOGY

a.m. or **A.M.** is an abbreviation of Latin *ante meridiem,* meaning "before noon."

p.m. or **P.M.** is an abbreviation of Latin *post meridiem,* meaning "after noon."

AM or **A.M.** amplitude modulation.

a·mal·gam (ə mal′gəm) *n* **1** an alloy of mercury with some other metal or metals. **2** a mixture or blend. <Latin, from Greek *malagma* softening substance>

a·mal·gam·ate (ə mal′gə māt′) *v* **a·mal·gam·at·ed, a·mal·gam·at·ing** combine or unite: *The two companies amalgamated to form one big one.* **a·mal′ga·ma′tion** *n.*

a·man·u·en·sis (ə man′yū en′sis) *n, pl* **a·man·u·en·ses** (ə man′yū en′sēz) a person who writes down spoken texts or copies written ones. <Latin (*servus*) *a manu* hand (= slave at handwriting) + *-ensis* belonging to>

am·a·ranth (am′ə ranth′) *n* an annual plant, especially the garden plant love-lies-bleeding. <Latin, from Greek *amarantos* not fading>

am·a·ryl·lis (am′ə ril′is) *n* a lilylike plant with clusters of large fragrant red, white, or pink flowers on a thick stalk, and long, narrow leaves that appear only after the flowers have withered. <Latin, from Greek, name for a country girl in pastoral poetry>

a·mass (ə mas′) *v* pile up or accumulate: *The miser amassed a fortune for himself.* <French, from Latin *massa* lump>

A·ma·te·ra·su (ä′mä te rä′sū) *Shintoism n* the sun goddess, to whom the imperial family of Japan has traditionally been traced.

am·a·teur (am′ə chər), (am′ə chůr′), *or* (am′ə tər′) *n* **1** a person who does something for pleasure, not for money or as a profession: *All the actors in this community theatre are amateurs.* **2** a person who does something with little skill: *This is clearly the work of an amateur.*
adj to do with an amateur or amateurs: *an amateur orchestra.* <French, from Latin *amare* to love>

am·a·teur·ish (am′ə chər′ish) *or* (am′ə chů′rish) *adj* inept or not very skilful. **am′a·teur′ish·ly** *adv.* **am′a·teur′ish·ness** *n.*

a·maze (ə māz′) *v* **a·mazed, a·maz·ing** fill with surprise and wonder: *The surprise party so amazed her that she could not speak.* <Old English *amasian*>
a·maze′ment *n.* **a·maz′ing** *adj.* **a·maz′ing·ly** *adv.*

Am·a·zon (am′ə zon′) *n* **1** *Greek myth* a member of a race of female warriors. **2** **amazon** a tall, strong, athletic woman.

Am·a·zo·ni·an (am′ə zō′nē ən) *adj* to do with the Amazon River in S America.

am·bas·sa·dor (am bas′ə dər) *n* **1** a high-ranking diplomat sent by one government or ruler to another. **2** an unofficial representative of a group: *Remember, at the tournament you are ambassadors of our school community.* <Old French, from Latin *ambasciator*> **am·bas′sa·do′ri·al** *adj.* **am·bas′sa·dor·ship** *n.*

am·ber (am′bər) *n* the translucent, fossilized, brownish yellow resin of ancient pine trees, used for making jewellery.
adj **1** made of amber. **2** brownish yellow. <Old French, from Arabic *anbar* ambergris>

am·ber·gris (am′bər grēs′) *or* (am′bər gris) *n* a waxlike, greyish substance secreted by sperm whales, used in making perfume. <French *ambre gris* grey amber>

am·bi·dex·trous (am′bə dek′strəs) *adj* able to use both hands equally well. <Latin *ambi-* on both sides + *dexter* right-handed> **am′bi·dex·ter′i·ty** *n.*

am·bi·ence (am′bē äns′) *or* (am′bē əns′) *n* the character or atmosphere of a place: *They felt uncomfortable in the formal ambience of the expensive restaurant.*
Also, **ambiance.** <See AMBIENT.>

am·bi·ent (am′bē ənt) *adj* surrounding: *the ambient temperature.* <Latin *ambi-* around + *ire* go>

a bat	e bed	i bid	o pot	u cup	th thin
ā cake	ē me	ī bite	ō go	ū rude	TH then
ä bar	ə about	ər over	ô for	ů put	zh measure

am·big·u·ous (am big′yū əs) *adj* **1** with more than one possible meaning. **2** vague or uncertain: *an ambiguous answer. She was left in an ambiguous position by her friend's sudden change of plans.* <Latin *ambi-* both ways + *agere* to drive> **am′bi·gu′i·ty** (am′bə gyū′ə tē) *n.* **am·big′u·ous·ly** *adv.* **am′big′u′ous′ness** *n.*

CONFUSABLES

Ambiguous means "unclear" or "indefinite": *His ambiguous answer left us confused.*

Ambivalent indicates being in a state of conflicting feelings or attitudes: *I am ambivalent about cola; it tastes good, but it keeps me awake at night.*

am·bi·tion (am bish′ən) *n* **1** a strong desire to be or do something: *Her ambition was to be a great actress.* **2** a strong inner drive for success: *With enough ambition, he could have been a politician.* <Old French, from Latin *ambire* canvass for votes> **am·bi′tion·less** *adj.*

am·bi·tious (am bish′əs) *adj* **1** with a strong desire and determination to succeed: *an ambitious person.* **2** requiring much skill or effort: *an ambitious plan.* **am·bi′tious·ly** *adv.* **am·bi′tious·ness** *n.*

am·biv·a·lent (am biv′ə lənt) *adj* with conflicting feelings about something: *I'm a bit ambivalent about it; it sounds like fun, but it's probably dangerous.* See AMBIGUOUS for confusable. <Latin *ambi-* in two ways + *valentia* value> **am·biv′a·lence** *n.* **am·biv′a·lent·ly** *adv.*

am·ble (am′bəl) *v* **am·bled, am·bling** walk at a slow, easy pace.
n this way of walking. <Old French, from Latin *ambulare* walk>

am·bro·sia (am brō′zhə) *n* **1** *Greek and Roman myth* the food of the gods. **2** anything especially delicious. <Latin, from Greek *a-* not + *brotos* mortal>

In Canada, some helicopters are equipped as air **ambulances** to transport critically ill patients from remote locations to urban centres for treatment. Helicopters can land next to a hospital, eliminating the need to transport a patient by ground ambulance to and from an airport.

am·bu·lance (am′byə ləns) *n* a vehicle, boat, or aircraft equipped to carry sick or wounded people. <French, from (*hôpital*) *ambulant* walking hospital>

am·bush (am′bůsh) *n* a surprise attack from a hidden position.
v attack someone who is unprepared for it. <Old French *en* in + *busche* wood, bush>

a·me·ba (ə mē′bə) AMOEBA.

a·mel·io·rate (ə mēl′yə rāt′) *v* **a·mel·io·rat·ed, a·mel·io·rat·ing** make or become better: *New housing ameliorated their living conditions.* <Old French, from Latin *ad-* to + *melior* better> **a·mel′io·ra′tion** *n.* **a·mel′io·ra′tive** *adj.*

a·men (ā′men′) *or* (ȧ′men′) *interj* **1** so be it, used as an exclamation after a Christian or Jewish prayer. **2** *Informal* used as an expression of approval or agreement: *Amen to that!*
n the saying, writing, or singing of "amen": *Several amens were heard from the crowd.* <Hebrew = truth, certainty>

a·me·na·ble (ə men′ə bəl) *or* (ə mē′nə bəl) *adj* (*with* ***to***) **1** open and responsive: *A reasonable person is amenable to persuasion.* **2** accountable; answerable: *People living in a country are amenable to its laws.* <Old French = answerable to the law, from Latin *minare* to drive (cattle) by shouting>

a·mend (ə mend′) *v* **1** change the wording of an official text such as a law, motion, or contract. **2** correct: *It is time you amended your poor table manners. A few inaccurate statistics were amended in the new edition.* Compare EMEND. <Old French *amender*, from Latin *ex-* out of + *menda* a fault> **a·mend′a·ble** *adj.* **a·mend′ment** *n.*

a·mends (ə mendz′) *pln* payment for loss or injury.
make amends, make up for what one has done: *After the quarrel he tried to make amends by giving her flowers.*

a·men·i·ty (ə men′ə tē) *or* (ə mē′nə tē) *n* usually, **amenities** *pl* **1** conveniences: *This house for rent has all the amenities.* **2** the things serving a community, such as stores, parks, schools, bus system, etc.: *a central location close to all the amenities.* <Old French, from Latin *amoenus* pleasant, agreeable>

A·men–Ra (a′mən ra′) *n* the chief god of the ancient Egyptians.

A·mer·i·ca (ə mer′ə kə) *n* **1** the United States. **2** usually, **the Americas** North, Central, and South America. **A·mer′i·can** *adj, n.*

A·mer·i·ca·na (ə mer′ə kan′ə) *n* objects or texts associated with the US, especially its history.

A·mer·i·can·ism (ə mer′ə kə niz′əm) *n* **1** a word, phrase, or custom originating in or typical of the US. **2** the qualities regarded as defining the US or its citizens.

A·mer·i·can·ize (ə mer′ə kə nīz′) *v* make American in nature or character.

American plan *n* a system used in hotels where one price covers room, meals, and service. Compare EUROPEAN PLAN.

American Sign Language *n* a language made up of hand and face gestures, used by much of the N American deaf and hearing-impaired community.
Abbrev. **Ameslan** or **ASL**

am·er·i·ci·um (am′ə rish′ē əm) *n* a radioactive metallic element obtained from plutonium. *Symbol* **Am**

Am·es·lan (am′e slan′) an abbreviation of *Ame*(rican) *S*(ign) *Lan*(guage).

am·e·thyst (am′ə thist) *n* a purple gemstone, a variety of quartz. <Old French, from Greek *amethystos* not drunk (i.e., sober). It was thought to prevent getting drunk.>

a·mi·a·ble (ā′mē ə bəl) *adj* good-natured and friendly: *a sweet, amiable girl.* <Latin *amicus* friend> **a′mi·a·bly** *adv.*

CONFUSABLES

Amiable means "good-natured": *The amiable dog made friends with everyone.*

Amicable means "peaceable": *The opponents shook hands in an amicable way when the race was over.*

am·i·ca·ble (am′ə kə bəl) *adj* peaceable and friendly: *Let's not quarrel; I'm sure we can settle our differences in an amicable way.* <Latin *amicus* friend> **am′i·ca·bly** *adv.*

a·mid (ə mid′) *prep* in the middle of; during. Also, **amidst**. <Old English *amidde*>

GRAMMAR AND USAGE

Amid is used for things that cannot be counted: *I lost my hat and gloves amid the confusion.*

Among is used with a plural noun: *The children played hide-and-seek among the trees.*

a·mid·ships (ə mid′ships) *adv* in or toward the middle part of a ship.

a·mi·no acid (ə mē′nō) *or* (am′ə nō′) *n* a complex organic compound of nitrogen that combines in various ways to form a protein.

am·ir (ā mēr′) EMIR.

Am·ish (ȧ′mish) *adj* to do with a strict Mennonite sect founded in the 1600s in Switzerland.
pl n the members of this sect, most of whom live in farming communities in S Ontario and parts of the US. <J. *Amen*, 17c Mennonite preacher>

a·miss (ə mis′) *adv, adj* not as it should be: *All our plans have gone amiss* (*adv*). *Even though you intended no harm, it would not be amiss to apologize* (*adj*). <Middle English *a mis* in a faulty manner>
take something amiss, be offended at something because one has misunderstood: *I meant it as a joke, but she took it amiss and got angry.*

am·i·ty (am′ə tē) *n, pl* **am·i·ties** a friendly relationship: *amity between nations.* <Old French, from Latin *amicus* friend>

am·me·ter (am′mē′tər) *n* an instrument measuring the strength of an electric current in amperes.

am·mo (am′ō) *Informal n* ammunition.

am·mo·nia (ə mō′nyə) *n* **1** a strong-smelling colourless gas consisting of nitrogen and hydrogen. **2** this gas dissolved in water, often used as a cleanser or to revive people who have fainted. <Latin, from Greek *ammoniakos* (salt) of Ammon, an Egyptian god. Ammonium chloride could be found near his shrine in Libya.>

am·mo·nite (am′ə nīt′) *n* the fossil shell of an extinct mollusc, coiled in a flat spiral and up to 2 m in diameter. <Latin (*cornu*) *Ammonis* (horn) of (the god) Ammon>

am·mo·nium (ə mō′nē əm) *n* a group of nitrogen and hydrogen atoms present in ammonia compounds.

am·mu·ni·tion (am′yə nish′ən) *n* **1** bullets or shells for guns or other weapons. **2** anything that can be shot, hurled, or thrown. **3** a means of attack or defence: *He used the evidence he had gathered as ammunition.* <French, from Latin *munire* fortify or secure>

am·ne·sia (am nē′zhə) *n* loss of memory, due to brain injury, disease, or shock. <Latin, from Greek *a-* not + *mnasthai* remember> **am·ne′sic** *adj.*

am·ne·si·ac (am nē′zē ak′) *n* a person who has amnesia.
adj suffering from amnesia.

am·nes·ty (am′nə stē) *n, pl* **am·nes·ties** a general pardon for past offences against authority: *After order was restored, the king granted amnesty to those who had plotted against him.* <French, from Greek *amnestia* forgetfulness>

am·ni·o·cen·te·sis (am′nē ō sen tē′sis) *n* a procedure for obtaining fluid from the amniotic sac of a fetus in order to diagnose any fetal abnormalities. <Latin, from Greek *amnion* fetal membrane + *kentein* to prick>

am·ni·on (am′nē ən) *n, pl* **am·ni·ons** or **am·ni·a** (am′nē ə) the lining of the sac that encloses the embryos of reptiles, birds, and mammals. <Greek = little lamb>

am·ni·ot·ic (am′nē ot′ik) *adj* to do with the amnion: *amniotic fluid.*

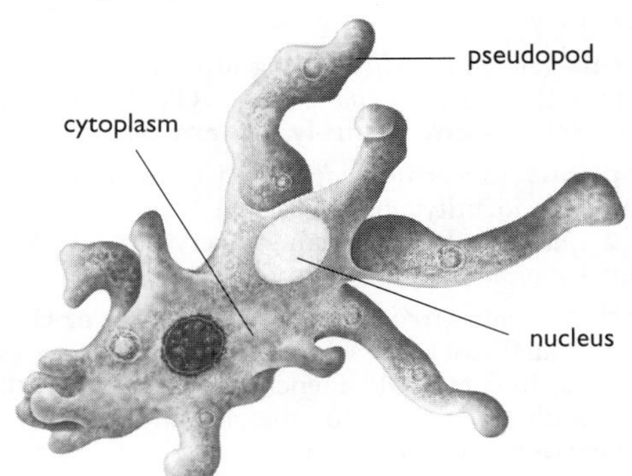

To feed, an **amoeba** forms a pair of projections called pseudopods that envelop an organism, the food. The amoeba also forms a cavity into which digestive enzymes are secreted to break down the food and then diffuse it into the cytoplasm.

a·moe·ba (ə mē′bə) *n, pl* **a·moe·bas** or **a·moe·bae** (ə mē′bē) *or* (ə mē′bī) a one-celled micro-organism that moves by forming temporary projections that constantly change. Also, **ameba**. <Latin, from Greek *amoibe* change> **a·moe′ba·like′** *adj.* **a·moe′bic** *adj.*

a bat	e bed	i bid	o pot	u cup	th **thin**
ā cake	ē me	ī bite	ō go	ū rude	ᴛʜ **then**
ȧ bar	ə about	ər over	ȯ for	ů put	zh measure

a·mok (ə muk′) *or* (ə mok′) *adv* in a frenzy; crazed. Also, **amuck.** <Malay *amok* rushing in a frenzy>
run amok, go out of control.

a·mong (ə mung′) *prep* (*only before plural nouns*) **1** surrounded by: *a house among the trees.* **2** one of: *Canada is among the largest countries of the world.* **3** so as to give some to each of (more than two): *Divide the money among the three of them.* **4** by, with, or through the whole of: *political unrest among the people.* **5** by the combined action or resources of: *Among us we had $85.* **6** in comparison or contrast with: *one among many.* Also, **amongst.** <Old English *on* in + *gemang* crowd>
among ourselves (or **yourselves** or **themselves**), **a** some with others: *They fought among themselves.* **b** as a group; each with all the others: *Settle it among yourselves.*
fall among, meet or become surrounded by: *The lone traveller fell among thieves.*

GRAMMAR AND USAGE

Among is used when giving something to more than two people: *Divide the wedding cake among all the guests.*

Between is used when there are just two: *Let's keep the secret between the two of us.*

a·mor·al (ā mô′rəl) *adj* **1** having nothing to do with questions of right and wrong: *an amoral issue.* **2** with no sense of right and wrong: *Psychopaths are amoral.* See IMMORAL for confusable. <Greek *a-* without + *moral*>
a′mor·al′ity *n.*

am·o·rous (am′ə rəs) *adj* **1** feeling love or sexual desire. **2** to do with love or sexual desire. <Old French, from Latin *amor* love> **am′o·rous·ly** *adv.* **am′o·rous·ness** *n.*

a·mor·phous (ə môr′fəs) *adj* **1** with no definite shape, structure, or identity: *an amorphous mass of locusts in flight.* **2** *Chemistry* not consisting of crystals. <Greek *a-* without + *morphe* shape>

am·or·tize (am′ər tīz′) *v* **am·or·tized, am·or·tiz·ing** repay the initial cost of an asset or mortgage by a series of regular instalments. <Old French, from Latin *ad-* to + *mortis* death (referring to the length of time of repayment)> **am′or·ti·za′tion** *n.*

a·mount (ə mount′) *n* a sum or quantity: *a small amount of money. Is this a sufficient amount of water?*
v (*with* ***to***) **1** add up to: *The loss amounted to a million dollars.* **2** be equivalent: *Borrowing without asking amounts to stealing.* <Old French, from Latin *ad-* to + *montem* mountain>

GRAMMAR AND USAGE

Amount is used to refer to a total in a general way: *A small amount of dust covered the desk.*

Number is used for items that can be counted: *A large number of students went to the concert.*

a·mour (ə mūr′) *n* a love affair, especially a secret one. <French = love>

amp[1] amplifier.

amp[2] ampere.

am·per·age (am′pə rij) *n* the strength of an electric current measured in amperes.

am·pere (am′pēr) *n* the SI unit for measuring the rate of flow of electric current. *Symbol* **A** <A. *Ampère,* 19c physicist>

am·pere–hour (am′pēr our′) *n* an amount of current with the strength of one ampere flowing through a conductor for one hour.

am·per·sand (am′pər sand′) *n* a symbol (&) meaning "and." <alteration of *and per se = and,* a printer's phrase>

am·phet·a·mine (am fet′ə mēn′) *n* a colourless, addictive, mood-altering drug that stimulates the nervous system.

Amphibians have smooth, moist skin, which they shed and regrow continually. Species of amphibians that live in cool regions like Canada hibernate through the winter because they are cold-blooded and must rely on external sources for warmth.

Salamanders and newts are tailed amphibians. They are often mistaken for lizards or other reptiles. Most tailed amphibians must stay close to water to survive. Frogs and toads are tailless amphibians that are better adapted to life on land.

Although there are over 4400 existing species of amphibians, their numbers are dwindling, as humans continue to destroy their habitat.

am·phib·i·an (am fib′ē ən) *n* **1** a cold-blooded vertebrate whose young breathe at first by means of gills. The young usually undergo a complete physical change as they grow, becoming land animals with lungs and legs. **2** an aircraft that can take off and come down on either land or water, or a motor vehicle that can travel across land or water.
adj to do with amphibians. <Latin, from Greek *amphi-* both + *bios* life>

am·phib·i·ous (am fib′ē əs) *adj* adapted to or involving both land and water: *amphibious creatures, amphibious vehicles.* **am·phib′i·ous·ly** *adv.* **am·phib′i·ous·ness** *n.*

am·phi·the·a·tre (am′fə thē′ə tər) *n* **1** a structure in which ascending rows of seats curve in a circle or U-shape around a central open space. **2** a level area of land surrounded by a steeply rising slope. Also, **amphitheater**. <Latin, from Greek *amphi-* on both (sides) + *theatron* theatre>

am·pho·ra (am fȯ′rə) *n, pl* **am·pho·rae** (am fȯ′rē) *or* (am fȯ′rī) a tall, two-handled jar used by the ancient Greeks and Romans. <Latin, from Greek *amphi-* on both (sides) + *phoreus* bearer>

am·ple (am′pəl) *adj* **am·pler, am·plest** **1** big: *ample closets.* **2** more than enough: *an ample supply of food. My allowance is ample for my needs.* <French, from Latin *amplus* large> **am′ply** *adv.*

am·pli·fi·er (am′plə fī′ər) *n* a device in or attached to a radio, CD player, electric musical instrument, or microphone, for strengthening electrical impulses in order to make the sound louder.

am·pli·fy (am′plə fī′) *v* **am·pli·fied, am·pli·fy·ing** **1** make greater or stronger. **2** *Electronics* increase the strength of an electrical impulse using an amplifier. **3** make fuller and more extensive: *to amplify a description, to amplify a point in an argument.* **4** write or talk at length: *to amplify on the details of a proposal.* <French, from Latin *amplus* large, wide> **am′pli·fi·ca′tion** *n.*

am·pli·tude (am′plə tyūd′) *or* (am′plə tūd′) *n* **1** breadth, width, or size. **2** *Physics* the maximum extent of a vibration or oscillation. **3** *Electricity* the peak strength of an alternating electric current in a particular cycle. <Latin *amplus* large>

amplitude modulation *Radio n* **1** a method of transmitting audio signals by changing the strength of the carrier waves to match the signal. **2** the broadcasting system that uses this method of transmission. *Abbrev.* **AM** or **A.M.** Compare FREQUENCY MODULATION.

am·pu·tate (am′pyə tāt′) *v* **am·pu·tat·ed, am·pu·tat·ing** cut off in a surgical operation: *The doctor amputated the soldier's wounded leg.* <Latin *amb-* about + *putare* to prune> **am′pu·ta′tion** *n.*

am·pu·tee (am′pyə tē′) *n* a person who has had an arm or leg amputated.

am·rit (ȧm′rit) *Sikhism n* a sweetened water used as a sacred drink and as baptismal water. <Sanskrit *amrta* immortal>

Am·rit·sar (ȧm rit′sȧr) *n* the site of the Golden Temple, centre of the Sikh religion.

amu atomic mass unit.

a·muck (ə muk′) AMOK.

am·u·let (am′yə lit) *n* an object worn as a magic charm against evil. <Latin *amuletum*>

a·muse (ə myūz′) *v* **a·mused, a·mus·ing** **1** cause to laugh or smile: *We were not amused by this joke.* **2** entertain; keep pleasantly interested: *The new toys amused the children.* <Old French *amuser* cause to be idle> **a·mus′ing** *adj.* **a·mus′ing·ly** *adv.*

a·muse·ment (ə myūz′mənt) *n* **1** the condition of being amused: *He could not hide his amusement and burst out laughing.* **2** fun or entertainment: *They often window-shop for amusement.* **3** something that amuses or entertains, such as a ride or game: *His favourite amusement is playing video games.*

amusement park *n* an outdoor area with rides such as roller coasters and Ferris wheels, games of chance, and refreshment stands.

am·y·lase (am′ə lās′) *n* an enzyme found in plants and animals that helps to change starch into sugar.

an (ən) *indefinite article* a form of the indefinite article A, used before a vowel or silent h: *an apple, an heir.*

An·a·bap·tist (an′ə bap′tist) *Christianity n* a member of a branch of Protestant Christianity that allows baptism only for adults on their confession of faith.
adj to do with this branch of Christianity. <Latin, from Greek *ana-* over again + *baptismos* baptism>

an·a·bol·ic steroid (an′ə bol′ik) *n* a synthetic male sex hormone used in medicine and illegally by some athletes to stimulate the growth of muscle and bone.

a·nab·o·lism (ə nab′ə liz′əm) *n* part of the process of metabolism that involves making complex molecules out of simple ones and changing food into living tissue. <Greek *ana-* backward + (*meta*)*bolism*> **an′a·bol′ic** *adj.*

a·nach·ro·nism (ə nak′rə niz′əm) *n* **1** something placed or occurring out of its proper time: *The phone in that movie about the War of 1812 was an anachronism; phones weren't invented then!* **2** the fact of putting a person, thing, or event in some time where it does not belong: *Much of the story's humour depends on anachronism.* <French, from Greek *ana-* backward + *chronos* time>
a·nach′ro·nis′tic *adj.*

Like amphibians, **anacondas** are cold-blooded animals. The anaconda, a non-venomous reptile, is considered the most powerful snake in the world. It suffocates its prey by wrapping itself around the victim and squeezing the life out of it.

an·a·con·da (an′ə kon′də) *n* a tropical American boa, living in trees and in water, considered the largest snake in the world. <Latin, from Sinhala (a language of Sri Llanka) *henakandaya* a type of snake>

a bat	e bed	i bid	o pot	u cup	th **thin**
ā cake	ē me	ī bite	ō go	ū rude	ᴛʜ **then**
ȧ bar	ə about	ər over	ȯ for	u̇ put	zh measure

a·nae·mi·a (ə nē′mē ə) ANEMIA.

an·aer·obe (an′ə rōb′) *or* (a ner′ōb) *n* a micro-organism that does not use oxygen from the air to convert food into energy. Compare AEROBE. <French, from Greek *an-* without + *aer* air + *bios* life> **an·aer·o′bic** *adj.*

an·aes·the·sia (an′əs thē′zhə) ANESTHESIA.

an·aes·thet·ic (ən′əs thet′ic) ANESTHETIC.

an·aes·the·tist (a′nēs′thə tist′) *or* (ə nes′thə tist′) ANESTHETIST.

an·aes·the·tize (ə nēs′thə tīz′) *or* (ə nes′thə tīz′) ANESTHETIZE.

an·a·gram (an′ə gram′) *n* a word or phrase formed from another by rearranging the letters. Example: *silent/listen.* <Latin, from Greek *ana-* back, anew + *gramma* letter>

a·nal (ā′nəl) *adj* to do with the anus. **a′nal·ly** *adv.*

an·a·lects (an′ə lekts′) *pln* a collection of short literary or philosophical extracts. <Latin, from Greek *ana-* up + *legein* gather>

an·al·ge·sic (an′əl jē′zik) *adj* to do with relieving pain: *an analgesic drug.*
n a painkiller. <Latin, from Greek *an-* not + *algeein* feel pain>

a·nal·o·gous (ə nal′ə gəs) *adj* **1** corresponding in some way: *The heart is analogous to a pump.* **2** *Biology* corresponding in function but not in origin. **a·nal′o·gous·ly** *adv.*

an·a·logue (an′ə lòg′) *adj* to do with a system in which information is linked to a physical change, as a watch with hands that move round a face. Compare DIGITAL.
n something or someone that is comparable to another: *Tofu is often advertised as an analogue to meat.* Also (*usually related to computers*), **analog**. <French, from Greek *analogia* proportion>

a·nal·o·gy (ə nal′ə jē) *n, pl* **a·nal·o·gies** **1** a likeness in some ways between things: *There is an analogy between the verbs "sink" and "ring" when it comes to forming the past tense "sank" and "rang."* **2** (*usually with the verb* **draw**) a comparison of such things, made to explain or illustrate something: *She drew an analogy between an atom and the solar system.* **3** the belief that things that are alike in some ways will be alike in others: *It is risky to argue by analogy.* **4** *Biology* similarity in function but not in origin.

SYNONYMS

An **analogy** describes what different things have in common: *He made an analogy between cars and horses.*

A **comparison** describes similarities and differences: *Make a comparison between spring and fall weather.*

A **contrast** focuses on differences: *The contrast in colour between the two trees is amazing.*

a·nal–re·ten·tive (ā′nəl ri ten′tiv) *adj* obsessively neat, fussy, or stingy, supposedly because of one's experiences as a toddler being toilet-trained. Often shortened to **anal**.

a·nal·y·sis (ə nal′ə sis) *n, pl* **a·nal·y·ses** (ə nal′ə sēz) **1** the process of analyzing. **2** psychoanalysis.
in the final analysis, when everything has been considered: *You can blame it on all kinds of things, but in the final analysis, you're responsible.*

an·a·lyst (an′ə list) *n* a person who analyzes something, especially a psychoanalyst or a systems analyst.

an·a·lyt·i·cal (an′ə lit′ə kəl) *adj* to do with analysis or tending to analyze: *analytical skills, an analytical thinker.* Also, **analytic**. **an′a·lyt′i·cal·ly** *adv.*

analytic geometry *Mathematics n* the use of algebra to solve problems in geometry, with coordinates representing points and equations representing lines and curves.

an·a·lyze or **an·a·lyse** (an′ə līz′) *v* **an·a·lyzed** or **an·a·lysed, an·a·lyz·ing** or **an·a·lys·ing** **1** examine carefully and in detail: *My essay analyzes the causes of World War II.* **2** separate into different components or elements and determine the nature and amount of each: *to analyze a blood sample.* **3** psychoanalyze. <Latin, from Greek *ana-* up + *lyein* loosen>

an·a·pest (an′ə pest′) *Poetry n* a metrical foot made up of two weakly stressed syllables followed by one strongly stressed one. Example: *From′ the′ cen′ tre′ all′ round′ to′ the′ sea′*. Compare DACTYL. <Latin, from Greek *anapaistos* reversed. An anapest is a reversed dactyl.>
an′a·pes′tic *adj.*

an·a·phase (an′ə fāz′) *Biology n* the third stage of asexual cell division, in which the chromatids of each chromosome separate and move toward either end of the cell. <Latin, from Greek *ana-* back + *phase*>

an·a·phy·lac·tic shock (an′ə fə lak′tik) *n* an acute, potentially fatal condition caused by a reaction to some substance, such as peanuts, to which a person is extremely sensitive. <Latin, from Greek *ana-* again + (*pro*)*phylassein* defend by taking measures in advance>

an·ar·chism (an′ər kiz′əm) *n* **1** the political theory that all systems of government should be replaced by voluntary co-operation. **2** lawlessness or terrorism. <See ANARCHY.>
an′ar·chist *n, adj.* **an′ar·chis′tic** *adj.*

an·ar·chy (an′ər kē) *n* **1** the absence of a system of government and law. **2** a state of political disorder and violence due to the absence of governmental authority. **3** disorder or confusion. <French, from Greek *an-* without + *archos* ruler>

a·nath·e·ma (ə nath′ə mə) *n* a person who or thing that is detested and condemned: *Messy writing is anathema to him.* <French, from Greek = thing devoted, especially to evil>

a·nat·o·my (ə nat′ə mē) *n, pl* **a·nat·o·mies** **1** the structure of an animal or plant: *The anatomy of an earthworm is much simpler than that of a human being.* **2** the science of the structure of animals and plants: *Anatomy is a part of biology.* **3** the structure of anything, or an analysis of this structure: *the anatomy of a city.* <Old French, from Greek *ana-* up + *temnein* to cut>

an·ces·tor (an′ses tər) *n* **1** a person from whom one is directly descended, such as a parent, grandparent, or great-grandparent: *My ancestors were Dutch.* **2** an original model or type from which others are developed: *The harpsichord is the ancestor of the piano.* **3** *Biology* an earlier species or type from which a later one evolved: *The horse and the donkey have a common ancestor.* Compare DESCENDANT. <Old French *ancestre*, from Latin *ante* before + *cedere* go> **an·ces′tral** *adj.* **an′ces·try** *n.*

an·chor (ang′kər) *n* **1** a heavy piece of iron, usually with hooks, fastened to a ship or boat by a chain or rope and dropped into the water to keep the vessel from drifting. See FLUKE for picture. **2** anything for holding something else in place: *A screw driven into a plaster wall won't hold unless you put in an anchor first.* **3** something that makes a person feel safe and secure. **4** *Radio, Television* the host or person who presents and co-ordinates a live broadcast, especially a newscast.
v **1** keep or stay in place with an anchor: *to anchor a ship. We'll anchor here until morning.* **2** fix firmly or make secure: *to anchor a tent to the ground with pegs. A child's self-esteem is anchored in the love of a family.* **3** *Radio, Television* work as an anchor on a broadcast. <Old English, from Greek *agkura*>
at anchor, held by an anchor.
cast anchor, drop an anchor in the water.
ride at anchor, be kept at some place by being anchored.
weigh anchor, pull up an anchor.

an·cho·rite (ang′kə rīt′) *n* in former times, a person who lived in isolation for purposes of religious meditation. <Latin, from Greek *ana-* back + *chorein* withdraw>

an·cho·vy (an′chō vē), (an′chə vē) *or* (an chō′vē) *n, pl* **an·cho·vies** a small fish related to the herring, used for food and for bait. <Spanish *anchova*>

an·cien régime (on sē ən′ rā zhēm′) *n* **1** the social and political structure of France before the Revolution of 1789. **2** a political or social system that has been replaced by another. <French = old rule>

an·cient (ān′shənt) *adj* **1** to do with times long past in history: *ancient civilizations.* **2** very old: *I heard an ancient song on the radio today.*
n **the ancients** *pl* people who lived in ancient times, especially the Greeks and Romans. <Old French *ancien*, from Latin *ante* before> **an′cient·ness** *n.*

an·cil·lar·y (an sil′ə rē) *or* (an′sə ler′ē) *adj* subordinate or supplementary: *Give any ancillary information on the back of this page.* <Latin *ancilla* handmaid>

and (and) *conj* **1** as well as: *windy and cold.* **2** used to introduce additional information: *It was warm and the sun was shining.* **3** added to or with: *He likes ham and eggs.* **4** then or next: *She came inside and took off her boots.* **5** as a result: *He fell and skinned his knee.* **6** whereas or on the other hand: *She is a homebody and he always wants to travel.* **7** *Informal* (*after* **try**) to: *Just try and stop me.* <Old English>

an·dan·te (än dän′tā) *Music adv, adj* at a moderately slow tempo, faster than ADAGIO but slower than **andantino** (an′dən tē′nō). <Italian = going, from Latin *ambulare* walk>

✱ **And·er·son chariot** (an′dər sən) *n* in the economic depression of the 1930s, a two-wheeled vehicle made from a dismantled car by farmers in the Prairies, and hitched up to horses because the owner could not afford gas, oil, or a licence. Also called **Anderson cart.** <J.T.M. *Anderson*, premier of Saskatchewan from 1929 to 1934>

An·des (an′dēz) *pl n* a mountain range that runs the length of the Pacific coast of S America. **An·de′an** *adj.*

and·i·ron (an′dī′ərn) *n* one of a pair of metal supports for wood in a fireplace. <Old French *andier*>

An·dor·ra (an dȯ′rə) *n* a tiny country between France and Spain. **An·dor′ran** *adj, n.*

an·drog·y·nous (an droj′ə nəs) *adj* **1** with both male and female characteristics. **2** *Botany* having flowers with stamens and flowers with pistils in the same cluster. <Latin, from Greek *andros* man + *gyne* woman>

an·droid (an′droid) *n* a robot built in the form of a human being. <Latin, from Greek *andros* man + *-oid*>

an·ec·dote (an′ik dōt′) *n* a short account of some interesting or amusing incident or event: *Many anecdotes are told about Sir John A. Macdonald.* <Latin, from Greek *anekdota* things not published> **an′ec·do′tal** *adj.*

a·ne·mi·a (ə nē′mē ə) *n* **1** a condition in which there are not enough red corpuscles or hemoglobin in the blood. **2** lack of strength and vitality in anything. Also, **anaemia.** <Latin, from Greek *an-* without + *haima* blood> **a·ne′mic** *adj.*

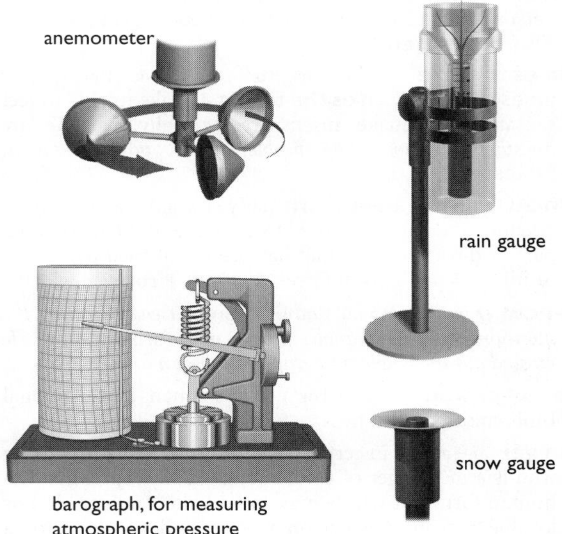

an·e·mom·e·ter (an′ə mom′ə tər) *n* an instrument for measuring wind speed. <French, from Greek *anemos* wind + *meter*>

a·nem·o·ne (ə nem′ə nē′) *n* **1** a flower of the buttercup family with large brightly coloured flowers. Also called **windflower.** **2** sea anemone. <Latin = windflower, from Greek *anemos* wind>

an·en·ceph·a·ly (an′ən sef′ə lē) *n* a birth defect in which all or part of the brain is missing. <Greek *an-* without + *enkephalos* brain> **an′en·ceph·al′ic** *adj.*

an·er·oid barometer (an′ə roid′) *n* an instrument for measuring atmospheric pressure that consists of a metal box containing a partial vacuum, enclosed by a flexible top that moves with changes in pressure.

a bat	e bed	i bid	o pot	u cup	th **thin**
ā cake	ē me	ī bite	ō go	ū rude	ᴛʜ then
ä bar	ə about	ər over	ȯ for	ů put	zh measure

an·es·the·sia (an′əs thē′zhə) *n* loss of sensation produced by drugs or hypnotism, or as the result of hysteria, paralysis, or disease. **General anesthesia** is loss of feeling in the whole body, causing complete or partial unconsciousness. **Local anesthesia** is loss of feeling in only part of the body. Also, **anaesthesia**. <Latin, from Greek *an-* without + *aisthesis* sensation>

an·es·the·si·ol·o·gy (an′əs thē′zē ol′ə jē) *n* the branch of medicine that studies anesthesia and the use of anesthetics. **an′es·the′si·ol′o·gist** *n.*

an·es·thet·ic (an′əs thet′ik) *n* a substance that causes total or partial loss of sensation, such as a **general anesthetic** used in medicine to make a patient unconscious, and a **local anesthetic** to make part of the body insensitive to pain or discomfort.
adj to do with anesthesia. Also, **anaesthetic**. **an′es·thet′i·cal·ly** *adv.*

an·es·the·tist (ə nēs′thə tist) *or* (ə nes′thə tist) *n* a trained person who gives a patient anesthetic during surgery. Also, **anaesthetist**.

an·es·the·tize (ə nēs′thə tīz′) *or* (ə nes′thə tīz′) *v* **an·es·the·tized, an·es·the·tiz·ing 1** make unable to feel sensations. **2** make insensitive or oblivious: *We are anesthetized to the problem of poverty.* Also, **anaesthetize**.

an·eu·rysm or **an·eur·ism** (an′yə riz′əm) *n* a permanent swelling of an artery, caused by pressure of the blood on a part of the artery wall that has been weakened by disease or injury. <Latin, from Greek *ana-* out + *eurynen* widen>

a·new (ə nyū′) *or* (ə nū′) *adv* **1** again: *At each meeting the question was raised anew.* **2** in a new form or way: *He crossed out the whole paragraph and began anew.*

an·ga·koq (ang′gə kok′) *n* a shaman in traditional Inuit culture. <Inuktitut>

an·gel (ān′jəl) *n* **1** in certain religions, a supernatural being who is a messenger of God, and is usually represented in human form but with wings and a halo. **2** a very kind or lovable person. **3** a person who provides money for a business venture such as the production of a play. <Latin, from Greek *angelos* messenger> **an·gel′ic** (an jel′ik) *adj.* **an·gel′i·cal·ly** *adv.*

an·gel·fish (ān′jəl fish′) *n, pl* **an·gel·fish·es** or (*especially collectively*) **an·gel·fish** a tropical marine fish, usually brightly coloured and with a deep, narrow body.

angel food cake *n* a light, springy, white sponge cake made with egg whites but no yolks or fat.

angel hair *n* long, silky white strings of spun glass used to trim a Christmas tree.

an·gel–hair pasta (ān′jəl her′) *n* very thin spaghetti.

an·ger (ang′gər) *n* the feeling of wanting to punish or retaliate against some person who or thing that offends, hurts, frustrates, or annoys.
v make or become angry: *Her rudeness angers me. He angers easily.* <Old Norse *angr* grief>

an·gi·na (an jī′nə) *n* in full, **angina pectoris** (pek′tə ris) a disease of the heart that causes sharp chest pains and a feeling of suffocation, caused by a sudden decrease in the flow of blood to the heart muscles. <Latin, from *angere* to choke and *pectoris* = of the chest>

an·gi·o·gram (an′jē ə gram′) *n* an X-ray picture of blood or lymph vessels. <Latin, from Greek *angeion* vessel + *-gram*>

an·gi·o·plas·ty (an′jē ə plas′tē) *n, pl* **an·gi·o·plas·ties** a procedure used to clear or repair a vein. <Latin, from Greek *angeion* vessel + *plastia* a forming>

an·gi·o·sperm (an′jē ə spərm′) *Botany n* any flowering plant whose seeds are enclosed in a fruit. <Latin, from Greek *angeion* vessel + *sperma* seed>

an·gle[1] (ang′gəl) *n* **1** *Mathematics* **a** the space between two lines extending in different directions from the same point or two surfaces extending from the same line. See ACUTE ANGLE for picture. **b** the figure formed by such lines or surfaces. **c** the difference in direction between two such lines or surfaces: *The roads lie at an angle of forty-five degrees.* **2** a corner. **3** a point of view or aspect: *From any angle, the job was excellent.*
v **an·gled, an·gling** move, place, turn, or bend at an angle: *Angle your chair so you can see the screen. A narrow path angled across the grass.* <Old French, from Latin *angulus* corner>

an·gle[2] (ang′gəl) *v* **an·gled, an·gling 1** fish with a hook and line for sport. **2** (*with* ***for***) try to get something by devious or subtle means: *to angle for an invitation.*
n a means or method, especially a devious one, of obtaining an advantage: *She always has an angle for getting the better of you.* <Old English *angul*>

An·gle (ang′gəl) *n* a member of a Germanic tribe that migrated from what is now southern Denmark to England in the 400s. **An′gli·an** *adj.*

angle brackets *n* brackets of the form < >.

angle of deviation *n* the angle made between a ray of light as it enters a prism or other optical medium and the ray that emerges.

angle of incidence *n* the angle made by a ray of light falling on a surface with a line perpendicular to that surface.

angle of reflection *n* the angle formed by a ray of light reflected from a surface with a line perpendicular to that surface.

angle of refraction *n* the angle made between a ray of light that is refracted at a surface, and a line perpendicular to the surface.

angle parking *n* a way of parking a vehicle so that it sticks out at an angle to the curb or to the direction of traffic.

an·gler (ang′glər) *n* **1** a person who fishes with a hook and line. **2** a fish that lives at the bottom of the coastal N Atlantic, with a long, spiny dorsal fin that it uses to attract other fish as prey.

An·gli·cism (ang′lə siz′əm) *n* a word or phrase that is peculiar to the English language.

an·gli·cize (ang′glə sīz′) *v* **an·gli·cized, an·gli·ciz·ing** make or become English in form, pronunciation, customs, or character: *Jan Schmidt decided not to anglicize his name to John Smith.* Also, **Anglicize**. <See ANGLO-.> **an′gli·ci·za′tion** *n.*

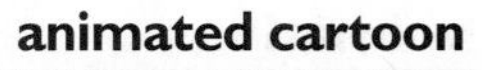

Ang·lo (ang′glō) *adj* English-speaking or of British descent.
n a person who is English-speaking or of British descent.

Anglo– *combining form* **1** English-speaking or of British birth or descent: *Anglo-Canadian.* **2** to do with both Britain (or only England) and some other nation: *Anglo-Irish interaction has often been been tense.*

An·glo–French (ang′lō french′) *adj* British (or English) and French: *an Anglo-French agreement.*

An·glo·phile (ang′glō fīl′) *n* a person who greatly admires any English-speaking people or culture.

An·glo·phobe (ang′glō fōb′) *n* a person who hates or fears any English-speaking people or culture.
An′glo·pho′bi·a *n.* **An′glo·pho′bic** *adj.*

❦ **An·glo·phone** or **an·glo·phone** (ang′glə fōn′) *n* a person whose native language is English.
adj speaking English as one's native language.

An·glo–Sax·on (ang′glō sak′sən) *n* **1** a member of the Germanic people who dominated England before the Norman Conquest in 1066, descended from tribes who arrived in the 400s. **2** Old English, the language spoken by this people. **3** a person of English descent.
adj to do with the Anglo-Saxons, their language, or their descendants.

An·go·la (an gō′la) *n* a country in southwest Africa.
An·go′lan *adj, n.*

an·go·ra (ang gȯ′rə) *n* **1** yarn made from the long hair of the Angora goat or Angora rabbit, used for knitting. **2 Angora a** the **Angora goat** a breed of goat with long, silky, curly white hair. **b** an animal with similar long hair such as the **Angora rabbit** or the **Angora cat.** <*Angora*, Turkey, origin of the goat>

An·gra Main·yu (ȧng′grə mīn′yū) *Zoroastrianism n* the evil spirit of the cosmos. <Avestan (the oldest Indo-European language) = destroying spirit>

an·gry (ang′grē) *adj* **an·gri·er, an·gri·est 1** feeling or showing anger: *an angry look. She was angry at her brother.* **2** raging or stormy: *an angry sky.* **3** inflamed and sore: *an angry cut on the chin.* **an′gri·ly** *adv.* **an′gri·ness** *n.*

angst (angst) *n* a feeling of anxiety or dread not related to any specific thing: *adolescent angst, midlife angst.* <German = fear>

ang·strom or **ång·ström** (ang′strəm) *n* a unit for measuring length, equal to 0.1 nanometres, or one ten-millionth of a millimetre. *Symbol* **Å** <A.J. *Angstrom*, 19c physicist>

an·guish (ang′gwish) *n* great pain, grief, suffering, or distress: *He was in anguish until the doctor had set his broken leg.* <Old French *anguisse* a strangling, from Latin *angustus* narrow> **an′guished** *adj.*

an·gu·lar (ang′gyə lər) *adj* **1** to do with angles and their measure: *angular distance.* **2** with sharp or prominent corners: *angular furniture.* **3** thin and bony: *He has a tall, angular body.* **an′gu·lar′i·ty** *n.*

an·hy·drous (an hī′drəs) *Chemistry adj* containing no water: *an anhydrous solution.* <Greek *an-* without + *hydor* water>

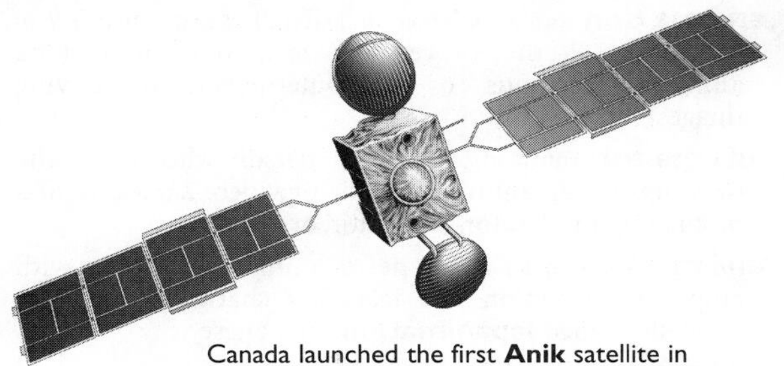

Canada launched the first **Anik** satellite in 1972. Since then, many versions of the Anik series have improved the area of coverage and the quality of radio, telephone, and TV signals.

❦ **An·ik** (an′ik) *n* a series of satellites launched by Canada to establish a domestic system of satellite communication. <Inuktitut = brother>

an·i·mal (an′ə məl) *n* **1** any of a KINGDOM (def. 3) of living things that feed on organic matter and usually have specialized sense organs and a nervous system. See also EUKARYOTE. **2** a living organism other than a human being: *birds, animals, and fish.* **3** a mammal. **4** a person thought of as being uncivilized, especially one who is cruel or violent.
adj **1** to do with animals: *animal communities.* **2** to do with the basic physical nature of human beings: *animal appetites.*

ETYMOLOGY

Animal comes from Latin *anima*, which means "breath." Although tiny organisms as well as humans are classified as animals, the word is often associated with mammals: *I love animals, but I can't stand bugs*

animal husbandry *n* the science of raising livestock.

animal magnetism *n* sexual attractiveness.

animal spirits *n* natural liveliness or healthy cheerfulness.

an·i·mate (an′ə māt′) *for v,* (an′ə mit) *for adj. v* **an·i·mat·ed, an·i·mat·ing 1** give life to or make alive. **2** add liveliness or zest to: *His high spirits animated the whole party.* **3** make into an animated cartoon: *to animate a story.* **4** inspire or motivate: *Ambition animated her.* **5** cause to act or work: *Windmills are animated by the wind.* **6** cause to move as if alive: *mechanically animated dolls.*
adj living or having life: *Stones are not animate.* <Latin *animare*, from *anima* life, breath> **an′i·mat′ed** *adj.* **an′i·ma′tion** *adj.*

animated cartoon *n* a series of drawings, paintings, or other art works arranged to be photographed and shown in rapid sequence as a movie or video to give the impression of motion.

a bat	e bed	i bid	o pot	u cup	th **thin**
ā cake	ē me	ī bite	ō go	ū rude	ᴛʜ **then**
ȧ bar	ə about	ər over	ȯ for	u̇ put	zh measure

an·i·ma·tion (an′ə mā′shən) *n* **1** liveliness: *a voice full of animation.* **2** the process or technique of making animated cartoons or computer-generated moving images.

an·i·ma·tor (an′ə mā′tər) *n* **1** a person who makes the drawings for an animated movie or video. **2** a leader of a discussion, moderator, facilitator, or host.

an·i·me (an′ə mā′) *n* a type of animated cartoon, with emphasis on action and featuring characters with big eyes. Also called **Japanimation.** <Japanese>

an·i·mism (an′ə miz′əm) *n* **1** a belief that some features of the natural world have living spirits. **2** a belief in spiritual beings that are separate from bodies. **an′i·mist** *n.* **an′i·mis′tic** *adj.*

an·i·mos·i·ty (an′ə mos′ə tē) *n* intense dislike: *I felt no animosity toward the person who beat me in the spelling contest.* <Latin *animus* spirit, feeling>

an·i·mus (an′ə məs) *n* **1** intense dislike or hostility. **2** a motivating thought or force: *Ambition was his animus.* <Latin = spirit, feeling>

an·i·on (an′ī ən) *Chemistry n* an atom or group of atoms with a negative charge. <Greek *an-* negative + *ion*>

an·ise (an′is) *or* (ə nēs′) *n* **1** a Mediterranean plant of the parsley family with fragrant, licorice-flavoured seeds. **2 aniseed** (an′i sēd′) the seed of this plant, used as a flavouring and in medicine. <Old French, from Greek *anison*>

A·nish·i·na·be (ə nish′ē nä′bā) *n, pl* **A·nish·i·na·beg 1** a member of a First Nations people living in the region around Lake Superior and adjacent areas. **2** their Algonquian language.
adj to do with this people or their language. Also called **Ojibway.**

ankh (ängk) *n* an ancient Egyptian symbol of life, in the form of a cross with a loop at the top instead of a vertical arm. <Egyptian *'nh* life, soul>

an·kle (ang′kəl) *n* **1** the joint formed by the lower leg bones and the highest bone of the foot, or the protruding part (the **anklebone**) on either side of this joint. <Old English *ancleow*>

an·klet (ang′klit) *n* **1** a chain or band worn around the ankle as an ornament. **2** a short sock.

an·ky·lo·saur (ang′kə lə sôr′) *n* a club-tailed, short-legged, plant-eating dinosaur that lived in West N America about 65 to 70 million years ago. <Greek *ankylos* crooked + *sauros* lizard>

an·nals (an′əlz) *pln* **1** the historical record: *That winning goal will find a permanent place in the annals of sport.* **2** a written account of events year by year. <Latin *annus* year>

an·neal (ə nēl′) *v* toughen glass or metals by heating and then cooling. <Old English *on-* on + *ælan* burn>

an·ne·lid (an′ə lid) *n* a worm or wormlike organism with a long, cylindrical body made up of ringlike segments. <French *annélide*, from Latin *anellus* very small ring>

an·nex (an′eks) *or* (an′iks) *for n;* (an′eks) *or* (ə neks′) *for v. n* a complete structure or area added to an existing larger one: *The store now has an annex for bargain items.*
v **1** join or add such a structure or area to a larger one: *Britain annexed Acadia in 1713.* **2** *Informal* take as one's own without permission: *My sister seems to have annexed my bedroom closet.* <Old French *annexer*, from Latin *ad-* to + *nectere* bind> **an′nex·a′tion** *n.*

an·nex·a·tion·ist (an′ik sā′shə nist) *n* **1** 🍁 in former times, a person supporting political union of Canada with the US. **2** a person who supports the joining of one city or nation with another, usually larger.
Also, **Annexationist.**

🍁 **Annexation Movement** *n* the name given to groups in Canada that have advocated political union with the US.

an·ni·hi·late (ə nī′ə lāt′) *v* **an·ni·hi·lated, an·ni·hi·lat·ing** destroy completely: *The earthquake annihilated more than thirty towns and villages.* <Latin *ad-* to + *nihil* nothing> **an·ni′hi·la′tion** *n.*

an·ni·ver·sa·ry (an′ə vər′sə rē) *n, pl* **an·ni·ver·sa·ries 1** a date on which an event occurred: *Tomorrow is the anniversary of the day we fell in love.* **2** a celebration of this: *They are planning their parents' 25th wedding anniversary.* <Old French *anniversarie*, from Latin *annus* year + *vertere* to turn>

an·no Dom·i·ni (an′ō dom′ə nē) a formula for introducing dates since the birth of Christ. *Abbrev.* **AD** See also CE. <Latin = in the year of the Lord>

an·no·tate (an′ə tāt′) *v* **an·no·tat·ed, an·no·tat·ing** provide with explanatory notes or comments: *an annotated edition of Shakespeare's plays.* <Latin *ad-* to + *nota* a mark> **an′no·ta′tion** *n.* **an′no·ta′tor** *n.*

an·nounce (ə nouns′) *v* **an·nounced, an·nounc·ing 1** give formal or public notice of: *to announce a wedding in the newspapers.* **2** make known in a definite and open manner: *She announced that she was going out for the evening.* **3** make known the presence of: *The butler announced each guest.* **4** be a sign of: *Dark clouds announced a coming storm.* **5** *Radio, Television* work as an announcer. <Old French *anoncier*, from Latin *ad-* to + *nuntiare* declare> **an·nounce′ment** *n.*

an·nounc·er (ə noun′sər) *n* a person who announces, especially a person who introduces something or gives information during a radio or TV broadcast.

an·noy (ə noi′) *v* anger, disturb, or irritate: *The baby annoys his sister by pulling her hair.* <Old French, from Latin *in odio* hateful> **an·noy′ance** *n.* **an·noyed′** *adj.* **an·noy′ing** *adj.*

an·nu·al (an′yū əl) *adj* **1** coming or happening once a year: *Your birthday is an annual event.* **2** in or for a year: *an annual salary of $45 000.* **3** of plants, living just one year or season.
n **1** a plant that lives one year or season. **2** a book or periodical published once a year. <Old French, from Latin *annus* year> **an′nu·al·ly** *adv.*

annual ring *n* a concentric circle that can be seen in the cross-section of a tree trunk, each ring being the layer of wood produced in one growing season.

an·nu·i·ty (ə nyū′ə tē) *or* (ə nū′ə tē) *n, pl* **an·nu·i·ties** a sum of money paid or received every year. <Old French, from Latin *annus* year>

an·nul (ə nul′) *Law v* **an·nulled, an·nul·ling** cancel or make void: *The judge annulled the contract because payments had not been made.* <Old French, from Latin *ad-* to + *nullum* nothing> **an·nul′ment** *n.*

an·nu·lar (an′yə lər) *adj* ringlike or ring shaped. <Latin *annulus*>

partial

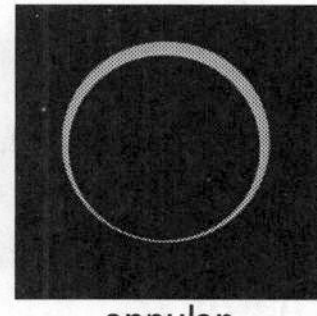
annular

total

An **annular eclipse** occurs when the moon is so far from the earth that it cannot completely block out the sun, as it does in a total solar eclipse. The result is that people on earth can still see a thin ring of light around the moon.

annular eclipse *n* a solar eclipse in which the sun appears as a ring of light surrounding the dark moon.

an·ode (an′ōd) *Electricity n* **1** the negatively charged electrode of a battery, through which the electrons leave the cell when the circuit is complete. **2** the positively charged electrode that attracts electrons from the cathode of an electrical device. Compare CATHODE. <Latin, from Greek *anhodos* way up (supposedly the path taken by the current>

a·noint (ə noint′) *v* **1** put oil or ointment on: *Sunburned skin should be anointed with cold cream.* **2** pour or smear oil on in a ceremony as a sign of consecration to an office: *The archbishop anointed the new king.* <Old French *enoint*, from Latin *in-* on + *unguere* smear> **a·noint′ed** *adj.*

a·nom·a·ly (ə nom′ə lē) *n, pl* **a·nom·a·lies** something that departs from the normal pattern or from the rule, often inexplicably: *Here's an anomaly—an apple with a core but no seeds.* <Latin, from Greek *an-* not + *homalos* even> **a·nom′a·lous** *adj.*

a·non (ə non′) *Poetic adv* soon. <Old English *on ane* in one, at once>

a·non·y·mous (ə non′ə məs) *adj* **1** to do with a person whose identity is not known: *a poem by an anonymous author. I wonder who could have sent this anonymous letter.* **2** without distinguishing features; characterless: *an anonymous face in a crowd. I prefer a large school where I can remain anonymous.* **3 Anonymous** part of the title of a support group for addicts that protects the privacy of its members: *Alcoholics Anonymous.* <Latin, from Greek *an-* without + *onyma* name> **an′o·nym′i·ty** (an′ə nim′ə tē) *n.* **a·non′y·mous·ly** *adv.*

🍁 **a·no·rak** (an′ə rak′) *n* **1** a waterproof, hooded outer coat of skins, often worn by Inuit when hunting. **2** a long hooded jacket, especially a waterproof one with a belt or drawstring at the waist. <Inuktitut *anoraq*>

an·o·rex·i·a (an′ə rek′sē ə) in full, **anorexia nervosa** (ner′vō′zə) a medical condition characterized by a refusal to eat. <Latin, from Greek *an-* without + *orexis* appetite> **an′o·rex′ic** *adj, n.*

an·oth·er (ə nuTH′ər) *adj* **1** one more: *Have another cookie.* **2** different: *That is another matter entirely.*
pron **1** one more: *He ate one candy and then asked for another.* **2** a different one: *I don't like this book; give me another.*
one after another, in quick succession: *eating chocolate bars one after another.*

an·swer (an′sər) *n* **1** words given in response to a question: *I didn't hear your answer.* **2** the solution to a problem: *The answer is to get more sleep.* **3** anything said or done in return: *A nod was her only answer.* **4** a counterpart, especially something produced in imitation or competition: *This new line of clothes is their answer to designer fashions.*
v **1** respond: *to answer a question. Answer me! I phoned but no one answered.* **2** act or move in response: *to answer a summons. Someone answer the door, please. The brake answers to the slightest touch.* **3** (*often with* ***to***) be responsible or accountable: *to answer for someone's safety. I answer to nobody.* **4** (*usually with* ***to***) correspond: *This house answers to his description.* **5** (*with* ***to***) recognize a name as one's or its own: *The dog answers to "Lucky."* **6** serve a purpose or meet a need: *This crate will answer until we get a table.* <Old English *andswaru*>
answer back, reply in a disrespectful way.
answer for, bear the consequences of: *They will answer for their crimes.*

an·swer·a·ble (an′sə rə bəl) *adj* **1** responsible and required to give an account: *The club treasurer is answerable to the members for the money given to him.* **2** that can be answered: *Is that an answerable question?*

answering machine *n* a machine that records telephone messages left by callers.

answering service *n* a company or agency that answers telephone calls on behalf of its clients and then reports on the calls received.

ant (ant) *n* a small insect that lives and works in organized groups called colonies. Most ants are wingless and live in tunnels in the ground or in wood. <Old English *æmete*> **ant′like′** *adj.*

ant·ac·id (an tas′id) *n* a substance that neutralizes acids, especially one that counteracts excess stomach acid.
adj tending to neutralize acids.

an·tag·o·nism (an tag′ə niz′əm) *n* active opposition and hostility. <Greek *anti-* against + *agonizesthai* struggle (to win a prize)> **an·tag′o·nis′tic** *adj.*

an·tag·o·nist (an tag′ə nist) *n* **1** one who opposes or struggles with another: *The knight defeated his antagonist.* **2** in a story, an unsympathetic character who opposes the main character. Compare PROTAGONIST.

an·tag·o·nize (an tag′ə nīz′) *v* **an·tag·o·nized, an·tag·o·niz·ing** cause somebody to be hostile: *Her unkind remarks antagonized all her classmates.* <See ANTAGONISM.>

a bat	e bed	i bid	o pot	u cup	th **thin**
ā cake	ē me	ī bite	ō go	ū rude	TH **then**
ä bar	ə about	ər over	ô for	ů put	zh measure

ant·arc·tic (an tärk′tik) *or* (an tär′tik) *adj* usually, **Antarctic** to do with the region south of the Antarctic Circle: *in Antarctic waters.*
n **the Antarctic** the region south of the Antarctic Circle. <Latin, from Greek *anti-* opposite + *arctic*>

An·tarc·ti·ca (an tärk′ti kə) *or* (an tär′ti kə) *n* the uninhabited continent covering the South Pole.

Antarctic Circle *n* **1** the imaginary circle enclosing the south polar region, parallel to the equator at 23 degrees 30 minutes (23°30′) north of the South Pole. **2** the polar region inside this circle.

an·te (an′tē) *n* in the game of poker, a stake that every player must put in, to be won or lost. <Latin = before>
up the ante, *Informal* increase what is risked or demanded: *The kidnappers have upped the ante by threatening to harm their captive.*

ante– *prefix* **1** before or earlier: *antedate.* **2** in front of: *anteroom.* <Latin>

CONFUSABLES

Ante– is a prefix that means "before" or "earlier": *Walk through the antechamber to get to the main room.*

Anti– is a prefix that means "against" or "opposed to": *Antisocial behaviour will not be tolerated.*

ant·eat·er (an′tē′tər) *n* a mammal of the tropical forests of Central and S America, with a tube-shaped head and a long, slender, sticky tongue with which it catches ants and termites to eat.

an·te·ced·ent (an′tə sē′dənt) *or* (an′tə sē′dənt) *n* **1** *Grammar* a word, phrase, or clause that is referred to by a pronoun or relative adverb. In *Although the car is old, it is in good shape,* the antecedent of *it* is *car.* **2** a previous thing or event. **3 antecedents** *pl* ancestors or family and social background: *No one knew the antecedents of the mysterious stranger.* **4** *Mathematics* the first term of a ratio.
adj coming or happening before. <Latin *ante-* before + *cedere* go>

an·te·cham·ber (an′tē chām′bər) ANTEROOM.

an·te·date (an′tē dāt′) *v* **an·te·dat·ed, an·te·dat·ing** come before in time: *Leif Erikson's discovery of the American continent antedates the voyage of Christopher Columbus by about 150 years.*

an·te·di·lu·vi·an (an′tē də lū′vē ən) *adj* **1** to do with the period before the Flood, as described in the Bible. **2** very old or old-fashioned. <Latin *ante-* before + *diluvium* flood>

an·te·lope (an′tə lōp′) *n, pl* **an·te·lopes** or (*especially collectively*) **an·te·lope 1** a hoofed, cud-chewing mammal found mainly in Africa, with horns that curve backwards and are not shed. See PREY for picture. **2** the **pronghorn antelope**, a hoofed, cud-chewing mammal of the N American plains whose horns have a permanent core and an outer layer that is shed every year. <Latin, from Greek *antholops*>

an·te me·rid·i·em (an′tē mə rid′ē əm) A.M.

an·ten·na (an ten′ə) *n, pl* **an·ten·nae** (an ten′ā) *or* (an ten′ī) *for 1,* **an·ten·nas** *for 2.* **1** one of two feelers on the head of an insect or on a crustacean such as the lobster. A small antenna may be called an **antennule. 2** *Television, Radio* a long wire or set of wires for sending out or receiving electromagnetic waves. <Latin *antennae*, a translation of Greek *keraioi* horns (of insects)>

an·te·pe·nul·ti·mate (an′tē pə nul′tə mit) *adj, n* third from the last: *The stress in "biographical" falls on the antepenultimate syllable.*

an·te·ri·or (an tē′rē ər) *adj* **1** located toward the front: *The anterior part of a fish contains the head and gills.* **2** earlier or previous. <Latin, comparative of *ante* before>

an·te·room (an′tē rūm′) *n* a small room leading to a larger one. Also called **antechamber**.

an·them (an′thəm) *n* a dignified song of praise, devotion, or patriotism: *"O Canada" is our national anthem. The choir sang an anthem during the service.* <Old English *antemne* hymn>

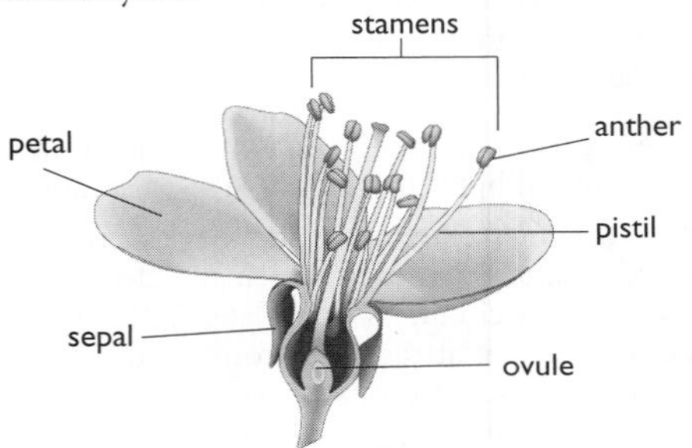

an·ther (an′thər) *n* the pollen-bearing part of the stamen of a flower. <Latin, from Greek *anthos* flower>

ant·hill or **ant hill** (ant′hil′) a heap of dirt piled up by ants or termites around the entrance to their nest.

an·thol·o·gy (an thol′ə jē) *n, pl* **an·thol·o·gies** a collection of writings by various authors, compiled by an editor or **anthologist**. <Latin, from Greek *anthos* flower + *legein* gather>

an·thra·cite (an′thrə sīt′) *n* a hard, shiny, black coal containing a high percentage of carbon and a low percentage of moisture. <Latin, from Greek *anthrax* charcoal>

an·thrax (an′thraks) *n* an infectious, often fatal, disease of sheep and cattle caused by a bacillus that can be transmitted to humans. <Latin, from Greek = charcoal, from the black scar tissue caused by the disease>

an·thro·po·cen·tric (an′thrə pə sen′trik) *adj* interpreting everything from the point of view of human beings: *I think hunting for sport depends on a very anthropocentric view of nature.* <Greek *anthropos* human being + *-centric*> **an′thro·po·cen′tri·cal·ly** *adv.*
an′thro·po·cen′trism *n.*

an·thro·po·gen·ic (an′thrə pə jen′ik) *adj* to do with substances added to the air, water, or soil by human activity, some of which are produced when pollutants react with chemicals already present. <Greek *anthropos* human being + *-genic*>

an·thro·poid (an′thrə poid′) *adj* resembling a human being in form, especially as part of the group of higher primates that includes monkeys, apes, and humans.
n APE (def. 1). <Greek *anthropos* human being + *-oid*>

an·thro·pol·o·gy (an′thrə pol′ə jē) *n* the science that studies the origin, development, races, customs, and beliefs of humans. **Cultural** or **social anthropology** studies and compares human societies and cultures. **Physical anthropology** studies humans as physical creatures, including their evolution and ecology. **an′thro·po·log′i·cal** *adj.* **an′thro·pol′o·gist** *n.*

an·thro·po·mor·phism (an′thrə pə mòr′fiz əm) *n* the practice of attributing human form or qualities to gods, animals, plants, etc. <Greek *anthropos* human being + *morphe* form> **an′thro·po·mor′phic** *adj.*

anti– *prefix* **1** against or opposed to: *antiwar.* **2** contrasting with the usual type: *antihero.* **3** preventing or counteracting: *antidepressant.* See ANTE- for confusable. <Greek>

an·ti–a·bor·tion (an′tē ə bor′shən) *adj* against abortion, or against unrestricted legal access to abortion.

an·ti–air·craft (an′tē er′kraft′) *adj* used in defence against enemy aircraft.

an·ti·bac·te·ri·al (an′tē bak tē′rē əl) *adj* counteracting or destroying bacteria.

an·ti·bal·lis·tic missile (an′tē bə lis′tik) *n* a ballistic missile designed to intercept and destroy an enemy missile. *Abbrev.* **ABM**

an·ti·bi·ot·ic (an′tē bī ot′ik) *n* an organic substance, such as penicillin, that can destroy or weaken harmful bacteria. *adj* to do with antibiotics: *antibiotic cream.* <*anti-* + *biotic*>

an·ti·bod·y (an′tē bod′ē) *n, pl* **an·ti·bod·ies** a protein produced in the blood that neutralizes or destroys foreign substances called antigens, thus providing immunity to diseases.

anti–choice *adj* anti-abortion. Compare PRO-CHOICE.

an·tic·i·pate (an tis′ə pāt′) *v* **an·tic·i·pat·ed, an·tic·i·pat·ing 1** expect: *The attack was not anticipated.* **2** look forward to: *to anticipate a holiday.* **3** take care of in advance: *The nurse anticipated all the patient's wishes.* **4** do, make, think of, or use something before someone else: *The invention of the abacus anticipated the electronic calculator.* **5** consider or mention prematurely: *to anticipate a point in an argument.* <Latin *ante-* before + *capere* take> **an·tic′i·pa·to′ry** *adj.*

an·tic·i·pa·tion (an tis′ə pā′shən) *n* **1** the act of anticipating: *The settler cut more wood than usual, in anticipation of a long winter.* **2** enjoyment in looking forward to something: *They eyed the cake with anticipation.*

an·ti·cler·i·cal·ism (an′tē kler′ə kə liz′əm) *n* opposition to the power and influence of the clergy, especially in politics. **an′ti·cler′i·cal** *adj.* **an′ti·cler′i·cal·ist** *n, adj.*

an·ti·cli·max (an′tē klī′maks) *n* **1** an event, remark, or act that represents a sudden drop in importance, tension, or excitement from a previous rise. **2** anything less exciting than one has been led to expect.
an′ti·cli·mac′tic (an′tē klə mak′tik) *adj.*

an·ti·cline (an′ti klīn′) *Geology n* an arch of stratified rock, in which the layers slope downward in opposite directions from the centre. Compare SYNCLINE. <Greek *anti-* against + *klinein* to lean> **an′ti·clin′al** *adj.*

an·ti·co·ag·u·lant (an′tē kō ag′yə lənt) *n* a substance that prevents or hinders blood from clotting.
adj preventing or hindering blood from clotting.

an·tics (an′tiks) *pln* funny, silly, or playful gestures or actions: *the antics of a clown.* <Italian *antico* grotesque>

an·ti·cy·clone (an′tē sī′klōn) *n* winds moving around and away from a centre of high pressure that is itself also moving. Compare CYCLONE. **an′ti·cy·clon′ic** *adj.*

an·ti·de·pres·sant (an′tē di pres′ənt) *n* a drug that relieves depression.
adj relieving depression.

an·ti·dote (an′tə dōt′) *n* **1** a medicine or remedy that counteracts a poison: *Milk is an antidote for some poisons.* **2** anything that counteracts or relieves: *Variety is the antidote to boredom.* <Old French, from Greek *anti-* against + *didonai* give>

an·ti·freeze (an′tē frēz′) *n* a substance, typically one based on alcohol, that is added to a liquid, especially the water in a car radiator, to lower its freezing point.

an·ti·gen (an′tə jən) *n* a substance that stimulates the production of antibodies in the immune system, or that reacts with existing antibodies. <*anti*(*body*) + *-gen*>

An·ti·gua and Bar·bu·da (an tē′gə and bär bū′də) a country in the Caribbean, named after the two main islands that make it up.

an·ti·he·ro (an′tē hē′rō) *n, pl* **an·ti·he·roes** a character in a story who, although the central character, has none of the qualities normally expected of a hero.
an′ti·he·ro′ic *adj.*

an·ti·her·o·ine (an′tē her′ō in) *n* a female character in a story who, although the central character, has none of the qualities normally expected of a heroine.
an′ti·he·ro′ic *adj.*

an·ti·his·ta·mine (an′tē his′tə mēn′) *n* a medicine used to treat colds and allergies by neutralizing histamines (a substance released by the body in allergic reactions).

an·ti·knock (an′tē nok′) *n* a substance added to the fuel of an internal combustion engine to reduce noise caused by too rapid combustion.

an·ti·lock braking system (an′tē lok′) *n* a computerized feature of motor vehicle brakes that prevents locking and improves stopping power.
Abbrev. **ABS**

an·ti·mat·ter (an′tē mat′ər) *Physics n* a form of matter that is not known to exist but is imagined in theory, composed of antiparticles.

anti·mis·sile (an′tē mis′īl) *or* (an′tē mis′əl) *adj* for use in defence against ballistic missiles or rockets.

an·ti·mo·ny (an′tə mō′nē) *n* a crystalline metallic element that occurs chiefly in combination with other elements. *Symbol* **Sb** <Latin *antimonium*>

an·ti·nov·el (an′tē nov′əl) *n* a novel-length work of fiction that lacks most of the basic features of the traditional novel, such as character development or plot.

a bat	e bed	i bid	o pot	u cup	th **thin**
ā cake	ē me	ī bite	ō go	ū rude	ᴛʜ **then**
ä bar	ə about	ər over	ò for	ů put	zh measure

an·ti·nu·cle·ar (an′tē nyū′klē ər) *or* (an′tē nū′klē ər) *adj* against the use of nuclear energy for any purpose: *antinuclear demonstrators.*

an·ti·par·ti·cle (an′tē pȧr′tə kəl) *Physics n* an elementary particle with the same mass as a given particle, but with opposite values for electric charge or magnetic effect. The **antineutron**, **antiproton**, and **positron** (poz′i tron′) are antiparticles of the neutron, proton, and electron. See also ANTIMATTER.

an·ti·pas·to (an′tē pas′tō) *n, pl* **an·ti·pas·tos** or **an·ti·pas·ti** (an′tē pas′tē) a dish consisting of small appetizers such as cold cuts and marinated vegetables. <Italian>

an·tip·a·thy (an tip′ə thē) *n, pl* **an·tip·a·thies** a strong or fixed dislike. <Latin, from Greek *anti-* against + *pathos* feeling> **an′ti·pa·thet′ic** *adj.*

an·ti·per·spi·rant (an′tē pər′spə rənt) *n* a substance applied to the skin, especially under the arms, to reduce perspiration.
adj reducing perspiration.

an·tip·o·des (an tip′ə dēz′) *pln* **1** two places on directly opposite sides of the earth: *The North Pole and the South Pole are antipodes.* **2** two opposites or contraries: *Forgiveness and revenge are antipodes.* **3 Antipodes** Australia and New Zealand, as viewed by those in the northern hemisphere. **an·tip′o·dal** *adj.*

an·ti·quar·i·an (an′tə kwer′ē ən) *n* a person who collects antiques or old books. Also called **antiquary**.
adj to do with antiques or old books, or the people who collect them: *an antiquarian bookstore.*

an·ti·quat·ed (an′tə kwā′tid) *adj* old-fashioned or out of date: *antiquated ideas, antiquated vehicles.*

an·tique (an tēk′) *adj* **1** made in an earlier period and considered valuable as a collectable object: *antique furniture.* **2** exhibiting or selling antiques: *an antique show.* **3** in the style of an earlier period: *an antique finish, antique manners.*
n an antique object: *He collects antiques.*
v **an·tiqued, an·tiqu·ing 1** cause to look antique by refinishing in the style of an earlier period. **2** hunt or shop for antiques: *Last weekend they went antiquing on Cape Breton Island.* <Old French, from Latin *ante* before> **an·tiqu′er** *n.*

an·tiq·ui·ty (an tik′wə tē) *n, pl* **an·tiq·ui·ties 1** ancient times: *We were impressed by the antiquity of the ruins.* **2 antiquities** *pl* things dating from ancient times.

an·ti–Sem·i·tism (an′tē sem′ə tiz′əm) *n* hatred against Jews. **an′ti-Se·mit′ic** (an′tē sə mit′ik) *adj, n.*

an·ti·sep·tic (an′tə sep′tik) *n* a substance that kills or prevents the growth of germs and prevents infection.
adj **1** preventing infection: *an antiseptic lotion.* **2** using or cleansed with antiseptics: *an antiseptic kitchen.* **3** unemotional: *an antiseptic way of arguing.* <Latin, from Greek *anti-* against + *septikos* rotten> **an′ti·sep′ti·cal·ly** *adv.*

an·ti·slav·er·y (an′tē slā′və rē) *adj* opposed to slavery.

an·ti·so·cial (an′tē sō′shəl) *adj* **1** against the principles upon which society is based: *Murder and stealing are antisocial acts.* **2** not wanting the society or companionship of others. See UNSOCIABLE for confusable.

an·ti·ter·ror (an′tē ter′ər) *adj* designed to prevent or counteract terrorism: *antiterror legislation.*

an·tith·e·sis (an tith′ə sis) *n, pl* **an·tith·e·ses** (an tith′ə sēz) **1** the direct opposite: *Hate is the antithesis of love.* **2** a contrast of ideas expressed by parallel arrangements of words or clauses. Example: *The more you have, the more you want.* **3** (*with* ***of*** *or* ***between***) an opposition or contrast: *the antithesis between theory and fact.* <Latin, from Greek *anti-* against + *tithenai* to place> **an′ti·thet′i·cal** (an′tə thet′ə kəl) *adj.*

an·ti·tox·in (an′tē tok′sin) *n* a substance formed in the body to counteract a disease or poison, or a serum containing such a substance. **an′ti·tox′ic** *adj.*

an·ti·trades (an′tē trādz′) *pln* winds that blow in a direction opposite to the trade winds but above them.

an·ti·trust (an′tē trust′) *adj* opposing the formation of large corporations that prevent fair competition: *antitrust legislation.*

an·ti·vi·ral (an′tē vī′rəl) *adj* counteracting or destroying viruses: *antiviral medication, antiviral software.*

an·ti·war (an′tē wȯr′) *adj* opposing armed combat between groups or nations: *an antiwar demonstration.*

Caribou shed their **antlers** every year. In the spring, as the new antlers are growing, they are covered with a velvety skin. Then, in the fall, when antler growth is complete, the animal rubs its antlers against bushes and trees to scrape away the dead skin.

ant·ler (ant′lər) *n* usually, **antlers** *pl* the branched horns of a deer or similar animal. <Old French *antoillier*> **ant′lered** *adj.*

ant lion *n* an insect that resembles a dragonfly, and whose larva catches small insects for food by lying in wait in a pit it has dug and seizing any insect that falls in.

an·to·nym (an′tə nim′) *n* a word that means the opposite of another word: *"Hot" is the antonym of "cold."* Compare SYNONYM. <Greek *anti-* opposite + *onyma* name>

GRAMMAR AND USAGE

Antonyms are words that are opposite in meaning.

Many antonyms are made by adding the prefixes *dis-*, *un-*, or *mis-*: *appear* and *disappear*, *known* and *unknown*, *behave* and *misbehave*.

ant·sy (ant′sē) *Slang adj* **ant·si·er, ant·si·est** nervous or restless due to anxiety, impatience, or excitement: *Don't get antsy; I've nearly finished my part of our project.*

a·nus (ā′nəs) *n* the opening at the lower end of the alimentary canal, through which solid waste and undigested food pass out of the body. <Latin = ring, from its shape> **a′nal** *adj.*

an·vil (an′vəl) *n* **1** an iron or steel block on which metals are hammered and shaped. **2** the **incus**, the middle of three small bones in the middle ear. See also HAMMER, STIRRUP. <Old English *anfilte*>

anx·i·e·ty (ang zī′ə tē) *or* (angk sī′ə tē) *n, pl* **anx·i·e·ties** **1** troubled thoughts or fears about what may happen: *We all felt anxiety when the dog was lost.* **2** an eager desire, accompanied by uneasiness: *In her anxiety to help, she kept getting in the way.* **3** *Psychiatry* a state of abnormal fear or mental tension: *He suffers from an anxiety disorder.* <See ANXIOUS.>

anxiety attack *n* a sudden feeling of intense anxiety, often accompanied by a fast heartbeat, shortness of breath, sweating, and trembling. Also called **panic attack**.

anx·ious (angk′shəs) *adj* **1** troubled by fears of what may happen: *I became anxious when you didn't arrive on time.* **2** causing worry: *an anxious time.* **3** eager, but with some uneasiness: *anxious to start school.* <Latin *anxius*, from *angere* choke> **anx′ious·ly** *adv.* **anx′ious·ness** *n.*

an·y (en′ē) *adj* **1** one, no matter which one, out of many: *Any book will do.* **2** (*in questions or conditional sentences, or with words with negative force*) **a** some: *Do you have any fresh fruit? If you see any weeds, tell me.* **b** even a single one: *She was forbidden to go to any movie.* **3** every: *Any child knows that.*
pron **1** (*in questions or conditional sentences, or with words with negative force*) **a** some: *I need paper; do you have any? I looked for paper, but didn't find any.* **b** a single one: *He didn't like any of my suggestions.* **2** no matter which: *I'm throwing these magazines out; take any that you want.*
adv (*in questions or conditional sentences, or with words with negative force*) in some degree: *Has the sick child improved any? If you jog any faster, you'll be running! Don't come any closer.* <Old English *ænig*>

an·y·bod·y (en′ē bud′ē) *pron* any person: *Is anybody there?*
n, pl **an·y·bod·ies** any important person: *Is she anybody?*

an·y·how (en′ē hou′) *Informal adv* **1** no matter how: *It's wrong anyhow you look at it.* **2** in any case: *She was tired but she got up anyhow. I can see better than you, anyhow.*

an·y·more (en′ē mòr′) *adv* (*in questions and conditional clauses, and with negatives*) any longer: *The book was not available anymore. Who walks to school anymore?*

CONFUSABLES

Anymore means "any longer": *I don't watch cartoons anymore.*

Any more means "additional": *He isn't allowed to have any more pets, since he now has four cats.*

an·y·one (en′ē wən) *pron* any person.

an·y·place (en′ē plās′) *Informal adv* anywhere.

an·y·thing (en′ē thing′) *pron* any thing.
adv in any way: *This isn't anything like what I expected.*
anything but, not in the least: *anything but poor.*
like anything, *Informal* to a great degree: *We worked like anything to finish in time.*

an·y·time (en′ē tīm′) *adv* at any time: *Call anytime.*

an·y·way (en′ē wā′) *adv* **1** no matter how: *It's wrong anyway you look at it.* **2** in any case: *I don't know just when, but anyway not now.* Also (*def. 2*), **anyways** (*Informal*).

an·y·where (en′ē wer′) *adv* **1** in, at, or to any place: *Put it down anywhere.* **2** at any point in some range: *I would guess her age to be anywhere between 30 and 50.*

A–OK *Informal adj, adv* perfectly good or well: *Your computer should be A-OK now.*

a·or·ta (ā òr′tə) *n* the main artery that carries blood from the left side of the heart to all parts of the body except the lungs. <Latin, from Greek *aorte* that which is attached>

a·pace (ə pās′) *Poetic adv* quickly: *Winter comes on apace.*

A·pach·e (ə pach′ē) *n, pl* **A·pach·es** or **A·pach·e** **1** a member of an Aboriginal people living in the southwestern US. **2** their Athapaskan language.
adj to do with these people or their language.

a·part (ə pàrt′) *adv* **1** in or into separate parts: *He took the watch apart.* **2** away from each other: *Keep the dogs apart.* **3** to one side: *The newcomer stood apart.* **4** excluded: *These few criticisms apart, it is a fine essay.* <Old French, from Latin *ad partem* to one side>
apart from, except for: *Apart from you, nobody knows.*
fall apart, a crumble or break into pieces: *This chair is falling apart. Their marriage has fallen apart.* **b** lose your mental or emotional balance: *When I heard the news I just fell apart; I couldn't stop crying.*
take apart, a separate into its parts: *She took the toaster apart to see how it worked.* **b** analyze: *In class we are taking apart World War II.*
tell apart, see the difference between: *The teacher sometimes can't tell us apart.*

a·part·heid (ə pàrt′hīt) *or* (ə pàrt′hāt) *n* racial segregation, especially as the former official policy in South Africa. <Afrikaans = separateness>

a·part·ment (ə pàrt′mənt) *n* a rented, self-contained room or set of rooms to live in, usually found in a building containing other such units. <French, from Italian *appartamento* (*a parte* apart)>

apartment block *n* a series of similar apartment buildings built by one developer.

apartment building *n* a building, often a tall one, containing a number of apartments.

ap·a·tet·ic (ap′ə tet′ik) *Biology adj* to do with protective colouring that works by camouflage. Compare APOSEMATIC. <Greek *apate* deceit>

a bat	e bed	i bid	o pot	u cup	th **thin**
ā cake	ē me	ī bite	ō go	ū rude	ᴛʜ **then**
à bar	ə about	ər over	ò for	ů put	zh measure

ap·a·thet·ic (ap′ə thet′ik) *adj* with little interest or enthusiasm. <French, from Greek *a-* without + *pathos* feeling> **ap′a·thet′i·cal·ly** *adv.* **ap′a·thy** *n.*

a·pat·o·saur·us (ə pat′ə sȯ′rəs) *n* a giant, land-dwelling, plant-eating dinosaur with a long neck, small head, and very long whiplike tail that lived in western N America about 145 to 156 million years ago. Formerly called **brontosaurus**. <Greek *apate* deceit + *sauros* lizard>

ape (āp) *n* **1** a large, tailless primate. Gorillas are apes. See GORILLA for picture. **2** a primate other than a human: *Monkeys are sometimes called apes.* **3** a large, clumsy, or stupid person. **4** a clumsy imitator of someone else.
v **aped, ap·ing** imitate or mimic. <Old English *apa*> **ape′like′** *adj.*

a·per·i·tif (ə per′i tēf′) *n* an alcoholic drink taken before a meal to stimulate the appetite. <French *apéritif*>

ap·er·ture (ap′ər chər) *n* **1** the opening through which light passes in a camera or telescope, or the diameter of this opening. **2** an opening, gap, or hole, especially an intended one. <Latin *apertura,* from *aperire* to open>

a·pex (ā′peks) *n, pl* **a·pex·es** or **a·pi·ces** (ā′pə sēz′) *or* (ap′ə sēz′) the highest point or tip of something: *the apex of a pyramid.* <Latin>

Ap·gar score (ap′gär) *n* a rating given to babies immediately after birth, based on their reflexes, breathing, cry, and other vital signs. <V. *Apgar,* 20c anesthesiologist>

a·pha·sia (ə fā′zhə) *n* a total or partial loss of the ability to use or understand words as a result of injury or disease. <Latin, from Greek *aphasia* (*a-* not + *phanai* speak)> **a·pha′sic** *adj, n.*

a·phe·li·on (ə fē′lē ən) *n, pl* **a·phe·li·ons** or **a·phel·i·a** (ē ə) the point in the orbit of a planet, comet, etc. where it is farthest from the sun. Compare PERIHELION, APOGEE. <Latin, from Greek *apo-* from + *helios* sun>

a·phid (ā′fid) *n* a tiny, soft-bodied insect that lives by sucking juices from plants. <Latin *aphidis*>

aph·o·rism (af′ə riz′əm) *n* a compressed statement expressing a general truth. Example: *There's no place like home.* <Latin, from Greek *aphorismos* definition> **aph′o·ris′tic** *adj.*

a·pho·tic (ā fō′tik) *adj* **1** *Botany* growing without light. **2** *Ecology* to do with the part of the ocean where there is too little light for photosynthesis to take place. <Greek *a-* without + *photos* light>

aph·ro·dis·i·ac (af′rə dē′zē ak′) *or* (af′rə dē′zhē ak′) *n* a substance that increases sexual desire.
adj increasing sexual desire. <Greek *Aphrodite,* love goddess>

a·pi·ar·y (ā′pē er′ē) *n, pl* **a·pi·ar·ies** a place where bees are kept in hives. <Latin *apis* bee>

a·pi·ces (ā′pə sēz′) *or* (ap′ə sēz′) a plural of APEX.

a·pi·cul·ture (ā′pə kul′chər) *n* the raising and care of bees. <Latin *apis* bee + *culture*> **a′pi·cul′tur·ist** *n.*

a·piece (ə pēs′) *adv* for, from, or by each: *These apples are 50 cents apiece.*

a·pla·cen·tal (ā′plə sen′təl) *Zoology adj* with no placenta in a mammal, such as in marsupials.

a·plen·ty (ə plen′tē) *Informal adv* in abundance: *We have corn aplenty right now.*

a·plomb (ə plom′) *n* self-confidence and assurance. <French *à plomb* = according to the plumbline, i.e., straight>

ap·ne·a (ap′nē ə) *n* a temporary failure to breathe, especially in sleep and occasionally lasting long enough to cause unconsciousness. <Latin, from Greek *a* without + *pnoie* breath>

a·poc·a·lypse (ə pok′ə lips′) *n* **1** *Christianity* **a** the future destruction of the world, especially as prophesied in the Bible. **b the Apocalypse** the book of Revelation in the Bible. **2** an event that involves great destruction and damage. <Latin, from Greek *apokalyptein* to reveal> **a·poc′a·lyp′tic** *adj.*

A·poc·ry·pha (ə pok′rə fə) *pln* **1** books that are not found in Hebrew scriptures but that are included in the Roman Catholic Bible. **2 apocrypha** writings of doubtful authority or authenticity. <Latin = hidden (writings), from Greek *apokryptein* to hide> **a·poc′ry·phal** *adj.*

ap·o·gee (ap′ə jē′) *n* **1** the point in the orbit of an earth satellite or earth-orbiting vehicle where it is farthest from the earth. Compare PERIGEE, APHELION. **2** the furthest or highest point. <French, from Greek *apo-* from + *ge* earth>

a·po·lit·i·cal (ā′pə lit′ə kəl) *adj* having nothing to do with politics: *an apolitical decision, an apolitical organization.* **a′po·lit′i·cal·ly** *adv.*

a·pol·o·get·ic (ə pol′ə jet′ik) *adj* **1** expressing regret or offering an excuse: *an apologetic reply.* **2** behaving uncertainly, as if in a weak position: *Don't be apologetic about your success; you deserved it.*
a·pol′o·get′i·cal·ly *adv.*

a·pol·o·gist (ə pol′ə jist) *n* a person who defends something in speech or writing: *an apologist for disarmament.*

a·pol·o·gize (ə pol′ə jīz′) *v* **a·pol·o·gized, a·pol·o·giz·ing** **1** acknowledge that one has done wrong and say that one is sorry. **2** speak as if one were in the wrong: *You don't have to apologize for exerting your authority; it's your job.*

a·pol·o·gy (ə pol′ə jē) *n, pl* **a·pol·o·gies** **1** a statement acknowledging that one has done wrong, expressing regret and asking pardon: *I said I was sorry, but she did not accept my apology.* **2** a defence in speech or writing: *an apology for universal medicare.* **3** a poor or inadequate substitute: *One piece of toast is a poor apology for a breakfast.* <Latin, from Greek *apo-* away + *legein* speak>

ap·o·plec·tic (ap′ə plek′tik) *adj* extremely angry or indignant. <Latin, from Greek *apoplessein* disable by a *stroke* (def. 6)>

ap·o·plex·y (ap′ə plek′sē) STROKE (def. 6).

ap·o·se·mat·ic (ap′ō si mat′ik) *Zoology adj* to do with protective colouring that works by warning off predators. <Greek *apo-* away from + *sema* sign>

a·pos·ta·tize (ə pos′ta tīz′) *v* **a·pos·ta·tized, a·pos·ta·tiz·ing** abandon or renounce a faith, belief, or principle. <Latin, from Greek *apostates* runaway slave> **a·pos′ta·sy** (ə pos′ta si) *n.* **a·pos′tate′** *adj, n.*

a·pos·tle (ə pos′əl) *n* **1 Apostle** *Christianity* each of the twelve chief disciples of Jesus Christ. **2** a person who strongly promotes a policy, idea, or cause: *an apostle of Marxism.* **3** *Mormonism* one of a council of twelve administrative officials. <Latin *apostolos* messenger, from Greek *apo-* off + *stellein* send>

ap·o·stol·ic (ap′ə stol′ik) *adj* **1** to do with an apostle or the Apostles. **2** to do with the Pope.

a·pos·tro·phe (ə pos′trə fē) *n* **1** the sign ['] used: **a** to show the omission of one or more letters in contractions, as in *can't* for *cannot.* **b** to show the possessive form: *the lions' den, everybody's business.* **c** to form certain plurals: *There are two o's in door, and four 9's in 9999.* **d** to show that certain sounds represented in the usual spelling have not been spoken: *'lectric.* **2** the addressing of words to an absent person, or to a thing or idea as if it could understand. Example: *Rain, rain, go away.* <Latin, from Greek *apostrephein* omit, digress (i.e., turn away)>

GRAMMAR AND USAGE

An **apostrophe** in contractions shows that one or more letters have been left out: *I'm* (I am), *don't* (do not), *she'd* (she would).

Another use for the apostrophe is to show possession: *the tree's leaves* (one tree), *the trees' leaves* (more than one tree).

An apostrophe also replaces missing numbers or missing letters in speech: *'05* (2005), *the 'hood* (neighbourhood), *'bout* (about).

a·pos·tro·phize (ə pos′trə fīz′) *v* **a·pos·tro·phized, a·pos·tro·phiz·ing** address emotionally some thing or absent person in a speech or poem.

a·poth·e·cary (ə poth′ə ker′ē) *Archaic n, pl* **a·poth·e·car·ies** a person who prepares and sells medicines. <Latin *apothecarius* warehouse keeper, from Greek *apotheke* storehouse>

ap·o·thegm (ap′ə them′) *n* a short, forceful saying. Example: *Beauty is only skin deep.* <Greek *apo-* forth + *phtheggesthai* speak out>

ap·pal or **ap·pall** (ə pol′) *v* **ap·palled, ap·pal·ling** fill with horror or dismay: *It appals me to think that our drinking water may be unsafe.* <Old French *a-* to + *palir* turn pale> **ap·pall′ing** *adj.* **ap·pall′ing·ly** *adv.*

ap·pa·loo·sa (ap′ə lū′sə) *n* a breed of horse with dark spots of varied size on a light skin. <perhaps *a Palouse horse,* named after the Palouse River country in Washington, where the breed is said to have been developed by the Nez Percé nation>

ap·pa·ra·tus (ap′ə rat′əs) *or* (ap′ə rāt′əs) *n, pl* **ap·pa·ra·tus** or **ap·pa·ra·tus·es 1** the equipment needed to carry out an activity: *the apparatus for an experiment in chemistry.* **2** a complex structure within an organization: *the apparatus of government.* <Latin *ad-* toward + *parare* make ready>

ap·par·el (ə per′əl) *n* clothing: *Does this store sell women's apparel?*
v **ap·par·elled** or **ap·par·eled, ap·parel·ling** or **ap·par·el·ing** clothe: *The horseback riders, colourfully apparelled, formed part of the circus parade.* <Old French *apareiller* clothe>

ap·par·ent (ə per′ənt) *adj* **1** easy to see or understand: *It was apparent that he was lying.* **2** according to appearances: *the apparent motion of the sun around the earth.* <Old French, from Latin *apparere* appear>
ap·par′ent·ly *adv.*

ap·pa·ri·tion (ap′ə rish′ən) *n* **1** a ghost or phantom. **2** any strange sight. <Old French, from Latin *apparere* appear>

ap·peal (ə pēl′) *v* **1** be attractive or enjoyable: *Bright colours appeal to young children.* **2** (*with* **to** *or* **for**) make a sincere and forceful request: *They appealed to their mother for help.* **3** resort to some principle to persuade a person or decide a matter in one's favour: *He appealed to her sense of duty, and finally she gave in.* **4** *Law* ask that a case be taken to a higher court to be reviewed.
n **1** the act of appealing: *an appeal for mercy, an appeal to the Supreme Court.* **2** an attraction or interest: *the appeal of fancy technology.* <Old French *appeler,* from Latin *appellare* approach, i.e., to ask for something>

ap·peal·ing (ə pē′ling) *adj* attractive or pleasing: *Ten hours on a bus is not an appealing prospect.*

ap·pear (ə pēr′) *v* **1** become visible: *One by one the stars appear.* **2** seem to the eyes or mind: *The apple appeared sound on the outside, but it was rotten inside.* **3** be presented to the public: *The sequel to that movie will appear this fall.* **4** present oneself publicly or formally: *to appear on the stage, to appear in court.* <Old French *apareir,* from Latin *ad-* to + *parere* come in sight>

ap·pear·ance (ə pē′rəns) *n* **1** the act or fact of appearing: *Her appearance in the doorway startled me. This is his first public appearance.* **2** the way a person or thing looks: *From the appearance of the house we guessed it was empty.* **3** a false show or pretence: *an appearance of truth.* **4 appearances** *pl* the impression given by something: *Don't judge by appearances.*
keep up appearances, act as though everything is fine.
make (or **put in**) **an appearance,** be present, even if only briefly: *I'd better at least make an appearance at the party.*
to all appearances, as far as one can see: *He was, to all appearances, asleep.*

ap·pease (ə pēz′) *v* **ap·peased, ap·peas·ing 1** make someone calm or content, especially by satisfying a demand: *to appease an angry crowd.* **2** satisfy an appetite or desire: *A good dinner will appease your hunger.* <Old French *apaisier,* from *a-* to + *pais* peace>
ap·pease′ment *n.*

ap·pel·lant (ə pel′ənt) *Law n* a person who appeals.
adj to do with appeals.

ap·pel·late court (ə pel′it) *n* a court with the power to re-examine and reverse the decisions of a lower court.

a bat	e bed	i bid	o pot	u cup	th thin
ā cake	ē me	ī bite	ō go	ū rude	ᴛʜ then
ȧ bar	ə about	ər over	ȯ for	u̇ put	zh measure

ap·pel·la·tion (ap′ə lā′shən) *n* a name or title: *He goes by the appellation "Chief Administrator."* <Latin *appelationis,* from *apellare* to address (someone)>

ap·pend (ə pend′) *v* add to a larger thing, especially something written: *A glossary is appended to that textbook.* <Latin *ad-* on + *pendere* hang>

ap·pend·age (ə pen′dij) *n* **1** something attached to some larger or more important thing. **2** an external or subordinate body part, such as an arm, tail, or fin.

ap·pen·dec·to·my (ap′ən dek′tə mē) *n, pl* **ap·pen·dec·to·mies** the removal of a person's appendix by a surgical operation. <Latin, from Greek *ek-* out + *tomia* cutting>

ap·pen·di·ci·tis (ə pen′də sī′tis) *n* a painful inflammation of the appendix.

ap·pen·dix (ə pen′diks) *n, pl* **ap·pen·di·ces** (ə pen′də sēz′) (*for 1*) *or* **ap·pen·dix·es** (*for 2*) **1** a separate section at the end of a book or document, containing additional material. **2** in full, **vermiform appendix** the small saclike growth attached to the large intestine, and that has no known function.

ap·per·tain (ap′ər tān′) *v* belong as a part: *Forestry appertains to geography, botany, and agriculture.* <Old French, from Latin *ad-* to + *pertinere* belong>

ap·pe·tite (ap′ə tīt′) *n* **1** a desire for food. **2** a desire: *an appetite for adventure.* <Old French, from Latin *appetitus* (*ad-* to + *petere* seek)>

ap·pe·tiz·er (ap′ə tī′zər) *n* something served before a meal to arouse the appetite: *Garlic bread was the appetizer.*

ap·pe·tiz·ing (ap′ə tī′zing) *adj* giving an appetite to those who see or smell it: *appetizing food.* **ap′pe·tiz′ing·ly** *adv.*

ap·plaud (ə plod′) *v* **1** clap the hands to show approval or praise. **2** strongly approve or praise. <Latin *ad-* to + *plaudere* to clap>

ap·plause (ə ploz′) *n* approval or praise expressed by clapping the hands.

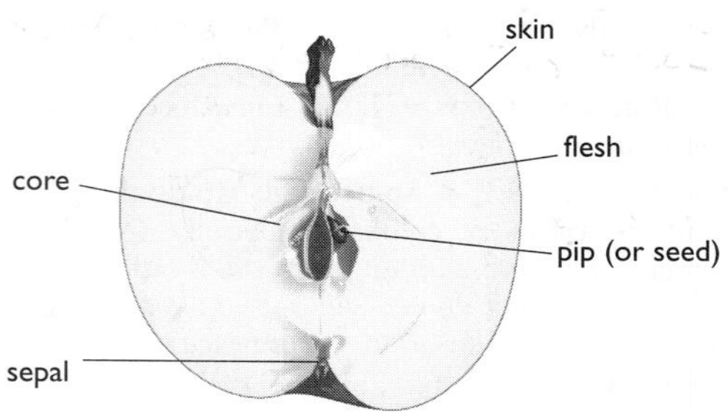

ap·ple (ap′əl) *n* the firm, fleshy fruit of a tree that grows in temperate climates. <Old English *æppel*>
apple of your eye, a person who or thing that you are fond of or proud of.
upset the apple cart, cause trouble.

apple butter *n* a smooth, jamlike spread made of apples and cider, with sugar and spices added.

apple–pie order (ap′əl pī′) *Informal n* perfect order or condition: *Everything is in apple-pie order for the wedding tomorrow.*

ap·ple–pol·ish (ap′əl pol′ish) *v* try to gain favour by flattering or doing things for a person. <from the tradition of children bringing a polished apple as a gift for the teacher> **ap′ple pol′ish·er** *n.*

ap·ple·sauce (ap′əl sos′) *n* apples cut up and cooked until soft, then often blended.

ap·plet (ap′lit) *Computers n* a small, specialized computer application. <*app*(*lication*) + *-let* (diminutive)>

ap·pli·ance (ə plī′əns) *n* a machine that runs by electricity and performs a specific task, especially a household one. <See APPLY.>

ap·pli·ca·ble (ap′lə kə bəl) *or* (ə plik′ə bəl) *adj* able to be applied in a certain situation: *If the question is not applicable in your case, just skip it.*

ap·pli·cant (ap′lə kənt) *n* a person applying for something, especially a job.

ap·pli·ca·tion (ap′lə kā′shən) *n* **1** the act, way, or result of applying: *This paint requires two applications. Technology is the application of science to practical problems.* **2** a form or letter used to apply for a job, loan, or position: *Fill out your application and send it in.* **3** *Computers* a program designed and written to serve a specific purpose: *an accounting application.* **4** consistent effort and close attention: *By continued application to her work she earned a promotion.* **5** a substance to be applied, such as an ointment or sealant.

ap·pli·ca·tor (ap′lə kā′tər) *n* a device used for applying a substance, such as polish, medicine, or cosmetics: *Rinse the applicator after each use.*

ap·plied (ə plīd′) *adj* **1** put to practical use: *Engineers study applied mathematics.* **2** in some school systems, to do with a program of study designed to be more practical than academic: *I am taking the applied course.* <See APPLY.>

ap·pli·qué (ap′lə kā′) *or* (ap′lə kā′) *n* **1** the art of sewing or gluing pieces of fabric in various shapes and colours onto a larger piece for decoration. **2** a cut-out piece of fabric attached to a larger piece in this way: *a skirt with butterfly appliqués.*
v **ap·pli·quéd, ap·pli·qué·ing** trim or ornament with appliqué: *to appliqué a skirt, to appliqué flowers on a skirt.* <French, from Latin *applicare.* See APPLY.>

ap·ply (ə plī′) *v* **ap·plied, ap·ply·ing** **1** put on as a treatment or coating to something: *to apply paint to a wall. Apply wet towels to the sick boy's face.* **2** put to practical use: *I understand the principle but am not sure how to apply it.* **3** come into effect: *English spelling rules do not apply to borrowed words.* **4** make a formal request: *to apply for a job.* **5** use for a special purpose: *to apply a sum of money to disaster relief.* <Old French *aplier,* from Latin *ad-* to + *plicare* attach>
apply yourself (**to**), give full attention to: *She applied herself to learning French.*

ap·point (ə point′) *v* **1** name to an office or position: *This man was appointed postmaster.* **2** decide on or set: *to appoint a time for the meeting.* **3** furnish or equip: *a well-appointed office.* <Old French, from Latin *ad-* to + *punctum* point> **ap·point′ee′** *n.*

ap·poin·tive (ə poin′tiv) *adj* filled by appointing rather than electing: *an appointive position on the town council.*

ap·point·ment (ə point′mənt) *n* **1** an arrangement to meet someone at a certain time and place: *I have an appointment with the doctor at four o'clock.* **2** the act of appointing someone: *The appointment of new officers happens before the annual meeting.* **3** an office or position to which someone is or will be appointed: *That's a good appointment to try for.*

ap·por·tion (ə pôr′shən) *v* divide and give out in shares: *His property was apportioned among his children after his death.* <Old French, from Latin *ad-* to + *portio* portion> **ap·por′tion·ment** *n.*

ap·po·site (ap′ə zit) *adj* apt or relevant: *an apposite quotation.* <Latin *appositus*, from *apponere* place nearby>

ap·po·si·tion (ap′ə zish′ən) *Grammar n* the relationship of two words or phrases when the one is added as an explanation to the other. In *Mr. Lee, our neighbour, has a new car*, the elements *Mr. Lee* and *neighbour* are in apposition. <French *apposer*, from Latin *apponere* put to>

ap·praise (ə prāz′) *v* **ap·praised, ap·prais·ing 1** estimate the value, worth, or quality of: *to appraise someone's work. The ring has been appraised at $600.* **2** set a price or value for: *Property is appraised for taxation.* <Old French *aprisier*, from Latin *appretiare* set a price on>
ap·prais′al *n.* **ap·prais′er** *n.* **ap·prais′ing** *adj.* **ap·prais′ing·ly** *adv.*

CONFUSABLES

Appraise means "estimate the value or quality": *She appraised the house at $300 000.*

Apprise means "inform": *The teacher will apprise you of the date of the test to give you time to study.*

ap·pre·ci·a·ble (ə prē′shə bəl) *adj* enough to be noticed: *an appreciable difference.* **ap·pre′ci·a·bly** *adv.*

ap·pre·ci·ate (ə prē′shē āt′) *v* **ap·pre·ci·at·ed, ap·pre·ci·at·ing 1** value or enjoy: *Almost everybody appreciates good food.* **2** feel thankful for: *I appreciate what you have done for me.* **3** have an informed opinion of the worth of: *to appreciate art.* **4** rise in value: *Land appreciates over time.* Compare DEPRECIATE. **5** be sensitive to: *to appreciate small differences. I appreciate how hard this is for you.* <Latin *appretiare* set a price on, from *ad-* to + *pretium* price> **ap·pre′ci·a′tion** *n.*

ap·pre·ci·a·tive (ə prē′shə tiv) *adj* showing appreciation: *She was appreciative of the smallest kindness.* **ap·pre′ci·a·tive·ly** *adv.*

ap·pre·hend (ap′ri hend′) *v* **1** understand: *I apprehended his meaning from his gestures.* **2** arrest: *The thief was apprehended and put in jail.* <Latin *apprehendere* take hold of, from *ad-* toward + *prehendere* seize>

ap·pre·hen·sion (ap′ri hen′shən) *n* **1** fear or uneasiness: *The roar of the hurricane filled us with apprehension.* **2** the act or fact of apprehending: *a clear apprehension of the facts, the apprehension of a thief.*

ap·pre·hen·sive (ap′ri hen′siv) *adj* fearful and anxious: *The risks involved are making me feel a little apprehensive.* **ap′pre·hen′sive·ly** *adv.*

ap·pren·tice (ə pren′tis) *n* **1** a person learning a trade or art from a skilled worker. **2** a beginner; a learner.
v **ap·pren·ticed, ap·pren·tic·ing** set to work as an apprentice: *He was apprenticed to a master carpenter for six years.* <Old French *aprentis* from *apprendre* learn (Latin *ad-* to + *prendere* seize)> **ap·pren′tice·ship** *n.*

ap·prise (ə prīz′) *v* **ap·prised, ap·pris·ing** inform or notify: *I received an e-mail apprising me of the extra charges.* See APPRAISE for confusable. <French *appris*, from *apprendre* learn, from Latin *apprehendere* take hold of>

ap·proach (ə prōch′) *v* **1** come near or nearer in space or time: *The train approached the station. Winter is approaching.* **2** come near or nearer to in character, quality, or amount: *The wind was approaching a gale.* **3** go to speak or negotiate with: *to approach the boss about a raise in pay.* **4** go about doing or dealing with: *I don't know how best to approach this problem.*
n the act, fact, or way of approaching: *the approach of night, a new approach to mathematics.* <Old French *aprochier*, from Latin *ad-* to + *prope* near>

ap·proach·a·ble (ə prō′chə bəl) *adj* **1** that can be approached: *Is the mountain approachable from the south?* **2** easy to approach: *He looks stern, but is really very friendly and approachable.* **ap·proach′a·bil′i·ty** *n.*

ap·pro·ba·tion (ap′rə bā′shən) *n* approval. <Latin *ad-* to + *probius* good>

ap·pro·pri·ate (ə prō′prē it) *for adj*, (ə prō′prē āt′) *for v.*
adj suitable or proper: *Jeans and a sweater are appropriate clothes for the hike. Write the appropriate word in the space.*
v **ap·pro·pri·at·ed, ap·pro·pri·at·ing 1** take for oneself: *My sister has appropriated half my wardrobe.* **2** set aside for some special use: *to appropriate public funds for road construction.* <Latin *ad-* to + *proprius* one's own> **ap·pro′pri·ate·ly** *adv.* **ap·pro′pri·ate·ness** *n.* **ap·pro′pri·a′tion** *n.*

ap·prove (ə prüv′) *v* **ap·proved, ap·prov·ing 1** (*with* ***of***) **a** be pleased with: *They approve of my work.* **b** consider proper or correct: *I don't approve of your staying up so late.* **2** consent to: *Parliament approved the bill.* <Old French *aprover*, from Latin *ad-* to + *probius* good> **ap·prov′al** *n.* **ap·prov′ing** *adj.* **ap·prov′ing·ly** *adv.*

ap·prox·i·mate (ə prok′sə mit) *for adj*, (ə prok′sə māt′) *for v.*
adj not exact, but close enough to be useful: *an approximate translation. The approximate area of New Brunswick is 73 000 km^2; the exact area is 73 437 km^2.*
v **ap·prox·i·mat·ed, ap·prox·i·mat·ing** come close to in quality, nature, or quantity: *This report approximates the truth. The crowd approximated a thousand people.* <Latin *ad-* to + *proximus* very near> **ap·prox′i·mate·ly** *adv.* **ap·prox′i·ma′tion** *n.*

a·près–ski (ap′rā skē′) *n* a social activity held in the evening after a day of skiing.
adj to do with such an activity: *an après-ski outfit.* <French *après* after + *ski*>

a bat	e bed	i bid	o pot	u cup	th thin
ā cake	ē me	ī bite	ō go	ü rude	ᴛʜ then
ȧ bar	ə about	ər over	ò for	ů put	zh measure

An **apricot** has the same fuzzy skin as a peach, but is much smaller. A nectarine is about the same size as a peach, but has a smooth skin.

ap·ri·cot (ap′rə kot′) *n* a small, soft, roundish fruit related to the peach.
adj pale orange-yellow. <Portuguese *albricoque*, from Latin *praecoquis* early ripe>

A·pril (ā′prəl) *n* the fourth month of the year, with 30 days. *Abbrev.* **Apr** <Latin *Aprilis*>

April fool *n* a person who gets fooled on **April Fools' Day**, April 1, a day sometimes traditionally observed by playing tricks and jokes. <After the adoption of the Gregorian calendar in 1582, New Year's Day changed from April 1 to January 1. Many people remained unaware of this and were regarded as fools.>

a pri·o·ri (ā′ prē ô′rē) *or* (ā′ prē ô′rī) *adj* involving deduction from a cause to an effect, and requiring no evidence. <Latin = from (something) previous, i.e., from a cause>

a·pron (ā′prən) *n* **1** a garment worn over the front of the body to protect one's clothes: *a chef's apron, a carpenter's apron.* **2** the part of a theatre stage in front of the curtain. **3** a paved area in front of a building. <Old French *naperon*, from Latin *mappa* napkin> **a′pron·like′** *adj.*
cut the apron strings, become or force to become independent.

ap·ro·pos (ap′rə pō′) *adj* fitting or suitable: *His remarks were very apropos.*
adv (*to introduce a related but new point*) incidentally: *Apropos, what are you doing tonight?*
prep with regard to; concerning: *Apropos our date tonight, I have to cancel.* <French *à propos* with regard to>

apse (aps) *n* in a Christian church, an alcove with an arched roof, usually at the east end. <Latin, from Greek *hapsis* arch>

apt (apt) *adj* **1** likely: *An overtired person is apt to make mistakes.* **2** suitable or fitting: *an apt reply.* **3** quick to learn: *an apt student.* <Latin *aptus* fitting, from *apere* fasten> **apt′ly** *adv.* **apt′ness** *n.*

ap·ter·ous (ap′tə rəs) *Zoology adj* wingless. <Greek *a-* without + *pteron* wing>

ap·ti·tude (ap′tə tyūd′) *or* (ap′tə tūd′) *n* a natural ability that suits a person for a certain kind of work: *an aptitude for fixing things.*

aq·ua (ak′wə) *or* (ȧ′kwə) *adj* light bluish green. <Latin = water>

aq·ua·lung (ak′wə lung′) *n* a diving apparatus consisting of cylinders of compressed air strapped to the diver's back and a watertight mask to cover the eyes and nose. <*Aqualung*, a trademark>

aq·ua·ma·rine (ak′wə mə rēn′) *n* a transparent, bluish green gemstone, a variety of beryl.
adj light bluish green.

aq·ua·relle (ak′wə rel′) *n* **1** a painting done with thin watercolours. **2** this method of painting. <French, from Latin *aqua* water>

a·quar·i·um (ə kwer′ē əm) *n, pl* **a·quar·i·ums** or **a·quar·i·a** (ə kwer′ē ə) **1** a tank or glass bowl in which living fish, water animals, and water plants are kept. **2** a building used for showing collections of such animals and plants. <Latin *aqua* water>

A·quar·i·us (ə kwer′ē əs) *n* **1** *Astronomy* a southern constellation suggesting a man with his left hand stretched upward and his right pouring a stream of water out of an urn. **2** *Astrology* **a** the eleventh sign of the zodiac. The sun enters Aquarius about January 21. **b** a person born under this sign. <Latin *aqua* water>

a·quat·ic (ə kwot′ik) *or* (ə kwat′ik) *adj* **1** growing or living in water: *aquatic plants.* **2** taking place in or on water: *aquatic sports.*
n **aquatics** (*with singular verb*) water sports, including diving, swimming, and water polo.

aq·ue·duct (ak′wə dukt′) *n* **1** an artificial channel or large pipe for bringing water from a distance. **2** a structure supporting such a channel or pipe. <Latin *aqua* water + *ductus*, from *ducere* to lead>

a·que·ous (ak′wē əs) *or* (ā′kwē əs) *adj* of, like, or containing water. <Latin *aqua* water>

aqueous humour or **humor** *n* the watery liquid that fills the space in the eye between the cornea and the lens.

aq·ui·fer (ak′wə fər) *n* an underground layer of porous rock or sand, holding water which can be tapped by wells. <Latin *aqua* water + *ferre* carry>

aq·ui·line (ak′wə līn′) *adj* **1** of or like an eagle. **2** curved like an eagle's beak: *an aquiline nose.* <Latin *aquila* eagle>

aq·ui·tard (ak′wə tard) *n* a layer of clay, silt, or rock, through which water cannot move quickly. <perhaps Latin *aqua* water + *tardus* slow>

a·quiv·er (ə kwiv′ər) *adj* trembling.

Ar·ab (er′əb) *n* **1** a member of a Semitic people who live throughout the Middle East and N Africa. **2** a member of an Arabic-speaking people.
adj to do with the Arabs.

GRAMMAR AND USAGE

Arab is commonly used in reference to the people or their culture: *the Arab world.*

Arabia is the original homeland of the Arabs.

Arabian is most often used for Arab home territory: *Arabian deserts.*

Arabic refers to the language: *Arabic literature.*

ar·a·besque (er′ə besk′) *n* **1** in ballet, a pose in which the dancer stands on one leg with the other extended behind and the arms stretched out. **2** an elaborate and fanciful design of flowing lines, especially of flowers and leaves. **3** *Music* a light, graceful, often elaborate composition or passage. <French = in Arab style>

A·ra·bi·an (ə rā′bē ən) *adj* to do with the peninsula between Africa and Asia, containing Saudi Arabia and other countries.
n a horse of a breed that originally came from Arabia.

Ar·a·bic (er′ə bik) *n* the Semitic language of the Arabs.
adj to do with the Arabs or their language.

Arabic numerals *pln* the figures 1, 2, 3, 4, 5, 6, 7, 8, 9, and 0. Compare ROMAN NUMERALS.

ar·a·ble (er′ə bəl) *adj* good for farming: *There is little arable land on the Canadian Shield.* <Old French, from Latin *arare* to plough>

Arab League *n* an association of Arab countries to foster social, political, and economic co-operation among themselves. Also called **League of Arab States**.

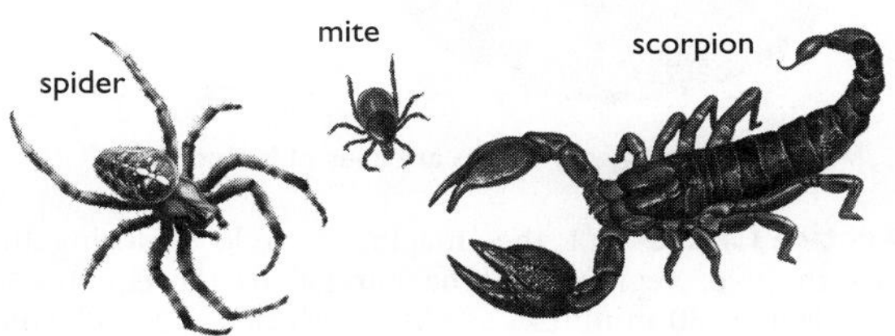

Most **arachnids** are harmless, but the stings of a few species of scorpions and the bites of some spiders are dangerously poisonous to humans.

a·rach·nid (ə rak′nid) *n* a small air-breathing arthropod, with no antennae or wings and four pairs of walking legs on a body divided into only two segments. Spiders, scorpions, and mites are arachnids. <Latin, from Greek *arachne* spider>

a·rach·no·pho·bi·a (ə rak′nə fō′bē ə) *n* an abnormal fear of spiders. <Latin, from Greek *arachne* spider + *phobia*>
a·rach′no·pho′bic *adj, n.*

ar·bi·ter (ȧr′bə tər) *n* a person with final authority to decide: *Who made her the arbiter of good taste?* <See ARBITRATE.>

ar·bi·trar·y (ȧr′bə trer′ē) *adj* **1** based on a whim rather than on sound reasoning: *an arbitrary decision.* **2** done or made at random: *an arbitrary selection.* **3** despotic: *an arbitrary regime.* **ar′bi·trar′i·ly** *adv.* **ar′bi·trar′i·ness** *n.*

ar·bi·trate (ȧr′bə trāt′) *v* **ar·bi·trat·ed, ar·bi·trat·ing** **1** decide a dispute as an impartial third party: *to arbitrate between two parties in a quarrel.* **2** submit to this method of settlement: *The two nations agreed to arbitrate their dispute.* <Latin *arbitrari* give judgement>
ar′bi·tra′tion *n.* **ar′bi·tra′tor** *n.*

ar·bo·re·al (ȧr bȯ′rē əl) *adj* **1** living in trees: *Squirrels are arboreal.* 2 to do with trees. <Latin *arbor* tree>

ar·bo·ri·cul·ture (ȧr bȯ′rə kul′chər) *n* the science of growing trees and bushes. <Latin *arbor* tree + *culture*>
ar·bor′i·cul′tur·ist *n.*

ar·bor·vi·tae (ȧr′bər vē′tī) *or* (vī′tē) *n, pl* **ar·bor·vi·tae** a large evergreen tree of the cypress family with very light wood that resists decay. <Latin = tree of life>

ar·bour or **ar·bor** (ȧr′bər) *n* **1** a shady place formed by trees or by vines growing on latticework. **2** the latticework.

ar·bu·tus (ȧr byū′təs) *n* **1** TRAILING ARBUTUS. **2** a broadleaf evergreen tree native to the pacific coast of N America. It is the only broadleaf evergreen native to Canada. <Latin>

arc (ȧrk) *n* **1** *Mathematics* any part of a circle or ellipse, or its angular measurement. See DIAMETER for picture. **2** a curved line or path. **3** a discharge of electricity seen as a curved stream of brilliant light, formed when a current jumps across a gap in a circuit or between electrodes.
v **arced, arc·ing** form an arc. <Old French, from Latin *arcus* bow>

ar·cade (ȧr kād′) *n* **1** a covered passageway, often with an arched roof. **2** a row of arches supported by columns. **3** a hall with video and other games, which people pay money to play. <French, from Latin *arcus* arch>

ar·cane (ȧr kān′) *adj* known or understood by only a few: *She uses all these arcane words I've never even heard of.* <Latin *arcanum* hidden>

arch[1] (ȧrch) *n* **1** an upright structure with a curved top that makes an opening, especially when used as a support for the weight of a bridge, roof, or wall. See TREFOIL for picture. **2** a curved upright structure that forms a passage or part of a monument. **3** the part of the sole of the foot that curves upward.
v bend into an arch: *The wind arched the trees over the road.* <French, from Latin *arcus* bow>

arch[2] (ȧrch) *adj* playful and teasing in an affected way: *The little girl gave her mother an arch look.* <a form of *arch-* >
arch′ly *adv.* **arch′ness** *n.*

arch– *prefix* chief or principal: *archbishop.* <Latin, from Greek *archos* ruler, chief>

ar·chae·a (ȧr′kē ə) *pln* a KINGDOM (def. 3) of one-celled micro-organisms that resemble bacteria, but whose molecules are organized differently. Archaea are found in volcanic vents and hot springs. See also BACTERIA, MONERA, PROKARYOTE. <Greek *archaios* ancient>

ar·chae·ol·o·gy (ȧr′kē ol′ə jē) *n* the study of life in ancient times by examining the remains of objects and settlements left by various civilizations. Also, **archeology**. <Greek *archaios* ancient>
ar′chae·o·log′i·cal *adj.* **ar′chae·ol′o·gist** *n.*

ar·cha·ic (ȧr kā′ik) *adj* very old or old-fashioned. A word or style of language no longer in everyday may be used for a special or a humorous effect. Example: *Gadzooks* (a mild oath), *I'm going to be late!* <Greek *archaikos*, from *arche* beginning>

ar·cha·ism (ȧr′kē iz′əm) *or* (ȧr′kā iz′əm) *n* a word or expression no longer in general use.
Example: *methinks* (= *I think*)

a bat	e bed	i bid	o pot	u cup	th **thin**
ā cake	ē me	ī bite	ō go	ū rude	ᴛʜ **then**
ȧ bar	ə about	ər over	ȯ for	ů put	zh measure

arch·an·gel (àr′kān′jel) *n* an angel of high rank.

arch·bish·op (àrch′bish′əp) *Christianity n* a bishop of the highest rank.

ar·che·go·ni·um (àr′kə gō′nē əm) *Botany n, pl* **ar·che·go·ni·a** (àr′kə gō′nē ə) the female reproductive organ in ferns, mosses, liverworts, and most conifers. <Greek *arche* beginning + *gonos* seed, race>

arch·en·e·my (àrch′en′ə mē) *n, pl* **arch·en·e·mies** a chief enemy.

ar·che·ol·o·gy (àr′kē ol′ə jē) ARCHAEOLOGY.

arch·er (àr′chər) *n* a person who shoots with a bow and arrow. See QUIVER for picture. <Old French, from Latin *arcus* bow>

arch·er·y (àr′chə rē) *n* the skill or art of shooting with bow and arrow at a target.

ar·che·type (àr′kə tīp′) *n* **1** an original model or pattern from which copies are made or later forms develop. **2** a typical example serving as a mental icon or image: *The robin is the archetype of a bird.* **3** a recurrent symbol or image found in the history of art, literature, or mythology. <Latin, from Greek *arche* beginning + *typos* print> **arch′e·typ′al** *adj.*

Ar·chi·me·des principle (àr′kə mē′dēz) *Physics n* the principle that the upward thrust of an object when partly or completely immersed in liquid is equal to the weight of the liquid it displaces. <*Archimedes*, scientist, 3c BCE>

Archimedes' screw *n* a device used by ancient peoples to raise water, consisting of a spiral tube around or inside a cylindrical shaft. The water was brought upward by manually turning the spiral. <See ARCHIMEDES PRINCIPLE.>

ar·chi·pel·a·go (àr′kə pel′ə gō′) *n, pl* **ar·chi·pel·a·gos** or **ar·chi·pel·a·goes** a group of many islands, such as the **Arctic** (or **Canadian**) **Archipelago** in the Arctic Ocean north of Canada's mainland. <Italian *arcipelago* the chief sea, probably a mistranslation of Greek *Aigaion pelagos* the (island-studded) Aegean Sea>

ar·chi·tect (àr′kə tekt′) *n* **1** a person whose profession is designing buildings and who often supervises their construction. **2** a designer, planner, or creator: *the architects of modern technology.*

ar·chi·tec·ture (àr′kə tek′chər) *n* **1** the science, art, or profession of designing buildings. **2** a particular style of building: *Greek architecture made much use of columns.* **3** the structure or design of anything: *computer architecture.* <Latin, from Greek *archi-* chief + *tekton* builder> **arch′itec′tur·al** *adj.*

ar·chive (àr′kīv) *v* **ar·chived, ar·chiv·ing** **1** place or store materials, especially historical documents or records, in a collection **2** *Computers* transfer data that is less frequently used to a special file or storage place in a computer system: *I have archived all my old e-mails.*
n usually, **archives** *pl* stored records or historical documents, or the place where they are kept: *The National Archives of Canada are in Ottawa.* <French, from Latin *archivum* (Greek *arche* government)> **ar·chi′val** *adj.*

arch·way (àrch′wā′) *n* **1** an entrance or passageway with an arch above it. **2** the arch itself.

arc lamp *n* a lamp whose light comes from an electric ARC (def. 3).

arc·tic (àrk′tik) *or* (àr′tik) *adj* **1 Arctic** to do with the region north of the Arctic Circle: *the Arctic fox.* **2** extremely cold: *arctic temperatures.*
n **the Arctic** the region north of the Arctic Circle. <Latin, from Greek *arktos* bear (the northern constellation Ursa Major)>

Arctic char *n* a food fish of the salmon family found throughout the Arctic.

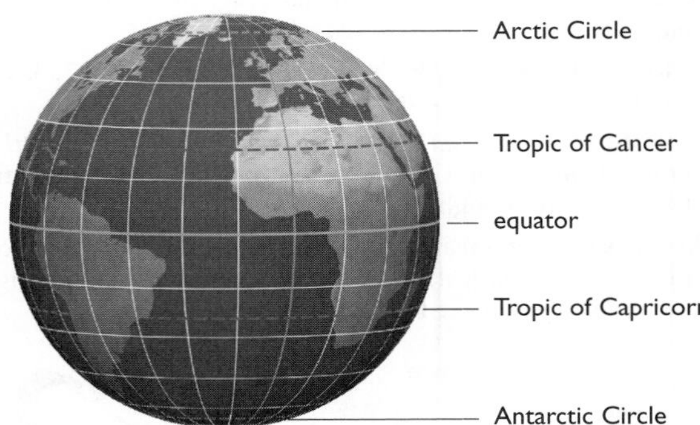

All of these imaginary circles are lines of latitude.

Arctic Circle *n* **1** the imaginary circle enclosing the north polar region, running parallel to the equator at 23 degrees 30 minutes (23°30′) south of the North Pole. **2** the polar region surrounded by this circle.

Arctic fox *n* a fox of the Arctic valued for its fur, which is grey in summer and white in winter. See FLYING FOX for picture.

✱ **Arctic hare** *n* a large hare of arctic Canada that is pure white in winter except for its black-tipped ears, and varies in summer from grey to almost white.

Arctic haze *n* a condition of the atmosphere in the Arctic, in which particles of pollutants suspended in air increase in concentration during the winter.

Arctic Ocean *n* the ocean covering the North Pole, much of it permanently frozen.

Arctic tern *n* a tern that breeds in the Arctic and migrates in the winter to the southern hemisphere.

arc welding *n* a method of welding using heat produced by an electric ARC (def. 3).

ar·dent (àr′dənt) *adj* very enthusiastic or passionate: *an ardent student of history.* <Old French *ardante,* from Latin *ardere* to burn> **ar′dent·ly** *adv.*

ar·dour or **ar·dor** (àr′dər) *n* great enthusiasm or passion: *patriotic ardour.*

ar·du·ous (àr′jū əs) *or* (àr′dyū əs) *adj* **1** requiring much effort: *an arduous task.* **2** intense or strenuous: *an arduous effort.* <Latin *arduus* steep> **ar′du·ous·ly** *adv.* **ar′du·ous·ness** *n.*

are[1] (àr) the plural and second person singular, present tense, of BE.

are[2] (er) *or* (àr) *n* a unit of area, equal to 100 m^2. *Symbol* **a** <French, from Latin *area* piece of level ground>

ar·e·a (er′ē ə) *n* **1** the measure or extent of a surface: *The area of this floor is 24 m^2.* **2** region: *a swampy area.* **3** a space devoted to a particular use: *a play area, a study area.* **4** a field of study or activity: *She works in the area of advertising.* <Latin *area* piece of level ground>

area code *n* a three-digit number identifying a particular area within a region served by a telephone system.

area rug *n* a rug covering only part of a floor.

a·re·na (ə rē′nə) *n* **1** a building for indoor sports, with a central space for players or competitors surrounded by tiered seats for spectators. **2** a sphere of public action, especially one involving conflict: *You have to have stamina to succeed in the political arena.* <Latin *arena* sand. Roman arenas had sand-covered floors.>

aren't (ärnt) *contraction* **1** are not. **2** (*in questions*) am not: *I'm too late, aren't I?*

Ar·gen·ti·na (är′jən tē′nə) *n* a country in S America. See the APPENDIX. **Ar′gen·tin′i·an** or **Ar′gen·tine′** *adj, n.*

ar·gon (är′gon) *n* an element that is a colourless, odourless, inactive gas forming a tiny part of the air. *Symbol* **Ar** <Latin, from Greek *a-* without + *ergon* work>

ar·got (är′gō), (är gō′), *or* (är′gət) *n* the specialized language of people in a particular group, especially the language of criminals. <French>

ar·gu·a·ble (är′gyū ə bəl) *adj* **1** able to be argued: *Whether or not he meant to do it is arguable.* **2** open to question; doubtful: *Whenever she finds her point of view is arguable, she changes the subject.*

ar·gue (är′gyū) *v* **ar·gued, ar·gu·ing** **1** exchange opinions with someone who disagrees: *to argue a question. She argued with her brother about who should wash the dishes.* **2** give reasons to support or oppose an idea, action, or theory: *He argued against the passage of the bill. Columbus argued that the world was round.* **3** persuade by giving reasons: *They argued me into going.* <Old French, from Latin *arguere* make clear> **ar′gu·er** *n.*
argue with, dispute; refute: *You can't argue with the facts.*

SYNONYMS

Argue means "oppose another's opinion": *He argued with his friend over who was stronger.*

Quarrel means "disagree angrily": *The brother and sister quarrelled over who should do the dishes.*

Debate means "argue logically": *The student council spent a long time debating the issue of mandatory school uniforms.*

ar·gu·ment (är′gyə mənt) *n* **1** an exchange of opposing views: *He won the argument by producing statistics to prove his point.* **2** an emotional disagreement or quarrel: *We had an argument about whose turn it was.* **3** a reasoned case for or against something: *the argument for subsidized daycare.* **4** the basic content of a speech or piece of text: *What is the main argument of the book?*

ar·gu·men·ta·tion (är′gyə mən tā′shən) *n* the process of building an argument.

ar·gu·men·ta·tive (är′gyə men′tə tiv) *adj* **1** fond of arguing. **2** using reasons for or against something. **ar′gu·men′ta·tive·ly** *adv.* **ar′gu·men′ta·tive·ness** *n.*

ar·gyle (är′gīl) *adj* to do with a diamond-shaped pattern that is knitted into socks and other garments. <*Argyll*, a county in Scotland, where this pattern originated>

a·ri·a (ä′rē ə) *n* a melody for a single unaccompanied voice, especially in an opera. <Italian, from Latin *aer* tune)>

ar·id (er′id) *adj* **1** with very little rainfall. **2** dull or uninteresting: *an arid style of writing.* <Latin *aridus*, from *arere* to be dry> **a·rid′i·ty** *n.*

Ar·ies (er′ēz) *n* **1** *Astronomy* a northern constellation shaped somewhat like a ram. **2** *Astrology* **a** the first sign of the zodiac. The sun enters Aries about March 20. **b** a person born under this sign.

a·right (ə rīt′) *Poetic adv* correctly: *Do I hear aright?*

a·rise (ə rīz′) *v* **a·rose, a·ris·en, a·ris·ing** **1** get up: *to arise early in the morning.* **2** move upward: *Smoke arose from the chimney.* **3** begin: *A great wind arose. Accidents arise from carelessness.* <Old English *arisan*>

ar·is·toc·ra·cy (er′i stok′rə sē) *n, pl* **ar·is·toc·ra·cies** **1** the highest class in some societies, typically one whose members have inherited their titles. **2** a class supposed to be superior because of birth, intelligence, culture, or wealth. **3** a system of government in which a privileged upper class holds power. <Latin, from Greek *aristos* best + *kratia* power>

a·ris·to·crat (ə ris′tə krat′) *n* a member of an aristocracy or elite. **a·ris′to·crat′ic** *adj.*

Ar·is·to·te·li·an (er′i stə tēl′yən) *or* (ə ris′tə tēl′yən) *adj* to do with the Greek philosopher Aristotle (384–322 BCE) or his philosophy.

a·rith·me·tic (ə rith′mə tik′) *for n,* (ər′ith mə′tik) *for adj.* *n* the branch of mathematics dealing with numbers, including adding, subtracting, multiplying, and dividing. *adj* to do with a progression in which a set amount is added or subtracted at each stage, rather than by multiplying quantities: *an arithmetic increase.* Also (*adj*), **arithmetical** (ər′ith mə′tik əl). <Old French, from Greek *arithmos* number> **ar′ith·met′i·cal·ly** *adv.*

arithmetic mean (ər′ith mə′tik) *Mathematics n* the average of a set of numerical values, obtained by adding them together and dividing by the number of terms in the set: *To obtain the arithmetic mean of 3, 9, 13, and 15, add them up and divide the total by 4.*

arithmetic progression (ər′ith mə′tik) *Mathematics n* a sequence in which there is always the same difference between any number and the next one: *The numbers 2, 4, 6, 8, 10 are in arithmetical progression; so are 8, 5, 2, -1.* Compare GEOMETRIC PROGRESSION. Also called **arithmetic sequence**.

arithmetic series (ər′ith mə′tik) *Mathematics n* the indicated sum of an arithmetic progression.
Example: 2 + 4 + 6 + 8 + 10

a bat	e bed	i bid	o pot	u cup	th **thin**
ā cake	ē me	ī bite	ō go	ū rude	ᴛʜ then
ä bar	ə about	ər over	ô for	ů put	zh measure

ark (ärk) *n* **1** in the Bible, the large boat in which Noah saved himself, his family, and a pair of each kind of animal from the Flood. **2 a Ark of the Covenant** the wooden box in which the ancient Hebrews kept the two tablets of stone containing the Ten Commandments. **b Holy Ark** the box in a Jewish synagogue that holds the Torah scrolls. <Old English *arc*>

arm[1] (ärm) *n* **1** each of the two parts of the human body that extends from the shoulder to the hand. **2** the forelimb of an animal that sometimes walks upright, such as a bear or gorilla. **3** anything shaped or used like an arm: *the arm of a chair.* **4** power or authority: *the strong arm of the law.* **5** a branch of an organization or government: *Parliament is the legislative arm of our system of government.* <Old English *earm*> **arm′ful′** *n.* **arm′less** *adj.*

an arm and a leg, *Informal* a very high price: *They charge an arm and a leg for repairs.*

arm in arm, with arms linked: *The two girls walked arm in arm.*

as long as your arm, *Informal* very long, especially tiresomely so: *a list of complaints as long as your arm.*

at arm's length, a as far as the arm can reach: *He held the picture up at arm's length to look at it.* **b** in a relationship that avoids contact or interference: *She was shy and kept everyone at arm's length. The police force and the Special Investigations Unit remain at arm's length.*

with open arms, in a warm, friendly way.

arm[2] (ärm) *n* **1** usually, **arms** *pl* weapons used for fighting. **2** the symbols and designs used in heraldry. See also COAT OF ARMS.

v **1** supply with weapons: *Who is arming the rebel forces?* **2** take up weapons: *The soldiers armed for battle.* **3** provide with equipment, tools, or other items as a preparation for some activity. *The lawyer entered court armed with plenty of evidence.* <Old French, from Latin *arma* weapons>

bear arms, a serve as a soldier. **b** own or carry a weapon.

take up arms, arm oneself for combat: *The settler took up arms against the invaders.*

under arms, equipped for fighting.

up in arms, very angry or indignant.

ar·ma·da (är mä′də) *or* (är mad′ə) *n* **1** an armed fleet of ships or aircraft. **2 the (Spanish) Armada** the Spanish fleet that was sent to attack England in 1588. <Spanish, from Latin *armare* to arm>

ar·ma·dil·lo (är′mə dil′ō) *n* a burrowing mammal mainly of Central and S America that has an armourlike covering of jointed, bony plates. <Spanish = little armed one>

Ar·ma·ged·don (är′mə ged′ən) *n* a huge and destructive conflict that is seen as likely to destroy the world or all of humanity. <Hebrew *har megiddon* hill of Megaddo (a site of great battles)>

ar·ma·ment (är′mə mənt) *n* **1** usually, **armaments** *pl* military weapons and equipment. **2** the guns on a ship, tank, airplane, etc. <French, from Latin *armare* to arm>

ar·ma·ture (är′mə chər) *n* **1** a piece of soft iron placed across the poles of a magnet to preserve its magnetic power. **2** *Electricity* **a** the revolving part of an electric motor. **b** the coils of wire that revolve in the magnetic field of a generator to produce an electric current. **3** a part of an animal or plant serving for offence or defence, such as claws or a shell. <French, from Latin *armare* to arm>

arm·band (ärm′band′) *n* a cloth band, often black, worn around the sleeve, usually as a sign of mourning.

arm·chair (ärm′cher′) *n* a chair with side pieces to support a person's arms or elbows.

armed forces *pln* the army, navy, and air force of a country.

Ar·me·ni·a (är mē′nē ə) *n* a country in southwest Asia. See the APPENDIX. **Ar·me′ni·an** *adj, n.*

arm·hole (ärm′hōl′) *n* the hole for the arm in a garment.

ar·mi·stice (är′mə stis) *n* an agreement by opposing sides to stop a war. <Latin *arma* arms + *-stitium* stoppage>

Armistice Day *n* in former times, REMEMBRANCE DAY.

arm·load (ärm′lōd′) *n* as much or many as a person's arms can carry at one time: *an armload of books.*

ar·moire (ärm wär′) *n* a large stand-alone cupboard or wardrobe. <Old French, from Latin *armarium* cabinet (originally for holding armour)>

ar·mo·ri·al bearings (är mô′rē əl) *pln* coat of arms.

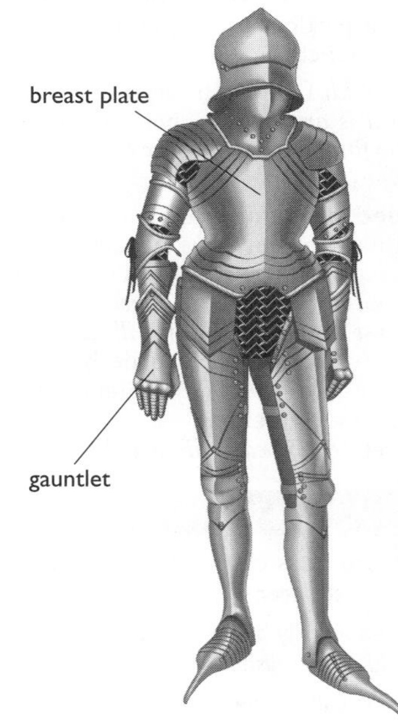

The earliest body **armour** was a wide belt worn by ancient Egyptians to protect the abdomen. Armour later evolved into a quilted garment that extended from the armpits to the knees and was held up by shoulder straps.

The medieval suit of armour, developed in the 1400s, weighed a maximum of 29 kg, to allow full mobility. Tournament armour, however, was twice as heavy for safety reasons.

ar·mour or **ar·mor** (är′mər) *n* **1** a suit, usually of metal, worn to protect the body in a fight. **2** a protective covering, such as steel plates on a warship, motor vehicle, etc. Also called **armour plate**. **3** anything that protects or defends: *A good education is the best armour against propaganda.* **4** the tanks and other armoured vehicles of an army.

v cover or protect with armour. <Old French *armeure*, from Latin *armare* to arm>

ar·mour·bear·er or **ar·mor·bear·er** (är′mər ber′ər) *n* in former times, an attendant who carried the armour and weapons of a knight or warrior.

ar·moured or **ar·mored** (är′mərd) *adj* covered with or using armour: *an armoured car, an armoured regiment.*

ar·mour·y or **ar·mor·y** (är′mə rē) *n, pl* **ar·mour·ies** or **ar·mor·ies 1** a place where weapons are kept.
2 🍁 **armouries** *pl* a place where reserve units of the armed forces have their headquarters and training area.
3 *US* a place where weapons are made.

arm·pit (ärm′pit′) *n* the hollow under the arm at the shoulder.

arm·rest (ärm′rest′) *n* the padded part of a chair or seat that supports a person's arm.

arms race *n* competition among different nations seeking to have the most weapons, or the most advanced weapons.

arm–twist·ing (ärm′twis′ting) *n* physical force or moral pressure on someone to do something: *It took a lot of arm-twisting, but he finally agreed to join the band.*

arm wrestling *n* a game in which two people facing each other rest their right or left elbows on a flat surface, clasp hands, and try to force each other's arm down sideways.

ar·my (är′mē) *n, pl* **ar·mies 1** a large, organized group of soldiers, trained and armed for war. **2** the part of such a group that operates on land, as opposed to on the sea or in the air; in Canada, **Mobile Command**. **3** a group organized along military lines: *The Salvation Army.* **4** a very large number: *an army of reporters.* <Old French *armee*, from Latin *armare* to arm>

army ant *n* a tropical ant that travels in large columns, preying mainly on insects and spiders.

army worm *n* the green-and-white-striped caterpillar of the **army worm moth** that sometimes travels across fields in N America, destroying crops.

a·ro·ma (ə rō′mə) *n* a pleasant and distinctive smell, especially of food: *the aroma of a cake in the oven.* <Old French, from Greek = spice> **ar′o·mat′ic** *adj.*

a·rose (ə rōz′) past tense of ARISE.

a·round (ə round′) *adv* **1** in a circle: *He spun around like a top.* **2** in circumference: *The tree measures 2 m around.* **3** on all sides: *A dense fog lay around.* **4** so as to face the other direction or form a different arrangement: *Turn around! I switched the furniture around.* **5** in or to a variety of places: *We walked around sightseeing.* **6** somewhere near: *He's around somewhere.* **7** on or to the far side of: *just around the corner.* **8** beside and past, so as to avoid: *Drive around that pothole.* **9** in such a way as to avoid conflicting with: *We planned the trip around my baby sister's nap times.* **10** having as a focus: *discussions around the issue of funding.* **11** through a circuit or cycle: *The seasons go around each year.* **12** over to a place, as for a brief visit: *I went around to see my mother yesterday.*
prep **1** following a circular route: *to travel around the world.* **2** closely wrapping or binding: *a coat around her shoulders, an elastic band around the papers.* **3** on all sides of: *Woods lay around the lake.* **4** approximately: *It cost around $25.* **5** here and there in: *She leaves her books around the room.* **6** somewhere in or near: *He stuck around the house all day.* **7** in existence: *Dinosaurs are no longer around.*
bring (or **come**) **around, a** bring (or come back) to consciousness: *He came around when we splashed water on his face.* **b** bring (or come) to the desired point of view: *She didn't want to go, but we soon brought her around.*
come around, a return to consciousness. **b** become convinced.
get around, a go from place to place: *It's difficult to get around with this hurt leg.* **b** avoid or overcome, sometimes by clever argument or manipulation: *She can get around any rule.* **c** be exposed to many sources of information: *"How did he know that?" "Oh, he gets around."*
have been around, *Informal* have a wide range of experience and understanding: *You'd think such a young guy might be a bit naive, but he's been around.*

a·rouse (ə rouz′) *v* **a·roused, a·rous·ing 1** bring about a feeling, emotion, or response: *to arouse interest. The kidnapping aroused the whole country.* **2** wake someone from sleep. **a·rous′al** *n.*

ar·peg·gio (är pej′ē ō) *Music n* the notes of a chord sounded one after another in quick succession, instead of all at once. <Italian *arpa* harp>

🍁 **ar·pent** (är′pənt) *n* an old French measure of land area, formerly used in Canada, equal to about 3400 square metres. <French>

ar·raign (ə rān′) *Law v* bring before a court to answer a charge: *She was arraigned on a charge of theft.* <Old French *arainer* accuse, from Latin *ad-* to + *rationis* response> **ar·raign′ment** *n.*

ar·range (ə rānj′) *v* **ar·ranged, ar·rang·ing 1** put in the desired order or position: *to arrange furniture in a room.* **2** plan, prepare, or set up: *to arrange transportation for a class trip. I've arranged to meet him tonight.* **3** adapt a piece of music to voices or instruments: *a book of songs arranged as piano solos.* <Old French *arangier* put in order> **ar·rang′er** *n.*

ar·range·ment (ə rānj′mənt) *n* **1** the result, manner, or act of arranging: *a class seating arrangement, an arrangement for violin. Arrangement of transportation is up to you.* **2** an agreed way of proceeding or doing business: *She has an arrangement with the bank to pay certain bills.* **3** usually, **arrangements** *pl* plans or preparations: *to make arrangements for a journey.*

ar·rant (er′ənt) *adj* of the worst kind: *an arrant liar, arrant foolishness.* <variant of *errant*>

ar·ray (ə rā′) *n* **1** a display of people or things: *a huge array of wedding gifts.* **2** a complete or impressive set: *The software provides an array of useful editing tools.* **3** order: *The troops were formed in battle array.* **4** *Mathematics* an arrangement of data in rows and columns. **5** *Computers* linked items sharing a common name and kept in consecutive positions in memory. **6** clothes, especially splendid ones: *in bridal array.*
v **1** arrange in order: *troops arrayed for battle.* **2** display or lay out attractively: *She arrayed the brochures on the table.* **3** dress in fine clothes: *arrayed like a queen.* <Old French *a* to + *rei* order>

a bat	e bed	i bid	o pot	u cup	th **thin**
ā cake	ē me	ī bite	ō go	ū rude	ᴛʜ **then**
ä bar	ə about	ər over	ô for	ů put	zh measure

ar·rears (ə rērz′) *pln* money due that should have been paid. <Old French, from Latin *ad-* toward + *retro* backwards>
in arrears, behind in payments.

ar·rest (ə rest′) *v* **1** seize a person by legal authority and take to jail: *Police arrested the thief.* **2** stop or check a process: *Filling a tooth arrests decay.* **3** attract someone's attention: *Our attention was arrested by the sound of a shot.*
n **1** the act of seizing a person by legal authority. **2** a stoppage: *cardiac arrest.* <Old French *arester,* from Latin *ad-* to + *restare* stay>
under arrest, held by the police.

ar·rest·ing (ə rest′ing) *adj* catching and holding the attention: *She has an arresting smile.*

ar·riv·al (ə rī′vəl) *n* **1** the act of arriving: *I'm waiting for the arrival of the train.* **2** a person who or thing that arrives: *The new arrivals were made welcome.* **3 Arrivals** *pl* the part of an airport where passengers arrive from a flight.

ar·rive (ə rīv′) *v* **ar·rived, ar·riv·ing 1** reach the end of a journey: *We arrived in Halifax a week ago.* **2** come or occur: *The time has arrived for us to speak out.* **3** be successful or reach one's goal. <Old French *ariver,* from Latin *ad ripam* (get) to the bank of the river>
arrive at, come to or reach: *You must arrive at a decision soon.*

ar·ri·viste (er′ə vēst′) *n* an ambitious or ruthless person who has recently acquired wealth, power, or status. <French>

ar·ro·gant (er′ə gənt) *adj* thinking too highly of oneself and disdainful of others. <Old French, from Latin *ad-* to + *rogare* claim for oneself> **ar′ro·gance** *n.* **ar′ro·gant·ly** *adv.*

ar·row (er′ō) *n* **1** a slender stick with a pointed or barbed tip and with feathers at the tail end, made to be shot from a bow. **2** anything fast, sharp, or straight like an arrow. <Old English *arwe*> **ar′row·like′** *adj.*
straight as an arrow, honest and moral.

ar·row·head (er′ō hed′) *n* the head or tip of an arrow, especially a separately made piece of stone or metal.

ar·row·root (er′ō rūt′) *n* an easily digested starch made from the roots of a tropical American plant. <Arawak (a language of S America) *aru-aru* = meal of meals>

ar·roy·o (ə roi′ō) *n* **1** a dry, steep-sided gully. **2** a small river. <Spanish>

ar·se·nal (år′sə nəl) *n* **1** a building for storing military weapons and equipment, or the weapons and equipment stored. **2** a stock of resources used for a particular purpose: *Humour was part of his debating arsenal.* <Italian, from Arabic *dar accina'ah* house of industry>

ar·se·nic (år′sə nik) *n* **1** a greyish white element that has a metallic lustre and evaporates when heated. *Symbol* **As** **2** a poison that is a compound of this element, in the form of a white, tasteless powder. <Latin, from Arabic *al-zaarnik* an arsenic compound>

ar·son (år′sən) *n* the crime of intentionally setting fire to a building or other property. <Old French *arson,* from Latin *arsionis* (*ardere* to burn)> **ar′son·ist** *n.*

art (årt) *n* **1** a human activity involving creativity and skill, such as poetry, music, and dancing, and especially painting, drawing, and sculpture: *to study art, to support the arts. Every civilization has art of some kind.* **2** works produced by such activity: *They collect art.* **3 the arts** *pl* a group of academic studies including languages and literature, history, and philosophy, and excluding the sciences and professional studies. **4** an activity that involves skill and a sense of style: *the household arts of cooking and sewing, the art of making friends.* **5** the pictures and other graphics in a printed work. **6** usually, **arts** *pl* cunning devices and tricks. <Old French, from Latin *artis*>

art dec·o (dek′ō) *n* a style of furniture, architecture, jewellery, etc. of the 1920s and 1930s that features geometrical, stylized forms. <shortened from French *art décoratif*>

ar·te·ri·ole (år tē′rē ōl′) *n* a blood vessel smaller than an artery, connecting it with even smaller blood vessels called capillaries. <French, from Greek *arteria*>

ar·te·ri·o·scle·ro·sis (år tē′rē ō sklə rō′sis) *n* a hardening of the walls of the arteries that hinders circulation of the blood.

ar·ter·y (år′tə rē) *n, pl* **ar·ter·ies 1** a blood vessel that carries blood from the heart to all parts of the body. Compare VEIN. **2** a main road or route: *Yonge Street is one of the main arteries of Toronto.* <Latin, from Greek *arteria*> **ar·te′ri·al** (år tē′rē əl) *adj.*

ar·te·sian well (år tē′zhən) *n* a deep-drilled well, especially one from which water gushes up without pumping. <French *artésien* of Artois (a former province of France, where these wells were common)>

art·ful (årt′fəl) *adj* **1** crafty or cunning. **2** skilful or clever. **art′ful·ly** *adv.* **art′ful·ness** *n.*

ar·thri·tis (år thrī′tis) *n* a disease causing inflammation and stiffness of the joints. <Latin, from Greek *arthron* joint> **ar·thrit′ic** *adj.*

ar·thro·pod (år′thrə pod′) *n* an animal belonging to a group of invertebrates with a segmented body and legs. Insects, spiders, and crustaceans are arthropods. <Greek *arthron* joint + *podos* foot>

Ar·thu·ri·an legend (år thū′rē ən) *n* a group of legends about Arthur, a supposed king in Britain, and his knights of the Round Table.

ar·ti·choke (år′tə chōk′) *n* the large flower head of a thistlelike plant native to Eurasia, cooked and eaten as a vegetable. <Italian *articiocco,* from Arabic *al-karsufa*>

ar·ti·cle (år′tə kəl) *n* **1** an informative piece of writing forming part of a magazine, newspaper, book, or website: *There are hundreds of articles on motorcycles on the Internet.* **2** a clause in a legal document: *The third article of the society's constitution dealt with member privileges.* **3** an item: *articles of clothing. Bread is an article of food.* **4** *Grammar* one of the words *a, an,* or *the,* that usually accompany nouns. The indefinite articles are *a* and *an;* the definite article is *the.*
v 🍁 **ar·ti·cled, ar·ti·cling** work under contract as part of one's training: *He is articling with a law firm now.* <Old French, from Latin *articulus* a small section (of a set of rules)>

article of faith *n* a central teaching, belief, or principle of a religion or ideology: *Responsible government was one of the politician's articles of faith.*

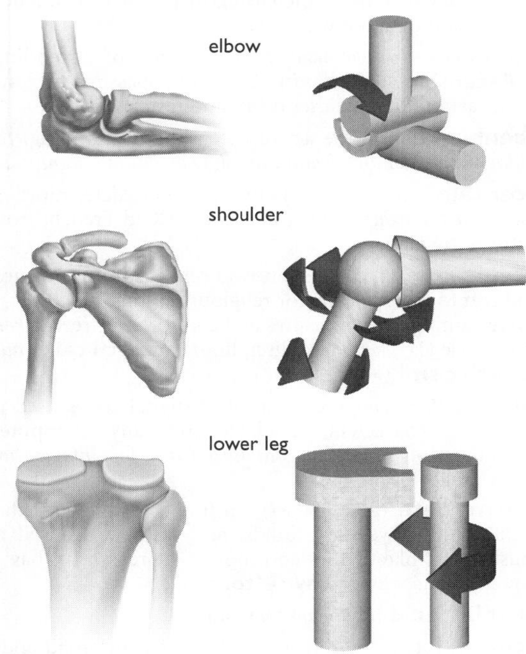

Whether it's the limbs of a human or animal body, or equipment connections, joints **articulate** to allow movement in different directions, depending on the kind of joint.

ar·tic·u·late (är tik′yə lit) *for adj,* (är tik′yə lāt′) *for v.* *adj* **1** good at putting one's thoughts into words: *She is the most articulate of the sisters.* **2** uttered as distinct words or syllables: *A baby coos and gurgles, but does not use articulate speech.* **3** able to use language: *Dogs are not articulate.* **4** *Biology* with limbs that are jointed or segmented, like arthropods and the higher vertebrates.
v **ar·tic·u·lat·ed, ar·tic·u·lat·ing 1** speak distinctly: *When speaking on stage you must be careful to articulate.* **2** express clearly in words: *to articulate your feelings.* **3** connect or allow to bend by a joint or joints: *an articulated streetcar. After her knee was injured, she was lame because the bones did not articulate well.* <Latin *articulus* small connecting part> **ar·tic′u·late·ly** *adv.* **ar·tic′u·la′tion** *n.*

ar·ti·fact (är′tə fakt′) *n* **1** an object made by a human being, especially an object of historical or cultural significance: *Clay pots and other artifacts were found in the tomb.* **2** a feature observed in a scientific experiment or examination that occurs only as a result of the procedure: *The dark patch on the X-ray was an artifact of the preparation method.* **3** *Computers* in computer graphics, unwanted collections of pixels that do not belong to the image. <Latin *artis* art + *facere* to make>

ar·ti·fice (är′tə fis) *n* a clever or cunning trick: *She will use any artifice to get her own way.* <Old French, from Latin *artis* art + *facere* make>

ar·ti·fi·cial (är′tə fish′əl) *adj* **1** produced by human skill or effort: *When you read at night, you read by artificial light.* **2** manufactured as an imitation: *artificial flowers.* **3** insincere or affected: *an artificial tone of voice.* <Old French, from Latin *artificium* something handcrafted> **ar′ti·fi′ci·al′i·ty** *n.* **ar′ti·fi′cial·ly** *adv.*

SYNONYMS

Artificial describes things that are made by human labour: *My sister has an artificial knee joint.*

Synthetic describes things that are manufactured by combining chemicals: *Polyester is a synthetic material that is commonly used to make fabrics.*

Imitation refers to something that is not real: *My jacket is imitation leather.*

artificial insemination *n* insemination by means other than sexual intercourse, using donor sperm. *Abbrev.* **AI**

artificial intelligence *n* the theory and technique of using computer systems to imitate tasks that normally require human intelligence. *Abbrev.* **AI**

artificial respiration *n* the process of restoring a person's breathing by rhythmically forcing air into and out of his or her lungs, such as by breathing directly into the mouth or applying and releasing pressure on the diaphragm.

artificial turf *n* a matlike synthetic material that looks like grass, used to cover playing fields.

ar·til·ler·y (är til′ə rē) *n* **1** large guns mounted on carriages. **2** the part of an army that uses them. <Old French *artillerie,* from *a-* to + *tire* order>

ar·ti·san (är′tə zən) *or* (är′tə zan′) *n* a person skilled in a craft, such as a cabinetmaker, mason, jeweller, or weaver. <French, from Latin *artis* art> **ar′ti·san′al** *adj.*

art·ist (är′tist) *n* **1** a person skilled in a fine art, such as painting, sculpture, music, or writing. **2** a person who works with skill, style, and good taste. <French, from Latin *artis* art> **ar′tist·ry** *n.*

ar·tiste (är tēst′) *n* a skilful performer or entertainer, especially a singer or dancer. <French>

ar·tis·tic (är tis′tik) *adj* **1** to do with art or artists: *the artistic imagination.* **2** done or made with imagination, a sense of style, and good taste: *an artistic design, an artistic presentation.* **3** with skill in art or an appreciation of art: *She is very artistic.* **ar·tis′ti·cal·ly** *adv.*

art·less (ärt′lis) *adj* **1** not artificial or affected: *She moved with artless grace.* **2** without ulterior motives: *artless questions.* **3** lacking skill, creativity, or style: *an artless piece of work.* **art′less·ly** *adv.* **art′less·ness** *n.*

art nou·veau (nū vō′) *n* a movement in art at the end of the 1800s featuring rounded stylizations of natural forms. <French = new art>

a bat	e bed	i bid	o pot	u cup	th **thin**
ā cake	ē me	ī bite	ō go	ū rude	ᴛʜ **then**
ä bar	ə about	ər over	ȯ for	ů put	zh measure

art·sy (ärt′si) *Informal adj* **art·si·er, art·si·est** artistic, often in a trendy, snobbish, or superficial way: *a street full of artsy boutiques.* Also, **arty**. **art′si·ness** *n.*

art·work (ärt′wərk′) *n* **1** ART (def. 2). **2** pictures and other graphics in a printed work.

Ar·y·an (er′ē ən) *n* **1** *Nazism* a person of Nordic descent who is not Jewish, Slav, or Gypsy and belongs to a supposed master race. **2** a member of an ancient people who invaded northern India and supposedly spoke a language that was the ancestor of modern Indo-European languages.
adj to do with one of these groups. <Sanskrit *arya* noble>

as (az) *adv* to the same degree or extent: *just as expensive, but not as good.*
conj **1** to the same degree or extent that: *She did only so much as she was told to.* **2** in the same way that: *Do as I do.* **3** while or when: *She sang as she worked.* **4** because: *I was already in bed, as it was quite late.* **5** though: *Brave as they were, they began to tremble.* **6** *Informal* if or whether: *I don't know as that's such a good idea.*
prep **1** in the character or role of: *As group leader, you are expected to set an example.* **2** like: *They treat their dog as a member of the family.* <Old English *alswa* similarly>
as for, (*to contrast someone or something with one already mentioned*) regarding: *We're leaving now; as for my sister, she'll have to go on her own.*
as is, *Informal* in the present condition: *to buy a used car as is.*
as it were, so to speak: *He is, as it were, the weakest link in the chain.*
as of, starting from: *As of April 7, I will be at this address.*
as to, about: *There is no information as to the cause of the explosion.*

GRAMMAR AND USAGE

As is often confused with **like**.

Use **as** to make a comparison when a whole clause follows, complete with its own subject and verb: *She was always quiet in class as the teacher requested.*

Use **like** if only a noun follows, with or without adjectives: *He swam quickly through the water like an otter.*

ASA ASPIRIN.

ASAP (ā′sap) as soon as possible: *Get that report to me ASAP, please.*

as·bes·tos (as bes′təs) *n* a mineral that does not burn or conduct heat, usually occurring in fibres. <Latin, from Greek *asbestos* unextinguishable (originally applied to a mythical stone, whose heat could not be put out)>

as·bes·to·sis (as′bes tō′sis) *n* a disease of the lungs caused by breathing in the dust and fibres of asbestos.

as·cend (ə send′) *v* **1** move upward: *We watched the plane ascend.* **2** climb or go to the top of: *to ascend a ladder.* <Old French, from Latin *ad-* to + *scandere* climb>
ascend the throne, become king or queen: *Queen Elizabeth II ascended the throne in 1953.*

as·cend·ant (ə sen′dənt) *adj* **1** increasing in power or influence. **2** dominant or supreme.
n dominance or supremacy. **as·cen′dan·cy** *n.*
in the ascendant, a increasing in power or influence. **b** dominant or supreme.

as·cen·sion (ə sen′shən) *n* **1** the act of ascending. **2 Ascension** *Christianity* the bodily passing of Jesus from earth to heaven after death and resurrection.

as·cent (ə sent′) *n* the act of ascending or climbing: *the sudden ascent of an elevator, the slow ascent of a mountain.*

as·cer·tain (as′ər tān′) *v* find out or determine: *to ascertain the exact time of departure.* <Old French, from Latin *certus* sure>

as·cet·ic (ə set′ik) *n* a person who refrains from pleasures and comforts, especially for religious reasons.
adj refraining from pleasures and comforts. <Greek *askein* to exercise (i.e., keep to a discipline)> **as·cet′i·cal·ly** *adv.* **as·cet′i·cism′** (ə set′i siz əm′) *n.*

ASCII (as′kē) *Computers n* a set of digital codes used to represent characters, readable by any computer. <acronym of *American Standard Code for Information Interchange*>

as·co·my·cete (as′kō mī′sēt) *n* a fungus of the class that includes most yeasts, moulds, and mildews as well as mushrooms like truffles and morels. <Greek *askos* bag + *myketes* fungi> **as′co·my·ce′tous** *adj.*

a·scor·bic acid (ə skör′bik) *n* vitamin C.

as·cot (as′kət) *or* (as′kot) *n* a neck scarf with broad ends, tied so that the ends may be laid flat one over the other. <*Ascot*, an English racetrack, where such scarves were probably firsty worn>

as·cribe (ə skrīb′) *v* **as·cribed, as·crib·ing** (*with* ***to***) **1** assign to something as a source or cause: *The police ascribed the accident to fast driving.* **2** consider as belonging to someone or something: *ascribing human characteristics to animals.* <Latin *ad-* to + *scribere* write> **as·crip′tion** *n.* **as·crip′tive** *adj.*

a·sep·tic (ə sep′tik) *or* (ā sep′tik) *adj* free from germs that cause infection. <Greek *a-* without + *septic*> **a·sep′sis** *n.*

a·sex·u·al (ā sek′shū əl) *adj* **1** without a sex or sexuality: *Angels are asexual beings.* **2** *Biology* independent of sexual processes: *Asexual reproduction is common in plants, but rare in animals.* **a·sex′u·al·ly** *adv.*

ash[1] (ash) *n* **1** (*often plural*) the remains of a thing that has been thoroughly burned or oxidized by chemical means: *We cleaned the ashes out of the fireplace.* **2 ashes** *pl* remains after burning: *The urn contained his best friend's ashes, a whole city in ashes.* <Old English *æsce*> **ash′y** *adj.*

ash[2] (ash) *n* a shade tree with greyish bark and straight-grained wood. <Old English *æsc*>

a·shamed (ə shāmd′) *adj* **1** feeling shame, for oneself or another: *She was ashamed of having cheated. Your temper tantrum made me ashamed.* **2** unwilling because of shame: *He was too ashamed to admit his mistake.*

as·hen (ash′ən) *adj* pale as ashes. <*ash*[1]>

Ash·ke·na·zi (ash′kə na′zi) *n, pl* **Ash·ke·naz·im** (ash′kə naz′im) a Jew of central and eastern Europe. Compare SEPHARDI. <Hebrew *Ashkenaz*, grandson of Noah in the Bible> **Ash′ke·naz′ic** *adj.*

a·shore (ə shȯr′) *adv* to or on the shore: *We rowed ashore.*

ash·ram (ash′rəm) *or* (ȧsh′rəm) *n* a place or community for Hindu instruction and retreat. <Sanskrit *asrama* hermitage>

ash·tray (ash′trā′) *n* a container for the ashes of cigarettes, cigars, and pipes.

A·sia (ā′zhə) *n* the continent east of Europe, bordered by the Pacific Ocean to the east and the Arctic Ocean to the north. Almost all of Asia is north of the equator. <Latin, from Greek>

Asia Minor *n* the part of Asia that is now the Asian part of Turkey.

A·sian (ā′zhən) *adj* **1** to do with Asia or its inhabitants. **2** with ancestors from Asia.
n **1** a native or inhabitant of Asia. **2** a person whose ancestors came from Asia. An **Asian-Canadian** is a Canadian of Asian descent or with some Asian ancestors.

Asian flu *n* **1** acute flu caused by a virus originating in Asia. **2** economic ill health which seems to spread from one Asian nation to another. **3** a computer virus.

Asian long–horned beetle *n* a black beetle with white spots, whose larvae tunnel deep inside a tree, then emerge as adults by chewing their way out. These beetles have destroyed many trees in British Columbia, where they arrived with imports from China.

A·si·at·ic (ā′zhē at′ik) *adj* to do with Asia.
n Offensive Asian.

a·side (ə sīd′) *adv* **1** on or to one side: *Move the table aside.* **2** out of one's thoughts or consideration: *Put your troubles aside.*
n a remark meant not to be heard by someone, especially an actor's speech meant to be heard by the audience but not by the other characters in the play.
aside from, except for.

as·i·nine (as′ə nīn′) *adj* stupid or silly: *asinine behaviour.* <Latin *asinus* ass>

ask (ask) *v* **1** try to find out by inquiring: *Why don't you ask? He asked about your health.* **2** seek the answer to: *Ask any questions you wish.* **3** address a question to: *Ask him how old he is.* **4** request: *Ask her to sing. I asked permission to leave the table.* **5** claim or demand: *to ask too high a price for a house.* **6** invite: *She asked ten guests to the party.* <Old English *ascian*>
ask after someone, ask about someone: *She asked after you, and seemed interested when I told her your plans.*
ask for (trouble or **it),** behave in a way that will cause difficulties: *Skipping school that day was just asking for it.*

SYNONYMS

Ask is a general term for inquiring about something: *I asked if he was enjoying his piano lessons.*

Request is often used as a somewhat more formal way to ask: *He requested a loan from the bank, but was turned down.*

Demand means "ask in a forceful way": *She demanded a raise or else she would quit her job.*

a·skance (ə skans′) *adv* to one side; sideways. <origin uncertain>
look askance at, regard with suspicion or disapproval: *They looked askance at the way she was dressed.*

a·skew (ə skyū′) *adv, adj* twisted or turned out of the proper position: *Her hat was pushed askew* (*adv*). *The bottom line of printing is askew* (*adj*).

ask·ing price *n* the price asked for something, especially property: *The asking price for the house was $250 000 but we got it for $240 000.*

ASL AMERICAN SIGN LANGUAGE.

a·sleep (ə slēp′) *adj* **1** sleeping: *The cat is asleep.* **2** numb from pressure or inactivity: *My foot is asleep.* **3** not alert: *asleep on the job.* **4** *Poetic* dead.
adv into a condition of sleep: *The tired boy fell asleep.*

asp (asp) *n* **1** the Egyptian cobra, a poisonous snake that was sacred to the Egyptians and became a symbol of royalty. **2** a small poisonous snake of Europe. <Latin, from Greek *aspis*>

as·par·a·gus (ə sper′ə gəs) *n* the stems of a perennial plant of the lily family, eaten as a vegetable. <Latin, from Greek *asparagos*>

as·par·tame (as′pər tām′) *or* (ə spȧr′tām) *n* an artificial sweetener with almost no calories. <*aspart*ic acid, an amino acid>

as·pect (as′pekt) *n* **1** one side, part, or view of a subject: *We must consider this plan in all its various aspects.* **2** appearance: *the stormy, frightening aspect of the ocean in winter.* **3** facial expression: *the solemn aspect of a judge.* **4** the direction in which a building faces: *This house has a western aspect.* <Latin *ad-* at + *specere* look>

as·pen (as′pən) *n* a kind of poplar tree whose leaves tremble and rustle in the slightest breeze. <Middle English>

as·per·i·ty (a sper′ə tē) *n, pl* **as·per·i·ties** severity or harshness: *We all noticed the asperity in our teacher's voice.* <Old French, from Latin *asper* rough>

as·per·sion (ə spər′zhən) *n* a damaging or false report. <Latin *ad-* to + *spargere* sprinkle (water, dust, etc. and so possibly damaging words)>
cast aspersions on, speak damagingly of.

as·phalt (as′folt) *or* (ash′folt) BITUMEN.

asphalt jungle *n* a densely populated, heavily built-up urban area thought of as breeding violent crime.

as·phyx·i·ate (as fik′sē āt′) *v* **as·phyx·i·at·ed, as·phyx·i·at·ing** suffocate through **asphyxia**, lack of oxygen and too much carbon dioxide in the blood: *The trapped coal miners were asphyxiated before help could reach them.* <Latin, from Greek *a-* without + *sphyxis* pulse> **as·phyx′i·a′tion** *n.*

as·pic (as′pik) *n* jelly made of meat or fish stock, often set in a mould with pieces of seafood or meat. <French>

a bat	e bed	i bid	o pot	u cup	th thin
ā cake	ē me	ī bite	ō go	ū rude	ᴛʜ then
ȧ bar	ə about	ər over	ȯ for	u̇ put	zh measure

as·pi·dis·tra (as′pə dis′trə) *n* an Asian plant with green leaves and small flowers, often used as a houseplant. <Latin, from Greek *aspidis* shield, from the shape of its leaves>

as·pi·rate (as′pə rāt′) *v* **as·pi·rat·ed, as·pi·rat·ing** **1** inhale, especially a small object: *Young children sometimes aspirate peanuts.* **2** pronounce with a puff of air or *h*-sound.

as·pi·ra·tion (as′pə rā′shən) *n* **1** a desire, hope, or ambition to do or be something: *Her aspiration was to be an artist.* **2** the act of aspirating.

as·pire (ə spīr′) *v* **as·pired, as·pir·ing** have an ambition to do or be something: *Scholars aspire after knowledge. He aspired to the position of captain.* <Old French *aspirer* inspire, from Latin *adspirare* = breathe into>

As·pi·rin (as′pə rin′) *Trademark n* a brand of tablets of acetylsalicylic acid, a drug commonly used to relieve pain and fever and reduce blood pressure. Also called **acetylsalicilic acid, ASA**.

ass (as) *n* **1** a donkey. **2** a hoofed wild mammal of Asia and Africa related to the horse but smaller, with long ears, and a very short mane. **3** *Informal* a foolish or stubborn person. <Old English, from Latin *asinus*>

as·sail (ə sāl′) *v* violently attack: *to assail a fortress, to assail a political opponent in a debate. My nostrils were assailed by a powerful stench.* <Old French *asalir,* from Latin *ad-* at + *salire* to leap> **as·sail′a·ble** *adj.* **as·sail′ant** *n.*

as·sas·sin (ə sas′ən) *n* **1** a murderer, especially of a politically important person. **2** a person who destroys or does serious damage: *a character assassin.* <Latin *assassinus,* from Arabic *hashhashin* hashish-eaters. The Assassins, an 11c Islamic order, were reputed to eat hashish in preparation for action.>

as·sas·si·nate (ə sas′ə nāt′) *v* **as·sas·si·nat·ed, as·sas·si·nat·ing** murder someone, especially a politically important person. **as·sas′si·na′tion** *n.*

as·sault (ə solt′) *n* **1** a sudden, violent attack. **2** *Law* the crime of threatening or attempting physical harm to another. Touching someone with hostile intent constitutes **assault and battery**.
v make an assault on.
adj automatic and designed for military use as a firearm: *assault rifle.* <Old French *asauter,* from Latin *ad-* at + *salire* to leap>

as·say (as′ā) *or* (ə sā′) *n* an analysis of a metal or ore by measuring its ingredients.
v perform an assay on. <Old French *essayer* to test>

as·sem·blage (ə sem′blij) *n* **1** a group of people or things gathered together: *An interesting assemblage of bicycle parts lay on the floor.* **2** the act or manner of assembling parts. **3** an art form in which a variety of objects are put together into a collage or sculpture.

as·sem·ble (ə sem′bəl) *v* **as·sem·bled, as·sem·bling** **1** come or bring together: *All the author's works are assembled in that book. The team members assembled in the gym for practice.* **2** put together the parts of: *to assemble a model airplane.* <Old French, from Latin *ad-* to + *simul* together>

as·sem·bler (ə sem′blər) *n* **1** *Computers* a program designed to convert ASSEMBLY LANGUAGE into MACHINE LANGUAGE. **2** a person who or thing that assembles parts into a whole.

as·sem·bly (ə sem′blē) *n, pl* **as·sem·blies** **1** a group of people gathered for some purpose: *We have an all-school assembly every Friday.* **2** ❁ **Assembly** in Québec, the NATIONAL ASSEMBLY. **3** the act of assembling. **4** a set of parts put together: *The entire wing assembly fell off the model plane.*

assembly language *Computers n* a low-level language using words and abbreviations that are then converted into the digital instructions of machine language.

assembly line *n* a row of workers and machines along which work is passed until the product, such as a car, is finished.

assembly member *n* in Prince Edward Island, one of 15 members of the Legislative Assembly.

❁ **Assembly of First Nations** *n* the political organization officially representing the First Nations in Canada. *Abbrev.* **AFN**

as·sent (ə sent′) *v* express agreement: *Everyone assented to the plan.*
n the act of assenting: *Parliament gave assent to the bill.* <Old French *assentir,* from Latin *ad-* along with + *sentire* feel> **as·sent′ing** *adj.*

as·sert (ə sərt′) *v* **1** state confidently or forcefully: *to assert your innocence. Columbus asserted that the earth was round.* **2** insist and act on a right or claim: *to assert your independence.* <Latin *asserere* join to oneself, from *ad-* to + *serere* join> **as·ser′tion** *n.*
assert yourself, insist on your rights or declare your views.

as·ser·tive (ə sər′tiv) *adj* confident and outspoken. **as·ser′tive·ly** *adv.* **as·ser′tive·ness** *n.*

as·sess (ə ses′) *v* **1** examine critically and evaluate the nature, ability, or quality of: *to assess a situation, to assess someone's work.* **2** estimate the value of something for taxation purposes: *A city official will assess the property.* **3** set the amount of a tax, fine, or damages. **4** put a tax on or call for a contribution: *Each employee was assessed ten dollars for the gift fund.* <Old French, from Latin *assidere* sit beside (as an assistant official)> **as·sess′ment** *n.* **as·sess′or** *n.*

as·set (as′et) *n* **1** something valuable: *Ability to get along with people is an asset in business.* **2** **assets** *pl* **a** all that a person or company owns of value: *Their assets include a condo, car, bonds, and jewellery.* **b** property that can be used to pay debts. <Old French (*aver*) *assez* (have) enough to pay, from Latin *ad satis* enough>

as·sid·u·ous (ə sij′ū əs) *adj* careful and attentive. <Old French *assiduité,* from Latin *assidere* sit beside> **as·sid′u·ous·ly** *adv.*

as·sign (ə sīn′) *v* **1** give a share, position, or task to: *She assigned an essay topic to each student. The captain assigned two officers to guard the door.* **2** set or appoint: *The judge assigned a day for the trial.* **3** set aside or allot: *More funds have been assigned to health care.* <Old French, from Latin *ad-* to + *signare* to sign>

as·sign·ment (ə sīn′mənt) *n* **1** something assigned, especially a piece of work to be done by a student: *Today's math assignment is ten problems.* **2** the act of assigning.

as·sim·i·late (ə sim′ə lāt′) *v* **as·sim·i·lat·ed, as·sim·i·lat·ing 1** digest and absorb, physically or mentally: *to assimilate information, to assimilate nutrients.* **2** adjust or become adjusted to existing within a larger group: *Many immigrants find it takes time to assimilate.* <Latin *ad-* to + *similis* like> **as·sim′i·la′tion** *n.*

as·sim·i·la·tion·ism (ə sim′ə lā′shə niz′əm) *n* a policy of trying to get a minority group to blend into the general population through education, employment, or intermarriage.

As·sin·i·boine (ə sin′ə boin′) NAKOTA.

as·sist (ə sist′) *v* help: *to assist in preparing a meal, to assist an injured person. I assisted on the second goal.*
n **1** *Sports* the credit given to a player who helps score a goal or put an opponent out. **2** an act of giving help: *With an assist from me, he soon climbed the fence.* <Old French, from Latin *ad-* by + *sistere* take a stand>

as·sist·ance (ə sis′təns) *n* help or aid.

as·sist·ant (ə sis′tənt) *n* a helper.
adj helping; assisting: *an assistant teacher.*

assisted suicide *n* death at one's own request, usually to end suffering, through the help of someone who agrees to give lethal drugs or other means of ending life.

as·size (ə sīz′) *n* **1** usually, **assizes** *pl* periodical sessions of a court of law. **2** a series of trials or lawsuits held before a travelling judge. <Old French, from Latin *assidere.* See ASSESS.>

as·so·ci·ate (ə sō′shē āt′) *or* (ə sō′sē āt′) *for v,* (ə sō′shē it) *or* (ə sō′sē it) *for n or adj. v* **as·so·ci·at·ed, as·so·ci·at·ing 1** mix socially (with): *She only associates with people of her own kind.* **2** connect automatically in thought: *We associate sailboarding with summer.* **3** connect in some formal way or join in a working relationship: *He is not associated with any political party.*
n **1** a companion or partner: *She and her associates on the organizing committee have done a great job.* **2** a member without full rights and privileges: *an associate in a law firm.*
adj being an associate or partner: *I am an associate editor of the school paper.* <Latin *ad-* to + *socius* sharing>

as·so·ci·a·tion (ə sō′sē ā′shən) *or* (ə sō′shē ā′shən) *n* **1** the act of associating, or the resulting relationship: *There is an association between the words "winter" and "snow." I have learned much through my association with other artists.* **2** (*often in names*) a group of people joined together by some shared interest: *the Young People's Association.*

as·so·ci·a·tive (ə sō′shyə tiv) *or* (ə sō′sē ā′tiv) *adj* **1** to do with association, especially of ideas or images. **2** *Mathematics* to do with a property of an operation, such as addition, in which the grouping of elements does not affect the result: Example: (7 + 3) + 8 = 7 + (3 + 8). See also DISTRIBUTIVE.

as·so·nance (as′ə nəns) *n* a partial rhyme in which the vowel sounds are alike but not the consonants.
Examples: *brave/vain, lone/show.* <French, from Latin *ad-* along with + *sonus* sound>

as·sort·ed (ə sôr′tid) *adj* of different kinds: *assorted cakes.* <Old French *a-* to + *sorte* sort>

as·sort·ment (ə sôrt′mənt) *n* a collection of various items: *an assortment of candies.*

as·suage (ə swāj′) *v* **as·suaged, as·suag·ing** relieve; ease: *to assuage your guilty conscience, to assuage your thirst.* <Old French, from Latin *ad-* to + *suavis* pleasant> **as·suage′ment** *n.*

as·sume (ə sūm′) *v* **as·sumed, as·sum·ing 1** take for granted: *She assumed the train would be on time.* **2** take or accept for oneself: *to assume a responsibility.* **3** adopt, often for effect: *to assume an air of superiority.* **4** pretend: *He assumed ignorance of the whole matter.* See PRESUME for confusable. <Latin *ad-* to + *sumere* take>

as·sumed (ə sūmd′) *adj* **1** pretended or false: *under an assumed name.* **2** supposed: *You and I are the assumed culprits.*

as·sum·ing (ə sū′ming) *conj* (*often with* ***that***) taking for granted (that): *Assuming I go to the party, will I get a drive back?*

as·sump·tion (ə sump′shən) *n* **1** the act or fact of assuming: *Court trials are based on the assumption of innocence.* **2** something assumed: *He took for granted he would win, but this was a false assumption.* **3** presumption; arrogance; unpleasant boldness. **4 Assumption** *Catholicism* the bodily taking up of the Virgin Mary to heaven after her death, or the festival in honour of this.

as·sur·ance (ə shůr′əns) *n* **1** sureness, certainty, or confidence: *We have the assurance of final victory.* **2** a definite statement meant to inspire confidence: *Despite assurances to the contrary on TV, it looks as if it will rain.*

as·sure (ə shůr′) *v* **as·sured, as·sur·ing 1** (*with reflexive pronoun*) make sure: *I assured myself that all the doors were locked.* **2** tell positively so as to inspire confidence: *The pilot assured the passengers that all was well.* <Old French, from Latin *ad-* to + *securus* safe>

CONFUSABLES

Assure means "instil confidence or certainty": *He assured me that he would pay back the loan quickly. The captain assured the passengers that the vessel was in no danger.*

Ensure means "make certain": *Before we left, I ensured we had enough food for our weekend camping trip.*

Insure means "arrange for money to be paid in case of loss, accident, or death": *They insured their car against accident, fire, and theft..*

as·sured (ə shůrd′) *adj* **1** sure or certain: *You may be assured that she is safe.* **2** confident or bold: *an assured manner.* **as·sur′ed·ly** (ə shū′ri dlē) *adv.*

a bat	e bed	i bid	o pot	u cup	th **thin**
ā cake	ē me	ī bite	ō go	ū rude	ᴛʜ **then**
ä bar	ə about	ər over	ô for	ů put	zh measure

as·ta·tine (as′tə tēn′) *n* a radioactive element produced artificially. It is the heaviest HALOGEN. *Symbol* **At** <Greek *a-* not + *statos* stable>

as·ter (as′tər) *n* a garden plant with flower heads surrounding a central disc of tiny, tube-shaped flowers. <Latin, from Greek = star>

as·ter·isk (as′tə risk) *n* a star-shaped mark (*) used in written or printed texts, usually to call attention to a footnote or to stand for omitted matter. <Latin, from Greek *asterikos* little star>

a·stern (ə stərn′) *adv* at or toward the rear of a ship or aircraft: *The captain went astern.*

as·ter·oid (as′tə roid′) *n* one of the group of very small planets whose orbits lie between the orbits of Mars and Jupiter. <Greek *aster* star + *-oid*>

asth·ma (az′mə) *n* a chronic disease that causes difficulty in breathing, a feeling of suffocation, and coughing. <Latin, from Greek *azein* breathe hard>
asth·mat′ic (az mat′ik) *adj, n.*

a·stig·ma·tism (ə stig′mə tiz′əm) *n* a defect of the eye or of a lens that makes it difficult to focus. See VISION for picture. <Greek *a-* without + *stigma* point, focus>
as′tig·mat′ic *adj.*

a·stir (ə stər′) *adv, adj* moving around: *A breeze set the leaves astir* (*adv*). *At dawn, the whole town was astir* (*adj*).

as·ton·ish (ə ston′ish) *v* amaze: *The gift of a new bicycle astonished the little boy.* <Old French *estoner*, from Latin *extonare* strike with thunder> **as·ton′ish·ing** *adj.* **as·ton′ish·ing·ly** *adv.* **as·ton′ish·ment** *n.*

as·tound (ə stound′) *v* fill with surprise and wonder. <Old French *estoner*, from Latin *extonare* strike with thunder> **as·tound′ing** *adj.* **as·tound′ing·ly** *adv.*

as·tral (as′trəl) *adj* to do with stars. <Latin *astrum* star, from Greek *astron*>

a·stray (ə strā′) *adv* off the correct path: *I hope she doesn't lead us astray.*
go astray, a take the wrong path: *Nothing has turned out right; where did we go astray?* **b** get lost or misplaced: *That glove of mine seems to have gone astray.*

a·stride (ə strīd′) *prep* with one leg on each side of something: *to sit astride a horse.*

as·trin·gent (ə strin′jənt) *adj* **1** causing the contraction of soft body tissues, especially the cells of the skin: *an astringent lotion for the face.* **2** severe or harsh: *astringent criticism.* **3** sharp or bitter in taste or smell.
n an astringent substance. <Latin *ad-* to + *stringere* pull tight>

astro– *combining form* to do with stars or with astronomy: *astrophysics.*

ETYMOLOGY

Astro– comes from the Greek word *astron*, meaning "star." An *astronaut* is a crew member on a spacecraft. *Astronomy* is the science that investigates the stars, sun, moon, and planets.

as·tro·dome (as′trə dōm′) *n* **1** an enclosed stadium with a domed roof. **2** a transparent domed structure for observing the sky, especially on an aircraft.

as·tro·ge·o·lo·gy (as′trō jē ol′ ə jē) *n* the science that studies the nature and history of rocks on other planets and the moon. **as′tro·ge·ol′ogist** *n.*

as·tro·labe (as′trə lāb′) *or* (as′trə lab′) *n* in former times, an instrument used to measure the altitude of the sun or stars. <Old French, from Greek *astron* star + *lambanein* take>

as·trol·o·gy (ə strol′ə jē) *n* the study of the stars and planets to reveal their supposed influence on people and events. <Old French, from Greek *astron* star> **as·trol′o·ger** *n.* **as′tro·log′i·cal** *adj.*

as·tro·naut (as′trə not′) *n* a pilot or member of the crew of a spacecraft. <*astro-* + Greek *nautes* sailor>

as·tro·naut·ics (as′trə not′iks) *n* (*with singular verb*) the science and technology of space flight.

as·tro·nom·i·cal (as′trə nom′ə kəl) *adj* **1** to do with astronomy. **2** enormous: *an astronomical sum of money.* **as′tro·nom′i·cal·ly** *adv.*

astronomical unit *Astronomy n* a unit of distance, equal to 149.6 million kilometres, the average distance from the centre of the earth to the centre of the sun. *Symbol* **AU**

astronomical year *n* a YEAR (def. 1).

as·tron·o·my (ə stron′ə mē) *n* the science that studies outer space and heavenly bodies. <Latin, from Greek *astron* star> **as·tron′o·mer** *n.*

as·tro·phys·ics (as′trō fiz′iks) *n* (*with singular verb*) the branch of astronomy that studies the physical and chemical characteristics of heavenly bodies.
as′tro·phys′i·cist *n.*

As·tro·Turf (as′trō tərf′) *Trademark n* a brand of artificial grass.

as·tute (ə styūt′) *or* (ə stūt′) *adj* **1** showing a keen, observant, discovering mind: *an astute remark.* **2** shrewd: *an astute business deal.* <Latin *astutus*, from *astus* cunning> **as·tute′ly** *adv.* **as·tute′ness** *n.*

a·sun·der (ə sun′dər) *Poetic adv* apart: *Lightning tore the tree asunder.* <Old English *on sundran* into a separate place>

a·sy·lum (ə sī′ləm) *n* **1** refuge or protection, especially if granted officially: *They faced persecution in their own country and sought asylum in Canada.* **2** in former times, an institution for the support and care of the mentally ill. <Latin, from Greek *a-* without + *sylon* right of seizure>

🍁 **a·sym·met·ri·cal federalism** (ā′sə met′rə kəl) *n* a view of federalism in which some provinces enjoy more powers than others.

a·sym·me·try (ā sim′ə trē) *n* **1** with parts that do not correspond to one another in shape, size, or arrangement. **2** a lack of equality or balance between people, groups, or forces within a system or relationship. **a′sym·met′ri·cal** (ā′sə met′rə kəl) *adj.* **a′sym·met′ri·cal·ly** *adv.*

as·ymp·tote (as′im tōt′) *Mathematics n* a straight line that approaches but does not meet a curve. <Greek *a-* not + *syn* together + *piptein* to fall>

at (at) *prep* **1** in, on, by, or near a certain place or time: *at school, at the door, at midnight.* **2** toward or in the direction of: *to aim at the mark. Look at me.* **3** in the position, manner, or condition of: *at right angles, at war.* **4** engaged in: *at work.* **5** with respect to; because of: *good at math. I'm amazed at your progress.* **6** for: *two books at a dollar each. Symbol* **@** <Old English *æt*>
at it, doing what one is supposed to or what one usually does: *Stop fooling around and get at it. Oh, no, he's been at it again—the furniture is rearranged!*

at·a·vism (at′ə viz′əm) *n* **1** the reappearance of an ancient pattern of behaviour after a long absence. **2** the reappearance of a characteristic in a plant or animal that has been absent for several generations. <Latin *atavus* ancestor> **at′a·vis′tic** *adj.*

a·tax·i·a (ə tak′si ə) *n* loss of full control of bodily movements. <Latin, from Greek *a-* without + *taxis* order>

ate (āt) past tense of EAT.

at·el·ier (at′əl yā′) *n* a workshop, especially an artist's or craftsperson's studio. <French>

a tem·po (ȧ tem′pō) *Music adj, adv* back to the previous speed. <Italian>

Ath·a·pas·kan (ath′ə pas′kən) *n* **1** a group of Aboriginal languages spoken in northwest Canada, Alaska, and the southwestern US, including Chipewyan, Dogrib, Sarcee, Slavey, and Navaho. **2** a member of any of the peoples that speak these languages.
adj to do with any of these languages or the peoples that speak them. Also, **Athapascan**, **Athabaskan**, **Athabascan**.

a·the·ism (ā′thē iz′əm) *n* the belief that there is no God. <French, from Greek *a-* no + *theos* god> **a′the·ist** *n.* **a′the·is′tic** *adj.*

Canadian **athletes** participate in a variety of sports. This sprinter is preparing for a block start. Her hands are positioned slightly wider than her shoulders, her arms are straight but not locked at the elbows, and her head and neck are in line with her spine. Next, she will raise her left knee off the track so she is ready to surge forward when the race begins.

ath·lete (ath′lēt) *n* a person who is proficient in sports or activities requiring physical strength, speed, and skill: *Canadian athletes did well in the last Winter Olympics.* <Latin, from Greek *athlon* prize>

athlete's foot *n* a contagious skin disease of the toes, caused by a fungus.

ath·let·ic (ath let′ik) *adj* **1** enjoying active games and sports and showing natural skill in them: *I'm not very athletic but I do enjoy swimming.* **2** to do with athletes or their activities: *an athletic association.*
n **athletics** (*with singular verb*) games and sports for individuals, rather than teams. Athletics is usually divided into **track** events (running, hurdling, steeplechasing), **field** events (jumping, pole vault, shot put, discus, javelin, hammer throw), and **road** events (marathon running, walking) **ath·let′i·cal·ly** *adv.*

athletic support *n* a belt and pouch worn by males to support and protect the genitals during athletic activity.

–athon *suffix* **1** raising funds in a campaign in which participants collect pledges from sponsors for taking part in some activity: *walkathon.* **2** *Informal* making an intense effort or spending a long time in some activity: *The Student Council meeting was a four-hour talkathon.* <(*mar*)*athon*>

at·i·gi (at′ə gē) *or* (ə tē′gē) *n* **1** a hooded, knee-length inner shirt traditionally made of caribou skins, with the hair inside against the body, used in winter especially by the Inuit. **2** a hooded outer garment of fur or other material. <Inuktitut>

At·lan·tic Ocean (at lan′tik) *n* the ocean separating the Americas from Europe and Africa.

Atlantic Provinces *pln* Newfoundland and Labrador, Prince Edward Island, Nova Scotia, and New Brunswick. See also MARITIME PROVINCES. Also called **Atlantic Canada**.

at·las (at′ləs) *n, pl* **at·las·es** a book of maps or charts.

ETYMOLOGY

The first **atlas** was published in 1578, named after *Atlas*, a giant from Greek mythology.

As a punishment for being the war leader in a rebellion against the gods, Atlas was condemned to hold the sky on his shoulders for eternity. (This myth explained why the sky does not fall.)

The first atlases had a picture of Atlas on them and the name **atlas** has traditionally been used ever since as a name for a book of maps.

ATM *n* in full, **automated teller machine** an electronic machine that allows bank customers to carry out transactions, such as making deposits, paying bills, or withdrawing cash. Also called **bank machine**.

at·man (ȧt′mən) *Hinduism n* **1** the soul, capable of reincarnation. **2** **Atman** the spiritual principle animating all creation. <Sanskrit = breath>

a bat	e bed	i bid	o pot	u cup	th thin
ā cake	ē me	ī bite	ō go	ū rude	TH then
ȧ bar	ə about	ər over	ȯ for	u̇ put	zh measure

at·mos·phere (at′məs fēr′) *n* **1** the air that surrounds the earth, consisting of oxygen and other gases and made up of different layers. Compare HYDROSPHERE, LITHOSPHERE. **2** the air in a certain place: *The atmosphere in the cave was damp.* **3** mental and moral environment, tone, or surrounding influence: *an atmosphere of love and acceptance.* **4** a pleasant effect produced by the décor of a place: *This café has a lot of atmosphere.* **5** a mass of gases surrounding any heavenly body. **6** standard atmosphere. <Latin, from Greek *atmos* vapour + *sphaira* sphere> **at′mos·pher′ic** (at′məs fer′ik) *adj.*

atmospheric pressure *n* the pressure exerted by the air on the earth's surface and everything on it, because of gravity.

at. no. atomic number.

at·oll (at′ol) *or* (ə tol′) *n* a ring of coral, or the top of a volcano, showing above the surface of the ocean and forming a pool in the centre called a LAGOON. <Dhivehi (a language of the Republic of Maldives) *atolu*>

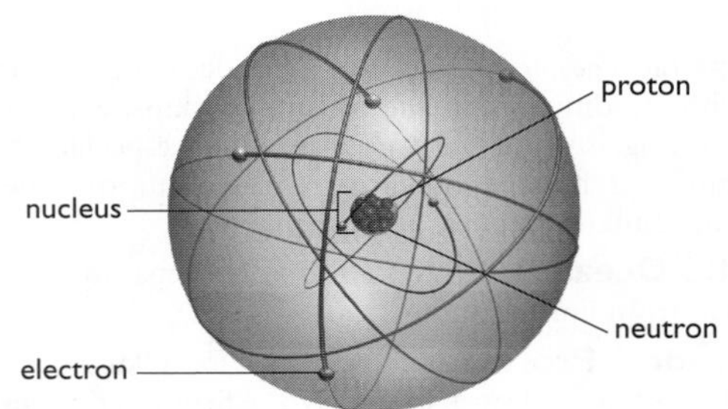

How small is small? A single drop of water contains more than a million million billion **atoms**. Now that's small.

a·tom (at′əm) *n* **1** the smallest part of an element that has all the properties of the element, made up of protons and neutrons forming the nucleus, and electrons orbiting this nucleus. **2** a tiny bit: *not an atom of strength left.* <Latin, from Greek *atomos* not divisible, from *a-* not + *temnein* to cut> **a·tom′ic** *adj.*

atom bomb *n* a bomb that uses the energy released by rapid splitting of atoms to cause an explosion of tremendous force. Also, **atomic bomb**.

atomic clock *n* an extremely accurate clock that keeps time according to the natural vibrations of atoms or molecules.

atomic energy *n* **1** the energy that exists naturally in atoms and that can be released in a reactor or bomb. **2** this energy used to generate power for practical uses.

atomic mass *n* the mass of an atom as expressed in atomic mass units.

atomic mass unit *n* a unit of mass equal to 1.6605×10^{-24} g. This is one-twelfth of the mass of an atom of carbon-12, which is the most common kind of carbon. *Symbol* **amu**

atomic number *n* the number used to describe an element and show its relation to other elements, consisting of the number of positive charges (protons) in the nucleus of one atom of the element. *Abbrev.* **at. no.**

at·om·ize (at′ə mīz′) *v* **at·om·ized, at·om·iz·ing** **1** change a liquid, such as perfume, into a fine spray. **2** separate into atoms or other small, distinct units. **at′om·i·za′tion** *n.* **at′om·iz′er** *n.*

atom smasher *n* an ACCELERATOR (def. 3).

a·ton·al (ā tō′nəl) *Music adj* not in a specific key or not with a keynote, and with all tones in equal relation to each other, as in the chromatic scale of twelve tones. **a′to·nal′i·ty** (ā′ tō nal′ ə tē) *n.* **a·ton′al·ly** *adv.*

a·tone (ə tōn′) *v* **a·toned, a·ton·ing** make up or make amends (for): *He atoned for his unkindness to me by taking me to the movies.* <Middle English *at onement* in harmony> **a·tone′ment** *n.*

a·top (ə top′) *prep* on the top of: *A bird sat atop the fencepost.*

a·tri·um (ā′trē əm) *n, pl* **a·tri·a** (ā′trē ə) **1** a high central hall or court in a large building, often with skylights or open to the sky. **2** either of the upper chambers of the heart that receive the blood. **3** the main room of an ancient Roman house. <Latin>

a·tro·cious (ə trō′shəs) *adj* **1** savage and brutal: *atrocious crimes.* **2** *Informal* very bad: *atrocious spelling, an atrocious pun.* <Latin *atrocitas,* from *atrox* cruel, fierce> **a·tro′cious·ly** *adv.* **a·troc′i·ty** (ə tros′ə tē) *n.*

at·ro·phy (at′rə fē) *v* **at·ro·phied, at·ro·phy·ing** waste away or fail to develop: *The disease had caused his leg muscles to atrophy. If you don't use a skill, it will atrophy.*
n the process of atrophying. <Latin, from Greek *a-* without + *trophe* nourishment>

at·tach (ə tach′) *v* **1** fasten: *She attached the boat to the pier using a rope.* **2** bind by affection: *He quickly became attached to the stray kitten.* **3** add, usually at the end of something: *to attach your name to a petition, a file attached to an e-mail.* **4** assign or give: *to attach importance to something.* **5** connect with for duty, etc.: *Later, he was attached to a different regiment.* <Old French *atachier* fasten> **at·tach′a·ble** *adj.*

at·ta·ché (ə tash′ā) *or* (at′ə shā′) *n* a specialist on the official staff of an ambassador to a foreign country: *a naval attaché, a cultural attaché.* <French>

attaché case *n* a briefcase shaped like a small, thin, rigid suitcase.

at·tach·ment (ə tach′mənt) *n* **1** the act or means of attaching. **2** something that is or can be attached: *I am sending my report as an attachment to this e-mail.* **3** affection or emotional ties.

at·tack (ə tak′) *v* **1** act aggressively toward someone or something in an attempt to injure, kill, damage, or destroy: *Their dog attacked our cat. The enemy attacked at dawn.* **2** criticize severely: *an article attacking big business.* **3** set to work vigorously on: *The hungry boy attacked his dinner.*
n **1** the act of attacking: *The enemy attack took them by surprise.* **2** a sudden episode of illness, pain, or discomfort: *an attack of malaria, an attack of remorse.* <French, from Italian *attaccare* join battle> **at·tack′er** *n.*

at·tain (ə tān′) *v* **1** arrive at or reach: *to attain the age of 80.* **2** achieve or accomplish: *to attain a goal.* <Old French, from Latin *ad-* to + *tangere* touch> **at·tain′a·ble** *adj.* **at·tain′ment** *n.*

attain to, succeed in coming to or getting: *to attain to a position of great influence.*

SYNONYMS

Attain means "arrive at": *The charity attained its goal of raising $500.*

Reach is a less formal way of saying "arrive at": *She reached her target of cycling 100 km each day.*

Accomplish means "carry out" or "complete": *He always accomplishes his goals.*

at·tar (at′ər) *n* a perfume made from the petals of roses or other flowers. <Persian, from Arabic *'itr* perfume>

at·tempt (ə tempt′) *v* **1** try to do: *to attempt the high jump. We attempted to study, but it was too noisy.* **2** make an effort to achieve or complete something: *to attempt a Mars landing.*
n **1** an effort to do or make something: *a pitiful attempt at bowling, an attempt to make us laugh.* **2** an attack: *an attempt on the king's life.* <Old French, from Latin *attemptare* to strive after>

at·tend (ə tend′) *v* **1** be present at: *to attend school, to attend a wedding.* **2** (*with* ***to***) do something about: *Attend to this matter right away.* **3** pay attention: *Attend to my instructions!* **4** accompany royalty or some other important person: *Noble ladies attended the queen.* **5** wait on or care for: *Nurses attended the sick.* <Latin *ad-* toward + *tendere* stretch, i.e., pay attention to>

at·tend·ance (ə ten′dəns) *n* **1** the act or fact of attending: *Your attendance at all classes is compulsory.* **2** the number of people attending: *Attendance at the play was over 200.*
in attendance, present: *How many were in attendance at the town hall meeting?*
take attendance, check to see if everyone is present who is supposed to be: *to take attendance every morning.*

at·tend·ant (ə ten′dənt) *n* a person who accompanies and serves another.
adj **1** staying with another to help or serve: *an attendant nurse.* **2** accompanying other things: *weakness attendant on illness.*

at·tend·ee (ə′ ten dē′) *n* a person who is present at a meeting, function, etc.: *attendees at a conference.*

at·ten·tion (ə ten′shən) *n* **1** careful looking or listening: *Please give me your undivided attention.* **2** notice: *He called my attention to the error. She's just acting up to get attention.* **3** thought and action to deal with something or someone: *The matter needs our immediate attention.* **4** thoughtfulness or consideration: *The boy shows his mother much attention.* **5 attentions** *pl* acts that show interest in another person, especially in a romantic or sexual way: *She responded to his attentions with indifference.* **6** *Military* a standing position taken by a soldier, with body straight, heels together, arms straight down at the sides, and eyes looking forward.
interj a command, especially to soldiers, to come to attention. <See ATTEND.>

attention deficit (hyperactivity) disorder ADD.

at·ten·tive (ə ten′tiv) *adj* **1** paying close attention: *an attentive student.* **2** eager to serve or help: *an attentive hostess.* **at·ten′tive·ly** *adv.* **at·ten′tive·ness** *n.*

at·ten·u·ate (ə ten′yū āt′) *v* **at·ten·u·at·ed, at·ten·u·at·ing** make or become thinner or weaker. <Latin *ad-* to + *tenuis* thin> **at·ten′u·a′tion** *n.*

at·test (ə test′) *v* **1** (*often with* ***to***) give proof or evidence of: *Your good health attests to your sensible eating habits.* **2** declare to be true or genuine: *The statement was attested by three witnesses.* <Old French, from Latin *ad-* to + *testis* witness> **at′tes·ta′tion** *n.*

at·tic (at′ik) *n* a room or space in a house just below the roof and above the other rooms. <French, from Greek *Atticus,* relating to Athens or Attica, where such architecture was found>

At·tik·a·mek (ə tik′ə mek′) *n* **1** a member of a First Nations people living in the St. Maurice River area in southwest Québec. **2** their Cree language.
adj to do with these people or their language.

at·tire (ə tīr′) *n* clothes or dress: *This is not suitable attire for school.*
v **at·tired, at·tir·ing** dress; array: *He was attired in full military uniform.* <Old French *a tire* in order, i.e., dressed>

at·ti·tude (at′ə tyūd′) *or* (at′ə tūd′) *n* **1** one's settled way of thinking or feeling about something or someone: *Her attitude toward school has changed from dislike to enthusiasm.* **2** a pose suggesting a particular intention or emotion: *standing in an attitude of defence.* **3 a** *Informal* a spirit of antagonism or defiance: *I don't like him; he has an attitude.* **b** *Slang* individuality, self-confidence, or flair: *a coffee shop with attitude.* <French, from Latin *aptitudo* fitness>
strike an attitude, pose for effect.

at·tor·ney (ə tər′nē) *n* **1** a person, typically a lawyer, with legal power to act for another. **2** *especially US* a lawyer. <Old French *atorner* prepare, appoint>

attorney general (ə tər′nē jen′rəl) *n, pl* **attorneys general** or **attorney generals** **1** a chief law officer in a government. **2** 🍁 **Attorney General** a member of a federal or provincial cabinet who is the chief law officer in charge of administering justice.

at·tract (ə trakt′) *v* **1** draw to oneself: *A magnet attracts iron.* **2** win attention, interest, or liking: *The street musician attracted a crowd.* <Latin *attractus,* from *ad-* toward + *trahere* draw>

at·trac·tion (ə trak′shən) *n* **1** the act or power of attracting: *The sea has a strong attraction for her.* **2** anything that delights or attracts people: *The acrobats were the main attraction at the circus.* **3** *Physics* the force exerted on one another by molecules, tending to draw or hold them together.

a bat	e bed	i bid	o pot	u cup	th **thin**
ā cake	ē me	ī bite	ō go	ū rude	ᴛʜ **then**
à bar	ə about	ər over	ȯ for	ů put	zh measure

at·trac·tive (ə trak′tiv) *adj* **1** pleasing in appearance: *an attractive outfit.* **2** to do with attracting: *the attractive force of a magnet.* **at·trac′tive·ly** *adv.* **at·trac′tive·ness** *n.*

SYNONYMS

Attractive is an overused adjective. Try to use words that make the description more visual: *a **glamorous** singer, a **colourful** basketball jersey, a **magnetic** personality, a **stunning** outfit, a **charming** smile, an **inviting** offer, a **catchy** tune.*

at·trib·ute (ə trib′yūt) *for v,* (at′rə byūt′) *for n.*
v **at·trib·ut·ed, at·trib·ut·ing** **1** consider as belonging (to): *They attribute enormous intelligence to their dog.* **2** assign to a particular cause or source: *I attribute his success to skill and hard work. This unsigned poem has been attributed to Earl Birney.*
n **1** a quality considered as belonging to a person or thing: *Kindness is an attribute of a good teacher.* **2** an object linked with a person, rank, or office as a symbol: *A crown is an attribute of a monarch.* <Old French, from Latin *ad-* to + *tribuere* assign> **at′tri·bu′tion** *n.*

at·trib·u·tive (ə trib′yə tiv) *adj* **1** *Grammar* used as an adjective before the noun it modifies, as *new* in *my new skates.* Compare PREDICATE ADJECTIVE. **2** to do with attributing.
n an attributive adjective: *"General" is an attributive in "general store."* **at·trib′u·tive·ly** *adv.*

at·tri·tion (ə trish′ən) *n* **1** a gradual process of wearing down: *a war of attrition.* **2** a gradual reduction in the number of employees or members due to events such as retirement and resignation. <Latin *attritionis,* from *ad-* against + *terere* rub>

at·tune (ə tyūn′) *or* (ə tūn′) *v* **at·tuned, at·tun·ing** (*with* ***to***) **1** adjust or bring into harmony: *He could not attune his ears to the sounds of the big city.* **2** make sensitive or responsive: *Her years in politics had attuned the minister to the shifts in public opinion.*

ATV all-terrain vehicle. See OFF-ROAD for picture.

a·typ·i·cal (ā tip′ə kəl) *adj* not typical: *an atypical example.*

AU astronomical unit(s).

au·ber·gine (ō′bər zhēn′) *n* an eggplant. <French, from Arabic *al-badinjan*>

au·burn (ob′ərn) *adj* reddish brown (*usually with reference to hair colour*). <Old French, from Latin *alburnus* whitish. Middle English spelling of this was *abroun,* which got confused with *brun* brown, and so the colour changed!>

au cou·rant (ō kū rong′) *adj, adv* up to date on current happenings. <French>

auc·tion (ok′shən) *n* a sale in which each thing is sold to the person who offers the most for it.
v (*often with* ***off***) sell at an auction. <Latin *auctionem,* from *augere* increase>

auc·tion·eer (ok′shə nēr′) *n* the person in charge at an auction.
v act as an auctioneer.

au·da·cious (o dā′shəs) *adj* **1** bold or daring. **2** so bold as to be rude. <Latin *audacitas,* from *audere* dare> **au·da′cious·ly** *adv.* **au·dac′i·ty** (o das′ə tē) *n.*

au·di·ble (od′ə bəl) *adj* loud enough to be heard: *Speak up; you are barely audible.* **au′di·bly** *adv.*

ETYMOLOGY

Audi– comes from the Latin word *audire,* meaning "hear." Words beginning with *audi-* deal with sound. An *audience* consists of people gathered to hear a performance. An *auditorium* is a room for an audience.

au·di·ence (od′ē əns) *n* **1** the people gathered to hear or see a performance or presentation: *The audience cheered the premier's speech.* **2** the people reached by a broadcast, magazine, book, advertisement, etc.: *The book is aimed at a young audience.* **3** a chance to be heard: *If you want to explain your idea, the board will give you an audience.* **4** a formal interview with a person of high rank: *The queen granted an audience to the famous singer.* <Old French, from Latin *audire* hear>

au·di·o (od′ē ō) *adj* to do with sound reproduction: *audio equipment.*
n sound that is recorded, received, or broadcast, etc. <Latin *audire* hear>

au·di·o·cas·sette (od′ē ō ka set′) *n* a cassette containing blank or pre-recorded audiotape.

audio frequency *n* a frequency corresponding to audible sound vibrations, from about 20 Hz to about 20 000 Hz for the normal human ear. *Abbrev.* **AF** or **A.F.**

au·di·ol·o·gy (od′ē ol′ə jē) *n* the branch of medicine that studies the sense of hearing. **au′di·ol′o·gist** *n.*

au·di·o·phile (od′ē ō fīl′) *n* a person who greatly values the quality of sound reproduction in a recording. <Latin *audio* + *-phile*>

au·di·o·tape (od′ē ō tāp′) *n* a magnetized tape for recording sound.
v **au·di·o·taped, au·di·o·tap·ing** record sound on such a tape.

au·di·o·vis·u·al (od′ē ō vizh′wəl) *adj* to do with both hearing and sight: *an audiovisual presentation.*

au·dit (od′it) *v* **1** officially and independently examine and check the accounts or tax returns of a business or organization. **2** informally attend a course as a listener, without earning a credit.
n an official and independent examination of business accounts, or the resulting report. <Latin *auditus* a hearing, from *audire* hear>

au·di·tion (o dish′ən) *n* a trial performance in which an actor or other performer demonstrates his or her skills.
v try out as a performer: *The director is auditioning singers for the musical.*

au·di·tor (od′ə tər) *n* **1** a person who audits business accounts. **2** a person who audits a course.

🍁 **auditor general** or **Auditor General** *n, pl* **auditors general** or **auditor generals** an officer appointed to examine the financial accounts of the federal government and make an annual report to Parliament.

au·di·to·ri·um (od′ə tȯ′rē əm) *n* a large room for an audience in a building. <Latin *audire* hear>

au·di·to·ry (od′ə tȯ′rē) *adj* to do with hearing, the sense of hearing, or the organs of hearing: *the auditory nerve.* <Latin *audire* hear>

au·ger (og′ər) *n* **1** a type of large drill, used to make holes in ice or in the ground. **2** a similar device with a continuous spiral channel inside a tube, used for moving large quantities of grain or snow. <Old English *nafu* hub + *gar* piercer>

aught (ot) *Archaic or Poetic n* anything. <Old English>

aug·ment (og ment′) *v* **1** increase or add to: *He had to augment his income by working nights.* **2** *Music* **a** raise by a halftone. **b** change a melody by increasing the time value of the notes. <Old French, from Latin *augere* increase> **aug′men·ta′tion** *n.* **aug·ment′ed** *adj.*

au grat·in (ō gra tong′) *adj* sprinkled with grated cheese and sometimes breadcrumbs, then browned in an oven. <French = by grating>

au·gur (og′ər) *v* **1** predict an outcome. **2** be a sign or promise of: *Clouds on the horizon augured rain.*
n in ancient Rome, a religious official who interpreted natural signs as an indication of whether the gods approved or disapproved of a proposed action. <Latin *augur* diviner, prophet>
augur ill (or **well**), be a bad (or good) sign.

au·gu·ry (og′yə rē) *n, pl* **au·gu·ries** a sign of what will happen in future: *Heavy rain is a bad augury for the game.*

au·gust (o gust′) *adj* impressive and inspiring respect: *The people were silent in the august presence of the queen.* <Latin *augustus* consecrated> **au·gust′ly** *adv.* **au·gust′ness** *n.*

Au·gust (og′əst) *n* the eighth month of the year, with 31 days. *Abbrev.* **Aug** <*Augustus* Caesar, first Roman emperor>

au jus (ō zhū′) *adj* served in its own juices or gravy. <French>

auk (ok) *n* a seabird of northern oceans, with a short neck, short legs set far back on a heavy body, and short, narrow wings. <Old Norse *alka*>

au lait (ō′ lā′) *adj, adv* prepared with milk. <French>

au na·tu·rel (ō′ na tū′rel′) *adj, adv* in the nude. <French = in the natural way>

aunt (ant) *or* (ȧnt) *n* **1** the sister of one's father or mother. **2** the wife of one's uncle. Also (*Informal*), **auntie**. <Old French, from Latin *amita*>

au·ra (ȯ′rə) *n, pl* **au·ras** or **au·rae** (ȯ′rē) *or* (ȯ′rī) **1** a distinctive atmosphere or quality that seems to be generated by a person: *An aura of dignity surrounded her.* **2** an invisible emanation that is supposed by some to surround a person's body: *She said that my aura was light blue in colour.* **3** *Medicine* a peculiar sensation that is a warning of a seizure or migraine about to begin. <Latin, from Greek = breeze, current>

au·ral (ȯ′rəl) *adj* to do with the ear or sense of hearing. <Latin *auris* ear> **au′ral·ly** *adv.*

au·re·ole (ȯ′rē ōl′) *n* **1** a ring of light surrounding the sun. **2** a halo. <Old French, from Latin *aurum* gold>

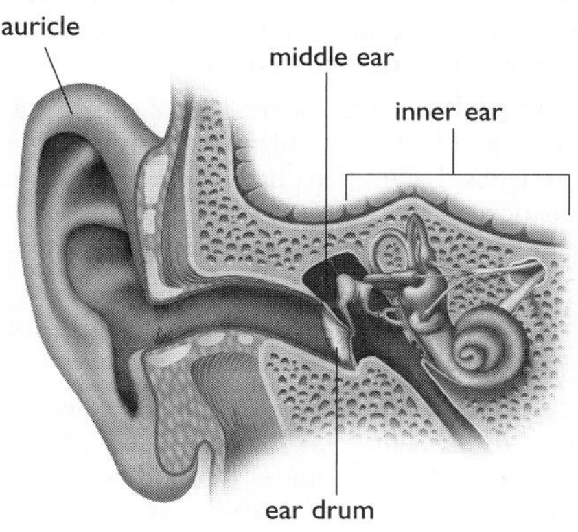

au·ri·cle (ȯ′rə kəl) *n* **1** the outer part of the ear. **2** either atrium of the heart. <Latin *auris* ear> **au·ric′u·lar** *adj.*

au·rochs (ȯ′roks) *n, pl* **au·rochs** a huge black ox, extinct in the 1600s, that was the wild ancestor of domestic varieties of cattle. <German *ur* wild bull + *ohso* ox>

au·ro·ra aus·tral·is (ə rȯ′rə os tral′is) *n* streamers or bands of light appearing in the southern sky at night. Also called **southern lights**. <Latin *Aurora* goddess of the dawn + *auster* the south wind>

aurora bo·re·al·is (bȯ′rē al′is) *n* streamers or bands of light appearing in the northern sky at night. Also called **northern lights**. <Latin *Aurora* goddess of the dawn + *boreas* the north wind>

aus·cul·tate (os′kəl tāt′) *Medicine v* **aus·cul·tat·ed, aus·cul·tat·ing** examine by listening with a stethoscope. <Latin *auscultare* listen> **aus′cul·ta′tion** *n.*

aus·pic·es (os′pə siz) *pln* support.
under the auspices of, through the sponsorship of: *The science fair was held under the auspices of the Board of Education.*

aus·pi·cious (o spish′əs) *adj* **1** favourable and seeming to be a good omen: *an auspicious first day in school.* **2** giving cause for celebration: *We welcome you on this auspicious occasion.* <Old French, from Latin *avis* bird + *specere* look. The Romans found omens by observing birds in flight.> **aus·pi′cious·ly** *adv.* **aus·pi′cious·ness** *n.*

Aus·sie (oz′ē) *Informal n* Australian.

aus·tere (o stēr′) *adj* **1** stern and strict: *the austere lifestyle of the Puritans. His father was a silent, austere man, very strict with his children.* **2** so simple as to be stark: *The tall, plain columns stood against the sky in austere beauty.* <Old French, from Greek *austeros,* from *auein* dry> **aus·tere′ly** *adv.* **aus·ter′i·ty** (o ster′ə tē) *n.*

Aus·tral·a·sia (os′trə lā′zhə) *n* the geographical region consisting of Australia, New Zealand, and the islands of the southwest Pacific. **Aus′tral·a′sian** *adj, n.*

a bat	e bed	i bid	o pot	u cup	th **thin**
ā cake	ē me	ī bite	ō go	ū rude	TH **then**
ȧ bar	ə about	ər over	ȯ for	u̇ put	zh measure

Aus·tral·ia (ə strāl′yə) *n* an island country and continent in the southwest Pacific. See the APPENDIX. <Latin *austral* the south wind> **Aus·tral′ian** *adj, n.*

Aus·tra·lo·pith·e·cine (os′trə lō pith′ə sēn′) *n* a member of a group of extinct primates with some human characteristics, believed to have lived in S Africa during the Pleistocene era.
adj to do with these primates. <Latin *australis* southern + *pithekos* ape>

Aus·tri·a (os′trē ə) *n* a country in central Europe. See the APPENDIX. **Aus′tri·an** *adj, n.*

au·then·tic (ə then′tik) *adj* genuine: *We serve authentic Japanese cuisine. Is this letter authentic, or is it a fake?* <Old French, from Greek *auto-* oneself + *hentes* doer> **au·then′ti·cal·ly** *adv.* **au′then·tic′i·ty** *n.*

au·then·ti·cate (o then′tə kāt′) *v* **au·then·ti·cat·ed, au·then·ti·cat·ing** **1** establish the genuineness of something, especially a claim or an art work. **2** *Computers* provide a name and a password in order to access a computer network. **au·then′ti·ca′tion** *n.*

au·thor (oth′ər) *n* **1** a writer of published works. **2** an author's published work: *Have you read this author?* **3** the creator or beginner of anything: *Are you the author of this scheme?* <Old French *autor*, from Latin *augere* originate> **au′thor·ship′** *n.*

au·thor·i·tar·i·an (ə thȯ′rə ter′ē ən) *adj* favouring or enforcing strict obedience to authority.
n a person with authoritarian views or practices. **au·thor′i·tar′i·an·ism′** *n.*

au·thor·i·ta·tive (ə thȯ′rə tā′tiv) *adj* **1** with or coming from an authority: *an authoritative statement, authoritative guidelines.* **2** commanding: *to speak in an authoritative tone.* **au·thor′i·ta′tive·ly** *adv.*

au·thor·i·ty (ə thȯ′rə tē) *n, pl* **au·thor·i·ties** **1** the right to decide or act, or to demand obedience from others: *Do you have the authority to detain this person?* **2** a person or organization with this right: *to rebel against authority.* **3** an influence that creates respect and confidence: *the authority of his voice and manner.* **4** a source of correct information or wise advice: *A good dictionary is an authority on word meanings. She is an authority on English history.* **5** **authorities** *pl* **a** government officials. **b** the people in control of something. **6** a government body that runs some activity or business on behalf of the public: *the St. Lawrence Seaway Authority.* <Old French *autorite*, from Latin *auctor* originator>

au·thor·ize (oth′ə rīz′) *v* **au·thor·ized, au·thor·iz·ing** **1** give the authority or right to: *The librarian is authorized to select and purchase books.* **2** approve or give permission for: *The principal authorized use of the gym for the dance.* **au′thor·i·za′tion** *n.*

au·tism (ot′iz əm) *n* a mental condition, present from early childhood, characterized by difficulty in understanding and responding to others, and in using language and concepts. <German, from Greek *autos* self> **au·tis′tic** *adj.*

au·to (ot′ō) *especially Commercial n* automobile.

auto– *combining form* **1** to do with oneself: *autobiography.* **2** self-propelled: *automobile.*

ETYMOLOGY

Auto– comes from the Greek word *auto*, meaning "self." Words beginning with *auto-* deal with *self.*
An *autobiography* is the story of a person's life, written by that person. An *autograph* is a person's own signature. *Automatic* can refer to something made to move or act by itself. *Autonomy* is self-government or independence.

au·to·an·ti·bod·y (ot′ō an′tə bod′ē) *Medicine n, pl* **au·to·an·ti·bod·ies** an antibody that reacts against substances in the body that produces it.

au·to·bi·og·ra·phy (ot′ə bī og′rə fē) *n, pl* **au·to·bi·og·ra·phies** the story of a person's life written by that person. **au′to·bi′o·graph′i·cal** *adj.*

au·toc·ra·cy (o tok′rə sē) *n, pl* **au·toc·ra·cies** **1** a government in which the ruler has absolute power over citizens. **2** unlimited power over others. <*auto-* + Greek *kratos* power>

au·to·crat (ot′ə krat′) *n* **1** a ruler with absolute power over his or her subjects. **2** a person who insists on total authority or control over others: *My friends think their parents are autocrats.* **au′to·crat′ic** *adj.*

au·to·graph (ot′ə graf′) *n* a person's signature: *Some people collect the autographs of movie stars.*
v write one's signature in or on: *The pitcher autographed my baseball.* <*auto-* + *-graph*>

au·to·harp (ot′ō härp′) *n* a stringed musical instrument with a series of padded bars that can be pressed down to silence certain strings, making it possible to play chords.

au·to·im·mune (ot′ō i myūn′) *adj* to do with the development of antibodies that are hostile to the body's own molecules: *an autoimmune reaction.*

au·to·mate (ot′ə māt′) *v* **au·to·mat·ed, au·to·mat·ing** **1** make a process automatic: *automated mail sorting.* **2** convert to automatic operation: *to automate a factory.* <*automation*>

automated teller machine ATM.

au·to·mat·ic (ot′ə mat′ik) *adj* **1** done without thought or attention, as from force of habit or a reflex: *Her automatic reply to questions from reporters was "No comment." Use of the seat belt soon became automatic.* **2** involuntary: *Your heartbeat is automatic.* **3** made to move or act by itself: *an automatic timer. Our car has an automatic transmission.* **4** repeatedly firing and reloading as a firearm as long as the trigger is pressed. **5** as a necessary consequence: *automatic promotion after a year of service.*
n **1** a motor vehicle equipped with an automatic transmission. Compare STANDARD. **2** an automatic firearm. <Greek *automatos* self-acting>
au′to·mat′i·cal·ly *adv.*

automatic pilot *n* **1** a device designed to keep an aircraft on a set course without human assistance.
2 *Informal* a mental state in which one carries out habitual activities automatically while thinking of something else: *She sat at the piano staring into space, her hands on automatic pilot.*

automatic transmission *n* a system in a motor vehicle for automatically altering the speed of the driving wheels relative to engine speed. Compare MANUAL TRANSMISSION.

au·to·ma·tion (ot′ə mā′shən) *n* the use of automatic controls to operate machines: *Automation has done away with many of the jobs formerly done by people.* <from *autom(atic)* + *(oper)ation*>

au·tom·a·ton (ə tom′ə ton′) *n, pl* **au·tom·a·ta** (ə tom′ə tə) **1** a robot. **2** a person or animal that acts or appears to act like a robot. <Greek = self-acting>

au·to·mo·bile (ot′ə mə bēl′) *n* a passenger vehicle with its own engine for use on roads. <*auto-* + French *mobile* moving>

au·to·mo·tive (ot′ə mō′tiv) *adj* to do with motor vehicles: *the automotive industry.*

au·to·nom·ic nervous system (ot′ə nom′ik) *n* the parts of the nervous system of vertebrates that control digestive and other involuntary functions of the body.

au·ton·o·my (ə ton′ə mē) *n* self-government or independence. <*auto-* + Greek *nomos* law>
au·ton′o·mous *adj.* **au·ton′o·mous·ly** *adv.*

au·to·pi·lot (ot′ō pī′lət) *n* automatic pilot.

au·top·sy (ot′op sē) *n, pl* **au·top·sies** an examination of a dead body to find the cause of death or the nature and extent of damage done by disease or injury. Compare BIOPSY. <Latin, from *auto-* + Greek *optos* seen, i.e., see for oneself>

au·to·tox·in (ot′ō tok′sən) *n* a substance, produced by an organism, that is poisonous to itself.

au·to·troph (ot′ə trof′) *Biology n* an organism that makes its own food from inorganic substances, such as a plant by photosynthesis. <*auto-* + Greek *trophe* food>
au′to·troph′ic *adj.*

au·tumn (ot′əm) *n* the season of the year between summer and winter. <Old French, from Latin *autumnus*>
au·tum′nal (ə tum′nəl) *adj.*

aux·il·ia·ry (og zil′ə rē) *or* (og zil′yə rē) *adj* helping or supporting: *an auxiliary engine on a sailboat. The main library has several auxiliary branches.*
n, pl **aux·il·ia·ries** **1** a supporting or helping organization, usually of volunteers: *The hospital auxiliary runs the gift shop.* **2** an auxiliary verb. **3 auxiliaries** *pl* troops that help the army of a nation at war. **4** a person who or thing that helps. <Latin *auxilium* aid>

auxiliary verb *Grammar n* a verb used to form the tenses, moods, or voices of other verbs, such as *will* in *He will go*, or *was* (a form of *be)* in *I was surprised.* The auxiliary verbs are: *be, can, do, have, may, must, shall,* and *will.*

GRAMMAR AND USAGE

An **auxiliary verb** precedes a main verb and shows its tense, mood, or voice:

I will go to school tomorrow. Here the auxiliary verb **will** shows that the action (*go*) is in the future.

The lost dog was found. Here the auxiliary verb **was** shows that the action (*find*) happened to the dog.

a·vail (ə vāl′) *v* **1** be of use or value to: *Money will not avail you after you are dead.* **2** accomplish: *Talk without work avails nothing.* <Old French, from Latin *valere* be strong, worthy>
avail yourself of, take advantage or make use of: *While in Québec, he availed himself of the opportunity to learn French.*
of no (or **little**) **avail,** useless or pointless: *Crying is of little avail now.*
to no (or **little**) **avail,** without effect: *He tried again and again, but to no avail.*

a·vail·a·ble (ə vā′lə bəl) *adj* **1** that can be obtained: *A few tickets are still available.* **2** willing or free to do something: *How soon would you be available for this job?* **3** ready or handy to be used: *an available water supply.*
a·vail′a·bil′i·ty *n.*

av·a·lanche (av′ə lanch′) *n* **1** a large mass of snow, ice, or rocks, sliding or falling down a mountainside. **2** an overwhelming quantity all at once: *an avalanche of work.* <French *la valanche*>

a·vant–garde (av′on gȧrd′) *n* the people who develop new and experimental ideas, especially in the arts: *a member of the literary avant-garde.*
adj to do with these people or their ideas: *an avant-garde artist, avant-garde ideas.* <French = advance guard>

av·a·rice (av′ə ris) *n* an extreme desire for money or possessions: *It was avarice, not thrift, that made them scrimp and save all those years.* <Old French, from Latin *avarus* greedy> **av′a·ri′cious** (av′ə ri′shəs) *adj.*

a·vast (ə vast′) *Nautical or Humorous interj* a command to stop: *"Avast, there, me hearties!" yelled the pirate.* <Dutch *houd vast* hold fast>

a·va·tar (av′ə tȧr′) *n* **1** *Hinduism* the descent or appearance of a deity in human or animal form. **2** an embodiment or manifestation of a person or idea. <Sanskrit *avatara* descent>

a·venge (ə venj′) *v* **a·venged, a·veng·ing** **1** take revenge for a wrong or injury: *to avenge an insult.* **2** take revenge on behalf of someone killed: *The clan avenged their slain chief.* <Old French, from Latin *ad-* to + *vindicare* punish>
a·veng′er *n.*
avenge yourself on someone, get revenge on someone: *He swore to avenge himself on those who had betrayed him.*

a·vens (ā′vənz) *n* a perennial plant of the rose family with divided leaves and seeds bearing small hooks, such as the MOUNTAIN AVENS. <Old French *avence*>

av·e·nue (av′ən yū′) *n* **1** a wide or main street. **2** a road or walk bordered by trees. **3** a way of approach or departure: *avenues to fame.* **4** in some cities, a main road running at right angles to streets. <French *avenir*, from Latin *ad-* toward + *venire* approach>

a·ver (ə vər′) *v* **a·verred, a·ver·ring** declare or state. <Old French, from Latin *ad-* to + *verus* true> **a·ver′ment** *n.*

a bat	e bed	i bid	o pot	u cup	th thin
ā cake	ē me	ī bite	ō go	ū rude	ᴛʜ then
ȧ bar	ə about	ər over	ȯ for	u̇ put	zh measure

av·er·age (av′rij) *n* **1** *Mathematics* the quantity found by dividing the sum of several amounts by the number of amounts. The average of 3, 5, and 10 is 6. **2** the usual rate, amount, or level of quality: *His work was far above the average.*
v **av·er·aged, av·er·ag·ing 1** find the average of. **2** amount to as an average: *Our phone bill averages about $50 a month.* **3** do or get on an average: *She averages six hours of work a day.*
adj **1** being an average: *the average temperature.* **2** unremarkable or ordinary: *average intelligence.* <French, from Arabic *'awar* damage to goods (referring to the equal distribution of loss among all the people concerned)>
average out, come to a certain average over time: *The heating bill varies with the season, but it averages out to about $150 a month.*
on (**the**) **average,** as an average amount: *He works six hours a day on average.*

a·verse (ə vərs′) *adj* (*with* ***to***) unwilling or reluctant to do something: *I am averse to fighting.* <Latin *aversus,* from *ab-* from + *vertere* to turn> **a·verse′ness** *n.*

a·ver·sion (ə vər′zhən) *n* **1** (*with* ***to***) a strong dislike: *an aversion to snakes.* **2** a thing or person that one dislikes: *Cooked tomatoes are an aversion of mine.*

a·vert (ə vərt′) *v* **1** prevent or avoid: *She averted an accident by swerving quickly.* **2** turn away or aside: *We averted our eyes from the wreck.* <Old French, from Latin *ab-* from + *vertere* to turn>

A·ves·ta (a ves′tə) *Zoroastrianism n* the sacred scriptures, compiled in the 300s, containing hymns and prayers, and instruction concerning rituals and ethics.

a·vi·ar·y (ā′vē er′ē) *n, pl* **a·vi·ar·ies** a place where birds are kept. <Latin *avis* bird>

a·vi·a·tion (ā′vē ā′shən) *n* the designing, building, and, especially, flying of aircraft. <French, from Latin *avis* bird>

a·vi·a·tor (ā′vē ā′tər) *n* a person who flies an aircraft.

av·id (av′id) *adj* enthusiastic or eager: *She is an avid reader.* <Latin *avidus,* from *avere* crave> **av′id·ly** *adv.*

a·vi·on·ics (ā′vē on′iks) *n* **1** (*with singular verb*) the application of electronic technology to aviation or space travel. **2** (*with plural verb*) equipment making use of this technology. <*avi*(*ation*) + (*electr*)*onics*>

av·o·ca·do (av′ə kå′dō) *n* a pear-shaped tropical fruit with a thin, dark green skin, a very large seed, and creamy yellowish green flesh. <Spanish, from Nahuatl (a language of Central and S America) *ahuacatl*>

av·o·ca·tion (av′ə kā′shən) *n* a hobby or minor occupation: *He is a lawyer, but writing is his avocation.* See VOCATION for confusable. <Latin *avocationis* distraction, from *ab-* away + *vocare* to call>

a·void (ə void′) *v* **1** keep away from: *We avoided large cities on our trip. She seems to be avoiding me.* **2** keep from doing or happening: *Avoid useless arguments. Avoid getting glue on your skin.* <Old French *avoider* quit, from *es-* out + *vuidier* empty> **a·void′a·ble** *adj.* **a·void′a·bly** *adv.* **a·void′ance** *n.*

av·oir·du·pois (ə vwår′dyū pwå′) *or* (av′ər də poiz′) *n* in full, **avoirdupois weight** a system of weights used in Canada before the change to the metric system. One pound in avoirdupois weight is equal to about 0.454 kilograms. <Old French *aveir* have + *peis* weight>

a·vow (ə vou′) *v* admit frankly or openly: *He avowed he could not sing.* <Old French, from Latin *ad-* to + *vocare* to call> **a·vow′al** *n.* **a·vow′ed·ly** (ə vou′id lē) *adv.*

a·vun·cu·lar (ə vung′kyə lər) *adj* to do with an uncle: *avuncular advice.* <Latin *avunculus* uncle>

a·wait (ə wāt′) *v* **1** look forward to: *We eagerly await your arrival.* **2** be in store for: *A surprise awaited them at home.* <Old French *a-* for + *waitier* wait>

a·wake (ə wāk′) *adj* **1** not asleep: *Are you still awake so late at night?* **2** alert and watchful: *awake to danger.*
v **a·woke, a·wok·en, a·wak·ing 1** rouse or be roused from sleep: *We awoke at dawn. The alarm clock awoke me.* **2** make or become active: *to awake old memories.* Also (*v*), **awaken**. <Old English *awacian*> **a·wak′en·ing** *n.*

a·ward (ə wórd′) *v* **1** give on the basis of merit: *A medal was awarded to the woman who saved the child.* **2** decide, in a court of law, that a certain sum is owing: *The court awarded damages of $5000 to the injured man.*
n **1** a prize for merit: *He won several academic awards.* **2** a sum awarded by a judge. <Old French *eswarder* decide after investigation>

a·ware (ə wer′) *adj* **1** knowing or perceiving a situation or fact: *Are you aware that the meeting was cancelled? She was not aware of her danger.* **2** alert and well-informed: *an aware teen.* <Old English *gewær*> **a·ware′ness** *n.*

a·wash (ə wosh′) *adj* (*never before the noun*) **1** flooded: *The deck of the sinking ship was already awash.* **2** floating: *Debris of all sorts was awash in the lake.*

a·way (ə wā′) *adv* **1** to or at a distance: *away from home. Get away from the door.* **2** in another direction: *She turned away.* **3** out of one's possession or use: *He gave his boat away.* **4** somewhere else, especially in a storage place: *Put these books away.* **5** out of existence: *The sound faded away.* **6** continuously: *She worked away at her job.* **7** beginning (an action): *Away we go!*
adj **1** at a distance: *I hate being away from home.* **2** absent or gone: *My mother is away today.* <Old English *onweg* on one's way>
away with ——! expressing a desire to get rid of a person or thing: *Away with you! Away with the GST!*
do away with, a put an end to. **b** kill.
send (or **write**) **away for,** order by mail.

awe (o) *n* **1** wonder and reverence inspired by something sacred, mysterious, or magnificent: *We gazed in awe at the mountains towering above us.* **2** respect or fear: *The stern old woman filled them with awe.*
v **awed, aw·ing** fill or overcome with awe: *We were awed by the vastness of space.* <Old English>
in awe of, awed or greatly impressed by: *I am in awe of your skill.*

a·weigh (ə wā′) *Nautical adj* of an anchor, no longer hooked to the seabed: *Anchors aweigh!*

awe·some (os′əm) *adj* **1** inspiring awe: *The starry sky is an awesome sight.* **2** *Slang* extremely good: *awesome desserts.*

awe·struck (o′struk′) *adj* overwhelmed with awe.

aw·ful (of′əl) *adj* **1** dreadful or terrible: *an awful storm.* **2** deserving great respect and reverence: *the awful power of God.* **3** *Informal* very bad: *His room was an awful mess.* <*awe*> **aw′ful·ness** *n.*

aw·ful·ly (of′ə lē) *adv* **1** dreadfully or terribly. **2** *Informal* very or extremely: *I know I'm late; I'm awfully sorry.*

a·while (ə wīl′) *adv* for a short time: *Please stay awhile.*

awk·ward (ok′wərd) *adj* **1** clumsy: *an awkward apology. Seals are awkward on land, but quite at home in the water.* **2** not easy to use or manage: *The handle of this mug has an awkward shape.* **3** embarrassing or embarrassed: *an awkward question. I feel awkward in her presence.* <*awk* the wrong way, from Old Norse *afugr* + *-ward*>
awk′ward·ly *adv.* **awk′ward·ness** *n.*

awl (ol) *n* a pointed tool for making small holes in leather or wood. <Old English *æl*>

awn (on) *n* a bristly hair extending from the ears of some cereal grains. <Old Norse *ogn* chaff>

awn·ing (on′ing) *n* a rooflike structure of metal, canvas, or plastic, extending out over a door or window as a protection from sun or rain. <origin uncertain>

a·woke (ə wōk′) past tense of AWAKE.

a·wok·en (ə wō′kən) past participle of AWAKE.

AWOL or **awol** (ā′wol) gone or away without explanation. <military acronym for *a*bsent *w*ith*o*ut *l*eave>

a·wry (ə rī′) *adv, adj* (*never before the noun*) **1** with a twist or turn to one side: *Her hair was blown awry by the wind* (*adv*). **2** wrong: *Something is awry here* (*adj*).

axe (aks) *n, pl* **ax·es 1** a tool for chopping wood, consisting of a long handle with a heavy, bladed head on the end. **2** a weapon of similar shape, such as a battle-axe.
v **axed, ax·ing** suddenly cancel, remove, or get rid of. Also, **ax.** <Old English *æx*> **axe′like′** *adj.*
have an axe to grind, have a special or private motive.
get the axe, *Informal* be removed, dismissed, or cancelled.
give the axe, *Informal* remove, dismiss, or cancel: *They gave half the plant workers the axe yesterday.*

There are several variations of the **axel**, which is the most difficult of all figure-skating jumps. After mastering the single axel, a skater can go on to learn to perform double and triple axels, like world-champion figure skater Elvis Stojko.

ax·el (ak′səl) *n* in figure skating, a jump in which the skater takes off from one foot, makes one and a half turns in the air, and lands on the other foot. <*Axel* Paulsen, skater>

ax·es[1] (ak′siz) plural of AXE.

ax·es[2] (ak′sēz) plural of AXIS.

ax·i·al (ak′sē əl) *adj* to do with an axis.

ax·i·om (ak′sē əm) *n* a concise statement that is seen or understood to be true without proof. <Latin, from Greek *axios* worthy, true> **ax′i·o·mat′ic** *adj.*

ax·is (ak′sis) *n, pl* **ax·es** (ak′sēz) **1** an imaginary or real line that passes through an object and around which the object turns, or seems to turn. **2** *Mathematics* a numbered line for positioning coordinates, such as on a graph. **3** a central or principal line around which parts are arranged in a balanced way: *axis of symmetry.* **4 the Axis** in World War II, Germany, Italy, Japan, and their allies. <Latin>

ax·le (ak′səl) *n* **1** a bar or shaft on which a wheel turns. **2** a horizontal shaft joining two wheels, as on a vehicle. Also, **axletree.** <Old Norse *oxultre* axle>

ax·on (ak′son) *n* the part of a nerve cell that carries impulses away from the body of the cell. <Latin, from Greek = axis>

a·yah (ȧ′yə) *n* in India and other former British colonies, a nanny or nursemaid employed by Europeans. <Portuguese *aia* nurse>

ay·a·tol·lah (ȧ′yə tō′lə) *Islam n* among Shiite Muslims, a high-ranking religious leader, chiefly in Iran. <Arabic *ayatu-llah* token of god>

aye[1] or **ay**[1] (ā) *Poetic adv* always or ever: *a love that lasts forever and aye.* <Old Norse *ei*>

aye[2] or **ay**[2] (ī) *especially Scottish adv* yes.
n a yes answer: *The ayes were in the majority when the vote was taken.* <origin uncertain>

Ay·ur·ve·da (ī′ůr vā′də) *n* a traditional Hindu system of medicine using diet, herbal treatments, and yogic breathing. <Sanskrit *ayus* life + *veda* knowledge>

a·zal·ea (ə zāl′yə) *n* a rhododendron with funnel-shaped flowers and leaves that drop off in the fall. <Latin, from Greek *azaleos* dry. The plant is supposed to prefer dry conditions.>

a·zan (ə zȧn′) *Islam n* the call to public prayer, proclaimed five times a day by a crier from the minaret of a mosque or played from a recording. <Arabic *adan* announcement>

Az·er·bai·jan (az′ər bī jȧn′) *n* a country in southeast Europe. See the APPENDIX. **Az′er·bai·ja′ni** *adj, n.*

az·i·muth (az′ə məth) *Astronomy n* the angular distance of a heavenly object east or west from true north. <Old French, from Arabic *al-samt* way, direction>

Az·tec (az′tek) *n* a member of the indigenous people who ruled Mexico before its conquest by the Spanish in the 1500s, or the language spoken by these people.
adj to do with the Aztecs or their language: *Aztec architecture.*

az·ure (azh′ər) *adj* bright blue. <Old French, from Persian *lazward* lapis lazuli (a blue gemstone)>

Bb

b or **B** (bē) *n, pl* **b's** or **B's** 1 the second letter of the English alphabet, or any speech sound represented by it. 2 the second thing in a list or series: *Do question 3, parts a and b.* 3 *Music* the seventh tone in the scale of C major, or a key based on a scale with B as its keynote. 4 **a** in school, a grade meaning good but not excellent: *I got a B on that test.* **b** a rating indicating relatively low quality: *a B movie.* **Plan B,** another, less desirable plan to follow in case the preferred plan does not work out.

B 1 one of the four main blood groups. The others are A, AB, and O. 2 boron.

baa (bȧ) *or* (ba) *n, v* bleat. <imitative>

bab·ble (bab′əl) *v* **bab·bled, bab·bling** 1 talk too much, too fast, or in a way that cannot be understood: *She babbled on and on about her great adventure. The baby babbled happily in his playpen.* 2 make a soft flowing or rippling sound: *The stream babbled over the stones.* 3 reveal foolishly: *to babble a secret.*
n 1 talk that is foolish or cannot be understood: *A confused babble filled the room.* 2 a soft flowing or rippling sound: *the babble of a brook.* <imitative> **bab′bler** *n.*

babe (bāb) *Poetic n* a baby.

ba·bel (bab′əl) *or* (bā′bəl) *n* 1 a confusion of many different sounds. 2 usually, **Babel** a place of noise and confusion. <*Babel,* biblical tower where God caused confusion in the language of the builders>

🍁 **ba·biche** (bə bēsh′) *n* rawhide in the form of strips or lacings, often used in making snowshoes. <Cdn French, from Algonquian>

babies' breath BABY'S BREATH.

ba·boon (bə bün′) *n* 1 a large monkey of Africa or Arabia with a heavy body, a large head with cheek pouches, a short tail, and a long muzzle. 2 *Informal* a clumsy or ignorant person. <Old French *babouin* stupid person> **ba·boon′ish** *adj.*

ba·by (bā′bē) *n, pl* **ba·bies** 1 a very young child or animal: *Some babies cry a lot.* 2 the youngest: *My sister is the baby of the family.* 3 a person who acts childishly or like a baby: *Don't be a baby.*
adj 1 very small or young: *a baby bird.* 2 suitable for a baby: *baby shoes, baby talk.* 3 smallest of its kind: *my baby finger.*
v **ba·bied, ba·by·ing** 1 pamper like a baby: *to baby a sick child.* 2 handle very carefully: *to baby a new bicycle.* <Middle English *babe*> **ba′by·hood′** *n.* **ba′by·ish** *adj.*

🍁 **baby bonus** *Informal n* in former times, a monthly payment from the government to a family for each child under the age of sixteen.

baby boom *n* a marked increase in the birth rate, especially, the one between 1945 and 1965 after the end of World War II. **baby boomer** *n.*

baby carriage *n* a light carriage used for wheeling a baby around. Also called **baby buggy** (*Informal*).

Bab·y·lon (bab′ə lon′) *n* 1 the capital of ancient Babylonia, on the Euphrates River. 2 any great, rich, corrupt city or place. **Bab′y·lo′ni·an** (bab′ə lō′nē ən) *adj, n.*

baby's breath *n* a plant of Europe, Asia, and Africa with tiny flowers on delicate branching stems, often added to flower arrangements. Also, **babies'-breath.**

ba·by·sit (bā′bē sit′) *v* **ba·by·sat, ba·by·sit·ting** take care of a child while family members are busy or away from home: *I'll babysit for the neighbours on Friday night. He babysat his little sister for two hours.* **ba′by·sit′ter** *n.*

baby tooth *n* one of the first set of teeth of a child or young animal that fall out to make room for the permanent teeth.

bac·ca·lau·re·ate (bak′ə lȯr′ē it) *n* 1 a bachelor's degree. See BACHELOR (def. 3). 2 a graduation speech.
adj to do with either of these. <Latin. See BACHELOR.>

bach (bach) *Slang v* usually, **bach it** keep house for oneself, especially temporarily while a spouse or others are away. <*bachelor*>

bach·e·lor (bach′ə lər) *n* 1 an unmarried man. 2 🍁 in full, **bachelor apartment** an apartment with a kitchen and a bathroom but no separate bedroom. 3 (*with the name of the field of study*) the first degree offered by a university or college: *She has a bachelor of arts from Memorial University.* <Old French *bacheler* squire, from Latin *baccalaureus* young man> **bach′e·lor·hood′** *n.*

ba·cil·lus (bə sil′əs) *n, pl* **ba·cil·li** (bə sil′ī) *or* (bə sil′ē) any of the rod-shaped bacteria. **ba·cil′lar** *adj.*

back (bak) *adv* 1 at, to, or toward the rear: *Please step back.* 2 in or toward the past: *We visited our cousins a few years back.* 3 in or to the place from which something or someone came: *Put the books back. Is Mom back yet?* 4 in return: *He hit me, but I didn't hit him back.*
n 1 the rear upper part of the body, or of an animal's body, from the neck to the end of the backbone: *She turned her back to the wind.* 2 the side opposite, under, or behind the front: *the back of a room, the back of a rug.* 3 the upper or outer side: *the back of my hand.* 4 the part of a piece of furniture or clothing that supports or covers a person's back: *This seat has no back.* 5 the last pages of a book, magazine, or newspaper. 6 *Football, etc.* a player whose position is behind the front line.
adj 1 opposite or behind the front: *the back seat of a car.* 2 directed or facing backwards: *The gymnast did a back flip.* 3 far from the main roads or towns: *back roads.* 4 old; previous: *a back issue of a magazine.*
v 1 move in reverse; move one way while facing the other way: *Mom backs the car into our parking spot.* 2 support or help: *to back a candidate in an election.* <Old English *baec*> **back′er** *n.*
back and fill, **a** in a vehicle, repeatedly go backwards and forwards to get out of mud or snow. **b** keep changing one's mind.
back away, **a** retreat or move away backwards. **b** withdraw an opinion: *I will not back away from my statement about school uniforms.*
back down, give up a claim: *When I challenged her to prove it, she backed down.*
back off, stop attacking.
back onto, faces with the back toward something: *Our farm backs onto a lake.*
back out, *Informal* decide not to do something after all: *He was going to go with us, but he backed out.*

back up, **a** move backwards. **b** support a claim, or the person making it: *If you complain to the teacher, I'll back you up.* **c** copy from a computer onto a disk, tape, CD, etc. **d** plug so that liquid collects and overflows: *The drain is backed up.*
behind someone's back, secretly in a way that betrays trust: *We shouldn't talk about him behind his back. I said no, but they went behind my back and did it anyway.*
get off someone's back, *Informal* stop nagging or criticizing someone.
get your (or **someone's**) **back up,** *Informal* make or become angry and stubborn: *She was only joking, so don't get your back up.*
go back on, *Informal* fail to keep a promise: *to go back on your word.*
have your back to the wall, be in a difficult or desperate situation.
in back of, *Informal* behind: *The football field is in back of the school.*
put your back into it, try hard to do something.
turn your back on, refuse, ignore, or reject: *My best friend would never turn her back on me if I needed help. The main character turned his back on success and returned to his hometown.*

back·ache (bak′āk′) *n* pain in the back.

❋ **back bacon** *n* bacon cut from the back of the pig rather than the sides. It has little fat and tastes like ham.

back·bench·er (bak′ben′chər) *n* in Parliament or a legislative assembly, a member who is neither part of the cabinet nor a leading member of an opposition party, said to be sitting on the **back bench**. Compare FRONTBENCHER. **back′bench′** *adj.*

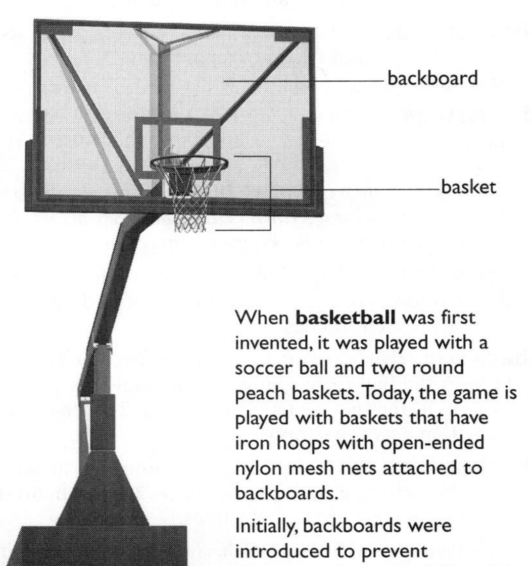

When **basketball** was first invented, it was played with a soccer ball and two round peach baskets. Today, the game is played with baskets that have iron hoops with open-ended nylon mesh nets attached to backboards.

Initially, backboards were introduced to prevent spectators from interfering with the play.

back·board (bak′bôrd′) *n* a board above and behind the basket on a basketball court.

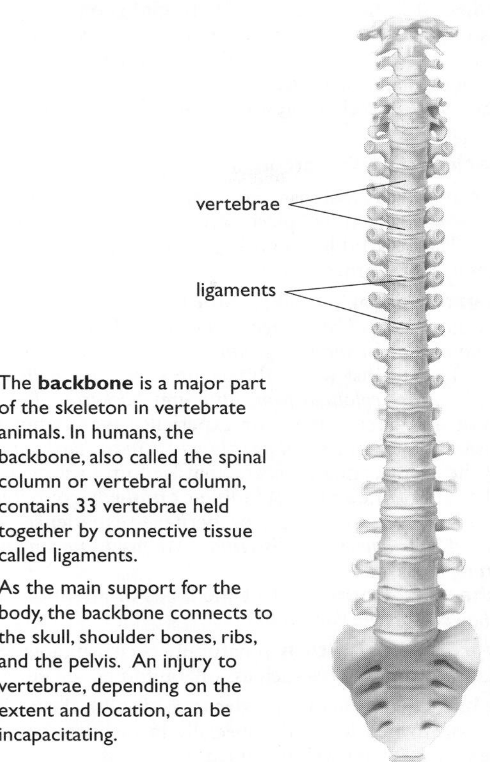

The **backbone** is a major part of the skeleton in vertebrate animals. In humans, the backbone, also called the spinal column or vertebral column, contains 33 vertebrae held together by connective tissue called ligaments.

As the main support for the body, the backbone connects to the skull, shoulder bones, ribs, and the pelvis. An injury to vertebrae, depending on the extent and location, can be incapacitating.

back·bone (bak′bōn′) *n* **1** the spine; a series of small bones along the middle of the back in humans and many other animals. **2** the main strength or support: *She is the backbone of our swim team.* **3** the courage to do or stand up for what one thinks is right.

back·break·ing (bak′brā′king) *adj* requiring very hard physical effort: *Digging this garden was backbreaking work.*

❋ **back channel** *n* a BACKWATER (def. 1) or side channel of a river.

back·check (bak′chek′) *Hockey v* skate back toward one's own defensive zone while trying to check or hinder an opponent who has the puck. **back′check′** *n.*

back·date (bak′dāt′) *v* **back·dat·ed, back·dat·ing** put a date on that is earlier than the actual date: *to backdate a cheque.*

back·drop (bak′drop′) *n* **1** a curtain or scenery at the back of a stage. **2** background: *The painting shows an old barn on a wintry backdrop. These events occurred against the grim backdrop of the war.*

❋ **back East** *adj, adv* in or to central or eastern Canada, from the perspective of those living west of it.

a bat	e bed	i bid	o pot	u cup	th thin
ā cake	ē me	ī bite	ō go	ū rude	ᴛʜ then
à bar	ə about	ər over	ȯ for	ů put	zh measure

back·fire (bak′fīr′) *v* **back·fired, back·fir·ing** 1 explode too soon or in the wrong place. 2 have an unexpected and unwanted result: *His plan backfired, so instead of getting an A, he got an F for cheating.*
n a fire set to check a forest or prairie fire by burning off the area in front of it.

back forty *n* the part of a farm farthest from the house.

back·gam·mon (bak′gam′ən) *Games n* a board game for two people who move pieces according to the throw of dice. <*back* + Middle English *gamen* game, because the pieces are sometimes set back>

back·ground (bak′ground′) *n* **1** the part of a scene farthest from the viewer: *The cottage stands in the foreground with the mountains in the background.* Compare FOREGROUND. **2** a surface against which things are seen: *The toolbar on this screen has coloured icons on a grey background.* **3** the part of any circumstance or experience that is not the focus of attention: *I could hear laughter in the background.* **4** all the events, situations, etc. that lead up to something or that affect one's understanding of it: *the background to the accident.* **5** upbringing or heritage, experience, and training: *Her background is Hindu. We need someone with a strong music background.*
in the background, out of the focus of attention: *The shy boy kept in the background.*

background radiation *n* naturally occurring low-level radiation from sources such as soil, buildings, air, etc.

back·hand (bak′hand′) *n* **1** a stroke made with the back of the hand turned forward, especially in racquet sports or table tennis. **2** handwriting which slants to the left.
adj, adv with the back of the hand turned forward: *a backhand serve in tennis* (*adj*). *to hit a ball backhand* (*adv*).

back·hand·ed (bak′han′did) *adj* **1** backhand. **2** slanting to the left. **3** double-edged; with the intention to ridicule as well as praise: *Praising an author for being good at spelling is a backhanded compliment.*

back·hoe (bak′hō′) *n* a large digging machine with a scoop at the end of a long, jointed arm. See EARTHMOVER for picture.

back·ing (bak′ing) *n* **1** support: *financial backing. The project has the backing of the student council.* **2** material that forms, covers, or reinforces the back of anything: *The backing on this bookcase is plywood.*

back·lash (bak′lash′) *n* a sudden hostile reaction to something that was originally approved or tolerated: *A rise in crime caused a backlash against lighter prison sentences.*

back·light (bak′līt′) *v* **back·lit, back·light·ing** light from behind.

back·log (bak′log′) *n* a number of things waiting to be done or dealt with: *The company hired high-school students to help clear the backlog of orders.*

back order *n* **1** an order for goods not currently in stock, to be filled when new stock comes in. **2** the status of such goods: *Your book is still on back order.* **back′-or′der** *v.*

back·pack (bak′pak′) *n* a light bag with straps for carrying it on your back. Bigger backpacks for hiking and camping are attached to a metal frame for support.
v travel while carrying all one's things in such a pack: *They backpacked through Gros Morne Park last summer.* **back′pack′er** *n.* **back′pack′ing** *n.*

back·ped·al (bak′ped′əl) *v,* **back·ped·alled** or **back·ped·aled, back·ped·al·ling** or **back·ped·al·ing** **1** move the pedals of a bicycle backwards, especially to brake or to change gears. **2** retreat from an earlier opinion, statement, policy, etc.: *The mayor quickly backpedalled from her careless remark.*

back·room (bak′rūm′) *Politics adj* happening or acting away from public view: *backroom policy-makers.*

back seat *n* **1** a seat at or in the back; especially, the rear passenger seat of a car. **2** a place of little power or influence: *She won't take a back seat to anybody.* **back-seat** (bak′sēt′) *adj.*

back–seat driver *n* **1** a passenger in a car who constantly tells the driver what to do. **2** a person who offers criticism or advice without assuming any responsibility.

back·side (bak′sīd′) *n* **1** the back of anything. **2** *Informal* the buttocks.

back·slash (bak′slash′) *especially Computers n* the character \.

back·slide (bak′slīd′) *v* **back·slid, back·slid·ing** go back to doing something wrong. **back′slid′er** *n.*

back·space (bak′spās′) *Computers v* **back·spaced, back·spac·ing** move the cursor backwards one character at a time, in text on a computer screen, using the **backspace key**.

back·spin (bak′spin′) *n* a reverse spin given to a ball, hoop, Frisbee, etc. giving it a shorter curved path or causing it to bounce off a surface at an unexpected angle.

back·stab·ber (bak′stab′ər) *n* a person who secretly betrays a supposed friend or an associate.
back′stab′bing *n, adj.*

back·stage (bak′stāj′) *adv* **1** in the dressing rooms of a theatre; behind the stage. **2** toward the back part of a stage.
adj **1** located or happening behind or toward the back of the stage: *a backstage conversation between actors.* **2** done secretly or privately: *backstage negotiations.*

back·stitch (bak′stich′) *n* a sewing stitch in which the thread doubles back each time on the preceding stitch.
v sew with such stitches.

back·stop (bak′stop′) *n* **1** *Sports* **a** a fence or screen used to keep the ball from going too far away. **b** a player who stops balls that get past another player. **2** a person who or thing that acts as a support.

back·stroke (bak′strōk′) *n* **1** a swimming stroke done with the swimmer on his or her back. **2** a backhand stroke in tennis and other racquet games.

back·swing (bak′swing′) *Golf, Tennis, etc. n* a raising of the club or racquet up and behind the player's hands to give power to a forward stroke.

back·talk (bak′tok′) *n* disrespectful, defiant answers.

back to back *adv* **1** with the backs facing each other: *We placed the chairs back to back.* **2** one after the other: *We watched three videos back to back.* **back′-to-back′** *adj.*

back·track (bak′trak′) *v* **1** go back over one's path: *We took a wrong turn and had to backtrack a few kilometres to reach the highway.* **2** retreat from an earlier statement, policy, or opinion. **3** return to a previous point or topic.

back·up (bak′up′) *n* **1** a person, group, or thing available for support or as a replacement: *If Plan A fails, we have Plan B as a backup.* **2** *Computers* a copy of programs or data, stored separately from the original.
v **back up** See BACK.

back·ward (bak′wərd) *adj* **1** toward the back or toward an earlier time: *a backward look.* **2** made with the back first or with the last part first: *a backward somersault.* **3** slow or behind others in development: *a backward community.* **4** shy or bashful: *Shake hands; don't be backward.*
adv backwards. **back′ward·ness** *n.*

back·wards (bak′wərdz) *adv* **1** toward the back or toward an earlier time: *to look backwards.* **2** with the back or the last part first: *to walk backwards. Count backwards from 100.* **3** opposite to the usual, natural, or logical way: *You're going at the whole thing backwards.* **4** toward the starting point: *The ball stopped and began to roll backwards.* **5** from better to worse: *He says education has gone backwards in this province.*
bend over backwards, *Informal* try extremely hard to help or please someone: *Our camp counsellor bent over backwards to make sure we had fun.*

USAGE

Backwards and **backward** can both be used as adverbs:

She skated backward with ease.

She skated backwards with ease.

Backward can also be used as an adjective, but **backwards** cannot:

He took a backward glance to make sure no one was following him.

back·wash (bak′wosh′) *n* **1** the water thrown back by oars, a passing ship, etc. **2** a backward current of air from something, especially the propellers of an aircraft.

back·wa·ter (bak′wot′ər) *n* **1** a stretch of still water that is held back or is not part of the current: *A backwater formed behind the beaver dam.* **2** a place thought of as slow, dull, or inactive: *Our town is a cultural backwater.*

back·woods (bak′wůdz′) *pl n* forests or thinly settled regions far from population centres.
adj **1** of the backwoods. **2** crude or rough.

back·yard (bak′yärd′) *n* a yard behind a house: *Our neighbour grows vegetables and flowers in her backyard.* Also, **back yard.**
in your own backyard, near or in your neighbourhood: *We have talented people right here in our own backyard.*
not in my backyard, *Informal* an expression of protest against something unwanted coming into one's neighbourhood. *Abbrev.* **NIMBY**

ba·con (bā′kən) *n* salted and smoked meat from the back and sides of a pig. <Old French>
bring home the bacon, *Informal* **a** earn an income. **b** be successful or victorious.

bac·te·ri·a (bak tē′rē ə) *pl n, sing* **bac·te·ri·um** a KINGDOM (def. 3) of one-celled micro-organisms that lack internal structures and an organized nucleus. Bacteria are found in the air, soil, water, and in the bodies of all plants and animals. See also ARCHAEA, MONERA, PROKARYOTE. <Latin, from Greek *bacterion* little stick, from the shape of many kinds of bacteria> **bac·te′ri·al** *adj.*

bac·te·ri·cide (bak tē′rə sīd′) *n* a substance that kills bacteria. <*bacteria* + *-cide*>

bac·te·ri·ol·o·gy (bak tē′rē ol′ə jē) *n* the science that studies bacteria. **bac·te′ri·o·log′i·cal** *adj.*
bac·te′ri·ol′o·gist *n.*

bad (bad) *adj* **worse, worst** **1** of poor quality: *bad writing, a bad cup of coffee.* **2** wrong, evil, or unjust: *bad laws. There are bad people in every society. Cheating is bad.* **3** harmful: *bad air, bad water.* **4** severe; serious: *a bad cold.* **5** rotten or decayed: *a bad egg.* **6** sick: *He felt so bad he had to lie down.* **7** unfavourable or unpleasant: *bad news, a bad mood. You have arrived at a bad time.* **8** worthless: *a bad cheque.* **9** with curses or rude words: *bad language.*
adv **worse, worst** *Informal* **1** sorry: *I feel bad about wrecking your skates.* **2** badly; severely: *My knee hurts bad.* <Middle English *badde*> **bad′ness** *n.*
be bad news, *Slang* be unwelcome or undesirable: *That kid is bad news.*
go bad, a become spoiled or rotten: *We forgot about the leftovers and they went bad.* **b** of a person, develop an immoral character. **c** fail or deteriorate suddenly; end in disaster: *a business deal that went bad.*
my bad, *Slang* my mistake; my fault.
not bad, good or better than expected.
not half bad, *Informal* better than average.
too bad, (*often ironic*) an expression of regret: *Too bad you weren't there.*
to the bad, in debt: *His winter vacation left him several hundred dollars to the bad.*

CONFUSABLES

Bad is an adjective that should be used with a linking verb, which does not express action: *He felt bad that the home team lost the game.* (*Felt* is a linking verb.)

Badly is an adverb that should be used to describe a verb: *She ran the race badly.* (*Ran* is a verb.)

In informal speech, many people use **badly** with a linking verb. To avoid this in formal speech, remember that you feel *mad* or *sad*, not *madly* or *sadly*.

bad blood *n* unfriendly or bitter feeling between people.

bade (bad) *or* (bād) a past tense of BID.

badge (baj) *n* **1** something worn on a person's clothes to show that he or she belongs to a certain occupation, organization, school, etc. **2** a symbol or sign: *He carried his scars as a badge of honour.* <Middle English *bage*>

a bat	e bed	i bid	o pot	u cup	th thin
ā cake	ē me	ī bite	ō go	ū rude	ᴛʜ then
ä bar	ə about	ər over	ô for	ů put	zh measure

badg·er (baj′ər) *n* a burrowing animal of the weasel family with long, coarse, grey fur and long front claws for digging. They are found in Europe, Asia, and N America.
v nag or pester: *He's badgering me to let him stay.* <perhaps *badge*, from the white spot on the animal's head>
badger a witness, *Law* harass a witness in court by persistent, aggressive questioning.

bad·lands (bad′landz′) *pl n* a region of barren land marked by ridges, gullies, and unusual rock formations caused by erosion, as found in southwest Saskatchewan and southeast Alberta: *The skeletons of prehistoric animals have been found in the badlands.*

bad·ly (bad′lē) *adv* **1** in a bad manner: *She sings badly.* **2** greatly: *a badly needed holiday.* See BAD for confusable.

bad·min·ton (bad′min tən) *n* a game for two or four players who use light racquets to hit a shuttlecock back and forth over a high net. <*Badminton* a place in England where this game was first played>

bad·mouth (bad′mouth′) *v* speak ill of: *She's always badmouthing her older sister.*

bad·tem·pered (bad′tem′pərd) *adj* easily angered.

baf·fle (baf′əl) *v* **baf·fled, baf·fling** be too hard for a person to understand or solve: *It baffles me how she can be so friendly one day and so mean the next.*
n a device to redirect the flow of air, water, or sound: *Baffles hung from the cafeteria ceiling keep kitchen smells out of the eating area.* **baf′fle·ment** *n.* **baf′fling** *adj.*

bag (bag) *n* **1** a loose container that can be pulled together or folded over at the top to close it. **2** a purse or suitcase. **3** something shaped like a bag, such as a sagging, swelling, or hollow part: *When I'm tired I get bags under my eyes.* **4** *Baseball* a base.
v **bagged, bag·ging 1** put into a bag or bags: *We bagged the cookies for the bake sale.* **2** sag or bulge: *These pants bag at the knees.* **3** *Informal* manage to capture, win, etc.: *Look at the stuffed lion I bagged at the fall fair!* <Old Norse *baggi* pack> **bag′ful′** *adj.* **bag′like′** *adj.*
bag and baggage, with all one's belongings: *Our house guest seems to have moved in, bag and baggage.*
in the bag, *Informal* sure to be achieved or obtained: *Don't worry, the championship's in the bag.*
leave someone holding the bag, *Informal* leave someone to take all the responsibility alone.

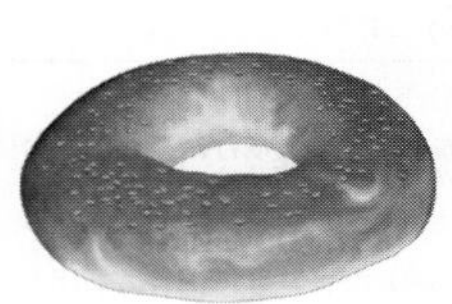

The **bagel,** around since the early 1600s, was introduced to North America by Jewish immigrants from Eastern Europe. It has the distinction of being the only type of bread that is boiled before it is baked, thus creating its distinctive chewy texture.

Both New York City and Montréal, places that welcomed large numbers of European immigrants, claim to have the world's best bagels.

ba·gel (bā′gəl) *n* a firm, doughnut-shaped bread roll. <Yiddish *beigel* ring>

bag·gage (bag′ij) *n* **1** the bags, suitcases, etc. packed with belongings that a person takes when travelling. **2** anything that burdens or hinders, especially harmful or unhelpful beliefs, ideas, or experiences.

bag·gy (bag′ē) *adj* **bag·gi·er, bag·gi·est** hanging loosely; baglike: *baggy pants.*

bag lady *n* a homeless woman who carries her belongings in shopping bags.

bag·pipes (bag′pīps′) *pl n* a musical wind instrument consisting of a bag with wooden pipes, played by applying pressure to the bag while blowing air in through a pipe and closing holes on another pipe with the fingers. **bag′pip′er** *n.*

ba·guette (ba get′) *n* a long, narrow loaf of bread. See CROISSANT for picture. <French, from Italian *bachetta* small stick>

bah (bä) *interj* an exclamation of scorn or contempt.

Ba·hai (bə hī′) *n* **1** a religion based on the teachings of **Bahaullah** (ba hä′ůl′a), that all people are united under God regardless of religion. **2** a follower of this religion.
adj to do with this religion or its followers.
Ba·ha′ism (bə hī′iz əm) *or* (bə hä′iz əm) *n.*

Ba·ha·mas (bə hä′məz) *pl n* a country of many small islands off the east Florida coast. See the APPENDIX. **Ba·ha′mi·an** (bə hā′mē ən) *or* (bə hä′mē ən) *adj, n.*

Bah·rain (bä rān′) *n* a country of several islands in the Persian Gulf. **Bah·rai′ni** *adj, n.*

bail[1] (bāl) *n* money paid as a security to release an arrested person until he or she is to appear in court: *Bail was set by the judge at $5000.* <French *baillier* hand over, give custody to>
bail out, a pay bail: *He bailed his son out of jail.* **b** help out of a difficulty: *I can't finish my report in time, and I hope that you can bail me out somehow.*
go (or **stand**) **bail for,** pay bail for someone.
jump bail, fail to appear at one's trial after being released on bail.

bail[2] (bāl) *v* scoop water out of the bottom of a boat.
n a container used for scooping water out of a boat. <Old French *baille* bucket>
bail out, a drop from an airplane by parachute: *When the plane caught fire, the pilot bailed out.* **b** scoop water out of a boat. **c** leave a place or situation as quickly as one can: *We need your help, so don't bail out now!*

bail·iff (bā′lif) *n* **1** any of various officials in a law court. **2** a creditor's agent who seizes goods in place of payment. <Old French *baillif*>

bail·i·wick (bā′lə wik′) *n* a person's field of knowledge, work, or authority. <Middle English *bailie* an official + *wick* village, i.e., area of authority>

bail·out (bāl′out′) *n* financial help given by a government to a business to keep it from going bankrupt.

Bai·ram (bī räm′) *Islam n* either of two annual festivals, the **lesser Bairam**, following immediately after Ramadan, or the **greater Bairam**, at the end of the Muslim year. <Turkish>

Bai·sak·hi or **Vai·sak·hi** (bī sä′kē) *or* (vī sä′kē) *Sikhism n* a harvest festival held April 13, the first day of the Hindu New Year. <Sanskrit *Baisakh*, the name of a month>

B

bait (bāt) *n* **1** food used to attract fish or other animals in order to catch them: *Worms are often used as bait in fishing.* **2** anything used to attract or to get a reaction: *They used a job ad in the paper as bait to get him to phone.* *v* **1** put bait on or in: *to bait a trap.* **2** tempt or attract. **3** try to get a reaction from someone by making annoying remarks, etc.: *Don't get angry, they're just baiting you.* **4** set dogs to attack or torment (a chained animal) for sport: *People used to bait bulls and bears, but it is illegal now.* <Old Norse *beita* cause to bite and *beita* food>

bake (bāk) *v* **baked, bak·ing 1** cook by dry heat in an oven: *to bake bread.* **2** dry or harden by heat: *to bake bricks or china.* **3** make or become very warm: *I'm going to lie in the sun and bake.* <Old English *bacan*>

🍁 **bake·ap·ple** (bāk′ap′əl) *especially Atlantic Provinces n* a creeping plant that grows in swampy areas, with amber-coloured, edible berries.

bak·er (bā′kər) *n* **1** a person who makes or sells bread, pies, cakes, etc. **2** a small portable oven.

baker's dozen *n* thirteen.

bak·er·y (bā′kə rē) *n, pl* **bak·er·ies** a baker's shop; a place where bread, pies, cakes, etc. are made or sold. Also called **bakeshop**.

bake sale *n* a sale of homemade cakes, pies, etc., to raise money.

baking powder *n* a white powdered mixture of baking soda, starch, and an acid compound such as cream of tartar, put in to make cakes rise.

baking soda SODIUM BICARBONATE.

bak·la·va (bȧ′klə və) *or* (bȧ′klə vȧ′) *n* a flaky Greek pastry made with nuts and honey. <Turkish>

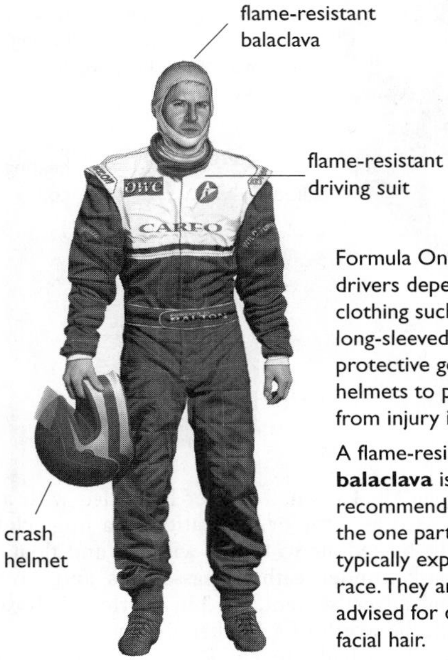

flame-resistant balaclava

flame-resistant driving suit

crash helmet

Formula One racing drivers depend on clothing such as long-sleeved tops, protective goggles, and helmets to protect them from injury in accidents.

A flame-resistant **balaclava** is also recommended to protect the one part of the body typically exposed during a race. They are especially advised for drivers with facial hair.

bal·a·cla·va (bal′ə klȧ′və) *n* a knitted cap covering most of the head and neck. <*Balaklava*, a battle site in the Crimean War where soldiers first wore such caps>

bal·ance (bal′əns) *n* **1** steadiness: *He lost his balance and fell off the ladder.* **2** a condition in which different things are the same in amount or importance: *a healthy balance of work and play.* **3** anything that counteracts the effect, weight, etc. of something else: *His humour serves as a balance to his strictness.* **4 a** remainder: *I'll be away for the balance of the week.* **b** the amount of money left in an account after all withdrawals: *He had a bank balance of $50.* **5** a weighing device consisting of a horizontal bar suspended by its centre, with a shallow pan hanging from each end.

v **bal·anced, bal·anc·ing 1** keep or put in a steady condition or position: *Can you balance a loonie on its edge?* **2** give equal importance to two or more things: *to balance schoolwork, hobbies, and social life.* **3** (*sometimes with* ***out***) have an equal effect: *Her generosity balances his selfishness.* **4** weigh or compare: *She balanced a trip to the Rockies against missing the soccer season.* <Old French, from Latin *bilanx* having two scale pans> **bal′anced** *adj.* **bal′anc·er** *n.*

balance out, be equal.

in the balance, undecided: *The outcome was in the balance until the last moment.*

off balance, a unsteady: *I was off balance and couldn't catch the ball.* **b** surprised or confused: *Her question caught me off balance.*

on balance, after considering all the facts: *On balance, I think it was a pretty good weekend.*

balance beam *n* a long, narrow piece of wood set up at some height from the floor, on which gymnasts perform exercises.

balance of nature *n* the stable state in which natural communities of animals and plants exist.

balance of power *n* **1** an even distribution of military and economic power among nations. **2** the power of a small group to give control to a larger group by joining forces with it.

balance of trade *n* the difference in value between a country's imports and its exports.

balance sheet *n* a written statement showing the profits and losses, assets and debts, and what a business is worth.

bal·co·ny (bal′kə nē) *n, pl* **bal·co·nies 1** an outside platform on the wall of a building, with an entrance from an upper floor. **2** in a theatre or hall, an overhanging level of seats above the main seating area. <Italian *balcone,* from *balco* scaffold> **bal′co·nied** *adj.*

bald (bold) *adj* **1** without hair on the head. Also called **baldheaded**. **2** bare: *a bald mountaintop, the bald prairie.* **3** plain: *The bald truth can be hard to take.* **4** with white on the head, found in some birds or mammals. <Middle English *balled* from *ball* white spot> **bald′ly** *adv.* **bald′ness** *n.*

a bat	e bed	i bid	o pot	u cup	th **thin**
ā cake	ē me	ī bite	ō go	ū rude	ᴛʜ **then**
ȧ bar	ə about	ər over	ȯ for	ů put	zh measure

bald eagle *n* a large, powerful, fish-eating eagle of N America, with dark brown feathers on the body and white feathers on the head, neck, and tail.

bal·der·dash (bol′dər dash′) *n* nonsense. <perhaps from 16c slang for a frothy mixture>

bald·ing (bol′ding) *adj* partly bald.

bald·pate (bold′pāt′) *n* **1** a wild duck found in western N America, the male of which has a white patch on the forehead and crown. **2** a bald person.

bale (bāl) *n* a large, tightly tied bundle of hay, straw, cotton, paper, used clothing, scrap metal, etc.
v **baled, bal·ing** make into bales: *to bale hay.* <Middle English> **bal′er** *n.*

ba·leen (bā lēn′) *n* in some whales, a tough, elastic substance that grows in large fringes from the roof of the mouth. It allows the whale to strain plankton as food from water it takes in. <Old French *baleine,* from Greek *phalaina* whale>

bale·ful (bāl′fəl) *adj* expressing hatred, anger, or a wish to harm someone: *a baleful glance.* <Old English *bealu* evil, harm> **bale′ful·ly** *adv.* **bale′ful·ness** *n.*

balk (bok) *or* (bolk) *v* **1** (*usually with* **at**) refuse to accept or do something; reject: *My horse balked at the third jump. The workers balked at the management's offer.* **2** *Baseball* cause a runner to advance one base because the pitcher has made an illegal motion. <Middle English *balkan* make ridges, i.e., obstacles> **bal′ky** *adj.*

bal·kan·ize (bol′kə nīz′) *v* **bal·kan·ized, bal·kan·iz·ing** divide a country or region into small independent units hostile to one another. <from political divisions in the *Balkan* Peninsula in Europe after World War I>

ball[1] (bol) *n* **1** a round or oval object that is thrown, kicked, bounced, etc. in a game. **2** a game in which you use a ball, especially baseball or softball. **3** anything round or roundish like a ball: *the ball of your thumb, a ball of string.* **4** *Baseball* a ball pitched too high, too low, or not over the plate, and which the batter does not swing at. **5** a ball thrown a certain way: *a curve ball.*
v form into a ball: *He balled his fists.* <Old Norse *böllr*>
get (or **keep**) **the ball rolling,** *Informal* get an activity started (or keep it going).
on the ball, alert, smart, or efficient.
play ball, a begin or resume a ballgame. **b** get started. **c** co-operate: *If everyone will play ball, we can succeed.*
the whole ball of wax, *Informal* everything.

ball[2] (bol) *n* **1** a large, formal party with dancing. **2** *Informal* a lot of fun: *We had a ball at camp!* <Old French *bal,* from Latin *ballare* to dance>

bal·lad (bal′əd) *n* **1** a simple poem that tells a story, often put to music. *The Wreck of the Edmund Fitzgerald* is a Canadian ballad by Gordon Lightfoot. **2** a pop song with a slow, gentle beat and sentimental lyrics. <Old French *balade* dancing song> **bal′lad·eer′** *n.*

ball–and–socket joint (bol′ən sok′ət) *n* a flexible joint formed by a ball fitting in a socket, such as the hip joint.

bal·last (bal′əst) *n* **1** something heavy carried in a ship to steady it, or in a BALLOON (def. 2) to control how high it rises. **2** anything that steadies a person or thing. **3** the gravel or crushed rock used in making the bed for a road or railway track. <Old Norse>

ball bearing *n* **1** a ring that has a groove around the inside with small metal balls rolling around in it, so that a rod passed through the ring can turn easily. **2** one of the small metal balls.

bal·le·ri·na (bal′ə rē′nə) *n* a female ballet dancer.

bal·let (bal ā′) *n* **1** an artistic dance that usually tells a story or expresses a mood, performed on stage by one or more dancers. **2** the art of creating or performing ballets: *He is studying ballet.* **3** a company of dancers that performs ballets. **4** ACRO. <French, from Latin *ballare* to dance>

ball·game (bol′gām′) *n* any game in which a ball is used, especially a baseball game.
a whole new ballgame, *Informal* a new or different situation.

ball hockey *n* HOCKEY played on a rink without ice or on pavement, with a ball instead of a puck.

🍁 **bal·li·cat·ter** (ba li ka′tər) *Newfoundland n* a ridge of ice formed along a shoreline by waves and freezing spray. <alteration of *barricade*>

bal·lis·tic (bə lis′tik) *adj* to do with the motion of any object that is thrown, launched, or shot.
n **ballistics** (*with singular verb*) the science that deals with this. <Latin, from Greek *ballein* throw>
go ballistic, *Slang* become extremely angry or excited.

ballistic missile *n* a missile that reaches its target as a result of aim at the time of launching, not by any homing device inside it.

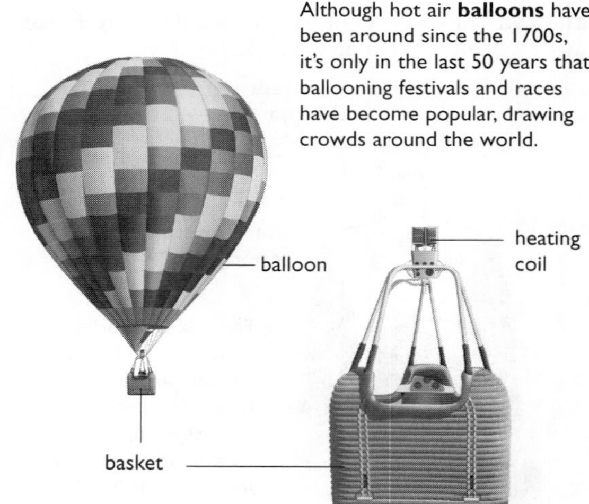

Although hot air **balloons** have been around since the 1700s, it's only in the last 50 years that ballooning festivals and races have become popular, drawing crowds around the world.

bal·loon (bə lūn′) *n* **1** a small rubber bag filled with air, helium, etc., used as a toy or decoration. **2** a huge cloth bag filled with heated air so that it will rise and float. It may have a basket underneath for passengers, and can be used as a signal, advertisement, etc. **3** in a cartoon, a boxed space in which the words of a speaker are written.
v **1** swell out like a balloon: *His jacket ballooned in the wind.* **2** travel by hot-air balloon.
adj puffed out like a balloon: *balloon sleeves.* <Italian *ballone,* from *balla* ball> **bal·loon′ist** *n.*
bal·loon′like′ *adj.*

bal·lot (bal′ət) *n* **1** a piece of paper for writing down or checking off one's vote. **2** a voting procedure using ballots for secrecy: *The question was decided by ballot.* **3** the list of candidates in an election: *He was too late to get on the ballot.* **4** the total number of votes cast.
v vote using a ballot or ballots.

ETYMOLOGY

Ballot comes from the Italian word *ballotta*, meaning "little round object." In medieval Venice, small white or black balls were placed into a box or urn to cast a vote.

The English shortened *ballotta* to *ballot*. The word came to mean any object—such as a ball, ticket, or piece of paper—used in casting a secret vote.

ballot box *n* the box into which voters put their ballots.

ball·park (bol′pärk′) *n* a park or stadium for playing baseball.
ballpark figure, a rough estimate.
in the ballpark, a reasonably close as an estimate or guess. **b** meeting minimum requirements.

ball·point (bol′point′) *n* in full, **ballpoint pen** a pen whose writing point is a small metal ball. The movement and pressure of writing make the ball turn against a cartridge of thick ink. See QUILL for picture.

ball·room (bol′rūm′) *n* a large room for dancing.

ballroom dancing *n* formal dancing in couples, with waltzes, tangos, etc.

bal·ly·hoo (bal′ē hū′) *n* **1** sensational advertising; hype. **2** an uproar or outcry. <origin uncertain>

balm (bom) *or* (bäm) *n* **1** a fragrant, oily resin obtained from some trees, used to heal or to lessen pain. **2** anything that heals or soothes: *My mother's praise was a balm to my hurt feelings.* **3** a fragrant plant of the same family as mint: *lemon balm.* <Old French *basme* balsam>

balm·y (bom′ē) *or* (bä′mē) *adj* **balm·i·er, balm·i·est** **1** mild, soft, or gentle: *a balmy breeze.* **2** barmy. **balm′i·ness** *n.*

ba·lo·ney (bə lō′nē) *Informal n* **1** nonsense: *That's a lot of baloney.* **2** BOLOGNA. <altered from *bologna*>

bal·sa (bol′sə) *n* a tropical American tree with very lightweight wood. <Spanish = raft. This light wood was often used to make rafts.>

bal·sam (bol′səm) *n* **1** a fragrant, oily substance obtained from some trees and shrubs, and used in cough syrups, perfumes, varnishes, etc. **2** in full, **balsam fir** an evergreen yielding this substance and found throughout eastern Canada and parts of the Prairies. **3** any other tree and shrub yielding fragrant resins. <Latin, from Greek *balsamon*>

bal·sam·ic vinegar (bol sam′ik) *n* an aged red-wine vinegar with a sweet taste.

Bal·tic (bol′tik) *adj* to do with the **Baltic Sea** in NE Europe, the countries near it (**Baltic States**), or any of their languages, such as Latvian or Estonian.

bam·boo (bam bū′) *n* a treelike tropical grass with stiff, hollow, woody stems that have hard, thick joints. Mature stems are used to make fishing rods, furniture, etc. and the young shoots are used as food. <Dutch *bamboes*, probably from Malay>

bam·boo·zle (bam bū′zəl) *Informal v* **bam·boo·zled, bam·boo·zling** **1** cheat or trick. **2** baffle or perplex. <origin uncertain> **bam·boo′zle·ment** *n.*

ban (ban) *v* **ban·ned, ban·ning** make a rule or law against something: *Smoking is banned on buses.*
n **1** a rule or law that forbids something: *There is a ban on parking in this street.* **2** *Christianity* a solemn condemnation. **3** a condition of being banished or declared an outlaw. <Old English *bannan* announce, proclaim>

ba·nal (bə nal′) *adj* commonplace; trite or trivial: *She made some banal remarks about the weather before coming to the point.* <Old French> **ba·nal′i·ty** *n.*

ba·nan·a (bə nan′ə) *n* the long, slightly curved fruit that grows in bunches on a treelike tropical plant. Bananas have thick, easily peeled yellow skin and creamy flesh.
adj **bananas** *Slang* crazy: *That noise is driving me bananas!* <Portuguese or Spanish>

banana split *n* a dessert consisting of a banana cut lengthwise so as to flank two or three scoops of ice cream in a row, topped with a sauce, fruit, nuts, etc.

band[1] (band) *n* **1 a** a group travelling or working together: *a band of robbers.* **b** a small group playing some combination of musical instruments: *He plays bass guitar in a rock band.* Compare ORCHESTRA. **c** a group of animals: *a band of muskox.* **2** 🍁 a group of First Nations people living on a reserve and officially recognized as a unit by the government. A single First Nation may be divided into many bands. <Old French *bande*>
band together, form a group: *The students banded together to buy a present for the teacher.*

band[2] (band) *n* **1** a relatively thin, flat strip: *a narrow band of lace, a band of forest at the edge of the property.* **2** a loop or ring of material used to secure something: *I put an elastic band around the rolled-up newspaper.* **3** a stripe: *a blue rug with bands of grey.* **4** a particular range of wavelengths of sound or light. **5** a plain finger ring: *a wedding band.*
v put a band on; mark with a band: *black wings banded with red. Scientists band birds' legs in order to identify them later.* <Middle English>

band·age (ban′dij) *n* a strip of cloth or other material to bind or cover a wound or injury.
v **band·aged, band·ag·ing** put a bandage on. <French>

band·aid (ban′dād′) *n* a quick, short-term solution, not dealing with an underlying problem: *A three-day suspension for bullying is only a bandaid.*
adj short-term and not addressing the real problem: *bandaid solutions.* <*Band-Aid*, a trademark for a small sticky bandage for minor wounds>

a bat	e bed	i bid	o pot	u cup	th **thin**
ā cake	ē me	ī bite	ō go	ū rude	ᴛʜ **then**
ä bar	ə about	ər over	ȯ for	u̇ put	zh measure

ban·dan·a or **ban·dan·na** (ban dan′ə) *n* a large, coloured handkerchief. <Hindi *bandhnu* to tie cloth for tie-dyeing>

B & B *Informal* bed and breakfast.

🍁 **band council** *n* the elected leaders of a First Nations band. **band councillor** *n.*

ban·di·coot (ban′də küt′) *n* in full, **bandicoot rat** a large rat of southeast Asia. <Telugu (a language of India) *pandikokku* pig-rat>

ban·dit (ban′dit) *n, pl* **ban·dits** or **ban·dit·ti** (ban dit′ē) a robber, especially a member of an armed gang. <Italian *bandito* = a banished man>

band·shell (band′shel′) *n* a platform for concerts with a shell-shaped rear wall to act as both a roof and a SOUNDING BOARD (def. 3).

band·stand (band′stand′) *n* an outdoor platform, usually roofed, for concerts.

B & W black and white.

band·wag·on (band′wag′ən) *n* a wagon that carries a musical band in a parade.
jump (or **climb**, or **get**) **on the bandwagon,** join what appears to be the winning or popular side in a political campaign, contest, public issue, etc.

band·width (band′width′) *n* **1** in telecommunications and radio, the range of frequencies needed to send or receive a certain signal. **2** *Computers* the rate at which digital information can flow over a hardware device or Internet channel, usually measured in megabytes per second.

ban·dy (ban′dē) *v* **ban·died, ban·dy·ing** toss casually back and forth: *to bandy words with someone. We bandied around some possible names for our cat.* <French *bander*>

bane (bān) *n* a source of great annoyance or irritation: *Noise through the wall was the bane of her existence.* <Old English *bana*, related to Old Norse *bani* death>

bang (bang) *n* **1** a sudden loud noise: *Don't pop balloons; the bang scares the dog.* **2** a violent, noisy blow: *Give the drum a good bang.* **3** *Slang* thrill or amusement: *They really got a bang out of the incident.*
v hit, close, etc. with a sudden, loud noise: *The baby was banging the pan with a spoon. The door banged shut.*
adv Informal **1** violently and noisily: *The car went bang into the tree.* **2** precisely: *The assembly began bang at ten.* <imitative>
bang around or **bang up,** damage by rough handling.
bang on, *Informal* exactly correct or on target: *Your answer is bang on.*
(**more**) **bang for your buck,** *Informal* (greater) good value for the effort, time, or money spent: *Posters are fine, but a TV ad will give you more bang for your buck.*
with a bang, with a burst of energy or excitement.

Bang·la·desh (bung′lə desh) *or* (bang′glə desh′) *n* a country in S Asia, forming part of the Indian subcontinent. It was formerly called East Pakistan. See the APPENDIX. **Bang′la·desh′i** *adj, n.*

ban·gle (bang′gəl) *n* a rigid bracelet, especially a shiny one. <Hindi *bangli* glass bracelet>

bangs (bangz) *pln* a fringe of hair on the forehead. <*bangtail* racehorse with cropped tail>

bang–up (bang′up) *Informal adj* first-rate; excellent: *You've done a bang-up job.*

ban·ish (ban′ish) *v* **1** send away, especially as a punishment: *She was banished from the game for cheating.* **2** get rid of: *Sunshine will banish the blues.* <Old French *banir*, from Latin *bannire* ban> **ban′ish·ment** *n.*

ban·is·ter (ban′i stər) *n* the handrail of a staircase together with its row of supports. Also, **bannister**. <French *balustre*>

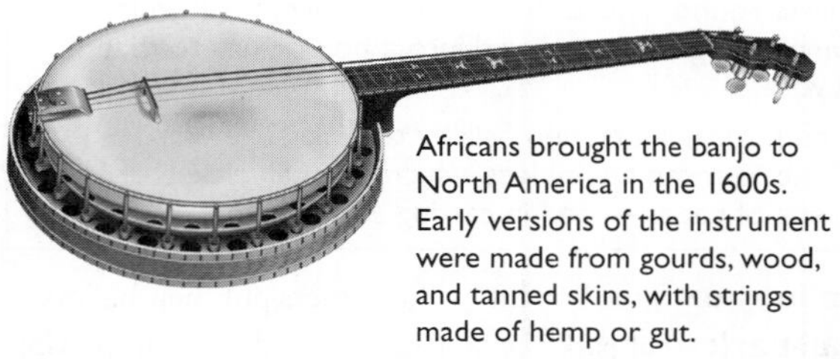

Africans brought the banjo to North America in the 1600s. Early versions of the instrument were made from gourds, wood, and tanned skins, with strings made of hemp or gut.

ban·jo (ban′jō) *n, pl* **ban·jos** or **ban·joes** a stringed musical instrument played with the fingers or a pick. <Spanish *bandore*> **ban′jo·ist** *n.*

bank[1] (bangk) *n* **1** a long pile or heap: *There was a bank of snow over a metre deep.* **2** the ground beside a river. **3** a shallow place in otherwise deep water. The Grand Banks are shallow places in the Atlantic off Newfoundland.
v **1** pile up; heap up: *The plows banked the snow by the side of the road. Clouds are banking on the horizon.* **2** tilt when turning: *The airplane banked as it turned south.* **3** cover a fire with ashes or with fresh fuel so it will burn slowly. **4** *Sports* hit a ball or puck so that it bounces off something. <Old Norse>

bank[2] (bangk) *n* **1** a business in which people save or borrow money. **2** a small container, often shaped like a pig or other object, for saving small sums of money. **3** a supply of anything, to be used as needed: *a blood bank, a food bank, a data bank, a word bank.*
v **1** do business at a bank: *My aunt banks at the branch near her office.* **2** put in a bank: *He banked most of the profits from his paper route.* <Italian *banca* bench, money changers' table> **bank′ing** *n.*
bank on, depend on: *I can bank on my brother's help.*

bank[3] (bangk) *n* a row or close arrangement: *a bank of machines, a bank of keys on a keyboard.*
v arrange in rows. <Old French, from Latin *bancus* bench>

🍁 **bank barn** *especially Ontario n* a two-storey barn built into a hill so the bottom level can be entered from one side and the top level from the other side.

bank·book (bangk′bük) PASSBOOK.

bank card *n* a card with a magnetic strip, issued by a bank as identification and allowing the holder to withdraw or put money into a bank or ATM.

bank·er[1] (bang′kər) *n* **1** a bank manager. **2** *Gambling* the dealer or player in charge of holding money used to place bets. <*bank*[2]> **bank′ing** *n.*

🍁 **bank·er**[2] (bang′kər) *Newfoundland n* a person who fishes off the Grand Banks, or the boat that he or she uses. <*bank*[1]>

bank machine ATM.

bank·note (bangk′nōt′) *n* a piece of paper money; a bill.

🍁 **Bank of Canada** *n* the agent of the Government of Canada that issues all Canadian banknotes and carries out policy for the government about how money is available for use. It also sets the **bank rate**, the minimum interest rate for short-term loans to banks.

bank·roll (bangk′rōl′) *n* the amount of money a person has available.
v supply the money: *A group of businesses bankrolled the theatre festival.*

bank·rupt (bangk′rupt) *adj* **1** legally declared as unable to pay one's debts. **2** having used up or spent all one's resources. **3** completely lacking in something: *morally bankrupt, bankrupt of new ideas.*
v use up all the resources: *That last business deal bankrupted them.*
n a bankrupt person. **bank′rupt·cy** (bangk′rəp sē) *n.*

ETYMOLOGY

Bankrupt comes from the Italian word *bancarotta*, which means "bank" + "broken."

The word in its current sense first came into use in English in the mid 1500s.

ban·ner (ban′ər) *n* **1** a flag. **2** a large piece of cloth, paper, or plastic with a design or words on it, used as a decoration or sign. **3** a newspaper headline in large type, usually extending across the entire width of a page. **4** *Computers* an advertisement on a web page, usually in the form of a horizontal rectangle.
adj outstanding: *a banner year in sports.* <Old French *baniere*>

ban·nis·ter (ban′i stər) BANISTER.

ban·nock (ban′ək) *n* **1** a flat, yeastless cake, made from oatmeal or barley flour and baked or fried. **2** 🍁 a similar cake made with wheat flour and sometimes baking powder, often cooked over an open fire on the end of a stick. <Old English *bannuc*, perhaps from Latin *panis* bread>

banns (banz) *pl n* a public notice, given in a Christian church, that two people are to be married. <Old French>

ban·quet (bang′kwit) *n* **1** a formal dinner, often with speeches. **2** any feast. <Old French>

ban·shee (ban′shē) *n* a spirit whose wails are supposed to be a death omen. <Irish *bean sidhe* woman of the fairies>

ban·tam (ban′təm) *n* **1** a breed of small chicken raised mainly as a hobby for its colourful feathers. **2** 🍁 *Sports* **a** a class for players under 15 years. **b** a member of this class: *This is his last year as a bantam in hockey.* **c** usually, **bantamweight** a boxer who weighs between 52 and 54 kilograms. **3** a small person who is fond of fighting.
adj small and light. <probably *Bantam*, a village in Java where the bird originated>

ban·ter (ban′tər) *n* playful conversation full of jokes and teasing: *I didn't mind their friendly banter about my freckles.*
v talk in a playful, teasing way. <origin unknown>

Ban·tu (ban′tū) *n, pl* **Ban·tu** or **Ban·tus** **1** a member of a group of peoples of central and southern Africa whose cultures are different but whose languages are related. **2** the group of African languages spoken by them, including Swahili, Zulu, and Kikuyu.
adj to do with any of these peoples or their languages.

ban·yan (ban′yən) *n* a tree of India and southeast Asia whose branches have hanging roots that grow down to the ground and start new trunks. <Sanskrit>

ba·o·bab (bā′ō bab′) *n* a tall, tropical African tree with a very thick trunk. <origin uncertain>

bap·tism (bap′tiz əm) *Christianity n* the ceremony of baptizing a person as a sign of welcoming him or her into a community of believers. <See BAPTIZE.> **bap·tis′mal** *adj.*
baptism of fire, a the first time a soldier is in active combat. **b** any severe trial or test; an ordeal.

Bap·tist (bap′tiz əm) *Christianity adj* to do with a church which advocates a baptism of total immersion.
n a member or follower of a church.

bap·tize (bap′ tīz) *or* (bap tīz′) *v* **bap·tized, bap·tiz·ing** **1** *Christianity* **a** dip into water or sprinkle with water as a sign of admission into the community of believing Christians. **b** give a first name to a person at baptism; christen: *He was baptized Jean-Pierre.* **2** purify or cleanse. <Old French *baptiser*, from Greek *baptein* dip>

bar[1] (bȧr) *n* **1** an evenly shaped, solid piece of something, longer than it is wide: *a bar of soap.* **2** a rod or rail, often one of a series that form a structure: *Don't stick things through the bars of the hamster's cage.* **3** anything that blocks the way or prevents progress; a barrier. **4** a band of colour; a stripe. **5** *Music* a unit of rhythm whose beginning and end is indicated on a staff by a vertical **bar line**: *The regular accent falls on the first note of each bar.* **6** a place where alcoholic drinks are served at a counter, or the counter itself. **7** any place where a specific kind of item is sold, usually with quick service: *a snack bar.* **8 the bar** the profession of lawyers; lawyers as a group. **9** a law court, or anything like a law court: *the bar of public opinion.* **10** in former times, the mouth of a harbour.
v **barred, bar·ring** **1** fasten or shut off with a bar or bars: *He bars the door every night.* **2** block or obstruct: *The exits were barred by chairs.* **3** forbid or exclude: *All talking is barred during study period. He was barred from the Olympics because he used steroids.* **4** mark with stripes: *barred feathers.* <Old French *barre*> **barred** *adj.*
bar none, nothing and no one excepted: *She is the best guitarist I know, bar none.*

bar[2] (bȧr) *n* a unit of pressure, equal to 100 kilopascals. *Symbol* **bar**

🍁 **bar·a·chois** (ba′ rə shwo′) *Atlantic Provinces n* a shallow coastal pond created behind a sandbar that has formed near a beach. <Cdn French>

barb (bȧrb) *n* **1** a point on an arrow, fishhook, etc. projecting back from the main point. **2** one of the hairlike branches on the shaft of a bird's feather. **3** a cutting or sarcastic remark. <Old French *barbe* point, from Latin *barba* beard> **barbed** *adj.*

a bat	e bed	i bid	o pot	u cup	th **thin**
ā cake	ē me	ī bite	ō go	ū rude	ᴛʜ **then**
ȧ bar	ə about	ər over	ȯ for	u̇ put	zh measure

Bar·ba·dos (bȧr bā′dōs) *n* an island country in the Caribbean. See the APPENDIX. **Bar·ba′di·an** *adj, n.*

bar·bar·i·an (bȧr ber′ē ən) *n* **1** a person belonging to a people thought to be uncivilized: *The Roman Empire was invaded by barbarians.* **2** in ancient and medieval times, any foreigner. **3** a person who cares nothing for beauty or the arts, or whose manners are crude.
adj to do with any of these kinds of people. <French, from Greek *barbaros* foreign>

SYNONYMS

Barbarian as an adjective is a general term and simply means "to do with barbarians."

Barbaric emphasizes crudeness: *His barbaric behaviour in class earned him a detention.*

Barbarous has a more negative connotation, and suggests cruelty: *She was arrested for her barbarous treatment of animals.*

bar·bar·ic (bȧr ber′ik) *adj* cruel or violent: *a barbaric act of terrorism.*

bar·ba·rism (bȧr′bə riz′əm) *n* **1** the condition or fact of being barbarian. **2** an act, custom, or expression thought of as crude or uneducated: *It's a very poorly written article full of all kinds of barbarisms.*

bar·bar·i·ty (bȧr ber′ə tē) *n, pl* **bar·bar·i·ties** brutal cruelty, or an act of such cruelty.

bar·ba·rous (bȧr′bə rəs) *adj* **1** not civilized or refined; primitive, rough, or crude in culture and customs. **2** cruelly harsh: *barbarous treatment.* **bar′ba·rous·ly** *adv.* **bar′ba·rous·ness** *n.*

Bar·ba·ry ape (bȧr′bə rē) *n* a tailless monkey of N Africa. <former name of this region, from *Berber*>

bar·be·cue (bȧr′bi kyū′) *n* **1** a grill or open fireplace for cooking food over coals or over an open flame. **2** a meal prepared on a barbecue, especially one prepared and eaten outdoors. **3** the flavour of the spicy sauce typically used in this style of cooking, often imitated in other foods: *barbecue chips.* **4 a** meat or a whole animal roasted over an open fire. **b** a feast at which such meat is eaten.
v **bar·be·cued, bar·be·cu·ing 1** cook over coals or an open fire. **2** cook in a spicy sauce. <American Spanish>

barbed wire *n* twisted wire with sharp points on it at short intervals, used for fences, etc.

bar·bel (bȧr′bəl) *n* a long, thin, whiskerlike growth hanging from the mouths of some fish, such as the Atlantic cod. <Old French, from Latin *barba* beard>

bar·bell (bȧr′bel′) *n* a long bar with weights at each end, used for lifting exercises.

bar·ber (bȧr′bər) *n* a person who cuts hair and shaves or trims beards for pay. <Old French, from Latin *barba* beard>

bar·ber·shop (bȧr′bər shop′) *n* a barber's place of business.
adj to do with or resembling a **barbershop quartet**, a quartet that sings popular sentimental songs in close harmony.

bar·bit·u·rate (bȧr bich′ə rit) *or* (bȧr bich′ə rāt′) *n* a drug derived from **barbituric acid**, and used as a sedative or hypnotic.

barb·wire (bȧrb′wīr′) *n* barbed wire.

bar code *n* a set of short vertical lines printed on an item by machine and readable by a computer. Bar codes are used on merchandise to encode the price and inventory number, as well as on mail for routing purposes.

bard (bȧrd) *n* **1** a poet and singer of long ago, especially in Celtic, Norse, and other northern cultures. Bards sang their own poems to music. **2** any poet. <Gaelic = poet>
Bard of Avon, Shakespeare, who came from Stratford-on-Avon in England.

bare (ber) *adj* **bar·er, bar·est 1** without covering or clothes: *bare feet, bare patches on the lawn.* **2** not disguised, and with nothing added: *the bare truth, bare facts.* **3** not furnished: *The room was bare.* **4** just enough and no more: *She earns a bare living as a hairdresser.*
v **bared, bar·ing** uncover: *to bare your feelings. The dog bared its teeth.* <Old English *bær*> **bare′ness** *n.*
lay bare, expose: *Their plot was laid bare.*
with your bare hands, without tools or weapons.

bare·back (ber′bak′) *adv, adj* without a saddle: *to ride bareback (adv), a bareback rider (adj).*

bare·bones (ber′bōnz′) *adj* basic, and with no extras: *She gave a barebones outline of her essay.*

bare·faced (ber′fāst′) *adj* **1** bold and shameless: *a barefaced lie.* **2** forthright and open. **3** with no covering for the face.

bare·foot (ber′fu̇t′) *adj, adv* without shoes or socks on: *a barefoot child (adj). If you go barefoot, watch out for broken glass (adv).*

bare·hand·ed (ber′han′did) *adj, adv* **1** without tools or weapons: *a barehanded attempt to climb a mountain (adj). He fought the lion barehanded (adv).* **2** wearing nothing on the hands.

bare·head·ed (ber′hed′id) *adj, adv* wearing nothing on the head.

bare·leg·ged (ber′leg′id) *or* (ber′legd′) *adj, adv* without stockings or long pants.

bare·ly (ber′lē) *adv* **1** by only a little: *He eats barely enough to survive.* **2** poorly or scantily: *The room was furnished barely but neatly.*

bar·gain (bȧr′gən) *n* **1** any agreement to trade or exchange: *We made a bargain: she pays for the movie and I pay for the popcorn.* **2** something offered at a low price, or any other agreement in which one gets good terms: *At half price, those shoes are a real bargain. Two days off in return for a few hours overtime is a bargain!*

v **1** negotiate: *She bargained for a lower price.* **2** (*often with* ***away***) give up in exchange for something else: *He bargained away his free time in order to take an after-school job.* See BARTER for confusable. <Old French *bargaigne*>
bargain for (or **on**)**,** be ready for and expect: *The rain wasn't so bad, but the hail was more than we bargained for.*
into the bargain, besides; also: *I've got a bad cold, and a backache into the bargain.*

barge (bárj) *n* **1** a large, flat-bottomed boat for carrying freight on rivers, canals, etc.: *a grain barge.* **2** a large boat furnished and decorated for use in excursions, pageants, and other special occasions.
v **barged, barg·ing 1** carry something by a barge. **2** move heavily or clumsily: *barging around, knocking things over.* **3** enter rudely or abruptly: *Everyone turned as she barged into the room.* <Old French, from Greek *baris* boat used on the Nile>
barge in, intrude: *Don't barge in where you're not wanted.*

bar graph *Mathematics n* a chart using bars of different lengths to represent different amounts for comparison.

bar·i·tone (ber′ə tōn′) *n* **1** a male singing voice with a range between TENOR and BASS[1], or a singer with such a range. **2** an instrument with a range between TENOR and BASS[1], in a family of musical instruments.
adj to do with a baritone. <Greek *barys* deep + *tonos* pitch>

bar·i·um (ber′ē əm) *n* **1** a soft, silvery-white metallic element used in alloys. *Symbol* **Ba** 2 *Informal* in full, **barium sulphate** a substance used in medicine to help in the X-ray diagnosis of diseases of the esophagus, stomach, and intestines. <coined by Sir. H. Davy, 19c chemist, from Greek *barytes* weight>

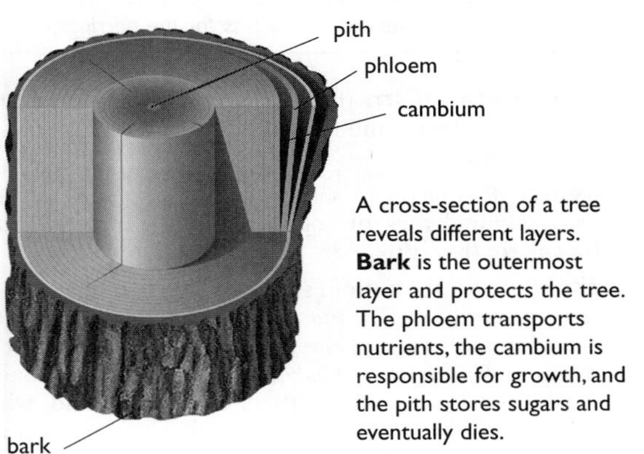

A cross-section of a tree reveals different layers. **Bark** is the outermost layer and protects the tree. The phloem transports nutrients, the cambium is responsible for growth, and the pith stores sugars and eventually dies.

bark[1] (bárk) *n* the tough outer covering of the stems and roots of woody plants.
v **1** scrape the skin from shins, knuckles, etc.: *I fell down the steps and barked my shins.* **2** strip bark from a tree. **3** treat or tan with bark. <Old Norse *börkr*>

bark[2] (bárk) *n* the short, sharp sound that a dog makes, or a sound like this.
v **1** make such a short, sharp sound: *The dog barked all night.* **2** speak sharply or gruffly: *The officer barked orders.* **3** stand outside a show, urging people to go in. <imitative> **bark′er** *n.*
be barking up the wrong tree, have the wrong idea.

bar·keep·er (bár′kē′pər) *n* a bartender. Also, **barkeep**.

bar·ley (bár′lē) *n* a cereal grass that has compact spikes of flowers. Its seed is used for food and for making malt. See GRAIN for picture.<Old English *bærlic*>

bar·maid (bár′mād′) *n* a woman who works in a bar, serving drinks to customers.

bar mitz·vah (bár mits′və) *Judaism n, pl* **bar mitz·vahs** or **mitz·voth** (mits′vōt) **1** a ceremony formally admitting a boy into the religious community, usually at age thirteen. **2** a boy who has reached this age.
v **bar mitz·vah′ed, mitz·vah′ing** admit to the Jewish religious community by a bar mitzvah. Compare BAT MITZVAH. <Hebrew = son of the divine law>

barm·y (barm′ē) *Slang adj* **barm·i·er, barm·i·est** insane. **barm′i·ness** *n.*

barn (bárn) *n* a large and usually tall building for sheltering farm animals and for storing hay, grain, and farm machinery. <Old English *bere* barley + *ærn* storing place> **barn′like′** *adj.*

bar·na·cle (bár′nə kəl) *n* a marine crustacean that spends its adult life attached to some underwater object like a rock, ship bottom, or sea creature. In the first two stages of its life, it has no shell and can swim around freely. <Old French *bernaque*> **bar′na·cled** *adj.*

barn owl *n* a brown and white owl that lives in barns and eats mice.

barn raising *n* in rural communities, a gathering of neighbours to build someone's barn. It is also a social event with food, drink, and dancing.

barn·storm (bárn′stôrm′) *Informal v* put on plays, shows, or concerts, make speeches, etc. in small towns and rural communities. **barn′storm′er** *n.*

barn swallow *n* a species of swallow that often nests in crevices of barns or caves. It has a deeply forked tail.

barn·yard (bárn′yárd′) *n* a yard, often fenced, adjoining a barn and used for livestock.
adj **1** typically found in a barnyard: *barnyard animals.* **2** crude or dirty: *barnyard humour.*

ba·rom·e·ter (bə rom′ə tər) *n* **1** an instrument for measuring atmospheric pressure. It is used to indicate probable weather changes and to determine height above sea level. **2** anything that indicates changes: *Newspapers can be a barometer of public opinion.* <Greek *baros* weight + *-meter*> **bar′o·met′ric** (ber′ə met′rik) *adj.*

bar·on (ber′ən) *n* **1** a nobleman of the lowest order. **2** a powerful merchant or financier: *a railway baron.* <Old French> **ba·ro′ni·al** (bə rō′nē əl) *adj.*

bar·on·ess (ber′ə nis) *n* **1** the wife or widow of a baron. **2** a noblewoman with the rank of a baron.

bar·on·et (ber′ən et′) *n* a nobleman of the lowest hereditary rank, below a baron.

a bat	e bed	i bid	o pot	u cup	th **thin**
ā cake	ē me	ī bite	ō go	ū rude	ᴛʜ **then**
á bar	ə about	ər over	ô for	ů put	zh measure

B

bar·o·ny (ber′ə nē) *n, pl* **bar·o·nies** the territory, rank, or title of a baron.

ba·roque (bə rōk′) *adj* **1** to do with a style of art, architecture, poetry, or music that developed in Europe especially in the 1600s, characterized by elaborate ornamentation. **2** overly fancy or complicated.
n the baroque style. <French, from Portuguese *barroco* irregular>

barque (bȧrk) *Poetic n* any boat or ship. <French, from Latin *barca*>

bar·racks (ber′əks) *pln* (*with singular or plural verb*) **1** a building or group of buildings for members of the armed forces to live in. **2** 🍁 **a** a building housing local detachments of the Royal Canadian Mounted Police. **b** *Informal* a training centre of the Royal Canadian Mounted Police. **3** any large, plain building housing many people. <Spanish *barracas* soldiers' huts or tents>

bar·ra·cu·da (ber′ə kū′də) *n, pl* **bar·ra·cu·da** or **bar·ra·cu·das** a fish found in tropical seas, with long, pointed jaws and razor-sharp teeth. A barracuda will pursue anything that moves in the water. <American Spanish>

bar·rage (bə rȧzh′) *n* **1** heavy, continuous artillery fire acting as a defensive or protective barrier. **2** an intense, continuous attack of any kind: *a barrage of questions from reporters.* <French, from *barrer* make a barrier>

barre (bȧr) *n* the supporting rail that ballet dancers use when practising. <French = bar>

bar·rel (ber′əl) *n* **1** a large container shaped like a cylinder, with a flat, round top and bottom and slightly bulging sides. It is usually made of boards called **staves**, held together by hoops. **2** any container or part shaped more or less like a cylinder: *the barrel of a drum.* **3** the tube of a gun, through which the bullet travels. **4** *Informal* a large quantity or number: *a barrel of fun.*
v **bar·relled** or **bar·reled, bar·rel·ling** or **bar·rel·ing** *Informal* move very fast, often with lack of control: *The car that passed us was barrelling down the highway.* <Old French, probably from Latin *barra* board, stave>
staring down the barrel of, facing something dangerous.

bar·ren (ber′ən) *adj* **1** not producing anything: *a barren desert.* **2** not able to bear offspring. **3** dull, empty, or lifeless.
n **1** 🍁 **the Barrens** *pl* the treeless, thinly populated region in N Canada, lying between Hudson Bay on the east and Great Slave Lake and Great Bear Lake on the west. Much of it is covered, in season, with short grass, moss, and small flowering plants. Also called the **Barren Ground** or **Barren Lands**. **2 barrens** any barren stretch of land. <Old French *baraine*> **bar′ren·ness** *n.*

bar·rette (bə ret′) *n* a decorative hair clip. <diminutive of *bar*[1]>

bar·ri·cade (ber′ə kād′) *n* **1** a temporary barrier: *They piled sandbags in the road to make a barricade.* **2** 🍁 large blocks of ice remaining frozen to the shore after spring breakup.
v **bar·ri·cad·ed, bar·ri·cad·ing** block or obstruct with a barricade: *We barricaded the doorway with furniture.* <Provençal (a language of S France) *barricada*, from *barrica* barrel. A barricade could be made quickly using barrels.>

bar·ri·er (ber′ē ər) *n* **1** a structure set up to block the passage of something or to keep two things separate. **2** anything that stops progress, blocks access, or keeps separate: *a barrier to success, a barrier between people.* **3** the starting gate in a horse race. <Old French, from Latin *barra* bar>

barrier reef *n* a long line of rocks or coral not far from the mainland, forming a barrier to ships.

bar·ring (bȧr′ing) *prep* except for: *Barring bad weather, the air show will start at twelve.*

bar·ris·ter (ber′i stər) *n* a lawyer, especially one who pleads in court as opposed to doing other legal tasks. Compare SOLICITOR. <*bar*[1] + *-ster*>

bar·room (bȧr′rūm′) *n* a room with a bar for the sale of alcoholic drinks.

bar·tend·er (bȧr′ten′dər) *n* a person who serves or mixes alcoholic drinks for customers at a bar.

bar·ter (bȧr′tər) *v* do business by exchanging goods or services without using money.
n the practice of exchanging goods and services without using money. <Old French *barater*>
barter away, give or trade without an equal return: *In his eagerness for fame, he bartered away his freedom.*

CONFUSABLES

Barter means "trade goods without using money": *He bartered his old bike for a dozen CDs.*

Bargain means "negotiate for a better price": *She bargained with the vendor to pay less for the earrings.*

bas·al metabolism (bā′səl) *or* (bā′zəl) *n* the amount of energy used by an animal or plant at rest to maintain its vital life processes.

bas·alt (bas′olt), (bā′solt), *or* (bə solt′) *n* a hard, dark-coloured rock of volcanic origin. <Latin *basaltes*> **ba·sal′tic** (bə sol′tik) *adj.*

base[1] (bās) *n* **1** the bottom surface or structure that a thing rests or stands on: *The machine rests on a base of steel.* See BASIS for confusable. **2** the most important element of a mixture: *This dog food has a meat base.* **3** *Baseball* one of the four stations at the corners of the diamond, where fielders and the catcher are stationed: *The player slid into third base.* **4** a centre of operations for an organization, expedition, the armed forces, etc. **5** *Biology* the part of an organ at or near its point of attachment: *the base of a leaf.* **6** *Chemistry* a compound that reacts with an acid to form a salt. **7** *Mathematics* **a** the line or surface considered to be the bottom of a geometrical figure: *the base of an isosceles triangle.* **b** the number that is the starting point for a numbering system: *The base of the decimal system is ten.*
v **based, bas·ing** (*often passive*) **1** locate the headquarters of an organization: *They decided to base the company in St John's.* **2** (*with* ***on***) form a basis for something: *The movie was based on a novel.* **3** assign to a centre of operations: *Troops were based in Germany.* <Old French, from Greek *basis*>

cover all the bases, pay attention to everything.

get to first base, *Informal* start making progress.

off base, *Informal* badly mistaken: *Your answer was way off base.*

touch base (or **bases**), make brief contact with someone after an absence.

base[2] (bās) *adj* **bas·er, bas·est 1** selfish and cowardly: *Only a base person would betray a friend.* **2** less valuable as a metal, such as lead or iron. <Old French, from Latin *bassus* low> **base′ly** *adv.* **base′ness** *n.*

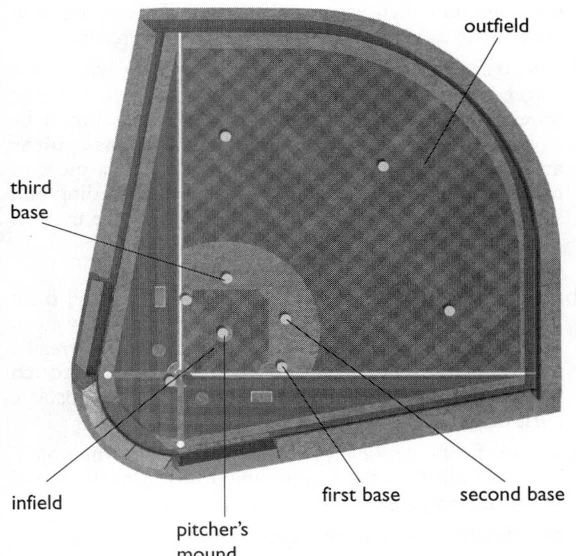

The playing area of a **baseball** field, which covers almost one hectare, is divided into the infield and the outfield. This area is known as fair territory. Beyond this area is foul territory.

The infield, also called the diamond, measures 27 m along each side, and is marked by the home plate and first, second, and third bases. Midway between second base and home plate is the pitcher's mound.

base·ball (bās′bol′) *n* **1** a game played with a bat and ball by two teams of nine players each on a diamond-shaped field with a base at each corner. **2** the ball used in this game.

base·board (bās′bȯrd′) *n* a line of boards around the walls of a room, next to the floor.

base·born (bās′bȯrn′) *adj* **1** *Archaic* in former times, born of slaves, peasants, an unmarried mother, or parents who had little money. **2** of low moral character.

base hit *Baseball n* a successful hitting of the baseball by a batter, enabling the player to reach first base.

base·less (bās′lis) *adj* without basis or foundation: *a baseless rumour.*

base·line (bās′līn) *n* **1** a line or amount used as a base or starting point. **2** *Baseball* a line between bases. **3** a standard of value against which things are measured or compared. **4** *Tennis, Basketball* a line marking the limit of play at either end of the court.

base·man (bās′mən) *Baseball n, pl* **base·men** a player stationed at one of the bases.

base·ment (bās′mənt) *n* the lowest storey of a building, partly or completely below ground.

bas·es[1] (bā′sēz) plural of BASIS.

bas·es[2] (bā′siz) plural of BASE[1].

bash (bash) *v* **1** strike with a smashing blow. **2** (*often in compounds, as* ***-bashing*** *and* ***-basher***) speak of with contempt: *I don't like the way she's always bashing Americans. The tabloids are full of celebrity-bashing.*
n **1** a smashing blow. **2** a party or celebration, especially a spectacular one. <probably imitative>
have a bash at, *Informal* try: *Here, you have a bash at it.*

bash·ful (bash′fəl) *adj* uncomfortable and awkward among others. **bash′ful·ly** *adv.* **bash′ful·ness** *n.*

ba·sic (bā′sik) *adj* **1** forming a basis or starting point for further thought or action: *basic beliefs about life, a basic course in drawing, a basic salary plus tips.* **2** *Chemistry* containing a BASE[1] (def. 6); alkaline.
n **basics** *pl* first, basic, or essential things: *Just teach me the basics; I'll figure it out from there.*

ba·si·cal·ly (bā′sik lē) *adv* **1** essentially: *The argument is basically flawed.* **2** putting it simply: *Basically, what he wants is for you to stop calling him.*

ba·sid·i·o·my·cete (bə sid′ē ō mī′sēt) *n* any fungus of the group that includes mushrooms and puffballs. <Latin *basidium* characteristic cell type + Greek *myketos* fungus>

bas·il (baz′əl) *or* (bā′zəl) *n* an annual herb of the mint family with aromatic leaves used as a seasoning. See HERB for picture. <Old French *basile*>

ba·sil·i·ca (bə sil′ə kə) *n* **1** a rectangular public building of ancient Rome with a row of columns along each side and a semicircular structure (**apse**) at one end. **2** a Christian church built in this form. <Latin, from Greek *basilike oikia* king's hall>

bas·i·lisk (baz′ə lisk′) *n* **1** *Greek and Roman myth* a lizardlike creature, hatched from a rooster's egg, whose breath and look were thought to be fatal. **2** a tropical lizard of the Americas belonging to the iguana family, with an inflatable head crest. <Latin *basiliscus* serpent, from Greek *basiliskos* = little king>

ba·sin (bā′sən) *n* **1** a wide, shallow bowl for holding liquids. **2** a bathroom sink. **3** the area of land drained by a river system: *the basin of the St. Lawrence.* **4** a bowl-shaped, low-lying area of land or the ocean floor: *the Annapolis Basin.* <Old French *bacin*, from Latin *bacca* water vessel>

a bat	e bed	i bid	o pot	u cup	th **thin**
ā cake	ē me	ī bite	ō go	ū rude	ᴛʜ **then**
ȧ bar	ə about	ər over	ȯ for	u̇ put	zh measure

ba·sis (bā′sis) *n, pl* **ba·ses** (bā′sēz) **1** the facts or ideas on which something is built: *Mutual respect is the basis of friendship.* **2** a way of operating or proceeding: *to pay on a monthly basis. She and I are on a first-name basis.* <Latin, from Greek *basis*>

CONFUSABLES

Basis applies to whatever supports an opinion or a belief: *Her argument had no basis in fact.* (The noun is figurative.)

Base applies to the bottom and supporting part of something: *The base of the lamp was heavy.* (The noun is concrete.)

bask (bask) *v* warm oneself pleasantly: *The cat was basking on the windowsill.* <Old Norse *bathask* bathe oneself>
bask in, spend time enjoying: *She basked in the praise of her friends.*

bas·ket (bas′kit) *n* **1** a container made of plastic, wire, wood, or grasses woven together, often with a handle arching over the top. **2** anything shaped or used like a basket: *a metal wastepaper basket.* **3** *Basketball* **a** a net open at the bottom hung from a metal ring through which the ball is thrown to score points. **b** a score made by putting the ball through the basket. **4** the structure beneath a balloon, for carrying passengers or ballast. <Middle English> **bas′ket·like′** *adj.*

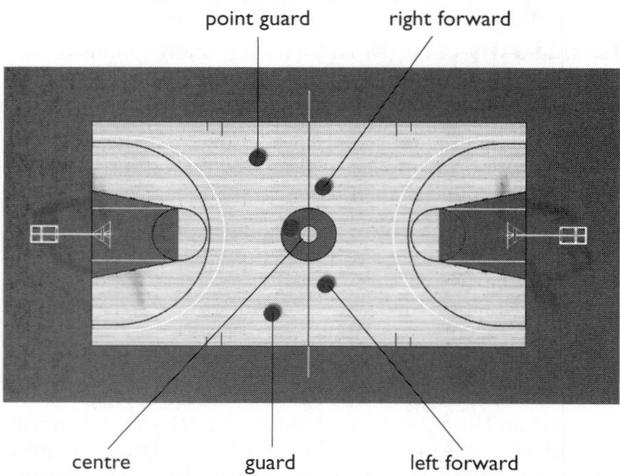

When **basketball** was first invented in 1891 by Canadian James Naismith, the basketball court had unspecified dimensions. Today, the playing area of a professional court measures 28.7 m long by 15.2 m wide.

bas·ket·ball (bas′kit bol′) *n* **1** a game played by two teams of five players with a large, round ball on an indoor court. Each team tries to put the ball through a high basketlike net at the opponents' end of the court. **2** the ball used in this game.

basket case *Slang n* a person who cannot deal even with simple situations because of a mental or emotional breakdown. <applied in World War I to a person who had lost all four limbs, as a form of humour to deal with the horrors of war.>

basket weave (bas′kit wēv′) *n* a weave in cloth that looks like the weave in a basket.

Basque (bask) *n* **1** a member of a people living in S France and N Spain. **2** the language of this people, apparently unrelated to any other known language.
adj to do with the Basques or their language.

bas–re·lief (bȧ′ri lēf′) *n* sculpture in which carved forms stand out only slightly from a background. Compare HIGH RELIEF. Also called **low relief.** <French = low relief>

bass[1] (bās) *n* **1** the lowest adult male singing voice, or a singer with such a range. **2 a** an instrument with the lowest range in a family of musical instruments, especially a DOUBLE BASS. See CELLO for picture. **b** in full, **bass guitar** an electric guitar for playing the bass line in a piece of music rather than chords. **3** especially in recording and sound reproduction, the lower half of the whole musical range. Compare TREBLE. **4** a deep male voice.
adj to do with a bass. <Italian *basso*> **bass′ist** *n.*

bass[2] (bas) *n, pl* **bass·es** or (*especially collectively*) **bass** **1** a marine fish found mostly in shallow tropical waters. **2** a freshwater sunfish native to eastern lakes and streams from Canada to Mexico. Species include the **largemouth bass**, **smallmouth bass**, and **spotted bass**. <obsolete *barse* perch (a freshwater fish)>

bass clef (bās) *Music n* the F CLEF that assigns the note F below middle C to the second line down from the top of the staff. Compare ALTO CLEF, TENOR CLEF, TREBLE CLEF.

bass drum (bās) *n* a large drum that makes a deep, low sound when struck.

bas·si·net (bas′ə net′) *or* (bas′ə net′) *n* a baby's basketlike cradle, usually with a hood and set on a stand. <French = little basin, from *bassin* basin>

bas·soon (bə sün′) *n* a deep-toned wind instrument with a double reed and a long wooden body. See DOUBLE BASSOON for picture. <Italian *basso* bass> **bas·soon′ist** *n.*

bas·tard (bas′tərd) *n* **1** in former times, a child whose parents were not married to each other. **2** *Slang* an unpleasant or inferior person or thing. <Old French, probably from *fils du bast* son of a packsaddle (i.e., not from a marriage bed)>

bas·tard·ize (bas′tər dīz′) *v* **bas·tard·ized, bas·tard·izing** corrupt or debase by mixing with different or inferior elements: *I think frozen yogurt is a bastardized version of ice cream!* **bas′tard·i·za′tion** *n.*

baste[1] (bāst) *v* **bast·ed, bast·ing** pour melted fat, butter, oil, etc. or a sauce on food while it is cooking, in order to keep it moist and improve its flavour. <Old French *basser* moisten> **bast′er** *n.*

baste[2] (bāst) *v* **bast·ed, bast·ing** sew pieces of cloth together temporarily with long running stitches to hold it until the final sewing. <Old French *bastir*> **bast′er** *n.*

bas·tion (bas′chən) *n* **1** a projecting part of a fortification, made so that the defenders can fire from as many angles as possible. **2** someone or something that acts as a strong defence: *The Charter of Rights is a bastion of justice.* <Italian *bastire* build> **bas′tioned** *adj.*

bat[1] (bat) *n* **1** *Baseball, Cricket* a specially shaped wooden stick or club used to hit the ball. **2** the act of batting, or one's turn at batting: *It's her bat next.* **3** a stroke or blow.
v **bat·ted, bat·ting 1** hit with or as if with a bat. **2** *Baseball* have a given BATTING AVERAGE: *He bats over 200.* <Old French *battre* hit, beat>
at bat, having a turn at batting.
go to bat for, *Informal* support something: *I'm sure she'll go to bat for you if you explain what happened.*
(**right**) **off the bat,** *Informal* without hesitation: *He accepted the offer right off the bat.*

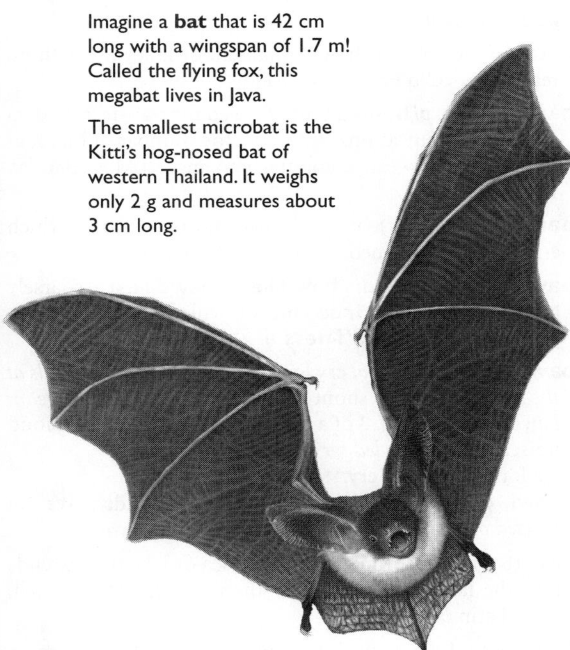

Imagine a **bat** that is 42 cm long with a wingspan of 1.7 m! Called the flying fox, this megabat lives in Java.

The smallest microbat is the Kitti's hog-nosed bat of western Thailand. It weighs only 2 g and measures about 3 cm long.

bat[2] (bat) *n* a flying mammal resembling a rat, but with leathery wings and a special radarlike sense by which it navigates. <Scandinavian> **bat′like′** *adj.*
blind as a bat, completely blind.

bat[3] (bat) *v* **bat·ted, bat·ting** blink or flutter (the eyes, eyelashes, eyelids). <from obsolete *bate* flutter>
not bat an eye, show no surprise or other reaction.

batch (bach) *n* **1** a quantity of anything made or dealt with as one lot or set: *a batch of cookies, a batch of websites to print.* **2** *Computers* a set of instructions or functions for a computer to perform in one run. <Middle English *bacche*>

bate (bāt) *v* (*now only in* ***bated breath***) hold back; lessen. <variant of *abate*>
with bated breath, holding the breath in great fear, awe, interest, etc.: *The children listened with bated breath to the adventure story.*

bath (bath) *n, pl* **baths** (baTHz) **1** a washing of the body while sitting in a bathtub filled with water. **2** the water or other liquid for a bath: *Your bath is cold.* **3** a tub, room, or other place for bathing: *House for rent with four bedrooms, two baths, finished basement.* **4** a liquid for rinsing or dipping something, such as a solution for developing photographic film.
v give a bath to a person or animal: *Mom baths the baby every day.* <Old English *bæth*>
take a bath, *Informal* lose a lot of money.

bathe (bāTH) *v* **bathed, bath·ing 1** take a bath: *to bathe every evening.* **2** wash with water or other liquid: *The doctor told her to bathe her eyes with the lotion.* **3** *Formal* go swimming for pleasure. **4** cover or surround: *The valley was bathed in sunlight.* <Old English *bathian*> **bath′er** *n.*

bathing cap (bā′THing) *n* a tight-fitting rubber cap worn to protect the hair while swimming.

bathing suit (bā′THing) *n* a garment worn for swimming. Also called **swimsuit**.

bath·robe (bath′rōb′) *n* a loose, belted garment worn when going to and from a bath or when resting or lounging.

bath·room (bath′rūm′) *n* **1** a room that has at least a toilet and a washbasin, and usually has a shower, a bathtub, or both. **2** any room with a toilet; a washroom.
go to the bathroom, *Informal* (*used as a euphemism*) use a toilet.

bath·tub (bath′tub′) *n* a tub to bathe in.

bath·wa·ter (bath′wȯ′tər) *n* water in a tub, for taking a bath in.
throw the baby out with the bathwater, reject good things by mistake while getting rid of the bad.

ba·tik (bə tēk′) *or* (bȧ tēk′) *n* **1** a method of making designs on cloth by dyeing all the parts that are one colour at one time while protecting the remainder with a removable coating of melted wax. **2** cloth dyed in this way. **3** a design formed in this way. <Malay>

bat mitz·vah (bȧt mits′və) *Judaism n, pl* **bat mitz·vahs** or **mitz·voth** (mits′vōt) a girl who has reached the age of twelve to fourteen, and has formally accepted her religious responsibilities. Compare BAR MITZVAH. <Hebrew = daughter of the divine law>

ba·ton (bə ton′) *n* **1** a stick passed from runner to runner in a RELAY RACE. **2** the stick used by the leader of an orchestra, choir, etc. to direct the performance. **3** a light, hollow metal rod twirled by a drum major or majorette as a display. **4** a staff or stick used as a symbol of office or authority. <French = stick>

bats·man (bat′smən) *Cricket n, pl* **bats·men** (bat′smen) a player who is batting.

batt (bat) *n* a thick sheet of cotton batting, fibreglass, or other pressed fibre: *a batt of insulation.* <related to *bat*[1], because cotton must be beaten before cleaning>

bat·tal·ion (bə tal′yən) *n* **1** *Military* a formation of four companies within an infantry regiment. **2** any large group organized to act together: *A battalion of volunteers helped to rescue the flood victims.* <Italian *battaglia* battle>

a bat	e bed	i bid	o pot	u cup	th thin
ā cake	ē me	ī bite	ō go	ū rude	TH then
ȧ bar	ə about	ər over	ȯ for	u̇ put	zh measure

bat·ten (bat′ən) *n* **1** a large, thick board used for flooring. **2** a strip of wood nailed across parallel boards to fasten, seal, or strengthen something.
v fasten down or strengthen with strips of wood. <variant of *baton*>
batten down the hatches, a on a ship, prepare for a storm by covering all entrances to the lower decks with boards, or with tarpaulins secured by boards. **b** prepare for any emergency or onslaught.

bat·ter[1] (bat′ər) *v* beat again and again so as to bruise, break, or damage: *The firefighter battered down the door with a heavy axe.* <Old French *batre* to beat>

bat·ter[2] (bat′ər) *n* a liquid mixture of flour, milk, eggs, etc. that becomes solid when cooked. Cakes, pancakes, etc. are made from batter.

> **ETYMOLOGY**
>
> **Batter** comes from Old French *bature*, meaning "a beating." In Middle English it became *bater*. Today, the word refers to a mixture of various ingredients that have been beaten together.

bat·ter[3] (bat′ər) *Baseball n* a player who is batting.

bat·tered (bat′ərd) *adj* **1** worn out; damaged by rough handling, harsh weather, or hard use: *a battered old book, battered backpacks.* **2** physically abused, especially over a period of time: *battered wives, battered children.*

bat·ter·ing ram (bat′ə ring) *n* **1** a war machine consisting of a heavy wooden beam with metal at one end, carried by many soldiers and pounded against walls, gates, etc. to break them down. **2** any heavy object used to break down a door, wall, etc.

bat·ter·y (bat′ə rē) *n, pl* **bat·ter·ies** **1** a device that produces electricity by the action of chemicals sealed inside it; a DRY CELL. A flashlight is a single cell; a car battery is made up of several cells. **2** a set of similar or connected things: *a battery of loudspeakers, a battery of medical tests.* **3** *Military* a set of machine guns or artillery pieces for combined action. **4** *Baseball* the pitcher and catcher together.

bat·ting (bat′ing) *n* sheets or layers of pressed cotton, wool, or synthetic fibre, used for lining quilts, stuffing mattresses, insulation, etc. <related to *bat*[1], because cotton must be beaten first before cleaning>

batting average *n* **1** *Baseball* a player's ratio of base hits to number of times at bat. **2** any record or indicator of performance: *Two promotions in two years is a pretty good batting average.*

bat·tle (bat′əl) *n* **1** a single encounter between opposing armed forces. A war may be made up of many battles. **2** fighting or war in general: *wounds received in battle.* **3** any fight or contest: *a battle of words.*
v **bat·tled, bat·tling** **1** take part in any battle or contest. **2** struggle against an opponent or opposing force: *battling a strong current.* <Old French, from Latin *battuere* beat>

bat·tle–axe (bat′əl aks′) *n* a kind of axe once used as a weapon of war.

bat·tle·field (bat′əl fēld′) *n* a place where a battle is fought or has been fought. Also called **battleground**.

bat·tle·front (bat′əl frunt′) *n* **1** the place where actual fighting between two armies is taking place. **2** the position of direct confrontation in any struggle: *In the war against cancer, medical researchers are on the battlefront.*

bat·tle·ment (bat′əl mənt) *n* in a castle or fort, a low wall for defence at the top of a tower, with indentations through which defending soldiers could shoot. **bat′tle·ment·ed** *adj.*

bat·tle·ship (bat′əl ship′) *n* the largest, most powerful, and most heavily armoured type of warship.

bat·ty (bat′ē) *Informal adj* slightly crazy. <*bat*[2]> **bat′ti·ness** *n.*

bau·ble (bob′əl) *n* a showy ornament or fancy toy with no real value. <Old French *baubel* toy>

baud (bod) *n, pl* **baud** a unit of speed for transferring data in telecommunications, especially the number of bits sent per second between computer systems. <J.M.E. *Baudot*, 19c engineer>

baux·ite (bok′sīt) *n* a claylike mineral from which aluminum is obtained. <from Les *Baux*, France>

bawd·y (bod′ē) *adj* **bawd·i·er, bawd·i·est** coarsely humorous, mildly indecent, or vulgar: *bawdy songs.* **bawd′i·ly** *adv.* **bawd′i·ness** *n.*

bawl (bol) *v* **1** *Informal* cry loudly: *My little brother bawls at the slightest thing.* **2** shout or call out noisily: *The sergeant bawled a command.* **3** of a calf, make its characteristic loud noise: *The calf bawled for its mother.*
n a loud bellowing cry. <Latin *baulare* bark>
bawl out, *Informal* scold severely or loudly: *We got bawled out for leaving our bicycles in the driveway.*

bay[1] (bā) *n* a wide indentation of a sea or lake that extends into the land, usually smaller than a gulf. <Old French, from Latin *baia*>

bay[2] (bā) *n* **1** a part projecting out from a wall, forming an alcove with a **bay window** (or set of windows) in it. **2** an alcove, platform, or other limited space set off for a specified purpose: *the bomb bay of a war plane. The truck backed up to the loading bay of the warehouse.* <Old French *baee* gap or recess in a wall, from Latin *batare* gape>

bay[3] (bā) *n* a long, deep howl or bark, especially as made by hounds pursuing prey. *The hunters heard the distant bay of the hounds.*
v utter a howl or prolonged barks: *The dogs sat and bayed at the moon.* <Old French *abayer* to bark>
at bay, a forced to face an enemy when escape is impossible: *The deer stood at bay on the edge of the cliff.* **b** being kept away or fought off: *The movie star's bodyguard held the reporters at bay.*
bring to bay, put in a position from which escape is impossible; hunt down.

bay[4] (bā) *n* a large shrub or small tree native to southern Europe and northern Africa, with aromatic, evergreen leaves used for flavouring food. Also called **laurel**. <Old French *baie* laurel berry, from Latin *baca* berry>

bay[5] (bā) *n* a reddish brown horse.
adj reddish brown. <Old French, from Latin *badius*>

bay·ber·ry (bā′ber′ē) *n, pl* **bay·ber·ries** a N American shrub with clusters of round fruits that are covered with greyish white wax. The wax is used to make fragrant candles.

bay·o·net (bā′ə net′) *or* (bā′ə nit) *n* a daggerlike blade for piercing or stabbing, attached to the end of a rifle. <French *bäionnette*, probably named after the town *Bayonne* where such blades were first made>

bay·ou (bī′ū) *especially US n* a marshy inlet or outlet of a lake, river, or gulf. <Louisiana French>

🍁 **Bay Street** *n* the money market or the financiers of Toronto, especially when contrasted with other areas of Canada. <a street in Toronto that is the site of many financial institutions>

ba·zaar (bə zär′) *n* **1** a sale of a wide variety of things, often second-hand goods or handcrafts that have been donated, held as a fundraiser. **2** in the Middle East and the Indian subcontinent, a market or shopping district. <Persian *bazar*>

ba·zoo·ka (bə zū′kə) *n* a rocket gun used against tanks. <named from the trombonelike musical instrument it resembled>

BB *n, pl* **BB's** a standard size of shot for use in a **BB gun** that works by compressed air and holds a single pellet.

BBS *Computers* bulletin-board system.

BC **1** before Christ; before the birth of Christ: *Julius Caesar died in 44* BC. See also BCE. **2** postal symbol for British Columbia.

BCE (*with dates*) before the Common Era, used in preference to BC: *Julius Caesar died in 44* BCE.

be (bē) *v, present sing* **am, are, is**; *pl* **are**; *past sing first and third person* **was**; *second person* **were**; *pl* **were**; *past participle* **been**; *present participle* **being**
1 have reality; live; exist: *The days of the pioneers are no more.* **2** have a particular position, quality, or condition: *The food is on the table. Are you sad?* **3** equal; represent: *Let x be the unknown quantity.* **4** belong to a particular group or class: *The new baby is a girl. Elephants and mice are mammals.* **5** happen: *The test was yesterday.* **6 a** with the present participle of another verb to make it progressive: *I am asking. He was asking.* **b** with the past participle of another verb to form the passive voice: *He was beaten.* **7** used to express future, duty, intention, and possibility: *I am to go to Regina next week.* <Old English *beon*>

be– *prefix* **1** thoroughly: *benumb.* **2** added to a verb or noun without an object to make it have one: *He bemoaned his fate.* **3** make or cause to seem: *belittle.* <Old English>

beach (bēch) *n* a flat, sandy or pebbly area at the shore of a lake or ocean.
v push or cause to drift up onto the shore: *a beached whale in need of rescue. We beached the boat in a little inlet.* <origin uncertain> **beach′less** *adj.*

beach·comb·er (bēch′kō′mər) *n* **1** a person who scavenges on beaches or in wharf areas. **2** 🍁 *British Columbia* a person or vessel that picks up logs broken loose from log booms and returns them to logging companies for a fee.

beach·head (bēch′hed′) *n* the first position established by an invading army on an enemy shore.

beach volleyball *n* a form of volleyball, played on sand by teams of two or more players each.

bea·con (bē′kən) *n* **1** a light used as a guide or warning signal, especially for ships or aircraft. **2** a tall tower for such a signal; a lighthouse. <Old English *beacn*>

bead (bēd) *n* **1** a small ball or bit of glass, metal, or plastic with a hole through it, so that it can be strung on a thread. **2** any small, round object like a bubble: *beads of sweat.* **3 beads** *pl* **a** a string of beads worn on the body. **b** a string of beads used in saying prayers.
v **1** ornament with beads: *I'm beading my old jacket to make it look different.* **2** form beads: *Water beaded on the glass.* <Old English *bedu* prayer> **bead′ed** *adj.* **bead′like′** *adj.*
draw a bead on, aim at.
say (or **tell**, or **count**) **your beads,** pray using a rosary.

bead·ing (bē′ding) *n* **1** a trimming made of beads threaded into patterns. Also called **beadwork**. **2** on woodwork, silver, etc., a border made up of small beads. **3** a narrow, semicircular moulding or strip of wood trim.

bead·y (bē′dē) *adj* **bead·i·er, bead·i·est** small, round, and shiny like beads: *beady eyes.*

bea·gle (bē′gəl) *n* a breed of small hunting dog with smooth hair, short legs, and drooping ears. <origin uncertain>

A beak used for catching insects must be fairly long and tapered enough to poke into holes in the bark of trees.

A beak used for eating grain must be strong enough to crack various seeds.

A beak used for tearing flesh must be very strong, and sharply pointed so as to be able to pierce the skin.

beak (bēk) *n* **1** a bird's mouth made of hornlike material, especially one that is strong and hooked and useful in striking or tearing. **2** a similar part in other animals, such as some turtles or dolphins. <Old French, from Latin *beccus*> **beaked** *adj.* **beak′like′** *adj.*

a bat	e bed	i bid	o pot	u cup	th **thin**
ā cake	ē me	ī bite	ō go	ū rude	ᴛʜ **then**
ä bar	ə about	ər over	ȯ for	u̇ put	zh measure

beak·er (bē′kər) *n* **1** a glass or metal container with a small lip for pouring and no handle, used in laboratories. **2** a plastic cup or drinking glass, especially a child's. <Old Norse *bikarr*, from Latin *bacarium*>

be–all and end–all (bē′ol ən en′dol) *Informal n* the most important person or thing: *She thinks she is the be-all and end-all.*

beam (bēm) *n* **1** a long, thick piece of wood, metal, concrete, etc. for use in building. **2** a ray or group of rays of light or heat: *the beam from a flashlight, a laser beam.* **3** in a set of weigh scales, the crosswise bar from which the pans are suspended. **4** the widest part of a ship.
v **1** send out rays of light; shine. **2** look very happy; smile brightly: *She beamed with pleasure.* **3** direct a radio or TV signal: *to beam programs at Yukon Territory.* <Old English> **beam′ing** *adj.*
off the beam, wrong; mistaken; not relevant.
on the beam, *Informal* correct; relevant.

bean (bēn) *n* **1** a plant of the pea family, producing edible, usually kidney-shaped seeds in long pods. There are numerous species of bean, many of them climbing plants. **2** the dried mature seed of a bean plant: *Baked beans are often eaten as a meal.* **3** the immature green or yellow pod of a bean plant, eaten as a vegetable. **4** some other seed or fruit related to or resembling a bean: *coffee beans.* <Old English> **bean′like′** *adj.*
full of beans, *Informal* lively and eager.

bean·bag (bēn′bag′) *n* a small cloth bag loosely filled with dry beans, tossed in various games.

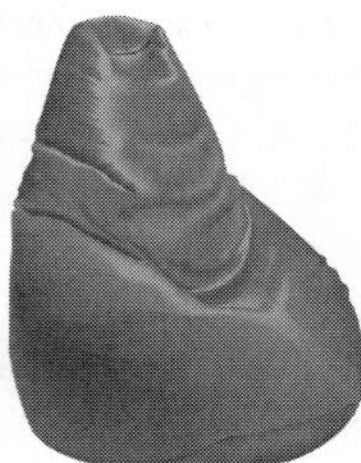

The **beanbag chair** was created by Italian designers in 1969 and called the "Sacco." This pear-shaped chair had a sturdy covering and was filled with tiny beads made of hard plastic. Real beans would have made the chair too heavy to be practical.

beanbag chair *n* a soft chair made of vinyl or strong cloth stuffed with polystyrene beads, allowing it to change shape to suit the user.

bean curd *n* tofu, a mild, protein-rich food with a cheeselike texture, made from soybeans.

bean·ie (bē′nē) *n* a small round cap, usually with no visor.

bean·pole (bēn′pōl′) *n* **1** a pole stuck in the ground for bean plants to climb on as they grow. **2** *Informal* a very thin, tall person.

bean sprouts *pln* the sprouts of various bean seeds eaten as a vegetable, either raw or cooked.

bean·stalk (bēn′stok′) *n* the main stem of a bean plant.

bear[1] (ber) *v* **bore, borne** or **born** (*for def. 4 when passive*), **bear·ing 1** carry or support: *She came into the bedroom bearing a tray of breakfast things. That board is too weak to bear your weight.* **2** tolerate or endure: *I can't bear cats. The pain was more than he could bear.* **3** produce or yield: *This tree bears excellent apples.* **4** give birth to; have offspring: *to bear a child. That woman has borne four boys. I was born on June 4.* **5** behave; conduct (oneself): *She bore herself with great dignity.* **6** bring forward or give: *to bear a hand, to bear witness to what happened.* **7** have: *I bear a scar on my knee. He bears the name of Lee.* **8** take on oneself: *to bear the cost, to bear the responsibility.* **9** move or go: *The ship bore north.* <Old English *beran*>
bear down (on), a press or push: *Don't bear down so hard on him.* **b** move relentlessly toward: *They watched helplessly as the ship bore down on the rowboat.*
bear in mind, remember or consider: *Bear in mind we have to leave early.*
bear on, have a connection with something: *Her comment was interesting, but did not bear on the topic.*
bear out, support or prove: *This conclusion is not borne out by the data.*
bear someone a grudge, resent an insult or injustice: *Do you still bear me a grudge for playing that joke on you?*
bear up, keep one's courage and hope: *bear up under the strain.*
bear with, be patient with someone or something: *Bear with me while I try to remember.*

Bears inhabit large areas of relative wilderness on all continents except Africa, Antarctica, and Australia. Today, their habitats are threatened by mineral and fuel exploration and land development.

bear[2] (ber) *n* **1** a large, heavily built mammal with thick, shaggy hair and powerful claws. Bears are omnivores, feeding on meat, fish, berries, young shoots, and buds. **2** a grumpy person. **3** a person who sells stocks expecting a fall in prices, in order to make a profit by buying them later at the lower price. In a **bear market**, prices are falling. Compare BULL (def. 2). <Old English *bera*>
a bear for punishment, a person who enjoys challenge.

bear·a·ble (ber′ə bəl) *adj* that can be borne; endurable: *The pain was severe but bearable.* **bear′a·bly** *adv.*

beard (bērd) *n* **1 a** the hair on a person's chin and cheeks, especially when left to grow. **b** something resembling or suggesting this, such as the tuft of hair on a goat's chin. **2** the tuft of bristly hairs on the heads of certain grains such as barley, wheat, etc.
v face boldly; defy someone or something on their own ground: *to beard the principal in his office.* <Old English>
beard′ed *adj.* **beard′less** *adj.* **beard′like′** *adj.*

bear·er (ber′ər) *n* **1** a person who or thing that carries or has a certain thing: *the bearer of good news, bearer of the title "Prince of the Realm."* **2** a person who holds or presents a cheque, ticket, or anything that entitles him or her to something: *Pay the bearer of this cheque.*

bear hug *n* a powerful, full-body hug.

bear·ing (ber′ing) *n* **1** a person's way of standing, sitting, or walking: *A queen should have a royal bearing.* **2** a connection in thought or meaning: *Her question has no bearing on the problem.* **3** a part of a machine on which another part turns or slides, such as a BALL BEARING. **4** one of the symbols in a coat of arms: *heraldic bearings.* **5 bearings** *pl* a position, especially according to some grid or system of locating things: *The pilot radioed his bearings.* **b** an understanding of one's position or situation: *Without a compass you'll lose your bearings in these woods. We'll give you a week to get your bearings and then see how the job is going.*

bear·ish (ber′ish) *adj* **1** rough or surly. **2** believing that prices in the stock market will fall. **3** pessimistic.

Bear·lake (ber′lāk′) *n, pl* **Bear·lake** **1** a member of a First Nations people living around the southwestern end of Great Bear Lake in the Northwest Territories. **2** their Athapaskan language.
adj to do with these people or their language.

✱ **bear·paw** *n* (ber′po′) a small round snowshoe.

bear·skin (ber′skin′) *n* **1** the skin of a bear with the fur attached. **2** a tall, black fur cap worn by members of certain regiments.

beast (bēst) *n* **1** any animal except a human being. **2** any four-footed animal. **3** a coarse or brutal person. <Old French, from Latin *besta*> **beast′like′** *adj.*

beast·ly (bēst′lē) *adj* **beast·li·er, beast·li·est** brutal or coarse. **beast′li·ness** *n.*

beast of burden *n* an animal used for carrying loads.

beat (bēt) *v* **beat, beat·en** or **beat, beat·ing** **1** strike hard again and again: *to beat a drum. The cruel man beat his horse.* **2** make a sound by being struck: *The drums beat loudly.* **3** throb: *Her heart beat fast with joy.* **4** defeat or overcome: *Their team beat ours 4–2.* **5** outdo or surpass: *Nothing beats hockey as a sport.* **6** mix by stirring vigorously: *to beat eggs.* **7** flatten by striking or pounding: *to beat gold into thin strips.* **8** move rapidly up and down: *The bird beat its wings.*
n **1** the act of beating, either once or repeatedly: *a single beat of a drum, the rhythmic beat of waves on a beach.* **2** *Music* a unit of time or accent: *three beats to a measure.* **3** a regular round or route, especially one taken by a police officer or sentry.
adj Informal worn out; exhausted: *I'm beat and I'm going to bed.* <Old English *beatan*> **beat′er** *n.*
beat about, try to discover: *She beat about in vain for a fitting answer.*
beat a retreat, **a** run away. **b** sound a retreat on a drum.
beat around (or **about**) **the bush,** approach a matter indirectly; avoid coming to the point: *Stop beating around the bush and tell me what you want.*
beat it, *Informal* go away.
beat out, *Informal* surpass: *He beat out his best friend by getting top marks.*
beats me, *Informal* used to express bafflement.
beat up, **a** hurt someone badly by hitting him or her. **b** *Informal* cause to feel very bad: *Don't beat yourself up over one small mistake.*
not miss a beat, be very alert and observant.

beat·en (bē′tən) *adj* **1** shaped by blows of a hammer: *beaten silver.* **2** much walked on or travelled: *a beaten path.* **3** discouraged by defeat or failure: *They were a beaten lot.*

beat·er (bē′tər) *n* a device or utensil for beating a liquid like eggs or cream: *an electric beater.*

be·a·tif·ic (bē′ə tif′ik) *adj* blessed or holy: *a beatific smile.* <Latin *beatus* happy + *facere* make> **be′a·tif′i·cal·ly** *adv.*

be·at·i·fy (bē at′ə fī′) *v* **be·at·i·fied, be·at·i·fy·ing** **1** make supremely happy. **2** *Catholicism* a stage in the process of declaring a person to be a saint.

beat·ing (bē′ting) *n* **1** punishment by being struck repeatedly. **2** a defeat: *They took a beating in the game.*

be·at·i·tude (bē at′ə tyūd′) *or* (bē at′ə tūd′) *n* **1** supreme happiness or blessedness. **2** a blessing.

beat·nik (bēt′nik) *n* a member of the **Beat Generation**, a group of people who, in the 1950s, rejected the prevailing standards and behaviour. Beatniks showed contempt for material wealth, traditional clothing, etc. by living in communes, using drugs, refusing to take regular employment, etc. <*beat* + Yiddish *-nik* one who is or does. The origin of this sense of *beat* is a combination of *tired, upbeat,* and *beatific.*>

beat–up (bēt′up′) *Informal adj* battered: *a beat-up old car.*

beau (bō) *n, pl* **beaus** or **beaux** (bōz) **1** a boyfriend. **2** a man who pays a lot of attention to his clothes. <French, from Latin *bellus* handsome>

beau·ti·cian (byū tish′ən) *n* a person who does cosmetic treatments like manicures, pedicures, and hairstyling.

beau·ti·ful (byū′tə fəl) *adj* very pleasing to see or hear; delighting the mind or senses: *a beautiful picture, beautiful music.* **beau′ti·ful·ly** *adv.*

beau·ti·fy (byū′tə fī′) *v* **beau·ti·fied, beau·ti·fy·ing** make beautiful or more beautiful. **beau′ti·fi·ca′tion** *n.*

beau·ty (byū′tē) *n, pl* **beau·ties** **1** a quality or combination of qualities that gives great pleasure to the senses or to the mind and spirit: *The richness and beauty of the great hall were almost beyond description. He wrote poetry of great beauty and power.* **2** a person who or thing that has beauty, especially a woman: *She is a renowned beauty.* **3** an excellent or pleasing feature: *the beauties of the countryside in spring. The beauty of her writing style is its simplicity.* **4** *Informal* a notable or exceptional example of its kind; often shortened to **beaut**. <Old French>

beauty salon *n* a place that provides such cosmetic services as hairstyling, manicures, and pedicures. Also called **beauty parlour**, **beauty shop**.

beaux (bōz) a plural of BEAU.

a bat	e bed	i bid	o pot	u cup	th **thin**
ā cake	ē me	ī bite	ō go	ū rude	ᴛʜ **then**
ȧ bar	ə about	ər over	ȯ for	u̇ put	zh measure

Beaver are social animals that live together in a community. They build cone-shaped lodges of sticks, grass, and moss woven together and plastered with mud. These lodges, which are repaired when necessary, are used year after year.

bea·ver (bē′vər) *n, pl* **bea·vers** or (*especially collectively*) **bea·ver** a large rodent of N America and northern Europe that lives in and around water, with a flat, scaly tail, webbed hind feet, soft fur, and chisel-like front teeth. The beaver is often considered an emblem of Canada. <Old English *beofor*>

Bea·ver (bē′vər) DUNNE-ZA.

🍁 **beaver fever** *n* an infection of the intestines, accompanied by diarrhea, usually caused by drinking water contaminated by the feces of beavers or other wildlife. The technical name is **giardiasis**.

bea·ver tail *n* **1** 🍁 **Beaver Tail** *Trademark* a flat, oval doughnut, sprinkled with sugar. **2** *Meteorology* a low, flat cloud found on the east or southeast side of a thunderstorm.

be·bop (bē′bop′) *n* a style of jazz that evolved in the 1940s, characterized by complex harmony and syncopation. <imitative>

be·calm (bi kom′) *v* prevent from moving by lack of wind: *Our boat was becalmed for several hours.*

be·came (bi kām′) past tense of BECOME.

be·cause (bi kuz′) *conj* for the reason that: *We play ball because we enjoy the game. Because we were late, we ran.* <Middle English *bi cause* by cause>
because of, by reason of: *Because of the rain, we stayed inside.*

beck (bek) *n* a motion of the head or hand meant as a call or command. <shortened from *beckon*>
at someone's beck and call, used as a servant by someone.

beck·on (bek′ən) *v* signal or call by a motion of the head or hand: *He beckoned me to follow him.* <Old English *becnen*>

be·come (bi kum′) *v* **be·came, be·come, be·com·ing** **1** come or grow to be: *At his words, she became angry. He became wiser as he grew older.* **2** be suitable for; suit: *Such rude comments do not become her position as chairwoman.* **3** look attractive on: *That outfit becomes her.* <Old English *becuman*>
become of, happen to: *What has become of my cookie?*

be·com·ing (bi kum′ing) *adj* **1** fitting; suitable; appropriate: *becoming conduct for a formal occasion.* **2** attractive on the person wearing it: *a becoming dress.* **be·com′ing·ly** *adv.*

bec·que·rel (bek′ə rel′) *n* the SI unit for measuring radioactivity, or the rate at which the atoms of radioactive elements disintegrate. One becquerel is equal to one disintegration per second. *Symbol* **Bq** <A.H. *Becquerel*, 19c physicist>

bed (bed) *n* **1** a piece of furniture to sleep or rest on, typically consisting of a mattress covered with sheets and blankets or quilts, etc. **2** any place where people or animals rest or sleep: *The cat made its bed by the fireplace.* **3** a flat base on which anything rests: *They set the pole in a bed of concrete.* **4** (*usually in compounds*) the ground under a body of water: *The riverbed is muddy.* **5** a prepared piece of ground in which plants are grown, especially in a garden. **6** a layer or stratum: *a bed of coal.*
v **bed·ded, bed·ding** **1** (*often with* **down**) provide with or put to bed: *The traveller bedded his horse on straw. After my little brother is bedded down, I'll phone you.* **2** set or plant in a bed: *Tulips should be bedded in rich soil.* <Old English *bedd*>
bed and board, sleeping accommodation and meals.
get up on the wrong side of the bed, *Informal* be irritable or bad-tempered.
put to bed, a cause someone to go to bed: *Put the baby to bed at six.* **b** finish preparing a newspaper or other publication for printing: *We can't add that photo, because the yearbook's already been put to bed.*
take to your bed, go to bed, especially when sick.

bed and breakfast *n* a private home offering travellers rooms for the night with breakfast served the next morning, often at a rate cheaper than that of a hotel.
adj **bed-and-breakfast** to do with this kind of accommodation: *a bed-and-breakfast tour of northern Ontario.*
v **bed-and-breakfast** travel, making use of this kind of accommodation: *We bed-and-breakfasted our way around Cape Breton Island. Abbrev.* **B & B**

bed·bug (bed′bug′) *n* a small, reddish brown bloodsucking bug, with a broad, flat, hairy body, small useless wings, and scent glands that give off a disagreeable odour. Bedbugs bite humans and can live in bedding.

bed·clothes (bed′klōz′) *or* (bed′klōᴛʜz′) *pl n* sheets, blankets, or quilts put on a bed.

bed·ding (bed′ing) *n* **1** sheets, blankets, or quilts put on beds. **2** material for an animal's bed: *Straw is used as bedding for cows.* **3** a foundation or bottom layer.

be·dev·il (bi dev′əl) *v* **be·dev·illed** or **be·dev·iled, be·dev·il·ling** or **be·dev·il·ing** **1** torment. **2** confuse completely. **3** put under a spell or bewitch. **be·dev′il·ment** *n.*

bed·fel·low (bed′fel′ō) *n* usually, **strange bedfellows** one of two or more ideas, things, or people that are found together, sometimes unexpectedly: *She said that hospitals and big business were strange bedfellows.*

bed·lam (bed′ləm) *n* uproar; confusion, or the place in which confusion occurs: *When the home team won, there was bedlam in the arena. The house was bedlam on moving day.* <Hospital of St. Mary of *Bethlehem*, a mental hospital in 19c England>

Bed·ou·in (bed′ū in) *n, pl* **Bed·ou·in** **1** an Arab nomad of the deserts, especially in the Middle East. **2** any wanderer or nomad.
adj to do with the Bedouins. Also, **Beduin.** <Old French *beduin*, from Arabic *badawin* desert dwellers>

bed·pan (bed′pan′) *n* **1** a specially designed pan used as a toilet by people who have to stay in bed. **2** in former times, a pan filled with hot coals for warming a bed.

be·drag·gled (bi drag′əld) *adj* wet and messy: *bedraggled hair.* <Old English *be-* thoroughly+ *dragan* drag>

bed·rid·den (bed′rid′ən) *adj* having to stay in bed for a long time because of illness or injury. <Old English *bedrida* bed rider>

bed·rock (bed′rok′) *n* **1** the solid rock beneath the soil and looser rocks. **2** the lowest level; the bottom: *We can't lower prices any further; we've hit bedrock.*

bed·roll (bed′rōl′) *n* blankets or a sleeping bag rolled up and tied for carrying.

bed·room (bed′rūm′) *n* a room in which to sleep.

bed·sheet (bed′shēt′) *n* a SHEET[1] (def. 1).

bed·side (bed′sīd′) *n* the side of a bed: *The mother sat by her sick child's bedside.*
bedside manner, a a doctor's manner, good or bad, of personally interacting with a patient. **b** a comforting, reassuring tone.

bed·sit·ting room (bed′sit′ing) *n* a large room doubling as a living room and a bedroom, with a sofa that can open out into a bed.

bed·sore (bed′sȯr′) *n* a sore caused by lying too long in the same position.

bed·spread (bed′spred′) *n* a cover spread over other sheets and blankets to keep them clean and neat.

bed·spring (bed′spring′) *n* **1** a set of springs in a frame supporting a mattress. **2** one of the springs in the frame.

bed·stead (bed′sted′) *n* the wooden or metal framework of a bed.

bed·time (bed′tīm′) *n* the usual time for going to bed: *His regular bedtime is nine o'clock.*

Bed·u·in (bed′ū in) BEDOUIN.

bed·wet·ting (bed′wet′ing) *n* lack of bladder control while sleeping, so that urine goes into the bed. **bed′wet′ter** *n.*

worker

queen

drone

Bees are social insects that live together in a colony. The queen lays the eggs, some of the male drones will mate with the queen, and the female worker bees collect pollen and nectar to provide food for the colony.

bee[1] (bē) *n* an insect with four wings that lives in large groups called hives. <Old English *beo*>
have a bee in your bonnet, *Informal* **a** be obsessed with a certain thing. **b** be slightly crazy.
the bee's knees, *Informal* the best there is.

bee[2] (bē) *n* a social gathering for work or competition: *a quilting bee, a spelling bee.* <perhaps *bean* neighbourly help, from Old English *ben* boon, favour>

beech (bēch) *n* a tree of N America and Europe, with edible **beechnuts**, and hard wood valued as timber. <Old English *bece*>

beef (bēf) *n, pl* (*def. 2*) **beef 1** the meat from a steer, cow, or bull. **2** a steer, cow, or bull when full-grown and fattened for food; such animals collectively: *They raise beef.* **3** *Informal* muscle; brawn: *This ought to put some beef on you.* **4** *Informal* a complaint: *What's your beef?*
v Informal complain; gripe. <Old French *bœf*, from Latin *bovis* ox>
beef up, *Informal* strengthen: *You could beef up your argument by adding more examples.*

beef·a·lo (bē′fa′lo) *n* an animal that is a cross between buffalo and domestic cattle, raised for meat.

beef·eat·er (bē′fē′tər) *n* the common nickname for a YEOMAN OF THE GUARD who acts as a guard and official guide of the Tower of London.

beef·steak (bēf′stāk′) *n* a slice of beef for broiling or frying.

beef tea *n* a strong beef broth, often given as a home remedy to sick people.

beef·y (bē′fē) *adj* **beef·i·er, beef·i·est 1** like beef: *The broth has a beefy taste.* **2** strong, muscular, heavy, or solid. **beef′i·ness** *n.*

bee·hive (bē′hīv′) *n* **1** a hive or house for bees. **2** a busy place with many people moving around.

bee·keep·ing (bē′kē′ping) *n* the art of managing colonies of honeybees so that they produce more honey than they need. The extra honey is collected for human use. **bee′keep′er** *n.*

bee·line (bē′līn′) *n* the most direct route between two places.
make a beeline for, *Informal* go as quickly and directly as possible: *The startled calf made a beeline for its mother.*

been (bin) *or* (bēn) past participle of BE.

beep (bēp) *n* a short, sharp, electronic sound.
v **1** make or cause to make such a sound: *to beep a car horn. When the microwave beeps, your soup is done.* **2** signal someone by means of such a sound, especially using a beeper: *Beep your grandmother if you need to be picked up from the mall.* <imitative>

beep·er (bee′pər) *n* a small, portable, radio-controlled device that beeps to tell the wearer to do something.

beer (bēr) *n* **1** an alcoholic drink made from malt and, usually, hops. **2** a drink made from roots or plants: *root beer, ginger beer.* <Old English *beor*>

✱ **beer parlour** or **parlor** *n* a room in a hotel or tavern where beer is sold and drunk.

a bat	e bed	i bid	o pot	u cup	th thin
ā cake	ē me	ī bite	ō go	ū rude	ᴛʜ then
ä bar	ə about	ər over	ȯ for	u̇ put	zh measure

section of a honeycomb

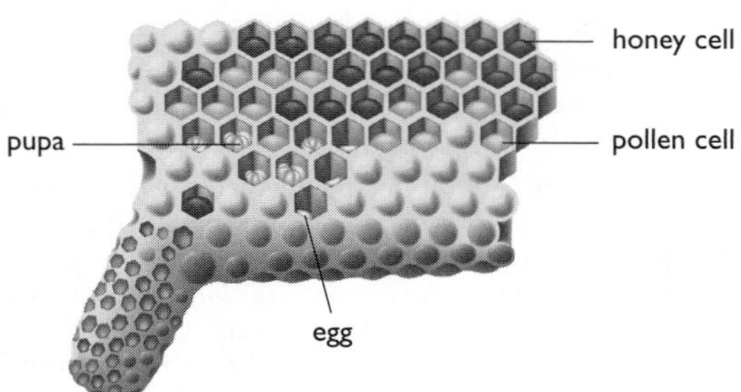

Bees produce honey from flower nectar and deposit it in honeycomb cells made of **beeswax**. Bees rely on this stored honey for food during the winter months. The queen bee's eggs are also stored in these beeswax cells.

bees·wax (bēz′waks′) *n* a yellowish, sweet-smelling wax produced by worker bees for constructing the cell walls of their honeycombs. It is processed for making candles, furniture polish, modelling wax, etc.

beet (bēt) *n* a biennial plant grown for its round, red or white fleshy root or edible leaves. The red roots of some varieties are eaten as a vegetable, while the white roots of other varieties yield sugar. See RADISH for picture. <Latin *beta*> **beet′like′** *adj.*
red as a beet or **beet red,** very red in the face, especially from blushing.

The **furniture beetle** lays its eggs in wooden furniture. The larvae (woodworms) feed on the wood until they are fully grown.

The **ladybug beetle** lives outdoors and eats aphids and other plant-eating insects, such as scales and mites.

bee·tle[1] (bē′təl) *n* **1** an insect with four wings, the front pair of which are modified into hard coverings that are folded along the back when at rest, hiding the rear pair of wings. **2** any similar insect. <Old English *bitela,* from *bitan* bite>

bee·tle[2] (bē′təl) *v* **bee·tled, bee·tling** project or overhang: *Great cliffs beetled above the narrow path.*
adj of eyebrows, shaggy and projecting: *fierce eyes beneath beetle brows.* <*beetle-browed*>

bee·tle–browed (bē′təl broud′) *adj* **1** with shaggy, projecting eyebrows. **2** scowling or sullen. <Middle English *bitel* biting + *brow*>

be·fall (bi fol′) *Archaic or Poetic v* **be·fell, be·fall·en, be·fall·ing** happen (to): *We will never surrender, whatever befalls.*

be·fit (bi fit′) *v* **be·fit·ted, be·fit·ting** be suitable or be proper for: *clothes that befit the occasion.*

be·fore (bi fôr′) *prep* **1** earlier than: *Be here before five o'clock.* **2** rather than: *He'd die before giving in.* **3** in the presence or sight of: *to stand before the king.* **4** being considered by: *The bill is before the House.* **5** in front of; in advance of; ahead of: *Walk before me and lead the way.*
conj **1** rather than: *I'll give up the trip before I'll go with them.* **2** earlier than the time when: *Before she goes, I must talk to her.*
adv **1** in front or ahead: *He went before to see if the road was safe.* **2** earlier: *Be here at five o'clock, not before.* **3** in the past: *I didn't know that before.* <Old English *beforan*>

be·fore·hand (bi fôr′hand′) *adv* earlier: *I'll get everything ready beforehand.*

be·friend (bi frend′) *v* be a friend to; help: *The children were eager to befriend the new girl.*

be·fud·dle (bi fud′əl) *v* **be·fud·dled, be·fud·dling** hopelessly confuse. <origin uncertain>

beg (beg) *v* **begged, beg·ging 1** ask for money or charity: *He was finally reduced to begging for a living. She begged a warm coat from a passerby.* **2** ask earnestly or humbly: *He begged his mother to forgive him.* <Middle English *beggen*>
beg off, ask to be released from an engagement or promise: *I was supposed to go along, but I begged off.*
beg the question, disregard the real question: *Arguing about how often you can borrow my bike begs the question whether you can borrow it at all.*
go begging, be available because something has not been taken: *There are still some cookies going begging.*

be·gan (bi gan′) past tense of BEGIN.

be·get (bi get′) *Archaic or Poetic v* **be·got, be·got·ten** or **be·got, be·get·ting 1** become the father of; father: *to beget children.* **2** cause to be; produce: *Hate always begets hate.* <Old English *begitan*>

beg·gar (beg′ər) *n* **1** a person who lives by begging. **2** *Informal* an affectionate term for a person or animal: *That puppy is a friendly little beggar.*
v make poor: *Your reckless spending will beggar your father.*
beg′gar·ly *adj.*
beggar description, difficult or impossible to describe: *The grandeur of Niagara Falls beggars description.*
beggars can't be choosers, used to express the idea that you have to accept what is available.

be·gin (bi gin′) *v* **be·gan, be·gun, be·gin·ning 1** start; start doing something: *We begin class at nine. Let's begin by introducing ourselves.* **2** come or bring into being: *This pain began two days ago. Two sisters began the fan club together.* **3** do something to even the least extent: *I can't begin to describe how I feel.* <Old English *beginnan*>

be·gin·ner (bi gin′ər) *n* **1** a person doing something for the first time; a person who lacks skill and experience. **2** the one who begins anything.
beginner's luck, unexpected success by a beginner.

be·gin·ning (bi gin′ing) *n* **1** a start: *to make a good beginning.* **2** the time when anything begins. **3** the first part: *The beginning of the book is good, but then it gets boring.* **4** a first cause, source, or origin: *That foolish act was the beginning of all his trouble.*
adj **1** just starting, new, or without experience: *a beginning student.* **2** first; earliest: *in the beginning days of the revolution.*

be·gone (bē gon′) *Archaic or Poetic interj* go away: *Sorrow and heartache, begone!*

be·go·nia (bi gō′nyə) *n* a plant with many varieties grown for its brightly coloured flowers and leaves. <M. *Bégon,* 17c colonial governor>

be·got (bi got′) past tense of BEGET.

be·got·ten (bi got′ən) past participle of BEGET.

be·grudge (bi gruj′) *v* **be·grudged, be·grudg·ing 1** be reluctant to give something: *She is so mean that she begrudges her dog decent food.* **2** resent somebody having something: *They begrudge us our new house.*

be·guile (bi gīl′) *v* **be·guiled, be·guil·ing 1** deceive or fool: *Her pleasant ways beguiled me into thinking she was my friend.* **2** cheat; take something from by cunning: *The crooked property owner beguiled the buyers of all their savings.* **3** entertain; amuse; charm: *a beguiling storyteller.* **4** pass or while away pleasantly: *We beguiled the time with reading.* **be·guil′ing** *adj.*

be·gun (bi gun′) past participle of BEGIN.

be·half (bi haf′) *n* interest, favour, or support: *She did a lot of work on their behalf.* <Middle English *behalve*>
on behalf of, as a representative of and in support of; for: *I gave the report on behalf of our group.*

be·have (bi hāv′) *v* **be·haved, be·hav·ing 1** act a certain way: *She behaved very badly in school. Water behaves in different ways at different temperatures.* **2** (*often reflexive*) do what is right: *Did you behave today? Behave yourselves!* <*be-* + *have*>

be·hav·iour or **be·hav·ior** (bi hāv′yər) *n* a way of acting: *His sullen behaviour showed he was angry. This section describes the behaviour of electrons.*
on your best behaviour, trying hard to be good.

be·hav·iour·ism or **be·hav·ior·ism** (bi hāv′yə riz′əm) *n* the theory that scientific psychology can deal only with objectively observed acts of people and animals, as opposed to thoughts, motives, and emotions. **be·hav′iour·ist** or **be·hav′ior·ist** *n.* **be·hav′iour·is′tic** or **be·hav′ior·is′tic** *adj.*

be·head (bi hed′) *v* cut off the head of.

be·held (bi held′) past tense of BEHOLD.

be·he·moth (bi hē′məth) *or* (bē′ə məth) *n* anything of very great size or power. <Hebrew *b'hemoth* huge beasts>

be·hest (bi hest′) *n* a command or order: *At the behest of her grandfather, she turned down the music.* <Old English *behœs* promise, from *be-* by + *hatan* command>

be·hind (bi hīnd′) *prep* **1** at the back of, to the rear of, or on the far side of: *I hid behind the sofa. A beautiful valley lies behind that hill.* **2** later than: *The letter carrier is behind his usual time today.* **3** hidden by: *Behind his smooth manners there is treachery.* **4** less advanced than: *She is behind the other children in her class.* **5** remaining after: *He left a family behind him when he died.* **6** in support of: *Her friends are all behind her.*
adv **1** at the back or in the rear: *The dog's tail hung down behind.* **2** farther back in place or time: *The rest of the hikers are far behind.* **3** slow; late: *The train is behind today.*
n Informal the buttocks. <Old English *be-* by + *hindan* from behind>

be·hind·hand (bi hīnd′hand′) *adj* **1** behind schedule or the due date; late: *You are always behindhand with your essays.* **2** behind others in progress: *He is behindhand in his schoolwork.*

be·hold (bi hōld′) *Poetic v* **be·held, be·hold·ing** see; look at: *Behold your new queen.* <Old English *behealden*> **be·hold′er** *n.*

be·hold·en (bi hōl′dən) *Archaic or Formal adj* in debt or under obligation to someone: *I am beholden to you.*

be·hoove (bi hūv′) *v* **be·hooved, be·hoov·ing** be necessary or proper for: *It behooves us to answer the challenge.* <Old English *behofian* need>

beige (bāzh) *adj* pale brown; light greyish brown. <French>

be·ing (bē′ing) *n* **1** life or existence: *This world came into being long ago.* **2** one's own nature or self: *Her whole being thrilled to the beauty of the music.* **3** a living person or creature: *human beings.*
for the time being, for now: *Let's leave that problem for the time being and come back to it later.*

bel (bel) *n* a unit for comparing levels of power, equal to ten decibels. <from A.G. *Bell,* 19c inventor>

be·la·bour or **be·la·bor** (bi lā′bər) *v* **1** repeat or work on longer than necessary: *to belabour a point in an argument.* **2** beat vigorously: *The man belaboured the poor donkey.* **3** abuse or ridicule: *The movie star was constantly belaboured by the press.*

Bel·a·rus (bel′ə rūs′) *n* a country in eastern Europe, formerly part of the Soviet Union. See the APPENDIX. **Bel′a·rus′sian** (bel′ə rush′yən) *adj, n.*

be·lat·ed (bi lā′tid) *adj* happening or coming too late: *a belated birthday card. Her belated attempt to apologize was rejected.* **be·lat′ed·ly** *adv.* **be·lat′ed·ness** *n.*

be·lay (bi lā′) *v* **be·layed, be·lay·ing 1** fasten a rope by winding it around a peg, piton, or cleat, as in rock climbing or on a sailboat. **2** *Nautical* stop: *Belay, there!*
n an object, such as a projecting piece of rock, to which a rope is secured. <Old English *belecgan*>

belch (belch) *v* **1** release gas from the stomach through the mouth. **2** erupt or explode: *The volcano belched fire, smoke, and ashes.*
n the act or sound of belching. <Old English *bealcian*>

be·lea·guer (bi lē′gər) *v* **1** surround or overpower: *Beleaguered by debts, she was finally forced into bankruptcy.* **2** surround and try to capture: *The beleaguered city refused to give in.* <Dutch *belegeren* besiege>

bel·fry (bel′frē) *n, pl* **bel·fries** a tower or other structure at the top of a building, containing a bell or bells. <Old French *berfrei*>
have bats in your belfry, *Informal* be slightly crazy.

Bel·gium (bel′jəm) *n* a country in western Europe, between France and the Netherlands. See the APPENDIX. **Bel′gian** *adj, n.*

a bat	e bed	i bid	o pot	u cup	th **thin**
ā cake	ē me	ī bite	ō go	ū rude	TH **then**
ä bar	ə about	ər over	ô for	ů put	zh measure

be·lie (bi lī′) *v* **be·lied, be·ly·ing 1** give a false idea of: *Her frown belied her usual good nature.* **2** show to be false; contradict: *Your actions belie your words. He cheated again, and so belied our hopes.* <Old English *beleogan*>

be·lief (bi lēf′) *n* **1** faith in a person or thing: *a belief in God, belief in a person's honesty.* **2** acceptance as true: *a belief that the earth is flat.* **3** a principle that one believes: *His beliefs are different from mine.* **4** an opinion: *It's my belief that we're in for a cold winter.* <Old English *bileafe*>

be·lieve (bi lēv′) *v* **be·lieved, be·liev·ing 1** (*usually with* ***in***) have faith or confidence in a person or thing: *All who believe are asked to pray for peace.* **2** (*sometimes with* ***in***) accept as true or real: *I don't believe her excuse.* **3** think that somebody tells the truth: *I believe him.* **4** think or suppose: *I believe we're putting on a play at graduation.* <Old English *belefan*> **be·liev′a·ble** *adj.* **be·liev′a·bly** *adv.*

SYNONYMS

To **believe** something is to think that it is true: *Do you believe the story he told us?*

To **know** something is to be certain that it is true: *I know that my eyes are brown.*

To **fathom** is to fully understand: *She's beginning to fathom the concept of algebra.*

be·liev·er (bi lē′vər) *n* a person who believes, especially a follower of a religion, philosophy, or set of political ideas.

be·lit·tle (bi lit′əl) *v* **be·lit·tled, be·lit·tling** speak of something as being small or unimportant: *Jealous people belittled the explorer's great discoveries.*

Be·lize (bə lēz′) *n* a country in Central America. **Be·li′ze·an** (bə lēz′ē ən) *adj, n.*

bell (bel) *n* **1** a hollow device, usually of metal, shaped more or less like a cup, that makes a continuing musical sound when struck. **2** a percussion instrument consisting of metal tubes or bars that produce bell-like tones when struck. **3** the sound of a bell: *You may leave on the second bell.* **4** on a ship, one to eight strokes of a bell to indicate a half hour of time.
v **1** put a bell on. **2** swell out like a bell. <Old English *belle*> **bell′-like′** *adj.*
bells and whistles, *Informal* extra features or accessories: *a brand-new TV with all the bells and whistles.*
bell the cat, do something dangerous or daring for the common good.
ring a bell, seem familiar: *I didn't recognize her at first, but the name rang a bell.*
saved by the bell, rescued at the last minute, usually by circumstances.
with bells on, *Informal* in full strength and high spirits: *My aunt doesn't usually show up at parties, but she was there with bells on.*

Bel·la Bel·la (bel′ə bel′ə) HEILTSUK.

Bel·la Coo·la (bel′ə kū′lə) NUXALK.

bel·la·don·na (bel′ə don′ə) *n* **1** a poisonous plant of Europe with black berries and red flowers. It belongs to the nightshade family. **2** a drug made from this plant. Also called **deadly nightshade.** <Italian = fair lady>

bell–bot·toms (bel′bot′əmz) *pln* pants that flare out widely at the ankle. **bell′-bot′tomed** *adj.*

bell·boy (bel′boi′) *n* a man or boy at a hotel or club who carries baggage and does errands for the guests.

bell buoy *n* a BUOY with a bell rung by the movement of the waves to alert ships to its presence.

bell curve *Statistics n* the symmetrical bell-shaped curve of a NORMAL DISTRIBUTION.

belle (bel) *n* **1** a beautiful woman or girl. **2** the prettiest or most admired woman or girl: *the belle of the ball.* <French, feminine of *beau,* from Latin *bellus* handsome>

belles let·tres (bel′let′rə) *pln* (*with singular verb*) writings considered as art rather than as giving information or teaching a lesson. <French = beautiful letters>

bell·hop (bel′hop′) *Informal n* a bellboy.

bel·li·cose (bel′ə kōs′) *adj* warlike. <Latin *bellum* war> **bel′li·cos′i·ty** (bel′ə kos′ə tē) *n.*

bel·lig·er·ent (bə lij′ə rənt) *adj* **1** eager to fight: *She gets very belligerent if you don't agree with her.* **2** at war: *belligerent nations.*
n **1** a country or group at war: *The belligerents agreed on a truce.* **2** a person fighting with another. <Latin *bellum* war + *gerere* wage> **bel·lig′er·ence** *n.* **bel·lig′er·ent·ly** *adv.*

bell jar *n* a glass bell-shaped cover used especially in scientific experiments that require reduced air pressure.

bel·low (bel′ō) *v* **1** roar as a bull does. **2** shout in a loud, full, or deep voice: *The lifeguard bellowed at the boys to stay near the shore.* **3** make a loud, deep noise: *We heard the waterfall bellowing in the distance.*
n the act or sound of bellowing. <Middle English *belwe*>

bel·lows (bel′ōz) *pln* (*with singular or plural verb*) a device with many folds that expand with the intake of air and then squeeze the air out, used to blow on a fire or to sound an accordion. <Old English *belgas* bags>

bell·weth·er (bel′weᴛʜ′ər) *n* **1** a sheep that wears a bell and leads the flock. **2** any person, group, or thing thought of as setting a standard or pattern: *The new magazine quickly became the bellwether of fashion.* <Old English>

bel·ly (bel′ē) *n, pl* **bel·lies 1** the lower part of the human body, containing the stomach and bowels. **2** the under front part of an animal's body. **3** the stomach: *a full belly.* **4** the bulging, hollow part of anything: *the belly of a sail.*
v **bel·lied, bel·ly·ing** bulge or swell out: *The ship's sails bellied in the wind.* <Old English *belg, belig* bag>
go belly up, *Slang* **a** die, as a fish in an aquarium does. **b** go bankrupt: *That new store has already gone belly up.*

bel·ly·ache (bel′ē āk′) *Informal n* **1** a pain in the abdomen. **2** something to complain about; grievance.
v **bel·ly·ached, bel·ly·ach·ing** complain or grumble, especially over trifles. **bel′ly·ach′er** *n.*

belly button *Informal n* the navel.

bel·ly·flop (bel′ē flop′) *v* **bel·ly·flopped, bel·ly·flop·ping 1** dive and strike the water with the chest or abdomen. **2** fall, lie, or throw oneself on one's stomach: *She bellyflopped on the bed.*
n a dive or movement made in this way.

bel·ly·ful (bel′ē fu̇l′) *Informal n* more than one wants or can stand: *After listening to complaints for two hours, the store clerk had had a bellyful.*

be·long (bi long′) *v* **1** have a proper place: *Books belong on this shelf.* **2** be accepted or included by a group: *Everyone needs to belong.* <Old English *gelang* belonging to>
belong to, a be the property of: *Does this cap belong to you?* **b** be a part of or be connected with: *That monitor belongs to this computer set-up.* **c** be a member of: *She belongs to the local figure-skating club.* **d** be the duty or concern of: *This responsibility belongs to the student.*

be·long·ings (bi long′ingz) *pln* things that belong to a person: *I can pack all my belongings in one suitcase.*

be·lov·ed (bi luv′id) *or* (bi luvd′) *adj* loved very much.
n (*often as a term of address*) a person who is loved.

be·low (bi lō′) *adv* **1** in or to a lower place: *From the airplane we could see the fields below.* **2** on or to a lower floor or deck: *The sailor went below.* **3** further on in a piece of writing: *See the note below.* **4** less than zero on a temperature scale: *It's ten below.*
prep lower or less than: *below the third floor. It is seven degrees below freezing.* <Middle English *biloghe* by low>

belt (belt) *n* **1** a strip of leather, cloth, etc. worn around the body to hold in or support clothing, to hold tools or weapons, or as a decoration. **2** any broad strip: *a belt of trees at the back of the property.* **3** (*often in compounds*) a region with distinctive characteristics: *the snowbelt.* **4** on a machine, an endless band that transfers motion from one wheel or pulley to another: *the fan belt in a car.* **5** *Informal* a sharp blow: *a belt on the chin.* **6** *Slang* a drink of liquor gulped hastily or greedily: *a belt of whisky.*
v **1** put a belt around; fasten with a belt. **2** (*with* ***out***) sing loudly and enthusiastically: *They belted out their favourite songs all the way home on the bus.* **3** *Informal* hit suddenly and hard. **4** beat with a belt. <probably from Latin *balteus*> **belt′ed** *adj.*
below the belt, unfair: *That remark was below the belt.*
tighten your belt, be more thrifty.
under your belt, a in your possession or experience: *I have two years as team captain under my belt.* **b** in your stomach: *With a good dinner under his belt, he felt happier and more relaxed.*

be·lu·ga (bə lū′gə) *n* **1** a white, toothed, Arctic whale, with no back fin. **2** a species of large white sturgeon, the world's largest freshwater fish and a source of caviar. <Russian *byelo-* white + *-uga* large>

be·moan (bi mōn′) *v* moan or complain about: *My friends and I were bemoaning the school's lack of air conditioning.*

be·muse (bi myūz′) *v* **be·mused, be·mus·ing** confuse; bewilder; daze. **be·muse′ment** *n.*

bench (bench) *n* **1** a long seat, usually of wood, stone, or plastic, with or without a back. **2** the worktable of a carpenter, or of any worker with tools and materials: *She worked at her bench in the basement.* **3** *Law* **a** the seat where judges sit in court. **b** a judge or group of judges presiding in court: *The witness was told by the bench to keep to the point.* **4** *Sports* **a** the place where team members sit who are not playing in a game, or are waiting to play: *on the bench.* **b** these players collectively.
v Sports take a player out of a game: *The coach benched me for arguing.* <Old English *benc*>

bench·mark (bench′märk′) *n* **1** a point of reference or standard of comparison. **2** in surveying, a mark used as a starting point or guide for the determination of altitude.

bend (bend) *v* **bent, bend·ing 1** make, be, or become curved or crooked: *He bent the iron bar as if it had been made of rubber. The branch began to bend as I climbed along it.* **2** direct or apply the mind or one's efforts: *Our steps were bent toward home. She bent her mind to the new work.* **3** (*often with* ***over*** *or* ***down***) stoop or bow: *The woman bent to pick up a stone.* **4** submit or force to submit: *to bend to someone's will.* **5** change slightly from the original intent, or interpret flexibly: *to bend the rules, to bend the meaning of a word.*
n **1** a part that is not straight; a curve or turn: *There is a sharp bend in the road here.* **2** the act of bending: *a bend of the knee.* **3 the bends** *Informal* decompression sickness. <Old English *bendan*> **bend′y** *adj.*
bend over backwards, make great effort or take great care: *We bent over backwards to please them.*
drive around (or **round**) **the bend,** *Slang* distracted; crazy: *That noise is driving me round the bend!*
on bended knee, *Poetic or Humorous* kneeling: *He proposed to her on bended knee.*

bend·er (ben′dər) *Slang n* a drinking spree.

be·neath (bi nēth′) *prep* **1** below or under: *The dog sat beneath the tree.* **2** unworthy of or not even worthy of: *a traitor beneath contempt. Telling lies is beneath you.*
adv below; underneath: *He dozed in the hammock, his cat lying beneath.* <Old English *be-* by + *neothan* below>

ben·e·dic·tion (ben′ə dik′shən) *n* **1** a blessing.
2 *Christianity* a prayer of blessing at the end of a service. <Latin *benedicere* bless>

ben·e·fac·tor (ben′ə fak′tər) *n* a person who has helped others, either by a gift or by some kind act: *It's a pity that the gift was anonymous; I'd like to know who my benefactor was.* Also, for a female, **benefactress**. <Latin *bene* well + *facere* do>

SYNONYMS

A **benefactor** helps others: *The benefactor brought the homeless man a hot meal and a blanket.*

A **patron** sponsors or supports a specific person or cause: *Her patron paid for her university education.*

A **humanitarian** tries to help humankind in general: *The humanitarian worked worldwide to end child labour.*

be·nef·i·cent (bə nef′ə sənt) *adj* **1** kind and good. **2** with good results: *beneficent acts.* <See BENEFACTOR.> **be·nef′i·cence** *n.*

ben·e·fi·cial (ben′ə fish′əl) *adj* favourable, helpful, or with good effects: *Sunshine and moisture are beneficial to plants.* <See BENEFACTOR.> **ben′e·fi′cial·ly** *adv.*

a bat	e bed	i bid	o pot	u cup	th thin
ā cake	ē me	ī bite	ō go	ū rude	ᴛʜ then
ä bar	ə about	ər over	ȯ for	u̇ put	zh measure

ben·e·fi·ci·ar·y (ben′ə fish′ə rē) *or* (ben′ə fish′ē er′ē) *n, pl* **ben·e·fi·ci·ar·ies 1** a person who receives a benefit: *All the children are beneficiaries of the new playground.* **2** a person who receives or is to receive money or property from an insurance policy or a will. <See BENEFACTOR.>

ben·e·fit (ben′ə fit) *n* **1** help, advantage, or profit: *Your talents are of no benefit to you if you don't develop them.* **2 benefits** *pl* payments received from an insurance plan administered by the government, an employer, or an insurance company: *health benefits.* **3** a performance, show, or game put on by professionals to raise money for a charitable cause.
v **1** be good for: *Rest will always benefit a sick person.* **2** gain: *She will benefit from extra time spent studying.* <Old French *benfet*, from Latin *benefactum*>
the benefit of the doubt, the act of believing someone without proof: *I said I had found the money on the street, and they gave me the benefit of the doubt.*

be·nev·o·lent (bə nev′ə lənt) *adj* kind; doing or intending good: *a benevolent smile, throughout the king's benevolent reign.* <Old French, from Latin *bene* well + *volere* wish> **be·nev′o·lence** *n.* **be·nev′o·lent·ly** *adv.*

be·night·ed (bi nī′tid) *adj* not knowing the truth or not knowing right from wrong.

be·nign (bi nīn′) *adj* **1** not diseased, especially, not cancerous: *a benign tumour.* Compare MALIGNANT (def. 1). **2** gentle and good-natured: *a benign question.* **3** favourable and mild: *a benign climate.* <Old French, from Latin *benignus* good-natured> **be·nign′ly** *adv.*

Be·nin (bə nēn′) *n* a country in west Africa.

🍁 **Ben·nett buggy** (ben′ət) *n* in the economic depression of the 1930s, a car hitched up to horses because the owner could not afford gas, oil, or a licence. <R.B. *Bennett*, prime minister of Canada from 1930 to 1935>

bent (bent) *v* past tense and past participle of BEND.
adj curved or crooked: *My grandmother's back is bent.*
n an inclination or tendency: *a bent for drawing.*
bent on, determined on: *bent on revenge. She is bent on becoming a doctor.*
bent out of shape, *Slang* angry or upset: *He's all bent out of shape because I said he was lazy.*

🍁 **bent·wood box** (bent′wůd) *n* a watertight box whose sides are made from one piece of cedar, bent by steam and pressure. First Nations peoples of British Columbia traditionally use these boxes for cooking and for storing.

be·numb (bi num′) *v* make numb, deaden, or stupefy: *A benumbing boredom had set in.*

ben·zene (ben zēn′) *or* (ben′zēn) *n* a colourless, flammable, and poisonous liquid hydrocarbon that has a pleasant odour and vaporizes easily. It is used to make such products as detergents, insecticides, and motor fuel. <German *Benzin*, coined by E. Mitscherlich, 19c chemist>

benzene ring *Chemistry n* the hexagonal shape taken by the six carbon atoms in a benzene molecule.

ben·zine (ben zēn′) *or* (ben′zēn) *n* a colourless, flammable liquid consisting of a mixture of hydrocarbons obtained by distilling petroleum, used mainly as a solvent and cleaning fluid. <See BENZENE.>

ben·zo·ic acid (ben zō′ ik) *n* a white crystalline solid used in the manufacture of **sodium benzoate**, a food preservative.

Be·oth·uk (bē oth′ək) *or* (bē ot′ək) *n, pl* **Be·oth·uk** or **Be·oth·uks 1** a member of an extinct people who were Aboriginal inhabitants of Newfoundland. The last Beothuk died in 1829. **2** their language.
adj to do with these people or their language.

be·queath (bi kwēth′) *or* (bi kwēᴛʜ′) *v* **1** give or leave property or money by a will: *He bequeathed the farm to his daughter.* **2** hand down to posterity: *One age bequeaths its civilization to the next.* <Old English *becwethan* give by will> **be·queath′al** *n.*

be·quest (bi kwest′) *n* **1** something bequeathed: *My grandfather died and left a bequest of ten thousand dollars to his favourite charity.* <Middle English *biqueste*>

be·rate (bi rāt′) *v* **be·rat·ed, be·rat·ing** scold sharply: *Our teacher berated us for arriving late.*

Ber·ber (bər′bər) *n* **1** a member of a N African people. **2** a group of languages spoken by peoples throughout N Africa, or any individual language of this group.

be·reave (bi rēv′) *v* **be·reaved** or **be·reft, be·reav·ing** (*usually passive*) **1** deprive by death: *Bereaved of their mother at an early age, the children learned to take care of themselves.* **2** deprive ruthlessly: *bereft of hope.*
n **the bereaved** the person or people whose loved one has died: *Close friends comforted the bereaved.* <Old English *be-* away + *reafian* rob> **be·reave′ment** *n.*

be·ret (bə rā′) *n* a floppy, round cap of wool, felt, etc. <French, from Latin *birrus* cloak>

berg (bərg) *Informal n* an iceberg.

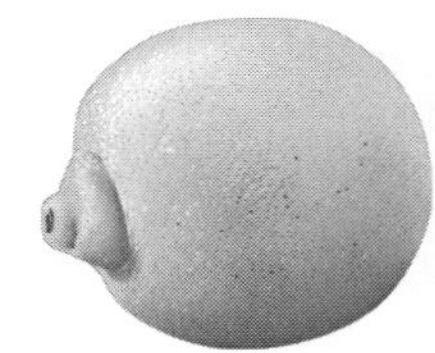

Bergamot oil is extracted from the rind when the fruit is nearly ripe. The oil has been used for hundreds of years as an antiseptic, and as a remedy for many ailments, ranging from acne to malaria. It was used to flavour gin, and it is still used to flavour tea.

ber·ga·mot (bər′gə mot′) *n* **1** a small citrus tree grown for the rind of its fruit, which yields a fragrant oil. **2** a plant of the mint family. <French *bergamote*, from Italian *bergamotta*>

be·rib·boned (bi rib′ənd) *adj* trimmed with many ribbons: *a beribboned hat.*

ber·ke·li·um (bər kē′lē əm) *n* a synthetic, radioactive element produced by nuclear reaction. *Symbol* **Bk** <*Berkeley*, California, where it was first produced>

Ber·mu·da (bər myū′də) *n* a UK Overseas Territory consisting of a group of islands off the southeast coast of the US. **Ber·mu′di·an** or **Ber·mu′dan** *adj, n.*

Bermuda shorts *pln* shorts, especially colourful ones, that reach to just above the knee.

Bermuda Triangle *n* a region of the Atlantic, bounded by Florida, Bermuda, and Puerto Rico, in which ships and planes are said to have mysteriously disappeared.

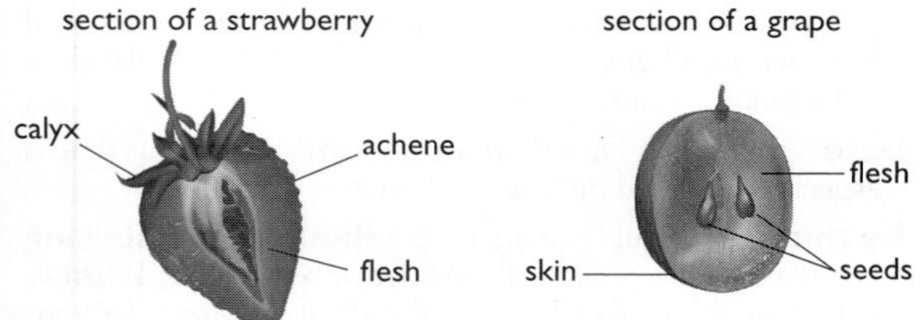

ber·ry (ber′ē) *n, pl* **ber·ries** **1** any small, juicy fruit with many seeds instead of a single stone or pit. Strawberries are berries. **2** *Botany* a small fruit with a skin or rind and with the seeds in the pulp. Grapes, tomatoes, currants, and bananas are all berries. **3** the dry seed, kernel, or fruit of certain kinds of grain or other plants: *a wheat berry.* **4** an egg of a lobster or fish.
v **ber·ried, ber·ry·ing** gather or pick berries. <Old English *berie*> **ber′ry·like′** *adj.*

ber·serk (bər zərk′) *adj* in a frenzy.

ETYMOLOGY

Berserk comes from the Icelandic word *berserkr,* meaning "wild warrior," from *ber* (bear) and *serkr* (shirt). These warriors, who were thought to wear bearskin shirts, became frenzied in battle. The word came to describe a person who becomes violent or loses control.

berth (bərth) *n* **1** a place to sleep on a ship, train, or aircraft. **2** the place reserved for a ship or boat at a dock, or for a vehicle being loaded or unloaded. **3** *Sports* a place or standing: *to win a berth in the finals.* **4** a position or job, especially a rather prestigious one. **5** 🍁 *Newfoundland* a stand of timber in which a person or business has the right to fell trees; a timber limit.
v **1** put in a berth; provide with a berth. **2** have or occupy a berth. <perhaps from *bear*[1]>
give a wide berth to, keep well away from: *I'd give a wide berth to that dog.*

ber·yl (ber′əl) *n* a hard mineral, usually green or greenish blue, a silicate of beryllium and aluminum used as a gemstone. Emeralds and aquamarines are beryls. <Old French, from Greek *beryllos*>

be·ryl·li·um (bə ril′ē əm) *n* a hard, strong, metallic element, used mainly in alloys as a hardening agent. *Symbol* **Be** <See BERYL.>

be·seech (bi sēch′) *Poetic v* **be·sought** or **be·seeched, be·seech·ing** beg earnestly: *Do not hurt her, I beseech you! She besought his forgiveness.* <Old English *be-* thoroughly + *sechen* ask, seek>

be·set (bi set′) *v* **be·set, be·set·ting** **1** attack on all sides: *In the swamp we were beset by mosquitoes.* **2** persistently trouble or threaten: *a task beset with difficulties. Laziness is my besetting sin.* <Old English *besettan* surround>

be·side (bi sīd′) *prep* **1** by the side of or near: *Grass grows beside the brook.* **2** compared with: *He seems dull beside his sister.* <Old English *be sidan* by side>
beside the point, with little to do with the most important point.

beside yourself, out of your mind or very upset: *He was beside himself with worry over his lost dog.*

be·sides (bi sīdz′) *adv* **1** also or moreover: *She didn't want to quarrel; besides, she wasn't completely sure she was right.* **2** in addition: *We tried two other ways besides.* **3** otherwise: *He is ignorant of music, whatever he may know besides.*
prep in addition to; over and above: *The picnic was attended by others besides our own family.*

be·siege (bi sēj′) *v* **be·sieged, be·sieg·ing** **1** surround with an army and try to capture: *For ten years, the Greeks besieged the city of Troy.* **2** crowd around: *Admirers besieged the famous astronaut.* **3** overwhelm with requests, questions, or complaints: *During the flood, the fire department was besieged with calls for help.* **be·sieg′er** *n.*

be·smirch (bi smərch′) *v* make dirty or stain.

be·sot·ted (bi sot′id) *adj* **1** foolish or infatuated. **2** dazed. **3** very drunk.

be·sought (bi sot′) past tense and past participle of BESEECH.

be·speak (bi spēk′) *v* **be·spoke, be·spo·ken** or **be·spoke, be·speak·ing** **1** show or indicate: *A neat appearance bespeaks care.* **2** anticipate: *Her early successes bespeak a great future.* **3** engage in advance; order; reserve: *to bespeak tickets to a play.*

be·spec·ta·cled (bi spek′tə kəld) *adj* wearing glasses.

Bes·se·mer process (bes′ə mər) *n* a method of making steel by using a blast of compressed air to burn the carbon and impurities out of molten iron. <H. *Bessemer,* 19c engineer>

best (best) *adj, superlative of* ***good*** **1** the most desirable, excellent, or beneficial: *the best players, the best thing to do.* **2** largest or most: *We spent the best part of a day just getting organized.* **3** *Informal* favourite: *my best colour.*
adv, superlative of ***well*** **1** in the most excellent way: *Who reads best?* **2** in the highest degree: *I like this book best.*
n **1** the person, thing, or quality that is best: *We want only the best. He is the best in the class.* **2** utmost: *I did my best to finish my homework early.*
v defeat: *Our team was bested in the final game.* <Old English *betst*>
(all) for the best, advantageous in the end: *At first we resisted the change, but it turned out to be all for the best.*
at best, even given the most favourable circumstances or interpretation: *Summer is at best rather short. It was a sad effort at best.*
at your (or **its**) **best,** showing all the best qualities of: *This show is TV at its best.*
get the best of, defeat.
had best, should; would be wise to: *We had best postpone the party.*
make the best of, do as well as possible with: *We'll just have to make the best of a bad job.*
with the best, as well as anyone: *She can swim with the best.*

a bat	e bed	i bid	o pot	u cup	th **thin**
ā cake	ē me	ī bite	ō go	ū rude	ᴛʜ **then**
ȧ bar	ə about	ər over	ȯ for	u̇ put	zh measure

bes·tial (bes′chəl) *or* (bes′tyəl) *adj* savagely cruel. <Old French, from Latin *bestia* beast> **bes′ti·al′i·ty** *n.* **bes′ti·al·ly** *adv.*

be·stir (bi stər′) *v* **be·stirred, be·stir·ring** (*usually with reflexive pronoun*) stir up, rouse, or exert: *to bestir oneself to action.*

best man *n* a person, usually male, who assists the bridegroom at a wedding, standing beside him during the ceremony.

be·stow (bi stō′) *v* (*with* ***on***) **1** give something as a gift: *You have bestowed so many kindnesses on us already.* **2** make use of: *She bestowed a great deal of thought on the plan.* <Middle English *bistowen*> **be·stow′al** *n.*

SYNONYMS

To **bestow** means "to award": *The mayor bestowed a medal on the heroic firefighter.*

To **endow** means "to give a permanent income": *He endowed the university with money for a trust fund.*

To **give** means "to hand over": *I'll give her a birthday present tomorrow.*

best·sell·er (best′sel′ər) *n* anything, especially a book, that sells very well. **best′sell′ing** *adj.*

bet (bet) *v* **bet** or **bet·ted, bet·ting** **1** promise money or something else to a person if that person is proved correct about the outcome of an event: *I bet you two dollars she'll be late.* **2** *Informal* be very sure: *I bet you are wrong about that.*
n **1** an agreement between two people or groups that the one who is proved wrong about the outcome of an event will give a certain thing or sum of money to the one who is correct: *I made a two-dollar bet that she would be late.* **2** the thing or sum of money risked in a bet. **3** a thing to bet on: *That horse is a good bet.* <origin uncertain>
a safe bet, a reliable or certain person or thing: *It's a safe bet we'll have rain before noon. I'll vote for her; she seems like a safe bet.*
bet on, a risk money on: *He bets on every hockey game.* **b** *Informal* depend on: *He might let us go, but don't bet on it.*
you bet, *Informal* definitely: *You bet I'm going to complain. "Want some cake?" "You bet!"*

be·ta (bā′tə) *n* the second thing in a series.
adj Computers to do with a stage of development of a piece of software that involves feedback from users: *a beta test. The beta version is on this CD.* <second letter of the Greek alphabet>

be·ta–block·er (bā′tə blo′kər) *Medicine n* a drug used to control high blood pressure and angina by decreasing the contraction and speed of the heart.

be·take (bi tāk′) *Poetic v* **be·took, be·tak·en, be·tak·ing** (*with a reflexive pronoun*) go: *He betook himself to the mountains.*

beta particle *n* a high-speed electron or positron given off by an atom in the process of radioactive decay. A stream of beta particles forms a **beta ray**.

be·tel (bē′təl) *n* **1** in full, **betel palm** a tropical Asian palm tree yielding an orange-coloured nut. **2** a climbing pepper plant of southeast Asia, whose leaves are chewed together with betel nuts as a mild stimulant. <Malayalam (a language of India) *vettila*>

bête noire (bet′ nwär′) *n* a person who or thing that is especially dreaded or hated. <French = black beast>

be·think (bi thingk′) *Archaic v* **be·thought, be·think·ing** (*with a reflexive pronoun*) consider or remember: *When he bethought himself of his dear friends back home, he grew sad.* <Old English *bethencan*>

be·tide (bi tīd′) *Archaic or Poetic v* **be·tid·ed, be·tid·ing** happen (to): *Our love shall endure, whate'er betide.* <Middle English *be-* + *tiden* happen>
woe betide, *Humorous* a severe warning to: *Woe betide anybody who touches my CD collection!*

be·to·ken (bi tō′kən) *v* indicate or show: *Dark clouds betoken a storm.*

be·took (bi tu̇k′) past tense of BETAKE.

be·tray (bi trā′) *v* **1** be unfaithful to: *She betrayed her friends. You have betrayed my trust.* **2** treacherously give away to an enemy: *The traitor betrayed his country to the invaders.* **3** reveal a secret or something hidden: *If I open my mouth, I'll betray my ignorance.* <Old French, from Latin *tradere* hand over> **be·tray′al** *n.* **be·tray′er** *n.*

be·troth (bi trōᴛʜ′) *v* promise in marriage; engage: *The princess and the duke were betrothed. He betrothed his daughter to a rich man.*
n **betrothed** fiancé or fiancée: *She gazed lovingly at her betrothed.* <Old English *treowth* pledge> **be·troth′al** *n.*

bet·ter (bet′ər) *adj, comparative of* **good** **1** more desirable, excellent, or useful, etc. than another: *a better idea, better bread.* **2** less sick or no longer sick: *The child is better today.* **3** larger: *Four days is the better part of a week.*
adv, comparative of ***well*** **1** more desirably, usefully, or in a more excellent way: *Do better another time.* **2** in a higher degree or more: *I like her cooking better than anyone else's.*
v **1** make or become better: *We can better our work by being more careful.* **2** do better than: *The other class cannot better our grades.*
n **1** a person, thing, or state that is better: *We'll take the better of the two roads.* **2** **betters** *pl* one's superiors: *Listen to the advice of your betters.* <Old English *betera*> **bet′ter·ment** *n.*
better off, in a better condition.
better yourself, improve your circumstances through effort.
for the better, to a more desirable state: *a change for the better. Her illness took a turn for the better.*
get (or **have**) **the better of,** defeat.
had better, should; would be wise to: *I had better go before it rains.*
think better of, think over and change one's mind.

GRAMMAR AND USAGE

In informal speech, people often use **better** instead of **had better**: *I better brush my teeth before I go see the dentist.*

In formal language and in writing, the correct usage is **had better**: *You had better remember to set your alarm clock before you go to bed.*

better half OTHER HALF.

be·tween (bi twēn′) *prep* **1** in or into the space or time separating: *Many cities lie between Calgary and Toronto. There is a paved highway between Flin Flon and The Pas. There are no more holidays between now and March break.* **2** in a range separating two quantities, conditions, times, or circumstances: *all the odd numbers between 9 and 25, somewhere between childhood and adulthood. She should arrive between noon and four o'clock.* **3** involving: *war between two nations. There was a strong bond of affection between them.* **4** by the joint ownership, action, or effort of: *We caught 12 fish between us.* **5** into portions for: *The estate was divided between the two grandchildren.* **6** restricted to: *We kept the matter between us.* **7** divided or shared by one thing and another: *to choose between death and dishonour. Between school and hockey practice, she had her hands full.*
adv in or into an intermediate space or time: *The speeches will seem long if there is no break between.* <Old English *betweonum*>
between the devil and the deep blue sea, in a predicament where the only choices are bad ones.
between you and me, confidentially.
in between, in the middle of.

GRAMMAR AND USAGE

Between is used when referring to only two things or people: *The tasks were divided between my science partner and me.*

Among is used when referring to more than two: *I think we should share the cash reward equally among all six of us.*

It is correct to say *between you and me*, rather than *between you and I,* because the pronoun is the object of the preposition.

For the same reason, say *between us two* rather than *between we two.*

be·twixt (bi twikst′) *Archaic n* between.
betwixt and between, in the middle.

bev·el (bev′əl) *n* **1** a sloping edge: *a wall plaque with a decorative bevel.* **2** a tool for measuring or drawing angles or for adjusting a surface in order to bevel it.
v **bev·elled** or **bev·eled, bev·el·ling** or **bev·el·ing** cut at an angle other than a right angle: *This mirror has bevelled edges.* <origin uncertain>

bev·er·age (bev′rij) *especially Commercial n* a drink of any kind. <Old French *bevrage*, from Latin *bibere* to drink>

bev·y (bev′ē) *n, pl* **bev·ies** a small group: *a bevy of quail, a bevy of children.* <Middle English>

be·wail (bi wāl′) *v* strongly lament or complain of: *to bewail your fate.*

be·ware (bi wer′) *v* (*infinitive or imperative only*) be on one's guard against or be careful of: *Beware! Danger!* <*be* + *ware* wary; careful>
beware of, be careful of; avoid: *Beware of the dog. Beware of swimming in a strong current.*

be·wil·der (bi wil′dər) *v* become confused or perplexed: *a bewildering assortment of clothes to choose from. The fireworks display bewildered the child.* <Old English *wilder* lead astray> **be·wil′der·ing** *adj.* **be·wil′der·ment** *n.*

be·witch (bi wich′) *v* **1** put under a magical spell. **2** charm, delight, or fascinate: *Her smile bewitches everybody.* **be·witched′** *adj.* **be·witch′ing** *adj.*

be·yond (bē yond′) *prep* **1** on or to the farther side of: *a foreign land beyond the sea.* **2** later or further on than: *They stayed beyond the set time.* **3** out of the reach or range of: *a beauty beyond description. He is beyond help. The meaning of this story is beyond me.* **4** in addition to: *I will do nothing beyond the job given me.*
adv farther away: *Beyond lay the mountains.*
conj more than: *The price of the jeans was beyond what she could pay.* <Old English *begeondan*>
the beyond or **the great beyond,** life after death.

Bha·ga·vad Gi·ta (bug′ə vəd gē′tə) *Hinduism n* a holy writing consisting of a philosophical and religious dialogue. <Sanskrit = Song of the Blessed One>

bhik·ku (bik′ū) *Buddhism n* a fully ordained monk. <Sanskrit *bhiksu*>

bhik·ku·ni (bi kū′nē) *Buddhism n* a fully ordained nun. <Sanskrit *bhiksu* + *-ni* feminine suffix>

BHT in full, **butylated hydroxytoluene** a common food preservative that helps to keep fats and oils from going rancid.

Bhu·tan (bū tän′) *n* a country between China and India, in the Himalayas. **Bhu′tan·ese′** *adj, n.*

bi– *combining form* **1** every two: *bimonthly.* **2** twice in a given period: *biannual.* **3** in two ways: *biconcave.* **4** joining or involving two: *bilateral.* <Latin>

bi·an·nu·al (bī an′yū əl) *adj* occurring twice a year: *a biannual visit to the dentist.* **bi·an′nu·al·ly** *adv.*

bi·as (bī′əs) *n* **1** a prejudice that interferes with fair judgment: *The newspaper account of the trial showed a bias in favour of the defendant.* **2** a slanting line. To cut cloth **on the bias** is to cut it diagonally across the weave.
v **bi·ased** or **bi·assed, bi·as·ing** or **bi·as·sing** cause to have a prejudice that interferes with fair judgment: *Several bad experiences have biased my mom against men drivers.*
adj slanting or diagonal: *a bias cut.*
bi′ased or **bi′assed** *adj.*

ETYMOLOGY

Bias comes from the French word *biais*, meaning "slant." In the late 1500s, its meaning in English changed, coming to mean a sense of prejudice or a slanted way of looking at something: *An illustration showing a mother, a father, a son, and a daughter is a biased example of a family. The doctor's bias against eating meat was evident in her speech on healthy living.*

a bat	e bed	i bid	o pot	u cup	th thin
ā cake	ē me	ī bite	ō go	ū rude	ᴛʜ then
ä bar	ə about	ər over	ô for	ů put	zh measure

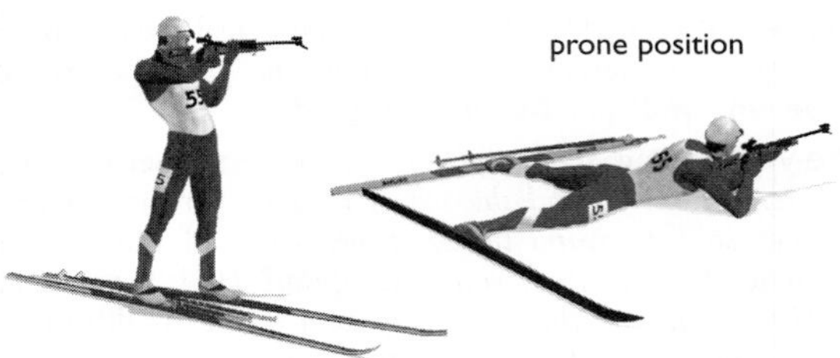

The **biathlon** combines an aerobic activity that requires strength, speed, and endurance, with a passive activity that needs a steady hand and concentration.

bi·ath·lon (bī ath′lon) *n* an Olympic event in which participants (**biathletes**) with rifles race on skis along a cross-country course, stopping to shoot at targets spaced along the way. <Latin *bi-* two + Greek *athlon* contest>

bib (bib) *n* **1** a specially shaped piece of cloth or plastic worn under the chin by babies and young children to protect their clothing, especially at meals. **2** the part of an apron or overalls above the waist. <Middle English = drink, from Latin *bibere*>
bib and tucker, *Informal* clothes: *Put on your best bib and tucker.*

Bi·ble (bī′bəl) *n* **1** the sacred writings of the Christian religion, consisting of the Old and New Testaments. **2** the Hebrew scriptures of Judaism, consisting of the Torah, the Prophets, and the Writings. **3 bible** any book accepted as an indisputable authority in a particular field: *The* Canada Year Book *is the Canadian geographer's bible.* <Old French, from Greek *biblia* books> **bib′li·cal** or **Bib′li·cal** *adj.*

bib·li·og·ra·pher (bib′lē og′rə fər) *n* a person who investigates the authorship, editions, dates, etc. of books or other publications or manuscripts.

bib·li·og·ra·phy (bib′lē og′rə fē) *n, pl* **bib·li·og·ra·phies** **1** a list of books and other publications about a subject or person, or by a certain author. **2** a list of references used in research. **3** the study of the history and description of books and other publications. **bib′li·o·graph′i·cal** *adj.*

bib·li·o·phile (bib′lē ə fīl′) *n* a lover of books, especially a collector of books. <Greek *biblion* book + *-philos* loving>

bi·cam·er·al (bī kam′ə rəl) *adj* **1** with two legislative assemblies. The Canadian Parliament is bicameral; it has both a Senate and a House of Commons. **2** with two parts that work together, like the human brain. <Latin *bi-* two + *camera* chamber>

bi·car·bo·nate (bī kär′bə nit) *or* (bī kär′bə nāt′) *n* any salt of CARBONIC ACID that contains a base and hydrogen.

bicarbonate of soda SODIUM BICARBONATE.

bi·cen·ten·a·ry (bī′sen ten′ə rē) *or* (bī′sen tē′nə rē) *n, pl* **bi·cen·ten·a·ries** **1** a period of two hundred years. **2** a two-hundredth anniversary or its celebration.
adj to do with a bicentenary.

bi·cen·ten·ni·al (bī′sen ten′yəl) *n* a two-hundredth anniversary or its celebration.
adj **1** to do with a period of 200 years or a 200th anniversary. **2** happening every 200 years.

bi·ceps (bī′seps) *n, sing or pl* any muscle with two points of origin, especially the large muscle at the front of the upper arm. <Latin *bi-* two + *caput* point, head>

bick·er (bik′ər) *v* argue about small things: *My brothers bickered all afternoon.* <Middle English *bikeren*>

bi·con·cave (bī kon′kāv) *or* (bī′kon kāv′) *adj* concave on both sides.

bi·con·vex (bī kon′veks) *or* (bī′kon veks′) *adj* convex on both sides.

bi·cul·tur·al (bī kul′chə rəl) *adj* **1** with two distinct cultures existing together. **2** 🍁 to do with the co-existence of English and French cultures in Canada, or policies and programs to promote their co-existence.
bi·cul′tur·al·ism′ *n.*

bi·cus·pid (bī kus′pid) *n* a double-pointed tooth. An adult human has eight bicuspids.
adj with two points. <Latin *bi-* two + *cuspis* point>

A pursuit **bicycle** weighs only about 8 kg, and has no brakes or gears—cyclists backpedal to slow down or stop. Races take place on an oval track with steeply banked corners that facilitate high speeds.

A mountain bike has straight handlebars, powerful brakes, and shift levers that control up to 24 gears. It also has low-pressure, knobby tires for extra traction in off-road racing on dirt paths and backwoods trails.

bi·cy·cle (bī′sə kəl) *n* a vehicle consisting of a metal frame with two wheels one behind the other, handles for steering, a seat for the rider, and pedals that drive a chain connected to the back wheel.
v **bi·cy·cled, bi·cy·cling** ride a bicycle. <Latin *bi-* two + Greek *kyklos* wheel> **bi′cy·clist** *n.*

bid (bid) *v* **bade** or **bid, bid·den** or **bid, bid·ding** (defs. 1–3)**; bid, bid·ding** (def. 4) **1** command or request: *Do as I bid you. They bade me stay overnight.* **2** say or tell: *I bid you goodbye.* **3** make an offer, stating the price one will pay or charge: *She bid $30 for the old table. Several companies will bid for the contract.* **4** in card games, state what one proposes to win.
n **1** an offer, or the amount stated in the offer: *Has anyone made a bid on the house yet? The lowest bid for building the bridge was $2 000 000.* **2** in card games, the act of bidding or the amount someone has bid. **3** an attempt to secure or obtain: *She made a bid for our sympathy.* <Old English *biddan*> **bid′der** *n.*
bid fair, seem likely: *The plan bids fair to succeed.*

bid·da·ble (bid′ə bəl) *adj* **1** willingly doing what one is told. **2** on which bids may be made.

bid·ding (bid′ing) *n* **1** a command or invitation. **2** the making of bids at an auction, in a card game, etc.: *The bidding at the auction was slow at first but soon became very lively.*
do someone's bidding, obey someone.

bid·dy (bid′ē) *Informal n, pl* **bid·dies** a talkative old woman. <origin uncertain>

bide (bīd) *Archaic* (*except in* **bide your time**) *v* **bode** or **bid·ed, bid·ed, bid·ing** **1** wait for. **2** abide. <Old English *bidan*>
bide your time, wait for a good chance: *If I bide my time, I will probably get those shoes at a bargain price.*

bi·det (bi dā′) *n* an oval bathroom fixture for bathing the genital and anal areas. <French>

bi·en·ni·al (bī en′ē əl) *adj* **1** lasting two years, as some plants do. **2** occurring every two years.
n **1** any plant that lives two years, usually producing flowers and seeds the second year: *Carrots and onions are biennials.* **2** an event that occurs every two years. <Latin *bi-* two + *annus* year> **bi·en′ni·al·ly** *adv.*

GRAMMAR AND USAGE

Biennial and **biannual** are easily confused, since they sound so much alike and both involve the number two.

Biennial means "occurring every two years": *The music festival is binennial.*

Biannual means "occurring twice a year": *I make biannual visits to the dentist.*

bier (bēr) *n* a movable stand on which a coffin or dead body is placed. <Old English *beran* bear[1]>

bi·fo·cal (bī fō′kəl) *adj* with two focuses. Bifocal eyeglasses have two parts: the upper part for far vision, the lower for near vision.
n **bifocals** *pl* eyeglasses with bifocal lenses.

bi·fur·cate (bī′fər kāt′) *or* (bī fər′kāt) *for v,* (bī fər′kit) *or* (bī′fər kit) *for adj. v* **bi·fur·cat·ed, bi·fur·cat·ing** divide into two parts or branches.
adj divided into two branches. <Latin *bi-* two + *furca* fork> **bi′fur·ca′tion** *n.*

big (big) *adj* **big·ger, big·gest** **1** large in width, length, height, or depth: *a big room, a big book, a big hole.* **2** great in extent or scope: *a big project.* **3** grown up: *He says he wants to be a firefighter when he's big.* **4** *Informal* important or significant: *This is big news.* **5** full; loud: *a big voice.* **6** *Informal* generous: *It was very big of you to help out.* **7** boastful: *big talk.* **8** ambitious and far-reaching: *big dreams, a big idea.* **9** *Informal* popular: *This hairstyle is very big right now.*
adv Informal in a big way or on a big scale: *to win big, to think big.* <Middle English> **big′ness** *n.*
be big on, *Informal* have a strong interest in or liking for: *I'm not big on action movies.*

big·a·my (big′ə mē) *n* the criminal offence of marrying someone while still legally married to someone else. <Latin *bi-* twice + Greek *gamos* married> **big′a·mist** *n.* **big′a·mous** *adj.*

big bang *n* the enormous explosion that is believed to have brought the universe into existence. The **big bang theory** attempts to explain how this happened.

big box store *n* a very large store, usually one of a chain, specializing in a certain kind of merchandise and set up like a warehouse. Big box stores are typically found in large retail parks or outdoor malls.

Big Brother *n* an adult male who, under the supervision of a social agency, befriends and guides a disadvantaged child.

big bucks *Slang pl n* a lot of money: *You'll pay big bucks for a sailboard like that one.*

big business *n* large, rich companies with great economic and political influence.

big deal *Informal n* (*often used ironically*) something or someone important, serious, or impressive: *Winning a Juno is a pretty big deal. You get up at 6 a.m.? Big deal! I get up at 4:30!*

Big Dipper *n* the seven principal stars in the constellation Ursa Major, arranged in a form that suggests a dipper.

Big·foot (big′fůt′) SASQUATCH.

big game *n* **1** large animals sought by hunters: *Elephants, tigers, lions, moose, and elk are big game.* **2** some important thing that is sought: *Running for premier? Wow, that's going after big game.*

big–heart·ed (big′härt′tid) *adj* kind and generous.

big·horn (big′hôrn′) *n, pl* **big·horns** or (*especially collectively*) **big·horn** a large wild sheep found mainly in the Rocky Mountains, with huge brown horns that curl back and down.

bight (bīt) *n* **1** a long inward curve in a coastline. **2** a bend, angle, or corner. **3** a loop of rope; the slack of rope between fastened ends. <Old English *byht*>

big·ot (big′ət) *n* an intolerant, prejudiced person; a person without respect for the views of others. <French> **big′ot·ed** *adj.* **big′ot·ry** *n.*

a bat	e bed	i bid	o pot	u cup	th thin
ā cake	ē me	ī bite	ō go	ū rude	ᴛʜ then
ä bar	ə about	ər over	ô for	ů put	zh measure

big picture *n* (*usually with* **the**) the view of anything as a whole, rather than in terms of details or separate aspects: *This book doesn't tell everything about the history of hockey, but it does give you the big picture.* **big-picture** *adj.*

big shot *Informal n* an important person.

Big Sister *n* an adult female who, under the supervision of a social agency, befriends and guides a disadvantaged child.

Big Smoke *Informal n* (*with* **the**) **1** 🍁 Toronto. **2** any big city.

big time *Informal n* the top level of advancement in an activity: *He's finally reached the big time.*
adv in an extreme way or to an extreme degree: *They were taken to court and lost big time.* **big′-time′** *adj.*

big wheel *Informal n* an influential or otherwise important person: *a big wheel in banking.*

big·wig (big′wig′) *Informal n* an important person.

bike (bīk) *Informal n, v* **biked, bik·ing** bicycle. <shortened from *bicycle*>

bik·er (bī′kər) *Informal n* **1** a motorcyclist, especially one who wears leather riding gear and belongs to a motorcycle club. **2** a bicyclist.

bi·ki·ni (bi kē′nē) *n, pl* **bi·ki·nis** **1** a brief two-piece bathing suit for women and girls. **2** brief, close-fitting underpants or men's swimming trunks. <*Bikini,* an atoll in the Pacific that was the site of a US atom bomb test. The swimsuit was advertised as having a similar devastating effect.>

bi·lat·er·al (bī lat′ə rəl) *adj* **1** with two sides. **2** existing on two sides. **3** affecting two sides or parties equally: *a bilateral agreement.* **bi·lat′er·al·ly** *adv.*

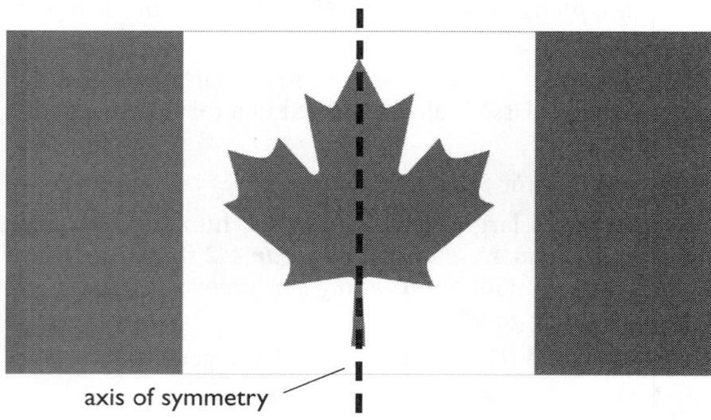

To picture **bilateral symmetry**, think of the axis of symmetry as a fold line. The two halves of the flag design would overlap exactly.

bilateral symmetry *Mathematics n* symmetry of two parts on either side of an axis. The Canadian flag has bilateral symmetry, about a vertical axis.

bile (bīl) *n* **1** a bitter yellow or greenish liquid secreted by the liver and stored in the gall bladder, discharged into the small intestine to aid digestion. **2** anger or irritability. <French, from Latin *bilis*>

bilge (bilj) *n* **1** the lowest part of a ship's hold, or the bottom of the hull. **2** usually, **bilge water** **a** the dirty water that collects there. **b** *Informal* nonsense. <origin uncertain>

bi·lin·gual (bī ling′gwəl) *or* (bī ling′gyə wəl) *adj* **1** able to speak two languages fluently. **2** using, containing, or expressed in two languages: *a bilingual dictionary, a bilingual meeting.* **3** 🍁 **a** able to speak both English and French. **b** using both English and French: *bilingual courts, a bilingual hospital.* <Latin *bi-* two + *lingua* language> **bi·lin′gual·ize′** *v.* **bi·lin′gual·ly** *adv.*

bi·lin·gual·ism (bī ling′gwə liz′əm) *or* (bī ling′gyə wə liz′əm) *n* **1** the ability to speak two languages fluently. **2** a policy of using or promoting two languages equally. **3** 🍁 **a** the ability to speak both English and French. **b** the policy of giving equal status to English and French.

bil·ious (bil′yəs) *adj* **1** to do with trouble involving the bile or the liver: *a bilious attack.* **2** cross or bad-tempered. **3** sickly-looking: *a bilious green.*

bi·li·ru·bin (bil′ə rū′bən) *n* an orange-yellow pigment in the bile, formed in the natural breakdown of hemoglobin. Excess amounts of bilirubin in the blood produce the yellow appearance associated with jaundice. <Latin *bilis* bile + *ruber* red>

bilk (bilk) *v* **1** defraud or cheat: *They bilked him of his entire inheritance.* **2** avoid paying bills or debts.
n **1** a fraud; deception. **2** a person who avoids paying his or her bills. <origin uncertain> **bilk′er** *n.*

bill[1] (bil) *n* **1** **a** a list or statement showing the payment owed for work done or things supplied: *We got the bill yesterday.* **b** the amount of money shown on such a statement: *Our grocery bill was high last week.* **2** a piece of paper money: *a five-dollar bill* **3** a proposed law presented to a lawmaking body for its approval: *In Canada, a bill becomes an act if it receives a majority vote in Parliament.* **4** a written or printed public notice, such as an advertisement or poster: *The sign on the wall says "Post no bills."* **5** the program of entertainment in a theatre.
v **1** send a statement of charges to: *The store will bill us on the first of the month.* **2** enter or list in a bill of any kind. **3** advertise or announce in a notice or poster: *The circus used to be billed as the greatest show on earth.* <Latin *bulla* document> **bill′er** *n.*
fill the bill, *Informal* satisfy requirements.
foot the bill, pay the costs for something.

bill[2] (bil) *n* the hard, hornlike part of a bird's jaws.
v touch bills or beaks: *Doves often bill in supposed affection.* <Old English *bile*>
bill and coo, behave or talk in an amorous or sentimental way.

🍁 **Bill 101** *n* a Québec law governing language use, enacted in 1977, that French would be the main language of business, employment, and education.

bill·board (bil′bôrd′) *n* a large board, usually outdoors, on which advertisements or notices are displayed.

bil·let (bil′it) *v* **bil·let·ed, bil·let·ing** give or assign lodging in a private home: *Members of the visiting choir were billeted by families in the community.*
n **1** a private home where a person is assigned to be lodged. **2** *Military* a written order to provide board and lodging for troops. <See BILL[1].>

bill·fold (bil′fōld′) *n* a folding wallet for paper money.

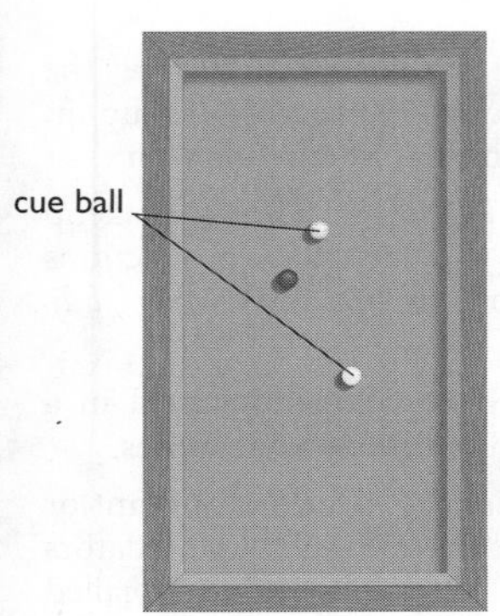

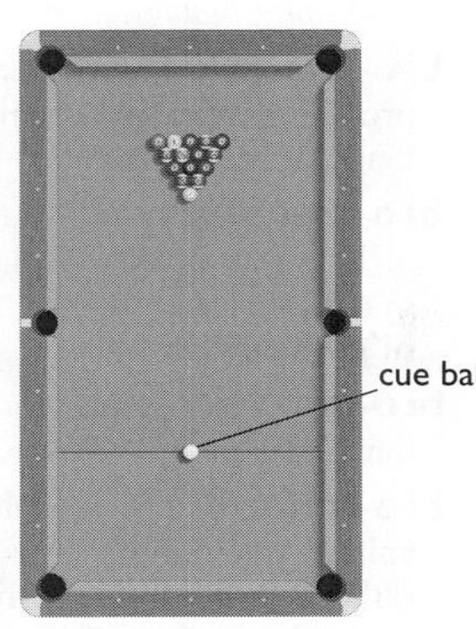

Billiards began in the 1300s as an outdoor game played on the ground with sticks and balls, but was eventually brought indoors. Although there have been a number of versions and different styles of play, the game has never lost its popularity. Technical advances have turned billiards into a game of precision and artistry.

bil·liard (bil′yərd) *n* **1 billiards** (*with singular verb*) **a** any of several games played with coloured balls on a special table with openings called pockets. A long stick called a cue is used to hit the balls. See also POOL, SNOOKER. **2 a carom billiards** a version of billiards played with two white balls and a red one. **b** in this game, a score made by striking one ball so that it hits the other two.
adj to do with the game of billiards: *a billiard table.* <Old French *billard* cue stick, from *bille* stick of wood>

bill·ing (bil′ing) *n* **1 a** the fact or action of being publicized in a specific order. **b** the position in such an order: *She received star billing.* **2** a listing of the total amount of money owed by a client or customer: *They thought the company's billings were too high.*

bil·lion (bil′yən) *n* **1** a thousand million; 1 000 000 000. <Latin *bi-* two (i.e., to the second power) + (*mi*)*llion*). Originally, a billion was a million million.>
bil′lionth *adj, n.*

bil·lion·aire (bil′yə ner′) *or* (bil′yə ner′) *n* a person whose wealth adds up to at least a billion dollars or other currency units.

bill of fare *n* a list of the dishes served at a meal or those that can be ordered; a menu.

bill of goods *n* a shipment of merchandise.
sell someone a bill of goods, mislead a person.

bill of health *n* a certificate stating whether or not there are infectious diseases on a ship or in the port from which it is leaving.
clean bill of health, an assurance that a person or thing is sound and in good health or condition.

bill of lading *n* a receipt given by a shipper that shows a list of goods received for transportation.

bill of rights *n* **1** a statement of the fundamental rights of the people of a nation. **2** ✱ **Bill of Rights** a statement of human rights and basic freedoms in Canada, passed by Parliament in 1960.

bill of sale *n* a written statement transferring ownership of something from the seller to the buyer.

bil·low (bil′ō) *n* **1** a great wave or surge of the sea. **2** any great wave: *billows of smoke.*
v **1** rise or roll in big waves: *On a windy day the surf billows.* **2** swell out: *The sheets on the clothesline billowed in the wind.* <Old Norse *bylgja*> **bil′low·y** *adj.*

bil·ly[1] (bil′ē) *n, pl* **bil·lies** a club or stick, such as is carried by some police officers. <diminutive of French *bille* log>

bil·ly[2] (bil′ē) *n, pl* **bil·lies** in full, **billycan** a can for boiling water or for holding hot liquids. <Australian Aborigine *billa* water>

billy goat *n* a male goat. <pet name *Billy*>

bi·me·tal·lic (bī′me ta′lik) *adj* made of two metals: *A toonie is a bimetallic coin.*

bi·month·ly (bī munth′lē) *adj, adv* **1** once every two months: *bimonthly meetings* (*adj*). *The newsletter is published bimonthly* (*adv*). **2** *Informal* twice a month.
n, pl **bi·month·lies** a magazine published bimonthly.

bin (bin) *n* a large container for holding loose things like potatoes, toys, bulk foods, etc. <Old English *binn*>

bi·na·ry (bī′nə rē) *adj* **1** to do with two. **2** *Mathematics, Computers* to do with binary digits, that is, only the digits 0 and 1. <Latin *bini* two at a time>

binary digit *n* either of the digits 0 or 1, the only digits in a binary system and the basic unit of information in computers. The two digits can be thought of as the *off* and *on* states of an electric circuit. Usually shortened to **bit**.

binary notation *Mathematics, Computers n* numbers written according to the binary system, using only the digits 0 and 1.

binary star *n* a pair of stars that revolve around a common centre of gravity, often appearing as a single object.

binary system *Mathematics n* a number system with a base of 2 instead of 10, so that the only digits available are 0 and 1. In the binary system, 1 is one, 10 is two, 11 is three, 100 is four, etc.

bind (bīnd) *v* **bound, bind·ing 1** tie together: *He bound the package with a bright ribbon.* **2** stick together: *Gravel can be bound by tar or cement.* **3** be too tight or limiting: *I don't like these tights; they bind.* **4** hold by a promise, agreement, or obligation: *I'd like to help you out, but I'm bound by school rules.* **5** put a bandage on: *to bind a wound.* **6** put a border on to strengthen or decorate: *They bound the frayed edge of the carpet.* **7** fasten pages inside a cover: *The pages were bound into a small book.*
n **1** anything that binds or ties. **2** *Informal* a situation that is difficult, inconvenient, or restrictive: *It'll put me in a real bind if she asks me to help out after school.* <Old English *bindan*>

a bat	e bed	i bid	o pot	u cup	th thin
ā cake	ē me	ī bite	ō go	ū rude	ᴛʜ then
ä bar	ə about	ər over	ô for	ů put	zh measure

bind·er (bīn′dər) *n* **1** a sturdy cover for holding loose pages together, usually with rings in the spine that go through holes in the margin of the pages. **2** a machine that cuts stalks of grain and ties them in bundles. **3** a person who binds, especially one who binds books.

🍁 **binder twine** *n* strong, coarse string originally used for binding grain into bales.

bind·ing (bīn′ding) *n* **1** the covering of a book, or the method used to bind a book. **2** a strip protecting or ornamenting an edge. **3 bindings** *pl Skiing* clips that join skis to boots, thus attaching the skis to the skier's feet.
adj **1** that binds, fastens, or connects. **2** with force or power to hold a person to some agreement or promise: *He signed the contract, so it's legally binding.*

binding energy *Physics n* the energy necessary to break an atomic nucleus into its smaller component particles.

bind·weed (bīnd′wēd′) *n* a plant with long runners that twine around the stems of other plants.

binge (binj) *n* a brief spree of overindulgence in anything, especially food or drink.
v **binged, binge·ing** have a binge: *to binge on doughnuts.* <uncertain origin>

bin·go (bing′gō) *n* **1** a game of chance in which each player has a card with randomly numbered squares, which are covered with markers as numbers are drawn and shouted out by a caller. A player with a full line of markers shouts "Bingo!" and wins the game. **2** an event at which people pay to play bingo for prizes, often as a fundraiser.
interj **1** the word called out by the winner of a bingo game. **2** an exclamation of pleased surprise when something turns out well. <origin uncertain>

bi·noc·u·lar (bə nok′yə lər) *or* (bī nok′yə lər) *adj* to do with two eyes.
n **binoculars** *pl* a pair of small telescopes joined as a unit for use with both eyes. **Field glasses** are binoculars. <Latin *bini* two at a time + *oculi* eyes>

bi·no·mi·al (bī nō′mē əl) *adj* consisting of two terms.
n **1** *Mathematics* an expression consisting of two terms connected by a plus or minus sign. **2** *Biology* the two-part Latin name identifying a plant or animal in binomial nomenclature. The binomial of the N American beaver is *Castor canadensis.* <Latin *bi-* two + *nomen* name>

binomial nomenclature *Biology n* the system of classification in which plants and animals are given two names, the first for the genus and the second for the species. These two names are usually printed in italics, with the genus name capitalized and the species name not capitalized, such as *Homo sapiens.*

GRAMMAR AND USAGE

While the two scientific names of plants and animals (genus and species) are usually italicized, the names of orders, phyla, families, and classes are not put into italics. *Sunflower* is known as *Helianthus annuus* in the **binomial nomenclature** system.

bio– *combining form* involving life or living things: *biography, biology.*

bi·o·ac·cu·mu·la·tion (bī′ō ə kyūm′yə lā′shən) *n* the process by which environmental poisons build up in living matter. Also called **biological accumulation**.

bi·o·chem·is·try (bī′ō kem′is trē) *n* the chemical makeup of living animals and plants, and the chemical reactions that go on inside them. **bi′o·chem′i·cal** *adj.* **bi′o·chem′ist** *n.*

bi·o·chip (bī′ō chip′) *n* a computer chip implanted in a living organism, for tracking or monitoring purposes.

bi·o·con·trol (bī′ō kən trōl′) *Ecology n* control of plant or animal populations by natural means such as predators rather than by chemicals or culling. Also called **biological control**.

bi·o·de·grad·a·ble (bī′ō di grā′də bəl) *adj* capable of being broken down, or decomposed, by a natural process such as the action of bacteria.

bi·o·di·ver·si·ty (bī′ō di vər′si tē) *or* (bī′ō dī vər′si tē) *Ecology n* the variety of plant and animal species found within a particular environment.

bi·o·en·gi·neer·ing (bī′ō en′jə nē′ring) *n* the application of engineering to living organisms, as in the development of artificial limbs or genetic manipulation.

bi·o·eth·ics (bī′ō eth′iks) *n* (*with singular verb*) the study of moral issues arising from research projects that involve human beings or live animals or their organs, or from the use of new genetic and medical procedures. **bi′o·eth′i·cal** *adj.* **bi′o·eth′i·cist** (bī′ō eth′ə sist) *n.*

bi·o·feed·back (bī′ō fēd′bak′) *n* the use of electronic monitoring devices to provide information about ordinary automatic body functions such as heart rate or blood pressure as a means of gaining voluntary control over them.

bi·og·ra·phy (bī og′rə fē) *n, pl* **bi·og·ra·phies** the written story of a person's life. <*bio-* + *-graphy*> **bi·og′ra·pher** *n.* **bi′o·graph′i·cal** *adj.*

bi·o·haz·ard (bī′ō haz′ərd) *Ecology n* any substance, condition, or activity that harms plant or animal life: *Dumping industrial waste in rivers creates a serious biohazard.* **bi′o·haz′ard·ous** *adj.*

biological accumulation BIOACCUMULATION.

biological clock *n* **1** the body's control of its own natural rhythms, especially those synchronized to the cycle of day and night. **2** *Informal* the natural process of aging, which may set a time limit on childbearing or other activities.

biological control BIOCONTROL.

biological warfare *n* the waging of war by using disease-producing bacteria or other micro-organisms to destroy crops, livestock, or human life.

bi·ol·o·gy (bī ol′ə jē) *n* the science of life or living matter in all its forms and activities; the study of the origin, reproduction, structure, etc. of plant and animal life. Botany and zoology are the main divisions of biology. **bi′o·log′i·cal** *adj.* **bi·ol′o·gist** *n.*

bi·o·lu·min·esc·ence (bī′ō lü′ mi nes′əns) the ability of certain living organisms, such as fireflies, to change chemical energy in the body into light.

bi·o·mass (bī′ō mas′) *n* **1** the amount of living matter in a given area, expressed as mass per unit area. **2** organic matter used as fuel, especially to generate electricity.

bi·ome (bī′ōm) *n* an extensive ecological community, especially one with one dominant type of vegetation; an ecozone. <Greek *bio-* life + *oma* mass>

bi·o·me·chan·ics (bī′ō me kan′iks) *n* (*with singular verb*) the study of mechanical laws as they apply to living organisms.

bi·o·med·i·cine (bī′ō med′ə sən) *n* the application of sciences such as biochemistry and biophysics to medicine, especially the human body's response to conditions outside its natural environment, such as during space or undersea travel. **bi′o·med′i·cal** *adj.*

bi·o·nic (bī on′ik) *adj* **1** *Medicine* to do with an artificial, electronic body part or a device that strengthens or replaces a natural body function: *a bionic arm.* **2** *Science fiction* to do with superhuman powers conferred by such a device. **3** to do with the science of bionics.
n **bionics** (*with singular verb*) the study of biological functions as models for the development of computers and other electronic devices or systems.

bi·o·phys·ics (bī′ō fiz′iks) *n* (*with singular verb*) the science that relates the principles of physics to biological problems. **bi′o·phys′i·cal** *adj.* **bi′o·phys′i·cist** *n.*

bi·o·pic (bī′ō pik′) *n* a movie about a real person's life. <*bio*(*graphy*) + *pic*(*ture*)>

bi·o poem (bī′ō) *n* a poem written about a real person's life. <*bio*(*graphy*) *poem*>

bi·op·sy (bī′op sē) *n, pl* **bi·op·sies** **1** an examination of tissue from a living body, to determine the cause or extent of a disease. Compare AUTOPSY. **2** the sample taken for this examination. <Greek *bio-* life + *opsis* a viewing>

bi·o·re·gion (bī′ō rē′jən) *n* a large area consisting of many related ECOREGIONS. The Arctic-Atlantic bioregion, for example, contains nearly 50 ecoregions. Bioregions are not dependent on any political boundaries, and often stretch across the borders of countries, provinces, states, etc. <*bio-* + *region*>

bi·o·rhythm (bī′ō riᴛʜ′əm) *n* a cycle of various bodily functions, such as the daily cycle of sleeping and waking.

bi·o·sphere (bī′ə sfēr′) *n* the parts of the earth and its atmosphere in which living things are found.

bi·o·ta (bī ō′tə) *n* all the living organisms of a particular place or time. <Greek *biote* way of life, from *bios* life>

bi·o·tech·no·lo·gy (bī′ō tek nol′ə jē) *n* **1** the use, including genetic manipulation, of living organisms or living matter for industrial and other purposes. **2** any science that deals with this.

bi·o·ter·ror·ism (bī′ō ter′ər iz′ əm) *n* **1** the use of disease that is deliberately spread to create terror in a population. **2** the terror caused in this way: *a nation in the grip of bioterrorism.* Also, **bioterror**. **bi′o·ter′ror·ist** *n.*

bi·ot·ic (bī ot′ik) *adj* involving living matter or organisms. The living or dead parts of an organism's surroundings are called **biotic factors**. <Greek *bios* life>

bi·par·ti·san (bī pȧr′tə zən) *or* (bī pȧr′tə zan′) *adj* **1** of or representing two political parties. **2** *US* involving both the Republican and the Democratic parties.

bi·par·tite (bī pȧr′tīt) *adj* with two parts: *the bipartite shell of an oyster.*

bi·ped (bī′ped) *n* an animal with two feet.
adj with two feet. <Latin *bi-* two + *pedis* foot>

bi·plane (bī′plān′) *n* an airplane with two sets of wings, one above the other.

bi·po·lar (bī pō′lər) *adj* **1** with two poles or extremes. **2** to do with both of the earth's polar regions.

bipolar (affective) disorder *Psychiatry n* a condition in which periods of depression and manic behaviour both occur. A person with this disorder may be called a **manic-depressive**.

bi·ra·di·al symmetry (bī rā′dē əl) *Mathematics n* an arrangement of equal parts both bilaterally (on either side of an axis) and radially (around a central point). A six-pointed star has biradial symmetry.

birch (bərch) *n* a tree or shrub found in the northern hemisphere, with peelable bark. This **birchbark** was traditionally used by First Nations peoples in making canoes. <Old English *bierce*>

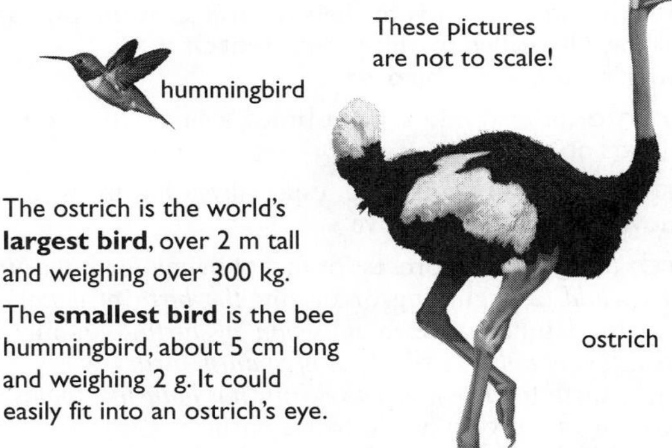
These pictures are not to scale!
hummingbird
The ostrich is the world's **largest bird**, over 2 m tall and weighing over 300 kg.
The **smallest bird** is the bee hummingbird, about 5 cm long and weighing 2 g. It could easily fit into an ostrich's eye.
ostrich

bird (bərd) *n* **1** a feathered, warm-blooded, egg-laying vertebrate with forelimbs modified into wings that allow most species to fly. See also THROAT for picture. **2** a shuttlecock. <Old English *bridd* bird> **bird′like′** *adj.*
a little bird told me, *Informal* an expression used to conceal the source of a rumour.
bird in the hand, something certain because you already have it.
birds of a feather, people sharing the same kinds of ideas or interests.
for the birds, *Informal* not worth considering: *That movie was for the birds.*
give someone the bird, *Informal* jeer or ridicule someone, especially a performer.
kill two birds with one stone, get two things done by one action.

a bat	e bed	i bid	o pot	u cup	th thin
ā cake	ē me	ī bite	ō go	ü rude	ᴛʜ then
ȧ bar	ə about	ər over	ȯ for	u̇ put	zh measure

bird·bath (bərd′bath′) *n* a shallow basin on a stand, filled with water for birds to bathe in or drink from.

bird call *n* **1** the sound that a bird makes, or an imitation of it. **2** an instrument for imitating the sound of a bird.

bird course *Slang n* a university or high school course that requires very little intelligence or work.

bird·house (bərd′hous′) *n* a small roofed box, hung in a tree or set on a pole for birds to nest in.

bird·ie (bər′dē) *n* **1** *Informal* a little bird. **2** *Golf* a score of one stroke less than PAR (def. 5) for any hole on a course. Compare BOGEY[1].

bird·ing (bər′ding) BIRDWATCHING.

bird of prey *n* any bird, such as an eagle, hawk, or owl, that kills animals and other birds for food.

bird·seed (bərd′sēd′) *n* a mixture of small seeds used to feed birds.

bird's–eye view (bər′dzī) *n* **1** a view from above: *We got a bird's-eye view of the Yukon River from the airplane.* **2** a general or overall view: *This summary will give you a bird's-eye view of the project.*

bird·song (bərd′song′) *n* the musical sounds of birds.

bird·watch·ing (bərd′woch′ing) *n* the observing and studying of wild birds in their natural surroundings as a hobby. Also called **birding**. **bird′watch** *v.* **bird′watch′er** or **bird′er** *n.*

bi·reme (bī′rēm) *n* in ancient times, a ship with two rows of oars on each side. <Latin *bi-* two + *remus* oar>

birl (bərl) *v* spin something, especially a log in water, by moving the feet. <imitative>

birth (bərth) *n* **1** the process or fact of being born: *the birth of a child.* **2** beginning or origin: *the birth of a nation.* **3** natural inheritance: *a musician by birth.* **4** family or ancestry: *of noble birth. She is of Spanish birth.*
v give birth to: *The maternity clinic has homelike rooms for birthing in.* <probably Old Norse *burthr*>
give birth to, a bear offspring. **b** be the origin or cause of: *to give birth to a new invention.*

birth canal *n* the passage followed by a baby during birth, from the uterus through the cervix and the vagina.

birth control *n* the use of special devices or other methods to prevent pregnancy.

birth·day (bərth′dā′) *n* **1** the day on which a person is born. **2** the day on which something began: *July 1 is Canada's birthday.* **3** the anniversary of either of these.

birth·ing centre (bərth′ing) *n* a ward in a hospital or clinic, where low-risk births take place in homelike surroundings. Mothers give birth in **birthing rooms**.

birth·mark (bərth′märk′) *n* a spot or mark on the skin that was there at birth.

birth mother *n* a woman who has given birth to a child, as distinguished from one who has adopted a child.

birth name *n* a woman's surname before marriage.

birth·place (bərth′plās′) *n* **1** the place where a person was born. **2** the place of origin of something: *Mesopotamia is the birthplace of civilization.*

birth rate *n* the proportion of the number of births per year to the total population.

birth·right (bərth′rīt′) *n* **1** a right enjoyed by a person because he or she was born in a certain country, or because of any other fact about his or her birth: *"Freedom is our birthright!" she shouted.* **2** in some cultures, the rights belonging to the eldest son.

birth·stone (bərth′stōn′) *n* a jewel associated with a certain month of the year.

bis·cuit (bis′kit) *n* **1** a small, soft cake made with baking powder or baking soda. **2** a crisp, somewhat thick cracker. **3** pottery or china that has been fired once but not glazed. <French *biscuit*, from *bis* twice + *cuit* cooked, in reference to how it was prepared>
have had the biscuit, *Slang* be good for nothing more: *I'm going home now; I've had the biscuit with this party.*

bi·sect (bī sekt′) *v* **1** divide or cut in two. **2** *Mathematics* divide (a line, figure, etc.) into two equal parts. <Latin *bi-* two + *secare* cut> **bi·sec′tion** *n.* **bi·sec′tor** *n.*

bi·sex·u·al (bī sek′shū əl) *adj* **1** to do with both sexes. **2** with male and female reproductive organs in the same organism. **3** sexually attracted to members of both sexes. **bi·sex′u·al·ism′** *n.* **bi·sex′u·al′i·ty** *n.*

bish·op (bish′əp) *n* **1** *Christianity* a member of the clergy who is in charge of a church district. **2** in chess, one of two pieces per player that may be moved diagonally across any number of unoccupied spaces of one colour. <Latin *espiscopus* overseer, from Greek *epi-* over + *skopos* watcher>

bis·muth (biz′məth) *n* a brittle metallic element. Some compounds are used in medicine. *Symbol* **Bi** <Greek>

bi·son (bī′zən) *or* (bī′sən) *n, pl* **bi·son** a large grazing animal of N America and Europe, belonging to the same family as domestic cattle and the buffalo of Africa and India. <Latin>

GRAMMAR AND USAGE

The North American **bison** is often called a buffalo. However, this is not strictly correct and should be avoided in careful speech and writing: *Both the plains and wood bison are found in Canada.*

bisque[1] (bisk) *n* a smooth, thick soup, often made from shellfish. <French>

bisque[2] (bisk) *or* (bēsk) *n* BISCUIT (def. 3), especially when purposely left unglazed for use in figurines, dolls, etc. <shortened from *biscuit*>

bis·tro (bēs′trō) *n* a small, informal restaurant serving wine and simple meals. <French>

bit[1] (bit) *n* **1** a small piece or part: *a bit of cake. The movie had some funny bits.* **2** a small degree or extent: *I'm a bit tired.* **3** a short time: *We'll rest for a bit.* **4** a certain typical set of actions or ideas: *the whole do-it-yourself bit.* <Old English *bita*>
bit by bit, a little at a time.
do your bit, do your share.
every bit, in every way: *He's every bit as skilled as you are.*
two bits, *Informal* a quarter; twenty-five cents.

bit[2] (bit) *n* **1** the part of a bridle that goes in a horse's mouth. **2** the biting or cutting part of a tool such as a drill. **3** the part of a key that goes in the lock. <Old English *bite*>

bit[3] (bit) past tense and a past participle of BITE.

bit[4] (bit) *Computers n* the basic unit of information in a computer, 0 or 1. See also BINARY DIGIT, BYTE. <*bi*(*nary*) + (*digi*)*t*>

bitch (bich) *n* **1** a female dog, wolf, fox, or otter. **2** *Slang* a malicious or bad-tempered woman. **3** *Informal* anything unpleasant or difficult.
v Informal complain persistently: *He's always bitching about something.* <Old English *bicce*> **bitch′y** *adj.*

bite (bīt) *v* **bit, bit·ten** or **bit, bit·ing 1** seize, cut into, or cut off with the teeth: *She bit the apple. Stop biting your fingernails.* **2** cut or pierce: *My dog never bites. A mosquito bit me. The sword bit the knight's helmet.* **3** cause a sharp, stinging pain to: *fingers bitten by frost.* **4** take a tight hold on: *The train wheels bite the rails.* **5** take bait: *The fish are biting well today.*
n **1** a piece bitten off; a mouthful: *Swallow that bite before taking more.* **2** a light meal; a snack: *I usually have a bite before going to bed.* **3** the act, result, or site of biting: *My uncle soon recovered from the snake bite.* **4** a sharp, stinging pain: *the bite of a cold wind.* **5** a tight grip. **6** *Dentistry* the way in which the upper and lower teeth meet when the mouth is closed. <Old English *bitan*> **bit′er** *n.*
bite off more than you can chew, attempt something too difficult.
bite someone's head off, be sharply angry with someone.
bite the dust, die, or be defeated.
bite the hand that feeds you, act ungratefully; behave badly to those who have helped you.
bite your tongue, keep from saying something.
bitten by the —— bug, be fascinated by or extremely involved in something: *to be bitten by the travel bug.*
once bitten twice shy, reluctant to try something because of a previous bad experience with it.
put the bite on, *Informal* demand money from.
take a bite out of, *Informal* use up a large part of: *That hotel stay sure took a bite out of our travel budget.*
What's biting you? *Slang* What's annoying you?

bit·ing (bī′ting) *adj* sharp, stinging, or cutting: *a biting wind, a biting remark.* **bit′ing·ly** *adv.*

bit·map (bit′map′) *Computers v* **bit·mapped, bit·map·ping** display an image or character digitally by attaching a bit value (0 or 1) to each pixel.
n such a display.

bit part *n* a small acting role in a play or movie.

bit·ten (bit′ən) a past participle of BITE.

bit·ter (bit′ər) *adj* **1** with a sharp, harsh, unpleasant taste: *bitter medicine.* **2** causing or expressing much pain or suffering, whether physical or mental: *bitter wounds, a bitter defeat* **3** showing anger or resentment because of a bad experience or unjust treatment: *Don't let this loss make you bitter.* **4** very cold: *a bitter January morning.* <Old English *biter* (related to *bite*)> **bit′ter·ly** *adv.* **bit′ter·ness** *n.*
to the bitter end, a until the very last. **b** to death.

bit·tern (bit′ərn) *n* a wading bird related to the herons, with a loud booming call. <Old French *butor*>

bit·ters (bit′ərz) *n* (*with singular verb*) a home remedy or drink, usually alcoholic, flavoured with some bitter plant.

bit·ter·sweet (bit′ər swēt′) *adj* **1** bitter and sweet at the same time: *bittersweet chocolate.* **2** pleasant, but including also some pain or regret: *bittersweet memories.*

bi·tu·men (bich′ə mən) *n* **1** any of various tarry substances obtained from the evaporation of petroleum. **2** a heavy, almost solid form of petroleum occurring in natural deposits, as in the Athabasca tar sands. Also called **asphalt**. <Latin> **bi·tu′mi·nous** *adj.*

bituminous coal *n* soft coal containing less carbon and more moisture than anthracite and burning with a smoky flame. It is the most plentiful type of coal.

bi·va·lent (bī vā′lənt) *adj* **1** *Chemistry* with a valence of two, or with two valences. **2** *Biology* with chromosomes arranged in pairs. <Latin *bi-* two + *valere* be worth> **bi·va′lence** *n.*

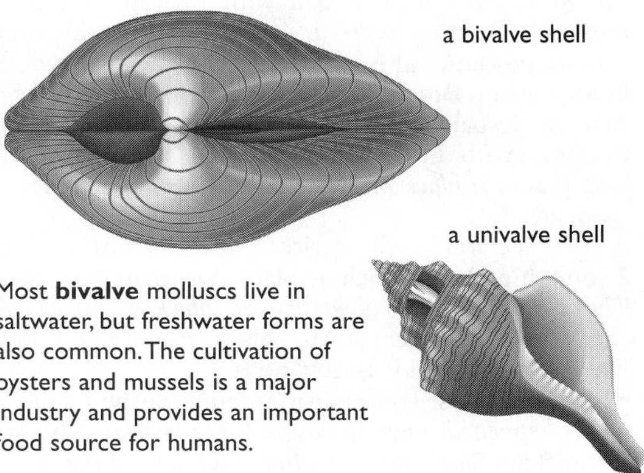

Most **bivalve** molluscs live in saltwater, but freshwater forms are also common. The cultivation of oysters and mussels is a major industry and provides an important food source for humans.

bi·valve (bī′valv′) *n* any mollusk, such as an oyster or clam, whose shell consists of two parts hinged together.
adj with two parts hinged together.

biv·ou·ac (biv′ū ak′) *n* a temporary camp outdoors, usually without tents: *The soldiers made a bivouac for the night in a field.*
v **biv·ou·acked, biv·ou·ack·ing** camp in a bivouac.

ETYMOLOGY

Bivouac is a French word that likely comes from the Swiss German *Beiwacht*, meaning "a patrol of citizens who assisted the town watch at night." In English, it originally meant "a night watch by an army to prevent a surprise attack."

a bat	e bed	i bid	o pot	u cup	th **thin**
ā cake	ē me	ī bite	ō go	ū rude	TH **then**
ȧ bar	ə about	ər over	ȯ for	u̇ put	zh measure

bi·week·ly (bī wēk′lē) *adj, adv* **1** once every two weeks: *biweekly updates (adj). New listings are issued biweekly (adv).* **2** *Informal* twice a week.
n, pl **bi·week·lies** a newspaper or magazine published biweekly.

bi·year·ly (bī yēr′lē) *adj, adv* **1** once every two years: *a biyearly visit (adj). The encyclopedia is updated biyearly (adv).* **2** *Informal* twice a year.

bi·zarre (bə zär′) *adj* odd, strange, or weird: *a bizarre dream.* <French *bizarre* odd, from Italian *bizzarro* angry> **bi·zarre′ly** *adv.* **bi·zarre′ness** *n.*

blab (blab) *Informal v* **blabbed, blab·bing 1** tell a secret: *Someone blabbed our game plan to the other team.* **2** talk too much: *blabbing on and on about nothing.*
n **1** excessive talk. **2** a person who blabs. <Middle English *blabbe*> **blab′ber** *v, n.*

blab·ber·mouth (blab′ər mouth′) *Informal n* a person who talks too much, especially one who reveals secrets.

black (blak) *adj* **1** caused by the absence or total absorption of light; the opposite of white: *The print in this dictionary is black.* **2** without any light; completely dark: *It was quite black outside.* **3 a** with African ancestry: *My mother is black; my father is Asian.* **b** to do with people of African descent, culture, or society: *black literature, black history.* Also, **Black**. **4** with tragic or disastrous events causing despair or misery: *a black day for all of us.* **5** covered with dirt or grime: *The windows were black with soot.* **6** angry: *black moods. She gave him a black look and stomped off.*
n **1** a person with African ancestry. Also, **Black**. **2** something black, such as black dye, paint, or clothing: *The old gentleman always wore black.* **3** in chess or checkers, the player of the black pieces.<Old English *blæc*> **black′ish** *adj.* **black′ness** *n.*
black out, a lose consciousness temporarily: *I don't know what happened next, because I blacked out.* **b** darken completely: *Black out the bedroom window so the sun won't wake you.* **c** prevent publication of; suppress: *The government blacked out all news of the invasion.* **d** cause electrical power to fail: *The Ottawa area was blacked out after the ice storm.* **e** prevent TV broadcasting of a local event: *The game will be blacked out in Vancouver.*
in the black, making a profit: *After a year of struggle the company is finally in the black.*

GRAMMAR AND USAGE

Compounds such as African-Canadian, or Jamaican-Canadian are acceptable to describe a black person, using that person's place of origin.

black and blue *adj* severely bruised. Also, before a noun, **black-and-blue**.

black and white *n* **1** writing or print: *I asked her to put her promise down in black and white.* **2** a colour scheme in which everything is represented in black, white, and shades of grey: *The movie was filmed in black and white.*
adj in black, white, and shades of grey: *black and white photographs.*

black arts *n* black magic.

black·ball (blak′bol′) *v* **1** vote against: *Some members of the club blackballed him, so he could not become a member.* **2** exclude from a group; boycott. <from the former practice of voting against a candidate by placing a black ball in the ballot box> **black′ball′er** *n.*

black bear *n* a N American bear with blackish fur and a lighter-coloured muzzle, found from Mexico north to the edge of the tundra, and able to swim and climb well. Most black bears are black, but lighter colours occur, especially in the western parts of Canada.

A person training in karate, judo, or other martial art wears a uniform called a *gi*. The colour of the belt indicates the level of achievement. A **black belt** has the highest skill, but in many martial arts there are different degrees of black belt, with tenth-degree usually being the highest.

black belt *n* **1** in martial arts, the highest level of skill, symbolized by a black belt or sash, or a person who has achieved this level of skill: *My sister is a black belt.* **2** the belt itself.

black·ber·ry (blak′ber′ē) *n, pl* **black·ber·ries** the small black or dark purple edible fruit of a bush or vine of the rose family, closely related to the raspberry.

black·bird (blak′bərd′) *n* **1** a black songbird of the same family as the meadowlarks. Canadian species include the **red-winged blackbird**, **rusty blackbird**, and **common grackle**. **2** a European bird of the thrush family, the male being black with an orange bill.

🍁 **black blizzard** *Prairie Provinces n* a storm of wind and dust.

black·board (blak′bòrd′) *n* chalkboard.

black·bod·y (blak′bo də) *Physics n, pl* **black·bod·ies** a theoretical surface or body that can absorb all the radiation that hits it, without reflecting any.

black book *n* **1** a book containing the names of people to be criticized or punished. **2 little black book** a private notebook, especially one for recording personal details about people one knows.
be in someone's black book(s), be out of favour with someone.

black box *n* **1** a self-contained electronic device that automatically records data, controls a mechanical process, etc. One type of black box is used to record all events in the flight of a plane. **2** something that carries out highly sophisticated functions, but whose inner workings are not understood or cannot be observed.

Black Death *n* a violent outbreak of the bubonic plague that spread through Asia and Europe in the 1300s, and in England killed one-third to one-half of the population in a few months.

black economy *n* a hidden sector of the economy where private cash transactions go unreported and therefore cannot be subject to tax.

black·en (blak′ən) *v* **black·ened, black·en·ing** **1** make or become black or very dark. **2** defame; damage the reputation or name of.

black eye *n* **1** a bruise around an eye. **2** *Informal* a cause of disgrace or discredit: *Garbage in the streets is this city's black eye.*

black–eyed Su·san (blak′īd′sū′zən) *n* a N American wildflower with bright yellow petals surrounding a cluster of dark brown florets.

black flag *n* a pirate's flag, usually with a white skull and crossbones on it.

black·fly (blak′flī′) *n* a small fly found throughout the world and with mouth parts adapted for sucking blood.

Black·foot (blak′fůt′) *n, pl* **Black·foot** **1** SIKSIKA. **2** a member of the Blackfoot confederacy.

Blackfoot confederacy *n* a confederacy of three Algonquian First Nations of the Plains, namely the Siksika (Blackfoot), Kainai (Blood), and Piikani (Peigan) peoples.

black gold *n* petroleum, viewed as a valuable resource.

black·guard (blag′ärd) *or* (blag′ərd) *n* a scoundrel. **black′guard·ly** *adj.*

black·hat (blak′hat′) *Computers n* any threat to a computer system, especially a hacker.

black·head (blak′hed′) *n* a small, black-tipped lump of dead cells and oil plugging a pore of the skin.

black hole *n* a region in space produced by the collapse of a star, with such a strong gravitational field that anything caught in this field, including light, can never escape.

black ice *n* **1** 🍁 thin ice on the surface of a road, appearing black because of its transparency. **2** similar thin ice on the surface of a body of water.

black·ing (blak′ing) *n* a black polish.

black·jack (blak′jak′) *n* **1** **a** a card game in which players try to get a count of 21. **b** in this game, a count of 21 with only two cards, namely an ace and a ten or any face card. **2** a club with a flexible handle, used as a weapon. **3** the black flag of a pirate.
v **1** hit a person with a blackjack. **2** coerce; strong-arm.

black·leg (blak′leg′) *Informal n* a worker who takes a striker's job. Also called **scab** (*Slang*).

black·list (blak′list′) *n* a list of people who are believed to deserve punishment, or are blamed for wrongdoing.
v put on such a list.

black lung (disease) *n* a disease common among coal miners, caused by long-term breathing of coal dust which settles in the lungs and hardens them. The technical name is **anthracosis**.

black magic *n* magic that supposedly uses the power of demons.

black·mail (blak′māl′) *v* **1** get or try to get money from someone by threatening to reveal something bad about him or her. **2** manipulate someone by unfair moral pressure, such as by threatening to hurt oneself or a loved one, or to withdraw one's friendship.
n **1** the act of blackmailing. **2** the money or other advantage obtained in this way. **black′mail′er** *n.*

black market *n* the selling of contraband or smuggled goods, or the selling of goods at illegal prices or in illegal quantities.

black·out (blak′out′) *n* **1** a failure of electrical power. **2** a temporary blindness or unconsciousness due to lack of blood circulation in the brain. **3** the act of putting out or hiding all the lights of a city or district as protection against an air raid. **4** the act of keeping news or other information from being broadcast: *News blackouts are common in wartime.* **5** a turning off of all the lights on the stage of a theatre to suggest the passing of time, or to mark the end of a scene.

black pepper *n* the dried unripe berries of the pepper plant, usually ground into a spicy powder to flavour food. Compare WHITE PEPPER.

black sheep *n* a person who is a disgrace to the family.

black·smith (blak′smith′) *n* a person who makes and repairs things out of iron, using a forge.

black·snake (blak′snāk′) *n* a harmless, swift-moving, glossy black snake of southeastern Canada and the eastern US, related to the garter snake.

black spruce *n* a northern spruce tree with small, egg-shaped cones, short, dark bluish green needles, and soft wood.

black tea *n* tea made from leaves that have been allowed to wither and ferment in the air for some time before being dried in ovens. Compare GREEN TEA.

black·thorn (blak′thôrn′) *n* **1** a thorny European shrub related to the plum tree, with small, bluish black fruits usually called **sloes**. **2** a walking stick or club made from the stem of this shrub.

black tie *n* formal dress for men, consisting of a dinner jacket or tuxedo, traditionally with a black bow tie: *Dress for the banquet is black tie.* Compare WHITE TIE.

black·top (blak′top′) *n* **1** asphalt mixed with crushed rock, used as paving material. **2** any surface so paved.
v **black·topped, black·top·ping** pave with blacktop.

black walnut *n* a N American walnut tree with round, edible nuts and heavy, hard wood used in making furniture.

black widow *n* an American spider, the female of which is mostly black and highly venomous. <named from its colour and the fact that the female often eats the male after mating>

a bat	e bed	i bid	o pot	u cup	th thin
ā cake	ē me	ī bite	ō go	ū rude	TH then
ä bar	ə about	ər over	ô for	ů put	zh measure

blad·der (blad′ər) *n* **1** a soft, thin, baglike organ in the body of humans and animals, which holds urine received from the kidneys until it is discharged. **2** any similar bag that holds liquid or air in a plant or animal: *the swim bladder of a fish.* **3** an artificial bag, often made of rubber, for holding gas or liquid. <Old English *blœdre*>

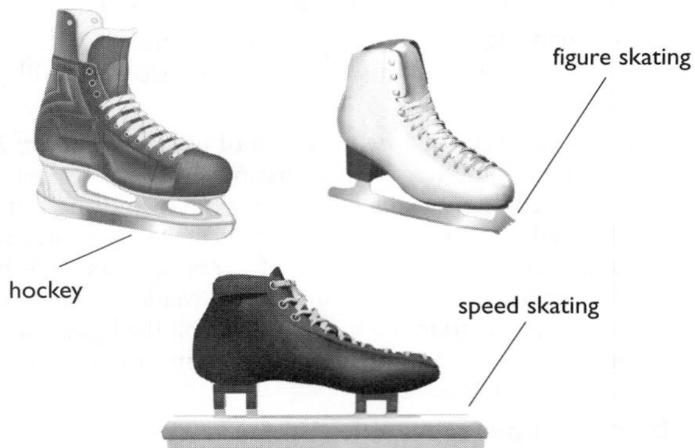

blade (blād) *n* **1** the cutting part of a tool or weapon: *A carving knife has a sharp blade.* **2** the runner on an ice skate. **3** a leaf of grass. **4** the flat, wide part of anything: *the blade of a leaf, the blade of a paddle, the shoulder blade.* **5** a sword, or a swordsman. **6** *Archaic or Humorous* a smart or dashing fellow.
v **blad·ed, blad·ing** *Informal* go inline skating. <Old English *blœd*> **blad′ed** *adj.* **blade′like′** *adj.*

blah (bla) *Slang adj* **1** dull, bland, or uninteresting: *a blah menu.* **2** feeling or causing low spirits and lack of energy: *blah weather. I was feeling kind of blah yesterday.*
n **1 the blahs** *pl* a feeling of boredom, dissatisfaction, or lack of energy. **2 blah-blah** tiresome or meaningless talk: *all that blah-blah about walking to school barefoot.*
interj **blah blah blah** an expression imitating tiresome or meaningless talk. <imitative>

blame (blām) *v* **blamed, blam·ing 1** hold responsible for something bad or wrong: *We blamed the fog for our accident.* **2** find fault with: *I don't blame you for being upset.*
n **1** the responsibility for something bad or wrong: *Haste deserves the blame for many mistakes.* **2** criticism or reproach: *a tone of blame.* <Old French, from Greek *blas-* false + *pheme* word> **blam′er** *n.*
be to blame, deserve blame: *Each person said somebody else was to blame.*
blame on, attribute to: *The accident was blamed on the icy road.*

SYNONYMS

Blame means "hold responsible": *She blamed her boss for her heavy workload.*

Accuse means "charge with wrongdoing": *That shopper has been accused of stealing a watch.*

Reprimand means "severely scold": *The students were reprimanded for dropping litter on school property.*

blame·less (blām′lis) *adj* deserving no blame. **blame′less·ly** *adv.* **blame′less·ness** *n.*

blame·wor·thy (blām′wər′ᴛʜē) *adj* deserving blame. **blame′wor′thi·ness** *n.*

blanch (blanch) *v* **1** turn white or become pale: *The boy blanched with fear when he saw the bear.* **2** loosen the skins of fruits and vegetables by plunging them first in boiling water and then in cold water. **3** make white; bleach. <Old French *blanc* white>

blanc·mange (blə mänzh′) *n* a sweet, jellylike dessert made of milk, eggs, sugar, etc., thickened with cornstarch or gelatin. <Old French *blanc* white + *manger* to eat>

bland (bland) *adj* **1** not spicy; with no strong flavours: *bland food.* **2** smooth, agreeable, and polite: *a bland manner.* **3** uninteresting: *Offices often have a bland interior design.* <Latin *blandus* soothing, pleasant> **bland′ly** *adv.* **bland′ness** *n.*

blan·dish (blan′dish) *v* coax by flattering. <Old French, from Latin *blandire* flatter> **blan′dish·ment** *n.*

blank (blangk) *n* **1** a space left empty or to be filled in: *Leave a blank after each word.* **2** an empty cartridge for a firearm: *He fired a few blanks into the air.* **3** an empty or vacant place or space: *She tried to read his face, but it was a complete blank.* **4** a partly formed piece, ready to be made into a finished object: *a key blank.*
adj **1** not written or printed on: *blank paper.* **2** with spaces to be filled in: *a blank application form.* **3** with or showing no idea or understanding: *His only answer was a blank stare. Her mind went blank in the middle of the exam.* **4** complete and absolute: *a blank refusal, blank dismay.* **5** empty; lacking some usual feature: *a blank disk.*
v **1** (*usually with* ***out***) become confused or distracted: *Just when I wanted to introduce them, I blanked out and couldn't remember their names.* **2** keep from scoring in a game: *They blanked their opponents 3–0.* <French *blanc* white> **blank′ly** *adv.* **blank′ness** *n.*
draw a blank, *Informal* fail completely, especially when trying to remember, find, or think of something: *I tried to remember our earlier decision, but drew a blank.*

blank cheque *n* **1** a cheque that has not been filled out, or on which the name or the amount has been left blank for another person to fill in. **2** permission to do as one pleases: *A majority in the House of Commons is not a blank cheque for the prime minister.*

blan·ket (blang′kit) *n* **1** a soft, heavy covering made of cloth or other material, used to keep people or animals warm. **2** anything like a blanket: *A blanket of mist covered the lake.*
v cover with a blanket or something like it: *Snow blanketed the ground.* <Old French *blankete,* from *blanc* white>

blanket statement *n* a broad, usually unfair, general statement about an entire group of people or things: *You can't make blanket statements about no-name products; some are good, some aren't.*

blank verse *n* unrhymed poetry with a metre based on five iambic feet in each line.

blare (bler) *v* **blared, blar·ing 1** make a loud, harsh sound: *The trumpets blared, announcing the queen's arrival.* **2** utter harshly or loudly.

n a loud, harsh sound: *The blare of the horn was startling.* <Dutch *blaren*>

blar·ney (blär′nē) *n* flattering talk.
v coax with flattery. <Kissing the *Blarney Stone,* a stone in a castle wall in Ireland, is said to give skill in flattery.>

bla·sé (blä zā′) *adj* **1** tired of pleasures, and bored. **2** unconcerned or unexcited by something: *You seem pretty blasé considering you just wiped out your hard drive!* <French *blaser* exhaust with pleasure>

blas·pheme (blas fēm′) *v* **blas·phemed, blas·phem·ing** speak about God or sacred things with abuse or contempt. <Latin, from Greek *blas-* false + *pheme* word>
blas′phe·mous (blas′fəm′əs) *adj.*
blas′phe·my (blas′fəm′ē) *n.*

blast (blast) *n* **1** a strong, sudden rush of wind or air: *the icy blasts of winter.* **2** the blowing of a trumpet, horn, or whistle, or the sound this makes. **3** an explosion: *We heard the blast from 2 km away.*
v **1** blow up with some explosive: *The old building was blasted with dynamite.* **2** wither, blight, or destroy: *The intense heat blasted the grapevines.* <Old English *blæst*>
blast off, take off from a launching site, especially for rockets and missiles: *Make ready to blast off.*
full blast, at top volume or capacity: *She played her stereo full blast.*

blast·ed (blas′tid) *adj* **1** *Poetic* withered or ruined: *blasted heath.* **2** *Informal* detestable or cursed: *This blasted pen won't write.*

blast furnace *n* a furnace for smelting ore, with a strong current of air blown into it from the bottom to make a very great heat.

blastoff (blast′ of′) *n* the moment or process of taking off from a launching site.

blas·tu·la (blas′chə lə) *Zoology n, pl* **blastulas** or **blastulae** (blas′chə lē) *or* (blas′chə lī′) the embryo of an animal, usually consisting of a hollow sphere formed by a single layer of cells. <Latin, from Greek *blastos* root, seed>

bla·tant (blā′tənt) *adj* obvious in an offensive way: *blatant lies.* <coined by E. Spenser, a 16c poet, probably influenced by Latin *blatire* to babble> **bla′tan·cy** *n.* **bla′tant·ly** *adv.*

blath·er (blaᴛʜ′ər) *v* talk nonsense.
n nonsensical talk. <Old Norse *blathr*>

blaze[1] (blāz) *n* **1** a bright flame or fire: *She could see the blaze of the campfire.* **2** intense light or glare: *the blaze of the noon sun.* **3** a bright display: *The tulips made a blaze of colour.* **4** a violent outburst: *a blaze of temper, a blaze of gunfire.*
v **blazed, blaz·ing 1** burn rapidly with a bright flame: *A fire blazed in the fireplace.* **2** show bright colours or lights: *On the evening of the party, the hall blazed with lights.* **3** burst out in anger: *She blazed at the insult.* <Old English *blæse*>
blaze away, fire ammunition rapidly and continuously.
blaze with, turn red in the face with: *His cheeks blazed with embarrassment.*

blaze[2] (blāz) *n* **1** a mark made on a tree by chipping off a piece of its bark. **2** a white mark on an animal's forehead.
v **blazed, blaz·ing** mark a tree in this way, or mark a trail by blazing trees. <German *bläse*>

blaz·er (blā′zər) *n* **1** a jacket styled like a suit coat, and usually worn as dressy but informal wear, or as part of a uniform. **2** a lightweight summer jacket, often part of a sports or school uniform.

bleach (blēch) *v* **1** whiten or lighten by exposing to sunlight or chemicals: *Bleached bones lay on the desert. We bleached the stains out of the shirt.* **2** cause to turn white or pale.
n a chemical used in bleaching. <Old English *blǣce* pale>

bleach·ers (blē′chərz) *pln* rows of staggered seats at outdoor games such as baseball and football, and at indoor games such as basketball. <because spectators supposedly got bleached by the sun while sitting there>

bleak (blēk) *adj* **1** bare, colourless, or harsh-looking: *a bleak landscape.* **2** chilly or cold: *a bleak wind.* **3** dreary or dismal: *With two minutes left in the game, the future looked bleak.* <Scandinavian> **bleak′ly** *adv.* **bleak′ness** *n.*

blear·y (blē′rē) *adj* **blear·i·er, blear·i·est** unable to see clearly, especially from tiredness or tears. <Middle English *bleren*> **blear′i·ness** *n.*

bleat (blēt) *n* **1** the cry made by a sheep, goat, or calf. **2** a sound like it.
v **1** make such a cry or sound. **2** complain, especially feebly or with a whine. <Old English *blǣtan*> **bleat′er** *n.*

bleed (blēd) *v* **bled** (bled), **bleed·ing 1** lose blood: *My foot is bleeding.* **2** suffer wounds or death: *He fought and bled for his country.* **3** take blood from: *Doctors used to bleed sick people.* **4** lose or take a fluid from a surface that has been cut or scratched: *The injured elm is bleeding.* **5** *Informal* get money by extortion. **6** run or spread, as colours do when wet. **7** empty liquid or gas from: *to bleed air from a hot-water radiator.* <Old English *blod* blood>
my heart bleeds, (*ironic*) I am filled with pity.

bleeding heart *n* **1** a common garden plant that has drooping clusters of heart-shaped flowers. **2** *Informal* an overly sentimental person who allows feelings of pity to override judgment.

blem·ish (blem′ish) *n* a stain, spot, or flaw: *A pimple is a blemish on a person's skin. A quick temper was the only blemish in her character.*
v stain or spoil (something): *blemished skin, to blemish a reputation.* <Old French *blemir* to make pale>

blend (blend) *v* **1** mix together so thoroughly that the mixed things cannot be distinguished or separated: *Oil and water will not blend. Blend the first three ingredients in a saucepan.* **2** make by mixing several kinds together: *to blend tea.* **3** shade into each other, little by little: *The colours of the rainbow blend into one another.* **4** go well together or harmonize: *Their voices do not blend.*
n **1** a thorough, even mixture made by blending. **2** something made by mixing several kinds: *a different blend of coffee.* <Old Norse *blanda*>

blend·ed family (blen′dəd) *n* a family formed by adoption or by remarriage of a parent.

a bat	e bed	i bid	o pot	u cup	th **thin**
ā cake	ē me	ī bite	ō go	ū rude	ᴛʜ **then**
ä bar	ə about	ər over	ȯ for	u̇ put	zh measure

blend·er (blen′dər) *n* a small household appliance for mixing ingredients, usually turning them into a liquid.

bless (bles) *v* **blessed** or **blest, bless·ing** 1 *Religion* **a** make holy or sacred: *to bless a church.* **b** ask favour or protection for someone or something: *Bless these little children.* **c** praise or glorify: *May Allah be blessed.* 2 be favoured with something good or desirable: *to be blessed with prosperity.* 3 feel or express gratitude to: *They blessed him for his kindness.* <Old English *bletsian*>
Bless you! an exclamation said to a person who has just sneezed.

bless·ed (bles′id) *for adj,* (blest) *for v. adj* 1 *Religion* holy; sacred. 2 *Catholicism* given as a title to someone who has been beatified: *the Blessed Marie-Anne Blondin.* 3 *Informal* used to express annoyance: *My kid sister wants to know about every blessed thing.*
v a past tense of BLESS. **bless′ed·ness** *n.*

bless·ing (bles′ing) *n* 1 *Religion* **a** a prayer asking for favour, or giving thanks for food: *At the end of the service, the bishop gave the blessing.* **b** a giving of favour: *May Allah's blessing be upon you.* 2 a wish for happiness or success. 3 approval or consent: *The marriage had the blessing of both families.* 4 anything that makes one happy: *A good temper is a great blessing.*
a blessing in disguise, something unpleasant which turns out to have good results.

blest (blest) *Poetic adj* blessed.
v a past tense of BLESS.

blew (blū) past tense of BLOW².

blight (blīt) *n* 1 a plant disease that causes leaves, stems, or other parts to wither and die. 2 something that causes this disease, such as mildew. 3 the condition of being spoiled or damaged: *urban blight.*
v 1 cause to wither and die: *Mildew blighted the June roses.* 2 destroy; ruin. <origin uncertain>

blimp (blimp) *Informal n* 1 a small airship that can be steered. 2 anything plump and rounded. <probably from *Type B limp*, which was the most common type of airship in World War I>

blind (blīnd) *adj* 1 not able to see: *The person with the white cane is blind.* 2 without thought, judgment, or good sense: *blind fury, a blind guess, blind prejudice.* 3 made without previous knowledge of a product: *a blind purchase.* 4 hard to see or hidden: *a blind seam, a blind curve on a highway.* 5 without an opening: *a blind wall.* 6 with only one opening: *a blind canyon.*
v 1 make unable to see: *The bright lights blinded me for a moment. She was blinded in an accident.* 2 take away the power to understand or judge: *Prejudice blinded him. His fine appearance blinded her to his faults.*
adv using instruments instead of the eyes: *to fly blind.*
n 1 a device on a roller that can be rolled down in front of a window as a screen: *We have blinds on our bedroom windows.* 2 a similar device made up of vertical or horizontal slats. 3 anything that conceals or covers: *Her joking was only a blind to hide her nervousness.* 4 a hiding place, often in the form of a small tent, for a hunter or photographer. <Old English> **blind′ly** *adv.* **blind′ness** *n.*

blind alley *n* 1 a passageway closed at one end. 2 anything that gives no chance for progress; a dead end: *That last job of his was a blind alley.*

blind date *n* 1 a date arranged by a third person for a couple who have not met. 2 either of the two people involved.

blind·er (blīn′dər) *n* 1 a leather flap designed to keep a horse from seeing to the side. 2 **blinders** *pl* an attitude or bias that keeps a person from having clear judgment: *She goes through life with blinders on.* Also called **blinker**.

blind·fold (blīnd′fōld′) *v* cover the eyes to prevent seeing: *I blindfolded my little sister when it was her turn to hit the piñata.*
n something covering the eyes to prevent seeing: *She put a blindfold on the horse and led it out of the burning barn.*
adv wearing a blindfold: *I can do it blindfold.*

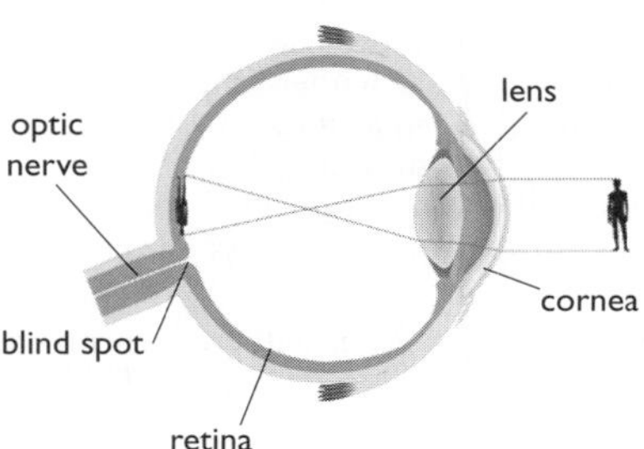

blind spot *n* 1 a spot on the retina of the eye that is not sensitive to light, where the optic nerve enters the eye. 2 the part on the edge of one's field of vision that is affected by this: *The motorist did not see the cyclist as he was in her blind spot.* 3 a matter on which a person does not know that he or she is prejudiced or poorly informed: *His blind spot is modern music; he refuses to listen to it.*

blink (blingk) *v* 1 close the eyes and open them again quickly: *We blink every few seconds.* 2 look with the eyes opening and shutting: *She blinked at the sudden light.* 3 flash on and off: *A lantern blinked through the darkness.* 4 be the first to give way or back down in a deadlock or standoff: *Negotiations are still stalled; neither party has blinked yet.*
n 1 the act or fact of blinking. 2 a glimpse. 3 in the Far North, a reflection of sunlight on cloud caused by ice or snow in the distance. <Middle English *blenken*>
blink at, ignore or overlook; pretend not to see (something bad).
on the blink, *Informal* out of order: *Our TV is on the blink again.*

blink·er (bling′kər) *n* 1 a flashing warning light, such as a turn signal on a vehicle. 2 BLINDER.

blintz (blints) *n* a thin, rolled pancake filled with cheese, fruit, jam, etc. <Ukrainian *blynci*>

blip (blip) *n* 1 a small dot of light on a radar screen, showing that radar waves are being reflected from an object: *The blip shows the location of the object and the direction in which it is moving.* 2 anything that has no permanent effect: *It looks like my low grade on the second test was was just a blip.* <imitative>

bliss (blis) *n* great happiness. <Old English *blithe* blithe>
bliss′ful *adj.* **bliss′ful·ly** *adv.*
bliss out, *Slang* become so happy that one can notice nothing other than the source of happiness: *He blissed out when she kissed him.*

blis·ter (blis′tər) *n* a small swelling of the skin that contains a watery fluid, and is caused by burning or irritation. **2** a raised bubble, as on a painted surface. **3** a rounded, transparent structure.
v cause a blister to form. <Old French *blestre*>

blithe (blīтн) *adj* **1** cheerful or light hearted: *a blithe and carefree spirit.* **2** casual and careless: *blithe indifference.* <Old English> **blithe′ly** *adv.* **blithe′ness** *n.*

blith·er·ing (blīтн′ə ring) *adj* talking nonsense; jabbering: *a blithering idiot.* <variant of *blathering*>

blitz (blits) *n* **1** a sudden, violent, and intense attack or onslaught. **2** any concerted effort or intense campaign: *The United Way launched a house-to-house blitz in a last attempt to meet its goal.*
v subject to a blitz. <German = lightning>

blitz·krieg (blits′krēg′) *n* warfare in which the offensive is extremely rapid, violent, and hard to resist. <German = lightning war>

bliz·zard (bliz′ərd) *n* a violent, long-lasting, blinding snowstorm. <origin uncertain>

bloat (blōt) *v* **1** swell up or puff up: *My hand was bruised and bloated after my fall.* **2** preserve herring by salting and smoking.
n a swelling of the abdomen of livestock after eating moist feed, caused by gases produced by the fermentation of the feed. <Old Norse *blautr* soft, swollen>

blob (blob) *n* **1** a small, soft drop or lump: *Blobs of wax covered the candlestick.* **2** a formless mass. <Middle English *blobe* a bubble>

bloc (blok) *n* a group of people, companies, or nations united for some purpose. <French = block>

block (blok) *n* **1** a solid piece of hard material: *The walls are made of cement blocks.* **2** a space in a city or town bounded by four streets: *one city block.* **3** the distance from one street to the next in a city or town: *Walk one block east.* **4** a group of things of the same kind: *a block of seats in a theatre.* **5** a large building containing a number of units: *an apartment block, an office block.* **6** 🍁 **Block** a number of townships, usually surrounded by land that has not been surveyed: *the Peace River Block in Alberta.* **7** *Computers* a collection of data identified and processed as a unit. **8** the platform where things are put up for sale at an auction. **9 a** the act of stopping something or someone by getting in the way. **b** something that does this. **10** in former times, the piece of wood put under the neck of a person being beheaded. **11** *Slang* a person's head. **12** a block and tackle.
v **1** fill a passage or opening so as to prevent progress: *The country roads were blocked with snow.* **2** obstruct, hinder, or prevent, often by putting things in the way: *He is always trying to block my plans.* **3** *Sports* hinder an opponent's play. **4** *Theatre* plan the moves of actors in a scene or play. <Old French *bloc*> **block′er** *n.*
block in, plan or sketch roughly without filling in the details.
block off, close off by blockading.
block out, a deliberately keep (something) out of your mind. **b** plan or sketch roughly.
go to the block, be put up for sale by auction.
on the block, being sold by auction.

block·ade (blok ād′) *n* **1** the closing off of a place or route by armed forces or police to keep people or supplies from getting through. **2** the people or things used for this. **3** anything set up to block or obstruct.
v **block·ad·ed, block·ad·ing** close off by a blockade: *We blockaded the doorway with furniture.* **block·ad′er** *n.*
run the blockade, try to get past a blockade.

block·age (blok′ij) *n* **1** the state of being blocked. **2** something that blocks: *We cleared the blockage from the pipe.*

block and tackle *n* an arrangement of pulleys and ropes used in lifting or pulling heavy weights.

block·bust·er (blok′bus′tər) *Informal n* a very popular or successful show, movie, video, or book: *The new musical is a blockbuster.* <nickname for a bomb able to destroy a large area, referring to the enormous effect of such shows>

block grant *n* a grant from a government or agency that may be used for several different purposes.

block·head (blok′hed′) *n* a stupid person.

block·house (blok′hous′) *n* **1** a military fortification built of heavy timbers or concrete, with openings to shoot from. **2** a heavily reinforced building used as a control centre and place of observation for operations involving danger: *The launching of space vehicles is controlled from a blockhouse.*

block letters *pl n* capital letters, usually hand printed: *Put your name in block letters at the top.*

🍁 **Bloc Québécois** (blok′kā bā kwa′) *n* one of the registered political parties of Canada. *Abbrev.* **BQ** **Blo·quiste′** (blo kēst′) *n.*

blog (blog) *Computers n* in full, **weblog** a website where users can post a journal entry of their thoughts. Each post usually contains a link, making the blog an open communication tool. **blog′ger** *n.*

bloke (blōk) *UK, Informal n* a man.

blond (blond) *adj* **1** with light-coloured hair: *two blond children.* **2** light-coloured: *blond hair, blond furniture.*
n a blond person. Also, for females (*especially n*), **blonde.** <French> **blond′ness** *n.*

GRAMMAR AND USAGE

As a noun, **blond** is more likely to be used for men and boys, while **blonde** is more commonly used for women and girls:
The blond's hair grew darker as he aged.
The blonde protected her skin from the sun.
As an adjective, **blond** is used for males and females.

a bat	e bed	i bid	o pot	u cup	th **thin**
ā cake	ē me	ī bite	ō go	ū rude	тн **then**
à bar	ə about	ər over	ȯ for	ů put	zh measure

blood (blud) *n* **1** the red liquid in the veins and arteries of vertebrates, carrying oxygen and nutrients to all parts of the body and taking away waste. **2** the corresponding liquid in other animals: *The blood of most insects looks yellow.* **3** family descent: *He is of Irish blood. Love of the sea runs in her blood.* **4** high lineage, especially royal lineage: *a prince of the blood.* **5 Blood** KAINAI. <Old English *blod*>
bad blood, feelings of ill will; resentment or a grudge: *There was bad blood between them.*
draw blood, a injure someone so as to cause bleeding. **b** deeply offend or provoke someone: *She really drew blood with her snide remark about his weight problem.*
in cold blood, on purpose and without emotion: *He lay in wait for the traitor and then shot him down in cold blood.*
make your blood boil, make you very angry.
make your blood run cold, fill you with terror.
new (or **fresh**) **blood,** new people seen as a source of fresh energy.

blood bank *n* a place for storing blood to be used in transfusions, or the blood stored.

blood·bath (blud′bath′) *n* a slaughter or massacre.

blood cell *n* See RED BLOOD CELL, WHITE BLOOD CELL.

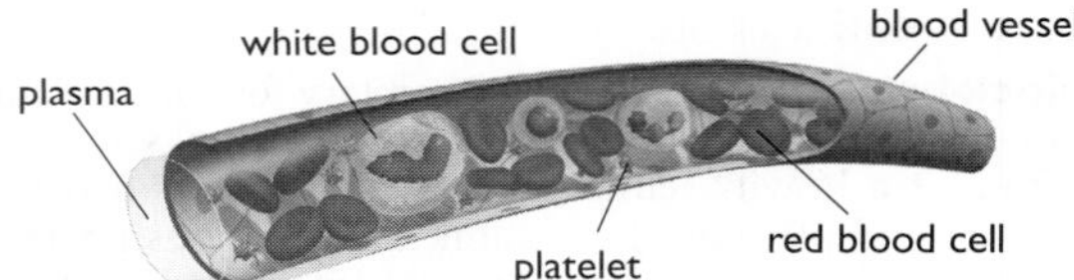

blood count *n* a count of the number of red and white cells in a sample of a person's blood.

blood·cur·dling (blud′kərd′ling) *adj* terrifying: *bloodcurdling screams, a bloodcurdling story.*

blood donor *n* a person who gives his or her blood to a blood bank.

🍁 **blood donor clinic** *n* a place, usually not in a hospital, where people can give blood.

blood group *n* blood type.

blood·hound (blud′hound′) *n* a large breed of hunting dog with a keen sense of smell and long ears.

blood·less (blud′lis) *adj* **1** without violence or killing: *a bloodless revolution.* **2** drained of blood; pale. **3** without life, spirit, or emotion.

blood·let·ting (blud′let′ing) *n* **1** in former times, a method of treating disease by taking blood from the veins in order to get rid of poison. **2** bloodshed or killing.

blood·line (blud′līn′) *n* a line of direct descent through the generations of a family.

blood money *n* **1** the money paid to a hired murderer. **2** in former times, the money paid as compensation to the family of a murdered person. **3** money paid for information about a murderer or murder. **4** money gained at the expense of someone else's life or livelihood.

blood poisoning *n* a diseased condition that occurs when the bloodstream is invaded by poisonous substances or disease-causing bacteria.

blood pressure *n* the pressure of the blood against the inner walls of the blood vessels, varying with exertion or excitement, health, or age.

blood·shed (blud′shed′) *n* killing.

blood·shot (blud′shot′) *adj* with the whites of the eyes tinged with blood from tiny swollen or burst blood vessels, usually as a result of tiredness or irritation.

blood sport *n* a sport, such as hunting or bullfighting, that involves the killing or injury of animals.

blood·stain (blud′stān′) *n* a mark or stain left by blood. **blood′stained** *adj.*

blood·stone (blud′stōn′) *n* a dark green, semiprecious stone with flecks of bright red through it.

blood·stream (blud′strēm′) *n* the blood flowing in the circulatory system of a living body.

blood·suck·er (blud′suk′ər) *n* a leech.

blood sugar *n* **1** the sugar (glucose) in one's blood. **2** the amount of this, used to diagnose diseases such as diabetes.

blood test *n* an examination of a sample of a person's blood, especially to determine a blood group or to diagnose illness.

blood·thirst·y (blud′thər′stē) *adj* violent, cruel, or murderous. **blood′thirst′i·ness** *n.*

blood type *n* any of the four main groups into which human blood is classified according to the presence or absence of certain genetically determined antigens. The four groups are A, AB, B, and O.

blood vessel *n* any tube in the body through which the blood circulates, such as an artery, vein, or capillary.

blood·y (blud′ē) *adj* **blood·i·er, blood·i·est 1** bleeding: *a bloody nose.* **2** covered or stained with blood: *a bloody bandage, a bloody sword.* **3** with much killing or violence: *a bloody battle.* **4** bloodthirsty. **5** *Slang* a word expressing frustration or irritation: *I can't find the bloody thing!*
adv Slang a word expressing frustration or irritation: *We worked bloody hard on this, so don't wreck it!*
v **blood·ied, blood·y·ing 1** cause to bleed: *His nose was bloodied in the fight.* **2** stain with blood. **blood′i·ness** *n.*

GRAMMAR AND USAGE

The slang use of **bloody** as an adjective or adverb is considered offensive or vulgar by some people. It is best avoided in formal writing and speech.

bloom (blūm) *v* **1** have flowers, or open as flowers: *Many plants bloom in the spring.* **2** develop and reach maturity: *Some people bloom later than others.* **3** glow with health and beauty.
n **1** a flower or blossom. **2** the condition or time of flowering: *in bloom.* **3** the peak of development. **4** a glow of health and beauty. **5** the powdery coating on some fruits and leaves, such as grapes, plums, and spruce needles. <Old Norse *blom*> **bloom′er** *n.*

bloom·ers (blū′mərz) *pln* **1** loose shorts gathered at the knee. **2** underwear or pyjamas made like these.
<A. *Bloomer*, 19c social reformer>

Bloquiste (blo kēst′) *n* a supporter of the Bloc Québécois.

blos·som (blos′əm) *n* **1** a flower, especially of a tree or plant that produces fruit: *apple blossoms.* **2** the condition or time of flowering: *a cherry tree in blossom.*
v **1** have flowers or open into flowers: *The apple trees are beginning to blossom.* **2** develop, flourish, or mature: *Her talent blossomed under the teacher's expert guidance.* <Old English *blostma*> **blos′som·y** *adj.*

blot (blot) *n* **1** a spot or stain: *an ink blot.* **2** a blemish: *a blot on his reputation, a blot on the landscape.*
v **blot·ted, blot·ting** **1** make blots on, stain, or spot. **2** dry ink or another liquid with paper or other absorbent material: *She blotted her signature so it wouldn't smear.* **3** blemish or disgrace: *His behaviour blotted his record.* <Middle English>
blot out, a hide or cover up. **b** wipe out or destroy: *to blot out an unpleasant memory.*

blotch (bloch) *n* a large, irregular patch of colour.
v cover or mark with blotches. **blotch′y** *adj.*

blot·ter (blot′ər) *n* **1** a piece of soft, absorbent paper used, especially in former times, to dry writing by soaking up excess ink. **2** a notebook for writing down a record, such as a police blotter that contains a record of arrests.

blouse (blouz) *n* **1** a light, loose or partly fitted garment for the upper body, worn by women and girls. **2** the upper part of the uniform of some armed forces. <Provençal *blouso* short> **blouse′like′** *adj.*

blow[1] (blō) *n* **1** a hard hit, knock, or stroke: *a blow with the fist, a hammer, etc.* **2** a misfortune, loss, setback, or severe shock: *His mother's death was a great blow to him.* <Middle English *blaw*>
come to blows, start fighting.

blow[2] (blō) *v* **blew, blown, blow·ing** **1** send forth a strong current of air: *Blow on the soup to cool it. A fan blew cool air into the room.* **2** move in a current, as air does: *A wind was blowing from the east.* **3** move or be moved by wind: *The papers blew off the table.* **4** produce or shape by means of a jet of air: *to blow bubbles, to blow glass.* **5** sound or cause to sound by a wind instrument or whistle: *to blow a trumpet. The whistle blew every day at noon.* **6** clear or empty by blowing air through: *to blow eggs, to blow your nose.* **7** explode; make or break by an explosion: *The dynamite blew the dam to pieces. Watch out; it'll blow in a second.* **8** *Informal* spend wastefully: *I blew a whole day on that project.* **9** burn out or otherwise wreck: *to blow a fuse. Driving without oil will blow the engine.* **10** *Informal* handle badly; bungle: *Don't blow this opportunity.* **11** be out of breath: *The horse was blowing at the end of the race.* **12** spout water and air, as whales do. **13** lay eggs in something, as some insects do. **14** *Informal* leave or get out of: *He blew town.*
n **1** the act or fact of blowing: *a blow of the whistle.* **2** a gale of wind: *Last night's big blow brought down several trees.* <Old English *blawan*> **blow′er** *n.*
blow away, *Slang* **a** impress deeply or astonish: *He blew me away with his generosity.* **b** kill or destroy by means of a weapon. **c** defeat utterly: *The home team was blown away 10–3.*
blow hot and cold, keep changing from a favourable opinion to an unfavourable one.
blow it, *Slang* fail, or make a serious mistake: *Oh, I blew it.*
blow off, *Informal* dismiss or reject advances: *I tried to invite her but she blew me off.*
blow out, a extinguish or be extinguished by wind: *to blow out a match. The flame blew out.* **b** stop blowing: *This wind will soon blow itself out.* **c** burst: *The tire blew out.*
blow out of the water, *Slang* do or be much better than: *The remake blows the original movie out of the water.*
blow over, a pass by or over: *The storm has blown over.* **b** be forgotten: *The scandal will soon blow over.*
blow up, a explode. **b** fill something with air, such as a balloon. **c** *Informal* become very angry. **d** begin: *A storm suddenly blew up.* **e** enlarge a photograph.
blow your mind, *Slang* amaze or overwhelm you: *It blows my mind how fast a computer can do this.*
blow your top (or **stack**), *Slang* become very angry.

blow–by–blow (blō′bī blō′) *Informal adj* very detailed: *a blow-by-blow account.*
n a detailed account or report: *Give me a blow-by-blow of last night's game.*

blow–dry·er (blō′drī ər) *n* a handheld electrical apparatus for drying the hair, often while styling it, by means of a current of hot air. **blow′-dry′** (blō′ drī) *v.*

blow·gun (blō′gun′) *n* a tube through which a person blows arrows or darts. Also called **blowpipe**.

blow·hard (blō′härd′) *Slang n* a braggart.

blow·hole (blō′hōl′) *n* **1** a hole for breathing, in the top of the head of whales and some other animals. **2** a hole in the ice where aquatic animals come to breathe. **3** a hole where air or gas can escape.

blown (blōn) *v* past participle of BLOW.
adj **1** shaped by blowing: *blown glass.* **2** out of breath or exhausted: *He was blown after climbing the steep hill.* **3** tainted by flies: *blown meat.*

blow·out (blō′out′) *n* **1** the bursting of a tire or some other inflated container. **2** the sudden, uncontrolled eruption of an oil or gas well. **3** the melting of an electric fuse caused by an overload in a circuit or line. **4** *Informal* a big celebration or sale.

blow·pipe (blō′pīp′) BLOWGUN.

blow·torch (blō′tôrch′) *n* a small torch that shoots out a hot flame, especially for welding, or to burn off paint.

blow·up (blō′up′) *n* **1** *Informal* **a** an outburst of anger. **b** a quarrel, fuss, or uproar. **2** an enlargement of a photograph. **3** an explosion.

blow·y (blō′ē) *adj* **blow·i·er, blow·i·est** windy.

blub·ber (blub′ər) *n* **1** the fat of whales and some other sea animals from which oil is extracted. **2** excessive fat on a human being. **3** noisy crying.
v cry noisily; speak while crying and sobbing: *Stop your blubbering. The child blubbered an apology.* <probably imitative> **blub′ber·y** *adj.*

bludg·eon (bluj′ən) *n* a short, heavy club used as a weapon.
v strike with a club. <origin unknown>

a bat	e bed	i bid	o pot	u cup	th **thin**
ā cake	ē me	ī bite	ō go	ū rude	ᴛʜ **then**
ä bar	ə about	ər over	ô for	ů put	zh measure

blue (blū) *adj* **blu·er, blu·est** **1** with the colour of the clear sky in daylight, between green and violet. **2** of the skin, pale or purplish with cold. **3** sad or discouraged: *feeling blue.*
n **1 the blue** the sky or the far distance: *way up in the blue, riding off into the blue.* **2 the blues** *pl* **a** *Informal* low spirits: *He's got the blues.* **b** *Music* a style of jazz characterized by a tendency to flatten certain notes, producing harmonies that give the music a melancholy sound. A **blue note** is such a flattened note. A **bluesy** song is done in the style of the blues. <Old French *bleu*> **blue′ness** *n.* **blu′ish** *adj.*
once in a blue moon, hardly ever: *Once in a blue moon we get an e-mail from him.*
out of the blue, completely unexpected and from an unknown source or for an unknown reason: *Suddenly, out of the blue, she announced she was quitting the team.*
sing (or **cry**) **the blues,** be unhappy.

Blue·beard (blū′bērd′) *n* a legendary character who murdered six of his wives and hid their bodies in a room which he forbade anyone to enter.

blue·bell (blū′bel′) *n* a plant with blue flowers shaped like bells, such as the wild hyacinth.

blue·ber·ry (blū′ber′ē) *n, pl* **blue·ber·ries** a small, sweet, dark blue berry that grows on a low shrub.

blue·bird (blū′bərd′) *n* a N American songbird of the thrush family. The male has mainly bright blue feathers.

blue blood *n* **1** aristocratic descent. **2 blueblood** an aristocrat. **blue′-blood′ed** *adj.*

blue·bot·tle (blū′bot′əl) *n* a large fly with a shiny blue body. It makes a loud buzzing sound in flight.

blue box *n* **1** a blue plastic box, used by households to hold recyclable waste. **2** in telecommunications, an illegal device once used to avoid paying for long-distance telephone calls.

blue cheese *n* cheese with streaks of mould in it, often somewhat crumbly.

blue–col·lar (blū′kol′ər) *adj* to do with industrial or manual workers, especially their way of life or attitudes: *He said he would prefer any blue-collar job to working in an office.* Compare WHITE-COLLAR. <Blue is a common colour for work clothes.>

blue·fish (blū′fish′) *n, pl* **blue·fish** a large blue-and-silver food fish of the Atlantic and Indian oceans.

blue flag *n* an iris with blue flowers.

blue·grass (blū′gras′) *n* **1** a N American grass with bluish green stems, especially **Kentucky bluegrass**, widely cultivated for pasture and lawns. **2** a type of country music with fast rhythms and bluesy harmony, making much use of the banjo.

blue–green algae (blū′grēn′) *n* a major division of bacteria that contain chlorophyll and produce their own food through photosynthesis. The technical name is **cyanobacteria.**

blue·ing (blū′ing) BLUING.

Blue jays are definitely not picky eaters. Their diet includes everything from nuts and seeds to small amphibians, insects, and the eggs of other birds.

blue jay *n* a N American bird with a crest on the head, a long tail, and a blue upper body and head. It is the provincial bird of Prince Edward Island.

blue laws *pl n* any strict and puritanical laws.

blue line *Hockey n* either of the two blue lines drawn midway between the centre red line and each goal, dividing the ice into three parts: defensive, neutral, and offensive.

Blue·nose (blū′nōz′) *n* **1** either of two famous schooners built in Nova Scotia. **2** *Informal* a Nova Scotian.

blue–plate special (blū′plāt′) *especially US n* at a restaurant, a complete meal featured at a low price.

blue·print (blū′print′) *n* **1** an exact photographic copy of an original drawing, especially of a building plan or machine design, usually showing white lines on a blue background. **2** a detailed plan for anything.
v make a blueprint of.

blue ribbon *n* the first prize or highest honour.

blue spruce *n* a spruce with bluish green needles, native to the western US but common as an ornamental tree throughout N America.

blue·stone (blū′stōn′) *n* copper sulphate.

blue streak *Informal n* anything very fast.
talk a blue streak, talk fast and excitedly.

blue whale *n* a greyish blue baleen whale, the largest animal that has ever existed on earth. It is an endangered species.

bluff[1] (bluf) *n* **1** a high, steep bank or cliff. **2** *Prairie Provinces* a clump of trees standing on the flat prairie: *The farmhouse was screened from the wind by a poplar bluff.*
adj frank and rough in a good-natured way: *He had a bluff, hearty way about him.* <probably Dutch *blaf* broad, flat> **bluff′ly** *adv.* **bluff′ness** *n.*

bluff[2] (bluf) *n* **1** a show of pretended confidence used to deceive or mislead. **2** a threat that cannot be carried out.
v **1** make a show of confidence in order to deceive. **2** make threats that cannot be carried out. <perhaps Dutch *bluffen* baffle, mislead> **bluff′er** *n.*
bluff your way through, proceed or succeed by bluffing: *He bluffed his way through this test, but he'll never pass the final exam.*
call someone's bluff, challenge or expose a bluff: *The bully backed down when I called her bluff.*

blu·ing or **blue·ing** (blū′ing) *n* a blue liquid or powder added to rinse water to keep white garments from turning yellow.

blun·der (blun′dər) *n* a stupid mistake.
v **1** make a stupid mistake. **2** move or act clumsily or blindly. <Middle English *blondren*> **blun′der·er** *n.*
blunder on, discover by chance.

blun·der·buss (blun′dər bus′) *n* in former times, a short shotgun with a wide, flared muzzle and a short range. <Dutch *donderbus* thunder gun>

blunt (blunt) *adj* **1** without a sharp edge or point. **2** frank, often so as to border on rudeness: *He thinks that blunt speech proves he is honest.*
v make or become less sharp or keen: *You will blunt the scissors if you use them to cut paper. All the delays have blunted their enthusiasm.* <Middle English> **blunt′ly** *adv.* **blunt′ness** *n.*

blur (blər) *v* **blurred, blur·ring 1** make or become unclear in form or outline: *Mist blurred the hills.* **2** make or become unable to see clearly: *Tears blurred my eyes.*
n something seen dimly or indistinctly: *The countryside was a blur through the rain on the windows.* <possibly a variant of *blear*> **blur′ry** *adj.*

blurb (blərb) *Informal n* a short written piece or endorsement used for promotional purposes, especially on the cover of a book or in an advertisement: *The blurb on the cover describes the book as "gently funny."* <coined by 20c humorist G. Burgess>

blurt (blərt) *v* (*often with* ***out***) say suddenly or without thinking: *In his anger, he blurted out the secret.* <imitative>

blush (blush) *v* **1** turn red in the face because of shame, embarrassment, or confusion: *She was so shy that she blushed every time she was spoken to.* **2** be ashamed: *I blush to confess I've done that too.* **3** be or become rosy.
n **1** a reddening of the skin caused by shame, confusion, or excitement. **2** a rosy colour: *The blush of dawn showed in the east.* **3** a reddish or pinkish cosmetic for applying to the cheeks. <Old English *blyscan*>
at first blush, at first glance or thought.
blush for, be ashamed of.

blus·ter (blus′tər) *v* **1** storm or blow noisily and violently: *a blustering wind.* **2** talk noisily and aggressively or arrogantly: *He blusters a lot but he's really kind.*
n **1** stormy noise and violence. **2** noisy and aggressive or arrogant talk: *I don't like her bluster.* <German *blüstern* blow violently> **blus′ter·er** *n.* **blus′ter·y** *adj.*

BMI body mass index.

BMX bikes are built for speed and manoeuvrability. They have small frames, and wheels with knobby tires for extra traction. BMX bikes are typically single speed with hand brakes or rear coaster brakes.

BMX *n* in full, **bicycle motocross** the sport of offroad bicycle racing.

BNA Act or **B.N.A. Act** British North America Act.

bo·a (bō′ə) *n* **1** a non-poisonous tropical snake that gives birth to live young, and that kills its prey by coiling around it and squeezing. One small species, the **rubber boa**, lives in valleys in the extreme south of British Columbia. **2** a woman's long, ornamental scarf made of fur or feathers. <Latin>

boa constrictor *n* **1** a large tropical American boa with tan skin and brown markings. **2** any large snake that kills its prey by squeezing it until it suffocates.

boar (bȯr) *n* **1** a tusked wild pig of Europe, N Africa, and Asia, hunted as a game animal. **2** an uncastrated domestic pig. <Old English *bar*>

board (bȯrd) *n* **1** a long, flat piece of lumber cut for use in building, etc.: *a deck made of cedar boards.* **2** (*often in compounds*) a flat piece of wood or other material used for some special purpose: *an ironing board, a chessboard, a snowboard, surfboard etc.* **3** a chalkboard, whiteboard, or blackboard: *Write the answers on the board.* **4** a group of people managing something: *a school board.* **5** meals provided for pay or as a form of pay: *Camp counsellors are paid a salary plus board.* **6** *Poetic* a dining table or the food served on it. **7 the boards a** the stage of a theatre. **b** the wooden barrier surrounding the ice of a hockey rink. **8** *Computers* a circuit board.
v **1** cover with boards: *We board up the windows of our cottage in the fall.* **2** get or give room and meals for pay: *He boards at our house. My grandmother boards two students.* **3** get onto some means of transport, such as a plane, ship, or train. **4** *Hockey* bodycheck an opposing player into the boards. **5** *Informal* snowboard, surfboard, etc. <Old English *bord*> **board′er** *n.* **board′ing** *n.*
across the board, affecting all people or things of a certain kind equally: *My grades have improved across the board.*
go by the board, be given up, discarded, neglected, or ignored: *Have school dress codes gone by the board?*
on board, on a plane, ship, train, etc.

board foot *n* a unit for measuring lumber, about 2500 cm^3.

boarding house *n* a house where rooms and meals are provided for pay.

boarding school *n* a school that provides lodging and food for some or all of its students during term.

board of education *n* a group of people, usually elected, who manage the schools in a certain area.

board of health *n* the department of a local government in charge of public health.

board·room (bȯrd′rūm′) *n* a meeting room regularly used by the directors (collectively, the **board of directors**) of an organization.

board·walk (bȯrd′wok′) *n* a sidewalk or raised walkway made of boards.

a **bat**	e **bed**	i **bid**	o **pot**	u **cup**	th **thin**
ā **cake**	ē **me**	ī **bite**	ō **go**	ū **rude**	ᴛʜ **then**
à **bar**	ə **about**	ər **over**	ȯ **for**	ů **put**	zh **measure**

boast (bōst) *v* **1** brag about oneself, one's relatives, or one's possessions: *He boasted that he was the best player on the team.* **2** have and be properly proud of: *Canada boasts many fine National Parks.*
n **1** something said in praise of oneself. **2** something to be proud of: *It was my little brother's boast that he could run faster than anyone in his class.* <Middle English *bosten*>
boast′er *n.* **boast′ful** *adj.* **boast′ful·ly** *adv.* **boast′ful·ness** *n.*

boat (bōt) *n* **1** a small, open vessel for travelling on water, such as a motorboat. **2** a ship. **3** a boat-shaped container with a spout for serving gravy or sauce.
v travel in a boat. <Old English *bat*> **boat′er** *n.* **boat′ing** *n.*
in the same boat, in the same position or condition: *We're all in the same boat, so stop complaining.*
miss the boat, miss an opportunity; lose one's chances.

SYNONYMS

In everyday speech, **boat** can mean a water vessel of any size: *That freighter is a big boat.*

A **ship** is a very large boat with a motor or sails: *My great-grandparents came to Canada across the ocean on a ship.*

A **yacht** is smaller than a ship, with sails and a motor, or just a motor: *She sailed her yacht in the race.*

boat·house (bōt′hous′) *n* a house or shed, usually built over the water, with a large opening in the floor for sheltering a boat or boats.

boat·load (bōt′lōd′) *n* as much or as many as a boat can carry.

boat people *pln* refugees who have escaped by boat and are seeking refuge in another country; originally, Asians who fled South Vietnam after it was conquered by North Vietnam in 1975.

🍁 **boat song** *n* a song used by the VOYAGEURS to help them maintain a steady rhythm with their paddles.

boat·swain (bō′sən); *less often,* (bōt′swān′) BOSUN.

bob[1] (bob) *v* **bobbed, bob·bing** **1** move up and down with short, quick motions: *The bird bobbed its head up and down. The boat bobbed on the waves.* **2** curtsy quickly. **3** try to catch a floating object with the teeth: *At the fall fair we bobbed for apples in a wooden bowl.*
n a bobbing motion. <Middle English>
bob up, surface suddenly.

bob[2] (bob) *n* **1** a short haircut. **2** a weight on the end of a pendulum or plumb line. **3** a float for a fishing line.
v **bobbed, bob·bing** cut (hair) short. <Middle English *bobbe* bunch>

bob·bin (bob′ən) *n* a small reel or spool for holding thread, wire, etc. <French *bobine*>

bob·by pin (bob′ē) *n* a clip for the hair, consisting of a thin strip of metal folded tightly in half.

bob·by·socks (bob′ē soks′) *Informal pln* girls' or women's ankle socks, usually with the tops folded over. <*bob*[2]>

bob·cat (bob′kat′) *n* a species of lynx found mostly in the US that has brown fur and a short tail. <*bob*[2] + *cat*>

bob·o·link (bob′ə lingk′) *n* a N American songbird, found in fields and meadows and with stiff, pointed tail feathers. <imitative of its call>

bob·skate (bob′skāt′) *n* a child's skate with a double set of blades, worn by strapping it to a regular boot or shoe. It has two sections so that the length can be adjusted. <*bob*[2] + *skate*>

bob·sled (bob′sled′) *n* a long sled with two sets of runners, a shaped seat for two or more people, a steering wheel, and brakes. A rigid covering at the front end covers the driver's hands and feet and the controls. Bobsled racing is an Olympic event.
v **bob·sled·ded, bob·sled·ding** ride or coast on a bobsled. Also (*UK*), **bobsleigh.** <*bob*[2] + *sled*>
bob′sled′der *n.*

bob·tail (bob′tāl′) *n* **1** a tail that has been cut short. **2** a horse or dog with such a tail. <*bob*[2]> **bob′tailed** *adj.*

bob·white (bob′wīt′) *n* a small quail found in S Ontario and the eastern US. <imitative of its call>

boc·ce (bo′chē) *n* a game similar to lawn bowling, but played on a dirt court. Also, **boccie, bocci.** <Italian>

bode (bōd) *v* **bod·ed, bod·ing** be a sign of; indicate beforehand: *Dark clouds boded rain.* <Old English *boda* messenger>
bode ill (or **well**)**,** be a bad (or good) sign.

bo·dhi (bō′dē) *Buddhism n* **1** the state of enlightenment attained by one who has achieved salvation. **2** the awakening into NIRVANA. <Sanskrit>

Bo·dhi·satt·va (bō′dē sut′və) *Buddhism n* one who has attained enlightenment but remains in the world for the sake of others. <Sanskrit>

bod·ice (bod′is) *n* **1** the part of a dress from the shoulders to the waist. **2** especially in former times, an outer garment for women and girls, worn over a blouse and laced up the front. It is still part of the traditional dress in some countries of Europe. <from *body*>

bod·i·ly (bod′ə lē) *adj* of or in the body: *bodily functions, assault causing bodily harm.*
adv **1** in person: *The man whom we thought dead walked bodily into the room.* **2** all together: *The audience rose bodily and cheered.* **3** by force and by taking hold of the body: *The noisy child was removed bodily from the room.*

bod·y (bod′ē) *n, pl* **bod·ies** **1** the whole material part of a human being, animal, or plant: *This girl has a strong, healthy body.* **2** the part of a human being or animal excluding the head and limbs; the torso. **3** the main mass of anything: *Tables are included in the body of the book instead of in an appendix.* **4** the outer or main structural part of something: *car body.* **5** a group of individuals or a mass of something, considered as a unit: *a legislative body. A lake is a body of water.* **6** *Informal* a person: *He is a good-natured body.* **7** a dead person. **8** density or thickness; volume: *This shampoo gives your hair extra body.* **9** richness and fullness of flavour or sound: *a voice with body.* <Old English *bodig*> **bod′i·less** *adj.*
in a body, all together.
keep body and soul together, have enough to eat to stay alive.

body bag *n* a large, zippered rubber bag used for carrying a dead body, especially in war.

bod·y·board (bod′ē bord′) *n* a short surfboard with one straight end, ridden usually by lying down rather than standing. **bod′y·board′** *v.* **bod′y·board′er** *n.*

Physical fitness through **bodybuilding** dates as far back as the 1000s in India. Athletes in those days lifted carved stone dumbbells, called *nals*, to build muscle.

bod·y·build·ing (bod′ē bil′ding) *n* advanced development of the muscles through weightlifting and other strenuous exercises. **bod′y·build′er** *n.*

bod·y·check (bod′ē chek′) *Hockey, Lacrosse v* use body contact to check or hinder an opponent's progress. **bod′y·check′** *n.*

bod·y·guard (bod′ē gȧrd′) *n* a person or group of people who accompany someone in order to protect him or her.

body language *n* gestures, posture, position of the body, and facial expression used to communicate an attitude, often unconsciously.

body mass index *n* a number arrived at by a formula based on one's weight and height, used to indicate whether one is overweight or not. *Abbrev.* **BMI**

body piercing *n* the piercing of one's body, especially in places other than the ears or nose, in order to wear studs or rings as ornaments.

body politic *n* the people in a politically organized community or country.

body shirt *n* a shirt or blouse for women or girls that ends in panties that fasten at the crotch. Also, **bodyshirt**.

body shop *n* a garage, or part of a garage, where repairs are done to BODYWORK.

body stocking *n* a lightweight, close-fitting, stretchy one-piece garment for the whole body. Also, **bodystocking**.

bod·y·surf (bod′ē sərf′) *v* ride waves without a surfboard. **bod′y·surf′er** *n.*

bod·y·work (bod′ē wərk′) *n* the outer shell of a vehicle, or any repairs done to it.

Boer (būr) *n* one of the Dutch settlers in South Africa, or one of their descendants. <Dutch = farmer>

bog (bog) *n* soft, wet, spongy ground.
v **bogged, bog·ging** (*used with* ***down***) **1** sink or get stuck in a bog. **2** hindered or slowed down: *bogged down in details.* <Gaelic = soft> **bog′gy** *adj.*

bo·gey[1] (bō′gē) *Golf n* a score of one stroke over PAR (def. 5): *He shot a bogey on the sixth hole.* <Colonel *Bogey,* a golfing character created by writer H. Hutchinson>

bo·gey[2] or **bo·gy** (bō′gē) *n, pl* **bo·geys** or **bo·gies** **1** an evil spirit, scary monster, or goblin. **2** a source of annoyance or fear; a bugaboo. <origin uncertain; probably related to *bug* an evil spirit>

bo·gey·man (bō′gē man) or (bū′gē man) *n* an imaginary, frightening being.

bog·gle (bog′əl) *v* **bog·gled, bog·gling** be astonished or overwhelmed by something: *The figures are so huge they boggle the mind. He boggled at the thought of so much responsibility.* <perhaps Scots *bogle*>

bo·gus (bō′gəs) *adj* not genuine: *a bogus twenty-dollar bill.* <origin unknown>

bo·he·mi·an (bō hē′mē ən) *adj* **1** not bound by rules and social conventions. **2** **Bohemian** concerning Bohemia, a region of the Czech Republic.
n **1** person who lives a bohemian lifestyle. **2** **Bohemian** a native or inhabitant of Bohemia, or its language. **bo·he′mi·an·ism′** *n.*

boil[1] (boil) *v* **1** of liquids, bubble up and begin to turn to steam or vapour, or cause to do this: *Water boils when heated to about 100°C. Boil some water for tea.* **2** put in boiling water to cook or sterilize: *to boil eggs, to boil a baby's bottles.* **3** have the contents of a container boil: *The kettle is boiling.* **4** be excited or angry: *She is still boiling over the incident.* **5** move violently: *The waves boiled among the rocks.*
n a boiling condition: *Bring the mixture to a boil.* <Old French, from Latin *bullire* to bubble>
boil down, a reduce the volume of a liquid by boiling: *to boil a sauce down.* **b** reduce to essentials: *He boiled down his notes to a list of important facts.*
boil over, a come to the boiling point and overflow. **b** let one's excitement or anger show.

boil[2] (boil) *n* a hard, round abscess in the skin consisting of pus around a hard core, usually caused by bacteria entering an oil or sweat gland. <Old English *byle*>

boil·er (boi′lər) *n* **1** a tank of water for making steam to heat buildings or drive engines. **2** a tank for holding hot water. **3** a container for heating liquids.

boil·ing point (boi′ling) *n* the temperature at which a liquid boils. The boiling point of water at sea level is 100°C.

bois·ter·ous (boi′stə rəs) *adj* **1** noisily cheerful: *a boisterous game.* **2** violent or rough: *a boisterous child.* <Middle English *boistrous*> **bois′ter·ously** *adv.* **bois′ter·ous·ness** *n.*

a bat	e bed	i bid	o pot	u cup	th thin
ā cake	ē me	ī bite	ō go	ū rude	ᴛʜ then
ȧ bar	ə about	ər over	ȯ for	u̇ put	zh measure

bold (bōld) *adj* **1** fearless; daring: *a bold explorer, bold deeds.* **2** cheeky or rude: *The bold little girl made faces at us. That was a rather bold request.* **3** vivid, forceful, or clear: *bold colours, bold brushstrokes. The mountains stood in bold outline against the sky.* **4** printed in boldface: *bold type.* <Old English *bald*> **bold′ly** *adv.* **bold′ness** *n.*
make bold, take the liberty; dare: *May I make so bold as to ask for the use of your pen?*

bold·face (bōld′fās′) *Printing n* a heavy type that stands out clearly: ***This sentence is in boldface.***

bole (bōl) *n* the trunk of a tree. <Old Norse *bolr*>

Bo·liv·i·a (bə liv′ē ə) *n* a country in central S America. See the APPENDIX. **Bo·liv′i·an** *adj, n.*

boll (bōl) *n* a rounded seed pod or capsule of a plant, especially cotton or flax. <variant of *bowl*>

boll weevil *n* a small brown or black beetle of Central America, Mexico, and the southern US. Both the larva and the adult feed on the buds and bolls of cotton plants, causing serious damage to crops.

bo·lo·gna (bə lō′nē) *n* a large, mildly flavoured sausage made of some mixture of beef, veal, pork, or poultry. Also, **baloney** (*Informal*). <*Bologna,* city in Italy>

bo·lo tie (bō′lō′) *n* a tie made of thin cord, the loose ends running through a sliding ornament which keeps the ends together. <American Spanish, altered from *bolas* weapon consisting of stone or metal balls tied to cords>

Bol·she·vik or **bol·she·vik** (bōl′shə vik′) *n* **1** in Russia, a member of a radical socialist party that seized power in 1917 and afterwards formed the Communist Party. **2** any extreme left-wing radical.
adj to do with Bolsheviks or their politics. <Russian> **Bol′she·vism′** or **bol′she·vism′** *n.* **Bol′she·vist** or **bol′she·vist** *n, adj.*

bol·ster (bōl′stər) *n* a long, cylindrical pillow or cushion.
v support or prop; reinforce: *to bolster someone's confidence.* <Old English>

bolt (bōlt) *n* **1** a small metal shaft made to hold parts together, with a head at one end and a thread at the other for screwing a nut onto it. **2** a sliding fastener for a door, window, or gate. **3** the part of a lock moved by a key. **4** a short arrow with a thick head, for shooting with a crossbow. **5** a stroke of lightning. **6** a sudden running away: *The prisoner made a bolt for freedom.* **7** a roll of cloth or wallpaper of a standard size.
v **1** fasten with a bolt. **2** dash away; run away: *The horse bolted.* **3** swallow without chewing: *The dog bolted its food.* <Old English = arrow>
a bolt from the blue, a complete surprise or sudden, unexpected happening.
bolt upright, stiff and straight up: *Awakened by a noise, he sat bolt upright in bed.*

bomb (bom) *n* **1** a container filled with an explosive charge or a chemical substance, that is exploded by a timing mechanism or by contact with something. **2** *Informal* a miserable failure. **3 the bomb** nuclear weapons: *Many nations have outlawed the bomb.*
v **1** attack, damage, or destroy with bombs, especially by dropping them from aircraft. **2** *Informal* fail completely and miserably: *All the jokes he made in his speech bombed.* <Old French, from Greek *bombos* deep sound>
drop a bomb, make an unexpected announcement.

bom·bard (bom bärd′) *v* **1** attack with bombs, grenades, or heavy guns: *The enemy bombarded the town all day.* **2** give or send a great many of something in quick succession: *TV bombards us with advertisements.* **3** *Physics* hit atomic nuclei with a stream of fast-moving particles, thus changing the structure of the nuclei. **bom·bard′ment** *n.*

bom·bar·dier (bom′bə dēr′) *or* (bom′bə dēr′) *n* **1** in the armed forces, a corporal who serves in the artillery. **2** the person in a bomber who aims and releases the bombs.

🍁 **Bom·bar·dier** (bom bär′dyā) *n* a large covered vehicle for travelling over snow and ice, usually equipped with tracked wheels at the rear and a set of skis at the front. <A. *Bombardier,* 20c Canadian inventor>

bom·bast (bom′bast) *n* flowery and overly complicated language that says little. <Old French, from Latin *bombax* padding material> **bom·bas′tic** *adj.*

bomb·er (bom′ər) *n* **1** an aircraft specially designed for dropping bombs. **2** a person who throws or drops bombs.

bomb·proof (bom′prūf′) *adj* strong or deep enough to be safe from bombs and shells: *a bombproof shelter.*

bomb·shell (bom′shel′) *n* **1** a bomb. **2** *Informal* an unexpected and usually unpleasant piece of news.

bo·na fi·de (bō′nə fīd′) *or* (bō′nə fī′dē) *adj* without pretence or fraud: *a bona fide signature on the document.* <Latin = in good faith>

bo·nan·za (bə nan′zə) *n* **1** a rich mass of ore in a mine. **2** *Informal* any rich source of profit.

ETYMOLOGY

Bonanza is a Spanish word meaning "fair weather" or "prosperity." It was first used in English to mean "a large quantity of ore," especially in the gold and silver mines of the United States in the mid 1800s.

bon·bon (bon′bon′) *n* a piece of candy. <French = candy>

bond (bond) *n* **1** anything that ties or unites: *a bond of trust between sisters.* **2** a certificate issued by a government or company promising to pay back borrowed money, together with interest. **3** *Law* a written agreement by which a person says he or she will pay a certain sum of money if he or she does not perform certain duties properly: *The judge put her under a bond to keep the peace.* **4** anything that creates an obligation. **5** a good quality of paper, made at least partly from rag pulp. **6** the sticking together of substances: *This glue provides an excellent bond.* **7** *Chemistry* the electrical forces that hold atoms and molecules together. **8 bonds** *pl Poetic* chains or shackles.
v **1** bind or stick firmly together. **2** develop strong emotional ties: *The baby needs a chance to bond with the mother.* **3** take out an insurance policy on an employee to pay for any losses caused by him or her: *The company bonds all its cashiers.* **4** put goods in bond in a warehouse. <variant of *band*[2]> **bond′ed** *adj.*
in bond, being held in a warehouse until taxes are paid.

bond·age (bon′dij) *n* slavery.

bond·hold·er (bond′hōl′dər) *n* a person who owns bonds issued by a government or company.

bond·serv·ant (bond′sər′vənt) *n* **1** a servant who works without pay, sometimes temporarily. **2** a slave.

bone (bōn) *n* **1** one of the parts of the skeleton of a human or other vertebrate: *the bones of the hand, a beef bone for soup.* **2** the hard substance of which bones are made. **3** anything like bone, such as ivory.
v **boned, bon·ing** take bones out of: *to bone fish.* <Old English *ban*>
bone of contention, the subject of argument.
bone up on, *Informal* study or get information on, especially at the last minute: *You'd better bone up on your facts before the test.*
feel in your bones, be sure without knowing why.
have a bone to pick, have a complaint or argument with someone.
make no bones, show no hesitation or embarrassment: *He makes no bones about skipping school to go shopping.*

bone china *n* a white, translucent type of china made by mixing bone ash or calcium phosphate with clay.

bone–dry (bōn′drī′) *adj* very dry.

bone·less (bōn′lis) *adj* with the bones removed: *boneless chicken.*

bone marrow *n* the fatty substance inside bones, where new red and white blood cells are formed.

bone meal *n* crushed or ground bones used as fertilizer or as animal feed.

bon·fire (bon′fīr′) *n* a large fire built on the ground outdoors. <Middle English *bonefire* bone fire; originally, a fire to burn corpses>

Bongos, played by musicians called *bongoseros*, are especially popular in Cuba. They originated in Africa, and have spread to Latin America and beyond.

bon·go (bong′gō) *n, pl* **bon·gos** or **bon·goes** one of a pair of small, connected drums, one slightly larger than the other, that are played with the hands, usually while being held between the knees. <American Spanish>

bonk (bongk) *Slang v* knock or hit *When he fell, he bonked his head against a tree.*
n a knock or hit: *a mighty bonk.* <imitative>

bon mot (bȯn mō′) *n, pl* **bons·mots** (bȯn mōz′) a witty remark. <French = good word>

bon·net (bon′it) *n* **1** a fitted, hoodlike hat for babies and little girls, usually tied under the chin and with a frill around the face. **2** a similar head covering in former times worn by girls and women. <Old French *bonet*, originally fabric for hats> **bon′net·ed** *adj.*

bon·sai (bon′sī) *n* **1** the art of dwarfing trees and shrubs by pruning the branches and roots. **2** a small potted tree or shrub of this kind. <Japanese *bon* basin + *sai* plant>

bon·spiel (bon′spēl′) *n* a curling tournament. <Dutch *bond* league + *spel* game>

bo·nus (bō′nəs) *n* a payment or gift in addition to what is usually due: *The company gave all its employees a bonus last year.* <Latin = good>

bon vivant (bȯn′ vē vȧn′) *n, pl* **bons vivants** (bȯn′ vē vȧn′) a person who is fond of good food and luxury. <French = good living>

bon vo·yage (bȯn′vwȧ yȧzh′) *n* a goodbye to someone going on a trip. <French = good trip>

bon·y (bō′nē) *adj* **bon·i·er, bon·i·est** **1** to do with or like bone. **2** full of bones. **3** with big bones that stick out. **4** very thin. **bon′i·ness** *n.*

boo (bū) *interj; n, pl* **boos** a sound made to show dislike or contempt or to frighten.
v **booed, boo·ing** show displeasure by saying "boo" at.

boob tube (būb) *Slang n* television. <*booby* foolish person + (*cathode ray*) *tube*, i.e, television>

boo·by (bū′bē) *n, pl* **boo·bies** **1** a stupid or foolish person. **2** a large seabird of the tropics. <Spanish *bobo* fool; probably from Latin *balbus* mumbling>

booby prize *n* a prize given to the person who does worst in a contest.

booby trap *n* **1** a trick arranged to annoy an unsuspecting person. **2** a bomb arranged to explode when an object is touched by an unsuspecting person.

boo·gie (bū′gē) *or* (bu̇g′ē) *Slang v* **boo·gied, boo·gy·ing** **1** dance to fast, lively music. **2** go or move fast: *I'm going to boogie on down to the mall.*
n rock, rock and roll, or jazz. <shortened from *boogie-woogie*>

boog·ie–woog·ie (bu̇g′ē wu̇g′ē) *Music n* a style of jazz with a repeating rhythmic pattern of notes in the bass, accompanying a melody that is often improvised.

book (bu̇k) *n* **1** a set of written or printed pages stitched or glued together along one edge, usually with attached front and back covers. **2** a long piece of written work, especially one that is published: *She writes books about her travels.* **3** a set of blank sheets bound together along one edge, used for taking notes, drawing, keeping records, etc. **4** a main division of a long literary work, or one volume in a series: *For most of book two, the setting is Nova Scotia.* **5** something fastened together like a book: *a book of tickets, a book of matches.* **6** **books** *pl* the records of all the transactions of a business. **7** the words of an opera or musical. **8** something thought of as giving knowledge if it is studied: *the book of life.* **9** a record of bets made by a BOOKMAKER. **10** in card games, a trick or number of tricks forming a set.
v **1** engage or reserve: *to book theatre tickets. We booked a deejay for the dance.* **2** record a charge against a person at a police station: *The officer booked him on a charge of theft.* <Old English *boc*>

a bat	e bed	i bid	o pot	u cup	th **thin**
ā cake	ē me	ī bite	ō go	ū rude	ᴛʜ **then**
ȧ bar	ə about	ər over	ȯ for	u̇ put	zh measure

by the book, strictly according to the rules: *The science experiment will work if it's done by the book.*
in my book, *Informal* in my opinion or judgment: *In my book, swearing is always unnecessary.*
keep books, keep a record of business accounts.
one for the book, a remarkable or memorable thing.
read someone like a book, guess accurately what a person is thinking or feeling.
throw the book at, *Informal* punish as severely as the law allows: *This is her third offence, so the judge will probably throw the book at her.*

book·bind·er (bu̇k′bīn′dər) *n* a person whose work or business is binding books.

book·case (bu̇k′kās′) *n* a piece of furniture with shelves for holding books.

book club *n* **1** a business or organization that regularly supplies selected books to subscribers. **2** a small informal group that meets to discuss books and related topics.

book·end (bu̇k′end′) *n* **1** a support, usually one of a matching pair, placed at either end of a row of books to hold them upright. **2** *Football* a player positioned at either of the ends of the defensive line.
v Informal occur on both sides or at either end of something: *I bookend my fitness workout with stretching exercises.*

book·ie (bu̇k′ē) *Informal n* a bookmaker.

book·ish (bu̇k′ish) *adj* devoted to reading or studying. **book′ish·ness** *n*

book·keep·ing (bu̇k′kē′ping) *n* the work of systematically recording, classifying, and summarizing data about the business transactions of a company according to certain rules. **book′keep′er** *n.*

book·let (bu̇k′lit) *n* a thin book, usually made of pages stapled together, and with paper covers.

book·mak·er (bu̇k′mā′kər) *n* a person who makes a business of accepting bets on horse races.

book·mark (bu̇k′märk′) *n* **1** a strip of some material put between book pages, or a clip attached to a page, to mark a place. **2** *Computers* a record of a place in a computer file or a page on the Internet. **book′mark′** *v.*

book·mo·bile (bu̇k′mə bēl′) *n* a large van or trailer that serves as a travelling branch of a public library.

book·plate (bu̇k′plāt′) *n* a label to paste in books, with the owner's name printed on it.

book·sell·er (bu̇k′sel′ər) *n* a person whose business is selling books.

book·shelf (bu̇k′shelf′) *n* a shelf for holding books.

book·stall (bu̇k′stol′) *n* a booth or counter where books are sold.

book·store (bu̇k′stôr′) *n* a store where books are sold. Also called **bookshop**.

book talk *n* an event usually held in a library, bookstore, or school, at which someone (often the author or a librarian, or a student) discusses a book and reads excerpts, so as to encourage reading. Also, **booktalk**.

book value *n* the value of something according to any official list or schedule of prices.

book·worm (bu̇k′wərm′) *n* **1** a person who is devoted to reading and studying. **2** an insect whose adult forms or larvae gnaw the bindings or pages of books, such as the silverfish.

Boo·le·an (bū′lē ən) *adj* to do with a mathematical system with only two values, usually 1 and 0, and the operators AND, OR, and NOT. It is used to program computers and solve problems in logic. <G. *Boole*, 19c mathematician>

boom[1] (būm) *n* **1** a deep, hollow, loud sound like that of a cannon or a bass drum. **2** rapid economic growth: *Dawson City enjoyed a boom during the Gold Rush.* **3** rapid growth or increase of any kind: *There was a baby boom after World War II.*
v **1** make a deep, hollow sound: *The big man's voice boomed out above the rest.* **2** increase suddenly in activity: *Business is booming.*

ETYMOLOGY

Boom comes from the Middle English *bommen*, meaning "hum." It is also an imitative word, which means that it reproduces a natural sound. Say the word "boom" out loud slowly and then compare it in your head to the sound of thunder.

There are many imitative words in English: *babble, bang, bark, bash, beep, blah, blip, blubber, bop, bump, burp, buzz*. How many more can you think of?

boom[2] (būm) *n* **1** a long pole used to extend the bottom of a sail. **2** the lifting or guiding pole of a crane. **3 a** a chain, cable, or other barrier used to keep logs from floating away. **b** a large raft of logs being floated over water. <Dutch = tree, pole>
lower the boom, suddenly become more strict or severe; crack down: *When she missed her curfew the third time, her mom lowered the boom.*

boom·box (būm′boks′) *Informal n* a powerful portable stereo.

boom·er (bū′mər) *Informal n* a person born during the BABY BOOM, especially with reference to the typical tastes, values, and attitudes of this age group.

boom·er·ang (bū′mə rang′) *n* **1** a curved piece of wood that can be thrown so that it will return to the thrower if it misses its target, originally used as a weapon to hunt game. **2** anything that recoils or reacts to harm the user.
v act as a boomerang. <Australian Aborigine>

boom town *n* a town that has quickly increased in size and wealth.

boon (būn) *n* **1** a great benefit. **2** something asked or granted as a favour. <Old Norse *bon* request>

boon·ies (būn′ēz) *Slang pln* in full, **boondocks** (būn′doks) wild or sparsely settled areas: *He lives in the boonies and comes into town twice a year.* <Tagalog (a language of the Philippines) *bundok* mountainous area>

boor (bu̇r) *n* **1** a person with bad manners. **2** a person of unrefined tastes who does not appreciate beauty, elegance, or the arts. <Old French *bovier* uncivilized person> **boor′ish** *adj.*

boost (būst) *n* **1** a push or lift that helps a person up or over: *a boost over the fence.* **2** an action that encourages: *The new amusement park gave a boost to the local tradespeople.* **3** an increase: *a boost in salary.*
v give a boost to: *to boost sales, to boost someone's spirits.* <blend of *boom* and *hoist*>

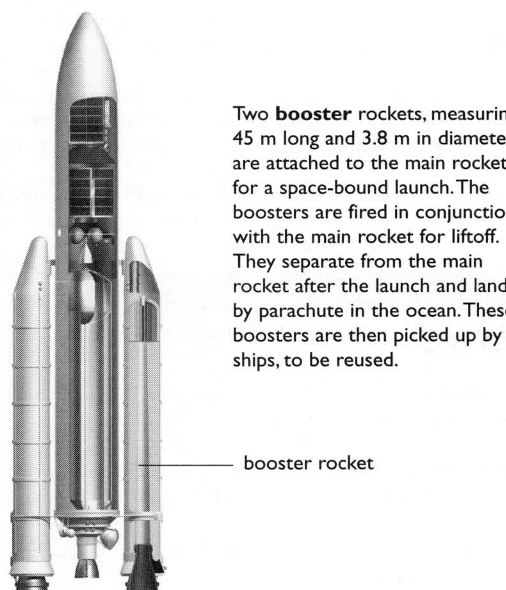

Two **booster** rockets, measuring 45 m long and 3.8 m in diameter, are attached to the main rocket for a space-bound launch. The boosters are fired in conjunction with the main rocket for liftoff. They separate from the main rocket after the launch and land by parachute in the ocean. These boosters are then picked up by ships, to be reused.

boost·er (bū′stər) *n* **1** the first stage of a multistage rocket. **2** the device used to put an artificial satellite into orbit. **3** in full, **booster shot** an injection given to reinforce an earlier inoculation.

booster cables *pln* cables used to connect the terminals of two car batteries, one of them low or dead, so that the dead one can get a charge from the other. Also called **jumper cables**.

boot[1] (būt) *n* **1** an outer covering for the foot and lower part of the leg. **2** *Informal* a kick: *She gave the ball a boot.* **3** *Computers* the start-up of a system or application.
v **1** *Informal* kick: *He booted the stone off the sidewalk.* **2** *Computers* (*usually with* ***up***) start up a computer or piece of software. <Old French *bote*>
bet your boots, *Informal* depend on it; be sure: *You can bet your boots our team will win.*
give someone (or **get**) **the boot,** *Slang* dismiss someone (or be dismissed) rudely or without ceremony.
lick someone's boots, flatter or obey slavishly in order to win favour.

boot[2] (būt) *Archaic* (*except in* ***to boot***) *n* **to boot** in addition; besides: *I got some great clothes for my birthday, and money to boot.* <Old English *bot* advantage>

boot·black (būt′blak′) *n* a person whose work is shining shoes and boots.

boot camp *n* **1** training camp for military recruits. **2** any strict training camp.

boot·ee (bū′tē) *for 1,* (bū tē′) *for 2.* *n* **1** a baby's soft shoe. **2** a woman's short boot. Also, **bootie**.

booth (būth) *n, pl* **booths** (būᴛʜz) *or* (būths) a small structure or partly enclosed space, such as one containing a public telephone, a private table in a restaurant, or a ballot box for voters. <Middle English *bothe*>

boot·jack (būt′jak′) *n* a device used for pulling off boots.

boot·leg (būt′leg′) *v* **boot·legged, boot·leg·ging** sell, transport, or make unlawfully.
adj made, transported, or sold unlawfully: *bootleg whisky, bootleg videotapes.*
n alcoholic liquor made, sold, or transported unlawfully.
boot′leg′ger *n.*

boot·lick (būt′lik′) *Informal v* try to win someone's favour by flattery or slavish obedience: *They would bootlick anyone with influence.* **boot′lick′er** *n.*

boot·strap (būt′strap′) *n* **1** a small strap or loop at the top of a boot, used for pulling it on. **2** *Computers* a short routine instructing the computer to take in other routines or information.
adj **1** done or attempted without outside help: *a bootstrap campaign.* **2** assuming that people can improve their situation solely by their own efforts without help: *bootstrap economic theory.*
lift (or **raise**) **yourself by your own bootstraps,** succeed or improve your life without outside help.

boo·ty (bū′tē) *n* **1** things taken from the enemy in war. **2** things seized by violence and robbery: *The pirates fought over the booty from the raided town.* **3** any valuable thing or things obtained; a prize. <*boot*[2]>

booze (būz) *Informal n* **1** any intoxicating liquor. **2** a drinking spree: *a three-day booze.*
v **boozed, booz·ing** drink heavily. <probably Middle Dutch *busen* to drink to excess> **booz′er** *n.*

bop[1] (bop) *Informal n, v* **bopped, bop·ping** hit; a clout: *a bop on the head* (*n*). *He bopped me with his baseball glove* (*v*). <imitative>

bop[2] (bop) *Informal v* **bopped, bop·ping** go about in a cheerful or easygoing way: *She's been bopping around downtown all morning.* <*bebop,* style of jazz>

bo·rax (bô′raks) *n* a white crystalline powder used as an antiseptic, in washing clothes, fusing metals, and preserving foods. <Persian *borah*>

bor·der (bôr′dər) *n* **1** a strip on or near the edge of anything, for strength or ornament: *a handkerchief with a lace border. Our lawn has a border of flowers.* **2** the line separating two countries, provinces, etc.; a boundary: *We entered the US by crossing the border at Windsor.*
v **1** form a boundary to: *A creek borders our property on the west.* **2** put a border on; edge: *We have bordered our lawn with shrubs.* <Old French *bord* side>
border on, a touch at the border; be next to. **b** be nearly the same as: *Extreme carelessness can border on criminal neglect.*

a bat	e bed	i bid	o pot	u cup	th **thin**
ā cake	ē me	ī bite	ō go	ū rude	ᴛʜ **then**
ä bar	ə about	ər over	ô for	ů put	zh measure

B

bor·der·land (bȯr′dər land′) *n* **1** land next to a border or forming a border. **2** a category that verges on another: *the borderland between sleeping and waking.*

bor·der·line (bȯr′dər līn′) *n* a boundary.
adj **1** on a border or boundary. **2** with uncertain status; near the dividing line between two categories: *He's not exactly failing, but his marks are borderline.*

bore[1] (bȯr) *v* **bored, bor·ing** make a hole or tunnel through something, with or without a tool such as a drill: *Bore a hole through the post and stick the bolt in. A mole has bored its way under our flower bed.*
n **1** the hollow space inside a pipe, tube, or gun barrel. **2** its diameter. <Old English *borian*> **bor′er** *n.*

bore[2] (bȯr) *v* **bored, bor·ing** make weary or uninterested by being dull or tiresome: *His stories bore me.*
n a dull, tiresome, or annoying person or thing. <origin unknown> **bored** *adj.* **bo′ring** *adj.* **bo′ring·ly** *adv.*

bore[3] (bȯr) past tense of BEAR[1].

bore[4] (bȯr) *n* a sudden, high tidal wave that rushes up a channel with great force. <Old Norse *bara* wave>

bo·re·al (bȯ′rē əl) *adj* northern. <Greek *Boreas* the north wind>

boreal forest *n* the northern forest, consisting mainly of spruce, fir, pine, and larch, with some birch, aspen, and elder. In Canada, it stretches from the tundra down to the mountains and prairies, the Great Lakes, and the Gaspé.

bore·dom (bȯr′dəm) *n* the state of being bored; weariness caused by dull, tiresome people or events.

bor·ic acid (bȯ′rik) *n* a crystalline substance used as a mild antiseptic or to preserve food. <from *boron*>

bor·ing (bȯ′ring) *adj* dull and tiresome: *Anything gets boring if you do it too often.*

born (bȯrn) *v* a past participle of BEAR[1].
adj **1** brought into life or existence; brought forth. **2** by birth; by nature: *a born athlete.*

born–a·gain (bȯrn′ə gen′) *adj* **1** *Christianity* with new spiritual life given by God. **2** *Informal* with renewed enthusiasm; committed: *a born-again jazz fan.*

borne (bȯrn) a past participle of BEAR[1]:

GRAMMAR AND USAGE

Borne is the past participle of **bear** for most of its meanings:

He had borne the hard work without complaint.

The feather was borne through the air by the wind.

For the meaning "give birth to," the past participle of **bear** is **born** in the usual passive voice: *She was born in Nova Scotia.* In the active voice, the correct spelling is **borne**: *She had borne one child.*

bo·ron (bȯ′ron) *n* a non-metallic element found in borax. *Symbol* **B** <*bor*(*ax*) + (*carb*)*on*>

bor·ough (bər′ō) *n* **1** ✱ in former times in Ontario, an urban community with the status of a township rather than a city: *Several former boroughs are now part of the megacity of Toronto.* **2** in the US and the UK, any of various other kinds of urban political unit. <Old English *burg* politically important town>

bor·row (bȯ′rō) *v* **1** get something from another person with the understanding that it will be returned: *Can I borrow your skates till tomorrow?* **2** take and use as one's own: *Rome borrowed many ideas from Greece.* **3** take a word or expression from another language and use it: *The word "kayak" was borrowed from Inuktitut.* **4** *Mathematics* in subtraction, decrease the digit in one column of the minuend by 1 in order to increase the value in the column on its right by 10. <Old English *borgian*> **bor′row·er** *n.*
borrow trouble, worry about something before there is reason to.
on borrowed time, longer than the expected time limit: *He's already living on borrowed time; a year ago they gave him six months to live.*

CONFUSABLES

Borrow means "get": *He borrowed the digital camera from his father.*

Lend means "give": *The man was nervous about lending the digital camera to his son.*

✱ **borrow pit** *Western Provinces n* a pit from which earth has been dug for use as fill, especially in road or rail construction.

borsch (bȯrsh) *n* a soup made from meat stock and beets. Also, **borscht**. <Russian *borshch*>

Bos·ni·a–Her·ze·go·vi·na (boz′nē ə herts′ə gō′vē nə) *n* a country in southeastern Europe, part of the former Yugoslavia. See the APPENDIX.

bos·om (bu̇z′əm) *n* **1** the human chest, especially the female breasts. **2** the most intimate place or part: *in the bosom of his family.* **3** the heart, considered as the site of a person's emotions: *He kept the secret in his bosom.*
adj close; intimate: *a bosom friend.* <Old English *bosm*>

boss[1] (bos) *n* a person who hires workers or tells them what to do; a manager.
v Informal direct; control by giving orders: *Who is bossing this job?* <Dutch *baas*>
boss around, give a lot of orders to: *Don't boss me around!*

boss[2] (bos) *n* a raised ornament of silver, ivory, or other material on a flat surface.
v decorate with bosses. <Middle English *boce*>

boss·y (bos′ē) *adj* **boss·i·er, boss·i·est** fond of telling others what to do and how to do it; domineering.

bo·sun (bō′sən) *n* a ship's officer in charge of the deck crew, the anchors, ropes, rigging, etc. Also, **boatswain**. <altered from *boatswain*>

bot (bot) *Computers n* (*often in compounds*) a short automatic program that accomplishes a specific function on the Internet: *infobot. There is a bot that will take you off their mailing list if you e-mail the word "off" to them.* Also called **agent**. <shortened from *robot*>

bot·a·ny (bot′ə nē) *n* the science that studies plants. <Greek *botane* plant> **bo·tan′i·cal** (bə tan′ə kəl) *adj.* **bot′an·ist** *n.*

botch (boch) *v* spoil by poor quality work; bungle. <Middle English *bocchen*> **botched** *adj.*

both (bōth) *adj* two, when only two are being considered: *Both books are good.*
pron the two together: *Both belong to her.*
adv, conj alike, equally, or together: *He can both sing and dance* (*adv*). *She is both strong and healthy* (*conj*). <Old Norse *bathir*>

both·er (boᴛʜ′ər) *n* worry, fuss, or trouble, or a source of any of these: *What a lot of bother about nothing. A broken zipper is such a bother!*
v **1** take trouble or concern oneself: *Don't bother about my breakfast; I'll eat whatever's here.* **2** make uneasy, worried, or annoyed: *Hot weather bothers me.* <perhaps Irish *bodhar* confused, annoyed>
be bothered, spend time or energy to do something: *I can't be bothered to go out tonight.*

both·er·some (boᴛʜ′ər səm) *adj* annoying or inconvenient.

Bot·swa·na (bot swon′ə) *n* a landlocked country in the south of Africa.

bot·tle (bot′əl) *n* **1** a container for liquids, usually without handles and with a narrow neck and mouth that can be closed with a cap or stopper. **2** specifically, such a container whose cap includes a rubber nipple, for the use of a baby. **3 the bottle** alcoholic liquor.
v **bot·tled, bot·tling 1** put into bottles: *to bottle pop.* **2** hold in; keep back; control: *to bottle your feelings.* <Old French, from Latin *butta* barrel> **bot′tler** *n.*
bottle up, hold in; keep back: *to bottle up your anger.*

bot·tle–feed (bot′əl fēd′) *v* **-fed** (fed), **-feeding** feed a baby milk, formula, etc. from a bottle.

bot·tle·neck (bot′əl nek′) *n* **1** the narrow neck of a bottle, or something like it such as a narrow passageway or street. **2** a situation in which progress is delayed: *They have hit a bottleneck that could hold up the decision for weeks.*

Bottlenosed dolphins are very fast swimmers. They can also dive to more than 300 m and jump up to 6 m out of the water.

These social animals live in pods of up to twelve members. Often, many pods will join together to form groups containing hundreds of dolphins.

bot·tle·nose (bot′əl nōz′) *n* in full, **bottlenosed dolphin** a species of dolphin found in tropical and temperate waters all over the world.

bot·tom (bot′əm) *n* **1** the lowest part: *The berries at the bottom of the basket were badly crushed.* **2** the underside: *The bottom of the shelf was left unpainted.* **3** the ground under a body of water: *the bottom of the sea.* **4** *Informal* the buttocks. **5 bottoms** *pl* the pants of pyjamas. **6** *Baseball* the second half of an inning: *the bottom of the ninth.* **7** the seat of a chair: *This chair needs a new bottom.* **8** the part farthest from the entrance: *the bottom of the garden.*
v touch or rest on the bottom: *The submarine bottomed on the ocean floor.*
adj lowest: *bottom prices.* <Middle English *botm*>
at bottom, basically or fundamentally: *At bottom, she's a kind person.*
at the bottom of, ultimately responsible for: *I think I know who's at the bottom of this joke.*
bet your bottom dollar, *Informal* bet all that you have; be absolutely certain: *I bet my bottom dollar he'll be late.*
bottom out, reach a low point and level off: *Attendance at that movie has bottomed out.*
bottoms up! *Informal* drain your glass! drink up!
get to the bottom of, solve; find out the cause or explanation for.

bot·tom–feed·er (bot′əm fē′dər) *n* **1** any water creature that lives and finds its food at the bottom of the ocean, river, etc. **2** *Slang* a person who profits from the misfortunes of others.

bot·tom·less (bot′əm lis) *adj* so deep that the bottom is or seems to be out of reach; extremely deep: *the bottomless depths of the sea.*

bottom line *n* **1** the final line of a financial statement, showing net profit or loss: *All they care about is the bottom line.* **2** the most fundamental point or principle: *The bottom line is that to become a veterinarian you must stay in school.*

bot·u·lism (boch′ə liz′əm) *n* an often fatal kind of food poisoning from poisons produced by certain bacteria in spoiled food. <Latin *botulus* sausage, because the illness was thought to come from eating sausages>

bou·doir (bū′dwȧr) *or* (bū dwȧr′) *n* a woman's private sitting room or dressing room. <French = a room for sulking in>

bou·gain·vil·le·a (bū′gən vil′ē ə) *n* a tropical American climbing shrub with small flowers surrounded by large, brilliantly coloured leaves. <L.A. de *Bougainville*, 18c explorer>

bough (bou) *n* **1** one of the main branches of a tree. **2** a branch cut from a tree. <Old English *bog*>

bought (bot) past tense and past participle of BUY.

bouil·lon (būl′yən) *n* a clear, thin soup or broth, sometimes reconstituted by adding hot water to a dried, concentrated **bouillon cube**. <French, from Latin *bullire* boil>

boul·der (bōl′dər) *n* a large rock. <Scandinavian>

boul·e·vard (bůl′ə vȧrd′) *n* **1** a wide street, often one lined with trees or divided by a strip of grass down the middle. **2** this dividing strip; a median strip. <French>

a bat	e bed	i bid	o pot	u cup	th **thin**
ā cake	ē me	ī bite	ō go	ū rude	ᴛʜ **then**
ȧ bar	ə about	ər over	ȯ for	ů put	zh measure

bounce (bouns) *v* **bounced, bounc·ing** **1** spring or cause to spring back into the air, often repeatedly, after striking something, as a rubber ball does: *The baby likes to bounce on the bed. Bounce the ball against the wall.* **2** *Slang* **a** of a cheque, send or be sent back because of lack of funds in the account. **b** of an e-mail, send or be sent back to the sender. **3** come or go energetically or noisily: *She bounced out of the room.*
n **1** the act of bouncing. **2** springiness: *This ball has lots of bounce.* **3** energy and enthusiasm: *He was in hospital for a week, but now he is as full of bounce as ever.* <Middle English *bunsen*> **bounc′y** *adj.*
bounce something off someone, *Informal* try out an idea on someone to get his or her reaction.

bounc·er (boun′sər) *n* **1** *Informal* a person hired to eject unruly or unwanted people from a bar or other public place. **2** something that bounces.

bounc·ing (boun′sing) *adj* strong, healthy, and vigorous: *a bouncing baby girl.*

bound[1] (bound) *adj* **1** under some obligation: *bound by a contract. He felt bound to volunteer.* **2** certain: *It's bound to rain soon.* **3** (*especially in compounds*) confined; stuck: *housebound, snowbound.* **4** firmly intending: *She was bound and determined to go.* **5** (*often in compounds*) with a specified binding: *a leather-bound book.*
v past tense and past participle of BIND.
bound up in (or **with**), closely linked or involved with.

ETYMOLOGY

Bound[1] is a form of **bind**, from the Old English verb *bindan* with the same meaning.

Bound[2] is from French *bondir*, meaning "leap."

Bound[3] is from Old French *bounde*, from Latin *butina*, meaning "landmark."

Bound[4] is from Middle English *boun*, meaning *ready*, from Old Norse *buinn*, past participle of the verb *bua*, meaning "get ready."

bound[2] (bound) *v* **1** spring lightly along or leap along: *The deer bounded into the woods and was gone.* **2** of a ball, etc., spring back after striking a surface; bounce: *The ball bounded from the wall and hit the car.*
n an act of bounding; a leap or bounce: *With one bound, the cat was on the mouse.*

bound[3] (bound) *v* be or form the boundary of: *A river bounds the property to the north.*
n usually, **bounds** *pl* a limit or limiting line: *the farthest bounds of the ranch. Keep your spending within bounds.*
out of bounds, outside the area allowed by rules, custom, or law: *He kicked the ball out of bounds. The swings are out of bounds to the older students.*

bound[4] (bound) *adj* going; on the way: *I am bound for home. By midnight, they were homeward bound.*

bound·a·ry (boun′də rē) *n, pl* **bound·a·ries** a line forming a limit; a division line, especially between properties, provinces, countries, etc.: *The Ottawa River forms part of the boundary between Ontario and Québec.* <*bound*[3]>

bound·less (bound′lis) *adj* unlimited or seeming to be so: *boundless space, boundless optimism.* **bound′less·ly** *adv.* **bound′less·ness** *n.*

boun·te·ous (boun′tē əs) *Poetic adj* generous or abundant: *a bounteous harvest.* <Old French *bonte* bounty> **boun′te·ous·ly** *adv.* **boun′te·ous·ness** *n.*

boun·ti·ful (boun′tə fəl) *adj* **1** plentiful: *a bountiful supply of tomatoes.* **2** generous: *bountiful gifts.* See also BOUNTEOUS. <*bounty* + *-ful*> **bount′i·ful·ly** *adv.*

boun·ty (boun′tē) *n, pl* **boun·ties** **1** generosity or a generous gift. **2** a reward, especially one given by a government for catching an animal or a wanted criminal. <Old French, from Latin *bonitas* goodness>

bou·quet (bō kā′) *or* (bū kā′) *for 1;* (bū kā′) *for 2.* *n* **1** a bunch of flowers. **2** a fragrance; aroma, especially of wine. <French>

bour·bon (bər′bən) *n* whisky distilled from a grain mash that contains at least 51 percent corn. <*Bourbon* County, Kentucky, where it was originally made)

bour·geois (būr zhwä′) *adj* **1** of the middle class. **2** not sophisticated; ordinary: *He has very bourgeois tastes.*
n, pl **bour·geois** a bourgeois person. <Old French *borjois* citizen of a town, from Latin *burgus* castle>

bour·geoi·sie (būr′zhwä zē′) *n* the middle class.

bout (bout) *n* **1** a match or contest, especially in boxing. **2** a short, intense period of time, especially one involving illness, effort, or endurance: *a long bout of the flu, a bout of housecleaning.* <variant of *bought* a turn>

bou·tique (bū tēk′) *n* a small shop or a department in a large store, especially specializing in fashionable clothes, accessories, and cosmetics. <French>

bou·ton·niere or **bou·ton·nière** (bū′tə nēr′) *n* a flower or flowers worn in a man's buttonhole. <French = buttonhole>

bo·vine (bō′vīn) *n* a member of a group of cud-chewing mammals that includes buffalo, bison, the yak, and domestic cattle.
adj **1** to do with this group of animals. **2** slow, stupid, or emotionless. <Latin *bovis* ox, cow>

bow[1] (bou) *v* **1** lower the head or bend the body in greeting, respect, worship, or submission. **2** cause to stoop: *a tree branch bowed by its weight of fruit.* **3** submit or give in: *We must bow to necessity.*
n an act of bending the head or body in this way. <Old English *bugan*>
bow out, withdraw (from): *He sprained his wrist and had to bow out of the tennis tournament.*
take a bow, *Informal* accept praise or applause.

bow[2] (bō) *n* **1** a weapon for shooting arrows, usually consisting of a strip of springy wood with a string stretched tightly between the two ends. **2** a curved shape or part: *A rainbow is a many-coloured bow in the sky.* **3** a looped knot: *a bow of ribbon.* **4** a slender rod with horsehairs stretched between the ends, for playing a stringed instrument.
v **1** curve; bend. **2** play a stringed instrument with a bow. <Old English *boga*> **bow′like′** *adj.*

bow[3] (bou) *n* the forward part of a ship, boat, or aircraft. <Middle English>

bowd·ler·ize (boud′lə rīz′) *or* (boud′lə rīz′) *v* **bowd·ler·ized, bowd·ler·iz·ing** delete parts of a book considered unacceptably crude: *School dictionaries are sometimes bowdlerized.* <T. *Bowdler*, an editor who thought the works of Shakespeare contained too many crude references>

bow·el (bou′əlz) *n* **1** the large intestine. **2 bowels** *pl* the intestines. **3 bowels** *pl* the inner part: *Gold lies in the bowels of the earth.* <Old French *boel*, from Latin *botellus* sausage. The intestines look like a string of sausages.>

bow·el movement (bou′əl) *n* the waste matter discharged from the large intestine.

bow·er (bou′ər) *Poetic n* an arbour. <Old English>
bow′er·y *adj.*

bow·head (bō′hed′) *n* a species of RIGHT WHALE with a very large head that is almost one-third of its total length.

bowl[1] (bōl) *n* **1** a hollow, rounded dish, usually without handles. **2** a roughly bowl-shaped or concave part: *the bowl of a spoon.* **3** a bowl-shaped structure such as an amphitheatre or a stadium. <Old English *bolla*>
bowl′ful′ *n.* **bowl′-like′** *adj.*

bowl[2] (bōl) *v* **1** play the game of bowling: *I bowl regularly in a small league.* **2** roll or move along rapidly and smoothly: *bowling along the highway.* **3** *Cricket* **a** throw the ball to the batsman **b** (*also with* ***out***) dismiss a batsman, especially by knocking down a wicket.
n Bowling, Cricket a roll or throw of the ball. <Latin *bulla* ball>
bowl over, a knock over. **b** *Informal* overwhelm; stun: *I was bowled over by the bad news.*

bow·leg·ged (bō′leg′id) *adj* with **bowlegs**, legs that curve outward at or below the knee.

bowl·er[1] (bō′lər) *n* a person who bowls.

bowl·er[2] (bō′lər) *n* a man's hat with a small brim and a hard, round crown. <W. *Bowler*, 19c hatter>

The game of tenpin **bowling** is usually played by two teams of up to five bowlers each. Each player in turn rolls two successive balls, attempting to knock down all the pins. Each pin knocked over counts one point, with 300 being the highest score possible in a game. In Canada, we also play a similar game known as *five-pin*.

bowl·ing (bō′ling) *n* an indoor game in which a heavy ball is rolled down a LANE (def. 5) at five or ten bottle-shaped wooden pins in an effort to knock them over.

bowling alley *n* a public place with a number of lanes in it, designed for bowling.

bow·man (bō′mən) *n, pl* **bow·men** (bō′mən) a soldier or warrior armed with bow and arrows.

bow·sprit (bou′sprit) *n* a pole projecting forward from the bow of a ship. Ropes from the bowsprit help to steady sails and masts.

bow·string (bō′string′) *n* a strong cord stretched tight between the ends of a BOW[2] (def. 1).

bow tie *n* a necktie worn in a small bow.

box[1] (boks) *n* **1** a container, usually rectangular and often with a lid. **2** a rectangular space set off by lines. There are boxes in this dictionary for usage notes. **3** a receptacle in a post office reserved, for a fee, for the incoming mail of a certain person or organization. **4** a small, partly enclosed space, such as for the witness in a courtroom, or a group of seats in a theatre, etc. **5** a small shelter: *a sentry box.* **6** *Baseball* the place where the pitcher stands or where the batter stands. **7** 🍁 an enclosed area for playing lacrosse. **8 the box** *Informal* television.
v pack in a box; put into a box. <specialized meaning of *box*[3]. The strong wood of the box tree was a typical choice for making crates.> **box′like′** *adj.*
box in, confine: *He couldn't get out of the parking space because another car had boxed him in.*
box the compass, recite the points of the compass, in order.
outside the box, beyond the limits imposed by the usual way of thinking and doing things.

box[2] (boks) *v* **1** participate in the sport of boxing: *He had not boxed since he left school.* **2** strike with the open hand or the fist, especially on the side of the head.
n such a blow: *She gave him a box on the ear.* <Middle English>

box[3] (boks) *n* an evergreen shrub or small tree often used for hedges, borders, etc., and with hard, durable wood. Also called **boxwood**. <Greek *puxos*>

box–and–whisker plot (boks′ən whisk′ər) *n* a graph that shows how far apart and how evenly data are distributed. The box represents the central half of the data, and the whiskers the upper and lower quarters. Also called **boxplot, box plot**.

box·car (boks′kär′) *n* a railway freight car enclosed on all sides.

box·er (bok′sər) *n* **1** a person who engages in the sport of boxing. **2** a breed of medium-sized dog with a stocky body and a deep chest, short brownish hair, and a short, square muzzle. **3 Boxer** in former times in China, a member of a society opposed to foreigners which rose in armed rebellion in 1900 but was defeated by foreign soldiers.

box·ing (bok′sing) *n* the sport of fighting with the fists, using padded **boxing gloves**.

a bat	e bed	i bid	o pot	u cup	th **thin**
ā cake	ē me	ī bite	ō go	ū rude	ᴛʜ **then**
ȧ bar	ə about	ər over	ȯ for	ů put	zh measure

Boxing Day *n* in Canada, December 26, a legal holiday in all provinces and territories except Québec. <from the former custom of giving boxed gifts to servants or employees on this day>

box·la (boks′lə) *n* short for **box lacrosse** an indoor version of lacrosse.

box office *n* **1** the place where tickets are sold in a theatre, concert hall, etc. **2** the money taken in at the box office. **3** an entertainer or show that attracts a large audience: *Adventure movies are good box office.*

box social *n* a social gathering with an auction of boxed sandwiches or other food, usually to raise money for charity.

box spring *n* a base for a bed, designed for use under a mattress and consisting of coil springs set in a cloth-covered frame.

box·wood (boks′wůd′) BOX^{3}.

box·y (bok′sē) *adj* **box·i·er, box·i·est** more or less rectangular in shape, with straight lines and sharp edges or corners.

boy (boi) *n* **1** a male child. **2** a son: *My aunt has two boys.* **3** a male servant or employee who runs errands, carries things, and performs other tasks. **4** a familiar term for a man: *the boys at the office.*
interj Informal an exclamation of surprise, pleasure, etc.: *Boy, it's hot!* <Middle English> **boy′hood** *n.* **boy′ish** *adj.*

boy·cott (boi′kot) *v* combine against and have nothing to do with a person, business, nation, or product: *Many South African goods were boycotted during apartheid. My friends are boycotting the class party.*
n the act of boycotting. <C.C. *Boycott*, a 19c agent for the owner of an estate, who was the victim of such treatment at the hands of the tenants on the estate> **boy′cot·ter** *n.*

boy·friend (boi′frend′) *n* a male companion in whom one has a romantic interest.

Boyle's law (boilz) *Physics n* the principle that, at a constant temperature, the volume of a gas decreases as the pressure on it increases, and vice versa. <R. *Boyle*, 17c scientist and philosopher>

boy·sen·ber·ry (boi′zən ber′ē) *n, pl* **boy·sen·ber·ries** a purple berry that looks like a blackberry and tastes like a raspberry. <R. *Boysen*, 20c botanist who developed it>

BP or **B.P.** before the present day. By convention, 1950 is the start of the present day. Thus the year 5000 BP is roughly equivalent to the year 3000 BCE.

BQ **1** Bloc Québécois. **2** **Bq** becquerel(s).

bra (brȧ) in full, **brassiere** or **brassière** an undergarment worn by women to support the breasts. <French *bras* arm>

brace (brās) *n* **1** something that holds parts in place. **2** **braces** *pl* **a** elastic straps to hold up pants, worn over the shoulders and fastened to the pants at the back and front. **b** an arrangement of wires attached to crooked teeth in order to correct their position. **3** a device worn on a weak part of the body as a support: *She wears a brace on her leg.* **4** a handle for a manual drill. **5** either of these signs { } used to enclose words, figures, or musical staves. **6** a pair of ducks, rabbits, or other small game, especially when killed in hunting.
v **braced, brac·ing** **1** give strength or firmness to; support. **2** enliven; invigorate: *a bracing run.* **3** prepare psychologically: *I braced myself for the results of the test.* <Old French = the two arms (i.e., supported), from Greek *brachion* arm>
brace yourself or **brace up,** summon your strength or courage.

brace and bit *n* a hand drill consisting of a bit fitted into a cranklike handle.

brace·let (brās′lit) *n* **1** an ornament worn around the wrist or arm. **2** the band of a wristwatch, especially a metal one. **3** **bracelets** *pl Informal* handcuffs. <Old French, from Greek *brachion* upper arm>

brach·i·o·pod (brak′ē ə pod′) *n* a marine invertebrate, especially a fossil one, with hinged top and bottom shells. <Latin, from Greek *brakhion* arm + *podos* foot>

brac·ing (brā′sing) *adj* giving strength and energy. **brac′ing·ly** *adv.*

brack·en (brak′ən) *n* **1** a large fern, with large, triangular fronds and creeping underground stems. **2** a clump or field of such ferns. <Scandinavian>

brack·et (brak′it) *n* **1** an often decorative piece of hard material attached to a wall to support a shelf, electric fixture, or other weight. **2** **brackets** *pl* two marks that are used to enclose words or figures, such as **round brackets** ( ), **square brackets** [ ], **angle brackets** < >, or **brace brackets** { }. **3** a category: *That raise puts my brother in a higher income-tax bracket. She is in a different age bracket from you.*
v **1** support with a bracket. **2** enclose within brackets. **3** think of or treat as members of one category: *You can bracket all these items as "miscellaneous expenses."* <by confusion with Latin *brachia* arms, French *braguette*, from Latin *bracae* breeches.>

GRAMMAR

Round brackets ( ) are used within a sentence to add extra information for clarity. Usually, the information is not essential to the sentence: *The supplies (pens, markers, and paper) that we bought are on the shelf.*

Square brackets [ ] are used in quotations to insert missing details: *"No further cases [of malaria] have been reported since yesterday."*

brack·ish (brak′ish) *adj* of water, somewhat salty. <German *brac*> **brack′ish·ness** *n.*

bract (brakt) *n* a small leaf at the base of a flower or flower stalk. <Latin *bractea* gold leaf>

brad (brad) *n* a small, thin nail with a small head. <Old Norse *broddr* spike>

brag (brag) *v* **bragged, brag·ging** talk boastfully.
n such talk. <Middle English> **brag′ger** *n.*

brag·ga·do·cio (brag′ə dō′shyō) *n* a show of boasting or bragging.

brag·gart (brag′ərt) *n* a person who brags habitually.

Brah·ma (brȧ′mə) *Hinduism n* a god understood to be the creator of all things. <Sanskrit>

Brah·man (brȧ′mən) *n, pl* **Brah·mans** **1** *Hinduism* the eternal, supreme reality that is the basis of the universe. **2** a member of the highest Hindu caste, the priestly caste. **3** any of several breeds of humpbacked cattle first developed in India; a zebu. Also, **Brahmin**.

Brah·man·ism (brȧ′mə niz′əm) *n* a classical form of Hinduism in which the priestly caste has great power and prestige and sacrificial rituals are very important.

braid (brād) *n* **1** a narrow length of hair formed by weaving together three or more strands or bunches: *She looks good with braids.* **2** ribbon or cord consisting of interwoven strands, used to trim or bind clothing, etc.
v **1** weave together three or more strands, stems, or bunches of: *to braid hair, to braid vines into a wreath.* **2** form or make in this way: *to braid a rug.* **3** trim or bind with braid. <Old English *bregdan*> **braid′ed** *adj.*

braille or **Braille** (brāl) *n* a system of writing where groups of raised dots represent letters. People who are blind can read by feeling the dots with their fingertips. <L. *Braille*, 19c educator who invented it>

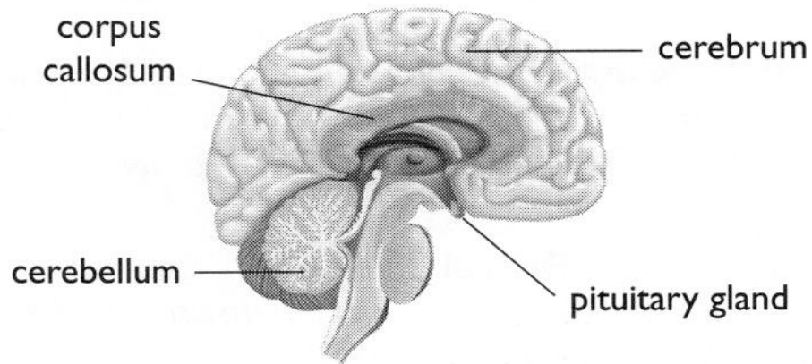

brain (brān) *n* **1** the mass of nerve tissue enclosed in the skull or head of vertebrate animals. The brain interprets sense data, controls and co-ordinates bodily activities, and is the centre of thought and emotions. **2** a corresponding part of the nervous system of invertebrates. **3** *Informal* a computer driving some complex piece of machinery. **4 brains** *pl* **a** intelligence: *He has more brains than anyone else in the family.* **b** the main planner of an organization or project: *She is the brains behind the whole thing.*
v kill by smashing the skull of: *The trapper brained the injured wolf with a large stone.* <Old English *brægan*>

brain·case (brān′kās′) BRAINPAN.

brain·child (brān′chīld′) *n* an original product of a person's imagination, especially an ingenious one that is a source of pride.

brain–dead (brān′ded′) *adj* **1** with irreversible brain damage that prevents a person from breathing on his or her own. **2** *Slang* very stupid. **brain death** *n.*

brain drain *n* a departure of the most highly trained or best-qualified people from a country or region because of better opportunities elsewhere.

brain·less (brān′lis) *adj* **1** without a brain. **2** stupid or foolish: *What a brainless thing to do!* **brain′less·ly** *adv.* **brain′less·ness** *n.*

brain·pan (brān′pan′) *n* the part of the skull that encloses the brain; the cranium. Also called **braincase**.

brain stem *n* the base of the human brain, beneath the cerebrum and the cerebellum, connecting the spinal cord with the forebrain.

brain·storm (brān′stȯrm′) *n* **1** *Informal* a sudden inspired idea. **2** a sudden, violent mental disturbance.
v gather as many ideas as possible from all members of a group. **brain′storm′ing** *n, adj.*

brain·teas·er (brān′tē′zər) *n* a tricky or difficult puzzle.

brain trust *n* a group of experts acting as advisers to a leader. Also, **brains trust**.

brain·wash (brān′wosh′) *v* change a person's beliefs by intensive forced drill, often with physical deprivation such as keeping the person from sleeping or eating: *to brainwash a political prisoner.* **brain′wash′ing** *n, adj.*

brain·wave (brān′wāv′) *n* **1** usually, **brainwaves** *pl* a rhythmic increase and decrease of voltage between parts of the brain, producing an electric current. **2** *Informal* a sudden inspiration or bright idea.

brain·y (brā′nē) *Informal adj* **brain·i·er, brain·i·est** intelligent; clever. **brain′i·ness** *n.*

braise (brāz) *v* **braised, brais·ing** brown meat quickly and then cook it long and slowly in a covered pan with very little water. <Old French *brese* embers, which were used to roast meat>

brake (brāk) *n* a device designed to slow or stop the motion of a wheel or other moving part.
v **braked, brak·ing** slow down or stop by using a brake or brakes: *He had to brake fast to avoid hitting the car ahead.* See BREAK for confusable. <Middle Dutch *braeke*>

brake·man (brāk′mən) *n, pl* **brake·men** (brāk′mən) **1** on a train, the person who helps the conductor or engineer by controlling the auxiliary brakes and inspecting the train. **2** the person at the back of a bobsled, who operates the brake.

bram·ble (bram′bəl) *n* a shrub belonging to the rose family. Many species, such as the blackberry, are prickly. <Old English *braembel*> **bram′bly** *adj.*

bran (bran) *n* the broken husk of the grains of wheat, etc., usually separated from the rest of the flour. <Old French>

branch (branch) *n* **1** on a tree or other large plant, a part growing out from the main stem. **2** any physical division or part resembling a branch of a tree: *the branches of a deer's antlers, a branch of a river.* **3** a division or part of a system or subject: *Botany is a branch of biology.* **4** a local office or subgroup of an organization: *The company's head office is in Moncton, but it has branches in several other cities.*
v **1** spread in branches. **2** divide into branches: *The road branches at the bottom of the hill.* <Old French, from Latin *branca* limb, supplement> **branch′less** *adj.* **branch′like** *adj.*
branch off, divide into branches.
branch out, expand an activity: *From watercolours, she branched out into other kinds of painting.*

a bat	e bed	i bid	o pot	u cup	th thin
ā cake	ē me	ī bite	ō go	ū rude	ᴛʜ then
ȧ bar	ə about	ər over	ȯ for	u̇ put	zh measure

branch plant *n* a business owned and controlled by a company with headquarters somewhere else.
adj **branch-plant** characterized by the existence of many branch plants: *a branch-plant economy.*

brand (brand) *n* **1** a product made by a particular company: *a popular brand of shampoo.* **2** a brand name; a trademark. **3** kind or sort: *I don't like his brand of humour.* **4** a mark in the skin of livestock to show who owns them, made by burning the skin with a hot iron. **5** a branding iron. **6** a mark of disgrace. **7** a burning piece of wood.
v **1** mark by burning the skin with a hot iron: *In former times, criminals were often branded.* **2** call by a term of disgrace: *He was branded a traitor.* <Old English>

brand·ing iron (brand′ing) *n* an iron stamp for burning an identification mark on wood, the hide of an animal, etc.

bran·dish (bran′dish) *v* wave or shake threateningly; flourish: *The knight brandished his sword at his enemy.* <Old French *brand* sword>

brand name *n* a name given to a product or service by its manufacturer or seller to distinguish it from similar ones produced or sold by others. **brand′-name′** *adj.*

brand new (brand′nyū′) *or* (brand′nū′) *adj* totally new.

bran·dy (bran′dē) *n, pl* **bran·dies** a strong alcoholic liquor distilled from wine or fermented fruit juice. <Dutch *brandewijn* burnt (i.e., distilled) wine> **bran′died** *adj.*

brant (brant) *n, pl* **brants** or (*especially collectively*) **brant** a small wild goose that breeds in the Arctic tundra and winters in temperate regions. It has a black head, neck, and breast, with a narrow white crescent on either side of the neck. <Middle English>

brash (brash) *adj* **1** loud, impetuous, and showing rather poor taste. **2** hasty or rash. **3** impudent or cheeky. <origin uncertain> **brash′ly** *adv.* **brash′ness** *n.*

brass (bras) *n* **1** a yellow metal that is an alloy of copper and zinc. **2** articles made of brass, such as door fittings or ornaments: *Polish the brass thoroughly.* **3 a** a brass musical instrument. **b brasses** *pl* such instruments forming a band or a section of an orchestra. **4** *Informal* high-ranking people in an organization. **5** *Informal* money. **6** *Informal* boldness: *Even though she had never acted in a play, she had the brass to audition for the lead part.*
adj made of brass. <Old English *bræs*>

brass band *n* a group of musicians with brass instruments.

bras·siere or **bras·sière** (brə zēr′) BRA.

brass instrument *n* a musical instrument made of brass or other metal and played by blowing, such as a trumpet, horn, trombone, or tuba.

brass knuckles *pln* a metal bar that fits across the knuckles, used in fighting.

brass tacks *Informal pln* (*usually with* ***get down to***) the actual facts or details: *Let's get down to brass tacks.*

brass·y (bras′ē) *adj* **brass·i·er, brass·i·est** **1** like brass in colour. **2** *Informal* impudent. **3** loud and harsh.
brass′i·ly *adv.* **brass′i·ness** *n.*

brat (brat) *n* a child, especially one who is badly behaved. <origin uncertain>

bra·va·do (brə vȧ′dō) *n* a great show of boldness or boastful defiance, without much real courage. <Spanish *bravo*>

brave (brāv) *adj* **brav·er, brav·est** **1** able to control one's fear and act firmly in the face of danger or difficulties; courageous: *One brave girl stood up to the bully.* **2** showing bravery: *brave deeds.* **3** fine; handsome; excellent.
n in former times, a First Nations or Native American warrior.
v **braved, brav·ing** **1** meet bravely: *Soldiers brave much danger.* **2** dare to defy: *She braved the king's anger.* <French, from Italian *bravo* bold> **brave′ly** *adv.* **brav′er·y** *n.*

bra·vo (brȧ′vō) *interj* **Bravo!** Well done! Excellent!
n, pl **bra·vos** a cry of "Bravo!" *The pianist rose and bowed to a chorus of bravos.* <Italian = excellent>

bra·vu·ra (brə vyū′rə) *n* **1** brilliance, dash, or spirit in a performance. **2** *Music* a passage giving the opportunity for such a display.
adj brilliant; showing dash and spirit. <Italian *bravura* bravery>

brawl (brol) *n* a noisy and disorderly fight: *The hockey game turned into a brawl.*
v fight in a noisy and disorderly way. <Middle English *brallen*> **braw′ler** *n.*

brawn (bron) *n* muscular strength: *He has brains as well as brawn.* <Old French *braon*> **brawn′y** *adj.*

bray (brā) *v* make a loud, harsh sound, as a donkey does. *He brayed with laughter.*
n the loud, harsh sound made by a donkey, or a noise like it. <Old French *braire*>

bra·zen (brā′zən) *adj* **1** openly rude or defiant: *brazen disregard for the rules.* **2** made of brass: *brazen trumpets.* <Old English *bræs* brass> **bra′zen·ly** *adv.*
bra′zen·ness *n.*
brazen it out, act as if one did not feel ashamed.

bra·zier (brā′zhər) *or* (brā′zē ər) *n* a metal container to hold burning charcoal or coal. <French *braise* hot charcoal>

Bra·zil (brə zil′) *n* a country in S America, the largest country on the continent. See the APPENDIX.
Bra·zil′ian *adj, n.*

Brazil nut *n* the large, triangular, edible nut of a tropical S American tree.

breach (brēch) *n* **1** a gap made by breaking through or breaking down: *a breach in a wall.* **2** a breaking, especially a breaking or neglect of a law, promise, or agreement: *She was sued for breach of contract.* **3** a breaking of friendly relations. **4** a whale's leap clear of the water.
v **1** break through: *The enemy's fierce attack finally breached the wall.* **2** leap clear of the water. <Old French>
step into the breach, fill a strategic position that has been left vacant in an organization, etc.

bread (bred) *n* a baked or fried food made of flour mixed with milk or water and, often, yeast.
v cover with breadcrumbs or flour before cooking. <Old English>
bread (**and butter**) food or livelihood: *to earn your bread.*
break bread, **a** share a meal. **b** *Christianity* take or give Communion.
cast your bread upon the waters, do good with little or no prospect of reward.
know which side your bread is buttered on, know what is to your advantage.

bread·bas·ket (bred′bas′kit) *n* **1** a basket for storing or serving bread. **2** a region that is the chief source of grain: *The Prairies are Canada's breadbasket.* **3** *Slang* the stomach.

bread·board (bred′bȯrd′) *n* **1** a board on which bread is cut. **2** a board on which bread dough is handled.

bread·crumb (bred′krum′) *n* a crumb of bread.

bread·fruit (bred′frūt′) *n* a large, round, starchy, tropical fruit of the Pacific islands.

bread·line (bred′līn′) *n* a line of people waiting to get food given as charity or relief: *My grandfather remembers the breadlines of the Great Depression.* Also, **bread line**.

bread stick *n* dough baked in the form of a crisp stick.

breadth (bredth) *n* **1** how wide a thing is: *the breadth of his shoulders.* **2** a piece of a certain width: *a breadth of cloth.* **3** freedom from narrowness in views or taste: *She is known for her breadth of mind.* **4** great extent or scope: *unusual breadth of learning.* <Old English *brad* broad>

bread·win·ner (bred′win′ər) *n* a member of a family who earns the family's living.

break (brāk) *v* **broke** (brōk), **bro·ken** (brōk′ən), **break·ing** **1** go or cause to go to pieces: *How did my glasses get broken? The plate fell and broke.* **2** stop or cause to stop working properly: *She broke her watch by overwinding it. The DVD player broke the first time we used it.* **3** injure by causing a bone to crack or come apart: *to break your arm.* **4** divide: *break a five-dollar bill. We have broken the presentation into two parts.* **5** fail to keep a promise or a law, or to fulfill an agreement: *break a contract.* **6** force one's way (into or out of): *to break into a house. They broke through the barricade.* **7** pause for rest or recreation: *Let's break for lunch.* **8** begin or end, often suddenly: *The storm will break within a few minutes. Her fever broke after midnight.* **9** decrease the force or impact of: *The bushes broke his fall.* **10** crush or be crushed by disappointment, grief, etc.: *You have broken my heart. His spirit broke when his wife died.* **11** ruin the health or finances of: *Buying all these clothes is going to break me.* **12** dig or plough land, especially for the first time: *The pioneers had to work hard to break the ground.* **13** tell or be told important news: *to break bad news gently.* **14** train away from a habit: *He's trying to break himself of nail biting.* **15** solve a code.
n **1** the act of breaking or the place where something breaks: *There's a break in the dam.* **2** a change, usually abrupt. **3** an interruption: *a break in traffic.* **4** a rest from work or effort, or a relief from hardship. **5** a good chance; an opportunity: *Finding that money was a lucky break.* <Old English *brecan*> **break′a·ble** *adj.* **break′age** *n.*
break a record, See RECORD.
break away, **a** leave or get free, especially suddenly or with effort: *He broke away from his captors.* **b** start before the signal: *The horse was disqualified for breaking away.* **c** *Hockey, Lacrosse, Soccer* make a breakaway.
break down, **a** stop functioning. **b** collapse: *She finally broke down under the strain of it all.* **c** begin to cry. **d** separate into components: *Water can be broken down into oxygen and hydrogen.*
break even, finish with the same amount one started with; gain or lose nothing.
break in, **a** train a beginner: *to break in the new player.* **b** bring to a comfortable condition by use: *My new shoes are not yet broken in.* **c** enter illegally or by force: *The thieves broke in through the basement.* **d** interrupt someone speaking: *He broke in with a funny remark.*
break into, **a** enter suddenly, by force, or illegally: *Someone broke into the school and stole computers.* **b** begin suddenly: *The horse broke into a gallop.* **c** interrupt: *to break into a conversation.* **d** enter a profession or activity, especially with some difficulty: *She's been trying to break into the advertising business.*
break off, **a** stop suddenly: *He broke off in the middle of a sentence.* **b** stop being friends or romantic partners.
break out, **a** begin or arise suddenly or unexpectedly: *Fire broke out in the basement.* **b** begin to show a rash, pimples, etc.: *The child broke out in measles.* **c** escape from prison: *Ten convicts have broken out in the last year.*
break the ice, See ICE.
break through, **a** appear from behind clouds: *At noon the sun broke through.* **b** overcome a barrier or opposition.
break trail, 🍁 go ahead of a dog team, vehicle, or person, to make a way through deep snow.
break up, **a** scatter: *The fog is breaking up.* **b** end: *Our meeting broke up early today.* **c** upset; disturb greatly: *She was very broken up about it.* **d** break into pieces: *to break up lumps of earth.* **e** stop being friends or partners: *The band has broken up.*
break (**up**) **with,** stop associating with (someone).

CONFUSABLES

Break means "come apart": *Move the vase gently or it will break.*

Brake means "slow down" or "stop": *He had to brake quickly when he suddenly saw the stop sign through the fog.*

a bat	e bed	i bid	o pot	u cup	th **thin**
ā cake	ē me	ī bite	ō go	ū rude	ᴛʜ **then**
ȧ bar	ə about	ər over	ȯ for	ủ put	zh measure

break·a·way (brāk′ə wā′) *n* **1** *Hockey, Lacrosse, Soccer* a play in which one person gains possession of the puck or ball and rushes forward alone. **2** the start of a race or other contest: *Three horses got well ahead at the breakaway.* **3** the act of separating from a group or from the usual pattern. **4** a small group that has separated from a larger one: *They are a breakaway from the Liberal Party.* **5** something designed to break off easily and harmlessly when struck, as a theatre prop.
adj being a breakaway: *a breakaway group.*

break·danc·ing (brāk′dan′sing) *n* an acrobatic style of dancing in which a single dancer makes abrupt turns, bends, flips, and spins, performed to music with a strong rock beat. **break′dance** *n, v.* **break′danc·er** *n.*

break·down (brāk′doun′) *n* **1** a failure to work: *a breakdown in machinery.* **2** a complete loss of health or strength: *a mental breakdown.* **3** the division of anything into its separate elements or steps.

break·er (brā′kər) *n* **1** a large wave that breaks into foam on the shore or on rocks. **2** a machine for breaking things into smaller pieces. **3 a** circuit breaker. **4** a breakdancer.

break·fast (brek′fəst) *n* the first meal of the day.
v eat breakfast: *We breakfasted at 7:30 a.m.* <*break* + *fast*[2]>

break–in (brāk′in′) *n* a burglary.

breaking and entering *Law n* the use of force or stealth to enter a room or building, especially to steal something.

break·neck (brāk′nek′) *adj* especially fast and dangerous: *breakneck speed.*

break of day *n* dawn.

break·out (brāk′out′) *n* **1** a rash or pimples on the skin. **2** the act of escaping from prison.

break·through (brāk′thrū′) *n* the solution of a problem, especially in science or technology, that has an important effect on all future research and development: *The development of the transistor was a major breakthrough in electronics.*

break·up or **break–up** (brāk′up′) *n* **1** the end of a relationship: *the breakup of a marriage.* **2** a scattering or separation. **3** collapse or decay. **4** 🍁 *especially North* the breaking of the ice on a river or lake in spring, or the time when this happens: *They planned to start work on the new road after breakup.*

break·wa·ter (brāk′wot′ər) *n* a wall or barrier built near the shore to break the force of waves and make an area of calm water for a harbour or beach.

bream (brēm) *n, pl* **breams** or (*especially collectively*) **bream 1** a European freshwater fish of the minnow family. **2** the common freshwater sunfish. **3** a sea bream. <Old French *bresme*>

breast (brest) *n* **1** either of the two milk-producing glands on the chest of the human female. **2** the chest, or a corresponding part in an animal: *The robin has a red breast.* **3** the part of a garment that covers the chest. **4** *Poetic* the heart, considered as the centre of emotions. **5** anything suggesting the human breast in shape or position.
v advance against: *to breast the current. He breasted each trouble as it came.* <Old English *breost*>
make a clean breast of (it), confess fully; tell everything.

breast·bone (brest′bōn′) *n* the thin, flat bone in the front of the chest to which the ribs are attached.

breast·feed (brest′fēd′) *v* **breast·fed** (brest′fed′), **breast·feed·ing** feed a baby at the mother's breast.

breast·plate (brest′plāt′) *n* a piece of armour for the chest.

breast·stroke (brest′strōk′) *n* a swimming stroke performed while face down in the water, bringing both arms forward from the breast, and then sweeping them out and down again while kicking the legs.

breast·work (brest′wərk′) *n* a low wall for defence.

breath (breth) *n* **1** air drawn into or forced out of the lungs: *Hold your breath a moment. His breath smells fresh. You can see your breath on a very cold day.* **2** a single act of breathing: *With every breath, she grew calmer.* **3** the ability to breathe easily: *That fall made me lose my breath.* **4** a trace or suggestion: *a breath of air. The slightest breath of scandal can ruin her.* <Old English *brǣth* odour, steam>
catch your breath, a stop for breath; rest. **b** gasp.
in the same breath, at the same time or almost the same time.
out of breath, breathing very hard as a result of exertion.
save your breath, avoid useless effort in trying to convince: *He won't listen, so you might as well save your breath.*
take your breath away, leave you breathless because of awe, suspense, or delight.
under your breath, in a whisper.
waste your breath, talk or argue uselessly.

Breath·a·lyz·er (breth′ə lī′zər) *Trademark n* a device for measuring the alcohol in a person's blood by testing the breath. <*breath* + *analyzer*>

breathe (brēᴛʜ) *v* **breathed, breath·ing 1** draw air into or expel air from the lungs, or both: *breathe in through the nose, breathe out heavily. If you breathe lightly on a mirror, it fogs up. The dragon breathed fire.* **2** whisper or make a sound softly: *"Don't move," she breathed. They breathed a sigh of relief.* **3** be alive. **4** rest after effort: *I need a moment to breathe.* **5** give or inspire: *Her enthusiasm breathed new life into the team.* **6** show clearly and naturally: *His whole appearance breathes confidence.* <Middle English *brethen*>
breathe again (or **freely**)**,** be relieved.
breathe a word of, tell a secret: *Don't breathe a word that we met. If you breathe a word of this, I'll never speak to you again!*
breathe down someone's neck, watch someone closely: *The supervisor breathed down their necks every step of the way.*
breathe new life into, enable to make a fresh start.
breathe your last, die.

breath·er (brē′ᴛʜər) *n* a short stop for rest or recreation.

breathing space *n* enough space or time to feel comfortable, not rushed or crowded.

breath·less (breth′lis) *adj* **1** gasping for breath: *breathless from a run.* **2** holding one's breath because of some strong emotion: *The beauty of the scenery left us breathless.* **breath′less·ly** *adv.* **breath′less·ness** *n.*

breath·tak·ing (breth′tā′king) *adj* thrilling: *a breathtaking ride on a roller coaster.*

bred (bred) past tense and past participle of BREED.

breech (brēch) *n* **1** in a firearm, the opening directly behind the barrel where the shells are inserted. **2** the rump or buttocks, especially of a child being born. In a **breech birth**, the rump emerges first instead of the head. <Old English *broc* breech>

breech·cloth (brēch′kloth′) *n* a covering for the loins consisting of a length of cloth or leather passed between the legs and fastened around the waist.

breech·es (brich′iz) *or* (brē′chiz) *pln* **1** short pants fastened snugly just below the knees. **2** *Informal* any pants.

breed (brēd) *v* **bred, breed·ing 1** mate and produce young: *Rabbits breed rapidly. Polar bears breed every other year.* **2** develop different types of an animal or plant by mating selected individuals: *to breed horses for harness racing.* **3** bring about; cause: *Despair often breeds violence.* **4** rear and train someone: *That's how I was bred.* **5** *Nuclear physics* produce fissionable material by nuclear reaction.
n **1** within an animal species, a particular type with certain inherited characteristics resulting from selective mating over time: *The wolfhound was originally a hunting breed.* **2** kind or sort: *It takes a tough breed of person to survive here.* <Old English *bredan*> **breed′er** *n.*

breeder reactor *n* a nuclear reactor that produces at least as much fissionable material as it uses.

breed·ing (brē′ding) *n* **1** upbringing: *Politeness is a sign of good breeding.* **2** the action of any person who or thing that breeds.

breeze (brēz) *n* **1** a light wind. **2** *Informal* something very easy to do: *That math test was a breeze.*
v **breezed, breez·ing** move easily or briskly: *She breezed into the room.* <probably from Spanish *briza* NE wind>
breeze through, perform or complete with ease: *She breezed through her homework.*
shoot the breeze, *Slang* chat or talk casually.

breeze·way (brēz′wā′) *n* a roofed passage, open at the ends, between two buildings.

breez·y (brē′zē) *adj* **breez·i·er, breez·i·est 1** with light winds blowing. **2** lively and jolly: *We like her breezy, joking manner.* **breez′i·ly** *adv.* **breez′i·ness** *n.*

breth·ren (breᴛʜ′rən) *Archaic or Poetic* a plural of BROTHER.

Bret·on (bret′ən) *n* **1** a native or inhabitant of Brittany, a region in northwest France. **2** the Celtic language of Brittany.
adj to do with Brittany, its people, or their language.

brev·i·ty (brev′ə tē) *n* briefness, conciseness, and exactness.

brew (brū) *v* **1** make a beverage by steeping, boiling, or fermenting. **2** be made in this way: *Your tea is brewing.* **3** plan or plot: *to brew mischief.* **4** begin to form: *A storm is brewing.*
n **1** a drink made by brewing. **2** the quantity brewed at one time. <Old English *breowan*> **brew′er** *n.*

brew·er·y (brū′ə rē) *n, pl* **brew·er·ies** a company that produces beer and ale, or the place where this is done.

🍁 **brew·is** (brūz) *or* (brū′is) *Newfoundland n* **1** a stew made by boiling hard biscuit in water. **2** FISH AND BREWIS. <variant of *brose* soaked bread>

bri·ar (brī′ər) BRIER.

bribe (brīb) *n* **1** anything given or offered to someone in order to get him or her to do something wrong. **2** a reward or incentive for doing something that one does not want to do: *She should not need a bribe to study.*
v **bribed, brib·ing** give or offer a bribe to: *The smugglers tried to bribe the customs officials.* <Old French *briber* to beg> **brib′a·ble** *adj.* **brib′er·y** *n.*

bric–a–brac or **bric–à–brac** (brik′ ə brak′) *n* a collection of interesting knick-knacks or small ornaments: *They have a cabinet for all their bric-a-brac.* <French>

brick (brik) *n* **1** a block of baked clay used in building. **2** such blocks taken together as building material: *a fireplace made of brick.* **3** anything shaped like a brick: *a brick of ice cream.* **4** *Informal* a dependable person.
v build, pave, or line with bricks. <Middle Dutch *bricke*>
brick in (or **up**), close or fill up with bricks: *The workers bricked up the old doorway.*
hit the bricks, *Informal* go on strike.
one brick short of a load, *Slang* **a** a little crazy **b** a little stupid.

GRAMMAR AND USAGE

The expression **one brick short of a load** has many variations: *a few sandwiches short of a picnic, one tomato short of a thick sauce, one card short of a full deck, one egg short of an omelette, a few cents short of dollar*, etc. All these phrases have the same meaning. Similar expressions are being created all the time. Try to come up with some yourself.

brick·bat (brik′bat′) *Informal n* an insult. <obsolete *brickbat* a piece of broken brick used as a missile>

brick·lay·er (brik′lā′ər) *n* a person whose work is building with bricks. **brick′lay′ing** *n.*

bricks–and–mortar (briks′ən môr′tər) *adj* to do with traditional retail businesses in stores, rather than electronic retailing via the Internet: *a bricks-and-mortar company.* Retailing through both traditional stores and the Internet is described as **bricks-and-clicks.**

brick·work (brik′wərk′) *n* any part or thing made of bricks: *They sandblasted all the brickwork on the house.*

bride (brīd) *n* a woman just married or about to be married. <Old English *bryd*> **brid′al** *adj.*

bride·groom (brīd′grūm′) *n* a man just married or about to be married.

brides·maid (brīdz′mād′) *n* a young, usually unmarried woman who attends the bride at a wedding.

a bat	e bed	i bid	o pot	u cup	th thin
ā cake	ē me	ī bite	ō go	ū rude	ᴛʜ then
à bar	ə about	ər over	ô for	ù put	zh measure

suspension bridge

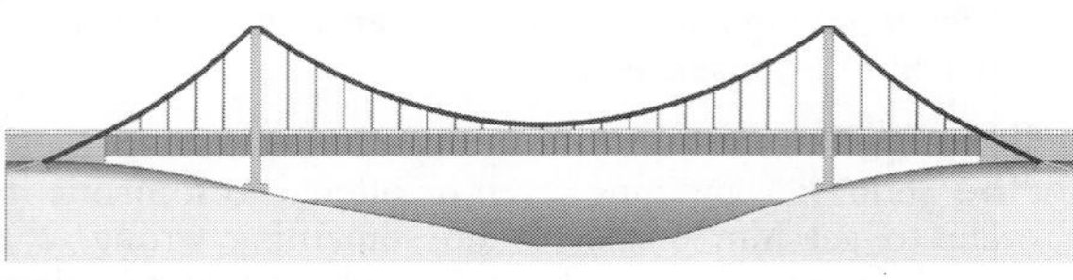

arch bridge

cantilever bridge

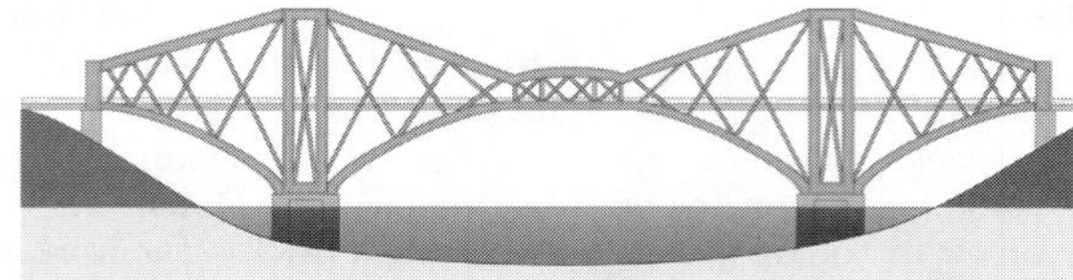

long beam bridge

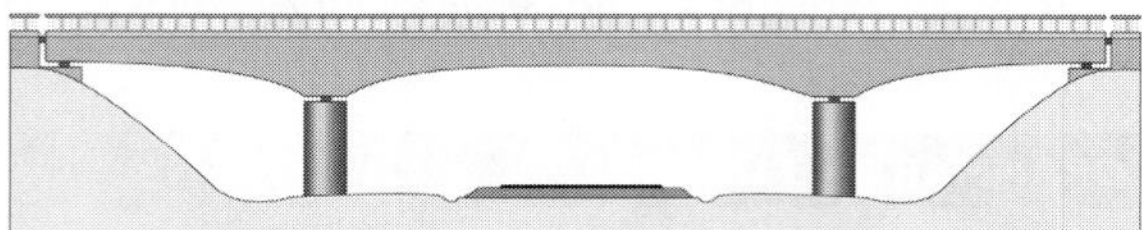

Two **suspension bridges** in Nova Scotia connect the cities of Halifax and Dartmouth.

In Ontario, the Peace Bridge over the Niagara River is an **arch bridge**.

The Québec Bridge, connecting Québec City and the south shore of the St. Lawrence River, is the largest **cantilever bridge** in the world.

Confederation Bridge is a **long beam bridge** between New Brunswick and Prince Edward Island. It is the longest bridge in Canada.

bridge[1] (brij) *n* **1** a structure built over a road or body of water so that traffic can get across. **2** anything that serves to connect things or people. **3** a platform above the deck of a ship for the officer in command. **4** the upper, bony part of the nose. **5** the part of a pair of eyeglasses that rests on the nose. **6** a mounting for a false tooth or teeth, fastened to the real teeth nearby. **7** a piece of wood on the box of a musical instrument over which the strings are stretched. **8** *Music* a passage connecting two similar parts of a piece of music.
v **bridged, bridg·ing** build or form a bridge over: *The engineers bridged the river. Logs bridged the swampy part of the valley. Politeness bridges many difficulties.* <Old English *brycg*>
burn your bridges, See BURN.

bridge[2] (brij) *n* a card game for two teams of two players each, played with a deck of 52 cards. There are two forms, **contract bridge** and **duplicate bridge**. <origin uncertain>

bridge·head (brij′hed′) *n* **1** a position obtained and held by advance troops within enemy territory, used as a starting point for further attack. **2** a fortification protecting the end of a bridge nearest to the enemy.

bridge·work (brij′wərk′) *n* false teeth in a mounting fastened to real teeth nearby.

bri·dle (brī′dəl) *n* **1** a harness fitted around a horse's head, consisting of a series of straps to hold it on, a bit made of metal to go in the horse's mouth, and reins for the rider. **2** anything that restrains or controls. **3** 🍁 a loop on a snowshoe for the toe of a boot or moccasin.
v **bri·dled, bri·dling 1** put a bridle on. **2** hold back or control: *Bridle your tongue.* **3** react with pride, scorn, or indignation by a gesture of holding the head high with the chin drawn back: *She bridled when we made fun of her new shoes.* <Old English *brigdels*, from *bregdan* to braid>

Brie (brē) *n* a variety of soft white cheese with a rind. <*Brie*, France, where it originated>

brief (brēf) *adj* **1** lasting only a short time: *a brief meeting.* **2** using few words: *a brief summary.* **3** barely covering: *a brief halter top.*
n **1** a formal statement of opinion for submission to an authority: *She submitted a brief to the Royal Commission on Taxation.* **2** *Law* a statement of the facts and the points of law of a case to be pleaded in court. **3 briefs** *pl* short, fitted underpants.
v give instructions or background information to: *She briefed him on how to approach the new client.* Compare DEBRIEF. <Old French, from Latin *brevis* short>
brief′ing *n.* **brief′ly** *adv.* **brief′ness** *n.*
in brief, in few words.

brief·case (brēf′kās′) *n* a flat case with a handle, for carrying books and papers.

bri·er[1] (brī′ər) *n* any of various kinds of thorny or prickly bush, especially the wild rose. Also, **briar**. <Old English *brer*>

bri·er[2] (brī′ər) *n* **1** an evergreen shrub of S Europe with a hard, woody root used for making tobacco pipes. **2** a tobacco pipe made of this root. Also (*especially def. 2*), **briar**. <French *bruyère* heath plant>

🍁 **Bri·er** (brī′ər) *Curling n* the Canadian national championship. <name of a trophy>

brig (brig) *n* **1** a square-rigged ship with two masts. See SCHOONER for picture. **2** the prison on a warship. <*brigantine*>

bri·gade (bri gād′) *n* **1** a part of an army, usually two or more regiments. **2** any group of people organized for some purpose: *Fire brigades fight fires.* **3** 🍁 in former times, a fleet of canoes, carts, or dog sleds used to carry goods and supplies to and from inland trading posts. <Italian *brigare*>

brig·a·dier general (bri′gə dēr′jen′ə rəl) *n*, *pl* **brigadier generals** an army officer ranking next above a colonel and below a major general. Also called **brigadier**. <French *brigade*>

brig·and (brig′ənd) *n* a highway robber; a bandit. <Italian *brigante* fighter>

brig·an·tine (brig′ən tēn′) *n* a two-masted ship with the foremast sails set across the ship and the mainmast sails set lengthwise to the ship. <French, from Italian *brigantino* pirate ship, from *brigante* pirate>

bright (brīt) *adj* **1** giving or reflecting much light: *the bright sun, bright silver.* **2** very light or clear: *a bright morning.* **3** quick-witted; clever: *She's a bright girl and learns quickly.* **4** vivid and glowing: *bright colours.* **5** lively and cheerful: *a bright smile.* **6** favourable: *a bright outlook.*
adv Poetic in a bright manner: *The fire shines bright.* <Old English *beorht*> **bright′en** *v.* **bright′ly** *adv.*
bright′ness *n.*
bright-eyed and bushy-tailed, *Informal* alert and lively.

bril·liant (bril′yənt) *adj* **1** bright; sparkling; shining: *brilliant jewels, brilliant sunshine.* **2** impressive; outstanding: *a brilliant scholar, a brilliant performance.*
n a diamond or other gem cut to sparkle brightly. <French *briller* shine> **bril′liance** *n.* **bril′liant·ly** *adv.*

brim (brim) *n* **1** the edge of a cup or container: *I filled my glass to the brim.* **2** the projecting edge of something, especially of a hat: *The wide brim shaded her eyes.*
v **brimmed, brim·ming** fill or be full to the top: *Her eyes brimmed with tears.* <Middle English *brimme*>
brim′less *adj.*
brim over, overflow.

brim·ful (brim′fůl′) *adj* full to the brim or to the very top.

brim·stone (brim′stōn′) *Poetic n* sulphur. <Old English *brynstan* = burn-stone>

brin·dle (brin′dəl) *adj* usually, **brindled** grey or tawny with darker streaks and spots. <Middle English *brended*>

brine (brīn) *n* **1** very salty water used for pickling. **2** the salt water of a sea or ocean. <Old English *bryne*>

bring (bring) *v* **brought, bring·ing 1** carry or take along to a place: *I didn't bring enough money. He brought his cousin to the party.* **2** cause to come: *What brings you home so early?* **3** cause or motivate: *Desperation brought them to do foolish things.* **4** present before a law court: *She brought a charge against me.* **5** sell for: *Eggs are bringing a high price this week.* <Old English *bringan*>
bring about, cause: *The flood was brought about by high winds and heavy rains.*
bring around, See AROUND.
bring down, a destroy or defeat. **b** lower or reduce a price, mark, or level. **c** make someone reduce a price: *He was asking $50 for the skis, but I brought him down to $45.* **d** officially present: *to bring down new legislation.*
bring forth, bring out and show: *He reached into his pocket and brought forth two rather grubby mints.*
bring forward, a *Accounting* carry over from one page to another. **b** produce for consideration: *In his talk, he brought forward several new ideas.*
bring home to someone, make someone understand something.
bring in, a earn. **b** call on someone for help: *They brought in an arbitrator to settle the strike.*
bring low, humiliate, defeat, or subdue.
bring something off, carry out successfully: *It's a good plan, but can we bring it off?*
bring on, cause to start: *My cold was brought on by lack of sleep.*
bring out, a reveal: *Her paintings bring out the loneliness of the North.* **b** offer to the public: *The band has brought out a new CD.*
bring to, restore to consciousness: *We tried to bring him to by loosening his clothing.*
bring to nothing, destroy or ruin.
bring up, a care for a child: *He was brought up by his grandparents.* **b** suggest for action or discussion: *You've brought up an important point.* **c** vomit. **d** stop suddenly: *He brought his horse up at the fence.*

CONFUSABLES

Bring means "carry to": *Please bring my duffel bag upstairs to me.*

Take means "carry away": *They hired a taxi to take them to the airport.*

Think of it this way: If it is coming *here*, someone is *bringing* it. If it is going *there*, someone is *taking* it.

brink (bringk) *n* an edge from which one can fall, such as that of a cliff, pit, body of water, etc.: *He stood on the brink and looked down.* <Middle English>
on the brink of, very near some event or act: *on the brink of a great discovery, on the brink of ruin.*

brink·man·ship (bringk′mən ship′) *n* **1** *Politics* the practice of maintaining or promoting a policy to the brink of open conflict or war. **2** a practice of pursuing any dangerous situation or agenda to the very limits of safety. <from *brink*>

brin·y (brī′nē) *adj* **brin·i·er, brin·i·est** salty, like brine.
brin′i·ness *n.*

bri·oche (brē′osh) *or* (brē osh′) *n* a soft, light bread roll. <French>

bri·quette or **bri·quet** (bri ket′) *n* a block of pressed charcoal or coal dust used for fuel. <French *brique* brick>

brisk (brisk) *adj* **1** acting, moving, or happening quickly: *a brisk walk, a brisk business.* **2** businesslike and matter-of-fact: *a brisk explanation.* **3** keen or sharp: *brisk weather.* <French *brusque*> **brisk′ly** *adv.* **brisk′ness** *n.*

bris·ket (bris′kit) *n* the breast of an animal, especially as a cut of meat. <Old French *bruschet*>

bris·tle (bris′əl) *n* **1** any short, stiff hair of an animal or plant. **2** such a hair, or a synthetic substitute, used in a brush: *My toothbrush has nylon bristles.*
v **bris·tled, bris·tling 1** stand up, as hair may: *The angry dog's hair bristled.* **2** show that one is ready to fight: *The whole country bristled with indignation.* <Old English *byrst*> **bris′tly** *adj.*
bristle with, be crowded or thickly set with: *The harbour bristled with boats and ships.*

bris·tol·board (bris′təl bȯrd′) *n* a heavy, stiff, smooth cardboard used for printing, drawing, and painting on. <*Bristol*, city in England where it was first made>

Brit·ain (brit′ən) n the United Kingdom.

brit·ches (brich′iz) *Informal pln* breeches.
too big for your britches, *Informal* conceited.

a bat	e bed	i bid	o pot	u cup	th thin
ā cake	ē me	ī bite	ō go	ū rude	ᴛʜ then
à bar	ə about	ər over	ȯ for	ů put	zh measure

Brit·i·cism (brit′ə siz′əm) *n* a British expression, such as *lorry* for *truck.*

Brit·ish (brit′ish) *adj* to do with the United Kingdom or its people. **Brit′ish·er** *n.*

British Co·lum·bi·a (kə lum′bē ə) *n* the westernmost province of Canada. *Abbrev.* **B.C.**; postal symbol **BC**; URL **www.gov.bc.ca**
adj to do with British Columbia: *British Columbia apples.* **Brit′ish Co·lum′bi·an** *n.*

British Commonwealth of Nations COMMONWEALTH (def. 1).

British Isles *pln* the islands off the northwest coast of Europe, among them Great Britain, Ireland, the Isle of Man, and the Channel Islands.

CONFUSABLES

British Isles is a geographical term and refers to the island group as a whole.

United Kingdom is a political term, and excludes the southern part of Ireland, which is an independent republic.

British North America Act *n* the Act of the British Parliament that in 1867 created the Dominion of Canada by the union of Ontario, Québec, Nova Scotia, and New Brunswick, later extended to the other provinces. Since 1981, it has been called the **Constitution Act, 1867**. *Abbrev.* **BNA Act**

British thermal unit *n* a nonmetric unit of the amount of heat needed to raise the temperature of one pound of water by one Fahrenheit degree. It is equivalent to about 1.06 kilojoules. *Abbrev.* **BTU**

Brit·on (brit′ən) *n* **1** a native or inhabitant of Britain. **2** a member of a Celtic people who lived in southern Britain at the time of the Roman conquest.

brit·tle (brit′əl) *adj* **1** rigid but easily broken. **2** tense and nervous: *a brittle voice.* **3** not flexible or adaptable; unstable: *a brittle personality. The software has such a brittle design that it crashes with every little error.* <Old English *breotan* break> **brit′tle·ness** *n.*

broach (brōch) *v* **1** open by making a hole: *to broach a barrel of cider.* **2** begin to speak of a topic, especially something sensitive or difficult: *I'm afraid to broach the subject with her.* <Old French *broche* pointed implement, from Latin *broccus* sticking out>

broad (brod) *adj* **1** wide: *a broad road.* **2** inclusive: *a broad rule, a broad range. He has broad experience in education.* **3** open or tolerant: *broad ideas, a broad interpretation.* **4** general and without details: *Give a broad outline of the speech.* **5** clear; unmistakeable: *broad daylight, a broad hint, a broad accent.* <Old English *brad*> **broad′en** *v.* **broad′ly** *adv.* **broad′ness** *n.*

broad·band (brod′band′) *adj* **1** *Radio* operating simultaneously over a wide range of frequencies. **2** *Computers* capable of transferring large amounts of data at high speed. **broad′band′** *n.*

broad·cast (brod′kast′) *v* **broad·cast** or (*sometimes for def. 1*) **broad·cast·ed, broad·cast·ing 1** send out by radio or TV: *The show will be broadcast tonight.* **2** scatter or spread widely: *to broadcast seed.* **3** make widely known: *He broadcast that story all over the school.*
adj **1** sent out by radio or TV: *a broadcast message.* **2** scattered or spread widely: *broadcast sowing.*
n a radio or TV program: *This broadcast is coming from St. John's.*
adv over a wide surface: *He scattered the seed broadcast.* **broad′cast′er** *n.*

broad·cloth (brod′kloth′) *n* a fine, closely woven cloth with a smooth finish. <originally from woollen cloth made wider than usual>

broad–gauge (brod′gāj′) *adj* with a railway track wider than the standard.

broad jump *n* the long jump.

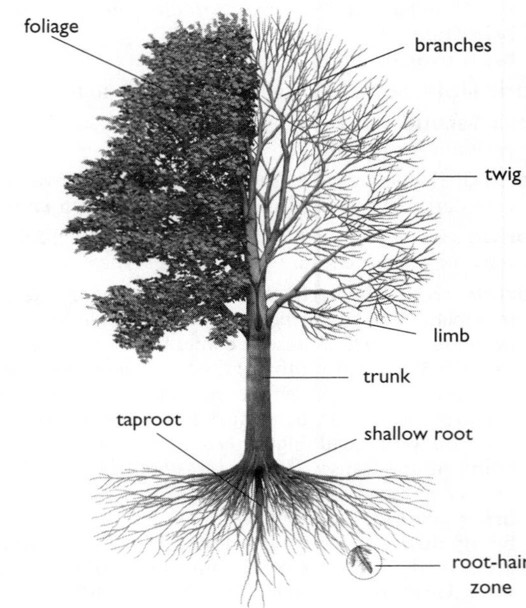

Chestnut, maple, and oak trees are examples of **broadleaf** deciduous trees. In the fall, these trees withdraw chlorophyll from their leaves. This process turns the leaves brilliant red, orange, or gold before they fall.

broad·leaf (brod′lēf′) *adj* of a tree or bush, with leaves rather than needles.
n, pl **broad·leafs** such a tree or bush.

broad·loom (brod′lūm′) *n* carpeting sold by the square metre or square yard and cut to fit the exact size and shape of a room.

broad–mind·ed (brod′mīn′did) *adj* able to appreciate and respect opinions, customs, or beliefs that differ from one's own. **broad′-mind′ed·ly** *adv.* **broad′-mind′ed·ness** *n.*

broad·sheet (brod′shēt′) *n* **1** a large sheet of paper printed on one side with information. **2** a newspaper printed on large pages. Compare TABLOID.

B

broad·side (brod′sīd′) *n* **1** a violent attack in words: *He was met with a broadside from his sister the minute he got home.* **2** the whole side of a ship above the water line. **3** the firing of all the guns on one side of a ship at the same time. **4** a large sheet of paper printed on one or both sides: *Girls were distributing broadsides announcing a big sale.*
adv with the side turned toward an object or point: *The ship drifted broadside to the pier.*
v **broad·sid·ed, broad·sid·ing** hit straight on from the side: *I was broadsided by another car turning left.*

broad–spec·trum (brod′spek′trəm) *adj* with a wide range of use or application: *a broad-spectrum drug.*

broad·sword (brod′sȯrd′) *n* a sword with a broad, flat blade.

Broad·way (brod′wā′) *n* the New York commercial theatre. <name of a street in New York famous for its theatres>

bro·cade (brō kād′) *n* heavy cloth woven with a raised design on it: *silk brocade, velvet brocade.* <Spanish *brocar* embroider>

broc·co·li (brok′ə lē) *n* a plant closely related to the cabbage and cauliflower, whose green branching stems and unopened flower heads are eaten as a vegetable.

ETYMOLOGY

Broccoli is an Italian word, meaning "little cabbage sprouts." It comes from the word *brocco*, meaning "sprout."

bro·chure (brō shūr′) *n* a printed booklet or folder, usually with colourful pictures, that advertises or gives information: *The provincial government puts out a brochure on each of its parks.* <French *brocher* stitch, in reference to the way they were originally made>

brogue (brōg) *n* an Irish accent. <origin uncertain>

broil (broil) *v* **1** cook by placing on a rack directly under a source of heat. **2** make or be very hot: *You'll broil in this hot sun!* <Old French *bruiller* burn>

broil·er (broi′lər) *n* **1** a pan, rack, or burner for broiling food. **2** a young chicken, often used for broiling.

broke (brōk) *v* past tense of BREAK.
adj Informal with no money.
go for broke, *Informal* **a** stake everything on a risky venture. **b** do something lavishly or without holding back.

bro·ken (brō′kən) *v* past participle of BREAK.
adj **1** cracked or shattered: *a broken cup.* **2** no longer functioning: *The alarm on this clock is broken.* **3** much weakened in strength: *He was a broken man after his long illness.* **4** rough or uneven: *broken ground, a broken voice.* **5** imperfectly spoken: *broken French.* **bro′ken·ly** *adv.* **bro′ken·ness** *n.*

bro·ken–heart·ed (brō′ken hȧr′tid) *adj* overwhelmed by disappointment or grief.

broken–line graph (brō′kən līn′) *Mathematics n* a graph in which points representing different values are joined by a broken straight line.

bro·ker (brō′kər) *n* a person who acts as an agent for others in arranging contracts, purchases, or sales in return for a fee. <Old French *brocour* wineseller, broker>

bro·ker·age (brō′kə rij) *n* **1** the business of a broker. **2** the fee or commission charged by a broker.

bro·mide (brō′mīd) *n* **1** a compound of bromine with another element or radical. **2** in full, **potassium bromide** a drug formerly used as a sedative. **3** a commonplace idea or trite remark.

bro·mine (brō′mēn) *or* (brō′mīn) *n* a heavy, non-metallic element that evaporates quickly, resembling chlorine and iodine. It is used in drugs and dyes and in developing film. *Symbol* **Br** <French *brome*, Greek *bromos* stench, in reference to the smell of this element>

bronc (brongk) *Informal n* a bronco.

bron·chi (brong′kī) *or* (brong′kē) *pl*n, *sing* **bron·chus** (brong′kəs) **1** the two main branches of the windpipe, one going to each lung. **2** the smaller, branching tubes in the lungs. <Latin, from Greek *bronchos* windpipe>

bron·chi·a (brong′kē ə) *pl*n usually, **bronchial tubes** the branching tubes of the windpipe, especially the smaller branches. **bron′chi·al** *adj.*

bron·chi·ole (brong′kē ōl′) *n* one of the tiny tubes into which the bronchi are divided.

bron·chi·tis (brong kī′tis) *n* an inflammation of the lining of the bronchial tubes, usually with much coughing and phlegm. **bron·chit′ic** (brong kit′ik) *adj.*

bron·cho·di·la·tor (brong′kō dī lā′tər) *n* a drug that causes widening of the bronchial tubes by relaxing the bronchial muscles, used to relieve asthma.

bron·co (brong′kō) *n* a wild or partly tamed horse or pony of western N America.

ETYMOLOGY

Bronco is a Spanish word meaning "rough." It was first used with reference to a half-tamed (and therefore rough) horse in California and New Mexico in the 1800s.

bron·co·bust·er (brong′kō bus′tər) *Western Canada and US, Informal n* a person who trains wild horses to carry a rider.

bron·to·sau·rus (bron′tə sȯ′rəs) *n* an old name for the APATOSAURUS. <Latin, from Greek *bronte* thunder + *sauros* lizard>

bronze (bronz) *n* **1** a brown alloy of copper and tin. **2** a similar alloy of copper with zinc or other metals. **3** a statue or medal made of bronze: *She won a bronze in the swimming competition.*
adj **1** made of bronze. **2** yellowish or reddish brown.
v **bronzed, bronz·ing** **1** make or become reddish brown: *The sailor was bronzed from the sun.* **2** cover with bronze to preserve as a decorative souvenir: *to bronze a pair of baby shoes.* <Italian *bronzo*>

a bat	e bed	i bid	o pot	u cup	th thin
ā cake	ē me	ī bite	ō go	ū rude	ᴛʜ then
ȧ bar	ə about	ər over	ȯ for	ů put	zh measure

Bronze Age *n* the prehistoric period after the Stone Age, when bronze tools, weapons, and other objects were first made. It began between 4000 and 3000 BCE.

brooch (brōch) *n* an ornamental pin with the point secured by a clasp or catch. <variant of *broach*>

brood (brūd) *n* **1** the young birds hatched at one time in the nest or cared for together: *a brood of chicks.* **2** *Informal* all the children in one family: *They brought their whole brood along to the party.*
v **1** sit on eggs in order to hatch them. **2** think a long time about something, especially something gloomy or grim: *to brood vengeance. She broods a lot these days.*
adj (*in compounds*) kept for breeding: *a broodmare.* <Old English *brod*>
brood over, a keep thinking about. **b** hover over.

brood·er (brū′dər) *n* **1** a closed place that can be heated, especially used for raising chicks. **2** a hen that is brooding or ready to brood. **3** a person who spends much time brooding about things.

brood·y (brū′dē) *adj* **1** sitting on eggs in order to hatch them, as hens do. **2** inclined to worry about things.

brook[1] (bru̇k) *n* a small freshwater stream; a creek. See RIVER for picture. <Old English *broc*>

brook[2] (bru̇k) *v* put up with; endure; tolerate: *Her pride would not brook such insults.* <Old English *brucan*>

Brook trout live in clean, clear, cold streams. In the fall, the female makes a depression with her tail fin in stream gravel and then deposits between 100 and 5000 eggs, depending on her size. Once fertilized, the eggs incubate throughout the winter and hatch in early spring.

brook trout *n* a freshwater food and game fish of N America, greenish brown, with a large head and a square tail. Also called **speckled char**, **mud trout**.

broom (brūm) *n* **1** a long-handled brush for sweeping floors or paved areas. **2** a shrub of the same family as the pea, with slender branches, small leaves, and yellow flowers. <Old English *brom*>

🍁 **broom·ball** (brūm′bol) *n* a game played on an ice rink in which players, with or without skates, use brooms and volleyballs instead of hockey sticks and pucks. A similar game is played in a gymnasium, without skates.

broom·stick (brūm′stik′) *n* the long handle of a broom; according to superstition, the vehicle of a witch.

broth (broth) *n* the water in which meat, fish, or vegetables have been boiled, often used as a thin soup or as a base for soup.

ETYMOLOGY

Broth and **brew** come from related words in Old English. They illustrate a frequent pattern in English, in which nouns are made from verbs or adjectives by adding *th*, often with a change in the vowel sound. Other examples of this pattern: *steal* and *stealth*, *long* and *length*, *bear* and *birth*.

broth·el (broth′əl) *n* a place where prostitutes can be hired. <Old English *breothan* to become worthless>

broth·er (bruŧH′ər) *n, pl* **broth·ers** or (*Poetic*) **breth·ren** **1** a son of the same parents as another; sometimes used for a son with either the same mother or the same father (a **half-brother**). **2** a male who fills the role of a brother: *My cousin is a brother to me.* **3** a male united to others by something shared: *The two soldiers were brothers in arms.* **4** a monk. <Old English> **broth′er·li·ness** *n.* **broth′er·ly** *adj.*

broth·er·hood (bruŧH′ər hu̇d′) *n* **1** the relationship between brothers. **2** an association of men with some common aim, characteristic, belief, or occupation: *the brotherhood of locomotive engineers.*

broth·er–in–law (bruŧH′ər in lo′) *n, pl* **broth·ers-in-law** **1** the brother of one's spouse. **2** the husband of one's sister or of one's sister-in-law.

brought (brot) past tense and past participle of BRING.

brou·ha·ha (brū′hȧ hȧ) *n* uproar; fuss. <French; imitative>

brow (brou) *n* **1** the forehead: *a wrinkled brow.* **2** the arch of hair over the eye; eyebrow. **3** the edge of a steep place; the top of a slope or cliff: *on the brow of a hill.* <Old English *bru*>

brow·beat (brou′bēt′) *v* **brow·beat, brow·beat·en, brow·beat·ing** (*often with* ***into***) frighten or intimidate by overbearing looks or words; bully.

brown (broun) *adj* **1** with the colour produced by mixing red, yellow, and black, including such shades that coffee or cinnamon have. **2** tanned: *She was brown from a summer in the sun.*
v make or become brown: *Brown the onions in butter.* <Old English *brun*> **brown′ish** *adj.* **brown′ness** *n.*

brown algae *pln* a division of multicellular marine algae that appear dark brownish green because their chlorophyll is partly masked by a brown pigment.

brown bear *n* the most widespread species of bear, found in northern parts of the world, with a thick coat of fur varying in colour from cream to blue-black. Grizzlies are brown bears. Compare BLACK BEAR.

brown betty *n* a baked pudding made of apples, breadcrumbs, sugar, and spices.

brown bread *n* bread made from whole-wheat flour, often mixed with white flour

Brown·i·an movement or **motion** (brou′nē ən) *Physics n* a rapid back-and-forth motion often observed in very tiny particles suspended in water or other liquid, caused by collision of the particles with molecules of the liquid. <R. *Brown,* 19c botanist>

brown·ie (brou′nē) *n* **1** a small square or bar of a rich, dense chocolate cake usually containing nuts. **2** a good-natured, helpful elf or fairy.

brownie points *Informal pln* credit earned for good behaviour, especially to gain favour with a superior: *He runs errands for the principal just to collect brownie points.*

ETYMOLOGY

Brownie points likely comes from the idea of credits earned for various achievements by Brownies, a division of the Girl Guides for younger girls. The term came into general use in the mid 1900s.

brown·out (broun′out′) *n* a partial failure of hydro power, so that lights dim or flicker without going off completely.

brown rice *n* unpolished rice with the outer layer containing the bran still on the grains.

brown·stone (broun′stōn′) *n* **1** a reddish brown sandstone used as a building material. **2** a building, especially a house, made from this.

brown study *n* a state of being absorbed in serious thought.

brown sugar *n* **1** refined sugar in which the crystals are coated with dark molasses-flavoured syrup. **2** sugar that is only partly refined and so retains the original brown colour.

brown toast *n* whole-wheat toast.

browse (brouz) *v* **browsed, brows·ing 1** feed on growing plants, especially the tender parts of trees and bushes: *The deer browsed on young shoots and leaves.* **2** read here and there in a book or in books. **3** look casually at articles for sale in a store. **4** *Computers* **a** look through a series of data files by having sets of them displayed successively. **b** search for material of interest on the Internet or another network.
n tender shoots, leaves, and twigs of trees and shrubs considered as food for animals: *The gorillas in the zoo were fed browse in the morning.* <French *broust* a bud, shoot>

browser *n* **1** *Computers* a piece of software enabling a user to access and browse on the Internet or other network. **2** a person, animal, or thing that browses.

bru·in (brū′ən) *Poetic n* a bear, especially a brown bear. <Dutch *bruin* brown>

bruise (brūz) *n* **1** a minor injury, caused by a fall or blow, that discolours the skin by breaking the blood vessels under the surface. **2** a slight injury to the surface of a fruit, vegetable, or plant.
v **bruised, bruis·ing 1** make or cause a bruise on: *I bruised my leg. Handle the tomatoes carefully so you don't bruise them.* **2** hurt someone's feelings. **3** become bruised: *I bruise easily.* <Old English *brysan* crush and Old French *bruisier* break>

bruis·er (brū′zər) *Informal n* **1** a big, muscular person. **2** a bully.

bruit (brūt) *v* spread a report or rumour of: *The princess's engagement was bruited about.* <Old French *bruire* roar>

bru·lé or **bru·le** (brū lā′) *n* **1** a forest area that has been destroyed by fire. **2** rocky land. <French *brûlé* burnt>

brunch (brunch) *n* a meal taken in the late morning, combining breakfast and lunch. <*br(eakfast)* + *(l)unch*>

Bru·nei (brū nī′) *n* in full, **Brunei Darussalam** a country in northwest Borneo.

bru·nette (brū net′) *n* a dark-haired female.
adj with dark hair and eyes. <French>

brunt (brunt) *n* the main force or violence; the worst effects: *This area got the brunt of the hurricane.* <Middle English>

brush[1] (brush) *n* **1** a tool for cleaning, sweeping, scrubbing, or to apply paint, with bristles, hair, or wires set into a stiff back or fastened to a handle. **2** a rub with a brush: *He gave his puppy a good brush.* **3** a light touch in passing: *Give the desk a brush with the cloth.* **4** an encounter or conflict: *The protesters had a brush with the police.* **5** the bushy tail of a fox. **6** *Electricity* a piece of carbon or metal used to conduct electricity from the revolving part of a motor or generator to the outside circuit. **7** the style of an artist: *She paints with a bold brush.*
v **1** clean, sweep, paint, etc. with a brush; use a brush on. **2** wipe away with a light stroke: *The child brushed the tears from his eyes.* **3** touch lightly in passing: *No harm was done; your bumper just brushed ours.* <Old French *broisse,* from Latin *bruscia* a bunch of twigs used to sweep>
brush aside (or **away**), refuse to consider.
brush off, *Informal* refuse or dismiss a person in a curt way: *He brushed us off when we asked for his autograph.*
brush up (on), refresh one's memory of by study: *I still have to brush up on some dates for the history test.*

brush[2] (brush) *n* **1** shrubs, bushes, and small trees growing thickly together. **2** branches broken or cut off. <Old French *broce* bushes> **brush′y** *adj.*

brush·off (brush′of′) *Informal n* (*usually with* **the**) a curt or careless dismissal of a person or request: *When I asked for an appointment, I got the brushoff.*

brush·stroke (brush′strōk′) *n* a movement of the brush in painting, or a particular technique of using the brush: *This artist has a heavy brushstroke.*

brush wolf *n* a coyote.

brush·wood (brush′wu̇d′) *n* BRUSH[2].

brush·work (brush′wərk′) *n* the application of paint with a brush, or a special technique used for this.

brusque (brusk) *or* (brūsk) *adj* abrupt, sharp, or overly direct in manner or speech. <French, from Italian *brusco* rough, coarse> **brusque′ly** *adv.* **brusque′ness** *n.*

Brus·sels sprouts (brus′əlz) *pln* a plant closely related to broccoli and cabbage, with many small heads that are eaten as a vegetable. Also, **brussels sprouts.**

a bat	e bed	i bid	o pot	u cup	th thin
ā cake	ē me	ī bite	ō go	ū rude	ᴛʜ then
ȧ bar	ə about	ər over	ȯ for	u̇ put	zh measure

bru·tal (brū′təl) *adj* cruel and savage. **bru·tal′i·ty** *n.* **bru′tal·ly** *adv.*

bru·tal·ize (brū′tə līz′) *v* **bru·tal·ized, bru·tal·iz·ing** 1 make brutal: *War brutalizes people.* 2 treat brutally: *to brutalize traitors.* **bru′tal·i·za′tion** *n.*

brute (brūt) *n* 1 an animal, especially with reference to its inability to reason. 2 a cruel, coarse, or savage person.
adj 1 without the power to reason: *brute creatures.* 2 cruel; coarse; savage. 3 not influenced by reason or emotion: *brute force.* <French, from Latin *brutus* heavy, dull> **brut′ish** *adj.*

SYNONYMS

A **brute** refers to a person who is cruel or savage: *He was a brute in the wrestling ring.*

A **bully** is someone who specifically picks on weaker people: *She was a bully to the younger children in the schoolyard.*

A **ruffian** often describes a violent person: *The ruffian dragged the tourist into the alley and stole his wallet.*

bry·o·phyte (brī′ə fīt′) *n* any of a major division of rootless, non-flowering plants that reproduce by spores. Mosses are bryophytes. <Latin, from Greek *bryon* tree moss + *phyton* plant>

BTU or **Btu** British thermal unit(s).

btw or **BTW** *Informal (in writing, especially e-mail)* by the way.

bub·ble (bub′əl) *n* 1 a thin, round film of liquid enclosing air or gas: *A soap bubble landed on my nose. The surface of boiling water is covered with bubbles.* 2 a pocket of air or gas inside a liquid such as pop, or a solid such as ice. 3 the process or sound of bubbling: *I hear the bubble of boiling water.* 4 something shaped like a bubble, such as a domed skylight or a compartment protecting a person who has many acute allergies.
v **bub·bled, bub·bling** 1 have or form bubbles: *Water bubbled between the stones.* 2 be full of enthusiasm: *She bubbled on and on about their trip.* <Middle English *bobel*> **bub′bly** *adj.*
bubble over, a overflow. **b** be very enthusiastic: *The girls were bubbling over with ideas for the canoe trip.*

bubble bath *n* 1 a liquid or gel added to bathwater while it is running, in order to produce a mass of bubbles. 2 a bath with a mass of bubbles on the surface.

bubble chamber *Physics n* an apparatus containing a superheated liquid, usually liquid hydrogen, in which the trail of a subatomic particle can be seen as a line of bubbles. Compare CLOUD CHAMBER.

bubble gum *n* chewing gum that can be stretched and blown into bubbles from the mouth.

bu·bon·ic plague (byū bon′ik) *n* a dangerous, contagious disease, accompanied by fever, chills, and swelling of the lymphatic glands (in the armpit and groin). It is carried by rats or squirrels and transmitted to humans by fleas. <Greek *boubon* groin>

buc·ca·neer (buk′ə nēr′) *n* a pirate. <French *boucaner* to smoke meat, from Tupi (a language of S America) *boucan* barbecue. Pirates probably smoked meat to preserve it for voyages.>

buck[1] (buk) *n* 1 an adult male of the deer, hare, rabbit, ferret, rat, or kangaroo. 2 *Informal* a man, especially a young man who is lively and bold. <Old English *buc*>
buck naked, *Informal* completely naked.

buck[2] (buk) *v* 1 *Informal* resist stubbornly: *The swimmer bucked the current with strong strokes. You can't buck progress.* 2 jump into the air with back curved and come down with the front legs stiff, as a horse does: *Her horse began to buck, but she managed to stay on.* 3 throw or attempt to throw a rider in this way: *The cowboy was bucked from the bronco.* 4 *Football* charge into the opposing line with the ball.
n an act of bucking. <special use of *buck*[1]> **buck′er** *n.*
buck up, *Informal* cheer up: *Buck up; everything will be all right.*

buck[3] (buk) *n* in former times, a marker placed before a poker player to show whose turn it is to deal. <origin uncertain>
pass the buck, *Informal* shift the responsibility or blame to someone else.
the buck stops here, *Informal* the ultimate responsibility lies with me or with us.

buck[4] (buk) *Informal n* a dollar. <origin uncertain>
a fast (or **quick**) **buck,** *Slang* profits earned quickly and often in a questionable way.

buck·a·roo (buk′ə rū′) *Slang n* a cowboy.

buck·et (buk′it) *n* 1 a metal or wooden pail used for carrying a liquid. 2 **buckets** *pl Informal* large quantities. 3 the scoop of a dredging machine. <Old French *buket*> **buck′et·ful** *n.*
a drop in the bucket, See DROP.
kick the bucket, *Slang* die.

bucket brigade *n* a line of people passing buckets of water hand to hand from the source, to put out a fire.

bucket seat *n* a low, contoured seat with a rounded back, for one person, used especially in sports cars.

buck·le[1] (buk′əl) *n* 1 a device used to fasten a belt or strap, usually consisting of a metal or plastic frame through which the end of the belt or strap is pulled. 2 a metal ornament, especially one for a shoe.
v **buck·led, buck·ling** fasten with a buckle. <Old French, from Latin *buccula* cheek strap on helmet>
buckle down (to), begin to work hard at: *She promised to buckle down to her homework right after supper.*

buck·le[2] (buk′əl) *v* **buck·led, buck·ling** bend out of shape: *The heavy snowfall caused the roof of the arena to buckle.*
n a bulge, kink, or wrinkle. <French *boucler* bulge>

buck·ler (buk′lər) *n* 1 a small, round shield. 2 *Poetic* a protection; a defence. <Old French *boucler*>

buck–pass·ing (buk′pas′ing) *n* avoidance of responsibility or blame by shifting it to another person. <possibly from *buck*[3]>

buck·saw (buk′so′) *n* a two-handed saw for wood, set in a light H-shaped frame.

buck·shot (buk′shot′) *n* large lead pellets for shotgun shells, used for hunting big game such as deer.

buck·skin (buk′skin′) *n* **1 a** the skin of a male deer. **b** a soft but heavy, tough, yellowish or greyish leather made from this, usually with a suede finish. **2** a similar leather made from sheepskin. **3 buckskins** *pl* clothing, especially pants, made from buckskin.

buck·teeth (buk′tēth′) *pl n* top front teeth that stick out. **buck′toothed′** (buk′tūthd′) *adj.*

buck·thorn (buk′thȯrn′) *n* a thorny tree or shrub with bluish black berries, some species of which yield pigments and medicinal compounds.

buck·wheat (buk′wēt′) *n* a plant native to N Asia, whose seeds are used as cereal grains or ground into flour. See GRAIN for picture. <Old English *boc* beech + *wheat*>

bu·col·ic (byū kol′ik) *adj* peaceful and rustic or rural.
n a poem about shepherds. <Latin, from Greek *boukolous* shepherd>

bud (bud) *n* **1** a small swelling on a plant that will develop into a flower, leaf, or branch. **2** a partly opened flower or leaf. **3** a taste bud.
v **bud·ded, bud·ding 1** put forth buds: *The rosebush has budded.* **2** begin to grow or develop. **3** *Biology* reproduce asexually by forming an outgrowth that eventually separates to become a new organism. <Middle English *budde*>
in bud, budding: *The pear tree is in bud.*
nip in the bud, stop at the very beginning.

Bud·dha (bu̇d′ə) *or* (bū′də) *n* **1** the title of Siddhartha Gautama, the Indian philosopher and religious teacher who founded Buddhism. **2** a statue of Buddha. <Sanskrit = enlightened one>

Bud·dhism (bu̇d′iz əm) *or* (bū′diz əm) *n* a religion based on the teaching of Buddha that through meditation and by leading a moral life one can eventually reach nirvana. **Bud′dhist** *n, adj.*

bud·ding (bud′ing) *adj* in an early stage of development: *My teacher says I'm a budding physicist.*

bud·dy (bud′ē) *Informal n, pl* **bud·dies 1** a friend; a comrade; a pal. **2** (*used as a form of address*) fellow: *Say, buddy, can you change a dollar?* Also, **bud** (*Informal*). <origin uncertain>

buddy system *n* in certain types of work or sport, an arrangement for safety whereby two people stay together to help each other in case of trouble or an accident.

budge (buj) *v* **budged, budg·ing** move or cause to move a little: *He wouldn't budge from his chair, even to get something to eat.* <French *bouger* to stir, from Latin *bullire* to bubble>

budg·et (buj′it) *n* an estimate of the amount of money that will be spent for various purposes in a given time: *We made a budget for our holiday trip so we wouldn't run out of money before the end.*
v make a plan for spending or using: *to budget your time. She budgets her money carefully.* <Old French *bouge* leather (money) bag, from Latin *bulga*>
budg′et·ar′y *adj.*
budget for, allot money for a particular purpose: *I forgot to budget for extras so I couldn't buy a souvenir.*

budg·ie (buj′ē) *n* in full, **budgerigar** a small parrot, kept as a cage bird but found wild only in dry regions of Australia.Wild budgies are mostly green, but the birds have been bred to have different colours. <Australian Aborigine *budgeri* good + *gar* cockatoo>

🍁 **bud run** *n* the third run of sugar maple sap, which makes syrup or sugar of a poor quality. Compare FROG RUN, ROBIN RUN.

buff[1] (buf) *n* **1** a strong, soft, dull yellow leather, made from the hide of a buffalo or ox. **2** a polishing wheel or stick covered with leather.
adj **1** dull yellow. **2** made of buff.
v polish with a cloth, chamois, etc. <French *buffle* buffalo>
in the buff, *Informal* naked.

buff[2] (buf) *Informal n* a fan; an enthusiast: *a hockey buff, a theatre buff.* <origin uncertain>

American buffalo

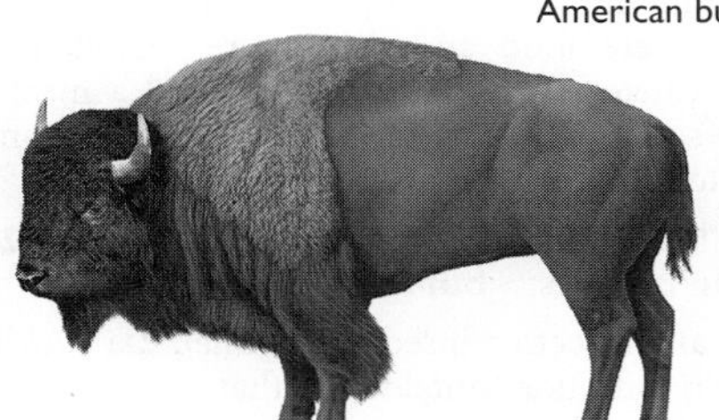

African buffalo

buf·fa·lo (buf′ə lō′) *n* **buf·fa·loes, buf·fa·los,** or (*especially collectively*) **buf·fa·lo 1** a powerful grazing animal of the N American plains with a large hump at the shoulders, shaggy, dark brown hair, short curved horns, and a large head that is carried low. The buffalo is a species of bison. **2** any of several species of bovine found in Africa and Asia, generally with long horns that curve up and back. Some species have been domesticated.
v **buf·fa·loed, buf·fa·lo·ing** *Informal* make unable to answer or proceed: *We were all buffaloed by the last question on the exam.* <Italian, from Greek *boubalos* ox>

🍁 **buffalo jump** *n* a place where buffalo were killed by stampeding them over a precipice.

a bat	e bed	i bid	o pot	u cup	th thin
ā cake	ē me	ī bite	ō go	ū rude	TH then
ȧ bar	ə about	ər over	ȯ for	u̇ put	zh measure

buff·er[1] (buf′ər) *n* **1** anything that softens the shock of a blow or lessens some other negative effect. **2** buffer zone. **3** *Chemistry* in a solution, a neutralizing substance that acts to maintain the alkalinity or acidity of the solution regardless of what is added. <Old French *buffe* a blow>

buff·er[2] (buf′ər) *n* a person who or thing that polishes, especially a device covered with leather or cloth for polishing or buffing.

buffer state *n* a small country between two larger ones that are enemies or that often experience friction, thought of as lessening the danger of open conflict between them.

buffer zone *n* a neutral area established as a barrier between two enemy or potentially competing forces.

buf·fet[1] (buf′it) *v* **1** strike with the hand or fist. **2** knock repeatedly and hard against: *The waves buffeted him.*
n a hard knock or blow. <Old French *buffe* blow>

buf·fet[2] (bə fā′) *n* **1** a low cabinet for storing dishes, silver, and table linen. Often the flat top serves as a sideboard. **2** a counter where food and drinks are served, or a restaurant or cafeteria with such a counter. **3** a meal at which guests serve themselves from food laid out on a table or counter. <French>

buf·foon (bə fūn′) *n* **1** a fool or ridiculous person. **2** a clown. <Italian *buffa* jest> **buf·foon′er·y** *n.*

bug (bug) *n* **1** any insect or insectlike animal. **2** a sucking insect, generally with horizontal wings that overlap on the body when at rest. There are many species. **3** *Informal* a germ or virus: *the flu bug.* **4** *Informal* a defect or error that interferes with proper function: *a bug in a piece of software.* **5** *Informal* a fan or enthusiast: *a camera bug.* **6** a small hidden microphone for secret recording. **7** *Informal* a passion or obsessive interest, thought of as being the result of a bite or sting: *bitten by the motorcycle bug.*
v **bugged, bug·ging 1** *Informal* annoy or irritate: *Her constant grumbling bugs me. You seem upset; what's bugging you?* **2** record secretly with a small hidden microphone: *to bug a telephone conversation. Be careful what you say; the room may be bugged.* <origin uncertain>

bug·a·boo (bug′ə bū′) *n, pl* **bug·a·boos** a cause of fear, usually unwarranted; something, often imaginary, that frightens: *The child was frightened by tales of monsters, ghosts, and other bugaboos.*

bug·bear (bug′ber′) *n* **1** bugaboo. **2** something that causes difficulties. **3** something that one especially hates.

bug–eyed (bug′īd′) *Informal adj* with eyes wide open and bulging, especially from wonder or excitement.

bug·gy[1] (bug′ē) *n, pl* **bug·gies 1** a light, open, four-wheeled horse-drawn carriage. **2** a wheeled cart used for shopping. **3** a baby carriage. <origin uncertain>

bug·gy[2] (bug′ē) *adj* **bug·gi·er, bug·gi·est** swarming with bugs.

bu·gle (byū′gəl) *n* a metal musical instrument like a small trumpet, usually without keys or valves.
v **bu·gled, bu·gling** blow a bugle. <Old French, from Latin *buculus* wild ox, in reference to early hunting horns> **bu′gler** *n.*

build (bild) *v* **built, build·ing 1** make by putting parts or materials together: *to build a tree house. I'm building a model airplane.* **2** put up a building or hire someone to do so: *Once you buy the land you have to build within the year. The construction company's sign read "Will build to suit."* **3** form or develop gradually: *They built that business out of nothing. Tension builds throughout the story until the climax.* **4** establish or base: *to build an argument on facts.*
n the size and arrangement of parts in a structure, including that of a person's or animal's body: *An elephant has a heavy build.* <Old English *bold* dwelling> **build′er** *n.*
build up, a increase gradually: *Ice is building up on the window sills. The firm has built up a reputation for fair dealing.* **b** encourage or affirm: *Say things that build other people up.* **c** fill with buildings: *This area used to be farmland, but now it's all built up.*

build·ing (bil′ding) *n* **1** a permanent structure built for people to live or work in, or to store things. **2** the process, art, or business of making houses, bridges, ships, and other large structures.

SYNONYMS

Building is a non-specific word. Try to be specific when describing the type of building in question.

A **bungalow** is a one-storey house, often small: *The street was lined with bungalows built in the 1950s.*

A **palace** is a splendid or spacious building: *The royal family lives in a palace.*

A **skyscraper** is a very tall building: *She worked in one of the skyscrapers downtown.*

build·up or **build–up** (bild′up′) *n* **1** the act or process of building up: *Stop the buildup of nuclear weapons.* **2** a mass that has built up: *a buildup of plaque on the teeth.* **3** publicity that creates anticipation: *The movie got such a buildup that we were disappointed when we finally saw it.*

built (bilt) past tense and past participle of BUILD.

built–in (bilt′in′) *adj* made in the course of building a larger structure and forming a part of it; not portable or detachable: *a built-in closet, built-in cupboards.*

built–up (bilt′ up′) *adj* with many buildings: *a built-up area.*

bulb (bulb) *n* **1** a round, underground bud from which certain plants grow, such as onions and tulips. **2** the thick part of an underground stem resembling a bulb: *a crocus bulb.* **3** an electric light bulb. See INCANDESCENT for picture. **4** a rounded or swelling end of anything: *the bulb of a thermometer.* <Latin, from Greek *bolbos* onion> **bulb′like′** *adj.*

bulb·ous (bul′bəs) *adj* **1** shaped like a bulb: *a bulbous nose.* **2** producing or growing from bulbs. Daffodils and tulips are bulbous plants.

Bul·gar·i·a (bul ger′ē ə) *n* a country in southeastern Europe. See the APPENDIX. **Bul·gar′i·an** *adj, n.*

bulge (bulj) *v* **bulged, bulg·ing** swell or cause to swell outward: *His pockets bulged with apples and candy.*
n **1** an outward swelling. **2** a slight temporary increase: *The graph shows a bulge in the birth rate.* <Old French, from Latin *bulga* bag> **bulg′y** *adj.*

bul·gur (bul′gər) *n* a Middle Eastern dish made from cracked wheat, or the wheat itself. Also, **bulghur.** <Turkish>

bu·li·mi·a (bū lē′mē ə) *n* in full, **bulimia nervosa** an eating disorder in which the affected person overeats and then purges by means of a laxative or self-induced vomiting. **bu·li′mic** *adj.*

bulk (bulk) *n* **1** size, especially large size: *He had a hard time finding clothes because of his bulk.* **2** the largest part or main mass: *The oceans form the bulk of the earth's surface.* *v* **1** be of importance. **2** grow or seem to be larger or looming up. <Old Icelandic *bulki* heap>
bulk large, seem important.
in bulk, a loose in bins, not packaged. **b** in large quantities: *We buy rice in bulk, because we use so much.*

bulk·head (bulk′hed′) *n* **1** one of the upright partitions dividing the hull of a ship into watertight compartments. **2** a similar partition in an aircraft. **3** any wall or partition built to hold back water, earth, rocks, air, etc. **4** a boxlike structure covering the top of a staircase or other opening.

bulk·y (bul′kē) *adj* **bulk·i·er, bulk·i·est 1** taking up much space: *Bulky shipments are often sent by freight.* **2** large and awkwardly shaped for carrying: *She dropped the bulky package twice.* **bulk′i·ness** *n.*

bull[1] (bu̇l) *n* **1** the adult male of cattle, buffalo, other bovine animals, and some large animals such as the moose, whale, or elephant. **2** a person who believes that prices in the stock market will rise. Compare BEAR[2] (def. 3). **3** *Slang* foolish or insincere talk: *Don't give me that bull.* <Old Norse *boli*>

bull[2] (bu̇l) *Catholicism n* a formal announcement from the Pope. <Latin *bulla* seal, sealed document>

Bulldogs were initially developed in England for bull baiting. When that sport became illegal in 1835, the dogs were bred to eliminate viciousness.

bull·dog (bu̇l′dog′) *n* a breed of dog with a heavy, muscular build, a large head, and short hair.
v **bull·dogged, bull·dog·ging** *Western Canada and US* throw a steer to the ground by grasping its horns and twisting its neck.

bull·doze (bu̇l′dōz′) *v* **bull·dozed, bull·doz·ing 1** move, clear, or level with a bulldozer. **2** *Informal* bully by manipulation or threats: *They bulldozed him into signing the statement.*

bull·doz·er (bu̇l′dō′zər) *n* a powerful tractor with a wide steel blade in front for clearing ground. See EARTHMOVER for picture.

bul·let (bu̇l′it) *n* **1** a round or pointed piece of lead or other metal designed to be shot from a rifle, pistol, or other small gun. **2** a fairly large round or square dot used to highlight items in a printed list. <French *boule* ball>
bite the bullet, brace oneself to endure or accept something without a fuss.

ETYMOLOGY

The expression **bite the bullet** comes from the days when wounded soldiers were treated on the battlefield without anesthetic. They were given a bullet to bite on to distract them from the pain.

bul·le·tin (bu̇l′ə tən) *n* **1** a short statement of news: *The hospital has issued a bulletin about the condition of the Prime Minister.* **2** a magazine or newspaper appearing regularly, especially one published by a club or society for its members. <Italian *bulla* bull[2]>

bulletin board *n* **1** a board made of cork or similar material attached to a wall, for putting up notices or other items. **2** in full, **bulletin-board system** *Computers* a system allowing networked users to post notices or messages, and share data or programs. *Abbrev.* **BBS**

bul·let·proof (bu̇l′it prūf′) *adj* made so that a bullet cannot go through: *a bulletproof jacket.*

bull·fight (bu̇l′fīt′) *n* in some countries, a traditional public performance in which a person, called a **bullfighter** or **matador**, confronts a fierce bull in an arena and baits it to charge while avoiding its horns. The bull is usually killed. **bull′fight′ing** *n.*

bull·finch (bu̇l′finch′) *n* a small bird, a woodland species of finch of Europe and Asia.

bull·frog (bu̇l′frog′) *n* a large green or brown frog of N America, Africa, and India, the male having a loud call a bit like the bellow of a bull.

bull·head·ed (bu̇l′hed′id) *adj* stupidly stubborn. **bull′head′ed·ly** *adv.* **bull′head′ed·ness** *n.*

bull·horn (bu̇l′hȯrn′) *n* a megaphone with an electric amplifier.

bul·lion (bu̇l′yən) *n* bricks or bars of gold or silver. <Old French *bouillir* to boil; refers to the practice of melting down gold and silver before it is cast into bars>

bull·ish (bu̇l′ish) *adj* **1** like a bull. **2** believing that prices in the stock market will rise. **3** optimistic. **bull′ish·ly** *adv.* **bull′ish·ness** *n.*

bull·ock (bu̇l′ək) *n* **1** a young bull or ox, often used as a draft animal. **2** STEER[2].

bull·pen (bu̇l′pen′) *n* **1** *Baseball* **a** a place outside the playing limits in which pitchers warm up during a game. **b** the group of pitchers in this area. **2** any place in which a group meets to prepare or confer.

bull·ring (bu̇l′ring′) *n* an enclosed arena for bullfights.

a bat	e bed	i bid	o pot	u cup	th thin
ā cake	ē me	ī bite	ō go	ū rude	TH then
ȧ bar	ə about	ər over	ȯ for	u̇ put	zh measure

bull's–eye (bůl′zī′) *n* **1** the centre of a target. **2** a shot that hits the centre: *She had three bull's-eyes in a row.*
hit the bull's-eye, be exactly correct or successful.

bull terrier *n* a strong breed of dog with a long head and stiff, usually white hair, originally bred as a cross between a bulldog and a terrier.

bul·ly (bůl′ē) *n, pl* **bul·lies** **1** a person who teases, frightens, or hurts smaller or weaker people. **2** anyone in a position of power who tries to control people by intimidation.
v **bul·lied, bul·ly·ing** intimidate or force by threats, ridicule, belittling, etc.: *They bullied her into going.*
adj Informal first-rate; excellent.
interj Informal well done! <perhaps Dutch *boele* loudmouthed coward>

bul·rush (bůl′rush′) *n* **1** a tall marsh plant of N America, Europe, and Asia with fuzzy brown flower spikes. **2** a grasslike marsh plant found in N America, Europe, and Asia, with long, spongy, usually leafless stems, often used for weaving. **3** PAPYRUS (def. 1). <Middle English *bule* bull + Old English *rysc* rush>

bul·wark (bůl′wərk) *n* **1** a wall for defence. **2** any person who or thing that defends, supports, or safeguards: *Free speech is a bulwark of democracy.* **3** a wall to break the force of waves. **4** **bulwarks** *pl* the part of a ship's side that extends above deck level. <Middle English *bulwerke* wooden fortress>

bum[1] (bum) *Informal n* **1** a tramp or loafer. **2** being a tramp or vagrant, or the period during which this happens: *on the bum.*
v **bummed, bum·ming** **1** loaf or loiter. **2** live off the kindness of others, either generally or for something in particular: *to bum a ride.*
adj **bum·mer, bum·mest** of poor quality. <perhaps from German *bummeln* stroll, loaf about>
bum around, *Informal* be lazy or do little.
bummed (out), *Slang* disappointed, annoyed, or upset.

bum[2] (bum) *Informal n* the buttocks. <Middle English>

bum·ble (bum′bəl) *v* **bum·bled, bum·bling** do things awkwardly. <Middle English> **bum′bling** *adj.*

bum·ble·bee (bum′bəl bē′) *n* a large bee closely related to the honeybees. Bumblebees live in colonies. <Middle English *bumbe* buzz + *bee*[1]>

🍁 **bum·ble·ber·ry** (bum′bəl be′rē) *n* a mixture of fruit, usually raspberries, blueberries, and strawberries, often with apples and other fruit, used as a pie filling, or to make jam. <probably Old English *braembel* bramble>

bump (bump) *v* **1** push or strike against something solid: *He bumped my elbow and I spilled my drink. The children all bumped against one another in their eagerness to be first.* **2** move or proceed with bumps: *Our car bumped along the rough road.* **3** *Informal* remove from an assigned spot to make room for someone or something else: *His act was bumped from the program when they found someone better.*
n **1** **a** a heavy blow or knock. **b** the resulting swelling. **2** any swelling or lump: *She swerved to avoid the bump in the road.* <imitative> **bump′y** *adj.*
bump into, meet accidentally.
bump off, *Slang* murder.
bump up, increase: *to bump up interest rates.*

bump·er (bum′pər) *n* **1** the wide bar of metal, rubber, etc. across the front and back of a vehicle, protecting it from damage if bumped. **2** a similar strip on the side of a boat or dock. **3** a cup or glass filled to the brim.
adj unusually large: *a bumper crop of wheat.*

bumper cars *pl n* an amusement ride where small electric cars with rubber bumpers and unreliable steering systems are driven by riders who try to bump into one another while avoiding being bumped into.

bumper sticker *n* a sticker with a slogan or emblem on it, for sticking on the bumper of a vehicle.

bump·kin (bump′kin) *n* an unsophisticated person from the country. <Dutch *bommekyn* little barrel, in reference to a short and stumpy man>

bump·tious (bump′shəs) *adj* unpleasantly assertive or conceited. <from *bump*> **bump′tious·ly** *adv.* **bump′tious·ness** *n.*

bun (bun) *n* **1** a small bread roll, often sweetened. **2** hair arranged in a thick coil or knot at the back of the head. <Middle English *bunne*>

bunch (bunch) *n* **1** a group of items of one kind, growing, fastened, placed, or dealt with together: *a bunch of grapes, a bunch of flowers.* **2** any group: *They're a friendly bunch.* **3** *Informal* a lot; a large number: *You can do this in a bunch of different ways.*
v come or put together in a bunch: *The sheep bunched in the shed to keep warm.* <Middle English *bunche*> **bunch′y** *adj.*

bun·dle (bun′dəl) *n* **1** a number of things tied or wrapped together: *a bundle of old newspapers, a bundle of clothing.* **2** *Informal* a large number or amount; a lot: *They gave us a bundle of new ideas.* **3** *Biology* a collection of fibres that perform a specific function. **4** a number of related items marketed together as a unit.
v **bun·dled, bun·dling** make into a bundle. <Middle English *bundel*> **bun′dler** *n.*
be a bundle of nerves, be very nervous.
bundle off, send away in a hurry: *We bundled her off to school even though she was late.*
bundle up, dress warmly: *Bundle up; it's cold outside.*

bung (bung) *n* a stopper closing the hole in the side or end of a barrel, keg, etc. <Middle Dutch *bonghe*>
bung up, **a** close with a bung. **b** clog or choke up. **c** *Informal* wreck or damage.

bun·ga·low (bung′gə lō′) *n* a small, one-storey house.

ETYMOLOGY

Bungalow comes from the Hindi word *bangla*, meaning "belonging to Bengal." Bungalows are built in a style that is based on a kind of one-storey house found in rural India.

bun·gee (bun′jē) *n* in full, **bungee cord** a strong, heavy elastic cable used to secure loads, or for other uses where tension or elasticity is required. <origin unknown>

bungee jumping *n* the sport of jumping from a high place with a bungee attached to one's ankles to keep one from hitting the ground.

bung·hole (bung′hōl′) *n* a hole in the side or end of a barrel, keg, etc. for filling and emptying it.

bun·gle (bung′gəl) *v* **bun·gled, bun·gling** spoil by doing or making in a clumsy, unskilful way.
n a clumsy, unskilful performance or piece of work. <origin uncertain> **bun·gler** *n.* **bun′gling·ly** *adv.*

bun·ion (bun′yən) *n* an enlargement of the first joint of the big toe, causing the toe to be permanently bent inward. <perhaps from obsolete *bunny* a swelling>

bunk[1] (bungk) *n* **1** a narrow bed attached to a wall like a shelf, or built in a unit that includes two beds (**bunk beds**) one above the other. **2** *Informal* any place to sleep.
v **1** spend the night; sleep, sometimes in a makeshift bed: *We bunked in an old barn.* **2** provide with a bunk or bed: *This cabin bunks three people.* <perhaps from *bunker*>

bunk[2] (bungk) *Informal n* insincere talk; nonsense. Also, **bunkum**. <*Buncombe*, the name of a US constituency, whose congressman F. Walker often made pointless speeches>

bunk·er (bung′kər) *n* **1** a fortified shelter built partly or entirely below ground. **2** a sandy hollow or mound of earth on a golf course, used as an obstacle. **3** a bin or other place for storing fuel on a ship. <Scots = bench>

bunk·house (bungk′hous′) *n* a building equipped with bunks for sleeping, as at a lumber camp.

bun·ny (bun′ē) *n, pl* **bun·nies** a pet name or child's word for a rabbit. <origin uncertain>

🍁 **bun·ny·hug** (bun′ē hug) *Saskatchewan n* a hooded sweatshirt.

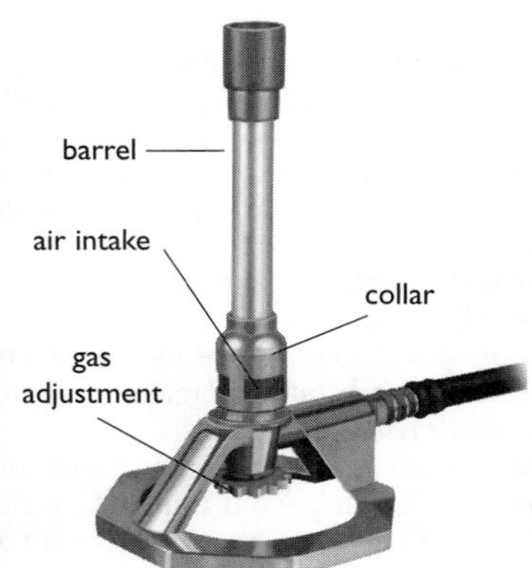

A **Bunsen burner** works by mixing gas with air *before* the point of combustion. Air is drawn in through an intake near the base, which can be opened and closed by turning a metal collar. When the collar is completely open, the flame can reach a temperature of 1500°C.

Bun·sen burner (bun′sən) *n* a gas burner that can be adjusted to give a very hot blue flame, used in laboratories. <R. *Bunsen*, 19c chemist>

bunt (bunt) *v* **1** *Baseball* hit the ball lightly so that it goes to the ground and rolls only a short distance. **2** strike with the head or horns as a goat does.
n an act of bunting. <from *butt*[3]> **bunt′er** *n.*

bun·ting[1] (bun′ting) *n* **1** a thin cloth used for flags. **2** long pieces of cloth with the colours and designs of a flag, or strips consisting of many flags or pennants hanging down side by side, used as outdoor decoration. **3 bunting bag** an infant's outer winter garment shaped like a hooded bag. <Middle English>

bun·ting[2] (bun′ting) *n* a small bird of N America, a type of finch, including the **snow bunting** and **indigo bunting**. <origin uncertain>

buoy (boi) *or* (bū′ē) *n* **1** an anchored object floating on the water as a warning or guide to ships or swimmers. **2** a cork or plastic belt or ring, used to keep a person from sinking.
v **1** mark with a buoy. **2** keep from sinking: *Her life jacket buoyed her up until rescuers came.* **3** (*often with* ***up***) support in trouble or encourage: *Hope buoys him up when things go wrong.* <Old French *boie*>

buoy·ant (boi′ənt) *adj* **1** able to float: *Wood and cork are buoyant in water. Helium balloons are buoyant.* **2** able to keep things afloat: *Salt water is more buoyant than fresh water.* **3** cheerful and hopeful: *Even in the hospital, her spirits were buoyant.* <perhaps Spanish *boyante*>
buoy′an·cy *n.* **buoy′ant·ly** *adv.*

bur·ble (bər′bəl) *v* **bur·bled, bur·bling 1** make a bubbling noise. **2** speak in a confused, excited manner. <probably imitative>

burbs (bərbz) *Slang pl n* the suburbs.

bur·den (bər′dən) *n* **1** something carried; a load. **2** anything difficult to carry or bear; a heavy load: *a burden of debts. Don't give a party if it'll be a burden to you.* **3** the main content or gist: *The burden of his argument was that hockey was too rough for girls.*
v **1** put a burden on or load. **2** load too heavily or weigh down. <Old English *byrthen*> **bur′den·some** *adj.*

burden of proof *n* the obligation of proving a statement or accusation that has been made: *In any court case, the burden of proof lies with the accuser.*

bur·dock (bər′dok′) *n* a coarse weed with prickly BURRS[1] (def. 1) and heart-shaped leaves. <*burr* + *dock*[4]>

bu·reau (byů′rō) *n, pl* **bu·reaus** or **bu·reaux** (byů′rōz) **1** a dresser; a chest of drawers. **2** a desk or writing table with drawers. **3** a certain kind of office or business: *a travel bureau.* **4** *especially US* a branch of a government department. <French = desk>

bu·reauc·ra·cy (byə rok′rə sē) *n, pl* **bu·reauc·ra·cies** **1** the officials administering the government or any large organization. **2** a governing system that has an excessive concentration of power in administrative offices rather than in the real or elected leaders. **3** a system with an excessive insistence on rigid routine; red tape. <French, from *bureau* desk + Greek *kratia* rule>

bu·reau·crat (byů′rə krat′) *n* **1** an official in a bureaucracy. **2** a formal, pretentious official who follows a routine. **bu′reau·crat′ic** *adj.*

burg or **burgh** (bərg) *Informal n* a town or city. <variant of *borough*>

bur·geon (bər′jən) *v* **1** bud or sprout: *burgeoning leaves.* **2** grow quickly or flourish: *The critics applauded as his talent burgeoned.* <Old French *burjon*>

a bat	e bed	i bid	o pot	u cup	th **thin**
ā cake	ē me	ī bite	ō go	ū rude	ᴛʜ **then**
ä bar	ə about	ər over	ô for	ů put	zh measure

bur·ger (bər′gər) *Informal n* a HAMBURGER (def. 2).

–burger *combining form* **1** a fried or grilled patty of a specified kind, served in a split bun: *fishburger, veggieburger.* **2** a HAMBURGER (def. 2) with a particular topping: *cheeseburger.*

bur·gess (bər′jis) *n* **1** 🍁 *Saskatchewan* a property owner entitled to vote on money bylaws in a municipality. **2** the citizen of a BOROUGH. <Old French, from Latin *burgensis* citizen>

burgh·er (bər′gər) *n* a citizen or inhabitant of a town, especially a middle-class person.

bur·glar (bər′glər) *n* a person who breaks into a building, especially at night, to steal or commit some other crime. <Old French *burgler,* probably from Latin *burgare* to thieve> **bur′glar·proof′** (bər′glər prūf′) *adj, v.*

bur·glar·ize (bər′glə rīz) *v* **bur·glar·ized, bur·glar·iz·ing** commit burglary.

bur·glar·y (bər′glə rē) *n, pl* **bur·glar·ies** the act of breaking into a room, apartment, or building, especially at night, to steal or commit some other crime.

bur·gle (bər′gəl) *Informal v* **bur·gled, bur·gling** break into a room, apartment, or building.

bur·gun·dy (bər′gən dē) *n, pl* **bur·gun·dies** **1** a wine, especially red, from eastern France. **2** **Burgundy** a region in eastern France.
adj dark purplish red. <*Burgundy,* the region where the wine was first made> **Bur·gun′di·an** (bər gun′dē ən) *adj, n.*

bur·i·al (ber′ē əl) *or* (bər′ē əl) *n* the act of burying, or a ceremony accompanying this.
adj to do with burying: *a burial service.*

Bur·ki·na Fa·so (bər kē′nō fȧ′sō) *n* a country in west Africa.

bur·lap (bər′lap) *n* a coarse, plain-woven fabric made of jute, hemp, or cotton, used mainly for sacks. <Middle English *borel* coarse cloth + *lappa* garment flap>

bur·lesque (bər lesk′) *n* **1** a literary or dramatic composition in which a serious subject is treated ridiculously, or with mock seriousness. **2** a cheap, vulgar kind of theatrical entertainment.
v **bur·lesqued, bur·les·quing** imitate so as to ridicule. <Italian *burla* jest>

bur·ly (bər′lē) *adj* **bur·li·er, bur·li·est** big, heavy, and strong; husky. <Middle English *burli* noble, tall> **bur′li·ness** *n.*

Bur·ma (bər′mə) *n* the former name of Myanmar, a country in southeast Asia.

Bur·mese (bər mēz′) *n* **1** a person who was born or comes from Burma (Myanmar), or a person of Burmese descent. **2** the official language of Myanmar. **3** a short-haired cat of Asian origin.
adj to do with Myanmar, its people, or its language.

burn (bərn) *v* **burned** or **burnt, burn·ing** **1** be consumed while giving off heat, light, and gases while on fire: *The campfire burned all night.* **2** go dry while being cooked, so that food turns crisp and black: *She forgot about the chicken and it burned to a crisp.* **3** cause to destroy, damage, or injure by fire, heat, radiation, acid, etc.: *to burn old papers. He burned his finger on the hot pan. That drain cleaner is so powerful it burned my hand.* **4** become sunburned: *I burn easily.* **5** use as fuel: *The stove burns wood or coal. Mom says our car burns too much gas. You burn calories even while asleep.* **6** make or produce by burning: *The candle fell and burned a hole in the carpet.* **7** shine by fire, electricity, oil, etc.: *Lamps were burning in every room.* **8** be or feel very hot: *the burning sands of the desert, burning with fever.* **9** have or produce a stinging sensation: *My hands were burning from the cold. That ointment burns.* **10** *Computers* prepare a CD so that it can it can be recorded on or read. **11** be or become very excited: *burning with enthusiasm, burning with resentment.* **12** *Informal* disappoint, hurt, or cheat: *He got burned trading in his old car.*
n **1** an injury or damage caused by fire, friction, acid, the sun, extreme cold, etc. On the skin, a **first-degree burn** causes pain and redness, a **second-degree burn** results in blisters, and a **third-degree burn** destroys skin: *How do you treat a burn? What made those burns on the rug?* **2** **prescribed burn** a fire deliberately set and controlled by forest management, to reduce fire hazards, keep insects in check, etc. Also called **controlled burn**. **3** *Space* a controlled firing of a rocket's engine to adjust course or position. **4** *Informal* a sensation of burning that occurs during strenuous exercise, and the positive psychological sensation associated with it: *Go for the burn!* <Old English *beornan*>

burn down, a burn to the ground: *The house burned down, but most of their possessions were saved.* **b** burn less strongly as fuel gets low: *Get more wood; the fire is beginning to burn down.*

burn off, a get rid of by burning or using up as fuel: *Go for a run to burn off some calories.* **b** use flame or acid to remove: *to burn off warts.*

burn out, a destroy the inside or contents of by burning: *The store was completely burned out, leaving just a shell.* **b** cease to burn: *The campfire had burned out and we were in darkness.* **c** wear out or exhaust through long service or hard use: *to burn out a motor. He burned himself out with worry and overwork.*

burn the candle at both ends, See CANDLE.

burn the midnight oil, See MIDNIGHT.

burn up, a burn completely: *By the time the police got there, the papers were burned up.* **b** *Informal* make angry or annoyed: *Her smug attitude really burns me up.*

burn your bridges (or **boats**), cut off all chance of retreat; make it impossible to change your mind: *It is wise to leave on good terms rather than burn your bridges with a bitter quarrel.*

burn your fingers or **get your fingers burned,** suffer from having interfered or been rash.

do a slow burn, have a hidden, steady anger.

have something to burn, have far more than enough of something: *She won the lottery and now has money to burn.*

GRAMMAR AND USAGE

The past tense and past participle of **burn** can be either **burned** or **burnt**.

Many people use **burned** for the verb: *He burned the firewood.* They use **burnt** when the participle is used as an adjective: *a burnt marshmallow.*

burn·er (bər′nər) *n* **1** the part of an object or appliance in which the flame or heat is produced. **2** any thing or part that burns or works by heat: *a charcoal burner.* **3** *Computers* usually, **CD burner** a computer device that prepares a CD so that it can be recorded on or read.
on the back burner, temporarily not part of activity or attention: *We'll keep that suggestion on the back burner while we deal with more urgent things.*

bur·nish (bər′nish) *v* polish; shine. <Old French *burnir* make brown, polish>

burn·out (bərn′out) *n* **1** mental and physical exhaustion due to overwork: *The volunteers were cautioned against burnout.* **2** a failure due to burning or overheating. **3** the stopping of a jet or rocket engine because the fuel has been either used up or shut off.

burnt (bərnt) a past tense and past participle of BURN[1].

burp (bərp) *v* **1** send out gas from the stomach through the mouth: *After drinking pop, I always have to burp.* **2** cause (a baby) to do this, by patting its back, etc.
n an instance of burping. <imitative>

burr[1] (bər) *n* **1** the prickly, clinging seed case, fruit husk, or flower of certain plants. **2** a rough ridge or edge left by a tool on a material after cutting or drilling it. **3** any of several kinds of cutting tool, such as a dentist's drill, with a rough head.
v remove burrs from. <probably Scandinavian>

burr[2] (bər) *n* **1** an accent in which *r* sounds are trilled: *a Scottish burr.* **2** a whirring sound. <imitative>

bur·ri·to (bə rē′tō) *n* a tortilla rolled around a filling of ground beef, beans, etc., often topped with melted cheese. <Spanish *burro* = young donkey>

bur·ro (bər′ō) *n* a kind of small, agile donkey. <Spanish, from Latin *burricus* small horse>

bur·row (bər′ō) *n* **1** a hole or tunnel dug in the ground by an animal for refuge or shelter: *Rabbits live in burrows.* **2** a dark or confined place like this, used as a refuge or shelter: *She made a burrow under her blankets.*
v **1** dig a hole or tunnel: *We burrowed through the snowbank at the end of the lane.* **2** hide; crawl into a dark, confined place: *The cat burrowed under the pile of dirty laundry.* **3** search with the hands: *He burrowed in his pockets for a dime.* <Middle English>

bur·sar (bər′sər) *n* a treasurer, especially of a college or university. <Latin *bursa* purse>

bur·sa·ry (bər′sərē) *n, pl* **bur·sa·ries** a grant of money to a college or university student.

bur·si·tis (bər sī′tis) *n* inflammation of a sac (**bursa**) of lubricating fluid located between the joints, usually in the hip or shoulder. <Latin, from Greek *byrsa* skin pouch>

burst (bərst) *v* **burst, burst·ing 1** break or cause to break open or fly apart suddenly and with force: *The balloon burst when it touched the light bulb. She burst the lock with a screwdriver.* **2** be as full as possible: *The granaries were bursting with grain.* **3** do something suddenly or violently: *to burst into a room, to burst into tears. The trees burst into bloom after the rain.* **4** suffer the bursting of: *He burst a blood vessel.*
n **1** a sudden display of activity or energy: *a burst of speed, a burst of laughter.* **2** a series of shots fired by one press of the trigger of an automatic weapon. <Old English *berstan*>

Bu·run·di (bə ru̇n′dē) *v* a country in central Africa. **Bu·run′di·an** *n, adj.*

bur·y (ber′ē) *or* (bər′ē) *v* **bur·ied, bur·y·ing 1** cover up with earth or some other material: *The dog buried its bone in the garden. We found the essay buried under a lot of papers.* **2** put a dead body in the earth, a tomb, or the sea. **3** hide from view: *He buried his face in his hands. The story was buried in the back pages of the newspaper.* **4** occupy oneself with great concentration: *She buried herself in her work.* **5** put out of mind: *They buried their differences and became friends.* <Old English *byrgan*> **bur′i·al** *n.*

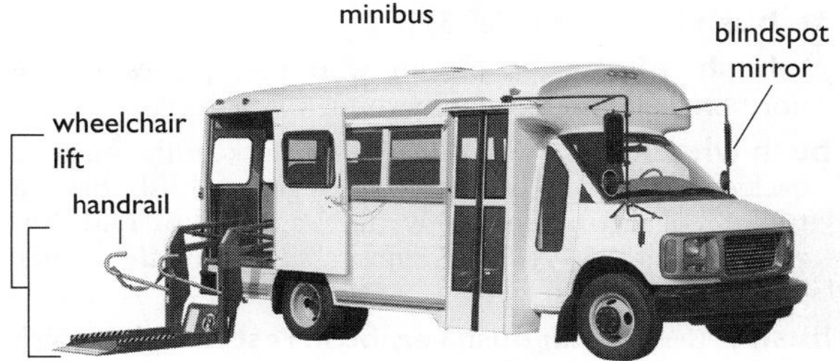

Buses can be specially equipped with lifts and other features to ensure that people who use wheelchairs have access to public transportation.

bus (bus) *n, pl* **bus·es** a large motor vehicle for carrying many passengers, often along a regular route.
v **bused, bus·ing 1** transport or travel by bus: *We were bused to the airport terminal.* **2** serve as a busboy. <short for *omnibus,* from French *voiture omnibus* = conveyance for the public>

bus·bar (bus′bȧr′) *n* an electrical conductor or set of conductors to which several circuits are connected.

bus·boy (bus′boi) *n* a server's assistant who clears tables.

bus·by (buz′bē) *n, pl* **bus·bies 1** a tall fur hat with a cloth bag hanging from the top over the right side, worn by hussar regiments. **2** BEARSKIN (def. 2). <origin uncertain>

bush (bu̇sh) *n* **1** a woody plant, usually smaller than a tree, with many separate branches starting at or near the ground. **2** forest, especially a forested wilderness. **3** 🍁 a tree-covered area on a farm: *They have a bush from which they get firewood.* Also called **bush lot**. **4** wild or uncultivated country.
v spread out like a bush; grow thickly. <Old Norse *buskr*>
beat around the bush, take a long time to get to the point: *Stop beating around the bush and tell me straight.*

bushed (bu̇sht) *Informal adj* **1** exhausted. **2** 🍁 acting strangely as a result of isolation in the wilderness.

a bat	e bed	i bid	o pot	u cup	th **th**in
ā cake	ē me	ī bite	ō go	ū rude	ŦH **th**en
ȧ bar	ə about	ər over	ȯ for	u̇ put	zh measure

bush·el (bu̇sh′əl) *n* a nonmetric unit of volume for grain, fruit, vegetables, and other dry things, equal to about 0.036 m^3. There are 32 quarts in a bushel. <Old French *boisse* a measure>

Bu·shi·do or **bu·shi·do** (bū′shē dō′) *or* (bū′shē dō′) *n* in medieval Japan, the moral code of the feudal knights and warriors; chivalry.

bush·ing (bu̇sh′ing) *n* a removable metal lining used to protect machine parts from wear. <Dutch *busse* box>

bush league *Informal n* **1** *Baseball* a minor league. **2** any second-rate group or organization: *Her brilliant performance in court shows that this lawyer is no longer in the bush league.* **bush leaguer** *n.*

✱ **bush line** *n* an airline that transports freight and passengers into the northern bush country and beyond.

✱ **bush lot** *n* BUSH (def. 3)

✱ **bush pilot** *n* a person who flies planes in the northern BUSH (def. 4) and beyond.

bush·whack (bu̇sh′wak′) *v* **1** live or work in the bush or backwoods. **2** hack one's way through the bush; blaze a trail. **3** engage in guerrilla warfare; ambush or raid: *The village had been bushwhacked several times.* **bush′whack′er** *n.*

bush·y (bu̇sh′ē) *adj* **bush·i·er, bush·i·est 1** with a thick growth: *a bushy beard.* **2** overgrown with bush; forested: *a bushy area.* **bush′i·ness** *n.*

busi·ness (biz′nis) *n* **1** activities of buying and selling goods or services for profit; trade; commerce. **2** a company or firm engaged in such activities: *a bakery business. They sold their business and retired last year.* **3** work: *A carpenter's business is building with wood. Business before pleasure!* **4** the right to act; responsibility: *It's not your business to decide what she should do. What is your business here?* **5** *Theatre* an incidental movement or action, such as bumping into furniture, by an actor to establish atmosphere, reveal character, etc. Also called **stage business**. **6** a matter; an affair: *That accident was a bad business.* <Middle English>

business as usual, the normal routines or attitudes, especially despite exceptional circumstances: *For pioneer women, it was business as usual the day after childbirth.*

mean business, be serious: *Don't argue; I mean business.*

mind your own business, avoid interfering in the affairs of others.

on business, travelling or present for the purpose of doing business: *My mom's in Vancouver on business.*

take care of business, *Informal* do whatever one finds necessary.

business college *n* an institution for high school graduates, giving training in business-related subjects, especially secretarial skills and office procedures.

busi·ness·like (biz′nis līk′) *adj* efficient, well-managed, and practical: *They pitched the tent in a businesslike manner.*

busi·ness·per·son (biz′nis pər′sən) *n,* *pl* **busi·ness·peo·ple** (biz′nis pē′pəl) a person who makes a living through commerce. Also, **businessman** or **businesswoman**.

busk·er (bus′kər) *n* a person who plays music, does tricks, or provides other entertainment for passersby on the street, in a subway station, etc. <perhaps Spanish *buscar* look for (money)> **busk′ing** *n.*

bus·man's holiday (bus′mənz) *n* a holiday spent doing something similar to what one does at work, as when a letter carrier goes for a walk on his or her day off.

buss (bus) *Informal n, v* kiss. <probably from Gaelic *bus*>

bus shelter *n* a shelter in which to wait for the bus.

bust[1] (bust) *n* **1** a piece of sculpture representing a person's head, shoulders, and chest. **2** the breasts of a woman. **3** the measurement around a woman's body at the level of the breasts. <French, from Latin *bustum* funeral ornament>

bust[2] (bust) *Informal v* **1** break: *Don't bust my watch.* **2** make or become bankrupt. **3** punch or hit: *He busted me on the nose.* **4** arrest: *She was busted for armed robbery.* **5** reduce to a lower rank: *He was busted to private.*
n **1** *Informal* a total failure: *The show was a complete bust.* **2** a punch: *I gave him a bust on the arm.*
<variant of *burst*>

go bust, *Slang* become bankrupt.

–buster *Informal combining form* one that defeats, destroys, or removes: *dustbuster.* **-busting** *adj, n.*

bus·tle[1] (bus′əl) *v* **bus·tled, bus·tling 1** move around busily and hurriedly. **2** make others hurry or get busy.
n busy, energetic, or noisy activity: *There was a great bustle as we got ready for the party.* <Middle English>

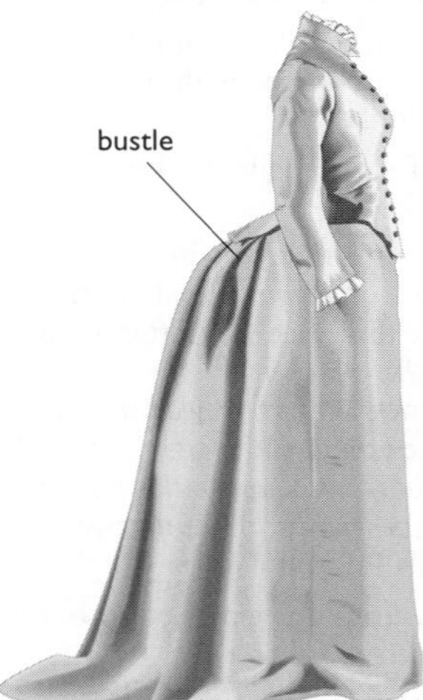

A Victorian fashion, **bustles** first became popular in 1870 and again in 1883. They were made of whalebone or steel strips and inserted in the back of the petticoat at the waist. An overskirt was then draped elaborately over the frame.

bus·tle[2] (bus′əl) *n* in former times, a padded framework worn under the upper back part of a woman's skirt to puff it out. <possibly special use of *bustle*[1]>

bus·y (biz′ē) *adj* **bus·i·er, bus·i·est 1** working or active: *I'm busy making supper.* **2** working or active most of the time; with little free or quiet time: *He's such a busy person that we rarely see him.* **3** in use: *I tried to phone her but her line was busy.* **4** full of work or activity: *a busy day, a busy street.* **5** very detailed or ornate: *a busy wallpaper pattern.*
v **bus·ied, bus·y·ing** make or keep busy: *The children busied themselves making valentines.* <Old English *bisig*> **bus′i·ly** *adv.*

bus·y·bod·y (biz′ē bod′ē) *or* (biz′ē bud′ē) *n, pl* **bus·y·bod·ies** a person who pries into other people's affairs; a meddler.

bus·y·work (biz′ē wərk′) *n* work done or given merely to fill time or look busy.

but (but) *conj* **1** however, yet, or still: *It rained, but I went anyway.* **2** on the contrary: *He is not snobbish but merely shy.* **3** used to indicate surprise or anger: *But I want to go too!* **4** used as part of an apology: *I'm sorry, but I don't agree with you.* **5** without something else also happening: *It never rains but it pours.* **6** *Informal* that: *I don't doubt but she'll be on time.*
prep other than: *No one knows it but me.*
adv only or merely: *He is but a boy.*
n an objection: *No buts! Just do as you're told!* <Old English *butan* without, unless>
all but, nearly or almost: *The book was all but finished when the author died.*

bu·ta·di·ene (byū′tə dī′ēn) *n* a colourless, flammable gas obtained from petroleum, used in making synthetic rubber. <*butane*>

bu·tane (byū′tān) *n* a colourless, flammable gas obtained from natural gas or petroleum, used as a fuel. <*but(yl)* + *ane*, from *butyric acid*, a by-product of rancid butter>

butch·er (bu̇ch′ər) *n* **1** a person whose work is killing animals to be sold for food, or who cuts up and sells meat. **2** a brutal killer or murderer.
v **1** kill or cut up killed animals for food. **2** kill savagely: *Many villagers were butchered in the raid.* **3** spoil; ruin: *He butchered the song by singing it much too loudly.* <Old French *boc*> **butch′er·y** *n.*

bu·te·o (byū′tē ō) *n* a hawk with a thickset body, broad wings, and a short, broad tail. <Latin>

but·ler (but′lər) *n* the chief male servant of a household. <Old French *bouteille* wine bottle; originally the butler was in charge of the wine>

but·su·dan (būt sū dȧn′) *Buddhism n* **1** the altar in a temple upon which statues are enshrined. **2** a household shrine containing statues, pictures, and memorial tablets of family ancestors.

butt[1] (but) *n* **1** the thicker end of anything: *the butt of a rifle.* **2** the end that is left; a stub or stump: *the butt of a cigarette.* **3** *Informal* the buttocks. **4** *Informal* an unsmoked cigarette.
v join end to end.
butt out, *Informal* **a** extinguish a cigarette. **b** stop smoking permanently.

ETYMOLOGY

Butt[1], **butt**[2], and **butt**[3] are all from different Old French words which are similar, but have different meanings.

Butt[1] is from *bout*, meaning "end."

Butt[2] is from *but*, meaning "goal."

Butt[3] is from *bouter*, meaning "thrust."

butt[2] (but) *n* **1** a target or the mound on which it is set. **2** an object of ridicule or scorn: *She was the butt of their jokes.* **3 butts** *pl Shooting, Archery* a place with targets for shooting practice; a shooting range.

butt[3] (but) *v* strike or push by knocking hard with the head.
n a push or blow with the head.
butt in, *Informal* meddle; interfere.
butt out, *Informal* stop interfering.

🍁 **butte** (byūt) *n* a steep, often flat-topped hill standing alone. Buttes are common in southern Alberta. See DESERT for picture. <French>

but·ter (but′ər) *n* **1** the solid, yellowish fat obtained by churning cream or whole milk, used in cooking or as a spread. **2** something like butter in consistency or use: *peanut butter, apple butter.*
v put butter on. <Latin *butyrum*, from Greek *boutyron*>
but′ter·less *adj.*
butter up, *Informal* flatter, especially in order to get something.

butt·er·cup (but′ər kup′) *n* a wildflower found especially in meadows and damp places, with yellow flowers.

but·ter·fat (but′ər fat′) *n* the fatty content of milk, from which butter is made.

but·ter·fin·gers (but′ər fing′gərz) *Informal n* a clumsy person who drops things: *Don't let her handle the china; she's a real butterfingers.* **but′ter·fin′gered** *adj.*

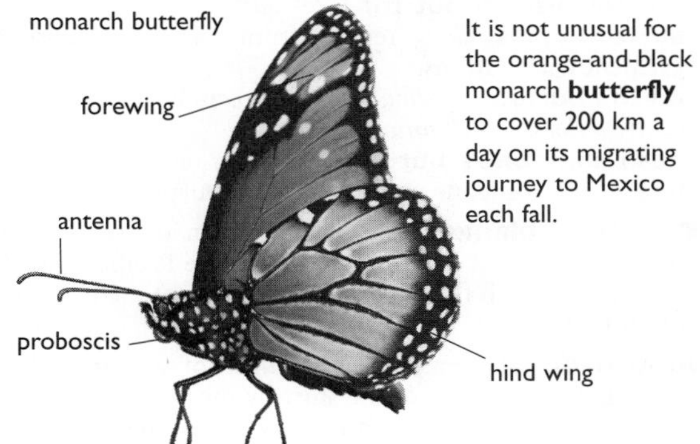

It is not unusual for the orange-and-black monarch **butterfly** to cover 200 km a day on its migrating journey to Mexico each fall.

but·ter·fly (but′ər flī′) *n, pl* **but·ter·flies** **1** an insect with a slender body and four large, often brightly coloured wings. **2** a person who flits from one thing to another. **3** a swimming stroke performed face down, in which the outstretched arms move together in a circular motion while the legs kick up and down together. **4** *Hockey* a defensive move in which the goalie drops to the knees and angles the legs out to either side, blocking the net. **5 butterflies** *pl* a queasy feeling in the stomach caused by nervous anxiety about something that is to happen: *I get butterflies just thinking about speaking in front of all those people.* **6** the butterfly-shaped metal clasp securing the post of an earring in a pierced ear. **7** a wing nut.

a bat	e bed	i bid	o pot	u cup	th **thin**
ā cake	ē me	ī bite	ō go	ū rude	ᴛʜ **then**
ȧ bar	ə about	ər over	ȯ for	u̇ put	zh measure

but·ter·milk (but′ər milk′) *n* the sour, fat-free liquid left after butter has been churned from cream.

but·ter·nut (but′ər nut′) *n* an oily kind of edible walnut grown in N America, or the tree it grows on.

butternut squash *n* a winter squash with orange skin and pulp, eaten as a vegetable.

but·ter·scotch (but′ər skoch′) *n* **1** a candy or syrup made from brown sugar and butter. **2** a flavouring that imitates this.

butter tart *n* a rich, sweet tart with a runny or firm filling made from butter, brown sugar, raisins, etc.

but·tock (but′ək) *n* usually, **buttocks** *pl* the fleshy part at the back of the body where the legs join the back. <Old English *buttuc* end>

but·ton (but′ən) *n* **1** a small knob or disc attached to fabric and serving as a fastening when passed through a specially made slit or loop. **2** a knob or small disc that is pushed or turned to open or close an electric circuit: *Push that button to start the machine.* **3** a badge with a slogan or logo printed on it and a pin at the back for attaching it to clothing. **4** *Computers* **a** an icon, dialogue box option, or other graphic that a user clicks in order to designate, cancel, confirm, etc. an action. **b** a small BANNER (def. 4). **5** anything resembling a button, such as the knob on the end of a fencing foil.
v close or fasten with buttons. <Old French *bouter*>
but′ton·less *adj.* **but′ton·like′** *adj.*
button up, a *Slang* refrain from talking. **b** close a garment with buttons.
on the button, *Informal* exactly; precisely: *She was there at five o'clock on the button.*
push someone's buttons, *Slang* do or say the things that irritate someone most, usually on purpose.

button blanket *n* a blanket worn on ceremonial occasions by First Nations peoples of the Pacific coast. It is decorated with figures or family crests outlined by rows of buttons.

but·ton–down (but′ən doun′) *adj* **1** of a shirt collar, fastening to the body of the shirt by means of buttons at the collar tips. **2** conventional and unimaginative: *a button-down mind.*

but·ton·hole (but′ən hōl′) *n* the slit through which a button is passed in fastening something.
v **but·ton·holed, but·ton·hol·ing 1** make or finish buttonholes in. **2** force someone to listen, as if by holding him or her by the buttonhole of the coat: *A man doing a survey buttonholed me in the street.* **but′ton·hol′er** *n.*

but·tress (but′ris) *n* **1** a structure built against a wall or building to strengthen or support it. **2** any support; a prop: *The experience was a buttress to her confidence.*
v **1** support with a buttress. **2** support and strengthen; bolster: *an argument buttressed by statistical data.* <Old French *bouter*>

bux·om (buk′səm) *adj* of a woman, plump and full-bosomed. <Old English *bugan* curve>

buy (bī) *v* **bought, buy·ing 1** get in exchange for money or, sometimes, for goods or services: *You can buy a pencil for 50 cents. You can't buy happiness.* **2** shop: *I won't buy there anymore.* **3** bribe: *The prosecution claimed that two jury members had been bought.* **4** *Informal* accept; believe: *I don't buy that excuse!*
n Informal something bought, especially at a bargain: *That book was a real buy.* <Old English *bycgan*>
buy off, get rid of by paying money to.
buy out, buy all parts of a business.
buy time, stall or delay in hopes of gaining an advantage.
buy up, buy all there is of.

CONFUSABLES

Buy is a verb that means "purchase": *Tomorrow I will buy a birthday present for my friend.*

By is a preposition that often means "beside": *You left your shoes by the back door.*

buy·er (bī′ər) *n* **1** a person who buys. **2** a person whose job is to buy goods for a business or organization.

buyer's market *n* an economic situation in which the buyer has the advantage because goods are plentiful and prices tend to be low. Compare SELLER'S MARKET.

buy·out (bī′out′) *n* the purchase of a company by its employees, by a partner or shareholder, by a larger company or creditor, etc.

buzz (buz) *n* **1** a humming sound made by flies, mosquitoes, or bees. **2** a low, indistinct, murmuring sound of many people talking quietly: *The buzz of conversation stopped when she entered the room.* **3** a state of high excitement or activity. **4** *Informal* news; rumour: *The buzz is that the vice-principal is retiring.* **5** *Slang* a slight euphoric effect: *She gets a buzz from eating licorice.* **6** *Informal* a telephone call: *I'll give you a buzz tonight.* **7** in full, **buzz cut** *Slang* a very short haircut, usually done with clippers.
v **1** make a humming or indistinct murmuring sound: *This radio buzzes when you turn it on.* **2** be full of talk or activity: *The whole room buzzed with excitement.* **3** approach quickly and closely with an aircraft or a small boat: *A pilot buzzed our school yesterday.* **4** signal by pressing a buzzer: *She buzzed her assistant.* **5** *Informal* to telephone: *I'll buzz you when I find out.* **6** *Slang* give a short haircut to. <imitative>
buzz off, *Informal* go away.

Buzzards rarely hunt when they are on the move because they are slow fliers. Instead, they perch motionless on a branch of a large tree and wait for a mouse or a rabbit to pass beneath. They then swoop down and pick up the prey.

buz·zard (buz′ərd) *n* a bird of prey, usually with broad wings and a soaring flight. <Old French, from Latin *buteo* hawk>

buzz·er (buz′ər) *n* an electrical device that makes a buzzing sound as a signal, or the sound it makes: *At the buzzer, they all rushed from the room.*

buzz saw *n* a circular saw.

buzz·word (buz′wərd′) *n* a trendy piece of jargon.

by (bī) *prep* **1** beside: *Sit here by me.* **2** through the action or means of: *The thief was captured by a police officer. We travelled by train.* **3** along, over, or through: *to go by the bridge.* **4** according to: *to play by the rules.* **5** not later than: *Be there by noon.* **6** in units of: *Eggs are sold by the dozen.* **7** during: *to travel by night.* **8** to the extent of: *Your room is larger than mine by half.* **9** combined with in multiplication or dimensions: *a room 4 m by 8 m.* **10** taken as separate units or groups in a series: *two by two. Algebra must be mastered step by step.* **11** in relation to: *She did well by her children.* See BUY for confusable.
adv **1** at hand: *close by.* **2** past: *A car dashed by. Years went by.* **3** aside or away: *I'll put the leftover food by for later.* <Old English *bi*>
by and by, after a while: *You'll feel better by and by.*
by and large, in general: *It has some faults, but by and large it is a good book.*
by the by, incidentally.
by the way, a incidentally; aside from the main point: *By the way, I still haven't found that book you mentioned.* **b** at the side of the road or path: *We stopped by the way to eat.*
by yourself, (*often preceded by* ***all***) without others or without help: *He was sitting in a room by himself. My little sister can read all by herself.*

by– *prefix* **1** secondary; on the side; less important: *by-product.* **2** nearby: *bystander.*

by–and–by (bī′ən bī′) *n* the future.

bye[1] (bī) *n* **1** *Sports* **a** the position of the odd player or team that does not play in a round involving pairs. **b** the player or team not required to play a round. **2** *Golf* the holes not played after one player has won. **3** *Cricket* a run made on a missed ball. <variant of *by*>

bye[2] or **'bye** (bī) *Informal interj* goodbye. Also, **bye-bye**.

by–e·lec·tion (bī′ ə lek′shən) *n* an election held in a single riding because of the death or resignation of its Member of Parliament or legislative body.

by·gone (bī′gon′) *adj* past or former: *in bygone days.*
n something in the past.
let bygones be bygones, let the past be forgotten.

by·law (bī′lo′) *n* **1** a law made by a municipality, company, or organization for the control of its own affairs: *Our city has bylaws to control parking, traffic, and building practices.* **2** a secondary law or rule, not one of the main rules.

by·line (bī′līn′) *n* a line at the beginning or end of a newspaper or magazine article giving the name of the writer.

by·pass (bī′pas′) *n* **1** a road or other passage leading off the main route, around some obstruction, and back to the main route: *Drivers use the bypass when there is a lot of traffic.* **2** *Medicine* a surgical operation in which a section of blood vessel is grafted onto a blocked one, usually a coronary artery, to carry blood around the obstruction. **3** *Electricity* a shunt.
v **1** go around: *to bypass a city.* **2** skip, set aside, or ignore; not bother with: *to bypass regulations. He bypassed the sales manager and took his complaint straight to the president.*

by–prod·uct (bī′prod′əkt) *n* **1** something useful that is produced in making or doing another thing: *Kerosene is a by-product of petroleum refining.* **2** a side effect: *One by-product of civilization is pollution.*

byre (bīr) *n* a shed for sheltering cows.

by·road (bī′rōd′) *n* a secondary road; a side road.

by·stand·er (bī′stan′dər) *n* a person who stands near or looks on but does not take part.

byte (bīt) *Computers n* a unit of computer memory equal to eight bits or binary digits (see BIT[4]). One keyboard character takes one byte of memory. <probably a blend of *bit*[4] and *bite*>

by·way (bī′wā′) *n* a side path or road, not much used.

by·word (bī′wərd′) *n* **1** a common saying; a proverb. **2** a person or thing taken as representing a certain characteristic, especially an unfavourable one: *The courts were a byword for corruption.* **3** an object of scorn or contempt: *The bully had become a byword throughout the school.*

Byz·an·tine (biz′ən tēn′) *or* (bi zan′tin) *adj* to do with **Byzantium** (bi zan′tē əm), an ancient city on the site of present-day Istanbul, or a style of art or architecture developed there. Byzantine architecture uses round arches, crosses, circles, domes, and mosaics.

Cc

c or **C** (sē) *n, pl* **c's** or **C's** **1** the third letter of the English alphabet, or any speech sound represented by it. **2** the third thing in a list or series: *I understood the first two sections, but Part C was not so easy.* **3** *Music* the first tone in the scale of C major, or a key based on a scale with C as its keynote. **4** a grade that rates a person or thing as average: *I got a C on the test.* **5** the Roman numeral for 100.

c **1** centi- (an SI prefix). **2** cent(s). Also, **¢**. **3** approximately (for Latin *circa*). Also, **ca.** **4** *Sports* catcher. **5** copyright. Also, ©. **6** century.

C **1** Celsius. **2** carbon. **3** coulomb(s).

cab (kab) *n* **1** a taxi. **2** in former times, a horse-drawn carriage hired with a driver. **3** the driver's compartment on a truck, bus, or train. <shortened from *cabriolet*>

ca·bal (kə bal′) *n* a small group of people working or plotting in secret. <French *cabale*, from Hebrew *qaballah* secret tradition>

cab·al·le·ro (kab′ə ler′ō) *or* (kab′əl yer′ō) *n* a Spanish gentleman. <Spanish, from Latin *caballus* horse>

ca·ba·na (kə ban′ə) *n* a shelter for changing clothes or for shade on the beach or at a swimming pool. <Spanish, from Latin *capana* cabin>

cab·a·ret (kab′ə rā′) *n* a restaurant or nightclub where entertainment is performed, or the entertainment itself. <Old French = wooden structure>

cab·bage (kab′ij) *n* a plant related to broccoli and cauliflower, eaten as a vegetable. It has large leaves folded into a compact head. <Old French *caboce*, from Latin *caput* head>

cab·in (kab′ən) *n* **1** a small, roughly built house. **2** a room for passengers or crew in a ship, boat, or aircraft. <Old French, from Latin *capanna*>

cabin crew *n* aircraft crew who attend to passengers.

cab·i·net (kab′ə nit) *n* **1** an upright piece of furniture, sometimes attached to a wall, with shelves or drawers to store or display things: *a china cabinet, a medicine cabinet.* **2** an upright case holding a radio, TV, or other electronic equipment. **3** a group of senior ministers who advise the head of a government. **4** 🍁 **Cabinet a** an executive committee of the Federal Government, chosen by the prime minister from members of the majority party in the House of Commons. **b** a similar committee of a provincial government or territory. <*cabin*>

cab·i·net·mak·er (kab′ə nit mā′kər) *n* a person skilled in making fine wooden furniture. **cab′i·net·mak′ing** *n.*

cabinet minister *n* in certain countries, including Canada, the head of a government department and member of the cabinet.

🍁 **cabin fever** *n* depression, restlessness, or irritability resulting from long isolation and confinement, such as may occur in the Far North toward the end of the long, dark winter.

ca·ble (kā′bəl) *n* **1** a strong, thick rope, usually made of wires twisted together. **2** a bundle of insulated electric wires bound together in one casing: *The cable between the telephone pole and the house has come down.* See COAXIAL CABLE for picture. **3** *Informal* cable television. **4** in former times, a telegram sent by means of a cable under the ocean. *v* **ca·bled, ca·bling** send a message or signal by cable. <Old French, from Latin *capulum* rope>

cable car *n* a passenger car that is pulled by a moving cable operated by a motor, usually up and down a steep hill.

cable television *n* a system by which signals from various TV stations are picked up by a central antenna and sent by cables to subscribers. Also, **cable TV**. *Abbrev.* **CATV**

ca·boo·dle (kə bū′dəl) *Informal n* a crowd; a pack; a lot. <Dutch *boedel* possessions>
the whole (kit and) caboodle, everything or everyone.

The observation windows on the top of a **caboose** were designed to help train crews see along the length of the train to look for safety problems.

With advances in technology, railways now have more sophisticated ways to monitor safety, and many railway companies no longer use the caboose.

ca·boose (kə būs′) *n* **1** a small car on a freight train, usually at the end, where a train crew can work, eat, and sleep. **2** 🍁 *especially North* a cabin or a loggers' bunkhouse or cookhouse, pulled along on runners. <Dutch *kabuis* hut, cabin>

cab·ri·o·let (kab′rē ə lā′) *n* **1** a small car with a folding top. **2** a light two-wheeled carriage, often with a folding top, drawn by one horse. <French *cabrioler* leap (from its bouncing motion)>

ca·ca·o (kə kā′ō) *or* (kə kȧ′ō) *n* a tropical American evergreen tree whose seeds (called **cacao beans** or **cocoa beans**) are processed into chocolate, cocoa, and cocoa butter. <Spanish, from Nahuatl (a language of Central and S America) *cacauna*>

cache (kash) *n* **1 a** a hiding place for storing valuable items, provisions, or ammunition. **b** 🍁 a place for storing supplies away from foraging animals and the weather. In the North, a cache is usually a structure built on poles. **3** the things hidden or stored in a cache: *We found a cache of acorns in the hollow tree.* **3** *Computers* a section of computer memory where frequently used instructions or data are stored for speedy retrieval.
v **cached, cach·ing** **1** deposit in a cache. **2** deposit or hold in a cache. <French *cacher* to hide>

ca·chet (ka shā′) *n* **1** a distinguishing mark. **2** stylish distinction or prestige: *These no-name jeans don't have the cachet of the designer brands.* <French>

cack·le (kak′əl) *v* **cack·led, cack·ling** 1 of a hen, make a harsh, broken sound, especially after laying an egg. 2 laugh or talk with shrill or harsh sound.
n a cackling sound. <Middle English *cakelen*>

ca·coph·o·ny (kə kof′ə nē) *n, pl* **ca·coph·o·nies** a mixture of harsh, clashing sounds. <Latin, from Greek *kakos* bad + *phone* sound> **ca·coph′o·nous** *adj.*

cac·tus (kak′təs) *n, pl* **cac·tus·es** or **cac·ti** (kak′tī) *or* (kak′tē) a plant of hot, dry regions, with a thick fleshy stem and spines, but no leaves. <Latin, from Greek *kaktos*>

cad (kad) *n* a man who behaves badly, especially toward a woman. <from *caddie*> **cad′dish** *adj.*

CAD computer-aided (or -assisted) design.

ca·dav·er (kə dav′ər) *n* a dead body, especially a human body to be dissected for scientific study. <Latin> **ca·dav′er·ous** *adj.*

🍁 **Cad·bo·ro·saur·us** (kad′bə rə sȯ′rəs) *n* a sea monster supposed to live in the waters off Victoria, B.C. Its nickname is **Caddy**. <*Cadboro* Bay>

cad·die or **cad·dy** (kad′ē) *Golf n* a person who helps a player by carrying the clubs, and provides advice and other assistance.
v **cad·died, cad·dy·ing** help a player in this way: *I caddy for my dad sometimes.* <French *cadet* younger son>

cad·dis fly (kad′is) *n* a mothlike insect whose larva, the **caddis worm**, lives under water in a case made of sand, bits of leaves, and other particles. <origin uncertain>

cad·dy (kad′ē) *n, pl* **cad·dies** a small box, often used to hold tea. <Malay *kati* a small unit of weight>

ca·dence (kā′dəns) *n* 1 a rhythmic rise and fall of sounds, especially the voice: *She speaks with a pleasant cadence.* 2 *Music* a sequence of notes or chords that close a passage or composition. <Old French, from Latin *cadere* to fall>

ca·den·za (kə den′zə) *Music n* an elaborate passage for an unaccompanied voice or solo instrument. <Italian = conclusion of a movement in music>

ca·det (kə det′) *n* 1 a person training to be an officer in the armed forces or police force. 2 an adolescent undergoing basic military training in an organization associated with the armed forces: *I am joining the air cadets next year.* <French = younger son, from Latin *capitellum* small head. In former times, officers in the French army were younger sons.> **ca·det′ship** *n.*

cad·mi·um (kad′mē əm) *n* a soft, bluish white metallic element resembling tin, used in making certain alloys and in plating to prevent rust. *Symbol* **Cd** <Latin, from Greek *kadmeia* zinc ore (a source of cadmium)>

ca·dre (kä′drā) *or* (kad′rā) *n* a group of people forming the core of an organization. <French, from Latin *quadrus* square>

cae·cum (sē′kəm) *n, pl* **cae·ca** (sē′kə) the large pouch, closed at one end, that forms the beginning of the large intestine. Also, **cecum**. <Latin = blind (thing), because of its closed end>

Cae·sar (sē′zer) *n* a title of the Roman emperors from Augustus to Hadrian. <Julius *Caesar*, a leading Roman statesmen>

Cae·sar·e·an (si zer′ē ən) *or* (si zar′ē ən) *n* in full, **Caesarean section** a method of delivering a baby by cutting through the wall of the mother's abdomen.
adj 1 done by Caesarian section: *a Caesarean delivery.* 2 to do with Julius Caesar or the Caesars. Also, **Caesarian**. <Julius *Caesar* was allegedly born this way>

C

cae·si·um (sē′zē əm) CESIUM.

cae·sur·a (si zyü′rə) *or* (si zhü′rə) *Poetry n* a pause at or near the middle of a line of poetry. <Latin *caedere* to cut>

ca·fé (ka fā′) *n* a small, informal restaurant selling drinks and light meals. <French>

café au lait (ka fā′ō lā′) *n* coffee made with hot milk. <French = coffee with milk>

caf·e·te·ri·a (kaf′e tē′rē ə) *n* a restaurant, such as in a school, store, or other institution, where people serve themselves or are served at a counter and then carry their meals to tables to eat. <Mexican Spanish = coffee shop>

caf·feine (kaf ēn′) *n* a stimulating drug found in coffee, tea, chocolate, and cola. <French *café* coffee>

Caftans were popular with both men and women in Western countries during the mid 1960s. The westernized versions were usually made of brightly coloured cotton or silk.

caf·tan (kaf′tən) *n* 1 a loose, ankle-length garment, worn especially in Middle Eastern Mediterranean countries. 2 a similar garment worn in western countries for lounging or recreation. Also, **kaftan**. <Turkish, from Persian *kaftan*>

cage (kāj) *n* 1 a frame or box closed in with wires or bars, such as for keeping a bird or animal in: *We keep our canary in a cage.* 2 something shaped or used like a cage, such as a prison cell or the platform of a mine elevator.
v **caged, cag·ing** put or keep in a cage. <Old French, from Latin *cavea* cell>
rattle someone's cage, *Informal* provoke someone.

cage·y (kā′jē) *adj* **cag·i·er, cag·i·est** 1 *Informal* shrewd: *a cagey lawyer.* 2 cautious; wary: *She was too cagey to commit herself completely.* **cag′i·ly** *adv.* **cag′i·ness** *n.*

a bat	e bed	i bid	o pot	u cup	th thin
ā cake	ē me	ī bite	ō go	ü rude	ᴛʜ then
ä bar	ə about	ər over	ȯ for	u̇ put	zh measure

ca·hoots (kə hūts′) <origin uncertain>
in cahoots, *Informal* involved in a secret plot: *The bank teller was in cahoots with the thief.*

cai·man (kā′mən) CAYMAN.

cairn (kern) *n* a pile of stones heaped up as a memorial, tomb, or landmark. <Scots Gaelic *carn* heap of stones>

🍁 **caisse pop·u·laire** (kes pop′yə ler′) *n* especially in Québec, a credit union. Also, **caisse**. <Cdn. French>

cais·son (kā′son) *or* (kā′sən) *n* a watertight chamber in which construction work may be carried out under water. <French, from Italian *cassone*>

ca·jole (kə jōl′) *v* **ca·joled, ca·jol·ing** persuade by flattery; coax: *His older sister cajoled him into cutting the lawn.* <French *cajoler*> **ca·jol′er·y** *n.*

Ca·jun (kā′jən) *n* a native or inhabitant of a French-speaking area of Louisiana, descended from French settlers of Acadia (now the Maritimes) who were deported by the British in 1763.
adj to do with the Cajuns or their culture, including their language, music, and cuisine. <*Acadian*>

cake (kāk) *n* **1** a baked dessert made from a mixture of flour, sugar, eggs, flavouring, and other ingredients: *a sponge cake, a fruit cake.* **2** a batter that has been fried or baked in a small, flat, usually round shape: *buckwheat cakes.* **3** a small, flat mass of food fried or baked on both sides: *a fish cake.* **4** a solid, shaped mass: *a cake of soap.*
v **caked, cak·ing** dry, harden, and form into a crust: *Mud cakes as it dries.* <Old Norse *kaka*>
have your cake and eat it (too), have two desirable but mutually exclusive things.
piece of cake, *Informal* something easy: *This so-called brainteaser is a piece of cake!*
take the cake, *Informal* be the last or greatest in a series of disappointments or surprises.

cake·walk (kāk′wok′) *n* **1** in former times, among blacks in the US, a strutting dance, with a prize of a cake for the best or most original steps, or the music for it. **2** something easy to do or succeed at: *This election was a cakewalk.*
v do a cakewalk.

cal·a·bash (kal′ə bash′) *n* a large tropical gourd whose dried shell is used to make hollow objects. <French, from Spanish *calabaza*>

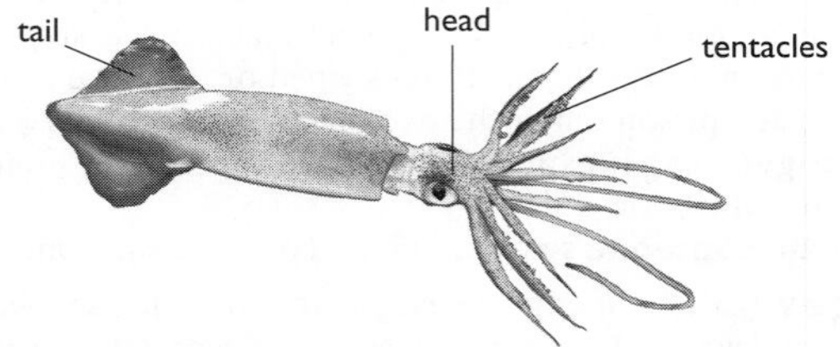

Calamari, or squid, range in size from 2.5 cm to 24 m. Those served as food, however, are usually between 15 and 30 cm long.

cal·a·ma·ri (kal′ə mä′rē) *n* squid served as food. <Italian, from Greek *kalamos*>

cal·a·mine (kal′ə mīn′) *n* a pink powder consisting mainly of ZINC OXIDE, used in skin lotions and ointments. <Old French, from Greek *kadmeia*>

ca·lam·i·ty (kə lam′ə tē) *n, pl* **ca·lam·i·ties** serious trouble or misfortune: *floods, plane crashes, and other calamities. Calamity may happen to anyone.* <French, from Latin *calamitas*> **ca·lam′i·tous** *adj.*

cal·car·e·ous (kal ker′ē əs) *adj* to do with or containing lime, limestone, or calcium.

ETYMOLOGY

Calcareous is one of several closely related words that can be traced back to Latin *calcis*, meaning "lime" or "limestone." Other related words include *calcify*, *calcine*, *calcite*, and *calcium*.

Chalk comes from the same root, but, as a less scientific word, it comes by way of Old English *cealc*.

cal·ci·fy (kal′sə fī′) *v* **cal·ci·fied, cal·ci·fy·ing** make or become hard by the deposit of lime. <See CALCIUM.> **cal′ci·fi·ca′tion** *n.*

cal·cine (kal′sīn) *v* **cal·cined, cal·cin·ing** heat an inorganic substance in order to reduce, dry, or oxidize it. **cal′ci·na′tion** *n.*

cal·cite (kal′sīt) *n* calcium carbonate.

cal·ci·um (kal′sē əm) *n* a soft, silvery white metallic element that is found in chalk, limestone, milk, and bone. *Symbol* **Ca** <Latin *calcis* lime>

calcium carbide *n* a heavy, grey crystalline compound that reacts with water to form acetylene gas.

calcium carbonate *n* a mineral occurring in rocks as marble and limestone, and as shells and stony corals.

calcium chloride *n* an absorbent compound of calcium and chlorine.

calcium hydroxide *n* a compound produced by the action of water on lime.

cal·cu·late (kal′kyə lāt′) *v* **cal·cu·lat·ed, cal·cu·lat·ing** **1** figure out by adding, subtracting, multiplying, or dividing: *to calculate the cost of the school trip to the theatre.* **2** figure out by any process of reasoning: *Calculate the day of the week on which your birthday will fall.* **3** plan or intend: *That remark was calculated to hurt my feelings.* <Latin *calculus* pebble for counting> **cal′cu·la·ble** *adj.* **cal′cu·la′tion** *n.*
calculate on, estimate or expect: *We calculated on ten guests, but only two arrived.*

cal·cu·lat·ed (kal′kyə lā′tid) *adj* **1** deliberate or conscious: *a calculated insult.* **2** arrived at by calculation: *How close was your estimate to the calculated total?*

cal·cu·lat·ing (kal′kyə lā′ting) *adj* cunning and scheming for personal advantage.

cal·cu·la·tor (kal′kyə lā′tər) *n* a device that performs mathematical calculations mechanically or electronically.

cal·cu·lus (kal′kyə ləs) *n, pl* (*def. 2*) **cal·cu·li** (kal′kyə lī′) *or* (kal′kyə lē′) **1** *Mathematics* a method of reasoning using a specialized system of notation. The two main types are differential calculus and integral calculus. 2 *Medicine* a stone or hard mass formed in the body. 3 *Dentistry* tartar.

> **ETYMOLOGY**
>
> **Calculus** is a Latin word meaning "pebble." People once used pebbles for counting on a device called an abacus. An abacus is a frame with rows of counters (pebbles, stones, or beads) that slide back and forth in grooves or on wires. You can perform calculations by moving the counters.

ca·lèche (kə lesh′) *n* a light, two-wheeled, one-horse carriage for two passengers, with a seat in front for the driver and, usually, a folding top: *In Québec City, we rode in a calèche.* <French, from Polish *kolo* wheel>

cal·en·dar (kal′ən dər) *n* **1** a chart dividing each month of the year into weeks and days, showing what day of the week each numbered day of the month falls on. **2** a system by which years are numbered and the beginning, length, and divisions of the year are fixed: *A lunar calendar has thirteen months. Most countries now use the Gregorian calendar.* **3** a schedule or other ordered list: *The trial had to be delayed; the court calendar was full.* **4** an annual booklet issued by a college or university listing its rules, courses offered, and other information. <Old French, from Latin *calendae* calends (the day bills were due)>

calendar day *n* the 24 hours from one midnight to the next midnight.

calendar month *n* one of the twelve named parts into which a year is divided.

calendar year *n* a period of 365 days (or in leap year, 366 days) that begins January 1 and ends December 31.

cal·en·der (kal′ən dər) *n* a machine in which cloth or paper is pressed between rollers to smooth and glaze it.
v make smooth and glossy by pressing in a calender. <French *calendre*, from Greek *kylindros* cylinder>

calf[1] (kaf) *n, pl* **calves** (kavz) **1** the young of the domestic cow or of a related animal such as the buffalo. **2** the young of a large mammal, such as the elephant, whale, seal, rhinoceros, deer, or antelope. <Old English *cælf*>

calf[2] (kaf) *n, pl* **calves** (kavz) the thick, fleshy part of the back of the leg, below the knee. <Old Norse *kalfi*>

calf·skin (kaf′skin′) *n* leather made from the skin of a calf.

cal·i·brate (kal′ə brāt′) *v* **cal·i·brat·ed, cal·i·brat·ing** check or adjust the scale of a thermometer or other measuring instrument by comparing it with a standard scale. <See CALIBRE.>**cal′i·bra′tion** *n.* **cal′i·bra′tor** *n.*

cal·i·bre (kal′ə bər) *n* **1** diameter, especially the inside diameter of a tube such as a gun barrel. **2** quality of character or level of ability: *He provides leadership of a very high calibre.* Also, **caliber.** <French, from Arabic *kalib* mould>

cal·i·co (kal′ə kō′) *n, pl* **cal·i·coes** or **cal·i·cos** a cotton cloth, usually with coloured patterns printed on one side.
adj **1** made of calico. **2** with patches of colour: *a calico cat.* <*Calicut*, India>

calico salmon CHUM[3].

cal·i·for·ni·um (kal′ə fôr′nē əm) *n* a radioactive synthetic element produced by bombarding curium with helium isotopes. *Symbol* **Cf** <*California*, where it was produced>

cal·i·pers (kal′ə pərz) *pln* an instrument used to measure the diameter or thickness of something. Also, **callipers.** <alteration of *calibre*>

ca·liph (kā′lif) *or* (kal′if) *Islam n* in former times, the person regarded as the chief Muslim civil and religious ruler. Also **calif, khalif.** <Old French, from Arabic *kalamfa* succeed> **cal′iph·ate** (kā′li fāt) *or* (kal′i fāt) *n.*

cal·is·then·ics (kal′is then′iks) *n* **1** (*with plural verb*) exercises without the use of special equipment, designed to develop a strong and graceful body. **2** (*with singular verb*) the practice or art of calisthenics: *Calisthenics is part of our training program.* Also, **callisthenics.** <Greek *kallos* beauty + *sthenos* strength>

call (kol) *v* **1** shout to get someone's attention *Her brother called from downstairs.* **2** order to come or respond: *My mom is calling me for dinner.* **3** announce: *to call a ceasefire.* **4** give a name or label to: *They called the baby John. She called me a coward.* **5** telephone: *Call me tomorrow morning.* **6** waken: *Call me at seven o'clock.* **7** visit: *Relatives had come to call.* **8** cancel: *The game was called on account of rain.* **9** demand payment of: *The bank called his loan.* **10** rule on as an umpire: *to call a foul.*
n **1** an act of calling: *a call for help.* **2** the characteristic sound of a bird or other animal. **3** a claim or demand: *The store doesn't stock that item since there is no call for it.* **4** a right or responsibility: *You have no call to meddle in other people's business.* **5** a spiritual urge: *a call to join a religious community.* <Old Norse *kalla* summon loudly> **call′er** *n.*
call attention to, bring to people's notice.
call away, call to another place: *I'm sorry, she's not here; she's been called away.*
call back, a ask a person to return: *Call him back before it's too late.* **b** take back or retract: *Can I call back that decision?* **c** telephone someone who has called earlier.
call down, *Informal* scold.
call for, a go and pick up: *You can call for the pictures any time after three o'clock.* **b** need or deserve: *This event calls for a celebration!* **c** ask for: *to call for the waiter. Some students are calling for more study periods.*
call forth, inspire emotion, energy, etc.: *a play that calls forth strong emotions.*
call in, ask someone to come and help: *Call in the experts.*
call off, a order to stop doing something: *Call off your dog.* **b** cancel: *We called off our trip.* **c** read aloud from a list: *The names were called off alphabetically.*
call on, a visit. **b** appeal to: *We called on you for help.*
call up, a bring to mind; remember. **b** telephone. **c** draft into military service.
on call, available at any time: *There are three doctors on call tonight.*
within call, close enough to hear a call or to be heard calling: *If you go exploring, please stay within call.*

a bat	e bed	i bid	o pot	u cup	th thin
ā cake	ē me	ī bite	ō go	ū rude	ᴛʜ then
ä bar	ə about	ər over	ô for	ů put	zh measure

cal·la (kal′ə) *n* **1** a bog plant with large spear-shaped or heart-shaped leaves and a greenish spathe around a yellow spadix. **2 calla lily** a S African plant with a large spathe surrounding a yellow spadix. <Latin>

call display *n* a telephone service identifying the source of an incoming call by displaying the caller's phone number and sometimes his or her name on a screen. Also called **caller ID**.

call girl *n* a prostitute with whom appointments are made by telephone.

cal·lig·ra·phy (kə lig′rə fē) *n* decorative writing or lettering done by hand. <Greek *kallos* beauty + *-graphy*> **cal′li·graph′ic** *adj.*

call·ing (kol′ing) *n* **1** a person's business or occupation, especially one that suits one's temperament and abilities: *He has found his calling in medicine.* **2** a spiritual or divine urging toward a special service or office: *Be sure of your calling before you enter the ministry.*

calling card *n* **1** a small card with one's name on it, used especially in former times when making a formal visit, or acknowledging a gift. **2** a characteristic object or mark left behind: *The burglar's calling card was a rose laid on the kitchen counter.*

cal·li·o·pe (kə lī′ə pē′) *n* a musical instrument consisting of a series of steam whistles played by a keyboard like that of an organ. <Latin, from Greek *kallos* beauty + *ops* voice>

cal·li·pers (kal′ə pərz) CALIPERS.

cal·lis·then·ics (kal′is then′iks) CALISTHENICS.

call letters *pln* the letters identifying a radio or TV station.

call number *n* a series of letters or numbers identifying a library book according to a special classification system.

cal·lous (kal′əs) *adj* **1** hardened on the skin from frequent pressure or friction. **2** unfeeling or insensitive: *Only a callous person can see suffering without trying to help.* **cal′lous·ly** *adv.* **cal′lous·ness** *n.*

SYNONYMS

Callous means "uncaring" or "lacking sensitivity": *She called him callous when he ignored her tears.*

Heartless means "hard-hearted": *It was heartless to leave the dog outside in the snow.*

Pitiless means "unkind" or "unsympathetic": *The pitiless coach yelled at the tired runners.*

cal·low (kal′ō) *adj* young and inexperienced. <Old English *calu* bald (i.e., unfeathered, like a baby bird)> **cal′low·ness** *n.*

cal·lus (kal′əs) *n, pl* **cal·lus·es** a hard, thickened place on the skin: *calluses on the hands from shovelling snow.* <Latin> **cal′lused** *adj.*

call waiting *n* a telephone service signalling to the user that there is an incoming call.

calm (kom) *or* (kåm) *adj* **1** peaceful and still: *a calm sea, a calm day.* **2** not excited or upset: *Although frightened, she answered in a calm voice.*
n a calm state: *After the storm came the calm.*
v make or become calm: *The sea has calmed. She soon calmed the baby.* <Latin *cauma*, from Greek *kauma* heat of the day; hence, time for rest> **calm′ly** *adv.* **calm′ness** *n.*

cal·o·rie (kal′ə rē) *n* **1** either of two nonmetric units for measuring heat. A **small calorie** is the amount of heat (about 4.18 J) needed to raise the temperature of a gram of water one Celsius degree. A **large calorie** is a thousand times this amount of heat. **2** a unit corresponding to a large calorie, used to measure the heat or energy produced by food as it is burned in the body: *About 100 calories are produced by 30 g of brown sugar.* <French, from Latin *calor* heat> **ca·lor′ic** *adj.*

cal·o·rif·ic (kal′ə rif′ik) *adj* producing heat.

🍁 **cal·u·met** (kal′yə met′) *n* a long, ornamented tobacco pipe formerly used by First Nations peoples of the plains and eastern woodlands, especially in formal peacemaking ceremonies. <French, from Latin *calamus* little reed>

cal·um·ny (kal′əm nē) *n, pl* **cal·um·nies** a slander. <French, from Latin *calumnia* trickery> **ca·lum′ni·ate** *v.* **ca·lum′ni·ous** *adj.*

calve (kav) *v* **calved, calv·ing 1** give birth to a calf. **2** set loose a smaller mass of ice from an iceberg or glacier.

calves (kavz) plural of CALF.

ca·lyp·so (kə lip′sō) *n* a lively style of music that originated in Trinidad, characterized by improvisation and usually satirical or humorous lyrics.
adj to do with calypso music. <origin uncertain>

ca·lyx (kā′liks) *or* (kal′iks) *n, pl* **ca·lyx·es** or **cal·y·ces** (kā′lə sēz′) *or* (kal′ə sēz′) the covering of outer leaves that surround an unopened flower bud. See COROLLA for picture. <Latin, from Greek *kalyptein* to hide>

cam (kam) *n* a projection on a wheel or shaft that changes a regular circular motion into an irregular circular motion or back-and-forth motion. <Dutch *kam* comb>

CAM computer-aided manufacturing.

ca·ma·ra·de·rie (kå′mə rå′də rē) *n* friendliness and loyalty among people who spend a lot of time together. <French *camarade*>

cam·as or **cam·ass** (kam′əs) *n* a N American herb of the lily family with sweet, edible bulbs traditionally gathered by First Nations people. <Chinook Jargon *kamass*>

cam·ber (kam′bər) *n* an upward bend or curve in the middle of a surface, such as the curve of a ship's deck or a road. <French, from Latin *camurus* curved inward>

cam·bi·um (kam′bē əm) *n* the layer of soft, growing tissue between the bark and the wood of trees, from which new bark and new wood grow. <Latin = exchange>

Cam·bo·di·a (cam bō′dē ə) *n* a country in southeast Asia. See the APPENDIX. **Cam·bo′di·an** *adj, n.*

Cam·bri·an (kam′brē ən) *or* (kām′brē ən) *n* the geological period lasting from about 600 million to 500 million years ago, when fish first appeared. See also PALEOZOIC.
adj to do with this period or the rocks formed then. <Latin, from Welsh *Cymru* Wales>

cam·bric (kām′brik) *n* a fine, thin linen or cotton cloth. <*Cambrai*, France>

cam·cord·er (kām′kȯr′dər) *n* a handheld video camera. <*cam(era)* + *(re)corder*>

came (kām) past tense of COME.

cam·el (kam′əl) *n* a large, cud-chewing desert mammal of Africa or Asia, with broad, padded feet, and one or two humps on the back in which they store fat. See DROMEDARY for picture. <Old English, from Greek *kamelos*>

camel hair *n* a heavy, fuzzy fabric, usually yellowish brown, made from or imitating the hair of a camel and used for making coats.

cam·el·lia (kə mēl′yə) *n* an ornamental shrub native to E Asia, with waxy, roselike flowers and glossy leaves. <G.J. *Kamel*, 17c botanist>

Cam·e·lot (kam′ə lot′) *n* a legendary place in England where King Arthur had his palace and court.

Cam·em·bert (kam′əm ber′) *n* a rich, soft cheese. <*Camembert*, France>

cam·e·o (kam′ē ō′) *n* **1** a small piece of jewellery consisting of a carving in relief against a background of a different colour. **2** a brief appearance by a famous actor in a minor but distinctive movie role: *In this movie, he has a cameo as an eccentric landlord.* **3** a short literary sketch of a character or event. <Old French, from Italian *cammeo*>

cam·er·a (kam′ə rə) *n* **1** a device for taking photographs or recording movies or videos, consisting of a lightproof box in which film or plates are exposed and the image is formed by means of a lens. **2** a device that records images digitally without using film. **3** *Television* the part of the transmitter that converts images into electronic impulses for transmitting. <Latin, from Greek *kamara* curved (as lenses are)>

cam·er·a·man (kam′rə man′) *n, pl* **cam·er·a·men** (kam′rə mən) a person who operates a camera, especially a movie or TV camera.

cam·e·ra–shy (kam′rə shī′) *adj* reluctant to have one's picture taken.

Cam·e·roon (kam′ə rūn′) *n* a country in central Africa. Also, **Cameroun.**

cam·i·sole (kam′ə sōl′) *n* a sleeveless undershirt worn by women and girls. <French, from Latin *camisa* shirt>

cam·o·mile (kam′ə mīl′) *n* a plant whose leaves and daisylike flowers are often dried and used in herbal teas and medicine. Also, **chamomile.** <Old English, from Greek *chamaimelon* earth apple>

cam·ou·flage (kam′ə flȧzh′) *n* **1** an outward natural appearance that makes a person, animal, or thing blend into natural surroundings. **2** the artificial disguising of something to make it blend into its surroundings: *A camouflage of branches hid the tent.*
v **cam·ou·flaged, cam·ou·flag·ing** conceal or disguise by camouflage: *The hunters were camouflaged with shrubbery.* <French, from Italian *camuffare* to disguise>

camp[1] (kamp) *n* **1** a temporary shelter such as a tent, trailer, or lean-to, or the ground on which it is set up: *Her camp was right in the bush.* **2** a temporary community of people living in cabins or tents in the forest or country, usually with a structured program of activities for recreation or for training of some kind: *a hockey camp, I go to camp for two weeks in July.* **3** the people in a camp: *You'll wake up the whole camp!* **4** the group of people who support a party, theory, or doctrine: *the liberal camp.*
v **1** make a camp or live in a camp: *We decided to camp by the river the first night.* **2** live simply without comforts for a time: *We had to camp in the house until our furniture arrived.* <French, from Latin *campus* field> **camp′er** *n.*
break (or **strike**) **camp,** pack up tents and equipment and leave.
camp out, live in a tent or trailer.
make camp, set up a camp: *We hiked until sunset and then made camp beside a creek.*

camp[2] (kamp) *n* a style of humour based on the exaggeration of what is corny, trite, lowbrow, etc.
adj using this kind of humour: *a camp comedy routine.* <origin uncertain>

cam·paign (kam pān′) *n* **1** a series of military operations: *The general planned a campaign to capture the enemy's most important city.* **2** a series of planned activities or tactics to get or accomplish something: *a campaign to raise money for a new hospital, an election campaign.*
v take part in or serve in a campaign: *She's campaigning in Saskatchewan this week.* <French *campaign* open country, from Latin *campus* field> **cam·paign′er** *n.*
on the campaign trail, travelling from place to place making speeches, etc. for an election.

cam·pan·u·la (kam pan′yə lə) *n* a bluebell or other similar plant with bell-shaped flowers. <Latin = little bell>

camp·craft (kamp′kraft′) *n* the skills needed for successful camping, such as pitching a tent or building a fire.

camp·er (kam′pər) *n* **1** a person who camps or attends a camp. **2** a vehicle equipped for camping, such as a small trailer or van, often with built-in beds and cupboards.

camp·fire (kamp′fīr′) *n* a fire in a camp for warmth, cooking, or as a focal point for social activity.

camp·ground (kamp′ground′) *n* **1** a parklike place where people pay a fee to pitch tents or park trailers for the night in individually marked sites. **2** the grounds of a camp.

cam·phor (kam′fər) *n* a white crystalline compound with a strong odour and a bitter taste. <Old French, from Sanskrit *karpura*>

camp·ing (kamp′ing) *n* the practice of living outdoors in a tent or trailer, especially for recreation: *Camping has always been part of our summer vacation.*

cam·pi·on (kam′pē ən) *n* a wild herb of the northern hemisphere with red or white flowers. <perhaps *champion*, because the leaves were used to make a crown for athletic champions>

🍁 **camp robber** CANADA JAY.

camp·site (kamp′sīt′) *n* **1** a place marked off for a person or group to camp, such as in a provincial park or private campground. **2** a place where someone camps or has camped: *We made our campsite under some pine trees.*

a bat	e bed	i bid	o pot	u cup	th thin
ā cake	ē me	ī bite	ō go	ū rude	ᴛʜ then
ȧ bar	ə about	ər over	ȯ for	u̇ put	zh measure

cam·pus (kam′pəs) *n* the grounds of a university, college, or school. <Latin = field>

cam·shaft (kam′shaft′) *n* a rotating rod on which a cam is fastened.

can[1] (kan) *auxiliary verb (followed by an infinitive without **to**), past tense* **could** **1** be able: *Can you swim? We could hear someone at the door.* **2** be allowed or have the right: *We can cross the street here. You can leave now.* **3** must (not): *You can't really think that!* **4** does, is, or will sometimes: *Bullying can occur in the schoolyard.* <Old English *cunnan* know>

GRAMMAR AND USAGE

Can means "be able to"; **may** means "be allowed to":
*Although I **can** skateboard, Mom says I **may** do so only until it gets dark.*

can[2] (kan) *n* **1** a small metal container in which foods are sealed to preserve them for later use: *a can of soup.* **2** a metal container taller than it is wide, usually with a lid: *a garbage can.* **3** *Slang* a washroom. **4** *Slang* jail.
v **canned, can·ning** preserve by putting in airtight cans or jars: *to can fruit.* <Old English *canne* container>
can of worms, (*often with **open***) a complicated, messy problem: *Don't mention his girlfriend, or you'll open a can of worms.*
in the can, *Informal* of a movie or other work, finished and ready to be broadcast or released.

Can·a·da (kan′ə də) *n* the second-largest country in the world, occupying most of the northern half of N America. See the APPENDIX. **Ca·na′di·an** (kə nā′dē ən) *adj, n.*

ETYMOLOGY

There are different theories about the origin of the name **Canada**. The main one is that it comes from Iroquoian *kanata*, meaning "village" or "cluster of dwellings."

Canada Act *n* **1** **Canada Act 1791** the act that divided the province of Québec into Upper and Lower Canada. Also called **Constitutional Act**. **2** **Canada Act 1982** CONSTITUTION ACT 1982.

Canada Council *n* a group established by Parliament in 1957 to administer funds encouraging the arts and other cultural activities. *Abbrev.* **C.C.**

Canada Day *n* July 1, Canada's national holiday, commemorating the establishment of the Dominion of Canada on July 1, 1867. Until 1982, it was called Dominion Day.

Canada goose *n* a large wild goose of North America, grey-brown with a black head and neck and white throat.

Canada jay *n* a species of jay common throughout Canada and the northern US, with loose, fluffy grey feathers on the body and a white and black head without a crest. Also called **camp robber**, **grey jay**, **moosebird**, **whisky-jack**.

Canada lynx *n* a lynx found mainly in Canada and Alaska, with tufted ears and a thick coat of long, silky, greyish fur.

Canada Medal *n* an award for bravery to civilians or military personnel, established in 1943.

🍁 **Ca·na·darm** (kan′ə darm′) *Trademark n* an extension of a spacecraft, allowing astronauts to move and handle objects in space. It was invented and built in Canada. <*Canada* + *arm*>

Canada thistle *n* a thistle introduced from Europe that has become a common weed in Canada.

Ca·na·di·an·a (kə nā′dē an′ə) *n* objects or texts associated with Canada or its history, especially early Canadian artifacts, or Canadian art and literature.

Canadian Action Party *n* one of the registered political parties of Canada.

Canadian Broadcasting Corporation *n* a crown corporation that does radio and TV broadcasting, established by Parliament in 1936. *Abbrev.* **CBC**

Canadian Charter of Rights and Freedoms CHARTER OF RIGHTS AND FREEDOMS.

Canadian crutch *n* See CRUTCH (def. 1).

Canadian Forces *n* the combined land, air, and naval forces of Canada. Also called **Canadian Armed Forces**.

Ca·na·di·an·ism (kə nā′dē ə niz′əm) *n* a word, usage, or custom originating in, characteristic of, or peculiar to Canada: *"Muskeg" and "caribou" are among many Canadianisms borrowed from Aboriginal languages.*

Ca·na·di·an·ize (kə nā′dē ə nīz′) *v* **Ca·na·di·an·ized, Ca·na·di·an·iz·ing** make Canadian in character, content, or ownership: *to Canadianize a TV program, to Canadianize a corporation.* **Ca·na′di·an·i·za′tion** *n.*

Canadian Labour Congress *n* a national federation of trade unions in Canada. *Abbrev.* **CLC**

Canadian Radio–television and Telecommunications Commission *n* a Federal Government body established in 1968 to regulate radio and TV broadcasting and its distribution. *Abbrev.* **CRTC**

Canadian Security and Intelligence Service *n* a government agency whose objective is to investigate and report on threats to the security of Canada. It is informally known as Canada's secret service.
Abbrev. **CSIS**

Canadian Shield *n* a region of ancient rock, chiefly granite, encircling Hudson Bay and covering nearly half the mainland of Canada.

ca·nal (kə nal′) *n* **1** a waterway dug across land. **2** a passageway in the body or in a plant: *the birth canal.* **3** any of the long, narrow markings on the surface of Mars. <Old French, from Latin *canalis* trench, pipe>

can·a·pé (kan′ə pā′) *or* (kan′ə pā′) *n* a cracker, piece of bread, or pastry spread with a topping and often eaten at a party. <French; originally a couch with a mosquito net>

ca·nard (kə närd′) *n* a false rumour. <French = duck, probably from *vendre un canard à moitié* = to half-sell a duck, i.e., not to sell it at all but rather deceive>

ca·nar·y (kə ner′ē) *n, pl* **ca·nar·ies** a small yellow songbird native to Africa.
adj light yellow.

> **ETYMOLOGY**
>
> **Canaries** were first seen in the Canary Islands. One of these islands was named *Canaria insula*, which, in English, means "Island of the Dogs." Sailors named the island because of the packs of large dogs that lived there.

ca·nas·ta (kə nas′tə) *n* a card game similar to rummy, played by two to six players using two decks of cards. <Spanish = basket)

can·can (kan′kan′) *n* a dance marked by extravagant kicking and leaping, performed by women in a chorus line and originating in nineteenth-century Paris. <French>

can·cel (kan′səl) *v* **can·celled** or **can·celed, can·cel·ling** or **can·cel·ing** 1 decide not to do or have: *to cancel an order, to cancel a meeting.* 2 take away the value of: *This evidence cancels your argument.* 3 mark, stamp, or punch something so that it cannot be used or used again: *to cancel a stamp.* 4 **a** compensate, make up for, or neutralize each other: *Your 20 points cancel 20 of mine. The pros and cons cancel out.* **b** *Mathematics* (*often with* **out**) divide a numerator and a denominator by a common factor. <Old French, from Latin *cancelli* crossed bars>
can′cel·la′tion *n.*

can·cer (kan′sər) *n* 1 an uncontrolled growth of new tissue or cells in the body that tends to spread and destroy healthy tissue. 2 a disease marked by such harmful growths. 3 **Cancer a** *Astronomy* a northern constellation shaped somewhat like a crab. **b** *Astrology* the fourth sign of the zodiac. The sun enters Cancer about June 21. **c** a person born under this sign. 4 **tropic of Cancer** an imaginary circle around the globe, about 23° north of the equator. <Old English, from Latin = crab; creeping tumour> **can′cer·ous** *adj.*

🍁 **Can·con** (kan′kon′) *Informal n* Canadian content, as determined by government regulations, especially in broadcasting or in school textbooks.

can·de·la (kan del′ə) *n* the SI unit for measuring the intensity of light. *Symbol* **cd** <Latin = candle>

can·de·la·bra (kan′də lab′rə) *pln* (*with singular verb*) a candlestick with several branches, or an electric light fixture imitating this. Also, **candelabrum** (*sing*). <Old English, from Latin *candere* to shine>

can·did (kan′did) *adj* 1 frank and honest; showing candour: *a candid reply.* 2 not posed as a photograph or movie, or that is taken without the person's knowledge: *a candid photo of children playing.* <Latin *candidus* white (i.e., clear, pure)> **can′did·ly** *adv.*

can·di·date (kan′də dāt′) *or* (kan′də dit) *n* 1 a person who applies or is proposed for a position, electoral office, honour, or prize: *There were three possible candidates for the award. She was one of five candidates in the student council election.* 2 a person who seems likely to gain a certain position, or receive a certain treatment: *Violent behaviour made him a likely candidate for prison.* <Latin *candidatus* dressed in white. Roman candidates were dressed in white togas.> **can′di·da·cy** *n.*

can·died (kan′dēd) *adj* glazed, soaked, or cooked with sugar: *a candied fruit.*

can·dle (kan′dəl) *n* 1 a stick of wax or tallow with a wick in it, burned to give light. 2 anything shaped like a candle: *The water in this tank is filtered through charcoal candles.*
v **can·dled, can·dling** test eggs for freshness or fertility by holding them in front of a light in order to see inside them. <Old English, from Latin *candere* to shine>
burn the candle at both ends, try to do more than one's energy or resources will allow.
not hold a candle to, not compare with: *The bread from the bakery can't hold a candle to the bread my sister makes.*

can·dle·hold·er (kan′dəl hōl′dər) *n* a holder for a candle, especially a small or sturdy one.

🍁 **candle ice** *n* ice on a body of water whose internal structure has fragmented into candlelike shapes, usually occurring shortly before breakup of the ice.

can·dle·light (kan′dəl līt′) *n* the light from a candle or candles. **can′dle·lit** *adj.*

can·dle·pow·er (kan′dəl pou′ər) *n* the intensity of a light source, measured in candelas.

can·dle·stick (kan′dəl stik′) *n* a holder for a candle, especially a tall and thin one.

can·dour or **can·dor** (kan′dər) *n* the quality of being candid, that is, frank and honest.

🍁 **CANDU** (kan dū′) *n* a nuclear reactor made in Canada. <*Can*(*ada*) + *d*(*euterium*) + *u*(*ranium*)>

can·dy (kan′dē) *n, pl* **can·dies** 1 a sweet snack food made with sugar or syrup and flavouring: *He doesn't eat much candy.* 2 a piece of this: *She took a candy from the box.* 3 something with no real function or value except to attract attention or amuse: *These flashy images are just eye candy. Many TV shows are pure brain candy.*
v **can·died, can·dy·ing** 1 cook or soak in sugar, or glaze with sugar. 2 crystallize into sugar. <French, from Arabic *sukkar* sugar>

candy apple *n* an apple on a stick, dipped in melted toffee that is then allowed to harden.

candy cane *n* a stick of hard candy typically eaten at Christmas, with spiralling stripes and shaped like a walking stick with a curved end.

candy floss *n* a light, fluffy candy made by spinning melted sugar with food colouring. Also called **cotton candy**.

can·dy·strip·er (kan′dē strī′pər) *n* a teenage girl who does volunteer work in a hospital. <from a former striped uniform>

can·dy·tuft (kan′dē tuft′) *n* a plant of the mustard family, with clusters of white, purple, or pink flowers.

a bat	e bed	i bid	o pot	u cup	th **thin**
ā cake	ē me	ī bite	ō go	ū rude	ᴛʜ **then**
ä bar	ə about	ər over	ô for	ů put	zh measure

C

cane (kān) *n* **1** a stick to help a person in walking. **2** a long, jointed stem like that of bamboo, or a plant with such stems: *sugar cane.* **3** such stems cut and used to make furniture. **4** in former times, a stick used to discipline schoolchildren by beating them with it.
v **caned, can·ing 1** beat with a cane. **2** make or repair with cane: *to cane a chair seat.* <Old French, from Greek *kanna* reed>

cane sugar *n* sugar from sugar cane.

ca·nine (kā′nīn) *adj* **1** to do with dogs. **2** to do with a family of animals that includes the domestic dog, wolf, coyote, dingo, and jackal.
n **1** a dog. **2** a member of the dog family. **3** in full, **canine tooth** one of the four pointed teeth next to the incisors. <French, from Latin *canis* dog>

can·is·ter (kan′i stər) *n* a small box or can with a lid, especially one for keeping tea, flour, sugar, and other dry products, or a similar container used for other purposes. <Latin, from Greek *kanastron* wicker basket>

can·ker (kang′kər) *n* **1** a spreading sore, especially one in the mouth. **2** a fungal disease of plants that causes slow decay. **3** anything that destroys by a gradual eating away. <Old French, from Latin *cancer* creeping tumour>

🍁 **Can·Lit** (kan′lit′) *Informal n* Canadian literature.

can·na (kan′ə) *n* a tropical American plant with large, pointed leaves and large red, pink, or yellow flowers. <Latin = reed>

can·na·bis (kan′ə bis) *n* **1** a tall plant with divided serrated leaves. Its resin or dried flowering tops are smoked as a recreational drug or for use in medicine. **2** a closely related plant that is a source of hemp fibre. <Latin, from Greek *kannabis*>

canned (kand) *adj* **1** preserved by being put in airtight cans or jars. **2** pre-recorded and then used in a broadcast or performance, or as a background to live events: *canned laughter. She sang to canned accompaniment.*

can·nel·lo·ni (kan′ə lō′nē) *n* pasta in the shape of large tubes stuffed with meat or cheese and baked in sauce. <Italian = large tubes>

can·ner (kan′ər) *n* a person or company that cans food. **can′ner·y** *n.*

can·ni·bal (kan′ə bəl) *n* **1** a person who eats human flesh. **2** an animal that eats others of its own kind.
adj to do with cannibals. <Spanish *Canibales* Carib people> **can′ni·bal′ism** *n.* **can′ni·bal·is′tic** *adj.*

can·ni·bal·ize (kan′ə bə līz′) *v* **can·ni·bal·ized, can·ni·bal·iz·ing** take usable parts from a vehicle or machine to assemble or repair another: *They cannibalized the wrecked car to fix ours.*

can·ning (kan′ing) *n* the process of preserving food by putting it in airtight cans or jars.

can·non (kan′ən) *n, pl* **can·non** or **can·nons** a big gun fixed to the ground or mounted on a carriage, especially the type that fires cannonballs.
v **1** fire at with a cannon. **2** collide with a rush: *to cannon against a tree.* **3** carom. <French, from Latin *canna* tube>

can·non·ade (kan′ə nād′) *n* a continuous firing of heavy guns.

can·non·ball (kan′ən bol′) *n* **1** in former times, a large iron or steel ball fired from a cannon. **2** a jump into water with the body in a curled-up position. **3** *Tennis* a forceful serve.
v **1** perform a cannonball jump or serve. **2** move with great force and speed.

cannon fodder *n* soldiers regarded as expendable in war.

can·not (kan′ot) *or* (kə not′) *v* can not.

can·ny (kan′ē) *adj* **can·ni·er, can·ni·est** shrewd and showing good judgment, especially in business matters. <from *can*[1]> **can′ni·ly** *adv.* **can′ni·ness** *n.*

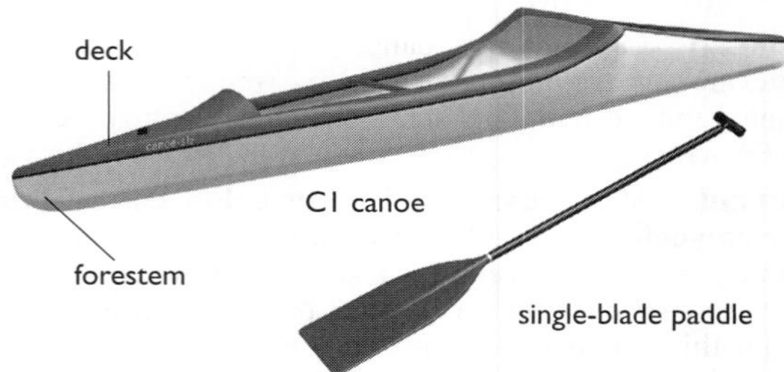

Historically, the **canoe** has been made of a variety of materials, including hollowed-out tree trunks, birchbark, bound bulrushes, and whalebone covered with animal skins.

Today, canoes are constructed of plastic, fiberglass, and other materials. The C1 canoe is specially made for competitive events on whitewater courses.

ca·noe (kə nū′) *n* a light, narrow boat with low, curving sides that come to a point at each end, moved by paddles.
v **ca·noed, ca·noe·ing** travel or carry by canoe. <Spanish, from Carib (a group of languages of the Caribbean) *canaoua*> **ca·noe′ing** *n.* **ca·noe′ist** *n.*

🍁 **canoe cedar** WESTERN RED CEDAR.

🍁 **Ca·no·la** (kə nō′lə) *Trademark n* a type of rape plant whose seeds are pressed to yield cooking oil and as a livestock feed. <*Can(ada)* + *ola*, from Latin *oleum* oil>

can·on[1] (kan′ən) *n* **1** *Christianity* a law of a church or a body of church law. Also, **canon law**. **2** a rule by which things are judged: *the canons of good taste.* **3** an official list. **4** a list of the works of an author considered as genuine or of the highest quality: *the canon of Shakespeare.* **5** *Music* a song in which different voice parts start and end the same melody at different times, so that they overlap in a harmonious way. <Latin, from Greek *kanon* rule>

can·on[2] (kan′ən) *n* **1** a member of the Christian clergy who is on the staff of a cathedral. **2** a member of a Roman Catholic order of clergy who lives in a religious community. <Old French, from Latin *canonicus* according to rule>

ca·non·i·cal (kə non′ə kəl) *adj* **1** according to or prescribed by the laws of a Christian church. **2** authorized or officially accepted. **ca·non′i·cal·ly** *adv.*

can·on·ize (kan′ə nīz′) *Catholicism v* **can·on·ized, can·on·iz·ing** officially declare a person to be a saint: *Joan of Arc was canonized in 1920.* **can′on·i·za′tion** *n.*

can·o·py (kan′ə pē) *n, pl* **can·o·pies 1** a covering fixed over a bed, throne, or entrance, or carried on poles over a person: *There is a striped canopy over the entrance to the hotel.* **2** a rooflike covering: *The trees formed a canopy over the old road.*
v **can·o·pied, can·o·py·ing** make a canopy over. <Latin, from Greek *konops* mosquito>

cant[1] (kant) *n* **1** hypocritical and high-sounding talk, especially of a political, religious, or moral kind. **2** the special vocabulary of a particular group: *The undercover cop had to learn the gang's cant.*
adj to do with such talk or vocabulary. <probably Latin *cantus* song>

cant[2] (kant) *v* cause something to be in a slanting position: *She canted her head to look out the window.*
n a slope or tilt. <Old French, from Latin *cantus* side>

can't (kant) *contraction* cannot.

can·ta·bi·le (kən tä′bə lā) *Music adj, adv* in a smooth, flowing, songlike style. <Italian, from Latin *cantare* to sing>

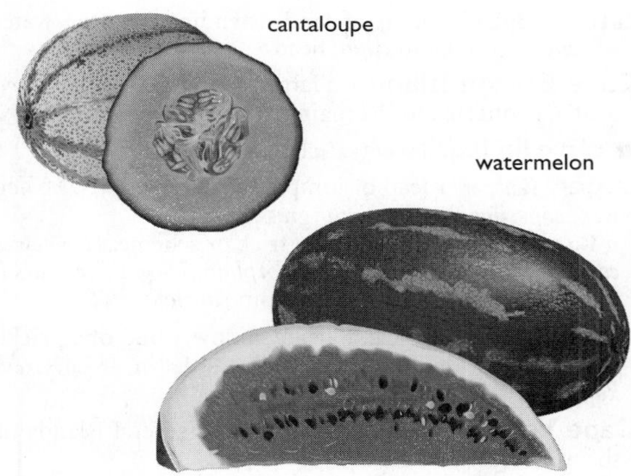

Melons are juicy and sweet, but vary greatly in size. Compare the weighty, oval, red-fleshed watermelon to the smaller, round **cantaloupe** with its orange-coloured pulp.

can·ta·loupe (kan′tə lōp′) *n* a melon with a rough, greyish rind and sweet, juicy, orange flesh. Also called **muskmelon**. <French, from Italian *Cantaluppi*, where first grown>

can·tan·ker·ous (kan tang′kə rəs) *adj* disagreeable and bad-tempered. <origin uncertain>
can·tan′ker·ous·ly *adv.* **can·tan′ker·ous·ness** *n.*

can·ta·ta (kən tä′tə) *or* (kən tat′ə) *n* a musical composition telling a story, sung without acting by a chorus and soloists, usually accompanied by an orchestra. <Italian *cantare* sing>

can·teen (kan tēn′) *n* **1** a small container, especially a flat, round one, for carrying water or other drinks. **2** a place in a school, camp, or factory where food and, sometimes, other articles are sold or given out. **3** a store, recreation hall, or club for members of the armed forces. <French, from Italian *cantina* cellar>

can·ter (kan′tər) *n* a horse's gait faster than a trot but slower than a gallop.
v move with this gait. <the pace of pilgrims riding to *Canterbury*, England>

cant–hook (kant′ hu̇k′) *n* a pole with a hinged hook near the end, used to catch and roll logs. A logger can use a chopping motion to dig the hook into a log. Compare PEAVEY. <See CANT[2].>

can·ti·cle (kant′ə kəl) *n* a song, hymn, or chant. <Latin *canere* sing>

can·ti·le·ver (kan′tə lē′vər) *n* a large bracket or beam fastened to a wall or base at one end only, supporting a structure that projects outward, such as a balcony or either end of a bridge. See BRIDGE for picture.
v **1** build with cantilevers. **2** stick out like a cantilever. <origin uncertain>

can·tle (kan′təl) *n* the part of a saddle that sticks up at the back. <Old French, from Latin *cantus* corner>

can·to (kan′tō) *n* one of the main divisions of a long poem. <Italian, from Latin *cantus* song>

can·ton (kan′ton) *n* **1** a political division of Switzerland. **2** in heraldry, a rectangular section in the upper corner of a shield or flag. <Old French>

Can·ton·ese (kan′tə nēz′) *n, pl* **Can·ton·ese 1** the language spoken in or near Guangzhou, formerly called Canton, a city in southern China. **2** a native or inhabitant of Guangzhou.
adj to do with Canton, its people, their language, cooking style, etc.

can·tor (kan′tər) *or* (kan′tôr) *Judaism n* a soloist in a synagogue who leads the congregation in prayer. <Latin *canere* sing>

Ca·nuck (kə nuk′) *Informal n, adj* Canadian.

ETYMOLOGY

Canuck was used in the northeastern American states as a derogatory name for French Canadians who went to these states to find work. This was viewed as "stealing" American jobs. Used in this way, the term was, and is, offensive. It is not surprising, therefore, that many French Canadians are sensitive to the word.

can·vas (kan′vəs) *n* **1** a strong cloth made of cotton, flax, or hemp, used to make tents, sails, running shoes, etc., and for painting pictures on. **2** a piece of canvas for painting a picture on, or on which one has been painted, especially in oils: *She's got seven canvases ready for the show.* **3** a sail or sails. **4** the floor of a boxing ring. <Old French, from Latin *cannabis* hemp>
under canvas, a with sails spread: *The boat left the harbour under canvas.* **b** in tents.

a **bat**	e **bed**	i **bid**	o **pot**	u **cup**	th **thin**
ā **cake**	ē **me**	ī **bite**	ō **go**	ū **rude**	TH **then**
ä **bar**	ə **about**	ər **over**	ô **for**	u̇ **put**	zh **measure**

C

can·vas·back (kan′vəs bak′) *n* a wild duck of North America, with a greyish back and a sloping forehead.

can·vass (kan′vəs) *v* **1** go around asking for subscriptions, votes, or orders, or to request opinions on some subject: *to canvass your neighbours for contributions to the food bank.* **2** examine: *He canvassed the papers in search of job ads.* **3** discuss thoroughly. <*canvas* originally = toss someone in a sheet, then perhaps = shake someone thoroughly, that is, harass> **can′vass·er** *n.*

can·yon (kan′yən) *n* a narrow valley with high, steep sides, usually with a stream at the bottom.
v participate in the sport of **canyoning**, going down a fast-flowing stream or waterfall in protective clothing. <Spanish *callon*, perhaps from Latin *callis* narrow path>

cap (kap) *n* **1** a close-fitting, brimless head covering, often with a visor. **2** a special head covering worn to show a rank, status, or occupation: *a soldier's cap.* **3** a small lid or protective cover for the top or end of something: *a bottle cap.* **4** the top part of something. **5** an upper limit or imposed maximum: *to place a cap on enrolment.* **6** a small quantity of explosive in a wrapper.
v **capped, cap·ping 1** put a cap on: *to cap an oil well, to cap spending.* **2** be or put on the top of: *Whipped cream capped the dessert.* **3** match or answer with something better: *capping each other's jokes.* **4** be the finishing touch to. <Old English, from Latin *cappa*> **cap′less** *adj.* **cap′like′** *adj.*
cap in hand, humbly or repentantly: *I went cap in hand to ask her forgiveness.*

ca·pa·bil·i·ty (kā′pə bil′ə tē) *n, pl* **ca·pa·bil·i·ties 1** the quality of being capable: *We rely daily on our bus driver's capability.* **2** the ability or power to do a specific thing.

ca·pa·ble (kā′pə bəl) *adj* able to do things well: *a capable teacher.* <French, from Latin *capabilis* able to take in> **ca′pa·ble·ness** *n.* **ca′pa·bly** *adv.*
capable of, a with ability or fitness for: *capable of hard work. This dog is not capable of learning tricks.* **b** open to: *a statement capable of many interpretations.*

ca·pa·cious (kə pā′shəs) *adj* able to hold much: *a capacious closet.* **ca·pa′cious·ness** *n.*

ca·pac·i·tance (kə pas′ə təns) *Electricity n* the ability of a capacitor to collect and store an electric charge.

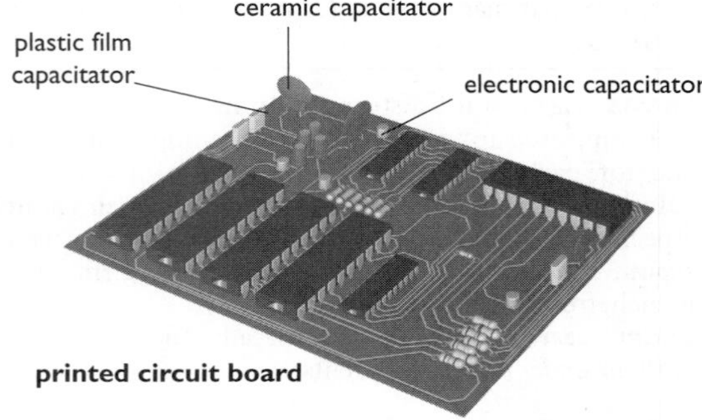

ca·pac·i·tor (kə pas′ə tər) *Electricity n* a device used in an electric circuit to temporarily collect and store an electric charge.

ca·pac·i·ty (kə pas′ə tē) *n, pl* **ca·pac·i·ties 1** the amount of room or space inside something: *This jug has a capacity of 4L. The theatre has a capacity of 400.* **2** ability: *a great capacity for learning. This book has the capacity to change your life.* **3** a position or role: *acting in the capacity of guardian. I say that in my capacity as a friend, not as your instructor.*
adj equal to the maximum capacity: *a capacity crowd.* <French, from Latin *capere* to hold>
filled to capacity, completely full.

cap and bells *n* a jester's cap trimmed with bells.

cap and gown *n* a flat-topped cap and loose gown worn by graduates and university professors on certain occasions.

ca·par·i·son (kə per′ə sən) *n* **1** an ornamental covering for a horse. **2** rich clothing or equipment.
v dress richly. <French, from Spanish *caparazon* saddlecloth>

cape[1] (kāp) *n* a sleeveless outer garment, or part of one, that falls loosely from the neck over the shoulders and back. <French, from Latin *cappa* covering for the head>

cape[2] (kāp) *n* a point of land extending into the water. <French, from Latin *caput* head>

Cape Breton Island *n* a large island northeast of Nova Scotia, connected to the mainland by a causeway.

🍁 **cap·e·lin** (kap′lin) *or* (kā′plin) CAPLIN.

ca·per[1] (kā′pər) *v* leap or jump around playfully: *The dogs were capering happily on the grass.*
n **1** a playful leap or jump. **2** a trick or scheme: *Her newest caper is to tell everyone she's an orphan. He got five years in jail for that caper.* <shortened from *capriole*>

ca·per[2] (kā′pər) *n* the edible green flower bud of a prickly shrub of the Mediterranean region. <Latin, from Greek *kapparis*>

Cape Ver·de (ver′dē) *n* a country of several islands off the west coast of Africa.

cap gun *n* a toy gun with a hammer action for setting off a small explosive charge.

cap·il·lar·y (kə pil′ə rē) *or* (kap′ə ler′ē) *n, pl* **cap·il·lar·ies** one of the network of tiny blood vessels connecting the arteries with the veins.
adj **1** to do with capillaries. **2** very slender. <French, from Latin *capillus* hair>

capillary action *Physics n* the force that makes a liquid rise against a vertical surface when the attraction between the molecules of liquid is less than the attraction between them and a solid surface. It is this force that allows a porous material to soak up a liquid.

capillary tube *n* a tube with a very slender opening, used in laboratories.

cap·i·tal[1] (kap′ə təl) *n* **1** the city where the government of a country, province, territory, or state is located: *Victoria is the capital of British Columbia.* **2** a letter of the alphabet of the size and form used to begin sentences and names. Also, **capital letter**. **3 a** the amount of money or property that a company or a person uses in carrying on a business: *The business has a capital of $150 000.* **b** money that is or can be invested. **c** *Accounting* the net worth of a business after deducting liabilities.

adj **1** to do with capital or a capital: *capital expenditures. What is the capital city of Manitoba?* **2** main or leading: *The invention of the telephone was a capital advance in communications.* **3** punishable by death: *Murder is a capital offence in some countries.* **4** *UK* excellent. <Old French, from Latin *caput* head>
make capital of, use to one's own advantage.

cap·i·tal[2] (kap′ə təl) *n* the top part of a column or pillar. <Old French *capitel*, from Latin *caput* head>

capital gain *n* profit from the sale of property or an investment.

capital goods *pl n* goods such as machinery or equipment that can be used to produce other goods. Compare CONSUMER GOODS.

cap·i·tal–in·ten·sive (kap′ə təl in ten′səv) *adj* requiring a lot of money as an investment.

cap·i·tal·ism (kap′ə tə liz′əm) *n* an economic system in which the means of production, such as land or factories, are privately owned by individuals or companies, and anyone may compete to produce goods and services for profit in a free market. Compare COMMUNISM, SOCIALISM. **cap′i·tal·is′tic** *adj.*

cap·i·tal·ist (kap′ə tə list) *n* a person with money and property used in carrying on business.
adj to do with capitalism.

cap·i·tal·ize (kap′ə tə līz′) *v* **cap·i·tal·ized, cap·i·tal·iz·ing 1** write or print with an upper-case initial letter: *Names are usually capitalized.* **2** (*with* ***on***) take advantage of: *They capitalized on the heat by setting up lemonade stands.* **3** turn into or use as CAPITAL[1] (*n* def. 3a). **cap′i·tal·i·za′tion** *n.*

capital letter CAPITAL[1] (*n* def. 2).

capital punishment *n* the death penalty for a crime.

ca·pit·u·late (kə pich′ə lāt′) *v* **ca·pit·u·lat·ed, ca·pit·u·lat·ing** surrender, give in, or give up: *She capitulated when she realized that arguing was useless.* <Latin *capitulare* arrange under several headings, i.e., set out conditions for surrender> **ca·pit′u·la′tion** *n.*

cap·let (kap′lit) *n* a solid pill that is shaped like a capsule, with a smooth coating on it. <*cap*(*sule*) + (*tab*)*let*>

🍁 **cap·lin** or **cape·lin** (kap′lin) *or* (kā′plin) *n* a small fish of the N Atlantic, used for food and as bait for cod. <French>

ca·po (kā′pō) *n* a clamp fastened over all the strings of a guitar to change key. <Italian = head>

ca·pon (kā′pon) *or* (kā′pən) *n* a rooster that has been neutered and fattened for eating. <Old English, from Latin *capo*, related to Greek *koptein* to cut off>

cap·puc·ci·no (kap′ə chē′nō) *n* coffee, especially espresso, served with hot, frothy milk, sometimes flavoured. <Italian = Capuchin, from its colour, light brown like a Capuchin monk's habit>

ca·price (kə prēs′) *n* a sudden decision or change of mind, for no reason: *By some caprice of the emperor, parties were outlawed.* <French, from Italian *capriccio*>

ca·pri·cious (kə prish′əs) *adj* likely to change suddenly and without reason: *a spoiled and capricious child, capricious weather.* **ca·pri′cious·ly** *adv.* **ca·pri′cious·ness** *n.*

Cap·ri·corn (kap′rə kôrn′) *n* **1** *Astronomy* a southern constellation shaped somewhat like a goat. **2** *Astrology* **a** the tenth sign of the zodiac. The sun enters Capricorn about December 22. **b** a person born under this sign.
3 tropic of Capricorn an imaginary circle around the globe, about 23° south of the equator. <Latin *Capricornus*, from *caper* goat + *cornu* horn>

cap·si·cum (kap′sə kəm) *n* a small tropical shrub, widely grown for its edible fruit called a pepper. Sweet peppers and pimentos are among such fruits. <Latin *capsa* case>

cap·size (kap′sīz) *or* (kap sīz′) *v* **cap·sized, cap·siz·ing** turn upside down in the water, especially as a boat: *The sailboat nearly capsized in the squall. He capsized the canoe when he stood up in it.* <origin unknown>

cap·stan (kap′stən) *n* a device that rotates on an upright shaft in order to pull or lift something attached to it by a cable. <Latin *capistrum*, from *capere* grab>

cap·stone (kap′stōn′) *n* the top stone of a wall or other structure.

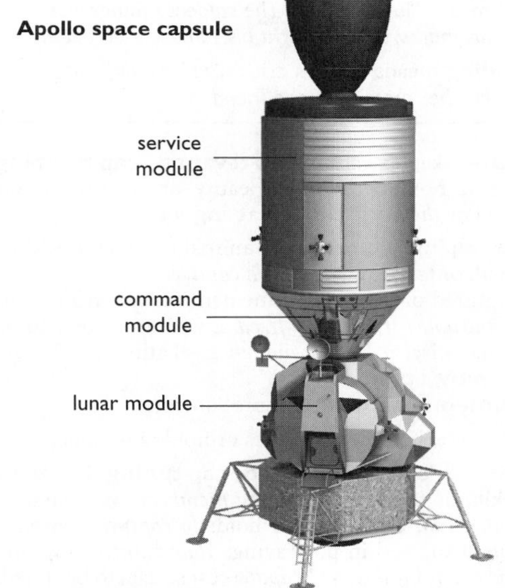

The Apollo space **capsule** held three astronauts, and they spent most of their journey in the command module. On July 20, 1969, Neil Armstrong became the first person to walk on the moon.

cap·sule (kap′səl) *n* **1** a tiny case or container of gelatin or other soluble substance enclosing a single dose of medicine and swallowed whole. **2** a detachable section of a rocket, made to carry instruments or astronauts into space. Also, **space capsule. 3** *Botany* a dry seedcase that opens when ripe.
adj condensed or concise: *The movie review gave a capsule version of the plot.*

a bat	e bed	i bid	o pot	u cup	th **thin**
ā cake	ē me	ī bite	ō go	ū rude	ᴛʜ **then**
ä bar	ə about	ər over	ô for	u̇ put	zh measure

cap·tain (kap′tən) *n* **1** a commander of a ship or pilot of a commercial aircraft. **2** a leader or chief: *She was chosen to be captain of the hockey team.* **3** *Military* a commissioned officer ranking above a lieutenant and below a major.
v lead or command as captain: *to captain a ship.* <Old French, from Latin *caput* head> **cap′tain·cy** *n.*

cap·tion (kap′shən) *n* **1** an explanation or title accompanying a picture or diagram. **2** a title or heading at the beginning of a page, article, or chapter.
v put a caption on. <Latin *captio*, from *capere* take, seize>

cap·tious (kap′shəs) *adj* hard to please; apt to look for trivial faults. <French, from Latin *capere* catch (i.e., catch someone making an error)> **cap′tious·ly** *adv.* **cap′tious·ness** *n.*

SYNONYMS

Captious can mean "petty": *The manager's captious attitude was evident in the way she loved to point out even the smallest mistake.*

Critical means "judgmental": *The student's father was critical of his marks, as he thought his son could do better.*

Faultfinding means "always critical": *Her faultfinding habit has lost her more than one friend.*

cap·ti·vate (kap′tə vāt′) *v* **cap·ti·vat·ed, cap·ti·vat·ing** attract and hold because of beauty or interest: *I was captivated by the story.* **cap′ti·vat′ing** *adj.*

cap·tive (kap′tiv) *n* a person or animal taken and held by force, skill, or trickery: *to tie up a captive.*
adj **1** captured or kept in confinement: *a captive bird. The captive journalist was finally freed.* **2** with no choice to be or do otherwise: *a captive audience.* <Latin *capere* seize, take> **cap·tiv′i·ty** *n.*
take someone captive, capture someone.

cap·tor (kap′tər) *n* one who takes or holds a prisoner.

cap·ture (kap′chər) *v* **cap·tured, cap·tur·ing** **1** seize by force, skill, or trickery: *Two gang members were captured during the raid.* **2** attract and hold: *to capture someone's attention.* **3** succeed in portraying: *Your painting captures the mood of a rainy day.* **4** *Computers* cause data to be stored.
n **1** anything captured. **2** the act or fact of capturing.
cap·ture–re·cap·ture (kap′chər rē′kap′chər) *Statistics* *n* a sampling method used to estimate the number of animals in a region. In this process, some animals are captured, marked, and released. After some time, some animals are again captured. The proportion of marked (i.e., recaptured) animals in this group is assumed to be the same as the proportion of marked animals in the whole population.

cap·u·chin (kap′yū shin′) *or* (kap′yū chin′) *n* a S American monkey whose head is covered with black hair that looks like a hood. <Italian *capuccio* hood>

cap·y·ba·ra (kap′ə bȧ′rə) *n* a S American mammal that lives near water. It is the largest living rodent. <Portuguese, from Tupi (a language of S America)>

car (kȧr) *n* **1** a motorized passenger vehicle driven on roads. **2** a long, narrow vehicle that carries people or freight, and moves on wheels or rails, or is pulled by a cable. **3** the closed platform of an elevator. <Latin *carrum* two-wheeled cart>

ca·rafe (kə raf′) *n* a tall, open-topped container for pouring water, wine, or coffee. <French, probably from Arabic *garafa* draw water>

car·a·ga·na (ker′ə gan′ə) *n* a shrub or small tree with feathery, pale green foliage and yellow flowers that appear in early spring. <Latin>

car·a·mel (ker′ə məl) *or* (kȧr′məl) *n* **1** sugar browned or burned over heat, used for colouring and flavouring food. **2** a small block of chewy candy flavoured with this sugar.
adj the colour of browned sugar. <Spanish *caramelo*> **car′a·mel·ize′** *v.*

car·a·pace (ker′ə pās′) *n* the hard upper shell of a tortoise or crustacean. <French, from Spanish *carapacho*>

car·at (ker′ət) *n* a unit of mass for precious stones, equal to 200 mg. <French, from Greek *keration* carob bean used as a unit of mass>

car·a·van (ker′ə van′) *n* **1** a group of people travelling together across land, with their vehicles or animals. **2** a large camper or recreational vehicle, or a large van such as used by a circus. <French, from Persian *karwan*>

car·a·vel (ker′ə vel′) *n* a small, fast sailing ship, used in the 1400s and 1500s. <Portuguese *caravela* little ship>

car·a·way (kar′ə wā) *or* (ker′ə wā′) *n* a plant of the parsley family with fragrant, spicy seeds. <Latin, from Arabic *al-karawiya*>

car·bide (kȧr′bīd) *n* a compound of carbon with a metal, especially CALCIUM CARBIDE. <Latin *carbo* coal>

car·bine (kȧr′bīn) *or* (kȧr′bin) *n* a light automatic rifle, originally a short rifle or musket designed for cavalry use. <French *carabin* mounted rifleman>

car·bo·hy·drate (kȧr′bō hī′drāt) *n* a compound made up of carbon, hydrogen, and oxygen that takes part in the chemical processes in living plants and animals, providing energy. <*carbon* + *hydrate*>

car·bol·ic acid (kȧr bol′ik) *n* a poisonous, corrosive, white crystalline compound with a strong odour. Also called **phenol**.

car·bon (kȧr′bən) *n* a non-metallic element found in combination with others in all living things and their products. Diamonds and graphite are pure carbon; coal and charcoal are impure carbon. *Symbol* **C** <French, from Latin *carbo* coal>

carbon–14 *n* a radioactive isotope of carbon produced by the bombardment of nitrogen atoms. The rate of decay of carbon-14 in organic matter is used to date archaeological objects or geological formations.

car·bo·na·ceous (kȧr′bə nā′shəs) *adj* of or containing carbon.

car·bon·ate (kȧr′bə nāt′) *v* **car·bon·at·ed, car·bon·at·ing** add carbon dioxide to. **Carbonated water**, also called **soda water** or **sparkling water**, is fizzy and forms the basis of many soft drinks.

carbon copy *n* **1** a copy made by using carbon paper. **2** anything that seems to be an exact duplicate: *His ideas are a carbon copy of his father's.*

carbon cycle *Biology n* the circulation of carbon in nature between living things and their environments.

carbon dating *n* the process of finding out how old an object is by measuring how far the CARBON-14 in it has decayed. **car′bon-date′** *v.*

carbon dioxide *n* a heavy, colourless, odourless gas present in the atmosphere. The air breathed out by people and animals contains carbon dioxide; plants absorb it from the air and use it to make tissue. *Symbol* **CO_2**

car·bon·ic acid (kȧr bon′ik) *n* the acid produced when carbon dioxide dissolves in water.

Car·bon·if·er·ous (kȧr′bə nif′ə rəs) *n* the geological period lasting from about 360 million to 280 million years ago, when the warm, moist climate produced a lush plant growth. See also PALEOZOIC.
adj **1** to do with this period or the rocks formed then. **2 carboniferous** containing coal. <*carbon* + Latin *ferre* to carry>

car·bon·ize (kȧr′bə nīz′) *v* **car·bon·ized, car·bon·iz·ing 1** change into carbon by burning. **2** cover or combine with carbon. **car′bon·i·za′tion** *n.*

carbon monoxide *n* a colourless, odourless, poisonous gas formed when carbon burns with an insufficient supply of air.

carbon paper *n* thin paper coated with a preparation of carbon or other inky substance on one surface that is placed between sheets of ordinary paper to make a copy of whatever is on the top sheet.

carbon tet·ra·chlo·ride (tet′rə klȯr′īd) *n* a poisonous, colourless, nonflammable liquid often used as a solvent.

car·bo·run·dum (kȧr′bə run′dəm) *n* a hard compound of carbon and silicon, used for grinding and polishing. <*Carborundum*, a trademark>

car·boy (kȧr′boi) *n* a large glass bottle, usually enclosed in basketwork or in a wooden box or crate. <Persian *karaba* large flagon>

car·bun·cle (kȧr′bung kəl) *n* a large, infected cluster of multiple boils. <Old French, from Latin *carbo* coal>

car·bu·retor (kȧr′bə rāt′ər) *n* a device in an internal combustion engine that mixes air with a fine spray of liquid fuel to produce an explosive mixture. <archaic *carburet* combine with a hydrocarbon>

🍁 **car·ca·jou** (kȧr′kə zhū′) *n* a wolverine. <Cdn French, from Algonquian>

car·cass (kȧr′kəs) *n* **1** the dead body of an animal. **2** the remains of something discarded, abandoned, or emptied. <Old French>

car·cin·o·gen (kȧr sin′ə jən) *n* a substance or agent that causes cancer. <Greek *karkinos* creeping tumour + *-gen*> **car′ci·no·gen′ic** *adj.*

car·ci·no·ma (kȧr′sə nō′mə) *n, pl* **car·ci·no·mas** or **car·ci·no·ma·ta** (kȧr′sə nō′mə tə) a cancerous growth, especially in the skin or the lining of a tube or cavity in the body.

card[1] (kȧrd) *n* **1** a piece of stiff paper, thin cardboard, or plastic, usually small and rectangular: *a business card, a credit card, playing cards.* **2** a piece of stiff paper, usually folded, containing a message and usually an illustration, sent to someone to mark a special occasion: *Did you send her a birthday card?* **3** *Informal* an amusing person. **4** *Computers* a circuit board to be inserted into a special slot inside a computer to give the computer additional capabilities: *a sound card.* **5 cards** *pl* a game played with a set of cards: *Let's play cards.* <Old French, from Greek *chartes* papyrus leaf (from which paper can be made)>
a card up your sleeve, a plan kept in reserve: *She doesn't look worried; she must have a card up her sleeve.*
hold all the cards, have complete control.
in (or **on**) **the cards,** sure to happen: *It was in the cards that it would rain; nothing has gone right all day.*
play the —— card, use a certain issue or fact to one's advantage: *The candidate played the language card, making all her speeches in Greek as well as English and French.*
play your cards right, act cleverly; use strategy: *If we play our cards right, we can get him on our side.*
put (or **lay**) **your cards on the table,** show what you feel or intend to do; be open and frank.
show your cards, reveal your plans, intentionally or not.

card[2] (kȧrd) *n* a toothed tool or wire brush used to separate, clean, and straighten wool or hemp fibres.
v clean or comb with this. <Old French, from Latin *carere* to card> **card′er** *n.* **card′ing** *n.*

car·da·mom or **car·da·mum** (kȧr′də məm) *n* the aromatic seed of a plant of the ginger family. <Old French, from Greek *kardamomon*>

card·board (kȧrd′bȯrd′) *n* a fairly thick kind of stiff paper, used to make cards, boxes, and packaging.

card–car·ry·ing (kȧrd′ker′ē ing) *adj* being an official member of an organization, or a firm believer in some idea or doctrine: *a card-carrying environmentalist.*

card catalogue or **file** *n* a set of index cards individually listing books and other items in a library or collection.

car·di·ac (kȧr′dē ak′) *adj* to do with the heart. A **cardiac arrest** is heart failure. <Greek *kardia* heart>

car·di·gan (kȧr′də gən) *n* a sweater or knitted jacket that opens down the front. <Earl of *Cardigan*, who wore such a jacket>

car·di·nal (kȧr′də nəl) *adj* main or principal: *a cardinal point in the argument.*
n **1** *Catholicism* a high official who is appointed by the Pope and belongs to a body that elects succeeding popes. Cardinals wear bright red robes. **2** a N American songbird, the male bright red and the female mainly brownish. **3** a cardinal number. <Old French, from Latin *cardo* hinge (on which something depends)>

cardinal number *n* a whole number, such as one, two, or three, that shows quantity. Compare ORDINAL NUMBER.

cardinal points *pl n* north, south, east, and west, the four main directions of the compass.

a bat	e bed	i bid	o pot	u cup	th **thin**
ā cake	ē me	ī bite	ō go	ū rude	TH **then**
ȧ bar	ə about	ər over	ȯ for	u̇ put	zh measure

C

cardinal virtues *pln* prudence, fortitude, temperance, and justice, traditionally considered to be the four basic qualities of a good character.

cardio– *combining form* to do with the heart: *cardiogram, cardiovascular.* <Greek *kardia* heart>

car·di·o·gram (kȧr′dē ə gram′) *n* a curving line on a graph showing the strength and nature of movements of the heart as recorded by a cardiograph.

car·di·o·graph (kȧr′dē ə graf′) *n* an instrument that records the electrical impulses representing the movements of the heart, by means of electrodes placed on the skin.

car·di·ol·o·gy (kȧr′dē ol′əjē) *n* the branch of medicine that studies diseases of the heart. **car′di·ol′o·gist** *n.*

car·di·o·pul·mo·na·ry (kȧr′dē ō pul′mə ner′ē) *adj* to do with the heart and lungs.

cardiopulmonary resuscitation CPR (def. 1).

car·di·o·vas·cu·lar (kȧr′dē ō vas′kyə lər) *adj* to do with the heart and blood vessels: *Hardening of the arteries is a cardiovascular disease.*

care (ker) *v* **cared, car·ing 1** be concerned or feel an interest: *He cares about the environment. I don't care what they said.* **2** pay kind attention to the needs of others: *doctors who care.* **3** (*usually with negatives or in questions*) to object: *They don't care if we're late once in a while.* **4** want or wish: *She didn't care to reply.*
n **1** safekeeping or responsibility: *The photos were left in his sister's care.* **2** provision of what is needed for health and safety, such as food, shelter, or protection: *I was given the best of care.* **3** serious attention to doing things properly and safely: *A good cook works with care.* **4** concern, worry, or anxiety: *Few people are totally free from care.* **5** an object of worry, concern, or attention: *weighed down by many cares. Keeping records is the care of the secretary of the club.* <Old English *caru*>
care for, a give or do what is needed for: *The nurse will care for her during the night.* **b** like: *She doesn't care for him.* **c** want or wish: *I don't care for any dessert tonight.*
care of (or **in care of**)**,** at the address or in the charge of: *Send it care of his father. Abbrev.* **c/o**
could care less, *Informal* not care at all: *I could care less what you do!*
couldn't care less, not care at all: *I couldn't care less how you spend your money.*
take care, a be careful: *Take care or you'll fall.* **b** a casual expression of farewell.
take care of, a attend to or take charge of: *This waiter will take care of you.* **b** look after: *Who took care of her while she was sick?* **c** be careful with: *Take care of your money.*

ca·reen (kə rēn′) *v* **1** lean or tilt a ship to one side: *The ship careened in the strong wind.* **2** rush along with an uncontrolled, leaning movement: *The waitress careened among the tables, balancing a heavy tray.* <French, from Latin *carina* keel>

ca·reer (kə rēr′) *n* **1** a way of making a living, especially when done with commitment: *She planned to make law her career.* **2** a general course of action through life: *I like to read about the careers of explorers.*
adj seriously following a certain occupation for the long term: *a career athlete.*
v rush along wildly: *The runaway horse careered through the streets.* <French *carrière* race course, from Latin *carrus* wagon>

care·free (ker′frē′) *adj* without worry or responsibility.

care·ful (ker′fəl) *adj* **1** paying attention to what one says and does: *Be careful around the pool. He is careful to tell the truth at all times.* **2** done with thought or attention and effort: *careful work, a careful investigation.* **3** avoiding risk: *a careful answer.* **4** considerate or protective: *always careful of the feelings of others.* **care′ful·ly** *adv.* **care′ful·ness** *n.*

care·giv·er (ker′giv′ər) *n* a person who looks after someone else, whether paid to do so or not.

care·less (ker′lis) *adj* **1** showing little attention to what one is saying or doing: *careless remarks, a careless worker.* **2** indifferent or unconcerned: *careless of the needs of others.* **3** (*usually before the noun*) carefree or untroubled. **care′less·ly** *adv.* **care′less·ness** *n.*

SYNONYMS

Careless can mean "inconsiderate": *The girl, with her careless movements, kept bumping into people.*

Casual can mean "unconcerned about appearance": *His casual way of dressing embarrassed his grandparents.*

Heedless can mean "thoughtless" as well as "careless": *Heedless of the blizzard, he went outside without a coat.*

Neglectful means "giving little attention to": *She was neglectful and didn't water the plants, so they died.*

ca·ress (kə res′) *n* **1** a gentle, loving touch, stroke, or kiss. **2** a light or gentle touch from something: *the caress of a summer breeze.*
v touch or stroke gently, lightly, or lovingly: *He talked to the kitten softly as he caressed it. The wind caressed the treetops.* <French, from Latin *carus* dear>

car·et (ker′ət) *n* a proofreader's mark [‸] to show where something should be inserted. <Latin = is lacking>

care·tak·er (ker′tā′kər) *n* **1** a person who is employed to look after a property or another person. **2** a person or group who holds power temporarily before another takes or resumes charge.
adj holding power temporarily: *a caretaker government.*

care·worn (ker′wȯrn′) *adj* showing the effects of continuous worry and care.

car·fare (kȧr′fer′) *n* the money to pay for riding on a streetcar, bus, or subway.

car·go (kȧr′gō) *n, pl* **car·goes** or **car·gos** the load of goods carried on a ship, aircraft, or motor vehicle: *a cargo of wheat.* <Spanish, from Latin *carrus* wagon>

cargo pants *pln* baggy casual pants with many large pockets closed by flaps or zippers, including on the side of the leg.

Car·ib·be·an (ker′ə bē′ən) *adj* to do with the Caribbean Sea, the islands in it, or the adjacent coasts of North, Central, and South America.
n the region that includes the Caribbean Sea.

C

car·i·bou (ker′ə bū′) *n, pl* **car·i·bou** or **car·i·bous** a reindeer of northern areas of North America, especially the Barren Lands. Its skin is used to make traditional parkas and moccasins. Also called **tuktu**. See ANTLER for picture. <Cdn French, from Algonquian *xalibu* an animal that paws things, from its habit of pawing snow in search of grass>

Caribou Inuit *n* a group of Inuit living on the west side of Hudson Bay.

GRAMMAR AND USAGE

Caribou Inuit is the English name to describe one Inuit community. However, the Inuit have their own Inuktitut names for their communities. *Ahiarmiut* is one such name for Caribou Inuit.

car·i·ca·ture (ker′ə kə chər) *n* **1** a picture, cartoon, or description that deliberately exaggerates peculiarities or characteristics: *In political caricatures, his large chin appears enormous.* **2** the art of making such pictures or descriptions. **3** a stereotype or oversimplification: *The movie reduces the characters to mere caricatures.*
v **car·i·ca·tured, car·i·ca·tur·ing** make or be a caricature of. <Italian *caricatura* distortion, from Latin *carricare* load up, exaggerate> **car′i·ca·tur′ist** *n.*

car·ies (ker′ēz) *or* (ker′ē ēz′) *n* the decay of teeth or bones: *Caries of the teeth is caused by bacteria.* <Latin>

car·il·lon (ker′ə lon′) *n* a set of bells arranged for playing melodies: *There is a carillon in the Peace Tower in Ottawa.* <French> **car′il·lon·neur′** (ker′ə lə nər′) *n.*

car·ing (ker′ing) *adj* displaying kindness and concern for others.

car·i·ole or **car·ri·ole** (ker′ē ōl′) *n* **1** a one-horse sleigh. **2** a dogsled, equipped to carry one person lying down: *The injured trapper was brought to the cabin in a cariole.* <French, from Latin *carrus* wagon>

car·jack (kår′jak′) *v* force or threaten a driver into giving up his or her car. <*car* + (*hi*)*jack*> **car′jack′er** *n.* **car′jack′ing** *n.*

car·load (kår′lōd′) *n* the number or amount that a car can carry: *a carload of people bound for the party, a train carrying several carloads of grain.*

car·mine (kår′mən) *or* (kår′mīn) *n* a deep red colouring matter found in COCHINEAL.
adj vivid deep red. <French, from Arabic *kirmiz*>

car·nage (kår′nij) *n* great slaughter or destruction. <French, from Latin *carnis* flesh>

car·nal (kår′nəl) *adj* to do with the desires and pleasures of the body, especially sexual ones: *carnal instincts.* <Latin *carnis* flesh> **car·nal′i·ty** *n.* **car′nal·ly** *adv.*

car·na·tion (kår nā′shən) *n* a flowering plant with large, fragrant flowers whose many petals have a jagged edge. <origin uncertain>

car·na·u·ba (kår no′bə) *or* (kår nū′bə) *n* a Brazilian palm tree whose leaves yield a yellowish wax. <Portuguese>

car·nel·ian (kår nēl′yən) *n* a red or reddish brown variety of quartz used in jewellery. <Old French>

car·nie (kår′nē) *Informal n* a person who works or performs in a carnival.

car·ni·val (kår′nə vəl) *n* **1** an amusement fair with rides, sideshows, games of chance, and other entertainments. **2** an organized program of events involving a particular sport, season, or place: *a winter carnival.* **3** in some Roman Catholic cultures, a time of feasting and merrymaking just before Lent.

ETYMOLOGY

Carnival comes from Italian *carnevale*. It in turn comes from Latin *carnelevamen* or *carnelevarium*, the name for the day just before Lent, which means, literally, "the giving up of meat-eating."

Carnivals are still held throughout the world in the two-week period prior to Lent.

car·ni·vore (kår′nə vôr′) *n* an animal that feeds on the flesh of other animals. <French, from Latin *carnis* flesh + *vorare* devour> **car·niv′o·rous** *adj.*

car·ob (ker′əb) *n* a brown, floury powder, tasting somewhat like chocolate, made from the beans of a Mediterranean evergreen tree. <Old French, from Arabic *karruba*>

car·ol (ker′əl) *n* a song or hymn of joy, especially a seasonal one: *Christmas carols.*
v **car·olled** or **car·oled, car·ol·ling** or **car·ol·ing** sing carols. <Old French *carole*> **car′ol·ler** or **car′ol·er** *n.*

car·om (ker′əm) *n* **1** *Billiards* a shot in which the ball, when struck with the cue, hits two balls one after the other. **2** a striking and rebounding of something.
v make a carom. <Spanish *carambola*>

car·o·tene (ker′ə tēn′) *n* a red or yellow pigment found in the carrot and other plants, and in animal tissues that is converted in the body into vitamin A. <German, from Latin *carota* carrot>

ca·rot·id (kə rot′id) *n* either of two large arteries, one on each side of the neck, that carry blood to the head.
adj to do with these arteries. <French, from Greek *karoun* become unconscious. This happens when the artery is pressed.>

ca·rouse (kə rouz′) *v* **ca·roused, ca·rous·ing** take part in noisy drinking parties.
n usually, **carousal** a noisy drinking party. <German *gar aus* (*trinken*) (drink) all up> **ca·rous′er** *n.*

car·ou·sel (ker′ə sel′) *n* **1** a merry-go-round. **2** in an airport, a revolving platform onto which the baggage of arriving passengers is delivered by a chute. **3** a round, rotating tray on a slide projector. It holds photographic slides and successively drops each in front of the light source and raises it again. <French, from Italian *carosello*>

a bat	e bed	i bid	o pot	u cup	th **thin**
ā cake	ē me	ī bite	ō go	ū rude	TH **then**
å bar	ə about	ər over	ô for	ů put	zh measure

carp[1] (kärp) *v* complain or find fault. <Old Norse *karpa,* related to Latin *carpere* tear to pieces>

carp[2] (kärp) *n, pl* **carps** or (*especially collectively*) **carp** a bony freshwater fish with barbels on the upper jaw, large scales, and a long dorsal fin. Goldfish and minnows are carp. <Old French, from Latin *carpa*>

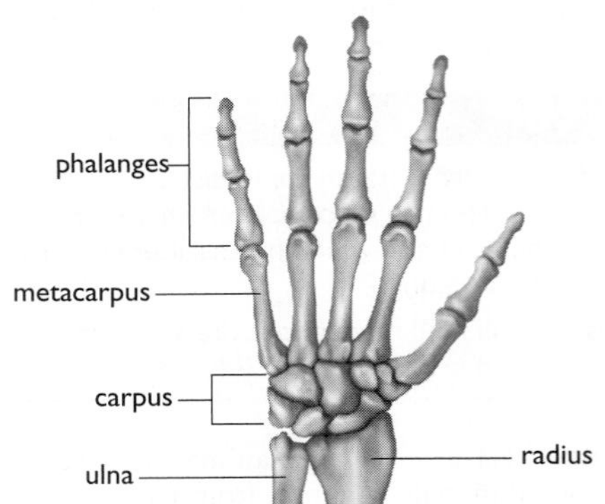

car·pal (kär′pəl) *adj* to do with the **carpus**, the group of short bones in the wrist. Pain or numbness in the hand and wrist due to highly repetitive movements, especially in keyboarding, is called **carpal tunnel syndrome**. <Greek *karpos* wrist>

car·pel (kär′pəl) *n* the central part of a flower containing the ovules, which develop into seeds. <French, from Greek *karpos* fruit>

carpenter ant *n* a large ant that burrows into wood to make its nest.

car·pen·try (kär′pən trē) *n* the trade or art of building, finishing, and repairing structures made of wood. <Old French, from Latin *carpentarius* wagon-maker>
car′pent·er *n.*

car·pet (kär′pit) *n* **1** a thick, heavy, woven covering for floors and stairs. **2** a thing resembling a carpet: *A carpet of grass stretched down to the lake.*
v cover with a carpet: *Violets carpeted the ground in spring.* <Old French, from Latin *carpere* to pluck>
on the carpet, *Informal* being scolded or rebuked.

car·pet·bag·ger (kär′pit bag′ər) *n* **1** a ruthless person who takes advantage of others. **2** a politician who seeks office in a place where he or she has no real connection. <in the US, a person who went to the South after the Civil War in order to make a profit from the situation. Such a person often carried a travelling bag made of carpeting or similar fabric.>

car·pet–bomb (kär′pit bom′) *v* drop many bombs in a short time over a wide area.

car·pet·ing (kär′pi ting′) *n* carpets or the fabric they are made from.

car·pool (kär′pül′) *n* an arrangement by which people take turns providing transportation in their own cars, especially to and from work. **car′pool′** *v.* **car′pool′ing** *n.*

car·port (kär′pört′) *n* a roofed space attached to a house and open on two or three sides, used as a garage.

car·ra·geen (ker′ə gēn) *n* an edible purplish seaweed, found along rocky coasts of the N Atlantic, that yields **carrageenan**, a substance that keeps liquids combined. <Irish *carraigín*>

car·rel (ker′əl) *n* an enclosed space for individual study in a library, usually with a desk and bookshelves. Also, **carrell**. <origin uncertain>

car·riage (ker′ij) *n* **1** a wheeled horse-drawn passenger vehicle. **2** a moving part of a machine that carries or supports some other part: *a lathe carriage.* **3** a manner of holding one's head and body; bearing: *She has a queenly carriage.* <Old French, from Latin *carrus* cart>

carriage bolt *n* a bolt with a square part just under the head, in former times used mainly to join parts of a carriage.

carriage trade *n* rich customers of a business. <In former times, rich customers arrived by carriage.>

car·ri·er (ker′ē ər) *n* **1** a company or person that carries or transports: *airlines, trucking companies, and other carriers. The post office employs letter carriers.* **2** an organism that carries and can pass on a disease or gene, often without being affected itself. **3** *Radio* a radio-frequency wave used to transmit, or carry, the waves that represent the sounds being broadcast. Also, **carrier wave**. **4** anything designed to carry something in or on.

Car·rier (ker′ē ər) WET'SUWET'EN.

carrier pigeon *n* a homing pigeon, usually one trained to fly home carrying written messages.

car·ri·ole (ker′ē ōl′) CARIOLE.

car·ri·on (ker′ē ən) *n* dead and decaying flesh: *Buzzards and vultures live on carrion.* <Old French, Latin *caro* flesh>

car·rot (ker′ət) *n* **1** a cultivated plant of the parsley family that has a tapering, usually orange, root that is eaten as a vegetable. **2** a promised reward used to motivate someone, from the supposed practice of dangling a carrot in front of a donkey's nose to make it go forward. **Carrot and stick** indicates reward and punishment. <French, from Greek *karoton*>

car·ry (ker′ē) *v* **car·ried, car·ry·ing 1** take from one place to another: *Buses carry passengers. Mom carried the sleepy child to bed.* **2** bear the weight of or hold up: *Those pillars carry the roof.* **3** (*with a reflexive pronoun*) **a** hold one's body and head in a certain way when moving: *She carries herself like a queen.* **b** behave or conduct oneself: *He knows how to carry himself in any situation.* **4** keep in stock: *This store carries men's clothing.* **5** pass or adopt a motion at a meeting: *The motion to adjourn was carried.* **6** have the power to cover or reach a certain distance: *Your voice carries easily to the back of the room.* **7** bear the main responsibility for: *In any group effort, he carries everyone else.* **8** have as an attribute: *The title "director" carries authority.* **9** have and potentially pass on a disease or gene. **10** *Mathematics* in adding, transfer a number from one place or column in the sum to the one on the left. <Old French, from Latin *carrus* cart>
carry a tune, keep to the correct notes in a melody.
carry away, influence beyond reason by strong feelings or enthusiasm: *carried away by excitement.*

carry on, **a** do or conduct: *to carry on a business.* **b** continue: *Carry on from where you left off. We must carry on the struggle for justice.* **c** *Informal* behave wildly or foolishly: *Stop carrying on.* **d** *Informal* talk, argue, or complain at length: *What's she carrying on about now?*
carry out, do or accomplish: *to carry out an order. He carried out his job well.*
carry over, continue or extend.
carry the day, win or be victorious.

SYNONYMS

Carry means "take something from one place to another": *Please carry this tray to your sister.*

Haul means "move" and suggests strength: *He hauled the huge bundle of newspapers in a wagon behind him.*

Transport is often used in reference to vehicles: *The furniture was transported by truck to our cottage.*

car·ry·all (ker′ē ol′) *n* a large, sturdy bag or case.

carrying charge *n* the interest charged on the balance owed when paying in instalments.

car·ry·ing–on (ker′ē ing on′) *Informal n, pl* **car·ry·ings-on** **1** loud disturbance or fuss: *What's all this carrying-on about?* **2** boldly inappropriate behaviour, especially in romantic involvement.

car·ry–o·ver (ker′ē ō′vər) *n* something continued or kept from a previous time or an earlier set of conditions: *This filing system is a carry-over from a time before computers.*

car seat *n* **1** a fixed seat for a passenger or driver in a car. **2** a safety seat for a baby or small child to use in a car, with straps to hold the child in.

carsick (kär′sik′) *adj* nauseated by the motion of a car. **car′sick′ness** *n.*

cart (kärt) *n* **1** a wagonlike vehicle with two wheels for carrying heavy loads, pulled by oxen, horses, etc., or by a motorized vehicle. **2** a small, wheeled vehicle moved by hand: *a grocery cart, a baggage cart.*
v **1** carry in a cart or other vehicle. **2** carry or go with effort: *I don't want to cart all my books around.* <Old Norse *kartr*>
put the cart before the horse, reverse the proper order or way to do something.

cart·age (kär′tij) *n* the business of transporting goods, or a fee charged for this.

carte blanche (kärt blänsh′) *n* complete freedom to use one's own judgment. <French = white card>

car·tel (kär tel′) *n* **1** a combination of businesses formed to control the production and marketing of goods. **2** an alliance of political groups for a common cause. <German, from Greek *chartes* papyrus leaf>

Car·te·sian coordinates (kär tē′zhən) *Mathematics pln* an ordered set of numbers that can plot the location of any point in space from a given starting point. <*Cartesius*, Latinized surname of R. *Descartes*, 17c philosopher and mathematician>

Car·tha·gin·i·an (kär′thə jin′ē ən) *adj* to do with Carthage, an ancient city and seaport in N Africa.
n a native or inhabitant of Carthage.

cart·horse (kärt′hors) *n* a horse used to pull carts or wagons.

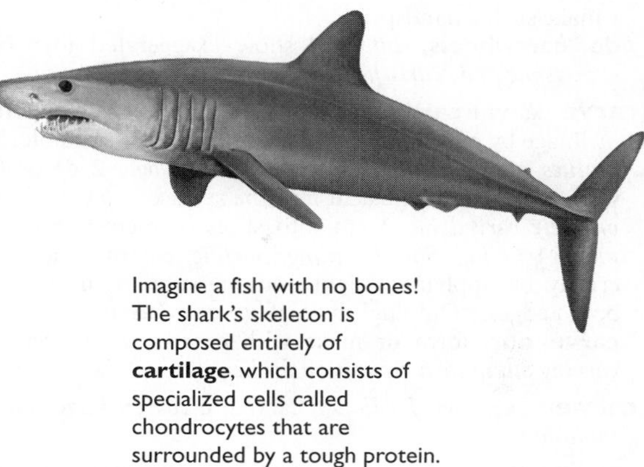

Imagine a fish with no bones! The shark's skeleton is composed entirely of **cartilage**, which consists of specialized cells called chondrocytes that are surrounded by a tough protein.

car·ti·lage (kär′tə lij) *n* a tough, elastic tissue found at the ends of long bones, between vertebrae, and in the nose. It is widespread in young vertebrates, later being converted into bone. <French, from Latin *cartilago*> **car′ti·lag′i·nous** (kär′tə laj′ə nəs) *adj.*

cart·load (kärt′lōd′) *n* as much as a cart can hold or carry.

car·tog·ra·phy (kär tog′rə fē) *n* the science or practice of making maps. <French, from Latin *carta* map + *-graphy*> **car·tog′ra·pher** *n.*

car·ton (kär′tən) *n* a box or other container made of cardboard: *a one-litre carton of milk. Pack the books in cartons.* <French, from Greek *chartes* papyrus leaf>

car·toon (kär tūn′) *n* **1** a humorous drawing, often with a caption: *The editorial page of our paper has a political cartoon every day.* **2** a comic strip. **3** a movie or TV show made up of a series of drawings shown in rapid sequence. **4** a caricature, stereotype, or oversimplification: *The plot is okay, but unfortunately all the characters are cartoons.* **5** a full-size drawing made by an artist as a design for a work of art.
v draw cartoons. <Italian, from Greek *chartes* papyrus leaf> **car·toon′ish** *adj.* **car·toon′ist** *n.*

car·touche (kär tūsh′) *n* **1** on ancient Egyptian monuments, a rectangular or oval figure framing the name of a ruler. **2** an elaborate frame in the shape of a scroll for a painted or carved inscription on a building. <French = scroll, from Greek *chartes* papyrus leaf (from which paper can be made)>

car·tridge (kär′trij) *n* **1** a metal or plastic tube containing a charge of explosive and pellets or a bullet, for use in a firearm. **2** a case containing a refill of some substance, such as toner for a printer or photocopier. **3** a sealed plastic case containing a spool of film together with a take-up spool, for use in a camera. <variant of *cartouche*>

a bat	e bed	i bid	o pot	u cup	th **thin**
ā cake	ē me	ī bite	ō go	ū rude	ᴛʜ **then**
ä bar	ə about	ər over	ȯ for	u̇ put	zh measure

cart·wheel (kärt′wēl′) *n* **1** a sideways handspring made with the arms and legs stretched out stiffly like the spokes of a wheel. **2** the wheel of a cart.
v make such a handspring.
do cartwheels, *Informal* show exaggerated joy: *He expects me to do cartwheels every time he smiles at me.*

carve (kärv) *v* **carved, carv·ing 1** make a design, letters, or image by cutting into a surface or out of a solid block: *Statues are often carved from stone or wood.* **2** decorate with figures or designs cut into the surface: *a box with an ornately carved lid.* **3** cut into slices or pieces: *to carve meat.* **4** *Skiing, Snowboarding, Surfing, etc.* make a turn crisply by applying weight and pressure to the ski or board edges. <Old English *ceorfan*> **carv′er** *n.*
carve out, form or make with care or effort: *She is carving out quite a reputation for herself.*

carv·en (kär′vən) *Poetic adj* carved: *a carven image on a tombstone.*

carving (kärv) *n* **1 a** a design cut into a surface or a figure cut out of a solid block of wood, stone, etc. **b** making such designs or figures. **2** the cutting of meat, poultry, etc. into slices or pieces.

carving knife *n* a knife for cutting cooked meat.

car·y·at·id (kar′ē a′tid) *or* (ker′ē a′tid) *n, pl* **car·y·at·ids** or **car·y·at·ides** (-tidz) a stone carving of a female figure, used as a pillar for the upper part of a building in ancient Greek architecture. <Latin, from Greek *Karyatides,* priestesses in Karyai, a village in Greece>

ca·sa·ba or **cas·sa·ba** (kə sä′bə) *n* a winter muskmelon with yellow rind and pale flesh. <*Kasaba,* former name of a town in Turkey>

Cas·a·no·va (kas′ə nō′və) *n* a man who has many romantic involvements with women. <G.J. *Casanova,* 18c adventurer>

cas·cade (kas kād′) *n* **1** a small waterfall. **2** an arrangement or hanging of material that resembles a small waterfall: *a cascade of windows on a computer screen. Her hair fell in a cascade of curls.* **3** a process by which each of a series of things sets off the next: *a cascade of practical jokes.*
v **cas·cad·ed, cas·cad·ing** fall in a cascade. <Old French, from Latin *casus* fall>

case[1] (kās) *n* **1** an example: *It was a clear case of reckless driving.* **2** a set of circumstances: *What would you do in such a case? She said she was alone, but that was not the case.* **3** an instance of a disease or injury: *a case of measles.* **4** a person requiring professional attention, such as from a doctor or social worker: *She handles ten cases a day.* **5** a matter for a law court to decide. **6** a set of arguments or supporting facts for or against something: *a good case against the use of cellphones in cars.* **7** *Informal* somebody of a particular kind or in a particular condition, especially an unfortunate one: *a hopeless case.* **8** *Grammar* the role of a noun, pronoun, or adjective in a sentence, shown by a particular form. English has case for personal pronouns only: *I, we, he, she, they,* and *who* are forms used only as subjects of a sentence, while *me, us, him, her, them,* and *whom* are forms of the same pronouns used as objects. <Old French, from Latin *casus* a fall>
in any case, a no matter what else is true: *It may have been Monday or Tuesday; in any case, it was this week.* **b** in spite of circumstances: *It was chilly, but we went swimming in any case.*
in case, so as to be prepared if: *Keep the receipt in case you need to return the jacket.*
in case of, in the event of: *In case of fire, walk quietly to the nearest door.*
in no case, under no circumstances: *In no case should you get into a stranger's car.*
on (or **off**) **someone's case,** *Informal* nagging or criticizing someone (or no longer doing so): *She's always on my case about getting too little sleep. Get off my case!*

case[2] (kās) *n* **1** a box or crate: *a packing case, a case of pop.* **2** a boxlike container with a handle, specially designed for carrying something. **3** a sheath or other specially fitted covering: *Put the knife back in its case.* **4** an outer protective part or framework holding the working parts: *My watch has a steel case.* **5** the fact of a letter being in **lower case** (small letters such as a, b, c) or **upper case** (large letters such as A, B, C): *This e-mail address is not sensitive to case.*
v **cased, cas·ing 1** enclose in a material or substance: *concrete cased in marble.* **2** *Informal* examine a place secretly, with a view to committing a crime there: *The meter reader was really a robber casing the computer lab.* <Old French, from Latin *capsa* box>

case·hard·en (kās′här′dən) *v* **1** harden iron or steel on the surface. **2** make a person hard or insensitive: *a soldier casehardened by years of civil war.*

case history *n* all the facts about a person, group, or series of events that may be useful in deciding what medical treatment or social services are needed.

ca·sein (kā′sēn) *or* (kā′sē in) *n* the protein found especially in milk and cheese. <French, from Latin *caseus* cheese>

case law *n* law based on previous decisions by judges rather than on statutes.

case·load (kās′lōd′) *n* the number of cases handled by a court, a social worker, or lawyer in a given time.

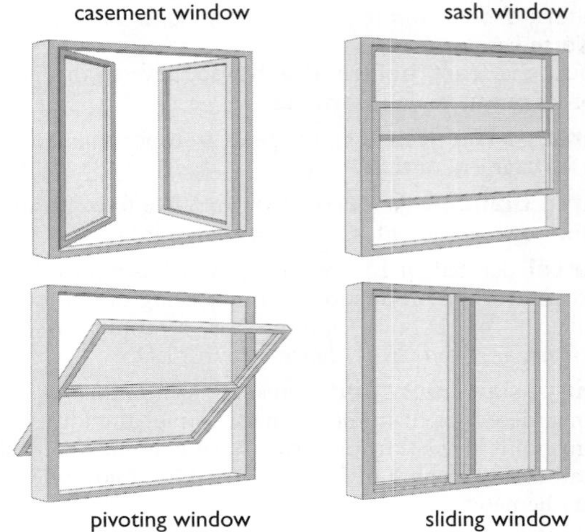

case·ment (kās′mənt) *n* a window opening on vertical hinges, like a door.

case study *n* **1** in social sciences, ecology, or medicine, an intensive study of a single case to illustrate general principles. **2** the method of research that makes use of such studies. **3** a suitable example: *That company is a case study in poor management.*

cash (kash) *n* **1** money in the form of coins and bills. **2** money, or something that equals money, such as a cheque or instant electronic debit, paid at the time of buying: *He doesn't like charge accounts, and prefers to pay cash.* **3** 🍁 *Informal* a checkout; a cash register.
v get or give cash for a cheque, money order, etc.: *Cash that refund cheque as soon as possible. That teller will cash your cheque.* <French, from Latin *capsa* (money) box>
cash in, change into cash.
cash in on, *Informal* **a** make a profit from. **b** take advantage of.

cash and carry *adj* with immediate payment for goods that are then taken away at once.

cash bar *n* a bar where one pays for one's own drinks at a party, banquet, or reception.

cash·book (kash′bu̇k′) *n* a book in which a record is kept of money received and paid out.

cash cow *Slang n* a consistent source of income.

cash crop *n* a crop grown only for sale.

cash·ew (kash′ū) *n* a small, edible, kidney-shaped nut that grows on a tropical American tree. <Portuguese, from Tupi (a language of S America) *acaju*>

cash flow *n* the ongoing movement of funds into and out of a business or household: *Our clients' failure to pay has created problems with cash flow.*

cash·ier[1] (ka shēr′) *n* an employee who handles payments and receipts in a store, bank, or business. <*cash*>

cash·ier[2] (ka shēr′) *v* dismiss from the armed forces for some dishonourable act: *The officer was deprived of his rank and cashiered.* <Flemish, from Latin *quassare* quash>

cash·mere (kash′mēr) *n* a fine, soft woollen cloth made from the downy undercoat of a breed of goats raised in Kashmir and Tibet. <*Kashmir*>

cash on delivery *n* payment when goods are delivered. *Abbrev.* **C.O.D.**

cash register *n* a machine that records and shows the amount of a sale and has a drawer for keeping money in.

cas·ing (kā′sing) *n* **1** a cover, shell, or container that fits or encloses something: *Animal intestines are sometimes used as sausage casing.* **2** a frame around a door or window.

ca·si·no (kə sē′nō) *n* **1** a public building where gambling takes place. **2** CASSINO. <Italian, from Latin *casa* house>

cask (kask) *n* a barrel, often a small one. <Spanish *casco* helmet>

cas·ket (kas′kit) *n* **1** a coffin. **2** a small box used to hold jewellery, letters, or other small items. <origin uncertain>

cas·sa·ba (kə så′bə) CASABA.

cas·sa·va (kə så′və) *n* a plant of tropical America with a large, edible, starchy root. <Arawak (a language of S America) *casavi*>

cas·se·role (kas′ə rōl′) *n* **1** food baked and served in the same dish, generally a mixture of ingredients forming a meal in itself: *a chicken-and-rice casserole.* **2** the dish in which such food is baked and served. <French *casse* ladle, from Greek *kyathos* cup>

cas·sette (kə set′) *n* **1** a sealed plastic case containing magnetic tape on a reel together with a take-up reel, for audio, video, or computer use. **2** a small, boxlike container. <French = little case>

C

cas·si·a (kash′ə) *or* (kas′ē ə) *n* **1** a spice resembling cinnamon, taken from the bark of a tropical Asian tree. **2** a tropical plant whose leaves or pods yield senna and other products. <Latin, from Hebrew *qesiah*>

cas·si·no or **ca·si·no** (kə sē′nō) *n* a card game in which the ten of diamonds and the two of spades have special counting value. <variant of *casino*>

cas·sock (kə sok′) *n* a full-length garment worn by some members of the Christian clergy, and by some choirs. <French, from Italian *cassaca* riding coat>

cas·so·war·y (kas′ə wer′ē) *n, pl* **cas·so·war·ies** a large, flightless bird, found mainly in the forests of New Guinea, with glossy black plumage and a bony growth on the head. <Malay *kasuari*>

cast (kast) *v* **cast, cast·ing** **1** throw forcefully in a particular direction. **2** throw one end of a fishing line out into the water. **3** direct or aim: *He cast a look of surprise at me.* **4** shape by pouring or squeezing into a mould to harden: *Metal is first melted and then cast.* **5** assign actors and parts in a play or movie: *Our drama teacher cast me as the villain.* **6** shed or let fall off: *The snake cast its skin.*
n **1** an act of casting: *The angler made a skilful cast from the riverbank.* **2** something made by casting, or the mould used for this: *A bronze cast of Sir Wilfrid Laurier.* **3** a rigid support for a broken bone to keep it in place while it heals: *His leg was in a cast for a month.* **4** the actors in a play or movie. **5** a slight squint: *a cast in one eye.*
adj made by casting: *cast iron.* <Old Norse *kasta* throw>
cast′er *n.*
cast a ballot, vote.
cast about, search; look.
cast down, make sad or discouraged: *Our hearts were cast down by the bad news.*
cast lots, decide something by lot: *We cast lots for first chance to try out the skateboard.*
cast off, a untie a boat from its moorings: *As soon as everyone was in, we cast off.* **b** in knitting, make the last row of stitches, removing the knitted fabric from the needle. **c** get rid of: *to cast off a gloomy feeling.*
cast on, in knitting, make the first row of stitches.
cast out, drive away or banish.

cas·ta·nets (kas′tə nets′) *pl n* a small, handheld rhythm instrument consisting of two wooden or plastic concave shells held together by string. The shells are clicked together in time, and are especially used in flamenco dancing. <Spanish, from Latin *castanea* a chestnut, which castanets resemble>

a bat	e bed	i bid	o pot	u cup	th **thin**
ā cake	ē me	ī bite	ō go	ū rude	ᴛʜ **then**
å bar	ə about	ər over	ȯ for	u̇ put	zh measure

cast·a·way (kas′tə wā′) *adj* shipwrecked.
n a shipwrecked person.

caste (kast) *n* **1** a hereditary Hindu social class. **2** a social class system based on strict divisions of birth, rank, wealth, or education. <Spanish and Portuguese, from Latin *castus* pure>

cast·er (kas′tər) *n* **1** a small swivelling wheel on the bottom of a piece of furniture or other heavy object to make it easier to move. Also, **castor**. **2** a person who or thing that casts.

cas·ti·gate (kas′tə gāt′) *v* **cas·ti·gat·ed, cas·ti·gat·ing** criticize severely. <Latin *castigare* punish>
cas′ti·ga′tion *n.* **cas′ti·ga′tor** *n.*

Cas·til·ian (kə stil′yən) *n* **1** the standard form of Spanish spoken and written in Spain, originally the dialect of the Castile region. **2** a native or inhabitant of Castile.
adj to do with Castile or this dialect of Spanish.

cast·ing vote (kas′ting) *n* a vote by the chairperson at a meeting or assembly to break a tie on an issue.

cast iron *n* a hard, brittle form of iron, made by remelting pig iron and pouring it into moulds to harden.

cast–i·ron (kast′ī′ərn) *adj* **1** made of cast iron: *a cast-iron frying pan.* **2** hard, strong, or tough: *a cast-iron stomach.*

cas·tle (kas′əl) *n* **1** a building or group of buildings with thick walls, towers, and other defences against attack. See MEDIEVAL for picture. **2** a palace or other large, impressive residence. **3** ROOK[2].
v **cas·tled, cas·tling** in chess, move the rook (castle) next to the king and then move the king to the other side of the rook. <Old French, from Latin *castrum* fort>
castle in the air (or **in Spain**)**,** an impossible dream.

cast·off (kast′of′) *n* something thrown away or put aside as no longer useful: *These old gloves are castoffs, but they're good enough for gardening.*
adj thrown away or abandoned.

cast·or (kast′or) CASTER (def. 1)

cas·tor oil (kas′tər) *n* a yellow oil obtained from the beans of a tropical plant.

cas·trate (kas′trāt) *v* **cas·trat·ed, cas·trat·ing 1** remove the testicles of: *A steer is a castrated bull.* **2** take away the strength or effectiveness of. <Latin *castrare*>
cas·tra′tion *n.*

cas·u·al (kazh′ū əl) *adj* **1** happening by chance or unplanned: *a casual meeting.* **2** not seeming to care very much: *a casual approach to your work. He gave the painting only a casual glance.* **3** informal: *casual manners, casual clothes.* **4** not involving serious commitment: *a casual interest in the arts. She's just a casual acquaintance.* **5** happening, active, or employed on an irregular basis only: *casual employment, a casual labourer.* <Old French, from Latin *casualis* happening by chance>
cas′u·al·ly *adv.* **cas′u·al·ness** *n.*

cas·u·al·ty (kazh′wəl tē) *or* (kazh′əl tē) *n, pl* **cas·u·al·ties** a person injured or killed in a war or accident.

cas·u·ist·ry (kazh′ū is trē) *n, pl* **cas·u·ist·ries** reasoning that is clever and subtle but false. <French, from Latin *casus* an instance or example. In former times, a casuist was a person who studied and resolved examples of right and wrong.> **cas′u·ist** *n.* **cas′u·is′tic** *adj.*

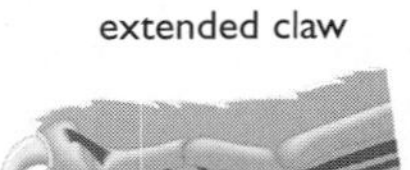

cat[1] (kat) *n* **1** a small domestic mammal with retractable claws, short pointed ears, and soft fur. **2** a wild animal belonging to the same family as the domestic cat. Lions, tigers, leopards, jaguars, lynxes, wildcats, and cougars are cats. **3** *Slang* a person: *A cool cat keeps calm all the time. Fat cats have too much money.* <Old English> **cat′like′** *adj.*
let the cat out of the bag, tell a secret.
rain cats and dogs, rain very hard.

cat[2] (kat) *Informal n* a Caterpillar.

ca·tab·o·lism (kə tab′ə liz′əm) *Biology n* the process of producing energy by breaking down living tissues into simpler substances or waste matter. <Greek *kata-* down + *ballein* to throw> **ca·tab′o·lize′** *v.*

cat·a·clysm (kat′ə kliz′əm) *n* **1** a violent change or upheaval: *World War II was a cataclysm in world history.* **2** a great flood, earthquake, or any other violent event with geological consequences. <French, from Greek *kataklyzmos* deluge> **cat′a·clys′mic** *adj.*

cat·a·comb (kat′ə kōm′) *n* usually, **catacombs** *pl* an underground gallery forming a burial place. <Old English, from Latin *catacumbus*>

cat·a·lep·sy (kət′ə lep′ si) *Medicine n* a medical condition in which a person loses consciousness, the body becoming rigid. <Latin, from Greek *katalepsis* a fit>
cat′a·lep′tic *adj.*

cat·a·logue (kat′ə log′) *n* a list of items in a collection, such as books in a library, works of art in a museum, or articles stocked by a store, usually with a brief description of each.
v **cat·a·logued, cat·a·logu·ing** make a catalogue of or put in a catalogue: *She catalogued all the insects in her collection.* Also (*especially US*), **catalog**. <Old French, from Greek *kata-* down + *legein* count>

ca·tal·pa (kə tal′pə) *n* a N American tree with large, heart-shaped leaves, clusters of bell-shaped flowers, and long pods. <Greek *katalpa*>

ca·tal·y·sis (kə tal′ə sis) *Chemistry n, pl* **ca·tal·y·ses** (kə tal′ə sēz′) the speeding of a reaction by the presence of a catalyst. <Greek *katalyein* dissolve, from *kata-* down + *lyein* loosen> **cat′a·lyze′** or **cat′a·lyse′** *v.*

cat·a·lyst (kat′ə list) *n* **1** *Chemistry* a substance that speeds up a reaction without itself being permanently changed. **2** a person who or thing that begins or speeds up a process. **cat′a·lyt′ic** *adj.*

catalytic converter *n* a device in the exhaust system of a motor vehicle, designed to act chemically on the exhaust so as to convert pollutants into harmless substances.

The **catamaran** has great stability, but it requires a large turning circle and is therefore slow in tacking.

cat·a·ma·ran (kat′ə mə ran′) *n* **1** a boat or raft consisting of two hulls or floats joined side by side by a frame. **2** 🍁 a type of platform on two runners used for hauling lumber or heavy objects. <Tamil *kattumaram* = tied wood>

cat·a·pult (kat′ə pult′) *n* **1** an ancient war machine for hurling rocks or arrows. **2 a** slingshot. **3** a device for launching a glider or other aircraft from a ship's deck.
v shoot a catapult, or fly as if shot from a catapult. <Latin, from Greek *kata-* down + *pallein* throw>

cat·a·ract (kat′ə rakt′) *n* **1** a large, steep waterfall. **2** a violent rush or downpour of water. **3** an opaque condition in the lens of the eye, sometimes covering the whole lens and causing blindness. <Latin, from Greek *kata-* down + *arassein* break into pieces>

ca·tarrh (kə tår′) *n* a cold in the head. <Latin, from Greek *kata-* down + *rhein* flow>

ca·tas·tro·phe (kə tas′trə fē) *n* a disaster or great misfortune: *If I ever lost my study notes, it would be a catastrophe.* <Greek *kata-* down + *strephein* to turn (i.e., overturn)> **cat′a·stroph′ic** *adj.*

cat·a·ton·ic (kat′ə ton′ik) *adj* awake but motionless and unresponsive, as if unconscious, often as a symptom of a mental illness. <Greek *kata-* down + *tonos* tension> **cat′a·to′ni·a** (kat′ə tō′nē ə) *n.* **cat′a·ton′i·cal·ly** *adv.*

cat·bird (kat′bərd′) *n* a dark grey N American songbird with a mewing call, belonging to the same family as the mockingbird.

catbird seat *n* a position of advantage or power. <perhaps from the fact that catbirds sit on high perches>

cat·boat (kat′bōt′) *n* a sailboat with a wide hull and one mast set far forward.

cat burglar *n* a stealthy burglar who enters a building by skilful feats of climbing.

cat·call (kat′kol′) *n* a yell or whistle expressing disapproval of a performer: *The stand-up comic's tasteless routine was greeted by catcalls from all sides.*
v make catcalls at.

catch (kach) *v* **caught** (kot), **catch·ing 1** stop and hold a moving person or thing: *to catch a ball, to catch your breath. He caught the child just as she reached the street.* **2** capture: *They finally caught the thief.* **3** become affected by: *to catch fire, to catch the spirit of the celebration. I think I've caught a cold.* **4** accidentally hook, pinch, or entangle: *My sleeve caught in the door. She caught her toe in the skate and fell.* **5** discover or notice, often something wrong or secret: *He caught me hiding his present. Did you catch the error before printing out your report?* **6** take or get briefly: *I caught a glimpse of her as she passed.* **7** attract: *Bright colours catch the eye.* **8** meet and board a bus, train, or aircraft: *to catch the next train.* **9** take suddenly and by surprise: *We were caught in the rain.* **10** *Baseball* act as catcher: *Who's catching for our team?*
n **1** an act of catching: *a fine catch with one hand, a catch in his voice as he described the accident.* **2** a game of throwing and catching a ball: *They're outside playing catch.* **3** something caught, or the total quantity caught: *Her catch was six trout.* **4** a part holding something else in place: *We can't fasten the windows because the catch is broken.* **5** *Informal* a person worth marrying or hiring for his or her excellent qualities or advantages. **6** a hidden meaning, trick, or difficulty: *There's a catch to that question, so think carefully before you answer.* <Old French, from Latin *capere* take>
catch as catch can, a grab or wrestle in any way, with no moves barred. **b** take whatever chances one gets.
catch at, try to grab: *He caught at the rope as it swung by.*
catch in the act (or **catch red-handed**), find someone in the process of doing something wrong.
catch it, *Informal* be scolded or punished: *We'll catch it if we're late again.*
catch on, a understand: *to catch on to a joke. You'll soon catch on to the rules.* **b** become popular: *The song never caught on.*
catch out, discover doing wrong: *He cheated, and was caught out.*
catch sight of, notice: *The dog suddenly caught sight of the cat.*
catch up, a come up even with a person or thing going the same way: *He ran hard to catch up with his sister.* **b** pick up suddenly: *She caught the laughing child up in her arms.* **c** (*followed by* ***with***) become too much for: *His late nights were beginning to catch up with him.* **d** bring or become up to date: *She's missed a lot of school, but it shouldn't take her too long to catch up. Drop over and catch me up on your news.*
caught up, a involved, especially unwillingly: *caught up in a scandal.* **b** with full attention: *We were caught up in the story and lost track of time.*

a bat	e bed	i bid	o pot	u cup	th **thin**
ā cake	ē me	ī bite	ō go	ū rude	ᴛʜ **then**
å bar	ə about	ər over	ȯ for	u̇ put	zh measure

catch–all (kach′ol′) *n* **1** a container for odds and ends: *That drawer is our kitchen catch-all.* **2** a term or category used to cover a number of possible examples: *The word "etc." in the definition is a catch-all.*

catch basin *n* **1** a sievelike receptacle at the entrance of a sewer to hold back anything that might block the flow of sewage. **2** a reservoir for catching and holding the surface water that drains from a large area of land.

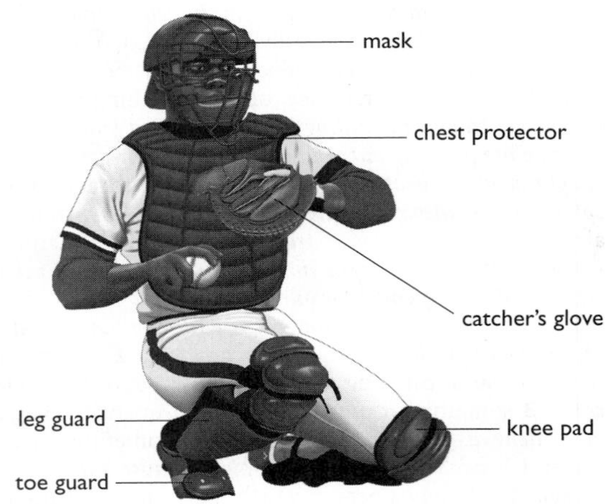

catch·er (kach′ər) *n* **1** *Baseball* the player who squats behind the batter to catch balls that are pitched but not hit. **2** a person who or thing that catches.

catch·ing (kach′ing) *adj* liable to spread from one to another: *Colds are catching.*

catch·ment (kach′mənt) *n* **1** a reservoir for catching drainage. **2 catchment area** the area drained by one river system or reservoir.

catch·word (kach′wərd′) *n* a popular word or phrase used often to represent a concept or notion: *"Canada first" was a catchword of a late nineteenth-century movement for cultural independence.* Also, **catchphrase**.

catch·y (kach′ē) *adj* **catch·i·er, catch·i·est** **1** attractive and easy to remember: *a catchy tune, a catchy title.* **2** tricky or misleading: *The third question on the test was catchy; we all gave the wrong answer.* **catch′i·ness** *n.*

cat·e·chism (kat′ə kiz′əm) *n* **1** *Christianity* a set of questions and answers, usually contained in a book, which is used for teaching religious doctrine. **2** any set of questions and answers used for instruction or testing.

cat·e·chize (kat′ə kīz′) *v* **cat·e·chized, cat·e·chiz·ing** **1** teach by questions and answers. **2** question closely and persistently: *Before I go anywhere, I get catechized on street safety.* <Greek *katechein* teach orally>
cat′e·chist (kat′ə kist′) or **cat′e·chiz′er** *n.*

cat·e·gor·i·cal (kat′ə gȯr′ə kəl) *adj* **1** without conditions or qualifications: *a categorical refusal.* **2** to do with a category or categories. **cat′e·gor′i·cal·ly** *adv.*

cat·e·gor·ize (kat′ə gə rīz′) *v* **cat·e·gor·ized, cat·e·gor·iz·ing** place in a category or classify: *Are fungi categorized as plants or animals?*

cat·e·go·ry (kat′ə gȯr′ē) *n, pl* **cat·e·go·ries** a group or division in any system of classification: *She groups people into two categories: those who like sports and those who don't.* <French, from Greek *kategoria* pronouncement>

ca·ter (kā′tər) *v* **1** provide food or supplies (for): *He caters weddings and parties. The restaurant can cater for parties of up to 50 people.* **2** (*with* ***to***) **a** provide what is needed or wanted by: *a TV show catering to people interested in crafts.* **b** try to satisfy in every respect: *They catered to her every wish.* <Old French *acater* buy>

ca·ter·er (kā′tə rər) *n* a person or company that provides food or supplies for special events or parties.

cat·er·pil·lar (kat′ər pil′ər) *n* the segmented, wormlike larva of a butterfly or moth. See CHRYSALIS for picture. <Old French *chatepelose* hairy cat>

Caterpillar *Trademark n* a tractor that can travel over rough land on wheels that run inside two endless belts of linked steel plates.

cat·er·waul (kat′ər wol′) *v, n* howl, screech, or wail. <Middle English *cat-* + imitative *waul* wail>

cat·fish (kat′fish′) *n, pl* **cat·fish** or **cat·fish·es** a scaleless fish with long, whiskerlike feelers around the mouth.

cat flap *n* an opening in the lower part of a door, filled by a hanging flap or swinging piece, so that a cat can enter either way.

cat·gut (kat′gut′) *n* tough cord used for strings of musical instruments and sports racquets, or for surgical stitches. It was originally made from the dried, twisted intestines of animals.

ca·thar·sis (kə thȧr′sis) *n* a release or expression of deep emotion, with a cleansing effect. <Latin, from Greek *katharos* pure> **ca·thar′tic** *adj, n.*

ca·the·dral (kə thē′drəl) *n* **1** the official church of a bishop. **2** a large church, especially an old one.
adj **1** to do with the place where a bishop is based: *a cathedral city.* **2** like that of a cathedral: *cathedral ceilings.* <Latin, from Greek *kathedra* seat (i.e., bishop's throne)>

cath·e·ter (kath′ə tər) *n* a slender tube inserted into a passage of the body, to drain urine from the bladder, widen a blood vessel, or deliver liquid nourishment to the stomach or veins. <Latin, from Greek *kata-* down + *hienai* send> **cath′e·ter·ize** *v.*

cath·ode (kath′ōd) *n* **1** *Electricity* **a** the positively charged electrode of a battery. **b** the negative electrode of an electrolytic cell, through which electrons enter the cell. **2** *Electronics* the electrode that is the main source of electrons in a vacuum tube. <Greek *kata-* down + *hodos* way. It was thought the current flowed down from the negative electrode.>

cathode ray *n* a high-speed, invisible stream of electrons from the heated cathode of a vacuum tube. Inside this **cathode-ray tube**, the rays produce a luminous image on a fluorescent screen, such as on a TV screen or computer monitor.

cath·o·lic (kath′lik) *adj* **1** broad, general, or all-inclusive: *Music has a catholic appeal.* **2** broad-minded and with wide-ranging sympathies. **3** to do with the whole Christian church, or all Christians. <Latin, from Greek *kata* in respect to + *holos* whole> **cath′o·lic′i·ty** *n.*

Cath·o·lic (kath′lik) *adj* in full, **Roman Catholic** to do with the Christian church that recognizes the Pope as its supreme head.
n a member of this church. **Ca·thol′i·cism′** or **Ro′man Catholicism** *n.* **Ca·thol′i·cize** *v.*

cat·i·on (kat′ī ən) *n* an ion with a positive charge. <*cat(hode)* + *ion*>

cat·kin (kat′kin) *n* the soft spike of the flowers of trees such as willows and hazels. <Dutch *katteken* kitten>

cat·nap (kat′nap) *v* **cat·nap·ped, cat·nap·ping** nap for a short time, as cats do. **cat′nap** *n.* **cat′nap·per** *n.*

cat·nip (kat′nip′) *n* a plant of the mint family, with scented leaves that cats like.

ETYMOLOGY

Catnip was called *catmint* in the 1200s. By the 1800s, it had become known as catnip.

Rather than being related to the word *nip*, meaning "bite," the *-nip* in catnip is a variant of the word *nep*, an earlier name for this plant, from the Latin name *nepeta*.

cat–o′–nine–tails (kat′ə nīn′tālz′) *n*, *pl* **cat-o′-nine-tails** a whip consisting of nine pieces of knotted cord fastened to a handle, used in former times to flog offenders, especially at sea.

CAT scan (kat) *n* **1** an examination of the soft tissues of the body, especially the brain, using a special X-ray process called **Computerized Axial Tomography**. Many X-rays are taken while the patient lies in a machine called a **CAT scanner**. **2** the resulting image of the X-rays, combined by computer. Also, **CT scan**.

cat's cradle *n* a game in which a loop of string, stretched over the fingers in an intricate pattern, is passed from one player to another, forming a new pattern each time.

cat's eye *n* **1** a playing marble with a green or blue swirl in the middle. **2** a row of small reflectors set on a road or curb to serve as guides. **3** a gem showing beautiful changes of colour suggesting a cat's eye.

cats·paw or **cat's paw** (kats′po′) *n* **1** a light breeze that ruffles a small stretch of water. **2** a person used by another to do something unpleasant or dangerous.

cat·sup (kat′səp) KETCHUP.

cat·tail or **cat–tail** (kat′tāl′) *n* a tall marsh plant with long, flat leaves, and flowers that form thick brown spikes.

cat·tle (kat′əl) *pln* domesticated cud-chewing animals with cloven hoofs that are used to produce milk or meat; cows and oxen. <Old French *catel*, from Latin *capitale* wealth>

🍁 **cattle crossing** *n* wooden boards or metal strips bridging a piece of ground that has been dug out, used to prevent cattle from entering or leaving an area.

cat·tle·man (kat′əl mən) *n*, *pl* **cat·tle·men** (kat′əl mən) a person who raises or takes care of cattle.

🍁 **cat–train** (kat′ trān′) *n* a series of large sleds pulled by a Caterpillar, used in the North for hauling goods over the frozen muskeg. Also, **cat-swing**.

cat·ty (kat′ē) *adj* **cat·ti·er, cat·ti·est** **1** mean or spiteful. **2** to do with cats: *The old carpet had a catty smell.* **cat′ti·ly** *adv.* **cat′ti·ness** *n.*

CATV cable television.

cat·walk (kat′wok′) *n* a high, narrow place to walk.

Cau·ca·sian (ko kā′zhən) *adj* **1** white-skinned or of European descent. **2** to do with the **Caucasus**, a mountainous region in southeastern Europe between the Black and Caspian Seas.
n **1** a white person or person of European descent. **2** a native or inhabitant of the Caucasus.

cau·cus (kok′əs) *n*, *pl* **cau·cus·es** **1 a** a group of people who are members of a political party, or who hold seats in a legislature, and who meet to discuss policy or select candidates. **b** a meeting in which such people take part. **2 a** a group of people who share common concerns within a larger organization: *the feminist caucus.* **b** a meeting in which such people take part. <perhaps Algonquian *cau′-cau-as′u* adviser>

cau·dal (kod′əl) *Zoology adj* to do with the tail. <Latin *cauda* tail>

Caugh·na·waug·a (kok′nə wog′ə) KAHNAWAKE.

caught (kot) past tense and past participle of CATCH.

caul (kol) *n* a membrane sometimes covering the head of a child at birth. <perhaps Old French *cale* head covering>

caul·dron (kol′drən) *n* a very large pot for heating water, food, etc. <Latin *calidus* warm>

cau·li·flow·er (kol′ē flou′ər) *n* a plant related to cabbage and broccoli, eaten as a vegetable. Its flower clusters form a solid white head. <French, probably from Latin *caulis* cabbage + *floris* flower>

cauliflower ear *n* an ear that is misshapen as a result of injuries, especially from boxing or rugby.

caulk or **calk** (kok) *v* fill up a seam, crack, or joint, often with a puttylike mixture called **caulking**, so that it will not leak. <Old French, from Latin *calcare* tread, press in>

caus·al (koz′əl) *adj* **1** to do with a cause. **2** *Grammar* introducing a cause or reason: *"Because" is a causal conjunction.* **cau·sal′i·ty** *n.* **caus′al·ly** *adv.*

cause (koz) *n* **1** a person, thing, or event that makes something else happen: *the causes of World War I. What is the cause of all this damage?* **2** a reason for action: *angry without cause.* **3** a goal, movement, etc. to which people give their support: *She has spent much energy in the cause of world peace.*
v **caused, caus·ing** produce or bring about: *What caused the fire? Extreme heat caused her to faint.* <Old French, from Latin *causa*> **cau·sa′tion** *n.* **cause′less** *adj.*
make common cause, join efforts.
plead the cause of, argue in favour of.

cause cé·lè·bre (kōz′sə leb′) *n*, *pl* **caus·es cé·lè·bres** (kōz′əz sə leb′) a famous or notorious case or incident. <French>

a bat	e bed	i bid	o pot	u cup	th thin
ā cake	ē me	ī bite	ō go	ü rude	ᴛʜ then
à bar	ə about	ər over	ȯ for	ů put	zh measure

cause·way (koz′wā′) *n* a raised road or path, usually built across wet ground or shallow water.

ETYMOLOGY

Causeway comes from the Old English word *causey*, which ultimately comes from the Latin word *calx*, meaning "limestone." The Romans used limestone for paving roads.

caus·tic (kos′tik) *adj* **1** able to burn or eat away by chemical action. **2** sarcastic, stinging, or cutting: *caustic remarks, a caustic tone.*
n a caustic substance. <Latin, from Greek *kaiein* to burn> **caus′ti·cal·ly** *adv.*

caustic soda SODIUM HYDROXIDE.

cau·ter·ize (kot′ə rīz′) *v* **cau·ter·ized, cau·ter·iz·ing** destroy defective tissue or seal a wound by burning: *Doctors often remove warts by cauterizing them.* <Old French, from Greek *kaiein* to burn> **cau′ter·i·za′tion** *n.*

cau·tion (kosh′ən) *n* **1** the practice of being careful and not taking chances: *Use caution in crossing streets.* **2** a warning: *A caution has been posted about the poison ivy.* **3** *Soccer* a warning against dangerous or unsportsmanlike behaviour, given by the referee holding up a **yellow card** to the player. Two yellow cards in one game earns the player a **red card**, and automatic removal from the game.
v urge to be careful: *He cautioned us to stay off the ice.* <Latin *cavere* beware> **cau′tion·ar′y** *adj.*

cau·tious (kosh′əs) *adj* careful and not taking chances: *a cautious driver.* **cau′tious·ly** *adv.* **cau′tious·ness** *n.*

SYNONYMS

Cautious means "prudent and wary": *He was cautious not to walk on the thin ice that covered the lake.*

Careful means "mindful" or "thoughtful": *She was careful not to disturb her father while he was sleeping.*

Deliberate means "careful" or "methodical" in deciding what to do: *I made a deliberate decision to say no if my friend ever asked me to smoke a cigarette.*

cav·al·cade (kav′əl kād′) *n* **1** a procession of vehicles or of people on horseback. **2** a series of scenes or events: *a cavalcade of sports.* <French, from Latin *caballus* horse>

cav·a·lier (kav′ə lēr′) *adj* too casual or easygoing: *a cavalier disregard for danger.*
n **1** *Poetic* a courteous gentleman. **2 Cavalier** in England, a person who supported the King in the Civil War with Parliament, 1642–1652. See also ROUNDHEAD. <French = knight, from Latin *caballus* horse> **cav′a·lier′ly** *adv.*

cav·al·ry (kav′əl rē) *n, pl* **ca·val·ries** army troops trained to fight in armoured vehicles or, formerly, on horses. <French, from Latin *caballus* horse>

cave (kāv) *n* a hollow place underground, often with an opening in the side of a hill or cliff.
v **caved, cav·ing 1** explore caves as a sport. **2** *Informal* give in under pressure or strain: *If you argue with her long enough, she'll cave.* <Old French, from Latin *cava* hollow>
cave′like′ *adj.*
cave in, a fall in or give way: *The roof of the shed caved in from the weight of the snow.* **b** give in to an argument, strain, or hardship.

cav·e·at (kav′ē at′) *n* **1** a warning: *I would recommend this movie, with the one caveat that the opening scene is very scary.* **2** *Law* a notice to some legal authority not to act until the person giving notice can be heard. <Latin *caveat* let (someone) beware>
caveat emptor, let the buyer beware.

cave dweller *n* **1** a person who lived in a cave in prehistoric times. **2** a person who lives in a cave. **cave-dwelling** *adj.*

cave–in (kāv′in′) *n* a collapse of a roof structure, especially in a mine, tunnel, or the place where it occurred.

cav·ern (kav′ərn) *n* a large cave. <Old French, from Latin *cavus* hollow>

cav·ern·ous (kav′ər nəs) *adj* large, dark, hollow, and echoing: *cavernous hallways.*

cav·i·ar (kav′ē är′) *n* the salted eggs of sturgeon or other fish, usually eaten as an appetizer. <Italian, probably from Greek *chaviari*>

cav·il (kav′əl) *v* **cav·illed** or **cav·iled, cav·il·ling** or **cav·il·ing** raise trivial or unnecessary objections.
n such an objection. <French, from Latin *cavilla* mockery>

cav·ing *n* the sport or pastime of exploring caves. Also called **spelunking**. **cav′er** *n.*

cav·i·ty (kav′ə tē) *n, pl* **cav·i·ties 1** a hole in a tooth, caused by decay. **2** an empty or hollow space within something solid, especially the human body: *the four cavities of the heart.* <Latin *cavus* hollow>

ca·vort (kə vȯrt′) *v* prance or jump around: *The colt cavorted in the pasture.* <origin uncertain>

ca·vy (kā′vē) *n, pl* **ca·vies** a rat-sized S American rodent with a short tail and rough grey or brown hair. Guinea pigs are cavies. <Carib (a group of languages of the Caribbean) *cabiai*>

caw (ko) *n* the harsh cry made by a crow or raven.
v make this cry.

cay·enne (kī en′) *or* (kā en′) *n* a hot-tasting, red seasoning made from the fruit of a variety of pepper plant. <Tupi (a language of S America) *kyynha,* later associated with *Cayenne* in French Guiana>

cay·man (kā′mən) *n* a reptile closely related to the alligator. Caymans are found in Central and South America. Also, **caiman**. See ALLIGATOR for picture. <Spanish, from Carib (a group of languages of the Caribbean) *acayuman*>

Cayman Islands *n* a country of several islands in the Caribbean Sea.

Ca·yu·ga (kə yū′gə) *n, pl* **Ca·yu·ga 1** a member of a First Nations or Native American people living mainly in New York State and, later, in Ontario. **2** their Iroquoian language.
adj to do with these people or their language. Also called **Kayonkwe'haka**.

cay·use (kī yūs′) *n* a small horse or pony of Western Canada and the US. <after the *Cayuse* Native Americans>

CB 1 in full, **Citizens' Band** a range of radio frequencies for public use. 2 a radio, especially in a motor vehicle, using such a frequency.

🍁 **CBC** Canadian Broadcasting Corporation.

CC 1 closed captioning; closed-captioned. Also, **cc**. 2 🍁 Companion of the Order of Canada.

🍁 **C.C.** Canada Council.

🍁 **CCF** or **C.C.F.** *n* in full, **Co-operative Commonwealth Federation** a Canadian political party established in 1932. It joined with the CANADIAN LABOUR CONGRESS to form the NEW DEMOCRATIC PARTY in 1961.

C clef *Music n* See CLEF.

cd candela(s).

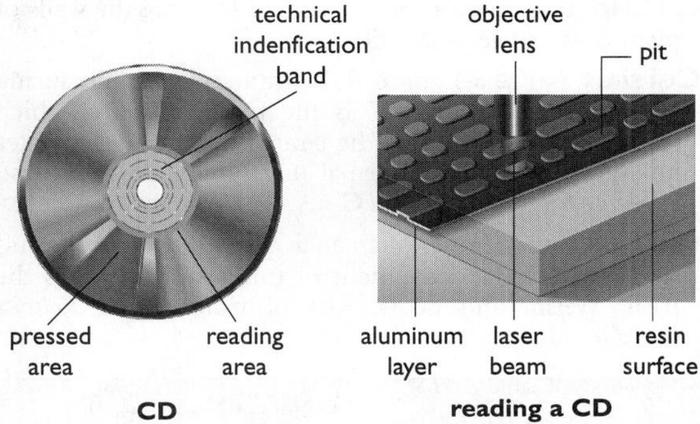

In direct digital recording, electronic pulses are placed on a **CD** and protected by a plastic coating. When a CD is played, the coded information is read by a laser beam and converted to analog signals for playback through conventional speakers.

CD *n* a disc whose finely pitted surface digitally encodes music or other data, which is readable by a laser beam in a CD or DVD player, or the CD-ROM drive of a computer. <*C*ompact *D*isc>

🍁 **Cdn** Canadian.

CD–ROM (sē′dē′ rom′) *Computers n* in full, **compact disc read-only memory** an optical storage technology that uses CDs to store and play back data. "Read-only" means the data cannot be altered. A user can store data once on a **CD-R** (compact disc-recordable), or more than once on a **CD-RW** (compact disc-rewritable).

CE (*with dates*) Common (or Christian) Era, the time since the birth of Christ; used as a preferred alternative to AD: *The empire of ancient Rome lasted from 27* BCE *to 476* CE *(or* AD *476)*.

cease (sēs) *v* **ceased, ceas·ing** stop: *The group is going to cease giving live concerts. The music ceased abruptly.* <Old French, from Latin *cedere* to yield> **cease′less** *adj.* **cease′less·ly** *adv.*
without cease, without stopping.

cease·fire (sēs′fīr′) *n* a stopping of combat, especially for the purpose of discussing peace.

ce·cum (sē′kəm) CAECUM.

ce·dar (sē′dər) *n* 1 a N African or Asian evergreen tree of the pine family, with long cones and short, sharp needles that grow in spirals. 2 an evergreen tree, especially of the cypress family, such as the **eastern white cedar** and the **eastern red cedar**. 3 the durable, fragrant, usually reddish wood of such trees. <Old French, from Greek *kedros*>

cedar waxwing *n* a small N American bird with a crest and small red markings on its wings.

cede (sēd) *v* **ced·ed, ced·ing** give up power or territory: *France ceded Louisiana to Spain by the Treaty of Paris in 1763.* <Latin *cedere* to surrender>

ce·dil·la (sə dil′ə) *n* a mark resembling a comma, put under *c* in certain words to show that it has the sound of *s* before *a*, *o*, or *u*. Example: *façade* <Spanish, from Greek *zeta*>

🍁 **CEGEP** (sā zhep′) *Québec n* an educational institution offering a course of study between the high school and university levels. <*C*ollège d'*E*nseignement *G*énéral *E*t *P*rofessionel (General and Vocational College)>

cei·lidh (kā′lē) *n* a social gathering featuring traditional Scots or Irish music, stories, and dances. <Old Irish *ceile* companion>

ceil·ing (sē′ling) *n* 1 the interior top surface of a room, opposite the floor. 2 the greatest altitude to which an aircraft can go under certain conditions: *That jet has a ceiling of more than 15 000 m.* 3 the distance between the earth and the lowest clouds. 4 an upper limit: *to place a ceiling on rents.* <perhaps Middle English *ceil* to line the interior of a room>
hit the ceiling, *Informal* react with an angry outburst: *When she saw the phone bill she hit the ceiling.*

cel·e·brant (sel′ə brənt) *n* 1 the person who performs a ceremony, such as a priest who leads a Mass. 2 a person who celebrates.

cel·e·brate (sel′ə brāt′) *v* **cel·e·brat·ed, cel·e·brat·ing** 1 observe a special time or day with ceremonies or festivities: *to celebrate Canada Day, to celebrate a birthday.* 2 have a joyful time: *The people celebrated when the war ended.* 3 praise or honour highly: *a poem celebrating the glory of nature.* 4 publicize extensively: *Jesse James was a celebrated outlaw.* 5 perform a ceremony or rite: *The priest celebrates Mass.* <Latin *celeber* honoured> **cel′e·bra′tion** *n.* **cel′e·bra′tor** *n.* **cel′e·bra·to′ry** *adj.*

ce·leb·ri·ty (sə leb′rə tē) *n, pl* **ce·leb·ri·ties** 1 a famous person. 2 the condition of being famous.

ce·ler·i·ac (sə ler′i ak′) *n* a type of celery with a large, white, turniplike root, eaten as a vegetable. <*celery*>

ce·ler·i·ty (sə ler′ə tē) *n* swiftness or speed. <French, from Latin *celer* swift>

cel·er·y (sel′ə rē) *n* a plant of the carrot family with crisp, pale green stalks, eaten as a vegetable. <French, from Greek *selinon* parsley>

a bat	e bed	i bid	o pot	u cup	th thin
ā cake	ē me	ī bite	ō go	ū rude	ᴛʜ then
à bar	ə about	ər over	ȯ for	ů put	zh measure

ce·les·ta (sə les′tə) *n* a musical instrument with a keyboard that produces tones by means of hammers that strike steel plates. <French *céleste* heavenly>

ce·les·tial (sə les′chəl) *adj* **1** to do with the sky or the heavens: *The sun, moon, planets, and stars are celestial bodies.* **2** very good or beautiful: *celestial music.* <Old French, from Latin *caelum* heaven> **ce·les′tial·ly** *adv.*

celestial sphere *Astronomy n* the imaginary sphere that encloses all celestial objects, assuming the observer is at the centre. The **celestial pole** is either of the two points at which the earth's axis, if extended, would intersect the celestial sphere. The **celestial equator** is the imaginary great circle that represents the intersection of the plane of the earth's equator with the celestial sphere.

cel·i·bate (sel′ə bit) *adj* unmarried and not sexually active, especially because of a religious vow.
n a celibate person. <Latin *caelebs* unmarried>
cel′i·ba·cy *n.*

cell (sel) *n* **1** the smallest structural unit of living things that can function independently. Most cells consist of protoplasm, have a nucleus near the centre, and are enclosed by a cell membrane. **2** a small room in a prison, convent, or monastery. **3** a small compartment: *Bees store honey in the cells of a honeycomb.* **4** a small battery. **5** *Computers* **a** in a spreadsheet or table, the space where a row and a column intersect and where a single entry is stored. **b** a unit of memory in which a single data item can be stored. **6** a cellphone. <Old English, from Latin *cella* storeroom>

cel·lar (sel′ər) *n* **1** an underground room or space, usually the unfinished basement of a building, used for storage. **2** such a room used for storing wines, or the supply of wines in it: *He keeps a sensational cellar.* <Old French, from Latin *cellarium* storeroom>

cell·block (sel′blok′) *n* an individual building or part of a complex of cells in a prison.

cell body *n* the nucleus of a neuron.

cell·mate (sel′māt′) *n* a person who shares a prison or jail cell with someone.

cel·lo (chel′ō) *n* a large instrument of the violin family, played by a seated person who rests it upright on the floor between his or her knees. <shortened from *violoncello*>
cell′ist *n.*

cel·lo·phane (sel′ə fān′) *Trademark n* a transparent, thin, crackly sheet made from cellulose, used as commercial packaging. <*cellulose* + Greek *phanein* shine>

cell·phone (sel′fōn′) *n* a wireless mobile telephone that makes use of cellular radio. <*cell(ular)* *(tele)phone*>

cel·lu·lar (sel′yə lər) *adj* to do with or consisting of cells.

cellular radio *n* a mobile telephone system that uses a number of small-range radio stations to cover the area it serves, the signal passed from one station to another as the user travels.

cell·u·lite (sel′yə līt′) *n* fatty deposits on the hips and buttocks, causing dimpling of the skin. <French, from Latin *cellula* small cell>

cel·lu·loid (sel′yə loid′) *n* a hard, transparent plastic made from cellulose and camphor, formerly used for movie film.
adj **1** made of celluloid. **2** to do with movies. <*cellulose*>

cel·lu·lose (sel′yə lōs′) *n* a substance forming the walls of plant cells and vegetable fibres.

Cel·si·us (sel′sē əs) *adj* to do with a scale for measuring temperature in which 0° is the temperature at which water freezes and 100° is the temperature at which water boils at sea level under normal atmospheric pressure. Also called **centigrade**. *Symbol* **C** <A. *Celsius*, 18c astronomer>

Celt (kelt) *n* a member of an ancient people of Europe and Asia Minor, or a descendant of this people, such as the Irish, Welsh, and Scots. <Latin, from Greek *Keltoi*>
Celt′ic *adj, n.*

GRAMMAR AND USAGE

Celt is always pronounced (kelt).

Celtic is pronounced (kel′tik) except in the case of the name of the Boston *Celtics* basketball team, in which case the word is pronounced (sel′tiks).

ce·ment (sə ment′) *n* **1** a fine, grey powder made by burning clay and limestone. **2** this substance mixed with water and sand or gravel to form concrete. **3** a soft substance used as an adhesive that hardens when it dries: *rubber cement.* **4** something that joins or keeps things together: *Sharing is the cement of friendship.*
v **1** stick together with cement. **2** pour or spread concrete for: *They are cementing the sidewalk.* **3** join firmly: *The wilderness adventure cemented their friendship.* <Old French, from Latin *caementum* stone cut from a quarry>

cem·e·ter·y (sem′ə ter′ē) *n, pl* **cem·e·ter·ies** a place for burying the dead. <Latin, from Greek *koimeterion* a room for sleeping>

cen·o·taph (sen′ə taf′) *n* a monument to a dead person whose body is buried elsewhere, or a monument to many dead, such as those killed in a war. <French, from Greek *kenos* empty + *taphos* tomb>

Ce·no·zo·ic (sē′nə zō′ik) *or* (sen′ə zō′ik) *Geology n* the era extending from the appearance of the first mammals, about 70 million years ago, to the present time. It covers the TERTIARY and QUATERNARY periods. Compare MESOZOIC, PALEOZOIC.
adj to do with this era or the rocks formed then. <Greek *kainos* recent + *zoion* animal>

cen·ser (sen′sər) *n* a container for burning incense in. <Old French, from Latin *incensum* incense>

cen·sor (sen′sər) *v* examine material such as news, books, or movies and perhaps change or delete parts in order to ensure they contain nothing offensive or harmful to the public interest: *Two scenes in the movie had been censored.* *n* **1** a person whose responsibility is censoring material. **2** in ancient Rome, a magistrate who took the census and supervised the conduct of citizens. <Latin *censere* evaluate> **cen′sor·ship** *n.*

cen·so·ri·ous (sen sôr′ē əs) *adj* critical or judgmental. **cen·so′ri·ous·ly** *adv.* **cen·so′ri·ous·ness** *n.*

cen·sure (sen′shər) *n* an expression of strong disapproval, often one issued officially or publicly as a form of protest or discipline: *a vote of censure against the mayor.*
v **cen·sured, cen·sur·ing** express formal disapproval of: *The press censured the government for failure to disclose all the facts.* <Old French, from Latin *censere* evaluate> **cen′sur·a·ble** *adj.*

CONFUSABLES

Censure means "criticize severely": *The student was censured for poor marks on the essay.*

Censor means "delete" or "ban all or part of something considered unsuitable for the public": *The violent video game was censored for teens.*

cen·sus (sen′səs) *n* an official count of the people living somewhere, usually combined with a collection of basic data about their age, occupation, income, and language. <Latin *censere* evaluate>

cent (sent) *n* a unit of money in Canada and several other countries, equal to one-hundredth of a dollar. *Symbol* **¢** <Old French, Latin *centum* hundred>

cen·taur (sen′tôr) *Greek myth n* a creature with the head, arms, and chest of a man and the body and legs of a horse. <Latin, from Greek *kentauros*>

cen·te·nar·i·an (sen′tə ner′ē ən) *n* a person who is one hundred years old or more.
adj one hundred years old or more. <See CENTENARY.>

cen·ten·a·ry (sen ten′ə rē) *or* (sen tē′nə rē) *n,*
pl **cen·ten·a·ries** **1** a hundredth anniversary or its celebration. **2** a period of one hundred years.
adj to do with a hundredth anniversary or a period of one hundred years. <Latin *centum* hundred>

cen·ten·ni·al (sen ten′yəl) *adj* to do with one hundred years or a hundredth anniversary: *Canada's centennial year was 1967.*
n a hundredth anniversary or its celebration. <Latin *cent*(*um*) hundred + (*bi*)*ennial*>

cen·ter (sen′tər) CENTRE.

centi– *combining form* **1** one-hundredth (an SI prefix): *centimetre. Symbol* **c** **2** one hundred: *centipede.* <French, from Latin *centum* hundred>

cen·ti·grade (sen′tə grād′) CELSIUS.

cen·ti·me·tre (sen′tə mē′tər) *n* a unit of length, equal to one-hundredth of a metre, or ten millimetres. Also, **centimeter**. *Symbol* **cm**

cen·ti·pede (sen′tə pēd′) *n* a small, wormlike creature with a long, flat, segmented body and many pairs of legs. <Latin *centum* hundred + *pedis* foot>

cen·tral (sen′trəl) *adj* **1** at the centre: *the central part of the city.* **2** being a roughly equal distance away from all points or for everyone involved: *They live in a central location. Barrie was a central meeting place for all the committee members.* **3** main or chief: *What is the central idea in the story?* **cen·tral′i·ty** *n.* **cen′tral·ly** *adv.*

Central African Republic *n* a country in central Africa.

Central America *n* the narrow piece of land joining North America and South America. It contains several countries. **Central American** *adj, n.*

central heating *n* a system for heating a building, with one main furnace or boiler and a set of ducts or pipes to carry the heated air or water into all the rooms.

cen·tral·ize (sen′trə līz′) *v* **cen·tral·ized, cen·tral·iz·ing** **1** collect or concentrate at a centre. **2** manage directly from a centre or headquarters instead of distributing power to local branches or agencies: *a centralized government.* **cen′tral·i·za′tion** *n.*

central nervous system *n* in vertebrates, the brain and spinal cord.

central processing unit CPU.

🍁 **Central Provinces** *pln* Ontario and Québec. Also called **Central Canada**.

central tendency See MEASURES OF CENTRAL TENDENCY.

cen·tre (sen′tər) *n* **1** a part or place in the middle: *the centre of the forehead, the centre of the stage.* **2** *Mathematics* a point within a circle or sphere, equally distant from all points of the circumference. **3** the chief object of interest: *She was the centre of attention. The new city hall was the centre of a huge controversy.* **4** a place of influence or activity: *a shopping centre.* **5** *Sports* the player in the middle position of a forward line in some sports such as hockey or basketball. **6** a political position characterized by compromise between extreme views: *Which candidate best represents the centre?*
v **cen·tred, cen·tring** **1** place in or at the centre: *She centred the title on the page.* **2** **be centred** have as its centre or headquarters: *The troops were centred at a temporary camp.* **3** aim or focus: *She centred the camera on the interviewer.* Also, **center**. <Old French, from Greek *kentron* sharp point> **cen′tred** *adj.*
centre on, have as the main theme or focus: *a report that centres on the health issues.*

GRAMMAR AND USAGE

It is preferable to use **centre on** instead of **centre around**, which is considered to be non-standard:
His speech centred on the topic of child labour.

a bat	e bed	i bid	o pot	u cup	th **thin**
ā cake	ē me	ī bite	ō go	ū rude	ᴛʜ **then**
ȧ bar	ə about	ər over	ȯ for	u̇ put	zh measure

centre·board (sen′tər bôrd′) *n* a movable keel for a sailboat, lowered through a slot to prevent drifting.

centre field *Baseball n* the section of the outfield behind second base. **centre fielder** *n.*

cen·tre·fold (sen′tər fōld′) *n* a large illustration that covers the two facing pages at the middle of a magazine.

centre ice *Hockey n* **1** the centre of the ice surface, from which play begins at the start of each period. **2** the whole of the ice surface between the blue lines.

centre of gravity *n* the point in any object around which its mass is evenly balanced.

cen·tre·piece (sen′tər pēs′) *n* **1** a decorative object for the centre of a table. **2** the main item in a display or collection: *A black skirt is the centrepiece of her wardrobe.*

cen·trif·u·gal force (sen trif′yə gəl) *n* a force tending to move things away from the centre around which they revolve. Compare CENTRIPETAL FORCE. <French, from Latin *centrum* centre + *fugere* flee>

cen·tri·fuge (sen′trə fyūj′) *n* a machine with a spinning chamber inside it that uses centrifugal force to separate cream from milk, serum from clot in blood samples, etc. <French, from Latin *centrum* centre + *fugere* flee>

cen·tri·ole (sen′trē ōl′) *Biology n* in most animal cells, one of a pair of cylindrical bodies near the nucleus.

cen·trip·e·tal force (sen trip′ə təl) *n* a force that tends to move things toward the centre around which they are turning. Compare CENTRIFUGAL FORCE. <Latin *centrum* centre + *petere* seek>

cen·trist (sen′trist) *n* a person with moderate political opinions.
adj to do with such people or their views.

cen·tro·mere (sen′trə mēr′) *Biology n* the structure or point joining two sister chromatids to each other and to a spindle during cell division. <Greek *kentron* centre + *meros* part>

cen·tro·some (sen′trə sōm′) *Biology n* in a cell, a small region of cytoplasm close to the nucleus that splits into two when the cell divides and that attracts the divided chromosomes, one group to each part. Also called **centrosphere**. <Greek *kentron* centre + *soma* body>

cen·tro·sphere (sen′trə sfēr′) *n* **1** a centrosome. **2** *Geology* the central core of the earth.

cen·tu·ple (sen tū′pəl) *or* (sen tup′əl) *adj* a hundred times as much or as many.
v **cen·tu·pled, cen·tu·pling** make 100 times as much or as many.

cen·tu·ri·on (sen chū′rē ən) *n* in the ancient Roman army, the commander of a group of about a hundred soldiers. <Latin *centrum* hundred>

cen·tu·ry (sen′chə rē) *n, pl* **cen·tu·ries** **1** each period of 100 years, starting at 1 and counting from some reference point. **2** a period of a hundred years: *The century from 1880 to 1980 was a very eventful one.* **3** a group of a hundred people or things. **4** in ancient Rome, **a** a body of about a hundred soldiers. **b** a division of the people for voting. **5** *Cricket* a score of a hundred runs. <Latin *centum* hundred>

CEO chief executive officer.

ceph·a·lo·pod (sef′ə lə pod′) *n* a mollusc, characterized by long, armlike tentacles and a sharp beak. Squid are cephalopods. <Greek *kephale* head + *podis* foot>

ce·ram·ics (sə ram′iks) *n* **1** (*with plural verb*) objects made from baked clay: *Many beautiful ceramics were on display.* **2** (*with singular verb*) the art of making such objects: *Ceramics is taught in art class.* <Greek *keramos* pottery> **ce·ram′ic** *adj.*

ce·re·al (sē′rē əl) *n* **1** a grass that produces a seed used as food, such as wheat, rice, and barley. **2** a food made from the seeds of such a grass, usually a breakfast food.
adj to do with grain or the grasses producing it: *cereal crops.* See SERIAL for confusable. <Latin *Ceres* goddess of agriculture>

cer·e·bel·lum (ser′ə bel′əm) *n, pl* **cer·e·bel·lums** or **cer·e·bel·la** (ser′ə bel′ə) a part of the brain located below the CEREBRUM, responsible for balance and muscle co-ordination. <Latin *cerebrum* brain>

cer·e·bral (se rē′brəl) *or* (ser′ə brəl) *adj* **1** to do with the brain: *cerebral hemorrhage.* **2** to do with the cerebrum: *The cerebral cortex is the outer layer of the cerebrum.* **3** involving or appealing to thought and reason: *She enjoys cerebral games like chess.*

cerebral palsy *n* a condition caused by brain damage, especially before or at birth, characterized by impaired muscle control and lack of co-ordination.

cer·e·brate (ser′ə brāt′) *v* **cer·e·brat·ed, cer·e·brat·ing** use the brain. <Latin *cerebrum* brain> **cer′e·bra′tion** *n.*

cerebro– *combining form* to do with the brain and something else: *cerebrospinal.*

cer·e·bro·spi·nal (sə rē′brō spī′nəl) *or* (ser′ə brō spī′nəl) *adj* of or affecting both the brain and spinal cord.

cer·e·bro·va·scu·lar (sə rē′brō vas′kyū lər) *adj* to do with the blood vessels of the brain.

cer·e·brum (sə rē′brəm) *or* (ser′ə brəm) *n, pl* **cer·e·brums** or **cer·e·bra** (sə rē′brə) **1** the part of the human brain, divided into two hemispheres, that controls memory, understanding, and logic, as well as voluntary activity in the body. **2** the part of the brain in other vertebrates that corresponds to this. <Latin *cerebrum* brain>

cer·e·mo·ni·ous (ser′ə mō′nē əs) *adj* very formal and polite: *He greeted us with a ceremonious bow.*
cer′e·mo′ni·ous·ly *adv.* **cer′e·mo′ni·ous·ness** *n.*

cer·e·mo·ny (ser′ə mō′nē) *n, pl* **cer·e·mo·nies** **1** a special form or set of acts to be done on special occasions. **2** very polite or formal manners: *The old man showed us to the door with a great deal of ceremony.* <Old French, from Latin *caerimonia*> **cer′e·mo′ni·al** *adj.*
not stand on ceremony, not insist on formalities.

SYNONYMS

A **ceremony** is a formal ritual: *The students received their diplomas at the graduation ceremony.*

A **celebration** is less formal than a ceremony or rite: *The twins' birthday celebration was on Saturday.*

A **rite** is a solemn ceremony: *Marriage rites differ from religion to religion.*

ce·rise (se rēz′) *or* (se rēs′) *adj* bright pinkish red. <French = cherry, from Greek *kerasos*>

ce·ri·um (sē′rē əm) *n* a greyish metallic element. *Symbol* **Ce** <*Ceres* an asteroid named after a Roman goddess>

cer·tain (sər′tən) *adj* **1** specific and known, but not named: *to arrive at a certain hour. Classroom activities will receive a certain percentage of the final mark.* **2** established beyond any doubt: *That he was here is certain, because I saw him.* **3** sure to; sure to happen: *She is certain to do well in her career. Death is certain.* **4** confident and positive: *Are you certain of your facts?* **5** that is indefinite or hard to describe: *She has a certain charm. To a certain extent we are all to blame.*
pron Formal a definite but unspecified number: *Certain of the students will be asked to give a detailed report.* <Old French, from Latin *certus* sure>
for certain, without doubt: *It will rain for certain.*

cer·tain·ly (sər′tən lē) *adv* **1** without doubt. **2** used to express complete agreement with what has just been said: *"May I start?" "Certainly."*

cer·tain·ty (sər′tən tē) *n, pl* **cer·tain·ties** **1** freedom from doubt: *She spoke with such certainty that we believed her.* **2** a sure or true fact: *Are there any real certainties?*

cer·ti·fi·a·ble (ser′tə fī′ə bəl) *or* (ser′tə fī′ə bəl) *adj* **1** that can be certified. **2** officially recognized as requiring treatment for a mental disorder.

cer·tif·i·cate (sər tif′ə kit) *n* a written or printed form officially declaring something to be a fact or giving a person certain status or rights: *a birth certificate. You can't teach in Canada without a teaching certificate.*

certified cheque *n* a cheque guaranteed by a bank because there is enough money in a bank account.

cer·ti·fy (ser′tə fī′) *v* **cer·ti·fied, cer·ti·fy·ing** **1** officially declare something to be true or correct, usually in writing: *The doctor certified the cause of death as a heart attack.* **2** legally recognize that a person requires treatment for a mental disorder. **3** guarantee the quality or value of: *All the meat we buy in the stores has to be certified by the government.* **4** give a certificate to a person, stating that he or she has a certain status or certain rights. <Old French, from Latin *certus*> **cer′ti·fi′er** *n.*

cer·ti·tude (ser′tə tyūd′) *or* (ser′tə tūd′) *n* total certainty that something is the case.

ce·ru·le·an (sə rū′lē ən) *adj* sky blue. <Latin *caeruleus*, from *caelum* sky>

cer·vi·cal cap (sər′və kəl) *n* a contraceptive device worn by a woman, shaped like a flexible cap and fitted over the cervix to prevent the entry of semen.

cer·vix (sər′viks) *n, pl* **cer·vix·es** or **cer·vi·ces** (sər′və sēz) the narrow opening of the uterus. <Latin> **cer′vi·cal** *adj.*

ce·si·um or **cae·si·um** (sē′zē əm) *n* a soft, silvery, metallic element found as a trace element in some rocks and minerals. *Symbol* **Cs** <Latin *caesius* bluish grey>

ces·sa·tion (sə sā′shən) *n* the fact of ceasing: *We still hope for a cessation of fighting.* <Old French, from Latin *cedere* to yield>

ces·sion (sesh′ən) *n* the formal act of giving up rights, property, or territory: *the cession of lands by a conquered nation.* <Latin *cedere* surrender>

cess·pool (ses′pūl′) *n* a pit or underground tank for sewage. <origin uncertain>

northern right whale

Cetaceans have larger brains than humans and demonstrate considerable capacity for learning. They even seem to have a language of their own. Whales are still hunted by some nations, and they are often hurt or killed when they become entangled in fishing nets. The northern right whale is the most endangered of the large cetaceans.

ce·ta·cean (si tā′shən) *n* a marine fishlike mammal. Whales and dolphins are cetaceans.
adj to do with cetaceans. <Greek *ketos* whale> **ce·ta′ceous** *adj.*

cf. compare. <Latin *confer*>

🍁 **CF** Canadian Forces.

🍁 **CFB** Canadian Forces Base.

CFC *n, pl* **CFCs** in full, **chlorofluorocarbon** a gaseous compound of carbon with hydrogen, chlorine, or fluorine, formerly used in aerosol cans and refrigerators. CFCs are harmful to the earth's ozone layer.

🍁 **CFL** or **C.F.L.** Canadian Football League.

CFS chronic fatigue syndrome.

Cha·bad (chab′ad) LUBAVITCH.

cha–cha (chà′ chà′) *n* a ballroom dance with a strong, fast rhythm, originally Latin American.
v **cha-cha'ed, cha-cha'ing** dance the cha-cha. Also, **cha-cha-cha.** <imitative>

Chad (chad) *n* a country in north central Africa.

cha·dor (chud′ər) *n* a large piece of cloth used as a long cloak and veil by some Muslim women. <Persian *chadar* veil, sheet>

chafe (chāf) *v* **chafed, chaf·ing** **1** make or become annoyed or impatient: *We chafed at the long delay. Their teasing began to chafe him.* **2** cause discomfort by rubbing: *I can't wear this skirt; the waistband chafes.* **3** wear or be worn away by rubbing: *The shoes had chafed the skin from his heels.* **4** warm the hands, feet, etc. by rubbing them. <Old French, from Latin *calere* be warm + *facere* make>

a **bat**	e **bed**	i **bid**	o **pot**	u **cup**	th **thin**
ā **cake**	ē **me**	ī **bite**	ō **go**	ū **rude**	ŦH **then**
à **bar**	ə **about**	ər **over**	ȯ **for**	u̇ **put**	zh **measure**

chaff[1] (chaf) *n* **1** husks of grain, especially when separated from the kernel by threshing. **2** hay or straw chopped for feeding cattle. **3** worthless stuff. <Old English *ceaf*>

chaff[2] (chaf) *v* tease good-naturedly: *The girls chaffed him about his new haircut.*
n good-natured teasing. <origin uncertain>

chaf·finch (chaf′inch) *n* a European songbird with a pleasant, short song. <Old English *ceaf* chaff[1] + *finc* finch>

chaf·ing dish (chā′fing) *n* a dish with a heating apparatus under it, for keeping food warm or for cooking at the table. <*chafe*>

cha·grin (shə grin′) *n* a feeling of embarrassment or disappointment.
v cause to feel this way. <French = melancholy>
cha·grined′ *adj.*

chain (chān) *n* **1** a connected series of links or rings used to attach, secure, or decorate: *a gold chain around her neck. The chain across the path warned us not to go ahead.* **2** a series of things joined or linked together in any way: *a chain of mountains, a chain of events, a chain of fast-food restaurants.* **3** **chains** *pl* **a** imprisonment. **b** something that binds or restrains: *the chains of poverty.* **4** *Chemistry* several atoms of one element, bonded together. **5** *Surveying* a measuring instrument 66 ft. (about 20 m) long, consisting of 100 LINKS (def. 4).
v join, fasten, or bind with a chain. <Old French, from Latin *catena*>

chain gang *n* a group of convicts chained together while at work outdoors.

chain letter *n* a letter that each recipient is asked to copy and send to others in order to get some supposed benefit.

chain·link (chān′lingk′) *adj* of a fence, made of interwoven steel links.

chain mail *n* a flexible armour made of small metal rings linked together.

chain reaction *n* **1** *Chemistry, Nuclear physics* a process that sustains itself once it has been started because it yields energy or products that cause further reactions of the same kind: *A nuclear reactor is designed to produce a controlled chain reaction.* **2** a series of events or happenings, each caused by the one that precedes it: *The dog spotted a squirrel, and there began a chain reaction that ended with our whole family needing medical attention.*

chain·saw (chān′sȯ′) *n* a portable power saw whose teeth are linked together in a moving chain.

chain store *n* one of a group of retail stores all owned and operated by the same company.

chair (cher) *n* **1** a single seat with four legs and a back and, sometimes, arms. **2** in full, **chairperson** the leader of a meeting, department, or committee: *If the chair is absent, the vice-chair runs the meeting.* **3** the position of such a person: *No one occupies the chair of Philosophy at the moment.* **4** the electric chair.
v be the chairperson of: *She chaired the committee for two years.* <Old French, from Greek *kathedra* seat>

chair·lift (cher′lift) *n* an apparatus consisting of a number of seats suspended from an endless cable, for carrying people through the air up a slope or between two points.

chair·man (cher′mən) *n, pl* **chair·men** (cher′mən) a male CHAIR (def. 2).

chair·wom·an (cher′wu̇m′ən) *n, pl* **chair·wom·en** (cher′wim′ən) a female CHAIR (def. 2).

GRAMMAR AND USAGE

Although chairman can be used to refer to a male or a female, many people prefer either **chair** or **chairperson**, which are gender-free terms to use instead of **chairwoman** or **chairman**.

chaise (shāz) *n* **1** in former times, a light horse-drawn carriage, often with a folding top. **2** in full, **chaise longue** (long) or **chaise lounge** a chair with a reclining back and a long seat, in which a person can sit with outstretched legs. <French *chaise longue* = long chair>

chal·ced·o·ny (kal sed′ə nē) *or* (kal′sə dō′nē) *n, pl* **chal·ced·o·nies** a quartz with a waxy lustre, occurring in various colours and forms, such as agate and onyx. <Greek *chalkedon*>

cha·let (sha lā′) *n* **1** a house of a style found in the Swiss Alps, with a steep roof and wide, overhanging eaves. **2** a house, cottage, or ski lodge with this design. <Swiss French>

chal·ice (chal′is) *n* a cup shaped like a large wine glass, especially one used in a Christian Communion service. <Old French, from Latin *calicis* cup>

chalk (chok) *n* **1** a soft white or grey limestone made up mostly of tiny fossilized seashells. **2** a substance like chalk, used for writing or drawing on a chalkboard. **3** a stick of this substance.
v **1** write or draw with chalk. **2** mark, rub, or whiten with chalk. <Old English, from Latin *calcis* lime> **chalk′y** *adj.*
chalk up, a score or earn: *We chalked up twenty points in that game.* **b** attribute or assign by way of explanation: *Chalk it up to simple human error.*

chalk·board (chok′bȯrd′) *n* a board with a smooth, hard surface for writing or drawing on with chalk.

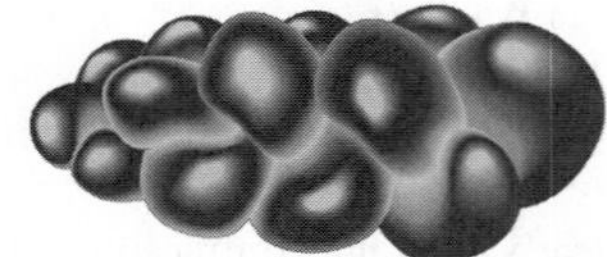

This bread was named for the tradition of separating a small piece of the dough, called the **challah**, before baking. In Jewish tradition, this piece is burnt and then thrown away after a special prayer.

chal·lah (hul′ə) *n* the braided loaf of rich white bread, made with yeast and eggs, traditionally eaten on the Jewish Sabbath. <Hebrew>

chal·lenge (chal′ənj) *v* **chal·lenged, chal·leng·ing** **1** call to engage in a fight or contest: *to challenge someone to a duel. I challenged her to a game of chess.* **2** question, dispute, or defy: *to challenge someone's statement.*

3 require or get serious effort from: *This assignment ought to challenge you.* 4 stop a person to demand his or her name or purpose: *When she tried to enter the camp, the guard challenged her.*

n 1 a statement challenging someone: *The sentry called out a challenge as we approached.* 2 something hard to do: *Training the puppy was a challenge.* <Old French, from Latin *calumnia* (false) accusation> **chal′leng·er** *n.* **chal′leng·ing** *adj.*

chal·lenged (chal′ənjd) *adj* (*often in compounds*) with more difficulties to overcome in some area than most other people: *A person in a wheelchair may be mobility-challenged.*

GRAMMAR AND USAGE

Some people use the word **challenged** playfully as a way of describing weaknesses that are not actual disabilities:
Dad is height-challenged.
Mom is punctuality-challenged.
I am sometimes sports-challenged.

chal·lis (shal′ē) *n* a lightweight, usually printed fabric of wool, wool and cotton, or a synthetic fibre, used for clothing. <origin uncertain>

cham·ber (chām′bər) *n* 1 an enclosed space in machinery, or in the body of an animal or plant, that contains some part or process: *the left chamber of the heart.* 2 a specially equipped room or hall, reserved for a particular activity: *the Senate Chamber, the decompression chamber on a submarine.* 3 **chambers** *pl* the office of a lawyer or judge. 4 *Archaic or Poetic* a room in a house, especially a bedroom. <Old French, from Greek *kamara* object with an arched cover (i.e., vaulted room)>

cham·ber·lain (chām′bər lin) *n* the person who manages the household of a monarch or lord.

cham·ber·maid (chām′bər mād′) *n* a person who makes the beds, and cleans bedrooms and bathrooms, now mainly in hotels.

chamber music *n* music suited to a room or small hall.

Chamber of Commerce *n* an organization of people involved in commerce, whose aim is to promote and protect the local business community.

chamber pot *n* a container used as a toilet in the bedroom during the night.

cham·bray (sham′brā) *n* a fine cloth in a plain weave, combining coloured threads with white threads in various designs. <*Cambrai*, France>

cha·me·le·on (kə mē′lē ən) *n* a lizard that can change its colour to blend with different backgrounds. <Old French, from Greek *chamai* on the ground + *leon* lion>

cham·ois (sham′ē); *for n def. 2,* (sham wȧ′) *or* (sham′wȧ) *n, pl* **cham·ois** 1 **a** a soft leather made from the skin of sheep, goats, or deer. **b** a piece of this, used for wiping and polishing. 2 a small, goatlike antelope that lives in the mountains of Europe and southwest Asia.

v **cham·oised, cham·ois·ing** wipe or polish with a chamois. <French>

cham·o·mile (kam′ə mīl′) CAMOMILE.

champ[1] (champ) *v* chew or bite noisily. <probably imitative>

champ (at) the bit, be restless or impatient: *After months with her leg in a cast, she was champing at the bit to go skiing again.*

champ[2] (champ) *Informal n* a champion.

cham·pagne (sham pān′) *n* a sparkling or bubbly wine made from a blend of grapes.

adj light brownish gold. <*Champagne*, France >

cham·pi·on (cham′pē ən) *n* 1 the winner of first place in a series of games or contests: *the school swimming champion.* 2 a person who promotes or speaks for another or for a cause: *a great champion of peace.* 3 a brave warrior or fighter.

adj that is a champion: *a champion figure skater.*

v promote or speak in behalf of: *She always championed the underdog.*

ETYMOLOGY

Champion is an Old French word that means "a man who fights on behalf of another." It comes from Latin *campio*, meaning "warrior," which in turn comes from *campus*, meaning "field of battle." Today's common meaning, "a person who has won a competition," did not develop until the 1800s.

cham·pi·on·ship (cham′pē ən ship′) *n* 1 the position or title of a champion in a competition. 2 a competition or series of competitions to decide a winner.

chance (chans) *n* 1 an opportunity: *a chance to make some money.* 2 the likelihood of something happening; probability: *There's a good chance we'll find him here.* 3 circumstances occurring by accident: *Chance led to their first meeting.* 4 a risk: *She took a chance when she swam across Lake Erie.*

adj not expected or planned: *a chance visit.*

v **chanced, chanc·ing** 1 happen: *He chanced to notice a coin in the gutter.* 2 risk: *I wouldn't chance sailing without a life jacket.* <Old French *cheance*, from Latin *cadere* happen>

by chance, a not having planned it so: *By chance, we ended up in the same hotel.* **b** by some possibility: *If by chance the weather clears, we can go for a swim.*

chance it, *Informal* take a risk.

chances are, *Informal* it is likely: *Chances are it'll rain.*

chance upon (or **on**), happen to find or meet: *He chanced upon an old friend.*

on the off chance, hoping for good luck: *She brought her skates on the off chance that the lake would be frozen.*

chan·cel (chan′səl) *n* the space around the altar of a Christian church, used by the clergy and the choir and often separated from the rest of the church by a railing. <Old French, from Latin *cancelli* crossbars>

a **bat**	e **bed**	i **bid**	o **pot**	u **cup**	th **thin**
ā **cake**	ē **me**	ī **bite**	ō **go**	ū **rude**	ᴛʜ **then**
ȧ **bar**	ə **about**	ər **over**	ȯ **for**	u̇ **put**	zh **measure**

chan·cel·lor (chan′sə lər) *n* **1** a high official, such as the secretary of a monarch or noble, the secretary of an embassy, or the head of government of some European countries. **2** the honorary head of a university. <See CHANCEL.> **chan′cel·lor·ship′** *n.*

chan·cre (shang′kər) *n* a hard, reddish, painless ulcer, especially on the genitals. <French, from Latin *cancer*>

chanc·y *Informal adj* **chan·ci·er, chan·ci·est** risky.

chan·de·lier (shan′də lēr′) *n* a light fixture with branches for individual lights, usually hanging from the ceiling. <Old French, from Latin *candere* to shine>

chan·dler (chan′dlər) *n* **1** a maker or seller of candles. **2** a dealer in supplies: *a ship's chandler.* <Old French, from Latin *candere* to shine>

change (chānj) *v* **changed, chang·ing 1** make or become different: *She changed her hairstyle. A caterpillar changes into a butterfly. He changed from an enemy to a friend.* **2** replace one thing with another or others: *to change your clothes, to change to a new format.* **3** exchange, trade, or switch: *I changed seats with my brother.* **4** get or give small units of money that equal a larger unit: *Can you change a five-dollar bill for me?* **5** put other clothes or coverings on: *to change the baby, to change the bed. I want to change before we go.* **6** transfer from one means of transport to another: *Since it's not a direct flight, you have to change at Winnipeg.*

n **1** the act, fact, or practice of changing, or the resulting condition: *a change in plans. Change is healthy.* **2** a fresh set: *a change of clothes.* **3** smaller units of money given for a larger unit or when a person has paid more than is due. **4** coins: *a five-dollar bill and some change.* <Old French, from Latin *cambire* exchange> **chang′er** *n.*

change around, rearrange or reverse.

change for the better, improve.

change over, switch to a new system, method, or owner: *Canada changed over to the metric system years ago.*

change places with, have someone else's lifestyle or job.

for a change, for the sake of variety.

SYNONYMS

Change can mean "transform": *Over the years, he changed his behaviour to become more considerate.*

Convert often means "change one thing into another": *I converted Canadian dollars into euros for my trip.*

Modify means "change somewhat": *I modified the recipe by slightly reducing the amount of sugar.*

change·a·ble (chān′jə bəl) *adj* **1** likely to change or frequently changing: *April weather is changeable.* **2** that can be changed: *a changeable clause in a contract.* **change′a·bil′i·ty** *n.* **change′a·bly** *adv.*

change·less (chānj′lis) *adj* unchanging. **change′less·ly** *adv.* **change′less·ness** *n.*

change·ling (chānj′ling) *n* in some fairy or folk tales, a child secretly substituted for another.

change of heart *n* a change of feeling or attitude.

change of life MENOPAUSE.

change·o·ver (chān′jō′vər) *n* a shift or switch to a different system or method, owner, or group of workers.

change·room (chānj′rūm′) *n* a room near a pool, beach, gym, or rink where people can change their clothes.

change table *n* a table on which to lay a baby for changing a diaper, often with storage space underneath and a device to keep the baby from rolling off.

chan·nel (chan′əl) *n* **1** a narrow band of frequencies used by a radio or TV station. **2** the bed of a stream or river. **3** a body of water joining two larger ones: *The Minas Channel lies between the Minas Basin and the Bay of Fundy.* **4** a passage for anything to flow or slide in. **5** a means of communication or expression: *to get information through secret channels.* **6** an outlet for a talent or emotion: *to find a suitable channel for your enthusiasm.*

v **chan·nelled** or **chan·neled, chan·nel·ling** or **chan·nel·ing 1** direct into or along a particular course: *She decided to channel her energies into her schoolwork. This trough channels rainwater out onto the lawn.* **2** form a channel in: *The river had channelled through the rocks.* <Old French, from Latin *canna* reed>

channel surfing *n* the practice of continually switching channels on the TV or radio to find something of interest.

chant (chant) *n* **1** a song, usually religious, in which several syllables or words are sung on one tone. **2** something repeated in a rhythmic way: *The demonstrators kept up their chant of "Save the trees!"*

v **1** sing a chant. **2** repeat rhythmically: *We chanted, "Go team, go!"* <Old French, from Latin *canere* sing>

chant·er (chan′tər) *n* **1** someone who chants, especially the singer of a liturgy. **2** the pipe on which the melody is played on a bagpipe.

The **chanterelle**, which has a nutlike flavour, has been popular in Europe since ancient Roman times.

The *oyster* mushroom gets its name from its oysterlike flavour when it is cooked.

Shitake mushrooms are a favourite in Japanese cooking, but only the cap is eaten.

Cultivated mushrooms are grown in dark cellars or mushroom houses, where temperature and humidity are controlled.

chan·te·relle (chan′tə rel′) *n* an edible woodland mushroom with an orange funnel-shaped cap. <French, from Greek *kantharos* drinking container>

C

chant·ey or **chant·y** (shan′tē) *or* (chan′tē) SHANTY[2].

chan·ti·cleer (chan′tə klēr′) *Poetic n* rooster. <Old French *Chantecler,* the name of the rooster in an old story called *Reynard the Fox*>

Cha·nu·kah (ḥȧ′nə kə) *or* (hȧ′nə kə) HANUKKAH.

cha·os (kā′os) *n* **1** great confusion or disorder: *The tornado left chaos behind it.* **2** the infinite space or formless matter formerly thought to have existed before the universe came into being. <Greek> **cha·ot′ic** *adj.* **cha·ot′i·cal·ly** *adv.*

chap[1] (chap) *v* **chapped, chap·ping** crack or roughen the skin: *My lips chap every winter. The cold wind had chapped her hands.* <Middle English *chappen* cut>

chap[2] (chap) *UK, Informal n* a fellow.

chap·ar·ral (shap′ə ral′) *n* in southwestern North America, a dense thicket of evergreen oaks or other small trees and shrubs. <Spanish *chaparro* evergreen oak>

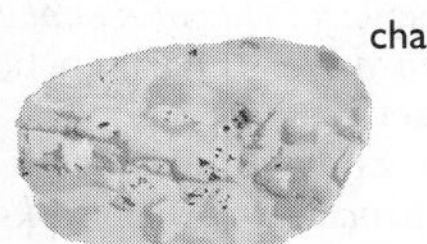

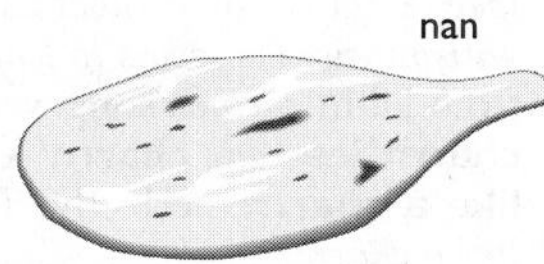

Chapati is popular in India and in east Africa, especially among Swahili Africans. It is often served with food flavoured with curry.

cha·pa·ti (chə pȧ′tē) *n* a flat, unleavened bread like a pancake, made of whole-wheat flour, common in Indian cooking. <Hindi *capana* flatten>

chap·book (chap′bu̇k′) *n* a small, inexpensive, softcover book, especially of poetry or short stories. <In former times, these books were sold by *chapmen* = peddlers.>

chap·el (chap′əl) *n* **1** a small church, either by itself or as part of a larger church. **2** a room for worship in an airport, hotel, hospital, or school. **3** a religious service in a chapel: *She was late for chapel.* <Old French, from Latin *cappella.* Originally, this meant the shrine in which was preserved a saint's *cappa* cape>

chap·er·one or **chap·er·on** (shap′ə rōn′) *or* (shap′ə rōn′) *n* **1** an adult who supervises young people's parties or student dances. **2** in former times, a married or older woman who accompanied a young unmarried woman in public for the sake of good form and protection.
v **chap·er·oned, chap·er·on·ing** act as a chaperone to. <French, from Latin *cappa* cape>

chap·lain (chap′lən) *n* a member of the clergy serving a public institution, unit in the armed forces, royal family, or other organization. <See CHAPEL.> **chap′lain·cy** *n.*

chap·let (chap′lit) *n* **1** a wreath worn on the head. **2** a string of beads used for counting prayers, or as a necklace. <Old French, from Latin *cappa* cape, hood>

chaps (chaps) *or* (shaps) *pl n* backless leggings of tough leather, worn by cowhands to protect their legs when riding. <Mexican Spanish>

chap·ter (chap′tər) *n* **1** a main division of a book. **2** a part of anything thought of as a story: *The development of radio is an interesting chapter in modern science.* **3** a local branch of a club or society. <Old French, from Latin *caput* head>

chapter and verse, a detailed written authority, quoted in an argument: *He cited chapter and verse of the Charter of Rights and Freedoms.* **b** an exact biblical reference.

char[1] (chȧr) *v* **charred, char·ring** burn slightly so as to blacken the surface: *The meat was charred.* <*charcoal*>

char[2] (chȧr) *n, pl* **char** a freshwater food fish belonging to the salmon family. Brook trout are char. <origin uncertain>

char[3] (chȧr) *Informal n* a charwoman.
v **charred, char·ring** work as a charwoman.<*charwoman*>

char·ac·ter (ker′ək tər) *n* **1** the combination of qualities that distinguishes one thing from another: *The character of the soil determines what can grow in it.* **2** the combined moral, emotional, and mental qualities of a person or group: *a person of moody character.* **3** moral strength or integrity: *It takes character to endure hardship for very long.* **4** a person or animal portrayed in a play, movie, or story: *The main character is a rancher.* **5** *Informal* an unusual person: *I hear he's quite a character.* **6** *Biology* a distinctive structure, function, or quality determined by heredity. **7** a letter, numeral, or other symbol of similar size, or a meaningful space in a series of these. <Old French, from Greek *charakter* stamping tool, which makes a distinguishing symbol or character (See def. 7.)> **char′ac·ter·less** *adj.*
in (out of) character, consistent (not consistent) with a person's known character: *Her stinging remark was entirely in character. It was out of character for her to go off without letting anyone know.*

char·ac·ter·is·tic (ker′ək tə ris′tik) *adj* **1** distinctive, special, or unique: *Bananas have a characteristic smell.* **2** typical or usual for a certain person or thing: *He prepared his presentation with characteristic thoroughness.*
n a quality or trait: *Cheerfulness is a characteristic I admire in people.* **char′ac·ter·is′ti·cal·ly** *adv.*

char·ac·ter·ize (ker′ək tə rīz′) *v* **char·ac·ter·ized, char·ac·ter·iz·ing 1** list the special qualities or features of a person or thing: *I would characterize our teacher as a very friendly person.* **2** be a distinguishing or typical feature of: *a disease characterized by a red rash and muscle cramps.* **char′ac·ter·i·za′tion** *n.*

character sketch *n* a brief description of a person or of a character in a book or story.

cha·rade (shə rād′) *n* **1** a very obvious pretence: *I don't know why she carries on this charade of being an invalid.* **2 charades** *pl* (*with singular verb*) a party game in which one acts out a word, title, or proverb for others to guess. <French = entertainment, from Provençal *charra* chatter>

char·broil (chȧr′broil′) *v* cook over burning charcoal.

char·coal (chȧr′kōl′) *n* **1** a form of carbon made by partly burning wood or bones in a place that is nearly airtight. **2** a stick, pencil, or crayon made of charcoal, for drawing. **3** a drawing made with such a tool.
adj very dark grey. <Middle English *charcole*>

a **bat**	e **bed**	i **bid**	o **pot**	u **cup**	th **thin**
ā **cake**	ē **me**	ī **bite**	ō **go**	ū **rude**	ᴛʜ **then**
ȧ **bar**	ə **about**	ər **over**	ȯ **for**	u̇ **put**	zh **measure**

chard (chȧrd) *n* in full, **Swiss chard** a white beet whose leaves are eaten as a vegetable.

charge (chȧrj) *v* **charged, charg·ing 1** ask as a price; require payment for: *They charge five cents per page for photocopying. They charge for hot water in the cafeteria.* **2** record a purchase as a debt to be paid later. *Cash or charge?* **3** load or fill: *The atmosphere was charged with emotion.* **4** restore or have restored the active materials in a battery: *Let your new cordless phone charge before the first use.* **5** give a task or responsibility to: *The law charges police officers with keeping order.* **6** accuse, especially in a court of law: *She was charged with assault.* **7** attack with a rush: *The troops charged the enemy.* **8** *Hockey* try to stop an opposing player illegally by taking more than two steps toward him or her in a direct attack.
n **1** the price or fee asked for something. **2** a debt or debit: *There are several charges against your account.* **3** whatever a thing is loaded or filled with: *The truck dumped its charge of gravel.* **4** an amount of electricity. **5** a responsibility or duty: *Arresting criminals is the charge of the police.* **6** care or management, or the person or thing under care: *Doctors and nurses have charge of sick people. The babysitter put her young charge to bed.* **7** *Informal* pleasure or fun: *I get a real charge out of playing with our cat.* **8** an accusation: *He admitted the charge and paid the fine.* **9** an attack: *The charge drove the enemy back.* <Old French *chargier* to load up, from Latin *carrus* wagon>
charge′a·ble *adj.*
charge up, assign as a credit or loss: *That was an unfortunate choice; well, charge it up to experience.*
in charge, in authority: *Who's in charge here?*
in charge of, with control or management of: *A new doctor is in charge of the case.*
in the charge of, under the control or management of: *The class was in the charge of a senior student.*
take charge, take control of a situation.

charge account *n* an arrangement with a business firm for buying goods or services on credit.

charge card CREDIT CARD.

char·gé d'af·faires (shȧr zhā′da fer′) *n, pl* **char·gés d'af·faires** (shȧr zhā′ da fer′) an official who takes the place of an ambassador or other diplomat. <French>

charg·er (chȧr′jər) *n* **1** a person who or thing that charges: *a battery charger.* **2** a warhorse.

char·i·ot (cher′ē ət) *n* a two-wheeled, horse-drawn vehicle used in ancient times in battles, races, and processions. <Old French, from Latin *carrus* wagon>
char′i·ot·eer′ *n.*

char·is·ma (kə riz′mə) *n, pl* **cha·ris·ma·ta** (kə riz′mə tə) **1** great power to attract and inspire people and win their loyalty. **2** *Christianity* a spiritual gift or grace. <Greek *charis* favour, grace> **cha′ris·ma′tic** (ker′iz mat′ik) *adj.*

char·i·ta·ble (cher′ə tə bəl) *adj* **1** for the purpose of helping those in need: *Many hospitals began as charitable establishments.* **2** generous and kind to people in need. **3** forgiving and thinking the best of others.
char′i·ta·bly *adv.*

char·i·ty (cher′ə tē) *n, pl* **char·i·ties 1** help given to people in need. **2** a fund, institution, or organization for helping people in need. **3** love for other people. **4** kindness in judging other people. <Old French *charite*, from Latin *caritas* affectionate care>

char·la·tan (shȧr′lə tən) *n* a person who pretends to have more knowledge or skill than he or she really has in order to swindle people. <French, from Italian *ciarlatre* to babble> **char′la·tan·ism′** *n.*

char·ley horse (chȧr′lē) *Informal n* a painful muscle cramp, especially of the leg or arm, caused by strain. <19c baseball slang, likely referring to a lame racehorse>

charm (chȧrm) *n* **1** very pleasant manners: *We were much impressed by the grace and charm of our host.* **2** a delightful or fascinating quality or feature: *The quaint old inn and its many charms are described in this brochure.* **3** a small ornament hanging on a chain or bracelet. **4** words, an action, or an object supposed to have magic power.
v **1** delight or fascinate: *I was charmed by the view of the lake.* **2** act on or protect as if by magic: *to charm a snake with music. He seems to lead a charmed life.* <Old French, from Latin *carmen* song, verse> **charm′er** *n.*
charm′less *adj.* **charm′less·ly** *adv.* **charm′less·ness** *n.*
like a charm, perfectly: *This new pencil sharpener works like a charm.*

charm·ing (chȧr′ming) *adj* (*often ironic*) delightful or fascinating. **charm′ing·ly** *adv.*

chart (chȧrt) *n* **1** a table, graph, or diagram presenting information. **2** a detailed record of the care a medical patient has received. **3** usually, **charts** *pl* a listing of the bestselling musical recordings: *That song is number three on the charts.* **4** a map, especially for navigating a ship or aircraft. **5** an outline map for recording special facts: *a weather chart.*
v **1** make a chart or map of: *to chart a course. Explorers charted the coast of North America.* **2** plan in detail. <French, from Greek *chartes* papyrus leaf (from which paper can be made)> **chart′less** *adj.*

char·ter (chȧr′tər) *n* **1** a royal or legislative grant to a group of people, specifying the form of organization: *All Canadian banks have charters from the Federal Government.* **2** a document setting out the basic principles and aims of a nation or organization: *the Canadian Charter of Rights and Freedoms.* **3 a** an arrangement whereby a bus, aircraft, or boat is hired, with a driver or pilot, for temporary private use by a group. **b** the bus, aircraft, or boat hired in this way.
v **1** give a charter to. **2** hire a bus, aircraft, or boat for private use. <Old French, from Latin *charta* papyrus leaf. See CHART.> **char′ter·less** *adj.*

chartered accountant *n* a licensed member of an accountants' organization. *Abbrev.* **CA**

🍁 **chartered bank** *n* a privately owned bank holding a charter from the Federal Government.

charter member *n* an original member of a club, society, or company.

🍁 **Charter of Rights and Freedoms** *n* in full, **Canadian Charter of Rights and Freedoms** a formal declaration written into the Constitution Act, 1982, guaranteeing basic freedoms and various rights (democratic, mobility, legal, equality, and minority language educational) to all Canadians.

char·treuse (shȧr trůz′) *or* (shȧr trūz′) *n* a green, yellow, or white liqueur first made by monks.
adj light yellowish green. <French = Carthusian (monk)>

char·wom·an (chȧr′wům′ən) *UK n, pl* **char·wom·en** (chȧr′wim′ən) a woman hired to clean a home or office. Usually shortened to **char**. <Old English *cerr* work + *woman*>

char·y (cher′ē) *adj* **char·i·er, char·i·est** (*with of*) shy or cautious: *chary of strangers. Cats are chary of wetting their paws.* <Old English *caru* care> **char′i·ly** *adv.* **char′i·ness** *n.*

Cha·ryb·dis (kə rib′dis) *Greek myth n* a dangerous whirlpool, opposite the cave of the sea monster Scylla.
between Scylla and Charybdis, between two dangers, one of which must be dealt with.

chase (chās) *v* **chased, chas·ing 1** run after or follow to catch or kill: *to chase a ball. The police are chasing a suspect.* **2** drive off: *The dog chased the squirrels from the garden.* **3** travel in order to see: *to chase eclipses.*
n **1** the act of chasing: *The thieves were caught after a short chase.* **2** hunting as a sport: *He was very fond of the chase.* <Old French, from Latin *capere* capture>
chase after, pursue.
chase around, *Informal* hurry from place to place.
chase up (or **down**)**,** look for and find or get: *We have to chase up a few more chairs.*
cut to the chase, get to the main point.
give chase, *Formal or Poetic* chase a person or thing.

chas·er (chā′sər) *n* **1** a drink taken after a drink of another kind, as, for example, beer after whisky. **2** a person who or thing that chases, such as a small, fast aircraft or ship used in war. **3** a horse for steeplechasing.

Chas·id (ha′sēd) HASID.

chasm (kaz′əm) *n* a deep opening or crack in the earth. <Latin, from Greek *chasma*>

chas·sis (shas′ē) *or* (chas′ē) *n, pl* **chas·sis** (shas′ēz) *or* (chas′ēz) a supporting framework; a frame supporting the body of a car or aircraft, the working parts of a radio or TV set, etc. <French, from Latin *capsa* box>

chaste (chāst) *adj* **1** virtuous; especially, refraining from sex outside of marriage. **2** simple in taste or style. <Old French, from Latin *castus* pure> **chaste′ly** *adv.* **chaste′ness** *n.*

chas·ten (chā′sən) *v* **1** admonish, with the intention of improving. **2** make more subdued or humble: *The frightening experience chastened them.* <Old French, from Latin *castus* pure>

chas·tise (chas tīz′) *v* **chas·tised, chas·tis·ing 1** punish. **2** criticize severely: *The coach chastised the players for being late.* **chas·tise′ment** *n.*

SYNONYMS

Chastise means "scold": *The teacher chastised the student for disrupting the class.*

Reprimand can mean "scold with anger": *Her dad severely reprimanded her for pushing her brother.*

Reproach means "blame": *The goalie was unfairly reproached for the loss.*

chas·ti·ty (chas′tə tē) *n* the quality of being chaste.

chat (chat) *v* **chat·ted, chat·ting 1** talk together in an easy, familiar way: *We sat chatting by the fire after supper.* **2** *Computers* converse in real time over the Internet by typing one's remarks on the keyboard so that they appear simultaneously on another user's screen.
n **1** easy, familiar conversation: *a pleasant chat about old times.* **2** *Computers* a real-time conversation over the Internet, using a computer keyboard. <*chatter*>

châ·teau or **cha·teau** (sha tō′) *n, pl* **châ·teaux** (sha tōz′) **1** a castle or large country house in France. **2** a building resembling this kind of house, such as a grand hotel. **3** in former times, in French Canada, the residence of a governor or a seigneur. **4 Château** 🍁 in former times, the Château St Louis in Québec City, residence of the Governor of Québec. <Old French, from Latin *castellum* castle>

🍁 **Château Clique** *n* the nickname given to the governing class of Lower Canada; the French equivalent of Upper Canada's **Family Compact**. <named after the *Château*, residence, in former times, of the Governor of Québec>

chat·e·laine (shat′ə lān′) *or* (shat′ə lān′) *n* the woman in charge of a castle, château, or a large, fashionable household. <French, from Latin *castellum* castle>

chat room or **chatroom** *Computers n* an Internet site where users can converse online in real time by typing on their computer keyboards. Compare INSTANT MESSAGING. Also called **chat line**, **chat site**.

chat·tel (chat′əl) *n* a piece of property that is not real estate, such as a piece of furniture, a vehicle, or a domestic animal. <Old French, from Latin *capitale* wealth>

chat·ter (chat′ər) *v* **1** talk constantly, rapidly, or foolishly. **2** make rapid, sharp sounds: *Monkeys chattered in the trees.* **3** rattle the teeth when one shivers violently.
n **1** rapid, foolish talk. **2** rapid, sharp sounds: *the chatter of her keyboard as she typed.* <Middle English; imitative> **chat′ter·er** *n.*

chat·ter·box (chat′ər boks′) *n* a person who talks a lot.

chat·ty (chat′ē) *adj* **chat·ti·er, chat·ti·est 1** talkative. **2** in the style of friendly, informal conversation: *a nice, chatty letter about his trip.* **chat′ti·ly** *adv.* **chat′ti·ness** *n.*

chauf·feur (shō fər′) *for n,* (shō′fər) *for v. n* a hired driver for a wealthy person or important official.
v act as a chauffeur to. <French *chauffer* = stoker (i.e., one who tends the fire for a steam engine)>

chau·vin·ism (shō′və niz′əm) *n* an arrogant, reasonless belief in the natural superiority of one's own nation, sex, cause, or group: *male chauvinism, political chauvinism.* <N. *Chauvin*, enthusiastic supporter of Napoleon I> **chau′vin·ist** *n.* **chau′vin·is′tic** *adj.*

🍁 **chaw** (cho) *North interj* a call directing a team of sled dogs to swing to the left.

a bat	e bed	i bid	o pot	u cup	th thin
ā cake	ē me	ī bite	ō go	ū rude	ᴛʜ then
ȧ bar	ə about	ər over	ȯ for	ů put	zh measure

cheap (chēp) *adj* **1** costing little money: *Eggs are cheap now.* **2** costing little effort or sacrifice: *a cheap victory.* **3** of little value; or treated as of little value: *cheap jewellery. Life was cheap in those days.* **4** morally low: *a cheap trick.* **5** stingy: *He was too cheap to leave a tip.*
adv cheaply: *After the accident, he sold his car cheap.* <Old English, from Latin *caupo* small trader> **cheap′en** *v.* **cheap′ly** *adv.* **cheap′ness** *n.*
feel cheap, feel inferior and ashamed.
hold something cheap, have little respect for the value of something.
on the cheap, at low cost: *to travel on the cheap.*
talk is cheap, promises are easily made and broken.

cheap shot *n* a mean or unfair remark.

cheap·skate (chēp′skāt′) *n* a stingy person.

cheat (chēt) *v* **1** unfairly trick into paying or giving: *That phony home renovation company cheated her of her life savings.* **2** act in a dishonest or unfair way to gain an advantage: *to cheat at cards, to cheat in an exam.* **3** deprive as if by cheating: *The flight delay cheated us of a day's sightseeing.* **4** escape; foil: *to cheat death.* **5** (*often with* ***on***) be sexually unfaithful to: *to cheat on one's spouse.*
n **1** one who cheats. **2** a fraud or trick. <variant of *escheat* to confiscate land. This later came to be used for any deceptive action.> **cheat′er** *n.*

cheat sheet *Slang n* a paper with information giving one an unfair advantage, such as notes taken into a test.

check (chek) *v* **1** examine something to see whether it is true or correct: *We should check her statement before we trust her.* **2** (*often with* ***on***) investigate; find out the status of: *Check your phone messages. When he checked, he found the money was gone. Excuse me while I check on my little brother.* **3** mark as correct or done: *Check one answer for each multiple-choice question.* **4** *Hockey* hinder or stop the puck-carrier by using the stick or the body. **5** stop, especially so as to prevent something: *The bushes checked her fall.* **6** hold back or control: *to check your anger.* **7** leave for safekeeping: *to check your coat.* **8** hand over one's baggage to be sent to a destination. **9** in chess, put the opponent's king in danger.
n **1** an act of checking: *an illegal hockey check. Do a thorough check to see that nothing has been stolen.* **2** something that checks: *A system of checks and balances keeps any part of the government from getting too powerful.* **3** a check mark. **4** a ticket given in return for baggage or other checked item to show ownership. **5** *especially US* **a** the bill in a restaurant: *Bring the check, please.* **b** a cheque. **6** a pattern of squares, or a fabric or wallpaper with such a pattern, or one of these squares: *The checks are smaller in this pattern.*
interj **1** in chess, a call made when one has put the opponent's king in danger. **2** *Informal* OK; all right. <Old French, from Persian *sah* king> **check′a·ble** *adj.*
check in, a register at a hotel or campground, or for a flight. **b** make a brief visit to see how things are going.
check off, mark as completed or correct.
check out, a leave a hotel or campground and pay the bill: *We have to check out by noon.* **b** in a store, bring one's purchases to the cashier and pay for them: *It took ages to check out.* **c** verify: *Check out your facts before printing them.* **d** borrow from a library: *I checked out two books.* **e** *Informal* look at: *Check out my new boots!* **f** turn out to be true when checked: *Her alibi checks out.*
check over, inspect.
check up on, seek more information on, especially secretly: *The police were checking up on her.*
in check, a held back; restrained: *Keep your impatience in check.* **b** in chess, threatened with checkmate.

checked (chekt) *adj* **1** marked in a pattern of squares. **2** stowed as baggage in the cargo compartment rather than carried by hand: *On arrival it took us a while to collect our checked baggage.*

check·er[1] (chek′ər) *v* **1** mark or arrange in a pattern of alternating squares or patches of contrasting colours: *a wall checkered with blue and white tiles. The ground under the trees was checkered with sunlight and shade.* **2** vary or have ups and downs: *a checkered career as an actor.*
n a piece used in checkers. <Old French, from Latin *scaccarium* chessboard> **check′ered** *adj.*

check·er[2] (chek′ər) *n* (*often in compounds*) a person who or thing that checks: *a spell-checker.*

check·er·board (chek′ər bòrd′) *n* a square board marked in a pattern of 64 squares of two alternating colours and used in playing checkers or chess.

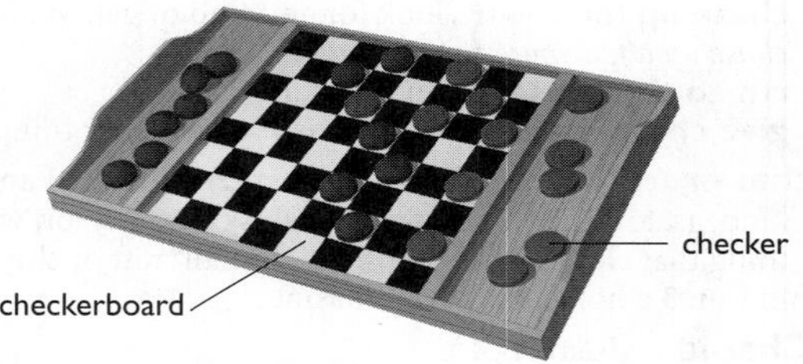

Checkers has been around for over 3000 years and has undergone many transformations. Perhaps the most extraordinary change of all is the most recent—humans playing against computers.

check·ers (chek′ərz) *n* a game played by two people, each with twelve round, flat pieces to move on a checkerboard.

check·list (chek′list′) *n* a complete list of things, such as names, items in an inventory, or steps in a procedure, used for checking or comparing.

check mark *n* a mark [√] to show that something is correct or has been dealt with or checked.

check·mate (chek′māt′) *v* **check·mat·ed, check·mat·ing 1** in chess, put an opponent's king in danger which no move can avert, and so win the game. **2** defeat completely.
n **1** in chess, a move that ends the game in this way. **2** a complete defeat.
interj in chess, a call indicating to one's opponent that his or her king is in danger which no move can avert. <Old French, from Persian *shah mat* king is dead>

check·out (chek′out′) *n* **1** in a store, the counter where shoppers present their purchases to the cashier and pay for them: *Go to the express checkout.* **2** the process of checking out: *Checkout was quick today.* **3** the time by which one must leave and pay at a hotel or campground: *We missed the checkout and had to pay for an extra day.*

check·point (chek′point′) *n* a place where a check is made, especially a place on a road where vehicles or people are inspected by authorities.

check·room (chek′rūm′) *n* a place where coats, hats, or baggage can be left until called for later.

check·up (chek′up′) *n* **1** a careful examination or inspection. **2** a thorough physical examination: *She made an appointment with the doctor for a checkup.*

Ched·dar or **ched·dar** (ched′ər) *n* a hard, dense, white or orange cheese. <*Cheddar*, England, where it was originally made>

🍁 **chee·cha·ko** (chē chȧk′ō) *n* a newcomer: *It took the cheechako many months to learn our ways.* <Chinook Jargon *chee* new + *chako* come>

cheek (chēk) *n* **1** the side of the face below either eye. **2** *Informal* rude, disrespectful talk or behaviour: *Enough of your cheek!* **3** *Slang* a buttock. <Old English *ceoce*>
cheek by jowl, side by side; close together.
turn the other cheek, take no revenge for wrong.

cheek·bone (chēk′bōn′) *n* the bone just below either eye.

cheek·y (chē′kē) *Informal adj* **cheek·i·er, cheek·i·est** disrespectful or impudent. **cheek′i·ly** *adv.* **cheek′i·ness** *n.*

SYNONYMS

Cheeky means "impertinent" or "ill-mannered": *The salesclerk's cheeky attitude insulted some customers.*

Brazen is more forceful and means "shameless" or "rude": *The brazen reporter pushed through the crowd.*

Insolent means "rude" and "bold": *The insolent child was constantly talking back to adults.*

cheep (chēp) *v* make a short, high-pitched sound like a young bird.
n a short, high-pitched sound like that of a young bird. <imitative> **cheep′er** *n.*

cheer (chēr) *n* **1** a spirit of gladness, hope, or courage: *A warm fire and a good meal brought cheer to our hearts again.* **2** a shout of encouragement, approval, or praise: *A cheer went up when she scored the winning goal.*
v **1** fill with cheer: *Our visit cheered the old woman.* **2** shout encouragement, approval, or praise to someone or at something: *We cheered loudly. Everyone cheered our team.* <Old French, from Greek *kara* head (i.e., welcoming face)>
cheer on, urge on with encouraging shouts.
cheer up, make or become happier.
of good cheer, *Archaic or Poetic* happy or hopeful.

cheer·ful (chēr′fəl) *adj* **1** full of gladness and optimism: *She is always cheerful no matter what.* **2** pleasant and bright: *a cheerful, sunny room.* **3** willing: *a cheerful worker.* **cheer′ful·ly** *adv.* **cheer′ful·ness** *n.*

cheer·i·o (chē′rē ō′) *UK, Informal interj* goodbye. <*cheer*>

cheer·lead·er (chēr′lē′dər) *n* **1** a person in a group that leads organized cheering at athletic events, often while performing acrobatics and dancelike steps. **2** one who rallies people in support of a cause: *This reporter is nothing but a cheerleader for whatever party is in power.*

cheer·less (chēr′ləs) *adj* depressing; gloomy: *a cold, cheerless room.* **cheer′less·ly** *adv.* **cheer′less·ness** *n.*

cheers *interj* **1** used to make a toast before drinking. **2** *Informal* **a** used to close a casual letter or an e-mail. **b** used to say goodbye.

cheer·y (chē′rē) *adj* **cheer·i·er, cheer·i·est** cheerful and pleasant: *a cheery voice, a cheery decor.* **cheer′i·ly** *adv.* **cheer′i·ness** *n.*

cheese (chēz) *n* a solid or semi-solid food made from the pressed curds of milk. <Old English, from Latin *caseus*> **cheese′like′** *adj.*

cheese·burg·er (chēz′bər′gər) *n* a hamburger with a slice of melted cheese on top of the meat.

cheese·cake (chēz′kāk′) *n* a baked or unbaked dessert, usually made with cream cheese, eggs, and sugar, often with a crumb crust on the bottom.

cheese·cloth (chēz′kloth′) *n* a thin, loosely woven cotton cloth, originally used for wrapping freshly made cheese.

chees·y (chē′zē) *adj* **chees·i·er, chees·i·est** **1** like or containing cheese: *a cheesy sauce.* **2** *Informal* **a** corny or unsophisticated: *a cheesy movie.* **b** cheap and of low quality: *cheesy knick-knacks.*

chee·tah (chē′tə) *n* a large, slender animal of the cat family, reddish yellow with black spots and a small head. It is the fastest mammal on earth. See PREY for picture. <Hindi *cita*>

chef (shef) *n* a skilled professional cook, especially the head cook in a large restaurant. <French *chef* = head>

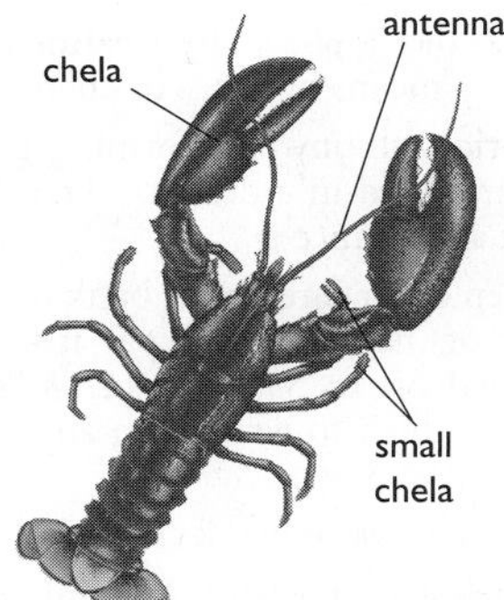

Lobsters have six **chelae**, but it's the two largest chelae that look like they could cause a nasty pinch. Each of these two claws has a different function. One is bigger and is used for crushing prey, while the other is smaller and is meant for seizing and for cutting.

che·la (kē′lə) *n, pl* **che·lae** (kē′lē) *or* (kē′lī) a pincerlike claw such as that of a lobster, crab, or scorpion. <Latin, from Greek *chele* claw>

chem·i·cal (kem′ə kəl) *adj* **1** to do with chemistry: *chemical experiments, a chemical compound.* **2** to do with chemicals: *the chemical industry.*
n a substance produced in a laboratory or in the body, using the principles of chemistry. <French, from Latin *alchimia*> **chem′i·cal·ly** *adv.*

a bat	e bed	i bid	o pot	u cup	th **thin**
ā cake	ē me	ī bite	ō go	ū rude	ᴛʜ **then**
ȧ bar	ə about	ər over	ȯ for	u̇ put	zh measure

chemical abuse *n* habitual use or overuse of alcohol, narcotics, drugs, or chemicals.

chemical change *Chemistry n* a change in which one substance is converted into one or more substances with different properties.

chemical element *n* an ELEMENT (def. 1).

chemical engineering *n* the science or profession of using chemistry for industrial purposes.

chemical warfare *n* the use of poison gas or any chemicals other than explosives as weapons.

chem·i·lu·mi·nes·cence (kem′ə lūm′ə nes′əns) *n* luminescence resulting from chemical action, not heat. The light from fireflies is a form of chemiluminescence. **chem′i·lu′mi·nes′cent** *adj.*

che·mise (shə mēz′) *n* an undershirt worn by women and girls. <Old French, from Latin *camisia* shirt>

chem·ist (kem′ist) *n* a person trained in CHEMISTRY (def. 1). <Old French, from Latin *alchimia* alchemy>

chem·is·try (kem′i strē) *n, pl* **chem·is·tries** **1** the science that studies the elements, the simplest substances making up the universe, and how they interact and combine under various conditions. **2** the application of this science to a certain subject: *the chemistry of foods.* **3** chemical processes, properties, or phenomena: *Some teenagers have acne because of their body chemistry.* **4** the dynamics of interaction between people: *the chemistry of love. The arrival of new members changed the chemistry of the group.*

che·mo·syn·thes·is (kē′mō sin′thə sis) *n* the use of chemical reaction as an energy source in some organisms to produce compounds.

che·mo·ther·a·py (kē′mō ther′ə pē) *n* the treatment of disease, especially cancer, by means of drugs or chemicals.

che·nille (shə nēl′) *n* a fabric with tiny tufts forming a soft, fuzzy surface and often arranged in a design. <French = caterpillar (from its fuzzy appearance)>

cheque (chek) *n* **1** a written order directing a bank to take money from the account of the signer and pay it to the person or company named on it: *She pays her bills by cheque.* **2** a blank form on which to write such an order. <special use of *check*>

cheque·book (chek′ing) *n* a book of blank cheques.

chequ·ing account (chek′ing) *n* a bank account from which money may be paid by cheque.

cher·ish (cher′ish) *v* **1** regard with deep affection: *They cherished their only child.* **2** cling to in the mind: *to cherish a hope.* <Old French, from Latin *carus* dear>

cher·no·zem (cher′nə zəm) *n* a fertile, dark topsoil, typical of cool-to-temperate areas like the North American prairie. <Russian = black earth> **cher′no·zem′ic** *adj.*

Cher·o·kee (cher′ə kē′) *n, pl* **Cher·o·kee** or **Cher·o·kees** **1** a member of an Aboriginal people now living mostly in Oklahoma and North Carolina. **2** their Iroquoian language.
adj to do with these people or their culture or language.

che·root (shə rūt′) *n* a cigar cut square at both ends. <Tamil *churuttu* roll of tobacco>

cher·ry (cher′ē) *n, pl* **cher·ries** a small, round, edible red fruit with a stone in the centre.
adj bright red. <Old French, from Greek *kerasos*>

cherry bomb *n* a round, red firecracker.

cherry picker *n* a crane with a large bucket at the end, in which a person can stand to carry out operations high above the ground, such as repairs to power lines.

cherry tomato See TOMATO.

cher·ub (cher′əb) *n, pl* **cher·u·bim** (cher′ə bim′) *for 1,* **cher·ubs** *for 2.* **1** among Christians, Jews, and Muslims, an angelic being, often shown as a child with wings, or as a child's head with wings but no body. **2** a person like a cherub, such as a child with a round, innocent face. <Old English, from Hebrew *kerub*> **che·ru′bic** (chə rū′bik) *adj.*

cher·vil (chər′vəl) *n* a herb of the parsley family with small white flowers and delicate fernlike leaves. <Old English, from Greek *chairein* rejoice + *phyllon* leaf>

Chesh·ire cat (chesh′ər) *n* anybody with a fixed grin. <the grinning cat in *Alice in Wonderland* by L. Carroll>

The king moves in any direction, but only one square at a time.

The queen moves in any direction.

The two bishops move diagonally.

The two rooks (also called castles) move horizontally or vertically.

The two knights move diagonally across a rectangle measuring two squares by three squares.

The eight pawns move vertically, usually one square at a time.

chess (ches) *n* a game played on a special board by two people, each of whom uses 16 chess pieces to try to capture the other's chess pieces until the other's king is in a position of no escape. See also CHECK, CHECKMATE. <Old French *eschec* a check>

chess·board (ches′bôrd′) *n* a checkered board marked in a pattern of 64 squares, used in playing chess.

chest (chest) *n* **1** the top front part of a person's or an animal's body. **2** a large storage box with a lid: *a linen chest, a tool chest, a treasure chest.* **3** a chest of drawers. **4** a small wall cabinet for first-aid supplies and drugs: *a medicine chest.* <Old English *cest*, from Greek *kiste* box>
get something off your chest, get a feeling of relief by talking about some problem.
play (or **keep**) **your cards close to your chest,** be secretive or cautious about revealing your intentions or motives.

ches·ter·field (ches′tər fēld′) *n* a long, upholstered seat with a back and arms. <19c Earl of *Chesterfield*, who popularized it>

chest·nut (ches′nut′) *n* **1** the sweet, edible nut of a large tree related to the beech. Chestnuts have prickly outer shells. Compare HORSE CHESTNUT. **2** a reddish brown horse. **3** *Informal* a old and stale joke or story.
adj reddish brown. <Old French *chastaigne*, from Greek *kastanea*>

chest of drawers *n* a piece of furniture with several drawers for keeping clothes in.

che·val glass (shə val′) *n* a tall mirror mounted in a frame so that it swings between its supports. <French *cheval* frame>

chèv·re (shev′rə) *n* cheese made from goat's milk. <French, from Latin *caper* goat>

chev·ron (shev′ron) *n* any V or inverted V shape, especially a stripe worn on the sleeve of a uniform to show rank or years of service. <Old French, from Latin *caper* goat. The inverted V-shape was supposed to look like a jumping goat.>

chew (chū) *v* **1** crush or grind with or as if with the teeth. **2** *Informal* (*often with* **over**) think over or consider.
n **1** an act of chewing: *The puppy gave the stick a good chew.* **2** the piece that is chewed: *a chew of tobacco.* <Old English *ceowan*>
chew out, *Informal* scold.
chew the fat, *Slang* chat; converse casually: *Now and then she calls me up and we chew the fat for a while.*

chewing gum *n* a preparation of chicle, or some artificial substitute, usually sweetened and flavoured, for chewing.

chew·y (chū′ē) *adj* becoming sticky and soft or stretchy when chewed.

Chey·enne (shī en′) *n, pl* **Chey·enne** or **Chey·ennes** **1** a member of an Aboriginal people now living in Montana and Oklahoma. **2** their Algonquian language.

ch'i (chē) *n* in Chinese philosophy, the life force that inhabits the body and breath. <Mandarin = breath>

chi·a·ro·scu·ro (kyȧ′rō skū′rō) *n* **1** the treatment of light and shade in a picture, or the effect produced by this. **2** stylistic effects of contrast or variation used in any of the arts. <Italian *chiaro* light + *oscuro* dark>

chic (shēk) *n* fashionable style.
adj stylish. <French>

chi·can·er·y (shi kā′nə rē) *n* clever, dishonest argument. <French *chicaner* to quibble>

Chi·ca·no (chi kȧ′nō) *n* an American born in Mexico or of Mexican descent. The feminine is **Chicana**. <Mexican alteration of Spanish *mejicano* Mexican>

chi–chi (shē′shē) *Informal adj* smart and stylish in a pretentious or affected way: *a chi-chi little restaurant.* <French, imitative>

chick (chik) *n* **1** a young chicken or other bird, especially one newly hatched. **2** *Slang* a girl or young woman. <from *chicken*>

chick·a·dee (chik′ə dē′) *n* a small N American songbird with a plump body, long tail, and a large black or brown patch on the top of the head. The **black-capped chickadee** is the provincial bird of New Brunswick. <imitative of its call>

chick·en (chik′ən) *n* **1** a domestic hen or rooster, especially a young one. **2** *Slang* a coward.
adj Slang cowardly. <Old English *cicen*>
chicken out, *Slang* back out or give up because of fear: *At the last minute she chickened out and refused to go bungee jumping.*
play chicken, *Informal* take part in a game in which each person takes a bold risk on the assumption that the other person will give up or back down first.

chicken feed *n* **1** food for chickens. **2** *Informal* a small or insignificant amount of money: *The pay is chicken feed.*

chick·en–heart·ed (chik′ən hȧr′tid) *adj* fearful or timid.

chick·en–liv·ered (chik′ən liv′ərd) *Informal adj* cowardly.

chicken pox *n* a contagious disease accompanied by a fever and a severe rash that usually occurs in childhood.

chicken wire *n* a light wire netting, used for fencing, pet cages, or to protect young trees.

chick flick *Slang n* a movie that is supposed to appeal especially to women's tastes. <*chick* = young woman + *flick* = movie>

chick lit *Slang n* fiction that is supposed to appeal to women's tastes. <*chick* = young woman + *lit*(*erature*)>

chick pea *n* the roundish, edible yellow seed of an annual plant of the pea family. Also called **garbanzo**.

chick·weed (chik′wēd′) *n* a white-flowered, low-growing plant that is a common garden weed.

chic·le (chik′əl) *n* a tasteless substance prepared from the milky juice of an evergreen tree of tropical America. Chicle is the main ingredient of chewing gum. <American Spanish, from Nahuatl (a language of Central and S America) *tzictli*>

chic·o·ry (chik′ə rē) *n, pl* **chic·o·ries** a blue-flowered plant of the daisy family with edible leaves. Its carrot-shaped root can be roasted and ground and used as a coffee substitute, or to flavour coffee. <Old French, from Greek *kichorion*>

chide (chīd) *v* **chid·ed, chid·ing** reproach, blame, or scold: *She chided her son for getting his sweater dirty.* <Old English *cidan*> **chid′ing·ly** *adv.*

a bat	e bed	i bid	o pot	u cup	th **thin**
ā cake	ē me	ī bite	ō go	ū rude	TH **then**
ȧ bar	ə about	ər over	ȯ for	u̇ put	zh measure

chief (chēf) *n* **1** the person highest in rank or authority in a group. **2 a** the head of a First Nations or Native American band. **b** the head of a tribe or clan.
adj **1** leading: *the chief engineer of a building project.* **2** main or most important: *The chief attraction of the fair was the roller coaster.* <Old French, from Latin *caput* head> **chief′dom** *n.* **chief′ly** *adv.*
in chief, a (*usually in compounds*) at the head or in the highest position: *editor-in-chief.* **b** mainly or primarily.

🍁 **chief electoral officer** *n* an official appointed to oversee federal and provincial or territorial elections.

chief executive officer *n* the leader of policy-making in a company. *Abbrev.* **CEO**

🍁 **chief justice** *n* a senior Supreme Court judge.

chief of staff *n* **1** in the armed forces, an officer at the head of a group of senior officers. **2** the principal adviser to the head of a government.

chief operating officer *n* the leader of day-to-day operations in a company. *Abbrev.* **COO**

chief·tain (chēf′tən) *n* the chief of a tribe or clan. <Old French, from Latin *capitaneus*>

chif·fon (shi fon′) *n* **1** a very thin, soft fabric. **2** in full, **chiffon cake** a cake made with beaten egg whites, giving it a light texture. <French *chiffe* rag>

chif·fo·nier (shif′ə nēr′) *n* a high chest of drawers, often with a mirror. <French>

chig·ger (chig′ər) *n* a tropical flea whose larvae stick to the skin and cause severe itching. <Carib (a group of languages of the Caribbean) *chigo*>

chi·hua·hua (chə wȧ′wȧ) *n* a very small dog of an ancient Mexican breed, with large, protruding eyes and large, erect ears. <*Chihuahua*, state and city in N Mexico>

chil·blain (chil′blān′) *n* usually, **chilblains** *pl* an itchy redness on the hands or feet, caused by prolonged cold. <*chill* + Old English *blain* blister>

Chil·co·tin (chil kō′tin) TSILHQOT'IN.

child (chīld) *n, pl* **chil·dren 1** a boy or girl, especially one up to the early or mid teens. **2** a son or daughter of any age: *All their children are married.* **3** an adult who behaves in a childish way: *My brother is such a child when he is sick.* **4** a person thought of as belonging to a particular period: *a child of the computer age.* <Old English *cild*> **child′hood** *n.* **child′less** *adj.* **child′less·ness** *n.*

child·bear·ing (chīld′ber′ing) *n* the act or process of conceiving and giving birth to children.
adj to do with this: *Her childbearing days are over.*

child·birth (chīld′bərth′) *n* the act or process of giving birth to a child.

child care *n* the care of a child or children, especially by a paid caregiver, usually in the child's home. Compare DAYCARE.

child·ish (chīl′dish) *adj* of or like a child, especially in being silly and immature: *childish speech, a childish person. It was childish of her to make such a fuss.* **child′ish·ly** *adv.* **child′ish·ness** *n.*

child labour or **labor** *n* paid work done by children.

child·like (chīld′līk′) *adj* of or like a child, especially in being innocent and honest: *He was almost childlike in his optimism. She laughed with childlike abandon.*

> **CONFUSABLES**
>
> **Childlike** means "innocent, like a child": *She had a childlike wonder at the beauty of the snowfall.*
>
> **Childish** means "immature, like a child": *The childish soccer player whined about receiving a penalty.*

child·proof (chīld′prūf′) *adj* arranged so as to prevent damage by or to a young child: *Is your home childproof?*
v make safe from or for a child.

chil·dren (chil′drən) plural of CHILD.

child's play *n* something very easy to do: *Writing computer programs was child's play to her.*

🍁 **child tax benefit** *n* in full, **Canada child tax benefit** a tax-free monthly payment from the Federal Government, made to eligible families to help with the cost of raising children under age 18. Formerly called **family allowance**.

Chi·le (chē′lā) *or* (chil′ē) *n* a country in S America. See the APPENDIX. **Chi·le′an** (chi lā′ən) *adj, n.*

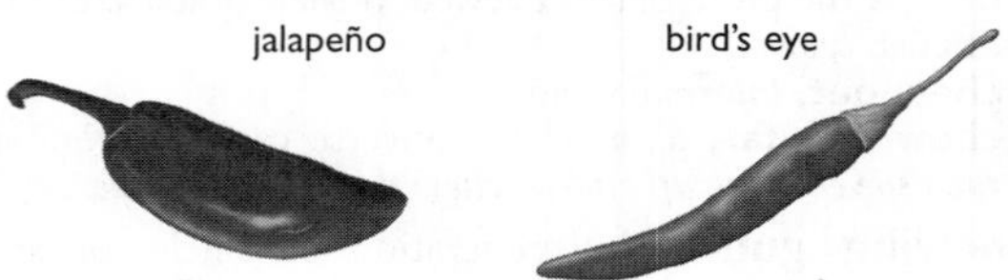

The seeds of the **chili**, also known as capsicum, are the hottest part of the fruit.

chil·i (chil′ē) *n, pl* **chil·ies 1** the small, hot-tasting pod or fruit of certain varieties of the pepper plant, used for seasoning. Also, **chile**. **2** in full, **chili con carne** (chil′ē kən kȧr′nē) a dish consisting of ground or cubed beef cooked with chilies or chili powder and kidney beans. <Nahuatl (a language of Central and S America) *chilli*>

chili dog *n* a hot dog with CHILI (def. 2) on it.

chili powder *n* dried ground chili pods mixed with herbs and spices, used as a seasoning.

chili sauce *n* a tomato-based sauce containing peppers, onions, spices, and various other ingredients.

chill (chil) *n* **1** a moderate but unpleasant coldness: *a chill in the air.* **2** a sudden coldness of the body with shivering: *She was very sick with chills and fever.* **3** unfriendliness: *I felt the chill in his greeting.* **4** a feeling of discouragement or dread: *The announcement of a surprise test cast a chill over the class.* **5 a** a pleasurable, thrilling sensation: *That music sends chills up my spine.* **b** a shiver or other unpleasant sensation, especially one caused by fear: *The thought of climbing the cliff gave me a chill.*
adj **1** unpleasantly cold: *a chill wind.* **2** unfriendly.
v **1** make or become cold: *Chill the juice in the fridge. His manner chilled as soon as he figured out who we were.* **2** have a discouraging or alarming effect on. <Old English *ciele*> **chilled** *adj.* **chill′ing** *adj.* **chill′ing·ly** *adv.*

chill·y (chil′ē) *adj* **chill·i·er, chill·i·est 1** unpleasantly cool: *a chilly day.* **2** unfriendly: *a chilly greeting.* **chill′i·ness** *n.*

CONFUSABLES

Chilly means "uncomfortably cool": *The people in the audience complained about the chilly auditorium.*

Chill, metaphorically, can mean "unpleasantly cold": *There was a chill atmosphere after the argument.*

Chilling means "frightening": *The survivors told a chilling story about the tornado's fury.*

chime (chīm) *n* **1** the musical sound made by a small bell, or any other pleasantly harmonious sound: *the chime of a grandfather clock.* **2 chimes** *pl* a set of small bells tuned to the musical scale, usually played by hammers or simple machinery.
v **chimed, chim·ing 1** ring out musically: *The bells chimed at midnight.* **2** say in a bright or musical voice.
chime in, join in a conversation, especially to agree: *"It's my favourite too!" chimed in the littlest brother.*

ETYMOLOGY

Both **chime** and **cymbal** come from the same Greek word *kymbalon*, from *kymbe*, meaning "hollow." However, **cymbal** came first into Old English, and then **chime** came into Middle English.

chi·me·ra or **chi·mae·ra** (kə mē′rə) *n* **1** *Greek myth* a fire-breathing monster with a lion's head, a goat's body, and a serpent's tail. **2** a strange or horrible creature of the imagination. **3** a wild but unrealistic idea or hope. **4** *Biology* an organism composed of cells from genetically different tissues. <Greek *chimaira* she-goat>
chi·mer′ic (kə mer′ik) *adj.*

chim·ney (chim′nē) *n* **1** an upright structure, part of a building, used to make a draft for a fire and carry away smoke. **2** a glass tube put around the flame of a lamp. **3** a crack or opening in a rock, mountain, or volcano. <Old French, from Greek *kaminos* oven>

chimney pot *n* a metal or earthenware pipe fitted on top of a chimney to increase the draft.

chimney sweep *n* a person who cleans out chimneys.

🍁 **chi·mo** (chē′mō) *or* (chī′mō) *especially North interj* a call or exclamation of greeting. <Inuktitut>

chim·pan·zee (chim′pan zē′) *or* (chim pan′zē) *n* a highly intelligent ape native to Africa that has large ears and is mainly black, with lighter coloration on the face. Also, **chimp**. <Bantu (a group of languages of Africa)>

chin (chin) *n* the outside of the lower jaw, especially the front part below the mouth.
v **chinned, chin·ning** (*used reflexively*) hang by the hands from a bar and pull oneself up until one's hands reach the bar. <Old English *cinn*> **chin·less** *adj.*
keep your chin up, remain cheerful or hopeful during hard times.
take it on the chin, endure hardship or injustice without complaining.

chi·na (chī′nə) *n* **1** a fine, white, translucent ceramic ware made of pure clay fired at high temperatures. **2** dishes, ornaments, and other objects made of china or a similar ceramic material. <Persian *chini*, referring to China, where china was originally made>

Chi·na (chī′na) *n* a large country in eastern Asia, the most populous country in the world. See the APPENDIX; see also CHINESE.

Chi·na·town (chī′nə toun′) *n* a part of a city with many Chinese restaurants and shops.

chinch bug (chinch) *n* a small black and white insect that damages grain plants, including grass, by feeding on their juices. <Spanish, from Latin *cimex* bug>

chin·chil·la (chin chil′ə) *n* **1** a small S American rodent that resembles a squirrel. It is farmed for its soft grey fur. **2** a cat or rabbit of a breed that has silver-grey fur. <Spanish, from Aymara or Quechua (languages of S America)>

Chi·nese (chī nēz′) *adj* to do with China, its people, or their language.
n **1** *pl* **Chinese** a native or inhabitant of China, or a person of Chinese descent. **2** any of the main languages of China.

Chinese cabbage *n* a plant related to cabbage but with looser leaves, eaten as a vegetable.

Chinese calendar *n* the ancient lunar calendar formerly used in China that had cycles of 60 years, with 12 months in a year, 29 or 30 days in a month, and an extra month added every 30 years.

Chinese lantern *n* **1** a lantern of thin, coloured paper that can be folded up accordion-style, often suspended with others in a row from a cord. **2** a perennial plant cultivated for its hollow, papery, red fruit casing.

chink[1] (chingk) *n* a narrow opening, crack, or slit: *The arrow entered through a chink in his armour.*
v fill up the chinks in: *The cracks in the walls of the log cabin were chinked with mud.* <Old English *cine*>

chink[2] (chingk) *n* a short, sharp, ringing sound like coins or glasses hitting together.
v make or cause to make such a sound. <imitative>

chi·no (chē′nō) *or* (shē′nō) *n* **1** a cotton or cotton-blend fabric with a smooth, almost shiny surface. **2 chinos** *pl* pants made of this material. <American Spanish = toasted, referring to its colour>

🍁 **chi·nook** (shi nu̇k′) *n* **1** a warm wind that blows from the southwest across British Columbia and Alberta and into Saskatchewan, often bringing high temperatures in winter. **2** in full, **chinook salmon** a large salmon of the Pacific, introduced into the Great Lakes and elsewhere. Also called **king salmon**, **spring salmon**. <*Chinook*>

Chi·nook (chi nu̇k′) *or* (shi nu̇k′) *n, pl* **Chi·nook** or **Chi·nooks 1** a member of a Native American people who lived along the Columbia River in the northwestern US. **2** the language of this people. **3** Chinook Jargon.
adj to do with the Chinook or their language.

a bat	e bed	i bid	o pot	u cup	th thin
ā cake	ē me	ī bite	ō go	ū rude	TH then
à bar	ə about	ər over	ȯ for	u̇ put	zh measure

chinook arch *n* an archlike cloud formation over blue sky above the western horizon, often seen just before or during a chinook.

Chinook Jargon *n* in former times, a language of the Pacific coast of North America based on Chinook, used in trading between First Nations or Native American peoples and Europeans.

chintz (chints) *n* a firm, colourfully printed cotton fabric used mostly for draperies and slipcovers. <Hindi *chimt* spattering, stain>

chint·zy (chint′sē) *adj* **chint·zi·er, chint·zi·est 1** like or decorated with chintz. **2** *Informal* cheap and gaudy.

chin–up (chin′ up) *n* the exercise of hanging by the hands from a bar and pulling oneself up until one's chin is level with the bar.

chin·wag (chin′wag) *Informal n* a conversation or chat.
v **chin·wagged, chin·wag·ging** chat or gossip.

chip (chip) *n* **1** a small, thin piece cut from wood or broken from stone or china: *I like the smell of wood chips.* **2** the flaw left by such a missing piece: *One of the cups has a chip in it.* **3** a small or thin piece of food: *chocolate chips, dried banana chips, potato chips.* **4** a French fry: *fish and chips.* **5** *Electronics* a small wafer of semiconductor material such as silicon, with many tiny electric circuits in it: *a memory chip in a computer.* **6** *Golf* in full, **chip shot** a short or medium-range shot played to the green, usually hit with a spin. **7** a counting disc used in games such as poker. **8** a piece of dried dung, used for fuel in some regions: *buffalo chips.*
v **chipped, chip·ping 1** cut, break, or lose a small piece from: *You chipped the edge of the table when you took it through the doorway. These plates chip easily.* **2** remove in small pieces: *We chipped off the old paint before repainting.* **3** shape by cutting at the surface or edge with an axe or chisel. **4** *Golf* give the ball a short lobbing shot: *She chipped from the sand trap onto the green.* <Old English *(for)cippian*>
cash in your chips, a in the game of poker, exchange chips for cash. **b** *Slang* close or sell a business. **c** *Slang* die.
chip in, *Informal* **a** join with others in giving money or help: *We all chipped in to buy your present.* **b** put in a remark when others are talking.
chip off the old block, *Informal* a person who is very much like his or her parent.
chip on your shoulder, *Informal* **a** a permanent sense of having been ill-treated. **b** a readiness to quarrel or fight.
when the chips are down, *Informal* when the crisis comes.

chip·board (chip′bȯrd′) PARTICLEBOARD.

Chip·e·wy·an (chip′ə wī′ən) *n, pl* **Chip·e·wy·an** or **Chip·e·wy·ans 1** a member of a First Nations people, one of the DENE, living in northern Manitoba and Saskatchewan, and the Northwest Territories. **2** their Athapascan language.
adj to do with these people or their language.

chip·munk (chip′mungk) *n* a small N American rodent of the squirrel family that lives mainly on the ground, mostly brown with black and beige stripes along the back. <perhaps Ojibway *atchitamon* headfirst (from its way of climbing down a tree)>

chip·per (chip′ər) *Informal adj* lively and cheerful: *You're very chipper this morning!* <origin uncertain>

Chip·pe·wa (chip′ə wȯ′) ANISHINABE.

chip·py (chip′ē) *adj* **2** with much aggressive play: *a chippy lacrosse game. She became a chippy hockey player.* <probably from the idiom *a chip on your shoulder*>

chip shot *Golf n* a short, somewhat high shot used to get the ball onto the green.

chip wagon *n* a vehicle or movable stand for selling French fries, hamburgers, etc. <UK *chips* = French fries>

chi·rop·o·dy (kə rop′ə dē) *n* the branch of medicine that treats foot ailments such as corns and bunions. Also called **podiatry**. <Greek *cheir* hand + *podis* foot>
chi·rop′o·dist *n.*

chi·ro·prac·tic (kī′rə prak′tik) *n* the treatment of disorders of the bones, muscles, and nerves by manipulation of the bony segments of the body, especially the spine.
adj to do with such treatment. <Greek *cheir* hand + *prakitkos* of practice> **chi′ro·prac′tor** *n.*

chirp (chərp) *n* a short, sharp sound such as certain birds and insects make.
v **1** make such a sound: *The crickets were chirping loudly.* **2** say quickly in a high voice. <imitative>

chir·rup (chir′əp) *or* (chər′əp) *v* **chir·rupped** or **chir·ruped, chir·rup·ping** or **chir·rup·ing 1** chirp again and again: *He chirrupped to his horse to make it go faster.* **2** utter with chirps or sounds like this.
n the sound of chirrupping. <imitative>

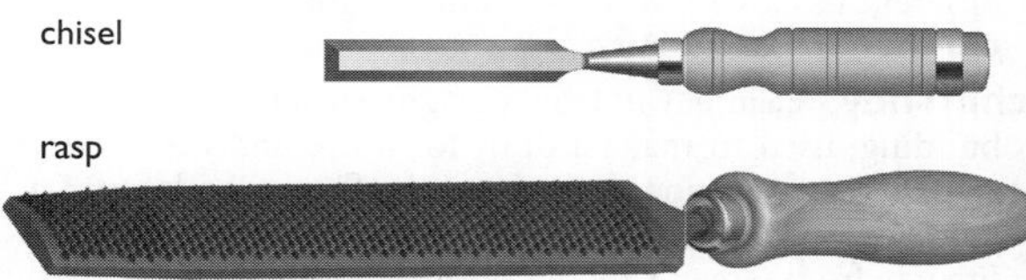

A **chisel** can be worked by hand or tapped with a mallet, depending on the material being shaped.

A *rasp* looks a bit like a chisel, but removes wood through abrasion, not by cutting and gouging.

chis·el (chiz′əl) *n* a cutting tool with a long, thick blade that ends in a sharp, bevelled edge, used to cut or shape wood, stone, or metal.
v **chis·elled** or **chis·eled, chis·el·ling** or **chis·el·ing 1** cut or shape with or as if with a chisel. **2** be dishonest in business. <Old French, from Latin *caedere* to cut> **chis′el·ler** or **chis′el·er** *n.*

chis·elled (chiz′əld) *adj* **1** cut or shaped with a chisel. **2** with clear, sharp outlines as if cut with a chisel: *chiselled features.*

chit[1] (chit) *n* **1** an immature or disrespectful girl. **2** a child. <Middle English = kitten>

chit[2] (chit) *n* a voucher, receipt, or stub related to a purchase. <Hindi *citthi* note>

C

chit·chat (chit′chat′) *n, v* **chit·chat·ted, chit·chat·ting** talk about trivial things.

ETYMOLOGY

Chitchat is an example of the process known as *reduplication*, where a word is formed by repeating a root, often with a change of vowel. The effect is usually to intensify the word. In this case, the new word implies repeated or lengthy chatting.

Other examples of this process are *crisscross* and *zigzag*.

chi·tin (kī′tin) *n* a semi-transparent, hornlike substance forming the hard outer covering of beetles, lobsters, and crabs, and the cell walls of fungi. <French, from Greek *chiton* tunic> **chi′tin·ous** *adj.*

chit·ter (chit′ər) *v, n* twitter or chatter as birds, squirrels, and monkeys do. <imitative>

chit·ter·lings (chit′ər lingz) *pln* parts of the small intestines of pigs, cooked as food. <Middle English>

chiv·al·ry (shiv′əl rē) *n* **1** qualities like those of an ideal medieval knight, including bravery, honour, and courtesy. **2** the medieval system of knighthood. <Old French, from Latin *caballus* horse. A knight had to have a horse.>
chiv′al·ric (shiv′əl rik) *or* (shə val′rik) *adj.*
chiv′al·rous *adj.*

chive (chīv) *n* usually, **chives** *pl* a plant of the onion family, with long, slender, hollow leaves that are used as flavouring. See ONION for picture. <Old French, from Latin *cepa* onion>

chiv·vy or **chiv·y** (chiv′ē) *v* **chiv·vied** or **chiv·ied, chiv·vy·ing** or **chiv·y·ing** nag or harass repeatedly: *They chivvied her into removing her nose ring.* <origin uncertain>

chla·myd·ia (klə mid′ē ə) *n* **1** a bacterium that causes various infections of the eyes, lungs, and genitals. **2** a sexually transmitted disease caused by one of these bacteria. <Greek *chlamus* cloak, from its effect on the eyesight>

chlo·ride (klô′rīd) *n* a chemical compound, classified as a salt, containing chlorine and a metal.

chlo·rin·ate (klô′rə nāt′) *v* **chlo·rin·at·ed, chlo·rin·at·ing** treat with chlorine to bleach or disinfect: *Paper pulp is chlorinated to bleach it. The water in the city reservoirs is chlorinated.* **chlo′ri·na′tion** *n.*

chlo·rine (klô rēn′) *or* (klô′rēn) *n* a poisonous, greenish yellow element, typically a gas. It has a sharp, unpleasant smell, and is irritating to the nose, throat, and lungs. *Symbol* **Cl** <Greek *chloros* green> **chlo′ric** (klô′rək) *adj.*

chlo·ro·fluo·ro·car·bon (klô′rō flô′rō kar′bən) CFC.

chlo·ro·form (klô′rə fôrm′) *n* a colourless liquid with a sweetish smell, used as a solvent and formerly as an anesthetic.
v **1** anesthetize or make unconscious by giving chloroform. **2** kill with chloroform. <*chlor*(ine) + *form*(*yl*). Formyl is a group of atoms containing hydrogen, oxygen, and carbon.>

chlo·ro·phyl or **chlo·ro·phyll** (klô′rə fil′) *n* the green colouring matter of plants that uses light to convert carbon dioxide and water into carbohydrates such as starch. <French, from Greek *chloros* green + *phyllon* leaf>

chlo·ro·plast (klô′rə plast′) *n* the part of a plant cell that contains chlorophyl. Also, **chloroplastid.** <Greek *chloros* green + *plastos* formed>

chock (chok) *n* **1** a block or wedge used to secure or support something, or to keep something from rolling away. **2** on a ship or boat, a heavy piece of metal or wood with two arms curving inward for a rope to pass through. <Old French *couche* log>

chock·a·block (chok′ə blok′) *adv, adj* crowded or packed close together: *The cars were parked chockablock in the lot* (*adv*). *The lot is chockablock with cars* (*adj*). <nautical sense: *with blocks drawn close together*>

chock–full (chok′fůl′) *adj* as full as can be.

choc·o·hol·ic (chok ə hol′ik) *n* a person who is very fond of eating chocolate Also, **chocaholic.** <Old French *couche* log>

choc·o·late (chok′lit) *n* finely ground and roasted cacao seeds mixed with other ingredients as a base or flavouring for candies, drinks, spreads, and syrups, and as unsweetened baking chocolate.
adj **1** made of or flavoured with chocolate: *chocolate cake.* **2** dark brown. <Nahuatl (a language of Central and S America) *chocolatl*> **choc′o·lat·ey** or **choc′o·lat·y** *adj.*

chocolate bar *n* a bar of candy made of solid sweetened chocolate, or a mixture of ingredients coated with chocolate.

choice (chois) *n* **1** the act or fact of choosing. **2** the right or opportunity to choose: *She had a choice between swimming and piano lessons. He had no choice but to accept their statement.* **3** the person or thing chosen: *My choice was cabbage rolls.* **4** a quantity and variety to choose from: *There's a wide choice of vegetables in this market.*
adj **choic·er, choic·est** excellent: *the choicest wines. She soon convinced them with a few choice arguments.* <Old French *choisir* choose> **choice′ness** *n.*
of choice, preferred or favourite: *Ice cream seemed to be the dessert of choice at our table.*

CONFUSABLES

Choice is a noun: *It was a difficult choice between vanilla and chocolate ice cream.*

Choose is a present-tense verb: *Think about it before you choose which ice cream you want.*

Chose is a past-tense verb: *She chose the chocolate ice cream over the vanilla.*

choir (kwīr) *n* **1** a large, organized group of singers. **2** the part of a church set apart for such a group. <Old French, from Latin *chorus*>

a bat	e bed	i bid	o pot	u cup	th **thin**
ā cake	ē me	ī bite	ō go	ū rude	TH **then**
ä bar	ə about	ər over	ô for	ů put	zh measure

choir loft *n* a balcony for a choir in a church.

choke (chōk) *v* **choked, chok·ing 1** keep from breathing by squeezing or blocking the windpipe: *The tight collar almost choked her.* **2** (*often with* ***on***) be kept from breathing: *He choked on a fishbone.* **3** cut off or lessen the air supply to a fire or engine. **4** block or clog: *Sand is choking the river.*
n **1** the act or sound of choking. *She gave a slight choke, but then got her breath.* **2** a valve, as on an internal combustion engine, that cuts off or lessens the air supply. <Old English *aceocian*>
choke back, hold back with difficulty: *She choked back her angry words.*
choke down, swallow with difficulty: *He choked down the dry bread and said nothing.*
choke off, stop by blocking or clogging: *The rock slide choked off our water supply.*
choke up, be or cause to be on the verge of tears: *People in the audience were choked up when the heroine died.*

choke chain *n* a collar for training a dog to heel that tightens around its neck whenever the dog pulls on the attached chain. Also called **choke collar**.

choke·cher·ry (chōk′cher′ē) *n, pl* **choke·cher·ries** a small, edible but bitter wild cherry that grows in clusters on a N American shrub.

choke·damp (chōk′damp′) *n* a heavy, suffocating gas, mainly carbon dioxide and nitrogen, that gathers in mines or old wells.

chok·er (chō′kər) *n* a necklace or ornamental band that fits closely around the neck.

chol·er·a (kol′ə rə) *n* an acute, infectious, potentially fatal disease of the stomach and intestines, characterized by vomiting and diarrhea. It usually results from drinking infected water supplies. <Latin, from Greek *chole* bile>

chol·er·ic (kol′ə rik) *adj* **1** easily angered. **2** showing or arising from anger: *a choleric outburst.*

ETYMOLOGY

Choleric can be traced back to the Greek word *chole*, meaning "bile." In ancient physiology, four bodily fluids were thought to determine a person's general nature, according to which fluid was the one most present in the person's system. Bile was thought responsible for a tendency toward anger.

cho·les·ter·ol (kə les′tə rol′) *or* (kə les′trəl) *n* a crystalline fatty alcohol produced by vertebrates, concentrated in the brain and nervous system and used to make digestive acids and hormones. <Greek *chole* bile + *stereos* stiff>

chomp (chomp) *v* chew noisily: *Don't chomp your food.* <variation of *champ*[1]>

choose (chūz) *v* **chose, chos·en, choos·ing 1** select from a group: *She chose a book from the library.* **2** prefer and decide on: *She chose not to go.* **3** make a choice: *the right to choose.* See CHOICE for confusable. <Old English *ceosan*>
choos′er *n.*
cannot choose but, have to: *Since the last bus has gone, I cannot choose but walk.*

choos·y (chū′zē) *Informal adj* **choos·i·er, choos·i·est** picky or fussy.

SYNONYMS

Choosy is an informal word meaning "demanding": *The choosy customer rejected all the outfits.*

Fastidious means "meticulous": *The fastidious child was upset when his boots got muddy.*

Particular means "discriminating": *The swimmers are particular about the kind of goggles they use.*

chop[1] (chop) *v* **chopped, chop·ping** cut by hitting with something sharp: *to chop wood with an axe, to chop cabbage with a knife.*
n **1** a vigorous cutting stroke: *He split the wood in one chop.* **2** a slice of meat from the rib, loin, or shoulder. **3** a short, sharp stroke in martial arts. **4** a broken motion of water, typically because of the action of wind against the tide. <Middle English *choppen*>
chop back, severely reduce.
chop down, make fall by cutting: *to chop down a tree.*
chop up, cut into small pieces: *to chop up vegetables.*

chop[2] (chop) *v* **chopped, chop·ping** shift quickly, especially as a direction of the wind: *The wind chopped around from west to north.* <obsolete *chap* buy and sell. *Chop* originally meant *barter.*>
chop and change, make frequent changes.

chop·per (chop′ər) *n* **1** a person who or thing that chops. **2** *Informal* helicopter.

chopping block *n* a hard wooden surface on which food or firewood is chopped up.
on the chopping block, being cut from a budget, schedule, contract, or other plan: *The band program is on the chopping block due to government cutbacks.*

chop·py (chop′ē) *adj* **chop·pi·er, chop·pi·est** of water, moving in short, irregular, broken waves: *The lake is choppy today.* <*chop*[1]>

chops (chops) *pl n* the cheeks or jaws, especially the fleshy covering of an animal's jaws: *The cat is licking the milk off its chops.* <special use of *chop*[1]>

chop·stick (chop′stik′) *n* either of a pair of small, shaped sticks used to raise food to the mouth. <Chinese pidgin English *chop* quick + *stick*>

chop su·ey (sū′ē) *n* a Chinese-style dish consisting of small pieces of meat cooked with vegetables. <Cantonese *tsap sui* odds and ends>

cho·ral (kȯ′rəl) *adj* to do with a choir or chorus: *a choral arrangement of a piece of music, a choral reading.*

cho·rale (kə ral′) *n* **1** a slow, stately hymn tune, especially a simple one sung in unison. **2** a choir or choral society. <German *Choral(gesang)*>

chord[1] (kȯrd) *Music n* a combination of two or more notes sounded together.
v **1** play a keyboard or guitar using chords only, without a melody line. **2** provide harmony for a melody by adding chords. <Middle English *cord*, shortened from *accord*>

chord[2] (kȯrd) *n* **1** *Mathematics* a straight line or segment between two points on a curve. **2** something in a person that produces an emotional response: *to touch a sympathetic chord.* <Latin, from Greek *chorde* string>

chor·date (kȯr′dāt) *n* a member of a PHYLUM of animals that includes vertebrates. <*chord*[2]>

chore (chȯr) *n* **1** a minor task, especially one that must be done daily: *Our chores on the farm are milking the cows and feeding the chickens.* **2** an unpleasant task: *She finds cooking quite a chore.* <Old English *cierr* a turn (of work)>

cho·re·a (kȯ rē′ə) *n* a nervous disease characterized by involuntary twitching of the muscles. Also called **St. Vitus's dance**. <Greek *choreia* dance>

cho·re·o·graph (kȯ′rē ə graf′) *v* **1** arrange the movements for a dance or any complex footwork. **2** arrange the details of anything complicated: *She choreographed the whole conference.* <Greek *choreia* dance + *-graphy*>
cho′re·og′ra·pher *n.* **cho′re·og′r·a·phy** *n.*

cho·ri·on (kȯ′rē on′) *n* **1** the outermost membrane of the sac that holds the embryo or fetus in higher vertebrates and eventually forms the placenta. **2** the shell or membrane enclosing the egg of an insect or other invertebrate. <Greek *chorion*> **cho′ri·on′ic** *adj.*

chor·is·ter (kȯ′rə stər) *n* a singer in a choir, especially a child. <Old French, from Latin *chorus*>

chor·tle (chȯr′təl) *v* **chor·tled, chor·tling** chuckle and snort at the same time.
n a combined chuckle and snort.

ETYMOLOGY

Chortle, invented by author Lewis Carroll, first appeared in his book *Through the Looking Glass.* It is a blend of two words, ***chuckle*** and *snort*. Carroll also created the word *galumphing* from ***galloping*** and *triumph*.

More common word blends are *smog* from ***smoke*** and ***fog***, *brunch* from ***breakfast*** and ***lunch***, and *motel* from ***motor*** and ***hotel***.

cho·rus (kȯ′rəs) *n, pl* **cho·rus·es** **1** the part of a song that is repeated after each verse. **2** a piece of music to be sung by a choir in full harmony: *The opera ends in a splendid chorus.* **3** something spoken by many at the same time: *My suggestion was met by a chorus of boos.* **4** a group of singers and dancers forming part of a musical. **5** in classical drama, **a** an actor or group of actors who comment on the action of a play. **b** the part of a play performed by the chorus.
v **cho·rused, chor·us·ing** sing or speak all at the same time. <Latin, from Greek *choros* dance, band of dancers>
in chorus, all together at the same time.

chorus line *n* a line of dancers and singers performing in a musical.

chose (chōz) past tense of CHOOSE.

cho·sen (chō′zən) *v* past participle of CHOOSE.
adj specially selected: *a privilege of the chosen few.*

chow (chou) *n* **1** *Informal* food, or the time when it is served. **2** a medium-sized breed of dog with a large head and thick coat. <Chinese pidgin English>
chow down, *Slang* start eating with a hearty appetite.

chow·der (chou′dər) *n* a thick soup or stew, often made of seafood with potatoes and onions, in a milk base. <French *chaudière*, from Latin *calidus* hot>

chow mein (chou′ mān′) *n* a Chinese-style dish of onions, celery, and meat, served over fried noodles. <Cantonese *chao mian* fried noodles>

Christ (krīst) *n* Jesus of Nazareth, regarded as divine Redeemer and the fulfilment of ancient Jewish prophecy about the Messiah. <Old English *Crist*, from Greek *khristos* the anointed one> **Christ′like′** *adj.*

chris·ten (kris′ən) *v* **1 a** baptize a child as a Christian. **b** give **Christian names** (that is, first names) at baptism: *The child was christened Lee Adrien.* **2** give a name to: *The new ship was christened before it was launched.* <Old English, from Latin *Christus* Christ> **chris′ten·ing** *n.*

Chris·ten·dom (kris′ən dəm) *n* all Christians.

Chris·tian (kris′chən) *n* a believer in **Christianity** (kris′chē an′ə tē), the religion based on the person and example of Jesus of Nazareth, or the beliefs and practices of this religion.
adj based on or following the teachings of Christ: *the Christian church, a Christian family.* **Chris′tian·like′** *adj.* **Chris′tian·ly** *adj, adv.*

Christian Era *n* the period of history since the birth of Jesus Christ; another name for Common Era. *Abbrev.* **CE** Compare BCE.

🍁 **Christian Heritage Party** one of the registered political parties of Canada.

Christian Science *n* a religious sect teaching that physical healing is possible through spiritual healing, founded by Mary Baker Eddy in the US in 1879.
Christian Scientist *n.*

Christ·mas (kris′məs) *n* **1** *Christianity* the yearly celebration of the birth of Jesus of Nazareth, in western Christianity reaching its peak on **Christmas Eve**, December 24 and **Christmas Day**, December 25. **2** the season around this celebration, generally ending at New Year. Traditionally, homes are decorated with a real or artificial evergreen **Christmas tree**, and **Christmas stockings** are hung up and filled with small gifts, candy, etc. for the children or other family members: *Christmas seems to start earlier and earlier.* Also called **Christmastime**. <Old English *Cristes mæsse* Christ's mass> **Christ′mas·sy** *adj.*

chro·mat·ic (krō mat′ik) *adj* **1** to do with colour. **2** *Music* to do with the **chromatic scale** that divides the octave into twelve halftones.
n **chromatics** (*with singular verb*) the scientific study of colour. <Greek *chroma* colour> **chro·mat′i·cal·ly** *adv.*

chro·ma·tid (krō′mə tid) *Biology n* either of the two portions of a chromosome that has doubled in preparation for cell division, joined at the middle by a CENTROMERE. <See CHROMATIN.>

a bat	e bed	i bid	o pot	u cup	th thin
ā cake	ē me	ī bite	ō go	ū rude	ᴛʜ then
ȧ bar	ə about	ər over	ȯ for	u̇ put	zh measure

chro·ma·tin (krō′mə tin) *Biology n* the substance in the nucleus of a cell other than bacteria, consisting of DNA, RNA, and proteins. <Greek *chromatos* colour. Chromatin is easily stained (that is, coloured) by basic dyes.>

chro·ma·tog·raph·y (krō′mə tog′rə fē) *Chemistry n* a process of separating a mixture or solution into its components by passing it through an adsorbent material. <German, from Greek *chromatos* colour + *-graphy*>

chrome (krōm) *n* **1** chromium. **2** a hard, strong steel containing chromium.

chro·mi·um (krō′mē əm) *n* a shiny, hard, white metallic element that resists rust and does not dull easily.
Symbol **Cr** <French, from Greek *chroma* colour. Chromium compounds make excellent paint pigments and dyes.>

chro·mo·some (krō′mə sōm′) *Biology n* a long, thin strand in the nucleus of every living cell, made up of protein and DNA, carrying genes. and forming pairs in cell division. <See CHROMATIN.>

chro·mo·sphere (krō′mə sfēr′) *n* a red-coloured layer of gas around the sun, mainly consisting of hydrogen, which forms the lower part of the sun's atmosphere. <Greek *chroma* colour + *sphere*>

chron·ic (kron′ik) *adj* **1** lasting a long time as a disease, or recurring often: *chronic bronchitis. Rheumatoid arthritis is a chronic disease.* **2** constant or habitual: *a chronic liar.* **chron′i·cal·ly** *adv.*

ETYMOLOGY

Words beginning with **chron–** come from the Greek root *chronos*, meaning "time." They all have to do with recording or measuring time, tracking events in time, or duration in time. For example, a ***chronology*** is a table or list of the dates or times of events, in the order in which they happened.

chronic fatigue syndrome *n* a medical disorder, sometimes following a viral infection, in which the affected person feels abnormally tired all the time.
Abbrev. **CFS**

chron·i·cle (kron′ə kəl) *n* a record of happenings in the order in which they occurred.
v **chron·i·cled, chron·i·cling** write or tell the story of. <Old French, from Greek *chronos* time> **chron′i·cler** *n.*

chron·o·log·i·cal (kron′ə loj′ə kəl) *adj* arranged in the order in which the events happened: *It would be easier to understand your story if you told it in chronological order.* **chron′o·log′i·cal·ly** *adv.*

chro·nol·ogy (krə nol′ə jē) *n, pl* **chro·nol·o·gies** **1** a table or list giving the dates or times of events in the order in which they happened. **2** the study of historical records to establish the dates at which events occurred.

chro·nom·e·ter (krə nom′ə tər) *n* a very accurate clock or watch. <Greek *chronos* time + *-meter*>

chrys·a·lid (kris′ə lid) *n* a CHRYSALIS (def. 1).
adj to do with a chrysalis.

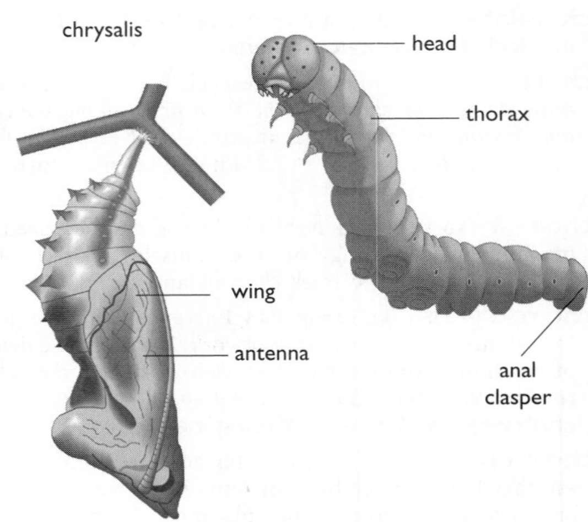

The life cycle of a butterfly or moth has four stages: egg, larva or caterpillar, pupa or **chrysalis**, and adult.

During pupation, the caterpillar is totally transformed within the chrysalis. Its internal system is reorganized and the external structures of the adult develop.

chrys·a·lis (kris′ə lis) *n, pl* **chrys·a·lis·es** or **chry·sal·i·des** (krə sal′ə dēz′) **1** a butterfly or moth in the resting stage, during which it develops into a winged adult. **2** the hard outer covering of the butterfly or moth during this stage, which splits to release the adult. **3** a stage of development or change, or a person or thing in such a stage. <Latin, from Greek *chrysalis* golden sheath>

chry·san·the·mum (krə san′thə məm) *n* a plant with large flowers, most commonly in shades of brownish yellow, that bloom in late summer or fall. <Latin, from Greek *chrysos* gold + *anthemon* flower>

chub (chub) *n, pl* **chubs** or (*especially collectively*) **chub** a freshwater game fish of the minnow family, including the **lake chub**, found throughout Canada and parts of the northern US. <Middle English *chubbe*>

chub·by (chub′ē) *adj* **chub·bi·er, chub·bi·est** round and plump. <perhaps from *chub*, with reference to its plump shape> **chub′bi·ness** *n.*

chuck[1] (chuk) *v* **1** throw; toss. **2** *Informal* abandon: *He's chucked his job.* **3** pat or tap, especially under the chin.
n **1** a light tap under the chin. **2** a careless throw or toss. <probably imitative>

chuck[2] (chuk) *n* **1** a device for holding a tool or piece of work in a machine. **2** a cut of beef between the neck and shoulder. <variant of *chock*>

chuck[3] (chuk) *West Coast n* a large body of water, such as a river; now usually the ocean. <Chinook Jargon, from *ch'a'ak* fresh water>

chuck·le (chuk′əl) *v* **chuck·led, chuck·ling** laugh softly with mild amusement: *I chuckled at the puppy's antics.*
n a quiet laugh. <Middle English *chuck* to cluck>

chuck·wag·on (chuck′wag′ən) *Western Canada and US n* a wagon that carries food and cooking equipment for cowboys, or farm or ranch hands. <from *chuck*[2]>

🍁 **chuckwagon race** *Western Provinces n* a race between chuckwagons drawn by horses, an event at rodeos and stampedes. Also, **chuck race**.

chug (chug) *n* a short, loud, explosive sound: *the chug of an engine.*
v **chugged, chug·ging 1** make such sounds. **2** go or move with such sounds: *The steam engine chugged up the hill.* **3** *Informal* make slow but steady progress: *"How's that report going?" "Oh, it's chugging along."* <imitative>

chum[1] (chum) *Informal n* a close friend or buddy.
v **chummed, chum·ming** be close friends: *They've chummed for years.* <perhaps *chamber* a room + *mate*>

chum[2] (chum) *n* fish cut up and scattered on the water as bait for other fish. <origin unknown>

🍁 **chum**[3] (chum) *n* in full, **chum salmon** a Pacific salmon found especially along the coasts of British Columbia and Alaska, metallic blue and silver in colour and with pale pink flesh. Also called **keta**, **calico salmon**. <Chinook Jargon *tsum* spotted>

chum·my (chum′ē) *Informal adj* **chum·mi·er, chum·mi·est** very friendly or familiar in manner. **chum′mi·ly** *adv.* **chum′mi·ness** *n.*

chump (chump) *Informal n* **1** a stupid or boorish person. **2** a person who is easily taken advantage of. <origin uncertain>

chunk (chungk) *n* a thick, solid piece or lump: *a chunk of earth.* <variant of *chuck*[2]>

chunk·y (chung′kē) *adj* **chunk·i·er, chunk·i·est 1** *Informal* short and sturdy. **2** containing chunks. **chunk′i·ness** *n.*

church (chərch) *n* **1** a building for Christian worship or services. **2** a public worship service in a church: *They go to church every week.* **3** a group of Christians who regularly worship together: *She is a member of our church.* **4 the church a** the organized leadership of a church. **b** all Christians. **5 Church** a specific Christian denomination: *the Anglican Church.* <Old English *cirice*, from Greek *kyriakon doma* the lord's house> **churched** *adj.* **church′y** *adj.*

church·go·er (chərch′gō′ər) *n* a person who attends church regularly. **church′go′ing** *adj.*

church·yard (chərch′yȧrd′) *n* the ground belonging to a church, especially a part used as a burial ground.

churl (chərl) *n* a rude, surly person. <Old English *ceorl* a man of low rank> **churl′ish** *adj.*

churn (chərn) *n* **1** a container or machine in which butter is made from cream or milk by beating and shaking. **2** a violent stirring.
v **1 a** stir or shake cream or milk in a churn. **b** make butter in this way. **2** stir or move violently: *The motorboat's propeller churned the water. The excited fans churned around the stage.* <Old English *cyrn*>
churn out, produce quickly and in large quantities.

chute[1] (shūt) *n* **1** a sloping shaft, trough, or tube, down which things are dropped to a lower level: *a garbage chute in an apartment building. They have a laundry chute in their house.* **2** a narrow waterfall or rapids in a river. <Old French *cheoite* to fall, influenced by English *shoot*>

chute[2] (shūt) *Informal n, v* **chut·ed, chut·ing** parachute.

chut·ney (chut′nē) *n* a relish made of fruits and spices: *tomato chutney.* <Hindi *chatni*>

C

chutz·pah (hu̇t′spə) *or* (hu̇t′spə) *n* bold self-confidence. <Yiddish>

chyle (kīl) *n* the milky fluid formed in the small intestine, consisting of lymph and fats. <Latin, from Greek *chulos* juice squeezed from a plant>

chyme (kīm) *n* the thick, semiliquid mass of partly digested food produced by the first stage of digestion in the stomach. <Latin, from Greek *chumos* juice>

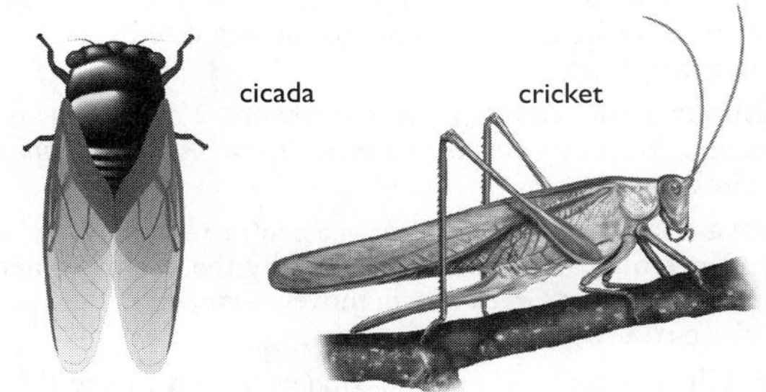

A **cicada** makes its characteristic buzzing song by vibrating two drumlike membranes on its abdomen. The *cricket* makes its chirping song by rubbing its wings together.

ci·ca·da (sə kā′də) *n* an insect noted for the loud buzzing sound the male makes. <Latin>

cic·a·trix (sik′ə triks′) *n, pl* **cic·a·tri·ces** (sik′ə trī′sēz) **1** the scar left by a healed wound. **2** the scar left on part of a plant where another part, such as a leaf or pod, used to be attached. <Latin>

–cide *combining form* **1** the act of killing a certain kind of person or thing: *homicide.* **2** a person who or thing that does this: *insecticide.* <Latin *caedere* kill>

ci·der (sī′dər) *n* a drink made from the juice pressed out of apples. **Hard cider** is fermented; **sweet cider** is not. <Old French, from Hebrew *sekar* liquor>

ci·gar (sə gȧr′) *n* a tight, thick roll of dried tobacco leaves for smoking. <Spanish *cigarro*>

cig·a·rette (sig′ə ret′) *or* (sig′ə ret′) *n* a slender roll of finely cut tobacco enclosed in a thin sheet of paper for smoking. <French, diminutive of *cigare* cigar>

ci·lan·tro (sə lan′trō) *n* coriander used as a seasoning or garnish, especially the feathery greens of the plant. <Spanish, from Latin *coliandrum* coriander>

cil·i·a (sil′ē ə) *Biology pl n, sing* **cil·i·um** (sil′ē əm) tiny hairlike growths on the surface of some cells. <Latin=eyelashes>

a bat	e bed	i bid	o pot	u cup	th **thin**
ā cake	ē me	ī bite	ō go	ū rude	TH **then**
ȧ bar	ə about	ər over	ȯ for	u̇ put	zh measure

cinch (sinch) *n* **1** a strong belt, usually of leather, for fastening a saddle or pack on a horse. **2** *Informal* something sure and easy: *Making brownies is a cinch.*
v bind firmly. <Spanish, from Latin *cincta* belt>

cin·cho·na (sing kō′nə) *n* a S American evergreen tree or shrub. Some species are cultivated for their bark which yields quinine and similar drugs. <Countess of *Chinchón*, who introduced it to Spain in the 1600s>

cin·der (sin′dər) *n* a piece of wood or coal that is partly burned but no longer flaming. <Old English *sinder*>

cinder block *n* a lightweight building block made of cement mixed with cinders, or a group of these blocks: *walls made of cinder block.*

Cin·der·el·la (sin′də rel′ə) *n* a person who suddenly gains fame after being poor, ignored, or neglected. <character in a fairy tale>

cin·e·ma (sin′ə mə) *n* **1** a movie theatre. **2** movies as an art form: *to study cinema at university.* <*cinema(tography)*>
cin′e·mat′ic *adj.*

cin·e·ma·tog·ra·phy (sin′ə mə tog′ra fē) *n* the art and science of making movies, especially the use of cameras. <French, from Greek *kinein* move + *-graphy*>
cin′e·ma·tog′ra·pher *n.*

🍁 **Cin·e·plex** (sin′ə pleks′) *Trademark n* a movie theatre holding several separate cinemas. <*cine(ma) (com)plex*, coined by entrepreneur Nat Taylor and his son Philip, 1979>

cin·e·rar·i·um (sin′ə rer′ē əm) *n, pl* **cin·e·rar·i·a** a place for keeping the ashes of cremated bodies. <Latin *cinerarius* of ashes>

cin·e·rar·y (sin′ə rer′ē) *adj* used to hold the ashes of a cremated body: *a cinerary urn.*

cin·na·bar (sin′ə bär′) *n* a bright red mineral that is the chief source of mercury and is sometimes used as a pigment. <Latin, from Greek *kinnabari*>

cin·na·mon (sin′ə mən) *n* a fragrant reddish brown spice, ground from the dried inner bark of a S Asian tree. <Old French, from Greek *kinnamon*>

cin·quain (sing′kān) *Poetry n* a five-line poem, usually unrhymed. The lines have 2, 4, 6, 8, 2 syllables or 1, 2, 3, 4, 1 words, respectively. <French *cinq* five>

cinque·foil (singk′foil′) *n* **1** a plant of the rose family that has flowers with five roundish petals. **2** *Architecture* an ornament made of five connected arcs or semicircles. <Old French, from Latin *quinque* five + *folium* leaf>

ci·pher (sī′fər) *n* **1** a secret code, or a coded message. **2** a thing whose meaning is hidden. **3** zero. **4** an insignificant person or thing.

ETYMOLOGY

Cipher comes from Old French *cifre*, meaning "zero," which originated from Arabic *sifr*, meaning "zero" or "empty." From about the 1500s, the English word was also used to refer to any Arabic numeral. It eventually came to mean "code," because early codes used numerals for letters. However, it is used increasingly rarely for all of these senses.

cir·ca (sər′kə) *prep* about or approximately: *Muhammad was born circa 570* CE. *Abbrev.* **c** or **ca** <Latin = around>

cir·ca·di·an (sər kā′dē ən) *adj* occurring naturally on a cycle of about 24 hours. An example of **circadian rhythm** is the opening and closing of flowers. In humans, examples are changes in temperature, blood pressure, and urine production. For diurnal animals, activity increases in daylight; for nocturnal animals, the main activity is at night. <Latin *circa* around + *dies* day>

cir·cle (sər′kəl) *n* **1** *Mathematics* **a** a curved line in which every point is equally distant from a point called the centre. **b** a plane figure bounded by such a line. **2** anything shaped like a circle: *The full moon was a bright circle in the night sky.* **3** a number of people or things arranged to form a circle: *a circle of chairs. We sat in a circle around the fire.* **4** a group of people held together by the same interests: *a circle of friends.* **5** a sphere of influence or activity: *He moves in different circles from you and me.*
v **cir·cled, cir·cling 1** go around in a circle: *The moon circles the earth. An airplane circles before it lands.* **2** form a circle or ring around: *A wooden fence circled the ranch house.* **3** draw a circle around: *Circle the answer you think is correct.* <Old English, from Latin *circus* ring>
come full circle, arrive back at a starting point after many stages or changes: *Fashion has come full circle and miniskirts are back in.*

circle graph PIE CHART.

cir·clet (sər′klit) *n* a round ornament worn on the head.

cir·cuit (sər′kit) *n* **1** the complete path followed by an electric current, or the arrangement of components forming this path. **2** a complete journey that is more or less circular: *It takes a year for the earth to make its circuit of the sun.* **3 a** a regular route followed by a touring theatre company, an itinerant preacher or judge, or travelling salesperson. **b** the area or region covered in this way. <Old French, from Latin *circum* around + *ire* go>

circuit board *n* a flat board of insulating material, with the parts of an electronic circuit etched or mounted on it.

circuit breaker *n* a switch that automatically interrupts an electric circuit when the current gets too strong.

cir·cu·i·tous (sər kyū′ə təs) *adj* roundabout; indirect: *To avoid unpaved roads, we took a circuitous route home.*
cir·cu′i·tous·ly *adv.* **cir·cu′i·tous·ness** *n.*

cir·cuit·ry (sər′kə trē) *n* **1** the component parts of a circuit. **2** a system or set of circuits.

cir·cu·lar (sər′kyə lər) *adj* **1** to do with circles. **2** shaped like a circle: *The full moon is circular.* **3** sent to each of a number of people on a regular list: *a circular letter.* **4** illogical because it depends on the very idea it is trying to prove: Example: *Exercising is good because exercise is good for you.*
n a letter or notice sent to each person on a list.
cir′cu·lar′i·ty *n.* **cir′cu·lar·ly** *adv.*

circular saw *n* a power saw in the form of a thin, toothed steel disc turned at high speed by machinery.

cir·cu·late (sər′kyə lāt′) *v* **cir·cu·lat·ed, cir·cu·lat·ing 1** move around so as to return to the starting point: *The blood circulates through the body.* **2** pass or send from place to place or person to person: *to circulate a rumour. The new five-dollar bills are just beginning to circulate.*

3 move around interacting with various people: *to circulate at a party.* 4 be published and sent to subscribers: *This magazine circulates across Canada.* <Old French, from Latin *circulus* small ring> **cir′cu·la′tor** *n.* **cir′cu·la′to·ry** (sər′kyə lə tô′rē) *adj.*

circulating library *n* a library whose materials may be taken off the premises.

cir·cu·la·tion (sər′kyə lā′shən) *n* **1** the fact or act of circulating: *the circulation of the blood. Open windows increase the circulation of air in a room.* **2** the number of copies of a periodical sold or distributed to readers: *The magazine has a circulation of 50 000.*

circulatory system *n* all the organs involved in the circulation of the blood in the body, including the heart, arteries, and veins.

circum– *prefix* around: *circumnavigate.* <Latin>

cir·cum·cise (sər′kəm sīz′) *v* **cir·cum·cised, cir·cum·cis·ing** **1** cut off the foreskin of the penis, either for medical reasons or as a religious rite. **2** perform one of a variety of mutilations on female genitalia. The removal of the external part of the clitoris compares to male circumcision. <Old French, from Latin *circum* around + *caedere* cut> **cir′cum·ci′sion** *n.*

cir·cum·fer·ence (sər kum′fə rəns) *n* **1** the boundary line of a circle, or the length of this line. **2** the distance around anything roughly circular in shape: *a big tree with a circumference of three metres.* See DIAMETER for picture. <Latin *circum* around + *ferre* carry>

cir·cum·flex (sər′kəm fleks′) *n* a mark [^] used especially over a vowel in certain languages and phonetic spelling systems.
adj written with such a mark.

cir·cum·lo·cu·tion (sər′kəm lō kyū′shən) *n* a roundabout expression: *"The wife of your mother's brother" is a circumlocution for "aunt."*

cir·cum·nav·i·gate (sər′kəm nav′ə gāt′) *v* **cir·cum·nav·i·gat·ed, cir·cum·nav·i·gat·ing** sail completely around: *Magellan circumnavigated the world.* **cir′cum·nav′i·ga′tion** *n.* **cir′cum·nav′i·gat′or** *n.*

cir·cum·po·lar (sər′kəm pō′lər) *adj* around the North Pole or South Pole.

cir·cum·scribe (sər′kəm skrīb′) *v* **cir·cum·scribed, cir·cum·scribing** **1** draw a line around. **2** restrict: *A prisoner's activities are severely circumscribed.* **3** *Mathematics* draw a circle around a polygon so as to pass through each vertex, or be so drawn: *A circle can circumscribe a square.* **4** inscribe around the edge of something round: *The medal was circumscribed with the words "For Outstanding Achievement."* <*circum* around + Latin *scribere* write> **cir′cum·scrip′tion** *n.*

cir·cum·spect (sər′kəm spekt′) *adj* careful or cautious. <Latin *circum* around + *specere* to look>
cir′cumspec′tion *n.* **cir′cum·spect′ly** *adv.*

cir·cum·stance (sər′kəm stans′) *n* **1** a happening, especially a chance one: *The arrival of a taxi just then was a fortunate circumstance.* **2** the way things happen to turn out: *a victim of circumstance.* **3 circumstances** *pl* **a** the details of time and place: *It was her success, not the circumstances of the achievement, that interested her family.* **b** all the conditions that influence or contribute to an act or event, or that give it a certain meaning: *You ought to consider all the circumstances before you judge her action.* **c** financial condition: *in reduced circumstances.* <Latin *circum* around + *stare* stand>
pomp and circumstance, splendid or impressive display, ceremony, or formality.
under no circumstances, never.
under the circumstances, in view of the situation.

cir·cum·stan·tial (sər′kəm stan′shəl) *adj* **1** pointing indirectly toward guilt but not conclusively proving it. **Circumstantial evidence** depends on the circumstances of a crime rather than the **direct evidence** of witnesses. **2** described in detail: *a circumstantial report of an accident.*
cir′cum·stan′tial·ly *adv.*

cir·cum·vent (sər′kəm vent′) *v* **1** avoid by going around: *We can circumvent the heavy traffic by taking side streets.* **2** defeat or get the better of by skilful manoeuvres: *to circumvent the law.* <Latin *circum* around + *venire* come>
cir′cum·ven′tion *n.*

cir·cus (sər′kəs) *n* **1** a travelling show that may include acrobats, clowns, and trained animals. **2** in ancient Rome, a kind of round or oval stadium. <Latin = ring>

cirque (sərk) *Geology, Geography n* a large bowl-shaped depression in a mountain, formed by glacial erosion and often containing a small lake or glacier. <French, from Latin *circus* ring>

cir·rho·sis (sə rō′sis) *n* a chronic disease of the liver caused by alcohol, poor diet, chronic infection, etc. <Latin, from Greek *kirrhos* orange-yellow, referring to the colour of the diseased liver>

cir·ro·cu·mu·lus (sēr′ō kyūm′yə ləs) *n, pl* **cir·ro·cu·mu·li** (sēr′ə kyūm′yə lī′) a cloud made up of rows or groups of small, fleecy clouds. See ALTOCUMULUS for picture. <*cirrus* + *cumulus*>

cir·ro·strat·us (sēr′ə strat′əs) *n, pl* **cir·ro·strat·i** (sēr′ə strat′ī) a thin, high cloud. See ALTOCUMULUS for picture. <*cirrus* + *stratus*>

cir·rus (sēr′əs) *n, pl* **cir·ri** (sēr′ī) *or* (sēr′ē) a thin, curling, wispy cloud very high in the air. See ALTOCUMULUS for picture. <Latin = curl>

CIS Commonwealth of Independent States.

🍁 **cis·co** (sis′kō) *n, pl* **cis·coes** or **cis·cos** a freshwater whitefish found in northern N America and northern Eurasia. <Cdn. French, from Ojibway *bemideswikawed* the fish with oily skin>

cis·tern (sis′tərn) *n* **1** a large tank, often underground, for storing water. **2** the water tank belonging to a toilet. <Old French, from Latin *cista* box>

cit·a·del (sit′ə dəl) *n* **1** a fortress commanding a city: *Halifax has a famous citadel.* **2** a strongly fortified place. <Old French *citadelle*, from Latin *civitas* city>

a bat	e bed	i bid	o pot	u cup	th thin
ā cake	ē me	ī bite	ō go	ū rude	TH then
ä bar	ə about	ər over	ô for	ů put	zh measure

cite (sīt) *v* **cit·ed, cit·ing 1** quote, especially as an authority: *She cited the dictionary and Shakespeare to prove her statement.* **2** mention as an example: *The lawyer cited another case similar to the one being tried.* **3** mention publicly for outstanding service. **4** summon to appear before a law court. <Old French, from Latin *ciere* to call> **ci·ta′tion** *n.* **cite′a·ble** *adj.*

cit·i·zen (sit′ə zən) *n* **1** a legally recognized member of a country, by birth or by immigration, with accompanying rights and responsibilities: *Many immigrants have become citizens of Canada.* **2** an inhabitant of a city or town. <Old French *citesein*, from Latin *civitas* city> **cit′i·zen·ship** *n.*

cit·i·zen·ry (sit′ə zən rē) *n* citizens as a group.

citizen's arrest *n* the lawful arrest of a criminal by an ordinary member of the public, not a police officer.

citizens' band CB.

cit·ric acid (sit′rik) *n* an odourless, sour-tasting acid found in citrus fruits.

cit·ron (sit′rən) *n* **1** a pale yellow citrus fruit resembling a lemon but larger and less acidic. **2** a small, round variety of watermelon whose rind is used in preserves. **3** the preserved or candied rind of either of these fruits.

cit·ron·el·la (sit′rə nel′ə) *n* a fragrant oil made from a tropical grass and used in perfumes and soaps. <from *citron* (because of its smell)>

cit·rus (sit′rəs) *n* **1** any of a related group of trees or shrubs growing in warm climates and bearing sweet or tart edible fruit. **2** the fruits of these trees collectively: *Include a lot of citrus in your winter diet.*
adj to do with any of these trees or their fruit. Oranges, lemons, limes, grapefruit, and citrons are citrus fruits. <Latin = citron tree> **cit′rous** *adj.* **cit′rus·y** *adj, adv.*

cit·y (sit′ē) *n, pl* **cit·ies 1** a large urban community, usually with more financial and social responsibilities and more sources of revenue than a town. **2** the people of a city: *The whole city celebrated when their team won the Stanley Cup.* **3** the government of a city: *The city of Yellowknife has decided to make more land available for parks.* **4** *Slang* an environment full of or characterized by a certain thing: *Our garden is vegetable city. This discount store is junk city.* <Old French, from Latin *civis* citizen>

city council *n* the elected government of a city.
city councillor *n.*

city hall *n* **1** the headquarters of a city government. **2** the local government itself: *He says you can't fight city hall.*

cit·y·scape (sit′ē skāp′) *n* a view, photograph, or painting of a city or part of one, or a city viewed as scenery.

city slicker *Informal n* a city person who is looked on with scorn or suspicion by country people: *The poor city slicker didn't even know how to chop wood.*

city–state (sit′ē stāt′) *n* an independent state consisting of a city and the territories depending on it. Athens in ancient Greece was a city-state.

civ·et cat (siv′it) *n* a small, spotted, catlike mammal of Africa, Europe, and Asia, whose anal glands secrete **civet**, a yellowish substance with a musky odour used in perfume. <French, from Arabic *zabad*>

civ·ic (siv′ik) *adj* **1** to do with a city. **2** to do with citizens or citizenship: *civic duties. If you have any civic pride, help keep your city clean.*

civic centre *n* the headquarters of a city government, often also housing a public library or other public facilities.

civ·ic–mind·ed (siv′ik mīn′did) *adj* taking one's social and political responsibilities seriously.

civ·ics (siv′iks) *n* (*with singular verb*) the study of the duties, rights, and privileges of citizens.

civ·il (siv′əl) *adj* **1** courteous: *She answered in a very civil way.* **2** to do with citizens: *civil rights.* **3** to do with the government or state: *civil servants.* **4** not connected with the military or the church: *a civil court, a civil marriage.* **5** *Law* to do with **civil law**, dealing with transactions between private individuals as opposed to crimes against society: *a civil lawsuit.* Compare CRIMINAL (def. 2). <Old French, from Latin *civis* citizen> **civ′il·ly** *adv.*

civil disobedience *n* refusal to obey laws that violate one's moral principles.

civil engineering *n* the planning, construction, and maintenance of bridges, roads, harbours, and dams.
civil engineer *n.*

ci·vil·ian (sə vil′yən) *n* a person who is not in the armed forces or police force.
adj to do with such people: *civilian life.*

ci·vil·i·ty (sə vil′ə tē) *n, pl* **ci·vil·i·ties** courtesy.

civ·i·li·za·tion (siv′ə lī zā′shən) *n* **1** a stage of social organization, scientific development, technology, and activity in the arts that is considered advanced. **2** the nations and peoples thought of as having reached such a stage. **3** the total culture of a nation or people at a given time: *Inuit civilization, 19th-century Canadian civilization.* **4** the process of civilizing or socializing.

civ·i·lize (siv′ə līz′) *v* **civ·i·lized, civ·i·liz·ing 1** change a social system to a more complex one by advancing knowledge of the arts and sciences and use of technology: *The Romans civilized a great part of their world.* **2** improve in culture and good manners: *We were given the job of trying to civilize our cousin.* **civ′i·lized′** *adj.*

civil liberty *n* the right of a person to do and say what he or she pleases as long as he or she does not harm anyone else or break established laws.

civil rights *pl n* the rights of a citizen.

civil service *n* the appointed officials, clerks, and other government employees who do the day-to-day work of government departments. **civil servant** *n.*

civil war *n* **1** a war between two groups of citizens of one nation. **2 Civil War a** in England, the war between King and Parliament, from 1642 to 1652. **b** in the US, the war between the northern and southern states, from 1861 to 1865.

civ·vies (siv′ēz) *Informal pl n* ordinary civilian clothes as opposed to a military, police, or other uniform.

clack (klak) *n* a short, sharp sound: *I heard the clack of your heels on the floor.*
v make or cause to make such a sound: *Her needles clacked as she knitted.* <imitative> **clack′er** *n.*

clad[1] (klad) a past tense and a past participle of CLOTHE.

clad[2] (klad) *v* **clad, clad·ding** cover in some protective material: *to clad the bottoms of stainless steel pots with copper.* <Old English *clæthan* clothe>

claim (klām) *v* **1** say that one has a right, possession, or title, and demand that others recognize it: *to claim a tract of land.* **2** identify as one's own and take: *to claim your baggage at the airport.* **3** declare despite possible opposition: *She claimed we ignored her. He claims to be a genius.* **4** require or demand: *I tried to keep studying, but the noise from the other room claimed my attention.*
n **1** the act of claiming or the thing claimed: *That is a ridiculous claim. Their claim to the estate was denied.* **2** a right to demand something: *She has no claim on us.* **3** something that requires a person's attention: *He has many claims on his time.* **4** a piece of public land chosen and marked out by a settler or prospector, who must buy it when it is offered for sale. <Old French, from Latin *clamare* proclaim> **claim′a·ble** *adj.*
jump a claim, illegally seize a piece of land that has been staked for mining by another, but not yet formally recorded.
lay claim to, declare one's ownership of or right to: *Nobody laid claim to the jacket.*
stake (out) a claim, a claim a piece of land for mining rights by setting out stakes to mark its boundaries and registering it at a government office. **b** claim a share or piece of territory, especially in advance: *Our new home has three bedrooms; I've staked my claim to the smallest one.*

claim·ant (klā′mənt) *n* one who claims something, especially in a lawsuit or from a government.

clair·voy·ant (kler voi′ənt) *adj* **1** with very keen insight. **2** with a supernatural ability to perceive things beyond the natural range of the senses.
n a person who has, or claims to have, such power: *The clairvoyant claimed to be able to locate lost articles.* <French *clair* clear + *voyant* from *voir* see> **clair·voy′ance** *n.*

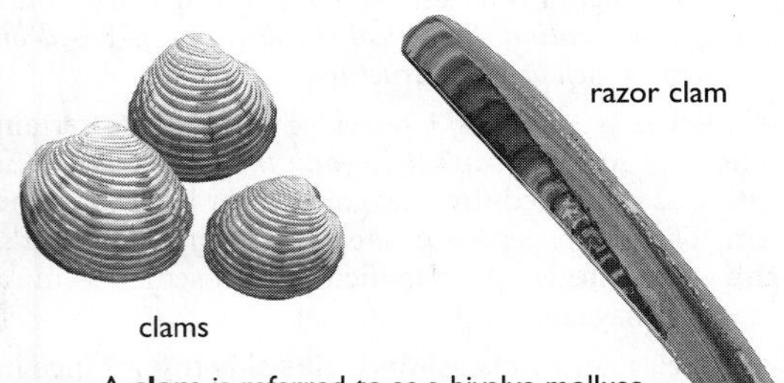

A **clam** is referred to as a bivalve mollusc because of the two valves, or shells, that enclose the body. The growth rings on the outside surface of the shells can help determine the age of a clam.

clam (klam) *n* a shellfish with a soft body and a hinged double shell, living in sand along the seashore or at the edges of lakes and rivers.
v **clammed, clam·ming** dig for clams. <*clamshell* (i.e., shell that clamps shut), from Old English *clamm* bond> **clam′like′** *adj.*
clam up, *Informal* stop talking.

clam·bake (klam′bāk′) *n* **1** a picnic at which clams are baked or steamed. **2** *Informal* a noisy social gathering.

clam·ber (klam′bər) *v* climb awkwardly or with difficulty.
n an act of clambering. <Middle English>

clam·my (klam′ē) *adj* **clam·mi·er, clam·mi·est** unpleasantly cold and damp. <probably Old English *clam* clay> **clam′mi·ness** *n.*

clam·our or **clam·or** (klam′ər) *n* **1** a loud, continual, and confused noise. **2** a noisy demand or complaint.
v **1** make a loud noise or uproar. **2** (*with* **for**) demand noisily: *The children were clamouring for candy.* <Old French, from Latin *clamare* cry out> **clam′or·ous** *adj.* **clam′our·er** or **clam′or·er** *n.*

clamp (klamp) *n* a brace, band, wedge, or other device for holding things tightly together: *She used a clamp to hold the joint until the glue dried.*
v put in a clamp to fasten together or strengthen. <Middle English>
clamp down (on), take strict measures (against): *The police are clamping down on drunk driving.*

clamp·down (klamp′doun′) *n* a sudden strict enforcement of laws or restriction of freedoms.

clan (klan) *n* **1** a large group of families descended from a common ancestor. **2** an extended family: *The clan always gets together for Thanksgiving.* **3** a group of people joined by a common interest: *Writers are not a wealthy clan.* <Gaelic, from Latin *planta* sprout> **clan′like′** *adj.* **clans′man** *n.* **clans′wo·man** *n.*

clan·des·tine (klan des′tən) *or* (klan des′tīn) *adj* secret or hidden: *clandestine visits.* <French, from Latin *clam* secretly> **clan·des′tine·ly** *adv.*

clang (klang) *n* a loud, harsh sound, as of metal striking metal: *The clang of the fire bell roused the town.*
v make or cause to make such a sound. <imitative>

clan·gour or **clan·gor** (klang′ər) *or* (klang′gər) *n* a continuous clanging: *the clangour of bells.* <Latin *clangere* resound>

clank (klangk) *n* a harsh, metallic sound like the rattle of a heavy chain.
v make or cause to make such a sound: *The sword clanked against his armour.* <imitative>

clan·nish (klan′ish) *adj* closely united as a group and tending not to like outsiders. **clan′nish·ly** *adv.* **clan′nish·ness** *n.*

clap (klap) *v* **clapped, clap·ping 1** strike together loudly: *to clap your hands.* **2** show appreciation by striking the hands together. **3** strike lightly with a quick blow: *She clapped her friend on the back.* **4** place quickly and effectively: *The police clapped the thief in jail.*
n **1** a sudden, loud, sharp noise, such as a burst of thunder or the sound of hands struck together. **2** an act of clapping: *He gave me a clap on the back.* <Old English *clappan*>
clap eyes on, *Informal* look at: *I liked her from the first time I clapped eyes on her.*

a bat	e bed	i bid	o pot	u cup	th **thin**
ā cake	ē me	ī bite	ō go	ū rude	TH **then**
à bar	ə about	ər over	ȯ for	u̇ put	zh measure

clap·board (klap′bôrd′) *or* (klab′ərd) *n* siding for outer walls, consisting of thin boards laid horizontally so they overlap, or one of these boards.

clap·per (klap′ər) *n* **1** the movable part inside a bell that strikes the outer part, causing it to ring. **2** a noisemaker used at parties. **3** a person who or thing that claps.

clap·trap (klap′trap′) *Informal n* foolish or insincere talk or ideas.

clar·et (kler′ət) *or* (klȧ rā′) *n* a dry red wine originally made in Bordeaux, France. <Old French, from Latin *clarus* clear>

clar·i·fy (kler′ə fī′) *v* **clar·i·fied, clar·i·fy·ing 1** explain clearly: *Could you clarify that statement, please?* **2** purify and make clear in colour: *to clarify butter. We clarified the syrup by filtering it.* <Old French, from Latin *clarus* clear + *facere* make> **clar′i·fi·ca′tion** *n.*

clar·i·net (kler′ə net′) *n* a wind instrument consisting of a straight metal or wooden tube with a slightly flared end, a single reed, and holes and keys for producing tones. <French, from Latin *clarus* clear> **clar′i·net′tist** or **clar′i·net′ist** *n.*

clar·i·on (kler′ē ən) *adj* clear and bright or sharp in tone. <Latin *clarus* clear>

clar·i·ty (kler′ə tē) *n* clearness. <Latin *clarus* clear>

clash (klash) *n* **1** a loud, harsh, discordant sound like that of two hard things colliding, metal striking metal, or bells that are not in harmony. **2** a strong disagreement or conflict: *a clash of opinion, a clash of colours.*
v **1** make a loud, harsh sound. **2** disagree or conflict strongly: *Our expectations often clash with reality. I think orange and pink clash.* <imitative>

clasp (klasp) *v* **1** hold close with the arms or hands: *The mother clasped her baby to her breast.* **2** grip firmly with the hand.
n **1** a fastening device, usually with a hook of some kind: *a suede belt with a gold clasp.* **2** an act of clasping: *a warm clasp of the hand.* <Middle English>

class (klas) *n* **1 a** a group of students taught together. **b** a meeting of students and teacher for instruction: *The class starts at nine o'clock.* **c** a group of students graduating in a certain year: *the class of 2012.* **2** a division of society based on birth, wealth, or some other criterion, or this system: *the middle class. Class is a feature of every human society.* **3** a grade of service or quality: *First class is the most costly way to travel.* **4** elegance, style, or honourable character: *You showed real class by refusing to take revenge.* **5** a group of people or things alike in some way: *Squares and rectangles belong to the class of quadrilaterals.* **6** *Biology* a category in the classification of living things. A class is more specific than a PHYLUM and more general than an ORDER. See also KINGDOM, DIVISION, FAMILY, GENUS, and SPECIES.
v put or be in a class or group: *Humans are classed with the other mammals.* <Latin *classis*>

class act *n* a person or group that achieves a high standard of general behaviour.

class action *n* a lawsuit on behalf of all who directly suffer loss from some cause: *The travellers who missed connecting flights brought a class action against the airline.*

class–con·scious (klas′kon′shəs) *adj* viewing all people in terms of their social class. **class′-con′scious·ness** *n.*

clas·sic (klas′ik) *adj* **1** outstanding or excellent and therefore established as a standard: *a classic example of dramatic irony.* **2** elegant and simple in a way that never loses its appeal: *Blue jeans are classic.* **3** famous in literature or history: *the classic smile of the Mona Lisa.* Compare CLASSICAL.
n **1** a work of literature or art long considered to be of the highest quality: *Gabrielle Roy's* The Tin Flute *is a Canadian classic.* **2 the classics** *pl* the literature of ancient Greece and Rome. <Latin *classis* class> **clas′si·cal·ly** *adv.*

clas·si·cal (klas′ə kəl) *adj* **1** to do with ancient Greece and Rome, especially their art, literature, and educational ideals: *classical studies, a classical scholar.* **2** accepted, but not new or up to date: *Classical physics doesn't include Einstein's theory of relativity.* **3** to do with the European tradition of written music, especially of the last 300 to 400 years: *She prefers classical music to jazz.* **4 Classical** to do with music by composers such as Mozart, as distinct from the later Romantic music of Chopin or the earlier Baroque music of Bach. Compare CLASSIC (*adj*).
clas′si·cal·ly *adv.*

🍁 **classical college** *n* in former times in French Canada, a private educational institution that offered a course over eight years in the classics and liberal arts and led to a bachelor's degree.

clas·si·cism (klas′ə siz′əm) *n* the principles of the literature and art of ancient Greece and Rome, followed by many artists and writers since: *Simplicity and regularity are principles of classicism.* **clas′si·cist** *n.*

clas·si·fi·ca·tion (klas′ə fə kā′shən) *n* the act or manner of classifying things: *I can't get the hang of this video store's system of classification. Biological classification is based on characteristics such as body structure.*

clas·si·fied (klas′ə fīd′) *adj* **1** secret, or restricted to certain people: *I'm sorry, I can't tell you; that information is classified.* **2** arranged by category according to some system: *The newspaper has a whole section of classified ads.*
n **the classifieds** *pl* classified advertisements in a newspaper, magazine, or the Internet.

clas·si·fy (klas′ə fī′) *v* **clas·si·fied, clas·si·fy·ing** arrange in classes or groups according to some system based on shared characteristics: *In the post office, they classify mail by destination.* **clas′si·fi′a·ble** *adj.*

class·mate (klas′māt′) *n* a fellow member of a class.

class·room (klas′rūm′) *n* a room where lessons take place, especially in a school or college.

clas·sy (kla′sē) *adj* **clas·si·er, clas·si·est 1** elegant, stylish, or refined: *a classy restaurant, a classy outfit.* **2** honourable, gracious, or noble: *Giving her your concert ticket was a classy thing to do.*

clat·ter (klat′ər) *n* a rattling noise: *the clatter of dishes.*
v make a rattling noise: *The horses clattered over the stones.* <Old English *clatrian*; imitative>

clause (kloz) *n* **1** *Grammar* a unit formed by a subject and predicate, and smaller than a sentence. **2** a single provision of a law, contract, treaty, or any other written agreement: *A clause in our lease says we may not keep a dog in this building.* <Old French, from Latin *claudere* close>

GRAMMAR AND USAGE

A **main** (or **independent**) clause can stand alone as a sentence, but a **subordinate** (or **dependent**) clause cannot, since it generally functions only to modify the main clause. Example: In *He arrived before we left*, the main clause is *He arrived* and the subordinate clause is *before we left*.

claus·tro·pho·bi·a (klos′trə fō′bē ə) *n* **1** an abnormal fear of enclosed spaces. **2** a feeling of being locked in or smothered. <Latin *claustrum* lock + *-phobia*>
claus′tro·pho′bic *adj, n.*

clav·i·chord (klav′ə kòrd′) *n* an early stringed musical instrument with a keyboard. <Latin *clavis* key + *chorda* string>

clav·i·cle (klav′ə kəl) *n* the collarbone.

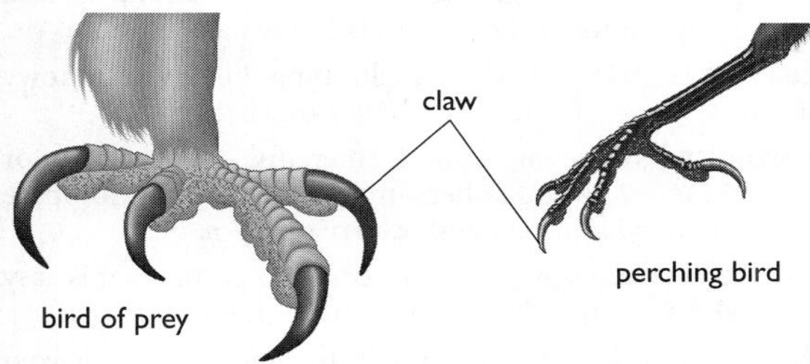

The **claws** of birds and other animals reveal a good deal about their habitat, how they find and capture food, and how they protect their young.

Hawks, eagles, and owls, for example, have sharp claws, or talons, to kill their prey. Sparrows, thrushes, and other perching birds have a special tendon that locks their claws around the branch they are sitting on so they can't fall off, even when they are asleep.

claw (klo) *n* **1** a sharp, hooked nail on each toe of an animal. **2** one of the pincers of a lobster, crab, etc. **3** anything like a claw, such as the end of a claw hammer. *v* scratch, tear, seize, or pull with the claws or fingernails. <Old English *clawu*> **claw′like′** *adj.*

claw·back (klo′bak′) *n* a tax, deduction, or fee imposed by a government, that has the effect of taking back what the government had previously paid out. **claw back** *v.*

claw hammer *n* a hammer with one end of the head tapered, forked, and curved like a claw for pulling nails.

clay (klā) *n* **1** a stiff, sticky kind of earth with little or no animal or vegetable matter in it, that can be easily shaped when wet and hardens after drying or baking: *Bricks and dishes may be made from clay.* **2** *Poetic* **a** earth. **b** the human body. <Old English *clæg*> **clay′ey** (klā′ē) *adj.*

clay·ma·tion (klā mā′shən) *n* movie animation using clay figures instead of drawings.

clay·more (klā′mòr′) *n* a heavy, two-edged sword used in former times by Scottish Highlanders. <Gaelic *claidheamh* sword + *mor* great>

clay pigeon *n* a saucerlike clay disc thrown in the air as a flying target for shooting.

🍁 **CLC** Canadian Labour Congress.

clean (klēn) *adj* **1** free of dirt or litter: *clean clothes, clean streets.* **2** with the habit of keeping clean: *Cats are clean animals.* **3** free of guilt: *a clean conscience.* **4** not obscene: *clean jokes.* **5** made swiftly and smoothly: *a clean cut.* **6** simple and elegant: *I likes the clean lines of that car.* **7** having or giving complete safety and freedom: *Once over the border, they'll be clean.* **8** honest, especially in sports: *a clean contestant.* **9** free of corrections: *a clean copy.* **10** blank or new: *a clean page.* **11** *Informal* not using drugs: *She has been clean for two years.* **12** acceptable under dietary law: *Not all meat is clean for Jews and Muslims.* **13** causing little or no radioactive fallout.
adv **1** completely: *I clean forgot.* **2** in a clean manner: *to fight clean.*
v **1** make clean: *to clean a pair of boots.* **2** prepare fish, game, or poultry for cooking by removing entrails, or the scales or feathers: *to clean a fish.* **3** do housecleaning: *I'm going to clean my room.* <Old English *clæne*>
clean′ly *adv.* **clean′ness** *n.*
clean house, get rid of any unnecessary things or people: *The principal cleaned house when he took over.*
clean out, a make clean by emptying: *Clean out your desk.* **b** empty or use up: *We cleaned out that whole package of cookies.*
clean up, a make clean or tidy: *Clean up the yard.* **b** get rid of mess left by some event: *to clean up an oil spill. When you've finished painting, don't forget to clean up.* **c** *Informal* make a large profit.
come clean, a *Informal* confess the truth: *You'd better come clean; lying only makes it worse.* **b** become clean as a result of washing: *This shirt will never come clean.*

clean and jerk *n* in weightlifting, a lift in which the barbell is raised to the shoulders in one movement, and then lifted above the head with the arms straight.

clean–cut (klēn′kut′) *adj* **1** with a neat and wholesome appearance: *a clean-cut young man.* **2** clear and distinct: *clean-cut features.*

clean·li·ness (klen′lē nis) *n* the habit of keeping oneself and one's surroundings clean.

clean room *n* a sterilized laboratory.

cleanse (klenz) *v* **cleansed, cleans·ing** make thoroughly clean, especially by removing contamination. <Old English *clæne* clean>

cleans·er (klenz′ər) *n* a substance that cleans, especially a soap, detergent, disinfectant, or bleach.

clean·shav·en (klēn′shā′vən) *adj* with the face shaved.

clean·up (klē′nup′) *n* a process of cleaning up.

a bat	e bed	i bid	o pot	u cup	th **thin**
ā cake	ē me	ī bite	ō go	ū rude	ᴛʜ **then**
ȧ bar	ə about	ər over	ȯ for	u̇ put	zh measure

clear (klēr) *adj* **1** free of cloud or haze: *a clear day.* **2** easy to see through: *clear glass.* **3** easy to understand or hear: *a clear idea, a clear voice.* **4** free from blockage or clutter: *a clear view, a clear path.* **5** free of blemishes: *clear skin.* **6** obvious or definite: *It is clear that changes are needed.* **7** with a pure, even colour: *a clear blue.* **8** (*with* ***of***) not caught; safely out of the way: *The ship was clear of the iceberg.* **9** free from blame or guilt: *a clear conscience.* **10** free of debt or deductions: *clear profit.*
v **1** make or become clear: *to clear your throat. By noon the sky had cleared.* **2** (*often with* ***away*** *or* ***off***) remove so as to leave a space: *Clear away the dishes.* **3** get by or over without touching or getting caught: *to clear a hurdle.* **4** make as profit: *The charity car wash cleared $200.* **5** get through an approval process with an authority: *It took us half an hour to clear customs. The plane has been cleared for landing.* **6** be eventually debited from the account a cheque was drawn on: *He can't withdraw any money till that cheque clears.*
adv completely: *The snowball went clear through the window.* <Old French, from Latin *clarus*> **clear′ly** *adv.* **clear′ness** *n.*
clear as a bell, very clear or clearly: *I heard my name clear as a bell. Your explanation was clear as a bell.*
clear out, make clear by emptying: *to clear out a drawer.*
clear out (or **off**), *Informal* leave: *You have to clear out of the gym by four because we need it for practice. She cleared off when she heard there was work involved.*
clear up, a clean up. **b** finish completely: *Clear up your breakfast.* **c** explain or solve: *Your explanation clears up that mystery.*
in the clear, a free of guilt or blame: *Her report shows that the suspect is in the clear.* **b** free of debt.
make clear, state definitely: *She made clear that she disapproved.*

clear·ance (klēr′əns) *n* **1** clear space, especially the distance allowing free movement between objects: *The underpass has a clearance of four metres.* **2** permission to go ahead: *Before taking off, a pilot must get clearance from the control tower.* **3** in full, **clearance sale** a sale to get rid of unwanted or old stock and make way for new.

clear–cut (klēr′kut′) *adj* **1** clear and definite: *He had clear-cut ideas about the work.* **2** cleared of all standing timber in a forest area.
v clear all standing timber from a forest area.

clear–head·ed (klēr′hed′id) *adj* showing clear thought. **clear′-head′ed·ly** *adv.* **clear′-head′ed·ness** *n.*

clear·ing (klē′ring) *n* an open space in a forest.

clearing house *n* a place where banks exchange cheques and bills and settle their accounts.

clear–sight·ed (klēr′sī′tid) *adj* able to see, understand, or think clearly. **clear′-sight′ed·ly** *adv.* **clear′-sight′ed·ness** *n.*

cleat (klēt) *n* **1** a stud or point attached to the sole of a shoe to prevent slipping. **2** a strip of wood, plastic, etc. fastened across something for sure footing: *A ramp has cleats to keep people from slipping.* **3** a fixture with projecting ends, attached to a boat, wharf, or flagpole for securing ropes by winding them around it. <Middle English>

cleav·age (klē′vij) *n* **1** a split or division, especially that between a woman's breasts as revealed by a low neckline. **2** the manner or direction in which something splits.

cleave[1] (klēv) *Poetic v* **cleft, cleaved,** or **clove; cleft, cleaved,** or **clo·ven; cleav·ing 1** cut, divide, or split open: *With one blow of the axe he cleft the log in two.* **2** pierce or penetrate: *We watched the airplane cleave the clouds and disappear.* **3** make by cutting: *to cleave a path through the wilderness.* <Old English *cleofan*>

cleave[2] (klēv) *Poetic v* **cleaved, cleav·ing** (*with* ***to***) hold fast or cling: *to cleave to an idea.* <Old English *cleofian*>

cleav·er (klē′vər) *n* a cutting tool with a wide, heavy blade and a short handle.

clef (klef) *Music n* a symbol that assigns a certain note to a certain line on the staff. The BASS CLEF 𝄢 assigns F to the line that falls between the two dots. The TREBLE CLEF 𝄞 assigns G to the line where the spiral begins. See also ALTO CLEF, TENOR CLEF. <French, from Latin *clavis* key>

cleft (kleft) *v* a past tense and a past participle of CLEAVE[1].
adj split or divided: *a cleft stick.*
n a space or opening made by splitting; a crack.

cleft lip *n* a congenital split in the upper lip.

cleft palate *n* a congenital split in the roof of the mouth, caused by failure of the two parts of the palate to join.

cle·mat·is (klə mat′is) *n* a climbing vine with showy flowers. <Latin, from Greek *klema* vine branch>

clem·ent (klem′ənt) *adj* **1** merciful in judging or punishing. **2** of weather, mild and clear. Compare INCLEMENT. <Latin *clemens*> **clem′en·cy** *n.*

clem·ent·ine (klem′ən tīn′) *n* a small tangerine that is easy to peel. <French *Clément* a personal name>

clench (klench) *v* **1** close tightly together: *to clench your fists, to clench your teeth.* **2** grip tightly: *The police officer clenched the prisoner's arm.*
n a tight grip: *I felt the clench of his hand on my arm.* <Old English *clencan* hold fast>

clere·sto·rey (klēr′stȯ′rē) *Architecture n, pl* **clere·sto·reys 1** the upper part of the wall of a church, with windows in it above the roofs of the aisles. **2** any similar structure. <Middle English *clere* clear + *storie* storey>

cler·gy (klər′jē) *n, pl* **cler·gies** a group of people specially trained and ordained to perform religious services, especially in the Christian church. Compare LAITY. <Old French, from Greek *kleros* clergy> **cler′gy·man** *n.* **cler′gy·wo′man** *n.*
without benefit of clergy, without a religious rite performed by an ordained person: *married without benefit of clergy.*

🍁 **Clergy Reserves** *n* lands set aside in Upper and Lower Canada in 1791 for the support of the Church of England clergy.

cler·ic (kler′ik) *n* a member of the Christian clergy. <Latin, from Greek *kleros* clergy>

cler·i·cal (kler′ə kəl) *adj* **1** to do with a clerk or office assistant: *clerical jobs such as filing and bookkeeping.* **2** to do with the clergy: *clerical robes.* **cler′i·cal·ly** *adv.*

clerical collar *n* a stiff white collar fastened at the back, worn by some members of the Christian clergy.

clerk (klərk) *n* **1** a salesperson or cashier in a store. **2** an office assistant: *a law clerk.* **3** an official who keeps records and takes care of regular business in a law court, legislature, or government office: *a county clerk.*
v work as a clerk in a store: *He clerks in a drugstore.* <See CLERIC.> **clerk′ship** *n.*

clev·er (klev′ər) *adj* **1 a** quick to learn and good at solving problems. **b** skilful or expert: *a clever carpenter, clever fingers.* **2** giving evidence of such inventiveness or skill: *a clever tool.* **3** annoyingly witty or sophisticated: *Enough of your clever remarks.* <Middle English> **clev′er·ly** *adv.* **clev′er·ness** *n.*

cli·ché (klē shā′) *n* an expression or idea used so often that it becomes dull or tiresome. Example: *last but not least.* <French *clicher* to stereotype>

click (klik) *n* **1** a light, short, sharp sound: *We heard the click as she turned the key in the lock.* **2** *Computers* the act of clicking (see *v* def. 4): *A few clicks and I am at my favourite web page.*
v **1** make or cause to make such a sound: *to click your heels. The clock clicks just before it chimes.* **2** *Informal* get along well together: *We clicked from the start.* **3** *Informal* suddenly make sense: *Then it clicked—all I had to do was lift the lid.* **4** *Computers* press and release the button on a mouse. To **double-click** is to press the button twice, quickly. To **right-click** is to press and release the button on the right side of the mouse: *Click on the icon to save the changes. Double-click to open the attachment. Right-click to see shortcut options.* **5** *Informal* go or do well: *This movie should click, since it has a popular theme.* <imitative>

cli·ent (klī′ənt) *n* **1** a person or organization served by a professional person or company: *She had few clients in her first year as a lawyer.* **2** *Computers* a computer that relies on a server. <Latin *cluere* hear or obey> **cli′ent·less** *adj.*

cli·en·tele (klī′ən tel′) *n* **1** customers or potential customers, regarded as a group of a certain kind: *We serve a very wealthy clientele.* **2** the total number of clients: *Our clientele is about 300 right now.*

client–server network (klī′ənt sər′vər) *Computers n* to do with a network in which one or more computers (**clients**) have access to data, programs, and peripherals such as a printer, through another, more powerful computer (**server**).

cliff (klif) *n* a place where the ground makes a steep, sharp drop, especially beside the sea. <Old English *clif*> **cliff′like′** *adj.*

cliff·hang·er (klif′hang′ər) *Informal n* **1** a movie, chapter, or episode in a serial that ends with a character in an extremely dangerous situation, to be resolved in the next chapter or episode or in a sequel. **2** a race, election, or other contest whose result is in doubt until the very end.

cli·mac·tic (klī mak′tik) *adj* to do with a climax.

CONFUSABLES

Climactic means "with a climax," as in dramatic action: *At the climactic moment of the film, the truth about the main character was revealed.*

Climatic refers to climate or weather: *The climatic research showed a trend of global warming.*

cli·mate (klī′mit) *n* **1** the pattern of weather a place has over a long period: *The climate of the Prairies is different from that of the West Coast.* **2** a region with a certain climate: *to go to a warmer climate.* **3** moral, social, or emotional atmosphere: *raised in a climate of love and acceptance.* **4** prevailing state or trend: *the climate of public opinion.* <Old French, from Greek *klinein* slope> **cli·mat′ic** *adj.* **cli·mat′i·cal·ly** *adv.*

C

cli·ma·tol·o·gy (klī′mə tol′ə jē) *n* the science dealing with climate. **cli′ma·to·log′i·cal** *adj.* **cli′ma·tol′o·gist** *n.*

cli·max (klī′maks) *n* **1** the point of greatest interest or excitement: *The battle is the climax of the story.* **2** the peak of any development: *Inflation reached a climax in the 1980s.* **3** the peak of sexual arousal.
v bring or come to a climax. <Latin, from Greek *klimax* ladder>

climb (klīm) *v* **climbed, climb·ing 1** go up, especially by using the hands or feet or both: *to climb a ladder. We had to climb for hours to reach the top of the hill.* **2** get in or out with effort: *She climbed awkwardly out of the car.* **3** rise or go up gradually or with steady effort: *climbing gas prices. The road climbed for more than a kilometre before it levelled off. It took her two years to climb to the position of team captain.* **4** grow upward by holding on or twining around: *The ivy has climbed up the porch railing.*
n **1** the act or fact of climbing: *a climb in bus fares. Our climb took two hours.* **2** a place to be climbed: *They took me to an easy climb for starters.* <Old English *climban*>
climb down, go down by using the hands and feet.

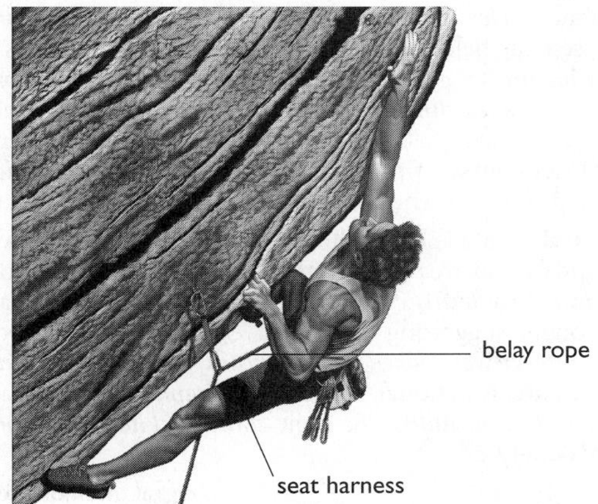

Rock climbing began as a technique used in mountain climbing, but has since developed into its own sport.

A **climber** uses rope-handling techniques and special equipment for protection and safety.

climb·er (klī′mər) *n* **1** a person who or thing that climbs. See also ADZE for picture. **2** *Informal* a person who is always trying to get ahead socially. **3** a climbing plant.

a bat	e bed	i bid	o pot	u cup	th **thin**
ā cake	ē me	ī bite	ō go	ū rude	ᴛʜ **then**
à bar	ə about	ər over	ȯ for	ů put	zh measure

clime (klīm) *Poetic n* climate.

clinch (klinch) *v* **1** settle decisively: *A deposit of twenty dollars clinched the bargain.* **2** grasp each other tightly in boxing or wrestling: *When the wrestlers clinched, the crowd booed.* **3** fasten a driven nail or rivet firmly after driving it in, by bending over or flattening the end that projects from the other side. **4** *Slang* hug.
n **1** an act of clinching: *The referee broke the boxers' clinch.* **2** a knot used to fasten ropes or fishing lines. <variant of *clench*>

clinch·er (klin′chər) *n* an argument, statement, or fact that decides or settles an issue.

cling (kling) *v* **clung, cling·ing 1** hold on tightly to: *The child clung to his mother.* **2** stick firmly to: *The static electricity makes my pants cling to my legs.* **3** remain committed to a belief, hope, or other emotion: *They clung to the dream of freedom.* **4** hang around a person, seeking attention.
v **1** the ability to cling: *This plastic wrap has good cling.* **2** static cling. <Old English *clingan*>

cling·stone (kling′stōn′) *n* a peach whose flesh clings to the stone.

cling·y (kling′ē) *adj* **cling·i·er, cling·i·est 1** clinging as clothing to the body so as to reveal its shape. **2** needing always to be with someone: *a clingy child.*

clin·ic (klin′ik) *n* **1** a part of a hospital where people are treated without staying overnight. **2** a place, separate from a hospital, where a group of doctors or dentists work together: *He is a heart specialist in the new clinic.* **3** a session held to treat or prevent certain illnesses or injuries, or to provide a special service: *a blood donor clinic, a rabies clinic for pets.* **4 a** *Medicine* a class where students watch doctors examine and treat patients. **b** a brief course of practical instruction: *a soccer clinic, a writing clinic.* <French, from Greek *kline* bed>

clin·i·cal (klin′ə kəl) *adj* **1** to do with a clinic. **2** to do with diagnosis and treatment rather than research or theory: *clinical psychiatry.* **3** detached, unemotional, and thorough, suggesting a medical examination or report: *The interviewer looked the applicant over with a clinical eye.* **4** bare, functional, and sterile: *Grandma's kitchen was rather clinical, unlike the cozy, cluttered kitchen at home.* **clin′i·cal·ly** *adv.*

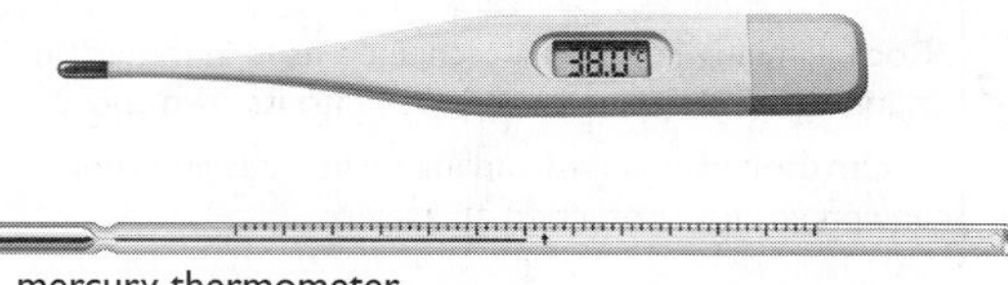

A **clinical thermometer** is sensitive to very small changes in temperature. The digital thermometers used today give a reading more quickly, store temperatures in memory—and some even talk.

clinical thermometer *n* a thermometer for measuring body temperature.

cli·ni·cian (klə nish′ən) *n* a doctor specializing in the treatment of patients rather than in medical research.

clink[1] (klingk) *n* a light, high, ringing sound like that of glasses hitting together.
v make or cause to make such a sound. <Middle English>

clink[2] (klingk) *Slang n* jail; prison: *five years in the clink.* <*Clink* St. in London, UK, site of former prison>

clip[1] (klip) *v* **clipped, clip·ping 1** cut; cut off, cut out, or cut short: *to clip your nails. I often clip newspaper articles and save them.* **2** cut or trim the hair or fleece of an animal: *Our dog gets clipped every summer.* **3 a** omit sounds in pronouncing. **b** shorten a word by leaving off syllables at the end. Such a word is called a **clipped form**. Example: *ad* for *advertisement.* **4** *Informal* hit or punch sharply. **5** *Football* illegally blocking a player on an opposing team by hitting that player with the body from behind. **6** *Slang* cheat, especially by overcharging.
n **1** the act of clipping. **2** a section of a movie or video. Also, **clipping**. **3** *Informal* (*often with* **good**) a fast pace: *moving along at a good clip.* <Old Norse *klippa*>

clip[2] (klip) *n* **1** a fastener that works by pressing things tightly together between two parts: *a paper clip, a hair clip.* **2** on some firearms, a metal holder for cartridges.
v **clipped, clip·ping** fasten with a clip: *to clip papers together.* <Old English *clyppan*>

clip art *n* pre-drawn pictures, usually stored in a computer program, that can be copied and used with no charge.

clip·board (klip′bôrd′) *n* **1** a small board with a heavy spring clip at one end for holding papers while writing. **2** *Computers* a temporary memory area, used to transfer data. The user can move data from a document to the clipboard (**cut**) and/or copy it to the clipboard (**copy**), then insert it somewhere else (**paste**).

clip–on (klip′on′) *adj* designed to be attached by means of a clip: *clip-on earrings.*
n something attached in this way, especially an earring.

clip·per (klip′ər) *n* **1** a very fast sailing ship of the mid 19th century. **2 clippers** *pl* a tool for cutting: *hedge clippers.*

clip·ping (klip′ing) *n* a piece cut from something, such as a piece cut out of a newspaper or magazine.

clique (klēk) *n* a small, tight circle of friends within a larger group, who exclude and ignore others: *Some of us complained that the student council was being run by a clique.* <French, perhaps from Old French *cliquer* click (the noise of a door being shut, to keep people out)> **cliqu′ey** *adj.* **cliqu′ish** *adj.*

clit·o·ris (klit′ə ris) *n* the erectile part of the female genitals, at the front of the vulva.

clo·a·ca (klō ā′kə) *Zoology n, pl* **clo·a·cae** (klō ā′sē) *or* (klō ā′sī) a cavity in the body of most vertebrates and some invertebrates into which the intestinal, urinary, and generative canals open.

cloak (klōk) *n* **1** a long, loose outer garment, usually without sleeves, hanging to the knees or ankles. **2** something that hides or conceals: *to act cruelly under the cloak of friendship.*
v **1** cover with a cloak: *The rider was hooded and cloaked.* **2** hide or conceal: *evil purposes cloaked by friendly words.* <Old French, from Latin *clocca* bell (because of its flared shape)>

cloak–and–dagger (klōk′ ən dag′ər) *adj* to do with or suggesting the intrigue and thrilling adventures of spies.

cloak·room (klōk′rūm′) *n* a room in a public building, such as a theatre, where coats, hats, and other belongings can be left for a time.

clob·ber (klob′ər) *Informal v* **1** hit very hard. **2** defeat severely. <origin unknown>

cloche (klōsh) *n* **1** a bell-shaped glass cover used to protect tender plants. **2** a woman's close-fitting hat popular in the 1920s and 1930s. <French = bell>

clock (klok) *n* an instrument for measuring and showing time, especially one not meant to be carried around.
v **1** measure or record the time of: *The coach clocked us to see who was the fastest runner.* **2** reach a certain speed, distance, or number, as recorded mechanically: *The racing car clocked 240 km/h.* <Dutch, from Latin *clocca* bell> **clock′er** *n.*
against the clock, under great pressure from a deadline: *working against the clock to deliver newspapers by six.*
around the clock, all day and all night.
turn (or **put**) **the clock back,** go back to an earlier time or an earlier way of doing things.

clock·mak·er (klok′mā′kər) *n* a person whose business is making or repairing clocks.

clock radio *n* a radio with a built-in clock that can be set to turn the radio on or off automatically at a certain time, for use as an alarm.

clock·wise (klok′wīz′) *adv, adj* in the direction in which the hands of a clock move: *Turn the lid clockwise to close it.*

clock·work (klok′wərk′) *n* **1** the gears, wheels, and springs that run some clocks. **2** any machinery like this, such as in a mechanical toy.
like clockwork, with great regularity or smoothness: *He stops for a bagel every morning, like clockwork. The graduation ceremony went off like clockwork.*

clod (klod) *n* **1** a lump or chunk of earth. **2** *Informal* a dull or stupid person. <Old English>

clod·hop·per (klod′hop′ər) *n* **1** a large, heavy shoe or boot. **2** *Informal* a clumsy or unsophisticated person.

clog (klog) *v* **clogged, clog·ging** block or become blocked by filling up: *Leaves clogged the drain. The drain has clogged.*
n **1** a shoe or sandal with a wooden sole. **2** something that blocks or hinders. <Middle English>

clog dance *n* a dance in which the dancer wears clogs to beat time.

cloi·son·né (kloi′zə nā′) *n* enamelware with designs made up of different colours of enamel separated by thin metal strips set into the surface.
adj enamelled in this way. <French = partitioned, from *cloison* partition>

clois·ter (kloi′stər) *n* **1** a covered walk along the outer wall of a building, with a row of pillars on the open side, often built around a courtyard: **2** a convent or monastery.
v shut away in a monastery or other secluded place. <Old French, from Latin *claustrum* closed space>
clois′tered *adj.*

clone (klōn) *n* **1** all the cells or organisms derived from a single individual by means such as cuttings or bulbs, by fission, or by the development of an unfertilized ovum. **2** an organism produced in such a way, genetically identical to the original. **3** a person who or thing that seems to be an exact copy of another: *He is a clone of his father!*
v **cloned, clon·ing** make a clone of. <Greek *klon* twig>

clop (klop) *n* a hard, hollow sound like that of a horse's hoof striking a paved road.
v **clopped, clop·ping** make this sound. <imitative>

close[1] (klōz) *v* **closed** (klōzd), **clos·ing** **1** shut: *The door closed with a bang. Close the book.* **2** fill or block: *to close a gap.* **3** end, or end something: *The day closed with a magnificent sunset. He closed the meeting with a speech.* **4** stop doing business (in): *They closed the shop and went home. That firm has closed for good.* **5** connect all the parts of an electric circuit so current will flow. **6** of a sale or other agreement, complete or be completed: *Our house closes on July 31 and we move in the next day.* **7** *Computers* take a file, application, or window out of use. **8** move in and begin to make contact during a fight.
n an end or finish: *the close of the day.* <Old French, from Latin *claudere* to shut> **clos′er** *n.*
close down, stop or cause to stop operating: *The town practically closes down whenever there's a snowstorm.*
close in (**on**), approach from all sides: *The thief gave up as the police closed in. The walls seem to be closing in on me.*
close on, start catching up to: *The other school's sprinter is closing on ours and will soon take the lead.*
close ranks, a of troops or any group fending off attack, move close together so as to leave no gaps. **b** co-operate in resisting something: *At any criticism of their dog, the family closes ranks.*
close up, a close completely or permanently. **b** heal a wound through the closing of the skin.

close[2] (klōs) *adj* **clos·er, clos·est** **1** with very little distance or time in between: *close to home, close to death.* **2** fitting tightly because there is little space between: *a close weave.* **3** intimate or dear: *a close friend.* **4** careful and strict: *Pay close attention.* **5** stifling or stuffy: *With the windows shut, the room soon became hot and close.* **6** not talkative. **7** strictly guarded: *a close secret.* **8** stingy: *She was close with her money.* **9** nearly equal or even: *a close contest.* **10** almost ending in misfortune: *That was close! I nearly missed the bus.*
adv in a close manner: *Hold me close.*
n **1** a cul-de-sac or other enclosed place. **2** the grounds around a cathedral or abbey. <Old French, from Latin *claudere* close> **close′ly** *adv.* **close′ness** *n.*
(**sail**) **close to the wind, a** with the ship pointed as nearly as possible in the direction from which the wind is blowing. **b** *Informal* just barely following rules or laws.
close up, at close range, with details clearly visible: *I've never seen a wolf close up.*

close call (klōs) *Informal n* a narrow escape from disaster: *I had a close call this morning when a car went through a red light and almost hit me.*

a bat	e bed	i bid	o pot	u cup	th **thin**
ā cake	ē me	ī bite	ō go	ū rude	ᴛʜ **then**
ä bar	ə about	ər over	ô for	ů put	zh measure

closed captioning *n* a system for hearing-impaired people that displays text with the image on a TV screen, visible only with the aid of a special device issued to users. *Abbrev.* **CC** or **cc**. **closed′-cap′tioned** *adj.*

closed–cir·cuit (klōzd′sər′kit) *adj* to do with TV broadcasting that is limited to a certain audience, such as in a school, or for security monitoring of buildings, etc.

closed shop *n* a factory or business that employs only members of a specific labour union. Compare OPEN SHOP.

close–fit·ting (klōs′fit′ing) *adj* fitting tightly.

close–knit (klōs′nit′) *adj* firmly united by affection or by shared interests: *a close-knit family.*

close–mouthed (klōs′mouTHd′) *adj* talking little.

close quarters (klōs) *n* a place or position with little space: *They were living in very close quarters.*
at close quarters, close to or at close range: *I had never seen a bear at close quarters before.*

close shave (klōs) *Informal n* a narrow escape.

clos·et (kloz′it) *n* a small room or built-in cupboard for storing clothes or household supplies: *The linen closet is next to the bathroom.*
adj doing or being a certain thing only in secret or in private: *a closet smoker.*
v shut in a room for a private talk: *The prime minister was closeted with his advisers for several hours.* <Old French *clos* closed>

close–up (klōs′up′) *n* **1** a picture taken at close range. **2** a detailed description or portrayal.

clo·sure (klō′zhər) *n* **1** the act of closing or the condition of being closed or ended. **2** a means of closing something: *The closure is broken on this jewellery box.* **3** a means of ending a debate in a legislative body in order to force an immediate vote.

clot (klot) *n* a half-solid lump or thickened mass: *A clot of blood formed in the cut and stopped the bleeding.*
v **clot·ted, clot·ting** form clots: *Milk clots when it turns sour.* <Old English *clott*>

cloth (kloth) *n, pl* **cloths** (kloTHz) *or* (kloths) **1** material made from wool, cotton, silk, linen, hair, or synthetic fibres by weaving, knitting, or rolling and pressing. **2** a piece of such material used for a special purpose: *a dusting cloth.* **3 the cloth** the Christian clergy: *a man of the cloth.* <Old English *clath*>

CONFUSABLES

Cloth is a noun meaning "a kind of fabric": *He used a cloth to dust the furniture.*

Clothe is a verb meaning "put clothes on someone": *She clothed the baby warmly.*

cloth·bound (kloth′bound′) *adj* bound as a book with a hard cover with a thin layer of fabric over it.

clothe (klōTH) *v* **clothed** or **clad, cloth·ing 1** put clothes on someone. **2** provide with clothes: *It costs a lot to clothe a family of six.* **3** cover as if with clothes: *evil intentions clothed in friendship. The sun clothes the earth with light.* **4** provide or equip: *A judge is clothed with authority by the state.* <Old English *clath*>

clothes (klōz) *or* (klōTHz) *pln* coverings for a person's body: *summer clothes. Our clothes were dirty after the hike.*

clothes·horse (klōz′hôrs′) *or* (klōTHz′hôrs′) *n* **1** a frame to hang clothes on in order to dry or air them. **2** *Informal* a person who cares much about clothing and is always fashionably dressed.

clothes·line (klōz′līn′) *or* (klōTHz′līn′) *n* a rope or wire to hang clothes on for drying or airing.

clothes·peg (klōz′peg′) *or* (klōTHz′peg′) *n* **1** a peg for hanging clothes on. **2** a clothespin.

clothes·pin (klōz′pin′) *or* (klōTHz′pin′) *n* a clip, often wooden, to hold clothes on a clothesline.

cloth·i·er (klōTH′yər) *n* a seller or maker of clothes or cloth.

cloth·ing (klō′THing) *n* clothes or a covering like clothes.

cloud (kloud) *n* **1** a white, grey, or almost black mass in the sky, made up of tiny drops of water or ice particles. See ALTOCUMULUS for picture. **2** a mass of smoke or dust or other suspended particles. **3** a great number of things close together in the air: *a cloud of mosquitoes.* **4** a blemish or spot on a polished stone or gem. **5** something that causes trouble, fear, or disgrace: *Fear of failure was a constant cloud over her.*
v **1** fill with clouds: *The sky clouded.* **2** make or become gloomy or anxious: *His face clouded as he sat thinking.* <Old English *clud*> **cloud′less** *adj.* **cloud′like′** *adj.*
have your head in the clouds, be impractical.
under a cloud, a under suspicion. **b** in gloom or trouble.

🍁 **cloud·ber·ry** (kloud′ber′ē) *n, pl* **cloud·ber·ries** **1** a berry that grows on a creeping bush in northern regions and resembles a small raspberry. **2** a bakeapple.

cloud·burst (kloud′bərst′) *n* a short, sudden, heavy rain.

cloud chamber *Physics n* an apparatus containing supersaturated vapour, for observing the movements of subatomic particles. Droplets condense on the paths left by these particles, making their movements visible.

cloud cover *n* the percentage of the sky covered by clouds when seen from a particular place: *If the cloud cover is more than 50 percent, I'm not going on the picnic.*

cloud forest *n* a forested, mountainous region, usually in the tropics, that receives much of its moisture in the form of dew condensed from the clouds that cover it most of the time.

cloud nine *n* a condition of great happiness: *She still hasn't come down from cloud nine.*

cloud seeding *n* the scattering (usually from an airplane) of particles of carbon dioxide or other chemicals in clouds to produce rain.

cloud·y (klou′dē) *adj* **cloud·i·er, cloud·i·est 1** to do with clouds: *a cloudy day. A cloudy veil of mist hid the mountaintop.* **2** as a liquid, murky or not clear: *cloudy pond water.* **3** streaked or spotted: *cloudy marble.* **4** unclear or vague: *I had a cloudy, half-formed idea, but no real plan.* **5** full of gloom, trouble, or uncertainty: *a cloudy future.* **cloud′i·ness** *n.*

clout (klout) *Informal v* hit hard: *He clouted the ball into the stands.*
n Informal **1** a hard hit. **2** power and influence: *She has a lot of clout around here.* <Old English = a blow with a sword or fist, probably from *clut* a patch of metal (i.e., something to be struck)>

clove[1] (klōv) *n* **1** (*usually in the plural*) the fragrant dried flower bud of a tropical tree, used as a spice either whole or ground. <Old French, from Latin *clavus* nail, from the shape>

clove[2] (klōv) *n* a small, separable section of a bulb of garlic or similar plant: *a clove of garlic.* <Old English *clufu*>

clove[3] (klōv) a past tense of CLEAVE[1].

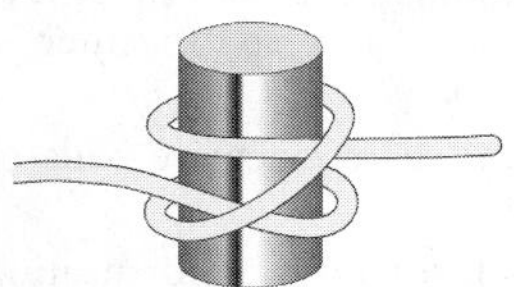

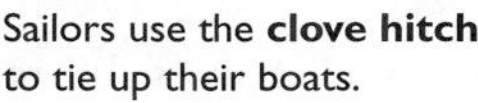

Sailors use the **clove hitch** to tie up their boats.

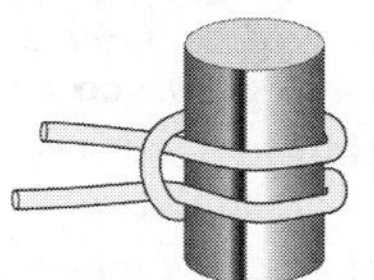

The **cow hitch** is named for its original use—tethering a cow to a pole.

clove hitch *n* a knot for tying a rope around a pole, spar, or another rope.

clo·ven (klō′vən) *v* a past participle of CLEAVE[1].
adj split or divided: *Cows and sheep have cloven hoofs.*

clo·ver (klō′vər) *n* a low-growing herb of the pea family with rounded flower heads and three leaflets, often used as fodder. <Old English *clafre*>
in clover, *Informal* enjoying a life of pleasure and luxury without work or worry.

clo·ver·leaf (klō′vər lēf′) *n* a series of access roads and ramps at an intersection of two highways, so arranged that traffic may move from one highway to the other without having to cross in front of other traffic. From above, this looks like a leaf of clover.

clown (kloun) *n* **1** a professional entertainer in a ridiculous costume whose show consists of amusing antics, tricks, and jokes. **2** a person who likes to get attention and entertains by acting silly: *the class clown.* **3** a foolish or bad-mannered person.
v act like a clown: *clowning around on the lawn.* <origin uncertain> **clown′ish** *adj.*

cloy (kloi) *v* make sick of something originally pleasant by giving or doing too much of it: *Her constant helpfulness soon begins to cloy. I was cloyed with sweets by the time the party was over.* <Old French *encloer*, from Latin *clavare* to nail (i.e. make an obstruction)>

club (klub) *n* **1** a heavy stick of wood, thick at one end, used as a weapon. **2** a specially shaped stick used in some games to hit a ball: *golf clubs.* **3** a group of people joined together for some purpose, usually recreation: *a tennis club.* **4** the building or rooms used by a club. **5 a** a playing card with one or more black ♣ designs on it. **b clubs** *pl* the suit of cards marked with this design.
v **clubbed, club·bing** beat or hit with a club. <Middle English, from Old Norse *klubba*>
club together, unite for some joint effort.
join the club! *Informal* I'm in the same situation as you.

club car *n* the former name for a railway passenger coach for day travel, more luxurious than ordinary coaches.

club·foot (klub′fu̇t′) *n, pl* **club·feet** a deformity of the foot present at birth, in which the foot is twisted and misshapen, often resembling a club. **club′foot′ed** *adj.*

club·house (klub′hous′) *n* a building used by a club.

club sandwich *n* a sandwich consisting of three layers of bread or toast with different kinds of meat in between (especially chicken and bacon), lettuce, and tomato.

club soda *n* carbonated water, often used in mixed drinks.

cluck (kluk) *n* **1** the short, guttural sound made by a hen calling her chicks. **2** a sound like this.
v make such a sound: *She clucked her disapproval.* <imitative>

clue (klü) *n* **1** a found object or piece of information that helps to solve a mystery: *Detectives look for clues.* **2** a hint given with a puzzle, riddle, etc. to help in solving it: *I'll give you a clue: he won a Juno award last year.* **3** (*with a negative*) any knowledge (about): *She hasn't a clue about talking to teenagers.*
v Informal (*usually with* ***in***) give information to: *She promised to clue me in later.*

ETYMOLOGY

Clue comes from Old English *cliewen*, meaning "ball of string." By following a trail of string unrolled from a ball, a person can find his or her way, much as a *clue* can lead a person to a destination.

clue·less (klü′lis) *Informal adj* knowing nothing: *I always feel clueless about politics.*

clump (klump) *n* **1** a tight group: *a clump of trees.* **2** a lump: *clumps of earth.* **3** the sound of heavy steps.
v **1** form a clump or clumps. **2** walk noisily and heavily. <Middle English = heap or lump>

clump·y (klump′ē) *adj* **clum·pi·er, clum·pi·est 1** to do with a clump or clumps: *The clay soil in the yard is clumpy.* **2** heavy and clumsy: *clumpy shoes.* **clum′pi·ly** *adv.* **clum′pi·ness** *n.*

clum·sy (klum′zē) *adj* **clum·si·er, clum·si·est 1** not graceful or skilful in moving, expressing oneself, or dealing with others: *The clumsy boy bumped into the kitchen table. That was a clumsy apology.* **2** not well-made or well-shaped: *The rowboat was a clumsy thing, made of old boxes.* <obsolete *clumse* numb with cold (and therefore awkward)> **clum′si·ly** *adv.* **clum′si·ness** *n.*

clung (klung) past tense and past participle of CLING.

clunk (klungk) *n* a dull sound like that of something hard hitting the ground.
v move or fall with such a sound: *Something clunked on the floor above.* <imitative>

a bat	e bed	i bid	o pot	u cup	th **thin**
ā cake	ē me	ī bite	ō go	ü rude	ᴛʜ **then**
ä bar	ə about	ər over	ȯ for	u̇ put	zh measure

C

clunk·y (klungk′ē) *Informal adj* **clunk·i·er, clunk·i·est** 1 making a dull, heavy sound: *clunky footsteps.* 2 bulky and heavy: *clunky shoes.* 3 dull, unsophisticated, or badly created: *a clunky movie.*

clus·ter (klus′tər) *n* a number of things of one kind, forming a small, closely set group: *a cluster of grapes. There was a little cluster of houses in the valley.*
v gather or be gathered into a cluster: *The data clustered around the average value.* <Old English *clyster*>

clutch[1] (kluch) *v* grasp tightly: *She clutched her doll.*
n **1** a tight grasp. **2 a** a mechanism for connecting and disconnecting the engine of a manual-drive motor vehicle from the transmission system. **b** the lever or pedal that operates such a device. **3 clutches** *pl* the control or power of a hostile person or thing: *in the clutches of drug addiction.* <Old English *clyccan* clench>
clutch at, try eagerly to grab or hold: *She clutched at the branch, but missed it and fell.*

clutch[2] (kluch) *n* **1** a nest of eggs. **2** a brood of chicks. <Old Norse *klekja* to hatch>

clutch purse *n* a purse without a handle or shoulder strap, meant to be carried under the arm.

clut·ter (klut′ər) *n* a lot of separate items, usually unnecessary, filling up space: *Get this clutter out of the hall.*
v fill or cover with a lot of unnecessary things: *Her desk was cluttered with books and papers. I find this flowered wallpaper too cluttered.* <Middle English, from dialect *clotter* to clot> **clut′tered** *adj.*

Clydes·dale (klīdz′dāl′) *n* a large, strong breed of horse.

cm centimetre(s). The symbol for cubic centimetres is **cm**^{3}.

🍁 **CN** Canadian National Railways, formerly abbreviated to **CNR**.

🍁 **CNE** Canadian National Exhibition, informally called **the Ex**, held in Toronto at the end of summer.

c/o in care of. (*used in addresses*)

co– *prefix* **1** with or together: *co-operate.* **2** joint: *co-author.* **3** equally: *co-extensive.* <Latin *com-* with; together; completely>

CO or **C.O.** Commanding Officer.

coach (kōch) *n* **1** in former times, a large, closed, horse-drawn carriage, driven by a **coachman**. **2** a passenger car of a railway train, with adjustable seats but no sleeping accommodation. **3** a bus, especially a tour bus or one that travels between cities. **4** a cheap class of air or rail travel. **5 a** a person who trains or instructs athletes or sports teams: *a hockey coach.* **b** a private instructor, especially one who prepares another for specific events such as an exam or concert.
v **1 a** be a coach for an athlete or sports team: *Who is coaching basketball next year?* **b** be a private instructor: *to coach mathematics.* **2** give or prompt with instructions: *His mother coached him in how to greet the prime minister.* <French, from Hungarian *Kocs*, town where coaches were made. In the sense *teach*, probably from the idea of an instructor carrying her or his students.>

co·ag·u·late (kō ag′yə lāt′) *v* **co·ag·u·lat·ed, co·ag·u·lat·ing** change from liquid form into a thickened mass: *Cooking coagulates the white of an egg. Blood coagulates in air.* <Latin *colagulum* rennet>
co·ag′u·lant *n.* **co·ag′u·la′tion** *n.*

coal (kōl) *n* **1** a hard, black substance containing carbon, formed in the earth over millions of years from the decomposition of plant matter, and used as a fuel. **2** a piece of burning or charred coal or wood. <Old English *col*>
rake over the coals, scold or question severely.

co·a·lesce (kō′ə les′) *v* **co·a·lesced, co·a·lesc·ing** **1** grow together from separate parts into a single mass. **2** unite into one body, group, etc.; combine: *Two political parties coalesced to form a new party.* <Latin *co-* together + *alescere* grow> **co′a·les′cence** *n.*

coal·field (kōl′fēld′) *n* a region where extensive beds of coal are found.

coal gas *n* a mixture of gases formerly used for heating and lighting, made by distilling coal.

co·a·li·tion (kō′ə lish′ən) *n* **1** a combination of different groups or parts into one. **2** *Politics* a formal agreement between parties to work together for a certain period or a special purpose, such as when no party has a sufficient majority to govern without the support of another party. <Latin *co-* together + *alescere* grow>

coam·ing (kō′ming) *n* the raised edge around a hatch or opening in a ship's or yacht's deck to keep water from running down below. <origin uncertain>

coarse (kòrs) *adj* **coars·er, coars·est** **1** heavy and rough in appearance or texture, or made up of fairly large parts: *coarse sand.* **2** rough, crude, or vulgar: *coarse manners, coarse language.* <origin uncertain> **coarse′ly** *adv.* **coars′en** *v.* **coarse′ness** *n.*

CONFUSABLES

Coarse describes something that or someone who is rough: *a coarse fabric, a coarse character.*

Course has many meanings, none of which have to do with roughness: *a golf course, a ship's course.*

coarse–grained (kòrs′grānd′) *adj* **1** with a coarse texture or grain: *coarse-grained wood.* **2** crude in manner or speech.

coast (kōst) *n* **1** the part of the land at the edge of a sea or ocean. **2** an act of moving without the use of power.
v **1** ride or slide down a hill without using power, as on a toboggan. **2** allow a vehicle or boat to continue to move without using power: *He cut the engine and the car coasted into the garage.* <Old French, from Latin *costa* side> **coast′al** *adj.*
the coast is clear, the danger is gone; one may proceed.

coast·er (kō′stər) *n* **1** a little mat to put a glass or bottle on so as not to stain the surface of a table. **2** a roller coaster. **3** a person who or thing that coasts.

coast guard *n* **1** 🍁 a government agency that does search-and-rescue operations at sea, establishes and maintains lighthouses and other navigation aids, and breaks ice and moves cargo in the North. **2** a coastal patrol and police force, often part of a country's armed forces, whose work is preventing smuggling and protecting lives and property along the coast, or a member of such a patrol.

coast·line (kōst′līn′) *n* the contour of a coast: *the rugged coastline of Labrador.*

Coast Salish *n* **1** informal name covering a number of First Nations peoples living in southwest British Columbia and Vancouver Island. **2** their Salishan language.
adj to do with these peoples or their language.

coat (kōt) *n* **1** an outer garment, usually fairly heavy, of cloth, fur, or leather, with sleeves. **2** an animal's covering of fur or hair: *a leopard's spotted coat.* **3** a layer, especially one of two or more, covering a surface: *a coat of paint.*
v cover with a layer: *coated with dust.* <Old French *cote*> **coat′less** *adj.*

coat check *n* a room where one can leave one's coat and other things with an attendant and pick them up later.

coat hanger *n* a specially shaped piece of strong wire, plastic, or wood on which to hang clothes. It has a hook at the top for hanging on a rod.

co·a·ti (kō ȧ′tē) *n* in full, **coatimundi** (kō ȧ′tə mu̇n′dē) a small mammal of Central and South America that resembles a raccoon. <Tupi (a language of S America) *cua* belt + *tim* nose>

coat·ing (kō′ting) *n* a layer covering a surface: *a coating of slime.*

coat of arms *n, pl* **coats of arms** an arrangement, usually in the shape of a shield, of symbols or designs showing the marks of distinction of a particular family or city and adopted as its emblem.

coat·tail (kōt′tāl′) *n* the back part of a coat below the waist, or one of a pair of flaps on this part of a coat.
ride on someone's coattails, get ahead by associating with a more successful or more popular person.

co–au·thor (kō oth′ər) *n* a person who shares the job of writing a book, article, etc. **co-auth′or** *v.* **co-auth′or·ship′** *n.*

coax (kōks) *v* **1** persuade by soft, reassuring words: *She coaxed her father to let her go to the party.* **2** get by coaxing: *We coaxed a smile from the baby.* **3** get anything from a source by careful, persistent effort: *I was finally able to coax a few notes from my new flute.* <origin unknown> **coax′ing·ly** *adv.*

coaxial cable

A twisted-pair cable is used to connect a telephone to the local telephone carrier.

A fibre-optic cable transmits data rapidly along very thin fibres of glass using pulses of light.

coax·i·al cable (kō ak′sē əl) *n* a cable containing two or more insulated conductors, one wrapped around another, for transmitting computer, telephone, and TV signals.

cob (kob) *n* **1** a corncob. **2** a strong horse with short legs, often used for riding. **3** a male swan. <Middle English>

co·balt (kō′bolt) *n* a silver-white metallic element used especially in alloys and for making pigments. A radioactive form of cobalt is a source of gamma rays used in medicine for radiation therapy. *Symbol* **Co**
adj in full, **cobalt blue** a bright blue. <German *Kobalt* goblin. In ancient times, it was thought that goblins stole silver and left cobalt behind.>

C

cob·ble[1] (kob′əl) *v* **cob·bled, cob·bling** **1** mend footwear. **2** put together clumsily. <origin unknown>

cob·ble[2] (kob′əl) *n* a cobblestone.
v **cob·bled, cob·bling** pave with cobblestones. <Middle English *cobel*>

cob·bler (kob′lər) *n* **1** a fruit pie baked in a deep dish, usually with a crust on top only: *peach cobbler.* **2** an iced drink made of wine and fruit juice. **3** a person who makes and mends shoes. <origin unknown>

cob·ble·stone (kob′əl stōn′) *n* a deep, rounded stone formerly much used in paving.

co–bel·lig·er·ent (kō′ bə lij′ə rənt) *n* a nation that helps another nation carry on a war.

CO·BOL (kō′bol) *n* in full, **Common Business Oriented Language** a computer language.

The **cobra's** venom destroys the victim's nervous system. The venom is used in medical research because it dissolves cell walls and even the membranes that enclose a virus.

co·bra (kō′brə) *n* a poisonous snake of Asia and Africa that spreads its upper ribs when excited, causing the skin just below the head to expand into a hoodlike form. <Portuguese, from Latin *colubra* snake>

cob·web (kob′web′) *n* **1** a spider's web, especially when it has gathered dust. <Middle English, from obsolete *coppe* spider + *web*> **cob′web′by** *adj.*
blow away the cobwebs, get rid of a feeling of dullness or drowsiness: *A fast walk will blow away the cobwebs.*

co·ca (kō′kə) *n* the dried leaves of a small tropical shrub of S America that are a source of cocaine and other alkaloids. <Spanish, from Quechua (a language of S America) *koka*>

co·caine (kō kān′) *n* an addictive drug prepared from coca and used to deaden pain and as an illegal stimulant. <*coca*>

a bat	e bed	i bid	o pot	u cup	th **thin**
ā cake	ē me	ī bite	ō go	ū rude	ᴛʜ **then**
ȧ bar	ə about	ər over	ȯ for	u̇ put	zh measure

coc·cus (kok′əs) *n, pl* **coc·ci** (kok′sī) *or* (kok′sē) **1** a ball-shaped bacterium. **2** a seed in the compound pistil of such plants as the carrot, which breaks away when the fruit is mature. <Latin, from Greek *kokkos* berry>

coc·cyx (kok′siks) *n, pl* **coc·cy·ges** (kok sī′jēz) a small triangular bone at the bottom of the spinal column. <Latin, from Greek *kokkyx* cuckoo (being shaped like a cuckoo's beak)>

coch·i·neal (koch′ə nēl′) *or* (koch′ə nēl′) *n* a bright red dye originally made from the dried body of the **cochineal insect** of tropical America. <Spanish *cochinilla* red, from Greek *kokkos* berry>

coch·le·a (kok′lē ə) *n, pl* **coch·le·ae** (kok′lē ē′) *or* (kok′lē ī′) a spiral-shaped cavity of the inner ear, containing the sensory ends of the auditory nerve. <Latin, from Greek *kochlias* snail>

cock[1] (kok) *n* **1 a** an adult male chicken. **b** the adult male of other birds, especially game birds. **2** a tap used to turn the flow of a liquid or gas on or off. **3** the hammer of a gun or rifle.
v **1** tilt the head in a particular direction: *She cocked her head to get a better view out the window.* **2** pull back the hammer of a gun or rifle. <Old English *cocc*>
cock of the walk, the person believing himself or herself to be in charge.

cock[2] (kok) *n* a small pile of hay, rounded on top.
v make such piles. <Middle English>

cock·ade (kok ād′) *n* a knot of ribbon or a rosette worn on the hat. <French *cocarde*>

cock·a·ma·mie (kok′ə mā′mē) *adj* ridiculously fake: *a cockamamie story.* <probably *decalcomania* the process of applying (cheap) decals to china, glass, etc.>

cock·a·tiel (kok′ə tēl′) *n* a small Australian parrot with a crest and a long tail. <Dutch *kaketielje*>

cock·a·too (kok′ə tū′) *n* a large parrot of Australia and southeast Asia, with mainly white plumage and a crest on the head. See MACAW for picture. <Dutch *kaketoe*, from Malay *kakatua*>

cock·a·trice (kok′ə tris) *n* a mythical creature, half snake and half cock, whose look was supposed to cause death. <Old French, from Latin *calcatrix* trampler>

cock·chaf·er (kok′chā′fər) *n* a large European beetle whose larvae feed on the roots of plants. The adult feeds on the green parts. <Old English>

cocker spaniel *n* a breed of small dog with long, silky hair and drooping ears. <*cocking* = hunting woodcock (a small game bird)>

cock·eyed (kok′īd′) *adj* **1** tilted or off-balance. **2** foolish or silly.

cock·fight (kok′fīt′) *n* a fight between roosters. **Cockfighting** is sometimes conducted as a sport, but is illegal in Canada and some other countries.

cock·le (kok′əl) *n* a saltwater clam whose heart-shaped shell has ridges radiating out from the hinge. <Old French, from Greek *konche* conch>
warm the cockles of your heart, (*usually humorous*) make you feel glad or encouraged.

Cock·ney (kok′nē) *n* a native or inhabitant of the East End of London, England, or the accent or dialect spoken by this person.
adj to do with Cockneys or their accent or dialect. <Middle English>

cock·pit (kok′pit′) *n* **1** the compartment where the pilot sits in an aircraft. **2** a similar place for the driver of a racing car, or at the helm of a small yacht. **3** an enclosed place for cockfights.

The **cockroach** is a cursorial insect, which means that its legs aren't useful for digging or grasping, but are ideal for running. The cockroach's ability to scurry from danger makes it hard to eliminate.

The *termite* does not move quickly, but is a major pest because its mouth has developed to allow it to eat wood. Over time, termites can bring a wooden structure tumbling to the ground.

cock·roach (kok′rōch′) *n* an insect with long feelers and a long, flat, shiny body. It scavenges for food. <Spanish *cucaracha*>

cocks·comb (koks′kōm′) *n* the fleshy, red crest on the head of a rooster.

cock·sure (kok′shůr′) *adj* annoyingly overconfident. **cock′sure′ness** *n.*

cock·tail (kok′tāl′) *n* **1** a mixed alcoholic drink, often with juice in it and a garnish of some sort. **2** any of various appetizers served in a glass: *shrimp cocktail.* **3** mixed diced fruits. **4** a mixture of juices, chemicals, or drugs.
adj **1** to do with the serving and drinking of cocktails: *a cocktail party.* **2** semiformal in clothing: *a cocktail dress.*

cock·y (kok′ē) *Informal adj* **cock·i·er, cock·i·est** conceited: *a cocky fellow.* **cock′i·ly** *adv.* **cock′i·ness** *n.*

co·co (kō′kō) *n* the fibres of coconut husks, used for weaving: *coco mats.*

co·coa (kō′kō) *n* **1** a reddish brown powder made from CHOCOLATE by pressing out most of the fat. It is used in baking and for making drinks. **2** a hot drink made from this, with milk or water and sugar.
adj medium reddish brown. <alteration of *cacao*>

cocoa bean *n* the seed of the CACAO. Also, **cacao bean.**

cocoa butter *n* a fatty substance obtained from CHOCOLATE, used in soap, cosmetics, and candy.

co·co·nut (kō′kə nut′) *n* the large, roundish fruit of the **coconut palm** tree, with edible white meat within a hard brown shell.

coconut milk *n* a sweet, whitish liquid found in the hollow centre of an unripe coconut.

co·coon (kə kün′) *n* **1** a covering prepared by the larva of many kinds of insect, including the ant and the moth, to protect itself while it is changing into an adult. **2** a cozy place that protects and isolates.
v **1** wrap or enclose in a cocoon or cocoonlike thing: *We lay cocooned in our sleeping bags.* **2** protect and isolate. **3** engage in cocooning. <French, from Provençal *coca* shell>

co·coon·ing (kə kün′ing) *n* the practice of staying at home in comfortable, familiar surroundings instead of going out to seek social life, dining, or entertainment. **co·coon′er** *n.*

cod (kod) *n, pl* **cod** **1** a food fish of the colder parts of the N Atlantic, with a barbel on the chin and a square tail. Also, **codfish**. See BARBEL for picture. **2** a family of fishes found in cold and temperate waters that includes cod, haddock, and pollock. <Middle English>

C.O.D. or **c.o.d.** cash (or collect) on delivery.

co·da (kō′də) *Music n* a separate passage at the end of a movement or composition, designed to bring it to a close. <Italian, from Latin *cauda* tail>

🍁 **cod·der** (kod′ər) *Atlantic Provinces n* **1** a boat used for cod fishing. **2** a cod fisherman.

cod·dle (kod′əl) *v* **cod·dled, cod·dling** pamper or indulge: *He has always been coddled and doesn't know how to look after himself.* <origin uncertain>

code (kōd) *n* **1** a system of secret writing. **2** a special alternative vocabulary; a code word: *"Maybe later" is code for "no."* **3** a system of signals for sending messages: *Morse code.* **4** *Computers* the set of instructions forming a program, written in a programming language. **5** a collection of laws: *Canada's criminal code.* **6** a set of rules: *a dress code.*
v **cod·ed, cod·ing** write or express in code. <Old French, from Latin *codex*>

co·deine (kō′dēn) *n* a white crystalline drug obtained from opium, used to relieve pain and cause sleep. <Greek *kodeia* poppy head>

co–de·pen·dent (kō′di pen′dənt) *adj* finding security in being with or serving another person, with an unhealthy loss of one's own interests and initiative.
n a co-dependent person. **co′-de·pen′den·cy** *n.*

code word *n* a word used to make something seem more acceptable, or to have a secret meaning known only to some people: *"Facilities" is a code word for "washroom." "Cobwebs" was the spies' code word for "microphones."*

co·dex (kō′deks) *n, pl* **co·di·ces** (kō′də sēz′) *or* (kod′ə sēz′) a manuscript or volume of manuscripts. <Latin = block of wood, split into tablets for writing on>

cod·fish (kod′fish′) COD (def. 1).
codfish cakes, a fried patty of cod or a mixture of cod and mashed potato.

codg·er (koj′ər) *Informal n* a peculiar, usually older person. <origin uncertain>

co·di·ces (kō′də sēz′) *or* (kod′ə sēz′) plural of CODEX.

cod·i·cil (kod′ə sil′) *or* (kod′ə səl) *n* something added to a will to change it, add to it, or explain it. <Latin *codicullus*, diminutive of *codex*>

cod·i·fy (kō′də fī′) *or* (kod′ə fī′) *v* **cod·i·fied, cod·i·fy·ing** arrange laws or a set of principles according to a system: *French law was codified between 1804 and 1810 by order of Napoleon I.* <from *code*> **cod′i·fi·ca′tion** *n.*

cod·ling moth (kod′ling) *n* a small moth whose larva feeds on fruit, especially apples. <Middle English>

cod–liv·er oil (kod′liv′ər) *n* the oil extracted from the liver of cod, used as a source of vitamins A and D.

co–ed or **co·ed** (kō′ed′) *n* especially in former times, a female college or university student.
adj co-educational. <*co-ed*(*ucation*)>

co–ed·u·ca·tion (kō′ej ə kā′shən) *n* the education of male and female students together in the same school or classes. **co′-ed·u·ca′tion·al** *adj.*

co·ef·fi·cient (kō′ə fish′ənt) *Mathematics n* a number or symbol put before and multiplying an unknown quantity. In the expression $3x$, 3 is the coefficient of x, and in the expression ax, a is the coefficient of x.

coe·la·canth (sē′lə kanth′) *n* a fish considered extinct until 1938, when a live specimen was caught. <Greek *koilos* hollow + *akantha* spine>

coe·len·ter·ate (si len′tə rāt′) *n* an aquatic invertebrate with a saclike body. Jellyfish and coral are coelenterates.
adj belonging to this division of invertebrates. <Latin, from Greek *koilos* hollow + *enteron* intestine>

co·erce (kō ərs′) *v* **co·erced, co·erc·ing** force by physical means or by unfair pressure or manipulation: *That confession was coerced and should not be trusted. They coerced him into signing the contract.* <Latin *co-* together + *arcere* restrain> **co·er′cion** *n.* **co·er′cive** *adj.*

co–ex·ist (kō′eg zist′) *v* exist together: *Fruit and flowers co-exist on an orange tree. Many different cultures co-exist in Canada.* **co′-ex·ist′ence** *n.* **co′-ex·ist′ent** *adj.*

co–ex·ten·sive (kō′ek sten′siv) *adj* covering the same space or time.

cof·fee (kof′ē) *n* **1** a drink or flavouring made from the roasted, ground beans of a tropical evergreen shrub. **2** the beans of this shrub, especially when roasted and ground: *a bag containing a kilo of coffee.* <Turkish *kahveh*, from Arabic *kahwa*>

coffee break *n* a brief rest from work, with coffee or other refreshments.

coffee cake *n* **1** a cake made of sweetened bread dough, usually with a glaze, nuts, raisins, and cinnamon. **2** a cake flavoured with coffee.

coffee house *n* a small, informal restaurant serving coffee and other refreshments, often with live entertainment: *She got her start as a musician by playing in coffee houses.*

coffee pot *n* a covered container for making or serving coffee.

a bat	e bed	i bid	o pot	u cup	th **thin**
ā cake	ē me	ī bite	ō go	ü rude	ᴛʜ **then**
ä bar	ə about	ər over	ô for	ů put	zh measure

coffee shop *n* a small, informal restaurant where coffee and other light refreshments are served.

coffee table *n* a low table, usually placed in front of a chesterfield, for serving refreshments and displaying ornaments or books.

cof·fee–ta·ble book (kof′ē tāb′əl) *n* a large book with many glossy pictures and not much text, meant for display or browsing.

cof·fer (kof′ər) *n* **1** a box or chest, especially one for money or other valuables. **2 coffers** *pl* funds or financial resources: *The ski trip has almost exhausted the school coffers.* **3** a sunken ornamental panel in a ceiling. <Old French *cofre,* from Greek *kophinos* basket>

cof·fer·dam (kof′ər dam′) *n* a watertight enclosure built in a shallow river or lake and pumped dry so that a bridge may be built or construction work done.

cof·fin (kof′ən) *n* a box in which the body of a dead person is put to be buried. <Old French *cofin,* from Greek *kophinos* basket>

cog (kog) *n* **1** one of the teeth on the edge of a **cogwheel**. These teeth fit into another cogwheel, so that one can cause the other to turn. **2** a person who plays a small but necessary part in a large, complex organization. <Middle English *cogge*> **cogged** *adj.* **cog′like** *adj.*

co·gen·e·ra·tion (kō jen′ə rā′shən) *n* a process in which an industry uses its waste energy to produce heat or electricity,

co·gent (kō′jənt) *adj* forceful and convincing in reasoning: *a cogent argument.* <French = essential, from Latin *co-* together + *agere* act> **co′gen·cy** *n.* **co′gent·ly** *adv.*

cog·i·tate (koj′ə tāt′) *v* **cog·i·tat·ed, cog·i·tat·ing** think carefully and deeply. <Latin *co-* together + *agitare* consider> **cog′i·ta′tion** *n.*

SYNONYMS

Cogitate is a formal word that means "reflect seriously": *Every day, the scientist would cogitate on how to improve his research.*

Contemplate means "think for a long time": *He will contemplate his future education over the summer.*

Ponder means "consider carefully": *She pondered the math problem.*

co·gnac (kon′yak) *or* (kō′nyak) *n* a fine brandy originally made in France. <*Cognac,* town and region in France>

cog·nate (kog′nāt) *adj* **1** related by family or origin and hence similar. **2** with a common source of language: *Dutch and German are cognate languages.*
n a person, word, or thing related to another by having a common source: *German "Wasser" and English "water" are cognates.* <Latin *co-* together + *natus* born>

cog·ni·tive (kog′nə tiv) *adj* to do with **cognition**, the mental process of receiving and using knowledge through thought, experience, and the senses. <Latin *co-* together + *gnoscere* know> **cog′ni·tive·ly** *adv.*

cognitive science *n* the study of thought and learning, which uses some aspects of psychology, philosophy, linguistics, and computer science.

cog·ni·zant (kog′nə zənt) *adj* aware: *The general was cognizant of the enemy's movements.* **cog′ni·zance** *n.*

co·hab·it (kō hab′it) *v* **1** live together, especially in a sexual relationship, without being legally married. **2** share the same habitat: *Many species cohabit the earth.* <Latin *co-* together + *habitare* dwell> **co·hab′i·ta′tion** *n.*

co·here (kō hēr′) *v* **co·hered, co·her·ing 1** hold together as a unit or mass: *That paragraph does not cohere well. Sand coheres better when wet.* **2** be logically consistent in an argument. <Latin *co-* + *haerere* to stick>

co·her·ent (kō hē′rənt) *adj* consistent in structure and thought and hence able to be understood: *His report was not very coherent because he was so excited.*
co·her′ence *n.* **co·her′ent·ly** *adv.*

co·he·sion (kō hē′zhən) *n* **1** the fact or quality of holding together as a unit or mass: *Shared experiences add to a family's cohesion. Beaten egg improves the cohesion of meatballs.* **2** *Physics* an attraction between molecules of the same kind. Compare ADHESION (def. 2).
co·he′sive (kō hē′siv) *adj.* **co·he′sive·ness** *n.*

co·ho (kō′hō) *n, pl* **co·hoes** or (*especially collectively*) **co·ho** in full, **coho salmon** a species of Pacific salmon found along the coast from southern California to Alaska. <origin uncertain>

co·hort (kō′hȯrt) *n* **1** in the army of ancient Rome, a group of 300 to 600 soldiers, one-tenth of a legion. **2** a group moving or working together. **3** *Informal* a companion or associate. **4** *Statistics* an age group or similarly well-defined group. <Old French, from Latin *cohors* company of soldiers>

co–host (kō′hōst′) *n* one of two or more people who present or sponsor an event together.
v be a co-host: *She co-hosts the morning newscast.*

coif (kwȧf) *v* arrange or dress the hair. <Old French, from Latin *cofia* helmet>

coif·fure (kwȧ fyūr′) *n* the art or a particular style of arranging the hair. <French; see COIF.>

coil (koil) *v* **1** wind around and around in a series of circles so as to form a spiral or tube: *The sailor coiled the rope so it would take up less space. A spring is a coiled piece of wire.* **2** move in a winding or twisting course: *The river coils through the jungle.*
n **1** one of a series of connected circles forming a spiral or tube, or a series of such circles: *the coils of a phone cord.* **2** a series of connecting pipes arranged somewhat like a coil, as in a hot-water radiator. **3** *Electricity* a spiral of wire used to induce a current, charge, or magnetic change. <Old French, from Latin *com-* together + *legere* collect>

coin (koin) *n* **1** a piece of metal stamped by a government for use as money. **2** metal money: *to mint coin from silver.*
v **1** manufacture money by stamping metal. **2** invent a word or phrase: *The word "chortle" was coined by Lewis Carroll.* <Old French = a wedge-shaped stamping die, from Latin *cuneus* wedge> **coin′age** *n.*
the other side of the coin, the opposite or contrasting aspect of something: *Linen clothes feel cool, but the other side of the coin is they wrinkle easily.*

C

co·in·cide (kō′in sīd′) *v* **co·in·cid·ed, co·in·cid·ing** **1** occupy the same space: *If these triangles* ∆ ∆ ∆ ∆ *were placed one on top of the other, they would coincide exactly.* **2** occur at the same time, often by chance: *My study periods coincide with hers.* **3** correspond exactly: *Our opinions coincide.* <Latin *co-* together + *incidere* happen> **co·in′ci·dent** *adj.*

co·in·ci·dence (kō in′sə dəns) *n* **1** the chance occurrence of two things happening together: *My friend and I were born on the very same day. Isn't that a coincidence?* **2** the fact of coinciding. **co·in′ci·den′tal** *adj.*

co·i·tus (kō′i təs), (koi′təs) *or* (kō ī′təs) *n* sexual intercourse. <Latin *coire* go together>

coke[1] (kōk) *n* a fuel made from coal by heating it in a closed oven until gases have been removed. <Middle English>

coke[2] (kōk) *Slang n* cocaine.

col (kol) *n* a gap or low place in a mountain range, usually providing a pass through the range. <French, from Latin *collum* neck>

col– *prefix* together or altogether; a form of the prefix COM- occurring before the letter *l*: *collinear.*

co·la (kō′lə) *n* a carbonated soft drink flavoured with kola nuts, the fruit of a tree related to the cacao. <*Coca-Cola,* a trademark>

col·an·der (kol′ən dər) *n* a bowl with many small holes in it for draining foods. <Latin *colare* to strain>

cold (kōld) *adj* **1** much less warm than one's body: *Snow and ice are cold.* **2** not as warm as usual, or as desired: *This coffee is cold.* **3** indifferent or unresponsive: *The audience seemed rather cold.* **4** not influenced by emotion: *cold logic.* **5** no longer fresh or easy to follow as a scent or trail. **6** not primed or prepared by previous activity or interaction: *a cold engine.* **7** feeling uncomfortable from lack of warmth: *If you're cold, we can go inside.*
n **1** the lack of heat or warmth: *sensitive to cold.* **2** a common viral infection that produces a stuffy or runny nose and, often, a cough or sore throat. <Old English *cald*> **cold′ly** *adv.* **cold′ness** *n.*
break out in a cold sweat, sweat from fear or shock.
catch (or **take**) **cold,** become sick with a cold.
cold comfort, something that might be expected to cheer you up, but does not: *She got a refund, but that was cold comfort when she had been looking forward to going to the concert.*
cold feet, sudden loss of one's nerve or courage: *He suddenly got cold feet and refused to go on stage.*
leave someone cold, be completely unappealing to someone: *I'm afraid jazz leaves me cold.*
out cold, unconscious.
(**out**) **in the cold,** alone, neglected, or ignored.
throw (or **pour**) **cold water on,** actively discourage or belittle: *She was always throwing cold water on his ideas.*

cold–blood·ed (kōld′blud′id) *adj* **1** with blood whose temperature varies with that of the surroundings: *Unlike mammals and birds, reptiles are cold-blooded.* Compare WARM-BLOODED. **2** without pity or remorse: *deliberate, cold-blooded murder.* Compare HOT-BLOODED. **cold′-blood′ed·ly** *adv.* **cold′-blood′ed·ness** *n.*

cold cash *n* ready money in coins and bills. Also, **cold hard cash.**

cold chisel *n* a strong steel chisel for cutting cold metal.

cold cream *n* a creamy, oil-based ointment for cleansing and softening the skin.

cold cuts *pl n* cooked, smoked, or otherwise prepared meats, sliced and served cold.

cold front *Meteorology n* the front edge of a cold air mass advancing into and replacing a warm one. See WARM FRONT for picture.

cold fusion *Physics n* a hypothetical form of nuclear fusion without the use of extreme temperatures or pressure.

cold hard cash COLD CASH.

cold–heart·ed (kōld′hȧr′tid) *adj* insensitive or unkind. **cold′-heart′ed·ly** *adv.* **cold′-heart′ed·ness** *n.*

cold light *n* light with little or no heat, such as phosphorescence and fluorescence.

cold shoulder *n* deliberately unfriendly or indifferent treatment: *to get the cold shoulder.* **cold′-shoul′der** *v.*

ETYMOLOGY

Although it is commonly thought that **cold shoulder** originally referred to *mutton* (meat from sheep), it probably did not. Sir Walter Scott used the term in novels he wrote in 1816 and 1824. In the first novel, a countess *showed the cold shoulder* to someone she disliked. Within a decade or two, it became a popular term in Britain.

cold snap *n* a sudden spell of cold weather.

cold sore *n* a sore on or near the lips, caused by a virus and consisting of a group of small blisters.

cold storage *n* storage at low temperature, to keep perishable goods from spoiling.

cold turkey *Slang n* sudden, total withdrawal from something to which one is addicted: *She said the only way she could quit smoking was cold turkey.*
adv using this method: *to quit cold turkey.* <origin uncertain; perhaps from the goose bumps, which look like turkey skin, experienced by addicts in withdrawal>

cold war *n* a prolonged campaign of hostility between nations that stops short of open warfare, especially the **Cold War** between the Soviet bloc and the Western powers after World War II, which ended about 1990. Compare HOT WAR.

cole·slaw (kōl′slo′) *n* a salad made of shredded raw cabbage. <Dutch *kool* cabbage + *salade* salad>

col·ic (kol′ik) *n* a condition involving painful and fluctuating spasms in the stomach, often affecting young babies. <Latin, from Greek *kolon* colon> **col′ick·y** *adj.*

a bat	e bed	i bid	o pot	u cup	th thin
ā cake	ē me	ī bite	ō go	ū rude	ᴛʜ then
ȧ bar	ə about	ər over	ȯ for	u̇ put	zh measure

col·i·se·um (kol′ə sē′əm) *n* **1** a large building or stadium for games and other events. **2 Coliseum** COLOSSEUM. <Latin, from Greek *colossus* huge statue>

co·li·tis (kə lī′tis) *n* inflammation of the lining of the colon, causing severe pain in the abdomen.

col·lab·o·rate (kə lab′ə rāt′) *v* **col·lab·o·rat·ed, col·lab·o·rat·ing** **1** work together: *to collaborate on a book.* **2** co-operate traitorously: *to collaborate with the enemy.* <Latin *com-* together + *laborare* to work> **col·lab′o·ra′tion** *n.* **col·lab′o·ra′tive** *adj.* **col·lab′o·ra′tor** *n.*

col·lage (kə läzh′) *n* an artistic arrangement of items of different textures, colours, and shapes attached or glued to a background. <French, from Greek *kolla* glue>

col·la·gen (kol′ə jən) *n* fibrous protein found in connective tissue such as skin, bone, or cartilage. <French, from Greek *kolla* glue>

col·lapse (kə laps′) *v* **col·lapsed, col·laps·ing** **1** fall down as a result of outside pressure or loss of support: *They escaped from the burning building just before it collapsed.* **2** fail suddenly: *Both his health and his business collapsed within a year.* **3** fold or slide parts together into a smaller format: *You can collapse this telescope to just 10 cm.*
n the fact of collapsing: *a mental collapse. A heavy flood caused the collapse of the bridge.* <Latin *com-* together + *labi* to slip> **col·laps′i·ble** *adj.*

col·lar (kol′ər) *n* **1** a band of cloth attached to the neckline of a garment, designed to stand up around the neck or lie flat over the shoulders. **2** a wide piece of jewellery worn around the neck or over the chest and shoulders. **3** a band for the neck of a dog or other pet animal. **4** a distinctive marking around the neck of an animal or bird. **5** a ring, disc, or flange around the end of a pipe or shaft.
v **1** put a collar on. **2** *Informal* seize or arrest. <Old French, from Latin *collum* neck> **col′lar·less** *adj.* **col′lar·like′** *adj.*

col·lar·bone (kol′ər bōn′) *n* the bone connecting the breastbone and the shoulder blade.

col·late (kō′lāt) *or* (kə lāt′) *v* **col·lat·ed, col·lat·ing** **1** assemble and compare data from different sources. **2** arrange pages or other items in proper order. <Latin *com-* together + *ferre* bring> **col·la′tion** *n.*

col·lat·er·al (kə lat′ə rəl) *adj* **1** descended in a family from the same stock but by a different line: *My cousins are collateral descendants of my mother.* **2** related but additional and less important: *The car was badly scratched, and there was collateral scratching on the garage door.* **3** side by side: *a pair of collateral parallel lines.* **4** secured by assets pledged against it: *a collateral loan.*
n assets pledged as security for a loan. <Latin *com-* together with + *lateris* side> **col·lat′er·al·ly** *adv.*

collateral damage *n* a euphemism for unintended harm to civilians and their property as a result of military attack.

col·league (kol′ēg) *n* a fellow worker or, sometimes, fellow student: *He gets along well with his colleagues.* <French, from Latin *com-* together + *ferre* bring>

col·lect (kə lekt′) *v* **1** gather or be gathered together: *The teacher collected the test papers. A crowd soon collects at the scene of an accident.* **2** form into a mass: *Drifting snow collects behind snow fences.* **3** gather as a hobby: *to collect baseball cards.* **4** call for and take away: *He's gone to collect his clothes from the cleaners.* **5** ask and receive payment for debts, dues, or taxes. **6** regain control of oneself: *Let me collect my thoughts a moment.*
adj, adv to be paid for by the recipient: *a collect call* (*adj*). *Phone him collect* (*adv*). <Old French, from Latin *com-* together + *legere* choose or collect> **col·lec′tor** *n.*

col·lect·ed (kə lek′tid) *adj* **1** gathered together into a set, or into a single volume: *the author's collected works.* **2** calm and in control of one's emotions.

col·lect·i·ble or **col·lect·a·ble** (kə lek′tə bəl) *adj* of interest or attractive to collectors.
n an item suitable for a collection: *a store window full of old picture frames, bottles, and other collectibles.*

col·lec·tion (kə lek′shən) *n* **1** the act of collecting: *Who is responsible for the collection of garbage?* **2** an act of collecting money, especially for charity. **3** something that has collected or been collected: *a collection of leaves on the porch, a coin collection, The collection taken for the refugees was larger than expected.*

col·lec·tive (kə lek′tiv) *adj* **1** belonging to or done by a group: *a collective decision. They thought the newspaper article harmed their collective reputation.* **2** run co-operatively by a group: *a collective farm.*
n a farm, factory, or other organization operated co-operatively by a group. **col·lec′tive·ly** *adv.*

collective bargaining *n* negotiation with an employer or employers by a labour union on behalf of all its members.

collective farm *n* a farm operated co-operatively by a group of people.

collective noun *Grammar n* a noun that is singular in form but refers to a group of things or people. Examples: *team, set, company, family*

GRAMMAR AND USAGE

There are many special **collective nouns** that apply to certain groups of animals. Some are more familiar than others: *an army of ants, a murder of crows, a band of gorillas, a watch of nightingales, a colony of beavers, a float of crocodiles, a pack of wolves, a school of fish.*

col·lec·tiv·ism (kə lek′ti viz′əm) *n* an economic system in which production of goods and distribution of wealth are controlled by the state or groups of people, not by individuals. **col·lec′tiv·ist** *n.* **col·lec′ti·vis′tic** *adj.*

col·lec·ti·vize (kə lek′tə vīz′) *v* **collectivized, collectivizing** transfer ownership and management of property or a business from an individual to a group or, especially, to the state.

collector's item *n* a collectible of high quality.

col·lege (kol′ij) *n* **1** an institution that offers training in one or more occupations and gives degrees or diplomas: *the Victoria College of Art. She took a course in computers at a community college.* **2** *Informal* a school that offers advanced instruction. **3** a division of a university. **4** an organization governing members of a profession: *the College of Physicians.* **5** a building used by a college. <Old French, from Latin *com-* together with + *legare* depute>

col·le·giate (kə lē′jit) *n* 🍁 in full, **collegiate institute** in some provinces, a secondary school with facilities or specialized staff beyond those in a high school.
adj **1** 🍁 to do with a collegiate institute. **2** to do with college or college students: *collegiate life.*

col·lide (kə līd′) *v* **col·lid·ed, col·lid·ing** **1** strike together with force: *Two ships collided in the harbour.* **2** come into conflict. <Latin *com-* together + *laedere* to strike>

col·lie (kol′ē) *or* (kō′lē) *n* a breed of dog originating in Scotland to herd sheep, like the **Highland collie**, with a tawny coat, and the **Border collie**, usually with a black and white coat. <origin uncertain>

col·lier (kol′yər) *n* **1** a ship for carrying coal. **2** a coal miner. <Middle English *col* coal>

col·lier·y (kol′yə rē) *n, pl* **col·lier·ies** a coal mine with its buildings and equipment.

col·lin·e·ar (kə lin′ē ər) *Mathematics adj* lying in the same straight line: *collinear points.*

col·li·sion (kə lizh′ən) *n* **1** a violent striking together: *an automobile collision.* **2** a clash or conflict: *a collision of ideas.* <Latin *com-* together + *laedere* to strike>
on a collision course, headed for conflict or a disaster: *She is on a collision course with school authorities. Economically, the country is on a collision course.*

col·loid (kol′oid) *n* **1** a substance made up of tiny particles that will remain suspended in another medium without dissolving. **2** such a substance together with the medium in which it is suspended. <Greek *kolla* glue>
col·loid′al *adj.*

col·lo·qui·al (kə lō′kwē əl) *adj* used mainly in informal conversation: *Colloquial language is quite acceptable in writing e-mails to friends.* <Latin *com-* together + *loquoi* speak> **col·lo′qui·al·ly** *adv.*

col·lo·qui·al·ism (kə lō′kwē ə liz′əm) *n* a word or phrase that is used in conversation but is too informal to be used in formal speech or writing.

GRAMMAR AND USAGE

Although a person, in conversation, might say, "She was so, like, angry," in formal speech or writing it is preferable to use "She was very angry."

Instead of "And she goes 'nuthin',' and I go 'really?' " one might say or write, "She said nothing was going on, but I didn't believe her."

col·lo·quy (kol′ə kwē) *n, pl* **col·lo·quies** **1** a conference to discuss and exchange ideas. **2** a written scholarly dialogue. <See COLLOQUIAL.>

col·lude (kə lūd′) *v* **col·lud·ed, col·lud·ing** act together in a secret plot. <Latin *com-* together + *ludere* to play> **col·lu′sion** *n.*

co·logne (kə lōn′) *n* a fragrant liquid for use on the body, not as strong as perfume. <French, from *Cologne,* Germany, where it was first made>

Co·lom·bi·a (kə lum′bē ə) *n* a country in northwestern S America. See the APPENDIX. **Co·lom′bi·an** *adj, n.*

co·lon[1] (kō′lən) *n* a punctuation mark [:] used after an introductory sentence, heading, or definition to show that a list, explanation, illustration, or quotation follows. <Latin, from Greek *kolon* limb, clause>

GRAMMAR AND USAGE

A **colon** is used to introduce a list: *I brought three pairs of shoes: sandals, high heels, and running shoes.*

A **colon** can also introduce an explanation of a statement: *Her advice was this: don't forget to brush your teeth before seeing the dentist.*

co·lon[2] (kō′lən) *n, pl* **co·lons** or **co·la** (kō′lə) the main part of the large intestine, from the caecum to the rectum. <Latin, from Greek *kolon*>

colo·nel (kər′nəl) *n* a military officer ranking below a brigadier general and above a lieutenant colonel. <French = leader of a regiment, from Latin *columna* column (of soldiers)>

co·lo·ni·al (kə lō′nē əl) *adj* **1** to do with the original 13 colonies that became the US, or the time when they were colonies: *colonial furniture.* **2** to do with a colony or with the policy of colonialism.
n a person living in a colony. Also, **Colonial.**
co·lo′ni·al·ly *adv.*

co·lo·ni·al·ism (kə lō′nē ə liz′əm) *n* the policy of a nation that seeks to make other countries into colonies and rule over them. **co·lo′ni·al·ist** *n.*

col·o·nist (kol′ə nist) *n* a person who helps to establish a colony or who settles in a newly established colony.

🍁 **colonist car** *n* in former times, a railway coach with wood seats, rough berths, and sometimes cooking facilities.

col·o·nize (kol′ə nīz′) *v* **col·o·nized, col·o·niz·ing** establish a colony or colonies: *France colonized parts of Canada.* **col′o·ni·za′tion** *n.* **col′o·niz′er** *n.*

col·on·nade (kol′ə nād′) *n* a row of evenly spaced pillars. <French, from Latin *columna* column>

col·o·ny (kol′ə nē) *n, pl* **col·o·nies** **1 a** a country or territory ruled by another country, usually more developed and far away. **b** such a group of people or the settlement they make. **2** a community of people of one culture, faith, or occupation living in the midst of a larger population: *a nudist colony. There are several Doukhobour colonies in British Columbia.* **3** a group of organisms of the same kind, living or growing together: *an ant colony, a colony of coral.* **4 the Colonies a** the 13 British colonies that became the US. **b** in former times, the colonies, as opposed to sovereign nations, in the Commonwealth of Nations. <Latin *colere* cultivate>

a bat	e bed	i bid	o pot	u cup	th **thin**
ā cake	ē me	ī bite	ō go	ū rude	TH **then**
ä bar	ə about	ər over	ô for	ů put	zh measure

col·o·phon (kol′ə fon) *n* an emblem of a publisher, especially one put on the title page. <Latin, from Greek *kolophon* finishing touch>

col·or (kul′ər) COLOUR.

GRAMMAR AND USAGE

Colour is the spelling used by most Canadians, although **color** is acceptable, and is sometimes preferred. Most media in Canada use *color.*

The *u* in colour is always dropped when a suffix is added that comes from a Latin source: *coloration.*

With other suffixes, the *u* is kept: *colour-blind, colourfast, colourless.*

col·or·a·tion (kul′ə rā′shən) *n* the way in which something is coloured: *The coloration of a polar bear is like that of its surroundings.*

col·o·ra·tu·ra (kul′ə rə tū′rə) *Music n* **1** ornamental passages such as trills or runs. **2** a soprano who specializes in singing such music. <Italian, from Latin *colorare* to colour>

co·los·sal (kə los′əl) *adj* **1** huge: *Building the St Lawrence Seaway was a colossal undertaking.* **2** (*especially of something bad*) remarkable; outstanding: *a colossal failure.* <French, from Greek *kolossos* huge statue>

Col·os·se·um (kol′ə sē′əm) *n* a large outdoor theatre in ancient Rome, completed in 80 CE. Also, **Coliseum.** <Latin, from Greek *kolossos* huge statue>

co·los·sus (kə los′əs) *n, pl* **co·los·sus** or **co·los·si** (kə los′ī) *or* (kə los′ē) **1** a huge statue. **2** a gigantic person or thing. <Greek *kolossos*>

co·los·to·my (kə los′tə mē) *n, pl* **colostomies** surgery to shorten the colon and divert the cut end to make an opening in the wall of the stomach. <*colon* + Greek *stoma* mouth>

co·los·trum (kə los′trəm) *n* the thin, yellowish milk secreted by a mammal for the first few days after giving birth. It helps establish digestion and natural immunity in newborn children. <Latin>

col·our or **col·or** (kul′ər) *n* **1** the effect of light waves of different lengths striking the retina of the eye: *Some people are not able to tell the difference between the colour red and the colour green.* **2** red, yellow, blue, or any combination of them other than black, white, or grey. **3** a paint, dye, or pigment: *oil colours.* **4** the natural healthy colour of a person's face: *The colour drained from his face and he nearly fainted.* **5** redness of the skin due to blushing: *The colour rushed to her face when her mistake was pointed out.* **6** vividness, detail, or interest: *Her gift for description adds colour to her stories.* **7** emotional quality: *His piano playing is precise but lacks colour.* **8** the part of a sports commentary that provides background information. **9 colours** *pl* **a** a badge, uniform, or other coloured marker worn to show allegiance. **b** the flag of a nation or regiment: *She carried the colours in the parade.*
v **1** give colour to or change the colour of. **2** draw or fill in pictures with coloured crayons or markers, etc. as a pastime: *My little sister likes to colour.* **3** become red in the face. **4** present so as to give a specific, especially false, impression: *The general coloured his report to make his mistake seem the fault of his officers.* **5** give a distinguishing quality to: *Love of nature colours all of Wordsworth's writing.* <Old French, from Latin *color*>
colour outside the lines, *Informal* experiment; be unconventional.
lose colour, become pale: *He lost a lot of colour during his long illness.*
of colour, non-white in skin colour: *a woman of colour.*
with flying colours, with great success: *She passed the examination with flying colours.*
your true colours, your real character: *In the fight, the bully showed his true colours and ran away.*

col·our–blind or **col·or–blind** (kul′ər blīnd′) *adj* **1** unable to tell certain colours apart. **2** indifferent to the colour of people's skin. **col′our-blind′ness** or **col′or-blind′ness** *n.*

col·our–code or **col·or–code** (kul′ər kōd′) *v* **-cod·ed, -cod·ing** use colours to identify: *We colour-code our class library books with a red sticker for science fiction, and a blue one for mysteries.*

col·oured or **col·ored** (kul′ərd) *adj* **1** with colour, other than black, white, or grey: *coloured pictures.* **2** *Offensive* with African ancestors. **3** *South Africa, in former times* **Coloured** of racially mixed descent. **4** biased: *a coloured analysis.*

GRAMMAR AND USAGE

Coloured in the sense of *of African descent* was once used innocently and is still used by some. However, today it is considered offensive and should be avoided.

col·our·fast or **col·or·fast** (kul′ər fast′) *adj* not losing or changing colour by fading or washing. **col′our·fast′ness** or **col′or·fast′ness** *n.*

col·our·ful or **col·or·ful** (kul′ər fəl) *adj* **1** with bright colours or many colours: *a colourful garden, a colourful design.* **2** picturesque or vivid: *a colourful description.* **col′our·ful·ly** or **col′or·ful·ly** *adv.* **col′our·ful·ness** or **col′or·ful·ness** *n.*

col·our·ing or **col·or·ing** (kul′ə ring) *n* **1** the pattern, kind, or amount of colour or colours that a person or thing has: *Her colouring is much better now that she is getting outside more.* **2** a substance used to colour something: *food colouring.* **3** a false appearance: *His lies have a colouring of truth.*

colouring matter or **coloring matter** *n* a substance used to colour something.

col·our·ize or **col·or·ize** (kul′ər īz′) *v* **col·our·ized** or **col·or·ized, col·our·iz·ing** or **col·or·iz·ing** convert black-and-white photographs or movies to colour. **col′our·i·za′tion** or **col′or·i·za′tion** *n.*

col·our·less or **col·or·less** (kul′ər lis) *adj* **1** without colour: *Water is a colourless liquid.* **2** without distinctive character: *a colourless personality.*
col′our·less·ly or **col′or·less·ly** *adv.*
col′our·less·ness or **col′or·less·ness** *n.*

colour wheel *Theatre n* a wheel attached to the front of a spotlight that has openings for different colour filters, used for making colour changes. It can be turned by hand or driven by motor.

colt (kōlt) *n* a young horse, especially a male under four or five years old. <Old English> **colt′ish** *adj.*

col·um·bine (kol′əm bīn′) *n* a plant related to the buttercup, with drooping, trumpet-shaped flowers.

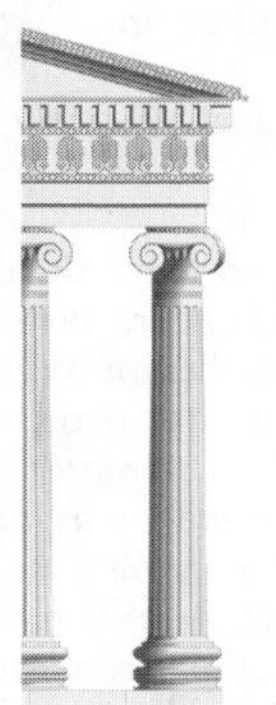

Three types of **columns** were used in classical Greek architecture: The oldest, the Doric, had a simple abacus (a flat stone) at the top and no base. The more ornate Ionic column, like the one shown here, had a base and a capital (top) made of scroll-shaped ornaments beneath the abacus. The Corinthian, the most ornate of all, had a capital with carved acanthus leaves ending in spiral ornaments.

col·umn (kol′əm) *n* **1** a narrow division of a page reading from top to bottom, set off by a line or a blank space: *The school newspaper has two columns per page.* **2** a regular part of a newspaper or magazine devoted to a special subject or contributed by a certain writer: *a sports column.* **3** a vertical section of a table of data, as opposed to a horizontal row. **4** a pillar. **5** anything narrow and tall or long: *a column of smoke rising from the chimney.* **6** in the armed forces, an arrangement of troops in rows one behind another. <Old French, from Latin *columna*> **co·lum′nar** *adj.* **col′umned** *adj.*

col·um·nist (kol′əm nist) *n* a person who writes or selects the material for a special column in a newspaper or magazine.

com– *prefix* **1** (*before the letters **b**, **m**, **p**, and sometimes **f***) with or together: *commingle.* **2** completely. **3** similar. <Latin>

GRAMMAR AND USAGE

The prefix **com–** is from the Latin preposition *cum*, meaning "with."

Com– takes other forms, depending on the initial sound in the rest of the word. It becomes **co–** before vowels and *h* (*coincide, cohabit*), **col–** before *l* (*collect*), and **cor–** before *r* (*correct*). In all other cases, the form is **con–**.

co·ma[1] (kō′mə) *n* a condition of prolonged unconsciousness caused by disease, injury, or poison. <Latin, from Greek *koma* deep sleep>

co·ma[2] (kō′mə) *n, pl* **co·mae** (kō′mē) *or* (kō′mī) a cloudlike mass around the nucleus of a comet. <Latin, from Greek *kome* hair of the head>

co·ma·tose (kō′mə tōs′) *adj* in a coma.

comb (kōm) *n* **1** a tool for arranging the hair, consisting of a narrow strip of material with many fine teeth and, often, a handle. A more decorative-looking type is used to keep the hair in place. **2** something shaped or used like a comb, such as a tool for cleaning and untangling wool or flax fibres. **3** the thick, red, fleshy piece on the top of the head in some fowls. **4** HONEYCOMB (def. 1).
v **1** use a comb to tidy or clean hair, fur, etc.: *to comb your hair, to comb a dog's fur.* **2** search thoroughly: *We combed the neighbourhood for our lost kitten.* <Old English> **comb′like′** *adj.*
with a fine-toothed comb, very carefully and inspecting every detail: *They searched her room with a fine-toothed comb, but didn't find the ring.*

com·bat (kəm bat′) *for v,* (kom′bat) *for n. v* **com·bat·ted** or **com·bat·ed, com·bat·ting** or **com·bat·ing** fight against: *Doctors combat disease.*
n **1** active fighting between armed forces: *My grandfather was wounded in combat.* **2** a fight or struggle. <Latin *com-* together + *battuere* to fight>

com·ba·tant (kəm bat′ənt) *or* (kom′bə tənt) *n* a fighter, especially a soldier who takes part in actual combat.
adj battling; fighting.

combat fatigue *n* mental exhaustion that sometimes affects soldiers as a result of warfare in the front lines.

com·bat·ive (kəm bat′iv) *or* (kom′bə tiv) *adj* fond of arguing or fighting. **com·bat′ive·ly** *adv.* **com·bat′ive·ness** *n.*

com·bi·na·tion (kom′bə nā′shən) *n* **1** the act or fact of combining different things or qualities: *The combination of shrewdness and good luck made her a millionaire before she was 30.* **2** something made by combining two or more different things: *I was drinking a combination of juice and pop.* **3** a series of numbers or letters used to open a combination lock: *I forgot the combination for my locker.* **4** *Mathematics* the arrangement of members of a set into groups of a given size, without regard to order. Example: Possible combinations of *a*, *b*, and *c*, taken two at a time, are *ab*, *ac*, and *bc*.

combination lock *n* a lock opened either by turning a dial through a pre-selected sequence of numbers or by setting a series of dials at pre-selected numbers.

combination square *n* a carpenter's measuring tool, usually in the shape of a right triangle, that combines an adjustable TRY SQUARE with a SPIRIT LEVEL.

com·bine (kəm bīn′); (kom′bīn) *for n and for v def. 3. v* **com·bined, com·bin·ing 1** join or mix together: *to combine work and play. The two classes were combined for the field trip.* **2** *Chemistry* unite to form a compound: *Two hydrogen atoms combine with one oxygen atom to form water.* **3** use a COMBINE (*n* def. 1) on: *We combined the wheat last week.*
n **1** a harvesting machine that cuts and threshes grain in one operation. **2** a group of people joined together for business or political purposes: *The companies formed a combine to keep prices up.* <Old French, from Latin *com-* together + *bini* two by two> **com·bin′a·ble** *adj.*

a bat	e bed	i bid	o pot	u cup	th **thin**
ā cake	ē me	ī bite	ō go	ū rude	TH **then**
ä bar	ə about	ər over	ô for	ü put	zh measure

C

combining form *n* a word element used to make compounds in combination with other word elements or with words. Examples: *socio-*, as in *socioeconomic*, or *-phone*, as in *Anglophone*.

com·bo (kom′bō) *Informal n* **1** a combination of things sold together, especially dishes on a menu to form a meal: *I'll have the breakfast combo, please.* **2** a small group of jazz musicians. <shortening of *combination*>

com·bust (kəm bust′) *v* burn; ignite. <Latin *comburere* burn up> **com·bus′ti·ble** *adj, n.* **com·bus′tion** *n.*

come (kum) *v* **came, come, com·ing** **1** move toward or with the person who is speaking: *Come here a minute. Come with us.* **2** reach a place or a time: *They come home from hockey camp today. The great day has come.* **3** be experienced or noticed: *The pain comes and goes.* **4** reach or extend: *The dress comes to her knees.* **5** (*often with* **along**) progress: *How is your project coming?* **6** take a certain position in a series: *He came second in the high jump. B comes after A in the alphabet.* **7** have a certain source: *Milk comes from cows.* **8** happen: *Come what may.* **9** be brought into a particular state: *This button has come undone.* **10** result: *Nothing good comes of interfering.* **11** occur to the mind: *Poems just come to me.* **12** be available: *This sofa comes in blue or green.* **13** amount or add up: *The bill comes to $50.* <Old English *cuman*>

as good (**strong**, **big**, etc.) **as they come,** one of the best (strongest, biggest, etc.).

come about, take place or happen: *How did the accident come about?*

come a cropper, *Informal* fail.

come across, **a** meet or find by chance: *I came across this book in my office.* **b** be communicated effectively: *The actor's portrayal of joy didn't really come across.* **c** give a certain impression: *He comes across as being very tough, but he's not really.* **d** meet a demand or need: *She came across with a donation.*

come along, **a** arrive on the scene, by chance or as if by chance: *When you came along, my life changed.* **b** progress: *She is coming along well now.* **c** accompany someone: *I'm going out; want to come along?*

come around, **a** return to consciousness: *She fainted but came around after a few minutes.* **b** give in or be persuaded: *Make him come around.* **c** change direction, especially of the wind. **d** come for a visit: *Come around more often.*

come back, **a** respond or retort: *He came back with an equally clever pun.* **b** be remembered: *The name came back to her the next day.* **c** return to popularity: *Bright colours are coming back.*

come between, cause unfriendly feeling between: *We won't let anything come between us.*

come by, **a** get or acquire: *How did you come by that bruise?* **b** visit: *Come by anytime.*

come down, **a** lose position, money, or status: *He's certainly come down in the last year.* **b** be passed along: *Many fables have come down through the ages.* **c** get sick (with): *I came down with the flu.*

come down on, scold or punish: *You don't have to come down so hard on her.*

come forward, volunteer.

come from, **a** be born in or descended from: *She comes from a large family.* **b** be a native or former resident of: *They come from Manitoba.*

come in, **a** be brought into use or fashion: *Scooters first came in when I was a kid.* **b** arrive: *The train came in at 6 p.m.* **c** win a certain place in a competition: *I came in fourth.*

come in for, *Informal* get or receive: *He came in for a lot of criticism on the essay he wrote.*

come into, acquire, especially by inheriting: *She has come into some money.*

come off, **a** happen or occur: *When does the party come off?* **b** succeed: *His plan didn't come off.*

come off it! *Informal* you can't be serious!

come on, **a** approach people in a given way: *She comes on too strong.* **b** meet by chance: *When I opened the door, I came on a strange sight.* **c** approach or begin: *Winter is coming on. I feel a sneeze coming on.* **d** appear on stage, screen, or TV, or be heard on radio: *The murderer comes on in the second act. My favourite show comes on at four.*

come on! *Informal* **a** hurry: *Come on! We'll be late!* **b** used to express impatience or disbelief: *A million dollars for that house? Come on!* **c** (*used to beg or coax*) please! **d** be reasonable! listen! stop!: *Come on! Don't be so silly!*

come on to, *Informal* show sexual interest in.

come out, **a** be revealed or made public: *The details of the scandal never came out.* **b** be offered to the public: *A new model came out last year.* **c** end up or result: *How did your pictures come out?* **d** put in an appearance or offer to take part: *Quite a few students came out for drama this year.* **e** state one's opinion publicly: *The mayor came out strongly in favour of the expressway.* **f** reveal one's homosexuality.

come out with, **a** say openly: *That child comes out with the strangest questions.* **b** offer to the public: *The record company has come out with a digitally remastered version.*

come over, **a** happen to and strongly affect: *A strange feeling came over me.* **b** visit: *When are you coming over?*

come through, **a** endure hardship successfully: *She has come through a lot.* **b** do or supply what was required or expected: *Thanks; you really came through for us.* **c** be released by an administration: *Have your visas come through yet?* **d** show through: *The print comes through from the page underneath.*

come to, return to consciousness: *When I came to, I was in hospital.*

come true, become reality or happen.

come up, **a** be mentioned: *The question is sure to come up in class.* **b** rise in status: *They've come up in the world.* **c** approach someone: *She came up and hugged me.*

come upon, meet or find by chance.

come up with, **a** supply: *Can you come up with the money?* **b** produce with the mind or imagination: *You come up with the weirdest ideas.*

have coming (**to you**), deserve: *Too bad he lost his girlfriend, but really, he had it coming.*

see coming, anticipate or expect: *I didn't see that coming. Did you?*

to come, in the future: *in years to come, for generations to come.*

come·back (kum′bak′) *Informal n* **1** a return to a former level of success or status: *The group made a comeback.* **2** a clever reply: *She's always ready with a good comeback.*

co·me·di·an (kə mē′dē ən) *n* **1** an entertainer who tells jokes or funny stories as an occupation. **2** a person who amuses others with funny talk and actions: *You're quite a comedian.* **3** an actor of comic parts.

co·me·di·enne (kə mē′dē en′) *n* a female comedian.

come·down (kum′doun′) *Informal n* a loss of position, money, or status.

com·e·dy (kom′ə dē) *n, pl* **com·e·dies** **1** a humorous or satirical play, movie, broadcast, or book, or one that has a happy ending. **2** the branch of drama concerned with such plays, movies, or broadcasts. **3** a funny incident or series of funny incidents. <Old French, from Greek *komoidos* comic poet + *aoidos* singer>

come–hith·er (kum′hiᴛʜ′ər) *Informal adj* flirtatious or seductive: *a come-hither look.*

come·ly (kum′lē) *Poetic adj* **come·li·er, come·li·est** good-looking or attractive. <Old English *cymlic*> **come′li·ness** *n.*

come–on (kum′on′) *Informal n* **1** something offered to attract: *The offer of a free sample is just a come-on.* **2** an expression of sexual interest.

com·er (kum′ər) *Informal n* a person who shows promise or seems likely to succeed.

co·mes·ti·ble (kə mes′tə bəl) *Formal n* a thing to eat.
adj edible. <Old French, from Latin *com-* altogether + *edere* eat>

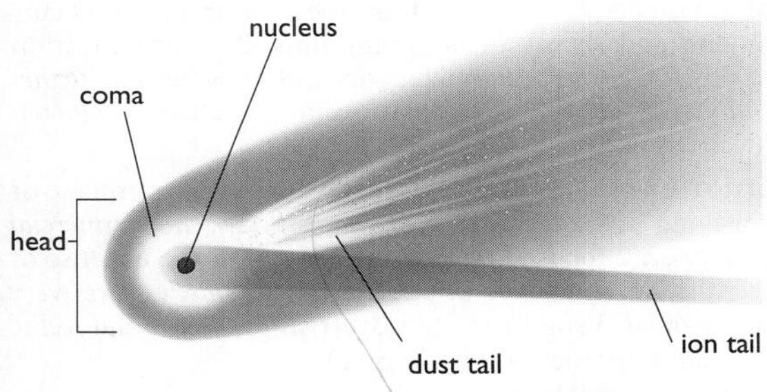

As a **comet** is warmed by solar radiation, the frozen substances become gases and it brightens enormously. The comet may develop a glowing tail composed of ionized molecules, and may also contain tails of fine dust blown from the coma by the pressure of solar radiation.

com·et (kom′it) *n* a starlike object that orbits the sun, consisting of a nucleus of frozen gases, ice, and dust, surrounded by a hazy cloud and often with a long, shining tail. <Old English, from Greek *kome* hair, from the look of the tail>

come·up·pance (kə mup′əns) *Informal n* a punishment that is deserved.

com·fort (kum′fərt) *v* lessen the sadnesss or fear of; reassure: *to comfort a sobbing child.*
n **1** a thing or person that makes trouble or sorrow easier to bear: *to bring comfort to a grief-stricken family. His sister is a great comfort to him.* **2** freedom from pain or hardship: *to live in comfort.* **3** a thing that makes life pleasant or easier: *a cottage with all the modern comforts.* <Old French, from Latin *com-* together + *fortis* strong> **com′fort·ing** *adj.* **com′fort·less** *adj.*

com·fort·a·ble (kum′fər tə bəl) *adj* **1** giving a feeling of ease: *a comfortable chair. The temperature in here is comfortable.* **2** feeling no pain or awkwardness: *Are you comfortable on that sofa? Are you comfortable going by yourself?* **3** enough for one's needs: *a comfortable income.* **com′fort·a·ble·ness** *n.* **com′fort·a·bly** *adv.*

com·fort·er (kum′fər tər) *n* **1** a person who or thing that comforts. **2** a padded or quilted covering for a bed.

comfort station *n* a public washroom, especially one with toilets and showers in a campground.

com·fy (kum′fē) *Informal adj* **com·fi·er, com·fi·est** comfortable: *comfy chairs.*

com·ic (kom′ik) *adj* **1** to do with comedy: *a comic actor.* **2** amusing or funny: *for comic effect.*
n **1** a comedian. **2** a comic book or comic strip. **3** **comics** *pl* the section of a newspaper containing comic strips.

com·i·cal (kom′ə kəl) *adj* amusing. **com′i·cal·ly** *adv.*

comic book *n* a magazine containing comic strips.

comic strip *n* a series of drawings that tell a joke or story.

com·ing (kum′ing) *n* an arrival or approach: *the coming of a new era.*
adj **1** now approaching or next: *this coming Friday.* **2** *Informal* on the way to importance or fame.

com·ma (kom′ə) *n* a punctuation mark [,] used to show a slight separation of words, phrases, or clauses within a sentence. <Latin, from Greek *koptein* to cut off>

GRAMMAR AND USAGE

Commas are used to indicate a short pause between different elements within a sentence:

After we filled the birdfeeder, the jays flocked to it.

We took sandwiches, milk, and fruit on our picnic.

com·mand (kə mand′) *v* **1** give an order to: *The captain commanded the soldiers to advance.* **2** have authority or control of: *to command a ship.* **3** control by virtue of location: *A hilltop commands the plain around it.* **4** have ready for use: *She commands enough knowledge to answer almost any question on Canadian history.* **5** ask for and get or cause to be given: *His manner commands respect. Imported shoes command a high price.*
n **1** an order or direction: *to obey a command.* **2** a position of authority or control: *Who is in command of this ship?* **3** the military unit controlled by an officer: *The captain knew every man in his command.* **4** 🍁 **Command** (*in compounds*) a tactical formation of the Canadian Forces: *Maritime Command.* **5** skill in using: *good command of the language.* **6** *Computers* an instruction to an operating system. <Old French, from Latin *com-* with + *mandare* commit, command>

a bat	e bed	i bid	o pot	u cup	th **thin**
ā cake	ē me	ī bite	ō go	ū rude	ᴛʜ **then**
ä bar	ə about	ər over	ô for	ů put	zh measure

com·man·dant (kom′ən dant′) *or* (kom′ən dȧnt′) *n* the officer in charge of a military base or training school.

command economy *n* an economy under direct control of a central government.

com·man·deer (kom′ən dēr′) *v* **1** seize private property for military or public use: *All vehicles in the town were commandeered by the army.* **2** *Informal* take by force.

com·mand·er (kə man′dər) *n* **1** a person who commands. **2** a commissioned officer in the armed forces.

com·mand·er–in–chief (kə man′dər in chēf′) *n, pl* **com·mand·ers-in-chief** one with complete command of the armed forces of a country.

com·mand·ing (kə man′ding) *adj* **1** in command. **2** with or giving control: *commanding influences, a commanding location.* **3** authoritative: *a commanding voice.* **com·mand′ing·ly** *adv.*

com·mand·ment (kə mand′mənt) *n* an order or law, especially a divine or religious one.

command module *n* the main section of a spacecraft, designed to carry the crew and equipment.

com·man·do (kə man′dō) *n* **1** a soldier who makes brief, daring raids in enemy territory and does close-range fighting. **2** a group of such soldiers.

command performance *n* a play, concert, or other entertainment given before royalty by request or order.

comma splice *Grammar n* the joining of two main clauses with a comma but without a co-ordinating conjunction. Also called **comma fault**.

GRAMMAR AND USAGE

To avoid a **comma splice**, separate main clauses with a co-ordinating conjunction, a semicolon, or a period:

Wrong: *We tried to help her, we couldn't.*

Correct: *We tried to help her, but we couldn't.*

com·mem·o·rate (kə mem′ə rāt′) *v* **com·mem·o·rat·ed, com·mem·o·rat·ing** honour the memory of: *a stamp commemorating the first space flight.* <Latin *com-* altogether + *memor* mindful> **com·mem′o·ra′tion** *n.* **com·mem′o·ra·tive** *adj.*

com·mence (kə mens′) *v* **com·menced, com·menc·ing** start: *The ceremony will commence at two o'clock.* <Old French, from Latin *com-* together + *initiare* begin>

com·mence·ment (kə mens′mənt) *n* **1** a beginning. **2** a graduation ceremony for students.

com·mend (kə mend′) *v* **1** praise: *The mayor commended the volunteers.* **2** entrust: *He commended the baby girl to her aunt's care.* <Latin *com-* together + *mandare* commit> **com′men·da′tion** *n.* **com·mend′a·to′ry** *adj.*

com·mend·a·ble (kə men′də bəl) *adj* deserving approval. **com·mend′a·bly** *adv.*

com·men·sal·ism (kə men′səl iz′əm) *n* a symbiotic relationship between two organisms of different species in which one derives some benefit while the other is unaffected. In one example of this kind of relationship, vultures eat the leftovers from animals killed by lions.

com·men·su·rate (kə men′shə rit) *or* (kə men′sə rit) *adj* **1** in the proper proportion: *The pay should be commensurate with the degree of skill and responsibility.* **2** of the same size, extent, or mass. <Latin *com-* together + *mensurare* to measure> **com·men′su·rate·ly** *adv.*

com·ment (kom′ent) *n* **1** a short note that explains, or makes a criticism or observation: *The teacher wrote comments in the margin of the essay. Prime Minister, do you have a comment on the proposed law?* **2** a remark. **3** talk or gossip: *Their activities are the subject of much comment.*
v make a comment or comments: *Everyone commented on his strange behaviour.* <Latin *com-* together + *minisci* invent>

com·men·tar·y (kom′ən ter′ə) *n, pl* **com·men·tar·ies** **1** a series of notes explaining something, or giving background: *an edition of the play with detailed commentary. The newscast follows up each news item with commentary.* **2** a description of a game or other live event, especially on radio or TV. **3** an explanatory article or essay.

com·men·ta·tor (kom′ən tā′tər) *n* **1** a person who describes and discusses sporting or other live events, especially for radio or TV: *a sports commentator, a fashion-show commentator.* **2** a person who gives or writes any other sort of commentary. **com′men·tate** *v.*

com·merce (kom′ərs) *n* **1** business or trade, especially buying and selling in large amounts. **2** communication between people: *After what he said, I want no further commerce with him.* <Latin *com-* together + *mercis* merchandise>

com·mer·cial (kə mər′shəl) *adj* **1** to do with commerce or engaging in commerce: *commercial law, a commercial enterprise.* **2** focused on making a profit at the expense of artistic or moral values: *Her recent movies are very commercial.* **3** supported by advertising: *commercial radio.*
n an advertisement on radio or TV.
com·mer′cial·ly *adv.*

commercial art *n* graphic art for commercial uses such as advertising and marketing. **commercial artist** *n.*

com·mer·cial·ism (kə mər′shə liz′əm) *n* the methods, attitudes, and aims of commerce, especially, the pursuit of profit, usually at the expense of artistic merit or moral values: *Commercialism has ruined him as a director.*

com·mer·cial·ize (kə mər′shə līz′) *v* **com·mer·cial·ized, com·mer·cial·iz·ing** practise or promote commercialism. **com·mer′cial·i·za′tion** *n.*

com·min·gle (kə ming′gəl) *v* **com·min·gled, com·min·gling** mingle together.

com·mis·er·ate (kə miz′ə rāt′) *v* **com·mis·er·at·ed, com·mis·er·at·ing** sympathize with each other. <Latin *com-* together + *miser* unhappy> **com·mis′er·a′tion** *n.*

com·mis·sar (kom′ə sȧr′) *n* in the former Soviet Union, the head of a government department called a **commissariat** (kom′ə ser′ē ət) <Russian>

com·mis·sar·y (kom′ə ser′ē) *n, pl* **com·mis·sar·ies** **1** a store or restaurant in a mining, logging, or military camp, a prison, or a movie studio. **2** a deputy or representative. <Latin *commisarius* official in charge>

com·mis·sion (kə mish′ən) *n* **1** a payment to a salesperson or agent, consisting of a percentage of the amount of a sale: *She gets a commission of 15 percent on every sale she makes.* **2** a custom piece of art or music ordered by a patron: *His last painting was a commission for the Town Council.* **3 a** a group of people given authority to manage a certain thing: *A commission studied the ecological effect of the proposed hydro project.* **b** the task entrusted to such a group. **4** *Military* rank and authority as an officer: *My brother received his commission as a lieutenant.* **5** the act of committing a crime or injury.
v **1** pay a commission to. **2** order a custom piece of art from an artist. **3** prepare and put into service: *to commission a warship.* <Old French, from Latin *com-* with + *mittere* put or send> **com·mis′sioned** *adj.*
in (or **out of**) **commission,** (not) ready for use.

com·mis·sion·er (kə mish′ə nər) *n* **1** a member of a COMMISSION (def. 3a). **2** an official in charge of some department of a government: *a police commissioner.* **3** 🍁 **Commissioner a** the highest ranking officer of the Royal Canadian Mounted Police. **b** the Federal Government's senior representative in a Territory.

com·mit (kə mit′) *v* **com·mit·ted, com·mit·ting 1** hand over for safekeeping or care: *He committed himself to the doctor's care.* **2** promise one's support by a definite statement: *volunteers who will commit for at least a year. The mayor did not commit herself on the issue of housing. We are committed to protecting the environment.* **3** force or oblige: *Signing this commits you to obeying the rules.* **4** put officially in the care of an institution such as a mental hospital or prison: *The judge committed the accused for psychiatric assessment.* **5** do something that is an offence: *to commit a crime.* <Latin *com-* together + *mittere* put>
commit to memory, learn by heart.
commit to paper (or **writing**)**,** write down.

com·mit·ment (kə mit′mənt) *n* **1** the act of committing. **2** a promise: *He made a commitment to be here.* **3** dedication or long-term involvement: *Learning to play an instrument takes commitment.* **4** an official order committing a person to prison or to a mental institution.

com·mit·tal (kə mit′əl) *n* **1** the act of committing something for safekeeping. **2** the burial of a dead person, with an accompanying ceremony.

com·mit·ted (kə mit′id) *adj* dedicated to something over the long term.

com·mit·tee (kə mit′ē) *n* a group of people appointed or elected to investigate or manage certain matters, and report back. A **standing committee** is permanent, while an **ad hoc** committee serves for one specific purpose: *The school board has appointed a committee to study safety on field trips.* <from *commit*>

com·mode (kə mōd′) *n* **1** a chest of drawers. **2** a washstand in a bedroom. **3** a special chair housing a chamber pot. **4** a toilet. <French, from Latin *commodus* convenient>

com·mo·di·ous (kə mō′dē əs) *adj* roomy.
com·mo′di·ous·ness *n.*

com·mod·i·ty (kə mod′ə tē) *n, pl* **com·mod·i·ties 1** something bought, sold, or traded. **2** a useful thing. <Old French, from Latin *commodus* convenient>

com·mo·dore (kom′ə dôr′) *n* **1** a naval officer ranking next above captain. **2** the chief officer of a merchant fleet or yacht club. <probably Dutch, from French *commandeur* commander>

com·mon (kom′ən) *adj* **1** shared by both or all: *The two of us have a lot of common interests. The house was the common property of the three sisters.* **2** belonging to or affecting the general public: *common knowledge, the common good.* **3** familiar to or used by most people: *common salt, common courtesy. The common name for "Equus caballus" is "horse."* **4** often found or encountered: *a common weed. Blizzards are common on the Prairies.* **5** without special status or title: *the common people, a common soldier.* **6** *especially UK* of poor class or quality: *common manners.*
n land used by all the people of a town or village. <Old French, from Latin *communis*> **com′mon·al′i·ty** *n.* **com′mon·ly** *adv.* **com′mon·ness** *n.*
in common, shared as an interest, experience, or property: *We three have a lot in common.*

common denominator *n* **1** *Mathematics* a denominator that is a COMMON MULTIPLE of all the denominators of a group of fractions. A common denominator of 1/2, 1/3, and 3/4 is 12, because 2, 3, and 4 all divide evenly into 12. The three fractions can then be expressed as 6/12, 4/12, and 9/12. **2** a quality or opinion shared by all the members of a group: *A desire to preserve the local park was the common denominator that brought the residents together.*

common divisor *Mathematics n* a number that will divide two or more other numbers without a remainder. A common divisor of 4, 6, 8, and 10 is 2. Compare COMMON MULTIPLE.

GRAMMAR AND USAGE

Common Era is a relatively new term. It is being used to replace the term AD, an abbreviation of *anno Domini,* meaning "in the year of Our Lord" (after the birth of Christ). Using this term avoids involving religion in citing dates.

com·mon·er (kom′ə nər) *n* a person who is not a member of the nobility.

Common Era *n* the period of history since the birth of Jesus Christ; another name for Christian Era. *Abbrev.* **CE** Compare BCE.

common factor *Mathematics n* a number that is a factor of each member of a group of numbers.
Example: 3 is a common factor of 3, 6, and 15.

common fraction *Mathematics n* a fraction in which both the numerator and the denominator are whole numbers. Examples: 5/8, 213/500, 15/4. Compare COMPLEX FRACTION, DECIMAL FRACTION.

a bat	e bed	i bid	o pot	u cup	th thin
ā cake	ē me	ī bite	ō go	ū rude	ᴛʜ then
ä bar	ə about	ər over	ô for	ů put	zh measure

common law *n* law recognized by the judgments of courts that is based on common custom, as opposed to law created by legislatures. **com′mon-law′** *adj.*

com·mon–law marriage (kom′ən lo′) *n* a marriage not confirmed by an official ceremony but established over time by the fact of living together as partners (**common-law spouses**), and legally recognized.

Common Market *n* the European Union.

common multiple *Mathematics n* a number that can be divided by two or more other numbers without a remainder. A common multiple of 2, 3, 4, and 6 is 12. Compare COMMON DIVISOR.

common noun *Grammar n* a noun that is not a proper noun, especially one that is not a name. Compare PROPER NOUN.

GRAMMAR AND USAGE

Common nouns name a class of things (an *airport*), or a particular person, place, or thing (our *doctor*, the *hotel*, that *pencil*). Common nouns are not usually capitalized unless they are used to begin a sentence or are part of a proper name (*Arctic Ocean*).

com·mon·place (kom′ən plās′) *adj* **1** not unusual or remarkable: *The use of our street for movie shoots is now commonplace.* **2** not original or interesting: *The speech was commonplace.*
n **1** an ordinary or everyday thing: *Sixty years ago, TV was a novelty; today it is a commonplace.* **2** an ordinary or obvious remark. **com′mon·place′ness** *n.*

common room *n* a room in a school, college, or student residence for students or staff to socialize and relax.

com·mons (kom′ənz) *n* (*with singular verb*) a dining hall where food is served to a large group seated at long tables. **2** ✽ **the Commons** the House of Commons.

common sense *n* good judgment in practical matters: *It's just common sense to carry a spare tire in the car.*

common stock *n* ordinary stock in a company, without a definite dividend rate. Compare PREFERRED STOCK.

com·mon·wealth (kom′ən welth′) *n* **1** in full, the **Commonwealth of Nations** an association of sovereign states, most of whom are or were ruled by the UK. **2** the people who form the whole of a nation or other large group. **3** an independent state or community.

Commonwealth of Independent States *n* a loose confederation of most of the countries that belonged to the former Soviet Union, including Azerbaijan, Armenia, Belarus, Georgia, Kazakhstan, Kyrgyzstan, Moldova, Russia, Tajikistan, Turkmenistan, Ukraine, and Uzbekistan. *Abbrev.* **CIS**

com·mo·tion (kə mō′shən) *n* a great deal of noise or movement: *Hearing a commotion in the hall, we went out and found two boys fighting.* <Latin *com-* altogether + *movere* move>

com·mu·nal (kə myū′nəl) *adj* **1** used or participated in by all members of a group or community: *The whole village fetches water from a communal well.* **2** to do with a COMMUNE[2]. **com·mu′nal·ly** *adv.*

com·mune[1] (kə myūn′) *v* **com·muned, com·mun·ing** **1** share one's innermost thoughts and feelings, with complete understanding but often without words. **2** interact with in a mystical or spiritual way: *to commune with nature.* <Old French, from Latin *communis*>

com·mune[2] (kom′yūn) *n* **1** a group of people living together on one piece of jointly-held property, sharing goods and expenses. **2** a unit of local government in China. **3** the smallest division of local government in France and some other European countries. <French, from Latin *communis*>

com·mu·ni·ca·ble (kə myū′nə kə bəl) *adj* **1** infectious or contagious: *Scarlet fever is a communicable disease.* **2** that can be communicated: *Some ideas are not communicable.*

com·mu·ni·cant (kə myū′nə kənt) *Christianity n* a person who receives Communion.

com·mu·ni·cate (kə myū′nə kāt′) *v* **com·mu·ni·cat·ed, com·mu·ni·cat·ing** **1** exchange information by talk, writing, or gestures: *The searchers communicated by two-way radio. It was impossible to communicate with my family during the storm.* **2** pass along; transmit: *to communicate a disease. A stove communicates heat to a room.* **3** exchange messages in a way that produces understanding: *The teacher could not communicate with some of the students.* **4** be connected from a room or passageway: *The dining room communicates with the kitchen.* <Old French, from Latin *communis* common, shared> **com·mu′ni·ca′tor** *n.*

SYNONYMS

Communicate can mean "convey information": *After school, my friend and I communicate by chat room.*

Announce means "make known," sometimes in a public way: *My brother's birth was announced in our local paper.*

Inform means "provide information": *You need to inform me if you can't come to my party.*

com·mu·ni·ca·tion (kə myū′nə kā′shən) *n* **1** the act or fact of communicating. **2** message: *Your communication came too late for me to change my plans.* **3** **communications** *pl* **a** a system for sending or receiving messages, such as by telephone, TV, radio, or Internet: *Communications are down, so we can't talk to her.* **b** (*with singular verb*) the art and technology of communicating, especially by mechanical or electronic means: *Communications is a rapidly expanding field.* **4** a connection or passageway.

communications satellite *n* an artificial satellite that receives radio and TV signals from earth and transmits them back to other places on earth.

com·mu·ni·ca·tive (kə myū′nə kə tiv) *or* (kə myū′nə kā′tiv) *adj* willing and able to give information.
com·mu′ni·ca·tive·ly *adv.* **com·mu′ni·ca·tive·ness** *n.*

com·mun·ion (kə myūn′yən) *n* **1** the sharing or exchanging of intimate thoughts and feelings, especially on a mental or spiritual level. **2** **Communion** or **Holy Communion** *Christianity* the ceremony that commemorates Christ's Last Supper and death.

com·mu·ni·qué (kə myū′nə kā′) *or* (kə myū′nə kā′) *n* an official statement or news bulletin.

com·mu·nism (kom′yə niz′əm) *n* a political, social, and economic system in which all property belongs to the community, and each person contributes and receives according to his or her ability and requirements. Compare CAPITALISM, SOCIALISM. <French, from Latin *communis*> **com′mu·nist** *n, adj.* **com′mu·nis′tic** *adj.*

Communist Party *n* in Canada, one of the registered political parties.

com·mu·ni·ty (kə myū′nə tē) *n, pl* **com·mu·ni·ties** **1** a group of people living in the same area under one government, interacting with one another, or sharing history and resources. **2** a group with a common bond of any kind: *the arts community, the Italian community in Toronto.* **3** a group of people living together, often sharing possessions and following certain rules: *a community of nuns.* **4** the public: *the approval of the community.* **5** *Ecology* a group of interacting populations of two or more species of animals and plants living in a particular region under similar conditions. <Old French, from Latin *communis* common>

community care *n* the care of ill or elderly people, or people with a disability, in their own homes with the help of visiting professionals or volunteers, rather than in institutions.

community centre *n* a building, hall, or arena used for recreation, entertainment, or public meetings.

Community Chest *n* a fund of money contributed voluntarily by people, to support various charitable organizations in their community.

community college *n* an institution for post-secondary and adult education, especially for practical training in an occupation or skill or for courses of personal interest.

com·mu·ta·tive (kə myū′tə tiv) *or* (kom′yə tā′tiv) *Mathematics adj* to do with an operation in which the order of the elements does not affect the result. Addition and multiplication are commutative because it does not matter which quantity is placed first.

com·mu·ta·tor (kom′yə tā′tər) *n* **1** a device for reversing the direction of an electric current. **2** a revolving part in a motor that carries the current to or from the brushes.

com·mute (kə myūt′) *v* **com·mut·ed, com·mut·ing** **1** travel regularly back and forth between one's home and workplace: *She commutes from a small town to her job in Regina.* **2** change a penalty to a lesser one: *His prison sentence was commuted to 800 hours of community service.* **3** reverse the direction of an electric current. **4** exchange: *to commute foreign currency into Canadian dollars.*
n a regular journey back and forth between your home and school or workplace. <Latin *com-* altogether + *mutare* change> **com′mu·ta′tion** *n.* **com′mu·ta′tor** *n.*

Com·o·ros (kom′ə rōz′) *n* a country of several islands off southeast Africa. **Com′o·ran** *adj, n.*

comp (komp) *n* **1** a complimentary ticket or voucher. **2** *Informal* compensation.
v give something away free, usually as part of a promotion: *to comp concert tickets.*
adj complimentary or free.

com·pact[1] (kom′pakt) *or* (kəm pakt′) *for adj,* (kəm pakt′) *for v,* (kom′pakt) *for n. adj* **1** firmly packed together: *Cabbage leaves form a compact head.* **2** with all necessary parts neatly arranged in a small space: *a compact kitchen.*
n **1** a small car. **2** a small case containing face powder and a mirror.
v **1** pack firmly together. **2** condense. <Latin *com-* together + *pangere* fasten> **com·pact′ly** *adv.* **com·pact′ness** *n.*

compact[2] (kom′pakt) *n* a formal agreement, or the people united by it. <Latin *com-* with + *pacisci* to contract>

compact disc CD.

com·pact·or (kəm pak′tər) *n* an electrically powered device that crushes garbage to less than its original volume.

com·pan·ion (kəm pan′yən) *n* **1** a person who goes along or stays with another, especially as a friend. **2** a person paid to live or travel with another, to provide friendly interaction and help. **3** anything that matches or goes with another in kind, size, or colour: *This thesaurus is a companion to my dictionary; they form a set.* **4 Companion** 🍁 a member of the highest grade of the ORDER OF CANADA. **5 Companion** a member of the lowest rank in an order of knighthood. <Old French, from Latin *com-* together + *panis* bread, i.e., someone you share food with> **com·pan′ion·less** *adj.* **com·pan′ion·ship′** *n.*

com·pan·ion·a·ble (kəm pan′yə nə bəl) *adj* **1** sociable and pleasant to be with: *a companionable young lady.* **2** spent enjoying one another's company: *a companionable evening.* **com·pan′ion·a·bly** *adv.*

com·pan·ion·way (kəm pan′yən wā′) *n* a staircase leading from the deck of a ship to the rooms below.

com·pa·ny (kum′pə nē) *n, pl* **com·pa·nies** **1** a group of people travelling or working together: *an opera company, a company of actors.* **2** a business organization: *a publishing company.* **3** the presence of other people: *He's quite shy in company.* **4** companions: *You are known by the company you keep.* **5** the fact of being with someone in friendly companionship: *They enjoy each other's company.* **6** one or more guests or visitors: *We'd better clean up; company's coming.* **7** a part of an army or a ship's crew, commanded by a captain. **8** associates not named in the title of a business firm: *Lamack and Company.*
adj provided for employee use: *a company car.*
keep company, carry on a romantic relationship: *They have been keeping company for several months.*
keep someone company, stay with someone for companionship, so that he or she will not be alone: *I was at home sick, with my sister keeping me company.*
part company, a split up, temporarily or permanently. **b** differ in outlook or opinion: *The two candidates part company on the issue of educational funding.*

a bat	e bed	i bid	o pot	u cup	th thin
ā cake	ē me	ī bite	ō go	ū rude	ᴛʜ then
à bar	ə about	ər over	ȯ for	u̇ put	zh measure

Company of New France *n* a company founded in 1627 by Cardinal Richelieu to develop New France. It ceased to function in 1657.

company town *n* a town built by a company for its workers, to whom it rents houses and provides services.

com·pa·ra·ble (kom′pə rə bəl) *or* (kəm per′ə bəl) *adj* **1** able to be compared: *A fire is comparable with the sun; both give light and heat.* **2** more or less equal: *a better product at a comparable price.* **com′pa·ra·ble·ness** *n.* **com′pa·ra·bly** *adv.*

com·par·a·tive (kəm per′ə tiv) *adj* **1** measured by comparison with something else: *to live in comparative peace.* **2** that involves making comparisons: *comparative anatomy.* **3** to do with the second degree of comparison of an adjective or adverb.
n Grammar the second degree of comparison of an adjective or adverb, or a form that shows this degree. **com·par′a·tive·ly** *adv.*

GRAMMAR AND USAGE

The most common way to form a **comparative** adjective is by adding the ending *-er*. This shows that something possesses a quality to a greater degree than what it is being compared with:

She is ***stronger*** *than I am.*

com·pare (kəm per′) *v* **com·pared, com·par·ing** **1** examine people or things to show or find out how they are alike and how they differ: *She compared the two books to see which one had the better pictures. We compared the fins of a fish and the wings of a bird.* **2** (*with* ***to***) treat as similar: *to compare life to a winding road.* **3** consider or be considered equal: *Artificial light cannot compare with daylight. You can't compare pearls and diamonds.* <Old French, from Latin *com-* with + *par* equal>
beyond compare, without an equal: *Their chocolate cakes are beyond compare.*

com·par·i·son (kəm per′ə sən) *n* **1** the process of comparing things, or a statement or explanation that compares: *to draw a comparison between the human heart and a pump. The teacher frequently uses comparison to make concepts clearer.* **2** similarity: *There is no comparison between these two cameras; one is excellent and the other is junk.* **3** *Grammar* a change in an adjective or adverb to show differences of degree. The three degrees of comparison are positive (*good, fast, helpful*), comparative (*better, faster, more helpful*), and superlative (*best, fastest, most helpful*).
in comparison with, when compared with: *Even a large lake is small in comparison with an ocean.*

comparison shop *v* compare the prices and quality of an item in different stores in order to find the best product at the lowest price before buying.

com·part·ment (kəm pärt′mənt) *n* a separate section of anything, closed off from others: *The cutlery tray is divided into compartments for knives, forks, and spoons.* <French, from Latin *compartiri* divide>

com·part·men·tal·ize (kəm pärt′men′tə līz′) *v* **com·part·men·tal·ized, com·part·men·tal·iz·ing** divide into isolated categories: *He has a tendency to compartmentalize his life into "work" and "family."* **com·part′ment′al·i·za′tion** *n.*

com·pass (kum′pəs) *n* **1** an instrument for showing direction, consisting of a magnetized pivoting needle that always points to the North Magnetic Pole, near the North Pole. **2** an instrument used in geometry for drawing circles and curved lines and for measuring distances. **3** a boundary or circumference: *The castle had a garden within the compass of its walls.* **4** a range: *Such things are outside the compass of my experience.*
v Poetic go or be around: *a farm house compassed by trees.* <Old French, from Latin *passus* pace, i.e., measure out>

com·pas·sion (kəm pash′ən) *n* kindness arising from sympathy with those who are suffering or in need. <Old French, from Latin *com-* with + *pati* suffer> **com·pas′sion·ate** *adj.* **com·pas′sion·ate·ly** *adv.*

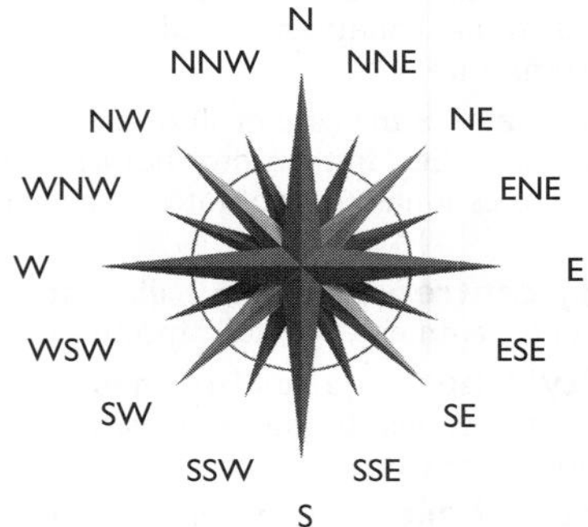

compass rose *n* a circle or decorative design on a map that shows the points (directions) of the compass.

com·pat·i·ble (kəm pat′ə bəl) *adj* **1** able to exist together in harmony: *My two sisters don't seem to be compatible; they're always arguing.* **2** (*often in compounds*) able to be used together with another, especially as a piece of technology: *That keyboard is not compatible with your operating system. My old video games are not PC-compatible.* <French, from Latin *com-* with + *pati* be in sympathy> **com·pat′i·bil′i·ty** *n.* **com·pat′i·bly** *adv.*

com·pa·tri·ot (kəm pā′trē ət) *n* another person from the same country: *Members of the Canadian Olympic team cheered their compatriots.*
adj from the same country. <French, from Latin *com-* with + Greek *patris* fatherland>

com·pel (kəm pel′) *v* **com·pelled, com·pel·ling** **1** force: *The cold finally compelled us to go in. The robber compelled the employees to lie face down.* **2** produce in a way that is irresistible: *Her voice compels obedience.* <Latin *com-* with + *pellere* to drive>

CONFUSABLES

Compel usually involves an outside force: *You can't compel me to like cats.*

Impel implies the action of an inner force: *A feeling of increasing cold impelled her to put on a sweater.*

C

com·pel·ling (kəm pel′ing) *adj* **1** forcing attention or interest: *compelling beauty.* **2** strongly persuasive or convincing: *a compelling argument.* **com·pel′ling·ly** *adv.*

com·pen·di·ous (kəm pen′dē əs) *adj* brief but giving a lot of information. <See COMPENDIUM.>

com·pen·di·um (kəm pen′dē əm) *n, pl* **com·pen·di·ums** or **com·pen·di·a** (kəm pen′dē ə) a summary that gives much information in relatively little space. <Latin = a saving>

com·pen·sate (kom′pən sāt′) *v* **com·pen·sat·ed, com·pen·sat·ing** **1** pay, especially for loss, damage, or effort: *The hunter agreed to compensate the farmer for shooting her cow.* **2** balance with equal weight or value: *A hockey player who is not a very fast skater can sometimes compensate by good positional play.* **3** make amends: *He brought me a bouquet of roses to compensate for being late.* **4** *Psychology* relieve one's insecurity about a real or imagined weakness by some other kind of ability or achievement, often unconsciously: *All that clowning is a way of compensating for his shyness.* <Latin *com-* together + *pendere* weigh> **com′pen·sa′tion** *n.* **com·pen′sa·to′ry** *adj.*

com·pete (kəm pēt′) *v* **com·pet·ed, com·pet·ing** **1** try hard to get something wanted by others: *Different species compete for food.* **2** try hard to do or be better than others or than someone else: *He is always competing with his brother academically.* **3** take part in a contest: *An injury kept her from competing in today's race.* <See COMPETENT.> **com·pet′i·tor** (kəm pet′ə tər) *n.*

com·pe·tent (kom′pə tənt) *adj* **1** able to do an acceptable job at something; with an adequate level of skill: *a competent cook.* **2** legally qualified: *The court ruled that the witness was not competent to judge the sanity of the accused.* <Latin *competere* agree, from *com-* together + *petere* seek> **com′pe·tence** *n.* **com′pe·tent·ly** *adv.*

com·pe·ti·tion (kom′pə tish′ən) *n* **1** the act or fact of competing against others: *I quit gymnastics because there was too much emphasis on competition.* **2** any contest. **3** significant challenge or opposition: *He's no competition; I can easily run twice as fast.* **4** those against whom one competes: *We beat the competition last year.*
in competition with, competing against: *He was in competition with five other dancers.*

com·pet·i·tive (kəm pet′ə tiv) *adj* **1** to do with or involving competition: *a competitive tryout for a place on the team.* **2** anxious to do better than others: *a competitive spirit.* **com·pet′i·tive·ly** *adv.* **com·pet′i·tive·ness** *n.*

com·pile (kəm pīl′) *v* **com·piled, com·pil·ing** **1** collect and bring together in one list or account: *He compiled the data for the report.* **2** make a book or report out of various materials: *to compile an encyclopedia.* **3** *Computers* translate data into MACHINE LANGUAGE for a computer. <Old French, from Latin *com-* together + *pilare* press> **com′pi·la′tion** (kom′pə lā′shən) *n.* **com·pil′er** *n.*

com·pla·cent (kəm plā′sənt) *adj* **1** pleased with oneself: *The winner's complacent smile annoyed the rest of us.* **2** too content with the way things are. See COMPLAISANT for confusable. <Latin *com-* with + *placere* please> **com·pla′cent·ly** *adv.*

com·plain (kəm plān′) *v* **1** talk about one's pains, troubles, or anything one does not like: *to complain of a headache, to complain that the room is too cold. He is always complaining.* **2** bring a formal accusation to an authority: *She complained to the police about her neighbour's dog.* <Old French, from Latin *com-* with + *plangere* lament> **com·plain′er** *n.*

com·plaint (kəm plānt′) *n* **1** an act of complaining: *Her e-mails are filled with complaints about how much studying she has to do.* **2** a cause for complaining. **3** a sickness or ailment: *Backache is a common complaint.*

com·plai·sant (kəm plā′zənt) *adj* eager to please or to accept a situation without complaint. <French, from Latin from *com-* with + *placere* please> **com·plai′sance** *n.*

CONFUSABLES

Complaisant means "eager to please": *The complaisant student enjoyed the teacher's praise.*

Complacent means "too pleased with oneself": *He became complacent and stopped attending practices.*

com·ple·ment (kom′plə mənt) *for n,* (kom′plə ment′) *for v.* *n* **1** something that completes: *Ice cream on the beach was the perfect complement to the day.* **2** the full quantity or number: *The ship has its full complement of crew.* **3** *Grammar* a word or phrase used after a verb, forming a necessary part of the predicate and giving further information about the subject or object. Examples: *old* in *The man is old,* or *queen* in *They made her queen.* **4** *Mathematics* either of a pair of angles that together measure 90°: *The complement of a 70° angle is a 20° angle.* **5** either of a pair of complementary colours. **6** *Music* either of two intervals that together make up an octave.
v supply a lack of any kind; make complete: *The salad dressing needs some oil to complement the sharpness of the vinegar.* <Latin *com-* with + *plere* fill> **com′ple·men′ta·ry** *adj.*

CONFUSABLES

To **complement** means "to complete by adding something": *The ice cream complemented the cake perfectly.*

To **compliment** means "to recognize in a positive way": *He complimented me on my skill in gymnastics.*

complementary angles *Mathematics pln* two angles that together total 90°.

complementary colours or **colors** *pln* **1** two colours of the spectrum, such as red and blue-green, that produce white light when combined in the correct proportions. **2** two pigments that produce dark grey or black, when combined in the correct proportions.

a **bat**	e **bed**	i **bid**	o **pot**	u **cup**	th **thin**
ā **cake**	ē **me**	ī **bite**	ō **go**	ū **rude**	ᴛʜ **then**
ä **bar**	ə **about**	ər **over**	ô **for**	ů **put**	zh **measure**

com·plete (kəm plēt′) *adj* **1** with all the parts included: *a complete set of hockey cards.* **2** thorough or total: *a complete surprise, a complete stranger.* **3** ended, done, or finished: *My journey is complete.*
v **com·plet·ed, com·plet·ing 1** make complete, full, or perfect: *She needs one more baseball card to complete the set. The good news completed our happiness.* **2** finish: *to complete a task.* <Old French, from Latin *com-* with + *plere* fill> **com·plete′ly** *adv.* **com·plete′ness** *n.* **com·ple′tion** *n.*

com·plex (kom′pleks)*; also, for adj,* (kom pleks′)
adj **1** including many parts, steps, relationships, or levels of structure: *complex social issues. The instructions for assembling the wheelbarrow were too complex for us to follow.* **2** made up of a number of connected parts: *A complex sentence has one or more subordinate clauses besides the main clause.*
n **1** something made up of many interconnected parts: *Once inside the hospital, I got lost in the complex of corridors.* **2** a group of related or connected units such as buildings: *The new civic complex includes a library and an auditorium.* **3** *Psychology* a system of related ideas, feelings, and memories, of which a person is usually not aware, that strongly influence behaviour, especially in abnormal or harmful ways: *a guilt complex.* **4** *Informal* an exaggerated mental tendency: *a complex about neatness.* <Latin *com-* together + *plectere* twine> **com·plex′i·ty** *n.* **com·plex′ly** *adv.*

complex fraction *n* a fraction with a fraction in the numerator, in the denominator, or in both. Compare COMMON FRACTION.

com·plex·ion (kəm plek′shən) *n* **1** the colour, quality, and general appearance of the skin, particularly of the face. **2** nature or character: *The complexion of the war was changed by two great victories.* <Old French = physical composition, from Latin *com-* together + *plectere* braid>

complex sentence *Grammar n* a sentence with one main clause and at least one subordinate clause. Compare SIMPLE SENTENCE, COMPOUND SENTENCE, COMPOUND-COMPLEX SENTENCE.

GRAMMAR AND USAGE

In a **complex sentence**, words such as *although, because, if, unless,* and *while* often introduce the subordinate clause.

It will take an hour to get there, ***unless*** *we get a ride.*

If *we don't get a ride, it will take an hour to get there.*

com·pli·ance (kəm plī′əns) *n* **1** the act of complying with a request or command. **2** willingness to comply; a tendency to yield to others. **com·pli′ant** *adj.*

com·pli·cate (kom′plə kāt′) *v* **com·pli·cat·ed, com·pli·cat·ing 1** make hard to understand or deal with by adding details, steps, etc.: *Too many rules complicate a game.* **2** make a disorder, injury, or problem worse by adding another one: *a headache complicated by eye trouble.* <Latin *com-* together + *plicare* fold> **com′pli·ca′tion** *n.*

com·plic·i·ty (kəm plis′ə tē) *n* co-operation in a crime or scheme: *Knowingly receiving stolen goods is complicity in theft.* <See COMPLICATE.>

com·pli·ment (kom′plə mənt) *for n,* (kom′plə ment′) *for v.*
n **1** praise said about a person. **2 compliments** *pl* greetings: *Give my compliments to your family.*
v praise or congratulate. See COMPLEMENT for confusable. <French, from Latin *complere* be fitting, i.e., polite>
with compliments, free of charge.
(with the) compliments of, provided free by: *Memo pads and pens are compliments of the hotel.*

com·pli·men·ta·ry (kom′plə men′tə rē) *adj* **1** expressing admiration, congratulation, or praise. **2** free: *complimentary tickets to a concert.*

com·ply (kəm plī′) *v* **com·plied, com·ply·ing** act in agreement with a request or a command: *to comply with the doctor's orders. When we asked them to turn down the music, they complied.* <Italian, from Latin *com-* with + *plere* fill>

com·po·nent (kəm pō′nənt) *n* one of the parts or elements making up a whole: *Separate the mixture into its components. A monitor is one of the components of a computer system.*
adj forming a part: *Blade and handle are the component parts of a knife.* <Latin *com-* together + *ponere* put>

com·port (kəm pôrt′) *Formal v* **comport oneself** behave: *She comported herself with dignity throughout the trial.* <Latin *com-* together + *portare* carry> **com·port′ment** *n.*

com·pose (kəm pōz′) *v* **com·posed, com·pos·ing 1** create works of music: *a symphony composed by Beethoven.* **2** write or write up: *to compose an essay.* **3** arrange parts in an effective way: *to compose the arguments and evidence for a debate. The photograph is clear, but poorly composed.* **4** (*usually passive*) make up a whole or mixture: *The ocean is composed of salt water. Parliament is composed of the House of Commons and the Senate.* <Old French, from Latin *com-* with + *ponere* put>
compose yourself, a calm your mind: *He tried to compose himself before speaking.* **b** prepare oneself: *I composed myself for a long wait.*

com·posed (kəm pōzd′) *adj* calm and self-controlled. **com·pos′ed·ly** (kəm pō′zid lē) *adv.*

com·pos·er (kəm pō′zər) *n* a person who composes, especially a writer of music.

com·pos·ite (kom′pə zit) *or* (kəm poz′it) *adj* **1** made up of various parts: *a composite photo made by joining parts of other photos, a composite figure made by basing a triangle on one side of a square.* **2** *Botany* to do with a large family of plants with flower heads made up of many tiny flowers bunched together, so that they appear to be single blooms.
n **1** something made up of distinct parts. **2** *Botany* a composite plant: *Many common weeds are composites.* See DISC FLOWER for picture. <French, from Latin *com-* together + *ponere* put> **com′pos·ite·ly** *adv.*

composite number *Mathematics n* a whole number that can be factored into two or more other whole numbers. Example: The number 6 has factors 2 and 3. Compare PRIME NUMBER.

composite school COMPREHENSIVE SCHOOL.

com·po·si·tion (kom′pə zish′ən) *n* **1** the set of ingredients of anything: *What is the composition of this fabric?* **2** the act or manner of composing. **3** something composed, such as a painting, or a piece of music or writing. **4** a mixture, especially a manufactured substance: *countertops made from a composition resembling marble.*

com·post (kom′pōst) *n* a mixture of decayed vegetable matter, used to fertilize and condition soil.
v **1** convert into compost. **2** fertilize with compost. <Old French, from Latin *com-* together + *ponere* put, i.e., mix> **com′post·er** *n.*

com·po·sure (kəm pō′zhər) *n* calmness and self-control.

com·pote (kom′pōt) *n* stewed, sweetened fruit. <French, from Latin *com-* together + *ponere* put, i.e., mix>

com·pound[1] (kom′pound) *for n or adj,* (kom pound′) *for v.*
n **1** a word made by joining together two or more separate words. Examples: *highway, snowball.* **2** *Chemistry* a substance formed by the chemical combination of two or more elements in fixed proportions. A compound has properties that are different from those of its individual elements: *Water is a compound of hydrogen and oxygen.* Compare MIXTURE (def. 2). **3** a combination or mixture: *This paste is a compound of flour and water.*
adj made up of two or more similar parts: *Clover has a compound leaf.*
v **1** increase or complicate by adding a new element: *The visitors compounded the space problem at our cottage by bringing along their dog.* **2** mix or combine: *to compound ingredients. Water is compounded of hydrogen and oxygen.* **3** calculate interest on the amount of a loan plus the accumulated unpaid interest: *The interest is compounded semi-annually.* **4** *Law* accept payment not to prosecute: *It is unlawful to compound an indictable offence.* <Old French, from Latin *com-* together + *ponere* put>

com·pound[2] (kom′pound) *n* an enclosed area with buildings in it. <Portuguese or Dutch, from Malay *kampong* enclosure>

compound–complex sentence (kom pound′kom pleks′) *Grammar n* a sentence made up of two or more main clauses, and at least one subordinate clause. Example: *If I go to the party, you must go too, and you must walk home with me, whether you want to or not.* Compare COMPOUND SENTENCE, COMPLEX SENTENCE, SIMPLE SENTENCE.

The **compound eyes** of the honeybee allow it to see in almost every direction simultaneously. These compound eyes have a great many facets, each functioning as a single lens. Only more distant objects will be in clear focus.

compound eye *Zoology n* an eye made up of many similar sections, each of which is sensitive to light and forms a part of the total image, and that is found in most insects and some crustaceans.

compound fracture *n* a fracture in which a broken bone cuts through the flesh and sticks out.

compound interest *n* interest calculated on both the amount of the original loan and on the accumulated unpaid interest.

compound number *n* a quantity expressed in two or more kinds of related units. Example: 2 h 30 min

compound sentence (kom′pri hend′) *Grammar n* a sentence made up of two or more main clauses. Examples: *He went, but I stayed home. The wind blew, lightning flashed, and the rain fell.* Compare COMPLEX SENTENCE, COMPOUND-COMPLEX SENTENCE, SIMPLE SENTENCE.

com·pre·hend (kom′pri hend′) *v* **1** understand fully: *They did not comprehend the news at first.* **2** include: *The Golden Horseshoe comprehends the whole urbanized area around the west end of Lake Ontario.* <Latin *com-* together + *prehendere* grasp>

com·pre·hen·si·ble (kom′pri hen′sə bəl) *adj* able to be understood: *He writes in comprehensible English.* **com′pre·hen′si·bly** *adv.*

com·pre·hen·sion (kom′pri hen′shən) *n* the ability to understand: *ideas beyond my comprehension.*

com·pre·hen·sive (kom′pri hen′siv) *adj* covering everything or nearly everything: *The teacher led the class in a comprehensive review before the exam.* **com′pre·hen′sive·ly** *adv.* **com′pre·hen′sive·ness** *n.*

✱ **comprehensive school** *n* a secondary school offering academic, commercial, and technical programs. Also called **composite school**.

com·press (kəm pres′) *for v;* (kom′pres) *for n.* *v* **1** make smaller and more compact by pressure or as if by pressure: *Paper is compressed into bales for recycling. Can you compress your speech down to two minutes?* **2** squeeze together: *Her compressed lips were a sign she was angry.*
n a pack or pad applied to the body to stop bleeding or reduce swelling. <Old French, from Latin *com-* together + *premere* to press> **com·press′i·ble** *adj.* **com·press′ion** *n.*

compressed air *n* air put under high pressure so that it has a great deal of force when released. It is used to inflate tires and to operate some brakes and machinery.

com·pres·sor (kəm pres′ər) *n* a thing that compresses; especially, a machine or engine part that compresses air or a gas.

com·prise (kəm prīz′) *v* **com·prised, com·pris·ing** consist of or include: *Atlantic Canada comprises four provinces.* <French, from Latin *com-* together + *prehendere* grasp>

CONFUSABLES

Sometimes people erroneously use *comprised of* instead of **comprises.** Think of it this way: since *comprised* means "consists of," by saying *comprised of,* you are really saying *consists of of.*

a bat	e bed	i bid	o pot	u cup	th thin
ā cake	ē me	ī bite	ō go	ū rude	TH then
ä bar	ə about	ər over	ô for	ů put	zh measure

com·pro·mise (kom′prə mīz′) *v* **com·pro·mised, com·pro·mis·ing 1** settle a dispute by agreeing that each side will give up a part of its demands. **2** risk or sacrifice unwisely: *to compromise public safety. Never compromise your self-respect to please others.*
n **1** a settlement of a dispute in which each side gives up something. **2** the act of compromising or a willingness to compromise. **3** anything halfway between two different things. <Old French, from Latin *compromittere* accept an arbiter's decision>

comp·trol·ler (kən trō′lər) CONTROLLER (def. 1).

com·pul·sion (kəm pul′shən) *n* **1** the fact of being or feeling compelled or forced, whether by others or by duty: *He claimed he had signed the confession under compulsion. Don't donate from a sense of compulsion.* **2** *Psychology* an irresistible, irrational impulse to act in a certain way. <Old French, from Latin *com-* with + *pellere* drive>

com·pul·sive (kəm pul′siv) *adj* acting as a result of an obsession or COMPULSION (def. 2): *a compulsive liar. He was compulsive about cleanliness.* **com·pul′sive·ly** *adv.* **com·pul′sive·ness** *n.*

com·pul·so·ry (kəm pul′sə rē) *adj* required by some rule or law: *In Ontario, the wearing of seat belts is compulsory.* **com·pul′so·ri·ly** *adv.*

com·punc·tion (kəm pungk′shən) *n* (*usually negative*) a moral or a sense of guilt that prevents or follows an action: *The software had a defect, so I had no compunction in asking for a refund.* <Old French, from Latin *com-* with + *pungere* to sting (as one's conscience is supposed to)>

com·pute (kəm pyūt′) *v* **com·put·ed, com·put·ing 1** find out by doing arithmetic: *to compute an average mark.* **2** *Slang* be comprehensible or conceivable to a person: *I told him the situation, but it didn't compute.* <Latin *com-* up + *putare* settle an account> **com·put′a·ble** *adj.* **com′pu·ta′tion** *n.*

com·put·er (kəm pyū′tər) *n* an electronic device that stores digitally coded information and can be programmed to perform mathematical and logical operations at high speed, or to run other machines. See SERIAL PORT for picture.

com·pu·ter·ese (kəm pyū′tər ēz′) *n* the specialized vocabulary of computer technology and programming.

computer graphics *n* (*with singular verb*) the use of a computer to produce designs, images, or scenes.

com·put·er·ize (kəm pyū′tə rīz) *v* **com·pu·ter·ized, com·pu·ter·iz·ing 1** store or manage by means of computers: *The bank has computerized all savings accounts.* **2** equip with computers: *to computerize an office.*

computer literacy *n* familiarity with computers and their operation. **computer literate** *adj.*

computer science *n* the science that studies the design and use of computer hardware and software.

com·rade (kom′rad) *or* (kom′rəd) *n* **1** a companion, friend, or fellow worker or union member. **2 Comrade** a title used for one another by members of a communist or socialist party. <French, from Latin *camera* room (i.e., a room shared by a group of soldiers)> **com′rade·ly** *adj.* **com′rade·ship** *n.*

con[1] (kon) *Informal n, v* **conned, con·ning** trick or swindle: *It's a con, so don't fall for it (n). He was conned into buying a worthless car (v).* <*con(fidence game)*>

con[2] (kon) *Informal n* a convict.

con[3] (kon) *adv* against: *The two debating teams argued the question pro and con.*
n a reason against: *She weighed the pros and cons carefully before choosing.* <Latin *contra* against>

con– *prefix* a form of COM- occurring before all consonants except *b*, *m*, and *p* and sometimes *f*: *converge, confederation.*

con artist *n* a person who wins people's confidence and then swindles them.

con·cat·e·nate (kon kat′ə nāt′) *v* **con·cat·e·nat·ed, con·cat·e·nat·ing** link or be linked together: *a series of concatenated events.* <Latin *com-* together + *catena* chain> **con·cat′e·na′tion** *n.*

con·cave (kon′kāv) *adj* hollow and curved like the inside of a bowl: *That concave object is a satellite dish.* Compare CONVEX. <Latin *com-* together + *cavus* hollow> **con·cav′i·ty** (kon kav′ə tē) *n.* **con·cave′ly** *adv.*

con·ca·vo–con·vex (kon kā′vō kon veks′) *adj* concave on one side and convex on the other, as some lenses. The curvature on the concave side is usually greater than on the convex side.

con·ceal (kən sēl′) *v* hide or keep secret. <Latin *com-* completely + *celare* hide> **con·ceal′a·ble** *adj.* **con·ceal′ment** *n.*

SYNONYMS

Conceal means "hide," and suggests secrecy: *He concealed his hockey cards under the bed, so that his younger brother would not find them.*

Disguise means "hide by changing the look of": *The money was in a box that had been disguised as a book.*

Shroud means "conceal by covering": *The box was shrouded in a blanket.*

con·cede (kən sēd′) *v* **con·ced·ed, con·ced·ing 1** admit as true, especially while disagreeing on other points: *I concede that you tried your best, but I think you took the wrong approach.* **2** give up something, often reluctantly or as a compromise: *to concede victory to an opponent. She conceded us the right to cross her land.* <Latin *com-* completely + *cedere* yield>

con·ceit (kən sēt′) *n* **1** too high an opinion of oneself or of one's ability or importance: *In his conceit, the track star thought no one could outrun him.* **2** in full, **literary conceit** a complicated image or far-fetched comparison: *Life is a mountain, and I am a climber with the wrong kind of boots.* <*conceive*, on analogy with *deceit*>
con·ceit′ed *adj.*

con·ceiv·a·ble (kən sē′və bəl) *adj* able to be imagined: *We should take every conceivable precaution against fire. It is conceivable that she left without us, but not likely.* **con·ceiv′a·bly** *adv.*

con·ceive (kən sēv′) *v* **con·ceived, con·ceiv·ing 1** think up, invent, or devise: *He has conceived a design for a house* that uses solar heating. **2** (*often with* ***of***) imagine: *It's hard to conceive of that happening nowadays.* **3** develop a feeling, taste, or inclination: *I conceived a dislike for her.* **4** become pregnant with: *to conceive a child. Some women have difficulty conceiving.* **5** put in words: *The warning was conceived in the plainest language.* <Old French, from Latin *com-* together + *capere* take>

con·cen·trate (kon′sən trāt′) *v* **con·cen·trat·ed, con·cen·trat·ing 1** (*with* ***on***) give close and unwavering attention (to): *He concentrated on his studies.* **2** direct at some specific area: *Where should we concentrate our efforts?* **3** bring or come together to one point: *A convex lens is used to concentrate rays of light.* **4** make stronger or more intense: *We concentrated the solution by boiling off some of the water. Listening to excuses only concentrated his rage.*
n something that has been concentrated: *lemon juice concentrate.* <French, from Latin *com-* together + *centrum* centre>

con·cen·tra·tion (kon′sən trā′shən) *n* **1** the fact of concentrating or being concentrated. **2** close attention: *We gave the problem our full concentration. Their sudden arrival broke my concentration.* **3** the strength of a solution or intensity of an effect.

concentration camp *n* a camp where political enemies, prisoners of war, and interned foreigners are held.

con·cen·tric (kən sen′trik) *adj* with the same centre. Compare ECCENTRIC (def. 2). **con·cen′tri·cal·ly** *adv.*

con·cept (kon′sept) *n* **1** an idea or abstract category: *the concept of equality.* **2** a design or basic plan: *She was responsible for the concept; others carried it out.* <Old French, from Latin *com-* together + *capere* take> **con·cep′tu·al** (kən sep′chū əl) *adj.* **con·cep′tu·al·ly** *adv.*

con·cep·tion (kən sep′shən) *n* **1** a way of seeing or thinking about something: *His conception of the problem is different from mine.* **2** the act of conceiving or fact of being conceived: *This diagram shows a fetus 18 weeks after conception.* **3** a design, plan, or idea.

concept map *n* See MAP (def. 4.)

con·cep·tu·al·ize (kən sep′chū ə līz′) *v* **con·cep·tu·al·ized, con·cep·tu·al·iz·ing** form an idea of: *Can an animal conceptualize freedom?*

con·cern (kən sərn′) *v* **1** make anxious or become a cause for worry: *She didn't want to concern us with details of the illness.* **2** have to do with: *The e-mail concerns the new safety measures.* **3** involve or affect: *The new rules concern all of us.*
n **1** worry, anxiety, or uneasiness: *The father's concern for his sick child kept him awake all night.* **2** whatever has to do with a person or thing: *How I spend my money is my concern, not yours.* **3** a business company: *She works for a big manufacturing concern in Hamilton.* **4** something dealt with or to be dealt with: *The special concern of this book is how to study effectively.* <French, from Latin *com-* with + *cernere* sift, discern>
as concerns, with reference to.
concern yourself, a worry or take trouble: *Don't concern yourself; I have everything under control.* **b** be busy: *She will concern herself with the water-sports program.*
of concern, of importance: *a matter of concern.*

con·cerned (kən sərnd′) *adj* **1** troubled, worried, or anxious. **2** interested: *Concerned students should attend the meeting on recycling.* **3** involved with: *Everyone concerned in the play will have time off for rehearsal.*

con·cern·ing (kən sər′ning) *prep* having to do with: *There were questions concerning the accident.*

con·cert (kon′sərt) *for n or adj,* (kən sərt′) *for v.*
n a musical performance.
adj used in concerts: *a concert orchestra.*
v plan or make together: *The rebels concerted a plan for seizing the town.* <French, from Latin *com-* together + *certare* strive>
in concert, a performing publicly: *Our school choir appears in concert tonight at the stadium.* **b** all together or in agreement: *The class acted in concert to raise money.*

con·cert·ed (kən sər′tid) *adj* planned or made together by more than one person or group: *a concerted attack, a concerted effort.*

con·cer·ti·na (kon′sər tē′nə) *n* a musical instrument like a small accordion, with a set of buttons at each end.

con·cert·mas·ter (kon′sərt mas′tər) *n* the leader of an orchestra, usually the first violinist, ranking next to the conductor.

con·cer·to (kən cher′tō) *n* a musical composition, usually in three parts, for one or more solo instruments such as a violin or piano, accompanied by an orchestra. <Italian *concertare* harmonize>

con·ces·sion[1] (kən sesh′ən) *n* **1** an act of conceding or the thing conceded: *As a concession, his mother allowed him to stay out an hour longer.* **2** a space leased for special use on private or public property, such as a refreshment stand in a park. **3** land or rights granted by a government. <Latin *concessio,* from *com-* completely + *cedere* yield>

🍁 **con·ces·sion**[2] (kən sesh′ən) *n* **1** mainly in Ontario and Québec, a subdivision of land in township surveys, formerly one of the 200-acre (about 81-hectare) lots into which each new township was divided. **2** concession road. <Cdn. French>

con·ces·sion·aire (kən sesh′ə ner′) *n* the operator or holder of a CONCESSION[1] (def. 2).

🍁 **concession road** *especially Ontario and Québec n* a rural road using the road allowance between concessions, connected to other concession roads by side roads.

conch (konch) *or* (kongk) *n, pl* **conch·es** (kon′chiz) or **conchs** (kongks) a large, plant-eating sea snail with a spiral shell and with a wide lip often curled back, revealing a smooth, pearly lining. <Latin, from Greek *konche*>

con·cierge (kon syerzh′) *or* (kon′ sē erzh′) *n* a person employed at a hotel, condominium, or apartment building to help the guests or residents by dealing with luggage, making travel arrangements, delivering messages, etc. <French>

a bat	e bed	i bid	o pot	u cup	th **thin**
ā cake	ē me	ī bite	ō go	ū rude	TH **then**
ä bar	ə about	ər over	ô for	ů put	zh measure

con·cil·i·ate (kən sil′ē āt′) *v* **con·cil·i·at·ed, con·cil·i·at·ing** win back the good will of; renew good relations with someone after or in the midst of a conflict: *He conciliated his angry little sister by promising to take her to the zoo.* <Latin *conciliare*, from *com-* together + *calare* call> **con·cil′i·a′tion** *n.* **con·cil′i·a·to′ry** *adj.*

con·cise (kən sīs′) *adj* expressing much in few words: *He gave a concise report of the meeting.* <Latin *concisus*, from *com-* completely + *caedere* to cut> **con·cise′ly** *adv.* **con·cise′ness** or **con·ci′sion** (kən sizh′ən) *n.*

con·clave (kon′klāv) *n* **1** a private meeting. **2** *Catholicism* a meeting of the cardinals for the election of a pope, or the place where they meet. <Latin = place that may be locked, from *com-* with + *clavis* key>

con·clude (kən klūd′) *v* **con·clud·ed, con·clud·ing 1** end: *She concluded her speech with a funny story.* **2** arrange or settle: *The two countries concluded a trade agreement.* **3** arrive at a decision, judgment, or opinion by thinking: *From the clues they found, the police concluded that the thief left in a hurry.* <Latin *com-* completely + *claudere* close>

con·clu·sion (kən klū′zhən) *n* **1** end: *at the conclusion of the game.* **2** the last part of a speech or text, summing up the important points. **3** a final result. **4** the act of concluding: *the conclusion of a peace treaty.* **5** a decision, judgment, or opinion reached by reasoning: *The conclusion of the jury was that the accused was not guilty.*
in conclusion, as a final point.

con·clu·sive (kən klū′siv) *adj* leading clearly to a definite conclusion: *a conclusive argument, conclusive evidence.* **con·clu′sive·ly** *adv.* **con·clu′sive·ness** *n.*

con·coct (kən kokt′) *v* **1** prepare by putting together ingredients: *The chef concocts the most delicious sauces.* **2** make up, especially something complicated, far-fetched, or whimsical: *What fantastic moneymaking scheme have you concocted this time?* <Latin *com-* together + *coquere* cook> **con·coc′tion** *n.*

SYNONYMS

Concoct can mean "mix ingredients": *He concocted a salad from a dozen vegetables.*

Compound means "mix ingredients scientifically": *She compounded the ingredients to make a sugar solution.*

Mix means "combine ingredients or other items": *The teacher mixed the three classes into two groups.*

con·com·i·tant (kon kom′ə tənt) *adj* happening or appearing together with something else: *Earning privileges has concomitant responsibilities.*
n an accompanying thing, quality, or circumstance. <Latin *com-* with + *comes* companion>
con·com′i·tant·ly *adv.*

con·cord (kon′kôrd) *n* **1** agreement or harmony: *concord between friends.* **2** a harmonious combination of tones. **3** a treaty. <Old French, from Latin *com-* together + *cordis* heart> **con·cord′ant** *adj.*

con·cord·ance (kən kôr′dəns) *n* **1** an alphabetical list of all the important words occurring in a particular body of writing, along with an indication of where each one occurs: *a concordance of Shakespeare, a concordance of the Bible.* **2** agreement or harmony.

Concord grape *n* a round, bluish black variety of grape used for making jelly, juice, or wine.

con·course (kon′kôrs) *n* **1** a running, flowing, or coming together: *the concourse of two rivers.* **2** a crowd or large gathering. **3** a large area, usually covered, where people can wait or walk around: *the main concourse of a railway station, a shopping concourse below ground level.* <Latin *com-* together + *currere* run>

con·crete (kon′krēt); *also,* (kon krēt′) *for adj*
n a mixture of crushed stone or gravel, sand, cement, and water that hardens as it dries, used as a building and paving material.
adj **1** made of this mixture: *a concrete sidewalk.* **2** existing as a real object, not as an idea, category, or quality: *A painting is concrete, but its beauty is abstract.* **3** specific and actual: *concrete examples. Explain it in concrete terms.* **4** *Grammar* naming a material thing when used as a noun. Examples: *sugar* and *people* are concrete nouns. **con·crete′ly** *adv.* **con·crete′ness** *n.*

ETYMOLOGY

Concrete comes from Latin *concretus*, the past participle of *concrescere*, meaning "grow together into a solid mass." It in turn comes from *com-* meaning "together" and *crescere* meaning "grow." When the building material was invented, it was called *concrete* because it was the ideal example of something that grows together into a solid mass.

con·cre·tion (kən krē′shən) *n* **1** the process of forming into a hard mass. **2** a solidified lump: *Gallstones are concretions in the gall bladder.*

con·cu·bine (kong′kyə bīn′) *n* in certain societies where polygamy was or is accepted, a woman of lower social and legal status than a wife, but who lives with the husband. <Old French, from Latin *com-* with + *cubare* to lie>

con·cur (kən kər′) *v* **con·curred, con·cur·ring 1** be of the same opinion: *The judges all concurred in giving him the prize.* **2** act together or have a combined effect: *The events of the week concurred to make it a great holiday.* **3** come or happen together. <Latin *com-* together with + *currere* to run> **con·cur′rence** *n.* **con·cur′rent** *adj.* **con·cur′rent·ly** *adv.*

SYNONYMS

Concur means "agree": *After weighing the pros and cons, his parents concurred that he could stay up late to finish his homework.*

Acquiesce can mean "concede by not making an objection": *We acquiesced to their suggestion for the group project, although we weren't sure that it was the best idea.*

Assent means "consent": *She assented to be the director of the school play.*

con·cus·sion (kən kush′ən) *n* **1** an injury to the brain or spine caused by a blow, fall, or violent shaking. **2** a sudden, violent shock, such as from an explosion. <Latin *concussus,* from *concutere* disturb greatly> **con·cuss′** *v.*

con·demn (kən dem′) *v* **1** express strong disapproval of: *We condemn cruelty and violence.* **2** show to be guilty: *Her actions are enough to condemn her.* **3** pass a judicial sentence on: *He was condemned to life imprisonment.* **4** officially declare unsound or unsuitable for use: *This bridge has been condemned because its surface is crumbling.* **5** put into an unpleasant condition: *Poverty condemned them to a life of frustration.* <Old French, from Latin *com-* with + *damnare* cause loss to> **con′dem·na′tion** *n.* **con′dem·na′to·ry** *adj.* **con·demned′** *adj.*

con·den·sate (kon′dən sāt′) *or* (kən den′sāt) *n* a substance formed or produced by condensation.

con·den·sa·tion (kon′dən sā′shən) *n* **1** the fact or process of condensing: *I have read a condensation of that book, the condensation of steam into water.* See STATE for picture. **2** something condensed, especially water droplets appearing on a surface that is colder than the air next to it: *The windowsill was wet from the condensation dripping down off the glass.*

con·dense (kən dens′) *v* **con·densed, con·dens·ing** **1** change state from a gas or vapour to a liquid by cooling. Steam condenses to water when it comes into contact with a cold surface. Compare EVAPORATE. **2** shorten: *He condensed the paragraph into one sentence.* **3** make denser or stronger: *Lenses can be used to condense light.* <Old French, from Latin *com-* completely + *densus* dense>

condensed milk *n* sweetened milk from which part of the water has been evaporated before being canned.

con·dens·er (kən den′sər) *n* **1** a device for receiving and holding a charge of electricity. **2** an apparatus for changing gas or vapour into a liquid. **3** something that condenses something else, such as a lens or set of lenses used to concentrate light.

con·de·scend (kon′di send′) *v* **1** show that one is or feels superior to another: *The general condescended to march with the troops. Wow, she actually condescended to help me with my chores.* **2** do something that is beneath one's status or dignity: *She would not condescend to taking a bribe.* <Old French, from Latin *com-* together + *descendere* descend> **con′de·scen′sion** *n.*

con·de·scend·ing (kon′di sen′ding) *adj* showing good will, while making it obvious that one feels superior: *I can't stand the condescending manner of that store manager.* **con′de·scend′ing·ly** *adv.*

con·di·ment (kon′də mənt) *n* something used to give flavour and zest to food, such as ketchup or mustard. <Latin *condire* to pickle>

con·di·tion (kən dish′ən) *n* **1** the condition in which a person or thing is: *The accident victim was in critical condition. My ski boots are several years old, but still in very good condition.* **2** **conditions** *pl* circumstances that affect an activity: *poor driving conditions. The working conditions at the fast-food restaurant are good.* **3** an ailment or disease: *a heart condition.* **4** **a** anything that is required in order for something else to happen or exist: *Willingness to travel is a condition of employment as a sales representative.* **b** a statement or demand that expresses such a requirement: *This warranty is limited by certain conditions.* **5** physical fitness or good health: *I work out every day to keep in condition.* **6** status or social position: *people of humble condition.*

v **1** put or keep in good condition: *a rinse to condition the hair. Exercise conditions your muscles.* **2** cause to depend on something: *The increase in his allowance was conditioned on his willingness to help more around the house.* **3** train by repeatedly following up certain behaviour with pleasant or unpleasant consequences: *This dog has been conditioned to expect food when it obeys a command.* **4** make accustomed to: *Many years of cleaning houses had conditioned her to hard work.* <Old French, from Latin *com-* together + *dicere* say (i.e., agree)> **con·di′tioned** *adj.*

on condition that, provided that: *I'll go on condition that you will too.*

on no condition, never: *On no condition will I do your homework for you.*

con·di·tion·al (kən dish′ə nəl) *adj* **1** depending on something else: *Permission to go out is conditional on your finishing your homework first. Love should not be conditional. A conditional equation is only true for certain values of the variable.* **2** *Grammar* expressing or containing a CONDITION (*n* def. 4). A **conditional clause** begins with *if, unless, provided that,* etc. **con·di′tion·al·ly** *adv.*

con·di·tion·er (kən dish′ə nər) *n* **1** a lotion or cream used to improve the condition of the hair or skin. **2** any person who or thing that conditions: *an air conditioner.*

con·do (kon′dō) *Informal n* condominium.

con·dole (kən dōl′) *v* **con·doled, con·dol·ing** (*with* ***with***) express sympathy; sympathize, especially at a death: *The widow's friends condoled with her at the funeral.* <Latin *com-* with + *dolere* grieve, suffer> **con·do′lence** *n.*

con·dom (kon′dəm) *n* a thin, usually rubber sheath worn over the penis during sexual intercourse to prevent infection and as a contraceptive. <origin unknown>

con·do·min·i·um (kon′də min′ē əm) *n* **1** an individually owned suite or townhouse on land that is jointly owned by all residents, who also share or pay for common facilities and maintenance services. **2** a building containing such suites. <Latin *com-* together with + *dominium* right of ownership>

con·done (kən dōn′) *v* **con·doned, con·don·ing** **1** accept or approve of behaviour that some regard as wrong: *We must put up with such behaviour, but we do not condone it.* **2** overlook an offence or fault: *His parents had always condoned his tantrums when he was small.* <Latin *condonare* forgive a debt, from *com-* together + *donare* give>

con·dor (kon′dôr) *n* a large black and white vulture that lives in mountainous areas. It has a massive wingspan. See BUZZARD for picture. <Spanish, from Quechua (a language of S America) *kuntur*>

a **bat**	e **bed**	i **bid**	o **pot**	u **cup**	th **thin**
ā **cake**	ē **me**	ī **bite**	ō **go**	ū **rude**	TH **then**
ä **bar**	ə **about**	ər **over**	ô **for**	ů **put**	zh **measure**

con·du·cive (kən dyū′siv) *or* (kən dū′siv) *adj* (*with* **to**) helpful or favourable: *Exercise is conducive to health.* <Old French, from Latin *com-* together + *ducere* lead>

con·duct (kon′dukt) *for n,* (kən dukt′) *for v*
n **1** behaviour or way of acting: *a medal for good conduct.* **2** direction or management: *the conduct of an office.*
v **1** direct or manage: *to conduct the affairs of a business, to conduct your life.* **2** direct a musical group as leader: *a performance of Beethoven, with Ms Bell conducting.* **3** go along with and show the way to: *The doorman conducted me to the elevator.* **4** transmit heat, electricity, or sound: *Those pipes conduct steam to the radiators upstairs.* <Old French, from Latin *com-* together + *ducere* lead>
conduct yourself, behave: *She conducted herself with great dignity throughout the ceremony.*

con·duc·tion (kən duk′shən) *n* the transmission of energy (heat, electricity, or sound) through a medium without bulk movement of the medium itself. The base of a cooking pot is heated by conduction. Compare CONVECTION. **con·duct′ive** *adj.* **con′duc·tiv′i·ty** *n.*

con·duc·tor (kən duk′tər) *n* **1** the director of a musical group. **2** the person in charge of a train or streetcar, who collects the tickets or fares from the passengers. **3** anything that transmits heat, electricity, or sound: *Copper is a good conductor of heat and electricity.* **4** a person who conducts something.

con·duit (kon′dyū it), (kon′dū it), *or* (kon′dit) *n* **1** a pipe, shaft, or other passage for carrying liquids, air, or electrical cables over long distances. **2** a channel for anything. <Old French, from Latin *com-* together + *ducere* lead>

pine cone

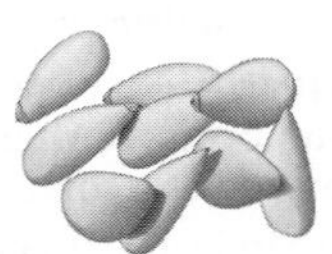
pine seeds

Pine trees produce no flowers or fruit, but instead make woody **cones** that contain their seeds.

Cones vary greatly in size, depending on the type of pine. Watch your head if you're walking underneath the Coulter pine. Its cones can weigh more than two kilograms!

cone (kōn) *n* **1** an object that tapers from a more or less circular base to a narrow point: *an ice cream cone, the cone of a volcano.* **2** *Mathematics* a figure generated by straight lines that pass from a closed curve to a single point not in the same plane as the curve. **3** the seed-bearing structure, made of overlapping woody scales, that grows on a pine or other evergreen tree. **4** one of a number of cone-shaped cells in the retina of the eye. These cells are sensitive to light and colour. <French, from Greek *konos*>

co·ney (kō′nē) *n* **1** *UK* a wild rabbit. **2** a pika. **3** a hyrax. Also, **cony.** <Old French, from Latin *cuniculus* rabbit>

con·fab (kon′fab) *Informal n* in full, **confabulation** (kon′fab yū lā′shən) a casual talk or consultation. <Latin *com-* together + *fabula* fable>

con·fec·tion (kən fek′shən) *n* a piece of candy, candied fruit, or fudge. <Old French, from Latin *com-* completely + *facere* produce>

con·fec·tion·er·y (kən fek′shə nər′ē) *n, pl* **con·fec·tion·er·ies** **1** candies or sweets. **2** a store that sells them. **con·fec′tion·er** *n.*

con·fed·er·a·cy (kən fed′ə rə sē) *n, pl* **con·fed·er·a·cies** **1** a union of countries or states, with most of the political authority centralized. **2** a number of individuals, groups, or nations, joined together for a special purpose. **3** a conspiracy. **4** **Confederacy** Confederate States of America.

con·fed·er·ate (kən fed′ə rit) *for adj or n,* (kən fed′ə rāt′) *for v.*
adj **1** joined together for a special purpose. **2** **Confederate** to do with the Confederate States of America: *the Confederate uniform.*
n **1** a country, group, or person, joined with another for a special purpose. **2** an accomplice in crime: *The thief was arrested, but his confederate escaped.* **3** **Confederate** a person who lived in and supported the Confederate States of America.
v enter a union or alliance: *Four provinces of Canada confederated in 1867.* <Latin *com-* together + *foederis* league>

Confederate States of America *n* the group of eleven southern states that seceded from the US in 1860 and 1861.

con·fed·er·a·tion (kən fed′ə rā′shən) *n* **1** the act of joining together in an alliance. **2** a group of countries or states, joined together for a special purpose; a league.
3 🍁 **Confederation a** the name given to the agreement and the event that joined Ontario, Québec, Nova Scotia, and New Brunswick as a nation in 1867, and later included the present provinces and territories. **b** *Newfoundland and Labrador* the political union of Newfoundland and Labrador with Canada in 1949.

con·fer (kən fər′) *v* **con·ferred, con·fer·ring** **1** consult together: *The prime minister often confers with his advisers.* **2** (*with* **on**) give, grant, or bestow: *The mayor conferred a medal on the brave firefighter.* <Latin *com-* together + *ferre* bring> **con·fer′ral** *n.*

con·fer·ee (kon′fə rē′) *n* **1** a person attending a conference: *A schedule was issued to all the conferees.* **2** a person on whom something, such as a university degree, is conferred.

con·fer·ence (kon′frəns) *n* **1** a meeting to discuss a particular subject: *a parent-teacher conference to discuss a student's progress.* **2** a formal event where many delegates, scholars, or members of an association gather to exchange ideas and recent findings: *My mother is giving a speech at a conference on women's health.* **3** an association of schools, sports teams, or churches.
v **con·fer·enced, con·fer·enc·ing** hold or participate in a conference.
in conference, in a meeting.

conference call *n* a telephone call involving three or more people at the same time, often in different places.

con·fess (kən fes′) *v* **1** admit to something wrong: *to confess your guilt, to confess to a crime. I must confess I forgot all about your call.* **2** *Christianity* **a** tell one's sins, especially to a priest, in order to receive forgiveness. **b** listen to a person tell his or her sins in one's capacity as a priest. **3** state (one's faith or beliefs) openly. <Old French, from Latin *com-* altogether + *fateri* declare> **con·fes′sor** *n.*

con·fes·sion (kən fesh′ən) *n* **1** the act of confessing. **2** a statement in which a person confesses something: *a signed confession.* **3** *Christianity* the act of telling one's sins, especially to a priest, in order to receive forgiveness. **4** usually, **confessions** *pl* an autobiography that includes personal reflections and intimate revelations. **5** a set of stated beliefs: *people of many different confessions.*

con·fes·sion·al (kən fesh′ə nəl) *n* a small booth where a priest hears confessions.
adj to do with confession or engaging in confession.

con·fet·ti (kən fet′ē) *n* the bits of coloured paper thrown at weddings and some other festive events.

ETYMOLOGY

Confetti is a borrowed Italian word meaning "candies." It comes from the same source as the English word *confection.* Originally, Italians threw candies at weddings and carnivals.

con·fi·dant (kon′fə dont′) *or* (kon′fə dont′) *n* a person to whom one tells one's secrets. A female in this role is a **confidante.** <See CONFIDE.>

con·fide (kən fīd′) *v* **con·fid·ed, con·fid·ing 1** tell as a secret: *He confided his troubles to me.* **2** give to another to take care of: *The collection of donations is confided to the treasurer.* <Latin *com-* altogether + *fidere* trust>
confide in, a tell a secret to: *She always confides in her sister.* **b** trust.

con·fi·dence (kon′fə dəns) *n* **1** a firm belief or trust: *I have no confidence in such a liar.* **2** a firm belief in oneself and one's abilities: *Her confidence shows in the way she does her work.* **3** bold optimism: *We face the future with confidence.* **4** an understanding that a piece of information is private: *The story was told to me in strict confidence.* **5** something told as a secret: *I listened to his confidences for half an hour.*

confidence game *n* a scheme in which someone wins people's confidence and then cheats them.

con·fi·dent (kon′fə dənt) *adj* **1** believing in oneself and one's abilities: *Each little victory made him more confident. I am confident that our team will win.* **2** sure (of): *confident of success.* **con′fi·dent·ly** *adv.*

con·fi·den·tial (kon′fə den′shəl) *adj* **1** to be kept secret: *The details of the report are confidential.* **2** expressing intimacy or secrecy: *He spoke in a confidential tone of voice.* **3** trusted with secrets: *a confidential adviser.* **con′fi·den′ti·al′i·ty** (kon′fə den′shē al′ i tē) *n.* **con′fi·den′tial·ly** *adv.*

con·fig·ure (kən fig′yər) *or* (kən fig′ər) *v* **con·fig·ured, con·fig·ur·ing 1** arrange or lay out: *Geographers study how the surface of the earth is configured.* **2** *Computers* set up a system or application to function in a certain way, choosing and installing various options. <Latin *com-* together + *figura* form> **con·fig′u·ra′tion** *n.*

con·fine (kən fīn′) *for v,* (kon′fīn) *for n.*
v **con·fined, con·fin·ing 1** keep within certain limits: *They confined the dog to the basement. This program is confined to children aged seven and under. Let's confine this discussion to the first book in the trilogy.* **2** shut in or lock up. **3** hamper the activity of: *She found the guidelines they had given her for the project very confining.*
n **confines** *pl* limits: *These people have never been beyond the confines of their own valley.* <French, from Latin *com-* together + *finis* end, border> **con·fin′ing** *adj.*
be confined, begin the process of childbirth.

con·fined (kən fīnd′) *adj* small or limited in space or area.

con·fine·ment (kən fīn′mənt) *n* **1** the act of confining or the condition of being confined. **2** the period for which a mother is confined to bed during and after childbirth.

con·firm (kən fərm′) *v* **1** show or declare to be true or correct: *to confirm a rumour.* **2** check and make certain: *The travel agent confirmed the flight reservation.* **3** strengthen a belief or way of life: *His experiences in wartime confirmed him as a pacifist.* **4** *Christianity* admit to full membership in a church by a ceremony at which one declares one's intention to follow the beliefs of the church. <Old French, from Latin *com-* altogether + *firmus* firm> **con′fir·ma′tion** *n.* **con·firmed′** *adj.*

con·fis·cate (kon′fi skāt′) *v* **con·fis·cat·ed, con·fis·cat·ing** seize by a government or other authority: *The police confiscated the stolen property. The teacher confiscated my chewing gum.* <Latin *com-* together + *fiscus* public treasury. Originally, the meaning was confined to assets seized by the government.> **con′fis·ca′tion** *n.*

con·fla·gra·tion (kon′flə grā′shən) *n* a great, destructive fire: *A conflagration destroyed most of the city.* <Latin *com-* altogether + *flagrare* burn>

con·flict (kon′flikt) *for n,* (kən flikt′) *for v. n* **1** a fight or struggle: *armed conflict.* **2** a direct opposition or disagreement: *a conflict of opinions. I have a conflict in my schedule; my music lesson is at the same time as baseball practice.*
v be directly opposed: *Their stories of the accident conflict.* <Latin *com-* together + *fligere* to strike>

con·flict·ed (kən flik′tid) *adj* filled with opposing feelings or desires: *My brother is quite conflicted about whether to quit his job or not.*

conflict of interest *n* a potential clash, or opposition, between the private interests and the public responsibilities of a person in a position of trust, such as a government official.

con·flu·ence (kon′flū əns) *n* **1** a flowing together: *the confluence of two rivers.* **2** a coming together of people or things: *a huge confluence of people at the Canada Day celebrations.* <Latin *com-* together + *fluere* flow> **con′flu·ent** *adj.*

a bat	e bed	i bid	o pot	u cup	th thin
ā cake	ē me	ī bite	ō go	ū rude	TH then
ä bar	ə about	ər over	ô for	u̇ put	zh measure

con·form (kən fôrm′) *v* **1** follow a law, standard, custom, fashion, etc.: *to conform to tradition, to conform to the rules of a club. Her bizarre clothing is part of her general refusal to conform.* **2** be or make similar: *The path conforms to the shoreline of the lake.* <Latin *com-* similar + *formare* shape> **con·form′ance** *n.* **con·form′i·ty** *n.*

con·form·a·ble (kən fôr′mə bəl) *adj* **1** similar. **2** in basic agreement: *The committee felt that the proposal was not conformable to their interests.* **con·form′a·bly** *adv.*

con·form·a·tion (kən fôr mə′ shən) *n* the shape or structure of something.

con·form·ist (kən fôr′mist) *n* a person who tends to conform to prevailing customs or ways of life. **con·form′ism** *n.*

con·found (kən found′) *v* **1** be confused or puzzled (by): *The shock confounded her. The general was confounded by the violence of the enemy attack.* **2** (*used as a mild curse*) damn: *Confound this pen! It never works!* <Old French, from Latin *com-* together + *fundere* pour>

con·found·ed (kən foun′did) *or* (kon foun′did) *adj* (*used as a mild curse*) detestable: *Where did I put the confounded thing?* **con·found′ed·ly** *adv.*

con·front (kən frunt′) *v* **1** meet or face: *We were immediately confronted with a problem.* **2** face boldly: *to confront danger. She whirled round and confronted the bully.* **3** force to see or recognize something: *The lawyer confronted the accused with the forged cheque.* <French, from Latin *com-* together + *frons, front-* face>

con·fron·ta·tion (kon′frən tā′shən) *n* **1** the act or fact of confronting. **2** an open conflict: *a confrontation between demonstrators and police.* **3** direct challenge as a way of handling disagreement: *a policy of confrontation. He doesn't believe in confrontation.* **con′fron·ta′tion·al** *adj.*

Con·fu·cian·ism (kən fyū′shə niz′əm) *n* a philosophical and religious system developed from the teachings of **Confucius** (kən fyū′shəs), a Chinese philosopher and teacher (551–479 BCE). **Confucian** philosophy emphasizes practical moral values. **Con·fu′cian·ist** *n, adj.* **Con·fu′cian·ist′·ic** *adj.*

con·fus·a·ble (kən fyūz′ə bəl) *n* two or more items so similar that they are easily mistaken for one another.

con·fuse (kən fyūz′) *v* **con·fused, con·fus·ing 1** throw into disorder: *His room was a confused jumble of clothes and books.* **2** make unable to think clearly: *So many people talking to me at once confused me.* **3** be unable to tell apart, or mistake one thing for another: *Even their own mother sometimes confused the twins.* <Old French, from Latin *com-* together + *fundere* to pour, i.e., mix> **con·fus′a·ble** *adj.* **con·fu′sion** *n.*

conga (kong′gə) *n* **1** a Cuban dance of African origin, usually performed by a group of people moving one behind the other in a single line. **2** a tall, narrow, low-toned drum beaten with the hands.
v **con·gaed** or **con·ga'd, con·ga·ing** dance the conga.

con·geal (kən jēl′) *v* **1** harden or make solid by cold. **2** thicken; clot: *The blood around the wound had congealed.* <Old French, from Latin *com-* together + *gelu* frost> **con·geal′ment** *n.*

con·ge·ni·al (kən jēn′yəl) *adj* **1** friendly and comfortable: *a congenial atmosphere.* **2** pleasant because matching one's tastes and interests: *congenial work, congenial companions.* <Latin *com-* together + *genitus* spirit> **con·ge′ni·al′i·ty** *n.* **con·ge′ni·al·ly** *adv.*

con·gen·i·tal (kən jen′ə təl) *adj* present at birth, but not necessarily inherited: *congenital deafness, a congenital heart defect.* Compare HEREDITARY. <Latin *com-* with + *genitus* born> **con·gen′i·tal·ly** *adv.*

con·ger eel (kong′gər) *n* a large, scaleless, marine eel found along the coasts of Eurasia and Africa and the Atlantic coast of America. <Old French, from Greek *gongros*>

con·gest (kən jest′) *v* **1** overcrowd or clog: *congested classrooms, traffic congesting the streets.* **2** cause too much blood or mucus to gather in the body: *congested nasal passages.* <Old French, from Latin *com-* together + *gerere* bring> **con·gest′ed** *adj.* **con·ges′tion** *n.*

con·ges·tive heart failure (kən jest′iv) *n* ongoing failure of the heart to pump enough blood from the ventricles, so that some veins and organs are congested with blood while others have an inadequate supply.

con·glom·er·ate (kən glom′ə rāt′) *for v,* (kən glom′ə rit) *for n or adj. v* **con·glom·er·at·ed, con·glom·er·at·ing** gather into a mass or cluster.
n **1** a mass formed of fragments stuck together. **2** *Geology* a sedimentary rock consisting of boulders or pebbles held together by a natural cementing material. **3** a large corporation made up of several companies dealing in different products or services.
adj **1** gathered into a mass or cluster. **2** made up of miscellaneous materials gathered from various sources. <Latin *com-* together + *glomus* ball> **con·glom′er·a′tion** *n.*

Con·go (kong′gō) *n* usually, **the Congo** a country in central Africa. **Con′go·lese′** *adj, n.*

con·grat·u·late (kən grach′ə lāt′) *v* **con·grat·u·lat·ed, con·grat·u·lat·ing 1** express pleasure at someone's happiness or success: *I congratulated my friend on making the honour roll.* **2** (*used reflexively*) take pride in one's own ability or luck: *He congratulated himself on having won the argument.* <Latin *com-* together + *gratus* pleasing> **con·grat′u·la′tion** *n.* **con·grat′u·la′to·ry** *adj.*

con·grat·u·la·tions (kən grach′ə lā′shənz) *pln or interj* an expression of pleasure at another's happiness or good fortune: *Congratulations are due to all our graduates* (*pln*). *Congratulations! You won* (*interj*).

con·gre·gate (kong′grə gāt′) *v* **con·gre·gat·ed, con·gre·gat·ing** come together into a crowd: *Thousands of people congregated in the town square to see the queen. The class test results congregate around the 67 percent mark.* <Latin *com-* together + *grex, greg-* flock>

con·gre·ga·tion (kong′grə gā′shən) *n* **1** a group of people gathered together for religious worship or instruction, or all the people that regularly gather in this way. **2** a gathering or collection of people or things: *A small congregation of unmatched socks lay in the laundry basket.* **3** the act of coming together or assembling. **con′gre·ga′tion·al** *adj.*

con·gre·ga·tion·al·ism (kong′grə gā′shə nə liz′əm) *Christianity n* **1** a system or philosophy of church government in which each local congregation governs itself independently. **2 Congregationalism** a Protestant movement favouring this system. **con′gre·ga′tion·al** or **Con′gre·ga′tion·al** *adj.* **con′gre·ga′tion·al·ist** or **Con′gre·ga′tion·al·ist** *n, adj.*

con·gress (kong′gris) *n* **1** a formal meeting of representatives of interested groups to discuss some subject: *delegates to an international congress on conservation.* **2** an organization of people for the purpose of promoting a common concern: *the Canadian Labour Congress.* **3 Congress a** the lawmaking body of a nation, especially of a republic, such as the US. **b** a session of such a body. **4** the act of meeting together: *a congress of cultures.* <Latin from *com-* together + *gradi* walk> **con·gres′sion·al** or **Con·gres′sion·al** *adj.*

con·gress·man (kong′gris mən) *n, pl* **con·gress·men** (*capitalized when used with a name*) in the US, a male member of Congress, especially of the House of Representatives.

con·gress·wom·an (kong′gris wu̇m′ən) *n, pl* **con·gress·wom·en** (*capitalized when used with a name*) in the US, a female member of Congress, especially of the House of Representatives.

con·gru·ent (kong′grū ənt) *or* (kən grū′ənt) *adj* **1** in agreement or harmony. **2** *Mathematics* exactly the same in size and shape, so that all parts match: *congruent triangles.* Compare SIMILAR. <Latin *com-* together + *ruere* fall or rush> **con′gru·ence** or **con·gru′en·cy** *n.* **con′gru·ent·ly** *adv.*

con·gru·ous (kong′grū əs) *adj* **1** in agreement or harmony. **2** fitting or appropriate. **con·gru′i·ty** *n.* **con′gru·ous·ly** *adv.*

con·i·cal (kon′ə kəl) *adj* **1** cone-shaped or like a cone: *The clown wore a conical hat.* **2** usually, **conic** *Mathematics* to do with a CONE (def. 2). **con′i·cal·ly** *adv.*

con·ic section (kon′ik) *Mathematics n* a curve forming the edge of the flat surface produced when a piece is cut off across a cone.

co·ni·fer (kon′ə fər) *n* a tree or shrub, most species of which have small, needle-shaped, evergreen leaves and all of which carry their seeds in cones. Compare DECIDUOUS. **co·nif′er·ous** (kə nif′ə rəs) *adj.*

con·jec·ture (kən jek′chər) *n* **1** an opinion formed without evidence or proof: *There were many conjectures about where she went, but no one knew for certain.* **2** opinions of this kind, or the process of forming them.
v **con·jec·tured, con·jec·tur·ing** form an opinion based on guesswork: *He conjectured that they were talking about him behind his back.* <Old French, from Latin *com-* together + *jacere* throw> **con·jec′tur·a·ble** *adj.* **con·jec′tur·al** *adj.*

con·join (kən join′) *v* join together. **Conjoined twins** are twins born joined together. <Old French, from Latin *com-* together + *jungere* to join>

con·ju·gal (kon′jə gəl) *adj* to do with marriage or with a spouse. <Latin *com-* together + *jugum* yoke> **con′ju·gal·ly** *adv.*

con·ju·gate (kon′jə gāt′) *for v,* (kon′jə git) *for adj.*
v **con·ju·gat·ed, con·ju·gat·ing** **1** give all the forms of a verb according to a systematic arrangement. **2** join together.
adj joined together. **con′ju·ga′tion** *n.*

con·junc·tion (kən jungk′shən) *n* **1** a joining or being joined together: *A headache in conjunction with the hot weather has me feeling miserable.* **2** *Grammar* a word that connects two grammatical units of the same kind, such as two nouns, two adjectives, two clauses, etc. Examples: *and, but, if, because, although.* See also CO-ORDINATING CONJUNCTION, SUBORDINATING CONJUNCTION, CORRELATIVE CONJUNCTION. **3** the apparent nearness of two or more heavenly bodies: *the Sun is in conjunction with Mars.* <Old French, from Latin *com-* together + *jungere* join>

GRAMMAR AND USAGE

Conjunctions are sometimes called *joining words.* They join two words or two parts of a sentence:

*We bought marshmallows **and** chocolate.*

*She walks to school **but** I take the bus.*

*The student will fail the test **if** he does not study.*

con·junc·tive (kən jungk′tiv) *adj* **1** joining together. **2** like a conjunction. The word *then* is a **conjunctive adverb**.
n a conjunctive word. **con·junc′tive·ly** *adv.*

GRAMMAR AND USAGE

Conjunctive adverbs are words that are ordinarily adverbs but, at times, are used to connect main clauses. In formal writing they are preceded by a semicolon:

I didn't get much sleep; ***consequently*** *I'm really tired.*

Some common conjunctive adverbs: *also, anyway, besides, however, indeed, likewise, nevertheless, then.*

con·junc·ti·vi·tis (kən jungk′tə vī′tis) *n* an inflammation of the **conjunctiva** (kon′jungk tī′və), the mucous membrane covering the front of the eyeball and the inner surface of the eyelids.

con·jure (kon′jər) *v* **con·jured, con·jur·ing** **1** (*sometimes with **up***) cause to appear as if by magic: *The magician conjured a rabbit from a hat.* **2** supposedly do magic or sorcery. **3** (*with **up***) bring an image or memory to the mind: *The melody conjures up visions of the sea.* <Old French *conjurer* plot (in secret), from Latin *com-* together + *jurare* swear> **con′jur·er** or **con′jur·or** *n.*
a name to conjure with, a person who or thing that has great importance or influence.

conk (konk) *Slang v, n* hit or punch. <possibly *conch*>
conk out, *Slang* stop functioning: *The air conditioner always conks out on the hottest day. By four o'clock, I'm about ready to conk out.*

a bat	e bed	i bid	o pot	u cup	th thin
ā cake	ē me	ī bite	ō go	ū rude	ᴛʜ then
à bar	ə about	ər over	ȯ for	u̇ put	zh measure

con·nect (kə nekt′) *v* **1** link or fasten two things together: *The plumber has to connect the pipes before the water can be turned on.* **2** think of one thing together with another: *We usually connect spring with sunshine and flowers.* **3** (*usually passive*) bring into a relationship: *This organization is not connected with any political party.* **4** put into communication, especially in a telephone system or computer network: *Please connect me with the Parts Department. Are you connected to the Internet?* **5** plug into an electrical power supply: *Don't try to repair the toaster while it is connected.* **6** relate to one another in a meaningful way: *We had a conversation, but never really connected.* **7** be scheduled so that passengers can transfer from one means of transport to another: *a connecting flight.* <Latin *com-* together + *nectere* tie> **con·nect′er** or **con·nec′tor** *n.*

con·nect·ed (kə nek′tid) *adj* **1** linked, associated, or joined. **2** hooked up or plugged in. **3** with useful social and business ties: *She is well connected.*

con·nec·tion (kə nek′shən) *n* **1** the act of connecting or the state of being connected. **2** something that connects people or things. **3** a relative: *She is a connection of ours by marriage.* **4** **connections** *pl* people with whom one has business or social ties: *She'll probably be able to get tickets through her connections in the city.* **5** *Computers* the line of communication between a computer (or any other device) and the Internet. *How fast is your connection?*
in connection with, in regard to.
in this (or **that**) **connection,** with regard to this (or that) matter.

con·nec·tive (kə nek′tiv) *adj* connecting or to do with connection.
n a word used to connect words, phrases, and clauses.

GRAMMAR AND USAGE

Connectives are words used to link ideas and help the flow of writing.

Some useful connectives: *afterward, although, as if, as long as, as soon as, even if, even though, first, in addition to, in spite of, provided that, similarly, since, so that, yet.*

connective tissue *n* tissue that forms tendons and ligaments, and supports or encloses other tissues and organs in the body.

con·ning tower (kon′ing) *n* a tower on the deck of a submarine, used as an entrance and as a place for observation. Also called (*especially US*) **sail**.

con·nip·tion (kə nip′shən) *Informal n* a tantrum or fit of rage or hysteria. Also, **conniption fit**, **conniptions**. <pseudo-Latin coining>

con·nive (kə nīv′) *v* **con·nived, con·niv·ing** **1** (*with at*) assist wrongdoing by ignoring it: *The mayor was accused of conniving at the misuse of public funds.* **2** co-operate secretly (with): *The traitor connived with the enemies of his country.* <Latin *com-* together + *nictare* to wink> **con·niv′ance** *n.* **con·niv′er** *n.*

con·nois·seur (kon′ə sər′) *n* an expert who is able to make fine distinctions and critical judgments, especially in art and matters of taste: *a connoisseur of wine, a connoisseur of antique furniture.* <French, from Latin *com-* altogether + *gnoscere* recognize>

con·note (kə nōt′) *v* **con·not·ed, con·not·ing** give a word other associations in addition to its basic meaning. Example: *plump* and *obese* both mean *fat*; but *plump* connotes attractive fullness, while *obese* connotes an unhealthy and unpleasant excess. Compare DENOTE. <Latin *com-* together + *notare* to make a note> **con′no·ta′tion** (kon′ə tā′shən) *n.*

con·quer (kong′kər) *v* **1** win control of by war: *to conquer territory.* **2** overcome or be victorious over: *to conquer an enemy, to conquer a bad habit.* **3** win someone's affections. <Old French, from Latin *com-* altogether + *quaerere* seek (i.e., collect)> **con′quer·a·ble** *adj.* **con′quer·or** *n.*

con·quest (kon′kwest) *or* (kong′kwest) *n* **1** the act of conquering. **2** the land or people who are conquered. **3** a person whose love or favour has been won: *You made a conquest of my brother—he can't stop talking about you.*

con·quis·ta·dor (kən kis′tə dȯr′) *or* (kən kwis′tə dȯr′) *n, pl* **con·quis·ta·dors** or **con·quis·ta·dor·es** (kən kis′tə dȯr′āz) one of the Spanish conquerors who went to the Americas in the 1500s to look for gold, conquering and even exterminating some native peoples. <Spanish = conqueror>

con·science (kon′shəns) *n* **1** the awareness of moral right and wrong, and the feeling that one ought to do right: *Her conscience prompted her to return the CD she had stolen.* **2** the habit of following one's conscience: *a person of conscience.* <Old French, from Latin *com-* with + *scire* know> **con′science·less** *adj.*
on your conscience, making you feel guilty: *That lie had been on her conscience for a long time.*

CONFUSABLES

Conscience means "knowing right from wrong": *Because of my conscience, I told the truth.*

Conscious means "aware": *I was conscious of someone looking at me.*

con·science–strick·en (kon′shəns strik′ən) *adj* overcome by a feeling of having done wrong.

con·sci·en·tious (kon′shē en′shəs) *adj* careful and thorough: *a conscientious worker.*
con′sci·en′tious·ly *adv.* **con′sci·en′tious·ness** *n.*

conscientious objector *n* a person whose beliefs prevent him or her from fighting in a war.

con·scion·a·ble (kon′shə nə bəl) *adj* acceptable to one's conscience. **con′scion·a·bly** *adv.*

con·scious (kon′shəs) *adj* **1** aware: *She was conscious of a sharp pain.* **2** awake: *He fainted, but he is now conscious again.* **3** capable of thought, will, or feeling: *A human being is a conscious animal.* See CONSCIENCE for confusable. **4** known to oneself: *conscious guilt.* **5** deliberate: *She's making a conscious effort to improve her writing.* **6** (*in compounds*) paying attention to: *clothes-conscious.* <Latin *com-* altogether + *scire* know> **con′scious·ly** *adv.*

con·scious·ness (kon′shəs nis) *n* **1** the state, fact, or degree of being conscious; awareness: *A blow to the head* *made him lose consciousness. We are trying to raise people's consciousness of the plight of refugees.* **2** all the thoughts, sensations, and emotions that a person is aware of having.

con·scious·ness–rais·ing (kon′shəs nis rā′zing) *n* the process of making people aware of issues, conditions, needs, or opportunities, in order to bring about change: *The main job of the campaign was consciousness-raising about mental illness.*
adj to do with this process: *consciousness-raising activities.*

con·script (kən skript′) *for v,* (kon′skript) *for adj or n. v* force by law to join the armed forces; draft.
n a person who has been drafted into the armed forces.
adj drafted into the armed forces. <Latin *com-* altogether + *scribere* write in a list> **con·scrip′tion** *n.*

con·se·crate (kon′sə krāt′) *v* **con·se·crat·ed, con·se·crat·ing** **1** set apart as sacred: *to consecrate a church for worship.* **2** devote to a purpose: *He has consecrated his life to music.* <Latin *com-* altogether + *sacer* sacred> **con′se·cra′tion** *n.*

con·sec·u·tive (kən sek′yə tiv) *adj* following one after another without interruption: *She was absent for three consecutive days, from Tuesday to Thursday.* <French, from Latin *com-* with + *sequi* follow> **con·sec′u·tive·ly** *adv.*

con·sen·sus (kən sen′səs) *n* **1** the opinion of all or most of the people consulted: *The consensus in our class was that the teacher had been quite fair.* **2** a policy of working toward general agreement of everyone or of the majority before taking action: *government by consensus.* <Latin = agreement>

GRAMMAR AND USAGE

It is best to avoid the phrase *consensus of opinion*, since **consensus** already has *of opinion* in its meaning. Just say *consensus*.

con·sent (kən sent′) *v* give permission or approval: *His father would not consent to his leaving school. She consented to run for class president.*
n approval or permission: *We have Mom's consent to go on the ski trip.* <Old French, from Latin *com-* together + *sentire* feel>

con·se·quence (kon′sə kwəns) *n* **1** a result or effect: *The consequence of his fall was a broken leg.* **2** importance: *The loss of that old coat is a matter of little consequence. She is a person of consequence in the community.*
in consequence, as a result.
suffer the consequences, accept any undesirable results of your actions: *Do it your way, but you'll have to suffer the consequences if it doesn't work out.*

con·se·quent (kon′sə kwənt) *adj* following as a natural result or effect: *His illness and consequent absence put him behind in his schoolwork.* <Old French, from Latin *com-* altogether + *sequi* follow> **con′se·quent·ly** *adv.*

con·ser·va·tion (kon′sər vā′shən) *n* **1** the act or policy of conserving: *the conservation of energy.* **2** the protection and care of the natural environment.
con′ser·va′tion·ist *n.*

conservation area *n* a forest or other undeveloped natural area placed under official protection and care, and usually open for recreational use.

conservation of energy *Physics n* the principle that the total amount of energy in the universe does not change, although energy can be converted from one form to another.

conservation of matter *Physics n* the principle that the total mass of any closed system remains unchanged by reactions within the system.

C

con·serv·a·tism (kən sər′və tiz′əm) *n* conservative policy or practice.

con·ser·va·tive (kən sər′və tiv) *adj* **1** inclined to keep things as they are, or as they were in the past. **2 Conservative** in Canada, **a** to do with the Conservative Party. **b** to do with the Progressive Conservative Party. **3** avoiding risks, extremes, novelties, or exaggeration: *a conservative estimate of the size of the crowd, shoes of a conservative style.* **4** to do with conserving.
n **1** a conservative person. **2 Conservative** in Canada, a supporter of the Conservative Party or the Progressive Conservative Party. **con·serv′a·tive·ly** *adv.* **con·serv′a·tive·ness** *n.*

Conservative Party *n* **1** one of the registered political parties of Canada. **2** 🍁 Progressive Conservative Party.

con·serv·a·to·ry (kən sər′və tô′rē) *n, pl* **con·serv·a·to·ries** **1** a greenhouse or sunroom for growing and displaying plants. **2** a school for instruction in music.

con·serve (kən sərv′) *for v,* (kon′sərv) *or* (kən sərv′) *for n.* *v* **con·served, con·serv·ing** **1** protect the natural environment from harm. **2** keep from being wasted or used up: *to conserve water. Conserve your strength for the end of the race.* **3** cook and can fruit with sugar.
n fruit cooked and preserved with sugar: *strawberry conserve.* <Old French, from Latin *com-* together + *servare* preserve>

con·sid·er (kən sid′ər) *v* **1** think about in order to make a decision: *The committee is considering the proposal. Would you consider going to the dance with me?* **2** think carefully: *He considered for a while before answering.* **3** think to be: *We consider her our best player.* **4** take into account: *This skateboard is in very good shape, if you consider how old it is.* **5** be thoughtful of others and their feelings. **6** look at closely. <Old French, from Latin *considerare* examine>

SYNONYMS

Consider means "think over": *He considered his travel options and chose the train.*

Meditate can mean "reflect quietly": *She meditated alone in her room before making her decision.*

Mull means "give careful thought to": *He mulled over the problem for hours.*

a bat	e bed	i bid	o pot	u cup	th thin
ā cake	ē me	ī bite	ō go	ū rude	ᴛʜ then
ä bar	ə about	ər over	ô for	ů put	zh measure

con·sid·er·a·ble (kən sid′ə rə bəl) *adj* enough, or good enough, to be worth thinking about or taking seriously: *a considerable sum, considerable political influence. She is a very considerable poet.* **con·sid′er·a·bly** *adv.*

con·sid·er·ate (kən sid′ə rit) *adj* thoughtful of others and their feelings. **con·sid′er·ate·ly** *adv.*
con·sid′er·ate·ness *n.*

con·sid·er·a·tion (kən sid′ə rā′shən) *n* **1** careful thought about something before making a decision: *Please give careful consideration to this question.* **2** something to be considered: *Price and quality are two considerations in buying anything.* **3** money or other payment: *He said he would cut the grass for a small consideration.* **4** thoughtfulness for others and their feelings: *Thank you for your consideration.* **5** importance: *a matter of some consideration.*
in consideration of, a because of: *In consideration of his wife's poor health, he moved to a milder climate.* **b** in return for: *She gave him a present in consideration of his helpfulness.*
on no consideration, not at all.
take into consideration, take into account: *The judge took the accused's mental state into consideration.*
under consideration, being discussed or thought about: *The length of your suspension is under consideration by the principal.*

con·sid·ered (kən sid′ərd) *adj* carefully thought out: *in my considered opinion.*

con·sid·er·ing (kən sid′ə ring) *prep* making allowances for: *Considering her age, she doesn't read very well.*
adv taking everything into consideration: *He does very well, considering.*

con·sign (kən sīn′) *v* **1** deliver, often to an undesirable fate: *The man was consigned to prison. That writer's books will be consigned to oblivion.* **2** deliver goods for sale, without being paid for them until another sells them. Such goods are said to be delivered **on consignment**. <Latin *com-* with + *signum* a seal) **con·sign′ment** *n.*

con·sist (kən sist′) *v* **1** (*with* ***of***) be made up of: *A week consists of seven days.* **2** (*with* ***in***) have its existence or being in: *Happiness for him consists in being left alone.* <Latin *com-* with + *sistere* stand>

con·sist·en·cy (kən sis′tən sē) *n, pl* **con·sist·en·cies** **1** degree of firmness: *Icing for a cake must be of the correct consistency to spread easily without dripping.* **2** the fact of being consistent: *There is little consistency between the two reports. Consistency is important in training pets.*

con·sist·ent (kən sis′tənt) *adj* **1** keeping to the same principles, rules, or course of action: *Whatever verb tense you choose for your story, be consistent.* **2** in agreement: *Such fast driving is not consistent with safety.* **3** of the same quality at all times: *The team has given a consistent performance this season.* **con·sist′ent·ly** *adv.*

con·so·la·tion (kon′sə lā′shən) *n* comfort, or a source of comfort: *Your presence was a consolation when I was sad.*
adj between losers in an earlier round of a tournament: *a consolation match.*

consolation prize *n* a prize given to a person or team that has not won, but has done well.

con·sole[1] (kən sōl′) *v* **con·soled, con·sol·ing** comfort. <French, from Latin *com-* with + *solari* soothe>
con·sol′a·ble *adj.* **con·sol′er** *n.*

con·sole[2] (kon′sōl) *n* **1** a panel of buttons, switches, or dials, used to control equipment. **2** *Music* the part of an organ containing the keyboard, stops, and pedals. **3** a cabinet for a TV set or stereo system. <French>

con·sol·i·date (kən sol′ə dāt′) *v* **con·sol·i·dat·ed, con·sol·i·dat·ing** **1** combine or merge: *to consolidate your debts.* **2** make secure or strengthen: *The army spent a day consolidating its advance by digging trenches.* <Latin *com-* together + *solidus* solid> **con·sol′i·da′tion** *n.*

🍁 **consolidated school** *n* a school for students from several school districts, especially in rural areas.

con·som·mé (kon′sə mā′) *n* a clear soup made by boiling meat, fish, or vegetables in water, and then straining the liquid. <French, from Latin *com-* completely + *summare* finish (with all the goodness taken from the meat, etc.)>

con·so·nance (kon′sə nəns) *n* **1** harmony; agreement. **2** *Music* harmony of tones. Compare DISSONANCE.

con·so·nant (kon′sə nənt) *n* **1** a speech sound formed by completely or partially blocking the breath. **2** a letter of the alphabet representing such a sound.
adj **1** in agreement: *Her cheerful manner is consonant with her happy nature.* **2** *Music* harmonious in tone. **3** to do with a consonant. <Old French, from Latin *com-* together + *sonus* sound> **con′so·nan′tal** *adj.*
con′so·nant·ly *adv.*

con·sort (kən sȯrt′) *for v,* (kon′sȯrt) *for n. v* keep company with: *Do not consort with hypocrites.*
n **1** a spouse, especially of a monarch. **2** an associate or companion. <French, from Latin *consortis* partner>

con·sor·tium (kən sȯr′shəm) *n, pl* **con·sor·tia** (kən sȯr′shə) or **con·sor·tiums** a partnership or association, especially among several companies or nations, for a specific undertaking. <Latin *com-* together with + *sortis* luck, destiny>

con·spic·u·ous (kən spik′yū əs) *adj* **1** easily seen: *Post the warning in a conspicuous location.* **2** attracting attention: *a conspicuous lack of manners, conspicuous by her absence.* <Latin *com-* altogether + *specere* look at>
con·spic′u·ous·ly *adv.* **con·spic′u·ous·ness** *n.*

con·spir·a·cy (kən spēr′ə sē) *n, pl* **con·spir·a·cies** **1** the act of scheming or plotting together to do wrong. **2** the plot or scheme itself, or the people involved in making it: *the leader of the conspiracy.* **3** the fact of occurring together as if by evil design: *There seemed to be a conspiracy of events to ruin our weekend.*

con·spire (kən spīr′) *v* **con·spired, con·spir·ing** **1** plan secretly with others to do something wrong; plot. **2** act together, as if by design: *The rain, the cold, and the mosquitoes conspired to ruin the concert in the park. All things conspired to make her birthday a happy one.* <Old French, from Latin *com-* together + *spirare* whisper>
con·spir′a·tor (kən spēr′ə tər) *n.*

con·sta·ble (kon′stə bəl) *n* a low-ranking police officer. <Old French, from Latin *comes stabuli* count of the stable; later, chief household officer>

C

con·stab·u·lary (kən stab′yə ler′ē) *n,* *pl* **con·stab·u·lar·ies** the group of constables of a particular police force.

con·stant (kon′stənt) *adj* **1** happening all the time or again and again: *three days of constant rain, his constant complaints.* **2** always the same: *travelling at a constant speed.* **3** loyal: *A constant friend is always there when you need help.*
n **1** *Mathematics* a quantity that does not change. **2** something unchanging. <Old French, from Latin *com-* with + *stare* stand> **con′stan·cy** (kon′stən sē) *n.* **con′stant·ly** *adv.*

con·stel·la·tion (kon′stə lā′shən) *n* a group of stars: *The Big Dipper is the easiest constellation to locate.* <Old French, from Latin *com-* together + *stella* star>

con·ster·na·tion (kon′stər nā′shən) *n* great dismay: *To our consternation, the dog raced out of sight.* <Latin *com-* altogether + *sternere* lay prone>

con·sti·pate (kon′stə pāt′) *v* **con·sti·pat·ed, con·sti·pat·ing** interfere with the regular movement of the bowels, so that it becomes difficult or impossible for the person to pass solid waste: *Bananas constipate me.* **con′sti·pa′tion** *n.*

con·stit·u·en·cy (kən stich′ū ən sē) *n,* *pl* **con·stit·u·en·cies** **1** a voting district represented by a member of a legislature. **2** the voters in this district: *Our MP pays careful attention to the needs of his constituency.* **3** a group of supporters or customers: *The newspaper hired more columnists to appeal to a broader constituency.*

con·stit·u·ent (kən stich′ū ənt) *adj* helping to make up a whole or compound: *Hydrogen and oxygen are constituent elements of water.*
n **1** a part of a whole, especially an essential one: *Sugar is the main constituent of candy.* **2** a person who votes: *Few of the MLA's constituents failed to vote.* <See CONSTITUTE.>

con·sti·tute (kon′stə tyūt′) *or* (kon′stə tūt′) *v* **con·sti·tut·ed, con·sti·tut·ing** **1** make up or form: *Seven days constitute a week. Hailstorms constitute a serious threat to standing crops.* **2** *Formal* appoint or elect: *He was constituted president of the Home and School Association.* **3** set up or establish: *Courts are constituted by law to dispense justice.* **4** make by putting parts together: *The cabin is well constituted and will withstand the severest weather.* <Latin *com-*together + *statuere* set up>

con·sti·tu·tion (kon′stə tyū′shən) *or* (kon′stə tū′shən) *n* **1** a person's physical makeup: *He has a sound constitution and is rarely sick.* **2** the way in which something is put together, or the act or fact of doing this. **3** the set of fundamental principles by which a nation, state, or group is governed, or a document stating these principles. <See CONSTITUTE.>

🍁 **Constitution Act 1867** *n* since 1981, the name of the British North America Act.

🍁 **Constitution Act 1982** *n* the document setting forth Canada's basic principles of government. It includes the CHARTER OF RIGHTS AND FREEDOMS, provisions from the British North America Act (now the **Constitution Act 1867**), and a clause governing future amendment of the constitution. Also called **Canada Act 1982**.

con·sti·tu·tion·al (kon′stə tyū′shə nəl) *or* (kon′stə tū′shə nəl) *adj* **1** to do with the physical makeup of a person or thing: *A constitutional weakness makes him subject to colds.* **2** to do with the constitution of a nation or organization: *an expert in constitutional law, the constitutional obligations of the government.* **3** for one's health.
n a walk or other exercise taken for one's health. **con′sti·tu′tion·al′i·ty** *n.* **con′sti·tu′tion·al′ly** *adv.*

🍁 **Constitutional Act** CANADA ACT 1791.

constitutional monarchy *n* a system of government in which the ruler's powers are limited by the constitution and the laws of the nation. Compare ABSOLUTE MONARCHY. Also called **limited monarchy**.

con·strain (kən strān′) *v* **1** force or compel by authority, by moral means, or by circumstances: *My father was constrained to accept his employer's decision or leave the job.* **2** place under certain limits: *ambition constrained by family responsibility.* **3** make stiff and unnatural because of tension or anxiety: *constrained attempts at conversation.* <Old French, from Latin *com-* together + *stringere* pull tightly> **con·straint′** *n.*

con·strict (kən strikt′) *v* squeeze or make narrower: *Apply a tourniquet to constrict the blood vessels and stop the bleeding.* <See CONSTRAIN.> **con·stric′tion** *n.* **con·stric′tive** *adj.*

con·stric·tor (kən strik′tər) *n* **1** a snake that kills its prey by squeezing it with its coils. **2** a muscle that constricts a part of the body.

con·struct (kən strukt′) *v* **1** put together or build: *Sentences are constructed of words. The house is constructed of brick.* **2** *Mathematics* draw a geometrical figure so as to fulfill given conditions. <Latin *com-* together + *struere* pile>

con·struc·tion (kən struk′shən) *n* **1** the act or manner of constructing. **2** something constructed: *The doll's house was a construction of wood and paper.* **3** an arrangement of words in a sentence, clause, or phrase. **4** an interpretation: *He put an unfair construction on what she said.*

GRAMMAR AND USAGE

In formal writing, it is best to use balanced or parallel **construction.** Adjectives should parallel adjectives, phrases should parallel phrases, etc.

Instead of saying *Your speech was informative, and it entertained us,* it is more balanced to write:
Your speech was informative and entertaining, or
Your speech informed and entertained us.

construction paper *n* heavy coloured paper, used for arts and crafts.

con·struc·tive (kən struk′tiv) *adj* **1** helpful or improving a situation: *constructive criticism. It is not constructive to have too many rules.* **2** to do with construction. **con·struc′tive·ly** *adv.* **con·struc′tive·ness** *n.*

a bat	e bed	i bid	o pot	u cup	th **thin**
ā cake	ē me	ī bite	ō go	ū rude	ᴛʜ **then**
ȧ bar	ə about	ər over	ȯ for	u̇ put	zh measure

con·strue (kən strū′) *v* **con·strued, con·stru·ing** 1 interpret: *Different lawyers may construe the same law differently.* 2 analyze the syntax of a text, sentence, or word. <Latin *com-* together + *struere* arrange>

con·sul (kon′səl) *n* 1 an official appointed by the government of a country to look after its business interests in a foreign city and to help any of its own citizens who may be in that city. 2 either of the two chief magistrates of the ancient Roman republic. 3 one of the three chief magistrates of the first French Republic (1799–1804). <Latin> **con′su·lar** *adj.* **con′sul·ship** *n.*

con·su·late (kon′sə lit) *n* 1 the official residence or offices of a consul: *He visited the Canadian consulate in New York.* 2 the position or term of office of a consul. 3 a government led by consuls: *France was governed by a consulate from 1799 to 1804.*

con·sult (kən sult′) *v* 1 seek information or advice from: *to consult a dictionary, to consult a doctor.* 2 (*with* ***with***) talk things over: *He is consulting with his lawyer.* 3 work as a professional consultant: *She consults for the school board.* <French, from Latin *consulere* take counsel>
con′sul·ta′tion *n.* **con·sult′ing** *adj.*

con·sult·ant (kən sul′tənt) *n* a person who gives professional or business advice: *a financial consultant.*

consulting room *n* the room in which a doctor, lawyer, or other professional meets with clients.

con·sum·a·ble (kən sū′mə bəl) *adj* intended to be used up: *Paper is a consumable product.*
n an article intended to be used up: *Government offices have been told to cut expenditures on pens, pencils, and other consumables.*

con·sume (kən sūm′) *v* **con·sumed, con·sum·ing** 1 eat or drink: *We consumed the whole bowl of fruit.* 2 destroy, especially by fire: *A fire can consume a forest.* 3 use up: *Homework consumes a lot of my evening.* 4 absorb the full attention of: *This problem has been consuming him for weeks.* <Latin *com-* altogether + *sumere* take up>
consumed with, preoccupied with: *consumed with envy.*

con·sum·er (kən sū′mər) *n* 1 a person who buys and uses goods produced by others: *A reduction in cost for the manufacturer should lead to a lower price for the consumer.* 2 *Ecology* an organism that feeds on other organisms or on materials they produce. 3 any person who or thing that consumes.

consumer goods *Economics pln* goods that people buy and use or consume. Food and clothing are two kinds of consumer goods. Compare CAPITAL GOODS.

con·su·mer·ism (kən sū′mə riz′əm) *n* the belief that prosperity can be measured by the amount of goods consumed.

consumer price index *n* a measure of the change in the cost of living, expressed as the percentage of increase or decrease in the cost of certain consumer goods.

con·sum·ing (kən sū′ming) *adj* 1 taking up all or most of a person's time and attention: *The school yearbook is a consuming interest of his right now.* 2 (*in compounds*) using up something in great quantities: *time-consuming, energy-consuming.*

con·sum·mate (kon′sə māt′) *for v,* (kon′sə mit) *or* (kən sum′it) *for adj.*
v **con·sum·mat·ed, con·sum·mat·ing** 1 complete a marriage by sexual union. 2 fulfil: *to consummate a lifelong ambition.*
adj complete or perfect: *consummate skill as an athlete.* <Latin *com-* altogether + *summus* highest, supreme>
con′sum·mate·ly *adv.* **con′sum·ma′tion** *n.*

con·sump·tion (kən sump′shən) *n* 1 the act or extent of using up: *Bring food for consumption on the trip. Our hydro consumption was up again last month.* 2 a former name for tuberculosis. **con·sump′tive** *adj.*

con·tact (kon′takt) *n* 1 the condition of touching: *Soap should not come in contact with the eyes. The disease is spread through contact.* 2 communication: *He has kept in contact with his old friends. The control tower lost contact with the pilot.* 3 a person one knows and can call on, especially for business purposes: *She has a useful contact in an advertising agency.* 4 an unknown person to be met by another in a secret operation or to relay a message: *Your contact will be wearing a blue anorak.* 5 *Medicine* a person through whom one is exposed to a contagious disease. 6 a part connecting two conductors of electricity in a circuit: *The contacts must be dirty because the light is flickering.* 7 **contacts** *pl* contact lenses.
v communicate with: *We could not contact them.* <Latin *com-* together with + *tangere* to touch>
make contact (with), a communicate successfully. **b** touch or hit: *If that wire makes contact with this terminal, the whole thing will explode. With his third swing, the batter made contact.*

contact flying *n* the flying of an aircraft within sight of the ground, using known points or objects on the ground to navigate. Compare INSTRUMENT FLYING.

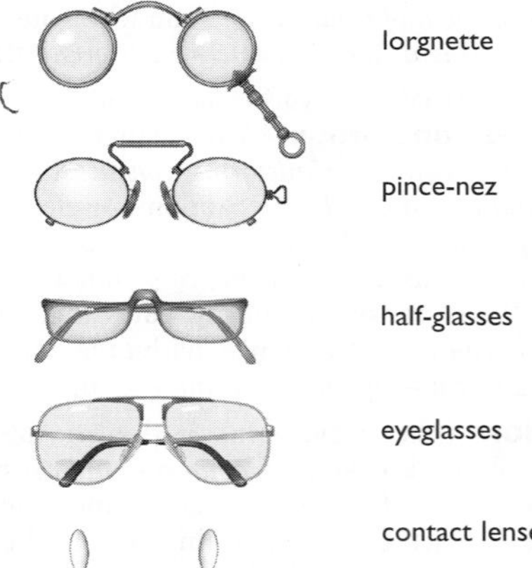

contact lens *n* a small, thin plastic lens made according to an optical prescription and worn directly over the pupil of the eye to correct vision.

con·ta·gion (kən tā′jən) *n* 1 the spreading of disease by contact. 2 a disease spread in this way. 3 a spreading influence or emotional state, especially a bad one: *A contagion of fear swept through the crowd and caused a panic.* <Latin *com-* together + *tangere* touch>

con·ta·gious (kən tā′jəs) *adj* 1 spreading by contact: *Chicken pox is a contagious disease.* 2 liable to pass on a disease by contact: *She has not fully recovered, but she is no longer contagious.* Compare INFECTIOUS. **3** easily spread from one person to another: *Yawning is often contagious.* **con·ta′gious·ly** *adv.* **con·ta′gious·ness** *n.*

con·tain (kən tān′) *v* **1** have within itself: *Books contain information. This purse contains no money.* **2** be capable of holding: *a jug containing one litre.* **3** control or restrain: *He contained his anger.* <Old French, from Latin *com-* altogether + *tenere* hold> **con·tain′a·ble** *adj.*
con·tain′ment *n.*

con·tain·er (kən tā′nər) *n* **1** a box, can, or jar used to hold or contain something. **2** a very large, boxlike receptacle of a standard size for transporting cargo: *The flatbed truck was carrying a container.*

container car *n* a railway flatcar adapted for carrying a CONTAINER (def. 2).

con·tam·i·nate (kən tam′ə nāt′) *v* **con·tam·i·nat·ed, con·tam·i·nat·ing** pollute or make impure: *Runoff from grazing land can contaminate ground water.* <Latin *com-* together with + *tangere* touch> **con·tam′i·na′tion** *n.*

con·tem·plate (kon′təm plāt′) *v* **con·tem·plat·ed, con·tem·plat·ing** **1** look at steadily or for a long time: *They sat there for some time, contemplating the evening sky.* **2** consider thoughtfully: *He contemplated his past life, with its successes and failures.* **3** meditate: *I sometimes like to sit and contemplate.* **4** consider as a possible course of action: *My sister is contemplating a change of career.* <Latin *com-* with + *templum* place for observation>
con′tem·pla′tion *n.*

con·tem·pla·tive (kən təm′plə tiv) *adj* **1** thoughtful. **2** devoted to religious meditation and prayer: *The Trappist monks are a contemplative order.*

con·tem·po·rar·y (kən tem′pə rer′ē) *adj* **1** to do with the present time: *contemporary theatre, contemporary attitudes.* **2** existing or living in the same period of time: *Maurice Richard and Pierre Trudeau were contemporary Canadians.*
n, pl **con·tem·po·rar·ies** a person who belongs to the same period of time as another or others: *Wolfe and Montcalm were contemporaries.* <Latin *com-* together + *temporis* time>

con·tempt (kən tempt′) *n* **1** the feeling that a person or thing is unworthy of any respect: *We feel contempt for a liar.* **2** the condition of being scorned or despised: *A liar is held in contempt.* <Old French, from Latin *com-* altogether + *temnere* disdain>
beneath contempt, unworthy of notice of any kind.

con·tempt·i·ble (kən temp′tə bəl) *adj* deserving contempt or scorn: *a contemptible act.* **con·tempt′i·bly** *adv.*

con·temp·tu·ous (kən temp′chū əs) *adj* full of or showing contempt: *a contemptuous sneer. He is contemptuous of anyone weaker than himself.* **con·temp′tu·ous·ly** *adv.* **con·temp′tu·ous·ness** *n.*

con·tend (kən tend′) *v* **1** fight or struggle: *The Arctic explorers had to contend with extreme cold, hunger, and loneliness.* **2** take part in a contest: *Five runners were contending in the first race.* **3** maintain as a fact in the face of opposition: *Columbus contended that the earth was round.* <Old French, from Latin *com-* with + *tendere* stretch, strive> **con·tend′er** *n.*

con·tent[1] (kon′tent) *n* **1** the facts or ideas in a book, speech, or text, as opposed to the way in which the facts are presented: *The content of her speech was good, but the form was not.* **2** the proportion of a certain substance contained in something else: *Cream has a higher fat content than milk.* **3 contents** *pl* what a thing contains: *She drained the contents of the glass in one gulp.* **4** the amount something can hold: *What is the content of the gas tank of this car?* <Old French, from Latin *com-* altogether + *tenere* hold>

con·tent[2] (kən tent′) *adj* not desiring more or other than what one has: *In spite of their small income, they were content. He was content to sit and read by himself.*
n a feeling of being satisfied and needing nothing more.
v satisfy or please: *Nothing contents her; she is always complaining.* <Old French, from Latin *com-* altogether + *tenere* hold>
content yourself, be satisfied.
to your heart's content, as much or as long as you please: *When summer comes you can swim to your heart's content.*

con·tent·ed (kən ten′tid) *adj* happy with things as they are. **con·tent′ed·ly** *adv.* **con·tent′ed·ness** *n.*

con·ten·tion (kən ten′shən) *n* **1** a statement that one argues for: *a contention that teenagers ought to be allowed to sleep until noon.* **2** arguing or disputing: *The main subject of contention was the proposed change in the school curriculum.*

con·ten·tious (kən ten′shəs) *adj* **1** quarrelsome or fond of arguing: *a contentious person.* **2** characterized by much arguing or conflict: *a contentious election campaign.* **conten′tious·ly** *adv.* **con·ten′tious·ness** *n.*

con·tent·ment (kən tent′mənt) *n* the condition of being happy with things as they are: *A cat asleep on the hearth is a picture of contentment.*

con·test (kon′test) *for n,* (kən test′) *for v.*
n **1** a competition, especially one in which entries or performances are rated by judges: *an essay contest, a pie-eating contest.* **2** a fight or dispute.
v **1** compete for: *The teams contesting the championship are both excellent.* **2** fight for: *The soldiers contested every spot of ground.* **3** argue against: *to contest a will, to contest the court's decision.* <Latin *com-* together + *testis* to witness> **con·test′a·ble** *adj.*

con·test·ant (kən tes′tənt) *n* a person taking part in a game or contest: *The contestant whose name is selected will win a trip to Paris.*

con·text (kon′tekst) *n* the text or situation in which a word, statement, or act occurs and that helps determine its meaning: *In today's high-tech context, speed is essential. In the context of the other speakers, his remarks were very mild.* <Latin *com-* together + *texere* weave>
con·tex′tu·al *adj.*

a bat	e bed	i bid	o pot	u cup	th thin
ā cake	ē me	ī bite	ō go	ū rude	ᴛʜ then
ȧ bar	ə about	ər over	ȯ for	u̇ put	zh measure

con·tig·u·ous (kən tig′yū əs) *adj* touching or adjoining: *The two farms are contiguous.* <Latin *com-* with + *tangere* touch> **con′ti·gu′i·ty** (kon′tə gyū′ə tē) *n.* **con·tig′u·ous·ly** *adv.*

con·ti·nent[1] (kon′tə nənt) *n* one of the seven great land masses on the earth: Africa, Antarctica, Asia, Australia, Europe, N America, S America. <See CONTINENT[2].>

con·ti·nent[2] (kon′tə nənt) *adj* **1** able to control one's bladder and bowels. **2** showing restraint or self-control, especially sexually. <Old French, from Latin *com-* together + *tenere* hold> **con′ti·nence** *n.*

con·ti·nen·tal (kon′tə nen′təl) *adj* **1** to do with a continent: *continental rivers.* **2 Continental** to do with the mainland of Europe, from the point of view of the UK: *Continental habits.*
n **Continental** a person living on the mainland of Europe, as opposed to a resident of the UK.

Continental breakfast *n* a light breakfast of various kinds of bread, croissants, and muffins, with butter, jam, and coffee.

Continental Divide *n* in N America, the ridge of the Rocky Mountains that separates water flowing toward the Pacific from water flowing toward the Atlantic or the Arctic.

continental drift *n* the gradual movement of the continents over the surface of the earth on a layer of magma. See also PLATE TECTONICS.

continental shelf *n* the submerged shallow shelf of land that borders most continents and ends in a steep slope (the **continental slope**) to deep water.

con·tin·gen·cy (kən tin′jən sē) *n, pl* **con·tin·gen·cies** **1** the fact of an event being uncertain or depending on chance. **2** an accidental or unexpected event: *The explorer carried supplies for every contingency.*

con·tin·gent (kən tin′jənt) *adj* **1** depending on something not certain: *Our plans for tomorrow's picnic are contingent on the weather.* **2** that may or may not happen: *Fifteen dollars a day should cover contingent expenses.*
n a group that is part of a larger group: *The Kingston contingent had seats together at the convention. Canada sent a large contingent of troops to France in World War I.* <Latin *com-* with + *tangere* to touch, happen> **con·tin′gent·ly** *adv.*

con·tin·u·al (kən tin′yū əl) *adj* **1** repeated many times: *Dancing requires continual practice.* **2** never stopping: *the continual flow of the river.* **con·tin′u·al·ly** *adv.*

CONFUSABLES

Continual means "often repeated": *Her continual complaining got on our nerves.*

Continuous means "without interruption": *The continuous rain created flood conditions.*

con·tin·u·ance (kən tin′yū əns) *n* **1** *Law* an adjournment or postponement. **2** the fact of continuing.

con·tin·ue (kən tin′yū) *v* **con·tin·ued, con·tin·u·ing** **1** go on or go on with: *The noise continued for almost an hour. We continued eating.* **2** go on after stopping: *She had lunch and then continued her studies. After a commercial, the program continued.* **3** stay: *We continue in school till the end of June.* **4** *Law* put off until a later time: *The judge has continued the case until next month.* <Old French, from Latin *com-* with + *tenere* join> **con·tin′u·a′tion** *n.*

con·ti·nu·i·ty (kon′tə nyū′ə tē) *or* (kon′tə nū′ə tē) *n, pl* **con·ti·nu·i·ties** **1** the quality of being a connected whole: *The story lacked continuity. Having the same tutor for each session provides continuity for the student.* **2** a detailed plan of a motion picture. **3 a** *Radio, Television* a connecting comment or announcement between parts of a program. **b** a script for these.

con·tin·u·ous (kən tin′yū əs) *adj* without a stop or break: *a continuous line, a continuous racket, a continuous flow of traffic.* **con·tin′u·ous·ly** *adv.*

con·tin·u·um (kən tin′yū əm) *n, pl* **con·tin·u·ums** or **con·tin·u·a** (kən tin′yū ə) **1** an unbroken whole or series; a gradual progression: *the continuum of time.* **2** a line representing a range between two extremes: *On the continuum between careless and uptight, he's about halfway.*

con·tort (kən tôrt′) *v* twist or bend out of shape: *a face contorted by rage.* <Latin *com-* together + *torquere* twist> **con·tor′tion** *adv.*

con·tor·tion·ist (kən tôr′shən ist) *n* an entertainer who twists or bends his or her body into odd and unnatural positions.

con·tour (kon′tūr) *n* **1** the outline of something: *The Atlantic coast of Canada has an irregular contour.* **2** a line on a contour map.
adj following the contours of something. In **contour ploughing**, the furrows are made horizontally around the slopes of a hill instead of from top to bottom.
v shape to fit the outline of something: *The car has bucket seats contoured to fit the body.* <French, from Latin *com-* with + *tornare* turn>

contour map *n* a map showing the outline of hills, mountains, and valleys by a series of lines made at regular intervals. These **contour lines** join all points that are at the same height, both above and below sea level.

con·tra·band (kon′trə band′) *adj* **1** that may not legally be imported or exported: *Articles made from endangered species are contraband in Canada.* **2** smuggled.
n contraband goods: *The customs official was looking for contraband.* <Spanish, from Latin *contra-* against + *bando* proclamation>

con·tra·cep·tion (kon′trə sep′shən) *n* the prevention of conception. <Latin *contra-* against + (*con*)*ception*> **con′tra·cep′tive** *adj, n.*

con·tract (kən trakt′) *for v, also* (kon′trakt) *for v def. 5;* (kon′trakt) *for n.*
v **1** make or become narrower or shorter: *If you stretch a rubber band and let it go, it contracts again. When you move a part of your body, the muscles contract.* **2** shorten a word by dropping some of the letters or sounds: *"Do not" is often contracted to "don't."* **3** get or catch a disease: *She contracted malaria in the tropics.* **4** enter into a legal agreement: *The builder contracted to build the new library.*
n an agreement, especially a written agreement that can be enforced by law: *All professional hockey players sign*

contracts, agreeing to play for a certain salary. <Old French, from Latin *com-* together + *trahere* draw>

con·trac·tile (kən trak′tīl) *adj* able to contract or causing things to contract: *Muscle is contractile tissue. Cooling is a contractile force.*

con·trac·tion (kən trak′shən) *n* **1** the act or process of contracting: *Cold causes the contraction of liquids, gases, and metals, whereas heat causes expansion.* **2** something contracted, especially, a shortened form of a word: *"It's" is a contraction of "it is."*

GRAMMAR AND USAGE

A **contraction** is a shortened form of one word (*ma'am* and *madam*), or a combination of two words (*don't* and *do not*; *there's* and *there is*; *I'm* and *I am*), in which an apostrophe indicates where one or more letters have been omitted.

con·trac·tor (kon′trak tər) *for 1,* (kən trak′tər) *for 2.* *n* **1** a person who agrees to do a piece of work for a certain price, especially for the construction of buildings: *The renovator had to deal with electricians, plumbers, and other contractors.* **2** a muscle that draws together some part or parts of the body. Compare EXTENSOR.

con·trac·tu·al (kən trak′chū əl) *adj* to do with or with the nature of a contract: *contractual obligations, a contractual relationship.*

con·tra·dict (kon′trə dikt′) *v* **1** declare to be false or untrue: *She contradicted his version of the accident.* **2** deny the statement of another person in this way: *It is rude to contradict a guest.* **3** be contrary to or inconsistent with: *His outburst contradicted his claim that he never lost his temper.* <Latin *contra-* against + *dicere* say>
con′tra·dic′tion *n.* **con′tra·dic′to·ry** *adj.*

con·tra·dis·tinc·tion (kon′trə dis tingk′shən) *n* a difference shown by opposition or contrast: *I am very disorganized, in contradistinction to my brother, who knows where everything is.*

con·trail (kon′trāl) *n* the trail of vapour left by an aircraft flying at high altitude. <*condensation* + *trail*>

con·tra–in·di·cate (kon′trə in′ di kāt′) *Medicine v* (*usually in the passive*) **con·tra-in·di·cat·ed, con·tra-in·di·cat·ing** declare to be unsafe or unwise: *Drinking alcohol is contra-indicated during pregnancy.*

con·tral·to (kən tral′tō) *or* (kən trol′tō) *n* the lowest female singing voice, or a singer with such a range.
adj to do with a contralto. See also ALTO. <Italian, from Latin *contra-* counter to + *alto* high>

con·trap·tion (kən trap′shən) *usually Humorous n* an odd or badly made device or gadget: *They invented a crazy contraption for removing the shells from boiled eggs.* <perhaps from *contrive*>

con·tra·pun·tal (kon′trə pun′təl) *Music adj* to do with or involving COUNTERPOINT (def. 1). <Italian *contrapunto* counterpoint>

con·tra·ry (kon′trer ē); *also, for adj 3,* (kən trer′ē) *adj* **1** being or meaning the opposite: *In debating, the other side must have a contrary opinion.* **2** unfavourable: *A contrary wind delayed the start of the boat race.* **3** opposing others only in order to be difficult: *Don't listen to her; she's just being contrary.*
n **the contrary** the opposite: *That's the contrary of what we heard yesterday.* <Old French, from Latin *contra-* against> **con′tra·ri·ly** *adv.* **con′tra·ri·ness** *n.*
contrary to, in opposition or contrast to: *Criminals act contrary to the law. Contrary to expectation, the party went off without a hitch.*
on the contrary, exactly opposite to what has been said: *He doesn't dislike the idea; on the contrary, he's keen on it.*
to the contrary, with the opposite effect or meaning: *Despite forecasts to the contrary, it did rain today.*

con·trast (kon′trast) *for n,* (kən trast′) *for v. n* **1** a great difference: *the contrast between black and white, the contrast between good and evil.* **2** something that shows such a difference when compared to something else: *Black hair is a sharp contrast to light skin.*
v **1** compare two things so as to show their differences: *My essay contrasts the climate of Pacific Canada with that of Atlantic Canada.* **2** show striking difference(s) when compared or put side by side: *Blue and yellow contrast beautifully in that design. Her awkward efforts at making speeches contrasted oddly with the naturalness of her conversation.* <French, from Latin *contra-* against + *stare* stand> **con·trast′ing** *adj.*
in contrast (to), in a way that is opposite or very different: *In contrast to most dogs, it dislikes meat. He is a homebody; she, in contrast, loves to travel.*

con·tra·vene (kon′ trə vēn′) *v* **con·tra·vened, con·tra·ven·ing** violate or conflict with: *His actions contravene Bylaw 412. A dictatorship contravenes the freedom of individuals.* <Latin *contra-* against + *venire* come> **con′tra·ven′tion** *n.*

con·trib·ute (kən trib′yūt) *v* **con·trib·ut·ed, con·trib·ut·ing** **1** give money or help, along with others: *to contribute to charity. Everyone was asked to contribute ideas for the party.* **2** help to bring something about: *Hard work contributed to her success.* **3** supply an article or other writing for a newspaper or magazine. <Latin *com-* with + *tribuere* bestow> **con′tri·bu′tion** *n.* **con·trib′u·tor** *n.* **con·trib′u·to′ry** *adj.*

con·trite (kon′trīt) *or* (kən trīt′) *adj* showing genuine sorrow for a wrong one has done and a desire to put it right. <Latin *contritus* crushed, from *com-* completely + *terere* wear down> **con·trite′ly** *adv.*
con·tri′tion (kən trish′ən) *n.*

con·triv·ance (kən trī′vəns) *n* **1** something contrived or invented. **2** the act or manner of planning or designing: *By careful contrivance she managed to fit all her errands into one afternoon.*

con·trive (kən trīv′) *v* **con·trived, con·triv·ing** **1** invent or design: *to contrive a new kind of can opener.* **2** scheme or plot: *to contrive a robbery.* **3** carefully or cleverly arrange to have something happen: *Contrive to be there by ten.* <Old French, from Latin *contropare* search out>

a bat	e bed	i bid	o pot	u cup	th **thin**
ā cake	ē me	ī bite	ō go	ū rude	ᴛʜ **then**
â bar	ə about	ər over	ȯ for	ů put	zh measure

C

con·trived (kən trīvd′) *adj* seeming unnatural or artificial, especially in a story: *The movie wasn't bad, but the ending struck me as very contrived.*

con·trol (kən trōl′) *n* **1** authority or management: *A child is under the control of a parent or guardian.* **2** the power or ability to restrain or keep in check: *He lost control of his temper.* **3** a means of restraint: *The new law was not an effective control against smuggling.* **4** a device, knob, or switch that regulates or adjusts a machine's functioning: *The control for our furnace is in the front hall. Where is the volume control on this stereo?* **5 a** a standard of comparison for testing the results of scientific experiments. **b** one of a series of repeats of an experiment in order to check results, changing one variable at a time and comparing the result with the standard. **6 controls** *pl* the instruments and devices by which a car, aircraft, or other means of transport is operated: *The pilot seated herself at the controls.* **7** a means of regulating or limiting something: *controls on spending.*
v **con·trolled, con·trol·ling 1** have power or authority over: *A captain controls his ship and its crew.* **2** restrain: *She controlled her frustration.* **3** regulate: *to control prices and wages.* <Old French *controler* check, from Latin *contra-* against + *rotulus* a list> **con·trol′la·ble** *adj.*

controlled substance *n* a substance, such as a drug, whose use is banned or restricted by law.

con·trol·ler (kən trō′lər) *n* **1** a person employed by a company to supervise its expenditures or manage its financial affairs. **2** a person who or thing that controls or regulates: *an air traffic controller.* Also, **comptroller. con·trol′ler·ship′** *n.*

control panel *n* a panel containing all the switches, dials, and buttons necessary to control and operate a complex machine such as an aircraft.

control room *n* **1** a soundproof room from which the transmission of a broadcast is controlled in a radio or TV studio. **2** a room containing all the instruments necessary to control a complex operation, such as the launching of a rocket.

control tower *n* the building from which the taking off and landing of aircraft is controlled at an airfield.

con·tro·nym (kon′trə nim) *n* a word that has two opposite meanings. Examples: *cleave* (split up/cling to), *sanction* (approve/penalize).

con·tro·ver·sy (kon′trə vər′sē) *n, pl* **con·tro·ver·sies** disagreement, especially when prolonged and public: *The decision to make school uniforms compulsory caused a great deal of controversy.* <Latin *contra-* against + *vertere* turn> **con′tro·ver′sial** (kon′trə vər′shəl) *adj.*

con·tro·vert (kon′trə vərt′) *v* contradict, deny, or argue against: *The statement of the last witness controverts the evidence of the first.* <See CONTROVERSY.>

con·tu·sion (kən tyū′zhən) *or* (kən tū′zhən) *n* a bruise: *He suffered contusions in the accident, but no broken bones.* <French, from Latin *com-* completely + *tundere* pound>

television control room

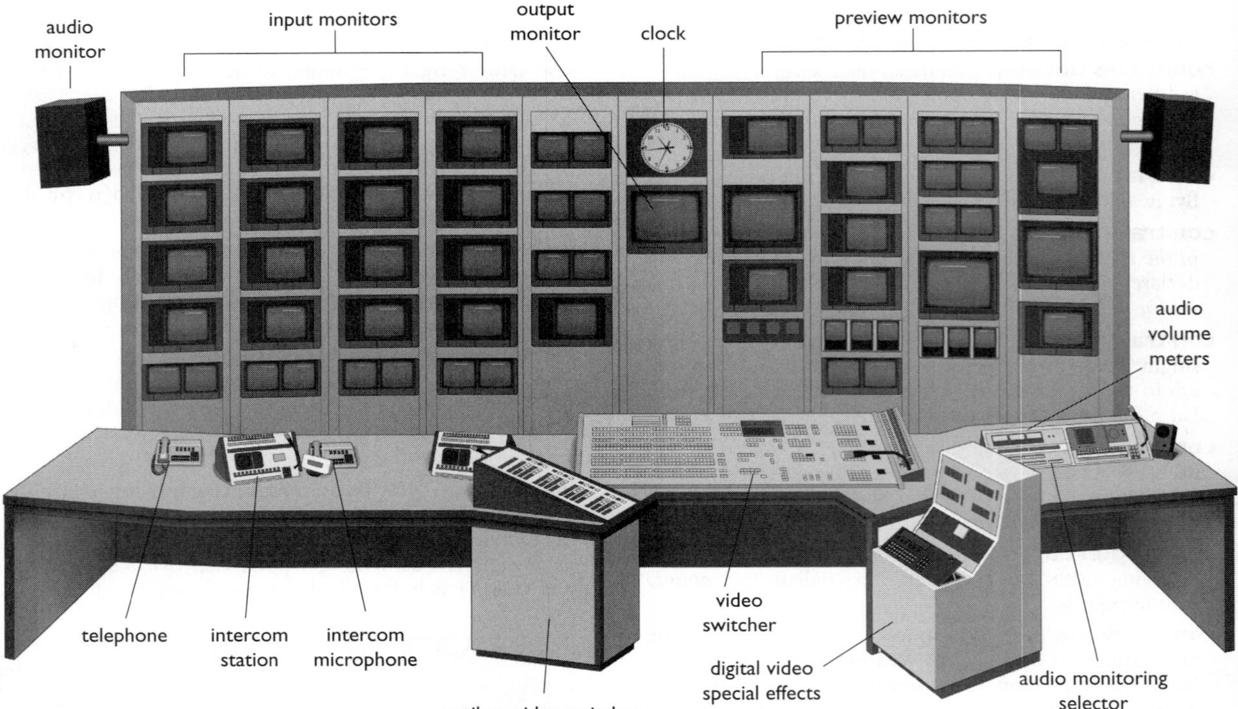

co·nun·drum (kə nun′drəm) *n* **1** a puzzling problem. **2** a riddle. <origin uncertain>

con·va·lesce (kon′və les′) *v* **con·va·lesced, con·va·lesc·ing** regain strength after illness; make progress toward health. <Latin *com-* altogether + *valere* be well>
con′va·les′cence *n.* **con′va·les′cent** *adj, n.*

con·vec·tion (kən vek′shən) *n* the transfer of heat from one place to another by a circulating **convection current** of heated particles of air or water. Liquid in a cooking pot is heated by convection. Compare CONDUCTION. <Latin *com-* together + *vehere* carry>

convection oven *n* an oven that cooks food by the forced circulation of hot air, reducing cooking time.

con·vene (kən vēn′) *v* **convened, con·ven·ing 1** have a meeting: *Parliament convenes in Ottawa at least once a year.* **2** call people together for a meeting or other activity: *Any member may convene the club in an emergency.* <Latin *com-* together + *venire* come>

con·ven·ience (kən vēn′yəns) *n* **1** the fact or quality of being convenient: *Many people appreciate the convenience of fast-food restaurants.* **2** comfort or advantage: *Many provincial parks have camping places for the convenience of tourists.* **3** something that increases comfort and saves trouble or work: *a house full of electrical appliances and other modern conveniences. A folding table is a convenience in a small room.* **4** usually, **conveniences** *pl* a washroom.
adj intended or prepared for people's convenience: *He lives on convenience foods.*
at your convenience, whenever and wherever you find it convenient: *Write at your convenience.*
marriage of convenience, a marriage whose main purpose is to gain legal, economic, or social benefit.

convenience store *n* a small store that is open every day for 24 hours or until late evening and specializes in basic food items, such as milk and bread, and a variety of small household articles.

con·ven·ient (kən vēn′yənt) *adj* **1** saving trouble, well arranged, or handy and easy to use: *a convenient tool, a convenient method.* **2** (*sometimes with* **to**) within easy reach of other places: *a convenient location. The library is convenient to my home.* **3** easily done: *Would it be convenient for you to give me a ride home?* <Latin *conveniens* appropriate, from *com-* together + *venire* come> **con·ven′ient·ly** *adv.*

con·ven·or (kən vē′nər) *n* a person who is responsible for calling people together for meetings or activities. Also, **convener**.

con·vent (kon′vent) *n* **1** a community of nuns. **2** the building or buildings in which they live. <Old French, from Latin *com-* together + *venire* come>

con·ven·tion (kən ven′shən) *n* **1** a large meeting for some purpose: *The NDP is holding a convention to choose a new leader.* **2** custom or tradition: *to dress according to convention.* **3** a rule based on common consent: *The convention is to use your right hand for shaking hands.* **4** something commonly accepted as having a certain meaning or working a certain way: *It is a convention of the theatre that asides are not heard by any of the other characters on stage.*

con·ven·tion·al (kən ven′shə nəl) *adj* **1** customary: *"Hello" is a conventional greeting.* **2** not original or interesting: *conventional clothes.* **con·ven′tion·al′i·ty** *n.*
con·ven′tion·al·ly *adv.*

con·ven·tion·al·ized (kən ven′shə nə līzd′) *adj* drawn in a simplified style rather than according to nature: *The sky in her picture was full of conventionalized birds in flight, like floating m's.*

conventional wisdom *n* what most people generally think is true: *The conventional wisdom is that you catch cold as a result of being cold and wet.*

con·verge (kən vərj′) *v* **con·verged, con·verg·ing**
1 meet in a point: *The two roads converge at Hamilton.*
2 come together from different directions to meet in one place: *Tourists converge on this resort town every summer.*
3 be or become more similar: *The policies of the two parties converge where education is concerned.* <Latin *com-* together + *vergere* slant> **con·ver′gence** *n.*
con·ver′gent *adj.*

con·ver·sant (kən vər′sənt) *adj* familiar with a field of knowledge: *The keyboard player is thoroughly conversant with modern music.*

con·ver·sa·tion (kon′vər sā′shən) *n* friendly talk: *a brief conversation over lunch, a lot of lively conversation.*
con′ver·sa′tion·al *adj.* **con′ver·sa′tion·al·ly** *adv.*
make conversation, find things to talk about with someone, just to be polite and friendly.

con·ver·sa·tion·al·ist (kon′vər sā′shə nə list′) *n* a person who is good at conversation and enjoys it.

con·verse[1] (kən vərs′) *for v,* (kon′vərs) *for n.* *v* **con·versed, con·vers·ing** talk informally together: *The two old veterans conversed about their experiences in the last war.*
n Formal conversation. <Old French *converser* keep company with, from Latin *com-* with + *vertere* to turn>

con·verse[2] (kon′vərs)*; also, for adj,* (kən vərs′) *n* something that is opposite or reversed: *"Honest but poor" is the converse of "Poor but honest."* Compare INVERSE.
adj opposite or reversed: *"Happy" and "sad" are converse adjectives.* <See CONVERT.> **con·verse′ly** *adv.*

con·vert (kən vərt′) *for v,* (kon′vərt) *for n.* *v* **1** change or turn into: *These machines convert pulp into paper.* **2** change or cause to adopt a religion or to change from one religion, political party, or belief to another: *He recently converted to Catholicism.* **3** exchange for an equivalent: *I converted my Canadian dollars into Euros before I left.* **4** take and use unlawfully: *The dishonest treasurer converted the club's money to his own use.* **5** *Football* kick a goal after a touchdown.
n **1** a person who has converted. **2** *Football* a goal kicked after a touchdown, or the point scored in this way. <Old French, from Latin *com-* altogether + *vertere* turn>
con·ver′sion (kən vər′zhən) *n.*

a bat	e bed	i bid	o pot	u cup	th **th**in
ā cake	ē me	ī bite	ō go	ū rude	ᴛʜ **th**en
ä bar	ə about	ər over	ô for	ù put	zh measure

con·vert·er (kən vər′tər) *n* **1** *Electricity* a device for changing alternating current into direct current. **2** a device for adapting a TV set to receive more channels. **3** a furnace in which pig iron is changed into steel by the BESSEMER PROCESS. **4** any person who or thing that converts.

con·vert·i·ble (kən vər′tə bəl) *n* a car with a roof that can be folded down or detached.
adj capable of being converted: *Paper money is convertible into coins.*

con·vex (kon veks′) *or* (kon′veks) *adj* curved outward, like the outside of a bowl: *Touch only the convex surface of a contact lens.* Compare CONCAVE. <Latin *convexus* vaulted> **con·vex′i·ty** *n.* **con·vex′ly** *adv.*

con·vex·o–con·cave (kon vek′sō kon kāv′) *adj* convex on one side and concave on the other, as some lenses. The curvature on the convex side is usually greater than on the concave side.

con·vey (kən vā′) *v* **1** carry or transport: *He was conveyed to his door by taxi.* **2** transmit or conduct: *a wire conveying an electric current.* **3** express or make known: *Her words convey no meaning to me.* **4** transfer ownership of property from one person to another. <Old French *conveier* escort, from Latin *com-* with + *via* way> **con·vey′a·ble** *adj.* **con·vey′or** *n.*

con·vey·ance (kən vā′əns) *n* **1** the act of conveying, or carrying. **2** anything that carries people or goods: *Trains and buses are public conveyances.*

conveyor belt *n* a mechanical device that carries things from one place to another by means of a moving endless belt or a series of rollers.

con·vict (kən vikt′) *for v,* (kon′vikt) *for n. v* prove or declare guilty: *The evidence will surely convict him. The jury convicted the prisoner of murder.*
n a person convicted by a court, especially one serving a prison sentence. <See CONVINCE.>

con·vic·tion (kən vik′shən) *n* **1** the act of convicting or state of being convicted: *a conviction for theft.* **2** a firm belief, often especially a moral or religious one: *It was his conviction that war was avoidable.* **3** evidence of strong belief, as in one's voice or expression: *She spoke with conviction on the need for increased educational funding.*

con·vince (kən vins′) *v* **con·vinced, con·vinc·ing** persuade by argument or proof: *The reviews convinced us that the movie wasn't worth seeing.* <Latin *convincere* prove without doubt, from *com-* with + *vincere* conquer> **con·vin′ci·ble** *adj.*

SYNONYMS

Convince means "bring around to the same way of thinking": *His slide show presentation helped convince us that his idea was valid.*

Persuade means "urge in a fairly strong way": *The salesclerk repeatedly tried to persuade me to buy the pants.*

Sway can mean "cause to change an opinion": *Each debate team tried to sway the audience to its position.*

con·vinc·ing (kən vin′sing) *adj* **1** that convinces: *a convincing argument.* **2** realistic or believable: *Her display of affection was not very convincing.* **con·vinc′ing·ly** *adv.* **con·vinc′ing·ness** *n.*

con·viv·i·al (kən viv′ē əl) *adj* **1** cheerful and friendly. **2** friendly, lively, and enjoyable: *a convivial gathering.* <Latin *convivium* a feast, from *com-* with + *vivere* live together> **con·viv′i·al′i·ty** *n.* **con·viv′i·al·ly** *adv.*

con·vo·ca·tion (kon′və kā′shən) *n* **1** the action of calling people together to a large assembly. **2** an assembly meeting together in answer to a summons. **3** in universities, **a** a ceremony at which degrees are conferred. **b** the officials and graduates at the ceremony.

con·voke (kən vōk′) *v* **con·voked, con·vok·ing** call together as an assembly.

con·vo·lut·ed (kon′və lū′tid) *adj* **1** complicated or intricate, especially unnecessarily so: *a convoluted theory. That paragraph is so convoluted; can't you simplify it?* **2** coiling, winding, or twisting: *the convoluted course of a river.* <Latin *com-* together + *volvere* roll> **con′vo·lu′tion** *n.*

con·voy (kon′voi) *n* a group of ships or vehicles travelling together, either as an escort, or while being escorted: *A convoy of police cars conducted the procession through town.* <Latin *com-* together + *via* way>

con·vulse (kən vuls′) *v* **con·vulsed, con·vuls·ing 1** throw into a fit or violent spasm: *The feverish child was convulsed.* **2** shake or disturb violently: *An earthquake convulsed the island. Rage convulsed his face.* **3** throw into a fit of laughter: *The clown convulsed us all with his funny costume.* <Latin *convulsus* torn up, from *com-* together + *vellere* to pull> **con·vul′sion** *n.* **con·vul′sive** *adj.* **con·vul′sive·ly** *adv.*

co·ny (kō′nē) CONEY.

coo (kū) *n* a soft, murmuring sound made by doves or pigeons.
v **cooed, coo·ing 1** make this sound. **2** murmur in a soft, loving manner. **3** make open vowel sounds, the first outward signs of language development in a baby. <imitative>

cook (ku̇k) *v* **1** prepare food for eating by applying heat, as in boiling, baking, frying, etc. **2** undergo cooking: *Let the meat cook slowly.* **3** work as a cook: *He cooked in the school cafeteria.* **4** *Informal* feel very hot: *You must be cooking! Take off your coat!* **5** *Informal* tamper with or falsify accounts: *She was caught cooking the company's books.*
n a person who cooks. <Old English, from Latin *coquus*>
cook someone's goose, *Informal* ruin everything for someone: *If you tell his mother, you'll cook his goose for sure.*
cook up, *Informal* **a** produce by cooking. **b** make up something false: *She had cooked up a story to explain her absence from band practice.*
what's cooking? *Slang* what's happening?

cook·book (ku̇k′bu̇k′) *n* a book of directions for preparing and cooking food.

cook·er (ku̇k′ər) *n* an apparatus or container to cook things in: *an electric rice cooker.*

cook·er·y (ku̇k′ə rē) *n* the art or occupation of cooking.

cook·house (ku̇k′hous′) *n* a room or building for cooking, especially in a large camp.

cook·ie (ku̇k′ē) *n* **1** a small, sweet, dense, firm, flattish cake. **2** *Computers* a small file containing information about an Internet user, sent automatically to a browser and stored there to make future transactions easier. <Dutch *koek* cake>
smart cookie, *Informal* a clever person.

cook·out (ku̇k′out′) *n* a picnic where the food is cooked and eaten outdoors.

cook·stove (ku̇k′stōv′) *n* a stove used for cooking.

cook·ware (ku̇k′wãr′) *n* cooking utensils.

cool (kūl) *adj* **1** somewhat cold: *We sat in the shade where it was cool.* **2** allowing or giving a cool feeling: *cool clothing.* **3** calm and unemotional: *He was always cool in an emergency.* **4** with little enthusiasm or interest: *a cool greeting.* **5** *Slang* **a** excellent. **b** acceptable or agreeable. **c** fashionable. **6** *Music* in jazz, restrained and relaxed. **7** *Informal* without exaggeration or qualification: *a cool million dollars.* **8** suggesting coolness or calmness in colour: *The room was painted a cool blue.*
n **1** a cool part, place, or time: *the cool of the evening.* **2** *Informal* control of one's actions or feelings: *to lose your cool. She kept her cool even though she was angry.*
v make or become cool: *Let the cake cool before icing it. Cool the ginger ale with ice.* <Old English *col*>
cool′ish *adj.* **cool′ly** *adv.* **cool′ness** *n.*
cool down (or **off**), lose one's enthusiasm, especially for a person.
cool it, *Slang* (*usually as a command*) calm down.

cool·ant (kū′lənt) *n* a substance circulated through machinery to absorb and carry off excess heat.

cool·er (kū′lər) *n* **1** an apparatus or container that cools things such as food or drink, or keeps them cool. **2** a drink containing a small amount of wine or other alcohol.

coo·lie (kū′lē) *Offensive n* an unskilled labourer in parts of Asia, especially a porter. <Hindi *kuli* day-labourer>

coon (kūn) *Informal n* a raccoon.

coon·skin (kūn′skin′) *n* the skin of a raccoon, used in making hats and other clothing.

co–op (kō′ op) *Informal n* a co-operative.

coop (kūp) *n* a small cage or pen, especially for chickens or rabbits.
v (*usually with* ***up***) **1** keep or put in a coop. **2** confine, especially in a small space: *The children were cooped up indoors by the rain.* <Latin *cupa* barrel>
fly the coop, *Informal* escape or run away.

coop·er (kū′pər) *n* especially in former times, a maker of barrels and casks. <See COOP.>

co–op·er·ate (kō op′ə rāt′) *v* **co-op·er·at·ed, co-op·er·at·ing** **1** work together: *If we co-operate, we can get the yard cleaned up quickly.* **2** comply with an order or request: *I asked him to leave, but he won't co-operate.* Also, **cooperate**. <Latin *co-* together + *operari* to work>
co-op′er·a′tion *n.*

co–op·er·a·tive (kō op′ə rə tiv) *adj* willing to work together with others: *Be helpful and co-operative.*
n a business owned jointly by a group of people and operated for their mutual benefit: *The daycare my mother works at is a co-operative.* Also, **cooperative**.
co-op′er·a·tive·ly *adv.* **co-op′er·a·tive·ness** *n.*

Co–operative Commonwealth Federation CCF.

co–opt (kō opt′) *v* **1** take for one's own use or purpose by neutralizing the opposition of another: *Though he was against us at first, we co-opted him by approving some of his ideas.* **2** invite a person to join a committee as a new member. <Latin *co-* with + *optare* choose>

co·or·di·nate (kō ȯr′də nit) *for adj or n;* (kō ȯr′də nāt′) *for v.*
adj **1** equal in importance. **2** equal in rank and with identical functions: *A compound sentence contains two or more coordinate clauses.* **3** *Chemistry* to do with a chemical bond in which one atom shares two electrons with another atom.
n **1 coordinates** *pl* **a** matching items of clothing, accessories, luggage, etc. **b** *Geography* a pair of references, such as latitude or longitude, that fix a position on a map. **2** *Mathematics* any of an ordered pair or triple of numbers or letters that fixes a position on a grid.
v **co·or·di·nat·ed, co·or·di·nat·ing** arrange in proper order or relation or cause to work together efficiently: *to coordinate the movements of your arms and legs.* Also, **co-ordinate.** <*co-* + Latin *ordo* order>
coor′di·nate·ly *adv.* **coor′di·na′tor** *n.*

coordinating conjunction *Grammar n* a conjunction joining two main clauses. Examples: *and, but, or.*

coor·di·na·tion (kō ȯr′də nā′shən) *n* **1** the act of coordinating: *She is responsible for the coordination of all the fundraising events at our school.* **2** the ability to control the movements of one's muscles so that they work together efficiently: *The more she swam, the more her coordination improved.* Also, **co-ordination**.

coot (kūt) *n* **1** a dark grey marsh bird of the rail family, resembling a duck but with a smaller bill. **2** a scoter. <perhaps Dutch *koet*>

coot·ie (kū′tē) *Slang n* (*used mostly by children or humorously*) **1** an imaginary germ carried by an undesirable person. **2** a louse. <perhaps Malay *kutu* biting insect>

cop (kop) *Informal n* a police officer.
v **copped, copping** **1** steal. **2** capture or seize. <perhaps Old French, from Latin *capere* catch>
cop out, avoid responsibility or challenge by failing to act or by withdrawing from a situation.

co·pa·cet·ic (kō′pə set′ik) *Slang adj* satisfactory: *Just checking to make sure everything's copacetic.* <origin unknown>

cope (kōp) *v* **coped, cop·ing** (*often with* ***with***) handle things successfully: *He said he just couldn't cope any more. Can you cope with the extra reading assignment?* <Old French *coup* strike (i.e., fight with, deal with), from Greek *kolaphos* a punch>

Co·per·ni·can (kə pər′nə kən) *adj* to do with the astronomer N. Copernicus (1473–1543), or his system of astronomy. The **Copernican system** is the theory that the planets move in orbits around the sun.

a bat	e bed	i bid	o pot	u cup	th **thin**
ā cake	ē me	ī bite	ō go	ū rude	ᴛʜ **then**
ȧ bar	ə about	ər over	ȯ for	u̇ put	zh measure

C

cop·i·er (kop′ē ər) *n* **1** a machine that makes copies. **2** a person who copies. **3** a person who makes written copies.

co–pi·lot (kō′pī′lət) *n* the assistant or second pilot in an aircraft.
v be the co-pilot of an aircraft.

cop·ing (kō′ping) *n* **1** the top layer of a brick or stone wall, usually sloped so as to shed water. **2** *Skateboarding* the rail at the top of the sloping section of the ramp. <Old French, from Greek *kolaphos* a strike with the fist>

coping mechanism *n* a way of behaving or thinking that allows one to cope with or deal with difficulties.

coping saw *n* a narrow saw in a U-shaped frame, used to cut curves.

co·pi·ous (kō′pē əs) *adj* **1** plentiful: *a copious supply of paper.* **2** containing much material or many words. <Old French, from Latin *copla* plenty> **co′pi·ous·ly** *adv.* **co′pi·ous·ness** *n.*

co·pla·nar (kō plā′nər) *Mathematics adj* lying in the same plane as a point, line, or figure.

cop–out (kop′out′) *Informal n* **1** an act or means of avoiding responsibility or challenge. *Pretending to be asleep just to avoid doing something is a cop-out.* **2** a person who does this.

cop·per (kop′ər) *n* a reddish brown metal element that resists rust and is easily shaped into thin sheets or fine wire. *Symbol* **Cu**
adj **1** made of copper. **2** reddish brown. <Old English, from Latin *Cyprium aes* metal from Cyprus (where copper was found)> **cop′per·y** *adj.*

cop·per·head (kop′ər hed′) *n* a poisonous N American snake with a reddish brown head, related to the water moccasin and the rattlesnake.

Copper Inuit *n* a group of Inuit living along the Arctic coast near the Coppermine River.

copper sulphate *n* a poisonous copper salt, usually seen in the form of a blue solid. It is used in agriculture and textile dyeing.

cop·ra (kop′rə) *or* (kō′prə) *n* the dried meat of ripe coconuts that yields **coconut meal** (a food for livestock) and coconut oil. <Malayalam (a language of India) *koppara* coconut>

Copt (kopt) *n* **1** a native of Egypt who is descended from the ancient Egyptians. **2** a member of the **Coptic Church**, the native Christian church of Egypt. <French, from Greek *Aigyptios* Egyptian>

cop·ter (kop′tər) *Informal n* a helicopter.

cop·u·la (kop′yə lə) *Grammar n* a linking verb. <Latin = bond, connection>

cop·u·late (kop′yə lāt′) *v* **cop·u·lat·ed, cop·u·lat·ing** have sexual intercourse. <See COPULA.> **cop′u·la′tion** *n.*

cop·y (kop′ē) *n, pl* **cop·ies** **1** something made to be as like another as possible: *This picture is an exact copy of the one hanging on the wall.* **2** a book, newspaper, etc. made with others in the same printing: *Can I read your copy of the newspaper?* **3** text to be printed in a book, newspaper, or magazine: *She writes advertising copy. He edits copy for a publisher.* **4** a source of material for an article or news report: *Movie stars are always good copy.*
v **cop·ied, cop·y·ing** **1** make a copy of: *Copy this page.* **2** follow as a pattern or model: *My little brother copies my way of walking.* **3** steal ideas or answers from someone and pass them off as one's own: *You won't get far in school by copying.* <Old French, from Latin *copia* plenty>

co·py·cat (kop′ē kat′) *Informal n* a person who habitually copies others.
adj done in imitation of someone else: *a copycat robbery.*

copy desk *n* the desk in a newspaper office where stories and articles are edited before being processed for printing.

co·py·ed·it (ko′pē ed′it) *v* read written material and correct it for publication Also, **copy-edit**. **co′py·ed′it·ing** *n.* **co′py ed′it·or** *n.*

copy protection *Computers n* features in software, designed to prevent copies of it from being created without authorization. **cop′y-pro·tect′** *v.* **cop′y-pro·tect′ed** *adj.*

cop·y·right (kop′ē rīt′) *n* a legal right given to artists, writers, etc. to protect their work from being copied, performed, filmed, etc. without permission. Artists, writers, etc. usually give such permission in exchange for payment. Most copyrights are held for a certain length of time, after which the work falls into the PUBLIC DOMAIN.
v protect by copyright.
adj protected by copyright.

cop·y·writ·er (kop′ē rī′tər) *n* a person whose work is writing advertisements and other promotional material.

co·quette (kō ket′) *n* a woman who flirts. <French, diminutive of *coq* rooster> **co′quet·ry** (kō′kə trē) *n.* **co·quet′tish** *adj.*

co·qui·na (kō kē′nə) *n* **1** a small clam native to tidal waters of eastern and southern US. **2** a soft, whitish rock made up of tiny fragments of limestone. <Spanish = shellfish>

cor– *prefix* a form of COM- occurring before *r*: *correspond.*

cor·a·cle (kô′rə kəl) *n* a light, bowl-shaped boat traditionally used in Wales and Ireland for river fishing, originally made of woven reeds, grasses, or branches with a covering of animal hides. <Welsh *corwg*>

cor·al (kô′rəl) *n* **1** a hard substance that is the skeleton of tiny sea animals called polyps. Generations of coral polyps build on these skeletons, and over time form a **coral reef** or a **coral island. 2** the unfertilized roe of a lobster or scallop, which turns red when cooked.
adj **1** to do with coral: *coral reefs.* **2** deep, slightly yellowish pink. <Old French, from Greek *korallion*>

coral snake *n* a poisonous snake of tropical and subtropical America, usually marked with red, black, and yellow or white bands around the body.

cord (kôrd) *n* **1** string made of several strands or fibres twisted tightly together. **2** an insulated electric wire with a plug at one end, connecting an electrical appliance to a source of power. **3** a similar cable connecting a telephone to the main telephone line. **4** a structure in an animal body that resembles a cord: *the vocal cords.* **5 cords** *pl* pants made of corduroy. **6** a unit for measuring cut firewood. A **standard cord** is a stack 8 feet long by 4 feet high by 4 feet deep (about 2.4 m by 1.2 m by 1.2 m). A **face cord** is equal to a stack 8 feet long by 4 feet high of logs roughly 12 to 16 inches long (about 30 to 40 cm). A face cord is about a third of a standard cord. <Old French, from Greek *chorde* gut, string> **cord′like** *adj.*

cord·age (kôr′dij) *n* a quantity of wood measured in cords.

cor·dial (kôr′dē əl) *or* (kôr′jəl) *adj* **1** warm and friendly: *a cordial welcome.* **2** heartfelt and sincere: *a cordial dislike.*
n **1** a drink or herbal medicine that strengthens or stimulates. **2** a fruit liqueur. <Latin *cordis* heart> **cor′di·al′i·ty** *n.* **cor′dial·ly** *adv.*

cor·dil·le·ra (kôr dil′ə rə) *or* (kôr′də ler′ə) *or* (kôr′dəl yer′ə) *n* a group or string of parallel mountain ranges and their geographical features, especially in the Andes or Rockies. <Spanish, from Greek *chorde* string>

cord·less (kôrd′lis) *adj* without a cord, especially as a device, battery-operated and not needing to be plugged in: *a cordless phone.*

cor·don (kôr′dən) *n* **1** a line or circle of soldiers, police, or ships, placed at intervals around an area to guard it. **2** a rope with the same function. **3** a cord, braid, or ribbon worn as a badge of honour.
v (*usually with* ***off***) put a protective line or barrier around: *The crime scene was cordoned off.* <French, from Greek *chorde* gut, string>

cordon bleu (kôr′dong blü′) *n* **1** a chef highly skilled in fine French cuisine. **2** fine French cuisine. <French = blue ribbon (awarded to the best in many kinds of contest)>

cor·du·roy (kôr′də roi′) *n* **1** cloth, usually of cotton, with a thick, velvety pile cut in wide or narrow ridges called **wales. 2 corduroys** *pl* corduroy pants.
adj with ridges like corduroy. <*cord* + obsolete *duroy*, a woollen cloth>

🍁 **corduroy bridge** *n* a temporary bridge made of logs laid crosswise.

🍁 **corduroy road** *n* a temporary road made of logs laid crosswise, often across low, wet land.

cord·wood (kôrd′wu̇d′) *n* **1** wood sold or stacked in cords. **2** wood or standing timber suitable for use as firewood.

core (kôr) *n* **1** the tough central part of fruits such as apples, that contains the seeds. **2** the central or essential part of anything: *the core of an argument.* **3** the central part of the earth, beginning at a depth of about 2880 km and with a radius of about 3400 km, believed to consist of iron and nickel. **4** an interior or basic layer of material over which some other material is laid or wound: *The bookcase is made of pine veneer on a plywood core.* **5** *Electricity* a bar of soft iron forming the centre of an electromagnet or induction coil. **6** the area in the centre of a nuclear reactor, where the reaction takes place. **7** in full, **core sample** a cylindrical piece of rock or other material extracted by cutting or drilling.
v **cored, cor·ing** take out the core of: *to core apples.* <Middle English>

cor·gi (kôr′gē) *n* in full, **Welsh corgi** a dog with short legs, ears that stick up straight, and a foxlike head. <Welsh *corr* dwarf + *ci* dog>

co·ri·an·der (kô′rē an′dər) *n* an annual herb of the parsley family with tiny seedlike fruits that are used as a spice and flavouring. See HERB for picture. <Old French, from Greek *koriannon*>

Co·rin·thi·an (kə rin′thē ən) *adj* to do with the most elaborate of the three types of classical Greek architecture. See also DORIC, IONIC.

Co·ri·o·lis force (kô′rē ō′lis) *n* the effect resulting from the earth's rotation that causes a moving body on or above the earth's surface to drift to the right in the northern hemisphere and to the left in the southern hemisphere. <G.G. de *Coriolis*, 19c mathematician>

cork (kôrk) *n* **1** the light, thick, somewhat spongy outer bark of a species of oak. **2** a bottle stopper, especially one made from cork. **3** the layers of dead tissue in the bark of a woody plant, serving as a protective covering.
v stop up with or as if with a cork. <Dutch, from Latin *quercus* cork oak>

cork·board (kôrk′bôrd′) *n* small bits of cork pressed together into sheets, or a notice board made of this.

corked (kôrkt) *adj* with the flavour of wine affected by the cork having too much tannin in it.

cork·screw (kôrk′skrü′) *n* a tool for pulling corks out of bottles, often ending in a sharp-pointed spiral.
adj shaped like a corkscrew: *a corkscrew dive.*
v move in a spiral course.

corm (kôrm) *n* a fleshy, round underground stem that has leaves and buds on the upper surface and roots usually on the lower. <Latin, from Greek *kormos* a bare tree trunk>

a bat	e bed	i bid	o pot	u cup	th thin
ā cake	ē me	ī bite	ō go	ū rude	ᴛʜ then
ȧ bar	ə about	ər over	ô for	u̇ put	zh measure

C

cor·mo·rant (kôr′mə rənt) *n* a large, black seabird that has a hooked bill with a skin pouch underneath for holding captured fish. <Old French, from Latin *corvus marinus* sea raven>

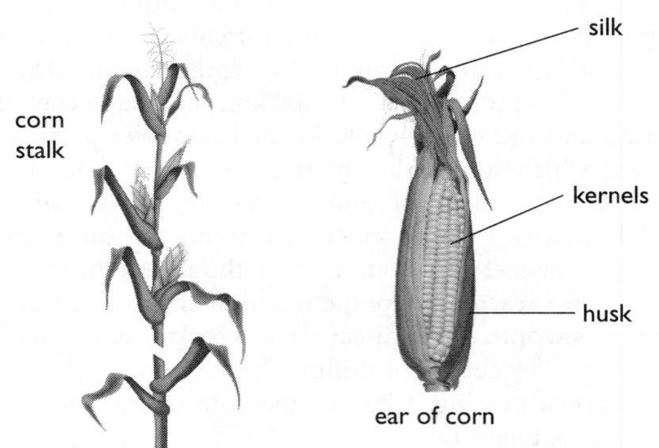

corn[1] (kôrn) *n* **1** a tall cereal plant whose kernels (seeds) grow in rows on a core called a cob. **2** *Informal* anything trite, unsophisticated, or too sentimental.
v preserve (meat) with salt: *corned beef.* <Old English>

corn[2] (kôrn) *n* a hardening and thickening of the skin, usually on a toe, caused by pressure or rubbing. <Old French, from Latin *cornu* horn>

corn·bread (kôrn′bred′) *n* bread made of cornmeal.

corn chip *n* a salty chip similar to a potato chip, but made with corn flour.

corn·cob (kôrn′kob′) *n* **1** the central, woody part of an ear of corn, on which the kernels grow. **2** a tobacco pipe with a bowl hollowed out of a piece of dried corncob.

corn·crib (kôrn′krib′) *n* a bin, rack, or small, open-sided building for storing CORNCOBS (def. 1).

corn dog *n* a wiener dipped in cornmeal batter and deep fried, usually on a stick.

cor·ne·a (kôr′nē ə) *n* the transparent, skinlike part over the front of the eyeball. The cornea covers the iris and the pupil. See EYEBALL for picture. <Latin *cornu* web of horn (skin)> **cor′ne·al** *adj.*

cor·ner (kôr′nər) *n* **1** the point or place where lines or surfaces meet: *A diagonal joins two opposite corners of a rectangle. There was a bookcase in the far corner of the room.* **2** the place where two streets meet. **3** something that forms, protects, or decorates a corner: *The leather wallet has gold corners.* **4** a small place that is hard to find: *The money was hidden in odd corners all over the house.* **5** an awkward or difficult position: *His enemies had driven him into a corner.* **6** a monopoly: *a corner in copper on the stock market. No one has a corner on truth.*
v **1** drive or force into a corner, or into a difficult situation from which escape is impossible: *I cornered our dog and got the leash on it.* **2** gain a monopoly in a commodity or stock: *Some speculators have tried to corner wheat.* <Old French, from Latin *cornu* point> **cor′nered** *adj.*
cut corners, a shorten the way by going across corners. **b** save money, effort, or time at the expense of quality.
turn a corner, pass a dangerous or critical point.

cor·ner·back (kôr′nər bak′) *Football n* a defensive player who covers offensive plays running toward the sidelines.

corner kick *Soccer n* a free kick from the corner awarded to the other side when a player has sent the ball behind his own goal line.

cor·ner·stone (kôr′nər stōn′) *n* **1** a large stone at the corner of two walls, forming part of each. **2** an important part on which something rests: *Clear thinking is the cornerstone of good writing.*

cor·net (kôr net′) *n* a valved brass wind instrument resembling a trumpet. <Old French, from Latin *cornu* horn> **cor·net′ist** or **cor·net′tist** *n.*

corn·field (kôrn′fēld′) *n* a field of growing corn.

corn·flow·er (kôrn′flou′ər) *n* an annual plant native to Europe and Asia, usually with blue flowers.

cor·nice (kôr′nis) *Architecture n* an ornamental moulding around the top of a wall. <French, perhaps from Latin *cornix* crow, from its curved beak or feet>

Cor·nish (kôr′nish) *adj* to do with Cornwall, a county in southwest England, its people, or the language formerly spoken by them.
n the ancient Celtic language of Cornwall.

corn·meal (kôrn′mēl′) *n* ground corn, not as fine as flour.

corn roast *n* a picnic, usually in the late summer or fall, where corn is roasted or boiled and eaten off the cob.

corn silk *n* the long, glossy fibres that emerge in a silky tuft from the tip of an ear of corn.

corn snow *n* snow consisting of granular particles suggesting cornmeal, formed by alternate periods of thawing and freezing.

corn·stalk (kôrn′stok′) *n* the stalk of a corn plant.

corn·starch (kôrn′stärch′) *n* a starchy flour made from corn, used as a thickener in cooking.

corn syrup *n* syrup made from corn.

cor·nu·co·pi·a (kôr′nyə kō′pē ə) *n* a large curved horn overflowing with fruits and flowers, used as a symbol of a good harvest or a time of prosperity. Also called **horn of plenty**. <Latin *cornu copiae* horn of plenty>

corn·y (kôr′nē) *Informal adj* **corn·i·er, corn·i·est** too sentimental or unsophisticated: *corny jokes. That movie has some corny scenes.*

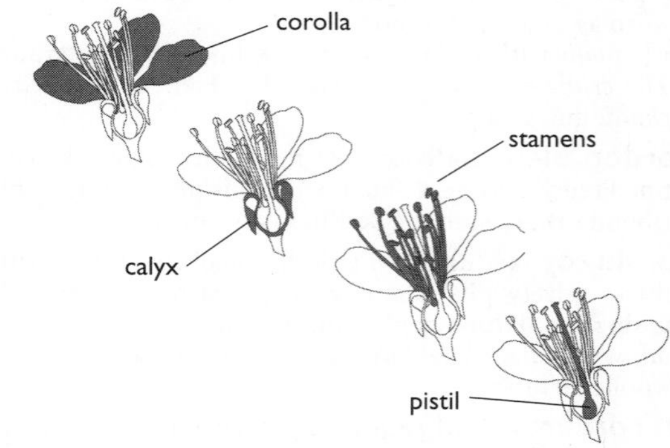

co·rol·la (kə rōl′ə) *Botany n* the structure formed by the petals of a flower, usually of some colour other than green. <Latin *corona* wreath >

cor·ol·lar·y (kə rol′ə rē) *or* (kȯ′rə ler′ē) *n, pl* **cor·ol·lar·ies** 1 something proved by proving something else. 2 a logical conclusion or deduction. 3 a natural consequence: *She says her good health is a corollary of her way of life.* <Latin *corollarium* money paid for a small wreath, i.e., a tip>

co·ro·na (kə rō′nə) *n, pl* **co·ro·nas** or **co·ro·nae** (kə rō′nē) *or* (kə rō′nī) 1 *Meteorology* a ring of usually coloured light visible around a shining object such as the moon seen through water droplets or dust particles. 2 *Astronomy* a layer of gases forming the outer part of the sun's atmosphere, visible only when the direct rays of the sun are blocked during a total eclipse. See SUNSPOT for picture. <Latin = crown>

cor·o·nar·y (kȯ′rə ner′ē) *adj* to do with either or both of the two arteries branching from the aorta that supply blood to the muscular tissue of the heart.
n, pl **cor·o·nar·ies** in full, **coronary thrombosis** the blocking of a branch of a coronary artery by a blood clot.

cor·o·na·tion (kȯ′rə nā′shən) *n* the ceremony of crowning a monarch. <See CORONA.>

cor·o·ner (kȯ′rə nər) *n* a doctor appointed by a provincial government to investigate the cause of a sudden or unexpected death that may be the result of a crime or of a situation that could be dangerous to other people. <Old French = official of the Crown, from Latin *corona* crown>

cor·o·net (kȯ′rə net′) *n* 1 a small crown worn by a noble other than a monarch. 2 a circle of gold, jewels, or flowers worn around the head as an ornament.

cor·po·ral[1] (kȯr′pə rəl) *adj* to do with the body: *Spanking is a form of corporal punishment.* <French, from Latin *corpus* body> **cor′po·ral·ly** *adv.*

cor·po·ral[2] (kȯr′pə rəl) *n* 1 the lowest-ranking non-commissioned officer in the armed forces. 2 🍁 in the RCMP, a rank next above constable. <French *caporale*, from Latin *caput* head>

corporal punishment *n* physical punishment, such as spanking, strapping, or whipping.

cor·po·rate (kȯr′pə rit) *adj* 1 to do with or being a corporation: *a corporate decision.* 2 to do with a group as a unified whole: *our corporate responsibility.*

cor·po·ra·tion (kȯr′pə rā′shən) *n* a business or other organization with rights and privileges distinct from those of its individual members.

cor·po·re·al (kȯr pȯ′rē əl) *adj* to do with the body: *Food and water are corporeal nourishment.* <French, from Latin *corpus* body> **cor·po′re·al′i·ty** *n.* **cor·po′re·al·ly** *adv.*

corps (kȯr) *n, pl* **corps** (kȯrz) 1 a formation made up of more than one division in the armed forces. 2 a branch of the armed forces that provides special services: *the Signal Corps.* 3 a group of people organized for working together: *a corps of volunteers.* <French = body, from Latin *corpus*>

corps de bal·let (kȯr′ də ba′lā) *n* the dancers in a ballet company who dance together as a group.

corpse (kȯrps) *n* a dead body, especially of a human being. <Old French, from Latin *corpus* body>

cor·pu·lent (kȯr′pyə lənt) *adj* excessively fat. <Latin *corpus* body> **cor′pu·lence** *n.*

cor·pus (kȯr′pəs) *n, pl* **cor·po·ra** (kȯr′pə rə) 1 a complete collection of written texts, especially the works of one author or on a particular subject. 2 a collection of written or spoken texts in machine-readable form so that frequency of words may be determined and other linguistic data studied. <Latin *corpus* body>

C

corpus callosum (kə lō′səm) *n, pl* **corpora callosa** (kə lō′sə) a bundle of nerves connecting the left and right hemispheres of the brain. <Latin = tough body>

cor·pus·cle (kȯr′pus əl) *or* (kȯr′pə səl) *n* a tiny body or cell of an organism, especially a red or white blood cell in a vertebrate. See BLOOD COUNT for picture. <Latin *corpus* body>

cor·ral (kə ral′) *n* 1 an outdoor pen on a farm or ranch for livestock, especially horses. 2 in former times, a circular camp formed by wagons for defence against attack.
v **cor·ralled, cor·ral·ling** 1 drive into and keep in a corral. 2 gather a group of people or things together. <Spanish, perhaps from Latin *currere* to run>

cor·rect (kə rekt′) *adj* 1 free from mistakes: *the correct answer.* 2 conforming to a general standard: *correct manners. "Humankind" is a politically correct term for "mankind."*
v 1 remove mistakes from: *Correct any wrong spellings you find.* 2 point out or mark the errors of: *to correct test papers. Stop correcting my grammar.* 3 adjust to account for some factor: *Archers must correct their aim for wind.* 4 rebuke or punish: *The mother corrected the child.* 5 remedy or overcome: *to correct a bad habit, to correct an injustice.* <Latin *com-* completely + *regere* guide> **cor·rec′tion** *n.* **cor·rect′ly** *adv.* **cor·rect′ness** *n.*

cor·rec·tion·al (kə rek′shə nəl) *adj* to do with correction, especially the rehabilitation of criminals: *Prisons are correctional facilities.*

🍁 **correction line** *n* on the Prairies, any of the north-south survey lines spaced six miles apart (about ten kilometres) perpendicular to an east-west baseline.

cor·rec·tive (kə rek′tiv) *adj* tending to correct or for the purpose of correcting: *corrective lenses to overcome short-sightedness.*
n something that tends to correct or set things right. **cor·rec′tive·ly** *adv.*

cor·re·late (kȯ′rə lāt′) *v* **cor·re·lat·ed, cor·re·lat·ing** 1 have a mutual relationship, in which one thing affects or depends on another: *For the average male, weight correlates fairly closely to height.* 2 show the connection or relation between: *The chart correlates readers' responses with their age and income.* <Latin *com-* together + *referre* bring back> **cor′re·la′tion** *n.*
cor′rel′a·tive (kə rel′ə tiv) *adj.*

correlative conjunction *Grammar n* one of a pair of words used together to join similar elements and depending on each other for meaning. Examples: *either...or; both...and.*

a bat	e bed	i bid	o pot	u cup	th thin
ā cake	ē me	ī bite	ō go	ū rude	ᴛʜ then
ä bar	ə about	ər over	ȯ for	u̇ put	zh measure

cor·re·spond (kô′rə spond′) *v* **1** have the same function, value, or effect as another: *The arms of a human correspond to the wings of a bird.* **2** write letters or e-mail to one another. <Old French, from Latin *com-* together + *respondere* answer> **cor′re·spond′ing** *adj.*

cor·re·spond·ence (kô′rə spon′dəns) *n* **1** the act, fact, or condition of corresponding: *We got to know each other well over the course of our long correspondence. There is an amazing correspondence between the careers of the two women.* **2** letters, or communication by exchanging letters: *She found a pile of correspondence on her desk when she returned from her holidays. Their correspondence went on over several years.* **3** *Mathematics* a matching of the members of one set of objects with the members of a second set of objects.

cor·re·spond·ent (kô′rə spon′dənt) *n* **1** a person who exchanges letters with another: *They have been correspondents for over two years.* **2** a person employed by a newspaper, magazine, or broadcaster to send news from a distant place: *a foreign correspondent for a national newspaper.* **3** something that corresponds to something else.

corresponding angles *Mathematics pln* a pair of angles formed on the same side of two lines and a transversal line that intersects them. The four angles at one of the two intersections correspond in turn to the four angles at the other intersection.

cor·ri·dor (kô′rə dôr′) *n* **1** a long hallway from which doors lead into rooms: *The gym is at the end of the corridor.* **2** something like this, such as a major road or transportation route, or a strip of land connecting two parts of a country: *Many trucks travel the Montreal-Toronto corridor. We need measures to relieve traffic jams along the city's main corridors.* <French, from Latin *currere* to run>

cor·ri·gen·dum (kô′rə jen′dəm) *n, pl* **cor·ri·gen·da** (kô′rə jen′də) an error to be corrected, especially in a book. <Latin *com-* together + *regere* to guide>

cor·rob·o·rate (kə rob′ə rāt′) *v* **cor·rob·o·rat·ed, cor·rob·o·rat·ing** back up or confirm: *Witnesses corroborated the police officer's statement.* <Latin *com-* together + *robur* strength> **cor·rob′o·ra′tion** *n.* **cor·rob′o·ra·tive** *adj.*

cor·rode (kə rōd′) *v* **cor·rod·ed, cor·rod·ing** **1** eat or wear away gradually, especially by rust or acid: *Acid rain had corroded the gravestones, making it difficult to read the names.* **2** become corroded: *Iron corrodes quickly.* <Latin *com-* altogether + *redere* gnaw> **cor·rod′i·ble** *adj.* **cor·ro′sion** (kə rō′zhən) *n.* **cor·ro′sive** (kə rō′ziv) *adj, n.*

cor·ru·gate (kô′rə gāt′) *v* **cor·ru·gat·ed, cor·ru·gat·ing** bend or shape a thin sheet of material into wavelike folds or ridges. <Latin *com-* altogether + *ruga* wrinkle> **cor′ru·ga′ted** *adj.* **cor′ru·ga′tion** *n.*

corrugated cardboard *n* cardboard consisting of two layers of paper with a sheet of corrugated paper between.

cor·rupt (kə rupt′) *adj* **1** influenced by bribes or personal interest, especially as a person in public office: *a corrupt judge, corrupt politicians.* **2** made unreliable by damage, miscopying, or alterations: *a corrupt manuscript.* **3** morally bad: *His corrupt desire for money led him to rob a corner store.* **4** *Computers* containing errors in a computer program or database. **5** *Archaic* rotten or decayed: *corrupt flesh.*
v make or become corrupt: *Too much power corrupts a leader. The original text had been corrupted by careless copying. He tried to corrupt the police officer by offering a bribe.* <Latin *com-* altogether + *rumpere* to break> **cor·rupt′i·ble** *adj.* **cor·rupt′ly** *adv.* **cor·rupt′ness** *n.*

cor·rup·tion (kə rup′shən) *n* **1** the act or process of corrupting or becoming corrupt. **2** a corrupt action or character. **3** *Archaic* rot or decay.

cor·sage (kôr säzh′) *n* a single flower or tiny bouquet to be worn on a blouse, dress, etc. <Old French *corsage* upper part of the body, from Latin *corpus* body>

cor·sair (kôr′ser) *n* a pirate or a pirate ship. <French *corsaire*, from Latin *currere* to run>

cor·set (kôr′sit) *n* a firm, close-fitting undergarment, worn (especially in former times) to support or shape the torso. <Old French, from Latin *corpus* body>

cor·tege or **cor·tège** (kôr tezh′) *n* a procession, especially for a funeral. <French, from Latin *cohors* attendants>

cor·tex (kôr′teks) *n, pl* **cor·ti·ces** (kôr′tə sēz′) **1** *Botany* **a** the layer of tissue between the epidermis and the vascular tissue of a stem or root. **b** the bark or rind of a plant. **2** **a** the outer part of an internal organ such as the kidneys (**renal cortex**). **b** the thin layer of grey matter that covers the cerebrum (**cerebral cortex**). <Latin *cortex* bark (of a tree)> **cor′ti·cal** (kôr′tə kəl′) *adj.*

cor·ti·sone (kôr′tə zōn′) *n* a hormone produced by the cortex of the adrenal glands, necessary for the regulation of many functions of the body, and made synthetically to treat diseases. <from elements of its long chemical name>

co·run·dum (kə run′dəm) *n* an extremely hard mineral, aluminum oxide, used as an abrasive in polishing and grinding. Sapphires and rubies are varieties of corundum. <Tamil *kuruntam*>

cor·us·cate (kô′rə skāt′) *v* **cor·us·cat·ed, cor·us·cat·ing** give off flashes of light; sparkle; glitter. <Latin *coruscare* to glitter> **cor′us·ca′tion** *n.*

cor·vette or **cor·vet** (kôr vet′) *n* **1** in former times, a warship with sails and one tier of guns. **2** a small, fast warship for use in antisubmarine and convoy work. <French, from Dutch *korf* a ship>

co·sign (kō′sīn) *or* (kō sīn′) *v* sign a document along with another person, so as to share a responsibility or right: *The accountant has to cosign all the company's cheques.* **co′sign·er** *n.*

cos·met·ic (koz met′ik) *n* a preparation for beautifying the skin, hair, or nails, such as lipstick or eyeshadow.
adj **1** to do with cosmetics. **2** improving only in a superficial way: *Cosmetic changes don't solve a problem.* <French, from Greek *kosmos* order>

cosmetic surgery *n* surgery performed to improve a person's appearance, especially of the face.

cos·me·tol·o·gy (koz′mə tol′ə jē) *n* the work or field of study of a beautician. **cos′me·tol′o·gist** *n.*

cos·mic (koz′mik) *adj* **1** to do with the universe: *Cosmic forces produce stars and meteors.* **2** vast: *a mistake of cosmic proportions.* <Greek *kosmos* world> **cos′mi·cal·ly** *adv.*

cosmic dust *n* fine particles of matter falling on the earth from outer space.

cosmic noise *n* radiation from sources outside the earth's atmosphere that can be detected at radio frequencies.

cosmic rays *n* streams of mostly electrically charged protons and alpha particles that travel through space at speeds nearly equal to that of light, some of which enter the earth's atmosphere.

cos·mog·o·ny (koz mog′ə nē) *n, pl* **cos·mog·o·nies** **1** the science that studies the origin of the universe, especially the solar system. **2** any theory of the origin of the universe. <Greek *kosmos* world + *gonos* birth>

cos·mog·ra·phy (koz mog′rə fē) *n, pl* **cos·mog·ra·phies** **1** the science that describes and maps the structure of the universe and bodies in the universe. **2** a general description of the universe or the earth.

cos·mol·o·gy (koz mol′ə jē) *n* **1** the philosophical study of the origin and nature of the universe. **2** a particular theory of the origin of the universe. **3** the branch of astrophysics that studies the origin, evolution, and structure of the universe.

cos·mo·naut (koz′mə not′) *n* a Russian astronaut. <Greek *kosmos* universe + *nautes* sailor>

cos·mo·pol·i·tan (koz′mə pol′ə tən) *adj* **1** feeling at home in or belonging to all parts of the world: *a cosmopolitan young woman. Music is one of the most cosmopolitan of the arts.* **2** showing the influence of many different cultures: *Vancouver is a cosmopolitan city.* **3** *Biology* found in many or all parts of the world: *Ants are cosmopolitan insects.* <French, from Greek *kosmos* world + *polites* citizen>

cos·mos (koz′mos) *n* **1** the universe thought of as an orderly, harmonious system. **2** a complete system that is orderly and harmonious. **3** a tall garden plant of the same family as the aster, with flowers that bloom in the fall. <Greek *kosmos* order>

Cos·sack (kos′ak) *n* a member of a people living in southern Russia, Ukraine, and Siberia, noted for their horsemanship and military skill.

cos·set (kos′it) *v* pamper or overprotect. <origin unknown>

cost (kost) *n* **1** the amount paid or to be paid for something: *The cost of this shirt was $38. The total cost of hosting the Olympics will be enormous.* **2** a loss or sacrifice: *The wolf escaped from the trap at the cost of a paw.* **3 costs** *pl* the expenses of a lawsuit or court case: *The defendant had to pay a $2000 fine plus costs.*
v **cost** or (*for def. 4*) **cost·ed, cost·ing** **1** have a certain price: *This shirt costs $38.* **2** require the spending of money, time, or effort. *Wasting time now is going to cost you later.* **3** cause someone the loss of: *His many absences finally cost him his part in the play.* **4** estimate or calculate the cost of: *The principal is costing upgrades to the school's computers.* <Old French, from Latin *com-* with + *stare* stand>
at all costs or **at any cost,** regardless of expense: *They had to go by taxi at all costs, or miss their flight.*
at cost, with no profit markup: *They got the tiles at cost because they were a charitable organization.*

cos·tal (kos′təl) *adj* to do with the ribs. <French, from Latin *costa* rib>

co–star (kō′ stȧr′) *n* one of two or more actors playing the leading roles in a movie or play.
v **co-starred, co-star·ring** feature or be featured as a co-star.

Cos·ta Ri·ca (kos′tə rē′kə) *n* a country in Central America. See the APPENDIX. **Cos′ta Ric′an** *adj, n.*

cost–ef·fec·tive (kost′i fek′tiv) *adj* bringing good results for a relatively low cost.

cost·ly (kost′lē) *adj* **cost·li·er, cost·li·est** **1** of great value: *costly jewels.* **2** causing serious loss: *costly mistakes.* **3** expensive: *a costly leather jacket.* **cost′li·ness** *n.*

cost of living *n* the average price paid by consumers for necessities such as food, rent, clothing, and transportation: *Wages were much lower in the nineteenth century, but so was the cost of living.*

cost price *n* a price equal to the cost of producing or distributing the item.

cos·tume (kos′chūm) *n* **1** an outfit representing a certain time or place, character, profession, or animal, worn on stage, at a masquerade party, etc.: *The actors wore Spanish costumes. He rented a pirate costume for the party.* **2** the style of dress of a time, place, or social class, including garments, hairstyles, jewellery, or other ornaments: *the traditional costume of a Swiss farmer.* **3** *UK* an outfit for a special purpose: *a bathing costume, a hunting costume.*
v **cos·tumed, cos·tum·ing** provide a costume for or dress in a costume. <French, from Latin *com-* with + *suescere* become accustomed>

costume jewellery *n* cheap, mass-produced, often colourful jewellery.

co·sy (kō′zē) COZY.

cot (kot) *n* **1** a narrow camp bed, usually made of canvas stretched over a frame that folds up when not in use. **2** a small bed with high barred sides for a baby or small child. <Hindi *khat* bedstead, hammock>

Côte d'Ivoire (kōt′ dē vwȧr′) *n* a country in west Africa.

co·te·rie (kō′tə rē) *n* a set or circle of acquaintances who often meet socially. <French, originally an association for tenants of one farm owner>

co·ter·mi·nous (kō tər′mə nəs) *adj* **1** with a common boundary: *Canada is coterminous with the United States.* **2** covering exactly the same area or territory: *Is present-day downtown Toronto coterminous with the old city of York?* <*co-* with + Latin *terminus* boundary>

co·til·lion (kə til′yən) *n* a dance with complicated steps and much changing of partners, led by one couple. <French, from Old French *cote*>

a bat	e bed	i bid	o pot	u cup	th thin
ā cake	ē me	ī bite	ō go	ū rude	TH then
ȧ bar	ə about	ər over	ȯ for	u̇ put	zh measure

cot·tage (kot′ij) *n* **1** a small house for holiday use, usually near a lake or in the woods. **2** a small rural home. <Old English *cot*> **cot′tag·er** *n.*

cottage cheese *n* a soft, white cheese made from the curds of sour skim milk.

cottage industry *n* **1** a business, often the production of goods, that is carried on in people's homes. **2** a small, loosely organized, but prosperous business or activity.

cot·ter pin (kot′ər) *n* a long metal pin used to fasten two small parts of machinery together.

cot·ton (kot′ən) *n* **1** cloth made from fibres obtained from the seed pods of the cotton plant. **2** the fibres themselves, which are attached to the seeds in a fluffy mass.
v Informal take a liking (to): *I cottoned to her at once.* <Old French, from Arabic *kutn*> **cot′ton·y** *adj.*
cotton on, *Informal* understand: *He still hasn't cottoned on that it was only a joke.*

cotton batting *n* soft, fluffy cotton fibres pressed into balls, wads, or thin layers, used as padding in quilting, for dressing wounds, or for applying cosmetics.

cotton candy CANDY FLOSS.

cotton gin *n* a machine for separating the fibres of cotton from the seeds.

cot·ton·mouth (kot′ən mouth′) WATER MOCCASIN.

cot·ton·seed (kot′ən sēd′) *n, pl* **cot·ton·seed** or **cot·ton·seeds** the seeds of cotton, used as fertilizer, cattle food, and a source of oil.

cot·ton·tail (kot′ən tāl′) *n* a wild rabbit of North America, with brownish or greyish fur.

cot·ton·wood (kot′ən wu̇d′) *n* a N American poplar tree with cottonlike tufts on the seeds.

cotton wool *n* **1** cotton batting. **2** raw cotton fibres.

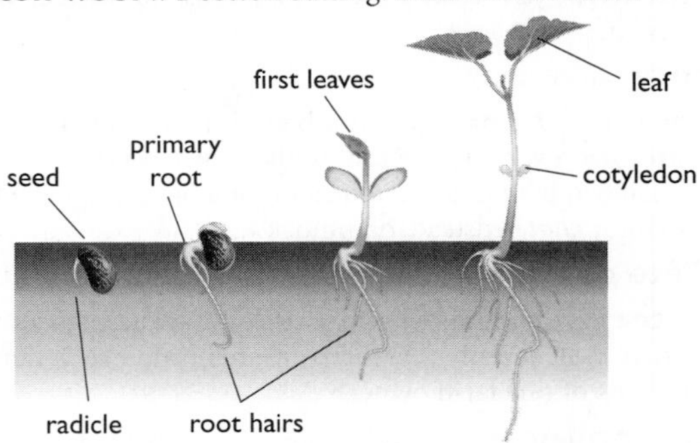

cot·y·le·don (kot′ə lē′dən) *Botany n* an embryo leaf, one or more of which is the first to appear from a seed when it germinates. <Latin, from Greek *kotyle* cup, from its shape>

couch (kouch) *n* a long piece of upholstered furniture for lying or sitting on, such as a sofa or chesterfield.
v express in a particular style of language: *insults couched in diplomatic language.* <Old French *couche* a bed, from Latin *com-* together + *locus* place> **couch′like′** *adj.*

couch grass (kouch) *or* (kūch) *n* a coarse perennial grass with underground stems by which it spreads. Also called **quack grass**. <Old English *cwice*>

couch potato *Slang n* someone who sits and watches TV a lot and gets little exercise.

cou·gar (kū′gər) *n* a large, usually sandy-coloured wild cat of N and S America, with short black ears and a very long black-tipped tail. Also called **puma, mountain lion**. See PUMA for picture.<French, from Tupi (a language of S America) *guaçuarana*>

cough (kof) *v* force air from the lungs suddenly with a short, harsh noise or series of noises.
n **1** the act or sound of coughing. **2** a condition or illness marked by frequent coughing: *She has a bad cough.* <Middle English *coghen*>
cough up, a expel from the throat or lungs by coughing: *to cough up phlegm.* **b** *Informal* hand over or pay: *I know you have my baseball glove. Cough it up!*

cough drop *n* a small candy containing medicine to relieve coughs or hoarseness.

could (ku̇d) past tense of CAN, used to express past time, a possibility, or a polite request: *Once she could sing beautifully. If you moved, I could visit more often. Could you lend me some money?* <Old English *cuthe*>

could·n't (ku̇d′ənt) *contraction* could not.

could·'ve (ku̇d′əv) *contraction* could have: *I could've gone if I'd known you wanted company.*

GRAMMAR AND USAGE

It is a mistake to rewrite the contraction **could've** in the form **could of**. Give the correct form, **could have**.

The same is true for *should've, would've,* and *must've.*

🍁 **cou·lee** (kū′lē) *n* especially on the Prairies, a deep ravine or gulch that is usually dry in summer. <Cdn French>

cou·lomb (kū′lōm) *or* (kū′lom) *n* the SI unit for measuring the quantity of electric charge carried by a current of one ampere flowing in one second. *Symbol* **C**
<C.A. de *Coulomb,* 18c physicist>

coun·cil (koun′səl) *n* **1** a group of people called together to give advice, talk things over, or settle questions: *a council of war.* **2** the small group of elected people who govern a township or city. **3** 🍁 in former times, the group of appointed or elected people governing a Territory. <Old English, from Latin *com-* together + *calare* call>
in council, in a meeting, especially a council meeting.

CONFUSABLES

Council is a noun that refers to a group of people:

The town council discussed a dog-leash bylaw.

Counsel means "advice" (noun) or "advise" (verb):

He gave me counsel on preparing for the competition.

The librarian counselled me on how to locate the resources I needed.

coun·cil·lor or **coun·ci·lor** (koun′sə lər) *n* **1** a member of the elected council of a village, town, or city. **2** 🍁 *Prince Edward Island* in former times, a member of the Legislative Assembly elected by property owners.

coun·sel (koun′səl) *n, pl* **coun·sel** **1** advice: *to seek the counsel of a friend.* **2** the process of talking things over: *There was little time for counsel.* **3** a lawyer or group of lawyers in court: *She is counsel for the defence.*
v **coun·selled** or **coun·seled, coun·sel·ling** or **coun·sel·ing** **1** advise or recommend: *He counselled immediate action. They counselled me to remain in school.* **2** act as a professional counsellor to: *She counsels high school students.* **3** exchange ideas or consult together. See COUNCIL for confusable. <Old French, from Latin *com-* together + *calare* call>
hold (or **take**) **counsel,** talk things over: *The stranded travellers held counsel to decide what they should do next.*

coun·sel·lor or **coun·se·lor** (koun′sə lər) *n* **1** a professional who gives guidance on personal, social, or psychological problems: *a guidance counsellor, a grief counsellor.* **2** *especially US* a lawyer. **3** a person who supervises children at a camp. **4** a person who gives advice, professionally or not.

count[1] (kount) *v* **1** name numbers in order: *Can you count to ten?* **2** find out how many: *He counted the books and found there were 50.* **3** include or be included in a total: *Let's not count that goal. Does this quiz count in our final grade?* **4** have importance or be of value: *I want to do something that counts with my life. It's who you know that counts.* **5** consider or think of as: *Count yourself lucky that you weren't hurt.*
n **1** an act of counting: *A careful count showed that 5019 votes had been cast.* **2** the total arrived at by counting: *The exact count was 173.* **3** *Law* each charge in a formal accusation. **4** the ten seconds counted to give a fallen boxer time to get up before being declared the loser. <Old French *counter*, from Latin *computare* calculate>
count for, be worth: *Her argument counted for little against theirs.*
count off, divide into equal groups by counting: *Count off in fours from the left.*
count on, a rely on or trust: *Can we count on you to help?* **b** plan on or expect: *I count on winning.*
count someone in, *Informal* (*usually as a command*) expect someone as a participant: *Count me in for the party!*
count someone out, a *Informal* (*usually as a command*) not expect to participate: *If you go skiing, count me out.* **b** declare a boxer the loser when he or she cannot get up after ten seconds: *The former champion was counted out in the third round.*
out for the count, a of a boxer, unable to get up after ten seconds have been counted. **b** *Informal* sound asleep.

count[2] (kount) *n* a European nobleman with a rank about the same as that of a British earl. <Old French *conte*, from Latin *comes* state official>

count·down (kount′doun′) *n* **1** the period just before a special event, such as the launch of a rocket, when people keep close track of the time left. **2** the act of counting days, hours, minutes, or seconds backwards to the moment of a special event, represented by zero.

coun·te·nance (koun′tə nəns) *n* **1** *Poetic* the face, or the expression on it: *a handsome countenance, an angry countenance.* **2** approval or encouragement: *He gave countenance to our plan, but no active help.*
v **coun·te·nanced, coun·te·nanc·ing** (*usually in the negative*) approve or encourage: *My mother would not countenance my plan to travel alone.* <Old French, from Latin *com-* altogether + *tenere* to hold>

count·er[1] (koun′tər) *n* **1** a fixture in a restaurant or store, with a long, flat top over which people are served or pay for things: *a lunch counter, a checkout counter.* **2** a similar fixture built against a wall of a kitchen or bathroom: *I left the groceries on the kitchen counter.* <Old French *compteur*, from Latin *computare* compute>
over the counter, without a prescription: *Vitamin pills are sold over the counter.*
under the counter (or **table**)**,** with no official record, in order to evade taxes or regulations.

count·er[2] (koun′tər) *n* **1** a person who or thing that counts. **2** a disc or other object used for counting and in some board games. **3** a slug or imitation coin. <Old French *conteor*, from Latin *computare* compute>

count·er[3] (koun′tər) *adv, adj* (*with* ***to***) opposite or contrary: *Such an idea runs counter to common sense* (*adv*). *What you say is counter to everything I believe* (*adj*).
v speak or act against and in response to: *She countered our every argument with one of her own. "You're so slow," I teased. "Maybe, but not sloppy like you," he countered.*
n something opposite or contrary to something else: *Her answer was a direct counter to his accusation.* <Old French *contre*, from Latin *contra* against>

counter– *combining form* **1** against or in opposition to: *counteract.* **2** in return: *counterattack.* **3** corresponding; correspondingly: *counterpart.* <See COUNTER[3].>

GRAMMAR AND USAGE

Authorities are divided on whether compounds with **counter–** should be hyphenated or not. In this dictionary, a hyphen is used before a following *r*.
A hyphen is also usually used when the second element of the compound carries the primary stress, or if the compound is more than three syllables long.

coun·ter·act (koun′tər akt′) *v* act against or neutralize the effect of. **coun′ter·ac′tion** *n.* **coun′ter·act′ive** *adj, n.*

coun·ter·at·tack (koun′tər ə tak′) *n* an attack made to respond to an attack.
v attack in return.

coun·ter·bal·ance (koun′tər bal′əns) *for v,* (koun′tər bal′əns) *for n.*
v **coun·ter·bal·anced, coun·ter·bal·anc·ing** offset or neutralize: *Their different personalities seem to counterbalance each other.*
n **1** a weight balancing another weight. **2** something that balances or offsets something else: *His stinginess is a counterbalance to her extravagance.*

coun·ter·charge (koun′tər chȧrj′) *n* a charge or accusation made in response to a charge.
v charge or accuse after being oneself charged.

a bat	e bed	i bid	o pot	u cup	th thin
ā cake	ē me	ī bite	ō go	ū rude	ᴛʜ then
ȧ bar	ə about	ər over	ȯ for	u̇ put	zh measure

coun·ter·claim (koun′tər klām′) *n* a claim made by a person to offset a claim made against him or her.

coun·ter·clock·wise (koun′tər klok′wīz′) *adv, adj* in the direction opposite to the movement of a clock's hands.

coun·ter·cul·ture (koun′tər kul′chər) *n* a movement or group that rejects the values of mainstream society and lives a very different lifestyle: *the hippie counterculture of the 1960s.* **coun′ter·cul′tur·al** *adj.*

coun·ter–es·pi·o·nage (koun′tər es′pē ə näzh′) *n* spy activity to hinder or prevent enemy spy activity.

coun·ter·feit (koun′tər fit) *adj* **1** fake, but being passed off as the real thing: *counterfeit money.* **2** pretended or insincere: *a counterfeit smile.*
n a copy made to deceive or defraud and passed off as genuine: *The cashier refused to accept the hundred-dollar bill, suspecting it was a counterfeit.*
v **1** copy money or pictures in order to deceive or defraud. **2** pretend or be insincere: *She counterfeited a grief she did not feel.* <Old French, from Latin *contra-* in opposition + *facere* make> **coun′ter·feit′er** *n.*

coun·ter–in·tel·li·gence (koun′tər in tel′ə jəns) *n* the work of tracking down and hindering or preventing enemy spy activity.

coun·ter–in·tu·i·tive (koun′tər in tū′ə tiv) *adj* opposite to the way one expects things to be: *English spelling is often counter-intuitive!*

coun·ter·mand (koun′tər mand′) *or* (koun′tər mand′) *for v;* (koun′tər mand′) *for n. v* withdraw or cancel an order or command: *The order to attack was countermanded and they were sent back to the base.*
n an order that cancels or is contrary to a previous order. <Old French, from Latin *contra-* against + *mandare* to order>

coun·ter·meas·ure (koun′tər mezh′ər) *n* an action taken against something: *Schoolyard bullying will continue unless we take stern countermeasures.*

coun·ter·of·fen·sive (koun′tər ə fen′siv) *n* an attack on a large scale to take the initiative back from an attacking force.

coun·ter·of·fer (koun′tər of′ər) *n* an offer made in response to an unsatisfactory offer: *Two hundred dollars is too much for that guitar; make him a counteroffer of $150.*

coun·ter·pane (koun′tər pān′) *n* an outer covering for a bed. <Old French, from Latin *culcita puncta* quilted mattress>

coun·ter·part (koun′tər pärt′) *n* **1** a person who or thing that corresponds to another: *The federal energy minister is holding talks with her provincial counterparts.* **2** a person who or thing that complements another: *Night is the counterpart of day.*

coun·ter·plot (koun′tər plot′) *n, v* **coun·ter·plot·ted, coun·ter·plot·ting** (a) plot to defeat another plot.

coun·ter·point (koun′tər point′) *n* **1** *Music* **a** a different melody added to another as an accompaniment. **b** the art of combining two or more distinct melodies so that they form a harmonious unit. **2** an element or theme that contrasts with or complements another: *This web page is an interesting counterpoint to our discussion about cloning.*

coun·ter·poise (koun′tər poiz) *n* **1** a factor, force, or influence that balances or offsets another. **2** a condition in which two things are balanced.
v **coun·ter·poised, coun·ter·pois·ing** have an opposing and balancing effect. <Old French, from Latin *contra-* against + *pendere* weigh>

coun·ter·pro·duc·tive (koun′tər prə duk′tiv) *adj* with an effect that hinders or is opposite to the desired effect: *Too strict an enforcement of rules can be counterproductive.*

coun·ter–rev·o·lu·tion (koun′tər rev′ə lū′shən) *n* a revolution against a regime established by a previous revolution. **coun′ter-rev′o·lu′tion·ary** *adj, n.*

coun·ter·sign (koun′tər sīn′) *v* sign something already signed by another, to confirm it.
n a password or secret signal given in answer to another: *The soldier had to give the countersign before he could pass the sentry.* <French, from Latin *contra-* against + *signum* sign>

coun·ter·sink (koun′tər singk′) *v* **coun·ter·sank, coun·ter·sunk, coun·ter·sink·ing** drive a screw, nail, or bolt in so that it is flush with or below the surface.
n a tool used for this.

coun·ter·ten·or (koun′tər ten′ər) *n* the highest adult male singing voice, or a singer with such a range.
adj to do with a countertenor.

count·ess (koun′tis) *n* **1** the wife or widow of a count. **2** a noblewoman equal to a count in rank.

counting house *n* in former times, a building or office used for keeping accounts and doing business.

count·less (kount′lis) *adj* too many to count: *the countless grains of sand on the seashore.*

coun·tri·fy (kun′tri fī′) *v* **coun·tri·fied, coun·tri·fy·ing** make typical of a rural style or way of life: *Whenever he's with his cousins, his accent becomes countrified.*

coun·try (kun′trē) *n, pl* **coun·tries** **1** a nation with a recognized government and territory: *There are three countries in North America: Canada, the US, and Mexico.* **2** the territory or the people only of such a nation: *I am leaving the country for a few weeks. The whole country supported the Olympic team.* **3** areas with farms and small villages rather than cities: *We went for a drive in the country.* **4** a region characterized by a certain geography, geology, or group of residents: *hill country, cottage country.* **5** in full, **country music** or **country and western** a style of music that developed from the traditional folk music of the rural southern US.
adj to do with the country: *country roads.* <Old French, from Latin *contrata* (land) spread out in front of one>

country club *n* a club on the outskirts of a city or in the suburbs, with a clubhouse and facilities for outdoor sports, especially a golf course.

country cousin *Informal n* a person from the country who finds the city confusing or frightening.

coun·try·man (kun′trē mən) *n, pl* **coun·try·men** (kun′trē mən) a person or man of one's own country: *They met many of their countrymen in their travels through Europe.*

country mile *Informal n* a long way.

coun·try·side (kun′trē sīd′) *n* **1** the land outside cities and towns, especially with reference to its scenic appearance: *The countryside looked beautiful in the fall sun.* **2** the people of a country or region: *The whole countryside was at work in the olive groves.*

country wife *n* in former times, the Aboriginal common-law wife of a European fur trader or pioneer.

coun·try·wom·an (kun′trē wu̇m′ən) *n, pl* **coun·try·wom·en** (kun′trē wim′ən) a woman of one's own country.

coun·ty (koun′tē) *n, pl* **coun·ties** a geographical area into which some countries, provinces, and states are divided for local government. <Old French = land belonging to a COUNT[2])>

county seat *n* the town or city where the government of a county is located.

coup (kū) *n* **1** in full, **coup d'état** (dā tȧ′) the sudden, violent overthrow of a government. **2** a sudden, brilliant or triumphant act. <French, from Greek *kolaphos* a blow with the fist>

coup de grâce (kū′də grȧs′) *n* **1** a finishing stroke: *The runner's final sprint gave the coup de grâce to her opponents.* **2** an action that kills a wounded animal or person. <French = stroke of grace>

GRAMMAR AND USAGE

Coup de grâce is an example of a French phrase that is now commonly used in English. Other examples are *bon voyage* (good trip), *c'est la vie* (that's life), and *déjà vu* (already seen).

coupe (kūp) *n* a two-door car, usually smaller than a sedan. Compare CONVERTIBLE. <French = cut-off (carriage), from *couper* to cut>

cou·ple (kup′əl) *n* **1** two people who are married, sexual or romantic partners, or on a date. **2** *Informal* (*with* ***of***) two or, more loosely, a few: *I'll be out for a couple of hours.* **3** the partners in a dance. **4** two things of the same kind that go together.
v **cou·pled, cou·pling 1** connect one thing to another to make a pair: *to couple freight cars.* **2** cause to happen together: *A rent increase coupled with layoffs meant hardship for her family.* **3** have sexual intercourse. <Old French, from Latin *co-* together + *apere* fasten>

SYNONYMS

Couple means "two": *I take the bus a couple of times each day.*

Few means "three," or "not many more than three": *A few ducks landed on the pond.*

Several usually means "more than a few, but not many more" (up to about seven): *She invited several friends to her birthday party.*

cou·pler (kup′lər) *n* a device used to connect two things, such as railway cars, electric circuits, or parts of machinery. Also called **coupling**.

cou·plet (kup′lit) *n* two successive lines of poetry that rhyme and have the same rhythm. Example: *Be not the first by whom the new are tried, Nor yet the last to lay the old aside.* <See COUPLE.>

cou·pon (kū′pon) *n* **1** a marked piece of paper that entitles the holder to get something in exchange: *a coupon for 50¢ off the price of a pizza slice.* **2** a printed statement of interest due on a bond that can be cut off and presented for payment. <Old French colpen a piece cut off, from Greek *kolaphos* a blow with the fist>

cour·age (kər′ij) *n* the inner strength to do what is right or necessary in spite of fear. <Old French, from Latin *cor* heart> **cou·ra′geous** (kə rā′jəs) *adj.* **cou·ra′geous·ly** *adv.*
have the courage of your convictions, act as you believe you should.

cou·reur de bois (kū rər′də bwȧ′) *n, pl* **cou·reurs de bois** (kū rər′də bwȧ′) in former times, a French or Métis fur trader or woodsman. <Cdn. French = forest runner>

cour·i·er (kər′ē ər) *n* **1** a person or agency whose work is delivering letters and parcels rapidly. **2** a messenger. **3** a person who goes with a group of travellers and takes care of hotel reservations, tickets, and other arrangements.
v Informal send by courier. <Old French, from Latin *currere* to run>

course (kȯrs) *n* **1** a series of classes or lessons: *a hairdressing course. She will take seven courses in grade 9.* **2** a part of a meal: *Soup was the first course.* **3** an area marked out for a game or sport: *a golf course, a racecourse.* **4** an onward movement through time: *the course of events.* **5** a line of action or response to a situation: *The only sensible course was to go home.* **6** a direction or route taken: *The ship's course was due east.* **7** a complete series: *a course of antibiotics.* **8** the regular or ordinary way of proceeding: *the course of nature.*
v **coursed, cours·ing** run or flow: *Blood courses through arteries.* See COARSE for confusable. <Old French, from Latin *currere* to run>
a matter of course, something to be expected: *People used to grow their own food as a matter of course.*
in due course, at the proper time: *I know he will be here in due course.*
in the course of, during: *in the course of our visit. In the course of cleaning my room I found $5.80 in loose change.*
of course, a as might be expected: *Of course it will rain on the weekend.* **b** certainly: *Of course I'll do it.*
on (**off**) **course,** going in (straying from) the correct direction: *It was hard to keep the canoe on course in the rough water.*
run (or **take**) **its course,** come to the end of its natural development: *With chicken pox, you just have to let it run its course.*

cours·er (kȯr′sər) *Poetic n* a swift warhorse.

course·ware (kȯrs′wer′) *Computers n* software that gives instruction in a variety of subjects.

a bat	e bed	i bid	o pot	u cup	th thin
ā cake	ē me	ī bite	ō go	ū rude	ᴛʜ then
ȧ bar	ə about	ər over	ȯ for	u̇ put	zh measure

C

court (kȯrt) *n* **1 a** a place where legal cases are heard and justice is administered. **b** the judge or judges and jury in a court: *The court found him guilty.* **2** a large enclosed space indoors or outdoors: *There are 20 fast-food restaurants in the mall's food court. The castle enclosed a grass court in the centre.* **3** a place marked or walled off for any of various games: *a tennis court, a basketball court.* **4 a** the residence of a monarch. **b** the family, household, or followers of a monarch: *The court of King Louis XVI was noted for its splendour.* **c** a formal assembly held by a monarch. **5** attention, often romantic, paid to win someone's favour.
v **1** pay attention to someone, often romantically, to gain his or her favour. **2** act so as to get: *You are courting disaster by such foolish behaviour.* <Old French, from Latin *cohors* enclosure>
hold court, receive or entertain people in a lordly way.
pay court to, try to win the love or favour of.

cour·te·ous (kər′tē əs) *adj* polite and thoughtful of others: *A courteous classmate helped me carry my books.* <Old French, from Latin *cohors* company of guards> **cour′te·ous·ly** *adv.* **cour′te·ous·ness** *n.*

cour·te·san (kȯr′tə zan′) *or* (kȯr′tə zən) *n* a prostitute whose clients are wealthy or of the nobility.

cour·te·sy (kər′tə sē) *n, pl* **cour·te·sies 1** polite or gracious behaviour. **2 courtesies** *pl* a polite or thoughtful gesture or remark: *They exchanged the usual courtesies and each went his own way.* <Old French *corteis,* from Latin *cohors* company of guards>
by courtesy of (or **through the courtesy of**)**,** with the permission or approval of: *The poem is included in the book by courtesy of the author.*
courtesy of, free of charge from someone or something: *Shampoo and soap are provided courtesy of the hotel.*

courtesy car *n* a car provided free of charge by a garage or insurance company while repairs are being made to one's own.

court·house (kȯrt′hous′) *n* a building where a law court holds hearings or trials.

cour·ti·er (kȯr′tē ər) *n* a person often present at a royal court as an official or attendant.

court·ly (kȯrt′lē) *adj* **court·li·er, court·li·est** polite and elegant: *courtly manners.* **court′li·ness** *n.*

court–mar·tial (kȯrt′ mär′shəl) *n, pl* **courts-mar·tial 1** a court that tries armed forces personnel accused of breaking military law. **2** a trial by such a court: *The captain's court-martial will be held next week.*
v **court-mar·tialled** or **court-mar·tialed, court-mar·tial·ling** or **court-mar·tial·ing** try by such a court.

court·room (kȯrt′rūm′) *n* a room where a law court is held.

court·ship (kȯrt′ship) *n* a time of romantic friendship, before marriage.

court·yard (kȯrt′yärd′) *n* a space enclosed by walls, in or next to a large building.

cous·cous (kūs′kūs) *n* a Mediterranean dish made from steamed pellets of semolina with a stew or sauce, or the pellets themselves. <French, from Arabic *kuskus*>

cous·in (kuz′ən) *n* **1** the son or daughter of one's uncle or aunt. **First cousins** have the same grandparents; **second cousins** have the same great-grandparents. Your father's or mother's first cousin is your **first cousin once removed**. **2** a distant relative. **3** a person or thing thought of as being related to another by similarity or common origin: *What a swimmer! He's cousin to a fish!* **4** in former times, a term used by royalty in speaking to another sovereign or to a great nobleman. <Old French, from Latin *com-* with + *soror* sister> **cous′in·ly** *adj.*

co·va·lent bond (kō vā′lənt) *Chemistry n* a chemical bond in which two or more electrons are shared by two atoms.

cove (kōv) *n* an inlet on the shore, such as is often formed by the mouth of a creek. <Old English *cofa* chamber>

cov·en (kuv′ən) *n* a group or gathering of witches. <Old French, from Latin *com-* together + *venire* come>

cov·e·nant (kuv′ə nənt) *n* **1** a solemn agreement between two or more people or groups. **2** a legal contract or agreement. **3** *Judaism, Christianity* a commitment between God and God's people.
v solemnly agree to do certain things. <Old French, from Latin *convenire* make an agreement> **cov′e·nant·er** or **cov′e·nan·tor** *n.*

cov·er (kuv′ər) *v* **1** put something over or around so as to protect, keep warm, or hide: *I covered my bike with a plastic sheet. Pull the blind to cover the window.* **2** lie all over the surface of: *Snow covered the ground.* **3** extend over or occupy: *Their farm covers about 120 hectares.* **4** travel over: *We covered more than 500 km the first day of our trip.* **5** deal with: *The review covered everything in the unit.* **6** insure against damage or loss: *The house is covered but not the contents. The insurance does not cover flood damage.* **7** be enough for: *My allowance won't cover the cost of a pair of jeans.* **8** act as a reporter or photographer of an event or subject: *She covers sports.* **9** *Sports* **a** watch and try to hinder an opposing player. **b** support a teammate in play. **10** protect, screen, or shelter: *to cover someone's retreat.* **11** aim a gun at: *One robber covered the cashier while the other emptied the cash drawer.*
n **1** anything that covers: *The cover of the book is torn. This plant is good ground cover.* **2** a blanket for a bed. **3** a false identity or other stratagem intended to hide: *Her office job was a cover for her spy activities.* **4** a table setting for one person. **5** cover charge. **6** *Music* a recording by a performer of a song that was first popularized by another performer. Also called **cover version**. **7** an envelope or wrapper with a stamp on it. <Old French *covrir,* from Latin *co-* up + *operire* cover> **cov′er·less** *adj.*
blow someone's cover, reveal someone's false identity.
break cover, come out of hiding, especially suddenly: *She broke cover and ran for the house.*
cover for, a substitute for someone who is absent: *He is covering for the manager while she is away.* **b** shield a guilty or incompetent person from discovery: *I can't keep covering for you; you'll have to shape up.*
cover up, a cover completely: *Cover up the baby; it's cold tonight.* **b** conceal error or wrongdoing through pretence or lies: *to cover up a scandal.* **c** cover or protect oneself: *The best defence against sunburn is to cover up.*
take cover, find shelter or protection: *We took cover from the rain in an old barn.*

under cover, secret or secretly: *to keep something under cover. Spies work under cover.*
under cover of, hidden by: *to attack under cover of darkness.*

cov·er·age (kuv′ər ij) *n* **1** the extent and quality of information provided by a reporter, newspaper, or newscast: *CBC had very good coverage of the Winter Olympics.* **2** the risks covered by an insurer, or the amount payable in case of loss: *to have $50 000 coverage in case of fire. Collision is not part of his insurance coverage.* **3** the audience reached by an advertising campaign or other media event. **4** the amount or extent covered by anything: *Our teacher was pleased at the good coverage of the discussion topic. This paint has better coverage than the cheaper brand.*

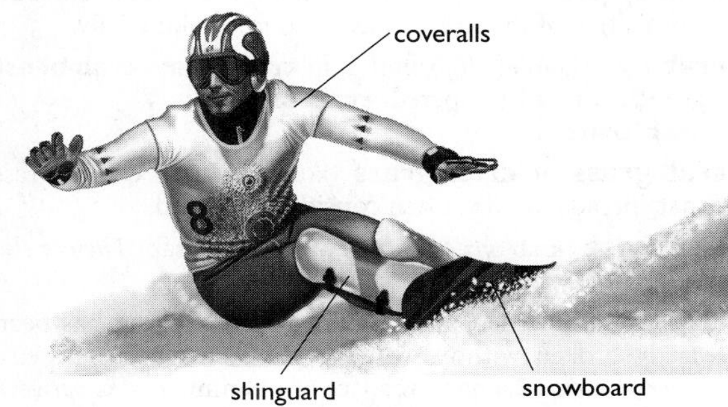

cov·er·alls (kuv′ə rolz′) *pln* a one-piece outer garment for the whole body, made of strong material and worn to protect other clothing.

cover charge *n* a charge made in some nightclubs and restaurants for service and entertainment in addition to what is charged for food and drink.

covered wagon *n* a large wagon with a removable, arched canvas cover, used especially by the pioneers.

cov·er·ing (kuv′ə ring) *n* anything that covers: *bed coverings.*

GRAMMAR AND USAGE

Covering can be a vague word. Try to use a more specific, descriptive noun. For example, a *hood* is a covering for the head and neck. A *sheath* is a covering for a blade. A *quilt* is a type of covering for a bed.

cov·er·let (kuv′ər lit) *n* an outer covering for a bed.

cover letter *n* a letter sent along with a résumé, application, or questionnaire. Also, **covering letter**.

co·vert (kō′vərt) *or* (kuv′ərt) *adj* done secretly or stealthily: *covert glances.* <Old French, form of *co-* altogether + *operire* to cover> **co·vert′ly** *adv.* **co·vert′ness** *n.*

cov·er–up (kuv′ər up′) *n* **1** an action meant to hide an error or wrongdoing. **2** a robe or wraplike garment for covering other clothing such as a swimsuit.

cov·et (kuv′it) *v* desire very much, especially something that belongs to another: *I must confess I've been coveting that new jacket of yours.* <Old French, from Latin *cupere* desire> **cov′et·ous** *adj.*

cov·ey (kuv′ē) *n, pl* **cov·eys** a brood or small flock, especially of partridges or quail. <Old French *covée,* from Latin *cubare* lie down (i.e., hatch)>

cow[1] (kou) *n* the adult female of cattle, buffalo, other bovine animals, and some large animals such as the moose, whale, or elephant. See UNGULATE for picture. <Old English *cu*>

C

cow[2] (kou) *v* (*usually passive*) frighten or intimidate: *Don't be cowed by his threats.* <probably Old Norse *kuga* oppress>

cow·ard (kou′ərd) *n* a person who lacks courage or avoids dangerous or unpleasant things. <Old French, from Latin *cauda* tail (perhaps suggesting a frightened animal with its tail between its legs)> **cow′ard·ice** (kou′ər dis) or **cow′ard·li·ness** *n.* **cow′ard·ly** *adj.*

cow·bell (kou′bel′) *n* a bell hung around a cow's neck so that the clanking sound will indicate where it is.

cow·bird (kou′bərd′) *n* a small N American blackbird, often found with cattle. It usually lays its eggs in other birds' nests.

cow·boy (kou′boi′) *n* **1** especially in Western Canada and the US, a man who looks after cattle on a ranch or on the range, doing much of his work on horseback. **2** *Informal* a person who ignores rules or proper methods.

cow·catch·er (kou′kach′ər) *n* a metal shelf at the bottom of the front of a locomotive, designed to push aside any obstruction on the tracks.

cow·er (kou′ər) *v* crouch or draw back in fear or shame: *The whipped dog cowered under the table. Don't cower at these bullies; stand up to them.* <German *kuren* lie in wait>

cow·girl (kou′gərl′) *n* especially in Western Canada and the US, a woman who looks after cattle on a ranch or on the range, doing much of her work on horseback.

cow·hand (kou′hand′) a cowboy or cowgirl.

cow·herd (kou′hərd′) *n* a person whose work is looking after cattle while they are grazing.

cow·hide (kou′hīd′) *n* the hide of a cow, or leather made from it.

Cow·i·chan (kou′i chən) *n, pl* **Cow·i·chan** *for 1,* **Cow·i·chans** *for 3.* **1** a member of a First Nations people living mainly on Vancouver Island. **2** their Salishan language. **3** 🍁 a heavy wool sweater knitted by the Cowichan people or in their traditional style, with symbolic designs on the front and back.
adj to do with the Cowichan or their language.

cowl (koul) *n* **1** a monk's hooded cloak, or the hood itself. **2** in full, **cowl neck** a wide neck on a woman's garment, consisting of loose folds of fabric somewhat resembling a lowered hood. **3** something shaped like a hood, such as a cover for machine parts. **4** the part of a car body that includes the windshield and the dashboard. **5** a cowling. <Old English *cule,* from Latin *cucullus* hood>

a bat	e bed	i bid	o pot	u cup	th **thin**
ā cake	ē me	ī bite	ō go	ū rude	TH **then**
ä bar	ə about	ər over	ȯ for	u̇ put	zh measure

cow·lick (kou′lik′) *n* a small tuft of hair that will not lie flat, usually just above the forehead.

ETYMOLOGY

Cowlick likely comes from its similarity to the look of the raised hairs on a cow's hide after the cow has licked them into that shape. The word was first recorded in 1598.

cowl·ing (kou′ling) *n* a removable metal covering over the engine of an aircraft.

co–work·er (kō wər′kər) *n* someone who works with another: *He likes his co-workers.*

cow·poke (kou′pōk′) *Informal n* a cowhand.

cow·pox (kou′poks′) *n* a disease of cows that causes pimples on their udders.

🍁 **cow·punch·er** (kou′pun′chər) *n* a cowhand.

cow·rie (kou′rē) *n* a glossy yellow seashell formerly used as money in some parts of Africa and Asia. <Hindi *kauri*>

cow·slip (kou′slip) *n* **1** a N American and European plant of the primrose family with drooping yellow flowers. **2** MARSH MARIGOLD.

cox (koks) *n* a coxswain.
v act as coxswain (for).

cox·comb (koks′kōm′) *Archaic n* a shallow, vain, empty-headed man. <variant of *cock's comb*>

cox·swain (kok′sən) *or* (kok′swān′) *n* a person who steers a racing boat and is in charge of its crew. <obsolete *cock* a ship's boat + *swain*>

coy (koi) *adj* **1** shy, modest, and bashful. **2** pretending to be shy: *The actress wore a coy smile.* <Old French *coi*, from Latin *quietus* quiet> **coy′ly** *adv.* **coy′ness** *n.*

coy·o·te (kī ō′tē) *or* (kī′ōt) *n* a N American wild animal of the dog family, resembling a small wolf and noted for its nighttime howls and barks. <Mexican Spanish, from Nahuatl (a language of Central and S America) *coyotl*>

coy·pu (koi′pū) *n, pl* **coy·pus** or (*especially collectively*) **coy·pu** a large beaverlike water rodent native to South America, with an undercoat of soft fur called **nutria** that is commercially valuable. <Spanish, from Araucanian (a language of S America) *koypu*>

co·zy or **co·sy** (kō′zē) *adj* **co·zi·er, co·zi·est 1** warm and snug or comfortable: *She liked to read in a cozy chair.* **2** familiar or intimate: *a cozy little gathering.*
n, pl **co·zies** a cover for a teapot, usually padded, to keep the tea hot. <origin uncertain> **co′zi·ly** *adv.* **co′zi·ness** *n.*
cozy up to, *Informal* get into favour with someone by flattery or pretended friendship: *She cozied up to the most popular person in the class.*

cpi *Computers* characters per inch.

CPR *n* **1** *Medicine* in full, **cardiopulmonary resuscitation** a method of saving life by combining mouth-to-mouth respiration with rhythmical pressure on the heart. **2** 🍁 Canadian Pacific Railway.

cps *Computers* characters per second.

CPU *Computers n* in full, **central processing unit** the main component of a computer system, which controls operations by interpreting and executing program instructions.

crab[1] (krab) *n* **1** a CRUSTACEAN that has a broad shell, four pairs of legs, and one pair of pincers. **2** a crustacean resembling the true crab, such as the hermit crab.
v **crabbed, crab·bing** catch crabs for eating. <Old English *crabba*> **crab′ber** *n.* **crab′like′** *adj.*

crab[2] (krab) *n* **1** crabapple. **2** a person who is always complaining or criticizing.
v **crabbed, crab·bing 1** complain or criticize: *It does no good to crab about the weather.* **2** act so as to spoil something. <German *krabben*> **crab′ber** *n.*

crab·ap·ple (krab′ap′əl) *n* the small, sour, applelike fruit from a tree of the rose family, used for making jelly.

crab·by (krab′ē) *Informal adj* **crab·bi·er, crab·bi·est** grouchy or bad-tempered. **crab′bi·ly** *adv.* **crab′bi·ness** *n.*

crab·grass or **crab grass** (krab′gras′) *n* a coarse grass that spreads rapidly, often considered a weed.

crab·wise (krab′wīz′) *adv* sideways like a crab: *The car slid crabwise into the fence.*

crack[1] (krak) *n* **1** a place or line where a thing has been partly broken without causing the pieces to separate: *a crack in a cup.* **2** a narrow space or opening: *cracks between the floorboards.* **3** a sudden, sharp noise, or a blow that makes such a noise: *the crack of a whip.* **4** *Informal* a try or attempt: *Let me take a crack at opening the jar.* **5** *Informal* a witty remark, often sarcastic: *What do you mean by that crack?*
v **1** break without separating into parts: *You have cracked the window.* **2** break with a sudden, sharp noise: *The tree cracked and fell.* **3** make or cause to make a sudden, sharp noise: *The whip cracked. He cracked the whip.* **4** change sharply in pitch or quality of the voice because of hoarseness or emotion. **5** give way or cause to give way: *He finally cracked under their persistent questioning.* **6** break into: *to crack a safe.* **7** solve a code or puzzle. **8** *Informal* open, especially for the first time: *to crack a bottle. He hasn't cracked a book since school began.*
adj Informal very skilled: *a crack golfer.* <Old English *cracian*>
crack a joke, say something funny.
crack a smile, smile, especially reluctantly.
crack down (on), impose much stricter discipline (on).
crack of dawn, the first light in the morning sky.
crack up, *Informal* **a** respond or cause to respond with a fit of laughter: *I almost cracked up during the last scene of the play. This TV show always cracks me up.* **b** suffer a breakdown in mental or physical health. **c** crash or smash.
fall through the cracks, be ignored or overlooked in a system, especially a large, impersonal system: *We can't let students with special needs fall through the cracks.*
get cracking, *Informal* hurry up or get started quickly: *We'd better get cracking if we want to catch that bus.*
not what it's cracked up to be, not living up to claims made by advertisers or others.

crack[2] (krak) *n* a very addictive crystalline form of cocaine. <origin uncertain>

crack·down (krak′doun′) *n* a sudden campaign of enforcement or disciplinary action: *The school board intensified their crackdown on bullying in the schoolyard.*

cracked (krakt) *adj* **1** broken without separating into parts. **2** of a voice, with harsh notes. **3** *Informal* crazy.

crack·er (krak′ər) *n* **1** a thin, crisp biscuit or wafer, usually not sweet: *a soda cracker, a graham cracker.* **2** a small paper roll used on festive occasions that explodes with a bang when it is pulled at both ends, revealing a message and trinket inside. **3** *Computers* a person who HACKS (def. 3) with the intention of destroying or damaging the systems or information accessed.
adj (*never before the noun*) **crackers** *Slang* crazy.

crack·er·jack (krak′ər jak′) *n* **1** caramel-coated popcorn. **2** a person or thing especially fine of its kind.
adj of superior ability or quality.

crack·head (krak′hed′) *Slang n* a person who is addicted to crack cocaine.

crack house *n* a place where crack cocaine is sold.

crack·ing (krak′ing) *Slang adv* (*with* ***good***) very: *a cracking good book.*

crack·le (krak′əl) *v* **crack·led, crack·ling** **1** make slight, sharp, snapping sounds: *A fire crackles.* **2** make many tiny cracks in the glaze of china.
n **1** a slight, sharp sound, such as paper makes when it is crushed. **2** very small cracks in a glaze. **crack′ly** *adj.*

crack·ling (krak′ling) *n* **1** the crisp rind of roasted pork. **2** **cracklings** *pl* the crisp remains of melted animal fat, especially from pork.

crack·pot (krak′pot′) *Slang n* an eccentric person.
adj eccentric or very impractical.

cra·dle (krā′dəl) *n* **1** a baby's little bed, usually on rockers or swinging in a frame. **2** the place where a thing begins its development: *Africa is called the cradle of civilization.* **3** the part of a telephone that supports the receiver. **4** a frame to support a ship, aircraft, or other large object while it is being built, repaired, lifted, etc. **5** a box on rockers, designed to wash gold from earth.
v **cra·dled, cra·dling** **1** hold as if in a cradle: *I cradled the child in my arms.* **2** rock in a cradle: *She cradled the baby to sleep.* <Old English *cradol*> **cra′dle·like′** *adj.*
from the cradle to the grave, for the whole length of your life.

🍁 **cra·dle·board** (krā′dəl bȯrd′) *n* a device for carrying a baby, in former times used by First Nations peoples, consisting of a thin board with a lace-up leather bag fastened to it.

cradle song *n* a lullaby.

cra·dle–to–grave (krā′dəl tə grāv) *adj* from birth to death.

craft (kraft) *n, pl* **crafts** (*defs. 1, 2*)**, craft** (*def. 3*)
1 a specific artistic skill, especially in handwork: *At camp they did knitting, woodcarving, and other crafts. To be a good writer you must work constantly at your craft.* **2** an article made skilfully by hand: *The store sells books and crafts.* **3** a boat, ship, or aircraft. **4** skill in deceiving others: *He used craft to get all their money from them.*
v make skilfully by hand: *The store is featuring oak furniture crafted in Québec. This quilt was crafted by hand.* <Old English *cræft*>

craft·er (kraf′tər) *n* a person who handcrafts things.

crafts·man (krafts′mən) *n, pl* **crafts·men** (krafts′mən) a man who is highly skilled in a craft.
crafts′man·like′ *adj.* **crafts′man·ship′** *n.*

crafts·per·son (krafts′pər′sən) *n, pl* **crafts·peo·ple** (krafts′pē′pəl) a craftsman or craftswoman.

crafts·wom·an (kraft′swu̇m′ən) *n, pl* **crafts·wom·en** (krafts′wim′ən) a woman who is highly skilled in a craft.

craft·y (kraf′tē) *adj* **craft·i·er, craft·i·est** skilful in deceiving others: *The crafty thief escaped by disguising himself as a waiter.* **craft′i·ly** *adv.* **craft′i·ness** *n.*

crag (krag) *n* a steep, rugged cliff or projecting rock. <Middle English>

crag·gy (krag′ē) *adj* **crag·gi·er, crag·gi·est** **1** with many crags: *a craggy hillside.* **2** suggesting the hardness and unevenness of crags: *a tall man with craggy features.* **crag′gi·ness** *n.*

cram (kram) *v* **crammed, cram·ming** **1** force or stuff into a small space: *He crammed all his clothes quickly into the bag.* **2** fill too full: *The hall was crammed with people.* **3** eat or feed too fast or too much. **4** *Informal* try to learn or study a lot in a short time: *cramming for her history exam.* <Old English *crimman* insert> **cram′mer** *n.*

cramp[1] (kramp) *n* **1** a painful muscle contraction: *The swimmer was seized with a cramp.* **2** temporary paralysis of a muscle or muscles as a result of overexercising: *writer's cramp.* **3** **cramps** *pl* sharp, continuous pains in the abdomen.
v cause a painful numbness or stiffness: *I was cramped from sitting in one position so long.* <German>

cramp[2] (kramp) *v* **1** confine in too small a space: *If the flowerpot is too small, it will cramp the roots of the plant. The three girls were cramped in one little tent.* **2** turn the wheels of a car or truck sharply. **3** fasten together with a cramp.
n **1** a small metal bar with both ends bent, used in building to hold timbers, or stone or concrete blocks permanently in place. **2** CLAMP. <German>
cramp someone's style, restrict or interfere with someone's natural or usual behaviour.

cramped (krampt) *adj* too small and confining: *a cramped apartment.*

cram·pon (kram′pən) *n* **1** a strong iron bar with hooks at one end, used to lift heavy objects. **2** a spiked plate fastened to the sole of a shoe to prevent slipping, often used by climbers. <Old French>

cran·ber·ry (kran′ber′ē) *n, pl* **cran·ber·ries** **1** a firm, edible, sour, red berry produced by any of several plants of the heath family. **2** any of several species of viburnum. The **highbush cranberry** has edible fruit. <German *kraanbere*>

a bat	e bed	i bid	o pot	u cup	th thin
ā cake	ē me	ī bite	ō go	ū rude	ᴛʜ then
ȧ bar	ə about	ər over	ȯ for	u̇ put	zh measure

C

tower crane

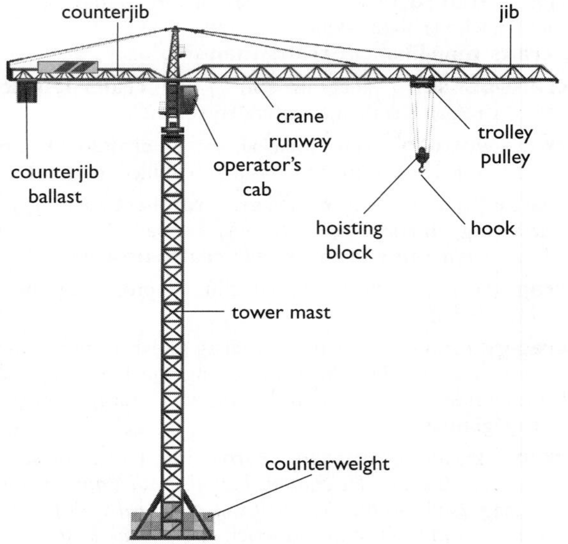

counterjib
jib
crane runway
trolley pulley
counterjib ballast
operator's cab
hoisting block
hook
tower mast
counterweight

crane (krān) *n* **1** a large machine with a long, horizontal swinging arm, for lifting and moving heavy weights, especially on construction sites. **2** a device consisting of a horizontal arm swinging on a vertical axis, such as a boom for a movie camera. **3** a tall wading bird with long legs and a long neck and bill. **4** a heron, especially the **great blue heron**.
v **craned, cran·ing** stretch the neck as a crane (def. 3) does: *He craned his neck, trying to see over the crowd.* <Old English *cran*>

crane fly *n* a large, delicate fly with a long slender body, two narrow wings, and very long legs.

cra·ni·um (krā′nē əm) *n, pl* **cra·ni·ums** or **cra·ni·a** (krā′nē ə) the skull of a vertebrate, especially the part enclosing the brain. <Latin, from Greek *kranion*> **cra′ni·al** *adj.*

crank (krangk) *n* **1** a part or handle of a machine, connected at right angles to a shaft to transmit motion: *to turn the crank of a pencil sharpener.* **2** *Informal* a person with odd habits, especially one possessed by some idea: *The police got a few calls from cranks when they asked for information about the robbery.* **3** *Informal* a bad-tempered person: *I wouldn't ask any favours of that old crank.*
v work or start by means of a crank: *to crank a window open. With the earliest cars, you had to crank the engine.*
crank up, *Informal* increase or raise: *to crank up prices, to crank up the volume on the CD player.*
turn someone's crank, *Slang* be or do exactly what excites or thrills someone.

ETYMOLOGY

The secondary, informal meaning of a **crank** is "a person with odd and unusual whims or habits." This meaning comes from the idea of someone being bent, just like a crank on a machine.

crank·case (krangk′kās′) *n* a heavy metal case forming the bottom part of an internal combustion engine and enclosing the crankshaft and connecting rods.

crank·shaft (krangk′shaft′) *n* a shaft turned by a crank in a machine.

crank·y (krang′kē) *adj* **crank·i·er, crank·i·est** bad-tempered or grumpy, especially as a result of tiredness or stress. **crank′i·ly** *adv.* **crank′i·ness** *n.*

cran·ny (kran′ē) *n, pl* **cran·nies** a small, narrow opening: *There were many nooks and crannies in the stone wall.* <French, from Latin *crena* notch>

crap (krap) *Slang n* **1** nonsense: *Don't give me that crap about it being everyone else's fault.* **2** dirt, junk, or garbage: *Who left all this crap in the hallway?* <perhaps Old French, from Latin *crappa* chaff> **crap′py** *adj.*

crap·pie (krap′ē) *n* a small, edible freshwater fish belonging to the sunfish family. <Cdn. French *crapet*>

craps (kraps) *n* a gambling game played with two dice. <perhaps Old English *crabba*>
shoot craps, play the game of craps.

crash (krash) *n* **1** a sudden, very loud, harsh noise: *a crash of thunder. There was a crash as the platform collapsed.* **2** a fall or collision with a violent impact: *a car crash.* **3** a sudden severe decline or failure, as in business: *a stock market crash.* **4** *Computers* the failure of a computer system: *I lost the last section of my report in a crash.*
v **1** make a sudden, loud, harsh noise: *The thunder crashed.* **2** fall, hit, break, or move with a loud noise: *The dishes crashed to the floor. He went crashing into the room.* **3** bump into or fall with force: *The plane crashed in a field.* **4** fail or decline suddenly: *The stock market crashed.* **5** *Informal* enter or attend without an invitation or ticket: *to crash a party.* **6** *Informal* go to sleep, especially after intense or prolonged activity. **7** *Computers* suddenly stop working as a computer system, due to a hardware or software error. **8** *Slang* come down quickly from a drug-induced state. <Middle English; imitative> **crash′er** *n.*

crash course *n* a course that compresses a lot of material into a very short time.

crash–land (krash′ land′) *v* make a forced landing of an aircraft in an emergency, usually suffering damage: *The glider crash-landed on the beach.* **crash landing** *n.*

crass (kras) *adj* **1** rude, tasteless, or vulgar: *crass humour.* **2** very obvious: *crass ignorance.* <Latin *crassus* thick> **crass′ly** *adv.* **crass′ness** *n.*

crate (krāt) *n* **1** a large, strong box, usually of wood, for packing things to be shipped or stored. **2** *Slang* an old, worn-out vehicle.
v **crat·ed, crat·ing** pack in a crate. <Middle English; origin unknown>

cra·ter (krā′tər) *n* **1** the depression around the opening at the top of a volcano. **2** a bowl-shaped hole: *craters made by meteors.* <Latin, from Greek *krater* bowl>

cra·vat (krə vat′) *n* **1** in former times, a scarf or cloth worn around the neck on the outside of a standing shirt collar. **2** an ascot. <French, from Croatian *Hrvat.* Croatians serving in the French army wore these.>

crave (krāv) *v* **craved, crav·ing 1** have strong desire for: *to crave attention, to crave certain foods during pregnancy.* **2** *Archaic or Formal* plead; beg: *I crave a favour from you.* <Old English *crafian* demand>

cra·ven (krā′vən) *adj* cowardly: *a craven act.*
n a coward. <Middle English *cravant* defeated>
cra′ven·ly *adv.* **cra′ven·ness** *n.*

crav·ing (krā′ving) *n* a strong desire: *She had a sudden craving for olives.*

craw (kro) *n* **1** the crop of a bird or insect. **2** the stomach of any animal. <Middle English>
stick in your craw, *Informal* be hard to accept or say: *He wanted to apologize, but the words stuck in his craw.*

crawl (krol) *v* **1** move with the body on or close to the ground, as worms, snakes, and insects do. **2** move on hands and knees: *to crawl through a hole in a fence. The baby can already crawl.* **3** move slowly: *The traffic crawled on the icy roads.* **4** to be or feel as if being covered with things that crawl or with things regarded as unpleasant: *The ground was crawling with ants. The place will be crawling with tourists. My flesh crawled at the thought of the huge snakes.* **5** behave or move in a cringing, pathetic way: *OK, do it yourself, but don't come crawling to me if it doesn't work.*
n **1** a slow pace: *The cafeteria line was moving at a crawl.* **2** a swimming style using alternate overarm strokes and a continuous kicking motion. <origin unknown>
make your skin (or **flesh**) **crawl,** fill you with horror or disgust.

crawl·er (krol′ər) *n* **1** someone or something that crawls. **2** a program that searches the Internet in order to locate new resources. These are added to a database that users can search by using a search engine. **3** printed text that moves across the bottom of a TV screen, as advertising, news headlines, sports results, etc. Also called **spider**.

crawl space *n* a low, narrow space in a house or other building, giving access to wiring or pipes, or used for storage.

crawl·y (krol′ē) *adj* **crawl·i·er, crawl·i·est 1** crawling: *crawly creatures.* **2** feeling as if things were crawling over the skin.

cray·fish (krā′fish′) *n, pl* **cray·fish·es** or (*especially collectively*) **cray·fish** a freshwater CRUSTACEAN resembling a small lobster. <Old French *crevice*>

cray·on (krā′on) *or* (krā′ən) *n* a pencil-shaped stick for drawing or writing with. It may be made of a waxlike substance, chalk, charcoal, or oil pastel.
v **cray·oned, cray·on·ing** draw or colour with crayons. <French, from Latin *creta*>

craze (krāz) *n* something about which people are enthusiastic for a short time: *Toe rings were a craze for a while.*
v **crazed, craz·ing 1** make crazy: *She was crazed with the pain.* **2** develop or cause to have a mesh of tiny cracks in the glaze of ceramics. <Middle English *crasen* crack>

cra·zy (krā′zē) *adj* **cra·zi·er, cra·zi·est 1** *Informal* insane. **2** temporarily irrational or wild: *crazy with fear.* **3** *Informal* ridiculous or foolish: *a crazy idea.* **4** *Informal* (*with* **for** *or* **about**) very enthusiastic or eager: *crazy for chocolate, crazy about sports cars. He's crazy about her.* **5** *Informal* unusual or bizarre: *She likes crazy jewellery.* **6** not following any pattern: *crazy paving, a crazy quilt.*
n, pl **cra·zies** *Informal* an insane or eccentric person.
cra′zi·ly *adv.* **cra′zi·ness** *n.*
like crazy, *Informal* to an extreme degree: *laughing like crazy, pedalling like crazy.*

C

creak (krēk) *v* make a harsh squeaking or croaking noise: *creaking hinges. The floorboards creaked when he stepped on them.*
n such a noise. <Middle English *creken*> **creak′i·ness** *n.* **creak′y** *adj.*

cream (krēm) *n* **1** the yellowish part of milk that contains fat. **2** a food made from cream, or with a consistency like cream: *ice cream, cream of mushroom soup.* **3** an oily preparation put on the skin to make it smooth and soft: *hand cream.* **4 the cream** the best part of anything: *the cream of the nation's youth.* **5** CREAMER (defs. 2, 3).
v **1** beat into a smooth mixture like cream: *to cream butter and sugar together.* **2** prepare with cream or a creamy sauce: *creamed potatoes.* **3** *Informal* defeat or beat soundly: *We got creamed in the semifinals.*
adj yellowish white. <Old French, blend of Latin *crama* cream and *chrisma* ointment>
cream off, *Informal* select the best from.
cream of the crop, the best of a group: *This company hires the cream of the crop from all the local universities.*

cream cheese *n* a soft, spreadable, mild cheese made from cream or milk and cream, often with flavouring added.

cream·er (krē′mər) *n* **1** a small pitcher for holding cream. **2** a liquid or powder used in coffee as a substitute for cream. **3** a small, disposable, sealed container holding one serving of cream for coffee. **4** a machine for separating cream from milk.

cream·er·y (krē′mə rē) *n, pl* **cream·er·ies 1** a place where butter and cheese are made or sold. **2** a room where milk is put until the cream rises to the top.

cream of tartar *n* a very sour, white powder used in baking, obtained from the deposit on the inside of wine casks.

cream puff *n* **1** a light pastry filled with whipped cream or custard. **2** *Slang* a weak, soft person.

cream soda *n* vanilla-flavoured pop, usually red.

cream·y (krē′mē) *adj* **cream·i·er, cream·i·est 1** smooth and soft or rich like cream. **2** with much cream in it. **3** with the colour of cream. **cream′i·ness** *n.*

crease (krēs) *n* **1** a line or mark made by folding. **2** *Hockey, Lacrosse* the small area marked off in front of each goal.
v **creased, creas·ing 1** make a crease or creases in. **2** become creased or wrinkled. <probably *crest*>

a bat	e bed	i bid	o pot	u cup	th **thin**
ā cake	ē me	ī bite	ō go	ū rude	TH **then**
à bar	ə about	ər over	ȯ for	ů put	zh measure

cre·ate (krē āt′) *v* **cre·at·ed, cre·at·ing 1** make something, especially something that has not existed before, using skill, intelligence, or power: *to create works of art.* **2** give rise to or cause: *Do not create a disturbance.* <Latin *creare*>

cre·a·tion (krē ā′shən) *n* **1** the act of creating. **2** the world and everything in it. **3** a created thing: *That painting is a magnificent creation.* **4 the Creation** in some belief systems, the creating of the universe by God.

cre·a·tion·ism (krē ā′shə niz əm) *n* the belief that the universe and everything in it were created by God according to the account given in the Bible, not the result of a physical process and of evolution. Also called **creation science**. **cre·a′tion·ist** *n.*

cre·a·tive (krē ā′tiv) *adj* **1** to do with creating or with the ability to create. **2** imaginative: *creative writing.* **3** resourceful, inventive, or original: *creative solutions to your problems.* **4** (*euphemistic*) ingenious but dishonest or wrong: *creative accounting, creative spelling.*
cre·a′tive·ly *adv.* **cre′a·tiv′i·ty** *n.*

creative sentencing *n* the practice of punishing people who break the law in the way that will be most meaningful and relevant to the individual, rather than by issuing a standard sentence in all cases.

cre·a·tor (krē ā′tər) *n* **1** a person who creates. **2 the Creator** God.

crea·ture (krē′chər) *n* **1** a living being or organism. **2** a person who is completely under the influence of another.

creature comforts *pln* the things that give bodily comfort, such as good food and comfortable clothing.

crèche (kresh) *n* **1** a nursery or daycare centre. **2** *Christianity* a model of the Christ child in the manger, often with other figures, displayed at Christmas. <French = cradle>

cre·dence (krē′dəns) *n* **1** belief: *Never give credence to gossip.* **2** credibility or believability: *The results of the experiment lend credence to her theory.* <Old French, from Latin *credere* believe>

cre·den·tials (kri den′shəlz) *pln* a qualification, quality, achievement, recommendation, or background that makes a person suitable for something: *He has pretty impressive credentials; let's interview him. She has ample credentials to speak on the subject.*

cre·den·za (kri den′zə) *n* **1** a piece of office furniture in the form of a long, low cupboard with doors. **2** a buffet or sideboard. <Italian, from Latin *credentia* trust, possibly from the practice of placing food and drink on a sideboard to be tasted by a servant to prove to guests that no poison had been added>

cred·i·ble (kred′ə bəl) *adj* believable or convincing: *a credible theory. You'll be much more credible as a coach if you've played a lot of hockey yourself.* <Latin *credere* believe> **cred′i·bil′i·ty** *n.* **cred′i·bly** *adv.*

CONFUSABLES

Credible means "believable": *She gave us a credible reason for being late.*

Creditable means "bringing praise": *The boy's creditable activities earned him a volunteer award.*

Credulous means "too ready to believe": *The credulous audience thought that everything the celebrity said was true.*

cred·it (kred′it) *n* **1 a** recognition or honour: *The person who does the work should get the credit.* **b** a source of honour or praise: *The author's latest novel is a credit to her.* **2** an entry on a student's record, showing that he or she has passed a course of study: *My brother needs two more credits to complete grade 12.* **3** usually, **credits** *pl* an acknowledgment of those who took part in making a movie or TV program, usually as a list scrolling down the screen. **4 a** the privilege of paying later for something one buys now: *She had no trouble getting credit for her purchase.* **b** one's reputation with respect to payment of debts: *If you pay your bills on time, your credit will be good.* **5** *Accounting* **a** an entry of money paid into an account. **b** a positive balance in an account: *He had a credit of $500 in his savings account.* Compare DEBIT. **6** belief or confidence in the truth of something: *I place little credit in what she says.*
v **1** believe to be true: *It was difficult to credit her excuses.* **2** deposit money into: *Do you want a cash refund, or shall we credit your account?* <French, from Latin *credere* believe, trust>
credit a person with, acknowledge something that a person has or does: *You have to credit her with some sense for not panicking during the fire.*
do credit to, bring honour or recognition to: *The team's performance did credit to our school.*
give someone credit for, acknowledge something that a person has or does: *Give him credit for some intelligence and let him try the job himself.*
on credit, on a promise to pay later: *She bought her car on credit.*
to someone's credit, in someone's favour: *It is to her credit that she accepted the criticism graciously.*

cred·it·a·ble (kred′ə tə bəl) *adj* bringing credit or honour: *a creditable performance.* See CREDIBLE for confusable. **cred′it·a·bly** *adv.*

credit bureau *n* a business that collects information on the ability of individuals or companies to pay debts and bills, then provides a **credit rating** based on this information.

credit card *n* a card that allows its holder to charge the cost of goods or services. Also called **charge card**.

Cred·i·tiste (kred′ə tēst′) *n* a supporter of the Québec wing of the SOCIAL CREDIT PARTY.

cred·i·tor (kred′ə tər) *n* a person to whom a debt is owed.

credit union *n* a financial co-operative that provides loans and offers savings accounts to its members.

cre·do (krā′dō) *n* a statement of beliefs or opinions on any subject: *Non-violence is part of her political credo.* Compare CREED. <Latin = I believe>

cred·u·lous (kred′yū ləs) *adj* too ready to believe whatever one is told. See CREDIBLE for confusable. <Latin *credere* believe> **cre·du′li·ty** (krə dyū′lə tē) *n.*

Cree (krē) *n, pl* **Cree** or **Crees** **1** a member of a First Nations people living mainly in central Canada and the Prairie Provinces, including the **Plains Cree** (central Alberta, Saskatchewan), the **Woodland Cree** (northern Saskatchewan, Manitoba), and the **Swampy Cree** (the lowlands around Hudson Bay and James Bay). Also called **Nehiyaw** (ne′hē yȧw′), *pl* **Nehiyawak** (ne′hē yȧ′wək). **2** any dialect of their Algonquian language.
adj to do with any of these people or their languages.

creed (krēd) *n* **1** a formal statement of the essential points of religious belief as authorized by a church: *to recite a creed.* **2** a system of religious belief: *people of every creed.* **3** a set of beliefs, principles, or opinions: *It was his creed that work should come before play.* <Old English, from Latin *credo*>

creek (krēk) *or, especially in Western Canada,* (krik) *n* **1** a small freshwater stream. **2** a narrow inlet in a shoreline or channel in a marsh. <Middle English *creke*>
up the creek or **up a creek,** *Slang* in difficulty: *If I don't hand in this assignment, I'll be up the creek.*

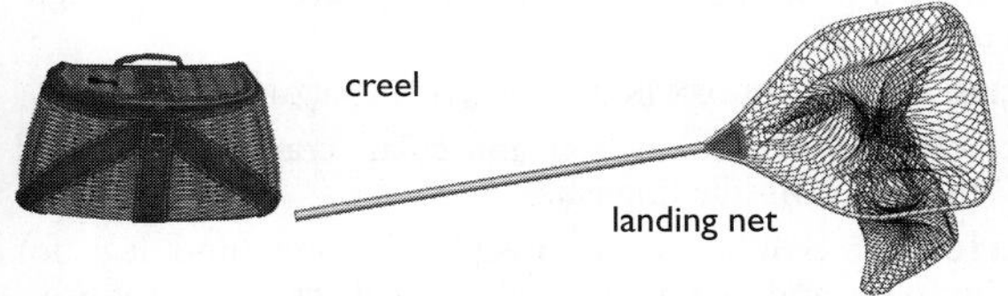

Traditionally, the fly-fishing **creel** had a kidney-shape design to sit on the hip so that it did not interfere with casting. The landing net comes in handy for scooping the hooked fish out of the water.

creel (krēl) *n* a basket, often made of wicker, for holding fish that have been caught. <Middle English *crele*>

creep (krēp) *v* **crept, creep·ing** **1** move in a timid or stealthy manner: *She crept out of the room on tiptoe.* **2** move with the body close to the ground or floor: *A cat crept across the lawn.* **3** move or expand slowly or gradually: *The traffic began to creep over the bridge. The Sahara Desert is creeping further south every year.* **4** grow as a plant along the ground or over a wall, etc., by means of clinging stems: *Ivy creeps.* **5** feel as if things were creeping over the skin: *Music in horror movies makes your flesh creep.* **6** slip slightly out of place: *The hall rug creeps.*
n **1** a movement like creeping. **2 the creeps** *pl Informal* an eerie feeling, or a feeling of fear and disgust. **3** *Informal* a person who gives one such a feeling. <Old English *creopan*>
creep up on, approach slowly and without being noticed: *Exam time crept up on me.*

creep·er (krē′pər) *n* **1** a plant that grows along a surface, sending out rootlets from the stem, such as the **Virginia creeper** and ivy. **2** a small brownish bird that climbs along the trunk and branches of trees looking for insects. **3** a person who or thing that creeps.

creep·y (krē′pē) *adj* **creep·i·er, creep·i·est** causing or having a feeling of fear or unease: *a creepy howl. The thick fog made me feel creepy.* **creep′i·ness** *n.*

creep·y–crawl·y (krē′pē krol′ē) *Informal adj* with or giving an unpleasant or frightening feeling.
n **creep·y-crawl·ies** *pl* **1** a small insect or other creature, especially when considered unpleasant or frightening. **2 the creepy-crawlies** *pl* an eerie feeling, or a feeling of fear and disgust.

Cree Syllabics *n* (*with singular verb*) a writing system used by the Cree, in which each symbol stands for a particular consonant-vowel combination.

cre·mate (kri māt′) *or* (krē′māt) *v* **cre·mat·ed, cre·mat·ing** burn a dead body to ashes. <Latin *cremare* burn> **cre·ma′tion** *n.*

cre·ma·to·ri·um (krē′mə tȯ′rē əm) *or* (krem′ə tȯ′rē əm) *n, pl* **cre·ma·to·ri·ums** or **cre·ma·to·ri·a** (krem′ə tȯ′rē ə) a furnace for cremation, or a place where this is done.

crème de la crème (krem′ də lə krem′) *n* the very best. <French = cream of the cream>

cren·el·lat·ed (kren′ə lā′tid) *adj* with indentations or openings in the wall through which to shoot at the enemy. Also, **crenelated.** <Old French, from Latin *crena* notch> **cren′el·la′tion** or **cren′e·la′tion** *n.*

cre·ole (krē′ōl) *n* a language that is based on two or more languages and is the native tongue of a community of speakers.
adj **1** to do with or typical of a creole language. **2** cooked in a sauce of stewed tomatoes, peppers, etc. <See CREOLE.>

Cre·ole (krē′ōl) *or* (krā′ōl) *n* **1** a descendant of the original French settlers of Louisiana. **2** a person of French or Spanish ancestry, or of mixed black and European ancestry, born in Spanish America or the Caribbean. **3** the variety of French spoken by some blacks in Louisiana. **4** the language spoken by blacks in Haiti, based on French, but with West African influences.
adj to do with the Creoles or with either of these languages. <French, from Latin *creare* create>

cre·o·sote (krē′ə sōt′) *n* an oily liquid with a penetrating odour, obtained by distilling coal tar. It is used to preserve wood and other materials.
v **cre·o·sot·ed, cre·o·sot·ing** treat with creosote. <German, from Greek *kreas-* flesh + *soter* preserver; originally an antiseptic>

crepe or **crêpe** (krāp) *n* **1** a type of cloth woven with a crinkled surface. Black crepe armbands are sometimes worn formally as a sign of mourning. **2** synthetic rubber with a crinkled surface, often used for the soles of shoes. **3** usually, **crêpe** a large, very thin pancake usually served folded or rolled up with a filling. <French, from Latin *crispus* curled>

a bat	e bed	i bid	o pot	u cup	th **thin**
ā cake	ē me	ī bite	ō go	ū rude	ᴛʜ **then**
ȧ bar	ə about	ər over	ȯ for	u̇ put	zh measure

crepe paper *n* thin, crinkled, stretchy paper, used for making party decorations, etc.

crept (krept) past tense and past participle of CREEP.

cre·pus·cu·lar (krə pus′kyə lər) *adj* **1** active by twilight, such as certain birds, animals, and insects. **2** of or like twilight: *the crepuscular light in a dense forest.* <Latin *crepusculum* twilight>

cre·scen·do (krə shen′dō) *n* **1** *Music* a gradual increase in force or loudness, or a passage to be played or sung in this way. **2 a** any gradual increase in force, loudness, or intensity. **b** the peak or climax of such an increase: *The rage within him finally reached a crescendo.*
adj, adv Music with a gradual increase in force or loudness. Compare DIMINUENDO. <Italian, from *crescere* increase>

cres·cent (kres′ənt) *n* **1** the shape of the moon as seen from the earth in its first or last quarter. **2** something shaped more or less like this, such as a bread roll, or a curved street. <Old French, from Latin *crescere* grow>
cres′cent·like′ *adj.*

cress (kres) *n* a plant such as **watercress**, whose leaves have a peppery taste, used as a garnish or in salads. <Old English *cresse*>

crest (krest) *n* **1** the top part of something, especially a mountain, wave, or ridge. See SUMMIT for picture. **2** a decoration at the top of a coat of arms: *The duke's family crest was painted on the carriage door.* **3** an emblem worn attached to clothing by members of an organization or team, or awarded for achievement: *a hockey crest.* **4** among First Nations peoples of the West Coast, **a** the symbol of a clan or similar social group. **b** the clan or group it identifies. **5** a tuft of hair or feathers or growth of skin on the top of a bird's or animal's head.
v **1** form or rise into the crest of a wave. **2** in a river, flood, etc., reach its highest point. **3** reach the crest or summit of: *When we crested the hill, we were met with a breathtaking view.* **4** serve as a crest for: *Snow crested the mountains.* <Old French, from Latin *crista* tuft of hair>
crest′ed *adj.*

crest·fall·en (krest′fol′ən) *adj* badly disappointed or discouraged: *He came home crestfallen because he had not made the team.*

Cre·ta·ceous (krə tā′shəs) *n* the geological period lasting from about 140 million to 70 million years ago, when most of the earth's chalk deposits were made. See also MESOZOIC.
adj to do with this period or the rocks formed then. <Latin *creta* chalk>

Crete (krēt) *n* a Greek island in the Mediterranean Sea.
Cre′tan *adj, n.*

cre·tin (kret′ən) *or* (krē′tən) *n* in former times, a person considered to be severely mentally retarded because of a congenital thyroid deficiency called **cretinism**. <French, from Latin *Christianus* human being>

cre·vasse (krə vas′) *n* a deep, often wide crack in the ice of a GLACIER. <French, from Latin *crepare* to crack>

crev·ice (krev′is) *n* a narrow crack: *Tiny ferns grew in crevices in the stone wall.* <Old French, from Latin *crepare* to crack>

crew (krū) *n* **1** a group of people who work together: *a road repair crew, the camera crew in a movie studio.* **2** the people who operate a ship, boat, aircraft, or spacecraft. **3** *Informal* a group or crowd: *The whole crew came to our place for dinner.*
v **1** supply a ship, spacecraft, etc. with a crew. **2** work as a member of a crew: *He had never crewed on an ocean voyage before.* <Old French *creue* military reinforcements, from Latin *crescere* grow>

crew·cut (krū′kut′) *n* a very short haircut, usually for males.

crew·neck (krū′nek′)*n* a plain, round neckline on a sweater or T-shirt, fitting closely around the base of the neck.

crib (krib) *n* **1** a small bed for a baby, with high, barred sides to keep him or her from falling out. **2** a stall for a farm animal. **3** a bin, manger, or racklike structure for storing grain: *a corn crib.* **4** a framework of logs or timbers used in building or as a raft. **5** *Informal* a set of notes or translations, sometimes for cheating with in a test or exam.
v **cribbed, crib·bing** *Informal* copy another's ideas or work to pass off as one's own. <Old English *cribb*>

crib·bage (krib′ij) *n* a card game for two, three, or four people in which the score is kept on a narrow board with holes into which small movable pegs are placed. <origin uncertain>

crib death SUDDEN INFANT DEATH SYNDROME.

crick (krik) *n* a sudden muscular cramp or painful stiffness. <Middle English>

crick·et[1] (krik′it) *n* an insect with long hind legs for jumping, and two pairs of wings. Male crickets produce a characteristic chirping noise. See CICADA for picture. <Old French *criquet*>

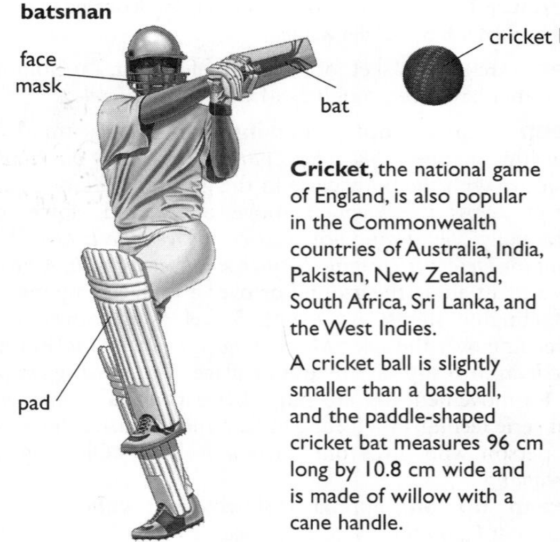

Cricket, the national game of England, is also popular in the Commonwealth countries of Australia, India, Pakistan, New Zealand, South Africa, Sri Lanka, and the West Indies.

A cricket ball is slightly smaller than a baseball, and the paddle-shaped cricket bat measures 96 cm long by 10.8 cm wide and is made of willow with a cane handle.

crick·et[2] (krik′it) *n* **1** an outdoor game played by two teams of eleven players each, with ball, bats, and wickets. See also WICKETKEEPER for picture. **2** *Informal* (*usually with a negative*) fair play or good sportsmanship: *That's not cricket.* <origin uncertain> **crick′et·er** *n.*

cri·er (krī′ər) *n* **1** an official who shouts out public announcements: *a town crier.* **2** a person who cries or shouts.

crime (krīm) *n* **1** a particular act, or activity in general, that is against the law: *Murder and theft are crimes. There has been a decrease in crime since last year.* **2** an immoral act: *It is a crime to waste all that good food.* <Old French, from Latin *crimen* judgment, offence>

crim·i·nal (krim′ə nəl) *n* a person who has committed a crime.
adj **1** to do with crime; illegal: *a criminal act.* **2** *Law* to do with **criminal law**, dealing with crimes against society: *criminal court.* Compare CIVIL (def. 5). **3** *Informal* immoral; senseless; disgraceful: *It's criminal to charge such high prices.* **crim′i·nal·ly** *adv.*

🍁 **Criminal Code** *n* a federal statute that lists criminal offences as well as the procedures and penalties related to them.

crim·i·nal·ize (krim′ə nəl īz′) *v* **crim·i·nal·ized, crim·i·nal·iz·ing** give an activity the status of a crime: *They haven't yet criminalized smoking.*

crim·i·nol·o·gy (krim′ə nol′ə jē) *n* the scientific study of crime and criminals and ways of dealing with them. **crim′i·nol′o·gist** *n.*

crimp (krimp) *v* press into small, narrow folds: *to crimp your hair, to crimp the edges of a pie crust.*
n a fold or wave made by crimping. <Old English *gecrympan*> **crimp′er** *n.*
put a crimp in, hinder: *That will put a crimp in his plan.*

crim·son (krim′zən) *adj* deep red. <Arabic *kirmiz*>

cringe (krinj) *v* **cringed, cring·ing** **1** bend one's head or body in fear, or from an inward sense of embarrassment or disgust. **2** behave or move in an overly humble manner.
n an act of cringing. <Old English *cringan* give way> **cring′er** *n.*

crin·kle (kring′kəl) *v* **crin·kled, crin·kling** **1** make or become full of small creases on the surface of something, such as the skin of the face as a result of smiling: *Her pants were crinkled from being left on the floor.* **2** crackle or rustle, such as wrapping paper when it is crushed or folded.
n **1** a crease or wrinkle, especially one of many small ones. **2** a crinkling sound. <Old English *crincan* bend> **crin′kly** *adj.*

cri·noid (krī′noid) *or* (krin′oid) *n* a flowerlike sea animal with a cup-shaped body and long feathery arms.
adj to do with or belonging to such an animal. <Greek *krinon* lily>

crin·o·line (krin′ə lin) *or* (krin′ə lēn′) *n* **1** in former times, a stiffened or hooped petticoat, made from a stiff fabric. **2** a hoop skirt. <Latin *crinis* hair + *linum* thread>

crip·ple (krip′əl) *n* a person who or thing that is unable to function normally. It is offensive to use the word *cripple* to mean a person who has a physical disability that hampers mobility, but it can be used in the case of an animal: *The crippled dog limped quickly back to the side of the road.*
v **crip·pled, crip·pling** damage, disable, or weaken: *The horse twisted its leg and is now crippled. The ship was crippled by the storm.* <Old English *crypel*> **crip′pled** *adj.*

cri·sis (krī′sis) *n, pl* **cri·ses** (krī′sēz) **1** a state of urgent need or grave danger: *days of heavy snowfall caused a crisis on the East Coast.* **2** an event that is a turning or dividing point in one's life: *a midlife crisis, a crisis of faith.* **3** the turning point in a serious illness or injury. **4** a point in a story or drama when a conflict reaches its highest tension and must be resolved. <Latin, from Greek *krinein* decide>

C

crisp (krisp) *adj* **1** stiff but brittle, like dry toast or fresh celery. **2** cool, fresh, and bracing: *The day was crisp and bright.* **3** clear or decisive: *crisp sentences, a crisp tone of voice.* **4** neat and unwrinkled: *a crisp $20 bill.*
v make or become crisp. Also, especially of food, **crispy.** <Old English, from Latin *crispus* curled> **crisp′ly** *adv.* **crisp′ness** *n.*
burn to a crisp, burn or char completely.

crisp·er (krisp′ər) *n* a closed compartment in a refrigerator for storing fresh vegetables and fruit.

criss·cross (kris′kros′) *adj* made up of crossed lines: *Plaids have a crisscross pattern.*
adv so as to cross one another.
v **1** mark or cover with crossed lines. **2** come and go across: *Buses and cars crisscross the city.*
n a mark or pattern made of crossed lines. <*Christ's cross*>

cri·te·ri·on (krī tē′rē ən) *n, pl* **cri·te·ri·a** (krī tē′rē ə) a test or standard for making a judgment: *Money is only one criterion of success. My teacher explained the criteria he will use to assess the next assignment.* <Latin, from Greek *krinein* decide>

GRAMMAR AND USAGE

The word **criteria** is one of several words derived from Greek that are almost always used in the plural, but are often mistaken as singular:

One criterion for voting is being old enough.

There are many criteria for writing a good essay.

crit·ic (krit′ik) *n* **1** **a** an expert who judges the quality of something, especially in the arts: *I'm no music critic, but I didn't think much of that performance.* **b** a person whose profession is writing such judgments for a newspaper or magazine. **2** a person who disapproves or criticizes: *Critics of the new attendance rules say they will have little effect.* <Latin, from Greek *krinein* to judge>

crit·i·cal (krit′ə kel) *adj* **1** inclined to criticize or disapprove: *Must you always be so critical?* **2** using careful consideration to evaluate: *a critical judgment, critical thinking.* **3** to do with professional critics: *The movie received critical acclaim.* **4** determining the outcome of something: *a critical moment. Speed is critical in such cases.* **5** characterized by urgent need or grave danger: *She is in critical condition in the hospital.* **6** to do with the point at which some physical or chemical change takes place. **crit′i·cal·ly** *adv.* **crit′i·cal·ness** *n.*

a bat	e bed	i bid	o pot	u cup	th **thin**
ā cake	ē me	ī bite	ō go	ū rude	TH **then**
ä bar	ə about	ər over	ô for	ů put	zh measure

critical mass *n* **1** *Nuclear physics* the minimum quantity of fissionable material needed in a reactor to produce or maintain a chain reaction. **2** the minimum amount or size needed to start something off successfully: *When her business reached a critical mass, she started a second office in Calgary.*

crit·i·cism (krit′ə siz′əm) *n* **1** an expression of disapproval. **2** the practice of making such statements: *Their constant criticism wears me down.* **3** careful analysis and evaluation, or the rules and principles used for this: *She is an expert in literary criticism.*

crit·i·cize (krit′ə sīz′) *v* **crit·i·cized, crit·i·ciz·ing** **1** express disapproval of or find fault with: *Do not criticize him until you know all the facts.* **2** judge as a critic.

cri·tique (kri tēk′) *n* a detailed analysis, judgment, or evaluation of a theory or practice.
v **cri·tiqued cri·tiqu·ing** give a critique of: *For a fee, the editor will critique your manuscript.*

crit·ter (krit′ər) *Informal n* a creature.

croak (krōk) *n* a deep, hoarse sound, such as a frog, crow, or raven makes.
v **1** make a deep, hoarse sound. **2** speak in a deep, hoarse voice. **3** *Slang* die. <Middle English>

Cro·a·tia (krō ā′shə) *n* a republic in southeastern Europe, part of the former Yugoslavia. See the APPENDIX. **Cro′at** (krō′at) *n.* **Cro·a′tian** *adj, n.*

cro·chet (krō shā′) *n* lacy needlework made by interlocking loops of a single thread of fine or heavy yarn using a hooked needle.
v **cro·cheted** (krō shād′) **cro·chet·ing** (krō shā′ing) do crochet; make of crochet: *to crochet a blanket. I like to crochet.* <French, from Old Norse *krokr*>
cro·chet′er (krō shā′ər) *n.*

crock (krok) *n* **1** an earthenware pot or dish: *a crock of butter.* **2** *Slang* a falsehood or piece of nonsense. **3** *Informal* an old, broken-down vehicle. <Old English *crocca*>

crock·er·y (krok′ə rē) *n* dishes made of earthenware or china.

Crock–Pot (krok′pot′) *Trademark n* an insulated ceramic electric pot designed to cook food slowly at low temperatures and keep it hot during serving.

croc·o·dile (krok′ə dīl′) *n* a reptile closely related to the alligator, with a long, thick body and tail, four short legs, powerful jaws with sharp teeth, and eyes and nostrils set on top of the skull. Crocodiles are found in the warm parts of Africa, America, and Asia. Often shortened informally to **croc**. See ALLIGATOR for picture. <Old French, from Greek *kroke* pebble + *drilos* worm, referring to its habit of lying on pebbly river banks>

crocodile tears (tērz) *pl n* pretended sadness. It was once believed that crocodiles made weeping noises to attract prey, and so would cry tears over their victims.

cro·cus (krō′kəs) *n, pl* **cro·cus·es** or **cro·ci** (krō′sī) *or* (krō′sē) **1** a small plant of the iris family, growing from an underground stem and with a single cup-shaped flower. **2** a small wildflower of central N America, a species of anemone with a cup-shaped purple flower that blooms early in spring. The **prairie crocus** is the floral emblem of Manitoba. <Greek *krokos*>

croft (kroft) *UK n* a very small farm, rented and worked by a **crofter**. <Old English>

Crohn's disease (krōnz) *n* a chronic inflammation of the lower intestine that causes thickening of the walls of the colon. <B.B. *Crohn*, 20c doctor who described it>

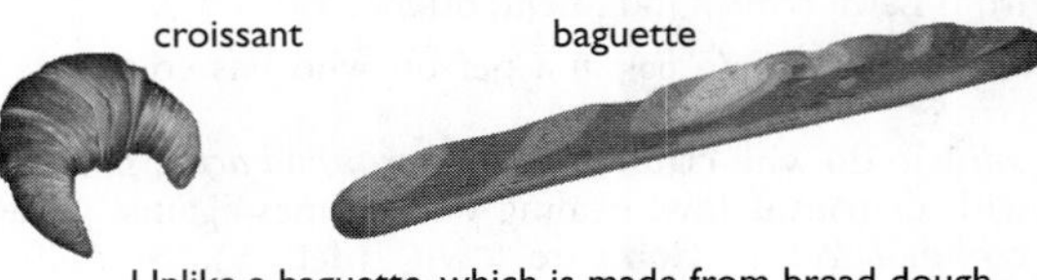

Unlike a baguette, which is made from bread dough, a **croissant** is made by layering pastry with butter and rolling and folding over several times.

crois·sant (krə sont′) *n* a small, flaky roll of rich bread shaped like a crescent. <French = crescent>

🍁 **cro·ki·nole** (krō′kə nōl′) *n* a table game in which each player tries to flick polished discs to the centre of a round board, at the same time trying to knock out the discs of opponents. <French *croquignole* flick>

Cro–Mag·non (krō mag′non) *adj* to do with a group of prehistoric people of southwestern Europe.
n a person of this group: *Some Cro-Magnons were skilled artists.* <*Cro-Magnon* cave in SW France, where remains were found>

crom·lech (krom′lək) *n* a set of upright stones erected in prehistoric times, usually in a circle and often with a large, flat stone laid horizontally across upright ones. <French, from Breton (a language of France) *krommlec'h*>

crone (krōn) *n* a shrivelled, wrinkled old woman. <Middle Dutch, from Old French *caroigne*>

cro·ny (krō′nē) *n, pl* **cro·nies** a close friend or companion, especially the associate of a criminal or other person being regarded unfavourably. <Greek *chronios* long-lasting>

crook (krůk) *n* **1** a thief or swindler. **2** a staff or stick with a hooked, curved, or bent part at the top, such as that carried by a bishop or shepherd. **3** a hooked, curved, or bent part of something: *the crook of a hockey stick. I held the baby in the crook of my arm.*
v **crooked** (krůkt), **crook·ing** bend or curve: *She beckoned to the people outside by crooking her finger at them.* <Old Norse *krokr*>

crook·ed (krůk′id) *adj* **1** bent, curved, or twisted: *narrow, crooked streets.* **2** slanted: *That picture on the wall is crooked.* **3** dishonest: *a crooked person, a crooked deal.* **crook′ed·ly** *adv.* **crook′ed·ness** *n.*

croon (krūn) *v* **1** sing softly and tenderly: *The mother was crooning to her baby.* **2** sing popular ballads in a sentimental manner.
n a soft or sentimental singing. <Dutch *kronen* groan>
croon′er *n.*

crop (krop) *n* **1 a** a product grown or gathered for use or for sale: *Wheat is the main crop of the Prairie Provinces.* **b** the total amount of it produced in one season: *The potato crop was small this year.* **2** a group of things of one kind appearing at the same time: *a crop of new paperbacks in the bookstore.* **3** the act or result of cutting or clipping.

4 *Zoology* the baglike swelling in a bird's food passage, where food is prepared for digestion. **5 a** a short whip used by horseback riders, with a loop instead of a lash: *a riding crop.* **b** the handle of a whip.
v **cropped, crop·ping 1** plant and cultivate a crop. **2** cut, clip, or bite off: *Sheep crop grass very short. The horse's tail was cropped.* <Old English *cropp*>
crop out, come through the earth's surface: *Great ridges of rock cropped out all over the hillside.*
crop up, appear or occur unexpectedly: *Even with a good plan, all sorts of difficulties can crop up.*

crop–dust·ing (krop′dus′ting) *n* the practice of spraying pesticides from a low-flying plane onto growing crops. **crop′-dust′er** *n.*

crop·land (krop′land′) *n* land used for growing crops. Also, **croplands**.

crop rotation *n* the system of growing a sequence of different crops on the same piece of ground, so as to keep the ground from becoming infertile.

cro·quet (krō kā′) *n* an outdoor game played on grass by knocking wooden balls through small wire arches by using mallets. <perhaps French *crochet* hook>

cro·quette (krō ket′) *n* a small ball or patty of chopped or ground cooked meat, fish, or vegetables, coated with crumbs and fried. <French *croquer* to crunch>

cross (kros) *n* **1 a** an upright post with another across it near the top, on which people were executed by the ancient Romans. **b** a representation of this in any of various styles, especially when used as the emblem of Christianity: *She wears a silver cross on her necklace.* **2** an X or similar mark made by crossing two lines. **3** a plant or animal that results from breeding or mating two breeds, varieties, or species: *Our dog is a cross between a spaniel and a poodle.* **4** something that is like a combination of two different things or is somewhere between them: *Documentary drama is a cross between theatre and journalism.* **5** a burden of duty or suffering that must be endured: *Her allergies are a cross that she must bear.*
v **1** go from one side to the other: *to cross a bridge.* **2** lie or extend across: *Second Avenue crosses Queen Street. The two streets cross.* **3** set or lay crosswise one over the other: *She crossed her arms. Don't cross those two wires!* **4** (*with* ***off*** *or* ***out***) draw a line through in order to cancel or delete: *Cross my name off the list. Why is this word crossed out?* **5** draw a line across: *You forgot to cross that "t."* **6** cause two different breeds, varieties, or species of animals or plants to mate in order to produce a new kind: *Canadian breeders have crossed domestic cattle with buffalo to produce the beefalo.* **7** *Christianity* (*with reflexive pronoun*) trace the form of a cross on one's body as an act of devotion: *He knelt and crossed himself.* **8** oppose or hinder: *If anyone crosses her, she gets very angry.*
adj **1** annoyed or grumpy. **2** moving or lying across: *the next major cross street.* <Old English, from Latin *crux*>
cross′ly *adv.* **cross′ness** *n.*
cross your fingers, a put one finger over another in a superstitious gesture intended to keep trouble away or to protect yourself while lying. **b** hope for the best.
cross your heart, swear that something is true, usually while saying "cross my heart," and making the sign of the cross over your heart.
cross your mind, be thought of: *It never crossed my mind that he might forget.*
cross someone's path, meet someone by chance.
cross swords, have an argument or conflict.
cross the floor, switch from one party to another in a legislature by moving from one's assigned seat to one in another part of the chamber.

cross·bar (kros′bȧr′) *n* a bar, line, or stripe going crosswise.

cross·beam (kros′bēm′) *n* a large beam that crosses another or extends from wall to wall.

cross·bones (kros′bōnz′) SKULL AND CROSSBONES.

cross·bow (kros′bō′) *n* a weapon consisting of a bow fixed sideways across a wooden stock that has a groove along the middle to direct the arrow, which is called a **quarrel**.

cross·breed (kros′brēd′) *v* **cross·bred, cross·breed·ing** breed by mating different species or varieties together.
n an individual animal or a breed produced by crossbreeding: *A mule is a crossbreed developed by crossing a horse and a donkey.*

cross·check (kros′chek′) *v* **1** check again or check against another source: *He checked his answers and then crosschecked them with mine to make sure they were correct.* **2** *Hockey, Lacrosse* check illegally by holding one's stick in both hands and pushing it in front of the opponent's face or body.
n the act of crosschecking.

Cross-country skiing is a low-impact, aerobically complete activity that provides skiers with an excellent workout. Depending on the technique used, both upper and lower body muscles are involved.

cross–coun·try (kros′kun′trē) *adj, adv* **1** across open country instead of by road or over a track: *a cross-country race* (*adj*). *The refugees fled cross-country* (*adv*). **2** skiing across countryside, as opposed to down slopes: *cross-country skis* (*adj*). *Can you ski cross-country* (*adv*)? **3** across a country: *a cross-country tour* (*adj*), *to fly cross-country from Vancouver to Halifax* (*adv*).

a bat	e bed	i bid	o pot	u cup	th thin
ā cake	ē me	ī bite	ō go	ü rude	ᴛʜ then
ȧ bar	ə about	ər over	ȯ for	u̇ put	zh measure

cross–cul·tur·al (kros′kul′chə rəl) *adj* to do with interaction between people of different cultures: *Life in Canada is enriched by many cross-cultural activities.*

cross·cur·rent (kros′kər′ənt) *n* a current, especially of air, flowing across another.

cross·cut saw (kros′kut′) *n* a saw used or made for cutting across the grain of wood.

cross–dres·sing (kros′dres′ing) *n* the practice of wearing the clothes typical of the other sex in order to try to look like a member of that sex. **cross-dres′ser** *n.*

cross–ex·am·ine (kros′eg zam′ən) *v* **cross-ex·am·ined, cross-ex·am·in·ing** 1 *Law* question a witness closely to test the truth of evidence given: *The defence counsel spent two hours cross-examining the first Crown witness.* 2 question closely or severely. **cross′-ex·am′i·na′tion** *n.* **cross′-ex·am′i·ner** *n.*

cross–eyed (kros′īd′) *adj* with one eye or both eyes turned in toward the nose.

cross–fer·ti·li·za·tion (kros′fər′tə lī zā′shən) *Botany n* the fertilization of one flower by pollen from another. **cross′-fer′ti·lize′** *v.*

cross·fire (kros′fīr′) *n* 1 gunfire coming from different directions so as to cross. 2 a verbal attack from different or opposing sources.

cross–grained (kros′grānd′) *adj* 1 in wood, with an irregular grain. 2 bad-tempered or hard to get along with.

cross·hairs (kros′hārz′) *pln* 1 fine crossed lines in the viewfinder of an optical instrument allowing one to focus accurately on an object. 2 **crosshair** *sing Computers* a cursor in the shape of a cross, indicating the starting point of a box.

cross·hatch (kros′hach′) *v* mark or shade with two sets of parallel lines crossing each other. **cross′hatch′ing** *n.*

cross·ing (kros′ing) *n* 1 a place where things cross each other: *The cars stopped at the railway crossing.* 2 a marked place where pedestrians may cross a street: *White lines mark the crossing.* 3 the act of crossing, especially a voyage across water.

crossing guard *n* a person who escorts children across busy streets.

cross–leg·ged (kros′leg′id) *or* (kros′legd′) *adv, adj* with the ankles crossed and the knees bent and spread wide apart: *We all sat cross-legged on the floor* (*adv*). *I find the cross-legged position uncomfortable* (*adj*).

cross·o·ver (kros′ō′vər) *n* 1 the act of crossing over or transferring: *The Conservative MP's crossover to the Liberal Party astonished everyone.* 2 a place or means of crossing, such as a bridge.

cross·piece (kros′pēs′) *n* a beam or bar that is placed across something.

cross–pol·li·na·tion (kros′pol′ə nā′shən) *Botany n* the transfer of pollen from the anther of one flower to the stigma of another: *Bees are agents of cross-pollination.* **cross′-pol′li·nate′** *v.*

cross–pur·pose (kros′pər′pəs) *n* an opposing or contrary purpose.

at cross-purposes, acting against one another, usually through misunderstanding.

cross–ques·tion (kros′kwes′chən) *v* question closely or severely.
n a question asked in cross-examining.

cross–ref·er·ence (kros′ref′ə rəns) *n* an instruction in one part of a book, essay, or index to go to another part for more information. Cross-references in this dictionary are printed in SMALL CAPITALS.
v connect by means of a cross-reference. Example: The entry "center" is cross-referenced to "centre." Also (*for v*), **cross-refer**.

cross·road (kros′rōd′) *n* 1 a road that crosses another. 2 a road connecting main roads. 3 **crossroads** *pl* **a** (*with singular or plural verb*) a place where roads cross: *We'll meet at the crossroads.* **b** (*with singular verb*) a critical point, especially where a decision has to be made: *Starting high school is a crossroads for many teenagers.*

cross–sec·tion (kros′sek′shən) *n* 1 a straight cut made right through from top to bottom or from side to side: *A cross-section is the intersection of a solid by a plane.* 2 a drawing or illustration of the surface exposed or that would be exposed by such a cut: *The diagram shows a cross-section of a volcano.* 3 a small selection of people or things of various kinds, taken to represent the larger group to which they belong: *to report the views of a cross-section of the community.*

cross–stitch (kros′stich′) *n* 1 one sewing stitch crossed over another, forming an X. 2 embroidery made with a series of such stitches.
v sew with such stitches. **cross′-stitch′ing** *n.*

cross·walk (kros′wok′) *n* a street crossing for pedestrians, marked by lines on the road.

cross·wind (kros′wind′) *n* a wind blowing across the path of a motor vehicle, aircraft, or other means of transport.

cross·wise (kros′wīz′) *adv* 1 so as to cross another thing. 2 in the form of a cross.

cross·word puzzle (kros′wərd′) *n* a puzzle with rows and columns of squares to be filled in with words, using numbered clues.

crotch (kroch) *n* 1 the place where the human body divides into its two legs. 2 the corresponding part of a garment. 3 a forked part, as where a tree divides into two branches. <origin uncertain>

crotch·et·y (kroch′ə tē) *adj* cranky and stubborn; bad-tempered. <Old French, from Old Norse *krokr*> **crotch′et·i·ness** *n.*

crouch (krouch) *v* 1 stoop low with legs bent, and the upper body brought forward and down, such as an animal ready to spring. 2 (*with* ***over***) bend over so as to be close to someone or something: *She crouched over me as I worked on the jigsaw puzzle.*
n a crouching position. <Middle English, perhaps from Old French *croche* hook>

croup[1] (krūp) *n* an inflammation of the throat and bronchial tubes characterized by a hoarse cough and difficult breathing. <imitative> **croup′y** *adj.*

croup[2] (krūp) *n* the rump of a horse, donkey, etc. <Old French *croupe*>

crou·ton (krū′ton) *n* a small cube of seasoned bread, toasted or fried. Croutons are usually served in soup or salad. <French, from Latin *crusta* crust>

crow[1] (krō) *v* **1** make the cry of a rooster. **2** show happiness and pride by boasting: *The winning team crowed over its victory.*
n the act or sound of crowing. <Old English *crawan*>

crow[2] (krō) *n* a large, glossy black bird that makes a harsh cry or caw. <Old English *crawe*>
as the crow flies, in a straight line: *The town is about 10 km away as the crow flies, but about 15 km by road.*
eat crow, *Informal* be forced to admit that you have been wrong.

crow·bar (krō′bȧr′) *n* a strong iron or steel bar with a bent, forked end, used as a lever to lift or pry things.

crowd (kroud) *n* **1** a large number of people together: *A crowd gathered to hear the speaker.* **2** the majority of people, with average tastes and intelligence: *TV programs that appeal to the crowd.* **3** *Informal* a circle of friends: *She and all her crowd went to the dance.* **4** a large number of things together.
v **1** collect or move in large numbers: *People crowded around the stage. Students began crowding into the gym for the last assembly of the year.* **2** fill a space almost completely: *Shoppers crowd the store at every sale.* **3** (*with* ***in, onto, into,*** *etc.*) get too close to or pack too closely together. *to be crowded into a bus.* **4** *Slang* pressure or harass: *Don't crowd me; wait till I've finished.* <Old English *crudan* to press> **crowd′ed** *adj.*
crowd out, leave no room or time for: *Don't let your friendships crowd out your family.*

SYNONYMS

Crowd means "many people": *A large crowd attended the Remembrance Day services.*

Drove can refer to either animals or people, moving along together: *The sheepdog guided the drove of sheep. A drove of spectators flooded out of the stadium.*

Flock can refer to people, but more often to animals or birds: *A flock of geese wandered along the shoreline.*

crown (kroun) *n* **1** headgear of precious metal and jewels, worn by a monarch. **2 the Crown** the monarchy as an office or institution. **3** anything like a crown. *In the ancient Greek Olympics, the winner of the race received a crown of leaves.* **4** the head. **5 a** the top or highest part: *the crown of a hat.* **b** the highest degree or state of anything. **6** the part of a tooth outside the gum, or an artificial substitute for this. **7** the leaves and branches of a tree: *The balsam fir has a pyramid-shaped crown.* **8** a coin or unit of money in various countries.
v **1** make someone into a king or queen. **2** honour or reward: *Her work was crowned with success.* **3** cover the highest part of: *A fort crowns the hill.* **4** make perfect or complete: *A visit to the ice cream parlour crowned the outing.* **5** *Informal* hit on the head. **6** begin to emerge while being born so that the top of the head shows. <Old French, from Latin *corona* wreath> **crown′ing** *adj, n.*

🍁 **Crown attorney** *n* in Canada, the lawyer representing the government in a trial involving a criminal case.

crown colony *n* a colony under the power and authority of the British government.

🍁 **Crown corporation** *n* an agency or company through which the Government of Canada or one of the provincial or territorial governments carries on certain activities.

crown fire *n* a forest fire that spreads from treetop to treetop.

Crown land *n* **1** 🍁 publicly owned land. **2** land that is the personal property of a monarch.

crown prince *n* the oldest living son of a king or queen, and who will inherit the throne.

crown princess *n* **1** the wife of a crown prince. **2** a girl or woman who is heir to the throne.

crow's feet *pl n* a series of wrinkles radiating from the outer corner of the eye.

crow's nest or **crows nest** *n* **1** a small, enclosed platform near the top of a ship's mast, used as a lookout. **2** a similar small, high place.

🍁 **CRTC** Canadian Radio-television and Telecommunications Commission.

cru·cial (krū′shəl) *adj* very important or decisive: *crucial information, a crucial point in an argument.* <French, from Latin *crux* cross> **cru′cial·ly** *adv.*

cru·ci·ble (krū′sə bəl) *n* a container in which metals or ores can be melted. <Latin *crux* cross>

cru·ci·fix (krū′sə fiks′) *n* a cross with a figure of the crucified Christ on it. <Old French, from *crux* cross + *figere* fasten>

cru·ci·fix·ion (krū′sə fik′shən) *n* **1** the act of crucifying. **2 the Crucifixion** the crucifying of Christ, often specifically as the subject of a work of art.

cru·ci·fy (krū′sə fī′) *v* **cru·ci·fied, cru·ci·fy·ing** **1** put to death by nailing or binding the hands and feet to a cross, as the ancient Romans did. **2** treat severely or torture. **3** blame and punish, often as a scapegoat: *The media will crucify anyone who lies to them.* <Old French, from Latin *crux* cross + *figere* fix>

crude (krūd) *adj* **crud·er, crud·est** **1** in a natural or raw state: *crude rubber, crude oil.* **2** rough, careless, or unfinished: *a crude shack, a crude attempt.* **3** lacking good taste or politeness: *a crude remark.*
n crude oil. <Latin *crudus* raw> **crude′ly** *adv.* **crude′ness** *n.* **cru′di·ty** *n.*

cru·di·tés (krū′di tā′) *pl n* small pieces of raw vegetables, eaten as an appetizer or snack. <French, from Latin *crudus* raw>

cru·el (krū′əl) *adj* **1** deliberately causing pain to others: *a cruel master, cruel words.* **2** causing pain and suffering: *a cruel war, a cruel winter.* <Old French, from Latin *crudus* rough> **cru′el·ly** *adv.* **cru′el·ty** *n.*

a bat	e bed	i bid	o pot	u cup	th **thin**
ā cake	ē me	ī bite	ō go	ū rude	ᴛʜ **then**
ȧ bar	ə about	ər over	ȯ for	u̇ put	zh measure

cru·et (krū′it) *n* **1** a glass bottle to hold vinegar or oil at the table. **2** a set of such bottles on a stand. <Old French, from Saxon *kruka*>

cruise (krūz) *v* **cruised, cruis·ing 1** sail from place to place on pleasure or business: *to cruise the Caribbean, to cruise along the coast.* **2** travel from place to place, with or without a special destination: *The taxi cruised in search of passengers. Police cars were cruising the streets.* **3** travel in an airplane or car at the speed of maximum efficiency. **4** 🍁 examine a tract of forest to estimate the value of the timber on it.
n a trip in which one sails from place to place. <Dutch *kruisen* sail across, from Latin *crux* cross>

cruise control *n* a device in a motor vehicle to maintain engine speed at a constant rate.

cruise missile *n* a guided missile that may be sent off from an aircraft or ship and travels at low altitudes in order to escape detection by radar.

cruis·er (krū′zər) *n* **1** a police car used for patrolling streets and highways. **2** a warship with less armour and more speed than a battleship. **3** usually, **cabin cruiser** a motorboat equipped with a cabin and facilities for living on board. **4** a person who or thing that cruises.

crul·ler (krul′ər), (krůl′ər), *or* (krū′lər) *n* a doughnut made of light dough twisted together. Also, **kruller**. <Dutch *krullen* to curl>

crumb (krum) *n* **1** a bit of bread or pastry. **2** the soft, inside part of bread as opposed to the crust. **3** the littlest bit of anything: *She didn't show even a crumb of gratitude for all my help.* <Old English *cruma*>

crum·ble (krum′bəl) *v* **crum·bled, crum·bling 1** break into very small pieces or crumbs: *to crumble dirt between your hands.* **2** fall to pieces gradually due to erosion or decay: *The old wall was crumbling away at the edges. Traditional social structures have begun to crumble.*

crumb·ly (krum′blē) *adj* **crumb·li·er, crumb·li·est 1** breaking, or tending to break, into very small pieces or crumbs: *a crumbly cookie.* **2** falling, or about to fall, into pieces gradually due to erosion or decay: *a crumbly old wall.*

crum·my[1] (krum′ē) *Slang adj* **crum·mi·er, crum·mi·est** unpleasant or of bad quality: *crummy food.* <*crumby*>

🍁 **crum·my**[2] (krum′ē) *n especially West Coast, Slang* in former times, an old railway car converted, by adding wooden benches, for loggers to use to get to work. They might have to travel many kilometres in these unheated cars. <US slang *crumb = body louse*>

crum·pet (krum′pit) *n* a round, flat cake, thicker than a pancake, baked on a griddle. <origin uncertain>

crum·ple (krum′pəl) *v* **crum·pled, crum·pling 1** crush something together so it becomes creased and wrinkled: *She crumpled the paper into a ball.* **2** fall down or collapse: *He crumpled to the floor.* <Old English *crump* bent>

crunch (krunch) *v* **1** crush something hard or crisp noisily with the teeth. **2** produce a loud crackling noise: *The snow crunched under our feet. We crunched through the snow.*
n **1** the act or sound of crunching. **2** *Informal* a crisis, shortage, or other difficult time: *an energy crunch. I hope she can hang in there when the crunch comes.* <earlier *cranch*, influenced by *crush, munch*>

crun·chy (krun′chē) *adj* **crunch·i·er, crunch·i·est** to do with anything that makes a crackling sound when bitten or otherwise crushed: *a crunchy apple.*

cru·sade (krū sād′) *n* **1** a vigorous campaign against something regarded as a public evil, or in favour of some new idea: *Everyone is joining the crusade against secondhand smoke.* **2 Crusade** any of several Christian military expeditions between the eleventh and the thirteenth centuries that sought to take the Holy Land from Muslim control. **3** a war with a religious purpose and approved by religious authorities.
v **cru·sad·ed, cru·sad·ing** take part in a crusade. <French, from Latin *crux* cross> **cru·sad′er** or **Cru·sad′er** *n.*

crush (krush) *v* **1** squeeze or press together with force so as to break or bruise: *My fingers got crushed in the door.* **2** flatten or crease by pressure: *His cap was crushed when he accidentally sat on it.* **3** grind or pound into fine pieces or into pulp. **4** put or keep down: *to crush a revolt.* **5** overwhelm with hurt or disappointment: *She was crushed when we refused her invitation.*
n **1** a violent pressure like grinding or pounding. **2** a mass of people crowded close together. **3** *Informal* **a** a sudden, strong liking for a person. **b** the object of such a liking. <Old French *cruissir* crack> **crushed** *adj.* **crush′er** *n.*

crust (krust) *n* **1** the firm, outer surface of baked bread. **2** a piece of this, especially a hard, dry piece of bread. **3** the baked outside covering of a pie. **4** a hard outside covering: *The snow had a crust that was thick enough to walk on.* **5** the outermost layer of the earth, about 30 to 50 km thick, mainly composed of rock.
v cover or become covered with a crust. <Old French, from Latin *crusta* rind> **crust′like′** *adj.*

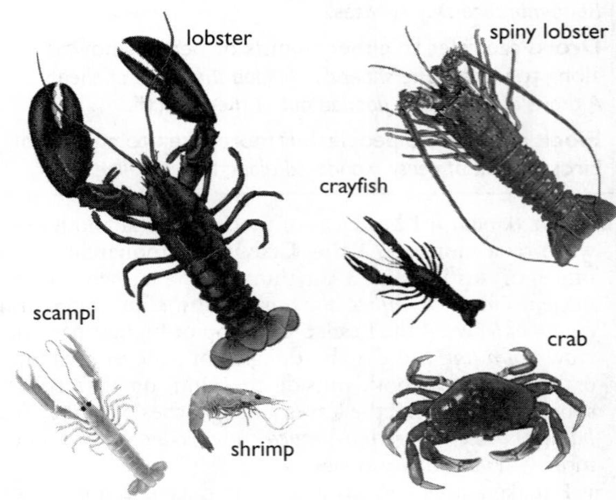

Crustaceans, abundant in the sea, also flourish in fresh water. A few, such as sowbugs, are common in moist land environments.

crus·ta·cean (krus tā′shən) *n* an animal with a segmented body and legs, usually living in water. Crustaceans have a hard shell, five pairs of legs, and two pairs of antennae.
adj to do with crustaceans.

crust·y (krus′tē) *adj* **crust·i·er, crust·i·est 1** with or characterized by a crust: *crusty bread, a crusty layer of dried mud.* **2** gruff or harsh in manner or speech. **crust′i·ly** *adv.* **crust′i·ness** *n.*

crutch (kruch) *n* **1** a tall support, usually used in pairs, that allows an injured person, or a person with a disability, to walk. An underarm crutch has a padded crosspiece at the top that fits under the armpit; a forearm crutch (also called a **Canadian crutch**) has a brace that attaches to the forearm. See UNDERARM for picture. **2** something that serves as a prop or support: *She is a poor manager who has to use her assistant as a crutch.* <Old English *crycc*>

crux (kruks) *n* the essential or most important point: *the crux of the problem.* <Latin = cross>

cry (krī) *v* **cried, cry·ing 1** weep. **2** (*often with* ***out***) make an involuntary sound that shows strong emotion, such as pain, sorrow, fear, or excitement. **3** call out loudly. **4** announce in public, especially in former times: *In former times, peddlers cried their wares in the street to sell them.* **5** make a bird's or animal's loud, characteristic call.
n, pl **cries 1** a loud call or shout: **2** an involuntary sound expressing strong emotion: *A startled cry escaped her lips.* **3** a period of weeping: *I buried my face in the pillow and had a good cry.* **4** the loud, characteristic call of an animal: *a gull's cry.* **5** a call to action: *a rallying cry, a war cry.* <Old French, from Latin *quiritare* raise a public outcry>
a crying shame, a very unfortunate situation.
a far cry, **a** a long way. **b** very different: *This is a far cry from what I expected.*
cry out for, need urgently and obviously: *This room cries out for a little colour.*
cry over spilled milk, be sad over something that cannot be undone.
cry your eyes out, *Informal* weep for a long time.
in full cry, in close pursuit.

SYNONYMS

Cry means "shed tears" and can vary in intensity: *He cried for hours when his best friend moved away. She cried with relief when her dog was found.*

Wail means "cry loudly for a long time": *The mourners wailed at the funeral and could not be comforted.*

Weep often means "cry gently or quietly": *No one noticed him weep at his son's graduation ceremony.*

cry·ba·by (krī′bā′bē) *n, pl* **cry·ba·bies** a person who cries easily or for attention, or who complains a lot.

cry·o·bi·ol·o·gy (krī′ō bī ol′ə jē) *n* the branch of biology that studies the effects of very low temperatures on organisms and tissues. <Greek *kryos* frost + *biology*> **cry′o·bi′o·log′i·cal** *adj.* **cry′o·bi·ol′o·gist** *n.*

cry·o·gen·ics (krī′ə jen′iks) *n* (*with singular verb*) the branch of physics that studies the production and effects of extremely low temperatures. <Greek *kryos* frost + *-genic*> **cry′o·gen′ic** *adj.*

cry·o·pre·serve (krī′ō pre zərv′) *v* **cry·o·pre·served, cry·o·pre·serv·ing** store living tissue, such as semen, eggs, embryos, and corneas, at very low temperatures in order to preserve them for later use. <Greek *kryos* frost + *preserve*> **cry′o·pres·er·va′tion** *n.*

crypt (kript) *n* an underground room or vault, especially, in former times, one beneath the main floor of a church, used as a burial place. <Latin, from Greek *kryptos* hidden>

cryp·tic (krip′tik) *adj* with a hidden meaning: *a cryptic message, a cryptic reply.* <Latin, from Greek *kryptos* hidden> **cryp′ti·cal·ly** *adv.*

cryptic crossword *n* a crossword puzzle whose clues are puzzling to figure out.

cryp·to·gram (krip′tə gram′) *n* something written in secret code.

cryp·tog·ra·phy (krip tog′rə fē) *n* the art or process of writing or deciphering secret codes. Also called **cryptology**. <Greek *kryptos* hidden + *-graphy*> **cryp·tog′ra·pher** *n.* **cryp′to·graph′ic** *adj.*

crys·tal (kris′təl) *n* **1** a solid whose parts are formed in a regular, three-dimensional pattern of atoms, ions, or molecules, and with fixed distances between the parts. **2** a clear, transparent mineral, a kind of quartz, that looks like ice. **3** a piece of crystal cut to a certain shape for use or ornament: *crystals hanging from a chandelier.* **4** clear glass of high quality: *wine glasses of fine crystal.* **5** a regular shape with angles and flat surfaces, into which a substance solidifies: *sugar crystals, crystals of snow.*
adj **1** made of crystal. **2** clear and transparent like crystal. <Old English, from Greek *kryos* frost>

crystal ball *n* a ball made of crystal or glass, used by psychics who gaze into it and supposedly see images of faraway or future events.

crystal clear *adj* perfectly clear: *The newly washed windows were crystal clear, a crystal-clear explanation.*

crystal gazing *n* **1** the practice of gazing into a crystal ball, supposedly to see images of faraway or future events. **2** guesswork about the future: *The candidate said she wasn't about to engage in crystal gazing about the election.* **crystal gazer** *n.*

crys·tal·line (kris′tə līn′) *or* (kris′tə lēn) *adj* **1** consisting or made of crystals: *Sugar and salt are crystalline.* **2** clear and transparent like crystal.

crys·tal·lize (kris′tə līz′) *v* **crys·tal·lized, crys·tal·liz·ing 1** form crystals: *Water crystallizes to form snow.* **2** take a clear, definite, and permanent form: *His vague ideas crystallized into a plan.* **3** coat and saturate with sugar: *crystallized fruits.*

🍁 **CSIS** Canadian Security and Intelligence Service.

CT scan (sē′tē′) CAT SCAN.

cu. (*used in nonmetric units of measure*) cubic.

cub (kub) *n* a young bear, fox, lion, etc.
adj inexperienced: *a cub reporter.* <origin uncertain>

Cu·ba (kyū′bə) *n* an island country in the Caribbean. See the APPENDIX. **Cu′ban** *n, adj.*

a bat	e bed	i bid	o pot	u cup	th **thin**
ā cake	ē me	ī bite	ō go	ū rude	ᴛʜ **then**
à bar	ə about	ər over	ô for	ů put	zh measure

cub·by·hole (kub′ē hōl′) *n* a small, enclosed space or compartment. <dialect *cub* shed + *hole*>

cube (kyūb) *n* **1** a solid with six identical square sides. **2** a mass of something, shaped more or less like a cube: *ice cubes.* **3** *Mathematics* the product obtained when a number is used three times as a factor. The cube of 5 is 125.
v **cubed, cub·ing 1** make or form into the shape of a cube: *The beets we had for supper were cubed instead of sliced.* **2** use a number three times as a factor: *Cube 5 and you get 125.* <Old French, from Greek *kybos*>

cube root *Mathematics n* a number that, when used three times as a factor, produces another number: *The cube root of 125 is 5.*

cu·bic (kyū′bik) *adj* **1** with the shape of a cube. Also, **cubical**. **2** to do with measuring volume or capacity. A **cubic metre** is the volume of a cube whose edges are each a metre long.

cu·bi·cle (kyū′bə kəl) *n* a small room, booth, or stall for one person, as in a public washroom, a large office room, or the reading room of a library. <Latin *cubare* lie>

cubic measure *n* a unit or series of units for measuring volume or capacity.

cub·ism (kyū′biz əm) *n* a style of art of the early 1900s that uses geometric shapes to represent people and objects. **cu′bist** *n, adj.*

cu·bit (kyū′bit) *n* an ancient unit of length, varying from about 45 to 50 cm, based on the length of the average arm from the elbow to the tip of the middle finger. <Latin *cubitum* forearm>

cu·boid (kyū′boid) *adj* shaped more or less like a cube.
n **1** a solid with six flat sides, each one a rectangle. **2** a bone of the foot between the heel and the instep.

cuck·old (kuk′əld) *Archaic n* a man whose wife is unfaithful.
v make a cuckold of. <Old English, from Old French *cucu* cuckoo, possibly from the cuckoo's habit of laying eggs in another's nest> **cuck′old·ry** *n.*

cuck·oo (kū′kū) *or sometimes for n,* (ku̇k′ū) *n* **1** a long, slender, brown and white bird. Many cuckoos lay their eggs in the nests of other birds. **2** the call of the cuckoo. **3** *Informal* an eccentric or mildly crazy person.
adj Informal crazy. <Old French *cucu*>

cuckoo clock *n* a clock with a toy bird that pops out of a little door and makes a sound like that of a cuckoo to mark intervals of time like the hour or half-hour.

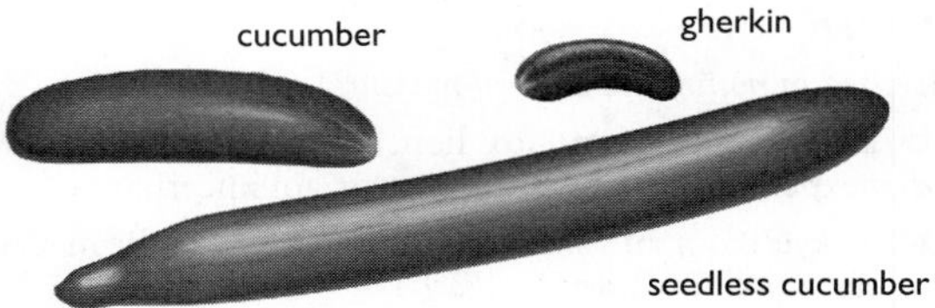

cu·cum·ber (kyū′kum bər) *n* the long, fleshy fruit of a vine of the gourd family, with a green skin, eaten as a raw or pickled vegetable. <Old French, from Latin *cucumis*>
cool as a cucumber, *Informal* calm and untroubled.

cud (kud) *n* food that has been brought up into the mouth from the first and second stomachs of cattle, deer, and other RUMINANTS, to be chewed and swallowed again. <Old English *cudu*>

cud·dle (kud′əl) *v* **cud·dled, cud·dling** hold or lie closely and lovingly: *The father cuddled his baby. The two sweethearts cuddled together in front of the fire.*
n a prolonged, affectionate hug. <origin uncertain>

SYNONYMS

Cuddle means "embrace affectionately": *The girl gently cuddled her baby sister.*

Huddle means "crowd closely together": *The skateboarders huddled in a doorway, waiting for the rain to end.*

Snuggle means "move close to" or "nestle": *The piglets snuggled against their mother.*

cud·dly *adj* **cud·dli·er, cud·dli·est 1** enjoying cuddling: *Don't try to hug my little brother; he's not cuddly.* **2** pleasant to cuddle: *a cuddly puppy.*

cudg·el (kuj′əl) *n* a short, thick stick used as a weapon.
v **cudg·elled** or **cudg·eled, cudg·el·ling** or **cudg·el·ing** beat with a cudgel. <Old English *cycgel*>
cudgel your brains, think very hard.

cue[1] (kyū) *n* **1** a hint or suggestion as to what to do or when to act. **2** an action or speech on or behind the stage that is the signal for a performer to enter or begin: *When he thumps the table, that's your cue to come running through the door.*
v **cued, cue·ing** or **cu·ing** give a cue to: *Don't forget to cue me when to start the song.* <origin uncertain>
cue in, give a cue to a performer.
on cue, at or as if at a signal: *They started on cue. I picked up the phone and, on cue, the the doorbell rang.*
take your cue from someone, be guided by someone else's action.

cue[2] (kyū) *Billiards, Pool n* a long tapered stick for striking the **cue ball**, which is usually the white one.

ETYMOLOGY

Both meanings of the word **cue** come from French *queue*, meaning "tail." The cue for an actor comes at the tail end of another actor's speech or action. A pool cue is shaped like a tail.

cue card *n* a card held out of the audience's sight, showing words or dialogue for a speaker or actor, usually in TV broadcasting.

cuff[1] (kuf) *n* **1** the part of a sleeve or glove that goes around the wrist. **2** a turned-up fold around the bottom of a pant leg. **3** the part of a blood-pressure measuring instrument that wraps around the arm. **4 cuffs** *pl Informal* handcuffs. <Middle English>
off the cuff, without preparation: *He spoke off the cuff, without notes.*

cuff[2] (kuf) *v, n* hit with the hand; slap. <origin uncertain>

cuff link *n* an ornamental link for joining together the open ends of a certain kind of shirt cuff.

Roman legionary

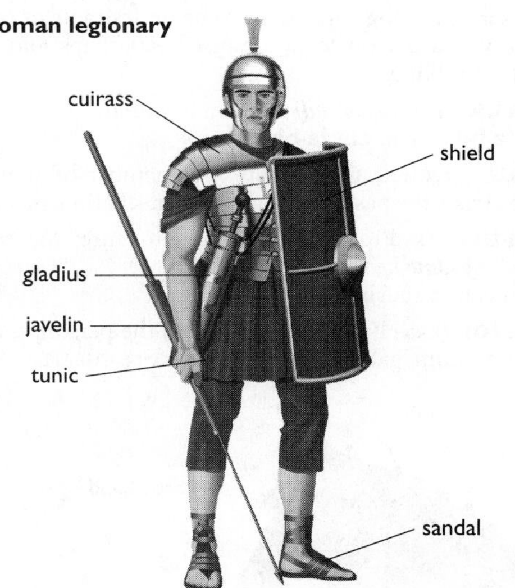

cui·rass (kwə ras′) *n* a piece of armour for the body, made of a breastplate and a plate for the back fastened together. <Old French, from Latin *coriam* leather>

cui·sine (kwi zēn′) *n* a style or method of cooking or preparing food: *local cuisine, Italian cuisine.* <French, from Latin *coquere* to cook>

cuke (kyūk) *Informal n* a cucumber.

cul–de–sac (kul′də sak′) *n* a street or passage open at only one end. <French = bottom of a bag>

cul·i·nar·y (kul′ə ner′ē) *or* (kyū′lə ner′ē) *adj* to do with cooking or the kitchen: *culinary herbs. He is often praised for his culinary skill.* <Latin *culina* kitchen>

cull (kul) *v* **1** pick out, either to keep or get rid of: *to cull important facts from a mass of evidence. The names of underage players were culled from the list.* **2** make selections from: *She culled her garden for the nicest blooms for a bouquet.* **3** reduce in number by selecting individuals for slaughter or removal: *The caribou herd is culled so the rest have a better chance of survival.*
n something picked out as inferior or worthless. <Old French, from Latin *com-* together + *legere* choose, collect>

cul·mi·nate (kul′mə nāt′) *v* **cul·mi·nat·ed, cul·mi·nat·ing** **1** rise to or end in a high point: *The tower had a long winding staircase that culminated in a lookout platform.* **2** reach a climax, decisive point, or end: *What would make a good culminating activity for this chapter? The dramatic action of the play culminates in a fight.* <Latin *culmen* summit> **cul′mi·na′tion** *n.*

cu·lottes (kū lots′), (kə lots′), *or* (kū′lots) *pln* women's or girls' pants or shorts cut with very wide legs to resemble a flared skirt. <French = knee breeches, from Latin *culus* rump>

cul·pa·ble (kul′pə bəl) *adj* deserving blame; guilty: *culpable neglect of duty. If you hit another vehicle from behind, you are culpable.* <Old French, from Latin *culpa* fault, blame> **cul′pa·bly** *adv.*

cul·prit (kul′prit) *n* **1** a person guilty of a crime or an offence. **2** the cause of any problem: *When people suffer from back pain, poor posture is usually the culprit.* <Old French *cul. prit.*, from *culpable* and *prist* ready (for trial)>

cult (kult) *n* **1** a system of religious worship, especially directed toward a particular figure or object. **2** a small, unorthodox religious group under the domination of a leader. **3 a** great admiration for or devotion to a person or thing: *the fitness cult.* **b** a group showing such admiration or devotion: *a movie director with a large cult.*
adj to do with a cult: *a cult movie. The author has acquired a cult following.* <Latin *colere* pay attention to>

cul·ti·va·ble (kul′tə və bəl) *adj* that can be cultivated.

cul·ti·vate (kul′tə vāt′) *v* **cul·ti·vat·ed, cul·ti·vat·ing** **1** prepare and use land to raise crops: *This whole region is cultivated.* **2** plant and help to grow by care and effort: *to cultivate roses.* **3** develop by care and effort: *to cultivate the mind, to cultivate a friendship.* <Latin *cultivare*>
cul′ti·va′tion *n.*

cul·ti·vat·ed (kul′tə vā′tid) *adj* **1** prepared and used to raise crops: *cultivated land.* **2** produced by cultivation: *cultivated blueberries.* **3** cultured, refined, and educated.

cul·ti·va·tor (kul′tə vā′tər) *n* **1** a tool or machine used to loosen the soil around growing plants: *A cultivator is pulled or pushed between rows of growing plants.* **2** a person who or thing that cultivates.

cul·ture (kul′chər) *n* **1** the customs, values, arts, and institutions characteristic of a particular community at a given time: *Modern Canadian culture is strongly influenced by TV and the other mass media.* **2** refinement of a person's tastes and interests, feelings, and manners. **3** the commercial raising of bees, fish, silkworms, etc. **4** *Biology* **a** the growth of living micro-organisms in a special medium for scientific study or medicinal use. **b** a colony of micro-organisms grown in this way.
v **cul·tured, cul·tur·ing** **1** educate in the arts and social graces. **2** *Biology* grow bacteria or other micro-organisms in a special medium. <French, from Latin *colere* cultivate> **cul′tur·al** *adj.* **cul′tur·al·ly** *adv.*

cul·tured (kul′chərd) *adj* **1** with civilized tastes and manners. **2** produced or raised under artificial conditions, as in a laboratory: *a necklace of cultured pearls.*

culture shock *n* the feeling of confusion or alienation caused by being suddenly exposed to a culture that is very different from one's own.

cul·vert (kul′vərt) *n* a small channel or drain that allows water to run under a road or railway. <origin uncertain>

cum (kum) *prep* (*usually in compounds*) combined with or together with: *an antique-cum-junk shop.* <Latin = with>

cum·ber·some (kum′bər səm) *adj* **1** difficult to carry or manage because of weight, shape, or size: *Medieval armour was cumbersome.* **2** burdensome or time-consuming: *long, cumbersome sentences. Rebooting is a cumbersome procedure.* <Old French *combrer* impede> **cum′ber·some·ly** *adv.* **cum′ber·some·ness** *n.*

a bat	e bed	i bid	o pot	u cup	th **thin**
ā cake	ē me	ī bite	ō go	ū rude	TH **then**
à bar	ə about	ər over	ȯ for	ů put	zh measure

cum·in or **cum·min** (kum′ən) *n* a plant of the parsley family whose aromatic, seedlike fruits are used in cooking and medicine. <Old English, from Greek *kyminon*>

cum lau·de (kům lou′dā) *adv* with honour: *To graduate cum laude is to graduate with high standing.* <Latin = with praise>

cum·mer·bund (kum′ər bund′) *n* a broad sash worn around the waist with a tuxedo. <Hindi, from Persian *kamar* waist + *band* band>

cu·mu·la·tive (kyū′myə lə tiv) *adj* increasing by successive additions in quality, degree, or force: *The cumulative effect of so many annoyances finally made her lose her temper.* <Latin *cumulus* a heap> **cu′mu·la·tive·ly** *adv.*

cu·mu·lo·nim·bus (kyū′myə lə nim′bəs) *n, pl* **cu·mu·lo·nim·bus·es** or **cu·mu·lo·nim·bi** (kyū′myə lə nim′bī) a massive cloud formation combining features of both cumulus and nimbus clouds and with peaks that resemble mountains. See ALTOCUMULUS for picture.

cu·mu·lus (kyū′myə ləs) *n, pl* **cu·mu·li** (kyū′myə lī′) *or* (kyū′myə lē) a cloud formation of rounded heaps with a flat base. See ALTOCUMULUS for picture.

cu·ne·i·form (kyū′nē ə fórm′) *or* (kyū nē′ə fórm′) *n* the wedge-shaped characters used in some ancient forms of writing, as in Babylonia, Assyria, and Persia.
adj wedge-shaped. <French, from Latin *cuneus* wedge>

cun·ning (kun′ing) *adj* **1** clever, especially in tricking or manipulating people: *a cunning rogue, a cunning plot.* **2** skilful: *cunning hands.* **3** ingenious: *a cunning device.*
n craftiness or slyness: *the natural cunning of the fox.* <perhaps Old Norse *kunna* know> **cun′ning·ly** *adv.*

cup (kup) *n* **1** a small, bowl-shaped container to drink from, usually with a handle. **2** an ornamental trophy in the shape of a deep, high cup: *Did a Canadian team win the Stanley Cup last year?* **3** a drink or mixture of food traditionally served in a cup or goblet: *I'll have the fruit cup for dessert.* **4** a nonmetric unit of volume, used especially in cooking, equal to about 250 mL. **5** something shaped like a cup, such as the corolla of some flowers, a hole on a golf course, or either of the two breast supports of a bra.
v **cupped, cup·ping** shape like a cup: *She cupped her hands to catch the ball.* <Old English, from Latin *cupa* tub> **cup′ful′** *n.* **cup′like′** *adj.*
in your cups, *Informal* drunk.
your cup of tea, the thing you enjoy.

cup·bear·er (kup′ber′ər) *n* in former times, in royal households, a person who tasted the wine before handing it to his master or mistress.

cup·board (kub′ərd) *n* a closet or cabinet with shelves for storing things, such as food and dishes.

cup·cake (kup′kāk′) *n* a small, sweet cake baked in a cup-shaped container.

cu·pid·i·ty (kyū pid′ə tē) *n* greed. <Old French, from Latin *cupere* to desire>

cu·po·la (kyū′pə lə) *n* **1** a round dome forming the roof or part of the roof of a building. **2** a small, domed structure on top of a roof. <Italian, from Latin *cupa* barrel>

cur (kər) *n* **1** a dog considered to be undesirable or of poor quality. **2** a person to be despised. <perhaps Old Norse *kurr* grumbling>

cur·a·ble (kyū′rə bəl) *adj* that can be cured.
cur′a·bil′i·ty *n.* **cur′a·bly** *adv.*

cu·rate (kyū′rət) *Christianity n* a member of the clergy who assists the pastor, rector, or vicar. <Latin *cura* care>

cur·a·tive (kyū′rə tiv) *adj* helping to cure: *the curative power of some herbs.*
n a means of curing.

cu·ra·tor (kyə rā′tər) *or* (kyůr′ā tər) *n* the person in charge of a museum, gallery, or collection. <See CURATE.>

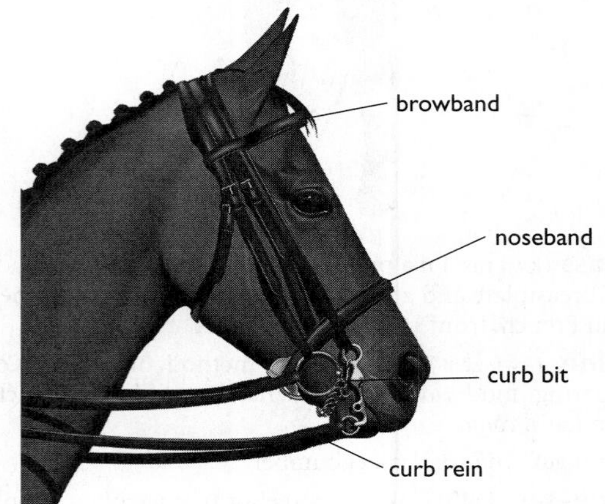

curb (kərb) *n* **1** a raised concrete border along the edge of a street or driveway. **2** a chain or strap fastened to a horse's bit and passing under its lower jaw that, when pulled tight, keeps the horse under control. **3** something that restrains or keeps under control: *Having no money really acts as a curb on spending!*
v **1** control or restrain: *Curb your anger.* **2** provide with a curb. <Old French, from Latin *curvus* bent>

curd (kərd) *n* **1** the thick part of milk that separates from the watery part (the **whey**) when milk sours. **2** a single blob of this. **3** a food with a similar consistency: *bean curd.* <Middle English>

cur·dle (kər′dəl) *v* **cur·dled, cur·dling 1** separate into soft blobs in the process of souring: *You left the milk out last night and it's already starting to curdle.* **2** thicken.
curdle the blood, horrify; terrify.

cure (kyūr) *v* **cured, cur·ing 1** bring back to health or to a sound or proper condition: *The sick child was soon cured. The punishment was meant to cure her of lying.* **2** get rid of: *to cure a cold, to cure a bad habit.* **3** preserve meat or fish by smoking, drying, or salting it. **4** prepare for use by a chemical or physical process: *to cure leather.*
n **1** the act or process of curing or treating: *medication for the cure of eye infections. Her cure took many months.* **2** a treatment or remedy that permanently gets rid of a disease or corrects a situation: *Researchers are seeking a cure for cancer. Wage cuts are not a cure for inflation.* <Old French, from Latin *cura* care> **cure′less** *adj.*

cure–all (kyůr′ol′) *n* a remedy supposed to cure any disease or evil.

curling

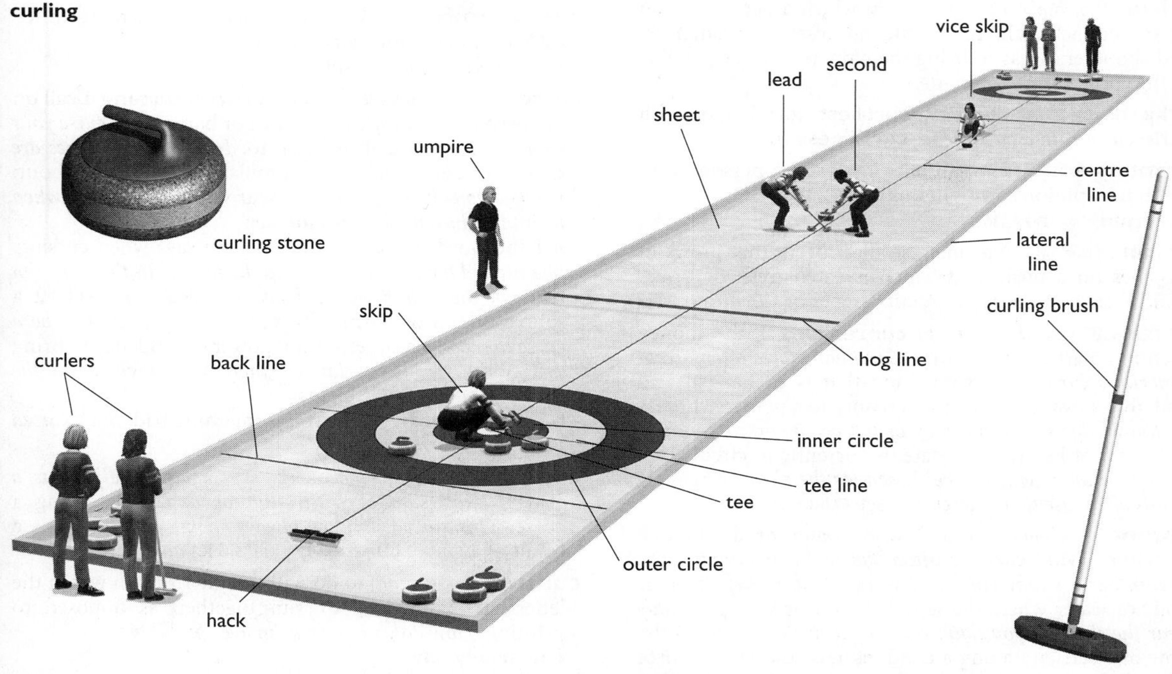

cur·few (kər′fyū) *n* **1** a time by which one is required to be home at night, imposed by others: *My curfew is 11 p.m.* **2** a law forbidding people to be on the streets after a certain hour. **3** a signal, such as a bell or whistle, given to mark a curfew. <Old French *covrir* cover + *feu* fire. In the Middle Ages, a bell would ring to signal that it was time to put out lights and cover fires for the night.>

cu·rie (kyů′rē) *or* (kyə rē′) *n* a unit for measuring radioactivity, equal to 37 gigabecquerels. *Symbol* **Ci** <P. *Curie*, 19c physicist and chemist>

cu·ri·o (kyů′rē ō′) *n* a rare, unusual, or interesting object, usually small: *Their living room was full of curios from their travels overseas.* <*curiosity*>

cu·ri·os·i·ty (kyů′rē os′ə tē) *n, pl* **cu·ri·os·i·ties 1** an eager desire to know: *Her curiosity made her rip open the package.* **2** a strange, rare, or unusual thing.

cu·ri·ous (kyů′rē əs) *adj* **1** eager to know or learn something: *a curious student.* **2** strange, odd, or unusual: *curious notions, a curious old book.* <Old French, from Latin *cura* care> **cu′ri·ous·ly** *adv.* **cu′ri·ous·ness** *n.*

cu·ri·um (kyů′rē əm) *n* an element made by the bombardment of plutonium and uranium by helium ions. *Symbol* **Cm** <M. *Curie*, 20c scientist>

curl (kərl) *v* **1** form into rolls, coils, or spirals: *to curl your hair. The dying leaves began to curl.* **2** form into a curve or twist: *Her lip curled in a sneer.* **3** move in spirals, curves, or twists: *Smoke curled slowly from the chimney.* **4** play the game of curling. **5** lift a weight in a weight-training exercise by using only the hands, wrists, and forearms.
n **1** a curled lock of hair. **2** something shaped like this: *a curl of birchbark.* **3** curliness: *His hair has lost its curl.* **4** a weight-training exercise using only the hands, wrists, and forearms. <Dutch *krul* curly>
curl up, a roll automatically into a tight curl or ball: *Some bugs curl up when you touch them. The paper curled up as it burned.* **b** take a comfortable position sitting or lying down with one's knees drawn up: *She curled up in the big chair and went to sleep.*
make your hair curl, be shocking or horrifying.

curl·er (kər′lər) *n* **1** a device around which hair is twisted to make it curl. **2** a person who plays the game of curling.

cur·lew (kər′lū) *n* a wading bird with a long, thin bill that has a distinctive two-note call. <Old French *courlieu*, imitative of its cry>

curl·i·cue (kər′lē kyū′) *n* a fancy twist, curl, or flourish: *Her handwriting is full of curlicues.* <*curly* + *cue*>

curl·ing (kər′ling) *n* a game played on ice, in which players slide heavy, round, polished stones fitted with a handle toward a marked circle at the end of the rink.

curling iron *n* an instrument for curling hair. It has a metal rod that heats up, around which the user winds one lock of hair at a time.

curling stone or **rock** *n* the object, usually made of polished granite and fitted with a handle, that is slid down the ice in the game of curling.

a bat	e bed	i bid	o pot	u cup	th thin
ā cake	ē me	ī bite	ō go	ū rude	ᴛʜ then
à bar	ə about	ər over	ȯ for	ů put	zh measure

curl–up (kərl′up′) *n* an exercise in which a person lies on his or her back with knees bent, and raises the head, neck, and shoulders so as to bring the chin as close as possible to the chest. Compare SIT-UP.

curl·y (kər′lē) *adj* **curl·i·er, curl·i·est** forming or with curls: *curly hair, a curly head.* **curl′i·ness** *n.*

cur·mudg·eon (kər muj′ən) *n* a rude person with stubborn opinions. <origin unknown>
cur·mudg′eon·ly *adj.*

cur·rant (kər′ənt) *n* a small, seedless berry that grows in bunches on a bush, and which is eaten fresh or dried. <Old French *raysons of Corauntz* grapes of Corinth>

cur·ren·cy (kər′ən sē) *n, pl* **cur·ren·cies 1** the money used in a particular country: *Canadian stores often accept American currency.* **2** something that is exchanged and that gives power, status, or acceptance to a person who has it: *Knowledge is the currency of the academic community.* **3** the fact of being up-to-date or currently in circulation: *Topics for the magazine are chosen for their currency. Slang words often lose their currency.* <See CURRENT.>

cur·rent (kər′ənt) *n* **1** a flow of water or air in one direction: *Wind currents affect the flight of aircraft. The stream has a strong current.* **2** the part of a river or other body of water where the flow is fastest or strongest: *Stay near the shore so you don't get caught in the current.* **3** the flow of electricity along a conductor, or the rate or force of such flow: *Heating requires more current than lighting.*
adj **1** happening or in effect now: *current prices, your current address.* **2** most recent: *the current issue of a magazine.* **3** being used, talked about, or circulated by people in general: *A rumour is current that we are getting a substitute teacher for the next two weeks. Many slang expressions of the 1980s are no longer current.* <Old French, from Latin *currere* run> **cur′rent·ly** *adv.*

current events *n* **1** (*with plural verb*) newsworthy things presently going on in the world: *Current events have necessitated postponement of the awards ceremony.* **2** (*with singular verb*) a subject in school during which students report on current events and discuss them: *I think current events is my favourite subject.*

cur·ric·u·lum (kə rik′yə ləm) *n, pl* **cur·ric·u·lums** or **cur·ric·u·la** (kə rik′yə lə) **1** the range of studies offered in a school or college, or at a certain level: *the university curriculum. Our school curriculum includes English as well as an Aboriginal language.* **2** the prescribed content of a course of study, or a document outlining it: *The government has issued a new math curriculum.* <Latin = racecourse (and so a course of study), from *currere* run>
cur·ric′u·lar *adj.*

curriculum vi·tae (vī′tē) *n* a summary of one's education, jobs held, special skills, and distinctions earned. It often accompanies a job application. *Abbrev.* **c.v.**

cur·ry[1] (kər′ē) *v* **cur·ried, cur·ry·ing** rub and clean a horse with a brush or currycomb. <Old French *correier* tidy up>
curry favour, seek favour by flattery or grovelling.

cur·ry[2] (kər′ē) *n, pl* **cur·ries 1** a hot-tasting sauce or powder containing a mixture of spices. **2** a dish flavoured with curry.
v **cur·ried, cur·ry·ing** prepare or flavour with curry: *curried rice, curried lamb.* <Tamil *kari*>

cur·ry·comb (kər′ē kōm′) *n* a brush with metal teeth for rubbing and cleaning a horse.
v brush with a currycomb.

curse (kərs) *v* **cursed** or (*Poetic*) **curst, curs·ing 1** call on a supernatural being to bring evil or harm to: *to curse your enemies.* **2** bring evil or harm to: *In folk tales, heroes are sometimes cursed by gods.* **3** complain bitterly at or about: *to curse your bad luck.* **4** use swear words: *He cursed when he hit his thumb with the hammer.*
n **1** the word or words that a person says when cursing: *She uttered a curse and hung up the phone. In the story I'm reading, the villain had a book of curses and spells.* **2** a source of evil or harm: *The stolen money proved to be a curse to them.* **3** a supernatural power or tendency to bring evil or harm: *They claimed there was a curse on the diamond.* <Old English *curs*>
be cursed with, suffer from something bad: *She's cursed with a fierce temper.*

curs·ed (kər′sid) *for def. 1,* (kərst) *for def. 2. adj* **1** (*as a general expression of frustration or anger*) deserving a curse: *This cursed window always sticks!* **2** suffering as a result of a curse. **curs′ed·ly** (kər′sid lē) *adv.*

cur·sive (kər′siv) *adj* to do with handwriting in which the letters are connected or run together, as opposed to printing: *How do you make a cursive capital N?*
cur′sive·ly *adv.*

ETYMOLOGY

Cursive comes from Medieval Latin *cursiva* from Latin *currere curs*, meaning "run." The idea is of *writing with a running hand*, that is, without raising the pen from the paper. The word was first used in the late 1700s.

cur·sor (kər′sər) *Computers n* a mark on the video display that indicates where the next character will be placed.

cur·so·ri·al (kər sȯ′rē əl) *Zoology adj* having legs used for running: *The ostrich is a cursorial bird.*

cur·so·ry (kər′sə rē) *adj* hasty and superficial: *Even a cursory reading of the book report showed many errors.* **cur′so·ri·ly** *adv.*

curt (kərt) *adj* speaking or spoken so briefly as to be rude; abrupt: *Her curt answer made him angry.* <Latin *curtus* cut short> **curt′ly** *adv.* **curt′ness** *n.*

cur·tail (kər tāl′) *v* reduce in extent or quantity: *to curtail someone's freedom. We must curtail the discussion for lack of time.* <French, from Latin *curtus* cut short>
cur·tail′ment *n.*

SYNONYMS

Curtail means "decrease": *Mom has curtailed the amount of television we may watch each day.*

Abbreviate means "make briefer": *I abbreviated my explanation when I saw he was losing interest.*

Cease means "come to an end": *The rain finally ceased, but it was too wet to play baseball.*

C

cur·tain (kər′tən) *n* **1** a piece of cloth or other similar material hung over a window or doorway to decorate, separate, hide, or darken. **2** *Theatre* **a** a movable hanging screen or drapery that, when closed, hides most of the stage from the audience. **b** the opening of the curtain at the beginning of an act or scene, or the closing of the curtain at the end. **3** something that hides or acts as a barrier: *a curtain of mist.* **4 curtains** *pl Slang* death or doom: *If I don't get this done in time, it's curtains for me!*
v **1** provide with a curtain: *We have yet to curtain the bedroom window.* **2** hide or cover with or as if with a curtain: *Fog curtained the city.* <Old French, from Latin *cortina* court>
curtain off, separate or partition with a curtain
lower (**raise**) **the curtain on,** end (begin): *Let's lower the curtain on the discussion. It's time to raise the curtain on the debate.*

curtain call *n* a call for a performer or performers to return to the stage and acknowledge the applause.

curt·sy (kərt′sē) *n, pl* **curt·sies** a formal bow of respect or greeting by women, made by bending the knees and lowering the body slightly.
v **curt·sied, curt·sy·ing** make a curtsy. <*courtesy*>

cur·va·ceous (kər vā′shəs) *adj* of a girl or woman, with an attractive, well-developed figure. <from *curve*>

cur·va·ture (kər′və chər) *n* the fact or condition of being curved: *the curvature of the earth's surface, abnormal curvature of the spine.*

curve (kərv) *n* **1** a line that has no straight part. **2** a thing or part in the shape of a curve: *I had to slow down for the curves in the road.* **3** a line on a graph, usually representing statistical data: *the cost-of-living curve, a bell curve.* **4** *Baseball* a ball pitched with a spin that causes it to swerve just before it reaches the batter. Also, **curveball. 5** *Mathematics* a line, straight or curved, whose path can be defined by an equation.
v **curved, curv·ing** bend or extend so as to form a curve: *The highway curves north just outside our town. A stone walkway curved up to the door.* <Latin *curvus* bent> **curv′y** *adj.*
grade on a curve, assign marks on a relative basis, so that a consistent proportion of people get a certain grade.
throw someone a curve, *Informal* do or say something surprising and unexpected.

cur·vi·lin·e·ar (kər′və lin′ē ər) *adj* to do with a curved line or lines.

cush·ion (kůsh′ən) *n* **1** a soft pillow or pad to sit, lie, or kneel on. **2** something used or shaped like a cushion, such as a layer of air supporting a hovercraft. **3** something that makes for greater comfort or lessens the effect of hardship: *a cushion of savings against long-term illness.* **4** the padded lining of the sides of a billiard table. **5** 🍁 the enclosed ice surface, especially an outdoor one, on which hockey is played.
v **1** soften or lessen a blow, impact, or shock: *The snowbank cushioned his fall.* **2** support or protect as if with a cushion. *Nothing could cushion my disappointment when our team lost.* <Old French, from Latin *coxa* hip, thigh> **cush′ion·like′** *adj.*

cush·y (kůsh′ē) *Informal adj* **cush·i·er, cush·i·est** extremely comfortable: *a cushy job, a cushy life.* <Urdu, from Persian *kus* pleasure>

cusk (kusk) *n* a large food fish of the N Atlantic, related to the cod.

cusp (kusp) *n* **1** a pointed end where two curves meet: *A crescent has two cusps.* **2** a point or raised blunt part at the top of a tooth. <Latin *cuspis* point>
on the cusp of, about to experience: *on the cusp of fame.*

cus·pid (kus′pid) *n* a tooth with one cusp.

cus·pi·dor (kus′pə dȯr′) *n* a container to spit into. <Portuguese = spitter, from Latin *conspuere* to spit>

cuss (kus) *Informal v* curse: *Quit your cussing.*
n **1** an odd or troublesome person or animal: *Tell that cuss to get over here now.* **2** a curse. <variant of *curse*>
cuss out, scold by using swear words.

cus·tard (kus′tərd) *n* a baked, boiled, or frozen dessert or sweet sauce made of eggs and milk. <Old French *crustado* pie (and so dessert), from Latin *crusta* crust>

custard apple *n* a large, dark brown fruit with soft, sweet pulp, that grows on a tropical American tree.

cus·to·di·an (kus tō′dē ən) *n* **1** the person in charge of a building; caretaker. **2** the person who looks after or is responsible for something: *the custodian of a museum.*

cus·to·dy (kus′tə dē) *n* **1** protective care of someone or something: *Young children must be in the custody of a guardian.* **2** imprisonment: *He was arrested and taken into custody.* <Latin *custos* guardian> **cus·to′di·al** *adj.*

cus·tom (kus′təm) *n* **1** a personal habit: *It was her custom to rise early.* **2** an established or traditional way of behaving in a certain community: *Different cultures have different customs.* **3 customs** *pl* **a** a duty paid to the government on imported goods. **b** the government department that collects this duty, or its station at a seaport, international airport, or border-crossing point. **4** a customer's regular business: *If you can't deliver, I'll take my custom elsewhere.*
adj to do with goods specially made to order for individual customers: *custom clothes, a custom tailor.* <Old French, from Latin *com-* altogether + *suescere* become accustomed>

GRAMMAR AND USAGE

Custom and **habit** have similar meanings but are used in different situations. A *custom* is a way of doing things that a person or a group of people always follows. A *habit* is something you do all the time without thinking.

cus·tom·ar·y (kus′tə mer′ē) *adj* following a custom or habit: *She sat in her customary place. It is customary to wait till everyone is seated before starting to eat.*
cus′to·mar′i·ly *adv.*

a bat	e bed	i bid	o pot	u cup	th **thin**
ā cake	ē me	ī bite	ō go	ū rude	TH **then**
ä bar	ə about	ər over	ȯ for	ů put	zh measure

cus·tom–built (kus′təm bilt′) *adj* built to order for individuals: *a custom-built games room.*

cus·tom·er (kus′tə mər) *n* **1** a person who buys goods or services. **2** *Informal* a person of a certain character: *Don't get mixed up with him, because he's a tough customer.*

cus·tom·ize (kus′tə mīz′) *v* **cus·tom·ized, cus·tom·iz·ing** make or change according to individual requirements: *to customize a van.*

cus·tom–made (kus′təm mād′) *adj* made specially for individuals: *These boots were custom-made for me.*

cut (kut) *v* **cut, cut·ting 1 a** open, remove part of, or divide with something sharp: *to cut meat, timber, grass, your nails, etc.* **b** be cut: *Very fresh bread does not cut well.* **2** make or shape by cutting: *to cut a hole in the wall, to cut stars out of gold foil. She cut her initials into the table.* **3** injure with something sharp: *I cut my finger on the broken glass.* **4 a** reduce: *to cut expenses. Cut your speech down to four minutes.* **b** remove or delete: *Cut that scene.* **5** divide by crossing: *A brook cuts the field in two.* **6** go by a more direct way: *Let's cut across the field to save time.* **7** change direction suddenly: *She cut to the right to avoid the oncoming car.* **8** hurt as if with something sharp: *The cold wind cut me to the bone. Their words cut her deeply.* **9** refuse to recognize socially: *They all cut the boy who kept lying.* **10** *Informal* stay away from without permission: *to cut class.* **11 a** dissolve: *This detergent cuts grease.* **b** dilute or be diluted by: *latex paint cut with water.* **12** in film or video, **a** switch suddenly to another scene. **b** stop filming briefly. **13** stop or take a break: *Let's cut for lunch.* **14** *Sports* hit with a slicing stroke.

n **1** an act of cutting or something cut. **2** a wound, notch, slit, or hole made by cutting. **3** a reduction: *a cut in free time.* **4** a piece of meat taken from a certain part of an animal's body: *We prefer to buy the leaner cuts.* **5** the style or shape of a garment: *I like the cut of those pants.* **6** a haircut. **7** a share: *Each partner has a cut of the profits.* <Middle English *cutten*>

a cut above, superior in quality to.

cut and dried, settled or arranged in advance.

cut and run, leave hastily.

cut and thrust, the give-and-take of vigorous debate.

cut back, a go back suddenly. **b** prune a plant. **c** reduce output or expenses.

cut both ways, a apply to both sides of a conflict: *That argument cuts both ways.* **b** have good and bad effects.

cut down, a cause to fall by cutting: *to cut down a tree.* **b** (*often with* ***on***) do or have less of: *to cut down expenses, to cut down on sweets.*

cut down to size, *Informal* humiliate.

cut in, a break in or interrupt: *to cut in with a remark.* **b** move suddenly into a line of moving traffic or waiting people. **c** interrupt a dancing couple to take the place of one of them. **d** use a knife or knives to work butter, shortening, or lard into a mixture.

cut it, *Informal* be good enough: *Her work just doesn't cut it.*

cut it fine, *Informal* leave oneself a very narrow margin for error, especially with regard to time: *You land at 2:15 and have to catch a train at 3? That's cutting it pretty fine!*

cut it out, *Informal* stop it.

cut off, a stop, block, or shut off: *The power was cut off for an hour.* **b** break or interrupt. **c** isolate: *to feel cut off from the world.* **d** force another driver to brake by suddenly driving in front of his or her vehicle. **e** permanently end a relationship; *I cut off my best friend after she lied to me.*

cut out, a delete or remove in editing. **b** stop doing, using, or making: *to cut out candy. Cut out the teasing.* **c** suddenly stop functioning: *The engine keeps cutting out.* **d** *Informal I was bored, so I cut out early from the party.*

cut out for, suited to: *I'm not cut out for a career as an actor.*

cut short, stop before the end.

cut teeth, have baby teeth grow through the gums.

cut up, a cut into small pieces. **b** *Informal* show off or be silly: *The father was annoyed because his daughter was cutting up.*

cut your teeth on, a learn, use, or be often exposed to something when very young: *Her family was musical, so she cut her teeth on Mozart and jazz.* **b** do as the first stage of a career: *He cut his teeth on TV sitcoms before moving on to movies.*

make the cut, *Informal* be one of a limited number selected for some purpose: *My poem didn't make the cut for the school year book.*

SYNONYMS

Cut can mean "slice with something sharp": *She cut the vegetables with a knife.*

Chisel means "cut using a specific tool with a bevelled edge." *He chiselled a face out of the piece of wood.*

Dissect means "cut," but is most often used in a scientific sense: *The students dissected frogs and studied the organs.*

cut–and–paste (kut′ən pāst′) *n* **1 a** a the process of cutting out shapes and pasting them on a background. **b** a piece of artwork made in this way. **2** *Computers* the act of removing data from one spot and placing it in another.

v **cut and paste, cut and pasted, cutting and pasting,** engage in any of these processes.

cu·ta·ne·ous (kyū tā′nē əs) *adj* to do with the skin. <Latin *cutis* skin>

cut·a·way (kut′ə wā′) *n* **1** a diagram or model of something, with part of the outside cut away to show its internal structure. **2** a man's formal coat with the lower part cut back from the waist in front to the tails in back.

adj to do with either of these.

cut·back (kut′bak′) *n* a reduction in output or expenses: *budget cutbacks, a cutback in production due to slow sales.*

cute (kyūt) *adj* **cut·er, cut·est 1** lovable: *a cute puppy, a cute baby.* **2** *Informal* good-looking: *cute guys.* **3** witty, stylish, or clever in a self-conscious and irritating way: *The play is full of cute dialogue.* <variant of *acute*>

cute′ly *adv.* **cute′ness** *n.*

cute·sy (kyūt′sē) *Slang adj* **cutesier, cutesiest** cute in an exaggerated or deliberate way: *I can't stand the cutesy little drawings in some kids' books.*

cut glass *n* glass shaped or decorated by cutting into it, then grinding and polishing.

cu·ti·cle (kyū′tə kəl) *n* **1** the strip of skin at the base of a fingernail or toenail. **2** the outer layer of skin of vertebrates. <Latin *cutis* skin>

cu·tie (kyū′tē) *Informal n* a cute person or thing.

cut·lass (kut′ləs) *n* a short, slightly curved sword with a single-edged blade. <French, from Latin *culter* knife>

cut·ler·y (kut′lə rē) *n* knives, forks, and spoons for table use. <Old French, from Latin *culter* knife>

cut·let (kut′lit) *n* a slice of meat for broiling or frying: *a veal cutlet.* <French *côtelette* little rib, from Latin *costa* rib>

cut·off (kut′of′) *n* **1** the limit set for something, such as an activity. **2** an exit ramp from a highway: *Take the Main St. cutoff.* **3 cutoffs** *pl* shorts made by cutting off the legs of pants and not hemming them. **4** the act of cutting off a process, or a mechanism that does this. **5** *Baseball* the interception by an infielder of a throw to home plate from the outfield.
adj **1** to do with a limit: *the cutoff date.* **2** cutting off a flow or process: *cutoff controls.* **3** isolated or without access: *cutoff climbers.* Also, **cut-off.**

cut·out (kut′out′) *n* **1** a shape or design that has been cut out or is to be cut out. **2** a device that allows the exhaust gases of an internal combustion engine to pass straight into the air instead of going through a muffler. **3** a device for breaking an electric current.
adj to do with a cutout. Also, **cut-out.**

cut–rate (kut′rāt′) *adj* extremely inexpensive and often of low quality.

cut·ter (kut′ər) *n* **1** a person who or tool that cuts: *a paper cutter.* **2** a horse-drawn sleigh. **3** a light, fast, coastal patrol boat: *a coastguard cutter.*

cut·throat (kut′thrōt′) *adj* **1** murderous or bloodthirsty. **2** fierce and merciless: *cutthroat competition.*
n a cutthroat person.

cut·ting (kut′ing) *n* **1** a small shoot cut from a plant to grow a new plant. **2** a newspaper or magazine clipping. **3** a place or way cut through high ground for a road or track.
adj **1** that cuts: *the cutting edge of a knife.* **2** that hurts the feelings: *a cutting remark.* **cut′ting·ly** *adv.*

cutting edge *n* **1** the most recent or adventurous developments in some field: *on the cutting edge of computer technology.* **2** the most effective part: *The drummer is the cutting edge of that band.*
cut′ting-edge′ *adj.*

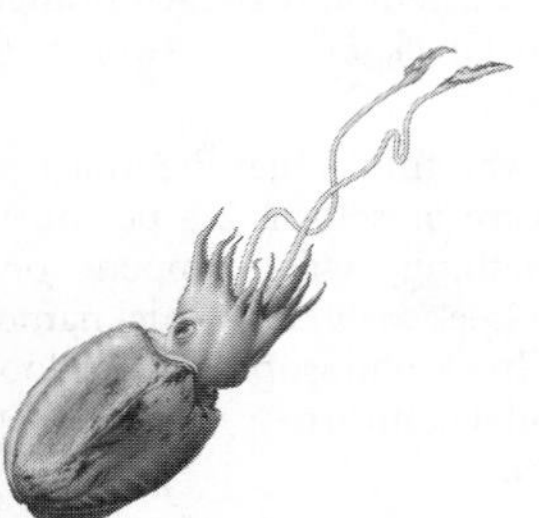

Cuttlefish, closely related to the squid, range in size from about 15 to 25 cm, have flattened bodies, and arms that are arranged in pairs around the mouth. When frightened, they eject a black, inky liquid.

cut·tle·fish (kut′əl fish′) *n, pl* **cut·tle·fish·es** or (*especially collectively*) **cut·tle·fish** a saltwater mollusc with ten sucker-bearing arms and a hard internal shell. <Old English *cudele*>

cut·up (kut′up′) *Informal n* **1** a person who behaves like a clown. **2** something funny done by such a person. Also, **cut-up.**

cut·worm (kut′wərm′) *n* a moth caterpillar that feeds on the stalks of young plants, cutting them off near or below the surface of the ground.

C

c.v. curriculum vitae.

–cy *suffix* **1** rank or status: *captaincy.* **2** state or condition: *infancy, bankruptcy.*

cy·an (sī an′) *adj* greenish blue. <Greek *kyaneos* dark blue>

cy·a·nide (sī′ə nīd′) *n* in full, **potassium cyanide** an extremely poisonous white crystalline salt.

cy·a·no·bac·te·ria (sī′ə nō bak tē′rē ə) *pl n, sing* **cy·a·no·bac·te·ri·um** (sī′ə nō bak tē′rē əm) bacteria that contain chlorophyll and produce their own food through photosynthesis.

cyber– *combining form* **1** to do with computers: *cybercafé.* **2** existing in cyberspace: *cybersex.* <*cybernetics*>

GRAMMAR AND USAGE

Words beginning with **cyber–** all have to do with computers or the Internet: *cyberspace, cyberart.*

cy·ber·bul·ly (sī′bər bū′lē) *Computers v* **cy·ber·bul·lied, cy·ber·bul·ly·ing** make demands and threats by computer, text messaging, cellphone, etc. in order to intimidate someone.
n a person who does this. **cy′ber·bul′ly·ing** *n.*

cy·ber·ca·fé (sī′bər ka fā′) *Computers n* a coffee shop with computers so customers can use the Internet while eating or drinking.

cy·ber·net·ics (sī′bər net′iks) *n* (*with singular verb*) the science that compares communication and control mechanisms in living organisms and in machines. <Greek *kybernan* to control>

cy·ber·sex (sī′bər seks′) *Computers n* explicit sexual conversation carried out online.

cy·ber·space (sī′bər spās′) *Computers n* the Internet, especially when thought of as an environment in which things may exist that have no existence in the real world: *When you shop in cyberspace, you don't need to get dressed!*

cy·ber·ter·ror·ism (sī′bər ter′ə riz′əm) *Computers n* the use of computers to terrorize a society by causing chaos in institutions, destroying national security, or sabotaging communication. Also, **cyberterror. cy′ber·ter′ror·ist** *n.*

cy·borg (sī′borg) *Science fiction n* a person or animal whose bodily functions are extended to an extraordinary level by electronic parts. <*cyber-* + *org*(*anism*)>

cy·cla·men (sī′klə mən) *n* a plant of the primrose family with heart-shaped leaves and showy flowers whose five petals bend backwards. <Latin, from Greek *kyklaminos*>

a bat	e bed	i bid	o pot	u cup	th thin
ā cake	ē me	ī bite	ō go	ū rude	ᴛʜ then
ä bar	ə about	ər over	ô for	ů put	zh measure

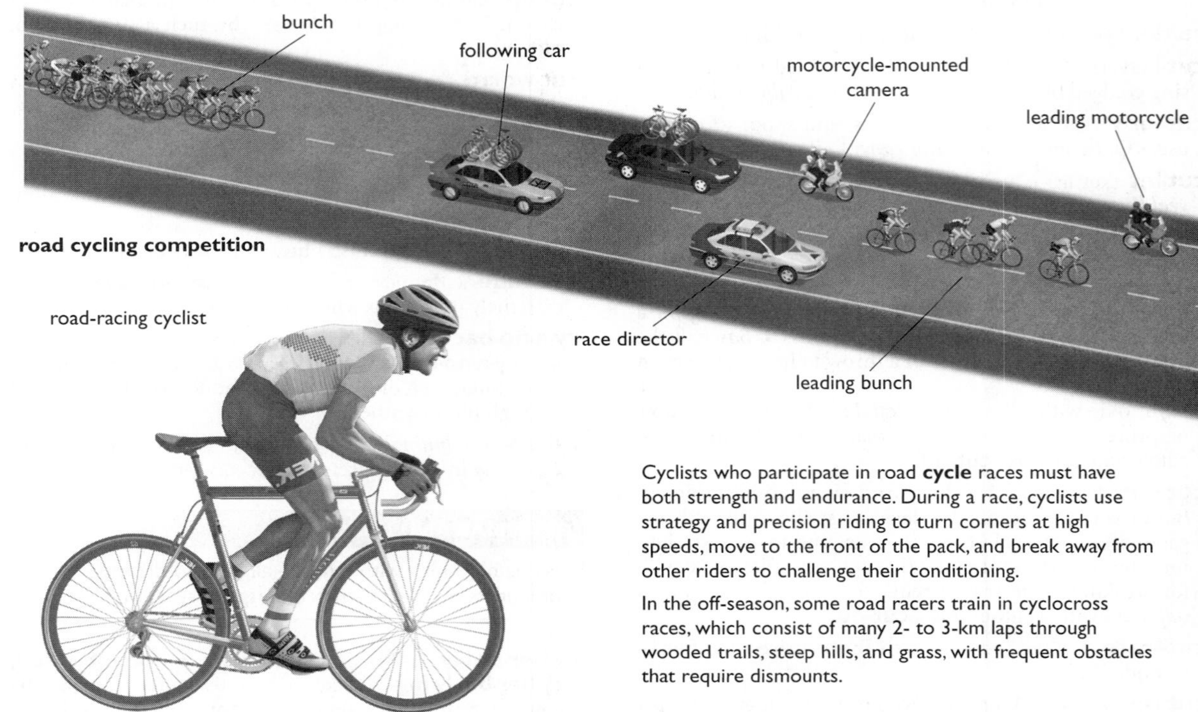

Cyclists who participate in road **cycle** races must have both strength and endurance. During a race, cyclists use strategy and precision riding to turn corners at high speeds, move to the front of the pack, and break away from other riders to challenge their conditioning.

In the off-season, some road racers train in cyclocross races, which consist of many 2- to 3-km laps through wooded trails, steep hills, and grass, with frequent obstacles that require dismounts.

cy·cle (sī′kəl) *n* **1** a complete process of development, movement, or action that repeats itself: *the cycle of the seasons, the life cycle of an organism.* **2** *Physics* one complete or double reversal of an alternating electric current, or one complete sound vibration. Frequency is measured in **cycles per second**. **3** *Astronomy* one full revolution in orbit. **4** a complete set or series, especially all the novels, stories, or poems on some topic: *the Harry Potter cycle.* **5** a bicycle, tricycle, unicycle, or motorcycle.
v **cy·cled, cy·cling 1** pass through a cycle; occur again and again in the same order. **2** ride a cycle, especially a bicycle. <Old French, from Greek *kyklos* wheel> **cyc′li·cal** (sik′lə kəl) or **cyc′lic** *adj.* **cyc′ling** *n.* **cyc′list** *n.*

cy·clone (sī′klōn) *n* **1** a severe windstorm resulting from a condition of low pressure, with winds moving in a spiral toward the centre where the air pressure is lowest. **2** a low-pressure weather system that can produce such storms. Compare ANTICYCLONE. **3** a violent windstorm with spiralling winds, such as a tornado. <probably Greek *kyklos* circle> **cy·clon′ic** (sī klon′ik) *adj.*

cy·clo·ram·a (sī′klə ram′ə) *n* **1** a large mural on the wall of a circular room. **2** *Theatre* a curved screen providing a background to a scene. <*cycle* + Greek *horama* spectacle>

cy·clo·tron (sī′klə tron′) *Physics n* a type of particle accelerator that accelerates the charged particles to very high speeds, used to cause changes in atomic nuclei. <*cycle* + (*elec*)*tron*>

cyg·net (sig′nit) *n* a young swan. <Old French, from Greek *kyknos* swan>

cyl·in·der (sil′ən dər) *n* **1** *Mathematics* a solid bounded by two equal, parallel circles and a curved surface. **2** a long, round object, solid or hollow, with flat or open ends, such as a tin can, or a mailer for a poster. **3** the part of a revolver that contains chambers for cartridges. **4** the piston chamber of an engine. <Old French, from Greek *kylindros* roller> **cy·lin′dri·cal** *adj.*

cym·bal (sim′bəl) *n* a slightly concave metal plate used as a musical instrument. Cymbals are struck together to make a ringing sound; a single cymbal may be struck with a drumstick or wire brush. See PERCUSSION INSTRUMENT for picture. <Latin, from Greek *kymbe* the hollow part of a bowl>

cyme (sīm) *Botany n* a flower cluster in which there is a flower at the top of the main stem and at each branch of the cluster. <French, from Greek *kyein* be swollen (i.e., sprout)>

cyn·ic (sin′ik) *n* **1** a person who thinks that the motives for people's actions are insincere or selfish. **2** a person who questions whether something will happen or is worthwhile. <Latin, from Greek *kyon* dog, a nickname for a member of a group of Greek philosophers who looked down on wealth and personal comfort>
cyn′i·cal *adj.* **cyn′i·cism** *n.*

cy·press (sī′prəs) *n* an evergreen tree of N America, Europe, and Asia, with round, upright cones. <Old French, from Greek *kyparissos*>

Cy·prus (sī′prəs) *n* an island country in the Mediterranean Sea. **Cyp′ri·ot** (sip′rē ət) *adj, n.*

Cy·ril·lic (si ril′ik) *adj* to do with the Slavic alphabet used for Russian, Ukrainian, and some other languages.

ETYMOLOGY

Cyrillic comes from St. *Cyril*, an apostle to the Slavs in the 800s, who is traditionally supposed to have invented the Cyrillic alphabet.

cyst (sist) *n* **1** an abnormal, bubblelike growth in plants or animals, including humans, usually containing fluid and with no opening to the outside of the body. **2** a saclike structure in animals or plants. <Latin, from Greek *kystis* bladder> **cys′tic** *adj.*

cys·tic fib·ro·sis (fi brō′sis) *n* a disease of some children, present from birth, causing frequent respiratory infections and malfunction of the pancreas.

–cyte *combining form* mature cell: *lymphocyte.* <Greek *kytos* anything hollow>

cy·tol·o·gy (sī tol′ə jē) *n* the branch of biology that deals with the formation, structure, and function of cells. <See –CYTE.> **cy·tol′o·gist** *n.*

cy·to·plasm (sī′tə plaz′əm) *n* the living substance or protoplasm of a cell, apart from the nucleus. <Greek *kytos* hollow thing + *plasma* something formed or moulded> **cy′to·plas′mic** *adj.*

czar (zär) *n* **1** the title of the former emperors of Russia. **2** a person with great power: *a czar of crime.* Also, **tsar**. <Russian, from Latin *Caesar* Emperor>

cza·ri·na (zä rē′nə) *n* a Russian empress. Also, **tsarina**.

czar·ist (zär′ist) *adj* to do with or supporting the Russian czars or their regime.

n a supporter of the government of the czars in Russia. Also, **tsarist**.

Czech Republic (chek) *n* a country in central Europe, part of the former Czechoslovakia. See the APPENDIX. **Czech** *adj, n.*

C

Dd

d or **D** (dē) *n, pl* **d's** or **D's** **1** the fourth letter of the English alphabet, or any speech sound represented by it. **2** the fourth thing in a list or series. **3** *Music* the second tone in the scale of C major, or a key based on a scale with D as its keynote. **4** in school, a grade meaning below average and barely acceptable. **5** **D** the Roman numeral for 500.

dab (dab) *v* **dabbed, dab·bing** **1** (*used with* ***at***) pat with something soft or moist in order to wipe away, spread, or apply something: *He dabbed at the spot with a napkin.* **2** apply with light, short strokes: *She dabbed a bit of ointment on the bee sting.*
n **1** a small, soft or moist mass: *a dab of butter.* **2** an act of dabbing. <Middle English> **dab′ber** *n.*

dab·ble (dab′əl) *v* **dab·bled, dab·bling** **1** dip one's hands or feet into water and splash lightly. **2** do something in a casual, superficial way: *to dabble at painting, to dabble in the stock market.* <Dutch *dabbelen*> **dab′bler** *n.*

da ca·po (də kap′ō) *Music adv* from the beginning, a direction to repeat a passage. *Abbrev.* **D.C.** or **d.c.** <Italian = from the head>

dachs·hund (dash′hůnd) *n* a breed of small dog with a long body, drooping ears, and very short legs. <German *Dachs* badger + *Hund* dog. It was first bred to hunt badgers.>

dac·tyl (dak′til) *Poetry n* a metrical foot made up of one strongly stressed syllable followed by two weakly stressed ones. Example: *Take′ her′ up′ ten′der′ly′.* Compare ANAPEST. <Latin, from Greek *daktylos* finger, a comparison of the three joints of the finger to the three syllables> **dac·tyl′ic** *adj.*

dad (dad) *Informal n* a father. Also (*especially among young children*), **daddy**. <baby talk>

dad·dy–long·legs (dad′ē long′legz′) *n* a small animal related to the spider, with a rounded body and eight very long, thin, bent legs.

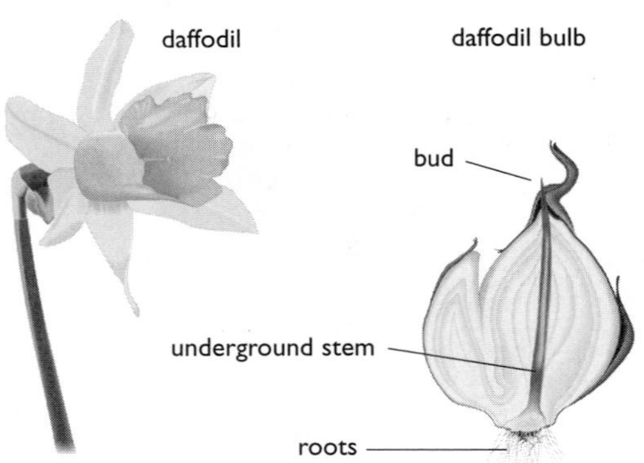

daf·fo·dil (daf′ə dil′) *n* a plant that grows from a bulb and has a flower with a trumpet-shaped corona growing out from the centre of its petals. <Latin, from Greek *asphodelos*>

daft (daft) *adj* silly or crazy. <Old English *gedæfte* gentle, foolish> **daft′ly** *adv.* **daft′ness** *n.*

SYNONYMS

Daft suggests not making sense: *He came up with a daft scheme to earn money that would never work.*

Ridiculous means "inviting mockery": *They laughed at her ridiculous attempts to keep her cap on in the wind.*

Silly means "foolish": *It was a silly idea for us to go swimming with our clothes on, because we had to walk home soaking wet.*

dag·ger (dag′ər) *n* **1** a small weapon with a short, pointed blade. **2** *Printing* a sign [†] referring the reader to a footnote or a note at the end of an essay or book. <Middle English from earlier *dag* stab>
look daggers at, look at with hatred or anger.

dahl·ia (dāl′yə) *or* (dal′yə) *n* a tall perennial plant with large, bright flowers that blooms in late summer and fall. <A. *Dahl*, 18c botanist>

dai·ly (dā′lē) *adv* every day, or every day except weekends: *His health is improving daily. The mail arrives daily at 11:00.*
adj done, happening, or appearing every day, or every day except weekends or Sundays: *a daily visit, a daily report.*
n, pl **dai·lies** a newspaper published every day, or every day except weekends or Sundays.

dain·ty (dān′tē) *adj* **dain·ti·er, dain·ti·est** **1** small or fine, pretty, and graceful: *a dainty flower, dainty lace curtains.* **2** prim or fussy: *taking dainty sips from her teacup.* **3** attractive and delicious: *dainty snacks.*
n, pl **dain·ties** a delicious and attractive-looking treat. <Old French *deinte*, from Latin *dignitas* beauty> **dain′ti·ly** *adv.* **dain′ti·ness** *n.*

dai·qui·ri (dak′ə rē) *n* a cocktail made from rum, lime juice, and sugar. <*Daiquiri*, Cuba>

dair·y (der′ē) *n, pl* **dair·ies** **1** a business that processes and sells milk and milk products. **2** a place where milk and cream are kept and made into butter and cheese. **3** milk products: *I can't eat dairy.*
adj **1** to do with milk and milk products: *dairy foods.* **2** producing milk or milk products: *dairy cattle, a dairy farm.* <Old English *dæge* = kneader of dough>

da·is (dā′is) *n* a raised platform at one end of a hall or large room, such as for a throne, seats of honour, or a podium or lectern. <Old French, from Latin *discus* little table>

dai·sy (dā′zē) *n, pl* **dai·sies** a plant with a tall, leafy stem and a flower with a yellow centre surrounded by petal-like flowers. <Old English *dæges eage* = day's eye. The ray flowers around the central disc resemble eyelashes around an eye, and they close up at night> **dai′sy·like′** *adj.*

Da·ko·ta (də kō′tə) *n, pl* **Da·ko·ta** or **Da·ko·tas**
1 a member of a First Nations or Native American people living on the plains of southern Canada and the northern US. **2** the language of these people.
adj to do with these people or their language. Also called **Lakota, Sioux**.

hydroelectric complex

D

dal (dȧl) *n* a dried, split legume, especially the lentil, used in Indian cooking. Also, **dhal**. <Hindi *daal*>

Da·lai La·ma (dȧ′lī lȧ′mə) *n* the spiritual leader of Tibetan Buddhism and, until the establishment of Chinese communist rule, the religious and temporal ruler of Tibet.

dale (dāl) *Poetic n* a valley. <Old English *dæl*>

dal·li·ance (dal′ē əns) *n* the action of taking part in a casual romantic relationship.

Dall sheep (dol) *n* a white sheep of the western Rockies, found from northern British Columbia to the Arctic Ocean. Also, **Dall's sheep**. <W.H. *Dall*, 20c naturalist>

dal·ly (dal′ē) *v* **dal·lied, dal·ly·ing** 1 move slowly, especially in wasting time: *He was late for school because he dallied along the way.* 2 have a casual romantic relationship. 3 be casually interested in something: *I dallied with the idea of joining the school band.* <Old French *dalier* chat>

Dal·ma·tian (dal mā′shən) *n* a breed of medium-sized, short-haired dog, usually white with black spots. <*Dalmatia*, a region in Croatia>

dam[1] (dam) *n* 1 a wall built to hold back flowing water. 2 the water held back by a dam: *They used to go swimming in the dam.* 3 something resembling a dam, such as a beaver lodge or a barrier to a flow.
v **dammed, dam·ming** 1 hold back by means of a dam: *Beavers have dammed the stream.* 2 hold back or block: *He tried to dam up his tears.* <Dutch>

dam[2] (dam) *n* the female parent of a four-footed animal, especially a domestic animal. <variant of *dame*>

dam·age (dam′ij) *v* **dam·aged, dam·ag·ing** harm something in a way that makes it less valuable, beautiful, or useful: *to damage a work of art. His habit of lying damaged his reputation.*
n 1 harm that lessens value, beauty, or usefulness: *The building has suffered major flood damage.* 2 **damages** *pl* money claimed by law or paid to make up for harm done to a person or property: *The injured man asked for $50 000 damages.* <Old French, from Latin *damnum* loss, hurt>

dam·ask (dam′əsk) *n* linen, silk, or cotton cloth with designs woven into it, especially when used for tablecloths and napkins.
adj 1 made of damask. 2 *Poetic* rosy or pink: *damask cheeks.*

ETYMOLOGY

Damask is a Middle English word that comes from Latin *Damascus*. It came into use in the mid 1200s, meaning "cloth from Damascus" (a Syrian city famous at the time for its silk).

a bat	e bed	i bid	o pot	u cup	th thin
ā cake	ē me	ī bite	ō go	ū rude	ᴛʜ then
ȧ bar	ə about	ər over	ȯ for	u̇ put	zh measure

dame (dām) *n* **1** *Slang* a woman. **2 Dame** the title of a woman belonging to an order of knighthood. <Old French, from Latin *domina* mistress>

damn (dam) *v* **1** declare to be bad: *The critics damned the new movie.* **2** prove the guilt of: *damning evidence.* **3** send to eternal punishment. **4** curse someone.
n **1 a damn** *Slang* the least amount: *not worth a damn. They don't give a damn.* **2 the damned** the souls in hell.
interj Slang an exclamation of anger or frustration: *Damn! Missed again!*
adj Slang used to express anger or frustration: *The damn thing won't work.* Also, **damned**. <Old French, from Latin *damnum* loss, damage>
damn with faint praise, praise so half-heartedly as to condemn.

dam·na·ble (dam′nə bəl) *adj* detestable. **dam′na·bly** *adv.*

dam·na·tion (dam nā′shən) *n* **1** the act of damning or condemning. **2** eternal punishment.
interj an expression of annoyance.

damp (damp) *adj* slightly wet: *The basement is damp in winter.*
n **1** slight wetness: *I could feel the damp in the morning air.* **2** foul or explosive gas that collects in mines.
v **1** dampen. **2** *Music* stop a string from vibrating. <Middle English> **damp′ly** *adv.* **damp′ness** *n.*
damp down, slow the burning of a fire by reducing the air supply: *She damped down the fire for the night.*

damp·en (dam′pən) *v* **1** make slightly wet: *Dampen the shirt before ironing it.* **2** depress or discourage: *The bad news dampened our spirits.*

damp·er (dam′pər) *n* **1** a movable plate to control the flow of air in a stove or furnace. **2** a piano part that stops the vibration of strings.
put a damper on, make more subdued: *Her father's illness put a damper on the birthday celebrations.*

dam·sel (dam′zəl) *Archaic or Poetic n* a young unmarried woman. <Old French, from Latin *domina* mistress>

dance (dans) *v* **danced, danc·ing** **1** move the body in rhythm, usually to music. **2** do a particular form of dancing: *Can you dance the tango?* **3** move in a lively or graceful way: *leaves dancing in the wind, sailboats dancing on the water.* **4** lead someone by dancing: *He danced her across the gymnasium floor.*
n **1** a special set of rhythmic movements done to music: *a folk dance. The waltz is a ballroom dance.* **2** a party where people dance: *Are you going to the school dance?* **3** one round of dancing: *I'm going to sit out this dance.* **4** the art of moving in rhythm to music: *to take lessons in dance.* **5** a lively or graceful movement: *the dance of the waves.* <Old French> **danc′er** *n.*

danc·er·cise (dan′sər sīz′) *n, v* **danc·er·cised, danc·er·cis·ing** exercise in the form of dancing. <*dance* + *exercise*>

dan·de·lion (dan′dē lī′ən) *n* a plant with long, notched leaves growing out from the base and a bright yellow flower head. It is a common weed but is also grown for its edible leaves and flowers. <French, translation of Latin *dens leonis* lion's tooth, from the appearance of the flower's leaves>

dan·der (dan′dər) *n* allergy-causing fragments of an animal's skin or hair. <origin uncertain>
get your dander up, *Informal* get angry.

dan·dle (dan′dəl) *v* **dan·dled, dan·dling** move a child up and down on one's knees or in one's arms. <origin uncertain>

dan·druff (dan′drəf) *n* small scales or flakes of dead skin that fall off the scalp. <*dand-* origin uncertain + perhaps Middle English *rufe* scab>

dan·dy (dan′dē) *n, pl* **dan·dies** **1** *Informal* an excellent or remarkable thing: *That last question was a dandy.* **2** a man unduly concerned with dress and appearance.
adj **dan·di·er, dan·di·est** *Informal* (*often ironic*) excellent or first-rate: *Everything is just dandy.* <perhaps pet form of personal name *Andrew*> **dan′di·fy** (dan′də fī) *v.*

Dane (dān) *n* a native of Denmark, or a person of Danish descent.

dan·ger (dān′jər) *n* **1** a chance of harm: *A firefighter's life is full of danger.* **2** something that may cause harm: *Hidden rocks are a danger to ships.* <Old French *dangier* power to harm, from Latin *dominus* lord> **dan′ger·ous** *adj.* **dan′ger·ous·ly** *adv.*
in danger of, near to some harmful or unwanted event: *The bridge is in danger of collapse. You are in danger of failing math.*

dan·gle (dang′gəl) *v* **dan·gled, dan·gling** **1** hang and swing loosely: *a dangling curtain cord.* **2** hold or carry something so that it swings loosely: *She dangled the toy in front of the baby.* **3** hold up to a person as a temptation: *to dangle false hopes before a person.* <Scandinavian> **dan′gler** *n.*

dangling modifier MISPLACED MODIFIER.

dangling participle MISPLACED MODIFIER.

Dan·ish (dā′nish) *adj* See DENMARK.
n in full, **Danish pastry** a rich, flaky pastry, often with cream cheese or fruit in it.

dank (dangk) *adj* unpleasantly damp, cool, and musty: *a dark, dank cave.* <perhaps from Old Norse>

dap·per (dap′ər) *adj* neat and trim in dress or appearance. <probably Dutch = strong>

dap·ple (dap′əl) *v* **dap·pled, dap·pling** mark or become marked with spots or patches of colour: *Sunlight dappled the forest floor.*
adj usually, **dappled** spotted or mottled. <origin uncertain>

dare (der) *v* **dared, dar·ing** **1** have the necessary courage: *He doesn't dare dive from the bridge.* **2** face boldly: *She dared the dangers of the Arctic.* **3** urge someone to do something risky: *I dare you to jump across the stream.*
n a suggestion to do something risky: *She took the dare and jumped across the stream.* <Old English *durran*>
I dare say, I would imagine: *I dare say he can outrun eveyone in the class.*

dare·dev·il (der′dev′əl) *n* a recklessly adventurous person.
adj reckless or very risky: *a daredevil stunt.*

dar·ing (der′ing) *n* the willingness to take risks: *She was known for her daring.*
adj involving or enjoying risk: *a daring move, a daring criminal.* **dar′ing·ly** *adv.*

dark (dȧrk) *adj* **1** without light or with very little light: *a dark, moonless night.* **2** keeping light out: *dark glasses.* **3** closer in colour to black than white: *dark green.* **4** mysterious or hidden: *a dark secret.* **5** full of sadness or suffering; gloomy: *These are dark times. His novels are very dark.* **6** sinister or evil: *dark deeds.* **7** angry or threatening: *She gave him a dark look.*
n **1 the dark** darkness or dark places: *Are you afraid of the dark?* **2** the time when night begins: *Be home before dark.* **3** dark colours: *the contrast between light and dark in a painting.* <Old English *deorc*> **dark′en** *v.* **dark′ly** *adv.* **dark′ness** *n.*
in the dark, not knowing or understanding: *I'm still in the dark about how to do my Science report.*
keep dark, keep secret.

Dark Ages *n* the early part of the Middle Ages in Europe, from the 500s to the 1100s, thought of by some as a time of poverty and little learning.

dark horse *n* a relatively unknown person who wins a contest or attracts notice unexpectedly.

dark·room (dȧrk′rūm′) *n* a room with very dim, coloured light, for developing photographs in.

dar·ling (dȧr′ling) *n* **1** used as a form of address for someone who is much loved: *Darling, could you get me a coffee?* **2** a favourite: *He's the darling of the drama club.*
adj **1** beloved. **2** *Informal* charming and attractive: *What a darling necklace!* <Old English *deore* dear>

darn[1] (dȧrn) *v* mend by weaving rows of thread or yarn across a hole, using a large needle: *to darn socks.* <perhaps Old English *diernan*> **darn′ing** *n.*

darn[2] (dȧrn) *Informal v, n, adj, adv, interj* a less offensive substitute for DAMN, used to express annoyance or anger. Also, **darned**.

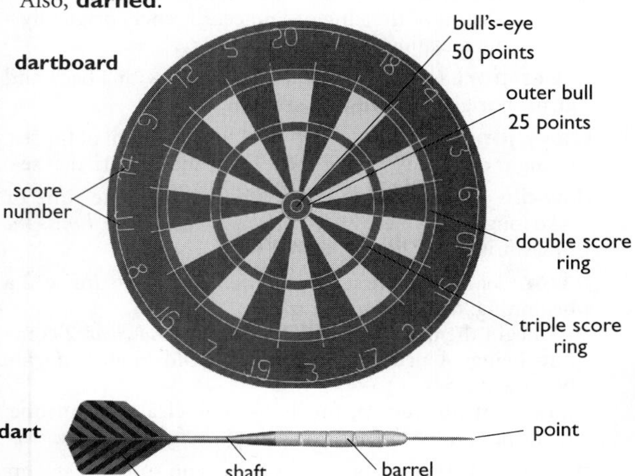

dart (dȧrt) *n* **1** a small, slender, pointed weapon thrown by hand or shot from a tube or gun. **2 darts** (*used with a singular verb*) an indoor game in which players throw darts at a round target. **3** a tapered fold or tuck sewn in a garment to shape it to the body. **4** *Mathematics* a concave trapezium with two sets of adjacent sides congruent. **5** a sudden, quick movement: *He made a dart to the right to avoid the oncoming cyclist.*
v **1** move suddenly and quickly: *She darted across the street.* **2** direct or send suddenly or sharply: *I darted an angry glance at my sister.* <Old French = spear, lance>

Dar·win·ism (dȧr′wə niz′əm) *n* a theory that, over time, plants and animals develop slight mutations that make them better adapted to their environment, and hence more likely to survive in a process of natural selection. <C. *Darwin*, 19c biologist>
Dar·win′i·an or **Dar′win·ist** *adj, n.*

dash (dash) *v* **1** rush: *They dashed by on rollerblades.* **2** strike violently against something: *She dashed her head against the cupboard door.* **3** smash; shatter: *dashed hopes. The boat was dashed to bits on the rocks.* **4** splash; spatter: *Passing cars dashed mud on our pants.*
n **1** a small amount: *Add a dash of pepper.* **2** in writing or printing, a mark [—] used to show a break in the flow or structure of a sentence. **3** a sudden rush: *He made a dash for the finish line.* **4** a short race: *the hundred-metre dash.* **5** liveliness or style. **6** in Morse code, a long sound or signal that represents a letter or part of a letter. Compare DOT (*n* def. 4). **7** a dashboard. <Middle English *daschen*>
dash off, write hastily: *to dash off an e-mail.*

GRAMMAR AND USAGE

The **dash** marks a strong break in a sentence:

I could beat her in a race any time—if I wanted to.

He brought fruit—an apple and a plum—for lunch.

Too many dashes in writing can be distracting. Consider using commas or parentheses for variety.

dash·board (dash′bȯrd′) *n* in a motor vehicle, a panel with controls and gauges, in front of the driver.

dash·ing (dash′ing) *adj* full of liveliness and style: *a handsome, dashing young man.* **dash′ing·ly** *adv.*

das·tard (das′tərd) *Archaic n* a coward or wicked person. <Middle English, a stupid person, probably from *dazed*> **das′tard·ly** *adj.*

DAT digital audiotape.

da·ta (dat′ə) *or* (dā′tə) *n* (*with singular verb or, more formally, plural verb*) **1** information or facts: *She has gathered a lot of data about drug abuse.* **2** *Computers* recorded information such as images, numbers, text, or sounds. <Latin *datum* (thing) given, from *dare* give>

GRAMMAR AND USAGE

Data is actually plural, but it is often used as a singular word: *The data on weather conditions is now available.*

In formal English, data should be treated as plural: *The data are presented in the form of a graph.*

data bank *n* a large, central body of information stored, especially electronically, and available for retrieval.

a bat	e bed	i bid	o pot	u cup	th **thin**
ā cake	ē me	ī bite	ō go	ū rude	ᴛʜ **then**
ȧ bar	ə about	ər over	ȯ for	u̇ put	zh measure

da·ta·base (dat′ə bās′) *or* (dā′tə bās′) *Computers n* **1** a body of information organized systematically according to a set structure, stored in a computer. **2** in full, **database management system** a piece of software used to enter, organize, store, retrieve, and perform operations on a body of information.

data entry *Computers n* the process in which a human operator enters data into a computer system, usually in large quantities and without manipulating or formatting the data.

data processing *Computers n* the operations performed on data, especially by or with a computer, especially in order to organize it or produce reports of various kinds. **data processor** *n.*

date[1] (dāt) *n* **1** a specific day, month, or year identified by a name or number: *Today's date is April 19, 2006. The date of Columbus's voyage to America was 1492.* **2 a** an arrangement to get together for a social activity, especially with a romantic partner: *I have a date with him for Saturday night.* **b** the social activity itself: *How was your date? He's out on a date.* **c** *Informal* the person with whom one has such an appointment: *Who's your date for the dance?*

v **dat·ed, dat·ing 1** mark with a date: *Date your papers, please.* **2** find out the date of: *to date a fossil.* **3** become old or old-fashioned, or cause to seem that way: *Encyclopedias date quickly these days. That expression dates you; I haven't heard it for years.* **4** go out socially with someone or with each other as romantic partners: *Those two have been dating for years. Are you still dating him?* <Old French, from Latin *data Romae* given at Rome (on a certain day)>

date back to or **date from,** belong to a certain time: *That courthouse dates from the 1700s. Such customs date back to colonial days.*

out of date, no longer current or fashionable.

to date, so far: *There have been no problems to date.*

up to date, in the latest style or using the latest information: *Make sure your sources are up to date. Our methods are up to date.*

GRAMMAR AND USAGE

A **date** can be written in a variety of ways:

a comma between the day, the day of the month, and the year: *Friday, May 13, 2005.*

a comma between the day of the month and the year: August 21, 2006.

no comma in dates like *April 2006* or *14 April 2007.*

For dates that use numbers only:

Canadian style is year-month-day. Thus *14 April 2007* would be written *07–04–14.*

American style is month/day/year: *04/14/07.*

date[2] (dāt) *n* the soft, sweet fruit of a **date palm** tree. <Old French, from Greek *daktylos* finger, because the leaves and fruit are shaped like fingers>

dat·ed (dā′tid) *adj* **1** out of date. **2** marked with a date.

date·line (dāt′līn′) a phrase at the beginning of a newspaper or magazine article that gives the date and place of its origin.

Date Line *n* in full, **International Date Line** an imaginary line agreed to be the place where each calendar day begins. It runs north and south through the Pacific, mostly along the 180th meridian. When it is Sunday just east of the date line, it is Monday just west of it.

date rape *n* rape by a person that the victim is going out with on a date.

daub (dob) *v* smear a moist, greasy, or sticky substance onto a surface: *The walls of the hut were daubed with cow dung.* **2** paint unskilfully.

n **1** a blob or streak daubed on a surface: *daubs of plaster.* **2** a badly painted picture. <Old French, from Latin *de-* not + *albus* white> **daub′er** *n.*

daugh·ter (dot′ər) *n* **1** a girl or woman in relation to either or both of her parents. **2** a female descendant. **3** a girl or woman thought of as being produced or formed by some person or thing: *daughters of the Revolution. She is a true daughter of France.* **4** a product: *Success is the daughter of hard work.* <Old English *dohtor*> **daugh′ter·ly** *adj.*

daugh·ter–in–law (dot′ər in lo′) *n,* *pl* **daugh·ters-in-law** the wife of one's son.

daunt (dont) *v* frighten or discourage: *Danger did not daunt the explorer.* <Old French, from Latin *domare* to tame, intimidate>

daunt·less (dont′lis) *adj* not frightened or discouraged by anything: *a dauntless sea captain.* **daunt′less·ly** *adv.* **daunt′less·ness** *n.*

dau·phin (dof′ən) *or* (dō fɴ′) *n* in former times, the title of the oldest son of the king of France. <French, originally a nickname meaning *dolphin*>

dav·en·port (dav′in pȯrt′) *n* a long couch with a back and arms. <origin uncertain>

Da·vy Jones' locker (dā′vē jōnz′) *n* the bottom of the sea, thought of as the grave of those drowned or buried at sea.

daw·dle (dod′əl) *v* **daw·dled, daw·dling** waste time or take longer than necessary: *Don't dawdle or you'll miss the bus.* <origin uncertain> **dawd′ler** *n.*

dawn (don) *n* **1** the first light in the sky before sunrise. **2** a beginning: *the dawn of civilization.*

v **1** begin the day: *Friday dawned bright and clear.* **2** come into being: *A new era is dawning.* <Old English *dagian* become day>

dawn on someone, finally become clear to someone: *It dawned on me that he was waiting for further instructions.*

day (dā) *n* **1** the time between sunrise and sunset: *Days are longer in summer than in winter.* **2 a** the 24 hours of day and night, the time it takes the earth to turn once on its axis. **b** *Astronomy* the time for any celestial body to turn once on its axis. **3** a special day on which something happens or is celebrated: *Canada Day, graduation day.* **4** the hours set aside for work: *Salary is based on a seven-hour day.* **5** a period in history: *the present day, in days of old.* **6 days** *pl* lifetime: *to spend your days in peace.* **7** the conflict or contest of a particular day: *Our team won the day.* <Old English *dæg*>

call it a day, *Informal* quit: *I'm tired; let's call it a day.*
day in and day out, every day, especially when tiresome or difficult: *I like corn, but I wouldn't want it day in and day out.*
from day one, from the very beginning: *This computer has not worked properly from day one.*
have had your day, be no longer active, powerful, or influential.
have your day in court, have a chance to give your side of the story.
in this day and age, in these modern times.

day·bed (dā′bed′) *n* a bed designed to be convertible for use as a couch or sofa during the day.

day·break (dā′brāk′) *n* dawn.

day camp *n* a camp for children, where they stay only for the day and go home at night.

day·care (dā′ker′) *n* **1** care provided outside the home during the day, especially of babies and preschool children: *Many believe that more funds are needed for daycare.* Also, **day care**. **2** a facility that provides this service. Also, **daycare centre**.
adj to do with this service: *daycare staff.*

day·dream (dā′drēm′) *v* **day·dreamed** or **day·dreamt** (dā′dremt′), **day·dreaming** think absent-mindedly or dreamily about pleasant or impractical things.
n **1** something pleasant that one thinks about but that is unlikely to come true: *I'm afraid my career as an artist is nothing but a daydream.* **2** a time of thinking dreamily or absent-mindedly: *A phone call startled him out of his daydream.*

day·light (dā′līt′) *n* **1** the natural light of day. **2** dawn: *She was up at daylight.* **3** daytime: *I'm not going to bed; it's still daylight.*
scare (or **beat, knock,** etc.) **the daylights out of,** *Informal* frighten or beat severely.
see daylight, a approach the end of a long and tiresome job. **b** understand. **c** come into being or into public knowledge: *His invention never saw daylight.*

day·light–sav·ing time (dā′līt′sā′ving) *n* the time in the spring and summer when clocks have been moved forward one hour ahead of standard time in order to give more daylight in the evening.

day lily *n* a plant of the lily family whose flowers last about a day.

Day of Atonement *Judaism n* Yom Kippur.

day·time (dā′tīm′) *n* the time between sunrise and sunset.

day–to–day (dā′tə dā′) *adj* ordinary or everyday: *day-to-day interaction with classmates.*

day·trad·ing (dā′trād′ing) *n* the practice of buying stocks and selling them within one day in order to take advantage of short-term price changes. **day′trad′er** *n.*

day trip *n* a trip lasting no longer than a day.
day′ trip′per *n.* **day′ trip′ping** *n, adj.*

daze (dāz) *v* **dazed, daz·ing** cause to feel stupid or confused: *She was so dazed by her fall that she didn't know where she was.*
n a confused state of mind: *He was in a daze from the accident and couldn't understand what was happening.* <Old Norse *dasathr* weary>

daz·zle (daz′əl) *v* **daz·zled, daz·zling 1** overpower the eyes with light that is too bright: *When I came out of the cave I was dazzled by the sun.* **2** impress or amaze with brilliance, beauty, or excellence: *The young violinist's performance dazzled the critics.*
n overpowering brightness, splendour, or glamour: *the dazzle of car headlights, the dazzle of show business.* <from *daze*> **daz′zling** *adj.* **daz′zling·ly** *adv.*

D

dB decibel.

DC or **D.C. 1** direct current. **2 D.C.** or **d.c.** *Music* da capo.

D–day (dē′dā) *n* **1** in World War II, the day when the Allies landed in France, on June 6, 1944. **2** the day on which a planned military attack or other decisive operation is to happen. <*D*, first letter of *day*>

DDT *n* a poisonous chemical compound formerly used as an insecticide. <*d*ichloro-*d*iphenyl-*t*richloro-ethane>

de– *prefix* **1** do the opposite of; not: *deactivate.* **2** down: *depress.* **3** away or off: *defrost.* **4** entirely: *despoil.* **5** around; about: *delineate.* <Latin>

de·ac·ces·sion (dē′ak sesh′ən) *v* remove an item from the collection in an art gallery, museum, or library.

dea·con (dē′kən) *Christianity n* **1** an ordained minister in the Roman Catholic, Anglican, and Orthodox churches, usually ranking below a priest. **2** an officer in some Protestant churches who helps the minister in many church duties. <Latin, from Greek *diakonos* servant of the church>

de·ac·ti·vate (dē ak′tə vāt′) *v* **de·ac·ti·vat·ed, de·ac·ti·vat·ing** make inactive: *to deactivate a bomb, to deactivate a bank account.*

dead (ded) *adj* **1** no longer alive: *a dead spider.* **2** without power, spirit, or feeling: *feeling dead inside.* **3** inactive and dull: *This town is dead in the summer.* **4** like death: *dead silence.* **5** *Informal* very tired. **6** no longer in use: *Latin is a dead language.* **7** *Sports* out of play: *a dead ball.* **8** exact; precise: *dead centre.* **9** total; complete: *a dead certainty.*
adv Informal completely: *You're dead wrong.*
n **1** people who have died: *to bury the dead.* **2** the time of greatest darkness, quiet, or cold: *the dead of night, the dead of winter.* <Old English> **dead′en** *v.* **dead′ness** *n.*
dead in the water, *Slang* utterly defeated: *We're dead in the water if we're late with our report.*
dead set against, *Informal* firmly opposed to: *My dad is dead set against letting me stay out late.*
dead to the world, *Informal* fast asleep.
over my dead body, *Informal* I will resist that plan or course of action to the end.
would not be caught dead, *Informal* be unwilling to do or be, under any circumstances, especially because of pride: *I wouldn't be caught dead wearing those jeans.*

dead·beat (ded′bēt′) *Informal n* a person who avoids paying debts, taking responsibility, or working.
adj to do with or being such a person.

a bat	e bed	i bid	o pot	u cup	th **thin**
ā cake	ē me	ī bite	ō go	ū rude	ᴛʜ **then**
ä bar	ə about	ər over	ô for	ů put	zh measure

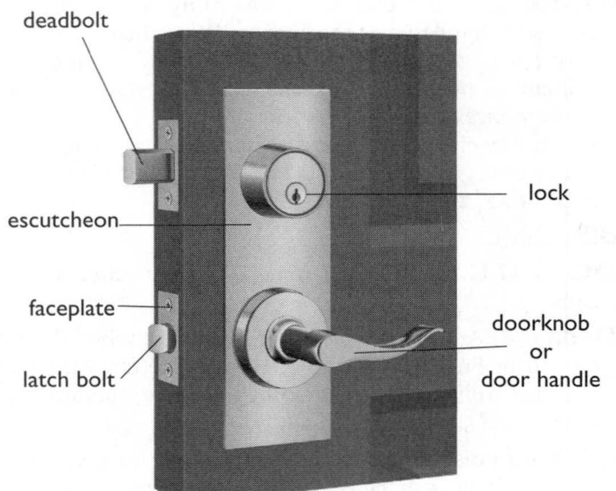

A **deadbolt** is a very secure lock. The bolt slides deeply into a slot in the frame of a door, and can't be opened easily from the outside—unless you have the key.

dead·bolt (ded′bōlt′) *n* a type of lock with a bolt that is turned with the key.

dead end *n* **1** a street or passage closed at one end. **2** a point beyond which there can be no more progress: *That job is a dead end. Discussion of that topic has reached a dead end.* **dead′-end′** *adj.*

dead·head (ded′hed′) *n* **1** *Slang* a stupid or lazy person. **2** *Informal* a dead bloom on a flowering plant: *Pick off the deadheads to encourage more blooms.* **3** 🍁 a log or fallen tree partly or entirely under water in a lake or river, usually with one end stuck into the bottom.

dead heat *n* a race or contest that ends in a tie or looks as if it will end in a tie.

dead letter *n* a letter that cannot be delivered or returned because the address is wrong, incomplete, or impossible to read.

dead·line (ded′līn′) *n* the latest possible time to do something: *April 30 is the deadline for sending in your income tax.*

dead load *n* the fixed weight of a structure like a bridge, or of a piece of machinery, not including any load it may be carrying. Compare DYNAMIC LOAD.

dead·lock (ded′lok′) *n* a position in which it is impossible to act because of disagreement: *The striking workers and their employer were at a deadlock.*
v bring or come to such a position: *The talks were deadlocked for weeks.*

dead·ly (ded′lē) *adj* **dead·li·er, dead·li·est** **1** causing death; able or likely to cause death or other great damage: *deadly poison, a deadly wound.* **2** like death: *deadly paleness.* **3** extreme or intense: *deadly enemies, deadly boredom.* **4** very dull: *The party was a deadly affair.*
adv extremely.

deadly nightshade BELLADONNA.

dead·pan (ded′pan′) *adj, adv* without expression or showing no emotion: *His face was completely deadpan. You have to do this scene deadpan or it's not funny.*
v **dead·panned, dead·pan·ning** act or tell in a totally expressionless manner: *She deadpanned every joke.*
n an expressionless face.

dead weight *n* the heavy weight of any lifeless object, or of a sleeping or unconscious person.

dead·wood (ded′wůd′) *n* dead branches or trees.

deaf (def) *adj* **1** not able to hear. **2** not listening or not willing to hear: *They were deaf to our cries for help.* <Old English> **deaf′en** *v.* **deaf′en·ing** *adj.* **deaf′ness** *n.*

deal (dēl) *v* **dealt** (delt), **deal·ing** **1** distribute, especially playing cards. **2** do business by buying and selling: *This shop deals mainly in imported goods. That company deals with overseas clients.* **3** sell illegal drugs. **4** behave: *Deal fairly with everyone.* **5** give; deliver: *One fighter dealt the other a powerful blow.*
n **1** a bargain, agreement, or contract: *We made a deal; I promised to do the dishes if she helped me with my homework. Ninety dollars for that TV set was a good deal.* **2** **a** a player's turn to distribute cards: *It's your deal.* **b** the cards received: *I got a lousy deal.* **3** *Informal* the way things work: *So, what's the deal here?* **4** a kind of treatment: *a rough deal.* <Old English *daelan*>
a good (or **great**) **deal,** much: *a great deal of money, a good deal farther away.*
deal out, distribute in portions or shares: *She dealt out two caramels to each child.*
deal with, **a** to do with: *We don't deal with that here, sorry. This book deals with social issues.* **b** resolve an issue or situation: *You'd better deal with this before it gets out of hand.*

deal·er (dē′lər) *n* **1** a person engaged in buying and selling: *a car dealer.* **2** a person who sells illegal drugs. **3** the player who deals in a game of cards.

deal·er·ship (dē′lər ship′) *n* a dealer's place of business: *You'll pass a row of car dealerships on your right.*

deal·ing (dē′ling) *n* **1** a manner of doing business or behaving: *She is respected by everyone for her fair dealing.* **2** **dealings** *pl* actions or business relations: *He has been honest in all his dealings with us.*

dealt (delt) past tense and past participle of DEAL.

dean (dēn) *n* **1** in a college or university: **a** the head of a division or school: *the Dean of Graduate Studies.* **b** a senior member of the teaching staff in charge of the studies or behaviour of students. **2** the most senior or respected member of an association, profession, or other group: *Robertson Davies was considered by many to be the dean of Canadian novelists.* <Old French, from Latin *decanus*, commander of ten soldiers> **dean′ship** *n.*

dear (dēr) *adj* **1** much loved or precious: *His sister is very dear to him.* **2** (*as a polite opening to a letter*) highly valued or esteemed: *Dear Esther, Dear Sir or Madam.* **3** expensive or high-priced: *Their produce is good, but it's very dear.*
n a beloved or lovable person: *You're such a dear!*
adv Poetic with a high price: *to pay dear.*
interj an exclamation of mild dismay: *Oh, dear! I've lost my key.* <Old English *deore*> **dear′ly** *adv.* **dear′ness** *n.*
hold dear, value highly or regard as precious: *We hold our freedom dear.*

dearth (dərth) *n* an extreme scarcity. <Old English *deore* costly>

death (deth) *n* **1** the act or fact of the ending of life: *a dignified death. Death came early to the president.* **2** the state of being dead: *It was quiet as death at midnight.* **3** any ending that is like dying; total destruction: *the death of an empire, the death of all our dreams.* **4** a cause of death: *Careless driving was the death of her.* **5** bloodshed or killing: *The battlefield seemed to have a smell of death.* <Old English> **death′like** *adj.*

at death's door, almost dead.

be death on, be very much against: *My parents are death on junk food.*

catch your death, *Informal* (*usually in warnings*) get a severe cold: *Get your jacket done up before you catch your death!*

do to death, a kill. **b** do or say the same thing so often that it becomes boring: *Scrap that idea; it's been done to death already.*

like death warmed over, *Informal* looking, sounding, or feeling very sick or tired.

put to death, kill.

to death, a to the point of dying: *flowers baked to death in the sun.* **b** almost beyond endurance: *bored to death.*

to the death, to the very end of life or of one's resources: *We will fight to the death.*

death·bed (deth′bed′) *n* the bed on which a person dies.
adj made during the last hours of life: *a deathbed confession.*

on your deathbed, in your last hours of life.

death·blow (deth′blō′) *n* **1** a blow that kills. **2** something that puts an end to something else: *The arrival of the calculator was a deathblow to the slide rule.*

death camp *n* a place to which large numbers of people are brought and then killed or allowed to die of overwork and malnutrition.

death knell *n* **1** a bell rung slowly to announce a death. **2** something that signals the end of something else: *User fees would sound the death knell for our community centre.*

death·less (deth′lis) *adj* **1** never dying or where there is no death. **2** never losing its power or beauty: *deathless prose.*

death·ly (deth′lē) *adj* **1** like that of death: *a deathly silence.* **2** causing death: *a deathly illness.*
adv **1** as if dead: *deathly pale.* **2** extremely: *deathly cold.*

death penalty *n* the punishment of a crime by death.

death rate *n* the ratio of the number of deaths per year to the total population, or to some other stated number.

death row *n* a section of prison cells for prisoners awaiting execution.

death squad *n* a group employed by an oppressive government to kill its opponents.

death·trap (deth′trap′) *n* an unsafe place where the risk of fire or other danger is great: *With all these oily rags, this shed is a deathtrap. That abandoned mine is a deathtrap.*

death warrant *n* **1** an official order for a person's death. **2** anything that spells the fall or ruin of a person or thing: *Talking pictures were the death warrant for silent movies.*

sign the death warrant of, cause the defeat or end of.

de·ba·cle (di bȧ′kəl) *n* **1** a complete and embarrassing failure. **2** the overthrow or downfall of some person or thing. **3** the breaking up of ice in a river. **4** a violent rush of water carrying debris. <Old French *desbacler* to unbar, to free, from Latin *de-* not + *bacler* to bar>

de·bar (dē bȧr′) *v* **de·barred, de·bar·ring** exclude, prohibit, or expel officially: *to be debarred from a competition for cheating.* <French *des-* reversing + *barrer* to bar>

D

de·base (di bās′) *v* **de·based, de·bas·ing 1** make lower in quality or character: *to debase oneself by telling lies.* **2** lower the value of: *debased currency.* <*de-* down + *base* bring down completely> **de·base′ment** *n.*

de·bate (di bāt′) *v* **de·bat·ed, de·bat·ing 1** think about the reasons for and against: *I am debating buying this DVD.* **2** argue logically about something, especially formally, publicly, or competitively: *City Council debated the clean water issue for three hours.*
n a formal, public, competitive discussion of opposing viewpoints; reasoned argument: *The election candidates are having a televised debate tonight.* <Old French, from Latin *de-* not + *battere* fight> **de·bat′a·ble** *adj.* **de·bat′er** *n.*

de·bauch (di boch′) *v* lead away from virtue into immoral behaviour: *debauched by bad companions.* <French *débaucher* lure away from duty> **de·bauched′** *adj.* **de·bauch′e·ry** *n.* **de·bauch′ment** *n.*

de·ben·ture (di ben′chər) *n* an investment bond, especially one issued by a corporation and backed by the general assets of the corporation. <Latin *debere* owe>

de·bil·i·tate (di bil′ə tāt′) *v* **de·bil·i·tat·ed, de·bil·i·tat·ing** weaken or make feeble: *a debilitating disease. This hot, humid weather is debilitating.* <Latin *debilis* weak> **de·bil′i·ta′tion** *n.*

de·bil·i·ty (di bil′ə tē) *n, pl* **de·bil·i·ties** weakness: *Long-term illness may cause general debility.* <Old French, from Latin *debilis* weak>

deb·it (deb′it) *n* **1** an amount owed on an account or subtracted from it as payment. **2** use of or a charge on a debit card: *to pay via debit. I made three debits already today.*
v **1** subtract from an account as payment: *We have debited your account $40.* **2** make a notation of this on a statement. Compare CREDIT.

ETYMOLOGY

Debit and **debt** come via different routes from the Latin word *debitum*, meaning "something owed," which, in turn, is a form of *debere*, meaning "to owe."

However, *debt* lost a syllable by coming through French first on its way into English.

a bat	e bed	i bid	o pot	u cup	th **thin**
ā cake	ē me	ī bite	ō go	ū rude	ᴛʜ **then**
ȧ bar	ə about	ər over	ȯ for	u̇ put	zh measure

debit card *n* a card used by a consumer to buy goods or services at businesses linked to a large network shared by several banks.

deb·o·nair (deb′ə ner′) *adj* elegant, sophisticated, and charming, especially in a man. <Old French *de bon aire* of good disposition> **deb′o·nair′ly** *adv.*

de·bone (dē bōn′) *v* **de·boned, de·bon·ing** remove the bones from meat or fish.

de·brief (dē brēf′) *v* **1** question someone who has returned from a mission or some other event, to find out its results and anything else the person has learned: *The fighter pilot was debriefed by the prime minister herself.* Compare BRIEF (*v*). **2** submit to such a questioning: *Debrief as soon as you've rested.* **de·brief′ing** *n.*

de·bris (də brē′) *n* **1** scattered fragments: *The street was covered with debris from the explosion.* **2** fragments of rock or wood, carried or left behind by a glacier or flood. <French obsolete *débriser* break down>

debt (det) *n* **1** something owed to another: *I've paid off my debts.* **2** the state of owing something: *to be in debt. Avoid debt.* <Old French, from Latin *debere* owe>

debt of honour *n* (*used as a euphemism, especially in former times*) a gambling debt.

debt·or (det′ər) *n* a person who owes something to another: *to collect payment from a debtor.*

de·bug (dē bug′) *v* **de·bugged, de·bug·ging** **1** find and get rid of errors or malfunctions in: *to debug software.* **2** find and remove hidden microphones in: *First we'd better debug the hotel room.* **de·bug′ger** *n.*

de·bunk (di bungk′) *v* expose as false, exaggerated, or not credible: *to debunk a theory, to debunk a popular hero.* **de·bunk′er** *n.*

de·but or **dé·but** (dā byū′) *n* **1** a first public appearance or performance: *The band is making its debut at the folk festival.* **2** in former times, among wealthy people, the first formal appearance of a girl in fashionable society. <French *dé-* from + *but* starting point>

deb·u·tante or **dé·bu·tante** (deb′yə tont′) *n* a girl or woman making her DEBUT (def. 2). <French>

deca– *combining form* ten: *decagon.* <Greek *deka* ten>

dec·ade (dek′ād) *n* **1** ten years. **2** any group of ten. <Latin, from Greek *deka* ten>

dec·a·dent (dek′ə dənt) *adj* **1** morally corrupt: *a decadent society.* **2** *Informal* giving so much pleasure that it is probably bad for one's character: *decadent chocolate cake.* *n* a morally corrupt person. <French, from Latin *de-* down + *cadere* fall> **dec′a·dence** *n.* **dec′a·dent·ly** *adv.*

de·caf (dē′kaf) *n* coffee with the caffeine removed: *A cup of decaf, please.* <*decaffeinated*>

de·caf·fein·ate (di kaf′ə nāt′) *v* **de·caf·fein·at·ed, de·caf·fein·at·ing** remove the caffeine from.

dec·a·gon (dek′ə gon′) *n* a plane figure with ten angles and ten sides. <*deca-* + Greek *gonia* corner, angle> **de·cag′on·al** (di kag′ə nəl) *adj.*

dec·a·he·dron (dek′ə hē′drən) *n, pl* **dec·a·he·drons** or **dec·a·he·dra** a solid with ten faces or surfaces. <*deca-* + Greek *hedra* base>

de·cal (dē′kal) *or* (dek′əl) *n* a design or picture meant to be stuck on a surface as a decoration or logo. <French *décalquer* transfer, a tracing>

de·camp (dē kamp′) *v* **1** leave quickly, secretly, or without ceremony. **2** leave a campsite or take down a camp <French *dé-* removal + *camp* camp> **de·camp′ment** *n.*

de·cant (di kant′) *v* **1** pour off a liquid gently, without disturbing any sediment at the bottom. **2** pour from one container to another. <Latin, from Greek *kanthos* corner of the eye. The corner of the eye, where tears form, bears a resemblance to the spout of a jug.>

de·cant·er (di kan′tər) *n* a glass bottle with a stopper, used for serving wine or liquor.

de·cap·i·tate (di kap′ə tāt′) *v* **de·cap·i·tat·ed, de·cap·i·tat·ing** cut off the head of. <Latin *de-* away + *caput* head> **de·cap′i·ta′tion** *n.*

dec·a·pod (dek′ə pod′) *n* **1** a crustacean with five pairs of limbs, one or more pairs being modified into pincers. Lobsters, shrimps, and crabs are decapods. **2** a mollusc with ten arms, such as a squid or cuttlefish. <*deca-* + Greek *podos* foot>

de·cath·lon (di kath′lon) *n* an athletic contest consisting of ten separate running, throwing, and jumping events, in which the winner is the person with the highest point total. Participants are called **decathletes.** <*deca-* + Greek *athlon* contest>

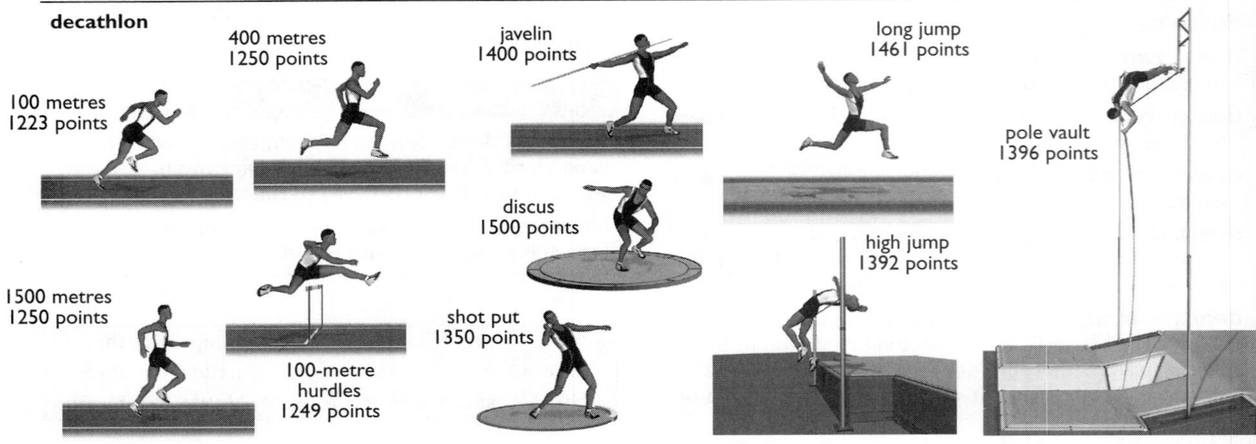

de·cay (di kā′) *v* **1** rot: *Fruits and vegetables decay. Teeth decay if they are not taken care of.* **2** *Physics* **a** disintegrate from one subatomic particle into others. **b** grow less as a radioactive substance through disintegration of its nuclei. **3** grow less in strength, beauty, goodness, or value.
n **1** the process of decaying, or a decayed condition: *the decay of civilization.* **2** decaying matter: *The tooth was so full of decay they had to pull it.* <Old French, from Latin *de-* away + *cadere* to fall> **de·cayed** *adj.*

de·cease (di sēs′) *Formal n* death: *his unexpected decease.* *v* **de·ceased, de·ceas·ing** die. <Old French, from Latin *de-* away + *cedere* to fall>

de·ceit (di sēt′) *n* **1** the act of lying or giving a false impression: *It was pure deceit to give her the impression you knew nothing about this.* **2** willingness to deceive: *a heart full of treachery and deceit.* <See DECEIVE.> **de·ceit′ful** *adj.* **de·ceit′ful·ly** *adv.*

CONFUSABLES

Deceit suggests a deliberate intention to mislead: *She used deceit to avoid doing her chores.*

Deception does not always imply ill will: *We used deception to get him to his surprise party.*

de·ceive (di sēv′) *v* **de·ceived, de·ceiv·ing** cause someone to believe something that is false: *It is illegal to deceive the public through false advertising. Appearances can deceive!* <Old French, from Latin *decipere* cheat> **de·ceiv′er** *n.*

de·cel·er·ate (dē sel′ə rāt′) *v* **de·cel·er·at·ed, de·cel·er·at·ing** slow down. <*de-* down + *accelerate*> **de·cel′er·a′tion** *n.* **de·cel′er·a′tor** *n.*

De·cem·ber (di sem′bər) *n* the twelfth and last month of the year, with 31 days. *Abbrev.* **Dec** <Latin *decem* ten. It was the tenth month in the early Roman calendar.>

de·cent (dē′sənt) *adj* **1** honourable, respectable, or morally proper: *a decent burial, decent people. The decent thing to do is apologize.* **2** not vulgar or obscene: *decent jokes.* **3** dressed in presentable clothes: *Don't look. I'm not decent.* **4** adequate or meeting minimum accepted standards: *a decent wage, a decent meal.* **5** kinder than one is obligated to be: *She was very decent about my coming in late for work.* <Latin *decere* proper> **de′cen·cy** *n.* **de′cent·ly** *adv.*

de·cen·tral·ize (dē sen′trə līz′) *v* **de·cen·tral·ized, de·cen·tral·i·zing** spread authority or responsibility or activity among groups, branches, or local governments, instead of concentrating it in one place. **de·cen′tral·i·za′tion** *n.*

de·cep·tion (di sep′shən) *n* **1** the act of deceiving or state of being deceived. **2** something that deceives. See DECEIT for confusable. **de·cep′tive** *adj.* **de·cep′tive·ly** *adv.*

deci– *combining form* one-tenth: *decimetre.* <Latin *decem* ten>

dec·i·bel (des′ə bel′) *or* (des′ə bəl) *n* a unit for measuring loudness of sound. *Symbol* **dB** <*deci-* + *bel* unit of intensity of power, after A.G. *Bell*, 20c inventor>

de·cide (di sīd′) *v* **de·cid·ed, de·cid·ing** **1** make up one's mind: *I decided to take piano this year. We've decided it's not wise to stay.* **2** settle an issue by giving victory to one side: *The whole war was decided by that one battle. The jury decided in favour of the defendant.* **3** cause to make up one's mind: *In the end, it was your argument that decided us.* <French, from Latin *decidere* terminate, from *de-* off + *caedere* to cut>

de·cid·ed (di sī′did) *adj* **1** clear and definite: *The home team had a decided advantage.* **2** firm or fixed: *She has very decided opinions.* **de·cid′ed·ly** *adv.*

D

CONFUSABLES

Decided means "distinct" or "unquestionable": *I notice a decided improvement in my grades when I study more.*

Decisive means "having or giving a clear result": *The candidate showed a decisive lead in the polls.*

de·cid·u·ous (di sid′yū əs) *adj* **1** shedding the leaves of a tree annually: *Maples and oaks are deciduous.* **2** falling off at a particular season or stage of growth: *deciduous antlers, deciduous leaves.* <Latin *de-* off + *cadere* to fall>

dec·i·mal (des′məl) *n* **1** a numeral that includes a fraction with a denominator of 10, 100, 1000, etc., separated from the whole number by a dot. Examples: 0.2, 9.93, 4000.07 Compare COMMON FRACTION. **2** in full, **decimal point** the dot in such a number. *Put the decimal between the units and the tenths.*
adj based on the number 10: *The SI is a decimal system of measurement. Canada uses a decimal currency.* <Latin *decimus* tenth> **dec′i·mal·ize′** *v.* **dec′i·mal·ly** *adv.*

decimal fraction *n* **1** DECIMAL (*n* def. 1). **2** a decimal less than one, such as 0.7 or 0.53.

dec·i·mate (des′ə māt′) *v* **dec·i·mat·ed, dec·i·mat·ing** reduce greatly in number: *War and famine had decimated the population.* **dec′i·ma′tion** *n.*

ETYMOLOGY

Decimate has the same root as *decimal.* The Latin word *decimus* means "tenth."

Originally, *decimate* meant "to select and remove" or "destroy every tenth member of a group," such as a group of prisoners or a herd of animals. Somehow it was turned around to mean "leaving only a tenth of the group."

dec·i·me·tre (des′ə mē′tər) *n* a unit of length, equal to one-tenth of a metre, or ten centimetres. A **cubic decimetre** is equal to a litre. *Symbol* **dm**

de·ci·pher (di sī′fər) *v* **1** make out what something says or means: *to decipher poor handwriting, to decipher legal jargon.* **2** change from secret code to ordinary language. **de·ci′pher·a·ble** *adj.*

a bat	e bed	i bid	o pot	u cup	th **thin**
ā cake	ē me	ī bite	ō go	ū rude	ᴛʜ **then**
ȧ bar	ə about	ər over	ȯ for	u̇ put	zh measure

de·ci·sion (di sizh′ən) *n* **1** the act or process of deciding: *The decision took a long time.* **2** the judgment reached by one who decides: *The court has handed down its decision.* **3** a clear outcome in a contest or conflict. **4** the winning of a boxing match on points or by the verdict of judges, rather than by a knockout.

de·ci·sive (di sī′siv) *adj* **1** with or giving a clear outcome: *a decisive victory.* **2** showing an ability to make a quick and firm decision: *a decisive answer, decisive leadership.* See DECIDED for confusable. **de·ci′sive·ly** *adv.* **de·ci′sive·ness** *n.*

deck (dek) *n* **1** the platform of a ship, extending from side to side and often from end to end. **2** a raised platform, usually with no roof, against an outside wall of a house. **3** a platform or shelf, such as the area surrounding a swimming pool. **4** a set of playing cards.
v **1** decorate or trim: *The hall was decked with flags.* **2** *Slang* knock a person down: *She decked the bully with a good hard punch.* <Dutch *dekken* to cover>
clear the deck, prepare for action.
deck out, dress splendidly: *She was all decked out in satin.*
hit the deck, *Slang* **a** drop to the ground. **b** prepare for action. **c** get out of bed.
not playing with a full deck, *Slang* stupid or crazy.
on deck, present and ready for work: *We were all on deck for the cleanup.*

deck·hand (dek′hand′) *n* an ordinary sailor who works on the deck of a ship.

de·claim (di klām′) *v* **1** speak in a loud, impressive, or emotional way: *I listened for an hour to my uncle declaiming about the beauty of hard work.* **2** make a formal speech. <French, from Latin *de-* away + *clamare* to call> **dec′la·ma′tion** *n.* **de·clam′a·to′ry** *adj.*

Declaration of Independence *n* the public statement signed on July 4, 1776, in which the American colonies declared themselves independent of Britain.

de·clar·a·tive (di kler′ə tiv) *Grammar adj* expressing a statement, as opposed to a question, wish, or command: *"I have two legs" is a declarative sentence.*

de·clare (di kler′) *v* **de·clared, de·clar·ing** **1** say strongly; assert: *They declared they would win or die trying.* **2** announce publicly or formally: *to declare bankruptcy. Parliament has declared a holiday.* **3** deliver a certain judgment about: *The jury declares the defendant guilty. He was declared Athlete of the Year by a sports magazine.* **4** officially report that one has: *to declare income on a tax form. You must declare all imported goods at the border.* <Latin *de-* entirely + *clarus* clear> **dec′la·ra′tion** *n.*
declare war (on), announce that one is at war or in open conflict with someone or something.
declare yourself, make your opinion or position clearly known: *They declared themselves in favour of stiffer environmental laws.*
I declare! I am amazed.

de·claw (dē klo′) *v* surgically remove the claws of an animal, especially a cat.

dec·li·na·tion (dek′lə nā′shən) *n* **1** a downward bend or slope. **2** the deviation of a compass needle away from true north or south.

de·cline (di klīn′) *v* **de·clined, de·clin·ing** **1** refuse, especially politely or formally: *to decline an invitation. She declined to comment.* **2** decrease gradually: *School enrolment is declining.* **3** fall in strength, value, or quality. *He feels that moral standards have declined.* **4** bend or slope down.
n the act or fact of declining: *a decline in the birth rate, the decline of the Roman Empire.* <Old French, from Latin *de-* down + *clinare* to bend>
your declining years, old age: *I want to spend my declining years in peace.*

de·code (dē kōd′) *v* **de·cod·ed, de·cod·ing** **1** translate from code into ordinary language. **2** get the meaning of anything expressed in symbols: *Different parts of the brain are used in decoding speech and writing.* **3** unscramble an electronic signal. **4** *Computers* convert encoded data back to its original form: *Decoding will let you see the image you've just downloaded.* **de·cod′er** *n.*

de·com·pose (dē′kəm pōz′) *v* **de·com·posed, de·com·pos·ing** **1** decay; rot. **2** break down or separate into parts. **de′com·po·si′tion** *n.*

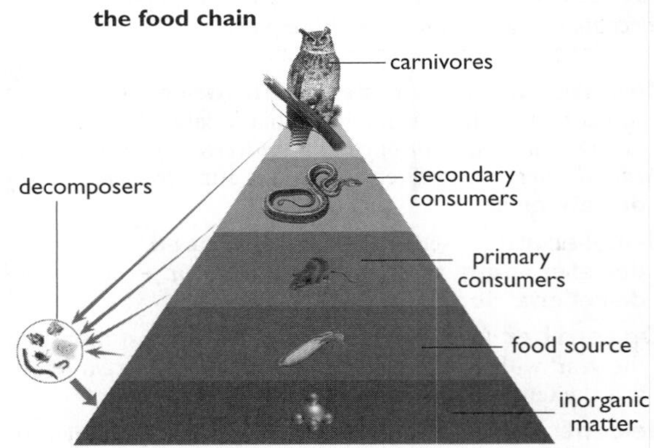

Insects, bacteria, and fungi are **decomposers** that feed on dead materials, breaking down the decaying matter. They then return the nutrients to the soil for plants to use again. Decomposers occupy several positions in the food chain.

de·com·pos·er (dē′kəm pō′zər) *n* **1** an organism that feeds on the wastes and dead tissues of other organisms, converting these materials to simpler forms. **2** anything that decomposes or speeds decomposing.

de·com·press (dē′kəm pres′) *v* **1** release from pressure. **2** remove pressure from a diver gradually by means of a decompression chamber. **de′com·pres′sion** *n.*

decompression chamber *n* an airtight compartment in which people can gradually readjust from abnormal to normal air pressure.

decompression sickness *n* a condition of severe headache, pain in the muscles and joints, cramps, and nausea after nitrogen bubbles form in body tissues after too rapid decompression. Also informally called **the bends**.

de·con·ges·tant (dē′kən jes′tənt) *n* a medication used to relieve congestion of the lungs, sinuses, and nasal cavities.

de·con·tam·i·nate (dē′kən tam′ə nāt′) *v* **de·con·tam·i·nat·ed, de·con·tam·i·nat·ing** make free of contamination such as dangerous substances, harmful bacteria, or radioactivity. **de′con·tam′i·na′tion** *n.*

dé·cor or **de·cor** (dā kôr′) *n* **1** the colours in a room and the overall style and arrangement of the furnishings. **2** a stage setting.

dec·o·rate (dek′ə rāt′) *v* **dec·o·rat·ed, dec·o·rat·ing** **1** add things in order to make more beautiful or interesting, often for a particular occasion: *to decorate tables for a banquet, to decorate a birthday cake.* **2** paint or paper a room or house: *We haven't decorated the family room since we moved in.* **3** plan the style, colour, and furnishings for: *The firm that decorated these offices is no longer in business.* **4** give a medal, ribbon, etc. to a person as a mark of honour: *The soldier was decorated for bravery.* <Latin *decoris* adornment> **dec′o·ra·tive** *adj.* **dec′o·ra·tive·ly** *adv.*

dec·o·ra·tion (dek′ə rā′shən) *n* **1** anything used to add beauty or interest. **2** a medal, badge, or ribbon awarded as a mark of honour. **3** the act or process of decorating.

dec·o·ra·tor (dek′ə rā′tər) *n* one who plans colour schemes, and the style and arrangement of furnishings for rooms or houses.
adj favoured by or made for decorators: *decorator fabrics, decorator colours.*

de·co·rum (di kôr′əm) *n* **1** the quality of behaving politely: *to behave with decorum.* **2** a requirement of etiquette: *She was taught to observe all the little decorums of polite society.* <Latin *decorus* seemly> **dec′o·rous** *adj.*

de·cou·page or **dé·cou·page** (dā′kū päzh′) *n* **1** the art of pasting cutout pictures or designs on a surface and then lacquering it. **2** a piece of work done by this technique. <French *dé-* out + *couper* cut>

de·coy (dē′koi) *for n,* (di koi′) *or* (dē′koi) *for v.*
n **1** an artificial or live bird or other animal used as a lure by hunters or trappers. **2** a person or thing used to lead into danger or onto the wrong track: *Don't follow that guy; he's a decoy leading us into an ambush.* **3** a place into which wild birds or animals are lured.
v **1** lure wild birds or animals into a trap or within gunshot range. **2** lead into danger. <Dutch, from Latin *cavea* cage>

de·crease (di krēs′) *for v,* (dē′krēs) *for n.*
v **de·creased, de·creas·ing** make or become less: *to decrease prices. Hunger decreases as you eat.*
n the fact, process, or amount of decreasing: *a decrease in crime, a decrease of 20 percent.* <Old French, from Latin *de-* down + *crescere* grow>

SYNONYMS

Decrease involves lessening, whether by a small or large amount: *The water decreased his thirst.*

Pare suggests lessening little by little: *She pared down the clothes she was packing so she could get them into one suitcase.*

Slash suggests reducing by a large amount: *The regular prices were slashed in half.*

de·cree (di krē′) *n* an official decision or order: *The dates of holidays are fixed by government decree.*
v **de·creed, de·cree·ing** decide or order by authority: *He had planned to go to Africa, but fate decreed otherwise.* <Old French, from Latin *de-* entirely + *cernere* decide>

de·crep·it (di krep′it) *adj* broken down or weakened by age or long use: *This old table is so decrepit I think it'll collapse soon.* <Latin *de-* down + *crepare* creak> **de·crep′i·tude** *n.*

D

de·cre·scen·do (dā′krə shen′dō) *Music n* a gradual decrease in loudness.
adv, adj with a gradual decrease in loudness. Compare CRESCENDO. <Italian = decreasing>

de·crim·i·nal·ize (dē krim′ə nə līz′) *v* **de·crim·i·nal·ized, de·crim·i·nal·iz·ing** remove something from the list of criminal offences: *Canada has decriminalized abortion.*

de·cry (di krī′) *v* **de·cried, de·cry·ing** express strong disapproval of: *We decry the use of animals for testing cosmetics.* <French *dé-* down + *crier* shout>

de·crypt (dē kript′) *v* **1** put a coded message into readable form. **2** *Computers* undo the encryption of (a message).

ded·i·cate (ded′ə kāt′) *v* **ded·i·cat·ed, ded·i·cat·ing** **1** set apart for a sacred or solemn purpose: *to dedicate a new altar. The monument is dedicated to the memory of our war dead.* **2** give up wholeheartedly to some person or cause: *He dedicated his life to the arts.* **3** use exclusively for one function: *We should dedicate one of the school printers for staff use. My computer has a dedicated phone line so I can use the Internet.* **4** as an author, address a book or other work to someone as a mark of affection, respect, or gratitude. **5** celebrate the official opening of an institution, bridge, etc. with a ceremony. <Latin *de-* entirely + *dicare* proclaim> **ded′i·ca·to′ry** *adj.*

ded·i·cat·ed (ded′ə kā′tid) *adj* **1** wholly committed. **2** kept or used for one function only: *The database is stored on a dedicated server.*

ded·i·ca·tion (ded′ə kā′shən) *n* **1** the act of dedicating, or a ceremony or inscription that does this. **2** faithful, wholehearted effort and commitment: *The dedication of the staff keeps the school running smoothly.*

de·duce (di dyūs′) *or* (di dūs′) *v* **de·duced, de·duc·ing** figure out from evidence or from a general rule or principle: *From all the the books in her room, I deduced that she read a lot.* <See DEDUCT.> **de·du′ci·ble** *adj.*

de·duct (di dukt′) *v* subtract: *Two marks will be deducted for lateness.* <Latin *de-* down + *ducere* lead> **de·duct′i·ble** *adj.*

de·duc·tion (di duk′shən) *n* **1** the act of deducting: *No deduction in salary is made for absence due to illness.* **2** an amount deducted: *a $50 deduction from each paycheque.* **3 a** the act of deducing from a general rule and evidence: *I solved the mystery by simple deduction.* **b** the conclusion reached in this way: *A brilliant deduction, Sherlock!*

a bat	e bed	i bid	o pot	u cup	th **thin**
ā cake	ē me	ī bite	ō go	ū rude	ᴛʜ **then**
ä bar	ə about	ər over	ô for	ů put	zh measure

de·duc·tive (di duk′tiv) *adj* to do with the process of deducing from a general rule to a particular situation, or from cause to effect: *deductive reasoning.* Compare INDUCTIVE. **de·duc′tive·ly** *adv.*

deed (dēd) *n* **1** an act, especially one that is remarkable or morally significant: *Feeding the hungry is a good deed.* **2** a document proving ownership: *A person who buys real estate gets a deed to the property.*
v transfer to someone by giving a DEED (def. 2): *He deeded the land to his daughter.* <Old English *dǣd*>

dee·jay (dē′jā) *Informal n* a disc jockey.

deem (dēm) *v* think, believe, or consider: *The lawyer deemed it unwise to take the case to court.* <Old English *dom* judgment>

de–em·pha·size (dē em′fə sīz′) *v* **de-em·pha·sized, de-em·pha·siz·ing** put less emphasis on: *She de-emphasized the risks involved in the adventure.*

deep (dēp) *adj* **1** going far down, back, or in: *a deep cut, a deep breath.* **2** absorbed or engrossed: *deep in thought.* **3** with a certain depth: *a puddle five centimetres deep, a lineup three deep to see the movie.* **4** low in pitch: *a deep voice.* **5** rich and dark in colour: *a deep red.* **6** intense, strong, or extreme: *deep sorrow, a deep sleep, a deep discount.* **7 a** requiring much thought to understand: *a deep book.* **b** very intellectual: *a deep thinker.* **8** *Baseball* farther from home plate or one of the bases than is usual: *deep left field.* **9** *Football, Soccer, etc.* nearer to the goal a team is defending than the goal it is attacking: *a deep defender.*
adv far down, back, or in: *to dig deep, to study deep into the night.*
n Poetic **the deep 1** the deepest or most intense part: *in the deep of winter.* **2** the sea. <Old English *deop*> **deep′en** *v.* **deep′ly** *adv.*
deep down, in one's innermost feelings: *Deep down she likes you, although she may not show it.*
go off the deep end, *Informal* **a** go to extremes; get carried away by one's feelings. **b** become insane.
in deep water, in serious difficulty or danger: *After all that spending, they were in deep water financially.*
in (too) deep, involved, or too involved, in a dangerous or compromising situation.

deep–dish (dēp′dish′) *adj* baked in a container with high sides: *deep-dish pizza, a deep-dish pie.*

deep–freeze (dēp′frēz′) *n* **1** a large freezer chest for freezing foods rapidly and storing them frozen for long periods. **2** the state of being frozen this way.
v **-froze** or **-freezed, -fro·zen, -freez·ing 1** freeze food rapidly or for long-term storage. **2** keep in a state of inactivity.

deep–fry (dēp′frī′) *v* **-fried, -fry·ing** fry in deep fat or oil.

deep–root·ed (dēp′rū′tid) *adj* **1** firmly fixed, intense, and of long standing: *a deep-rooted distrust of advertising.* **2** with deep roots.

deep–sea (dēp′sē′) *adj* done in the deepest parts of the ocean: *deep-sea diving.*

deep–seat·ed (dēp′sē′tid) *adj* established over time and mostly unconscious, such as in a feeling or belief: *deep-seated anxiety.*

deep–set (dēp′set′) *adj* set deeply in: *deep-set eyes.*

deep space *n* space beyond the earth's atmosphere.

deer (dēr) *n, pl* **deer 1** a cud-chewing animal with long, slender legs and small, split hoofs. The males (and in some species, the females) have solid, bony antlers that are shed each year. **2** an animal belonging to the same family as the true deer, such as moose, wapiti (elk), or caribou. **3** 🍁 *North* a caribou. <Old English *deor* animal>

deer

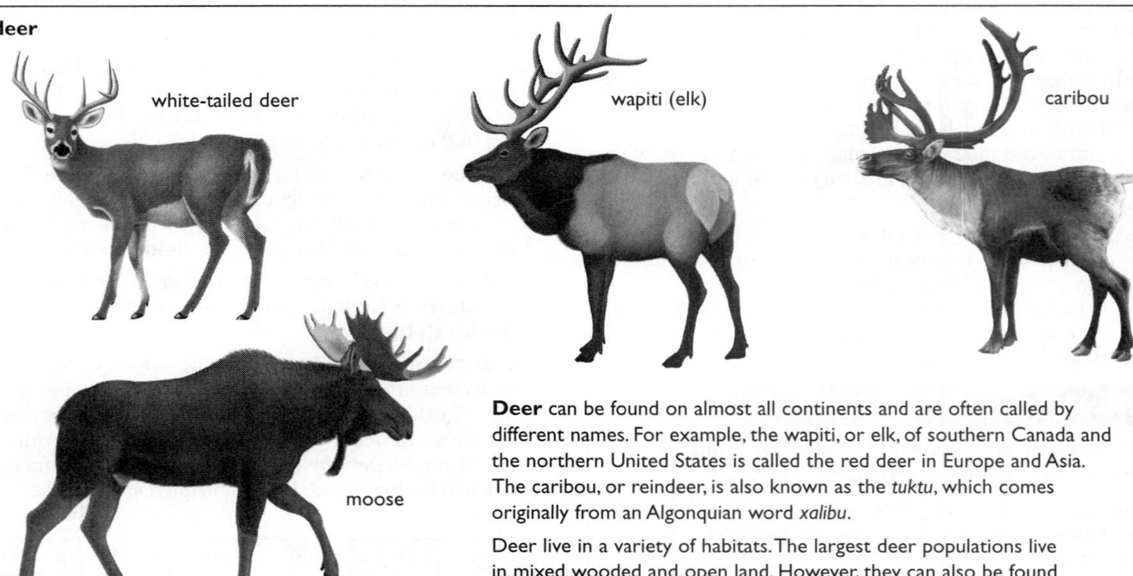

Deer can be found on almost all continents and are often called by different names. For example, the wapiti, or elk, of southern Canada and the northern United States is called the red deer in Europe and Asia. The caribou, or reindeer, is also known as the *tuktu*, which comes originally from an Algonquian word *xalibu*.

Deer live in a variety of habitats. The largest deer populations live in mixed wooded and open land. However, they can also be found on mountains, in swamps, and on tundra areas of North America, Scandinavia, and northern Asia.

deer·fly (dēr′flī′) *n, pl* **deer·flies** a small blood-sucking fly related to the horsefly.

deer mouse *n* a small N American mouse with white feet and large ears.

deer·skin (dēr′skin′) *n* **1** the hide of a deer, or leather made from it. **2 deerskins** *pl* clothes made from this.

deer·stalk·er (dēr′stok′ər) *n* a soft cloth cap with earflaps, originally worn by hunters.

de·face (di fās′) *v* **de·faced, de·fac·ing** spoil the appearance of: *Scribbled notes defaced the book's pages.* <Old French *des-* removal + *face* face> **de·face′ment** *n.*

de fac·to (di fak′tō) *adj* **1** in fact. **2** actually existing, whether recognized or not: *a de facto government.* <Latin = from the fact>

de·fame (di fām′) *v* **de·famed, de·fam·ing** attack the good reputation of someone: *The candidate tried to defame his opponent.* **def′a·ma′tion** *n.* **de·fam′a·to′ry** *adj.*

de·fault (di folt′) *n* **1** a failure to do something, or appear somewhere when due: *If a team does not show up, it loses by default.* **2** something done automatically if there are no other instructions: *Unless you write down another country, they register you as Canadian; that's the default.* **3** *Computers* a pre-selected option adopted when no alternative is given.
v **1** fail to do or appear when due: *They defaulted on their loan.* **2** assume a certain status automatically if there are no other instructions: *The "hours of overtime" field defaults to zero if left blank.*
adj automatically assigned or carried out if there are no other instructions: *The default screen setting is black on white.* <Old French *defaute* failure, from Latin *de-* entirely + *fallere* disappoint>
in default of, in the absence of: *In default of proper tools, she used a hairpin and a nail file.*

de·feat (di fēt′) *v* **1** win a victory over: *to defeat another team in hockey, to defeat a bad habit.* **2** block or thwart: *The bill was defeated in Parliament, to defeat someone's plans.*
n the act of defeating or the fact of being defeated. <Old French, from Latin *dis-* un- + *facere* do>

de·feat·ism (di fē′tiz əm) *n* an attitude of expecting defeat. **de·fea′tist** *n, adj.*

def·e·cate (def′ə kāt′) *v* **def·e·cat·ed, def·e·cat·ing** have a bowel movement. <Latin *de-* away + *faex* dregs> **def′e·ca′tion** *n.*

de·fect (dē′fekt) *for n,* (di fekt′) *for v. n* a flaw or weakness: *surgery to correct a heart defect. Jealousy was the only defect in her character.*
v abandon one's own country, party, or group for another. <Old French, from Latin *deficere* to fall short, fail> **de·fec′tion** *n.* **de·fec′tor** *n.*

de·fec·tive (di fek′tiv) *adj* with a noticeable defect or not working properly: *We returned the toaster because it was defective.*

de·fence (di fens′) *n* **1** the act of protecting or guarding against attack or harm: *The armed forces are responsible for the nation's defence.* **2** anything that protects or guards against attack: *walls, moats, and other defences. Your best defence against their lies is the truth.* **3** *Sports* **a** all efforts made to keep an opponent from scoring. **b** the player or players primarily responsible for this, or the position that they play. **4** a statement arguing in favour of something: *He has written a defence of standardized tests.* **5** *Law* **a** the argument of an accused person who pleads not guilty: *Her defence was temporary insanity.* **b** an accused person and his or her lawyers: *a witness for the defence.* Also (*especially US*), **defense.** <Old French, from Latin *defendere* defend> **de·fence′less** *adj.* **de·fence′less·ness** *n.*

D

de·fend (di fend′) *v* **1** protect from attack or harm: *She defended her little brother against the bullies.* **2** justify with arguments: *The company defended its policy in a letter to the editor.* **3** *Sports* try to keep opponents away from the goal. **4** try to keep a position by taking on a challenger: *to defend a championship title. She is defending her seat in the next provincial election.* **5** *Law* **a** act as counsel for an accused person in court. **b** resist a charge or claim in court: *Is he going to defend the speeding charge?* <Old French, from Latin *de-* off + *fendere* to strike> **de·fend′er** *n.*

de·fend·ant (di fen′dənt) *n* a person accused or sued in a law court.

de·fen·si·ble (di fen′sə bəl) *adj* **1** able to be defended from attack. **2** able to be argued for.

de·fen·sive (di fen′siv) *adj* **1** for defence: *defensive strategy.* **2** trying to avoid being harmed by others: *defensive driving.* **3** acting or speaking as if one is being attacked or accused: *There's no need to get defensive; I'm just making a suggestion.* **de·fen′sive·ly** *adv.*
on the defensive, a fighting off an attack. **b** acting or speaking as if attacked or accused: *He's been criticized so often that he's always on the defensive now.*

de·fer[1] (di fər′) *v* **de·ferred, de·fer·ring** put off or postpone: *The track meet has been deferred for another week.* <Old French, from Latin *dis-* apart + *ferre* bring> **de·fer′ment** *n.*

de·fer[2] (di fər′) *v* **de·ferred, de·fer·ring** submit to another's judgment or wishes: *He deferred to his father and put on the news instead of a sitcom.* <Old French, from Latin *de-* down + *ferre* carry>

def·er·ence (def′ə rəns) *n* **1** submission to the judgment or wishes of another. **2** respect or honour: *As a mark of deference, he stood up when she entered.*
def′er·en′tial *adj.* **def′er·en′tial·ly** *adv.*
in deference to, out of respect for: *In deference to local custom, they kept their heads covered.*

de·fi·ance (di fī′əns) *n* the act or attitude of openly challenging or opposing: *Rebellion is defiance against authority.* <Old French, from Latin *dis-* reversing + *fidus* faithful> **de·fi′ant** *adj.* **de·fi′ant·ly** *adv.*
in defiance of, in open disregard for: *In defiance of the subzero weather, she left her coat open.*

a bat	e bed	i bid	o pot	u cup	th **thin**
ā cake	ē **me**	ī bite	ō **go**	ū **rude**	ᴛʜ **then**
ä bar	ə about	ər over	ô for	ů put	zh measure

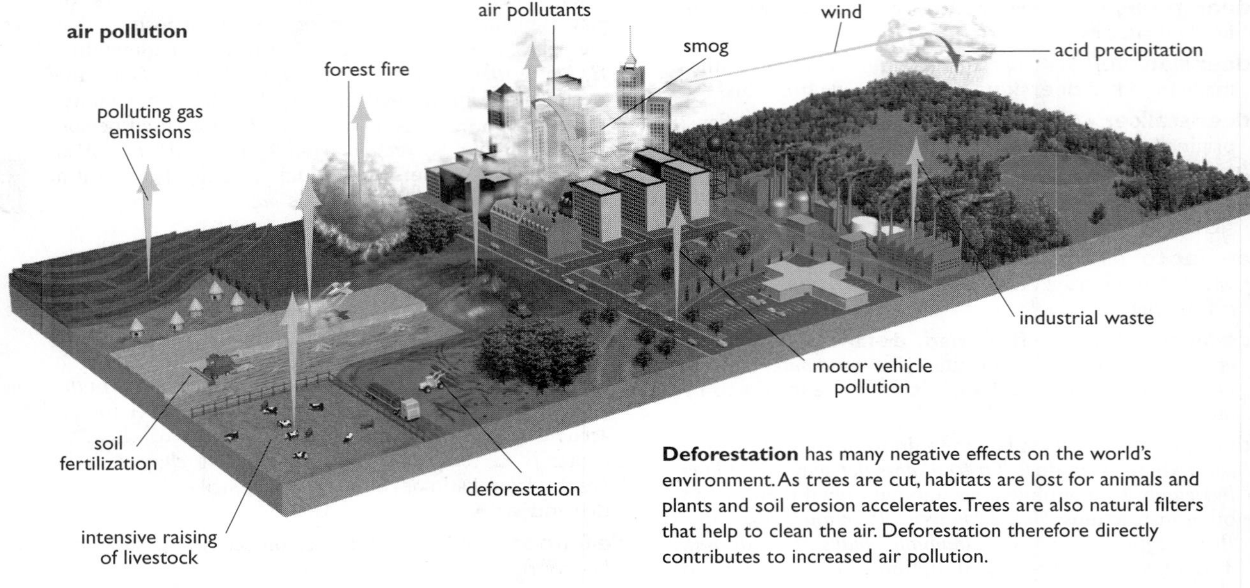

Deforestation has many negative effects on the world's environment. As trees are cut, habitats are lost for animals and plants and soil erosion accelerates. Trees are also natural filters that help to clean the air. Deforestation therefore directly contributes to increased air pollution.

de·fib·ril·late (dē fib′rə lāt′) *v* **de·fib·ril·lat·ed, de·fib·ril·lat·ing** stop the fibrillation or twitching of a muscle by applying electric shock. **de·fib′ril·la′tor** *n.*

de·fi·cient (di fish′ənt) *adj* **1** having or being too little: *My diet is deficient in iron.* **2** not up to standard: *His knowledge of geography is deficient.* <Latin *deficere* to fall short, fail> **de·fi′cien·cy** *n.*

def·i·cit (def′ə sit) *n* **1 a** the fact of having more expenses than income: *If we don't do some fundraising our swim club will end up with a deficit.* **b** the amount of this shortage. **2** a falling short in any area. <Latin = it is lacking>

de·file[1] (di fīl′) *v* **de·filed, de·fil·ing** violate something sacred or holy: *Raiders defiled the churches and temples.* <Old French *defouler* trample> **de·file′ment** *n.*

de·file[2] (dē′fīl) *n* a place so narrow that people must travel in single file, such as a steep and narrow valley. <French *dé-* off + *file* row>

de·fine (di fīn′) *v* **de·fined, de·fin·ing 1** give the meaning of: *A dictionary defines words.* **2** be the meaning or essence of: *Love defines real parenthood. Your life is defined by the choices you make.* **3** make sharp and distinct: *The mountain peaks were clearly defined against the sky.* **4** fix the limits of: *The powers of the courts are defined by law.* <Old French, from Latin *de-* entirely + *finire* limit> **de·fin′a·ble** *adj.*

def·i·nite (def′ə nit) *adj* **1** positive, sure, and clear: *She was very definite about the time of the shot. Is it definite that you're going?* **2** with stated limits: *within a definite time period.* <See DEFINE.>

definite article *Grammar n* in English, the word *the*, used to introduce a noun phrase and to refer to a person or thing that is known about, that has just been mentioned, or about which details will be given.

def·i·nite·ly (def′ə nit lē) *adv* **1** clearly and specifically: *The law very definitely forbids assault.* **2** certainly: *I definitely can't afford designer shoes.*

def·i·ni·tion (def′ə nish′ən) *n* **1** a statement that gives the meaning of a word or phrase: *Write a definition for each of the following words.* **2** the act of defining. **3** clearness or distinctness of image or sound: *You get better definition with this monitor.*
by definition, because of the very meaning or nature of the thing: *A son is by definition somebody's child.*

de·fin·i·tive (di fin′ə tiv) *adj* conclusive, final, or authoritative: *to issue a definitive statement on something.* **def·in′i·tive·ly** *adv.*

de·flate (di flāt′) *v* **de·flat·ed, de·flat·ing 1** let air out of a balloon or tire. **2** reduce the amount of: *to deflate prices. When a currency is deflated, its value increases.* **3** reduce confidence, excitement, or enthusiasm: *I was quickly deflated by their scornful laughter.* <Latin *de-* down + *flare* to blow> **de·fla′tion** *n.* **de·fla′tion·ar′y** *adj.*

de·flect (di flekt′) *v* cause to go off in another direction: *The gladiator used his shield to deflect his opponent's blows.* <Latin *de-* away + *flectere* to bend> **de·flec′tion** *n.*

de·flow·er (dē flou′ər) *v* **1** mar the beauty or innocence of. **2** end the virginity of.

de·fog (dē fog′) *v* **de·fogged, de·fog·ging** remove condensation from a window or mirror. **de·fog′ger** *n.*

de·fo·li·ate (dē fō′lē āt′) *v* **de·fo·li·at·ed, de·fo·li·at·ing** remove leaves from a plant, especially by means of a chemical spray. <Latin *de-* away + *folia* leaves> **de·fo′li·ant** *n, adj.* **de·fo′li·a′tion** *n.*

de·for·est (dē fô′rist) *v* clear the trees from an area: *Intense logging has deforested this region.* **de·for′es·ta′tion** *n.*

de·form (di fôrm′) *v* **1** distort the form or shape: *Shoes that are too tight deform the feet.* **2** make ugly: *a face deformed by rage.* **de′for·ma′tion** *n.* **de·formed′** *adj.* **de·form′i·ty** *n.*

de·fraud (di frod′) *v* cheat or swindle: *The criminals defrauded the widow of her savings.*

de·fray (di frā′) *v* pay costs or expenses: *The expenses of national parks are defrayed by taxpayers.* <French, from Latin *fredum* a fine for breach of the peace> **de·fray′al** *n.*

de·frost (di frost′) *v* **1** remove frost or ice from: *to defrost the windshield.* **2** thaw frozen food.
n a feature in a motor vehicle or freezer that removes frost: *The rear window defrost doesn't work.* **de·frost′er** *n.*

deft (deft) *adj* skilful or nimble: *the deft fingers of a surgeon.* <variant of *daft*> **deft′ly** *adv.* **deft′ness** *n.*

de·funct (di fungkt′) *adj* dead or extinct. <Latin *defunctus* dead>

de·fuse (dē fyūz′) *v* **de·fused, de·fus·ing** **1** remove the fuse or triggering device from an explosive device. **2** remove a source of possible trouble, conflict, or violence: *to defuse a tense situation.* See DIFFUSE for confusable.

de·fy (di fī′) *v* **de·fied, de·fy·ing** **1** set oneself openly against authority or danger: *to defy the law, to defy death.* **2** be too strong, great, or difficult for: *beauty that defies description.* **3** dare or challenge: *I defy you to stop us.* <Old French, from Latin *dis-* away + *fidus* faithful>

SYNONYMS

Defy often suggests acting against some type of control: *He defied his parents by sneaking out after being grounded.*

Oppose means "resist": *I opposed my cousin's plans for the evening because I don't like dancing.*

Withstand means "oppose successfully": *Our small tent managed to withstand the harsh wind and rain.*

de·gen·er·ate (di jen′ə rāt′) *for v,* (di jen′ə rit) *for adj or n. v* **de·gen·er·at·ed, de·gen·er·at·ing** grow worse in physical, mental, or moral condition.
adj having degenerated, especially morally: *Only a truly degenerate person would commit such a crime.*
n a degenerate person: *I want nothing to do with this degenerate.* <Latin *de-* away + *generus* race, kind> **de·gen′er·a·cy** *n.* **de·gen′er·a′tion** *n.*

de·gen·er·a·tive (di jen′ə rə tiv) *adj* causing or resulting from degeneration, especially physical or mental: *a degenerative disease, degenerative symptoms.*

de·grade (di grād′) *v* **de·grad·ed, de·grad·ing** **1** make or cause to seem unworthy: *Is it degrading to beg for money?* **2** lower the value of: *Any bruises will degrade the apple crop.* **deg′ra·da′tion** *n.*

de·gree (di grē′) *n* **1** a unit of temperature on a scale: *It's three degrees above freezing.* **2** a title given by a college or university to a student who fulfils certain academic requirements, or as an honour recognizing someone's life accomplishment: *to earn a bachelor's degree. She has an honorary degree from Simon Fraser University.* **3** amount, intensity, or extent: *To what degree is his complaint true?* **4** *Mathematics* **a** a unit for measuring angles. There are 360 degrees in a circle and 90 in a right angle. *Symbol* ° **b** of a vertex, the number of edges that meet at the vertex. **5** a unit of distance from the equator or from the PRIME MERIDIAN, used to locate places on the earth in terms of latitude and longitude. **6** rank or level: *Queens, lords, and other people of high degree, murder in the first degree, third-degree burns.* **7** a stage or step in a scale or process: *The sky grew darker by degrees. "Good," "better," and "best" are the three degrees of the adjective "good."* <Old French, from Latin *de-* down + *gradus* step, degree>

deg·ree–day (di grē′dā′) *n* a unit used to measure energy requirements for heating. It represents one degree of deviation from a reference point (usually 18°C) in the outdoor temperature.

de·his·cent (di his′ənt) *Botany adj* bursting open to release seeds or pollen. <Latin *dehiscere* to split open, from *de-* entirely + *hiare* gape> **de·hisce′** *v.*

de·hu·man·ize (dē hyū′mə nīz′) *v* **de·hu·man·ized, de·hu·man·iz·ing** cause to seem less than human. **de·hu′man·i·za′tion** *n.*

de·hu·mid·i·fy (dē′ hyū mid′ə fī′) *v* **de·hu·mid·i·fied, de·hu·mid·i·fy·ing** remove moisture from the air. **de′hu·mid′i·fi·ca′tion** *n.* **de′hu·mid′i·fi′er** *n.*

de·hy·drate (dē hī′drāt) *v* **de·hy·drat·ed, de·hy·drat·ing** **1** remove water or moisture from: *Dehydrated foods are good for wilderness camping.* **2** lose too much water or moisture from the body: *Drink while exercising or you'll dehydrate.* **3** *Chemistry* remove water or its elements from a chemical compound. <*de-* away+ Greek *hydor* water> **de′hy·dra′tion** *n.*

de–ice (dē īs′) *v* **-iced, -ic·ing** remove ice from: *We had to wait on the ground while the plane was de-iced.* **de-ic′er** *n.*

de·i·fy (dē′ə fī′) *v* **de·i·fied, de·i·fy·ing** treat or worship as a god: *The ancient Egyptians deified their Pharaohs.* <Old French, from Latin *deus* god> **de′i·fi·ca′tion** *n.*

deign (dān) *v* (*usually ironic*) be gracious enough to people whom one considers below one's status: *The waiter finally deigned to notice us.* <Old French, from *dignus* worthy>

de·i·on·ize (dē ī′ə nīz′) *v* **de·i·on·ized, de·i·on·iz·ing** remove ions from water, especially salt ions. **de·i′on·i·za′tion** *n.*

de·ism (dē′iz əm) *n* the belief that a supreme being has created the universe but does not have a relationship with human beings, influence their lives, or intervene in the world in any way. <Latin *deus* god> **de′ist** *n.* **de·is′tic** *adj.*

de·i·ty (dē′ə tē) *n, pl* **de·i·ties** **1** a god or goddess. **2** the fact of being a god: *The Babylonians believed in the deity of the emperor.* <Latin *deus* god>

dé·jà vu (dā′zhȧ vū′) *n* the feeling that one has already experienced the present situation. <French = already seen>

a bat	e bed	i bid	o pot	u cup	th thin
ā cake	ē me	ī bite	ō go	ū rude	ᴛʜ then
ȧ bar	ə about	ər over	ô for	u̇ put	zh measure

de·ject·ed (di jek′tid) *adj* discouraged and sad. <Latin *deicere* to cast down, from *de-* down + *-iecere* to throw> **de·ject′ed·ly** *adv.* **de·jec′tion** *n.*

deke (dēk) *Informal n* especially in hockey, a movement, such as a fake shot, intended to draw a defending player out of position.
v **deked, dek·ing 1** make such a movement. **2** (*often with* ***out***) draw a defending player out of position in this way. <*decoy*>

de·lay (di lā′) *v* **1** hinder or slow down the progress of: *The accident delayed the train for two hours.* **2** hesitate or go slowly: *Go at once; don't delay.* **3** postpone.
n the act of delaying or fact of being delayed: *We can afford no further delay.* <Old French *delayer* postpone>

de·lec·ta·ble (di lek′tə bəl) *adj* delicious or delightful: *We ate some delectable pastries.* <Old French, from Latin *delectare* to charm> **de·lec′ta·bly** *adv.*

del·e·gate (del′ə gāt′) *v* **del·e·gat·ed, del·e·gat·ing** appoint someone to take over a task or area of responsibility: *to delegate authority. She delegated a committee member to do the phoning.*
n a person appointed in this way, especially one sent somewhere as a representative: *Sixty delegates from across Canada attended the meeting.* <Latin *de-* down + *legare* instruct someone to act on one's behalf>

del·e·ga·tion (del′ə gā′shən) *n* **1** the act of delegating. **2** a group of delegates or representatives sent to some event: *The Winnipeg delegation sat together.*

de·lete (di lēt′) *v* **de·let·ed, de·let·ing** strike out or remove something written or printed: *Delete her name from the list.* <Latin *delere* destroy> **de·le′tion** *n.*

del·e·te·ri·ous (del′ə tē′rē əs) *adj* harmful: *Overwork has a deleterious effect on your health.* <Latin, from Greek *deleterios* harmful>

del·i (del′ē) *Informal n* delicatessen.
adj to do with or sold in such a store: *deli meats.*

de·lib·er·ate (di lib′ə rit) *for adj,* (di lib′ə rāt′) *for v. adj* **1** made or done on purpose: *a deliberate lie.* **2** slow and careful or purposeful: *deliberate steps.*
v **de·lib·er·at·ed, de·lib·er·at·ing 1** think something over carefully: *She deliberated awhile before stating her opinion.* **2** debate or discuss, especially in a legislative body: *Parliament is deliberating the tax hike.* <Latin *de-* entirely + *librare* weigh> **de·lib′er·ate·ly** *adv.* **de·lib′er·ate·ness** *n.* **de·lib′er·a·tive** *adj.*

de·lib·er·a·tion (di lib′ə rā′shən) *n* **1** careful thought or discussion. **2** slowness and care: *She took aim with great deliberation.*

del·i·ca·cy (del′ə kə sē) *n, pl* **del·i·ca·cies 1** a fine or choice food: *caviar and other delicacies.* **2** the fact or quality of being delicate: *the delicacy of lace. This is a matter of great delicacy, so be discreet.*

del·i·cate (del′ə kit) *adj* **1** light, fine, or subtle: *a delicate fragrance.* **2** finely fashioned or textured: *delicate woodcarving, delicate silk.* **3** easily broken, hurt, or made ill: *delicate china. He has a delicate constitution and is often sick.* **4** responding to very slight changes: *delicate instruments.* **5** requiring skill or tact: *a delicate heart operation, a delicate situation.* **6** showing tact and good taste: *How can I put this in a more delicate way?* <Latin *delicatus* pampered> **del′i·cate·ly** *adv.*

del·i·ca·tes·sen (del′ə kə tes′ən) *n* **1** a store that sells prepared foods, such as cooked meats, smoked fish, cheese, and salads. **2** such foods. <German *Delikatesse* fine food, from French *délicatesse* delicate>

de·li·cious (di lish′əs) *adj* very pleasing or delightful, especially to taste or smell: *delicious apples, a delicious excitement.* <Old French, from Latin *deliciae* delight, pleasure> **de·li′cious·ly** *adv.* **de·li′cious·ness** *n.*

SYNONYMS

Delicious usually describes something good to eat or that has an appealing aroma: *The meal was delicious.*

Delightful means "enjoyable": *It was a delightful movie because of the happy ending.*

Gratifying means "pleasing": *It was gratifying to see my artwork displayed.*

de·light (di līt′) *n* **1** great pleasure or joy. **2** something that gives great pleasure: *The resort offers good food, lovely scenery, and other delights.*
v **1** please greatly: *His stories delighted the audience.* **2** find pleasure: *She delights in playing practical jokes.* <Old French, from Latin *delectere* to charm> **de·light′ed** *adj.* **de·light′ed·ly** *adv.* **de·light′ful** *adj.* **de·light′ful·ly** *adv.*

de·lim·it (di lim′it) *v* fix or define the limits of: *School policy delimits the responsibilities of the Student Council.* **de·lim′i·ta′tion** *n.*

de·lin·e·ate (di lin′ē āt′) *v* **de·lin·e·at·ed, de·lin·e·at·ing 1** trace, draw, or outline: *a face with finely delineated features.* **2** describe carefully in words. <Latin *de-* about + *linea* line> **de·lin′e·a′tion** *n.*

de·link (dē lingk′) *v* cause to be no longer linked.

de·lin·quent (di ling′kwənt) *adj* **1** failing to do what is required by law or duty. **2** due and not paid: *delinquent taxes.*
n a delinquent person. <Latin *delinquere* to disobey> **de·lin′quen·cy** *n.*

del·i·ques·cent (del′ i kwe′ sənt) *adj* tending to become liquid by absorbing moisture from the air. <Latin *deliquescere*, from *liquere* be liquid> **del′i·ques′cence** *n.*

de·lir·i·ous (di lēr′ē əs) *adj* **1** temporarily with a disturbed mind and body resulting from illness or intoxication, and marked by restlessness, illusions, and confused thoughts: *a delirious fever. The patient was delirious.* **2** wildly excited: *delirious with joy.* <Latin *delirare* to be crazy, from *de-* off + *lire* = to go off the furrow> **de·lir′i·ous·ly** *adv.* **de·lir′i·um** *n.*

de·liv·er (di liv′ər) *v* **1** bring to the proper person, people, or place: *to deliver newspapers. Deliver these documents to the lawyer.* **2** help in the birth of: *A midwife delivered the baby.* **3** make, produce, or do for or to someone: *to deliver a speech, to deliver a good day's work. I delivered a swift kick to his knee.* **4** set free or rescue: *She was delivered from a life of homelessness.* **5** hand over or give up: *to deliver a fort to the enemy.* <Old French, from Latin *de-* away + *liberare* to free> **de·liv′er·er** *n.*

de·liv·er·ance (di liv′ə rəns) *n* the act of setting free.

de·liv·er·y (di liv′ə rē) *n, pl* **de·liv·er·ies** 1 the act, process, or manner of delivering: *mail delivery, the delivery of a baby. The content of his speech was good, but his delivery was poor.* 2 anything that is delivered: *The shipping department receives all deliveries.*

dell (del) *n* a small, sheltered valley, usually with trees in it. <Old English>

del·phin·i·um (del fin′ē əm) *n* a plant of the buttercup family that bears tall spikes of flowers. Also called **larkspur**. <Latin, from Greek *delphin* dolphin, from the shape of the flower>

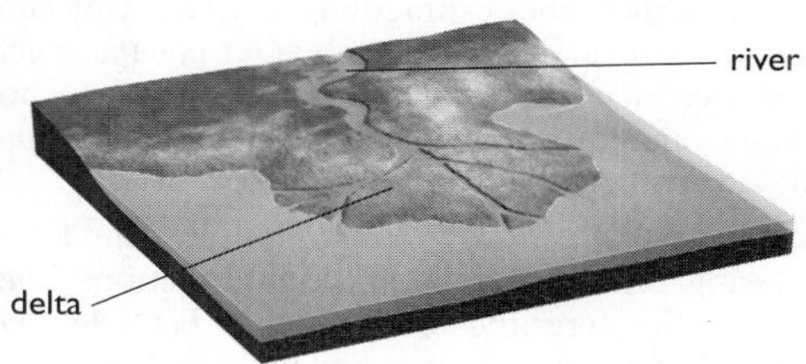

The world's largest **deltas** are those of the Nile River in Egypt, the Mississippi River in the United States, and the Ganges and Brahmaputra Rivers in India.

del·ta (del′tə) *n* 1 a deposit of earth and sand, usually three-sided, at the mouth of some rivers. 2 a code word representing the letter D, used in radio communications. <fourth letter of the Greek alphabet, shaped like a triangle>

de·lude (di lūd′) *v* **de·lud·ed, de·lud·ing** mislead or deceive, especially unintentionally: *He deluded himself into thinking study was unnecessary.* <Latin *de-* down + *ludere* to play>

del·uge (del′yūj) *n, v* **del·uged, del·ug·ing** flood. <Old French, from Latin *dis-* away + *luere* wash>

de·lu·sion (di lū′zhən) *n* 1 a completely false and often unreasonable belief, sometimes resulting from mental illness: *The king suffered from the delusion that his food was being poisoned.* 2 the act of deluding or the fact of being deluded. **de·lu′sion·al** *adj.*

de·luxe (di luks′) *adj* with many extras or luxurious additions: *a deluxe hotel suite. The deluxe model has power windows and leather seats.* <French *de luxe* of luxury>

GRAMMAR AND USAGE

Deluxe is sometimes used after the noun as in French, especially as an affectation of elegance. In that case, it is usually spelled as two French words: *I want the ice cream de luxe, with nuts and sprinkles.*

delve (delv) *v* **delved, delv·ing** reach inside something and search for: *delving in his pockets for some change. She delved for information in every library and on the Internet.* <Old English *delfan* dig>

de·mag·net·ize (dē mag′nə tīz′) *v* **de·mag·net·ized, de·mag·net·iz·ing** remove magnetism from. **de·mag′net·i·za′tion** *n.*

dem·a·gogue (dem′ə gog′) *n* a popular leader who stirs up the people by appealing to their emotions and prejudices: *He's no statesman; he's nothing but a demagogue.* **dem′a·gogu′e·ry** *n.*

de·mand (di mand′) *v* 1 ask for with authority or as if one has authority: *to demand someone's ID, to demand to be served. "Who are you?" he demanded.* 2 call for or require: *Training a puppy demands a lot of patience.*
n 1 an insistent request: *My frequent demands for money annoyed my mom.* 2 a situation that requires a response: *As a father of three, he has many demands on his time.* 3 the amount wanted or needed: *When the worldwide supply of oil exceeds the demand, the price goes down.* <Old French, from Latin *de-* entirely + *mandare* to order>
in (great) demand, wanted by many people: *Trained teachers are in great demand these days.*
on demand, whenever asked for: *video on demand.*

de·mand·ing (di man′ding) *adj* that requires or demands a lot of effort or attention: *a demanding job, a demanding child.* **de·mand′ing·ly** *adv.*

de·mar·cate (dē′mär kāt′) *or* (di mär′ kāt) *v* **de·mar·cat·ed, de·mar·cat·ing** 1 set and mark the limits of. 2 mark as different. <Spanish *de-* off + *marcar* to mark> **de′mar·ca′tion** *n.*

de·mean (di mēn′) *v* belittle or humiliate: *We were all demeaned by his sexist humour.* <*de-* down + *mean*[2], on the model of *debase*> **de·mean′ing** *adj.*

de·mean·our (di mē′nər) *n* the way a person looks and acts: *a boy of quiet, solemn demeanour.* <Old French, from Latin *de-* away + *minare* drive animals on with threats>

de·ment·ed (di men′tid) *adj* insane. <Old French, from Latin *de-* away + *mentis* mind> **de·ment′ed·ly** *adv.*

de·men·tia (di men′shə) *n* partial or total loss of mental powers such as memory, or the ability to distinguish reality from unreality. <See DEMENTED.>

de·mer·it (di mer′it) *n* 1 a mark against a person's record for violation of a rule or law: *He already has five demerits on his driving record.* 2 a fault or defect: *The two biggest demerits of this plan are expense and delay.*

dem·i·god (dem′ē god′) *Mythology n* a god that is partly human, the offspring of a deity and a human being: *Hercules was a demigod.*

dem·i·john (dem′ē jon′) *n* a large glass or earthenware bottle enclosed in wicker, sometimes used for wine. <French *dame-jeanne* Lady Jane, from the appearance of the bottle, which looks like a woman in a full skirt>

de·mil·i·tar·ize (dē mil′ə tə rīz′) *v* **de·mil·i·tar·ized, de·mil·i·tar·iz·ing** remove military control from a place. **de·mil′i·ta·ri·za′tion** *n.*

de·mise (di mīz′) *n* a death, end, or disappearance: *My mom bewailed the demise of the full-service gas station. After her father's demise, she took over the business.* <Old French, from Latin *dis-* away + *mittere* send>

a **bat**	e **bed**	i **bid**	o **pot**	u **cup**	th **thin**
ā **cake**	ē **me**	ī **bite**	ō **go**	ū **rude**	ᴛʜ **then**
ä **bar**	ə **about**	ər **over**	ô **for**	ů **put**	zh **measure**

dem·i·tasse (dem′ē tas′) *n* **1** a very small cup for serving black coffee. **2** a serving of espresso in such a cup. <French = half cup>

dem·o (dem′ō) *n* **1** a car, machine, or other product used for demonstration or for testing by customers: *I got this DVD player cheap because it was a demo.* **2** a sample of a computer program or recorded work by a musician: *I downloaded a demo of the game from a Web site. Send the radio station a demo with your résumé.* **3** a demonstration of a product and how it is used: *She's doing demos of their new laptop at the trade fair.*
adj used for demonstration purposes: *a demo CD.*

de·mo·bi·lize (dē mō′bə līz′) *v* **de·mo·bi·lized, de·mo·bi·liz·ing 1** disband an army. **2** release a person from military service. **de·mo′bi·li·za′tion** *n.*

de·moc·ra·cy (di mok′rə sē) *n, pl* **de·moc·ra·cies** **1 a** a system of government in which the people either vote directly on issues or elect representatives to do so. **b** the ideals and principles underlying this system, such as equality of rights and opportunities and the rule of the majority. **2** a country or a community with such a government: *Canada is a democracy.* <French, from Greek *demos* people + *kratos* rule>

dem·o·crat (dem′ə krat′) *n* **1** a person who believes in democracy as a form of government, or who upholds equality of rights and opportunities and the rule of the majority. **2** a person, especially one in authority, who treats others as equals. **3 Democrat** *US* a member of the Democratic Party.

dem·o·crat·ic (dem′ə krat′ik) *adj* **1** to do with democracy; consistent with the principles of democracy. **2** treating others as one's equals. **3 Democratic** *US* to do with the Democratic Party. **de·moc′ra·tize′** *v.*

de·mod·u·late (dē moj′ə lāt′) *Electronics v* **de·mod·u·lat·ed, de·mod·u·lat·ing** separate an output signal from a radio wave whose frequency has been varied.

de·mo·graph·ics (dem′ə graf′iks) *n* **1** (*with plural verb*) the statistics about a certain population, such as age, sex, average income, language, family size, or area of residence. **2** (*with singular verb*) the science of collecting and dealing with such statistics. <Greek *demos* people + *graphein* write> **de′mo·graph′ic** *adj.*

de·mol·ish (di mol′ish) *v* tear down; wreck; destroy completely: *to demolish an old building, to demolish an argument.* <French, from Latin *de-* down + *moles* mass> **dem′o·li′tion** *n.*

demolition derby *n* a contest using old cars to smash up other old cars, to see which can do the most damage.

de·mon (dē′mən) *n* **1** an evil spirit or devil. **2** a wicked or cruel person. **3** an evil influence: *the demon alcohol, the demon of greed.* **4** a person of great energy, speed, or skill: *a demon for work. Behind the wheel, she's a demon.* <Latin, from Greek *daimon* divinity, spirit> **de·mon′ic** *adj.* **de·mon′i·cal·ly** *adv.*

de·mon·ize (dē′mə nīz′) *v* **de·mon·ized, de·mon·iz·ing** **1** represent or think of as evil: *The article unfairly demonizes video games.* **2** have a demonic influence on. **de′mon·i·za′tion** *n.*

de·mon·stra·ble (di mon′strə bəl) *adj* able to be proved: *That's not merely a theory, it's a demonstrable fact.* **de·mon′stra·bly** *adv.*

dem·on·strate (dem′ən strāt′) *v* **dem·on·strat·ed, dem·on·strat·ing 1** show how something is done or how it works, by actually using or doing it in front of someone: *to demonstrate how to get on a horse, to demonstrate a new product.* **2** give evidence of or show by action: *He demonstrates his love by generous giving.* **3** express one's opinion publicly about something, such as by picketing or taking part in a rally or march: *Outside the embassy a crowd was demonstrating against the war.* **4** show by evidence and reasoning. <Latin *de-* entirely + *monstrare* show> **dem′on·stra′tion** *n.*

de·mon·stra·tive (di mon′strə tiv) *adj* **1** openly expressing one's feelings, especially affection: *The girl's demonstrative greeting embarrassed her shy brother.* **2** *Grammar* pointing out a certain one (or more than one). *This, that, these,* and *those* are demonstrative words.
n Grammar a demonstrative pronoun or adjective. **de·mon′stra·tive·ly** *adv.*

dem·on·stra·tor (dem′ən strā′tər) *n* **1** a person who takes part in a public demonstration: *The street in front of the embassy was crowded with angry demonstrators.* **2** a person who demonstrates how a piece of equipment works or how something is done. **3** an article or product used in a demonstration; a demo.

de·mor·alize (di môr′ə līz′) *v* **de·mor·al·ized, de·mor·al·iz·ing 1** weaken the spirit, hope, or discipline of: *The troops were demoralized by the loss of their beloved leader.* **2** corrupt or undermine the morals of: *The drug habit demoralizes people.* **3** throw into confusion or disorder: *Threats of war demoralized the stock market.* **de·mor′a·li·za′tion** *n.*

de·mote (di mōt′) *v* **de·mot·ed, de·mot·ing** put back to a lower rank or position: *She was demoted from sergeant to private.* <*de-* down + *promote*> **de·mo′tion** *n.*

de·mur (di mər′) *v* **de·murred, de·mur·ring** object or protest about something: *When asked to do her brother's chores, she demurred.* <Old French, from Latin *de-* entirely + *morari* to delay, i.e., stop, refuse> **de·mur′ral** *n.*

de·mure (di myūr′) *adj* **de·mur·er, de·mur·est** quiet and modest in behaviour, or pretending to be so: *She gave a demure smile.* <perhaps Old French, from Latin *matures* ripe> **de·mure′ly** *adv.* **de·mure′ness** *n.*

de·my·thol·o·gize (dē′mə thol′ə jīz′) *v* **de·my·thol·og·ized, de·my·thol·og·iz·ing** strip the mystical, supernatural, or mythical elements from: *The author attempts to demythologize Joan of Arc.*

den (den) *n* **1** a wild animal's home: *The bear made its den in a cave.* **2** a room in a home where a person can read, work, or think in privacy. **3** a room, building, etc. where disreputable people gather: *The abandoned warehouse was a drug dealers' den.* <Old English *denn*> **den′like′** *adj.*

de·na·tion·a·lize (dē nash′ə nə līz′) *v* **de·na·tion·al·ized, de·na·tion·al·iz·ing** take from national government control and put under private control or ownership.

de·na·ture (dē nā′chər) *v* **de·na·tured, de·na·tur·ing** 1 change the essential qualities or properties of: *denatured proteins, denatured DNA samples.* 2 make unfit for drinking or eating without destroying its usefulness for other purposes: *denatured alcohol.*

den·drite (den′drīt) *n* 1 a stone or mineral with branching, treelike markings. 2 such a marking. 3 the branching part at the receiving end of a nerve cell. <French, from Greek *dendron* tree> **den·drit′ic** (den drit′ik) *adj.*

De·ne Nation (den′ā) *n* the official organization representing the Athapaskan peoples of the Northwest Territories. <Athapaskan *dene* people, men>

De·nen·deh (den′en de′) *n* the homeland of the Athapaskan peoples in the Northwest Territories.

De·ne–thah (den′ā tȧ′) *n, pl or sing* 1 a member of a First Nations people of the Northwest Territories living between the Rockies and Great Slave Lake. 2 their Athapaskan language.
adj to do with these people or their language. Also called **Slavey**, **Slave**, or **Acha'otinne**.

den·gue (deng′gā) *n* an infectious tropical fever with skin rash and severe pain in the joints and muscles. <Spanish, from Swahili (a language of Africa) *dinga*>

de·ni·al (di nī′əl) *n* 1 the act of denying something: *the denial of a request, the denial of a previous statement.* 2 *Psychology* a state of ignoring the effects of something unpleasant, or acting as if it is not true: *He is still in denial over the death of his father.*

den·i·grate (den′ə grāt′) *v* **den·i·grat·ed, den·i·grat·ing** attack the reputation of; belittle: *You shouldn't denigrate the other team just because they had one bad game.* **den′i·gra′tion** *n.* **den′i·gra′tor** *n.*

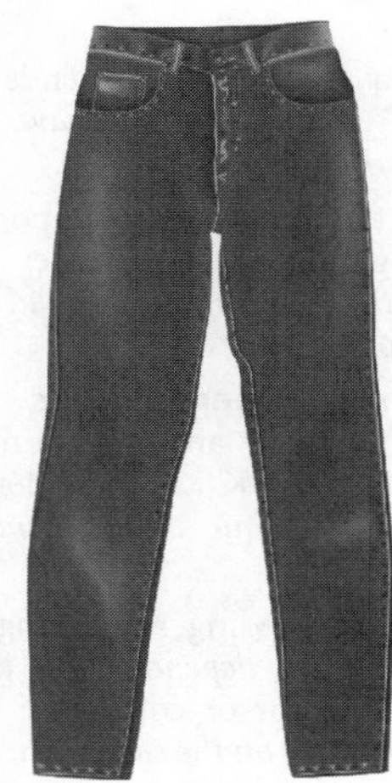

In the late 1800s, a man by the name of Levi Strauss added copper rivets to "waist overalls," and modern jeans were born. His original purpose was to provide a sturdy work garment made of strong, durable fabric. The fabric, of course, was **denim**. Over the years, denim jeans have gradually changed from being strictly work clothing to extremely popular wear for leisure activities.

den·im (den′əm) *n* a heavy cotton cloth with a diagonal weave, of the kind that jeans are made of. <French *de Nîmes* of Nîmes, where it was first made>

den·i·zen (den′ə zən) *n* 1 one that lives or spends a lot of time in a certain place: *denizens of the video arcade. Fish are the denizens of the sea.* 2 a foreigner who is given certain rights. 3 a foreign plant or animal that has been naturalized: *Many English birds are now denizens of North America.* <Old French, from Latin *de-* entirely + *intus* within>

Den·mark (den′mark) *n* a country in Europe. See the APPENDIX. **Dane** *n.* **Dan′ish** *adj.*

de·nom·i·na·tion (di nom′ə nā′shən) *n* 1 a group of religious congregations sharing a certain way of interpreting and practising their faith: *Presbyterian and Baptist are two large denominations of Christians.* 2 a category based on units of value: *The gift certificates come in denominations of $10 and $25.* 3 a name, especially for a class or category: *He didn't like to go by the denomination of "secretary"; he preferred "archivist."* <Latin *de-* entirely + *nominis* to name> **de·nom′i·na′tion·al** *adj.*

de·nom·i·na·tor (di nom′ə nā′tər) *Mathematics n* the number below the line in a fraction, giving the total number of equal parts into which a whole is divided. In 3/4, 4 is the denominator, and 3 is the numerator.

de·no·ta·tion (dē′nə tā′shən) *n* the bare, literal meaning of a word, apart from any associations or emotional overtones it may have: *The denotation of "home" is "the place where one lives," but it expresses much more than that.* Compare CONNOTATION.

de·note (di nōt′) *v* **de·not·ed, de·not·ing** mean, especially literally: *The word "stool" denotes a small backless seat. The symbol "&" denotes "and."* <Latin *denotare*, from *de-* entirely + *notatare* to mark>

de·noue·ment or **dé·noue·ment** (dā′nū mȧɴ′) *n* the way things are worked out, with no questions or surprises remaining, at the end of a play, film, opera, or story. <French, from Latin *de-* not + *nodare* to knot>

de·nounce (di nouns′) *v* **de·nounced, de·nounc·ing** 1 express strong disapproval of: *The judge denounced drinking and driving.* 2 inform against or accuse: *She denounced her own brother to the police as a thief.* <Old French, from Latin *de-* down + *nuntiare* to announce> **de·nun′ci·a′tion** (di nun′sē ā′shən) *n.*

dense (dens) *adj* **den·ser, den·sest** 1 closely packed together: *dense population, a dense forest, dense fog.* 2 with much matter per unit of volume: *Ironwood is denser than other woods.* 3 dull witted or slow thinking: *He's too dense to get that joke.* <Latin *densus*> **dense′ly** *adv.* **dense′ness** *n.*

den·si·ty (den′sə tē) *n, pl* **den·si·ties** 1 the fact or degree of being dense: *The density of the forest hampered our progress.* 2 the quantity of mass per unit of volume of a substance, especially relative to another substance.

dent (dent) *n* a place where a surface has been knocked or pushed inward: *There was a dent in the fender where the car had been hit.*
v make a dent in or acquire a dent: *Don't pack the melon on top of the bread; it'll dent the loaf. This thin metal dents easily.* <Middle English> **dent′ed** *adj.*
make a dent in, reduce noticeably: *The new carpet sure made a dent in our savings.*

a bat	e bed	i bid	o pot	u cup	th thin
ā cake	ē me	ī bite	ō go	ū rude	ᴛʜ then
ȧ bar	ə about	ər over	ȯ for	u̇ put	zh measure

D

den·tal (den′təl) *adj* to do with the teeth or dentistry: *dental hygiene, a dental appointment.*

ETYMOLOGY

Dental is one of a series of words in English that come from the Latin root *dentis*, a form of *dens*, meaning "tooth."

Dentine, *dentist*, and *denture* are all from the same source and all have to do with teeth.

dental floss *n* a thin, strong, smooth thread used to remove food particles from between the teeth.

dental hygienist *n* a trained technician who cleans people's teeth, takes X-rays, and other tasks related to dental health.

den·tine (den′tēn), (den′tin), *or* (den tēn′) *n* the hard, bony material beneath the enamel of the tooth, forming the main part of a tooth. Also, **dentin.** <See DENTAL.>

den·tist (den′tist) *n* a person trained to treat tooth decay and other problems and diseases of the teeth and gums. <See DENTAL.> **den′tist·ry** *n.*

den·ture (den′chər) *n* a full or partial set of artificial teeth, fitted by a trained **denturist.**

de·nu·cle·ar·ize (dē nyū′klē ə rīz′) *or* (dē nū′klē ə rīz′) *v* **de·nu·cle·ar·ized, de·nu·cle·ar·i·zing** make free of nuclear weapons.

de·nude (di nyūd′) *or* (di nūd′) *v* **de·nud·ed, de·nud·ing** make bare: *The denuded maples swayed in the winter wind.*

de·nun·ci·a·tion (di nun′sē ā′shən) *n* the act of denouncing or a statement that denounces. **de·nun′ci·a·to′ry** *adj.*

de·ny (di nī′) *v* **de·nied, de·ny·ing 1** declare that something is not true: *to deny an accusation. He denied that he had been in the computer lab.* **2** refuse to give: *to deny a request, to deny someone a fair trial.* <Old French, from Latin *de-* away + *negare* say no>
deny yourself, do without the things you want.

de·o·dor·ant (dē ō′də rənt) *n* a substance that destroys, prevents, or masks an unpleasant odour, especially such a substance used on the body.
adj destroying, preventing, or masking undesirable odours: *deodorant soap.*

de·o·dor·ize (dē ō′də rīz′) *v* **de·o·dor·ized, de·o·dor·iz·ing** remove undesirable odours from: *to deodorize a cat's litter box.* **de·o′dor·iz′er** *n.*

de·ox·y·ri·bo·nu·cle·ic acid (dē ok′sē rī′bō nyū klē′ik) DNA.

🍁 **dé·pan·neur** (de′pə nər′) *Québec n* a convenience store.

de·part (di pårt′) *v* **1** go away or leave: *The train departs at 5:04 p.m.* **2** turn away from a habit or standard; think or do things differently: *In this movie the director departs from the usual conventions.* <Old French, from Latin *dispertire* to divide>
depart this life, *Formal or Poetic* die.

de·part·ed (di pår′tid) *adj* dead or gone: *We fondly remember our dear departed brother.*
n a dead person or persons: *a poem in honour of the departed.*

de·part·ment (di pårt′mənt) *n* **1** a division of an organization, warehouse, or store devoted to a certain thing: *the math department of a high school, the furniture department of a store.* **2** a person's area of activity or influence: *Sorry, yard work is not my department.* **3** in some countries, an administrative district similar to a province. <See DEPART.>

de·part·men·tal (di pårt′men′təl) *adj* to do with departments or divided into departments.
n 🍁 in former times, a standardized examination held at the end of high school.

department store *n* a large store that sells many different kinds of items arranged in separate departments.

de·par·ture (di pår′chər) *n* **1** the act of departing or leaving. **2** a change from the usual: *Having sushi today was a real departure for her; she normally eats vegetables.* **3 Departures** *pl* the part of an airport where passengers depart on a flight.

de·pend (di pend′) *v* **1** be controlled or influenced by: *The success of the School Fair depends partly on the weather.* **2** rely on or trust: *You can depend on us to get you there safely.* **3** be supported by: *Children depend on their parents. Their conclusion depends on two very strong arguments.* **4** hang down. <Old French, from Latin *de-* down + *pendere* hang>
that (or **it**) **depends,** *Informal* the answer will be determined by certain conditions not yet definitely known: *"Can we have pizza tonight, Mom?" "That depends. What did you have for lunch?"*

de·pend·a·ble (di pen′də bəl) *adj* reliable or trustworthy. **de·pend′a·bil′i·ty** *n.*

de·pend·ant (di pen′dənt) *n* a person who depends on someone else for support: *My aunt and uncle have two incomes and no dependants, so they're pretty well off.*

de·pend·ence (di pen′dəns) *n* the fact of being supported or controlled by something or someone else: *the dependence of crops on the weather. Getting a job would end her dependence on her grandmother.*

de·pend·en·cy (di pen′dən sē) *n, pl* **de·pend·en·cies 1** a country or territory controlled by another country: *Gibraltar is a dependency of the UK.* **2** dependence. **3** addiction to a substance: *This clinic treats chemical dependency.*

de·pend·ent (di pen′dənt) *adj* **1** needing something or someone else for support: *Pets are dependent on their owners.* **2** determined by some factor or condition: *The student council's decision is dependent on the staff's reaction to the idea.* **3 a** addicted to a substance: *chemically dependent.* **b** excessively involved with or controlled by another person: *Even as an adult he was emotionally dependent on his mother.*

dependent clause SUBORDINATE CLAUSE.

dependent variable *Mathematics n* a variable whose value is determined by the value of some other variable forming part of its definition. In $y = 5x$, y is the dependent variable; its value depends on the value of x.

de·per·son·al·ize (dē pər′sə nə līz′) *v* **de·per·son·al·ized, de·per·son·al·iz·ing 1** make impersonal: *to depersonalize health care.* **2** treat impersonally: *Does online business depersonalize customers?* **de·per′son·al·i·za′tion** *n.*

de·pict (di pikt′) *v* create or be an image of: *The* Mona Lisa *depicts a woman smiling. The author depicts life on the Prairies during the Depression.* <Latin *de-* entirely + *pingere* to paint> **de·pic′tion** *n.*

de·pil·a·to·ry (di pil′ə tȯ′rē) *n, pl* **de·pil·a·to·ries** a preparation for removing unwanted hair.
adj for removing hair: *depilatory cream.* <Latin *de-* off + *pilus* hair>

de·plane (dē plān′) *v* **de·planed, de·plan·ing** leave an airplane: *It was raining as we deplaned at Pearson airport.*

de·plete (di plēt′) *v* **de·plet·ed, de·plet·ing** use up: *to deplete natural resources. All this printing has depleted our paper supply.* <Latin *de-* not + *plenus* full> **de·ple′tion** *n.*

de·plore (di plȯr′) *v* **de·plored, de·plor·ing** be very sorry about or appalled by; regret deeply: *We deplore these acts of violence.* <French, from Latin *de-* entirely + *plorare* regret> **de·plor′a·ble** *adj.* **de·plor′a·bly** *adv.*

de·ploy (di ploi′) *v* **1** use strategically: *to deploy your talents to the best possible advantage.* **2** distribute troops, staff, or resources in strategic positions for action: *The general deployed his troops along the southern border.* <French, from Latin *displicare* to scatter> **de·ploy′ment** *n.*

de·pop·u·late (dē pop′yə lāt′) *v* **de·pop·u·lat·ed, de·pop·u·la·ting** get rid of the people living in a place: *War and famine have virtually depopulated the region.* **de·pop′u·la′tion** *n.*

de·port (di pȯrt′) *v* send a non-citizen out of the country, usually back to his or her homeland: *Illegal immigrants may be deported.* <Latin *de-* away + *portare* carry> **de′por·ta′tion** *n.*

de·port·ment (di pȯrt′mənt) *n* graceful movement and proper etiquette: *Young women used to take lessons in deportment.*

de·pose (di pōz′) *v* **de·posed, de·pos·ing 1** remove from power: *The dictator was deposed by the revolution.* **2** *Law* **a** testify under oath as a witness, usually in writing to be used later in court. **b** receive or take down the sworn testimony of a witness: *Lawyers came to depose each staff member after the accident.* <Old French *de-* down + *poser* put>

de·pos·it (di poz′it) *v* **1** put in a place for safekeeping, especially money into a bank account: *She deposited most of each paycheque. They deposited a copy of their will with the lawyer.* **2** set or lay down: *He deposited his books on the table. The flood deposited a layer of mud in the streets.* **3** pay as a deposit.
n **1** the act of depositing, especially money or other valuables: *You can use the bank machine for deposits and withdrawals.* **2** a sum of money put in a bank account. **3** material laid down or left lying by natural means: *mineral deposits in the earth.* **4** something paid or given as a pledge that one will return a rented item, or pay or give more later: *To use the mall strollers you have to pay a refundable deposit of $10. Your real birthday gift is a personal stereo; this CD is just the deposit.* <Latin *de-* away, down + *ponere* put> **de·pos′i·tor** *n.*

dep·o·si·tion (dep′ə zish′ən) *n* **1** the act or fact of removal from power: *the deposition of a monarch by a political coup.* **2** *Law* **a** a testimony given under oath, usually in writing to be used later in court. **b** the act of giving or taking down such a testimony. **3** the process of depositing, especially the settling of eroded material: *River deltas are formed by the deposition of sediment.* <Latin *de-* away, down + *ponere* put>

D

dep·ot (dē′pō) *n* **1** a bus or railway station. **2** a warehouse or distribution centre: *a military supplies depot. There's a big discount footwear store called Shoe Depot.* <French, from Latin *depositum*>

de·prave (di prāv′) *v* **de·praved, de·prav·ing** make morally bad or corrupt: *Prison life often further depraves a criminal's character.* **de·praved′** *adj.* **de·prav′i·ty** (dep′rav′ə tē) *n.*

dep·re·cate (dep′rə kāt′) *v* **dep·re·cat·ed, dep·re·cat·ing 1** express disapproval of: *Environmental groups have deprecated the use of pesticides.* **2** (*especially in* ***self-deprecating***) belittle. <Latin *de-* away + *precari* pray> **dep′re·ca′tion** *n.* **dep′re·ca′tor** *n.* **dep′re·ca·to′ry** (dep′rə kə tȯr′ē) *adj.*

de·pre·ci·ate (di prē′shē āt′) *v* **de·pre·ci·at·ed, de·pre·ci·at·ing 1** go down or cause to go down in market value: *Cars depreciate by about half in the first year. The badly kept lawn and tumbledown shed depreciate this property.* **2** disparage or belittle: *She depreciates every effort I make.* <Latin *de-* down + *pretium* price> **de·pre′ci·a′tion** *n.* **de·pre′cia·to′ry** *adj.*

dep·re·da·tion (dep′rə dā′shən) *n* the act of plundering or robbery. <French, from Latin *de-* off + *praeda* booty>

de·press (di pres′) *v* **1** make very sad or gloomy: *Goodbyes depress me.* **2** press down: *If you depress this key, the cursor moves up.* **3** reduce, slow down, or weaken a process: *Some drugs depress heart action. Threats of war have depressed the economy.* **de·pressed′** *adj.* **de·press′ing** *adj.*

de·pres·sant (di pres′ənt) *n* anything that slows vital functions or causes mental depression: *Failing a course can be a powerful depressant.*

de·pres·sion (di presh′ən) *n* **1** *Psychiatry* a condition characterized by loss of interest in normal activities, loss of appetite, difficulty sleeping, feelings of hopelessness or sadness, and other symptoms. **2** a sad or gloomy feeling. **3** the act of pressing down: *Depression of these keys will lock the computer.* **4 a** a time of low economic activity and high unemployment. **b the Depression** or **the Great Depression** such a time in the 1930s, during which there was a prolonged and severe weakening of the economy. **5** a low place or hollow: *Depressions in the lawn were filled with water after the heavy rain.*

de·press·ive (di pres′iv) *adj* tending toward, suggesting, or caused by depression: *a depressive mood disorder, typical depressive behaviour.*
n a person who is clinically or chronically depressed.

a b**a**t	e b**e**d	i b**i**d	o p**o**t	u c**u**p	th **th**in
ā c**a**ke	ē m**e**	ī b**i**te	ō g**o**	ū r**u**de	ᴛʜ **th**en
ȧ b**a**r	ə **a**bout	ər ov**er**	ȯ f**o**r	u̇ p**u**t	zh mea**s**ure

de·press·or (di pres′ər) *n* **1** an instrument for pressing down: *That flat wooden stick is a tongue depressor.* **2** a person who or thing that depresses.

de·prive (di prīv′) *v* **de·prived, de·priv·ing** keep from having or doing something: *to be deprived of privileges because of bad behaviour. Worry deprived her of sleep.* <Old French, from Latin *de-* away + *privare* exempt> **dep′ri·va′tion** *n.*

> **SYNONYMS**
>
> **Deprive** suggests something is being denied: *The boy was deprived of his candy after he ate too much and became sick.*
>
> **Deny** can mean "refuse to give": *The reporters were denied access to the scene of the accident.*
>
> **Dispossess** means "deprive by taking away": *She was dispossessed of her land to make way for the new road.*

de·prived (di prīvd′) *adj* lacking the usual comforts or learning experiences: *a deprived childhood.*

de·pro·gram (dē prō′gram) *v* **de·pro·grammed, de·pro·gram·ming** help someone get rid of beliefs produced by brainwashing.

depth (depth) *n* **1** the quality or extent of being DEEP (def. 7): *depth of mind. Her writing is good but it lacks depth.* **2** the distance from top to bottom or from front to back: *the depth of a hole. The depth of our house lot is 50 m.* **3** the deepest part or place: *in the depth of winter, in the depths of the earth.* <Old English *deop* deep>
in depth, in a thorough and detailed way: *We studied Canadian history in depth.*
out of your depth, a involved in things you cannot understand or cope with. **b** in water so deep that you cannot touch bottom while keeping your head out.

depth charge *n* a bomb dropped from a ship or airplane into the water and set to explode at a certain depth.

depth perception *n* the ability to perceive and estimate the distance between nearer and farther objects and the distance between oneself and those objects.

dep·u·ta·tion (dep′yə tā′shən) *n* **1** a group sent or appointed to act for others: *The Fair Funding lobby sent a deputation to present their case to the Minister of Education.* **2** the act of appointing or sending someone in this way, or the work done by those appointed.

de·pute (di pyūt′) *v* **de·puted, de·put·ing** appoint to act in one's place: *The teacher deputed a student to take charge of the class while she was gone.* <Old French, from Latin *deputare* to allot>

dep·u·tize (dep′yə tīz′) *v* **dep·u·tized, dep·u·tiz·ing** act or appoint as deputy.

dep·u·ty (dep′yə tē) *n, pl* **dep·u·ties 1** a person appointed or sent to act in another's place: *A deputy attended the ceremony on behalf of the mayor.* **2** *Lacrosse* a player who enters the goal circle when the goalie is out of the goal circle and his or her team is in possession of the ball. <See DEPUTE.>

🍁 **deputy minister** *n* a senior public servant who is the chief assistant to a cabinet minister.

de·rail (dē rāl′) *v* **1** go or cause to go off the rails of a train track: *The engine derailed and pulled several cars off with it. An avalanche derailed the train.* **2** stray or cause to stray from a purpose, resulting in failure: *A major disagreement derailed the committee.*

de·rail·leur (di rā′lər) *n* a mechanism that changes gears on a bicycle by moving the chain from one sprocket to another. <French>

de·range (di rānj′) *v* **de·ranged, de·rang·ing 1** make insane: *deranged by greed.* **2** disturb, upset, or put into disorder: *The airline strike deranged our holiday plans.* <Old French *désrengier* move from orderly rows> **de·range′ment** *n.*

der·by (dər′bē) *n* **1** a contest or race: *a fishing derby.* **2** a man's stiff hat with a rounded top and narrow brim. **3 Derby** an annual horse race: *The Kentucky Derby.* <Earl of *Derby*, founder in 1780 of a famous horse race in England, still held yearly>

de·reg·u·late (dē reg′yə lāt′) *v* **de·reg·u·lat·ed, de·reg·u·lat·ing** remove restrictions or controls from: *to deregulate the distribution of hydro.* **de·reg′u·la′tion** *n.*

der·e·lict (der′ə likt′) *adj* **1** abandoned or deserted: *a derelict ship.* **2** failing to do one's duty.
n a derelict person or thing, especially a homeless person or an abandoned ship. <Latin *de-* entirely + *relinquere* forsake> **der′e·lic′tion** *n.*

de·ride (di rīd′) *v* **de·rid·ed, de·rid·ing** make fun of. <Latin *de-* down + *ridere* laugh>

de ri·gueur (də ri gər′) *adj* required by custom or polite behaviour: *Black is no longer de rigueur at funerals.* <French = strictly>

de·ri·sion (di rizh′ən) *n* ridicule or scornful laughter: *He stuck to his principles despite the derision of his peers.* <See DERIDE.> **de·ri′sive** (di rī′siv) *or* (di riz′iv), *adj.* **de·ri′sive·ly** *adv.* **de·ri′so·ry** *adj.*

der·i·va·tion (der′ə vā′shən) *n* **1** the act or process of deriving: *the derivation of new words by adding suffixes, the derivation of gasoline from petroleum.* **2** a source or origin: *Many English words are of French derivation.* **3** a statement of how a word was derived: *This dictionary puts the derivation at the end of the entry.*

de·riv·a·tive (də riv′ə tiv) *adj* seeming to be copied from other people's work or ideas.
n **1** something derived from a certain source: *"Collection" is a derivative of "collect." Many drugs are plant derivatives.* **2** *Mathematics* the rate of change of one quantity with respect to another.

de·rive (di rīv′) *v* **de·rived, de·riv·ing 1** get or come from a source: *to derive pleasure from music, to derive a conclusion from the data. The word "table" derives from Latin "tabula."* **2** make a new thing out of something else by a specific process: *Gasoline is derived from petroleum by distilling.* **3** trace the development or origin of: *I derive all her present troubles from her original career choice.* <Old French, from Latin *derivere*>

der·ma·ti·tis (dər′mə tī′tis) *n* inflammation of the skin. <See DERMIS.>

der·ma·tol·o·gy (dər′mə tol′ə jē) *n* the branch of physiology or medicine that deals with the skin and its diseases. <See DERMIS.> **der′ma·to·log′i·cal** *adj.* **der′ma·tol′o·gist** *n.*

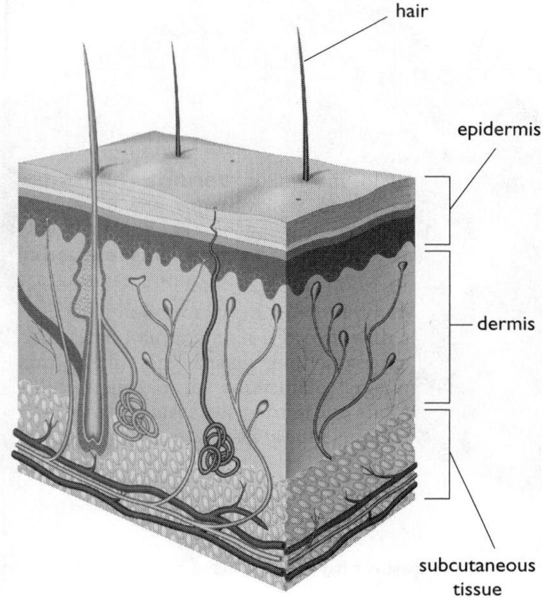

der·mis (dər′mis) *n* the sensitive layer of skin under the outer layer or epidermis. <Latin, from Greek *derma* skin>

der·o·gate (der′ə gāt′) *v* **der·o·gat·ed, der·o·gat·ing** **1** take away or detract: *The king thought that having a parliament would derogate from his authority.* **2** disparage: *Don't derogate other people's religion.* **3** deviate, especially in becoming worse. <Latin *derogare* take away from> **der′o·ga′tion** *n.*

de·rog·a·to·ry (di rog′ə tȯr′ē) *adj* disparaging or contemptuous: *"Cur" is a derogatory term for a dog.* Also, **derogative**.

der·rick (der′ik) *n* **1** a towerlike framework, such as over an oil well or gas well, that holds the drilling and hoisting machinery. **2** a large machine with a long, movable, horizontal arm for lifting and moving heavy objects; a crane. <*Derrick*, a 17c hangman>

der·ring–do (der′ing dū′) *Archaic or Humorous n* daring deeds. <Middle English>

der·vish (dər′vish) *Islam n* a member of a religious order dedicated to a life of poverty. Some dervishes practise rites that include whirling and dancing. <Turkish, from Persian *darvis* poor>

de·sal·i·nate (dē sal′ə nāt′) *v* **de·sal·i·nat·ed, de·sal·i·nat·ing** remove salt from, especially from seawater. <*de-* not + *saline*> **de·sal′i·na′tion** *n.*

des·cant (des′kant) *for n,* (di skant′) *for v.*
n Music a separate melody or counterpoint sung or played above the basic melody.
v talk or write at length and enthusiastically: *to descant upon the wonders of nature.* <Latin *dis-* away + *cantus* song>

de·scend (di send′) *v* **1** go or come down: *to descend a staircase. The river descends to the sea.* **2** pass from an earlier time or generation to a later one: *customs descending from the Middle Ages.* **3** go in sequence from greater to smaller: *Arrange the numbers in descending order.* **4** usually, **be descended from** trace one's origin to a certain ancestor: *His family is descended from the Vikings.* **5** lower oneself and commit some unworthy act: *He was so desperate to win that he actually descended to cheating.* **6** (*with* ***on*** *or* ***upon***) make a sudden attack or appearance: *Wolves descended on the sheep and killed them. Thousands of tourists descend on Prince Edward Island every summer.* <French, from Latin *de-* down + *scandere* climb> **de·scend′ing** *adj.*

D

de·scend·ant (di sen′dənt) *n* **1** a person or animal with a certain ancestor or group of ancestors: *She is a direct descendant of Attila the Hun.* **2** something developed from an earlier thing: *The piano is a modern descendant of the harpsichord.*

de·scend·er (di sen′dər) *n* the part of a letter, such as *p* or *g*, that goes below the line. Compare ASCENDER.

de·scent (di sent′) *n* **1** the act, process, or means of descending: *The climbers made their slow descent back to base camp.* **2** a downward slope: *The lot ends in a steep descent to the river.* **3** a family line; ancestry: *They are of Dutch descent.*

de·scram·ble (dē skram′bəl) *v* **de·scram·bled, de·scram·bling** restore a scrambled electronic signal to an intelligible state. **de·scram′bler** *n.*

de·scribe (di skrīb′) *v* **de·scribed, de·scrib·ing** **1** tell in words what a person or thing is like: *Critics describe the movie as "slow-moving but fascinating."* **2** trace the outline of: *The skater described a figure 8 on the ice.* <Latin *de-* about + *scribere* write>

de·scrip·tion (di skrip′shən) *n* **1** the act of describing. **2** words that do this: *Write a one-page description of your neighbourhood.* **3** a kind or sort: *games of every description.* **de·scrip′tive** *adj.* **de·scrip′tive·ly** *adv.*

de·scry (di skrī′) *v* **de·scried, de·scry·ing** catch sight of: *The castaway at last descried a ship on the horizon.* <Old French, from Latin *describere* write down>

des·e·crate (des′ə krāt′) *v* **des·e·crat·ed, des·e·crat·ing** violate the sacredness or beauty of: *to desecrate gravestones with graffiti.* <*de-* not + *consecrate*> **des′e·cra′tion** *n.*

de·seg·re·gate (dē seg′rə gāt′) *v* **de·seg·re·gat·ed, de·seg·re·gat·ing** abolish a law or practice that isolates one part of a population from another on grounds of race, ethnicity, or religion: *A century after slavery ended, schools in the southern US were finally desegregated.* **de·seg′re·ga′tion** *n.*

de·sen·si·tize (dē sen′sə tīz′) *v* **de·sen·si·tized, de·sen·si·tiz·ing** make insensitive or less sensitive: *Do action films desensitize people to violence?* **de·sen′si·ti·za′tion** *n.*

a bat	e bed	i bid	o pot	u cup	th thin
ā cake	ē me	ī bite	ō go	ū rude	ᴛʜ then
ȧ bar	ə about	ər over	ȯ for	u̇ put	zh measure

desert

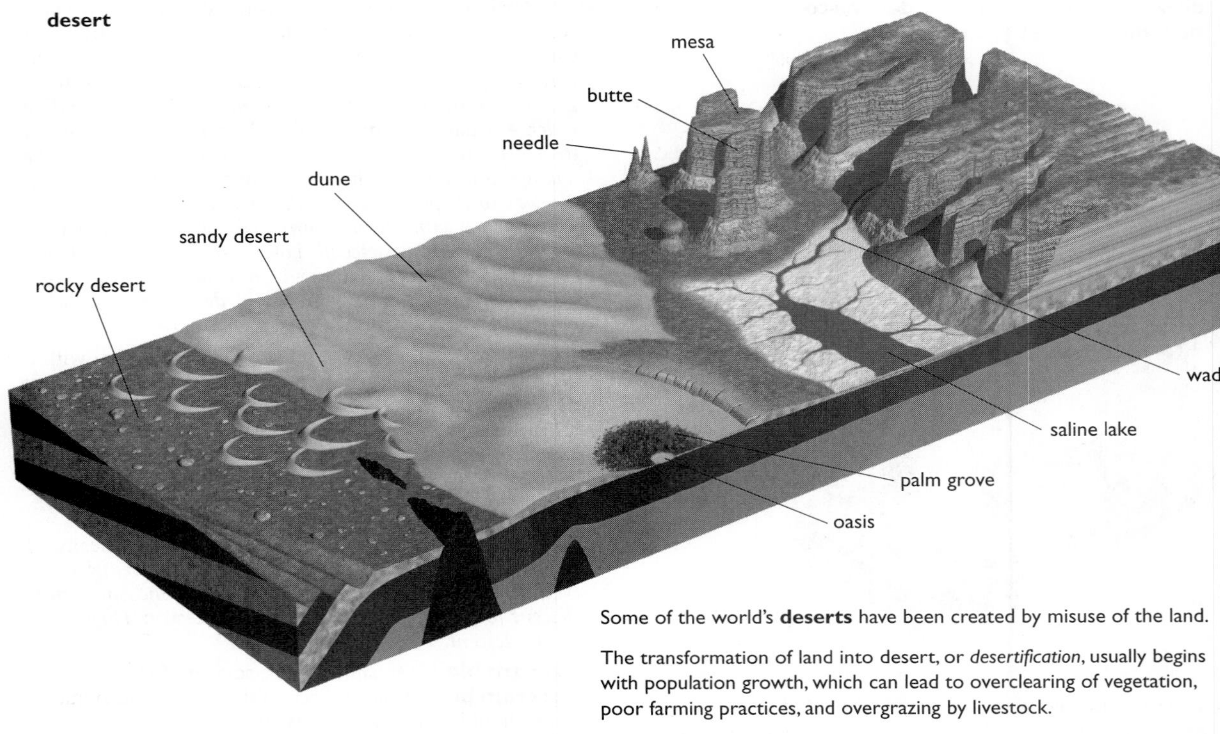

Some of the world's **deserts** have been created by misuse of the land.

The transformation of land into desert, or *desertification*, usually begins with population growth, which can lead to overclearing of vegetation, poor farming practices, and overgrazing by livestock.

des·ert[1] (dez′ərt) *n* **1** a dry, barren region, typically rocky or sandy and without trees. **2** a region that is not settled or cultivated; wilderness. **3** a place thought of as lacking some feature: *This town is a cultural desert.*
adj **1** dry and barren. **2** uninhabited and uncultivated: *a desert island.* <Old French, from Latin *deserere* abandon>

CONFUSABLES

A **desert** is a place with little water and not much plant or animal life.

A **dessert** is something sweet to eat that is served after the main part of a meal.

de·sert[2] (di zərt′) *v* **1** leave, especially when one has an obligation to stay: *She deserted her family.* **2** leave the army without permission and with no intention of returning: *He didn't believe in the war and finally deserted.* <Old French, from Latin *deserere* abandon> **de·sert′er** *n.* **de·ser′tion** *n.*

de·sert[3] (di zərt′) *n* usually, **deserts** *pl* a suitable reward or punishment: *So that thug has gone to jail—well, he got his just deserts.* <Old French, from Latin *deservire* serve well>

de·sert·i·fi·ca·tion (di zər′tə fə kā′shən) *n* the deterioration of a dry region into desert as a result of climate change or overuse by people and animals. **de·sert′i·fied′** *adj.* **de·sert′i·fy′** (di zər′tə fī) *v.*

de·serve (di zərv′) *v* **de·served, de·serv·ing** have a claim or right to: *Good work deserves praise. She doesn't deserve to be treated so harshly.* <Old French, from Latin *deservire* serve well> **de·serv′ed·ly** *adv.*

de·serv·ing (di zər′ving) *adj* having earned a privilege or special treatment: *The scholarship is awarded to a deserving student.*

des·ic·cate (des′ə kāt′) *v* **des·ic·cat·ed, des·ic·cat·ing** dry completely, often as a means of preservation: *desiccated fruit.* <Latin *de-* entirely + *siccus* dry> **des′ic·cant** *n, adj.* **des′ic·ca′tion** *n.*

de·sid·er·a·tum (di zid′ə rȧ′təm) *n, pl* **de·sid·er·a·ta** a desirable thing. <Latin, *desiderare* long for>

de·sign (di zīn′) *n* **1** an arrangement of lines or shapes and often colours: *Ornate designs had been carved into the wood.* **2** an idea of how something should be made or should work: *She explained the design she had in mind for the database. These shoes have a comfortable design.* **3** a drawing or sketch used as a pattern for making something: *He showed me his most recent car design.* **4** the art or act of designing: *evidence of intelligent design in the universe. Architects are skilled in design.* **5** plan; intention: *It wasn't my design to get him fired.*
v **1** figure out how a thing will work or what it will look like: *We've designed a way to make the factory more efficient.* **2** make a sketch or drawing to be used as a pattern for making something: *He designs clothes.* **3** intend

for a certain purpose: *That remark was designed to stir up trouble.* <Latin *de-* entirely + *signum* mark> **de·sign′er** *n.*

by design, on purpose.

have designs on, (*often used humorously*) have a plan or scheme for getting or using: *Does anyone have designs on that last doughnut?*

des·ig·nate (dez′ig nāt′) *v* **des·ig·nat·ed, des·ig·nat·ing** **1** mark out, point out, or show: *Red lines designate main roads on this map.* **2** name or call: *The food they were given could hardly be designated a "meal."* **3** appoint: *She was designated team captain.* <Latin *de-* entirely + *signum* mark> **des′ig·na′tion** *n.*

designated driver *n* a person who drinks no alcohol so as to be able to drive others home from a party or other social event.

de·sign·ing (di zī′ning) *adj* scheming or plotting: *a designing scoundrel.*

de·sir·a·ble (di zī′rə bəl) *adj* **1** worth having or wishing for. **2** sexually attractive. **de·sir′a·bil′i·ty** *n.* **de·sir′a·bly** *adv.*

de·sire (di zīr′) *v* **de·sired, de·sir·ing** **1** wish for, especially strongly. **2** want someone sexually. **3** request formally: *The Governor General desires your presence at the ceremony.*
n a strong wish: *a desire for lasting peace, a desire to see the world.* <Old French, from Latin *desiderare* long for>

de·sir·ous (di zī′rəs) *adj* (*used with* ***of, to,*** *or* ***that***) wanting; having desire: *desirous of fame, desirous to learn more. He was desirous that his identity be kept secret.*

de·sist (di sist′) *v* stop doing something: *The judge ordered him to desist from fighting.* <Old French, from Latin *de-* off + *sistere* stop>

desk (desk) *n* **1** a piece of furniture with a flat or sloping top on which to write, draw, set a computer, or rest books and papers. **2** a department or service counter: *the complaints desk, the copy desk of a newspaper office.* <Latin *desca* table, from Greek *diskos* disc>

desk·top (desk′top′) *n* **1** the top of a desk. **2** *Computers* **a** in certain operating systems, a screen displaying icons and a status bar, from which one opens files or applications. **b** a computer, usually not portable, for use at a desk.
adj **1** designed to be put on a desk: *desktop computer.* **2** using desktop computers exclusively: *a desktop operation.*
v **desk·topped, desk·top·ping** produce and print on a desktop computer instead of a printing press: *The company desktops its newsletters.*

desktop publishing *Computers n* the use of a desktop computer to prepare books, magazines, etc. for printing.

des·o·late (dez′ə lit) *for adj,* (dez′ə lāt′) *for v. adj* **1** barren or laid waste: *a desolate land.* **2** empty or deserted: *After they left, the house stood desolate for many years.* **3** miserable or hopeless: *a desolate life, a ragged, desolate child.*
v **des·o·lat·ed, des·o·lat·ing** make desolate: *The Vikings desolated the lands they attacked. He was desolated to hear that his best friend was moving away.* <Latin *de-* entirely + *solus* alone> **des′o·late·ly** *adv.* **des′o·la′tion** *n.*

de·spair (di sper′) *n* **1** a complete loss of hope: *Despair seized them as they felt the boat sinking.* **2** a cause of this feeling: *The rebellious girl was the despair of her parents.*
v lose or give up hope: *She despaired when she saw the mangled car. Doctors despaired of saving the injured man's life.* <Old French, from Latin *de-* away + *sperare* to hope> **de·spair′ing** *adj.*

des·per·a·do (des′pə rä′dō) *n, pl* **des·per·a·does** or **des·per·a·dos** a reckless or dangerous criminal. <Spanish = desperate>

des·per·ate (des′pə rit) *adj* **1** having lost all hope: *She would have to be desperate before she asked for help.* **2** reckless because of a feeling that things cannot get any worse: *a desperate criminal, a desperate attempt to flee.* **3** extremely serious or urgent: *in desperate need. The situation is desperate.* **4** with an extreme need or desire: *desperate for something to do, desperate for affection.* <Old French, from Latin *de-* down from + *sperare* to hope> **des′per·ate·ly** *adv.* **des′per·a′tion** *n.*

de·spic·a·ble (di spik′ə bəl) *adj* worthy of the greatest contempt: *despicable actions, a despicable coward.* <Latin *despicari* despise> **de·spic′a·bly** *adv.*

de·spise (di spīz′) *v* **de·spised, de·spis·ing** look down on; feel contempt for: *I despise people who cheat.* <Old French, from Latin *de-* down + *specere* look at>

de·spite (di spīt′) *prep* in spite of; without regard for: *They went hiking despite the rain.* <Old French, from Latin *de-* down + *specere* look at>

de·spoil (di spoil′) *v* rob or plunder. <Old French, from Latin *despoliare*> **de·spo′li·a′tion** (di spō′lē ā′shən) *n.*

de·spond·ent (di spon′dənt) *adj* totally discouraged. <Latin *despondere* to give up> **de·spond′en·cy** *n.*

des·pot (des′pət) *n* **1** a ruler whose power is absolute or oppressive. **2** anyone who uses his or her power to control others: *I can't work for that despot any longer.* <French, from Greek *despotes* master> **des·pot′ic** *adj.* **des·pot′i·cal·ly** *adv.* **des′pot·ism′** *n.*

des·sert (di zərt′) *n* **1** a sweet course served at the end of a meal. **2** food suitable for this course: *This store stocks frozen desserts.* See DESERT for confusable. <French *des-* away + *servir* to serve>

de·sta·bil·ize (dē stā′bə līz′) *v* **de·sta·bil·ized, de·sta·bil·iz·ing** make unstable: *to destabilize a government, to destabilize a person emotionally.* **de·sta′bil·i·za′tion** *n.*

des·ti·na·tion (des′tə nā′shən) *n* the place to which a person or thing is going.

des·tine (des′tin) *v* **des·tined, des·tin·ing** (*usually passive*) cause by fate: *My e-mail was destined never to reach her.* <Old French, from Latin *destinare* to appoint>
destined for, a headed for: *ships destined for England.* **b** intended or fated for: *destined for failure.*

des·ti·ny (des′tə nē) *n, pl* **des·ti·nies** **1** all that is supposedly predetermined to happen to someone or something in spite of all efforts to change or prevent it. **2** **Destiny** a force or agency that supposedly predetermines what will happen.

a bat	e bed	i bid	o pot	u cup	th thin
ā cake	ē me	ī bite	ō go	ū rude	ᴛʜ then
ä bar	ə about	ər over	ô for	ů put	zh measure

D

des·ti·tute (des′tə tyūt′) *or* (des′tə tūt′) *adj* lacking basic necessities such as food, clothing, and shelter. <Latin *destituere* abandoned> **des′ti·tu′tion** *n.*
destitute of, entirely without: *a region destitute of trees. The bully was destitute of pity.*

de·stroy (di stroi′) *v* **1** ruin completely: *to destroy a building, a life destroyed by crime.* **2** bring to nothing: *to destroy someone's confidence.* **3** kill: *The injured dog had to be destroyed.* <Old French, from Latin *de-* not + *struere* build>

SYNONYMS

Destroy means "wreck completely": *Fire destroyed the abandoned building.*

Demolish means "pull or tear down": *The bridge was demolished to make way for a new one.*

Dissolve means "break up" or "terminate": *They dissolved their friendship because they were arguing all the time.*

de·stroy·er (di stroi′ər) *n* **1** a small, fast warship equipped with guns, torpedoes, and other weapons. **2** a person who or thing that destroys.

de·struc·tion (di struk′shən) *n* **1** the act of destroying: *We watched the destruction of the old building.* **2** destroyed things, or the condition of being destroyed: *The storm left destruction behind it.* **3** the cause or means of destroying: *That letter was the destruction of all her hopes.* <Old French, from Latin *de-* not + *struere* build>
de·struc′tive *adj.*

des·ul·to·ry (des′əl tòr′ē) *or* (dez′əl tòr′ē) *adj* going constantly from one thing or place to another without a plan or purpose: *desultory thoughts, a desultory ramble through the town.* <Latin *de-* entirely + *salire* leap> **des′ul·to′ri·ly** *adv.* **des′ul·to′ri·ness** *n.*

de·tach (di tach′) *v* **1** unfasten and remove: *She detached a charm from her bracelet to show me.* **2** set apart a group of people or vehicles from the main body for some special duty: *A squad of soldiers was detached to watch the camp.* **3** make emotionally distant or uninvolved: *He tried to detach himself from the horrible scene he had just witnessed.* <French, from Old French *des-* reversing + *tache* nail> **de·tach′a·ble** *adj.* **de·tached′** *adj.*

de·tach·ment (di tach′mənt) *n* **1** the act of detaching. **2** emotional uninvolvement: *He listened to their story with an air of detachment.* **3** a group of troops or ships assigned to some special duty. **4** 🍁 the smallest organizational unit in the Royal Canadian Mounted Police or other police force.
on detachment, assigned to some special duty.

de·tail (dē′tāl) *or, especially for military senses,* (di tāl′) *n* **1** a single small or minor fact: *She gave a basic explanation, leaving out the details. The two drawings were alike in every detail.* **2** the fact of including or dealing with small things one by one: *This map has more detail than mine. There's a lot of detail involved in accounting.* **3** a reproduction, often enlarged, of part of a work of art: *The picture on the card is a detail of a painting by da Vinci.* **4** **a** a small group selected for special duty: *The captain sent a detail of six soldiers to guard the road.* **b** the special task or duty itself.
v **1** give all the facts of: *He detailed all he had seen on his trip.* **2** select for or send on a special duty: *Officers were detailed to restrain the crowd.* <Old French, from Latin *de-* entirely + *taillier* to cut in pieces> **de′tailed** *adj.*
go into detail, give all the facts one by one: *There's no time to go into detail; just give me a general idea.*
in detail, fully, giving all the parts or facts: *He described the scene in detail.*

de·tain (di tān′) *v* **1** hold back or delay: *I would have been on time, but I was detained by problems at home.* **2** keep in a place by some authority: *The police detained the suspect for questioning. Misbehaving students will be detained after class.* <Old French, from Latin *de-* away + *tenere* to hold> **de′tain·ee′** *n.* **de·tain′ment** *n.*

de·tect (di tekt′) *v* **1** notice or discover the existence of: *She detected an odour in the room.* **2** uncover and investigate: *to detect a crime.* <Latin *de-* not + *tegere* to cover> **de·tect′a·ble** *adj.* **de·tect′a·bly** *adv.* **de·tec′tion** *n.*

de·tec·tive (di tek′tiv) *n* **1** a police officer whose work is investigating crimes. **2** a person who works for a private person or organization as an investigator.
adj used in detecting: *the detective powers of a police dog.*

de·tec·tor (di tek′tər) *n* a device that registers the presence of something such as smoke or radioactivity, and alerts people to it by some signal.

dé·tente (dā tànt′) *n* the loosening of tensions between nations or political groups. <French *détendre* relax>

de·ten·tion (di ten′shən) *n* **1** a school punishment consisting of being kept in during recess or after school. **2** the act of keeping in prison: *Jails are for the detention of arrested people.* <Old French, from Latin *de-* away + *tenere* to hold>

de·ter (di tər′) *v* **de·terred, de·ter·ring** discourage or restrain: *We were going to go out, but the extreme heat deterred us. Does the probability of punishment deter people from crime?* <Latin *de-* away + *terrere* frighten> **de·ter′rence** *n.*

de·ter·gent (di tər′jənt) *n* a chemical compound that acts like a soap, used for cleansing: *dishwashing detergent, laundry detergent.*
adj cleansing: *the detergent action of suds.* <Latin *de-* off + *tergere* wipe>

de·te·ri·o·rate (di tē′rē ə rāt′) *v* **de·te·ri·o·rat·ed, de·te·ri·o·rat·ing** become worse or fall into bad condition: *His health is deteriorating. Machinery soon deteriorates if not properly maintained.* <Latin *deterior* worse> **de·te′ri·o·ra′tion** *n.*

de·ter·mi·na·tion (di tər′mə nā′shən) *n* **1** a fixed purpose or intention: *She went with the determination to see every exhibit in the art show.* **2** firmness in carrying out a purpose: *You need real determination to get through this training program.* **3** the process of determining: *the determination of the amount of gold in a sample of ore.*

de·ter·mine (di tər′mən) *v* **de·ter·mined, de·ter·min·ing** **1** make up one's mind firmly: *He determined to become the best player in the league.* **2** decide some issue or question: *The judge will determine your* *sentence.* **3** find out: *They used carbon dating to determine the age of the fossil.* **4** be the deciding factor in something: *Tomorrow's events will determine whether we go or stay.* **5** limit or define: *The amount of walking we do tomorrow will be determined by the weather.* **de·ter′min·a·ble** *adj.*

de·ter·mined (di tər′mənd) *adj* with firmness of purpose: *a determined effort. She was determined to finish the race no matter how tired she felt.* **de·ter′mined·ly** *adv.*

SYNONYMS

Determined means "being firmly resolved": *She was determined to win the race.*

Obstinate suggests being too determined: *The obstinate boy refused to stop talking.*

Resolute can include an element of zeal: *He was resolute in his plan to collect more money in the fundraiser than his classmates.*

de·ter·min·er (di tər′mə nər) *Grammar n* a modifying word such as *the, a, her,* or *this,* that comes before a noun or noun phrase.

de·ter·min·ism (di tər′mə niz′əm) *n* the doctrine that all events, including all human thoughts and acts, are the necessary results of earlier events. **de·ter′min·ist** *n.* **de·ter′min·is′tic** *adj.*

de·ter·rent (di tər′ənt) *n* something that deters or discourages people from acting a certain way: *Fear of punishment is a common deterrent from wrongdoing.*
adj deterring or restraining: *A mere detention has little deterrent effect.*

de·test (di test′) *v* dislike intensely. <Latin *detestari* to curse, from *de-* down + *testiari* to witness>
de·test′a·ble *adj.* **de·test′a·bly** *adv.* **de′tes·ta′tion** *n.*

de·throne (dē thrōn′) *v* **de·throned, de·thron·ing** remove from a throne or deprive of power: *The rebels dethroned the monarch.* **de·throne′ment** *n.*

det·o·nate (det′ə nāt′) *v* **det·o·nat·ed, det·o·nat·ing** explode or cause to explode with a loud noise: *to detonate a charge of dynamite. The bomb detonated a moment later.* <Latin *de-* down + *tonare* thunder> **det′o·na′tion** *n.* **det′o·na′tor** *n.*

de·tour (dē′tūr) *n* **1** a way around, taken to avoid traffic or obstacles: *We had to take a detour because of the road construction.* **2** a trip out of one's way to do some errand: *He made a quick detour to pick up his friend.*
v use or make a detour: *She detoured around the flooded area.* <French, from *dé-* off + *tour* a turn>

de·tox·i·fy (dē tok′sə fī′) *v* **de·tox·i·fied, de·tox·i·fy·ing** make free of a poisonous or harmful substance or its effects: *to detoxify an alcoholic.* <*de-* not + *toxin*> **de·tox′i·fi·ca′tion** *n.* (Both noun and verb are often shortened informally to **detox**.)

de·tract (di trakt′) *v* take away from the quality, value, or beauty of something: *The ugly frame really detracts from the picture.* <Latin *de-* away from + *trahere* draw> **de·trac′tion** *n.*

de·tract·or (di trak′tər) *n* one who speaks negatively about a person or thing: *Every good theory has its detractors.*

det·ri·ment (det′rə mənt) *n* harm, or a source of harm: *She worked long hours, apparently without detriment to her health. Too little sleep is a detriment to the quality of my work.* <Old French, from Latin *de-* away + *terere* wear> **det′ri·men′tal** *adj.*

de·tri·tus (di trī′təs) *n* **1** particles of rock or other material worn away from a mass. **2** debris of any kind: *Detritus left by the flood littered the highway.* <French, from Latin *de-* away + *terere* wear>

deuce[1] (dyūs) *or* (dūs) *n* **1** the number two in a game of cards or dice. **2** *Tennis* a score tied at 40 each. <Old French, from Latin *duos* two>

deuce[2] (dyūs) *or* (dūs) *Informal n* a word used to express annoyance or surprise: *What the deuce does he want now?* <German, probably from *deuce*[1], an unlucky throw at dice>

de·us ex ma·chi·na (dā′əs eks mak′ə nə) *n* a person, god, or unexpected event in a story or play that comes just in time to neatly solve a difficulty. <Latin, translation of Greek *theos ek mechanes* = god from the machinery. It originally referred to a mechanical stage device in ancient Roman theatre, used to represent divine intervention in the action.>

deu·te·ri·um (dyū tē′rē əm) *or* (dū tē′rē əm) *n* an isotope of hydrogen whose mass is double that of ordinary hydrogen. Also called **heavy hydrogen**. *Symbol* **D** <Latin, from Greek *deuteros* second>

de·val·ue (dē val′yū) *v* **de·val·ued, de·val·u·ing** **1** lower the value or importance of: *Some cultures devalue punctuality, whereas our culture overvalues it.* **2** officially declare a lower value for currency in relation to other currencies or to gold: *Some countries have had to devalue their currency several times.* **de·val′u·a′tion** *n.*

dev·as·tate (dev′ə stāt′) *v* **dev·as·tat·ed, dev·as·tat·ing** **1** make desolate or lay waste: *A long war devastated the border towns.* **2** hurt or humiliate very much: *I was devastated by her cruel remark.* <Latin *de-* entirely + *vastare* lay waste> **dev′as·ta′tion** *n.*

de·vel·op (di vel′əp) *v* **1** come or bring into existence gradually, by stages of growth and change: *Did land animals develop from sea animals? to develop a taste for olives. The power loom was developed from a simple hand loom.* **2** become or cause to become more mature or complete, or bigger: *Seedlings develop into tall trees. Hardship develops character.* **3** happen as a result of earlier events: *Let's see what develops and then decide.* **4** change from a natural state to one that serves another purpose: *to develop natural resources.* **5** build new housing, commercial structures, and roads on a piece of land: *The plan to develop the ravine was strongly opposed by the community.* **6 a** treat a photographic plate or film with chemicals to bring out the image recorded on it. **b** produce prints in this way. <French *développer* unwrap>

a bat	e bed	i bid	o pot	u cup	th thin
ā cake	ē me	ī bite	ō go	ū rude	ŦH then
ä bar	ə about	ər over	ȯ for	ů put	zh measure

de·vel·op·er (di vel′ə pər) *n* **1** a person or company that buys up land, builds on it, and then sells the homes, factories, and commercial structures that have been built. **2** a person who or thing that develops: *a job as a software developer. Give her time; some children are slow developers.* **3** the chemical used to bring out the image on an exposed photographic film or plate.

developing nation *n* a nation that has not yet achieved a significant degree of industrialization relative to its population, and which has a low overall standard of living.

de·vel·op·ment (di vel′əp mənt) *n* **1** the process of developing. **2** a group of buildings made by the same builder: *The new development will have homes and a school.* **3** an event resulting from a previous event: *Have there been any developments in the transit strike?*

de·vel·op·men·tal (di vel′əp men′təl) *adj* **1** to do with the process of developing anything. **2** to do with the physical and psychological development of a child.

de·vi·ant (dē′vē ənt) *adj* departing from an accepted standard: *deviant behaviour.*
n a person who departs from an accepted standard of behaviour. **de′vi·ance** *n.*

de·vi·ate (dē′vē āt′) *v* **de·vi·at·ed, de·vi·at·ing** depart from a way, a rule or standard, the facts, or the truth: *to deviate slightly from the truth. Her case deviates from the normal pattern.* <Latin *de-* off + *via* road> **de′vi·a′tion** *n.*

de·vice (di vīs′) *n* **1** a mechanical, electrical, or electronic invention used for some special purpose: *a device for lighting a barbecue.* **2** a scheme or trick: *By some device he managed to get past the guards.* **3** a stylistic or technical feature in a piece of literature, music, or other artistic work to produce a certain effect: *This poet uses a lot of formal devices such as alliteration, internal rhyme, and oxymoron.* **4** a motto or emblem: *The flag bore the device of King Arthur.* <Old French, from Latin *dividere* divide>
leave someone to his or **her own devices,** let someone do as he or she pleases.

CONFUSABLES

A **device** is a noun: *The telephone is a device I use every day.*

Devise is a verb: *I devised a new route that takes less time to cycle to school.*

de·vil (dev′əl) *n* **1 a** an evil spirit or demon. **b the Devil** in some belief systems, the supreme spirit of evil and the enemy of God. Also called **Satan**. **2** a wicked or cruel person. **3** *Informal* a very dashing, energetic, mischievous, or reckless person. **4** *Informal* an unfortunate or wretched person: *The poor devil didn't even hear the warning.* <Latin, from Greek *diabolos* enemy>
between the devil and the deep blue sea, with only two choices, equally bad.
devil of a, *Informal* **a** very difficult or awkward: *We had a devil of a time getting the piano into the basement.* **b** very: *She did a devil of a fine job.*
give the devil his due, be fair, even to a bad or disliked person.
go to the devil, go to ruin.
like the devil, *Informal* with great force and energy: *working like the devil.*
the devil to pay, much trouble as a consequence: *If we get it wrong now, there'll be the devil to pay later.*

dev·il·fish (dev′əl fish) MANTA.

dev·il·ish (dev′ə lish) *adj* **1** like that of a devil: *a devilish scheme.* **2** *Informal* very great or extreme: *She's always in such a devilish hurry.*
adv Informal very or extremely: *They worked devilish hard.* **dev′il·ish·ly** *adv.*

dev·illed (dev′əld) *adj* prepared with hot seasoning: *devilled ham, devilled eggs.*

de·vil–may–care (dev′əl mā ker′) *adj* easygoing and carefree.

de·vil·ry (dev′əl rē) *n* mischievous behaviour. Evil or wicked behaviour is usually called **deviltry**. Also, **devilment**.

devil's advocate *n* **1** a person who argues for an unpopular position, often just to be contrary, or to force the other person to examine his or her own position. **2** *Catholicism* an official whose job is to argue against a proposal to beatify or canonize someone, so as to ensure that the evidence in the person's favour is strong enough.

devil's food cake *n* a rich, dark chocolate cake.

de·vi·ous (dē′vē əs) *adj* **1** subtle, crafty, or underhanded: *a devious character, a devious plan.* **2** winding or twisting: *a devious route.* <Latin *de-* off + *via* road> **de′vi·ous·ly** *adv.* **de′vi·ous·ness** *n.*

de·vise (di vīz′) *v* **de·vised, de·vis·ing** think up or invent: *We must try to devise a way of escape.* See DEVICE for confusable. <Old French, from Latin *dividere* to divide>

de·vi·tal·ize (dē vī′tə līz′) *v* **de·vi·tal·ized, de·vi·tal·iz·ing** drain the life or vigour from: *a devitalized economy. They warned that cutbacks have devitalized the education system.*

de·void (dē void′) *adj* (*used with* ***of***) lacking: *a speech completely devoid of humour.* <Old French *devoidier*>

de·volve (di volv′) *v* **de·volved, de·volv·ing** hand down or be handed down to someone else as a responsibility, right, or piece of property: *If the student council president is unable to handle her duties, they devolve upon the vice-president.* <Latin *de-* down + *volvere* to roll> **de′vo·lu′tion** (dē′və lū′shən) *n.*

De·vo·ni·an (de vō′ni ən) *n* the geological period lasting from about 400 million to 360 million years ago, when forests became widespread. See also PALEOZOIC.
adj to do with this period or the rocks formed then. <Latin *Devonia* Devonshire, an area in England>

de·vote (di vōt′) *v* **de·vot·ed, de·vot·ing** give or set apart for a specific person, purpose, or service: *The mother devoted herself to her children. We should devote a whole day to this discussion.* <Latin *de-* entirely + *vovere* vow>

de·vot·ed (di vō′tid) *adj* faithful and deeply committed: *a devoted friend.*

dev·o·tee (dev′ō tē′) *or* (di vō′tē′) *n* an enthusiastic admirer of something: *a devotee of the opera.*

de·vo·tion (di vō′shən) *n* **1** deep, faithful, self-giving love: *the devotion of a lifelong friend.* **2** whole-hearted commitment: *his devotion to the arts.* **3 devotions** *pl* informal, often private religious worship. **4** the act of devoting or setting apart for a purpose: *the devotion of much time to study.*

de·vo·tion·al (di vō′shə nəl) *adj* to do with or used for worship and meditation.
n a short, informal sermon or spiritual talk.

de·vour (di vour′) *v* **1** eat greedily: *The hungry girls devoured the pizza.* **2** take in eagerly or greedily with the mind or senses: *to devour a book.* **3** consume: *Sports devoured his free time.* **4** completely absorb the attention or emotions of: *devoured by curiosity.* <Old French, from Latin *de-* down + *vorare* gulp>

de·vout (di vout′) *adj* **1** deeply religious. **2** earnest and sincere: *devout thanks, a devout fan.* <See DEVOTE.> **de·vout′ly** *adv.* **de·vout′ness** *n.*

dew (dyū) *or* (dū) *n* **1** the moisture from the air that condenses and collects on cool surfaces during the night. **2** *Poetic* a sort of moisture in small drops, like sweat.
v make wet with small drops: *His forehead was dewed with sweat.* <Old English *deaw*> **dew′less** *adj.* **dew′y** *adj.*

dew·drop (dyū′drop′) *or* (dū′drop′) *n* a drop of dew.

Dew·ey decimal system (dyū′ē) *or* (dū′ē) *n* one of the two main systems for classifying nonfiction in libraries. Specific numbers and decimals are assigned to each subject and its subdivisions. Examples: History 900, Canadian History 971, Canadian Northwest History 971.2 <M. *Dewey*, 19c librarian who invented it>

dew·lap (dyū′lap′) *or* (dū′lap′) *n* a loose fold of skin under the throat of cattle and some other animals.

DEW Line (dyū) *or* (dū) *n* a network of radar stations set up across the Arctic regions of North America, designed to give an early warning of approaching enemy aircraft and missiles. <*D*istant *E*arly *W*arning>

dew point *n* the temperature at which water vapour in the air begins to condense as dew.

🍁 **dew worm** *n* a large earthworm that comes to the surface at night when there is dew on the grass.

dex·ter·i·ty (dek ster′ə tē) *n* skill, quickness, or cleverness in using the hands or mind: *the dexterity of a surgeon, the mental dexterity of a mathematician.* <French, from Latin *dexter* skillful> **dex′ter·ous** *adj.* **dex′ter·ous·ly** *adv.*

dex·trose (dek′strōs) *n* a form of glucose that is less sweet than cane sugar. <Latin *dexter* right + *glucose*, from its rightward rotation of the plane of polarization>

dhal (dȧl) DAL.

dhar·ma (dȧr′mə) *Buddhism, Hinduism n* the eternal spiritual or moral law that is shown by correct behaviour. <Sanskrit>

Dhar·ma·pa·da (dȧr′mə pud′ə) *Buddhism n* a sacred book covering aspects of Buddhist teaching about truth, duty, and enlightenment. <Sanskrit>

dho·ti (dō′tē) *n* a garment for the lower body worn mostly by Hindu men. It consists of a single large piece of cloth passing between the legs and secured at the waist. <Hindi>

dhur·rie (dùr′ē) *n* a woven cotton rug. <Hindi>

di–[1] *prefix* **1** twice; double: *dicotyledon.* **2** with two atoms of the substance specified: *dioxide.* <Greek *dis* twice>

di–[2] *prefix* a form of **dis-** occurring before certain consonants: *divert, direct.*

di·a·base (dī′ə bās) *n* a fine-textured igneous rock used for monuments and as crushed stone. <French>

di·a·be·tes (dī′ə bē′tis) *or* (dī′ə bē′tēz) *n* a chronic disease in which the digestive system is unable to absorb normal amounts of sugar and starch. It is caused by a failure to produce insulin. <Latin, from Greek *dia-* through + *bainein* go> **di′a·bet′ic** (dī′ə bet′ik) *adj, n.*

di·a·bol·i·cal (dī′ə bol′ə kəl) *adj* devilish or fiendish. <Greek *diabolos* devil> **di′a·bol′i·cal·ly** *adv.*

di·a·crit·ic (dī′ə krit′ik) *n* a mark placed over or under a letter to indicate pronunciation. Examples: *é* as in *Québec*, or *ç* as in *soupçon.* <Greek *dia-* through + *krinein* to separate>

di·a·dem (dī′ə dem′) *n* a crown. <Old French, from Greek *dia-* around + *dein* tie>

di·ag·nose (dī′əg nōs′) *v* **di·ag·nosed, di·ag·nos·ing** determine what is wrong with a patient or situation by a careful examination of symptoms: *to diagnose a disease. He was recently diagnosed with cancer. Teachers can use tests to diagnose gaps in students' understanding.* <Latin, from Greek *dia-* apart + *gignoskein* learn to know> **di′ag·no′sis** *n.* **di′ag·nos′tic** (dī′əg nos′tik) *adj.*

di·ag·o·nal (dī ag′ə nəl) *adj* **1** slanting. **2** *Mathematics* connecting two corners that are not next to each other in a polygon with four or more sides.
n a diagonal line. <Latin, from Greek *dia-* through + *gonia* angle>
on the diagonal, in a diagonal direction: *The wooden planks were set on the diagonal.*

di·a·gram (dī′ə gram′) *n* a drawing showing important parts of a thing and how they are related and work together: *a labelled diagram of a car engine, a diagram showing how actors should move during a scene.*
v **di·a·grammed, di·a·gram·ming** draw a diagram of: *Using a stick in the sand, he diagrammed our escape route.* <Latin, from Greek *dia-* through + *graphein* write>

SYNONYMS

A **diagram** is an illustration or a graph or chart: *The diagram showed how the machine worked.*

A **blueprint** is a drawing of a building plan: *The blueprint showed the layout of the house.*

A **sketch** is a drawing done quickly: *His sketch had few lines, but was a good likeness of the model.*

di·a·gram·mat·ic (dī′ə grə mat′ik) *adj* in the form of a diagram. **di′a·gram·mat′i·cal·ly** *adv.*

a bat	e bed	i bid	o pot	u cup	th thin
ā cake	ē me	ī bite	ō go	ū rude	ᴛʜ then
ȧ bar	ə about	ər over	ȯ for	ů put	zh measure

di·al (dī′əl) *n* **1** a surface, especially one in the shape of a circle or arc, with marks indicating measures of some kind: *This dial shows rate of flow in litres per minute. The dial on a radio shows the station frequencies.* **2** a round knob or other device that can be turned or moved to regulate or select something: *Use this dial to adjust the volume.* **3** on older telephones, a rotating disc turned with the finger in order to enter each digit of a telephone number.
v **di·alled** or **di·aled, di·al·ling** or **di·al·ing** **1** enter a telephone number, whether by means of a dial or buttons: *to dial the police, to dial 911. I must have dialled the wrong number.* **2** use a dial in order to operate, adjust, or select: *to dial a combination on a lock.* <Latin *diale* clock-dial, from *dies* day>
dial direct, make a telephone call without the help of an operator.

di·a·lect (dī′ə lekt′) *n* a particular form of a language that is characteristic of a certain region or social group: *the Newfoundland dialect of English.* <French, from Greek *dia-* between + *legein* speak> **di′a·lect′al** *adj.*

GRAMMAR AND USAGE

There can be many different dialects of the same language. Often one dialect is perceived as more "correct" than the others and is held up as the standard. But each dialect is a valid form of the language, with its own grammatical rules.

di·a·log (dī′ə log′) *US n* dialogue.

di·a·logue (dī′ə log′) *n* **1 a** conversation, especially between characters in a story, play, or movie: *It was a good plot, but the dialogue was totally unrealistic.* **b** a piece of writing that consists entirely of a conversation. **2** the friendly exchange of ideas or opinions, especially between individuals or groups of very different views: *dialogue between members of different faiths.*
v **di·a·logued, di·a·logu·ing** engage in dialogue, especially to exchange opinions: *to dialogue about possible solutions.* <Old French, from Greek *dia-* through + *legein* speak>

GRAMMAR AND USAGE

Dialogue, the words that people say, is shown by the use of quotation marks. If a different person begins to speak, start a new paragraph:

The coach said, "You all played a great game."

"Thanks, Coach," we responded.

dialogue box *Computers n* an onscreen box prompting the user to enter certain information: *In the "Print" dialogue box you can specify printer, pages, and number of copies.*

dial tone *n* the humming sound heard on a telephone, showing that the line is in service and not currently in use.

dial–up (dī′əl up′) *Computers adj* requiring the entry of a telephone number each time: *dial-up Internet access.*

di·al·y·sis (dī al′ə sis) *n, pl* **di·al·y·ses** (dī al′ə sēz) **1** the separation of waste matter from the blood in an artificial kidney. **2** the process by which this works, that is, the separation of substances in solution using a membrane as a filter. <Latin, from Greek *dia-* apart + *lyein* set free>
di′a·lyt′ic (dī a lit′ik) *adj.*

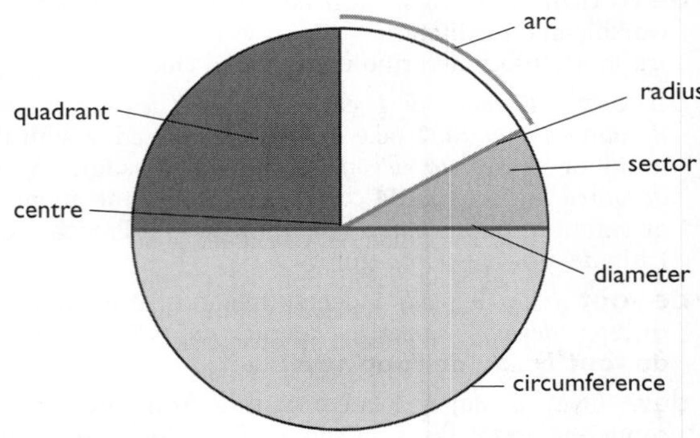

di·am·e·ter (dī am′ə tər) *n* **1** *Mathematics* a straight line connecting two points on the circumference of a circle, and passing through its centre. **2** the distance from one side to the other of anything, measured straight through the centre; thickness: *The tree trunk was almost 60 cm in diameter.* <Old French, from Greek *dia-* across + *metron* measure>

di·a·met·ric (dī′ə met′rik) *adj* **1** of or along a diameter. **2** showing complete difference between two or more things: *Their two opinions are in diametric opposition to each other.* Also, **diametrical**. **di′a·met′ri·cal·ly** *adv.*

di·a·mond (dī′mənd) *n* **1** a colourless or tinted precious stone made of pure carbon in crystals. Diamond is the hardest known substance. **2** a piece of jewellery with a diamond or diamonds in it. **3** a shape like this ◆. **4 a** a playing card with one or more red diamond-shaped designs on it. **b diamonds** *pl* the suit of cards marked with this design. **5** *Baseball* the space inside the lines that connect the bases.
adj to do with a 60th or 75th anniversary. <Old French, from Greek *adamas* the hardest metal. Diamond is the hardest known substance.> **dia′mond·like′** *adj.*
diamond in the rough, a person with poor manners or behaviour which may often hide admirable or undeveloped qualities.

dia·mond·back (dī′mənd bak′) *n* **1** a large, dangerous rattlesnake of the southern US, with diamond-shaped markings. **2** in full, **diamondback terrapin** a turtle whose shell is marked with diamond shapes, found in salt water in N America.

di·a·per (dī′pər) *n* a piece of folded cloth or other absorbent material, used as underpants for a baby.
v put a diaper on (a baby). <Old French, from Greek *diaspros* white (cloth)>

di·aph·a·nous (dī af′ə nəs) *adj* sheer and very light: *diaphanous fabric.* <Latin, from Greek *dia-* through + *phainein* show>

di·a·phragm (dī′ə fram′) *n* **1** a partition of muscles and tendons in mammals separating the chest cavity from the abdominal cavity. **2** a thin disc or cone that vibrates rapidly when sound waves or electrical impulses are directed at it, used in telephone receivers, microphones, earphones, and similar instruments. **3** a contraceptive device in the form of a flexible cap fitted over the entrance to the uterus. **4** a device that controls the amount of light entering a camera or microscope. <Latin, from Greek *dia-* across + *phragma* fence>

di·ar·rhe·a or **di·ar·rhoe·a** (dī'ə rē'ə) *n* the condition of having too many and too loose bowel movements. <Latin, from Greek *dia-* through + *rheein* to flow>

di·a·ry (dī'ə rē) *n, pl* **di·a·ries** **1** an account written down of one's experiences during each day. **2** a book made for this purpose, usually with a space for each day of the year. <Latin *dies* day> **di'a·rist** *n.*

di·as·po·ra (dī as'pə rə) *n* **1 Diaspora a** the dispersion of the Jews living in Israel at various points in history, especially after the sack of Jerusalem in 70 CE. **b** the Jews thus scattered. Also called **Dispersion**. **2** a people widely dispersed from the land that they traditionally regard as their home. <Greek *dia-* through + *sperein* scatter>

di·as·to·le (dī as'tə lē) *n* the normal, rhythmic dilation of the heart, especially that of the ventricles. Compare SYSTOLE. <Latin, from Greek *dia-* apart + *stellein* to place> **di'as·tol'ic** *adj.*

di·a·tom (dī'ə tom') *n* a microscopic alga with a hard shell. <Latin, from Greek *dia-* through + *temnein* cut> **di'a·to·ma'ceous** (dī'ə to mā' shəs) *adj.*

di·a·ton·ic scale (dī'ə ton'ik) *Music n* a standard major or minor scale of eight tones. <Latin, from Greek *dia-* through + *tonos* tone>

di·a·tribe (dī'ə trīb') *n* a bitter and violent speech or written commentary against some person or thing. <Latin, from Greek *diatribe* lecture>

dibs (dibz) *Informal pl n* a stated claim on a desired object: *I have first dibs on the ice cream bar.* <origin uncertain>

dice (dīs) *pl n, sing* **die** (dī) **1** small cubes with a different number of spots (usually one to six) on each side, used in games and gambling. Dice are often used in pairs. **2** *Informal* a single one of these cubes. **3** (*with a singular verb*) a gambling game played with such cubes.
v **diced, dic·ing** **1** cut into small cubes: *to dice carrots.* **2** rolling dice to see how many spots there will be on the sides turned up. **3** gamble: *dicing with death by going skydiving. She diced away her inheritance.* <Old French, from Latin *dare* to play>
load the dice, influence an outcome unfairly in advance.
no dice, *Slang* an expression of failure or refusal.

dic·ey (dī'sē) *Informal adj* **dic·i·er, dic·i·est** risky.

di·chlo·ride (dī klôr'īd) *n* a compound composed of chlorine and one other element or radical, with two atoms of chlorine for each atom of the other element or radical.

di·chot·o·my (dī kot'ə mē) *n, pl* **di·chot·o·mies** a division into two distinct parts or opposite categories: *a dichotomy between living and nonliving things.* <Latin, from Greek *dicho-* in two + *temnein* cut> **di·chot'o·mize'** *v.* **di·chot'o·mous** *adj.*

Dick·en·si·an (di ken'zē ən) *adj* to do with the nineteenth-century English novelist Charles Dickens, or with his style or the time and place in which he lived.

dick·er (dik'ər) *v* argue about small amounts in bargaining or negotiating: *I'm not going to dicker about a measly dollar here or there.* <originally, ten hides as a unit of trade, from Latin *decem* ten>

dick·ie (dik'ē) *n* a false shirt or blouse front to be worn under a vest, suit, or low-cut dress or sweater. Also, **dickey** or **dicky**. <perhaps *Dick*, proper name>

D

di·cot·y·le·don (dī'kot ə lē'dən) *Botany n* a flowering plant that has two leaves when it first sprouts from the seed. Compare MONOCOTYLEDON. Often shortened informally to **dicot**. **di·cot'y·le'don·ous** *adj.*

dic·ta (dik'tə) a plural of DICTUM.

dic·tate (dik'tāt) *v* **dic·tat·ed, dic·tat·ing** **1** say or read something aloud for another person to write, type, or enter on a keyboard: *The teacher dictated a spelling list.* **2** give orders that must be obeyed: *to dictate terms of peace to a defeated enemy. No one is going to dictate to me!*
n a direction or order given with authority: *Follow the dictates of your conscience.* <Latin *dicere* say, tell> **dic·ta'tion** *n.*

dic·ta·tor (dik'tā tər) *n* **1** the absolute ruler of a nation or empire, especially one who has illegally seized control of the government. **2** someone who tries to exercise absolute authority or control over others: *The staff says their new boss is a dictator.* **dic'ta·to'ri·al** *adj.*

dic·ta·tor·ship (dik tā'tər ship') *n* **1** a country, institution, or organization ruled by a dictator. **2** the position or rule of a dictator.

dic·tion (dik'shən) *n* **1** the choice and use of words and phrases in speaking and writing. **2** the distinctness of pronunciation in speech or singing; enunciation: *clear diction.* <Latin *dicere* to say>

dic·tion·ar·y (dik'shə ner'ē) *n, pl* **dic·tion·ar·ies**
1 a reference book of words and terms arranged alphabetically, with information about their meanings and, often, pronunciation, history, and usage: *a medical dictionary, an intermediate dictionary.* **2** a book of this kind that gives the equivalent of each word or expression in another language, with short definitions: *a French-English dictionary.* <See DICTION.>

dic·tum (dik'təm) *n, pl* **dictums** or **dic·ta** a formal comment or opinion intended to be authoritative: *I pay no attention to the dictums of movie reviewers.* <Latin = thing said, from *dicere* say>

did (did) past tense of DO[1].

di·dac·tic (dī dak'tik) *adj* **1** intended to teach or give a lesson of some kind: *The fables of Aesop are didactic in that each one has a moral.* **2** inclined to instruct others: *This writer's didactic style gets on my nerves.* <Greek *didaskein* teach> **di·dac'ti·cal·ly** *adv.* **di·dac'ti·cism'** *n.*

did·n't (did'ənt) *contraction* did not.

a bat	e bed	i bid	o pot	u cup	th **thin**
ā cake	ē me	ī bite	ō go	ū rude	TH **then**
ȧ bar	ə about	ər over	ȯ for	u̇ put	zh measure

die[1] (dī) *v* **died, dy·ing 1** stop living: *My rosebush died.* **2** stop functioning: *The car engine sputtered and died. We started up a stamp club, which died soon afterwards.* **3** *Informal* suffer mental anguish: *If he asks me that in public, I will just die.* <Old English, from Old Norse *deyja*>

be dying for (or **to**), *Informal* See DYING.

die away (or **out**), become gradually less or weaker until it stops: *The echoes died away. The noise eventually died out.*

die down, become calmer or less violent or extreme: *The storm died down after a while.*

die hard, resist to the very end.

die off (or **out**), die one after another until all are dead: *The whole herd of cattle died off in the epidemic. Dinosaurs died out ages ago.*

to die for, *Informal* (*especially of food*) excellent or superb: *This cheesecake is to die for!*

GRAMMAR AND USAGE

Die is generally followed by *of* when illness is the cause of death: *He died of cancer.* However, *from* is sometimes used when injury is the cause: *She died from a wound.* When a process is referred to, *by* is used: *The victim died by drowning.*

die[2] (dī) *n* a tool for cutting or stamping things that is used to make the thread on pipes, bolts, and screws, and to make machine parts. <from DIE[3]. A die is often in the form of a block with the desired shape cut out of the centre.> **die′mak′er** *n.*

die[3] (dī) singular of DICE.

the die is cast, the decision is made and cannot be changed.

die·back (dī′bak′) *n* a disease of trees and other woody plants in which the twigs and tips of branches die first.

die·hard (dī′härd′) *adj* supporting and resisting all attacks, to the very end.
n a person who is like this.

die·sel (dē′zəl) *n* **1** in full, **diesel engine** an internal combustion engine that burns fuel oil ignited by heat from compressed air instead of by an electric spark as in a gasoline engine. **2** a vehicle powered by such an engine. **3** the fuel required by such an engine. <R. *Diesel,* 20c inventor of the diesel engine>

di·et (dī′ət) *n* **1** the usual food and drink of a person or animal: *a rich diet. A giraffe's diet consists of young leaves and shoots.* **2** a special selection of food and drink eaten for a special purpose, such as to lose or gain weight. **3** something given or used habitually: *A steady diet of TV is boring.*
v eat special food and drink as a treatment for disease or in order to gain or lose weight: *You don't need to diet; your weight is fine.* <Old French, from Greek *diaita* way of life> **di′e·tar′y** *adj.* **di′et·er** *n.*

on a diet, dieting.

di·e·tet·ics (dī′ə tet′iks) *n* (*with singular verb*) the science that deals with the amount and kinds of food needed for good health. **di′e·tet′ic** *adj.*

di·e·ti·tian or **di·e·ti·cian** (dī′ə tish′ən) *n* a person trained to plan healthy meals with the correct kinds and amounts of different foods.

dif·fer (dif′ər) *v* **1** be unlike: *Results will differ according to temperature. My answer differed from hers.* **2** have or express a disagreement. <Old French, from Latin *dis-* apart + *ferre* carry>

I beg to differ, a polite formula expressing disagreement.

dif·fer·ence (dif′rəns) *n* **1** the fact or condition of being unlike: *We are not afraid of difference.* **2** a specific way in which things are different: *There are three main differences between these two theories.* **3** what is left after subtracting one quantity from another: *He subtracted the cost of the jeans from his savings, leaving a balance of $90.* **4** usually, **differences** *pl* disagreement or dispute: *Let us put aside our differences.*

make a difference, a matter or be important: *It doesn't make any difference who did it; it got done.* **b** have an effect or influence: *Here's how you can make a difference in the world.* **c** give different treatment: *The law makes no difference between rich and poor.* **d** distinguish or see a difference: *I make no difference between lying and hiding the truth.*

make all the difference, be very important to an outcome.

same difference or **same diff,** *Slang* it makes no difference.

split the difference, a divide what is left in half: *My meal was $6.50 and yours was $8.00; let's split the difference and each pay $7.25.* **b** compromise.

dif·fer·ent (dif′rənt) *adj* **1** not alike: *We have different opinions. Cars are different from vans.* **2** separate or distinct: *I warned her on three different occasions.* **3** various: *There are different ways you can do this.* **4** not like most others: *His style of dress is rather different.* **dif′fer·ent·ly** *adv.* **dif′fer·ent·ness** *n.*

GRAMMAR AND USAGE

In formal English, the standard expression is **different from**. In informal usage, **different than** is often used. Either one can be used before a clause:

This story is different from others written by the author.
That shirt's different than what I thought you'd wear.

dif·fer·en·tial (dif′ə ren′shəl) *adj* **1** differing according to conditions or circumstances: *differential rates of pay. The cliff shows signs of differential erosion.* **2** to do with distinguishing between similar things. A **differential diagnosis** tells which of two or more diseases with similar symptoms is the one from which a patient is suffering, based on an analysis of the clinical data. **3** *Physics* to do with the difference of two or more motions or pressures.
n **1** a systematic difference: *There's still an alarming pay differential for men and women.* **2** an arrangement of gears in a car allowing one rear wheel to turn faster than the other in rounding a corner or curve. **dif′fer·en′tial·ly** *adv.*

dif·fer·en·ti·ate (dif′ə ren′shē āt′) *v* **dif·fer·en·ti·at·ed, dif·fer·en·ti·at·ing 1** be the thing that distinguishes: *acts of kindness that differentiate real compassion from mere politeness.* **2** recognize or see a difference: *to differentiate* *between truth and fiction.* **3** become different: *The cells of an embryo eventually differentiate to form specific kinds of tissue.* **dif′fer·en′ti·a′tion** *n.*

differently a·bled (ā′bəld) *adj* with some disability.

dif·fi·cult (dif′ə kəlt) *adj* **1** hard to do or understand: *Moving the piano was difficult work. I find algebra difficult.* **2** hard to please or get along with: *Don't be difficult.* <See DIFFICULTY.>

dif·fi·cul·ty (dif′ə kul′tē) *n, pl* **dif·fi·cul·ties** **1** the fact or condition of being difficult: *Time required for the task depends on the level of difficulty.* **2** a hard time or trouble: *I have difficulty with spelling.* **3** something that makes things difficult: *One of our biggest difficulties is finding time to do everything.* **4** financial trouble. <Latin *dis-* reverse + *facilis* easy>
in difficulties, in trouble, especially money trouble.
make difficulties, raise unnecessary objections.

dif·fi·dent (dif′ə dənt) *adj* shy or timid. <Latin *dis-* reversing + *fidere* to trust> **dif′fi·dence** *n.* **dif′fi·dent·ly** *adv.*

dif·frac·tion (di frak′shən) *Physics n* **1** the process of breaking up a ray of light into a series of lighter and darker bands or into coloured bands of the spectrum. **2** a similar breaking up of sound waves or electricity. <Latin *dis-* away from + *frangere* to break> **dif·fract′** *v.*

dif·fuse (di fyūz′) *for v,* (di fyūs′) *for adj. v* **dif·fused, dif·fus·ing** **1** spread out so as to cover a larger space or surface: *The fan diffuses heat from the fireplace throughout the room. His friendly manner diffused good humour among the team.* **2** *Physics* mix fluids together by spreading into one another.
adj **1** not concentrated together at a single point: *diffuse light.* **2** using many words where a few would do: *a diffuse writer.* <Latin *dis-* away + *fundere* pour> **dif·fu′sion** *n.*

CONFUSABLES

To **diffuse** is to make something spread: *The air freshener diffused a pine scent throughout the room.*

To **defuse** is to neutralize: *The peacekeepers defused the bomb.*

dig (dig) *v* **dug** (dug) **, dig·ging** **1** use a tool or part of the body to make a hole or passageway in the ground or to turn over soil: *to dig a hole, to dig for earthworms, to dig under a fence.* **2** get by digging: *to dig potatoes.* **3** search deeply and thoroughly: *to dig for information. He dug in his pockets for a quarter.* **4** jab, thrust, or poke: *She dug her spurs into the horse's side.* **5** *Tennis, Volleyball* strike a ball just before it hits the ground. **6** *Slang* **a** understand: *I don't dig how this works.* **b** like or enjoy.
n **1** an archaeological expedition or excavation: *We went to Alberta on a dig.* **2** a jab, thrust, or poke: *He gave me a dig in the ribs.* **3** *Informal* a sarcastic remark: *She made a few nasty little digs about my cooking.* <perhaps Old English *dic* ditch> **dig′ger** *n.*
dig in (or **into**), **a** begin to eat heartily. **b** begin to work hard at: *He took one look at the mess, rolled up his sleeves, and dug in.* **c** secure your position as if by digging a trench.
dig up, a find or get by digging: *Squirrels have dug up the tulip bulbs.* **b** find by thorough search, often in obscure places: *He dug up his old report cards.*

❦ **Dig·by chicken** (dig′bē) *n* a small, smoke-cured herring. <*Digby*, Nova Scotia>

di·gest (dī jest′) *for v,* (dī′ jest) *for n. v* **1 a** break down food in the stomach so that it can be taken into the blood to nourish the body: *I can't digest pork very well.* **b** undergo this process: *Some foods digest more easily than others.* **2** think through and integrate with the rest of one's knowledge: *It takes me a long time to digest new ideas.*
n information condensed and systematically arranged: *a digest of Canadian criminal law.* <Latin *dis-* apart + *gerere* carry> **di·gest′i·ble** *adj.* **di·ges′tion** *n.* **di·gest′ive** *adj.*

dig·it (dij′it) *n* **1** a single numeral: *There are three digits in 329.* **2** a finger or toe, or some corresponding part in an animal. <Latin *digitus* finger>

dig·i·tal (dij′ə təl) *adj* **1** giving information in the form of numerals only, or to do with this kind of information: *a digital watch.* **2** using information processed electronically as binary digits: *a digital recording, digital images.* Compare ANALOGUE. **dig′i·tal·ly** *adv.*

digital audiotape *n* a magnetic audiotape with digitally recorded sound. *Abbrev.* **DAT**

digital camera *Computers n* a camera whose lens projects images onto photoelectric cells, digitally stores them, and can have them loaded into a computer for printing as an image, or stored on a disk.

dig·i·tal·is (dij′ə tal′is) *n* a medicine for stimulating the heart, obtained from the dried leaves of the purple foxglove. <See DIGIT. The corolla of the foxglove is shaped like a finger.>

dig·i·tize (dij′ə tīz′) *Computers v* **dig·i·tized, dig·i·tiz·ing** convert images, data, or sound to digital form for processing by computer. **dig′i·ti·za′tion** *n.* **dig′i·tiz′er** *n.*

dig·ni·fied (dig′nə fīd′) *adj* with or showing dignity.

dig·ni·fy (dig′nə fī′) *v* **dig·ni·fied, dig·ni·fy·ing** **1** give dignity to: *Work and leisure dignify human life.* **2** treat as worthy: *I won't dignify that impertinent question with an answer.*

dig·ni·tar·y (dig′nə ter′ē) *n, pl* **dig·ni·tar·ies** a person of high or honourable position: *The funeral was attended by the prime minister, the archbishop, and other dignitaries.*

dig·ni·ty (dig′nə tē) *n, pl* **dig·ni·ties** **1** behaviour that shows self-respect and commands the respect of others: *He answered with dignity that he wanted no part of their scam. She carries herself with dignity.* **2** seriousness or formality: *the dignity of a funeral service. Casual dress is not in keeping with the dignity of your position.* **3** an honourable or worthy quality: *the dignity of labour.* **4** proper pride or self-esteem: *Don't trample on her dignity by treating her like a slave.* <Old French, from Latin *dignus* worthy>
beneath your dignity, humiliating: *He thinks doing dishes is beneath his dignity.*

a bat	e bed	i bid	o pot	u cup	th thin
ā cake	ē me	ī bite	ō go	ū rude	TH then
ä bar	ə about	ər over	ô for	ů put	zh measure

di·graph (dī′graf) *n* **1** two letters used together to spell a single sound, as *ea* in *each* or *th* in *with*. **2** a single symbol consisting of two joined letters, such as *æ* or *œ*. <Greek *di-* two + *graphe* a writing>

di·gress (dī gres′) *v* get off the main subject in talking or writing. <Latin *di-* aside + *gradi* to walk> **di·gres′sion** *n.* **di·gres′sive** *adj.*

Di·jon mustard (dē zhōɴ′) *n* mustard containing white wine. <*Dijon*, France, where it was originally made>

dike (dīk) *n* a bank of earth or wall built as a defence against attack, flooding, etc. Also, **dyke**. <Old Norse *dik*>

di·lap·i·dat·ed (di lap′ə dā′tid) *adj* falling to pieces. <Latin *di-* apart, abroad + *lapidis* stone> **di·lap′i·da′tion** *n.*

dil·a·ta·tion (dī′lə tā′shən) *or* (di′lə tā′shən) *n* **1** *Mathematics* a transformation in which the image is an enlargement or a reduction of the original. **2** *Medicine* an enlargement of a part of the body. <Old French, from Latin *di-* apart + *latus* wide>

di·late (dī lāt′) *or* (dī′lāt) *v* **di·lat·ed, di·lat·ing 1** make or become larger in an opening: *The pupils of your eyes dilate when the light gets dim.* **2** speak or write at great length and in great detail: *to dilate on a subject.* <Old French, from Latin *di-* apart + *latus* wide> **di·la′tion** *n.*

dil·a·to·ry (dil′ə tòr′ē) *adj* tending to stall or delay. <Latin *differre* defer, delay>

di·lem·ma (di lem′ə) *n* a difficult problem, especially a situation requiring a choice between two equally bad or good things. <Latin, from Greek *di-* two + *lemma* premise, term>

GRAMMAR AND USAGE

In formal English, **dilemma** should be used when there are only two choices, because *di–* means "two." In informal usage, dilemma means any problem that doesn't seem to have a solution.

dil·et·tante (dil′ə tont′) *or* (dil′ə tan′tā) *n, pl* **dil·et·tantes** or **dil·et·tan·ti** (dil′ə tan′tē) a person whose interest in art or some other subject is for fun or for social status only, without putting in serious effort or time. <Italian, from Latin *delectare* to charm> **dil′et·tan′tish** *adj.* **dil′et·tan′tism** *n.*

dil·i·gent (dil′ə jənt) *adj* carefully and steadily doing one's duty: *I haven't been very diligent about my homework lately.* <Latin *diligentem* careful, from *di-* apart + *legere* read> **dil′i·gence** *n.* **dil′i·gent·ly** *adv.*

dill (dil) *n* **1** a tall plant of the parsley family grown for its flavourful seeds and leaves. See HERB for picture. **2** in full, **dill pickle** a pickle flavoured with dill: *a jar of dills.* <Old English *dile*>

dil·ly–dal·ly (dil′ē dal′ē) *v* **dil·ly-dal·lied, dil·ly-dal·ly·ing** waste time or dawdle. <reduplication of *dally*>

di·lute (dī lūt′) *or* (di lūt′) *v* **di·lut·ed, di·lut·ing 1** make weaker or thinner by adding water or some other liquid. **2** weaken or lessen: *The effect of his argument was diluted by the use of poor examples.*

adj Chemistry diluted: *dilute acid.* <Latin *di-* apart + *luere* wash> **di·lu′tion** *n.*

dim (dim) *adj* **dim·mer, dim·mest 1** without much light: *a dim hallway, dim light.* **2** not clear or distinct: *dim outlines, a dim memory.* **3** poor or weak in eyesight. **4** not favourable or hopeful: *a dim future. His chances of winning are dim.* **5** *Informal* stupid.

v **dim·med, dim·ming** make or become dim or dimmer: *The theatre lights dimmed. Dim your headlights for oncoming traffic.* <Old English *dimm*> **dim′ly** *adv.* **dim′ness** *n.*

take a dim view of, disapprove of: *My parents take a pretty dim view of unsupervised parties.*

dime (dīm) *n* a ten-cent coin of Canada or the US. <Old French, from Latin *decem* ten>

a dime a dozen, easy to get or commonplace: *Poorly written paperback dictionaries are a dime a dozen.*

on a dime, within very limited time or space: *to turn or stop on a dime.*

di·men·sion (di men′shən) *n* **1** the property of length, area, or volume. A line has only one dimension, a plane figure has two dimensions, and a solid has three. **2** the measure of length, width, or thickness: *The dimensions of my room are 4 m by 3 m.* **3** an aspect, element, or characteristic: *Her work adds a new dimension to the art of filmmaking.* **4 dimensions** *pl* size, extent, or scope: *a project of huge dimensions.* <Old French, from Latin *di-* out + *metiri* to measure> **di·men′sion·al** *adj.*

dime store *n* especially in former times, a store selling a wide variety of cheap items, now often called a dollar store. **dime′-store′** *adj.*

di·min·ish (di min′ish) *v* **1** make or become less or smaller: *The heat diminished as the sun went down. Such cowardly behaviour diminishes a person.* **2** *Music* reduce a major or minor interval by a halftone: *a diminished seventh.* <Latin *minutus* small)> **di·min′ish·ing** *adj.*

diminishing returns *n* less and less profit or output relative to the amount of money, time, or labour invested.

di·min·u·en·do (di min′yū en′dō) *Music adj, adv* with a gradual lessening in force or loudness. <Italian = diminishing, from Latin *deminuere* lessen>

dim·i·nu·tion (dim′ə nyū′shən) *n* the act or fact of diminishing: *the diminution of natural resources.* <See DIMINISH.>

di·min·u·tive (di min′yə tiv) *adj* **1** very small. **2** *Grammar* expressing smallness: *In English, -ie is a diminutive suffix.*

n Grammar a word, form, or affix expressing smallness: *"Doggie" is a diminutive of "dog."* <Old French, from Latin *deminuere* lessen> **di·min′u·tive·ness** *n.*

dim·mer (dim′ər) *n* in full, **dimmer switch** a device operated by a knob or switch for adjusting the brightness of an electric light, usually gradually.

dim·ple (dim′pəl) *n* **1** a small natural hollow in the surface of a plump part of the body, such as the cheek, chin, or the back of the hand. **2** a dent or a small, hollow place: *the dimples on a golf ball.*

v **dim·pled, dim·pling** form dimples in the surface: *The large, heavy raindrops dimpled the sand. Her cheeks dimple when she smiles.* <Middle English *dympull*>

dim sum (dim′ sum′) *n* Chinese food consisting of steamed dumplings and other small dishes of food, served in a restaurant from a passing cart or ordered from a waiter. <Cantonese>

dim·wit (dim′wit′) *Slang n* a stupid person.
dim′wit′ted *adj.*

din (din) *n* a loud, confused, continuous noise.
v **dinned, din·ning 1** make a din. **2** say over and over: *He was always dinning into our ears the importance of good grammar.* <Old English *dyne*>

dine (dīn) *v* **dined, din·ing 1** eat dinner. **2** give a dinner to or for: *We dined our host family as thanks for their kindness.* <Old French, from Latin *dis-* undo + *jejunium* starve>
dine on, eat for dinner: *to dine on shellfish.*

din·er (dī′nər) *n* **1** a person eating a meal, especially in a restaurant. **2** a railway car in which meals are served. **3** a small, inexpensive restaurant, especially one near a highway or one shaped and decorated like a railway dining car.

di·nette (dī net′) *n* **1** a small dining room in a home. **2** a compact set of a table and chairs for such a room.

ding (ding) *v* **1** make a sound like a small bell. **2** strike and dent slightly: *Somebody dinged my car in the parking lot.*
n **1** the sound of a small bell. **2** a small dent. <imitative>

ding·bat (ding′bat′) *n* **1** *Printing* an ornamental character, symbol, or icon in a special font. **2** *Slang* a stupid or crazy person. <origin uncertain>

din·ghy (ding′ē) *n, pl* **din·ghies** a small rowboat, life raft, or sailboat. <Hindi *dingi*>

din·go (ding′gō) *n, pl* **din·goes** a wolflike wild dog of Australia. <native Aborginal name>

din·gy (din′jē) *adj* **din·gi·er, din·gi·est** dirty or dull-looking; not bright and fresh: *frayed, dingy curtains, a dingy hallway.* <perhaps Old English *dynge* dung>

dining room *n* a room in which meals are served.

dink·y (din′kē) *Informal adj* **din·ki·er, din·ki·est** small and insignificant; cute. <Scots neat, trim>

din·ner (din′ər) *n* **1** the main meal of the day. **2** a social event including this meal: *The community centre holds a dinner for seniors the third Friday of each month.* **3** a packaged meal designed for quick, convenient preparation: *TV dinners, a macaroni and cheese dinner.* <Old French, from Latin *dis-* undo + *jejunium* starve >

dinner jacket *n* a man's short jacket worn on formal occasions.

dinner theatre *n* a restaurant offering a show during or after dinner.

din·ner·time (din′ər tīm′) *n* the time when dinner is served.

di·no·flag·el·late (dī′nō flaj′ə lit) *n* a single-celled, chiefly marine organism that in large numbers is a main ingredient of plankton. <Greek *dinos* whirling + Latin *flagellum* whiplike tail, with reference to a characteristic of some bacteria>

di·no·saur (dī′nə sȯr′) *n* **1** an extinct four-limbed reptilian or birdlike creature that often reached an enormous size. **2** a person who or thing that is hopelessly outdated. <Latin, from Greek *deinos* terrible + *sauros* lizard>

dint (dint) *n, v* dent. <Old English *dynt*>
by dint of, by means of: *By dint of changing the schedule, we managed to keep the deadline.*

di·o·cese (dī′ə sēs′) *Christianity n* the district over which a bishop has authority. <Old French, from Greek *dioikein* keep house>

D

di·ode (dī′ōd) *Electronics n* in full, **semiconductor diode** an electronic device or component consisting of a semiconductor with two electrodes, used especially to convert alternating current to direct current. <*di-*[1] + *electrode*>

di·o·ram·a (dī′ə ram′ə) *n* **1** a picture, or a three-dimensional scene with a painted backdrop and often specially lit, to be looked at through a small opening. **2** a miniature three-dimensional scene made in a box with an open front: *For school, we had to build a diorama of Canadian pioneer life.* <French, from Greek *dia-* through + *horama* sight>

di·ox·ide (dī ok′sīd) *Chemistry n* a compound with two atoms of oxygen per molecule and one atom of a metal or other element.

dip (dip) *v* **dipped, dip·ping 1 a** put or go into water or a liquid and then quickly out again: *I dipped my toe into the pool to test the water.* **b** wash, rinse, dye, or coat by doing this: *to dip candles.* **2** put one's hand, or a container, into something and take a little out: *to dip soup out of a pot with a ladle.* **3** lower and raise again quickly: *to dip a flag in salute.* **4** drop or go down slightly: *My grades dipped a little last month. The road dips on the other side of the bridge.*
n **1** a short swim. **2** a creamy mixture eaten by dipping into it with a piece of food: *chips and dip.* **3** a sudden drop: *a dip in the road, a dip in prices.* **4** a liquid in which to dip something. **Sheep dip** is a disinfectant bath for sheep. **5** an act of dipping. <Old English *dyppan*>
dip into, a read or look at briefly. **b** use a little of: *I dipped into my savings to buy my friend a birthday gift.*

diph·the·ri·a (dif thē′rē ə) *or* (dip thē′rē ə) *n* a dangerous, infectious disease of the throat, usually with a high fever and the formation of membranes that interfere with breathing. <Latin, from Greek *diphthera* hide, leather, from the membranes that form on the affected parts>

diph·thong (dif′thong) *or* (dip′thong) *n* a vowel sound that is made up of two vowels pronounced in smooth succession as one syllable. The words *house* and *noise* both contain a diphthong. Compare MONOPHTHONG. <French, from Greek *di-* double + *phthongos* sound>

di·plod·o·cus (di plod′ə kəs) *n* a plant-eating dinosaur with a long, slender neck and tail that lived in western North America about 145 to 155 million years ago. <Latin, from Greek *diplo-* double+ *dokos* beam, from its appearance>

a bat	e bed	i bid	o pot	u cup	th **thin**
ā cake	ē me	ī bite	ō go	ū rude	ᴛʜ **then**
ȧ bar	ə about	ər over	ȯ for	u̇ put	zh measure

di·plo·ma (di plō′mə) *n* a certificate given by a school, college, or university to its graduating students. <Latin = letter folded double, from Greek *diplous* double>

di·plo·ma·cy (di plō′mə sē) *n* **1** the management of relations between nations. **2** skill and tact in dealing with others. <French, from Greek *diploma* letter of introduction (which diplomats traditionally carry)>

dip·lo·mat (dip′lə mat′) *n* **1** a nation's representative located in another country for the purpose of looking after his or her own country's interests there. Such representatives are members of the **diplomatic corps**. **2** a person who is skilful and tactful in dealing with others. **dip′lo·mat′ic** *adj.* **dip′lo·mat′i·cal·ly** *adv.*

diplomatic immunity *n* special privileges given to diplomats and their families and staffs by international agreement, including freedom from arrest, search, and taxation.

dip·per (dip′ər) *n* **1** a deep, long-handled cup or larger container for scooping out water and other liquids. **2** either of two constellations in the northern sky that are shaped like dippers, the Big Dipper or the Little Dipper. **3** a group of wading and diving songbirds.

dip·stick (dip′stik′) *n* a rod for measuring the level of liquid in a narrow container, such as the oil in a car's crankcase.

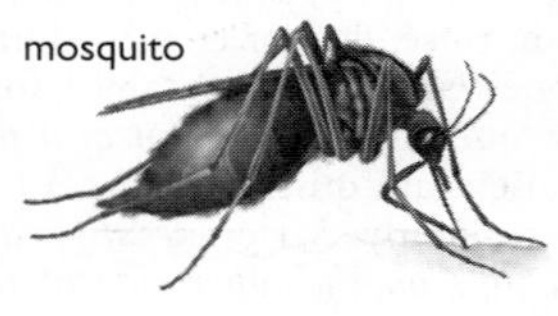

housefly

Dipterous insects like the mosquito and housefly can transmit diseases such as malaria, yellow fever, dengue, encephalitis, typhoid fever, cholera, dysentery, trachoma, and anthrax.

Female mosquitoes infect their victims by biting them, whereas flies normally transmit diseases by contaminating food with organisms that they pick up on their hairy legs.

dip·ter·ous (dip′tə rəs) *adj* to do with a large group of insects with sucking or piercing mouths and one pair of wings, including houseflies and mosquitoes. <Greek *di-* two + *pteron* wing>

dire (dīr) *adj* **dir·er, dir·est** **1** causing great fear or suffering: *dire news, a dire enemy.* **2** desperate, urgent, or extreme: *in dire need.* <Latin *dirus* fearful, threatening> **dire′ly** *adv.* **dire′ness** *n.*

di·rect (də rekt′) *or* (dī rekt′) *v* **1** manage, control, guide, or lead: *The teacher directs the work of students. Who directs this organization?* **2** command: *The officer directed us to wait.* **3** tell or show the way: *Can you direct me to the nearest bus stop?* **4** point or aim: *They directed the hose at the burning building.* **5** address words, a letter, or other communication: *to direct a request to your MP.*
adj **1** following a straight line without stops or turns: *a direct route.* **2** by an unbroken line of descent: *a direct descendant of Queen Victoria.* **3** without anyone or anything in between: *direct access, a direct purchase from the supplier.* **4** straightforward or plain: *a direct answer.* **5** exact or absolute: *the direct opposite.*
adv directly: *We fly to Winnipeg direct, without changing planes.* <Latin *de-* down + *regere* set straight>
di·rect′ness *n.*

direct current *n* a steady electric current that flows in one direction only. *Abbrev.* **DC** or **D.C.** Compare ALTERNATING CURRENT.

di·rec·tion (də rek′shən) *or* (dī rek′shən) *n* **1** the way that something points, faces, or travels: *What direction are we driving—north or south?* **2** guidance, management, or control: *The school is under the direction of a good principal.* **3** **directions** *pl* information about what to do, how to do something, or where to go: *I have lost the directions for assembling this thing.* **4** a command. **5** a line of action: *The criminal investigation has taken a new direction.*

di·rec·tion·al (də rek′shə nəl) *or* (dī rek′shə nəl) *adj* **1** to do with the direction of movement. **2** used for determining the direction from which radio signals come, or for picking up or sending radio signals in one direction only: *a directional microphone, a directional antenna or transmitter.*

direction finder *n* a radio receiver used to determine the direction of incoming signals.

di·rec·tive (də rek′tiv) *or* (dī rek′tiv) *n* an official instruction about procedure: *We have to comply with government directives.*

di·rect·ly (də rekt′lē) *or* (dī rekt′lē) *adv* **1** in a direct manner. **2** immediately.

direct mail *n* advertising material sent directly to large numbers of people at their home or business addresses.

direct object *Grammar n* in a sentence, the word or phrase that stands for the person or thing undergoing the action expressed by the verb. In *The car struck me*, the direct object is *me*. Compare INDIRECT OBJECT.

di·rec·tor (də rek′tər) *or* (dī rek′tər) *n* **1** the leader or chief manager of an organization or major project. **2** a person who belongs to a group of people chosen to oversee the affairs of a company or institution: *She is on the board of directors of a large corporation.* **3** the person who plans, guides, and rehearses the staging of a play, opera, movie, or TV show. **di·rec·to′ri·al** *adj.* **di·rec′tor·ship** *n.*

di·rec·tor·ate (də rek′tə rit) *or* (dī rek′tə rit) *n* **1** the office or position of a director. **2** directors as a group.

di·rec·to·ry (də rek′tə rē) *or* (dī rek′tə rē) *n, pl* **di·rec·to·ries** **1** a list of names, arranged alphabetically or in some other systematic way, telling the user where to find or how to reach the people or things named: *a telephone directory. This book of maps includes a street directory.* **2** *Computers* a list of the folders and files stored on a particular disk or drive.

directory assistance *n* a service offered by a telephone company allowing users to call and ask the operator for a listed phone number.

direct proportion *n* a relation between two quantities in which one of them increases or decreases at the same rate that the other does: *Your chances of getting higher grades are in direct proportion to the amount of time you study.* Compare INVERSE PROPORTION.

direct question *Grammar n* a person's question quoted in his or her exact words, as in *Her father asked, "Would you like a ride to school?"* Compare INDIRECT QUESTION.

direct speech *Grammar n* a quote of what a person says, in his or her exact words, as in *She said, "Let's go now."* Compare INDIRECT SPEECH.

direct tax *n* a tax collected by the government directly from the people who actually pay it, such as income tax, property tax, or inheritance tax.

dirge (dərj) *n* a slow, mournful piece of funeral music. <contracted from Latin *dirige!* direct!, from the first word in the ceremony for the dead>

dir·i·gi·ble (də rij′ə bəl) *or* (dēr′ə jə bəl) *n* a kind of aircraft shaped like a fat cigar and filled with a gas that keeps it airborne, with a steering and propelling mechanism attached to the bottom.
adj capable of being steered. <Latin *dirigere* to direct>

dirn·dl (dərn′dəl) *n* **1** the traditional dress of a peasant girl of the Alps, consisting of a blouse, a tight, laced bodice, and a full skirt gathered at the waist. **2** a dress imitating this. <Swiss German dialect *Dirne* girl>

dirt (dərt) *n* **1** mud, dust, or anything else unwanted that marks or stains clothing, furniture, walls, or skin. **2** loose earth or soil: *There was a pile of dirt beside the hole.* **3** obscene talk, writing, or images. **4** *Informal* **a** information or news: *Have you heard the latest dirt on my favourite movie star?* **b** information that discredits a person: *to spread dirt about someone.* <Old Norse *drit* excrement>
eat dirt, submit to a humiliating experience, such as making an apology or taking back what you have said.
treat someone like dirt, treat someone with contempt; treat very badly.

dirt bike *n* a small motorcycle designed for riding over rough ground.

dirt cheap *Informal adj* very cheap.

dirt poor *Informal adj* very poor.

dirt·y (dər′tē) *adj* **dirt·i·er, dirt·i·est 1** stained with dirt or exposing one to dirt: *dirty socks. Gardening can be dirty work.* **2** unfair or dishonourable: *a dirty trick.* **3** obscene or indecent: *a dirty joke.* **4** angry or hostile: *a dirty look.* **5** not clear or pure in colour: *a dirty red.* **6** unpleasant or disagreeable: *dirty weather, a dirty job.*
adv in a dirty way: *to fight dirty, to talk dirty.*
v **dirt·ied, dirt·y·ing** make dirty. **dir′ti·ness** *n.*
do someone dirty, *Slang* behave dishonourably toward someone, as by swindling or slandering.

dirty laundry *n* private or intimate matters that are somewhat shameful, will cause embarrassment if made public.
air (or **hang** or **wash**) **your dirty laundry in public,** publicize family or private quarrels or misdeeds.

Dirty Thirties *n* the drought years of the 1930s, that coincided with the (Great) Depression.

dirty word *n* **1** an obscene or vulgar word. **2** a politically incorrect word, or a word for something very unpopular: *"Homework" is a dirty word around here.*

dis or **diss** (dis) *Slang v* **dissed, dis·sing** show disrespect or contempt for.
n a put-down or other show of disrespect. <*disrespect*>

dis– *prefix* **1** not: *dishonest.* **2** do the reverse of: *disentangle.* **3** away, apart, or off: *discard.* <Latin>

GRAMMAR AND USAGE

The prefix **dis–** can be used to show the opposite of the root word:

appear and *disappear*, *advantage* and *disadvantage*, *respect* and *disrespect*, *trust* and *distrust*.

dis·a·bil·i·ty (dis′ə bil′ə tē) *n, pl* **dis·a·bil·i·ties 1** lack of normal function in some part of the body or mind: *a hearing disability, a learning disability.* **2** a disadvantage in some situation: *I'm afraid honesty is a real disability in this business, kid.* **3** *Law* something that disqualifies: *Her relationship to the accused was a disability that kept her from serving on the jury.*

dis·a·ble (dis ā′bəl) *v* **dis·a·bled, dis·a·bling 1** disrupt normal function in some part of the body or mind: *A fall like that could disable your ability to walk.* **2** make ineffective or keep from functioning: *Pull the switch to disable the alarm. The power failure has disabled public transport.* **dis·a′bled** *adj.*

GRAMMAR AND USAGE

It is offensive to use **disabled** as a noun or adjective when referring to a person or people.

Instead of *a disabled person,* say *a person with a disability*. Rather than *the disabled*, say *people with a disability*, or *people with disabilities*.

It is acceptable to use **disabled** when referring to a machine or machinery.

dis·a·buse (dis′ə byūz′) *v* **dis·a·bused, dis·a·bus·ing** free a person from false notions: *Education is supposed to disabuse people of prejudice.*

dis·ad·van·tage (dis′əd van′tij) *n* a fact or quality that makes success more difficult: *Lack of a computer is a definite disadvantage in this society.* **dis·ad′van·ta′geous** *adj.*
at a disadvantage, having to deal with a disadvantage: *People who can't read are at a disadvantage.*
to someone's disadvantage, leading to loss or difficulty for someone: *It is to your own disadvantage to cheat.*

dis·ad·van·taged (dis′əd van′tijd) *adj* suffering from severe economic or social disadvantage.

a bat	e bed	i bid	o pot	u cup	th thin
ā cake	ē me	ī bite	ō go	ū rude	TH then
ä bar	ə about	ər over	ȯ for	u̇ put	zh measure

dis·af·fect·ed (dis′ə fek′tid) *adj* **1** discontented or dissatisfied. **2** no longer loyal to an ideology or cause: *a new party made up mostly of disaffected Communists.* **dis′af·fec′tion** *n.*

dis·a·gree (dis′ə grē′) *v* **dis·a·greed, dis·a·gree·ing 1** fail to agree: *The two witnesses disagreed on the time of the shot. I disagree with you; the movie's not as bad as you say. Her words and her actions disagree.* **2** have an argument. **3** have a harmful effect: *Eggs disagree with him.* **dis′a·gree′ment** *n.*

SYNONYMS

Disagree means "differ in opinion": *My sister and I disagree on temperature; I like it hotter than she does.*

Contest means "challenge": *The student contested his essay mark, because he thought it was too low.*

Object means "argue": *The lawyer objected to the ruling against her client.*

dis·a·gree·a·ble (dis′ə grē′ə bəl) *adj* **1** unpleasant: *a disagreeable task, disagreeable weather.* **2** bad-tempered. *She's very disagreeable when she is tired.* **dis′a·gree′a·bly** *adv.*

dis·al·low (dis′ə lou′) *v* refuse to allow or accept. **dis′al·low′ance** *n.*

dis·ap·pear (dis′ə pēr′) *v* **1** move out of sight: *In the story, putting on the magic ring makes you disappear. The little dog disappeared down the road.* **2** pass out of existence: *Dinosaurs have disappeared.* **3** (*a euphemism or code word*) be secretly killed or imprisoned: *Under his regime, political protestors disappear every day.* **dis′ap·pear′ance** *n.*

dis·ap·point (dis′ə point′) *v* **1** fail to satisfy or please: *The movie disappointed me because the acting was poor.* **2** break a promise to; be unfaithful to: *You said you'd be there, so don't disappoint me.* <Old French *disappointer*> **dis′ap·point′ing** *adj.* **dis′ap·point′ment** *n.*

dis·ap·pro·ba·tion (dis ap′rə bā′shən) *n* disapproval.

dis·ap·prove (dis′ə prūv′) *v* **dis·ap·proved, dis·ap·prov·ing** believe or say that something is bad or not good enough: *When I ate the bacon with my fingers, I could see by her face that she disapproved.* **dis′ap·prov′al** *n.* **dis′ap·prov′ing·ly** *adv.*

dis·arm (dis årm′) *v* **1** take weapons away from: *The police captured the bandits and disarmed them.* **2** reduce or limit military forces and equipment: *Peace groups are urging the government to disarm.* **3** get rid of someone's suspicion or anger: *Her friendly smile disarmed the defiant little boy and he began to warm up.* **4** make harmless: *to disarm a bomb.* **dis·arm′ing** *adj.* **dis·arm′ing·ly** *adv.*

dis·ar·ma·ment (di sår′mə mənt) *n* the act of reducing military forces and equipment.

dis·ar·range (dis′ə rānj′) *v* **dis·ar·ranged, dis·ar·rang·ing** put out of order: *The wind disarranged her hair.* **dis′ar·range′ment** *n.*

dis·ar·ray (dis′ə rā′) *n* disorder or confusion.

dis·as·sem·ble (dis′ə sem′bəl) *v* **dis·as·sem·bled, dis·as·sem·bling** take apart. **dis′as·sem′bly** *n.*

dis·as·ter (də zas′tər) *n* **1** an event that causes great suffering and loss, such as an earthquake, flood, plane crash, or collapse of a mine. **2** an utter failure: *The play was a disaster.* <Old French *désastre* without a star. The supposed bad position of a star was thought to cause calamities.> **dis·as′trous** *adj.* **dis·as′trous·ly** *adv.*

disaster area *n* an area officially declared to have suffered some kind of disaster and to be in need of aid.

dis·a·vow (dis′ə vou′) *v* deny that one knows about, approves, or is responsible for: *She disavowed writing graffiti on the wall, even though her hands were covered in paint.* **dis′a·vow′al** *n.*

dis·band (dis band′) *v* cease to exist as a group or organization: *The photography club has disbanded; we all got too busy.* **dis·band′ment** *n.*

dis·bar (dis bår′) *v* **dis·barred, dis·bar·ring** take away a lawyer's right to practise law: *The lawyer was disbarred for unethical practices.* **dis·bar′ment** *n.*

dis·be·lieve (dis′ bə lēv′) *v* **dis·be·lieved, dis·be·liev·ing** be unable or unwilling to believe: *She stared, disbelieving, at her winning raffle ticket.* **dis′be·lief′** *n.* See UNBELIEF for confusable.

dis·burse (dis bərs′) *v* **dis·bursed, dis·burs·ing** pay out from a fund: *Our city treasurer disburses thousands of dollars each week.* **dis·burse′ment** *n.*

disc (disk) *n* **1** a round, thin, flat object, or one that appears to be so: *a compact disc, plastic coloured discs used in a game. The sun's disc appeared above the horizon.* **2** *Anatomy, Zoology* a round, flat mass of cartilage between the spinal vertebrae in humans or animals. **3** *Botany* the round central part of the flower head of most composite plants, composed of tiny florets. Also (*especially US*) **disk.** <Latin discus, from Greek *diskos*>

dis·card (di skård′) *for v,* (dis′kård) *for n. v* **1** throw away as no longer needed or wanted: *to discard worn-out clothing, to discard outdated ideas.* **2** get rid of an unwanted playing card.
n something rejected as no longer needed or wanted: *She gets free books from the library's bin of discards.* <dis- + card>

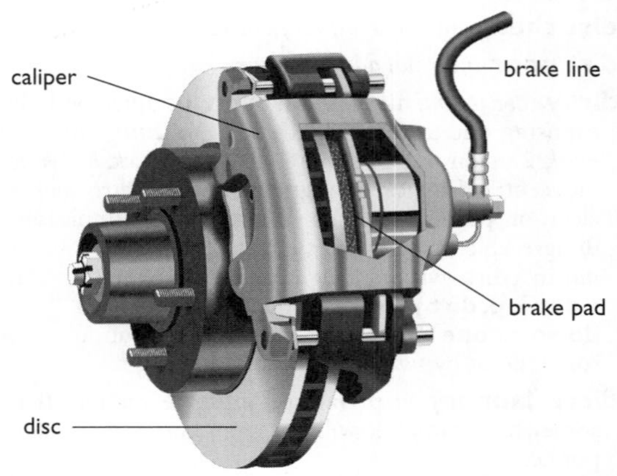

disc brake *n* a brake in a motor vehicle that works by pressing flat pads against both sides of a disc attached to the wheel.

dis·cern (di sərn′) *v* see, especially something that is not obvious: *I could just discern a shape through the fog. It can be difficult to discern the truth.* <Old French, from Latin *dis-* apart + *cernere* to separate> **dis·cern′i·ble** *adj.*

dis·cern·ing (di sər′ning) *adj* showing insight and keen judgment; able to see and recognize what is not obvious: *Discerning moviegoers will see through the movie's plot at once.* **dis·cern′ment** *n.*

Composite plants like the sunflower are quite complicated. What looks like one big flower is really a collection of tiny tubular flowers grouped in a central disc and surrounded by ray flowers (the petals).

disc flower *Botany n* one of the tiny flowers that make up the central disc of the flower head of a composite plant.

dis·charge (dis chärj′) *for v,* (dis′chärj) *for n. v* **dis·charged dis·charg·ing 1** release or dismiss: *to discharge a patient from hospital, to discharge a soldier from the army.* **2** fire or shoot: *to discharge a rifle.* **3** unload or empty: *to discharge cargo. The river discharges into the bay.* **4** give off or let out: *The wound was still discharging pus.* **5** *Electricity* **a** use up or lose the electric charge of: *A battery discharges slowly.* **b** give off electricity suddenly in the form of a spark. **6** pay or settle: *to discharge a debt.* **7** perform or carry out: *He discharged his duty with ease.*
n **1** the act of discharging. **2** something that is discharged: *A watery discharge oozed from the sore.* **3** a certificate showing that a person has been dismissed or released from the armed forces, a hospital, or other institution.

disc harrow *n* a low frame pulled behind a tractor over ploughed land, that turns and loosens the soil by means of rows of revolving, saucer-shaped blades set at an angle.

dis·ci·ple (də sī′pəl) *n* **1** a person who believes in, lives by, and helps to spread the ideas and teachings of another. **2** *Christianity* one of the 12 earliest followers of Jesus Christ. <Old English, from Latin *discere* learn> **dis·ci′ple·ship′** *n.*

dis·ci·pli·nar·i·an (dis′ə plə ner′ē ən) *n* a person who believes in and enforces strict discipline.
adj believing in and enforcing strict discipline.

dis·ci·pline (dis′ə plən) *n* **1 a** training to obey rules: *Parents see to the discipline of their children.* **b** the resulting condition of order or self-control: *The class showed excellent discipline while the teacher was out of the room.* **2 a** the business of enforcing rules or administering punishment: *The vice-principal is in charge of discipline.* **b** punishment intended to correct behaviour. **3** a branch of study or education: *Scholars of various disciplines met to discuss co-operative research.*
v **dis·ci·plined, dis·ci·plin·ing 1** bring to a condition of order and responsibility. **2** punish: *The students who were caught skipping class were severely disciplined.* <Old French, from Latin *discere* learn> **dis′ci·pli·nar′y** *adj.*

disc jockey *n* a person who chooses, introduces, and plays recorded music for a radio program, party, or dance. Also informally called **deejay**. *Abbrev.* **DJ**

dis·claim (dis klām′) *v* refuse to take as one's own: *The motorist disclaimed responsibility for the accident. She disclaimed any credit for the invention.*

dis·claim·er (dis klā′mər) *n* a statement intended to deny responsibility: *A disclaimer at the end of the movie says that any resemblance to real persons or events is purely accidental.*

dis·close (dis klōz′) *v* **dis·closed, dis·clos·ing** make known or lay open to view: *The curtain rose, disclosing a scene in a typical 1940s home. For reasons of privacy, participants' names will not be disclosed.* **dis·clo′sure** *n.*

dis·co (dis′kō) *n* **1** in full, **discothèque** a type of nightclub where one may listen and dance to recorded music. **2** the style of music or dancing characteristic of such a nightclub.
adj to do with such a place or such a style.

dis·col·our or **dis·col·or** (dis kul′ər) *v* change or spoil the colour of: *Smoke had discoloured the walls. Many materials discolour when exposed to sunlight.* **dis·col′or·a′tion** *n.*

dis·com·bob·u·late (dis′kəm bob′yə lāt′) *Informal v* **dis·com·bob·u·lat·ed, dis·com·bob·u·lat·ing** disconcert or confuse: *The household was discombobulated by the renovations.* <perhaps from *discomfit*> **dis′com·bob′u·la′tion** *n.*

dis·com·fort (dis kum′fərt) *n* **1** pain or uneasiness: *She felt some discomfort after the operation. I expressed my discomfort with the new school rules.* **2** a cause of pain, uneasiness, or inconvenience: *Outhouses are one of the discomforts of camping.*

dis·com·pose (dis′kəm pōz′) *v* **dis·com·posed, dis·com·pos·ing** disturb the calm or confidence of: *The student making the speech seemed discomposed by the grins of those in the front row.* **dis′com·po′sure** *n.*

dis·con·cert (dis′kən sərt′) *v* confuse or embarrass. **dis′con·cert′ing** *adj.*

dis·con·nect (dis′kə nekt′) *v* **1** undo or unfasten. **2** unplug: *Disconnect the toaster oven before trying to clean it.* **dis′con·nec′tion** *n.*

dis·con·nect·ed (dis′kə nek′tid) *adj* **1** not joined to something else. **2** not plugged in: *The printer doesn't work because it's disconnected!* **3** without logical order: *a disconnected account of events, disconnected paragraphs.* **dis′con·nect′ed·ly** *adv.*

dis·con·so·late (dis kon′sə lit) *adj* unable to be comforted: *She was disconsolate when her best friend moved away.* <Latin *consolari* to console> **dis·con′so·late·ly** *adv.*

a bat	e bed	i bid	o pot	u cup	th **thin**
ā cake	ē me	ī bite	ō go	ū rude	TH **then**
ä bar	ə about	ər over	ȯ for	u̇ put	zh measure

D

dis·con·tent (dis′kən tent′) *n* a dislike of what one has and a desire for something different. Also, **discontentment**.
v dissatisfy or displease: *It greatly discontented him that they had not laughed at any of his jokes.*
dis′con·tent′ed *adj.*

dis·con·tin·ue (dis′kən tin′yū) *v* **dis·con·tin·ued, dis·con·tin·u·ing 1** put an end or stop to: *That TV series has been discontinued. Once the dog was well, the vet discontinued the treatment.* **2** stop using or taking: *You may discontinue the medicine after three days.* **dis′con·tin′u·a′tion** *n.*

dis·con·tin·u·ous (dis′kən tin′yū əs) *adj* not continuous or connected. **dis′con·ti·nu′i·ty** *n.*

dis·cord (dis′kȯrd) *n* **1** disagreement or unfriendly relations: *a meeting spoiled by discord.* **2** a clashing of sounds or tones. <Old French, from Latin *dis-* apart + *cordis* heart> **dis·cord′ant** *adj.*

disc·o·thèque (dis′kə tek′) See DISCO (def. 1). <French>

dis·count (dis′kount) *for n,* (dis kount′) *for v. n* an amount or percentage deducted from a price: *Seniors get a 15 percent discount on everything in the store.*
v **1** deduct a certain amount or percentage from a price: *All the swimwear has been discounted. The store discounts 3 percent on all bills paid early.* **2** consider as unreliable: *He loves to exaggerate, so you have to discount most of what he tells you.*
adj sold or selling at prices less than the current average retail price: *discount merchandise, a discount store.*

dis·cour·age (di skər′ij) *v* **dis·cour·aged, dis·cour·ag·ing 1** take away the hope or confidence of: *Repeated failures discouraged her.* **2** make someone less willing or interested in doing something: *Traffic congestion discourages people from visiting the city. The colder weather soon discouraged our picnics.* **3** try to talk out of doing something: *They discouraged her from swimming alone.* **dis·cour′age·ment** *n.*

dis·course (dis′kȯrs) *for n,* (di skȯrs′) *for v. n* **1** a formal speech or piece of writing. **2** a conversation.
v **dis·coursed, dis·cours·ing 1** speak or write formally. **2** converse or talk. <Old French, from Latin *discursus* running or travelling around (a topic)>

dis·cour·te·ous (dis kər′tē əs) *adj* impolite.
dis·cour′te·ous·ly *adv.* **dis·cour′te·sy** *n.*

dis·cov·er (di skuv′ər) *v* see or learn for the first time: *We discovered a great ski hill near our new home. I discovered that the new girl was a lot nicer than I had thought.* **dis·cov′er·a·ble** *adj.* **dis·cov′er·er** *n.* **dis·cov′er·y** *n.*

dis·cred·it (dis kred′it) *v* **1** show to be unworthy of belief: *Recent data has discredited this theory.* **2** refuse to believe. **3** harm the reputation of: *This season's slump has done much to discredit the team's coach.*
n **1** reason for disbelief or doubt: *The new evidence casts discredit on her version of events.* **2 a** the loss of good reputation: *His conduct brought discredit on his firm.* **b** a person who or thing that causes this: *She was a discredit to the school.*

dis·cred·it·able (dis kred′ə tə bəl) *adj* bringing discredit or causing disgrace. **dis·cred′it·a·bly** *adv.*

dis·creet (di skrēt′) *adj* **1** showing tact and good judgment in speech or conduct: *The discreet servant never let on that he had heard the quarrel.* **2** not lavish or overdone: *discreet elegance.* <Old French, from Latin *discernere* discern>
dis·creet′ly *adv.*

CONFUSABLES

Discreet means "careful" or "prudent": *She was discreet enough never to repeat gossip.*

Discrete means "dissimilar" or "unconnected": *The interviewer asked questions about three discrete topics.*

dis·crep·an·cy (di skrep′ən sē) *n, pl* **dis·crep·an·cies** inconsistency or disagreement between two or more facts: *Why is there such a discrepancy in your grades between first and second term?* <Latin *discrepare* differ>

dis·crete (di skrēt′) *adj* separate or distinct. See DISCREET for confusable. <See DISCREET.> **dis·crete′ly** *adv.* **dis·crete′ness** *n.*

dis·cre·tion (di skresh′ən) *n* **1** the freedom to judge or choose: *Making final plans was left to the president's discretion.* **2** the quality of being discreet: *This is a sensitive situation, to be handled with discretion.*
age of discretion, the age at which one is legally able to manage one's own activities.
at someone's discretion, as someone sees fit.

dis·cre·tion·ar·y (di skresh′ə ner′ē) *adj* with freedom to judge or choose: *The law gives the mayor certain discretionary powers.*

dis·crim·i·nate (di skrim′ə nāt′) *for v,* (di skrim′ə nit) *for adj.* *v* **dis·crim·i·nat·ed, dis·crim·i·nat·ing 1** see or recognize a difference: *to discriminate between exaggeration and lying. You learn to discriminate good books from bad by reading a lot.* **2** make a biased distinction or unfair decision based on prejudice: *Employers must not discriminate on the basis of race. This policy discriminates against the poor.*
adj making the proper choice or distinction: *You need to be more discriminate in your choice of videos.* <Old French, from Latin *dis-* apart + *cernere* to separate>
dis·crim′i·nate·ly *adv.*

dis·crim·i·nat·ing (di skrim′ə nā′ting) *adj* **1** with or showing the ability to make proper distinctions and choices: *The discriminating reader will immediately see that this essay is poorly written.* **2** characteristic or identifying: *The discriminating mark of measles is a rash on the skin.*

dis·crim·i·na·tion (di skrim′ə nā′shən) *n* **1** the act of making or recognizing differences and distinctions: *Don't make purchases without discrimination.* **2** the ability to recognize differences, especially subtle differences: *Her discrimination in such matters is well-known.* **3** the act of making an unfair distinction or making decisions based on prejudice.

dis·crim·i·na·to·ry (di skrim′ə nə tȯr′ē) *adj* making an unfair distinction based on prejudice: *a discriminatory policy.*

dis·cur·sive (di skər′siv) *adj* wandering from one topic to another. <Old French, from Latin *dis-* away + *currere* to run> **dis·cur′sive·ly** *adv.* **dis·cur′sive·ness** *n.*

swing

gripping the discus

release

The **discus** throw is an Olympic event that goes all the way back to ancient Greece. The first discuses were made of stone, but iron, lead, and bronze proved to be more durable.

In today's competitions, men throw a discus that weighs 2 kg, while females use one that weighs 1 kg.

dis·cus (dis′kəs) *n* a heavy, circular stone or metal plate used in a throwing contest. The **discus throw** is a FIELD EVENT. <Latin, from Greek *diskos*>

dis·cuss (di skus′) *v* **1** talk about together, bringing in various points of view: *The class discussed the first two chapters of the novel.* **2** present various sides of an issue: *Her new book discusses the future of Québec in Canada.* <Latin *dis-* apart + *quatere* to shake> **dis·cus′sion** *n.*

dis·dain (dis dān′) *n* scorn or contempt.
v refuse with scorn: *He disdained the offer of a bribe. The woman disdained to answer their ridiculous question.* <Old French, from Latin *de-* not + *dignus* worthy> **dis·dain′ful** *adj.* **dis·dain′ful·ly** *adv.*

dis·ease (di zēz′) *n* **1** a condition in which an organ, system, or part of the body does not function properly: *All living things are subject to disease.* **2** a particular illness or disorder: *Cancer and alcoholism are diseases.* <Old French *des-* without + *aise* comfort> **dis·eased′** *adj.*

dis·em·bark (dis′əm bårk′) *v* get off or cause to get off a ship or aircraft: *to disembark passengers. We disembarked at Halifax.* **dis′em·bar·ka′tion** *n.*

dis·em·bod·y (dis′əm bod′ē) *v* **dis·em·bod·ied, dis·em·bod·y·ing** without or separate from the body: *disembodied spirits, a disembodied head.* **dis′em·bod′i·ment** *n.*

dis·em·bow·el (dis′əm bou′əl) *v* **dis·em·bow·elled** or **dis·em·bow·eled, dis·em·bow·el·ling** or **dis·em·bow·el·ing** take or rip out the intestines of. **dis′em·bow′el·ment** *n.*

dis·en·chant (dis′ən chant′) *v* **1** cause one to stop liking or admiring something: *The bad weather disenchanted us with England.* **2** free from a magic spell or illusion. **dis′en·chant′ed** *adj.* **dis′en·chant′ment** *n.*

dis·en·fran·chise (dis′ən fran′chīz) *v* **dis·en·fran·chised, dis·en·fran·chis·ing** **1** take the rights of citizenship away from. **2** leave powerless: *seeking to empower the poor and disenfranchised.* **dis′en·fran′chise·ment** *n.*

dis·en·gage (dis′ən gāj′) *v* **dis·en·gaged, dis·en·gag·ing** **1** loosen things that are meshed or intertwined; unlink: *The mother gently disengaged her hand from that of her sleeping child.* **2** withdraw from a commitment or obligation, or relationship: *Over the years he disengaged himself from his family by immersing himself in his career.* **dis′en·gage′ment** *n.*

dis·en·tan·gle (dis′ən tang′gəl) *v* **dis·en·tan·gled, dis·en·tan·gling** **1** release from tangles or from being tangled up. **2** sort out something complex and confused: *It's difficult to disentangle all the related issues.* **3** release from a messy situation. **dis′en·tan′gle·ment** *n.*

dis·fa·vour or **dis·fa·vor** (dis fā′vər) *n* **1** a negative opinion about something or someone: *He looked with disfavour on any attempt to change the routine.* **2** a state of being looked on with disapproval or dislike: *Since she was already in disfavour with her friends, she continued to defend her point of view.*

dis·fig·ure (dis fig′yər) *v* **dis·fig·ured, dis·fig·ur·ing** spoil the beauty or appearance of: *Large billboards disfigured the countryside.* **dis·fig′ure·ment** *n.*

dis·gorge (dis gȯrj′) *v* **dis·gorged, dis·gorg·ing** **1** throw up what has been swallowed. **2** pour out with force: *The swollen streams disgorged their waters into the river.* <Old French *des-* reverse of + Latin *gurges* throat>

dis·grace (dis grās′) *n* **1** a loss of respect or honour: *The boy brought disgrace to his family by his behaviour. She is still in disgrace for having cheated on the test.* **2** a source or cause of dishonour and shame: *Their laziness is a disgrace to this company.*
v **dis·graced, dis·grac·ing** cause to lose honour or respect: *They disgraced themselves by booing during the national anthem.* **dis·grace′ful** *adj.* **dis·grace′ful·ly** *adv.*

dis·grun·tle (dis grun′təl) *v* **dis·grun·tled, dis·grun·tling** make discontented: *travellers disgruntled by the delay, disgruntled customers.* <*dis-* down, off + Old English *grunettan* to grunt> **dis·grun′tle·ment** *n.*

dis·guise (dis gīz′) *v* **dis·guised dis·guis·ing** **1** make changes in appearance so as not to be recognized: *The spy disguised herself as an old man.* **2** try to make a thing seem like something better: *This is just elitism disguised as academic excellence.*
n **1** the act of disguising: *She resorted to disguise in order to get past the guards.* **2** the clothes, behaviour, makeup, or other false appearance used to hide what a person or thing really is: *A wig was part of his disguise. That friendly smile is just a disguise for her hostility.* <Old French *des-* down + *guise* guise>
in disguise, disguised as someone or something else.

a bat	e bed	i bid	o pot	u cup	th **thin**
ā cake	ē me	ī bite	ō go	ū rude	TH **then**
å bar	ə about	ər over	ȯ for	u̇ put	zh measure

dis·gust (dis gust′) *n* **1** the sense that something is ugly or horrible: *The smell filled me with disgust. We expressed our disgust at the media's graphic coverage of the accident.* **2** the state of being annoyed and angry; the feeling that one cannot put up with any more: *His excuses were so silly that she finally turned away in disgust.*
v cause to feel disgust: *His rudeness disgusted me.* <Latin *dis-* reversing + Latin *gustus* taste> **dis·gust′ed** *adj.* **dis·gust′ing** *adj.*

dish (dish) *n* **1** a fairly shallow, flat-bottomed container for holding or serving food; a shallow bowl: *The jelly beans were in a dish on the table.* **2 dishes** *pl* tableware: *Whose turn is it to wash the dishes after supper?* **3** a particular kind of food: *My favourite dish is lasagna.* **4** a satellite dish or dish antenna.
v put food in a dish or dishes for serving. <Latin *discus* disc> **dish′ful′** *n.*
dish out, *Informal* give, especially freely: *to dish out punishment, to dish out insults.*
dish up, a serve food in dishes: *to dish up a delicious meal. Seat the guests; I'm ready to dish up now.* **b** present neatly or in a pleasing way: *to dish up a good argument.*

dish antenna *n* a radio or TV antenna with a reflector shaped like a dish.

dish·cloth (dish′kloth′) *n* a small cloth for washing dishes.

dis·heart·en (dis hȧr′tən) *v* take away the confidence or optimism of. **dis·heart′ened** *adj.* **dis·heart′en·ing** *adj.*

di·shev·elled or **di·shev·eled** (di shev′əld) *adj* rumpled or untidy: *They could tell by her dishevelled appearance that she had just got up.* <Old French *des-* away + *chevel* hair> **di·shev′el·ment** *n.*

dis·hon·est (di son′ist) *adj* **1** lacking honesty or integrity: *dishonest merchants, dishonest business practice.* **2** designed to give a false impression or result: *dishonest weigh scales.* **dis·hon′es·ty** *n.*

dis·hon·our or **dis·hon·or** (di son′ər) *n* **1** a loss of honour or good reputation. **2** the cause of this: *That violent player is a dishonour to the sport of hockey.*
v **1** cause or bring dishonour to: *You have dishonored the family by your reckless behaviour.* **2** refuse to accept as valid: *to dishonour a movie pass.*

dis·hon·our·a·ble or **dis·hon·or·a·ble** (di son′ə rə bəl) *adj* causing or deserving dishonour: *dishonourable conduct, dishonourable people.* **dis·hon′our·a·ble·ness** *n.* **dis·hon′our·a·bly** *adv.*

dish·pan (dish′pan′) *n* a large pan or basin in which to wash dishes.

dish·rag (dish′rag′) *n* **1** a dishcloth. **2** *Informal* a person with no energy or vitality.

dish·tow·el (dish′tou′əl) *n* a cloth for drying dishes.

dish·wash·er (dish′wosh′ər) *n* **1** a machine for washing, rinsing, and drying dishes in one continuous operation. **2** a person whose job is washing dishes, as in a restaurant.

dish·wa·ter (dish′wot′ər) *n* water in which dishes are being or have been washed.

dis·il·lu·sion (dis ə lū′zhən) *v* destroy a person's ideals or pleasant illusions by deeply disappointing him or her: *His early experience with politics had disillusioned him and he gave it up.*
n the resulting state of disappointment. **dis′il·lu′sioned** *adj.* **dis′il·lu′sion·ment** *n.*

dis·in·cline (dis′in klīn′) *v* **dis·in·clined, dis·in·clin·ing** make unwilling or reluctant: *The salesperson's pushiness disinclined me to buy from him.* **dis′in·cli·na′tion** *n.*

dis·in·fect (dis′in fekt′) *v* make free of disease-producing germs: *A doctor's instruments are disinfected before use.* **dis′in·fect′ant** *n, adj.*

dis·in·gen·u·ous (dis′in jen′yū əs) *adj* not completely frank or sincere. **dis′in·gen′u·ous·ly** *adv.* **dis′in·gen′u·ous·ness** *n.*

dis·in·her·it (dis′in her′it) *v* exclude from an inheritance: *Her father disinherited her because she quit school.* **dis′in·her′it·ance** *n.*

dis·in·te·grate (di sin′tə grāt′) *v* **dis·in·te·grat·ed, dis·in·te·grat·ing** **1** break up into small pieces. **2** be reduced to nothing or to ruins: *His courage had completely disintegrated.* **3** *Physics* undergo a change in nuclear structure through bombardment by charged particles. **dis·in′te·gra′tion** *n.*

dis·in·ter (dis′in tər′) *v* **dis·in·terred, dis·in·ter·ring** dig up something buried, especially a dead body: *The body had to be disinterred for a forensic examination.* **dis′in·ter′ment** *n.*

dis·in·ter·est (di sin′trist) *n* **1** fairness and impartiality. **2** indifference or lack of interest.

dis·in·ter·est·ed (di sin′tris tid) *adj* **1** impartial and not biased or influenced by one's own interests: *We need a disinterested party to help us resolve this dispute.* Compare UNINTERESTED. **2** not caring or paying attention. **dis·in′ter·est′ed·ly** *adv.*

CONFUSABLES

A **disinterested** person is unbiased and does not try to get an advantage out of a particular situation.

An **uninterested** person doesn't care about, or is indifferent to, a situation.

dis·join (dis join′) *v* separate or detach.

dis·joint·ed (dis join′tid) *adj* broken or disconnected: *disjointed paragraphs.* **dis·joint′ed·ly** *adv.* **dis·joint′ed·ness** *n.*

disjoint set (dis joint′) *Mathematics n* one of two or more sets that have no members in common.

disk (disk) *n* **1** *Computers* a round, thin, flat, usually rewritable plate used for storing data. A **magnetic disk**, such as a floppy disk, is covered with a magnetic coating on which digital information is stored in the form of microscopically small, magnetized needles. An **optical disk** has pits etched in it and is read with a laser that scans the surface. **2** DISC.

disk drive *Computers n* the part of a computer that reads the data on magnetized disks.

disk·ette (di sket′) FLOPPY DISK.

dis·like (dis līk′) *v* **dis·liked, dis·lik·ing** find unpleasant or irritating: *I dislike country music. He dislikes studying.*

n **1** a feeling that something or someone is unpleasant or irritating: *She has a strong dislike for cats.* **2** something that one does not like: *Liver is one of my worst dislikes.*

dis·lo·cate (dis′lə kāt′) *or* (dis′lə kāt′) *v* **dis·lo·cat·ed, dis·lo·cat·ing 1** cause the bones of a joint to be shifted out of place: *He dislocated his shoulder when he fell.* **2** put out of order: *Our plan to hike through Fundy National Park was dislocated by the bad weather.* **dis′lo·ca′tion** *n.*

dis·lodge (dis loj′) *v* **dis·lodged, dis·lodg·ing** force out of a place or position: *We used a crowbar to dislodge the heavy stone. Heavy gunfire dislodged the enemy from the fort.* **dis·lodg′ment** or **dis·lodge′ment** *n.*

dis·loy·al (dis loi′əl) *adj* failing to be loyal to a person or thing. **dis·loy′al·ly** *adv.* **dis·loy′al·ty** *n.*

dis·mal (diz′məl) *adj* depressing, dreary, or miserable: *dismal weather, a dismal failure, a dismal future.* <Old French, from Latin *dies mali* evil days> **dis′mal·ly** *adv.*

dis·man·tle (dis man′təl) *v* **dis·man·tled, dis·man·tling 1** take apart piece by piece: *We had to dismantle the bookcases to move them.* **2** destroy, remove, or discontinue by gradual steps: *The opposition accused the government of dismantling social programs.* <Old French = to remove a cloak, from Latin *des-* off + *manteler* to cloak>

dis·may (di smā′) *n* loss of courage or hope: *Reports that her son had been caught skipping class filled her with dismay.*

v alarm and sadden: *We were all dismayed by the news about his accident.* <Old French>

dis·mem·ber (dis mem′bər) *v* pull apart; cut, tear, or otherwise separate into pieces: *The lynx killed and dismembered the rabbit. The Austro-Hungarian Empire was dismembered after World War I.* **dis·mem′ber·ment** *n.*

dis·miss (di smis′) *v* **1** allow to go: *At noon, the teacher dismissed the class.* **2** remove from a job or office: *I was dismissed from reading the announcements because of constantly being late.* **3** refuse to consider: *She dismissed my objections with a wave of her hand and continued speaking.* <Latin *dimittere* send away> **dis·miss′al** *n.* **dis·miss′ive** *adj.*

dis·mount (dis mount′) *v* **1** get off something one is riding, such as a horse or bicycle. **2** remove something from its setting or support: *The jewel was dismounted so they could repair the ring itself.*

dis·o·be·di·ence (dis′ə bē′dē əns) *n* failure or refusal to obey. **dis′o·be′di·ent** *adj.*

dis·o·bey (dis′ə bā′) *v* fail to follow orders or rules.

dis·or·der (dis ȯr′dər) *n* **1** confusion or chaos: *The room was in such disorder that it was impossible to find anything.* **2** a sickness or disease: *a stomach disorder.* **3** public disturbance.

v destroy the order or arrangement of: *lives disordered by war.* **dis·or′dered** *adj.* **dis·or′der·ly** *adj.*

dis·or·gan·ize (dis ȯr′gə nīz′) *v* **dis·or·gan·ized, dis·or·gan·iz·ing** upset the order and arrangement of: *Heavy snowstorms disorganized the bus schedules.*

dis·or·gan·ized (dis ȯr′gə nīzd′) *adj* lacking an orderly arrangement or system: *If you weren't so disorganized you could get your homework done on time.*

dis·o·ri·ent (dis ȯr′ē ent′) *v* cause to lose one's sense of direction or time, or one's sense of identity: *Waking up in a strange place disorients me.* **dis′or·i·en·ta′tion** *n.* **dis·or′i·ent·ed** *adj.* **dis·or′i·ent·ing** *adj.*

dis·own (dis ōn′) *v* refuse to recognize as one's own: *to disown your family. The mayor has disowned her earlier statements on the subject.*

dis·par·age (di sper′ij) *v* **dis·par·aged, dis·par·ag·ing** express lack of respect or appreciation for: *Don't disparage her work; it is of quite acceptable quality.* <Old French, from Latin *dis-* not + *par* equal> **dis·par′age·ment** *n.*

dis·pa·rate (dis′pə rit) *adj* essentially unlike and diverse: *The peace movement has brought together very disparate groups of people.* <Latin *dis-* apart + *parare* prepare>

dis·par·i·ty (di sper′ə tē) *n, pl* **dis·par·i·ties** inequality or difference: *a disparity of income. There were some disparities in the two accounts of the event.*

dis·pas·sion·ate (dis pash′ə nit) *adj* free from emotion or prejudice: *a dispassionate defence of school policy.* **dis·pas′sion·ate·ly** *adv.*

dis·patch (di spach′) *for v,* (dis′pach) *for n. v* **1** send off: *to dispatch a messenger, to dispatch a taxi to pick up a customer.* **2** kill: *He dispatched the deer with his first shot.* **3** get something done promptly or speedily: *As soon as we had dispatched our morning chores we went to the fair.* **4** eat up, especially quickly: *She dispatched three pieces of pie at one sitting.*

n **1** a written message such as a news report or report to a government by an official: *This dispatch has been two days on the way.* **2** the act or fact of dispatching: *Please speed the dispatch of this package.* **3** promptness and speed: *She works with neatness and dispatch.* <Spanish *despachar*>

mention in dispatches, *Military* **a** commend for bravery, distinguished service, etc. in the official report of an action. **b** the fact of being commended in this way: *He received three mentions in dispatches.*

dis·patch·er (di spach′ər) *n* a person who dispatches, especially one whose work is to dispatch taxis, couriers, or ambulances.

dis·pel (di spel′) *v* **dis·pelled, dis·pel·ling** drive away and scatter: *to dispel a person's doubts and fears.* <Latin *dis-* away + *pellere* to drive>

dis·pen·sa·ble (di spen′sə bəl) *adj* easy to replace or do without: *He treats his employees as if they were dispensable.*

dis·pen·sa·ry (di spen′sə rē) *n, pl* **dis·pen·sa·ries** a place where medicines are stored and given out, especially one that is part of a hospital or clinic.

dis·pen·sa·tion (dis′pən sā′shən) *n* **1** rule or management: *England under the dispensation of Elizabeth I.* **2** *Catholicism* special permission to disregard a law or obligation without penalty. **b** a similar exemption or release.

a bat	e bed	i bid	o pot	u cup	th **thin**
ā cake	ē me	ī bite	ō go	ū rude	ᴛʜ **then**
ä bar	ə about	ər over	ȯ for	u̇ put	zh measure

dis·pense (di spens′) *v* **dis·pensed, dis·pens·ing** 1 distribute, especially in measured amounts: *The aid workers dispensed food and clothing to the refugees. This machine dispenses paper cups one at a time.* 2 put in force or apply: *The courts dispense justice.* 3 prepare and give out: *Pharmacists dispense medicines.* <Old French, from Latin *dis-* out + *pendere* weigh>
dispense with, a get rid of, or make unnecessary: *The new evaluation system dispenses with oral exams.* **b** get along without: *He found he could dispense with rich food when he began to eat properly.*

dis·pen·ser (di spen′sər) *n* 1 a machine or container that releases its contents one at a time or in measured amounts: *a soap dispenser.* 2 a person who gives out or distributes something.

dis·perse (di spərs′) *v* **dis·persed, dis·pers·ing** 1 send or go in different directions: *The police dispersed the rioters. The crowd dispersed when the game was over.* 2 *Physics* separate white light into its coloured rays. <Latin *dis-* apart + *spargere* scatter> **dis·per′sal** *n.*

dis·per·sion (di spər′zhən) *n* 1 *Physics* the separation of white light into its coloured rays. 2 **Dispersion** DIASPORA (def. 1).

dis·pir·it (di spē′rit) *v* depress or discourage. **dis·pir′it·ed** *adj.* **dis·pir′it·ed·ly** *adv.*

dis·place (dis plās′) *v* **dis·placed, dis·plac·ing** 1 take over the place or position of: *The car has displaced the horse and buggy. The chief of police was displaced by a younger man.* 2 *Physics* move as a solid object a certain volume or mass of fluid out of place: *The water displaced by the stones we dropped in made the beaker overflow.* 3 *Psychology* transfer the focus of a negative emotion to some other person or thing: *displaced anger.*
dis·place′ment *n.*

displaced person *n* a person forced out of his or her home by war, natural disasters, or political unrest.

dis·play (di splā′) *v* 1 put out in clear view, especially in an attractive or interesting way: *to display paintings in a gallery, to display merchandise in a store window.* 2 show or demonstrate: *She displayed great tact in handling that situation.* 3 *Computers* present electronic data in visual form, as on the screen of a computer.
n 1 an arrangement of things put out for viewing: *On the table was a display of imported handcrafts.* 2 an act that demonstrates, or is intended to demonstrate, some quality: *a shocking display of bad temper.* 3 the act of showing off or purposely attracting attention to oneself: *Her fondness for display led her to buy the showiest clothes.* 4 **a** *Computers* a device, such as a screen, for presenting electronic data in visual form. **b** the data so presented. 5 *Zoology* especially among certain birds, a dancelike set of movements performed by the males just before breeding. <Old French, from Latin *dis-* out + *plicare* fold>
on display, being displayed: *Our paintings are on display at the back of the classroom.*

dis·please (dis plēz′) *v* **dis·pleased, dis·pleas·ing** offend, annoy, or be unacceptable to: *I was displeased by their lack of respect. The new playground rules displeased my little sister.* **dis·pleas′ure** (dis plezh′ər) *n.*

dis·port (di spȯrt′) *v* (*used with the reflexive pronoun*) play or amuse oneself: *We laughed at the otters disporting themselves in the water.* <Old French *des-* away + *porter* carry>

dis·pos·able (di spō′zə bəl) *adj* 1 meant to be thrown out after use: *disposable plates.* 2 available for use: *a family's disposable income.*

dis·pos·al (di spō′zəl) *n* 1 the act, process, or manner of disposing of something: *The city looks after the disposal of garbage.* 2 a grinder, compactor, chute, or other unit for disposing of garbage. 3 the act of assigning things to certain places: *the disposal of furniture in a room, the disposal of scarce resources.*
at someone's disposal, available for someone's use or service at any time: *My computer is at your disposal while you are here.*

dis·pose (di spōz′) *v* **dis·posed, dis·pos·ing** 1 arrange in or assign to certain places: *The battleships were disposed in a straight line.* 2 make ready or willing: *His friendly manner disposed her to look kindly on his suggestions.* 3 make liable or subject: *A weak immune system disposes you to catching cold.* <Old French, from Latin *dis-* apart + *ponere* to place>
dispose of, a get rid of, as by throwing out, selling, or giving away: *Where can I dispose of these empty paint cans?* **b** eat or drink up: *Among us we disposed of a whole watermelon.* **c** arrange or settle: *The club disposed of its business in an hour.*

dis·posed (di spōzd′) *adj* with a particular attitude or inclination: *How were they disposed toward the plan? Did they approve? She is disposed to get upset at the least thing.*

dis·po·si·tion (dis′pə zish′ən) *n* 1 one's usual way of behaving or thinking: *She has a cheerful disposition.* 2 a tendency or inclination: *a disposition to take offence.* 3 the act, process, or manner of arranging or distributing: *the disposition of troops in battle.*

dis·pos·sess (dis′pə zes′) *v* 1 force to give up possession of something: *Families dispossessed by war are living in refugee camps. The farmer was dispossessed for not paying her rent.* 2 deprive: *Fear had dispossessed him of his senses.*
dis′pos·ses′sion *n.*

dis·proof (dis prūf′) *n* 1 the act of disproving. 2 a particular fact or argument that disproves something.

dis·pro·por·tion (dis′prə pȯr′shən) *n* lack of balance or symmetry. **dis′pro·por′tion·ate** *adj.*
dis′pro·por′tion·ate·ly *adv.*

dis·prove (dis prūv′) *v* **dis·proved, dis·prov·ing** prove something to be false: *The evidence disproves your claim.*
dis·prov′a·ble *adj.*

dis·pu·ta·tion (dis′pyə tā′shən) *n* 1 the act, process, or manner of disputing: *After years of bitter disputation, the will was finally settled.* 2 a dispute or controversy.
dis′pu·ta′tious *adj.*

dis·pute (di spyūt′) *n* a debate or quarrel.
v **dis·put·ed, dis·put·ing** 1 debate or quarrel: *disputing about who had to mow the lawn.* 2 disagree with: *The insurance company disputed the family's claim.* 3 fight for or over: *The soldiers disputed every inch of ground.* <Old French, from Latin *dis-* separately + *putare* to consider>
dis·put′a·ble *adj.* **dis·put′a·bly** *adv.* **dis·put′ant** *n.*

beyond dispute, not to be questioned or argued about. **in dispute,** being argued about: *Ownership of the property is still in dispute.*

dis·qual·i·fy (dis kwol′ə fī′) *v* **dis·qual·i·fied, dis·qual·i·fy·ing 1** make unfit or unable to do something: *His injury disqualified him from playing football.* **2** declare unfit to do something: *She was disqualified from the contest because she was not old enough to participate.* **3** declare illegitimate because some rule or criterion is not met: *That last goal was disqualified by the referee.* **dis·qual′i·fi·ca′tion** *n.*

dis·qui·et (dis kwī′it) *v* make uneasy or anxious: *Rumours of revolution disquieted the king.*
n uneasiness or anxiety. Also, **disquietude**.
dis·qui′et·ing *adj.*

dis·re·gard (dis′ri gärd′) *v* pay no attention to: *Disregard that last e-mail I sent you.*
n **1** lack of attention: *His disregard for the critics gave him more freedom in writing.* **2** lack of proper respect: *You can't treat people's property with such blatant disregard.*

dis·re·pair (dis′ri per′) *n* bad condition or a state of needing repairs: *The house was in disrepair.*

dis·rep·u·ta·ble (dis rep′yə tə bəl) *adj* **1** with a bad reputation: *a disreputable part of town.* **2** giving one a bad reputation: *He was suspended for disreputable conduct.* **dis·rep′u·ta·bly** *adv.*

dis·re·pute (dis′ri pyūt′) *n* the condition of being no longer respected: *This theory has fallen into disrepute.*

dis·re·spect (dis′ ri spekt′) *n* lack of respect: *Don't answer in that tone of disrespect.* **dis′re·spect′ful** *adj.* **dis′re·spect′ful·ly** *adv.*

GRAMMAR AND USAGE

Disrespect is a noun that is sometimes used as an informal verb, or shortened to the slang verb *dis*: *He dissed me when he said that my cap looked stupid.*

dis·robe (dis rōb′) *v* **dis·robed, dis·rob·ing** undress.

dis·rupt (dis rupt′) *v* **1** break off: *Telephone service has been disrupted temporarily.* **2** disturb or destroy the order or continuity of: *Your behaviour is disrupting the class.* <Latin *dis-* apart + *rumpere* break> **dis·rup′tion** *n.* **dis·rup′tive** *adj.*

dis·sat·is·fied (dis sat′is fīd′) *adj* not pleased or contented: *If you're dissatisfied with your report, talk to your teacher.* **dis′sat·is·fac′tion** *n.* **dis·sat′is·fy′** *v.*

dis·sect (dī sekt′) *or* (di sekt′) *v* **1** cut up into parts in order to study the structure: *We dissected a frog in biology class.* **2** examine carefully part by part: *The lawyer dissected the testimony to show where the contradictions were.* **dis·sec′tion** *n.* **dis·sec′tor** *n.*

dis·sem·ble (di sem′bəl) *v* **dis·sem·bled, dis·sem·bling 1** pretend: *The bored listener dissembled an interest she did not feel.* **2** disguise or hide one's real feelings or thoughts: *She dissembled her disgust with a smile.* <Old French, from Latin *dissimulare* disguise, conceal> **dis·sem′bler** *n.*

dis·sem·i·nate (di sem′ə nāt′) *v* **dis·sem·i·nat·ed, dis·sem·i·nat·ing** distribute widely: *to disseminate information.* <Latin *dis-* away + *semen* seed> **dis·sem′i·na′tion** *n.* **dis·sem′i·na′tor** *n.*

dis·sen·sion (di sen′shən) *n* disagreement, or hard feelings caused by this: *The unity of the party was threatened by dissension.* <See DISSENT.>

dis·sent (di sent′) *v* **1** express a difference of opinion, especially with a majority or established view: *Two of the judges dissented from the decision of the other three.* **2** refuse to conform to the rules and doctrines of a religious or political institution: *Some clergy have decided they must dissent from official church doctrine.*
n the act or fact of dissenting. <Latin *dis-* separately + *sentire* feel, think> **dis·sent′er** *n.* **dis·sent′ing** *adj.*

D

dis·ser·ta·tion (dis′ər tā′shən) *n* a long, formal discussion of a subject, often a major scholarly work written as part of the requirements for a graduate university degree. <Latin *disserere* to examine>

dis·serv·ice (dis sər′vis) *n* an unfair or harmful act, often one committed unconsciously: *You do yourself a disservice when you cheat, you know. To call this a "garden" does it a disservice; it's a floral masterpiece!*

dis·si·dent (dis′ə dənt) *adj* disagreeing or dissenting: *a dissident opinion.*
n a person who disagrees or dissents: *The dictator jailed all political dissidents.* <Latin *dis-* apart + *sedere* sit> **dis′si·dence** *n.*

dis·sim·i·lar (di sim′ə lər) *adj* different: *They come from very dissimilar backgrounds.* **dis·sim′i·lar·ly** *adv.* **dis·sim′i·lar′i·ty** *n.*

dis·si·pate (dis′ə pāt′) *v* **dis·si·pat·ed, dis·si·pat·ing 1** spread in different directions: *The crowd soon dissipated.* **2** disappear or cause to disappear: *When darkness fell, her courage dissipated.* **3** spend foolishly: *My sister dissipated her savings in one afternoon at the mall.* **4** weaken oneself morally by indulging too much in foolish or harmful pleasures. <Latin *dis-* apart + *supare* to throw> **dis′si·pa′tion** *n.*

dis·so·ci·ate (di sō′shē āt′) *or* (di sō′sē āt′) *v* **dis·so·ci·at·ed, dis·so·ci·at·ing 1** break the connection or association with: *When he discovered his friends were shoplifting, he dissociated himself from them.* **2** *Chemistry* **a** separate the molecules of a compound into atoms. **b** separate the molecules of an electrolyte into ions. <Latin *dis-* apart + *socius* companion> **dis·so′ci·a′tion** *n.*

dis·sol·u·ble (di sol′yə bəl) *adj* capable of being dissolved: *The partnership is dissoluble with the consent of both parties.* **dis·sol′u·bil′i·ty** *n.*

dis·so·lute (dis′ə lūt′) *adj* living an immoral life. <Latin *dissolvere* loosen up> **dis′so·lute·ly** *adv.* **dis′so·lute·ness** *n.*

dis·so·lu·tion (dis′ə lū′shən) *n* **1** the act or fact of dissolving: *the dissolution of a partnership.* **2** ruin, destruction, or death.

a bat	e bed	i bid	o pot	u cup	th **thin**
ā cake	ē me	ī bite	ō go	ū rude	ᴛʜ **then**
ä bar	ə about	ər over	ȯ for	ů put	zh measure

dis·solve (di zolv′) *v* **dis·solved, dis·solv·ing 1** mix completely with liquid so as to form a solution: *Salt or sugar will dissolve in water. Dissolve one bouillon cube in a cup of water.* **2** end a joint activity such as a relationship or meeting: *to dissolve a partnership. Parliament is dissolved before an election.* **3** fade away: *The dream dissolved when she woke up.* **4** in films, TV, or videos, fade gradually into the next image or scene. <Latin *dis-* apart + *solvere* loosen>
dissolve in tears, give way to intense weeping.

dis·so·nance (dis′ə nəns) *n* **1** *Music* a combination of tones that are not in harmony, often for effect and often resolved in a following chord. **2** a clashing or conflict of views or opinions. <Old French, from Latin *dis-* differently + *sonare* sound> **dis′so·nant** *adj.*

dis·suade (di swād′) *v* **dis·suad·ed, dis·suad·ing** (*used with* ***from***) persuade not to do something: *They dissuaded us from heading out in the snowstorm.* <Latin *dis-* against + *suadere* to urge> **dis·sua′sion** (di swā′zhən) *n.* **dis·sua′sive** (di swā′siv) *adj.*

dis·tance (dis′təns) *n* **1** the space between things: *The distance from here to town is five kilometres.* **2** a long way: *The farm is quite a distance from the highway.* **3** a point that is far away in space or time: *From a distance it looks like a blob. It was last year; at this distance it's hard to remember details.* **4** lack of friendliness, warmth, or intimacy: *When we met again after that incident, there was a certain distance between us.* **5** emotional detachment or objectivity: *We need someone with enough distance from the event to be more rational about it.*
v **dis·tanced, dis·tanc·ing 1** keep unconnected or separate: *The government has tried to distance itself from the scandal surrounding the minister.* **2** keep oneself from being friendly or intimate with someone: *She has distanced herself from me since that argument.* **3** leave far behind: *The black horse distanced all the others.*
go the distance, a *Sports* go through an entire game or match without being taken out of play or knocked out. **b** endure anything to the end.
in the distance, far away: *Can you see hills in the distance?*
keep at a distance, refuse to be friendly with.
keep your distance, a remain some distance away: *The dog might be dangerous, so keep your distance.* **b** be not too friendly or intimate: *He prefers to keep his distance with me.*
put some distance between, a separate in space or time. **b** lessen involvement between: *I'd like to put some distance between me and that organization.*

distance learning *n* education for students working at home with no instructor present. Learning material is provided by mail, e-mail, television, and the Internet. Also called **distance education**.

dis·tant (dis′tənt) *adj* **1** far away in space: *distant lands. Areas that are distant from large cities have poorer access to services.* **2** away: *a town six kilometres distant.* **3** far apart in time, relationship, or likeness: *distant memories. A second cousin is a distant relative.* **4** cool in manner: *a distant nod.* Old French, from Latin *dis-* apart + *stare* stand> **dis′tant·ly** *adv.*

dis·taste (dis tāst′) *n* the fact of not enjoying, or not being attracted to, something: *His distaste for work makes him hard to motivate.* **dis·taste′ful** *adj.* **dis·taste′ful·ly** *adv.*

dis·tem·per (dis tem′pər) *n* **1** an infectious viral disease of animals, causing a short, dry cough and general weakness. **2** disease or disorder of the mind, body, or society: *Greed is the distemper of our times.* <Old French, from Latin *dis-* not + *temperare* mix in proper proportion>

dis·tend (di stend′) *v* swell out: *Her cheeks distended with each blast on the bugle. A distended stomach is a sign of malnutrition or worms.* <Latin *dis-* apart + *tendere* stretch> **dis·ten′sion** or **dis·ten′tion** *n.*

dis·til or **dis·till** (di stil′) *v* **dis·tilled, dis·til·ling 1** heat a liquid or other substance so that it evaporates, and then condense the vapour, usually as a means of separating a solution. **2** obtain by distilling: *Gasoline is distilled from crude oil.* **3** purify, intensify, or obtain the essence of: *to distil the truth from the testimony of several witnesses.* **4** give off or let fall in drops: *Flowers distil nectar.* <Latin *de-* down + *stilla* a drop> **dis′til·la′tion** *n.*

dis·til·late (dis′tə lit) *n* a distilled liquid.

dis·till·er (di stil′ər) *n* a person who or thing that distils, especially a person or company that makes whisky, rum, brandy, and other hard liquors. **dis·till′er·y** *n.*

dis·tinct (di stingkt′) *adj* **1** separate and different: *These are two distinct issues. Mice are distinct from rats.* **2** clear and unmistakable: *distinct outlines, a distinct lisp, a distinct advantage.* <Latin *dis-* apart + *stinguere* put out> **dis·tinct′ly** *adv.* **dis·tinct′ness** *n.*

dis·tinc·tion (di stingk′shən) *n* **1** the fact or quality of being different: *There is little distinction between a small motorcycle and a large scooter.* **2** a feature that makes something different: *There are only minor distinctions between the standard and deluxe models.* **3** the act of treating or regarding as different: *She rewarded all the students equally, without distinction.* **4** honour or excellence above that of others: *The badge is given as a mark of distinction. His writing has true distinction.*

dis·tinc·tive (di stingk′tiv) *adj* clearly distinguishing one from others: *RCMP officers wear a distinctive uniform.* **dis·tinct′ive·ly** *adv.* **dis·tinct′ive·ness** *n.*

🍁 **distinct society** *n* in constitutional discussions, a status proposed for Québec based on its unique cultural identity, giving it certain powers of self-government not available to other provinces.

dis·tin·guish (di sting′gwish) *v* **1** tell apart or notice the difference: *He cannot distinguish red from orange. I find it hard to distinguish between her voice and her sister's.* **2** see or hear clearly: *It was too dark to distinguish the outline of the house.* **3** make different: *The ability to talk distinguishes humans from animals.* **4** win fame or honour for: *She distinguished herself by winning all three competitions.* <Latin *dis-* apart + *stinguere* put out>
dis·tin′guish·a·ble *adj.* **dis·tin′guish·a·bly** *adv.*

dis·tin·guished (di sting′gwisht) *adj* **1** showing excellence, honour, or greatness: *a distinguished artist, a medal for distinguished conduct.* **2** giving an impression of greatness or dignity; impressive or unusual in an attractive way: *a distinguished profile. He was tall and distinguished.*

dis·tort (di stôrt′) *v* **1** pull or twist out of shape, especially in an unattractive way: *a face distorted by rage.* **2** twist the intent or meaning of; change from the truth: *a distorted account of events. To call that painting "art" is to distort the* *meaning of the word.* <Latin *dis-* apart + *torquere* to twist> **dis·tor′tion** *n.*

dis·tract (di strakt′) *v* **1** draw away the attention of someone: *I distracted my kid sister while the doctor gave the injection. Playing in the band distracted him from his schoolwork.* **2** confuse by drawing the attention in too many directions: *Too many people talking at once distracts me.* **3** (*used only after the verb **be***) make frantic or crazed: *She was distracted with grief.* <Latin *dis-* apart + *trahere* draw> **dis·tract′ed** *adj.* **dis·tract′ing** *adj.* **dis·trac′tion** *adj.*

dis·traught (di strot′) *adj* in a state of great anxiety, mental or emotional anguish, or confusion: *The distraught mother could neither eat nor sleep till her child was found.* <Latin *distrahere* pull in different directions>

dis·tress (di stres′) *n* **1** great mental or physical pain: *I tried to comfort him in his distress.* **2** a dangerous or desperate situation: *a call from a ship in distress.* **3** misfortune or trouble: *economic distress.*
v cause distress to: *It distresses me to hear that you are switching to another school.* <Old French, from Latin *distringere* pull apart> **dis·tres′sing** *adj.*

dis·tressed (di strest′) *adj* **1** feeling distress. **2** slightly damaged: *distressed furniture, distressed produce.* **3** characterized by a low standard of living: *a distressed area of town.*

dis·trib·ute (di strib′yūt) *v* **dis·trib·ut·ed, dis·trib·ut·ing** **1** give out: *The teacher distributed textbooks to the class.* **2** put in different places: *Distribute the paint evenly over the wall. The students' artwork is distributed throughout the school.* **3** supply to the public or to consumers: *This firm distributes books produced by several different publishers.* **4** divide up and assign to categories: *The class was distributed into three groups for the tour.* <Latin *dis-* separately + *tribuere* assign> **dis′tri·bu′tion** *n.*

dis·trib·u·tive (di strib′yū tiv) *adj* **1** *Mathematics* to do with a property by which an operation has the same result when applied to a set of quantities as it has when applied to individual members of the set. **2** to do with distribution.

dis·trib·u·tor (di strib′yə tər) *n* **1** a company that markets or supplies goods to consumers. **2** the part of a gasoline engine that distributes electric current to the spark plugs. **3** a person who or thing that distributes.

dis·trict (dis′trikt) *n* **1** an area of a country, town, or city with a certain character or feature: *a mining district in northern Québec, a fashionable district of Vancouver.* **2** an area marked off as an administrative unit for some purpose: *a school district. Sault Ste. Marie is in Algoma district in northern Ontario.* <French, from Latin *distringere* stretch apart>

dis·trust (dis trust′) *n* a lack of trust or confidence: *She could not overcome her distrust of the stranger.*
v be suspicious of. **dis·trust′ful** *adj.* **dis·trust′ful·ly** *adv.*

dis·turb (di stərb′) *v* **1** destroy the quiet or rest of: *The noise of my brother's music disturbed us so much that we couldn't study.* **2** break in on or interrupt: *Don't disturb him; he's in a meeting.* **3** make uneasy or worry: *My mom was disturbed by the comments on my report card.* **4** put out of order: *Someone has disturbed my papers.* **5** cause to be emotionally or mentally unbalanced. <Old French, from Latin *dis-* utterly + *turba* tumult> **dis·turb′ance** *n.* **dis·turbed′** *adj.*

di·sul·phide or **di·sul·fide** (dī sul′fīd) *n* a compound consisting of two atoms of sulphur combined with another element or radical.

dis·u·ni·ty (dis yū′nə tē) *n* lack of unity; conflict.

dis·use (dis yūs′) *n* lack of use: *a word that has fallen into disuse. Her German was rusty from long disuse.*
dis·used′ (dis yūzd′) *adj.*

ditch (dich) *n* a narrow trench dug in the earth, usually to carry off water, and often along the side of a road.
v **1** *Informal* abandon or get rid of: *She ditched her boyfriend. I'm going to ditch these jeans and get a new pair.* **2** drive a vehicle into a ditch: *He ditched his car in the snowstorm.* <Old English *dic*>

dith·er (diᴛʜ′ər) *Informal n* a state of nervous excitement or indecision: *We were all in a dither, waiting for the contest results.*
v **1** be nervously indecisive: *Stop dithering and make a choice!* **2** *Computers* improve a screen image by getting rid of the jagged appearance of computer-generated curved lines. <origin uncertain>

dit·to (dit′ō) *n* **1** usually, **ditto mark** a pair of quotation marks ["] used in lists or tables to stand for the same as whatever is written above. **2** especially in former times, an inked stencil used for making copies on a duplicating machine.
v copy or repeat: *She simply dittoed what I had said.*
adv as was just said or written before: *"I like the chocolate ones best." "Ditto for me."* <Italian, from Latin *dicere* say>

dit·ty (dit′ē) *n, pl* **dit·ties** a short, simple song or poem. <Old French, from Latin *dictare* speak>

di·u·ret·ic (dī′ə ret′ik) *adj* causing the body to produce more urine.
n any drug or other substance that does this. <Old French, from Greek *dia-* through + *ouron* urine>

di·ur·nal (dī ər′nəl) *adj* **1** occurring every day: *the diurnal course of the sun.* **2** of or belonging to the daytime, such as of animals and flowers that are active or open during the day and not at night. **3** lasting a day. **di·ur′nal·ly** *adv.*

di·va (dē′və) *n* a famous female singer. <Italian, from Latin *diva* goddess>

di·va·lent (dī vā′lənt) *Chemistry adj* with a valence of two.

Di·va·li (dē vȧ′lē) DIWALI.

di·van (di van′) *n* a long, low, soft couch or sofa, often armless or even backless.

ETYMOLOGY

Divan comes from Persian *devan*, first meaning "a collection of documents," then "court" or "council," then "the room in which the court is held," and finally "a piece of furniture" from such a room.

a bat	e bed	i bid	o pot	u cup	th **thin**
ā cake	ē me	ī bite	ō go	ū rude	ᴛʜ **then**
ȧ bar	ə about	ər over	ȯ for	ů put	zh measure

D

diving
In the **head-first dive**, the arms are swung forward over the head and the hands are brought together so that they break the water before the body. The legs, body, and outstretched arms should be in perfect vertical alignment on entry into the water.
In the **feet-first dive**, in the straight position, the body must be perfectly extended.
In competitive diving, takeoff is usually from a springboard or platform.
In a **synchronized dive**, two divers dive at the same time, each using a separate board. This style of dive was added as a medal sport for the 2000 Olympic games held in Sydney, Australia. The judging of this event gives marks for each diver's execution as well as for the synchronization of the pair of divers.

dive (dīv) *v* **dived** or **dove, dived, div·ing** 1 jump downward headfirst, especially into water. 2 go down sharply and swiftly: *The aircraft began diving suddenly. My grades have dived in the last six months.* 3 go under water, especially as a submarine or water bird. 4 plunge the hand suddenly into something: *He dived into his pocket and pulled out a loonie.* 5 go down or out of sight suddenly: *She dived into a back alley.*
n 1 the act of diving: *He did a perfect head-first dive into the pool, a dive in popularity.* 2 *Informal* a cheap, disreputable, or poorly maintained place: *She lives in a dive at the other end of town. That coffee shop is a dive.* <Old English *dyfan* immerse>
dive into, apply oneself fully to a task or other activity.
take a dive, 1 fall suddenly, especially in price or value. 2 in sports like boxing, fall down deliberately, or pretend to be knocked out.

GRAMMAR AND USAGE

Dived and **dove** are both used for the past tense.

Dived seems to be preferred in written and formal English, but **dove** is very common in spoken and informal English.

dive bomber *n* a bomber that dives toward the target and then drops the bomb before pulling out of the dive. **dive′-bomb′** *v.*

div·er (dī′vər) *n* 1 **a** person who or thing that dives. 2 a person whose hobby or job is to explore or work under water. 3 a water bird that frequently dives under the water, such as the loon.

di·verge (dī vərj′) *v* **di·verged, di·verg·ing** 1 move or extend in different directions from one point: *Their paths diverged at the fork in the road.* 2 differ or vary: *Our opinions diverge on this issue.* 3 turn away from a set course: *We took a direct route, diverging from it only once to look in a shoe store.* <Latin *dis-* apart + *vergere* slope> **di·ver′gence** *n.* **di·ver′gent** *adj.*

di·verse (dī vərs′) *adj* 1 made up of unlike parts: *a diverse group of people.* 2 different from one another: *The six of us have quite diverse views.* 3 various: *a person of diverse interests, lectures on diverse topics.* <Old French, from Latin *diversus* diverse> **di·verse′ly** *adv.*

di·ver·si·fy (di vər′sə fī′) *v* **di·ver·si·fied, di·ver·si·fy·ing** 1 give variety to: *You need to diversify your interests.* 2 expand business activity into different areas: *The publishing company has recently diversified and now also produces software.* **di·ver′si·fi·ca′tion** *n.*

di·ver·sion (di vər′zhən) *or* (dī vər′zhən) *n* 1 an act of diverting or turning aside: *Closing the museum will cause a diversion of tourists to other attractions in the city.* 2 an activity intended to draw attention away from something else: *You create a diversion while I go stick this surprise gift on his chair.* 3 an amusement or pastime. 4 an alternative route for use by traffic. <Latin *dis-* aside + *vertere* turn> **di·ver′sion·ar′y** *adj.*

di·ver·si·ty (di vər′sə tē) *n* variety: *The cultural diversity in Canada is exciting. There's a diversity of opinion on the latest referendum.*

di·vert (di vərt′) *or* (dī vərt′) *v* **1** turn aside: *to divert someone's attention, to divert water from a stream into a field.* **2** amuse or entertain: *The woman next to me used toys to divert the baby on the long flight.* <French, from Latin *dis-* aside + *vertere* turn> **di·vert′ing** *adj.*

di·vest (dī vest′) *v* **1** deprive or strip of: *Under the dictator's rule, citizens were divested of their voting rights.* **2** (*with reflexive pronoun*) get rid of: *I shall divest myself of all the trappings of modern society and lead a simpler life.* <Old French, from Latin *dis-* off + *vestire* clothe> **di·vest′i·ture** *n.* **di·vest′ment** *n.*

di·vide (di vīd′) *v* **di·vid·ed, di·vid·ing** **1** separate into parts: *Here the river divides into two streams. This partition divides the room into two work areas.* **2** *Mathematics* break into equal amounts: *Divide 8 by 2 and you get 4. Symbol* ÷ **3** mark off into units: *a ruler divided into centimetres.* **4** give some to each: *The four children divided the candy among themselves.* **5** disagree or cause to disagree: *The school divided on the choice of a motto. Envy divided us.*
n **1** a ridge of land separating the regions drained by two different river systems. **2** a point or line that separates one space, group of people, or period in history from another. <Latin *dividere* force apart> **di·vid′er** *n.*

divided highway *n* a road, especially an expressway, with a median strip or boulevard between lanes of traffic going in opposite directions.

div·i·dend (div′ə dend′) *n* **1 a** a sum of money, especially profit from a business or an investment, to be shared by participants or shareholders: *The company has announced a shareholder dividend.* **b** a share of this money. **2** a benefit or advantage gained from something: *Travel brings important dividends.* **3** *Mathematics* a number or quantity to be divided by another. In 8 ÷ 2, the dividend is 8. Compare DIVISOR. <Old French, from Latin *dividere* force apart>

di·vine (di vīn′) *adj* **1** to do with God or a god: *divine wisdom, divine revelation, divine service.* **2** *Informal* delightful or excellent: *These brownies are simply divine!*
n a theologian, minister, or priest.
v **di·vined, di·vin·ing** **1** find out by intuition or by guessing: *She divined their plan and immediately set out to stop them.* **2** find out by supernatural means: *Fortunetellers claim to divine the future.* **3** locate water or minerals underground using a divining rod. **div′i·na′tion** (di′vin ā′shən) *n.* **di·vine′ly** *adv.* **di·vin′er** *n.*

diving bell *n* a large, hollow, bell-shaped container supplied with air, in which a person can work under water.

diving board *n* a horizontal board for diving from, mounted over a swimming pool.

diving suit *n* a waterproof suit for working under water, with a helmet into which air is pumped from a tank through a tube.

divining rod *n* a forked stick, usually of willow or hazel, that is used to locate water or metal underground.

di·vin·i·ty (di vin′ə tē) *n, pl* **di·vin·i·ties** **1** a divine being. **2** divine nature or quality. **3** theology.

di·vi·si (di vē′zē) *Music pln* divided parts, as opposed to unison. <Italian = divided>

di·vis·i·ble (di viz′ə bəl) *adj* **1** capable of being divided: *The atom is divisible.* **2** *Mathematics* capable of being divided evenly without leaving a remainder: *Any even number is divisible by 2.* **di·vis′i·bil′i·ty** *n.*

D

di·vi·sion (di vizh′ən) *n* **1** the act or process of dividing, or the fact of being divided. **2** a part; a section: *the sales division of a company.* **3** a military unit in various armed forces. **4** disunity or conflict: *The new political party is already threatened by division.* **5** *Biology* a category in the classification of plants, corresponding to the PHYLUM for animals. A division is more specific than a KINGDOM and more general than a CLASS.

division of labour *n* **1** a condition in society under which work is divided among various specialized trades and professions. **2** a system in which different tasks are systematically assigned to different people, such as on an assembly line.

di·vi·sive (di vī′siv) *or* (di viz′iv) *adj* tending to cause disunity: *a divisive issue.*

di·vi·sor (di vī′zər) *Mathematics n* a number or quantity by which another is divided. In 8 ÷ 2, the divisor is 2. Compare DIVIDEND.

di·vorce (di vórs′) *n* **1** the legal ending of a marriage. **2** complete separation: *One cause of global warming is the divorce of business from environmental concerns.*
v **di·vorced, di·vorc·ing** **1** legally end one's marriage: *She divorced her husband a year ago. My aunt and uncle are divorcing.* **2** legally end the marriage of: *The judge refused to divorce them.* **3** separate or detach completely: *Our studies should not be divorced from everyday life.* <Old French, from Latin *divertere* to separate>

di·vor·cee (di vór′sē′) *n* a divorced person.

div·ot (div′ət) *n* a small piece of turf or earth dug up by a golf club in hitting, or trying to hit, the ball. <origin uncertain>

di·vulge (di vulj′) *or* (dī vulj′) *v* **di·vulged, di·vulg·ing** reveal something secret: *The traitor divulged secret plans to the enemy.* <Latin *di-* widely + *vulgus* to spread among people>

div·vy (div′ē) *Informal v* **div·vied, div·vy·ing** divide into shares: *The work will go faster if we divvy it up.* <variant of *dividend*>

Di·wa·li (dē vá′lē) *Hinduism n* a festival celebrated in the fall, dedicated to Lakshmi and also known as the **Festival of Lights**. Also, **Divali**. <Hindi, from Sanskrit *dipa* lamp + *vali* row>

a bat	e bed	i bid	o pot	u cup	th **thin**
ā cake	ē me	ī bite	ō go	ū rude	TH **then**
á bar	ə about	ər over	ó for	ů put	zh measure

Dix·ie (dik′sē) *n* the southern states of the US as a group, especially those that formed the Confederacy during the Civil War. <*Dixie's Land,* song by D. Emmett, 19c songwriter>

DIY do-it-yourself.

diz·zy (diz′ē) *adj* **diz·zi·er, diz·zi·est 1** feeling as if things are whirling or spinning around and that one is about to fall: *The midway rides make me dizzy.* **2** confused or bewildered: *dizzy from the rush of the holiday season.* **3** causing or likely to cause dizziness: *dizzy heights, a dizzy round of social activities.*
v **diz·zied, diz·zy·ing** make dizzy. <Old English *dysig* foolish> **diz′zi·ly** *adv.* **diz′zi·ness** *n.*

DJ disc jockey.

Dji·bou·ti (ji bū′tē) *n* a country in east Africa.

djinn (jin) JINN.

dm decimetre(s).

DNA *n* a long, often double-stranded molecule, made up of acids and containing the genetic codes that determine heredity. <*d*eoxyribo*n*ucleic *a*cid>

DNA fingerprint or **profile** *n* the unique pattern of DNA strands of an individual, used for identification.

DNS *Computers n* in full, **Domain Name System** a system that stores information about domain names on networks such as the Internet. It provides a numeric address for each name.

do[1] (dū) *v, 3rd person singular* **does; did, done 1** carry out or perform: *to do work. Words can't do justice to how I feel. That's easy to do.* **2** complete; produce: *I haven't quite done my assignment. The band recently did a CD in a different style.* **3** act or behave: *You have done wisely.* **4** have as a livelihood or occupation: *What does his mother do?* **5** deal with as is required: *to do the dishes, to do your hair.* **6** get along or manage: *How is she doing these days?* **7** be good enough: *This copy is a bit rough, but it'll do.* **8** *Informal* travel at a specified speed: *That van must be doing about 120 km/h.* **9** *Informal* spend time in prison: *He did six years for that bank robbery.* **10** *Informal* use, especially an illicit drug: *She does cocaine.* **11** *Informal* happen or go on: *What's doing at the SkyDome tonight?* **12** used as an auxiliary verb, **a** in asking questions: *Do you like milk?* **b** in negatives with ***not***: *I did not believe him.* **c** to emphasize the main verb: *We do want to go, but not today.* **d** to stand for a verb already used: *He knows as much as I do.* **e** in inverted constructions after certain adverbs: *Rarely did she laugh.*
n Informal **1** a hairdo. **2** a social function, party, or celebration. **3** (*especially in **do's and don'ts***) something that is expected or prescribed. <Old English *don*> **do′a·ble** *adj.*
do away with, a abolish or get rid of: *We should do away with that stupid rule.* **b** kill or destroy.
do by, act or behave toward: *He did well by his children. I was very well done by, despite the circumstances.*
do for, look after the needs of: *Who did for her while she was sick?*
do in, *Informal* **a** ruin or kill. **b** tire out completely: *That hike did me in.*
do up, a close or fasten a zipper, button, or laces: *He had trouble doing up the top button. Do up your jacket or you'll freeze.* **b** make ready: *to do up a room for guests, to do up a report.* **c** style one's hair so that it is off one's neck or face.
do with, (*after **could** or **can***) enjoy or use: *I could do with a cold drink right now. My bedroom could do with a good cleaning!*
do without, get along or manage without: *I can do without desserts for a while.*
have (or **be**) **to do with,** be related to or involve: *Academic success has little to do with intelligence. The article is to do with recent events in Asia.*
How do you do? (*used in formal introductions*) Pleased to meet you.
it isn't done, it is not proper or in good taste.

SYNONYMS

Do is a neutral word that has a variety of meanings. More specific verbs may be better for the meaning you require.

Achieve suggests getting something done: *She achieved all that she had planned.*

Create suggests using imagination in doing something: *Did he create that sculpture in one day?*

Practise emphasizes doing something again and again in order to do it well: *He had practised his lines so often that he was not nervous before the performance.*

Arrange suggests doing something with care: *She arranged her hair in a different style.*

do[2] (dō) *Music n* **1** the first and last tones of an eight-tone scale, especially as sung to sol-fa syllables: *do, re, mi, fa, sol, la, ti, do.* **2** the tone C. Also, **doh.** <Middle English>

Do·ber·man (dō′bər mən) *n* in full, **Doberman pinscher** a large, slender dog with black and tan markings and a short, smooth coat, often kept as a watchdog. <L. *Doberman,* dog breeder + German *Pinscher* terrier>

do·cile (dō′sīl) *or* (dos′īl) *adj* easily accepting control or instruction. <Latin *docere* teach> **do′cile·ly** *adv.* **do·cil′i·ty** *n.*

dock[1] (dok) *n* **1** a platform built along the shore or out from the shore, at which boats or ships can be loaded or unloaded. **2** the water between two such platforms, allowing ships to enter. **3** dry dock. **4** a place on a space station to accommodate a spacecraft.
v **1** bring or come alongside or into a dock: *The ship docks at 10:30 a.m. The crew docked the ship and began to unload.* **2** join spacecraft together in space. <Dutch *docke*>

dock[2] (dok) *v* **1** cut the end off: *Horses' and dogs' tails are sometimes docked.* **2** deduct part of: *The company docked employees' wages if they arrived late.* <Middle English>

dock[3] (dok) *n* the place where an accused person stands in criminal court. <perhaps Flemish *dok* pen, coop>
in the dock, on trial.

dock·et (dok′it) *n* **1** a list of tasks or matters to be considered by someone, such as a list of the cases to be tried by a court, a list of tests to be done in a lab, or an agenda for a meeting: *What's on the docket for today?*

2 a label indicating the contents of a package or sealed document.
v **1** write on a docket. **2** attach a docket to. <perhaps *dock*[1]>

dock·yard (dok′yärd′) *n* a place with docks, workshops, and warehouses, where ships are built, equipped, and repaired.

doc·tor (dok′tər) *n* **1** a person qualified to treat injuries and physical or mental disorders. **2** a person who has received the highest degree possible in a university: *She is a Doctor of Philosophy.*
v **1** give medical treatment to: *He doctors his children when they have colds or stomach aches.* **2** *Informal* practise medicine: *She spent years doctoring in northern Manitoba.* **3** alter for a dishonest purpose: *to doctor accounts. The whisky had been doctored with water.* <Old French, from Latin *docere* teach>

doc·tor·al (dok′tə rəl) *adj* to do with a **doctorate**, the highest degree given by a university: *She still has to complete her doctoral thesis.*

doc·trine (dok′trən) *n* **1** a specific teaching of a religion, moral system, political ideology, or scientific theory: *One of the doctrines of democracy is that voting is a right.* **2** a whole body of such teachings: *a course in Darwinian doctrine.* <Old French, from Latin *docere* teach>
doc·tri·nal (dok trī′nəl) *or* (dok′trə nəl) *adj.*

doc·u·dra·ma (dok′yə dram′ə) *or* (dok′yə drä′mə) *n* a film that is basically factual, but that contains fictional elements for added dramatic interest. <*documentary* + *drama*>

doc·u·ment (dok′yə mənt) *n* **1** an official paper such as a passport, deed of ownership, diploma, or licence. **2** something written or printed that is meant to give authoritative information or evidence. **3** *Computers, Printing* **a** a formatted electronic text file. **b** a printed text generated from an electronic file.
v **1** prove or support by means of documents: *These facts are well documented, so there is no point in disputing them.* **2** provide with official papers. **3** cite the sources for: *Her article on mood disorders is good but not very thoroughly documented.* **4** demonstrate or illustrate in a book, movie, or TV program: *The film documents the changing face of the North.* **5** explain or describe a piece of software or other technology systematically, such as in a manual, or online tutorial. <Old French, from Latin *docere* teach>

doc·u·men·ta·ry (dok′yə men′tə rē) *n, pl* **doc·u·men·ta·ries** a film, radio, or TV program that presents factual information in an entertaining or artistic way.
adj **1** presenting factual information: *a documentary film.* **2** consisting of documents: *documentary evidence.* **doc′u·men′ta·rist** *n.*

doc·u·men·ta·tion (dok′yə mən tā′shən) *n* **1** material that explains the use of a piece of software or other technology: *The program comes with full documentation.* **2** **a** the act or an instance of supplying supporting references. **b** the documents or references so supplied: *Do you have documentation to support your statement?*

dod·der (dod′ər) *v* move or walk unsteadily: *The man doddered around as if he were 100 years old.* <Middle English>

A **pentagon** has 5 sides.
A **hexagon** has 6 sides.
A **septagon** has 7 sides.
An **octagon** has 8 sides.
A **nonagon** has 9 sides.
A **decagon** has 10 sides.
A **hendecagon** has 11 sides.

As the number of sides of a polygon increases, the figure begins to look like a circle.

dodecagon

D

do·dec·a·gon (dō dek′ə gon′) *n* a plane figure with twelve sides. <Greek *dodeka* twelve + *gonia* angle>

do·dec·a·he·dron (dō′dek ə hē′drən) *n* a solid with 12 faces. The faces of a dodecahedron are regular pentagons. <Greek *dodeka* twelve + *hedra* seat, base>

dodge (doj) *v* **dodged, dodg·ing** **1** move quickly to one side: *I dodged into the shadow of the house.* **2** avoid something by moving quickly to one side: *He dodged the ball as it came flying toward him.* **3** avoid something difficult or embarrassing by trickery or clever talk: *She dodged the question by faking a coughing fit and running out of the room.*
n **1** a quick movement to one side. **2** a trick or clever answer used to avoid something. <origin uncertain>
dodg′er *n.*

dodge·ball (doj′bol′) *n* a game in which players form a circle or two opposite lines and try to hit opponents in the centre with a large ball.

dodg·em (doj′əm) *n* a small electrically powered car with rubber bumpers all around it, driven inside an enclosure at a midway or carnival. Drivers try to bump each other's cars as much as possible. <*Dodgem*, a trademark>

do·do (dō′dō) *n* an extinct bird, big and heavy with a large hooked bill and small flightless wings, that lived on islands in the Indian Ocean. <Portuguese *doudo* fool, from the awkward appearance of the bird>
dead as a dodo, *Informal* extinct or obsolete, with no chance of returning.
go the way of the dodo, die out.

doe (dō) *n* the female of a deer, antelope, rabbit, hare, ferret, or kangaroo. <Old English *da*>

do·er (dū′ər) *n* **1** a person who does something: *a doer of great deeds.* **2** a person of action: *She is a dreamer, but her brother is a doer.*

does (duz) *v* third person singular, present tense, of DO[1].

doe·skin (dō′skin′) *n* **1** the skin of a female deer, especially when made into soft leather. **2** a smooth, soft, thick fabric with a slightly fuzzy surface.

does·n't (duz′ənt) *contraction* does not.

doff (dof) *v* take off: *to doff your clothes. He doffed his hat to her in greeting.* <Middle English, contraction of *do off*>

a bat	e bed	i bid	o pot	u cup	th **thin**
ā cake	ē me	ī bite	ō go	ū rude	ᴛʜ **then**
ä bar	ə about	ər over	ȯ for	u̇ put	zh measure

dog (dog) *n* **1 a** a domesticated mammal related to the wolf, kept as a pet or for such uses as guarding people or property, leading the blind, or hunting. **b** a member of the family that includes these animals as well as wolves, coyotes, jackals, and foxes. **c** a male of these animals. The female is called a bitch. **2** an animal that more or less resembles the domesticated dog, such as the prairie dog. **3** *Informal* a hot dog: *a chili dog.* **4** *Informal* **a** an ugly or contemptible person. **b** (*with* ***lucky, handsome,*** *and certain other adjectives*) a person.
v **dogged, dog·ging** hunt or follow like a dog: *The Mounties dogged her footsteps until they caught her.* <Old English *docga*> **dog′gy** *adj.* **dog′like** *adj.*
a dog's age, *Informal* a very long time: *I haven't seen her for a dog's age.*
a dog's life, a miserable life.
dog in the manger, someone who will not let others use something that he or she cannot use anyway.
every dog has his day, everyone gets some luck or attention in his or her life eventually.
go to the dogs, be ruined.
let sleeping dogs lie, avoid stirring up unnecessary trouble.
put on the dog, *Informal* behave or dress in an affected way.
teach an old dog new tricks, get an older person to accept new ideas or ways.

dog·cart (dog′kärt′) *n* **1** a small cart pulled by dogs. **2** a small, open, usually two-wheeled carriage with two seats set back to back.

dog days *pl n* in the northern hemisphere, a period of very hot, humid weather during July and August. <in reference to the rising of Sirius, also called the *Dog Star*>

doge (dōj) *or* (dō′jā) *n* the chief magistrate of Venice or Genoa, in former times. <French, from Latin *ducis* leader>

dog–ear (dog′ēr′) *n* a folded-over corner of a page.
v make such a fold on a page, often with the effect of making the book look shabby. **dog′-eared′** *adj.*

dog–eat–dog (dog′ēt dog′) *adj* marked by ruthless or vicious competition.

dog·fight (dog′fīt′) *n* **1** a fight between dogs. **2** combat between individual fighter planes.

dog·fish (dog′fish′) *n, pl* **dog·fish·es** or (*especially collectively*) **dog·fish** a small shark found in temperate and warm seas.

dog·ged (dog′id) *adj* stubborn or persistent: *dogged determination, dogged attempts.* **dog′ged·ly** *adv.* **dog′ged·ness** *n.*

dog·ger·el (dog′ə rəl) *n* verse that is trivial or trite and has too-obvious rhymes. <Middle English>

dog·gie (dog′ē) *n* a pet name or child's word for a dog, especially a small dog.

doggie bag *n* food left over from a restaurant meal, given to the customer to take home, usually in a bag.

dog·gone (dog′gon′) *Informal adj, adv, interj, v* damn or damned. <probably alteration of *God damn*>

dog·house (dog′hous′) *n* a small house for a dog.
be in the doghouse, *Informal* be in disfavour with somebody: *I'm in the doghouse because I spilled pop all over the rug.*

do·gie (dō′gē) *n* in the western parts of Canada and the US, a motherless calf on the range. <origin uncertain>

dog·leg (dog′leg′) *n* a sharp bend, especially in a road.
v **dog·legged, dog·leg·ging** make a sharp bend: *The road doglegs before it crosses the railway.*

dog·ma (dog′mə) *n* doctrine, especially when asserted strictly, with authority and without compromise. <Latin, from Greek *dokein* think>

dog·mat·ic (dog mat′ik) *adj* **1** asserting beliefs in a forceful, arrogant, or uncompromising way: *dogmatic statements based on mere opinion. You don't need to be so dogmatic about it.* **2** to do with dogma or doctrine. **dog·mat′i·cal·ly** *adv.* **dog′ma·tism′** *n.*

do–good·er (dū′gůd′ər) *Informal n* a well-intentioned person who tries to correct wrongs or help those in need, sometimes considered to be interfering or unrealistic.

dog–pad·dle (dog′pa′dəl) *n* a simple swimming stroke in which the arms pump up and down one at a time, and the legs move as if running.

Dog·rib (dog′rib′) *n, pl* **Dog·rib** or **Dog·ribs 1** a member of a First Nations people who live in the Northwest Territories, one of the Dene peoples. **2** their Athapaskan language.
adj to do with these people or their language.

dogs·bo·dy (dogz′bod′ē) *Slang n, pl* **dogs·bod·ies** a person who does routine or unskilled work. <UK naval slang for a junior officer>

dog·sled (dog′sled′) *n* a sled pulled by dogs, used especially in the Far North.

dog–tired (dog′tīrd′) *adj* exhausted.

dog·tooth violet (dog′tūth′) *n* a plant of the lily family with lilylike flowers and long, pointed, oval leaves.

dog·wood (dog′wůd′) *n* a tree, shrub, or herb with clusters of small flowers and red, dark blue, or white fruit. The **Pacific** (or **western**) **flowering dogwood** is the floral emblem of British Columbia.

doh (dō) DO [2].

doi·ly (doi′lē) *n, pl* **doi·lies** a decorative piece of lace or cloth, or a paper imitation of this, used on a plate, or under a vase or centrepiece. <name of a 17c cloth dealer>

do·ings (dū′ingz) *pln* things that are done: *The monthly newsletter reports all the doings of the club.*

do–it–your·self (dū′ it yər self′) *adj* done by, or designed for, people acting without professional help: *a do-it-yourself plumbing book. This tile floor looks like it was a do-it-yourself job. Abbrev.* **DIY do′-it-your·self′er** *n.*

do·jo (dō′jō) *n* a gymnasium or studio where martial arts are taught. <Japanese *do* pursuit + *jo* a place>

Dol·by (dōl′bē) *Trademark n* an electronic circuit that reduces noise from recorded and other audio signals. <R.M. *Dolby*, its inventor>

dol·ce (dōl′chā) *Music adj, adv* sweet or sweetly. <Italian>

dol·drums (dol′drəmz) *pln* (*used with* ***the***) **1** certain regions of the Atlantic near the equator with very light or constantly shifting winds. Sailing ships caught in the doldrums were often unable to move for days. **2** a feeling of boredom, low spirits, and lack of energy. <perhaps *dull*>

dole (dōl) *n* **1** a portion of money, food, or supplies carefully measured out and given. **2 the dole** *Informal* welfare or, sometimes, employment insurance.
v **doled, dol·ing** give out in carefully measured portions: *She doled out candy to each child.* <Old English *dal* part>

dole·ful (dōl′fəl) *adj* sad or mournful: *a doleful expression on her face.* <Old French, from Latin *dolere* to grieve> **dole′ful·ly** *adv.* **dole′ful·ness** *n.*

doll (dol) *n* **1** a toy in the shape of a human being. **2** *Slang* a very good-looking or likeable person.
v **doll up** *Informal* dress or decorate in a stylish or showy way; make fancy: *They were all dolled up for the party.* <pet form of the name *Dorothy*> **doll′-like′** *adj.*

dol·lar (dol′ər) *n* **1** a unit of money in Canada, the US, and some other countries, divided into 100 cents. **2** a coin or bill worth one dollar: *Have you got four quarters for a dollar?*

ETYMOLOGY

Dollar comes from the Low German word *daler*, from German *thaler*, which is short for *Joachimsthaler*, meaning "a silver coin." The coin had this name because the silver was mined in a valley called the *Joachimsthal*, in Bohemia.

The dollar sign ($) is said to derive from the image on a Spanish coin called a *piece of eight*.

dollar diplomacy *n* the practice by a rich country, especially the US, of using financial aid to win allies or further its own economic interests abroad.

dollar store *n* a store selling a wide variety of small items for about a dollar.

doll·house (dol′hous′) *n* a miniature house used as a toy.

dol·lop (dol′əp) *n* a portion or serving of something soft or liquid: *a dollop of mashed potatoes, another dollop of cream.* <perhaps Scandinavian>

doll·y (dol′ē) *n, pl* **doll·ies 1** a child's word for a doll. **2** a low platform on wheels for moving heavy things. **3** a wheeled structure on which a movie or TV camera can be moved around.
v **dol·lied, dol·ly·ing** move a camera on a dolly: *The cameraman dollied in for the final scene.*

dol·men (dōl′mən) *n* a prehistoric monument made by laying a large, flat stone across several upright ones. <French, perhaps from Breton *tol* table + *men* stone>

dol·o·rous (dol′ə rəs) *adj* full of grief or pain. <Old French, from Latin *dolere* to grieve> **dol′or·ous·ly** *adv.* **dol′or·ous·ness** *n.*

dol·phin (dol′fin) *n* a small toothed whale with a snout shaped like a beak. Dolphins are known for their intelligence and sociability. See BOTTLENOSE for picture. <Old French, from Greek *delphin*>

dolt (dōlt) *n* a stupid person. <perhaps Old English *dol* stupid> **dolt′ish** *adj.*

–dom *suffix* **1** the position, rank, or realm of: *kingdom.* **2** the condition of being a certain thing: *freedom.* <Old English = decree, judgment>

do·main (dō mān′) *n* **1** the territory or land under one ruler, government, leader, or owner: *The chef claims the kitchen as his domain. The just queen brought peace to all her domain.* **2** a field of thought or activity: *the domain of science.* **3** *Computers* a group of addresses on the Internet that share a common suffix, such as for a country or for the type of user. The domain name for Canada ends in *.ca.* For an educational institution, it ends in *.edu.* <French, from Latin *dominus* lord>

domain name *Computers n* the sequence of words, abbreviations, or characters that identifies a computer network connection on the Internet and serves as its address. Compare IP ADDRESS, HOST NAME, URL.

The first **domes** were developed about 6000 years ago. They are a prominent part of many religious buildings—Buddhist temples, Muslim mosques, and Christian cathedrals.

dome (dōm) *n* **1** a large, rounded roof on a circular or many-sided base. **2** a building with such a roof, especially one used for sports. **3** anything that is or appears high and rounded: *the dome of the sky, the dome of a hill.* **4** a clear, bubblelike projection in the roof of a railway car, enhancing the view for passengers. <French, from Latin *domus* house> **domed** *adj.*

a bat	e bed	i bid	o pot	u cup	th thin
ā cake	ē me	ī bite	ō go	ū rude	TH then
à bar	ə about	ər over	ò for	ù put	zh measure

🍁 **dome fastener** *n* a metal or plastic fastener made up of two parts, one with a small, round bump in the centre that snaps into a hole in the centre of the other. Also called **snap**, **snap fastener**.

do·mes·tic (də mes′tik) *adj* **1** to do with the home or with family activities: *domestic quarrels, domestic chores.* **2** fond of home and family life: *Since his marriage, he has become quite domestic.* **3** having lived as animals among humans for generations as pets, farm animals, or work animals. **4** to do with one's own country: *domestic wines.*
n a household servant. <French, from Latin *domus* house> **do·mes′ti·cal·ly** *adv.* **do′mes·tic′i·ty** *n.*

do·mes·ti·cate (də mes′tə kāt′) *v* **do·mes·ti·cat·ed, do·mes·ti·cat·ing** bring animals or plants from a wild to a tame or cultivated state. **do·mes′ti·ca′tion** *n.*

dom·i·cile (dom′ə sīl′) *Formal n* **1** one's permanent residence, as officially registered with a government for legal purposes. **2** a dwelling place. <Old French, from Latin *domus* house> **dom′i·ciled′** *adj.*

dom·i·nant (dom′ə nənt) *adj* **1** controlling, strongest, or most influential: *The dominant force in her life has been her grandmother.* **2** rising high above its surroundings; more prominent than others. **3** *Biology* to do with a gene in one chromosome that dominates over the corresponding gene in a matching chromosome and is therefore expressed as a trait in the organism. Compare RECESSIVE (def. 2). **4** *Ecology* to do with or being the most extensive and characteristic species in a plant or animal community.
n Music the fifth tone in an eight-tone scale. <See DOMINATE.> **dom′i·nance** *n.* **dom′i·nant·ly** *adv.*

dom·i·nate (dom′ə nāt′) *v* **dom·i·nat·ed, dom·i·nat·ing** **1** command or rule by strength, numbers, or power: *A person of strong will can often dominate others. Dandelions will dominate over grass if they're not kept out.* **2** rise high above: *The mountains dominate the landscape.* **3** have the foremost place in: *The new hockey team already dominates the league.* <Latin *dominus* lord> **dom′i·na′tion** *n.*

dom·i·neer (dom′ə nēr′) *v* exercise authority in an overbearing, arrogant way: *He tried to domineer over the other student council members.* <Dutch, from Latin *dominus* lord> **dom′i·neer′ing** *adj.*

Dom·i·ni·ca (də min′i kə) *n* an island country in the Caribbean. **Dom·in′i·can** *adj, n.*

Dominican Republic *n* a country in the Caribbean, part of the island of Hispaniola. The other part is the country of Haiti.

do·min·ion (də min′yən) *n* **1** authority or rule: *The British had dominion over a large part of the world.* **2** a territory under the control of a ruler or government: *The king divided his dominion between his children.* **3** **Dominion** especially in former times, a name for certain self-governing Commonwealth nations, such as Canada and New Zealand. <Old French, from Latin *dominus* lord>

🍁 **Dominion Day** *n* the former name for Canada Day.

Dominoes are like cards, because you can use the same pieces to play many different games, each of which has its own set of rules. But there's another use for dominoes, too. It's fun to stand them on end, positioning them so when the first one is tipped over it causes the whole pattern to fall—a pastime that gave rise to the expression *the domino effect.*

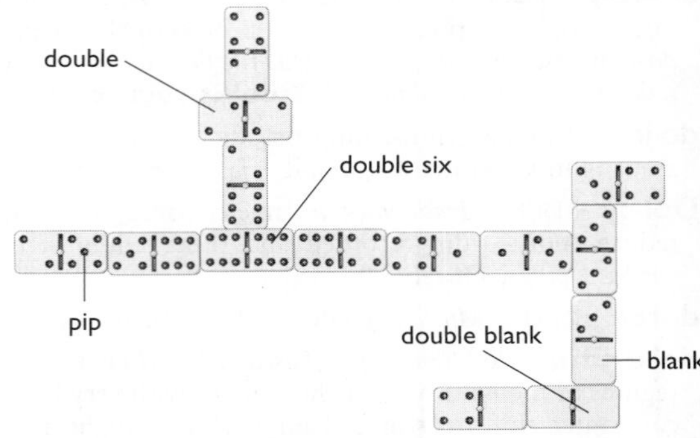

dom·i·no (dom′ə nō′) *n, pl* **dom·i·noes** or **dom·i·nos** **1 a** **dominoes** *pl* (*with singular verb*) a game played with flat, rectangular pieces of wood, bone, or plastic that are either blank or marked with dots on one side. **b** a piece used in this game. **2** a hooded cloak and mask, worn as a disguise, especially at masquerades, or the mask itself.

ETYMOLOGY

Although **domino** originally meant "priest's hooded cloak," it may have come to mean "piece of wood" as used in the game, because the white dots on the black tiles were like eyes peering out of the black mask of a masquerade costume.

domino effect *n* the effect of an action or event that triggers a whole series of similar ones: *Shortly after he quit the club, the others did too, one after another; it was a domino effect.*

don[1] (don) *v* **donned, don·ning** put on: *The knight donned his armour.* <Middle English, contraction of *do on*>

don[2] (don) *n* **1 a** 🍁 in some Canadian universities and colleges, an official in charge of a student residence. **b** in the UK, a university teacher, especially a head, fellow, or tutor of a college of Oxford or Cambridge. **2 a** a Spanish gentleman. **b** **Don** a Spanish title meaning Mr. or Sir. **3** a leader in the Mafia. <Spanish, from Latin *dominus* lord> **don′nish** *adj.*

do·nair (dō′ner) *n* lamb moulded and cooked on a vertical spit, from which pieces are shaved off and served in a pita.. <Turkish *döner* turn>

do·nate (dō nāt′) *or* (dō′nāt) *v* **do·nat·ed, do·nat·ing** contribute money, goods, etc. as a gift: *to donate food for the food bank, to donate blood. She has donated many hours of work to the hospital.* <Old French, from Latin *donum* gift> **do·na′tion** *n.*

GRAMMAR AND USAGE

Although ***donator*** can be formed from **donate**, the usual term for someone who donates is ***donor***.

done (dun) *v* past participle of DO[1].
adj **1** finished: *Day is done.* **2** cooked thoroughly: *These burgers don't look done.* **3** following the established custom: *the done thing.* **4** tired out.
done for, *Informal* finished, ruined, or doomed.
done in, *Informal* **a** tired out. **b** ruined or killed.
have done with, give up or abandon: *I've decided to have done with that whole lifestyle.*

SYNONYMS

Done is a neutral word that means "ended": *Her work was done before noon.*

Performed means "carried out": *He performed his nightly task of locking all the doors.*

Executed means "carried out with formality": *The mayor executed the duties of her office with great dignity.*

Accomplished also has a sense of formality: *I have accomplished all that was asked of me..*

Concluded has a sense of finality: *Once your signature is on the contract, our business is concluded.*

Don Juan (don′hwon′) *n* a man who leads an irresponsible life and has affairs with many women. <legendary Spanish nobleman>

don·key (dong′kē) *n* an animal related to the horse but smaller and with larger ears. <perhaps a nickname for *Duncan*>
talk the hind leg off a donkey, *Slang* talk constantly.

donkey's years *Informal pl n* a very long time: *I haven't heard from them in donkey's years.* <Donkeys have a fairly long lifespan.>

don·ny·brook (don′ē brůk′) *n* a brawl or riot. <*Donnybrook*, a suburb of Dublin, Ireland, formerly the site of a fair that was notorious for brawls>

do·nor (dō′nər) *n* a person who donates.

Don Qui·xo·te (don′ kē hō′tē) *n* an idealistic and impractical person. <hero of a satirical novel by 17c author M. de Cervantes>

don't (dōnt) *contraction* do not.

do·nut (dō′nut′) *Commercial or Informal n* a doughnut.

doo·dad (dū′dad) *Informal n* a fancy little ornament. <origin uncertain>

doo·dle (dū′dəl) *v* **doo·dled, doo·dling** make little drawings, patterns, or other marks while thinking of something else: *He doodled while talking on the phone.*
n such a drawing or pattern. <perhaps English dialect *doodle* fool, i.e., waste time> **doo′dler** *n.*

doo·hick·ey (dū′hik ē) *Informal n* a small mechanical device or gadget whose name one has forgotten or cannot bother to say. <perhaps blend of *doodad* and *hickey*>

doom (dūm) *n* an unhappy or terrible fate: *The soldiers marched to their doom.*
v **1** destroy all hopes for: *Bad weather doomed our picnic plans.* **2** destine to an unhappy or terrible fate: *He was doomed to a life of loneliness.* <Old English *dom* law, judgment> **doomed** *adj.*
doom and gloom, constant bad news or dreadful predictions.

doom·say·er (dūm′sā′ər) *n* a person who is always predicting disaster.

dooms·day (dūmz′dā′) *n* the end of the world; in some belief systems the day of God's final judgment of humankind.
(from now) till doomsday, for an extremely long time, or forever: *You can argue from now till doomsday, but I won't change my mind.*

door (dȯr) *n* **1** **a** a hinged, sliding, or revolving structure made of wood, metal, or another material for entering or leaving a building, room, or vehicle. **b** a similar structure that can be opened or closed in a cupboard, cabinet, or other piece of furniture. **2** an opening where a door is: *He just now walked through the door.* **3** the room or building to which a certain door belongs: *The washroom is the third door on the left.* **4** a means of getting in or out: *The new highway is a door to the interior of Labrador.* <Old English *duru*>
lay at someone's door, blame for: *The new premier laid the weak economy at the door of the previous government.*
leave the door open, allow for the possibility: *Let's leave the door open on whether changes to school policy are needed.*
out of doors, outside.
show someone the door, **a** ask or order a person to leave. **b** dismiss from a job.

door·bell (dȯr′bel′) *n* a bell or buzzer to be rung by a person outside a door as a signal to those inside.

door·keep·er (dȯr′kē′pər) *n* doorman.

door·knob (dȯr′nob′) *n* a knob on a door that releases the latch of the door when turned.

door·man (dȯr′man′) *or* (dȯr′mən) *n, pl* **door·men** (dȯr′mən) a person whose job is opening the door of a hotel, store, restaurant, or apartment building for people going in or out.

door·mat (dȯr′mat′) *n* **1** a mat at the door of a house for wiping one's shoes or boots on. **2** *Slang* a person who allows others to take advantage of him or her.

door·nail (dȯr′nāl′) *n* in former times, one of a set of nails used to reinforce and decorate a door.
dead as a doornail, *Informal* entirely dead.

door·post (dȯr′pōst′) *n* one of the vertical parts of a door frame.

door prize *n* a prize awarded to a person whose name is drawn at random from those attending a party or other social event.

door·step (dȯr′step′) *n* **1** a step leading from an outside door to the ground or other flat surface. **2** in the absence of such a step, the space immediately in front of an outside door.
on your doorstep, very close to home: *We have the world on our doorstep in this multicultural city.*

a bat	e bed	i bid	o pot	u cup	th **thin**
ā cake	ē me	ī bite	ō go	ū rude	ᴛʜ **then**
ȧ bar	ə about	ər over	ȯ for	ů put	zh measure

door·stop (dȯr′stop′) *n* a device to hold a door open or to keep it from opening too far.

door to door *adv* **1** calling at each address in turn in a particular neighbourhood: *We went door to door selling chocolates.* **2** from the original starting point to the final destination: *Door to door, it takes me 20 minutes to walk to school.* **door′-to-door′** *adj.*

door·way (dȯr′wā′) *n* **1** an opening that can be closed by a door: *She stood in the doorway.* **2** a point giving access to some place: *Our town is called "the doorway to the North."*

dope (dōp) *n* **1** *Informal* **a** a harmful narcotic drug, such as heroin or opium. **b** athletic steroids. **c** an anesthetic or other medication that reduces a person's alertness. **2** *Slang* a stupid person. **3** *Slang* information: *What's the latest dope on that scandal?*
v **doped, dop·ing** *Informal* give dope to or put dope in: *to dope someone's drink.* <Dutch *doop* thick sauce. Prepared opium looks like a thick sauce.> **dop′er** *n.* **dop′ey** *adj.*
dope up, *Slang* give or take enough of a drug to impair thinking.

dop·pel·gäng·er (dup′əl geng′ər) *n* a living person's ghostly double. <German *doppel* double + *Gänger* goer>

Dop·pler effect (dop′lər) *Physics n* the shift in the frequency of sound or other waves as the wave source and the observer move closer or farther apart, for example, causing an apparent change in pitch in a passing siren. <C. *Doppler*, 19c physicist>

🍁 **do·ré** (dȯr′ā) *or* (dȯr′ē) *n* the yellow walleye. <French = golden>

Dor·ic (do′rik) *adj* to do with the plainest of the three types of classical Greek architecture. See also CORINTHIAN, IONIC.

dorm (dȯrm) *Informal n* dormitory.

dor·mant (dȯr′mənt) *adj* **1** sleeping or in a state like sleep: *Bears are dormant during the winter.* **2** inactive: *a dormant volcano.* <Old French, from Latin *dormire* to sleep> **dor′man·cy** *n.* **dor′mant·ly** *adv.*

dor·mer (dȯr′mər) *n* **1** in full, **dormer window** an upright window that projects from a sloping roof. **2** the projecting part of a roof that contains such a window. <Old French, from Latin *dormire* to sleep>

dor·mi·to·ry (dȯr′mə tȯr′ē) *n, pl* **dor·mi·tor·ies** **1** a building containing many small private suites for people to live in temporarily, as at a college. **2** a large sleeping room containing a number of beds. <Latin *dormire* to sleep>

dor·mouse (dȯr′mous′) *n, pl* **dor·mice** a small rodent with big black eyes and a long tail. <Middle English>

dor·sal (dȯr′səl) *adj* on, in, or to do with the back: *dorsal fins, a dorsal nerve.* <Latin *dorsum* back> **dor′sal·ly** *adv.*

do·ry (dȯr′ē) *n, pl* **do·ries** a rowboat with a flat bottom and high sides, often used for fishing. <origin uncertain>

DOS (dos) *Computers n* in full, **Disk Operating System** a program that controls a computer's internal functions and enables the user to manage the computer's operations and run applications.

dos·age (dō′sij) *n* **1** the amount and frequency of the usual dose of a certain medicine. **2** the intensity or duration of X-rays in radiation therapy.

dose (dōs) *n* **1** the amount of a medicine to be given or taken at one time. **2** an amount of anything given at one time as a punishment, remedy, or treatment: *She needs a good dose of exercise.* **3** *Informal* a lot of anything, especially something unpleasant: *I've had a dose of trouble with that dog.*
v **dosed, dos·ing** give medicine to in doses: *The doctor dosed the boy with quinine.* <Latin, from Greek *dosis* something given>

do–si–do (dō′sē dō′) *n* in square dancing, a move in which two partners start out facing each other, revolve around each other back to back, and return to their original positions.
v **-do′ed, -do′ing** perform a do-si-do. <French *dos-à-dos* back to back>

dos·si·er (dos′ē ā′) *n* a collection of papers or documents on some person or subject. <French, from Latin *dorsum* back. A dossier was originally a file with a label on the back.>

dot (dot) *n* **1** a tiny, round mark: *The balloon floated up and up until it was nothing but a dot in the sky.* **2** a small, round spot in a pattern: *bright blue curtains with white dots.* **3** *Music* **a** a tiny, round mark after a note or rest, increasing its length by half. **b** a similar mark under a note, indicating that it is to be played or sung staccato. **4** a short sound used in Morse code. Compare DASH. **5** a period in an e-mail address or URL.
v **dot·ted, dot·ting** **1** mark with a dot or dots: *You forgot to dot that j.* **2** be here and there in: *Trees and bushes dotted the broad lawn.* <Old English *dott* head of a boil> **dot′ter** *n.*
dot your i's and cross your t's, be very accurate or careful about details.
on the dot, (*often with* **of** *and a specific time*) exactly at the specified time: *at six on the dot, on the dot of six.*

dot·age (dō′tij) *n* a period of life in which a person is old and may be weak-minded: *My great-grandfather is in his dotage.* <from *dote*> **do′tard** *n.*

dot–com (dot′kom′) *adj* to do with a business on the Internet: *dot-com millionaires.* <from the suffix *.com* on web addresses>

dote (dōt) *v* **dot·ed, dot·ing** (*used with* **on**) be foolishly or excessively fond: *He dotes on his children.* <Middle English *doten* act or talk foolishly>

dot matrix printer *Computers n* especially in former times, a printer producing characters made up of tiny dots.

dotted line *n* a line made up of dots, especially for writing one's signature on, or as a guide for cutting or folding.
sign on the dotted line, commit oneself fully.

dou·ble (dub′əl) *adj* **1** twice as much or twice as many: *double pay.* **2** for two: *a double bed.* **3** made up of two similar parts or sets of parts: *double doors. A double rose has two sets of petals.* **4** made up of two different parts: *a double career in dentistry and photography. Puns depend on words that have a double meaning.*

adv **1** as a pair or by pairs: *to ride double on a horse.* **2** twice: *His vote counts double.*
n **1** twice as much or twice as many: *I get paid double on Saturdays.* **2** a person or thing exactly or almost exactly like another: *I saw your double on the subway yesterday.* **3** an understudy or substitute: *She always uses a double to do the stunts for her.* **4** *Baseball* a hit that allows the batter to get to second base. **5 doubles** *pl* a game with two players on each side, as in tennis.
v **dou·bled, dou·bling 1** make or become twice as much or as many: *The town's population has doubled in twenty years.* **2** in place of: *I'll double for you at the presentation.* **3** serve two purposes: *The maid doubles as a cook.* **4** fold or bend: *to double your fists.* **5** *Baseball* make a two-base hit. <Old French, from Latin *duplus*> **dou′bly** *adv.*
double back, a go back the same way that one came: *The fox doubled back over his trail to confuse the dogs.* **b** fold over: *Double the cloth back to make a hem.*
double up, a share a room or other accommodation: *The brothers had to double up whenever guests stayed overnight.* **b** bend the body sharply at the waist: *She doubled up with laughter. He was doubled up in pain.* **c** fold up.
on the double, at a run.
see double, see two of everything.

double agent *n* a spy who pretends to be working for one side but is actually working for the other, or even deceiving both sides.

double bar *Music n* a vertical double line on a staff, marking the end of a movement or of an entire piece of music.

dou·ble–bar·relled or **dou·ble–bar·reled** (dub′əl ba′reld) *adj* **1** with two linked purposes or parts: *a double-barrelled approach to health care, combining prevention and treatment.* **2** with two barrels in a firearm.

double bass (bās) *n* a stringed instrument with a deep bass tone, the largest member of the modern violin family. It has four strings and is played standing upright on the floor with the player standing behind it.

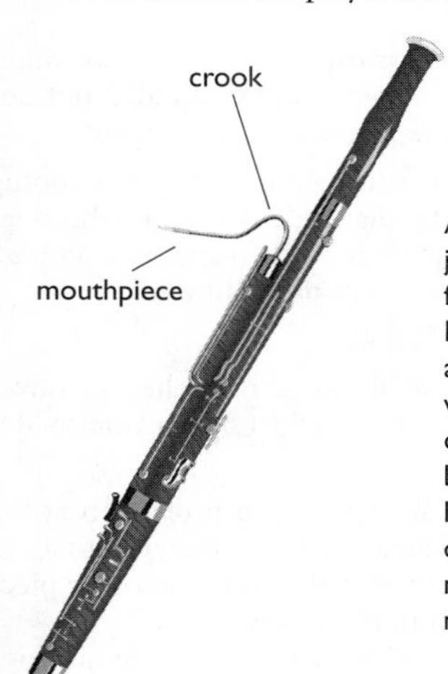

A **double bassoon** is just over a metre long from top to bottom. But if you could unwind all its wooden tubing, it would stretch out to over 5 metres. A double bassoon can make the lowest sound in an orchestra, a sound that is more like a rattle than a musical note.

double bassoon *n* a large bassoon, an octave lower in pitch than the ordinary bassoon.

double bill *n* two movies, plays, or other entertainments presented one after the other as part of a single program.

double boiler *n* a pair of cooking pots, one fitting into the other so that food in the upper pot is cooked gently by the heat from hot water in the lower one.

dou·ble–breast·ed (dub′əl bres′tid) *adj* overlapping enough to make two thicknesses across the chest of a coat or jacket, and with two rows of buttons.

dou·ble–check (dub′əl chek′) *v* check twice: *The police double-checked the man's story before releasing him.*
n the act of checking twice.

double chin *n* a soft fold of flesh under the chin.

dou·ble–click (dub′əl klik′) *Computers v* See CLICK.

dou·ble–cross (dub′əl kros′) *v* act like a friend or ally and then prove to be an enemy.
n **double cross** an act of treachery or betrayal. **dou′ble-cross′er** *n.* **dou′ble-cross′ing** *adj.*

double date *n* an outing for two couples.
dou′ble-date′ *v.*

dou·ble–deck·er (dub′əl dek′ər) *n* a structure with two levels or layers: *Some buses are double-deckers.*
adj with two floors, levels, or layers: *a double-decker sandwich.*

double digits *n* the range of numbers from 10 to 99: *Inflation is in the double digits now.* **doub′le-dig′it** *adj.*

dou·ble–edged (dub′əl ejd′) *adj* **1** with two sharpened edges. **2** accomplishing two things at once. **3** helpful and harmful at the same time.

double en·ten·dre (on ton′drə) *n* a word or expression used with two meanings, one of which is often potentially offensive. <French = double understanding>

double exposure *n* **1** the exposing of the same piece of photographic film twice. **2** a print made from two negatives superimposed.

double feature *n* a showing of two full-length movies one after the other for one price.

dou·ble–glazed (dub′əl glāzd′) *adj* having two layers of glass, with the space in between acting as insulation. **double glazing** *n.*

dou·ble·head·er (dub′əl hed′ər) *n* **1** two baseball games between the same teams on the same day, one right after the other. **2** a set of two similar events, one closely following the other.

double helix *Zoology n* the two-stranded, spiral character of a molecule of DNA, the base sequence on one strand being complementary to the sequence on the other strand.

dou·ble–joint·ed (dub′əl join′tid) *adj* with very flexible joints that allow one's fingers, arms, or legs to bend in unusual ways.

double negative *Grammar n* the use of two negatives by mistake in a sentence that is supposed to be negative, as in *I don't have no pen* for *I don't have a pen* or *I have no pen.*

a bat	e bed	i bid	o pot	u cup	th thin
ā cake	ē me	ī bite	ō go	ū rude	ᴛʜ then
ȧ bar	ə about	ər over	ȯ for	u̇ put	zh measure

D

dou·ble–park (dub′əl pärk′) *v* park a vehicle beside another that is occupying the legitimate parking space.

double play *Baseball n* a play in which two base runners are put out one just after the other.

dou·ble–quick (dub′əl kwik′) *adj, adv* **1** to do with a marching step that is very fast, but not as fast as a run. **2** very quick or very quickly.

dou·ble–space (dub′əl spās′) *v* **dou·ble-spaced, dou·ble-spac·ing** write or type text on every other line. Compare SINGLE-SPACE.

dou·ble·speak (dub′əl spēk′) *n* talk that is purposely made confusing so as to hide ignorance or dishonesty.

double standard *n* rules that are stricter for one set of people than another, especially rules for sexual behaviour that are stricter for women than for men.

doublet (dub′lit) *n* a man's close-fitting jacket, worn in Europe from the 1300s to the 1600s.

double take *n* a slightly delayed reaction to a surprising situation or joke, often used for comic effect by actors.

dou·ble·think (dub′əl thingk′) *n* acceptance or defence of contradictory ideas, whether unconscious, or deliberate and intended to mislead. <coined by G. Orwell in his novel *1984*>**double time** *n* **1** payment at twice the normal rate: *They get double time for working on Sundays or holidays.* **2** *Music* **a** a rhythm in which there are two main beats to the bar. **b** a tempo twice as fast as the previous tempo, with each note being given half its normal value. **3** a rate of marching in which 180 paces, each about one metre, are taken in a minute.

double vision *n* an abnormal condition in which one sees two images of every object.

doubling time *n* **1** *Zoology* the time taken for a cell to complete a cell cycle. **2** the time taken for a population to double in size.

doubt (dout) *v* not believe or trust: *I doubt he can get here that fast. Why do you doubt me? Have I ever failed you?*
n **1** lack of belief, faith, or confidence: *plagued by doubt.* **2** a particular point about which one is uncertain: *A thousand doubts crowded his mind.* <Old French, from Latin *dubius* doubtful> **doubt′er** *n.* **doubt′ing** *adj.*
beyond doubt, certain.
in doubt, unsure: *I am in some doubt about this proposal; it sounds risky. The outcome was in doubt until the very end.*
no doubt, a certainly. **b** probably.
without doubt, certainly.

GRAMMAR AND USAGE

In negative statements, *that* follows the verb **doubt**: *I don't doubt that she's sick.*

In positive statements, use *whether* or *if* to show uncertainty: *I doubt whether he can pass the exam.*

To show disbelief, use *that,* or no conjunction at all: *I doubt (that) she can answer this question.*

doubt·ful (dout′fəl) *adj* **1** unclear or disputable: *It is doubtful whether he even received the e-mail.* **2** feeling uncertain: *You sound doubtful.* **3** open to suspicion: *people of doubtful character.* **doubt′ful·ly** *adv.* **doubt′ful·ness** *n.*

doubt·less (dout′lis) *adv* **1** certainly. **2** probably: *He'll doubtless find an excuse not to go.*

douche (dūsh) *n* a jet of water squirted or sprayed into a part of the body.
v **douched, douch·ing** apply or take a douche. <French = shower>

dough (dō) *n* **1** a soft, thick mixture of flour, liquid, and other ingredients for baking into bread or pastry. **2** *Slang* money. <Old English *dag*>

dough·nut (dō′nut′) *n* a small cake, especially a ring-shaped one, made with or without yeast and fried in deep fat.

dough·ty (dou′tē) *Poetic adj* **dough·ti·er, dough·ti·est** brave and strong: *King Arthur's doughty knights.* <Old English *dohtig*> **dought′i·ly** *adv.* **dought′i·ness** *n.*

dough·y (dō′ē) *adj* **dough·i·er, dough·i·est 1** of or like dough. **2** not fully cooked when made of dough: *These dumplings are still a little doughy.* **dough′i·ness** *n.*

Doug·las fir (dug′ləs) *n* a very tall evergreen tree of the pine family found in western N America, with long cones and flat needles growing singly along the stem.
<D. *Douglas,* 19c botanist and explorer>

Douglas Treaties *n* a series of fourteen treaties made by governor James Douglas in the 1850s with various First Nations on Vancouver Island.

Douk·ho·bour or **Douk·ho·bor** (dū′kə bôr′) *n* a member of a Christian sect, originally from Russia, that believes in pacifism and simplicity of worship. <Russian *dukh* spirit + *borcy* wrestlers>

dour (dūr) *or* (dour) *adj* gloomy, severe, or stern. <probably from Gaelic, perhaps from Latin *durus* hard> **dour′ly** *adv.* **dour′ness** *n.*

douse (dous) *v* **doused, dous·ing 1** throw water or other liquid over. **2** plunge into water or other liquid. **3** put out a light or fire: *Douse the candles.* <origin uncertain>

dove[1] (duv) *n* **1** a seed- or fruit-eating bird with a cooing voice, closely related to the pigeon. **2** a person who does not believe in the use of force to settle disputes. Compare HAWK (def. 2). <Old Norse *dufa*> **dove′like** *adj.*

dove[2] (dōv) a past tense of DIVE.

dove·cote (duv′kōt′) *n* a small house or shelter for doves or pigeons. <*dove* + *-cote,* from Old English *cote* shelter for animals>

dove·tail (duv′tāl′) *n* **1** a wedge-shaped projection at the end of a piece of wood, metal, or other material that fits into a corresponding opening at the end of another piece to form a joint. **2** the joint made in this way.
v **1** fasten or join together with wedge-shaped projections that fit into matching openings. **2** fit together exactly: *Our strengths and weaknesses dovetail to make us a great team.*

dow·a·ger (dou′ə jər) *n* **1** a widow who holds some title or property from her dead husband. **2** *Informal* a dignified elderly lady. <Old French, from Latin *dotare* endow>

dow·dy (dou′dē) *adj* **dow·di·er, dow·di·est** dull, unimaginative, or unstylish in appearance: *a dowdy coat, a rather dowdy individual.* <origin uncertain> **dow′di·ly** *adv.* **dow′di·ness** *n.*

dow·el (dou′əl) *n* **1** a cylindrical peg made to fit into a corresponding hole so as to form a joint between two things. **2 a** wood in the form of slender cylindrical rods of various thicknesses, for making dowels. **b** one of these rods: *The banner was hung by means of a dowel inserted through a hem at the top edge.* Also, **dowelling, doweling.** <perhaps German *dovel* plug of a barrel>

down[1] (doun) *adv* **1** to do with a lower place, level, rank, or condition: *They ran down from the top of the hill. Down in the valley the fog lingered. Gas prices are down again.* **2** from an earlier to a later time or person: *The house was handed down from one generation to the next.* **3** to do with a place or condition thought of as lower, at a lesser height, or farther south: *We go down to Florida in winter.* **4** actually or really: *Get down to work. When it comes down to the practical details, you might need some help.* **5** in writing: *Take down this message.* **6** at the time of purchase: *He paid $500 down and took out a loan for the rest.* **7** to a position or condition that prevents escape or loss: *to pin something down, to track down a criminal.* **8** to a quieter or less intense state: *Settle down.*

adj **1** going or pointing lower: *the down escalator, the down arrow.* **2** sick or ill: *She's down with a cold.* **3** sad or discouraged: *He's pretty down about the breakup with his girlfriend.* **4** of a computer or other machine, not functioning. **5** behind by a certain amount: *Our team is down two goals.* **6** done or completed as one of a series of tasks: *One exam down, two to go!*

prep to a lower position or level: *to ride down a hill, to sail down the river.*

n **1** *Football* a chance to move the ball forward. In Canadian football, a team is allowed three downs in which to move the ball forward ten yards. **2** a period of bad luck or unhappiness: *the ups and downs of life.*

v put or get down: *I downed the medicine in one swallow. He downed his opponent and sat on top of him.* <Old English *adune* downward>

come down with, get sick with a short-term illness: *She's come down with the flu.*

down and out, a with many misfortunes, such as a lack of money, friends, a home, or health. **b** of a boxer, knocked out.

down on, *Informal* **a** angry at or with a grudge against. **b** critical or disapproving of.

down with someone (or **something**)**,** an exclamation calling for the removal or end of some person or thing: *Down with the tyrant! Down with TV!*

down[2] (doun) *n* **1** the short, soft, fluffy feathers covering baby birds and lying under the outer feathers of adult birds. **2** fuzz or hair like this. <Old Norse *dunn*>
down′y *adj.*

down[3] (doun) *n* usually, **downs** *pl* a stretch of high, rolling, grassy land. <Old English *dun* hill>

down·beat (doun′bēt′) *Music n* **1** the first beat in a measure. **2** the downward gesture of the conductor's hand to indicate this.

adj Informal **1** casual and relaxed: *One day she had a stiff manner, the next she had a downbeat approach.* **2** depressed or depressing.

down·cast (doun′kast′) *adj* **1** directed downward: *Ashamed, he stood with downcast eyes.* **2** dejected or discouraged.

down·draft (doun′draft′) *n* a current of air coming down something, usually a chimney.

down East *n* **1** the Atlantic Provinces. **2** anywhere to the east of Winnipeg, Manitoba.

down·er (dou′nər) *Informal n* **1** a disappointing or depressing thing or person: *That piece of news was a real downer.* **2** a depressant drug, such as a tranquillizer.

down·fall (doun′fol′) *n* **1** the ruin, overthrow, or failure of some person or institution: *the downfall of a hero, the downfall of an empire.* **2** the cause of this: *Gambling was her downfall.* **down′fall′en** *adj.*

down·grade (doun′grād′) *n* **1** a downward slope. **2** a decline toward a lower or worse status: *She didn't make the team and has been on the downgrade ever since.*

v **down·grad·ed, down·grad·ing 1** lower the status and rate of pay of a job or person: *The position has been downgraded.* **2** speak scornfully of: *Don't downgrade the novel; it's a good first attempt.*

down·heart·ed (doun′hȧr′tid) *adj* discouraged or sad. **down′heart′ed·ly** *adv.*

The slalom is a **downhill** race that requires both good technique and speed. Skiers must quickly zigzag between flexible poles called *gates,* placed along the course.

down·hill (doun′hil′) *adv* down the slope of a hill: *walking downhill.*

adj **1** sloping down: *the downhill portion of the hike.* **2** to do with skiing down slopes as opposed to cross-country: *downhill skis.* **3** *Informal* smooth and easy: *Once we had done the research, the rest of the project was all downhill.*

go downhill, fall into a bad or worse condition: *The business went downhill once the new owner took over.*

a bat	e bed	i bid	o pot	u cup	th **thin**
ā cake	ē me	ī bite	ō go	ū rude	ᴛʜ **then**
ȧ bar	ə about	ər over	ȯ for	u̇ put	zh measure

Down·ing Street (dou′ning) *n* the British government. <a street in London, UK, where the prime minister's home and office is located>

down·link (doun′lingk′) *n* **1** the sending of signals from a satellite or spacecraft to a receiver on earth. **2** such a receiver.

down·load (doun′lōd′) *Computers v* transfer data from a server to another computer: *to download files from the Internet.*
n the body of data transferred in this way, or the process of transferring it: *The download took about 20 seconds.* Compare UPLOAD.

down payment *n* a deposit or partial payment made at the time of purchase, with the remainder on credit.

down·play (doun′plā′) *or* (doun′plā′) *v* treat as unimportant: *Her speech downplayed the recent increase in unemployment.*

down·pour (doun′pôr′) *n* a heavy fall of rain.

down·right (doun′rīt′) *adv* nothing other than: *That behaviour was downright sleazy.*
adj **1** nothing other than: *You're a downright genius!* **2** plain and straightforward: *Her downright answer left no room for doubt.*

down·riv·er (doun′riv′ər) *adv, adj* to do with a point nearer the mouth of a river: *They live downriver from us* (*adv*). *Is your boat downriver from here?* (*adj*)

down·scale (doun′skāl′) *adj* not fancy or expensive.
v **down·scaled, down·scal·ing** reduce the size or scope of: *The Fall Fair has been downscaled for lack of funds.*

down·shift (doun′shift′) *v* **1** shift from a higher to a lower gear. **2** switch to a slower pace or reduced scope: *They're downshifting the fundraising effort now that building is underway.*
n the act of downshifting.

down·side (doun′sīd′) *n* (*with* ***the***) disadvantage: *It's a good plan, but the downside is we'll have to pay more.*

down·size (doun′sīz′) *v* **down·sized, down·siz·ing** **1** make smaller. **2** reduce the number of employees of a company or organization.

down·stage (doun′stāj′) *adj, adv* at or toward the front of the stage in a theatre.

down·stairs (doun′sterz′) *adv* **1** down a set of stairs: *The baby can crawl downstairs backwards.* **2** on or to a lower floor: *Who lives downstairs? I yelled downstairs for someone to make tea.*
adj located on a lower floor: *the downstairs bathroom.*
n a lower floor: *The downstairs is usually cooler.*

down·stream (doun′strēm′) *adj, adv* in the direction of flow of a stream or river: *downstream villages* (*adj*), *to sail downstream* (*adv*).

down·swing (doun′swing′) *n* a fairly sharp downward movement or trend: *a downswing in sales.*

Down syndrome *n* a condition caused at birth by a change in a chromosome that results in a person having skin folds on the upper eyelids and delayed mental development. <L. *Down,* 19c physician>

down·time or **down time** (doun′tīm′) *n*
1 *Computers* time during which a computer or other machine is not working. **2** time to relax.

down–to–earth (doun′ tū ərth′) *adj* practical and realistic.

down·town (doun′toun′) *adj, adv* in or to the lower, central, or main part of a town: *a downtown office* (*adj*). *We went downtown to do some errands* (*adv*).
n the lower, central, or main part of a town: *They are renovating the downtown.*

down·trend (doun′trend′) *n* a downturn.

down·trod·den (doun′trod′ən) *adj* without rights or power.

down·turn (doun′tərn′) *n* a decline in business or other activity.

Down Under *n* Australia and New Zealand.

down·ward (doun′wərd) *adj, adv* toward a lower place or a worse condition: *a downward trend in the economy* (*adj*), *sliding downward* (*adv*). Also (*adv*), **downwards**.

down·wind (doun′wind′) *adj, adv* in the same direction as the wind is blowing.

down·y (dou′nē) *adj* **down·i·er, down·i·est** soft, fine, light, and fuzzy like DOWN[2].

dow·ry (dou′rē) *n, pl* **dow·ries** **1** in some cultures, the money, property, or goods that a bride brings to her husband in marriage. **2** a natural gift, talent, or quality: *a dowry of good health and intelligence.* <Old French, from Latin *dotare* endow>

dowse (douz) *v* **dowsed, dows·ing** locate water, minerals, or other things using a divining rod. <origin uncertain> **dows′er** *n.*

doze (dōz) *v* **dozed, doz·ing** sleep lightly or be half asleep: *The cat is dozing on the windowsill.*
n a light sleep or nap.
doze off, fall into a light sleep: *He dozed off while watching the news.*

doz·en (duz′ən) *n, pl* **dozens** a group of twelve: *I've been to Saskatoon dozens of times.* <Old French, from Latin *duodecim* twelve> **doz′enth** *adj, n.*

GRAMMAR AND USAGE

After a number, the singular **dozen** is used: *Five dozen doughnuts might be too many.*

dpi *Computers n* in full, **dots per inch** a measure of the density of the image on a computer screen or produced by a printer.

drab (drab) *adj* **drab·ber, drab·best** **1** lacking brightness, colour, or interest: *drab curtains, a drab storefront.* **2** dull brownish grey.
n a khaki drill uniform: *The soldiers wore drab on manoeuvres.* <Old French *drap* cloth> **drab′ly** *adv.* **drab′ness** *n.*

dra·co·ni·an (drə kō′nē ən) *or* (drā kō′nē ən) *adj* harsh or severe: *a draconian regulation, draconian penalties.* <*Draco,* a legislator of the 7c BCE>

draft (draft) *n* **1** a current of air inside a building or other enclosed space. **2** a device for controlling the flow of air in a furnace or stove: *Open the draft so the fire will burn*

faster. **3** a rough, unpolished version of a piece of writing: *This is only the first draft of my essay, so it still has mistakes in it.* **4** a written order for a certain amount of money to be paid by one bank to another. **5 a** in some countries, such as in former times in the US, a system for selecting people for compulsory military service. A person selected is called a **draftee. b** the group of people selected in this way at one time. **6** the depth of water that a ship needs for floating, especially when loaded. **7** the act of drinking or inhaling, or the amount drunk or inhaled: *She emptied the glass in one draft. He took in a large draft of fresh air.* **8** a plan drawn on paper: *The architect showed my dad a draft of the new house.*
v **1** draw a plan or design of: *He drafted a floor plan for the new wing.* **2** write a first version of: *to draft new legislation, to draft a report.* **3** select for compulsory military service. *He was drafted in the middle of the Vietnam war.*
adj **1** drawn from a keg of beer, ale, or cider: *Some people prefer draft beer to bottled.* **2** used for pulling loads: *Oxen are draft animals.* Also, **draught.** <Old English, from Old Norse *drattr* something drawn>
on draft, of beer, ale, etc., available for drawing directly from a keg when ordered.

GRAMMAR AND USAGE

It can be useful to make more than one **draft** of a piece of writing, to improve it at each stage.

Make sure your *first draft* contains all the ideas that you want to include. Don't check grammar, spelling, or punctuation just yet.

In your *second draft*, check that all the information is correct, and organize your ideas so that they flow from one to the next.

In the *third draft*, check and fix any errors in grammar, punctuation, or spelling.

Proof your *final version*. It should be clean and free of errors.

draft–dod·ger (draft′doj′ər) *n* a person who avoids compulsory military service.

draft horse *n* a large, strong, heavily built horse for pulling heavy loads, such as a plough.

drafts·man (drafts′mən) *n, pl* **drafts·men** (drafts′mən) **1** a person who makes plans or sketches of things to be built. **2** an artist with special skill in drawing. **3** a person who drafts official documents. Also, **draughtsman. drafts′man·ship′** or **draughts′man·ship′** *n.*

draft·y (draf′tē) *adj* **draft·i·er, draft·i·est** letting in or exposed to currents of air: *a drafty window, drafty rooms.* **draft′i·ness** *n.*

drag (drag) *v* **dragged, drag·ging 1** pull along heavily or slowly: *A team of horses dragged the big log out of the forest.* **2** trail along the ground: *Your scarf is dragging.* **3** go too slowly: *Time drags when you have nothing to do.* **4** search or clear by pulling a net or hook along: *to drag a lake for a drowned person's body.* **5** go or cause to go wearily or reluctantly: *We needed a rest after dragging around town all day. I dragged myself out of bed at six.* **6** involve someone or something unnecessarily: *Don't drag me into your quarrel.* **7** *Computers* move an object on the screen using a MOUSE (def. 3). **8** *Informal* challenge or compete in a drag race: *I'll drag you to the corner.* **9** *Informal* inhale on a cigarette.
n **1** *Informal* something boring or disappointing: *It's a real drag that you can't go to the movies with us.* **2** *Informal* a long puff on a cigarette. **3** *Slang* (*especially in* ***the main drag***) a street. **4** characteristic women's clothing worn by a man. **5** a net or hook used in dragging. **6** the act of dragging. **7** the force acting on a moving body in a direction opposite to the body's movement, produced by friction. See AIRPLANE for picture. **8** a kind of brake that slows motion by causing friction. **9** a person who or thing that hinders or holds back: *Such attitudes are a drag on progress.* **10** *Slang* social or political influence: *He has a lot of drag at city hall.* <Old Norse *draga* or Old English *dragan* to draw>
drag′gy *adj.*
drag in, bring something irrelevant into a discussion: *Whatever we talk about, you drag in hockey.*
drag on, be boringly long: *The speech dragged on and on.*
drag your feet (or **heels**), act or work slowly on purpose: *The government is dragging its feet on the new legislation.*

drag and drop *Computers n* a feature of an application or operating system that lets users select and move onscreen objects with a mouse. **drag-and-drop** *adj.*

drag·net (drag′net′) *n* **1** a net pulled over the bottom of a body of water or along the ground. **2** a systematic, careful search, using many people to cover a large area at once: *A police dragnet rounded up three members of the drug ring.*

drag·on (drag′ən) *n* **1** a mythological fire-breathing creature like a large lizard with wings and claws. **2** a fierce or fearsome person. <Old French, from Greek *drakon* serpent> **drag′on·like′** *adj.*

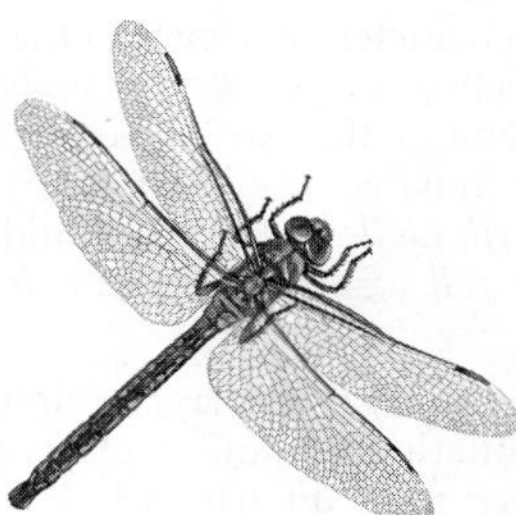

In spite of its ferocious name, the **dragonfly** cannot bite or sting. In fact, it spends a great part of its life not even flying. The eggs are usually laid on water, and the larvae stay in water for as long as several years. Eventually, this insect leaves the water as the adult dragonfly.

drag·on·fly (drag′ən flī′) *n, pl* **drag·on·flies** a large insect with a long, slender body and two pairs of very thin wings. Dragonflies eat flies, mosquitoes, and other insects.

dra·goon (drə gūn′) *n* **1** in former times, a mounted soldier with a musket. **2** a soldier in a cavalry regiment.
v force by violence: *He was dragooned into signing a false statement.* <French *dragon* dragon>

drag race *n* a contest between motor vehicles to see which can accelerate fastest.

a bat	e bed	i bid	o pot	u cup	th thin
ā cake	ē me	ī bite	ō go	ū rude	TH then
à bar	ə about	ər over	ȯ for	u̇ put	zh measure

D

drain (drān) *v* **1** gradually draw liquid off, or flow off: *to drain a swamp, to drain water from a swamp. The meltwater drains from the field into the creek.* **2** lose liquid by a gradual flowing off: *The clean dishes were draining in the sink. This whole region drains into Lake Ontario.* **3** take or be taken away gradually: *War had drained the country of its resources. The colour drained from her cheeks at the news.* **4** empty by drinking: *He drained his glass.* **5** use up the strength of a person: *I was drained by the experience.*
n **1** an opening, often attached to a pipe or channel, for water or other liquid to flow out: *There's a drain in the middle of the laundry room floor.* **2 a** a gradual outflow or loss: *Lack of opportunity caused a serious drain of talent to other regions.* **b** anything that causes such an outflow or loss: *Repairing the old car was a drain on their finances.* <Old English *dreahnian*> **drained** *adj.* **drain′er** *n.* **drain′ing** *adj.*
down the drain, lost or wasted: *That used TV was just fifty dollars down the drain.*

drain·age (drā′nij) *n* **1** the process of draining. **2 a** a system of pipes, ditches, etc for carrying water or waste. **b** what is drained off: *The drainage flows into the river.*

drain·board (drān′bȯrd′) *n* **1** a section of a countertop, usually with a different surface, that slopes slightly into a sink so as to drain the water off washed dishes. **2** a rubber mat or pan used for the same purpose.

drain·pipe (drān′pīp′) *n* a pipe for carrying off water or other liquid.

drake (drāk) *n* an adult male duck. <Middle English>

dram (dram) *n* **1** a unit of weight equal to one-sixteenth of an ounce (about 1.77 g). **2** a small drink of liquor. <Old French, from Greek *drachme* coin and unit of weight>

dra·ma (dram′ə) *or* (drȧ′mə) *n* **1** a story written to be acted out on a stage. **2** a play or movie that deals with serious issues of morality, personal character, or society. **3** the art of writing, acting, or directing plays: *She is studying drama.* **4** a series of happenings that seem like a play because they are exciting or moving: *The history of Arctic exploration is a great and thrilling drama.* **5** an emotional or exciting quality: *a story full of drama.* <Latin, from Greek *dran* to do>

dra·mat·ic (drə mat′ik) *adj* **1** to do with plays or drama: *the dramatic arts.* **2** like or imitating a drama or play: *After a dramatic pause, my father went on with his lecture.* **3** vibrant, colourful, or making a forceful impression: *a dramatic evening dress, a dramatic personality.* **dra·mat′i·cal·ly** *adv.*

dram·a·tis per·so·nae (dram′ə tis pər sō′nē) *or* (pər sō′nī) *n* a list of characters in a play, novel, or story. <Latin = people in the play>

dram·a·tist (dram′ə tist) *or* (drȧ′mə tist) *n* a writer of plays.

dram·a·tize (dram′ə tīz′) *or* (drȧ′mə tīz′) *v* **dram·a·tized, dram·a·tiz·ing 1** put into the form of a play: *to dramatize a novel.* **2** show or express in a dramatic way: *to dramatize an insignificant event.* **dram′a·ti·za′tion** *n.*

drank (drangk) past tense of DRINK.

drape (drāp) *v* **draped, drap·ing 1** cover or hang with cloth falling loosely in graceful folds, often as a decoration: *The painters had draped the furniture with large dropcloths.* **2** arrange or fall in graceful folds: *The designer draped the robe around the model's shoulders. Soft fabrics drape well.* **3** stretch out and allow to hang: *He draped his legs over the arm of the sofa.*
n **1 drapes** *pl* large, heavy curtains made to hang in folds: *We got new drapes for the living room window.* **2** the fact or manner of hanging in loose folds. <Old French, from Latin *drappus* cloth>

drap·er·y (drā′pə rē) *n, pl* **drap·er·ies 1** clothing or hangings arranged in graceful folds, especially on figures in paintings or sculpture. **2 draperies** *pl* drapes.

dras·tic (dras′tik) *adj* extreme or radical: *drastic changes. The police took drastic measures to curb gang violence.* <Greek *dran* to do> **dras′ti·cal·ly** *adv.*

drat (drat) *Informal interj, v* darn or damn. <alteration of *God rot*> **drat′ted** *adj.*

draught (draft) DRAFT.

draughts·man (drafts′mən) DRAFTSMAN.

draw (dro) *v* **drew, drawn, draw·ing 1** make a picture of something with pencil, pen, crayon, etc: *She draws very well for her age. I drew a picture of my house.* **2** pull: *A horse draws a wagon. He drew a wallet from his pocket.* **3** choose at random: *to draw names.* **4** attract: *A parade draws a crowd. May I draw your attention to a little problem?* **5** take out a sword or other weapon for use. **6** get or take: *to draw a conclusion from the evidence. I draw strength from your friendship.* **7** move toward: *We drew nearer to the fire to get warm. Day is drawing to a close.* **8** take out of a banking account: *to draw money from a bank.* **9** make a current of air to carry off smoke: *This chimney won't draw; it's getting smoky in here.* **10** take in: *to draw a breath.* **11** of a ship, boat, etc., float at a certain depth: *A ship draws more water when loaded than when empty.*
n **1** a tie in certain games. **2** a random selection of names or numbers for a prize: *She won a quilt in the draw.* **3** the act of pulling out a sword or other weapon for use. **4** *Golf* a deliberate shot that curves from left to right for a right-handed golfer. <Old English *dragan*>
beat to the draw, *Informal* manage to do something before someone else: *I was going to invite her to the dance, but he beat me to the draw.*
draw a blank, fail completely to find out, figure out, or remember.
draw and quarter, in medieval times, execute a person by tying the limbs to four horses and sending the horses in different directions.
draw on, get resources from or use as a resource: *to draw on your savings, to draw on someone's expertise.*
draw out, a extend too much: *Don't draw out the story so much; it gets boring.* **b** persuade to talk or respond freely: *Knowing he was a bit shy, we tried to draw him out.*
draw the line, set a limit or boundary: *She doesn't know where to draw the line in playing practical jokes.*
draw up, a write out in a certain form: *to draw up a list of candidates, to draw up a will.* **b** come or bring to a stop: *The taxi drew up in front of the house.*
quick on the draw, *Informal* quick to react.

draw·back (dro′bak′) *n* a disadvantage: *One drawback of having a paper route is that it makes going on holiday difficult.*

draw·bridge (dro′brij′) *n* a bridge that can be lifted or moved to one side, such as in castles.

draw·er (drȯr) *for 1 and 2,* (dro′ər) *for 3 and 4. n* **1** a box built to slide in and out of a dresser, desk, or other piece of furniture: *I keep my socks in a drawer in the dresser.* **2 drawers** *pl Informal* short or long underpants. **3** a person who writes an order to pay money. **4** a person who or thing that draws.

draw·ing (dro′ing) *n* **1** the art or act of making a picture with lines on a surface, using pencil, pen, chalk, or crayon. **2** a picture made in this way.

drawing board *n* a board used as a support for drawing or drafting on paper.
(go) back to the drawing board, (go) back to the beginning to try a new approach.
on the drawing board, in the planning or designing stage.

drawing card *n* a feature or event that or performer who will attract people: *Two Juno winners are performing at our music festival—that's a pretty big drawing card.*

drawing room *n* especially in former times, a room for receiving or entertaining guests. <shortened from *withdrawing room*, a room where, in former times, people withdrew after dinner>

drawl (drol) *v* talk in a slow way, making the vowels of words very long: *He drawled a lazy answer.*
n a way of talking that is slow and draws out the vowels. <Dutch *dralen* delay, linger>

drawn (dron) *v* past participle of DRAW.
adj **1** distorted with pain, anxiety, or tiredness: *Her face looked tired and drawn.* **2** melted as butter for use as a sauce.

draw·string (dro′string′) *n* a cord or string running through a hem or eyelets so that it can be pulled tight to close or narrow an opening, as on a hood, in the waist of a pair of pants, or at the top of a duffel bag.

dread (dred) *v* look ahead to something with fear or extreme uneasiness: *She dreaded the interview.*
n **1** fear, especially of something that will or may happen: *The old man lived in dread of winter.* **2** a person who or thing that inspires such fear: *The final test was the dread of the whole class.*
adj Poetic feared: *the dread tyrant.* **dread′ed** *adj.*

dread·ful (dred′fəl) *adj* **1** causing dread or great fear: *The dragon was a dreadful creature.* **2** very bad or unpleasant: *a dreadful headache, dreadful grammar.* **dread′ful·ly** *adv.* **dread′ful·ness** *n.*

SYNONYMS

Dreadful can mean "frightening": *Her first time diving was a dreadful experience for the young swimmer.*

Hideous often means "ugly and frightful": *She wore a hideous mask that scared the children.*

Horrifying is a strong word, meaning "terrifying": *The news of the approaching hurricane was horrifying.*

dread·locks (dred′loks′) *pl n* a hairstyle in which the hair is twisted into tight braids or ringlets.

dread·nought or **dread·naught** (dred′not′) *n* in former times, a big, powerful battleship with heavy armour and large guns.

dream (drēm) *n* **1** something imagined during sleep. **2** a vision of what might be accomplished. **3** a daydream. **4** something or someone beautiful or perfect.
v **dreamed** or **dreamt, dream·ing 1** have a dream or dreams: *You only dream during certain phases of sleep. I dreamed I was a lion tamer. We dream of the day when justice shall reign.* **2** (*usually in the negative*) suppose or think of as possible: *I never dreamed I would actually win!* <probably Old English *dream* joy, music>
dream′less *adj.* **dream′less·ly** *adv.* **dream′like** *adj.*
a dream come true, exactly what one would have wanted or hoped for.
a ——'s dream, the ideal thing for a certain kind of person: *This hardware store is a renovator's dream.*
dream of, (*used in the negative*) consider at all: *I wouldn't dream of hurting an animal.*
dream on! *Informal* that is only wishful thinking.
dream up, have an idea, especially an unusual one: *She was always dreaming up fanciful machines.*
in your dreams! *Informal* you may wish for that, but it will never happen.
like a dream, perfectly.

dream catcher *n* among some First Nations, a round frame with a knotted web of strings or leather strips, often decorated. Only good dreams are supposed to pass through; bad ones get caught.

dream·er (drē′mər) *n* **1** a person whose goals seem unrealistic. **2** a person who daydreams a lot instead of concentrating on the task at hand.

dream·land (drēm′land′) *n* an imaginary place where a person seems to be when dreaming or sleeping.
in dreamland, *Informal* asleep.

dreamt (dremt) a past tense of DREAM.

dream·y (drē′mē) *adj* **dream·i·er, dream·i·est 1** like something in a dream: *a dreamy recollection.* **2** soft and soothing: *dreamy music.* **3** impractical and fond of pleasant fantasies: *a dreamy person.* **4** *Slang* wonderful or lovely. **dream′i·ly** *adv.* **dream′i·ness** *n.*

drear·y (drē′rē) *adj* **drear·i·er, drear·i·est 1** gloomy and depressing: *dreary weather, in a dreary frame of mind.* **2** dull or boring: *long, dreary speeches.* <Old English *dreorig*> **drear′i·ly** *adv.* **drear′i·ness** *n.*

dredge (drej) *n* a machine with a scoop or series of buckets for removing mud, sand, or other things from the bottom of a river, harbour, or other body of water.
v **dredged, dredg·ing** clean out or deepen with a dredge: *They're dredging the harbour because it has silted up.* <Middle English *dreg-*>
dredge up, a bring up or gather with a dredge. **b** bring up or discover information, especially things that have been hidden or forgotten: *to dredge up an old scandal.*

a bat	e bed	i bid	o pot	u cup	th **thin**
ā cake	ē me	ī bite	ō go	ū rude	ŦH **then**
ȧ bar	ə about	ər over	ȯ for	u̇ put	zh measure

dregs (dregz) *pln* **1** the solid bits that settle to the bottom of a liquid: *After pouring the tea, she rinsed the dregs out of the teapot.* **2** the most worthless part: *the dregs of society.* <Middle English, from Scandinavian>

drei·del (drā′dəl) *n* a four-sided spinning top with Hebrew letters on each side, used in a game played during Hanukkah. <Yiddish *dreyen* spin>

drench (drench) *v* wet thoroughly: *We were drenched in a sudden rainstorm.* <Old English *drenc* a drink>
drench′ing *adj, n.*

dress (dres) *n* **1** a one-piece garment typically worn by women and girls, consisting of a top and skirt. **2** clothing: *sixteenth-century dress, casual dress.*
v **1** put clothes on: *to dress a doll. It's time to dress for the banquet.* **2 a** wear clothes, especially of a certain kind: *to dress in black, to dress formally.* **b** wear clothes attractively and with style or flair: *She really knows how to dress.* **3** put on formal clothes: *Some people dress for dinner, even when they're home alone.* **4** cause to wear clothes, especially of a certain kind: *They dress their daughters in fine clothing.* **5** decorate: *The store windows were dressed for Canada Day.* **6** clean or treat a wound. **7** add a dressing to a salad. **8** clean and prepare food for use, especially poultry or shellfish: *dressed crab.* **9** form in a straight line: *The captain ordered the soldiers to dress their ranks.*
adj **1** worn on formal or semiformal occasions: *dress shoes.* **2** requiring formal clothing: *This is a dress occasion.* <Old French, from Latin *directus* straight> **dressed** *adj.*
dress down, a wear casual clothes, especially in contrast to what is usual or expected: *The teachers dress down on Track and Field Day.* **b** scold.
dress up, a put on one's best or formal clothes: *You have to dress up to go to the opera.* **b** wear a costume: *We dressed up for the theme party.* **c** make something seem more interesting or exciting: *That poster is a bit drab; how can we dress it up a little?*

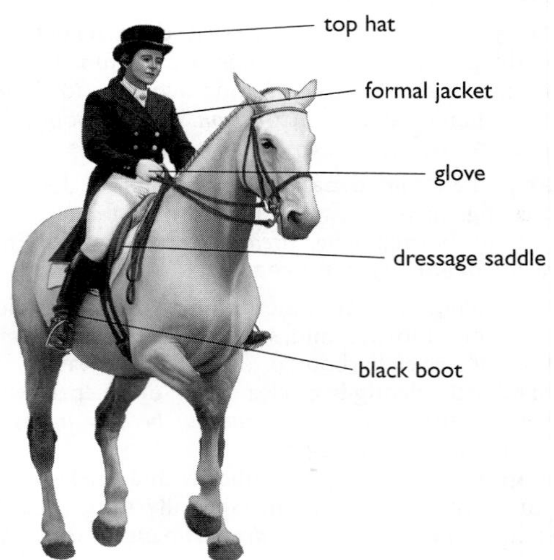

dres·sage (dre sȧzh′) *n* the training of a horse to respond to its rider and carry out certain manoeuvres typically used in competitions. <French *dresser* to train>

dress code *n* a set of rules, often unofficial, about what sort of clothing is acceptable in a certain place: *Does your school have a dress code?*

dress·er[1] (dres′ər) *n* **1** a person who dresses in a particular way: *He's a smart dresser.* **2** a person who dresses another, especially one who helps actors or entertainers dress for their performances. **3** a person whose work is arranging displays: *a window dresser.* <from *dress*>

dress·er[2] (dres′ər) *n* a piece of furniture with drawers for clothes and, often, a mirror. <Old French *dresser* prepare, train>

dress·ing (dres′ing) *n* **1** a sauce for salad. **2** a stuffing of crumbs, seasoning, and other ingredients for roast poultry or game. **3** the medicine or bandage put on a wound or sore. **4** fertilizer for soil, especially organic.

dress·ing–down (dres′ing doun′) *n* a severe scolding.

dressing gown *n* a loose robe worn over nightclothes, or while resting.

dress·mak·er (dres′mā′kər) *n* a person, especially a woman, whose work is making women's clothing. **dress′mak′ing** *n.*

dress rehearsal *n* a rehearsal of a play or other performance with costumes, scenery, and lighting just as for a regular performance.

dress·y (dres′ē) *adj* **dress·i·er, dress·i·est** fancy or formal: *That outfit is too dressy for a corn roast.*

drew (drü) past tense of DRAW.

drib·ble (drib′əl) *v* **drib·bled, drib·bling 1** flow or let flow in drops or in a thin stream: *Gasoline dribbled from the leak in the tank. Dry yourself off, you're dribbling water on the carpet.* **2** let spit run from the mouth. **3** *Basketball, Soccer* move a ball along by bouncing it or giving it short kicks.
n **1** a very slight flow: *All we could get out of the hose was a dribble.* **2** the act of dribbling a ball. <*drib*, variant of *drip*> **drib′bler** *n.*

dribs and drabs (dribz) *pln* small and incomplete amounts: *Pay me back all at once, not in dribs and drabs.*

dried (drīd) *v* past tense and past participle of DRY.
adj preserved by having moisture removed, sometimes with a change of form to powder, flakes, or crystals: *dried fruits, dried mashed potato.*

dri·er (drī′ər) DRYER.
adj comparative of DRY.

drift (drift) *v* **1** carry or be carried along by currents of water or air: *The wind drifted the boat onto the rocks. A raft drifts if it is not steered.* **2** heap or be heaped up by the wind: *The snow had drifted against the fence. The wind is drifting the sand.* **3** move or act seemingly without aim or intention: *Some people have a purpose in life; others just drift.* **4** go or come one at a time or in small groups: *The students drifted into class.* **5** move gradually from a certain position: *If you let go of the steering wheel, this car drifts to the left.*
n **1** a mass of snow, sand, or soil heaped up by the wind. **2** the basic meaning or general line of thought: *I caught the drift of her speech, but couldn't understand all the details.* **3** a tendency or trend: *The drift in public opinion was against war.* **4** the sand, gravel, or rocks moved from

one place to another by a river or glacier. **5** the fact, amount, or direction of drifting. <Old Norse *drift* snowdrift>
drift apart, gradually cease to be friends or romantic partners.

drift·er (drift′ər) *n* **1** a wanderer; someone who does not stay in the same place or job for long. **2** a fishing boat that uses a **drift net**, that is, a net that is allowed to drift along with the current.

drift·wood (drift′wu̇d′) *n* wood drifting in water or washed ashore, especially with the bark off and the wood worn smooth.

drill[1] (dril) *n* **1** a tool or machine for making holes. **2 a** a process of teaching by having people do a thing over and over again: *Military training involves regular drill in marching.* **b** a particular exercise of this kind: *The teacher gave us a quick arithmetic drill.*
v **1** pierce: *to drill a hole. Stop drilling in the desktop with your compass point.* **2** teach by doing or saying the same thing over and over: *My mother drilled us in basic manners. He drilled it into them that good work was its own reward.* <Dutch *drillen* bore, turn in a circle>
know the drill, be familiar with the way things are done: *You know the drill—you can't go out till your room is clean.*

drill[2] (dril) *n* a machine for planting seeds in rows that makes a small furrow, drops the seeds, and then covers the furrow. <perhaps from *drill*[1]>

drill[3] (dril) *n* a strong cotton cloth with a diagonal weave similar to denim. <German, from Latin *tri-* three + *licium* thread>

dri·ly (drī′lē) DRYLY.

drink (dringk) *v* **1** swallow liquid: *to drink milk. She drank the whole glass.* **2** absorb: *The dry ground drank up the rain.* **3 a** use alcohol: *No, thanks, I don't drink.* **b** use alcohol to excess. **c** spend on alcohol: *She drinks most of her paycheque.* **4** (*often with* **to**) drink in honour or approval of: *They drank his health. I'll drink to that!*
n **1** liquid meant for drinking. **2** alcoholic liquor. **3** the excessive drinking of liquor: *Unfortunately he's taken to drink.* **4 the drink** *Informal* the water of a lake, ocean, etc.: *The canoe tipped and she fell in the drink.* <Old English *drincan*> **drink′a·ble** *adj.* **drink′er** *n.*
drink in, experience or receive eagerly: *drinking in the beauty of nature.*

🍁 **drink box** *n* a small carton holding a single portion of a drink, with a straw attached for piercing the carton and drinking. Also, **drinking box**.

drip (drip) *v* **dripped, drip·ping** **1** fall or let fall in drops: *Rain dripped from her umbrella. You're dripping coffee on my magazine.* **2** be so wet that drops fall: *I'm dripping with sweat.* **3** have an obvious excess of some quality: *The movie is dripping with nostalgia.*
n **1** a drop that is falling or has fallen. **2** a falling in drops: *Can you fix the drip in the bathtub?* **3** the constant dispensing of liquid medicine or nourishment intravenously, or the substance dispensed in this way. <Old English *dropa* a drop> **drip′py** *adj.*

drip–dry (drip′drī′) *v* **drip-dried, drip-dry·ing** hang wet and allow to drip until dry.
adj meant to be hung up after washing and allowed to drip until dry, with little or no ironing: *drip-dry curtains.*

drip·ping (drip′ing) *n* usually, **drippings** *pl* the melted fat and juices that drip from roasting meat.
adj very wet.

drive (drīv) *v* **drove, driv·en, driv·ing** **1** operate or manage a vehicle, especially a motor vehicle: *to drive a truck, to drive a horse and buggy. Can you drive? What is your sister driving these days?* **2** travel by motor vehicle: *She drove 50 km each way. Airfare was too expensive, so we drove.* **3** transport as a passenger in a motor vehicle: *He drove me all the way to Toronto.* **4** cause to go or move: *to drive nails into wood, to drive away flies.* **5** send or force into some condition or behaviour: *Hunger drove him to steal. That noise drives me crazy.* **6** cause to work: *Their boss drives them so hard.* **7** get or bring by being forceful, clever, or shrewd: *to drive a bargain, to drive a point home in an argument.* **8** strike or hit hard: *The little boat drove onto the rocks in the high wind.* **9** 🍁 float logs in large numbers down a river.
n **1** a trip, usually short, taken in a car or other vehicle: *a Sunday drive.* **2** (*mainly in street names*) a road: *Greenleaf Drive.* **3** a driveway. **4** capacity for hard work and persistence: *Her success was largely due to her drive and energy.* **5** something that forces one to act a certain way: *The craving for approval is a strong drive in people.* **6** a special, organized effort for some purpose: *a fundraising drive, a drive to get more low-cost housing built.* **7** *Computers* an electronic device in a computer that holds a disk, CD, or tape and reads data from it. **8** a part or arrangement of parts that produces or controls motion: *Our van has four-wheel drive.* **9** *Baseball* a stroke of a ball hit low and hard, usually slanting or in a straight line. **10** *Golf* the stroke that hits the ball from the tee. **11** the process of moving a herd of cattle overland. **12** 🍁 the act of floating a large number of logs down a river, or the logs themselves. <Old English *drifan* urge to go forward>
be driving at, mean or intend: *I didn't understand what she was driving at.*

drive–by (drīv′bī′) *n* in full, **drive-by shooting** a shooting attack done by someone riding by in a vehicle.

drive–in (drīv′in′) *n* a theatre or fast-food outlet where patrons can watch movies on an outdoor screen or eat while seated in their cars.
adj to do with such a place: *a drive-in movie.*

driv·el (driv′əl) *n* stupid, foolish talk or writing. <Old English *dreflian* dribble>

driv·en (drivən) past participle of DRIVE.

driv·er (drī′vər) *n* **1** a person who drives a vehicle. **2** *Golf* a club with a large head for hitting the ball from the tee. **3** a person who makes other people work very hard.
the driver's seat, *Informal* the position of power or control.

drive·shaft (drīv′shaft) *n* a shaft that transmits power or motion, such as the shaft in a motor vehicle that connects the transmission to the axle of the driving wheels.

a bat	e bed	i bid	o pot	u cup	th **thin**
ā cake	ē me	ī bite	ō go	ū rude	ᴛʜ **then**
ȧ bar	ə about	ər over	ȯ for	u̇ put	zh measure

D

drive–through (drīv′thrū′) *n* a service window or machine at a bank, fast-food restaurant, or other business that allows customers to drive to and be served without leaving their cars.
adj to do with such a facility.

drive·train or **drive train** (drīv′trān′) *n* a mechanical system that sends turning power from an engine to the drive axles.

drive·way (drīv′wā′) *n* a private lane leading from a house, garage, or other building to the street.

driv·ing (drī′ving) *adj* very forceful and steady: *a driving rain, music with a driving beat.*

driz·zle (driz′əl) *v* **driz·zled, driz·zling 1** rain in very small drops: *It's drizzling out.* **2** let fall in drops or small bits: *Drizzle the shaved chocolate over the cake.*
n very small drops of rain resembling mist: *The drizzle lasted all day.* <possibly Old English *dreosan* to fall> **driz′zly** *adj.*

droll (drōl) *adj* odd or quaint in a comical way. <French> **droll′er·y** *n.*

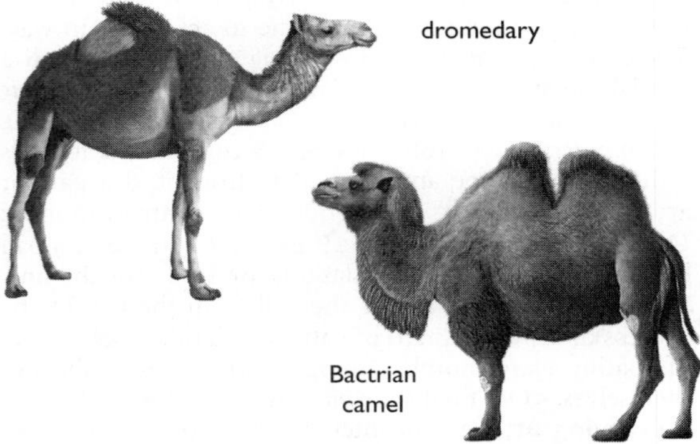

drom·e·dar·y (drom′ə der′ē) *n, pl* **drom·e·dar·ies** the one-humped Arabian camel. <Old French, from Greek *dromos* runner>

drone (drōn) *n* **1** a continuous humming sound: *the drone of an airplane engine.* **2** a monotonous speaking voice. **3** a male bee, especially the honeybee. It has no sting and does not gather honey. See BEE for picture. **4** a person who does no work. **5** a pipe on a bagpipe that with others makes a continuous sound.
v **droned, dron·ing 1** make a continuous humming sound: *Bees droned among the flowers.* **2** speak or say in a monotonous voice: *She droned on and on about her boyfriend.* <Old English *dran* male bee>

drool (drūl) *v* **1** let spit run from the mouth. **2** make an excessive show of pleasure or enthusiasm: *drooling over the new computer equipment.*
n spit running from the mouth. <contraction of *drivel*>

droop (drūp) *v* **1** hang down or bend down limply: *These flowers are drooping because they haven't been watered for days.* **2** become weak: *As the day grew hotter, we began to droop.* <Old Norse *drupa* hang the head> **droop′y** *adj.*

drop (drop) *n* **1** a very small, roundish mass of liquid: *a drop of rain, drops of sweat.* **2** the very smallest amount of liquid: *I haven't had a drop of water all day.* **3 drops** *pl* liquid medicine dispensed with a dropper. **4** a small, round, smooth mass, such as a candy: *a cough drop.* **5** a sudden fall or decrease i *a drop in temperature. The lake is shallow at first; then there's a sudden drop.* **6** the act of letting supplies or other things fall from an aircraft. **7 a** a secret place where illegal goods are left. **b** these goods.
v **dropped, drop·ping 1** fall or let fall: *The leaves dropped one by one. I dropped a toonie on the floor.* **2** fall dead or exhausted: *Shop till you drop.* **3** go or fall down, or cause to do so: *The sun dropped below the horizon. Drop your voice.* **4** omit: *Drop the final "e" before adding "ing."* **5** abandon: *to drop a friend. Let's drop the subject.* **6** say, send, or give casually: *to drop a hint.* **7** let passengers off a vehicle: *You can drop me at the corner.* **8** *Informal* lose: *Our team has just dropped six straight games.* **9** *Informal* spend, especially a lot at once: *They just dropped a thousand on car repairs.* **10** give birth as an animal: *Has the cow dropped her calf yet?* <Old English *dropa*> **drop′like′** *adj.*
at the drop of a hat, willingly and at once: *I'd change places with her at the drop of a hat.*
drop a brick, make a tactless or tasteless comment.
drop behind (or **back**)**,** begin to go more slowly or do less well than others.
drop by (or **in, over, around**)**,** visit briefly.
drop dead! *Slang* a dismissive expression of disbelief, annoyance, or contempt.
drop in the bucket (or **ocean**)**,** a tiny amount compared with all the rest.
drop names, try to impress someone by mentioning important people in a way that suggests one knows them personally.
drop off, a fall asleep. **b** become less: *Sales have dropped off.* **c** stop on one's way: *I have to drop off at my mom's office.* **d** stop to let a passenger out or deliver something: *Can you drop this book off at the library on your way?*
drop out, leave school or a course of instruction without finishing.
drop the ball, *Informal* make a mess of what you are doing; fail.
have the drop on, get or have an advantage over, especially by acting first.

drop·cloth (drop′kloth′) *n* a large sheet of cloth or plastic used to protect floors and furnishings from paint or dust.

drop–dead (drop′ded′) *Slang adv* very impressively; extremely; spectacularly: *In that outfit, you are drop-dead gorgeous.*
adj **1** very impressive; spectacular: *a drop-dead hairdo.* **2** to do with a deadline that cannot be changed: *Friday is the drop-dead date for handing in the essay.*

drop–down menu (drop′doun′) *Computers n* a vertical list of options that appears below a word or icon selected by the user. Compare PULL-DOWN MENU.

drop–in centre (drop′in′) *n* an informal place for people to come for help, recreation, or companionship: *a drop-in centre for parents with preschoolers.*

drop kick *n* **1** *Football* a kick given to the ball after it is dropped to the ground and bounces. **2** a flying kick in martial arts made while dropping to the ground. **drop′-kick′** *v.*

drop leaf *n* a hinged section of a tabletop, meant to be folded down when not in use. **drop′-leaf′** *adj.*

drop·let (drop′lit) *n* a tiny drop.

drop–off (drop′of′) *n* **1** a decrease: *a drop-off in sales.* **2** a sudden, sharp slope: *Watch out for the drop-off beyond the buoys.* **3** the act or site of dropping off a person or thing: *The coffee shop is a convenient drop-off because it's a central location.*

drop·out (drop′out′) *n* a person who has quit school or some other program without finishing.

drop pass *Hockey n* a pass on which a player leaves the puck behind on the ice for a teammate to pick up.

drop·per (drop′ər) *n* a small glass or plastic tube with a hollow rubber bulb at one end and a small opening at the other, for taking up liquid and letting it fall, or squeezing it out, in drops.

drop·pings (drop′ingz) *pln* the dung of animals and birds.

dross (dros) *n* **1** the waste or scum that comes to the surface when metals are melted. **2** something regarded as worthless. <Old English *dros*>

drought (drout) *n* **1** a long period of dry weather resulting in a shortage of water. **2** a prolonged shortage of something, or a long period of being unproductive. <Old English *drugath*>

drove[1] (drōv) past tense of DRIVE.

drove[2] (drōv) *n* **1 droves** *pl* large groups of people: *droves of tourists.* **2** a group of cattle or other livestock being herded along together: *We had to stop for a drove of cattle crossing the road.* <Old English *draf*>

drown (droun) *v* **1** die or cause to die in water or other liquid through lack of air to breathe. **2** put too much water or liquid on: *You're drowning that pancake in syrup!* **3** (*usually with* ***out***) be louder and so keep something from being heard: *The firecrackers drowned out what she was saying.* **4** get rid of by overpowering with something else: *He tried to drown his sorrows in work.* <Middle English>

drowse (drouz) *v* **drowsed, drows·ing** lie around sleepily: *drowsing in a hammock.*
n a state of sleepiness: *His pleasant drowse was cut short by a yapping dog.* <probably Old English *drusian* sink, become slow>

drow·sy (drou′zē) *adj* **drow·si·er, drow·si·est** sleepy: *a drowsy child, a drowsy afternoon.* **drow′si·ly** *n* **drow′si·ness** *n.*

drub (drub) *v* **drubbed, drub·bing 1** thrash (someone). **2** defeat by a large margin in a game. <perhaps from Arabic *daraba* beat>

drudge (druj) *n* a person who does hard, boring work.
v **drudged, drudg·ing** do hard, boring work: *My grandmother drudged for that company for 30 years.* <Middle English> **drudg′er·y** *n.*

drug (drug) *n* **1** a chemical substance that is taken into the body to correct a problem. **2** a substance that dulls the nerves, causes euphoria or hallucinations, or affects rational thought, especially one that is harmful, such as alcohol, nicotine, or heroin.
v **drugged, drug·ging** give drugs to or put drugs in, especially drugs that are harmful or cause sleep: *to drug someone's drink. The witch drugged the princess with a magic apple.* <Old French>
drug on the market, an article that is too plentiful or sells too slowly.

drug·gist (drug′ist) *n* a person who runs a drugstore or pharmacy.

drug·store (drug′stȯr′) *n* a store that sells medicines and, often, a variety of items such as candy and cosmetics.

D

Dru·id (drū′id) *n* among the ancient pagan Celts, a member of an order of priests who gave religious and social leadership. <Latin> **Dru·id′ic** *adj.* **Dru′id·ism′** *n.*

drum (drum) *n* **1** a musical instrument that makes a sound when struck with sticks or the hands, used to create a percussion sound and for rhythm. See PERCUSSION INSTRUMENT for picture. **2** a large cylindrical container, spool, reel, or anything else of cylindrical shape.
v **drummed, drum·ming 1** play a drum. **2** tap or strike again and again: *Stop drumming your fingers on the table.* **3** make a loud, rhythmic sound like a drum: *He could hear his own pulse drumming in his ears.* **4** force into someone's mind by many repetitions: *Basic school rules are drummed into children from the first day of kindergarten.* <German *trammel*, imitative> **drum′like′** *adj.* **drum′mer** *n.*
drum up, get or gather by making many requests or invitations: *to drum up support for a project, to drum up enough players for a game.*

drum·beat (drum′bēt′) *n* the beat of a drum.

🍁 **drum dance** *n* a dance of the Inuit or of the First Nations, accompanied by drums and often by singing. **drum dancer** *n.*

drum·lin (drum′lin) *n* a ridge or oval hill formed by deposit from a glacier. See SUMMIT for picture. <Gaelic *druim* ridge>

drum·stick (drum′stik′) *n* **1** a stick for beating a drum. **2** the lower part of the leg of a cooked chicken, turkey, or other fowl.

drunk (drungk) *v* past participle of DRINK.
adj **1** overcome by alcohol, so that one can no longer move, think, or talk normally. **2** overcome by pleasure, excitement, or happiness: *drunk with success.*
n **1** a person who is drunk. **2** a person who is habitually drunk. **3** *Informal* time spent drinking liquor: *a three-day drunk.*

GRAMMAR AND USAGE

The form of the adjective is usually **drunk** after a verb and **drunken** before a noun: *The woman was drunk. The drunken man fell down.*

Exceptions: *drunk driver* and *drunk driving.*

drunk·ard (drung′kərd) *n* a person who is often drunk.

drunk·en (drung′kən) *adj* **1** DRUNK (*adj* def. 1). **2** resulting from being drunk: *a drunken quarrel.* **drunk′en·ly** *adv.* **drunk′en·ness** *n.*

a bat	e bed	i bid	o pot	u cup	th **thin**
ā cake	ē me	ī bite	ō go	ū rude	TH **then**
ȧ bar	ə about	ər over	ȯ for	ů put	zh measure

drupe (drūp) *Botany n* a soft, fleshy fruit with a thin skin and a hard pit or stone in the centre containing the seed. A cherry is a drupe; a raspberry is a mass of tiny drupes or **drupelets.** <Latin, from Greek *druppa* ripe olive>

druth·ers (druTH′ərz) *Informal pln* one's own way or what one wants: *If I had my druthers, I'd quit the band tomorrow.* <shortening of *I'd rather*>

dry (drī) *adj* **dri·er, dri·est 1** not wet or moist: *dry bread. Hang the clothes out till they are dry.* **2** with little or no rain: *a dry climate.* **3** containing no liquid: *a dry well. The kettle is dry.* **4** with no tears: *a dry sob.* **5** thirsty. **6** solid as opposed to liquid: *dry measure, on dry land.* **7** dull: *a dry speech.* **8** seemingly matter-of-fact, but actually ironic: *dry humour.* **9** of wine, not sweet. **10** having laws against making and selling liquor: *a dry township.*
v **dried, dry·ing** make or become dry: *to dry the dishes. The towels soon dried in the breeze.* **dry′ly** *adv.*
dry′ness *n.*
dry out, a make or become completely dry, especially over time. **b** *Informal* take or cause to take treatment for alcoholism.
dry up, a disappear or cause to disappear by drying: *The creek dried up in midsummer. The sun dried up all the rain.* **b** *Slang* stop talking.
suck dry, use up all the vitality or resources of: *Wars have sucked the nation dry.*

dry·ad (drī′ad) *Greek myth n* a nymph that lives in a tree. <Old French, from Greek *dryas* tree>

dry cell *n* a battery in which the electrolyte is in the form of a paste so it cannot spill.

dry cleaning *n* **1** the cleaning of fabrics without water, using a chemical solvent, usually done professionally in a special store. **2** something cleaned or to be cleaned by this method: *I have to pick up the dry cleaning today.* **dry′-clean′** *v.* **dry′-clean′able** *adj.* **dry cleaner** *n.*

dry dock *n* an area set between two piers, built watertight so that water can be pumped out and ships or boats can be built or repaired there. **dry′-dock′** *v.*

dry·er or **dri·er** (drī′ər) *n* **1** a machine for drying things quickly, especially by heat or blowing air: *a clothes dryer, a hair dryer.* **2** a stand or rack for hanging clothes on to dry. **3** usually, **drier** a substance added to oil paint or varnish to make it dry faster.

dry–eyed (drī′īd′) *adj* not crying: *She remained dry-eyed at the funeral.*

dry goods *pln* textiles, clothing, ribbons, and lace as sold commercially.

dry ice *n* a very cold, white solid formed from compressed and cooled carbon dioxide. It is used for cooling because it evaporates without melting first, and in the theatre to create the effect of fog.

dryland (drī′land) *Ecology n* usually, **drylands** *pl* areas of severe drought, such as deserts and savannas. Compare WETLAND.

dry law *n* a law prohibiting the making and selling of liquor.

dry measure *n* a system for measuring pourable solids like grain or berries, in which two pints equal a quart, eight quarts equal a peck, and four pecks equal a bushel. A quart is about a litre.

dry rot *n* **1** the decay of seasoned wood due to various fungi, causing it to crumble to a dry powder. **2** decay in living plants, caused by the same fungi.

dry run *n* a practice test or session.

dry·wall (drī′wol′) *n* **1** a building material in thin sheets, made of plaster between layers of pressed felt covered with paper. **2** a method of construction that uses this material.
v make interior walls or ceilings with this material: *The contractors have finished building the addition, but it still needs to be drywalled.* **dry′wal·ler** *n.* **dry′wal·ling** *n.*

du·al (dyū′əl) *or* (dū′əl) *adj* involving or made up of two: *Driving lessons are given in a car with dual controls, one set for the driver and one for the instructor.* <Latin *duo* two>
du·al′i·ty *n.* **du′al·ly** *adv.*

dub[1] (dub) *v* **dubbed, dub·bing 1** make a person a knight by striking his shoulder lightly with a sword and giving him a title: *I dub thee Sir Galahad.* **2** call or name: *Because of her orange hair, they dubbed her "Carrots."* <Old French *adober* equip with armour>

dub[2] (dub) *v* **dubbed, dub·bing 1** add or replace a soundtrack, or part of one: *The Italian film was dubbed with English dialogue.* **2** (*usually with* **in**) add sounds to a film or other recording: *We still have to dub in the violin.* **3** copy a recording: *They made a video of the graduation and dubbed it for each family.*
n **1** the sounds added to a film or other recording. **2** a copy of a recording. <*double*> **dub′ber** *n.*

du·bi·ous (dyū′bē əs) *or* (dū′bē əs) *adj* **1** doubtful or uncertain: *The book is of dubious authorship. He was a little dubious, but agreed in the end.* **2** arousing suspicion and probably bad: *a dubious moneymaking scheme.* <Latin *dubius*> **du′bi·ous·ly** *adv.* **du′bi·ous·ness** *n.*

dub poetry *n* performance poetry using the rhythms and speech styles of Caribbean English. <from disc jockeys dubbing their own words onto records>

du·cat (duk′ət) *n* in former times, a gold or silver coin used in some European countries. <Old French, from Latin *ducis* duke, after the duke who issued the coin>

duch·ess (duch′is) *n* **1** the wife or widow of a duke. **2** a woman with a rank equal to that of a duke. <Old French, from Latin *ducis* leader>

duch·y (duch′ē) *n, pl* **duch·ies** the territory under the rule of a duke or duchess; a dukedom. <Old French, from Latin *ducis* leader>

duck[1] (duk) *n* **1** a small or medium-sized swimming bird with a flat bill and webbed feet. **2** the female of this animal. Compare DRAKE. **3** *Informal* a person: *lucky duck. He's a strange old duck.* <Old English *duce*>
duck′like′ *adj.*
like water off a duck's back, without having an effect.

duck[2] (duk) *v* **1** lower the head or bend the body suddenly, especially to keep from being hit or seen. **2** avoid or evade: *to duck responsibility.* **3** move quickly, suddenly, and stealthily: *She ducked into an alleyway.* **4** dip or plunge suddenly under water and out again.
n an act of ducking. <Middle English *duken*>
duck out, *Informal* go out quickly and for a short time,

often without being noticed: *She's just ducked out for a minute; can you call back later?*

duck[3] (duk) *n* a strong cotton or linen cloth like canvas but with a lighter, finer weave, used for clothing, small sails, etc. <Dutch *doek* linen cloth>

duck·billed platypus or **duck·bill** (duk′bild) PLATYPUS.

ducking stool *n* in former times, a stool on which a person was tied and ducked into water as a punishment.

duck·ling (duk′ling) *n* a young duck.

duck·weed (duk′wēd′) *n* a tiny stemless plant that grows in water, often covering the surface of still water.

duct (dukt) *n* **1** a tube, pipe, or channel for carrying liquid, air, wires, etc.: *a heating duct.* **2** a tube in the body for carrying a bodily fluid: *tear ducts.* <Latin *ductus* liquid-carrying>

duc·tile (duk′tīl) *adj* capable as a metal of being hammered out thin or drawn into a wire: *Gold and copper are ductile metals.* <See DUCT.> **duc·til′i·ty** *n.*

duct tape *n* strong, wide, very sticky plastic tape reinforced with a mesh of thread, used for minor repairs.

dud (dud) *n* **1** a firecracker, grenade, or shell that fails to explode. **2** a failure.
adj useless or unsatisfactory: *a dud cheque.* <Middle English *dudde*>

dude (dūd) *n* **1** a city person who spends a holiday on a ranch and knows nothing about ranch life. **2** *Slang* any man or boy. **3** a man who pays a great deal of attention to his clothes. <probably German *Dude* fool>

dude ranch *n* a ranch that is run as a tourist resort.

dudg·eon (duj′ən) *n* (*Archaic except in the expression* ***in high dudgeon***) anger or resentment. <origin unknown>

duds (dudz) *Slang pl n* clothes.

due (dyū) *or* (dū) *adj* **1** owed or deserved as a right: *Money is due her for her work. Respect is due to older people.* **2** proper or suitable: *Use due care when crossing the street.* **3** expected: *Her flight is due at noon. Your book report is due tomorrow.*
n **1** something owed as a debt or deserved as a right: *Give every person his or her due.* **2** **dues** *pl* a membership fee or similar charge payable at regular intervals to a club or other organization: *Union dues were deducted from his paycheque.*
adv directly: *The wind was blowing due east.* <Old French, from Latin *debere* owe>
due to, a caused by. **b** as a result of.
fall due, be required to be paid or given at a certain time: *The next instalment falls due on March 14.*
pay your dues, work hard and experience difficulties before gaining success: *She's a star now, but she's paid her dues.*

du·el (dyū′əl) *or* (dū′əl) *n* **1** especially in former times, a formal fight between two men armed with swords or guns, in the presence of witnesses, usually to settle a quarrel. **2** a fight or contest between two opponents: *a duel of words.*
v **du·elled** or **du·eled, du·el·ling** or **du·el·ing** fight or compete in a duel. <Latin *bellum* war> **du′el·list** or **du′el·ist** *n.*

due process *n* **1** *Law* proper, fair treatment by the justice system, in accord with the law and people's established rights: *No matter how extreme the crime, due process cannot be bypassed.* **2** proper, fair procedures for dealing with an accusation or complaint: *Due process requires that we listen to both sides.*

du·et (dyū et′) *or* (dū et′) *n* **1** a piece of music to be sung or played by two people. **2** two singers or players performing together. <Italian, from Latin *duo* two>

duf·fel bag or **duf·fle bag** (duf′əl) *n* a long bag of heavy cloth, often used by campers, sailors, soldiers, etc. to carry their belongings. <*Duffel,* a town in Belgium, where the cloth for it was first made>

duffel coat or **duffle coat** *n* a knee-length, usually hooded overcoat made of coarse woollen cloth with a fuzzy surface. See TOGGLE for picture.

duf·fer (duf′ər) *Informal n* **1** (*with* **little** *or* **old**) used to express endearment or familiarity to or about a small boy or an old man: *Let me have a look at the little duffer. Is the old duffer still hale and hearty?* **2** a clumsy or inept person or player. <Scots *dowfart* stupid person, from *douf* spiritless>

dug (dug) past tense of DIG.

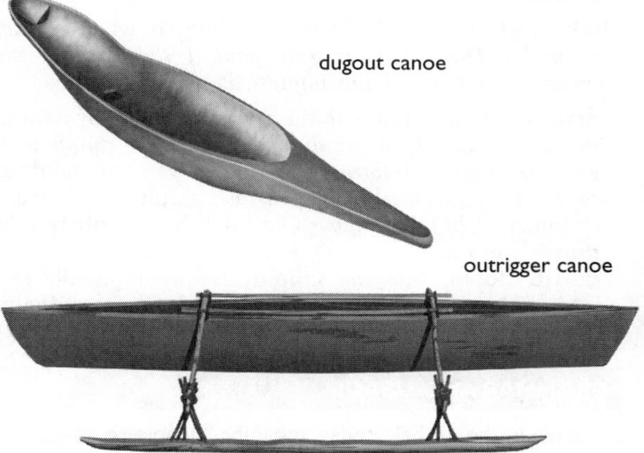

Many of Canada's Aboriginal peoples used **dugout** canoes. Pacific Coast bands, such as the Haida, hollowed out giant red cedars for seagoing vessels.

In some cultures, an attachment to the dugout, called an *outrigger*, was added to the canoe to provide stability in choppy waters. This invention seems to have originated in the area of the Indian Ocean or possibly east Africa.

dug·out (dug′out′) *n* **1** a canoe made by hollowing out a large log. **2** *Baseball* a small shelter near the diamond, used by players who are not at bat or not in the game. **3** in war, a trench made by digging into the side of a hill for protection against shells and bombs. **4** 🍁 a large excavation used to hold water for irrigation or for watering livestock.

a bat	e bed	i bid	o pot	u cup	th **thin**
ā cake	ē me	ī bite	ō go	ū rude	ᴛʜ **then**
ä bar	ə about	ər over	ô for	u̇ put	zh measure

duke (dyūk) *or* (dūk) *n* **1** a nobleman ranking just below a prince. **2** a prince who rules a small state or country called a duchy. <Old French, from Latin *ducis* leader> **du′cal** *adj.* **duke′dom** *n.*
duke it out, *Slang* settle something by fighting or arguing.

dul·cet (dul′sit) *adj* soothing and sweet-sounding. <French, from Latin *dulcis* sweet>

dul·ci·mer (dul′sə mər) *n* **1** a musical instrument with metal strings, played by striking them with two hammers. **2** a similar instrument of the S Appalachians in the US, held in the lap and played by plucking. <Old French, probably from Latin *dulcis* sweet + *melos* song>

dull (dul) *adj* **1** not sharp: *a dull knife, a dull pencil, a dull ache.* **2** not bright: *a dull day, dull colours.* **3** tiresome or boring: *a dull book.* **4** with little energy or spirit: *"I don't care," he answered in a dull voice.* **5** slow to understand.
v make or become dull: *Here is some medication to dull the pain.* <Old English *dol* stupid> **dull′ness** *n.* **dul′ly** *adv.*

dull·ard (dul′ərd) *n* a stupid or slow-witted person.

dulse (duls) *n* a coarse, edible seaweed with red fronds, found in the N Atlantic. There are several species. <Gaelic *duileasg*>

du·ly (dyū′lē) *or* (dū′lē) *adv* according to what is due; properly: *The debt was duly paid. I showed him my invention and he was duly impressed.*

dumb (dum) *adj* **1** not with the power of speech by nature: *dumb animals.* **2** silent: *dumb grief. I was dumb with embarrassment.* **3** *Informal* stupid: *That was a dumb thing to say!* **4** *Archaic* unable to speak as a result of a disorder or injury: *deaf and dumb.* <Old English> **dumb′ly** *adv.* **dumb′ness** *n.*
dumb down, *Informal* simplify for a supposedly less informed or less skilled audience, often losing meaningful content or insulting people's intelligence.

GRAMMAR AND USAGE

Dumb in the archaic sense, meaning "unable to speak as a result of a disorder or injury," is offensive in today's English, because of the current informal use of *dumb* to mean "stupid."

dumb·bell (dum′bel′) *n* **1** a short bar with heavy, ball-shaped ends, for weightlifting. Dumbbells are usually used in pairs. **2** *Slang* a stupid person.

dumb·found (dum′found′) *or* (dum′found′) *v* amaze to the point of speechlessness. Also, **dumfound**. <*dumb* + (*con*)*found*> **dumb′found′ed** *adj.*

dumb show *n* gestures without words.

dumb·struck (dum′struk′) *adj* speechless with surprise.

dumb·wait·er (dum′wā′tər) *n* especially in big, old houses, a small box with shelves that is pulled up and down a shaft inside a wall, carrying things such as food or dishes from one floor to another.

dum·my (dum′ē) *n, pl* **dum·mies** **1** a figure of a person, used to display clothing in stores, as a target in shooting practice, or to take the place of a real passenger in a vehicle crash test. **2** *Informal* a stupid person. **3** an item made to resemble the real thing and used in its place for display or testing, or as a prop, etc.: *The ventriloquist's dummy was a sheep made from a sock.* **4** a person supposedly acting on his or her own, but really controlled by another.
adj **1** made to resemble the real thing and used in its place: *The actors used dummy swords for the battle scene.* **2** supposedly real and intended to mislead: *a dummy corporation set up to avoid paying tax.* <from *dumb*>

dump (dump) *v* **1** empty out, throw down, or unload in a mass: *She dumped her books on the sofa. Dump the topsoil in the driveway.* **2** unload garbage: *The sign says, "No dumping."* **3** *Informal* get rid of or abandon: *to dump an impractical plan.* **4** put goods on the market in large quantities and at a low price, especially in a foreign country at a price lower than in the home country. **5** *Computers* **a** copy stored data to another location or application, especially to avoid loss. **b** print out data.
n **1** a place for unloading garbage. **2** a heap of garbage. **3** *Informal* a shabby, untidy, or depressing house, town, or place: *Life in this dump is unbearable.* **4** a place for storing military supplies: *an ammunition dump.* **5** *Computers* the process of copying or printing out data. A **screen dump** is a printout of whatever is displayed on the screen. <perhaps Old Norse>
dump on, *Informal* **a** criticize severely: *In her article, she dumps on lack of funding for the arts.* **b** vent one's frustration on: *So you lost the race! Don't dump on me!*

dump·ling (dum′pling) *n* **1** a ball of boiled or steamed dough. **2** such a piece of dough with a filling inside it. **3** a person or animal with a fat, round shape. <earlier *dump* doughy + *-ling*>

dumps (dumps) *Informal pln* sad or gloomy feelings.
down in the dumps, feeling gloomy or sad.

ETYMOLOGY

Rather than a reference to a place for garbage, the expression **down in the dumps** probably comes from the Dutch word *domp*, meaning "haze" or "dullness."

Dump·ster (dump′stər) *Trademark n* a large metal container used to hold trash, especially for apartment buildings, malls, or construction sites.

dump truck *n* a truck whose back section tips up and opens at the bottom end to dump its load. See TRUCK for picture.

dump·y (dum′pē) *Informal adj* **dump·i·er, dump·i·est** **1** short and stout. **2** like a dump. **dump′i·ness** *n.*

dun[1] (dun) *adj* greyish brown. <Old English>

dun[2] (dun) *v* **dunned, dun·ning** harass somebody persistently for payment of a debt. <perhaps obsolete *dunnen* to make a lot of noise>

dunce (duns) *n* **1** a stupid person. **2** in former times, a child who was slow at learning his or her lessons in school, often made to wear a tall, cone-shaped **dunce cap** as punishment. <*Dunsman*, name applied by critics to followers of J. *Duns Scotus*, a medieval theologian>

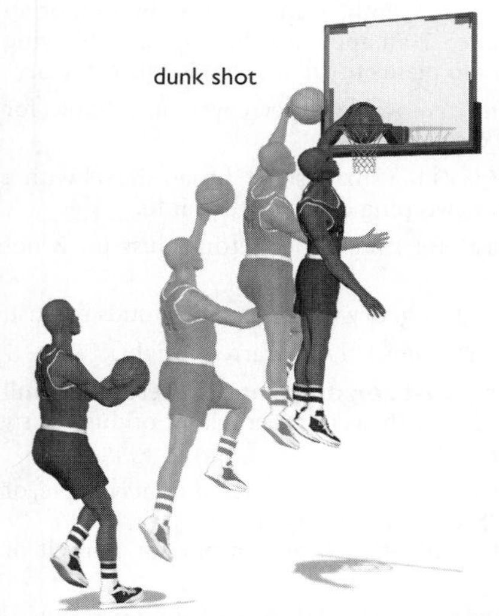

The **dunk** and the **slam dunk** provide some of the most exciting moments in basketball. With a powerful leap, the player lifts into the air. The player's hands actually rise above the level of the hoop, and then drive the ball down through the basket. Keep in mind that the hoop is 3 m above the ground, and that some players execute a dunk while spinning or flying through the air backwards.

layup

dun·der·head (dun′dər hed′) *n* a foolish person. <origin uncertain> **dun′der·head′ed** *adj.*

dune (dyūn) *or* (dūn) *n* a large mound or ridge of loose sand heaped up by the wind. See DESERT for picture. <French, from Dutch>

dune buggy *n* a small, open vehicle for driving on sand or rough terrain.

dung (dung) *n* the solid waste of animals. <Old English>

dun·ga·rees (dung′gə rēz′) *pln* pants made of coarse cotton cloth such as denim. <Hindi *dungri*>

dung beetle *n* a beetle that feeds on dung as larva or as adults, or both.

dun·geon (dun′jən) *n* a dark, underground room, as in a castle, to keep prisoners in. <Old French, from Latin *dominus* lord (of the castle)> **dun′geon·like′** *adj.*

dunk (dungk) *v* **1** dip something, especially food, into a liquid: *to dunk doughnuts in coffee.* **2** push somebody under or into water. **3** *Basketball* push the ball through the basket from above by jumping up above the rim. In a **slam dunk**, the ball is thrown down very hard through the basket. <German *tunken* dip, plunge> **dunk′er** *n.*

dunk shot *Basketball n* a shot in which the player jumps up high and scores by dropping the ball through the basket.

Dun·ne–za (dů′nə zȧ′) *n* **1** a First Nations people of the Peace River Valley in Alberta. **2** the language of this people. Also called **Beaver**.

du·o (dyū′ō) *or* (dū′ō) *n* any group of two acting together; a pair. <Italian, from Latin>

du·o·dec·i·mal (dyū′ə des′məl) *or* (dū′ə des′məl) *Mathematics adj* to do with twelfths or twelves. The **duodecimal system** of numbering uses twelve as a base instead of ten as in the decimal system. <Latin *duo* two + *decem* ten>

du·o·de·num (dyū′ə dē′nəm) *or* (dū′ə dē′nəm) *n* the first part of the small intestine, just below the stomach. <Latin *duodeni* twelve each, with reference to its length, about twelve finger breadths> **du′o·de′nal** *adj.*

dupe (dyūp) *or* (dūp) *v* **duped, dup·ing** deceive or trick.
n a person who is or is likely to be deceived or tricked: *The young politician's inexperience made her the dupe of every interest group.* <French *dupe* hoopoe (a bird thought to be particularly stupid)>

du·plex (dyū′pleks) *or* (dū′pleks) *n* **1** 🍁 **a** a building consisting of two homes under one roof, either side by side or, more often, one above the other. **b** one of the homes in such a building. **2** *US* a self-contained apartment with rooms on two floors.
adj double. <Latin, from *duo* two + *-plex* times as many parts>

du·pli·cate (dyū′plə kāt′) *or* (dū′plə kāt′) *for v,* (dyū′plə kit) *or* (dū′plə kit) *for n or adj. v* **du·pli·cat·ed, du·pli·cat·ing** **1** make an exact copy of: *to duplicate a document.* **2** repeat: *to duplicate an experiment. I've done that already, so you'll just be duplicating my work.*
n an exact copy: *Use a duplicate of the application form for your rough copy.*
adj **1** exactly alike: *duplicate keys for the front door.* **2** with or consisting of two similar parts: *A person's lungs are duplicate.* <Latin *duplicare* to double> **du′pli·ca′tion** *n.* **du′pli·ca′tor** *n.*
in duplicate, in two identical copies: *This application form must be submitted in duplicate.*

a bat	e bed	i bid	o pot	u cup	th **thin**
ā cake	ē me	ī bite	ō go	ū rude	ᴛʜ **then**
ȧ bar	ə about	ər over	ȯ for	ů put	zh measure

du·plic·i·ty (dyū plis′ə tē) *or* (dū plis′ə tē) *n* pretending to do one thing while really doing another. <Old French, from Latin *duplex* twofold> **du·plic′i·tous** *adj.*

du·ra·ble (dyu̇′rə bəl) *or* (du̇′rə bəl) *adj* able to last a long time: *toys made of durable plastic.* <Old French, from Latin *durus* hard> **du′ra·bil′i·ty** *n.* **du′ra·bly** *adv.*

du·ra·tion (dyə rā′shən) *or* (də rā′shən) *n* the length of time that something lasts: *The strike was of short duration.* <Old French, from Latin *durare* to last>
for the duration, until the end, especially of a war or other struggle.

du·ress (dyə res′) *or* (də res′) *Law n* force or coercion: *A confession made under duress is not legally valid.* <Old French, from Latin *durus* hard>

Dur·ga Pu·ja (du̇r′gə pū′jə) *Hinduism n* a festival in honour of Durga, the goddess of power, that lasts nine days in recognition of her nine different forms.

Dur·ham boat (dər′əm) *n* a large boat propelled by sails or poles, used in the early 1800s on the St. Lawrence and its tributaries for carrying goods and passengers. <R. *Durham*, 19c boatbuilder>

dur·ing (dyu̇′ring) *or* (du̇′ring) *prep* **1** through the entire time or process of: *Students must remain on the premises during school hours.* **2** at some point in the course of: *Drop it off during noon hour.* <Old French, from Latin *durus* hard>

du·rum (dyu̇′rəm) *or* (du̇′rəm) *n* a hard wheat from which flour is made, especially for pasta. <Latin = hard>

dusk (dusk) *n* **1** the time just before dark. **2** dim light. <Old English *dox* dark>

dusk·y (dus′kē) *adj* **1** dimly lit: *a dusky room.* **2** rather dark in colour: *dusky skin.*

dust (dust) *n* **1** fine particles of dry earth or other material: *Dust lay thick on the porch. His clothes were covered with coal dust.* **2** *Poetic* human flesh or its remains, especially when regarded as weak and mortal: *He shall return to the dust from whence he sprung. We are but dust.*
v **1** remove dust from: *to dust the furniture.* **2** sprinkle with dust or powder of some kind: *to dust crops with an insecticide.* <Old English> **dust′less** *adj.*
dust off, a brush or shake the dust from something. **b** restore to use: *Dust off your German; we're going to Austria!*
make the dust fly, move very quickly.
shake the dust off your feet, go away feeling angry or scornful.
throw dust in someone's eyes, deceive or mislead someone.

dust bowl *n* a region that suffers from severe dust storms due to long periods of drought.

dust bunny *n* a small mass of dust, hair, or cobwebs, especially under furniture or in a corner of a room.

Dust·bust·er (dust′bust ər) *Trademark n* **1** a small electrical home appliance for sucking up dust and dirt. **2 DustBuster** *Computers* software for removing unwanted files from a hard drive.

dust devil *n* a small whirlwind that stirs up a spiral of dust or leaves as it moves along.

dust·er (dus′tər) *n* **1** something used for removing dust from things, such as a cloth, a small feather broom, or an electrical appliance. **2** an apparatus for sifting or blowing dry chemicals onto plants to kill insects. **3** a dust storm.

dust jacket *n* a removable paper cover on a book, for protection and display.

dust·pan (dust′pan′) *n* a small, short, broad shovel with a straight edge, for sweeping dust or debris into.

dust·proof (dust′prūf′) *adj* **1** not letting dust in. **2** not damaged by dust.

dust storm *n* a strong, dry wind carrying clouds of dust.

dust–up (dust′ up′) *Informal n* a quarrel or fight.

dust·y (dus′tē) *adj* **dust·i·er, dust·i·est 1** covered with, full of, or like dust. **2** greyish, as if under a layer of dust: *dusty pink.* **dust′i·ness** *n.*

Dutch (duch) *adj* to do with the Netherlands, its people, or their language. See also NETHERLANDS.
go Dutch, *Informal* let each person pay for himself or herself.

Dutch elm disease *n* a fatal disease of elm trees, caused by a fungus and carried by insects.

Dutch oven *n* a large metal cooking pot.

Dutch treat *Informal n* a meal or entertainment where each person pays for himself or herself.

du·ti·a·ble (dyū′tē ə bəl) *or* (dū′tē ə bəl) *adj* requiring payment of a duty or tax: *Perfumes imported into Canada are dutiable goods.*

du·ti·ful (dyū′tə fəl) *or* (dū′tə fəl) *adj* showing a willingness to do one's duty: *a dutiful child, dutiful words.* **du′ti·ful·ly** *adv.* **du′ti·ful·ness** *n.*

du·ty (dyū′tē) *or* (dū′tē) *n* **1** the thing that a person ought to do: *It is your duty to obey the laws of the land.* **2** a feeling of having to do what is correct: *She acted out of duty more than love.* **3 duties** *pl* the tasks or functions that make up a person's job: *Duties for this position include setting up meetings.* **4** a government tax, especially on imported or exported goods. <Old French *deu*>
above and beyond the call of duty, more or further than one's duty requires: *Medals are awarded to those whose efforts are above and beyond the call of duty.*
do duty for, serve in place of: *This wooden crate can do duty for a table.*
(in) duty bound, compelled to do something as a duty.
off duty, away from one's work or job: *He's off duty till six o'clock.*
on duty, at one's post or job: *There were two security guards on duty.*

du·ty–free (dyū′tē frē′) *or* (dū′tē frē′) *adj* exempt from any tax due at a country's border.

du·vet (dū vā′) *n* a lightweight comforter with a removable cover, used instead of a top sheet and blankets. <French = down>

DVD *n, pl* **DVDs** in full, **DVD-ROM** or **digital video disc read-only memory** a compact disc with the capacity to hold a larger quantity of video, audio, or other information than a CD. "Read-only" means the information on the disc may be displayed or used but not altered. A user can store data once on a **DVD-R** (digital video disc-recordable), and can store data more than once on a **DVD-RW** (digital video disc-rewritable).

dwarf (dwôrf) *n, pl* **dwarfs** or **dwarves** (dwôrvz) **1** a person, animal, or plant much smaller than usual for its kind. **2** in fairy tales, one of a race of tiny people, often ugly, with magic powers.
adj much smaller than usual for its kind.
v **1** cause to seem very small by contrast: *The house was dwarfed by the gigantic home next door.* **2** stunt the growth of. <Old English *dweorg*> **dwarf′ism** *n.*

dwarf star *n* a star of relatively low mass and brightness.

dwell (dwel) *Poetic v* **dwelt** or **dwelled, dwel·ling** live in a certain place: *The princess dwelt in a beautiful castle.* <Old English *dwellan* stay, delay> **dwell′er** *n.*
dwell on, think, write, or speak about for a long time: *Don't dwell on your misfortunes.*

dwel·ling (dwel′ing) *Poetic or Formal n* a place in which people live: *a two-family dwelling.* Also (*Poetic*), **dwelling place**.

dwin·dle (dwin′dəl) *v* **dwin·dled, dwin·dling** become smaller and smaller or less and less: *Their supply of food dwindled rapidly.*

dye (dī) *n* **1** colouring matter: *hair dye. This weaver uses only plant-based dyes for her yarns.* **2** the colour produced by treatment with such a liquid: *The dye faded after only two washings.*
v **dyed, dye·ing 1** colour cloth, textiles, or hair by treating with colouring matter: *I'm going to dye my hair green.* **2** take on colour by this method: *Cotton fabrics dye easily.* **3** colour or stain something: *The blueberries had dyed his fingers purple.* <Old English *deag*> **dy′er** *n.*

dyed–in–the–wool (dīd′ in ᴛʜə wůl′) *adj* unchanging in a belief or opinion: *He's a dyed-in-the-wool conservative.*

dye·stuff (dī′stuf′) *n* a substance yielding a dye or used as a dye.

dy·ing (dī′ing) present participle of DIE[1].
dying for (or **to**)**,** *Informal* extremely eager or anxious to have or do something: *I'm dying for a cold drink. We're dying to see you!*

dyke (dīk) DIKE.

dy·nam·ic (dī nam′ik) *adj* **1** involving change, growth, or interaction: *Building a team is a dynamic process.* **2** active, energetic, or forceful: *a dynamic teaching style.* **3** *Physics, Music* to do with dynamics.
n a process of change, growth, or interaction, or a force that produces it: *There's an interesting dynamic going on here.* <French, from Greek *dynamis* power>
dy·nam′i·cal·ly *adv.* **dy′na·mism′** *n.*

dynamic load *n* a load that varies, like the weight of traffic crossing a bridge. Compare DEAD LOAD.

dy·nam·ics (dī nam′iks) *n* **1** (*with singular verb*) **a** a branch of study dealing with forces of change, growth, or interaction: *the dynamics of family life, an expert in population dynamics.* **b** the branch of physics that studies the motion of bodies and the forces that produce motion and balance. Compare STATICS. **2** (*with plural verb*) *Music* the effect of variation and contrast in loudness and style.

D

dy·na·mite (dī′nə mīt′) *n* **1** a powerful explosive in the form of round sticks made of nitroglycerin mixed with an absorbent material. **2** *Informal* something spectacular or likely to provoke a strong reaction: *A speech like that is potential dynamite in Canadian politics.*
v **dy·na·mit·ed, dy·na·mit·ing** charge or blow up with dynamite.
adj spectacular or impressive: *What a dynamite idea! We have a dynamite new lacrosse team.* <Greek *dynamis* power>

dy·na·mo (dī′nə mō′) *n* **1** GENERATOR (def. 1). **2** an energetic and forceful person.

dy·nas·ty (dī′nə stē) *n, pl* **dy·nas·ties 1** a succession of rulers who belong to the same family: *The Windsor dynasty.* **2** the time during which they rule. <French, from Greek *dynasthai* be powerful> **dy·nas′tic** *adj.*

dyne (dīn) *n* a former unit for measuring force. One dyne is the force required to give an acceleration of 1 cm/sec. <French, from Greek *dynamis* power>

dys– *prefix* bad or abnormal: *dysfunction.* <Greek *dys-* bad>

dys·en·ter·y (dis′ən ter′ē) *or* (dis′ən trē) *n* an infection of the intestines, producing diarrhea with blood and mucus that is caused by consuming contaminated food or water. <Latin, from Greek *dys-* bad + *entera* intestines>

dys·func·tion (dis fungk′shən) *n* a failure to function normally: *the dysfunction of social institutions.* <Greek *dys-* bad + *function*> **dys·func′tion·al** *adj.*

dys·lex·i·a (dis lek′sē ə) *n* a learning disability that mainly affects one's ability to read or to process written information. <Greek *dys-* bad + *lexis* speech>
dys·lex′ic *adj, n.*

dys·pep·tic (dis pep′tik) *adj* **1** irritable or bad-tempered. **2** to do with or suffering from **dyspepsia**, poor digestion or indigestion. <Greek *dys-* bad + *pep-* digest>

dys·pro·sium (dis prō′zē əm) *n* a rare chemical element, the most magnetic substance known. *Symbol* **Dy** <Greek *dysprositos* hard to get at>

Ee

e or **E** (ē) *n, pl* **e's** or **E's** **1** the fifth letter of the English alphabet, or any speech sound represented by it. **2** the fifth thing in a list or series. **3** *Music* the sixth tone in the scale of C major, or a key based on a scale with E as its keynote. **4** a grade rating a person or thing as inadequate.

e **1** *Physics* erg. **2** *Baseball* error.

e– *combining form* carried on or published electronically over the Internet: *e-commerce, e-mail, e-zine.* <from *electronic*>

E east; eastern.

each (ēch) *adj, pron* every one of two or more people or things considered separately: *Each dog has a name (adj). Each of us can play a part (pron).*
adv for each or to each: *These pencils cost fifty cents each.* <Old English *aelc*>

> **GRAMMAR AND USAGE**
>
> As a pronoun, **each** is singular and takes a singular verb: *Each of us has specific duties.*
>
> When *each* is used together with a noun, the noun decides if the verb that follows is singular or plural:
> *Each member performs her duties.* (singular)
> *The members each perform their duties.* (plural)

each other *pron* each in relation to the other or others: *They gave each other a pat on the back.*

ea·ger (ē′gər) *adj* **1** wanting to do or have something very much: *eager for information. I am eager to meet her.* **2** showing keen desire or anticipation: *eager looks.* <Old French, from Latin *acer* keen> **ea′ger·ly** *adv.* **ea′ger·ness** *n.*

eager beaver *Informal n* an especially enthusiastic person.

ea·gle (ē′gəl) *n* **1** a large, strong bird of prey with keen eyes, a hooked beak, sharp claws, and powerful wings. **2** *Golf* two strokes less than par for any hole on a course. <Old French, from Latin *aquila*>

eagle eye *n* **1** keen vision. **2** a careful watch: *Keep an eagle eye out for trouble.* **ea′gle-eyed′** *adj.*

eagle feather *n* among some First Nations, a feather of an eagle, which gives the person holding it the right to speak in a group. Compare TALKING STICK.

ea·glet (ē′glit) *n* a young eagle.

ear[1] (ēr) *n* **1** the organ by which human beings and animals hear. See AURICLE for picture. **2** the part of the ear on the outside of the head. **3** the ability to hear, especially to detect small differences in sounds: *A musician must have a good ear.* **4** anything like an ear in being attached at the side or edge. <Old English *eare*>
be all ears, *Informal* listen eagerly.
believe your ears, believe what you have heard.
be up to your ears in something, *Informal* have as much of something as you can possibly cope with: *I'm up to my ears in homework.*
fall on deaf ears, be ignored: *Their pleas have fallen on deaf ears.*
give ear, listen favourably: *Give ear to my request.*
go in one ear and out the other, *Informal* make no impression.
have (or **keep**) **an ear to the ground,** pay close attention.
have coming out (**of**) **your ears,** *Informal* have more of something than you can possibly use or manage: *I have three younger sisters, so we have toys coming out of our ears.*
have the ear of, be able to influence: *If you have the ear of the Student Council, try to get its support.*
lend an ear, pay attention.
play by ear, a play music without having it in written form. **b** *Informal* see what happens and act accordingly: *I don't know when to serve the food; let's just play it by ear.*
talk someone's ear off, *Informal* go on and on talking to someone.
turn a deaf ear to, ignore.
wet behind the ears, *Informal* inexperienced.

ear[2] (ēr) *n* the mature spike of a cereal plant, containing the seeds or kernels. <Old English *ear*>

ear·ache (ēr′āk′) *n* a pain in the ear.

ear·drum (ēr′drum′) *n* the thin membrane that stretches across the middle ear and vibrates when sound waves strike it. See AURICLE for picture.

ear·flap (ēr′flap′) *n* a part of a cap that can be turned down over the ear to keep it warm.

ear·ful (ēr′fu̇l′) *n* **1** as much as one can stand to hear: *I've had an earful of your complaining.* **2** a scolding. **3** a piece of gossip.

earl (ərl) *n* a British nobleman ranking below a marquis and above a viscount. <Old English *eorl*> **earl′dom** *n.*

ear·lobe (ēr′lōb′) *n* the smooth, soft part at the bottom of the ear.

ear·ly (ər′lē) *adv* **1** before the usual or expected time: *We arrived early.* **2** near the beginning: *I do my best work early in the day.*
adj **ear·li·er, ear·li·est** **1** coming or happening before the usual or expected time: *an early dinner, an early spring.* **2** happening or coming near the beginning: *early civilizations, the early chapters of the book.* **3** happening or coming soon: *an early trial.* <Old English *ǣr* ere + *lice* -ly> **ear′li·ness** *n.*
early on, at an early stage: *They learned to help themselves early on.*

early bird *Informal n* a person who gets up or arrives early.

ear·mark (ēr′mȧrk′) *v* **1** set aside for some special purpose: *A large sum of money has been earmarked for library books.* **2** be an identifying feature: *Careful work earmarks a good student.* **3** identify an animal by marking its ear.
n **1** a mark made on the ear of an animal to show who owns it. **2** an identifying feature.

ear·muffs (ēr′mufs′) *pl n* a pair of coverings to wear over the ears to keep them warm.

Earth and the planets

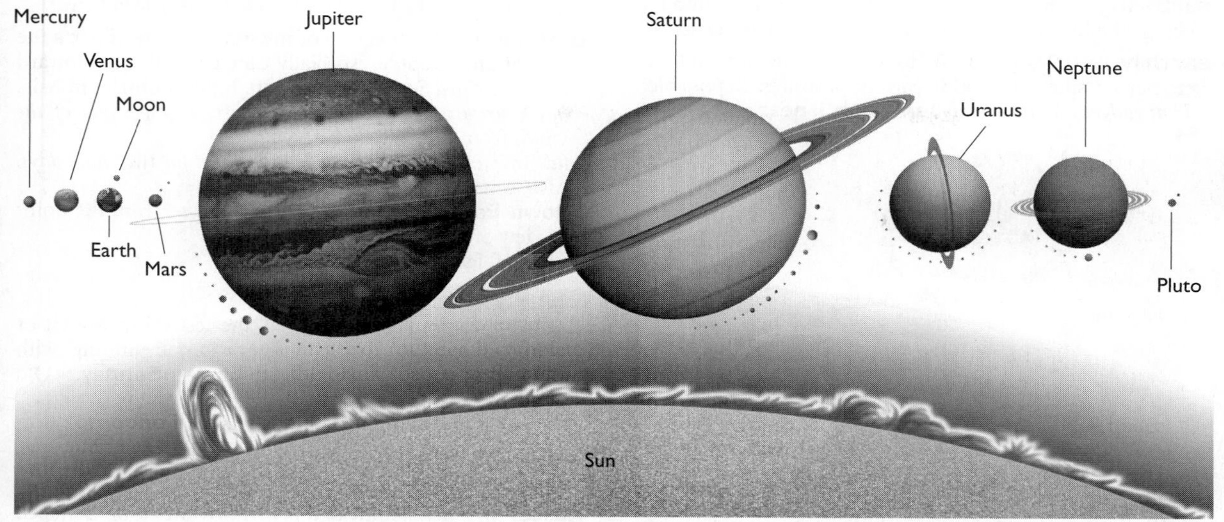

E

earn (ərn) *v* **1** be paid for work or service, or have a paying job: *She earns $100 a week from her part-time job. Now that two of them are earning, they can afford more things.* **2** bring or get as deserved: *Her courage earned her the respect of all who knew her.* <Old English *earnian*> **earn′er** *n.*

earned run *Baseball n* a run that is not the result of an error or a passed ball.

earned run average *Baseball n* the average number of runs scored against a pitcher in nine innings. *Abbrev.* **ERA**

ear·nest (ər′nist) *adj* sincere and serious: *an earnest desire to help others.* <Old English *eornost*> **ear′nest·ly** *adv.* **ear′nest·ness** *n.*
in earnest, a serious: *We could see she was in earnest about the request.* **b** seriously: *We had felt a few drops before, but now it began to rain in earnest.*

earn·ings (ər′ningz) *pl n* wages or profits.

ear·phone (ēr′fōn′) *n* a device inserted into or worn over the ear, by which electric signals are made audible.

ear·piece (ēr′pēs′) *n* a part of something that covers or fits over the ear: *the earpiece of a telephone.*

ear–pierc·ing (ēr′pēr′sing′) *adj* so loud, sharp, or shrill that it hurts the ears: *The little girl jumped up and gave an ear-piercing scream, then began to laugh when her brother took off the gorilla mask.*

ear·plug (ēr′plug′) *n* a piece of soft material inserted into the ear to keep out water or noise.

ear·ring (ēr′ring′) *n* an ornament for the ear, held in place by a screw or clip, or a wire passed through a hole pierced in the earlobe.

ear·shot (ēr′shot′) *n* the distance a sound can be heard: *He was out of earshot and could not hear our shouts.*

ear·split·ting (ēr′split′ing) *adj* extremely loud or shrill.

earth (ərth) *n* **1** the planet on which we live; the third planet from the sun, and the fifth in size. **2** this world in contrast with an eternal or spiritual world. **3** dry land. **4** soil: *The earth in the garden is soft.* **5** the ground: *The arrow fell to earth 100 m away.* **6** the hole of a fox or other burrowing animal.
v Electricity connect a wire or other conductor with the earth. <Old English *eorthe*>
come back to earth, stop daydreaming; get back to practical matters.
down to earth, seeing things as they really are; practical.
on earth, (*to add stress to question words*) ever: *What on earth have you done with my boots?*

GRAMMAR AND USAGE

Earth is spelled with a capital when it is used without "the" as the name of the planet, in reference to astronomy:
Jupiter is much bigger than Earth.
Many different species live on earth.

earth·bound (ərth′bound′) *adj* **1** headed for the earth: *earthbound spacecraft.* **2** unable to leave the earth.

Earth Day *n* since 1970, April 22, a day devoted to promoting environmental issues and awareness.

earth·en (ər′thən) *adj* made of baked clay: *an earthen jar.*

a bat	e bed	i bid	o pot	u cup	th thin
ā cake	ē me	ī bite	ō go	ū rude	ᴛʜ then
à bar	ə about	ər over	ȯ for	u̇ put	zh measure

earth·en·ware (ər′thən wer′) *n* pottery made of baked clay; pottery.

earth·ling (ərth′ling) *especially Science Fiction n* a human being who lives on Earth, not a creature from outer space.

earth·ly (ərth′lē) *adj* **1** to do with this world, not an eternal or spiritual world: *earthly pleasures.* **2** possible: *That gadget is of no earthly use.* **earth′li·ness** *n.*

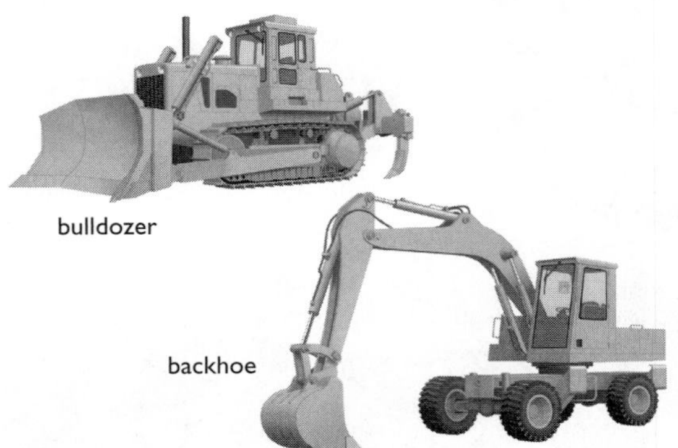

earth·mov·er (ərth′mū′vər) *n* a bulldozer or backhoe.

earth·quake (ərth′kwāk′) *n* a shaking of the earth's surface due to the sudden movement of masses of rock or to changes beneath the earth's surface. See QUAKE for picture.

earth science *n* one of the sciences that relate to the study of the planet Earth. Geology is an earth science.

earth–shak·ing (ərth′shā′king) *adj* extremely important.

earth·ward (ərth′wərd) *adj, adv* toward the earth. Also (*adv*), **earthwards**.

earth·work (ərth′wərk′) *n* a bank of earth piled up as a fortification.

earth·worm (ərth′wərm′) *n* a long, reddish brown worm that lives in the soil.

earth·y (ər′thē) *adj* **earth·i·er, earth·i·est 1** to do with earth or soil. **2** practical, everyday, and simple. **3** direct and uninhibited. **earth′i·ness** *n.*

ear·wax (ēr′waks′) *n* the sticky, yellowish substance that collects in the canal of the outer ear.

ear·wig (ēr′wig′) *n* an insect with a pair of appendages at the tail end that are like forceps. <Old English *eare* ear + *wicga* beetle, worm>

ease (ēz) *n* **1** freedom from pain, worry, or hardship: *She was rich enough to live a life of ease.* **2** a relaxed manner.
v **eased, eas·ing 1** give relief or comfort to: *This news ought to ease your mind.* **2** lessen: *to ease pain.* **3** loosen or relax: *to ease a tight shoe.* **4** move slowly and carefully: *She eased the big box through the narrow door.* <Old French *aise* comfort>
at ease, a comfortable: *I don't feel at ease in their company.* **b** *Military* with the hands behind the back, the feet apart, and the body somewhat relaxed.
ease off (or **up**), lessen.
with ease, easily.

ea·sel (ē′zəl) *n* an upright support for an artist's work. <Dutch *ezel*>

ease·ment (ēz′mənt) *Law n* a right to make limited use of another's property.

eas·i·ly (ē′zə lē) *adv* **1** in an easy manner: *She solved the puzzle easily.* **2** beyond question: *He is easily the best singer in the choir.* **3** likely: *These events may easily lead to war.*

east (ēst) *n* **1** the direction of the sunrise. **2 the East a** the part of any country, especially Canada or the US, toward the east: *Nova Scotia is in the East.* **b** the countries in Asia.
adj **1** toward, in, or facing the east. **2** (*especially of the wind*) from the east: *an east wind.*
adv toward the east: *They travelled east for two more days.* Also, **easterly**. <Old English *east*>
down East, ✱ in the Atlantic Provinces, from the point of view of provinces to the west.
east of, farther east than.

east·bound (ēst′bound′) *adj* going east.

East·er (ē′stər) *Christianity n* **1** the festival in March or April celebrating Christ's resurrection, beginning with **Good Friday** and ending with **Easter Sunday**. <Old English *eastre*>

Easter egg *n* a decorated egg, either real or made of chocolate, plastic, or glass, used as a gift or ornament at Easter.

Easter lily *n* **1** a cultivated lily with white flowers shaped like trumpets. **2** a wildflower of the lily family found in southern British Columbia and the northwestern US, with white flowers that bloom in early spring.

east·er·ly (ēs′tər lē) *adj* east.
adv from the east: *The wind blew easterly.*
n, pl **east·er·lies** a wind or storm from the east.

east·ern (ēs′tərn) *adj* **1** to do with the east: *Halifax is an eastern port.* **2 Eastern** to do with the countries of Asia and their cultures: *Eastern religions.*

east·ern·er (ēs′tər nər) *n* a person born in or living in the eastern part of the country. Also, **Easterner**.

east·ern·most (ēs′tərn mōst′) *adj* farthest east.

✱ **Eastern Townships** *pl n* the part of Québec lying south of the St. Lawrence River Valley and west of a line drawn southeast from Québec City to the US border.

East Indian *adj* to do with the Indian subcontinent or its inhabitants.
n a native or inhabitant of the Indian subcontinent, or one whose recent ancestors came from there.

east·ing (ēst′ing) *n* **1** the distance eastward of a point from a certain meridian, given by the first part of a map grid reference. **2** a longitudinal grid line. Compare NORTHING.

east–north·east (ēst′nôrth′ēst′) *n* a direction midway between east and northeast.
adj, adv in, toward, or from this direction. *Abbrev.* **ENE**

east–south·east (ēst′south′ēst′) *n* a direction midway between east and southeast.
adj, adv in, toward, or from this direction. *Abbrev.* **ESE**

East Ti·mor (tē′mōr) *n* a country occupying the eastern part of the island of Timor in the S Pacific.
East Ti′mo·rese′ *adj, n.*

east·ward (ēst′wərd) *adj, adv* toward the east: *an eastward route* (*adj*), *to ride eastward* (*adv*). Also (*adv*), **eastwards**.
east′ward·ly *adj, adv.*

eas·y (ē′zē) *adj* **eas·i·er, eas·i·est 1** requiring little effort: *easy work.* **2** free from pain, worry, or trouble: *an easy life.* **3** not harsh or severe: *That teacher is an easy marker.* **4** *Informal* **a** flexible: *Choose whichever one you want; I'm easy.* **b** easily seduced or tricked. **5** natural, smooth, and relaxed: *an easy conversational style.* **6** not tight: *These jeans are an easy fit.*
adv Informal with ease.
easy come, easy go, *Informal* easily obtained and easily lost.
easy does it, *Informal* **a** act gently. **b** relax.
go easy on, *Informal* **a** treat gently: *Go easy on him; he's new and doesn't know the ropes.* **b** (*sometimes without* **go**) use sparingly: *Go easy on the mustard.*
on easy street, *Informal* well off.
take it easy, relax.

GRAMMAR AND USAGE

Although **easy** usually is an adjective, it can be used as an adverb in phrases like *take it easy* or *easy does it.* Similarly, the adjective **hard** can be used as an adverb in phrases like *don't take it so hard.*

easy chair *n* a soft, comfortable chair with arms.

eas·y·go·ing (ē′zē gō′ing) *adj* tending not to worry or get upset.

easy mark *n* a person who is easily taken advantage of.

eat (ēt) *v* **ate, eat·en, eat·ing 1** take into the mouth, chew, and swallow. **2** have a meal: *Have you eaten yet?* **3** destroy as if by eating: *The acid has eaten through the metal.* **4** make by eating: *Moths ate holes in my coat.* <Old English *etan*> **eat′er** *n.*
eat out, have a meal in a restaurant.
eat out of someone's hand, be easily led or influenced by someone.
eat up, a eat all of. **b** use up: *The trip to Igloolik ate up all our savings.*
eat your words, admit that you were wrong.

eat·a·ble (ē′tə bəl) *adj* fit to eat.
n **eatables** *pl Informal* food.

eat·er·y (ē′tə rē) *Informal n, pl* **eat·er·ies** a restaurant.

eat·ing disorder *n* a psychological disorder in which the person has a much greater or smaller appetite than normal, eats very irregularly, or deliberately interferes with the digestive process.

eats (ēts) *Slang pln* food.

eau de Cologne (ō′də kə lōn′) *n* See COLOGNE. <French = water of Cologne, the city where it was first made>

eaves (ēvz) *pln* the lower edges of a roof, projecting beyond the wall of a building. <Old English *efes*>

eaves·drop (ēvz′drop′) *v* **eaves·dropped, eaves·drop·ping** listen secretly to private conversation. <Old English *efesdrype* the ground under the eaves (where a person might stand to listen to a conversation inside the house)> **eaves′drop′per** *n.*

eaves·trough (ēvz′trof′) *n* a gutter placed under the eaves of a roof to catch rainwater and carry it away.

ebb (eb) *n* **1** the receding of the tide away from the shore. **2 a** any process of growing less or weaker: *an ebb in political involvement among youth.* **b** a point in this process: *Her fortunes were at their lowest ebb.*
v **1** recede: *We waded farther out as the tide ebbed.* **2** grow less or weaker: *His courage began to ebb.* <Old English *ebba*>
ebb and flow, a the falling and rising of the tide. **b** the regular rise and fall of anything.

E·bo·la virus (i bō′lə) *n* an often fatal virus native to Africa, spread by direct contact with an infected person's bodily fluids.

E

eb·on·y (eb′ə nē) *n, pl* **eb·on·ies** a hard, usually black wood of a tropical tree, valued especially for ornamental use.
adj **1** made of ebony. **2** black; very dark. <Latin *ebeninus*>

e–book (ē′bu̇k′) *n* a book published on the Internet, or stored in and retrieved by an electronic device.

e·bul·li·ent (i bul′yənt) *adj* full of cheerfulness and energy. <Latin *ebuillire* to burst out, from *ex-* out + *bullire* to bubble> **e·bul′li·ence** *n.*

e–busi·ness (ē′biz′nis) *n* business carried out over the Internet.

EC See EUROPEAN UNION.

ec·cen·tric (ek sen′trik) *adj* **1** odd or peculiar: *eccentric clothes.* **2** not with the same centre. Compare CONCENTRIC. **3** not with a perfectly circular path or shape. **4** slightly away from the centre.
n an eccentric person or thing. <Latin, from Greek *ek-* out + *kentron* centre> **ec·cen′tri·cal·ly** *adv.*
ec′cen·tric′i·ty (ek′sen tris′ə tē) *n.*

ec·cle·si·as·tic (i klē′zē as′tik) *Christianity n* a member of the clergy.
adj usually, **ecclesiastical** to do with the church or clergy. <Latin, from Greek *ekklesia* church>
ec·cle′si·as′ti·cal·ly *adv.*

ECG *n* in full, **electrocardiogram** a record of the electric current produced by the action of the heart muscle, used in the diagnosis and treatment of heart disease. The machine that records it is called an **electrocardiograph**.

ech·e·lon (esh′ə lon′) *n* **1** a level in a set of rankings: *the upper echelons of a large company.* **2** a tiered or steplike arrangement of aircraft, troops, or vehicles. <French *échelle* ladder>

e·chid·na (i kid′nə) *n* a small, egg-laying, ant-eating mammal of Australia. <Latin, from Greek = viper>

e·chi·na·cea (ek′ə nā′shə) *n* a N American plant whose flowers consist of florets surrounding a central cone. Extracts from its roots are used as a herbal remedy. Its common name is **coneflower**. <Latin, from Greek *echinos* sea urchin. The flower cone looks like a sea urchin.>

a bat	e bed	i bid	o pot	u cup	th **thin**
ā cake	ē me	ī bite	ō go	ū rude	ᴛʜ **then**
ä bar	ə about	ər over	ȯ for	u̇ put	zh measure

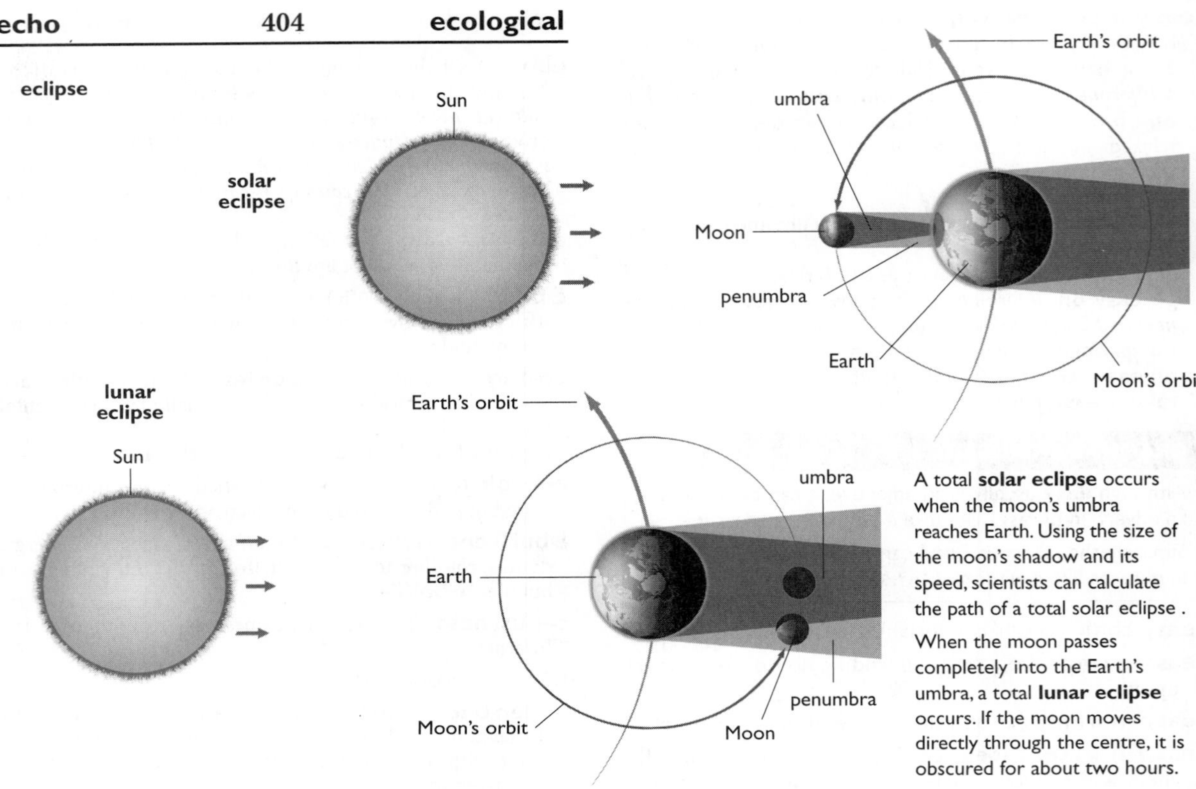

A total **solar eclipse** occurs when the moon's umbra reaches Earth. Using the size of the moon's shadow and its speed, scientists can calculate the path of a total solar eclipse .

When the moon passes completely into the Earth's umbra, a total **lunar eclipse** occurs. If the moon moves directly through the centre, it is obscured for about two hours.

ech·o (ek′ō) *n, pl* **ech·oes** **1** the repeating of a sound as it bounces back from a surface. **2 a** a repeating or imitating. **b** a person who or thing that does or seems to do this.
v **1** send back or repeat as sound: *The hills echoed the sound of the explosion.* **2** be repeated in sound: *The boom echoed through the valley.* **3** repeat the words or imitate the feelings or acts of another: *The premier's speech echoes the one made earlier by the prime minister.* <Latin, from Greek *eche* sound> **e·cho′ic** *adj.*

echo chamber *n* a room or microphone that produces hollow or echolike sound effects.

ech·o·lo·ca·tion (ek′ō lō kā′shən) *n* the process of finding the position of an object by bouncing sound waves off it, based on the time it takes for the sound waves to return (echo) and the direction from which they return.

echo sounding *n* the process of determining the depth of water or the location of an underwater object by means of an **echo sounder**, a device which emits sound waves and measures the time it takes for them to return.

é·clair (ē kler′) *or* (ā kler′) *n* a long pastry filled with whipped cream or custard and topped with chocolate icing. <French = lightning, possibly because, like lightning, an éclair is spectacular and does not last long>

ec·lec·tic (i klek′tik) *adj* selecting from various sources, kinds, or styles: *an eclectic taste in music.*
n a follower of an eclectic method. <Greek *ek-* out of + *legein* pick> **e·clec′ti·cism′** (i klek′ti siz′əm) *n.*

e·clipse (ē klips′) *n* a darkening of one celestial body, such as the sun or moon, when another body is in a position that cuts off its light as seen from the earth. A **solar eclipse** occurs when the moon passes between the sun and the earth. A **lunar eclipse** occurs when the moon enters the earth's shadow. See also ANNULAR for picture.
v **e·clipsed, e·clips·ing** **1** darken or obscure. **2** make less important by comparison: *Napoleon eclipsed other generals of his time.* <Old French, from Greek *ek-* out + *leipein* leave>

eco– *combining form* to do with the environment or habitats: *ecosystem.*

ETYMOLOGY

Eco– comes from the Greek word *oikos*, meaning "environment."

e·co·cide (ē′kə sīd′) *n* large-scale destruction of the environment or of a specific habitat.

E. co·li (ē′ kō′lī) *n* a species of bacteria (*Escherichia coli*) found in manure and human waste, which can contaminate drinking water. <T. *Escherich*, 19c physician + Latin *coli* of the colon>

e·co·log·i·cal footprint *n* an approximation of the amount of land it takes to sustain one group of humans, based on their use of energy, food, water, etc.: *The footprint of a town may be as much as 200 times the area covered by that town.*

e·co·log·i·cal terrorism ECOTERRORISM.

e·col·o·gy (ē kol′ə jē) *n* the science that studies the relation of living things to their environment and to each other. <Greek *oikos* habitation + *logos* study>
e′co·log′i·cal *adj.* **e·col′o·gist** *n.*

e–com·merce (ē′kom′ərs) *n* business carried out over the Internet.

GRAMMAR AND USAGE

E-commerce is one of many words that developed as use of the Internet increased. The **e–** is an abbreviation of *electronic*. Other such words are *e-learning, e-mail, e-trading, and e-zine.*

Similar computer-related words are being introduced all the time, such as *e-tail.*

ec·o·nom·ic (ek′ə nom′ik) *or* (ē′kə nom′ik) *adj* to do with economics or the economy: *an economic upswing.* **ec′o·nom′i·cal·ly** *adv.*

ec·o·nom·i·cal (ek′ə nom′ə kəl) *or* (ē′kə nom′ə kəl) *adj* avoiding waste: *It is more economical to buy paper in bulk.* **ec′o·nom′i·cal·ly** *adv.*

CONFUSABLES

Economical means "saving" or "avoiding waste": *Travelling by bus is an economical way to get to the city.*

Economic means "having to do with economics": *Economic issues deal with the production, distribution, and consumption of wealth.*

ec·o·nom·ics (ek′ə nom′iks) *or* (ē′kə nom′iks) *n* (*with singular verb*) the science that studies the production, distribution, and transfer of wealth. **e·con′o·mist** *n.*

e·con·o·mize (i kon′ə mīz′) *v* **e·con·o·mized, e·con·o·miz·ing 1** manage a resource so as to avoid waste. **2** cut down expenses.

e·con·o·my (i kon′ə mē) *n, pl* **e·con·o·mies 1** a system of managing the production, distribution, and transfer of wealth in a society: *the feudal economy.* **2 a** careful management to avoid waste: *Greater economy is needed in our use of energy.* **b** an example of this: *Many little economies were necessary.* **3** an organization of parts for maximum efficiency: *In the economy of a household each person has a role.*
adj relatively low in price: *The cheapest air fare available was economy class.* <Latin, from Greek *oikos* house + *nemein* manage>

ec·o·re·gion (ē′kō rē′jən) *n* an area defined by its environmental conditions. Climate, soil, and geographical features are so similar that the same kinds of plants and animals are able to live and interact anywhere in the region. See also BIOREGION. <*eco*(*logical*) + *region*>

e·co·sphere (ē′kō sfēr′) BIOSPHERE.

e·co·sys·tem (ē′kō sis′təm) *n* the system formed by the interaction of all the living things of a specific environment with one another and with their habitat: *Ecosystems are a network of interactions linking biotic and abiotic factors.*

e·co·ter·ror·ism (ē′kō ter′ər izm) *n* the use of violence by radical environmentalists to achieve their goals. Also, **ecological terrorism, ecoterror. e′co·ter′ror·ist** *n.*

e·co·tour·ism (ē′kō tūr′izm) *n* travel to areas of ecological interest, for the purpose of observing wildlife and learning about the environment. **e′co·tour′ist** *n.*

e·co·zone (ē′kō zōn′) *n* a broad geographic area, such as a desert or a wetland, in which there are characteristic climate patterns, ocean conditions, types of landscapes, and species of plants and animals.

ec·sta·sy (ek′stə sē) *n, pl* **ec·sta·sies 1** thrilling or overwhelming delight: *Speechless with ecstasy, the little girl gazed at the toys.* **2 Ecstasy** an illegal drug causing euphoria and hallucinations. <Old French, from Greek *ekstasis* trance> **ec·stat′ic** *adj.* **ec·stat′i·cal·ly** *adv.*

ECT electroconvulsive therapy.

ec·to·derm (ek′tə dərm′) *Zoology n* the outer layer of cells formed when animal embryos develop, from which the skin, hair, nails, and parts of the nervous system grow. <Greek *ektos* outside + *derma* skin>

ec·top·ic pregnancy (ek top′ik) *n* a condition in which a fertilized egg becomes implanted in a Fallopian tube instead of in the uterus, so that it cannot develop into a fetus and must be removed surgically.

ec·to·plasm (ek′tə plaz′əm) *Biology n* the outer portion of the cytoplasm of a cell. <Greek *ektos* outside + *plasma* something moulded>

Ec·ua·dor (ek′wə dȯr′) *n* a country on the northwest coast of S America. See the APPENDIX. **Ec′ua·do′re·an** *adj, n.*

ec·u·mene (ek′yə mēn′) *n* the settled or inhabited portion of a country or continent. <Greek *oikos* house>

ec·u·men·i·cal (ek′yə men′ə kəl) *adj* **1** to do with the whole Christian community. **2** promoting unity among all Christians or Christian denominations. **3** representing all faiths or promoting unity among them. <Latin, from Greek *oikoumene ge* the inhabited world>
ec′u·men·ism′ *n.*

ec·ze·ma (ek′sə mə), (eg zē′mə), *or* (eg′zə mə) *n* an inflammation of the skin, characterized by redness, itching, and the formation of scaly patches. <Latin, from Greek *ek-* out + *zeein* to boil. The sores sometimes ooze a fluid.>

ed·dy (ed′ē) *n, pl* **ed·dies** a small whirlpool or whirlwind. *v* **ed·died, ed·dy·ing** whirl against the main current: *The water eddied among the rocks.* <perhaps Old English *ed-* turning + *ea* stream>

e·del·weiss (ā′dəl vīs′) *n* a small plant of the Alps with small white flowers. <German *edel* noble + *weiss* white>

e·de·ma (i dē′mə) *n* swelling caused by an abnormal accumulation of fluid in body tissues. <Latin, from Greek *oidos* tumour>

a bat	e bed	i bid	o pot	u cup	th **thin**
ā cake	ē me	ī bite	ō go	ū rude	ᴛʜ **then**
à bar	ə about	ər over	ȯ for	ů put	zh measure

E·den (ē′dən) *n* **1** in the Bible, the garden where Adam and Eve first lived. **2** any beautiful, blissful spot. <Hebrew *eden* pleasure>

edge (ej) *n* **1** the line or place where something ends: *the edge of the page.* **2** the place near a steep drop: *to look over the edge of a cliff.* **3** a border: *a white quilt with a blue edge all around.* **4** a thin, sharp side that cuts: *a blade with two edges.* **5** an advantage: *We have a slight edge on the other team.* **6** *Mathematics* the line formed by the intersection of two faces of a solid: *A cube has 12 edges.*
v **edged, edg·ing 1** put an edge on: *She edged the path with white stones.* **2** move little by little: *He edged his chair nearer to the fire.* **3** win a narrow victory over: *Our hockey team edged the visitors 3–2.* <Old English *ecg*>
edge out, a defeat by a narrow margin: *Montréal edged out Toronto in the playoffs.* **b** gradually take the place of: *His obsession with sports is edging out all his other interests.*
on edge, nervous and tense: *She was a little on edge as she waited for the test to begin.*
set on edge, make nervous, tense, or anxious.
set your teeth on edge, irritate you very much.
take the edge off, take away the sharpness of: *A cup of herbal tea took the edge off her headache.*

edge·wise (ej′wīz′) *adv* with the edge forward. Also, **edgeways.**
get a word in edgewise, manage to say a few words during a conversation.

edg·ing (ej′ing) *n* anything forming an edge or put along an edge.

edg·y (ej′ē) *adj* **edg·i·er, edg·i·est 1** sharply defined: *edgy outlines.* **2** impatient and irritable. **3** *Slang* boldly innovative.

The destroying angel mushroom is deadly poisonous.

The fly agaric mushroom is poisonous.

Many poisonous mushrooms look similar to other mushrooms that are **edible**. Eat only those mushrooms that are known to be harmless.

ed·i·ble (ed′ə bəl) *adj* fit to eat: *Not all mushrooms are edible.*
n **edibles** *pl* food. <Latin *edere* eat>

e·dict (ē′dikt) *n* a command to the public by some authority; a decree. <Latin *ex-* out + *dicere* say>

ed·i·fice (ed′ə fis) *n* a building, especially a large or imposing one. <Latin *aedis* building + *facere* to make>

ed·i·fy (ed′ə fī′) *v* **ed·i·fied, ed·i·fy·ing** improve or strengthen morally or spiritually. <Old French, from Latin *aedificare* build (up). See EDIFICE.> **ed′i·fi·ca′tion** *n.*

ed·it (ed′it) *v* **1** correct, condense, or change a text for publication or a speech for delivery: *to edit an essay.* **2** have charge of a publication and decide what will be printed in it: *Who edits this newspaper?* **3** prepare a final version of a film or tape by cutting and splicing. <Latin *edere* publish, from *ex-* out + *dare* give>

GRAMMAR AND USAGE

Edit your writing to make it better.

Vary sentences by making some sentences short, and others long.

To give your writing more energy, use the active voice instead of the passive voice: *Father cooked dinner,* rather than *Dinner was cooked by Father.*

Use specific and lively adjectives: *The icy wind flung the snow against their faces.*

e·di·tion (i dish′ən) *n* **1** all the copies of a publication printed alike and issued at or near the same time: *Errors appearing in the book were corrected in the next edition.* **2** the format of a publication: *a pocket edition.*

ed·i·tor (ed′ə tər) *n* **1** a person who edits, especially professionally: *a dictionary editor, a film editor.* **2** a person responsible for a certain part of a publication: *a sports editor.* **ed′i·tor·ship** *n.*

ed·i·to·ri·al (ed′ə tò′rē əl) *adj* to do with editing or editors: *editorial skills.*
n a piece in a publication or broadcast presenting an opinion on some topic. **ed′i·to′ri·al·ly** *adv.*

ed·i·to·ri·al·ize (ed′ə tò′rē ə līz′) *v* **ed·i·to·ri·al·ized, ed·i·to·ri·al·iz·ing** insert opinion into what is meant to be a factual report: *This is a straight news story; don't editorialize.*

ed·i·tor–in–chief (ed′ə tər in chēf′) *n, pl* **ed·i·tors-in-chief** the head of a staff of editors for a publication or a publishing company.

EDP electronic data processing.

ed·u·cate (ej′ə kāt′) *v* **ed·u·cat·ed, ed·u·cat·ing 1** develop in knowledge or understanding, skill, and character by instruction, study, or experience: *Schools help to educate the young. Parents are responsible for educating their children.* **2** teach or train: *We have to educate people to drink responsibly.* **3** send to school. <Latin *educare* bring up, raise>

educated guess *n* a guess based on experience.

ed·u·ca·tion (ej′ə kā′shən) *n* **1** the process of educating or the experience of being educated: *Where did you get your education?* **2** a social science that studies methods and styles of teaching and learning.

ed·u·ca·tion·al (ej′ə kā′shə nəl) *adj* **1** to do with education: *an educational association.* **2** having the aim or effect of teaching something: *an educational film. That was an educational experience!* **ed′u·ca′tion·al·ly** *adv.*

ed·u·ca·tor (ej′ə kā′tər) *n* **1** a teacher. **2** an authority on methods and principles of education.

Ed·war·di·an (ed wòr′dē ən) *adj* to do with King Edward VII or his reign (1901–1910).
n a person who lived during the reign of this king.

–ee *suffix* **1** one who is or does something: *absentee.* **2** one to whom something is done, or who receives something: *appointee.* <French *-é* suffix on past participles>

EEC See EUROPEAN UNION.

EEG *n* in full, **electroencephalogram** a record of the brain's electrical activity, used in diagnosis. The machine that produces it is an **electroencephalograph**.

eel (ēl) *n* **1** a fish with a long, usually scaleless, snakelike body. **2** any of certain other fishes with a similar shape, such as the electric eel or the LAMPREY. <Old English *ael*>

–eer *suffix* a person who makes, works with, or is concerned with: *auctioneer.* <French *-ier*>

e'er (er) *Poetic adv* ever.

ee·rie (ē′rē) *adj* **ee·ri·er, ee·ri·est** strange in a frightening way: *an eerie scream.* <Old English> **ee′ri·ly** *adv.* **ee′ri·ness** *n.*

ef·face (ə fās′) *v* **ef·faced, ef·fac·ing** erase: *The inscription on the old gravestone had been effaced.* <French, from Latin *ex-* away + *facies* form> **ef·face′a·ble** *adj.*

ef·fect (i fekt′) *n* **1** whatever is brought about by a cause: *The overturned boats were the effect of the gale.* **2** influence: *The medicine had an immediate effect.* **3** an impression produced: *The sun coming through the leaves creates a lovely effect. I forget her exact words, but the main effect was "No."* **4** *Physics* a phenomenon in nature, usually named for its discoverer: *Doppler effect.* **5 effects** *pl* belongings: *He lost all his personal effects in the fire.*
v bring about: *to effect a change.* <Latin *effectus*, from *efficere* work out, accomplish>
for effect, as a way to impress others.
in effect, in fact or in operation, even if not explicitly stated: *The new rules are now in effect. In effect, he said he was giving up.*
put into effect, put into force or operation: *We immediately put our plan into effect.*
take effect, begin to operate: *The new prices will take effect on January 1st.*
to the effect (that), with a certain meaning, although not necessarily in those words: *He made a rule to the effect that no one could leave early.*

CONFUSABLES

Effect is usually a noun, meaning "a result": *What effect did the storm have?*

Affect is a verb meaning "influence": *How did the storm affect you?*

Sometimes, especially in formal texts, **effect** is a verb meaning "cause" or "bring about."

ef·fec·tive (i fek′tiv) *adj* **1** producing the desired effect: *an effective treatment for acne.* **2** in operation or force: *Effective today, my e-mail address has changed. The new law will become effective on January 1st.* **3** for practical purposes: *Increases in the cost of living have reduced our family's effective income.* **ef·fec′tive·ly** *adv.* **ef·fec′tive·ness** *n.*

ef·fec·tu·al (i fek′chū əl) *adj* actually accomplishing something: *taking effectual steps to reduce poverty.* **ef·fec′tu·al·ly** *adv.*

ef·fem·i·nate (i fem′ə nit) *adj* of a male, showing qualities supposed to be typical of a woman. <Latin *effeminare* make a woman of, from *ex-* out + *femina* woman> **ef·fem′i·na·cy** *n.* **ef·fem′i·nate·ly** *adv.*

ef·fer·ves·cent (ef′ər ves′ənt) *adj* **1** giving off bubbles of gas. **2** lively and high-spirited. <Latin *ex-* out + *fervescere* start to boil> **ef′fer·ves′cence** *n.*

ef·fete (i fēt′) *adj* **1** no longer productive. **2** over-refined and unproductive. <Latin *effetus* unproductive, from *ex-* out of + *fetus* offspring> **ef·fete′ness** *n.*

E

ef·fi·ca·cious (ef′ə kā′shəs) *adj* able to produce the desired effect: *Vaccination for flu is usually efficacious.* <Latin *efficere*> **ef′fi·ca′cious·ly** *adv.* **ef′fi·ca·cy** (ef′ə kə sē) *n.*

ef·fi·cien·cy (ə fish′ən si) *n* **1** the fact of being efficient. **2** *Physics* the ratio of work output to work input.

ef·fi·cient (ə fish′ənt) *adj* not wasting time or effort: *an efficient worker. A more efficient furnace uses less gas.* <Latin *ex-* out + *facere* do, make> **ef·fi′cient·ly** *adv.*

ef·fi·gy (ef′ə jē) *n, pl* **ef·fi·gies** a figure meant to represent a person. <Latin *effigies* copy of an object>
burn (or **hang**) **in effigy,** burn (or hang) a stuffed image of a person to show hatred or contempt.

ef·flu·ent (ef′lū ənt) *n* something flowing out, especially liquid waste or sewage. <Latin *ex-* out + *fluere* flow>

ef·flu·vi·um (i flū′vē əm) *n, pl* **ef·flu·vi·a** or **ef·flu·vi·ums** an unpleasant odour. <Latin *ex-* out + *fluere* flow>

ef·fort (ef′ərt) *n* **1** the use of mental energy or physical strength to do something: *Climbing a steep hill takes effort.* **2** a serious try: *You could at least make an effort to be on time.* **3** something produced by effort: *His latest effort, a detective novel, is worth reading.* **4** *Physics* the amount of energy required to perform a certain amount of work. <French, from Latin *ex-* out + *fortis* strong>

ef·fort·less (ef′ərt lis) *adj* involving little or no effort. **ef′fort·less·ly** *adv.* **ef′fort·less·ness** *n.*

ef·fron·ter·y (ə frun′tə rē) *n, pl* **ef·fron·ter·ies** insolent or insulting behaviour: *After refusing to lend me money, she had the effrontery to laugh.* <Old French *esfronté*, barefaced, i.e., shameless, from Latin *ex-* without + *frons* forehead>

ef·ful·gent (i ful′jənt) *adj* shining brightly. <Latin *ex-* forth + *fulgere* shine> **ef·ful′gence** *n.* **ef·ful′gent·ly** *adv.*

ef·fu·sive (i fyū′siv) *adj* gushing; showing too much emotion. <Latin *effundere* pour out> **ef·fu′sive·ly** *adv.* **ef·fu′sive·ness** *n.*

EFT *n* in full, **electronic funds transfer** a means of transferring money between bank accounts by computer.

e.g. for example. See I.E. for confusable. <Latin = *exempli gratia*>

e·gal·i·tar·i·an (i gal′ə ter′ē ən) *adj* believing in or based on treating people fairly and equally: *an egalitarian approach to management.*
n a person with egalitarian attitudes. <French *égal* equal>

a bat	e bed	i bid	o pot	u cup	th **thin**
ā cake	ē me	ī bite	ō go	ū rude	ᴛʜ **then**
à bar	ə about	ər over	ô for	ů put	zh measure

egg[1] (eg) *n* **1** a roundish object that is covered with a shell or membrane and usually contains a developing embryo. It is laid by the female of birds, reptiles, fish, or invertebrates. See ALBUMEN for picture. **2** something resembling an egg in shape. **3** a female reproductive cell. <Old English *eggian*> **egg′less** *adj.* **egg′like′** *adj.* **eg′gy** *adj.*
have egg on your face, *Informal* be embarrassed.
put all your eggs in one basket, risk everything on one chance.

egg[2] (eg) *v* (*with* ***on***) encourage to do something foolish or wrong: *The other boys egged him on to fight.* <Old Norse *egg* edge, point>

egg·beat·er (eg′bē′tər) *n* a kitchen utensil for beating a liquid, especially a hand-operated one with rotary blades.

egg cell *n* the mature female reproductive cell produced by the ovary of a plant or animal and developing into a new plant or animal if fertilized.

egg cup *n* a small cup in which a boiled egg is placed to be eaten.

egg·head (eg′hed′) *Informal n* an intellectual.

egg·nog (eg′nog′) *n* a drink made of eggs beaten with milk, spices, and sugar, often containing some alcoholic beverage. <*egg* + *nog* strong ale>

egg·plant (eg′plant′) *n* the egg-shaped fruit of a plant of the nightshade family, eaten as a vegetable.

egg roll *n* a small, deep-fried pastry containing chopped vegetables and, often, pieces of meat or seafood.

egg·shell (eg′shel′) *n* the shell covering an egg.
adj **1** thin and delicate, like an eggshell.

egg timer *n* a device, often shaped like a miniature hourglass, for timing the boiling of an egg.

egg tooth *n* a small projection in the upper part of a bird's beak or reptile's jaw, used by the embryo to break the eggshell when hatching.

egg white *n* the clear part of an egg surrounding the yolk. It turns white during cooking.

e·go (ē′gō) *n* **1** a person's sense of self-esteem: *He has an ego the size of Lake Superior.* **2** in psychoanalysis, the part of the personality that governs personal identity. <Latin = I>

e·go·cen·tric (ē′gō sen′trik) *adj* thinking only of oneself.

e·go·ma·ni·a (ē′gō mā′nē ə) *n* extreme self-centredness. **e′go·ma′ni·ac′** *n.* **e′go·ma·ni′a·cal** (ē′gō mə nī′ə kəl) *adj.*

e·go·tism (ē′gə tiz′əm) *n* excessive attention paid to oneself, and one's own needs and interests. **e′go·tist** *n.* **e′go·tis′ti·cal** *adj.*

ego trip *n* something done to enhance feelings of power and prestige: *That newspaper column of his is just an ego trip.* **e′go-trip′** *v.* **e′go-trip′per** *n.*

e·gre·gious (i grē′jəs) *adj* remarkably or extraordinarily bad: *an egregious lie.* <Latin *egregius* = standing out from the herd, from *ex-* out of + *gregis* flock, herd>
e·gre′gious·ly *adv.* **e·gre′gious·ness** *n.*

e·gress (ē′gres) *n* the action, means, or right of going out; exit: *With rubble blocking the opening, there was no egress from the cave. The hostages were denied egress.* Compare INGRESS. <Latin *egredi*, from *ex-* out + *gradi* step, go>

e·gret (ē′gret) *n* a heron that in mating season grows long plumes. <French *aigrette*>

E·gypt (ē′jipt) *adj* a country in northeast Africa. See the APPENDIX. **E·gyp′tian** *adj, n.*

eh (ā) *interj* **1** 🍁 used to invite agreement, explanation, or to confirm that something is heard: *It sure is hot, eh? He was just minding his own business, eh, when this guy started yelling at him.* **2** used to express doubt, surprise, or failure to hear exactly: *Eh? What did you say?*

EI EMPLOYMENT INSURANCE.

Eid al–Fitr (ēd′ ȧl fit′rə) *Islam n* one of the two main festivals, celebrated at the end of the month-long fast of Ramadan. The other is **Eid ul-Adha** (ēd′ ūl ȧ′də).

ei·der (ī′dər) *n* a large northern sea duck, the female having soft feathers on its breast. <Icelandic *æthr*>

ei·der·down (ī′dər doun′) *n* **1** the soft breast feathers from eider ducks, used to stuff pillows and bedding. **2** a quilt stuffed with these feathers.

eight (āt) *n* **1** a cardinal number that is one more than seven. **2** the numeral 8.
adj **1** one more than seven: *She sneezed eight times.* **2** (*after the noun*) eighth in a series: *Section Eight is missing.*
eighth *adj, adv.*
behind the eight ball, *Informal* in most unfavourable circumstances: *That delay has really put us behind the eight ball, and I don't know if we'll make the deadline.*

ETYMOLOGY

Eight is from Old English *ehta, eahta*, related to German *acht*, Latin *octo*, and Greek *okto*.
By comparing similar words in different languages, we can learn a lot about the history of those languages and the peoples who speak them.

eight·een (ā′tēn′) *n* **1** a cardinal number that is eight more than ten. **2** the numeral 18.
adj **1** eight more than ten: *I sent eighteen invitations.* **2** (*after the noun*) eighteenth in a series: *Chapter Eighteen.* <Old English *eahtatene*> **eight′eenth′** *adj, adv.*

eight·eenth (ā′tēnth′) *n* **1** next after the seventeenth: *I am eighteenth in the movie line.* **2** one of eighteen equal parts: *an eighteenth part of the profit.*
adj, adv See EIGHTEEN.

eight·fold (āt′fōld′) *adj, adv* **1** eight times as much or as many. **2** consisting of eight parts.

eighth (ātth) *adj, n* **1** next after the seventh: *on the eighth day* (*adj*), *eighth in line* (*n*). **2** one, or being one, of eight equal parts: *an eighth part of the total amount* (*adj*). *An eighth of the population left the town* (*n*). **eighth′ly** *adv.*

eighth note *Music n* a note lasting one eighth of a whole note, written with a tail. Symbol ♪

eight·i·eth (ā′tē əth′) *n* **1** next after the seventy-ninth. **2** one of eighty equal parts.
adj, adv See EIGHTY.

eight·y (ā′tē) *n, pl* **eight·ies** **1** eight times ten. **2** **eighties** *pl* the years from eighty through eighty-nine, especially of a century or of a person's life: *My great-grandmother is in her eighties.*
adj **1** eight times ten: *eighty years old.* **2** (*after the noun*) eightieth in a series: *page eighty.* <Old English *eahtatig*> **eigh′ti·eth** *adj, adv.*

ein·stein·i·um (īn stī′nē əm) *n* a rare, radioactive artificial element, a by-product of nuclear fission. *Symbol* **Es** <A. *Einstein*, 20c physicist>

ei·ther (ē′ᴛʜər) *or* (ī′ᴛʜər) *adj* **1** one or the other of two: *She can write with either hand.* **2** each of two: *On either side of the river lie cornfields.*
pron one or the other of two: *Either of us will be there.*
conj one or the other of two actions: *Either come in or go out.*
adv (*with a negative*) also: *If you don't go, I won't go either.* <Old English *a* always + *gehwæther* each of two>

GRAMMAR AND USAGE

In informal use, when **either** is followed by a plural noun, the verb can be plural, too: *Either of these CDs are worth listening to.* In formal speech or writing, however, the verb should be singular: *Either of the first two volumes is superior to the last of the trilogy.*

e·jac·u·late (i jak′yə lāt′) *v* **e·jac·u·lat·ed, e·jac·u·lat·ing** **1** say suddenly and briefly. **2** eject semen. <Latin *ex-* out + *jacere* throw> **e·jac′u·la′tion** *n.*

e·ject (i jekt′) *v* **1** throw out with force: *The volcano ejected lava and ashes.* **2** force to leave: *The landlady ejected the tenant who did not pay his rent.* <Latin *ex-* out + *jacere* throw> **e·jec′tion** *n.* **e·jec′tor** *n.*

ejection seat *n* in an aircraft, a seat that can be instantly ejected with its occupant, to be parachuted to earth. Also, **ejector seat**.

eke (ēk) *v* **eked, ek·ing** (*with* **out**) add to something or use it sparingly to make it go further: *He eked out his income by working evenings. They eked out their powdered milk supply by using extra water with it.* <Old English *eaca* addition>
eke out a living, barely make a living.

e·lab·o·rate (i lab′ə rit) *for adj,* (i lab′ ə rāt′) *for v. adj* in great detail: *He gave his parents an elaborate description of the video game he wanted.*
v **e·lab·o·rat·ed, e·lab·o·rat·ing** work out, talk, or write with great care or in detail: *My sister spent months elaborating her wedding plans. Could you elaborate on your answer?* <Latin *ex-* out + *labor* work>
e·lab′o·rate·ly *adv.* **e·lab′o·rate·ness** *n.*

é·lan (ā län′) *n* flair and enthusiasm. <French *élancer* rush forward>

e·land (ē′lənd) *n* a large, heavily built African antelope with spiral horns. <Dutch = elk>

e·lapse (i laps′) *v* **e·lapsed, e·laps·ing** slip away or glide by: *Several hours elapsed while she slept.* <Latin *ex-* away + *labi* glide>

e·las·tic (i las′tik) *n* **1** a thin circular strip of stretchy rubber, used to hold things together. **2** tape or fabric woven partly of rubber threads to make it stretchy: *You need a piece of elastic for the waistband.*
adj **1** able to be stretched and then spring back to its original shape: *Balloons are elastic.* **2** flexible and adaptable: *an elastic schedule.* <Latin, from Greek *elastos* flexible> **e·las′ti·cal·ly** *adv.* **e·las′tic′i·ty** (i las′tis′ə tē) *n.*

e·las·ti·cize (i las′ti sīz′) *v* **e·las·ti·cized, e·las·ti·ciz·ing** make stretchy with elastic: *an elasticized waistband.*

e·lat·ed (i lā′tid) *adj* proud and joyful. <Latin *elatus* elevated> **e·lat′ed·ly** *adv.* **e·la′tion** *n.*

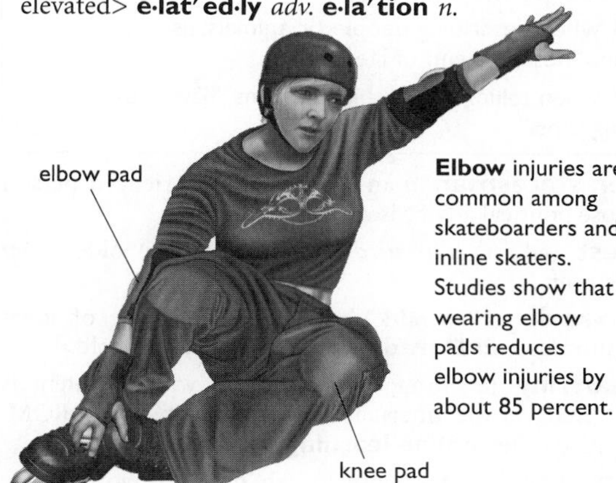

Elbow injuries are common among skateboarders and inline skaters. Studies show that wearing elbow pads reduces elbow injuries by about 85 percent.

el·bow (el′bō) *n* **1** the joint connecting the upper arm and forearm. **2** the outer part of this joint, especially the point formed by the bent arm. **3** anything resembling a bent elbow in shape or position.
v **1** push or jab someone with the elbow: *They elbowed me off the sidewalk.* **2** proceed by pushing with the elbows: *He elbowed his way to the front.* <Old English *eln* length of lower arm + *boga* bow[2]>
at your elbow, close by: *When I do my homework, a dictionary is always at my elbow.*
rub elbows with, mingle with: *At the rock festival, musicians rubbed elbows with fans.*

elbow grease *n* hard work.

elbow room *n* enough space to move or work in.

eld·er (el′dər) *adj* (*used mainly of people; never in a comparison with* **than**) older: *my elder sister.*
n **1** a person older than oneself: *Show respect for your elders.* **2** one of the older and more influential people of a community who help lead or govern it. **3** *Christianity* an official with spiritual or pastoral duties. <Old English *eldra*, from *eald* old>

GRAMMAR AND USAGE

Use **elder** and **eldest** when you're talking about the ages of people within families. Use *older* and *oldest* when referring to the ages of other people or things.

a bat	e bed	i bid	o pot	u cup	th **thin**
ā cake	ē me	ī bite	ō go	ū rude	ᴛʜ **then**
ä bar	ə about	ər over	ô for	ů put	zh measure

el·der·ber·ry (el′dər ber′ē) *n, pl* **el·der·ber·ries** a shrub or tree with flat clusters of white **elderflowers** and tiny edible purple berrylike fruits. <Old English *ellærn* + *berry*>

eld·er·ly (el′dər lē) *adj* old or growing old.

GRAMMAR AND USAGE

Elderly is used only to describe people, and means "past middle age and getting old."

Old, when describing people or animals, usually means "near the end of life."

Old, when telling about things, means "having existed a long time."

elder statesman *n* an influential, experienced person whose political advice is respected.

eld·est (el′dist) *adj* (*used mainly of people*) oldest: *her eldest son.*

El·do·ra·do (el′də rä′dō) *n* a legendary place of great wealth. Also, **El Dorado**. <Spanish = place of gold>

e–learn·ing (ē′lərn ing) *n* learning in which content is delivered via the Internet, audiovisual tapes, CD-ROM, etc. Also called **online learning**.

e·lect (i lekt′) *v* **1** choose for an office by voting: *The students elect a new class representative each year.* **2** choose: *We elected to play baseball.*
adj **1** (*in compounds, after the noun*) elected but not yet in office: *the president-elect.* **2** specially chosen.
n **the elect** people who belong to a specially chosen, privileged group. <Latin *ex-* out + *legere* choose>

e·lec·tion (i lek′shən) *n* **1** the process of electing members to a legislative body or council. **2** any act of electing or choosing.

e·lec·tion·eer (i lek′shə nēr′) *v* work for a candidate or political party in an election.

e·lec·tive (i lek′tiv) *adj* **1** optional: *elective surgery, an elective school subject.* **2** to do with election rather than appointment: *an elective office.*
n an optional course or school subject.

e·lec·tor (i lek′tər) *n* **1** a person who has the right to vote in an election. **2** in former times, a prince who had the right to elect the emperor of the Holy Roman Empire. **e·lec′tor·al** *adj.*

electoral college *US n* a group of people chosen by individual states to formally elect the president and vice-president in keeping with the results of a national election.

e·lec·tor·ate (i lek′tə rit) *n* all the people who have the right to vote in an election.

e·lec·tric (i lek′trik) *adj* **1** charged with, using, or producing electricity: *an electric train, an electric guitar.* **2** capable of giving an electric shock: *an electric eel.* **3** thrilling: *an electric performance.* <Latin *electricus,* from Greek *elektron* amber. Amber is a resin that generates an electrostatic charge when it is rubbed.>
e·lec′tri·cal·ly *adv.*

e·lec·tri·cal (i lek′trə kəl) *adj* to do with electricity: *an electrical charge, electrical equipment.*

ETYMOLOGY

Electrical and other words beginning with **electr–** can all be traced back to Greek *elektron,* meaning "amber." In early experiments, scientists rubbed amber in order to get an electrostatic charge.

The word *electrical* was first used in 1635. Other words with this root include *electricity, electrician, electrify,* and *electronic.*

electrical engineering *n* the branch of engineering dealing with electricity, especially in its practical applications.

electrical storm or **electric storm** *n* a storm accompanied by much thunder and lightning.

electric chair *n* the chair used for electrocuting convicted criminals.

electric eel *n* a large fish of S America, capable of giving strong electric shocks.

electric eye *n* a photoelectric cell.

e·lec·tri·cian (i lek′trish′ən) *n* a person who installs, repairs, or maintains electrical equipment.

e·lec·tric·i·ty (i lek′tris′ə tē) *n* **1** a form of energy created by the behaviour of charged particles, such as electrons or protons, that is expressed in such phenomena as light, heat, and magnetism. **2** a supply of electric current. **3** a feeling of excitement.

electric ray *n* a fish found in warm seas that stuns its prey or predators by means of shocks produced by an electrical organ.

e·lec·tri·fy (i lek′trə fī′) *v* **e·lec·tri·fied, e·lec·tri·fy·ing** **1** charge with electricity. **2** equip to use electricity: *Some railways once run by steam are now electrified.* **3** excite or thrill: *The speaker electrified her audience.*
e·lec′tri·fi·ca′tion *n.*

electro– *combining form* to do with electricity: *electromagnet, electrotherapy.*

e·lec·tro·car·di·o·gram (i lek′trō kär′dē ə gram′) ECG.

e·lec·tro·chem·i·cal cell (i lek′trō kem′ə kəl) *n* a battery that produces an electric current by means of chemical action.

e·lec·tro·con·vul·sive therapy (i lek′trō kon vul′səv) *n* the treatment of mental disorders, especially depression, by means of electric shock. *Abbrev.* **ECT**

e·lec·tro·cute (i lek′trə kyūt′) *v* **e·lec·tro·cut·ed, e·lec·tro·cut·ing** kill by means of an electric current. <*electro-* + (*exe*)*cute*> **e·lec′tro·cu′tion** *n.*

e·lec·trode (i lek′trōd) *n* a metal conductor through which an electric current flows into or out of a conducting medium. <*electro-* + *-ode,* on the pattern of anode and cathode>

e·lec·tro·en·ceph·a·lo·gram (i lek′trō en sef′ə lə gram′) EEG.

e·lec·trol·o·gist (i lek′trol′ə jist) *n* a person who removes warts, moles, unwanted hair, etc. by electrolysis.

electronic and electric instruments

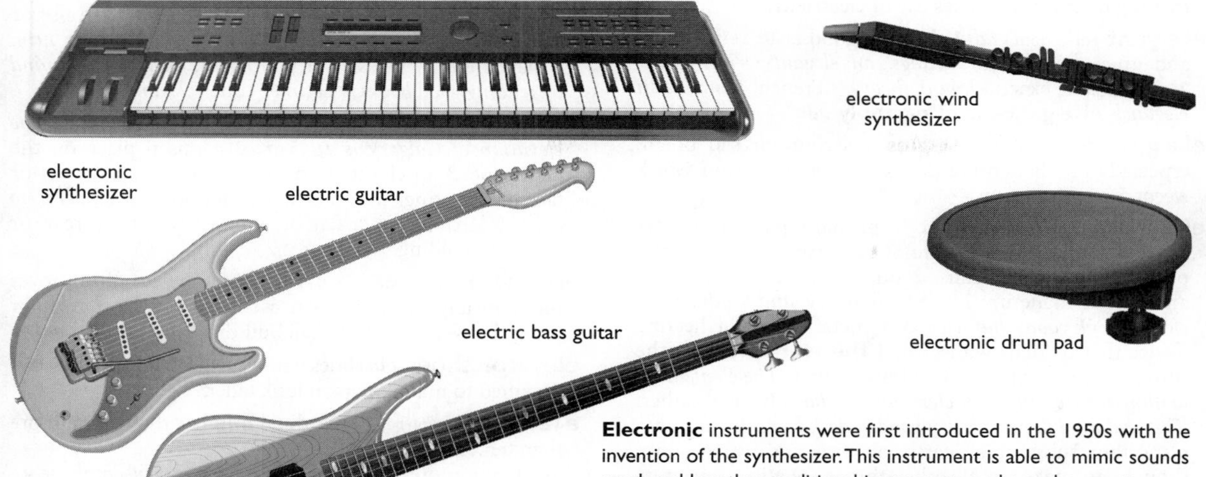

Electronic instruments were first introduced in the 1950s with the invention of the synthesizer. This instrument is able to mimic sounds produced by other traditional instruments and can also create sounds that no other instrument can make.

An electronic instrument produces sound in a different way from the traditional instrument it looks like. For example, an electronic drum doesn't have a skin that vibrates. When the stick contacts the pad it triggers a programmed sound that is heard through speakers.

E

e·lec·tro·lyse (i lek′trə līz′) *v* **e·lec·tro·lysed, e·lec·tro·lys·ing** break down into chemical components by ELECTROLYSIS (def. 1).

e·lec·trol·y·sis (i lek′trol′ə sis) *n* **1** the breakdown of a chemical compound into ions by passing an electric current through a solution containing it. **2** the removal of excess hair or small blemishes by destroying tissue with an electrified needle. <*electro-* + Greek *lysis* a loosening, from *lyein* to set free>

e·lec·tro·lyte (i lek′trə līt′) *n* **1** a solution of water and a chemical compound that will conduct an electric current. See ELECTROLYSIS (def. 1). **2** an ion, such as potassium or sodium, that a body cell requires to regulate the electric charge and flow of water molecules.

e·lec·tro·lyt·ic (i lek′trə lit′ik) *adj* to do with electrolysis or with an electrolyte. **e·lec′tro·lyt′i·cal·ly** *adv.*

e·lec·tro·mag·net (i lek′trō mag′nit) *n* a strong magnet made by coiling wire around an iron core and applying an electric current to the coil. **e·lec′tro·mag·net′ic** *adj.* **e·lec′tro·mag′net·ism′** *n.*

electromagnetic wave *n* a wave of energy, such as a radio wave, light wave, or X-ray that can travel through space or matter.

e·lec·tro·mo·tive force (i lek′trō mō′tiv) *n* the amount of energy derived from an electric source when a unit of current passes through the source.

e·lec·tron (i lek′tron) *Chemistry, Physics n* an elementary particle carrying one unit of negative electric charge. See ATOM for picture.

electron beam *n* a stream of electrons moving in the same direction at the same speed.

e·lec·tron·ic (i lek′tron′ik) *adj* to do with electronics and related technology, especially computers.
n **electronics 1** (*with singular verb*) the branch of physics that studies the production, activity and effects of electrons. **2** (*with plural verb*) technology making use of the principles of electronics, such as radio, TV, radar, and computers. **e·lec′tron′ic·al·ly** *adv.*

electronic banking *n* banking activities carried out at a bank machine or over the Internet from one's computer.

electronic flash *n* a flash lamp, often attached to a camera.

electronic mail E-MAIL.

electron microscope *n* a microscope that uses beams of electrons instead of beams of light and has much higher power than any ordinary microscope.

electron tube *n* a device producing a controlled flow of electrons between electrodes within a sealed glass or metal tube.

e·lec·tron·volt (i lek′tron vōlt′) *n* a unit of the kinetic energy of electrons, equal to about 1.6×10^{-19} joules. *Symbol* **eV**

e·lec·tro·plate (i lek′trə plāt′) *v* **e·lec·tro·plat·ed, e·lec·tro·plat·ing** coat with a metal by means of ELECTROLYSIS (def. 1). **e·lec′tro·plat′er** *n.*

e·lec·tro·stat·ic (i lek′trō stat′ik) *adj* to do with electric charges that are stationary instead of flowing as a current.

a bat	e bed	i bid	o pot	u cup	th **thin**
ā cake	ē me	ī bite	ō go	ū rude	ᴛʜ **then**
à bar	ə about	ər over	ȯ for	u̇ put	zh measure

e·lec·tro·ther·a·py (i lek′trō ther′ə pē) *n* any method of treating disease that makes use of electricity.

el·e·gant (el′ə gənt) *adj* **1** showing good taste, refinement, and grace: *elegant furnishings, an elegant writing style.* **2** simple and exact: *elegant theory.* <French, from Latin *elegans*> **el′e·gance** *n.* **el′e·gant·ly** *adv.*

el·e·gy (el′ə jē) *n, pl* **el·e·gies** a serious or sad poem, especially one lamenting the dead. <French, from Greek *elegos* mournful poem>

el·e·ment (el′ə mənt) *n* **1** a primary part of matter composed of atoms that cannot be separated into simpler parts by chemical means. **2** one of the parts of which anything is made up: *Honesty, industry, and kindness are elements of good character.* **3** a metal coil in a heating device that reddens with heat. **4 the elements** *pl* **a** the simple, necessary parts to be learned first: *The elements of arithmetic are taught in elementary school.* **b** the weather: *This sealant will protect the wooden deck from the elements.* **c** the four substances—earth, air, fire, and water—once thought to make up all other things. <Latin *elementum* rudiment, first principle>
in your element, in the environment or activity to which you are best suited and which you like best.

el·e·men·tal (el′ə men′təl) *adj* **1** basic, simple, and rooted in nature: *The need for love is elemental in humans.* **2** essential: *an elemental ingredient in a recipe.*

el·e·men·ta·ry (el′ə men′tə rē) *adj* to do with the first, basic, or simplest aspects of a subject: *elementary physics*

elementary particle *Physics n* a basic component of matter found within an atom, such as an electron, positron, or photon.

elementary school *n* a school of five to eight grades for children aged six and over. Also called **grade school**.

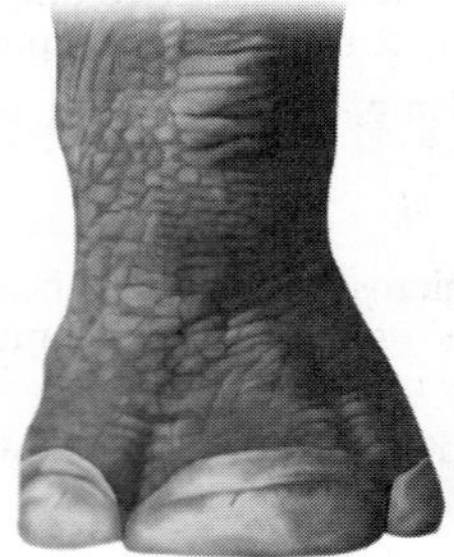

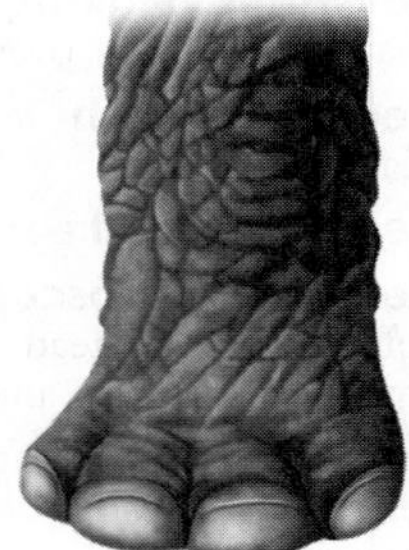

three toes

four toes

African **elephants** have three toes on their hind legs, and four or five toes on their front legs. Indian elephants have four toes on their hind legs, and five toes on their front legs.

el·e·phant (el′ə fənt) *n* a huge animal of Africa and Asia, with almost hairless grey skin, large ears, and a long, flexible snout called a trunk. They are the largest land animals now living. See also UNGULATE for picture. <Old French, from Greek *elephantis* elephant, ivory>
el′e·phan′tine (el′ə fan′tēn) *adj.*

el·e·phan·ti·a·sis (el′ə fan tī′ə sis) *n* a disease caused by parasitic worms that block the flow of lymph. Parts of the body, usually the legs, become greatly enlarged.

el·e·vate (el′ə vāt′) *v* **el·e·vat·ed, el·e·vat·ing 1** raise or lift up: *The physiotherapist told her to elevate her arm.* **2** make more impressive or important: *to elevate the mind by reading good books.* <Latin *ex-* out + *levare* raise>

el·e·va·tion (el′ə vā′shən) *n* **1** height above sea level: *The elevation of Calgary is 1045 m.* **2** a raised place on the landscape. **3** an elevated position or quality. **4** the act or fact of elevating: *the elevation of the Roman emperor to deity.* **5** *Architecture* a flat drawing of the front, rear, or side of a building.

el·e·va·tor (el′ə vā′tər) *n* **1** a compartment that moves mechanically up and down a shaft, carrying people or things between levels. **2** a tall building for storing grain.

elevator shoes *pln* shoes with very thick soles or insoles, designed to make a person look taller.

e·lev·en (i lev′ən) *n* **1** a cardinal number that is one more than ten. **2** the numeral 11.
adj **1** one more than ten: *There were eleven empty seats.* **2** (*after the noun*) eleventh in a series: *Section Eleven.* <Old English *endleofan* one left (over ten)>
e·lev′enth *adj, adv.*
(at) the eleventh hour, (at) the very last moment.

e·lev·enth (i lev′ənth) *n* **1** next after the tenth: *eleventh in line at the checkout.* **2** one of eleven equal parts: *an eleventh of 22 is 2.*
adj, adv See ELEVEN.

elf (elf) *n, pl* **elves** a mythological being of folk tales, often portrayed as having pointed ears, a mischievous personality, and magical powers. <Old English *ælf*>
elf′ish or **elv′ish** *adj.* **elf′like′** *adj.*

elf·in (el′fən) *adj* like an elf: *an elfin smile.*

e·lic·it (i lis′it) *v* get from someone: *to elicit a reply.* <Latin *ex-* out + *lacere* persuade> **e·lic′i·ta′tion** *n.*

e·lide (i līd′) *v* **e·lid·ed, e·lid·ing** omit or slur over in pronunciation. <Latin *ex-* out + *laedere* to strike>

el·i·gi·ble (el′ə jə bəl) *adj* **1** meeting requirements set by law or a rule: *Only those 12 to 16 years of age are eligible for the contest.* **2** suitable and desirable: *an eligible candidate.* <French, from Latin *eligere* choose> **el′i·gi·bil′i·ty** *n.*

e·lim·i·nate (i lim′ə nāt′) *v* **e·lim·i·nat·ed, e·lim·i·nat·ing 1** get rid of: *to eliminate a problem, to eliminate salt from your diet.* **2** put out of a competition by defeating: *Our team was eliminated in the first round of the hockey playoffs.* **3** *Mathematics* get rid of an unknown quantity by combining equations. **4** expel waste from the body. <Latin *eliminare* thrust outside, remove, from *ex-* out + *limen* doorway> **e·lim′i·na′tion** *n.*

e·li·sion (i lizh′ən) *n* the omission of a vowel or syllable in pronunciation.

e·lite or **é·lite** (i lēt′) *or* (ā lēt′) *n* a group of people with a privileged status because of talent, power, wealth, or social position: *He is a member of the sporting elite.*
adj to do with an elite; exclusive; distinguished: *Olympic medal winners are an elite group.* <French, from Latin *eligere*>

e·lit·ism or **é·lit·ism** (i lē′tiz əm) *or* (ā lē′tiz əm) *n* **1** a policy of serving or catering to the elite only: *Do all private schools practise elitism?* **2** awareness of belonging to an elite: *Her attitude shows her elitism.* **e·lit′ist** or **é·lit′ist** *adj, n.*

e·lix·ir (i lik′sər) *n* a magical or medicinal substance supposed to have special power. <Arabic *al-iksir*>

E·liz·a·be·than (i liz′ə bē′thən) *adj* to do with the period during which Queen Elizabeth I reigned (1533–1603).
n a person who lived during this period.

Elizabethan sonnet *n* a form of sonnet used by Shakespeare and other writers of the same period. Its rhyme scheme is *abab cdcd efef gg.* Also called **Shakespearean sonnet**. Compare ITALIAN SONNET, PETRARCHAN SONNET.

elk (elk) *n, pl* **elks** or (*especially collectively*) **elk** **1** a large N American mammal that is brown with a light-coloured rump patch, long shaggy hair covering the neck and shoulders, and, in the adult male, large antlers. See DEER for picture. **2** a large deer of Europe and Asia, considered to be of the same species as the moose. <Old English *eolh*>

el·lipse (i lips′) *Mathematics n* an oval with both ends alike. Any plane surface formed by cutting through a cone at an angle to the base, but not passing through the base, is an ellipse. <See ELLIPSIS.>

el·lip·sis (i lip′sis) *n, pl* **el·lip·ses** (i lip′sēz) **1** *Grammar* the leaving out of a word or words in a sentence, without losing the meaning. In *She is as strong as I am, but not as fast,* there is an ellipsis of the words *as I am* after the word *fast.* **2** a series of dots [...], used to show words left out in writing or printing. <Latin, from Greek *elleipein* leave out>

el·lip·ti·cal (i lip′tə kəl) *adj* **1** shaped like or to do with an ellipse. **2** omitting words that can be figured out from context: *This writer has an elliptical style.*
el·lip′ti·cal·ly *adv.*

elm (elm) *n* a tall hardwood tree of the northern hemisphere with rough serrated leaves. <Old English>

El Ni·ño (el nēn′yō) *n* a warm ocean current sometimes occurring off the west coast of N America that changes global weather patterns. Compare LA NIÑA. <Spanish = the boy, i.e., the Christ child, with reference to its appearance at Christmas time>

el·o·cu·tion (el′ə kyū′shən) *n* the art of speaking or reading clearly and effectively in public. <Latin *ex-* out + *loqui* speak> **el′o·cu′tion·ar·y** *adj.* **el′o·cu′tion·ist** *n.*

e·lon·gate (i long′gāt) *v* **e·lon·gat·ed, e·lon·gat·ing** lengthen; stretch: *A rubber band can be elongated to several times its normal length.* <Latin *ex-* out + *longus* long> **e′lon·ga′tion** *n.*

e·lope (i lōp′) *v* **e·loped, e·lop·ing** run away with a lover: *Juliet planned to elope with Romeo.* <Middle English *lopen* run> **e·lope′ment** *n.*

el·o·quent (el′ə kwənt) *adj* **1** expressing ideas in graceful, powerful language. **2** very expressive: *eloquent eyes.* <Old French, from Latin *ex-* out + *loqui* speak>
el′o·quence *n.* **el′o·quent·ly** *adv.*

El Sal·va·dor (el sal′və dôr′) *n* a country in Central America. See the APPENDIX. **El Sal′va·dor′e·an** *adj, n.*

else (els) *adj* **1** other; different: *What else could I say?* **2** in addition: *I'm here; are you expecting anyone else?*
adv **1** differently: *How else can it be done?* **2** (*usually preceded by* ***or***) otherwise; if not: *Hurry or else you will be late.* <Old English *elles*>
or else! *Informal* or there will be serious consequences: *You'd better be back on time, or else!*

else·where (els′wer′) *adv* in or to some other place.

e·lu·ci·date (i lū′sə dāt′) *v* **e·lu·ci·dat·ed, e·lu·ci·dat·ing** make clear; explain: *to elucidate a theory.* <Latin *elucidare* make clear> **e·lu′ci·da′tion** *n.*

e·lude (i lūd′) *v* **e·lud·ed, e·lud·ing** **1** slip away from; avoid or escape: *The sly fox eluded the dogs.* **2** fail to be found by: *Success has eluded the team again.* <Latin *ex-* out + *ludere* play>

CONFUSABLES

Elude means "escape" or "slip away from": *So far, the the thief has eluded the police.*

Allude means "mention" or "refer to": *She alluded briefly to a painful experience in her past.*

e·lu·sive (i lū′siv) *adj* hard to capture, find, pin down, etc.: *an elusive idea, an elusive runaway.* **e·lu′sive·ness** *n.*

el·ver (el′vər) *n* a young eel.

elves (elvz) plural of ELF.

elv·ish (el′vish) *adj* elfish; elflike.

E·lys·i·an Fields (i lizh′ē ən) *or* (i lizh′ən) *Greek myth n* a place where heroes and virtuous people lived after death. Also called **Elysium**. <Latin, from Greek *Elysion*>

em (em) *Printing n* a unit for measuring the width of type, usually based on the width of the capital M.

em– *prefix* a form of EN- occurring before the letters *b* or *p: emboss, empathy.*

e·ma·ci·at·ed (i mā′sē ā′tid) *or* (i mā′shē ā′tid) *adj* very thin from starving or losing too much weight. <Latin *ex-* extreme + *macies* leanness> **e·ma′ci·a′tion** *n.*

e–mail (ē′māl′) *Computers n* in full, **electronic mail** messages sent from one computer to another over a network. Compare INSTANT MESSAGING. Also, **email**.

em·a·nate (em′ə nāt′) *v* **em·a·nat·ed, em·a·nat·ing** come forth: *a rumour emanating from Ottawa.* <Latin *ex-* out + *manare* flow> **em′a·na′tion** *n.*

e·man·ci·pate (i man′sə pāt′) *v* **e·man·ci·pat·ed, e·man·ci·pat·ing** set free, especially from restrictions imposed by law or society. <Latin *ex-* away + *manus* hand + *capere* take> **e·man′ci·pa′tion** *n.* **e·man′ci·pa′tor** *n.*

e·mas·cu·late (i mas′kyə lāt′) *v* **e·mas·cu·lat·ed, e·mas·cu·lat·ing** destroy the force of; weaken: *The editor emasculated the speech by cutting out its strongest passages.* <Latin *ex-* away + *masculus* male> **e·mas′cu·la′tion** *n.*

a bat	e bed	i bid	o pot	u cup	th **thin**
ā cake	ē me	ī bite	ō go	ū rude	ᴛʜ **then**
à bar	ə about	ər over	ȯ for	ů put	zh measure

em·balm (em bom′) *v* **1** treat a dead body with chemicals to keep it from decaying. **2** keep in memory: *fine sentiments embalmed in poetry.* **em·balm′er** *n.*

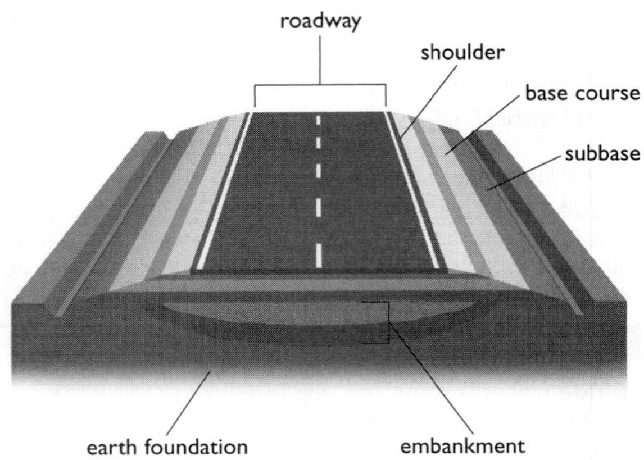

em·bank·ment (em bangk′mənt) *n* a raised bank of earth or stones, used to hold back water or to support a roadway.

em·bar·go (em bȧr′gō) *n, pl* **em·bar·goes** a ban on trade or other commercial activity with another country. <Spanish, from Latin *in-* upon + *barra* bar, ban>

em·bark (em bȧrk′) *v* go on board a ship or plane: *We embarked at Halifax for Europe.* <French *en-* in + *barque* boat> **em′bar·ka′tion** *n.*
embark on, begin or enter upon: *After graduating, she embarked on a business career.*

em·bar·rass (em ber′əs) *v* **1** make someone feel socially uneasy or self-conscious and slightly ashamed: *Their personal questions embarrassed her, and she blushed.* **2** burden with debt. <French *embarras* obstacle, from Latin *barra* bar, ban> **em·bar′rassed** *adj.* **em·bar′rass·ing** *adj.* **em·bar′rass·ment** *n.*

em·bas·sy (em′bə sē) *n, pl* **em·bas·sies** the official residence or offices of an ambassador in a foreign country. <Old French *ambassee*>

em·bed (em bed′) *v* **em·bed·ded, em·bed·ding** set, stick, or enclose in a surrounding mass: *A splinter has embedded itself in my finger. Every detail is embedded in my memory, embedded journalists in a war zone.*

em·bel·lish (em bel′ish) *v* **1** make fancier or more beautiful: *to embellish a room with colourful furnishings.* **2** make more interesting by adding details, usually imaginary: *to embellish a story.* <Old French, from Latin *bellus* handsome> **em·bel′lish·ment** *n.*

em·ber (em′bər) *n* (*usually plural*) a piece of wood or coal still glowing in the ashes of a fire. <Old English *æmerge*>

em·bez·zle (em bez′əl) *v* **em·bez·zled, em·bez·zling** secretly use for oneself money that belongs to others and has been put in one's safekeeping: *The treasurer embezzled $2000 from the club's funds.* <Old French *beseiller* to steal> **em·bez′zle·ment** *n.* **em·bez′zler** *n.*

em·bit·ter (em bit′ər) *v* make bitter: *She was embittered by her loss.*

em·bla·zon (em blā′zən) *v* **1** display conspicuously, in bright colours or large letters, etc.: *The school's motto was emblazoned on a banner across the gym wall.* **2** decorate or adorn in this way: *The knight's shield was emblazoned with his coat of arms.* <Old French *blason* shield>

em·blem (em′bləm) *n* an object or image adopted as a symbol, either formally or by custom: *A logo is the emblem of a company. The dove is an emblem of peace.* <Latin *emblema* inlaid work, from Greek *emblema* embossed ornament> **em′blem·at′ic** *adj.*

em·bod·y (em bod′ē) *v* **em·bod·ied, em·bod·y·ing** **1** put into material form: *The architect's vision was embodied in the new building.* **2** bring together into a single unit or organized system: *The British North America Act embodies the conditions of Confederation.* **em·bod′i·ment** *n.*

em·bold·en (em bōl′dən) *v* make bold or confident: *Emboldened by their positive reaction, she risked a few more daring suggestions.*

em·bol·ism (em′bə liz′əm) *n* the blocking of a blood vessel by a clot of blood or an air bubble. <Latin, from Greek *emballein*>

em·boss (em bos′) *v* cause a design or lettering to stand out from the surface, by carving or moulding: *She ran her finger over the letters to see if they had been embossed.* <Old French *en-* in + *boce* swelling>

em·bou·chure (om′bə shər) *or* (om′bə shůr′) *Music n* **1** the shape and use of the lips and tongue on the mouthpiece of a wind instrument. **2** the mouthpiece itself. <French *en-* in + *bouche* mouth>

em·brace (em brās′) *v* **em·braced, em·brac·ing** **1** hold closely in one's arms. **2** accept or welcome wholeheartedly: *to embrace an idea, to embrace an opportunity.* **3** include: *Palliser's Triangle embraces much of southern Alberta.*
n **1** a hug. **2** wholehearted acceptance. <Old French, from Latin *em-* in + Greek *brachion* arm>
em·brace′a·ble *adj.*

em·bra·sure (em brā′zhər) *n* a slanting of a wall at an oblique angle, especially on the inner sides of a window or door. <Old French *embraser* to cut at a slant>

em·broi·der (em broi′dər) *v* **1** sew a design on cloth with stitches: *She embroidered stars on her blue dress.* **2** add imaginary details: *to embroider the truth.* <Old French *broder*> **em·broi′dered** *adj.* **em·broi′der·y** *n.*

em·broil (em broil′) *v* involve someone in a quarrel or other confused situation: *She did not wish to become embroiled in the dispute.* <French *en-* in + *brouiller* to disorder> **em·broil′ment** *n.*

em·bry·o (em′brē ō′) *n* **1** the unborn young of an animal or human from the time the egg is fertilized. **2** an undeveloped plant within a seed. **3** the earliest stage of development of anything, before it really takes shape: *an embryo of a plan.* <Latin, from Greek *en-* in + *bryein* swell> **em′bry·on′ic** (em′brē on′ik) *adj.*
in embryo, in an undeveloped stage.

em·cee (em′sē′) *Informal n* a master of ceremonies.
v **em·ceed, em·cee·ing** act as master of ceremonies. Also, **M.C.** <the initials *M.C.*>

e·mend (i mend′) *v* correct a text. Compare AMEND. <Latin *ex-* out of + *mendum* fault>
e′men·da′tion (ē′men dā′shən) *n.*

em·er·ald (em′rəld) *n* a bright green precious stone, a variety of beryl.
adj bright green. <Old French *esmeralde*, from Greek *smaragdos*>

e·merge (i mərj′) *v* **e·merged, e·merg·ing 1** come out or into view: *He emerged dripping wet from the shower.* **2** be noticed or recognized: *After the military coup, a new dictator emerged.* <Latin *emergere* to rise up from> **e·mer′gence** *n.* **e·mer′gent** *adj.*

e·mer·gen·cy (i mər′jən sē) *n, pl* **e·mer·gen·cies** a serious or dangerous situation that arises suddenly and requires immediate action: *I keep a fire extinguisher in my car for use in an emergency.*
adj to do with an emergency: *an emergency operation.*

emergency brake *n* an extra brake, usually hand operated, to hold a vehicle in place.

e·mer·i·tus (i mer′ə təs) *adj* (*after* ***professor***) retired but still holding one's rank and title. <Latin *emerere* to complete one's service, from *e-* out + *merere* to serve>

em·er·y (em′rē) *n* a hard, dark mineral used for grinding, smoothing, and polishing. <French, from Greek *smyris* abrasive powder>

emery board *n* a strip of strong cardboard coated with fine particles of emery, used especially to file the nails.

emery paper *n* a fine grade of sandpaper, used for final smoothing.

e·met·ic (i met′ik) *adj* causing vomiting.
n a substance that causes vomiting. <Latin, from Greek *emeein* to vomit>

em·i·grate (em′ə grāt′) *v* **em·i·grat·ed, em·i·grat·ing** leave one's own country or region to settle in another: *Many people emigrated from Russia during the revolution.* Compare IMMIGRATE. <Latin *ex-* out + *migrare* move> **em′i·grant** *n, adj.* **em′i·gra′tion** *n.*

CONFUSABLES

Emigrate means "move out of a country or region": *My family emigrated from China to Canada in 1990.*

Immigrate means "move into a country or region": *My family immigrated to Canada from China in 1990.*

é·mi·gré (em′ə grā′) *n* a person who emigrates from somewhere, usually for a political reason. <French>

em·i·nence (em′ə nəns) *n* **1** a high rank or position above others: *Alexander Graham Bell won eminence as an inventor.* **2** a high or lofty location. **3 Eminence** *Catholicism* the title given to a cardinal. <Latin *ex-* out + *minere* jut>

em·i·nent (em′ə nənt) *adj* **1** distinguished or ranking above others: *The Governor General is an eminent person.* **2** outstanding or noteworthy: *The judge was a woman of eminent fairness.* **em′i·nent·ly** *adv.*

e·mir (ə mēr′) *Islam n* a title given to rulers. <Arabic *amir* commander>

e·mir·ate (em′ə rit) *Islam n* the rank or the domain of an emir.

em·is·sar·y (em′ə ser′ē) *n, pl* **em·is·sar·ies** a person sent on a mission. <Latin *emissarius*, from *emittere.* See EMIT.>

e·mis·sion (i mish′ən) *n* **1** the act or fact of emitting: *the emission of light from the sun.* **2** the thing emitted: *carbon monoxide and other deadly emissions.*

emission control *n* a device attached to a vehicle with an internal combustion engine to reduce pollution from its exhaust system.

e·mit (i mit′) *v* **e·mit·ted, e·mit·ting** give off, send out, or discharge: *The machine emits a high-pitched beep in the presence of radiation.* <Latin *ex-* out + *mittere* send> **e·mit′ter** *n.*

Em·my (em′ē) *n, pl* **Em·mies** a statuette awarded annually in the US by the Academy of Television Arts and Sciences for outstanding achievement in the field of television. <from *Immy*, slang shortening of *image orthicon*, part of a TV camera>

e·mol·lient (i mol′yənt) *adj* softening or soothing.
n something that softens and soothes: *Hand lotion is an emollient for the skin.* <Latin *emollire* to soften, from *mollis* soft>

e·mol·u·ment (i mol′yə mənt) *n* any salary, fee, or profit from a job or office. <Latin *emolumentum* profit (originally, payment to a miller for grinding corn), from *molere* to grind>

e·mote (i mōt′) *Informal v* **e·mot·ed, e·mot·ing** display emotion freely or excessively.

e·mo·ti·con (i mō′tə kon′) *Computers n* an icon conveying emotion through a facial expression made up of punctuation marks. Tilt your head to the left to see the emoticon for a smile **:)**. <*emot(ion)* + *icon*>

e·mo·tion (i mō′shən) *n* **1** a strong feeling that is accompanied by physical changes which may or may not be shown outwardly; *My voice shook with emotion.* **2** one's feelings as opposed to one's reason or will. <Old French, from Latin *emovere* to disturb>

e·mo·tion·al (i mō′shə nəl) *adj* **1** to do with the emotions: *emotional balance.* **2** quick to feel or show emotion: *He is quite emotional and cries easily.* **3** appealing to the emotions: *an emotional plea for money to help starving children.* **e·mo′tion·al·ly** *adv.*

e·mo·tive (i mō′tiv) *adj* to do with the emotions.

em·pa·thize (em′pə thīz′) *v* **em·pa·thized, em·pa·thiz·ing** (*followed by* ***with***) understand and share in the feelings of another: *A good listener must be able to empathize with the other person.*

empathy (em′pə thē) *n* the ability to understand and share in the feelings of others, or the act of doing so. <Greek *en-* in + *pathos* feeling> **em′pa·thet′ic** *adj.* **em′pa·thet′i·cal·ly** *adv.*

a **bat**	e **bed**	i **bid**	o **pot**	u **cup**	th **thin**
ā **cake**	ē **me**	ī **bite**	ō **go**	ū **rude**	ᴛʜ **then**
ȧ **bar**	ə **about**	ər **over**	ȯ **for**	u̇ **put**	zh **measure**

E

em·per·or (em′pə rər) *n* a ruler of great rank, especially of an empire. <Old French, from Latin *imperator* commander>

em·pha·sis (em′fə sis) *n, pl* **em·pha·ses** (em′fə sēz) **1** special force or attention given to something: *There is an increased emphasis on basic literacy skills in school.* **2** special force given to a particular syllable or word by a speaker, or by a writer through using an italic, underlined, or bold typeface. <Latin, from Greek *emphasis* significant stress>

em·pha·size (em′fə sīz′) *v* **em·pha·sized, em·pha·siz·ing** put emphasis on; stress, accent, or highlight: *to emphasize a word in speaking, to emphasize the need to stay in school.*

em·phat·ic (em fat′ik) *adj* **1** expressed with force or emphasis: *Her answer was an emphatic "No!"* **2** expressing oneself strongly or with force: *He was most emphatic on this point.* **em·phat′i·cal·ly** *adv.*

em·phy·se·ma (em′fə zē′mə) *n* a chronic condition of the lungs in which the air sacs become swollen and breathing is difficult. <Latin, from Greek>

em·pire (em′pīr) *n* **1** a group of countries or states under the same supreme ruler, government, or authority: *Queen Victoria reigned over the British Empire for more than 60 years.* **2** a very large business or group of businesses under the same ownership or management. <Old French, from Latin *imperium*>

em·pir·i·cal (em pē′rə kəl) *adj* based mainly on concrete data from experience as opposed to reasoning or pure logic: *an empirical observation, empirical evidence.* <Latin, from Greek *en-* in + *peira* experience> **em·pir′i·cal·ly** *adv.*

em·pir·i·cism (em pē′rə siz′əm) *n* **1** the gathering and use of data based on experience and observation, especially as practised in the natural sciences. **2** the belief that the only basis of knowledge is sense experience. **em·pir′i·cist** *n.*

em·ploy (em ploi′) *v* **1** use the services of or give work and pay to: *The mall employs many workers.* **2** use: *to employ a different strategy, to employ your talents.*
n the state of being a paid worker for someone: *Many people are in the employ of the government.* <French, from Latin *implicare* involve> **em·ploy′a·ble** *adj.* **em·ploy′ment** *n*

em·ploy·ee (em ploi′ē) *n* a person who works for some person or company for pay.

em·ploy·er (em ploi′ər) *n* a person or company for whom someone works.

🍁 **employment insurance** *n* **1** (*often unofficially called by its former name,* ***unemployment insurance***) a Federal Government program providing regular payments to people who have had a job but who are currently unemployed, paid for through the contributions of employees, employers, and the Federal Government. **2** benefits paid through this program. *Abbrev.* **EI**

em·po·ri·um (em pό′rē əm) *n, pl* **em·po·ri·ums** or **em·po·ri·a** (em pό′rē ə) a place where many different things are sold. <Latin, from Greek *emporos* merchant, traveller, from *poros* voyage>

em·pow·er (em pou′ər) *v* **1** give power, or a specific power: *The principal was empowered to suspend students for being late to school.* **2** help someone develop the strength and confidence needed to act freely.

em·press (em′pris) *n* **1** a woman who is a ruler of great rank, especially of an empire. **2** the wife of an emperor.

emp·ty (emp′tē) *adj* **emp·ti·er, emp·ti·est** **1** with nothing or no one in it: *The birds had gone, and their nest was empty.* **2** meaningless: *empty promises, empty words.*
v **emp·tied, emp·ty·ing** **1** make or become empty: *I emptied the fridge so I could clean it. After class, the room emptied quickly.* **2** pour or put the entire contents of: *Empty the can onto a plate.* **3** flow out: *The Credit River empties into Lake Ontario.*
n, pl **emp·ties** *Informal* an empty bottle or other container. <Old English *æmtig*> **emp′ti·ly** *adv.* **emp′ti·ness** *n.*

SYNONYMS

Empty can suggest having no one or nothing inside: *The arena was empty soon after the hockey game ended.*

Bare can mean "empty by being not furnished" or "unoccupied": *On moving day, the apartment was bare except for a few leftover boxes.*

Barren can mean "empty because of being sterile": *The ground was barren because of the polluted soil.*

emp·ty–hand·ed (emp′tē han′did) *adj* bringing or taking nothing.

empty nest syndrome *n* depression or disorientation felt by a parent (**empty nester**) whose children have become independent and left home.

empty set *Mathematics n* a set that has no members. Also called **null set.**

e·mu (ē′myū) *n* a large, flightless, Australian bird resembling an ostrich but smaller. <Portuguese *ema* ostrich>

em·u·late (em′yə lāt′) *v* **em·u·lat·ed, em·u·lat·ing** **1** strive to be like: *to emulate a hero.* **2** be an imitation of: *This program emulates software produced by another major company.* **3** try to equal or outdo. <Latin *aemulus* striving to be equal> **em′u·la′tion** *n.* **em′u·la′tor** *n.*

e·mul·si·fy (i mul′sə fī′) *v* **e·mul·si·fied, e·mul·si·fy·ing** make into an emulsion. **e·mul′si·fi·ca′tion** *n.* **e·mul′si·fi′er** *n.*

e·mul·sion (i mul′shən) *n* **1** a mixture of liquids that do not dissolve in each other, so that very fine drops of one liquid are evenly distributed throughout. **2** a coating on a camera film or plate that is sensitive to light. <Latin *emulsus*, from *emulgere* to squeeze out a milky fluid>

en (en) *Printing n* half the width of an EM.

en– *prefix* **1** cause to become: *enfeeble.* **2** put into or on: *encircle, enthrone.* **3** cause to have: *encourage.* **4** used to make a verb more emphatic: *entangle.* **5** used to form verbs with the suffix *–en*: *enliven.* Also, before *b, p,* and sometimes *m,* **em-** <Latin *in-* in, into>

–en[1] *suffix* develop, create, or intensify something: *deepen, loosen.* <Old English>

–en[2] *suffix* made of: *wooden, woollen.* <Old English>

en·a·ble (en ā′bəl) *v* **en·a·bled, en·a·bling** make able: *Airplanes enable us to travel through the air.*

en·act (en akt′) *v* **1** make into law: *to enact legislation.* **2** act out: *to enact a scene from a play.* **en·act′ment** *n.*

e·nam·el (i nam′əl) *n* **1** a coloured, glasslike substance melted and then cooled to make a smooth, hard, glossy surface, often used to cover or decorate metal or pottery. **2** a paint or varnish used to make a smooth, hard, glossy surface. **3** the smooth, hard, glossy outer layer of the teeth. *v* **e·nam·elled** or **e·nam·eled, e·nam·el·ling** or **e·nam·el·ing** cover or decorate with or as if with enamel. <Old French *en-* on + *amayl* enamel> **e·nam′el·ler** or **e·nam′el·er** *n.* **e·nam′el·ware** *n.*

en·am·our or **en·am·or** (en am′ər) *v* (*in the passive*) arouse love, delight, or enthusiastic approval in someone: *The boss was greatly enamoured with our clever proposal.* <Old French, from Latin *amor* love> **en·am′oured** or **en·am′ored** *adj.*

en·camp (en kamp′) *v* make, stay, or put in a camp: *They encamped by the river. The troops were encamped in tents.* **en·camp′ment** *n.*

en·cap·su·late (en kap′sə lāt′) *v* **en·cap·su·lat·ed, en·cap·su·lat·ing** capture the essence of something and present it in brief form, as if enclosing it in a capsule: *This story encapsulates the world of the pioneers.* **en·cap′su·la′tion** *n.*

en·case (en kās′) *v* **en·cased, en·cas·ing** put into a case or rigid covering: *a knight encased in armour. Videotapes are encased in a plastic cassette.*

en·ceph·a·li·tis (en sef′ə lī′tis) *n* an inflammation of the brain caused by a virus. <Latin, from Greek *en-* in + *kephale* head>

en·chant (en chant′) *v* **1** in fiction, put under a magic spell: *In this fairy story, the witch enchants the princess.* **2** delight greatly: *The musical enchanted us all.* <French, from Latin *cantare* chant> **en·chant′er** *n.* **en·chant′ing** *adj.* **en·chant′ment** *n.*

en·chan·tress (en chan′tris) *n* in fiction, a woman who makes magic spells.

en·chi·la·da (en′chə lá′də) *n* a tortilla rolled around a filling of meat or cheese, served with a spicy sauce. <Spanish *en-* in + Nahuatl *chili* chili>

en·cir·cle (en sər′kəl) *v* **en·cir·cled, en·cir·cling** form a circle around: *Trees encircled the pond. We encircled the flower bed with stones.* **en·cir′cle·ment** *n.*

en·clave (on′klāv) *or* (en′klāv) *n* **1** a group forming a distinct community, enclosed within a different, larger one: *an enclave of Canadians in an American city.* **2** a district surrounded by the territory of another country. <French *enclaver* enclose>

en·close (en klōz′) *v* **en·closed, en·clos·ing** **1** surround or shut in on all sides: *The farmer enclosed her pasture with a rail fence.* **2** include in an envelope or package along with something else: *A cheque was enclosed with the birthday card.* <Old French>

en·clo·sure (en klō′zhər) *n* **1** a structure that encloses: *walls, fences, and other enclosures.* **2** something enclosed, especially additional material enclosed in an envelope with a letter. **3** the act of enclosing.

en·code (en kōd′) *v* **en·cod·ed, en·cod·ing** **1** put into a secret code: *The spy encoded his message before sending it.* **2** express in a symbolic system: *to encode computer instructions in a programming language.*

en·com·i·um (en kō′mē əm) *n* an elaborate expression of praise: *flowery encomiums by reviewers.* <Latin, from Greek *en-* in + *komos* celebration>

en·com·pass (en kum′pəs) *v* **1** surround completely: *The atmosphere encompasses the earth.* **2** include: *The forest encompasses two thirds of the estate.*

en·core (on′kȯr) *n* **1** a demand by the audience for another appearance of a performer: *Encore! Encore!* **2** an additional part of a performance given in response to such a demand. <French = again>

en·coun·ter (en koun′tər) *v* **1** meet, face, or confront: *to encounter difficulties, to encounter an enemy.* **2** meet by accident: *I encountered an old friend on the street.*
n a meeting or confrontation: *an encounter with the law.* <Old French, from Latin *incontra* in front of>

en·cour·age (en kər′ij) *v* **en·cour·aged, en·cour·ag·ing** **1** give courage, hope, or confidence to: *Your kind words encouraged me when I was down.* **2** urge, advise, or recommend: *The teacher encouraged us to read more.* **3** be favourable to: *Fair pricing for fresh produce encourages farming.* <Old French *en-* cause to have + *corage* courage> **en·cour′age·ment** *n.*

en·croach (en krōch′) *v* **1** trespass on the property or rights of another: *He is a good salesman and will not encroach upon his customer's time.* **2** go beyond existing or usual limits: *The desert encroaches farther southward each year.* <Old French *encrochier* to grab> **en·croach′ment** *n.*

en·crust (en krust′) *v* **1** cover with a crust or hard coating: *The inside of the kettle is encrusted with lime.* **2** decorate with jewels or other hard, sharp objects: *a crown encrusted with gems.* **en′crus·ta′tion** *n.*

en·crypt (en kript′) *v* **1** *Computers* send or store data in a coded form to prevent access by the wrong people. **2** put into a secret code: *The seemingly innocent conversation may have been encrypted.* **en·crypt′ed** *adj.* **en·cryp′tion** *n.*

en·cum·ber (en kum′bər) *v* **1** hamper or hinder the movements of: *Encumbered by the heavy pack, she could only climb slowly.* **2** block or clutter: *Empty boxes encumbered the fire escape.* **3** weigh down or burden: *encumbered with cares.* **4** put a property under a mortgage or a legal claim: *The farm was encumbered with a heavy mortgage.* <Old French *en-* in + *combre* barrier> **en·cum′brance** *n.*

a bat	e bed	i bid	o pot	u cup	th **thin**
ā cake	ē me	ī bite	ō go	ū rude	TH **then**
á bar	ə about	ər over	ȯ for	ů put	zh measure

E

en·cy·clo·pe·di·a or **en·cy·clo·pae·di·a** (en sī′klə pē′dē ə) *n* a book or series of books giving information, usually arranged alphabetically, on all branches of knowledge, or on many aspects of one subject: *a medical encyclopedia.* <Latin, from Greek *enkyklios paideia* well-rounded education> **en·cy′clo·pe′dic** or **en·cy′clo·pae′dic** *adj.*

end (end) *n* **1** the very last part: *He read through to the end of the book.* **2** the edge or boundary: *Those trees mark the end of their property.* **3** the point where something stops: *Every stick has two ends.* **4** a purpose or object: *This ridiculous exercise serves no useful end.* **5** a final result or outcome: *It is hard to tell what the end will be.* **6** death or destruction: *My dog met his end in an accident.* **7** a stub or fragment: *the end of a loaf of bread.* **8** *Football* the player at either end of the line. **9** *Curling* one of the divisions of a game: *We were beaten in the last end.*
v bring or come to an end: *to end an argument, to end on a happy note. Where does the property end?* <Old English *ende*>
at loose ends, not involved in doing anything in particular: *My appointment was cancelled, so I'm at loose ends this afternoon.*
end to end, with the end of one thing next to the end of another: *Lay the dominoes end to end.*
end up, do or be eventually, after various developments: *She ended up as a judge. We ended up staying home.*
hold (or **keep**) **your end up,** carry your share of responsibility.
in the end, finally: *Everything will turn out fine in the end.*
jump (or **go**) **off the deep end,** *Informal* act rashly without thinking: *Think the situation through and don't jump off the deep end.*
make both ends meet, spend no more than one has.
no end, very much or very many: *We had no end of trouble with that car. I respect him no end.*
on end, **a** in an upright position: *She stood the dominoes on end.* **b** one after another: *I've been doing chores on end all day.*

en·dan·ger (en dān′jər) *v* cause danger to: *Drunk driving endangers people's lives.*

endangered species *n* any species of life that is threatened with extinction.

en·dear (en dēr′) *v* make dear: *Her kindness endeared her to all of us.* **en·dear′ing** *adj.*

en·dear·ment (en dēr′mənt) *n* **1** the act or process of endearing. **2** an act or word showing love or affection.

en·deav·our or **en·deav·or** (en dev′ər) *v* try hard: *We endeavour to treat all people with kindness.*
n **1** an earnest attempt or effort. **2** an undertaking or project: *Preparing my science project was no small endeavour.* <Middle English *put in dever* make it one's duty>

en·dem·ic (en dem′ik) *adj* regularly found among a certain people or in a certain environment: *Cholera is endemic in that country. Corruption is endemic in this government.*
n an endemic disease. Compare EPIDEMIC. <Greek *en-* in + *demos* people>

end·ing (en′ding) *n* **1** the last part: *The story had a sad ending.* **2** *Grammar* a suffix that does not change the part of speech of a word but has a purely grammatical function such as, in English, *-ed* showing tense or *-s* showing number.

en·dive (en′dīv) *n* a leafy green plant related to chicory, eaten as a vegetable. <Old French, from Greek *entybon*>

end·less (end′lis) *adj* **1** with or seeming to have no end: *the endless motion of the sea, an endless task.* **2** forming a continuous loop: *A bicycle chain is an endless chain.* **end′less·ly** *adv.* **end′less·ness** *n.*

end·note (end′nōt′) *n* a note like a footnote, but placed at the end of a text rather than at the bottom of the page.

> **GRAMMAR AND USAGE**
>
> There are various standard formats for **endnotes** as for footnotes. Check with your teacher to confirm the preferred style for assignments.

en·do·carp (en′dō kärp′) *Botany n* the inner layer of a fruit or ripened OVARY (def. 2). <Greek *endo-* inside + *karpos* fruit>

en·do·crine gland (en′dō krin) *or* (en′dō krīn′) *n* a gland, such as the thyroid, that produces hormonal secretions influencing other organs in the body and passing directly into the bloodstream or lymph. Such glands and their secretions form the **endocrine system.**

🍁 **end of steel** *n* the limit to which tracks have been laid for a railway, especially going north.

en·dor·phin (en dôr′fin) *n* a protein produced in the nervous system that has several functions, including the relief of pain. <*endo(genous)* generated within + *(m)orphine*>

en·dorse (en dôrs′) *v* **en·dorsed, en·dors·ing** **1** sign the back of a cheque or other document to show that one is entitled to receive a stated amount of cash or credit: *She had to endorse the cheque before cashing it.* **2** approve or support, especially publicly; promote: *Parents endorsed the plan for a new playground. The Olympic medallist now endorses a line of swimwear in a series of TV ads.* <Old French *endosser*, from Latin *dorsum* back>
en·dorse′ment *n.* **en·dors′er** *n.*

en·dor·see (en dôr′sē′) *n* a person to whom a cheque or other document is signed over.

en·do·skel·e·ton (en′dō skel′ə tən) *Zoology n* the internal supporting structure of all vertebrates. Compare EXOSKELETON. <Greek *endo-* inside + *skeleton*>

en·do·sperm (en′dō spərm′) *Botany n* the nourishment for an embryo, enclosed with it in the seed of a plant. <Greek *endo-* inside + *sperm*>

en·dow (en dou′) *v* **1** furnish at birth with some quality, trait, or asset: *Nature endowed her with both intelligence and good looks.* **2** give money or property to provide an ongoing income for: *The rich man endowed the college he had attended.* <Old French *endouer*, from Latin *dotare* give as a gift> **en·dow′ment** *n.*

end run *n* **1** *Football* a play in which a ball carrier attempts to run wide around the end of the opposing team's defensive line. **2** an attempt to evade opposition to an action or idea by finding an indirect way to achieve a desired result.

end table *n* a small table set beside a chair or at either end of a sofa.

en·due (en dyū′) *or* (en dū′) *v* **en·dued, en·du·ing** provide with a quality or power: *He believed he was a prophet endued with wisdom.* <Old French, from Latin *inducere* lead into>

en·dur·ance (en dyů′rəns) *or* (en dů′rəns) *n* **1** the power to last or continue: *You need endurance to run a marathon.* **2** the act of bearing something unpleasant or difficult: *His endurance of pain was impressive.*

en·dure (en dyūr′) *or* (en dūr′) *v* **en·dured, en·dur·ing** **1** continue through time: *These statues have endured for a thousand years.* **2** suffer and survive: *Those brave people endured much pain.* <Old French, from Latin *indurare* to harden> **en·dur′a·ble** *adj.*

end–user (end′yū′zər) *n* the person who actually makes use of a product developed by others.

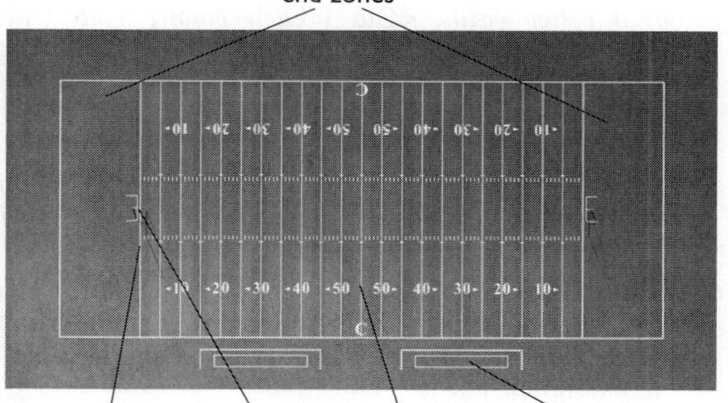

end zone *n* **1** *Football* the part of the field between each end of the field and the nearest goal line. **2** *Hockey* the ice between each end of the rink and the nearest blue line.

ENE east-northeast.

en·e·ma (en′ə mə) *n* an injection of liquid into the rectum to flush the bowels. <Greek *en-* in + *hienai* send>

en·e·my (en′ə mē) *n, pl* **en·e·mies** **1** a person or group that hates and fights or works against another. **2** anything that harms or that prevents success: *Frost is an enemy of plants. Fear is our worst enemy.* <Old French, from Latin *in-* not + *amicus* friendly>

en·er·get·ic (en′ər jet′ik) *adj* **1** active and eager to do things: *Cool fall days make some people feel energetic.* **2** forceful and strong: *an energetic warning.* **en′er·get′i·cal·ly** *adv.*

en·er·gize (en′ər jīz′) *v* **en·er·gized, en·er·giz·ing** fill with energy: *She felt energized after her nap.*

en·er·gy (en′ər jē) *n, pl* **en·er·gies** **1** the will or strength to act: *Surprisingly, exercise gives you more energy.* **2** force or intensity: *Put more energy into your singing.* **3** *Physics* the capacity for doing work, such as lifting or moving an object, or causing change. **4** natural resources such as oil, coal, or nuclear or hydroelectric power needed to make things work, especially machinery and heating and lighting systems: *We must conserve energy.* <Latin, from Greek *energos* active, working>

en·er·vate (en′ər vāt′) *v* **en·er·vat·ed, en·er·vat·ing** weaken: *A hot, humid climate enervates people who are not used to it.* <Latin *enervare* to weaken>

en·fee·ble (en fē′bəl) *v* **en·fee·bled, en·fee·bling** make weak or feeble. **en·fee′ble·ment** *n.*

en·fold (en fōld′) *v* **1** surround or envelop: *I kept myself enfolded in the blanket to keep warm.* **2** hold or embrace: *The mother enfolded her baby in her arms.*

E

en·force (en fòrs′) *v* **en·forced, en·forc·ing** **1** put into force: *Police officers and judges enforce the law.* **2** get by force: *Obedience enforced by threats is not true obedience.* **3** impose; thrust on someone: *You can't enforce your values on me.* **en·force′a·ble** *adj.* **en·force′ment** *n.* **en·forc′er** *n.*

en·fran·chise (en fran′chīz) *v* **en·fran·chised, en·fran·chis·ing** **1** give the right to vote: *All adult Canadian citizens are enfranchised.* **2** set free. **en·fran′chise·ment** *n.*

en·gage (en gāj′) *v* **en·gaged, en·gag·ing** **1** promise in marriage: *My sister is engaged to a medical student.* **2** catch and hold: *Bright colours engaged the baby's attention.* **3** involve fully: *We tried to engage him in conversation, but we failed.* **4** hire or reserve: *They engaged a hall and a band for the reception.* **5** fit together: *The teeth of one gear engage with the teeth of another.* **6** enter into combat with: *to engage the enemy.* **7** put into operation: *Flipping this switch engages the alarm system.* <French *en gage* under pledge>
engage in, take part in: *She engages in many sports.*

en·gaged (en gājd′) *adj* **1** promised in marriage: *an engaged couple.* **2** *UK* in use: *That signal on the phone means the line is engaged.*
engaged in, busy at: *She was engaged in repairing the car.*

en·gage·ment (en gāj′mənt) *n* **1** the period during which one is engaged: *They were married after an engagement of six months.* **2** an appointment or commitment: *A previous engagement prevented her from coming to our party.*

en·gag·ing (en gā′jing) *adj* winning the attention, interest, and liking of others: *an engaging smile, an engaging conversational style.* **en·gag′ing·ly** *adv.*

en·gen·der (en jen′dər) *v* bring into existence: *Filth engenders disease.* <Old French, from Latin *generare* create>

en·gine (en′jən) *n* **1** a machine that supplies energy to other moving parts of a larger machine. **2** the machine that pulls a railway train. **3** *Archaic or Poetic* a machine, device, or instrument: *battering rams, catapults, and other ancient engines of war.* <Old French *engin* cleverness, i.e., clever machine, from Latin *ingenium* natural talent>

a bat	e bed	i bid	o pot	u cup	th **thin**
ā cake	ē me	ī bite	ō go	ū rude	ᴛʜ **then**
ȧ bar	ə about	ər over	ȯ for	ů put	zh measure

engine block *n* the main mass of an internal combustion engine, holding the cylinders.

en·gi·neer (en′jə nēr′) *n* **1** a person who takes care of or runs engines, especially the driver of a locomotive. **2** a person trained in a branch of engineering.
v manage or guide: *Although many opposed his plan, he engineered it through to completion.*

en·gi·neer·ing (en′jə nē′ring) *n* the application of science and technology to practical uses, such as the design, use, and building of engines and machines (**mechanical engineering**), as well as systems and structures (**computer engineering, civil engineering**).

Eng·land (ing′glənd) *n* a country occupying, along with Scotland and Wales, the largest island in the UK.

Eng·lish (ing′glish) *n* the language first spoken in England, beginning with Old English or Anglo-Saxon (before 1100 CE) and including Middle English (about 1100–1500) and Modern English (from about 1500). English is now spoken throughout the world.
adj **1** to do with or using English. **2** to do with England or its people. <Old English *Engle* the English people>

🍁 **English Canada** *n* **1** Canadians whose first or main language is English or whose ancestors came from the UK, considered as a group. **2** the part of Canada inhabited mainly or entirely by such Canadians, as distinct from Québec. **English Canadian** *adj, n.*

The English horn is a woodwind instrument, and the French horn is a brass instrument.

English horn *n* a wooden musical instrument resembling an oboe, but larger and with a lower tone.

English muffin *n* a small, flat cake made with bread dough, cooked on a griddle.

en·gorge (en gȯrj′) *v* **en·gorged, en·gorg·ing 1** fill too full. **2** *Medicine* congest with blood or other bodily fluid.

en·grave (en grāv′) *v* **en·graved, en·grav·ing 1** cut into the surface of: *initials engraved on the inside of a ring. The back of the watch is engraved with his name.* **2** cut a design on a metal plate or block of wood for printing. **3** impress deeply in the mind: *His mother's face was engraved on his memory.* <French *engraver*> **en·grav′er** *n.*

en·grav·ing (en grā′ving) *n* **1** something engraved. **2** an engraved plate or block or the picture printed from it.

en·gross (en grōs′) *v* take up all the attention of: *She was engrossed in a book.* <French *en gros* in a lump, in large amounts> **en·gross′ing** *adj.*

en·gulf (en gulf′) *v* swallow up or overwhelm: *engulfed in sorrow. A wave engulfed the small boat.*

en·hance (en hans′) *v* **en·hanced, en·hanc·ing** improve or add to: *Gardens enhanced the beauty of the old house.* <Old French *enhauncer* raise, from Latin *altus* high> **en·hance′ment** *n*

e·nig·ma (i nig′mə) *n* a riddle or puzzle. <Latin, from Greek *ainos* fable> **en′ig·mat′ic** *adj.*

en·jamb·ment or **en·jambe·ment** (en jam′mənt) *Poetry n* the continuation of a sentence without pause from one line to the next. <French = a straddling>

en·join (en join′) *v* **1** order, direct, or urge: *Parents enjoin good behaviour on their children. We were strictly enjoined to observe all local customs.* **2** issue a court injunction to: *Through an injunction, a judge may enjoin a person to do some act.* <Old French, from Latin *injungere* to impose>

en·joy (en joi′) *v* **1** experience with pleasure: *to enjoy a performance. We enjoy her sense of humour.* **2** have as an advantage or benefit: *Farmers using organic fertilizer enjoyed better yields.* <Old French *enjoir*, from Latin *gaudere* rejoice> **en·joy′a·ble** *adj.* **en·joy′a·bly** *adv.* **en·joy′ment** *n.*
enjoy yourself, have a good time; have pleasure: *Enjoy yourself at the party.*

en·large (en lȧrj′) *v* **en·larged, en·larg·ing** make larger.
enlarge on, talk or write more about: *In her speech she enlarged on her earlier statement to the press.*

en·large·ment (en lȧrj′mənt) *n* **1** anything that has been enlarged, especially a photographic print. **2** an addition: *They built an enlargement on the back of their house.* **3** the act of enlarging.

en·light·en (en lī′tən) *v* give someone greater knowledge and understanding.

en·light·en·ment (en lī′tən mənt) *n* **1** the act of enlightening. **2 the Enlightenment** from the late 1600s to the mid-1700s in Europe, an intellectual movement marked by belief in the power of reason and emphasis on the freedom of speech and ideas.

en·list (en list′) *v* **1** enrol in a branch of the armed forces. **2** join or persuade to join in some cause or undertaking: *The mayor enlisted the local schools in cleaning up the parks.* **3** secure or obtain: *She enlisted the support of her parents.* **en·list′ment** *n.*

en·liv·en (en lī′vən) *v* make more entertaining, appealing, or interesting: *to enliven a speech with humour. Bright curtains enliven a room.*

en masse (on′mas′) *adv* in a large group or mass. <French>

en·mesh (en mesh′) *v* catch in a net or involve in a complex situation.

en·mi·ty (en′mə tē) *n, pl* **en·mi·ties** the feeling of hatred or hostility that exists between enemies. <Old French, *ennemistie*, from Latin *in-* not + *amicus* friendly>

en·no·ble (en nō′bəl) *v* **en·no·bled, en·no·bling 1** raise in quality or moral stature: *a character ennobled by suffering.* **2** give the title of nobility to; raise to the rank of a noble. **en·no′ble·ment** *n.*

en·nui (on wē′) *n* a feeling of being weary or bored of life. <French = boredom>

e·nor·mi·ty (i nȯr′mə tē) *n, pl* **e·nor·mi·ties 1** the act or fact of great wrongdoing: *The enormity of his crime turned the whole country against him.* **2** enormous size, scope, or significance: *The sheer enormity of the project daunted her.*

e·nor·mous (i nȯr′məs) *adj* of great size, quantity, or extent: *an enormous sum of money, an enormous success.* <Latin *ex-* out of + *norma* pattern, norm>
e·nor′mous·ly *adv.* **e·nor′mous·ness** *n.*

e·nough (i nuf′) *adj, n* as much or as many as needed or wanted: *Is this enough food* (*adj*)*? I've had enough to eat* (*n*). *adv* (*after the adj or v*) **1** as much as needed or wanted: *Have you played enough? I'm not tall enough to reach that.* **2** quite or rather: *He was willing enough when I asked for his help.* <Old English *genog*>

en·quire (en kwīr′) INQUIRE.

en·quiry (en kwī′rē) INQUIRY.

en·rage (en rāj′) *v* **en·raged, en·rag·ing** make furious.

en·rap·ture (en rap′chər) *v* **en·rap·tured, en·rap·tur·ing** fill with great delight: *The audience was enraptured by the singer's beautiful voice.*

en·rich (en rich′) *v* improve or enhance: *to enrich flour with vitamins and minerals, to enrich soil with fertilizer. An education enriches your mind.* **en·rich·ment** *n.*

en·rol or **en·roll** (en rōl′) *v* **en·rolled, en·rol·ling 1** enter in a list of members or participants: *A guidance counsellor enrols all the students in their courses.* **2** become a member or participant: *I've just enrolled in a book club.* <Old French *enroller,* from Latin *inrotulare* write in a roll. Names were originally written on a roll of parchment.>

en·rol·ment or **en·roll·ment** (en rōl′mənt) *n* **1** the act of enrolling. **2** the number enrolled, especially of students: *The school has a higher enrolment this year.*

en route (on rūt′) *adv* on the way: *We'll stop at Toronto en route from Montréal to Winnipeg.* <French>

en·sconce (en skons′) *v* **en·sconced, en·sconc·ing** settle comfortably and firmly: *The cat ensconced itself in the armchair.* <origin uncertain>

en·sem·ble (on som′bəl) *n* **1** a group of singers or musicians performing together: *Two violins, a cello, and a harp make up the string ensemble.* **2** any complete, harmonious set, such as a suit of clothing. **3** all the parts of a thing considered together. <French, from Latin *in-* in + *simul* at the same time>

SYNONYMS

An **ensemble** refers to an unspecified number of musicians: *The brass ensemble consisted of two trumpets, two trombones, and one tuba.*

A **quartet**, as the word implies, always refers to four musicians: *The quartet was composed of one cello and three violins.*

A **troupe** suggests a number of entertainers—singers, actors, and so on: *During summer vacation, a dozen teenagers performed together in a troupe to earn money.*

en·shrine (en shrīn′) *v* **en·shrined, en·shrin·ing 1** enclose in a shrine: *A holy relic is enshrined in the cathedral.* **2** keep safe and sacred: *Basic human rights are enshrined in the Charter of Rights and Freedoms.* **en·shrine′ment** *n.*

en·sign (en′sīn) *or* (en′sən) *n* **1** a flag or banner: *the Red Ensign.* **2** any of various low-ranking military officers in different armed forces. <Old French, from Latin *insignia* badge>

en·si·lage (en′sə lij) *n* the preservation of green fodder by packing it in a silo or pit. <French>

en·slave (en slāv′) *v* **en·slaved, en·slav·ing** make a slave of: *enslaved by drugs.* **en·slave′ment** *n.*

en·sue (en sū′) *or* (en syū′) *v* **en·sued, en·su·ing** come after in time: *in the ensuing weeks. My brother refused to help me with the dishes, and a quarrel ensued.* <Old French *ensuivre,* from Latin *sequi* follow>

en·suite (on′swēt′) *adj* attached as a bathroom to another larger room such as a bedroom. <French *en suite* = in a series>

en·sure (en shūr′) *v* **en·sured, en·sur·ing** make sure or certain: *Please ensure that all doors are locked.*

CONFUSABLES

Ensure means "make sure" or "be certain": *Please ensure you have my correct phone number.*

Insure means "arrange for money payment in case of loss, accident, or death": *I insured my car against theft.*

en·tail (en tāl′) *v* **1** require: *Taking care of a pet entails more work than I had expected.* **2** limit the inheritance of property to a specified line of heirs so that future owners cannot leave it to anyone else. <Old French *taillier* cut to shape, from Latin *taliare* to split> **en·tail′ment** *n.*

en·tan·gle (en tang′gəl) *v* **en·tan·gled, en·tan·gling 1** get twisted up and caught: *Loose string is easily entangled.* **2** get into difficulty or trouble: *The villain tried to entangle the heroine in an evil scheme.* **en·tan′gle·ment** *n.*

en·tente (on tont′) *n* an understanding or agreement, especially between nations. <French *entendre* understand>

en·ter (en′tər) *v* **1** go or come in or into: *to enter a room. Let them all enter.* **2** (*often with* **on** *or* **upon**) begin: *to enter a position at a company, to enter on a career.* **3** take part in or join, or cause to take part in or join: *to enter a competition. Parents enter their children in school.* **4** include in a record or list: *Enter your score on the sheet provided.* **5** *Theatre* come on stage. **6** *Computers* input data or instructions. <Old French, from Latin *intra* within>
enter into, a begin to take part in: *He entered into conversation with the woman.* **b** be relevant to: *That question doesn't enter into the problem.*

a bat	e bed	i bid	o pot	u cup	th thin
ā cake	ē me	ī bite	ō go	ū rude	ᴛʜ then
ȧ bar	ə about	ər over	ȯ for	u̇ put	zh measure

en·ter·i·tis (en′tə rī′tis) *n* inflammation of the intestines, usually with diarrhea and fever. <Greek *entera* intestines>

en·ter·prise (en′tər prīz′) *n* **1** a project or undertaking, especially an important or challenging one: *Raising children is quite an enterprise.* **2** a business project. **3** courage, initiative, and energy in starting and carrying out projects: *His spirit of enterprise led him to achieve much with little.* <Old French *entreprise*, from Latin *prehendere* to undertake>

en·ter·pris·ing (en′tər prī′zing) *adj* showing courage, initiative, and energy in starting and carrying out projects.

en·ter·tain (en′tər tān′) *v* **1** amuse: *The toys entertained the children.* **2** have as guests: *She entertained ten people at dinner. They entertain a great deal.* **3** consider: *I refuse to entertain such a foolish idea.* **4** hold in the mind: *Even after failing twice, we still entertained a hope of success.* <Old French *entretenir* hold together, from Latin *tenere* to hold>

en·ter·tain·er (en′tər tā′nər) *n* a person who performs publicly for the enjoyment of others.

en·ter·tain·ing (en′tər tā′ning) *adj* amusing or pleasantly interesting.
n the practice of having guests. **en′ter·tain′ing·ly** *adv.*

en·ter·tain·ment (en′tər tān′mənt) *n* **1** something fun to do or see, or such things generally. **2** the act of entertaining.

en·thral or **en·thrall** (en throl′) *v* **en·thralled, en·thral·ling** fascinate: *We were enthralled by the performance.* **en·thral′ment** or **en·thrall′ment** *n.*

en·throne (en thrōn′) *v* **en·throned, en·thron·ing** **1** make into a monarch. **2** place in a high position: *Sir Wilfrid Laurier is enthroned in the hearts of his countrymen.* **en·throne′ment** *n.*

en·thuse (en thūz′) *v* **en·thused, en·thus·ing** **1** show or speak with enthusiasm. **2** fill with enthusiasm.

en·thu·si·asm (en thū′zē az′əm) *n* eager excitement and interest: *A good coach fills players with enthusiasm for the sport.* <Latin, from Greek *entheos* inspired, god-possessed, from *theos* god> **en·thu′si·as′tic** *adj.*
en·thu′si·as′ti·cal·ly *adv.*

en·thu·si·ast (en thū′zē ast′) *n* a person who is filled with enthusiasm for a particular thing: *a baseball enthusiast.*

en·tice (en tīs′) *v* **en·ticed, en·tic·ing** tempt or attract by offering some pleasure or reward: *The little boy, enticed by the prospect of a lollipop, allowed the doctor to vaccinate him.* <Old French *enticier* stir up, from Latin *intitare* to urge> **en·tice′ment** *n.* **en·tic′ing·ly** *adv.*

en·tire (en tīr′) *adj* with all the parts: *The tea set emerged dusty but entire from the moving crate. The entire class passed the test.* <Old French *entier*, from Latin *integer* whole> **en·tire′ly** *adv.*

en·tire·ty (en tīr′tē) *or* (en tī′rə tē) *n, pl* **en·tire·ties** **1** wholeness or completeness. **2** a complete thing.
in its entirety, as a whole; with all its parts: *He enjoyed the concert in its entirety.*

en·ti·tle (en tī′təl) *v* **en·ti·tled, en·ti·tling** **1** call by a certain title; name: *She read a poem entitled "Trees."* **2** give the right to have or do a certain thing: *This coupon entitles you to one free ride. Your position doesn't entitle you to order me around.* **en·ti′tle·ment** *n.*

en·ti·ty (en′ti tē) *n, pl* **en·ti·ties** a thing with real and separate existence, either actually or in the mind: *Borders and governments are political entities.* <Latin *entis* being>

en·tomb (en tūm′) *v* lay or shut up in a tomb or tomblike place: *to entomb a body.* **en·tomb′ment** *n.*

en·to·mol·o·gy (en′tə mol′ə jē) *n* the branch of zoology that studies insects. <Greek *en-* in + *temnein* cut, in reference to their segmented bodies>
en′to·mo·lo′gi·cal *adj.* **en′to·mol′o·gist** *n.*

en·tou·rage (on′tə räzh′) *or* (on′tə räzh′) *n* the group of attendants or other people that usually accompany someone: *the queen and her entourage.* <French *entour* surround>

en·tr'acte (on trakt′) *n* **1** a break between two acts of a play, ballet, or opera. **2** a piece of music or other entertainment performed during this break. <French = between-act>

en·trails (en′trālz) *or* (en′trəlz) *pln* intestines, especially when exposed. <Old French, from Latin *intralia* intestines>

en·trance[1] (en′trəns) *n* **1** the act of coming or going in: *The actor's entrance was greeted with applause.* **2** a place by which to enter or an open area in front of or around it. Also, **entranceway**. **3** the freedom or right to enter; admission: *A family membership gives entrance to the art gallery as often as you want.* <French *entrer* to enter>

en·trance[2] (en trans′) *v* **en·tranced, en·tranc·ing** **1** fill with joy and wonder: *The girl was entranced by her new book.* **2** put into a trance. <*en-* in + *trance*>
en·trance′ment *n.* **en·tranc′ing·ly** *adv.*

en·trant (en′trənt) *n* a person who enters: *Contest entrants must be 18 or over.*

en·trap (en trap′) *v* **en·trapped, en·trap·ping** **1** catch in a trap or difficult situation: *By clever questioning, the lawyer entrapped the witness into contradicting himself.* **2** trick someone into committing a crime in order to arrest him or her. **en·trap′ment** *n.*

en·treat (en trēt′) *v* ask earnestly or beg: *The captives entreated the enemy not to kill them.* <Old French *en-* cause + *traitier* to discuss> **en·treat′y** *n.*

en·tree or **en·trée** (on′trā) *n* the main dish at a meal. <French *entrer* enter. In former times, this course was served after a course called the *relevé* remove.>

en·trench (en trench′) *v* **1** establish firmly: *Your rights as a Canadian citizen are entrenched in the Charter.* **2** surround or fortify with trenches: *Our soldiers were entrenched opposite the enemy.* **3** (*with* ***on*** *or* ***upon***) trespass or encroach: *Do not entrench upon the rights of others.*
en·trench′ment *n.*

en·tre·pre·neur (on′trə prə nər′) *n* a person who finances, sets up, and sometimes runs a business enterprise. <Old French one who undertakes, from *entreprendre* to undertake> **en′tre·pre·neur′i·al** *adj.*
en′tre·pre·neur′ship *n.*

en·tro·py (en′trə pē) *n* **1** *Physics* in any closed mechanical system, a measure of the energy that is lost as heat and is therefore not available to do work. **2** a gradual decline into disorder. <German *Entropie*, probably from Greek *en-* in + *trope* transformation>

en·trust (en trust′) *v* trust a person with a responsibility: *to entrust someone with a task, to entrust something precious to someone.*

en·try (en′trē) *n, pl* **en·tries** **1** the act or right of entering. **2** a place by which to enter, or an open area around or in front of it. Also, **entryway**. **3** something entered in a list, record, or database. **4** a thing sent in to a contest. **5** *Law* the act of taking possession of lands or buildings by entering or setting foot on them. <Old French, from Latin *intra* inside>

entry word *n* in a dictionary, one of the words listed in alphabetical order and followed by information about it.

en·twine (en twīn′) *v* **en·twined, en·twin·ing** **1** twine together. **2** twine around: *Roses entwined the little cottage.*

e·nu·mer·ate (i nyū′mə rāt′) *or* (i nū′mə rāt′) *v* **e·nu·mer·at·ed, e·nu·mer·at·ing** **1** name one by one: *She enumerated the capitals of each province and territory.* **2** count. **3** 🍁 include in a list of eligible voters in an area. <Latin *e-* out + *numerare* to count> **e·nu′mer·a′tion** *n.* **e·nu′mer·a′tor** *n.*

e·nun·ci·ate (i nun′sē āt′) *v* **e·nun·ci·at·ed, e·nun·ci·at·ing** **1** pronounce words distinctly: *Actors learn to enunciate.* **2** state definitely and clearly: *to enunciate a new theory.* <Latin *e-* out + *nuntiare* announce> **e·nun′ci·a′tion** *n.*

en·vel·op (en vel′əp) *v* **en·vel·oped, en·vel·op·ing** wrap or cover completely; surround: *The baby lay in the carriage, enveloped in blankets. Fog enveloped the island.* <Old French *en-* in + *voloper* wrap> **en·vel′op·ment** *n.*

en·ve·lope (en′və lōp′) *or* (on′və lōp′) *n* **1** a paper cover in which a letter or anything flat and thin can be sealed for mailing or storage. **2** any covering or wrapper. **push the envelope,** *Informal* go to the extreme limit of what is usual.

en·vi·a·ble (en′vē ə bəl) *adj* worth having: *She has an enviable school record.* **en′vi·a·bly** *adv.*

en·vi·ous (en′vē əs) *adj* feeling or showing envy: *envious glances. I'm envious of your new boots.* **en′vi·ous·ly** *adv.*

en·vi·ron·ment (en vī′ərn mənt) *n* **1** the earth, water, and air as the home of living things: *We must care for the environment.* **2** all the surrounding conditions and influences that affect the development of a living person or thing: *He was raised in an environment of love and acceptance.* **3** physical setting: *You can't do that in a classroom environment.* <Old French *en-* in + *viron* circle> **en·vi′ron·men′tal** *adj.*

en·vi·ron·men·tal·ism (en vī′ərn men′tə liz′əm) *n* **1** social and political activism in favour of protecting the environment. **2** the theory that environment is the most powerful influence determining a person's development. **en·vi′ron·men′tal·ist** *n.*

en·vi·rons (en vī′rənz) *pln* the surrounding area or districts: *We visited Medicine Hat and its environs.*

en·vis·age (en viz′ij) *v* **en·vis·aged, en·vis·ag·ing** foresee: *I envisage no difficulty with our plans.* <French, from Latin *visus* a vision>

en·vi·sion (en vizh′ən) *v* have a mental picture of: *It is difficult to envision spring flowers when the snow is on the ground.*

en·voy (en′voi) *n* **1** a messenger. **2** a diplomat ranking below an ambassador and above a minister. <Old French, from Latin *in via* on the way>

en·vy (en′vē) *n, pl* **en·vies** **1** a strong desire for what another person has: *I was overcome with envy when I saw his new computer.* **2** the object of such feeling: *She was the envy of the younger girls in the school.*
v **en·vied, en·vy·ing** **1** feel envy toward: *Some people envy the rich.* **2** feel envy because of: *He envied his friend's success.* <Old French *envie*, from Latin *invidere* to look with ill will upon>

en·zyme (en′zīm) *n* a chemical substance, produced in living cells that can cause changes in other substances in the body without being changed itself. <German *Enzym*, from Greek *en-* in + *zyme* leaven>

E·o·cene (ē′ə sēn′) *Geology n* the geological epoch lasting from about 60 million to 40 million years ago, when mammals were the dominant species. See also CENOZOIC, TERTIARY.
adj to do with this epoch. <Greek *eos* dawn + *kainos* recent>

e·on (ē′on) *n* a very long period of time. Also, **aeon.** <Latin, from Greek *aion* lifetime, age>

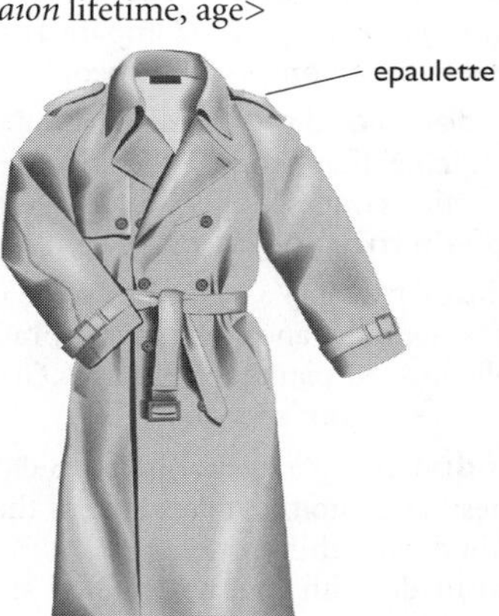

The trench coat is modelled on military coats worn in World War I (1914–1918), during which much of the fighting took place in and around trenches. Originally, all trench coats had **epaulettes**.

ep·au·lette or **ep·au·let** (ep′ə let′) *or* (ep′ə let′) *n* a decoration or flap of cloth on the shoulder of a coat or jacket, often seen on uniforms worn by officers in the armed forces. <French *épaule* shoulder>

é·pée or **e·pee** (ā pā′) *n* a narrow fencing sword with no edge and a blunted point. <French>

a bat	e bed	i bid	o pot	u cup	th thin
ā cake	ē me	ī bite	ō go	ū rude	ᴛʜ then
à bar	ə about	ər over	ò for	ů put	zh measure

e·phem·er·a (i fem′ə rə) *pln* printed items meant for short-term use, such as posters, playbills, or tickets, often collected by fans: *She collects Beatles ephemera.* <Greek *ephemeros* living only a day, from *epi-* upon + *hemera* day>

e·phem·er·al (i fem′ə rəl) *adj* lasting only a very short time; fleeting.

ep·ic (ep′ik) *n* **1** a long, dignified, or majestic poem about heroic adventures. **2** a novel or movie with similar qualities.
adj to do with or being an epic, or like an epic: *epic deeds.* <Latin, from Greek *epos* word, story> **ep′i·cal·ly** *adv.*

ep·i·cen·tre (ep′ə sen′tər) *n* **1** the point directly above something, especially the centre of the earthquake. **2** the focal point of a disturbance: *the epicentre of a tropical storm, the epicentre of a revolt.* Also, **epicenter**. <Greek *epi-* on, in + *centre*>

ep·i·cure (ep′ə kyūr′) *n* a person of refined tastes in eating and drinking. <*Epicurus*, a philosopher who taught that the avoidance of pain is the greatest good>

ep·i·cu·re·an (ep′ə kyə rē′ən) *adj* **1** like an epicure; fond of pleasure and luxury. **2** fit for an epicure: *an epicurean banquet.*
n a person fond of pleasure and luxury.

ep·i·dem·ic (ep′ə dem′ik) *n* **1** the rapid spread of a disease so that many people have it at the same time: *a flu epidemic.* **2** the rapid spread of anything bad: *an epidemic of burglaries.*
adj affecting many people at the same time; widespread: *an epidemic disease. The wild rumours had reached epidemic proportions.* Compare ENDEMIC. <French, from Greek *epi-* among + *demos* people>

ep·i·de·mi·ol·o·gy (ep′ə dē′mē ol′ə jē) *n* the branch of medicine that studies the spread and containment of infectious disease. **ep′i·de′mi·o·log′i·cal** *adj.* **ep′i·de′mi·ol′o·gist** *n.*

ep·i·der·mis (ep′ə dər′mis) *n* **1** the outer layer of the skin of vertebrates, and some invertebrates. **2** a skinlike layer of cells in seed plants and ferns. <Greek *epi-* over + *derma* skin> **ep′i·der′mal** *adj.*

ep·i·du·ral (ep′ə dyū′rəl) *or* (ep′ə dū′rəl) *n* an injection of anesthetic into the membrane of the spinal cord to relieve pain during childbirth.
adj to do with this part of the spinal cord and similar membranes protecting other parts of the nervous system. <Greek *epi-* on + Latin *dura mater* = hard mother, the membrane's technical name>

ep·i·glot·tis (ep′ə glot′is) *n* a thin, triangular plate of cartilage covering the entrance to the windpipe during swallowing, so that food does not enter the lungs. <Latin, from Greek *epi-* on + *glotta* tongue>

ep·i·gram (ep′ə gram′) *n* **1** a short, pointed or witty saying. Example: *I can resist everything but temptation.* **2** a short poem ending in a witty or clever thought. <Latin, from Greek *epi-* on + *graphein* write> **ep′i·gram·mat′ic** *adj.*

ep·i·lep·sy (ep′ə lep′sē) *n* a disorder of the nervous system causing periodic convulsions and total or partial loss of consciousness. <Latin, from Greek *epi-* on + *lepsia* seizing> **ep′i·lep′tic** *adj, n.*

ep·i·logue (ep′ə log′) *n* a section added at the end of a book, poem, or speech and serving to round out or interpret the work. Also, **epilog**. <French, from Greek *epi-* in addition + *legein* speak>

e·piph·a·ny (i pif′ə nē) *n, pl* **e·piph·a·nies** **1** a sudden, significant understanding: *My first airplane flight was an epiphany, and I am determined to become a pilot.* **2 Epiphany** *Christianity* the festival celebrating the visit of the Wise Men to Christ at Bethlehem, in Western churches, January 6, in Orthodox churches, January 19. <Old French, from Greek *epiphainein* to show>

ep·i·phyte (ep′ə fīt′) *Botany n* any of various plants that grow on other plants for support but not for nourishment. Mosses and lichens are epiphytes. <Greek *epi-* on + *phyton* plant>

e·pis·co·pal (i pis′kə pəl) *adj* to do with or governed by a group of bishops. <Latin *episcopus* bishop, from Greek *episkopos* overseer>

ep·i·sode (ep′ə sōd′) *n* **1** an incident or experience that stands out from others: *The year in France was an important episode in her life.* **2** a set of events forming a unit in the plot of a novel or story. **3** a portion of a serial TV show or movie: *The final episode will be shown next week.* **4** an attack of a disease. <Greek *episod* commentary between two parts of a Greek tragedy>

ep·i·sod·ic (ep′ə sod′ik) *adj* **1** containing a series of separate parts or elements: *The episodic style of writing makes it difficult to follow the plot of the story.* **2** occurring at irregular intervals: *episodic attacks.*

e·pis·tle (i pis′əl) *n* a letter, especially a long, formal, or instructive letter, or a piece of literature written in the form of a letter to someone. <Latin, from Greek *epi-* to + *stellein* send> **e·pis′to·lar′y** (i pis′tə ler′ē) *adj.*

ep·i·taph (ep′ə taf′) *n* a short statement in memory of a dead person, especially one put on a tombstone. <Latin, from Greek *epi-* on + *taphos* tomb>

ep·i·the·li·um (ep′ə thē′lē əm) *Biology n, pl* **ep·i·the·li·ums** or **ep·i·the·li·a** (ep′ə thē′lē ə) a thin layer of cells forming a tissue that covers surfaces and lines hollow organs. <Latin, from Greek *epi-* on + *thele* nipple, a term originally applied to tissue with a nipplelike surface> **ep′i·the′li·al** *adj.*

ep·i·thet (ep′ə thit) *n* **1** a descriptive expression used as a name or forming part of a name. Example: *Richard the Lion-Hearted.* **2** a word or phrase, sometimes very insulting, used in place of a person's name. Example: *Hey, Fatty, come here!* <Latin, from Greek *epi-* on + *tithenai* to place>

e·pit·o·me (i pit′ə mē) *n* a person who or thing that is an ideal or typical example of some quality: *With all his education, he is the very epitome of wisdom.* <Latin, from Greek *epitome* summary, essence>

e·pit·o·mize (i pit′ə mīz′) *v* **e·pit·o·mized, e·pit·o·miz·ing** be an epitome of: *Robin Hood epitomizes basic social justice.*

e·poch (ē′pok) *or* (ep′ək) *n* a long period of time, especially one in which important events happened: *The years leading to Confederation were an epoch in Canada's history.* <Latin, from Greek *epoche* fixed point of time>

ep·och·al (ep′ə kəl) *or* (ē′pok əl) *adj* beginning an epoch; causing important changes: *Starting high school is an epochal event in your life.* Also, **epoch-making**.

ep·o·nym (ep′ə nim′) *n* a person after whom something is named: *Romulus is the eponym of Rome.* <Greek *epi-* to + *onyma* name> **e·pon′y·mous** *adj.*

e·pox·y (i pok′sē) *n, pl* **e·pox·ies** a resin containing oxygen as a bond between two different atoms already united in another way.
adj to do with or being an epoxy. <Greek *epi-* on + *oxy(gen)*>

EPROM (ē′prom) *Computers n* a PROM chip that can be erased by ultraviolet light and reprogrammed. <*e* from *erasable* + *PROM*>

Ep·som salts (ep′səm) *n* a bitter, white, crystalline powder used as a laxative. <*Epsom*, a town in England, where these salts were originally obtained>

eq·ua·ble (ek′wə bəl) *or* (ē′kwə bəl) *adj* steady or even, especially in mood or temper: *He has an equable disposition.* **eq′ua·bly** *adv.*

e·qual (ē′kwəl) *adj* the same in amount, size, or degree, neither more nor less: *These two fish are equal in weight. Men and women have equal rights.*
n a person or thing equal to another: *In spelling she had no equal.*
v **e·qualled** or **e·qualed, e·qual·ling** or **e·qual·ing** **1** be the same in amount or value: *Four times five equals twenty. Symbol* **=** **2** make or do something as good as: *I tried hard to equal the scoring record.* <Latin *aequus* even, just> **e·qual′i·ty** (i kwol′ə tē) *n.* **e′qual·ize** *v.* **e′qual·ly** *adv.*
equal to, a the same as: *Ten dimes are equal to one dollar.* **b** capable of; strong enough or brave enough for: *She is equal to the task.*

✱ **e·qual·i·za·tion payment** (ē′kwə lī′zā′shən) *n* money paid to less wealthy provinces by the Federal Government in order to make the level of services to citizens equal in all provinces.

e·qual·iz·er (ē′kwə lī′zər) *n* **1** a network of coils, resistors, or capacitors that controls the response of frequencies in an audio system and lets the user adjust the tone. **2** a person who or thing that makes things or people equal: *She scored the equalizer to make the score 2–2.*

equal opportunity *n* **1** the policy of giving everyone the same chances or treatment in employment or promotion. **2** operating under such a policy: *an equal opportunity employer.*

equal sign *n* the sign =.

e·qua·nim·i·ty (ē′kwə nim′ə tē) *n* evenness of mind or temper: *to bear disappointment with equanimity.* <Latin *aequus* even + *animus* mind, temper>

e·quate (i kwāt′) *v* **e·quat·ed, e·quat·ing** declare to be the same; treat or consider as equivalent: *Don't equate academic success with intelligence.* <Latin *aequus* equal>

e·qua·tion (i kwā′zhən) *n* **1** a statement that quantities are equal. Example: (4 x 8) + 12 = 44. **2** a formula for calculating something, or a set of factors to be considered: *Don't forget to include weather in the equation, because if it rains, we'll need an indoor location.* **3** an expression using chemical formulas and symbols to show the substances used and produced in a chemical change. Example: $NaOH + HCl = NaCl + H_2O$. **4** the act of equating things.

E

e·qua·tor (i kwā′tər) *n* **1** an imaginary circle around the middle of the earth, halfway between the North Pole and the South Pole. **2** a similarly situated circle on any celestial body. <Latin *aequator* equalizer (of day and night)>

e·qua·to·ri·al (ek′wə tô′rē əl) *or* (ē′kwə tô′rē əl) *adj* **1** of, at, or near the equator: *equatorial countries.* **2** like conditions at or near the equator: *This heat is almost equatorial.*

Equatorial Guinea *n* a country in west central Africa.

Equestrians who participate in the Olympic event of Jumping must complete the course consisting of a series of 15 to 20 obstacles, while accumulating as few penalties as possible. A competitor loses four points if the horse knocks down an obstacle, puts a foot in the water jump, or refuses to jump. If a horse refuses to jump a second time, the penalty is eight points.

e·ques·tri·an (i kwes′trē ən) *adj* **1** to do with horseback riding: *equestrian skill. The three Olympic equestrian sports are dressage, eventing, and jumping.* **2** showing someone mounted on horseback: *an equestrian statue.*
n a rider or performer on horseback. <Latin *equus* horse>

a bat	e bed	i bid	o pot	u cup	th thin
ā cake	ē me	ī bite	ō go	ū rude	ᴛʜ then
à bar	ə about	ər over	ô for	ů put	zh measure

e·qui·an·gu·lar (ē′kwē ang′gyə lər) *Mathematics adj* with all angles equal: *A rectangle is equiangular.*

e·qui·dis·tant (ē′kwə dis′tənt) *adj* equally far: *All points on the circumference of a circle are equidistant from the centre.* **e′qui·dis′tant·ly** *adv.*

e·qui·lat·er·al (ē′kwə lat′ə rəl) *or* (ek′wə lat′ə rəl) *adj* with all sides equal: *A square is equilateral.*

e·qui·lib·ri·um (ē′kwə lib′rē əm) *or* (ek′wə lib′rē əm) *n* **1** a state in which opposing forces are equal or parts of a system are in balance. **2** one's physical or mental sense of balance: *Don't let little annoyances upset your equilibrium.* <Latin *aequus* equal + *libra* a balance>

e·quine (ē′kwīn) *or* (ek′wīn) *adj* to do with horses.
n horse. <Latin *equus* horse>

e·qui·nox (ē′kwə noks′) *or* (ek′wə noks′) *n* either of the two times in the year when day and night are of equal length. The **vernal** or **spring equinox** occurs near March 21, the **autumnal** or **fall equinox** near September 22. See VERNAL for picture. <Latin *aequus* equal + *nox* night> **e′qui·noc′tial** *adj.*

e·quip (i kwip′) *v* **e·quipped, e·quip·ping** furnish with what is needed: *The school equips each player with a complete hockey outfit. We are equipped to handle any emergency.* <Old Norse *skip* ship>

e·quip·ment (i kwip′mənt) *n* the things needed or used for a certain task or activity: *Writing equipment includes pen and paper.*

eq·ui·ta·ble (ek′wə tə bəl) *adj* fair and just: *equitable treatment for all.* <Latin *aequus* equal> **eq′ui·ta·bly** *adv.*

eq·ui·ta·tion (ek′wə tā′shən) *n* horseback riding. <Latin *equus* horse>

eq·ui·ty (ek′wə tē) *n, pl* **eq·ui·ties** **1** fairness or justice. **2** the amount that a property is worth, minus what is still owed on it. <Latin *aequus* equal>

e·quiv·a·lent (i kwiv′ə lənt) *adj* **1** equal in value, measure, effect, or meaning: *Nodding your head can be equivalent to saying "yes."* **2** *Mathematics* with the same extent although not the same form: *A triangle and a square of equal area are equivalent.*
n something equivalent: *What's the English equivalent of "bonjour"?* <Latin *aequus* equal + *valere* be worth> **e·quiv′a·lence** *n.* **e·quiv′a·lent·ly** *adv.*

e·quiv·o·cal (i kwiv′ə kəl) *adj* **1** intentionally vague or ambiguous: *His equivocal answer left us unsure of his real position on the issue.* **2** uncertain: *The result of the experiment was equivocal and proved nothing.* **3** rousing suspicion: *equivocal behaviour.* <See EQUIVOCATE.> **e·quiv′o·cal·ly** *adv.*

e·quiv·o·cate (i kwiv′ə kāt′) *v* **e·quiv·o·cat·ed, e·quiv·o·cat·ing** use deliberately vague expressions in order to mislead or avoid committing oneself: *Don't equivocate; just give me a straight answer.* <Latin *aequivocus* vague> **e·quiv′o·ca′tion** *n.* **e·quiv′o·ca′tor** *n.*

–er[1] *suffix* a person who or thing that makes or does something, lives in a certain place, or has a certain attribute: *admirer, Newfoundlander, complainer.* <Old English>

–er[2] *suffix* more. This suffix forms the comparative degree of adjectives and adverbs: *smaller, oftener.* <Old English>

GRAMMAR AND USAGE

Usually you can add **–er**, meaning "more," and **–est**, meaning "most," to adjectives and adverbs that have only one syllable: *higher, softest.*

With adjectives and adverbs of two or more syllables, you usually use "more" and "most": *more interesting, most valuable.*

e·ra (er′ə) *or* (ē′rə) *n* **1** a historical period distinguished by certain important events or ideas: *the era of space travel, the Depression era.* **2** any of five long periods of time in geological history: *the Cenozoic era.* <Latin *era* a point from which time is calculated>

ERA earned run average.

e·rad·i·cate (i rad′ə kāt′) *v* **e·rad·i·cat·ed, e·rad·i·cat·ing** destroy completely: *Yellow fever has been eradicated in some countries.* <Latin *eradicare* to pull up by the roots> **e·rad′i·ca·ble** (i rad′ə kə′ bəl) *adj.* **e·rad′i·ca′tion** *n.*

e·rase (i rās′) *v* **e·rased, e·ras·ing** **1** rub out; wipe out: *She erased the wrong answer and wrote in the correct one.* **2** remove marks or recorded information from: *to erase a chalkboard, to erase a disk.* **3** remove all trace of: *The blow on his head erased all memory of the accident.* <Latin *ex-* out + *radere* scrape> **e·ras′a·ble** *adj.*
e·ra′sure (i rā′zhər) *n.*

e·ras·er (i rā′sər) *n* a piece of rubber, felt, or plastic for erasing marks made with pencil, ink, or chalk.

er·bi·um (ər′bē əm) *n* a rare metallic element of the yttrium group. *Symbol* **Er** <*Ytterby*, Sweden, where it was discovered>

ere (er) *Poetic prep, conj* before: *ere nightfall* (*prep*), *ere I return* (*conj*). <Old English *ær*>

e·rect (i rekt′) *adj* **1** upright: *to stand erect. The cat faced the dog with fur erect.* **2** engorged with fluid in a bodily organ, especially the penis, so as to become rigid.
v **1** set up; cause to stand upright: *to erect a flagpole.* **2** build: *That house was erected forty years ago.* <Latin *ex-* up + *regere* keep straight> **e·rect′ly** *adv.*

e·rect·ion (i rek′shən) *n* **1** the act of erecting or building something. **2** something that has been erected. **3** the state of a bodily organ, especially the penis, that has become engorged with fluid and is rigid.

erg[1] (erg) *n* a unit of work or energy, equal to 0.1 microjoules. *Symbol* **e** <Greek *ergon* work>

erg[2] (erg) *n* a large area of sand dunes in the desert. <Arabic *irq*>

er·go (er′gō) *or* (ər′gō) *adv, conj* therefore. <Latin = therefore>

er·go·nom·ics (ər′gə nom′iks) *n* (*with singular verb*) the science that studies the relationship between the human body and the working environment in order to maximize efficiency and minimize strain. <Greek *ergon* work + (*econ*)*omics*> **er′go·nom′ic** *adj.*
er′go·nom′i·cal·ly *adv.*

Er·i·tre·a (er′ə trē′ə) *or* (er′ə trā′ə) *n* a country in northeast Africa. **Er′i·tre′an** *adj, n.*

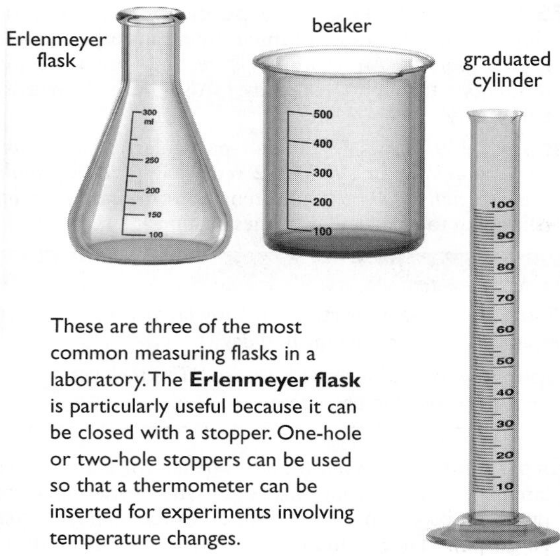

These are three of the most common measuring flasks in a laboratory. The **Erlenmeyer flask** is particularly useful because it can be closed with a stopper. One-hole or two-hole stoppers can be used so that a thermometer can be inserted for experiments involving temperature changes.

Er·len·mey·er flask (ər′lən mī′ər) *n* a laboratory flask with a broad base and a narrow neck, shaped like a cone. <E. *Erlenmeyer*, 19c chemist>

er·mine (ər′mən) *n, pl* **er·mines** or (*especially collectively*) **er·mine 1** a weasel of northern climates, brown in summer but white with a black-tipped tail in winter. **2** the fur of this animal, used for trimming garments. <probably from Latin *Armenius* Armenian rat>

e·rode (i rōd′) *v* **e·rod·ed, e·rod·ing 1** wear away gradually: *The stream eroded a channel in the solid rock.* **2** deteriorate or cause to deteriorate gradually: *Failure to make the team eroded his confidence.* <Latin *ex-* away + *rodere* gnaw>

e·ro·sion (i rō′zhən) *n* the gradual wearing away and movement of rock or soil caused, for example, by water, wind, or ice. **e·ro′sive** (i rō′siv) *adj.*

e·rot·ic (i rot′ik) *adj* to do with sexual desire. <Greek *eros* sexual love> **e·rot′i·cal·ly** *adv.* **er′o·ti·cize** *v.*

e·rot·i·ca (i rot′ə kə) *n* literature or art with erotic content.

err (er) *or* (ər) *v* **1** make a mistake: *He seems to have erred when reporting the time, because it couldn't have been that early.* **2** do wrong: *He admitted that he had erred in his youth.* <Latin *errare* to stray (from normal behaviour) i.e., to make a mistake> **err′ing** *adj.*

er·rand (er′ənd) *n* a small job that involves a short journey: *He rakes leaves and does other errands for his parents.* <Old English *ærende*>
run errands, do small jobs that involve going somewhere.

er·rant (er′ənt) *adj* (*especially in* ***knight errant***) travelling in search of adventure.

er·ra·ta (ə rȧ′tə) *or* (ə rā′tə) *pl n, sing* **er·ra·tum** a list of errors found in a printed text, usually listed on a separate sheet.

er·rat·ic (ə rat′ik) *adj* **1** irregular: *an erratic heartbeat.* **2** behaving strangely or unpredictably. <Latin *errare* wander> **er·rat′i·cal·ly** *adv.*

er·ro·ne·ous (ə rō′nē əs) *adj* mistaken or incorrect: *an erroneous belief.* **er·ro′ne·ous·ly** *adv.*

er·ror (er′ər) *n* **1** something wrong or incorrect: *a spelling error, errors in counting.* **2** wrongdoing. **3** *Baseball* a mistake in fielding or throwing that allows a runner to advance.
in error, a wrong or mistaken: *I'm afraid you are in error.* **b** by mistake: *He got on the westbound bus in error.*

er·satz (er zats′) *adj* substituting, often in a poor way, for the real thing: *ersatz coffee.* <German>

erst·while (ərst′wīl′) *adj* former; past: *erstwhile classmates.* <Old English *aerest* earliest>

er·u·dite (er′yə dīt′) *or* (er′ə dīt′) *adj* scholarly and well-informed. <Latin *erudire* instruct, from *ex-* away + *rudis* unlearned> **er′u·dite′ly** *adv.* **er′u·di′tion** *n.*

e·rupt (i rupt′) *v* **1** burst forth: *Hot water erupted from the geyser. The volcano last erupted in 1807.* **2** break out in a rash: *Her skin erupted after she ate mangoes.* **3** break through the gums during the normal development of a tooth. <Latin *ex-* out + *rumpere* burst> **e·rup′tion** *n.*

e·ryth·ro·cyte (ə rith′rə sīt′) *n* a red blood cell that carries oxygen to cells and tissues, and carbon dioxide back to the lungs. Compare LEUCOCYTE. <Greek *erythros* red + *-cyte*>

es·ca·late (es′kə lāt′) *v* **es·ca·lat·ed, es·ca·lat·ing** increase steadily and quickly in amount or in scope: *Small battles can easily escalate into major wars.* <See ESCALATOR.> **es′ca·la′tion** *n.*

es·ca·la·tor (es′kə lā′tər) *n* a continuous moving staircase that runs by electricity, as in malls, subway stations, etc. <*Escalator*, a trademark, from Latin *scala* ladder + (*elev*)*ator*>

es·ca·pade (es′kə pād′) *n* a wild adventure or prank: *Dad told us about some of his foolish escapades as a high school student.* <French = prank, from Latin *excappare* escape (e.g., from rules of good behaviour)>

es·cape (e skāp′) *v* **es·caped, es·cap·ing 1** get free: *to escape from prison.* **2** manage to avoid or evade: *to escape responsibility, to escape punishment. We all escaped the flu this year.* **3** come out, especially unintentionally or in small amounts: *A cry escaped her lips. A leak in the hose was allowing gas to escape.* **4** fail to be noticed or remembered by: *That tiny error escaped my eye. His name escapes me right now.*
n **1** an act or means of escaping. **2** the act or means of finding distraction from a routine: *to find escape in mystery stories.* <Old French, from Latin *excappare* to slip out of one's cloak, i.e., to free oneself>

escape artist *n* a performer who entertains people by getting free from chains or other confinement.

escape clause *n* a clause in a contract that frees a signer from certain responsibilities under specified circumstances.

a bat	e bed	i bid	o pot	u cup	th thin
ā cake	ē me	ī bite	ō go	ū rude	ᴛʜ then
ȧ bar	ə about	ər over	ȯ for	u̇ put	zh measure

escape velocity *n* the velocity that must be reached by an object, such as an artificial satellite, in order to escape the gravitational pull of the earth, sun, or moon.

es·cap·ism (e skā′piz əm) *n* the tendency to avoid unpleasant realities or routines through entertainment or fantasy. **es·cap′ist** *n, adj.*

es·car·got (es′kȧr gō′) *n* an edible snail. <French>

es·ca·role (es′kə rōl′) *n* a green plant related to endive and eaten as a vegetable, usually in salads. <French>

es·carp·ment (e skȧrp′mənt) *n* a high area of land that drops off sharply; a cliff. <French *escarpe* steep slope>

es·chew (es chū′) *v* refuse to do, use, or have anything to do with: *A wise person eschews bad company.* <Old French *eschiver*>

es·cort (es′kȯrt) *for n,* (e skȯrt′) *for v. n* **1** a person, vehicle, or group of people or vehicles accompanying someone to guard, guide, or to show honour or courtesy: *an escort of ten Mounties.* **2** a man or boy who accompanies a woman or girl to a social event: *Her escort to the party was a tall young man.* **3** the act of going with another as an escort.
v accompany as an escort: *Motorcycles escorted the parade.* <Italian *scorgere* guide>

escort service *n* a business that provides companions for hire.

es·crow (es′krō) *or* (e skrō′) *n* a deed, bond, or other written agreement kept by a third person until certain conditions are fulfilled by the two parties to the agreement. <Old French *escroue* roll of parchment>
in escrow, held by a third party in accordance with an agreement.

es·cutch·eon (e skuch′ən) *n* a shield or shield-shaped surface on which a coat of arms is put. <Old French, from Latin *scutum* shield>

ESE east-southeast.

es·ker (es′kər) *n* a winding ridge of sand or gravel, deposited by meltwater streams flowing inside the retreating glaciers of the Ice Age. <Irish *eiscer*>

Es·ki·mo (es′kə mō′) *n* **1** See INUIT and YUPIK (def. 1). **2** See INUKTITUT, INUPIAT, and YUPIK (def. 2).

GRAMMAR AND USAGE

Eskimo, which probably comes from a word in an Algonquian language, is a disparaging name applied to the Inuit and Yupik by Europeans. In Canada, it is considered offensive.

ESL *n* in full, **English as a Second Language** English as studied by those whose first language is not English.

e·soph·a·gus (i sof′ə gəs) *n, pl* **e·soph·a·gi** (i sof′ə jī′) the passage carrying food from the mouth to the stomach. Also, **oesophagus**. <Latin, from Greek *oiso* carry + *phagein* eat>

es·o·ter·ic (ez′ə ter′ik) *or* (es′ə ter′ik) *adj* understood only by a select few. <Greek *eso* within>
es′o·ter′i·cal·ly *adv.*

ESP *n* in full, **extrasensory perception** the supposed ability to become aware of things by means other than the normal senses. An example is reading other people's thoughts through telepathy. Also called **mental telepathy**.

es·pe·cial·ly (e spesh′ə lē) *adv* **1** particularly: *That book is hard, especially for children.* **2** remarkably: *These candies are especially good.* <Old French, from Latin *specialis* belonging to a particular species or kind>

CONFUSABLES

Especially means "particularly": *My brother was especially nice to me on my birthday.*

Specially means "for one purpose": *This tool was specially designed to open boxes.*

Es·pe·ran·to (es′pə rȧn′tō) *or* (es′pə ran′tō) *n* an artificial language for international use, with vocabulary and grammar based on forms common to the main European languages. <Dr. *Esperanto*, pseudonym of its inventor, 19c physician L.L. Zamenhof>

es·pi·o·nage (es′pē ə nȧzh′) *n* the practice of spying in other countries to find out their military or political secrets. <French *espion* spy>

es·pla·nade (es′plə nād′) *or* (es′plə nȧd′) any open, level space used for public walks or drives. <French, from Latin *ex-* out + *planus* level>

es·pouse (es pouz′) *v* **es·poused, es·pous·ing 1** marry. **2** adopt as one's own: *to espouse a new theory.* <Old French, from Latin *spondere* to betroth>
es·pous′al *n.*

es·pres·so (e spres′ō) *n* coffee brewed from dark-roasted beans under steam pressure. <Italian>

es·prit de corps (es prē′ də kȯr′) *n* a sense of unity and shared purpose in a group. <French = group spirit>

–esque *suffix* similar in style to: *statuesque.* <French>

es·quire (es kwīr′) *or* (es′kwīr) *n* **1** in the Middle Ages, a young man of noble family who attended a knight until he himself was made a knight. **2 Esquire** (*now mostly humorous*) an old formal title of respect placed after a man's last name instead of placing *Mr.* before: *John Jones, Esquire.* <Old French, from Latin *scutiarus* shield bearer, from *scutum* shield>

–ess *suffix* female: *lioness.* <French, from Greek *-issa*>

GRAMMAR AND USAGE

The feminine suffix **–ess** used in names of occupations (*actress*, *waitress*, *hostess*, etc.) is widely regarded as sexist. Neutral terms such as *actor*, *server*, and *host* are preferred.

es·say (es′ā) *for n; also, for def. 3,* (e sā′); (e sā′) *for v.*
n **1** a short literary piece of nonfiction, usually expressing personal opinions: *The author has written a collection of essays on Canadian politics.* **2** a fairly lengthy written work assigned as a learning exercise. **3** an attempt.
v attempt: *She essayed a very difficult jump.* <Old French *essai*, from Latin *exagium* a weighing> **es′say·ist** *n.*

estuary

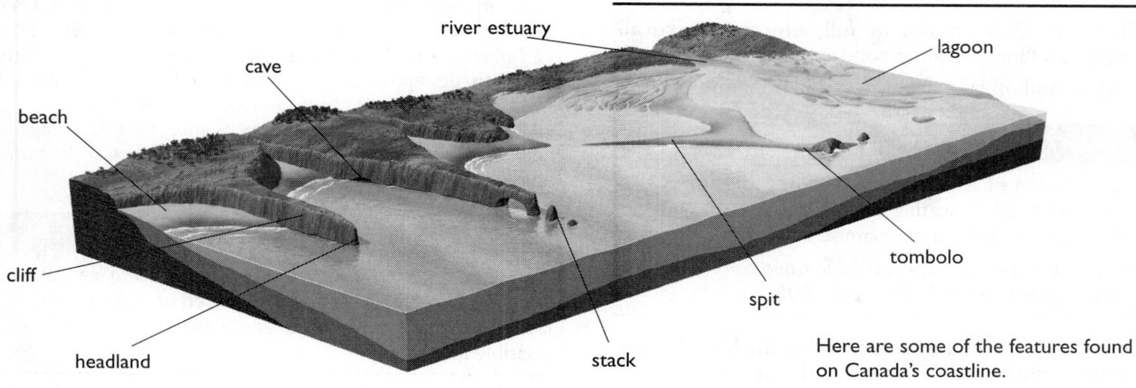

Here are some of the features found on Canada's coastline.

es·sence (es′əns) *n* **1** the defining or core feature of something: *Kindness is the essence of politeness.* **2** a concentrated substance obtained from a plant or fruit with its characteristic flavour, fragrance, or effect. <Old French, from Latin *esse* be>
in essence, basically: *So, in essence, what you are saying is that it's too expensive.*
of the essence, essential.

es·sen·tial (i sen′shəl) *adj* **1** necessary: *It is essential that you book your seat early.* **2** making a thing what it is: *Fairness is an essential feature of justice.*
n a necessary part: *Leave out extra details and just stick to the essentials.*

es·sen·tial·ly (i sen′shə lē) *adv* basically: *Essentially, plagiarism is stealing.*

essential oil *n* an oil that gives a plant or fruit its characteristic flavour, fragrance, or effect, and is extracted for use in perfume, flavouring, or medicine.

–est *suffix* most. This suffix forms the superlative degree of adjectives and adverbs: *smallest, oftenest.* <Old English *-est, -ost*>

es·tab·lish (e stab′lish) *v* **1** set up permanently: *to establish a business, to establish a colony, to establish a set of rules.* **2** (*with a reflexive pronoun*) start living or working: *A new doctor has established herself on our street.* **3** cause to be generally accepted over the long term: *to establish a custom.* **4** show to be true: *to establish a fact.* <Old French, from Latin *stabilis* stable, firm> **es·tab′lished** *adj.*

es·tab·lish·ment (e stab′lish mənt) *n* **1** the act of establishing. **2** something, especially an institution, that is established: *A household, business, church, or army may be called an establishment.* **3 the Establishment** the people traditionally holding power in a society.

es·tate (e stāt′) *n* **1** a large piece of land belonging to a person: *He has a beautiful country estate with a house and a pool.* **2** all that a person owns: *When she died, her estate was divided up among her children.* **3** a condition or stage in life: *to reach adult's estate.* **4** a class in a politically organized community. From feudal times, the **first estate** consists of senior members of the clergy; the **second estate** is the nobility; the **third estate** is the common people. The press is sometimes called the **fourth estate**. <Old French, from Latin *status* state>

es·teem (e stēm′) *v* have a high opinion of: *We esteem people of good character.*
n high regard: *Courage is held in esteem.* <Old French, from Latin *aestimare* value>

es·ter (es′tər) *Chemistry n* a compound resulting from the reaction of an acid with an alcohol. <German *es*(*sig*) vinegar + (*ä*)*ther* ether>

es·thet·ic (es thet′ik) AESTHETIC.

es·ti·ma·ble (es′tə mə bəl) *adj* **1** worthy of esteem. **2** capable of being estimated or calculated. <See ESTEEM.>

es·ti·mate (es′tə mit) *for n,* (es′tə māt′) *for v. n* **1** a rough judgment of size, quantity, or time: *By my estimate, the room was about 7 m long, and it actually measured 6.9 m.* **2** a contractor's official statement of what a certain piece of work is expected to cost: *The estimate for painting the house was $4000.*
v **es·ti·mat·ed, es·ti·mat·ing** make or give an estimate: *She estimated that it would take four hours to weed the garden.* <See ESTEEM.> **es′ti·ma′tor** *n.*

es·ti·ma·tion (es′tə mā′shən) *n* **1** judgment or opinion: *In my estimation, your plan will not work.* **2** the act of estimating.

Es·to·ni·a (es tō′nē ə) *n* a country in N central Europe, on the Baltic Sea. **Es·to′ni·an** *adj, n.*

es·trange (e strānj′) *v* **es·tranged, es·trang·ing** cause to turn from love or friendship to indifference or hatred: *His long absences had estranged him from his family.* <Old French *estranger*> **es·trange′ment** *n.*

es·tro·gen (es′trə jen) *n* a female sex hormone. <*estrus* the time in which most mammals are receptive to copulation>

es·tu·ar·y (es′chū er′ē) *n, pl* **es·tu·ar·ies** **1** a broad river mouth flowing into the sea, where its current meets the tide and is influenced by it. **2** an inlet of the sea. <Latin *aestus* tide>

a bat	e bed	i bid	o pot	u cup	th **thin**
ā cake	ē me	ī bite	ō go	ū rude	TH **then**
ä bar	ə about	ər over	ô for	ů put	zh measure

e–tail (ē′tāl) *Computers n* in full, **electronic retail** buying and selling consumer goods via the Internet.

et al. (et′al) and others (an abbreviation of Latin *et alii*).

> **GRAMMAR AND USAGE**
>
> The abbreviation **et al.** is used in bibliographies or lists of works cited, indicating that an entry has several authors besides those named:
>
> Brugmann, Stefan et al., *Explorations in Canadian Literature*, Bentfield Press, Vancouver, 2006.

etc. (et set′ə rə) in full, **et cetera** and so forth; and so on; and other similar things. <Latin = and others>

et·cet·er·as (et set′ə rəz) *pl n* miscellaneous extra things.

etch (ech) *v* **1** use acid to engrave a design or drawing on a metal plate, which can then be printed. *The artist etched only a few copper plates.* **2** make a vivid impression on the mind: *The event remains etched in my memory.* <German *ätzen*> **etch′er** *n.* **etch′ing** *n.*

e·ter·nal (i tər′nəl) *adj* **1** without beginning or ending; existing beyond time and therefore not limited or affected by time. **2** seeming to go on forever: *I wish they would stop that eternal racket.* <Old French, from Latin *aeternalis*> **e·ter′nal·ly** *adv.*

e·ter·ni·ty (i tər′nə tē) *n, pl* **e·ter·ni·ties** **1** existence without beginning or end. **2** time that goes on forever. **3** the fact of being eternal. **4** a very long time: *I waited an eternity for him.*

eth·a·nol (eth′ə nol′) ETHYL ALCOHOL.

e·ther (ē′thər) *n* **1** in full, **ethyl ether** a colourless, strong-smelling liquid that burns and evaporates readily, used as a solvent for fats and resins. **2** *Poetic* the clear sky or outer space. **3** in ancient thought, the invisible, stretchy substance believed to be distributed evenly throughout space. Also (defs. 2, 3), **aether**. <Latin, from Greek *aither* upper air>

e·the·re·al (i thē′rē əl) *adj* **1** light, airy, and delicate: *ethereal beauty, ethereal voices.* **2** to do with the ETHER (defs. 2, 3). Also, **aethereal**. **e·the′re·al·ly** *adv.*

E·ther·net (ē′thər net′) *Trademark n* a system for exchanging messages between computers on a local area network.

eth·i·cal (eth′ə kəl) *adj* **1** to do with standards of right and wrong: *ethical issues.* **2** in accordance with a set of professional honourable standards: *It is not considered ethical for a doctor to treat a family member.* **eth′i·cal·ly** *adv.*

eth·ics (eth′iks) *n* **1** (*with singular verb*) the branch of philosophy that studies moral principles, or questions of right and wrong. **2** (*with plural verb*) rules of right and wrong forming a social or professional code of behaviour: *medical ethics, business ethics.* **3** **ethic** a particular set of moral values, or a single moral value forming the basis of a moral system: *the work ethic.* <Latin, from Greek *ethos* moral character> **eth′i·cist** (eth′i səst) *n.*

E·thi·o·pi·a (ē′thē ō′pē ə) *n* a country in northeast Africa, on the Red Sea. See the APPENDIX. **E′thi·o′pi·an** *adj, n.*

eth·nic (eth′nik) *adj* **1** to do with national tradition and identity, including a shared culture and language: *There are 46 different ethnic groups represented in our school.* **2** *Informal* **a** to do with members of a minority in society. **b** 🍁 to do with people whose first language is neither English nor French: *ethnic dances, the ethnic vote.*
n 🍁 *Informal* an immigrant whose first language is neither English nor French. <Latin, from Greek *ethnos* nation> **eth·nic′i·ty** (eth′ni′sə tē) *n.*

> **GRAMMAR AND USAGE**
>
> Many people avoid using **ethnic** in its *Informal* senses because they feel it is sometimes used as a negative label. The words *multicultural* and *immigrant* are two possible substitutes.

ethnic cleansing *n* the forced removal or wholesale killing of people of a certain ethnic group in an area.

eth·no·cen·tric (eth′nə sen′trik) *adj* regarding everything from the point of view of a certain ethnic group, as though it were the norm. **eth′no·cen′tri·cal·ly** *adv.* **eth′no·cen·tric′i·ty** (eth′nə sen′tri′sə tē) *n.*

e·thos (ē′thos) *n* the essential, distinctive character or spirit of a particular people, community, or period: *Individualism is part of the ethos of modern Western society.* <Latin, from Greek *ethos* character, nature>

eth·yl alcohol (eth′əl) *n* alcohol made by the fermentation of grain, fruits, vegetables, or sugar. Also called **ethanol**. <from *ether*>

eth·yl·ene (eth′ə lēn′) *n* a colourless, flammable gas, used as an anesthetic, in making organic compounds, and for colouring and ripening citrus fruits. <from *ether*>

et·i·quette (et′ə kit) *n* the conventional rules for polite behaviour, especially in formal settings: *business etiquette, wedding etiquette.* <French *étiquette* ticket (giving instructions)>

e–trad·ing (ē′trā′ding) *n* the buying and selling of stocks, bonds, and other securities over the Internet. **e′-trad′er** *n.*

E·trus·can (i trus′kən) *adj* to do with Etruria, an ancient country in western Italy, or its people, their language, or culture.
n **1** a native or inhabitant of Etruria. **2** the language of Etruria.

é·tude (ā tyūd′) *Music n* a short musical piece, usually for a single instrument, often intended to develop the player's skill. <French = study>

et·y·mol·o·gy (et′ə mol′ə jē) *n, pl* **et·y·mol·o·gies** **1** an explanation of the origin and development of a word. **2** the study of the history of individual words and of general historical trends in languages. <Latin, from Greek *etymon* original sense or form of a word> **et′y·mo·log′i·cal** *adj.* **et′y·mol′o·gist** *n.*

EU EUROPEAN UNION.

eu·ca·lyp·tus (yū′kə lip′təs) *n, pl* **eu·ca·lyp·tus·es** or **eu·ca·lyp·ti** (yū′kə lip′tī) a tree that grows in Australia and elsewhere, valued for its timber and for the oil from its leaves. <Latin, from Greek *eu-* well + *kalyptos* covered, from the covering on the tree's buds>

eu·ca·ry·ote (yū ker′ē ət) EUKARYOTE.

Eu·cha·rist (yū′kə rist) *Christianity n* Holy Communion. <Old French, from Greek *eucharistia* thankfulness> **Eu′cha·ris′tic** *adj.*

eu·chre (yū′kər) *n* a simple card game for two to four players, using the 32 highest cards in the deck. <German>

Eu·clid·e·an (yū klid′ē ən) *Mathematics adj* to do with Euclid, a mathematician of ancient Greece, or his principles of geometry.

eu·gen·ics (yū jen′iks) *n* (*with singular verb*) the science of improving the human race by a careful selection of parents in order to develop traits considered desirable. **eu·gen′ic** *adj.* **eu·gen′i·cal·ly** *adv.*

eu·ka·ry·ote (yū kar′ē ət) *n* an organism whose cells have a membrane-bound nucleus, as found in animals, plants, fungi, and protists. Compare PROKARYOTE. Also, **eucaryote.** <Greek *eu-* true + *karyote* cell nucleus, from Greek *karyon* kernel> **eu·ka·ry·o′tic** *adj.*

eu·la·chon (ū′lə kən) OOLICHAN.

eu·lo·gy (yū′lə jē) *n, pl* **eu·lo·gies 1** a speech or piece of writing in praise of someone who has died, usually one delivered at the person's funeral. **2** any expression of high praise. <Latin, from Greek *eu-* well + *legein* speak> **eu′lo·gist** *n.* **eu′lo·gize′** *v.*

eu·nuch (yū′nək) *n* **1** a castrated man, especially one supervising a harem or performing some religious service. **2** an ineffectual person. <Latin, from Greek *eune* bed + *echein* keep. Originally, a eunuch referred to a guard of the bed chamber.>

eu·phe·mism (yū′fə miz′əm) *n* a mild or indirect expression substituted for one that is harsh or unpleasantly direct. Example: *pass away* is a euphemism for *die.* <Greek *eu-* good + *pheme* speaking> **eu′phe·mis′tic** *adj.* **eu′phe·mis′ti·cal·ly** *adv.*

eu·pho·ni·ous (yū fō′nē əs) *adj* pleasing in sound. <Latin, from Greek *eu-* good + *phone* sound> **eu·pho′ni·ous·ly** *adv.* **eu′pho·ny** *n.*

eu·pho·ri·a (yū fô′rē ə) *n* a powerful feeling of well-being or happiness. <Greek = good ability to endure> **eu·pho′ric** *adj.*

Eur·a·sia (yů rā′zhə) *n* the land mass that includes Europe and Asia. **Eu·ra′sian** *adj, n.*

eu·re·ka (yů rē′kə) *interj* used to express joy at having found or discovered something. <Greek *heuriskein* I have found it>

eu·rhyth·mics (yů rɪᴛʜ′miks) EURYTHMICS.

flag of the European Union

eu·ro (yů′rō) *n* the unit of currency shared by most members of the European Union. <*European*>

Euro– *combining form* (**Eur-** *before a vowel*) Europe or European: *Eurasia.*

Eu·rope (yů′rəp) *n* the continent bounded by the Atlantic on the west, the Ural and Caucasus Mountains and the Black Sea on the east, and the Mediterranean Sea on the south. All of Europe is north of the equator. <Greek *Europa*>

Eu·ro·pe·an (yů′rə pē′ən) *adj* **1** to do with Europe or its inhabitants. **2** with ancestors from Europe.
n **1** a native or inhabitant of Europe. **2** a person with ancestors who came from Europe.

European plan *n* a hotel system by which guests pay for only room and service, meals being extra. Compare AMERICAN PLAN.

European Union *n* a group of European nations, formerly called the **European Economic Community** (**EEC**), the **European Community** (**EC**), and (informally) the **Common Market**, that form an economic and political association. These nations have adopted free trade among themselves, and most members share a common currency, the euro.

eu·ro·pi·um (yə rō′pē əm) *n* a rare metallic element of the same group as cerium. *Symbol* **Eu** <Greek *Europa*>

eu·ryth·mics (yů rɪᴛʜ′miks) *n* (*with singular verb*) a system of bodily movements done to music, designed to develop rhythm and grace. Also, **eurhythmics.** <Greek *eu-* good + *rhythm*> **eu·ryth′mic** *adj.*

Eu·sta·chi·an tube (yū stā′shən) *n* a slender canal between the pharynx and the middle ear, which equalizes the air pressure on the two sides of the eardrum. <B. *Eustachio,* 16c anatomist>

eu·tha·na·sia (yū′thə nā′zhə) *n* the painless killing of a person in order to end a pain or distress caused by an incurable disease. <Greek *eu-* easy, good + *thanatos* death>

eu·troph·ic (yū trof′ik) *or* (yū trō′fik) *adj* with excessive plant growth in a lake or river due to a high concentration of nutrients, resulting in a decrease in oxygen and hence a decrease in the number of organisms such as fish. Compare OLIGOTROPHIC. <Greek *eu-* good, well + *trophe* nourishment> **eu′tro·phy** *n.*

eV electronvolt(s).

e·vac·u·ate (i vak′yū āt′) *v* **e·vac·u·at·ed, e·vac·u·at·ing 1** remove people from an area: *Efforts were made to evacuate all foreign residents from the war zone. When the alarm bell rings, the building has to be evacuated.* **2** make or leave empty. <Latin *ex-* out + *vacuus* empty> **e·vac′u·a′tion** *n.* **e·vac′u·ee′** (i vak′yū ē′) *n.*

e·vade (i vād′) *v* **e·vad·ed, e·vad·ing 1** get away from or avoid by cleverness or trickery: *to evade income tax. The thief evaded his pursuers and escaped.* **2** avoid answering, or answer in a misleading way: *Don't evade the question by changing the subject.* <Latin *ex-* away + *vadere* go> **e·vad′er** *n.*

a bat	e bed	i bid	o pot	u cup	th **thin**
ā cake	ē me	ī bite	ō go	ū rude	ᴛʜ **then**
ä bar	ə about	ər over	ô for	ů put	zh measure

E

e·val·u·ate (i val′yū āt′) *v* **e·val·u·at·ed, e·val·u·at·ing** judge the worth, quality, truth, or importance of: *The teacher is evaluating our essays. The ring was evaluated at $800.* **e·val′u·a′tion** *n.* **e·val′u·a′tor** *n.*

ev·a·nes·cent (ev′ə nes′ənt) *adj* tending to disappear or fade away quickly: *The colours of the rainbow are evanescent.* **ev′a·nes′cence** *n.*

e·van·gel·i·cal (ē′van jel′ə kəl) *Christianity adj* to do with churches that emphasize salvation by faith and preaching over ritual. <Latin, from Greek *euangelistes* bringer of good news>

e·van·gel·ism (i van′jə liz′əm) *Christianity n* any effort to teach people about the Christian faith or convert them to it. **e·van′gel·ist** *n.* **e·van′gel·is′tic** *adj.* **e·van′gel·i·za′tion** *n.*

e·vap·o·rate (i vap′ə rāt′) *v* **e·vap·o·rat·ed, e·vap·o·rat·ing** 1 change from a liquid into a gas: *Boiling water evaporates rapidly.* Compare CONDENSE. See STATE for picture. 2 condense by removing moisture, especially water: *Evaporated milk is much thicker than fresh milk.* 3 disappear: *Her good resolutions evaporated soon after New Year's Day.* <Latin *ex-* out + *vapor* vapour> **e·vap′o·ra′tion** *n.* **e·vap′o·ra′tor** *n.*

evaporated milk *n* canned milk prepared by evaporating some of the water from ordinary milk.

e·va·sion (i vā′zhən) *n* the act or a means of evading or avoiding a responsibility or obligation: *guilty of tax evasion.* <Latin *evasionem,* from *evadere* to escape> **e·va′sive** *adj.*

eve (ēv) *n* 1 the evening or day before a holiday or some other special day: *New Year's Eve.* 2 the time just before: *the eve of a revolution.* <Old English *æfen*>

e·ven (ē′vən) *adj* 1 level and smooth: *A tabletop is an even surface.* 2 at the same level: *The snow was even with the windowsill.* 3 the same always or throughout: *an even motion, an even distribution of paint.* 4 equal: *They divided the food in even shares.* 5 with no remainder when a number is divided by two: *Eight is an even number.* 6 neither more nor less: *an even dozen.* 7 not easily disturbed or angered: *an even temper.*
v make even: *to even the score. She evened the edges by trimming them.*
adv 1 contrary to or beyond what might be expected: *Even though I was exhausted, I kept on working.* 2 (*with a comparative*) still or yet: *You can do even better if you try.* 3 exactly: *She left even as you came.* 4 indeed: *He is ready, even eager to go.* <Old English *efen*> **e′ven·ly** *adv.* **e′ven·ness** *n.*
be even, a owe nothing. b have revenge.
break even, have equal gains and losses.
even out, become more even, level, or balanced: *After a rough stretch, the path evens out.*
get even, take revenge.

e·ven–hand·ed (ē′vən han′did) *adj* impartial and fair. **e′ven-hand′ed·ly** *adv.* **e′ven-hand′ed·ness** *n.*

eve·ning (ēv′ning) *n* the last part of day, just before night. *adj* to do with the evening. <Old English *æfen* evening>

evening dress *n* 1 men's formal clothes worn in the evening. 2 an evening gown.

evening gown *n* a woman's long formal or semiformal dress.

evening star *n* a bright planet seen in the western sky after sunset: *Venus is often the evening star.*

even number *n* a number that has no remainder when divided by 2, such as 2, 4, 6, or 8.

e·vent (i vent′) *n* 1 a happening: *current events.* 2 an important happening: *His grandma's 100th birthday was quite an event.* 3 an item in a series of contests or some other program: *The long jump was the last event.* <Latin *eventus* from, *evenire* to happen>
in any event or **at all events,** in any case.
in the event of, in the case of: *In the event of rain, the party will be held indoors.*
in the event that, if it should happen that: *In the event that the roads are icy, we will not come.*

e·ven–tem·pered (ē′vən tem′pərd) *adj* not easily upset or angered; calm.

e·vent·ful (i vent′fəl) *adj* containing unusual or important events: *Our trip to northern Alberta was an eventful one.* **e·vent′ful·ly** *adv.* **e·vent′ful·ness** *n.*

e·vent·ing (i vent′ing) *n* one of the three equestrian disciplines contested at the Olympics. **Jumping** (or **show jumping**) consists of negotiating a series of obstacles without disturbing the fences. **Dressage** is a sort of ballet on horseback in which the rider guides the horse to perform certain intricate manoeuvres. Eventing combines the above two disciplines, and adds a third competition of riding a cross-country course on horseback.

e·ven·tu·al (i ven′chū əl) *adj* happening in the end: *Her eventual success after several failures surprised us.* **e·ven′tu·al·ly** *adv.*

e·ven·tu·al·i·ty (i ven′chū al′ə tē) *n, pl* **e·ven·tu·al·i·ties** a possible event: *We hope for sunshine but are ready for the eventuality of rain.*

ev·er (ev′ər) *adv* 1 at any time: *Is she ever at home?* 2 at all times: *ever at your service.* 3 *Informal* (*in exclamations, with inverted subject and verb*) very: *Is it ever hot!* <Old English *æfre*>

ev·er·green (ev′ər grēn′) *adj* of leaves, trees, etc., staying green all year.
n 1 a tree or shrub that keeps its leaves or needles all year. 2 **evergreens** *pl* evergreen branches used for decoration.

ev·er·last·ing (ev′ər las′ting) *adj* 1 lasting forever. 2 lasting too long: *his everlasting whining.* **ev′er·last′ing·ly** *adv.*

ev·er·more (ev′ər môr′) *adv* always.

eve·ry (ev′rē) *adj* 1 all, regarded singly or separately: *Every room in the house is carpeted.* 2 all possible: *We showed her every consideration.* 3 at a regular interval: *A bus leaves every two hours.* <Old English *æfre* ever + *ælc* each>
every now and then or **every so often,** from time to time: *We hear from him every now and then.*
every other, at intervals of two: *The magazine comes out every other month.*
every which way, *Informal* in all directions: *The marbles fell out and rolled every which way.*

eve·ry·bod·y (ev′rē bud′ē) *or* (ev′rē bod′ē) *pron* every person: *Everybody likes the new teacher.*

eve·ry·day (ev′rē dā′) *adj* **1** happening every day: *Accidents are everyday occurrences.* **2** for every ordinary day: *my everyday clothes.* **3** not exciting or unusual: *He's just an everyday guy.*

GRAMMAR AND USAGE

Everyday is written as one word when it is an adjective, but when ***day*** is a noun modified by **every**, they are two separate words: *Just wear everyday clothes to the picnic. Every day is a good day for a holiday.*

Everyone is written as one word when it is a pronoun, but as two words when ***one*** is a pronoun modified by **every**: *Everyone should read this book. Every one of you should read this book.*

Everything is usually written as one word. It is written as two words when ***thing*** is a noun modified by **every** and an adjective, for emphasis: *Everything in this box is broken. Every single thing in this box is broken.*

Eve·ry·man (ev′rē man′) *n* a typical human being. <chief character in a 16c play, symbolizing humanity>

eve·ry·one (ev′rē wən) *pron* every person: *Everyone went home.*

eve·ry·thing (ev′rē thing′) *pron* all things: *I do everything I can to help my mother.*
n Informal most important thing: *You are my everything.*
mean (or **be**) **everything,** *Informal* be more important than anything else.

eve·ry·where (ev′rē wer′) *adv* in every place: *We looked everywhere for our lost dog.*

e·vict (i vikt′) *v* legally force a tenant out of a building or off a piece of land: *The tenant was evicted for not paying his rent.* <Latin *evincere* regain property, from *e-* out + *vincere* conquer> **e·vic′tion** *n.*

ev·i·dence (ev′ə dəns) *n* **1** whatever makes clear that a thing is true or false: *There is plenty of evidence that smoking causes cancer.* **2** facts established and accepted in a court of law: *The jury hears all the evidence.* **3** an indication or sign: *A smile is evidence of pleasure.*
v **ev·i·denced, ev·i·denc·ing** show clearly: *His face evidenced his displeasure.* <Old French, from Latin *evidentia* proof>
in evidence, easily seen or noticed.

ev·i·dent (ev′ə dənt) *adj* easy to see or understand: *It is evident that she loves her little brother.*

ev·i·dent·ly (ev′ə dən tlē) *adv* **1** according to the information available: *Evidently you passed your history test, otherwise you wouldn't look so happy.* **2** clearly or plainly: *He was very evidently impressed.*

e·vil (ē′vəl) *adj* **1** very morally wrong: *evil deeds, an evil character.* **2** wicked and threatening: *an evil smile.* **3** bringing disaster: *Those were evil days.* **4** disgusting or repulsive: *an evil smell.*
n **1** great moral wrongdoing. **2** a cause of suffering or misery: *War is one of many evils.* <Old English *yfel*> **e′vil·ly** *adv.*

e·vil·do·er (ē′vəl dū′ər) *n* one who does evil.

evil eye *n* the supposed power of some people to cause harm to others by looking at them.

e·vince (i vins′) *v* **e·vinced, e·vinc·ing** show clearly: *to evince dislike.* <French, from Latin, from *evincere* prove, conquer>

e·vis·cer·ate (i vis′ə rāt′) *v* **e·vis·cer·at·ed, e·vis·cer·at·ing** **1** remove the guts or inner parts from. **2** deprive of something essential: *He thinks cutbacks have eviscerated the armed forces.* <Latin *e-* out + *viscera* entrails> **e·vis′cer·a′tion** *n.*

E

ev·o·ca·tion (ev′ō kā′shən) *n* the act of evoking.

e·voc·a·tive (i vok′ə tiv) *adj* producing or arousing a strong emotional response or a vivid mental image: *an evocative poem.* <See EVOKE.>

e·voke (i vōk′) *v* **e·voked, e·vok·ing** bring to mind a memory, image, or emotion: *The poem evokes the days of childhood.* <Latin *e-* out + *vocare* call>

ev·o·lu·tion (ev′ə lū′shən) *or* (ē′və lū′shən) *n* **1** any process of gradual change or development: *the evolution of a flower from a bud.* **2** something that has evolved from earlier things: *Do you want to hear the latest evolution of my idea?* **3** *Biology* the scientific theory that all living things developed from a few simple forms of life, or from a single form, by a process of natural selection. <Latin *evolutionem* unrolling of a book, from *evolvere* to unroll, to evolve> **ev′o·lu′tion·ar′y** *adj.*

ev·o·lu·tion·ism (ev′ə lū′shə niz′əm) *or* (ē′və lū′shə niz′əm) *n* **1** belief in the theory of biological evolution. **2** the belief that everything, including physical life, society, human thought, etc., is in a constant process of evolution toward something better or more advanced. **ev′o·lu′tion·ist** *n.*

e·volve (i volv′) *v* **e·volved, e·volv·ing** **1** develop gradually: *Their casual acquaintance evolved into a great friendship.* **2** *Biology* reach a more highly organized condition by a gradual process of change through natural selection. <See EVOLUTION.>

ewe (yū) *n* a female sheep. <Old English *eowu*>

ex (eks) *Informal n* a former spouse or partner: *I saw my ex in the mall yesterday.*

ex– *prefix* **1** out of; from; out: *export.* **2** completely: *exterminate.* **3** former or formerly: *ex-member.*

ETYMOLOGY

The prefix **ex–** comes from Latin and is usually joined to a Latin root. Therefore it follows Latin rules for combining elements, and takes different forms depending on what it is joined to. It becomes **e–** before the letters *b, d, g, j, l, m, n, r,* and *v.*

🍁 **Ex** (eks) *n* usually, **the Ex**, in full, the **Canadian National Exhibition**, held in Toronto at the end of summer. Also abbreviated to **the CNE**.

a bat	e bed	i bid	o pot	u cup	th **thin**
ā cake	ē me	ī bite	ō go	ū rude	TH **then**
ȧ bar	ə about	ər over	ȯ for	u̇ put	zh measure

ex·ac·er·bate (eg zas′ər bāt′) *v* **ex·ac·er·bat·ed, ex·ac·er·bat·ing** make worse: *Nagging him will only exacerbate the situation.* <Latin *ex-* completely + *acerbus* harsh, bitter> **ex·ac′er·ba′tion** *n.*

ex·act (eg zakt′) *adj* **1** accurate and precise: *an exact measurement, the exact amount.* **2** specific: *Don't just say "one day." Give me an exact date.*
v **1** demand and get: *If he does the work, he can exact payment for it.* **2** require: *This work exacts effort and patience.* <Latin *exactus,* from *ex-* out + *agere* weigh> **ex·ac′tion** *n.* **ex·act′ly** *adv.* **ex·act′ness** *n.*

ex·act·ing (eg zak′ting) *adj* requiring much effort and attention: *an exacting employer, exacting work.*

ex·act·i·tude (eg zak′tə tyūd′) *or* (eg zak′tə tūd′) *n* exactness.

exact science *n* a science in which facts can be accurately observed and results accurately predicted: *Mathematics and physics are exact sciences.*

ex·ag·ger·ate (eg zaj′ə rāt′) *v* **ex·ag·ger·at·ed, ex·ag·ger·at·ing 1** make something out to be more than it is: *She exaggerated the dangers of the trip in order to appear brave. If you exaggerate, people will not trust you.* **2** overdo: *exaggerated emotion.* <Latin *ex-* up + *agger* heap> **ex·ag′ger·a′tion** *n.*

ex·alt (eg zolt′) *v* **1** place high in rank, honour, or character: *our exalted leader.* **2** fill with pride, joy, or noble feeling. <Latin *ex-* up + *altus* high> **ex′al·ta′tion** *n.*

ex·am (eg zam′) *Informal n* an examination.

ex·am·i·na·tion (eg zam′ə nā′shən) *n* **1** a thorough test of knowledge or skills, as at the end of an academic course: *a math examination.* **2** a careful inspection, especially by a doctor: *You should go for an eye examination.* **3** the act of examining.

ex·am·ine (eg zam′ən) *v* **ex·am·ined, ex·am·in·ing 1** look at closely and carefully: *The doctor examined the wound.* **2** test the knowledge or skills of. <French *examiner,* from Latin *exigere* weigh accurately> **ex·am′i·nee′** *n.* **ex·am′in·er** *n.*

ex·am·ple (eg zam′pəl) *n* **1** a specific item taken to show what similar items are like: *Here is an example of my work.* **2** a model or pattern to be imitated or avoided: *That mother is a good example to her daughters.* <Old French *essample,* from Latin *exemplum* a sample>
for example, as an illustration: *Children play many games—baseball, for example.*
make an example of, punish sternly in order to show others the result of misbehaviour: *The judge made an example of the graffiti artist by imposing a very large fine.*
set an example, behave in a way that others may imitate.

ex·as·per·ate (eg zas′pə rāt′) *v* **ex·as·per·at·ed, ex·as·per·at·ing** irritate or annoy very much: *The child's endless questions exasperated her father.* <Latin *ex-* thoroughly + *asper* rough> **ex·as′per·a′tion** *n.*

Ex·cal·i·bur (eks kal′ə bər) *n* in Arthurian legend, King Arthur's magic sword.

ex ca·the·dra (eks kə thē′drə) *n* with authority. <Latin = from the chair (of a bishop)>

ex·ca·vate (ek′skə vāt′) *v* **ex·ca·vat·ed, ex·ca·va·ting 1** make a large hole by removing earth or rocks.: *The construction company will excavate tomorrow.* **2** make by digging: *The tunnel was excavated through solid rock.* **3** get or uncover by digging: *to excavate an ancient buried city.* <Latin *ex-* out + *cavus* hollow> **ex′ca·va′tion** *n.* **ex′ca·va′tor** *n.*

ex·ceed (ek sēd′) *v* go beyond: *Motorists are fined for exceeding the speed limit.* <French, from Latin *ex-* out + *cedere* go>

ex·ceed·ing·ly (ek sē′ding lē) *adv* extremely: *an exceedingly hot day.*

ex·cel (ek sel′) *v* **ex·celled, ex·cel·ling** do very well, and better than others: *The old king excelled in wisdom. She excelled all her classmates in history.* <French, from Latin *ex-* up + *celsus* lofty>

Ex·cel·len·cy (ek′sə lən sē) *n, pl* **Ex·cel·len·cies** a title of honour used in addressing or referring to the Governor General, an ambassador, and other high officials: *Her Excellency Adrienne Clarkson.*

ex·cel·lent (ek′sə lənt) *adj* extremely good: *an excellent musician, excellent work.* **ex′cel·lence** *n.* **ex′cel·lent·ly** *adv.*

ex·cept (ek sept′) *prep* **1** other than: *every day except Sunday.* Also, **excepting**. **2** with any purpose other than: *He hardly ever goes out except to visit his brother.*
conj Informal (*often with **that***) only; but: *I'd like to go with you, except I can't swim.*
v leave out: *All the children, the baby excepted, were helping to clean up the backyard.* <Latin *ex-* out + *capere* take>

> **CONFUSABLES**
>
> **Except** means "other than": *Everyone went skiing except me.*
>
> **Accept** means "receive": *I will gladly accept your donation for our charity.*
>
> Note that ***accept*** is a verb and ***except*** is a preposition.

ex·cep·tion (ek sep′shən) *n* a person who or thing that does not follow the rule: *She usually comes on time; today was an exception.*
take exception to, object to or protest against: *He took exception to the editorial and wrote a letter to the newspaper about it.*
with the exception of, except: *I like all music, with the exception of country.*

ex·cep·tion·al (ek sep′shə nəl) *adj* unusual: *This warm weather is exceptional for January.* **ex·cep′tion·al·ly** *adv.*

ex·cerpt (eg′zərpt) *for n,* (eg zərpt′) *for v. n* a passage taken from a longer text: *The article included excerpts from several books.*
v select passages from a longer text. <Latin *ex-* out + *carpere* pull>

ex·cess (ek ses′) *or, especially for adj,* (ek′ses) *n* **1** an amount beyond what is normal or allowed: *an excess of emotion. He had to pay for an excess of five kilos on his baggage.* **2** the act of going beyond reasonable limits: *The newspaper report criticized the excesses of the rock band's behaviour.*

adj more than is normal or allowed: *excess weight.* <Latin *excessus* beyond the bounds of reason, from *excedere* go beyond> **ex·ces′sive** *adj.* **ex·ces′sive·ly** *adv.*
in excess of, more than: *Contributions were in excess of $5000.*
to excess, too much: *to drink to excess.*

ex·change (eks chānj′) *v* **ex·changed, ex·chang·ing 1** trade for something else: *She would not exchange her house for a palace.* **2** give and receive things of the same kind: *to exchange letters.* **3** switch or trade: *to exchange seats with someone.* **4** replace (a purchase): *Sorry, we cannot exchange swimsuits.*
n **1** the act of exchanging: *Ten dimes for a dollar is a fair exchange.* **2** the thing exchanged. **3** a place where things are traded: *a stock exchange.* **4** the act of changing one currency into another. <Old French *eschangier,* from Latin *ex-* out + *cambiare* change> **ex·change′a·ble** *adj.*

exchange rate *n* the ratio at which the currency of one country can be exchanged for that of another: *The exchange rate on the Canadian dollar today is 75 cents US.*

exchange student *n* a student who changes places with another in a different province or country in order to learn a language or find out about life in that place.

ex·cheq·uer (eks chek′ər) *n* the treasury of a state or nation.

ETYMOLOGY

Exchequer is a Middle English word from Old French *escheker,* meaning "chessboard." Originally, a checkered cloth covered a table on which accounts of revenue were tallied with counters.

ex·cise[1] (ek′sīz) *n* a tax on the manufacture, sale, or use of certain articles: *There is an excise on tobacco.* <Old French, from Latin *ad-* to + *census* tax>

ex·cise[2] (ek sīz′) *v* **ex·cised, ex·cis·ing** cut out: *to excise a tumour, to excise passages from a text.* <Latin *excisus,* from *ex-* out + *caedere* cut> **ex·ci′sion** *n.*

ex·cit·a·ble (ek sī′tə bəl) *adj* easily excited: *Our dog is excitable and will bark at anything.* **ex·cit′a·bil′i·ty** *n.* **ex·cit′a·bly** *adv.*

ex·cite (ek sīt′) *v* **ex·cit·ed, ex·cit·ing 1** cause enthusiasm and eagerness: *It excites me just to think of winning the contest.* **2** leading to emotion, energy, or activity: *His new jacket excited envy in some of the other boys. Don't excite the dogs.* **3** produce a response in an organism: *to excite a nerve.* **4** *Physics* raise an atom, nucleus, or molecule to a higher level of energy. <Latin *ex-* out + *ciere* set in motion> **ex·cit′ed** *adj.*

ex·cite·ment (ek sīt′mənt) *n* **1** the state of being eager and enthusiastic: *The baby's first steps caused great excitement in the family.* **2** something that excites: *There's no excitement in that game.* **3** the act of exciting.

ex·cit·ing (ek sī′ting) *adj* causing eagerness and enthusiasm: *an exciting piece of news, an exciting game.*

ex·claim (ek sklām′) *v* say something suddenly, and often loudly, with strong feeling: *"You're finally home!" exclaimed his mother.* <French, from Latin *ex-* out + *clamare* cry out>

ex·cla·ma·tion (ek′sklə mā′shən) *n* something said with strong feeling. **ex·clam′a·to′ry** (ek′sklə′mə′to rē) *adj.*

exclamation mark *n* a mark [!] of punctuation used after a word or sentence to show strong feeling.

GRAMMAR AND USAGE

Take care not to overuse exclamation marks. If too many are used in a piece of writing, they quickly lose their effectiveness. Except in very informal writing, don't use more than one exclamation mark after any single word, phrase, or sentence.

ex·clude (ek sklūd′) *v* **ex·clud·ed, ex·clud·ing 1** shut out or keep out: *Professional athletes are excluded from this competition.* **2** keep out of consideration: *The invitation excludes children.* <Latin *ex-* out + *claudere* shut>

ex·clud·ing (ek sklū′ding) *prep* except: *The cost is $500, excluding taxes.*

ex·clu·sion (ek sklū′zhən) *n* the act or fact of excluding or being excluded: **ex·clu′sion·a·ry** *adj.*

ex·clu·sive (ek sklū′siv) *adj* **1** excluding most people for social, financial, or other reasons: *an exclusive club.* **2** single or sole: *Our firm has the exclusive right to manufacture this product.* **3** not available elsewhere or to anyone else: *an exclusive interview.* **4** shutting out all other things: *He demanded our exclusive attention.* **5** that cannot both be true at the same time: *"Baby" and "adult" are exclusive terms.*
n an item or news story that is published or broadcast by only one source. **ex·clu′sive·ly** *adv.* **ex·clu′sive·ness** *n.*
exclusive of, excluding: *The dress is 100% cotton, exclusive of trimming.*

ex·clu·siv·ism (ek sklū′sə viz′əm) *n* the attitude of a group that tends to reject all but a narrow class of people. **ex·clu′siv·ist** *adj, n.*

ex·com·mun·i·cate (ek′skə myū′nə kāt′) *Christianity v* **ex·com·mu·ni·cat·ed, ex·com·mu·ni·cat·ing** expel formally from a church. <Latin *ex-* out of + *communitas* community> **ex′com·mu′ni·ca′tion** *n.*

ex·co·ri·ate (ek skó′rē āt′) *v* **ex·co·ri·at·ed, ex·co·ri·at·ing 1** strip or rub off the skin. **2** denounce violently: *The politician was excoriated in the media.* <Latin *ex-* off + *corium* hide, skin> **ex·co′ri·a′tion** *n.*

ex·cre·ment (ek′skrə mənt) *n* solid waste from the body. <See EXCRETE.>

ex·cres·cence (ek skre′səns) *n* an unattractive addition or feature. <Latin *excrescentia* abnormal growths, from *ex-* out + *crescere* grown>

ex·crete (ek skrēt′) *v* **ex·cret·ed, ex·cret·ing** discharge waste matter from the body: *The pores of the skin excrete sweat.* <Latin *ex-* out + *cernere* sift> **ex·cre′tion** *n.* **ex′cre·to′ry** *adj.*

a bat	e bed	i bid	o pot	u cup	th thin
ā cake	ē me	ī bite	ō go	ū rude	TH then
à bar	ə about	ər over	ó for	ù put	zh measure

E

ex·cru·ci·at·ing (ek skrū′shē ā′ting) *adj* extremely painful: *an excruciating toothache.* <Latin *ex-* completely + *cruciare* torture>

ex·cur·sion (ek skər′zhən) *n* **1** a short pleasure trip: *an excursion to the mountains.* **2** a round trip at a reduced fare, usually with certain restrictions. <Latin *excursionem,* a running forth, from *excurrere* run out>

ex·cuse (ek skyūz′) *for v,* (ek skyūs′) *for n. v* **ex·cused, ex·cus·ing 1** overlook a fault, pardon, or forgive: *Please excuse my lateness.* **2** give a reason or apology for: *She excused her own faults by blaming others.* **3** be a reason or explanation for: *No amount of tiredness excuses such nasty behaviour.*

n **1** a real or pretended reason or explanation: *She had many excuses for not doing her work.* **2** a legitimate reason or explanation: *There's no excuse for cheating.* <Latin *excusare* release from an accusation, from *ex-* away + *causa* accusation> **ex·cus′a·ble** *adj.* **ex·cus′a·bly** *adv.*

a poor excuse for, a poor example of: *That was a poor excuse for a meal.*

be excused from, be permitted to miss: *You are excused from today's practice.*

excuse me, used to politely apologize, or request that someone repeat what he or she has just said.

excuse yourself, a say "excuse me." **b** say that you are leaving.

make your excuses, politely explain that you cannot come or stay.

ex·e·cra·ble (ek′sə krə bəl) *or* (eg′zə krə bəl) *adj* extremely bad: *an execrable crime, execrable taste in art.* <Latin *ex-* completely + *sacer* horrible> **ex′e·cra·bly** *adv.*

ex·e·cute (ek′sə kyūt′) *v* **ex·e·cut·ed, ex·e·cut·ing 1** carry out or perform: *to execute orders, to execute a figure skating routine.* **2** punish with death: *In wartime, spies may be executed.* **3** make according to a plan or design: *The tapestry was executed with great skill.* **4** *Law* complete a deed, contract, or will by signing or doing whatever is necessary. **5** *Computers* follow an instruction or run a program. <Old French *executeur* executor>
ex′e·cu′tion *n.*

ex·e·cu·tion·er (ek′sə kyū′shə nər) *n* a person who carries out a death penalty according to law.

ex·ec·u·tive (eg zek′yə tiv) *n* **1** a person in upper management in business: *She is a highly paid executive.* **2** the branch of a government with the duty and power to put laws into effect. **3** a group of leaders who manage the affairs of an organization: *He's on the executive of the student council.*

adj **1** carrying out decisions or managing affairs: *an executive committee. The principal of a school has an executive position.* **2** suitable or designed for executives: *an executive suite, executive toys.* **3** with the duty and power to put laws into effect: *The Cabinet is the executive branch of our Federal Government.*

🍁 **Executive Council** *n* the cabinet of a provincial or territorial government.

ex·ec·u·tor (eg zek′yə tər) *n* a person named in a will to carry out the provisions of the will.

ex·em·plar (eg zem′plər) *n* an ideal or typical example: *They looked on him as the exemplar of courage.* <Latin *exemplarium,* from *exemplium* example>

ex·em·pla·ry (eg zem′plə rē) *adj* serving as a worthy example: *exemplary conduct.*

ex·em·pli·fy (eg zem′plə fī′) *v* **ex·em·pli·fied, ex·em·pli·fy·ing** be an example of: *She exemplifies courage.*

ex·empt (eg zempt′) *v* release from an obligation or rule: *The teacher exempted me from the test because I had missed the lesson.*

adj not subject to an obligation or rule: *Food is exempt from sales tax.* <Latin *eximere* release, from *ex-* out + *emere* take> **ex·emp′tion** *n.*

Clothing worn for **exercise** is designed to allow freedom of movement. Synthetic fabrics quickly draw moisture away from the body to minimize the chilling effect of sweat evaporating on the surface of the skin.

ex·er·cise (ek′sər sīz′) *n* **1** vigorous physical activity: *Go outside and get some exercise.* **2** a particular activity designed to train the body or mind to develop some skill: *Do the exercise on page 40 of your math text.* **3** the act of using or performing: *the exercise of a person's right to vote.* **4 exercises** *pl* a routine set of activities: *graduation exercises.*

v **ex·er·cised, ex·er·cis·ing 1** take part or cause to take part in vigorous physical activity: *to exercise your dog. I exercise daily.* **2** use or carry out: *to exercise your freedom, to exercise care in crossing the street.* **3** develop by active use: *to exercise your imagination.* **4** (*usually in the passive*) make angry, anxious, or excited: *I don't think we need to get exercised about this issue.* <Old French, from Latin *exercere* not allow to rest> **ex′er·cis′er** *n.*

ex·ert (eg zərt′) *v* put into action: *to exert your authority.* <Latin *exserere* put forth> **ex·er′tion** *n.*

exert yourself, try hard: *I think he never exerts himself because he's too lazy.*

ex·er·tion (eg zər′shən) *n* **1** strenuous physical effort. **2** the application of pressure or influence.

ex·fo·li·ate (eks fō′lē āt′) *v* **ex·fo·li·at·ed, ex·fo·li·at·ing** remove or cast off flakes or scales from, especially from the skin. <Latin *ex-* out + *folium* leaf> **ex·fo′li·ant** *n, adj.*

ex·hale (eks hāl′) *v* **ex·haled, ex·hal·ing** breathe out: *to exhale air from the lungs. Exhale completely.* <French, from Latin *ex-* out + *halare* breathe> **ex′ha·la′tion** *n.*

ex·haust (eg zost′) *v* **1** tire out: *The climb up the hill exhausted us.* **2** use up completely: *to exhaust your supplies.* **3** drain of strength or resources: *The long war exhausted the country.* **4** say all there is to be said about: *I think we have exhausted that subject.* **5** expel steam or gas.
n **1** waste gases that escape from a machine. **2** the act or means of releasing waste gases. <Latin *exhaurire* use up, from *ex-* out + *haurire* to drain>

ex·haust·ed (eg zos′tid) *adj* **1** extremely tired. **2** used up. **ex·haus′tion** *n.*

ex·haus·tive (eg zos′tiv) *adj* leaving out nothing: *an exhaustive study of the subject.* **ex·haus′tive·ly** *adv.*

ex·hib·it (eg zib′it) *v* **1** give evidence of: *to exhibit nervousness.* **2** put on public display: *You should exhibit your roses in the flower show.*
n **1** something displayed publicly: *His pottery exhibit won the prize.* **2** a public show, often part of a museum, art gallery, or fair: *Did you look at the Emily Carr exhibit?* **3** *Law* something shown in court as evidence: *She held up Exhibit A, the ransom note.* <Latin *ex-* out + *habere* hold> **ex·hib′i·tor** *n.*
on exhibit, being displayed publicly.

ex·hi·bi·tion (ek′sə bish′ən) *n* **1** the act of exhibiting: *I have never seen such an exhibition of bad manners.* **2** a public show: *The art school holds an exhibition every year.* **3** a large fair with exhibits of livestock, produce, manufactured goods, as well as rides and games.

ex·hi·bi·tion·ism (ek′sə bish′ə niz′əm) *n* **1** a tendency to seek attention or show off. **2** a compulsion to expose the genitals in public. **ex′hi·bi′tion·ist** *n.*

ex·hil·a·rate (eg zil′ə rāt′) *v* **ex·hil·a·rat·ed, ex·hil·a·rat·ing** **1** refresh or invigorate: *We were exhilarated by our morning swim.* **2** put into high spirits: *He was exhilarated by the prospect of getting home a day early.* <Latin *ex-* completely + *hilaris* merry> **ex·hil′a·ra′tion** *n.*

ex·hort (eg zôrt′) *v* urge strongly: *The teacher exhorted his class to work harder.* <Latin *ex-* completely + *hortari* urge strongly> **ex′hor·ta′tion** *n.*

ex·hume (eg zyūm′) *or* (eks hyūm′) *v* **ex·humed, ex·hum·ing** **1** take out of a grave or the ground. **2** reveal or disclose. <Latin *ex-* out of + *humus* ground> **ex′hu·ma′tion** *n.*

ex·ile (eg′zīl) *or* (ek′sīl) *v* **ex·iled, ex·il·ing** banish a person from his or her country: *After the revolution, the former dictator was exiled.*
n **1** the condition or period of being exiled: *Napoleon's exile to Elba was brief.* **2** an exiled person: *He has been an exile for ten years.* **3** any prolonged absence from one's country. <Old French, from Latin *exiliare* banish>

ex·ist (eg zist′) *v* **1** have objective reality or being: *The earth has existed a long time.* **2** live: *She exists on coffee and doughnuts.* <Latin *existere* exist> **ex·ist′ence** *n.*

ex·is·ten·tial·ism (eg′zə sten′shə liz′əm) *n* the philosophy that the point of existence is for people to make moral choices in a world that has no purpose or objective values. **ex′is·ten′tial** *adj.* **ex′is·ten′tial·ist** *adj, n.*

ex·it (eg′zit) *or* (ek′sit) *v* **1** go out or leave: *to exit a building, to exit the highway.* **2** a stage direction telling an actor to leave the stage.
n **1** a way out: *The museum has six exits.* **2** the act of exiting: *a graceful exit.* <Latin = goes out>

E

exit poll *n* a survey of voters leaving a polling booth.

ex li·bris (eks′ lē′bris) an inscription used on a bookplate, followed by the owner's name. <Latin = from the library (of)>

ex·o·dus (ek′sə dəs) *n* **1** the departure of a large number of people: *Every summer there is an exodus from the city.* **2** **Exodus** the departure of the Hebrews from Egypt under Moses. <Latin, from Greek *exodos* departure>

ex·on·er·ate (eg zon′ə rāt′) *v* **ex·on·er·at·ed, ex·on·er·at·ing** prove or declare innocent: *Witnesses of the accident completely exonerated the driver of the truck.* <Latin *ex-* off + *oneris* burden> **ex·on′er·a′tion** *n.*

ex·or·bi·tant (eg zôr′bə tənt) *adj* beyond what is reasonable: *an exorbitant price, exorbitant demands.* <Latin *exorbita* deviate, go out of the track, from *ex-* out of + *orbita* wheel, track> **ex·or′bi·tance** *n.* **ex·or′bi·tant·ly** *adv.*

ex·or·cise (ek′sôr sīz′) *v* **ex·or·cised, ex·or·cis·ing** drive an evil spirit out of a person or place by prayers or ceremonies: *to exorcise a demon.* <Old French *exorciser*, from Greek *exorkizein*> **ex′or·cism′** *n.* **ex′or·cist′** *n.*

ex·o·skel·e·ton (ek′sō skel′ə tən) *n* the hard, external structure that protects and supports the bodies of many invertebrates, such as oysters, lobsters, or insects. Compare ENDOSKELETON. <Greek *exo-* outside + *skeleton*>

ex·ot·ic (eg zot′ik) *adj* **1** from a very different part of the world: *exotic foods.* **2** strange or unusual in a way that is fascinating or beautiful: *Her clothes had an exotic glamour.* <Latin, from Greek *exo-* outside> **ex·ot′i·cal·ly** *adv.*

ex·ot·i·ca (eg zot′ə kə) *pl n* things that are different, strange, or unusual in an intriguing way.

ex·pand (ek spand′) *v* **1** increase in size: *The balloon expanded as it was filled with air. Heat expands metal.* **2** spread out: *The bird expanded its wings.* **3** speak or write in greater detail: *She expanded on the theme in the second chapter.* **4** *Mathematics* express a quantity as a sum of terms or product of terms. The **expanded form** of 2(x + y) is 2x + 2y. <Latin *ex-* out + *pandere* spread> **ex·pand′a·ble** *adj.* **ex·pan′sion** *n.*

ex·panse (ek spans′) *n* a large, unbroken area or surface: *An ocean is a vast expanse of water.* <See EXPAND.>

a bat	e bed	i bid	o pot	u cup	th **thin**
ā cake	ē me	ī bite	ō go	ū rude	ᴛʜ **then**
à bar	ə about	ər over	ô for	ù put	zh measure

ex·pan·sile (ek span′sīl) *or* (ek span′səl) *Physics adj* capable of being expanded. Also, **expansible**.

expansion card *Computers n* a CARD[1] (def. 4) inserted into an **expansion slot** in the central processing unit of a computer to add to its capacity or function.

ex·pan·sion·ism (ek span′shə niz′əm) *n* a policy of expanding one's territory or sphere of power, usually at the expense of others: *political expansionism, economic expansionism.*

ex·pan·sive (ek span′siv) *adj* **1** wide or broad. **2** showing one's feelings freely and openly: *He is a very expansive and hospitable person.* **ex·pan′sive·ly** *adv.*
ex·pan′sive·ness *n.*

ex·pa·ti·ate (ek spā′shē āt′) *v* **ex·pa·ti·at·ed, ex·pa·ti·at·ing** write or talk at length: *She expatiated on the thrills of her trip.* <Latin *expatiatus* to wander, digress> **ex·pa′ti·a′tion** *n.*

ex·pa·tri·ate (eks pā′trē ət′) *for adj or n,* (eks pā′trē āt′) *for v. adj* living outside of one's own country for a long period: *There are many expatriate Canadians in New York.*
n an expatriate person.
v **ex·pa·tri·a·ted, ex·pa·tri·at·ing 1** banish from a country. **2** renounce one's citizenship. <Latin *ex-* out + *patria* homeland> **ex′pa·tri·a′tion** *n.*

ex·pect (ek spekt′) *v* **1** think likely to come or happen: *He's expecting a phone call. I expect she will be late as usual.* **2** plan or intend: *I expect to visit my cousins this summer.* **3** count on as reasonable or required: *You are expected to do your homework.* **4** suppose or guess: *I expect they haven't told him yet.* **5** look forward to the arrival of: *We'll expect you for dinner on Thursday. My sister is expecting her first baby.* <Latin *expectare* await, from *ex-* out + *specere* look>

ex·pect·an·cy (ek spek′tən sē) *n, pl* **ex·pect·an·cies 1** the feeling of hopefulness, anticipation, or eagerness: *There was a look of expectancy on his face.* **2** an expected amount based on statistics: *a life expectancy of 82 years.*

ex·pect·ant (ek spek′tənt) *adj* **1** feeling or showing hope, anticipation, or eagerness: *He opened his birthday present with an expectant smile.* **2** expecting a baby: *an expectant mother.* **ex·pect′ant·ly** *adv.*

ex·pec·ta·tion (ek′spek tā′shən) *n* **1** the fact or feeling of expecting: *The ad creates an expectation that buying will make you happy.* **2** what is expected: *Contrary to her expectation, the house was tidy.* **3** usually, **expectations** *pl* the standard that a person or thing is expected to meet: *The movie did not live up to my expectations.*

ex·pect·ing (ek spek′ting) *adj* pregnant.

ex·pec·to·rate (ek spek′tə rāt′) *v* **ex·pec·to·rat·ed, ex·pec·to·rat·ing** cough up and spit out. <Latin *ex-* out + *pectoris* chest> **ex·pec′to·ra′tion** *n.*

ex·pe·di·en·cy (ek spē′dē ən sē) *n, pl* **ex·pe·di·en·cies 1** the fact of being expedient: *I question the expediency of this course of action.* **2** personal advantage: *Her offer to help was motivated by expediency, not kindness.*

ex·pe·di·ent (ek spē′dē ənt) *adj* **1** useful or suitable under the circumstances: *She decided it would be expedient to take an umbrella.* **2** prompted by self-interest.
n a means of achieving a certain result: *With no ladder or rope, he escaped by the expedient of tying bedsheets together.* <Latin *expedire* prepare, make ready, from *ex-* out + *pedis* foot. Originally, expedient meant to free from chains, i.e., to free from difficulties.> **ex·pe′di·ent·ly** *adv.*

ex·pe·dite (ek′spə dīt′) *v* **ex·pe·dit·ed, ex·pe·dit·ing 1** make easy and quick: *If everyone helps, that will expedite matters.* **2** complete quickly. <See EXPEDIENT.>

ex·pe·di·tion (ek′spə dish′ən) *n* **1 a** a journey for some special purpose: *a fishing expedition.* **b** a group making such a journey: *a well-equipped expedition.* **2** efficient and prompt action: *He completed his work with expedition.*

ex·pe·di·tious (ek′spə dish′əs) *adj* efficient and prompt. **ex′pe·di′tious·ly** *adv.*

ex·pel (ek spel′) *v* **ex·pelled, ex·pel·ling 1** force to leave: *The demonstrators were expelled from city hall.* **2** dismiss permanently: *Violent students may be expelled from school.* **3** force out: *to expel air from the lungs.* <Latin *ex-* out + *pellere* drive>

ex·pend (ek spend′) *v* spend or use up energy or resources. <Latin *ex-* out + *pendere* weigh, pay>

ex·pend·a·ble (ek spen′də bəl) *adj* **1** normally consumed or used up in service: *Pencils, paper, stamps, etc. are expendable items.* **2** not essential: *If you take the expendable items out of your suitcase, you'll be able to close it.* **3** that may be sacrificed if necessary: *In that regime, soldiers were considered expendable.*
n **expendables** *pl* expendable items.

ex·pend·i·ture (ek spen′də chər) *n* **1** the act of spending or using up: *Such a task requires the expenditure of much time and effort.* **2** an amount of money spent: *Keep a record of your expenditures.*

ex·pense (ek spens′) *n* **1** the fact of bearing a cost: *He travelled at his uncle's expense.* **2** a cause of spending: *A car is an expense.* **3** usually, **expenses** *pl* **a** the charges incurred in running one's business or doing one's job. **b** the money to repay such charges: *Because my mom has to travel a lot as a consultant, she gets expenses besides her salary.* <See EXPEND.>
at the expense of, a with the loss of: *He achieved prosperity, but it was at the expense of his health.* **b** so as to cause harm, loss, or discredit to someone or something: *They had many a laugh at my expense.*

expense account *n* a record of money spent in the course of doing one's job, to be repaid by the employer.

ex·pen·sive (ek spen′siv) *adj* costing a lot: *expensive clothes.* **ex·pen′sive·ly** *adv.* **ex·pen′sive·ness** *n.*

ex·pe·ri·ence (ek spē′rē əns) *n* **1 a** something that happens to a person: *The safari was an exciting experience for her.* **b** all such things taken together: *I have never encountered such kindness in all my experience.* **2** active participation or observation: *to learn by experience.* **3** skill, practical knowledge, or wisdom gained by observing, doing, or living through things: *Salesperson wanted; experience required.*
v **ex·pe·ri·enced, ex·pe·ri·enc·ing** have happen to one: *to experience a car accident, to experience joy.* <Latin *experiri* try out> **ex·pe′ri·en′tial** *adj.*

ex·pe·ri·enced (ek spē′rē ənst) *adj* with considerable skill or knowledge gained by experience: *an experienced driver.*

ex·per·i·ment (ek sper′ə mənt) *v* try things in order to see what happens: *He has been experimenting with dyes to get the colour he wants.*
n **1** a test or trial to find out or show what happens: *We did an experiment in class to show how electricity produces magnetism.* **2** experiments in general as a method of research: *Scientists test theories by experiment and observation.* **ex·per′i·men·ta′tion** *n.*

ETYMOLOGY

Experiment comes from Latin *experimentum* (*a trial, or a test*) from *experiri*, meaning "to try out."

The same Latin root is in the word *experience*, which came into use later.

ex·per·i·men·tal (ek sper′ə men′təl) *adj* **1** used for, based on, or undergoing experiments: *an experimental lab, an experimental science. The new drug is still in the experimental stage.* **2** using new techniques or ideas: *His art is very experimental and is difficult to understand.* **ex·per′i·men′tal·ly** *adv.*

ex·pert (ek′spərt) *n* a person with a great deal of knowledge, skill, and experience in some area.
adj to do with being an expert: *an expert carpenter, an expert opinion.* <Latin *expertus* known by experience> **ex′pert·ly** *adv.* **ex′pert·ness** *n.*

ex·per·tise (ek′spər tēz′) *n* the knowledge and skill of an expert: *We can use your expertise on this project.*

ex·pi·ate (ek′spē āt′) *v* **ex·pi·at·ed, ex·pi·at·ing** make amends for: *We cannot expiate all the offences of our ancestors.* <Latin *ex-* completely + *piare* satisfy> **ex′pi·a′tion** *n.*

ex·pire (ek spīr′) *v* **ex·pired, ex·pir·ing** **1** cease to be valid or usable: *This movie pass has expired.* **2** die. <Latin *ex-* out + *spirare* breathe> **ex′pi·ra′tion** *n.*

ex·pi·ry (ek spī′rē) *n, pl* **ex·pi·ries** often, **expiry date** the date when something has ceased to be valid or usable.

ex·plain (ek splān′) *v* **1** make clear or understandable: *Can you explain how to use this software?* **2** tell how or why something happened: *Nobody could explain his strange behaviour. Explain your absence!* <Latin *explanare* to make clear, from *ex-* out + *planus* flat, clear> **ex·plain′a·ble** *adj.* **ex·plan′a·to′ry** (ek splan′ ə to′rē) *adj.*
explain away, get rid of or make insignificant by giving reasons or excuses: *to explain away someone's fears.*
explain yourself, **a** make your meaning clear. **b** justify or give reasons for your behaviour: *Why did you go off without telling us? Explain yourself.*

SYNONYMS

Explain emphasizes making something clear: *He tried to explain to his parents the difference between an MP3 player and a CD player.*

Define involves making clear the meaning of something: *The teacher helped us define the scientific words.*

Illustrate suggests making clear through tools such as stories, examples, or comparisons: *She illustrated her point with a story from her past.*

ex·pla·na·tion (ek′splə nā′shən) *n* **1** the act or process of explaining: *Her explanation of electricity was easy to follow.* **2** something that explains: *These shoes are the explanation for my sore feet!*

ex·ple·tive (ek splē′tiv) *or* (ek′splə tiv) *n* **1** an oath or exclamation, often containing an offensive word or words, expressing surprise or anger, such as *I'll be damned!* **2** *Grammar* a word used to fill out a statement without adding to its sense. The word *There* in *There is a book on the table* is an expletive because the sentence could have been phrased *A book is on the table.* <Latin *expletivus* for filling out, from *ex-* out + *plere* fill>

ex·plic·a·ble (ek splik′ə bəl) *or* (ek′splə kə bəl) *adj* explainable.

ex·pli·cate (ek′splə kāt′) *v* **ex·pli·cat·ed, ex·pli·cat·ing** **1** thoroughly analyze the meaning of a principle, doctrine, or text. **2** explain. <Latin *explicare* unfold, explain, from *ex-* out + *plicare* fold> **ex·plic′a·ble** *adj.* **ex′pli·ca′tion** *n.*

ex·plic·it (ek splis′it) *adj* **1** clearly expressed and stated openly: *explicit orders, an explicit statement of your intentions.* Compare IMPLICIT. **2** sparing no details, however shocking: *The account of the accident was so explicit I couldn't bear to read it.* < Latin *explicare* unfold, explain, from *ex-* out + *plicare* fold> **ex·plic′it·ly** *adv.* **ex·plic′it·ness** *n.*

ex·plode (ek splōd′) *v* **ex·plod·ed, ex·plod·ing** **1** blow up, either as a result of pressure from within or as a chemical or nuclear reaction: *The building was destroyed when the defective boiler exploded. The bomb exploded.* **2** cause to explode: *to explode dynamite.* **3** react suddenly with noise or violence: *His mistake was so funny that the audience exploded with laughter.* **4** increase rapidly in an uncontrolled way: *an exploding population.* <Latin *explodere* to drive off by clapping. Originally used in the theatre, meaning to drive an actor off the stage by making a loud noise.>

ex·ploit (ek′sploit) *for n,* (ek sploit′) *for v. n* a bold, remarkable deed: *tales about the exploits of famous heroes.*
v **1** use profitably: *A mine is exploited for its minerals.* **2** use unfairly, greedily, or selfishly. <See EXPLICIT.> **ex·ploit′a·tive** *adj.* **ex′ploi·ta′tion** *n.*

ex·plore (ek splȯr′) *v* **ex·plored, ex·plor·ing** **1** go to a new place in order to see what it is like, or what may be found there: *Champlain explored the Ottawa River and Georgian Bay. Let's explore the attic.* **2** examine something closely: *We explored several possible solutions before choosing.* **3** examine by touch: *The doctor explored the wound.* <Latin *explorare* search out, from *ex-* out + *plorare* cry. Originally thought to be a hunter's term meaning a loud cry to scare an animal from its hiding place.> **ex′plo·ra′tion** *n.* **ex·plor′a·to′ry** *adj.* **ex·plor′er** *n.*

a bat	e bed	i bid	o pot	u cup	th thin
ā cake	ē me	ī bite	ō go	ū rude	ᴛʜ then
ȧ bar	ə about	ər over	ȯ for	u̇ put	zh measure

ex·plo·sion (ek splō′zhən) *n* the act, fact, or sound of exploding: *the explosion of a bomb, an explosion of laughter.*

ex·plo·sive (ek splō′siv) *adj* **1** capable of exploding: *explosive chemicals.* **2** tending to burst forth noisily: *an explosive temper.*
n a substance that is capable of exploding: *Explosives are used in making fireworks.* **ex·plo′sive·ly** *adv.* **ex·plo′sive·ness** *n.*

ex·po·nent (ek spō′nənt) *n* **1** someone who believes in and explains an idea or theory: *an exponent of socialism.* **2** a person who develops or has a specific skill: *an exponent of jazz.* **3** *Mathematics* a small number written above and to the right of a quantity or symbol to show how many times it is to be used as a factor. Examples: $2^2 = 2 \times 2$; $a^3 = a \times a \times a$. <Latin *ex-* up + *ponere* put>

ex·po·nen·tial (ek′spō nen′shəl) *adj* **1** *Mathematics* to do with algebraic exponents. **2** happening at an ever greater and greater rate: *an exponential increase in population.* **ex′po·nen′tial·ly** *adv.*

ex·port (ek spôrt′) *or* (ek′spôrt) *v* **1** send goods out of one country to be sold in another: *Canada exports wheat to many parts of the world.* **2** *Computers* send from one application into another: *Data can be exported and imported between word processing programs.*
n **1** the act of selling or shipping goods to another country: *to manufacture products for export.* **2** something sold or shipped in this way: *Clothing is an important export of Québec.* <Latin *ex-* away + *portare* carry> **ex′por·ta′tion** *n.* **ex·port′er** *n.*

ex·pose (ek spōz′) *v* **ex·posed, ex·pos·ing** **1** display or make visible: *They stripped off the paint, exposing the original surface.* **2** lay open to harm, risk, or any influence or effect: *His foolish actions exposed him to ridicule.* **3** make something known that was hidden: *to expose a liar, to expose a takeover plot.* **4** allow light to reach and act on sensitive photographic film, plate, or paper. **5** put out without shelter: *To expose unwanted pets is shameful.* <Old French *ex-* forth + *poser* put>

ex·po·sé (ek′spō zā′) *n* an article or report that exposes a crime or a scandal.

ex·po·si·tion (ek′spə zish′ən) *n* **1** a large public fair; an exhibition. **2** **a** the act of expounding, or explaining in detail: *an exposition of a scientific theory.* **b** a speech or piece of writing that does this. <See EXPOUND.> **ex·pos′i·tor** *n.* **ex·pos′i·to′ry** *adj.*

expository paragraph *n* a paragraph giving facts, explaining ideas, or giving directions. Some topics for expository paragraphs might be: *My Favourite Sport; Why I Like Candy; How to Use a Camera.*

ex·post·u·late (ek spos′chə lāt′) *v* **ex·pos·tu·lat·ed, ex·pos·tu·lat·ing** argue or reason with a person against something he or she means to do or has done: *They expostulated with her about the foolishness of leaving school.* <Latin *expostulare* to demand urgently, from *ex-* from + *postulare* demand> **ex·pos′tu·la′tion** *n.* **ex·pos′tu·la·to′ry** *adj.*

ex·po·sure (ek spō′zhər) *n* **1** the act or instance of exposing, or the state of being exposed: *Years of exposure to the rain had rusted the machinery.* **2** appearance in public, especially in the media: *His campaign manager thought he needed more TV exposure.* **3** a position relative to the sun and wind: *a house with a southern exposure.* **4** **a** the time during which light reaches and acts on sensitive photographic film, plate, or paper: *A longer exposure is needed to take a picture in shade.* **b** one of the pictures on a photographic film.
die of exposure, die from hypothermia due to lack of shelter or adequate clothing.

ex·pound (ek spound′) *v* explain or teach something thoroughly: *to expound a principle.* <Old French, from Latin *ex-* forth + *ponere* put>

ex·press (ek spres′) *v* **1** put into words: *to express your opinion.* **2** show by look, voice, or action; communicate: *Her radiant face expressed her joy.* **3** press out: *Oil is expressed from olives by machine.*
adj **1** fast and making few stops: *an express train, an express courier.* **2** to do with quick transport: *an express company.* **3** clearly stated: *It was his express wish that we go without him.* **4** for a particular purpose: *I'm here for the express purpose of seeing you.* **5** exact: *She is the express image of her mother.*
n **1** a system or means of sending things quickly and directly: *to send a package by express.* **2** a fast train, bus, or elevator making few stops.
adv by express: *Send it express.* <Latin *expressus*, from *ex-* out + *premere* press> **ex·press′i·ble** *adj.*
express yourself, communicate your feelings or ideas.

ex·press·i·ble (ek spres′ə bəl) *adj* capable of being put into words: *a feeling of unhappiness too strong to be expressible.*

ex·pres·sion (ek spresh′ən) *n* **1** the act of expressing, or something that expresses: *We encourage the free expression of feelings.* **2** a word or group of words used as a unit: *"Eye candy" is a slang expression.* **3** a look on one's face: *We could tell by his expression that he was confused.* **4** an effort to communicate meaning or emotion: *Put more expression into the song.* **ex·pres′sion·less** *adj.* **ex·pres′sion·less·ly** *adv.*

ex·pres·sion·ism (ek spresh′ə niz′əm) *n* a movement in the arts in the late 1800s and early 1900s, marked by the attempt to express feelings without regard for accepted forms or tradition. **ex·pres′sion·ist** *n, adj.*

ex·pres·sive (ek spres′iv) *adj* showing much feeling or meaning: *an expressive pause. He has a very expressive face.* **ex·pres′sive·ly** *adv.* **ex·pres′sive·ness** *n.*
expressive of, expressing: *a poem expressive of joy.*

ex·press·ly (ek spres′lē) *adv* **1** by a clear statement: *You were expressly forbidden to touch it.* **2** for the particular purpose: *She left expressly to avoid seeing you.*

ex·press·way (ek spres′wā′) *n* a divided highway for fast driving without stops, using ramps to enter and exit and overpasses for roads that cross the highway.

ex·pro·pri·ate (ek sprō′prē āt′) *v* **ex·pro·pri·at·ed, ex·pro·pri·at·ing** take property away from an owner, especially for public use: *The provincial government expropriated five hectares of land for a public housing development.* <Latin *ex-* away from + *proprius* one's own> **ex·pro′pri·a′tion** *n.*

ex·pul·sion (ek spul′shən) *n* **1** the act of expelling or forcing out: *The threat of expulsion from school might change her bad behaviour.* **2** ✱ **Expulsion** the eviction of the francophone Acadians in 1755.

ex·punge (ek spunj′) *v* **ex·punged, ex·pung·ing** delete or erase: *The club secretary was directed to expunge certain items from the agenda.* <Latin *expungere* to blot out, from *ex-* out + *pungere* prick>

ex·pur·gate (ek′spər gāt′) *v* **ex·pur·gat·ed, ex·pur·gat·ing** remove objectionable parts or words from a text: *This is the expurgated version of the novel.* <Latin *ex-* out + *purgare* purge>

ex·qui·site (ek skwiz′it) *or* (ek′skwi zit) *adj* **1** lovely in a delicate way: *exquisite lace.* **2** of the highest excellence: *a person of exquisite taste.* **3** sharp and intense: *exquisite pain, exquisite joy.* <Latin *exquisitus* carefully chosen, from *ex-* out + *quaerere* seek> **ex·quis′ite·ly** *adv.* **ex·quis′ite·ness** *n.*

ex·tant (ek′stənt) *or* (ek stant′) *adj* currently existing: *Some of Sir John A. Macdonald's letters are still extant.* <Latin *exstare* stand out>

ex·tem·po·ra·ne·ous (ek stem′pə rā′nē əs) *adj* spoken or done without preparation; ad lib: *an extemporaneous speech.* **ex·tem′po·ra′ne·ous·ly** *adv.* **ex·tem′po·ra′ne·ous·ness** *n.*

ex·tem·po·re (ek stem′pə rē) *adj, adv* without preparation: *an extempore speech* (*adj*). *Each student will be called on to speak extempore* (*adv*). <Latin *ex tempore* according to the moment>

ex·tem·po·rize (ek stem′pə rīz′) *v* **ex·tem·po·rized, ex·tem·po·riz·ing** speak, sing, or play, making up what's being expressed as one goes along: *The pianist was extemporizing.* **ex·tem′po·ri·za′tion** *n.*

ex·tend (ek stend′) *v* **1** stretch out or reach out: *Extend your hand.* **2** continue in time or space: *The beach extends for more than a kilometre in each direction.* **3** straighten out: *Extend both arms in front of you.* **4** cause to go on longer or farther: *to extend a show for two more weeks. They have extended the ski trail another three kilometres.* **5** go as far as: *Your authority does not extend to my personal life.* **6** offer or give: *to extend help to someone in need, to extend a warm welcome.* <Latin *ex-* out + *tendere* stretch> **ex·tend′i·ble** *adj.*

ex·tend·ed (ek sten′did) *adj* long: *He stayed away for an extended period of time.*

extended family *n* a family including relatives other than one set of parents and children. Compare NUCLEAR FAMILY.

ex·ten·sile (ek sten′sīl) *or* (ek sten′səl) *adj* in scientific use, capable of being extended. Also, **extensible**.

ex·ten·sion (ek sten′shən) *n* **1 a** an addition that increases area, operation, contents, etc.: *a new extension built onto the school, an extension for the vacuum cleaner.* **b** an extra telephone connected to a line: *He was listening in on an extension.* **2** an increase in the time given for something: *I got an extension on my essay because I had been sick.* **3** a post-secondary education program for people who cannot attend regular courses: *She has a full-time job, but is completing her degree by extension.* **4** *Computers* the set of characters, such as *doc, jpg,* or *exe,* following the dot in a file name, indicating what kind of file it is. **5** the act of extending: *Extension of your hand is a sign of friendship.*

extension cord *n* an electrical cord with a plug at one end and a socket at the other, used to lengthen the cord attached to an appliance.

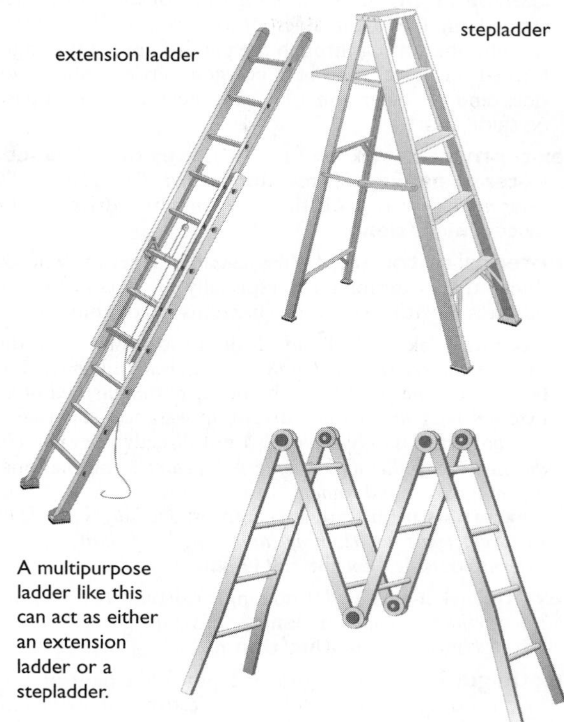

A multipurpose ladder like this can act as either an extension ladder or a stepladder.

extension ladder *n* a ladder with a movable part that makes it longer.

ex·ten·sive (ek sten′siv) *adj* **1** large: *Their property is quite extensive.* **2** covering a wide area, a lot of material, or many different things: *extensive research, extensive changes.* **ex·ten′sive·ly** *adv.* **ex·ten′sive·ness** *n.*

ex·ten·sor (ek sten′sər) *n* a muscle that extends or straightens out a limb or other part of the body. Compare CONTRACTOR (def. 2).

ex·tent (ek stent′) *n* **1** the area, distance, or degree to which something reaches or goes: *The extent of a judge's power is limited by law.* **2** an extended space or time: *a vast extent of prairie.*

ex·ten·u·ate (ek sten′yū āt′) *v* **ex·ten·u·at·ed, ex·ten·u·at·ing** make someone's guilt or offence seem less: *Ignorance of the law does not extenuate the crime.* <Latin *extenuare* lessen> **ex·ten′u·a′tion** *n.*
extenuating circumstances, facts or conditions that partly excuse a person's offence.

a bat	e bed	i bid	o pot	u cup	th thin
ā cake	ē me	ī bite	ō go	ū rude	ᴛʜ then
à bar	ə about	ər over	ȯ for	ů put	zh measure

ex·te·ri·or (ek stē′rē ər) *n* an outer surface or part: *The exterior of the house was brick. He has a harsh exterior but a kind heart.*
adj on or for the outside: *exterior paint for a house.* <Latin = farther outside>

exterior angle *Mathematics n* **1** any of the four angles formed on the outer sides of two parallel lines by a straight line cutting through the parallel lines. **2** the angle formed on the outside of a polygon between one of its sides and an extension of a side next to it. Compare INTERIOR ANGLE.

ex·ter·mi·nate (ek stər′mə nāt′) *v* **ex·ter·mi·nat·ed, ex·ter·mi·nat·ing** destroy completely: *This poison will exterminate rats.* <Latin *exterminare* drive out> **ex·ter′mi·na′tion** *n.*

ex·ter·mi·na·tor (ek stər′mə nā′tər) *n* a person who or thing that exterminates, especially a person whose business is getting rid of unwanted insects or animals.

ex·ter·nal (ek stər′nəl) *adj* **1** on or coming from the outside: *the external part of the ear, external influences.* **2** to be used on the outside of the body: *ointments and other external remedies.* **3** for outward appearance; superficial: *Her politeness is only external.* **4** not directly relevant: *His decision was influenced by external factors.* **5** international or foreign: *external trade.*
n **externals** *pl* outward appearances: *She judges people by such externals as clothing and length of hair.* <Latin *externus* outside> **ex·ter′nal·ly** *adv.*

ex·tinct (ek stingkt′) *adj* **1** no longer existing: *The dinosaur is an extinct animal.* **2** no longer active: *an extinct volcano.* <See EXTINGUISH.> **ex·tinc′tion** *n.*

ex·tin·guish (ek sting′gwish) *v* **1** put out a light or fire: *Water extinguished the blaze.* **2** destroy: *to extinguish someone's hopes.* <Latin *ex-* out + *stinguere* quench> **ex·tin′guish·a·ble** *adj.* **ex·tin′guish·er** *n.*

ex·tir·pate (ek′stər pāt′) *v* **ex·tir·pat·ed, ex·tir·pat·ing** **1** remove or destroy completely: *to extirpate a prejudice.* **2** pull up (plants) by the roots. <Latin *ex-* out + *stirps* root> **ex′tir·pa′tion** *n.*

ex·tol or **ex·toll** (ek stōl′) *v* **ex·tolled, ex·tol·ling** praise highly: *The article extols the virtues of the simple life.* <Latin *ex-* up + *tollere* raise>

ex·tort (ek stôrt′) *v* obtain money or a promise by threats, force, fraud, or illegal use of authority: *Blackmailers try to extort money from their victims.* <Latin *extortus* yank away, twist away, from *ex-* out + *torquere* twist> **ex·tor′tion** *n.* **ex·tor′tion·ist** *n.*

ex·tor·tion·ate (ek stôr′shə nit) *adj* characterized by or seeming like extortion: *extortionate demands, an extortionate price.* **ex·tor′tion·ate·ly** *adv.*

ex·tra (ek′strə) *adj* **1** more than what is usual or needed: *extra time to complete the test. Do you have an extra pencil?* **2** not included in the basic cost: *Batteries are extra.*
n **1** something for which an additional charge is made: *Gravy for your fries is considered an extra. Her bill for extras was $30.* **2** an extra thing or amount; something beyond the basic or required amount: *The drink costs extra. If anyone needs another copy, I have a few extras here.* **3** a special edition of a newspaper. **4** an extra worker, especially a person hired by the day to act in crowd scenes in a movie.
adv more than usual: *They like their coffee extra strong.* <probably short for *extraordinary*>

extra– *prefix* beyond; outside: *extraordinary, extracurricular.* <Latin>

🍁 **ex·tra–bill·ing** (ek′strə bil′ing) *n* the practice of a doctor charging patients a direct fee in addition to the standard payment from a provincial health plan.

ex·tract (ek strakt′) *for v,* (ek′strakt) *for n. v* **1** pull or take out: *to extract a tooth. He extracted a key from his pocket.* **2** obtain by pressing, distilling, or by a chemical process: *to extract oil from olives.* **3** get from someone by force or pressure: *to extract payment, to extract a confession.* **4** derive; obtain: *to extract pleasure from a situation, to extract a generalization from a set of data.* **5** take a passage from a text: *He extracted some bits of dialogue from the play for his review.*
n **1** a passage taken from a text: *The magazine published an extract from her new novel.* **2** a concentrated preparation of a substance, usually from a plant: *maple extract.* <Latin *ex-* out + *trahere* draw> **ex·trac′tor** *n.*

ex·trac·tion (ek strak′shən) *n* **1** the act or process of extracting: *the extraction of a tooth.* **2** descent or origin: *Her father is of Spanish extraction.*

ex·tra·cur·ric·u·lar (ek′strə kə rik′yə lər) *adj* outside of and in addition to one's classes, job, or other chief obligations: *His extracurricular activities are football and debating.*

ex·tra·dite (ek′strə dīt′) *v* **ex·tra·dit·ed, ex·tra·dit·ing** **1** hand over a fugitive or prisoner to another nation or legal authority for trial or punishment: *The criminal, a native of Toronto, was caught in the US and extradited to Canada.* **2** get another nation or authority to hand over such a person. <Latin *ex-* out + *tradere* hand over> **ex′tra·di′tion** *n.*

ex·tra·mar·i·tal (ek′strə mer′ə təl) *adj* outside the marriage relationship: *an extramarital affair.*

ex·tra·mu·ral (eks′trə myů′rəl) *adj* **1** between schools, colleges, or universities: *extramural hockey.* **2** occurring or done off the premises of a school, college, or university: *extramural activities.* <Latin *extra muros* outside the walls>

ex·tra·ne·ous (ek strā′nē əs) *adj* **1** coming from outside and not belonging: *Sand or some other extraneous matter had got into the butter.* **2** not essential to what is under consideration: *interesting but extraneous remarks.* <Latin *extra* outside>

ex·tra·net (ēks′tra net) *Computers n* the part of a corporate network available to customers, suppliers, etc., usually using password-protected access.

ex·traor·di·nar·y (ek strôr′də ner′ē) *adj* **1** far beyond what is ordinary: *an extraordinary child, perhaps a genius.* **2** outside of or additional to the regular schedule: *an extraordinary session of Parliament.*
ex·traor′di·nar′i·ly *adv.*

ex·trap·o·late (ek strap′ə lāt′) *v* **ex·trap·o·lat·ed, ex·trap·o·lat·ing** **1** draw a conclusion or make a prediction based on incomplete evidence, assuming that it forms part of a pattern: *to extrapolate the year's sales figures. We don't know what their response will be, but we can extrapolate from past situations.* **2** *Mathematics* project new values or terms of a series from those already known: *If you know the first four terms of this series, you should be able to extrapolate the fifth.* <extra- + (inter)polate>

ex·tra·sen·so·ry perception (ek′strə sen′sə rē) ESP.

ex·tra·ter·res·tri·al (ek′strə tə res′trē əl) *adj* coming from another planet or outer space: *extraterrestrial beings.*
n a supposed creature from another planet.

ex·trav·a·gant (ek strav′ə gənt) *adj* **1** costing or spending more than is proper or sensible: *an extravagant lifestyle, extravagant gifts.* **2** going beyond what is proper or sensible: *extravagant praise, an extravagant imagination.* <Latin *extravagari* wander beyond> **ex·trav′a·gance** *n.* **ex·trav′a·gant·ly** *adv.*

ex·trav·a·gan·za (ek strav′ə gan′zə) *n* a lavish or spectacular show, party, meal, or sales event.

ex·treme (ek strēm′) *adj* **1** much more than usual: *extreme poverty.* **2** very severe or harsh: *The government took extreme measures to protect the population.* **3** farthest from the centre: *the extreme suburbs of a city.* **4** totally uncompromising in opinions or policies: *She's a member of the extreme right.* **5** defying usual conventions or limits: *extreme sports such as bungee jumping.*
n **1** one of two things as far or as different as possible from each other: *Love and hate are two extremes of feeling. What are the two extremes in the range of data?* **2** a maximum degree: *Bliss is happiness in the extreme.* **3** *Mathematics* the first or last term in a proportion or series. In the proportion, 2 : 4 = 8 : 16, the extremes are 2 and 16; the numbers 4 and 8 are the means. <Latin *extremus* farthest ouside> **ex·treme′ly** *adv.* **ex·treme′ness** *n.*
go to extremes, go beyond reasonable limits.

extremely high frequency *n* the highest range of frequencies in the radio spectrum, between 30 and 300 gigahertz. *Abbrev.* **EHF**

extremely low frequency *n* the lowest range of frequencies in the radio spectrum, between 30 and 300 hertz. *Abbrev.* **ELF**

ex·trem·ist (ek strē′mist) *n* a person who goes to extremes, especially one with extreme opinions or policies.
adj extreme in opinions or policies: *He is too extremist to get elected in this riding.*

ex·trem·i·ty (ek strem′ə tē) *n, pl* **ex·trem·i·ties** **1** the farthest possible place or point: *the southern extremity of Africa.* **2** extreme need, danger, or suffering: *In their extremity, the refugees clung to hope.* **3** the highest degree: *in an extremity of joy.* **4** an extreme action: *Police were forced to the extremity of using tear gas to stop the riot.* **5 the extremities** *pl* the hands and feet or fingers and toes.

ex·tri·cate (ek′strə kāt′) *v* **ex·tri·cat·ed, ex·tri·cat·ing** set free from entanglements, difficulties, or embarrassing situations: *He extricated his younger brother from the barbed-wire fence.* <Latin *extricare* disentangle> **ex′tri·ca·ble** *adj.* **ex′tri·ca′tion** *n.*

ex·trin·sic (ek strin′sik) *adj* **1** not essential. **2** being, coming, or acting from outside of a thing. Compare INTRINSIC. <Latin *extrinsecus* from outside>
ex·trin′si·cal·ly *adv.*

ex·tro·vert (ek′strə vərt′) *n* an outgoing person who spends little time alone. Compare INTROVERT. <Latin *extra* outside + *vertere* turn> **ex′tro·vert′ed** *adj.*

ex·trude (ek strūd′) *v* **ex·trud·ed, ex·trud·ing** **1** push out. **2** give something a shape by forcing it through a screen or set of holes. <Latin *ex-* out + *trudere* thrust> **ex·tru′sion** *n.*

E

ex·u·ber·ant (eg zū′bə rənt) *adj* **1** with or showing eagerness and enthusiasm: *an exuberant welcome.* **2** growing abundantly: *the exuberant vegetation of the rainforest of British Columbia.* <Latin *exuberare* be abundant, from *ex-* completely + *uber* fertile> **ex·u′ber·ance** *n.* **ex·u′ber·ant·ly** *adv.*

ex·ude (eg zūd′) *v* **ex·ud·ed, ex·ud·ing** **1** come or send out in drops: *Sweat is exuded through the pores in the skin.* **2** be overflowing with some quality: *She exudes self-confidence.* <Latin *ex-* out + *sudare* sweat>

ex·ult (eg zult′) *v* rejoice greatly: *The winners exulted in their victory.* <Latin *exsultare*, from *ex-* out + *salire* leap> **ex·ult′ant** *adj.* **ex′ul·ta′tion** *n.*

eye (ī) *n* **1 a** either of the two organs of the body by which people and animals see. See BLIND SPOT, VISION for pictures. **b** the coloured part of this: *He has brown eyes.* **c** this organ and all the visible structures on and around it, including the eyelids and eyelashes: *The blow gave him a black eye.* **2 eyes** *pl* the sense of sight: *She has very good eyes.* **3** sensitivity and judgment with regard to visual details or effects: *A good artist has an eye for colour.* **4** a look or glance: *He cast an eye in her direction.* **5** something like or suggesting an eye: *the eye of a needle, the eye of a potato.* **6** the calm, clear area at the centre of a hurricane or cyclone.
v **eyed, eye·ing** or **ey·ing** look at, especially look at watchfully or sharply: *The dog eyed the stranger. She was eyeing my brownie.* <Old English *eage*> **eye′less** *adj.*
an eye for an eye, punishment or revenge that matches the offence.
be all eyes, watch eagerly and attentively: *We were all eyes as he unwrapped the box.*
catch your eye, attract your attention: *An ad in the paper caught my eye.*
feast your eyes on, admire something beautiful: *Feast your eyes on the gorgeous fall colours!*
have eyes for, be interested in, especially romantically: *I was her escort, but all evening she had eyes only for my best friend.*
in the eye(s) of, in the judgment or opinion: *In the eyes of her parents, she can do no wrong.*
in the public eye, often seen or mentioned in the media: *She was very much in the public eye during the Olympics.*
keep an eye on, watch and take care of: *Keep an eye on your little brother.*

a bat	e bed	i bid	o pot	u cup	th **thin**
ā cake	ē me	ī bite	ō go	ū rude	TH **then**
à bar	ə about	ər over	ô for	ů put	zh measure

keep an eye out for, be alert for: *Keep an eye out for bargains.*
keep your eyes peeled, *Informal* watch alertly and intently: *Keep your eyes peeled for anything unusual.*
look someone in the eye, look straight at someone's eyes, especially as a sign of honesty.
make eyes at, *Informal* look at in a flirtatious way.
open your eyes, make you see what is really happening: *The incident opened our eyes to his real character.*
run your eye over, look through something quickly: *Run your eye over this answer and tell me if it's OK.*
see eye to eye, agree: *They often don't see eye to eye, but they never actually fight.*
set eyes on, see: *I liked him the minute I set eyes on him.*
shut your eyes to, refuse to see or consider: *You can't shut your eyes to the problem forever.*
under the eye of, supervised or watched by: *The toddler played under the watchful eye of the babysitter.*
up to your (or **the**) **eyes in,** with as much of something as you can cope with: *I'm up to my eyes in homework tonight.*
with an eye to, with the possible intention of: *He looked over the catalogue with an eye to upgrading his computer.*
with your eyes shut, easily: *She can make lasagna with her eyes shut.*

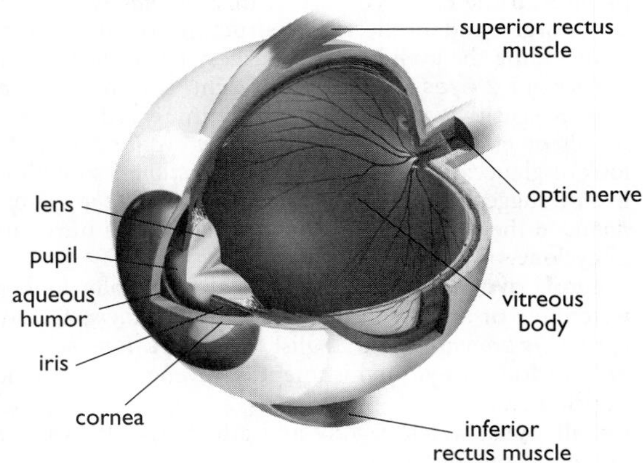

eye·ball (ī′bol′) *n* the ball-shaped part of the eye without the surrounding lids and bony socket.
v Slang look at, especially closely.

eye·brow (ī′brou′) *n* **1** the arch of hair above the eye. **2** the bony ridge that this hair grows on.
raise eyebrows, arouse interest or disapproval: *His outlandish clothes raised a few eyebrows, but that was all.*

eye candy *Slang n* an extra feature whose only value is to increase visual appeal.

eye–catch·ing (ī′kach′ing) *adj* appealing and attracting attention.

eye contact *n* the act of meeting someone's gaze with one's own: *A good speaker makes eye contact with her audience.*

eye·drop·per (ī′drop′ər) a dropper for putting medication or other liquid into the eye.

eye·ful (ī′fu̇l′) *n* **1** as much as the eye can see at one time. **2** *Informal* a good look.

eye·glass·es (ī′glas′iz) *pln* a pair of glass or plastic lenses in a frame, worn in front of the eyes to help vision. See CONTACT LENS for picture.

eye·lash (ī′lash′) *n* one of the hairs on the edge of the eyelid.

eye·let (ī′lit) *n* **1** a small, round hole for a lace or cord to go through, as on a shoe. **2** a small, round hole edged with fine stitches, used as a decorative pattern in embroidery. **3** cloth with a pattern of such eyelets.

eye·lid (ī′lid′) *n* the movable fold of skin over the eye.

eye·lin·er (ī′lī′nər) *n* a coloured cosmetic applied as a fine line along the base of the lashes to emphasize the eyes.

eye–o·pen·er (ī′ō′pə nər) *n* something that comes as an unpleasant surprise: *That documentary on fast food was an eye-opener; I wasn't aware of the issues before.*
eye′-op′en·ing *adj.*

eye·piece (ī′pēs′) *n* the lens or set of lenses nearest the user's eye in a telescope or microscope.

eye rhyme *n* words that appear to rhyme because they are spelled the same at the end, but don't because they are pronounced differently, such as *cough, tough,* and *though.*

eye·shad·ow (ī′shad′ō) a cosmetic applied to the eyelids to accent the eye. Also, **eye shadow**.

eye·sight (ī′sīt′) *n* **1** the power of seeing: *He has good eyesight.* **2** the range of vision; the view: *within eyesight.*

eye socket *n* the bony cavity in which the eyeball is set.

eye·sore (ī′sȯr′) *n* something unpleasant to look at: *Your room is an eyesore.*

eye·spot (ī′spot′) *n* an organ for seeing, found in many invertebrates, consisting of a spot of pigment that is sensitive to light.

eye·stalk (ī′stok′) *n* a slender stalk with an eye on the end, especially in lobsters or shrimp.

eye·strain (ī′strān′) *n* a tired or weak condition of the eye muscles due to overuse or an uncorrected defect, such as shortsightedness.

eye·tooth (ī′tūth′) *n, pl* **eye·teeth** an upper canine tooth.
would give your eyeteeth for (or **to**), *Informal* want very much: *I'd give my eyeteeth to be able to skate like that.*

eye·wit·ness (ī′wit′nis) *n* a person who actually sees some act or happening, and can hence give testimony concerning it.

ey·rie (ī′rē) *or* (ēr′ē) *n* **1** the nest of an eagle or other bird of prey high on a mountain or cliff. **2** a house or castle built in a high place. Also, **aerie**. <Old French *aire,* from Latin *area* a piece of level ground>

e–zine (ē′zēn′) *Informal n* a regular publication on the Internet that caters to a particular interest. <*e-*+ (*maga*)*zine*>

Ff

f or **F** (ef) *n, pl* **f's** or **F's 1** the sixth letter of the English alphabet, or any speech sound represented by it. **2** the sixth thing in a list or series: *Do all six parts of the question, from (a) to (f).* **3** *Music* the fourth tone in the scale of C major, or a key based on a scale with F as its keynote. **4** a grade indicating a person's work or performance as failing:. *I got an F on the last test, so I have to do a lot better next time.*

f 1 female. **2** *Grammar* feminine. **3** *Music* forte. **4** *Mathematics* function. **5** *Physics* frequency.

F 1 Fahrenheit. **2** fluorine. **3** farad(s).

fa (fȧ) *Music n* **1** the fourth tone of an eight-tone scale, especially as sung to sol-fa syllables: *do, re, me, fa, so, la, ti, do.* **2** the tone F. Also, **fah.** <Middle English>

fa·ble (fā′bəl) *n* **1** a story made up to teach a lesson, such as a short one with animals for characters. **2** an untrue story. **3** a legend; a myth. <Latin *fabula* story, from *fari* speak>

fa·bled (fā′bəld) *adj* legendary or told about in fables.

fab·ric (fab′rik) *n* **1** a woven or knitted material, used for clothing, curtains, etc. **2** a structure made up of connected parts: *the fabric of society.* <Latin *fabrica* something skilfully produced>

fab·ri·cate (fab′rə kāt′) *v* **fab·ri·cat·ed, fab·ri·cat·ing 1** manufacture. **2** invent an excuse or lie. **3** forge a document. <Latin *fabricare* build> **fab′ri·ca′tion** *n.*

fab·u·lous (fab′yə ləs) *adj* **1** wonderful or excellent. *I had a fabulous time at the party.* **2** extraordinary: *That clothing store charges fabulous prices.* **3** imaginary; found only in stories: *The dragon is a fabulous creature.* <Latin *fabulosos* celebrated in fable, from *fabula* fable> **fab′u·lous·ly** *adv.* **fab′u·lous·ness** *n.*

fa·çade (fə sȧd′) *n* **1** the front part of a building. **2** a false outward appearance that conceals something: *That friendly smile of hers is just a façade.* <French *face* face>

face (fās) *n* **1** the front part of the head, from forehead to chin: *a beautiful face, a wide face.* **2** an expression or look: *a sad face.* **3** a distortion of the face that is meant to be funny: *We made faces at the baby to cheer him up. She made a face at her dinner but ate it anyway.* **4** outward appearance: *This new information puts a different face on the matter.* **5** the outer surface of something: *the face of the earth.* **6** the front or main side: *the face of a clock, the face of a playing card.* **7** *Mathematics* a plane surface of a solid: *A cube has six faces.* **8** dignity, self-respect, or prestige: *He tried to save face by changing the subject.*

v **faced, fac·ing 1** have or turn the face or front part toward: *Please face the wall. Our classroom faces east.* **2** present itself to: *A difficult decision is facing us.* **3** meet bravely or boldly: *She has the courage to face her problems.* **4** be opposite to: *Look at the picture facing page 60.* **5** cover the surface of with a layer of different material: *a wooden house faced with brick.* <French, from Latin *facies* form>

face down (or **up**)**,** with the front or main side down (or up): *Lay your tests face down on the desk.*

face off, *Hockey, Lacrosse* put a puck or ball into play by dropping it between the sticks of two players facing each other.

face someone down, confront or challenge, causing someone to feel embarrassed or lose confidence.

face to face, a with faces toward each other: *The players were lined up face to face for the singing of* O Canada. **b** in person: *I finally met him face to face.*

face up to, meet bravely and boldly, especially after avoiding: *to face up to the truth.*

face with, present with a problem: *They faced him with an impossible request.*

get (or **be**) **in someone's face,** *Informal* be aggressive: *She won't listen unless you get in her face about it.*

in the face of, a in the presence of: *The firefighter showed no fear in the face of danger.* **b** in spite of: *to succeed in the face of great hardship.*

on the face of it, going by appearances or by the first impression: *On the face of it, it seemed a pretty easy task.*

pull a long face, *Informal* look sad or disapproving.

put a good (or **brave**, etc.) **face on it,** make the best of a situation.

to someone's face, boldly, in the presence of: *He called her "Carrots" to her face.*

SYNONYMS

Face can refer strictly to the front portion of the head: *The man had a very round face.*

Countenance suggests a facial expression: *The spoiled child often had a sulky countenance.*

Visage also suggests a facial expression, but is a literary or poetic term: *The queen had a proud and noble visage.*

face card *n* the king, queen, or jack of a suit of playing cards.

face·cloth (fās′kloth′) *n* a small cloth for washing the face or body.

face·less (fās′lis) *adj* without any personal or individual character: *a faceless bureaucrat.*

face·lift (fās′lift′) *n* **1** a surgical operation that tightens the skin of the face to remove wrinkles. **2** a change that improves the appearance of something: *The whole mall needs a facelift.*

face·off (fās′of′) *Hockey, Lacrosse n* the act of putting a puck or ball into play: *The last goal was scored from the faceoff.*

face–sav·ing (fās′sā′ving) *adj* keeping or with the intention of keeping one's dignity or self-respect: *That was just a face-saving gesture.*

fac·et (fas′it) *n* **1** a small polished surface of a cut gem. **2** a feature of something: *Selfishness was a facet of his character that we seldom saw.* <French *facette*>

fa·ce·tious (fə sē′shəs) *adj* speaking or spoken in fun: *facetious remarks. I was just being facetious.* <Latin *facetus* witty> **fa·ce′tious·ly** *adv.* **fa·ce′tious·ness** *n.*

a bat	e bed	i bid	o pot	u cup	th thin
ā cake	ē me	ī bite	ō go	ū rude	ᴛʜ then
ȧ bar	ə about	ər over	ȯ for	u̇ put	zh measure

F

face value *n* 1 the value marked on a bond, cheque, coin, or bill: *He paid much more than the face value for the silver quarters in his collection.* 2 the obvious meaning: *I took the compliment at face value without worrying about hidden sarcasm.*

fa·cial (fā′shəl) *adj* of or for the face: *facial features, facial tissue.*
n a massage or cosmetic treatment of the face.

fa·cile (fas′īl) *adj* 1 moving, acting, or working with ease: *more stories from the facile pen of one of my favourite authors.* 2 showing little thought, effort, or depth: *facile answers to complex questions.* <Latin *facilis* easy, from *facere* do> **fac′ile·ly** *adv.* **fac′ile·ness** *n.*

fa·cil·i·tate (fə sil′ə tāt′) *v* **fa·cil·i·tat·ed, fa·cil·i·tat·ing** 1 make easier: *Modern appliances facilitate many everyday tasks.* 2 give specialized leadership to a discussion or meeting: *A consultant facilitated the planning sessions.* **fa·cil′i·ta′tor** *n.*

fa·cil·i·ty (fə sil′ə tē) *n, pl* **fa·cil·i·ties** 1 a building or centre specially equipped to serve a certain purpose: *The town has built a new sports facility.* 2 usually, **facilities** *pl* **a** equipment or furnishings that make an action or activity possible or easier: *The library provides facilities for studying.* **b** the washrooms in a public building. 3 ease in doing something: *Practice will give him greater facility in reading.* 4 a particular ability or skill: *a facility with words.*

fac·ing (fā′sing) *n* 1 a protective or decorative layer covering a surface: *The front of the museum has a marble facing.* 2 a lining along the inside of a garment's edge to reinforce it.

fac·sim·i·le (fak sim′ə lē′) *n* 1 a copy or reproduction: *Send in the attached entry form or a reasonable hand-drawn facsimile.* 2 a FAX (def. 3). <Latin *fac* make + *simile* like>

fact (fakt) *n* 1 a specific thing known to be true or to have real existence: *You can't ignore the fact of gravity. It is a fact that he was there; we all saw him.* 2 something believed or presented as a fact: *Check your facts before you present your argument.* 3 an act or deed: *She was charged with being an accessory after the fact.* <Latin *factum* something done, from *facere* do>
as a matter of fact, in fact, or **in point of fact,** in truth: *I'm kind of hungry; in fact, I haven't eaten all day.*
facts and figures, detailed factual information: *You need facts and figures to prove your theory.*

> **GRAMMAR AND USAGE**
>
> **The fact that** is a roundabout phrase that is worth avoiding in writing and speech. Using **that** by itself is more straightforward.
>
> Compare the following sentences:
> *He was well aware of **the fact that** he had missed the school bus.*
> *He was well aware **that** he had missed the school bus.*

fact–find·ing (fakt′fīn′ding) *n* the process of investigating the facts of a situation.
adj existing for this purpose: *a fact-finding committee, a fact-finding mission.*

fac·tion (fak′shən) *n* a group of people within a larger group, holding views that differ from those of the majority: *A radical faction is threatening to take over the leadership of the organization.* <Latin *factionem* class of persons>

fac·tious (fak′shəs) *adj* causing or fond of causing conflict: *a few factious employees.* **fac′tious·ly** *adv.* **fac′tious·ness** *n.*

fac·ti·tious (fak tish′əs) *adj* produced artificially: *Advertising can cause a purely factitious demand for an item.* <Latin *facticius* artificial, from *facere* make> **fac·ti′tious·ly** *adv.*

fact of life *n* 1 a part of life that cannot be changed or ignored: *Hard work is a fact of life for most people.* 2 **facts of life** *pl* basic information about sex.

fact·oid (fak′toid) *n* 1 something generally accepted as fact, but unproven. 2 *Informal* a trivial or useless piece of information.

fac·tor (fak′tər) *n* 1 an element, condition, or quality that contributes to a result: *Luck is usually a factor in success.* 2 *Mathematics* one of two or more quantities that divides a given quantity with no remainder: *The factors of 30 are 2, 3, and 5.* 3 🍁 in former times, a representative of a company, such as the Hudson's Bay Company.
v Mathematics separate into factors. <Latin *factor* maker, from *facere* make>
factor in (or **out**), include in (or leave out of) one's calculation or analysis: *When you factor in the number of times I'll wear this jacket, the cost isn't so high.*

fac·to·ri·al (fak tô′rē əl) *Mathematics n* the product of a certain whole number and all the positive whole numbers below it, down to 1. Example: 4 factorial = $4 \times 3 \times 2 \times 1 = 24$ *Symbol* ***n!*** (where *n* is the start number).
adj to do with factors or factorials.

fac·to·ry (fak′tə rē *or* fak′trē) *n, pl* **fac·to·ries** 1 a place where things are manufactured: *a button factory.* 2 🍁 in former times, a trading post, but now found only in place names: *Moose Factory, Ontario.* <Latin *factoria*, from *factor* maker>

fac·tu·al (fak′chū əl) *adj* to do with facts: *factual information. My teacher wants a factual report on global warming, not my opinion on the matter.* **fac′tu·al·ly** *adv.*

fac·ul·ty (fak′əl tē) *n, pl* **fac·ul·ties** 1 a power of the mind or body: *the faculty of hearing. At 95 years of age she still has all her faculties.* 2 a special ability: *He has an amazing faculty for mental arithmetic.* 3 the teaching staff of a college or university. 4 a department of learning in a university: *the faculty of law.* <Latin *facultatem* ability>

fad (fad) *n* something many people are very interested in for a short time: *The scooter fad came and went.* <origin uncertain> **fad′dish** *adj.*

fade (fād) *v* **fad·ed, fad·ing** 1 lose colour or brightness: *My bedroom curtains have faded a lot.* 2 lose freshness or strength: *Most of the garden flowers had faded by September.* 3 slowly disappear: *At his words, her smile faded. The sound of the train faded in the distance.* 4 cause to fade: *Sunlight will fade some dyes.* 5 *Golf* of a ball, deviate from a straight course. <Old French *fade* pale>
fade in (**out**), slowly become more (less) distinct, as a movie image or electronic signal.

fade–in (fād′in′) *n* the process of becoming gradually more distinct as a movie image or electronic signal.

fade–out (fā′dout′) *n* the process of becoming gradually fainter as a movie image or electronic signal until it disappears.

fae·ces (fē′sēz) FECES.

fag (fag) *v* **fagged, fag·ging** work hard or until weary or tire out with hard work: *The horse was fagged.*
n a person who does hard work; a drudge. <origin uncertain>

fag·got or **fag·ot** (fag′ət) *n* **1** a bundle of wooden or metal rods, sticks, or twigs. **2** *Offensive slang* a male homosexual. Also, **fag**.
v tie or fasten together into bundles. <Old French *fagot*>

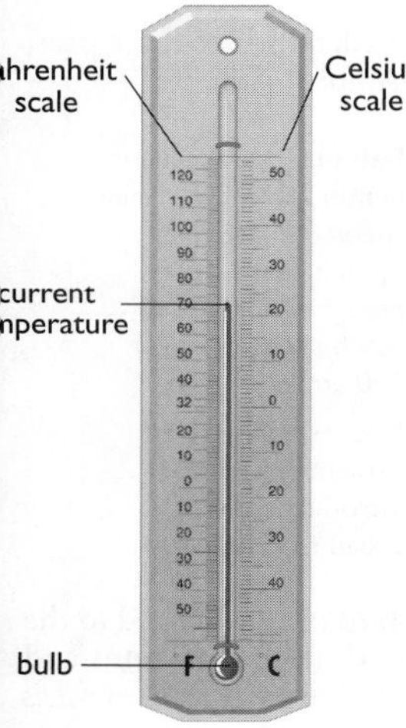

The **Fahrenheit** scale, devised in 1714 by Gabriel Fahrenheit, was based on measuring temperature changes in a thermometer using mercury. Before that (in 1709), he had constructed an alcohol thermometer, but his newer invention was more accurate.

Most English-speaking countries now use the Celsius scale. Another temperature scale is the Kelvin scale, which uses absolute zero (–273°C) as its zero point.

Fahr·en·heit (fer′ən hīt′) *adj* to do with a temperature scale in which 32° marks the freezing point of water (0°C) and 212° marks the boiling point (100°C). *Symbol* **F** <G.D. *Fahrenheit*, 18c physicist>

fai·ence (fī ons′) *n* glazed earthenware or porcelain of fine quality. <French, probably after *Faenza*, Italy, where it originated>

fail (fāl) *v* **1** try to do something and not succeed: *He failed to achieve his goal. I fail to understand why you didn't show up.* **2** not remember or bother to do; neglect: *He failed to read the instructions.* **3** in school, get or give a mark that is too low for a pass or a credit: *She failed her first year. The teacher failed a third of the class.* **4** fall far short of what is wanted or expected: *My science experiment failed. The crops failed again this year.* **5** be of no use to when needed: *Her courage suddenly failed her. His friends failed him when he was in trouble.* **6** come to an end as a supply: *A rescue party found them just before their supplies failed.* **7** break down: *Her health is failing. The engine has failed.* **8** go bankrupt: *That company will fail.* <Old French *faillir* not succeed, from Latin *fallere* to disappoint>
without fail, for sure: *She promised to be there without fail.*

fail·ing (fā′ling) *n* a fault or weakness: *He is a lovable person despite his failings.*
adj indicating failure: *a failing grade.*
prep in the absence of: *Failing good weather, the party will be held indoors.*

fail–safe (fāl′sāf′) *adj* **1** automatically returning to a safe condition, or switching to a backup, whenever there is a failure in a system. **2** impossible to fail: *a fail-safe recipe for banana bread.*

fail·ure (fāl′yər) *n* **1** the act or fact of failing. **2** a person who or thing that has failed: *The play was considered a failure because only a few tickets were sold.*

faint (fānt) *adj* **1** not clear or distinct: *a faint idea, a faint outline of the Peace Tower through the fog.* **2** weak: *a faint voice, a faint attempt.* **3** ready to lose consciousness: *I feel faint.* **4** lacking in courage: *A few faint hearts did not dare to go skydiving and stayed behind.* **5** remote or slight: *a faint chance, faint hope of success.*
n a condition in which a person is briefly unconscious because too little blood is flowing to the brain: *She fell to the floor in a faint.*
v lose consciousness temporarily: *He fainted at the sight of blood.* <Old French *faindre* to be idle> **faint′ly** *adv.* **faint′ness** *n.*

F

faint–heart·ed (fānt′hår′tid) *adj* lacking courage. **faint′-heart′ed·ly** *adv.* **faint′-heart′ed·ness** *n.*

fair[1] (fer) *adj* **1** just and impartial: *a fair judge, a fair mark.* **2** according to the rules: *fair play.* **3** average: *She has a fair understanding of the subject.* **4** blond. **5** clear and sunny: *The weather will be fair today.* **6** *Poetic* beautiful: *a fair lady.* **7** of considerable size or amount: *They own a fair piece of property.* **8** helpful, especially to a ship's course: *We had fair winds all the way.*
adv **1** honestly and according to the rules: *Play fair.* **2** directly: *The stone hit her fair on the head.* <Old English *faeger*> **fair′ness** *n.*
bid fair, seem likely: *This young man bids fair to succeed.*
fair and square, *Informal* just(ly); honest(ly): *They won fair and square.*
fair enough, *Informal* an expression of agreement.
fair to middling, *Informal* average.
no fair, *Informal* (*often used as an interjection, especially by children*) unfair.

fair[2] (fer) *n* **1** a gathering for the purpose of showing local produce and livestock, crafts, and manufactured goods, often with other attractions such as games, rides, shows, and refreshments. **2** a gathering of people in a certain industry to buy and sell and to trade ideas: *a computer fair, a book fair.* **3** a fundraising event with entertainment and things for sale: *The school holds a fair every spring.* <Old French, from Latin *feria* market fair, holiday>

fair game *n* **1** animals or birds that can be legally hunted. **2** a person or thing considered a legitimate target of attack or ridicule: *She was fair game for political cartoonists because of her odd way of dressing.*

a bat	e bed	i bid	o pot	u cup	th thin
ā cake	ē me	ī bite	ō go	ū rude	TH then
à bar	ə about	ər over	ȯ for	u̇ put	zh measure

fair·ground (fer′ground′) *n* an open outdoor space where fairs are held.

fair–haired (fer′herd′) *adj* with light-coloured hair.

fair·ly (fer′lē) *adv* 1 in a fair manner: *She judged all entries fairly.* 2 somewhat: *The pay was fairly good.* 3 almost: *He was fairly bursting with pride.*

fair–mind·ed (fer′mīn′did) *adj* not prejudiced or biased. **fair′-mind′ed·ly** *adv.* **fair′-mind′ed·ness** *n.*

fair play *n* 1 behaviour that follows the rules. 2 just treatment for all.

fair shake *Informal n* honest or just treatment: *All I want is a fair shake.*

fair–spo·ken (fer′spō′kən) *adj* speaking smoothly and pleasantly.

fair·way (fer′wā′) *n* 1 the part in a golf course where the grass is kept short, between the tee and the putting green. 2 an unobstructed passage or way: *a fairway for ships in a harbour.*

fair–weath·er friend (fer′weᴛʜ′ər) *n* a person who stops being a friend during difficult times.

fair·y (fer′ē) *n, pl* **fair·ies** an imaginary being of folklore and myth with power to help or harm human beings, often pictured as small and delicate.
adj to do with fairies: *fairy tales.* <Old French *faerie*>

fair·y·land (fer′ē land′) *n* 1 the imaginary place where the fairies live. 2 any charming and seemingly magical place.

fairy tale *n* 1 a story involving fairies, elves, ogres, or other imaginary beings with magical powers. 2 an untrue story.

fait ac·com·pli (fet′ ə kom plē′) *n* something completed and therefore no longer worth opposing. <French = accomplished fact>

faith (fāth) *n* 1 belief without proof, based on someone's word: *We have faith in our friends.* 2 confident belief in supernatural or spiritual things. 3 a particular religion: *the Islamic faith, the Catholic faith.* 4 confidence in something: *If you think this will work, you have more faith than I do.* <Old French, from Latin *fides*>
break faith, break one's promise.
in bad faith, insincerely and with bad intentions.
in good faith, sincerely and with good intentions: *Although the boys had done the wrong thing, they had acted in good faith.*
keep faith, keep one's promise.
keep the faith, stay true to a principle, ideal, or cause.

faith·ful (fāth′fəl) *adj* 1 loyal and reliable: *a faithful friend, a faithful servant.* 2 true: *a faithful account of what happened, a translation that is faithful to the original.*
n **the faithful** loyal followers or supporters.
faith′ful·ly *adv.* **faith′ful·ness** *n.*

faith healing *n* the healing of an illness or injury through prayer and the use of physical touch, based on faith in God working through the healer. **faith healer** *n.*

faith·less (fāth′lis) *adj* 1 unable to be trusted. *a faithless friend.* 2 without religious faith: *He was a faithless, godless man.* **faith′less·ly** *adv.* **faith′less·ness** *n.*

fa·ji·tas (fə hē′təs) *pln* strips of grilled meat and chopped vegetables with grated cheese and other toppings, rolled up in a soft tortilla. <Spanish = little strips>

fake (fāk) *v* **faked, fak·ing** 1 make or set up dishonestly and pass off as true or real: *The picture was faked by digitally combining two photos. They faked the whole argument in order to create a distraction.* 2 pretend to have or do: *to fake an illness.*
n 1 something made to deceive: *That ten-dollar bill is a fake.* 2 a person who tries to impress others falsely.
adj intended to deceive: *a fake testimonial.* <origin uncertain> **fak′er** *n.*
fake it, *Informal* bluff or improvise: *If you forget the words to the song, just fake it.*

fa·kir (fā′kər) *or* (fə kēr′) *n* a Muslim holy man who lives by begging. <Arabic *faqir* poor>

fa·la·fel (fə lä′fəl) *n* ground, seasoned, and fried chick peas, usually eaten with or in a pita. <Arabic *falafil*>

Falcons are excellent hunters, noted for their speed and accuracy in pursuit of prey. The peregrine falcon can reach speeds of over 200 km/h.

Falcons will nest on skyscrapers when introduced into an urban environment.

fal·con (fal′kən) *or* (fol′kən) *n* 1 a bird of prey related to the hawk and eagle. 2 a falcon or hawk trained to hunt and kill birds and small game. <Old French, from Latin *falcis* sickle. The falcons's hooked claws resemble a sickle.>

fal·con·er *n* a breeder and trainer of falcons, or a person who hunts with trained falcons. **fal′con·ry** *n.*

fall (fol) *v* **fell, fall·en, fall·ing** 1 drop down from a higher place: *Snow was falling fast. The leaves have fallen from the trees.* 2 lower oneself suddenly from an erect position: *He fell to his knees.* 3 hang down: *Her hair fell to her shoulders.* 4 become less or lower: *CD prices have fallen. The lake fell about half a metre. Her voice fell when she told him the news.* 5 lose status, power, or honour: *The dictator fell from the people's favour.* 6 be captured, overthrown, or destroyed: *The fort fell to the enemy.* 7 be wounded or killed, especially in battle: *a monument to those who fell in the last war.* 8 look or become sad or disappointed: *His spirits fell when he heard they weren't going. Her face fell when I told her the news.* 9 pass into a certain condition: *to fall asleep.* 10 happen: *My birthday falls on a Sunday this year.* 11 occur as a right or responsibility: *It falls to you to ensure that supper is made on time.* 12 divide into or be arranged as: *The story falls into five parts. This question falls into a different category.*
n 1 the season of the year between summer and winter. 2 the act or distance of falling: *The fall from his horse hurt him.* 3 the amount that falls: *a heavy fall of snow.* 4 usually, **falls** *pl* a waterfall: *We sat and ate lunch by the falls.* 5 the way something falls or hangs: *I don't like the fall of this coat.* 6 a hairpiece of long hair, usually worn at the back of the head. <Old English *feallan*>

fall (all) over yourself, *Informal* be extremely eager.
fall apart, **a** crumble; break down. **b** lose your composure.
fall back, retreat: *The soldiers fell back to a stronger position.*
fall back on, **a** use a strategy or argument that is not one's first choice. **b** turn to for help or support: *He knew he could fall back on his father.*
fall behind, fail to keep up: *Before the race was half over, he had fallen a lap behind. Don't let your homework fall behind.*
fall down, fail to turn out or perform as expected or required: *to fall down on the job.*
fall for, a be fooled by: *Don't fall for that old trick.* **b** fall in love with: *She's really fallen for him.*
fall in, a collapse: *The roof fell in from the weight of the snow.* **b** *especially Military* take one's place in line.
fall in with, a meet and start keeping company with: *to fall in with the wrong crowd.* **b** agree to: *They fell in with our plans.*
fall off, decline: *My grades have fallen off.*
fall on (or **upon**)**, a** attack: *Thieves fell on the man and stole his money.* **b** be the responsibility of: *It falls on me to thank the speaker publicly.*
fall out, a *especially Military* step out of one's place in a line or orderly formation. **b** quarrel and stop being friends. **c** happen by chance: *We didn't plan to, but it fell out that we both arrived at the party at the same time.*
fall short (of), be less than a standard or required amount: *Last year's amount of sunshine fell short of the annual average.*
fall through, fail: *Her plans fell through.*
fall to, begin to fight, attack, eat, etc.: *The swordsmen fell to with great enthusiasm.*

GRAMMAR AND USAGE

Falls is usually used with a plural verb: *The falls are most spectacular in the spring.*

Falls as part of a place name is used with a singular verb: *Niagara Falls is a popular tourist attraction.*

fal·la·cy (fal′ə sē) *n, pl* **fal·la·cies** **1** a mistaken belief: *It is a fallacy to suppose that money always bring happiness.* **2** a mistake in reasoning. <Latin *fallere* deceive>
fal·la′cious (fə lā′shəs) *adj.*

fall·back (fol′bak′) *n* **1** an alternative plan or response. **2** an act of retreating: *fallback in wages.*

fall·en (fol′ən) *v* past participle of FALL.
adj **1** that fell down: *a fallen tree. They picked up some fallen apples.* **2** defeated: *a fallen city.* **3** deemed by a religion to have sinned.
n **the fallen** *pl* all those killed in battle: *The memorial commemorates the fallen.*

fall fair *n* in some communities, a fair held in the fall for the showing and judging of livestock, produce, and crafts, often with contests and entertainment.

fall guy *Informal n* a scapegoat.

fal·li·ble (fal′ə bəl) *adj* capable of being wrong or mistaken. <Latin *fallere* betray, deceive> **fal′li·bil′i·ty** *n.*

fall·ing–out (fol′ing out′) *Informal n, pl* **fallings-out** a quarrel.

falling star *n* a meteor.

Fal·lo·pi·an tubes (fə lō′pē ən) *pl n* in female mammals, a pair of slender tubes through which eggs pass from the ovaries to the uterus. <*Fallopius,* 16c anatomist>

fall·out (fol′out′) *n* **1** the radioactive particles that fall to the earth after a nuclear explosion. **2** any incidental result of something, especially a negative result.

fal·low (fal′ō) *or, especially in the Prairie Provinces,* (fol′ō) *adj* **1** ploughed and left unseeded to restore nutrients to the land: *fallow fields.* **2** inactive: *a fallow imagination.*
n **1** the state of being fallow. **2** land left to lie fallow: *Twenty hectares of fallow.* <Old English *fealh* fallow land>

false (fols) *adj* **fals·er, fals·est** **1** not true or not truthful; lying: *false statements, a false witness.* **2** not loyal: *a false friend.* **3** made or done so as to deceive: *false pretences, false identification.* **4** inaccurate: *to play a false note.* **5** not genuine: *false eyelashes.* **6** based on wrong ideas: *false pride, a false sense of security.* **7** not structurally essential but for some purpose: *They put in a false ceiling to hide the pipes.* <Latin *fallere* trick> **false′ly** *adv.* **false′ness** *n.*
false step, a a stumble: *One false step and the climber would fall to her death.* **b** a mistake or blunder: *The police were waiting for the suspect to make a false step.*
play someone false, cheat or betray someone.

false alarm *n* **1** a warning signal given when no actual danger exists. **2** a situation arousing some strong reaction that turns out to be unjustified: *Oops, false alarm—the key isn't lost, it's here in my pocket.*

false·hood (fols′hůd) *n* **1** a false statement or idea. **2** the practice of lying. **3** the fact of being false.

false memory syndrome *Medicine n* a condition resulting from suggestions made by a therapist during hypnosis or psychoanalysis, in which a patient mistakenly believes that he or she has experienced a trauma in the past that was later forgotten.

false ribs *pl n* the ribs not attached to the breastbone.

false teeth *pl n* a set of artificial teeth used after a person's real teeth have been taken out.

fal·set·to (fol set′ō) *n, pl* **fal·set·tos** **1** an adult male voice pitched artificially high, especially a singing voice that goes above the normal register. **2** a singer who uses falsetto.
adv in falsetto: *He sang the part falsetto.* <Italian, from Latin *fallere* deceive>

fal·si·fy (fol′sə fī′) *v* **fal·si·fied, fal·si·fy·ing** **1** make false or misrepresent: *to falsify data in a report.* **2** disprove: *That theory has been falsified by further research.* **fal′si·fi·ca′tion** *n.*

fal·si·ty (fol′sə tē) *n, pl* **fal·si·ties** **1** the fact of being false: *Experience showed him the falsity of his superstitions.* **2** something false; a lie.

a bat	e bed	i bid	o pot	u cup	th **thin**
ā cake	ē me	ī bite	ō go	ū rude	ᴛʜ then
ȧ bar	ə about	ər over	ȯ for	ů put	zh measure

fal·ter (fol′tər) *v* **1** lose courage or strength: *The soldiers faltered for a moment as their captain fell.* **2** move unsteadily. **3** say in hesitating, broken words: *Greatly embarrassed, he faltered out his thanks.*
n the act or sound of faltering. <Middle English *faltren*>
fal′ter·ing *adj.*

fame (fām) *n* **1** the fact of being receiving much public attention: *to achieve fame.* **2** what is said about one: *Her fame has gone around the world.* **famed** *adj.*

ETYMOLOGY

Fame comes from Latin *fama*, meaning "talk." (*Fama* was the goddess of fame and rumour in Roman mythology.) A person who has achieved fame is someone that people will talk about.

fa·mil·iar (fə mil′yər) *adj* **1** often seen or experienced: *a familiar tune, a familiar face.* **2** well acquainted: *She is familiar with fire drill procedures.* **3** personal and intimate: *They are on familiar terms.* **4** more friendly or casual than one has a right to be: *They didn't like his familiar manner.*
n **1** a close friend. **2** a spirit or demon supposed to serve a particular person: *A black cat was thought to be a witch's familiar.* <Old French, from Latin *familia* family>
fa·mil′i·ar′i·ty *n.* **fa·mil′iar·ize′** *v.* **fa·mil′iar·ly** *adv.*

fam·i·ly (fam′ə lē) *or* (fam′lē) *n, pl* **fam·i·lies** **1** a group of people who are related, especially a parent or guardian, his or her partner if there is one, and their children. **2** the children of a father and mother: *My uncle and aunt don't have a family yet.* **3** all of a person's relatives. **4** a clan or tribe. **5** *Biology* a category in the classification of living things. A family is more specific than an ORDER and more general than a GENUS. See also KINGDOM, DIVISION, PHYLUM, CLASS, and SPECIES. **6** any group of related or similar things, such as languages with a common origin. <Latin *familia*> **fa·mil′ial** *adj.*
in the family way, *Informal* pregnant.

Family Allowance CHILD TAX BENEFIT.

🍁 **Family Compact** *n* the nickname given to the governing class of Upper Canada; the English equivalent of Lower Canada's **Château Clique**.

family name *n* **1** in some cultures, the last name of all members of a particular family. **2** a family's reputation: *to uphold the family name.*

family planning *n* the practice of limiting the number of children one has, or of controlling the intervals between births.

family room *n* a room in a home, used by the whole family for general relaxation.

family tree *n* **1** a diagram showing the relationships and descent of all the members of a family, especially over several generations. **2** all the individuals represented by such a diagram.

fam·ine (fam′ən) *n* **1** an extreme lack of food in a place at a particular time: *Many people died during the famine in India.* **2** a very great shortage of anything: *a coal famine.* <French, from Latin *fames* hunger>

fam·ished (fam′isht) *adj* extremely hungry. <Old French, from Latin *fames* hunger>

fa·mous (fā′məs) *adj* receiving much public attention: *a famous writer.* <Latin *fama* rumour> **fa′mous·ly** *adv.*

fan[1] (fan) *n* **1** a machine with revolving blades that stirs the air for cooling or ventilation. **2** a flexible, handheld device that cools the air when it is waved back and forth. **3** anything spread out like an open handheld fan.
v **fanned, fan·ning** **1** stir the air with a fan or one's hand. **2** direct a current of air toward something: *Fan the fire to make it burn faster.* **3** drive away with a fan or one's hand: *She fanned the flies from the sleeping child.* **4** make more intense: *The website fanned my desire to visit Nunavut.* **5** *Baseball slang* strike out: *The pitcher fanned five batters.* <Latin *vannus*> **fan′like′** *adj.* **fan′ner** *n.*

fan[2] (fan) *n* someone who likes and takes a great interest in a certain person or thing: *a hockey fan. She is one of Mike Myer's greatest fans.* <*fanatic*>

fa·nat·ic (fə nat′ik) *n* **1** a person who carries his or her beliefs beyond reasonable limits: *She was such a fanatic about fresh air that she wouldn't stay in any room with the windows closed.* **2** an enthusiastic FAN[2].
adj usually, **fanatical** enthusiastic or zealous beyond reason. <Latin *fanaticus* mad, inspired (by a god), from *fanum* temple> **fa·nat′i·cal·ly** *adv.* **fa·nat′i·cism′** *n.*

fan belt *n* the belt that drives the fan to cool a car engine or other machine.

fan·ci·er (fan′sē ər) *n* a person who is especially interested in and knowledgeable about something, especially the growing or breeding of a particular kind of plant or animal: *a dog fancier, an orchid fancier.* <See FANCY.>

fan·ci·ful (fan′si fəl) *adj* **1** creative in an unusual or playful way: *fanciful designs. He must have been in a fanciful mood when he wrote this delightful story.* **2** existing only in the imagination: *a fanciful account of the events.*
fan′ci·ful·ly *adv.* **fan′ci·ful·ness** *n.*

fan club *n* a group of people devoted to a certain (usually famous) person: *She was my friend, but I'm not part of her fan club now.*

fan·cy (fan′sē) *adj* **fan·ci·er, fan·ci·est** **1** showing great technical skill and grace: *He showed us some fancy moves on the ice.* **2** highly decorative: *a fancy tablecloth.* **3** expensive and elegant: *a fancy restaurant.* **4** of high quality: *Canada Grade A Fancy peaches.*
n, pl **fan·cies** **1** imagination, especially of a whimsical or playful kind. **2** something imagined: *Is it just fancy, or do I hear a sound?* **3** an impulse: *She had a sudden fancy to go for a swim.* **4** a liking or fondness: *a fancy for gold jewellery.*
v **fan·cied, fan·cy·ing** **1** imagine: *Can you fancy yourself living in that house?* **2** like or be fond of: *He fancies ice cream on a hot day.* <*fantasy*>
strike someone's fancy, seem attractive to someone: *Do whatever strikes your fancy.*
take a fancy to, develop a fondness for: *He took a fancy to her right away.*

fancy dress *n* a costume for a masquerade party.

fan·fare (fan′fer) *n* **1** a short tune sounded by a brass musical instrument. **2** a lot of activity or talk leading up to or accompanying some event. <Arabic *farfar* talkative>

fang (fang) *n* **1** a long, sharp tooth by which certain animals such as dogs or wolves seize and hold their prey: *The wolf buried its fangs in the caribou's neck.* **2** a hollow or grooved tooth of a poisonous snake, by which it injects poison into its prey. See ADDER for picture. <Old English>

fan mail *n* mail received by a celebrity from fans.

fan·ny pack (fa′nē) *Informal n* a container for money or small personal items, in the form of a small pouch worn on a strap around the waist. <*fanny*, slang for buttocks>

fan·ta·sia (fan tā′zhə) *Music n* a composition following no fixed form or style.

fan·ta·size (fan′tə sīz′) *v* **fan·ta·sized, fan·ta·siz·ing** daydream about impractical or unlikely things: *He often fantasized about being a rock star.*

fan·tas·tic (fan tas′tik) *adj* **1** extremely good: *We had a fantastic vacation in Labrador.* **2** not possible in the real world: *The idea of space travel seemed fantastic a hundred years ago.* **3** appealing to or produced by the imagination: *There are many fantastic creatures in* The Lord of the Rings. *The firelight cast weird, fantastic shadows on the walls.* **fan·tas′ti·cal·ly** *adv.*

fan·ta·sy (fan′tə sē) *n, pl* **fan·ta·sies 1** something existing only in the imagination: *Space travel was once thought to be pure fantasy.* **2** daydreaming, or a specific daydream: *living in a world of fantasy, fantasies about sudden wealth and fame.* **3 a** a story involving things that could never be real, often set in an entirely imaginary world: *The* Harry Potter *books are fantasies.* **b** such stories as a class: *He reads a lot of fantasy.* <Old French, from Greek *phantazesthai* picture to oneself>

fan·wise (fan′wīz′) *adv* like an open FAN[1] (def. 2).

fan·zine (fan′zēn′) *Informal n* a magazine that caters to fans of someone or something. <*fan* + (*maga*)*zine*>

FAQ (fåk) *Computers n* in full, **frequently asked questions** a list of common questions about a topic or product, posted on a website.

far (får) *adj* **far·ther** or **fur·ther, far·thest** or **fur·thest** **1** a long way away: *a far country.* **2** least near to the speaker: *the far side of the room.*
adv very much: *It is far better to fail than never to have tried at all.* <Old English *feorr*>
a far cry, See CRY.
by far, very much: *She was by far the better swimmer.*
far and away, very much: *He was far and away the best student.*
far and wide, everywhere; even the most distant places.
far be it from me, I do not dare or want: *Far be it from me to question her expert opinion.*
far from it, by no means; not at all: *Tired? Far from it! I'm full of energy!*
far out, a *Slang* excellent. **b** unusual or unconventional: *His style of dress is pretty far out.*
go far, a last long: *That new shampoo doesn't go very far.* **b** help very much: *A little humility goes far toward mending a relationship.* **c** get ahead: *She has talent and should go far.*
in so far as, to the extent that.
so far, a up to a certain limit: *He accepts teasing just so far, and then he gets angry.* **b** up to this point: *Our team has won every game so far this season.*
so far so good, until now everything has been fine.

far·ad (fer′əd) *n* the SI unit of electrical capacity, such that one coulomb of charge causes a potential difference of one volt. *Symbol* **F** <M. *Faraday*, 19c scientist>

far·a·way (får′ə wā′) *adj* **1** distant: *faraway countries.* **2** dreamy and wistful: *a faraway look in her eyes.*

farce (fårs) *n* **1** a comic dramatic work full of ridiculous or absurd situations. **2** the kind of humour found in such plays. **3** a mockery or pretence: *The trial was a mere farce.* <French = stuffing, from Latin *farcire* to stuff. Refers to comic acts that were often inserted into a play during an intermission.> **far′ci·cal** *adj.*

F

fare (fer) *n* **1** the price paid to ride in a vehicle or airplane. **2** a paying passenger, especially in a taxi. **3** food provided or eaten: *party fare.*
v **fared, far·ing** *Formal, Archaic, or Humorous* **1** do well or badly: *How did you fare at the tryouts?* **2** turn out: *It will not fare well with the thief if he is caught.* <Old English *faran*>

Far East *n* (*with* ***the***) China, Japan, and other parts of eastern Asia.

fare·well (fer′wel′) *interj* an expression of good wishes at parting.
n **1** an act of saying goodbye. **2** a departure, or a social event held in honour of the person departing: *We're having a little farewell for him on Sunday.*
adj saying goodbye: *a farewell wave, a farewell performance.*

SYNONYMS

Farewell is a somewhat formal expression: *He bid me farewell at the end of the evening.*

Goodbye is more commonly used in speech: *She shouted "Goodbye!" as she got on the train.*

Bye is an informal way to say "Goodbye."

far–fetched (får′fecht′) *adj* very unlikely: *That story ending was a little far-fetched.*

far–flung (får′flung′) *adj* covering a large area: *a far-flung empire.*

far·i·na·ceous (fer′ə nā′shəs) *adj* consisting of flour or meal made of cereal grains or starchy roots. <Latin *farina* flour>

farm (fårm) *n* **1** a piece of land, usually with a house and barn on it, used for growing crops and/or raising animals. **2** any place or arrangement for cultivating some animal or plant: *a fish farm.*
v **1** grow crops and/or raise animals on a farm: *My aunt farms for a living.* **2** cultivate land: *They farm 100 hectares.* <Old French *ferme* rented land, from Latin *firmare* to settle> **farm′er** *n.* **farm′ing** *n.*
farm out, turn over to another, usually under a contract: *She farms out certain parts of the work. They farmed the kids out to various relatives while they went on vacation.*

a bat	e bed	i bid	o pot	u cup	th **thin**
ā cake	ē me	ī bite	ō go	ū rude	TH **then**
å bar	ə about	ər over	ȯ for	u̇ put	zh measure

farmstead

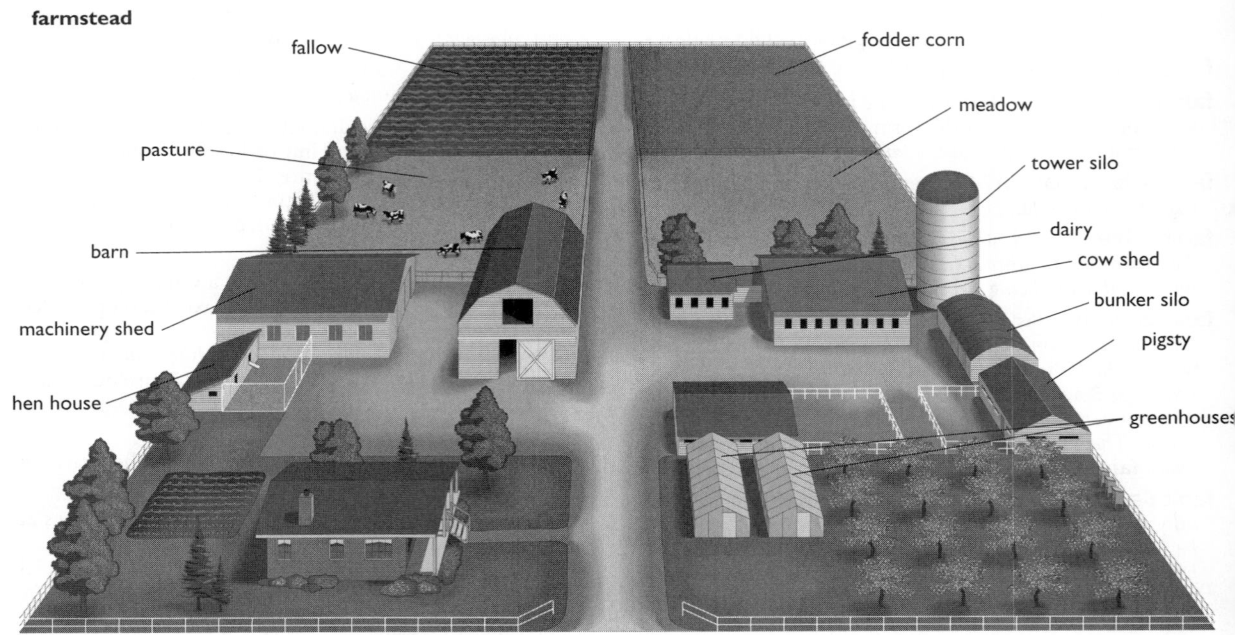

farm·hand (fȧrm′hand′) *n* a person hired to work on a farm.

farm·house (fȧrm′hous′) *n* the dwelling on a farm.

farm·land (fȧrm′land′) *n* land suitable for or used for growing crops or raising animals.

farm·stead (fȧrm′sted′) *n* a farm with its buildings.

farm team or **club** *Sports n* a minor-league team that trains players for the major leagues.

farm·yard (fȧrm′yȧrd′) *n* the yard attached to the buildings of a farm or enclosed by them.

Far North *n* (*with **the***) arctic and subarctic regions.

far–off (fȧr′of′) *adj* far away: *far-off lands across the ocean.*

far–rang·ing (fȧr′rān′jing) *adj* covering a wide area of thought, subject, influence, etc.: *a far-ranging discussion.*

far–reach·ing (fȧr′rē′ching) *adj* with important effects or implications: *far-reaching influence.*

far·ri·er (fer′ē ər) *n* a blacksmith who shoes horses. <French, from Latin *ferrum* iron. A blacksmith uses iron to shoe horses.>

far·row (far′ō *or* fer′ō) *n* a litter of pigs.
v of a pig, give birth: *The sow farrowed yesterday. She farrowed a litter of six.* <Old English *fearh*>

far–see·ing (fȧr′sē′ing) *adj* planning wisely for the future.

Far·si (far′sē) *n* a language, formerly called Persian, spoken in Iran and Afghanistan.

far–sight·ed (fȧr′sī′tid) *adj* **1** having a condition of the eyes in which nearby objects are out of focus. Compare NEAR-SIGHTED. See VISION for picture. **2** planning wisely for the future. **far′-sight′ed·ly** *adv.* **far′-sight′ed·ness** *n.*

far·ther (fȧr′ᴛʜər) *adj, adv* a comparative of **far 1** a longer distance: *Three kilometres is farther than two* (*adj*). *I can see farther than you* (*adv*). **2** at or to a more advanced point: *He has investigated the subject farther than most people* (*adv*). **3** onward or ahead: *Let's walk a bit farther* (*adv*). <Middle English *ferther*>

GRAMMAR AND USAGE

In formal English, **farther** is used for physical distance, and **further** for abstract senses:

They had farther to walk. Let's discuss this further.

far·thest (fȧr′ᴛʜist) *adj, adv* a superlative of **far 1** most distant: *to the farthest reaches of the galaxy* (*adj*). **2** to or at the greatest distance: *Who lives farthest from the town centre* (*adv*)*?*

far·thing (fȧr′ᴛʜing) *n* a former British coin worth a quarter of a penny. < Old English *feortha* fourth >

fas·cia (fā′shə) *for 1,* (fash′ə) *for 2. n* **1** *Architecture* a flat, horizontal piece of material covering the ends of rafters or on the underside of a roof overhang. **2** *Biology* **a** a sheath of connective tissue enclosing a muscle or organ. **b** a broad band of contrasting colour. <Latin>

fas·ci·cle (fas′ə kəl) *n* **1** one of the parts of a book published in instalments. **2** a small bundle, especially of stems, flowers, or leaves. <Latin *fascis* bundle>

fas·ci·nate (fas′ə nāt′) *v* **fas·ci·nat·ed, fas·ci·nat·ing** interest very strongly: *Her stories fascinated everyone. I am absolutely fascinated by butterflies.* <Latin *fascinare* enchant, from *fascinum* spell> **fas′ci·na′tion** *n.*

fas·cism (fash′iz əm) *n* **1** a system of government that closely regulates industry and culture, believes in the purity and supremacy of one race and the importance of one supreme leader. **2** any expression of extreme right-wing authoritarian or nationalistic views. Also, **Fascism. fas′cist** or **Fas′cist** *n, adj.*

ETYMOLOGY

Fascism comes from Italian *fascio,* meaning "bundle," from Latin *fasces.* In ancient Rome, the *fasces* was a bundle of rods containing an axe, carried by a magistrate as a symbol of authority. In Italy, the fascists (1922–1943) chose this symbol as their emblem.

fash·ion (fash′ən) *n* **1** the current style: *Such pointed shoes are no longer the fashion.* **2** current styles or trends: *He follows fashion very closely.* **3** a garment in the current style: *That shop carries all the latest fashions.* **4** manner or way: *I won't be treated in this fashion.*
v makes or shape: *She fashioned a whistle out of a stick.* <Latin *factio,* from *facere* make>
after a fashion, in some way or other.
fashion after (or **on**), model after: *My costume is fashioned after clothing worn in the nineteenth century.*
in fashion, being the current style: *Black is always in fashion.*

fash·ion·a·ble (fash′ə nə bəl) *adj* **1** in fashion or stylish: *Her clothes are fashionable, but they do not always suit her.* **2** prestigious or trendy: *a fashionable resort.*
fash′ion·a·bly *adv.*

fash·ion·is·ta (fash′ə nē′stə) *n* a person who is keenly interested in the latest fashion trends in clothes.

fashion plate *n* **1** a person who always wears stylish clothes. **2** a picture of a model wearing the latest styles.

fast[1] (fast) *adj* **1** doing, going, or happening in a very short time: *a fast car, a fast worker, fast Internet access.* **2** showing a time ahead of the correct time: *My watch is fast.* **3** wild in lifestyle: *He led a fast life, drinking and gambling.* **4** close and faithful: *fast friends.* **5** not fading easily: *fast colours.* **6** *Informal* tricky and smooth: *a fast talker.* **7** in photography, taking less time to be exposed: *Fast film is used in dim light or for action shots.*
adv **1** do a lot, go far, or happen in a short time: *to travel fast, to think fast.* **2** firmly or tightly: *caught fast in a trap. She held fast to the bar on the roller coaster.* **3** thoroughly or completely: *He was fast asleep.* <Old English *fæst*>
a fast one, *Informal* (*usually with* ***pull***) a trick.
play fast and loose, *Informal* be tricky, insincere, or unreliable: *to play fast and loose with the truth.*

fast[2] (fast) *v* go without food, sometimes as an act of spiritual discipline: *Followers of some religions fast on certain days. The doctor said to fast for 24 hours before this test.*
n an act or time of going with little or no food. <Old English *fæstan*>

fastball (fast′bol) *Baseball n* a pitch thrown at high speed.

fast buck *Informal n* a sum of money made easily and quickly, and often in a questionable manner.

fast day *n* a day observed by fasting, especially a day regularly set apart for this purpose by a religion.

fas·ten (fas′ən) *v* **1** firmly close, attach, or put in place, usually by means of a small device: *to fasten a dress, to fasten papers together, to fasten a shelf to the wall.* **2** lay or impose blame: *He tried to fasten the blame on his companions.* **3** direct the gaze: *The dog fastened its eyes on the girl.* <Old English *fæstnian* make firm>
fasten on (or **upon**), **a** take hold of. **b** decide on.

fas·ten·er (fas′ə nər) *n* a small device used to fasten something.

fas·ten·ing (fas′ə ning) *n* an arrangement, part, or attachment by which something is fastened: *The window fastening has broken.*

fast food *n* casual restaurant food prepared quickly, often for takeout.

fast–for·ward (fast′for′wərd) *n* **1** a mode on a tape recorder that winds the tape ahead at high speed. **2** a jump to a much later point in a story, movie, or play. **fast-forward** *v.*

fas·tid·i·ous (fa stid′ē əs) *or* (fə stid′ē əs) *adj* very concerned about details, especially about cleanliness, and hard to please: *a fastidious eater. He's fastidious about clothes.* <Latin *fastidiosus* scornful, from *fastidium* loathing> **fas·tid′i·ous·ly** *adv.* **fas·tid′i·ous·ness** *n.*

fast lane *n* **1** a lane on a highway that is reserved for fast traffic. **2** a hectic, busy way of life: *living in the fast lane.*

fast·ness (fast′nis) *n* **1** *Poetic* a strong, safe place: *The bandits hid in their mountain fastness.* **2** the quality of being fast.

fast talk *n* smooth, persuasive talk meant to deceive or to overcome suspicion. **fast-talk** *v.*

fast track *n* **1** a career path promising quick promotion. **2** an alternative schedule devised so that a project may be completed more quickly than usual. **fast-track** *v.*

fat (fat) *n* **1** a white or yellow greasy or oily substance naturally formed in the bodies of animals and in the fruits, seeds, and nuts of some plants. **2 a** any animal tissue mainly composed of such a substance: *There is a layer of fat under the skin.* **b** an excess of this: *Running will get rid of the fat on my legs.* **3** unnecessary and unwanted parts or elements: *to get rid of the fat in an organization. Cut the fat from this essay and hand it in again.* **4** an organic chemical compound not soluble in water.
adj **fat·ter, fat·test 1** with too much flesh because of an excess of stored fat: *His rich diet and lack of exercise have made him quite fat. Some people are fat because their metabolism is not working properly.* **2** thick or lengthy: *I don't read many fat books.* **3** rich; fertile; plentiful: *fat land, a fat profit.*
v **fat·ted, fat·ting** *Archaic or Poetic* make or become fat. <Old English *fæt*> **fat′ness** *n.* **fat′ty** *adj.*
chew the fat, See CHEW.
fat chance, (*ironic*) no chance.
live off the fat of the land, have the best of everything.
the fat is in the fire, matters have been made worse.

a bat	e bed	i bid	o pot	u cup	th thin
ā cake	ē me	ī bite	ō go	ū rude	ᴛʜ then
ȧ bar	ə about	ər over	ȯ for	ů put	zh measure

fa·tal (fā′təl) *adj* **1** causing death: *a fatal accident.* **2** causing destruction or ruin: *The delay was fatal to their plans.* **3** fateful: *He would find out if he passed as soon as the fatal day arrived.* **4** to do with fate. <See FATE.> **fa′tal·ly** *adv.*

> **SYNONYMS**
>
> **Fatal**, **mortal**, **deadly**, and **lethal** can all mean "causing death."
>
> **Fatal** and **mortal** are used when something, especially a condition, has caused death or is sure to cause it: *a fatal disease, a mortal wound.*
>
> **Deadly** and **lethal** describe something that could cause death: *a deadly weapon, a lethal poison.*

fa·tal·ism (fā′tə liz′əm) *n* **1** the belief that everything that happens is a result of fate. **2** an attitude of submitting to everything that happens as if it were inevitable.
fa′tal·ist *n.* **fa′tal·is′tic** *adj.*

fa·tal·i·ty (fə tal′ə tē) *n, pl* **fa·tal·i·ties** **1** an occurrence of a fatal illness or injury: *There were several fatalities on the highways last weekend.* **2** fatal influence or effect: *Treatment helps to reduce the fatality of diseases.*

fat cat *Informal n* a person who is rich and privileged or powerful.

fate (fāt) *n* **1** a power believed to control everything that happens: *Fate is beyond human control. She does not believe in fate.* **2** the outcome of something, especially if unpleasant: *He deserved a better fate. The poor animal suffered a cruel fate.* **3 the Fates** *pl Greek and Roman myth* the three goddesses believed to control human life. **4** death; ruin.
v **fat·ed, fat·ing** (*always passive*) control by fate: *She was fated to be a great leader.* <Latin *fatum* thing spoken by the gods, from *fari* speak>

fate·ful (fāt′fəl) *adj* determining what is to happen, especially in a highly significant way: *a fateful battle, a fateful day.* **fate′ful·ly** *adv.* **fate′ful·ness** *n.*

fat farm *Slang n* a resort or camp where people go to lose weight through special diets and exercise.

fa·ther (foᴛʜ′ər) *n* **1** a male parent, or a male who has the responsibilities of a parent. **2** a male ancestor: *the customs of our fathers.* **3** a man who was the creator of something: *Alexander Graham Bell was the father of the telephone.* **4** an Anglican or Catholic priest, or the title of respect given this person. **5 the Father** *Christianity* God.
v **1** sire children: *He has fathered three children.* **2** create or originate: *Edison fathered many inventions.*
adj being or resembling a father: *a father figure.* <Old English *fæder*> **fa′ther·hood** *n.* **fa′ther·ly** *adj.*

fa·ther–in–law (foᴛʜ′ər in lo′) *n, pl* **fa·thers-in-law** the father of one's spouse.

fa·ther·land (foᴛʜ′ər land′) *n* one's native country.

Fathers' Day *n* the third Sunday in June, an unofficial day to honour fathers.

🍁 **Fathers of Confederation** *pln* the men, led by Sir John A. Macdonald, who brought about the confederation of the original provinces of Canada in 1867.

fath·om (faᴛʜ′əm) *n, pl* **fath·oms** or (*especially collectively*) **fath·om** a nonmetric unit of measure equal to about 1.8 m, used mostly in measuring the depth of water.
v **1** measure the depth of. **2** understand fully: *I can't fathom why you did that.* <Old English *fæthm* width of outstretched arms> **fath′om·a·ble** *adj.*

fath·om·less (faᴛʜ′əm lis) *adj* **1** too deep to measure or to reach the bottom. **2** impossible to fully understand: *the fathomless riddle of the universe.*

fa·tigue (fə tēg′) *n* **1** physical or mental tiredness. **2** any hardship, effort, or condition producing tiredness: *The doctor has not yet recovered from the fatigues of the epidemic.* **3** a state of mental exhaustion resulting from too much of something: *combat fatigue, compassion fatigue.* **4** a weakening of metal or some other material due to long-continued use or strain. **5 a** in full, **fatigue duty** unskilled labour done by members of the armed forces, sometimes as a punishment. **b fatigues** *pl* clothes worn for this.
v **fa·tigued, fa·ti·guing** **1** make tired or weary. **2** weaken by much use or strain. <French, from Latin *fatigare* to tire>

fat·ten (fat′ən) *v* (*often with* **up**) make or become fat: *Pigs are fattened for market. The turkeys have fattened up a lot in the last month.* **fat′ten·ing** *adj.* **fat′tish** *adj.*

fat·u·ous (fach′ū əs) *adj* stupid but self-satisfied. <Latin *fatuus* foolish> **fat′u·ous·ly** *adv.* **fat′u·ous·ness** *n.*

fat·wa (fȧ′twə) *Islam n* a ruling made by a high authority in religious law. <Arabic>

fau·cet (fos′it) *especially US or Commerical n* a device containing a valve to control the flow of water or other liquid from a pipe, tank, or barrel, by opening or closing; a tap. <Old French *fausset* plug for a barrel, from *falser* to drill>

fault (folt) *n* **1** a cause for blame: *This whole mess is your fault.* **2** a flaw or defect: *Sloppiness is my greatest fault.* **3** a mistake. **4** *Geology* a break in a mass of rock, with the segment on one side of the break pushed up or down. **5 a** *Tennis* a penalty point imposed for an error in serving. **b** *Show jumping* a penalty point imposed on a rider for an error.
v **1** find fault with: *Her work could not be faulted.* **2 a** *Tennis* fail to serve the ball into the correct place. *She faulted twice and lost the match.* **b** *Show jumping* make an error. <Old French, from Latin *fallere* to fail>
fault′less *adj.* **fault′less·ly** *adv.* **fault′less·ness** *n.* **fault′y** *adj.*
at fault, deserving the blame.
find fault, (*often with* ***with***) criticize: *She always finds fault with everything I do.*
to a fault, to a great degree: *generous to a fault.*

fault·find·ing (folt′fin′ding) *n* habitual criticism.
adj engaging in this habit. **fault′find′er** *n.*

faun (fon) *n* a mythical creature often depicted as a human with the ears, horns, tail, and legs of a goat. See FAWN for confusable. <Latin *Faunus* a rural god>

fau·na (fon′ə) *n* all the animals of a particular region or time: *the fauna of the Maritimes.* <Latin *Fauna* a rural goddess, wife of Faunus>

faux (fō′) *adj* imitation: *faux leather, faux pearls.* <French = false>

faux pas (fō′pȧ′) *n, pl* **faux pas** a slip or blunder in speech, conduct, or manners. <French = false step>

fa·vour or **fa·vor** (fā′vər) *n* **1** an act of kindness: *Will you do me a favour?* **2** liking or approval: *They looked with favour on our suggestion.* **3** the condition of being liked or approved: *He is out of favour with me since we argued.* **4** a small gift or token of friendship: *party favours.*
v **1** be on the side of: *to favour legal reform.* **2** treat better than others: *The teacher favours you.* **3** be to the advantage of; help: *The longer daylight hours favour plant growth.* **4** approve of or prefer: *I favour the other team.* **5** show kindness to: *Would you favour us with a song?* **6** use gently because of injury or weakness: *to favour a sore foot.* **7** look like: *She favours her mother.* <Old French, from Latin *favere* show kindness to>
find favour with, win the approval of; please.
in favour of, a supporting: *He is in favour of a longer school year.* **b** to the benefit or advantage of: *an accounting error in favour of the bank.* **c** to be paid to: *Make the cheque out in favour of the company, not the sales rep.*
in your favour, to your benefit or advantage.

fa·vour·a·ble or **fa·vor·able** (fā′və rə bəl) *or* (fāv′rə bəl) *adj* **1** showing or giving approval: *a favourable answer.* **2** being to one's advantage: *a favourable wind.* **3** likely to be good: *It was a favourable time to go to the cottage, since the mosquitoes would be gone by then.* **fa′vour·a·bly** or **fa′vor·a·bly** *adv.*

fa·voured or **fa·vored** (fā′vərd) *adj* preferred: *a favoured method.*

fa·vour·ite or **fa·vor·ite** (fāv′rit) *adj* liked best of all or very much: *What is your favourite dessert?*
n **1** a person or thing liked best of all or very much: *He is a favourite with everybody. This song is my favourite.* **2** a contestant expected to win: *Featherfoot is the favourite in today's horse race.*

fa·vour·it·ism or **fa·vor·it·ism** (fāv′rə tiz′əm) *n* the practice of favouring one or certain ones more than others.

fawn[1] (fon) *n* a deer less than a year old.
adj greyish brown. <Old French, from Latin *fetus* offspring> **fawn′like′** *adj.*

CONFUSABLES

Fawn is a *noun* meaning "a very young deer" and an *adjective* for the greyish brown colouring of that animal. It is also a *verb* that means "flatter," in the sense of paying a compliment to someone.

Faun is a mythical creature that is half human and half goat.

fawn[2] (fon) *v* (*with **on***) flatter or show exaggerated affection, often to gain personal advantage: *Greedy relatives fawned on the rich woman.* <Old English *fægen* glad, originally an expression of delight> **fawn′ing** *adj.*

fax (faks) *n, pl* **fax·es** **1** a system for transmitting written or printed material by which text and images are converted to digital signals and transmitted by a special machine, then reconverted and printed out at the other end. **2** the machine used for this: *Does your office have a fax?* **3** the material sent: *Here is the fax you expected.*
v **faxed, fax·ing** send a message to someone using the system: *I'll fax you the permission form today.* <facsimile>

faze (fāz) *v* **fazed, faz·ing** (*usually in the negative*) disturb or impress: *A scolding doesn't faze her. He wasn't fazed at all by your great show of skill.* <variant of *feeze*, from Old English *fesian* frighten>

F

F clef *Music n* See CLEF.

fe·al·ty (fē′əl tē) *n, pl* **fe·al·ties** **1** the loyalty and duty owed by a vassal to his feudal lord: *The nobles swore fealty to the king.* **2** formal loyalty and allegiance. <Old French, from Latin *fidelitas*>

fear (fēr) *n* **1** a feeling of being afraid of a danger, pain, or threat: *In spite of his fear, he stepped out onto the log bridge.* **2** a cause for being afraid: *There is no fear of our losing.* **3** doubt or anxiety: *She has no fears about driving all that way in the winter.*
v **1** feel afraid of something: *to fear failure, to fear loud noises.* **2** have an uneasy feeling or anxious thought: *I fear it may already be too late.* <Old English *fær* danger>
fear for, worry about.
for fear of, in order to prevent: *We went as quietly as we could for fear of waking the dog.*

SYNONYMS

Fear involves a feeling of anxiety and concern: *The dog's fear of thunder sent it scampering under the bed.*

Apprehension suggests uneasiness: *We waited with apprehension for the roller coaster to start moving.*

Dread suggests great fear: *My dread of exams causes my hands to shake.*

fear·ful (fēr′fəl) *adj* **1** feeling or showing fear: *fearful of the dark. She cast a fearful glance at the huge dog.* **2** causing fear: *The explosion was a fearful sight.* **3** *Informal* very bad or unpleasant: *I have a fearful cold.* **fear′ful·ly** *adv.* **fear′ful·ness** *n.*

fear·less (fēr′lis) *adj* afraid of nothing. **fear′less·ly** *adv.* **fear′less·ness** *n.*

fear·some (fēr′səm) *adj* scary or frightening in appearance: *monsters and other fearsome creatures.* **fear′some·ly** *adv.* **fear′some·ness** *n.*

fea·si·ble (fē′zə bəl) *adj* **1** that can be done: *The dance committee chose the plan that seemed most feasible.* **2** likely: *That sounds like a feasible explanation.* **3** suitable or convenient: *The road was too rough to be feasible for car travel.* <Old French, from Latin *facere* do>
fea′si·bil′i·ty *n.*

a bat	e bed	i bid	o pot	u cup	th **thin**
ā cake	ē me	ī bite	ō go	ü rude	ᴛʜ **then**
ȧ bar	ə about	ər over	ȯ for	u̇ put	zh measure

feast (fēst) *n* **1** a big, elaborate meal prepared for some special occasion and for a number of guests: *a wedding feast.* **2** an enjoyable or abundant meal. **3** something that gives pleasure or joy: *Beauty is the soul's feast.* **4** a religious festival or celebration: *Every religion has its special feasts.*
v **1** have or celebrate with a feast. **2** provide with a feast: *The queen feasted the ambassadors.* <Old French, from Latin *festa*> **feast′er** *n.*
feast on, eat with great pleasure and in large quantities: *We feasted on fruit, nuts, and chocolate.*
feast your eyes (on), *Informal* enjoy looking at something.

feat (fēt) *n* an act showing great skill, daring, or strength. <*factum* (thing) done>

feath·er (feᴛʜ′ər) *n* a flat, light, thin, often soft outgrowth from a bird's skin.
v **1** cut in different lengths to give a featherlike texture to: *She asked the stylist to feather her hair.* **2** turn an oar or paddle after a stroke so that the blade is horizontal, keeping it that way until the next stroke begins. **3** apply brakes on and off, giving light pressure, to avoid locking or skidding. **4** touch the strings of a violin very lightly with a bow. **5** *Printing* adjust the space between lines so that the page is evenly filled. **6** of a bird, grow feathers. <Old English *fether*> **feath′ered** *adj.* **feath′er·y** *adj.*
feather in your cap, something to be proud of.
feather your nest, take advantage of chances to get rich.
in feather, covered with feathers.

feath·er·bed (feᴛʜ′ər bed′) *n* a mattress stuffed with feathers.

feath·er·weight (feᴛʜ′ər wāt′) *n* **1** a very light thing or person. **2** an unimportant person or thing: *He is a featherweight on the political scene.* **3** a boxer who weighs between 55 and 57 kilograms.
adj to do with a featherweight.

fea·ture (fē′chər) *n* **1 features** *pl* the parts of the face and their shape: *childish features, rugged features.* **2** a distinctive characteristic or quality: *One outstanding feature of Alberta and British Columbia is the Rocky Mountains.* **3** a full-length movie or other show. **4** a special article or story in a newspaper or magazine.
v **fea·tured, fea·tur·ing** give or have special prominence: *The store was featuring videos in its sale. She has featured in several recent movies.* <Old French, from Latin *factura* a formation>

feature film *n* a full-length movie.

fea·ture·less (fē′chər lis) *adj* without distinctive or impressive features or character: *a featureless landscape.*

fe·brile (fē′brīl) *or* (feb′rīl) *adj* **1** with or caused by fever: *a febrile illness.* **2** with or showing nervous excitement: *a febrile look.* <Latin *febris* fever>

Feb·ru·ary (feb′rū er′ē) *or* (feb′yū er′ē) *n, pl* **Feb·ru·ar·ies** the second month of the year. It has 28 days except in leap years, when it has 29. *Abbrev.* **Feb** <Latin *februa* Roman feast of purification, held on February 15>

fe·ces (fē′sēz) *n. pl* solid body waste from the intestines. Also, **faeces**. <Latin *faeces* dregs>
fe′cal or **fae′cal** (fē′kəl) *adj.*

feck·less (fek′lis) *adj* **1** ineffective or feeble. **2** careless and irresponsible: *feckless behaviour.* <obsolete *feck* effect + *-less*>

fe·cund (fē′kənd) *or* (fek′ənd) *adj* fertile: *a fecund imagination.* <French, from Latin *fecundus*>
fe·cun′di·ty *n.*

fed[1] (fed) *v* past tense and past participle of FEED.
fed up, tired, bored, or frustrated.

fed[2] (fed) *Slang n* **1** usually, **feds** *pl* a federal government or any of its agencies: *The feds have cut health funding. Is the fed going to raise interest rates?* **2** a member or official of a federal government. <*federal*>

fed·er·al (fed′ə rəl) *adj* **1 a** to do with the central or national government of any country that is a FEDERATION: *a federal parliament, a federal court.* **b** 🍁 sometimes, **Federal** to do with the central or national government of Canada. **2** to do with any federation: *Some unions representing large industries are actually federal organizations.* <See FEDERATE.>

🍁 **Federal Government** *n* **1** the government of Canada, located in Ottawa, and all its agencies and ministries. Its responsibilities are specified by the Constitution Act, 1867. **2** the prime minister and his or her Cabinet.

fed·er·al·ism (fed′ə rə liz′əm) *n* **1** the principles of the system of government by which a FEDERATION operates. **2** the support or promotion of these principles or this system. **fed′er·al·ist** *n, adj.*

fed·er·ate (fed′ə rāt′) *v* **fed·er·at·ed, fed·er·at·ing** unite into a FEDERATION. <Latin *foederatus* having a treaty, from *foederis* contract>

fed·er·a·tion (fed′ə rā′shən) *n* **1** an organization uniting a number of groups in which overall rights and responsibilities belong to a central administration, while each group retains control of its internal affairs. **2** the act of forming such an organization: *Several local unions are contemplating federation.*

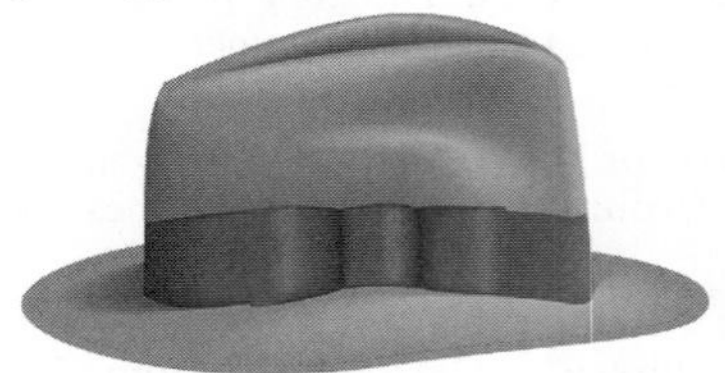

The **fedora** got its name from a nineteenth century play whose heroine was a Russian princess called Fedora Romanoff. The actress Sarah Bernhardt, who played the lead, was a notorious cross-dresser, and wore such a hat during her performances.

fe·do·ra (fi dô′rə) *n* a soft felt hat with a curved brim and a crown creased lengthwise.

fee (fē) *n* **1** a sum of money paid for a service or privilege: *I've raised my fee for babysitting. What is the annual membership fee for the health club?* **2 fees** *pl* money paid for instruction at a private school, college, or university. **3** the right to keep and use land in a feudal society, or the land held in this way. <Old French, from Latin *feodum* property>

fee·ble (fē′bəl) *adj* **fee·bler, fee·blest** 1 lacking strength or force: *feeble from long illness, a feeble mind, a feeble cry.* 2 involving little effort or energy: *a feeble attempt.* <Old French, from Latin *flebilis* to be wept over>
fee′ble·ness *n.* **fee′bly** *adv.*

fee·ble–mind·ed (fē′bəl mīn′did) *adj* not intelligent: *a feeble-minded approach to the problem.*
fee′ble-mind′ed·ly *adv.* **fee′ble-mind′ed·ness** *n.*

feed (fēd) *v* **fed, feed·ing** 1 give food to or help to eat: *It's time to feed the baby. The cattle were feeding in the barn.* 2 provide food for: *enough to feed six people.* 3 give as food: *to feed grain to chickens.* 4 supply, especially continuously *to feed a furnace with fuel. The paper feeds into the printer from beneath.* 5 encourage or cause to grow: *Don't feed his vanity by flattering him. The sunshine fed her happy mood and she laughed aloud.*
n 1 food for animals: *Give the chickens their feed.* 2 *Informal* a meal: *a good feed of corn on the cob.* 3 **a** the act or means of supplying a machine or furnace with material. **b** the material supplied. <Old English, from *foda* food> **feed′er** *n.*
feed on (or **off**)**,** live at the expense of: *The artist feeds on admiration from the public.*
off your feed, *Informal* too unwell to eat.

feed·back (fēd′bak′) *n* 1 the return to a system or machine of part of its output, either as an unwanted effect or in order to adjust future output. 2 the unwanted return of a signal to a sound amplification system, causing it to produce a loud, high-pitched tone. 3 information on the results of one's actions that will influence one's future decisions or actions.

feel (fēl) *v* **felt, feel·ing** 1 be aware of by the sense of touch: *I felt something wet on my arm.* 2 touch in order to see what the texture or temperature is like: *Feel this cloth.* 3 try to find by touch: *She felt her way across the dark room. He felt in his pockets for a loonie.* 4 have a feeling within oneself: *I feel sick. The air feels cold. This whole place feels strange.* 5 experience an emotion: *to feel intense joy.* 6 think or believe, often by intuition: *I feel that my team will win.*
n 1 the way something feels to the touch: *This soap has a greasy feel.* 2 an instinctive understanding of, or talent for, something: *She has a real feel for music.* <Old English *felan*>
feel for (or **with**), sympathize or empathize with.
feel like, *Informal* **a** have a desire for: *I feel like an ice-cream cone.* **b** seem as if it is going to: *It feels like rain.*
feel out, find out about in a cautious way; test for possible reactions or effects: *to feel out an opportunity.*
feel up to, feel able to do something.

feel·er (fē′lər) *n* 1 a special part of an animal's body for touching, such as an insect's antenna. 2 a suggestion, remark, hint, or question, made to find out what others are thinking or planning: *She has put out some feelers to see how people like the idea.*

feel–good (fēl′gu̇d′) *adj* arousing good or pleasant feelings: *a feel-good movie.*

feel·ing (fē′ling) *n* 1 the sense of touch: *She had no feeling in her left hand.* 2 a sensation experienced within oneself or by touching: *a feeling of dampness, a sick feeling in one's stomach.* 3 a quality that something seems to have: *There was a happy feeling about the place.* 4 emotion: *a voice full of feeling, a mix of joy and other feelings. He was guided by feeling rather than thought.* 5 an opinion or belief: *Her feeling is that we should act immediately.* 6 an inner sense that something will happen: *I had a feeling the package would arrive today.* 7 **feelings** *pl* emotional sensitivity: *The remark hurt her feelings. Our feelings were touched by his sad story.*
adj sensitive or emotional: *a feeling heart, a feeling rendition of a song.* **feel′ing·ly** *adv.*

feet (fēt) *n* plural of FOOT.
feet of clay, a character flaw that is not immediately apparent.
get (or **have**) **cold feet,** lose courage: *I wanted to dive from the high board, but I got cold feet and just sat by the pool.*
get to your feet, stand up.
get your feet wet, try a new experience or activity.
have your feet on the ground, be sensible, practical, and clear-headed.
keep your feet, keep from falling.
stand on your own (**two**) **feet,** be independent.

feign (fān) *v* pretend: *to feign ignorance. He feigned a headache so he could go home.* <Old French, from Latin *fingere* to make up> **feigned** *adj.*

feint (fānt) *n* 1 a pretended blow or stroke. 2 a pretence: *She made a feint of studying while actually listening to her CDs.*
v make a pretended blow: *The boxer feinted with his right hand and struck with his left.* <See FEIGN.>

feist·y (fī′stē) *adj* **feist·i·er, feist·i·est** 1 aggressively energetic, brave, or determined. 2 quarrelsome.

ETYMOLOGY

The word **feisty** is often used to describe a person or animal that is small but surprisingly fearless or aggressive. Feisty comes from American English *feist*, meaning "small dog," from *fysting curre*, meaning "stinking cur" in Middle English.

feld·spar (feld′spȧr′) *n* a crystalline mineral composed mostly of aluminum silicates, used for making glass and pottery. <German *Feldspath*>

fe·lic·i·ta·tion (fə lis′ə tā′shən) *n* (*often plural*) a formal expression of good wishes.

fe·lic·i·tous (fə lis′ə təs) *adj* 1 fortunate and happy: *on this felicitous occasion.* 2 well chosen or unusually appropriate: *"Snowy" is a felicitous name for the white cat.*
fe·lic′i·tous·ly *adv.* **fe·lic′i·tous·ness** *n.* **fe·lic′i·ty** *n.*

fe·line (fē′līn) *adj* to do with cats or the cat family: *She moved with feline grace.*
n a member of the cat family: *leopards, lions, and other felines.* <Latin *felinis* cat>

a bat	e bed	i bid	o pot	u cup	th **thin**
ā cake	ē **me**	ī **bite**	ō **go**	ū **rude**	TH **then**
ȧ bar	ə **about**	ər **over**	ȯ **for**	u̇ **put**	zh measure

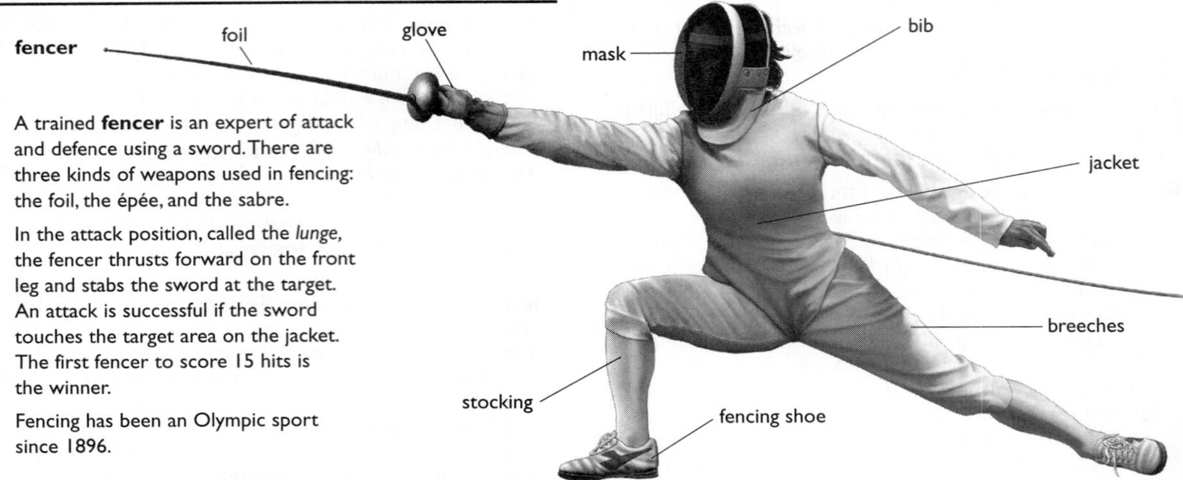

A trained **fencer** is an expert of attack and defence using a sword. There are three kinds of weapons used in fencing: the foil, the épée, and the sabre.

In the attack position, called the *lunge,* the fencer thrusts forward on the front leg and stabs the sword at the target. An attack is successful if the sword touches the target area on the jacket. The first fencer to score 15 hits is the winner.

Fencing has been an Olympic sport since 1896.

fell[1] (fel) past tense of FALL.

fell[2] (fel) *v* **1** knock down: *He felled the enemy with one blow.* **2** cut down a tree.
n all the trees cut down in one season. <Old English *feallan* fall> **fell′er** *n.*

fell[3] (fel) *Poetic adj* cruel; fierce; terrible; deadly; destructive: *a fell blow, a fell disease.* <Old French *felon*>
in (or **at**) **one fell swoop,**

fel·low (fel′ō); *often* (fel′ə) *for defs. 1, 2, and 3.*
n **1** *Informal* a man, boy, or male animal: *Never mind, old fellow. Poor fellow!* **2** a companion or colleague: *She gets along well with all her fellows at school.* **3** a graduate student who has a FELLOWSHIP (def. 3) in a university or college. **4** a member of an academic or professional society.
adj belonging to the same group, doing the same thing, or being in the same condition: *fellow citizens, fellow students.* <Old English *feolaga* partner>
hail fellow well met, very friendly.

fellow feeling *n* shared feeling.

fel·low·ship (fel′ō ship′) *n* **1** the fact of having things in common, or the bond of mutual understanding that results from this: *She enjoys the fellowship of other hockey players.* **2** a group of people with similar tastes or interests: *He belongs to a national writers' fellowship.* **3** a teaching or research position or a sum of money given to a person, especially a graduate student, in order to continue his or her studies.

fel·on (fel′ən) *n* a person who has committed a felony. <Old French *felon*>

fel·o·ny (fel′ə nē) *n, pl* **fel·o·nies** a serious crime, typically involving violence. **fe·lo′ni·ous** (fel ō′ nē əs) *adj.*

felt[1] (felt) past tense and past participle of FEEL.

felt[2] (felt) *n* **1** a cloth that is made by rolling and pressing together fibres of wool, hair, or fur. **2** something made of felt: *The hammers in the piano need new felts.* <Old English>

felt pen or **felt–tip pen** (felt′tip′) *n* a pen that has a point or tip made of felt.

fe·male (fē′māl) *adj* **1** belonging to the sex that gives birth to young or produces eggs. **2** to do with women and girls: *a female contraceptive.* **3** *Botany* with pistils and no stamens. **4** with a hollow or cavity in a machine or fitting into which a corresponding projecting part can be inserted.
n a female person, animal, or plant. <Old French, from Latin *femina* woman>

fem·i·nine (fem′ə nin) *adj* **1** to do with women and girls: *a feminine hairstyle, a feminine name, feminine instinct.* **2** *Grammar* to do with a class of noun that includes nouns for female people and animals. Examples: *princess, cow.*
n Grammar the feminine gender, or a word or form in this gender: *"Lioness" is the feminine of "lion."* <Old French, from Latin *femina* woman> **fem′i·nin′i·ty** *n.*

fem·i·nism (fem′ə niz′əm) *n* a philosophy and social movement advocating independence, rights, and opportunities for women. **fem′i·nist** *n, adj.*

fe·mur (fē′mər) *n, pl* **fe·murs** or **fem·o·ra** (fem′ə rə) the thighbone. <Latin = thigh>

fen (fen) *UK n* a marsh or swamp. <Old English *fenn*>

fence (fens) *n* **1** a barrier or railing, usually wood or wire, that encloses an area of ground to show its boundaries or to prevent people or animals from going in or out. **2** a similar barrier meant to stop snow from drifting, or rocks or soil from sliding. **3** a person or establishment that buys and sells stolen goods.
v **fenced, fenc·ing** **1** enclose with a fence. **2** fight with long, slender swords that have knobs on the end instead of sharp tips to avoid injury. **3** avoid giving frank, direct answers: *Don't fence with me; I want the truth.* **4** buy and sell stolen goods. <variant of *defence*>
fence in, keep in with a fence: *Fence in the chickens.*
mend your fences, renew neglected relationships.
on the fence, not having made up one's mind or taken a side in a debate.

fenc·ing (fen′sing) *n* **1** the art of fighting, now only as a sport or in theatre or film, with swords or foils. **2** a fence or fences, or material for making them. **fenc′er** *n.*

fend (fend) *v* <variant of *defend*>
fend for yourself, provide for yourself: *A young child cannot fend for itself.*
fend off, resist an attack or attacker: *to fend off blows with your arm.*

fend·er (fen′dər) *n* **1** the part of a motor vehicle that curves around a wheel. **2** a guard, made of rubber, thick rope, or plastic, hung over the side of a boat or attached to a dock to protect a boat while docking. **3** a metal frame or screen in front of a fireplace to keep hot coals and sparks from the room.

fend·er–bend·er (fen′dər ben′dər) *Informal n* a minor car accident.

feng shui (fung′shway′), (fong′shoi′), *or* (fung′shwē′) *n* a Chinese method of maintaining harmony by regulating the flow of energy through arrangement of objects, often applied to interior design. <Mandarin = wind and water>

Fen·i·an (fen′ē ən) *n* a member of an Irish secret organization in the 1800s, founded to overthrow British rule in Ireland.
adj to do with the Fenians. <Old Irish *fian* band of warriors>

fen·nel (fen′əl) *n* a herb of the parsley family. See KOHLRABI for picture. <Latin *fenum* hay>

fe·ral (fer′əl) *or* (fē′rəl) *adj* **1** wild; undomesticated: *Our cat spends so much time outdoors that it is becoming feral.* **2** fierce or savage. **3** resembling a wild animal. <Latin *fera* beast>

fer·ment (fər ment′) *for v,* (fər′ment) *for n. v* **1** undergo a gradual chemical change caused by yeast or bacteria that breaks down a compound into simpler substances, producing heat and giving off gas bubbles. **2** cause this chemical change. **3** make or become excited, restless, or agitated.
n **1** the process or condition of fermenting. **2** excitement, agitation, or unrest: *Rumours that movie scenes were to be filmed in our street created a ferment.* <Latin *fervere* boil>
fer′men·ta′tion *n.*

fer·mi·um (fər′mē əm) *n* a radioactive metallic element, produced artificially. *Symbol* **Fm** <E. *Fermi*, 20c nuclear physicist>

fern (fərn) *n* a plant that has roots, stems, and leaves, but no flowers, and reproduces by spores instead of seeds. See FIDDLEHEAD for picture. <Old English *fearn*> **fern′y** *adj.*

fe·ro·cious (fə rō′shəs) *adj* savagely cruel and violent. <Latin *ferocis* fierce> **fe·ro′cious·ly** *adv.*
fe·roc′i·ty (fə ros′ə tē) *n.*

fer·ret (fer′it) *n* a white or yellowish white weasel sometimes used to kill rats or rabbits, but more often kept as a pet.
v hunt with ferrets. <Old French, from Latin *fur* thief i.e., something stealthy>
ferret out, find by persistent searching: *to ferret out the truth, to ferret out a criminal.*

fer·ric (fer′ik) *adj* to do with iron, especially iron with a valence of three. Compare FERROUS. <Latin *ferrum* iron>

Fer·ris wheel (fer′is) *n* an amusement park ride consisting of a large, revolving framework of steel like an upright wheel with swinging seats that hang from its rim. <19c engineer G.W.G. *Ferris*, its inventor>

fer·rous (fer′əs) *adj* to do with iron, especially iron with a valence of two. Compare FERRIC. <Latin *ferrum* iron>

fer·ry (fer′ē) *n, pl* **fer·ries** **1** a boat that carries people and goods back and forth across a river or stretch of water. Also, **ferryboat**. **2** a service that regularly transports people or goods back and forth over a route. **3** the delivery of aircraft to a destination by flying them there.
v **fer·ried, fer·ry·ing** **1** carry back and forth on a ferry, especially as a regular service: *Every day, hundreds of cars are ferried from Vancouver to Victoria and back.* **2** travel or cross by ferry: *They ferried over to Wolfe Island.* **3** transport goods or people back and forth over a regular route: *My dad ferries us to school and back every day.* **4** deliver an aircraft to a destination by flying it there. <Old English *ferian* to carry>

fer·tile (fər′tīl) *or* (fər′təl) *adj* **1** rich in nutrients and capable of producing healthy plants or crops: *Sand is not very fertile.* **2** capable of conceiving young or producing seed. **3** producing or yielding much: *The Internet is a fertile source of information.* <Latin *fertilis* productive, from *ferre* to produce>

Fertile Crescent *n* a fertile, crescent-shaped strip of land extending from the eastern shore of the Mediterranean to the valley of the Tigris and Euphrates Rivers to the Persian Gulf.

fer·til·i·ty (fər til′ə tē) *n* **1** the condition of being fertile. **2** everything connected with producing young or crops: *a goddess of fertility, a festival celebrating fertility.*

fer·ti·lize (fər′tə līz′) *v* **fer·ti·lized, fer·ti·liz·ing** **1** make fertile or productive: *Some plants fertilize the soil by adding nitrates to it.* **2** put fertilizer on: *I help my mom fertilize the lawn every spring and fall.* **3** unite a male reproductive cell, or sperm, with an egg cell. **fer′ti·li·za′tion** *n.*

fer·ti·liz·er (fər′tə lī′zər) *n* a chemical or natural substance put on land to make it able to produce more: *Manure makes good fertilizer.*

fer·vent (fər′vənt) *adj* earnest and intense: *a fervent plea.* <Latin *fervere* burn, i.e., be eager> **fer′ven·cy** *n.* **fer′vent·ly** *adv.*

fer·vid (fər′vid) *adj* showing exaggerated excitement or intensity: *a fervid speech.* <See FERVENT.> **fer′vid·ly** *adv.*

fer·vour or **fer·vor** (fər′vər) *n* intense emotion: *His voice trembled with the fervour of his love.* <See FERVENT.>

fes·cue (fes′kyū) *n* a tough grass of the northern hemisphere, used for pasture or lawn mixtures. <Old French, from Latin *festuca*>

a bat	e bed	i bid	o pot	u cup	th **thin**
ā cake	ē me	ī bite	ō go	ū rude	ᴛʜ **then**
ä bar	ə about	ər over	ô for	ů put	zh measure

–fest *combining form* **1** an event celebrating an art, season, or activity, often involving competitions: *dramafest, Winterfest.* **2** *Slang* an excessive display of a certain kind of activity: *talkfest, slugfest.* <German *Fest* festival>

fes·tal (fes′təl) *Formal or Poetic adj* to do with a feast or festival: *on this festal day.*

fes·ter (fes′tər) *v* **1** form pus: *The neglected wound festered and became very painful.* **2** cause increasing pain or bitterness: *Resentment festered in his heart.* **3** decay or rot. <Old French, from Latin *fistula* ulcer>

fes·ti·val (fes′tə vəl) *n* **1** a day or special time set aside for celebrating, often in memory of some event or person: *a harvest festival.* **2** an event or series of events focusing on an art or activity, often involving competitions: *a high-school drama festival. Every year Ottawa has a tulip festival.* <Latin *festum* feast>

fes·tive (fes′tiv) *adj* to do with a celebration: *A birthday or wedding is a festive occasion.* **fes′tive·ly** *adv.*

fes·tiv·i·ty (fes tiv′ə tē) *n, pl* **fes·tiv·i·ties** (*usually plural*) a festive activity; something done to celebrate: *We joined in the local festivities on Canada Day.*

fes·toon (fe stūn′) *n* a hanging decoration of flowers, leaves, ribbons, etc.: *The flags were hung on the wall in colourful festoons.*
v **1** decorate with festoons: *The gym was festooned with tinsel for the dance.* **2** form into or like festoons: *Draperies were festooned over the window.* <Italian *festa* festival>

fet·a (fet′ə) *n* a firm, crumbly cheese made from goat's or sheep's milk. <Greek *tyri pheta*>

fe·tal or **foe·tal** (fē′təl) *adj* to do with a fetus.

fetal alcohol syndrome *n* a group of physical or brain disorders in a fetus, resulting from the consumption of alcohol during pregnancy.

fetch (fech) *v* **1** bring or send for: *Please fetch me my glasses. Fetch the doctor.* **2** provoke a reaction: *That joke fetches a good laugh every time.* **3** be sold for: *Apples were fetching a good price that year.* <Old English *feccan*>
fetch up, *Informal* arrive: *He fetched up in front of the library.*

fetch·ing (fech′ing) *Informal adj* attractive or charming: *The bridesmaids wore very fetching outfits.*

fete or **fête** (fet) *n* a party or celebration: *A large fete was given to benefit the town hospital.*
v **fet·ed** or **fêt·ed, fet·ing** or **fêt·ing** honour with a fete: *The winning team was feted by their fans.* <French = feast>

🍁 **Fête nationale** (fet′ nas yə nal′) *n* June 24, a holiday in the province of Québec celebrating French-Canadian culture, formerly (and still unofficially) called **St. Jean Baptiste Day**.

fet·id (fet′id) *or* (fē′tid) *adj* smelling very bad. <Latin *foetere* to smell>

fet·ish (fet′ish) *n* **1** a material object supposed to contain a spirit or have magic power. **2 a** an unreasonable attachment, devotion, or reverence: *a fetish for shoes.* **b** the object of this: *Some people make a fetish of fashionable clothes.* <Latin *facticius* artificial>

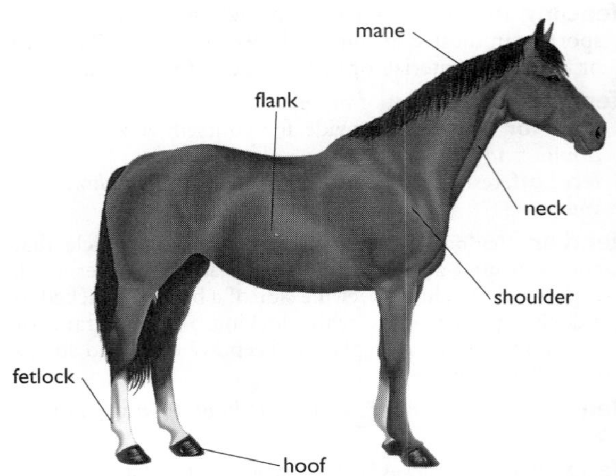

fet·lock (fet′lok) *n* **1** the tuft of hair above a hoof of an animal on the back part of the leg. **2** the joint or part of the leg where this tuft grows. <Middle English *fetlok*>

fet·ter (fet′ər) *n* usually, **fetters** *pl* chains or shackles, or anything that binds or restrains.
v bind or restrain with or as if with fetters. <Old English *feter*>

fet·tle (fet′əl) *n* <Old English *fetel* belt>
in fine fettle, in an excellent condition and mood: *The horse is in fine fettle and should win the race.*

fet·tu·ci·ne (fet′ə chē′nē) *n* narrow, flat strips of pasta. Also, **fettuccine**, **fettucini**. <Italian>

fe·tus or **foe·tus** (fē′təs) *n* an embryo of a human being, animal, or bird, especially during the later stages of its development in the womb or in the egg. <Latin>

feud (fyūd) *n* **1** a long and deadly quarrel between families or tribes, often passed down from generation to generation. **2** any long, ongoing quarrel.
v engage in a feud: *They have been feuding with their neighbours for years.* <German *vede*>

feu·dal·ism (fyū′də liz′əm) *n* **1** a social system of medieval western Europe, by which peasants gave military and other services to a lord in return for protection and the use of land for farming. Also called **feudal system.** **2** any social, economic, or political system that suggests or resembles this. <Latin *feudum*> **feu′dal** *adj.* **feu′dal·is′tic** *adj.*

fe·ver (fē′vər) *n* **1** an unhealthy condition of the body in which the temperature is higher than normal. **2** a disease that causes fever, such as scarlet fever. **3** an excited, restless condition: *spring fever.* **4** a fad or enthusiasm for something or for some person: *The rush to find gold in the Yukon was called Klondike fever.* <Latin *febris*>
fe′vered *adj.* **fe′ver·ish** *adj.*

fever blister *n* a cold sore.

fe·ver·few (fē′vər fyū′) *n* a perennial plant with small, white, daisylike flowers, formerly used as a medicine for fever. <Latin *febris* fever + *fugare* drive away, >

fever pitch *n* a state of intense excitement or frenzied activity.

few (fyū) *adj* not many: *Few girls are more than 185 cm tall.*
n **1** a small number: *Only a few of the boys had bicycles.* **2 the few** the minority, especially a small, privileged group. <Old English *feawe*>
few and far between, very few or rare.
quite a few, a fairly large number of people or things: *We caught ten fish, but quite a few got away.*

> **CONFUSABLES**
>
> **Fewer** means "not so many," and usually refers to countable things: *I have fewer cookies than you.*
>
> **Less** means "not so much," and mostly refers to what cannot be counted: *He had less work to do than you did.*

fey (fā) *adj* strange or unusual in a way that suggests psychic powers. <Old English *fæge* touched by fate>

fez (fez) *n, pl* **fez·zes** a high felt cap, usually red, with a flat top and a long, black tassel: *The fez was formerly the national headdress of Turkish men.* <Turkish, after the town of *Fez* in Morocco>

fi·an·cé (fē ȧn′sā) *or* (fē′ȧn sā′) *n* the man to whom one is engaged to be married. A woman in this role is one's **fiancée**. <French *fiancer* betroth>

fi·as·co (fē as′kō) *n, pl* **fi·as·cos** or **fi·as·coes** a complete failure, especially a scandalous or embarrassing one: *Breakfast was a fiasco—the toast was burnt and the milk had gone sour.* <Italian = flask>

fi·at (fē′ət) *or* (fī′at) *n* an authoritative order or command: *The emperor's fiat must be obeyed.* <Latin = let it be done>

fib (fib) *Informal n* a lie about some small matter.
v **fibbed, fib·bing** tell such a lie: *Remember I said I had baked these cookies? I was fibbing.* <possibly *fibble-fabble* nonsense> **fib′ber** *n.*

Fi·bo·nac·ci sequence or **series** (fib′ə nȧ′chē) *Mathematics n* an infinite sequence of numbers, each number being the sum of the two previous ones. <L. *Fibonacci*, 13c mathematician>

fi·bre (fī′bər) *n* **1 a** a slender, threadlike strand which, with others, can form body or plant tissue, a mineral substance, or a textile: *muscle fibres.* **b** a substance made up of such threadlike strands: *Hemp fibre can be woven into a coarse cloth.* **2** texture: *cloth of coarse fibre.* **3** one's essential character or nature: *His smile stirred the very fibre of her being, a person of strong moral fibre.* **4** roughage. Also, **fiber**. <French, from Latin *fibra*>

fi·bre·board (fī′bər bȯrd′) *n* a building material made by compressing fibres, especially of wood, into flat sheets: *Fibreboard is often used in constructing partitions between rooms.* Also, **fiberboard**.

fi·bre·fill (fī′bər fil′) *n* synthetic fibres, usually polyester, used as a filling for clothing, pillows, sleeping bags, etc. Also, **fiberfill**.

fi·bre·glass (fī′bər glas′) *n* a strong, fireproof material made from fine threads of glass used in insulation, boats, textiles, etc. Also, **fiberglass**.

fibre optics *n* (*with singular verb*) the use of long, fine, flexible glass or acrylic fibres to transmit light signals. **Fibre-optic cables** are often used in telecommunications.

fi·bril (fī′brəl) *n* a small or slender fibre. <Latin *fibra* fibre>

fib·ril·late (fib′rə lāt′) *v* **fib·ril·lat·ed, fib·ril·lat·ing** undergo abnormal, rapid, irregular twitching or contraction in a muscle, especially the muscles of the heart. **fib′ril·la′tion** *n.*

fi·broid (fī′broid) *adj* made up of fibres.
n a benign tumour made up of fibres or fibrous tissue.

fi·brous (fī′brəs) *adj* made up of fibres.

fib·u·la (fib′yə lə) *n, pl* **fib·u·las** or **fib·u·lae** (fib′yə lē′) *or* (fib′yə lī′) **1** the outer and thinner of the two bones in the human lower leg, extending from knee to ankle. **2** a similar bone in the hind leg of an animal. <Latin = clasp. The bone resembles a safety pin clasp.> **fib′u·lar** *adj.*

F

fick·le (fik′əl) *adj* unreliable and likely to change without any reason: *fickle weather, a fickle friend.* <Old English *ficol* tricky, dishonest> **fick′le·ness** *n.*

fic·tion (fik′shən) *n* **1** a prose writing that tells a story about characters and events that are partly or completely imaginary. **2** unreal or made-up facts or events: *She exaggerated so much that it was impossible to separate fact from fiction.* **3** a made-up story: *That excuse of his is a complete fiction.* <Latin *fingere* to make up>
fic′tion·al *adj.*

fic·ti·tious (fik tish′əs) *adj* **1** imaginary: *Characters in novels are usually fictitious.* **2** false and intended to deceive: *to make a fictitious claim. The criminal used a fictitious name.* **fic·ti′tious·ly** *adv.* **fic·ti′tious·ness** *n.*

fid·dle (fid′əl) *n* a violin.
v **fid·dled, fid·dling 1** play the violin, especially folk music. **2** play nervously or restlessly with something: *The embarrassed boy fiddled with his cap.* **3** (*often with* ***around***) **a** tinker with something or make minor adjustments: *He fiddled around with the bicycle chain, trying to fix it.* **b** waste time: *She fiddled away the whole afternoon.* <Old English *fithele*> **fid′dler** *n.*
fit as a fiddle, in excellent physical condition.
play second fiddle, take a secondary part.

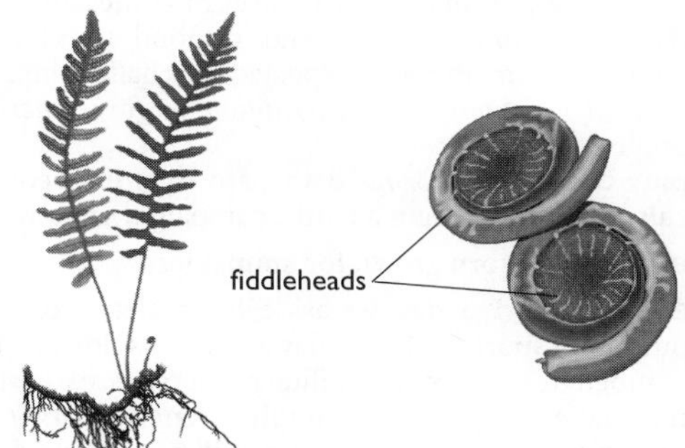

fid·dle·head (fid′əl hed′) *n* a young, curled frond of certain ferns, eaten as a delicacy.

a bat	e bed	i bid	o pot	u cup	th thin
ā cake	ē me	ī bite	ō go	ū rude	ᴛʜ then
ȧ bar	ə about	ər over	ȯ for	u̇ put	zh measure

fiddler crab *n* a small burrowing crab of American coastlines. On the male, one claw is greatly enlarged.

fid·dle·sticks (fid′əl stiks′) *interj* nonsense! rubbish!

fi·del·i·ty (fə del′ə tē) *n, pl* **fi·del·i·ties** 1 faithfulness or loyalty. 2 accuracy or exactness of a copy, sound reproduction, or translation. <Latin *fides* faith>

fidg·et (fij′it) *v* move around or play aimlessly with things because one is restless: *The children, who had been sitting still for two hours, began to fidget.*
n 1 a person who moves about restlessly. 2 **the fidgets** *pl* a fit of restlessness or uneasiness. <obsolete *fidge* move restlessly> **fidg′et·y** *adj.*

fie (fī) *Archaic or Humorous interj* shame on you! <Old French *fi*>

fief (fēf) *n* in feudal times, a piece of land held from a lord in return for military and other services. <Old French, from Latin *feodum* property>

field (fēld) *n* 1 a piece of land used for crops or pasture: *a wheat field.* 2 an area of land used for some special purpose: *a playing field.* 3 an area of land yielding some product: *the coal fields of Alberta.* 4 a large, flat area or surface of a specified kind: *a field of ice.* 5 an area of activity or study: *He is an expert in the field of literature.* 6 the place where a battle is or has been fought, or where military manoeuvres are carried out. 7 all the places, other than a laboratory, where scientific observations are made. A **field study** is a piece of research undertaken in such a place: *Archeologists do much of their work in the field.* 8 *Physics* the space throughout which a force operates: *a magnetic field.* 9 *Sports* in full, **field events** the jumping and throwing competitions that take place in the area enclosed by a running track. 10 the area covered by something: *My field of vision was blocked by several tall people. That is outside my field of knowledge.* 11 the background against which something appears: *His coat of arms has a lion on a green field.* 12 all other participants in an outdoor contest: *At the halfway mark in the marathon, a Canadian was leading the field.*
v 1 *Baseball, Cricket* stop and return the ball after it has been hit. 2 put forward as a player or contestant: *to field a top-notch team.* 3 accept and respond to as required, especially something unexpected or challenging: *to field difficult questions about corruption in government.* <Old English *feld*>
play the field, *Informal* date many different people.
take the field, begin a battle, campaign, or game.

field corn *n* corn grown for animal feed.

field day *n* 1 a day set aside for athletic contests and outdoor sports. 2 a day when soldiers practise manoeuvres or other military exercises. 3 a time of unusual activity, or of triumph or enjoyment: *If you say that in public, the news reporters will have a field day.*

field·er (fēl′dər) *Baseball, Cricket n* a player stationed inside the playing area to stop a hit ball and throw it in.

field glasses *n* binoculars.

field goal *Football n* a goal counting three points, scored by kicking the ball between the uprights and above the crossbar of the goal post.

field hockey *n* a game similar to ice hockey, played on a grass field with curved sticks and a hard ball.

field hospital *n* a temporary hospital near a battlefield.

field marshal *n* the officer of highest rank in the armies of certain countries.

Field mice are related to rats, but a large rat is about ten times the size of a large field mouse. Both rats and mice can carry harmful diseases, and both are therefore treated as pests.

field mouse *n* a small mouse or vole found in meadows and fields.

field of view *n* the area visible through the eyepiece of a microscope or other optical instrument.

field·stone (fēld′stōn′) *n* rough stones found lying around and used just as they are for building.

field test *n* a test of a new product or system in the places and by the users for which it is intended. **field-test** *v.*

field trip *n* a class trip to give students a chance to learn outside the school by observation or practical experience.

field·work (fēld′wərk) *n* scientific or technical work done in the FIELD (def. 7) rather than in a laboratory or office. **field′work′er** *n.*

fiend (fēnd) *n* 1 an evil spirit or demon. 2 (*often used humorously*) a very wicked or cruel person: *People who mistreat animals are fiends. My younger brother plays tricks all the time, the little fiend!* 3 *Informal* a person who indulges excessively in some habit, practice, or game: *a tennis fiend.* <Old English *feond* enemy> **fiend′ish** *adj.*

fierce (fērs) *adj* **fierc·er, fierc·est** 1 savage and liable to attack: *a fierce lion.* 2 violent or raging: *a fierce wind.* 3 intense, and asserted forcefully: *fierce pride, fierce determination.* 4 extreme: *The heat was fierce.* <Old French, from Latin *ferus* wild> **fierce′ly** *adv.* **fierce′ness** *n.*

fier·y (fī′rē) *adj* **fier·i·er, fier·i·est** 1 containing or consisting of fire. 2 very hot or bright: *a fiery red. His forehead was fiery and he felt sick.* 3 full of feeling: *a fiery speech.* 4 easily aroused or excited: *a fiery temper.* <Old English *fyr*> **fier′i·ness** *n.*

fi·es·ta (fē es′tə) *n* a festival or party. <Spanish = feast>

fife (fīf) *n* a small flutelike instrument used in marching bands.
v **fifed, fif·ing** play on a fife. <German *Pfeife* pipe>
fif′er *n.*

fif·teen (fif′tēn′) *n* 1 five more than ten: *We need between fifteen and twenty copies.* 2 the numeral 15.
adj 1 five more than ten: *Fifteen people arrived.* 2 (*after the noun*) fifteenth in a series: *Chapter Fifteen.* <Old English *fiftene*> **fif′teenth′** *adj, adv.*

fif·teenth (fif′tēnth′) *n* **1** next after the fourteenth: *You're fifteenth in line.* **2** one of fifteen equal parts: *A fifteenth isn't much.*
adj, adv See FIFTEEN.

fifth (fifth) *adj* **1** next after the fourth: *on the fifth day.* **2** being one of five equal parts: *a fifth part of the group.*
n **1** next after the fourth: *Today is the fifth.* **2** one of five equal parts: *I've read a fifth of the book.* **3** *Music* an interval stretching from one note to another five notes higher, or the sound made when both these notes are played simultaneously. <alteration of Old English *fifta*>
fifth′ly *adv.*

fifth column *n* the people in a country who secretly aid that country's enemies. **fifth columnist** *n.*

fifth wheel *Informal n* a person who or thing that is in the way or not needed.

fif·ti·eth (fif′tē əth′) *n* **1** next after the forty-ninth. **2** one of fifty equal parts.
adj, adv See FIFTY.

fif·ty (fif′tē) *n, pl* **fif·ties 1** five times ten. **2** a fifty-dollar bill: *She asked the bank teller for two fifties.* **3 fifties** *pl* the years from fifty through fifty-nine, especially of a century or of a person's life: *Her father is in his fifties.*
adj **1** five times ten: *fifty dollars.* **2** (*after the noun*) fiftieth in a series: *page fifty.* <Old English *fiftig*>
fif′ti·eth *adj, adv.*

fif·ty–fif·ty (fif′tē fif′tē) *Informal adv, adj* forming two equal shares.

fig (fig) *n* the small, edible fruit of a tree that grows in warm regions. Figs are often dried for eating. <Old French, from Latin *ficus*>
not give (or **care**) **a fig,** *Informal* not care at all.

fight (fīt) *v* **fought, fight·ing 1** try to defeat or get rid of: *to fight your fear of heights, to fight crime.* **2** carry on a violent struggle, conflict, or war: *Two men were fighting in the street. Soldiers were sent to fight overseas.* **3** disagree angrily: *They were fighting over whose turn it was to unload the dishwasher.* **4** compete in a sport such as wrestling, boxing, or a martial art. **5** proceed by vigorously pushing, hacking, or forcing things out of one's way: *She fought her way through the dense brush.*
n **1** a struggle, conflict, or dispute. **2** the power or will to fight: *There is fight in the old dog yet.* <Old English *feohtan*> **fight′er** *n.*
fight back, a offer resistance or return an attack: *They had no strength to fight back.* **b** struggle to control: *I fought back my tears.*
fight down, suppress; hold back: *to fight down a feeling of fear.*
fight it out, fight until one side wins.
fight off, a turn back or repel: *Fight off an enemy attack.* **b** overcome or stop the progress of: *to fight off a cold.*
fight shy of, keep away from.
put up a fight, a protest vigorously: *He puts up a fight every time he's asked to help.* **b** defend yourself physically.

fighter plane *n* a heavily armed airplane that is highly manoeuvrable, used in warfare.

fighting chance *Informal n* the possibility of success after a hard struggle.

fig·ment (fig′mənt) *n* something imagined; a made-up story. *a figment of her wild imagination.* <Latin *figmentum* creation, from *fingere* to shape>

fig·ur·a·tive (fig′yə rə tiv) *or* (fig′ə rə tiv) *adj* **1** going beyond the ordinary meaning of words in order to add force, beauty, or interest. Example: *There is more than one way to skin a cat* means *There is more than one way to do something.* It has nothing to do with skinning cats. **2** full of language used in this way: *Much poetry is figurative.*
fig′ur·a·tive·ly *adv.* **fig′ur·a·tive·ness** *n.*

fig·ure (fig′yər) *or* (fig′ər) *n* **1** a numeral, such as 1, 2, 3, etc. **2** an amount or value given in figures: *The figures for government salaries were listed in the newspaper article.* **3 figures** *pl* arithmetic: *He was never very good at figures.* **4** a form or shape, especially of a person: *In the darkness she saw dim figures moving.* **5** a person or character: *Samuel de Champlain is a great figure in Canadian history.* **6** a person considered from the point of view of appearance or manner: *The crying child was a figure of distress.* **7** a diagram, illustration, or graph: *This figure shows how a digital camera works.* **8** a set of movements in dancing or skating.
v **fig·ured, fig·ur·ing 1** appear in or be part of: *Nellie McClung figures largely in the history of women's rights.* **2** expect or suppose: *I figure he'll eat before he gets here.* **3** do arithmetic. **4** represent something in a design or pattern: *figured wallpaper.* <Latin *fingere* to shape>
figure in, include in one's calculations or analysis: *As well as fees for skating lessons, you have to figure in the cost of equipment.*
figure on, *Informal* expect and take into consideration when planning: *We are figuring on your help in painting the house.*
figure out, a calculate; find out using arithmetic: *She soon figured out how much it would cost.* **b** understand by thinking: *I can't figure out what he's doing.*
it figures, it make sense, or it is as expected.

figure eight *n* the shape of the numeral 8, as traced by a person, object, or movement.

fig·ure·head (fig′yər hed′) *or* (fig′ər hed′) *n* **1** a person who is the leader or ruler in name only, and has no real authority or responsibility. **2** a statue or carving decorating the bow of a ship.

figure of speech *n* an expression in which words are used with a figurative meaning or in unusual combinations to add beauty, force, or interest.

GRAMMAR AND USAGE

Using a figure of speech can add interest to writing and often makes it more concise. Instead of a character saying "*Don't even bother trying to talk to me about it anymore,*" that person could simply say "*Save your breath!*"

a bat	e bed	i bid	o pot	u cup	th thin
ā cake	ē me	ī bite	ō go	ū rude	ᴛʜ then
à bar	ə about	ər over	ȯ for	ů put	zh measure

F

figure skating
ice dancing
A **figure skating** routine is judged on technical merit and presentation. Judges consider a number of elements in these categories, including footwork, variations in speed, ice coverage, jump skills, originality, harmony, and overall performance.
figure skating blades
Pairs skating requires synchronization through a routine of lifts and jumps.
Competitive **ice dancing** requires great technical skills and the performance of difficult steps and turns.

figure skating *n* the art of performing figures and dance routines on ice wearing **figure skates**, usually to music. **figure skate** *v.* **figure skater** *n.*

fig·ur·ine (fig′yə rēn′) *or* (fig′ə rēn′) *n* a small ornamental figure, often made of stone or pottery.

Fi·ji (fē′jē) *n* a country consisting of a group of islands in the S Pacific. **Fi′ji·an** *adj, n.*

fil·a·ment (fil′ə mənt) *n* **1** a thread or very fine wire, often the conducting wire that glows in a light bulb. **2** *Botany* the stalklike part of the stamen of a flower, supporting the ANTHER. <Latin *filum* thread>

fil·bert (fil′bərt) *n* a hazelnut. <St. *Philibert.* The nuts ripen around the time of his feast day, August 22.>

filch (filch) *v* steal things of little value: *He filched apples from the basket.* <origin uncertain> **filch′er** *n.*

file[1] (fīl) *n* **1** a set of papers on some subject, kept in order, usually in a folder. **2** *Computers* a collection of data or programs with a unique name and stored as a unit in one place in memory or on a storage device. **3** a line of people or things one behind another: *a long file of cars.*
v **filed, fil·ing 1** put papers away in the proper file or files: *Please file this printout.* **2** move in a line: *The class filed quietly into the gym.* **3** submit an official document: *Have you filed your income tax return yet?* **4** apply to an authority: *to file for divorce.* **5** send in a report to a newspaper or news organization: *to file a story.* <French, from Latin *filum* thread, referring to the former practice of hanging documents on a wire for future reference>
in single file, one after another in a line: *We walked in single file.*
on file, kept in a file: *The principal keeps all our school reports on file.*

file[2] (fīl) *n* a steel tool with many small ridges or teeth on it, for smoothing away rough edges.
v **filed, fil·ing** smooth or wear away with a file. <Old English *fīl*>

file clerk *n* a person whose work is taking care of the files in an office.

file extension *n* an EXTENSION (def. 4).

fi·let (fi lā′) FILLET.

filet mi·gnon (mēn yōN′) *n* a small, round, thick piece of tender beef, cut from the tenderloin.

fil·i·al (fil′ē əl) *adj* of or from a son or daughter: *filial respect, filial duty.* <Latin *filius* son, *filia* daughter>

fil·i·bus·ter (fil′ə bus′tər) *n* an act of deliberately hindering the passage of a bill in a legislature by making long speeches or other delaying tactics.
v carry out a filibuster in a legislature. <French *flibustier*> **fil′i·bus′ter·er** *n.*

fil·i·gree (fil′ə grē′) *n* **1** delicate, lacelike, ornamental work of gold or silver wire. **2** a lacy or delicate pattern in any material: *a filigree of frost on the windowpane.* <Italian, from Latin *filum* thread + *granum* wood grain. The swirling patterns made in filigree look somewhat like the grain of wood.>

filing cabinet *n* a piece of furniture containing drawers for storing FILES (def. 1).

fil·ings (fī′lingz) *pln* the particles that have been removed by a file.

Fil·i·pi·no (fil′ə pē′nō) *n, female* **Fil·i·pi·na** (fil′ə pē′nə) a native or inhabitant of the Philippines.

fill (fil) *v* **1** keep putting something in until there is no room for more or for anything else: *to fill a cup, to fill your mouth.* **2** cause to have an intense emotion or quality: *The news filled us with joy.* **3** go into all parts of: *A sweet fragrance filled the room.* **4** take up all the space in, or become full: *The crowd filled the auditorium. The room filled rapidly.* **5** stop up or close by putting something in: *to fill a cavity in a tooth.* **6** supply what is needed for: *to fill a prescription at the drugstore.* **7** hold a position or office. *Cabinet positions are filled by appointment.*
n **1** (*with a possessive*) all that is needed or wanted: *Eat and drink your fill.* **2** earth or rock used to raise land or to make it level. <Old English *fyllan*>
fill in, fill a space or opening: *Fill in the blank with the correct word. Fill in the missing word.*
fill in for, substitute for: *Can you fill in for me tonight?*
fill out, a make or become bigger or rounder. **b** complete by writing information in the blank spaces: *to fill out an application form.*
fill someone in, bring someone up to date: *Fill me in on the latest news.*
fill the bill, *Informal* be just what is needed.

filled gold *n* a base metal plated with gold.

fill·er (fil′ər) *n* anything put in to fill something, such as paper for a binder, or a preparation to fill cracks in wood.

fil·let (fi lā′) *or* (*always for n def. 2*) (fil′ət) *n* **1** a slice of fish or meat without bones or fat. Also, **filet**. **2** a narrow band or strip of any material.
v cut fish or meat into fillets. <French, from Latin *filum* thread, i.e., narrow strip>

fill·ing (fil′ing) *n* anything put in to fill something: *a filling for a cavity in a tooth, pie filling.*
adj quickly making one feel as if one's stomach is full.

fil·lip (fil′əp) *n* anything that rouses, revives, or stimulates: *A compliment is a fillip to your self-confidence.* <Middle English>

fil·ly (fil′ē) *n, pl* **fil·lies** a young female horse less than four years old. <Old Norse *fylja*>

film (film) *n* **1** a very thin layer or surface: *A film of tears blurred my eyes. The spilled oil formed a film on the water.* **2 a** thin, flexible material with a special light-sensitive coating, used in a camera to make photographs or movies. **b** a roll or sheet of this, sometimes in a sealed cartridge. **3** a movie: *Have you seen his latest film?*
v **1** cover or become covered with a film: *Her eyes filmed with tears.* **2** make a movie of: *They filmed the story of Grey Owl.* **3** photograph for a movie: *They filmed the scene three times.* <Old English *filmen* membrane, i.e., thin coating>
film′y *adj.*
film over, become covered with or as if with a film: *The lenses of my glasses are filmed over with moisture.*

film·mak·er *n* a movie director or producer, or a company that makes movies.

film noir (nwär) *n* a style of movie shot in dark tones, with a cynical or despairing mood.

filmstrip (film′strip) *n* a piece of developed photographic film containing a series of images that can be projected one at a time onto a screen.

fil·ter (fil′tər) *v* **1** put a liquid or gas through something that traps unwanted substances or will not let them pass: *We have to filter our drinking water here.* **2** trap or strain out unwanted substances: *Charcoal will filter bacteria from water.* **3** flow or pass very slowly: *Water filters through the sandy soil into the well.* **4** separate unwanted elements from desired elements in a selection process: *We use this questionnaire to filter job applicants.*
n **1** a device for removing impurities from a liquid or gas: *an air filter on a furnace. The coffee drips through a filter.* **2** a device for controlling light rays, or sound and electric currents. **3** a thing or person that separates wanted from unwanted elements: *All movies must pass through the filter of censorship.* **4** *Computers* a piece of software that processes text, removing unwanted data. <Latin *filtrum* felt (a kind of thick cloth)> **fil′ter·a·ble** *adj.*
filter out, a remove or control by a filter: *Filter out the dirt before using the water.* **b** pass or leak slowly out.

filth (filth) *n* **1** foul, disgusting dirt: *The alley was littered with garbage and other filth.* **2** obscene words, images, or thoughts. **filth′i·ness** *n.* **filth′y** *adj.*

ETYMOLOGY

Filth is from Old English *fylth*, meaning "foulness," from *ful*, meaning "foul." These words illustrate the English pattern of making a noun out of an adjective or verb by adding *-th*, often changing the vowel sound: *wide* and *width*; *steal* and *stealth*.

fil·trate (fil′trāt) *n* liquid that has been passed through a filter.
v **fil·trat·ed, fil·trat·ing** pass through a filter. <Latin *filtrum* felt (a kind of thick cloth)>

fil·tra·tion (fil trā′shən) *n* the act or process of filtering.

fin (fin) *n* **1** a movable, winglike part of a fish's body, enabling it to swim, steer, and balance itself in the water. **2** anything shaped or used like a fin, such as a part on the side of an airship that aids balance. **3** a FLIPPER (def. 2). <Old English *finn*> **fin′less** *adj.* **fin′like′** *adj.*

fi·na·gle (fə nā′gəl) *Informal v* **fi·na·gled, fi·na·gling** manage to do or get by cunning means. <origin unknown> **fi·na′gler** *n.*

fi·nal (fī′nəl) *adj* **1** coming last of all: *He is in his final year of high school.* **2** settling the question permanently: *The judges' decision is final.*
n **1** something that happens last of all, such as the last examination of a school term: *I have to study for my English final.* **2 finals** *pl* the last set of games or contests in a championship series, deciding the ultimate winner. <Latin *finis* end> **fi·nal′i·ty** *n.*

fi·na·le (fə nal′ē) *or* (fə nä′lē) *n* the last part of a performance, usually impressive or forming a climax. <Italian = final>

a bat	e bed	i bid	o pot	u cup	th **thin**
ā cake	ē me	ī bite	ō go	ū rude	TH **then**
ä bar	ə about	ər over	ô for	ů put	zh measure

F

fi·nal·ist (fī′nə list) *n* a person who or team that takes part in the last set of competitions.

fi·nal·ize (fī′nə līz′) *v* bring to a final or firm state: *The committee hopes to finalize the conference schedule this week.*

fi·nal·ly (fī′nə lē) *adv* **1** at the end, especially after many other things or after a long wait. **2** in such a way as to decide or settle a question permanently.

fi·nance (fī′nans) *or* (fə nans′) *n* **1** the management of money: *The minister of finance prepares the government's budget.* **2 finances** *pl* money or funds: *Our finances are rather low right now.*
v **fi·nanced, fi·nanc·ing** provide the funds for: *His friends helped him finance a new business.* <Old French, from Latin *finis* settle by payment> **fi·nan′cial** *adj.* **fi·nan′cial·ly** *adv.*

finance company *n* a firm that deals in loans and mortgages.

fin·an·cier (fī′nən sēr′), (fin′ən sēr′), *or* (fə nan′sē ər) *n* a person who is skilled in matters of finance or who manages large sums of money.

fin·back (fin′bak′) *n* a whale with a fin on its back.

finch (finch) *n* a small songbird with a cone-shaped bill. Sparrows are finches. <Old English *finc*>

find (find) *v* **found, find·ing 1** discover by chance: *She found a dime in the road.* **2** look for and eventually see or get: *After searching the whole house, I finally found my key.* **3** discover or learn: *We found that he could not swim.* **4** become aware by experience: *He found that he was growing sleepy.* **5** decide and declare: *The jury found the accused man guilty.*
n something found, especially something worth finding. <Old English *findan*> **find′er** *n.*
find yourself, a figure out your purpose or goal in life. **b** consider your abilities and decide how to use them.
find out, get to know, often by deliberate effort: *I found out where she lives.*

find·ing (fīn′ding) *n* **1** the act of discovering or the thing discovered: *Learning who had been at the scene of the crime was an important finding.* **2** often, **findings** *pl* the conclusion reached after an examination of data by a commission, judge, or scholar: *The Commission will publish its findings next spring.* **3 findings** *pl* the tools and incidental supplies used by a shoemaker, dressmaker, or other artisan: *A jeweller's findings include clasps and wire.*

fi·ne (fē′nā) *Music n* a direction marking the end of a passage. <Italian = end>

fine[1] (fīn) *adj* **fin·er, fin·est 1** of very high quality: *a fine piece of writing, a fine view.* **2** very small or thin: *fine mesh, fine sand.* **3** in good health: *I feel fine.* **4** delicate: *fine linen.* **5** clear, pleasant, or bright: *fine weather.* **6** fancy, sophisticated, or elegant: *fine cooking.* **7** subtle: *There's a fine distinction between "most" and "almost all."* **8** sharp or precise. *Sharpen the pencil to a fine point.*
adv very well; excellently: *I can see just fine, thanks.* <Old French, from Latin *finire* end, peak i.e., of the highest quality> **fine′ly** *adv.* **fine′ness** *n.*

fine[2] (fīn) *n* a sum of money paid as a punishment.
v **fined, fin·ing** cause to pay a fine: *The judge fined him $120 for vandalism.* <Old French, from Latin *finis* end>

fine arts *pln* the arts that depend on taste and originality and appeal to the sense of beauty, especially the visual arts of painting and sculpture.

fine print *n* details printed in small type on a contract or other document: *Read the fine print before you sign anything.*

fin·er·y (fī′nə rē) *n, pl* **fin·er·ies** showy, elegant clothes and accessories.

fi·nesse (fə nes′) *n* **1** delicacy, skill, and expert judgment in the way one works: *Her finesse as an artist is apparent in all her paintings.* **2** the skilful or crafty handling of a delicate situation to one's advantage: *A good diplomat must be a master of finesse.*
v **fi·nessed, fi·ness·ing 1** do something in a delicate and refined way. **2** slyly attempt to avoid blame or an unpleasant situation. **3** in some card games such as bridge, take a trick with a lower card while holding a higher card for later use. <French = fineness>

fine–tune (fīn′tyūn′) *or* (fīn′tūn′) *v* **fine-tuned, fine-tun·ing 1** tune a radio or musical instrument precisely. **2** make small adjustments and improvements to: *to fine-tune a piece of writing, to fine-tune an engine.*

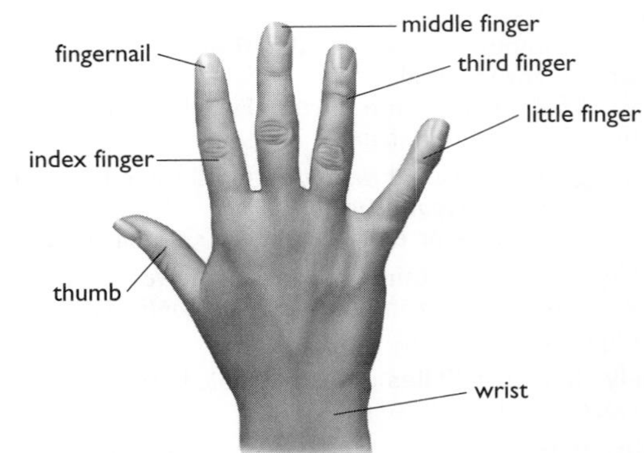

fin·ger (fing′gər) *n* **1** any of the five slender jointed parts of the hand, especially the four other than the thumb. **2** the part of a glove that covers a finger. **3** the breadth or the length of a finger.
v **1** touch or handle with the fingers. **2** *Music* perform or mark a passage of music with a certain FINGERING. **3** *Slang* inform on someone to the police. <Old English>
burn your fingers, get into trouble by meddling.
have a finger in every pie, be involved in many activities or enterprises: *The new principal showed he had a finger in every pie.*
keep your fingers crossed, wish for good luck.
lay a finger on, touch to the least degree: *If you lay a finger on that cake, you'll be sorry!*
lift a finger, do the least bit of work: *She doesn't lift a finger around the house.*
put your finger on, identify or find something.
twist around your little finger, manage easily; control completely: *He has you twisted around his little finger.*

finger bowl *n* a small bowl to hold water for rinsing the fingers after or during a meal.

finger food *n* food that can be easily eaten with the fingers.

fin·ger·ing (fing′gə ring) *Music n* **1** a way of using the fingers on certain musical instruments. **2** markings on a piece of music to show which fingers are to be used for which notes.

fin·ger·nail (fing′gər nāl′) *n* the hard layer of hornlike substance at the end of a finger.

fin·ger·paint (fing′gər pānt′) *v* paint with the fingers and other parts of the hands instead of with brushes.
n thickened watercolour designed for finger painting.
fin′ger·paint′ing *n.*

fin·ger·print (fing′gər print′) *n* an imprint of the pattern of ridges on the inner surface of the last joint of a finger, often used to identify a person: *Her fingerprints were found on the doorknob.*
v take the fingerprints of: *They took him to the police station and fingerprinted him.*

fin·ger·tip (fing′gər tip′) *n* the tip of a finger.
at your fingertips, able to be reached or produced instantly: *Keep your dictionary at your fingertips. He has all the answers at his fingertips.*

fin·ick·y (fin′ə kē) *adj* **1** picky or fussy: *She's finicky about her food.* **2** too delicate or precise: *Embroidery is too finicky for me.* <probably *fine*[1]>

fin·ish (fin′ish) *v* **1** bring to or be at an end: *The meeting finished early. She finished speaking and sat down.* **2** do the last part of and complete: *He started the race but did not finish it.* **3** use up completely: *to finish a bag of cookies.* **4** treat the surface of, for protection or beauty: *to finish a piece of furniture.* **5** ruin, destroy, tire out, or kill: *That long climb nearly finished me.*
n **1** an end: *to fight to the finish.* **2** the way a surface looks or feels after treating it with something: *a smooth finish.* **3** a polished condition or quality: *There is an expert finish to this photographer's work.* **4** something used to finish a surface. <Old French, from Latin *finis* end>
fin′ished *adj.*
finish off, a finish completely; get rid of by finishing. **b** overcome completely, destroy, or kill.
finish up, finish the last part of.
finish with or **be finished with,** finish using, doing, or having dealings with.

finishing school *n* a private college that prepares young women for social life rather than for business or a profession.

finish line *n* the line marking the end of a race.

fi·nite (fī′nīt) *adj* with limits or bounds, and with an end: *The number of words in a language, though great, is finite.* <Latin *finire* finish>

fink (fingk) *Slang n* **1** an informer. **2** a strikebreaker. **3** any unpleasant person.
v be an informer to the authorities. <German = bird, slang for a person not belonging to a university fraternity, or not part of a union or a gang>

Fin·land (fin′lənd) *n* a country in N Europe on the Baltic Sea. See the APPENDIX. **Finn** *n.* **Finn′ish** *adj.*

fiord (fyôrd) FJORD.

fir (fər) *n* **1** an evergreen tree found in northern temperate regions, with flat needles and upright cones. Canadian species include the **balsam fir**, **alpine fir**, **amabilis fir**, and **grand fir**. **2** another tree of the pine family, such as the Douglas fir. See SITKA SPRUCE for picture. <probably Old Norse *fyri*>

fire (fīr) *n* **1** the flame, heat, and light caused by something burning. **2** a mass of fuel, burning or arranged for burning: *Put more wood on the fire. A fire was laid in the fireplace.* **3** the process of burning: *The building was destroyed by fire.* **4** anything hot or bright: *If the curry needs a little more fire, add a chili or two, a determined fire in her eye.* **5** intense or passionate emotion: *Their hearts were filled with patriotic fire.* **6** the shooting of weapons: *enemy fire.*
v **fired, fir·ing 1** shoot: *to fire a missile. The official fired the starter pistol to signal the start of the race..* **2** dismiss from a job or office. **3** arouse or enthuse: *Stories of adventure fire the imagination.* **4** dry or harden with heat; bake in a kiln: *to fire clay.* **5** supply fuel to: *to fire the furnaces on an old steamship.* <Old English *fyr*>
catch fire, begin to burn.
fight fire with fire, respond to an attack with similar behaviour.
fire away, *Informal* go ahead and ask or speak.
fire up, a put into operation: *Fire up your engines.* **b** fill with eagerness: *Her speech fired up the listeners, and many began shouting for justice.*
go through fire and water, endure many troubles or dangers, usually for another's sake.
hang fire, be slow to take action.
light a fire under, *Informal* encourage or force someone to act more quickly.
play with fire, meddle with something dangerous.
under fire, a being shot at. **b** being criticized or blamed.

fire alarm *n* **1** the signal that a fire has broken out. **2** a device that gives such a signal.

fire·arm (fīr′ârm′) *n* a gun, rifle, pistol, or other handheld weapon to shoot with.

fire·ball (fīr′bol′) *n* a mass of fire, such as is produced by an explosion: *The oil tanker exploded in a fireball.*

fire·ball·er (fīr′bol′ər) *Baseball, Slang n* a pitcher who usually throws fastballs.

fire·boat (fīr′bōt′) *n* a boat equipped for putting out fires on a dock or ship.

fire·bomb (fīr′bom′) *n* a bomb designed to start a fire where it lands.
v attack with such bombs.

fire·brand (fīr′brand′) *n* **1** a person who stirs up angry or passionate feelings in others. **2** a piece of burning wood.

fire·break (fīr′brāk′) *n* a strip of land that has been cleared of trees or on which the sod has been turned over so as to prevent the spreading of a fire.

a bat	e bed	i bid	o pot	u cup	th **thin**
ā cake	ē me	ī bite	ō go	ū rude	TH **then**
â bar	ə about	ər over	ô for	ů put	zh measure

fire brigade *n* a group of people organized to fight fires, often temporarily or as volunteers.

fire·bug (fīr′bug′) *Informal n* a person who purposely sets houses or property on fire; an arsonist; a pyromaniac.

fire chief *n* the head of a fire department.

fire·crack·er (fīr′krak′ər) *n* a paper roll containing gunpowder and a fuse, which explodes with a loud noise, used for recreation or as part of a celebration.

fire·damp (fīr′damp′) *n* methane gas formed in coal mines, or an explosive mixture of methane and air.

fire department *n* a municipal department in charge of fighting and preventing fires.

fire drill *n* a practice exercise in a school or building to train people how to respond in case of fire.

fire–eat·er (fīr′ē′tər) *n* **1** an entertainer who pretends to eat fire. **2** a person who is too ready to fight or quarrel.

fire engine *n* a truck with water hoses, chemicals, ladders, and other equipment used to put out fires. Also called **fire truck**.

fire escape *n* a staircase, door, or ladder, often on the outside of a building, to use in case of fire.

fire extinguisher *n* a container filled with chemicals that can be sprayed on a fire to extinguish it.

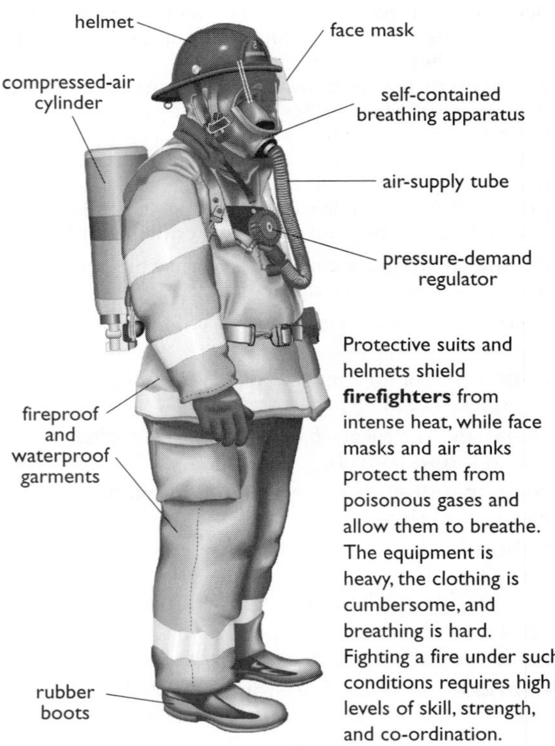

Protective suits and helmets shield **firefighters** from intense heat, while face masks and air tanks protect them from poisonous gases and allow them to breathe. The equipment is heavy, the clothing is cumbersome, and breathing is hard. Fighting a fire under such conditions requires high levels of skill, strength, and co-ordination.

fire·fight·er (fīr′fī′tər) *n* a specially trained and equipped person whose job is putting out fires.

fire·fight·ing (fīr′fī′ting) *n* the act or process of putting out fires.

fire·fly (fīr′flī′) *n, pl* **fire·flies** a small, night-flying beetle that gives off flashes of light that can be seen in the dark.

✱ **fire hall** *n* the headquarters of a fire department, or any other building for keeping firefighting equipment.

fire irons *pl n* tools, such as a poker, tongs, and shovel, needed for tending a fire and kept beside a fireplace.

fire·light (fīr′līt′) *n* the light from a fire.

fire·man (fīr′mən) *n, pl* **fire·men** (fīr′mən) **1** a man who tends the fire in a furnace, boiler, or locomotive. **2** a male firefighter.

fire·place (fīr′plās′) *n* a place built in the wall of a room or outdoors to hold a fire.

fire·pow·er (fīr′pou′ər) *n* the amount of ammunition that a gun can shoot, or the total amount available to a group of people.

fire·proof (fīr′prūf′) *adj* that will not or is almost impossible to burn: *A building made entirely of steel and concrete is fireproof.*
v make fireproof.

fire ranger *n* a government employee engaged in preventing and putting out forest fires.

fire screen *n* a screen placed in front of a fireplace as protection against heat or flying sparks.

fire·side (fīr′sīd′) *n* the space around a campfire or fireplace.
adj **1** beside the fire. **2** cozy or intimate, as if beside a home fireplace: *a fireside chat.*

fire station *n* a fire hall.

fire·storm (fīr′stôrm′) *n* **1** a large fire with strong winds, such as one started by a big explosion. **2** a violent outburst, especially from many people: *a firestorm of protest.*

fire tower *n* a tower in which a ranger keeps watch for forest fires.

fire·trap (fīr′trap′) *n* a building that will burn very easily, or is hard to escape from in case of fire.

fire·truck (fīr′truk′) FIRE ENGINE.

fire·wall (fīr′wol′) *n* **1** a fireproof wall, plate, or other built-in barrier to keep a fire from spreading. **2** *Computers* a software feature that blocks the passage of unwanted data or unauthorized access to an Internet site.

fire warden *n* an official whose duty is preventing and putting out fires in forests or camps.

fire·wa·ter (fīr′wot′ər) *Archaic n* a strong alcoholic drink. <Ojibway *ishkodew* fire + *aaboo* water>

fire·weed (fīr′wēd′) *n* a tall, fast-growing plant that grows especially in newly burned areas, with long spikes of purple flowers. It is the floral emblem of Yukon Territory.

fire·wood (fīr′wůd′) *n* wood for burning in a stove or fireplace.

fire·work (fīr′wərk′) *n* **1** a firecracker, small bomb, or rocket that makes a loud noise or display of lights or sparks in the sky. **2 fireworks** *pl* **a** a fireworks display. **b** *Informal* a violent quarrel or outburst.

firing line *n* **1** a line where soldiers are stationed to shoot at the enemy, or the soldiers themselves. **2** the foremost position in a campaign for a cause.

firing squad *n* a group of soldiers assigned to execute someone by shooting.

fir·kin (fər′kən) *n* **1** a quarter of a barrel, formerly used as a measure of capacity. **2** a small wooden cask used for butter, fish, or liquids. <Dutch *vierde* fourth part + *-kin*>

firm[1] (fərm) *adj* **1** not yielding easily to pressure or force: *firm flesh, firm ground.* **2** tightly fastened or fixed: *a tree firm in the earth.* **3** showing determination and confidence: *a firm purpose, a firm belief.* **4** not changing: *a firm price, a firm date.*
v (*usually with* **up**) make or become firm: *Can we firm up the date for our meeting?* <Latin *firmus*> **firm′ly** *adv.* **firm′ness** *n.*

firm[2] (fərm) *n* a company or partnership of two or more people in business together: *an old and trusted law firm.* <Italian, from Latin *firmus* firm[1]>

fir·ma·ment (fər′mə mənt) *Archaic or Poetic n* the sky. <Latin *firmus* firm[1]>

firm·ware (fərm′wer′) *Computers n* system programs stored permanently on a computer's ROM chip.

first (fərst) *adj* **1** coming before all others in time, rank, or importance: *the first day of summer. He is first in his class in math.* **2** *Music* playing or singing the highest part: *first violin, first soprano.* **3** to do with the lowest gear in a standard transmission.
adv **1** before all others in time, rank, or importance: *to put safety first. Women and children go first.* **2** before some other thing or event: *First bring me some tea.* **3** for the first time: *when I first visited the Northwest Territories.* **4** rather; instead: *I'll go to jail first.* **5** as a first point: *First, you're too young, and second, it's too dangerous.*
n **1** a person who or thing that is first: *She was the first to arrive.* **2** the winning position in a race or contest: *to finish first.* **3** beginning: *It was like that from the first.* **4** the lowest gear in a standard transmission. <Old English *fyrst*> **first′ly** *adv.*
at first, in the beginning: *At first I did not like school.*
first and foremost, above all; before everything else.
first and last, taking all together.
first thing, a at the earliest possible moment: *I'll do it first thing Monday morning.* **b** (*with* **the** *and a negative*) even the most basic facts: *I don't know the first thing about baseball.*
first things first, what is most important must be put first.

GRAMMAR AND USAGE

First and **last** refer to items in a series, usually of more than two: *Her first day at camp was a bit scary. We had to leave before the last inning ended.*

Latest refers to a series that is still continuing: *Have you seen the band's latest video?*

first aid *n* emergency treatment given to an ill or injured person. **first′-aid′** *adj.*

first base *Baseball n* the base to the left of the pitcher, that must be touched first by a runner.
get to first base, *Informal* (*usually with a negative*) make the first step toward success: *You'll never get to first base if you don't work hard.*

first–born (fərst′ bȯrn′) *adj* born first.
n a person's first-born child.

first class *n* **1** the highest class or best quality: *a poet of the first class.* **2** in the most expensive accommodations on an airplane, ship, train, etc.: *We have booked first class.* **first′-class′** *adj, adv.*

first cousin *n* the child of one's parent's sister or brother. See also COUSIN.

first–day cover (fərst′dā′) *Stamp collecting n* an envelope with a commemorative stamp on it, mailed on its first day of issue and prized by some collectors.

first degree *n* **1** the least serious category of burns to the human body, affecting only the top layer of skin. **2** *Law* the most serious category of certain crimes, such as murder. **3** the highest, purest, or most serious category of anything: *That is a lie in the first degree!* **first-degree** *adj.*

first estate *n* senior members of the clergy. See also ESTATE.

first–hand (fərst′hand′) *adj, adv* from the original source: *first-hand information, to hear first-hand.*

First Lady *n* the wife of the US president.

🍁 **First Meridian** *n* the basic north-south line from which lands were surveyed in the Northwest Territories and from which they are now surveyed in the Prairie Provinces.

🍁 **First Ministers** *pln* the prime minister and all the provincial premiers.

first name *n* a person's first given name or, sometimes, the name that he or she is usually known by: *Her first name is Alicia.*

🍁 **First Nation** *n* a group of Aboriginal people that make up a community sharing the same culture and heritage, usually one that is recognized as a BAND[1] (def. 2) by the Federal Government.
adj **First Nations** to do with any of these groups: *a First Nations school.*

GRAMMAR AND USAGE

Although **First Nation**, technically, is a band on a reserve, it is often used more generally (as in this dictionary) to refer to an ethnic or cultural community. It is best to use specific First Nations names such as *Cree* whenever possible.

first night *n* **1** the night of the opening performance of a play or other live show. **2 First Night** New Year's Eve, especially celebrated with an outdoor party or concert.

first offender *n* someone convicted of having broken the law for the first time.

🍁 **First Peoples** *pln* the Aboriginal peoples living in Canada, including the First Nations, Inuit, and Métis.

a bat	e bed	i bid	o pot	u cup	th **thin**
ā cake	ē me	ī bite	ō go	ū rude	ᴛʜ **then**
ȧ bar	ə about	ər over	ȯ for	u̇ put	zh measure

F

first person *Grammar n* **1** the category to which a pronoun or verb belongs when used to refer to the speaker or speakers. *I, me, my,* and *we, us, our* are pronouns of the first person. **2** the form of a pronoun or verb indicating this. Example: *am* is the first person singular of the verb *be.*

first quarter *n* **1** the first three months of a year, especially a fiscal year. **2** the period between a new moon and the first half moon after it.

first–rate (fərst′rāt′) *adj* of the highest class or quality.

First World War WORLD WAR I.

firth (fərth) *n* especially in Scotland, a narrow inlet of the sea. <Old Norse *fjörthr*>

fis·cal (fis′kəl) *adj* financial. <Latin *fiscalus* belonging to the state treasury, from *fiscus* public money>

fiscal year *n* a year for tax or accounting purposes, which may not correspond to the calendar year: *March is always very busy in the accounting department, because that's when the company's fiscal year ends.*

fish (fish) *n, pl* **fish** or **fish·es** a cold-blooded vertebrate that lives in water and has gills instead of lungs for breathing.
v **1** catch or try to catch fish: *to fish for salmon, to fish a river.* **2** (*with* **for**) try to get or pick up as if with a hook: *We fished for the fallen wallet with a stick.* **3** search by groping inside something: *She fished in her backpack for pencil.* **4** find and take out: *He fished the map from the back of the drawer.* **5** (*with* **for**) try to get, usually by indirect means: *fishing for compliments, fishing for information.* <Old English *fisc*> **fish′ing** *n.* **fish′like′** *adj.*
a fish out of water, a person who is uncomfortable or ill at ease in unfamiliar surroundings.
drink like a fish, *Informal* drink (usually alcoholic beverages) a lot.
fish in troubled waters, take advantage of confusion or trouble to get what one wants.
fish or cut bait, either do something decisive or abandon a task altogether.
fish out, fish until there are no more fish worth catching.
have other fish to fry, have other and more important things to do.

GRAMMAR AND USAGE

The plural of **fish** is usually *fish*, but *fishes* is used when referring to different kinds of fish, especially in a technical or scientific context: *She caught six fish. Salmon is one of our most important food fishes.*

🍁 **fish and brewis** (brūz) *especially Newfoundland and Labrador n* a dish of cooked salt cod mixed with soaked hard bread (brewis). Cubes of fried salt pork (called scrunchions) can be poured on top. Also, **brewis.**

fish and chips *pln* pieces of fish fried in batter and served with French fries.

fish·bowl (fish′bōl′) *n* **1** a deep, roundish glass container for keeping small fish. **2** any lifestyle in which one is always being watched by the public: *The princess had to learn to cope with life in the fishbowl.*

fish·er (fish′ər) *n* **1** an animal or bird that catches fish for food. **2** a slender, dark-coloured weasel that lives in the forests of Canada and the northern US. **3** one who catches fish for a living or as a hobby.

fish·er·man (fish′ər mən) *n, pl* **fish·er·men** (fish′ər mən) a person who fishes for a living or for pleasure.

fish·er·y (fish′ə rē) *n, pl* **fish·er·ies 1** the business or industry of catching fish. **2** a place where fish are caught or farmed.

fish–eye lens (fish′ī′) *n* a wide-angle camera lens that covers a field of vision of about 180°, producing a circular, distorted image.

fish farm *n* a place where fish are bred for the market.

fish flake *n* a slatted platform used for drying fish.

fish hawk *n* an osprey.

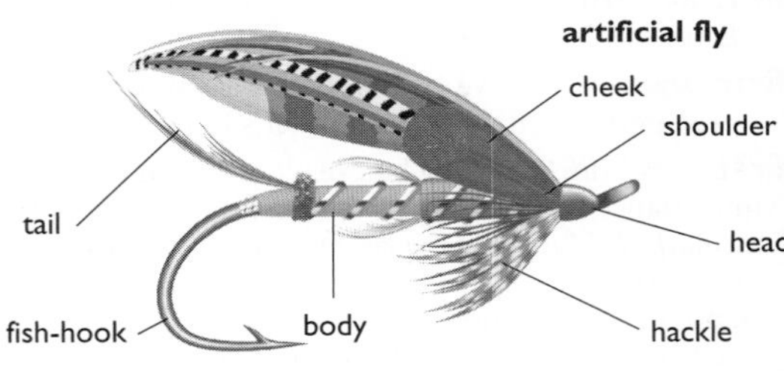

One type of **fish-hook** used in sport fishing is called a *fly*. A fly consists of a hook with feathers, hair, and artificial materials attached, made to resemble an insect. The type of fly used depends on what the fish are feeding on at the time.

fish–hook (fish′hůk′) *n* a hook used for catching fish.

fishing ground *n* a place in the ocean where fish are plentiful and a lot of fishing is done.

fishing line *n* a long, strong thread used in fishing.

fishing rod or **pole** *n* a long, slender rod to which a fishing line is attached.

fishing tackle *n* rods, lines, and hooks used in catching fish.

fish meal *n* dried fish, ground up and used as feed for animals or as fertilizer.

fish·pond (fish′pond′) *n* a pond with fish in it, especially an ornamental pool where fish are kept.

fish stick *n* **1** a piece of fish frozen in the form of a short, rectangular stick. **2** a small portion of fish, usually precooked and ground, shaped into a stick, breaded, and frozen.

fish story *Informal n* an exaggerated, unbelievable story.

fish·tail (fish′tāl′) *v* **1** swing from side to side, especially uncontrollably, while moving forward in a motor vehicle: *The van fishtailed on the icy road.* **2** move the tail of an airplane from side to side in order to reduce speed.

fish·way (fish′wā′) *n* a special waterway built to enable fish, such as salmon, to swim past waterfalls on their way to their spawning grounds upriver.

fish·wife (fish′wīf′) *n, pl* **fish·wives** a woman who uses coarse and abusive language. <originally a woman who sold fish in the street, hence a woman of low social class>

fish·y (fish′ē) *adj* **fish·i·er, fish·i·est 1** like a fish in smell, taste, or shape. **2** *Informal* arousing suspicion.
fish′i·ly *adv.* **fish′i·ness** *n.*

fis·sile (fis′īl) *adj* **1** capable of nuclear FISSION. **2** easily split as rocks.

fis·sion (fish′ən) *n* **1** the act of splitting apart. **2** *Physics* the splitting that occurs when the nucleus of an atom under bombardment absorbs a neutron, releasing tremendous energy. <Latin *findere* break up> **fis′sion·a·ble** *adj.*

fis·sure (fish′ər) *n* a long, narrow, deep split or crack: *a fissure in a rock.*
v **fis·sured, fis·sur·ing** split; crack.

fist (fist) *n* a hand tightly closed or holding something. <Old English *fyst*> **fist′like′** *adj.*

fist·fight (fist′fīt′) *n* a fight using only the fists.

fist·i·cuffs (fis′ti kufs′) *pl n* a fight with the fists.

fit[1] (fit) *adj* **fit·ter, fit·test 1** with the necessary or desirable qualities: *This food is not fit to eat.* **2** in good health and physical condition: *She works out every day to keep fit.* **3** ready or prepared: *Boots, mitts, and coat; now you're fit for winter.*
v **fit·ted, fit·ting 1** have the correct size or shape: *These pants don't fit. That puzzle piece doesn't fit this space.* **2** be or make suitable or appropriate: *Let the punishment fit the crime. Fit your response to the situation.* **3** put something in or on a place designed for it: *You have to fit this tab into that slot. Fit the pieces together.* **4** design or adjust to fit well or snugly: *to fit a garment.* **5** take someone's measurements for this purpose: *Tomorrow I'll fit you for your uniform.* **6** make ready or prepare: *courses that fit students for the workplace.* **7** install something: *to fit a store with shelves.*
n **1** the way in which one thing fits another: *the fit of a jacket, a tight fit.* **2** something that fits or is suitable: *This program is a good fit for you.* <Middle English> **fit′ly** *adv.*
fit out, supply with what is needed.
fit to be tied, *Informal* overwhelmed with frustration.
see (or **think**) **fit,** consider suitable or appropriate.

fit[2] (fit) *n* **1** a sudden, sharp attack of some uncontrollable symptom or emotion: *a coughing fit, a fit of depression.* **2** a short period of uncontrolled activity or emotion: *a fit of laughter, a fit of rage.* **3** a seizure with sudden loss of consciousness or convulsions: *an epileptic fit.* <Old English *fitt* conflict>
by (or **in**) **fits and starts,** irregularly: *The group project took a long time because we did it in fits and starts.*

fit·ful (fit′fəl) *adj* stopping and starting many times: *a fitful sleep, fitful conversation.* **fit′ful·ly** *adv.* **fit′ful·ness** *n.*

fit·ness (fit′nəs) *n* **1** suitability or appropriateness: *His poor performance calls into question his fitness for this job.* **2** good physical health, including muscle tone, endurance, flexibility, and proper body weight.

fitness club HEALTH CLUB.

fit·ted (fit′id) *adj* shaped to fit snugly the contours of something: *a fitted shirt, a fitted sheet.*

fit·ter (fit′ər) *n* **1** a person who fits garments on people. **2** a person who adjusts parts of machinery. **3** a person who supplies and installs a certain kind of equipment: *a gas fitter.*

fit·ting (fit′ing) *adj* correct, proper, or suitable: *It is only fitting to reward him for his honesty. The banquet was a fitting end to the day's festivities.*
n **1** a trying on of unfinished clothes to see if they will fit. **2 fittings** *pl* removable furnishings or fixtures.
fit′ting·ly *adv.*

five (fīv) *n* **1** a cardinal number that is one more than four: *Count to five.* **2** the numeral 5. **3** a playing card or side of a die with five spots: *the five of hearts.* **4** a five-dollar bill.
adj **1** one more than four: *We ordered five tickets.* **2** (*after the noun*) fifth in a series: *Lesson Five.* <Old English *fif*>
fifth *adj, adv.*

five·fold (fīv′fōld′) *adj, adv.* **1** five times as much or as many. **2** consisting of five parts.

Five Nations *pl n* a former confederacy of Iroquois nations, consisting of the Mohawk, Oneida, Onondaga, Cayuga, and Seneca. See also SIX NATIONS.

five o'clock shadow *n* the light growth of hair seen in the evening on the face of a man who shaved that morning.

✱ **five–pin** (fīv′pin′) *n* in full, **five-pin bowling** a type of indoor bowling using five rather than ten pins, and with a smaller ball.

five–star (fīv′stȧr′) *adj* of the best quality in a hotel, resort, or restaurant.

five W's *pl n* the group of questions reporters use to organize information: who, what, when, where, and why.

fix (fiks) *v* **fixed, fix·ing 1** mend or repair: *to fix a broken watch.* **2** prepare or arrange: *to fix your hair, to fix a meal.* **3** fasten, set, or hold firmly or permanently: *She fixed the new shelf to the wall. I have fixed his name in my memory.* **4** settle a price or date definitely: *We fixed the price at one dollar. I want to fix the party date for the first Sunday in June.* **5** direct and hold steady the gaze or attention: *He fixed a suspicious eye on the stranger.* **6** make or become rigid: *eyes fixed in death.* **7** *Informal* sterilize an animal: *We got the cat fixed.* **8** treat to keep from changing or fading: *A dye or photograph is fixed with chemicals.* **9** influence the outcome of an event dishonestly: *The jury had been fixed.* **10** *Informal* get revenge on: *Just you wait; I'll fix you.* **11** *Chemistry* change to a more permanent form or state.
n Informal a difficult situation from which it is hard to get out: *If you keep lying, you'll get yourself into a fix.* <French, from Latin *figere* fix> **fix′a·ble** *adj.*
fix on (or **upon**), decide on.
fix up, a do repairs or make improvements on. **b** arrange: *My uncle fixed me up with a summer job.*

fix·ate (fik′sāt) *v* **fix·at·ed, fix·at·ing** (*with **on***) become obsessed: *As soon as she finds some error, she fixates on it.*
fix′at·ed *adj.*

a bat	e bed	i bid	o pot	u cup	th **thin**
ā cake	ē me	ī bite	ō go	ū rude	ᴛʜ **then**
ȧ bar	ə about	ər over	ȯ for	ů put	zh measure

fix·a·tion (fik sā′shən) *n* **1** an obsession: *He has a fixation with movies.* **2** the act or process of fixing chemically. **3** the process by which soil bacteria convert atmospheric nitrogen into nitrates or nitrites.

fix·a·tive (fik′sə tiv) *n* a chemical used to keep something from fading or changing.
adj that prevents fading or change.

fixed (fikst) *adj* **1** not changeable: *a fixed rate, a fixed arrangement, to have fixed opinions.* **2** not moving: *a fixed stare.* **3** with its outcome prearranged dishonestly: *a fixed game.* **fix′ed·ly** *adv.*
be fixed for, *Informal* be in a certain condition with regard to something: *How are you fixed for cash? I think we're pretty well fixed for the party now.*

fixed star *n* a star whose position in relation to other stars appears not to change.

fix·ings (fik′singz) *Informal pln* ingredients needed for something: *She gathered all the fixings for a chocolate cake.*

fix·i·ty (fik′sə tē) *n* the fact of being fixed in condition or quality.

fix·ture (fiks′chər) *n* **1** a piece of furniture or equipment put in place to stay: *bathroom fixtures, light fixtures.* **2** a person or institution that seems always to have been there: *The caretaker had become a fixture in the school.*

fizz (fiz) *v* produce tiny bubbles and a hissing sound in a drink or other liquid.
n the bubbles and hissing sound produced by a drink or other liquid: *This pop has lost its fizz.* <imitative>
fizz′y *adj.*

fiz·zle (fiz′əl) *v* **fiz·zled, fiz·zling** (*sometimes with* ***out***) **1** hiss or sputter weakly and go out: *The firecracker fizzled instead of exploding.* **2** *Informal* end in failure: *The chess club fizzled.*
n **1** the act or sound of fizzling. **2** *Informal* failure. <Middle English>

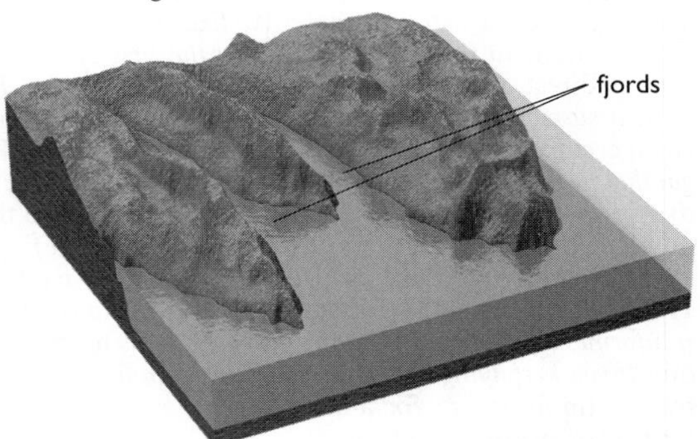

fjord or **fiord** (fyörd) *n* a long, narrow inlet of the sea between cliffs. <Norwegian>

flab (flab) *n* **1** flesh or muscle that is fatty and lacks firmness: *I have to exercise to get rid of some of this flab.* **2** weakness, lack of rigour, or useless elements that hinder effectiveness: *The new CEO will cut some of the flab from the organization.* <back-formed from *flabby*>
flab′by *adj.*

flab·ber·gast (flab′ər gast′) *v* amaze. <origin uncertain>

flac·cid (flak′sid) *or* (flas′id) *adj* soft, limp, and weak: *flaccid muscles, a flaccid will.* <Latin *flaccus* flabby>
flac·cid′i·ty *n.*

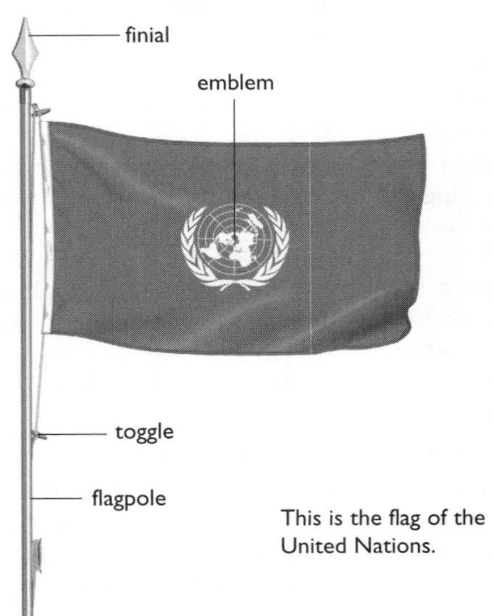

This is the flag of the United Nations.

flag[1] (flag) *n* **1 a** a piece of cloth, usually rectangular, showing the emblem of a country, unit of the armed forces, or other organization: *the Canadian flag, a regimental flag.* **b** a picture, sticker, or pin bearing this emblem. **2** a brightly coloured piece of cloth, usually triangular and strung together with others, used as a decoration: *The circus tent was decorated with flags.* **3** a piece of cloth, paper or metal tab of a certain colour or design that has a special meaning: *a white flag for surrender, a red flag for warning. When the flag on the mailbox is up, it means mail is inside.* **4** something that suggests a flag, such as the tail of certain animals.
v **flagged, flag·ging 1** put a flag or flags on. **2** stop or signal, especially by waving a flag or other object: *to flag down a cab.* <origin uncertain>

flag[2] (flag) *n* **1** a plant with swordlike leaves, such as the blue flag or the sweet flag. **2** the flower or leaf of such a plant. <Scandinavian>

flag[3] (flag) *v* **flagged, flag·ging** get tired, weak, or less enthusiastic: *After digging for three hours he began to flag.* <origin uncertain>

flag[4] (flag) *n* a flagstone.
v **flagged, flag·ging** pave with flagstones. <Scandinavian>

flag·el·late (flaj′ə lāt′) *for v,* (flaj′ə lit) *for adj. v* **flag·el·lat·ed, flag·el·lat·ing** whip or flog.
adj Biology with flagella. <Latin *flagellum* small whip>
flag′el·la′tion *n.*

fla·gel·lum (flə jel′əm) *Biology n, pl* **fla·gel·la** (flə jel′ə) a long, threadlike structure that allows certain cells, bacteria, or protozoa to move.

flag football *n* a game following the rules of US or Canadian football in which a ball carrier is stopped when an attached flag or handkerchief is snatched from his or her clothing.

flag·on (flag′ən) *n* **1** a container for liquids, usually with a handle and spout, and often a cover. <Old French, from Latin *flasca*>

flag·pole (flag′pōl′) *n* a pole from which a flag is flown.

fla·grant (flā′grənt) *adj* outrageously or scandalously offensive: *flagrant disregard for the law.* <obsolete *flagrant* burning, from Latin *flagrare* burn> **fla′gran·cy** *n.* **fla′grant·ly** *adv.*

flag·ship (flag′ship′) *n* **1** the ship that carries the officer in command of a fleet or squadron. **2** the most outstanding member of any group or collection.
adj main; leading: *The chain's flagship store is in Toronto.*

flag·staff (flag′staf′) *n* a flagpole.

flag·stick (flag′stik′) *Golf n* a pole with a small flag on top, placed in the hole to show the hole's location.

flag·stone (flag′stōn′) *n* **1** a large, flat stone used for paving walks, yards, or patios. **2** such stones collectively, or the rock from which they are cut.

flag·wav·ing (flag′wā′ving) *n* a display of patriotism, or activity or speeches designed to arouse patriotic enthusiasm.
adj engaging in such behaviour, especially to an excessive degree.

flail (flāl) *v* **1** wave or swing one's limbs or an object in a violent and confused way: *She flailed her arms at the officer to get his attention. He was flailing around in the snowbank, trying to climb out.* **2** strike with a flail.
n an instrument for threshing grain by hand, consisting of a wooden handle with a short, heavy stick fastened at one end by a thong. <Old English *fligel*>

flair (fler) *n* **1** a natural talent: *The poet had a flair for making clever rhymes.* **2** bold creativity or individuality. **3** good taste and style: *to dress with flair.* **4** an uncanny ability to find: *She had a flair for bargains.* <French *flair* scent, from Latin *fragrare* smell sweet, refers to perceptiveness, i.e., someone with a keen sense of smell>

flak (flak) *n* **1** gunfire from the ground against airplanes. **2** strong criticism. <German, acronym for *Fl(ieger) a(bwehr)k(anone)* anti-aircraft gun>

flake[1] (flāk) *n* **1** a small, thin piece of something, especially of paint, dead skin, pastry, or stone: *flakes of rust. The paint was coming off in flakes.* **2** a snowflake. **3** *Informal* an odd or eccentric person.
v **flaked, flak·ing** **1** peel off in flakes: *The skin on my back is flaking where it was burnt by the sun.* **2** break or separate into flakes: *a can of flaked tuna.* <Middle English>
flak′y *adj.*

flake[2] (flāk) *n* a slatted platform or shelf used for drying fish or other foods. <possibly Scandinavian>

flake[3] (flāk) *Informal v* (*with* ***out***) fall into a deep sleep; faint: *He flaked out on the couch, and we couldn't wake him.* <obsolete *flack*>

flam·bé (flȧm bā′) *adj* (*after the noun*) served with liquor poured over it and ignited: *crêpes flambé.*
v **flam·béd** or **flam·béed, flam·bé·ing** pour liquor over and set on fire.
n a dish prepared in this way: *a peach flambé.* <French>

flam·boy·ant (flam boi′ənt) *adj* **1** doing and saying things that attract attention: *The film director was a flamboyant individual who was often in the news.* **2** gorgeously brilliant: *flamboyant colours.* **3** showy or ornate: *flamboyant architecture.* <French, from Latin *flamma* flame. *Flamboyant* originally referred to something that was brilliantly or flamingly coloured.> **flam·boy′ance** *n.* **flam·boy′ant·ly** *adv.*

flame (flām) *n* **1** a glowing red or yellow tongue of light that shoots out from a blazing fire: *The house burst into flames.* **2** the state of burning with flames: *The glowing ember suddenly burst into flame.* **3** *Slang* an insulting e-mail message.
v **flamed, flam·ing** **1** burn with flames: *The dying fire suddenly flamed brightly.* **2** be or become hot or red: *Her cheeks flamed.* **3** be full of bright light or passionate feeling: *His eyes flamed with hatred.* **4** burst out quickly and hotly: *She flamed with indignation.* **5** *Slang* write insulting things in an e-mail message: *I've been flamed.* <Old French, from Latin *flamma*> **flame′like′** *adj.*

fla·men·co (flə meng′kō) *n* **1** a style of vigorous Spanish dance performed with castanets to a very fast rhythm. **2** a piece of music in this style, or for such a dance.

ETYMOLOGY

Flamenco in Spanish means "gypsylike," but literally means "Flemish." In medieval times, the Flemish in Holland, Belgium, and France were famous for their bright, flamboyant clothes, and thus *Flemish* in Spanish became the same as *gypsylike*.

flame·proof (flām′prüf′) *adj* not liable to catch fire.
v treat with a substance that does not catch fire.

flame retardant *n* a substance used to treat materials so they will be slower to ignite and burn.
flame-retardant *adj.*

flame–throw·er (flām′thrō′ər) *n* a weapon or device that directs a jet of burning fuel through the air.

flam·ing (flā′ming) *adj* **1** burning with flames. **2** very bright or hot: *flaming orange, flaming cheeks.* **3** extremely passionate or vehement: *a flaming idealist.*

fla·min·go (flə ming′gō) *n, pl* **fla·min·gos** or **fla·min·goes** a tropical wading bird with thin long legs and neck, and feathers that vary from pink to scarlet. <Spanish, early form of *flamenco*>

flam·ma·ble (flam′ə bəl) *adj* easily set on fire.

GRAMMAR AND USAGE

Flammable and **inflammable** mean the same, but *inflammable* is sometimes misunderstood because it looks like a negative. The word *flammable* is preferred for the sake of clarity, but whichever form is used, the opposite is *nonflammable*.

a bat	e bed	i bid	o pot	u cup	th **thin**
ā cake	ē me	ī bite	ō go	ū rude	ᴛʜ **then**
ȧ bar	ə about	ər over	ȯ for	ů put	zh measure

F

flan (flan) *n* **1** a baked custard topped with caramelized sugar. **2** an open pie with a fruit or other filling. <Old French, from Latin *flado* flat cake>

flange (flanj) *n* a projecting edge or rim on an object to attach it to another object or to strengthen it, or to keep a wheel in place on a railway track. <origin uncertain>

flank (flangk) *n* **1** the part of the body between the hips and the ribs, especially on an animal. **2** a piece of meat cut from this part of an animal. **3** the side of anything, especially of a mountain or an army formation: *No one had ever climbed the northern flank before. The left flank bore the brunt of the enemy attack.*
v **1** be at the side or both sides of: *High buildings flanked the narrow alley.* **2** attack or get around the far right or left side of: *to flank the enemy's troops.* <Old French *flanc*>

flan·nel (flan′əl) *n* **1** a soft, warm, fuzzy woollen fabric. **2 flannelette** a similar fabric made of cotton. **3 flannels** *pl* clothes, especially pants or thermal underwear, made of flannel. <probably from Welsh *gwlan* wool>

flap (flap) *v* **flapped, flap·ping 1** swing or sway about loosely: *The curtains flapped in the wind.* **2** move the wings or arms up and down: *The crow flapped its wings.* **3** fly by moving wings up and down: *The bird flapped away.* **4** strike noisily with something broad and flat: *The beaver flapped the water with its tail as a warning.*
n **1** a broad, flat piece fastened at one edge only: *a coat with flaps on the pockets.* **2** a small, movable section of an airplane wing, near the fuselage, that can be lowered to increase lift. **3** the act or sound of flapping. <Middle English, probably imitative>
in a flap, *Informal* upset, agitated, or flustered: *It's just a game, so there's no need to get all in a flap about it.*

flap·jack (flap′jak′) *n* a pancake.

flap·per (flap′ər) *n* in the 1920s, a fashionable and unconventional young woman who was fond of pleasure. <origin uncertain>

flare (fler) *v* **flared, flar·ing 1** flame up briefly or unsteadily, sometimes with smoke: *A gust of wind made the torches flare.* **2** spread out in the shape of a bell: *The jeans flare at the ankles.* **3** burst out passionately: *Suddenly her temper flared.* **4** signal by means of flares: *The rockets flared a warning.*
n **1** a bright but brief or unsteady flame or blaze: *The flare of a match showed us his face.* **2** a chemical light that burns for a short time, used for signalling or warning: *The police had put flares around the accident scene.* **3** a sudden outburst. **4** the fact of spreading out in a bell shape: *the flare of a skirt.* <Scandinavian>
flare up, a burst into sudden flame: *The dying fire flared up briefly.* **b** become suddenly more intense or active: *My rash was almost gone but it has flared up again today.*

flare–up (fler′up′) *n* **1** a sudden outburst of flame. **2** a sudden increase or return of intensity or activity.

flash (flash) *n* **1** a sudden light that lasts only an instant: *a flash of lightning, the flash of sparks.* **2** a sudden, brief feeling, outburst, or display: *a flash of hope, a flash of wit.* **3** a very brief time: *It all happened in a flash.* **4** a brief news report of current developments, often interrupting regular programming: *a news flash.* **5** a bright, showy display: *a flash of colour.*
v **1** give out or cause to give out flashes: *to flash the headlights. The warning light was flashing.* **2** communicate by flashes: *to flash a warning.* **3** arrive suddenly: *A thought flashed through my mind.* **4** *Informal* briefly expose the genitals to: *He was caught flashing young women in the park.* **5** *Informal* show off jewellery or money: *Stop flashing your cash or we'll be mugged.* <Middle English, probably imitative>
flash back (**forward**)**,** switch briefly to an earlier (later) time in a story.
flash in the pan, a success that ends quickly or is not followed by further successes.

flash·back (flash′bak′) *n* a brief return to an earlier time in a story.

flash·bulb (flash′bulb′) *n* in former times, a bulb used to give a bright light for taking photographs in low light. It has mostly been replaced by an ELECTRONIC FLASH.

flash burn *n* a severe burn caused by sudden thermal radiation, such as from an atomic bomb.

flash card *n* one of a set of cards displaying letters, words, numbers, or pictures, shown briefly for drill in reading, arithmetic, vocabulary, or other skills.

flash·er (flash′ər) *n* **1** a light that flashes as a signal, especially on a vehicle. **2** *Informal* a person who gains sexual pleasure from publicly exposing the genitals.

flash flood *n* a very sudden, violent flooding of a river or stream.

flash–for·ward (flash′fôr′wərd) *n* a brief switch to a later time in a story.

flash·ing (flash′ing) *n* sheet metal used to cover and protect the joints and angles of a building to make them watertight.

flash·light (flash′līt′) *n* a portable electric light operated by batteries.

flash·point (flash′point′) *n* **1** *Chemistry* the lowest temperature at which vapour from a combustible substance such as gasoline will ignite if exposed to flame. **2** the point at which anger or frustration bursts out into action or violent speech.

flash·y (flash′ē) *adj* **flash·i·er, flash·i·est** attractive or impressive in a showy way: *a flashy performance. He tries to impress people by wearing flashy clothes.* **flash′i·ly** *adv.* **flash′i·ness** *n.*

flask (flask) *n* **1** a small glass, plastic, or metal bottle with flat sides, made to be carried in the pocket. **2** a narrow-necked container made of thin glass, used in chemical laboratories. <Old English *flasce*>

flat[1] (flat) *adj* **flat·ter, flat·test 1** smooth and level: *flat land.* **2** not very deep or thick: *A plate is flat.* **3** spread out at full length: *Lie flat on the floor.* **4** with little or no air in it: *a flat tire.* **5** definite and direct: *a flat refusal.* **6** dull; without zest or interesting character: *flat food, a flat voice.* **7** not shiny or glossy: *flat paint.* **8** no longer fizzy: *flat pop.* **9** *Music* **a** singing or playing slightly below the correct pitch: *Sopranos, you are flat.* **b** lowered by a halftone from the natural pitch: *B flat.*

n **1** something flat, such as a flat tire, the palm of the hand, or flat land: *to fix a flat on a bicycle. I can skateboard well enough on the flat; it's hills that are the problem.* **2** a shallow box: *I helped to plant three flats of petunias in the garden.* **3** a piece of stage scenery. **4** land covered with shallow water, often next to a river. **5** *Music* **a** a note lowered by a halftone from the natural pitch: *Does this song have any flats in it?* **b** the sign (♭) that shows such a tone or note in music.
adv Music below the true pitch: *to sing flat.* <Old Norse *flatr*> **flat′ly** *adv.* **flat′ness** *n.* **flat′tish** *adj.*
fall flat, fail completely: *One actor forgot her lines, and the scene fell flat.*
flat out, a bluntly or directly: *He refused flat out.* **b** at maximum speed or effort: *We've been working flat out for days now.*
that's flat, that's final: *You're not going and that's flat.*

flat² (flat) *n* an apartment or set of rooms on one floor. <Old English *flet* floor>

flat·bed (flat′bed′) a truck or trailer without sides, especially one used for carrying heavy machinery.

flat·bread (flat′bred′) *n* bread made with little or no leavening agent, often in a round, flat shape.

flat·car (flat′kȧr′) *n* a railway freight car with no roof or sides.

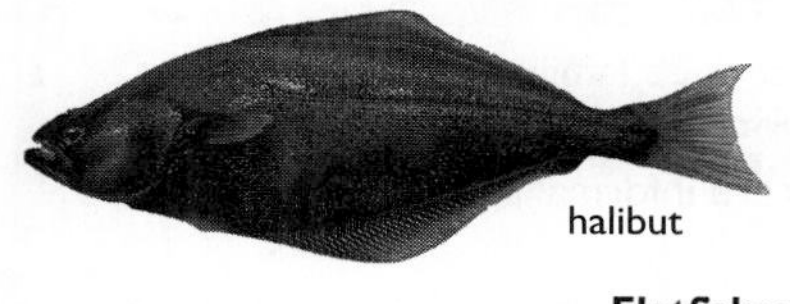
halibut

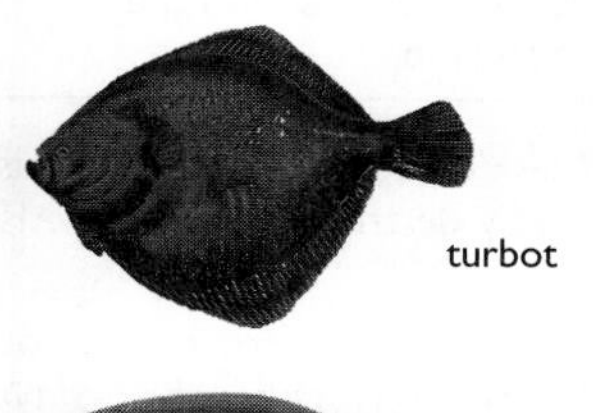
turbot

sole

Flatfish are found in the Atlantic and Pacific Oceans, where they swim near the bottom and feed on small marine life. Many species can change colour to blend with their surroundings.

Flatfish such as halibut, turbot, sole, and flounder are important to the Canadian food fishing industry.

flat·fish (flat′fish′) *n, pl* **flat·fish** or **flat·fish·es** a saltwater fish with a flat body and with both eyes on the side that is kept uppermost when lying flat. Halibut, turbot, and sole are flatfish.

flat–foot·ed (flat′fu̇t′id) *adj* **1** having feet with flattened arches. **2** *Informal* clumsy. **flat′-foot′ed·ness** *n.*
catch flat-footed, catch unprepared.

flat·line (flat′līn′) *n* a horizontal line on a graph indicating a total lack of change or activity, as in a patient's vital signs, economic growth, or business performance.
v **flat·lined, flat·lin·ing 1** reach a level of zero activity or change: *Interest rates have flatlined.* **2** show complete lack of vital signs on a monitor attached to a patient.

flat–out (flat′out′) *adj* blunt, direct, or absolute: *a flat-out insult, a flat-out refusal.*
adv (*modifying an adjective*) absolutely: *You are flat-out mistaken.*

flat rate or **fee** *n* a charge that is the same in all cases: *There's a flat rate for the rental no matter how long you keep the canoe.*

flat–screen TV (flat′skrēn′) *n* **1** an extremely thin TV with a PLASMA SCREEN. **2** a traditional cathode-ray tube TV with a screen made of flat glass.

flat·ten (flat′ən) *v* **1** press or become flat: *Flatten cans before recycling them.* **2** destroy or ruin: *to flatten someone's hopes, to flatten a city.*

flat·ter (flat′ər) *v* **1** praise too much or more than is true. **2** show to be better looking than is really the case: *That picture flatters her.* **3** cause to feel pleased or honoured: *I'm flattered that you asked for my opinion.* <Middle English> **flat′ter·er** *n.* **flat′ter·ing** *adj.* **flat′ter·y** *n.*
flatter yourself, a congratulate yourself: *She flattered herself that she was the only student to earn an A plus in math.* **b** overestimate yourself: *You think you can beat him? Don't flatter yourself.*

flat·u·lent (flach′ə lənt) *adj* **1** with much gas in the stomach or intestines. **2** pompous in speech or behaviour. <French, from Latin *flare* to blow> **flat′u·lence** *n.*

flat·ware (flat′wer′) *n* knives, forks, and spoons.

flat·worm (flat′wərm′) *n* a worm with a flat body that lives in water or as a parasite on some animal.

flaunt (flont) *v* show off: *He's always flaunting his knowledge of Latin.* <origin uncertain> **flaunt′ing·ly** *adv.*

CONFUSABLES

Flaunt means "show off": *He had a tendency to flaunt his expensive tastes.*

Flout means "show contempt for authority": *She had been warned not to flout the rules.*

flau·tist (flout′ist) *or* (flot′ist) FLUTIST.

fla·vour or **fla·vor** (flā′vər) *n* **1** a taste, especially a characteristic taste, and usually a good one: *Chocolate and vanilla have different flavours.* **2** anything used to give a certain taste to food or drink. **3** a distinctive or interesting quality: *He lives in Labrador, and all his stories have a flavour of the sea.*
v give a flavour to: *She flavoured the sauce with lemon. Add some description to your story to flavour it a little.* <Old French *flaor*> **fla′vour·ful** *adj.* **fla′vour·less** *adj.* **fla′vour·less·ness** *n.*

fla·vour·ing or **fla·vor·ing** (flā′və ring) *n* something added to give a certain taste to food or drink: *vanilla flavouring, chocolate flavouring.*

flaw (flo′) *n* a fault, defect, or imperfection: *a character flaw, a flaw in an argument, a flaw in a piece of pottery.*
v (*usually passive*) make defective or imperfect. <probably related to Swedish *flaga*> **flawed** *adj.* **flaw′less** *adj.* **flaw′less·ly** *adv.* **flaw′less·ness** *n.*

a bat	e bed	i bid	o pot	u cup	th **thin**
ā cake	ē me	ī bite	ō go	ü rude	ᴛʜ **then**
ȧ bar	ə about	ər over	ȯ for	u̇ put	zh measure

flax (flaks) *n* a plant with small, narrow leaves, blue or yellow flowers, and slender stems whose seeds are the source of linseed oil and whose stem fibres are used to make linen. <Old English *fleax*>

flax·en (flak′sən) *adj* **1** made of flax or linen. **2** pale yellow: *flaxen hair.*

flay (flā) *v* **1** strip the skin or outer covering from someone or something by whipping or lashing: *The tyrant had his enemies flayed alive.* **2** scold or criticize mercilessly. <Old English *flean*>

Both the **flea** and the louse are blood-sucking parasites, but there are differences. For example, the flea has powerful legs for jumping, while the louse has short legs adapted for clinging to the host.

flea (flē) *n* a small, wingless, jumping insect that lives as a parasite on animals, sucking their blood. <Old English *fleah*>
put a flea in someone's ear, *Informal* give someone a tip or suggestion.

flea collar *n* a collar for a dog, cat, or other pet, treated with insecticide to kill fleas and other pests.

flea market *n* a market where vendors at individual booths sell a mixture of cheap or unusual items, second-hand goods, or antiques.

fleck (flek) *n* **1** a small particle or flake. **2** a small spot of colour, light, or dirt.
v sprinkle with spots or patches of colour or light: *yellow fabric flecked with orange.* <Middle English>

fled (fled) past tense and past participle of FLEE.

fledge (flej) *v* **fledged, fledg·ing 1** grow the feathers needed for flying. **2** bring up a young bird until it is able to fly. <Old English>

fledg·ling or **fledge·ling** (flej′ling) *n* **1** a young bird just able to fly. **2** a young, inexperienced person.

flee (flē) *v* **fled, flee·ing 1** run away from: *to flee from danger. The suspect fled police.* **2** move or be driven swiftly: *The clouds are fleeing before the wind.* **3** vanish: *The darkness flees at dawn. The colour fled from her cheeks.* <Old English *fleon*>

fleece (flēs) *n* **1** the wool that covers a sheep or goat. **2** the quantity of wool cut from a sheep or goat at one time. **3** soft, warm fabric that has a fuzzy or fluffy surface on one side. **4** something resembling fleece: *a fleece of newly fallen snow.*
v **fleeced, fleec·ing 1** cut the fleece from. **2** *Informal* cheat of money or belongings: *The gamblers fleeced him of a large sum.* <Old English *fleos*>

fleec·y (flē′sē) *adj* **fleec·i·er, fleec·i·est 1** soft, fluffy, and white like fleece: *fleecy clouds.* **2** made of or covered with fleece.

fleet[1] (flēt) *n* **1** a group of ships sailing together, engaged in the same activity, or under one command: *the Canadian fleet.* **2** a group of motor vehicles or aircraft operating together or owned by one company: *a fleet of trucks.* <Old English>

fleet[2] (flēt) *Poetic adj* swift or rapid: *a fleet messenger.* <probably Old Norse *fljotr*> **fleet′ly** *adv.* **fleet′ness** *n.*

fleet·ing (flē′ting) *adj* short-lived: *Her anger was intense but fleeting.* **fleet′ing·ly** *adv.*

Flem·ish (flem′ish) *adj* to do with a Dutch language that is an official language of Belgium, or its speakers.

flesh (flesh) *n* **1** the soft substance of a human or animal body, consisting mostly of muscles and fat, that covers the bones and is covered by skin. **2** one's family or relatives by birth: *my own flesh and blood.* **3** the soft or inner part of fruits or vegetables: *The McIntosh apple has crisp, juicy flesh.* **4** fatness: *He's put on a lot of flesh.* **5 the flesh** the body or physical part of a person, as opposed to the soul or spirit: *The flesh is weak.* <Old English *flæsc*>
in the flesh, in person: *There she stood in the flesh.*
press the flesh, *Informal* shake hands with many people, especially as a political campaigner.

SYNONYMS

Flesh can suggest one's family or relatives: *That famous actor is my own flesh and blood—my cousin.*

Kin and **kinfolk** are informal and also mean "relatives."

Clan refers to a group of related families with the same ancestry, especially in Scotland.

flesh–eat·ing disease (flesh′ē′ting) *n* an acute disease caused by bacteria that rapidly destroy body tissue. Also called **necrotizing fasciitis**.

flesh·pots (flesh′pots′) *pl n* places offering sensuous pleasure, entertainment, or luxurious living: *the fleshpots of the city.*

flesh wound *n* a wound that breaks the skin but does not damage bones or vital organs.

flesh·y (flesh′ē) *adj* **flesh·i·er, flesh·i·est 1** with much flesh: *The calf is the fleshy part of the lower leg.* **2** somewhat fat. **flesh′i·ness** *n.*

fleur–de–lys or **fleur–de–lis** (flər′də lē′) *n,* *pl* **fleurs-de-lys** or **fleurs-de-lis** (flər′də lē′) *or* (flər′də lēz′) *for both spellings.* **1** a design or device used in heraldry, representing a lily, an emblem of the province of Québec. **2** the former royal coat of arms of France. **3** the iris flower or plant. <French = flower of the lily>

GRAMMAR AND USAGE

The spelling **fleur-de-lis** is actually more common in English, but since most Canadian references are to the Québec emblem, the spelling used in Québec, **fleur-de-lys**, is preferred.

flew (flū) a past tense of FLY[2].

flex (fleks) *v* **1** bend, usually with a return to the original position: *He slowly flexed his stiff arm. With each step the cat made, the tree branch flexed slightly.* **2** tighten and relax muscles alternately: *The muscles in his jaw flexed. She flexed her biceps.* <Latin *flectere* to bend>

flex·i·ble (flek′sə bəl) *adj* **1** bending easily: *flexible wire.* **2** able to move the body easily and in many different ways: *Yoga exercises will make you more flexible.* **3** easily adjusted to fit various uses or purposes: *a flexible schedule. An actor must have a flexible voice.* **4** willing to adapt or submit: *You choose where to go for lunch; I'm flexible.* **flex′i·bil′i·ty** *n.* **flex′i·bly** *adv.*

flex·time (fleks′tīm′) *n* a system with flexible working schedules, so that employees can choose their starting and finishing times provided they put in the required number of hours.

flick (flik) *n* **1** a quick, light blow: *By a flick of her whip, she drove the fly from the horse's head.* **2** the light, snapping sound of such a blow or stroke. **3** a sudden jerk: *The fisherman made a short cast with a flick of his wrist.* **4** *Slang* a movie.
v **1** strike lightly with a quick, snapping blow: *He flicked the dust from his shoes with a handkerchief.* **2** make a sudden, snapping stroke with: *The childrens flicked wet towels at each other.* **3** make short, quick movements with: *The snake flicked its tongue in and out.* <imitative>

flick·er[1] (flik′ər) *v* **1** shine or cause to shine with a wavering, unsteady light: *The candle flickered in the breeze.* **2** make small, quick movements, especially with the eyes: *His gaze flickered a moment.*
n **1** a wavering, unsteady light or flame. **2** a brief appearance, flash, or spark: *a flicker of hope.* **3** a fluttering or small, quick movement: *the flicker of an eye.* <Old English *flicorian*>

flick·er[2] (flik′ər) *n* a woodpecker of the Americas with a brown or buff-coloured back and a long bill. <perhaps imitative of its movement>

fli·er (flī′er) FLYER.

flight (flīt) *n* **1** the act, manner, or phenomenon of flying or of travelling by air: *the flight of a bird through the air, a book on the physics and history of flight.* **2** a trip through the air or in an aircraft: *How was your flight?* **3** the act of fleeing or running away: *The only option was flight.* **4** a set of stairs or steps between landings or storeys. **5** a soaring above or beyond what is ordinary: *a flight of the imagination.* **6** a group flying through the air together: *a flight of six birds.* <Old English *flyht*> **flight′less** *adj.*
put to flight, force to flee.
take flight, begin flying.
take to flight, flee or run away.

flight attendant *n* a person employed by an airline to look after passengers during a flight.

flight recorder *n* a device in an aircraft that records all the sounds in the cockpit including the pilots' voices and engine noise, in order to provide clues to what went wrong in the case of a crash or hijacking.

flight test *n* a test of an aircraft by actually flying it. **flight-test** *v.*

flight·y (flī′tē) *adj* **flight·i·er, flight·i·est** fickle and irresponsible: *You're too flighty to be reliable.*
flight′i·ness *n.*

flim·flam (flim′flam′) *Informal n* **1** nonsensical or insincere talk. **2** a swindle or trick.
v **flim·flammed, flim·flam·ming** swindle someone. <obsolete *flam* deceptive trick>

flim·sy (flim′zē) *adj* **flim·si·er, flim·si·est** **1** light and thin: *This fabric is too flimsy for a jacket.* **2** not strong or sturdy: *a flimsy structure.* **3** not adequate or convincing: *a flimsy excuse.* <probably from *flimflam*> **flim′si·ly** *adv.*
flim′si·ness *n.*

F

flinch (flinch) *v* make a quick, nervous movement away from difficulty, danger, or pain: *The toddler flinched when she touched the hot radiator.*
n the act of flinching: *He took his punishment without a flinch.* <Old French *flenchir*>

fling (fling) *v* **flung, fling·ing** **1** throw carelessly or violently: *I usually fling my backpack into the closet.* **2** move impulsively or without restraint: *He flung his arms happily around his mother's neck. She flung angrily out of the room.*
n **1** a violent or careless throw. **2** a time of doing as one pleases, without restraint: *He had his fling when he was younger, but now he must work.* **3** a lively Scottish dance: *the Highland fling.* **4** a short-lived romantic affair. <possibly Old Norse *flengja* to beat>
have (or **take**) **a fling at,** *Informal* try or attempt.

flint (flint) *n* **1** **a** a very hard grey or brown stone, a kind of quartz. **b** a piece of this, struck against steel to make a spark. A **flintlock** (flint′lok′)is an old-fashioned pistol, or a rifle, that is fired using such a mechanism. **2** anything very hard or unyielding: *a heart of flint.* <Old English>
flint′y *adj.*

flip (flip) *v* **flipped, flip·ping** **1** toss or move with a flick of a finger and thumb: *She flipped a coin onto the counter.* **2** toss a coin in order to decide something: *We'll flip to see who pays.* **3** turn or move with a sudden quick movement: *The branch flipped back in my face.* **4** turn over: *to flip pages, to flip a fried egg.* **5** invert, switch, or reverse: *If you flip "stop" you get "pots."* **6** *Slang (sometimes with* **out***)* **a** react with anger or surprise: *I flipped when I saw he was wearing my jacket.* **b** suddenly become enthusiastic: *I just flipped out when I heard that song.*
n an act of flipping: *I gave the pancakes a flip.*
adj **flip·per, flip·pest** flippant. <probably a contraction of *fillip*>

flip–flop (flip′flop′) *Informal v* **flip-flopped, flip-flop·ping** suddenly change one's opinion: *She flip-flopped on the issue of free trade.*
n **1** a sudden change of opinion. **2** **flip-flops** *pl* rubber or plastic sandals held on by a strap between the toes.

a bat	e bed	i bid	o pot	u cup	th **thin**
ā cake	ē me	ī bite	ō go	ū rude	ᴛʜ **then**
à bar	ə about	ər over	ȯ for	u̇ put	zh measure

flip·pant (flip′ənt) *adj* too casual or smart-alecky in speech or attitude: *a flippant answer.* <*flip*> **flip′pan·cy** *n.* **flip′pant·ly** *adv.*

flip·per (flip′ər) *n* **1** a broad, flat fin especially adapted for swimming, such as seals and walrus have. **2** a broad, flat blade of rubber that fits onto the foot, used by swimmers to give extra power when swimming.

flip side *Informal n* the reverse and often less obvious side or point of view: *to look at the flip side of an issue.*

flirt (flərt) *v* **1** try to win a person's romantic interest but without serious intentions: *Her friends advised her not to flirt so much.* **2** (*with* ***with***) consider in a half-serious way: *She flirted with the idea of going to Europe, though she couldn't afford it.*
n a person who flirts habitually. <origin uncertain> **flir·ta′tion** *n.* **flir·ta′tious** *adj.*

flit (flit) *v* **flit·ted, flit·ting** fly or pass by lightly and quickly: *Birds flitted from tree to tree. Many idle thoughts flitted through her mind as she lay there.*
n a light, quick movement. <Old Norse *flytja*>

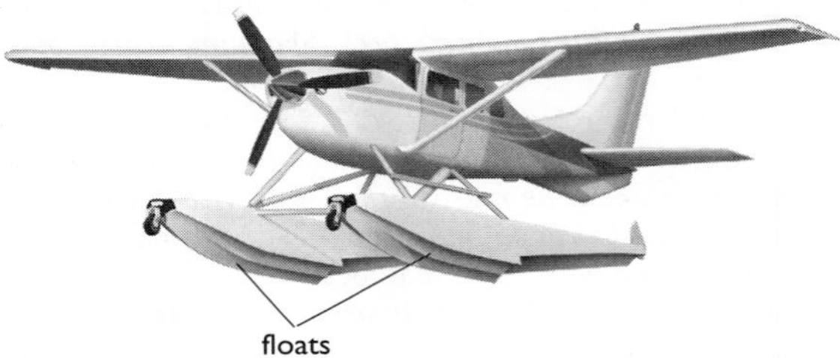

float (flōt) *v* **1** stay on top or be held up by a fluid, such as air or water: *A cork floats in water, but a stone sinks. The helium in the balloon makes it float.* **2** rest or move along in a liquid or the air: *The little boat floated out to sea. Dandelion seeds floated on the breeze.* **3** cause to float: *The tide gently floated the canoe out to sea.* **4** be employed without a specific assignment, doing whatever is necessary. **5** put forward an idea in order to get some reaction.
n **1** anything that stays up or holds up something else in water, such a bob on a fishing line, or one of the hollow supports on a seaplane. **2** a position of the body that allows one to float easily in water: *He has learned the starfish float.* **3** a hollow floating ball, attached to a valve by a movable rod, that regulates the level of a liquid in a tank by opening or closing the valve when it reaches a certain height. **4** a low, flat vehicle carrying an exhibit in a parade. **5** a drink consisting of pop with ice cream in it. **6** a sum of money supplied to a store, restaurant, etc., in order to make change. <Old English *flotian*>
float′a·ble *adj.*

float·er (flō′tər) *n* **1** a person who or thing that floats. **2** an employee not assigned to a specific job, who fills in wherever needed.

floating ribs *n* the two ribs that are not attached to the breastbone.

floc·cu·late (flok′yū lāt′) *v* **floc·cu·lat·ed, floc·cu·lat·ing** cause particles suspended in water to gather into clumps or masses that then sink or can be removed by filtering.

flock (flok) *n* **1** a group of animals of one kind, moving around and feeding together, especially sheep, goats, or birds. **2** any large group: *a flock of tourists.* **3** a group of people for whom one is responsible: *The priest tended his flock well. The kindergarten teacher led her little flock out to the bus.*
v go or gather in a flock: *Sheep usually flock together. The children flocked around the storyteller.* <Old English *flocc*>

floe (flō) *n* **1** a field or sheet of floating ice. **2** a floating piece broken off from such a field or sheet. <probably Old Norse *flo* layer>

flog (flog) *v* **flogged, flog·ging** **1** beat with a whip, stick, etc.. **2** *Informal* sell or offer for sale, especially in an aggressive way. <origin uncertain> **flog′ger** *n.*
flog a dead horse, *Informal* pursue a useless cause or argument.
flog to death, *Informal* overdo to the point of ineffectiveness.

flood (flud) *n* **1** a flow of water over what is usually dry land. **2** any great rush of water, such as a huge wave, a river that is higher than usual, or the tide. **3** a great outpouring of anything: *a flood of joy, a flood of words.* **4 the Flood** in the Bible, the water that covered the earth in the time of Noah.
v **1** flow over or into: *The river rose and flooded the fields.* **2** become covered or filled with water: *During the rainstorm our basement flooded.* **3** fill or cover with water: *They flood the ice before every hockey game.* **4** pour, flow, or stream like a flood: *Sunlight flooded through the window.* **5** fill, cover, or overcome like a flood: *The rich woman was flooded with requests for money. The room was flooded with moonlight.* <Old English *flod*>
in flood, filled to overflowing: *The river was in flood.*

flood·gate (flud′gāt′) *n* **1** a gate in a canal, river, or stream to control the flow of water. **2** anything that controls the flow or passage of something else.

flood·light (flud′līt′) *n* **1** a lamp giving a broad beam of bright light: *Several floodlights were used to illuminate the stage.* **2** the light from such a lamp.
v **flood·lit** (flud′lit′), **flood·light·ing** illuminate with floodlights.

flood plain *n* a plain next to a river, made of soil laid down by floods. See RIVER for picture.

flood tide *n* the flowing in of the tide.

floor (flôr) *n* **1** the horizontal part of a room, that people walk on. **2** a storey of a building: *Our apartment is on the fourth floor.* **3** a flat surface at the bottom of anything: *the floor of the ocean.* **4** the right or privilege to speak in a group: *The chairperson gave her the floor.*
v **1** knock down: *He floored his opponent with one punch.* **2** *Informal* confuse completely: *Her question floored me.* <Old English *flor*>

floor·board (flôr′bôrd′) *n* **1** a strip of wood used in a wooden floor. **2** usually, **floorboards** *pl* the floor of a car.

floor hockey *n* an indoor game derived from hockey, in which the players use a long stick to carry and pass a plastic ring or puck.

floor·ing (flô′ring) *n* material for making floors: *Tile is often used as flooring for bathrooms.*

floor plan *n* a diagram of one floor of a building, showing all the parts of it.

floor show *n* an entertainment of music, singing, dancing, etc., presented at a casino, hotel, etc., rather than at a theatre.

floor·walk·er (flôr′wok′ər) *n* a person employed in a large store to oversee sales or to help customers find what they want.

flop (flop) *v* **flopped, flop·ping 1** fall or move around loosely and heavily: *The fish flopped helplessly on the deck. Exhausted, she flopped down into a chair.* **2** *Informal* fail. **3** *Slang* go to a place to sleep: *to flop at a friend's house.*
n **1** the act or sound of flopping. **2** *Informal* failure: *The new play was a flop.* <variant of *flap*>

flop·house (flop′hous′) *n* a cheap, rundown hotel or rooming house.

flop·py (flop′ē) *adj* **flop·pi·er, flop·pi·est** limp or hanging loosely: *a sunhat with a floppy brim.*
n, pl **flop·pies** floppy disk. **flop′pi·ness** *n.*

floppy disk *Computers n* a round, magnetized plate made of thin, flexible plastic, used for storing data or programs.

flo·ra (flô′rə) *n* the plants of a particular region or time: *The Sahara Desert has few flora.* <Latin *floris* flower>

flo·ral (flô′rəl) *adj* **1** to do with flowers: *floral arrangements.* **2** representing flowers: *a floral design.*

Flor·en·tine (flô′rən tēn′) *adj* **1** to do with Florence, a city in Italy. **2** cooked with spinach.
n a native or inhabitant of Florence.

flo·ret (flô ret′) *or* (flô′rit) *n* a small flower, especially one of the small flowers making up the flower head of a composite plant such as the aster or cauliflower. <Old French *flor* flower >

flor·id (flô′rid) *adj* **1 a** reddish in complexion. **b** with such a complexion: *a florid young man.* **2** flowery, showy, or ornate: *florid language, florid architecture.* <Latin *floris* flower> **flor′id·ly** *adv.* **flor′id·ness** *n.*

flo·rist (flô′rist) *n* one who raises or sells flowers.

floss (flos) *n* **1** shiny, untwisted silk thread: *floss for embroidery, dental floss for cleaning between the teeth.* **2** soft, silky fluff or fibres of any kind: *Spun sugar is candy floss. Milkweed pods contain white floss.*
v to clean between the teeth using dental floss. <Old French *flosche* tuft of wool> **floss′y** *adj.*

flo·ta·tion (flō tā′shən) *n* the act or fact of floating. <Old English *flotian*>

flo·til·la (flə til′ə) *n* a small fleet, or a fleet of small ships. <Spanish *flota* fleet>

flot·sam (flot′səm) *n* the wreckage of a ship or its cargo found floating on the sea. <Old French *floter* to float>
flotsam and jetsam, a wreckage or cargo found floating on the sea or washed ashore. **b** useless or discarded things.

flounce[1] (flouns) *v* **flounced, flounc·ing** go with an angry or impatient movement of the body: *She flounced out of the room in a huff.*
n an angry or impatient movement of the body. <Scandinavian>

flounce[2] (flouns) *n* a wide strip of cloth, gathered along the top edge and sewn to a dress or skirt as trimming. <Old French *fronce* gather, from Frankish *hrunkja* wrinkle>

floun·der[1] (floun′dər) *v* **1** struggle awkwardly without making progress: *Men and horses were floundering in the deep snowdrifts.* **2** be clumsy or confused and make mistakes: *When the actor forgot her lines she began to flounder.* **3** struggle against failure: *My brother is floundering in math.*
n a floundering movement or action. <Old French *flondre*> **floun′der·ing** *adj.*

> **CONFUSABLES**
>
> **Flounder** means "struggle without making progress": *The sailboat floundered about in the crashing waves.*
>
> **Founder** means "sink in water or in soft ground": *The ship foundered in the sea, and all aboard drowned.*

floun·der[2] (floun′dər) *n, pl* **floun·der** or **floun·ders** a flatfish with a large mouth. <Scandinavian>

flour (flour) *or* (flou′ər) *n* a fine, powdery substance made by grinding and sifting wheat, corn, soybeans, etc.
v sprinkle with flour. <Middle English *flur* = best part of the grain> **flour′y** *adj.*

flour·ish (flər′ish) *v* **1** grow or develop vigorously: *Her newspaper business grew and flourished.* **2** be in the most vigorous time of life or activity: *Chivalry flourished in the twelfth and thirteenth centuries.* **3** wave something in the air: *He ran toward us, flourishing the concert tickets.*
n **1** the act of waving something in the air: *He removed his hat with a flourish.* **2** a small decoration in handwriting or a decorative passage in a piece of music. **3** a display of enthusiasm or heartiness: *My little brother showed us around his classroom with much flourish.* <Old French, from Latin *floris* flower> **flour′ish·ing** *adj.*

flout (flout) *v* treat with contempt: *to flout the rules. He flouted his parents' advice.* See FLAUNT for confusable. <origin uncertain>

flow (flō) *v* **1** move in a current or stream like water. **2** move or cause to move smoothly, with no abrupt stops or changes: *a flowing movement in a dance, flowing verse. Just flow that paragraph into the next one.* **3** hang long and loose so as to move freely: *flowing robes, her flowing hair.* **4** be full: *His mind is always flowing with ideas.* **5** (*with* ***from***) follow naturally or logically as a result: *All sorts of wrong ideas flow from this assumption.*
n **1** the act, manner, or rate of flowing: *a flow of blood.* **2** any continuous movement like that of water in a river: *a rapid flow of speech.* **3** the coming in of the tide. <Old English *flowan*>
go with the flow, *Informal* take things as they are without fussing or resisting.

a bat	e bed	i bid	o pot	u cup	th **thin**
ā cake	ē me	ī bite	ō go	ü rude	ᴛʜ then
à bar	ə about	ər over	ô for	ù put	zh measure

flow chart *n* a diagram showing the order of operations in a complex system. Also, **flowchart**.

flow·er (flou′ər) *n* **1** the usually colourful part of a plant that produces the seed: *The rose is my favourite flower.* See ANTHER for picture. **2** a plant grown for its blossoms: *to plant flowers.* **3** the finest part: *in the flower of her life. The flower of the country's youth was killed in the war.* **4** any of several kinds of reproductive structures in lower plants, such as the mosses.
v **1** have or produce flowers. **2** be at one's best. <Old French, from Latin *floris* flower> **flow′er·ing** *adj.*
in flower, flowering.
in full flower, a with all the blossoms open. **b** at the peak of development or excellence: *The novel showed that the author's talent was in full flower.*

flower bed *n* a strip or patch of earth in a garden in which flowers are grown.

flower child *n* a hippie.

flow·ered (flou′ərd) *adj* decorated with flowers: *The fabric was a flowered print.*

flower girl *n* **1** a very young girl who attends the bride at the wedding ceremony. **2** in former times, a girl or woman who sold flowers on the street.

flower head *n* a bloom composed of many tiny flowers grouped together so that they appear to be a single flower.

flow·er·pot (flou′ər pot′) *n* a pot to hold soil for a plant to grow in.

flow·er·y (flou′ə rē) *adj* **flow·er·i·er, flow·er·i·est 1** full of or covered with flowers. **2** containing many fine words and fancy expressions: *a flowery speech.* **flow′er·i·ness** *n.*

flown (flōn) a past participle of FLY[2].

🍁 **FLQ** *n* in full, the **Front de libération du Québec** a separatist terrorist organization active in Canada from 1963–1971.

flu (flū) *n* in full, **influenza** a contagious viral infection that often causes severe aches, fever, or vomiting. <Italian *influenza* epidemic>

flub (flub) *Informal v* **flubbed, flub·bing** do clumsily or badly: *He flubbed his lines in the first scene.*
n a clumsy blunder or failure.

fluc·tu·ate (fluk′chū āt′) *v* **fluc·tu·at·ed, fluc·tu·at·ing** change or vary continually: *The temperature fluctuates from day to day.* <Latin *fluctus* wave, from *fluere* to flow> **fluc′tu·a′tion** *n.*

flue (flū) *n* a tube, pipe, or other enclosed passage for conveying smoke or hot air. <Middle English>

flu·ent (flū′ənt) *adj* **1** flowing smoothly or easily: *She speaks fluent French.* **2** speaking or writing easily and rapidly: *He is a fluent lecturer.* <Latin *fluere* flow> **flu′en·cy** *n.* **flu′ent·ly** *adv.*

fluff (fluf) *n* soft, light, fuzzy or downy fibres: *Woollen blankets often have fluff on them.*
v I fluffed the pillows when I made the bed. <perhaps Latin *vellus* fleece> **fluff′y** *adj.*

flu·id (flū′id) *n* a liquid or gas that has no fixed shape and responds to external pressure.
adj **1** in the state of a fluid: *He poured the fluid mass of hot candy into a dish to harden.* **2** to do with fluids: *fluid mechanics.* **3** changing easily and continuously: *Languages are fluid.* <Latin *fluere* flow> **flu·id′i·ty** *n.* **flu′id·ly** *adv.*

fluid ounce *n* a nonmetric unit of liquid volume, equal to about 28.4 mL.

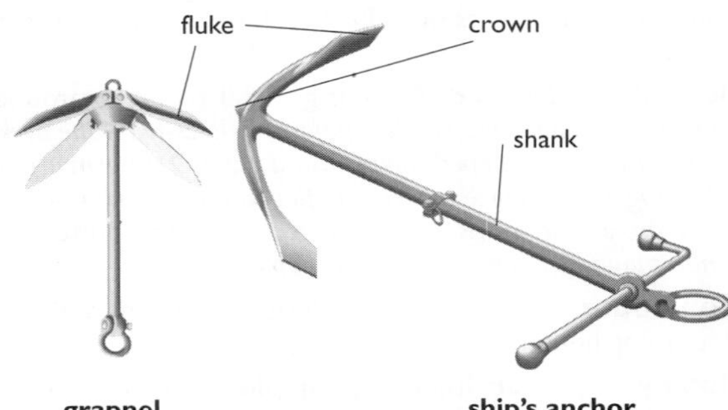

grapnel **ship's anchor**

fluke[1] (flūk) *n* **1** the pointed part of an anchor that catches in the ground. **2** either half of a whale's tail. <perhaps from *fluke*[3] because of the shape>

fluke[2] (flūk) *n* an unlikely chance occurrence, especially a fortunate one: *By some fluke, she managed to get there before us.* <origin uncertain>

fluke[3] (flūk) *n* **1** a flatfish. **2** a parasitic flatworm. <Old English *floc*>

flume (flūm) *n* **1** a deep, narrow valley with a stream running through it. **2** a large, sloped trough or chute for carrying water. <Old French, from Latin *fluere* flow>

flum·mox (flum′əks) *Informal v* bewilder or greatly perplex. <origin uncertain> **flum′moxed** *adj.*

flung (flung) past tense and past participle of FLING.

flunk (flungk) *Informal v* **1** fail in schoolwork: *He flunked his geography test.* **2** mark or grade as having failed: *The teacher flunked her.* <origin uncertain>
flunk out, *Informal* leave or be dismissed from school, college, or university because one is failing.

flunk·ey (flung′kē) *n* a low-ranking assistant, especially someone who tries to please and impress a boss. Also, **flunky**. <origin uncertain>

fluo·res·cent (flə res′ənt) *or* (flȯ res′ənt) *adj* **1** giving off light while exposed to radiation such as X-rays or ultraviolet rays. **2** to do with the light given off in this way. <*fluor(ite)* + *(phosphor)escent.* See FLUORINE.>
fluo·res′cence *n.*

fluorescent lamp *n* a type of electric lamp in which a low-pressure gas in a sealed glass tube is acted upon by an electric current.

fluor·i·date (flȯ′rə dāt′) *v* **fluor·i·dat·ed, fluor·i·dat·ing** add small amounts of a fluoride to a drinking water supply, especially to decrease tooth decay in children. **fluor′i·da′tion** *n.*

fluor·ide (flȯ′rīd) *n* a compound of fluorine and another element or radical.

fluor·ine (flȯ′rēn) *n* a poisonous, greenish yellow, gaseous element. *Symbol* **F** <*fluorite* the mineral in which fluorine is found>

fluor·o·car·bon (flọ′rō kär′bən) *n* a synthetic compound formed by replacing some of the hydrogen atoms in a hydrocarbon with fluorine atoms.

fluor·o·scope (flọ′rə skōp′) *n* a device containing a fluorescent screen for examining objects exposed to X-rays or other radiation.

flur·ry (flər′ē) *n, pl* **flur·ries** **1** a light fall of snow. **2** a sudden gust of wind: *A flurry upset the small sailboat.* **3** a sudden rush: *a flurry of activity.* <obsolete *flurr* to scatter>

flush[1] (flush) *v* **1** briefly empty a toilet with a downward rush of water, or be emptied in this way: *After using the toilet, flush it.* **2** cleanse or clear out with a rapid flow of water: *The streets were flushed every night. He flushed the debris from the eavestrough.* **3** blush or glow: *He flushed red when we mentioned her name. She was flushed from running.* **4** excite; make joyful and proud: *The team was flushed with its first victory.*
n **1** a blush or glow: *the first flush of dawn in the east.* **2** an act of flushing: *It took two flushes to clear the drain.* **3** glowing vigour or freshness: *the flush of youth.* **4** a period of feeling very hot. <Middle English *flusshen*>

flush[2] (flush) *adj* **1** exactly level: *The edge of the new shelf must be flush with the old one.* **2** well supplied: *She was always flush with money.* **3** plentiful: *Money is flush when times are good.*
adv **1** so as to be level. **2** directly or squarely: *The hammer landed flush on the nail.* <origin uncertain>

flush[3] (flush) *v* fly up or cause to fly up suddenly, as some birds do when startled: *The dog flushed a partridge in the woods.* <origin uncertain>

flush[4] (flush) *n* in some card games, a hand all of one suit. <Old French, from Latin *fluxus* flow>

flus·ter (flus′tər) *v* (*in the passive*) confuse through nervousness or excitement: *I was flustered at your sudden appearance, and forgot what to say.*
n confusion due to nervousness or excitement. <Old Norse> **flus′tered** *adj.*

flute (flūt) *n* a long, slender musical instrument, played by blowing across a hole near one end.
v **flut·ed, flut·ing** **1** sing or whistle so as to sound like a flute. **2** make long, round grooves in. <Old French *fleute*> **flut′ist** *n.*

flut·ed (flū′tid) *adj* with long, rounded grooves: *fluted pillars.* **flut′ing** *n.*

flut·ter (flut′ər) *v* **1** wave back and forth quickly and lightly: *The flag fluttered in the breeze.* **2** fly, run, or fall with quick movements of the wings: *The chickens fluttered excitedly when they saw the dog. The young birds fluttered to the ground.* **3** tremble or beat quickly, feebly, or unevenly: *Her pulse fluttered.*
n **1** the act of fluttering. **2** a confused or excited condition: *The appearance of the Queen caused a great flutter in the crowd.* <Old English *flotoriant*>

flutter kick *n* a swimming movement in which the legs are held rigid and alternately make small, rapid, up-and-down movements. In training, the arms may hold a floating **flutter board**, while the legs do all the work.

flu·vi·al (flū′vē əl) *adj* to do with a river: *A delta is a fluvial deposit.* <Latin *fluvius* river, from *fluere* flow>

flux (fluks) *n* **1** the act or rate of flowing. **2** a state of continuous change: *Atomic science is in a state of flux.* **3** an unnatural discharge of blood or other fluid from the body. **4** a substance used to help metals or minerals melt together.
v melt together; heat with a substance of this kind. <Latin *fluere* to flow>

fly[1] (flī) *n, pl* **flies** **1** a housefly. **2** an insect that has two wings. Mosquitoes are flies. **3** a flying insect, such as a butterfly. **4** a fish-hook with feathers or other materials on it to make it look like an insect: *Some fishermen make their own flies.* See FISH-HOOK for picture. <Old English *fleogan* to fly[2]>
fly in the ointment, *Informal* a small problem that spoils a situation.
no flies on ——, *Slang* the person named is mentally quick and alert.

fly[2] (flī) *v* **flew, flown, fly·ing** (defs. 1–6); **flied, fly·ing** (def. 7) **1** move through the air, especially with wings: *Birds fly.* **2** float or wave in the air, or cause to do so: *to fly a kite. The Canadian flag flies every day on Parliament Hill.* **3 a** travel or carry through the air in an aircraft: *We're flying from Edmonton to Whitehorse. He flew us to James Bay in his little Cessna.* **b** control or pilot an airplane or airship in the air. **c** use a particular airline: *They often fly Air North.* **4** move swiftly: *Clouds fly before the wind.* **5** *Informal* of new ideas or inventions, be successful: *I doubt that idea will fly.* **6** *Poetic* run away from: *Fly, you fools!* **7** *Baseball* hit the ball high into the air: *The batter flied into left field.*
n, pl **flies** **1** in full, **fly ball** *Baseball* a ball hit high into the air: *She enjoys catching flies.* **2** a piece of fabric that serves as an extra outer flap or roof for a tent. **3** an opening in a garment to aid in putting it on, especially in the front of pants. <Old English *fleogan*>
fly at, attack violently.
fly in the face of, disobey or contradict openly.
fly out, *Baseball* be put out when the ball you hit is caught by a fielder.
let fly, a aim or shoot: *The hunter let fly an arrow.* **b** say violently.
on the fly, hastily, while going somewhere: *He had to have lunch on the fly.*

fly·a·way (flī′a′wā) *adj* of hair, so fine and dry that it floats up at the ends.

fly·blown (flī′blōn′) *adj* **1** dirty or contaminated, especially by the eggs or larvae of flies. **2** covered with flyspecks.

fly–by–night (flī′bī nīt′) *adj* not reliable, especially in business: *Don't buy from a fly-by-night computer store.*
n *Informal* an unreliable or irresponsible person, especially one who avoids paying debts.

fly·catch·er (flī′kach′ər) *n* a bird that feeds on flying insects.

fly·er or **fli·er** (flī′ər) *n* **1** a sheet of paper with advertising on it. **2** a person who flies something, especially an aircraft pilot. **3** a person who or thing that flies.

a bat	e bed	i bid	o pot	u cup	th thin
ā cake	ē me	ī bite	ō go	ū rude	TH then
ä bar	ə about	ər over	ȯ for	u̇ put	zh measure

F

fly–fish·ing (flī′fish′ing) *n* fishing with artificial flies as bait. **fly′-fish′er** *n.*

fly·ing (flī′ing) *adj* **1** moving through the air or floating or waving in the air. **2** short and quick: *Our aunt paid us a flying visit last week.* **3** wavy in the letters on cattle brands: *Any steer with a flying H belongs to the Hendersons' ranch.* **with flying colours,** triumphantly: *to pass an exam with flying colours.*

flying buttress *n* an arched support or brace built out from the wall of a building to bear some of the weight of the roof.

flying fish *n* a fish mainly of tropical seas that has winglike pectoral fins that help them glide for some distance through the air after leaping from the water.

flying fox *n* a large fruit-eating bat native to tropical Africa, Asia, and Australia, with a face like that of a fox.

flying jib *n* on a sailboat, a small triangular sail set in front of the regular jib.

flying saucer *n* a disclike object that some people claim to have seen, and which is supposed to be a spacecraft used by extraterrestrials.

flying squirrel *n* a squirrel that can make long, gliding leaps through the air.

✱ **flying wing** *Football n* a player whose position is variable behind the line of scrimmage.

fly·leaf (flī′lēf′) *n, pl* **fly·leaves** a blank sheet of paper at the beginning or end of a book or pamphlet.

fly·pa·per (flī′pā′pər) *n* a sticky strip of paper, usually hung from the ceiling to catch flies.

fly·past (flī′past′) *n* a display in which aircraft in formation fly over a reviewing stand located on the ground: *We were thrilled by the flypast at the air show.*

fly·speck (flī′spek′) *n* a piece of fly dung that flies leave as a dark spot on a surface.

fly swatter *n* a device for killing flies, usually consisting of a long handle with a flexible piece of mesh attached to the end.

fly·trap (flī′trap′) *n* **1** a plant that traps insects. **2** a trap to catch flies.

fly·way (flī′wā′) *n* an established route followed by migrating birds.

fly·weight (flī′wāt′) *n* a boxer who weighs between 49 and 51 kilograms.

fly·wheel (flī′wēl′) *n* a heavy wheel attached to machinery to keep the speed even.

FM or **F.M.** frequency modulation.

foal (fōl) *n* a horse, pony, or donkey under one year old. *v* give birth to a foal. <Old English *fola*>

foam (fōm) *n* **1** a mass of very small bubbles. **2** a spongy, flexible material made from plastic or rubber.
v form or cause to form foam: *The stream foams over the rocks.* <Old English *fam*> **foam′y** *adj.*
foam at the mouth, *Informal* be enraged or go into a frenzy.

foam rubber *n* a firm, spongy foam of natural or synthetic rubber, used for mattresses and upholstery.

fob[1] (fob) *n* **1** a small pocket in pants or in a vest, for a watch, etc. **2** a short watch chain, or ribbon that hangs out of a watch pocket, or an ornament on the end of it. <origin uncertain>

fob[2] (fob) *v* **fobbed, fob·bing** (*with off*) **1** put off or deceive by a trick: *He was asking too many questions, so we fobbed him off with a story about being late for class.* **2** get rid of by a trick: *Don't try to fob that piece of junk off on me.* <Middle English>

fo·cal (fō′kəl) *adj* to do with a focus.

focal length *n* a FOCUS (def. 3b).

focal point *n* a FOCUS (defs. 2, 3a).

fo'c'sle (fōk′səl) *Nautical n* **1** the upper deck in front of the foremast of a ship or boat. **2** the forward part of a ship below the deck, traditionally housing the ship's crew. Also, **forecastle**.

GRAMMAR AND USAGE

Fo'c'sle is an example of the language of sailors where sounds are dropped in quick speech. *Forecastle* is thus reduced to *fo'c'sle*. Similarly, *gunwale* is pronounced *gunnel.*

fo·cus (fō′kəs) *n, pl* **fo·cus·es** or **fo·ci** (fō′sī) **1** the correct adjustment of a lens or the eye to make a clear image: *You must have been holding the camera too close, because this picture is out of focus.* **2** the central point of attention or activity: *The focus of this presentation will be developing good study habits.* **3 a** a point where rays of light or heat meet, appear to meet, or should meet after being bent by a lens or curved mirror. **b** the distance of this point from the lens or curved mirror: *A near-sighted eye has a shorter focus than a normal eye.*
v **fo·cus·es** or **fo·cus·ses, fo·cused** or **fo·cussed, fo·cus·ing** or **fo·cus·sing** **1** make an image clear by adjusting a lens, the eye, etc.: *I'm near-sighted, so I don't focus well on distant objects.* **2** concentrate on: *to focus your attention on something. Let's focus on the task at hand.* **3** bring or arrive together at one point in a ray of light or heat: *The lens focused the sun's rays on a piece of paper so that they burned a hole in it.* <Latin *focus* fireplace, originally referred to the burning point of a lens or mirror>

fod·der (fod′ər) *n* **1** coarse food for livestock, such as dried hay or straw. **2** fuel or material for anything: *fodder for debate, fodder for news stories.* <Old English *foda* food>

foe (fō) *Poetic n* an enemy. <Old English *fah* hostile>

foehn (fān) *n* a hot, dry wind that blows in the lee of a mountain range, especially on the northern slopes of the Alps. <German, from Latin *Favonius* the west wind>

foe·tus (fē′təs) FETUS.

fog (fog) *n* **1** a cloud of fine droplets of water that forms just above the earth's surface. **2** a film of fine water droplets that forms on a surface as it condenses from the air: *When he entered the warm house, his glasses quickly covered with fog.* **3** a blurriness or dimness in an image: *What's responsible for this fog in the middle of the photo?* **4** a confused or bewildered condition: *His mind was in a fog for most of the exam.*
v **fogged, fog·ging 1** cover or fill with fog. **2** dim or blur: *Something fogged six of our photographs.* **3** confuse or bewilder. <origin uncertain> **fog′gy** *adj.*

fog bank *n* a dense mass of fog.

fog·bound (fog′bound′) *adj* unable to travel because of fog.

fo·gey (fō′gē) *n* a person who is considered to be old-fashioned or conservative. Also, **fogy**. <origin uncertain>

fog·horn (fog′hôrn′) *n* a loud horn or siren used in foggy weather to warn ships of danger.

foi·ble (foi′bəl) *n* a minor weakness in character: *Talking too much is one of her foibles.* <Old French *fieble*>

foil[1] (foil) *v* prevent from carrying out a plan or succeeding: *The heroine foiled the villain.* <Old French *fouler* trample, i.e., mislead by walking over someone's trail, from Latin *fullo* cloth cleaner. In ancient Rome, cloth was cleaned by trampling it in a cleaning liquid.>

foil[2] (foil) *n* **1** metal beaten, hammered, or rolled into a very thin sheet: *gold foil, aluminum foil.* **2** a person who or thing that complements or enhances another by contrast: *The dark green dress was a foil for her red hair.* <Old French, from Latin *folium* leaf>

foil[3] (foil) *n* **1** a long, narrow sword with a knob or button on the point to prevent injury, used in fencing. **2 foils** *pl* the sport of fencing. See FENCE for picture. <origin uncertain>

foist (foist) *v* **1** force someone to accept something that is unwanted: *Mom's always foisting my sister's old clothes on me.* **2** do this secretly or dishonestly: *The author discovered that the translator had foisted several passages of his own into her book.* <Dutch *vuisten* enclose in the hand, from the practice of hiding a false die in the palm of the hand in order to cheat at dice>

fold[1] (fōld) *v* **1** bend or double over on itself: *She folded the paper, tore it in two, and gave me half.* **2** bring together with the parts in or around one another: *She folded the camp stool and packed it in the trunk.* **3** put one over the other: *He folded his arms across his chest.* **4** hold closely and tenderly: *She folded her child to her breast.* **5** wrap: *Fold the pills in a piece of blue paper.* **6** close up permanently because of failure: *The restaurant folded after only three months.* **7** break down or collapse from physical or mental strain: *The overworked student finally folded from the pressure.*
n **1** a form or shape, such as a groove or line, made by folding. **2** a layer of something folded: *a fold of cloth.* **3** *Geology* a bend in a layer of rock. <Old English *fealdan*>
fold in, in cooking, mix ingredients gently, by turning one part of the mixture over another with a spoon: *Fold in the beaten egg whites.*
fold up, a make or become smaller by folding. **b** close a business, or have a business fail.

fold[2] (fōld) *n* **1** an enclosure to keep sheep in. **2** the sheep kept in it. **3** a close-knit community, especially a religious group, that shares aims and values.
v put or keep sheep in a pen. <Old English *falod*>
return to the fold, return to active membership in a close-knit community.

–fold *suffix* **1** in an amount multiplied by: *He planted one bushel of potatoes and harvested tenfold.* **2** consisting of a specified number of parts: *My reason for refusing is twofold: no time and no money.* <Old English *-feald*>

fold·er (fōl′dər) *n* **1** a holder for papers, consisting of a folded piece of cardboard. **2** a person who or thing that folds. **3** *Computers* a collection of files, traditionally shown on screen as a small file folder.

folding door *n* a door made of parts hinged to one another so that it opens and closes by folding and unfolding.

fold·out (fōld′out′) *n* an extra-wide page inserted into a magazine or book, such as for a picture or map, which the reader unfolds to look at.
adj to do with such a page.

fo·li·age (fō′lē ij) *n* the leaves of a plant, especially of a tree. <French, from Latin *folia* leaves>

fo·li·a·tion (fō′lē ā′shən) *n* the act of putting forth leaves: *foliation of trees in the spring.*

fo·lic acid (fō′lik) *n* a crystalline compound of the vitamin B complex, found in green leaves, mushrooms, and some animal tissue. <Latin *folium* leaf>

fo·li·o (fō′lē ō′) *Printing n* **1** a large sheet of paper folded once to make two leaves, i.e., four pages, of a book. **2** a book formed from such sheets of paper. **3** a page number of a printed book. <Latin *folium* leaf>

folk (fōk) *pl n* **1** people as a group: *Most city folk know very little about farming.* **2 folks** *Informal* **a** people: *Well, folks, I guess we should get started.* **b** the members of one's own family, especially one's parents: *How are your folks?*
adj **1** to do with the common people of a region or country and their shared beliefs, legends, and customs, handed down through generations: *folk tales, folk tunes.* **2** to do with FOLK MUSIC: *a folk festival.* <Old English *folc*>

folk dance *n* a dance originating among and shared by the common people of a region or country, or the music for such a dance.

a bat	e bed	i bid	o pot	u cup	th thin
ā cake	ē me	ī bite	ō go	ū rude	TH then
ä bar	ə about	ər over	ô for	ů put	zh measure

folk etymology *n* a popular misunderstanding about the origin of a word, sometimes resulting in a change to its sound or spelling.

folk hero *n* a popular hero, often fictitious or legendary: *Terry Fox and Anne of Green Gables are both folk heroes.*

folk·lore (fōk′lôr′) *n* the beliefs, legends, or customs of a people. **folk′lor′ic** *adj.* **folk′lor′ist** *n.*

folk medicine *n* popular remedies, often herbal, passed down through generations.

folk music *n* **1** music originating among and shared by the people of a region or country. **2** a style of modern popular music that resembles traditional folk music.

folk song *n* a piece of FOLK MUSIC with lyrics.

folk·sy (fōk′sē) *Informal adj* **folk·si·er, folk·si·est** friendly, plain, and unpretentious: *just a nice, folksy evening.*

folk tale *n* a story or legend usually originating among the people of a region or country.

folk·way (fōk′wā′) *n* a custom or tradition that has developed in a certain cultural group.

fol·li·cle (fol′ə kəl) *Biology n* a small cavity, sac, or gland that secretes a substance. <Latin *follis* = leather bag for inflating>

fol·low (fol′ō) *v* **1** go or happen after in time or space: *Night follows day. She took a few steps and waited for us to follow.* **2** result from: *Misery follows war. If you eat too much, a stomachache may follow.* **3** travel along a certain route: *Follow this road to the corner.* **4** act according to: *Follow good advice.* **5** believe in and order one's life on the principles of: *to follow Islam.* **6** keep the eyes or attention on: *It's hard to follow the ball in a fast game of table tennis.* **7** keep up with and understand: *He was able to follow the conversation in French.* **8** keep informed about: *Do you follow current events?* **9** take as one's work or profession: *She expects to follow medicine.* <Old English *folgian*>
fol′low·er *n.*
as follows, a the following: *The duties of the various officers are as follows.* **b** in the following way: *Assemble the wheelbarrow as follows.*
follow suit, a in some card games, play a card of the same suit as that first played. **b** follow someone's example.
follow through, a continue a stroke or motion: *Most golfers follow through after hitting the ball.* **b** carry out fully: *When you begin a job, you should try to follow it through.*
follow up, complete or increase the effect of by further action: *He followed up his first request by asking again a week later.*

fol·low·ing (fol′ō ing) *adj* coming after or as a result of: *on the following day.*
n **1** a group of followers or attendants: *The charismatic leader attracted a large following.* **2 the following** the people or things about to be named or described: *Please read the following carefully. Do the following questions: 2, 3, 7, 9, and 12.*

fol·low–through (fol′ō thrū′) *n* **1** *Sports* the smooth completion of a swing or stroke after the moment of contact with the ball. **2** the logical continuation and completion of any action.

fol·low–up (fol′ō up′) *n* an action or thing intended to reinforce an original effort.
adj done for this purpose: *a follow-up call.*

fol·ly (fol′ē) *n, pl* **fol·lies** **1** foolishness or unwise behaviour. **2** a foolish act, practice, or idea. <Old French *fol* fool>

fo·ment (fō ment′) *v* promote or foster trouble, rebellion, or discontent. <Latin *fovere* to encourage>
fo′men·ta′tion *n.* **fo·ment′er** *n.*

fond (fond) *adj* **1** showing or feeling much affection: *a fond look.* **2** loving foolishly or too much: *Her fond father let her get away with anything.* **3** *Archaic* foolishly optimistic: *fond hopes.* <Middle English> **fond′ly** *adv.* **fond′ness** *n.*

fon·dant (fon′dənt) *n* a creamy, fudgelike candy usually used as a filling or coating for other candies. <French = melting>

fon·dle (fon′dəl) *v* **fon·dled, fon·dling** **1** caress lovingly: *Most people like to fondle puppies.* **2** touch or caress someone in an aggressive or unwelcome way; sexually molest. <obsolete *fonding* much-loved person>
fon′dler *n.*

fon·due (fon dū′) *n* **1** a dish made by dipping small pieces of bread into melted cheese, or fruit into melted chocolate. **2** a dish made by dipping small pieces of meat or vegetables into hot oil or broth. <French *fondre* melt>

font[1] (font) *n* **1** an abundant source: *He is a font of wisdom.* Also, **fount.** **2** a container holding holy water or water for baptism. <Latin *fontis* fountain>

font[2] (font) *Printing, Computers n* **1** a complete set of type or characters of one size and style. Compare TYPEFACE. **2** the file containing this set of characters, accessed or used by a computer application: *The fonts you'll need are on this disk.* <French *fonte,* from *fondre* melt. Type used to be made by melting metal and pouring into shapes.>

food (fūd) *n* **1** what an animal or plant takes in to enable it to live and grow. **2** things that one eats, as opposed to liquids that one drinks: *Give him food and drink.* **3** a particular kind or item of food or a dish prepared a certain way: *What is your favourite food?* **4** anything that serves as fuel or material for some activity: *This magazine article is food for thought.* <Old English *foda*>

food bank *n* an organization that collects donated food, to be given free or at low cost to the unemployed, homeless, or those with low incomes.

food chain *n* a set of organisms and substances, thought of as a linked series with each one using the next as food: *Foxes, mice, cereals, and minerals form a food chain.* Also called **food pyramid.** See DECOMPOSER for picture.

food court *n* a large space in an indoor mall, with tables in the centre for eating at, and fast-food counters along each side.

food group *n* one of several categories into which similar foods are grouped according to their nutritional value. Traditionally, the four basic food groups are: meat; dairy; vegetables; grain.

food poisoning *n* sickness from eating contaminated food, usually characterized by vomiting or diarrhea.

food processor *n* a small electric kitchen appliance for slicing, grating, chopping, mixing, and blending food.

food pyramid *n* **1** FOOD CHAIN. **2** *especially US* in full, **food guide pyramid** recommendations as to how much of various food groups one should eat each day.

food·stuff (fūd′stuf′) *Commercial n* any material used for food: *Milk, vegetables, and meat are foodstuffs.*

food web *n* the interdependent feeding patterns of a community of living things.

foo·fa·raw (fū′fə ro′) *n* **1** fuss, uproar, or disturbance. **2** unnecessary frills or any other ornamental trim. <origin uncertain>

fool (fūl) *n* **1** an unwise or silly person. **2** in former times, a clown employed by a king or lord to amuse people. **3** a person who has been deceived or tricked.
v **1** tease by saying things without meaning them: *Don't believe her, she's fooling.* **2** deceive or trick: *He tried to fool me by disguising his voice.* <Old French *fol* madman, from Latin *follis* empty-headed>
be nobody's fool, be clever and sharp-witted.
fool around, *Informal* **a** behave in a playful or silly way. **b** engage in casual sexual activity.
fool away, *Informal* waste foolishly: *to fool away the day.*
fool with, *Informal* meddle with: *Don't fool with my day.*
play the fool, clown around; act silly.

fool·er·y (fū′lə rē) *n, pl* **fool·er·ies** foolish behaviour.

fool·har·dy (fūl′hȧr′dē) *adj* **fool·har·di·er, fool·har·di·est** foolishly bold or impulsive. **fool′har′di·ness** *n.*

fool·ish (fū′lish) *adj* ridiculous, silly, or unwise. **fool′ish·ly** *adv.* **fool′ish·ness** *n.*

SYNONYMS

Foolish can mean "unwise": *He was foolish to try the advanced slope when he had never skied before.*

Inane means "senseless": *It is inane to try to travel around a strange city without a map.*

Witless suggests a great lack of intelligence: *You would have to be witless to stand in an open field in a lightning storm.*

fool·proof (fūl′prūf′) *adj* so safe or simple that anyone can use or do it: *a foolproof piece of software, a foolproof plan.*

fools·cap (fūl′skap′) *n* lined writing paper in long sheets. <originally, this type of paper had a watermark that showed a jester's cap>

fool's gold *n* a mineral that looks like gold, such as iron pyrites or copper pyrites.

foot (fůt) *n, pl* **feet 1** the end part of a leg that a person, animal, or thing stands on. **2** the end of a bed where the feet are placed. **3** the end of a table opposite the person in the seat of honour at the top of the table. **4** the lowest part, bottom, or base: *the foot of a hill, the foot of a page.* **5** the part that covers the foot: *a hole in the foot of my tights.* **6** a nonmetric unit of length equal to about 30.5 cm. There are 12 inches in a foot. *Symbol* **′ 7** a unit in a line of poetry that is made up of a combination of syllables. <Old English *fot*>
foot the bill, accept responsibility for paying.
have a (or **your**) **foot in the door,** have a good chance of success.
my foot! *Informal* I don't believe that!
on foot, walking.
put your best foot forward, do your best; try hard to make a good impression.
put your foot down, make up your mind and act firmly.
put your foot in it, *Informal* get into trouble by saying or doing an inappropriate thing.
set foot in (or **on**), (*usually in the negative*) enter: *I've never set foot in her house.*
(**with**) **one foot in the grave,** near death.

foot·age (fůt′ij) *n* movie film, whether shot, processed, or shown: *We shot some good footage today. The local newscast included some footage of our canned food drive.*

foot–and–mouth disease (fůt′ən mouth′) *n* a dangerous contagious disease of cattle and some other animals, causing blisters in the mouth and around the hoofs.

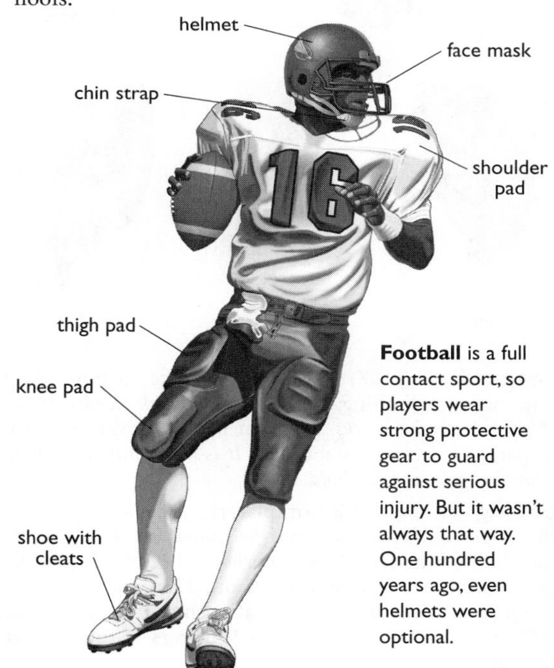

Football is a full contact sport, so players wear strong protective gear to guard against serious injury. But it wasn't always that way. One hundred years ago, even helmets were optional.

foot·ball (fůt′bol′) *n* **1** chiefly in N America, a game in which an inflated ball of roughly oval shape is kicked, passed, or carried toward a goal. Opponents try to stop the ball carrier by tackling him or her. **2** in the UK and many other countries, soccer. **3** the ball used in either game.

a bat	e bed	i bid	o pot	u cup	th thin
ā cake	ē me	ī bite	ō go	ū rude	ᴛʜ then
ȧ bar	ə about	ər over	ȯ for	ů put	zh measure

foot·board (fu̇t′bȯrd′) *n* **1** an upright piece across the foot of a bed. **2** a board or small platform to be used as a support for the feet.

foot·bridge (fu̇t′brij′) *n* a bridge for pedestrians only.

foot·er (fu̇t′ər′) *n* a line of text such as a title or date, especially one that is automatically inserted by word-processing software, appearing at the foot of each page of a document, book, etc. Compare HEADER (def. 1).

foot·fall (fu̇t′fol′) *n* the sound of a footstep.

foot·hill (fu̇t′hil′) *n* a low hill at the base of a mountain or mountain range: *a ranch in the foothills of the Rockies.*

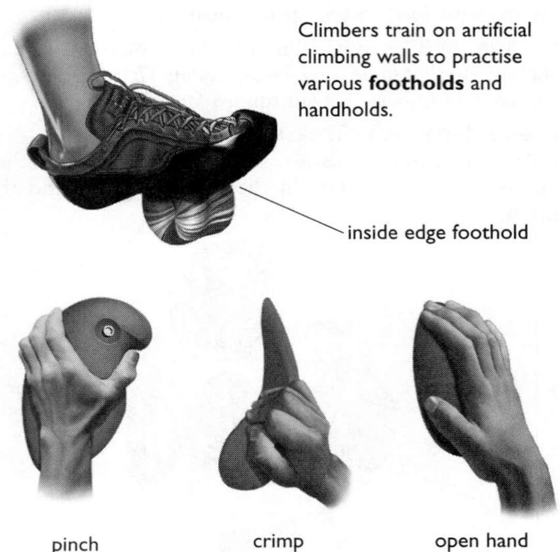

Climbers train on artificial climbing walls to practise various **footholds** and handholds.

foot·hold (fu̇t′hōld′) *n* **1** a secure place to put a foot, especially in climbing: *She climbed the rock face by finding footholds in the cracks.* **2** a firm position from which to expand or become established: *It is hard to break a habit that has gained a foothold.*

foot·ing (fu̇t′ing) *n* **1** a firm placement or position of the feet: *He lost his footing and fell down on the ice.* **2** the position of the feet: *When he changed his footing, he lost his balance.* **3** a surface to stand on: *The steep cliff gave us no footing.* **4** the basis of a relationship: *Canada and the US are on a friendly footing.* **5** **footings** *pl* the concrete foundations of a building or wall.

foot·lets (fu̇t′lits) *pln* very short socks sometimes worn by women or girls.

foot·lights (fu̇t′līts′) *pln* **1** a row of lights at the front of a stage. **2** the profession of acting.

foot·lock·er (fu̇t′lok′ər) *n* a small chest in which personal belongings are kept, designed to stand at the foot of a bed.

foot·loose (fu̇t′lūs′) *adj* free to go anywhere or do anything.

foot·man (fu̇t′mən) *n, pl* **foot·men** (fu̇t′mən) a uniformed male servant who admits visitors and serves meals.

foot·note (fu̇t′nōt′) *n* **1** a note at the bottom of a page about text above it, usually giving the source of a quotation. **2** a minor comment or event connected with something bigger and more important: *In a footnote to his speech, he mentioned that he had once visited Vancouver.*

foot·path (fu̇t′path′) *n* a path for pedestrians.

foot·print (fu̇t′print′) *n* a mark made by a foot: *The children left footprints in the snow.*

foot·rest (fu̇t′rest′) *n* a support on which to rest the feet.

foot·sie (fu̇t′sē) *Informal n* (*especially a child's term*) foot.
play footsie, *Informal* **a** touch feet or knees in a flirtatious way while seated. **b** toy or flirt with: *Don't play footsie with someone's emotions.*

foot soldier *n* a soldier who fights on foot.

foot·sore (fu̇t′sȯr′) *adj* with sore feet from much walking.

foot·step (fu̇t′step′) *n* **1** a person's step, or the distance covered by it. **2** the sound of someone taking a step. **3** the mark left by this. **4** a step on which to go up or down.
follow in someone's footsteps, do as another has done.

foot·stool (fu̇t′stūl′) *n* a low stool on which to rest the feet when sitting.

foot·wear (fu̇t′wer′) *n* outer covering for the feet, such as shoes and boots.

foot·work (fu̇t′wərk′) *n* **1** the way of using the feet, as in boxing or dancing. **2** skilful manoeuvring: *It took some fancy footwork to avoid answering the question.*

fop (fop) *n* a vain man who is fond of fine clothes and has fancy manners. <Middle English *foppe*> **fop′per·y** *n.* **fop′pish** *adj.*

for (fȯr) *prep* **1** to be given to or used by: *I made this for you.* **2** in the support, favour, or interest of: *She voted for Laurier. A lawyer acts for his or her client.* **3** in payment or consideration of: *These apples are two for a dollar. We thanked him for his kindness.* **4** with the purpose of taking, finding, getting, or keeping: *to go for a walk, to run for your life. He had an interview for the job.* **5** in order to go to: *She has just left for school.* **6** meant to be used with: *a shelf for books.* **7** because of: *shout for joy. He was punished for lying.* **8** in honour of: *A party was given for her.* **9** with respect or regard to: *Eating too much is bad for your health.* **10** as far or as long as: *He worked for an hour.* **11** as: *We used boxes for chairs.* **12** in proportion to: *For every poisonous snake, there are many harmless ones.* **13** in the amount of: *His sister gave him a cheque for $100.* **14** considering what is typical of: *It is warm for March.* **15** scheduled at or on: *an appointment for two o'clock.*
conj Poetic because: *Make haste, for the hour is near.* <Old English>
oh for, *Poetic or Humorous* I wish that I could have: *Oh for the wings of a bird right now!*

for·age (fȯ′rij) *n* **1** food for horses or cattle. **2** a hunt or search for something, especially food: *We went on a forage for supplies.* **3** food found by searching for it.
v **for·aged, for·ag·ing 1** hunt or search, especially for food: *We foraged in the kitchen till we found some cookies. He made a living foraging for scrap metal.* **2** get by hunting or searching: *The campers foraged some dry wood for the fire.* <Old French *fourrage*> **for′ag·er** *n.*

for·ay (fô′rā) *n* an excursion for the purpose of raiding and plundering.
v make a foray: *to foray into enemy territory.* <Old French *forrer* to forage>

for·bade (fər bad′) *or* (fər bād′) past tense of FORBID. Also, **forbad.**

for·bear (fər ber′) *v* **for·bore, for·borne, for·bear·ing** **1** keep from doing or saying: *He forbore to hit back because the other boy was smaller.* **2** be patient and control oneself. <Old English *forberan*> **for·bear′ance** *n.* **for·bear′ing·ly** *adv.*

for·bid (fər bid′) *v* **for·bade** or **for·bad, for·bid·den, for·bid·ding** **1** order someone not to do something: *She forbade us to leave.* **2** make or be a rule against: *to forbid smoking on school premises.* **3** keep from happening: *God forbid that you should get hurt! High prices forbid us from going to the best concerts.* **4** command to keep away from something: *I'm forbidden chocolate because I'm allergic to it.* <Old English *forbeodan*>

for·bid·ding (fər bid′ing) *adj* inspiring fear or discouragement: *The coast was rocky and forbidding. The castle was surrounded by huge, forbidding walls.* **for·bid′ding·ly** *adv.*

for·bore (fər bôr′) past tense of FORBEAR.

for·borne (fər bôrn′) past participle of FORBEAR.

force (fôrs) *n* **1** strength or power. **2** strength used against a person or thing: *The rebels captured the village by force.* **3** a quality that has the power to impress, persuade, or evoke a feeling: *She writes with force.* **4** *Physics* a cause that produces, changes, or stops the motion of a body: *the force of gravity.* **5** an agency, influence, or source of power: *social forces at work.* **6** a group of people working or acting together: *our sales force, members of the police force.* **7** **the forces** *pl* the armed forces. **8** total meaning: *No two synonyms have quite the same force.*
v **forced, forc·ing** **1** make someone do something against his or her will: *Give it to me at once, or I will force you to.* **2** get, take, or put by force: *He forced the toy out of the dog's mouth. She forced the lid shut.* **3** break open or through by force: *to force a locked door.* **4** produce by great effort in spite of one's feelings: *The tearful boy forced a polite smile.* **5** make someone listen, obey, or accept: *You can't force your opinion on me.* **6** hurry the growth of by artificial means: *The rhubarb was forced by growing it in a dark, warm place.* **7** *Baseball* create a run by walking a batter when the bases are full. <French, from Latin *fortis* strong> **force′ful** *adj.* **force′ful·ly** *adv.* **force′ful·ness** *n.*
in force, a in effect or operation: *The old rules are still in force.* **b** with full strength: *The enemy attacked us in force.*

SYNONYMS

Force is a neutral word that does not indicate the degree of strength or power used: *He could not exert much force in his weakened condition.*

Vigour suggests energetic action: *She showed her vigour through the great amount of work she finished.*

force–feed (fôrs′fēd′) *v* **force-fed, force-feed·ing** **1** feed by forcible means, such as by passing a tube through the mouth into the stomach, or holding the mouth open and putting food in: *They used to force-feed geese to fatten them.* **2** force someone to accept: *Don't try to force-feed me your beliefs.*

for·ceps (fôr′seps) *n, pl* **for·ceps** a pair of small pincers or tongs used by surgeons or dentists for seizing, holding, and pulling. <Latin>

for·ci·ble (fôr′sə bəl) *adj* **1** made or done by force: *The burglars were charged with forcible entry.* **2** effective or powerful: *forcible words, forcible arguments.* **for′ci·bly** *adv.*

CONFUSABLES

Forcible applies to what is done by force or violence: *The forcible removal of the protestors was covered in the news.*

Forceful refers to being effective by means of force: *The forceful speech moved the students to action.*

ford (fôrd) *n* a place where a river or stream is shallow enough to cross by going through the water.
v cross in this way: *They were looking for a place to ford the river.* <Old English> **ford′a·ble** *adj.*

fore (fôr) *adj, adv* (*adjective usually in compounds*) at or toward the front: *a dog's forelegs* (*adj*). *There is lots of stowage fore-and-aft in this boat* (*adv*).
n the forward part, especially of a ship or boat.
interj Golf a shout of warning to people ahead who are liable to be struck by the ball. <Old English>
to the fore, into a conspicuous place or position.

fore– *prefix* **1** to do with the front: *foremost.* **2** before; beforehand: *foresee.* <Old English *fore* before>

fore–and–aft (fôr′ən aft′) *adj, adv* lengthwise on a ship, taking in the front or rear: *a ship rigged fore-and-aft.*

fore·arm[1] (fô′rärm′) *n* the part of the arm between the elbow and wrist.

fore·arm[2] (fô rärm′) *v* prepare for trouble ahead of time.

fore·bear (fôr′ber′) *n* an ancestor: *He is proud of his pioneer forebears.* <*fore-* + *be* + *-er*[1]>

fore·bode (fôr bōd′) *v* **fore·bod·ed, fore·bod·ing** give or be a warning of: *Black clouds forebode a storm.*

fore·bod·ing (fôr bō′ding) *n* **1** a warning of something bad or unpleasant in the future: *A strange silence lay about the house, full of foreboding.* **2** a feeling that something bad is going to happen: *She had a foreboding that her son would not return.*

fore·brain (fôr′brān′) *n* the front section of the brain, where the cerebrum is. See BRAIN for picture.

fore·cast (fôr′kast′) *v* **fore·cast** or **fore·cast·ed, fore·cast·ing** **1** predict, especially the weather: *Rain is forecast for tomorrow.* **2** be a sign of something that will happen: *They say a large berry crop forecasts a hard winter.*
n a prediction. **fore′cast′er** *n.*

a bat	e bed	i bid	o pot	u cup	th thin
ā cake	ē me	ī bite	ō go	ū rude	ᴛʜ then
ä bar	ə about	ər over	ô for	ů put	zh measure

fore·cas·tle (fōk′səl) *or* (fôr′kas′əl) FO'C'SLE.

fore·check (fôr′chek) *Hockey v* play aggressive defence, checking opposing players before they can form an attack. **fore′check·er** *n.* **fore′check·ing** *n.*

fore·close (fôr klōz′) *v* **fore·closed, fore·clos·ing** seize a mortgaged property because mortgage payments have not been made. <Old French *forclore* exclude, from Latin *foris* out + *clore* to shut> **fore·clo′sure** *n.*

fore·fa·ther (fôr′foтн′ər) *n* a male ancestor.

fore·fing·er (fôr′fing′gər) *n* the finger next to the thumb.

fore·front (fôr′frunt′) *n* the place of greatest importance or activity.

fore·go (fôr gō′) FORGO.

fore·go·ing (fôr′gō′ing) *adj* preceding or previous: *The experiment is described in the foregoing pages.*
n **the foregoing** the preceding text or comments.

fore·gone conclusion (fôr′gon′) *n* a fact or result that was expected: *It was a foregone conclusion that she would ace the exam.*

fore·ground (fôr′ground′) *n* **1** the part of a picture or scene nearest the viewer. **2** the centre of attention by being prominent.
v place in the foreground.

fore·hand (fôr′hand′) *adj, adv* with the palm of the hand turned forward: *a forehand stroke* (*adj*). *She returned my serve forehand* (*adv*).
n a stroke made with the palm of the hand turned forward.

fore·hand·ed (fôr′han′did) *adj* **1** providing for the future. **2** using a forehand stroke.

fore·head (fôr′hed′) *or* (fô′rid) *n* the part of the face above the eyebrows. <Old English *forheafod*>

for·eign (fô′rən) *adj* **1** outside one's own country: *foreign currency. She has travelled in foreign cities.* **2** carried on or dealing with other countries: *foreign trade.* **3** not natural or meant to be there: *Sitting still all day is foreign to a healthy child's nature. A tiny piece of foreign material got stuck in my eye.* <Latin *foras* outside> **for′eign·er** *n.*

foreign affairs *n* a country's relations with other countries.

foreign correspondent *n* a journalist or reporter of one country who sends news from another.

foreign exchange *n* **1** the changing of funds from one currency to another. **2** a place, such as in an airport, providing this service: *Where's the foreign exchange?*

foreign policy *n* a government's stated position and practice with regard to other nations.

fore·knowl·edge (fôr nol′ij) *n* knowledge of a thing before it happens.

fore·leg (fôr′leg′) *n* one of the front legs of a four-legged animal.

fore·limb (fôr′lim′) *n* one of the front limbs of an animal.

fore·man (fôr′mən) *n, pl* **fore·men** (fôr′mən) **1** a man in charge of a group of workers, or of some part of a factory. **2** the CHAIR (def. 2) of a jury. See also FOREWOMAN.

fore·mast (fôr′mast′) *n* the front mast of a ship.

fore·most (fôr′mōst′) *adj, adv* chief, leading, or most notably: *the nation's foremost thinkers* (*adj*). *He thinks foremost of his own comfort* (*adv*). <Old English *formest*>

fore·noon (fôr′nūn′) *n* the time between early morning and noon.
adj between early morning and noon.

fo·ren·sic (fə ren′sik) *adj* to do with the application of medical and other sciences to police work, or their use in court trials: *forensic evidence. The lawyer got a forensic psychiatrist to testify that the defendant was insane.*
n **forensics** (*with singular verb*) scientific techniques or tests used in police work. <Latin *forensis* public, from *forum* forum>

fore·paw (fôr′po′) *n* a front paw.

fore·play (fôr′plā′) *n* physical stimulation intended to arouse one's partner sexually before intercourse.

fore·quar·ter (fôr′kwôr′tər) *n* the front leg, shoulder, and associated ribs of animals slaughtered for food.

fore·run·ner (fôr′run′ər) *n* **1** the first sign of something coming: *A tickly throat is often the forerunner of a cold.* **2** a predecessor: *The electric organ was the forerunner of the synthesizer.*

fore·see (fôr sē′) *v* **fore·saw, fore·seen, fore·see·ing** see or predict ahead of time: *That was one problem we didn't foresee.* <Old English *foreseon*> **fore·see′a·ble** *adj.*

fore·shad·ow (fôr shad′ō) *v* be a hint or symbol of future events: *The dying of the rosebush foreshadowed the heroine's tragic end.* **fore·shad′ow·ing** *n.*

fore·short·en (fôr shôr′tən) *v* show or seem to be shorter, giving perspective or a three-dimensional effect: *Taking a photo from above foreshortens the model's legs.* **fore·short′en·ing** *n.*

fore·sight (fôr′sīt′) *n* the power or act of seeing beforehand what is likely to happen or what will be needed: *A little foresight could have prevented this problem.* **fore′sight′ed** *adj.*

fore·skin (fôr′skin′) *n* the fold of skin that covers the end of the penis.

for·est (fô′rist) *n* **1** a large area of land densely covered with trees and undergrowth. **2** a large number or dense mass of objects: *a forest of apartment buildings.* <Latin *foris* = out of doors> **for′est·ed** *adj.* **for′est·less** *adj.*

fore·stall (fôr stol′) *v* **1** prevent by acting first: *The mayor forestalled a riot by having the police ready.* **2** deal with in advance; anticipate: *I had a question ready, but she forestalled me.*

for·est·a·tion (fô′ri stā′shən) *n* the planting or maintenance of forests.

forest ranger *n* a government official in charge of patrolling and guarding a public forest and its wildlife.

for·est·ry (fô′ri strē) *n* the science of planting, managing, and protecting forests. **for′est·er** *n.*

fore·taste (fôr′tāst′) *n* a preliminary sample or experience: *The boy got a foretaste of business life by working during the summer vacation.*

fore·tell (fôr tel′) *v* **fore·told, fore·tell·ing** predict: *to foretell the future.*

fore·thought (fôr′thot′) *n* careful thought about what may happen or be needed: *A little forethought will often prevent mistakes.*

fore·told (fôr tōld′) past tense and past participle of FORETELL.

for·ev·er (fə rev′ər) *adv* **1** without ever coming to an end: *Do you think the universe will last forever?* **2** constantly: *That air conditioner is forever running.*

for·ev·er·more (fə rev′ər môr′) *adv* from a certain time onward, without ever ending.

fore·warn (fôr wôrn′) *v* warn beforehand: *The exam will be tough; consider yourselves forewarned.*

fore·wom·an (fôr′wu̇ m′ən) *n, pl* **fore·wom·en** (fôr′wi mən) **1** a woman in charge of a group of workers, or of some part of a factory. **2** the CHAIR (def. 2) of a jury. See also FOREMAN.

fore·word (fôr′wərd′) *n* a short introduction to a text, usually one written by someone other than the author.

for·feit (fôr′fit) *v* lose or have to give up as a penalty for some act, neglect, or fault: *to forfeit a game by failing to show up. Return the canoe, or forfeit your deposit.*
n **1** something unpleasant that happens because of some act, neglect, or fault: *A headache was the forfeit she paid for staying up late.* **2** the act of forfeiting.
adj lost or given up as a penalty. <Old French *forfait* penalty for a crime> **for′fei·ture** *n.*

for·fend (fôr fend′) *Archaic or Humorous v* prevent; avert.
heaven forfend, may it never happen!

for·gave (fər gāv′) past tense of FORGIVE.

forge[1] (fôrj) *n* **1** a furnace or open fireplace where metal is heated to a high temperature to soften it before being hammered into shape: *The blacksmith took the white-hot horseshoes out of the forge.* **2** a blacksmith's shop.
v **forged, forg·ing 1** heat metal to a high temperature and then hammer it into shape, or to make something in this way: *to forge a bar of iron into a hook. The blacksmith forged a horseshoe from iron.* **2** form, especially through effort or commitment: *They forged a strong and lasting friendship.* **3** make or write something false or counterfeit: *to forge a will, to forge someone else's signature.* <Old French, from Latin *fabrica* workshop> **forg′er** *n.*

forge[2] (fôrj) *v* **forged, forg·ing** (*usually with* ***ahead***) move forward slowly but steadily: *Researchers are forging ahead in the battle against cancer.* <origin uncertain>

for·ger·y (fôr′jə rē) *n, pl* **for·ger·ies 1** the action, usually a crime, of forging a signature, document, banknote, or work of art. **2** something made in this way: *The painting, supposedly by Picasso, was actually a forgery.*

for·get (fər get′) *v* **for·got, for·got·ten, for·get·ting 1** fail or be unable to remember: *I couldn't introduce her because I had forgotten her name.* **2** omit or neglect without meaning to: *Don't forget to lock the door.* **3** leave behind unintentionally: *She had to return home because she had forgotten her homework.* **4** pay no attention to: *Forget the danger and just do it.* <Old English *forgietan*>
for·get′ful *adj.* **for·get′ful·ly** *adv.* **for·get′ful·ness** *n.*
for·get′ta·ble *adj.* **for·get′ta·bly** *adv.*
forget it, *Informal* **a** don't concern yourself about it: *"What do I owe you for that?" "Forget it, I'll take care of it."* **b** absolutely not: *"Can I borrow the car?" "Forget it."*
forget yourself, a fail to think before speaking or acting. **b** not think of your own interests.

for·get–me–not (fər get′mē not′) *n* a low-growing plant with hairy leaves and clusters of small flowers. <translation of Old French *ne m'oubliez mye*, said to have the quality of ensuring that the wearer of the flower would never be forgotten>

for·give (fər giv′) *v* **for·gave, for·giv·en, for·giv·ing 1** give up being angry or resentful toward someone for an offense or mistake: *She forgave us for losing her CD. Please forgive my mistake.* **2** give up all claim to or not demand payment for: *to forgive a debt.* <Old English *forgiefan*>
for·giv′a·ble *adj.* **for·giv′a·bly** *adv.* **for·give′ness** *n.*

F

SYNONYMS

Forgive involves giving up being angry or resentful: *I forgive you because you're my best friend.*

Acquit involves being declared not guilty of an offence and involves no emotions: *The jury acquitted him of the crime.*

Condone can mean "overlook an offense or fault": *She condoned her sister's outbursts, because they never lasted long.*

for·giv·ing (fər giv′ing) *adj* **1** willing to forgive. **2** allowing for the making of mistakes: *Track pants are very forgiving, because I can gain weight and still wear them.*
for·giv′ing·ly *adv.*

for·go (fôr gō′) *v* **for·went, for·gone** (fôr gon′)**, for·go·ing** do without or give up: *He chose to forgo the movies and do his work.* Also, **forego.** <Old English *forgan*>

for·got (fər got′) past tense of FORGET.

for·got·ten (fər got′ən) past participle of FORGET.

fork (fôrk) *n* **1** an instrument for eating, with a handle and two or more long, pointed prongs at one end. See SOUP SPOON for picture. **2** a tool of similar shape but bigger: *a garden fork, a tuning fork.* **3** the place where a tree, road, or stream divides into two branches: *Follow this road until it becomes a fork.* **4** one of the branches: *Take the left fork.*
v **1** lift or throw with a fork: *to fork hay.* **2** divide into branches: *There is a general store where the road forks.* <Latin *furca*> **fork′like′** *adj.*
fork out, *Slang* pay.
fork over, *Slang* give or give up what is demanded: *OK, mister, fork over the cash.*

forked (fôrkt) *adj* divided into branches. *forked lightning.*

fork·lift (fôrk′lift′) *n* a power-operated vehicle with a horizontal, forklike device that can be raised and lowered for lifting and moving heavy objects.

for·lorn (fôr lôrn′) *adv* **1** left alone, neglected, or deserted: *I will not leave you forlorn.* **2** looking pitifully sad, abandoned, or lonely: *The lost kitten looked scared and forlorn.* **3** very unlikely to succeed: *a forlorn attempt at reconciliation.* <Old English *forloren* lost>
for·lorn′ly *adv.* **for·lorn′ness** *n.*

a bat	e bed	i bid	o pot	u cup	th **thin**
ā cake	ē me	ī bite	ō go	ū rude	ᴛʜ **then**
ȧ bar	ə about	ər over	ȯ for	u̇ put	zh measure

form (fôrm) *n* **1** shape or configuration: *A cookie is roughly circular in form.* **2** the particular shape of a certain person, animal, or thing: *She saw his tall form in the doorway.* **3** a structure or an arrangement of parts: *The appeal of a good poem is in its form as well as its content.* **4** a document with blank spaces to be filled in: *To get a licence, you must fill out a form.* **5** the particular condition or character in which a thing exists or shows itself: *Water in the form of ice or steam is still water. "Went" is the past form of the verb "go."* **6** something that gives shape to something else: *a cake form.* **7** a correct or incorrect manner of doing something: *He is a fast skater, but needs to work on his form.* **8** a customary social behaviour: *Being late is bad form.*
v **1** give shape to or take shape: *Form the dough into loaves. Using the modelling clay, she formed a lion. Clouds form in the sky.* **2** become: *Water forms ice when it freezes.* **3** make up or compose: *Fresh bread and cheese formed her customary lunch.* **4** set up, organize, or establish: *We formed a club.* **5** develop: *Form good habits while you are young.* **6** arrange in some order: *Each class formed a line.* <Old French, from Latin *forma* shape> **form′less** *adj.* **form′less·ly** *adv.* **form′less·ness** *n.*

for·mal (fôr′məl) *adj* **1** paying attention to rules and ceremonies: *a formal introduction. A court trial is a formal proceeding.* **2 a** requiring correct, elegant dress: *a formal dance.* **b** suitable for a formal occasion: *a formal gown.* **3** clear, definite, and recognized by all involved: *a formal offer of employment. A written contract is a formal agreement to do something.* **4** to do with the outward form, not the meaning or the content: *formal aspects of poetry such as rhyme and metre. Her religion was purely formal.*
n **1** a social gathering at which formal dress is worn. **2** a gown worn to formal social gatherings: *She was dressed in her first formal.* <Latin *forma* form> **for′mal·ize′** *v.* **for′mal·ly** *adv.*

form·al·de·hyde (fôr mal′də hīd′) *n* a colourless gas with a sharp odour, used in solution as a disinfectant and preservative. <*form(ic acid)* = an acid that occurs naturally in ants + *al(cohol) dehyd(rogenatum)* = alcohol with the hydrogen removed>

for·ma·lin (fôr′mə lin) *n* a solution of formaldehyde in water.

for·mal·ism (fôr′mə liz′əm) *n* **1** strict attention to form as opposed to content: *formalism in art.* **2** emphasis on outward forms and ceremonies. **for′mal·is′tic** *adj.*

for·mal·i·ty (fôr mal′ə tē) *n, pl* **for·mal·i·ties**
1 a procedure required by custom or rule: *the formalities of a wedding. The voting is just a formality, since you're the only candidate for class rep.* **2** strict attention to forms and customs: *Visitors at the court of a queen are received with formality.*

for·mat (fôr′mat) *n* **1** the shape, size, and general layout: *the format of a magazine.* **2** the design, plan, or arrangement of a program or activity: *the format of a TV show, the format of a course.* **3** *Computers* a particular arrangement or system of handling or presenting data: *Is that movie available in DVD format?*
v **1** *Computers* prepare a disk for use by having the operating system write certain essential data on it. Also called **initialize**. **2** design or make with a particular format: *He didn't like how the physics course was formatted.* <French, from Latin *formare* to form>

for·ma·tion (fôr mā′shən) *n* **1** the act, process, or manner of forming or being formed: *the formation of steam from water.* **2** a particular arrangement or order: *troops in battle formation. Geese fly in formation.* **3** the thing formed: *Clouds are formations of tiny drops of water in the sky.*

form·a·tive (fôr′mə tiv) *adj* to do with development: *School is a formative influence in a child's life.*

for·mer (fôr′mər) *adj* **1** the first of two mentioned: *North America includes Canada and the US; the former country lies north of the latter.* Compare LATTER. **2** earlier or past: *in former times. She's a former teacher of mine.*
n **the former** the first of two mentioned: *When offered ice cream or pie, I always choose the former.* <Middle English *formere*> **for′mer·ly** *adv.*

form–fit·ting (fôrm′fit′ing) *adj* closely following the contours of the body.

For·mi·ca (fôr mī′kə) *Trademark n* a laminated plastic material with a hard, smooth, heat-resistant surface.

for·mi·da·ble (fôr′mə də bəl) *adj* inspiring fear or respect: *a formidable opponent.* <Latin *formidare* to fear> **for′mi·da·bly** *adv.*

form letter *n* a letter worded so that it may be sent to many different people.

for·mu·la (fôr′myə lə) *n, pl* **for·mu·las** or **for·mu·lae** (fôr′myə lē′) *or* (fôr′myə lī′) **1** a nutritious mixture for an infant to drink from a bottle, made to imitate breast milk as much as possible. **2** a recipe or prescription: *a formula for making soap. What you are doing is a formula for disaster.* **3** an expression using chemical symbols to show the composition of a compound: *The formula for water is* H_2O. **4** an expression using algebraic symbols to show a rule or principle of how one quantity is related to others. The equation $(a + b)^2 = a^2 + 2ab + b^2$ is an algebraic formula. **5** a set form of words, especially one that has partly lost its meaning through use: *"How do you do?" is a polite formula.* **6** a fixed way of doing or presenting something: *All the books in that detective series follow a set formula.* <Latin *formula* rule>

for·mu·late (fôr′myə lāt′) *v* **for·mu·lat·ed, for·mu·lat·ing**
1 state definitely and systematically: *Our ideas of fair treatment for all Canadians are formulated in the Charter.* **2** give definite form to in the mind: *to formulate a plan.* **3** express in a formula.

for′mu·la′tion *n.*

for·ni·cate (fôr′nə kāt′) *Archaic v* **for·ni·cat·ed, for·ni·cat·ing** have sexual intercourse with someone who is not a marriage partner. <Latin *fornix* arch. In ancient Rome, prostitutes solicited their business under building arches.> **for′ni·ca′tion** *n.*

for–prof·it (fôr prof′it) *adj* existing in order to make money for its owners or shareholders: *a for-profit organization.*

for·sake (fər sāk′) *v* **for·sook** (fər su̇k′), **for·sak·en, for·sak·ing** **1** abandon someone or something: *He ran away from home, forsaking his family.* **2** permanently give up: *to forsake old habits.* <Old English *forsacan*>

for·sooth (fôr sūth′) *Archaic or Humorous adv* in truth or indeed. <Old English *for* for + *soth* truth>

for·swear (fȯr swer′) *v* **for·swore** (fȯr swōr′), **for·sworn** (fȯr swōrn′), **for·swear·ing** 1 swear or promise solemnly to give up: *The coach asked the team to forswear smoking.* 2 deny solemnly or on oath: *He forswore all connection with the gang's activities.* 3 *Archaic* (*with reflexive pronoun when active*) be untrue to one's sworn word or promise: *She first made the promise, then forswore herself. By breaking that promise, she is forsworn.* <Old English *for-* away + *swerian* swear>

for·syth·i·a (fȯr sith′yə) *n* a shrub with many bell-shaped yellow flowers in early spring before its leaves come out. <W. *Forsyth*, 18c horticulturalist>

fort (fȯrt) *n* 1 a strong building or walled place that can be defended against an enemy. 2 in the early days of the fur trade, a trading post with stockades or walls to protect it against attack: *Winnipeg is built on the site of Fort Garry, an old Hudson's Bay Company post.* <French, from Latin *fortis* strong>
hold the fort, a make a defence. b *Informal* keep things functioning.

for·te[1] (fȯr′tā) *n* something a person does very well: *Cooking is her forte.* <French, from Latin *fortis* strong>

for·te[2] (fȯr′tā) *Music adj, adv* loud or loudly. *Symbol* **f** <Italian, from Latin *fortis*>

forth (fȯrth) *adv* 1 forward or onward: *From that day forth she lived alone.* 2 *Archaic or Formal* into view: *The sun burst forth from behind the clouds.* 3 into consideration: *to bring forth a topic for discussion.* <Old English>
and so forth, and so on: *We ate cake, candy, and so forth.*
back and forth, backwards and forwards, especially many times.

forth·com·ing (fȯrth′kum′ing) *for 1 and 3,* (fȯrth kum′ing) *for 2. adj* 1 about to appear: *You can read about it in my forthcoming book.* 2 ready when wanted: *She needed help, but none was forthcoming.* 3 giving help or information when wanted: *The person I interviewed was not very forthcoming.*

forth·right (fȯrth′rīt′) *adj* frank and direct: *He made forthright objections to the proposal.* **forth′right′ly** *adv.* **forth′right′ness** *n.*

forth·with (fȯrth′with′) *adv* immediately: *She said she would be there forthwith.*

for·ti·eth (fȯr′tē əth′) *n* 1 next after the thirty-ninth. 2 one of forty equal parts.
adj, adv See FORTY.

for·ti·fi·ca·tion (fȯr′tə fə kā′shən) *n* 1 anything used to fortify a place, such as a wall, ditch, or stockade. 2 a fortified place. 3 the act of fortifying: *The nutritional value of some foods is improved by fortification with vitamins.*

for·ti·fy (fȯr′tə fī′) *v* **for·ti·fied, for·ti·fy·ing** 1 strengthen against attack by building structures and placing troops. 2 give support to or strengthen. 3 add something that strengthens or enriches: *Breakfast cereal is often fortified with vitamins.*

for·tis·si·mo (fȯr tis′ə mō′) *Music adj, adv* very loud or loudly. *Symbol* **ff** <Italian = loudest>

for·ti·tude (fȯr′tə tyūd′) *or* (fȯr′tə tūd′) *n* courage and endurance. <Latin *fortis* strong>

for·tress (fȯr′tris) *n* a large and well-protected fort.

for·tu·i·tous (fər tyū′ə təs) *or* (fər tū′ə təs) *adj* accidental but good: *a fortuitous meeting. Penicillin was a fortuitous discovery.* <Latin *fortis* chance> **for·tu′i·tous·ly** *adv.*

for·tu·nate (fȯr′chə nit) *adj* having or bringing good luck or happiness: *a fortunate turn of events. You were fortunate to escape unharmed.* **for′tu·nate·ly** *adv.*

for·tune (fȯr′chən) *n* 1 a great deal of money or property: *He made a fortune in the oil industry.* 2 what is supposed to be going to happen to a person: *to tell someone's fortune.* 3 good luck, prosperity, or success: *to achieve fame and fortune.* <Old French, from Latin *fortuna*>

fortune cookie *n* a small, crisp, hollow cookie served at the end of a Chinese meal, containing a slip of paper with a proverb, piece of advice, or prediction on it.

fortune hunter *n* 1 a person who tries to get a fortune by marrying someone rich. 2 anybody who seeks wealth.

for·tune·tell·er (fȯr′chən tel′ər) *n* a person who tries to predict what will happen to people, usually for payment. **for′tune·tell′ing** *n.*

for·ty (fȯr′tē) *n, pl* **for·ties** 1 four times ten. 2 **forties** *pl* the years from forty through forty-nine, especially of a century or of a person's life: *She achieved success as a playwright in her forties.*
adj 1 four times ten: *forty years.* 2 (*after the noun*) fortieth in a series: *page forty.* <Old English *feowertig*>
for′ti·eth *adj, adv.*

forty–ninth parallel (fȯr′tē nīnth′) *n* the parallel of LATITUDE that forms part of the border between Canada and the US. It is 49° north of the equator.

forty winks *n* a short nap.

fo·rum (fȯ′rəm) *n* 1 in ancient Rome, the public square or marketplace of a town, used for public assemblies and business. 2 any place, gathering, or online discussion group in which issues are discussed publicly. <Latin>

for·ward (fȯr′wərd) *adv* 1 toward the front: *He leaned forward. Walk forward.* 2 onward or further ahead: *We are moving forward in our struggle for justice.* 3 out; into view or consideration: *In his talk, he brought forward several new ideas.* 4 earlier in time: *The meeting has been moved forward.* 5 so as to show later time: *We put the clocks forward in spring.* Also, **forwards**.
adj 1 toward the front: *the forward part of a ship.* 2 too bold or familiar: *Don't be so forward as to ask; wait for them to offer.* 3 eager or quick, often too much so: *He knew his lesson and was forward with his answers.*
v 1 send on to another person or address: *Please forward my mail to my new address.* 2 try to help succeed: *He did all he could to forward our plans.*
n in certain games, a player whose position is in the front line. <Old English *forweard*> **for′ward·ness** *n.*
bring (or **carry**) **forward,** *Accounting* enter a current or outstanding amount again at the beginning of the next record or statement.

a bat	e bed	i bid	o pot	u cup	th thin
ā cake	ē me	ī bite	ō go	ū rude	ᴛʜ then
ȧ bar	ə about	ər over	ȯ for	u̇ put	zh measure

forwarding address *n* an address to which a person's mail can be sent.

for·ward–look·ing (fȯr′wərd lůk′ing) *adj* looking to and preparing for the future.

for·went (fȯr went′) past tense of FORGO.

fos·sil (fos′əl) *n* the petrified remains of a prehistoric animal or plant. <French, from Latin *fodere* dig up> **fos′sil·ize′** *v.* **fos′sil-like′** *adj.*

fossil fuels *n* fuels obtained from the earth, such as coal, petroleum, and natural gas, all of which are derived from what was originally plant material.

fos·ter (fos′tər) *v* help and encourage the growth or development of: *Ignorance fosters superstition.*
adj to do with an arrangement by which a child is cared for temporarily in a family other than his or her natural one: *my foster brother.* <Old English *fostrian* nourish>

fought (fot) past tense and past participle of FIGHT.

foul (foul) *adj* **1** offensive to the senses, especially to the smell, taste, or sight: *Open the windows and let out the foul air.* **2** extremely immoral: *foul deeds.* **3** played so as to break a rule or go out of bounds: *a foul ball.* **4** unfavourable or stormy: *foul weather.*
v **1** make dirty or impure: *Exhaust fumes fouled the air.* **2** hit a ball or make a play in a way that breaks a rule. **3** (*often with* ***up***) tangle or clog: *Hair fouled the drain. The rope fouled up the anchor chain.*
n Sports **1** something done contrary to the rules. **2** a ball that is hit so as to break a rule. <Old English *ful*>
foul′ly *adv.* **foul′ness** *n.*
fall (or **run**) **foul of, a** get into conflict with: *You don't want to fall foul of the referee, so be careful.* **b** collide or get tangled up with.
foul out, a *Baseball* be put out by hitting a ball that is caught outside the foul line. **b** *Basketball* be put out of a game for having committed too many fouls.
foul up, make a mess of: *He fouled up the whole project.*

SYNONYMS

Foul can refer to smell, taste, or sight: *The sight and smell of the rotting garbage heap was foul.*

Fetid refers specifically to a very bad smell: *He didn't know how long the fetid socks had been in his gym bag.*

Putrid means "rotting" or "decaying": *She found some putrid meat in the back of the refrigerator.*

foul ball *Baseball n* a ball hit so that it falls outside the area of play.

foul line *n* **1** *Baseball* either of the boundary lines extending from home plate. **2** *Basketball* either of the lines from which a FREE THROW is taken.

foul–mouthed (foul′mouᴛʜd′) *or* (foul′moutht′) *adj* habitually using profane or offensive language.

foul play *n* **1** *Sports* play that is against the rules. **2** treachery or violence, especially in criminal activity: *The man seems to have died in his sleep, but foul play is suspected.*

foul–up (foul′up′) *Informal n* a mistake that causes confusion or loss.

found[1] (found) past tense and past participle of FIND.

found[2] (found) *v* **1** establish or set up: *Champlain founded Québec City in 1608.* **2** provide support or a foundation for: *He founded his claim on facts. Her theory is very poorly founded.* <Old French, from Latin *fundus* foundation>

foun·da·tion (foun dā′shən) *n* **1** the part of a thing, especially a building, that forms a support or base for the rest: *the foundation of a house.* **2** the basis of a belief, idea, or argument: *The report has no foundation in fact.* **3** a cosmetic applied to the face as a base before other cosmetics are applied. **4** an institution, usually charitable, founded and given money or property by someone so it will have a steady income: *The Heart and Stroke Foundation.* **5** the act of founding or establishing.

foun·der[1] (foun′dər) *v* **1** fill with water and sink: *The ship foundered in the storm.* **2** become bogged down in soft ground. **3** stumble or fall from exhaustion: *Her horse foundered.* **4** fail. See FLOUNDER for confusable. <Old French *fondrer* fall to the bottom, from Latin *fundus* bottom>

foun·der[2] (foun′dər) *n* a person who founds or establishes something.

Founder's Day *Buddhism n* the October festival commemorating the introduction of Buddhism to Canada in 1905.

found·ling (found′ling) *n* a baby or child found abandoned.

found·ry (foun′drē) *n, pl* **found·ries** a place where metal is melted and made into objects. <perhaps French *fondre* melt>

fount (fount) *n* **1** *Poetic* a fountain. **2** FONT[1] (def. 1) <Latin *fontis* fountain>

foun·tain (foun′tən) *n* **1** a decorative structure, as in an ornamental pool or garden, through which water is forced into the air in a stream or spray. **2** a device in a public place from which to drink water. **3** any stream or spray of water rising into the air: *We all jumped into the pool, sending fountains of water into the air.* **4** a spring of water coming up out of the earth. **5** an abundant source: *My grandmother is a fountain of wisdom.*

foun·tain·head (foun′tən hed′) *n* **1** the source of a stream. **2** an original or ultimate source.

fountain pen *n* a pen that automatically supplies liquid ink to the nib from a tube inside. See QUILL for picture.

four (fȯr) *n* **1** a cardinal number that is one more than three. **2** the numeral 4. **3** a playing card or side of a die with four spots: *He threw a four.*
adj **1** one more than three: *She saw the movie four times.* **2** (*after the noun*) fourth in a series: *I don't understand Section Four of the manual.* <Old English *feower*>
fourth *adj, adv.*
on all fours, on hands and knees.

four–flush·er (fȯr′flush′ər) *Informal n* a treacherous person; a cheat. **four′–flush′ing** *adj.*

four·fold (fōr′fōld′) *adj, adv* **1** four times as much or as many. **2** consisting of four parts.

four–foot·ed (fȯr′fůt′id) *adj* with four feet.

four–let·ter word (fȯr′let′ər) *n* an obscene or vulgar word.

🍁 **four·plex** (fȯr′pleks′) *n* a building containing four apartments.

four·score (fȯr′skȯr′) *Archaic adj* eighty. <*score* = twenty>

four·some (fȯr′səm) *n* **1** a group of four people. **2** *Sports, Games* two opposing teams of two people.

four·square (fȯr′skwer′) *adj* square and solid.

four–stroke (fȯr′strōk′) *adj* to do with an internal combustion engine that takes four piston strokes to complete a fuel cycle.

four·teen (fȯr′tēn′) *n* **1** four more than ten: *Count to fourteen.* **2** the numeral 14.
adj **1** four more than ten: *fourteen days.* **2** (*after the noun*) fourteenth in a series: *Lesson Fourteen.* <Old English *feowertene*> **four′teenth′** *adj, adv.*

four·teenth (fȯr′tēnth′) *n* **1** next after the thirteenth. *I am fourteenth in line at the checkout.* **2** one of fourteen equal parts: *The grandchildren each get a fourteenth of the inheritance.*
adj, adv See FOURTEEN.

fourth (fȯrth) *adj* **1** next after the third: *on the fourth day.* **2** *Formal* being one of four equal parts; a quarter: *She was given a fourth part of the inheritance.*
n **1** next after the third: *I'm fourth in line.* **2** *Formal* being one of four equal parts; a quarter: *He donated a fourth of his art collection to the local library.* **3** *Music* an interval stretching from one note to another four notes higher, or the sound made when both these notes are played simultaneously. **fourth′ly** *adv.*

fourth estate *n* the press and other news media, and all those employed by them. See also ESTATE.

four–wheel drive (fȯr′wēl′) *n* **1** in a motor vehicle, a system in which power is transmitted to all four wheels at once. **2** a vehicle equipped with such a system.

The thickets and scrub in the arid regions of Somalia and sub-Saharan Africa are the natural habitat for the Vulturine Guinea **fowl**.

This bird is smaller than a chicken, with red eyes, a bright blue breast, and a hackle of black-and-white striped feathers.

fowl (foul) *n, pl* **fowls** or (*especially collectively*) **fowl** **1** a large bird, raised for meat and eggs. Chickens, geese, and turkeys, or wild birds related to these, are fowls. **2** (*usually in compounds*) any bird: *a waterfowl.* <Old English *fugol*>

fox (foks) *n* **1** a small wild animal of the dog family, with a pointed muzzle and a bushy tail. **2** a sly, crafty person. **3** *Slang* an attractive woman or girl.
v Informal outwit by being sly and crafty. <Old English> **fox′like′** *adj.*

fox·glove (foks′gluv′) *n* a plant with tall stalks and many bell-shaped flowers. Digitalis, an important drug, is obtained from the leaves and seeds of the foxglove.

fox·hole (foks′hōl′) *n* a hole in the ground used by soldiers for protection against enemy fire.

fox·trot (foks′trot′) *n* a dance with short, quick steps, or the music for such a dance.
v **fox·trot·ted, fox·trot·ting** dance the foxtrot.

fox·y (fok′sē) *adj* **fox·i·er, fox·i·est** **1** sly and crafty. **2** *Slang* seductive or sexy. **fox′i·ly** *adv.* **fox′i·ness** *n.*

foy·er (foi′ā) *n* an entrance hall, especially a large one where people wait or gather. <French, from Latin *focus* hearth. Entrance halls used to be large rooms with fireplaces.>

fra·cas (frak′əs) *or* (frā′kəs) *n* a noisy quarrel or fight. <French, from Italian *fracassare* make an uproar>

frac·tal (frak′təl) *adj* to do with curves or geometrical figures that show a pattern, but with small irregular or fragmented variations so that no two parts are alike.
n a fractal form. <Latin *fractus*, from *frangere* fragment>

frac·tion (frak′shən) *n* **1** *Mathematics* one or more of the equal parts of a whole. Examples: 3/4; 0.2 **2** a small part: *He ate only a fraction of his lunch.* <Latin *fractionem* a breaking into pieces, from *frangere* break>
frac′tion·al *adj.*

frac·tious (frak′shəs) *adj* **1** bad-tempered. **2** unruly, especially in a group or organization. <obsolete *fraction* discord> **frac′tious·ly** *adv.* **frac′tious·ness** *n.*

frac·ture (frak′chər) *v* **frac·tured, frac·tur·ing** break: *fractured relationships. The boy fell from a tree and fractured his arm.*
n **1** the act, fact, or place of breaking. **2** the breaking of a bone. <French, from Latin *frangere* break>

frag·ile (fraj′īl) *or* (fraj′əl) *adj* easily broken, damaged, or destroyed. <Latin *frangere* to break> **frag′ile·ly** *adv.* **fra·gil′i·ty** (frə jil′ə tē) *n.*

frag·ment (frag′mənt) *for n,* (frag ment′) *for v.* *n* **1** a part broken off. **2** an incomplete or disconnected part: *fragments of a conversation, fragments of an ancient manuscript.*
v break or divide into fragments: *Regionalism fragments the nation.* <Latin *frangere* break> **frag′men·tar′y** *adj.* **frag′men·ta′tion** *n.*

fra·grance (frā′grəns) *n* **1** a sweet smell. **2** a sweet-smelling preparation for the body, such as perfume or cologne. <Latin *fragrare* smell sweet> **frag′rant** *adj.* **fra′grant·ly** *adv.*

frail (frāl) *adj* **1** weak and prone to injury or sickness: *a frail child.* **2** likely to break or collapse: *Be careful, those branches are a very frail support.* **3** morally weak. **frail′ty** *n.*

a bat	e bed	i bid	o pot	u cup	th **thin**
ā cake	ē me	ī bite	ō go	ū rude	ᴛʜ **then**
ä bar	ə about	ər over	ȯ for	ů put	zh measure

frame (frām) *n* **1** a supporting structure over which something is stretched or built: *the frame of a house.* **2** anything made of parts fitted and joined together. **3** a person or animal's physical build: *a man of heavy frame.* **4** the border in which a thing is set: *a window frame, a picture frame.* **5** a separate picture on a strip of movie, video, or photographic film, or in a comic strip, or one image transmitted by TV. **6** one turn or round of turns in bowling, or in snooker, one game. **7 frames** *pl* a metal or plastic structure that holds the lenses in eyeglasses.
v **framed, fram·ing 1** put a border around; enclose with a frame: *to frame a picture.* **2** set things up so as to make someone seem guilty: *If he was framed, then the real criminal is still free.* **3** build the frame of a house or other building. **4** put together or compose: *carefully framed sentences.* <Old English *framian* profit, be helpful, have a plan> **fram′er** *n.*
frame of mind, a way of thinking or feeling: *You have to be in the proper frame of mind to enjoy this music.*

frame–and–shell structure (frām′ən shel′) *n* a building made of a framework plus an outer shell. Houses and apartment buildings are frame-and-shell structures.

frame house *n* a house made of a wooden framework covered with boards.

frame of reference *n* **1** the entire set of circumstances within which something exists. **2** a point of view. **3** the set of criteria used to make a judgment.

frame–up (frām′up′) *n* a scheme to make a person appear guilty and cause him or her to be falsely accused.

frame·work (frām′wərk′) *n* **1** a support over which a thing is stretched or built and which gives it its shape: *A bridge often has a steel framework.* **2** the way in which anything is ordered or arranged. **3** a set of parameters or limits within which something must be done.

France (frans) *n* a country in western Europe. See the APPENDIX. See also FRENCH.

fran·chise (fran′chīz) *n* **1 a** the legal right to sell the products or services of a certain company in a given area. **b** a business operating on this basis, often part of a chain. **c** a similar privilege or right granted by a government: *The city granted the company a franchise to operate buses on the city streets.* **2** authorization to own a team of a professional sports league. **3** the right to vote: *In 1920, Canada established a universal franchise for persons of 21 years and over.*
v **fran·chised, fran·chis·ing 1** grant a franchise to. **2** convert a business or company to a franchise. <Old French *franche* free>

fran·ci·um (fran′sē əm) *n* a radioactive element of the alkali metal group. *Symbol* **Fr** <Latin, after *France*, the discoverer's native country>

🍁 **fran·cize** (fran′sīz) *v* **fran·cized, fran·ciz·ing** make or become French or French-speaking; specifically, in Québec, cause to meet regulations protecting the French language. **fran′ci·za′tion** *n.*

Franco– or **franco–** *combining form* French and ______: *Franco-Albertan, the Franco-Prussian war.*

fran·co·phobe (frang′kə fōb′) *n* a person who hates or fears the people and culture of France or French-speaking Canada. Also, **Francophobe**. **fran′co·pho′bi·a** *n.* **fran′co·pho′bic** *adj.*

🍁 **fran·co·phone** (frang′kə fōn′) *n* a person whose native language is French.
adj **1** with French as one's native language. **2** made up of francophones: *francophone Canada.* Also, **Francophone**.

🍁 **Fran·glais** (frång gle′) *Informal n* French spoken with many English words and expressions. Also, **Franglish**. <French *français* French + *anglais* English>

frank[1] (frangk) *adj* open, clear, and undisguised: *frank talk.* <Old French *franc* sincere> **frank′ly** *adv.* **frank′ness** *n.*

CONFUSABLES

Being **frank** often involves being outspoken and direct: *She gave her frank opinion of the plan, which upset the others.*

Being **candid** suggests being sincere and honest: *We appreciated his candid answer to the question, although it was not what we wanted to hear.*

Being **forthright** suggests being straightforward: *The teacher was forthright in her expectations of the students.*

frank[2] (frangk) *Informal n* a frankfurter.

Frank (frangk) *n* a member of a group of peoples who crossed the Rhine and invaded the Roman Empire in the fourth century CE, gradually conquering most of Gaul and Germany. **Frank′ish** *adj, n.*

Frank·en·stein (frang′kən stīn′) *n* a creation that causes the ruin of its creator, or any monstrous creation. <in a 19c novel by M. Shelley, a character who creates an uncontrollable monster>

frank·furt·er (frangk′fər tər) *n* a lightly seasoned sausage made of beef and pork. <German = of the town of Frankfurt>

frank·in·cense (frang′kin sens′) *n* a fragrant resin from certain Asiatic or African trees that gives off a sweet, spicy odour when burned. <Old French *franc encens* pure incense>

fran·tic (fran′tik) *adj* extremely excited or agitated: *She made frantic motions to stop the approaching car. I was frantic when I couldn't find my study notes.* <Old French, from Greek *phrenetikos* inflammation of the brain> **fran′ti·cal·ly** *adv.*

frap·pé (fra pā′) *adj* iced or chilled.
n fruit juice sweetened and frozen. <French *frapper* to chill>

frat (frat) *Informal n* a university fraternity.

fra·ter·nal (frə tər′nəl) *adj* **1** brotherly. **2** to do with a fraternity. **3** of twins, coming from two separately fertilized egg cells. Compare IDENTICAL (def. 3). <Latin *frater* brother> **fra·ter′nal·ly** *adv.*

fra·ter·ni·ty (frə tər′nə tē) *n, pl* **fra·ter·ni·ties 1** a group of people joined together for social interaction or some other purpose, often living together: *a student fraternity at a university.* **2** a group of people sharing similar interests or work, and providing mutual support. **3** brotherly feeling

frat·er·nize (frat′ər nīz′) *v* **frat·er·nized, frat·er·niz·ing** 1 associate in a friendly way. 2 associate in a friendly way with people of an enemy country.
frat′er·ni·za′tion *n.*

fraud (frod) *n* 1 deceit or dishonesty; the practice of cheating or swindling. 2 a trick or swindle. 3 a person who is not what he or she pretends to be. <Old French, from Latin *fraudis* cheating> **fraud′u·lent** *adj.* **fraud′u·lent·ly** *adv.*

fraught (frot) *adj* 1 (*followed by* ***with***) loaded or filled with something bad: *A battlefield is fraught with horror.* 2 *Informal* full of difficulties or problems: *a fraught relationship.* <Dutch *vracht* freight>

fray[1] (frā) *n* a battle or fight. <Old French *affrei*, from Latin *exfridare* take out of peace>

fray[2] (frā) *v* 1 make or become ragged or worn along the edge. 2 cause strain or wear on something: *Their constant arguing frayed my nerves.* <French, from Latin *fricare* rub>

🍁 **fraz·il** (fraz′əl) *or* (frə zēl′) *n* ice crystals or flakes formed in the rushing waters of rivers or rapids, often building up as ice banks along the shore. <French *fraisil* coal cinders, from its look>

fraz·zle (fraz′əl) *v* **fraz·zled, fraz·zling** 1 bring to a state of nervous exhaustion or confused agitation. 2 char or burn food beyond recognition.
n a frazzled condition: *nerves worn to a frazzle, steak burnt to a frazzle.* <origin uncertain>

freak (frēk) *n* 1 a person, plant, or animal with an abnormal physical trait: *Look, a freak of nature—a green leaf growing in the middle of a rose.* 2 an extreme enthusiast: *a hockey freak.* 3 a person with bizarre habits or behaviour. 4 a sudden, seemingly random twist or turn of events or change of mind.
adj odd or unusual: *a freak blizzard in June.*
v Slang 1 (*often with* ***out***) react or cause to react strongly, especially with fear or alarm: *She freaked when I told her the price. The ride on the roller coaster really freaked him out.* 2 (*with* ***out***) behave in a wild or irrational way from the effects of taking a psychedelic drug. <origin uncertain> **freak′ish** *adj.* **freak′y** *adj.*

freck·le (frek′əl) *n* a small, light-brown spot on the skin that occurs naturally.
v **freck·led, freck·ling** 1 become marked or spotted with freckles: *I freckle when I spend time in the sun.* 2 cover with freckles. <Old Norse *freknur*> **freck′ly** *adj.*

freck·le–faced (frek′əl fāst′) *adj* with many freckles on the face.

free (frē) *adj* **fre·er, fre·est** 1 able to act or behave without being under the control of someone or something else: *a free citizen, free speech. You are free to do as you wish.* 2 with a government that is not subject to the rule of a tyrant or the control of a foreign country: *a free country.* 3 with no payment required or expected: *free tickets to a movie, a free clinic.* 4 not shut up, restrained, or confined: *The hostages are now free.* 5 not strained, held back, or hampered by anything: *to walk with a free step. Make sure the rope hangs free.* 6 saying frankly and openly what one thinks: *a free discussion.* 7 generous or lavish: *He is very free with his money.* 8 not rigidly following rules, conventions, or formal structure: *a free translation.* 9 too bold or familiar in one's manner: *Don't be too free with me in public.* 10 not combined with something else: *Oxygen exists free in air.*
adv without cost or payment: *Children under 12 attend free.*
v **freed, free·ing** make free: *to free a boat from weeds, to free a caged animal.* **free′ly** *adv.* **free′ness** *n.*
a free hand, a freedom to act as one sees fit: *When it came to preparing speeches, students were given a free hand.* **b** generosity: *to give with a free hand.*
for free, at no cost: *They're handing these out for free.*
free and easy, paying little attention to rules and customs: *His free and easy manner was not typical of the diplomatic service.*
make free, act as if one had complete rights.
no free lunch, *Informal* you can't get something for nothing.

ETYMOLOGY

Free is from Old English *freo*, which can be traced to much earlier Germanic and Indo-European forms meaning "dear" or "loved." The people who were dear to each other in a household were the members of the family, the free people as opposed to the slaves.

The word is also related to Old English *frigu*, meaning "love."

–free *combining form* not containing a thing considered undesirable or inconvenient: *fat-free, problem-free.*

free agent *n* 1 *Sports* a professional athlete who is free to sign with any team. 2 someone with the power to make choices without interference.

free·base (frē′bās′) *n* a highly addictive form of cocaine specially prepared for smoking.
v **free·based, free·bas·ing** smoke this form of cocaine.

free·bie (frē′bē) *Informal n* a small free gift or benefit.

free·boot·er (frē′bū′tər) *n* a pirate or lawless adventurer. <Dutch *vrijbuiten* to rob, from *vrij* free + *buit* loot> **free′boot′ing** *n.*

free·born (frē′bôrn′) *adj* not born in slavery.

free·dom (frē′dəm) *n* 1 the condition of not being restrained or controlled by another person or thing: *political freedom, freedom of movement.* 2 the right or privilege of doing something: *the freedom to choose, the freedom to speak your mind.* 3 the fact of being without something unwanted: *comparative freedom from noise and stress.* 4 free use: *We give our guests the freedom of our home.*

free enterprise *n* an economic system in which a private individual has the right to own and operate a business for profit with a minimum of government control.

F

a bat	e bed	i bid	o pot	u cup	th **thin**
ā cake	ē me	ī bite	ō go	ū rude	ᴛʜ **then**
à bar	ə about	ər over	ô for	ů put	zh measure

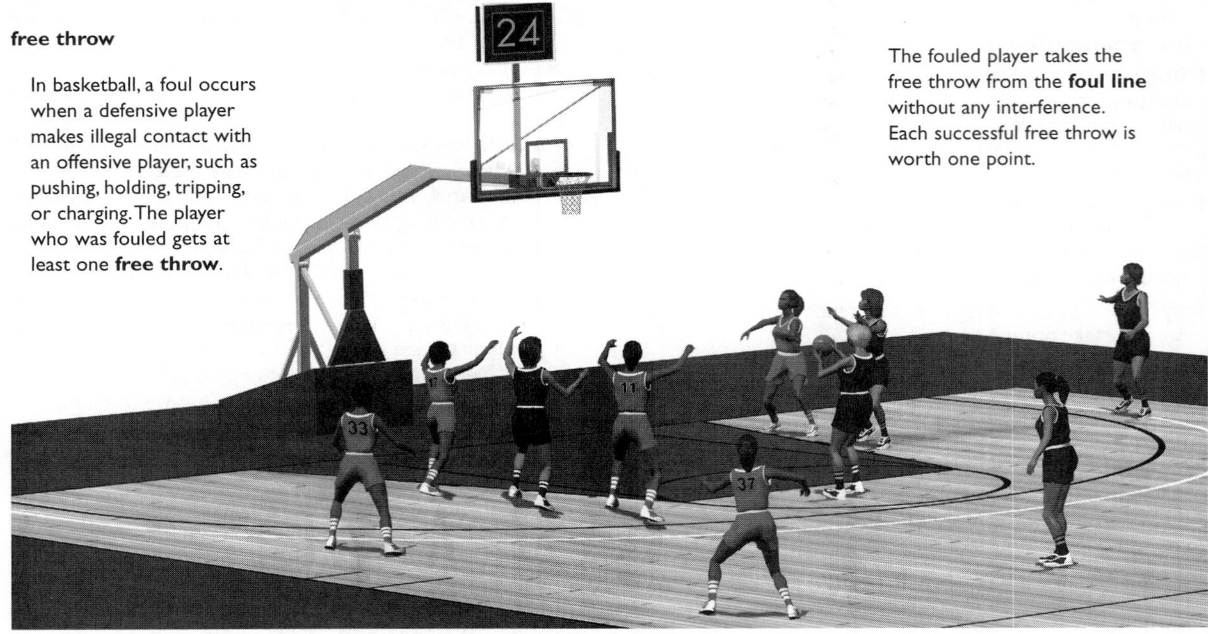

free throw

In basketball, a foul occurs when a defensive player makes illegal contact with an offensive player, such as pushing, holding, tripping, or charging. The player who was fouled gets at least one **free throw**.

The fouled player takes the free throw from the **foul line** without any interference. Each successful free throw is worth one point.

free fall *n* **1** the fall of a body when it is unrestrained by anything except gravity, such as in parachuting, the period between jumping and the opening of the parachute. **2** any rapid, unchecked decline: *Interest rates are in free fall. My grades are in free fall.*

free–for–all (frē′fər ol′) *n* a situation in which no rules are followed and anyone participates who wants to.

free·hand (frē′hand′) *adj, adv* by hand without using instruments, measurements, or a pattern: *a freehand sketch* (*adj*). *I drew it freehand* (*adv*).

free·hold (frē′hōld′) *n* **1** a piece of land held for life or with the right to transfer it to one's heirs. **2** the holding of land in this way.
adj held in this way: *freehold townhouses.*

free kick *Soccer n* a kick at a stationary ball, having no opponent within 10 yards (about 3 m), awarded to a player for a foul committed by the other team.

free·lance (frē′lans′) *v* **free·lanced, free·lanc·ing** work independently as a writer, artist, or other professional, selling one's work or services to clients under a contract.
adj, adv to do with this kind of work arrangement: *a freelance translator* (*adj*). *He worked freelance for three years* (*adv*).
n usually, **freelancer** a freelance worker. <originally, *free lance*, in medieval times a soldier or knight who fought for anyone who would pay him>

free·load (frē′lōd′) *Informal v* live at the expense of others, or take advantage of hospitality, without contributing anything in return. **free′load′er** *n.* **free′load′ing** *adj.*

free·man (frē′mən) *n, pl* **free·men** (frē′mən) in former times, a person who was not a slave or serf.

free press *n* **1** newspapers and other media not censored or controlled by the government. **2** *Informal* publicity gained from being written or talked about, rather than from paid advertising.

free–range (frē′rānj′) *adj* to do with poultry or livestock that are allowed to roam freely rather than being shut up in a small space: *free-range chickens, free-range beef.*

free·sia (frē′zhə) *n* a plant that grows from a bulb, with clusters of delicate, fragrant flowers. <F.H.T. *Freese*, 19c botanist>

free·stone (frē′stōn′) *n* **1** a stone, such as limestone or sandstone, that can be cut easily without splitting. **2** a fruit whose stone can be separated easily from the pulp when it is ripe.
adj with such a stone: *freestone peaches.*

free·style (frē′stīl′) *adj* **1** *Sports* to do with a performance or competition in which one is not required to follow a specific style or set of rules: *She won gold in the women's freestyle skiing.* **2** *Swimming* to do with a swimming contest in which the competitors use their fastest swimming stroke, usually the front crawl.
n a performance or event of this kind: *The men's freestyle is tomorrow.*

free·think·er (frē′thing′kər) *n* a person who forms his or her opinions independently of authority or tradition. **free′think′ing** *adj.*

free throw *Basketball n* an undefended shot taken from one of the two foul lines. These lines are about 5 m from the backboard.

free trade *n* international trade with few or no restrictions from tariffs, customs, or protective duties. Compare PROTECTIONISM.

free verse *n* poetry without regular metre or rhyme.

free·ware (frē′wer′) *Computers n* software available at no charge.

free·way (frē′wā′) *especially US n* a high-speed highway on which no tolls are charged.

free·wheel·ing (frē′wē′ling) *adj* independent and unhampered by rules or established conventions.

free will *n* the power to make free choices, without being controlled by nature, history, fate, etc.

free·will (frē′wil′) *adj* voluntary: *a freewill offering.*

freeze (frēz) *v* **froze, fro·zen, freez·ing** **1** harden or turn from liquid to solid by cold: *to freeze meat. The water in the pail has frozen.* Compare MELT. **2** of the temperature, reach 0°C or colder: *It's going to freeze tonight.* **3** (*often with* ***over***) have a surface turn to ice: *The lake has frozen.* **4** be, feel, or become very cold: *You'll freeze in that thin jacket.* **5** kill or damage by frost; be so killed or damaged: *The tomato plants froze last night.* **6** make a part of the body numb by injecting or applying anesthetic: *The dentist froze my mouth before filling the tooth.* **7** fix or become stuck to something by freezing: *It was so cold that my fingers froze together.* **8** become fixed or motionless, out of terror or some other cause: *The mouse froze as the snake moved toward it, a frozen smile.* **9** *Sports* keep possession of the puck or ball and prevent the other team from attempting to score. **10** fix a price or rate at a certain amount, usually by government decree. **11** make funds or bank balances unusable and inaccessible: *Your account will be frozen until the cheque clears.* **12** stop all further activity or progress in: *Production of nuclear weapons has been frozen.*
n **1** a state of freezing or frost: *The freeze last night damaged the roses.* **2** a period during which there is freezing weather. <Old English *freosan*>
freeze out, *Informal* drive away or keep out by unfriendliness: *It was mean to freeze out the new student.*

SYNONYMS

Freeze involves hardening or making solid: *We need to freeze some ice cubes.*

Chill means "make cold": *We chilled the dessert in the refrigerator.*

Ice means "cool by surrounding with ice": *We iced the pop before the party.*

freeze–dry (frēz′drī′) *v* **freeze-dried, freeze-dry·ing** preserve food or a substance by quick-freezing it and then evaporating the frozen moisture in a vacuum.

freeze–frame (frēz′frām′) *n* a picture held still in a movie or TV show.

freez·er (frē′zər) *n* a refrigerated cabinet, especially for food, in which the temperature is below freezing point.

freezer burn *n* drying or discoloration of uncovered or inadequately covered frozen food due to evaporation of moisture from the parts left exposed.

🍁 **freeze–up** (frēz′up′) *n* the time of year when the rivers and lakes freeze over.

freez·ing (frē′zing) *n* the temperature at which water freezes: *It's below freezing outside.*
adj very cold: *It's freezing in here!*

freezing point *n* the temperature at which a liquid freezes: *The freezing point of water at sea level is 0°C.*

freight (frāt) *n* **1** the load of goods carried as cargo: *It took a whole day to unload the freight.* **2** the system of transporting goods: *She sent the box by freight.* **3** the charge for this.
v **1** load with goods. **2** carry or send by freight. <Dutch *vracht* freight>

freight car *n* a railway car for carrying freight.

freight·er (frā′tər) *n* a ship or aircraft for carrying freight.

French (french) *adj* **1** to do with France, its people, or their language. **2** 🍁 to do with French Canada, its people, or their language. <Old English *Frencisc*>

French and Indian War *n* the war (1754–1763) fought in N America between Britain and France, each having certain First Nations as allies, part of a larger conflict known as the **Seven Years' War**.

🍁 **French Canada** *n* **1** Canadians whose first or main language is French or whose ancestors came from France, considered as a group. **2** the part of Canada inhabited mainly or entirely by such Canadians, especially the province of Québec. **French Canadian** *adj, n.*

French doors *n* a pair of doors side by side, opening in the middle and with panes of glass all the way down.

French fry or **french fry** *n, pl* **French fries** or **french fries** a long strip of potato that has been cooked in boiling fat until crisp on the outside.

French horn *n* a brass wind instrument with a mellow tone. See ENGLISH HORN for picture.

🍁 **French immersion** *n* an educational program in which anglophone students are taught entirely and solely in French.

French press *n* a style of non-electric coffee maker with a fine screen that can be pushed down, trapping the coffee grounds.

🍁 **French Shore** *n* **1** the west coast of Newfoundland, where the French held fishing and other rights from 1713 to 1904. **2** an area originally settled by the Acadian French on the southwest coast of Nova Scotia.

French toast *n* a slice of bread dipped in egg or a mixture of egg and milk, and then fried.

fre·net·ic (frə net′ik) *adj* rushed, stressful, and uncontrolled: *a frenetic pace, a frenetic lifestyle.* <Greek *phrenetikos* inflammation of the brain>
fre·net′i·cal·ly *adv.*

fren·zy (fren′zē) *n, pl* **fren·zies** a state of very great excitement; a state of near madness: *There was a frenzy of activity in the gym as the students decorated it for the dance. The spectators were in a frenzy after the home team scored the winning goal.* **fren′zied** *adj.*

a **bat**	e **bed**	i **bid**	o **pot**	u **cup**	th **thin**
ā **cake**	ē **me**	ī **bite**	ō **go**	ū **rude**	ᴛʜ **then**
ä **bar**	ə **about**	ər **over**	ô **for**	ů **put**	zh **measure**

F

Fre·on (frē′on) *Trademark n* a nonflammable, inert gaseous or liquid fluorocarbon used especially as refrigerants and aerosol propellants. <f(*luorine*) + re(*frigerant*) + -on, modelled on *neon*>

fre·quen·cy (frē′kwən sē) *n, pl* **fre·quen·cies** **1** the number of times something happens: *He makes this mistake with alarming frequency.* **2** *Electronics, Radio* the number of complete cycles per second of an alternating current or any type of wave motion: *Different radio stations broadcast at different frequencies so their signals are distinct.*

frequency distribution *Statistics n* an arrangement of statistical data that shows how often a value occurs. The values are often arranged in a **frequency table**: *to study the frequency distribution of the number of cars per family unit in Hamilton. Make a frequency table of the ages of the students in the class.*

frequency modulation *Radio n* **1** a method of transmitting the sound signals of a broadcast by changing the frequency of the carrier waves to match those of the sound signals. **2** a broadcasting system that uses frequency modulation. *Abbrev.* **FM** or **F.M.** Compare AMPLITUDE MODULATION.

fre·quent (frē′kwənt) *for adj,* (fri kwent′) *for v. adj* **1** occurring often or close together: *Storms are frequent in March. Towns are not very frequent on the prairies.* **2** doing something often or habitually: *That airline gives special privileges to frequent flyers.*
v go often to or be often in: *She frequents the mall.* <Latin *frequentis* crowded> **fre·quent′er** *n.* **fre′quent·ly** *adv.*

fres·co (fres′kō) *n, pl* **fres·coes** or **fres·cos** **1** the art of painting with watercolours on damp, fresh plaster. **2** a picture or design so painted: *Beautiful frescoes covered the walls and ceiling of the cathedral.*
v **fres·coed, fres·co·ing** paint in fresco. <Italian = fresh>

fresh (fresh) *adj* **1** newly grown or produced: *fresh vegetables, fresh milk.* **2** newly made or obtained: *fresh footprints. Is there any fresh news from home?* **3** not preserved by drying, canning, freezing, etc.: *Fresh green beans taste so much better than canned ones.* **4** found as water without salt in lakes or rivers rather than salty, as in an ocean. **5** clean: *a fresh shirt, fresh air.* **6** pure, cool, and brisk: *a fresh breeze.* **7** creative and original: *a fresh approach to an old problem.* **8** rested and renewed for work or other activity: *fresh horses.* **9** new, without being affected by what has gone before: *to make a fresh start.* **10** disrespectful: *a fresh child. Don't be fresh with me!* <Old English *fresc*> **fresh′ly** *adv.* **fresh′ness** *n.*
fresh out of something, having just sold or used up the last of a supply of something.

SYNONYMS

Fresh can mean "new and creative": *We need a fresh approach to solving this problem.*

Novel suggests something that is new in an unusual way: *Her novel idea was to make footwear out of recycled automobile tires.*

fresh·en (fresh′ən) *v* make fresh or fresher: *to freshen the paint on the house.* **fresh′en·er** *n.*
freshen up, do something to make fresh or feel fresh: *He freshened up by taking a bath and changing his clothes.*

fresh·et (fresh′it) *n* **1** the rising or overflowing of a river due to heavy rains or melted snow. **2** a rush of fresh water flowing into the sea. <probably Old French *freis* fresh>

fresh·man (fresh′mən) *n, pl* **fresh·men** (fresh′mən) a student in the first year of university, college, or high school.

fresh·wa·ter (fresh′wot′ər) *adj* to do with lakes and rivers rather than the sea: *freshwater fish.*

fret[1] (fret) *v* **fret·ted, fret·ting** make or be irritable or whiny, agitated, or worried: *fretting about the time. The baby frets in hot weather. It fretted her to know that she had made a mistake.*
n a state of complaining or worry. <Old English *fretan* eat away at> **fret′ful** *adj.* **fret′ful·ly** *adv.* **fret′ful·ness** *n.* **fret′ter** *n.*

fret[2] (fret) *n* one of a series of ridges on the neck of some stringed instruments showing where to put the fingers to make the desired tones. <origin uncertain>

fret·saw (fret′so′)*n* a saw with a long, slender blade and fine teeth, used to cut thin wood into patterns.

fret·work (fret′wərk′) *n* ornamental design in wood done with a fretsaw.

Freud·i·an slip (froi′dē ən) *n* a slip of the tongue that may reveal what one is thinking. <S. *Freud,* 20c physician>

fri·a·ble (frī′ə bəl) *adj* easily crumbled: *Dry soil is friable.* <Latin *friare* crumble> **fri′a·bil′i·ty** *n.*

fri·ar (frī′ər) *n* a Roman Catholic monk, especially from an order that is supported solely by charity, such as the Franciscans. <Old French, from Latin *frater* brother. Monks use "brother" as a title.>

fric·as·see (frik′ə sē′) *n* meat cut up, stewed, and served in its own gravy.
v **fric·as·seed, fric·as·see·ing** prepare meat in this way. <French *fricasser* mince and cook in sauce>

fric·tion (frik′shən) *n* **1** a rubbing of one object against another: *The constant friction of her shoe against her heel produced a blister.* **2** *Physics* resistance of a moving body to the medium through which or surface on which it moves: *A sled slides more easily on smooth snow than on rough ground because there is less friction.* **3** conflict or unfriendly disagreement: *A difference of opinion caused friction between them.* <Latin *fricare* rub> **fric′tion·al** *adj.*

Fri·day (frī′dā′) *n* the day of the week after Thursday and before Saturday. *Abbrev.* **Fri** <Old English *Frigedæg* Frig's day. Frig was the Germanic goddess of love.>

fridge (frij) *Informal n* refrigerator.

fried (frīd) past tense and past participle of FRY[1].

friend (frend) *n* **1** a person who knows and likes another. **2** a person who favours and supports: *She was a friend to the poor.* **3** a person on the same side in a conflict: *Are you friend or foe?* **4** **Friend** a member of the religious Society of Friends; a Quaker. <Old English *freond*>
friend′less *adj.* **friend′ship** *n.*
be (or **make**) **friends,** have (or start) a close friendly relationship (with).

friend·ly (frend′lē) *adj* **friend·li·er, friend·li·est** **1** showing the attitude of a friend: *a friendly greeting. Be friendly to the newcomer, friendly faces.* **2** on good terms: *friendly relations between countries.* **3** wanting to be a friend: *a friendly dog.* **4** favourable or sympathetic: *friendly winds. That political party is not friendly to our cause.* **friend′li·ness** *n.*

SYNONYMS

Friendly means "having a sociable feeling toward another": *She gave a friendly wave to her neighbour.*

Amicable suggests being peaceable as well as friendly: *They ended the competition in an amicable way.*

Cordial can suggest being warm as well as friendly: *He welcomed her enthusiastically with a smile and a cordial handshake.*

–friendly *combining form* not harmful, offensive, or difficult for: *child-friendly literature, environment-friendly cleaning products.*

friendly fire *n* gunfire coming from one's own forces or from allies, not from the enemy.

fries (frīz) *Informal pln* French fries.

frieze (frēz) *n* a horizontal band of decoration around a room, building, or mantel of a fireplace, usually built into or forming part of the wall. <French, from Latin *Phrygium* coming from Phrygia>

frig·ate (frig′it) *n* **1** a modern warship smaller than a destroyer. **2** in former times, a three-masted sailing warship of medium size. <Italian *fregata*>

frigate bird *n* a tropical seabird with black plumage and a long, forked tail.

fright (frīt) *n* **1** fear or alarm. **2** a sudden onset of this feeling: *That mask was so realistic it gave me a fright.* **3** *Informal* a person who or thing that looks ugly, shocking, or ridiculous: *Your room is a fright; clean it up.* <Old English *fryhto*>
take fright, become alarmed.

fright·en (frī′tən) *v* make afraid, or become afraid: *You frighten me when you start yelling. The kitten frightens easily, so be gentle.* **fright′ened** *adj.* **fright′en·ing** *adj.*

fright·ful (frīt′fəl) *adj* **1** causing fright or horror: *frightful news.* **2** very unpleasant or ugly: *in this frightful heat, a frightful shirt.* **fright′ful·ly** *adv.* **fright′ful·ness** *n.*

frig·id (frij′id) *adj* **1** very cold: *a frigid climate.* **2** very formal, distant, and unfriendly in manner: *a frigid greeting.* **3** sexually unresponsive. <Latin *frigus* cold> **fri·gid′i·ty** *n.* **frig′id·ly** *adv.*

frill (fril) *n* **1** a ruffle. **2** anything added merely for show or as a luxury: *It was a plain house with few frills.* <origin uncertain> **frill′y** *adj.*

fringe (frinj) *n* **1 a** a border or trimming made of threads, either loose or tied together in small bunches: *My scarf has a fringe at both ends.* **b** anything that forms or looks like a border or trimming: *a fringe of hair.* **2** often,
fringes *pl* anything thought of as being far from the core or centre: *These remote islands are on the fringes of civilization. She belongs to the radical fringe of the labour movement.*
adj unconventional and not part of the mainstream: *Some of the skits performed at the fringe festival were quite offensive.*
v **fringed, fring·ing** make or form a fringe on: *Bushes fringed the road.* <Old French, from Latin *fimbria*>

fringe benefit *n* **1** a financial benefit given to an employee over and above regular wages, such as a pension, dental insurance, or a drug plan. **2** a desirable side effect: *One of the fringe benefits of living here is the chance to see good live theatre.*

frip·per·y (frip′ə rē) *n, pl* **frip·per·ies** showy or tawdry features, especially for foolish display. <Old French *friperie* old clothes, from *frepe* rag>

Fris·bee (friz′bē) *Trademark n* a plastic disc with edges that curve under to make throwing and catching easier.

ETYMOLOGY

Frisbee is thought to come from the name of a pie company in Bridgeport, Connecticut, called *Mother Frisbie's Pie Company.* Local college students began tossing the pie plates to each other as a game in the 1930s.

frisk (frisk) *v* **1** move about in a lively, playful way. **2** search a person for concealed weapons or stolen goods by running a hand quickly over the person's body. <Old French *frisque* lively> **frisk′y** *adj.*

frit·ta·ta (fri tȧ′tə) *n* an omelette cooked with pieces of meat and vegetables. <Italian = fried>

frit·ter[1] (frit′ər) *v* waste little by little: *She frittered away the afternoon trying to decide what to do.* <Old English> **frit′ter·er** *n.*

frit·ter[2] (frit′ər) *n* a small, deep-fried lump of batter, sometimes containing fruit or other food: *corn fritters, apple fritters.* <Old French, from Latin *frigere* to fry>

fritz (frits) *n* <origin unknown>
on the fritz, *Slang* broken; not in working order.

friv·o·lous (friv′ə ləs) *adj* **1** lacking in seriousness or common sense: *Frivolous behaviour is out of place at a funeral.* **2** of little worth, usefulness, or importance: *frivolous purchases. He wasted his time on frivolous matters.* <Latin *frivolus*> **fri·vol′i·ty** *n.* **friv′o·lous·ly** *adv.* **friv′o·lous·ness** *n.*

frizz or **friz** (friz) *v* **frizzed, frizz·ing** form hair into many small, tight curls.
n hair curled in small tight curls. <French *friser*> **frizz′y** *adj.*

fro (frō) *v* <Old Norse *fra*>
to and fro, first one way and then back again: *A rocking chair goes to and fro.*

frock (frok) *n* **1** a robe worn by a member of the clergy. **2** *UK* a girl's or woman's dress. **3** any loose, light, outer garment. <Old French *froc*>

a bat	e bed	i bid	o pot	u cup	th **thin**
ā cake	ē me	ī bite	ō go	ū rude	ᴛʜ **then**
ȧ bar	ə about	ər over	ȯ for	u̇ put	zh measure

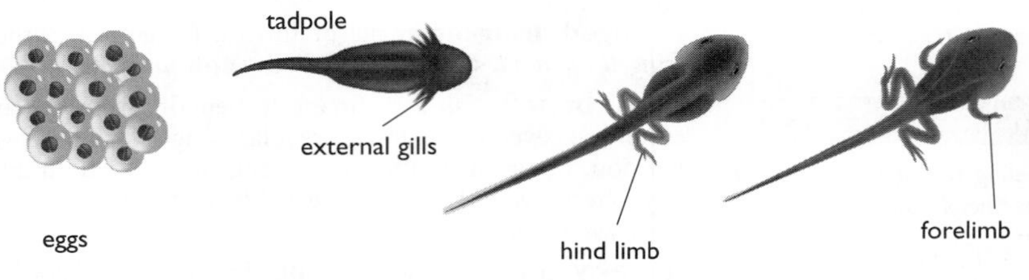

frog[1] (frog) *n* **1** a small, smooth-skinned, four-legged animal without a tail, living in or near water. **2** the part of the bow of a small stringed instrument, such as a violin, by which it is held for playing. <Old English *frogga*>
frog in the throat, *Informal* a slight hoarseness caused by soreness or swelling in the throat.

frog[2] (frog) *n* a decorative fastening for clothes, consisting of a loop of cord and a button, knot, or toggle that fits into the loop. <origin uncertain> **frogged** *adj.*

frog kick *n* in swimming, a leg movement done with the breaststroke, in which the swimmer draws the knees forward, then kicks out to the sides and brings both legs together again.

frog·man (frog′mən) *n, pl* **frog·men** (frog′mən) a skin diver, especially one working for the armed forces: *Most of the world's navies now have frogmen.*

frog·march (frog′märch′) *v* force someone to walk by grasping their arms from behind: *My brother frogmarched me over to the table and said, "Clean this up!"*

🍁 **frog run** *n* in sugaring-off operations, the second run of sap in the maple trees. Compare BUD RUN, ROBIN RUN.

frol·ic (frol′ik) *v* **frol·icked, frol·ick·ing** play and move about in a lively, cheerful way.
n a playful action, movement, game, or party. <Dutch *vrolijk* cheerful> **frol′ick·er** *n.* **frol′ic·some** *adj.*

from (frum) *prep* **1** using as a material: *Bricks are made from clay.* **2** starting out at or beginning with: *the train from Montréal. Study the lesson from page 10 to page 15.* **3** originating in or having as a source: *Milk comes from cows. Much of our clothing is from Québec.* **4** given or sent by: *a gift from me to you.* **5** because of: *weak from hunger, acting from a sense of duty.* **6** as being different: *Anyone can tell apples from oranges.* **7** off, out of, or out of the range or possession of: *Take a book from the table or from the box beside it. She took the toy from the baby.* <Old English *fram*>

frond (frond) *n* a divided leaf of a fern or palm. <Latin *frondis* leaf>

front (frunt) *n* **1** the part that faces or points forward: *the front of a car, the front of a building.* **2** the first part: *at the front of the book.* **3** in war, the place where most fighting is going on: *He spent many weeks at the front.* **4** a sphere of activity, especially one in which different groups are mostly in conflict: *the labour front.* **5** (*in compounds*) the land or part of a building facing a street, road, or body of water: *a storefront, the waterfront.* **6** an outward appearance meant to hide something or deceive others: *She put on a cheerful front, but inside she was torn by grief.* **7** a business or operation that serves as a cover for illegal activities. **8** *Meteorology* the dividing surface between two dissimilar air masses: *The weather report says there is a cold front approaching from the northwest.*
adj to do with the front: *the front page.*
v **1** (*usually with **on***) have the front toward: *Our house fronts on the park.* **2** put a front on or cover the front of: *A brick house fronted with stone.* **3** serve as a cover for illegal activities: *That store fronts for a drug-smuggling ring.* <Old French, from Latin *frontem* forehead. This was the original meaning in Old French and Middle English.>
up front, a in or to the front of something, especially a motor vehicle: *I want to sit up front.* **b** *Informal* frank(ly) and open(ly): *He was very up front about his earlier problem with drug abuse.* **c** paid right away: *The drug plan will cover prescription fees, but they have to paid up front.*

front·age (frun′tij) *n* **1** the part of a property next to a street, road, or body of water. **2** the length of this.

fron·tal (frun′təl) *adj* **1** of, on, in, or at the front: *a frontal attack, frontal nudity.* **2** of the forehead: *frontal bones.*

front·bench·er (frunt′ben′chər) *n* in a parliament or a legislative assembly, one of the leaders of any of the political parties, said to be sitting on the **front bench**. Compare BACKBENCHER. **front′bench′** *adj.*

fron·tier (fron tēr′) *or* (frun tēr′) *n* **1** the farthest part of a settled country, where the wilderness begins: *Yukon Territory is part of Canada's present-day frontier. Life on the frontier was often harsh.* **2** a part of one country touching on the border of another. **3** an unknown or undeveloped region: *the frontiers of science.*

fron·tis·piece (frun′tis pēs′) *n* a picture opposite the title page of a book or opposite the first page of one of its chapters or divisions. <Latin *frontis* forehead>

front line or **lines** *n* **1** in a war, the places closest to positions held by the enemy. **2** the part of any struggle involving the most activity: *on the front lines of the battle against cancer.* **front′line** *adj.*

front man *n* **1** a person who officially represents an organization. **2** a person who serves as a cover for illegal or secret activity: *The pleasant storekeeper was a front man for a gang of jewel smugglers.*

front–run·ner (frunt′run′ər) *n* the leader in any contest.

front–wheel drive (frunt′wēl′) *n* a transmission system in a motor vehicle in which power from the engine is transmitted to the front wheels.

frosh (frosh) *Informal n* a first-year student in university or college. <altered from *freshman*>

frost (frost) *n* **1** the feathery crystals of ice formed when water vapour in the air condenses at a temperature below freezing: *frost on the grass, frost on a window.* **2** temperature below the point at which water freezes: *There was frost in the air last night.* **3** an unfriendly manner: *I noticed a certain frost in her words to me.*
v **1** (*usually with* ***over***) cover or become covered with frost: *The car windows are frosted over.* **2** cover with icing: *to frost a cake.* **3** make glass opaque or translucent by doing something to the surface. **4** bleach or lighten selected strands of hair. <Old English> **frost′ed** *adj.* **frost′y** *adj.*

frost·bite (frost′bīt′) *n* injury to body tissues, caused by severe cold: *Experienced skiers take precautions against frostbite.* **frost′bit′ten** (frost′bit′ən) *adj.*

frost·ing (fros′ting) ICING (def. 1).

froth (froth) *n* a mass of tiny bubbles in a liquid: *The bottle of pop had been shaken so much that it was half froth.*
v **1** give out froth. **2** cause to foam by beating, pouring, producing saliva, or fermenting something. <Old Norse *frotha*> **froth′y** *adj.*

frown (froun) *n* a drawing together of the brows, often with a tightening of the mouth or jaw, often expressing deep thought or disapproval.
v **1** draw the brows together, as in deep thought or disapproval: *She frowned, trying to remember his phone number.* **2** express by frowning: *He frowned his annoyance.* <Old French *froignier* >

SYNONYMS

Frown expresses displeasure at something specific: *The teacher frowned when we came in late.*

Scowl means "look sullen or sour": *He is so grumpy that he scowls all day.*

frowz·y (frou′zē) *adj* **frowz·i·er, frowz·i·est** dirty and untidy. Also, **frowsy**. <origin unknown> **frowz′i·ly** *adv.* **frowz′i·ness** *n.*

froze (frōz) past tense of FREEZE.

fro·zen (frō′zən) *v* past participle of FREEZE.
adj **1** hardened, turned to ice, or preserved by freezing: *a frozen dessert. The water in the pail was frozen.* **2** very cold: *the frozen north.* **3** motionless from fear or shock.

fruc·tose (fruk′tōs) *n* a water-soluble sugar found especially in fruit juices and honey. Also called **fruit sugar**. <Latin *fructus* fruit>

fru·gal (frū′gəl) *adj* **1** avoiding any waste, luxury, or unnecessary spending: *A frugal person buys and uses food carefully.* **2** costing little and barely sufficient: *She ate a frugal supper of bread and milk.* <Latin *frugalis* profitable, from *frugis* fruit, profit> **fru·gal′i·ty** *n.* **fru′gal·ly** *adv.*

fruit (frūt) *n* **1** the fleshy, edible, usually seed-bearing product of a plant. **2** *Botany* the part of a plant that contains the seeds. **3** a useful product or result: *the fruits of your labour.*
v produce fruit. <Old French, from Latin *fructus* fruit> **fruit′like′** *adj.* **fruit′y** *adj.*

fruit bat *n* a bat that lives on fruit, especially in tropical or subtropical regions.

fruit·cake (frūt′kāk′) *n* **1** a rich cake usually made for weddings and other festive occasions, containing preserved and dried fruit, nuts, and spices. **2** *Slang* an eccentric or slightly crazy person.

fruit fly *n* a small, two-winged fly whose larva feeds on decaying fruits and vegetables.

fruit·ful (frūt′fəl) *adj* **1** producing or bearing much fruit: *a fruitful tree, a fruitful garden, fruitful soil.* **2** with good results: *a fruitful discussion, a fruitful use of your time.* **fruit′ful·ly** *adv.* **fruit′ful·ness** *n.*

fru·i·tion (frū ish′ən) *n* the state of being fulfilled or realized: *Her plans have at last come to fruition.* <*fruit*>

fruit·less (frūt′lis) *adj* **1** having no or worthless results: *fruitless efforts.* **2** producing no fruit; barren. **fruit′less·ly** *adv.* **fruit′less·ness** *n.*

fruit nap·pie or **nap·py** *n* a small bowl or dish designed for serving fruit or other dessert.

fruit sugar *n* **1** FRUCTOSE. **2** very fine white sugar crystals.

frump (frump) *n* a dowdy, unattractive woman or girl who wears unfashionable clothes. <origin uncertain> **frump′y** *adj.*

frus·trate (frus′trāt) *v* **frus·trat·ed, frus·trat·ing 1** prevent something from happening or succeeding: *Heavy rain frustrated our picnic plans.* **2** prevent someone from succeeding: *to frustrate an opponent.* **3** make someone discouraged or resentful: *What frustrates me is that he never listens to anything I say.* <Latin *frustra* in vain> **frus·tra′tion** *n.*

fry[1] (frī) *v* **fried, fry·ing 1** cook in a pan or on a griddle over direct heat, usually in hot fat or oil. **2** undergo frying: *While the hamburgers were frying, I set the table.* **3** *Slang* wreck or destroy, often by overuse or misuse: *You'll fry your brains if you try to write the essay all in one night. The power surge fried the hard drive on my computer.*
n, pl **fries 1** a short, narrow single strip of deep-fried potato. **2** a social gathering at which food is fried and eaten: *a fish fry.* <Old French, from Latin *frigere*>

fry[2] (frī) *n, pl* **fry 1** the young of fish. **2** small adult fish that live together in large groups, or schools: *Sardines are classed as fry.* **3** offspring or children. <Old French *froi* spawn, from *freier* to rub, in reference to fish that spawned by rubbing their belly on the sand>
small fry, *Informal* **a** children: *This movie is not for small fry.* **b** people or things with little importance: *The police raid netted only small fry.*

a bat	e bed	i bid	o pot	u cup	th **thin**
ā cake	ē me	ī bite	ō go	ū rude	ᴛʜ **then**
ä bar	ə about	ər over	ô for	ů put	zh measure

F

fry bread *n* QUICK BREAD cooked by deep-frying.

fry·er (frī′ər) *n* **1** a chicken young and tender enough for frying: *A fryer usually weighs less than 1.5 kg.* **2** an appliance or piece of equipment used to fry food.

frying pan *n* a shallow pan with a long handle, used for frying food.
out of the frying pan into the fire, straight from one danger or difficulty into a worse one.

FSH *n* in full, **follicle-stimulating hormone** a hormone produced by the pituitary gland, causing the female ova and the male testicles to mature.

f–stop (ef′stop) *n* a camera setting that determines how much light will fall on the film. <from *focal length*>

fuch·sia (fyū′shə) *n* a shrub or small tree with funnel-shaped, hanging flowers that are usually purple or red.
adj vivid purplish red. <L. *Fuchs*, 16c botanist>

fud·dle (fud′əl) *v* **fud·dled, fud·dling** make stupid or confused, often by alcohol. <origin uncertain>

fud·dy–dud·dy (fud′ē dud′ē) *n, pl* **fud·dy-dud·dies** a stuffy, old-fashioned person.
adj stuffy and old-fashioned. <origin uncertain>

fudge (fuj) *n* **1** a soft candy made of sugar, milk, butter, and a flavouring such as maple sugar, or vanilla, sometimes with nuts added. **2** nonsense; empty talk.
v **fudged, fudg·ing 1** avoid committing oneself: *Don't let him fudge on the issue.* **2** say misleading things. **3** produce or alter dishonestly: *The researchers fudged the results.* <origin uncertain>

fu·el (fyū′əl) *n* **1** something burned to provide heat or power: *Coal, wood, gas, and oil are fuels.* **2** a material from which atomic energy can be obtained, such as in a reactor. **3** material that supplies nutrients for a living organism: *Your body needs fuel to live and grow.* **4** anything that keeps something else going or increases it: *Her insults were fuel to his anger.*
v **fu·elled** or **fu·eled, fu·el·ling** or **fu·el·ing 1** supply with fuel. **2** get fuel. <Old French *fouaille* bundle of firewood, from Latin *focus* fireplace>

fuel cell *n* an electric cell, or battery, that produces electrical energy directly from the chemical reaction between oxygen and a fuel such as hydrogen.

fu·el–ef·fi·cient (fyūl′i fish′ənt) *adj* going a distance, heating a space, or doing work while using relatively little fuel: *a fuel-efficient car. This airtight wood stove is very fuel-efficient.* **fuel efficiency** *n.*

fuel injection *n* a system in an internal combustion engine by which vaporized fuel is injected under pressure directly into the cylinders for greater fuel efficiency. **fu′el-in·ject′ed** *adj.*

fu·gi·tive (fyū′jə tiv) *n* a person who has escaped from confinement or persecution and is trying to avoid capture: *a fugitive from the law.*
adj **1** fleeing from confinement or persecution: *a fugitive slave.* **2** quick to disappear: *fugitive thoughts, the fugitive hours.* <Old French, from Latin *fugere* flee>

fugue (fyūg) *Music n* a composition in which different voices or instruments repeat the same melody at different times with slight variations. <French, from Latin *fuga* flight>

Füh·rer (fyù′rər) *n* **der Führer** the title given to Adolf Hitler (1889–1945), Nazi dictator of Germany. Also, **Fuehrer**. <German = leader>

lever

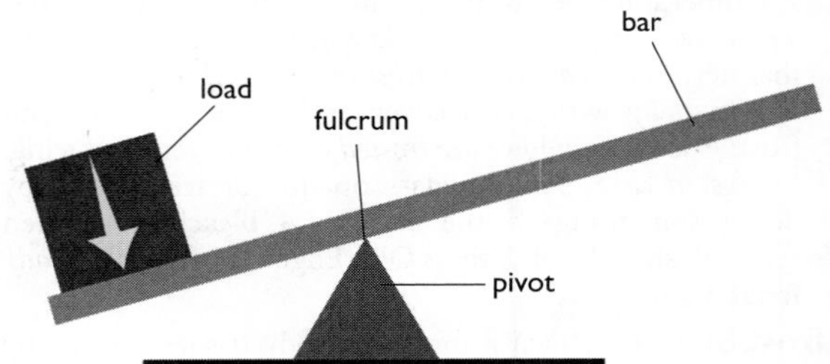

ful·crum (ful′krəm) *or* (fùl′krəm) *n, pl* **ful·crums** or **ful·cra** the support on which a lever turns or is supported. <Latin *fulcire* support>

ful·fill or **ful·fil** (fəl fil′) *v* **ful·filled, ful·fill·ing 1** cause to happen or take place: *to fulfill a lifelong dream, to fulfill a prophecy.* **2** do or perform: *to fulfill the terms of a contract. He fulfilled his duty.* **3** satisfy or meet: *to fulfill a need, to fulfill a requirement.* <Old English *fullfyllan*>
ful·fill′ment or **ful·fil′ment** *n.*
fulfill yourself, make the best of your potential.

ful·fill·ing (fəl fil′ing) *adj* satisfying, rewarding, or giving a feeling of accomplishment: *a fulfilling job.*

full (fùl) *adj* **1** filled and able to hold no more: *a full cup. The box is full of firewood.* **2** complete or entire: *a full supply, the full treatment. I waited a full hour.* **3** of the greatest size, amount, extent, or development: *at full speed, in full bloom.* **4** having had enough food: *He was full after the first course.* **5** plump and rounded: *full lips.* **6** made with a large amount of material, in gathers, folds, or pleats: *a full skirt.* **7** of the highest grade or rank: *a full professor.* **8** strong, deep, and rich in sound: *a full alto voice.*
adv **1** completely or entirely: *Fill the pail full.* **2** very: *He knew full well that he would have to go back.* **3** squarely or directly: *As he stepped outside, the wind hit him full in the face.*
n **the full** the greatest size, amount, or degree: *The moon is past the full. Enjoy life to the full.* <Old English>
full′ness *n.* **full′y** *adv.*
full of, a filled with: *a pail full of water, air full of the scent of the sea.* **b** having a great amount or number of: *Her writing is full of mistakes.* **c** completely absorbed in: *He's full of his latest project. She's so full of herself.*
in full, a to or for the complete amount: *The account has been paid in full.* **b** written or said with all the words: *Write your name in full.*

full·back (fùl′bak′) *Football n* a player whose position is farthest behind the front line.

full blast *Informal n* at highest speed or largest capacity: *The copy machine has been going full blast all day.*

ETYMOLOGY

The term **full blast** was used in the 1800s in reference to the large industrial furnaces that operated with blasts of hot air. A furnace that was burning as hot as it could was said to be at *full blast.*

full–blood·ed (fu̇l′blud′id) *adj* **1** of a pure race, breed, or variety. **2** vigorous and enthusiastic.

full–blown (fu̇l′blōn′) *adj* **1** in full bloom. **2** completely developed or matured.

full–bod·ied (fu̇l′bod′ēd) *adj* of wine, having considerable strength, flavour, etc.

full dress *n* formal clothes worn in the evening or on important occasions. **full′-dress′** *adj.*

full–fledged (fu̇l′flejd′) *adj* **1** fully developed. **2** of full rank or standing: *He is now a full-fledged auto mechanic.*

full–grown (fu̇l′grōn′) *adj* fully developed or mature.

full house *n* **1** the condition in which every seat is occupied, especially in a theatre. **2** in poker, a hand made up of three cards of one kind and two of another, such as three sixes and two kings.

full–length (fu̇l′length′) *adj* **1** showing the full length of the human figure: *a full-length portrait, a full-length mirror.* **2** of traditional or standard size, length, or duration: *a full-length novel, a full-length feature film.*

full moon *n* **1** the moon seen as a whole circle. **2** the time, once every four weeks, when this occurs.

full–scale (fu̇l′skāl′) *adj* **1** made in the original or actual size: *a full-scale drawing, a full-scale working model.* **2** using or involving all available resources: *a full-scale investigation, full-scale war.*

full–size (fu̇l′sīz′) *adj* of the standard size for its kind.

full stop PERIOD (def. 7)

full–time (fu̇l′tīm′) *adj, adv* for the full number of scheduled hours, especially working hours: *a full-time job* (*adj*). *I can't work full-time until I finish school* (*adv*).

ful·mi·nate (ful′mə nāt′) *v* **ful·mi·nat·ed, ful·mi·nat·ing** greatly object to something or someone: *The newspapers fulminated against the new law.* <Latin *fulmen* lightning, i.e., something that seems to be violently thrown> **ful′mi·na′tion** *n.*

ful·some (fu̇l′səm) *adj* so excessive as to be annoying or offensive: *fulsome detail, fulsome praise.* <*full* + *-some*[1]> **ful′some·ly** *adv.* **ful′some·ness** *n.*

fum·ble (fum′bəl) *v* **fum·bled, fum·bling** **1** fail to catch and hold a ball. **2** feel around clumsily: *He fumbled in his pockets for the ticket. She fumbled for words to express her thanks.* **3** handle awkwardly: *He fumbled the introduction.*
n **1** a failure to catch and hold a ball. **2** an awkward handling of a situation. <Middle English> **fum′bler** *n.* **fum′bling·ly** *adv.*

fume (fyūm) *n* usually, **fumes** *pl* a vapour, gas, or smoke, especially if harmful, stifling, stinging, or smelly: *The strong fumes of the acid nearly choked him.*
v **fumed, fum·ing** **1** give off fumes: *The kerosene lamp fumed and sputtered.* **2** be in a state of great irritation or impatience: *By the time we got there, he was fuming.* **3** treat wood with ammonia fumes: *to fume oak.* <Old French, from Latin *fumus* smoke>

fu·mi·gate (fyū′mə gāt′) *v* **fu·mi·gat·ed, fu·mi·gat·ing** expose to chemical fumes in order to kill vermin or to disinfect: *The whole apartment building needs to be fumigated.* **fu′mi·ga′tion** *n.* **fu′mi·ga′tor** *n.*

fun (fun) *n* **1** lively play or amusement: *an evening of fun.* **2** playfulness or humour: *She is always full of fun.* **3** ridicule: *He became a figure of fun.*
adj Informal amusing or entertaining: *It was a fun evening. This game is fun.* <Middle English *fonnen*>
for fun, for no other purpose than amusement: *I just did it for fun.*
in fun, as a joke: *She said it in fun, so you shouldn't take it seriously.*
like fun, *Slang* an expression used to contradict someone: *"It's your turn to vacuum; I did it last week." "Like fun you did!"*
make fun of or **poke fun at,** laugh at.

GRAMMAR AND USAGE

Fun, once strictly a noun, is now commonly used as an adjective: *We had a really fun time.*

However, the adjective forms *funner* and *funnest* and *more fun* and *most fun* are still regarded as non-standard and somewhat awkward. These usages should be avoided in formal writing.

func·tion (fungk′shən) *n* **1** the natural or proper purpose of something: *The function of the stomach is to digest food.* **2** (*usually plural*) duty: *He was too sick to carry out his regular functions.* **3** a public gathering for some purpose: *The class reps have planned several social functions for the upcoming year.* **4** *Mathematics* a quantity whose value depends on, or varies with, the value given to one or more related quantities: *The volume of a sphere is a function of the radius.*
v **1** work or operate: *This pen does not function very well.* **2** (*with* ***as***) serve or be used: *That heavy ornament functions as a doorstop now.* <Latin *fungi* perform>

func·tion·al (fungk′shə nəl) *adj* **1** to do with a function or functions. **2** working or operating properly: *My computer has not been functional for four days.* **3** strictly practical, with little regard for attractiveness: *functional shoes.* **func′tion·al·ly** *adv.*

functional illiteracy *n* lack of ability to read well enough for ordinary practical purposes. **functionally illiterate** *adj.*

func·tion·al·ism (fungk′shə nə liz′əm) *n* the principle that the design of a thing should be determined mainly by its purpose or function. **func′tion·al·ist′** *n, adj.*

a bat	e bed	i bid	o pot	u cup	th **thin**
ā cake	ē me	ī bite	ō go	ū rude	ᴛʜ **then**
ȧ bar	ə about	ər over	ȯ for	u̇ put	zh measure

func·tion·ar·y (fungk′shə ner′ē) *n, pl* **func·tion·ar·ies** an official, especially a low-ranking government official.

function key *Computers n* a key on the keyboard that causes some preprogrammed operation to take place, such as exiting an application, accessing a help program, etc.

function word *Grammar n* a word used mainly to show relationships between other words, such as prepositions, conjunctions, and articles. Words such as *the*, *of*, and *but* are function words.

GRAMMAR AND USAGE

Although the total number of **function words** in English is relatively low, they make up about half of any given text, whether spoken or written.

Their high frequency is one of the reasons they are usually short—for efficiency!

fund (fund) *n* **1** a sum of money set aside for a special purpose: *The school has a small fund to buy books for the library.* **2** a stock or store of something ready for use: *a fund of information.* **3 funds** *pl* money available for use: *He had to end his trip early because he ran out of funds.*
v **1** provide funds for: *This summer camp is funded by the community association.* **2 a** set aside a sum of money to pay interest on a debt. **b** change a debt from a short term to a long term. <French *fond* stock or capital, from Latin *fundus* piece of land> **fund′ing** *n.*

fun·da·men·tal (fun′də men′təl) *adj* **1** basic: *the fundamental principles of design, a fundamental change of attitude.* **2** principal or main: *The fundamental idea in my speech is that Canadians should lead the fight against air pollution.* **3** *Music* to do with the lowest note of a chord.
n **1** (*usually plural*) a principle, rule, or law that forms a foundation or basis: *the fundamentals of grammar.* **2** *Music* the lowest note of a chord. <Latin *funduse* bottom> **fun′da·men′tal·ly** *adv.*

fun·da·men·tal·ism (fun′də men′tə liz′əm) *n* a movement or tendency in religion or thought that insists on a strict, narrow interpretation of scriptures or basic documents. **fun′da·men′tal·ist′** *n, adj.*

SYNONYMS

Fundamental means "basic": *The right to a fair trial is fundamental to our system of justice.*

Essential also means "basic and necessary": *The ability to react quickly is essential to being a racing car driver.*

fund·rais·ing (fund′rā′zing) *n* the process of raising money for a special purpose or organization.
adj intended to raise money: *a fundraising event.*

fu·ner·al (fyū′nə rəl) *n* the ceremonies that accompany the burial or burning of the dead, often including a religious or memorial service and taking the body to the place of burial or burning.
adj to do with a funeral: *a funeral march.* <Latin *funeris*>

funeral director *n* an undertaker.

funeral home *n* a business that arranges or holds funeral services and has facilities for preparing dead bodies for burial or cremation. Also called **funeral parlour** or **parlor**.

fu·ner·ar·y (fyū′nə rer′ē) *adj* used for a funeral, cremation, or burial. A **funerary urn** holds the ashes of a dead person's body.

fu·ne·re·al (fyū nē′rē əl) *adj* mournful and solemn, as if to do with a funeral. **fu·ne′re·al·ly** *adv.*

fun·gi (fung′gī) *or* (fun′jī), (fung′gē) *or* (fun′jē) a plural of FUNGUS.

fun·gi·cide (fung′gə sīd′) *or* (fun′jə sīd′) *n* a substance that destroys fungus. **fun′gi·cid′al** *adj, n.*

fun·gus (fung′gəs) *n, pl* **fun·gi** or **fun·gus·es** **1** any of a KINGDOM (def. 3) of living things that reproduce by spores, live on other organic matter, and lack flowers, stems, and chlorophyll. Mushrooms, moulds, and mildews are fungi. See also EUKARYOTE. **2** a diseased condition of the skin caused by such an organism growing on or in it. <Latin> **fun′gal** *adj.* **fun′gous** *adj.*

CONFUSABLES

Fungus is the noun form: *Mould is a common type of fungus.*

Fungous is the adjective form: *Mildew is a fungous growth.*

fu·nic·u·lar (fyū nik′yə lər) *adj* hanging from or operated by a rope or cable. A **funicular railway** is a railway system in which the cars are moved by cables, such as some short railways that carry people up and down steep slopes. <Latin *funiculus* little rope>

funk[1] (fungk) *Informal n* a depressed mood: *He's been in a funk since he and his girlfriend broke up.* <origin uncertain>

funk[2] (fungk) *Informal n* **1** an originally black style of popular music combining rock, blues, and soul. **2** a strong, musty odour. <perhaps Old French *funkier* give off smoke, from Latin *fumus* smoke>

funk·y (fungk′ē) *adj* **funk·i·er, funk·i·est** **1** *Music* to do with FUNK[2] (def. 1). **2** offbeat, especially in an unconventional or striking way: *funky clothes, a funky restaurant décor.* <from *funk*[2]> **funk′i·ness** *n.*

fun·nel (fun′əl) *n* **1** a tube with a high, wide, cone-shaped mouth, used for pouring a liquid or powder into a container with a small opening: *She used a funnel to pour the gas into the tank.* **2** anything like a funnel, such as a wide road that leads into a narrower one. **3** a round smokestack or flue: *The steamship had two funnels.*
v **fun·nelled** or **fun·neled, funnel·ling** or **fun·nel·ing** pass or feed through a funnel. <Old French, from Latin *fundere* pour>

fun·ny (fun′ē) *adj* **fun·ni·er, fun·ni·est** **1** humorous; amusing or comical: *a funny story. My little brother was very funny the first time he tried to skate.* **2** trying or intending to amuse: *She was just being funny.* **3** strange, peculiar, or odd: *That's funny; I thought I left my wallet right here.* **4** deceptive or tricky: *Don't try anything funny or you might get hurt.*

n **funnies** *pl* comic strips, or the section of a newspaper devoted to comic strips: *Who's got the funnies?*
fun′ni·ly *adv.* **fun′ni·ness** *n.*
get funny with, *Informal* be impudent toward: *Don't get funny with me, young man.*

funny bone *n* the part of the elbow over which a nerve passes, causing a sharp tingling sensation if struck.
strike your funny bone, *Informal* seem amusing to you.

funny money *Informal n* counterfeit bills.

fur (fər) *n* **1** the thick covering of hair on the skin of **fur-bearing** animals. **2** any furlike coating: *There's fur on my tongue.* **3** often, **furs** *pl* a garment or garments made of fur.
v **furred, fur·ring 1** make, cover, trim, or line with fur. **2** cover or become covered with a furlike coating. <Old French *fuerre* covering> **fur′less** *adj.* **fur′ry** *adj.*
make the fur fly, *Informal* quarrel or fight.

fur·ball (fər′bol′) *n* a small mass coughed up by a cat, made up of hair it has swallowed in the process of cleaning itself.

fur·bish (fər′bish) *v* (*usually with* ***up***) restore to good condition: *Before going to Québec, he furbished up his French.* <Old French *forbir* polish>

🍁 **fur brigade** *n* in former times, a convoy of freight canoes, dog sleds, and boats that carried furs and other goods from remote trading posts.

fu·ri·ous (fyū′rē əs) *adj* **1** intensely violent: *a furious storm.* **2** full of fierce anger: *She was furious at me.* **3** showing unrestrained energy or speed: *furious activity.* <Latin *furia*> **fu′ri·ous·ly** *adv.* **fu′ri·ous·ness** *n.*

furl (fərl) *v* roll or fold up: *to furl a sail, to furl a flag.* <French, from Latin *firmus* firm + *ligare* bind>

fur·long (fər′long) *n* a nonmetric unit of distance equal to one-eighth of a mile (about 0.2 km), used mostly in horse races. <Old English *furh* channel + *lang* long>

fur·lough (fər′lō) *n* a leave of absence, usually for a member of the armed forces.
v give or take such a leave of absence. <Dutch *verlof* permission>

fur·nace (fər′nis) *n* **1** an enclosed structure in a building for heating water or air which then circulates through pipes, radiators, or registers to warm the building. **2** a similar structure providing intense heat for melting and refining ore or treating metal or minerals. **3** a very hot place: *This room is a furnace in summertime.* <Old French, from Latin *fornacis* oven>

fur·nish (fər′nish) *v* **1** supply with furniture or equipment: *to furnish a house.* **2** supply or provide: *The sun furnishes heat.* <Old French *fournir*> **fur′nished** *adj.*

fur·nish·ings (fər′ni shingz) *pln* the furniture or equipment for a room, house, apartment, office, etc.

fur·ni·ture (fər′nə chər) *n* the large movable articles needed for living or working in a house, office, or other space, such as tables and chairs. <French *fournir* furnish>

fu·ror (fyū′rər) *n* a wild or confused outburst of enthusiasm, anger, or excitement: *The announcement caused a furor.* <French, from Latin *furere* to rage>

fur·ri·er (fər′ē ər) *n* a dealer in furs, or whose work is preparing furs or making and repairing fur garments.

fur·row (fər′ō) *n* **1** a long, narrow groove cut in the ground, usually for planting seeds or seedlings in. **2** any long, narrow groove or track: *The wheels of heavy trucks made deep furrows in the muddy road.* **3** a deep wrinkle: *a furrow in your brow.*
v make furrows in: *His face was furrowed with age.* <Old English *furh*>

fur·ry (fər′ē) *adj* **fur·ri·er, fur·ri·est 1** like fur or consisting of fur: *furry material.* **2** having fur as its natural covering: *a little furry animal.* **3** having a furlike coating: *a furry tongue.* **fur′ri·ness** *n.*

fur seal *n* a seal whose thick coat with fine underfur is used commercially.

fur·ther (fər′ᴛʜər) *adj, adv,* a comparative of **far 1** farther: *Our house is on the further side* (*adj*). *Go no further* (*adv*). **2** additional or additionally: *I have no further need of it* (*adj*). *He refused to discuss it further* (*adv*). See also FARTHER.
v help forward; promote: *Let us further the cause of peace.* <Old English *furthra*> **fur′ther·ance** *n.*

fur·ther·more (fər′ᴛʜər mȯr′) *adv* moreover or also: *I'm tired, and furthermore, I'm annoyed.*

fur·ther·most (fər′ᴛʜərmōst′) *adj* most distant: *the furthermost parts of the earth.*

fur·thest (fər′ᴛʜist) *adj, adv,* a superlative of **far 1** farthest in space or time. **2** to the greatest degree or extent.

fur·tive (fər′tiv) *adj* trying not to be seen or caught: *She made a furtive attempt to read her sister's letter. His furtive manner makes it difficult to trust him.* <Latin *fur* thief>
fur′tive·ly *adv.* **fur′tive·ness** *n.*

fu·ry (fyū′rē) *n, pl* **fu·ries 1** wild, fierce anger. **2** violence or fierceness: *the fury of a hurricane.* **3** a fit of wild or fiercely energetic activity: *in a fury of housecleaning.* **4 Fury** *Greek and Roman myth* one of the three spirits of revenge. <Latin *furia*>
like fury, *Informal* violently or wildly and very rapidly.

furze (fərz) GORSE.

fuse[1] (fyūz) *n* a safety device in an electric circuit, consisting of a metal strip or wire that melts and breaks the connection when the current becomes dangerously strong.
v **fused, fus·ing 1** melt together: *to fuse metals. Fuse the patch to the fabric with a hot iron.* **2** blend or unite: *to fuse two styles of music.* <Latin, from *fundere* melt>
fus′i·ble *adj.*
blow a fuse, a trip the safety device in an electrical circuit by overloading or short-circuiting it. **b** *Informal* burst out in anger.

fuse[2] (fyūz) *n* a slow-burning wick or other device to detonate dynamite, a firecracker, grenade, or bomb from a safe distance. <Italian, from Latin *fusus* spindle, for the tube of explosive material which was spindle shaped>
have a short fuse, *Informal* have a quick temper.

a bat	e bed	i bid	o pot	u cup	th **thin**
ā cake	ē me	ī bite	ō go	ū rude	ᴛʜ **then**
ȧ bar	ə about	ər over	ȯ for	u̇ put	zh measure

fuse box *n* a compartment containing the fuses connected to a set of electrical circuits.

fu·se·lage (fyū′zə lȧzh′) *or* (fyū′zə lij) *n* the main body of an aircraft, apart from wings and tail. See AILERON for picture. <French *fuselé* spindle-shaped, from the shape of the body of the aircraft>

fu·sil·lade (fyū′zə lād′) *n* **1** a discharge of many guns at the same time or in rapid succession. **2** something that resembles this: *a fusillade of questions.* <French *fusil* musket>

fu·sion (fyū′zhən) *n* **1** a melting or blending together: *Bronze is made by the fusion of copper and tin. A new party was formed by the fusion of various right-wing groups.* **2** a type of popular music blending elements of jazz, funk, rock, and sometimes other forms. **3** a style of cuisine that blends dishes and techniques from various cultures. **4** *Nuclear physics* the combining of nuclei of light elements to create nuclei of greater mass and release tremendous amounts of energy. <Latin, from *fundere* melt>

fuss (fus) *n* **1** needless excitement, talk, activity, or worry: *Why make a fuss over the loss of a loonie?* **2** a show of enjoyment or pleasure: *They all made a fuss over the new baby.* **3** an uproar: *The announcement caused a fuss in educational circles.*
v **1** make a fuss: *He's always fussing about nothing.* **2** fret, be discontented, or whine: *The baby always starts fussing just before supper.* <origin uncertain> **fuss′er** *n.*

fuss·budg·et (fus′buj′it) *Informal n* a fussy person.

fuss·y (fus′ē) *adj* **fuss·i·er, fuss·i·est 1** hard to please about needs or requirements: *She is fussy about grammar.* **2** easily upset and irritable: *a fussy baby.* **3** elaborate or fancy: *a fussy blouse.* **4** full of details and requiring much care: *Proofing an essay is fussy work.* **fuss′i·ly** *adv.* **fuss′i·ness** *n.*

fust·y (fus′tē) *adj* **fust·i·er, fust·i·est 1** having a stale, musty, or mouldy smell. **2** old-fashioned: *fusty opinions.* <Old French *fust* wine cask, from Latin *fustis* barrel stave> **fust′i·ly** *adv.* **fust′i·ness** *n.*

fu·tile (fyū′tīl) *or* (fyū′təl) *adj* **1** not successful; useless: *a futile attempt.* **2** purposeless or pointless: *a futile existence.* <Latin *futilis*> **fu′tile·ly** *adv.* **fu·til′i·ty** (fyū til′ə tē) *n.*

fu·ton (fū′ton) *n* a quilted mattress, usually stuffed with cotton or other material. <Japanese>

fu·ture (fyū′chər) *n* **1** the time that is to follow the present: *She has not done very well so far, but hopes to do better in the future.* **2** events that will happen: *to predict the future.* **3** a chance or expectation of success and prosperity: *a young woman with a future.* **4 futures** *pl* contracts for commodities or stocks bought or sold to be received at a future date.
adj that is to come: *They wished him happiness in his future years.* <Latin *futurus*> **fu·tur′i·ty** *n.*

GRAMMAR AND USAGE

Unlike other languages, English has no simple **future tense**. One way to show that an action will happen in the future is to use the auxiliary verbs *will* or *shall* before the basic form of a verb:
She will brush her hair before she goes to bed.
I shall eat dinner after my guitar lesson.

future perfect *Grammar n* the verb tense used to express an action that will already have been completed at some future time. Example: *They will have finished their work by tomorrow.*

future shock *n* alienation and disorientation resulting from rapid change, especially technological change, with too little time for people to adjust. <coined by A. Toffler in his book *Future Shock*>

future tense *Grammar n* a verb tense that expresses occurrence in time to come. It is made up of the auxiliary *will* followed by the infinitive of the main verb. Examples: *He will go. I will be.*

fu·tur·is·tic (fyū′chə ris′tik) *adj* showing what is imagined for the future, especially very advanced technology and design: *a futuristic movie, set in the year 2050. The display featured futuristic designs in furnishings.*

fuzz (fuz) *n* **1** tiny, fine, light fibres or hairs: *Some caterpillars are covered with fuzz.* **2** an indistinct quality in sound or image reproduction such as blurriness or distortion. **3 the fuzz** *pl Slang* the police.
v make or become fuzzy. <origin uncertain>

fuzz·y (fuz′ē) *adj* **fuzz·i·er, fuzz·i·est 1** like or consisting of fuzz: *The baby's hair was just a fuzzy halo. My hair gets fuzzy when it's humid outside.* **2** covered with fuzz: *a fuzzy caterpillar.* **3** indistinct, blurry, or distorted as a sound or image. **4** vague or unclear: *That argument is an example of fuzzy thinking.* **fuzz′i·ly** *adv.* **fuzz′i·ness** *n.*

FX special effects.

–fy *suffix* forming verbs to do with causing or becoming: *petrify, falsify, horrify.* <French, from Latin *facere* do, make>

FYI for your information.

Gg

g or **G** (jē) *n, pl* **g's** or **G's** **1** the seventh letter of the English alphabet, or any speech sound represented by it. **2** the seventh thing in a list or series. **3** *Music* the fifth tone in the scale of C major, or a key based on a scale with F as its keynote.

g **1** gram(s). **2** a unit of acceleration equal to the force of gravity on a body at rest, used to measure the force exerted on an accelerating body.

G giga- (an SI prefix).

G7 *n* in full, **Group of Seven** seven economically powerful nations including Canada, the US, the UK, Japan, Germany, France, and Italy, whose representatives meet regularly to discuss policy.

G8 *n* in full, **Group of Eight** eight economically powerful nations, whose representatives meet regularly to discuss policy. They include the members of the Group of Seven, together with Russia.

gab (gab) *Informal v* **gabbed, gab·bing** talk casually, especially idly or too much.
n chitchat; idle talk. <Gaelic *gob* mouth>
gift of the gab, *Informal* fluency and ease in speaking.

gab·ar·dine (gab′ər dēn′) *n* a closely woven cloth with small, diagonal ribs on its surface, used for raincoats, suits, etc. Also, **gaberdine.** <Old French *gallevardine*>

gab·ble (gab′əl) *v* **gab·bled, gab·bling** **1** make unintelligible sounds like those a goose makes. **2** talk rapidly, without making much sense: *She was gabbling on excitedly about a movie she had seen.*
n rapid, nonsensical talk or unintelligible sounds: *the gabble of geese.* <Dutch *gabbelen*> **gab′bler** *n.*

gab·by (gab′ē) *Informal adj* **gab·bier, gab·bi·est** very talkative.

gab·fest (gab′fest′) *Slang n* a great deal of talking, especially idle conversation: *I hate to interrupt your gabfest, but we're trying to study here.*

ga·ble (gā′bəl) *n* **1** the end of a ridged roof, with the triangular upper part of the wall that it covers. **2** an end wall topped by a gable. **3** a triangular, canopylike ornament built over a door or window. <Old Norse *gafl*>
ga′bled *adj.*

Ga·bon (gə bōn′) *n* a country in west Africa.
Gab′o·nese′ *adj, n.*

gad (gad) *v* **gad·ded, gad·ding** (*with* ***about***) go around looking for pleasure or excitement: *She was always gadding about town.* <obsolete *gadling* wanderer>

gad·a·bout (gad′ə bout′) *Informal n* a person who goes around looking for pleasure or excitement.

gad·fly (gad′flī′) *n, pl* **gad·flies** **1** a large fly that stings livestock. Horseflies are gadflies. **2** a person who irritates others or rouses them from a state of self-satisfaction by calling attention to their faults. <obsolete *gad* goad + *fly*[1]>

gadg·et (gaj′it) *n* a small, ingenious or unusual mechanical device: *a handy gadget.* <origin uncertain>
gadg′et·ry *n.*

Gae·a (jē′ə) GAIA.

Gael·ic (gā′lik) *or* (gȧ′lik) *n* a language of the Celts.
adj to do with the speakers of the Gaelic language of Scotland. <Irish *Goidhel*>

gaff (gaf) *n* **1** a spar or pole extending along the upper edge of a fore-and-aft sail. **2** a strong hook or barbed spear for pulling large fish out of the water.
v hook or pull a fish out of the water with a gaff. <French *gaffe*>

gaffe (gaf) *n* a tactless remark, or other clumsy social mistake. <French *gaffe*>

gaf·fer (gaf′ər) *n* **1** *Informal* a humorous or affectionate term for an old man. **2** the chief electrician in the production of a movie or TV program. <alteration of *godfather*>

gag[1] (gag) *n* **1** something, especially a cloth, thrust into or put over a person's mouth to keep him or her from speaking or crying out. **2** anything used to silence a person or organization.
v **gagged, gag·ging** **1** put a gag in or on the mouth of: *The bandits bound and gagged the watchman.* **2** force to keep silent. **3** try or start to vomit: *I gagged on the pudding, which was far too sweet.* **4** cause to do this: *The fumes gagged me.* <probably imitative>

gag[2] (gag) *n* a joke or funny stunt; something said or done to cause a laugh: *A comedian has to keep thinking up new gags.* <origin uncertain>

ga·ga (gȧ′gȧ) *Informal adj* **1** wildly or foolishly enthusiastic: *They all went gaga over the new lead singer.* **2** senile. <French = foolish>

gage (gāj) GAUGE.

gag·gle (gag′əl) *n* **1** a flock of geese. **2** *Informal* a group or cluster of people: *A gaggle of autograph hunters waited outside the door.* <Middle English *gagelen*>

gag order or **rule** *n* a ruling that certain information must not be published or broadcast, so as to protect the integrity of a court trial.

Gai·a (gī′ə) *n* the goddess of the earth and mother of the Titans. Also, **Gaea.**

a bat	e bed	i bid	o pot	u cup	th **thin**
ā cake	ē me	ī bite	ō go	ū rude	TH **then**
ȧ bar	ə about	ər over	ȯ for	u̇ put	zh measure

gai·e·ty (gā′ə tē) *n, pl* **gai·e·ties** **1** cheerful liveliness: *Her gaiety helped the party.* **2** bright appearance or showiness, especially of clothing or decoration. <French *gaieté*>

gai·ly (gā′lē) *adv* in a lively, cheerful manner: *She ran gaily to meet them. The room was gaily decorated.*

gain (gān) *v* **1** get or obtain: *The rebels gained possession of the town.* **2** get as an increase or advantage: *I have gained 2 kg since last month.* **3** make progress: *The sick child is gaining and will soon be well.* **4** get to or arrive at: *The swimmer gained the shore.* **5** of a watch or clock, run too fast: *My watch gains about six minutes a week.* **6** *Archaic or Poetic* win: *to gain the battle.*
n **1** (*often plural*) a getting ahead; an advantage: *He has made a substantial gain over his opponent in this match.* **2** an increase in amount or degree: *a gain in speed, a gain of ten percent.* **3** **gains** *pl* profits; earnings; winnings. **4** the process of getting material wealth: *Greed is love of gain.* <Old French *gaigne*>
gain on, catch up to, in a race or pursuit: *The pirate ship was slowly gaining on them.*

gain·ful (gān′fəl) *adj* bringing in an income; profitable: *gainful employment.* **gain′ful·ly** *adv.*

gain·say (gān′sā′) *Archaic or Poetic v* **gain·said** (gān′sed′), **gain·say·ing** contradict or deny: *The facts cannot be gainsaid.* <obsolete *gain-* against + *say*> **gain′say′er** *n.*

gaits of a horse

When a horse **walks**, it moves its legs in the order of left front, rear right, right front, left rear.

When a horse **trots**, its diagonally opposite legs move nearly in unison. Trotting is a *symmetrical* gait; equal time intervals separate the touching of the ground by right and left legs.

When a horse **gallops**, one hind leg and then the other hind leg touch the ground, followed by one and then the other front leg. This is an *asymmetrical* gait, since the time intervals are not equal.

gait (gāt) *n* a particular style or manner of walking or running: *He has an unsteady gait because of his injured foot. A gallop is one of the gaits of a horse.* <Middle English>

gai·ter (gā′tər) *n* in former times, a cloth or leather covering worn by men on the lower leg and ankle, held on by buckles or buttons on the side and, often, a strap under the foot. <French *guêtre*>

gal. gallon(s).

ga·la (gal′ə) *or* (gā′lə) *n* a festive occasion or celebration.
adj of, for, or involving festivity: *a gala occasion.* <Old French *gale* rejoicing>

gal·ax·y (gal′ək sē) *n, pl* **gal·ax·ies** **1** a huge group of stars, as well as gas and dust, that is held together by gravitational attraction. **2** a brilliant or splendid group: *The queen was followed by a galaxy of brave knights and fair ladies.* **3** **the Galaxy** the Milky Way, the galaxy that contains the solar system, perceived as a faintly luminous band of countless stars that stretches across the sky. <Latin, from Greek *galaktos* milk, originally in reference to the Milky Way> **ga·lac′tic** *adj.*

gale (gāl) *n* **1** a very strong wind; technically, a wind with a velocity of 50–102 km/h (27–55 knots). **2** a noisy outburst, especially of laughter. <origin uncertain>

CONFUSABLES

A **gale** is just one kind of a strong wind.

A **hurricane** is a tropical cyclone with winds stronger than a gale—more than 120 km/h, usually with heavy rain.

A **storm** classification also has stronger winds than a gale—about 100–120 km/h. A storm can also mean violent rain with strong winds.

ga·le·na (gə lē′nə) *n* a grey or black metallic ore consisting of lead sulphide. <Latin>

ga·lette (ga let′) *n* a flat, unleavened cake made in a frying pan or by covering with hot ashes in a fireplace. <French>

gall[1] (gol) *n* **1** bile, especially animal bile used in medicines. **2** anything very bitter or harsh. **3** bitterness or hatred: *Her heart was filled with gall.* **4** rude boldness: *You had a lot of gall answering the principal in such a flippant way.* <Old English *gealla*>

gall[2] (gol) *v* **1** make or become sore by rubbing: *The rough strap galled the horse's skin.* **2** annoy or irritate: *His continual challenges galled the teacher.*
n **1** a sore spot on the skin caused by rubbing. **2** a source of annoyance or irritation. <extended use of *gall*[1]> **gall′ing** *adj.*

gall[3] (gol) *n* a growth, or tumour, on the leaves, stems, or roots of plants, caused by insects, fungi, or bacteria. <French, from Latin *galla*>

gal·lant (gal′ənt) *adj* **1** noble; brave; daring: *gallant knights, a gallant effort to save the building.* **2** grand; fine; stately: *a gallant ship.* **3** very polite and attentive to women. <Old French *galant* courteous, from *galer* make merry> **gal′lant·ly** *adv.* **gal′lant·ry** *n.*

gall bladder *n* a sac attached to the liver, in which excess bile is stored until needed.

gal·le·on (gal′ē ən) *n* in former times, a large, heavy sailing ship, usually with three or four decks, used in Europe as a warship and armed trading ship. <Spanish *galeón*>

gal·ler·y (gal′ə rē) *n, pl* **gal·ler·ies** **1** a room or building where works of art are shown. **2 a** a projecting upper floor, especially the highest one, in a church, theatre, etc., with seats for part of the audience. **b** the people sitting there. **3** a long, narrow room or passage such as a covered walkway or porch. **4** a room or building where an activity takes place, such as taking photographs.
play to the gallery, *Informal* do or say what will please most people in order to be popular.

> **ETYMOLOGY**
>
> **Play to the gallery** originally meant that actors would style their performances to suit the tastes of the people in the cheaper seats (the gallery).

gal·ley (gal′ē) *n, pl* **gal·leys** **1** a ship propelled mainly by one or more banks of oars, used in ancient times as a warship and a trading ship. See TRIREME for picture. **2** the kitchen of a ship or aircraft, or any very compact kitchen. **3** *Printing* a text whose print is set in long, single-columned strips to permit corrections before final printing. <Old French, from Greek *galea*>

galley slave *n* a person compelled or condemned to row a GALLEY (def. 1).

Gal·lic (gal′ik) *adj* to do with ancient Gaul or its people, the ancestors of the French. <Latin *Gallus* a Gaul>

gal·li·na·ceous (gal′ə nā′shəs) *adj* to do with a large group of heavy-bodied birds that nest on the ground and fly only short distances, including chickens, turkeys, pheasant, and grouse. <Latin *gallina* hen>

gal·li·nule (gal′ə nyūl′) *or* (gal′ə nūl′) *n* a marsh bird with long thin toes and a fleshy shield on the forehead.

gal·li·um (gal′ē əm) *n* a shiny, soft, bluish white metallic element with a low melting point. *Symbol* **Ga** <Latin *gallus* cock, translation of *coq*, the name of its discoverer, P.E. Lecoq de Boisbaudran, 20c physicist>

gal·li·vant (gal′ə vant′) *v* roam or go places for pleasure, often irresponsibly: *He was out gallivanting all weekend.* <perhaps altered from *gallant,* with reference to flirting> **gal′li·vant′er** *n.*

gal·lon (gal′ən) *n* a nonmetric unit of liquid volume, equal to four quarts. In the UK and Canada, it is equal to about 4.6 L; the US gallon is equal to about 3.8 L. *Abbrev.* **gal.** <Old French *galon*>

gal·lop (gal′əp) *v* **1** move at the fastest pace of a horse or other four-footed animal, with all feet off the ground together once in each stride: *The pony galloped up to the fence.* **2** ride a horse or pony at this gait: *The cowboy galloped across the field.* **3** cause to gallop: *She was galloping her horse down the road.* **4** go very fast: *He galloped downstairs to tell us the news.*
n **1** the gait or pace of a horse or other animal that gallops: *The mare approached at a gallop.* See GAIT for picture. **2** a ride taken at this gait: *We went for a gallop across the open fields.* **3** any fast rate or pace: *I did my chores at a gallop.* <Old French *galoper*>

gal·lows (gal′ōz) *n, pl* **gal·lows** or **gal·lows·es** **1** a wooden frame made of a crossbar on two upright posts, used for hanging people condemned to death. **2 the gallows** punishment by hanging: *The king sentenced him to the gallows.* <Old English *galga*>

gall·stone (gol′stōn′) *n* a pebblelike mass that forms in the gall bladder or its duct, causing a painful illness if it stops the flow of bile.

ga·lore (gə lôr′) *adj* (*after the noun*) in abundance: *The apartment was decorated with balloons galore for the party.* <Irish *go leor* enough>

ga·losh·es (gə losh′iz) *pln* high rubber or plastic overshoes worn in wet or snowy weather. <French *galoche,* probably from Latin *gallica* (*solea*) = Gallic (shoe)>

ga·lumph (gə lumf′) *v* move or run heavily and clumsily: *He went galumphing up the stairs in his clunky boots.* <L. Carroll, 19c writer, perhaps *gal*(*lop*) + (*tri*)*umph*>

gal·van·ic (gal van′ik) *adj* **1** to do with a direct current of electricity, especially one resulting from chemical action. **2** startling or stimulating: *a galvanic personality.* **3** produced as if by an electric shock: *a galvanic reaction.* <L. *Galvani,* 18c physicist>

gal·va·nize (gal′və nīz′) *v* **gal·va·nized, gal·va·niz·ing** **1** apply an electric current to. **2** suddenly stimulate into action: *galvanized into action. The nation was galvanized by the threat of war.* **3** cover iron or steel with a thin coating of zinc to prevent rust. **gal′va·ni·za′tion** *n.*

gal·va·nom·e·ter (gal′və nom′ə tər) *n* an instrument for detecting and measuring a small electric current.

Gam·bia (gam′bē ə) *n* a country in west Africa. Its full name is **Republic of the Gambia**, often shortened to **The Gambia**. **Gam′bi·an** *adj, n.*

gam·bit (gam′bit) *n* **1** a way of beginning a game of chess by purposely sacrificing a pawn or another piece to gain some advantage. **2** a somewhat risky move or tactic intended to gain an advantage. **3** an opening move, such as in a conversation. <Italian *gambetto* = tripping up>

gam·ble (gam′bəl) *v* **gam·bled, gam·bling** **1** make bets or play games of chance for money or some other prize. **2** take a risk in order to gain some advantage: *She decided to gamble by refusing the job offer and hoping for a better one.* **3** (*often with* **away**) use or use up in gambling: *He gambled away his inheritance.*
n **1** a risky undertaking: *Investing money in newly discovered mines is a gamble.* **2** a bet. <obsolete *gamel* play games, from *game*[1]> **gam′bler** *n.*

> **SYNONYMS**
>
> To **gamble** means "to take a risk," especially with the possibility of winning a prize or money.
>
> To **bet** involves risking something, such as money, on the outcome of a particular event.
>
> To **speculate** involves the buying or selling of something in the hope of making a profit, but with great risk attached to the venture.

a bat	e bed	i bid	o pot	u cup	th thin
ā cake	ē me	ī bite	ō go	ū rude	ᴛʜ then
à bar	ə about	ər over	ô for	ù put	zh measure

G

gam·bol (gam′bəl) *v* **gam·bolled** or **gam·boled, gam·bol·ling** or **gam·bol·ing** run and jump around in play: *Lambs gambolled in the meadow.*
n a time of lively play. <Old French *gambade* leap of a horse, from Greek *kampe* bend>

gam·brel roof (gam′brəl) *n* a two-sided roof with two slopes on each side, with the lower slope steeper than the upper one.

game[1] (gām) *n* **1** an activity done for entertainment or amusement: *a game of catch. My brother and sister play games with their action figures.* **2 a** a physical or mental activity with certain rules, played either alone or with another person or group, usually in competition: *Scrabble and hockey are games.* **b** a specific instance or occasion of such an activity, with a beginning and end, often forming part of a series: *We played a quick game of pool. The tennis champion won four games out of six.* **3** the equipment needed to play a particular game, especially a table or video game: *This store stocks a lot of different games.* **4** the accounting of the score in a game: *At the end of the first period the game was 6 to 3 in our favour.* **5** a particular manner of playing a game: *He plays a mean game of squash.* **6** an activity or undertaking carried on as if under set rules and requiring skill and strategy: *the game of life.* **7** *Informal* a line of work or business: *She's in the acting game.* **8** a plan or scheme: *He tried to trick us, but we saw through his game.* **9 a** wild animals, birds, or fish hunted or caught for sport or for food. **b** anything that is hunted or pursued.
adj **gam·er, gam·est 1** to do with hunting or fishing: *Game laws protect wildlife.* **2** brave: *The losing team put up a game fight.* **3** willing to do something new or challenging: *She was game for any adventure.*
v **gamed, gam·ing** play video or computer games. <Old English *gamen* fun> **game′ly** *adv.* **game′ness** *n.*
ahead of the game, winning rather than losing.
game over, *Informal* final defeat or failure, often, death: *If he doesn't stop speeding, it'll soon be game over for him.*
off your game, not playing well.
play the game, *Informal* follow the rules or be a good sport.
the game is up, *Informal* the plan or scheme has failed.

game[2] (gām) *adj* lame: *The veteran had a game leg.* <origin uncertain>

game bird *n* a bird hunted for sport or food.

game·keep·er (gām′kē′pər) *n* a person who works on a large estate, looking after game animals and birds and preventing anyone from stealing or killing game without permission.

game law *n* a law made to restrict and regulate hunting and fishing in order to preserve or protect game animals, birds, and fish.

game plan *n* a course of action for achieving some purpose.

game point *n* a final point needed to win a game, especially in tennis.

game preserve or **reserve** *n* a large area of land set aside by the government for the protection of wildlife.

game show *n* a program on radio or especially TV in which contestants play a game and win prizes.

games·man·ship (gāmz′mən ship′) *n* the art or practice of defeating an opponent, such as in a game, by tactics that seek to gain a psychological advantage: *political gamesmanship.*

gam·ete (gam′ēt) *or* (gə mēt′) *Biology n* a mature reproductive cell capable of uniting with another to form a fertilized cell that can develop into a new plant or animal. <Latin, from Greek *gamos* marriage>

game warden *n* an official whose duty is to enforce the game laws in a certain district.

game·y (gā′mē) GAMY.

gam·ine (ga mēn′) *n* a slender girl or young woman with boyish looks and behaviour. <French, feminine of *gamin* street urchin>

gam·ma decay (gam′ə) *Physics n* the decay of a radioactive substance, during which it gives off rays. <*gamma*, third letter of the Greek alphabet>

gamma globulin (gam′ə glo′byū lən) *Chemistry n* the constituent of blood plasma that contains the most antibodies.

gamma rays *Physics n* electromagnetic radiation of very high frequency and great penetrating power, given off by radioactive substances.

gam·ut (gam′ət) *n* **1** the entire range of anything: *This book covers the whole gamut of poetry from children's rhymes to* Paradise Lost. **2** *Music* the whole series of recognized notes, or the complete scale of any key, especially the major scale. <contraction of Latin *gamma ut*, notes of the medieval scale>
run the gamut, go through the whole range of something: *Her emotions ran the gamut from despair to joy.*

gam·y (gā′mē) *adj* **gam·i·er, gam·i·est** with a taste or smell characteristic of the meat of wild animals or birds when it is too strong, as when the meat is tainted or improperly cooked. Also, **gamey**.
gam′i·ness *n.*

gan·der (gan′dər) *n* an adult male goose. <Old English *gandra*>
take a gander, *Informal* look: *Take a gander at this outfit.*

Ga·nesh·a (gə nā′shə) *Hinduism n* the god of wisdom and success, depicted as a small fat man with an elephant's head. Also, **Ganesh**.

gang (gang) *n* **1** a group of people engaged in crime together or attempting to control a certain neighbourhood or territory by means of threats and violence. **2** a group of people working together under one supervisor: *Two gangs of workers were repairing the road.* **3** a group of friends who are often together: *Let's have the gang over for pizza after the show.*
v (*usually with* ***together***) form a gang. <Old English = journey>
gang up, come together into a group for some purpose: *We ganged up to give a party for our coach.*
gang up on, join forces against: *to gang up on a bully.*

gang·land (gang′land′) *n* the world of organized criminal gangs.
adj to do with this world: *gangland violence.*

gan·gli·on (gang′glē ən) *n, pl* **gan·gli·a** (gang′glē ə) a mass of nerve cells forming a nerve centre outside the brain or spinal cord. <Greek = cystic tumor>

gan·gly (gang′glē) *adj* **gan′gli·er, gan′gli·est** awkwardly tall and thin, with long limbs. Also, **gangling.** <Old English *gangan*>

gang·plank (gang′plangk′) *n* a movable bridge used in getting on and off a ship or boat. <Old English *gang* a journey + *plank*>

gan·grene (gang′grēn) *or* (gang grēn′) *n* the decay of tissue in part of a living person or animal when the blood supply is interfered with by injury, infection, or freezing.
v **gan·grened, gan·gren·ing** affect or become affected with gangrene: *The wounded leg gangrened and had to be amputated.* <Latin, from Greek *gangraina*>
gan′gre·nous (gang′grə nəs) *adj.*

gang·ster (gang′stər) *n* a member of a gang of violent criminals.

gang·way (gang′wā′) *n* **1** a raised passageway or corridor, especially on a ship. **2** a gangplank.
interj Informal Get out of the way! Stand aside and make room!

gan·net (gan′it) *n* a large, white, fish-eating sea bird with long, black-tipped wings, and webbed feet. <Old English *ganot*>

gant·let (gant′lit) GAUNTLET[1].

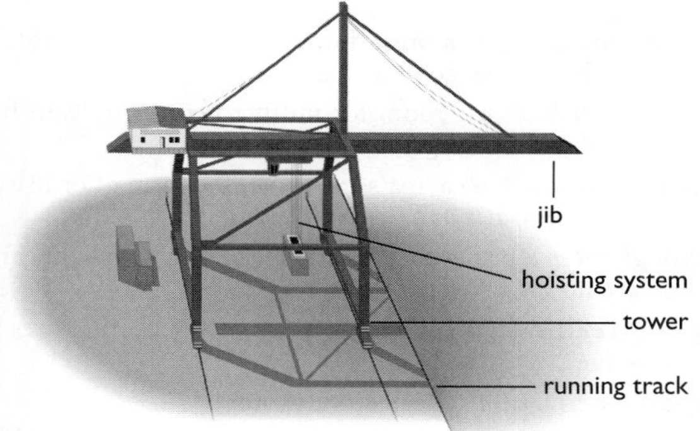

gan·try (gan′trē) *n, pl* **gan·tries** **1** a towerlike, movable framework with platforms at different levels, used for servicing a rocket on its launching pad. **2** a bridgelike structure that moves along on parallel tracks, for carrying a travelling crane. <Middle English>

gap (gap) *n* **1** a hole or opening, such as in a fence, wall, or a row of teeth. **2** a place where something is missing: *There are gaps in her knowledge of Canadian history, a gap in the data.* **3** a wide difference of opinion, situation, or way of life: *the generation gap.* **4** the space crossed by an electric spark. <Old Norse *gapa*>

gape (gāp) *v* **gaped, gap·ing** **1** stare with the mouth open: *The children gaped when they saw the huge birthday cake.* **2** open wide: *A deep crevasse gaped before us.*
n **1** an open-mouthed stare. **2** a wide opening. <Old Norse *gapa*>

gap·toothed (gap′tūtht′) *adj* with a gap or gaps between the teeth, especially at the front.

ga·rage (gə räzh′) *or* (gə raj′) *n* **1** a shelter for cars next to a house or building. **2** a business where motor vehicles are serviced and repaired. <French *garer* put in shelter>

garage sale *n* an informal sale of used household items, typically held in a private garage or driveway.

garb (gärb) *n* **1** the way one is typically dressed: *a judge's garb, dressed in the garb of a painter.* **2** the outward covering, form, or appearance: *She arrived in the garb of a friend but she was really my enemy.*
v clothe: *The doctor was garbed in white.* <French *garbe* graceful outline, from Italian *garbo* elegance>

gar·bage (gär′bij) *n* **1** waste material that is thrown away: *We threw out several boxes of garbage when we cleaned out the garage.* **2** *Informal* inferior, worthless, or offensive speech or writings: *That argument is a lot of garbage.* <Old French *garbelage* removal of discarded matter>
garbage in, garbage out, *Informal* **a** *Computers* See GIGO. **b** you get out of something what you put into it.

G

gar·ban·zo (gär ban′zō) CHICK PEA.

gar·ble (gär′bəl) *v* **gar·bled, gar·bling** **1** confuse or mix up messages, words, or electronic signals. **2** misrepresent intentionally by taking things out of context or omitting parts: *The newspapers gave a garbled account of his speech.* <Old French, from Arabic *gharbala* to sift, nowadays in the sense of select words unfairly from a statement>

gar·den (gär′dən) *n* **1** a piece of ground used for growing plants. **2** a park with many attractively arranged beds of plants: *Hamilton has a fine botanical garden.*
v make, take care of, or work in a garden: *He loves to garden.* <Old French *gardin*> **gar′den·ing** *n.*
gar′den·like′ *adj.*
lead up (or **down**) **the garden path,** *Informal* lure or deceive.

gar·den·er (gär′də nər) *n* **1** a person hired to take care of a garden. **2** a person who likes to garden as a hobby or who is good at gardening: *I'm no gardener.*

gar·de·nia (gär dēn′yə) *n* a tropical or subtropical tree or shrub that has fragrant flowers with waxy petals. <A. *Garden*, 18c botanist>

gar·den–va·ri·e·ty (gär′dən və rī′ə tē) *adj* common or ordinary: *a garden-variety fantasy novelist.*

gar·fish (gär′fish′) *n* a freshwater fish of North and Central America with an alligator-like snout, and many sharp teeth.

gar·gan·tu·an (gär gan′chū ən) *adj* huge. <*Gargantua*, a giant in a story by Rabelais, 16c writer>

gar·gle (gär′gəl) *v* **gar·gled, gar·gling** **1** wash or rinse the inside of the throat with liquid while breathing out, so that the air flowing out keeps the liquid in motion. **2** utter with a sound like gargling.
n **1** a liquid used for gargling. **2** an act of gargling. <French *gargouille* throat>

a bat	e bed	i bid	o pot	u cup	th **thin**
ā cake	ē me	ī bite	ō go	ū rude	ᴛʜ **then**
ȧ bar	ə about	ər over	ȯ for	u̇ put	zh measure

gar·goyle (går′goil) *n* a projection, usually a drainage spout, on a Gothic-style building, with the form of a grotesquely shaped animal or imaginary creature.

> **ETYMOLOGY**
>
> **Gargoyle** comes from Old French *gargoyle*, meaning "throat" or "waterspout." Gargoyles were originally used to decorate the end of a spout carrying rainwater from a gutter on a roof. The water poured out of the gargoyle's mouth. *Gargle* comes from the same root.

gar·ish (ger′ish) *adj* **1** unpleasantly bright or glaring: *a garish yellow.* **2** too showy: *a garish shirt.* <origin uncertain> **gar′ish·ly** *adv.* **gar′ish·ness** *n.*

gar·land (går′lənd) *n* a wreath of flowers and leaves, worn on the head, around the neck, or hung as a decoration: *Garlands are often used as symbols of peace or victory.*
v decorate with garlands. <Old French *garlande*>

gar·lic (går′lik) *n* a plant with a strong-smelling bulb made up of small sections called cloves, used to flavour food. See ONION for picture. <Old English *garleac*>

gar·ment (går′mənt) *n* any item of clothing. <Old French *garnir* adorn>

gar·ner (går′nər) *v* **1** gather and store away: *to garner wheat. Squirrels garner nuts in the fall.* **2** earn: *He has garnered a reputation for honesty.* <Old French *gernier* storehouse, from Latin *granum* seed>

gar·net (går′nit) *n* a brittle silicate mineral occurring mainly in red crystals, often polished and used as a semi-precious stone.
adj deep red. <Old French *grenat* dark red, from *pomegranate*, because the garnet is similar in colour to the seeds of the fruit>

gar·nish (går′nish) *n* something edible laid on or around food as a decoration or to add a stimulating flavour: *a garnish of parsley.*
v add a garnish to food: *pudding garnished with chocolate shavings.* <Old French *garnir* to adorn>

gar·nish·ee (går′ni shē′) *Law v* **gar·nish·eed, gar·nish·ee·ing** take money, especially wages, or property from a person by court authority in payment of a debt.

gar·ret (ger′it) *n* a space in a house just below a sloping roof. <Old French *garite* watchtower>

gar·ri·son (ger′ə sən) *n* **1** the soldiers stationed in a fort or town, usually for purposes of defending it. **2** a place where such troops are stationed.
v put troops in a place to defend it: *to garrison a fort.* <Old French *garir* defend>

gar·rote (gə rot′) *or* (gə rōt′) *n* a wire, cord, or apparatus used to strangle someone.
v **gar·rot·ed, gar·rot·ing** kill with a garrote. Also, **garotte, garrotte.** <Spanish>

gar·ru·lous (ger′ə ləs) *or* (ger′yə ləs) *adj* very talkative. <Latin *garrire* chatter> **gar′ru·lous·ly** *adv.* **gar·ru′li·ty** (gə rū′lə tē) *n.*

gar·ter (går′tər) *n* **1** an elastic strap attached to a band worn around the leg to hold up a stocking or sock. **2 a** the badge of the **Order of the Garter**, the oldest and highest-ranking British order of knighthood. **b** membership in this order. <Old French *garet* bend of the knee>

garter belt *n* a wide elastic belt worn around the waist, with elastic straps attached to it that snap onto the tops of stockings to hold them up.

garter snake *n* a small, harmless, brownish or greenish snake with long yellow stripes.

gas[1] (gas) *n* **1** a fluid substance that can expand without limit. Oxygen and nitrogen are gases. **2** a mixture of gases used as fuel, obtained from coal and other substances: *Does this stove use gas or electricity?* **3** air or other gases accumulated in the stomach as a result of indigestion: *She suffers from gas pains.* **4** a gas or vapour used to blind or kill, such as mustard gas, tear gas, or nerve gas. **5** an explosive mixture of accumulated methane with air. **6** *Slang* something or someone entertaining: *The party was a gas.* **7** *Slang* empty or boastful talk.
v **gassed, gas·sing 1** attack or subdue with gas: *The police gassed the violent demonstrators.* **2** *Slang* talk idly or boastfully. **3** treat with gas: *Some kinds of seeds are gassed to speed up sprouting.* <perhaps Greek *khaos* atmosphere>
gas′less *adj.* **gas′sy** *adj.*

gas[2] (gas) *n* gasoline.
v **gassed, gas·sing** (*with* ***up***) fill the tank of a motor vehicle with gasoline: *Dad gassed up before we left the city.* <*gasoline*>
step on the gas, a push down the gas pedal of a motor vehicle. **b** *Informal* go or act faster.

gas chamber *n* a room for putting people to death by means of poisonous gas.

gas·e·ous (gas′ē əs) *or* (gā′sē əs) *adj* in the form of or like a gas: *Steam is water in a gaseous condition.*

gas giant *n* a planet that is a huge ball of gas and appears to have no solid surface.

gas guzzler *Informal n* a car or other vehicle that uses a lot of fuel.

gash (gash) *n* a long, deep cut or wound.
v make a long, deep cut or wound in. <Old French, from Greek *kharassein* to scratch>

gas·ket (gas′kit) *n* a ring or strip of rubber, cork, or similar material packed around a piston, joint, pipe, etc. to make it leakproof. <origin uncertain>
blow a gasket, *Slang* get very angry.

gas·light (gas′līt′) *n* **1** in former times, light made by burning natural gas. **2** a burner or fixture for this purpose.
adj to do with a time when gas lighting was used: *a gaslight melodrama.*

gas mask *n* a helmet or mask that covers the mouth and nose and is supplied with a chemical filter to neutralize poisons.

gas·o·hol (gas′ə hol′) *n* a mixture of gasoline and alcohol used as a fuel for motor vehicles.

gas·o·line (gas′ə lēn′) *n* a motor fuel distilled from petroleum.

gasp (gasp) *n* **1** a sudden, short intake of breath through

the mouth, often indicating suspense, shock, or fear. **2** one of a series of short breaths taken when breathing is difficult: *After her hard run, her breath came in gasps.*
v breathe or speak with gasps. <Old Norse *geispa* yawn>
the last gasp, a the final moment; the moment just before death. **b** a last, usually futile, attempt to do something.

gas pedal *n* a pedal on the floor of a motor vehicle, which the driver presses in order to control the speed of the vehicle by adjusting the flow of fuel to the engine.

🍁 **gas·pe·reau** (gas′pə rō′) *n, pl* **gas·pe·reaux** (gas′pə rōz′) ALEWIFE. <Cdn French>

gas pump *n* a machine at a gas station for refilling the fuel tank of a vehicle. It draws fuel up out of an underground tank through a hose.

gas station *n* a place for supplying vehicles with gasoline, motor oil, or water.

gas·tric (gas′trik) *adj* to do with the stomach: *gastric pains.* <Greek *gastros* stomach>

gastric juice *n* the digestive fluid secreted by glands in the mucous membrane lining the stomach.

gas·tri·tis (gas trī′tis) *n* inflammation of the stomach, especially of the mucous membrane that lines it. <See GASTRIC.>

gas·tro·en·ter·i·tis (gas′trō en′tə rī′tis) *n* inflammation of the lining of the stomach and intestines, usually with vomiting and diarrhea. <Greek *gastros* stomach + *entera* intestines>

gas·tro·en·ter·ol·ogy (gas′trō en′tə rol′ə jē) *n* the branch of medicine that studies diseases of the stomach and intestines. <See GASTROENTERITIS.>
gas′tro·en·ter·ol′o·gist *n.*

gas·tro·in·tes·tin·al (gas′trō in tes′tə nəl) *adj* to do with the stomach and the intestines. <See GASTRIC.>

gas·tro·nome (gas′trə nōm) *n* a person who enjoys excellent food and drink. <Greek *gastros* stomach + *nomos* law>

gas·tron·o·my (gas tron′ə mē) *n* the art or practice of enjoying excellent food and drink. <Greek *gastros* stomach + *nomos* law> **gas′tro·nom′ic** *adj.* **gas′tro·nom′ic·al·ly** *adv.*

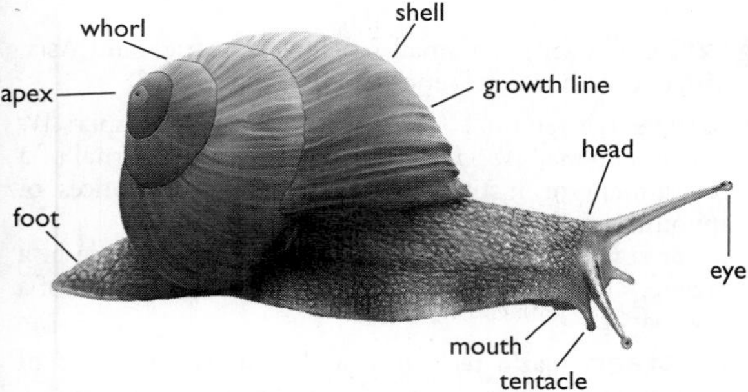

gas·tro·pod (gas′trə pod′) *n* a member of a large class of molluscs with one-piece shells or no shells that move by means of a disclike foot attached to the undersurface of their bodies. <Greek *gastros* stomach + *podos* foot>

gate (gāt) *n* **1 a** an opening in a wall or fence, fitted with a doorlike barrier on hinges. **b** the hinged, doorlike barrier itself. **2** a way to go in or out of any place. **3** a barrier, such as one stopping traffic at a level railway crossing, or a turnstile at which people must stop and pay before going through. **4** a door or valve for stopping or controlling the flow of water in a pipe, dam, or lock. **5 a** the number of people who pay to see an event: *The rink manager was expecting a good gate at the playoff game.* **b** the total amount of money received from these people: *The teams divided a gate of $3250.* <Old English *gæt*>
gat′ed *adj.* **gate′less** *adj.* **gate′like′** *adj.*

–gate *combining form* (*often with a proper name*) a political scandal or cover-up involving a certain person or thing: *Tunagate.* <*Watergate*, a building complex in Washington, DC, scene of a burglary in 1972 that gave rise to a series of political scandals>

G

gate–crash (gāt′krash′) *Informal v* attend an event, party, or other gathering without an invitation.
gate′-crash′er *n.* **gate′-crash′ing** *n.*

gate·house (gāt′hous′) *n* a house at or over a gate, especially of a castle or large estate, where a gatekeeper sits or lives.

gate·keep·er (gāt′kē′pər) *n* **1** a person hired to guard a gate and control passage through it. **2** a person who or thing that controls access to resources or information: *Librarians are gatekeepers of all sorts of information.*

gate·leg (gāt′leg′) *n* on a table, a hinged leg that swings out to support an extra section of tabletop that can be folded down when not in use.

gate·post (gāt′pōst′) *n* one of the posts on either side of a gate.

gate·way (gāt′wā′) *n* **1** an opening in a wall or fence, fitted with a gate or some other barrier. **2** *Computers* a system that that uses a combination of hardware and software to connect two different types of network so that information can be exchanged. **3** a way to get to or attain something: *Winnipeg is known as the "Gateway to the West." A college education is one of the gateways to success.*

gath·er (gaᴛʜ′ər) *v* **1** bring or come together into one place or group: *He gathered his books and left for school. A crowd gathered at the scene of the accident. Tears gathered in her eyes.* **2** pick and collect crops or a harvest. **3** gain or increase little by little: *The train gathered speed as it left the station. Darkness is gathering.* **4** collect one's strength, energies, or thoughts for an effort: *He gathered his thoughts before replying.* **5** draw a conclusion: *I gathered from his words that he was really upset.* **6** draw together or closer: *She gathered her cloak around her.* **7** pull together in little folds and stitch: *The sleeves are gathered at the wrist.*
n one of the little folds in cloth that is gathered. <Old English *gaderian* together>
gather yourself together, prepare yourself mentally.

a bat	e bed	i bid	o pot	u cup	th **thin**
ā cake	ē me	ī bite	ō go	ū rude	ᴛʜ **then**
à bar	ə about	ər over	ȯ for	ů put	zh measure

gath·er·ing (gaTH'ə ring) *n* **1** a meeting or assembly. **2** a swelling that comes to a head and forms pus. **3** the act of one that gathers, or that which is gathered.

ga·tor (gā'tər) *Informal n* an alligator.

GATT (gat) in full, **General Agreement on Tariffs and Trade** an agreement among many countries to promote free trade.

gauche (gōsh) *adj* socially awkward or clumsy. **gauche'ly** *adv.* **gauche'ness** *n.*

ETYMOLOGY

Gauche comes from French *gauche*, meaning "left-handed," from Middle French *gauchir*, meaning "turn aside" or "swerve." The meaning "socially awkward" came about in the mid 1700s.

gau·che·rie (gō'shə rē') *n* **1** awkwardness in social situations. **2** an awkward or tactless remark or act.

gau·cho (gou'chō) *n* a cowboy or herdsman in the plains of S America. <Spanish>

gaud·y (god'ē) *adj* **gaud·i·er, gaud·i·est** bright or ornate in a cheap and tasteless way: *gaudy costume jewellery.* <Middle English> **gaud'i·ly** *adv.* **gaud'i·ness** *n.*

gauge (gāj) *n* **1** a scale of standard measurements of a particular kind. **2** an instrument for measuring or showing a measurement: *a pressure gauge. The fuel gauge reads "Empty."* **3** a criterion or standard of comparison for estimating or judging anything. **4** diameter, size, or scope: *We need wire of a thicker gauge than this.* **5** the distance between the rails of a railway track or between the right and left wheels of a wagon or vehicle.
v **gauged, gaug·ing 1** measure: *She had a special instrument to gauge the width of the metal strip.* **2** estimate or judge: *It is difficult to gauge the character of a stranger.* Also, **gage**. <Old French> **gauge'a·ble** *adj.* **gaug'er** *n.*

Gaul (gol) *n* **1** a part of the Roman Empire that included modern N Italy, France, Belgium, and Switzerland. **2** one of the Celtic inhabitants of Gaul. <French, from Latin *Gallus*> **Gaul'ish** *adj.*

gaunt (gont) *adj* **1** very thin and bony with a starved look: *Hunger and suffering make people gaunt.* **2** looking desolate or grim: *The ancient castle stood gaunt on the hilltop.* <Middle English> **gaunt'ly** *adv.* **gaunt'ness** *n.*

gaunt·let[1] (gont'lit) *n* **1** a heavy glove, usually of leather covered with iron or steel plates, that was part of a knight's armour. **2** a heavy glove with a wide, flaring cuff, used for protection against injury. See GOGGLE for picture. <Old French *gantelet* little glove>
take up the gauntlet, accept a challenge.
throw down the gauntlet, issue a challenge.

gaunt·let[2] (gont'lit) *n* a former military punishment in which the offender had to run between two rows of men who struck him with clubs or other weapons as he passed. Also, **gantlet**. <Swedish *gatlopp*, from *gata* lane + *lopp* running>
run the gauntlet, a bravely pass through a danger that threatens on all sides: *During the war, convoys ran the gauntlet of enemy submarines.* **b** run between two rows of people, each of whom strikes the runner.

gaur (gour) *n* a large wild ox of southeast Asia and the Malay archipelago, with a dark coat and upward pointing horns. <Sanskrit *gaura*>

Gau·ta·ma (got'ə mə) *or* (gou'tə mə) *n* See BUDDHA.

gauze (goz) *n* very thin, sheer fabric. <French *gaze*> **gauze'like'** *adj.* **gauz'y** *adj.*

gave (gāv) past tense of GIVE.

gav·el (gav'əl) *n* a small mallet used to signal for attention or order, or by an auctioneer to announce that bidding is over. <origin uncertain>

ga·vi·al (gā'vē əl) *n* a large fish-eating crocodile-like reptile of India.

ga·votte (gə vot') *n* **1** a lively formal dance. **2** a piece of music for it. <Provençal (a language of S France) *gavoto*, from *Gavot* Alpine inhabitant. The dance originated in the Alps.>

gawk (gok) *v* stare rudely or stupidly.
n an awkward or shy person. <origin uncertain>

gawk·y (gok'ē) *adj* **gawk·i·er, gawk·i·est** awkward or clumsy. **gawk'i·ly** *adv.* **gawk'i·ness** *n.*

gay (gā) *adj* **gay·er, gay·est 1** homosexual. **2** happy and full of fun: *gay laughter.* **3** brightly coloured; showy: *gay decorations.*
n a homosexual. <French *gai*> **gai'e·ty** *n.* **gai'ly** *adv.* **gay'ness** *n.*

GRAMMAR AND USAGE

Currently, the most common meaning of **gay** is "homosexual." Many people therefore avoid using gay in the earlier senses of "full of fun" or "bright." You might encounter these senses in some older books.

The noun *gaiety* is related to these older meanings of gay, as well.

gaze (gāz) *v* **gazed, gaz·ing** look long and steadily: *She sat for hours gazing at the stars.*
n a long, steady look: *a loving gaze.* <Middle English>

ga·ze·bo (gə zē'bō) *n* a small, usually open structure in a garden or park. <supposedly from *gaze* + *-bo*, Latin future ending>

ga·zelle (gə zel') *n* a small antelope of Africa and Asia, with curved horns. <French, from Arabic *ghazal*>

ga·zette (gə zet') *n* **1** (*often in names*) a newspaper: *We subscribe to the "Weekly Gazette."* **2** an official journal of a government or institution, often containing notices of appointments and promotions.
v **ga·zet·ted, ga·zet·ting** publish, list, or announce in a gazette. <Italian *gazeta* small coin, originally the price of a newspaper>

gaz·et·teer (gaz'ə tēr') *n* **1** a dictionary or index of geographical names. **2** one who writes for or publishes a government gazette.

gaz·pa·cho (gə spä'chō) *n* a soup served cold, made with tomatoes, cucumbers, onions, peppers, bread, and olive oil. <Spanish>

GB gigabyte(s).

G clef *Music n* See CLEF.

GDP or **G.D.P.** gross domestic product.

gear (gēr) *n* **1** a wheel with teeth that fit into the teeth of another wheel, used in machinery to transmit or change motion. **2** an arrangement of such wheels, especially in a motor vehicle or bicycle, to control speed: *Put your bike in low gear to go up the hill.* **3** the equipment needed for some purpose: *poles, lines, hooks, and other fishing gear.*
v **1** connect by gears or equip with gears. **2** adjust, adapt, or design something for a particular audience or purpose: *This set of novels is geared to younger readers.* <Scandinavian>
gear up (or **down**), **a** shift to a higher (or lower) gear in a vehicle. **b** increase (or decrease) speed, intensity, or effort: *The team is gearing up for the playoffs.*
in gear, a connected to the motor or other source of power, making movement possible. **b** in working order.
in(to) high gear, in or into a state of increased speed, intensity, or effort: *Rehearsals for the school musical are in high gear now.*
out of gear, a disconnected from the motor or other source of power. **b** not in working order.
shift gears, a change from one gear to another. **b** switch to a different way of thinking or doing things.

gear·box (gēr′boks′) *n* an enclosed system of gears, especially in a motor vehicle.

gear ratio *n* the ratio of the speed of rotation of the powered gear of a gear train to that of the driven gear.

gear·shift (gēr′shift′) *n* a device for switching gears in a motor vehicle.

gear train *n* a system of interconnected gears.

gear·wheel (gēr′wēl) *n* a wheel with precisely manufactured identical teeth around the rim.

geck·o (gek′ō) *n, pl* **geck·os** or **geck·oes** a small, insect-eating lizard of the tropics, with suction pads on its toes for climbing. <Malay *gekok*>

gee[1] (jē) *interj* a command to horses or oxen directing them to turn to the right or to go faster. <origin uncertain>

gee[2] (jē) *interj* an exclamation or mild oath. <perhaps shortened form of *Jesus*>

geek (gēk) *Slang n* a socially inept person, especially one isolated by his or her high intelligence or extreme interest in some technical field: *computer geek.* **geek′ish** *adj.*

ETYMOLOGY

Geek comes from the Dutch word *gek*, meaning "fool" or "madman." It was originally a term for a circus performer. The word then came to mean "a generally odd or eccentric person," and in recent years its meaning has narrowed to a specific kind of oddness.

geese (gēs) plural of GOOSE.

gee·zer (gē′zər) *Slang n* an elderly person, especially a man who is cranky and set in his ways. <alteration of dialect *guiser* someone in disguise>

ge·fil·te fish (gə fil′tə) *n* balls of boneless, seasoned fish cooked in broth. <Yiddish *gefilte* filled + *fish* fish>

Gei·ger counter (gī′gər) *n* a device that detects and counts ionizing particles. It is used to measure radioactivity, test cosmic-ray particles, etc. <H. *Geiger*, 20c physicist>

gei·sha (gā′shə) *or* (gē′shə) *n, pl* **gei·sha** or **gei·shas** a Japanese girl or woman specially trained in singing, dancing, and the art of conversation, in order to act as a hostess or companion for men. <Japanese>

gel (jel) *n* **1** a jellylike substance formed from a solution in which fine particles are suspended but not dissolved. **2** such a substance used to style hair.
v **gelled, gel·ling** form a gel. <*gelatin*>

G

gel·a·tin or **gel·a·tine** (jel′ə tən) *n* **1** an odourless, tasteless substance obtained by boiling the skin, bones, and connective tissues of animals and used in certain foods, photographic processes, and glue. **2** a vegetable substance with similar properties. <French, from Latin *gelare* form a jelly> **ge·lat′i·nous** (jə lat′ə nəs) *adj.*

ge·la·to (jə lȧ′tō) *n, pl* **ge·la·ti** (jə lȧ′tē) Italian or Italian-style ice cream. <Italian *gelare* freeze>

geld (geld) *v* **geld·ed** or **gelt, geld·ing** remove the testicles of an animal, especially a horse. <Old Norse *geldr* barren>

geld·ing (gel′ding) *n* a gelded horse or other animal.

gem (jem) *n* a jewel. Diamonds and rubies are gems.
v **gemmed, gem·ming** set or adorn with gems or gemlike things: *Stars gem the sky.* <Old French, from Latin *gemma* precious stone> **gem′like′** *adj.*

Gem·i·ni (jem′ə nī′) *or* (jem′ə nē′) *pln* (*with singular verb*) **1** *Astronomy* a northern constellation containing the two bright stars Castor and Pollux. **2** *Astrology* the third sign of the zodiac. The sun enters Gemini about May 21. **3** a person born under this sign. <Latin = twins>

gem·mol·o·gy (jem ol′ə jē) *n* the study of gems. **gem·mol′o·gist** *n.*

gems·bok (gemz′bok′) *n* a large antelope of southern Africa, with long, straight horns and a long, tufted tail. <Afrikans (a language of South Africa), from German *Gemse* goat-antelope + *Bock* male goat>

gem·stone (jem′stōn′) *n* a precious or semiprecious stone that may be cut and polished for use in jewellery.

–gen *suffix* **1** denoting a substance that produces something: *oxygen, nitrogen.* **2** denoting a substance, disease, or plant that is produced: *carcinogen.* <Greek *-genes*, from *gignesthai* be born>

gen·darme (zhon dȧrm′) *n, pl* **gen·darmes** (zhon dȧrm′) in France or a French-speaking country, a police officer. <French>

a bat	e bed	i bid	o pot	u cup	th **thin**
ā cake	ē me	ī bite	ō go	ū rude	TH **then**
ȧ bar	ə about	ər over	ȯ for	u̇ put	zh measure

gen·der (jen′dər) *n* **1** a person's sex viewed as an aspect of his or her role or experience in society. **2** *Grammar* **a** in some languages, a system of grouping words such as nouns, pronouns, and adjectives into the masculine, feminine, or neuter classes. These groupings have less to do with sex differences than to relations with other words. **b** one of the classes in such a system. <Old French, from Latin *generis* kind, sort>

GRAMMAR AND USAGE

Historically, **gender** is a grammatical term, but it has also come to mean "the condition of being male or female." Use **sex** to refer to biological differences and **gender** to refer to cultural or social ones.

gen·der–neu·tral (jen′dər nyū′trəl) *or* (nū′trəl) *adj* applying or referring equally to males and females: *gender-neutral language, gender-neutral legislation.* **gender neutrality** *n.*

gene (jēn) *n* in a plant or animal cell, a part of a chromosome that determines the nature and development of an inherited characteristic. <German (*Pan*)*gen*, from Greek *pan-* all + *genos* race>

ge·ne·al·o·gy (jē′nē ol′ə jē) *n, pl* **ge·ne·al·o·gies 1** a record of the descent of a person from an ancestor or ancestors. **2** descent from an ancestor. **3** the study or investigation of lines of descent, especially of a family. <Greek *genea* generation> **ge′ne·a·log′i·cal** *adj.* **ge′ne·al′o·gist** *n.*

GRAMMAR AND USAGE

Genealogy does not end in *-ology* but it is pronounced that way.

gene map *Genetics n* a map of the set of chromosomes unique to a certain species, indicating the exact position of each gene that has been located by research. **gene mapping** *n.*

gene pool *n* the full set of genes in a population.

gen·er·a (jen′ə rə) a plural of GENUS.

gen·er·al (jen′ə rəl) *adj* **1** to do with most people or things: *A government takes care of the general welfare. These items are not for general use.* **2** broad and not limited to one subject, kind, department, or use: *general knowledge, general reading.* **3** not detailed or specific; indefinite or vague: *general instructions. She referred to her trip in a general way.* **4** applying to all members of a category or all cases of a certain kind: *a general rule about parenting. "Cat" is a general term covering all felines.* **5** (*in titles, usually after the noun*) chief; of the highest rank: *the Governor General.*
n **1** the highest-ranking officer in the Canadian Forces. **2** in other countries, a high-ranking military officer. <Latin *generalis* of a whole class> **gen′er·al·ly** *adv.* **gen′er·al·ship′** *n.*
in general, a referring to a category as a whole: *I like cats in general, but not this cat.* **b** usually: *In general, people get along fairly well here.*

General Assembly *n* the legislative body of the United Nations.

general delivery *n* a department of a post office that holds mail until it can be collected by the person to whom it is addressed.

general election *n* **1** an election involving all the voters of a country. **2** 🍁 a federal or provincial election in which all the seats of Parliament or the legislature are at stake.

gen·er·al·ist (jen′ə rəl ist) *n* a person who does not specialize in any one field of study but has wide general knowledge. **gen′er·al·ism′** *n.*

gen·er·al·i·ty (jen′ə ral′ə tē) *n, pl* **gen·er·al·i·ties 1** a general statement, word, or phrase: *The candidate spoke only in generalities; he mentioned no specific measures planned by his party.* **2** a general principle or rule. **3** the greater part: *The generality of people must work for a living.* **4** the fact of being general: *The extreme generality of the statement makes it almost meaningless.*

gen·er·al·ize (jen′ə rə līz′) *v* **gen·er·al·ized, gen·er·al·iz·ing 1** arrive at a general rule or conclusion from particular facts: *Canada is such a diverse country that it is impossible to generalize about its geography or its people. It is the business of science to generalize.* **2** state in a more general form: *The statement that 5 + 3 = 8 and 50 + 30 = 80 can be generalized to the form 5a + 3a = 8a.* **3** talk indefinitely or vaguely: *The commentator generalized because he knew no details.* **4** include in one general statement: *All men, women, and children can be generalized under the term "human being."* **5** bring into general use or knowledge: *Many expressions become generalized through being used on television.*

general practitioner GP.

gen·er·al–pur·pose (jen′rəl pər′pəs) *adj* suitable for a number of different uses.

general store *n* a small store that carries a wide variety of goods for sale but is not divided into departments. General stores are usually located in small communities and rural areas.

general strike *n* a labour strike involving many industries or trades.

gen·er·ate (jen′ə rāt′) *v* **gen·er·at·ed, gen·er·at·ing 1** produce: *Rubbing generates heat. Rabbits generate offspring at a high rate.* **2** *Mathematics* form a line, surface, figure, or solid by moving a point, line, or plane. <Latin *generare* to produce, from *generis* race>
gen′er·a·tive *adj.*

gen·er·a·tion (jen′ə rā′shən) *n* **1** all the people born at about the same time: *Your parents belong to one generation, and you belong to the following generation.* **2** the average time from the birth of one generation to the birth of their children: *Their family came from Europe eight generations ago.* **3** one step, or stage, in the history of a family: *The picture showed four generations—great-grandmother, grandmother, mother, and baby.* **4** one step, or stage, in the history or development of anything: *The manufacturer cleared up many problems in the second generation of this software.* **5** the act or process of generating: *Water power is used for the generation of electricity.* **6** *Biology* a form or stage of a plant, with reference to its method of reproduction: *the asexual generation of a fern.*

generation gap *n* the differences in attitudes and behaviour between young and older people, especially between children and their parents.

Generation X *n* the people born in the late 1960s and the 1970s, after the baby boom generation. Often shortened to **GenX**. <from the view that they lack roots, focus, or any distinguishing character> **Generation Xer** or **GenXer** *n.*

gen·er·a·tor (jen′ə rā′tər) *n* **1** a machine that changes mechanical energy into electrical energy. **2** an apparatus for producing gas or steam. **3** the originator or producer of something.

ge·ner·ic (jə ner′ik) *adj* **1** to do with a whole category or group of things: *Liquid is a generic term that includes gasoline, water, and milk.* **2** not a proper name or brand name: *"Cola" is generic; there are many brands of cola. "Boy" is a generic term, but "Anil" is a name.* **3** *Biology* to do with a genus of plants or animals: *Cats and lions show generic differences.* **ge·ner′i·cal·ly** *adv.*

ETYMOLOGY

Generic comes from Latin *generis*, meaning "kind" or "sort." Other words in this group include *general, generalize, generate, generation,* and *genre.*

gen·er·ous (jen′ə rəs) *adj* **1** willing to share with others. **2** willing to forgive or to think the best of others: *a generous mind.* **3** large or plentiful: *a generous harvest, a generous serving of pie.* <Latin *generosus* of noble birth (i.e., magnanimous), from *generis* race> **gen′er·os′i·ty** *n.* **gen′er·ous·ly** *adv.*

gen·e·sis (jen′ə sis) *n, pl* **gen·e·ses** (jen′ə sēz) origin or beginning. <Latin, from Greek>

gene therapy *n* the treatment of a genetic disease or disorder by inserting copies of normal genes into the patient's cells.

genetically modified GM.

genetic code *n* in DNA or RNA, the instructions by which an individual develops hereditary characteristics.

genetic engineering *n* the altering of genetic material by DNA so as to change the hereditary characteristics of an individual. **genetically engineered** *adj.*

ge·net·ics (jə net′iks) *n* **1** (*with singular verb*) the branch of biology that studies the principles of how characteristics are inherited. **2** (*with plural verb*) the genetic makeup of an individual organism or type or group. <Greek *genesis* origin> **ge·net′ic** *adj.* **ge·net′i·cal·ly** *adv.* **ge·net′i·cist** *n.*

Ge·ne·va Convention (jə nē′və) *n* an international agreement that provides for proper treatment and status of the wounded and captured in wartime.

ge·ni·al (jēn′yəl) *adj* **1** pleasantly cheerful and friendly: *a genial welcome.* **2** pleasantly mild: *genial sunshine.* <Latin *genialis* pleasant, from *genius* guardian spirit> **ge′ni·al′i·ty** *n.* **ge′ni·al·ly** *adv.*

–genic *combining form* producing or causing; triggering: *allergenic, pathogenic.* <Greek *gignesthai* be born>

ge·nie (jē′nē) *n* a spirit of Arabian folklore that makes one's wishes come true when it is summoned: *When Aladdin rubbed his lamp, the genie appeared.* Also called **jinn, djinn**. <Arabic *jinni*>

gen·i·tals (jen′ə təlz) *pl n* the external sex organs. Also, **genitalia** (jen′ə tā′lē ə). <Latin *genitalis* concerning birth, from *gignere* to produce> **gen′i·tal** *adj.*

ge·ni·us (jēn′yəs) *n* **1 a** a person with extraordinary mental or artistic ability: *Einstein was a genius; so was Shakespeare.* **b** such ability: *The genius of Mozart is often celebrated.* **2** a great natural ability of some special kind: *a genius for making people feel at ease.* **3** the special character or spirit of a person, nation, time, culture, or language: *Flexibility is the peculiar genius of English.* <Latin *genius* guardian spirit, from *gignere* to produce>

G

gen·o·cide (jen′ə sīd′) *n* the deliberate, systematic killing of a whole cultural or racial group. <Greek *genos* race + *-cide*> **gen′o·cid′al** *adj.*

ge·nome (jē′nōm) *n* the full DNA sequence containing all the genetic information for a gamete, an individual, a population, or a whole species. <*gen(e)* + *(chromos)ome*>

gen·o·type (je′nə tīp) *n* See PHENOTYPE.

gen·re (zhon′rə) *n* a kind or category of literature, music, or art: *The novel, drama, and poetry are three literary genres.* <French, from Latin *genus* kind>

gent (jent) *Informal n* gentleman.

gen·teel (jen tēl′) *adj* polite, refined, or respectable. <French *gentil* well-born> **gen·teel′ly** *adv.* **gen·teel′ness** *n.*

gen·tian (jen′shən) *n* a plant with funnel-shaped flowers, stemless leaves, and bitter juice. <Latin *gentiana*, named after an ancient king *Gentius*>

gentian violet *n* a crystalline substance that forms a violet solution in water. It is used as a dye, a chemical indicator, and an antiseptic.

gen·tile or **Gen·tile** (jen′tīl) *n* a person who is not Jewish. *adj* not Jewish. <Latin *gentilis* of the (foreign) people>

gen·til·i·ty (jen til′ə tē) *n* good manners; refinement: *The girl had an air of gentility.*

gen·tle (jen′təl) *adj* **gen·tler, gen·tlest** **1** mild in action, effect, or degree: *a gentle tap on the shoulder, a gentle breeze.* **2** mild, kind, or tender in manners or behaviour: *a strong and gentle man, a gentle horse.* **3** quiet and low: *a gentle sound.* **4** moderate: *a gentle slope.* **5** *Archaic* to do with the nobility: *of gentle birth.*
v **gen·tled, gent·ling** treat in a gentle, soothing way: *The rider gentled his excited horse.* <Old French *gentil*> **gen′tle·ness** *n.* **gen′tly** *adv.*

a bat	e bed	i bid	o pot	u cup	th **thin**
ā cake	ē me	ī bite	ō go	ū rude	ᴛʜ **then**
à bar	ə about	ər over	ȯ for	ů put	zh measure

gen·tle·folk (jen′təl fōk′) *Archaic pl n* people of the nobility or high social position.

gen·tle·man (jen′təl mən) *n, pl* **gen·tle·men** (jen′təl mən) **1** a man who belongs to the nobility or a high social class. **2** a man who is honourable, polite, and considerate of others. **3** a polite term for any man.
gen′tle·man-like′ *adj.* **gen′tle·man·ly** *adj.*

gentleman's agreement *n* an unwritten agreement that is not legally binding but depends only on the honour of the people that participate in it. Also, **gentlemen's agreement**.

gen·tle·wom·an (jen′təl wům′ən) *Archaic n, pl* **gen·tle·wom·en** (-wim′ən) a woman who belongs to the nobility or a high social class.

gen·tri·fy (jen′trə fī′) *v* **gen·tri·fi·ed, gen·tri·fy·ing** renovate or improve a house or neighbourhood to give it greater social prestige. <See GENTRY.>

gen·try (jen′trē) *n* **1** people of high social position, historically, in Britain, next below the nobility in rank. **2** high-ranking people of any kind or community: *the academic gentry.* <French *gentil*>

gen·u·flect (jen′yə flekt′) *v* bend the knee as an act of respect or worship. <Latin *genu* knee + *flectere* bend> **gen′u·flec′tion** *n.*

gen·u·ine (jen′yū ən) *or* (jen′yū īn) *adj* **1** actually being what it seems or is claimed to be: *genuine leather, genuine diamonds.* **2** sincere: *genuine sorrow.* <Latin *genuinus* natural, i.e., authentic> **gen′u·ine·ly** *adv.*
gen′u·ine·ness *n.*
the genuine article, the real thing.

ge·nus (jē′nəs) *n, pl* **gen·er·a** (jen′ə rə) or **ge·nus·es** **1** *Biology* a category in the classification of living things, consisting of SPECIES that share many characteristics and are considered to be closely related. See also BINOMIAL NOMENCLATURE. **2** any kind or sort. <Latin>

GenX (jen′eks′) *n* Generation X.

geo– *combining form* earth: *geophysics.* <Greek *ge*>

ge·o·cen·tric (jē′ō sen′trik) *adj* **1** with or representing the earth as the centre of the universe: *The people of medieval times had a geocentric view of the universe.* **2** as viewed or measured from the earth's centre. Compare HELIOCENTRIC. <*geo-* earth+ Greek *kentron* centre> **ge′o·cen′tri·cal·ly** *adv.*

ge·ode (jē′ōd) *n* **1** a rock with a cavity in it that is lined with crystals. **2** the cavity itself. <French, from Greek *ge* earth + *eidos* form>

ge·o·des·ic (jē′ə des′ik) *or* (jē′ə dēs′ik) *adj* **1** to do with the geometry of curved lines. **2** *Architecture* built as a dome with short, straight, lightweight struts forming a spherical grid of triangles.
n the shortest possible distance between two points along a surface, especially a curved surface. <Latin, from Greek *ge* earth + *daiein* divide>

ge·o·duck (jō′duk), (gō′ē duk′), *or* (gū′ē duk′) *n* a large, edible burrowing clam of the Pacific coast. <Chinook Jargon>

geographical information system GIS.

ge·og·ra·phy (jē og′rə fē) *n, pl* **ge·og·ra·phies** **1** the science that studies the earth's surface, its physical features and the effects of climate, and how these influence plant and animal life, peoples, resources, and industries. **2** the surface features of a place or region: *the geography of the Maritime Provinces.* **3** an account of this: *He has written a geography of Canada.* <Latin, from Greek *ge* earth +*graphein* describe> **ge·og′ra·pher** *n.* **ge′o·graph′i·cal** or **ge′o·graph′ic** *adj.*

geological time *n* time measured by developments in the earth and its crust, divided into **geological periods**, and often linked to the evolution of various forms of life.

ge·ol·o·gy (jē ol′ə jē) *n, pl* **ge·ol·o·gies** **1** the science that studies the earth's crust, the layers of which it is composed, and their history. **2** the features of the earth's crust in a specific region: *the geology of the Canadian Shield.* <Latin, from Greek *ge* earth + *-logos* treating of> **ge′o·log′i·cal** *adj.* **ge·ol′o·gist** *n.*

ge·o·met·ric (jē′ə met′rik) *adj* **1** to do with geometry: *a geometric proof.* **2** consisting of or characterized by regular lines and shapes: *a geometric design.* Also, **geometrical**.

geometric progression *Mathematics n* a sequence in which each following number is obtained by multiplying the preceding one by the same factor: *The numbers 2, 4, 8, 16, and 32 form a geometric progression; so do 4, 2, 1, 0.5, 0.25.* Compare ARITHMETIC PROGRESSION. Also called **geometric sequence**.

ge·om·e·trid (jē om′ə trid) *n* a grey or greenish moth whose larvae are called measuring worms or inchworms.

ge·om·e·try (jē om′ə trē) *n, pl* **ge·om·e·tries** **1** the branch of mathematics that studies lines, angles, surfaces, and solids, including the definition, comparison, and measurement of them. **2** a particular system of geometry, or a book about geometry.

ETYMOLOGY

Geometry is one of many English words (such as *geography* and *geology*) that contains the combining form *geo-*, borrowed from Greek, from *ge*, meaning "earth." In *geometry*, *geo-* is attached to another Greek word, *metron*, meaning "measure." *Geo-* is also attached to English words and stems, as in *geophysics*, *geopolitics*, and *geocentric*.

ge·o·phys·ics (jē′ō fiz′iks) *n (with singular verb)* the science that studies the relationship between the earth's features and the forces that produce them. **ge′o·phys′i·cal** *adj.* **ge′o·phys′i·cist** *n.*

ge·o·pol·i·tics (jē′ō pol′ə tiks) *n* (*with singular verb*) global or international politics. **ge′o·po·lit′i·cal** *adj.*

geor·gette (jôr jet′) *n* a thin, fine cloth having a slightly wavy surface and used for dresses, etc. <*Georgette* de la Plante, 20c dressmaker>

Geor·gia (jôr′jə) *n* a republic between Russia and Turkey on the Black Sea. **Geor′gian** *adj, n.*

Geor·gian (jôr′jən) *adj* **1 a** to do with any of four British kings named George who ruled from 1714 to 1830. **b** to do with the style of architecture that was popular during this period. **2 a** to do with the reigns of George V and George VI, who ruled during the period 1910 to 1952. **b** to do with the writing style that prevailed from 1910 to 1920.

ge·o·sta·tion·ary (jē′ō stā′shə ner′ē) *adj* moving as an object in outer space at the same speed as the earth, and therefore appearing not to move.

ge·o·tech·nol·o·gy (jē′ō tek nol′ə jē) *n, pl* **ge·o·tech·nol·o·gies** a tool or technique used to solve problems of a geographical nature, such as determining location. **ge′o·tech′no·log′i·cal** *adj.*

ge·o·tec·ton·ics (jē′ō tek ton′iks) *n (with singular verb)* the science that studies bodies of rock, and the forces and movements of the earth's crust that formed them. **ge′o·tec·ton′ic** *adj.*

ge·o·tro·pism (jē ot′rə piz′əm) *Biology n* an organism's response to gravity, as in the tendency of roots to grow downward into the earth. <*ge* earth + Greek *trope* a turning> **ge′o·trop′ic** *adj.*

ge·ra·ni·um (jə rā′nē əm) *or* (jə rā′nyəm) *n* **1** a cultivated plant with large clusters of showy flowers and fragrant leaves: *The geranium is often grown as a window plant.* **2** a wild flowering plant with deeply notched leaves and long, pointed pods. <Latin, from Greek *geranion* crane. The pod resembles a crane's bill.>

ger·bil (jər′bəl) *n* a rodent with long hind legs, native to Asia and Africa, often kept as a pet. <French, from Latin *gerbo* a small rodent>

ger·i·at·rics (jer′ē at′riks) *n* (*with singular verb*) the branch of medicine that studies old age and its diseases. Compare GERONTOLOGY. <Greek *geras* old age + *iatreia* healing> **ger′i·at′ric** *adj.* **ger′i·a·tric′ian** (jer′ē at ri′ shən) *n.*

G

germ (jərm) *n* **1** a microscopic organism, especially one that causes disease: *You've probably left flu germs all over that cup.* **2** the embryo in a cereal grain or other plant seed. **3** the earliest beginning of anything: *Counting was the germ of arithmetic.* <French, from Latin *germen* a sprout> **germ′less** *adj.* **germ′like′** *adj.*

ger·mane (jər mān′) *adj* relevant to a subject: *Your statement is not germane to the discussion.* <Middle English G*erman* German>

Ger·man·ic (jər man′ik) *n* a family of languages, including English, German, Dutch, and the languages of Scandanavia. *adj* **1** to do with this group of languages, or with the peoples speaking any of these languages. **2** to do with Germans or Germany.

ger·ma·ni·um (jər mā′nē əm) *n* a greyish white, brittle, metallic element. *Symbol* **Ge** <Latin *Germania* Germany>

German measles (jər′mən) RUBELLA.

German shepherd *n* a breed of large dog developed in Germany, often trained to work with police or to guide the blind. Also called **Alsatian**.

Ger·man·y (jər′mə nē) *n* a country in western and central Europe. See the APPENDIX. **Ger′man** *adj, n.*

germ cell *n* a cell that can produce a new individual, usually after union with another cell of the opposite sex.

ger·mi·cide (jər′mə sīd′) *n* a substance that kills germs, especially disease germs. **ger′mi·cid′al** *adj.*

ger·mi·nate (jər′mə nāt′) *v* **ger·mi·nat·ed, ger·mi·nat·ing** **1** sprout, or cause to sprout: *Seeds germinate in the spring. Warmth and moisture germinate seeds.* **2** start growing or developing: *An idea was germinating in his head.* **ger′mi·na′tion** *n.*

germ·plasm *n* (jərm′plaz əm) **1** the chromosomes and genes in a germ cell. **2** germ cells as a group, in contrast to body cells.

germ warfare *n* the spreading of germs to produce disease among the enemy in time of war.

a bat	e bed	i bid	o pot	u cup	th **thin**
ā cake	ē me	ī bite	ō go	ū rude	ᴛʜ **then**
ä bar	ə about	ər over	ô for	ů put	zh measure

ger·on·tol·o·gy (jer′ən tol′ə jē) *n* the branch of social science that studies the aging process and the particular problems of old people. Compare GERIATRICS. <Greek *geron* old man> **ger′on·tol′ogist** *n.*

ger·ry·man·der (jer′ē man′dər) *v* arrange the boundaries of a political riding or constituency so as to give the party in power an unfair advantage in an election.
n such an arrangement. <*Gerry* + (*sala*)*mander.* Massachusetts governor E. *Gerry* rearranged districts in 1812, and one district became salamander-shaped.>

ger·und (jer′ənd) *Grammar n* an *-ing* verb form used as a noun. Example: *Swimming is fun.* <Latin *gerundium,* from *gerere* to do>

GRAMMAR AND USAGE

A **gerund** is an *-ing* form that acts as a noun, including acting as the subject or object of a verb, or the object of a preposition: *Jogging is tiring. I like jogging. Some people have difficulty with jogging.*

A gerund can also take its own object: *Jogging laps is fun.*

ges·so (jes′ō) *n* a white plastic or liquid coating used by artists to give surfaces the correct finish for painting. <Italian, from Latin *gypsum* chalk>

Ge·sta·po (gə stä′pō) *n* in Nazi-ruled Europe, the secret state police. <German Ge(*heime*) Sta(*ats*)po(*lizei*) secret state police>

ges·tate (jes′tāt) *v* **ges·tat·ed, ges·tat·ing** carry young in the uterus from conception to birth: *The elephant gestates much longer than the human.* <Latin *gestare* carry> **ges·ta′tion** *n.*

ges·tic·u·late (jə stik′yə lāt′) *v* **ges·tic·u·lat·ed, ges·tic·u·lat·ing** make or use dramatic gestures: *The angry motorist gesticulated wildly at us.* <Latin *gestus* action> **ges·tic′u·la′tion** *n.*

ges·ture (jes′chər) *n* **1** a movement of the hands, arms, or any part of the body, used instead of words or with words to help express an idea or feeling: *Waving the hand is a gesture of greeting.* **2 a** an action that conveys an intention: *a friendly gesture.* **b** any action done insincerely or merely for effect: *Her refusal was only a gesture; she really wanted to go.*
v **ges·tured, ges·tur·ing** make or use gestures. <Latin *gerere* perform>

Ge·sund·heit (gə zůnt′hīt) *interj* a word said to someone who has just sneezed. <German = health>

get (get) *v* **got, got** or **got·ten, get·ting 1** come to have: *I got a new coat yesterday. She got first prize in the spelling contest.* **2** become: *to get sick.* **3** go and bring: *Get me a glass of water.* **4** reach or arrive: *I got home early last night.* **5** cause to be or do: *He got his hair cut yesterday. They got the fire under control.* **6** persuade or influence: *Try to get him to stop.* **7** prepare: *She helped her father get dinner.* **8** (*often with* **to**) begin: *We soon got talking about our days at camp.* **9** succeed in hitting or striking: *I got three people during the dodgeball game.* **10** cause a disadvantage or defeat: *I know how we can get them.* **11** *Informal* puzzle or annoy: *What gets me is, I've already told her twice and she's doing it again.* **12** understand: *I don't get your point.* **13** forming, together with a past participle, a passive verb. Example: *He got arrested.* <Old Norse *geta*>

as all get out, *Informal* to an extreme extent: *lazy as all get out.*

get across, make clear: *The teacher used diagrams to get the idea across.*

get after, *Informal* scold or nag: *She got after me for leaving the lights on.*

get along, a be on friendly terms: *He doesn't get along with his neighbours.* **b** manage: *I can't get along without you.* **c** make progress: *How are you getting along with that project?* **d** go away: *"Get along," said the officer to the vagrant. I'll have to be getting along now.*

get around, a go from place to place. **b** become widely known: *Word got around that he was in town.* **c** overcome by charm or flattery: *She knows how to get around her father.* **d** avoid by sly means: *to get around the law.*

get around to, take or have the time for: *I never get around to answering my e-mails.*

get at, a get access to: *to get at a file. I can't get at the stuff on the top shelf.* **b** find out: *to get at the truth.* **c** *Informal* unfairly influence: *The convicted woman protested that one of the jurors had been got at.*

get away, a escape. **b** start on a trip: *We should try to get away by noon.* **c** go away.

get away with, manage to take or do something without being caught or punished: *You can't get away with lateness here.*

get back, a return from a trip. **b** recover something lost. **c** respond; reply: *I'll get back to you tomorrow.*

get behind, a fail to keep up to a schedule. **b** support or endorse: *We must all get behind the recycling program.*

get by, a pass, usually through a small space: *Please let me get by.* **b** manage: *Some people seem to get by with very little sleep.*

get down, discourage or depress: *The hot weather was getting her down.*

get down to, a begin: *to get down to work.* **b** reach by removing what stands in the way: *to get down to the real issue.*

get even, take revenge: *He said he'd get even with her for tattling on him.*

get in, a go or put in: *The door's locked, so we can't get in. Open the bag wide so I can get the books in.* **b** arrive after travelling some distance. **c** (*with* **with**) become friendly or familiar: *I'd like to get in with that group.*

get into, a touch something and make a mess of it: *The baby keeps getting into things.* **b** become interested or involved in: *I've really gotten into running.*

get it, *Informal* **a** be scolded or punished: *I'll really get it if I'm late again.* **b** *Informal* understand: *Why are we doing this? I don't get it.*

get off, a come down from or out of: *Get off the couch.* **b** remove: *I can't get the lid off.* **c** escape or cause to escape with little or no punishment: *The naughty boy got off with a scolding. His lawyers got him off.* **d** send off or see off: *I just want to get this birthday card off.*

get off on, *Slang* find pleasure in: *She gets off on classical music.*

get on, a go up on or into: *Get on the bus!* **b** put on: *Get on your coat.* **c** See **get along**.

get out, a go or take out. **b** go away. **c** escape. **d** become known: *If this secret ever gets out, we're done for.*

get out (of here), *Slang* (*as an exclamation*) Don't be ridiculous; I don't believe you: *Fifty dollars for that thing? Get out of here!*
get over, a recover from: *to get over an illness, to get over your disappointment.* **b** stop being amazed at: *I can't get over how smart that kid is.* **c** overcome an obstacle.
get set, get ready or prepare.
get there, succeed or reach a goal.
get through, a complete or finish: *She always gets through her homework quickly.* **b** endure successfully: *to get through hard times. His friends' help got him through.* **c** make a telephone connection: *I tried to phone you but I couldn't get through.* **d** succeed in communicating: *No one can get through to her when she's angry.*
getting on for, be near a certain time: *It's getting on for six and I want to be home by seven.*
get to, a manage to reach. **b** affect emotionally: *Don't let her criticism get to you. Such generosity to a total stranger—that's what got to me.* **c** manage to find time for: *I finished my history assignment, but didn't get to my math homework.* **d** *Informal* have the privilege, opportunity, or good luck to: *How come they get to have cookies and I don't? We got to see the northern lights last night.*
get together, a bring or meet together. **b** come to an agreement.

GRAMMAR AND USAGE

The forms of **get** tend to be overused:
Our dog got a kilometre away before he was found.
She gets her vegetables from an organic farm.

The examples above could be rewritten as:
We found our dog a kilometre away.
She buys her vegetables from an organic farm.

get·a·way (get′ə wā′) *Informal n* **1** an act or means of getting away. **2** a place to go for a rest or a vacation: *a lovely getaway in the mountains.* **3** the start of a race.

get–go (get′gō′) *Informal n* (*with* ***from***) the very beginning: *I suspected him right from the get-go.*

get–to·geth·er (get′tə geтн′ər) *Informal n* an informal social gathering or party.

get·up (get′up′) *Informal n* an outfit or costume.

get–up–and–go (get′up ən gō′) *n Informal* energy or initiative.

gey·ser (gī′zər) *n* a spring that sends a column of hot water and steam into the air at intervals. <Icelandic *geysir* a gusher>

Gha·na (gȧ′nə) *n* a country in west Africa. See the APPENDIX. **Gha·na′ian** (gə nā′ən) *adj, n.*

ghast·ly (gast′lē) *adj* **ghast·li·er, ghast·li·est** horrible: *Murder is a ghastly crime.* <Old English> **ghast′li·ness** *n.*

ghee (gē) *n* a liquid butter used in Indian and Pakistani cooking, made from the milk of cows or buffaloes and clarified by heating. <Hindi>

gher·kin (gər′kən) *n* a small, prickly cucumber used for pickling. See CUCUMBER for picture. <Dutch *agurkje*, perhaps from Greek *angourion* cucumber>

ghet·to (get′ō) *n* **1** a part of a city, especially a slum area, inhabited mainly or entirely by a minority group. **2** a community isolated from mainstream influences or interaction. **ghet′to·ize′** *v.*

ETYMOLOGY

Ghetto is thought to come from Italian *borghetto*, meaning "settlement outside the city walls." The word was first used in Italy in the 1600s as a name for the part of a city to which Jews were restricted. By the end of the 1800s, the word ghetto had come to mean "a crowded urban slum."

ghost (gōst) *n* **1** the spirit of a dead person that is supposed to appear to living people as a pale, dim, shadowy form. **2** the slightest suggestion: *a ghost of a smile, not a ghost of a chance.* **3** a secondary or multiple image, such as results in television from the reflection of a transmitted signal.
v work as a ghostwriter: *Her autobiography was ghosted by a journalist.* <Old English *gast*> **ghost′like′** *adj.* **ghost′ly** *adv.*
give up the ghost, *Informal* die.

🍁 **ghost car** *Informal n* an unmarked police car.

ghost town *n* a town that has become deserted or lifeless: *When the gold rush was over, the once-flourishing community became a ghost town.*

ghost·writ·er (gōst′rī′tər) a person who writes something for another who pretends to be the author. **ghost′write′** *v.*

ghoul (gūl) *n* **1** a person who enjoys what is frightening, grisly, and horrible. **2** a horrible spirit who is supposed to rob graves and feed on corpses. <Arabic *ghul* monster> **ghoul′ish** *adj.*

GI *Informal n, pl* **GIs** a soldier in the US army. <*Government Issue*>

gi·ant (jī′ənt) *n* **1** a legendary being of human form, but of superhuman size and strength. **2** a person or thing of unusual size, strength, or importance: *This author is a literary giant.* Also, for a female, **giantess**.
adj like a giant. <Old French, from Greek *gigantos*>

giant panda PANDA (def. 1).

gib·ber (jib′ər) *v* speak rapidly and unintelligibly, often out of fear or shock: *The monkeys gibbered angrily at each other.*
n rapid and unintelligible speech. <imitative>

gib·ber·ish (jib′ə rish) *n* meaningless nonsense or unintelligible language: *This so-called poem is nothing but gibberish.* <*gibber*>

gib·bet (jib′it) *n* **1** an upright post with a projecting arm at the top, from which, in former times, the bodies of executed criminals were hung. **2** a gallows. <Old French *gibet* gallows>

a bat	e bed	i bid	o pot	u cup	th **thin**
ā cake	ē me	ī bite	ō go	ū rude	тн **then**
ȧ bar	ə about	ər over	ȯ for	u̇ put	zh measure

G

Gibbons are very agile. Using an arm-over-arm movement, they hook their hands on the limbs and swing from tree to tree. Gibbons are also the only anthropoid apes to walk on their hind legs only. To maintain balance, they raise their arms over their heads.

gib·bon (gib′ən) *n* a small, long-armed, tree-dwelling ape of southeast Asia. <French>

gib·bous (gib′əs) *adj* **1** curved out or bulging. **2** showing a phase in which more than half the disc of a moon or planet is illuminated, but less than the whole disc. <Latin *gibbus* hump>

gibe (jīb) *v* **gibed, gib·ing** jeer, scoff, or sneer.
n an insulting or mocking remark. Also, **jibe**. <Old French *giber* to treat roughly>

gib·lets (jib′lits) *pln* the heart, liver, and gizzard of poultry, usually cooked separately and used in making gravy. <Old French *gibelet* stew of game>

GIC *n* in full, **guaranteed investment certificate** a savings bond held for a predetermined term at a rate of interest higher than ordinary savings accounts.

gid·dy (gid′ē) *adj* **gid·di·er, gid·di·est 1** unable to keep one's balance: *Merry-go-rounds make me giddy.* **2** likely to make dizzy: *to look down from a giddy height.* **3** living for the pleasure of the moment: *Nobody can tell what that giddy girl will do next.* <Old English *gydig*, insane, with reference to the original sense of the word> **gid′di·ly** *adv.* **gid′di·ness** *n.*

gid·dy–up (gid′ē up′) *interj* a command to a horse to speed up.

gift (gift) *n* **1** a thing given to someone without expecting payment: *a birthday gift.* **2** a natural ability or special talent: *a gift for painting.* **3** the act, power, or right of giving.
v give a gift to: *Heredity has gifted him with an excellent sense of humour.* <Old Norse *gipt*>
look a gift horse in the mouth, be suspicious of a gift or something obtained free.

gift·ed (gif′tid) *adj* with great natural ability or talent: *a gifted musician.*

gift–wrap (gift′rap′) *v* **gift-wrapped, gift-wrap·ping** wrap decoratively for presentation as a gift.
n decorative paper suitable for wrapping gifts.

gig[1] (gig) *Informal n* an engagement for a band, singer, or other entertainer to perform. <origin uncertain>

gig[2] (gig) *n* in former times, a light, open, two-wheeled carriage drawn by one horse. <origin uncertain>

gig[3] (gig) *Informal n* a gigabyte.

giga– *combining form* **1 a** billion (an SI prefix): *gigavolt.* **b** *Computers* denoting 2^{30} (about a billion): *gigabyte. Symbol* **G 2** *Informal* to do with a very great degree or quantity: *a gigastar in the movie business.* <Greek *gigas* giant>

gig·a·byte (gig′ə bīt′) *Computers n* a unit of digital information, roughly equal to one billion bytes. *Symbol* **GB**

gig·a·hertz (gig′ə hərts′) *n* one billion hertz per second. *Symbol* **GHz**

gi·gan·tic (jī gan′tik) *adj* of great size or extent: *a gigantic building project.* **gi·gan′ti·cal·ly** *adv.*

ETYMOLOGY

Gigantic comes from Greek *gigas*, meaning "giant." The prefix *giga-* has come to mean "one billion," as in *gigabyte*, which means "one billion bytes" (of storage in a computer).

gig·a·volt (gig′ə vōlt′) *n* one billion volts.

gig·gle (gig′əl) *v* **gig·gled, gig·gling** laugh in a silly or nervous way.
n a silly or nervous laugh. <imitative> **gig′gler** *n.* **gig′gly** *adj.*

GIGO (gi′gō) *Computers* the acronym for Garbage In, Garbage Out; if unreliable data is fed into a computer, the output will also be unreliable.

gig·o·lo (jig′ə lō′) *n* a man who is a sexual partner or escort for an older woman, who pays him for his services. <French, perhaps a back formation from *gigolette* prostitute>

Gi·la monster (hē′lə) *n* a large, poisonous lizard found in the southwest US and northern Mexico. <*Gila* River, Arizona>

gild (gild) *v* cover with a thin layer of gold or gold-coloured material. <Old English *gyldan*>
gild the lily, praise or try to improve something that is beautiful or excellent enough on its own.

gill (gil) *n* **1** one of the pair of breathing organs of fish and those aquatic animals that use water to obtain oxygen. **2** a thin, leaflike radiating structure on the underside of the cap of a mushroom. **3 gills** *pl* **a** the flesh under a person's jaws. **b** the hanging flesh under the throat of a chicken, turkey, or goose. <Old Norse>

gill·net (gil′net) *n* a net suspended upright in the water, for catching fish by entangling their gills in its meshes.

gilt (gilt) *n* a thin layer of gold or gold-coloured material with which a thing is gilded.
adj gilded: *The pages in this huge old book have gilt edges.* <See GILD.>

gilt–edged (gilt′ejd′) *adj* **1** with gilded edges. **2** of the best quality: *gilt-edged qualifications.*

gim·crack (jim′krak′) *n* a showy but poorly made item.
adj showy but useless. <Middle English *gimcrake*>

gim·let (gim′lit) *n* **1** a small hand tool for piercing or boring holes. **2** a drink made from gin and lime juice. <Old French *guimble* drill>

gim·let–eyed (gim′lit īd′) *adj* with sharp, piercing eyes.

gim·me (gim′ē) *Informal contraction* (*used in speech*) give me: *Gimme that!*

gim·mick (gim′ik) *n* something whose only value is to attract attention or lure people into listening or buying: *That book of coupons they give out is just a sales gimmick; all the coupons are for things no one wants.* <origin uncertain> **gim′mick·y** *adj.*

gimp[1] (gimp) *n* cord or braid, sometimes stiffened with wire, used in crafts and for trimming clothing, curtains, or furniture. <Dutch>

gimp[2] (gimp) *Offensive slang n* a lame person <Dutch> **gimp′y** *adj.*

gin[1] (jin) *n* a strong, colourless, alcoholic drink, usually flavoured with juniper berries. <*geneva liquor*>

gin[2] (jin) *n* a machine for separating cotton from its seeds.
v **ginned, gin·ning** separate cotton from its seeds. <Old French *engin* engine>

gin[3] (jin) *n* gin rummy.

gin·ger (jin′jər) *n* **1** a plant of tropical southeast Asia. Its pungent root is made into a sweet, or pickled, or dried and powdered to be used as a spice. **2** *Informal* liveliness or energy: *That horse has plenty of ginger.*
adj light reddish or brownish yellow: *ginger hair.* <Latin *zingiber*, from Greek *zingiberis*> **gin′ger·y** *adj.*

ginger ale *n* a non-alcoholic, sweetened, carbonated drink flavoured with an extract of ginger. **Ginger beer** is similar to ginger ale, but stronger-tasting.

gin·ger·bread (jin′jər bred′) *n* **1** a densely textured cookie or cake, flavoured with ginger and sweetened with molasses. **2** intricate wooden decoration, such as fretwork or carving, on the gables of houses.

gin·ger·ly (jin′jər lē) *adv, adj* with extreme care or gentleness as if protecting something sensitive or fragile. **gin′ger·li·ness** *n.*

gin·ger·snap (jin′jər snap′) *n* a thin, crisp cookie flavoured with ginger and molasses.

ging·ham (ging′əm) *n* a cloth, usually cotton or part cotton, with a striped, plaid, or checked pattern. <Malay *genggang* striped>

gin·gi·vi·tis (jin′jə vī′tis) *n* inflammation of the gums. <Latin *gingiva* gum>

gink·go (ging′kō) *or* (jing′kō) *n, pl* **gink·goes** a deciduous tree with fan-shaped leaves and yellow fruit, widely cultivated in temperate regions as an ornamental tree. <Japanese>

gin rummy *n* a card game in which players form sequences and matching combinations.

gin·seng (jin′seng) *n* a plant found in N America and E Asia, with a branched root that is used as a medicine. <Mandarin *jen shen jen* man, from the two-legged shape of the root>

Every **giraffe** has chestnut brown blotches against a buff background. The pattern of blotches is unique to each individual animal. These markings offer ideal camouflage protection by blending with the shadows of tree branches.

gi·raffe (jə raf′) *n* a large African mammal, the tallest living animal, with a very long neck and legs and spotted skin. <Arabic *zarafa*>

gird (gərd) *v* **girt** or **gird·ed, gird·ing 1** get ready for action: *They girded themselves for battle.* **2** fasten with a belt or band. <Old English *gyrdan*>

gird·er (gər′dər) *n* a main supporting beam, usually horizontal, in the framework of a bridge or tall building. <*gird*>

gir·dle (gər′dəl) *n* **1** an elasticized undergarment worn around the hips or waist. **2** *Archaic* a ring of bark removed around a tree in order to kill it. **3** anything that surrounds or encloses: *a girdle of trees around the pond.*
v **gir·dled, gir·dling 1** cut away the bark so as to make a ring around a tree. **2** surround: *Wide roads girdle the city.* <See GIRD.>

a bat	e bed	i bid	o pot	u cup	th **thin**
ā cake	ē me	ī bite	ō go	ū rude	TH **then**
à bar	ə about	ər over	ȯ for	ů put	zh measure

G

girl (gərl) *n* **1** a female child. **2** a daughter: *My aunt has two girls.* **3** *Informal* **a** a young or relatively young woman. **b** a girlfriend. <Middle English> **girl′hood** *n.* **girl′ish** *adj.*

girl·friend (gərl′frend′) *n* **1** someone who is one's regular female companion, especially in a romantic relationship: *Do you have a girlfriend?* **2** a female who is one's friend.

girt (gərt) a past tense and a past participle of GIRD.

girth (gərth) *n* **1** the measure around anything: *a person of large girth, the girth of a tree.* **2** a strap or band that keeps a saddle or pack in place on a horse's back. <Old Norse *gjorth*>

GIS *n* in full, **geographical information system** a computerized system used to gather, store, process, and display data relating to physical location.

gist (jist) *n* the main idea expressed in speaking or writing: *The article is hard to read, but I got the gist of it.* <Old French, from Latin *jacet* it lies (on the surface), i.e., it is obvious>

git·chi manitou (gich′ē) *n* the supreme deity of the Ojibway, and other Algonquin peoples. <Algonquian = great spirit>

Git·xsan (git′ksan) *n, pl* **Git·xsan** **1** a member of a First Nations people living in central British Columbia. **2** either of their dialects of Nass-Gitxsan, a Tsimshian language.
adj to do with these people or their language.
Also, **Gitksan**.

give (giv) *v* **gave, giv·en, giv·ing** **1** make a present of: *My brother gave me a watch on my birthday.* **2** hand over or deliver: *Can I give you this book to return to the library?* **3** hand over in return for something: *I gave her $5 for a used CD.* **4** cause someone or something to have: *to give your approval, to give your word. This colour gives the room a brighter look.* **5** make a donation: *Please give to this cause.* **6** perform a certain action on: *She gave the ball a kick.* **7** offer, present, or make available: *This newspaper gives a full story of the game.* **8** produce a sound: *He gave a cry of pain.* **9** host: *to give a party.* **10** perform or do: *to give a lecture.* **11** yield to force: *The lock gave when she pushed hard against the door.* **12** provide a view or passage: *This door gives onto the deck.*
n the quality of yielding to force: *You need a fabric with lots of give.* <Old English *giefan*> **giv′er** *n.*
give away, a give without expecting payment: *I gave away all my toys to the local hospital.* **b** hand over a bride to a bridegroom as part of a wedding ceremony: *The bride's father gave her away.* **c** reveal or betray: *to give away a secret.*
give in, a stop resisting and admit defeat. **b** hand in: *He gave in his essay when it was due.*
give or take, *Informal* approximately: *I'll be there at 3 p.m., give or take.*
give out, a distribute to many people: *The agent gave out the travel vouchers.* **b** become used up or exhausted: *The food gave out during the famine.* **c** fail to operate: *The engine gave out.* **d** announce; make known: *The news was given out at midnight.*
give rise to, cause, create, or lead to: *Favouritism gives rise to jealousy.*
give up, a stop trying: *Don't give up now; we're almost there.* **b** hand over, deliver, or surrender: *The bandits were ordered to give up their weapons.* **c** stop having or doing: *to give up a bad habit, to give up chocolate.* **d** abandon: *I gave up that idea.* **e** devote entirely: *He gave himself up to his studies.*
what gives? *Slang* what's going on?

SYNONYMS

Give is an informal word for handing something over: *He was kind enough to give me valuable advice.* Other words also mean give, but with slight variations.

Donate suggests giving something officially: *I will donate some of my time and money to your charity.*

Grant involves giving something in response to a request: *The Queen had the power to grant him his wish.*

Present emphasizes giving something in a formal manner: *They presented the firefighter with an award for outstanding bravery.*

give–and–take (giv′ən tāk′) *n* **1** co-operation between people or groups, often involving concessions: *A good friendship will have lots of give-and-take.* **2** good-natured banter.

give·a·way (giv′ə wā′) *n* **1** the act of revealing or betraying something, especially unintentionally. **2** (*often preceded by* **dead**) an obvious clue: *Your handwriting on the Valentine card was a dead giveaway.* **3** anything given away or sold at a cheap price for promotional purposes.

giv·en (giv′ən) *v* past participle of GIVE.
adj **1** stated, fixed, or specified: *You must finish the test in a given time.* **2** assigned as a basis of calculating or reasoning: *Given that the radius is 19 cm, find the circumference.*
n something that can be taken for granted: *In high school, homework is a given.*
given to, inclined or disposed toward: *The fisherman was given to boasting.*

given name *n* a personal name other than a family name, especially a first name: *Glenna is the given name of Glenna Nelson.*

giz·mo (giz′mō) *n* an object whose name one cannot remember. <origin uncertain>

giz·zard (giz′ərd) *n* **1** a small, muscular part of a bird's stomach, where the food is ground up. **2** a muscular organ in some fish, insects, molluscs, and worms that serves to grind food. <Old French, from Latin *gigeria* cooked entrails of a fowl>

gla·cial (glā′shəl) *adj* **1** to do with ice, glaciers, an ice age, or any of their effects: *a glacial plain. During the last glacial period, much of the northern hemisphere was covered with great ice sheets.* **2** like ice: *a glacial stare.* <Latin *glacies* ice> **gla′cial·ly** *adv.*

glacial epoch *n* an ice age.

gla·ci·a·tion (glās′ē ā′shən) or (glā′shyā′shən) *adj* **1** the process of covering or being covered with glaciers or masses of ice. **2** change resulting from the action of glaciers or masses of ice. **gla′ci·ate** *v.*

glacier

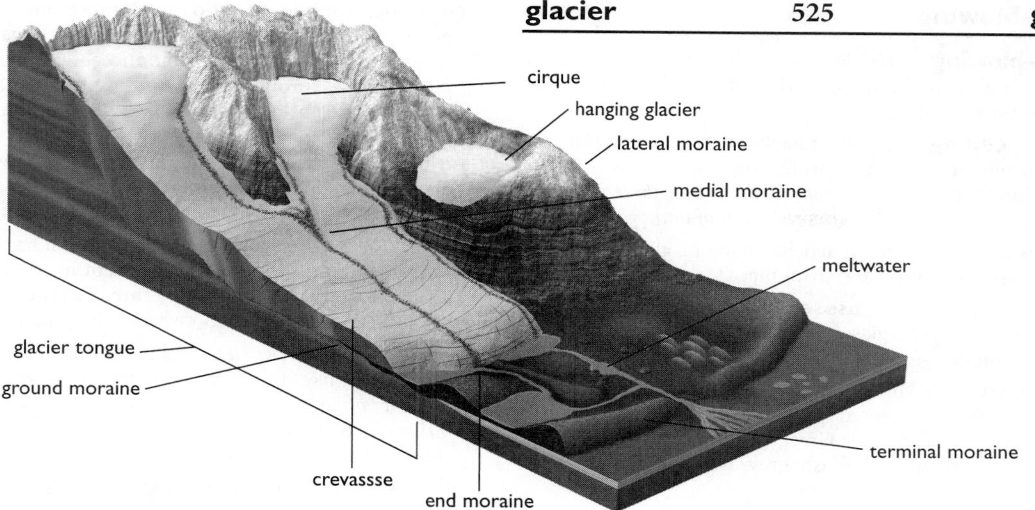

gla·cier (glā′shər) *or* (glās′yər) *n* a large, slowly moving mass of ice formed from snow on high ground wherever winter snowfall exceeds summer melting. Glaciers move under the influence of gravity.

glacier lily *n* a plant of the lily family found in the mountains of western N America; a dogtooth violet.

glad (glad) *adj* **glad·der, glad·dest 1** feeling, expressing, full of, or causing joy, often mixed with relief: *a glad shout, glad news. I'll be glad when exams are over.* **2** very willing: *I'd be glad to help.* **3** bright and cheerful. <Old English *glæd* bright> **glad′den** *v.* **glad′ly** *adv.* **glad′ness** *n.*

glade (glād) *n* an open space in a forest. <perhaps related to *glad* or *gleam*>

glad·i·a·tor (glad′ē ā′tər) *n* in ancient Rome, a slave, captive, or paid fighter who fought in public shows. <Latin *gladius* sword>

glad·i·o·lus (glad′ē ō′ləs) *n, pl* **glad·i·o·li** (glad′ē ō′lī) a plant of the iris family, with spikes of large flowers all growing on one side of the stem. <Latin *gladius* sword, in reference to the sword-shaped leaves>

glad rags *Slang pln* one's best clothes.

glam·our (glam′ər) *n* a romantic, fascinating, exciting, and fashionable quality: *the glamour of show business.* Also, **glamor**. **glam′or·ize′** *v.* **glam′or·ous** *adj.*

ETYMOLOGY

Glamour and **grammar** are ultimately the same word; glamour is a variant form. Since *grammar* originally referred mainly to Latin grammar, it meant knowledge of a kind that only few wise people had. From there, it acquired the meaning "occult learning" or "magic." This ingredient of magic was taken over by the variant *glamour*, as in a magical, alluring quality that holds people under a spell.

glance (glans) *v* **glanced, glanc·ing 1** look quickly: *He glanced in my direction.* **2** hit and bounce off: *The ball glanced off the wall and just missed him.*
n **1** a quick look: *I threw her a meaningful glance.* **2** a flash of light. **3** the act of hitting and bouncing off. <Old French *glacier* to slip>

gland (gland) *n* an organ in the body that takes certain substances, such as bile, from the blood and changes them into other substances for the body's use. <Latin *glandula* = little acorns, from the appearance of the organ>
glan′du·lar *adj.*

glare (gler) *n* **1** light that shines so brightly that it hurts the eyes: *She shielded her eyes from the glare of the ice.* **2** a fierce, angry stare. **3** too great brightness and showiness: *the glare of shopping malls at holiday time.*
v **glared, glar·ing 1** stare fiercely and angrily: *He glared sternly at the disobedient child.* **2** be so bright as to hurt the eyes. <German *glaren* to gleam>

glare ice *n* ice that has a thin, smooth, shiny surface.

glar·ing (gler′ing) *adj* **1** shining so brightly as to hurt the eyes: *glaring headlights.* **2** obvious and bad: *a glaring error.* **3** too bright and showy: *a glaring orange colour.*

glas·nost (glaz′nəst) *n* in the former Soviet Union just before its breakup, a government policy of greater freedom of speech and information. <Russian = openness>

glass (glas) *n* **1** a hard, brittle, usually transparent substance made by melting sand with soda, potash, lime, or other substances. **2** a drinking container made of glass or plastic, without a handle: *Fill this glass with water.* **3** something made of glass, such as the piece of glass in a picture frame. **4** a mirror. **5 glasses** *pl* **a** a pair of lenses to correct defective eyesight. **b** binoculars.
v put glass in; cover or protect with glass. <Old English *glæs*> **glass′ful** *n.*

a bat	e bed	i bid	o pot	u cup	th thin
ā cake	ē me	ī bite	ō go	ū rude	ᴛʜ then
à bar	ə about	ər over	ȯ for	ů put	zh measure

G

glass–blowing (glas′blō ing) *n* the art or process of shaping glass by blowing it while it is still hot and soft. **glass-blow·er** *n.*

glass ceiling *n* an unacknowledged barrier to advancement in a profession, due to unfair discrimination: *The reporter suggested that there is a glass ceiling that keeps visible minorities out of management.*

glass·ware (glas′wer′) *n* articles made of glass, especially those used for eating and drinking.

glass·y (glas′ē) *adj* **glass·i·er, glass·i·est 1** smooth or transparent like glass: *glassy water.* **2** fixed and expressionless: *glassy eyes, a glassy stare.*

glau·co·ma (glo kō′mə) *or* (glou kō′mə) *n* a disease of the eye, in which increased pressure in the eyeball causes gradual loss of sight. <Greek *glaukoma* cataract, from *glaukos* bluish green, bluish grey, with reference to the colour of the haze in the pupil>

glaze (glāz) *v* **glazed, glaz·ing 1** put a smooth, glossy, glasslike coating on a piece of china or earthenware. **2** cover food with a thin, clear, sugary coating. **3** (*usually with* ***over***) become smooth, glassy, or glossy. **4** put glass in or cover with glass: *to glaze a window or picture frame.*
n **1** a smooth, glassy surface or glossy coating: *the glaze on a china cup, a glaze of ice.* **2** a substance used to make such a surface or coating on things. <Old English *glæs*>

gla·zier (glā′zhər) *n* a person whose work is putting glass in windows or picture frames.

gleam (glēm) *v* shine with soft light.
n **1** a pale beam of light: *We saw the gleam of headlights through the fog.* **2** a brief or faint appearance: *a gleam of hope.* **gleam′ing** *adj.* **gleam′ing·ly** *adv.*

ETYMOLOGY

Gleam is one of a whole series of *gl-* words that have to do with light, including *glimmer, glint, glisten, glitter,* and *glow.* All of these words come from a Germanic source.

glean (glēn) *v* **1** gather grain left on a field by harvesters. **2** gather little by little or slowly: *The spy gleaned information from the soldier's talk.* <Old French, from Latin *glennare*> **glean′er** *n.* **glean′ings** *pln.*

glee (glē) *n* playful joy, delight, or merriment. <Old English *gleo*> **glee′ful** *adj.* **glee′ful·ness** *n.*

glee club *n* a society or group organized for singing songs in harmony, usually in trios or quartets.

glen (glen) *n* a small, narrow valley. <Gaelic *gleann*>

glen·gar·ry (glen ger′ē) *n, pl* **glen·gar·ries** a Scottish cap with straight sides and a lengthwise crease in the top, often with short ribbons at the back. <after *Glengarry*, a valley in Scotland>

glib (glib) *adj* **glib·ber, glib·best 1** speaking or spoken too smoothly and easily to be sincere: *a glib sales talk, glib excuses.* **2** showing little depth of understanding: *to offer glib solutions to age-old problems.* **3** 🍁 *especially P.E.I.* smooth; slippery: *glib ice.* <perhaps imitative>
glib′ly *adv.* **glib′ness** *n.*

glide (glīd) *v* **glid·ed, glid·ing 1** move along smoothly, evenly, and easily: *The canoe glided through the still water.* **2** pass gradually, quietly, or unnoticeably: *The years glided past.* **3** move through the air or come down slowly at a slant, without using engine power: *The airplane glided to the landing strip.* **4** fly by means of a glider.
n **1** an act of gliding or a gliding movement. **2** *Music* a slur. **3** a speech sound that has qualities of both consonants and vowels, such as a *y* or *w* sound. <Old English *glidan*>

glid·er (glī′dər) *n* **1** a motorless aircraft that has long wings in proportion to the body, and is kept in the air by rising air currents. See AILERON for picture. **2** a type of chair with a sliding base. **3** any person who or thing that glides.

glim·mer (glim′ər) *n* a faint or unsteady light, or something like this: *the glimmer of a distant star, a glimmer of hope.*
v shine with a faint or unsteady light: *A candle glimmered on the windowsill.* <Middle English>

glimpse (glimps) *n* a short, quick view: *I caught a glimpse of the falls as our train went by.*
v **glimpsed, glimps·ing** catch a short, quick view of. <Middle English>

glint (glint) *n* a gleam or flash, especially of something hard or metallic: *There was a glint of steel as the logger swung his axe.*
v produce such a gleam or flash: *Her eyes glinted fiercely in the light.* <Scandinavian>

glis·san·do (gli sän′dō) *Music adj, adv* with a continuous gliding or sliding effect between two notes.
n, pl **glis·san·di** (gli sän′dē) **1** a glissando passage. **2** a gliding effect. <French *glisser* slide>

glis·ten (glis′ən) *v* shine softly, especially with moisture: *The leaves glistened after the rain.* <Old English *glisnian*>

glitch (glich) *n* a sudden, minor problem: *Because of some glitch in the system, your timetable wasn't printed out.* <origin uncertain>

glit·ter (glit′ər) *v* **1** shine with a sparkling light: *Jewels and new coins glitter.* **2** be bright and showy.
n **1** a sparkling light. **2** a bright, showy display: *the glitter of an awards ceremony.* **3** 🍁 **glitter ice** the layer of clear ice that forms on everything outdoors after a rain that freezes. <Old Norse *glitra*> **glit′ter·y** *adj.*

glitz (glits) *Informal n* anything tastelessly extravagant. <*gl*(*itter*) + (*r*)*itz*> **glitz′y** *adj.*

gloam·ing (glō′ming) *n* twilight; the evening, just before dark. <Old English *glom*>

gloat (glōt) *v* **1** gaze intently with greedy pleasure: *The miser gloated over his gold.* **2** show enjoyment or triumph in a smug or mean way: *The winning team gloated over their victory.* <origin uncertain> **gloat′ing** *adj.* **gloat′ing·ly** *adv.*

glob (glob) *n* a blob of something liquid or semisolid. <*globule*>

glob·al (glō′bəl) *adj* **1** of the earth as a whole: *the threat of global warming.* **2** affecting or regarding anything as a whole: *The "Replace" function in the software allows you to make global changes in a document.* **3** shaped like a globe. **glob′al·ly** *adv.*

glob·al·ize (glō′bə līz′) *v* **glob·al·ized glob·al·iz·ing** develop worldwide influence and operations, especially in commerce. **glob′al·i·za′tion** *n.*

global positioning system GPS.

global village *n* the world considered as a community or as a network of tightly interdependent relationships. <M. McLuhan, 20c Canadian writer>

global warming *n* a gradual, steady increase in the average temperature experienced everywhere on the earth over the last century, thought to be chiefly the result of the greenhouse effect.

globe (glōb) *n* **1** the world. **2** a sphere with a map of the earth or sky on it. **3** anything round like a ball, such as certain kinds of light fixture. <French, from Latin *globus*>

globe·trot·ter (glōb′trot′ər) *n* a person who travels all over the world. **globe′trot′ting** *n, adj.*

glob·ule (glob′yūl) *or* (glob′yəl) *n* a tiny drop: *globules of sweat.* <French, from Latin *globus*> **glob′u·lar** *adj.*

glob·u·lin (glob′yə lin) *n* a protein, found in plant and animal tissues, that is soluble in weak salt solutions but insoluble in pure water.

glock·en·spiel (glok′ən spēl′) *n* a musical instrument consisting of a graduated series of small, tuned bells, metal bars, or tubes mounted in a frame and struck with two little hammers. <German *Glocke* bell + *Spiel* play>

gloom (glūm) *n* **1** darkness; deep shadow; dimness. **2** low spirits; sadness. <Middle English> **gloom′y** *adj.*

Gloo·scap (glū′skap) *n* a legendary trickster hero of the Mi'kmaw, Maliseet, and related Algonquin peoples. Also, **Gluskap**. <Algonquian>

glo·ri·fy (glȯ′rə fī′) *v* **glo·ri·fied, glo·ri·fy·ing 1** honour, exalt, or give a high position to: *to glorify the freedom of the individual above all else.* **2** praise or worship: *to glorify God.* **3** cause something to seem better than it is: *The first computers were just glorified electric typewriters.* **glo′ri·fi·ca′tion** *n.*

glo·ri·ous (glȯ′rē əs) *adj* **1** bringing great honour: *a glorious victory.* **2** magnificent; delightful: *a glorious parade. Isn't it a glorious day?* **glo′ri·ous·ly** *adv.*

glo·ry (glȯ′rē) *n, pl* **glo·ries 1** radiant beauty: *the glory of the sun on the mountain peaks.* **2** great praise and honour given in worship. **3** a source of great honour, pride, or joy: *My real glory will be finishing the marathon, whether I win or not.*
v **glo·ried, glo·ry·ing** (*with* ***in***) take great pride or delight: *Her father gloried in her success.* <Old French, from Latin *gloria*>
in your glory, in a state of the greatest satisfaction or enjoyment: *He's in his glory when pounding out a tune on the piano.*

gloss[1] (glos) *n* **1** a smooth, shiny surface: *The varnish produced a high gloss on the cupboard doors.* **2** an outward appearance or surface that covers faults underneath.
v put a smooth, shiny surface on. <origin uncertain> **gloss′y** *adj.*
gloss over, downplay, ignore, or try to excuse something that is wrong.

gloss[2] (glos) *n* a translation, explanation, or paraphrase, especially of words.
v provide a translation, explanation, or paraphrase. <Latin, from Greek *glossa* obscure word>

glos·sa·ry (glos′ə rē) *n, pl* **glos·sa·ries** a list of special, technical, or difficult words with explanations or comments: *a glossary to Shakespeare's plays, a glossary of chemistry terms at the end of the textbook.* <Latin *glossarium.* See GLOSS[2].>

GRAMMAR AND USAGE

A **glossary** is a list that explains or defines words that the reader of a text may not understand. It can usually be found at the end of the text, and the glossed words are usually in alphabetical order.

Glossaries are most often found in mathematics and science texts.

G

glot·tis (glot′is) *n* the opening at the upper part of the windpipe, between the vocal cords. <Latin, from Greek>

glove (gluv) *n* **1** a covering for the hand, with separate sections for each of the four fingers and the thumb. **2** a padded covering to protect the hand: *a baseball glove.* <Old English *glof*> **gloved** *adj.* **glove′less** *adj.*
handle with (**kid**) **gloves,** *Informal* treat carefully.

glove compartment *n* a compartment in the dashboard of a motor vehicle, for storing small items.

glow (glō) *n* **1** the shine from something very hot or from something phosphorescent or fluorescent. **2** any brightness that suggests warmth or energy: *the glow of sunset, a glow of excitement in her eyes.* **3** warmth of the body or colour in the skin showing good circulation: *the glow of health on his cheeks.* **4** a warm feeling, such as of affection, happiness, pride, etc.: *She felt a glow of pleasure from all their compliments.*
v **1** shine or radiate with a glow. **2** feel warm and happy. <Old English *glowan*>

glow·er (glou′ər) *v* stare angrily: *The fighters glowered at each other.*
n an angry or sullen look. <origin uncertain>
glow′er·ing *adj.* **glow′er·ing·ly** *adv.*

glow·ing (glō′ing) *adj* **1** shining with a glow. **2** enthusiastic: *a glowing description, glowing praise.* **glow′ing·ly** *adv.*

glow–worm (glō′wərm′) *n* a soft-bellied beetle or its larva, or the larva of a firefly, that glows in the dark.

glu·cose (glū′kōs) *n* **1** a sugar occurring naturally in fruits. **2** a syrup containing this and other sugars. <French, from Greek *gleukos* sweet wine>

glue (glū) *n* a substance used to stick things together.
v **glued, glu·ing** stick together with glue: *to glue pieces of wood.* <Old French, from Latin *glutis*> **glu′ey** (glū′ē) *adj.*
glued to, *Informal* **a** gazing fixedly at: *glued to the TV set.* **b** clinging firmly as if stuck with glue: *His hands felt glued to the steering wheel.*

a bat	e bed	i bid	o pot	u cup	th **thin**
ā cake	ē me	ī bite	ō go	ū rude	TH **then**
ȧ bar	ə about	ər over	ȯ for	u̇ put	zh measure

glue gun *n* a gunlike tool for applying glue to a surface by pressing a trigger.

glum (glum) *adj* **glum·mer, glum·mest** feeling or looking gloomy and dismal: *a glum face.* <Middle English> **glum′ly** *adv.* **glum′ness** *n.*

Glu·skap (glū′skap) GLOOSCAP.

glut (glut) *v* **glut·ted, glut·ting 1** satisfy with more than is wanted: *A year of travelling glutted her appetite for adventure.* **2** supply more than can be used: *The price of wheat dropped when the market was glutted with it.*
n too great a supply. <Old French, from Latin *gluttire*>

glu·ten (glū′tən) *n* a mixture of proteins found in cereal flours, especially wheat, that causes dough to be stretchable. <Latin = glue> **glu′te·nous** *adj.*

glu·ti·nous (glū′tə nəs) *adj* sticky.

glut·ton (glut′ən) *n* **1** a person who eats too much. **2** a person who never seems to have enough of something. *a glutton for work, a glutton for punishment.* <Old French, from Latin *glutto*> **glut′ton·ous** *adj.* **glut′ton·y** *n.*

glyc·er·ol (glis′ə rol′) *n* a colourless, syrupy, sweet liquid obtained from fats and oils as a by-product of making soap. Also called **glycerin, glycerine** (glis′ə rin). <French, from Greek *glykeros* sweet>

gly·co·gen (glī′kə jən) *n* a starchlike substance in body tissues that is changed into sugar when needed.

gly·col (glī′kol) *n* a colourless liquid obtained from certain compounds that contain ethylene. <*glyc*(*erin*) + (*alcoh*)*ol*>

glyph (glif) *n* a character or symbol in the form of a picture, especially one carved into a surface. <Greek *gluphe* carving>

GM *adj* in full, **genetically modified** to do with organisms, especially plants and animals used for food, whose genes have been changed by humans in order to increase or introduce some quality considered to be desirable: *genetically modified wheat.* Also, **genetically altered.**

GMT Greenwich Mean Time.

gnarled (närld) *adj* **1** with many knots or hard, rough lumps (**gnarls**): *a gnarled old oak tree.* **2** rough and hard; rugged and sinewy, such as the hands of a person who has done much hard, rough, manual work. <Middle English>

gnash (nash) *v* strike or grind the teeth together. <Middle English>

gnat (nat) *n* any of various small two-winged insects that suck blood, leaving an itchy bite. <Old English *gnætt*>

gnaw (no) *v* **1** wear away with the teeth or gradually chew through: *to gnaw a bone. The mouse has gnawed right through the oatmeal box.* **2** make distressed or anxious: *gnawed by a sense of guilt.* <Old English *gnagan*>

gneiss (nīs) *n* a layered metamorphic rock composed of quartz, feldspar, and mica or hornblende. <German>

gnoc·chi (nok′ē) *n* an Italian dish consisting of small boiled potato dumplings. <Italian>

gnome (nōm) *n* in folklore, a dwarf that lives in the earth and guards treasures of precious metals and stones. <French, from Latin *gnomus*>

GNP or **G.N.P.** gross national product.

gnu (nyū) *or* (nū) *n* a large African antelope with an oxlike head, curved horns, and a long tail. Also called **wildebeest.** <San (a language of Africa)>

go[1] (gō) *v* **went, gone, go·ing 1** move to some other place: *Go home.* **2** leave: *We must go now.* **3** operate or work: *I could hear the dishwasher going.* **4** get to be: *to go mad.* **5** progress or develop: *How are things going at school?* **6** have a certain result: *How did the game go?* **7** go regularly as a participant: *She's going to a vocational school.* **8** extend or reach: *My memory does not go back that far.* **9** circulate; pass from person to person: *A rumour went through my class.* **10** be spent or used up: *Rainy days go slowly. That bag of cookies went fast.* **11** be awarded or given to: *First prize goes to the winner. The painting goes to the highest bidder.* **12** have its place: *This book goes on the top shelf.* **13** remain: *to go hungry.* **14** have a certain tune, words, or rules: *How does that song go?* **15** die: *His wife went first.* **16** break down or stop functioning: *The brakes finally went. Her eyesight is going.* **17** be known: *She went under a false name.* **18** (*with* ***to***) take upon oneself as work or effort: *Don't go to any trouble for me.* **19** tend or lead to: *This goes to show that you must work harder.* **20** *Informal* make a certain sound: *The cow went "moo."* **21** *Informal* (*in the present tense only*) say: *So I smiled at her, and she goes, "What are you laughing at?"* **22** *Informal* urinate or defecate.
n, pl **goes** *Informal* **1** a try or attempt: *Let me have a go at it.* **2** spirit or energy: *She's got a lot of go.* <Old English *gan*> **go′er** *n.*
as people (or **things**) **go,** considering how people or things are in general.
from the word "go", *Informal* from the very beginning.
go about, a be busy at or work on. **b** choose a certain strategy or method in dealing with: *I'm not sure how to go about organizing all this stuff.*
go along, agree; co-operate.
go around, a go from place to place. **b** be served or given to everyone: *There's not enough cake to go around.* **c** *Informal* make a habit of: *You can't go around borrowing from people.* **d** associate with, as friends: *They've gone around together for years.*
go at, a attack: *With a snarl, the dog went at the intruder.* **b** make a start on: *The girls went at the task eagerly.*
go back on, a be disloyal to: *He went back on his friends.* **b** fail to live up to: *Don't go back on your word.*
go by, a pass. **b** be guided by: *He promised to go by the rules.* **c** be controlled or determined by. **d** be known by: *She goes by the nickname of "Red."*
go down, be defeated.
go for, *Informal* **a** try to get. **b** favour or support. **c** be attracted to. **d** attack.
go in for, take part in: *My sister goes in for a lot of sports.*
going on (**a certain time**), almost or nearly: *It is going on four o'clock.*
go into, a *Mathematics* be contained in: *Three goes into nine three times.* **b** investigate.
go in with, join or share with.
go it alone, *Informal* manage without help.
go off, a leave; depart. **b** be fired or explode: *The firework*

went off accidentally. **c** happen: *Did everything go off as planned?*
go on, a continue doing something or going somewhere: *He went on talking for another hour.* **b** happen: *What's going on here?*
go out, a stop burning or shining: *Don't let the candle go out.* **b** engage in social activity: *They don't go out much.* **c** date; keep company: *Are they still going out?* **d** cease to be fashionable.
go over, a look at carefully. **b** do again or read again. **c** be received (well or badly) by others: *The idea did not go over well.*
go someone one better, a outdo someone's performance or expectations in some way: *"Can you help me carry this outside?" "I'll go you one better: I'll tie it to your roof rack for you."* **b** accept a bet and offer to increase it.
go through, a consume or finish: *to go through a whole loaf of bread. I went through two books over the weekend.* **b** undergo or experience: *She went through some hard times.* **c** search thoroughly in: *to go through your pockets.* **d** be officially approved: *The new schedule did not go through.*
go through with, carry out something planned: *The plan to cheat on the exam bothered his conscience so much that he couldn't go through with it.*
go under, a sink or go below the surface. **b** be ruined or overwhelmed; fail: *The service was bad, so the restaurant failed.*
go with, a date: *He's been going with that girl for a long time.* **b** match or harmonize with: *That shirt doesn't go with those pants.*
it's a go, *Informal* it's approved or settled.
let something (or **someone**) **go, a** stop restraining or confining. **b** give up: *They had to let the house go; they couldn't pay the mortgage.* **c** fail to keep in good condition: *Don't let yourself go.* **d** ignore or overlook.
make a go of, *Informal* make a success of: *I see they're making a go of that bakery after all.*
no go, *Informal* not to be done or had.
on the go, *Informal* always busy or active: *He's tired because he's been on the go all day.*
to go, of food bought in a restaurant, for taking away to be eaten elsewhere: *She ordered two hamburgers to go.*

GRAMMAR AND USAGE

Go and is used informally to introduce or emphasize a verb: *Go and see for yourself. She went and dug the hole herself.*

Sometimes the phrase implies criticism: *He went and lost my new magazine.*

Try to avoid using this phrase in formal writing, except in dialogue.

go² (gō) *n* a game for two people, played on a gridded board with white and black pieces. The object is to surround one's opponent's pieces. <Japanese>

goad (gōd) *v* drive or urge on: *Her friends goaded her to ask for the star's autograph.*
n **1** a sharp stick for driving cattle. **2** anything that drives or urges a person on. <Old English *gad*>

go–a·head (gō′ə hed′) *Informal n* (*with* **the**) permission or approval.

goal (gōl) *n* **1** in certain games, the space between two posts into which a player tries to shoot a puck or kick a ball in order to score. **2** the act of scoring in such a manner, or the point earned by this. **3** what one is trying to achieve: *Her goal was to be a great doctor.* **4** a destination. <Middle English *gol*> **goal′less** *adj.*
play goal, be the goalie.

goal·ie (gōl′ē) *Sports n* in some games, the player who guards the goal to prevent the ball or puck from going in. Also called **goalkeeper, goaltender**.

goal·post (gōl′pōst′) one of a pair of posts with a bar across them, forming a goal in football, hockey, soccer, and lacrosse.
move (or **shift**) **the goalposts,** *Informal* make a task harder by continually changing the expectations.

goat (gōt) *n* a cud-chewing mammal with horns and, in the male, a beard. See UNGULATE for picture. <Old English *gat*> **goat′like′** *adj.*
get someone's goat, *Informal* make a person angry or annoyed by teasing.

goat·ee (gō tē′) *n* a small pointed beard.

goat·herd (gōt′hərd′) *n* a person who looks after goats.

goat·skin (gōt′skin′) *n* the hide of a goat, or leather made from it.

a bat	e bed	i bid	o pot	u cup	th thin
ā cake	ē me	ī bite	ō go	ū rude	ᴛʜ then
à bar	ə about	ər over	ȯ for	ů put	zh measure

G

gob (gob) *Informal n* **1** a lump or mass: *She put a big gob of honey on her bread.* **2 gobs** *pl Slang* a great quantity: *gobs of candy.* **3** *Slang* saliva; spit. <Old French *gobe* lump from *gober* to swallow>

gob·ble[1] (gob′əl) *v* **gob·bled, gob·bling 1** eat fast and greedily. **2** *Informal* (*with* **up**) seize upon eagerly: *He gobbled up every piece of information he could find on the rock group.* <probably *gob*>

gob·ble[2] (gob′əl) *v* **gob·bled, gob·bling** make the throaty sound that a turkey does.
n the throaty sound that a turkey makes. <imitative>

gob·ble·dy·gook or **gob·ble·de·gook** (gob′əl dē gūk′) *Informal n* speech or writing that is unnecessarily complicated or involved: *Official documents are often full of gobbledygook.* <probably imitative>

gob·bler (gob′lər) *n* **1** a male turkey. **2** someone or something that gobbles.

go–be·tween (gō′bi twēn′) *n* an impartial person who helps with negotiation in a conflict by speaking with both sides and taking messages from one side to the other.

gob·let (gob′lit) *n* a large drinking glass with a stem. <Old French *gobelet*>

gob·lin (gob′lən) *n* in folklore, a mischievous, ugly, dwarflike creature. <French *gobelin*>

go·by (gō′bē) *n, pl* **go·by** or **go·bies** a small, bony fish with a large head and two pelvic fins which form a cup-shaped suction pad that allows it to cling to rocks. <Latin, from Greek *kobios* type of small fish>

go–cart (gō′kårt′) GO-KART.

god (god) *n* **1** a male being thought of as above and beyond nature, greater than any human being, and worthy of worship. **2** an image or embodiment of a god. **3 God** in the Christian, Jewish, Muslim, and certain other religions, the sole creator and ruler of the universe. **4** a person or thing intensely admired and respected: *His father was a god to him.* <Old English> **god′like′** *adj.*

god·child (god′chīld′) *Christianity n, pl* **god·chil·dren** a child (**godson** or **goddaughter**) whose spiritual upbringing is made the responsibility of a godmother or a godfather, or both, at baptism.

god·dess (god′is) *n* **1** a female GOD (def. 1). **2** a woman adored for her beauty or other qualities.

god·for·sak·en (god′fər sā′kən) *adj* without any merit or appeal: *I'm not staying another day in this godforsaken place.*

god·less (god′lis) *adj* not believing in or obeying God. **god′less·ness** *n.*

god·ly (god′lē) *adj* **god·li·er, god·li·est** devoutly following God's way. **god′li·ness** *n.*

god·par·ent (god′per′ənt) *Christianity n* an adult (**godfather** or **godmother**) who is made responsible for the spiritual upbringing of a child, at baptism.

god·send (god′send′) *n* something very welcome: *Your visit was a godsend; I really needed someone to talk to.*

god·speed (god′spēd′) *n* success wished to a person starting a journey or other undertaking: *She wished him godspeed.* Also, **Godspeed**.

goes (gōz) third person singular, present tense, of GO.

go·fer (gō′fər) *Informal n* a person who runs errands. <altered from *go for* = fetch>

go–get·ter (gō′get′ər) *Informal n* an energetic or aggressive person.

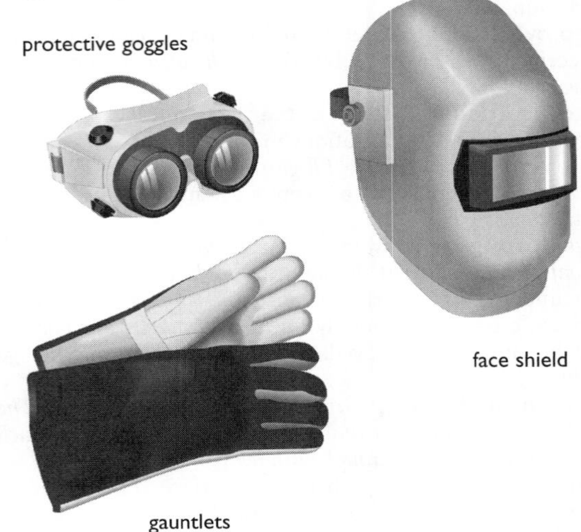

Welders wear special **goggles** and other heavy-duty protective clothing to guard against the dangers of intense light, heat, and sparking that they encounter in their work.

gog·gle (gog′əl) *v* **gog·gled, gog·gling** be wide-eyed with surprise, disbelief, or wonder: *We all goggled at the huge dog.*
n **goggles** *pl* a pair of glasses whose frames fit snugly to the head at all points, worn while swimming underwater or to protect the eyes: *She wore goggles while she was welding the broken steel rod.*
adj bulging: *A frog has goggle eyes.* <Middle English> **gog′gle-eyed′** *adj.*

go–go (gō′gō′) *adj* to do with a type of fast, sexy dance performed to popular music by one person for the entertainment of an audience.

going concern *n* a company or a person that is busy and thriving.

go·ing–o·ver (gō′ing ō′vər) *n, pl* **go·ings-o·ver 1** a thorough study, review, or examination. **2** *Informal* a scolding or beating.

go·ings–on (gō′ingz on′) *pl n* actions or events, especially questionable or unwanted ones: *We'll have to put a stop to such goings-on.*

goi·tre (goi′tər) *n* **1** a disease of the thyroid gland that often produces a large swelling in the neck, usually caused by a diet with too little iodine. **2** the swelling itself. Also, **goiter**. <French, from Latin *guttur* throat>

go–kart (gō′ kårt′) *n* a small four-wheeled racing vehicle, often homemade or custom-built, that consists of a bare chassis and a low-powered engine. Also **kart**, **go-cart**.

gold (gōld) *n* **1** a shiny, yellow, non-rusting precious metal and element that is soft and easily shaped. *Symbol* **Au** **2** great wealth. **3** anything beautiful or precious: *Wheat is sometimes called prairie gold.*
adj **1** made of gold. **2** bright, slightly brownish yellow. <Old English>

gold dust *n* gold in the form of fine powder.

gold·en (gōl′dən) *adj* **1** made or consisting of gold: *a golden goblet.* **2** shining or bright yellow, like gold: *golden hair.* **3** extremely favourable, valuable, or important: *a golden opportunity, golden deeds.* **4** to do with a fiftieth anniversary: *a golden wedding anniversary.*

Golden Age *n* **1** *Greek and Roman myth* the first age of the human race, an era of perfect prosperity, happiness, and innocence. **2** **golden age** any period like this.

golden eagle *n* a large eagle of the northern hemisphere. See NOCTURNAL for picture.

gold·en·eye (gōl′də nī′) *n, pl* **gol·den·eye** or **gol·den·eyes** a northern diving duck with yellow eyes.

golden handshake *n* a pension or a lump sum of money given to an employee at early or forced retirement.

golden mean *n* the avoidance of extremes.

golden old·ie (ōld′dē) *n* a song that has remained popular over a period of many years.

gold·en·rod (gōl′dən rod′) *n* a perennial plant with spikes of tiny yellow flower heads.

golden rule *n* the rule that people should behave toward others as they would want others to behave toward them: *The golden rule of wilderness camping is to leave the forest as you found it.*

golden wedding *n* the fiftieth anniversary of a wedding.

gold·eye (gōl′dī′) *n, pl* **gold·eye** or **gold·eyes** an edible freshwater fish of central N America whose eyes have golden irises.

gold–filled (gōld′fild′) *adj* made of cheaper metal covered with a layer of gold.

gold·finch (gōld′finch′) *n* **1** a small American songbird, the male of which is yellow marked with black. **2** a European songbird with yellow on its wings and, in the male, a red and white head.

gold·fish (gōld′fish′) *n, pl* **gold·fish** a small fish of the minnow family often kept in garden pools or glass bowls that, when kept, is orange or golden in colour.

gold leaf *n* gold hammered into very thin sheets.

gold mine *n* **1** a mine with ore that has gold in it. **2** the source of something valuable: *That online encyclopedia is a gold mine.*

gold–plate (gōld′plāt′) *v* **-plat·ed, -plat·ing** coat a metal object with gold, especially by electroplating.

gold rush *n* a sudden movement of people to a place where gold has just been found.

gold·smith (gōld′smith′) *n* an artisan who makes things out of gold.

gold standard *n* the use of gold as the standard of value for a country's currency, so that a unit of currency is officially declared to be equal to and exchangeable for a certain amount of gold.

golf (golf) *n* an outdoor game played with a small, hard **golfball** and a set of long-handled clubs. **golf′er** *n*
v play this game: *She golfs every Saturday.* <Scots>

golf course *n* a large grassy area designed for playing golf. See PAR for picture. Also called **golf links**.

gol·ly (gol′ē) *interj* an inoffensive substitute for GOD, used to express surprise or delight.

gon·ad (gō′nad) *n* an organ, such as an ovary or testicle, in which reproductive cells develop. <Latin, from Greek *gignesthai* be born>

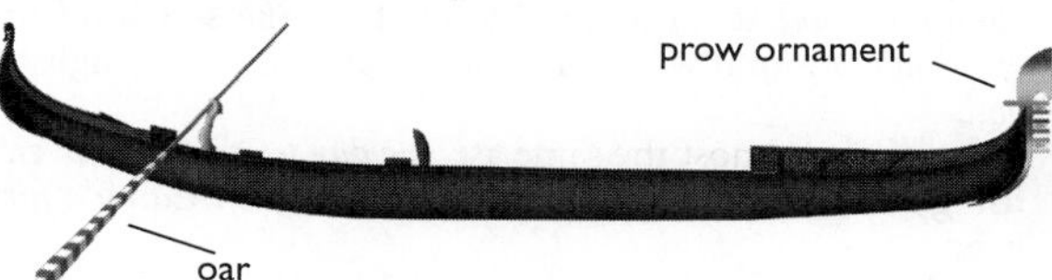

gon·do·la (gon′də lə) *n* **1** a long, narrow, flat-bottomed boat with a high peak at each end, used on the canals of Venice, or a boat that resembles it. **2** an enclosed compartment that hangs under a dirigible or a hot-air balloon. **3** a railway freight car that has low sides and no top. **4** 🍁 a broadcasting booth built high up in a hockey arena, near the roof. **5** a car that hangs from and moves along a cable: *We went up the mountain on the gondola.*

ETYMOLOGY

Gondola comes from the Italian word *gondolare*, meaning "to rock." The various definitions of gondola all have the implication of something that rocks or moves.

gon·do·lier (gon′də lēr′) *n* the person who rows a GONDOLA (def. 1).

gone (gon) *v* past participle of GO.
adj **1** no longer present. **2** *Informal* weak or faint: *a gone feeling.*
be gone on, *Informal* be in love with.
far gone, in a very advanced stage.

gon·er (gon′ər) *Informal n* a person who or thing that is dead, ruined, or past being helped.

gong (gong) *n* a large, round metal plate that makes a resonant sound when struck, used especially as a PERCUSSION INSTRUMENT. <Malay>

gon·or·rhe·a or **gon·or·rhoe·a** (gon′ə rē′ə) *n* a sexually transmitted disease that causes inflammation of the genital and urinary organs. <Latin, from Greek *gonos* semen + *rhoia* flow. It was believed that the discharge of mucus due to the disease was a discharge of semen.>

goo (gū) *Informal n* **1** any thick, sticky substance. **2** sentimental, gushy talk or writing. <origin uncertain> **goo′ey** *adj.*

a bat	e bed	i bid	o pot	u cup	th **thin**
ā cake	ē **me**	ī bite	ō **go**	ū **rude**	TH **then**
à bar	ə about	ər over	ȯ for	ů put	zh measure

good (gu̇d) *adj* **bet·ter, best 1** of high quality: *a good book, a good game.* **2 a** doing the morally correct things: *a good person.* **b** doing the correct things: *a good dog.* **3** favourable: *Say a good word for me.* **4** close or intimate: *a good friend.* **5** real or genuine: *It is hard to tell counterfeit money from good money.* **6** helpful or useful: *medicine good for a fever.* **7** enjoyable: *We had a good time.* **8** sound and undamaged: *a good apple.* **9** skilled or talented: *a good mechanic. She is good at math.* **10** fairly big or long: *a good while.*
n **1** benefit, advantage, or usefulness: *to work for the common good.* **2** an admirable quality: *She sees good in everyone.* **3** moral worth: *Do good, not evil.* <Old English *god*>
as good as, almost the same as: *The day is as good as over.*
for good, finally or permanently: *She has left Canada for good.*
good and ____, *Informal* thoroughly: *He was good and angry. Get the cloth good and wet.*
good for, a able to do, live, or last for: *This yogurt is good for another two days.* **b** able to pay or give: *He ought to be good for a few hundred dollars.* **c** able to be exchanged for: *a coupon good for one ride.*
make good, a pay for: *He made good the damage done by his car.* **b** fulfill or carry out: *to make good a promise.* **c** succeed or prosper: *His parents expected him to make good.*
to the good, on the side of profit or advantage: *He promised to quit gambling when he was $1000 to the good.*
up to no good, plotting or carrying out something wrong.

CONFUSABLES

Good is an adjective, and so always describes a noun: *She has a good appetite.*

Well is an adverb, and so always describes a verb: *He always dresses well.*

However, to make things rather confusing, **well** can also be used as an adjective to mean "in good health": *I'm not well.*

good·bye or **good–bye** (gəd bī′) *interj, n, pl* **good·byes** or **good-byes** something said when one is leaving or is ending a conversation.

good–for–noth·ing (gu̇d′fər nuth′ing) *adj* considered worthless or useless.
n a person who is considered worthless or useless.

Good Friday *Christianity n* the Friday before Easter Sunday, when Christ's crucifixion is commemorated.

good–heart·ed (gu̇d′här′tid) *adj* kind and generous. **good′-heart′ed·ly** *adv.* **good′-heart′ed·ness** *n.*

good–hu·moured or **good–hu·mored** (gu̇d′ hyū′mərd) *adj* cheerful and pleasant. **good′-hu′moured·ly** or **good′-hu′mored·ly** *adv.*

good·ish (gu̇d′ish) *Informal adj* **1** fairly good. **2** considerable: *a goodish amount of money.*

good looks *pln* a handsome or pleasing physical appearance. **good′-look′ing** *adj.*

good·ly (gu̇d′lē) *adj* **good·li·er, good·li·est** considerable: *a goodly quantity.*

good–na·tured (gu̇d′nā′chərd) *adj* friendly and cheerful. **good′-na′tured·ly** *adv.* **good′-na′tured·ness** *n.*

good·ness (gu̇d′nis) *n* **1** the quality or state of being good. **2** the valuable features or best part: *She cooked the goodness out of all the vegetables.*
interj used to express surprise: *Goodness, you have been working hard!*

goods (gu̇dz) *pln* **1** belongings: *They shipped their goods overseas.* **2** things to be bought or sold: *canned goods. Several merchants had goods on display at the fall fair.*
deliver the goods, *Slang* do what is wanted or expected.
get (or **have**) **the goods on,** *Slang* find out or know something bad about.

Good Samaritan *n* a person who unselfishly helps others, especially strangers. <in the Bible, a traveller who rescued and cared for another>

good–sized (gu̇d′sīzd′) *adj* large or fairly large: *Please give me a good-sized helping.*

good–tem·pered (gu̇d′tem′pərd) *adj* cheerful and easy to get along with. **good′-tem′pered·ly** *adv.*

good turn *n* a kind or friendly act.

good·will or **good will** (gu̇d′will′) *n* **1** a feeling of wanting to do good for others. **2** the established reputation that a business has with its customers.

good·y (gu̇d′ē) *Informal n* **1** usually, **good·ies** *pl* good things to eat, especially sweet things: *There were lots of goodies at the party.* **2** things eagerly desired by people and offered or given as a reward or incentive: *The store promises a free DVD player and other goodies to the first customer.*
interj used to express pleasure: *Are we going to the beach? Oh, goody!*

good·y–good·y (gu̇d′ē gu̇d′ē) *n, pl* **good·y-good·ies** a person who makes too much show of obeying rules and doing good deeds.
adj to do with such a person.

goof (gūf) *Informal n* **1** a foolish, silly, or ridiculous person. **2** an obvious or careless error.
v **1** (*with* ***around***) waste time. **2** (*with* ***up***) make a mess of. <origin uncertain> **goof′i·ly** *adv.* **goof′i·ness** *n.* **goof′y** *adj.*

goof·ball (gūf′bol′) *Slang n* an odd, peculiar, or crazy person.
adj stupid or silly.

goo·gle (gū′gəl) *Trademark v* to search for information on the web, particularly by using the Google search engine: *I googled* whales *and got a lot of great facts and ideas for a project!* <Google™ is a trademark identifying the search technology and services of Google Technologies Inc.>

goo·gol (gū′gəl) *n* a number represented by 1 followed by a hundred zeros; 10^{100}. A **googolplex** is a number represented by 1 followed by a googol zeros. <thought to have been named by M. Sirotta, the nine-year-old nephew of E. Kasner, 20c mathematician>

goon (gūn) *Slang n* a bully or thug, especially a member of an armed or security force. <perhaps obsolete *gooney* idiot>

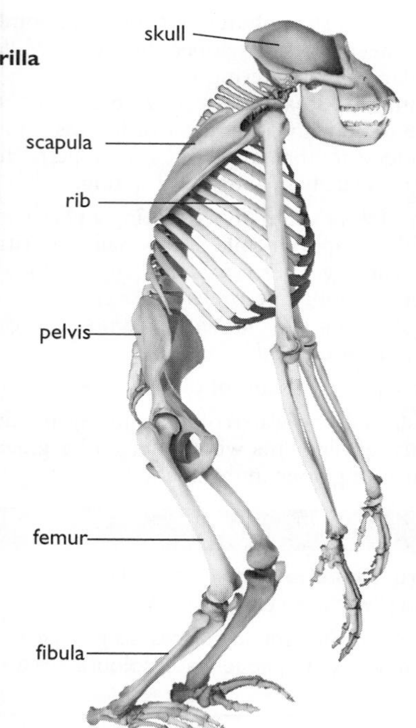

The human and the **gorilla** have similar skeletal structures, except the gorilla's bones are thicker, its arms are much longer, and its legs are shorter. The gorilla is unable to stand erect and moves in a stooped position, using its long arms and knuckles to support its weight.

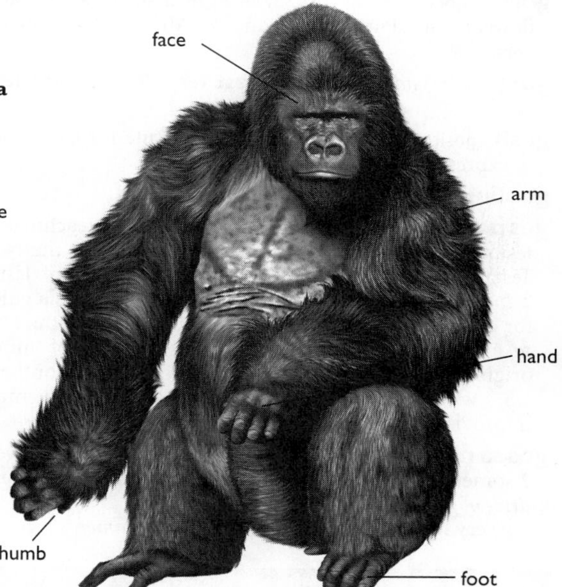

goose (gūs) *n, pl* **geese 1 a** a web-footed swimming bird with a short broad bill, resembling a duck, but larger and with a longer neck. **b** the female of this bird. The male is called a **gander**. **2** a silly person: *What a goose you are!* <Old English *gos*> **goose′like′** *adj.*
cook someone's goose, *Informal* ruin someone's chances.
kill the goose that lays the golden egg, foolishly sacrifice future good in order to satisfy present greed.

goose·ber·ry (gūs′ber′ē) *n, pl* **goose·ber·ries** a small, sour, edible, yellowish green berry that grows on a thorny shrub. <origin uncertain>

goose·bumps (gūs′bumps) *pln* a rough condition of the skin caused when the hairs stand up straight because of cold, fear, or extreme pleasure or excitement. Also called **goose pimples**, **gooseflesh**.

goose egg *Slang n* **1** a lump, especially on the head, from a hard blow. **2** zero.

goose step *n* a marching step in which the leg is swung high with straight, stiff knees. **goose′-step′** *v.*

go·pher (gō′fər) *n* a burrowing ground squirrel found in the central plains of N America. <perhaps Cdn French *gaufre* = honeycomb, from the structure of its burrow>

gore[1] (gȯr) *n* blood that has been shed, especially as a result of violence: *The battlefield was covered with gore.* <Old English *gor* dirt>

gore[2] (gȯr) *v* **gored, gor·ing** wound with a horn or tusk: *The bull gored the farmer to death.* <Middle English>

gore[3] (gȯr) *n* **1** 🍁 an unassigned tract of land remaining after a township has been surveyed and marked out into lots. **2** a long, tapered piece of cloth put in a skirt or sail to shape it or give it greater width. <Old English *gara* triangular piece of land>

gorge (gȯrj) *n* **1** a deep, narrow valley, usually steep and rocky. **2** an act of gorging or a gluttonous meal. **3** a mass stopping up a narrow passage: *An ice gorge blocked the river.*
v **gorged, gorg·ing** (*often with reflexive pronoun*) eat greedily: *He gorged himself on potato chips.* <Old French = throat>
your gorge rises, you are disgusted.

gor·geous (gȯr′jəs) *adj* beautiful in a rich, magnificent way: *a gorgeous sunset.* **gor′geous·ly** *adv.*
gor′geous·ness *n.*

ETYMOLOGY

Gorgeous comes from Old French *gorgias*, meaning "fashionable," which is from *gorge*, meaning "throat."

At one time, it was fashionable to wear a ruffle or some other adornment around the throat.

Gor·gon (gȯr′gən) *Greek myth n* any of three horrible sisters who had snakes for hair. Anyone who looked at a Gorgon would be turned to stone. <Latin, from Greek *gorgos* terrible>

go·ril·la (gə ril′ə) *n* an ape from the forests of central Africa. It is the largest living primate. <origin uncertain>

a bat	e bed	i bid	o pot	u cup	th **thin**
ā cake	ē me	ī bite	ō go	ū rude	TH **then**
ä bar	ə about	ər over	ȯ for	u̇ put	zh measure

gorse (gôrs) *n* a low, prickly evergreen shrub with yellow flowers, found in Europe and N Africa. <Old English *gorst*>

gor·y (gô′rē) *adj* **gor·i·er, gor·i·est** very bloody. **gor′i·ness** *n.*

gosh (gosh) *interj* an inoffensive substitute for GOD, used to express surprise, admiration, etc.

gos·ling (goz′ling) *n* a young goose.

gos·pel (gos′pəl) *n* **1** *Christianity* **a** the life and teachings of Jesus. **b Gospel** any of the first four books of the New Testament, telling about the life and teachings of Jesus. **2** *Informal* anything earnestly believed or taken as a guide for action: *the socialist gospel.* **3** the complete truth: *They take her words for gospel.* **4** a fervent style of music originating in African-American churches of the southern US, with devotional lyrics and sung with much improvisation. <Old English *god* good + *spel* story>

gos·sa·mer (gos′ə mər) *n* **1** a film or thread of cobweb. **2** something, such as cloth, that is very thin or delicate: *a dress of gossamer silk.*
adj very light and thin: *butterflies with gossamer wings.*

ETYMOLOGY

Gossamer is a Middle English word, likely from *gossomer*, meaning "Indian summer" (literally, *goose summer*, because this kind of bird was eaten at that time). The silk of spider webs, plentiful in Indian summer, may have shown a resemblance to the down off a goose.

gos·sip (gos′ip) *n* **1** casual talk about other people, typically involving reports that have not been confirmed. **2** a person who gossips a lot.
v **gos·siped, gos·sip·ing** talk casually about other people, passing on news or rumours about them. <Old English *godsibb* godparent, i.e., familiar acquaintance> **gos′sip·er** *n.* **gos′sip·y** *adj.*

gos·sip·mon·ger (gos′ip mong′gər) *n* a person who spreads gossip.

got (got) past tense and a past participle of GET.

GRAMMAR AND USAGE

Got and **gotten** are both past participles of the verb **get**:

Had you gotten your test results before Spring Break?

I had got the grass cut just before my parents returned.

Many people prefer **got** to **gotten**, and **got** is always used in sentences containing the idiom *have got*, meaning "have": *You can see that I have got more books than I can fit into my knapsack.*

Goth (goth) *n* **1** a member of a Germanic people that invaded the Roman Empire from the east between the 200s and the 400s. **2 a** a style of music that shares features of punk and heavy metal, dealing with grim or supernatural themes. **b** a person who wears black clothes and black and white makeup, and likes Goth music.

Goth·ic (goth′ik) *n* **1** a style of architecture using pointed arches and high, steep roofs, developed during the Middle Ages. **2** an angular style of lettering and type.
adj **1** to do with Gothic architecture. **2** to do with the ancient Goths. **3** to do with Goth music or its fans. **4** to do with a style of literature that emphasizes the supernatural and the grotesque, usually in a medieval setting.

go–to (go′tü) *adj* **1** *Football* to do with being a player who consistently makes important plays, especially in critical situations: *the team's go-to receiver.* **2** *Slang* to do with being something or someone preferred over others: *the go-to narcotic for wealthy Americans. She's the go-to member of the Student Council.*

got·ten (got′ən) a past participle of GET.

gouache (gwäsh) *n* **1** the watercolour painting medium obtained by mixing pigments with water and a gluelike substance. **2** a painting done in this medium.

ETYMOLOGY

The French word **gouache** came from Italian *guazzo*, originally meaning "watering place."

Watering holes tend to be muddy places, so *guazzo* came to mean "mud," and opaque watercolours are a little like mud.

gouge (gouj) *v* **gouged, goug·ing** **1** cut deeply into with a chisel or other sharp object: *to gouge a piece of wood. She gouged me with her nails.* **2** make by gouging: *He gouged a deep scratch in the desktop.* **3** dig or tear (*with* ***out***): *to gouge out a big splinter.* **4** *Informal* grossly overcharge.
n **1** a chisel with a concave blade, for cutting round grooves or holes. **2** a groove, trench, or hole made by gouging. **3** *Informal* an act of overcharging. <French, from Latin *gulbia*>

gou·lash (gū′lash) *n* a highly seasoned stew or soup of meat and vegetables, flavoured with paprika. <Hungarian *gulyas*>

gourd (gūrd) *or* (gôrd) *n* **1** the hard-shelled, inedible fruit of certain vines, often dried and hollowed out as a cup or bowl, or used as seasonal decorations in fall. **2** a container made from the dried shell of a gourd. <French, from Latin *cucurbita*>

gour·mand (gūr′mənd) *n* a person who is fond of good food and often eats too much. <Old French> **gour′mand·ism′** *n.* **gour′mand·ize′** *v.*

gour·met (gūr mā′) *n* a person who enjoys and is knowledgeable about fine foods and wines.
adj to do with fine foods and wines: *gourmet cooking.* <French = wine taster>

gout (gout) *n* **1** a painful disease of the joints, often characterized by a swelling of the big toe. **2** *Poetic* a large drop or clot of blood. <Old French, from Latin *gutta* a drop> **gout′y** *adj.*

gov·ern (guv′ərn) *v* **1** control and direct, especially a country, organization, or people. **2** hold back or restrain: *to govern your temper.* **3** influence or determine: *the motives governing a person's decision.* **4** be a rule or law for: *the principles governing a case.* <Old French, from Greek *kybernaein* to steer> **gov′ern·a·ble** *adj.*

gov·ern·ess (guv′ər nis) *n* especially formerly in upper-class families, a woman who was employed to teach children in a private household.

gov·ern·ment (guv′ərn mənt) *or* (guv′ər mənt) *n* **1** rule or authority over a country or community. **2** the person or people ruling a country or community: *The government was defeated in the general election.* **3** a system of ruling: *Canada has democratic government.*
gov′ern·men′tal *adj.*

✱ **Government House** *n* **1** the official residence of the Governor General in Ottawa. **2** in some provinces, the official residence of the Lieutenant-Governor.

gov·er·nor (guv′ər nər) *n* **1** the appointed ruler of a colony; the representative of a king or queen in a colony. **2** in the US, an elected official who is the executive head of a state government: *the governor of Pennsylvania.* **3** a person who manages or directs an institution: *A board of governors oversees this organization.* **gov′er·nor·ship′** *n.*

Governor General *n, pl* **Governors General** in Canada, the representative of the king or queen, appointed for a term of five years.
Also, **Governor-General**.

gown (goun) *n* **1** a woman's long formal dress. **2** a loose outer garment, such as that worn by a judge, member of the clergy, graduating student, choir member, or hospital patient. <Old French, from Latin *gunna*> **gowned** *adj.*

GP or **G.P.** *n* in full, **general practitioner** a physician with a family practice (as distinct from a consultant or specialist).

GPS *n* in full, **global positioning system** a navigational system allowing users to find out their exact position on the earth by means of information received from satellites.

grab (grab) *v* **grabbed, grab·bing 1** seize suddenly, hurriedly, or greedily: *The dog grabbed the meat and ran.* **2** take hold suddenly, such as in brakes or other mechanical device. **3** *Slang* attract the attention of: *How does that idea grab you?*
n an act of grabbing: *She made a grab for the apple.* <Dutch *grabben*> **grab′ber** *n.*
up for grabs, *Informal* **a** available free. **b** potentially able to be bargained away, given up, or changed.

grab bag *n* **1** a bag filled with a variety of things, one of which is to be picked out without seeing what it is. **2** a bag that people are invited to buy without knowing its contents. **3** a varied or seemingly random assortment.

grace (grās) *n* **1** beauty of form or movement: *the grace of a skater.* **2** a fine quality of speech, appearance, or behaviour: *She accepted her loss with grace and dignity.* **3** mercy or favour, such as shown by forgiving a fault. **4** an allowance of time: *The library gives you three days' grace before charging for overdue books.* **5** a short prayer of thanks before or after a meal. **6** a positive quality of a person or thing: *Hospitality is one of her many graces.* **7** *Christianity* God's favour toward people. **8** usually, **graces** *pl* behaviour put on for effect: *I am tired of her little airs and graces.* **9 Grace** a title used in speaking to or of a duke, duchess, or archbishop: *Welcome, Your Grace. He spoke to His Grace the Duke of Bedford.*
v **graced, grac·ing** do a favour or honour to: *She graced the banquet with her presence.* <French, from Latin *gratus* pleasing>
fall from grace, earn general disapproval by a serious error or misdeed.
have the grace, have the goodness or courtesy: *He had the grace to say he was sorry.*
in someone's good (or **bad**) **graces,** in (or out of) favour with someone.
with good (or **bad**) **grace,** in a pleasant and willing (or unpleasant and unwilling) manner.

grace·ful (grās′fəl) *adj* beautiful in form, movement, or manner: *a graceful apology, a graceful dancer.*
grace′ful·ly *adv.* **grace′ful·ness** *n.*

grace·less (grās′lis) *adj* lacking grace, elegance, or charm.
grace′less·ly *adv.* **grace′less·ness** *n.*

grace note *Music n* a quick note or group of notes added for ornament and not included in counting beats.

gra·cious (grā′shəs) *adj* **1** courteous and kindly: *She welcomed her guests in a gracious manner that made them feel at ease.* **2** characterized by wealth and elegance: *gracious living.*
interj used to express surprise. **gra′cious·ly** *adv.* **gra′cious·ness** *n.*

grack·le (grak′əl) *n* a N American blackbird whose black feathers have a bronze lustre.. <Latin *graculus* jackdaw, a small black bird found in Europe and Asia>

gra·da·tion (grə dā′shən) *n* **1** a step, stage, or degree in a series: *My ruler is marked off in gradations of 1 cm. The rainbow shows gradations of colour.* **2** a change that occurs by steps or stages: *a gradation of temperature from cold to hot.* <See GRADE.>

grade (grād) *n* **1** a division of a school arranged according to the students' progress, usually corresponding to one year's study: *grade seven.* **2** a degree in a scale of rank, quality, or value: *Grade A butter is the best in quality. My grade in Math was B.* **3** a step or stage in a process. **4** the slope of a road or railway track, or the amount of this slope: *a steep grade.*
v **grad·ed, grad·ing 1** arrange in categories according to quality or value: *These apples are graded by size.* **2** mark and assign a grade to: *The teacher graded the test papers.* **3** make more nearly level: *The workers graded the land around the new house.* **4** change gradually, by stages or degrees: *Red and yellow grade into orange.* <French, from Latin *gradus* step>
make the grade, a meet a standard. **b** overcome difficulties.

grad·er (grā′dər) *n* **1** a wheeled machine for levelling earth. **2** a person who or thing that grades. **3** (*only in compounds*) a person in a certain grade in school: *a sixth-grader.*

grade school ELEMENTARY SCHOOL.

a bat	e bed	i bid	o pot	u cup	th **thin**
ā cake	ē me	ī bite	ō go	ū rude	ᴛʜ **then**
à bar	ə about	ər over	ȯ for	ů put	zh measure

grain

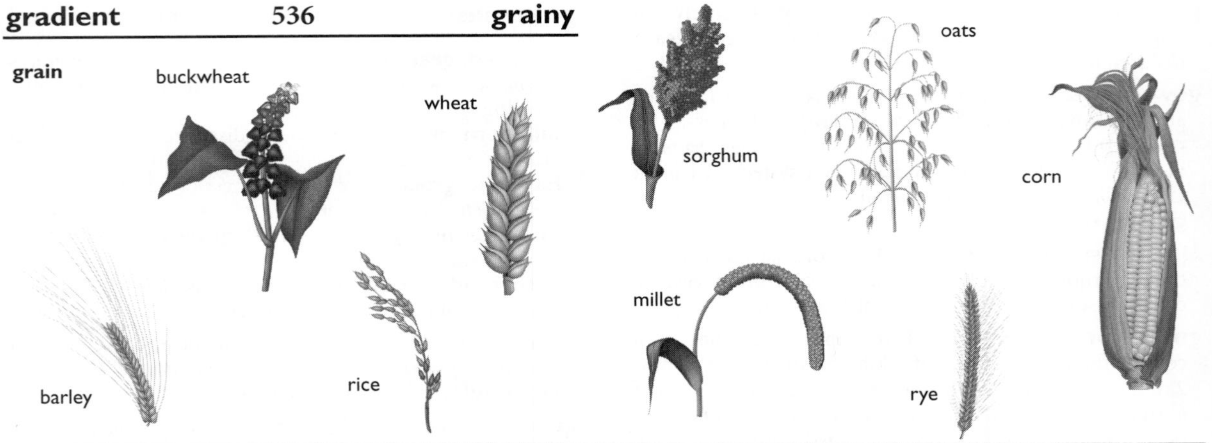

buckwheat wheat sorghum oats corn barley rice millet rye

gra·di·ent (grā′dē ənt) *n* **1** the sloping part of a road or railway track, or the rate at which it slopes. **2** a rate of increase or decrease, as of temperature or pressure. <Latin *gradus* step>

grad·u·al (graj′ū əl) *adj* by degrees too small to be separately noticed: *a gradual increase in sound, a gradual improvement. The hill had a gradual slope.* <Latin *gradus* step> **grad′u·al·ly** *adv.*

grad·u·ate (graj′ū āt′) *for v,* (graj′ū ət′) *for n, adj.* *v* **grad·u·at·ed, grad·u·at·ing 1** finish a course of study at a school, college, or university and receive a paper officially declaring that one has done so: *He graduated from high school last year.* **2** give a diploma to, for finishing a course of study: *They won't graduate you if you don't have enough credits.* **3** mark with units for measuring. **4** arrange in regular steps, levels, or degrees: *Income tax is graduated so that those whose income is highest pay the highest rate of tax.* **5** change gradually: *The colours in this scarf graduate from paler to darker shades.*
n a person who has graduated.
adj of or for graduates: *a graduate student, a graduate school.* <Latin *gradus* step>

🍁 **graduated licensing** *n* a process of becoming a licensed driver that involves several stages, each requiring a student to graduate from one stage before advancing to the next.

grad·u·a·tion (graj′ū ā′shən) *n* **1** the act or fact of graduating; especially, the act of graduating from a school, college, or university. **2** the ceremony that accompanies this.

graf·fi·ti (grə fē′tē) *pln, sing* **graf·fi·to** things written or drawn on a public surface such as a wall or fence. <Italian>

GRAMMAR AND USAGE

Although **graffiti** is a plural in the language it comes from—Italian, in English it can be used as either a singular or plural noun.

Its singular form, *graffito,* is not commonly used in informal writing or speech.

graft[1] (graft) *v* **1** insert a shoot or bud from one tree or plant into a slit in another so that it will grow there permanently. **2** transfer a piece of skin or bone from one part of the body to another so that it will grow there permanently.
n **1 a** the shoot, bud, or part of the body used in grafting. **b** the place on a plant or a person's body where grafting has been done. **2** a tree or plant that has had a shoot or bud grafted on it. <Old French, from Greek *grapheion* stylus, from the shape of the shoot> **graft′er** *n.*

graft[2] (graft) *n* **1** the taking of money dishonestly, especially in connection with government business. **2** money taken or obtained in this way. <origin uncertain>

gra·ham (grā′əm) *n* a finely ground, unsifted, whole-wheat flour: *graham crackers.* <S. *Graham,* 19c dietician>

Grail (grāl) *n* according to medieval tradition, the cup used by Christ at the Last Supper. Also called **Holy Grail.** <Old French, from Greek *krater*>

grain (grān) *n* **1 a** a single seed of wheat, oats, or similar cereal grasses: *a grain of wheat.* **b** the seeds of such plants considered as a mass: *a sack of grain.* **c** a plant that these seeds grow on, or such plants in general: *Oats and barley are grains. A lot of grain is grown in this area.* **2** a tiny, hard particle: *a grain of sand, a grain of sugar.* **3** a nonmetric unit of mass, equal to 0.065 grams. **4** the smallest possible amount: *a grain of truth.* **5** the arrangement or direction of the fibres in wood or layers in stone: *That mahogany table has a fine grain.*
v **1** give a rough texture or surface to something: *His fingers were grained with dirt.* **2** form into grains. **3** paint in imitation of the grain in wood or marble. <Old French, from Latin *granum* seed> **grain′less** *adj.*
go against the grain, be contrary to one's natural tendency: *Sitting still goes against the grain for my little brother.*

grain alcohol *n* ethyl alcohol.

grain elevator *n* a tall building for storing grain.

grain·field (grān′fēld′) *n* a field in which grain grows.

grain·y (grā′nē) *adj* **grain·i·er, grain·i·est** with a texture like grain.

gram (gram) *n* a unit of mass, equal to one-thousandth of a kilogram. *Symbol* **g** <French, from Latin *gramma* a small weight>

–gram *combining form* written or recorded: *telegram, electrocardiogram.* <Greek *graphein* write>

gram·mar (gram′ər) *n* **1 a** the rules by which words are used in the system and structure of a language. **b** the version of these rules considered to be the standard by educated users of a language. **c** a person's manner of using words and building sentences, relative to such rules: *He has such bad grammar.* **2** a book on grammar: *a German grammar.* <Old French, from Greek *gramma* thing written>

gram·mar·i·an (grə mer′ē ən) *n* an expert in grammar.

grammar school *UK n* a high school that prepares students for university.

gram·mat·i·cal (grə mat′ə kəl) *adj* **1** to do with grammar: *a grammatical error.* **2** correct according to the rules of grammar in a particular language: *"We is leaving now" is not a grammatical sentence.* **gram·mat′i·cal·ly** *adv.*

gram·o·phone (gram′ə fōn′) *n* an old name for a record player.

Gram's method (gramz) *n* a means of classifying bacteria, in which they are first stained with gentian violet and then treated with an agent that can remove colour. Some bacteria keep the stain (**Gram-positive**), while others lose it (**Gram-negative**). <H.C.J. *Gram*, 20c physician>

gran·a·ry (gran′ə rē) *or* (grā′nə rə) *n, pl* **gran·a·ries** a place or building where grain is stored. <Latin *granum* seed>

grand (grand) *adj* **1** impressive, splendid, or dignified: *grand music, to make a grand entrance onto the stage.* **2** highest or very high in rank: *a grand duchess, a grand master in chess.* **3** complete or comprehensive: *grand total.* **4** *Informal* excellent: *We had a grand time.*
n **1** a grand piano. **2** *Slang* a thousand dollars: *He won two grand in the lottery.* <French, from Latin *grandis* big> **grand′ly** *adv.* **grand′ness** *n.*

Grand Banks or **Grand Bank** *n* a shallow region of the ocean lying southeast of Newfoundland, famous as a fishing ground.

grand·child (gran′chīld′) *n, pl* **grand·chil·dren** a child of one's son or daughter.

grand·dad or **gran·dad** (gran′dad′) *Informal n* grandfather.

grand·dad·dy (gran′dad′ē) *Informal n, pl* **grand·dad·dies** **1** grandfather. **2** the largest one of its kind: *This fish is the granddaddy of them all.*

grand·daugh·ter (gran′dot′ər) *n* a daughter of one's son or daughter.

gran·deur (gran′jər) *or* (grand′yər) *n* greatness and impressiveness: *the grandeur of the Rocky Mountains.* <French>

grand·fa·ther (gran′foᴛʜ′ər) *n* **1** the father of one's father or mother. **2** an early male originator or founder of something.
v exempt from a new regulation those cases that existed before the regulation was made, often by means of a special clause called a **grandfather clause**. **grand′fa′ther·ly** *adj.*

grandfather clock *n* a clock in a tall wooden case.

gran·dil·o·quent (gran dil′ə kwənt) *adj* using pretentious or pompous words. <Latin *grandis* big + *loqui* speak> **gran·dil′o·quent·ly** *adv.*

gran·di·ose (gran′dē ōs′) *adj* grand in an exaggerated or pompous way. <Italian *grande* grand> **gran′di·ose′ly** *adv.*

grand·ma (gram′ə) *or* (gran′mə) *Informal n* grandmother.

grand mal (mal) *n* an epilepsy characterized by seizures and loss of consciousness. Compare PETIT MAL. <French = great illness>

grand·moth·er (gran′muᴛʜ′ər) *n* **1** the mother of one's father or mother. **2** an early female originator or founder of something. **grand′moth′er·ly** *adj.*

grand·neph·ew (gran′nef′yū) *n* the son of one's nephew or niece.

grand·niece (gran′nēs′) *n* the daughter of one's nephew or niece.

grand·pa (gram′pə) *or* (gram′på) *Informal n* grandfather.

grand·par·ent (gran′per′ənt) *n* grandfather or grandmother.

grand piano *n* a large, full-toned piano with a horizontal frame and strings. Compare UPRIGHT PIANO.

🍁 **Grand Portage** *n* in former times, a rendezvous point for fur traders at Lake Superior, used as the main exchange point between Montréal and the inland posts of the Northwest.

Grand Prix (grån′ prē′) *n* a road race for sports cars with a specified size of engine.

grand slam *n* **1** the act of winning all the tricks in a hand in a game of bridge. **2** *Tennis, Golf, Rugby* the act of winning a group of major tournaments in the same year. **3** *Baseball* a home run hit when each of the three bases is occupied, thereby scoring four runs.

grand·son (gran′sun′) *n* a son of one's son or daughter.

grand·stand (gran′stand′) *n* the main seating place, usually covered, for the spectators at an athletic field, racetrack, or parade.
v act or speak in a grand or fancy way to impress an audience: *Pay no attention to him, because he's just grandstanding.*

gran·ite (gran′it) *n* a hard, coarse-grained igneous rock consisting chiefly of quartz and feldspar, used for buildings and monuments. <Italian *granito* grained, from Latin *granum* grain>

gran·ite·ware (gran′it wer′) *n* kitchen or dining items made of iron covered with grey enamel.

gran·ny or **gran·nie** (gran′ē) *Informal n, pl* **gran·nies** grandmother.

a bat	e bed	i bid	o pot	u cup	th **thin**
ā cake	ē me	ī bite	ō go	ū rude	ᴛʜ **then**
å bar	ə about	ər over	ȯ for	ů put	zh measure

G

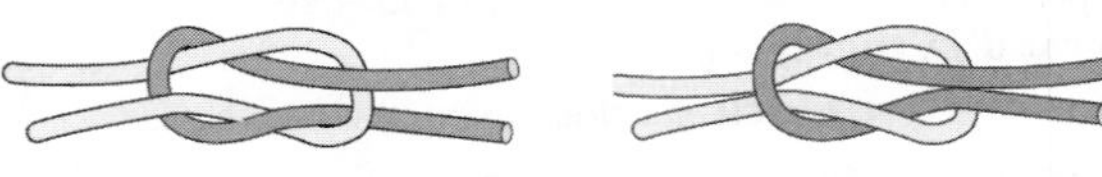

granny knot or **grannie knot** *n* a knot similar to a reef knot, but with ends crossed differently. It is not as secure as a reef knot.

Granny Smith *n* an eating apple with bright green skin and crisp flesh. <M.A. (*Granny*) *Smith*, 19c fruit grower who developed the variety>

gra·no·la (grə nō′lə) *n* a nutritious breakfast cereal or snack mix consisting of rolled oats, wheat germ, chopped nuts, seeds, etc. <*grano* grain + *-ola*>

grant (grant) *v* **1** give what is asked, especially if the giver has authority: *to grant a request, to grant permission.* **2** admit or accept, with a reservation: *I grant that she's clever, but she sure isn't very friendly.* **3** officially transfer ownership or some other right, especially by deed or writing.
n something granted by an authority, especially a sum of money: *He received a grant to allow him to carry out his research project.* <Old French, from Latin *credere* trust> **grant′er** *n.*
take (it) for granted, assume to be true without anyone saying so or without proof: *We took for granted that he would do well.*

gran·u·lar (gran′yə lər) *adj* consisting of, containing, or resembling grains or granules.

gran·u·late (gran′yə lāt′) *v* **gran·u·lat·ed, gran·u·lat·ing 1** form into grains or granules: *Granulated sugar is coarser than icing sugar.* **2** roughen on the surface. **3** form small grainlike bodies on the surface of a wound in the course of healing. **gran′u·la′tion** *n.*

gran·ule (gran′yūl) *n* **1** a small grain. **2** a small bit or spot like a grain, especially a brilliant spot that appears on the sun's surface and lasts only a few minutes.

grape (grāp) *n* a small, edible berry that grows in bunches on a vine. See BERRY for picture. **grape′like′** *adj.*

ETYMOLOGY

Grape comes from the Old French name for the hook used to pick grapes, from the Germanic *graper*, meaning "pick grapes."

Eventually, the name of the tool came to mean what you picked with the tool, namely, a bunch of grapes. In English, it became known as the individual fruit in the bunch.

grape·fruit (grāp′frūt′) *n, pl* **grape·fruit** or **grape·fruits** a large, pale yellow, round citrus fruit with an acid juicy pulp. <*grape* + *fruit*, probably because the fruit grows in clusters like grapes>

grape·shot (grāp′shot′) *n* a cluster of small iron balls formerly used as ammunition for cannons.

grape·vine (grāp′vīn′) *n* **1** a vine that bears grapes. **2** *Informal* (*usually with* ***through*** *or* ***from***) the informal spreading of news and rumours throughout a community: *She learned through the grapevine that her old boyfriend was back in town.*

graph (graf) *n* a line or diagram showing the relation of two or more quantities that vary. See also BAR GRAPH, BROKEN-LINE GRAPH, CIRCLE GRAPH, and LINE GRAPH.
v represent or show by such a line or diagram: *Take a survey of your classmates' opinions and graph the result.* <Greek *graphein* write>

–graph *combining form* **1** written, drawn, or recorded: *autograph, photograph.* **2** written, drawn, or recorded by a machine: *seismograph.* <See GRAPH.>

graph·ic (graf′ik) *adj* **1** vivid and including much realistic detail: *a graphic account of the battle. The movie contains graphic violence.* **2** to do with making two-dimensional images: *Drawing is a graphic art.* **3** to do with writing: *graphic symbols.* **4** to do with a graph or graphs.
n **1** *Computers* a drawing, illustration, or diagram displayed on a screen or stored as data. **2 graphics** (*with singular verb*) **a** the art or technique of producing graphic work, especially commercial design or illustration. **b** computer graphics. **graph′i·cal** *adj.* **graph′i·cal·ly** *adv.*

graph·i·cal user interface (graf′ə kəl) GUI.

graphic arts *pln* the arts that involve the making of two-dimensional images with lines and tones rather than with the use of colour or as three-dimensional work. Design is a graphic art. **graphic artist** *n.*

graphic organizer *n* a pictorial way of organizing notes and information, usually in the form of a diagram showing relationships between concepts.

graph·ite (graf′īt) *n* a soft, black form of carbon that has a metallic lustre, often used in pencils. <Greek *graphein* write>

graph·ol·o·gy (graf ol′ə jē) *n* the study of handwriting, especially as a means of analyzing character. <See GRAPH.> **graph·ol′o·gist** *n.*

graph paper *n* paper with small ruled squares for the drawing of diagrams or graphs.

–graphy *combining form* **1** indicating a form of writing or otherwise recording: *photography.* **2** indicating an art or a descriptive science: *choreography, geography.* <See GRAPH.>

grap·nel (grap′nəl) *n* **1** a grappling iron. **2** a small anchor with three or more hooks. <Old French *grapon*>

grap·ple (grap′əl) *v* **grap·pled, grap·pling 1** struggle or fight: *The wrestlers grappled in the centre of the ring.* **2** try to deal with: *to grapple with a problem.*
n an iron bar with hooks at one end for seizing an object and holding it. <Old French *grapon* hook i.e., something that can seize and hold tight>

grappling iron *n* an instrument with one or more hooks for seizing and holding something. Also called **grappling hook, grapnel.**

grasp (grasp) *v* **1** seize and hold firmly with the hand. **2** take eagerly: *to grasp an opportunity.* **3** understand: *a difficult concept to grasp.*
n **1** the act or power of seizing and holding firmly: *She has*

a strong grasp. Success is within his grasp. **2** control or possession. **3** understanding: *He has a good grasp of mathematics.* <Middle English> **grasp′a·ble** *adj.*

grasp·ing (gras′ping) *adj* greedy for money or property.

grass (gras) *n* **1** any of several low-growing green plants with long narrow leaves that grow wild or in lawns, pastures, and fields. **2** any of a large family of plants with jointed stems and long, narrow leaves. Wheat, corn, sugar cane, and bamboo are grasses. <Old English *græs*> **grass′less** *adj.* **grass′like′** *adj.* **grass′y** *adj.*
not let the grass grow under your feet, not waste time.
put out to grass, a cause livestock to graze in a pasture. **b** *Informal* force to retire.

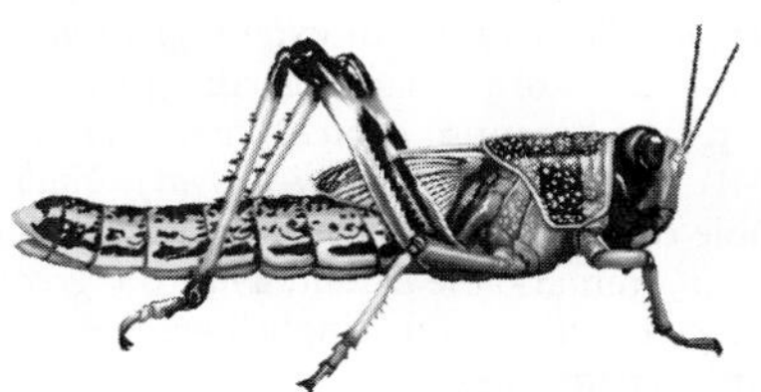

An adult **grasshopper** can jump over something that's about 500 times its own height.

grass·hop·per (gras′hop′ər) *n* a plant-eating insect with two pairs of wings and long, strong hind legs adapted for jumping.

grass·land (gras′land′) *n* land with grass on it, especially a region where grass is the natural vegetation.

grass·roots (gras′rūtz′) *pl n* ordinary people and organizations in a community at the local or most basic level.

grass snake *n* a harmless, greyish green snake living in marshy places.

grate[1] (grāt) *n* **1** a framework of iron bars, such as in a fireplace to hold the wood, or over a window or opening. **2** a fireplace. <Latin *grata* lattice, from *cratis* latticework> **grate′like′** *adj.*

grate[2] (grāt) *v* **grat·ed, grat·ing** **1** have an annoying or unpleasant effect: *His rude manners grate on people.* **2** make a harsh grinding sound. **3** move with a harsh sound: *The door grated on its old, rusty hinges.* **4** wear down or scrape off in small pieces: *to grate cheese.* <Old French *grater*>

grate·ful (grāt′fəl) *adj* feeling or showing gratitude or appreciation: *a grateful sigh. We were grateful for their help.* <Latin *gratus*> **grate′ful·ly** *adv.* **grate′ful·ness** *n.*

grat·er (grā′tər) *n* a device with a rough surface for wearing things down into shreds or particles by rubbing: *a cheese grater.*

grat·i·fy (grat′ə fī′) *v* **grat·i·fied, grat·i·fying** **1** give pleasure or satisfaction to: *He was very gratified by the rave reviews of his acting.* **2** satisfy or indulge: *Don't gratify every craving you have for sweets.* <French, from Latin *gratus* pleasing + *facere* make> **grat′i·fi·ca′tion** *n.* **grat′i·fy′ing** *adj.* **grat′i·fy′ing·ly** *adv.*

grat·ing[1] (grā′ting) *n* a framework of bars over a window or opening.

grat·ing[2] (grā′ting) *adj* **1** annoying or irritating. **2** harsh or jarring in sound: *a grating voice.*

grat·is (grat′is) *adv, adj* free of charge. <Latin, from *gratia* favour>

grat·i·tude (grat′ə tyūd′) *or* (grat′ə tūd′) *n* a thankful feeling because of a favour received. <Latin *gratus* thankful>

SYNONYMS

Gratitude is a thankful feeling: *He expressed his gratitude for his friend's help.*

Appreciation has the same meaning of thankfulness: *They gave her an award to show their appreciation for her outstanding community work.*

Indebtedness refers to the condition of owing gratitude: *The family's kindness caused a sense of indebtedness in their guests.*

gra·tu·i·tous (grə tyū′ə təs) *or* (grə tū′ə təs) *adj* **1** without reason or cause: *a gratuitous insult, gratuitous violence in a movie.* **2** freely given or obtained. <See GRATUITY.> **gra·tu′i·tous·ly** *adv.* **gra·tu′i·tous·ness** *n.*

gra·tu·i·ty (grə tyū′ə tē) *or* (grə tū′ə tē) *n, pl* **gra·tu·i·ties** a present of money in return for service: *Gratuities are often given to hairdressers.* <Latin *gratuitas* gift>

grave[1] (grāv) *n* **1** a hole dug in the ground where a dead body is to be buried. **2** the area on top when this hole is filled in after the burial: *She carefully tended his grave.* **3** any place in which what is dead can be located: *a watery grave.* **4** death: *an early grave.* <Old English *græf*>
have one foot in the grave, be near death.
make someone turn over in his or her grave, say or do something that someone who is now dead would have strongly disapproved of.

grave[2] (grāv) *adj* **grav·er, grav·est** **1** important and to be taken seriously: *a grave decision, grave issues.* **2** serious or likely to have bad consequences: *grave doubts, a grave illness.* **3** dignified or solemn: *a grave face.* <French, from Latin *gravis* serious> **grave′ly** *adv.* **grav′i·ty** *n.*

grave·dig·ger (grāv′dig′ər) *n* a person who digs GRAVES[1] (def. 1).

grav·el (grav′əl) *n* pebbles and small pieces of rock, sometimes used for the surface of roads and walks.
v **grav·elled** or **grav·eled, grav·el·ling** or **grav·el·ing** cover with gravel: *to gravel a road.* <Old French *grave* sand>

grav·el·ly (grav′ə lē) *adj* **1** consisting of or like gravel. **2** of a voice, deep and rough.

grave·side (grāv′sīd′) *n* the area around the edge of a grave, especially a new, open grave where people have gathered for a burial ceremony.

grave·stone (grāv′stōn′) *n* a small stone monument that marks a grave.

a bat	e bed	i bid	o pot	u cup	th thin
ā cake	ē me	ī bite	ō go	ū rude	ᴛʜ then
à bar	ə about	ər over	ȯ for	ů put	zh measure

grave·yard (grāv′yärd′) *n* a place for burying the dead.

graveyard shift *Informal n* of work, the shift from midnight to 8 a.m.

grav·i·tate (grav′ə tāt′) *v* **grav·i·tat·ed, grav·i·tat·ing** **1** move or tend to move by the force of gravity. **2** settle down, sink, or fall: *The sand and dirt in the water gravitated to the bottom of the bottle.* **3** move toward or be attracted to a place: *At noon hour, the students gravitated to the common room.* <See GRAVITY.> **grav′i·ta′tion** *n.* **grav′i·ta′tion·al** *adj.*

grav·i·ty (grav′ə tē) *n, pl* **grav·i·ties** **1 a** the movement or tendency that attracts objects toward the centre of the earth or some other physical mass. **b** the natural force of attraction in the universe that makes objects tend to move toward each other. **2** a serious matter, manner, or character: *a look of gravity. When she had explained the gravity of the situation, we were eager to help.* <Latin *gravis* heavy>

gra·vy (grā′vē) *n, pl* **gra·vies** **1** a sauce made from the fat and juice that comes out of meat in cooking. **2** *Informal* unearned or unexpected money.

ETYMOLOGY

Gravy comes from someone mistakenly thinking that the Old French word *grané* was actually *gravé*. The word *grané* meant "properly seasoned." It came from Latin *granum*, meaning "grain," because to season food was to put grains of spice in it.

gravy boat *n* a long, narrow, shallow jug used for serving gravy.

gravy train *Slang n* a situation in which a lot of money can be made with little effort: *to ride the gravy train.* <railroad slang for a short haul that paid well>

gray (grā) GREY.

gray·ling (grā′ling) *n* an edible freshwater fish that is silver-grey with horizontal violet stripes.

graze[1] (grāz) *v* **grazed, graz·ing** **1** feed on growing grass: *Cattle and sheep graze.* **2** put livestock to feed on growing grass or a pasture, or tend them while they do so: *They grazed their sheep on the mountain slopes.* <Old English *græs* grass>

graze[2] (grāz) *v* **grazed, graz·ing** **1** rub lightly against in passing: *The car grazed the garage door.* **2** scrape the skin from: *I fell and grazed my knee.*
n the act of grazing, or a slight wound made in this way. <origin uncertain>

gra·zi·o·so (grä′tsē yō′sō) *Music adv, adj* in a graceful style.

grease (grēs) *n* **1** fat that has been melted and then allowed to cool to a soft solid: *bacon grease.* **2** a thick, oily substance, especially one used to lubricate.
v **greased, greas·ing** **1** smear with grease: *Grease the cookie sheet well.* **2** lubricate with grease: *My dad took his car in to have it greased.* <Old French, from Latin *crassus* fat>

grease monkey *Slang n* a mechanic who works on motor vehicles.

grease·paint (grēs′pānt′) *n* a waxy substance used as makeup by actors in the theatre.

grease pencil *n* a pencil made of compressed and coloured grease for writing on smooth surfaces.

greas·er (grē′sər) *n* a young man, often much involved with cars or motorcycles, who wears his hair greased back.

greas·y (grē′sē) *adj* **greas·i·er, greas·i·est** **1** containing or coated with grease: *greasy food, greasy hair.* **2** slippery like grease: *The roads were greasy after the snowfall.*
greas′i·ly *adv.* **greas′i·ness** *n.*

greasy spoon *n* a small, cheap restaurant whose menu features quickly prepared fried foods.

great (grāt) *adj* **1** large in size or extent: *great mountains, a great crowd.* **2** more than usual: *great ignorance.* **3** important and famous: *a great composer.* **4** *Informal* excellent: *We had a great time in Calgary. You're a great cook!* **5** noble or generous: *a great heart.* **6** doing or being something to a remarkable extent: *That is a great habit of hers. He is a great talker.* <Old English *great*>
great′ly *adv.* **great′ness** *n.*

great ape *n* a large ape such as the chimpanzee.

great–aunt (grāt′ant′) *n* an aunt of one's mother or father.

great blue heron *n* a large heron with a long bill and greyish blue plumage.

Great Britain *n* the main island of the UK, including England, Scotland, and Wales.

great circle *n* a circle on the surface of a sphere, whose plane passes through the centre and represents the shortest distance between any two points on a sphere.

great·coat (grāt′kōt′) *n* a long, heavy overcoat for a man.

The **Great Dane**, a breed of working dog, was once used to hunt wild boar. Today, it is mainly a pet.

Great Dane *n* a very large, strong, short-haired breed of dog.

Great Divide *US n* the Continental Divide.

Great·er (grā′tər) *adj* (*in names of cities*) including neighbouring suburbs and towns: *Greater Vancouver, Greater Montréal.*

great–grand·child (grāt′gran′chīld′) *n, pl* **great-grand·chil·dren** a grandchild of one's son or daughter.

great–grand·daugh·ter (grāt′gran′dot′ər) *n* a granddaughter of one's son or daughter.

great–grand·fa·ther (grāt′gran′foᴛʜ′ər) *n* a grandfather of one's father or mother.

great–grand·moth·er (grāt′gran′muᴛʜ′ər) *n* a grandmother of one's father or mother.

great–grand·son (grāt′gran′sun′) *n* a grandson of one's son or daughter.

great–heart·ed (grāt′hȧr′tid) *adj* noble, generous, or fearless. **great′-heart′ed·ness** *n.*

Great Lakes *pln* the five large interconnected lakes in central N America, including Lakes Superior, Michigan, Huron, Erie, and Ontario, that are connected to the Atlantic by the St. Lawrence Seaway.

Great Spirit *n* an English name for the supreme deity worshipped by some First Nations peoples.

great–uncle (grāt′ung′kəl) *n* an uncle of one's father or mother.

Great Wall of China *n* a huge stone wall along the northern and northwestern boundary of China, separating it from Mongolia.

Great War *n* World War I, from 1914 to 1918.

grebe (grēb) *n* a diving water bird with a long neck and a pointed bill. <French *grèbe*>

Gre·cian (grē′shən) *adj* to with Greece.

start position in Greco-Roman wrestling

start position in freestyle wrestling

In **Greco-Roman** wrestling, all holds must be applied above the waist.

In **freestyle** wrestling, competitors are allowed to use their entire bodies, for a greater variety of holds.

Gre·co–Ro·man (grē′kō rō′mən) *adj* to do with the ancient Greeks and Romans.

Greece (grēs) *n* a country in southeast Europe. See the APPENDIX. **Greek** *adj, n.*

greed (grēd) *n* the fact of wanting more than one's share or more than one needs; extreme or excessive desire: *People get taken in by scams because of greed.* <Old English *grædig*>

greed·y (grē′dē) *adj* **greed·i·er, greed·i·est** **1** characterized by greed. **2** eager for something that one finds enjoyable: *greedy for new experiences.*
greed′i·ly *adv.* **greed′i·ness** *n.*

Greek fire (grēk) *n* a flammable substance whose flames could not be put out by water, used in warfare in ancient and medieval times. It was probably petroleum-based.

Greek Orthodox *Christianity adj* to do with the Orthodox Church, especially the traditional established church of Greece.

green (grēn) *adj* **1** with the colour between yellow and blue, like that of many growing plants. **2** with many growing plants: *green fields.* **3** not ripe, dried, cured, etc.: *green peaches, green tea.* **4** not experienced or not mature: *He is too green to know better.* **5** *Informal* helpful, or at least not harmful, to the natural environment: *green products.* **6** with a pale, sickly colour because of fear, jealousy, or sickness: *green with envy.*
n **1** a plot of grassy ground. **2** the part of a golf course with smooth, very short grass near a hole. **3 greens** *pl* parts of green plants used for food: *salad greens.*
v make or become green. <Old English *grene*>
green′ish *adj.* **green′ness** *n.*

green bean *n* a cultivated bean whose long green pods are eaten as a vegetable when young and tender.

green·belt (grēn′belt′) *n* a circle of parks and other open land around a city.

green·er·y (grē′nə rē) *n* green plants, grass, or leaves.

green–eyed monster (grē′nīd′) *Informal n* jealousy.

green·horn (grēn′hȯrn′) *Informal n* an inexperienced person.

green·house (grēn′hous′) *n* a building with a glass roof and glass sides, kept warm for growing plants.

greenhouse effect *n* the accumulation of gases in the earth's atmosphere that act to trap the heat from the sun.

greenhouse gas *n* a gas, such as water vapour, ozone, carbon dioxide, or methane, that acts to trap the heat from the sun in the earth's lower atmosphere, causing the greenhouse effect.

green light *Informal n* permission to proceed with a particular task or activity.

green onion *n* an onion pulled before it is mature, with long, tender green leaves and a small, undeveloped bulb.

Green Party *n* one of the registered political parties of Canada.

green pepper *n* the unripe, hollow fruit of a sweet pepper, eaten as a vegetable.

green tea *n* a pale, slightly bitter tea made from leaves that have been steamed and then crushed and dried in ovens. Compare BLACK TEA.

green thumb *n* skill in gardening, especially as a hobby.

Green·wich Mean Time (gren′ich) *n* the basis for setting standard time worldwide, reckoned from the meridian passing through Greenwich, England.
Abbrev. **GMT** Also, **Greenwich Time.**

a bat	e bed	i bid	o pot	u cup	th **thin**
ā cake	ē me	ī bite	ō go	ū rude	ᴛʜ **then**
ȧ bar	ə about	ər over	ȯ for	u̇ put	zh measure

greet (grēt) *v* **1** address a greeting to: *She greeted him happily.* **2** receive or respond to: *His speech was greeted with cheers.* **3** present itself to: *A strange sight greeted her eyes.* <Old English *gretan*> **greet′er** *n.*

greet·ing (grē′ting) *n* **1** the first words said on meeting or noticing a person, or beginning a conversation or letter. **2 greetings** *pl* friendly wishes, often on a special occasion: *birthday greetings. Give my greetings to your sister.*

greeting card *n* a card of usually folded stiff paper, illustrated and generally with some printed message to do with a special occasion or to acknowledge an important event in a person's life.

gre·gar·i·ous (grə ger′ē əs) *adj* **1** fond of being with others: *My sister is more gregarious than I am.* **2** of animals, living in flocks, herds, or other groups: *Sheep and cattle are gregarious.* <Latin *gregis* a flock> **gre·gar′i·ous·ly** *adv.* **gre·gar′i·ous·ness** *n.*

Gre·gor·i·an calendar (grə gȯ′rē ən) *n* the calendar now in use in most countries, with 365 days in an ordinary year, and 366 days in a leap year, that is, every fourth year. It was introduced by Pope Gregory XIII in 1582 as a correction to the Julian calendar.

Gregorian chant *n* church singing with a free rhythm and a single vocal line, introduced by Pope Gregory I in the 500s and still used in some churches. See also PLAINSONG.

grem·lin (grem′lən) *n* an imaginary, mischievous spirit or goblin, often humorously blamed for mechanical and other difficulties. <origin uncertain>

Gre·na·da (grə nā′də) *or* (grə nȧ′də) *n* an island country in the Caribbean. **Gre·na′di·an** *adj, n.*

gre·nade (grə nād′) *n* **1** a small bomb, usually thrown by hand. **2** a round, glass bottle filled with chemicals that scatter as the glass breaks, used to put out fires.

ETYMOLOGY

Grenade was borrowed from French, from Old French *pome grenate*, meaning "pomegranate," or, literally, "seedy fruit (or apple)." As the pomegranate is shaped somewhat like an apple and has many seeds, so a grenade has a shape similar to a pomegranate and is full of bits of shrapnel (metal and granules of powder).

gren·a·dier (gren′ə dēr′) *n* **1** in former times, a soldier who threw grenades. **2** a soldier in a special infantry regiment.

grew (grū) past tense of GROW.

grey (grā) *adj* **1** with the colour made by mixing black and white. **2** with grey hair: *She is already grey.* **3** overcast, gloomy, or dismal: *a grey day.* **4** not clearly defined or determined: *A mark of 47 percent lies in the grey area between passing and failing.*
n a grey horse.
v make or become grey. Also, **gray**. <Old English *græg*> **grey′ish** *adj.* **grey′ness** *n.*

grey·beard (grā′bērd′) *n* an old man.

🍁 **Grey Cup** *n* **1** a trophy awarded each year to the champion professional football team in Canada. It was first presented in 1909 by Earl Grey, then Governor General of Canada. **2** the game played to decide the winner of this trophy.

Dog racing is a popular sport in the United States. Races are held on a running track, where **greyhounds** can reach speeds of up to 64 km/h. Usually, eight or nine greyhounds compete in a race.

grey·hound (grā′hound′) *n* a breed of tall, slender, swift dog used for racing.

grey jay CANADA JAY.

grey matter *n* **1** the greyish tissue in the brain and spinal cord that contains nerve cells and some nerve fibres. **2** *Informal* intelligence.

grey power *n* the political power of elderly people, especially when organized.

grey·scale (grā′skāl′) *Computers adj* to do with a range of grey shades from white to black, especially in a monochrome display or a printout.

grey water *n* water that has been used for washing or industrial purposes but contains no sewage or radiation.

grey whale *n* a large, mottled grey and black baleen whale of the N Pacific.

grey wolf *n* a timber wolf.

grid (grid) *n* **1** a pattern of evenly-spaced lines crossing each other at right angles, especially such a pattern drawn on a map. **2** the system of survey lines (**grid lines**) running parallel to lines of latitude and longitude, used in dividing an area of land into parts. **3** the network of power lines by which hydroelectricity is distributed in an area. **4** the electrode in a valve or tube that controls the flow of current. <*gridiron*>

grid·dle (grid′əl) *n* a wide, heavy, flat metal plate on which food is cooked. <Old French, from Latin *craticula* small griddle, diminutive of *cratis* latticework>

grid·i·ron (grid′ī′ərn) *n* **1** a metal framework of crisscrossed bars, often with a handle, for broiling food. **2** a framework or network that looks like this. **3** a football field.

grid·lock (grid′lok′) *n* **1** total stoppage of traffic because key intersections are blocked by traffic. **2** a stopping of activity of any kind due to overloading or crowding.

🍁 **grid road** *n* a municipal road that follows a grid line established by survey.

grief (grēf) *n* **1** deep sadness caused by trouble or loss. **2** a cause of this: *Her son's incurable illness was a great grief to her.* <Old French *grever* to burden>
come to grief, have serious trouble: *If that lad doesn't watch out, he'll come to grief one of these days.*

grief–strick·en (grēf′strik′ən) *adj* overwhelmed by sorrow.

griev·ance (grē′vəns) *n* an injustice one has suffered, real or imagined.

grieve (grēv) *v* **grieved, griev·ing 1** feel or cause to feel grief: *She grieved over the death of her cat. His criminal activities grieved his family.* **2** officially file a grievance against a person or group: *The worker grieved his dismissal.* <Old French, from Latin *gravis* heavy>

griev·ous (grē′vəs) *adj* **1** causing or full of grief, pain, or suffering: *grievous wounds, a grievous loss.* **2** severe or serious: *grievous crimes.* **griev′ous·ly** *adv.*
griev′ous·ness *n.*

grif·fin (grif′ən) *n* a mythical creature with the head and wings of an eagle and the body of a lion. Also, **gryphon, griffon.** <Old French, from Greek *grups*>

grill (gril) *n* **1** a framework of parallel metal wires or bars to put food on over direct heat. **2** a dish consisting of grilled food. **3** a restaurant that specializes in grilled food.
v **1** grill food. **2** question severely and persistently: *The detective grilled the prisoner until he finally confessed.* <French, from Latin *craticula* small latticework>

grille (gril) *n* a metal grating or screen used in front of something as protection, to give ventilation, or to permit discreet observation. Also called **grillwork.** <French *grille* grating, from Latin *craticula* gridiron>

grim (grim) *adj* **grim·mer, grim·mest 1** stern, severe, or forbidding: *grim fortress walls.* **2** serious, desperate, or worrisome: *grim news. The situation is grim.* **3** suffering great losses or difficulty but not yielding: *The losing team fought on with grim resolve.* **4** dealing with horrible things: *grim humour. The second novel in the trilogy is quite grim.* <Old English *grimm* fierce> **grim′ly** *adv.* **grim′ness** *n.*

gri·mace (grim′əs) *n* an ugly or twisted distortion of the face: *a grimace caused by pain.*
v **gri·maced, gri·mac·ing** make grimaces. <Spanish *grima* fright>

gri·mal·kin (grə mal′kən) *n* a cat, especially an old female cat. <probably *grey* + *Malkin,* diminutive of *Maud,* feminine name>

grime (grīm) *n* accumulated dirt, rubbed deeply into a surface: *the grime on a coal miner's hands.*
v **grimed, grim·ing** cover with grime or dirt. <Middle English> **grim′y** *adj.*

grin (grin) *v* **grinned, grin·ning 1** smile broadly. **2** express by smiling broadly: *He grinned his approval of my suggestion.*
n a broad smile. <Old English *grennian*>
grin and bear it, put up with something cheerfully.

grind (grīnd) *v* **ground, grind·ing; 1** crush into little bits or into powder: *to grind flour. Your back teeth grind food. A mill grinds wheat into flour.* **2** sharpen, smooth, or wear by rubbing on something rough: *to grind an axe.* **3** rub harshly together or into or against a surface: *to grind your heel into the earth, to grind your teeth in anger.* **4** crush by harshness or cruelty: *Her confidence was ground down by his daily teasing.* **5** make lenses according to a prescription for eyeglasses. **6** *Informal* work or study long and hard: *He ground away at his algebra till midnight.* **7** (*with* ***out***) produce in great numbers by steady effort: *That novelist grinds out bestsellers at the rate of one a year.*
n **1 the grind** *Informal* a routine of long hours or hard work or study. **2** an act of grinding: *Give the soup a couple of grinds of pepper.* <Old English *grindan*> **grind′er** *n.*

grind·stone (grīn′stōn′) *n* **1** a flat, round stone set vertically in a frame and mounted so as to revolve and used to sharpen blades or to smooth and polish metal. **2** a millstone.
have (or **keep** or **put**) **your nose to the grindstone,** work long and hard.

grip (grip) *v* **gripped, grip·ping 1** seize and hold tight: *The dog gripped the stick with its teeth.* **2** get and keep the interest and attention of: *A good story grips the reader.*
n **1** a tight grasp. **2** the power of gripping: *My hand is so numb there's no grip left in it.* **3** a part to take hold of; a handle: *the grip of a suitcase.* **4** firm control: *The country is in the grip of winter.* **5** a small suitcase. **6** a special or secret handshake. **7** mental grasp: *I think I have a good grip on math now.* **8** a member of a film production crew who moves camera equipment. <Old English *gripan*> **grip′per** *n.*
come to grips with, begin to do something about: *It's time you came to grips with that problem.*
get a grip, *Slang* get control of oneself and look at things realistically.

gripe (grīp) *Informal v* **griped, grip·ing** complain or grumble, especially about something unimportant: *Quit griping.*
n a complaint.

> **ETYMOLOGY**
>
> **Gripe** started out as Old English *gripan*, which meant "hold tightly to something." It shifted to the idea of pinching or squeezing, and began to refer to the sharp, sudden pain of stomach cramps, and then to mean "repeated complaining of such pains."

grippe (grip) *n* an old-fashioned word for influenza. <French>

grip·ping (grip′ing) *adj* holding the attention or interest.

gris·ly (griz′lē) *adj* **gris·li·er, gris·li·est** frightful or horrible: *a grisly scene of a car crash.* <Old English *grislic*> **gris′li·ness** *n.* See GRIZZLY for confusable.

grist (grist) *n* grain to be ground into flour or that has been ground. <Old English *grindan* grind>
grist to your mill, something you can profitably make use of.

a bat	e bed	i bid	o pot	u cup	th **thin**
ā cake	ē me	ī bite	ō go	ū rude	ᴛʜ **then**
à bar	ə about	ər over	ȯ for	ủ put	zh measure

G

gris·tle (gris′əl) *n* cartilage, especially the tough, elastic tissue in meat. <Old English> **gris′tly** (gris′lē) *adj.*

grist mill *n* a mill for grinding grain.

grit (grit) *n* **1** very fine bits of stone or sand: *There was grit in the spinach.* **2** *Informal* courage: *The fighter showed plenty of grit.* **3** 🍁 **Grit** *Informal* a member of the Liberal party.
v **grit·ted, grit·ting** clench one's teeth in determination: *She gritted her teeth and plunged into the cold water.*
adj 🍁 **Grit** *Informal* to do with the Liberal party. <Old English *greot*>

grits (grits) *pl n* coarsely ground corn or oats with the husks removed, cooked in milk or water. <Old English *grytte*>

grit·ty (gri′tē) *adj* **1** containing or covered with grit. **2** showing courage and determination. **3** tough and realistic: *a gritty novel about life in the ghetto.*
grit′ti·ly *adv.* **grit′ti·ness** *n.*

griz·zled (griz′əld) *adj* with dark and white hairs mixed, especially in hair or fur. <Old French *gris* grey>

griz·zly (griz′lē) *n, pl* **griz·zlies** in full, **grizzly bear** a large, fierce, brownish grey bear of western N America.
adj **griz·zli·er, griz·zli·est** grizzled.

CONFUSABLES

Grizzly names a type of bear: *The grizzly is the second largest North American land carnivore.*

Grisly means "frightful" or "horrible": *The horror movie contained several grisly scenes.*

groan (grōn) *n* a deep-throated sound expressing grief, pain, disappointment, or disgust: *My friend gave a groan, so I knew that she was in pain.*
v **1** give a groan or groans: *We all groaned at her stupid pun.* **2** be loaded or overburdened: *The table groaned with food.* **3** suffer greatly: *The people groaned under the tyrant's cruel oppression.* <Old English *granian*>

gro·cer (grō′sər) *n* a merchant who sells food and small household supplies. <Old French *grossier* one who sells in bulk, from Latin *grossus* coarse (of food)>

gro·cer·y (grō′sə rē) *n* **1 groceries** *pl* food and small household supplies bought from a store. **2** usually, **grocery store** a store that sells food and household supplies.

grog (grog) *especially UK n* **1** a drink made of rum or any other strong liquor diluted with water. **2** any strong liquor. <origin uncertain>

grog·gy (grog′ē) *adj* **grog·gi·er, grog·gi·est** unsteady and not fully alert, such as from sleepiness, alcohol, or anesthetic. <*grog*> **grog′gi·ly** *adv.* **grog′gi·ness** *n.*

groin (groin) *n* the hollow on either side of the body where the thigh joins the abdomen. <Middle English *grynde*>

grok (grok) *Slang v* **grokked, grok·king** understand completely, by instinct. <coined by R. Heinlein, 20c writer of fantasy and SF>

grom·met (grom′it) *n* **1** a metal eyelet or ring for putting a lace or cord through. **2** a ring of rope, used as an oarlock or to hold a sail on its stays. <French *gourmette* chain linking the ends of a bridle>

groom (grūm) *n* **1** a bridegroom. **2** a person who takes care of horses. **3** an official of the British royal household.
v **1** brush and clean the coat of a horse, dog, or other animal. **2** take care of the appearance of: *She groomed herself carefully.* **3** prepare a person for a job, position, or political office: *The president's daughter is being groomed to take over his position.* <Middle English>

grooms·man (grūmz′mən) *n, pl* **grooms·men** (grūmz′mən) a man who attends the bridegroom at a wedding.

groove (grūv) *n* **1** a long, narrow channel or furrow, especially one cut by a tool: *The plates rest in a groove on the rack.* **2** any similar channel: *Wheels leave grooves in a dirt road.* **3** a fixed way of doing things: *It is hard to get out of a groove.*
v **grooved, groov·ing 1** make a groove in. **2** *Slang* (*often with* **to** *or* **on**) feel enjoyment or excitement: *grooving to the music.* <Dutch *groeve* ditch>
in the groove, *Slang* **a** proceeding smoothly and with skill. **b** fashionable.

groov·y (grū′vē) *adj* **groov·i·er, groov·i·est** *Slang, now usually humorous* **1** fashionable and exciting: *He thought it would be groovy to live in a van.* **2** excellent. <*groove*>

grope (grōp) *v* **groped, grop·ing 1** feel around with the hands: *She groped for a flashlight when the lights went out. Blindfolded, he groped his way to the door.* **2** search blindly and uncertainly: *The detectives groped for some clue to the crime.* **3** *Informal* touch sexually without permission. <Old English *grapian*> **grop′ing** *adj.* **grop′ing·ly** *adv.*

gros·beak (grōs′bēk′) *n* a N American or European finch with a large cone-shaped bill. <French *gros* large + *bec* beak>

gross (grōs) *adj* **1** *Informal* disgusting: *What is that gross smell?* **2** obviously bad: *gross misconduct, gross errors in calculation.* **3** coarse or vulgar: *gross table manners.* **4** with nothing deducted: *What is his gross income before taxes? That figure represents gross weight; it will be less after you subtract the weight of the container.*
n, pl **gross·es** *for 1,* **gross** *for 2.* **1** the whole sum or total amount. **2** a unit consisting of twelve dozen. <Old French, from Latin *grossus* coarse> **gross′ly** *adv.* **gross′ness** *n.*

gross domestic product *n* the market value of a nation's goods produced and services provided in one year, within the nation's borders. It is the standard measure of the overall size of the economy. *Abbrev.* **GDP** or **G.D.P.** Compare GROSS NATIONAL PRODUCT.

gross national product *n* the total income of a nation's goods produced and services provided in one year. It includes income received from exporting to other countries. *Abbrev.* **GNP** or **G.N.P.** Compare GROSS DOMESTIC PRODUCT.

gro·tesque (grō tesk′) *adj* **1** so bizarre or unnatural in appearance or manner as to be ugly or repellent: *The book had pictures of grotesque monsters.* **2** ridiculous or absurd: *The monkey's grotesque antics made the children laugh.* <Italian *grottesca*> **gro·tesque′ly** *adv.*
gro·tesque′ness *n.*

grot·to (grot′ō) *n, pl* **grot·toes** or **grot·tos** a small cave, especially an artificial one. <Italian, from Greek *krypte* vault>

grot·ty (grot′ē) *Informal adj* **grot·ti·er, grot·ti·est** dirty, ugly, or unpleasant. <*grotesque*>

grouch (grouch) *Informal n* a habitually sulky or grumpy person.
v be sulky or grumpy: *I feel like grouching about my extra homework.* <Old French *grouchier* to grumble>
grouch′y *adj.*

ground[1] (ground) *n* **1** the solid surface of the earth: *Snow covered the ground.* **2** earth or soil: *Dig the ground around the flowers.* **3** land used for some special purpose: *a camping ground, a breeding ground.* **4 grounds** *pl* **a** the reasons for a claim, complaint, or action: *There are no grounds for saying such a thing.* **b** the land, lawns, and gardens around a house or other building: *A gardener takes care of the hospital grounds.* **c** the small bits that sink to the bottom of a drink such as coffee. **5** the connection of an electrical conductor with the earth. **6** background: *a blue pattern on a white ground.*
v **1** hit ground or set on the ground: *The boat grounded in shallow water.* **2** put on a firm foundation or basis. **3** instruct in basic principles: *The class is well-grounded in arithmetic.* **4** connect an electric wire or other conductor with the earth. **5 a** prohibit a pilot or aircraft from flying. **b** punish a child or teenager by forbidding certain social or leisure activities, especially outside the home. <Old English *grund* bottom>
break ground, a dig or plough. **b** begin building; begin digging the foundation for a building.
break (new) ground, do something original and innovative that marks a significant advance.
cut the ground from under someone's feet, spoil a person's defence or argument by meeting it in advance.
from the ground up, completely or thoroughly: *She learned her mother's business from the ground up.*
gain ground, a go forward; advance; make progress: *During the second week of training, I began to gain ground as my stamina increased.* **b** become more common or widespread.
get off the ground, make a successful start.
give ground, retreat or yield: *Under our attack, the enemy was forced to give ground.*
ground out, *Baseball* be put out after hitting a ground ball that is fielded and thrown to first base.
lose ground, a be forced to yield or retreat. **b** give up what has been gained: *As soon as the runner became tired, she began to lose ground.* **c** become less common or widespread.
on the grounds of (or **that**), because of.
run something into the ground, *Informal* **a** mismanage or neglect to the point of complete collapse or failure: *They took a successful business and ran it into the ground.* **b** overdo.
shift your ground, change your position or approach on an issue.
stand (or **hold**) **your ground,** refuse to yield or retreat: *Stand your ground no matter how much she begs.*

ground[2] (ground) past tense and past participle of GRIND.

ground·break·ing (ground′brā′king) *adj* new or original and with important consequences.
n the first act of putting a shovel in the ground, marking the beginning of a building project and often accompanied by a ceremony.

ground control *n* the people and equipment on the ground that control an aircraft or spacecraft before, during, and after its flight.

ground cover *n* any of many low-growing, fast-spreading plants used to control weeds, anchor the soil, or provide interest between taller plants and shrubs.

ground crew *n* the non-flying personnel responsible for maintaining aircraft.

ground·er (groun′dər) *Baseball n* a ball hit or thrown so as to bounce or roll along the ground.

ground floor *n* the first floor of a building, at the same level as the street or ground.
on the ground floor, *Informal* **a** at the very beginning of a venture. **b** in a competitive or advantageous position for a relationship or a business deal.

The **groundhog** lives in a burrow underground. It digs the burrow with sharp claws, and in one day can complete its new home by removing up to 325 kg of soil!

ground·hog (ground′hog′) *n* a burrowing rodent of N America, with a thickset body and a flat head.

Groundhog Day *n* February 2. Supposedly, if a groundhog comes out of hibernation and sees its own shadow (i.e., the day is sunny), it returns to its hole for six more weeks of winter.

ground·less (ground′lis) *adj* without foundation, basis, or reason: *Your complaints are groundless.*
ground′less·ly *adv.* **ground′less·ness** *n.*

ground·nut (ground′nut′) *n* an edible underground tuber or nutlike seed. Peanuts are groundnuts.

ground rule *n* a basic principle: *Before you babysit for us, we have to lay down some ground rules.*

ground·sheet (ground′shēt′) *n* a waterproof sheet, especially of rubber or plastic, used under a tent or sleeping bag to protect against dampness from the ground.

ground squirrel *n* a chipmunk or other burrowing rodent of the squirrel family.

ground·swell (ground′swel′) *n* **1** the broad, deep waves caused by a distant storm or earthquake. **2** a great and steady increase: *a groundswell of public support for recycling garbage.*

a bat	e bed	i bid	o pot	u cup	th **thin**
ā cake	ē me	ī bite	ō go	ū rude	ᴛʜ **then**
à bar	ə about	ər over	ȯ for	ů put	zh measure

ground·water (ground′wot′ər) *n* water that flows or seeps through the ground into springs and wells.

ground wire *n* a wire connecting electric wiring with the ground.

ground·work (ground′wərk′) *n* the beginning part on which future efforts will be built.

ground zero *n* the exact point where a bomb strikes the ground or otherwise detonates.

group (grūp) *n* **1** a number of people or things together: *A group of children were playing tag.* **2** a number of people or things of a certain kind: *Wheat, rye, and oats belong to the grain group.*
v **1** form into a group or groups: *The children grouped themselves into two teams. Group the used toys according to size.* **2** put in a certain group: *We should group the students by grade.* <Italian *gruppo*>

group·er (grū′pər) *n* a large, heavy-bodied food fish of warm seas. <Portuguese *garupa*>

group home *n* a home where a small number of people live who require care, support, or supervision.

group·ie (grū′pē) *Slang n* a fan who follows members of touring music groups or sports teams, in the hope of meeting or getting to know them.

group·ing (grū′ping) *n* **1** a way of assigning people or things to groups. **2** a category in such a system.

Group of Eight G8.

Group of Seven *n* **1** 🍁 a group of seven landscape painters who organized themselves in 1920 to promote a specifically Canadian movement in painting. **2** G7.

grouse[1] (grous) *n, pl* **grouse** a wild bird often hunted for sport. The **sharp-tailed grouse**, also called the **prairie grouse**, is the provincial bird of Saskatchewan. <origin uncertain>

grouse[2] (grous) *Informal v* **groused, grous·ing** grumble or complain.
n **1** a complaint. **2** a person who often complains. <origin uncertain> **grous′er** *n.*

grout (grout) *n* thin mortar used to fill cracks between tiles or stones.
v fill or finish with this mortar. <Old English *grut*>

grove (grōv) *n* a group of trees, usually of the same kind: *an orange grove.* <Old English *graf*>

grov·el (grov′əl) *v* **grov·elled** or **grov·eled, grov·el·ling** or **grov·el·ing** **1** crawl at someone's feet in order to gain favour or avoid punishment. **2** be overly respectful in order to gain forgiveness or a favour. <Old Norse *grufu*> **grov′el·ler** or **grov′el·er** *n.*

grow (grō) *v* **grew, grown, grow·ing** **1** become bigger by taking in food and building new tissue, as plants and animals do. **2** live or be located as plants: *Palm trees grow in the tropics.* **3** become greater: *Her fame grew.* **4** get into a certain state by growth: *The separate parts of a baby's skull eventually grow together into one.* **5** become: *to grow angry.* **6** cause or allow to grow: *to grow corn, to grow a beard.* **7** develop or mature: *A person grows by meeting new experiences and challenges.* <Old English *growan*> **grow′er** *n.*
grow on, a have an increasing effect or influence on: *The habit grew on me.* **b** become gradually more attractive or pleasing to: *That music grows on you after a while.*
grow out of, grow too big or too old for.
grow up, a become an adult: *What will you be when you grow up?* **b** behave maturely. *Why don't you grow up?*

growing pains *pln* **1** pains during childhood and youth, supposed to be caused by growing. **2** troubles that arise when something is just developing or suddenly expanding.

growl (groul) *v* **1** make a deep, low, angry sound in the throat: *The dogs growled at each other.* **2** complain angrily: *The soldiers growled about the poor food.* **3** rumble: *Her stomach growled with hunger.*
n **1** the act or sound of growling. **2** an angry complaint. <Old French *grouller* to grumble> **growl′er** *n.*

grown (grōn) past participle of GROW.

grown–up (grō′nup′) *adj* **1** adult or mature: *a grown-up dog.* **2** typical of or suitable for adults: *grown-up tastes.*
n an adult: *A grown-up must supervise the field trip.*

🍁 **grow op** *n* in full, **marijuana grow operation** an illegal growing, often in a house or apartment, of large quantities of cannabis for sale.

growth (grōth) *n* **1 a** the fact, process, or amount of growing. **b** the characteristic of life that allows organisms to get bigger, to change, and to repair themselves. **2** something that has grown or is growing: *a cancerous growth on her thyroid. A thick growth of bushes covered the ground.*

grub (grub) *n* **1** the thick, smooth, wormlike larva of an insect, especially of a beetle. **2** *Informal* food.
v **grubbed, grub·bing** **1** dig or dig up: *to grub stumps from cleared land. Pigs grub for roots.* **2** drudge or toil: *to grub for a living.* <Middle English *grubben*> **grub′ber** *n.*

grub·by (grub′ē) *adj* **grub·bi·er, grub·bi·est** dirty or grimy: *grubby hands.* **grub′bi·ness** *n.*

grub·stake (grub′stāk′) *Informal n* the money supplied for a proposed project in exchange for a share in any profits.
v **grub·staked, grub·stak·ing** supply with a grubstake. **grub′stak′er** *n.*

ETYMOLOGY

Grubstake comes from the mid-1800s practice of investors providing a supply of food to gold prospectors in exchange for a share (a stake) in the gold that might be found.

grudge (gruj) *n* a lasting, sullen feeling against someone because of a real or imagined offence.
v **grudged, grudg·ing** **1** feel anger or dislike toward a person because of something he or she has or can do: *She grudged me my little prize even though she had won a bigger one.* **2** give or let have unwillingly: *The mean man grudged his horse its food.* <Old French *groucher* grumble> **grudg′ing** *adj.* **grudg′ing·ly** *adv.*
bear (or **carry**) **a grudge,** have and keep a grudge.

gru·el (grū′əl) *n* thin, almost liquid oatmeal porridge. <Old French>

gru·el·ling or **gru·el·ing** (grū′ə ling) *adj* demanding long, intense effort: *a gruelling contest.* <obsolete *gruel* exhaust, punish>

grue·some (grū′səm) *adj* horrible or frightful: *a gruesome sight.* <Scots *grue* shudder> **grue′some·ly** *adv.* **grue′some·ness** *n.*

gruff (gruf) *adj* **1** deep and harsh or raspy in a voice. **2** abrupt and uncommunicative in manner: *The gruff storekeeper ordered us to leave.* <Dutch *grof*> **gruff′ly** *adv.* **gruff′ness** *n.*

grum·ble (grum′bəl) *v* **grum·bled, grum·bling 1** mutter or complain in a bad-tempered way. **2** rumble: *My stomach is grumbling because I didn't eat breakfast.*
n an act or sound of grumbling. <perhaps Dutch *grommen* to rumble> **grum′bler** *n.*

grump (grump) *Informal n* a bad-tempered, crabby, or cranky person: *That grump finds fault with everything.*
v grumble or complain: *Must you grump about everything?* <origin uncertain> **grump′i·ly** *adv.* **grump′i·ness** *n.* **grump′y** *adj.*

grunge (grunj) *n* **1** dirt or grime. **2** a fashion movement featuring loose, layered clothing. **3** a style of rock music with a harsh guitar sound, influenced by punk and heavy metal. <*grungy*>

grun·gy (grun′jē) *adj* **grun·gi·er, grun·gi·est 1** messy, dirty, and unattractive: *a grungy little motel.* **2** characteristic of grunge music or fashion. <probably *grubby* + *dingy*>

grunt (grunt) *n* **1** the low, deep, rough sound that a pig makes. **2** a sound like this: *With a grunt, he pulled the stump out of the ground.*
v **1** make a grunt. **2** speak with barely articulate sounds. *She grunted an apology.* <Old English *grunettan*>

gry·phon (grif′ən) GRIFFIN.

🍁 **GST** *n* in full, the **Goods and Services Tax**, a federal sales tax paid by consumers on most goods and services.

G–string (jē′string) *n* **1** a narrow loincloth held up by a cord around the waist. **2** a string tuned to G on a musical instrument.

gua·ca·mo·le (gwȧ′kə mō′lē) *n* a Mexican dip or sauce made with a base of mashed avocado. <Spanish, from Nahuatl (a language of Central and S America) *a wakamo lli* avocado sauce>

gua·na·co (gwȧ nȧ′kō) *n* a wild mammal related to the llama, that lives in the mountains of S America. <Quechua *huancau*>

gua·no (gwȧ′nō) *n* **1** the manure of seabirds, found especially on islands near Peru and Chile, used as fertilizer. **2** an artificial fertilizer made from fish. <Quechua (a language of S America) *huana* dung>

guar (gwȧr) *n* a plant grown in warm, dry regions as food for livestock and for its seeds, which yield a gum (**guar gum**) used in food processing. <Hindi>

guar·an·tee (ger′ən tē′) *or* (gȧ′rən tē′) *n* **1** a pledge to replace or repair goods, or refund money, if the goods are defective or unsatisfactory. **2** a pledge, assurance, or promise: *Wealth is not a guarantee of happiness. I'll leave my ID as a guarantee that I will return.*
v **guar·an·teed, guar·an·tee·ing 1** give a guarantee for: *This company guarantees its watches for a year.* **2** pledge that something will be satisfactory or agree to take the consequences: *The mother guaranteed her son's future behaviour.* **3** promise: *I guarantee I'll be on time this time.* **4** make certain: *Wealth does not guarantee happiness. Paying a deposit guarantees the good faith of the purchaser.* **5** secure or protect legally or financially: *His insurance guarantees him against loss caused by fire.* <perhaps Spanish *garante* guarantor> **guar′an·tor** (ger′ən tôr′) *n.*

SYNONYMS

A **guarantee** is a general pledge or promise.

Bail is money paid as a guarantee that an arrested person will appear in court at the required time.

A **bond** is a lawful guarantee that a particular duty will be performed or money will be forfeited.

guard (gȧrd) *v* **1** watch over carefully to protect or defend: *The dog guards the house.* **2** watch over to keep from escaping or misbehaving: *The soldiers guarded the prisoners day and night.* **3** keep under control: *Guard your tongue.* **4** (*with* ***against***) take precautions: *We must guard against every emergency.*
n **1** a person or group that guards: *A guard was stationed at the gate.* **2** something that gives protection: *A guard in front of the fire keeps sparks off the rug. She wears shin guards when playing soccer.* **3** a careful watch: *to keep guard over a treasure.* **4** a defensive player or position in various sports. **5 Guards** certain British or Canadian regiments with special functions: *the Governor General's Horse Guards.* <Old French *guarder* to guard>
off guard, unprepared: *The pitcher was off guard when the ball was hit to him.*
on guard, ready to defend: *A dog stood on guard near the door.*
stand guard, do duty as a guard: *The soldier stood guard at the gate of the fort.*

guard·ed (gȧr′did) *adj* cautious and wary: *Her answers to our questions were very guarded.* **guard′ed·ly** *adv.* **guard′ed·ness** *n.*

guard·i·an (gȧr′dē ən) *n* **1** a person who takes care of another or of some special thing: *guardians of the royal jewels.* **2** a person who is legally responsible for the care and management of a child or other person who cannot look after his or her affairs independently.
adj protecting: *a guardian angel.* <Old French *garden*> **guard′i·an·ship′** *n.*

guard·rail (gȧrd′rāl′) *n* a protective rail or railing.

Gua·te·ma·la (gwȧ′tə mȧ′lə) *n* a republic in northern Central America. See the APPENDIX.
Gua′te·ma′lan *adj, n.*

gua·va (gwȧ′və) *n* the pear-shaped edible fruit of a tropical American tree or shrub. <Spanish *guayaba*>

a bat	e bed	i bid	o pot	u cup	th thin
ā cake	ē me	ī bite	ō go	ū rude	ᴛʜ then
ȧ bar	ə about	ər over	ȯ for	u̇ put	zh measure

gu·ber·na·to·ri·al (gū′bər nə tô′rē əl) *adj* to do with a governor, especially of a state of the US: *a gubernatorial election.* <Latin *gubernator* governor>

guer·ril·la (gə ril′ə) *n* a member of a small independent band of fighters who harass their enemy by sudden raids or ambushes.
adj of or by guerrillas: *guerrilla warfare.* <Spanish *guerra* war>

guess (ges) *v* **1** form an opinion of without really knowing: *to guess the height of a tree.* **2** be correct or find out by guessing: *to guess a riddle.* **3** believe or suppose: *I guess she is really sick after all.*
n **1** an opinion formed without really knowing: *My guess is that it will rain tomorrow.* **2** an attempt to guess something: *You only get three guesses.* <Middle English> **guess′er** *n.*

SYNONYMS

Guess suggests forming an opinion without knowing for sure: *I bet I can guess your weight.*

Conjecture suggests having some, but not enough, evidence for proof: *His conjecture was proved correct with further research.*

Hypothesis involves a likely explanation that has not yet been proved: *My hypothesis is that those seeds will grow the fastest.*

guess·ti·mate (ges′tə mət) *for n,* (ges′tə māt′) *for v. Informal n* an estimate based on guessing.
v **guess·ti·mat·ed, guess·ti·mat·ing** make a guesstimate of. <*guess* + (*es*)*timate*>

guess·work (ges′wərk′) *n* thinking, action, or results based on guessing: *There is a lot of guesswork involved in buying a used car.*

guest (gest) *n* a person who is invited to visit or stay in a place, or to take part in an event, process, or organization: *a guest at a hotel, a guest invited to speak at a school assembly. We are having overnight guests at home this weekend.*
v be or appear as a guest: *She guested on the new talk show last night.* <Old Norse *gestr*>
be my guest, *Informal* (*often sarcastic*) you are welcome to do as you wish: *"Can I use your phone?" "Be my guest." If you want to fail, be my guest; but I plan to study.*

guest of honour *n* the most important guest at a social event, in whose honour the event is held.

guff (guf) *Informal n* foolish talk or ideas, especially when intended to hide the real facts. <probably imitative>

guf·faw (gə fo′) *n* a loud, coarse burst of laughter.
v laugh loudly and coarsely. <imitative>

GUI (gū′ē) *Computers n* in full, **graphical user interface** the screens, icons, and dialogue boxes that allow a user to enter information and otherwise interact with a program.

guid·ance (gī′dəns) *n* **1** the act of guiding, leadership, or direction: *Under his mother's guidance, he learned how to cook.* **2** a school department offering the services of a **guidance counsellor**, who gives students advice and helps them plan for the future.

guide (gīd) *v* **guid·ed, guid·ing 1** show the way: *to guide a group of climbers.* **2** direct the work, actions, or decisions of: *You should be guided by your conscience.*
n **1** a person who or thing that shows the way: *Hunters sometimes hire guides. Let the map be your guide.* **2** a book or manual that gives instruction or advice, especially to travellers. Also called **guidebook**. **3** a part of a machine for directing or regulating a certain motion or action. **4 Guide** a member of the **Girl Guides**, an organization set up for girls to develop character and physical fitness.<Old French *guider*>

SYNONYMS

Guide suggests knowing the way and showing it to others: *I can guide you through the mall.*

Escort means "accompany" in a formal way: *The police on motorcycles escorted the funeral procession.*

Lead emphasizes going ahead, expecting to be followed: *The boy led his friend to the club's hideout.*

guide dog *n* a dog specially trained to guide a blind person.

guide·line (gīd′līn′) *n* a principle, rule, or standard given as a guide.

guide·post (gīd′pōst′) *n* a post with signs and directions on it for travellers.

guide word *n* in dictionaries and other reference works, either of the first and last entry words on a page, identified by being repeated at the top of the page.

guild (gild) *n* **1** a society for mutual aid or for some common purpose: *She volunteered for the Halton Literacy Guild.* **2** in the Middle Ages, a union of workers in a trade, formed to keep standards high and protect common interests. <Middle English *gylde*>

guild·hall (gild′hol′) *n* **1** the hall in which a guild meets. **2** *UK* a town hall or city hall.

guile (gīl) *n* crafty deceit: *A swindler uses guile; a robber uses force.* <Old French> **guile′less** *adj.* **guile′less·ly** *adv.*

guil·lo·tine (gil′ə tēn′) or (gil′ə tēn′) *n* a machine for beheading people, consisting of a heavy blade that slides down between two grooved posts.
v **guil·lo·tined, guil·lo·tin·ing** behead with this machine.

ETYMOLOGY

The **guillotine** is named after Joseph-Ignace *Guillotin*, a French doctor and member of the National Assembly in the 1700s, who advocated using the machine for merciful executions.

guilt (gilt) *n* **1** the fact or state of having done wrong: *The evidence proved his guilt.* **2** a feeling or awareness of having done wrong: *Overwhelmed by guilt, she confessed to the police.* <Old English *gylt* offence> **guilt′i·ness** *n* **guilt′less** *adj.* **guilt′less·ly** *adv.*

guilt·y (gil′tē) *adj* **guilt·i·er, guilt·i·est 1** (*sometimes with of*) deserving of blame or responsible for having done a wrong: *The jury pronounced the prisoner guilty of murder.* **2** feeling or showing that one has done wrong: *a guilty conscience, a guilty smile.* **guilt′i·ly** *adv.*

guin·ea (gin′ē) *n* in former times, a British gold coin. <*Guinea*, part of W Africa, where the gold was mined>

Guin·ea (gin′ē) *n* a country in west Africa.

Guin·ea–Bis·sau (gin′ē bi sou′) *n* a country in west Africa.

guinea fowl *n* a domestic bird resembling a pheasant. See FOWL for picture.

guinea pig *n* **1** a short-eared, short-tailed rodent kept as a pet and for scientific experiments. See HAMSTER for picture. **2** a person or thing serving as a subject for experiment or testing: *We were the guinea pigs for her new recipe.*

guise (gīz) *n* a deceptive outward appearance, usually adopted on purpose: *The spy entered the monastery in the guise of a monk. Under the guise of friendship, he plotted treachery.* <Old French *guise* clothing>

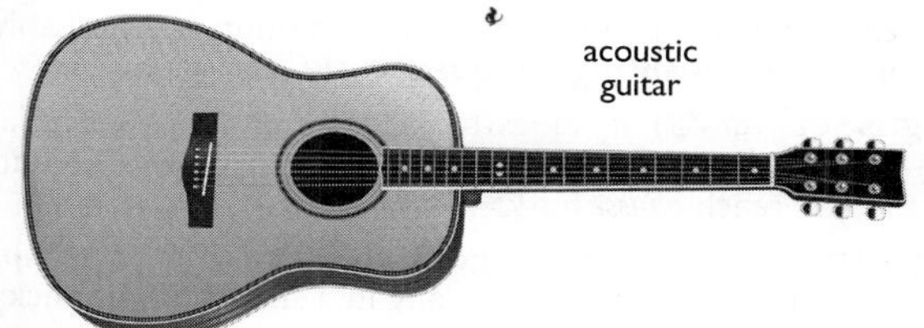

gui·tar (gə tär′) *n* a musical instrument, usually with six or twelve strings, played with the fingers or with a pick. <Spanish *guitarra*, from Greek *kithara* a stringed instrument> **gui·tar′ist** *n.*

gu·lag (gū′lag) *n* a system of forced labour camps in the former Soviet Union, or a camp in this system. <Russian G(*lavnoe*) u(*pravlenie ispravitel' no trudovykh*) lag(*erei*) Chief Administration of Corrective Labour Camps>

gulch (gulch) *n* a deep, narrow ravine with steep sides, especially one marking the course of a seasonal stream or torrent in a dry region. <origin uncertain>

gulf (gulf) *n* **1** a deep, wide inlet of an ocean or sea that has a narrow mouth, such as the Gulf of St. Lawrence or the Gulf of Mexico. **2** a deep, wide opening in the earth. **3** a wide separation between people, situations, or ideas: *The quarrel left a gulf between the old friends.* <Greek *kolpos*>

Gulf Stream *n* a current of warm water in the Atlantic, flowing north from the Gulf of Mexico along the US coast to Newfoundland and then northeast toward the UK.

gull[1] (gul) *n* a graceful grey and white bird with long wings, webbed feet, and a thick, strong beak, living on or near large bodies of water. There are numerous species of gull. <origin uncertain>

gull[2] (gul) *v* deceive; cheat.
n a person who is easily deceived or cheated. <origin uncertain>

gul·let (gul′it) *n* the esophagus; the passage carrying food from the mouth to the stomach. <Old French, from Latin *gula* throat>

gul·li·ble (gul′ə bəl) *adj* easily deceived. <*gull*[2]>
gul′li·bil·i·ty *n.* **gul′li·bly** *adv.*

gul·ly (gul′ē) *n, pl* **gul·lies** **1** a narrow gorge or small ravine. **2** a ditch made by heavy rains or running water: *After the storm, the newly seeded lawn was covered with gullies.* <French *goulet* gullet>

gulp (gulp) *v* **1** swallow eagerly, greedily, or with effort or force. **2** choke back: *to gulp down a sob.*
n **1** the act of gulping. **2** the amount swallowed at one time; a mouthful. <Middle English>

gum[1] (gum) *n* **1** a sticky juice secreted by certain trees and plants that hardens in the air and dissolves in water. **2** a similar secretion, such as a resin, for use in industry or the arts. **3** glue pre-applied to a stamp, sticker, or envelope flap that becomes sticky when moistened. **4** chewing gum. **5** a tree that yields gum, especially the eucalyptus.
v **gummed, gum·ming** **1** stick or stiffen with gum: *gummed stamps.* **2** make or become sticky: *My pocket was all gummed up with candy.* <Egyptian *kommi*>

gum[2] (gum) *n* (*usually pl*) the flesh around the roots of the teeth.
v **gummed, gum·ming** chew with toothless gums: *The baby gummed a biscuit.* <Old English *goma* jaw>

gum arabic *n* the gum obtained from acacia trees, used in making candy, medicine, or glue.

gum·bo (gum′bō) *n* **1** okra. **2** soup thickened with okra pods: *chicken gumbo.* **3** soil that contains much silt and becomes very sticky when wet.

ETYMOLOGY

Gumbo is from Louisiana French *gombo*, ultimately from a Bantu word *kingombo*, a name for the okra plant, which is native to Africa.

gum·drop (gum′drop′) *n* a small, stiff, jellylike piece of candy, sweetened and flavoured.

gum·my (gum′ē) *adj* **gum·mi·er, gum·mi·est** sticky like gum.

gump·tion (gump′shən) *Informal n* common sense combined with energy and initiative. <Scots>

gum·shoe (gum′shū′) *n* **1** a rubber overshoe. **2** *Informal* a detective.

gun (gun) *n* **1** a weapon with a long, metal tube for shooting bullets, shells, or shot. **2** anything resembling a gun in use or shape that ejects something when a trigger is pulled: *a spray gun, a staple gun.*
v **gunned, gun·ning** **1** (*usually with* ***down***) shoot with a gun. **2** cause to accelerate suddenly: *My mom gunned the engine in order to pass the other car.* <Middle English>
go great guns, *Informal* do something with intensity, enthusiasm, or speed.
gun for, *Informal* **a** support or cheer for: *Your friends are all gunning for you!* **b** try hard for: *gunning for victory.* **c** go after to try to hurt or destroy.
jump the gun, *Informal* **a** start running before the signal is given in a race. **b** act too early.
stick to your guns, refuse to yield.
under the gun, *Informal* having to defend one's position, decision, or action.

a bat	e bed	i bid	o pot	u cup	th **thin**
ā cake	ē me	ī bite	ō go	ū rude	ᴛʜ **then**
ä bar	ə about	ər over	ô for	ů put	zh measure

G

gun·boat (gun′bōt′) *n* a small, fast ship with mounted guns, often one that can be used in shallow water.

gun·fight (gun′fīt′) *n* a fight in which guns are used. **gun′fight·er** *n.*

gun·fire (gun′fīr′) *n* the act or sound of shooting a gun or guns.

gung–ho (gung′hō′) *Informal adj* eager and enthusiastic: *He's just starting high school this year and is very gung-ho.* <Mandarin *gonghe* work together. The US Marines used this term as a slogan during World War II.>

gunk (gungk) *Informal n* an unpleasant, heavy, oily or sticky substance. <*Gunk*, a trademark>
gunk′y *adj.*

gun·man (gun′mən) *n, pl* **gun·men** (-mən) a person who uses a gun to commit a crime.

gun·met·al (gun′met′əl) *n* a dark grey alloy of bronze and zinc.
adj dark blue-brown grey.

gun·ner (gun′ər) *n* a member of the military who operates or specializes in guns.

gun·ny sack (gun′ē) *n* a bag made out of strong, coarse fabric. <Sanskrit *goni* sack>

gun·point (gun′point′) *n* the tip of a gun barrel.
at gunpoint, a under threat of being shot: *The prisoners were herded through the camp at gunpoint.* **b** being forced by means of some other serious threat.

gun·pow·der (gun′pou′dər) *n* a powder that explodes when brought into contact with fire.

gun·run·ning (gun′run′ing) *n* the smuggling of guns and ammunition. **gun′run′ner** *n.*

gun·shot (gun′shot′) *n* **1** a shot fired from a gun. **2** the distance that a gun will shoot: *The target was within gunshot.*

gun–shy (gun′shī′) *adj* **1** afraid of the noise of guns. **2** wary and hesitant.

gun·sling·er (gun′sling′ər) *Slang n* a person who carries a gun. **gun′sling′ing** *adj.*

gun·smith (gun′smith′) *n* a person whose work is making or repairing small guns.

gun·stock (gun′stok′) *n* the wooden support or handle to which the barrel of a gun is fastened.

gun·wale (gun′əl) *n* the upper edge of a ship's or boat's side.

gur·dwa·ra (gər dwä′rə) *Sikhism n* a temple in which services of worship are held on Sundays and also serves as a community centre. <Sanskrit>

gur·gle (gər′gəl) *v* **gur·gled, gur·gling 1** flow or run with a bubbling sound, such as of water pouring out of a bottle or flowing over stones. **2** make a bubbling sound in the throat: *The baby gurgled happily.*
n a bubbling sound. <imitative>

Gur·kha (gər′kə) *n* a member of a Nepalese people famous for their military service.

gur·ney (gər′nē) *n* a stretcher on wheels, used in a hospital to move patients. <probably J. T.*Gurney*, 19c inventor>

gu·ru (gū′rū) *n* **1** *Hinduism* a revered spiritual teacher. **2** an influential teacher or popular expert: *The young activist was hailed as a guru of pop culture.* **3 Guru** *Sikhism* one of the ten founding teachers of Sikhism. <Hindi, from Sanskrit *guruh* teacher>

Guru Granth Sa·hib (gū′rū granth′ sä′hib) *Sikhism n* the sacred scriptures containing the teachings of the ten founding Gurus.

gush (gush) *v* **1** rush out suddenly: *A spring gushed from the earth.* **2** speak or write with a rush of exaggerated enthusiasm or emotion: *"It was absolutely the most splendid thing I ever saw," she gushed.* **3** have a sudden, abundant flow of something: *All at once the tap gushed water. His eyes gushed with tears.*
n **1** a rush of water or other liquid from an enclosed place: *a gush of blood from a wound.* **2** *Informal* talk that is full of exaggerated enthusiasm or emotion. <probably imitative> **gush′ing** *adj.* **gush′ing·ly** *adv.* **gush′y** *adj.*

gus·set (gus′it) *n* an extra piece or layer of material inserted in a garment or bag to strengthen or enlarge it. <Old French *gousse* husk>

gus·sy (gus′ē) *Informal v* **gus·sied, gus·sy·ing** (*with* **up**) make more attractive, especially in a showy or gimmicky way: *all gussied up for the party.* <origin uncertain>

gust (gust) *n* a sudden rush of strong wind: *A gust upset the small sailboat.*
v blow in gusts: *wind gusting from the south at 30 km/h.* <Old Norse *gustr*> **gust′i·ly** *adv.* **gust′i·ness** *n.* **gust′y** *adj.*

gus·to (gus′tō) *n* hearty enjoyment: *The hungry girl ate her dinner with gusto.* <Italian, from Latin *gustus* taste>

gut (gut) *n* **1** *Slang* belly. **2 guts** *pl* **a** intestines. **b** the inner parts or core elements of anything. **c** *Informal* courage. **3** a tough string, now usually synthetic, originally made from the dried and twisted intestines of sheep or other animals.
v **gut·ted, gut·ting 1** remove the intestines of. **2** destroy or remove the inner part of: *Fire gutted the building and left only the brick walls standing.*
adj **1** core or basic: *the gut issue.* **2** arising from one's basic impulses or instincts: *a gut reaction.* <Old English *guttas*>

gut·less (gut′lis) *Informal adj* cowardly: *gutless leaders.* **gut′less·ly** *adv.* **gut′less·ness** *n.*

gut·sy (gut′sē) *Informal adj* **gut·si·er, gut·si·est** bold, determined, or brave. **guts′i·ly** *adv.* **guts′i·ness** *n.*

gut·ter (gut′ər) *n* **1** a small ditch or low part along the side of a street, to carry off water. **2** a trough along the lower edge of a roof to carry off rainwater. **3** a channel or groove. **4** the environment of the homeless; the street as a home: *a child of the gutter.* **5** any wretched or vulgar environment: *Get your mind out of the gutter.*
v **1** of a candle flame, flicker before going out. **2** form channels or furrows in: *The spring runoff had guttered the fields.* <Old French *gutiere*, from Latin *gutta* a drop>

gut·ter·snipe (gut′ər snīp′) *Informal n* **1** an urchin who lives in the streets. **2** a person with coarse or vulgar manners.

gut·tur·al (gut′ə rəl) *adj* harsh and formed as speech far back in the throat: *a guttural voice.* <Latin *guttur* throat>
gut′tur·al·ly *adv.*

guy[1] (gī) *Informal n* **1** a male person. **2 guys** *pl* people of either sex: *Are you guys going to the movie?* <*Guy* Fawkes, leader of a plot to blow up the British parliament in 1605. A custom developed of burning dummy "Guys" on November 5, and *guy* came to refer first to any strange-looking person, then just to any person.>

guy[2] (gī) *n* in full, **guy rope** a rope, chain, or wire attached to something to steady or secure it.
v steady or secure with a guy or guys: *The mast was guyed by four ropes.* <Old French *guie* guide>

Guy·an·a (gī an′ə) *n* a country in S America. See the APPENDIX. **Guy′a·nese′** *adj, n.*

guy·ot (gē′ō) *n* a flat-topped underwater mountain, considered to be an extinct volcano. <A.H. *Guyot* 19c geologist>

guz·zle (guz′əl) *v* **guz·zled, guz·zling** drink greedily. <perhaps Old French *gosier* throat> **guz′zler** *n.*

Gwich'in (gwich′in) *n, pl* **Gwich'in** **1** a member of a First Nations people of the Northwest Territories. **2** their Athapascan language.
adj to do with these people or their language. Also called **Kutchin.**

gym (jim) *n* **1** a gymnasium. **2** a school subject involving physical exercise, sports, and games: *We have gym on alternate days.*

gym·nas·i·um (jim nā′zē əm) *n* a room or building equipped for physical exercise or training and for indoor athletic sports. <Latin, from Greek *gymnazein* to exercise naked, from *gymnos* naked>

gym·nast (jim′nəst) *or* (jim′nast) *n* a person trained or skilled in gymnastics.

gym·nas·tics (jim nas′tiks) *n* (*with singular verb*) athletic exercises that develop or display physical ability and co-ordination. The three main disciplines are **artistic gymnastics**, **rhythmic gymnastics**, and **trampoline**. <See GYMNASIUM.> **gym·nas′tic** *adj.*

gy·ne·col·o·gy (gī′nə kol′ə jē) *n* the branch of medicine that studies the functions and disorders specific to women, especially of their reproductive systems. <Greek *gyne* woman> **gy′ne·co·log′i·cal** *adj.* **gy′ne·col′o·gist** *n.*

gyp·sum (jip′səm) *n* a soft white or grey mineral that is used for making plaster of Paris and fertilizers. <Latin, from Greek *gypsos* chalk, plaster>

Gyp·sy (jip′sē) *n, pl* **Gyp·sies** **1** See ROMANY. **2 gypsy** a wandering or rootless person.

ETYMOLOGY

Gypsy comes from the word *Egyptian.* When the *Gypsies* first went to England in the 1500s, they were thought to have come from Egypt.

gy·rate (jī′rāt) *v* **gy·rat·ed, gy·rat·ing** move rapidly in a circle or spiral: *a gyrating top, the gyrating hips of a dancer.* <Latin, from Greek *gyros* a ring> **gy·ra′tion** *n.*

gyre (jīr) *n* a circular or spiral motion, especially a circular ocean current.

gyr·fal·con (jər′fal′kən) *or* (jər′fol′kən) *n* the largest falcon, found mainly in arctic and subarctic regions. It is the provincial bird of the Northwest Territories. <Old French *gerfaucon*>

gy·ro·com·pass (jī′rō kum′pəs) *n* a compass using a motor-driven gyroscope instead of a magnetic needle to point to the geographic north. <Greek *gyros* a ring + *compass*>

gy·ros (yē′rōs) *or* (yē′ros) *n* a Greek dish made of spiced meat, cooked by turning on an upright spit, then shaved off and served in a pita. <Greek *gyros* a turning>

gy·ro·scope (jī′rə skōp′) *n* a heavy wheel or disc mounted so that its axis can turn freely in one or more directions, used to keep ships and aircraft balanced. <Greek *gyros* a ring + *-scope*> **gy′ro·scop′ic** *adj.*

h or **H** (āch) *n, pl* **h's** or **H's** **1** the eighth letter of the English alphabet, or any speech sound represented by it. **2** the eighth thing in a list or series. **3** a symbol used on pencils to show the degree of hardness of the lead.

h **1** hour. **2** *Baseball* hit or hits.

H henry(s).

ha[1] (hä) *or* (ha) *interj* **1** used to express scorn or triumph: *Ha! I've caught you!* **2** used to express laughter: *"Ha! ha! ha!" laughed the girls.*

ha[2] hectare(s).

ha·be·as cor·pus (hā′bē əs kôr′pəs) *n* an order requiring that a person under arrest be brought before a judge to decide whether he or she is being held lawfully. <Latin = you may have the person>

hab·er·dash·er (hab′ər dash′ər) *n* a dealer in men's furnishings, such as hats, ties, shirts, socks, etc. <Middle English> **hab′er·dash′er·y** *n.*

hab·it (hab′it) *n* **1** a tendency to act a certain way: *He has a habit of correcting people's grammar.* **2** an addiction: *a caffeine habit.* **3** the distinctive garment worn by members of some religious orders. **4** a woman's riding outfit. <Latin *habitus* custom, from *habere* to have>
in the habit of, accustomed to doing something regularly: *He was in the habit of buying a chocolate bar on his way home.*

SYNONYMS

A **habit** is something that is often done without thinking: *My brother has a habit of biting his nails.*

A **custom** is a long-time practice of a group of people: *Our family's custom is to go camping once a year.*

A **quirk** is an odd, often irritating habit: *Her quirk of always cracking her knuckles irritates me.*

hab·it·a·ble (hab′ə tə bəl) *adj* fit to live in.

hab·i·tant (hab′ə tont′) *n* a French-Canadian farmer.
adj to do with rural French Canada, especially historically. <Cdn French, from Latin *habitare* live in>

hab·i·tat (hab′ə tat′) *n* the place where an animal or plant naturally lives: *Beavers prefer a wet habitat.* <Latin = it inhabits>

hab·i·ta·tion (hab′ə tā′shən) *n* **1** a place to live in. **2** the act of living in a place: *Is this house fit for human habitation?*

hab·it–form·ing (hab′it fôr′ming) *adj* causing the user to become addicted: *Caffeine can be habit-forming.*

ha·bit·u·al (hə bich′ü əl) *adj* **1** done, or doing something, as a habit: *a habitual liar.* **2** usual: *Ice and snow are habitual sights in arctic regions.* **ha·bit′u·al·ly** *adv.*

ha·bit·u·ate (hə bich′ü āt′) *v* **ha·bit·u·at·ed, ha·bit·u·at·ing** (*with* **to**) accustom: *Farmers are habituated to hard work.* **ha·bit′u·a′tion** *n.*

ha·bit·u·é (hə bich′ü ā′) *or* (hə bich′ ü ā′) *n* a person who has the habit of going to one place frequently: *a habitué of the theatre.*

ha·ci·en·da (hä′sē en′də) *n* a large ranch or rural estate, especially in the southwestern US. <Spanish>

hack[1] (hak) *v* **1** cut or chop roughly and unevenly with repeated strokes: *She began hacking away at the fallen tree.* **2** give short, dry coughs. **3** *Computers* experiment extensively with programming as a skilled amateur. See also CRACKER (def. 3). **4** *Slang* cope with: *I couldn't hack the having to practise, so I quit piano.*
n **1** a rough cut or cutting stroke. **2** a tool or instrument for hacking or cutting, such as an axe, pick, or hoe. **3** a short, dry cough. <Old English *haccian*> **hack′er** *n.*

hack[2] (hak) *n* **1** a person hired to do routine, unimaginative written work. **2** an undistinguished employee who does dull tasks. **3** **a** a horse used for riding or driving. **b** a worn-out horse that can be hired. **4** in former times, a carriage for hire. **5** *Informal* a taxi.
adj being or done by a hack (*n* def. 1) *a hack writer.* <See HACKNEYED.>

hack·le (hak′əl) *n* one of the long, slender feathers on the neck of some birds. <Middle English *hakell*>
raise the hackles of, *Informal* arouse suspicion or anger in someone.

hack·ma·tack (hak′mə tak′) *n* tamarack. <Algonquian>

hack·neyed (hak′nēd) *adj* used too often: *"White as snow" is a hackneyed comparison.* <*hackney* in former times, a hired carriage>

hack·saw (hak′so′) *n* a saw for cutting metal that has a narrow, fine-toothed blade fixed in a frame.

had (had) past tense and past participle of HAVE.

had·dock (had′ək) *n, pl* **had·docks** or *(especially collectively)* **had·dock** a bottom-dwelling food fish of the N Atlantic, related to the cod. <Middle English *haddok*>

Ha·des (hā′dēz) *n* **1** *Greek myth* the home of the dead, below the earth. **2** hell. <Greek *Haides*>

ha·dith (ha dēth′) *Islam n* a collection of the sayings of the prophet Muhammad, with accounts of his daily practice. <Arabic>

ha·fiz (hä′fiz) *Islam n* a Muslim who can recite the entire Koran from memory. <Arabic>

haf·ni·um (haf′nē əm) *n* a rare metallic element resembling zirconium. *Symbol* **Hf** <*Hafnia*, Latin form of *havn* from Danish *Kobenhavn* (Copenhagen), where it was discovered>

haft (haft) *n* the handle of a knife, sword, or dagger. <Old English *hæft*>

hag (hag) *n* **1** *Offensive* an ugly old woman, sometimes used as a term of abuse. **2** *Archaic* a witch. <Middle English *hagge*>

hag·fish (hag′fish′) *n, pl* **hag·fish** a small saltwater fish shaped like an eel.

Hag·ga·dah (hə gä′də) *Judaism n, pl* **Hag·ga·doth** (hə gä′dōth) **1** a story in the Talmud that explains or illustrates Jewish law, or the section of the Talmud containing such stories. **2** a text from this section, recited on the first two nights of Passover. <Hebrew = story>

hag·gard (hag′ərd) *adj* looking tired and tense. <French *hagard*> **hag′gard·ly** *adv.* **hag′gard·ness** *n.*

hag·gis (hag′is) *n* a food made from the heart, lungs, and liver of a sheep, chopped up and mixed with suet and oatmeal and boiled in the sheep's stomach. <probably Scots *hag* chop>

hag·gle (hag′əl) *v* **hag·gled, hag·gling** dispute about a price or the terms of something being bought. <perhaps from Old Norse> **hag′gler** *n.*

hah (hȧ) *interj* HA[1].

Hai·da (hī′də) *n, pl* **Hai·da** or **Hai·das 1** a member of a First Nations people living in western British Columbia. **2** the language of these people.
adj to do with these people or their language.

hai·ku (hī′kū) *or* (hī kū′) *n* a Japanese verse form consisting of three lines of five, seven, and five syllables respectively. <Japanese>

hail[1] (hāl) *v* **1** shout in welcome to; cheer: *He was hailed a hero.* **2** call or wave to in order to get someone's attention: *to hail a taxi.*
interj used as a shout of greeting, welcome, praise or congratulation. <Scandanavian>
hail from, *Informal* come from: *She hails from Montréal.*

hail[2] (hāl) *n* **1** small pellets of ice (**hailstones**) coming down from the clouds in a shower: *Hail fell with such violence that it broke windows.* **2** a heavy shower of anything: *a hail of insults.*
v **1** rain small pellets of ice: *Sometimes it hails during a summer thunderstorm.* **2** pour down like hail: *The angry mob hailed blows on the thief.* <Old English *hægel*>

Hail Mary (mārē) *Catholicism n* a prayer to Mary, mother of Jesus Christ.

hail·storm (hāl′stôrm′) *n* a storm with falling hail.

hair (her) *n* **1** a fine, threadlike strand growing from the skin of humans and animals or from the outer layer of a plant. See DERMIS for picture. **2** a mass of such strands, especially on the human head: *I have black hair.* **3** a tiny amount: *Could you move over just a hair?* <Old English *ær*> **hair′less** *adj.* **hair′less·ness** *n.* **hair′like′** *adj.*
get in someone's hair, *Informal* annoy; be a nuisance.
let your hair down, relax and behave informally.
make someone's hair stand on end, frighten, thrill, or horrify.
not turn a hair, show no sign of being disturbed or embarrassed.
split hairs, make too fine distinctions.

hair·brush (her′brush′) *n* a brush used for tidying the hair.

hair·cut (her′kut′) *n* **1** the act or service of cutting the hair of a person's head: *I have to get a haircut.* **2** a certain way of doing this, or the resulting appearance of the hair: *That's a cute haircut.*

hair·do (her′dū′) *n* a way of styling the hair.

hair·dress·er (her′dres′ər) *n* a person who cuts and styles people's hair. **hair′dress′ing** *n.*

hair·line (her′līn′) *n* **1** a very thin line. **2** the line where hair growth ends on the head or forehead.

hair·net (her′net′) *n* a net worn to keep one's hair in place.

hair·piece (her′pēs′) *n* a wig or partial wig.

hair·pin (her′pin′) *n* a U-shaped piece of wire bent tightly in half, used to keep the hair in place.
adj doubling back sharply like a hairpin: *a hairpin bend in a road.*

hair–rais·ing (her′rā′zing) *adj* terrifying or shocking: *hair-raising stories.*

hair's–breadth or **hairs·breadth** (herz′bredth′) *n* (*often metaphorical*) a very narrow space or distance: *I was a hair's-breadth from being run over.*
adj extremely close: *a hair's-breadth escape.*

hair·split·ting (her′split′ing) *n, adj* making unnecessary distinctions.

hair·spray (her′sprā′) *n* a substance sprayed onto the hair after styling, to keep it in place.

hair·style (her′stīl′) *n* a way of arranging the hair.

hair·styl·ist (her′stī′list) *n* a hairdresser.

hair trigger *n* a trigger that operates by slight pressure.
adj **hair-trigger** set off by the slightest provocation: *a hair-trigger temper.*

hair·y (her′ē) *adj* **hair·i·er, hair·i·est 1** with much hair: *hairy hands, a hairy ape.* **2** *Slang* alarming or very stressful: *a hairy adventure.* **hair′i·ness** *n.*

Hai·sla (hīs′lə) *n, pl* **Hais·la** or **Hais·las** a member of a Kwakiutl-speaking First Nations people living in northern British Columbia. Also called **Kitimat**.

Hai·ti (hā′tē) *or* (hȧ ē′tē) *n* a republic in the Caribbean. See the APPENDIX. **Hai′tian** (hā′shən) *adj, n.*

hajj (hȧj) *Islam n* a pilgrimage to the sacred shrine at Mecca, which all Muslims are expected to undertake at least once during their lifetime. A pilgrim who has been to Mecca is called a **haji**. <Arabic>

ha·lal (hȧ lȧl′) *Islam adj* in accordance with Islamic food laws: *a halal butcher.* <Arabic = lawful>

hal·cy·on (hal′sē ən) *adj* peaceful and happy: *halcyon days.* <Latin, from Greek *halkyon* kingfisher, a mythical bird that could calm rough seas>

hale (hāl) *adj* **hal·er, hal·est** (*especially in **hale and hearty***) strong and healthy. <Old English *hal*>

half (haf) *n, pl* **halves 1** one of two equal parts: *Half of four is two.* **2** one of two equal periods in certain games. **3** one of two nearly equal parts: *Which is the bigger half?*
adj (*often in compounds*) **1** forming a half: *a half-circle.* **2** partial: *A half-truth is no better than a lie.*
adv **1** to half of the full amount or degree: *The glass is half full.* **2** partly: *half cooked. She spoke half aloud.* **3** almost: *half dead from hunger.* <Old English *healf*>
half a ——, of even the least competence: *If he were half a plumber he'd know how to fix the leak.*
half past, thirty minutes after a specified hour: *It's half past six.*
not half bad, *Informal* reasonably good.
too —— by half, excessively: *He's too clever by half.*

a bat	e bed	i bid	o pot	u cup	th **thin**
ā cake	ē me	ī bite	ō go	ū rude	ᴛʜ then
ȧ bar	ə about	ər over	ȯ for	u̇ put	zh measure

H

half–and–half (haf′ən haf′) *adj* half one thing and half another.
adv in two equal parts: *Split it half-and-half.*

half·back (haf′bak′) *Football, Soccer, Field hockey n* a player whose position is behind the forward line.

half–baked (haf′bākt′) *Informal adj* showing poor planning or judgment: *half-baked ideas.*

half–broth·er (haf′bruᴛʜ′ər) *n* a brother related through one parent only.

half dozen *adj* usually, **half a dozen** or **a half dozen** six: *Bring me a half dozen nails.*

half–heart·ed (haf′härt′tid) *adj* lacking interest or enthusiasm: *a half-hearted attempt.*
half′-heart′ed·ly *adv.* **half′-heart′ed·ness** *n.*

half hitch *n* a type of knot used especially by sailors.

half–hour (haf′our′) *n* **1** thirty minutes. **2** the halfway point in an hour: *The bus leaves every hour on the half-hour.*
adj lasting one half-hour: *a half-hour meeting.* **half′-hour′ly** *adv.*

half–life (haf′līf′) *n* **1** the time needed for a radioactive substance to lose half its radioactivity. **2** the time it takes for a substance to lose half its strength through a natural process, such as in the body or in the environment.

half–light (haf′līt′) *n* twilight or other dim light.

half–mast (haf′mast′) *n* a position halfway or partway down from the top of a mast or staff: *When the princess died, flags were lowered to half-mast as a mark of respect.*

half moon *n* **1** the moon when only half of its surface appears bright. **2** something shaped like a half moon or crescent.

half note *Music n* a note held half as long as a whole note.

At the top of a **half-pipe,** the athlete "grabs some air," executes a stunt, and lands back in the pipe to repeat the process. A snowy version of the half-pipe is used by snowboarders.

half–pipe (haf′pīp′) *n* a wooden structure used in extreme sports such as freestyle BMX, inline skating, etc., consisting of two concave ramps facing each other.

🍁 **half–sec·tion** (haf′sek′shən) *n* a piece of land of about 130 hectares.

half–sis·ter (haf′sis′tər) *n* a sister related through one parent only.

half–time (haf′tīm′) *Sports n* the interval between two halves of a game.

half·tone (haf′tōn′) *n* **1 a** a process in photoengraving in which the subject is photographed through a fine screen, breaking the image into tiny dots. **b** a picture made by this process. **2** *Music* an interval equal to half a tone on the scale.

half–truth (haf′trūth′) *n* a statement that is only partly true, or that is technically true but gives a false impression.

half·way (haf′wā′) *adv* **1** half the way: *The rope reached only halfway to the boat.* **2** partially: *By the end of January, the school year is halfway finished.*
adj **1** located in the middle between two things or ends: *the halfway point.* **2** partial: *Halfway measures are never satisfactory.*
go (or **meet**) **halfway,** do one's share toward reaching an agreement or patching up a quarrel.

halfway house *n* a residence in which recently released convicts, recovering addicts, or street youth can gradually readjust to life in society.

half·wit (haf′wit′) *n* **1** *Offensive* a feeble-minded person. **2** a stupid, foolish person: *Only a halfwit would try to ski on that icy slope.* **half′wit′ted** *adj.*

hal·i·but (hal′ə bət) *n, pl* **hal·i·but** or **hal·i·buts** a large flatfish of the Atlantic and Pacific used for food. See FLATFISH for picture. <Middle English *haly* holy + *butte* flatfish, because it was traditionally eaten on holy days>

hal·ide (hal′īd *or* hā′līd) *n* a compound, such as sodium chloride, of a halogen with another element or radical.

hal·i·to·sis (hal′ə tō′sis) *n* bad or offensive breath. <Latin *halitus* breath>

hall (hol) *n* **1 a** a passageway through a building, with rooms leading off it: *Please don't run in the hall.* **b** a passageway or room at the entrance of a building: *Leave your umbrella in the hall.* Also, **hallway**. **2** a large room for parties, receptions, and banquets: *to rent a hall for the dance.* **3** a building used as a centre or for public functions: *a concert hall, a fire hall. The mayor's office is in the town hall.* **4** a large residence, such as for a school or college, or on a large estate. <Old English *heall*>

hal·le·lu·jah (hal′ə lū′yə) *n* **1** ALLELUIA. **2** any shout of praise. <Hebrew = praise Jehovah>

Hal·ley's comet (hal′ēz) *or* (hā′lēz) *Astronomy n* a recurring comet that can be observed about every 76 years, last observed in 1986. <E. *Halley*, 18c astronomer, who predicted the intervals of its reappearance>

hall·mark (hol′märk′) *n* **1** an official mark indicating a standard of purity, stamped on gold and silver articles. **2** a mark or sign of genuineness or good quality: *Loyalty is the hallmark of a friend.* <Goldsmiths' *Hall* in London, UK, seat of the Goldsmiths' Co., who regulated stamping>

Hall of Fame *n* **1** a group of people who are formally recognized as having made great achievements. **2** the room or building where photographs and other memorabilia of such people are kept.

hal·low (hal′ō) *v* **1** make holy or sacred. **2** honour as holy or sacred. <Old English *halig* holy> **hal′lowed** *adj.*

ETYMOLOGY

Hallow comes from Old English *halig*, meaning "holy." Formerly, **hallow** was also a noun meaning "saint." The feast of *Allhallows*, November 1, was a day to honour all saints.

See the etymology for *Halloween*, the evening before Allhallows, October 31.

Hal·low·een or **Hal·low·e′en** (hal′ə wēn′) *n* the evening of October 31, associated with ghosts and spirits and observed by dressing up in costume and masks, often by children who go from house to house collecting treats. <*Allhallow Even*, the eve of Allhallows (All Saints' Day), November 1>

hal·lu·ci·nate (hə lū′sə nāt′) *v* **hal·lu·ci·nat·ed, hal·lu·ci·nat·ing** see or hear things that are completely imaginary, as a result of fever, mind-altering drugs, or a mental disorder. <Latin *hallucinari*, from Greek *haluein* be delirious> **hal·lu′ci·na′tion** *n.*

hal·lu·cin·o·gen (ha lū′sə nə jən) *n* a drug or substance that causes people to hallucinate. <*hallucin*(*ate*) + *-gen*> **hal·lu′cin·o·gen′ic** *adj.*

hall·way (hol′wā′) HALL (def. 1).

ha·lo (hā′lō) *n, pl* **ha·los** or **ha·loes** **1** in paintings, a ring or circle of light around the head of a saint, angel, or divine being that represents holiness. **2** a series of coloured rings appearing around the sun or moon when it is seen through a cloud of ice crystals suspended in the atmosphere. <Latin, from Greek *halos* disk> **ha′loed** *adj.*

hal·o·gen (hal′ə jən) *n* any of the five elements iodine, bromine, chlorine, fluorine, and astatine, that combine directly with metals to form salts. <Greek *halos* salt + *-gen*>

hal·o·gen light *n* an electric light consisting of a thin, sealed quartz bulb containing a halogen gas and a tungsten filament.

halt[1] (holt) *n, v, interj* stop: *to ask for a temporary halt* (*n*). *The traffic halted at the red light* (*v*). <German *halten* stop>
call a halt, order a stop.

halt[2] (holt) *v* hesitate or waver: *a halting confession.*
n **the halt** *Archaic* people who limp or are lame. <Old English *haltian*> **halt′ing** *adj.* **halt′ing·ly** *adv.*

hal·ter (hol′tər) *n* **1** a rope or strap placed around the head of an animal, used for leading or tying the animal. **2** usually, **halter top** a backless and sleeveless blouse that fastens behind the neck and across the back. <Old English *hælftre*>

hal·vah or **hal·va** (hȧl′və) *n* a mixture of ground sesame seeds and honey, pressed into a block. <Arabic *halwa*>

halve (hav) *v* **halved, halv·ing** **1** divide into two equal parts: *The two girls agreed to halve expenses on their trip.* **2** reduce by half: *The new machine halves the time it takes to do the work.*
n **halves** plural of HALF. <Old English *healf*>
by halves, in an incomplete or half-hearted way.
go halves, share equally.

ham (ham) *n* **1** salted and smoked meat from the upper part of a pig's hind leg. **2** *Informal* a person who overacts or exaggerates his or her part in a play or show, or one who clowns for attention: *Look at him making faces at the camera; such a ham!* **3** *Informal* an amateur radio operator.
v **hammed, ham·ming** *Informal* (*often in the phrase* ***ham it up***) overact in order to get attention. <Old English *hamm* bend of the knee>

ham·burg·er (ham′bər gər) *n* **1** ground beef. **2** ground beef shaped into a patty and fried or grilled, especially when served in a split bun or roll. <*Hamburg* city in Germany, where this type of steak may have originated>

ham·let (ham′lit) *n* a very small rural community with no fixed boundaries and no local government of its own. <Old French *hamel* little village>

ham·mer (ham′ər) *n* **1** a tool with a handle and a metal head, used to drive nails and beat metal into shape. **2** a metal ball, linked to a handle by a steel wire, used in a throwing contest. The **hammer throw** is a field event. **3** the **malleus**, the outermost of three small bones in the middle ear. See also ANVIL, STIRRUP.
v **1** hit or beat into shape with a hammer: *to hammer nails, to hammer metal into ornaments.* **2** fasten or make with hammer and nails: *He hammered together a crude bookcase.* **3** pound again and again: *I hammered on the door with my fist.* <Old English *hamor*> **ham′mer·er** *n.* **ham′mer·like′** *adj.*
hammer and tongs, with all one's force and strength: *The two boys fought hammer and tongs.*
hammer (**away**) **at, a** work hard at: *She hammered away at her homework.* **b** nag at someone: *He hammered at his father till he got what he wanted.*
hammer out, a flatten or spread with a hammer. **b** clarify by much thinking or talking: *to hammer out plans for a trip.*

hammer and sickle *pl n* (*with singular verb*) a sickle and hammer crossed, used on the flag of the former Soviet Union, symbolizing the farmer and the industrial worker.

ham·mer·head (ham′ər hed′) *n* a shark whose wide head resembles a double-headed hammer.

ham·mer·lock (ham′ər lok′) *Wrestling n* a hold in which an opponent's arm is twisted and held behind his or her back.

ham·mock (ham′ək) *n* a swinging bed usually made of canvas or netted cord that is suspended at both ends. <Spanish *hamaca*, from Carib (a group of languages of the Caribbean)>

ham·per[1] (ham′pər) *v* hold back or hinder: *The heavy winter coat hampers my movements.* <Middle English *hampren*>

ham·per[2] (ham′pər) *n* a large container, often basketlike, usually with a cover: *a picnic hamper, a laundry hamper.* <Old French *hanapier* basket for documents>

a bat	e bed	i bid	o pot	u cup	th **thin**
ā cake	ē me	ī bite	ō go	ū rude	ᴛʜ **then**
ȧ bar	ə about	ər over	ȯ for	u̇ put	zh measure

It's believed that all **hamsters** in the West can be traced back to a brood of hamsters taken from Syria in the 1930s. Guinea pigs have been domesticated for over 400 years.

ham·ster (ham′stər) *n* a small, short-tailed rodent with large cheek pouches, often kept as a pet. <German>

ham·string (ham′string′) *n* **1** in human beings, one of the tendons at the back of the knee. **2** in four-footed animals, the great tendon at the back of the hock.
v **ham·strung, ham·string·ing 1** disable by cutting the hamstring. **2** seriously hamper: *to hamstring a project by cutting back its budget.* <Old English *hamm* bend of the knee>

Han[1] (hȧn) *n, pl* **Han 1** a member of a First Nations people living along the Yukon River. **2** their Athapascan language. *adj* to do with these people or their language. Also called **Tr'on Dek Hwech'in**.

Han[2] (hȧn) *n* **1** a Chinese dynasty that ruled from 206 BCE to 220 CE. **2** the largest ethnic group in modern China.

hand (hand) *n* **1 a** the end part of an arm, with fingers on it; the part used for picking up and holding things. **b** the end of an animal's limb that grasps, holds, or clings, such as a monkey's feet. **2** any of the long, thin parts that indicate the time on the face of a clock. **3** a hired worker who does physical work: *a factory hand, a farm hand.* **4 hands** *pl* control: *The town is in the hands of the enemy. Can I leave the matter in your capable hands?* **5** a share in doing something: *She had no hand in the matter.* **6** the left or right side: *At her left hand stood two men.* **7** one's style of handwriting: *She writes in a clear hand.* **8 a** skill: *The artist's work showed a master's hand.* **b** a person, with reference to skill or ability: *She is a great hand at thinking up new games.* **9** a round of applause: *The crowd gave the winner a big hand.* **10** a promise of marriage: *to ask for someone's hand.* **11** the width of a hand, used to measure horses, about 10 cm: *This horse is eighteen hands high.* **12** one round of a card game, or the cards held by a player in one such round.
v **1** pass to someone: *Please hand me the scissors.* **2** help someone by using the hand: *The paramedic handed the woman into the ambulance.* <Old English>
hand′like′ *adj.*
all hands, a all sailors of a ship's crew. **b** *Informal* all members of a group.
at first hand, from the original source: *I got the information at first hand.*
at hand, (*often preceded by* ***near*** *or* ***close***) near, in time or space: *Winter is at hand. I keep my notepad close at hand.*
at second (or **third**, etc.) **hand,** not directly from the original source: *I only heard the news at second hand.*
at the hands of, from or by a person: *We have received many favours at his hands. The accused claimed he was mistreated at the hands of the police.*
by hand, using the hands or hand tools, not machinery.
change hands, pass from one person to another: *During the sale a lot of money changed hands.*
force someone's hand, a make a person do something. **b** make a person reveal his or her real motives or plans.
(**from**) **hand to mouth,** without being able to put anything aside for the future: *During the long strike, many families lived hand to mouth.*
hand down, a pass to someone younger: *Her old clothes were handed down to her younger sister.* **b** deliver from a position of authority: *to hand down a decision.*
hand in, give or pass to a person in authority: *The tests were handed in to the teacher.*
hand in glove, in a close relationship with someone.
hand in hand, a holding hands. **b** together: *working hand in hand with someone.*
hand it to, *Informal* express admiration of: *I have to hand it to you for not losing your temper.*
hand on, pass along: *Read the note and hand it on to the next person.*
hand out, distribute: *The storekeeper handed out free suckers.*
hand over, give up to another: *When he asked for his book, I handed it over.*
hand over fist, fast and in large amounts: *They're making money hand over fist with that landscaping business.*
hands down, easily: *She won hands down.*
hands off, *Informal* do not touch: *Hands off my guitar.*
hand to hand, close together: *to fight hand to hand.*
have your hands full, have as much to do as you can manage.
in hand, under control: *We have everything in hand. The principal promised to take the matter in hand.*
keep your hand in, keep in practice.
lay hands on, a seize, take, or get. **b** attack physically.
lend (or **give**) **a hand,** help: *Can you lend me a hand with the dishes?*
off your hands, outside your responsibility: *The babysitter was glad when the child was taken off his hands.*
on hand, a available, ready, or in stock: *The supermarket has lots of oranges on hand.* **b** present: *I'll be on hand for the rehearsal.*
on (**the**) **one** (or **other**) **hand,** considering one or the other side of an issue or argument: *On the one hand, she's fast; but on the other hand, she's a bit sloppy.*
on your hands, for you to deal with: *Now I have this awkward situation on my hands.*
out of hand, a out of control: *The angry crowd soon got out of hand.* **b** at once; without hesitation: *The girl was expelled out of hand.*
show your hand, reveal your real motives and plans.
sit on your hands, do nothing, especially when it is important to act.
tie your hands, make you unable to do something: *If you won't speak up in your own defence, my hands are tied and I can't help you.*
try your hand, test your ability: *I'd like to try my hand at acting, but I'm nervous on stage.*
wait on someone hand and foot, do everything for someone.
wash your hands of, refuse to have anything more to do with.

hand·bag (hand′bag′) *n* **1** a purse. **2** a small travel bag.

hand·ball (hand′bol′) *n* a game played by hitting a small ball against a wall with the bare hand.

hand·bell (hand′bel′) *n* a bell with a handle, to be rung by hand, especially one of a set used as a musical instrument.

hand·bill (hand′bil′) *n* a printed advertisement or notice to be handed out to people.

hand·book (hand′bu̇k′) *n* a small book giving instructions or information for reference; a manual: *a car repair handbook.*

hand·breadth (hand′bredth′) *n* the width of a hand, used as a measure. Also, **hand's-breadth**.

hand·cart (hand′kȧrt′) *n* a small cart pulled or pushed by hand.

hand·craft (hand′kraft′) *n* HANDICRAFT.
v skilfully make by hand: *a finely handcrafted chair.*

hand·cuff (hand′kuf′) *n* usually, **handcuffs** *pl* a device to restrain a prisoner's hands, consisting of a lockable pair of metal bracelets joined by a short chain.
v fasten with handcuffs: *He was handcuffed to a chair.*

hand·ful (hand′fu̇l′) *n* **1** as much as the hand can hold: *a handful of candy.* **2** a small number or quantity: *A handful of men could defend this pass against hundreds.* **3** *Informal* a person who or thing that is hard to handle: *The puppy is quite a handful.*

hand·gun (hand′gun′) *n* a firearm, such as a revolver, that is held and can be shot with one hand.

hand·held (hand′held′) *adj* compact enough to hold in the hand while using: *a handheld computer.*

hand·hold (hand′hōld′) *n* **1** a secure place to hold on while climbing. **2** the kind of grip used in climbing. See FOOTHOLD for picture.

hand·i·cap (han′dē kap′) *n* **1** something that may put a person at a disadvantage: *A sore throat is a handicap to a singer.* **2** in a contest or game, a disadvantage imposed on a superior competitor in order to give other competitors a better chance.
v **hand·i·capped, hand·i·cap·ping** **1** put at a disadvantage: *The pitcher was handicapped by a lame arm.* **2** give a handicap to: *The Sports Committee handicapped me five metres.* <*hand in cap*, a betting game in which money was held in a cap>

GRAMMAR AND USAGE

The term **handicapped** may be used when referring to an environmental or attitudinal barrier:

A person will be handicapped by a set of stairs leading to the entrance.

The handicapped is an offensive term that should be avoided. Use *person with a disability* instead.

Disabled is used as an adjective, not a noun.

hand·i·craft (hand′i kraft′) *n* **1** a trade or art involving making things skilfully by hand, such as knitting, woodworking, weaving, or quilting. Also, **handcraft**. **2** an article made skilfully by hand: *a display of handicrafts for sale.*

hand·i·work (han′dē wərk′) *n* **1** work done with the hands. **2** anything that a person has produced or brought about: *All these destroyed relationships are her handiwork.*

hand·ker·chief (hang′kər chif′) *n* a square piece of fine cloth used for wiping one's nose or as an accessory for clothes.

han·dle (han′dəl) *n* a part for holding a thing by, such as on cooking pots or a tool.
v **han·dled, han·dling** **1** touch, lift, lower, pass, or hold with the hand: *Handle those plates carefully.* **2** cope with: *Can you handle that much stress?* **3** manage: *I like how that teacher handles the class.* **4** take care of: *The assistant handles some of the paperwork.* **5** behave or perform in a certain way when operated or used: *Mom says her new car handles well.* **6** deal in: *This store doesn't handle sports equipment.* <Old English *hand* hand> **han′dler** *n.*
fly off the handle, *Informal* lose one's temper.

H

han·dle·bars (han′dəl bȧrz′) *pl n* the bars in front of the rider on a bicycle or other vehicle for holding on and steering.

hand·made (hand′mād′) *adj* made by hand, not by machine.

hand·maid (hand′mād′) *n* a female servant or attendant. Also (*Poetic*), **handmaiden**.

hand–me–down (hand′mē doun′) *n* a previously used piece of clothing, especially one passed on from friends or family members: *I was always dressed in hand-me-downs.*
adj to do with such clothing.

hand·out (han′dout′) *n* **1** one or more printed sheets of information given out by a person or organization, especially by a speaker to an audience or a teacher to a class. **2** something given out free, often to people in need: *Flood victims were helped by a government handout.*

hand–pick (hand′pik′) *v* **1** choose carefully for some purpose: *to hand-pick a team of assistants.* **2** pick items or fruit and vegetables by hand. **hand′-picked′** *adj.*

hand·rail (han′drāl′) *n* a railing to hold onto for support or safety.

hand's·breadth (handz′bredth′) HANDBREADTH.

hand·set (hand′set′) *n* a phone with the keypad, receiver, and mouthpiece all in one handheld unit.

hand·shake (han′shāk′) *n* a clasping of hands by two people as a sign of friendship when meeting or parting, or to confirm an agreement.

hand·some (han′səm) *adj* **hand·som·er, hand·som·est** **1** good-looking: *my handsome boyfriend.* **2** substantial; generous; gracious: *a handsome sum of money, a handsome gift, handsome treatment.* <Middle English *handsom* easy to handle, in reference to the obsolete sense of the word> **hand′some·ly** *adv.* **hand′some·ness** *n.*

hands–on (hanz′on′) *adj* making use of personal, especially physical, involvement: *hands-on learning.*

a bat	e bed	i bid	o pot	u cup	th thin
ā cake	ē me	ī bite	ō go	ū rude	TH then
ȧ bar	ə about	ər over	ȯ for	u̇ put	zh measure

hand·spring (han′spring′) *n* a somersault made from a standing position, in which the person comes down first on the hands, turning the body forward or backward in a full circle and landing again on the feet.

hand·stand (han′stand′) *n* an act of supporting the body on the hands alone, while the torso and legs are stretched in the air.

hand–to–hand (han′tə hand′) *adj* close together: *hand-to-hand combat.*

hand–to–mouth (hand′tə mouth′) *adj* with nothing to spare or save for the future: *a hand-to-mouth existence.*

hand·work (hand′wərk′) *n* skilled work done by hand.

hand·writ·ing (hand′rī′ting) *n* **1** writing done by hand. **2** a particular style of writing by hand: *I recognized his handwriting on the card.* **hand′writ′ten** *adj.*
handwriting on the wall, a sign of approaching failure or ruin.

hand·y (han′dē) *adj* **hand·i·er, hand·i·est 1** easy to reach or use: *handy shelves, a handy tool.* **2** skilful: *She is handy with tools.* **hand′i·ly** *adv.* **hand′i·ness** *n.*
come in handy, be useful or convenient: *A cellphone comes in handy when you're stranded on the roadside.*

han·dy·man (han′dē man′) *n, pl* **han·dy·men** a person who does small tasks, such as building or fixing things around a house.

hang (hang) *v* **hung** or (def. 3) **hanged, hang·ing 1** attach or be attached at the top only: *Hang your coat on the hook.* **2** fasten or be fastened so as to swing or turn freely: *to hang a door on its hinges.* **3** put or be put to death by hanging with a rope around the neck: *He was hanged for treason.* **4** droop or let droop: *She hung her head in shame.* **5 a** attach wallpaper or pictures to walls. **b** cover or decorate with things that hang: *to hang a window with curtains. The walls were hung with pictures.* **6** depend: *Everything hangs on your early arrival.* **7** keep a jury from reaching a verdict: *One member hung the jury by refusing to agree with the others.* **8** *Informal* (*often with* **out**) spend relaxed time with a person or in a place: *Who do you hang with? Let's just hang out at the mall for a bit.* **9** *Slang* stop working suddenly and inexplicably: *My computer hangs whenever I try to close this file.*
n the way that a thing hangs: *I didn't like the hang of that coat, so I didn't buy it.* <Old English *hon* suspend and *hangian* be suspended>
get the hang of, *Informal* learn how to operate or do: *It didn't take her long to get the hang of the new software.*
hang a left (or **right**), *Informal* make a left (or right) turn.
hang around, a loiter or spend time aimlessly in a certain place or with a certain person. **b** wait near: *There's a small crowd hanging around the door.*
hang back, be unwilling to go forward.
hang fire, be slow or reluctant to take action.
hang heavily (or **heavy**), of time, pass slowly.
hang in (**there**), *Informal* be persistent; not give up.
hang in the balance, be undecided.
hang on, a hold tight: *She hung on to the railing until help arrived.* **b** be unwilling to let go, stop, give up, or leave: *The bad weather hung on for several days.* **c** wait: *Hang on a minute while I get my coat.*
hang on someone's words, listen with great attention.
hang out, *Informal* habitually spend time in a place or with someone: *Where do you guys hang out? Don't hang out with the wrong crowd.*
hang over, a seem likely to happen in a threatening way: *Worry over his grades hung over him until the results were given out.* **b** *Informal* remain from an earlier time or condition.
hang someone out to dry, leave someone in an unpleasant situation.
hang together, a be faithful to one another. **b** be coherent or consistent: *The story does not hang together.*
hang up, a hang on a hook or peg. **b** disconnect or end a phone conversation. **c** be delayed or detained: *We got hung up in traffic.*
hang up your skates, retire from some position or activity.
🍁 **hang your head,** be ashamed.

GRAMMAR AND USAGE

In formal English, the preferred form of the past tense and past participle of **hang**, for definition 3 only, is **hanged**: *The murderer was hanged.* In informal English, however, **hung** is often used: *He was hung for his crimes.*

hang·ar (hang′ər) *n* a shed for aircraft. <French, from Latin *angarium* shed for shoeing horses. *Hangar* was first used to describe a shed for aircraft in the early 20c.>

hang·dog (hang′dog′) *adj* looking ashamed or guilty: *a hangdog expression.*

hang·er (hang′ər) *n* **1** anything on which something else is hung: *a coat hanger, a hanger for a picture.* **2** a person, machine, or tool that hangs things.

hang·er–on (hang′ər on′) *n, pl* **hang·ers-on** someone who follows or depends on another, often as a way to gain personal advantage.

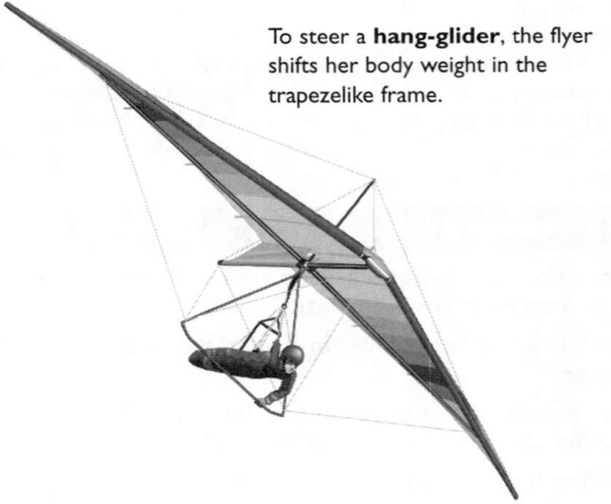

To steer a **hang-glider**, the flyer shifts her body weight in the trapezelike frame.

hang–glider (hang′glī′dər) *n* **1** a large, flat, usually triangular kite with an attached harness, designed to carry a person through the air for a short while. **2** a person who flies on one of these. Compare PARAGLIDER.
hang′-glid′ing *n.*

hang·ing (hang′ing) *n* **1** death by allowing to hang with a rope around the neck. **2** something made to hang, especially a decorative banner or tapestry.
adj deserving death by hanging: *a hanging offence.*

hang·man (hang′man′) *n, pl* **hang·men** an executioner who hangs people who have been sentenced to death by hanging.

hang·nail (hang′nāl′) *n* a bit of skin that hangs partly loose near a fingernail.

ETYMOLOGY

Hangnail comes from Old English *angnæl,* from *ang-*, meaning "painful" and *nægl*, meaning "nail." The influence from the word *hang*, as in a piece of skin hanging, came later.

hang·out (hang′out′) *Informal n* a place where a person or group spends a lot of time: *The library is a favourite hangout of hers.*

hang·o·ver (hang′ō′vər) *Informal n* **1** a sick state resulting from drinking too much alcohol. **2** something that remains from an earlier time or condition.

hang·up (hang′up′) *Informal n* a personal emotional difficulty: *That teacher helped me get over my hangup about public speaking.*

hank (hangk) *n* a coil or loop of hair, yarn, string, or rope. <Old Norse *honk*>

han·ker (hang′kər) *v* (*with* **for** *or* **after**) wish for or crave: *I'm hankering for pizza.* <origin uncertain>
han′ker·ing *n.*

hank·y (hang′kē) *Informal n, pl* **hank·ies** a handkerchief.

hank·y–pank·y (hang′kē pang′kē) *Informal n* improper behaviour that is kept secret: *There was no hanky-panky involved in his getting the contract.*

Han·sard (han′sərd) *n* the printed record of the proceedings of the Canadian, British, Australian, or New Zealand parliaments. <L. *Hansard*, 18c printer, who first compiled it>

Han·sen's disease (han′sənz) LEPROSY.

Ha·nuk·kah or **Ha·nuk·ka** (hä′nə kə) *Judaism n* the Feast of Dedication or the Feast of Lights, an eight-day festival falling in December, celebrating the rededication of the Temple in Israel in 165 BCE after its desecration. Also, **Chanukah**. <Hebrew = dedication>

hap·haz·ard (hap′haz′ərd) *adj* random or casual: *a haphazard system of management.* <Middle English *hap* chance + *hazard*> **hap′haz′ard·ly** *adv.*

hap·less (hap′lis) *adj* unlucky: *The hapless ship struck an iceberg on its maiden voyage.* <Middle English *hap* chance>

hap·pen (hap′ən) *v* **1** take place or occur: *Nothing interesting happens here.* **2** be or take place by chance: *I didn't do it; it just happened.* **3** do by chance: *I happened to sit next to a famous hockey player.* **4** be done to: *Something has happened to this lock; the key won't turn.* <Middle English *hap* chance>
as it happens, the truth is: *As it happens, I have no money with me.*
happen on (or **upon**), meet or find unexpectedly: *She happened on a loonie while looking for her keys.*
happen to, be experienced by someone: *Nobody knew what happened to the last explorer.*

hap·pen·ing (hap′ə ning) *n* **1** anything that happens. **2** an artistic or theatrical event in which the audience participates.
adj Informal exciting and fashionable: *a happening place.*

hap·pen·stance (hap′ən stans′) *n* a situation or circumstance that is the result of chance. <*happen* + (*circum*)*stance*>

hap·py (hap′ē) *adj* **hap·pi·er, hap·pi·est** **1** feeling or showing pleasure and joy: *a happy smile.* **2** fortunate: *By a happy chance, I found the lost money.* **3** clever and fitting: *a happy choice of words.* <Middle English, from *hap* luck>
hap′pi·ly *adv.* **hap′pi·ness** *n.*

hap·py–go–luck·y (hap′ē gō luk′ē) *adj* light-hearted and taking things easily.

happy hour *n* the part of each day when some bars or pubs lower the price of drinks.

ha·ra–ki·ri (hä′rə kē′rē) *n* ritual suicide by ripping open the abdomen with a knife, formerly considered in Japan as an honourable alternative to disgrace. Also, **hari-kari.** <Japanese *hara* belly + *kiri* cutting>

ha·rangue (hə rang′) *n* a long, aggressive speech.
v **ha·rangued, ha·rangu·ing** deliver a harangue: *He harangued the crowd at length.* <Old French *arenge*>

ha·rass (hə ras′) *or* (her′əs) *v* **1** trouble by repeated attacks: *Pirates harassed the villages along the coast.* **2** torment or bully: *I know someone who was sexually harassed by a co-worker.* <Old French *harasser* vex> **ha·rass′ment** *n.*

har·bin·ger (här′bin jər) *n* a person who or thing that goes ahead to announce or give a sign of something's approach: *The robin is a harbinger of spring.* <Old French *herbergere* provider of shelter, i.e., someone who goes ahead of a group>

har·bour or **har·bor** (här′bər) *n* **1** a naturally or artificially sheltered area of deep water where ships may dock or anchor. **2** any place of shelter or refuge.
v **1** provide a place to hide: *to harbour a criminal. The dog's shaggy hair harbours fleas.* **2** take shelter or refuge. **3** keep in the mind: *Don't harbour unkind thoughts.* <Old English *here* army + *beorg* shelter> **har′bour·less** *adj.*

SYNONYMS

Harbour refers to any place where ships can be anchored near shore.

Port suggests a town or city where ships regularly stop to take on or unload goods or passengers, or to obtain more supplies.

a bat	e bed	i bid	o pot	u cup	th **thin**
ā cake	ē me	ī bite	ō go	ū rude	ᴛʜ **then**
ä bar	ə about	ər over	ô for	u̇ put	zh measure

H

hard (hȧrd) *adj* **1** solid, rigid, and firm to the touch: *Rocks are hard.* **2** demanding much skill, effort, or time: *a hard problem, a hard job. She is hard to get along with.* **3** involving much suffering, trouble, or care: *hard times.* **4** showing much energy, vigour, force, or persistence: *a hard worker, a hard kick. There was a hard rain last night.* **5 a** strong and tough: *hard muscles.* **b** of a mineral, resistant to being scratched. **6** stern, harsh, or severe: *a hard boss, a hard face.* **7** containing mineral salts that interfere with the action of soap: *hard water.* **8** containing much alcohol: *hard liquor, hard cider.* **9** seriously addictive and harmful to health: *hard drugs.* **10** of wheat, with a hard kernel and high gluten content. **11** of currency, stable and with a high exchange value because it is backed by gold or silver. **12** dealing with facts that can be verified: *hard science.* **13** real and significant: *hard facts.* **14** *Phonics* of the consonants *c* and *g*, pronounced as in *corn* and *get*, not soft as in *city* and *gem*.
adv **1** firmly or tightly: *Grip it as hard as you can.* **2** with difficulty: *to breathe hard.* **3** with much energy, effort, or force: *Try hard. He hit me hard.* **4** earnestly; intently: *Listen hard.* <Old English *heard*> **hard′en** *v.* **hard′ness** *n.*
go hard with, be very difficult or unpleasant for: *It will go hard with the murderer if he is caught.*
hard and fast, not to be changed.
hard done by, treated unfairly, either in reality or in one's imagination.
hard of hearing, somewhat deaf.
hard pressed, subject to severe pressure, attack, etc.: *It was a struggle; we were hard pressed on every side. She was hard pressed to finish her essay by Friday.*
hard up, *Informal* needing money or anything very badly: *He is always hard up the day before he is paid. It rained all day, and we were hard up for things to do.*

hard·back (hȧrd′bak′) *n, adj* hardcover.

hard–boiled (hȧrd′boild′) *adj* **1** of eggs, boiled until firm. **2** *Informal* tough and skeptical.

hard cash *n* actual coins or bills as opposed to a cheque or other forms of payment.

hard cider *n* fermented cider, containing alcohol.

hard copy *n* written or printed material, as opposed to material in an electronic form.

hard–core (hard′kȯr′) *adj* **1** most solidly committed or established: *hard-core sci-fi fans, a hard-core Liberal.* **2** of pornography, illicit drugs, crime, etc., the worst, most serious, most damaging, etc.

hard·cov·er (hard′kuv′ər) *adj* with rigid covers of stiff cardboard.
n a book bound in such a way.

hard drive *Computers n* the internal storage device of a single computer terminal. The **hard disk** is the actual storage device, and the hard drive reads it.

hard feelings *n* (*usually with a negative*) resentment or hostility: *Even though we quarrelled, I had no hard feelings toward him.*

hard hat *n* **1** a hat made of rigid material, worn by construction workers or miners for protection against falling objects or other causes of injury. **2** *Informal* a construction worker.

hard–head·ed (hȧrd′hed′id) *adj* **1** not easily excited or deceived. **2** stubborn. **hard′-head′ed·ly** *adv.* **hard′-head′ed·ness** *n.*

hard–heart·ed (hȧrd′hȧr′tid) *adj* without pity. **hard′-heart′ed·ly** *adv.* **hard′-heart′ed·ness** *n.*

har·di·hood (hȧr′dē hu̇d′) *n* boldness; daring.

hard landing *n* **1** a rough or clumsy landing of an aircraft. **2** an uncontrolled landing of a spacecraft, in which the spacecraft is destroyed.

hard line *n* a stern, aggressive, or uncompromising attitude or policy: *taking a hard line against minority language rights.* **hard′line′** or **hard′-line′** *adj.* **hard′lin′er** *n.*

hard luck *n* misfortune.

hard·ly (hȧrd′lē) *adv* **1** only just or barely: *We hardly had time for breakfast.* **2** very probably not: *She will hardly leave now, just when the party is starting.* **3** with trouble or effort: *money hardly earned.*

hard–nosed (hȧrd′nōzd′) *adj* practical and unemotional, often to the point of ruthlessness: *a hard-nosed executive.*

hard·pan (hȧrd′pan′) *n* hard, firm earth underneath the topsoil.

hard return *Computers n* a return inserted by the user. Compare SOFT RETURN.

hard·scrab·ble (hȧrd′skrab′əl) *adj* involving much work for little return: *a hardscrabble existence on the farm.*

hard sell *Informal n* a forceful and direct method of advertising a product or service: *More and more companies are using the hard sell.* **hard′-sell′** *adj.*

hard·ship (hȧrd′ship) *n* suffering of any kind: *to endure much hardship.*

hard·tack (hȧrd′tak′) *n* a hard, dry biscuit formerly eaten on long ship voyages because it kept well.

hard·top (hȧrd′top′) *n* a car that looks like a convertible but has a rigid, sometimes removable, top.

hard·ware (hȧrd′wer′) *n* **1** relatively small items, often made of metal, used to build or repair other things. **2** *Computers* the mechanical or electronic parts of a computer. Compare SOFTWARE. **3** *Military* manufactured equipment such as guns, tanks, aircraft, or missiles.

hard–wired (hȧrd′wīrd′) *adj* made to perform tasks in permanently connected electrical circuits, without input from a user.

hard·wood (hȧrd′wu̇d′) *n* **1** any tree that has broad leaves instead of needles. **2** the wood of such a tree. Compare SOFTWOOD.

hard–work·ing (hȧrd′wər′king) *adj* working with energy and commitment: *She is a hard-working student.*

har·dy (hȧr′dē) *adj* **har·di·er, har·di·est** **1** able to deal with rough treatment or difficult conditions. **2** of plants, able to withstand the cold of winter in the open air. <Old French *hardir* become bold> **har′di·ness** *n.*

hare (her) *n* a wild rodent like a rabbit but bigger, with long ears and hind legs, a short tail, and a divided upper lip. See PIKA for picture.
v **hared, har·ing** (*usually with* ***off***) hurry away. <Old English *hara*>

harness racing

Trotting and pacing are the two types of **harness racing**. In a trotting race, the horse's left front and right rear legs move forward at the same time, and then the right front and left rear leg move.

In a pacing race, both of the horse's right legs move and then both left legs. Most pacers wear straps that connect the front and rear legs to help these legs move in unison.

Hare (her) *n, pl* **Hare** or **Hares** **1** a member of a First Nations people living in the Mackenzie Valley. **2** their Athapascan language.
adj to do with these people or their language.

hare·brained (her′brānd′) *adj* foolish and reckless: *a harebrained scheme.*

Ha·re Krish·na (hȧ′rā krish′nə) *n* a religious community (the International Society for Krishna Consciousness) founded in the US, that reveres the Hindu god Krishna.

hare·lip (her′lip′) *Offensive n* a cleft lip.

har·em (her′əm) *n* **1** in the ancient Middle East, all the wives and concubines of a ruler or other wealthy man, or the part of a household to which they were confined. **2** the female members of a polygamous household. <Arabic *harim* forbidden, because off limits to males>

ha·ri–ka·ri (hȧ′rə kē′rē) HARA-KIRI.

hark (hȧrk) *Poetic v* listen. <Middle English *herkian*>
hark back (to), return to a previous time or subject: *My father is always harking back to his childhood.*

Har·le·quin (hȧr′lə kwin′) *or* (hȧr′lə kin′) *n* **1** a character in comedy and pantomime who is usually masked and wears a costume of various colours. **2 harlequin** a mischievous or clownish person. **3** varied in colour. <French *Herlequin*, from Middle English *Herle King* (a mythical figure)>

har·lot (hȧr′lət) *Archaic or Poetic n* a prostitute. <Old French *herlot* tramp> **har′lot·ry** *n.*

harm (hȧrm) *n* **1** hurt or damage: *The accident did a lot of harm to the car.* **2** morally wrong: *What harm is there in borrowing a friend's bicycle?*
v damage or injure. <Old English *hearm*> **harm′ful** *adj.* **harm′ful·ly** *adv.* **harm′less** *adj.* **harm′less·ly** *adv.*

har·mat·tan (hȧr′mə tan′) *n* a dry wind that blows from the Sahara. <Twi (a language of Africa) *haramata*>

har·mon·ic (hȧr mon′ik) *Music adj* **1** to do with harmony as opposed to melody, rhythm, or dynamics. **2** to do with fainter and higher tones heard along with the main tones.
n **1** a fainter, higher tone heard along with the main tone. **2 harmonics** (*with singular verb*) the science that studies how musical sounds are made. <French, from Greek *harmonia* agreement of sounds>

har·mon·i·ca (hȧr mon′ə kə) *n* a small, rectangular musical instrument that vibrates when the player blows into any of a horizontal series of openings. Also called **mouth organ.**<See HARMONIC.>

har·mo·ni·um (hȧr mō′nē əm) *n* a small musical organ. <See HARMONIC.>

har·mo·nize (hȧr′mə nīz′) *v* **har·mo·nized, har·mo·niz·ing** **1** *Music* add tones to a melody to make pleasing chords. **2** go or put together in a pleasing way: *The colours in the room harmonize.* **3** bring into harmony or agreement: *to harmonize different points of view.*

har·mo·ny (hȧr′mə nē) *n, pl* **har·mo·nies** **1** *Music* **a** the pleasing sounding of notes together to form a chord. **b** the study of chords and their relationships to one another. **2** a sweet or musical sound. **3** an agreement of feeling, thought, or action: *The two brothers lived and worked in perfect harmony.* **4** any orderly and pleasing arrangement: *harmony of design and colour.* <See HARMONIC.> **har·mo′ni·ous** *adj.* **har·mo′ni·ous·ly** *adv.*

har·ness (hȧr′nis) *n* **1** a combination of leather straps and other pieces of hardware, used to hitch a horse or other animal to a carriage, wagon, or plough. **2** any arrangement of straps to fasten or hold: *a parachute harness.*
v **1** put a harness on: *Harness the horse.* **2** bring under management and control for some useful purpose: *to harness someone's youthful energy, to harness the energy in a waterfall to produce electric power.* <Old French *harneis*>
in harness, at one's regular work: *She was content to be back in harness after a good holiday.*

harness race *n* a horse race in which each horse pulls a small two-wheeled cart with a driver. **harness racer** *n.* **harness racing** *n.*

a bat	e bed	i bid	o pot	u cup	th **thin**
ā cake	ē me	ī bite	ō go	ū rude	ᴛʜ **then**
ȧ bar	ə about	ər over	ȯ for	u̇ put	zh measure

harp (hȧrp) *n* a large musical instrument with strings set in a roughly triangular frame, played by plucking the strings with the fingers.
v (*with* ***on***) keep on tiresomely talking or writing about. <Old English *hearpe*> **harp′ist** *n.*

har·poon (hȧr pūn′) *n* a barbed spear with a rope tied to it, used for catching large fish and other sea animals. Harpoons are thrown by hand or shot from a gun.
v strike, catch, or kill with a harpoon: *He skilfully harpooned the seal.* <Old French *harpon* clamp, from *harper* to grasp> **har·poon′ist** *n.*

harp seal *n* a seal of the Atlantic, mainly pale grey in colour.

Like a harp, the **harpsichord** has metal strings that are plucked to produce sound. Pressing a harpsichord key moves a piece of material called a plectrum that in turn plucks a string.

harp·si·chord (hȧrp′sə kȯrd′) *n* a musical instrument like a piano, used especially from the 1500s to the 1700s. <Old French *harpechorde* stringed instrument>

har·ri·dan (her′ə dən) *n* a bad-tempered old woman. <probably French *haridelle* worn-out horse>

har·row (her′ō) *n* a device pulled over ploughed land to break up earth, remove weeds, or cover seeds, consisting of a heavy frame with iron teeth or upright discs in it.
v **1** draw a harrow over. **2** cause to feel pain or agony, distress, or alarm. <Old Norse *herfi*> **har′row·ing** *adj.* **har′row·ing·ly** *adv.*

har·ry (her′ē) *v* **har·ried, har·ry·ing 1** raid and rob with violence: *The pirates harried the towns along the coast.* **2** torment or worry: *He was harried by fear of failing.* <Old English *herian*>

harsh (hȧrsh) *adj* **1** rough or sharp and unpleasant to the senses: *a harsh voice, a harsh climate.* **2** without compassion or gentleness: *harsh discipline.* <perhaps from Old Norse> **harsh′ly** *adv.* **harsh′ness** *n.*

hart (hȧrt) *n* a male deer. <Old English *heorot*>

har·te·beest (hȧr′tə bēst′) *n* a large African antelope with curved horns bent back at the tips. <Dutch *hert* hart + *beest* beast>

har·um–scar·um (her′əm sker′əm) *adj* reckless or rash: *a harum-scarum child.*
n a reckless person. <apparently *hare* frighten + *scare*>

har·vest (hȧr′vist) *n* **1** the gathering in of food crops, usually in late summer or early fall. **2** the time or season when this happens. **3** one season's yield of any crop: *The corn harvest was small this year.*
v **1** gather in for use: *to harvest wheat, to harvest fish from the sea.* **2** gather crops or other useful things from: *to harvest the fields.* <Old English *hærfest*> **har′vest·er** *n.*

harvest moon *n* the full moon in late September, nearest the time of the autumn equinox.

has (haz) third person singular, present tense of HAVE.

has–been (haz′bin′) *or* (haz′bēn′) *n* a person or thing no longer important or significant.

hash[1] (hash) *n* **1** a mixture of cooked meat and potatoes, chopped into small pieces and fried or baked. **2** a mixture or jumble.
v **1** chop into small pieces. **2** *Informal* (*with* ***over*** *or* ***out***) talk about in detail: *My friend and I hashed over the party plans for hours.* **3** mix up or mess up. <French *hache* axe>
make a hash of, make a mess of.
settle someone's hash, *Informal* subdue or silence someone completely.

hash[2] *Informal n* hashish.

hash browns *pl n* boiled potatoes that have been chopped and fried or deep-fried.

hash·ish (hash′ēsh) *or* (hash′ish) *n* an extract from dried hemp flowers that is smoked, chewed, or drunk for its intoxicating effect. Also, **hasheesh.** <Arabic>

Has·id (has′id) *or* (hə sēd′) *Judaism n, pl* **Has·id·im** (has′ə dim) *or* (hə sē′dim) a member of a mystical sect emphasizing personal devotion. Also, **Chasid.**
Ha·sid′ic *adj.*

hasn't (haz′ənt) *contraction* has not.

hasp (hasp) *n* a clasp or fastening for a door, window, or container, especially a hinged metal clasp that fits over a metal loop and is kept in place by putting a peg or padlock through the loop. <Old English *hæpse*>

has·sle (has′əl) *Informal n* **1** a struggle or argument: *There was a hassle about who was going to be first.* **2** trouble or annoyance: *Driving in city traffic is too much hassle.*
v **has·sled, has·sling 1** struggle over or argue. **2** annoy or make trouble for: *The movie star was being hassled by newspaper reporters.* <origin uncertain>

haste (hāst) *n* **1** efforts to be quick: *Some haste is required—the matter is urgent.* **2** quickness without thought or care: *She wrote in haste and didn't check her spelling. Do not make decisions in haste.* <Old French>
make haste, be quick.

has·ten (hā′sən) *v* **1** hurry or cause to hurry: *She hastened to explain. The babysitter hastened the kids off to bed.* **2** speed up: *Fertilizer hastens growth.*

hast·y (hās′stē) *adj* **hast·i·er, hast·i·est 1** hurried: *a hasty visit.* **2** not well thought out: *a hasty decision.* **3** quick-tempered. **hast′i·ly** *adv.* **hast′i·ness** *n.*

hat (hat) *n* a shaped covering, often with a brim, for the head. <Old English *hætt*> **hat′less** *adj.* **hat′like′** *adj.*

hats off to, congratulations to: *Hats off to the organizers for such a successful sports day!*
keep under your hat, *Informal* keep information to yourself.
old hat, already familiar and therefore uninteresting.
pass the hat, take up a money collection.
take off your hat to, congratulate; admire.
talk through your hat, talk foolishly or ignorantly.

hatch[1] (hach) *v* **1** break out of an egg: *Three new chicks hatched today.* **2** break open from an egg and reveal a baby animal: *Not all eggs hatch properly.* **3** keep an egg warm until the young come out: *The sun's heat hatches turtle eggs.* **4** arrange or develop, especially in secret: *to hatch an evil scheme.* <Middle English *hæchen*>

hatch[2] (hach) *n* **1** an opening in a ship's deck, especially one that leads to the hold. **2** the trapdoor covering such an opening. **3** an opening in the floor or roof of a building, etc.: *an escape hatch.* **4** the rear door of a hatchback, or the cargo compartment behind it. <Old English *hæcc* lower half of a divided door>

hatch[3] (hach) *v* draw, cut, or engrave fine parallel lines on: *If you hatch parts of a drawing, it gives the effect of shading.*
n one of such a set of lines. <Old French *hache* axe>

hatch·back (hach′bak′) *n* a car with a sloping back instead of a trunk, the whole of which swings up like a hatch to give access to the interior of the car.

hatch·er·y (hach′ə rē) *n, pl* **hatch·er·ies** a place where the eggs of fish or poultry are hatched.

hatch·et (hach′it) *n* a small axe with a short handle, for use with one hand. <Old French *hache* axe>
bury the hatchet, make peace.

hatchet job *Informal n* a vicious personal attack in speech or writing: *This columnist sure did a hatchet job on the mayor.*

hate (hāt) *v* **hat·ed, hat·ing** dislike extremely: *She hates everyone who disagrees with her. I hate sports.*
n extremely strong dislike, especially toward people: *a heart poisoned by hate.* <Old English *hatian*>

hate crime *n* a crime committed only to express hatred toward a specific group: *mosque burning and other hate crimes.*

hate·ful (hāt′fəl) *adj* **1** worthy of being hated: *a hateful job.* **2** feeling or showing hate: *hateful remarks.*
hate′ful·ly *adv.* **hate′ful·ness** *n.*

hate·mong·er (hāt′mong′gər) *n* a person who spreads hate.

hat·pin (hat′pin′) *n* a long pin used to fasten a hat to the hair.

ha·tred (hā′trid) *n* extremely strong dislike. <Old English *ræden* state>

GRAMMAR AND USAGE

The nouns **hate** and **hatred** mean the same thing.

However, **hate** is used in a more general way and is not usually followed by a prepositional phrase: *Hate can poison a person's life.*

When the object of the extreme dislike is mentioned, **hatred** is used: *Her hatred of snakes affected her enjoyment of the field trip.*

hat·ter (hat′ər) *n* a maker or seller of hats.

hat trick *n* **1** *Hockey, Soccer* three goals scored in a single game by the same player. **2** *Informal* any feat consisting of three or more successes in a row.

ETYMOLOGY

Hat trick comes from the game of cricket. To commemorate the taking of three wickets with three successive balls, a *hat* was presented to the bowler.

The term was later extended to other sports, especially hockey where, at games, fans throw hats onto the ice in celebration of one player scoring three goals in a game.

Hau·den·o·sau·nee (hou′də nō sou′nē) *n, pl* **Hau·den·o·sau·nee** **1** a member of any of the Iroquoian peoples of Ontario, Québec, and New York whose ancestors historically formed the Six Nations alliance. Also called **Iroquois**. **2** any of the Iroquoian languages spoken by these people.
adj to do with any of these people or their languages.

haugh·ty (hot′ē) *adj* **haugh·ti·er, haugh·ti·est** showing scorn for others: *a haughty girl, a haughty smile.* <Old French *haut,* from Latin *altus* high> **haugh′ti·ly** *adv.* **haugh′ti·ness** *n.*

haul (hol) *v* **1** pull or drag with force: *The logs were hauled by horses.* **2** transport by truck or rail. **3** change direction: *The wind hauled around to the east.*
n **1** the act of hauling or distance hauled. **2** the load hauled: *Big trucks are used for heavy hauls.* **3** the amount taken or won: *The fishing boats made a good haul today.* <Middle English> **haul′er** *n.*
for the short (or **long**) **haul,** for the near (or more distant) future: *That solution might do for the short haul, but you'll need something better eventually.*
haul off, a turn a ship away from an object. **b** *Informal* draw back one's arm to give a blow.
haul on (or **to**) **the wind,** sail closer to the direction of the wind.
long haul, something requiring long, hard effort: *Getting rid of the deficit is going to be a long haul.*

haunch (honch) *n* **1** usually, **haunches** *pl* **a** the part of the body around the hips. **b** the hindquarters of an animal: *A dog sits on its haunches.* **2** a cut of meat consisting of the leg and loin of the animal. <Old French *hanche*>

haunt (hont) *v* **1** be often or continually present in a place as a ghost: *They say ghosts haunt that old house.* **2** visit and spend much time in: *That crowd haunts the new sports centre.* **3** be persistently present in the mind: *haunted by memories.*
n a place one often visits and spends time in: *The swimming pool was our favourite haunt in the summer.* <Old French *hanter*> **haunt′ed** *adj.*

a bat	e bed	i bid	o pot	u cup	th **thin**
ā cake	ē me	ī bite	ō go	ū rude	ᴛʜ **then**
à bar	ə about	ər over	ò for	ù put	zh measure

H

haunt·ing (hon′ting) *adj* memorable and deeply felt: *a haunting melody, haunting memories.* **haunt′ing·ly** *adv.*

haute couture (ōt′ kū tūr′) *n* the world of high fashion; the most prestigious fashion houses and designers and their work. <French = high sewing>

haute cuisine (ōt′ kwi zēn′) *n* **1** cooking as a fine art, as practised by highly trained chefs. **2** food prepared in this style. <French = high cooking>

hau·teur (hō tər′) *n* a haughty manner. <French *haut* high>

haut–relief (ōt′rə lēf′) *n* sculpture in which carved forms stand well out from a background. Compare BAS-RELIEF. Also called **high relief**.

have (hav) *v*, **has** (*third person singular, present tense*), **had, hav·ing 1** hold: *I have a book in my hand.* **2** possess: *She has a new bicycle.* **3** be in a certain relation to: *She has three brothers. Our school has twelve teachers.* **4** cause somebody to do something or cause something to be done: *Please have your sister call me when she gets home. I had my cellphone replaced.* **5** experience: *to have a fever. They had trouble with this software.* **6** engage in; carry on: *Have a talk with her.* **7** take or get: *Have a seat. Let's go have lunch.* **8** be forced or required: *Everybody has to eat.* **9** allow: *She won't have any noise while she is reading.* **10** generate or produce: *to have an idea, to have a baby.* **11** *Informal* hold an advantage over: *You have him there.* **12** *Informal* outwit or cheat: *I've been had.* **13** also used with past participles to express completed action: *They have gone. She had already left.*

n a person or country that has property or wealth: *the haves and have-nots.* <Old English *habban*>

have had it, *Informal* **a** become fed up or frustrated: *I've had it with your laziness!* **b** come to an end; stop being effective: *I think this vacuum cleaner has had it.*

have it, a win in a vote: *The nays have it.* **b** believe or claim that: *She has it that some poverty is inevitable.*

have it in for, *Informal* have a grudge against.

have it out, argue or fight until a dispute is settled.

have nothing on someone (or **something**), be no better than: *That fancy expensive backpack has nothing on my sturdy old canvas one.*

have on, a be wearing: *She had her school uniform on.* **b** have scheduled: *Do you have anything on for tonight?*

have to do with, a be connected with. **b** have dealings with.

ha·ven (hā′vən) *n* **1** a harbour, especially one providing shelter from a storm. **2** any place of shelter and safety: *Home should be a haven.* <Old English *hæfen*>

have–not (hav′not′) *Informal n* a person, group, area, or country that has little property or wealth.

adj poor.

haven't (hav′ənt) *contraction* have not.

hav·er·sack (hav′ər sak′) *n* a backpack or knapsack. <German *Habersack* oat sack>

hav·oc (hav′ək) *n* great destruction or chaos: *A tornado can create widespread havoc.* <Old French *havot* devastation>

play havoc with, ruin or wreck.

haw[1] (ho) *n* the hawthorn or its red berry. <Old English *haga*>

haw[2] (ho) *v* See HEM[2].

haw[3] (ho) *interj, n* a command to a horse or ox to turn left. <origin uncertain>

Ha·waii (hə wī′ē) *n* a group of islands in the Pacific that together make up one of the states of the US.

Ha·wai′ian (hə wī′ən) *adj, n.*

hawk[1] (hok) *n* **1** a bird of prey with a strong hooked beak, large curved claws, and a long tail. **2** a similar bird of prey such as a buzzard or kite. **3** a person who preys on others. **4** a person who favours war or confrontation rather than peace and compromise. <Old English *hafoc*>

hawk′ish *adj.* **hawk′like′** *adj.*

watch like a hawk, watch very closely, especially to guard or control.

hawk[2] (hok) *v* peddle, especially by carrying goods outdoors and shouting that they are for sale. <probably German or Dutch> **hawk′er** *n.*

haw·thorn (ho′thôrn′) *n* a thorny shrub or tree with small red berries. <Old English *hagathorn*>

hay (hā) *n* grass and other plants cut and dried for use as food for livestock.

v **1** cut grass or other plants for making into hay: *Is anyone haying in the east field?* **2** supply with hay. <Old English *heg*>

hit the hay, *Informal* go to bed.

make hay (**while the sun shines**), *Informal* take advantage of some opportunity.

hay fever *n* an allergy with effects like those of a cold, caused by the pollen of some plants.

hay·field (hā′fēld′) *n* a field where grass, alfalfa, or clover is grown for hay.

hay·loft (hā′loft′) *n* the upper storey of a barn, where hay is stored. Also called **haymow** (hā′mō′) *or* (hā′mou′).

hay·ride (hā′rīd′) *n* a ride for fun on a wagon filled with bales of hay, pulled by horses or a tractor. **hay′rid′ing** *n.*

hay·seed (hā′sēd′) *n* **1** *Informal or Offensive* an unsophisticated person, especially one from or who lives in a rural area. **2** a seed or seeds shaken out of hay.

hay·stack (hā′stak′) *n* a large pile of hay.

hay·wire (hā′wīr′) *Informal adj* wrong, out of order, confused, or crazy. <The wire used to tie bales of hay typically gets tangled up.>

haz·ard (haz′ərd) *n* **1** a risk or danger: *The life of an explorer is full of hazards.* **2** chance: *By pure hazard, we ended up on the same bus.* **3** any obstruction designed to challenge players on a golf course.

v take a chance with: *to hazard a guess. I would hazard, my life on her honesty.* <Arabic *al-zahr* die (singular of *dice*). *Hazard* originally referred to a game of chance played with dice.> **haz′ard·ous** *adj.*

hazardous waste *n* waste that is harmful to people or the environment, such as radioactive material, paint, and some chemicals.

haze[1] (hāz) *n* **1** a small amount of mist, smog, or dust in the air: *A thin haze veiled the mountains.* **2** anything that keeps one from seeing or thinking clearly: *She saw everything through a haze of suspicion.* <origin uncertain> **ha′zy** *adj.*

haze[2] (hāz) *v* **hazed, haz·ing 1** force to do ridiculous or dangerous tasks, especially as a rite of initiation: *We resented being hazed by the older students.* **2** *Western Canada and US* drive cattle or horses from horseback. <origin uncertain> **haz′er** *n.*

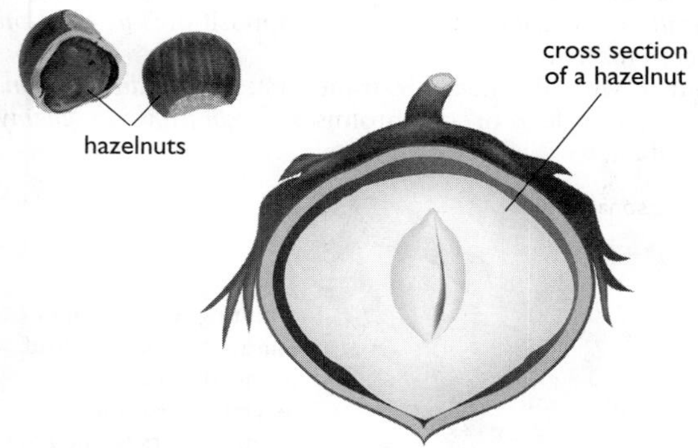

ha·zel (hā′zəl) *n* a shrub or small tree native to north temperate regions, with light-brown, edible **hazelnuts.** *adj* greenish brown: *hazel eyes.* <Old English *hæsel*>

H–bomb (āch′bom′) *n* a hydrogen bomb.

HDI *n* in full, **Human Development Index** a measure of a country's achievements in the areas of life expectancy, literacy, and standard of living. It has been used since 1993 in the annual report of the United Nations.

HDL *n* in full, **high-density lipoprotein** a fat and protein molecule complex found in the blood. It holds very little cholesterol. This is the so-called "good cholesterol." Compare LDL. <Greek *lipos* fat + *protein*>

HDTV *n* in full, **high-definition television** a television system that has a much sharper image, and a wide-screen format.

he (hē) *pron* a male person already referred to and identified: *My dad has to work hard, but he likes his job.* <Old English *he*>

GRAMMAR AND USAGE

The use of the third person singular pronoun **he** to mean *he or she* should be avoided. Try rewriting a sentence in the plural so that *they* can be used instead. Alternately, try substituting *he or she, his or her,* or *him or her.* Sometimes, by simply rewording, the difficulty can be resolved: *Will the winner please claim his prize?* could be rewritten as *Will the winner please claim the prize?*

head (hed) *n* **1** the upper part of a body, above the neck. **2** the top or front part of anything: *the head of a page, the head of a parade.* **3** a person in charge of something. **4** the position of leadership: *Who is at the head of this organization?* **5** the end of a bed where one puts one's head. **6** the end of a table where the host or most honoured person sits. **7** a unit used in counting animals: *She sold fifty head of cattle and ten head of horses.* **8** anything rounded like a head: *a head of cabbage, the head of a pin, a flower head.* **9** the source of a river or stream. **10** the part of a boil or pimple where pus is about to break through the skin. **11** the striking part of a tool such as an axe or hammer. **12** mind, understanding, or mental ability: *She has a good head for figures.* **13** a category or topic with a title: *He arranged his speech under four main heads.* **14** a headland. **15** pressure of water or steam. **16** the foam or froth on beer or fizzy drinks. **17** the device in an audio, video, or information system that records, reads, or deletes data on a magnetic tape or disc. **18** usually, **heads** the side of a coin bearing the likeness of a head, especially this side facing up when the coin is tossed: *Heads, you do the dishes.*
v **1** begin or cause to begin moving in a certain direction: *Let's head for home. They headed the boat toward the shore.* **2** be at the head, top, or front of: *to head a parade.* **3** be the leader or director of: *to head an organization.* **4** *Soccer* strike the ball with one's head: *He headed the ball away from his opponent.*
adj leading or in charge of: *Who's the head person here?* <Old English *heafod*> **head′less** *adj.* **head′ship** *n.*
come to a head, a of boils, pimples, etc., reach the stage where they are about to break through the skin. **b** reach a climax or decisive stage: *The international crisis came to a head and war was declared.*
give someone his or **her head,** let someone do as he or she pleases.
go (or **be**) **head to head,** be directly opposed.
go to your head, a make you dizzy or tipsy. **b** make you conceited.
hang your head, be ashamed and show it.
head off, get in front of and turn back or aside: *The cowboys tried to head off the stampeding herd.*
head on, with the head or front first: *The car crashed head on into the wall.*
head over heels, a hastily or rashly. **b** turning over in a somersault. **c** (*especially with* **in love**) completely or thoroughly.
heads will roll, someone will be punished.
keep your head, remain calm.
keep your head above water, survive or manage, especially financially.
lose your head, get excited and lose control of yourself.
make head or tail of, understand any of.
off (or **out of**) **your head,** *Informal* insane.
over someone's head, a beyond someone's understanding. **b** directly to a person higher in authority: *She threatened that she would go over the principal's head to the school board.*
put heads together, confer or discuss.
turn your head, a make you dizzy. **b** make you conceited.
—— your head off, *Informal* to an extraordinary or excessive extent: *working our heads off, shouting his head off.*

head·ache (hed′āk′) *n* **1** a pain in the head. **2** *Informal* a cause of annoyance, bother, or trouble.

a bat	e bed	i bid	o pot	u cup	th thin
ā cake	ē me	ī bite	ō go	ū rude	ᴛʜ then
ȧ bar	ə about	ər over	ȯ for	u̇ put	zh measure

H

head·band (hed′band′) *n* a band of fabric worn around the head.

head·board (hed′bòrd′) *n* a board or frame attached to the head of a bed.

head·cheese (hed′chēz′) *n* parts of the head and feet of pigs cooked, seasoned, and formed into a jellied loaf.

head cold *n* a form of the common cold mostly affecting the sinuses.

head count *n* a counting of individuals one at a time.

head·dress (hed′dres′) *n* a covering or decoration for the head, especially in ceremonies.

head·er (hed′ər) *n* **1** a line of text such as a title or date, especially one that is automatically inserted by word-processing software, appearing at the top of each page of a document, book, etc. Compare FOOTER. **2** *Informal* a plunge or dive headfirst: *She took a header into the water.* **3** *Soccer* a shot or pass made with the head.

head·first (hed′fərst′) *adv* **1** with the head first: *He slid headfirst down the hill.* **2** hastily, rashly: *to run headfirst into a dangerous situation.*

head·gear (hed′gēr′) *n* a covering for the head, especially a hat or helmet.

head·hunt·ing (hed′hun′ting) *n* **1** the recruitment of skilled employees, especially by luring away those already successfully employed elsewhere. **2** the practice, among certain preindustrial peoples, of collecting the heads of dead enemies as a symbol of triumph.
adj to do with either of these practices: *a headhunting agency, a headhunting tribe.* **head′hunt·er** *n.*

head·ing (hed′ing) *n* **1** something written or printed at the top of a page. **2** the title of a category, topic, or chapter: *Under the heading "indoor games," have you included bowling?* **3** the direction of a ship or aircraft as indicated by a compass.

head·lamp (hed′lamp′) *n* a small lamp worn on the cap or the forehead, especially by miners.

head·land (hed′lənd) *or* (hed′land′) *n* a point of land jutting out into water. See ESTUARY for picture.

head lettuce *n* a variety of lettuce whose leaves form a solid head.

head·light (hed′līt′) *n* one of two lights at the front of a motor vehicle.

head·line (hed′līn′) *n* the words printed at the top of an article in a newspaper or magazine to indicate the topic.
v **head·lined, head·lin·ing 1** furnish with a headline. **2** be mentioned in a headline.
make headlines, be noticed and reported by the media.

head·long (hed′long′) *adv* **1** headfirst: *to plunge headlong into the sea.* **2** with great speed and force: *to rush headlong into the crowd.* **3** recklessly: *She was always rushing headlong into trouble.*
adj done rashly or recklessly.

head–man (hed′man′) *Hockey* *v* **head·manned, head·man·ning** pass the puck forward to a teammate during an offensive rush.

head·man (hed′man′) *n, pl* **head·men** (hed′men′) a chief or leader of a community.

head·mas·ter (hed′mas′tər) *n* a principal of a private school or, in Great Britain, of any school.

head–on (hed′on′) *adj* **1** with the head or front first: *a head-on collision.* **2** in direct opposition: *a head-on confrontation.*
adv **1** with the head or front first: *to collide head-on.* **2** without fear or compromise: *to confront an enemy head-on.*

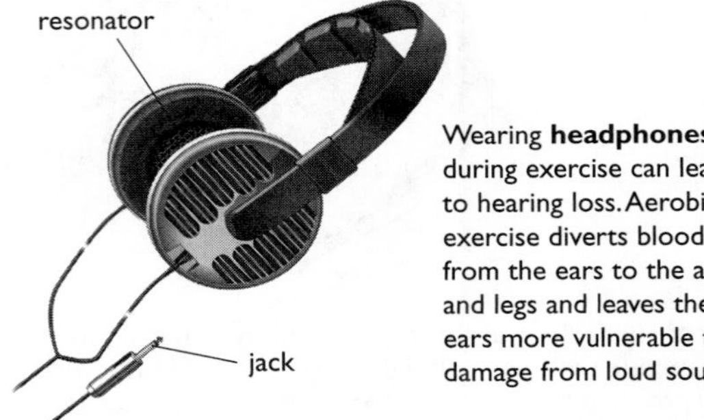

Wearing **headphones** during exercise can lead to hearing loss. Aerobic exercise diverts blood from the ears to the arms and legs and leaves the ears more vulnerable to damage from loud sound.

head·phones (hed′fōnz′) *pln* a pair of audio receivers joined by a band that holds them on the head against the ears, for private listening to a radio, CD, or tape player.

head·quar·ters (hed′kwòr′tərz) *n* (*with singular or plural verb*) the main office or centre from which any organization is controlled and directed: *The company's headquarters are in Ottawa. If you want excitement, headquarters is the place to be.*
v **headquarter** establish or provide with headquarters: *The company is headquartered in Ottawa.*

head·rest (hed′rest′) *n* a padded support for the head: *The dentist's chair has a headrest.*

head·room (hed′rūm′) **1** space above one's head; clearance. **2** overhead clearance for vehicles, such as under a bridge.

head·set (hed′set′) *n* **1** headphones. **2** a similar device for use with a telephone, with a mouthpiece as well as one or two earpieces.

head·stand (hed′stand′) *n* a gymnastics move in which the head is on the floor while the rest of the body, supported by the hands, is upright.

head start *n* **1** an advantage or lead allowed someone at the beginning of a race: *The smaller girl was given a head start.* **2** any advantage: *A good breakfast gives you a head start on the day.*

head·stone (hed′stōn′) *n* **1** a stone set at the head of a grave, with the person's name, etc. marked on it. **2** the main stone in a foundation; a cornerstone.

head·strong (hed′strong′) *adj* rashly or foolishly determined to have one's own way.

heads–up (hed′zup′) *Informal* *n* a warning or advance notice: *Give me a heads-up when you're about to leave.*
adj alert for possible opportunities.

head tax *n* a tax imposed on every person within a certain group, especially new immigrants.

head·wa·ters (hed′wot′ərz) *pln* the source or upper part of a river.

head·way (hed′wā′) *n* **1** forward motion: *The ship could make no headway against the strong wind and tide.* **2** progress with work or some other activity.

head·wind (hed′wind′) *n* a wind blowing straight against the front of a ship or aircraft.

head·y (hed′ē) *adj* **head·i·er, head·i·est 1** hasty or rash. **2** making one dizzy or exhilarated. **head′i·ly** *adv.* **head′i·ness** *n.*

heal (hēl) *v* **1** bring back to health: *Rest and proper food soon healed her.* **2** get rid of an illness, injury, or hurt: *to heal wounds, to heal a broken heart.* **3** become well, healthy, or sound again: *His cut finger soon healed.* <Old English *hal* well> **heal′er** *n.*

health (helth) *n* **1** the condition of being healthy. **2** a condition of body or mind: *My great-grandmother is in poor health.* **3** a toast drunk in someone's honour: *We all drank a health to the bride.* <Old English *hal* well>

🍁 **health card** *n* a card that identifies a person as eligible for provincially funded medical treatment.

health care *n* the provision of services by the medical profession, especially in the prevention and treatment of illness.

health club *n* an organization that provides the use of exercise facilities to its members. Also called **fitness club**.

health food *n* foods with few preservatives and minimum processing, thought to have extra nutritional value and a healthy effect on the body.

health·ful (helth′fəl) *adj* good for the health: *healthful exercise, a healthful diet.*

CONFUSABLES

Healthful means "good for the health."

Healthy means "in good health."

Places and food are healthful.

Persons and animals are healthy.

health·y (hel′thē) *adj* **health·i·er, health·i·est 1** with or showing good health: *a healthy baby. You have a healthy colour in your cheeks.* **2** *Informal* good for the health: *healthy living.* **health′i·ly** *adv.* **health′i·ness** *n.*

heap (hēp) *n* a pile of many things thrown or lying together: *a heap of stones.*
v **1** put or make into a heap: *I heaped the dirty clothes beside the washing machine.* **2** give generously or in large amounts: *They heaped compliments on him. She heaped my plate with mashed potatoes.* <Old English *heap*>

hear (hēr) *v* **heard** (herd)**, hear·ing 1** perceive with the ears: *I hear music. He can no longer hear well.* **2** listen to with special attention: *Please hear what I have to say.* **3** give a formal hearing to, such as a judge does: *to hear an appeal.* **4** find out by hearing: *I heard she got a new job.* <Old English *heran*> **hear′er** *n.*
hear from, a receive news or information from: *Have you heard from your friend?* **b** receive criticism or scolding from: *Any more silly behaviour, and you'll hear from me.*
hear! hear! an expression of approval or agreement, especially during a debate.
hear of, a have some knowledge of: *I've never heard of her.* **b** (*in the negative*) consider or agree to: *I tried to pay him but he wouldn't hear of it.*
hear out, listen to till the end.

CONFUSABLES

Hear is a noun that means "listen to": *Did you just hear that noise outside?*

Here is an adverb that means "at this place": *I'm glad that you came here to meet me.*

hear·ing (hē′ring) *n* **1** the sense by which sound is perceived: *The old man's hearing is poor.* **2** a formal or official presentation of evidence: *The Royal Commission has set a date for its next hearing. The judge gave both sides a hearing in court.* **3** a chance to be heard: *Give us a hearing.* **4** the distance that a sound can be heard: *Stay within hearing of the baby.*

hearing aid *n* a small battery-operated device worn in or behind the ear to amplify sounds for the wearer.

hear·ing–im·paired (hēr′ing im perd′) *adj* deaf or partly deaf.

heark·en (hȧr′kən) *Poetic v* listen; listen attentively: *Hearken to my plea.* <Old English *hercnian*>

hear·say (hēr′sā′) *n* **1** rumour or gossip. **2** in full, **hearsay evidence** *Law* evidence based on the testimony of another person, rather than on the witness's first-hand knowledge. Usually it is not accepted in court.

hearse (hərs) *n* a vehicle used in funerals to carry the dead body in a coffin. <Old French *herce*, a frame with teeth (it resembles a harrow) for holding candles over a coffin, from Latin *hirpicis* a harrow>

heart (hȧrt) *n* **1** the organ that pumps the blood throughout a body. **2** the emotional centre of a person: *She has a kind heart.* **3** one's love or commitment: *You have my heart.* **4** kindness or sympathy: *Have you no heart?* **5** courage and enthusiasm: *The losing team showed plenty of heart.* **6** the deepest or most essential part: *in the heart of the forest, the very heart of the matter.* **7** a shape like this ♥, often a symbol of love: *There was a big red heart on the front of the valentine card.* **8 a** a playing card with one or more red heart-shaped designs on it. **b hearts** *pl* the suit of cards marked with this design. <Old English *heorte*>
after my own heart, pleasing me perfectly.
at heart, in truth: *He is kind at heart, though he seems gruff.*
by heart, by memory.
change of heart, a reversal of one's opinion or attitude: *I was going to quit, but I've had a change of heart.*

a bat	e bed	i bid	o pot	u cup	th thin
ā cake	ē me	ī bite	ō go	ū rude	ᴛʜ then
ȧ bar	ə about	ər over	ȯ for	u̇ put	zh measure

eat your heart out, *Informal* feel great envy, disappointment, or worry.
from the (**bottom of my**) **heart,** with deep sincerity.
get to the heart of, understand the real character or cause of.
have a heart, *Informal* be kind, merciful, or sympathetic.
have a heart of gold, be very kind or generous.
have the heart, have the courage to do or say something: *She didn't have the heart to play anymore. I didn't have the heart to tell him the bad news.*
have your heart in the right place, have good intentions.
have your heart in your mouth, be very frightened.
heart and soul, with all your feeling and energy.
heart of gold, extremely kind and generous.
in your heart of hearts, in your deepest thoughts or feelings.
lose your heart to, fall in love with.
my heart goes out (**to**), I feel compassion (for).
near (or **dear**) **to my heart,** of great value or importance to me.
set my heart on, be determined to have or do: *I had my heart set on camping in Nunavut this summer.*
steal someone's heart, win someone's love or affection.
take heart, be encouraged.
take to heart, think seriously about or be deeply affected by.
wear your heart on your sleeve, show your feelings too plainly.
with all my heart, sincerely or completely.

heart·ache (härt′āk′) *n* anguish or grief.

heart attack *n* a sudden destruction of muscle tissue in the heart, especially because the blood supply has been interrupted by a clot in a coronary artery.

heart·beat (härt′bēt′) *n* **1** one pulsation of the heart, including one complete contraction and dilation. **2** the rate at which the heart is beating.

heart·break (härt′brāk′) *n* an overwhelming grief. **heart′break′ing** *adj.* **heart′break′ing·ly** *adj.*

heart·bro·ken (härt′brō′kən) *adj* overwhelmed with grief. **heart′bro′ken·ly** *adv.*

heart·burn (härt′bərn′) *n* a burning sensation in the chest caused by acidic digestive juices escaping from the stomach up into the esophagus.

heart·en (här′tən) *v* encourage or be made more confident: *We were heartened by the good news.* **heart′en·ing** *adj.* **heart′en·ing·ly** *adv.*

heart failure *n* especially as a cause of death, a condition in which one or both sides of the heart are unable to pump enough blood to meet the needs of the body.

heart·felt (härt′felt′) *adj* sincere: *heartfelt thanks.*

hearth (härth) *n* **1** the part of a floor directly in front of a fireplace. **2** home: *The traveller longed for his own hearth.* <Old English *heorth*>

heart·land (härt′land′) *n* the region that is central or most vital to an industry, nation, or institution: *Manitoba, the Métis heartland. British Columbia has become the heartland of Canada's logging industry.*

heart·less (härt′lis) *adj* without kindness or sympathy. **heart′less·ly** *adv.* **heart′less·ness** *n.*

heart rate *n* the number of heartbeats per minute, as an indication of exertion or stress.

heart–rend·ing (härt′ren′ding) *adj* causing emotional distress. **heart′-rend′ing·ly** *adv.*

heart·sick (härt′sik′) *adj* very depressed or disappointed.

heart·sore (härt′sôr′) *adj* feeling or showing grief.

heart–stop·ping (härt′stop′ing) *adj* giving a thrill of fear or suspense.

heart·strings (härt′stringz′) *pln* one's deepest feelings, especially of sympathy or compassion.

heart·throb (härt′throb′) *Informal n* a person with whom one is infatuated: *This young actor is the heart-throb of every teenage girl.*

heart–to–heart (härt′tə härt′) *adj* frank, sincere, and earnest: *a heart-to-heart talk.*
n Informal a heart-to-heart talk: *I'd better have a heart-to-heart with him.*

heart·warm·ing (härt′wôr′ming) *adj* stirring up warm, sympathetic, or glad feelings.

heart·wood (härt′wu̇d′) *n* the hard, central wood of a tree.

heart·y (här′tē) *adj* **heart·i·er, heart·i·est 1** warm and friendly: *a hearty welcome.* **2** strong and vigorous: *My great-grandmother is still hale and hearty.* **3** full of energy and enthusiasm: *He burst out in a loud, hearty laugh.* **4** plentiful and nourishing: *A hearty meal satisfied her hunger.*
n, pl **heart·ies** a vigorous and cheerful person, especially one interested in sports. **heart·i·ly** *adv.* **heart·i·ness** *n.*

heat (hēt) *n* **1** the fact, condition, degree, or sensation of being hot: *Test the heat of the water with your finger.* **2** *Physics* a form of energy consisting in the random motion of molecules, transferred in the form of conduction, convection, or radiation. **3** hot weather: *Are you ready for the heat?* **4** a system for warming the air indoors, such as a furnace or heater, or its output: *Turn up the heat.* **5** the most intense or passionate point or state: *In the heat of the argument, she lost her temper.* **6** intensity of feeling; anger or excitement: *He replied with great heat that he had never been so insulted.* **7** *Informal* **a** criticism: *We took some heat for that decision.* **b** pressure from others. **8** one trial in a race: *She won the first heat, but lost the final race.* **9** a recurring period of sexual receptiveness in female mammals: *Our dog is in heat right now.*
v make or become hotter or warmer. <Old English *hætu*>

heat capacity *Physics n* the heat needed to raise the temperature of a unit mass of some substance by one Centigrade degree, measured in joules.

heat·ed (hē′tid) *adj* **1** angry or excited: *a heated debate, a heated reply.* **2** artificially supplied with heat: *a heated pool.* **heat·ed·ly** *adv.*

heat·er (hē′tər) *n* a device that gives heat or warmth, especially one that is not part of a central heating system: *an electric heater for the cabin.*

heat exchanger *n* a device that transfers heat from one fluid to another, without mixing them, for purposes of heating or cooling or for use as a source of power.

heath (hēth) *especially UK n* open wasteland with heather or low bushes growing on it. <Old English *hæth*>

hea·then (hē′ᴛʜən) *n, pl* **hea·thens** or **hea·then** **1** a person thought to have no religion, as regarded by one who has. **2** a person who is considered uncivilized.
adj to do with heathens or being a heathen: *heathen idols.* <Old English *hæthen* people who live on open wasteland, i.e., uncivilized people> **hea′then·dom** *n.* **hea′then·ish** *n.*

GRAMMAR AND USAGE

Both **heathen** and **pagan** have an implied meaning of "ignorant" or "unbelieving." Many people regard these terms as offensive and it is therefore best to avoid them.

Except for informal or humorous usages, the words should be reserved for historical contexts:
Julius Caesar was a pagan.
The Goths were heathen.

heath·er (heᴛʜ′ər) *n* a shrub growing in wild open spaces in northern regions, often with clusters of tiny flowers. <probably from *heath*>

heat lightning *n* flashes of light without any thunder, seen near the horizon especially on hot summer evenings.

heat pump *n* a device using mechanical energy to transfer heat from a colder area to a warmer area, such as in a refrigerator.

heat shield *n* a covering of special material on the nose cone of a missile or spacecraft to protect it from the heat produced when it re-enters the earth's atmosphere.

heat sink *n* a device or substance that conducts or absorbs unwanted heat away from sensitive equipment or from a heat-generating process.

heat·stroke (hēt′strōk′) *n* a condition produced by exposure to extreme heat, in which the body temperature rises dangerously.

heat wave *n* a long period of very hot weather.

heave (hēv) *v* **heaved** or (*especially in nautical use*) **hove, heav·ing** **1 a** lift or pull with force or effort: *She heaved the heavy box into the wagon. They heaved on the rope.* **b** lift and throw with effort: *The sailors hove the anchor overboard.* **2** utter with effort: *to heave a sigh of relief.* **3** pant: *He was heaving from the exertion.* **4 a** rise and fall rhythmically: *The sea was heaving.* **b** rise and swell, bulge, or buckle: *The ground heaved during the earthquake.* **5** vomit.
n **1** the act or fact of heaving: *With a great heave, they got the dresser into the truck.* **2** **heaves** (*with singular verb*) a disease of horses, characterized by difficult breathing, coughing, and heaving of the flanks. <Old English *hebban*>
heave ho! a sailor's cry when pulling up the anchor, or pulling on any rope or cable.

heave–ho (hēv′hō′) *Informal n* (*with* ***the***) rejection: *She gave him the heave-ho.*

heav·en (hev′ən) *n* **1** for many religious believers, a place or condition in which God lives and with whom the truly good may achieve eternal life after death. Compare HELL (def. 1). **2** a place or condition of greatest happiness: *It was heaven just to be able to relax after the uproar.* **3** usually, **the heavens** *pl* the sky: *Millions of stars were shining in the heavens.* <Old English *heofon*>
for heaven's sake! or **good heavens!** an exclamation of surprise or protest.
move heaven and earth, do everything possible.

heav·en·ly (hev′ən lē) *adj* **1** of, from, or in heaven: *heavenly angels, heavenly wisdom.* **2** of more than human excellence: *heavenly beauty.* **3** *Informal* delightful: *a heavenly spot for a picnic, heavenly weather.* **4** of or in the heavens; in the sky: *stars, planets, and other heavenly bodies.* **heav′en·li·ness** *n.*

heav·en·ward (hev′ən wərd) *adv, adj* toward heaven.

heav·y (hev′ē) *adj* **heav·i·er, heav·i·est** **1** hard to lift or carry: *a heavy load.* **2** thicker, denser, or bigger than most: *heavy canvas, heavy shoes.* **3** happening or doing something to a greater than usual extent: *heavy rain, a heavy sleep.* **4** hard to do or to deal with: *a heavy responsibility.* **5** sorrowful, gloomy, or serious: *a heavy heart.* **6** involving much thought or deep emotion: *The story is a little too heavy for young kids.* **7** cloudy or stormy, or about to be so: *heavy weather.* **8** somewhat overweight. **9** clumsy, sluggish, or slow: *heavy movements.*
n, pl **heav·ies** **1** *Informal* the villain in a play. **2** *Slang* (*often plural*) somebody hired to persuade people, by threats or violence, to do something: *A couple of heavies were collecting gambling debts.* <Old English *hebban* heave> **heav′i·ly** *adv.* **heav′i·ness** *n.*
hang heavy, of time, pass slowly and boringly: *She had nothing to do, and time hung heavy on her hands.*

heav·y–du·ty (hev′ē dyū′tē) *or* (hev′ē dū′tē) *adj* **1** built to withstand unusual strain or hard use: *a heavy-duty vacuum cleaner.* **2** *Informal* serious, thorough, complex, or considerable: *a heavy-duty talk, heavy-duty changes.*

heav·y–hand·ed (hev′ē han′did) *adj* **1** clumsy or awkward: *a heavy-handed attempt at humour.* **2** harsh or cruel: *That penalty was a little heavy-handed.* **heav′y–hand′ed·ly** *adv.* **heav′y–hand′ed·ness** *n.*

heav·y–heart·ed (hev′ē hȧr′tid) *adj* sad and gloomy. **heav′y–heart′ed·ly** *adv.*

heavy hydrogen DEUTERIUM.

heavy industry *n* the manufacture of large objects, such as machines. Compare LIGHT INDUSTRY.

heavy metal *n* **1** any metal with high relative density, usually poisonous. **2** loud rock music with a pounding rhythm and often lyrics with violent imagery.

heav·y·set (hev′ē set′) *adj* with a solid, heavy build: *a heavyset man.*

a bat	e bed	i bid	o pot	u cup	th thin
ā cake	ē me	ī bite	ō go	ū rude	ᴛʜ then
ȧ bar	ə about	ər over	ȯ for	u̇ put	zh measure

H

heavy water *n* water composed of oxygen and heavy hydrogen, used in nuclear power plants to moderate and control nuclear reactions.

heav·y·weight (hev′ē wāt′) *n* **1** a person or thing of much more than average mass. **2** a boxer who weighs more than 88 kilograms. **3** *Informal* a person of great importance or influence: *a literary heavyweight.*

He·brew (hē′brū) *n* **1** a member of a Semitic people of ancient Palestine, especially an Israelite, or a descendant of such a person. **2** the ancient or modern form of the Semitic language of the Hebrews.
adj to do with the Hebrews or their language.
He·bra′ic *adj.*

heck (hek) *Informal interj, n* a mild form of the word HELL.

heck·le (hek′əl) *v* **heck·led, heck·ling** harass a public speaker or entertainer with interruptions or bothersome questions. <Middle English, from Dutch *hekele* prickle, irritate> **heck′ler** *n.*

hec·tare (hek′ter) *or* (hek′tår) *n* a unit of land area, equal to 10 000 m^2. *Symbol* **ha** <French, from Greek *hekaton* hundred>

hec·tic (hek′tik) *adj* filled with or characterized by great excitement, hurry, or confusion: *a hectic life. We spent three hectic days packing for the move.*

ETYMOLOGY

Hectic has a little-used meaning, referring to the cough, fever, flushed appearance, or other symptoms of diseases such as tuberculosis. It originally comes from Greek *hektikos*, meaning "habitual," because such diseases generally last a long time or recur in bouts. The "feverish" aspect was used as a metaphor to describe rushed, excited activity.

hecto– *combining form* hundred: *hectometre.* <French, from Greek *hekaton* hundred>

he'd (hēd) *contraction* **1** he had: *He'd better not be late.* **2** he would: *He'd always help out at home.*

hedge (hej) *n* **1** a thick row of bushes or small trees, planted as a fence or boundary. **2** any barrier or boundary. **3** the act of hedging.
v **hedged, hedg·ing 1** enclose or separate with a hedge; put a hedge around or along: *to hedge a garden.* **2** avoid giving a direct answer or taking a clear stand: *Stop hedging and tell us what you want.* **3** protect against loss from an investment or bet by making a counterbalancing bet or investment: *to hedge a bet.* <Old English *hecg*>
hedg′er *n.*
hedge in, a surround on all sides: *The town was hedged in by mountains and a forest.* **b** keep from getting away or from moving freely.
hedge your bets, avoid committing yourself.

hedge·hog (hej′hog′) *n* a small mammal of Europe, Asia, and Africa, with short, sharp spines on the back. When attacked or frightened, hedgehogs roll up into a bristling ball.

hedge·row (hej′rō′) *n* a thick row of bushes or small trees forming a hedge.

he·don·ism (hē′də niz′əm) *n* the philosophy that pleasure or happiness is the highest good. <Greek *hedone* pleasure> **he′don·ist** *n.* **he′don·is′tic** *adj.*

heed (hēd) *v* take notice of: *Heed what I say.*
n careful attention: *She paid no heed to their warning.* <Old English *hedan*> **heed′less** *adj.* **heed′less·ly** *adv.* **heed′less·ness** *n.*
take heed, be careful and pay attention.

hee·haw (hē′ho′) *n* **1** the braying sound made by a donkey. **2** a loud, coarse laugh.
v make either of these sounds. <imitative>

heel[1] (hēl) *n* **1** the back part of a person's foot, below the ankle. **2** the part of a shoe or boot that is under the heel or raises the heel. **3** *Informal* an untrustworthy or contemptible person. **4** anything shaped, used, or placed at an end like a heel, such as the end crust of a loaf of bread.
v **1** follow closely behind someone: *I'm teaching my dog to heel.* **2** put a heel or heels on: *to heel a shoe.* <Old English *hela*> **heel′less** *adj.*
cool your heels, *Informal* be kept waiting a long time: *She was left cooling her heels for an hour in the waiting room.*
down at the heel, a of a shoe or shoes, with the heels worn down. **b** in a shabby or run-down condition: *The whole place looked very down at the heel.*
kick up your heels, enjoy yourself in a light-hearted, exuberant way: *She really kicked up her heels at the party.*
out at the heels, a with the heel of the stocking, sock, or shoe worn through. **b** shabby and rundown.
take to your heels, run away.
to heel, a close behind: *The dog walked to heel.* **b** under control: *He soon brought the mutineers to heel.*

heel[2] (hēl) *v* lean over, especially of a sailboat or ship.
n the act of leaning over. <Old English *heald* inclined>

heft (heft) *Informal n* mass or heaviness.
v **1** judge the mass or heaviness of something by lifting: *She hefted the baseball bat to get the feel of it.* **2** lift or heave. <made up from *heave* in imitation of other pairs such as *thieve, theft* and *cleave, cleft*>

heft·y (hef′tē) *Informal adj* **heft·i·er, heft·i·est 1** heavy: *a hefty load.* **2** large or considerable: *a hefty repair bill.* **3** big and strong. **heft′i·ness** *n.*

he·gem·o·ny (hi jem′ə nē) *or* (hej′ə mō′nē) *n, pl* **he·gem·o·nies** a domination, especially political, of one group or state over others. <Greek *hegemon* leader>

He·gi·ra (hi jī′rə) *Islam n* **1** the flight of Muhammad from Mecca to Medina in 622 CE. **2** the Muslim era, whose calendar is reckoned from this date. Also, **Hejira**. <Arabic *hijrah* flight>

heif·er (hef′ər) *n* a young cow that has not had a calf. <Old English *heahfore*>

height (hīt) *n* **1** the measurement from top to bottom or from base to top: *My height is 167 cm.* **2** distance above ground or sea level. **3** a high point or place: *on the mountain heights. They stood on a height overlooking the river.* **4** the peak: *at the height of her career.* **5** the highest degree: *That idea is the height of folly.* <Old English *heah* high>

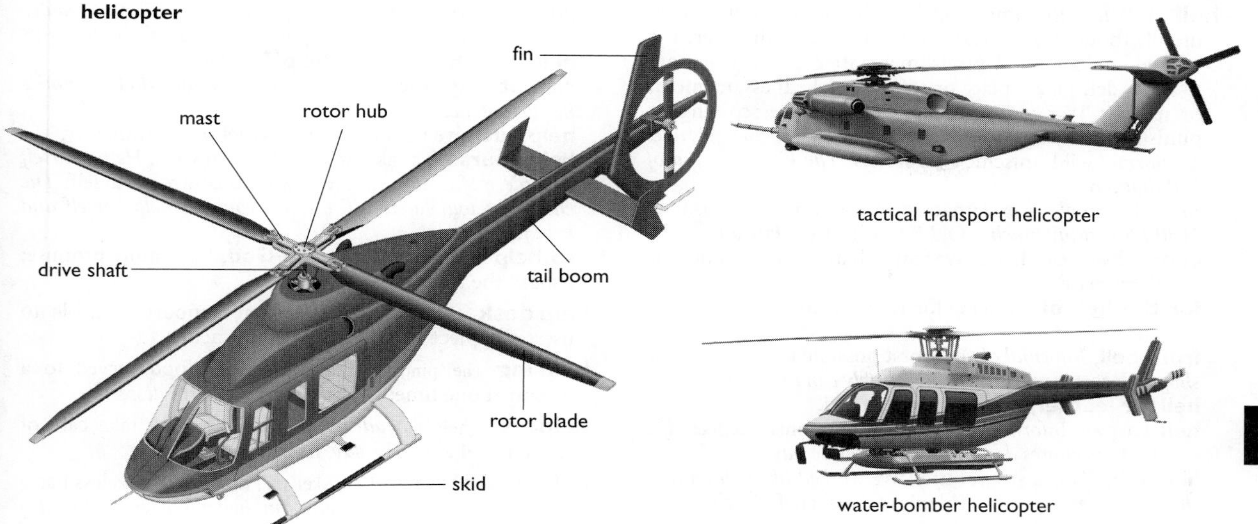

height·en (hī′tən) *v* make or become stronger, greater, or more intense: *The background music heightened the feeling of suspense.*

height of land *n* **1** any region higher than its surroundings. **2** 🍁 a DIVIDE (*n* def. 1): *A height of land marks the boundary between Labrador and Québec.*

Heil·tsuk (hīl′tsu̇k) *n, pl* **Heil·tsuk** **1** a member of a First Nations people living on the coast of British Columbia. **2** their Wakashan language. Also called **Bella Bella**.

Heim·lich manoeuvre (hīm′lik) *n* an emergency procedure used to dislodge food from a person's airway by pressing one's fist just below the rib cage and giving upward thrusts. <H. J. *Heimlich*, 20c physician>

hei·nous (hā′nəs) *adj* atrocious and abominable: *heinous crimes.* <Old French *hair* to hate> **hei′nous·ly** *adv.* **hei′nous·ness** *n.*

heir (er) *n* **1** a person who receives, or has the right to receive, someone's property or title after the owner's death. **2** a person who receives some trait, ideal, etc. from a predecessor. <Old French, from Latin *heres* heir>

heir apparent *n, pl* **heirs apparent** a person who is first in line to inherit a property or title: *The queen's oldest son is heir apparent to the throne.*

heir·ess (er′is) *n* a female heir, especially to a great fortune.

heir·loom (er′lūm′) *n* a special possession handed down from generation to generation: *This clock is a family heirloom.*

heist (hīst) *Slang n* a robbery.
v steal; rob. <*hoist*>

He·ji·ra (hi jī′rə) HEGIRA.

held (held) past tense and past participle of HOLD[1].

hel·i·cal (hel′ə kəl) *adj* in the form of a helix.

hel·i·ces (hel′ə sēz′) a plural of HELIX.

hel·i·cop·ter (hel′ə kop′tər) *n* an aircraft with one or more horizontal rotors by means of which it can hover, take off, and land vertically as well as move forward, backwards, or sideways in the air. <French, from Greek *helikos* spiral + *pteron* wing>

he·li·o·cen·tric (hē′lē ō sen′trik) *adj* with or representing the sun as the centre. Compare GEOCENTRIC. <Greek *helios* sun + *kentron* centre>

he·li·o·graph (hē′lē ō graf) *n* a signalling device that reflects sunlight in flashes from a flexible mirror. <Greek *helios* sun>

he·li·o·trope (hē′lē ə trōp′) *n* a herb or shrub with spikes or clusters of small white, lilac, or blue flowers that turn to face the sun. <Latin, from Greek *helios* sun + *tropos* a turning>

he·li·ot·ro·pism (hē′lē ot′rə piz′əm) *n* in some plants and other organisms, a tendency to turn toward or away from sunlight. <See HELIOTROPE.> **he′li·o·trop′ic** *adj.*

hel·i·pad (hel′ə pad′) *n* a small, level surface for helicopters to land on or take off from. <*heli*(*copter*) + (*landing*) *pad*>

hel·i·port (hel′ə pȯrt′) *n* a place for helicopters to land or take off. <*heli*(*copter*) + (*air*)*port*>

he·li·um (hē′lē əm) *n* a light, colourless, inert gas that will not burn, much used in balloons and dirigibles. *Symbol* **He** <Latin, from Greek *helios* sun. Helium was first detected from observations of the solar spectrum.>

he·lix (hē′liks) *n, pl* **hel·i·ces** (hē′li səs) or **he·lix·es** **1** a spiral form, such as a spring or the thread on a screw. **2** the rim of the outer ear. <Latin, from Greek>

a bat	e bed	i bid	o pot	u cup	th **thin**
ā cake	ē me	ī bite	ō go	ū rude	ᴛʜ then
ȧ bar	ə about	ər over	ȯ for	u̇ put	zh measure

hell (hel) *n* **1** in some religions, the home of the devil, usually thought of as below or within the earth, where the wicked suffer eternal punishment after death. Compare HEAVEN (def. 1). **2** a place or state of wickedness, torment, or misery: *War is hell.* **3** *Informal* a severe scolding or punishment: *His friends gave him hell for being so rude.* **4** *Informal* wild, mischievous spirits: *The kids were full of hell that day.*
interj Informal an exclamation of annoyance or dismay: *Hell! I forgot my lunch.* <Old English> **hell′ish** *adj.*
come hell or high water, whatever difficulties or problems arise.
for the hell of it, *Slang* for fun; not for any particular reason.
from hell, *Informal* of the worst possible kind: *This is the shopping cart from hell; you absolutely can't steer it.*
hell for leather, *Informal* at top speed.
hell to pay, *Informal* very unpleasant consequences: *If I don't get my chores done, there'll be hell to pay.*
like hell, *Slang* **a** strenuously: *We worked like hell on that thing.* **b** an expression of denial or disbelief: *"We're going to win." "Like hell you are!"*
raise hell, *Informal* cause trouble.
when hell freezes over, *Slang* never.

he'll (hēl) *contraction* **1** he will. **2** he shall.

hell·bent (hel′bent′) *adj* (*usually with* **on** *or* **for**) recklessly or stubbornly determined: *She was hellbent on getting that bike no matter what it cost.*
adv recklessly: *He came tearing hellbent around the corner.*

Hel·lene (hel′ēn) *n* a Greek. <Greek *Hellen* mythical father of the Greeks> **Hel·len′ic** (he len′ik) *adj.*

hell·fire (hel′fīr′) *n* the punishing fire supposed to exist in hell.

hell·hole (hel′hōl′) *Informal n* a place of great discomfort or squalor.

hel·lion (hel′yən) *Informal n* a very mischievous or troublesome person: *a little hellion.* <origin uncertain>

hel·lo (hə lō′) *interj* an exclamation used to attract attention or express a greeting or surprise.
n a call of greeting or surprise, or to attract attention: *By her loud hellos we figured out where she was.* <origin uncertain>

helm (helm) *n* **1** the handle or wheel by which a ship is steered. **2** a position of control or guidance: *There's a new principal at the helm this year.* <Old English *helma*> **helms′man** *n.*

hel·met (hel′mit) *n* a rigid metal or plastic covering worn to protect the whole head, such as by soldiers, cyclists, or hockey players. <Old French *helme* protective head covering> **hel′met·like′** *adj.*

help (help) *v* **1** provide with something needed or useful: *to help a person by lending money.* **2** work together with someone to make things go faster, better, etc.: *Help me set up the tent.* **3** wait on or serve in a store, etc.: *"May I help you?" asked the salesperson.* **4** improve or relieve: *This medicine might help your cough. More study would help your grades.* **5** prevent, stop, or avoid: *It can't be helped. I can't help yawning.*
n **1** the act of helping, or any person who or thing that helps: *Your advice is a great help. I need some help with my homework.* **2** a hired helper or group of hired helpers: *The restaurant owner treats his help well.* **3** a means of preventing or stopping: *There's no help for it once you've been exposed to chicken pox.* <Old English *helpan*> **help′er** *n.* **help′ful** *adj.* **help′ful·ly** *adv.*
cannot help but, cannot avoid: *I cannot help but admire her persistence.*
help out, give temporary help to get over a difficulty.
help yourself, a take or use what you wish: *Help yourself to a piece of candy while you wait.* **b** control yourself: *The child was told to sit still but she couldn't help herself and kept fidgeting.*
so help me or **so help me God,** I solemnly promise; I speak the truth.

help·desk (help′desk) *n* telephone support available to users of a piece of software or equipment.

help·ing (hel′ping) *n* the portion of food served to a person at one time: *He had two helpings of dessert.*

help·less (help′lis) *adj* unable to defend or take care of oneself. **help′less·ly** *adv.* **help′less·ness** *n.*

hel·ter–skel·ter (hel′tər skel′tər) *adv, adj* in careless haste or confusion: *The chickens ran helter-skelter as the dog bounded toward them* (*adv*). *The room had been ransacked and everything was helter-skelter* (*adj*). <imitative>

hem[1] (hem) *n* **1** a finished border or edge on a cloth article made by folding the cloth over and sewing it down. **2** a hemline.
v **hemmed, hem·ming** make a hem on: *I hemmed the dress by hand.* <Old English *hemm*>
hem in (or **around** or **about**), surround on all sides.

hem[2] (hem) *v* **hemmed, hem·ming** hesitate in speaking. <imitative>
hem and haw, hesitate in order to avoid committing oneself: *The committee hemmed and hawed and finally turned the problem over to a subcommittee.*

he–man (hē′man′) *Informal n* a man who is tough and rugged, or one who pretends to be so.
adj to do with such a man.

hem·a·tite (hem′ə tīt′) *n* an iron ore that is reddish brown or black when powdered. <Latin, from Greek *haimatites* bloodlike, from Greek *haimatos* blood, with reference to the colour of the ore>

he·ma·tol·o·gy (hē′mə tol′ə jē) *n* the branch of medicine dealing with the structure, function, and diseases of the blood. <See HEMATITE.> **he′ma·tol′o·gist** *n.*

hem·i·sphere (hem′əs fēr′) *n* **1** half of the earth's surface. The equator divides the earth into the northern and southern hemispheres, and an imaginary line passing through the North and South Poles divides it into the eastern and western hemispheres. **2** half of any sphere or globe. <French, from Greek *hemi-* half + *sphaira* sphere> **hem′i·spher′i·cal** *adj.*

hem·line (hem′līn′) *n* the bottom edge of a coat, skirt, or dress: *I like shorter hemlines.*

hem·lock (hem′lok) *n* **1** an evergreen tree of the pine family, with needles growing spirally along the stem. **2** a poisonous European plant related to parsley. <Old English *hymlice*>

hemo– *combining form* blood: *hemophilia.* <Greek *haima*>

he·mo·glo·bin (hē′mə glō′bən) *n* the protein in the red blood cells of vertebrates that carries oxygen from the lungs to the tissues, and carbon dioxide from the tissues to the lungs. <*hemo-* + Latin *globulus* globule>

he·mo·phil·i·a (hē′mə fil′ē ə) *n* an inherited condition in which the blood fails to clot normally, resulting in excessive bleeding after a cut or injury. <Latin, from *hemo-* + Greek *philia* tendency> **he′mo·phil′i·ac′** *n, adj.*

hem·or·rhage (hem′ə rij) *n* abnormally heavy or uncontrollable bleeding.
v **hem·or·rhaged, hem·or·rhag·ing** bleed heavily or uncontrollably. <Latin, from *hemo-* + Greek *rhegnynai* burst>

hem·or·rhoids (hem′ə roidz′) *pln* painfully swollen tissue near the anus, due to the dilation of blood vessels. <Latin, from *hemo-* + Greek *rhoos* flowing>

hemp (hemp) *n* a tall, Asiatic plant whose tough fibres are made into heavy string, rope, coarse cloth, etc. Some varieties are the source of hashish and marijuana. <Old English *henep*>

hen (hen) *n* **1** an adult female chicken. **2** the adult female of certain aquatic animals, such as the lobster, crab, salmon, and octopus. <Old English *henn*> **hen′like′** *adj.*
scarce as hens' teeth, *Informal* almost impossible to get.

hen·bane (hen′bān′) *n* a poisonous plant native to Europe and Asia, with large, sticky, hairy leaves, funnel-shaped yellowish flowers, and a strong, unpleasant smell.

hence (hens) *adv* **1** as a result or a logical conclusion of this: *He slept through his alarm and hence missed the bus.* **2** from this time onward: *A year hence, the incident will have been forgotten.* **3** away from here: *She lives a long way hence.* **4** from this source or origin: *Hence came several problems.* <Old English *heonan*>

GRAMMAR AND USAGE

The adverb **hence** is a more formal way to say "consequently," "therefore," or "so": *The garage sale was a great success; hence, I now have enough money to buy a new bike.*

hence·forth (hens′fôrth′) *adv* from now on.

hench·man (hench′mən) *n, pl* **hench·men** a follower or assistant of a criminal or a corrupt politician: *He had one of his henchmen collect the blackmail money.* <Old English *hengestman* horse attendant, squire>

hendeca– *combining form* eleven: *hendecagon* (a polygon with eleven sides). <Greek *hendeka*>

hen·house (hen′hous′) *n* a low shed for chickens to live in.

hen·na (hen′ə) *n* the dark orange-red dye made from the leaves of the henna shrub, used to colour fingernails and hair. <Arabic>

hen·pecked (hen′pekt′) *Informal adj* nagged or dominated by one's wife. **hen′peck′** *v.*

hen·ry (hen′rē) *n, pl* **hen·rys** the SI unit for measuring electrical inductance, equal to the electromotive force of one volt in a circuit when a current varies uniformly at the rate of one ampere per second. *Symbol* **H** <J. *Henry,* 19c physicist>

he·pat·ic (hi pat′ik) *adj* to do with the liver. <Latin, from Greek *hepatos* liver>

hep·a·ti·tis (hep′ə tī′tis) *n* inflammation of the liver. Hepatitis A, B, and C types are caused by viruses and may be spread by contaminated food and drink or infected blood. <See HEPATIC.>

hepta– *combining form* seven: *heptameter.* <Greek>

hep·tam·e·ter (hep tam′ə tər) *n* a line of poetry with seven feet. Example: And thrice/ he rout/ ed all/ his foes,/ and thrice/ he slew/ the slain.

hep·tath·lon (hep tath′lon) *n* an athletic contest for women, consisting of seven separate running, jumping, and throwing events, in which the winner is the person with the highest point total. Participants are called **heptathletes.** See TRACK AND FIELD for picture. <*hepta-* + Greek *athlon* contest>

her (hər) *pron* the objective form of SHE: *I like her.*
adj a possessive form of SHE: *She raised her hand.* <Old English *hire*>

her·ald (her′əld) *n* **1** especially in the Middle Ages, an officer who carried messages, made announcements, and had other ceremonial duties. **2** a person who delivers formal messages or announcements. **3** a person or thing viewed as a sign that something is about to happen: *Dawn is the herald of day.* **4** *UK* an officer in charge of coats of arms and pedigrees, who also has other royal ceremonial duties.
v show a sign that something is about to happen: *The robins heralded the arrival of spring.* <German *heriwald* army chief>

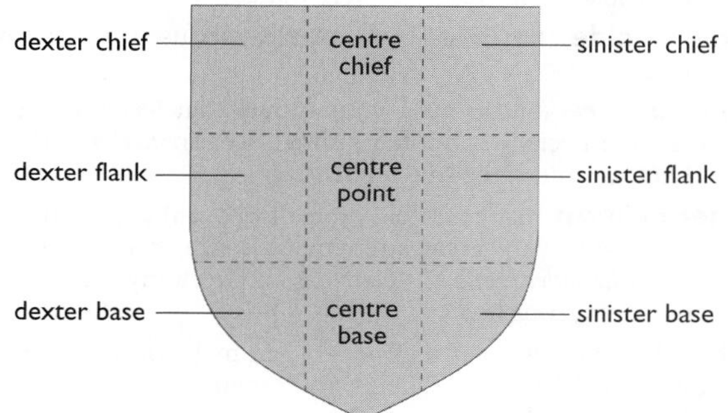

Heraldry originated in the Middle Ages when knights in battle needed to distinguish friend from foe. Unique marks on their shields made this possible. Note that dexter (right) and sinister (left) are named from the viewpoint of the person carrying the shield.

her·ald·ry (her′əld rē) *n* the science or art dealing with coats of arms. **he·ral′dic** *adj.*

a bat	e bed	i bid	o pot	u cup	th **thin**
ā cake	ē me	ī bite	ō go	ū rude	ᴛʜ **then**
ä bar	ə about	ər over	ô for	u̇ put	zh measure

herbs

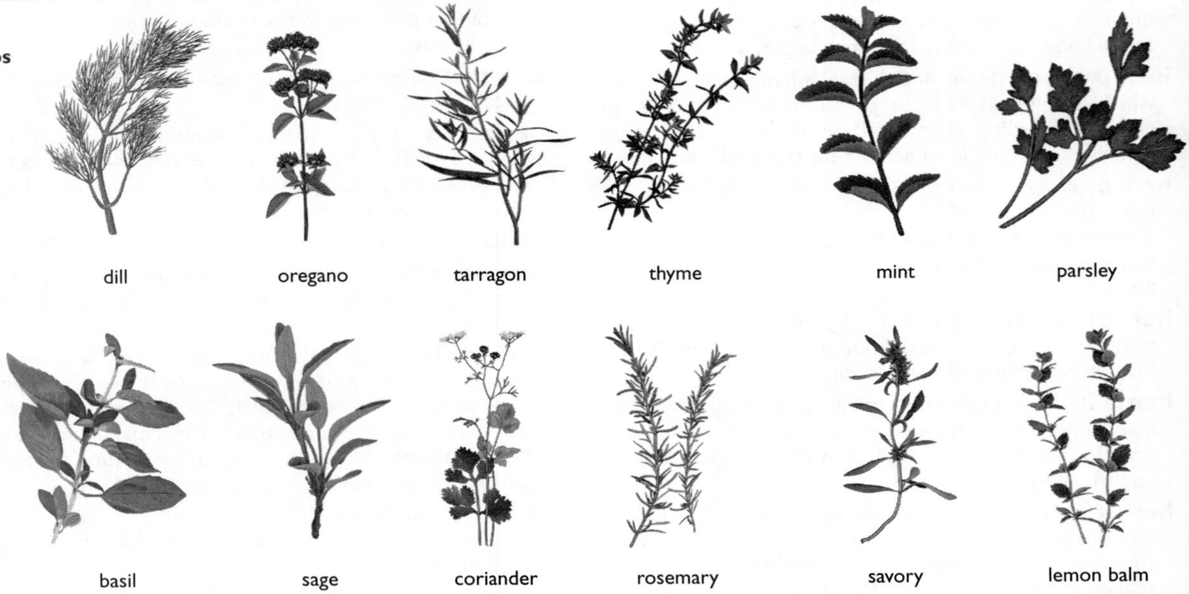

dill oregano tarragon thyme mint parsley

basil sage coriander rosemary savory lemon balm

herb (hərb) *or* (ərb) *n* **1** a flowering plant whose stem lives only one season and which therefore does not form woody tissue. **2** any of many aromatic herbs, such as sage and mint, used in medicine, food and drink, or perfumes. <Old French, from Latin *herba*> **herb′al** *adj.*

her·ba·ceous (hər bā′shəs) *Botany adj* with stems that are soft and not woody.

herb·al·ist (hər′bə list′) *n* an expert in herbs, especially one who sells or prescribes herbal medicines.

her·bi·cide (hər′bə sīd′) *n* a preparation used to destroy plants.

her·bi·vore (hər′bə vôr′) *n* an animal that feeds only on plants, especially a hoofed animal. <Latin *herba* herb + *vorare* devour> **her·biv′o·rous** *adj.*

her·cu·le·an (hər′kyə lē′ən) *or* (hər kyū′lē ən) *adj* requiring or showing very great strength or courage: *a herculean task, a herculean effort.* <*Hercules*, in Greek myth a strong and courageous hero>

herd (hərd) *n* **1** a number of animals of one kind, especially hoofed ones, living and moving together: *a herd of cows, a herd of elephants.* **2** people considered as a mass or mob: *the common herd.* **3** (*in compounds*) the keeper of a herd: *cowherd, goatherd.*
v **1** move or cause to move in a herd: *The cattle were herded into the corral. Many animals herd for protection.* **2** drive or take care of livestock: *His job is herding sheep.* <Old English *heord*> **herd′er** *n.* **herds′man** *n.*

here (hēr) *adv* **1** to do with this place or this point in time: *Put it here. Sit here. Here the speaker paused.* **2** a word used to call attention to the presence of a person or thing mentioned: *My friend here can probably give you a hand. Here is your scarf.*
n this place: *Fill the bottle up to here.*
interj an exclamation expressing indignation, rebuke, etc.: *Here! What do you think you're doing?* See HEAR for confusable. <Old English *her*>
here and there, in various places: *Here and there we saw an early crocus blooming.*
here goes, *Informal* an exclamation announcing something is about to be done: *Well, here goes! Wish me luck!*
here's to, a toast or congratulations to: *Here's to the best coach in the league!*
here, there, and everywhere, in many different places: *Toys lay here, there, and everywhere.*
here we go again, an unpleasant event is happening again.
here you are or **here you go,** a polite phrase used when giving something to someone.
neither here nor there, unimportant: *Why he left is neither here nor there; the question is, where is he?*

here·a·bouts (hē′rə bouts′) *adv* around here.

here·af·ter (hēr af′tər) *adv* **1** after this. **2** in life after death.
n **the hereafter** **1** the future. **2** life after death.

here·by (hēr bī′) *adv* (*in a document*) by this means: *The licence read, "You are hereby given the right to fish in Ontario."*

he·red·i·tar·y (hə red′ə ter′ē) *adj* **1** transmitted through the genes: *Colour blindness is hereditary.* Compare CONGENITAL. **2** coming by inheritance, such as a title, office, or right: *"Prince" is a hereditary title.* **3** derived from one's parents or ancestors; established by tradition: *a hereditary enemy, hereditary beliefs,*

he·red·i·ty (hə red′ə tē) *Biology n, pl* **he·red·i·ties** the transmission of physical or mental characteristics or qualities from parent to offspring through the genes. <Old French, from Latin *hereditat* inheritance>

here·in (hēr in′) *adv* in this place, thing, or document: *the parties named herein. Herein lies the difference.*

her·e·sy (her′ə sē) *n, pl* **her·e·sies** **1** a belief that strongly differs from the accepted belief of a church, political party, or profession. **2** the holding of such a belief, especially publicly. <Old French *heresie* school of thought, from Greek *haireisthai* choose>

her·e·tic (her′ə tik) *n* a person who holds a strong belief different from the accepted belief of a church, political party, or profession. <See HERESY.> **he·ret′i·cal** *adj.*

here·to·fore (hēr′tə fôr′) *or* (hēr′tə fôr′) *adv* before now.

here·with (hēr with′) *adv* with this.

her·it·a·ble (her′ə tə bəl) *adj* capable of being inherited.

her·it·age (her′ə tij) *n* **1** what is received from one's ancestors, especially traditions, values, language, or a home. **2** something that a person has as a result of having been born in a certain time, place, or condition: *a heritage of freedom.*

❦ **Heritage Day** *n* a day set aside to celebrate the history of Canada and the heritage of Canadians, the third Monday in February.

❦ **heritage language** *n* a language, other than French or English, which is that of a person's ethnic background.

her·maph·ro·dite (hər maf′rə dīt′) *n* **1** an animal or plant with the reproductive organs of both sexes. **2** a person who or thing that combines opposite qualities. <Latin, from *Hermaphroditos*, in Greek myth the son of *Hermes* and *Aphrodite*, who became united in body with a nymph> **her·maph′ro·dit′ic** (hər maf′rə dit′ik) *adj.*

her·met·ic (hər met′ik) *adj* **1** completely sealed, especially against the entry of air. **2** unable to be affected by outside interference. <Latin *hermeticus*, from *Hermes* Trismegistus, the mythical inventor of an airtight glass tube> **her·met′i·cal·ly** *adv.*

her·mit (hər′mit) *n* **1** a person who lives alone in some isolated place, often for religious reasons. **2** a spiced cookie, usually containing raisins and nuts. <Old French, from Greek *eremos* uninhabited> **her′mit·like′** *adj.*

her·mit·age (hər′mə tij) *n* the home of a hermit.

hermit crab *n* a small, soft-bodied crab found mainly in the ocean, with eyes on long stalks and living in the empty shells of snails or similar animals.

her·ni·a (hər′nē ə) *n* a condition in which part of an organ of the body pushes itself through a break in its surrounding walls. <Latin>

he·ro (hē′rō) *n, pl* **he·roes** **1** a person who does great and brave deeds and is admired for them: *the heroes of old, a hero in the field of science.* **2** anyone who is admired or looked up to: *The toddler's hero is his eight-year-old brother.* **3** the most important male character in a story, play, or movie. **4** in myth and legend, a man or boy of superhuman qualities: *Hercules was a hero.* <Latin, from Greek *heros*>

he·ro·ic (hə rō′ik) *adj* **1** like a hero or heroine in deeds or character: *the heroic deeds of our firefighters.* **2** of or about heroes and their deeds: *Homer's* Iliad *is a heroic poem.* **3** unusually daring or bold: *Only heroic measures could save the town from the flood.*
n **1** a heroic poem. **2** **heroics** *pl* talk, feelings, or actions that seem grand or noble but are only for effect: *We are all getting a little tired of his heroics.* **he·ro′i·cal·ly** *adv.*

heroic couplet *n* a pair of rhyming lines in iambic pentameter, used in the poems of Chaucer and in poetry of the 1600s and 1700s.

her·o·in (her′ō in) *n* a powerful, habit-forming, pain-killing drug made from morphine. <German *Heroin*, a former trademark>

her·o·ine (her′ō in) *n* **1** a woman or girl admired for her bravery or great deeds: *Laura Secord and Madeleine de Verchères are Canadian heroines.* **2** any female who is admired or looked up to: *The toddler's heroine is his eight-year-old sister.* **3** the most important female character in a story, play, or movie. **4** in myth and legend, a woman or girl of superhuman qualities.

her·o·ism (her′ō iz′əm) *n* the actions and qualities of a hero or heroine.

her·on (her′ən) *n* a large, freshwater wading bird with a long neck. <Old French *hairon*>

hero–wor·ship (hē′ro wər′ship) *n* **1** the idolizing of great people, or of people thought of as heroes. **2** in ancient Greece and Rome, the worship of ancient heroes as gods. **he′ro–wor′ship** *v.* **he′ro–wor′ship·per** *n.*

her·pes (hər′pēz) *n* a viral disease of the skin, mucous membranes, or nervous system, often characterized by clusters of blisters. **Herpes simplex** is marked by watery blisters on the mouth and lips or on the genitals. **Herpes zoster** is better known as SHINGLES. <Latin = a spreading skin disease, from Greek *herpein* creep>

her·pe·tol·o·gy (hər′pə tol′ə jē) *n* the branch of zoology that studies reptiles and amphibians. <Greek *herpeton* creeping animal, from *herpein* creep>
her′pe·tol′o·gist *n.*

her·ring (her′ing) *n, pl* **her·ring** or **her·rings** a small, silvery food fish of the Atlantic and Pacific. Sprats are herring. <Old English *hæring*>

her·ring·bone (her′ing bōn′) *n* **1** a zigzag pattern. **2** a fabric with a small, woven zigzag pattern: *He chose a herringbone for his suit.* **3** *Skiing* a method of going up a slope by pointing the front of the skis outward and putting the weight on the inner side.
v **her·ring·boned, her·ring·bon·ing** **1** arrange in a zigzag pattern. **2** go up a slope using the herringbone method.

❦ **herring choker** *Slang n* a person from the Maritimes, especially one from New Brunswick.

herring gull *n* a large gull of the northern hemisphere, white with black wing tips.

hers (hərz) *pron* a possessive form of SHE; that which belongs to her: *My answer was wrong; hers was correct.* <Old English *hire*>

a bat	e bed	i bid	o pot	u cup	th **thin**
ā cake	ē me	ī bite	ō go	ū rude	ᴛʜ then
à bar	ə about	ər over	ô for	ù put	zh measure

her·self (hər self′) *pron* 1 the object of a reflexive verb with *she* as subject: *She asked herself if it was really worth all the trouble.* 2 an intensive pronoun, used to emphasize the noun or pronoun it follows: *She herself told me.* 3 her usual self: *She is not herself today.*

hertz (hərts) *n, pl* **hertz** the SI unit for measuring the frequency of waves and vibrations, equal to one cycle per second. *Symbol* **Hz** <H. *Hertz,* 19c physicist>

he's (hez) *contraction* 1 he is: *He's tall.* 2 he has: *He's walked a long way.*

hes·i·tant (hez′ə tənt) *adj* tentative, unsure, or slow in speaking or acting. **hes′i·tan·cy** *n.* **hes′i·tant·ly** *adv.*

hes·i·tate (hez′ə tāt′) *v* **hes·i·tat·ed, hes·i·tat·ing** 1 be tentative, unsure, or slow in speaking or acting: *I hesitated about taking his side until I knew the whole story.* 2 (*with* ***to***) be reluctant to do something: *I hesitated to ask you because you were so busy.* 3 pause for a moment: *She hesitated before asking the question.* <Latin *haesitare* be undecided, from *haerere* to cling> **hes′i·ta′tion** *n.*

hetero– *combining form* other or different: *heterogeneous.* <Greek *heteros* other>

het·er·o·dox (het′ər ə doks′) *adj* to do with any belief or practice that differs from an accepted custom or standard. Compare ORTHODOX. <Latin, from *hetero-* + Greek *doxa* opinion> **het′er·o·dox′y** *n.*

het·er·o·ge·ne·ous (het′ə rə jē′nē əs) *adj* made up of unlike elements or parts: *a heterogeneous mixture of soil and water. We are a heterogeneous group.* Compare HOMOGENEOUS. <Latin, from *hetero-* + Greek *genos* kind> **het′er·o·ge·ne′i·ty** (het′ə rə jə nē′ə tē) *n.* **het′er·o·ge′ne·ous·ly** *adv.*

het·er·o·sex·ism (het′ə rə sek′siz əm) *n* discrimination in favour of heterosexuals and against homosexuals. **het′er·o·sex′ist** *adj, n.*

het·er·o·sex·u·al (het′ə rə sek′shū əl) *adj* 1 characterized by sexual attraction to a person of the opposite sex. Compare HOMOSEXUAL. 2 to do with different sexes.
n a heterosexual person. <Greek *heteros* other + *sex*> **het′er·o·sex′u·al′i·ty** *n.*

het·er·o·troph (het′ə rə trof′) *Biology n* an organism that obtains food from organic material only, and not from inorganic matter. <*hetero-* + Greek *trophe* food>

heu·ris·tic (hyə ris′tik) *adj* 1 guiding or helping one to discover things for oneself by personal investigation, observation, etc.: *a heuristic method of education.* 2 *Computers* to do with a technique or procedure used to solve a problem by trial and error or with loosely defined rules. <Greek *heuriskein* to discover>

hew (hyū) *v* **hewed, hewed** or **hewn, hew·ing** 1 chop or cut with an axe, pick, or other tool: *to hew down a tree.* 2 shape by cutting a material, especially wood or stone: *to hew stone for building, to hew logs into beams.* <Old English *heawan*>

hex (heks) *Informal v* bewitch or put a spell on.
n a magic spell. <German *Hexe* witch>

hex– (heks) *combining form* six: *hexagon.*

hex·a·gon (hek′sə gon′) *n* a plane figure with six interior angles and six sides. <Latin, from Greek *hex* six + *gonia* angle> **hex·ag′o·nal** *adj.*

hex·a·he·dron (hek′sə hē′drən) *n, pl* **hex·a·he·drons** or **hex·a·he·dra** a solid figure with six faces. <Greek *hex* six + *hedra* surface> **hex′a·he′dral** *adj.*

hex·am·e·ter (hek sam′ə tər) *n* a line of poetry with six feet. Example: He seeks/ out might/y charms,/ to trou/ble sleep/y minds. <Latin, from Greek *hex* six + *metron* measure>

hey (hā) *interj* an exclamation made to attract attention, to express surprise, interest, or annoyance, or to gain agreement: *"Hey! Stop!" "Hey, we got here, didn't we?"*

hey·day (hā′dā′) *n* the period of greatest power, status, vigour, or prosperity: *In her heyday, she was the best basketball player in the division.* <origin uncertain>

hi (hī) *Informal interj* a call used as a greeting; hello.

hi·a·tus (hī ā′təs) *n* 1 an empty space; a gap. *Someone interrupted us so there was a brief hiatus in our talk.* 2 a slight pause between two vowels that come together in successive syllables or word, such as the one between the two e's in *pre-eminent.* <Latin = gap, from *hiare* to gape>

hi·ba·chi (hi bá′chē) *n* a portable metal container for burning charcoal to heat or grill food. <Japanese>

hi·ber·nate (hī′bər nāt′) *v* **hi·ber·nat·ed, hi·ber·nat·ing** 1 spend the winter in sleep or in an inactive condition, as bears, groundhogs, and some other wild animals do. 2 be or become inactive or remain indoors for a period of time: *I think I'll just hibernate for the first week of my holidays.* <Latin *hibernus* winter> **hi′ber·na′tion** *n.*

hi·bis·cus (hə bis′kəs) *n* a herb, shrub, or small tree, often cultivated for large flowers of various colours. <Latin>

hic·cup (hik′up) *n* 1 a sudden, involuntary contraction of the diaphragm that causes the opening of the windpipe to close just when one is inhaling, producing a characteristic short clicking sound. 2 **hiccups** *pl* (*often with* ***the***) the condition of having one hiccup after another: *I've got the hiccups.* 3 a small, unexplained misfunction or hesitation: *Some hiccup in the program caused the dates on all the invoices to be off by one day.*
v **hic·cupped, hic·cup·ping** make or have a hiccup: *He hiccupped.* <probably imitative>

hick (hik) *Slang n* an unsophisticated person from a rural area or small town.
adj to do with such people: *a hick accent.* <*Hick,* form of Richard, a man's name>

hick·o·ry (hik′ə rē) *n, pl* **hick·o·ries** a N American tree with hard, edible nuts and tough wood, related to the walnut. <Algonquian>

hid (hid) past tense and a past participle of HIDE[1].

hid·den (hid′ən) *v* a past participle of HIDE[1].
adj 1 concealed or secret: *a hidden passageway.* 2 mysterious or obscure: *hidden meanings.*

hide[1] (hīd) *v* **hid, hid·den** or **hid, hid·ing** 1 put something where others will not see it: *She hid the presents in the attic. He hid his face in the pillow.* 2 keep secret: *to hide your laughter.* 3 go or stay where one will not be seen by others: *I'll hide, and you find me. The shy little boy hid behind his mother's skirt.* 4 shut off from sight: *Clouds hid the moon.* 5 (*with* ***from***) avoid: *to hide from trouble.* <Old English *hydan*>

hide out, keep oneself hidden so as to avoid notice or capture: *The bandits hid out in a mountain shack.*

hide[2] (hīd) *n* **1** the skin of an animal, either raw or tanned. **2** *Informal* a person's skin. <Old English *hyd*>
neither hide nor hair of, nothing at all of

hide–and–seek (hīd′ən sēk′) *n* a children's game in which one player has to find the others, who hide in different places. Also, **hide-and-go-seek**.

hide·a·way (hī′də wā′) *n* **1** a place to hide. **2** a quiet, restful, usually isolated place where one can go to be alone or escape one's busy routine for a while.

hide·bound (hīd′bound′) *adj* narrow-minded and stubborn: *He was too hidebound to accept new ideas.*

hid·e·ous (hid′ē əs) *adj* ugly, disgusting, or very unpleasant: *a hideous monster, a hideous story.* <Old French *hide* horror> **hid′e·ous·ly** *adv.* **hid′e·ous·ness** *n.*

hide·out (hī′dout′) *n* a place for hiding or escaping from others.

hid·ing[1] (hī′ding) *n* the condition of being hidden: *They went into hiding right after the robbery.*

hid·ing[2] (hī′ding) *Informal n* a physical beating.

hie (hī) *Archaic, Poetic, or Humorous v* **hied, hie·ing** or **hy·ing** go quickly: *Hie thee hence!* <Old English *higian*>

hi·er·ar·chy (hī′rȧr′kē) *n, pl* **hi·er·ar·chies** any organization of people or things in higher and lower ranks: *He has the lowest position in the office hierarchy.* <Latin, from Greek *hieros* sacred (one) + *archos* ruler. *Hierachy* originally referred to a ranked division of angels.> **hi′er·ar′chi·cal** *adj.*

hi·er·o·glyph·ic (hī′rə glif′ik) *n* **1** a picture or symbol standing for a word, idea, or sound: *He showed me the Egyptian hieroglyphic for "bird."* Also, **hieroglyph**. **2 hieroglyphics** *pl* a system of writing that uses such symbols.
adj to do with hieroglyphics. <Latin, from Greek *hieros* sacred + *glyphe* carving. Writing in ancient Egypt was done by priests.> **hi′er·o·glyph′i·cal·ly** *adv.*

hi–fi (hī′fī′) *for n,* (hī′fī′) *for adj. Informal n* sound equipment delivering high-fidelity sound reproduction.
adj high-fidelity.

hig·gle·dy–pig·gle·dy (hig′əl dē pig′əl dē) *adj, adv* in jumbled confusion: *On the shelf was a higgledy-piggledy arrangement of odds and ends* (*adj*). *They ran higgledy-piggledy out the door* (*adv*). <imitative>

high (hī) *adj* **1** at or reaching far above the ground or some base: *a high building, an airplane high in the sky.* **2** rising to a specified extent: *The mountain is 6100 m high.* **3** done from a height: *a high dive.* **4** above others in rank, position, or quality: *a high official, a person of high character.* **5** greater than average: *a high fever, high crimes, high treason.* **6** above normal pitch, degree, etc.: *a high voice, high water, high temperature.* **7** at its peak: *high summer.* **8** stinking, especially as a result of decay. **9** *Informal* intoxicated; under the influence of alcohol or drugs.
adv at or to a high point, rank, amount, degree, price, or pitch: *The eagle flies high.*
n the highest level reached or to be reached by something, especially a price or the daily temperature: *They've forecast a high of 19°C for Friday.* <Old English *heah*>
fly high, have big ideas, plans, hopes, ambitions, etc.: *She was flying high after winning the award.*
high and dry, a up out of the water: *The fish lay high and dry on the beach.* **b** all alone without help: *He has left me high and dry with all this work to do.*
high and low, everywhere: *I looked high and low for it.*
high and mighty, acting as though one is superior to others.
high time, the last or almost the last opportunity to do something: *If your test is tomorrow, it's high time you started studying.*
on high, a in or to a high place. **b** in a high rank. **c** in heaven.
run high, a of water, be rougher or higher and swifter than usual: *The seas ran high. Rivers run high in the spring.* **b** become emotionally heated: *Tempers ran high at the town meeting.*

high·ball (hī′bol′) *n* **1** a drink consisting of whisky or other liquor mixed with soda water or ginger ale and served with ice in a tall glass. **2** *Informal* a high bid, estimate, or asking price. **3** a railway signal to proceed.
v **1** *Informal* give a high bid, estimate, or asking price on something or to someone: *They deliberately highballed the estimate so they could bring the price down later.* **2** *Slang* move or drive very fast. **3** signal to a train engineer to proceed.

high beams *pl n* on a motor vehicle, headlights switched to a setting that directs them higher so that they shine farther: *At night, on poorly-lit roads, it's a good idea to use high beams.* Compare LOW BEAMS.

high·born (hī′bórn′) *adj* born into the nobility.

high·boy (hī′boi′) *n* a tall chest of drawers on legs.

high·brow (hī′brou′) *Informal n* a person interested in the arts and intellectual things.
adj of or suitable for highbrows: *highbrow music, a highbrow discussion.*

high·chair (hī′cher′) *n* a baby's raised seat for feeding, usually with a detachable feeding tray.

high–class (hī′klas′) *adj* of high quality or social status: *a high-class restaurant.*

High Commission *n* the embassy of one Commonwealth country in another.
High Commissioner *n.*

high–definition television HDTV.

high–density lipoprotein (lī′pō prō′tēn) HDL.

high·er (hī′ər) *adj* **1** further up or closer to the top. **2** more advanced: *higher mathematics, higher education.*

high·er–up (hī′ər up′) *Informal n* a person holding a superior position in an organization: *The change was vetoed by the higher-ups.*

a bat	e bed	i bid	o pot	u cup	th thin
ā cake	ē me	ī bite	ō go	ū rude	TH then
ȧ bar	ə about	ər over	ȯ for	u̇ put	zh measure

H

high jump

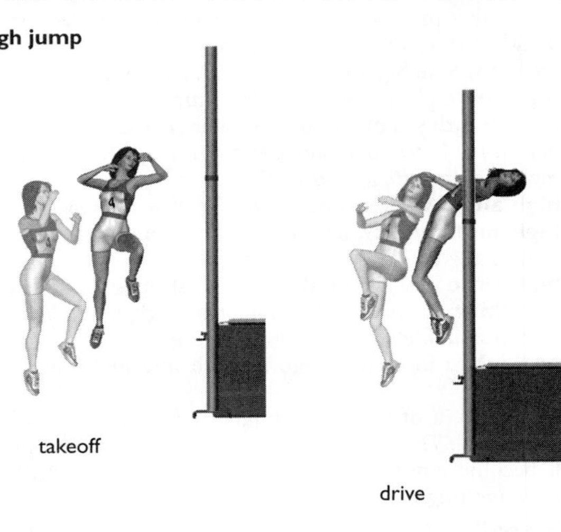

In the **high jump**, competitors can choose the bar height they wish to begin at. Once a height has been cleared, the other competitors may not start at a lower height. The bar is moved up usually by 3 or 5 cm, and often by just 1 cm for attempts at a world record.

high·fa·lu·tin (hī′fə lū′tən) *Informal adj* pompous or pretentious. <origin unknown>

high–fi·del·i·ty (hī′fə del′ə tē) *adj* to do with sound reproduction that delivers the full range of frequencies with little distortion.

high–five (hī′fīv′) *Slang n* a gesture of triumph or greeting in which two people each raise a hand above their heads and slap each other's palms.
v **high-fived, high-fiv·ing** make this gesture with (someone): *She high-fived me when I got the ball over the net.*

high–flown (hī′flōn′) *adj* attempting to be elegant or noble by using extravagant language: *high-flown compliments.*,

high frequency *n* the range of radio frequencies between 3 and 30 MHz, in the range next above medium frequency. **high′-fre′quen·cy** *adj.*

high–grade (hī′grād′) *adj* of fine or superior quality: *high-grade ore, a high-grade scholarship.*

high–hand·ed (hī′han′did) *adj* using one's authority in an overbearing way: *It is a bit high-handed of you to order people around like that.* **high′-hand′ed·ly** *adv.* **high′-hand′ed·ness** *n.*

high jump *n* an athletic contest in which people try to jump over a bar that keeps being raised higher and higher.

high·land (hī′lənd) *n* **1** an area that is higher and hillier than the neighbouring region. **2 the Highlands** *pl* a hilly region in north and west Scotland.
adj **1** to do with such an area: *a highland meadow.* **2 Highland** to do with the Highlands. **High′land′er** *n.*

Highland fling *n* a lively dance of the Scottish Highlands.

high life *n* a fashionable and luxurious lifestyle.

high·light (hī′līt′) *n* **1** the most interesting or most striking part, event, or scene: *The highlight of our trip was the drive along the Cabot Trail.* **2** an effect, such as in a painting or photograph, of bright light falling on something. **3 highlights** *pl* subtle streaks of lighter or brighter colour added to something, such as the hair, giving a warmer or more lustrous appearance.
v **high·light·ed, high·light·ing** **1** make prominent or treat as a special feature: *The fiftieth anniversary of our school was highlighted in the local paper.* **2** emphasize with lighting or colour: *The photographer highlighted the child's curly hair, to highlight sentences in a printout.*

high·light·er (hī′līt′ər) *n* a marking pen with coloured ink through which other writing can still be easily seen.

high·ly (hī′lē) *adv* **1** in a high or favourable degree: *highly suspicious.* **2** highly ranked: *a highly regarded scientist, a highly placed official.*

high–mind·ed (hī′mīn′did) *adj* with strong moral principles. **high′-mind′ed·ly** *adv.* **high′-mind′ed·ness** *n.*

🍁 **high muck·a·muck** (muk′ə muk′) *Slang n* a person in a position of power, especially one who is arrogant. <Chinook jargon *hyiu muckamuck* a good big meal>

high·ness (hī′nis) *n* **1** the condition of being high. **2 Highness** a title of honour given to members of royal families: *The Prince of Wales is addressed as "Your Highness" and spoken of as "His Royal Highness."*

high noon *n* exactly 12 o'clock in the daytime.

high–oc·tane (hī′ok′tān) *adj* **1** with a high percentage of octane in gasoline. **2** *Informal* with a powerful effect: *high-octane coffee.*

high–pitched (hī′picht′) *adj* **1** sounding shrill: *a high-pitched whistle.* **2** of a roof, steeply sloped. **3** showing intense feeling: *high-pitched excitement.*

high–pow·ered (hī′pou′ərd) *adj* with much power or energy: *a high-powered car, a high-powered sales talk.*

high–pres·sure (hī′presh′ər) *adj* **1** made by or involving the use of a relatively high pressure: *a high-pressure laminate.* **2** with or showing high barometric pressure: *There is a high-pressure area just to the south.* **3** *Informal* using or involving a strong, insistent approach or argument, especially in selling: *a high-pressure sales pitch.* **4** involving a lot of emotional tension or strain: *She has a high-pressure job.*
v **high-pres·sured, high-pres·sur·ing** use insistent argument or persuasion: *He was high-pressured into buying the more expensive model.*

high priest *n* a chief priest in some religions.

high relief *n* **1** HAUT-RELIEF. **2** a situation or condition in which something is strongly emphasized: *Recent accidents have brought the lack of pedestrian crossings into high relief.*

high–res·o·lu·tion (hī′rez′ə lū′shən) *adj* to do with very sharp, clear images: *a high-resolution computer monitor.* Often shortened informally to **high-res**.

high–rise (hī′rīz′) *adj* **1** with many storeys: *high-rise apartment buildings.* **2** higher than usual: *high-rise jeans.*
n a building with many storeys: *He lives in a high-rise downtown.* Compare LOW-RISE.

high road *n* a direct and certain way: *There is no high road to success.*

high school *n* a school that follows elementary or public school: *Some provinces have junior high schools, intermediate between elementary and high school.* **high′-school′** *adj.*

GRAMMAR AND USAGE

Capitalize **high school** only when using it as part of a proper name to refer to a particular school:
She graduated from high school last year.
He graduated from Gravenhurst High School in 2005.

high seas *pln* the open ocean, far from any coast: *The high seas are outside the authority of any country.*

high–sound·ing (hī′soun′ding) *adj* intended to sound noble or impressive: *high-sounding words.*

high–spir·it·ed (hī′spir′ə tid) *adj* **1** showing a bold, proud, or energetic spirit: *a high-spirited horse.* **2** happy and excited: *It took the babysitter a while to settle the high-spirited children.* **high′-spir′it·ed·ly** *adv.* **high′-spir′it·ed·ness** *n.*

high spirits *pln* liveliness and happiness.

high·stick·ing (hī′stik′ing) *Hockey, Lacrosse n* the act of illegally striking or hindering an opposing player with one's stick carried above shoulder level.

high–strung (hī′strung′) *adj* very sensitive, nervous, or easily excited.

high·tail (hī′tāl′) *Informal v* (*with **it***) run away at full speed.

high tech *n* in full, **high technology** sophisticated electronic equipment, especially computers and telecommunication systems. Also **hi tech**.
high′-tech′ *adj.*

high–ten·sion (hī′ten′shən) *adj* carrying a high voltage in electric power lines.

high–test (hī′test′) *adj* vaporizing at a low temperature in gasoline: *High-test gas is used in cars in winter because it forms a vapour in the engine quickly.*

high tide *n* the highest level of the tide.

high–toned (hī′tōnd′) *adj* **1** fancy and expensive: *a high-toned neighbourhood.* **2** morally superior.

high–wa·ter mark (hī′wȧ′tər) *n* **1** the highest level reached by a body of water. **2** any highest point: *This movie turned out to be the high-water mark of his career as an actor.*

high·way (hī′wā′) *n* **1** a main road or route connecting towns or cities. **2** a main road with few intersections and turns, designed for high speeds. **3** a direct way to some goal.

high·way·man (hī′wā′mən) *n, pl* **high·way·men** in former times, a man, usually on horseback, who robbed travellers on a public road.

high wire *n* a tightrope high above the ground, on which an acrobat performs balancing acts.
adj **high-wire** **1** to do with activities on a high wire: *an amazing high-wire act at the circus.* **2** to do with risky activities requiring great skill or judgment: *a high-wire career as a professional hockey player.*
Also (*adj*), **highwire**.

hi·jack (hī′jak′) *v* **1** stop a vehicle by force or threat and steal it or its cargo: *The truck was hijacked about 70 km out of the city. Several shipments have been hijacked.* **2** seize control of an aircraft in flight by force or threat, in order to obtain money or some other concession. **3** seize control of any process or interfere with it so that it fails: *Protesters keep hijacking the peace talks.* <origin uncertain> **hi′jack′er** *n.*

hi·jinks (hī′jingks) *Informal pln* lively fun or practical jokes. Also, **high jinks**. <origin uncertain>

hike (hīk) *v* **hiked, hik·ing** **1** take a long walk, especially through woods or fields: *The scouts hiked into the hills.* **2** pull up with a jerk: *He hiked himself up onto the platform.* **3** increase prices or wages.
n **1** a long walk, especially through woods or fields: *We're going on a hike today.* **2** an increase: *a hike in prices.* <possibly related to *hitch*> **hik′er** *n.*

hil·ar·i·ous (hə ler′ē əs) *adj* **1** very funny: *a hilarious joke.* **2** filled with laughter and high spirits: *It was a hilarious evening.* <Latin, from Greek *hilaros* merry> **hi·lar′i·ous·ly** *adv.* **hi·lar′i·ty** *n.*

hill (hil) *n* **1** a raised part on the earth's surface, smaller than a mountain. **2** a pile or mound of earth or sand: *Moles had made hills all over the lawn. The potatoes were planted in hills.* <Old English *hyll*> **hill′y** *adj.*
over the hill, *Informal* past one's peak of achievement.

a bat	e bed	i bid	o pot	u cup	th **thin**
ā cake	ē me	ī bite	ō go	ū rude	ᴛʜ **then**
ȧ bar	ə about	ər over	ȯ for	ů put	zh measure

hill·bil·ly (hil′bil′ē) *Informal or Offensive n, pl* **hill·bil·lies** an unsophisticated country or backwoods person, especially one from the mountains.
adj of or relating to such people: *hillbilly music.*

hill·side (hil′sīd′) *n* the side of a hill.

hill·top (hil′top′) *n* the top of a hill.

hilt (hilt) *n* the handle of a weapon or tool, especially a sword, dagger, or knife. <Old English>
to the hilt, thoroughly; completely. *She was up to the hilt in trouble.*

him (him) *pron* the objective form of HE: *I admire him.* <Old English>

Him·a·la·yas (him′ə lā′əz) *pln* a high mountain range along the border between India and Tibet. <Sanskrit *hima* snow + *alaya* home> **Him′a·lay′an** *adj, n.*

him·self (him self′) *pron* **1** the object of a reflexive verb with *he* as subject: *He asked himself what he really wanted.* **2** an intensive pronoun, used to emphasize the noun or pronoun it follows: *Just then the principal himself walked in.* **3** his usual self: *He hasn't been himself all week.*

hind[1] (hīnd) *adj* back or rear: *The mule kicked up its hind legs.* <Old english *hindrian*>

hind[2] (hīnd) *n, pl* **hind** or **hinds** a female deer, usually a female red deer after its third year. <Old English>

hin·der (hin′dər) *v* hold back or get in the way of: *She was hindered by deep snow. Don't let this disagreement hinder completion of the project.* <Old English *hindrian*>

Hin·di (hin′dē) *n* one of the official languages of India, and the one most widely spoken there. <Persian *Hind* India>

hind·most (hīnd′mōst′) *adj, n* farthest back or last.

hind·quar·ter (hīnd′kwôr′tər) *n* **1** the hind leg and loin of an animal butchered for food. **2 hindquarters** *pl* the rear end and back legs of an animal.

hin·drance (hin′drəns) *n* **1** a person who or thing that hinders: *The noise was a hindrance to our studying.* **2** the act of hindering.

hind·sight (hīnd′sīt′) *n* the ability to recognize, after the event is over, what should have been done.

Hin·du·ism (hin′dū iz′əm) *n* a religion and way of life with many forms, which share a belief in reincarnation. <Persian *Hindu,* from *Hind* India> **Hin′du** *adj, n.*

Hin·du·sta·ni (hin′dū stä′nē) *n* a group of languages spoken in northwest India, including Hindi and Urdu.
adj to do with these languages, their speakers, or with northwest India.

hinge (hinj) *n* **1** a jointed attachment by which a door, gate, or lid moves back and forth or up and down on its frame. **2** a natural joint with a similar function: *the hinge of a clam shell.* **3** the determining factor: *Her permission is the hinge on which this whole plan turns.*
v **hinged, hing·ing 1** furnish with or attach by a hinge or hinges. **2** depend: *The success of the event will hinge on the dedication of the people involved.* <Middle English *heng*>

hint (hint) *n* **1** a slight indication: *A small black cloud gave a hint of the coming storm.* **2** something expressed indirectly: *When she stood up, he took it as a hint that the discussion was over.* **3** a very small amount: *The soup has just a hint of garlic.* **4** a small piece of practical information or advice: *helpful hints for the traveller.*
v give or be a hint: *He yawned heavily to hint that he was tired. The unsettled weather hinted at a storm.* <Old English *hentan*>

hin·ter·land (hin′tər land′) *n* **1** a region far from major urban centres and outside their influence. **2** the interior part of a country. <German *hinter* behind + *Land* land>

hip[1] (hip) *n* **1** the projecting upper part of the pelvis and upper thigh bone on each side of the body: *She broke her hip.* **2** the parts on each side of the body between the waist and the upper thighs: *The safety belt should go around your hips.* **3** the corresponding part(s) of a four-legged animal's body, where a hind leg joins the trunk. <Old English *hype*>

hip[2] (hip) *n* the pod containing the ripe seed of a rose, especially a wild rose. <Old English *heope*>

hip[3] (hip) *Slang adj* aware of or following the latest trends and fashions. <origin uncertain>
hip to, *Slang* aware of or knowledgeable about: *She's obviously not hip to the new rules.*

hip·bone (hip′bōn′) *n* either of the large, irregular bones that form the main part of the pelvis.

hip hop *n* a style of rap music with an electronic backing that originated among black American inner-city youth. Also, **hip-hop**, **hiphop**. **hip′-hop′per** *n.*

hip·hug·gers (hip′hug′ərz) *pln* pants with a very low waist that fit tightly around the hips.

hip·pie (hip′ē) *n* a young person of the 1960s who rejected conventional society and its values. Also, **hippy**. <*hip*[3]>

hip·po (hip′ō) *Informal n* a hippopotamus.

hip pocket *n* a pocket on either side of the back of a pair of pants, just below the waist.

Hip·po·crat·ic oath (hip′ə krat′ik) *n* an oath taken by those about to become physicians, describing their duties and obligations. <*Hippocrates,* physician in ancient Greece>

hip·po·drome (hip′ə drōm′) *n* **1** in ancient Greece and Rome, an oval track for horse races and chariot races, surrounded by tiers of seats for spectators. **2** an arena or building for a circus or rodeo. <Latin, from Greek *hippos* horse + *dromos* race>

hip·po·pot·a·mus (hip′ə pot′ə məs) *n, pl* **hip·po·pot·a·mus·es** or **hip·po·pot·a·mi** (-mī′) a huge, thick-skinned, hairless mammal with an enormous mouth, found in and near the rivers of tropical Africa. See UNGULATE for picture. <Latin, from Greek *hippos* horse + *potamos* river>

hip waders *pln* rubber boots reaching to the hips, worn while wading in water.

hire (hīr) *v* **hired, hir·ing 1** take on as an employee: *The manager hired more student help.* **2** *especially UK* rent something: *We hired a car for the weekend.*
n the act or cost of hiring: *A good worker is worthy of his or her hire.* <Old English *hyrian*>
hire out, give one's services or those of another in return for payment: *to hire yourself out as a babysitter. He hired out as a carpenter.*

hire·ling (hīr′ling) *n* a hired worker, usually at a casual, menial, or disreputable task.

hir·sute (hər sūt′) *or* (hər′sūt) *adj* hairy. <Latin *hirsutus*>

his (hiz) *adj* a possessive form of HE: *He raised his hand.*
pron a possessive form of HE; that which belongs to him: *My jacket is black; his is dark blue.* <Old English>

hiss (his) *v* **1** make a sound like that of the *s* in *see*: *The cat hissed as we approached.* **2** show disapproval by using this sound: *The play was hissed by the audience.* **3** utter by hissing or as if by hissing: *"Sit up and listen!" she hissed.*
n a hissing sound: *There was a loud hiss as the water boiled over onto the stove.* <imitative>

his·ta·mine (his′tə mēn′) *n* a substance released by the body in allergic reactions. <Greek *histion* tissue + *-amine* any organic compound derived from ammonia>

his·to·gram (his′tə gram′) *Statistics n* a vertical bar graph representing a frequency distribution. <Greek *histos* mast (i.e., upright) + *-gram* something recorded>

his·to·ri·an (hi stȯ′rē ən) *n* a person who is an expert or specialist in history.

his·tor·ic (hi stȯ′rik) *adj* famous or important in history: *Halifax and Kingston are historic cities.*

CONFUSABLES

Historic means "famous in history": *The patriation of Canada's constitution was a historic event.*

Historical means "to do with history": *I enjoy reading historical novels. The fall of Rome is a historical fact.*

his·tor·i·cal (hi stȯ′rə kəl) *adj* **1** to do with a study of history: *historical research.* **2** according to or based on history: *a historical novel.* **3** known to be actual or true: *historical facts.* **his·tor′i·cal·ly** *adv.*

his·to·ric·i·ty (his′tə ris′ə tē) *n* the fact of having actually existed in time and space, as proven by records: *The historicity of King Arthur has not been established.*

his·to·ry (his′tə rē) *or* (his′trē) *n, pl* **his·to·ries** **1** all events that take place in time, especially those already past, taken as a whole. **2 a** the story or past of a particular person, thing, nation, or geographical area: *He knows a lot about the history of Canada. This ship has an interesting history.* **b** a systematic written account of this. **3** the branch of knowledge or study that deals with recording and explaining past events. <Latin, from Greek *historia* record, from *histor* judge>
make history, a influence or guide the course of history: *The Magna Carta made history.* **b** do something memorable: *Marilyn Bell made history by swimming across Lake Ontario.*

his·tri·on·ic (his′trē on′ik) *adj* overly melodramatic.
n **histrionics** *pl* exaggerated dramatic talk and display of emotions: *Don't be swayed by her histrionics.* <Latin *histrionis* actor>

hit (hit) *v* **hit, hit·ting** **1** strike something or someone quickly and forcefully: *She hit the ball with the bat. I hit my head against the shelf.* **2** get to or reach: *Her second arrow hit the bull's eye. When we hit Toronto, we'll look for a motel.* **3** occur suddenly: *As he bent down, a sharp pain hit him in the back. An idea just hit me.* **4** achieve something by hitting a ball with a bat, racquet, or stick: *She hit a double in baseball today.*
n **1** the act or fact of striking or being struck. **2** a very successful or popular person or thing: *That new song is sure to be a hit.* **3** a sharp attack or criticism: *The review ended with a hit at the producer.* **4** *Baseball* a successful hitting of the ball by a batter so that he or she can get to at least first base without the help of an error. **5** *Computers* a connection to a website on the Internet or other network. <Old Norse *hitta*> **hit′ter** *n.*
hit it off, *Informal* get along well: *The two of them hit it off right away.*
hit on, a discover by chance: *They've hit on a new idea for advertising the contest.* **b** *Slang* make sexual overtures to someone.
hit or miss, in a haphazard way.

hit–and–run (hit′ən run′) *adj* **1** to do with a driver who has an accident and drives away without stopping. **2** to do with any similar act: *a hit-and-run attack.*

To transport recreational vehicles like boats and snowmobiles, a trailer can be attached to a ball-mount **hitch** on an automobile or truck. This design allows the connection to pivot freely.

hitch (hich) *v* **1** fasten with a hook, ring, rope, or strap: *He hitched his horse to a post.* **2** (*with* ***up***) harness to a wagon or carriage: *She hitched up the team and drove to town.* **3** move or pull with a jerk: *He hitched his chair closer to the fire.* **4** *Informal* get by hitchhiking: *They hitched a ride home with a friend.*
n **1** a means of attaching or fastening: *There's a trailer hitch on the back of the car.* **2** a short, sudden pull or jerk: *The sailor gave his pants a hitch.* **3** something that delays progress: *A hitch in my plans made me miss the bus.* <Middle English *hychen*>
get hitched, *Slang* get married.
without a hitch, smoothly and successfully.

hitch·hike (hich′hīk′) *Informal v* **hitch·hiked, hitch·hik·ing** travel by asking for free rides from passing motorists: *Hitchhiking can be dangerous.* **hitch′hik′er** *n.*

hi tech HIGH TECH.

hith·er (hiᴛʜ′ər) *adv* to or toward this place.
adj nearer: *on the hither side.* <Old English *hider*>
hither and thither, here and there or back and forth, especially in haste or confusion.
hither and yon, to all sorts of places far and near.

hith·er·to (hiᴛʜ′ər tū′) *adv* up to this or that time: *Her talent as a writer, hitherto unknown, became clear when she won the short-story competition.*

a bat	e bed	i bid	o pot	u cup	th **thin**
ā cake	ē me	ī bite	ō go	ū rude	ᴛʜ **then**
à bar	ə about	ər over	ȯ for	ů put	zh measure

H

hit list *n* a list of people to be murdered, attacked in the media, or otherwise injured by some group or individual.

hit man *n* a hired murderer.

hit–or–miss (hit′ər mis′) *adj* haphazard or inconsistent: *The results of the experiment were useless because of our hit-or-miss methods.*

Hit·tite (hit′īt) *n* **1** a member of an ancient people of Asia Minor and Syria whose civilization lasted from about 2000 to 1200 BCE. **2** the Indo-European language of these people.
adj to do with the Hittites or their language.

HIV *n* in full, **human immunovirus** a virus that destroys the body's capacity to protect itself from diseases, and leads to AIDS. <*H*(*uman*) *I*(*mmuno*) *V*(*irus*)>

Beekeepers can harvest as much as 100 kg of honey in one summer from this kind of **hive**. The beekeeper draws the honey from each honeycomb using a machine called an extractor, which works by centrifugal force.

hive (hīv) *n* **1** a place in which bees live. **2** a large number of bees living together: *The whole hive came after him.* **3** a busy place full of people: *On Saturdays, the mall is a hive.*
v **hived, hiv·ing 1** put bees in a hive. **2** of bees, enter a hive. <Old English *hyf*>
hive off, separate or be separated from a larger group or unit: *They've hived off the three-year-olds into a separate class.*

hives (hīvz) *pln* an itchy rash with swollen patches, often an allergic reaction. <origin uncertain>

ho (hō) *interj* **1** an exclamation of surprise, joy, or scorn. **2** an exclamation used to attract attention: *Land ho!*

hoard (hȯrd) *v* save and store away: *He's a miser and hoards his money. Before the war started many people hoarded food and water.*
n what is saved and stored away: *The squirrel had a hoard of nuts in a hole in the tree.* <Old English *hord*>
hoard′er *n.*

CONFUSABLES

Hoard is a verb that means "gather or collect up and stockpile": *He hoards his car magazines in a pile under his bed.*

Horde is a noun that means "crowd" or "swarm": *She was surrounded by a horde of fans.*

hoard·ing (hȯr′ding) *n* a high wooden barrier around a building site. <probably Old French *hourd*>

hoar·frost (hȯr′frost′) *n* a film of tiny ice crystals that sometimes forms on a cold surface. <Old English *har* grey + *frost*>

hoarse (hȯrs) *adj* **hoars·er, hoars·est 1** rough and deep in sound: *Her voice was hoarse from shouting.* **2** with such a voice: *He's hoarse because of a cold.* <Old English *has*>
hoarse′ly *adv.* **hoarse′ness** *n.*

hoar·y (hȯ′rē) *Poetic adj* **hoar·i·er, hoar·i·est 1** greyish white: *hoary frost.* **2** old and overly used: *a hoary expression.* <Old English *har* grey> **hoar′i·ness** *n.*

🍁 **hoary marmot** *n* a large grey marmot found in the mountains of northwest N America. Also called **whistler**.

hoax (hōks) *n* a deception or false story intended to trick people: *That report about a new computer virus was a hoax.* <probably altered from *hocus* in *hocus-pocus*>

hob[1] (hob) *n* a shelf at the back or side of a fireplace, used for keeping things warm. <variant of *hub*>

hob[2] (hob) *n* a hobgoblin. <Middle English, nickname for *Robert*>
play (or **raise**) **hob,** *Informal* cause trouble.

hob·bit (hob′ət) *n* a member of an imaginary race who are smaller than humans, and have beardless faces and hairy feet. <created by J.R.R. Tolkien in his books *The Hobbit* and *Lord of the Rings*>

hob·ble (hob′əl) *v* **hob·bled, hob·bling 1** walk awkwardly or unsteadily: *She managed to hobble to the phone without her crutches.* **2** put a strap or rope, around the legs, especially of a horse, so that it can move a little but not run away. **3** cause to walk awkwardly or limp. **4** hinder or make ineffective.
n **1** an awkward or limping walk. **2** a rope or strap used to hobble a horse or other animal. <Middle English *hobelen*>

hob·by (hob′ē) *n, pl* **hob·bies** something a person especially likes to work at or study apart from his or her main business or job: *Collecting seashells is her hobby.* <Middle English *hoby*> **hob′by·ist** *n.*

hob·by·horse (hob′ē hȯrs′) *n* **1** a stick with a horse's head, used as a toy horse by children. **2** a rocking horse. **3** a favourite topic: *Dad is back on his neatness hobbyhorse.*

hob·gob·lin (hob′gob′lən) *n* **1** a mischievous elf. **2** something imaginary that one fears; a bogey. <*Hob* Middle English nickname for *Robert* + *goblin*>

hob·nail (hob′nāl′) *n* a short nail with a large head, used to protect the soles of boots. <obsolete *hob* peg + *nail*>
hob′nailed′ *adj.*

hob·nob (hob′nob′) *Informal v* **hob·nobbed, hob·nob·bing** mix socially, especially with people of higher social status: *to hobnob with royalty.* <Middle English *hæbbe* have + *næbbe* not have>

ho·bo (hō′bō) *n, pl* **ho·bos** or **ho·boes** a homeless person who lives outdoors and wanders from place to place. <origin uncertain>

Hob·son's choice (hob′sənz) *n* the choice of either taking the thing offered or having nothing. <T. *Hobson* 16c stables owner, who rented out horses and made his customers take whatever horse was nearest to the door>

In **hockey**, referees and linesmen monitor the play and make sure the players obey the rules. The referee uses arm and hand gestures to indicate specific penalties.

Ho·che·la·ga (hō′shə lä′gə) *n* the name of the Iroquois village on the site of Montréal before the arrival of Champlain.

hock[1] (hok) *n* the joint in the hind leg above the fetlock joint on certain animals: *pig hocks.* <Old English *hoh*>

hock[2] *v* get money from a pawnshop for something deposited, which may or may not be redeemed within a fixed period of time: *He hocked his watch to buy a plane ticket.* <Dutch *hok* debt>
in hock, a in the possession of a pawnshop until it can be redeemed: *His watch is in hock.* **b** in debt.

hock·ey (hok′ē) *n* **1** a game played on ice by two teams of six players on skates and carrying hooked sticks with which they try to shoot a black rubber disc, the puck, into the opposing team's goal. **2** a version of this game played on a different surface, such as field hockey, floor hockey, or road hockey.

ETYMOLOGY

Hockey is thought to come from Old French *hoquet*, meaning "shepherd's crook," since hockey sticks resembled shepherds' crooks.

ho·cus–po·cus (hō′kəs pō′kəs) *n* meaningless or insincere talk or activity designed to distract attention from what is important: *All her talk about our beautiful house and garden was just hocus-pocus.*
interj used as a word to distract audience attention while a magic trick is performed. <fake Latin *hax pax max Deus adimax*>

hod (hod) *n* a trough or tray with a long handle, used for carrying bricks or mortar on the shoulder. <perhaps Dutch *hodde* basket>

hodge·podge (hoj′poj′) *n* a mess or jumble. <variant of *hotchpotch*, from Old French *hochepot* stew>

Hodg·kin's disease (hoj′kinz) *n* a cancer in which the lymph nodes, spleen, and sometimes the liver are enlarged. <T. *Hodgkin*, 19c physician>

hoe (hō) *n* a tool with a small blade set across the end of a long handle, used to loosen soil and cut weeds.
v **hoed, hoe·ing** loosen, dig, or cut with a hoe: *to hoe the garden.* <Old French *houe*> **ho′er** *n.*

hoe·down (hō′doun′) *n* **1** a lively folk dance, especially a square dance, or the music for it. **2** a party featuring such dances.

hog (hog) *n* **1** a domestic pig, especially a full-grown, castrated male raised for meat. **2** *Informal* a selfish, greedy person.
v **hogged, hog·ging** *Informal* take more than one's share of: *Don't hog the blanket.* <Old English *hogg*>
hog′gish *adj.*
go whole hog, *Informal* do something thoroughly.
live high off the hog, *Informal* lead a luxurious life.

ho·gan (hō′gən) *n* a traditional Navajo dwelling with a roof of earth, usually built with the entrance facing east. <Navajo>

a bat	e bed	i bid	o pot	u cup	th thin
ā cake	ē me	ī bite	ō go	ū rude	TH then
ä bar	ə about	ər over	ȯ for	u̇ put	zh measure

H

hog·back (hog′bak′) *n* a low, sharp ridge of land with steep sides.

hogs·head (hogz′hed′) *n* an old unit of volume for wine or beer, the typical capacity of a large barrel. <probably from the shape of the cask>

🍁 **Hog·town** (hog′toun′) *Informal* Toronto.

hog·wash (hog′wosh′) *n* nonsense.

> **ETYMOLOGY**
>
> **Hogwash** is made up from *hog* and *wash,* but the original sense in the mid 1400s was "kitchen swill for pigs," that is, kitchen scraps mixed with water and fed to pigs.

hog–wild (hog′wīld′) *Slang adj* overcome by enthusiasm, excitement, or frustration.

ho–hum (hō′hum′) *Informal interj* used to express boredom by imitating a yawn.
adj **1** dull or boring: *The first few chapters are ho-hum.* **2** unenthusiastic or unmoved: *I don't know how you can be so ho-hum about it.* <imitative of yawning>

hoi pol·loi (hoi′pə loi′) *n* the ordinary people; most people. <Greek = the many>

hoist (hoist) *v* lift up, often with ropes and pulleys: *to hoist sails, to hoist blocks of stone.*
n **1** an act of lifting up: *She gave me a hoist up the wall.* **2** an apparatus for raising heavy loads: *The mechanic raised the car on the hoist so he could work underneath.* <Dutch *hijschen*>

hoi·ty–toi·ty (hoi′tē toi′tē) *adj* snobbish. <origin uncertain>

hok·ey (hō′kē) *adj* **hok·i·er, hok·i·est** *Slang* exaggerated or unrealistic, especially too sentimental. <from *hokum*>

hok·um (hō′kəm) *Slang n* **1** something that seems true but is in fact meaningless or false: *Most advertising is hokum.* **2** very melodramatic or comic elements in a story, play, etc., as an easy way to catch or regain the attention of the audience: *A little hokum will liven up the second act.* <probably *hocus-pocus* and *bunkum*>

hold[1] (hōld) *v* **held, hold·ing 1** grasp, carry, or support with the hands, arms, or mouth: *Please hold my books while I phone home.* **2** keep in a certain position or condition: *to hold someone hostage. Hold the ladder steady.* **3** stay in place: *The river bank held during the flood.* **4** keep from acting or continuing: *to hold your breath. Hold your fire!* **5** defend and keep against an enemy: *They managed to hold the border town.* **6** contain: *This theatre holds 500 people.* **7** have or possess: *to hold an office, to hold tickets to an event.* **8** have and take part in: *to hold a meeting.* **9** host or sponsor: *Who's holding the family reunion this year?* **10** have in the mind: *to hold a belief. People once held that the world was flat.* **11** wait on the telephone: *Please hold while I transfer your call.* **12** remain faithful or firm: *She held to her convictions.* **13** be in force or effect: *The rule holds in all cases.* **14** *Music* keep on singing or playing a note. **15** *Informal* leave out: *Hold the mayo on that sandwich, please.*
n **1** the act or state of holding: *to release your hold.* **2** something to hold on by: *She looked for a hold on the smooth rock but couldn't find any.* **3** a controlling force or influence: *Don't let that habit get a hold on you.* **4** a function on a telephone that temporarily cuts the connection: *The operator put me on hold.* **5** *Wrestling* a way of holding one's opponent. <Old English *healdan*>
hold′er *n.*
get hold of, a get or obtain: *I want to get hold of a copy of today's paper.* **b** grasp or get a grip on: *The ball was so slippery I couldn't get hold of it.* **c** get in contact with someone: *You can always get hold of me by cellphone.*
hold against, continue to resent for: *She will hold that remark against me forever.*
hold back, a hesitate and not commit yourself. **b** keep someone from acting freely.
hold down, keep a job or position.
hold forth, a talk at length: *He held forth on the merits of regular exercise.* **b** offer.
hold it! *Informal* stop! wait!
hold off, a defend oneself from: *They managed to hold off the enemy until reinforcements arrived.* **b** delay action: *I was going to call but I think I'll hold off for another day.*
hold on, a keep holding tightly: *She held on to the overturned boat till help came.* **b** keep on or endure. **c** *Informal* Stop! Wait a minute!
hold out, a last: *Our supplies will not hold out much longer.* **b** keep resisting: *The company of soldiers held out for six days until help arrived.* **c** offer. *I can't hold out much hope that the dog will come back.*
hold over, a keep longer than originally scheduled: *The musical was so popular that it was held over for another week.* **b** postpone: *The game has been held over until next week.*
hold the fort, be in charge to see that nothing goes wrong, especially while others are away.
hold up, a continue or endure: *How are you holding up?* **b** stop or delay: *What is holding up traffic?* **c** *Informal* stop by force and rob.
hold your own, maintain your strength or position.
lay (or **take**) **hold of, a** seize or grasp. **b** get control or possession of.
no holds barred, any method is acceptable.
on hold, a waiting on the telephone. **b** inactive or set aside until something decisive happens: *Put the celebrations on hold until we know the final score.*

hold[2] (hōld) *n* the interior of a ship below the deck, where cargo is carried. <variant of *hole*>

hold·ing (hōl′ding) *n* **1** a piece of land rented or owned by someone. **2** in certain sports, the illegal hindering of an opponent's movements. **3** usually, **holdings** *pl* property, especially in the form of stocks or bonds.

holding company *n* a company that owns the stocks or bonds of other companies and controls them.

holding pattern *n* **1** the circular pattern of movement of a plane waiting in the air for landing instructions. **2** a temporary way of dealing with things while waiting for an issue to be settled: *You should go into a holding pattern until your broken leg has healed*

hold·out (hōl′dout′) *n* a person or group that continues to resist after others have come to an agreement, given in, or given up.

hold·o·ver (hōl′dō′vər) *n* a person who or thing that is held over from another time or place: *She was a holdover from last year's team.*

hold·up (hōl′dup′) *n* **1** *Informal* the act of stopping and robbing a person by force. **2** a stop or delay: *She got out of her car to see what the holdup was.*

hole (hōl) *n* **1** an opening in or through something, often a break or tear: *a hole in a sock.* **2** a hollow place where something has been dug out or bashed in: *The holes in the road were full of water.* **3** a burrow: *Rabbits live in holes.* **4** *Informal* a small, dark, dreary, or dirty place: *I wouldn't want to live in that hole.* **5** *Informal* a flaw or defect: *There are a few holes in that argument.* **6** *Informal* an embarrassing, awkward, or difficult position: *The business got itself into a hole financially.* **7** *Golf* **a** a small round cavity, into which the ball is eventually hit. **b** a section of a golf course from a tee to a hole, one of a number into which the course is divided: *A regular golf course consists of 18 holes.*
v **holed, hol·ing** make a hole or holes in: *The side of the ship was holed by an iceberg.* <Old English *hol*>
hol′ey *adj.*
burn a hole in your pocket, *Informal* of money, make you want to spend; be easily spent: *Her allowance is burning a hole in her pocket.*
hole in one, *Golf* a single shot that takes the ball straight from the tee into the hole on the green.
hole in the wall, *Informal* a small, shabby, insignificant or unimpressive place.
hole up, *Informal* go into hiding for a time: *The robbers holed up in an old cabin.*
in the hole, *Informal* owing or having lost money: *The wedding left them several thousand dollars in the hole.*
make a hole in, *Informal* use up a large amount of: *The new radio made quite a hole in my savings.*
pick holes in, find fault with.

CONFUSABLES

Hole is a noun that means "empty space": *The dog dug a hole in the backyard.*

Whole is an adjective that means "entire": *I read the whole book in one afternoon.*

Ho·li (hō′lē) *Hinduism n* a popular spring fertility festival generally dedicated to Krishna. <Sanskrit *holika*>

hol·i·day (hol′ə dā′) *n* **1** a day on which general business is suspended, by law or custom: *July 1st is a holiday in Canada.* **2** a day for celebration or pleasure. **3 holidays** *pl* a period of rest or recreation: *the summer holidays. He gets three weeks of holidays a year.* **4** a holy day or religious festival.
v take or have a period of rest or recreation: *They are holidaying in France.* <Old English *haligdæg* holy day (of the Christian church), traditionally a day off work>
hol′i·day′er *n.*

ho·li·er–than–thou (hō′lē ər ᴛʜən ᴛʜou′) *Informal adj* considering oneself morally better than others.
n a person who thinks or acts this way.

ho·li·ness (hō′lē nis) *n* **1** the fact of being holy. **2 Holiness** a title used in speaking to or of the Pope.

ho·lis·tic (hō lis′tik) *adj* recognizing and emphasizing the relationships among all the different elements of a whole, especially of a whole human being: *holistic medicine. A holistic education develops students intellectually, physically, emotionally, morally, and socially.* <Greek *holos* whole>
ho′lism *n.*

Hol·land (hol′ənd) *n* a former name for the Netherlands.

hol·lan·daise sauce (hol′ən dāz′) *n* a creamy sauce made from egg yolks, butter, lemon juice, and seasoning.

hol·ler (hol′ər) *Informal n, v* shout; yell: *Give me a holler if you need help* (*n*). *We hollered at her to come back* (*v*).

ETYMOLOGY

Holler developed from an earlier dialect word *hollar*, which was a variant of *holla*, meaning "a cry used to attract attention." The word *holla* can be found in the works of Shakespeare. More recent versions, still found in some writing, are *hullo* and *halloa*; even **hello** has the same ultimate origin.

H

hol·low (hol′ō) *adj* **1** with a hole or cavity inside: *a hollow sphere. Some plants have hollow stems.* **2** sunken and with an inward curve: *hollow cheeks. There is a large hollow place in the lawn where the earth has settled.* **3** sounding as if coming from something hollow; deep-toned, and muffled: *a hollow voice.* **4** lacking real worth, truth, or significance: *hollow promises, a hollow victory.*
n **1** a bowl-shaped place or shallow hole: *a hollow in the road.* **2** a small valley: *They built their house in a hollow.*
v **1** make or become hollow. **2** (*usually with* **out**) make or form by hollowing: *He hollowed out a canoe from a log.* <Old English *holh*> **hol′low·ly** *adv.* **hol′low·ness** *n.*
beat (**all**) **hollow,** *Informal* be much better than.

hol·ly (hol′ē) *n, pl* **hol·lies** a tree or shrub with thick, shiny leaves with spiny points along the edges and clusters of bright red berries. <Old English *holegn*>

hol·ly·hock (hol′ē hok′) *n* a tall perennial plant widely grown for its spikes of large, showy flowers. <Old English>

Hol·ly·wood (hol′ē wůd′) *n* a district of Los Angeles, California, taken to symbolize the American movie industry and the people and lifestyles associated with it.

hol·mi·um (hōl′mē əm) *n* a metallic element belonging to the yttrium group. *Symbol* **Ho** <(*Stock*)*holm*, where it was discovered>

hol·o·caust (hol′ə kost′) *or* (hō′lə kost′) *n* **1** great or total destruction of life, especially by fire. **2 the Holocaust** the mass murder of Jews and other peoples by the Nazis during the World War II (1939–1945), chiefly in concentration camps. **3** in former times, a Jewish sacrificial offering that was burnt on an altar. <Latin, from Greek *holos* whole + *kaustos* burned>

a bat	e bed	i bid	o pot	u cup	th **thin**
ā cake	ē me	ī bite	ō go	ū rude	ᴛʜ **then**
ȧ bar	ə about	ər over	ȯ for	ů put	zh measure

Hol·o·cene (hol′ə sēn′) *n* the geological epoch lasting from about 10 000 years ago up to the present time. See also CENOZOIC, QUATERNARY.
adj to do with this epoch. <Greek *holos* whole + *kainos* recent>

hol·o·gram (hol′ə gram′) *or* (hō′lə gram′) *n* a three-dimensional photograph obtained by exposing a photographic plate near an object illuminated by a laser beam. <Greek *holos* whole (three dimensional)+ *-gram*>

ho·log·ra·phy (hə log′rə fē) *n* a photographic process for making three-dimensional pictures by means of laser light. <See HOLOGRAM.> **ho·lo·gra′phic** *adj.* **ho·lo·gra′phic·al·ly** *adv.*

hol·ster (hōl′stər) *n* a case for a pistol, usually of leather and attached to a belt. <Old English *heolster*, from *helustr* hiding place>

ho·ly (hō′lē) *adj* **ho·li·er, ho·li·est 1** recognized as sacred by religious use and authority: *Most religions have a holy book.* **2** worthy of reverence: *The Tomb of the Unknown Soldier is a holy place.* <Old English *halig*>

Holy Communion *Christianity n* a ceremony re-enacting Christ's Last Supper, in which bread and wine are taken as the body and blood of Christ or as symbols of them.

Holy Ghost HOLY SPIRIT.

Holy Grail GRAIL.

Holy Land *Christianity, Islam, Judaism n* the biblical region once called Palestine, on the eastern shore of the Mediterranean.

holy of ho·lies (hō′lēz) *Judaism n* **1 Holy of Holies** the inner, most sacred chamber of the ancient Jewish tabernacle and temple in Jerusalem. **2** any place that is reserved for the highest authority: *That parking spot is the principal's holy of holies.*

holy orders *Christianity pl n* the profession of a member of the clergy: *to be in holy orders.*

Holy Roman Empire *n* the empire that included western and central Europe, regarded both as a continuation of the Roman Empire and as a spiritual kingdom. It lasted from from about 800 CE to 1806.

Holy See *Catholicism n* the papal court; the people associated with the Pope in the Vatican.

Holy Spirit *Christianity n* God considered as spiritually active in the world. Also called **Holy Ghost**.

holy water *Catholicism n* water blessed by a priest and used in ceremonies.

hom·age (hom′ij) *or* (om′ij) *n* **1** anything done or given to show honour to someone: *Everyone paid homage to the great leader.* **2** in medieval times, a formal acknowledgment by a vassal that loyalty and service was owed to a lord. <Old French, from Latin *homo* man>

home (hōm) *n* **1** the place where a person, family, or creature lives permanently: *Her home is at 25 South Street.* **2** a privately owned house, townhouse, or condominium. *There are some lovely homes for sale in the new subdivision.* **3** the place where a person was born or brought up: *Ottawa is his home.* **4** a place where a thing belongs, is found, or is very common: *Toronto is the home of the CNE.* **5** an institution for people who need special help or care: *Great-grandfather has moved into a home for the aged.* **6** the finishing point or goal in a race or game, or a place where a player is free from attack. **7** *Baseball* home plate.
adv **1** at, to, or toward one's home: *Go home.* **2** to the desired place or position: *to hammer a nail home.*
v **homed, hom·ing** find and go toward one's home or toward a target: *a homing device.* <Old English *ham*>
at home, a in one's own home or country. **b** comfortable, as if at home: *I just don't feel at home in this city.* **c** ready to receive visitors.
bring (or **drive**) **home,** make clear, emphatic, or convincing to someone: *The documentary really brought home the importance of free speech.*
close to home, affecting one deeply or directly: *When my brother was sick, it brought the issue of donating blood a lot closer to home.*
hit (or **strike**) **home, a** reach a target: *The bullet hit home.* **b** make a forceful impression: *The plight of the children hit home when I saw them on TV.*
home free, sure of success or victory: *One more game like that and we'll be home free.*
home in on, a be guided toward a target by radar. **b** narrow one's attention to.
see someone home, escort someone to his or her home.
to write home about, worth mentioning or remarkable: *That's nothing to write home about.*

Home and School Association *n* an association of parents and teachers who meet from time to time to discuss the education of students.

home·bod·y (hōm′bod′ē) *or* (hōm′bud′ē) *n,*
pl **home·bod·ies** a person who likes to stay home or whose interests revolve around the home.

home·bound (hōm′bound′) *adj* headed for home.

home·brew (hōm′brū′) *n* an alcoholic drink made at home.

🍁 **home care** *n* medical care given at home.

home·com·ing (hōm′kum′ing) *n* **1** the fact of coming home. **2** an annual celebration held at many universities and colleges for former graduates.

home economics *n* (*with singular verb*) the science and art of managing a household, especially when taught as a school subject.

home fries *pl n* boiled potatoes, sliced and fried.

home front *n* **1** civilians and their activities during a war. **2** *Informal* one's home and family and related matters: *trouble on the home front. Who took care of the home front while you were away?*

home–grown (hōm′grōn′) *adj* grown or raised locally: *home-grown vegetables, a home-grown hero.*

home·land (hōm′land′) *n* **1** the country where one was born or where one lives. **2** a geographical area regarded as the home of a people. **3** in former times in South Africa, under apartheid, a partly self-governing region set aside for blacks.

home·less (hōm′lis) *adj* with no home.
home′less·ness *n.*

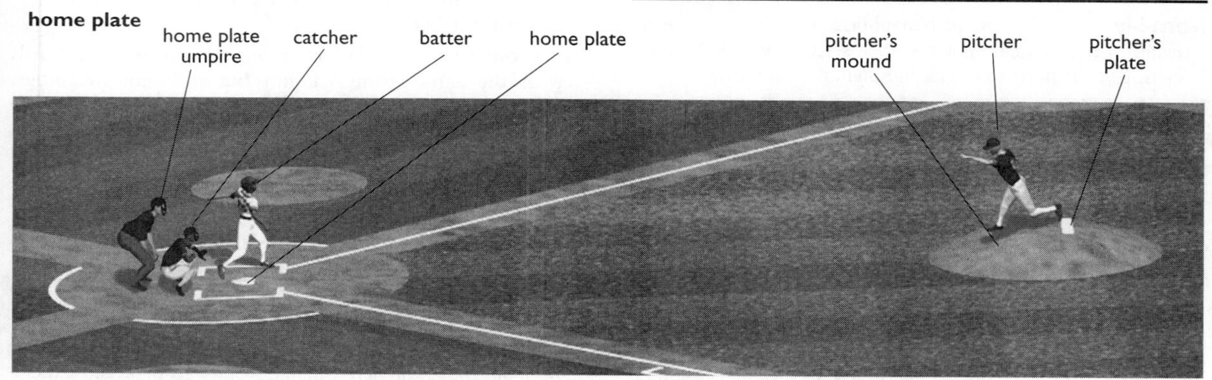

H

home·like (hōm′līk′) *adj* like home in being friendly, familiar, or comfortable: *a homelike atmosphere.*

home·ly (hōm′lē) *adj* **home·li·er, home·li·est** 1 plain or unattractive: *His homely face lit up in a smile.* 2 simple and unpretentious: *homely pleasures, homely food.* **home′li·ness** *n.*

home·made (hōm′mād′) *adj* made at home, not in a factory, commercial kitchen, etc: *homemade cookies.*

home·mak·er (hōm′mā′kər) *n* a person who manages a household for his or her family. **home′mak′ing** *n.*

ho·me·o·path (hō′mē ə path′) *n* a medical professional who treats diseases by giving tiny doses of a natural substance that in large quantities would produce symptoms of the disease. **ho′me·o·path′ic** *adj.* **ho′me·op′a·thy** (hō′mē op′ə thē) *n.*

home·own·er (hōm′ō′nər) *n* a person who owns a home.

home page *n* an introductory document for a site on the World Wide Web.

home plate *Baseball n* the base beside which a player stands to hit the ball, and to which he or she must return after hitting the ball and rounding the other bases, in order to score.

hom·er (hō′mər) *Informal n* a home run.

home·room (hōm′rūm′) *n* 1 the classroom in a school where a certain class meets first each day to be checked for attendance, and hear announcements, or where the class is taught most subjects, usually by the same teacher. 2 the period during which a class meets in the homeroom.

home rule *n* self-government by a colony, dependent country, or region.

home run *Baseball n* a run scored when the batter hits the ball and is able to run around all the bases without stopping or being stopped.

home–schooling (hōm′skū′ling′) *n* the practice of having a child taught in his or her own home, instead of in a school. **home′-school′** *v.* **home′school′er** *n.*

home·sick (hōm′sik′) *adj* depressed or sad because one is away from home. **home′sick′ness** *n.*

home·spun (hōm′spun′) *adj* 1 of yarn or fabric, spun or made at home. 2 plain; unsophisticated: *homespun manners.*
n 1 cloth made of yarn spun at home. 2 a strong, loosely woven cloth imitating this.

home·stead (hōm′sted′) *n* 1 a house with its land and any other buildings, especially when there is a lot of land or it is farmed. 2 in former times in western N America, a parcel of public land, usually consisting of a quarter section, 160 acres (about 65 hectares), granted to a settler by a government.
v settle and work a farm or land: *They homesteaded a farm south of the river.* **home′stead′er** *n.*

🍁 **Homestead Act** *n* the federal Act of 1872, under which settlers became homesteaders of the Canadian West.

home stretch *n* 1 the part of a track over which the last part of a race is run. 2 the last part of any journey or project.

home theatre *n* 1 a system of television and video equipment that attempts to reproduce the experience of attending a movie theatre. 2 the room or area in a home where this is located.

home·town (hōm′toun) *n* the town or city where one grew up or where one's home is. **home′town′** *adj.*

home·ward (hōm′wərd) *adv, adj* toward home: *to turn homeward (adv), the homeward road (adj).* Also (*adv*), **homewards**.

home·work (hōm′wərk′) *n* 1 schoolwork to be studied or prepared outside the classroom. 2 paid work done at home. 3 preparatory work or research: *The interviewer's good questions showed that she had done her homework.*

home·y (hō′mē) *adj* **hom·i·er, hom·i·est** cozy and comfortable: *The old inn had a very homey atmosphere.*

hom·i·cide (hom′ə sīd′) *n* the killing of one human being by another. <Old French, from Latin *homo* man + *-cidium* act of killing> **hom′i·cid′al** *adj.*

a bat	e bed	i bid	o pot	u cup	th **thin**
ā cake	ē me	ī bite	ō go	ū rude	ᴛʜ **then**
ȧ bar	ə about	ər over	ȯ for	u̇ put	zh measure

hom·i·ly (hom′ə lē) *n, pl* **hom·i·lies** 1 a short sermon, usually on practical matters. 2 a serious moral talk or writing. <Latin, from Greek *homilein* to talk with>

hom·ing device (hōm′ing) *n* an electronic device in a torpedo, missile, or other weapon that keeps it on a course toward its target.

homing pigeon *n* a pigeon trained to fly home, often from great distances: *Homing pigeons were often used for carrying written messages.*

hom·i·nid (hom′ə nid′) *n* a member of the family of primates that includes modern humans.
adj to do with hominids. <Latin *homo* man>

hom·i·ny (hom′ə nē) *n* dried corn with the hulls removed. Hominy that is coarsely ground and then boiled is called **hominy grits**. <Algonquian>

🍁 **ho·mo** (hō′mō) *Informal n* in full, **homogenized milk** milk that contains 3.25 percent butterfat.

ho·mo·ge·ne·ous (hō′mə jē′nē əs) *adj* 1 made up of similar elements or parts throughout: *a homogeneous rock, a homogeneous community.* 2 similar or of the same kind: *homogeneous interests.* Compare HETEROGENEOUS. Also, **homogenous** (hə moj′ə nəs). <Latin, from Greek *homos* same + *genos* kind> **ho′mo·ge·ne′i·ty** (hō′mə jə nē′ə tē) *n.* **ho′mo·ge′ne·ous·ly** *adv.*

ho·mog·e·nize (hə moj′ə nīz′) *v* **ho·mog·e·nized, ho·mog·e·niz·ing** 1 break up the fat globules in whole milk so that the fat remains emulsified and is distributed evenly throughout the milk. 2 make the same throughout: *The public school system is not intended to homogenize communities.*

hom·o·graph (hom′ə graf′) *n* one of two or more words with the same spelling but different meanings, origins, and, sometimes, pronunciations. *Mail* meaning *letters* and *mail* meaning *armour* are homographs; so are *tear* (ter) meaning *rip* and *tear* (tēr) meaning *drop of salt water from the eye.* See also HOMONYM, HOMOPHONE. <Greek *homos* same + *graphe* writing>

hom·o·nym (hom′ə nim′) *n* one of two or more words with the same pronunciation or spelling but different meanings and origins, such as *tail* and *tale,* or *rose* (past tense of *rise*) and *rose* (the flower). See also HOMOPHONE, HOMOGRAPH. <Latin, from Greek *homos* same + *onyma* name>

GRAMMAR AND USAGE

Homonyms are words that have the same sound or spelling, but have different meanings. For example, *bear* can mean "carry" or "large mammal."

Sometimes, words sound the same, but have different spellings and meanings, like *board* and *bored.* These are called **homophones**.

Some words look the same, but are pronounced differently, like *content* (what is contained in something) and *content* (satisfied). These are called **homographs**.

ho·mo·pho·bia (hō′mə fō′bē ə) *n* hatred or fear of homosexuals. <*homo(sexual)* + *phobia*>
ho′mo·pho′bic *adj, n.*

hom·o·phone (hom′ə fōn′) *n* one of two or more words with the same pronunciation but different meanings, origins, and, sometimes, spellings. *Pear, pair,* and *pare* are homophones. See also HOMOGRAPH, HOMONYM. <Greek *homos* same + *phone* sound>

Ho·mo sa·pi·ens (hō′mō sā′pē inz′) *n* the primate species to which all humans belong. <Latin = wise man>

ho·mo·sex·u·al (hō′mə sek′shū əl) *adj* sexually attracted to members of the same sex. Compare HETEROSEXUAL.
n a homosexual person. <Greek *homos* same + *sex*>
ho′mo·sex′u·al′i·ty *n.*

hon·cho (hon′chō) *Slang n* a leader or manager: *Who's the head honcho round here?* <Japanese *han* group + *cho* leader>

Hon·du·ras (hon dyů′rəs) *or* (hon dů′rəs) *n* a country in Central America. See the APPENDIX. **Hon·du′ran** *adj, n.*

hone (hōn) *n* a fine-grained stone on which to sharpen cutting tools, especially razors.
v **honed, hon·ing** 1 sharpen on a hone. 2 make sharper or more precise: *to hone your skills.* <Old English *han* a stone>

CONFUSABLES

Hone is often mistakenly used in place of **home** in the expression **home in on**, meaning "focus on" or "concentrate on." This is probably because the verb *hone*, meaning "sharpen on a special stone," does have an element of "sharpness" or "precision" to it, making the expression sound reasonable.

Although ***hone in on*** is popularly used, it is still regarded as incorrect and should be avoided.

hon·est (on′ist) *adj* 1 morally correct and truthful: *an honest person.* 2 obtained without lying, cheating, or stealing: *honest profits.* 3 expressed frankly or sincerely, without hiding anything: *honest criticism. I would like your honest opinion.* 4 genuine: *an honest mistake.* <Latin *honos* honour> **hon′es·ty** *n.*
honest to goodness, *Informal* I am telling the truth: *Honest to goodness, I didn't take it.*

hon·est·ly (on′ist lē) *adv* 1 in an honest manner. 2 (*as a sentence adverb*) speaking truthfully: *I honestly have no idea.*
interj used to express impatience: *Honestly! Act your age!*

hon·est–to–good·ness (on′ist tə gůd′nis) *Informal adj* 1 genuine and real: *We still haven't had an honest-to-goodness snowfall and it's the end of January.* 2 sincere and straightforward.

hon·ey (hun′ē) *n, pl* **hon·eys** 1 a thick, sweet liquid that bees make out of nectar collected from flowers, used as food by people and certain animals. 2 the drop of sweet liquid found in many flowers. 3 something sweet or agreeable. 4 *Slang* a particularly attractive person or thing: *His new car is a honey.*
v 1 sweeten with honey. 2 make more pleasant, especially deceptively: *honeyed words.* <Old English *hunig*>
hon′eyed *adj.* **hon′ey·like′** *adj.*

hon·ey·bee (hun′ē bē′) *n* a bee that makes honey and wax.

hon·ey·comb (hun′ē kōm′) *n* **1** a wax structure made by bees, containing rows of six-sided cells in which they store honey, pollen, and their eggs. **2** anything with a similar structure.
v make like a honeycomb, with many holes or tunnels: *Gophers had honeycombed the hillside.*

hon·ey·dew (hun′ē dyū′) *or* (hun′ē dū′) *n* **1** a variety of melon with sweet, green flesh and a smooth, whitish skin. **2** a sweet substance that oozes from the leaves of certain plants in hot weather. **3** a sweet, sticky substance deposited on leaves and stems by aphids.

honey locust *n* a thorny tree of eastern N America with large, flat pods containing sweet pulp.

hon·ey·moon (hun′ē mūn′) *n* **1** the holiday spent together by a newly married couple. **2** the initial period of marriage. **3** the initial period of any new relationship, arrangement, or situation in which things are harmonious and peaceful.
v spend or have a honeymoon. **hon′ey·moon′er** *n.*

hon·ey·suck·le (hun′ē suk′əl) *n* an upright or climbing shrub or vine of temperate regions with fragrant, tubular flowers.

honk (hongk) *n* **1** the cry of the wild goose. **2** a similar sound, as of a car horn or blowing the nose.
v make or cause to make this sound: *to honk a horn. The geese were honking overhead.* <imitative> **honk′er** *n.*

hon·ky–tonk (hong′kē tongk′) *n* **1 a** a cheap bar or nightclub. **b** a style of music, especially country music, played in such places. **2** jazz music with a heavy beat, played on an upright piano with a tinny sound. <origin unknown>

hon·or (on′ər) HONOUR.

hon·o·rar·i·um (on′ə rer′ē əm) *n, pl* **hon·o·rar·i·ums** or **hon·o·rar·i·a** money paid for professional services given as a token of thanks rather than as payment: *The guest speaker received an honorarium.* <Latin>

hon·or·ar·y (on′ə rer′ē) *adj* **1** given or done as an honour, whether or not the usual conditions have been fulfilled: *an honorary degree from a university.* **2** as an honour only: *an honorary secretary.*

hon·or·if·ic (on′ə rif′ik) *adj* showing respect or honour.
n a title of respect. *Sir* is an honorific.

hon·our or **hon·or** (on′ər) *n* **1** great respect or high regard: *to show honour to your guests.* **2 a** glory, fame, or renown. **b** a source or cause of honour: *She is an honour to her family and school.* **3** principles of correct and proper behaviour: *He has no sense of honour and never apologizes.* **4** a great privilege that makes one feel humble: *I consider it an honour to work with you on this project.* **5 honours** *pl* **a** special favours or courtesies. **b** special mention or recognition given to a student for unusually excellent work. **c** an advanced course or program of study. **6 Your** (**His, Her**) **Honour** a title used in speaking to (or of) a judge or mayor.
v **1** regard highly: *to honour your elders.* **2** dignify with a special privilege: *to be honoured by a royal visit.* **3** accept a cheque, currency, etc. when presented: *This store honours American money.* <Old French, from Latin *honor*>
do the honours, a act as host or hostess. **b** perform a required courtesy.
on (or **upon**) **your honour,** pledging to speak the truth and to do what is proper.

hon·our·a·ble or **hon·or·able** (on′ə rə bəl) *adj* **1** with or showing a sense of what is proper: *It was not honourable of you to cheat.* **2** worthy of honour: *my honourable companions, to perform honourable deeds.* **3** bringing honour to the one that has it: *honourable wounds received while defending her country.* **4** accompanied by honour or honours: *an honourable burial.* **5 a** with a title, rank, or position of honour. **b Honourable** in Canada, a title given to members of the Privy Council including the Cabinet, to the Speakers of the House of Commons and of the provincial legislatures, and to certain senior judges. **hon′our·a·ble·ness** or **hon′or·a·ble·ness** *n.* **hon′our·a·bly** or **hon′or·a·bly** *adv.*

honour roll or **honor roll** *n* a list of students who have achieved high marks.

honour system or **honor system** *n* a system of trusting people to obey the rules without being watched.

🍁 **hooch** or **hootch** (hūch) *Slang n* inferior or illegal liquor, especially cheap whisky. <*Hootchinoo*, Aboriginal settlement in Alaska, where such liquor was made>

hood (hu̇d) *n* **1** a soft, loose covering for the head and neck, usually attached to a coat or other garment. **2** anything like a hood in shape or use, like the part of a motor vehicle that covers the engine. **3** a fold of cloth worn over an academic gown, with a band or bands of colour to indicate the degree held and the university or college of the wearer.
v put a hood on. <Old English *hod*> **hood′ed** *adj.* **hood′less** *adj.* **hood′like′** *adj.*

hood[2] *Informal n* a hoodlum.

–hood *suffix* **1** state or condition: *childhood.* **2** showing people as a group: *neighbourhood.* <Old English *had* condition>

hood·ie (hu̇d′ē) *n* a sweatshirt or T-shirt with an attached hood. Also, **hoody**.

hood·lum (hu̇d′ləm) *n* a person who engages in crime and violence. <unknown origin>

hoo·doo (hū′dū) *n* **1** *Informal* bad luck or a person who or thing that brings bad luck. **2** *Geology* irregularly shaped rock columns or pinnacles caused by erosion, found especially in western N America. <perhaps *voodoo*>

hood·wink (hu̇d′wingk′) *v* mislead by a trick. **hood′wink′er** *n.*

ETYMOLOGY

Hoodwink originally meant "blindfold," and comes from the idea of covering someone's entire head with a *hood*, so as to have the effect of closing the eyes (as if causing the person to *wink*).

a bat	e bed	i bid	o pot	u cup	th thin
ā cake	ē me	ī bite	ō go	ū rude	ᴛʜ then
à bar	ə about	ər over	ȯ for	u̇ put	zh measure

H

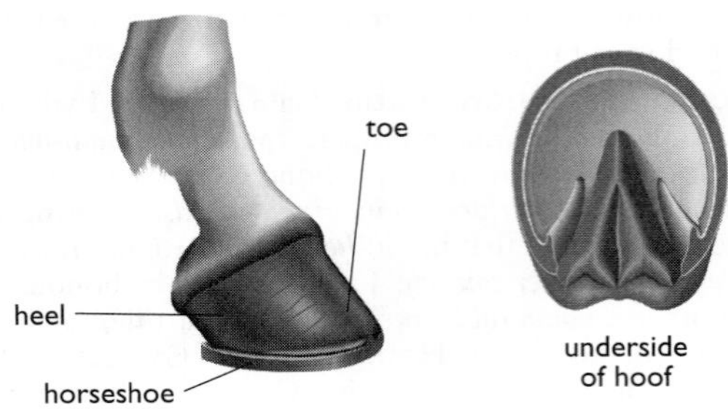

hoof (hūf) *or* (hůf) *n, pl* **hoofs** or **hooves** **1** a thick, hard covering made of a substance resembling horn, on the feet of horses, cattle, sheep, etc. **2** the whole foot of such animals. <Old English *hof*>
hoof it, walk.
on the hoof, of livestock, alive and moving freely.

hoof·beat (hūf′bēt′) *or* (hůf′bēt′) *n* the sound made by an animal's hoof on the ground as it walks or runs.

hook (hůk) *n* **1** a piece of metal, wood, or plastic, curved or with a sharp angle for catching or fastening something or for hanging things on: *a clothes hook. You attach the chain by putting the hook through this loop.* **2** a curved piece of wire, usually with a barb at the end, for catching fish. **3 a** a way of attracting interest or attention: *Giving away balloons is a sales hook.* **b** a catchy musical phrase in a pop song or advertising jingle. **c** an attention-getting fact or theme around which a story can be created. **4** *Hockey* an illegal check made by catching at an opponent's body with one's stick. **5** *Golf, Baseball* a stroke that causes the ball to curve away from the dominant hand. Compare SLICE (def. 3). **6** a short, swinging blow: *a right hook to the jaw.*
v **1** attach or fasten with a hook or hooks: *This part hooks into the other part.* **2** catch with a hook: *to hook a fish.* **3** curve or bend like a hook: *He hooked his ankle round the leg of the chair.* **4** cause to become addicted: *She's hooked on morphine.* **5** win attention, approval, or commitment, sometimes by trickery: *I was so hooked after the first chapter that I couldn't put the book down. Don't let them hook you with their scam.* **6** make rugs, etc., by pulling loops of yarn or strips of cloth through coarse fabric with a hook. **7** *Hockey* check an opponent illegally by catching at his or her body with one's stick. **8** *Golf, Baseball* hit a ball so that it curves away from the dominant hand. Compare SLICE (def. 3). **9** hit with a short, swinging blow. **10** *Informal* steal. <Old English *hoc*> **hook′like** *adj.*
by hook or by crook, in any way at all, whether fair or not.
hook, line, and sinker, a (*with* ***swallow, buy,*** etc.) accept or believe completely: *He swallowed my story hook, line, and sinker.* **b** the whole lot.
hook up, a connect an electric light or appliance, or arrange and connect parts of a telephone or electronic system. **b** *Informal* meet; get together: *We arranged to hook up later.*
off the hook, a *Informal* free of a responsibility or obligation. **b** of a telephone, in active use or not hung up properly.
on the hook, obligated in some way.

hook·ah or **hook·a** (hůk′ə) *or* (hū′kə) *n* a tobacco pipe with a long tube by which the smoke is drawn through water and cooled. <Arabic *huqqah*>

hook and eye *n* a fastener for a garment, consisting of a loop or bar and a hook that catches on it.

hooked (hůkt) *adj* **1** curved or bent like a hook: *a hooked nose.* **2** addicted. **3** thoroughly committed, engaged, or convinced: *It sounds like a good deal; I'm hooked.* **4** made with a hook: *a hooked rug.*

hook·er (hůk′ər) *Slang n* a prostitute.

hook shot *Basketball n* a twisting shot at the basket, made with a pivot of the body.

hook·up (hůk′up′) *n* the arrangement and connection of the parts of a TV set, telephone, or electronic system.

hook·worm (hůk′wərm′) *n* **1** a worm that gets into the intestines and feeds on blood. **2** a disease caused by this worm, often causing anemia.

hook·y (hůk′ē) *adv* being illegally absent, especially from school. <origin uncertain>

hoo·li·gan (hū′lə gən) *n* a violent young troublemaker, usually part of a gang. <origin uncertain>
hoo′li·gan·ism′ *n.*

hoop (hūp) *n* **1** a ring or flat band in the form of a circle, especially one that holds the staves of a barrel together. **2** a large wooden or plastic ring used as a toy by children: *The boy rolled his hoop along the ground.* **3** a circular frame formerly used to spread out a woman's skirt. **4** in the game of croquet, one of the metal arches through which players try to hit the balls. <Old english *hop*>
hoop′like′ *adj.*

hoop·la (hūp′lə) *Informal n* a big fuss about something, especially sensational advertising. <origin uncertain>

hoop skirt *n* a skirt worn over a framework of connected flexible hoops to make it spread out. Also called **crinoline**.

hoo·ray (hə rā′) HURRAH.

hoot (hūt) *n* **1** the deep, wavering sound that an owl makes. **b** a loud sound somewhat like this: *the hoot of an automobile horn, hoots of laughter.* **2** *Informal* something very funny: *Her clown costume was a hoot.* **3** *Informal* (*in the negative*) the tiniest amount: *She doesn't give a hoot what happens.*
v **1** make the sound that an owl makes or one like it. **2** express disapproval, scorn, or enjoyment by hooting: *They hooted him off the stage. We hooted with laughter.* <Middle English *huten*> **hoot′er** *n.*

hoo·te·nan·ny (hūt′nan′ē) *n, pl* **hoo·te·nan·nies** an informal gathering that features folk music. <*hoot*>

hooves (hūvz) *or* (hůvz) a plural of HOOF.

hop[1] (hop) *v* **hopped, hop·ping** **1** bounce or jump on one foot only. **2** move along by jumping on both feet, as many birds do, or on all four feet, as some animals do. **3** jump over: *to hop a ditch.* **4** move or jump quickly: *He hopped off his bicycle and ran inside.* **5** *Informal* quickly board a train or bus, sometimes by actually jumping onto it: *I can hop a bus and be there in 20 minutes.*
n **1** the act of hopping. **2** *Informal* a short trip. **3** *Informal* a dance party: *the annual spring hop.* <Old English *hoppian*>

a hop, skip, and a jump, a short distance: *My school is only a hop, skip, and a jump from home.*
hopping mad, *Informal* very angry.
hop to it, *Informal* hurry up.
keep someone hopping, *Informal* keep someone very busy.

hop² (hop) *n* a vine of the mulberry family whose ripened, dried flower clusters (**hops**) are used to flavour beer and other malt drinks. <Dutch *hoppe*>

hope (hōp) *n* **1** a feeling or belief that good things will happen: *His promise gave me hope.* **2** a person who or thing that is the source of this feeling: *She is the hope of the family.* **3** something hoped for: *Their one hope was to reach the shore before the storm hit.* **4** an attitude of optimism. *His promise gave me hope.* **5** a chance of success: *Without our goalie, we don't have a hope.*
v **hoped, hop·ing 1** wish that something one believes possible may in fact happen: *I hope they get here on time.* **2** wish and expect: *She hopes to travel across Canada next year.* <Old English *hopa*>
hope against hope, keep on hoping even though there is no good reason to have hope.

SYNONYMS

Hope suggests that what is anticipated will likely occur: *Her hope was that she would pass the driving test.*

Desire suggests a longing, regardless of its likeliness of occurring: *She desired peace in her country.*

Expectation suggests believing that something will occur: *We arrived home that night with the expectation of a good meal.*

hope chest *n* a chest in which a woman collects articles that will be useful after she marries.

hope·ful (hōp′fəl) *adj* **1** feeling or showing hope: *a hopeful smile. They were all in a hopeful frame of mind by morning.* **2** giving or inspiring hope: *The lessening of the fever was a hopeful sign.*
n a person who expects or is likely to achieve something: *The room was filled with young hopefuls waiting for auditions.* **hope′ful·ness** *n.*

hope·ful·ly (hōp′fə lē) *adv.* **1** in a hopeful manner: *The dog followed him hopefully to the cupboard.* **2** *Informal* (*as a sentence adverb*) it is to be hoped: *Hopefully, the weather will improve.*

hope·less (hōp′lis) *adj* **1** feeling no hope: *He was disappointed so often that he became hopeless.* **2** giving no hope: *a hopeless situation.* **3** *Informal* incompetent: *Let your brother do the ironing since you're so hopeless at it.* **hope′less·ly** *adv.* **hope′less·ness** *n.*

hop·lite (hop′līt) *n* a heavily armed foot soldier of ancient Greece. <Greek *hopla* weapons>

hop·per (hop′ər) *n* **1** a container into which grain, sand, or other material is poured into a grinder or mixer so as to feed evenly into the machine. **2** a person, animal, or thing that hops.

hop·scotch (hop′skoch′) *n* a children's game in which the players hop over the lines of a figure drawn on the ground.

ho·ra (hô′rə) *n* a folk dance with a lively rhythm, or the music for such a dance. <Hebrew *horah*, from Turkish>

horde (hôrd) *n* a crowd or swarm: *hordes of shoppers at the mall on Saturday, hordes of grasshoppers.* See HOARD for confusable. <Turkish *ordu* army>

ho·ri·zon (hə rī′zən) *n* **1** the line where the earth and sky seem to meet: *You cannot see beyond the horizon.* **2** usually, **horizons** *pl* the limit of one's thinking, experience, interest, or outlook: *She wanted to expand her horizons by travelling.* <Old French, from Greek *horizon kyklos* a circle forming a boundary>

hor·i·zon·tal (hô′rə zon′təl) *adj* **1** parallel to the line of the horizon. Compare VERTICAL. **2** flat and level: *You need a horizontal surface to work on.*
n a horizontal line, plane, direction, or position. **hor′i·zon′tal·ly** *adv.*

H

hor·mone (hôr′mōn) *n* **1** a substance, such as adrenalin or insulin, formed in the body and entering the bloodstream so as to stimulate cells and tissues: *growth hormones, sex hormones.* **2** a similar substance carried in the sap of plants. **3** a synthetic substance that has the effect of a hormone. **hor′mon′al** *adj.* <Greek *horman* set in motion, from *horme* impulse>

horn (hôrn) *n* **1 a** a hard outgrowth, usually curved, pointed, and in pairs, on the heads of cattle, sheep, goats, and some other animals. **b** the tough, fibrous material that horns are made of. **2** a brass musical wind instrument with a flared end, such as a trumpet or French horn. **3** a device sounded as a warning signal: *a foghorn, a car horn.* **4** anything that projects like a horn or is shaped like a horn: *a saddle horn.* <Old English> **horn′less** *adj.* **horn′like′** *adj.*
blow your own horn, praise yourself.
draw (or **pull**) **in your horns, a** restrain yourself. **b** back down or withdraw.
horn in (**on**), *Informal* meddle or intrude: *She kept trying to horn in on our conversation.*
lock horns, *Informal* get into a conflict or argument: *The two customers locked horns over who was first in line.*
on the horns of a dilemma, with two unpleasant choices, one of which must be taken.

horn·beam (hôrn′bēm′) *n* a tree or shrub of temperate regions with very hard wood and grey bark.

horn·bill (hôrn′bil′) *n* a large tropical bird with a very large bill with a horn or lump on it.

horn·blende (hôrn′blend′) *n* a black, dark green, or brown mineral found in granite and other rocks. <French>

horned toad (hôrnd) *n* a small insect-eating lizard of N America, with spines on the back and tail.

hor·net (hôr′nit) *n* a large wasp, mostly dark with white or yellow markings, that lives in colonies in large, roundish nests made of a papery material. <Old English *hyrnetu*]
hornet's nest, a situation likely to be troublesome or provoke strong reactions.

a bat	e bed	i bid	o pot	u cup	th thin
ā cake	ē me	ī bite	ō go	ū rude	ᴛʜ then
ä bar	ə about	ər over	ô for	ů put	zh measure

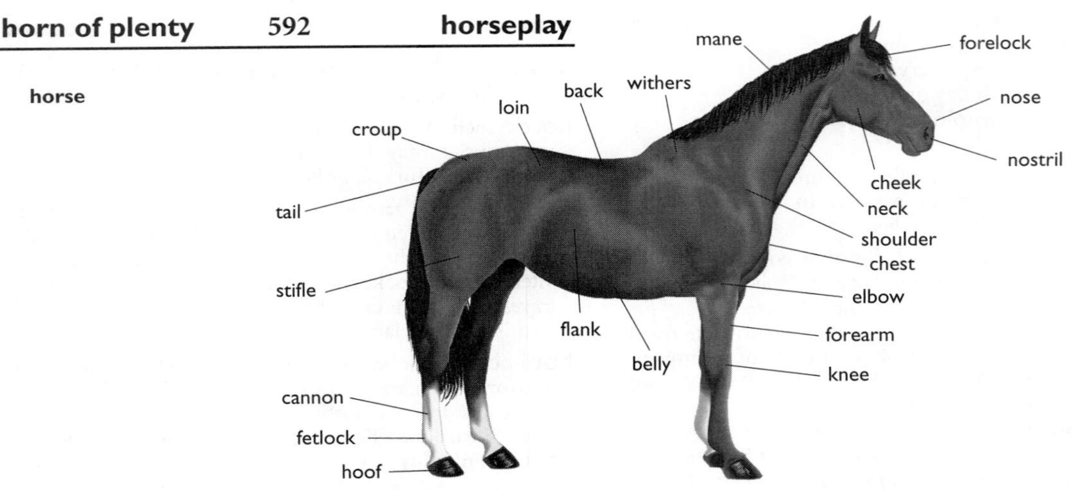

horn of plenty CORNUCOPIA.

horn·pipe (hòrn′pīp′) *n* a lively dance done by one person, formerly popular among sailors, or the music for it.

horn·swog·gle (hòrn′swog′əl) *v* **horn·swog·gled, horn·swog·gling** swindle or cheat. <origin unknown>

ho·ro·scope (hò′rə skōp′) *n* a forecast of a person's future supposedly based on the position of the planets and stars at the time of birth: *I read my horoscope in the paper every day.* <Latin, from Greek *hora* time + *skopos* watcher>

hor·ren·dous (hò ren′dəs) *adj* horrifying or terrible. **hor·ren′dous·ly** *adv.*

hor·ri·ble (hò′rə bəl) *adj* **1** causing horror: *horrible crimes, a horrible disease.* **2** extremely unpleasant: *a horrible noise.* **hor′ri·ble·ness** *n.* **hor′ri·bly** *adv.*

hor·rid (hò′rid) *adj* very unpleasant: *a horrid child, an absolutely horrid day.* <Latin *horridus*> **hor′rid·ly** *adv.* **hor′rid·ness** *n.*

hor·rif·ic (hò rif′ik) *adj* causing horror.

hor·ri·fy (hò′rə fī′) *v* **hor·ri·fied, hor·ri·fy·ing** cause to feel horror: *We were horrified by the news of the accident.*

hor·ror (hò′rər) *n* **1** a mixture of intense fear, shock, and disgust. **2** a great fear or dislike felt toward something: *a horror of snakes and spiders.* **3** a horrible or horrifying quality: *Oh, the horror of it!* **4** a cause of horror. **5** *Informal* a naughty or mischievous person, especially a child: *a little horror.*

ETYMOLOGY

Horror is a Latin word, derived from the verb *horrere*, meaning "to bristle." The image is of a fear and disgust so great that it causes a person's hair to stand on end.

hors d'oeu·vre (òr′dərv′) *n, pl* **hors d'oeu·vres** (òr′dərvz′) an appetizer or something small to eat with one's fingers, served before a meal or with drinks. <French = apart from the main work>

horse (hòrs) *n, pl* **hors·es** or (*especially collectively*) **horse** **1** a large four-legged animal with a coarse-haired mane and tail. **2** a piece of gymnastics equipment to jump or vault over. **3** a frame with legs to support something; a trestle. **4** soldiers on horses: *a troop of horse.* <Old English *hors*> **horse′less** *adj.*

back the wrong horse, make a prediction that turns out to be wrong.

hold your horses, *Informal* restrain yourself; have patience: *Hold your horses till we get there.*

horse around, *Informal* play in a rough, boisterous way.

horse of a different colour, something quite different.

on your high horse, behaving in an arrogant or pretentious way.

the horse's mouth, the original and well-informed source: *news straight from the horse's mouth.*

horse·back (hòrs′bak′) *n* the back of a horse: *We can go on horseback.*
adv on the back of a horse: *to ride horseback.*

horse chestnut *n* a large tree with compound leaves, and flower spikes that form inedible large brown seeds. Compare CHESTNUT (def. 1).

horse·flesh (hòrs′flesh′) *n* **1** horses for riding, driving, and racing. **2** meat from horses.

horse·fly (hòrs′flī′) *n, pl* **horse·flies** a large fly that sucks the blood of horses and cattle.

horse·hair (hòrs′her′) *n* **1** the hair from the mane or tail of a horse, used as stuffing, or to make bristles or fabric. **2** a stiff fabric made of this hair.

horse·hide (hòrs′hīd′) *n* the hide of a horse, or leather made from it.

horse latitudes *pl n* the two regions extending around the world at about 30°N and 30°S of the equator, where there is often calm weather.

horse laugh *Informal n* a loud, boisterous laugh.

horse·man (hòrs′mən) *n, pl* **horse·men** (-mən) **1** a man on horseback. **2** a man skilled in riding or managing horses. **horse′man·ship** *n.*

horse·play (hòrs′plā′) *n* rough, boisterous fun.

horse·pow·er (hôrs′pou′ər) *n* a nonmetric unit of power equal to 0.746 kilowatts, used for measuring the power of engines and motors. *Symbol* **hp**

horse·rad·ish (hôrs′rad′ish) *n* a white, hot-tasting condiment, made from the grated roots of a herb of the mustard family. See PARSNIP for picture.

horse sense *Informal n* practical good sense.

horse·shoe (hôrsh′shū′) *n* **1 a** a U-shaped piece of iron nailed to the bottom of a horse's hoof to protect it. **b** one of these pieces, mounted or hung as a symbol of good luck. **2 horseshoes** *pl* (*with singular verb*) a game in which the players throw horseshoes toward a stake some distance away.

horseshoe crab *n* a crablike sea animal with a body shaped like a horseshoe and a long, spiny tail. Also called **king crab**.

horse·whip (hôrs′wip′) *n* a whip for driving or controlling horses.
v **horse·whipped, horse·whip·ping** beat badly, especially with a horsewhip.

horse·wom·an (hôrs′wům′ən) *n, pl* **horse·wom·en** (-wim′ən) **1** a woman on horseback. **2** a woman skilled in riding or managing horses.

hors·y (hôr′sē) *adj* **hors·i·er, hors·i·est 1** to do with horses. **2** fond of horses or horse racing.

hor·ti·cul·ture (hôr′tə kul′chər) *n* the art or science of cultivating and managing gardens. <Latin *hortus* garden> **hor′ti·cul′tur·al** *adj.* **hor′ti·cul′tur·ist** *n.*

hose (hōz) *n, pl* (*def. 1*) **hos·es 1** a flexible tube made of rubber, plastic, or other tough material, used to carry water or other liquids over short distances. **2** (*with plural verb*) **a** stockings, tights, or socks. **b** an outer garment resembling tights, formerly worn by men.
v **hosed, hos·ing 1** (*usually with* ***down*** *or* ***off***) wash by spraying with a hose: *She hosed down the lawn furniture.* **2** *Slang* trick or deceive someone. <Old English *hosa*>

🍁 **hos·er** (hō′zər) *Slang n* an unintelligent, loud, opinionated, and usually beer-drinking man.

ho·sier·y (hō′zhə rē) *n* socks, stockings, tights, or pantyhose. <*hose*>

hos·pice (hos′pis) *n* **1** a residence to care for people who are dying. **2** a house where travellers can stay, especially one kept by a religious order: *the hospice of the monks of Saint Bernard in the Alps.*

hos·pit·a·ble (ho spit′ə bəl) *or* (hos′pə tə bəl) *adj* **1** welcoming to visitors: *My host family was very hospitable and made me feel at home.* **2** receptive or open: *hospitable to new ideas.* <See HOSPITAL.> **hos·pit′a·bly** *adv.*

hos·pi·tal (hos′pi təl) *n* a place where sick or injured people are treated and cared for.

ETYMOLOGY

Hospital and **hospice** come through Old French from Latin *hospes,* meaning "host" or "guest." In the 1400s, *hospital* meant "a place for looking after the poor." By the 1500s, it had the sense of being a place for people who were ill.

hos·pi·tal·i·ty (hos′pə tal′ə tē) *n* friendliness and generosity to guests or strangers.

hos·pi·tal·ize (hos′pi tə līz′) *v* **hos·pi·tal·ized, hos·pi·tal·iz·ing** put in a hospital to be treated or cared for. **hos′pi·tal·i·za′tion** *n.*

host[1] (hōst) *n* **1** a person who entertains guests. **2** the person who regularly leads a game show, talk show, or other program in which he or she talks directly to listeners or viewers. **3** a plant or animal in or on which a parasite lives: *The oak tree is the host of the mistletoe that grows on it.*
v act as host to or for: *to host a party, to host visitors.* <Old French, from Latin *hospitis* guest>

host[2] (hōst) *n* **1** a large number: *A host of stars glittered in the sky.* **2** *Archaic* an army. <Old French, from Latin *hostis* army>

hos·ta (hos′tə) *n* a plant of the lily family with large, often wavy and striped leaves, and spikes of flowers. Also called **plantain lily**. <N. *Host*, 19c physician>

hos·tage (hos′tij) *n* a person taken and held by an enemy as a way of forcing others to meet certain demands in exchange for the person's safe return. <Old French *hostage* person given as security, from *hoste* guest >

hos·tel (hos′təl) *n* **1** a place offering cheap, simple, dormitory-style accommodations for travellers. **2** a shelter for homeless people in a city. **3** a student residence at a boarding school.

ETYMOLOGY

Hostel and **hotel** are both English versions of Old French *hostel,* but *hotel* entered English later, after the *s* had dropped out in French. The origin of the Old French word is Latin *hospitalia,* meaning "guest rooms." Forgotten after the 1500s, the term began to be used again in the 1800s, thanks to the novelist and poet Sir Walter Scott.

🍁 **hostel school** *n* a residential school.

host·ess (hō′stis) *n* **1** a woman who entertains guests. **2** a woman who greets customers in a restaurant or nightclub and shows them to a table. **3** a female flight attendant. <Old French, from Latin *hospitis* guest>

hos·tile (hos′tīl) *or* (hos′təl) *adj* **1** being or belonging to an enemy: *a hostile army.* **2** showing active dislike or hatred: *a hostile look.* **3** actively and strongly opposed: *Groups hostile to the new policy are staging a demonstration.* **4** unfavourable or harsh: *a hostile climate.* <Latin *hostis* enemy> **hos′tile·ly** *adv.*

hos·til·i·ty (ho stil′ə tē) *n, pl* **hos·til·i·ties 1** a hostile feeling or attitude: *The mistreated child regarded everyone with hostility.* **2 hostilities** *pl* acts of warfare.

a bat	e bed	i bid	o pot	u cup	th **thin**
ā cake	ē me	ī bite	ō go	ū rude	TH **then**
ȧ bar	ə about	ər over	ȯ for	ů put	zh measure

host name *Computers n* the name which identifies a computer on a network. A computer may have more than one host name if it hosts more than one Internet site. Usually, the host name is the same as the DOMAIN NAME.

hot (hot) *adj* **hot·ter, hot·test 1** with a high degree of heat or a high temperature: *The fire is hot.* **2** with a relatively high temperature: *a hot day, hot coffee.* **3** with or giving a bodily sensation of being unpleasantly warm: *This sweater is too hot. I'm hot; let's go swimming.* **4** with a sharp or burning taste: *hot chili.* **5** full of a strong emotion, such as passion, anger, or excitement: *a hot temper, hot with enthusiasm.* **6** new and interesting: *hot news, on a hot scent.* **7** *Informal* **a** very fashionable or popular: *a hot new CD.* **b** *Slang* stolen: *a hot car.* **c** *Slang* sexy. **8** following closely: *in hot pursuit, hot on someone's trail.* **9** bright and intense in colour: *hot pink.* **10** radioactive.
v **hot·ted, hot·ting** (*with* ***up***) make or become more intense: *Things are hotting up.* <Old English *hat*>
hot′ly *adv.* **hot′ness** *n.*
all hot and bothered, *Informal* angry or upset, especially unnecessarily so.
blow hot and cold, keep reversing one's position on an issue.
hot under the collar, *Informal* angry.
in the hot seat, *Informal* **a** in a situation in which one is subject to aggressive and searching questioning. **b** in any embarrassing position.

SYNONYMS

Hot is a general word that refers to a high degree of heat: *It's so hot outside that I'm sweating.*

Boiling refers specifically to liquid that has become so hot it gives off vapour: *The soup was boiling.*

Scalding suggests something that is so hot it can burn: *The scalding liquid turned her skin red.*

hot air *Informal n* meaningless talk or writing: *The candidate's speech was just a lot of hot air.*

hot·bed (hot′bed′) *n* **1** any place favourable to rapid growth, often of something undesirable: *These slums are a hotbed of crime.* **2** a bed of earth covered with glass or plastic and kept warm for growing plants.

hot–blood·ed (hot′ blud′id) *adj* passionate or quick-tempered. Compare COLD-BLOODED (def. 2)

hot button *Informal n* a controversial or sensitive topic.

hot·cake (hot′kāk′) *n* a pancake.
go (or **sell**) **like hotcakes,** be sold quickly.

hot dog *n* **1** a wiener served hot in a long bun, usually with a topping. **2** the wiener alone. **3** a hot-dogger.

hot–dog (hot′dog′) *v* **hot-dogged, hot-dog·ging** do stunts while skiing, surfing, skateboarding, etc. **hot′-dog′ger** *n.* **hot′-dog′ging** *n.*

ho·tel (hō tel′) *n* a building where rooms may be rented and meals bought on a day-to-day basis, usually by travellers. <French *hôtel*, from Latin *hospitalia*>

hot flash *n* a sudden feeling of being too hot, experienced by women during menopause.

hot·foot (hot′fu̇t′) *Informal adv* in great haste: *She went hotfoot up the stairs with me after her.*
v (*usually with* ***it***) go in great haste: *We hotfooted it out to the airport.*

hot·head (hot′hed′) *n* an impetuous or quick-tempered person. **hot′head′ed** *adj.* **hot′head′ed·ness** *n.*

hot·house (hot′hous′) *n* **1** a greenhouse. **2** an environment that encourages the rapid growth of something desirable, sometimes in an overly intense way: *a business which claims to be a hothouse of technological innovation.*

hot·line (hot′līn′) *n* **1** a phone line which people can call anonymously, either to get advice in distress or to listen to recorded information: *a children's help hotline, the weather hotline.* **2** a phone line allowing listeners to call in to a radio or TV talk show to express their views or ask questions. **3** a direct means of communication for emergencies, especially between heads of countries.

hot·link (hot′lingk′) *Computers n, v* link using hypertext: *The Internet site has hotlinks to several others* (*n*). *Related entries in the online dictionary are hotlinked* (*v*).

hot·list (hot′list′) *Computers n* a list of frequently accessed websites, coded so the user can click on any name on the list to go to that site.
v add a website to such a list.

hot plate *n* **1** a small, portable cooking stove, usually with only one burner. **2** a heated metal plate for keeping food hot.

hot potato *Informal n* something controversial that no one wants to deal with: *Extending the school year? I'm not touching that hot potato.*

hot rod *n* a car that is rebuilt or modified to give it extra power and speed.

hot–rod (hot′rod′) *Informal v* **hot-rod·ded, hot-rod·ding** drive around in a hot rod: *hot-rodding around town.* **hot′ rod′der** *n.*

hot·shot (hot′shot′) *Slang n* a person who is skilful or competent in a showy, often aggressive way.
adj of or being such a person: *a hotshot basketball player.*

hot spot *n* **1** an exciting and fashionable bar, restaurant, nightclub, or resort. **2** an area of political or social unrest or violence. **3** a relatively small area showing significant radioactivity. **4** a point in the earth's crust where a volcano is likely to form. **5** the hottest place on a particular day.

hot spring *n* usually, **hot springs** *pl* a place where hot water gushes out of the earth.

hot–tem·pered (hot′tem′pərd) *adj* easily angered.

hot tub *n* a large, deep tub filled with circulating hot water, often outdoors, in which several people can soak at the same time. **hot′-tub′** *v.* **hot′-tub′bing** *n.*

hot war *n* a war involving actual fighting. Compare COLD WAR.

hot–wire (hot′wīr′) *Informal v* **hot-wired, hot-wir·ing** start a vehicle without a key by connecting wires so as to bypass the ignition lock.

hound (hound) *n* **1** a dog that hunts by scent, with large, drooping ears. **2** any dog. **3** *Informal* a person who is always trying to find or get a certain thing: *a news hound, an autograph hound.*
v **1** keep on chasing or tracking: *The police hounded the thief until they caught him.* **2** keep asking or urging: *Her parents hounded her to do her homework.* <Old English *hund*>
follow the hounds, go hunting on horseback with hounds.

hour (our) *n* **1** a unit of time, equal to 3600 seconds or 60 minutes. *Symbol* **h** **2** one of the twelve points that measure time from noon to midnight and from midnight to noon: *The clock chimes every hour on the hour.* **3** a particular or fixed time: *A bell signals the dinner hour for lodge guests.* **4** a short or limited space of time: *After his hour of glory, he was soon forgotten.* **5** the distance that can be travelled in one hour: *They live an hour east of Calgary.* **6 hours** *pl* **a** a period of time set aside for or marked by some activity: *The mall hours are 9 to 9.* **b** one's usual times for going to bed and getting up: *She keeps very odd hours.* <Old French *hure*, from Greek *hora*> **hour′ly** *adj, adv.*
of the hour, most important or receiving most attention at the present time: *He is the man of the hour.*

hour·glass (our′glas′) *n* a device for measuring time, requiring exactly an hour for its contents, usually sand, to go from a container on top, through a narrow neck, to an identical container below.

house (hous) *for n,* (houz) *for v.*
n, pl **hous·es** (hou′ziz) **1 a** a building designed for people to live in, especially one for a single family. **b** the people living in a house: *The whole house was awake by 7 o'clock.* **2** (*often in compounds*) a building for a certain kind of activity or thing, especially a public building: *a courthouse, a house of worship.* **3** a lawmaking assembly, or the place where it meets: *the House of Commons, both houses of Parliament.* **4** a business firm or its place of business: *a publishing house.* **5** a place of entertainment, or the audience in it: *They had a full house for the play.* **6** a family regarded as consisting of an ancestor and all his or her descendants: *He was a prince of the house of Hanover.* **7** *Curling* the goal or target.
v **housed, hous·ing** **1** provide with a home or place to stay: *Where can we house all these children?* **2** be the protective case or frame for: *This box houses the computer's main circuits.* **3** place in a secure or protected position: *The campers housed their provisions in a shack.* **4** take shelter.
adj prepared or favoured by a particular restaurant: *the house wine, salad with the house dressing.* <Old English *hus*>
bring down the house, *Informal* be loudly applauded.
clean house, a thoroughly clean a house. **b** get rid of bad conditions or practices, or useless people, in a business or other institution.
house of cards, something that is flimsy or shaky: *If we don't keep strictly to the schedule, our whole plan will come down like a house of cards.*
keep house, manage a home.
like a house on fire (or **afire**), very well or very fast: *We got along like a house on fire.*
on the house, free: *After visiting the candy factory, we were each given a box of chocolates on the house.*
put (or **set**) **your house in order, a** organize your activities. **b** resolve problems or get rid of bad elements in your life or in an organization.

house arrest *n* the state of being forbidden to leave one's house, by order of a court.

Houseboats have been around for centuries. The Chinese used them as permanent residences, the Romans used them as floating palaces and temples, and today, Canadians use them to holiday on Canada's many waterways.

house·boat (hous′bōt′) *n* a boat designed to be used as a place to live.

house·bound (hous′bound′) *adj* not able to leave one's house: *He is housebound because of his arthritis.*

house·break (hous′brāk′) *v* **house·broke, house·brok·en, house·break·ing** train a pet to urinate and defecate outdoors or only in certain places.

house call *n* a visit to a private home to give medical care or other professional services.

house·clean *v* clean a home. **house′clean′ing** *n.*

house·coat (hous′kōt′) *n* a woman's bathrobe or dressing gown.

house·fly (hous′flī′) *n, pl* **house·flies** a fly that lives around and in houses, feeding on food and garbage. Often shortened to **fly**. See DIPTEROUS for picture.

house·ful (hous′fu̇l) *n, pl* **house·fuls** the amount or number that a house can hold: *a houseful of guests. There seemed to be housefuls of old furniture in the garage.*

house·hold (hous′hōld′) *n* **1** all the people living in one dwelling. **2** a home and its activities: *I run the household when my mother is away.*

house·hold·er (hous′hōl′dər) *n* **1** a person who owns or lives in a house. **2** the head of a family.

household word *n* a familiar word or very famous name.

house·hus·band (hous′huz′bənd) *n* a man who stays at home to look after the house and, usually, children while his wife or partner goes out to work.

house·keep·er (hous′kē′pər) *n* a person who manages a home and its affairs and does the housework, especially one hired to do so.

house·keep·ing (hous′kē′ping) *n* **1** the work of managing a home and its activities. **2** the routine details of any operation.

a bat	e bed	i bid	o pot	u cup	th **thin**
ā cake	ē me	ī bite	ō go	ū rude	TH **then**
ȧ bar	ə about	ər over	ȯ for	u̇ put	zh measure

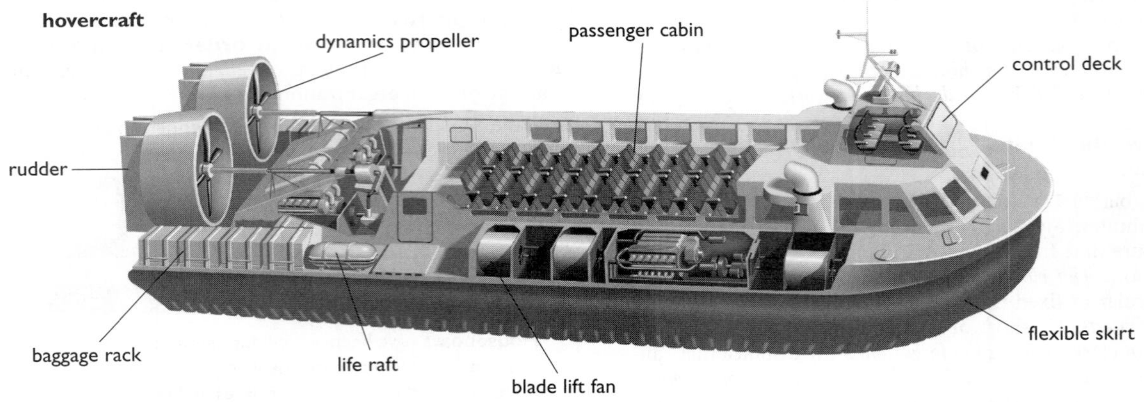

house lights *n* the lighting in the part of a theatre or auditorium where the audience sits, as opposed to the stage lights.

house·maid (hous′mād′) *n* a female servant who does housework.

✱ **House of Assembly** *n* in Newfoundland, the provincial legislature.

House of Commons *n* **1** the part of the federal Parliament made up of elected representatives, or the place in which they meet. **2** the corresponding body and meeting place in the UK.

House of Lords *UK n* the upper branch of Parliament, historically composed of nobles and high-ranking clergy, or the place in which they meet.

House of Representatives *n* **1** *US* the lower house of Congress, or of some state legislatures. **2** the lower branch of the lawmaking body of some other democracies. **3** the place where any of these groups meet.

house·plant (hous′plant′) *n* a plant kept indoors.

house–proud (hous′proud′) *adj* very proud of the appearance of one's house.

house–sit (hous′sit′) *v* **house-sat, house-sit·ting** live in a house to look after it while the owners are away.

house·top (hous′top′) *n* the outer surface of a house roof. **shout from the housetops,** make public to all: *He got an A, and kept shouting about it from the housetops.*

house–train (hous′trān′) *v* housebreak.

house·wares (hous′werz′) *especially Commercial pln* equipment for the home, such as dishes, small appliances, or cleaning utensils.

house·warm·ing (hous′wȯr′ming) *n* a party given when someone moves into a new home.

house·wife (hous′wīf′) *n, pl* **house·wives** (hous′wīvz′) a woman whose full-time job is taking care of the home and children, if any, for her family.

house·work (hous′wərk′) *n* the routine work to be done in a house.

hous·ing (hou′zing) *n* **1** houses or dwellings: *The city does not have enough housing.* **2** a frame or case holding and protecting the parts of a machine.

hove (hōv) a past tense and the past participle of HEAVE.

hov·el (hov′əl) *or* (huv′əl) *n* a small, unattractive, crudely built house. <Middle English>

hov·er (huv′ər) *or* (hov′ər) *v* **1** stay in one place in the air: *The hummingbird hovered next to the flower.* **2** (*often with* ***over***) hang around, waiting or watching: *The dogs hovered around the kitchen door at mealtime. Can't I surf the Net without you hovering over me?* **3** be in an unstable or uncertain condition: *The sick woman hovered between life and death.* <Middle English *hoveren*>

hov·er·craft (huv′ər kraft′) *or* (hov′ər kraft′) *n, pl* **hov·er·craft** a motorized vehicle capable of travelling just above the surface of water or land on a cushion of air created under the vehicle by powerful fans.

how (hou) *adv* **1** in what way or by what means: *Tell her how to do it.* **2** to what degree or extent: *How big is it?* **3** in what state or condition: *How is your sister?* **4** for what reason: *How is it you are so late?* **5** in what exact sense: *How do you mean?*
n the way or manner of doing something: *I'll leave the how up to you; just get it done.* <Old English *hu*>
and how! *Informal* an exclamation of emphatic agreement: "*This store is a little expensive.*" "*And how!*"
how come, *Informal* why: *How come you didn't call me?*
How so? In what way (or for what reason) is it so?
How's that? Pardon me? What did you say?

how·dah (hou′də) *n* a seat for riders on the back of an elephant. <Hindi *haudah*, from Arabic *haudaj*>

Howe Street (hou) *n* the money market or the financiers of Vancouver, especially when contrasted with other areas of Canada. <a street in Vancouver that is the site of many financial institutions>

how·ev·er (hou ev′ər) *adv* **1** but, though, or in spite of that: *It is his; however, you may borrow it. Not today; I can do it tomorrow, however.* **2** no matter how: *However you do it, it works out the same.* **3** (*emphatically, in questions*) how: *However did you get so dirty?*

how·itz·er (hou′it sər) *n* a weapon for firing shells in a high curve. <Czech *houfnice* catapult>

howl (houl) *v* **1** give a long, loud, mournful cry: *howling winds. The dog howled at the moon.* **2** yell or shout: *to howl with pain. We were howling with laughter.*
n **1** a long, loud, mournful cry. **2** a shout of scorn, pain, or amusement. **3** *Informal* something very funny: *Their skit was a howl.* <Middle English *houlen*>
howl down, drown out by howling: *The speaker was howled down by his opponents.*

howl·er (hou′lər) *n* **1** *Informal* a ridiculous mistake. **2** a person who or thing that howls.

how–to (hou′tü′) *adj* giving basic instructions for making or doing something: *a how-to book on building model airplanes.*

hoy·den (hoi′dən) *n* a boisterous, rough girl; a tomboy. <Dutch *heiden* a rustic person> **hoy′den·ish** *adj.*

Hoyle (hoil) *n* a standard book of rules and instructions for playing card games. <E. *Hoyle,* 18c writer on card games>
according to Hoyle, according to the rules or customs; fair; correct.

hp or **HP** horsepower.

HRH or **H.R.H.** His Royal Highness; Her Royal Highness.

HTML *Computers n* in full, **Hypertext Markup Language** a computer programming language for tagging text, used to create and display hypertext files on the Internet.

http *Computers n* in full, **hypertext transfer protocol** the basic protocol (standard) that allows documents to be delivered across the Internet.

hua·ra·che (wə rȧ′chē) *n* a flat Mexican sandal with leather straps to cover the upper foot. <Spanish>

hub (hub) *n* **1** the central part of a wheel. **2** a centre of activity, interest, or importance: *The office is the hub of the school.* **3** *Computers* a common connection point for devices in a network. <origin uncertain>

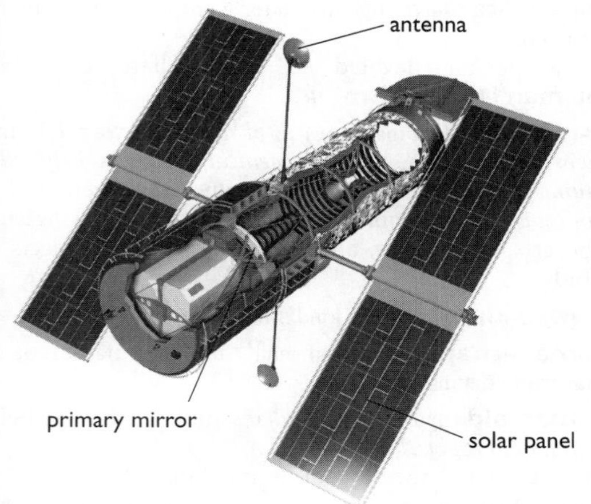

Hub·ble telescope (hub′əl) *n* a telescope mounted on a satellite that orbits around the earth and photographs distant parts of the universe. <E.P. *Hubble,* 20c astronomer>

hub·bub (hub′ub) *n* a lot of confused noise: *There was a hubbub when the crowd was told to move.* <perhaps Irish>

SYNONYMS

Hubbub means "disorderly commotion": *There was a hubbub when the rap star was spotted in the crowd.*

Riot suggests an uncontrolled disturbance created by a large number of people: *Property was damaged and stores were looted during the riot.*

hub·cap (hub′kap′) *n* the cover, often decorative, that fits over the hub of a wheel on a motor vehicle.

hu·bris (hyü′bris) *n* excessive pride or self-confidence. <Greek *hybris*>

huck·le·ber·ry (huk′əl ber′ē) *n, pl* **huck·le·ber·ries** a glossy, blackish, many-seeded berry related to the blueberry. <possibly *hurtleberry* whortleberry>

huck·ster (huk′stər) *n* **1** a person who sells or promotes something dishonestly and aggressively. **2** a peddler or seller of small items.
v **1** sell or advertise aggressively. **2** peddle or haggle. <Middle English> **huck′ster·ism′** *n.*

hud·dle (hud′əl) *v* **hud·dled, hud·dling** **1** crowd close together: *The sheep had huddled in a corner of the pen.* **2** crouch or curl up, especially for warmth: *The rescued swimmer sat huddled in a blanket by the fire.* **3** gather for a huddle (*n* defs. 1, 2).
n **1** *Football* during a game, a meeting of players in a small group behind the line of scrimmage to receive instructions on the next play. **2** *Informal* a secret conference, especially to plan strategy: *During the court recess, the lawyer went into a huddle with her partner.* **3** a confused mass of people or things crowded together. <German>

Hud·son Bay (hud′sən) *n* an inland sea in northern Canada. <H. *Hudson,* 16c explorer>

✱ **Hudson's Bay blanket** *n* a woollen blanket, typically cream-coloured, with wide green, red, yellow, and indigo stripes.

✱ **Hudson's Bay Company** *n* a company chartered in 1670 to trade in furs in N America.

ETYMOLOGY

Hudson's Bay Company is the popular and traditional name of *The Company of Adventurers of England Trading into Hudson's Bay.* The company's name was taken from Hudson Bay, an inland sea in northern Canada, named after the explorer Henry Hudson.

a bat	e bed	i bid	o pot	u cup	th **thin**
ā cake	ē me	ī bite	ō go	ü rude	TH **then**
ȧ bar	ə about	ər over	ȯ for	u̇ put	zh measure

H

hue (hyū) *n* a colour, shade, or tint: *all the hues of the rainbow.* <Old English *hiw*>

hue and cry *n* **1** shouts of alarm or protest: *There was a great hue and cry when the referee called a foul.* **2** in former times, an alarm raised to call people to chase a criminal, and the chase itself. <Old French *huer* to shout>

huff (huf) *n* a fit of anger or annoyance: *She went off in a huff, feeling insulted.*
v **1** puff or blow: *The old locomotive huffed along.* **2** sniff glue or other things as a form of substance abuse. <imitative>

huff·y (huf′ē) *adj* **huff·i·er, huff·i·est** quick to take offence. **huff′i·ly** *adv.* **huff′i·ness** *n.*

hug (hug) *v* **hugged, hug·ging** **1** put one's arms around and hold close, usually to show affection: *She hugged her little boy.* **2** keep or be close to: *The boat hugged the shore.*
n an act of hugging: *He gave his mother a quick hug.* <Scandinavian> **hug′ga·ble** *adj.*

huge (hyūj) *adj* **hug·er, hug·est** extremely large or great in quantity, scope, or degree: *a huge undertaking. A whale is a huge animal.* <Old French *ahuge*> **huge′ly** *adv.* **huge′ness** *n.*

SYNONYMS

Huge is one of several words that suggests something very large either in size or extent: *Her mother inherited a huge amount of money.*

Gigantic means "enormous": *The artist created a gigantic sculpture for display in the courtyard.*

Tremendous can mean "very great in size or scope": *There was a tremendous display of fireworks on Canada Day.*

hug·ger–mug·ger (hug′ər mug′ər) *Informal n* **1** confusion or disorder. **2** secrecy or concealment.
adj, adv **1** in confusion or disorder. **2** secret or concealed. <origin uncertain>

Hu·gue·not (hyū′gə not′) *or* (hyū′gə nō′) *n* a member of a group of French Protestants of the 1500s and 1600s. <French *eigenot*, from German *Eidgenoss* confederate>

huh (hu) *interj* a sound expressing surprise or contempt, or asking a person to repeat what he or she has just said.

hu·la (hū′lə) *n* a Hawaiian dance, with rhythmic hip movements and hand gestures that tell a story. <Hawaiian>

Hula Hoop *Trademark n* a plastic hoop designed to be spun around the body by swinging the hips.

hulk (hulk) *n* **1** the body of an old or worn-out ship. **2** a big, clumsy person or thing. <Old English *hulc* fast ship>

hulk·ing (hul′king) *adj* big and clumsy.

hull[1] (hul) *n* the main body of a ship or boat.
v pierce the hull of a ship with a shell or torpedo. <Middle English>

hull[2] (hul) *n* **1** the husk of grain or the outer covering of a fruit or vegetable, especially the pod of peas and beans. **2** the calyx of some fruits, such as the cluster of green leaves at the stem of a strawberry.
v remove the hulls from fruit, seeds, or grain. <Old English *hulu*> **hull′er** *n.*

hul·la·ba·loo (hul′ə bə lū′) *n* a loud noise or disturbance. <imitative>

hum (hum) *v* **hummed, hum·ming** **1** make a continuous murmuring or buzzing sound: *The sewing machine hummed away.* **2** sing with closed lips, not using words: *to hum a little tune.* **3** *Informal* be busy and active: *The workshop was humming as we built the stage sets.*
n **1** a humming sound: *the hum of bees, the hum of distant traffic.* **2** busy activity: *the hum of daily life.* <imitative> **hum′mer** *n.*

hu·man (hyū′mən) *adj* **1** to do with people: *Men, women, and children are human beings.* **2** to do with the natural character of all or most people: *human weaknesses.* **3** warm, understanding, and down-to-earth: *She is a very human person.*
n a human being. <Old French, from Latin *humanus*> **hu′man·ize′** *v.* **hu′man·like** *adj.* **hu′man·ly** *adv.*

CONFUSABLES

Human refers to qualities belonging specially to people as distinct from animals or deities.

Humane refers to a person's compassionate feelings toward animals or other people.

human being *n* a man, woman, or child.

Human Development Index HDI.

hu·mane (hyū mān′) *adj* decent and fair: *humane working conditions, the humane treatment of prisoners.* <human> **hu·mane′ly** *adv.* **hu·mane′ness** *n.*

hu·man·ism (hyū′mə niz′əm) *n* **1** a system of thought expressing the belief that human beings can provide meaning, values, and responsibilities to their lives through the power of reason alone. **2** **Humanism** during the Renaissance, a revival of interest in ancient Greece and Rome. **hu′man·ist** *n.* **hu′man·is′tic** *adj.*

hu·man·i·tar·i·an (hyū man′ə ter′ē ən) *adj* helping people in need.
n a person devoted to the welfare of others. **hu·man′i·tar′i·an·ism′** *n.*

hu·man·i·ty (hyū man′ə tē) *n, pl* **hu·man·i·ties** **1** human beings taken as a group: *Medical advances help all of humanity.* **2** the fact of being human. **3** humaneness: *Treat animals with humanity.* **4 the humanities** *pl* languages, the arts, philosophy, and social sciences as subjects for study.

hu·man·kind (hyū′mən kīnd′) *n* all human beings.

hu·man–made (hyū′mən mād′) *adj* manufactured; not naturally occurring.

hu·man·oid (hyū′mə noid′) *adj* resembling a human being: *humanoid robots.*
n **1** an early ancestor of humankind. **2** any creature resembling a human being: *Science fiction often deals with humanoids from other planets.*

human race *n* all human beings.

human resources *n* **1** (*with plural verb*) the employees in a business or organization. **2 Human Resources** (*with singular verb*) in a company, the department concerned with hiring, firing, salary levels, and other relations with employees. *Abbrev.* **HR**

human rights *n* the rights that are believed to belong to every individual in a society.

hum·ble (hum′bəl) *adj* **hum·bler, hum·blest 1** with or showing an awareness of one's own imperfections: *The occasional failure keeps us humble.* **2** deeply or courteously respectful: *in my humble opinion.* **3** lacking high social or economic status: *a humble dwelling, humble tasks.*
v **hum·bled, hum·bling** make humble: *humbled by defeat.* <Old French, from Latin *humilis* low, from *humus* ground> **hum′ble·ness** *n.* **hum′bly** *adv.*

humble pie *n* in former times, an inferior pie made of scraps of meat, intestines, etc.
eat humble pie, a admit one's mistake and say that one is sorry. **b** be forced to do something humiliating.

ETYMOLOGY

Humble pie is from *umble pie*, a pie made of *umbles* (worthless bits of meat), formerly given to servants. The expression has obviously been influenced by the word *humble*, whose source is completely different.

hum·bug (hum′bug′) *n* **1** nonsense or foolishness: *That argument is pure humbug.* **2** a person who claims to be something other than he or she is. **3** a fraud or hoax. **4** a hard candy, usually with stripes.
interj used to express disagreement or contempt. <origin unknown>

hum·ding·er (hum′ding′ər) *Slang n* a person who or thing that is remarkable in some way: *That last retort was a humdinger!* <origin unknown>

hum·drum (hum′drum′) *adj* dull or commonplace.
n a dull routine. <probably based on *hum*>

hu·mid (hyū′mid) *adj* with a relatively high level of water vapour in the atmosphere: *a hot, humid day.* <Latin *umere* be moist> **hu·mid′i·ty** *n.*

🍁 **hu·mi·dex** (hyū′mə deks′) *n* an index of discomfort resulting from a combination of humidity and heat.

hu·mid·i·fy (hyū mid′ə fī′) *v* **hu·mid·i·fied, hu·mid·i·fy·ing** increase the level of water vapour in the air in a building. **hu·mid′i·fi′er** *n.*

hu·mi·dor (hyū′mə dȯr′) *n* an airtight container for keeping cigars or pipe tobacco moist.

hu·mil·i·ate (hyū mil′ē āt′) *v* **hu·mil·i·at·ed, hu·mil·i·at·ing** lower someone's pride, dignity, or self-respect: *Don't humiliate her by criticizing her in public.* <Latin *humiliare*, from *humulis* humble>
hu·mil′i·a′tion *n.*

hu·mil·i·ty (hyū mil′ə tē) *n, pl* **hu·mil·i·ties** the quality of being humble.

hum·ming·bird (hum′ing bərd′) *n* a small, brightly coloured bird of the Americas, with wings that move so rapidly they make a humming sound. See BIRD for picture.

hum·mus (hum′əs) *n* a Middle Eastern paste or spread of ground chick peas and sesame seeds, lemon juice, garlic, and olive oil. <Arabic *hummus*>

hu·mong·ous or **hu·mung·ous** (hyū mong′gəs) *or* (hyū mung′gəs) *Slang adj* extremely huge. <possibly *huge* + *monstrous*>

hu·mor (hyū′mər) HUMOUR.

hu·mor·ist (hyū′mə rist) *n* a comic writer, performer, or artist.

hu·mor·ous (hyū′mə rəs) *adj* causing or meant to cause laughter or amusement. **hu′mor·ous·ly** *adv.*

GRAMMAR AND USAGE

Humorous is one example of a word in which the *u* is dropped from its stem word, *humour*, when the adjective is created. Other such words include:
glamorous and *glamour*
honorable and *honour*
tumorous and *tumour*

hu·mour or **hu·mor** (hyū′mər) *n* **1** an amusing quality: *I see no humour in your tricks.* **2** the ability to see or show the funny side of things: *a good sense of humour.* **3** funny material for reading, watching, or listening to: *She is one of the best writers of humour I know.* **4** a state of mind or mood: *Sunny weather puts me in a good humour.* **5** a fancy or whim: *It was a humour of the emperor to wear a crown at all times.* **6** *Archaic* one of four bodily fluids (blood, phlegm, choler, and melancholy) formerly supposed to determine a person's physical and mental qualities.
v give in to someone's desires or requests: *A sick person has to be humoured.* <Old French, from Latin *umor* fluid>
hu′mour·less *adj.*
out of humour, angry or in a bad mood.
sense of humour, the ability to laugh or be amused.

hump (hump) *n* a rounded lump sticking up from a surface: *Some camels have two humps on their backs.*
v bend upward into an arc: *The cat humped its back when it saw the dog.* <Dutch *homp* lump>
over the hump, past the most difficult part.

hump·back (hump′bak′) *n* **1** a hunchback. **2** a large baleen whale with a hump and long white flippers. **3** a small Pacific salmon with dark spots on the back.
hump′backed′ *adj.*

humph (humpf) *interj, n* used to express doubt, disgust, or contempt.

hu·mus (hyū′məs) *n* rich, dark soil made up of decayed leaves and other vegetable matter. <Latin = earth>

Hun (hun) *n* **1** a member of a nomadic Asiatic people who overran much of eastern and central Europe between the 300s and 400s CE. **2 hun** a wildly cruel or destructive person.

a bat	e bed	i bid	o pot	u cup	th **thin**
ā cake	ē me	ī bite	ō go	ū rude	TH **then**
ȧ bar	ə about	ər over	ȯ for	u̇ put	zh measure

hunch (hunch) *v* draw, bend, or form into a hump: *He sat hunched over with his chin on his knees.*
n **1** a hump, especially on one's back. **2** *Informal* a vague feeling or suspicion: *I had a hunch we would win.* <origin unknown>

hunch·back (hunch′bak′) *n* **1** a person with a crooked back that forms a hump at the shoulders. **2** a crooked back like this. **hunch′backed′** *adj.*

hun·dred (hun′drəd) *n, pl* **hun·dreds** or (*after a number*) **hun·dred** **1** ten times ten: *Count to a hundred.* **2** a 100-dollar bill. **3** **hundreds** *pl* the numbers between 100 and 999.
adj ten times ten: *two hundred pages.* <Old English *hund* 100 + *red* number> **hun′dredth** *adj, adv.*

hun·dredth (hun′drədth) *n* **1** next after the ninety-ninth: *You are the hundredth on the list!* **2** one of a hundred equal parts: *One cent is one-hundredth of a dollar.*
adj, adv See HUNDRED.

hun·dred·weight (hun′drəd wāt′) *n, pl* **hun·dred·weight** a nonmetric unit of mass, equal to 100 pounds (about 45 kg) in Canada and 112 pounds (about 51 kg) in the UK.

hung (hung) *v* a past tense and the past participle of HANG.
adj unable to agree on a verdict in a jury.
hung over, with a hangover.
hung up, *Informal* **a** delayed: *hung up at the office.* **b** (*with* ***on, about,*** *or* ***over***) anxious or preoccupied: *too hung up on the details. There's no need to get hung up about it.*

Hun·gar·y (hung′gə rē) *n* a country in central Europe. See the APPENDIX. **Hun·gar′i·an** (hung gā′ rē ən) *adj, n.*

hun·ger (hung′gər) *n* **1** an uncomfortable or painful sensation caused by lack of food. **2** lack of food, or the resulting illness or weakness: *the problem of hunger in the world.* **3** a strong desire; a longing: *a hunger for affection.*
v **1** endure hunger. **2** have a strong desire: *The lonely girl hungered for friends.* <Old English *hungor*>

hunger strike *n* a refusal to eat until certain demands are met.

hun·gry (hung′grē) *adj* **hun·gri·er, hun·gri·est** feeling or showing hunger or desire: *hungry beggars, a hungry look. He is hungry for power.* <Old English *hungrig*>
hun′gri·ly *adv.*

hunk (hungk) *n* **1** *Informal* a big lump, piece, or slice: *a hunk of cheese.* **2** *Slang* a handsome, strong-looking boy or man. <related to Flemish *hunke* hunk> **hun′ky** *adj.*

hun·ker (hung′kər) *v* (*with* ***down***) **1** squat on one's haunches. **2** get into a defensive position, ready for an attack. <origin uncertain>

hunk·y–dor·y (hung′kē dô′rē) *Slang adj* going well. <Perhaps obsolete *hunk* in a safe position, from Dutch *honc* hiding place. The origin of *dory* is unknown.>

hunt (hunt) *v* **1** go after wild animals or birds to catch or kill them. **2** go after or look for someone in order to hurt or persecute. **3** search thoroughly for someone or something: *to hunt through drawers, hunt for a missing child, hunt for clues.*
n **1** an act of hunting. **2** a trip or outing for the purpose of hunting: *We are going on a duck hunt.* <Old English *hunitian*> **hunt′er** *n.* **hunt′ing** *n.*
hunt down, a hunt until caught or killed. **b** look for until found.
hunt up, find by searching.

hunt·er–gath·er·er (hunt′ər gaᴛʜ′ə rər) *n* a member of a people that solely supports itself by hunting animals and gathering food from wild plants.
adj to do with this way of making a living: *a hunter-gatherer economy.*

hunting ground *n* a place or region for hunting.

hur·dle (hər′dəl) *n* **1** a barrier that must be jumped over in a race. **2** an obstacle or difficulty. **3** **hurdles** *pl* (*with singular verb*) a race in which the runners jump over hurdles. See TRACK AND FIELD for picture.
v **hur·dled, hur·dling** **1** jump over: *The horse hurdled both the fence and the ditch.* **2** overcome an obstacle or difficulty. <Old English *hyrdel* temporary fence>

hur·dy–gur·dy (hər′dē gər′dē) *n, pl* **hur·dy-gur·dies** a hand organ played by turning a handle.

hurl (hərl) *v* **1** throw with force: *He hurled the stone far out into the lake.* **2** utter violently: *to hurl insults.* **3** *Slang* vomit.
n a forcible or violent throw. <Middle English>
hurl′er *n.*

Hu·ron (hyůr′on) *n, pl* **Hu·rons** **1** in former times, a member of a First Nations people living in the region between Lake Huron and Lake Ontario. The descendants of these people now live in Québec. **2** their Iroquoian language.
adj to do with these people or their language.

hur·rah (hə rä′) *interj, n* a shout of joy or approval. Also, **hooray, hurray.**

hur·ri·cane (hər′ə kān′) *n* **1** a tropical cyclone that forms over the Atlantic or Caribbean, with winds of more than 120 km/h and, usually, very heavy rain. **2** a wind with a speed of more than 117 km/h. See GALE for confusable. **3** a sudden, violent outburst or commotion: *a hurricane of cheers.* <Arawak (a language of S America) *hurakán* god of the storm>

A **hurricane lamp** uses a cotton or flax wick and capillary action to draw up oil. When the lamp is lit, the oil burns at the end of the wick.

hurricane lamp *n* an oil lamp with a glass chimney to protect the flame from the wind.

hur·ried (hər′ēd) *adj* **1** done or made in a hurry: *a hurried reply.* **2** forced to hurry. **hur′ried·ly** *adv.*

hur·ry (hər′ē) *v* **hur·ried, hur·ry·ing 1** move or act faster than is easy or natural: *We'll have to hurry to make it on time.* **2** take or send quickly: *They hurried the sick child to the doctor.* **3** urge to hurry: *Don't hurry the driver.* **4** cause to happen faster than usual: *Please hurry dinner.*
n, pl **hur·ries 1** the state of hurrying: *In my hurry, I dropped the eggs.* **2** a state of eagerness: *She was in a hurry to see her father.* <imitative>

SYNONYMS

Hurry refers to action that is quicker than is usual, and often suggests rushing: *Despite her hurry, she missed her plane.*

Haste emphasizes trying to save time, and often suggests rushed action, sometimes too rushed: *In his haste to finish the essay, he made many errors.*

Rush suggests swift movement of people or things: *The horses went in a rush toward the fresh hay.*

hurt (hərt) *v* **hurt, hurt·ing 1** cause pain, suffering, harm, or damage: *to hurt your arm, to hurt someone's reputation. These new shoes hurt.* **2** feel pain: *My ankle hurts.*
n a wound or injury: *to kiss the hurt.* <Old French *hurter* to strike>
be hurting for, *Informal* need badly: *We're hurting for time, here, folks, so move fast.*

hurt·ful (hərt′fəl) *adj* causing pain or distress: *a mean and hurtful remark.* **hurt′ful·ly** *adv.*

hur·tle (hər′təl) *v* **hur·tled, hur·tling** move at a great speed, especially in a seemingly uncontrolled way: *The express train hurtled past. The car hurtled across the road into a fence.* <Middle English>

hus·band (huz′bənd) *n* a married man considered in relation to his spouse.
v manage carefully and economically: *to husband your resources.* <Old Norse *hus* house + *bondi* having a household> **hus′band·less** *adj.* **hus′band·ly** *adj.*

hus·band·ry (huz′bən drē) *n* **1** farming. **2** careful, economical management.

hush (hush) *v* make or become quiet: *The wind has hushed. Hush your dog.*
n a stopping of sounds: *There was a hush as he walked in.*
interj be quiet! calm down! <obsolete *husht*>
hush up, a keep secret. **b** *Informal* be silent!

hush–hush (hush′hush′) *adj* secret or confidential: *It's all very hush-hush.*

hush money *Informal n* money paid to keep a person from revealing information.

husk (husk) *n* **1** the dry outer covering of certain seeds or fruits. **2** the dry or rough outer layer of something.
v remove the husk from: *Husk the corn.* <perhaps Dutch *huuskyn* little house, from *huus* house> **husk′er** *n.*

husk·y[1] (hus′kē) *adj* **husk·i·er, husk·i·est 1** of a voice, low-pitched and slightly hoarse. **2** big, heavy, and strong: *a husky young man.* <*husk,* from the toughness of the corn husk> **husk′i·ly** *adv.* **husk′i·ness** *n.*

husk·y[2] (hus′kē) *n, pl* **hus·kies** in full, **Siberian husky** a powerful Arctic working dog with a thick coat. <variant of *Eskimo*>

hus·sar (hə zär′) *n* a light-armed cavalry soldier. <German, from Italian *corsaro* pirate>

hus·sy (hus′ē) *n, pl* **hus·sies** a poorly-mannered or immoral girl or woman. <Middle English>

hus·tings (hus′tingz) *n* an election campaign, tour, or meeting, thought of as a forum for speeches and debates.

ETYMOLOGY

Hustings comes from Old Norse *husthing,* meaning "council," from *hus* (house) + *thing* (assembly).

In England, candidates stood on the hustings (a platform) to address voters.

hus·tle (hus′əl) *v* **hus·tled, hus·tling 1** hurry: *We hustle to get ready for school in the morning.* **2** *Informal* go or work quickly or with tireless energy. **3** *Slang* **a** sell or get by dishonest or aggressive means: *to hustle used cars.* **b** work as a prostitute. **4** shove or push roughly: *They hustled him along the street.*
n **1** hurry: *It was done with much hustle and bustle.* **2** the act of hustling. <Dutch *hutselen* shake>

hus·tler (hus′lər) *n* **1** an energetic, resourceful, usually unscrupulous person. **2** a prostitute.

hut (hut) *n* a small, roughly built house. <German *hütte*> **hut′like′** *adj.*

hutch (huch) *n* **1** a box or cage in which rabbits or other small domesticated animals are kept. **2** a cupboard containing shelves for dishes and other items. <Old French, from Latin *hutica* chest>

🍁 **Hut·ter·ite** (hut′ə rīt′) *n* a member of a pacifist Protestant group that came to western Canada and the northwestern US in the 1800s, practising a simple way of life in farming communes.
adj to do with the Hutterites: *Hutterite communities.* <J. *Hutter,* 16c founder>

hy·a·cinth (hī′ə sinth′) *n* a plant related to the lily, growing from a bulb and with a spike of small, fragrant, bell-shaped flowers. <Latin, from Greek *hyakinthos*>

hy·brid (hī′brid) *n* **1** a plant or animal produced by crossbreeding two plants or animals of different species or varieties: *Most garden roses are hybrids.* **2** a product of blending different kinds of things: *Opera is a sort of hybrid of theatre and music.*
adj to do with a hybrid: *A mule is a hybrid animal.* <Latin *hybrida* mongrel>

hy·brid·ize (hī′bri dīz′) *v* **hy·brid·ized, hy·brid·iz·ing 1** crossbreed: *Botanists hybridize different kinds of plants to get new varieties.* **2** produce by crossbreeding. **hy′brid·i·za′tion** *n.*

a bat	e bed	i bid	o pot	u cup	th **thin**
ā cake	ē me	ī bite	ō go	ü rude	ᴛʜ **then**
ȧ bar	ə about	ər over	ȯ for	u̇ put	zh measure

hy·dra (hī′drə) *Greek myth n, pl* **hy·dras** or **hy·drae** (hī′drē) *or* (hī′drī) **1 Hydra** a monstrous serpent with nine heads, whose heads multiplied as they were cut off. **2** a freshwater polyp with a tubelike body and a ring of tentacles around the mouth. <Latin, from Greek *hydra* water snake>

hy·dran·gea (hī drān′jə) *n* a shrub with large clusters of small flowers. <Latin, from Greek *hydor* water + *angeion* vessel, from its cup-shaped seed>

hy·drant (hī′drənt) *n* a short, wide, capped pipe that is connected to the main underground water pipes of a town or city to provide a supply of water for fighting fires. <Greek *hydor* water>

hy·drate (hī′drāt) *v* **hy·drat·ed, hy·drat·ing 1** *Chemistry* combine with water. **2** moisturize: *Drinking plenty of water helps to hydrate the skin.*
n a compound produced when any of certain substances unites with water. <Greek *hydor* water> **hy·dra′tion** *n.*

hy·drau·lic (hī drol′ik) *adj* **1** to do with water or other liquid in motion. **2** operated by the pressure of water or other liquid: *hydraulic brakes, a hydraulic press.* **3** hardening under water: *hydraulic cement.* **4** specializing in hydraulics: *a hydraulic engineer.*
n **hydraulics** (*with singular verb*) the branch of science dealing with water and other liquids in motion and their uses in engineering. <Latin, from Greek *hydor* water + *aulos* pipe> **hy·drau′li·cal·ly** *adv.*

hydraulic fluid *n* an oil used in hydraulic systems such as power steering.

hy·dro (hī′drō) *n* **1** electricity produced by using the energy of falling water: *Niagara Falls provides hydro for many factories.* **2** electricity as a utility distributed by a power company: *The hydro was off for two hours during the storm.* <*hydro-electricity*>

hydro– *combining form* **1** to do with water: *hydroelectric.* **2** combined with hydrogen: *hydrochloric.*

ETYMOLOGY

All words beginning with **hydr–** came originally from a form of Greek *hydor*, meaning "water." Several such words came into English through Latin.

Other more recently invented words have been created as part of our modern technical vocabulary; for example: *hydrofoil*, *hydrometer*, *hydroplane*, *hydroponics*, and *hydrotherapy*.

hy·dro·car·bon (hī′drō kȧr′bən) *n* an organic compound containing only hydrogen and carbon, such as methane, benzene, and acetylene.

hy·dro·ceph·a·lus (hī′drō sef′ə ləs) *n* a condition, especially in infancy, in which fluid collects in the skull, often causing the head to become greatly enlarged. <*hydor* water + Greek *kephale* head> **hy′dro·ce·phal′ic** *adj, n.*

hy·dro·chlo·ric acid (hī′drə klȯ′rik) *n* a strong acid containing hydrogen and chlorine that is clear and colourless and has a strong, sharp odour. <*hydro*(*gen*) + *chlor*(*ine*)>

hy·dro–e·lec·tric·i·ty (hī′drō i lek′tris′ə tē) *n* electricity generated by using the energy of falling water, or by the friction of water or steam. See DAM for picture. **hy′dro-e·lec′tric** *adj.*

hy·dro·fluor·ic acid (hī′drə flȯ′rik) *n* a colourless, corrosive, volatile liquid containing hydrogen and fluorine. <*hydro*(*gen*) + *fluor*(*ine*)>

hy·dro·foil (hī′drə foil′) *n* **1** one of a set of blades or fins attached at an angle to the hull of a boat so that the boat, when moving, is lifted just clear of the water. **2** a boat equipped with hydrofoils.

hy·dro·gen (hī′drə jən) *n* an element that is a colourless, odourless gas, burning easily, and combining with oxygen to form water. *Symbol* **H** <French, from Greek *hydor* water + *-genes* born>

hy·dro·gen·ate (hī′drə jə nāt′) *v* **hy·dro·gen·at·ed, hy·dro·gen·at·ing** combine or treat with hydrogen; especially, combine hydrogen with an unsaturated organic compound, such as a vegetable oil, to produce solid fat. **hy′dro·gen·a′tion** *n.*

hydrogen bomb *n* a bomb that uses the nuclear fusion of atoms to cause an explosion of tremendous force.

hydrogen peroxide *n* a colourless, unstable liquid often used in solution as an antiseptic or bleaching agent.

hydrogen sulphide or **sulfide** *n* a flammable, poisonous gas with an odour like that of rotten eggs, found especially in mineral waters and decaying matter.

hy·drog·ra·phy (hī drog′rə fē) *n* **1** the branch of geography that studies bodies of water, especially with reference to their use for navigation and commerce. **2** the bodies of water in a certain region, especially as dealt with on a map, survey, or chart: *the hydrography of northern Saskatchewan.* **hydro·graph′ic** *adj.*

hy·dro·log·ic cycle (hī′drə loj′ik) *n* the process in which water evaporates from the ocean, falls to earth as precipitation, and returns to the ocean from rivers fed by rain, melting snow, etc.

hy·drol·y·sis (hī drol′ə sis) *n, pl* **hy·drol·y·ses** (hī drol′ə sēz) a chemical reaction between a compound and a water molecule, splitting up the compound and the water molecule and forming new compounds. <Greek *hydor* water + *lysis* a loosening, from *lyein* to loosen> **hy′dro·lyze′** or **hy′dro·lyse′** *v.*

hy·drom·e·ter (hī drom′ə tər) *n* an instrument for measuring the density of liquids.

hy·dro·pho·bi·a (hī′drə fō′bē ə) *n* rabies, especially in human beings. <Greek *hydro-* water + *phobos* fear>

hy·dro·plane (hī′drə plān′) *n* **1** a light, fast motorboat that glides on the surface of the water. **2** HYDROFOIL (def. 2).
v glide, often uncontrollably, on a wet surface.

hy·dro·pon·ics (hī′drə pon′iks) *n* (*with singular verb*) the science of growing plants in water containing the necessary nutrients instead of in soil. <*hydor* water + Latin *ponere* to place> **hy′dro·pon′ic** *adj.*

hy·dro·sphere (hī′drə sfēr′) *n* **1** all the water on the surface of the earth. **2** the water vapour in the atmosphere. Compare ATMOSPHERE, LITHOSPHERE.

hy·dro·stat·ics (hī′drō stat′iks) *n* (*with singular verb*) the branch of physics that studies the equilibrium and pressure of water and other liquids.

hy·dro·ther·a·py (hī′drō ther′ə pē) *n* the use of water to treat disease or rehabilitate injured people, such as by bathing or exercising in water.

hy·dro·tro·pism (hī drot′rə piz′əm) *n* the tendency of an organism to grow or turn in the direction of water. <Greek *hydor* water + *tropos* a turning>

hy·drous (hī′drəs) *Chemistry adj* containing water or combined with water.

The **hyena** has extremely powerful jaws, which it uses to crush the bones of its prey. The hyena can eat and digest a whole animal—bones, horns, and teeth included.

hy·e·na (hī ē′nə) *n* a wild, wolflike, flesh-eating mammal of Africa and Asia that lives mostly by scavenging. <Latin, from Greek *hyaina* pig>

hy·giene (hī′jēn) *n* the principles and practices, especially cleanliness, that help to prevent disease: *personal hygiene. Good hygiene helps prevent the spread of disease.* <French, from Greek *hygies* healthy> **hy·gien′ic** *adj.*

hy·gien·ist (hī′jē nist) *or* (hī jē′nist) *n* **1** a person trained in hygiene. **2** a dental hygienist.

hy·grom·e·ter (hī grom′ə tər) *n* an instrument for determining the amount of moisture in the air or in a gas. <Greek *hygros* wet + meter>

hy·men (hī′mən) *n* a fold of mucous membrane that extends partly across the opening of the vagina until ruptured. <Latin, from Greek *hymen* membrane>

hymn (him) *n* a religious song of praise, especially one sung as part of a service. <Latin, from Greek *hymnos*> **hymn′like′** *adj.*

hym·nal (him′nəl) *n* a book of hymns. Also, **hymnbook**.

hype (hīp) *Informal n* exaggerated, intense, or sensational publicity or promotion.
v **hyped, hyp·ing** (*usually with* ***up***) publicize or promote extravagantly. <origin uncertain>

hy·per (hī′pər) *Slang adj* **1** overexcited: *Don't get all hyper about it; it's not so bad.* **2** habitually excitable, or too talkative and active: *She's so hyper, I can't spend more than ten minutes with her.* <*hyperactive*>

hyper– *prefix* **1** too much; more than normal: *hyperacidity, hyperactive.* **2** *Computers* to do with hypertext. <Greek *hyper* beyond, excessive>

hy·per·a·cid·i·ty (hī′pər ə sid′ə tē) *n* more than the normal amount of acid, especially in the stomach juices, causing indigestion or heartburn.

hy·per·ac·tive (hī′pər ak′tiv) *adj* abnormally or extremely active. **hy′per·ac·tiv′i·ty** *n.*

hy·per·bo·la (hī pər′bə lə) *Mathematics n* a curve formed when a cone is cut by a plane that makes a larger angle with the base than the side of the cone makes. <Latin, from Greek *hyper-* beyond + *ballein* throw>

hy·per·bo·le (hī pər′bə lē′) *n* a figure of speech in which extravagant exaggeration is used for emphasis or effect. Examples: *I could listen to that record all night. That colour is so bright I need to wear sunglasses.* <Latin, from Greek. See HYBERBOLA.>

hy·per·crit·i·cal (hī′pər krit′ə kəl) *adj* extremely critical. **hy′per·crit′i·cal·ly** *adv.*

hy·per·link (hī′pər lingk′) *Computers n* a link from one Internet page, file, or document to another, embedded in a highlighted text or an image, so that by clicking on it a user can activate the link. See also HYPERTEXT.

hy·per·me·di·a (hī′pər mē′dē ə) *Computers pln* the hypertext system that allows the downloading of graphics, sound files, video files, and text.

hy·per·o·pi·a (hī′pə rō′pē ə) *n* farsightedness. Compare MYOPIA. <Latin, from Greek *hyper* beyond + *ops* eye>

hy·per·sen·si·tive (hī′pər sen′sə tiv) *adj* abnormally sensitive. **hy′per·sen′si·tiv′i·ty** *n.*

hy·per·ten·sion (hī′pər ten′shən) *n* abnormally high blood pressure.

hy·per·text (hī′pər tekst′) *Computers n* **1** a computer software system that allows related pages, files, or images to be linked. **2** an Internet page, file, or image that contains a highlighted link to another, activated by clicking on it. **3** the text or graphic material accessed by the link. See also HYPERLINK, PROTOCOL.

hy·per·ven·ti·late (hī′pər ven′tə lāt′) *v* **hy·per·ven·ti·lat·ed, hy·per·ven·ti·lat·ing** breathe too deeply and too rapidly, often as a result of extreme stress. **hy′per·ven′ti·la′tion** *n.*

hy·phen (hī′fən) *n* a mark [-] connecting the parts of certain compound words such as *low-spirited* or *re-enter*, or connecting the parts of a word divided at the end of a line of text. <Latin, from Greek>

GRAMMAR AND USAGE

Hyphens are used in compound numbers (sixty-six) and fractions (two-thirds).

They are often used in compound phrases that come before a noun: *easy-to-use instructions.*

There is an increasing tendency to omit hyphens in compound words: *goodbye, bodybuilding.*

a bat	e bed	i bid	o pot	u cup	th thin
ā cake	ē me	ī bite	ō go	ū rude	TH then
á bar	ə about	ər over	ȯ for	ů put	zh measure

H

hy·phen·ate (hī′fə nāt′) *v* **hy·phen·at·ed, hy·phen·at·ing** spell with a hyphen: *You have to hyphenate the word "four-legged."* **hy′phen·a′tion** *n.*

hy·phen·at·ed (hī′fə nā′tid) *adj* **1** spelled with a hyphen. **2** *Informal* emphasizing a dual heritage by using two nationalities as a description, such as in *Chinese-Canadian* or *Italian-American*: *a hyphenated Canadian.*

hyp·no·sis (hip nō′sis) *n, pl* **hyp·no·ses** (hip nō′sēz) a state of consciousness in which a person apparently has little will and little feeling, and responds to the suggestions or directions of the person who brought about the hypnosis. <Latin, from Greek *hypnos* sleep>

hyp·no·ther·a·py (hip′nō ther′ə pē) *n, pl* **hyp·no·ther·a·pies** the use of hypnosis to treat addictions or emotional or psychiatric disorders. **hyp′no·ther′a·pist** *n.*

hyp·not·ic (hip not′ik) *adj* **1** to do with hypnosis. **2** tending to have a compelling, fascinating or sleep-inducing effect: *the hypnotic monotone of his voice.*
n a sleep-inducing drug. **hyp·not′i·cal·ly** *adv.*

hyp·no·tize (hip′nə tīz′) *v* **hyp·no·tized, hyp·no·tiz·ing** **1** put into a hypnotic state. **2** *Informal* dominate or control the will or emotions of a person. **hyp′no·tism′** *n.* **hyp′no·tist** *n.*

hypo– *prefix* under or below normal: *hypothermia.* <Greek>

hy·po·al·ler·gen·ic (hī′pō al′ər jen′ik) *adj* unlikely to cause an allergic reaction: *These earrings are made of hypoallergenic materials.*

hy·po·chlo·rous acid (hī′pə klô′rəs) *n* a weak acid of chlorine dissolved in water, used in bleaching and water treatment. <Greek *hypo-* under + *chlor(ine)*>

hy·po·chon·dri·a (hī′pə kon′drē ə) *n* an unnatural anxiety about one's health, often taking the form of imaginary illness. <Latin, from Greek *hypo-* under + *chondros* cartilage. The cartilage referred to is that of the breastbone, which was supposed to be the place of low spirits.> **hy′po·chon′dri·ac′** *n, adj.*

hyp·o·crite (hip′ə krit′) *n* a person who pretends to be what he or she is not, especially one who has an appearance of goodness. <Latin, from Greek, from *hypokrinestha* play a part> **hy·poc′ri·sy** *n.* **hyp′o·crit′i·cal** *adj.*

hy·po·der·mic (hī′pə dər′mik) *adj* **1** under the skin. **2** for injecting under the skin: *a hypodermic needle.*
n **1** a dose of medicine given by injection: *The doctor gave her a hypodermic to make her sleep.* **2** a syringe used to inject medicine under the skin. <Latin, from *hypo-* under + Greek *derma* skin> **hy′po·der′mi·cal·ly** *adv.*

hy·po·gly·ce·mi·a (hī′pō glī sē′mē ə) *n* a condition caused by an abnormally low concentration of sugar in the blood. <*hypo-* under + *glyco-* relating to sugar+ *-emia* relating to blood> **hy′po·gly·ce′mic** *adj, n.*

hy·pot·e·nuse (hī pot′ə nyūs′) *or* (hī pot′ə nūs′) *Mathematics n* the longest side of a right-angled triangle, opposite the right angle. <Latin, from *hypo-* under + Greek *teinein* stretch, i.e., to stretch under the right angle>

hy·po·thal·a·mus (hī′pō thal′ə məs) *n* the part of the brain beneath the thalamus that controls hunger, thirst, temperature, and growth.

hy·po·ther·mi·a (hī′pō thər′mē ə) *n* a body temperature greatly below normal: *Shipwrecked in the icy sea, the sailors died of hypothermia.* <Greek *hypo-* under + *therme* heat>

hy·poth·e·sis (hī poth′ə sis) *n, pl* **hy·poth·e·ses** (hī poth′ə sēz) **1** a theory taken as likely to be true, subject to further investigation: *We did an experiment to test our hypothesis.* **2** an assumption used as a basis for reasoning. <Latin, from Greek *hypothesis* basis of an argument>

hy·poth·e·size (hī poth′ə sīz′) *v* **hy·poth·e·sized, hy·poth·e·siz·ing** suggest as a likely prediction or explanation.

hy·po·thet·i·cal (hī′pə thet′ə kəl) *adj* suggesting a possibility to be considered or imagined. **hy′po·thet′i·cal·ly** *adv.*

hy·rax (hī′raks) *n* a small mammal with a compact body and a very short tail found in dry parts of Asia and Africa. <Latin, from Greek = shrew-mouse>

hys·ter·ec·to·my (his′tə rek′tə mē) *n, pl* **hys·ter·ec·to·mies** the surgical removal of all or part of the uterus. <Greek *hystera* uterus>

hys·te·ri·a (hi ster′ē ə) *or* (hi stē′rē ə) *n* **1** a nervous disorder that causes violent swings of emotion and lack of self-control. **2** extreme excitement: *the hysteria of fans at a rock concert.* **3** overreaction: *Public hysteria surrounding the issue was fuelled by the media.* <Latin, from Greek *hystera* womb. It was formerly believed that more women than men were affected by this disorder.>

hys·ter·i·cal (hi ster′ə kəl) *adj* **1** suffering from or showing hysteria: *hysterical with grief.* **2** *Informal* extremely funny: *Your skit was absolutely hysterical!* **hys·ter′i·cal·ly** *adv.*

hys·ter·ics (hi ster′iks) *n* (*with singular verb*) behaviour that shows, or seems to show, that a person has HYSTERIA (def. 1).

Hz hertz.

Ii

i or **I** (ī) *n, pl* **i's** or **I's** **1** the ninth letter of the English alphabet, or any speech sound represented by it. **2** the ninth thing in a list or series: *Complete sections a to i of this form, please.* **3** the Roman numeral for 1.

I (ī) *pron* the person who is speaking or writing: *I like my dog. Where am I?* <Old English *ic*>

GRAMMAR AND USAGE

The pronoun **I** is written with a capital because in old handwritten manuscripts a small i was likely to be lost or get attached to a word next to it.

i·am·bic (ī am′bik) *Poetry adj* to do with a metrical foot consisting of two syllables, the first with a weak stress and the second with a strong one: *Iambic pentameter is a poetic metre based on five iambic feet in a line of verse.* <French, from Greek *iambos*>

i·at·ro·gen·ic (ī at′rə jen′ik) *adj* of an illness, caused by medical treatment. <Greek *iatros* doctor + *-genic* produced by>

I–beam (ī′bēm) *n* a BEAM (*n* def. 1) with a cross-section resembling the capital letter I.

I·be·ri·a (ī bē′rē ə) *n* the ancient name for the large peninsula in southwestern Europe that contains Spain and Portugal. **I·be′ri·an** *adj, n.*

i·bex (ī′beks) *n, pl* **i·bex·es** or (*especially collectively*) **i·bex** a wild mountain goat of Europe, Central Asia, or Ethiopia. <Latin>

ibid. *adv* an abbreviation for the Latin *ibidem*, meaning "in the same place."

GRAMMAR AND USAGE

The term **ibid.** is used in a footnote to save space by referring to a text (book, article, etc.) mentioned in the immediately preceding footnote.

i·bis (ī′bis) *n, pl* **i·bis·es** or (*especially collectively*) **i·bis** a long-legged wading bird resembling a heron. <Egyptian>

–ible *suffix* able to be, suitable for being, causing, or with the quality to: *convertible, reducible, terrible, edible.* <Old French, from Latin *-ibilis*>

i·bu·pro·fen (ī′byū prō′fən) *or* (ib′yū prō′fən) *n* a synthetic drug used to reduce inflammation and pain.

ICBM in full, **intercontinental ballistic missile** a ballistic missile with a long range (up to 8000 km).

ice (īs) *n* **1** frozen water. **2** a frozen surface for sports and recreation, such as skating, playing hockey, or curling. **3** a frozen dessert usually made of sweetened fruit juice. **4** 🍁 **the ice** *especially Newfoundland* the edge of the Arctic icefields where seal hunting takes place.
v **iced, ic·ing** **1** cover with icing: *Let's ice the cookies.* **2** chill with ice: *an iced drink.* **3** *Hockey* See ICING (def. 2). **4** 🍁 *Slang* choose a (hockey) player or team to play: *Our town iced a good hockey team.* **5** *Slang* make certain of winning: *We iced the game with a late field goal.* <Old English *is*> **ice′less** *adj.*
break the ice, *Informal* help people relax and begin talking or getting acquainted.
ice over, form a layer of ice on the surface: *Has the pond iced over yet?*
ice up, become covered or clogged with ice: *The windshield wipers have iced up.*
on thin ice, in a dangerous or difficult position.

ice age *n* **1** a geological period during which much of the earth was covered with glaciers. **2** **Ice Age** the most recent such time, when most of the northern hemisphere was covered with glaciers, from about 1 600 000 years ago until about 10 000 years ago.

🍁 **ice·bank** (īs′bangk) *n* a perpendicular ridge of ice along a river.

ice·berg (īs′bərg′) *n* a large mass of ice detached from a glacier and floating in the sea, most of it beneath the surface. <Dutch *ijs* ice + *berg* mountain>
tip of the iceberg, a small part of something much larger.

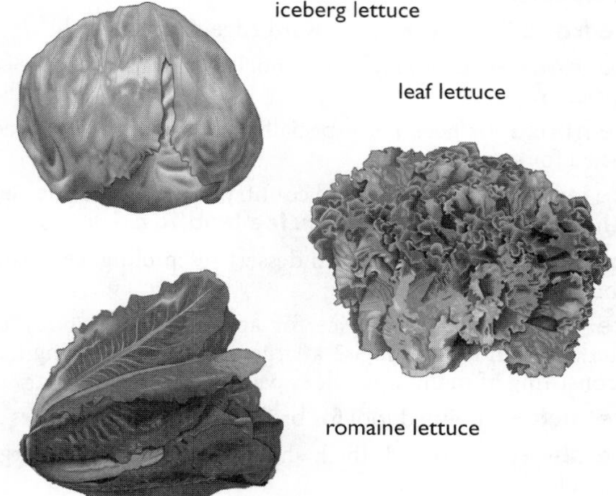

iceberg lettuce *n* a variety of lettuce with crisp, pale leaves forming a compact head like a small cabbage.

ice·boat (īs′bōt′) *n* **1** 🍁 a light frame, often triangular, set on runners and fitted with sails or a propeller for skimming along the frozen surface of a lake or river. **2** an ICEBREAKER (def. 1).

ice·bound (īs′bound′) *adj* **1** frozen in: *The ship was icebound for several weeks.* **2** blocked or made unusable by ice: *The port at Churchill is icebound for about ten months of the year.*

ice·box (īs′boks′) *n* an insulated chest or box with ice in it for keeping food cool.

a bat	e bed	i bid	o pot	u cup	th **thin**
ā cake	ē me	ī bite	ō go	ū rude	TH **then**
ä bar	ə about	ər over	ô for	ů put	zh measure

ice·break·er (īs′brā′kər) *n* **1** a ship designed for breaking a passage through ice. **2** an activity, or opening of a conversation, intended to help people relax and get acquainted. See SHIP for picture.

🍁 **ice bridge** *n* **1** a winter road over a frozen river or lake. **2** a bridge of ice formed by the jamming of ice in a river or other channel.

ice·cap (īs′kap′) *n* a permanent covering of ice over a large area, especially on the polar region of a planet.

ice–cold (īs′kōld′) *adj* thoroughly chilled.

ice cream *n* a frozen dessert made with cream and other ingredients: *an ice cream cone.*

ice cream parlour *n* a café selling ice cream to be eaten on the premises.

ice cube *n* a small block of ice, used for chilling drinks.

iced (īst) *adj* **1** cooled with ice: *iced tea.* **2** covered with icing: *iced cake.*

ice·field (īs′fēld) *n* a large sheet of ice, either on land or floating in the sea.

🍁 **ice fishing** *n* the act or practice of fishing through a hole cut in the ice.

ice·front (īs′frunt) *n* the seaward edge of an ice shelf.

ice hockey *especially UK n* hockey played on ice. See HOCKEY.

ice·house (īs′hous′) *n* especially formerly, an insulated shed for storing ice.

Ice·land (īs′lənd) *n* an island country in the N Atlantic. See the APPENDIX. **Ice′land′er** *n.* **Ice′land′ic** *adj, n.*

ice milk *n* a smooth, frozen dessert resembling ice cream but with less milk fat.

ice pack *n* **1** a bag of ice for applying to the body to reduce pain or swelling. **2** a large expanse of floating ice, consisting of many small floes packed together.

ice pick *n* a pointed tool for breaking ice.

ice sheet *n* a broad, thick sheet of ice covering a large area for a long time.

ice skate SKATE (*n* def. 1).

ice storm *n* a freezing rain that covers exposed surfaces with a layer of glistening ice.

ice time *n* **1** *Hockey* the time actually spent on the ice by a player during a game. **2** the time during which the ice at a rink is available to a team, group, or individuals.

ice water *n* **1** water cooled with ice. **2** melted ice.

ice·wine (īs′wīn) *n* a sweet wine made from grapes that have been allowed to freeze on the vine.

ice·worm (īs′wərm) *n* **1** a worm that feeds on algae in melting glacial ice. **2** 🍁 *North* a mythical creature, thought up as a joke.

I Ching (ē′ jing′) *n* a Chinese book that offers guidance about the future based on symbolic groups of characters and their accompanying commentary.

ich·neu·mon fly (ik nyū′mən) *or* (ik nū′mən) *n* a wasplike insect with long antennae whose larvae live as parasites in or on other insects.

ich·thy·ol·o·gy (ik′thē ol′ə jē) *n* the branch of zoology that studies fish. <Greek *ichthys* fish> **ich′thy·ol′o·gist** *n.*

ich·thy·o·saur (ik′thē ə sôr′) *n* an extinct sea reptile with a fishlike body, four flippers, and a long snout.

i·ci·cle (ī′sə kəl) *n* a pointed, hanging stick of ice formed by the freezing of dripping water.

ic·ing (ī′sing) *n* **1** a sweet, creamy mixture used as a coating for cakes, cookies, and pastries. Also called **frosting**. **2** *Hockey* the shooting or directing of the puck from within your own defensive zone (or from behind the redline) so that it crosses the opposition's goal line. It is not icing if the puck passes through the opposition's goal crease, or if your team is shorthanded.

icing sugar *n* fine powdered sugar.

i·con (ī′kon) *n* **1** *especially Christianity* a sacred picture or image. **2** *Computers* an image, such as a symbol on a screen representing a certain program, function, or window: *Click on the paintbrush icon for colour.* **3** a well-known person or thing regarded as a symbol of something important in a particular culture: *the great Canadian hockey icon, Wayne Gretzky.* <Latin, from Greek *eikon*>

i·con·ic (ī kon′ik) *adj* to do with an icon.

i·con·o·clast (ī kon′ə klast′) *n* **1** a person opposed to the use of images in religious worship. **2** a person who attacks or mocks cherished beliefs or institutions. <Latin, from Greek *eikon* image + *klan* to break> **i·con′o·clas′tic** *adj.*

i·co·sa·he·dron (ī′kō sə hē′drən) *n* a solid figure with twenty faces. <Greek *eikosi* twenty + *hedra* side>

ICT information and communication technologies.

ICU intensive care unit.

i·cy (ī′sē) *adj* **i·ci·er, i·ci·est** **1** very cold: *an icy blast of wind.* **2** with, consisting of, or covered with ice: *an icy road, icy precipitation.* **3** very unfriendly: *an icy stare.* **i′ci·ly** *adv.* **i′ci·ness** *n.*

id (id) *Psychoanalysis n* that part of the unconscious self that is the source of instinctive impulses. Compare EGO (def. 3), SUPEREGO. <Latin translation of German *es* it>

ID *n* identification or identity, especially an official document that serves to identify a person: *an ID card. Are you carrying any ID?*
v **ID'd, ID'ing** *Informal* **1** provide with official identification. **2** check someone's ID.

I'd (īd) *contraction* **1** I had: *I'd always wated to visit Nunavut.* **2** I would: *I'd like to go to Nova Scotia.*

i·de·a (ī dē′ə) *n* **1** a thought, opinion, or belief: *She is always ready to express her ideas. This is a difficult idea to understand.* **2** a plan or scheme: *We told them our idea for the yearbook advertising campaign.* **3** an image in the mind: *I have an idea how such a thing would look.* **4** the point or purpose: *The idea of a vacation is to get a rest.* **5** a suggestion or hint: *Can you give me an idea how to start?* <Latin, from Greek *idein* to see>
get ideas (into your head), *Informal* start planning, seeking, or expecting things you shouldn't.
have no idea, not know at all: *I have no idea where he is.*
the (very) idea! how outrageous!

i·de·al (ī dēl′) *n* a moral principle guiding behaviour: *He refused to abandon his ideals of honesty in order to win by cheating.*
adj **1** just as one would wish: *What a warm, sunny day—ideal for a picnic! The cafeteria is not ideal for studying, but it will do.* **2** existing only in one's mind or in theory, especially because it is too good or impractical for the real world: *You are never going to find your ideal friend.* <Latin *idea*> **i·de′al·ly** *adv.*

i·de·al·ism (ī dē′ə liz′əm) *n* **1** the fact of having high moral principles and following them regardless of circumstances, practical consequences, or the opinion of others. **2** the practice of representing imagined types rather than producing an exact copy of any individual person, thing, or situation. **3** a system of thought in which it is believed that the objects of our knowledge are entirely based on the activity of the mind and not on the external world. **i·de′al·ist** *n.* **i′de·al·is′tic** *adj.*

i·de·al·ize (ī dē′ə līz′) *v* **i·de·al·ized, i·de·al·iz·ing** think of or represent as perfect rather than as is actually the case: *Don't idealize movie stars just because they look good on the screen.* **i·de′al·i·za′tion** *n.*

i·dée fixe (ē dā′fēks′) *n* an obsession. <French = fixed idea>

i·den·ti·cal (ī den′tə kəl) *adj* **1** being the same exact person or thing: *The composer of this song is identical with the lyricist.* **2** exactly alike: *The two photos are identical. The copy is identical to the original.* **3** coming from a single fertilized egg cell as twins. Compare FRATERNAL. <Latin *idem* same> **i·den′ti·cal·ly** *adv.* **i·den′ti·cal·ness** *n.*

> **GRAMMAR AND USAGE**
>
> **Identical to** is used when there are two separate things that are alike in every detail:
> *The photocopy is identical to the original.*
>
> **Identical with** is used when there is really only one thing or person, seen on different occasions or known by different names, etc.:
> *Hogtown is identical with Toronto.*

i·den·ti·fi·ca·tion (ī den′tə fə kā′shən) *n* **1** the act of identifying or being identified. **2** anything used to identify a person or thing: *She showed her birth certificate as identification.*

i·den·ti·fy (ī den′tə fī′) *v* **i·den·ti·fied, i·den·ti·fy·ing** **1** tell, show, or prove that someone or something is a certain person or thing: *She identified the bag as hers by telling what it contained. His badge identified him as the store manager.* **2** recognize correctly: *a feeling I cannot identify. Can you identify all the provincial capitals?* **3** treat or regard as the same: *The good king identified his people's welfare with his own.* **4** (*usually with* ***with***) understand and relate to: *I can identify with you and your situation because I've had the same experience myself.* **i·den′ti·fi′a·ble** *adj.* **i·den′ti·fi′a·bly** *adv.* **i·den′ti·fi′er** *n.*

i·den·ti·ty (ī den′tə tē) *n, pl* **i·den·ti·ties** **1** who or what a person or thing is: *The writer concealed his identity under an assumed name.* **2** the fact of being identical: *The identity of the two sets of fingerprints indicated that they were from the same person.*

identity crisis *n* confusion about one's purpose in life or role in society, or one's basic personal values.

identity element *Mathematics n* a member of a set that can operate on *x*, another member of the set, to produce *x*. The identity element for addition is 0, since $x + 0 = x$. For multiplication, the identity element is 1, since $x \times 1 = x$.

identity theft *n* the stealing of another's personal information (name, address, date of birth, social insurance number, etc.) usually in order to impersonate and defraud that person. Identity theft is also used in other criminal activities like illegal immigration and terrorism.

id·e·o·gram (id′ē ə gram′) *n* a written symbol that represents a thing or idea directly, without representing the sounds of the word for it. Chinese characters are ideograms. Also called **ideograph**. <Greek *idea* form + *-gram*>

i·de·ol·o·gy (ī′dē ol′ə jē) *or* (id′ē ol′ə jē) *n, pl* **i·de·ol·o·gies** a set of beliefs or teachings about social, political, or economic systems: *Communist ideology.*
i′de·o·log′i·cal *adj.*

ides (īdz) *pln* (*with singular or plural verb*) in the Roman calendar, the fifteenth day of March, May, July, and October, and the thirteenth day of the other months.

id·i·o·cy (id′ē ə sē) *n, pl* **id·i·o·cies** **1** the quality or state of being idiotic. **2** idiotic talk or behaviour. <See IDIOT.>

id·i·om (id′ē əm) *n* **1** a phrase or expression whose meaning cannot be understood from the ordinary meanings of its individual words, or which seems to break usual grammatical patterns: *"How do you do?" and "like crazy" are English idioms.* **2** a particular dialect, language, or way of expressing oneself: *She speaks in the idiom of the Ottawa Valley.* <Latin, from Greek *idios* one's own> **id′i·o·mat′ic** *adj.*

> **GRAMMAR AND USAGE**
>
> **Idioms** are phrases that can make writing more colourful and interesting, but they can also be more difficult to understand than ordinary wording, especially for people from cultures not speaking the same language.
>
> Idioms may give writing a more casual tone, too, so they should be used with care. It is best not to use too many idioms in any one piece of writing.

id·i·o·syn·cra·sy (id′ē ə sing′krə sē) *n, pl* **id·i·o·syn·cra·sies** a personal peculiarity of behaviour or opinion: *He was an eccentric person with many idiosyncrasies.* <Greek *idiosynkrasia* one's own temperament> **id′i·o·syn·crat′ic** *adj.*

a bat	e bed	i bid	o pot	u cup	th thin
ā cake	ē me	ī bite	ō go	ū rude	ᴛʜ then
ä bar	ə about	ər over	ô for	ů put	zh measure

I

id·i·ot (id′ē ət) *n* a very stupid or foolish person: *He was an idiot to behave like that.* <Latin, from Greek *idiotes* lacking professional knowledge> **id′i·ot′ic** (id′ē ot′ik) *adj.* **id′i·ot′ic·al·ly** (id′ē ot′ik lē) *adv.*

idiot box *Slang n* television.

id·i·ot·proof (id′ē ət prūf′) *adj* almost impossible to break or to use incorrectly.

i·dle (ī′dəl) *adj* **i·dler, i·dlest** **1** not busy or in use: *idle hands. His computer sat idle for weeks while he was in the hospital.* **2** not willing to work. **3** serving no good purpose: *idle pleasures.* **4** with no good reason or cause: *idle fears, idle rumours.*
v **i·dled, i·dling** **1** waste time or do nothing: *Are you going to spend your whole vacation just idling?* **2** run without transmitting power in an engine: *Let the motor idle a bit first so it can warm up.* <Old English *idel* empty> **i′dle·ness** *n.* **i′dler** *n.* **i′dly** *adv.*
idle away, spend wastefully: *She idled away many hours lying in the hammock.*

i·dol (ī′dəl) *n* **1** an image or object worshipped as a god. **2** a thing or person that becomes the object of too much devotion or interest: *He has made an idol out of wealth.* **3** a person who is loved or admired very much: *The baby girl was the idol of her family.* <Old French, from Greek *eidolon* image>

i·dol·a·try (ī dol′ə trē) *n* **1** the worship of idols. **2** excessive devotion or interest paid to a person or thing.
i·dol′a·ter *n.* **i·dol′a·trous** *adj.*

i·dol·ize (ī′də līz′) *v* **i·dol·ized, i·dol·iz·ing** **1** worship as an idol: *The Romans idolized their emperor.* **2** love or admire very much: *She idolizes her big sister.* **i′dol·i·za′tion** *n.*

id·yll (ī′dəl) *or* (id′əl) *n* **1** a short description in poetry or prose, or a depiction in music, of a peaceful, charming scene or event, especially one connected with country life. **2** a peaceful and charming scene or event. <Latin, from Greek *eidyllion* short poem> **i·dyl′lic** *adj.*

–ie *suffix* a form of *–y.*

i.e. in other words: *I'll arrive the day after tomorrow, i.e., Friday.* <Latin *id est* that is>

CONFUSABLES

i.e. means "that is," and is used to restate or explain something just said or written: *State your full address, i.e., your street, town or city, province, and postal code.*

e.g. means "for example": *I eat fruit daily, e.g., apples.*

if (if) *conj* **1** supposing that: *If you had been here, things would have been different. I'll go if you will.* **2** whether: *I wonder if she'll be there.* **3** although; even though: *He is strong, if small.*
n a condition or supposition: *No ifs; just take it or leave it.* <Old English *gif*>
if not, a otherwise: *I'll assume he's coming; if not, let me know.* **b** even though not: *a wholesome meal, if not a very tasty one.* **c** probably even: *She should be disciplined for that, if not expelled.*

if·fy (if′ē) *Informal adj* **if·fi·er, if·fi·est** uncertain, risky, or undecided: *The weather looks iffy.*

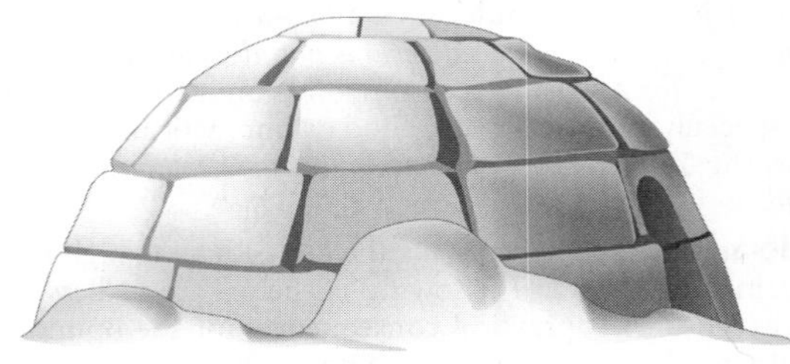

To make an **igloo**, the Inuit placed blocks of snow in a spiral pattern to form the dome shape. Body heat and small oil lamps heated the interior. A platform covered with animal hides and furs kept people comfortable while sleeping. Tents made from hide, sod, wood, or other available natural materials were the traditional Inuit summer shelters.

ig·loo (ig′lū) *n* **1** a traditional Inuit dwelling, especially a domed structure, built of blocks of snow. See also TEEPEE, WIGWAM. **2** any structure resembling this in shape. <Inuktitut *iglu* dwelling>

Ig·lu·lik (i glū′lik) *n, pl* **Ig·lu·lik** **1** a member of an Inuit people living in the eastern Arctic. **2** their Inuktitut language.
adj to do with these people or their language.

ig·ne·ous (ig′nē əs) *Geology adj* formed as rock by the solidification of molten matter. <Latin *ignis* fire>

ig·nite (ig nīt′) *v* **ig·nit·ed, ig·nit·ing** **1** set on fire or catch fire: *The match was ignited by scraping it against the sidewalk. Gasoline ignites easily.* **2** arouse a strong or intense emotion: *to ignite someone's passion.* <Latin *ignis* fire> **ig·nit′a·ble** *adj.*

ig·ni·tion (ig nish′ən) *n* **1** the system in an internal combustion engine for igniting the explosive vapour in the cylinders. **2** the act or fact of igniting.

ig·no·ble (ig nō′bəl) *adj* dishonourable: *To betray a friend is an ignoble deed.* <Latin *in-* not + *gnobilis* noble> **ig′no·bil′i·ty** *n.* **ig·no′bly** *adv.*

ig·no·min·i·ous (ig′nə min′ē əs) *adj* **1** bringing shame or disgrace: *We suffered an ignominious defeat in the final.* **2** contemptible. <Latin *ignominia* loss of good name, from *in-* not + *nomis* name> **ig′no·min′i·ous·ly** *adv.* **ig·nom′i·ny** *n.*

ig·no·ra·mus (ig′nə rā′məs) *or* (ig′nə ram′əs) an ignorant person. <Latin = we do not know, from *ignorare* not know>

ig·no·rant (ig′nə rənt) *adj* **1** knowing little or nothing: *City people are often ignorant about farm life.* **2** caused by or showing lack of knowledge: *an ignorant remark.* **3** uninformed or unaware: *He was ignorant of the fact that we had arrived.* <See IGNORE.> **ig′no·rance** *n.* **ig′no·rant·ly** *adv.*

ig·nore (ig nôr′) *v* **ig·nored, ig·nor·ing** pay no attention to or disregard: *The teacher ignored the noise her students were making.* <Latin *in-* not + *gno-* know>

There are three kinds of **iguanas**: the green iguana, which lives in trees; the rhinoceros iguana, which is terrestrial; and the marine iguana, which forages for food in the sea. Some authorities also classify the monitor lizard as an iguana.

i·gua·na (i gwä′nə) *n* a large climbing lizard with a crest of skin along the back, found in tropical America. <Arawak (a language of S America) *iwana*>

i·gua·na·don (i gwä′nə don′) *n* a large dinosaur of the early Cretaceous period, with a broad stiff tail. <*iguana* + Greek *odontis* tooth>

🍁 **ik·tas** (ik′täs) *West Coast pln* goods or belongings: *We've got food and all the iktas we need for now.* <Chinook Jargon>

il– *prefix* a form of IN-[1] or IN-[2] occurring before the letter *l*: *illegal, illuminate.*

i·le·i·tis (ĭ′lē ī′təs) *n* inflammation of the lower part of the small intestine (the **ileum**), partly or completely blocking the passage of food. <Latin *ilia* entrails>

ilk (ilk) *Informal n* a kind or sort: *doctors, lawyers, and people of that ilk.* <Old English *ilca* same>

ill (il) *adj* **worse, worst 1** sick: *ill with a fever.* **2** bad, harmful, or unkind: *ill deeds, ill will.* **3** unfavourable: *an ill wind.*
n **1** a sickness or disease: *She told us all the ills she had suffered.* **2** an evil: *poverty, war, and other social ills.* **3** harm: *to do someone ill.*
adv **1** (*often in compounds*) badly or poorly: *ill-equipped. Work done ill is best not done at all.* **2** with trouble or difficulty: *You can ill afford to waste time.* <Old Norse *illr*>
ill at ease, uncomfortable.
take ill, get sick.

I'll (īl) *contraction* **1** I will. **2** I shall.

ill–ad·vised (il′əd vīzd′) *adj* showing too little thought or caution.

ill–bred (il′bred′) *adj* badly brought up or rude.

ill breeding *n* lack of good upbringing; bad manners.

ill–con·ceived (il′kən sēvd′) *adj* not sensible or properly thought out: *an ill-conceived plan.*

ill–dis·posed (il′di spōzd′) *adj* unfriendly or unfavourable.

il·le·gal (i lē′gəl) *adj* against the law or against the rules: *illegal parking.* **il′le·gal′i·ty** *n.* **il·le′gal·ly** *adv.*

il·leg·i·ble (i lej′ə bəl) *adj* very hard or impossible to read: *His handwriting was nearly illegible.* **il·leg′i·bly** *adv.*

il·le·git·i·mate (il′i jit′ə mit) *adj* **1** against the law or the rules. **2** not valid or acceptable: *That is an illegitimate excuse.* **3** born of parents who are not married to each other. **il′le·git′i·ma·cy** (il′ə jit′ə mə sē) *n.* **il′le·git′i·mate·ly** *adv.*

ill–e·quipped (il′i kwipt′) *adj* poorly equipped .

ill fame *n* bad reputation.

ill–fat·ed (il′fā′tid) *adj* destined to have a bad end or result: *an ill-fated voyage, an ill-fated decision.*

ill–fa·voured or **ill–fa·vored** (il′fā′vərd) *adj* unattractive or offensive: *The actor wore very complicated makeup in order to look ill-favoured.*

ill feeling *n* dislike or mistrust: *There has been ill feeling between them ever since they quarrelled.*

ill–found·ed (il′foun′did) *adj* without a sound basis.

ill–got·ten (il′got′ən) *adj* acquired by evil or unfair means: *ill-gotten riches.*

ill humour or **humor** *n* a bad or irritable mood. **ill′-hu′moured** or **ill′-hu′mored** *adj.* **ill′-hu′moured·ly** or **ill′-hu′mored·ly** *adv.*

il·lic·it (i lis′it) *adj* illegal or immoral: *illicit traffic in drugs, an illicit sexual affair.* **il·lic′it·ly** *adv.* **il·lic′it·ness** *n.*

il·lim·it·a·ble (i lim′ə tə bəl) *adj* without limits. **il·lim′it·a·bil′i·ty** *n.* **il·lim′it·a·bly** *adv.*

il·lit·er·ate (i lit′ə rit) *adj* **1** unable to read or write. A person who does not read or write well enough to function independently in the world is termed **functionally illiterate**. **2** showing a lack of education: *He speaks in a very illiterate way.* **3** ignorant in a particular area: *I'm completely illiterate when it comes to sports.*
n an illiterate person. **il·lit′er·a·cy** (i lit′ə rə sē) *n.* **il·lit′er·ate·ly** *adv.*

ill–man·nered (il′man′ərd) *adj* with or showing bad manners. **ill′-man′nered·ly** *adv.*

ill–na·tured (il′nā′chərd) *adj* habitually irritable or nasty. **ill′-na′tured·ly** *adv.*

ill·ness (il′nis) *n* **1** poor health: *She suffered from long periods of illness.* **2** a particular sickness or disease: *Scarlet fever is a serious illness.*

il·log·i·cal (i loj′ə kəl) *adj* **1** not following the rules of logic: *illogical arguments.* **2** with no basis in fact: *an illogical fear of the dark.* **il·log′i·cal′i·ty** *n.* **il·log′i·cal·ly** *adv.*

ill–suit·ed (il′sū′tid) *adj* unsuitable: *A waiter's job is ill-suited to a clumsy person.*

ill–tem·pered (il′tem′pərd) *adj* with or showing a bad temper. **ill′-tem′pered·ly** *adv.*

ill–timed (il′tīmd′) *adj* done or happening at a bad time.

ill–treat (il′trēt) *v* treat badly. **ill′-treat′ment** *n.*

a bat	e bed	i bid	o pot	u cup	th thin
ā cake	ē me	ī bite	ō go	ū rude	ᴛʜ then
ä bar	ə about	ər over	ȯ for	ů put	zh measure

I

il·lu·mi·nate (i lū′mə nāt′) *v* **il·lu·mi·nat·ed, il·lu·mi·nat·ing 1** light up or make bright: *The room was illuminated by four large lamps.* **2** decorate with gold, colours, pictures, and designs: *Some old books and manuscripts were illuminated.* **3** make clear or explain: *a commentary illuminating the plays of Shakespeare.* **4** enlighten, inform, or instruct: *The police officer illuminated me on the advantages of walking home with a buddy.* <Latin *in-* in + *lumen* light>
il·lu′mi·na′tion *n.*

il·lu·mine (i lū′mən) *v* **il·lu·mined, il·lu·min·ing** bring light to: *a face illumined by hope.*

il·lu·sion (i lū′zhən) *n* **1** an appearance or feeling that misleads because it is not real or gives a false idea: *Beauty produced by makeup is a mere illusion.* **2** a false idea or belief: *He is under the illusion that he is smarter than everyone else.* <Latin *illusio* deceit, from *illudere* to sport with>

CONFUSABLES

An **illusion** is a misleading appearance: *The large car she drives gives an illusion of wealth.*

An **allusion** is an indirect reference or slight mention: *We gathered from his allusions to Mexico that he had been there recently.*

il·lu·sion·ist (i lū′zhən ist) *n* a magician.

il·lu·so·ry (i lū′sə rē) *or* (i lū′zə rē) *adj* due to or resulting in an illusion: *Their initial advantage proved to be illusory, as their opponents began to score points.*

il·lus·trate (il′ə strāt′) *v* **il·lus·trat·ed, il·lus·trat·ing 1** make clear or explain by stories, examples, or comparisons: *The teacher used a pump to illustrate the action of the heart.* **2** provide with pictures, diagrams, or maps that explain or decorate: *The Geography book is well illustrated.* <Latin *illustrationem* vivid representation, from *illustrare* embellish> **il′lus·tra′tion** *n.* **il′lus·tra′tor** *n.*

il·lus·tra·tive (i lus′trə tiv) *or* (il′ə strā′tiv) *adj* helping to explain: *an illustrative example.* **il·lus′tra·tive·ly** *adv.*

il·lus·tri·ous (i lus′trē əs) *adj* highly respected and admired: *our illustrious hero.* <See ILLUSTRATE.> **il·lus′tri·ous·ly** *adv.* **il·lus′tri·ous·ness** *n.*

ill will *n* unkind or unfriendly feeling.

im– *prefix* a form of IN-[1] or IN-[2] occurring before the letters *b, m,* or *p*: *imbalance, impart.*

IM instant messaging.

im·age (im′ij) *n* **1** a picture, statue, reflection, or any other visual likeness of something: *This software lets you create and animate images. He saw the image of himself in the mirror.* **2** a person or thing much like another: *She is the very image of her mother.* **3** a picture in the mind: *The image lingered in my memory for a long time.* **4** a description or figure of speech that helps the mind to form vivid or beautiful pictures. **5** the way a person or group is thought of: *If you have a poor self-image, you may be just shy. He wears a suit because he is trying to cultivate a conservative image.*
v **im·aged, im·ag·ing** form or be an image of. <Old French, from Latin *imago*>

im·age·ry (im′ij rē) *n* **1** the use of figurative language and vivid description to create a mental picture. **2** mental pictures or images in general.

i·mag·i·nar·y (i maj′ə ner′ē) *adj* existing only in the imagination: *The equator is an imaginary line circling the earth midway between the North and South Poles.*

i·mag·i·na·tion (i maj′ə nā′shən) *n* **1** the ability to form images in the mind: *The child's imagination filled the woods with strange animals.* **2** the ability to create new things or come up with new ideas or solutions: *Poets, artists, and inventors make use of their imagination.* **3** a creation of the mind. **i·mag′i·na·tive** *adj.*

i·mag·ine (i maj′ən) *v* **i·mag·ined, i·mag·in·ing 1** form a mental image of something that is not actually present or real: *We can hardly imagine life without electricity.* **2** guess: *I can't imagine what you mean. I imagine traffic would be bad at that hour.* **3** think or believe something that is not true: *She imagined someone was watching her.* <Old French, from Latin *imago* image> **i·mag′i·na·ble** *adj.* **i·mag′i·na·bly** *adv.*

i·mag·ing (i′mə jing) *n* the visualization of internal body parts using instruments and special techniques. Ultrasonic scans are a kind of imaging.

i·ma·go (i mā′gō) *n, pl* **i·ma·gos** or **i·mag·i·nes** (i maj′ə nēz′) an insect in the final adult stage. <Latin>

im·am (i mäm′) *Islam n* **1** a leader of prayer in a mosque. **2** a spiritual leader whose authority derives directly from the prophet Muhammad. <Arabic>

im·bal·ance (im bal′əns) *n* lack of balance, proportion, or co-ordination: *a chemical imbalance in the brain.*

im·be·cile (im′bə səl) *n* a very stupid or foolish person: *Don't be an imbecile.* <Latin *imbecillus* feeble (physically and mentally)> **im′be·cil′ic** *adj.* **im′be·cil′i·ty** *n.*

im·bibe (im bīb′) *v* **im·bibed, im·bib·ing 1** drink or take in: *to imbibe liquor. Roots imbibe moisture from the earth.* **2** take into one's mind: *Children often imbibe superstitions.* <Latin *in-* in + *bibere* drink>

im·bro·glio (im brōl′yō) *n* a complicated, confused, or difficult situation. <Italian *imbrogliare* confuse>

im·bue (im byū′) *v* **im·bued, im·bu·ing** fill; inspire: *The teacher imbued their minds with the ambition to succeed.* <French, from Latin *imbuere* moisten>

IMF International Monetary Fund.

im·i·tate (im′ə tāt′) *v* **im·i·tat·ed, im·i·tat·ing 1** follow the example of: *The little boy imitated his father in everything.* **2** act like, especially for amusement: *She made us laugh by imitating a bear.* **3** be or look like: *Plastic is often made to imitate wood.* <Latin *imitari* to copy> **im′i·ta′tor** *n.*

im·i·ta·tion (im′ə tā′shən) *n* **1** the act of imitating: *We learn many things by imitation.* **2** an act copying some person or thing for entertainment: *He did an imitation of the prime minister.*
adj made to look like something better: *imitation pearls, imitation leather.*

im·i·ta·tive (im′ə tā′tiv) *adj* **1** following an example, usually without an attempt at originality. **2** intended to make words sounds like what they mean, such as *bang* or *whiz*, **im′i·ta′tive·ly** *adv.* **im′i·ta′tive·ness** *n.*

im·mac·u·late (i mak′yə lit) *adj* **1** absolutely clean: *The newly washed shirts were immaculate.* **2** without fault: *His work was immaculate.* <Latin *in-* not + *macula* spot> **im·mac′u·late·ly** *adv.* **im·mac′u·late·ness** *n.*

im·ma·nent (im′ə nənt) *adj* existing or operating within. <Latin *in-* in + *manere* remain> **im′ma·nence** *n.* **im′ma·nent·ly** *adv.*

im·ma·te·ri·al (im′ə tē′rē əl) *adj* **1** irrelevant: *This error is immaterial.* **2** spiritual rather than material or physical.

im·ma·ture (im′ə chůr′) *adj* **1** not full-grown or fully developed. **2** acting as if younger than one is. **im′ma·ture′ly** *adv.* **im′ma·tur′i·ty** *n.*

im·meas·ur·a·ble (i mezh′ə rə bəl) *adj* too vast to be measured. **im·meas′ur·a·bil′i·ty** *n.* **im·meas′ur·a·ble·ness** *n.* **im·meas′ur·a·bly** *adv.*

im·me·di·ate (i mē′dē it) *adj* **1** coming or happening at once: *an immediate reply.* **2** direct: *the immediate result, in immediate contact.* **3** closest in relationship or location: *my immediate family, in the immediate neighbourhood.* **4** to do with the present or very near future: *our immediate plans.* <Latin *in-* not + *mediare* to be in the middle. The image is of two things or people with nothing "in the middle" or between them to interrupt the flow of events or communication.> **im·me′di·a·cy** *n.* **im·me′di·ate·ly** *adv.*

im·me·mo·ri·al (im′ə mô′rē əl) *adj* so far back it cannot be remembered: *time immemorial.*

im·mense (i mens′) *adj* huge or vast: *an immense task. The Pacific is an immense body of water.* <Latin *immensus* unmeasured, from *in-* not + *metiri* to measure> **im·mense′ly** *adv.* **im·mens′i·ty** *n.*

im·merse (i mərs′) *v* **im·mersed, im·mers·ing** **1** put completely under water or other liquid: *Do not immerse the electric kettle.* **2** involve deeply or absorb completely: *immersed in business affairs.* **3** surround by a certain environment in order to improve learning opportunities: *Students learn French best if they are immersed in a francophone environment.* <Latin *immersus*, from *in-* in + *mergere* plunge> **im·mers′i·ble** *adj.*

im·mer·sion (i mər′zhən) *n* **1** the act of immersing. **2** 🍁 a method of teaching a second language by means of intensive exposure to and practice in the language: *French immersion.*

im·mi·grate (im′ə grāt′) *v* **im·mi·grat·ed, im·mi·grat·ing** come into a country to live: *People have immigrated to Canada from many different nations.* <Latin *in-* into + *migrare* move> **im′mi·grant** *n, adj.*

CONFUSABLES

Immigrate means "move into a country or region": *My grandfather immigrated to Canada from Italy in 1960.*

Emigrate means "move out of a country or region": *My grandfather emigrated from Italy to Canada in 1960.*

im·mi·gra·tion (im′ə grā′shən) *n* **1** the act of immigrating. **2** a group or number of immigrants: *Immigration was low last year. The immigration of 1956 included many people from Hungary.* **3** the official formalities involved in immigrating or entering a country, or the government departments that take care of this: *It took us hours to get through Immigration on our arrival.*

im·mi·nent (im′ə nənt) *adj* likely to happen soon: *We could tell by the black clouds and thunder that a storm was imminent.* <Latin *imminere* overhang> **im′mi·nence** *n.* **im′mi·nent·ly** *adv.*

CONFUSABLES

Imminent means "expected soon": *We anxiously awaited the imminent arrival of our guests.*

Immanent means "naturally present" or "inherent": *The genius had an immanent intelligence.*

Eminent means "outstanding": *She is an eminent scholar, with many original theories.*

im·mo·bile (i mō′bīl) *or* (i mō′bəl) *adj* **1** not movable. **2** staying motionless. **im′mo·bil′i·ty** *n.* **im·mo′bil·ize′** *v.*

im·mod·er·ate (i mod′ə rit) *adj* without any restraint: *His immoderate appetite embarrassed the other guests.* **im·mod′er·ate·ly** *adv.* **im·mod′er·ate·ness** *n.*

im·mod·est (i mod′ist) *adj* not modest; flashy, conceited, indecent, improper, etc.: *immodest behaviour, immodest clothing.* **im·mod′est·ly** *adv.* **im·mod′es·ty** *n.*

im·mo·late (im′ə lāt′) *v* **im·mo·lat·ed, im·mo·lat·ing** offer or kill as a sacrifice: *Many soldiers' lives have been immolated on the altar of patriotism.* <Latin *immolare* sacrifice, from *im-* upon + *mola* sacrifical meal, ground-up grain. The ancient Romans sprinkled meal on their sacrifices as part of the offering.> **im′mo·la′tion** *n.*

im·mor·al (i mô′rəl) *adj* against the principles of proper living: *Lying and stealing are immoral.* **im′mo·ral′i·ty** *n.* **im·mor′al·ly** *adv.*

CONFUSABLES

Immoral refers to actions that go against accepted moral law or standards: *Cheating is immoral.*

Amoral describes behaviour not based on any moral standards: *The repeat offender was amoral.*

im·mor·tal (i mô′təl) *adj* **1** living forever. **2** to do with gods, angels, or other immortal beings; divine rather than human or earthly. **3** remembered or deserved to be remembered forever: *the immortal Elvis.*
n an immortal being or person. **im′mor·tal′i·ty** *n.* **im·mor′tal·ize** *v.* **im·mor′tal·ly** *adv.*

a bat	e bed	i bid	o pot	u cup	th thin
ā cake	ē me	ī bite	ō go	ū rude	TH then
ä bar	ə about	ər over	ô for	ů put	zh measure

im·mov·a·ble (i mū′və bəl) *adj* **1** that cannot be moved. **2** firm, steadfast, or unyielding: *Her immovable opinions made it impossible to reason with her.* **3** not able to be influenced emotionally.
n **immovables** *pl Law* land, buildings, and other property that cannot be moved from one place to another. **im·mov′a·bil′i·ty** *n.* **im·mov′a·bly** *adv.*

SYNONYMS

Immovable emphasizes being inflexible or determined: *She was immovable in her views, despite her friend's criticism of them.*

Obstinate suggests unreasonableness in refusing to give in: *The obstinate child refused to share the toy.*

Uncompromising indicates being unwilling to compromise: *The uncompromising owners would not drop the selling price of their house.*

im·mune (i myūn′) *adj* **1** resistant to an infection or toxin owing to the presence of the correct antibodies or responses: *I am immune to poison ivy, and never get a rash.* **2** not affected or influenced by something: *She is immune to insults.* **3** (*with* ***from***) free from an obligation or from something unpleasant: *immune from taxes. Diplomatic staff and their families are immune from arrest in the country where they work.* <Latin *immunis* exempt> **im·mu′ni·ty** *n.*

immune response *n* what the body does in reaction to the presence of a substance that is not recognized as belonging to it.

immune system *n* the body's system of defence against infection or a toxin, including organs, tissues, cells, and cell products such as antibodies.

im·mu·nize (im′yə nīz′) *v* **im·mu·nized, im·mu·niz·ing** make immune, especially by administering a vaccine or serum, etc.: *Schoolchildren in Canada must be immunized against certain diseases.* **im′mu·ni·za′tion** *n.*

im·mu·no·de·fi·cien·cy (i myū′nō di fish′ən sē) *n* lack of normal immune response. Also, **immune deficiency**.

im·mu·nol·o·gy (im′yə nol′ə jē) *n* the branch of medicine that studies the resistance to infection or toxins in human beings and animals. **im′mu·nol′o·gist** *n.*

im·mu·no·sup·pres·sion (i myū′nō sə pre′shən) *n* the reduction or elimination of the normal immune response, especially to prevent rejection of a transplant. Any drug used for this treatment is called an **immunosuppressant**. **im′mu·no·sup·pres′sive** *adj.*

im·mu·ta·ble (i myū′tə bəl) *adj* never changing: *the immutable laws of nature.* <Latin *in-* not + *mutare* change> **im·mu′ta·bil′i·ty** *n.* **im·mu′ta·bly** *adv.*

imp (imp) *n* **1** a mischievous child. **2** a young or small demon or malicious fairy. <Old English *impe* a bud of a plant, i.e., offspring> **imp′ish** *adj.*

im·pact (im′pakt) *n* **1** a striking of one thing against another: *The impact of the stone against the window shattered the glass.* **2** a forceful effect or influence: *Computers have had a strong impact on our lives.*
v **1** strike forcefully: *The cyclist impacted the fence and was thrown backward.* **2** have a forceful effect on: *The Internet has impacted everyday language.* <Latin *impingere* strike against>

im·pact·ed (im pak′tid) *adj* pressed firmly together in the body, such as a tooth pressed between the jawbone and another tooth.

im·pair (im per′) *v* **1** make bad or worse: *Poor food impaired her health.* **2 –impaired** (*in compounds*) with some degree of disability in a certain area: *hearing-impaired.* **3** 🍁 **impaired** *Law* under the influence of alcohol or narcotics: *The motorist was charged with impaired driving.* <Old French *empeirer* to make worse, from Latin *pejor* worse> **im·pair′ment** *n.*

im·pa·la (im pal′ə) *n, pl* **im·pa·las** or (*especially collectively*) **im·pa·la** a medium-sized antelope of Africa. Adult males have long S-shaped horns. <Zulu>

im·pale (im pāl′) *v* **im·paled, im·pal·ing** **1** pierce through with something pointed: *The butterflies on display were impaled on small pins stuck in a sheet of cork.* **2** in former times, torture or kill by thrusting on a pointed stake. **3** make helpless as if by piercing: *The teacher impaled the mouthy student with a look of ice.* <French, from Latin *in-* on + *palus* stake> **im·pale′ment** *n.*

im·part (im pärt′) *v* **1** give: *The furnishings imparted an air of elegance to the room.* **2** make information known: *The interviewer asked her to impart the secret of her success.* <Latin *impertire* share in>

im·par·tial (im pär′shəl) *adj* showing no more favour to one side than to the other: *A judge should be impartial.* **im·par′ti·al′i·ty** *n.* **im·par′tial·ly** *adv.*

im·pass·a·ble (im pas′ə bəl) *adj* not usable for travel: *Deep mud made the road impassable.* **im·pass′a·bil′i·ty** *n.* **im·pass′a·bly** *adv.*

im·passe (im′pas) *n* a point where no further progress is possible; a problem with no apparent solution; a dead end. <French>

im·pas·sioned (im pash′ənd) *adj* full of strong feeling: *an impassioned speech.*

im·pas·sive (im pas′iv) *adj* with or showing no feeling or emotion: *She listened with an impassive face.* **im·pas′sive·ly** *adv.* **im′pas·siv′i·ty** *n.*

im·pa·tiens (im pā′shəns) *n* an annual or biennial plant with pouch-shaped flowers and seed pods that burst open when ripe. <Latin = impatient, because the pods burst open easily when touched>

im·pa·tient (im pā′shənt) *adj* **1** showing an unwillingness to wait or to bear pain, trouble, or inconvenience: *She frequently gets angry in traffic because she is so impatient.* **2** restless, anxious, or eager: *I am impatient to see the new puppy.* **3** annoyed or exasperated: *He became impatient with her for asking so many questions.* **im·pa′tience** *n.* **im·pa′tient·ly** *adv.*

im·peach (im pēch′) *v* **1** bring a public official to trial for misconduct during office: *The judge was impeached for taking a bribe.* **2** call into question: *to impeach a person's honour, to impeach the testimony of a witness.* <Old French *empeechier* hinder, from Latin *impedicare* shackle. Those arrested or convicted of crimes were imprisoned with

shackles on their ankles. In English the sense narrowed to apply mainly to public officials.> **im·peach′a·ble** *adj.* **im·peach′a·bly** *adv.* **im·peach′ment** *n.*

im·pec·ca·ble (im pek′ə bəl) *adj* faultless. <Latin *in-* not + *peccare* to sin> **im·pec′ca·bil′i·ty** *n.* **im·pec′ca·bly** *adv.*

im·pe·cu·ni·ous (im′pi kyū′nē əs) *adj* with little or no money. <Latin *in-* not + *pecunia* money>

im·pede (im pēd′) *v* **im·ped·ed, im·ped·ing** hinder: *The deep snow impeded travel.* <Latin *impedire* = to shackle the feet>

im·ped·i·ment (im ped′ə mənt) *n* **1** a hindrance or obstruction. **2** a defect, especially in speech.

im·pel (im pel′) *v* **im·pelled, im·pel·ling** motivate or force in an irresistible way: *His desire for fashionable clothes impelled him to take a part-time job.* <Latin *impellere* to drive forward>

CONFUSABLES

Impel suggests urging to action: *Her affection for her brother impelled her to help him with his project.*

Compel suggests an element of force being applied: *The ice storm compelled us to cancel the trip to the farm.*

im·pend·ing (im pen′ding) *adj* especially of something unpleasant, about to happen; coming soon: *our impending departure. She dreaded the impending exams.* <Latin *in-* upon + *pendere* hang>

im·pen·e·tra·ble (im pen′ə trə bəl) *adj* **1** that cannot be entered, pierced, or passed through: *A thick sheet of steel is impenetrable by an ordinary bullet.* **2** not open to ideas or influences: *an impenetrable mind.* **3** impossible to explain or understand: *an impenetrable mystery.* **im·pen′e·tra·bil′i·ty** *n.* **im·pen′e·tra·ble·ness** *n.* **im·pen′e·tra·bly** *adv.*

im·pen·i·tent (im pen′ə tənt) *adj* feeling no sorrow or regret for having done wrong. **im·pen′i·tence** *n.* **im·pen′i·tent·ly** *adv.*

im·per·a·tive (im per′ə tiv) *adj* **1** urgent; necessary: *It is imperative that a very sick child stay in bed.* **2** *Grammar* expressing a command. *Go!* and *Don't touch that!* are in the imperative mood.

n **1** something that must be obeyed. **2** *Grammar* **a** the category or verb form to which commands belong. **b** a particular verb in this form. <Latin *imperare* command> **im·per′a·tive·ly** *adv.*

im·per·cep·ti·ble (im′pər sep′tə bəl) *adj* so slight as to be unnoticeable or hardly noticeable: *an imperceptible flaw.* **im′per·cep′ti·bly** *adv.*

im·per·fect (im pər′fikt) *adj* **1** with some defect or fault: *imperfect work.* **2** lacking some part. **3** *Grammar* in some languages, expressing continued or customary action in the past.

n *Grammar* the imperfect tense. **im′per·fec′tion** *n.* **im·per′fect·ly** *adv.*

im·pe·ri·al (im pē′rē əl) *adj* **1** to do with an empire or its ruler. **2** to do with a system in which one country rules over others and establishes colonies for itself. **3** to do with the traditional British system of weights and measures. <Latin *imperium* empire> **im·pe′ri·al·ly** *adv.*

imperial gallon *n* in the UK and formerly in Canada, a nonmetric unit of liquid volume equal to about 4.55 L. See also GALLON.

im·pe·ri·al·ism (im pē′rē ə liz′əm) *n* the policy of one country extending its rule over other countries and establishing colonies for itself. **im·pe′ri·al·ist** *n, adj.* **im·pe′ri·al·is′tic** *adj.*

im·per·il (im per′əl) *v* **im·per·illed** or **im·per·iled, im·per·il·ling** or **im·per·il·ing** put in danger: *He decided not to imperil his life by drinking and driving.*

im·pe·ri·ous (im pē′rē əs) *adj* arrogant and domineering. <Latin *imperiosus* commanding> **im·pe′ri·ous·ly** *adv.* **im·pe′ri·ous·ness** *n.*

im·per·ish·a·ble (im per′i shə bəl) *adj* that never decays or deteriorates. **im·per′ish·a·bil′i·ty** *n.*

I

im·per·ma·nent (im pər′mə nənt) *adj* not lasting. **im·per′ma·nence** *n.*

im·per·me·a·ble (im pər′mē ə bəl) *adj* not allowing fluid to pass through. **im·per′me·a·bil′i·ty** *n.*

im·per·son·al (im pər′sə nəl) *adj* **1** treating people as objects or cases to be dealt with rather than as people: *an impersonal bureaucracy. I found the clerk's manner very impersonal.* **2** *Grammar* to do with a verb that has no definite subject, but often is only used with *it.* Example: *It is raining.* **im·per′son·al′i·ty** *n.* **im·per′son·al·ly** *adv.*

im·per·son·ate (im pər′sə nāt′) *v* **im·per·son·at·ed, im·per·son·at·ing** pretend to be someone or something else, either to entertain or to deceive: *The robber gained entry to the house by impersonating a TV repairman. The stand-up comic impersonated a few famous politicians.* **im·per′son·a′tion** *n.* **im·per′son·a′tor** *n.*

im·per·ti·nent (im pər′tə nənt) *adj* cheeky; disrespectful: *Enough of your impertinent remarks.* <Latin *in-* not + *pertinere* belong> **im·per′ti·nence** *n.* **im·per′ti·nent·ly** *adv.*

im·per·turb·a·ble (im′pər tər′bə bəl) *adj* unable to be excited or upset. **im′per·turb′a·bil′i·ty** *n.* **im′per·turb′a·bly** *adv.*

im·per·vi·ous (im pər′vē əs) *adj* **1** not allowing fluid to pass through: *Rubberized cloth is impervious to moisture.* **2** not open to or affected by something: *She is impervious to being teased.* <Latin *in-* not + *per-* through + *via* way> **im·per′vi·ous·ly** *adv.* **im·per′vi·ous·ness** *n.*

im·pe·ti·go (im′pə tī′gō) *n* an infectious skin disease causing pimples filled with pus. <Latin *impetigo* skin eruption, from *impetere* to attack>

im·pet·u·ous (im pech′ū əs) *adj* **1** impulsive or rash and driven by emotion: *Children are usually more impetuous than adults.* **2** moving with great force or speed: *the impetuous rush of water over Niagara Falls.* <Latin *impetus* attack> **im·pet′u·os′i·ty** *n.* **im·pet′u·ous·ly** *adv.*

a **bat**	e **bed**	i **bid**	o **pot**	u **cup**	th **thin**
ā **cake**	ē **me**	ī **bite**	ō **go**	ū **rude**	ᴛʜ **then**
à **bar**	ə **about**	ər **over**	ò **for**	ù **put**	zh **measure**

im·pe·tus (im′pə təs) *n* **1** something that causes people or things to act: *A series of accidents provided the impetus for a full-fledged safety inquiry.* **2** *Physics* the force with which a moving body tends to maintain its velocity and overcome resistance. <Latin = attack>

im·pinge (im pinj′) *v* **im·pinged, im·ping·ing** (*with* ***on***) **1** have an effect or impact, especially an unfavourable one: *The tragedy greatly impinged on the family.* **2** advance into an area belonging to someone or something else: *Your stuff is impinging on my side of the room.* <Latin *in-* into + *pangere* to strike> **im·pinge′ment** *n.*

im·pi·ous (im′pi əs) *or* (im pī′əs) *adj* not showing due respect or reverence, especially for God or a god. **im·pi′ety** (im′pī ə tē) *n.* **im′pi·ous·ly** *adv.*

im·plac·a·ble (im plak′ə bəl) *adj* that cannot be soothed or satisfied: *an implacable enemy, implacable rage.* <Latin *in-* not + *placere* please> **im·plac′a·bil′i·ty** *n.* **im·plac′a·ble·ness** *n.* **im·plac′a·bly** *adv.*

im·plant (im plant′) *for v,* (im′plant) *for n.* *v* **1** insert more or less permanently: *a microchip implanted in a dog's ear.* **2** instil; fix deeply: *A good teacher implants ideas worth remembering.*
n something implanted, especially tissue or artificial support grafted into the body. **im′plan·ta′tion** *n.*

im·plaus·i·ble (im ploz′ə bəl) *adj* hard to believe: *By way of excuse, he offered an implausible story about meeting Prince Charles on the bus.* **im·plaus′i·bil′ity** *n.* **im·plaus′i·bly** *adv.*

im·ple·ment (im′plə mənt) *for n,* (im′plə ment′) *for v.* *n* a tool, instrument, or other piece of equipment: *The gardening implements are kept in the shed.*
v put into action or effect: *to implement a new policy. That's a great suggestion, and we should implement it right away.* <Latin *implementum,* from *in-* in + *plere* fill> **im′ple·men·ta′tion** *n.*

im·pli·cate (im′plə kāt′) *v* **im·pli·cat·ed, im·pli·cat·ing** **1** show to be involved in wrongdoing: *The thief's confession implicated two other people.* **2** involve as a consequence. <Latin *implicare* to involve, from *in-* in + *plicare* to fold>

im·pli·ca·tion (im′plə kā′shən) *n* **1** the act of implying something or implicating someone. **2** something implied: *I resent the implication that I don't work hard enough.*

im·plic·it (im plis′it) *adj* **1** without doubting, hesitating, or asking questions: *implicit trust, implicit obedience.* **2** meant, but not clearly expressed or distinctly stated: *Her silence gave implicit consent.* **3** involved as a necessary part or condition: *Confidentiality is implicit in the relationship between lawyer and client.* <See IMPLICATE.> **im·plic′it·ly** *adv.*

im·plied (im plīd′) *adj* involved, indicated, suggested, or understood without a clear statement: *an implied insult.*

im·plode (im plōd′) *v* **im·plod·ed, im·plod·ing** burst or cause to burst inward: *External pressure can cause a vacuum tube to implode.* <Latin *in-* in + (*ex*)*plode*> **im·plo′sion** *n.*

im·plore (im plȯr′) *v* **im·plored, im·plor·ing** beg a person to do something: *She implored her dad to let her stay up late on Saturdays.* <Latin *implorare* call for help> **im·plor′ing** *adj.* **im·plor′ing·ly** *adv.*

im·ply (im plī′) *v* **im·plied, im·ply·ing** **1** indicate without saying outright: *Her smile implied that she had forgiven us.* **2** involve as a necessary part or condition: *Communication implies the existence of a communicator and a message.* <See IMPLICATE.>

CONFUSABLES

Imply means "indicate without saying" or "suggest": *He implied by his smile that he knew the answer.*

Infer means "suppose": *They inferred from his smile that he knew the answer.*

im·po·lite (im′pə līt′) *adj* with or showing bad manners. **im′po·lite′ly** *adv.* **im′po·lite′ness** *n.*

SYNONYMS

Impolite means "ill-mannered": *She was impolite not to respond to the invitation.*

Insolent means "rude": *The insolent child ignored his parents, and continued to chatter during the movie.*

im·pol·i·tic (im pol′ə tik′) *adj* not wise from a political or social point of view: *It would be impolitic to offend him now that we need his help.*

im·pon·der·a·ble (im pon′də rə bəl) *adj* that cannot be analyzed completely or measured exactly: *Faith and love are imponderable forces.*
n something imponderable. **im·pon′der·a·bil′i·ty** *n.* **im·pon′der·a·bly** *adv.*

im·port (im pȯrt′) *for v,* (im′pȯrt) *for n.* *v* **1** bring in from a foreign country for sale or use: *Canada imports coffee.* **2** *Computers* bring from one application into another: *You can import tables from the spreadsheet into your text document.* **3** *Formal or Archaic* be important; matter: *It imports little what you do.*
n **1** anything imported: *Rubber is a useful import.* **2** importance: *It is a matter of great import.* **3** meaning or significance: *What is the import of this argument?* <Latin *in-* in + *portare* to carry> **im′por·ta′tion** *n.* **im·port′er** *n.*

im·por·tant (im pȯr′tənt) *adj* **1** worth taking seriously and caring about: *important business, an important occasion.* **2** with high social status or influence: *The mayor is an important person in our town.* **3** acting as if important: *He rushed around in an important manner, giving orders.* <See IMPORT.> **im·por′tance** *n.* **im·por′tant·ly** *adv.*

SYNONYMS

Important suggests something of great meaning, significance, or value: *Her graduation was an important event in her family.*

Consequence implies importance in rank or position: *He was a man of great consequence in the business world.*

Vital means "of the greatest importance": *Control of pollution is vital for the environment.*

im·por·tu·nate (im pôr′chə nit) *adj* persistent, especially in an annoying or intrusive way. **im·por′tu·nate·ly** *adv.*

im·por·tune (im′pôr tyün′) *or* (im′pôr tün′) *v* **im·por·tuned, im·por·tun·ing** ask urgently or repeatedly: *He importuned his mom until she gave in and bought him the jacket.* <Latin *importunus* tiresome> **im′por·tu′ni·ty** *n.*

im·pose (im pōz′) *v* **im·posed, im·pos·ing 1** apply a burden, tax, or punishment on someone: *to impose a fine of for not wearing a bike helmet.* **2** force one's wishes or one's company on others: *I don't want to impose, but could you give me a ride if it's not too much trouble?* <Old French, from Latin *in-* on + *ponere* put> **im·pos′er** *n.*
impose on, take advantage of selfishly: *to impose on the good nature of others.*

im·pos·ing (im pō′zing) *adj* impressive because of size, majesty, or dignity: *The Peace Tower of the Parliament Buildings is an imposing landmark.*

im·po·si·tion (im′pə zish′ən) *n* **1** the act or fact of imposing: *A war requires the imposition of heavy taxes.* **2** a tax or duty. **3** a demand, request, or expectation that burdens someone: *Would it be an imposition to ask you to mail this parcel?*

im·pos·si·ble (im pos′ə bəl) *adj* **1** that cannot be reached, done, or fulfilled: *an impossible task, an impossible goal.* **2** that cannot happen or be true: *an impossible story. It is impossible for two and two to be six.* **3** not to be tolerated or endured: *an impossible person.* **im·pos′si·bil′i·ty** *n.* **im·pos′si·bly** *adv.*

im·pos·tor (im pos′tər) *n* a person who pretends to be someone else in order to deceive people for his or her own advantage: *They discovered he wasn't the real prince but an impostor.* <See IMPOSE.>

im·po·tent (im′pə tənt) *adj* **1** powerless or helpless: *impotent rage. Without ammunition the soldiers were impotent.* **2** of males, unable to have an erection: *Alcohol abuse can make you impotent.* **im′po·tence** *n.* **im′po·tent·ly** *adv.*

im·pound (im pound′) *v* **1** shut up in a pen or pound: *to impound stray animals.* **2** put in the custody of a law court: *The court impounded the documents to use as evidence.* <Latin *in-* in + *pound*[3]>

im·pov·er·ish (im pov′ə rish) *v* **1** make very poor. **2** exhaust the strength, richness, or resources of: *Censorship impoverishes freedom of speech.* <Old French, from *em-* cause to be + *povre* poor> **im·pov′er·ished** *adj.* **im·pov′er·ish·ment** *n.*

im·prac·ti·ca·ble (im prak′tə kə bəl) *adj* impossible or too difficult or expensive to put into practice: *His suggestion was impracticable.* **im·prac′ti·ca·bil′i·ty** *n.* **im·prac′ti·ca·bly** *adv.*

im·prac·ti·cal (im prak′tə kəl) *adj* not practical or sensible: *Those fancy shoes are impractical for hiking in. She's clever, but so impractical.* **im·prac′ti·cal′i·ty** *n.* **im·prac′ti·cal·ly** *adv.*

im·pre·cate (im′prə kāt′) *v* **im·pre·cat·ed, im·pre·cat·ing** utter a curse or invoke evil on someone: *The prophet imprecated ruin on his enemies.* <Latin *in-* on + *precari* to pray> **im′pre·ca′tion** *n.*

im·pre·cise (im′pri sīs′) *adj* inexact or vague: *imprecise measurements, an imprecise term.* **im′pre·cise′ly** *adv.* **im′pre·ci′sion** *n.*

im·preg·na·ble (im preg′nə bəl) *adj* able to resist any attack: *an impregnable fortress, impregnable arguments.* <Old French, from Latin *in-* not + *prehendere* sieze> **im·preg′na·bil′i·ty** *n.* **im·preg′na·bly** *adv.*

im·preg·nate (im preg′nāt) *v* **im·preg·nat·ed, im·preg·nat·ing 1** make pregnant. **2** *Biology* fertilize: *to impregnate an egg cell.* **3** saturate or permeate: *Tar paper is heavy paper impregnated with tar.* <Latin *in-* in + *praegnare* to make pregnant> **im′preg·na′tion** *n.*

im·pre·sa·ri·o (im′prə sȧ′rē ō′) *n* an organizer or manager of operas, concerts, or other entertainments. <Italian = one who undertakes>

im·press (im pres′) *for v,* (im′pres) *for n.* *v* **1** have a strong effect on the mind or feelings of, especially, cause to have a high opinion of a person or thing: *His generosity is what impressed me most. I was not impressed by the performance.* **2** fix in the mind: *She repeated the list several times to impress it on her memory.* **3** mark by pressing or stamping: *to impress wax with a seal.*
n a special mark or quality: *An author leaves the impress of his personality on his work.* <Latin *impressus,* from *in-* in + *premere* press>

im·pres·sion (im presh′ən) *n* **1** an effect produced on a person: *Punishment seemed to make little impression on the child.* **2** a feeling or idea: *I have a vague impression that I left the house unlocked.* **3** something produced by pressure: *There was an impression of someone's foot in the cement.* **4** an impersonation of someone: *He can do a great impression of Pierre Trudeau.*

im·pres·sion·a·ble (im presh′ə nə bəl) *adj* easily impressed or influenced: *Children are usually more impressionable than adults.* **im·pres′sion·a·bil′i·ty** *n.*

im·pres·sion·ism (im presh′ə niz′əm) *n*
1 Impressionism a school of painting among French painters of the 1800s, characterized by the use of colour to suggest the visual effect of natural reflected light. **2** a style in any of the arts, characterized by subjective, often emotional, impressions of reality.

im·pres·sion·ist (im presh′ə nist) *n* **1 a Impressionist** a painter of the school of IMPRESSIONISM (def. 1). **b** a painter, writer, or composer who follows a style emphasizing subjective impressions of reality. **2** an entertainer who does impersonations of famous people.
adj **Impressionist** to do with IMPRESSIONISM (def. 1).

im·pres·sion·is·tic (im presh′ə nis′tik) *adj* **1** giving only a general or hasty impression. **2** in the style of impressionism.

im·pres·sive (im pres′iv) *adj* making a strong impression on the mind by excellence, size, or intensity: *an impressive accomplishment, an impressive storm.*
im·pres′sive·ly *adv.* **im·pres′sive·ness** *n.*

a bat	e bed	i bid	o pot	u cup	th thin
ā cake	ē me	ī bite	ō go	ü rude	ᴛʜ then
ȧ bar	ə about	ər over	ô for	u̇ put	zh measure

im·pri·ma·tur (im′pri mä′tər) *or* (im′pri mat′ər) *n* 1 *Catholicism* official authorization to print or publish as a religious book. 2 approval, especially for something written. <Latin = let it be printed>

im·print (im′print) *for n,* (im print′) *for v. n* 1 a mark made by pressure: *the imprint of a foot in the sand.* 2 a permanent mark: *Suffering left its imprint on her face.* 3 in or on a printed work, the publisher's or printer's name.
v 1 mark by pressing or stamping: *to imprint a postmark on an envelope.* 2 press or impress: *a scene imprinted on my memory.*

im·print·ing (im prin′ting) *Biology n* the process by which a very young animal recognizes that another animal, person, or thing is a parent or other object of trust. 2 other learning that occurs automatically in the first hours or days of life.

im·pris·on (im priz′ən) *v* put in prison or anything like prison. **im·pris′on·ment** *n.*

im·prob·a·ble (im prob′ə bəl) *adj* 1 not likely to happen: *It is improbable that they will win the most medals at the next Olympic games.* 2 not likely to be true: *an improbable story.* **im·prob′a·bil′i·ty** *n.* **im·prob′a·ble·ness** *n.* **im·prob′a·bly** *adv.*

im·promp·tu (im promp′tū) *adv, adj* without preparing or rehearsing beforehand: *an impromptu speech* (*adj*). *He delivered the speech impromptu* (*adv*).
n an impromptu speech or performance. <Latin *in promptu* in readiness>

im·prop·er (im prop′ər) *adj* 1 not according to the standards of good behaviour: *improper language.* 2 not suitable for the purpose or the circumstances: *improper clothing for a hike.* 3 incorrect: *improper methods, an improper argument.* **im·prop′er·ly** *adv.*

SYNONYMS

Improper suggests not suitable according to standard conventions: *Her jeans were improper attire at the wedding ceremony.*

Crude is more forceful than improper, suggesting vulgarity: *His crude language offended his grandfather.*

Unfitting suggests not proper or right: *The man's remarks about his employer's appearance were unfitting.*

improper fraction *Mathematics n* a fraction greater than 1, such as 3/2 or 27/4.

im·pro·pri·e·ty (im′prə prī′ə tē) *n, pl* **im·pro·pri·e·ties** 1 the fact or quality of being improper. 2 an improper remark or act.

im·prov (im′prov) *Informal n* 1 STANDUP. 2 role-playing without a script.
adj doing or featuring improvisation: *an improv group, improv theatre.*

im·prove (im prūv′) *v* **im·proved, im·prov·ing** make or become better: *You could improve your handwriting if you tried. His health is improving.* <Old French *en-* in + *prou* profit> **im·prov′a·ble** *adj.* **im·prov′a·bly** *adv.* **im·prove′ment** *n.*

improve on, do or be better than: *The edited version of your story should improve on your first draft.*

im·prov·i·dent (im prov′ə dənt) *adj* not careful in providing for the future. **im·prov′i·dence** *n.* **im·prov′i·dent·ly** *adv.*

im·pro·vise (im′prə vīz′) *v* **im·pro·vised, im·pro·vis·ing** 1 create and perform something without any preparation: *We improvised a skit for the school assembly.* 2 make or provide offhand, using whatever may be available: *The girls improvised a tent out of two blankets and some long poles.* <French *improviser,* from Latin *in-* not + *providere* foresee> **im′pro·vi·sa′tion** *n.* **im′pro·vis′er** *n.*

im·pru·dent (im prū′dənt) *adj* not showing care for the consequences of an action: *an imprudent decision.* **im·pru′dence** *n.* **im·pru′dent·ly** *adv.*

im·pu·dent (im′pyə dənt) *adj* so bold as to be rude: *The impudent girl made faces at the bus driver.* <Latin *in-* not + *pudere* be modest> **im′pu·dence** *n.* **im′pu·dent·ly** *adv.*

im·pulse (im′puls) *n* 1 a sudden desire to act, often based on instinct or emotion: *to buy something on an impulse.* 2 a signal transmitted by nerve cells, influencing muscle action and other changes in the body. 3 a pulse of electrical energy. 4 *Physics* a force acting briefly on a body and producing a limited change of momentum. 5 a sudden, driving force or influence: *the impulse of a wave.* <Latin *impellere* urge>

im·pul·sive (im pul′siv) *adj* 1 tending to act without thinking: *The impulsive child ran up and hugged the team mascot.* 2 coming from a sudden impulse: *an impulsive burst of laughter.* **im·pul′sive·ly** *adv.* **im·pul′sive·ness** *n.*

im·pu·ni·ty (im pyū′nə tē) *n* freedom from punishment, injury, or other unpleasant consequences: *You didn't think you could shoplift with impunity, did you?* <Latin *in-* without + *poena* punishment>

im·pure (im pyūr′) *adj* 1 dirty or polluted: *The air in cities is often impure.* 2 mixed with something, often something of lower value: *The salt we use is slightly impure. An impure substance consists of two or more pure substances mixed together.* 3 bad or immoral: *impure thoughts.* **im·pure′ly** *adv.* **im·pu′ri·ty** *n.*

im·pute (im pyūt′) *v* **im·put·ed, im·put·ing** blame on someone or something: *The crime had been imputed to the wrong person; he was innocent.* <Latin *in-* against + *putare* to think> **im′pu·ta′tion** *n.*

in (in) *prep* 1 inside: *in the box.* 2 completely surrounded by: *in water.* 3 using: *to paint in watercolours.* 4 among: *one in a hundred.* 5 motivated by: *to act in self-defence.* 6 about: *a course in Canadian history.* 7 during: *in April.* 8 after: *I will be back in an hour.* 9 by or through: *In giving we receive.* 10 while or when: *In cleaning my room, I found this book of yours.*
adv 1 on or to the inside: *Come in. Wear it with the fuzzy side in.* 2 arriving at a destination: *The plane got in late.* 3 as a tide, rising or at the highest level: *The tide is coming in right now.*
adj 1 present, especially in one's home or office: *The doctor is not in today.* 2 fashionable: *Baggy pants are in again. Blue is the in colour now.* <Old English>
in for, sure to get or have: *We are in for a storm.*

in on, involved in and informed about: *I'm not in on what the class did, since I wasn't at school yesterday.*
ins and outs, all the different parts; details: *He knew all the ins and outs of the rules of hockey.*
in that, in the sense or to the extent that: *Reading is beneficial in that it exposes you to new ideas.*
in with, friendly with.

GRAMMAR AND USAGE

In generally shows location: He was in the garage. (literal). *The child was in a rage* (figurative).

Into generally shows direction or change: *She came into the room. The rain changed into snow.*

in–[1] *prefix* not or without: *inexpensive, inattention.* Also, IL- before the letter *l*, IM- before the letters *b*, *m*, or *p*, and IR- before the letter *r*. <Latin>

in–[2] *prefix* in, into, toward, or within: *inscribe, induce, inborn.* Also, IL- before the letter *l*, IM- before the letters *b*, *m*, or *p*, and IR- before the letter *r*. <Latin>

in·a·bil·i·ty (in′ə bil′ə tē) *n* a lack of ability or power: *He was frustrated by their inability to understand.*

in ab·sen·tia (ab sen′shə) *adv* in the absence of (a person): *The traitor had escaped to another country, but he was tried and convicted in absentia.* <Latin = in absence>

in·ac·ces·si·ble (in′ək ses′ə bəl) *adj* **1** hard or impossible to reach, enter, or get at: *High cliffs made the castle inaccessible from the west.* **2** not open or available: *Those files are inaccessible to employees.* **in′ac·ces′i·bil′i·ty** *n.* **in′ac·ces′si·bly** *adv.*

in·ac·cu·rate (i nak′yə rit) *adj* **1** not exact or correct: *an inaccurate measurement.* **2** false: *inaccurate statements.* **in·ac′cu·ra·cy** *n.* **in·ac′cu·rate·ly** *adv.*

in·ac·tive (i nak′tiv) *adj* not doing anything or not in use: *an inactive account, an inactive volcano.* **in·ac′tion** *n.* **in·ac′tive·ly** *adv.* **in′ac·tiv′i·ty** *n.*

in·ad·e·quate (i nad′ə kwit) *adj* not enough or not good enough: *inadequate supplies, inadequate work.* **in·ad′e·qua·cy** *n.* **in·ad′e·quate·ly** *adv.*

in·ad·mis·si·ble (in′əd mis′ə bəl) *adj* that cannot be allowed or accepted: *Such a ridiculous excuse is inadmissible.* **in′ad·mis′si·bil′i·ty** *n.* **in′ad·mis′si·bly** *adv.*

in·ad·vert·ent (in′əd vər′tənt) *adj* done by mistake: *Sorry about the inadvertent omission of your name from the list.* <Latin *inadvertere*> **in′ad·vert′ence** *n.* **in′ad·vert′ent·ly** *adv.*

in·ad·vis·a·ble (in′əd vī′zə bəl) *adj* not recommended as a course of action: *It is inadvisable to keep an extra house key in the mailbox.* **in′ad·vis′a·bil′i·ty** *n.* **in′ad·vis′a·ble·ness** *n.* **in′ad·vis′a·bly** *adv.*

in·a·li·en·a·ble (i nāl′yə nə bəl) *adj* that cannot be given away or taken away: *Equality before the law is an inalienable right.* **in·al′ien·a·bly** *adv.*

in·al·ter·a·ble (i nol′tə rə bəl) *adj* that cannot be changed. **in·al′ter·a·bil′i·ty** *n.* **in·al′ter·a·bly** *adv.*

in·ane (i nān′) *adj* mindlessly silly or foolish: *an inane remark.* <Latin *inanis* empty> **in·ane′ly** *adv.* **in·an′i·ty** (i nan′ə tē) *n.*

in·an·i·mate (i nan′ə mit) *adj* without life: *A stone is an inanimate object.* **in·an′i·mate·ly** *adv.*

in·ap·pli·ca·ble (in′ə plik′ə bəl) *or* (i nap′lə kə bəl) *adj* not fitting a particular situation: *If any parts of the questionnaire are inapplicable in your case, leave them blank.* **in′ap·plic′a·bil′i·ty** *n.* **in·ap′plic·a·ble·ness** *n.* **in′ap·plic′a·bly** *n.*

in·ap·pro·pri·ate (in′ə prō′prē it) *adj* not proper or suitable: *Flip-flops are inappropriate footwear for rock climbing.* **in′ap·pro′pri·ate·ly** *adv.* **in′ap·pro′pri·ate·ness** *n.*

in·apt (i napt′) *adj* **1** not suitable or appropriate: *Daisy Cottage seems an inapt name for this huge mansion.* **2** without a natural aptitude for something: *an inapt student of music.* **in·apt′ly** *adv.* **in·apt′ness** *n.*

CONFUSABLES

Inapt, in addition to meaning "not fitting," can mean "without a natural aptitude": *The inapt job applicant failed most of the tests.*

Inept means "unskilful" or "incompetent": *The inept painter dripped blotches of paint all over the floor.*

in·ar·tic·u·late (in′är tik′yə lit) *adj* **1** not clearly forming spoken words: *an inarticulate mutter.* **2** unable to express oneself well: *I don't do well in discussions because I am so inarticulate.* **3** not with the natural power of spoken language: *Animals are inarticulate.* **4** without joints or articulations. **in′ar·tic′u·late·ly** *adv.* **in′ar·tic′u·late·ness** *n.*

in·as·much as (in′əz much′) *conj* in view of the fact that: *Inasmuch as he was smaller than the other boys, he was given a head start in the race.*

in·at·ten·tive (in′ə ten′tiv) *adj* not paying attention: **in′at·ten′tion** *n.* **in′at·ten′tive·ly** *adv.*

in·au·di·ble (i nod′ə bəl) *adj* that cannot be heard: *The street noises were almost inaudible at the back of the house.* **in·au′di·bil′i·ty** *n.* **in·au′di·bly** *adv.*

in·au·gu·rate (i nog′yə rāt′) *v* **in·au·gu·rat·ed, in·au·gu·rat·ing** **1** formally place someone in office by a special ceremony: *The new mayor will be inaugurated at noon tomorrow.* **2** make a formal beginning of: *The development of the airplane inaugurated a new era in transportation.* **3** open for use, often with a ceremony or celebration: *The new park was inaugurated with a community picnic and ball game.* <Latin *in-* + *augurare* read omens (at the start of a journey, project, etc.) In ancient Rome, the installation of a new officer, opening of a new institution, start of a journey, or any other major undertaking was always scheduled at a time considered favourable by interpreters of omens in the flight of birds.> **in·au′gu·ral** *adj.* **in·au′gu·ra′tion** *n.*

a bat	e bed	i bid	o pot	u cup	th **thin**
ā cake	ē me	ī bite	ō go	ū rude	TH **then**
ä bar	ə about	ər over	ô for	ů put	zh measure

in·aus·pi·cious (in′o spish′əs) *adj* seeming likely to produce failure: *Despite its inauspicious loss in the first game, the home team won the series.*
in′aus·pi′cious·ly *adv.* **in′aus·pi′cious·ness** *n.*

in–be·tween (in′bi twēn′) *adj* not quite one thing nor the other: *I hate my hair when it gets to that in-between stage, neither short nor long.*
n a person or thing of this kind: *He's neither a child nor an adult; he's an in-between.*

in·board (in′bȯrd′) *adv, adj* within a ship or boat: *an inboard motor.*
n **1** a motorboat with its motor within. **2** the motor itself.

in·born (in′bȯrn′) *adj* in a person from birth: *an inborn sense of rhythm.*

in·bred (in′bred′) *adj* **1** belonging to a person genetically or by virtue of upbringing: *an inbred courtesy.* **2 a** bred for generations from ancestors who were closely related: *an inbred strain of horses.* **b** showing genetic deterioration or lack of diversity as a result of this.

in·breed (in′brēd′) *v* **in·bred, in·breed·ing** breed or be bred from closely related people, animals, or plants.

In·ca (ing′kə) *n* **1** a member of an indigenous people of S America that held power in Peru before the Spanish conquest. **2** one of the rulers of these people. <Quechua *ynca* prince>

in·cal·cu·la·ble (in kal′kyə lə bəl) *adj* **1** too great to be counted: *of incalculable value.* **2** not able to be predicted or estimated beforehand. **in·cal′cu·la·bil′i·ty** *n.*
in·cal′cu·la·bly *adv.*

in camera *adj, adv* **1** *Law* in the privacy of a judge's chambers, rather than in open court. **2** in a closed session, such as of a committee. <Latin = in a room>

Light sources that produce a lot of heat are not efficient sources of light. Since fluorescent tubes produce much less heat than **incandescent** light bulbs, most schools and office buildings use fluorescent lighting.

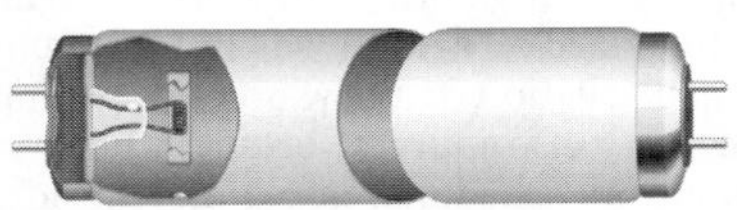

in·can·des·cent (in′kən des′ənt) *adj* **1** glowing with heat. **2** to do with a material that glows brightly when hot. **Incandescent light** is produced by an electric bulb with a very fine wire in it that becomes white-hot when current flows through it. <Latin *in-* in + *candere* gleam>

in·can·ta·tion (in′kan tā′shən) *n* a word or set of words used as a charm or magic spell. <Latin *in-* at, to + *cantare* chant>

in·ca·pa·ble (in kā′pə bəl) *adj* without the ability to do the thing required. **in·ca′pa·bil′i·ty** *n.* **in·ca′pa·bly** *adv.*
incapable of, a unable to do, by one's very nature: *She was incapable of lying.* **b** not legally qualified for: *Certain beliefs make a person incapable of serving on a jury.* **c** not able to undergo or receive: *Some qualities are incapable of exact measurement.*

in·ca·pac·i·tate (in′kə pas′ə tāt′) *v* **in·ca·pac·i·tat·ed, in·ca·pac·i·tat·ing 1** make powerless or unable to do things: *The man's injury incapacitated him for working.* **2** legally disqualify. **in′ca·pac′i·ta′tion** *n.*
in′ca·pac′i·ty *n.*

in·car·cer·ate (in kȧr′sə rāt′) *v* **in·car·cer·at·ed, in·car·cer·at·ing** put in prison. <Latin *in-* in + *carcer* jail> **in·car′cer·a′tion** *n.*

in·car·nate (in kȧr′nit) *for adj,* (in kȧr′nāt) *for v.*
adj embodied in flesh, especially in human form: *That villain is the devil incarnate.*
v **in·car·nat·ed, in·car·nat·ing 1** put into flesh: *Ancient Egyptian gods were incarnated as humans and as animals.* **2** give material form to: *The artist's vision has been incarnated in a breathtaking mural.* **3** be the physical realization of: *She incarnates all our ideals.* <Latin *in-* in + *carnis* flesh> **in′car·na′tion** *n.*

in·cau·tious (in kosh′əs) *adj* not cautious.
in·cau′tious·ly *adv.* **in·cau′tious·ness** *n.*

in·cen·di·ar·y (in sen′dē er′ē) *adj* **1** causing or used to start a fire: *incendiary bombs and shells.* **2** deliberately stirring up conflict or rebellion: *He was arrested for making incendiary speeches.*
n, pl **in·cen·di·ar·ies 1** a person who deliberately stirs up conflict or rebellion. **2** a shell or bomb containing chemical agents that cause fire. **3** an arsonist. <Latin *incendium* fire>

in·cense[1] (in′sens) *n* **1** a substance giving off a sweet smell when burned. **2** the perfume or smoke from it. <Latin *incendere* burn>

in·cense[2] (in sens′) *v* **in·censed, in·cens·ing** make very angry: *Her dishonesty incenses me.* <Latin *incendere* burn>

in·cen·tive (in sen′tiv) *n* something, especially a reward, that motivates a person to do something: *The fun of playing the game was a greater incentive than the prize.* <Latin *incinere* blow into a musical instrument (i.e., make encouraging noises)>

in·cep·tion (in sep′shən) *n* the starting point of something. <Latin *incipere* begin, *in-* on + *capere* take>

in·ces·sant (in ses′ənt) *adj* never stopping: *The incessant noise of highway traffic kept her awake all night.* <Latin *in-* not + *cessare* cease> **in·ces′sant·ly** *adv.*

in·cest (in′sest) *n* **1** sexual relations between people who are so closely related by blood that intercourse is forbidden by law or custom. **2** a relationship that is abnormally close. <Latin *in-* not + *castus* chaste> **in·ces′tu·ous** *adj.*

inch (inch) *n* **1** a nonmetric unit for measuring length, equal to about 2.54 cm. *Abbrev.* **in. 2** the smallest part, amount, or degree: *She would not yield an inch.*

v move slowly or little by little: *The worm inched along.* <Latin *uncia* a twelfth>

by inches, by degrees; gradually.

every inch, in every way: *He is every inch a Canadian.*

inch by inch, slowly.

within an inch of, very near: *The stray dog was within an inch of death when I found it.*

in·cho·ate (in kō′it) *adj* just begun; in an early stage; undeveloped. <Latin *incohare* begin>

inch·worm (inch′wərm′) *n* the thin, wormlike larva of a geometrid, a type of moth.

in·ci·dence (in′sə dəns) *n* **1** the act or fact of occurring: *Check each incidence of his name to ensure you have spelled it correctly.* **2** the manner, extent, or rate of occurring: *a high incidence of traffic accidents over the holiday weekend. In an epidemic, the incidence of a disease is widespread.* **3** *Physics* the falling of something, such as a ray of light, on a surface. <See INCIDENT.>

in·ci·dent (in′sə dənt) *n* **1** an event or occurrence. **2** a single complete piece of action in a narrative. <Latin *incidere* happen>

in·ci·den·tal (in′sə den′təl) *adj* **1** occurring or likely to occur as a minor thing along with something else: *Certain discomforts are incidental to wilderness hiking.* **2** unplanned and insignificant or seeming insignificant: *an incidental encounter with a friend on the street.*

n a minor expense coming as part of some undertaking: *In addition to meals, accommodations, and bus fare, we had to pay for incidentals such as snacks, magazines, and stamps.*

CONFUSABLES

Incidental means "not well thought out": *The premier's incidental remark about the homeless was tactless.*

Accidental means "happening by chance": *Some accidental discoveries turn out to be very important.*

in·ci·den·tal·ly (in′sə den′tə lē) *adv* **1** as a minor thing along with the main point: *She mentioned incidentally that she had had no dinner.* **2** (*as a sentence adverb*) by the way: *Incidentally, have you bought your ticket yet?*

in·cin·er·ate (in sin′ə rāt′) *v* **in·cin·er·at·ed, in·cin·er·at·ing** burn to ashes. <Latin *in-* into + *cineris* ashes> **in·cin′er·a′tion** *n.* **in·cin′er·a′tor** *n.*

in·cip·i·ent (in sip′ē ənt) *adj* just beginning or in an early stage: *A good rest got rid of my incipient cough.* <Latin *incipere* begin> **in·cip′i·ent·ly** *adv.*

in·ci·sion (in sizh′ən) *n* **1** a cut made in something: *The doctor made a small incision to remove the glass from her foot.* **2** the act of cutting or engraving. **in·cise′** (in sīz′) *v.*

ETYMOLOGY

Incise, incision, incisive, and **incisor** all come by way of Middle English and can be traced back to the Latin prefix *in-*, meaning "into," combined with the verb *caedere*, meaning "to cut."

in·ci·sive (in sī′siv) *adj* sharp, penetrating, or keen: *incisive criticism, incisive wit.* **in·ci′sive·ly** *adv.* **in·ci′sive·ness** *n.*

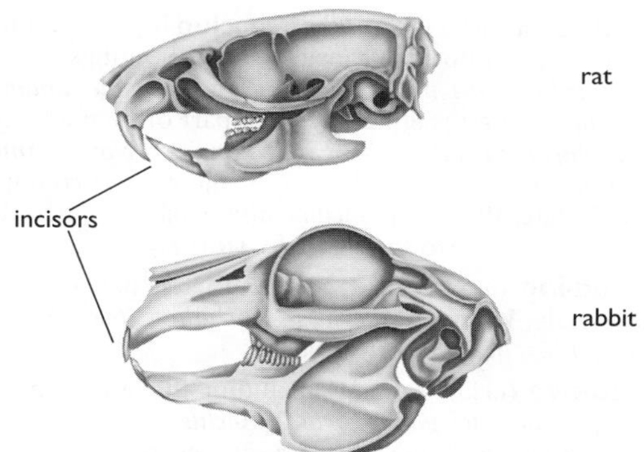

Rats have powerful incisors at the front of the mouth for gnawing through materials such as wood to get to stored food.

Rabbits, which are largely herbivores, use their incisors for cutting grassy foods.

Incisors are constantly worn down by gnawing, but continue to grow throughout the life of the animal.

in·ci·sor (in sī′zər) *n* a tooth at the front part of the mouth with a sharp edge for cutting.

in·cite (in sīt′) *v* **in·cit·ed, in·cit·ing** stir up or rouse: *to incite hatred in people. The captain's example incited the crew to bravery.* <Latin *in-* on + *ciere* cause to move> **in′ci·ta′tion** *n.* **in·cite′ment** *n.* **in·cit′er** *n.*

in·ci·vil·i·ty (in′sə vil′ə tē) *n, pl* **in·ci·vil·i·ties 1** rudeness that borders on hostility. **2** a rude or impolite comment.

in·clem·ent (in klem′ənt) *adj* of weather, uncomfortably cold or wet. **in·clem′en·cy** *n.* **in·clem′ent·ly** *adv.*

in·cli·na·tion (in′klə nā′shən) *n* **1** a preference or liking: *I have no inclination for sports.* **2** a vague desire or impulse: *My first inclination was to ask why, but on second thought, I kept quiet.* **3** a tendency: *One sign of a slower metabolism is an inclination to gain weight.* **4** a leaning, tilting, or sloping: *the inclination of a roof. He acknowledged her by a slight inclination of the head.* <See INCLINE.>

in·cline (in klīn′) *for v,* (in′klīn) *for n. v* **in·clined, in·clin·ing 1** tend: *He inclines toward excessive neatness.* **2** make favourable or willing: *The prisoner's unruliness did not incline the judge to reduce his sentence.* **3** slope, slant, or tilt: *That roof inclines steeply.*

n a slope or slant: *There is quite an incline to that roof.* <Latin *in-* in + *clinare* bend>

be inclined, feel disposed toward an action, belief, or attitude: *I'm inclined to agree with you on that. She is inclined to be critical, so watch out.*

a bat	e bed	i bid	o pot	u cup	th **thin**
ā cake	ē me	ī bite	ō go	ū rude	ᴛʜ **then**
ä bar	ə about	ər over	ô for	ů put	zh measure

I

inclined plane *n* a ramp or other thing placed at an oblique angle to a horizontal surface, especially used to move objects up or down.

in·clude (in klūd′) *v* **in·clud·ed, in·clud·ing 1** count into a total or put into a category with other things: *We have included the GST in the price. I don't include her among the nation's greatest poets.* **2** have as a part or be made up of: *The farm includes about 65 hectares. North America includes Canada and the US.* **3** allow or encourage to participate: *We tried to include him in our activities* <Latin *in-* in + *claudere* to shut> **in·clu′sion** *n.*

in·clud·ing (in klū′ding) *prep* counting as part of a group or total: *What is the cost, including tax? She took everything, including my wallet.*

in·clu·sive (in klū′siv) *adj* **1** including the outer limits in a range. Example: *pages 10 to 20 inclusive* means *pages 10 and 20 as well as all those in between.* **2** including everything possible: *Make an inclusive list of your expenses.* **3** not excluding any group of people: *One example of choosing inclusive language is to use "people" instead of "mankind."* **in·clu′sive·ly** *adv.* **in·clu′sive·ness** *n.*
inclusive of, including: *This shirt is 100% cotton, inclusive of trim.*

in·cog·ni·to (in′kog nē′tō) *adj, adv* with one's identity hidden: *The princess travelled incognito to avoid crowds and ceremonies (adv).* <Latin *incognitus,* from *in-* not + *cognoscere* know>

in·co·her·ent (in′kō hē′rənt) *adj* not making clear sense because of a lack of logical connectedness: *incoherent speech, an incoherent plot.* **in′co·her′ence** *n.*
in′co·her′ent·ly *adv.*

in·come (in′kum′) *n* all the money or valuable goods that a person has received, especially on a regular basis, for work or through investments.

in·come tax *n* a government tax on a person's yearly income.

in·com·ing (in′kum′ing) *adj* coming in: *the next incoming train.*
n a coming in: *the incoming of the tide.*

in·com·mu·ni·ca·do (in′kə myū′nə kȧ′dō) *adj* cut off from communication with others: *The prisoner was being held incommunicado.* <Spanish>

in·com·pa·ra·ble (in kom′prə bəl) *or* (in′kəm per′ə bəl) *adj* **1** without equal: *incomparable beauty.* **2** not to be compared or unsuitable for comparison: *The two works of art are so different as to be incomparable.* **in·com′pa·ra·bil′i·ty** *n.* **in·com′pa·ra·ble·ness** *n.* **in·com′pa·ra·bly** *adv.*

in·com·pat·i·ble (in′kəm pat′ə bəl) *adj* **1** not able to exist peacefully together: *My two cats are incompatible; they're always fighting.* **2** inconsistent: *Lack of rest is incompatible with health.* **in′com·pat′i·bil′i·ty** *n.*
in′com·pat′i·bly *adv.*

in·com·pe·tent (in kom′pə tənt) *adj* **1** lacking the skill or knowledge to do the work required. **2** not legally qualified.
n an incompetent person. **in·com′pe·tence** *n.*
in·com′pe·tent·ly *adv.*

in·com·plete (in′kəm plēt′) *adj* lacking some part. **in′com·plete′ly** *adv.* **in′com·plete′ness** *n.*

in·com·pre·hen·si·ble (in′kom pri hen′sə bəl) *adj* impossible to understand. **in′com·pre·hen′si·bly** *adv.* **in′com·pre·hen′sion** *n.*

in·con·ceiv·a·ble (in′kən sē′və bəl) *adj* very hard or impossible to imagine: *For her, a party without dancing was inconceivable.* **in′con·ceiv′a·bil′i·ty** *n.*
in′con·ceiv′a·bly *adv.*

in·con·clu·sive (in′kən klū′siv) *adj* not settling or deciding anything: *The jury, finding the evidence against the prisoner inconclusive, acquitted him.*
in′con·clu′sive·ly *adv.* **in′con·clu′sive·ness** *n.*

in·con·gru·ent (in′kən grū′ənt) *adj* **1** *Mathematics* not congruent. **2** incongruous.

in·con·gru·ous (in kong′grū əs) *adj* out of harmony or not appropriate: *Heavy boots would be incongruous with a swimsuit.* <Latin *in-* not + *congruere* agree> **in·con′gru·ous·ly** *adv.* **in·con′gru·ous·ness** *n.*

❋ **in·con·nu** (in′kə nū′) *n, pl* **in·con·nu** or **in·con·nus** a species of whitefish found in fresh water in northern Canada. <French = unknown>

in·con·se·quen·tial (in′kon sə kwen′shəl) *adj* unimportant or insignificant. **in·con′se·quen′tial·ly** *adv.*

in·con·sid·er·ate (in′kən sid′ə rit) *adj* not thoughtful of the rights and feelings of others.
in′con·sid′er·ate·ly *adv.* **in′con·sid′er·ate·ness** *n.*

in·con·sist·ent (in′kən sis′tənt) *adj* **1** failing to keep to the same principles or course of action: *Inconsistent enforcement of the rules creates confusion.* **2** not in agreement or harmony: *My science lab results were inconsistent with the findings of the rest of the class.* **3** not the same all the way through, especially, not equally good all the way through: *an inconsistent performance.* See INCONSTANT for confusable. **in′con·sist′en·cy** *n.* **in′con·sist′ent·ly** *adv.*

in·con·sol·a·ble (in′kən sō′lə bəl) *adj* not able to be comforted: *The children were inconsolable at the loss of their cat.* **in′con·sol′a·bil′i·ty** *adv.* **in′con·sol′a·bly** *adv.*

in·con·spic·u·ous (in′kən spik′yū əs) *adj* attracting little or no attention: *Test the stain remover on an inconspicuous part of the rug first.* **in′con·spic′u·ous·ly** *adv.* **in′con·spic′u·ous·ness** *n.*

in·con·stant (in kon′stənt) *adj* not dependable. **in·con′stan·cy** *n.* **in·con′stant·ly** *adv.*

CONFUSABLES

Inconstant means "erratic" or "changeable": *Her inconstant, moody behaviour ruined our friendship.*

Inconsistent means "not in harmony": *His actions are inconsistent with the promises he made.*

in·con·test·a·ble (in′kon test′ə bəl) *adj* not able to be disputed. <Old French, from Latin *in-* not + *contestari* call to witness> **in′con·test′a·bil′i·ty** *adv.* **in′con·test′a·bly** *adv.*

in·con·ti·nent (in kon′tə nənt) *adj* **1** unable to control one's bladder and bowel movements. **2** showing little or no self-restraint, especially sexually. **in·con′ti·nence** *n.* **in·con′ti·nent·ly** *adv.*

in·con·tro·vert·i·ble (in′kon trə vər′tə bəl) *adj* so certain or obviously true that it cannot be denied or argued against: *It is an incontrovertible fact that the earth is round.* **in′con·tro·vert′i·bly** *adv.*

in·con·ven·ience (in′kən vēn′yəns) *n* **1** a difficulty, usually involving extra work or effort. **2** a cause of this: *Typing in this password every time is such an inconvenience!*
v **in·con·ven·ienced, in·con·ven·ienc·ing** cause difficulty or bother to: *Will it inconvenience you to carry this package for me?*

in·con·ven·ient (in′kən vēn′yənt) *adj* causing bother or difficulty. **in′con·ven′ient·ly** *adv.*

in·cor·po·rate (in kȯr′pə rāt′) *v* **in·cor·po·rat·ed, in·cor·po·rat·ing** **1** make something a part of something else: *We'll incorporate your suggestion in this new plan.* **2** form into a corporation: *When the business got bigger, the owners decided to incorporate.* **3** give physical form to: *to incorporate your thoughts in an article.* <Latin *in-* into + *corpus* body> **in·cor′po·ra′tion** *n.*

in·cor·po·re·al (in′kȯr pȯ′rē əl) *adj* not made of any physical substance. **in′cor·po′re·al·ly** *adv.*

in·cor·rect (in′kə rekt′) *adj* **1** containing errors: *an incorrect spelling, an incorrect answer in math.* **2** against what is socially approved or expected: *The correct thing to do is sometimes the politically incorrect thing.* **in′cor·rect′ly** *adv.* **in′cor·rect′ness** *n.*

in·cor·ri·gi·ble (in kȯ′rə jə bəl) *adj* to do with behaviour that is so habitual and so firmly fixed as to be unchangeable: *an incorrigible liar, an incorrigible habit of wrinkling your nose.* <Latin *in-* not + *corrigere* to correct> **in·cor′ri·gi·bil′i·ty** *n.* **in·cor′ri·gi·bly** *adv.*

in·cor·rupt·i·ble (in′kə rup′tə bəl) *adj* **1** not giving in to corruption, especially by bribery: *The incorruptible woman could not be bribed.* **2** not capable of decay: *Diamonds are incorruptible.* **in′cor·rupt′i·bly** *adv.*

in·crease (in krēs′) *for v,* (in′krēs) *for n.* *v* **in·creased, in·creas·ing** make or become greater or more numerous: *to increase your speed, to increase prices. The population increases every year.*
n **1** the act or fact of increasing: *There was an increase in student enrolment last year.* **2** the part or amount that is added by increasing: *an increase of 20 percent. Every year she took the increase from her account and reinvested it.* <Latin *in-* in + *crescere* grow>
on the increase, increasing: *The movement of people to the cities is on the increase.*

in·creas·ing·ly (in krē′sing lē) *adv* more and more: *As we travelled south, the weather became increasingly warm.*

GRAMMAR AND USAGE

Increasingly already contains the idea of "more," so it is unnecessary to combine it with the comparative "more." Say or write *He grew increasingly depressed,* not *He grew increasingly more depressed.*

in·cred·i·ble (in kred′ə bəl) *adj* too extraordinary to be possible: *incredible courage. It is incredible that such a small thing should cost so much.* **in·cred′i·bly** *adv.*

CONFUSABLES

Incredible means "hard to believe": *He told his friends an incredible story about rescuing four children from drowning.*

Incredulous means "not able or willing to believe": *His incredulous friends demanded proof to back up what he said about rescuing the four children.*

in·cred·u·lous (in krej′ə ləs) *adj* showing an unwillingness or inability to believe: *an incredulous smile. When she told them she knew the famous actor, they were incredulous.* **in′cre·du′li·ty** *n.* **in·cred′u·lous·ly** *adv.*

in·cre·ment (in′krə mənt) *n* an increase, especially one of a series of regular increases: *Profits are growing by a yearly increment of about 8 percent.* <Latin *in-* in + *crescere* grow> **in′cre·men′tal** *adj.* **in′cre·men′tal·ly** *adv.*

in·crim·i·nate (in krim′ə nāt′) *v* **in·crim·i·nat·ed, in·crim·i·nat·ing** make someone appear to be guilty of a crime or wrongdoing: *The witness's testimony incriminated two other people besides the accused.* <Latin *in-* against + *crimen* charge> **in·crim′i·na′tion** *n.* **in·crim′i·na·to′ry** *adj.*

in·cu·bate (in′kyə bāt′) *v* **in·cu·bat·ed, in·cu·bat·ing** **1** sit on eggs in order to hatch them. **2** artificially keep eggs, bacteria, or embryos at a certain temperature so that they will develop. **3** develop in a disease from the point of infection to the appearance of the first symptoms: *They say this flu virus incubates for several days, so you may already have it and not know it.* <Latin *in-* upon + *cubare* to lie> **in′cu·ba′tion** *n.*

in·cu·ba·tor (in′kyə bā′tər) *n* a machine with an enclosed, artificially warmed chamber for keeping living things, such as premature babies, at a controlled temperature while they develop.

in·cul·cate (in kul′kāt) *or* (in′kəl kāt′) *v* **in·cul·cat·ed, in·cul·cat·ing** instil an attitude, idea, or habit by frequent repetition: *to inculcate good moral principles in children.* <Latin *inculcare* force upon> **in′cul·ca′tion** *n.*

in·cum·bent (in kum′bənt) *adj* **1** resting on a person as a duty: *She felt it was incumbent upon her to answer the letter at once.* **2** currently holding office, as opposed to being nominated or running for it: *the incumbent MP.*
n the person currently holding an office: *He defeated the incumbent by a landslide.* <Latin *in-* on + *cumbere* lie down>

in·cur (in kər′) *v* **in·curred, in·cur·ring** bring something unpleasant on oneself: *to incur many expenses, to incur serious injury.* <Latin *in-* into + *currere* run>

a bat	e bed	i bid	o pot	u cup	th thin
ā cake	ē me	ī bite	ō go	ū rude	ᴛʜ then
ä bar	ə about	ər over	ȯ for	ů put	zh measure

in·cur·a·ble (in kyū′rə bəl) *adj* that cannot be cured or got rid of: *incurable diseases, an incurable habit.* **in·cur′a·bil′i·ty** *n.* **in·cur′a·ble·ness** *n.* **in·cur′a·bly** *adv.*

in·cur·sion (in kər′zhən) *n* **1** a raid or sudden brief attack: *The pirates made incursions along the coast.* **2** a running or flowing in: *Dikes protected the lowland from incursions of the sea.*

in·cus (ing′kəs) ANVIL (def. 2). <Latin = anvil>

in·debt·ed (in det′id) *adj* owing money or gratitude: *I am indebted to you for all your help.* **in·debt′ed·ness** *n.*

in·de·cent (in dē′sənt) *adj* **1** showing lack of basic morals or manners: *He showed an indecent lack of gratitude to the woman who had saved his life.* **2** vulgar or obscene according to public standards: *indecent jokes, indecent pictures.* **in·de′cen·cy** *n.* **in·de′cent·ly** *adv.*

in·de·ci·pher·a·ble (in′di sī′fə rə bəl) *adj* incapable of being read, decoded, or understood. **in′de·ci′pher·a·bil′i·ty** *n.* **in′de·ci′pher·a·bly** *adv.*

in·de·ci·sion (in′di sizh′ən) *n* the inability to make a firm decision.

in·de·ci·sive (in′di sī′siv) *adj* **1** with the habit of putting off decisions or of changing one's mind. **2** that does not decide or settle anything: *an indecisive battle.* **in′de·ci′sive·ly** *adv.* **in′de·ci′sive·ness** *n.*

in·de·co·rum (in′di kȯ′rəm) *n* lack of social grace or manners. **in·dec′o·rous** *adj.*

in·deed (in dēd′) *adv* in fact, truly, or surely: *She is hungry; indeed, she is almost starving. War is indeed terrible.*
interj used to express surprise, skepticism, or agreement: *"It's a cold one today." "Indeed!"*

in·de·fat·i·ga·ble (in′di fat′ə gə bəl) *adj* never getting tired or giving up: *an indefatigable worker.* <Latin *in-* not + *de-* completely + *fatigare* to tire> **in′de·fat′i·ga·bil′i·ty** *n.* **in′de·fat′i·ga·bly** *adv.*

in·de·fen·si·ble (in′di fen′sə bəl) *adj* **1** that cannot be defended: *an indefensible island, an indefensible argument.* **2** not justifiable: *an indefensible lie.* **in′de·fen′si·bly** *adv.*

in·de·fin·a·ble (in′di fī′nə bəl) *adj* that cannot be defined or is hard to identify or explain exactly. **in′de·fin·a·bil′i·ty** *n.* **in′de·fin′a·bly** *adv.*

in·def·i·nite (in def′ə nit) *adj* **1** not clearly defined: *"Maybe" is an indefinite answer.* **2** *Grammar* not specifying a person, thing, or time in a word, inflection, or phrase: *In English, the indefinite article is "a" or "an."* **in·def′i·nite·ly** *adv.* **in·def′i·nite·ness** *n.*

SYNONYMS

Indefinite emphasizes something that is unclear: *Her indefinite answer showed that she had not read the book.*

Hazy suggests something that is confused or vague: *I asked him to clarify his hazy directions to the arena.*

Obscure suggests something not clearly expressed: *The presenter's obscure remarks about the proof of his theory confused his audience.*

indefinite article *Grammar n* an article used when the noun does not refer to a specific known individual, such as, in English, **a** or **an.**

in·de·his·cent (in′di his′ənt) *Biology adj* not opening as a pod or fruit at maturity. Acorns are indehiscent.

in·del·i·ble (in del′ə bəl) *adj* **1** that cannot be erased or removed: *indelible ink, an indelible impression on your memory.* **2** capable of making an indelible mark: *an indelible pencil.* <Latin *in-* not + *delere* delete> **in·del′i·bil′i·ty** *n.* **in·del′i·bly** *adv.*

in·del·i·cate (in del′ə kit) *adj* **1** coarse or crude: *indelicate manners.* **2** tactless or insensitive: *That was an indelicate question.* **in·del′i·ca·cy** *n.* **in·del′i·cate·ly** *adv.*

in·dem·ni·fy (in dem′nə fī) *v* **in·dem·ni·fied, in·dem·ni·fy·ing** **1** compensate for damage, loss, or expense incurred: *The court ruled she had to indemnify me for my losses.* **2** secure against damage or loss. <Latin *indemnis* without loss>

in·dem·nit·y (in dem′nə tē) *n, pl* **in·dem·ni·ties** **1** compensation for damage, loss, or expense incurred by someone else. **2** a security against damage or loss; insurance. **3** 🍁 the salary paid to an MP or an MLA. <Latin *indemnis* without loss>

in·dent (in dent′) *for v,* (in′dent) *for n.* *v* **1** begin a line of text farther in from the margin of the page than other lines: *Indent the first line of a paragraph.* **2** make notched or jagged: *an indented coastline.*
n the act of indenting or place where something is indented: *Use the ruler at the top of your screen to set the paragraph indent.* <See INDENTURE.> **in′den·ta′tion** *n.* **in′den′tion** *n.*

in·den·ture (in den′chər) *n* **1** a contract by which a person is bound to serve someone else. **2** any written agreement.
v **in·den·tured, in·den·tur·ing** bind by a contract to serve someone else: *Many people came to the colonies indentured for several years.* <Old French, from Latin *dentis* tooth. When a contract was written, a copy was put together with the original and a notch cut in the margin to produce matching indentations>

in·de·pend·ent (in′di pen′dənt) *adj* **1** not needing, wanting, or getting help from others: *She is a reliable, independent worker.* **2** not influenced, ruled, or controlled by others: *an independent thinker. Canada is an independent nation.* **3** not connected or aligned with a particular organization: *The committee reviewing the officer's conduct is independent of the police force.* **4** not resulting from or determined by another thing.
n **1** a person who is independent in thought or behaviour, especially one who votes without regard to any political party. **2 Independent** a person who stands for election or wins a seat in a legislature without belonging to any political party. **in′de·pen′dence** *n.* **in′de·pen′dent·ly** *adv.*

independent clause MAIN CLAUSE.

independent school PRIVATE SCHOOL.

independent variable *Mathematics n* in a statement, a variable whose value determines the value of a dependent variable. In $y = f(x)$, x is the independent variable; it determines the value of y.

in–depth (in′ depth′) *adj* comprehensive and detailed on some issue or topic: *an in-depth study of pollution in the Great Lakes.*

in·de·scrib·a·ble (in′di skrī′bə bəl) *adj* that cannot be described: *a scene of indescribable beauty.* **in′de·scrib·a·bil′i·ty** *n.* **in′de·scrib′a·bly** *adv.*

in·de·struct·i·ble (in′di struk′tə bəl) *adj* that cannot be destroyed: *This toy is so well made it is virtually indestructible.* **in′de·struct′i·bly** *adv.*

in·de·tect·a·ble (in′di tek′tə bəl) *adj* so slight or so well hidden that it cannot be noticed: *She made an indetectable adjustment to her hair and went out.* **in′de·tect·a·bil′i·ty** *n.* **in′de·tect′a·bly** *adv.*

in·de·ter·mi·nate (in′di tər′mə nit) *adj* vague, unknown, or indefinite: *Stuck to the desk were two wads of gum of indeterminate origin.* **in′de·ter′mi·nate·ly** *adv.*

in·dex (in′deks) *n, pl* **in·dex·es** or **in·di·ces** (in′də sēz′) **1** an alphabetical list of the names or subjects mentioned or discussed in a book, typically at the end of a text, and giving page or other references for where they occur. **2** another list, such as a list of items in a collection, or links to websites, etc. **3** a number indicating the amount, intensity, or value of something at a certain point in time: *a pollution index, the consumer price index.* **4** a sign or measure of some property or state of mind: *Facial expression is often an index of a person's mood.*
v **1** adjust an amount automatically and proportionately according to changes, such as in the cost of living, or the needs or expenses of the individual: *an indexed pension.* **2** provide with an index: *to index the items in a collection.* **3** enter in an index. <Latin *index* that which points out>

index card *n* a card of a standard size, used for making notes or for listing and describing the items in a collection: *He used index cards to organize the notes for his speech.*

index finger *n* the finger next to the thumb.

In·dia (in′dē ə) *n* a large country in southern Asia. Together with adjacent countries such as Pakistan, Nepal, and Bangladesh, it forms the **Indian subcontinent**. See the APPENDIX. **In′di·an** *adj, n.*

India ink *n* a liquid ink that contains carbon particles, such as soot from lamps, used for writing or drawing.

In·di·an (in′dē ən) *n* **1** a native or inhabitant of the Republic of India. **2** a name given by Europeans to any member of the groups of people who were living in North and South America, south of the Arctic coast region, when the Europeans arrived.
adj to do with any of these peoples or their languages.

GRAMMAR AND USAGE

The name **Indian** for the Aboriginal peoples of North and South America began with a mistake. When Christopher Columbus landed in the Americas in 1492, he thought he had reached India.

The name *Indian* is still common outside Canada, but it is offensive to some Canadians. Acceptable substitutes are *Aboriginal, Native, Indigenous,* and *First Peoples*, all of which include Indians, Métis, and Inuit.

🍁 **Indian agent** *n* in former times, an official in the Federal Government in charge of affairs relating to Aboriginal peoples, especially those living on reserves.

Indian corn *n* **1** CORN[1] (def. 1). **2** dried cobs of corn whose kernels are purple, brown, and orange, often used as a decoration in autumn.

🍁 **Indian Days** *n* a festival during which First Nations people celebrate their customs and heritage, often involving traditional dress and dances.

Indian Ocean *n* the ocean separating Africa and Australasia, south of India.

🍁 **Indian paintbrush** *n* a wild plant with spikes of flowers and bright red or orange leaves.

Indian summer *n* a time of mild, dry, hazy weather in October or early November, after the first frosts of autumn.

Indian wrestling *n* a contest in which a person places a foot against another's, grasps the corresponding hand, and tries to throw the opponent off balance.

in·di·cate (in′də kāt′) *v* **in·di·cat·ed, in·di·cat·ing** **1** point out or make known: *A thermometer indicates temperature. He indicated that he was ready to leave.* **2** be or give a sign or hint of: *Fever indicates sickness.* **3** declare to be needed as a remedy or treatment: *In cases of this nature, complete bed rest is indicated.* <Latin *in-* toward + *dicare* proclaim> **in′di·ca′tion** *n.*

in·dic·a·tive (in dik′ə tiv) *adj* **1** showing, suggesting, or being a sign of something: *A headache is often indicative of eyestrain.* **2** *Grammar* denoting a mood of a verb expressing a simple statement of fact. Examples: *I went, I did not go,* and *Did you go?* all contain verbs in the **indicative mood**.

in·di·ca·tor (in′də kā′tər) *n* **1** anything that indicates or points to something else: *A growling stomach is often an indicator of hunger.* **2** the pointer on the dial of a measuring instrument: *The indicator is pointing to 140 km/h.* **3** *Chemistry* a substance, such as litmus, that will indicate chemical changes or conditions by changing colour.

in·di·ces (in′də sēz′) a plural of INDEX.

in·dict (in dīt′) *v* **1** formally charge with a crime or serious offence. **2** *US Law* of a grand jury, find enough evidence against an accused person to justify a trial. <Old French, from Latin *indictare* express in writing> **in·dict′er** or **in·dict′or** *n.* **in·dict′ment** *n.*

🍁 **in·dict·a·ble offence** (in dī′tə bəl) *Law n* a criminal offence, such as armed robbery or murder, that is more serious than a SUMMARY OFFENCE.

in·die (in′dē) *Informal adj* to do with movies, music, etc. promoted by small, independent companies.
n such a movie, music, etc. or the group that produces it. <*independent*>

a bat	e bed	i bid	o pot	u cup	th thin
ā cake	ē me	ī bite	ō go	ū rude	ᴛʜ then
ä bar	ə about	ər over	ô for	ů put	zh measure

in·dif·fer·ent (in dif′rənt) *adj* **1** with no feeling for or against: *He admired her very much, but she was indifferent to him.* **2** unimportant: *It is indifferent to me where we eat.* **3** mediocre: *an indifferent ballplayer.* <Latin *indifferens*> **in·dif′fer·ence** *n.* **in·dif′fer·ent·ly** *adv.*

in·dig·e·nous (in dij′ə nəs) *adj* **1** native to a particular country or region: *The muskox is indigenous to Canada.* **2** coming from within a certain culture or language: *indigenous vocabulary, indigenous customs.* **3** 🍁 **Indigenous** to do with the original inhabitants of Canada: First Nations, Métis, and Inuit. <Latin *indigena* a native> **in·dig′e·nous·ly** *adv.*

in·di·gent (in′də jənt) *adj* very poor. <Latin *indigere* to need> **in′di·gence** *n.*

in·di·gest·i·ble (in′də jes′tə bəl) *adj* that cannot be properly digested. **in′di·gest′i·bil′i·ty** *n.*

in·di·ges·tion (in′də jes′chən) *n* pain or discomfort resulting from difficulty in digesting food: *If I eat too much or too quickly, I get indigestion.*

in·dig·nant (in dig′nənt) *adj* angry at something seen as an insult to one's dignity or honour, or to that of other people: *When I asked if he had taken the loonie out of my desk, he was indignant.* <Latin *indignare* regard as unworthy> **in·dig′nant·ly** *adv.* **in′dig·na′tion** *n.*

in·dig·ni·ty (in dig′nə tē) *n, pl* **in·dig·ni·ties** **1** lack of respect or proper treatment. **2** an insult. **3** humiliation.

in·di·go (in′də gō′) *n, pl* **in·di·gos** or **in·di·goes** a blue dye formerly obtained from certain plants, but now usually made artificially.
adj deep violet-blue. <Latin, from Greek *indikos* Indian (dye), after *Indos* the Indus River>

in·di·rect (in′də rekt′) *adj* **1** not direct or straight: *an indirect route.* **2** not immediately or directly connected: *an indirect consequence. I heard it from an indirect source.* **3** not straightforward and to the point: *an indirect answer.* **in′di·rect′ly** *adv.* **in′di·rect′ness** *n.*

indirect lighting *n* indoor lighting that uses reflected or diffused light, so that the actual source of the light cannot be seen.

indirect object *Grammar n* an object that is affected by the action but is not the primary object. Example: In *I gave my sister a book*, the indirect object is *my sister*, and the direct object is *book.*

indirect question *Grammar n* a question that is reported rather than quoted directly. Example: *She asked when we were leaving* is the indirect form of *She asked, "When are you leaving?"* Compare DIRECT QUESTION.

indirect speech *Grammar n* statements or questions that report a person's speech without directly quoting it. Example: *He said that he would go* is the indirect form of *He said, "I will go."* Compare DIRECT SPEECH. Also called **reported speech**.

indirect tax *n* a tax, such as sales tax, collected by a person or company, and then passed on to the government.

in·dis·creet (in′di skrēt′) *adj* **1** failing to respect other people's privacy or feelings: *It was indiscreet of you to reveal that without permission.* **2** morally questionable or mildly scandalous: *engaging in indiscreet activities with the opposite sex.* **in′dis·creet′ly** *adv.*
in′dis·cre′tion (in′di skresh′ən) *n.*

in·dis·crim·i·nate (in′di skrim′ə nit) *adj* **1** confused or jumbled: *He dumped everything out of his suitcase in an indiscriminate mass.* **2** not paying attention to important differences: *She is an indiscriminate reader who can't tell good books from bad ones.* **in′dis·crim′i·nate·ly** *adv.*

in·dis·pen·sa·ble (in′di spen′sə bəl) *adj* absolutely necessary: *Air is indispensable to life.*
in′dis·pen′sa·bil′i·ty *n.* **in′dis·pen′sa·ble·ness** *n.*
in′dis·pen′sa·bly *adv.*

in·dis·pose (in′di spōz′) *v* **in·dis·posed, in·dis·pos·ing** **1** make unwilling: *Hot weather indisposes a person to work hard.* **2** (*in the passive*) be slightly ill. **in′dis·posed′** *adj.* **in′dis·po·si′tion** *n.*

in·dis·put·a·ble (in′di spyū′tə bəl) *adj* not to be disputed, questioned, or denied: *indisputable evidence.* **in′dis·put′a·bil′i·ty** *n.* **in′dis·put′a·ble·ness** *n.* **in′dis·put′a·bly** *adv.*

in·dis·tinct (in′di stingkt′) *adj* not clear to the eye, ear, or mind: *an indistinct picture. We could hear an indistinct roar from the faraway ocean.* **in′dis·tinct′ly** *adv.* **in′dis·tinct′ness** *n.*

in·dis·tin·guish·a·ble (in′di sting′gwi shə bəl) *adj* so alike that one cannot be distinguished from the other: *The two photos are indistinguishable.* **in′dis·tin′guish·a·bil′i·ty** *n.* **in′dis·tin′guish·a·ble·ness** *n.* **in′dis·tin′guish·a·bly** *adv.*

in·di·um (in′dē əm) *n* a metallic element that is soft, white, malleable, and easily fusible. *Symbol* **In** <*ind*(*igo*) (because there are indigo lines in its spectrum) + *-ium*>

in·di·vid·u·al (in′də vij′ū əl) *n* **1** a person: *I was approached by an individual I had never met before.* **2** a single person, animal, or thing, in contrast to a group: *a herd of giraffes containing 30 individuals.* **3** an independent person; a person with distinct tastes, ideas, or habits: *I am an individual and can form my own opinions. I hear she is quite an individual.*
adj **1** to do with one only: *The package contains four individual portions. Students will spend one hour a day on individual work.* **2** special or unique: *He has a very individual style of handwriting.* <Latin *in-* not + *dividuus* separable> **in′di·vid′u·al′i·ty** *n.* **in′di·vid′u·al·ize′** *v.* **in′di·vid′u·al·ly** *adv.*

in·di·vid·u·al·ism (in′də vij′ū ə liz′əm) *n* **1** the belief that an individual's freedom of action is more important than any form of social or collective control. **2** the tendency to be independent and self-reliant. **in′di·vid′u·al·ist** *n, adj.* **in′di·vid′u·al·is′tic** *adj.*

in·di·vis·i·ble (in′də viz′ə bəl) *adj* **1** not capable of being divided or broken down: *Life is an indivisible whole, not a series of compartments.* **2** *Mathematics* not capable of being divided evenly, without a remainder. **in′di·vis′i·bil′i·ty** *n.*

Indo– *combining form* Indian: *an Indo-Canadian.*

industrial pollution

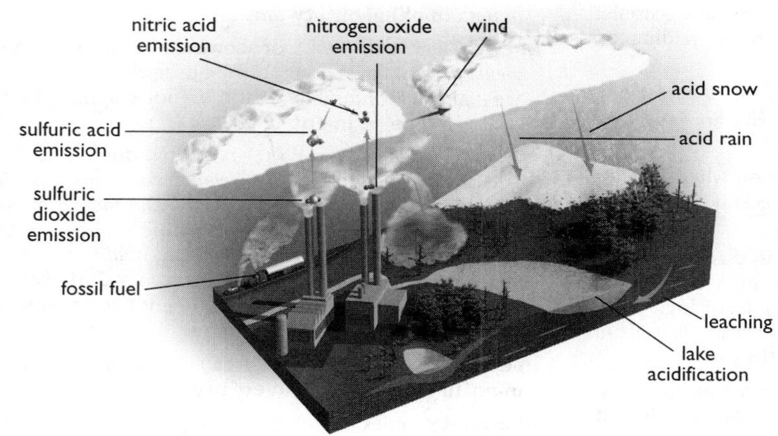

One negative aspect of an **industrial** society is the amount of pollution that industry generates. Sulphuric acid and nitric acid emissions pollute the atmosphere and fall to the ground as acid rain or snow. This precipitation pollutes the rivers and lakes and leaches into the groundwater through the soil.

Industries have also at times dumped waste chemicals into rivers and lakes, which pollute the water and kill fish and other organisms.

I

in·doc·tri·nate (in dok′trə nāt′) *v* **in·doc·tri·nat·ed, in·doc·tri·nat·ing** teach one or more people to uncritically accept a doctrine, belief, or principle. <Latin *in-* in + *doctrinare* teach> **in·doc′tri·na′tion** *n.*

In·do–Eu·ro·pe·an (in′dō yů′rə pē′ən) *n* **1** a reconstructed prehistoric language, the parent of a large number of related languages spoken in India, western Asia, and Europe. **2** a speaker of this language, or of any of the languages descended from it.
adj to do with Indo-European, its descendant languages, or speakers of any of these.

in·do·lent (in′də lənt) *adj* lazy. <Latin *in-* not + *dolere* suffer pain> **in′do·lence** *n.* **in′do·lent·ly** *adv.*

in·dom·i·ta·ble (in dom′ə tə bəl) *adj* that cannot be subdued or defeated: *indomitable courage.* <Latin *in-* not + *domare* to tame> **in′dom·it·a·bil′i·ty** *n.* **in·dom′it·a·ble·ness** *n.* **in·dom′i·ta·bly** *adv.*

In·do·ne·sia (in′dō nē′zhə) *n* a country of many islands in southeast Asia. See the APPENDIX. **In′do·ne′sian** *adj, n.*

in·door (in′dôr′) *adj* done, used, or located in a house or other building: *indoor tennis, an indoor pool.*
adv **indoors** in or into a house or other building: *Let's go indoors.*

in·du·bi·ta·ble (in dyū′bə tə bəl) *or* (in dū′bə tə bəl) *adj* known for certain: *Laziness was the indubitable cause of his failure.* <Latin *in-* not + *dubitare* doubt> **in′du·bit·a·bil′i·ty** *n.* **in·du′bi·ta·bly** *adv.*

in·duce (in dyūs′) *or* (in dūs′) *v* **in·duced, in·duc·ing** **1** influence or persuade to do something: *Advertising induces people to buy.* **2** cause or bring about: *Some drugs induce sleep.* **3** produce an electric current or charge or a magnetic field without direct contact. <Latin *in-* in + *ducere* to lead>

in·duce·ment (in dyūs′mənt) *or* (in dūs′mənt) *n* something offered to persuade a person to do something: *By various inducements I got my brother to do the dishes.*

in·duct (in dukt′) *v* formally admit a person to a position or organization: *The new minister was inducted in a special ceremony.* <Latin *in-* in + *ducere* lead>

in·duc·tion (in duk′shən) *n* **1** the process of passing on electrical or magnetic properties to a nearby object, without direct contact. **2** the act or result of reasoning from particular facts to a general rule or principle. **3** the act of formally admitting someone to a position or organization.

induction coil *n* a transformer for producing a high, pulsating voltage from a current of low, steady voltage, such as from a battery.

in·duc·tive (in duk′tiv) *adj* **1** to do with the process of arriving at a general principle from particular cases: *inductive reasoning.* **2** to do with the induction of electrical or magnetic properties. **in·duc′tive·ly** *adv.*

in·dulge (in dulj′) *v* **in·dulged, in·dulg·ing** **1** give in to the wishes of: *He wasn't feeling well, so we indulged him.* **2** (*with* ***in***) let oneself enjoy: *She indulges in fast food now and then.* <Latin *indulgere*>

in·dul·gence (in dul′jəns) *n* **1** the act or habit of giving in to desire, whether one's own or another's. **2** something that one indulges in: *Bacon and eggs is their traditional Saturday morning indulgence.* **3 a** a favour or privilege granted to someone. **b** *Catholicism* in former times, a partial or total cancelling of the time someone must spend being punished after death for a sin.
in·dul′gent *adj.* **in·dul′gent·ly** *adv.*

in·dus·tri·al (in dus′trē əl) *adj* **1** to do with industry, especially industry that delivers goods or raw materials rather than services: *industrial products, an industrial firm.* **2** dominated or driven by such industry or its products: *an industrial economy, industrial pollution.* **3** specially designed for use in industry rather than in households: *an industrial dishwasher, industrial adhesives.* **in·dus′tri·al·ly** *adv.*

a bat	e bed	i bid	o pot	u cup	th **thin**
ā cake	ē me	ī bite	ō go	ū rude	ᴛʜ **then**
à bar	ə about	ər over	ȯ for	ů put	zh measure

industrial arts *pln* (*with singular verb*) in some schools, a course in various manual skills such as welding or woodworking.

in·dus·tri·al·ism (in dus′trē ə liz′əm) *n* a social or economic system in which large industries are prevalent and important.

in·dus·tri·al·ist (in dus′trē ə list) *n* a person who manages or owns an industrial enterprise, especially a large or wealthy enterprise.

in·dus·tri·al·ize (in dus′trē ə līz′) *v* **in·dus·tri·al·ized, in·dus·tri·al·iz·ing** develop industries in a country or region, especially large-scale manufacturing: *The invention of new technology in the 1800s helped to industrialize Europe.* **in·dus′tri·al·i·za′tion** *n.*

industrial park *n* a suburban area reserved for factories, wholesale outlets, and other businesses, usually in low-rise buildings.

Industrial Revolution *n* the change from an agricultural to an industrial civilization that took place in England from about 1750 to about 1850, and later in other countries.

in·dus·tri·ous (in dus′trē əs) *adj* working hard and steadily: *an industrious student.* **in·dus′tri·ous·ly** *adv.* **in·dus′tri·ous·ness** *n.*

in·dus·try (in′də strē) *n, pl* **in·dus·tries 1** any branch of business, trade, or manufacture: *the steel industry, the publishing industry.* **2** all such enterprises thought of as a group: *Canadian industry is expanding.* **3** the production of goods; manufacturing in general: *He would rather be a teacher than work in industry.* **4** steady effort: *Industry and eagerness to learn helped my sister achieve top grades.* <Latin *industria* diligence>

in·e·bri·ate (i nē′brē āt′) *v* **in·e·bri·at·ed, in·e·bri·at·ing** make drunk. <Latin *in-* in + *ebrius* drunk> **in·e′bri·a′tion** *n.*

in·ed·i·ble (i ned′ə bəl) *adj* not fit to eat: *This cake is inedible.*

in·ef·fa·ble (i nef′ə bəl) *adj* too great or extreme to be expressed or described in words: *ineffable joy.* <Latin *in-* not + *effari* to speak> **in′ef·fa·bil′i·ty** *n.* **in·ef′fa·ble·ness** *n.* **in·ef′fa·bly** *adv.*

in·ef·fec·tive (in′ə fek′tiv) *adj* **1** not producing the desired effect: *The painkiller was ineffective and did not get rid of my headache.* **2** not able to do the work required: *an ineffective leader.* **in′ef·fec′tive·ly** *adv.* **in′ef·fec′tive·ness** *n.*

in·ef·fec·tu·al (in′ə fek′chū əl) *adj* useless or powerless: *The searchlights were ineffectual in the fog.* **in′ef·fec′tu·al·ly** *adv.*

in·ef·fi·cient (in′ə fish′ənt) *adj* **1** failing to make the best use of time or resources: *Using a watering can is an inefficient way to water a large garden.* **2** not able to get things done: *an inefficient housekeeper.* **in′ef·fi′cient·ly** *adv.*

in·el·e·gant (i nel′ə gənt) *adj* showing a lack of grace, elegance, or refinement. **in·el′e·gance** *n.* **in·el′e·gant·ly** *adv.*

in·el·i·gi·ble (i nel′ə jə bəl) *adj* not meeting a criteria or standard: *She is over age 16 and therefore ineligible for the contest.* **in·el′i·gi·bil′i·ty** *adv.*

in·ept (i nept′) *adj* **1** with or showing no skill: *That was an inept performance.* **2** foolish and useless: *inept ideas.* See INAPT for confusable. <Latin *in-* not + *aptus* apt> **in·ept′i·tude′** *n.* **in·ept′ly** *adv.*

in·e·qual·i·ty (in′ē kwol′ə tē) *n, pl* **in·e·qual·i·ties 1 a** a difference in amount, size, value, or rank: *Is there inequality between the salaries of men and those of women?* **b** an unfair difference in the opportunities, power, rights, or wealth available to people: *Social inequality need not be a fact of life.* **2** unevenness or inconsistency. **3** *Mathematics* an expression showing that two quantities are unequal, such as $a > b$ or $c < d$.

in·eq·ui·ta·ble (i nek′wə tə bəl) *adj* unfair or unjust. **in·eq′ui·ta·ble·ness** *n.* **in·eq′ui·ta·bly** *adv.*

in·eq·ui·ty (i nek′wə tē) *n, pl* **in·eq·ui·ties** unfairness or injustice.

in·ert (i nərt′) *adj* **1** with no power to move or act: *Stone is inert matter.* **2** without energy. **3** *Chemistry* with few or no active properties and therefore not reacting chemically: *Helium and neon are inert gases.* <Latin *inertis* idle>

in·er·tia (i nər′shə) *n* **1** a tendency to do nothing and remain unchanged: *He talks about exercising, but inertia keeps him from actually doing so.* **2** *Physics* the tendency of a motionless object to stay motionless, or of a moving object to keep moving at the same speed and in the same direction, unless acted on by some outside force. <See INERT.>

in·es·cap·a·ble (in′i skā′pə bəl) *adj* that cannot be escaped or avoided. **in′es·cap′a·bil′i·ty** *n.* **in′es·cap′a·ble·ness** *n.* **in′es·cap′a·bly** *adv.*

in·es·ti·ma·ble (i nes′tə mə bəl) *adj* too good, great, or valuable to be measured or estimated: *Your help has been of inestimable value to me.* **in·es′tim·a·ble·ness** *n.* **in·es′ti·ma·bly** *adv.*

in·ev·i·ta·ble (i nev′ə tə bəl) *adj* sure to happen. <Latin *in-* not + *evitare* avoid> **in·ev′i·ta·bil′i·ty** *n.* **in·ev′i·ta·bly** *adv.*

in·ex·act (in′ig zakt′) *adj* not exact, precise, or completely correct. **in′ex·act′i·tude′** *n.* **in′ex·act′ly** *adv.*

in·ex·cus·a·ble (in′ik skyū′zə bəl) *adj* that cannot be excused or justified: *Failing to thank your host is an inexcusable rudeness.* **in′ex·cus′a·bil′i·ty** *n.* **in′ex·cus′a·ble·ness** *n.* **in′ex·cus′a·bly** *adv.*

in·ex·haust·i·ble (in′ig zos′tə bəl) *adj* so abundant that it can never be completely used up: *Thanks to my teacher's inexhaustible patience, I finally learned how to write an essay.* **in′ex·haust′i·bil′i·ty** *n.* **in′ex·haust′ib·ly** *adv.*

in·ex·o·ra·ble (i neg′zə rə bəl) *or* (in′eg zô′rə bəl) *adj* impossible to stop or prevent: *The forces of nature are inexorable.* <Latin *inexorabilis* = unable to be talked out of something, from *in-* not + *ex-* out + *orare* beg, pray> **in·ex′o·ra·bil′i·ty** *n.* **in·ex′o·ra·bly** *adv.*

in·ex·pe·di·ent (in′ik spē′dē ənt) *adj* not practical, convenient, or wise: *It would be inexpedient to tell her that now; she'll only get angrier.* **in′ex·pe′di·en·cy** *n.*

in·ex·pen·sive (in′ik spen′siv) *adj* not expensive. **in′ex·pen′sive·ly** *adv.* **in′ex·pen′sive·ness** *n.*

SYNONYMS

Inexpensive emphasizes that something does not cost much, but does not refer to quality: *He saved some money by buying an inexpensive meal.*

Cheap can suggest something of poor quality as well as of little cost: *The cheap toy soon fell apart.*

Reasonable can mean "fairly priced": *The new shoe store has reasonable prices for leather boots.*

in·ex·pe·ri·ence (in′ik spē′rē əns) *n* lack of experience or of the skill gained from experience.
in′ex·pe′ri·enced *adj.*

in·ex·pert (i nek′spərt) *adj* with or showing a lack of experience or knowledge: *inexpert sewing, an inexpert musician.* **in·ex′pert·ly** *adv.* **in·ex′pert·ness** *n.*

in·ex·plic·a·ble (in′ik splik′ə bəl) *or* (i nek′splə kə bəl) *adj* impossible to explain or understand the cause of: *His inexplicable moodiness was starting to worry her.* **in′ex·plic′a·bil′i·ty** *n.* **in′ex·plic′a·bly** *adv.*

in·ex·press·i·ble (in′ik spres′ə bəl) *adj* that cannot be expressed. **in′ex·press′i·bly** *adv.*

in·ex·tin·guish·a·ble (in′ik sting′gwi shə bəl) *adj* that cannot be put out or stopped: *an inextinguishable fire.* **in′ex·tin′guish·a·bil′i·ty** *n.* **in′ex·tin′guish·a·bly** *adv.*

in·ex·tri·ca·ble (i nek′strə kə bəl) *or* (in′ik strik′ə bəl) *adj* **1** that one cannot get out of: *caught in an inextricable dilemma.* **2** that cannot be disentangled or solved: *an inextricable mess of relationships.* **in′ex·tri′ca·bil′i·ty** *n.* **in·ex′tri·ca·bly** *adv.*

in·fal·li·ble (in fal′ə bəl) *adj* **1** free from error: *No dictionary is an infallible authority.* **2** never failing and absolutely reliable: *an infallible method, infallible obedience.* **in·fal′li·bil′i·ty** *n.* **in·fal′li·bly** *adv.*

in·fa·mous (in′fə məs) *adj* **1** well-known for bad qualities or acts: *an infamous traitor.* **2** deserving or causing a bad reputation: *infamous crimes.* **in′fa·mous·ly** *adv.* **in′fa·my** *n.*

in·fan·cy (in′fən sē) *n, pl* **in·fan·cies** **1** the condition or time of being an infant. **2** the earliest stage of development of anything: *In the 1960s, space travel was still in its infancy.*

in·fant (in′fənt) *n* a baby, especially a very young one who cannot walk yet.
adj **1** of or for an infant: *infant food.* **2** just beginning to develop: *an infant industry.*

ETYMOLOGY

Infant came through Old French from Latin *infantis*, literally meaning "not speaking," from *in-*, meaning "not" + *fari*, meaning "speak."

in·fan·ti·cide (in fan′tə sīd′) *n* the killing of a baby.

in·fan·tile (in′fən tīl′) *adj* **1** like an infant: *We were disgusted with his infantile behaviour.* **2** to do with infants: *infantile diseases.*

in·fan·try (in′fən trē) *n, pl* **in·fan·tries** <Italian *infante* foot soldier; originally, young man. It was the youngest soldiers, sometimes little more than adolescents, who fought on foot.> **in′fan·try·man** *n.*

in·fat·u·at·ed (in fach′ū ā′tid) *adj* with sudden, unreasoning, and extreme admiration for someone. <Latin *infatuare* infatuate> **in·fat′u·a′tion** *n.*

in·fect (in fekt′) *v* **1** affect or contaminate with a disease-causing germ: *Dirt infects an open cut. She didn't want to stay home from school, and so infected us all with her cold.* **2** influence, especially in feeling or mood, by spreading from one person to another: *The team captain's enthusiasm infected all the players.* <Latin *infecere* to dye, from *in-* + *facere* put. Disease spreads like dye colours fabric.> **in·fect′ed** *adj.*

in·fec·tion (in fek′shən) *n* **1 a** the fact of causing or spreading disease with germs: *Keep the countertops clean to reduce infection.* **b** a diseased condition caused in this way: *He has a throat infection.* **2** an influence or feeling spreading from one to another.

in·fec·tious (in fek′shəs) *adj* **1** that spreads by passing on germs: *infectious diseases.* **2** of feelings, etc., easily spread to others: *She has an infectious laugh.* **in·fec′tious·ly** *adv.*

in·fer (in fər′) *v* **in·ferred, in·fer·ring** conclude by reasoning: *I inferred from her silence that she didn't agree with me.* <Latin *inferre* bring about, from *in-* in + *ferre* bring> **in′fer·ence** *n.*

CONFUSABLES

Infer means "suppose."

Imply means "indicate without saying" or "suggest."

The one who **infers** takes a hint, while the one who **implies** gives it.

in·fer·i·or (in fē′rē ər) *adj* **1** low in quality: *inferior work, an inferior grade of coffee.* **2** lower in position, rank, or importance: *an inferior officer.*
n a person who is lower in rank or importance: *A good leader gets along well with her inferiors.* <Latin = lower> **in·fe′ri·or′i·ty** *n.*

inferiority complex *n* a persistent feeling that one is inferior to other people, sometimes resulting in aggressive behaviour as a compensation.

in·fer·nal (in fər′nəl) *adj* **1** of or like hell: *infernal heat, the infernal fires.* **2** *Informal* irritating or tiresome: *Stop that infernal racket!* <See INFERNO.> **in·fer′nal·ly** *adv.*

in·fer·no (in fər′nō) *n* a place or thing that seems to be like hell, especially a big fire: *Within half an hour of the start of the fire, the whole building was a raging inferno.* <Italian, from Latin *infernus* hell>

a bat	e bed	i bid	o pot	u cup	th **thin**
ā cake	ē me	ī bite	ō go	ū rude	ᴛʜ **then**
á bar	ə about	ər over	ȯ for	ů put	zh measure

I

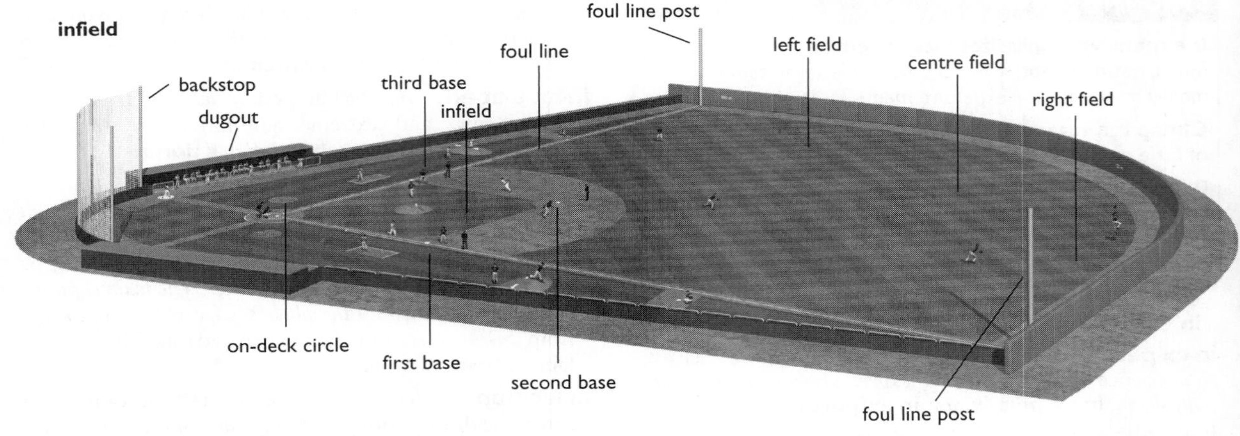

in·fer·tile (in fər′tīl) *or* (in fər′təl) *adj* **1** not fertile or fruitful: *infertile soil.* **2** unable to conceive offspring. **in′fer·til′i·ty** *n.*

in·fest (in fest′) *v* (*used of undesirable things*) be present in large numbers, often so as to cause damage or disease: *The warehouse was infested with cockroaches. Tourists infest our town every summer.* <Latin *infestare* to attack, from *infestus* hostile> **in′fes·ta′tion** *n.*

in·fi·del (in′fə dəl) *n* a person who does not believe in God or a god, or who does not accept a particular faith.
adj to do with infidels. <Latin *in-* not + *fidelis* faithful>

in·fi·del·i·ty (in′fə del′ə tē) *n, pl* **in·fi·del·i·ties** unfaithfulness, especially to a spouse or sexual partner.

in·field (in′fēld′) *Baseball n* **1** the part of the field within the baselines. **2** the part of a team consisting of the basemen and shortstop: *That team has a good infield.* **in′field′er** *n.*

in·fight·ing (in′fī′ting) *n* conflict between individuals or groups within a larger group: *The student council was nearly destroyed by infighting.*

in·fil·trate (in′fəl trāt′) *or* (in fil′trāt) *v* **in·fil·trat·ed, in·fil·trat·ing 1** enter or pass through unnoticed, like tiny particles through a filter: *Enemy troops infiltrated the front lines. Spies have infiltrated several government departments.* **2** filter into or through. **in′fil·tra′tion** *n.*

in·fi·nite (in′fə nit) *adj* **1** without limits or bounds: *the infinite reaches of space.* **2** extremely great in amount or degree: *With infinite care, the nurse removed the cast from my arm.*
n **the infinite** that which is infinite. <Latin *in-* not + *finis* boundary> **in′fi·nite·ly** *adv.* **in·fin′i·tude′** *n.*

in·fi·ni·tes·i·mal (in′fi nə tes′ə məl) *adj* so small as to be almost nothing: *an infinitesimal increase in temperature.* **in′fi·ni·tes′i·mal·ly** *adv.*

in·fin·i·tive (in fin′ə tiv) *Grammar n* the basic form of a verb, not limited by person, tense, or number and, in English, often preceded by *to.* <Latin *infinitis* unrestricted>

in·fin·i·ty (in fin′ə tē) *n, pl* **in·fin·i·ties 1** the state or quality of being infinite: *the infinity of space.* **2** an infinite distance, space, time, or quantity.

in·firm (in fərm′) *adj* physically or mentally weak, especially because of age or illness: *The woman was very old and infirm.* <Latin *infirmus*>

in·fir·ma·ry (in fər′mə rē) *n, pl* **in·fir·ma·ries 1** a place for the care of sick or injured people, especially in an institution such as a school or camp. **2** a hospital.

in·fir·mi·ty (in fər′mə tē) *n, pl* **in·fir·mi·ties 1** weakness or feebleness. **2** a sickness or illness. **3** a moral weakness or failing.

in·flame (in flām′) *v* **in·flamed, in·flam·ing 1** excite anger, hatred, passion, or some other violent emotion: *Her speech inflamed the crowd.* **2** make unnaturally hot, red, sore, or swollen: *The smoke had inflamed the firefighter's eyes.* <Old French, from Latin *in-* in + *flamma* flame>

in·flam·ma·ble (in flam′ə bəl) *adj* **1** easily set on fire: *Paper and gasoline are inflammable.* **2** easily excited or aroused: *an inflammable temper.* <See INFLAME.>
in·flam′ma·bil′i·ty *n.* **in′flam′ma·ble·ness** *n.*
in′flam′ma·bly *adv.*

GRAMMAR AND USAGE

Although it may not look like it, **inflammable** and **flammable** both mean "easily set on fire." Because *inflammable* sounds like it might mean "not flammable," *flammable* is preferred for the sake of clarity. Whichever form is used, the opposite is *nonflammable.*

in·flam·ma·tion (in′flə mā′shən) *n* a diseased condition of some part of the body, marked by heat, redness, swelling, and pain.

in·flam·ma·to·ry (in flam′ə tò′rē) *adj* **1** tending to stir up violent emotions: *inflammatory remarks.* **2** of, causing, or accompanied by inflammation: *an inflammatory condition of the tonsils.*

in·flate (in flāt′) *v* **in·flat·ed, in·flat·ing** **1** fill with air or gas: *to inflate a balloon.* **2** swell or puff out: *inflated with pride.* **3** increase prices or currency beyond a reasonable or normal amount. **4** exaggerate: *Reports of his success are rather inflated.* <Latin *in-* into + *flare* to blow> **in·flat′a·ble** *adj.* **in·flat′er** or **in·fla′tor** *n.*

in·fla·tion (in flā′shən) *n* **1** a general rise in prices and wages, and fall in the purchasing power of money. **2** the act of inflating. **in·fla′tion·ar′y** *adj.*

inflationary spiral *n* a cycle of repeated increases in prices and wages, each one causing the other to rise.

in·flect (in flekt′) *v* **1** change the tone or pitch of the voice. **2** *Grammar* change the form of a word to show number, gender, person, tense, comparison, or case. <Latin *inflectere* change> **in·flec′tion** *n.*

in·flex·i·ble (in flek′sə bəl) *adj* **1** not compromising or giving in to persuasion or influence: *inflexible determination. He's a hard worker, but often so inflexible that he can't work on a team with others.* **2** fixed and unchangeable. **3** not easily bent: *an inflexible piece of wire.* **in·flex′i·bil′i·ty** *n.* **in·flex′i·bly** *adv.*

in·flict (in flikt′) *v* give or impose something unwelcome: *to inflict a penalty on a player. She inflicted herself on her relatives for a long visit.* <Latin *infligere* to strike against> **in·flic′tion** *n.*

in·flight (in′flīt′) *adj* served, shown, or happening during a flight in an airplane: *an inflight movie.*

in·flo·res·cence (in′flə res′əns) *Botany n* **1** the flowering stage in a plant. **2** the particular arrangement of flowers on the stem. **3** a flower cluster. <Latin *in-* in + *floris* flower> **in′flo·res′cent** *adj.*

in·flow (in′flō′) *n* **1** the act of flowing in: *a sudden inflow of cold air.* **2** that which flows in.

in·flu·ence (in′flū əns) *n* **1** the power to cause any effect or change: *the influence of the moon on the tides.* **2** the power to affect people's decisions because of one's personality, social position, emotional impact, or wealth: *Use your influence to persuade your friends to join us.* **3** a person who or thing that has such power: *He was a good influence throughout the school because of his upbeat attitude.*
v **in·flu·enced, in·flu·enc·ing** have power over: *The moon influences the tides.* <Latin *influentem* a flowing in (from the stars). *Influence* originally referred to the power of the stars to influence the destiny and behaviour of people.> **in′flu·en′tial** *adj.* **in′flu·en′tial·ly** *adv.*

in·flu·en·za (in′flū en′zə) FLU.

in·flux (in′fluks) *n* **1** arrival or entry of large numbers of people or things: *the influx of immigrants into a country.* **2** that which flows in. <See INFLUENCE.>

in·fo (in′fō) *Informal n* information.

info– *combining form* information, often information using electronic media: *infomercial.*

in·fo·bot (in′fō bot′) *Computers n* an electronic message sent automatically, often as a standard reply to an inquiry: *I e-mailed a letter to the editor of the newspaper and got back an infobot thanking me.* <*info-* + (*ro*)*bot*>

in·fo·mer·cial (in′fō mər′shəl) *n* a TV program whose main function is to promote some product, organization, or service. <*info-* + (*com*)*mercial*>

in·form (in fòrm′) *v* **1** give knowledge, facts, or news to: *Inform the office if you must leave early.* **2** (*with* **on** *or* **against**) give information about someone to the police or other authority: *One gang member informed on the others.* <Latin *in-* in + *forma* form>

in·for·mal (in fòr′məl) *adj* **1** not done in a formally or officially recognized way: *an informal contract. He has no diploma, but has plenty of informal education in management.* **2** casual, relaxed, or unofficial: *an informal party, informal clothes.* **3** to do with language in everyday situations and in conversation, but not in formal speech or writing. **in′for·mal′i·ty** *n.* **in·for′mal·ly** *adv.*

GRAMMAR AND USAGE

Informal English is used in everyday speaking and writing. It ranges from the casual to the careful and precise. **Formal** English is used in legal documents, speeches, lectures, business correspondence, essays, and so on.

In this dictionary, **informal** is used to mean "acceptable in everyday use, but not appropriate in situations requiring formal language."

in·form·ant (in fòr′mənt) *n* a person who gives information to another: *My informant was an eyewitness.*

in·for·ma·tion (in′fər mā′shən) *n* **1** facts provided or acquired about something or someone: *An encyclopedia contains information about many things.* **2** a particular arrangement or sequence of things that is stored, conveyed, or presented: *Nerves carry information about smells to the brain. This disk holds about two megabytes of information.* **3** the act of informing someone.

information highway or **superhighway** *n* all electronic media and communication systems.

information science *n* the study of all the methods and technologies available for storing, processing, and retrieving various kinds of information.

information technology IT.

in·form·a·tive (in fòr′mə tiv) *adj* giving useful or interesting information: *This brochure is not very informative.* **in·form′a·tive·ly** *adv.*

in·form·er (in fòr′mər) *n* a person who gives confidential information about someone to the police or other authority.

in·fo·tain·ment (in′fō tān′mənt) *n* programs, movies, or games that are designed to be both informative and entertaining. <*info-* + (*enter*)*tainment*>

a bat	e bed	i bid	o pot	u cup	th **thin**
ā cake	ē me	ī bite	ō go	ū rude	ᴛʜ **then**
à bar	ə about	ər over	ò for	ù put	zh measure

in·frac·tion (in frak′shən) *n* a breaking or violation of a rule or law: *Jaywalking is an infraction rarely ticketed by the police.* <Latin *in-* in + *frangere* break>

in·fra·red (in′frə red′) *adj* to do with the electromagnetic waves whose length is greater than that of the red end of the colour spectrum. <Latin *infra* after + *red*>

in·fra·struc·ture (in′frə struk′shər) *n* **1** the basic physical structures necessary for a system to work **2 a** the roads, sewers, and power supply needed by a city. **b** the manufacturing, distribution, and selling facilities in an industrial economy. <Latin *infra* below + *structure*>

in·fre·quent (in frē′kwənt) *adj* happening seldom or far apart: *infrequent visits. Trees are infrequent on the prairies.* **in·fre′quen·cy** *n.* **in·fre′quent·ly** *adv.*

in·fringe (in frinj′) *v* **in·fringed, in·fring·ing 1** break a law or rule, or trespass on the legal right of another: *to infringe copyright.* **2** (*with* ***on***) unfairly limit or undermine something: *to infringe on someone's privacy.* <Latin *in-* in + *frangere* break> **in·fringe′ment** *n.*

in·fu·ri·ate (in fyū′rē āt′) *v* **in·fu·ri·at·ed, in·fu·ri·at·ing** make someone extremely angry and impatient: *She was infuriated by their insults.* <Latin *in-* into + *furia* fury> **in·fu′ri·at′ing** *adj.* **in·fu′ri·at′ing·ly** *adv.*

SYNONYMS

Infuriate means "make furious or extremely angry": *She was infuriated when her purse was stolen.*

Aggravate carries less force than infuriate, meaning "annoy" or "provoke": *The ball player was aggravated by the bee buzzing around his head.*

Enrage carries more force than infuriate, meaning "put into a rage": *The bull was enraged by the matador.*

in·fuse (in fyūz′) *v* **in·fused, in·fus·ing 1** pour in; put in: *The author infuses his own moral values into his writing. Her courage infused the survivors with hope.* **2** steep or soak in a liquid to draw out flavour or minerals: *to infuse tea.* <Latin *in-* in + *fundere* pour> **in·fu′sion** *n.*

in·ge·ni·ous (in jēn′yəs) *adj* showing cleverness and originality in making things or coming up with ideas: *What an ingenious device! The ingenious girl made a radio set from found materials.* <Latin *ingenium* natural talent> **in·gen′ious·ly** *adv.* **in·gen′ious·ness** *n.*

in·gé·nue (on′zhə nū′) *n* a simple, innocent girl or young woman, especially as represented on the stage. <French = ingenuous>

in·ge·nu·i·ty (in′jə nyū′ə tē) *or* (in′jə nū′ə tē) *n* cleverness and originality in making or inventing things or coming up with ideas.

in·gen·u·ous (in jen′yū əs) *adj* simple, sincere, and innocent: *The little boy gave an ingenuous account of his actions.* <Latin *ingenuus* noble character> **in·gen′u·ous·ly** *adv.* **in·gen′u·ous·ness** *n.*

in·gest (in jest′) *v* take food, drink, or medicine into the body through the mouth. <Latin *ingerere* to put into> **in·ges′tion** *n.*

in·glo·ri·ous (in glô′rē əs) *adj* bringing or with no glory: *inglorious acts.* **in·glo′ri·ous·ly** *adv.* **in·glo′ri·ous·ness** *n.*

in·got (ing′gət) *n* a mass of metal, such as gold, cast into a block or bar. <Old English *in-* in + *goten* poured>

in·grained (in grānd′) *adj* firmly fixed or deeply rooted in one's character: *ingrained habits.*

ETYMOLOGY

Ingrained comes from the verb *ingrain*, a term from the textile industry. To dye an item in *grain* was to dye it thoroughly and permanently.

in·grate (in′grāt) *n* a person who is not grateful. <Latin *in-* not + *gratus* thankful>

in·gra·ti·ate (in grā′shē āt′) *v* **in·gra·ti·at·ed, in·gra·ti·at·ing** gain favour through flattery or trying to please someone: *Don't try to ingratiate yourself with the teacher by giving him presents.* <Italian, from Latin *in gratium* into favour> **in·gra′ti·at′ing** *adj.* **in·gra′ti·at′ing·ly** *adv.*

in·grat·i·tude (in grat′ə tyūd′) *or* (in grat′ə tūd′) *n* a lack of gratitude or thankfulness.

in·gre·di·ent (in grē′dē ənt) *n* one of the parts of a mixture: *The ingredients for the cake are listed in the recipe.* <Latin *ingredi* to enter>

in·gress (in′gres) *n* the act, means, or right of entering: *A high fence prevented ingress to the field.* <Latin *ingredi* to enter>

in–group (in′grūp′) *n* a closed group of people with shared interests and background, who hold the power and prestige in an organization or society.

in·grown (in′grōn′) *adj* having grown within, especially of a toenail that has grown into the flesh.

in·hab·it (in hab′it) *v* live in a place: *Fish inhabit the sea.* <Latin *in-* in + *habitare* dwell> **in·hab′it·ed** *adj.*

in·hab·it·ant (in hab′ə tənt) *n* a person who or animal that lives in a place: *an inhabitant of Moncton.*

in·hal·ant (in hā′lənt) *n* a medicine to be inhaled, such as for the relief of asthma.

in·ha·la·tor (in′hə lā′tər) *n* an INHALER (def. 1).

in·hale (in hāl′) *v* **in·haled, in·hal·ing** draw air or smoke into the lungs. <Latin *in-* in + *halare* breathe>

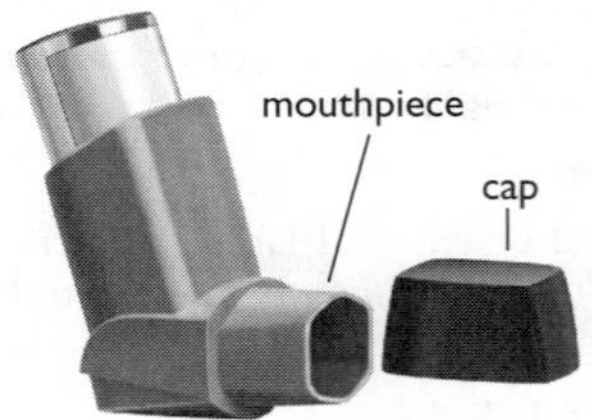

People who suffer from asthma or have other respiratory problems often need to take medication through an **inhaler**, which produces a controlled puff of mist that delivers medicine to the lungs.

in·hal·er (in hāl′ər) *n* **1** an apparatus for inhaling medicine, anesthetics, or oxygen. Also called **inhalator**. **2** a person or animal that inhales.

in·her·ent (in her′ənt) *or* (in hē′rənt) *adj* existing as a natural, essential, or basic quality of a person or thing: *inherent honesty. Certain problems are inherent in this design.* <Latin *inhaerentem* be closely connected with> **in·her′ent·ly** *adv.*

in·her·it (in her′it) *v* **1** receive rightfully after the owner dies: *Their nephew inherited the farm.* **2** acquire through heredity: *She inherited her green eyes from her dad.* **3** receive anything from an earlier situation, owner, etc.: *The new government inherited a financial crisis. My little sister inherited all my old toys.* <Latin *in-* in + *heredis* heir> **in·her′it·ance** *n.* **in·her′i·tor** *n.*

inheritance tax *n* a tax on inherited property.

in·hib·it (in hib′it) *v* **1** hinder or restrain: *His impulse to run away was inhibited by a strong sense of loyalty.* **2** fill with anxiety, shame, pride, or other feelings and attitudes that keep a person from relaxing and acting naturally. **3** slowing, preventing, or reducing the effect of an enzyme or other agent when taken as a drug or other substance. <Latin *in-* in + *habere* hold> **in′hi·bi′tion** (in′ə bish′ən) *or* (in′hi bish′ən) *n.*

in·hos·pit·a·ble (in′hə spit′ə bəl) *or* (in hos′pə tə bəl) *adj* **1** not making visitors welcome and comfortable: *They were too inhospitable to offer us anything to eat.* **2** harsh or providing no shelter or comfort: *an inhospitable landscape.* **in′hos·pit′a·bil′i·ty** *n.* **in′hos·pit′a·bly** *adv.*

in·hos·pi·tal·i·ty (in hos′pə tal′ə tē) *n* failure to make visitors welcome and comfortable.

in–house (in′hous′) *adj, adv* using an organization's own resources instead of the services of contractors: *an in-house publication* (*adj*). *This magazine gets all its photography done in-house* (*adv*).

in·hu·man (in hyū′mən) *adj* **1** without ordinary human kindness or decency: *inhuman treatment, inhuman living conditions.* **2** not human. **in′hu·man′i·ty** *n.* **in·hu′man·ly** *adv.*

CONFUSABLES

Inhuman refers to a lack of natural human kindness: *The revolutionaries were involved in the inhuman treatment of their enemies.*

Inhumane implies a lack of compassionate feelings: *It was inhumane to make them work all through the holidays.*

in·hu·mane (in′hyū mān′) *adj* not kind or compassionate. <variant of *inhuman*> **in′hu·mane′ly** *adv.*

in·im·i·cal (i nim′ə kəl) *adj* unfavourable; harmful: *Lack of ambition is inimical to success.* <Latin *in-* not + *amicus* friendly> **in·im′i·cal·ly** *adv.*

in·im·i·ta·ble (i nim′ə tə bəl) *adj* that cannot be imitated or copied: *the inimitable talent of Wayne Gretzky.* <Latin *in-* not + *imitari* imitate> **in′im′it·a·bil′i·ty** *n.* **in·im′i·ta·bly** *adv.*

in·iq·ui·ty (i nik′wə tē) *n, pl* **in·iq·ui·ties** greatly immoral or unjust behaviour. <Latin *in-* not + *aequus* just> **in·iq′ui·tous** *adj.*

i·ni·tial (i nish′əl) *adj* occurring at the beginning: *My initial feeling of shyness was soon over.*
n the first letter of a word: *The initials N.S. stand for Nova Scotia.*
v **i·ni·tialled** or **in·i·tialed, i·ni·tial·ling** or **i·ni·tial·ing** mark or sign with initials: *Juan Segovia initialled the note J.S.* <Latin *initium* beginning> **i·ni′tial·ly** *adv.*

i·ni·tial·ism (i nish′ə liz′əm) *n* an abbreviation for a phrase, made up of the first letter of each word and pronounced as a series of separate letters. Examples: *VIP, GST.*

i·ni·tial·ize (i nish′ə līz′) FORMAT (*v* def. 1).

i·ni·ti·ate (i nish′ē āt′) *for v,* (i nish′ē it) *for n. v* **i·ni·ti·at·ed, i·ni·ti·at·ing** **1** take the first step in doing something: *Who initiated this process?* **2** bring a new member into a group by special ceremonies: *The new team members were initiated at the first practice with a series of practical jokes.* **3** introduce to the knowledge of some subject: *Last summer I was initiated into the thrills of rock climbing.*
n a person who is initiated. <See INITIAL.>
i·ni′ti·a′tion *n.* **i·ni′ti·a′tor** *n.*

i·ni·ti·a·tive (i nish′ə tiv) *n* **1** the power or opportunity to act or lead before others do: *She is shy and does not take the initiative in making friends* **2** a strategy to resolve a problem or to improve a situation: *The mayor announced an initiative to improve the Toronto waterfront.*
on your own initiative, not as a result of anyone else's suggestion or action: *She set up the food drive on her own initiative.*

in·ject (in jekt′) *v* **1** force liquid into a passage, cavity, or tissue: *to inject fuel into an engine, inject a vein with medicine.* **2** introduce: *The stranger injected a remark into their conversation.* <Latin *in-* in + *jacere* throw> **in·jec′tion** *n.* **in·jec′tor** *n.*

in–joke (in′jōk′) *n* a joke understood only by members of a certain group.

in·ju·di·cious (in′jū dish′əs) *adj* showing lack of judgment. **in′ju·di′cious·ly** *adv.* **in′ju·di′cious·ness** *n.*

in·junc·tion (in jungk′shən) *n* **1** an order: *Injunctions of secrecy did not prevent the news from leaking out.* **2** a formal order issued by a law court: *A court injunction kept the protestors at least 5 m from the door of the building.* <Latin *injunctionem* a command, from *injungere* impose>

in·jure (in′jər) *v* **in·jured, in·jur·ing** **1** do harm or damage to: *Do not injure the young trees. Dishonesty injures a business.* **2** be unfair to. <Latin *in-* not + *juris* right>

in·ju·ry (in′jə rē) *n, pl* **in·ju·ries** **1** harm or damage endured by a person or thing: *She escaped from the train wreck without injury.* **2** unfairness or injustice: *You did me an injury when you said I lied.* **in·ju′ri·ous** *adj.*

in·jus·tice (in jus′tis) *n* **1** unfairness or lack of justice. **2** an unjust act: *To send an innocent person to jail is an injustice.*

a bat	e bed	i bid	o pot	u cup	th **thin**
ā cake	ē me	ī bite	ō go	ū rude	TH **then**
à bar	ə about	ər over	ȯ for	ů put	zh measure

A *flip* in **inline skating** is any move in which the skater rotates a full circle with the waist being the axis of rotation. To do a *misty flip*, the skater lifts knees to chin, which causes the feet to rise higher than the skater's head.

A *grind (rail slide)* involves jumping onto a hand rail or something similar and sliding down it on skates. A *soul grind* is having the front foot perpendicular and the back foot parallel to the handrail. It's best to wear protective gear for these and other moves.

ink (ingk) *n* **1** a coloured liquid used for writing, printing, or drawing. **2** a dark liquid ejected by cuttlefish, octopus, or squid to confuse an attacker. <Old French, from Greek *enkauton* reddish blue ink, used by Greek and Roman emperors for their signatures>
ink in, a fill in an outline with ink. **b** write something on a schedule in ink as something definite.

ink·blot test (ingk′blot′) RORSCHACH TEST.

ink·jet printer (ingk′jet′) *Computers n* a printer that forms characters and images by spraying ink onto the paper in the appropriate pattern.

ink·ling (ingk′ling) *n* a slight suggestion or hint. <Middle English>

ink·well (ingk′wel′) *n* a container used to hold ink, especially if recessed in a desk.

ink·y (ing′kē) *adj* **ink·i·er, ink·i·est 1** black or very dark like ink: *inky shadows.* **2** marked with or containing ink. **ink′i·ness** *n.*

in·laid (in′lād′) *or* (in lād′) *adj* **1** set in the surface as a decoration or design: *The desk had an inlaid design of light wood in dark.* **2** decorated with a design or material set in the surface: *The box had an inlaid cover.*

in·land (in′land′) *or* (in′lənd) *adj* away from the coast or border of a country: *an inland sea.*
n land away from the border or the coast.
adv in or toward the interior: *to travel inland.*

in–law (in′lo′) *n* a relative by marriage.

in·lay (in lā′) *or* (in′lā′) *for v,* (in′lā′) *for n. v* **in·laid, in·lay·ing 1** set as a decoration or design into a shallow recess in a surface: *to inlay strips of gold.* **2** decorate with something set into the surface: *to inlay a wooden box with silver.*
n **1** an inlaid decoration, design, or material. **2** a shaped piece of metal or porcelain cemented in a tooth as a filling.

in·let (in′let′) *or* (in′lət) *n* a narrow strip of water extending from a larger body of water into the land or between islands: *The fishing village was on a small inlet of the sea.* <Middle English>

in·line skate (in′līn′) *n* a roller skate with four wheels in a single row, one behind the other. **inline skating** *n.*

in loco parentis (lō′cō par ent′is) *adj, adv* said of a person who has responsibility for children, such as a teacher. <Latin = in the place of a parent>

in·mate (in′māt′) *n* a person who lives with others in an institution, especially a prison.

in me·mo·ri·am (mə mȯ′rē əm) (*in obituaries, epitaphs, etc.*) in memory (of). <Latin>

in·most (in′mōst′) *adj* **1** farthest or deepest in: *the inmost depths of a cave.* **2** most private or personal: *Her inmost desire was to be an artist.*

inn (in) *n* **1** a building that offers rooms and meals for travellers. **2** a tavern. <Old English>

in·nards (in′ərdz) *Informal pln* the internal organs of the body, especially the entrails. <variant of *inward*>

in·nate (i nāt′) *adj* natural or inborn: *an innate talent for drawing.* <Latin *in-* in + *natus* born> **in·nate′ly** *adv.* **in·nate′ness** *n.*

in·ner (in′ər) *adj* **1** farther in or inside: *an inner room.* **2** intimate or private: *your inner thoughts.* <Old English *inne* within>

inner child *n* the part of an adult person that is trusting, playful, or able to feel wonder, especially when it is repressed by work and responsibilities.

inner circle *n* in any group, the few people who have privileged access to power and information.

inner city *n* the older, central part of a large city, especially when densely populated and less well-off than the rest of the city. **in′ner-cit′y** *adj.*

inner ear *n* in humans, the part of the ear containing the organ that changes sound into nerve impulses and the organ for maintaining balance.

in·ner·most (in′ər mōst′) *adj* farthest in: *the innermost part of the earth is liquid.*

inner planet *n* in our solar system, any of the four small planets closest to the sun: Mercury, Venus, Earth, or Mars.

inner tube *n* a rubber tube that fits inside some tires and is inflated with air.

in·ning (in′ing) *Baseball, Cricket n* the period of play in which each team has a turn at bat. <Old English *innung* a taking in. *Inning* was first used in its current sense in the early 18c.>
have your innings, get a chance to act, accomplish something, or be recognized.

inn·keep·er (in′kē′pər) *n* a person who owns, manages, or keeps an inn.

in·no·cent (in′ə sənt) *adj* **1** not guilty or not involved in a particular wrongdoing: *An innocent bystander was hit in the shootout. The person they accused turned out to be innocent.* **2** without causing harm: *innocent amusements.* **3** free from pretence, craftiness, or ulterior motives: *an innocent question.* **4** without experience or worldly knowledge: *The innocent young child was ready to trust any stranger.*
n a person who becomes involved by chance in a dangerous situation, especially a crime or war: *When the bomb went off several innocents were killed.* <Latin *innocentem* harmless, from *in-* not + *nocere* to harm> **in′no·cence** *n.* **in′no·cent·ly** *adv.*

SYNONYMS

Innocent emphasizes having done no wrong: *The judge found her innocent of any criminal behaviour.*

Blameless means "not responsible," whether or not wrong has been done: *To the victim's dismay, the young offender was held blameless for his actions.*

Guiltless means "without guilt in thought, intention, or act": *The driver whose car was wrecked during a high-speed police chase was guiltless.*

in·noc·u·ous (i nok′yū əs) *adj* not likely to cause injury or offence: *an innocuous poke in the ribs, innocuous remarks.* <Latin *in-* not + *nocere* to harm> **in·noc′u·ous·ly** *adv.* **in·noc′u·ous·ness** *n.*

in·no·vate (in′ə vāt′) *v* **in·no·vat·ed, in·no·vat·ing** bring in something new or do something in a new way. <Latin *in-* in + *novus* new> **in′no·va′tion** *n.* **in′no·va′tive** *adj.* **in′no·va′tor** *n.*

In·nu (in′ū) *n, pl* **In·nu** **1** a member of a First Nations people living in northern Québec and the interior of Labrador, formerly known as the **Montagnais** and the **Naskapi.** **2** their Cree language.
adj to do with these people or their language.

in·nu·en·do (in′yū en′dō) *n, pl* **in·nu·en·does** an indirect hint or suggestion: *to spread scandal by innuendo.* <Latin = giving a nod to>

in·nu·mer·a·ble (i nyū′mə rə bəl) *or* (i nū′mə rə bəl) *adj* too many to count: *innumerable stars in the sky.* <Latin *in-* not + *numerabilis* countable> **in′num′er·a·bil′i·ty** *n.* **in·nu′mer·a·bly** *adv.*

in·nu·mer·ate (i nyū′mə rit) *or* (i nū′mə rit) *adj* unable to do the simple arithmetic needed for everyday life. Compare ILLITERATE. <Latin *in-* not + *numerus* number> **in·nu′mer·a·cy** *n.*

in·oc·u·late (i nok′yə lāt′) *v* **in·oc·u·lat·ed, in·oc·u·lat·ing** vaccinate a person or animal with a weak or dead disease-causing organism, in order to stimulate the production of protective antibodies by the immune system. <Latin *inoculare* to implant> **in·oc′u·la′tion** *n.*

in·of·fen·sive (in′ə fen′siv) *adj* not objectionable or harmful. **in′of·fen′sive·ly** *adv.* **in′of·fen′sive·ness** *n.*

in·op·er·a·ble (i nop′rə bəl) *adj* **1** not able to be cured or helped by surgery: *an inoperable tumour.* **2** impossible to carry out: *an inoperable plan.* **in·op′er·a·bil′i·ty** *n.* **in·op′er·a·ble·ness** *n.* **in·op′er·a·bly** *adv.*

in·op·er·a·tive (i nop′rə tiv) *adj* not functioning or operating. **in·op′er·a·tive·ly** *adv.* **in·op′er·a·tive·ness** *n.*

in·op·por·tune (i nop′ər tyūn′) *or* (i nop′ər tūn′) *adj* happening or done at the wrong time: *My mom said that the dinner hour would be an inopportune time to call.* **in·op′por·tune′ly** *adv.*

in·or·di·nate (i nôr′də nit) *adj* much too much: *He spends an inordinate amount of time on the phone.* <Latin *inordinatus* not kept inside limits> **in·or′di·nate·ly** *adv.*

in·or·gan·ic (in′ôr gan′ik) *adj* **1** made up of matter that does not have the organized structure of living things: *Minerals are inorganic.* **2** *Chemistry* **a** derived from minerals and not containing carbon. **b** to do with the branch of chemistry that studies such compounds and elements. **in′or·gan′i·cal·ly** *adv.*

in–pa·tient (in′pā′shənt) *n* a patient who stays in a hospital for treatment.
adj of or for such patients: *in-patient services.*

in·put (in′pu̇t′) *n* **1** anything that is put in or taken in. **2** the knowledge, ideas, effort, or leadership contributed to an undertaking: *I had very little input on our group project.* **3** the power or material supplied to a machine, or the place where it enters. **4** *Computers* information fed into a computer or computer application.
v **in·put, in·put·ting** *Computers* feed information into a computer or data processing system by means of an **input device** such as a keyboard, mouse, touchpad, joystick, trackball, scanner, etc.

in·quest (in′kwest) *n* **1** a legal inquiry led by a coroner, usually with a jury, to determine the cause of a sudden death. **2** a jury appointed to hold such an inquiry: *The inquest was told that a witness had been delayed.* **3** an investigation into the causes of an event or situation. <See INQUIRE.>

a bat	e bed	i bid	o pot	u cup	th **thin**
ā cake	ē me	ī bite	ō go	ū rude	TH **then**
ä bar	ə about	ər over	ô for	u̇ put	zh measure

in·quire (in kwīr′) *v* **in·quired, in·quir·ing 1** ask: *She phoned the hotel to inquire about a room.* **2** make an investigation or examination, especially by asking questions: *to inquire into someone's past.* Also, **enquire.** <Latin *in-* into + *quaerere* ask> **in·quir′er** *n.* **in·quir′ing** *adj.* **in·quir′ing·ly** *adv.*

SYNONYMS

Inquire is one of several words that mean "ask": *She kindly inquired about my health.*

Query is a more formal or more official way to ask: *The lawyer queried the reliability of the defence witness.*

Quiz suggests questioning closely: *My mother quizzed me on my whereabouts when I came home late.*

in·quir·y (in kwī′rē) *or* (in′kwə rē) *n, pl* **in·quir·ies 1** the act of inquiring. **2** a question. **3** an investigation or examination: *The authorities are conducting an inquiry into the cause of the explosion.* Also, **enquiry.**

in·qui·si·tion (in′kwə zish′ən) *n* **1** an official investigation or inquiry. **2** a very severe or intensive questioning. **3 the Inquisition** an ecclesiastical court of the Roman Catholic Church, active between the 1200s and the 1500s, that was established to suppress heresy. <See INQUIRE.> **in·quis′i·tor** *n.* **in·quis′i·to′ri·al** *adj.*

in·quis·i·tive (in kwiz′ə tiv) *adj* **1** very curious or asking many questions: *Children are usually inquisitive.* **2** unduly curious about other people: *He is an inquisitive person who asks very personal questions.* **in·quis′i·tive·ly** *adv.* **in·quis′i·tive·ness** *n.*

in·road (in′rōd′) *n* an attack or raid.
make inroads on, damage, weaken, or lessen: *The unexpected expenses made serious inroads on her savings.*

in·rush (in′rush′) *n* the act of rushing in or that which rushes in: *an inrush of water through a gap in the wall.*

in·sane (in sān′) *adj* **1** with a severe mental illness. **2** extremely foolish: *an insane plan.* **3** extremely distracting or annoying: *insane buzzing of the mosquitoes.* *n* (*with* ***the***) people with severe mental illness: *She spoke about humane treatment of the insane.* **in·sane′ly** *adv.* **in·san′i·ty** (in san′ə tē) *adv.*

in·sa·tia·ble (in sā′shə bəl) *adj* that cannot be satisfied and always wants more: *an insatiable appetite for science fiction.* **in·sa′tia·bil′i·ty** *n.* **in·sa′tia·ble·ness** *n.* **in·sa′tia·bly** *adv.*

in·scribe (in skrīb′) *v* **in·scribed, in·scrib·ing 1** engrave letters or words on a surface: *Her initials were inscribed on the bracelet.* **2** write a brief message or dedication in or on: *The book was inscribed "To Pauli, with love from Dad."* **3** impress deeply: *His mother's words are inscribed on his memory.* **4** *Mathematics* draw a figure inside another figure so that their boundaries touch in as many places as possible: *to inscribe a triangle in a circle.* <Latin *in-* on + *scribere* write> **in·scrib′er** *n.*

inscribed angle *n* an angle drawn inside a circle so that the vertex of the angle is on the circumference and the arms of the angle are chords of the circle.

in·scrip·tion (in skrip′shən) *n* the act of inscribing, or the words or letters inscribed: *The inscription on the coin reads "Elizabeth II* D.G. REGINA."

in·scru·ta·ble (in skrū′tə bəl) *adj* mysterious or hard to interpret: *an inscrutable look on his face.* <Latin *in-* not + *scrutari* examine> **in·scru′ta·bil′i·ty** *n.* **in′scru′ta·ble·ness** *n.* **in·scru′ta·bly** *adv.*

The praying mantis is named for the posture it assumes while waiting for its prey. This **insect** plays an important role in nature by eating pests such as mosquitoes and flies.

in·sect (in′sekt) *n* **1** a small invertebrate animal whose body is divided into three parts (head, thorax, and abdomen), with three pairs of legs and, usually, one or two pairs of wings. **2** a small animal that has its body divided into several parts and with several pairs of legs. <Latin *in-* into + *secare* to cut (from their segmented bodies)>

in·sec·ti·cide (in sek′tə sīd′) *n* a substance used for killing insects.

in·sec·ti·vore (in sek′tə vȯr′) *n* **1** an insect-eating animal, especially a small mammal such as a mole or shrew. **2** a plant that traps and consumes insects. <*insect* + Latin *vorare* devour> **in′sec·tiv′o·rous** (in sek tiv′ə rəs) *adj.*

in·se·cure (in′sə kyūr′) *adj* **1** lacking confidence: *Many insecure people seek constant attention from others.* **2** worried or anxious in general: *These rumours of war make us all rather insecure.* **3** not safe from danger, loss, failure, or breakage: *insecure investments, an insecure relationship.* **4** not firmly fixed or attached: *This ladder was insecure and wobbled when I tried to climb it.* **in′se·cure′ly** *adv.* **in′se·cu′ri·ty** *n.*

in·sem·i·nate (in sem′ə nāt′) *v* **in·sem·i·nat·ed, in·sem·i·nat·ing** introduce semen into a woman or female animal: *She finally conceived after being artificially inseminated.* <Latin *in-* into + *semen* seed> **in·sem′i·na′tion** *n.*

in·sen·sate (in sen′sāt) *adj* **1** without sensation: *the insensate stones.* **2** lacking sympathy or compassion: *insensate cruelty.* **3** unreasonable or stupid: *insensate folly.* <Latin *in-* not + *sensus* feeling>

in·sen·si·ble (in sen′sə bəl) *adj* **1** not able to perceive with the senses: *A blind person is insensible to colours.* **2** not able to respond emotionally: *We were thrilled by the view but she was insensible to it.* **3** not aware: *The children in the boat were insensible of the danger.* **4** not easily felt or realized; too gradual to be noticeable: *The room grew cold by insensible degrees.* **5** unconscious or completely numb. **in·sen′si·bil′i·ty** *n.* **in·sen′si·bly** *adv.*

in·sen·si·tive (in sen′sə tiv) *adj* **1** not noticing or caring about the feelings of others: *It was insensitive of her to laugh when he had obviously hurt himself.* **2** not aware of or able to respond to something: *The insensitive brute thought all art was a waste of time.* **3** numb or without physical feeling: *An injection makes the tooth insensitive so that the drilling won't hurt.* **in·sen′si·tive·ly** *adv.* **in·sen′si·tiv′i·ty** *n.*

in·sep·a·ra·ble (in sep′rə bəl) *adj* that cannot be separated or parted: *inseparable friends.* **in·sep′a·ra·bil′i·ty** *n.* **in·sep′a·ra·bly** *adv.*

in·sert (in sərt′) *for v,* (in′sərt) *for n. v* put or set in something or between other things: *to insert a key in a lock. Insert a space between these two paragraphs.*
n a piece or section put into something: *The newspaper had a special insert full of ideas for March break.* <Latin *inserere* put in> **in·ser′tion** *n.*

in·set (in′set) *for n,* (in set′) *or* (in′set) *for v. n* a small map, photograph, or illustration set within the border of a larger one, to show some part in detail or to give extra information.
v **in·set, in·set·ting** set or put in as an inset.

in·shore (in′shȯr′) *for adj,* (in′shȯr′) *for adv. adj* **1** near the shore: *inshore shoals.* **2** done or working near the shore: *the inshore fishery of Newfoundland.*
adv in toward the shore: *The wind blew them inshore.*

in·side (in′sīd′) *n* **1** the inner surface or part: *The inside of the box was lined with coloured paper. He looked at the magazine cover but didn't read the inside.* **2 insides** *pl* the parts inside the body, especially the stomach and intestines. **3** in an organization, the position of those with access to information, power, or influence.
adv **1** in or into the inner part: *Open the box and look inside.* **2** in one's inner thoughts or feelings: *I may look bored, but inside I'm excited.* **3** indoors: *Go inside if you're cold.*
prep within or contained in: *The nut is inside the shell.*
adj **1** located on the inside: *an inside seat.* **2** known only to a few: *inside information, an inside joke.* **3** working within a group or company as a spy or informant: *an inside man.* **4** indoor.
inside of, *Informal* within the limits of: *We'll be back inside of an hour.*
inside out, a with the inside showing or turned outward: *Your shirt is inside out.* **b** completely: *He knows his subject inside out.*
on the inside, a in your deeper feelings: *She seems like the life of the party, but she's very lonely on the inside.* **b** within an organization, especially in a position giving access to special information or influence.

inside job *n* a crime committed by someone closely associated with the victim, such as a robbery by an employee.

🍁 **Inside Passage** *n* a route followed by ships along the west coast of Canada, naturally protected by the shape of the coast.

in·sid·er (in′sī′dər) *n* a person recognized as having power, influence, or access to confidential information: *an insider's report on the workings of Parliament.*

insider trading *n* the illegal practice of using confidential information about stocks to trade on the stock market for one's own advantage.

inside track *n* **1** on a racetrack, the lane nearest the inside of the curve, hence the shortest way around. **2** an advantageous position: *I think I have the inside track in the music competition, because I practise every day.*

in·sid·i·ous (in sid′ē əs) *adj* working harm subtly or gradually without attracting attention: *an insidious disease, an insidious plot.* <Latin *insidiae* ambush> **in·sid′i·ous·ly** *adv.* **in·sid′i·ous·ness** *n.*

in·sight (in′sīt′) *n* **1** an understanding of something from a look at the inside or inner nature of it: *In science lab, we took a machine apart to get an insight into how it works.* **2** wisdom and understanding: *He has tremendous insight in the area of human relationships.* <Middle English> **in·sight′ful** *adj.* **in·sight′ful·ly** *adv.*

in·sig·ni·a (in sig′nē ə) *pl n* (*with singular or plural verb*) the distinguishing logo, badges, or other symbols or marks of a noble family, military order, team, or other organization: *Each player's jacket bears the insignia of the team.* <Latin *insigne* badge>

in·sig·nif·i·cant (in′sig nif′ə kənt) *adj* **1** with little importance, effect, or influence: *an insignificant error, an insignificant author.* **2** with little meaning: *insignificant chatter.* **in′sig·nif′i·cance** *n.* **in′sig·nif′i·cant·ly** *adv.*

in·sin·cere (in′sin sēr′) *adj* not honest or genuine. **in′sin·cere′ly** *adv.* **in′sin·cer′i·ty** (in′sin ser′ə tē) *n.*

in·sin·u·ate (in sin′yū āt′) *v* **in·sin·u·at·ed, in·sin·u·at·ing 1** suggest or hint at something, especially something unpleasant: *She made no charge, but insinuated that the mayor had accepted bribes.* **2** get or bring in by gradual and stealthy means: *The spy insinuated himself into the confidence of important army officers.* <Latin *insinuare* wind one's way into, from *in-* in + *sinus* a curve> **in·sin′u·a′tion** *n.*

in·sip·id (in sip′id) *adj* **1** without much taste: *The coffee was weak and insipid.* **2** uninteresting or dull: *insipid writing.* <Latin *in-* not + *sapidus* tasty> **in·sip′id·ly** *adv.* **in·sip′id·ness** *n.*

in·sist (in sist′) *v* keep firmly to some demand, statement, or position: *to insist on your rights. I insist that it be fixed at once.* <Latin *in-* on + *sistere* take a stand>

in·sist·ent (in sis′tənt) *adj* **1** continuing to make a strong, firm demand or statement: *Although it was raining, she was insistent about going for a walk.* **2** hard to ignore because it is vigorous and continues on and on: *My brother's insistent knocking on the door woke me up.* **in·sist′ence** *n.* **in·sist′ent·ly** *adv.*

in·so·far (in′sō fȧr′) *adv* (*usually with* **as**) to such a degree or extent: *He should be told the facts insofar as they concern him.*

a bat	e bed	i bid	o pot	u cup	th **thin**
ā cake	ē me	ī bite	ō go	ū rude	ᴛʜ **then**
ȧ bar	ə about	ər over	ȯ for	u̇ put	zh measure

in·sole (in′sōl′) *n* a shaped piece of material laid in the bottom of a shoe or boot for extra warmth, support, or control of odours.

in·so·lent (in′sə lənt) *adj* boldly rude or disrespectful: *The insolent boy was punished for yelling at his mother.* <Latin *insolentem* arrogant, from *in-* not + *solere* be accustomed> **in′so·lence** *n.* **in′so·lent·ly** *adv.*

in·sol·u·ble (in sol′yə bəl) *adj* **1** that cannot be dissolved: *Fats are insoluble in cold water.* **2** that cannot be solved or explained: *an insoluble mystery.* **in·sol′u·bil′i·ty** *n.* **in·sol′u·bly** *adv.*

in·sol·vent (in sol′vənt) *adj* not able to pay one's debts. **in·sol′ven·cy** *n.*

in·som·ni·a (in som′nē ə) *n* the inability to sleep, especially when the condition lasts a long time. <Latin *in-* not + *somnus* sleep> **in·som′ni·ac′** *adj, n.*

in·spect (in spekt′) *v* **1** examine carefully: *The mother inspected the boy's face to make sure it was clean.* **2** examine officially: *The factory is inspected annually by a government official.* <Latin *in-* on + *specere* look> **in·spec′tion** *n.*

in·spec·tor (in spek′tər) *n* **1** one who inspects, especially an official appointed to inspect. **2** a high-ranking police officer, often ranking next below a superintendent.

in·spi·ra·tion (in′spə rā′shən) *n* **1** uplifting ideas, feelings, or guidance that come from outside oneself and help to shape one's outlook on life: *Some people get inspiration from nature, some from art.* **2** ideas, or a source of ideas, that stimulate one's imagination and lead to works of art or inventions. *If you sit and wait for inspiration, you'll never get your story written. Her experience as a coach was the inspiration for a new design in figure skates.* **3** someone or something that motivates a person to do well: *The coach was an inspiration to the whole team.* **4** the act of inspiring. **in′spi·ra′tion·al** *adj.*

in·spire (in spīr′) *v* **in·spired, in·spir·ing** **1** fill with uplifting thoughts or feelings or noble intentions: *The speaker inspired the crowd.* **2** cause a particular thought or feeling in someone: *Her courage inspired confidence in all of us.* **3** make a person want or choose something: *What inspired you to become a nurse?* **4** stimulate by, or as if by, a divine force: *Inspired by the grandeur of the Rockies, he took some amazing photographs.* **5** give rise to: *Her last movie was inspired by a novel.* <Latin *inspirare* blow into, from *in-* in + *spirare* breathe>

in·sta·bil·i·ty (in′stə bil′ə tē) *n* the fact or state of being unstable: *the instability of the economy, emotional instability.*

in·stall or **in·stal** (in stol′) *v* **1** put something in place, ready for use: *to install a program on a computer, to install a new hardwood floor.* **2** place formally in a position or office: *to install a new judge.* **3** settle or establish in a place: *The cat installed itself in an easy chair.* <Latin *in-* in + *stallum* stall[1]>

in·stal·la·tion (in′stə lā′shən) *n* **1** the act of installing. **2** equipment or fixtures placed in position for use.

in·stal·ment or **in·stall·ment** (in stol′mənt) *n* **1** a part of a sum of money to be paid at certain regular times: *The bike will be mine once my mom pays the final instalment.* **2** any of several parts issued at different times as a series: *The magazine printed the story in six instalments.* **3** the process of installing something. <Old French *estaler* to fix, from *estal* something fixed>

in·stance (in′stəns) *n* an occurrence or example of something: *Her rude question was a clear instance of bad manners.*
v **in·stanced, in·stanc·ing** **1** refer to as an example: *He instanced the fly as a disease-carrying insect.* **2** be an example of. <Old French, from Latin *instantia* presence>
for instance, as an example: *Her many hobbies—for instance, skating and drawing—keep her very busy.*

in·stant (in′stənt) *n* **1** an exact moment in time: *At that very instant the phone rang.* **2** a very short period of time: *It will only take an instant.*
adj **1** happening right away: *The medicine gave instant relief from pain.* **2** prepared very quickly, often without cooking, from premixed or fully processed ingredients: *instant pudding, instant coffee.* <Latin *instantem* present, from *instare* to be at hand> **in′stant·ly** *adv.*
the instant, just as soon as: *The instant he walked in the door, everyone stopped talking.*

in·stan·ta·ne·ous (in′stən tā′nē əs) *adj* done, happening, or acting immediately: *His reaction was instantaneous.* **in′stan·ta′ne·ous·ly** *adv.*

instant messaging (mes′ə jing) *Computers n* a form of real-time conversation on a computer network. An instant messaging system alerts the user whenever someone on the user's contact list is online and trying to get in contact. *Abbrev.* **IM** Compare TEXT MESSAGING, CHAT ROOM.

instant replay *n* an immediate playback of part of a TV broadcast, typically one in slow motion of action in a sports event.

in·stead (in sted′) *adv* in place of someone or something else: *If you can't go, let him go instead.* <Middle English *in stede* in place (of)>

in·step (in′step) *n* the inner arch of the human foot between the toes and the heel.

in·sti·gate (in′stə gāt′) *v* **ins·ti·gat·ed, in·sti·gat·ing** start something, especially something undesirable: *She denied that she instigated the argument.* <Latin *in-* toward + *stigare* spur on> **in′sti·ga′tion** *n.* **in′sti·ga′tor** *n.*

in·stil or **in·still** (in stil′) *v* **in·stilled, in·still·ing** put in little by little: *Reading good books instils a love for fine literature.* <Latin *instillare* let drip in>

in·stinct (in′stingkt) *n* **1** a natural, inborn ability or fixed pattern of behaviour, like that which guides animals: *Birds build nests by instinct.* **2** a natural talent or sensitivity: *Even as a child, the artist had an instinct for colour.* <Latin *instinctus* drive from within, from *instinguere* urge> **in·stinc′tive** *adj.* **in·stinc′tive·ly** *adv.*

in·sti·tute (in′stə tyūt′) *or* (in′stə tūt′) *n* **1** (*usually in names*) an organization or society for the support or promotion of a particular cause: *the Institute for Technological Studies, the Canadian National Institute for the Blind.* **2** the building used by such an organization: *We spent the afternoon at the Art Institute.* **3** an educational institution: *a collegiate institute.*
v **in·sti·tut·ed, in·sti·tut·ing** set up or establish: *The*

police instituted an inquiry into the causes of the accident. <Latin *in-* in + *statuere* establish, from *status* position>

in·sti·tu·tion (in′stə tyū′shən) *or* (in′stə tū′shən) *n* **1** an organization or society established for some public or social purpose: *A church, school, college, hospital, or prison is an institution.* **2** a building used by such an organization or society. **3** an established law, custom, or system: *The birthday supper is an institution in our family.* **4** the act of establishing or setting up something.

in·sti·tu·tion·al (in′stə tyū′shə nəl) *or* (in′stə tū′shə nəl) *adj* **1** characteristic of institutions, especially in being impersonal, dull, inflexible or regimented: *institutional food. She hated the institutional life of the boarding school.* **2** intended for or carried out in institutions rather than private households or consumers: *institutional care of the elderly. Their main business is in institutional sales rather than retail trade.* **in′sti·tu′tion·al·ism′** *n.* **in′sti·tu′tion·al·ize′** *v.*

in·struct (in strukt′) *v* **1** teach a subject or skill: *to instruct someone in the basics of grammar.* **2** give directions or orders to: *He instructed the boys to clean up the yard.* **3** inform or tell: *Our teacher instructed us that the final test would be next Friday.* **in·struc′tor** *n.*

ETYMOLOGY

Instruct comes from Latin *instructus*, from *in-*, meaning "on" + *structus*, the past form of *struere*, meaning "pile" or "build." The same root appears in *construct, construe, destructive,* and *structure*.

in·struc·tion (in struk′shən) *n* **1** the teaching of a subject or skill: *instruction in drawing techniques.* **2 instructions** *pl* **a** orders: *She refuses to obey instructions.* **b** information provided with something, telling how to use it: *The kit comes with instructions for assembling the model.* **in·struc′tion·al** *adj.*

in·struc·tive (in struk′tiv) *adj* useful for learning: *A field trip is an instructive experience.* **in·struc′tive·ly** *adv.*

in·stru·ment (in′strə mənt) *n* **1** a device that a person plays in order to make music, such as a flute or guitar: *stringed instruments.* **2** a tool or mechanical device: *surgical instruments. A thermometer is an instrument for measuring temperature.* **3** a person or thing used by another to get something done: *Joan of Arc believed she was God's instrument.* **4** a formal legal document, such as a contract, deed, or grant. <Latin *instrumentum* a tool>

in·stru·men·tal (in′strə men′təl) *adj* **1** acting or serving as a means: *His uncle was instrumental in getting him a job.* **2** performed on or written for a musical instrument: *an instrumental arrangement. He prefers instrumental music to vocal.*

in·stru·men·tal·ist (in′strə men′tə list) *n* a person who plays a musical instrument.

in·stru·men·ta·tion (in′strə men tā′shən) *n* **1** the arrangement of music for instruments. **2** tools, etc. used in industry or science.

instrument flying *n* the piloting of an aircraft by the use of instruments only, without being able to see points or objects on the ground.

instrument panel *n* a panel displaying gauges, indicator lights, and switches on an aircraft, motor vehicle, or other machine so that the operator can check and control specific functions.

in·sub·or·di·na·tion (in′sə bȯr′də nā′shən) *n* defiance of authority: *The junior officer was disciplined for insubordination.* **in′sub·or′di·nate** *adj.*

in·sub·stan·tial (in′səb stan′shəl) *adj* **1** frail or flimsy: *as insubstantial as a cobweb.* **2** small or meagre: *a rather insubstantial meal.* **3** with no material reality: *Dreams are insubstantial.* **in′sub·stan·ti·al′i·ty** (in′səb stan shē al′ i tē) *n.* **in′sub·stan′tial·ly** *adv.*

in·suf·fer·a·ble (in suf′ə rə bəl) *adj* too extreme to tolerate: *insufferable rudeness.* **in·suf′fer·a·bil′i·ty** *n.* **in·suf′fer·a·ble·ness** *n.* **in·suf′fer·a·bly** *adv.*

in·suf·fi·cient (in′sə fish′ənt) *adj* less than is needed: *I get grumpy when I've had insufficient sleep.* **in′suf·fi′cien·cy** *n.* **in′suf·fi′cient·ly** *adv.*

in·su·lar (in′sə lər) *adj* **1** ignorant or uninterested in cultures, ideas, or peoples outside one's own experience: *an insular point of view.* **2** to do with an island or its inhabitants: *an insular climate, an insular people.* <Latin *insula* island> **in′su·lar′i·ty** *n.*

in·su·late (in′sə lāt′) *v* **in·su·lat·ed, in·su·lat·ing** **1** surround with a non-conducting material to keep from losing or transferring electricity, heat, or sound. **2** protect from hardship or negative influences, often by setting apart from others: *Private school is not meant to insulate you from life in the real world.* <Latin *insula* island>

in·su·la·tion (in′sə lā′shən) *n* **1** the material used in insulating: *We need quite a few batts of insulation for the garage.* **2** the act or means of insulating.

in·su·la·tor (in′sə lā tər) *n* a device to prevent contact between wires, electrical conductors, etc.

in·su·lin (in′sə lin) *n* **1** a hormone secreted in the pancreas, that enables the body to regulate the amount of sugar in the blood. **2** a preparation that contains this hormone, used especially to treat diabetes.

ETYMOLOGY

Insulin is related to *insular* and *insulate*; they all come from Latin *insula*, meaning "island."

Insulin is secreted by the pancreas in several masses of endocrine cells, and each mass of cells is thought of as a small island or *islet*; together, they are called the *islets of Langerhans*.

Canadians Frederick Grant Banting and John James Richard Macleod won the 1923 Nobel Prize for Medicine for discovering insulin.

insulin shock *n* a state of physical collapse caused by an excess of insulin in the blood.

a bat	e bed	i bid	o pot	u cup	th **thin**
ā cake	ē me	ī bite	ō go	ū rude	ᴛʜ **then**
ä bar	ə about	ər over	ȯ for	ů put	zh measure

in·sult (in sult′) *for v*, (in′sult) *for n. v* speak to or treat with contempt or great rudeness: *The rebels insulted the flag by throwing mud on it. Such a question insults my intelligence.*
n an act or remark that insults someone: *To be called a coward is an insult.* <Latin *insalire* jump on>
in·sult′ing *adj.*

in·su·per·a·ble (in sū′pə rə bəl) *adj* that cannot be passed over or overcome: *an insuperable barrier.* <Latin *in-* not + *superare* surmount> **in·su′per·a·bil′i·ty** *n.* **in·su′per·a·ble·ness** *n.* **in·su′per·a·bly** *adv.*

in·sup·port·a·ble (in′sə pȯr′tə bəl) *adj* **1** unbearable or intolerable: *insupportable living conditions.* **2** that cannot be defended or justified: *insupportable rudeness.* **in′sup·port′a·bil′i·ty** *n.* **in′sup·port′a·bly** *adv.*

in·sur·ance (in shů′rəns) *n* **1** a practice or arrangement by which regular payments are made in return for a guarantee that compensation will be paid should loss or damage occur: *accident insurance, health insurance.* **2** the business that provides such protection: *My aunt works in insurance.* **3** the amount of money for which a person or thing is insured: *Is $150 000 enough life insurance?* **4** the amount of money paid for insurance: *We pay our insurance in monthly instalments.* **5** a means of protection or security: *Good health habits are an insurance against illness.*

in·sure (in shūr′) *v* **in·sured, in·sur·ing** **1** arrange for money payment in case of loss or damage to property or health, or in case of death: *It costs a lot to insure a new car against collision, because the car costs so much to replace.* **2** make safe or secure. See ENSURE for confusable. <variant of *ensure*> **in·sur′a·ble** *adj.* **in·sur′er** *n.*

in·sur·gent (in sər′jənt) *n* a person who takes part in a revolt: *The insurgents captured the town.*
adj taking part in a revolt: *Insurgent forces captured the radio station.* <Latin *in-* against + *surgere* rise> **in·sur′gence** *n.*

in·sur·mount·a·ble (in′sər moun′tə bəl) *adj* that cannot be overcome: *insurmountable obstacles.*
in′sur·mount′·a·bil′i·ty *n.* **in′sur·mount′a·ble·ness** *n.* **in′sur·mount′a·bly** *adv.*

in·sur·rec·tion (in′sə rek′shən) *n* a revolt or rebellion. <Latin *in-* against + *surgere* to rise up>
in′sur·rec′tion·ist *n.*

in·tact (in takt′) *adj* with no part missing or damaged: *When we unpacked the dishes after the move, they were all intact.* <Latin *in-* not + *tangere* to touch>

in·tagl·io (in tal′yō) *n* a design cut into the surface of metal or stone. <Italian, from *in-* into + *tagliare* cut>

in·take (in′tāk′) *n* **1** the place where water, air, or some other substance enters a pipe, machine, or tank. **2** the process of taking in, or the substance or amount taken in: *The average daily intake from the water main was 10 m.*

in·tan·gi·ble (in tan′jə bəl) *adj* **1** not capable of being touched or handled: *Sound and light are intangible.* **2** not easily understood: *She had that intangible quality called charm.* **in·tan′gi·bil′i·ty** *n.*

in·te·ger (in′tə jər) *Mathematics n* any positive or negative whole number, or zero. <Latin = a whole>

in·te·gral (in′tə grəl) *or* (in teg′rəl) *adj* **1** necessary to the completeness of something: *The arts are an integral part of a person's education.* **2** entire or complete. **3** *Mathematics* involving whole numbers or zero. <Latin *integer* a whole>

in·te·grate (in′tə grāt′) *v* **in·te·grat·ed, in·te·grat·ing** **1** bring or be joined together into a whole: *Let's integrate all these suggestions into one master plan.* **2** bring in different individuals or groups to become a fully connected part of a larger group: *to integrate immigrants into Canadian society.* **3** unify or harmonize the parts of: *an integrated personality. Consumers and the packaging industry should integrate their plans to reduce the amount of garbage we make.* <Latin *integer* a whole> **in′te·gra′tion** *n.*

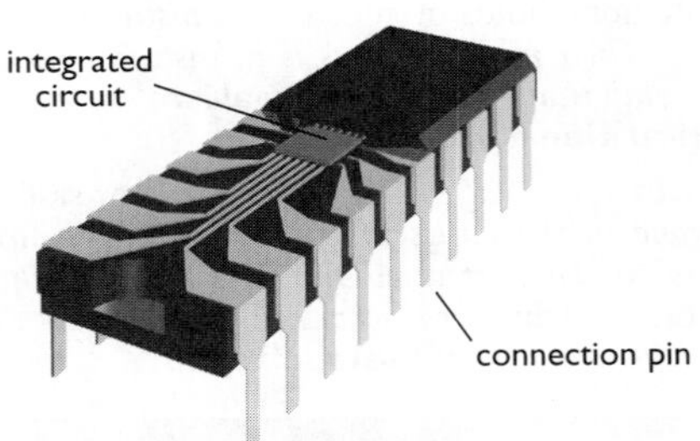

integrated circuit *n* an electronic circuit that incorporates many components in a single chip made from a semiconductor.

in·teg·ri·ty (in teg′rə tē) *n* **1** firm attachment to moral principles and to high standards: *Her poetry is too commercial to have integrity.* **2** the state of being whole and undivided, or the fact of being unbroken or undamaged: *Do cutbacks threaten the integrity of the health-care system?* <Latin *integer* whole>

in·teg·u·ment (in teg′jə mənt) *n* a natural outer covering of an animal or plant, like the skin of an animal.

in·tel·lect (in′tə lekt′) *n* **1** the power of reasoning and understanding: *Some people's actions are influenced more by emotion than by intellect.* **2** the mental powers of a particular person: *Einstein was one of the greatest intellects of all time.* <Latin *intelligere* understand, from *inter-* between + *legere* choose. Thinking was viewed as a process of choosing, in the sense of sorting through ideas or pieces of information to fit them together.>

in·tel·lec·tu·al (in′tə lek′chū əl) *adj* **1** to do with the intellect or mind: *Thinking is an intellectual process.* **2** enjoying or inclined toward things that involve or challenge the mind: *intellectual tastes, an intellectual person.*
n a person with a highly developed intellect: *a magazine designed for intellectuals.* **in′tel·lec′tu·al·ly** *adv.*

in·tel·li·gence (in tel′ə jəns) *n* **1** the ability to learn and know. **2** information, often secret, of military, commercial, or political value: *The government received secret intelligence of the enemy's plans.* **3 a** the work of getting or passing on secret information: *She worked in intelligence during the war.* **b** a group or agency engaged in this work: *Intelligence had failed to inform them of the planned attack.*

intelligence quotient IQ.

in·tel·li·gent (in tel′ə jənt) *adj* **1** with or showing a highly developed ability to learn and think: *an intelligent student, an intelligent remark.* **2** with intelligence or able to reason: *Is there intelligent life on other planets?* **3** with certain data storage or processing capabilities: *intelligent terminal.* <Latin *intelegere* understand> **in·tel′li·gent·ly** *adv.*

in·tel·li·gent·si·a (in tel′ə jent′sē ə) *or* (in tel′ə gent′sē ə) *n* (*with singular or plural verb*) intellectuals and highly-educated people considered as a group. <Russian, from Latin *intelligere* understand>

in·tel·li·gi·ble (in tel′ə jə bəl) *adj* capable of being understood: *He was so upset that his report was barely intelligible.* **in·tel′li·gi·bil′i·ty** *n.* **in·tel′li·gi·bly** *adv.*

in·tem·per·ate (in tem′pə rit) *adj* showing a lack of restraint or self-control, especially in the use of alcohol. **in·tem′per·ance** *n.* **in·tem′per·ate·ly** *adv.*

in·tend (in tend′) *v* **1** have in mind as a purpose or plan: *We intend to go home soon. When I said that, I intended no insult.* **2** design or set aside for a particular purpose or use: *That gift was intended for you.* <Old French, from Latin *intendere* turn one's attention to>

In·tend·ant (in ten′dənt) *n* the most important administrative officer in New France, eventually responsible for finance, justice, and police in the colony. <Latin *intendere* attend to>

in·tend·ed (in ten′did) *adj* planned or meant: *an intended insult. The medicine did not have the intended effect.*

in·tense (in tens′) *adj* **1** of a very high degree: *intense pain, an intense colour.* **2** strenuous, eager, or passionate: *intense thought. She lived an intense life.* **3** to do with strong or deep feelings, desires, or intentions: *an intense face. He is an intense person.* **in·tense′ly** *adv.* **in·ten′si·fy′** *v.* **in·ten′si·ty** *n.*

in·ten·sive (in ten′siv) *adj* **1** in-depth or detailed: *an intensive study of Shakespeare. After playing hockey for years, her knowledge of the game is intensive.* **2** (*in compounds*) using a lot of a certain kind of resource: *a labour-intensive job. Starting up a company is capital-intensive.* **3** *Grammar* adding emphasis. Example: In *You yourself said it,* the word *yourself* is an **intensive pronoun**.
n Grammar a word or prefix that adds emphasis. **in·ten′sive·ly** *adv.* **in·ten′sive·ness** *n.*

intensive care unit *n* a part of a hospital for patients who need **intensive care**, constant close monitoring of their medical condition. *Abbrev.* **ICU**

in·tent (in tent′) *n* **1** the goal of an action: *I took swimming lessons with the intent of becoming a lifeguard.* **2** meaning or significance: *What is the intent of that remark?*
adj **1** with the eyes or thoughts fixed on something: *an intent gaze.* **2** (*usually with* **on**) seriously engaged or much interested in: *She is intent on making money.* <Latin *intentus* intention, from *intendere* stretch toward> **in·tent′ly** *adv.*
to (or **for**) **all intents and purposes,** in almost every way; practically: *By the middle of June, the school year is finished, to all intents and purposes.*

in·ten·tion (in ten′shən) *n* **1** a determination to act in a certain way: *I'm sure she had no intention of hurting your feelings.* **2 intentions** *pl* **a** one's plans with respect to a particular situation or activity. **b** *Archaic* a man's plans regarding marrying a certain woman.

in·ten·tion·al (in ten′shə nəl) *adj* deliberate or planned with some purpose: *His insult was intentional; he wanted to hurt your feelings.* **in·ten′tion·al·ly** *adv.*

in·ter (in tər′) *v* **in·terred, in·ter·ring** bury a dead body in a grave or tomb. <Old French, from Latin *in-* in + *terra* earth>

CONFUSABLES

Inter means "bury": *They interred the dead woman.*

Intern means "confine (someone who might cause trouble)": *The police had to intern the angry suspect so that he wouldn't hurt anyone.*

inter– *prefix* **1** mutual: *interdependence.* **2** between or among: *intercontinental.* **3** involving more than one group or organization: *interbranch banking.* <Latin>

In·ter·ac (in′tə rak′) *Trademark n* an organization that administers a network of electronic financial services, including cash dispensing at bank machines and payment by debit card in stores.

in·ter·act (in′tə rakt′) *v* **1** take part in an exchange of some kind; have an effect on one another: *Students need time to interact with each other as well as with their teachers.* **2** *Computers* respond in a way that brings a response in turn from the program: *You can interact with this tutorial program so that it will spend more time on the things you need most help with.* **in′ter·ac′tion** *n.* **in′ter·ac′tive** *adj.* **in′ter·ac′tive·ly** *adv.*

in·ter·branch (in′tər branch′) *adj* between or involving different branches of a company, especially a financial institution: *interbranch banking, an interbranch memo.*

in·ter·breed (in′tər brēd′) *v* **in·ter·bred, in·ter·breed·ing** breed animals or plants by mating different varieties or species.

in·ter·cede (in′tər sēd′) *v* **in·ter·ced·ed, in·ter·ced·ing** **1** ask for help, mercy, or a favour on behalf of someone else: *Friends of the expelled student interceded with the authorities to give him a second chance.* **2** act as a mediator between parties in a conflict in order to help bring agreement. <Latin *inter-* between + *cedere* go>

in·ter·cel·lu·lar (in′tər sel′yə lər) *adj* between or among CELLS (def. 1).

in·ter·cept (in′tər sept′) *for v,* (in′tər sept′) *for n. v* seize or stop a person or thing on the way from one place to another: *On my way to class, the principal intercepted me with a message from home.*
n **1** *Mathematics* the distance on a graph from the origin to the point where a line crosses an axis. **2** an act or fact of intercepting something: *He studied the group of radio intercepts.* <Latin *inter-* between + *capere* catch> **in′ter·cep′tion** *n.* **in′ter·cep′tor** *n.*

a bat	e bed	i bid	o pot	u cup	th thin
ā cake	ē me	ī bite	ō go	ū rude	ᴛʜ then
ä bar	ə about	ər over	ȯ for	ů put	zh measure

in·ter·ces·sion (in′tər sesh′ən) *n* **1** the act or fact of interceding: *The judge's intercession saved the boy from a severe sentence.* **2** a prayer on behalf of someone else. **in′ter·ces′sor** *n.*

in·ter·change (in′tər chānj′) *for v,* (in′tər chānj′) *for n.* *v* **in·ter·changed, in·ter·chang·ing 1** put each of two things in the other's place: *The food processor has blades that can be interchanged for different purposes.* **2** cause to happen alternately: *to interchange work with play.*
n **1** a ramp or road leading from one highway or thoroughfare to another without crossing in front of other traffic: *Turn off at the next interchange.* **2** the act of interchanging: *an interchange of ideas between two groups.* **in′ter·change′a·ble** *adj.* **in′ter·change′a·bly** *adv.*

in·ter·com (in′tər kom′) *n* a system of radio or telephone communication, such as between rooms of a building, or parts of a ship or aircraft. <*intercommunication system*>

in·ter·con·nect (in′tər kə nekt′) *v* connect with each other. **in′ter·con·nect′ed** *adj.*

in·ter·con·ti·nen·tal (in′tər kon′tə nen′təl) *adj* involving more than one continent or capable of travelling between them: *intercontinental aircraft.*

intercontinental ballistic missile ICBM.

in·ter·course (in′tər kȯrs′) *n* **1** communications or dealings between people: *Intercourse between cultures has enriched our society.* **2** sexual intercourse. <Latin *inter-* between + *currere* to run>

in·ter·cul·tu·ral (in′tər kul′chər əl) *adj* between or involving different cultures.

in·ter·de·nom·i·na·tion·al (in′tər di nom′ə nā′shə nəl) *adj* between or involving different religious denominations.

in·ter·de·pend·ent (in′tər di pen′dənt) *adj* dependent on one another. **in′ter·de·pend′ence** *n.* **in′ter·de·pend′ent·ly** *adv.*

in·ter·dis·ci·plin·a·ry (in′tər dis′ə plə ner′ē) *adj* involving more than one academic subject or discipline: *The interdisciplinary unit "Agriculture Around the World" combines Geography and Life Sciences.*

in·ter·est (in′trist) *or* (in′trest) *n* **1** a feeling of wanting to know about something, or the quality that arouses such a feeling: *He has no interest in sports. The story lacks interest.* **2** something in which a person is involved: *My grandfather is retired, but has many interests that keep him busy.* **3** a fee paid for the use of someone else's money: *Banks charge interest when they give you a loan.* **4** a share in ownership: *She bought a half interest in the farm.* **5** advantage or benefit: *to look out for your own interest.* **6 interests** *pl* all those involved in a certain business: *mining interests.*
v **1** attract and hold the attention of: *Action movies do not interest me.* **2** cause a person to feel like doing something: *Can I interest you in something to eat?* <Old French, from Latin *interesse* be of importance>
in the interest of, a for the purpose of: *In the interest of keeping the peace, she let the matter rest.* **b** to the advantage of: *It is not in your interest to cheat; it only harms you.*

in·ter·est·ed (in′tris tid) *or* (in′tə res′tid) *adj* **1** feeling or showing interest: *a crowd of interested listeners. Are you interested in running for class president?* **2** involved or concerned: *A meeting will be held tonight for all interested parties.*

CONFUSABLES

Interested has two opposites:

Uninterested means "having no interest."

Disinterested means "impartial": *A disinterested onlooker offered to referee the game.*

in·ter·est·ing (in′tris ting) *or* (in′tə res′ting) *adj* attracting and holding one's attention: *an interesting book.* **in′ter·est·ing·ly** *adv.*

in·ter·face (in′tər fās′) *n* **1** an area where different systems, processes, or groups influence each other: *Taxation is the most important interface between government and business.* **2** a surface that forms a common boundary between two portions of matter or space: *the interface of air and water.* **3** *Computers* a device or program connecting computers or applications with each other, or connecting either of these with other machines.
v **in·ter·faced, in·ter·fac·ing 1** bring or come into contact or interaction: *Consultants must interface with clients on a regular basis.* **2** *Computers* connect with an interface.

in·ter·fac·ing (in′tər fā′sing) *n* a stiff material placed between two layers of fabric to give greater firmness.

in·ter·faith (in′tər fāth′) *adj* open to or involving people of different religious faiths: *interfaith dialogue.*

in·ter·fere (in′tər fēr′) *v* **in·ter·fered, in·ter·fer·ing 1** happen or act in such a way as to change or conflict with something else: *I will be there on Saturday if nothing interferes. El Niño interferes with the normal weather patterns.* **2** take part without being invited to, or without any need to do so: *This has nothing to do with you, so don't interfere.* **3** *Sports* hinder the action of an opponent in an illegal way. <Old French *enterferir* to collide, from Latin *inter-* between + *ferire* strike>

in·ter·fer·ence (in′tər fē′rəns) *n* **1** the act or fact of interfering: *I resent your interference in my plans for the weekend.* **2** something that interferes. **3** *Radio, Television* confusion of signals, such as that producing static or distortion of sound. **4** *Hockey* the illegal hindering of an opponent not in possession of the puck.
run interference (for), a *Football* clear the way for the ball carrier. **b** act as a go-between or screen, handling any problems: *She never has to deal directly with the public because her assistant runs interference for her.*

in·ter·fer·on (in′tər fē′ron) *n* a protein released by a body cell in response to a virus or other antigen and that helps to prevent the spread of infected cells. <*interfere*>

in·ter·ga·lac·tic (in′tər gə lak′tik) *adj* between galaxies: *intergalactic dust.*

in·ter·gen·er·a·tion·al (in′tər jen′ə rā′shə nəl) *adj* between different generations: *intergenerational conflict.*

in·ter·im (in′tə rim) *n* the time between: *The house won't be ready till September, so we'll be living with my grandparents in the interim.*
adj for the meantime; temporary: *The investigation is not complete, but we have an interim report.* <Latin = meanwhile>

in·te·ri·or (in tē′rē ər) *n* **1** the inner part or surface: *The interior of the house was beautifully decorated.* **2 a** the regions away from the coast or border, often those less developed: *The interior of the island is sparsely populated.* **3** 🍁 the inland area of British Columbia. **4** a picture or stage setting of the inside of a room or house: *The watercolour exhibit featured some landscapes and some interiors.*
adj **1** on the inside: *an interior wall.* **2** away from the coast or border: *the interior regions.* **3** to do with affairs within a country. **4** known only to oneself: *interior longings.* <Latin = inner>

interior angle *Mathematics n* **1** any of the four angles formed on the inner sides of two parallel lines by a straight line cutting through them. **2** the angle formed on the inside of a polygon between two adjacent sides. Compare EXTERIOR ANGLE.

interior decoration *n* the art and practice of planning furnishings and decorations for the interior of homes, offices, and other buildings. **interior decorator** *n.*

interior monologue *n* a part of a story or novel that expresses a character's thoughts.

in·ter·ject (in′tər jekt′) *v* say abruptly or as an interruption: *Every now and then the speaker interjected some witty remark.* <Latin *interjicere* to place between>

in·ter·jec·tion (in′tər jek′shən) *n* something interjected, such as a word or remark. **in′ter·jec′tion·al** *adj.*

GRAMMAR AND USAGE

An **interjection** is a word that expresses emotion such as shock, surprise, sadness, or excitement. Interjections often stand alone rather than as part of a sentence. Some common interjections: *ah, aha, excellent, hello, hey, oh, oops, ouch, sh, wow.*

Use an exclamation mark when an interjection expresses a very strong or sudden emotion: *Aha!*

in·ter·lace (in′tər lās′) *v* **in·ter·laced, in·ter·lac·ing** **1** cross threads, branches, etc., so that they go over and under each other: *Baskets are made by interlacing fibres.* **2** cross in an intricate manner: *interlacing highways.*

in·ter·lard (in′tər lärd′) *v* mix so as to give variety to: *The speaker interlarded her long speech with amusing stories.* <French, from Latin *inter-* between + *lardum* fat, from the custom of mixing strips or layers of lard with meat, to preserve the meat or make it tastier.>

in·ter·leave (in′tər lēv′) *v* **in·ter·leaved, in·ter·leav·ing** insert a leaf or leaves of paper between pages.

in·ter·lin·e·ar (in′tər lin′ē ər) *adj* inserted between the lines of a text.

in·ter·lin·ing (in′tər lī′ning) *n* an extra lining between the outer fabric of a garment and the lining: *The coat has a warm woollen interlining.*

in·ter·link (in′tər lingk′) *v* link together.

in·ter·lock (in′tər lok′) *v* join or fit tightly together: *The two stags interlocked their horns.*

in·ter·loc·u·tor (in′tər lok′yə tər) *n* a person who takes part in a conversation or dialogue. <Latin *inter-* between + *loqui* speak>

in·ter·lop·er (in′tər lō′pər) *n* a person who intrudes on or meddles in other peoples affairs. <*inter-* between + Dutch *lopen* to run>

in·ter·lude (in′tər lūd′) *n* **1** anything thought of as filling the time between two things: *There were only a few interludes of fair weather during the rainy season.* **2** a piece of music played between the parts of a song, religious service, or play. <Latin *inter-* between + *ludus* play>

in·ter·mar·riage (in′tər mar′ij) *or* (in′ter mer′ij) *n* **1** marriage between members of different religious, social, or ethnic groups. **2** marriage between close relatives. **in′ter·mar′ry** *v.*

in·ter·me·di·ar·y (in′tər mē′dē er′ē) *n,*
pl **in·ter·me·di·ar·ies** a person who deals with each side in settling a dispute or negotiating an agreement: *She acted as intermediary in the land deal between the city and the developer.*
adj **1** acting between two people or groups as an intermediary: *an intermediary agent.* **2** being between two things: *A chrysalis is an intermediary stage between caterpillar and butterfly.*

in·ter·me·di·ate (in′tər mē′dē it) *adj* being between extremes or in a middle stage: *Grey is intermediate between black and white. The language school offers only beginning and intermediate courses in French.*
v **in·ter·me·di·at·ed, in·ter·me·di·at·ing** act as an intermediary. <Latin *inter-* between + *medius* in the middle>

in·ter·ment (in tər′mənt) *n* the act of putting a dead body into a grave or tomb. <Old French, from Latin *in-* in + *terra* earth>

in·ter·mez·zo (in′tər met′sō) *or* (in′tər med′zō) *Music n, pl* **in·ter·mezzos** or **in·ter·mez·zi** (in′tər met′sē) *or* (in′tər med′zē) **1** a short dramatic, musical, or other entertainment of a light character between the acts of a drama or opera. **2** an independent composition of similar character. <Italian>

in·ter·mi·na·ble (in tər′mə nə bəl) *adj* endless or so long as to seem endless: *an interminable speech.* **in·ter′min·a·bil′i·ty** *n.* **in·ter′min·a·ble·ness** *n.* **in·ter′mi·na·bly** *adv.*

in·ter·mis·sion (in′tər mish′ən) *n* a break between periods of activity, especially, between acts of a play or musical performance: *The rain continued all day without intermission. There were two fifteen-minute intermissions in the performance.* <Latin *inter-* between + *mittere* put>

a bat	e bed	i bid	o pot	u cup	th thin
ā cake	ē me	ī bite	ō go	ū rude	ᴛʜ then
ä bar	ə about	ər over	ô for	ů put	zh measure

in·ter·mit·tent (in′tər mit′ənt) *adj* stopping and beginning again: *The intermittent noise of passing trucks kept her awake.* <Latin *inter-* between + *mittere* put> **in′ter·mit′tent·ly** *adv.*

in·tern (in tərn′) *n* a medical doctor who completes training by working in a hospital: *The new interns found the long hours exhausting.*
v **1** force to stay in a certain place, especially during a war: *Foreigners are sometimes interned in wartime.* **2** serve as an intern. See INTER for confusable. <French, from Latin *internus* within>

in·ter·nal (in tər′nəl) *adj* **1** of or on the inside: *internal injuries.* **2** to be taken inside the body: *internal remedies.* **3** coming from within: *The date of the author's death is unknown, but events in the story provide internal evidence that she was still alive in 1920.* **4** to do with activities within a country: *internal politics.* <Latin *internus* within> **in·ter′nal·ly** *adv.*

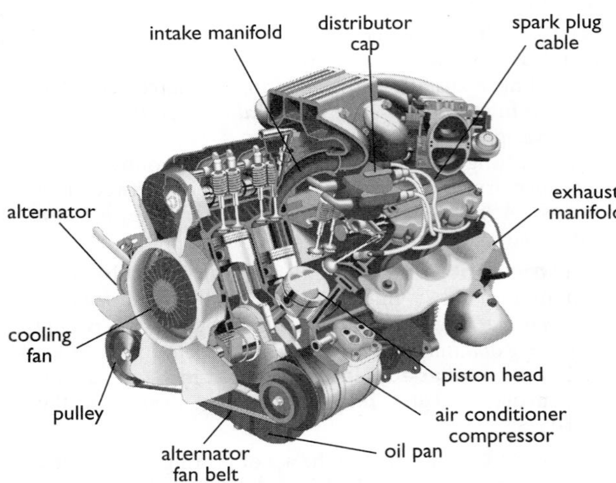

internal combustion engine *n* an engine in which the power is produced by gas or vapour exploding and expanding inside a cylinder and driving the piston: *Automobiles have internal combustion engines.*

in·ter·nal·ize (in tər′nə līz) *v* **in·ter·nal·ized, in·ter·nal·iz·ing** **1** learn so thoroughly that it becomes part of one's own thinking, attitudes, or character. **2** make subjective. **in·ter′nal·i·za′tion** *n.*

internal revenue *n* government income from taxes.

internal rhyme *n* a rhyme in which a rhyming syllable is in the middle of the line rather than at the end.

in·ter·na·tion·al (in′tər nash′ə nəl) *or* (in′tər nash′nəl) *adj* **1** between or among nations: *international trade.* **2** accepted by or agreed on by many or all nations: *an international driver's licence, an international unit of measure, international law.* **3** for the use of all nations: *international waters.* **in′ter·na′tion·al·ly** *adv.*

International Court of Justice *n* the official name of the World Court, the main judicial body of the United Nations, which settles disputes between member states. It is made up of representatives from various countries.

International Date Line DATE LINE.

in·ter·na·tion·al·ism (in′tər nash′ə nə liz′əm) *or* (in′tər nash′nə liz′əm) *n* **1** the state or process of existing between or among nations. **2** the principle of international co-operation for the good of all nations. **in′ter·na′tion·al·ist** *n.*

in·ter·na·tion·al·ize (in′tər nash′ə nə līz′ or in′tər nash′nə līz) *v* **in·ter·na·tion·al·ized, in·ter·na·tion·al·iz·ing** bring territory under the control of several nations: *internationalize commerce, an internationalized city.* **in′ter·na′tion·al·i·za′tion** *n.*

International Joint Commission *n* a committee set up by Canada and the US to settle possible disputes concerning boundary waters.

international law *n* the body of rules that most nations recognize as binding in international relations.

International Monetary Fund *n* an agency of the United Nations that is intended to stabilize the currencies of the world and that lends money to member nations. *Abbrev.* **IMF**

International Standards Organization ISO.

international unit IU.

in·ter·ne·cine (in′tər nē′sən) *or* (in′tər nē′sīn) *adj* destructive to both sides in a conflict. <Latin *inter-* between + *necere* kill>

in·tern·ee (in′tər nē′) *n* a person who is interned: *The prisoners of war became internees for several years.*

In·ter·net (in′tər nĕt) *Computers n* (*with* ***the***) a computer network that links smaller networks around the world, providing access to information, e-mail, and many other services. See also WORLD WIDE WEB. Also called **the Net**.

Internet café *Computers n* a place where one can pay to use a computer with Internet access, usually per hour or minute. It usually operates as a regular café as well.

in·tern·ment (in tərn′mənt) *n* the state of being forced to stay in a certain place, especially during a war.

in·tern·ship (in′tərn ship′) *n* a position of or period of service as an intern.

in·ter·of·fice (in′tər o′fis) *adj* between offices within an organization: *an interoffice memo.*

in·ter·per·son·al (in′tər pūr′sə nəl) *adj* between individuals: *interpersonal relations. His interpersonal skills leave something to be desired.*

in·ter·plan·e·tar·y (in′tər plan′ə ter′ē) *adj* existing or taking place between planets: *interplanetary space, interplanetary travel.*

in·ter·play (in′tər plā′) *n* the action or influence of things on each other: *the interplay of light and shadow.*

In·ter·pol (in′tər pol′) *n* in full, the **International Criminal Police Commission** an organization that co-ordinates the activities of police of participating nations to control international crime.

in·ter·po·late (in tər′pə lāt′) *v* **in·ter·po·lat·ed, in·ter·po·lat·ing** **1** insert text or other matter between fixed points, especially in a book. **2** *Mathematics* insert intermediate terms in a series. <Latin *inter-* between + *polare* alter>

in·ter·po·la·tion (in tər′pə lā′shən) *n* **1** the act of interpolating. **2** something interpolated: *an old manuscript with many interpolations of later date.*

in·ter·pose (in′tər pōz′) *v* **in·ter·posed, in·ter·pos·ing** **1** put between. **2** put forward as an interruption: *She interposed an objection.* **3** intervene in a dispute: *The teacher quickly interposed between the students who were arguing.* <French, from Latin *inter-* between + *ponere* put> **in′ter·pos′er** *n.*

in·ter·pret (in tər′prit) *v* **1** explain the meaning of: *to interpret a difficult passage in a book, to interpret a dream.* **2** perform in a certain way to bring out the meaning of a dramatic part, a character, or a piece of music. **3** understand according to one's own judgment: *We interpreted your silence as consent.* **4** translate as an interpreter: *She interprets for our Spanish visitors.* <Latin *interpretari* explain>

SYNONYMS

Interpret explains a meaning: *We interpreted his reply as an apology.*

Clarify makes a meaning clearer: *Can you clarify the problem for me?*

Construe analyzes a meaning: *How would you construe his answer?*

in·ter·pre·ta·tion (in tər′prə tā′shən) *n* **1** an explanation: *different interpretations of the same facts.* **2** a performance so as to bring out the meaning of a dramatic part or piece of music: *The critics praised the actor's interpretation of Hamlet.*

in·ter·pre·ta·tive (in tər′prə tə tiv) *or* (in tər′prə tā′tiv) INTERPRETIVE.

in·ter·pret·er (in tər′prə tər) *n* a person who interprets, especially one whose work is translating a language orally, as in a conversation between people who do not understand each other's language: *The government leaders spoke through an interpreter.*

in·ter·pre·tive (in tər′prə tiv) *adj* **1** explanatory. **2** performed in a way to bring out the meaning of a dramatic part, a character, or a piece of music: *interpretive dance.* Also, **interpretative**. **in·ter′pre·tive·ly** *adv.*

🍁 **in·ter·pro·vin·cial** (in′tər prə vin′shəl) *adj* between or among provinces, or connecting two or more provinces: *interprovincial agreements, an interprovincial highway.* **in′ter·pro·vin′cial·ly** *adv.*

in·ter·quart·ile range (in′tər kwor′tīl) *n* the difference between the upper quartile and the lower quartile.

in·ter·ra·cial (in′tər rā′shəl) *adj* between or involving different races. **in′ter·ra′cial·ly** *adv.*

in·ter·reg·num (in′tər reg′nəm) *n, pl* **in·ter·reg·nums** or **in·ter·reg·na** (in′tər reg′nə) **1** the time between the end of one ruler's reign and the beginning of the next one. **2** a time during which a nation is without its usual ruler or government. **3** a period of inactivity. <Latin *inter-* between + *regnum* reign>

in·ter·re·late (in′tər ri lāt′) *v* **in·ter·re·lat·ed, in·ter·re·lat·ing** relate to one another: *The two questions are interrelated.* **in′ter·re·la′tion** *n.* **in′ter·re·la′tion·ship** *n.*

in·ter·ro·gate (in ter′ə gāt′) *v* **in·ter·ro·gat·ed, in·ter·ro·gat·ing** ask questions of, especially formally and systematically: *The lawyer took two hours to interrogate the witness.* <Latin *inter-* between + *rogare* ask> **in′ter·ro·ga′tion** *n.* **in·ter′ro·ga′tor** *n.*

in·ter·rog·a·tive (in′tə rog′ə tiv) *adj* **1** having the form of a question: *an interrogative look or tone of voice.* **2** used in asking questions: *an interrogative pronoun.*
n an interrogative word, especially a pronoun: *The word* who *is an interrogative.*

GRAMMAR AND USAGE

Interrogatives are the words used in asking questions. Interrogative adverbs are *where, when, why,* and *how*, and their compounds (such as *wherever* and *however*). Interrogative pronouns are *who, which, what,* and *their* compounds (*whoever, whichever, whatever*).

The interrogatives *who, why, when, where,* and *what* are called the five W's.

in·ter·rupt (in′tə rupt′) *v* **1** stop the continuous progress of an activity: *A fire drill interrupted the lesson. It is not polite to interrupt when someone is talking.* **2** obstruct or break the continuity of: *A building interrupts the view from our window.* <Latin *inter-* between + *rumpere* to break> **in′ter·rupt′er** *n.*

in·ter·rup·tion (in′tə rup′shən) *n* **1** the act of interrupting or being interrupted: *The rain continued without interruption all day.* **2** something that interrupts: *It's hard to study when there are so many interruptions.*

in·ter·sect (in′tər sekt′) *v* **1** cut or divide by passing through or crossing. **2** cross each other: *Streets in Canada usually intersect at right angles.* <Latin *inter-* between + *secare* to cut>

in·ter·sec·tion (in′tər sek′shən) *or* (in′tər sek′shən) *n* **1** the process of intersecting: *the intersection of two lines. Bridges are used to avoid the intersection of a railway and a highway.* **2** a point, line, or place where two or more things, such as roads, cross each other: *The light changed just before we got to the intersection.* **3** *Mathematics* the set of elements common to two or more given sets.

in·ter·sperse (in′tər spərs′) *v* **in·ter·spersed, in·ter·spers·ing** **1** decorate or vary with other things put here and there: *The lawn was interspersed with beds of flowers.* **2** made diversified by being scattered here and there: *He interspersed jokes throughout his talk.* <Latin *inter-* between + *spargere* scatter>

in·ter·state (in′tər stāt′) *adj* between states: *an interstate highway.*

in·ter·stel·lar (in′tər stel′ər) *adj* **1** existing between or among the stars: *interstellar space.* **2** carried on between stars or star systems: *plans for interstellar travel.*

a bat	e bed	i bid	o pot	u cup	th **thin**
ā cake	ē me	ī bite	ō go	ū rude	ᴛʜ **then**
à bar	ə about	ər over	ô for	ù put	zh measure

in·ter·stice (in tər′stis) *n, pl* **in·ter·sti·ces** (in tər′stə sēz′) a small or narrow space between things or parts. <Latin *inter-* between + *-stare* to stand>

in·ter·trib·al (in′tər trī′bəl) *adj* between tribes.

in·ter·twine (in′tər twīn′) *v* **in·ter·twined, in·ter·twin·ing** twist or become twisted together: *Two vines intertwined on the wall.*

in·ter·val (in′tər vəl) *n* **1** the time or space between: *an interval of a week, intervals of freedom from pain. There are trees at intervals of ten metres.* **2** *Music* the difference in pitch between two tones. <Latin *inter-* between + *vallum* fence, originally referred to the space between the stakes of a fence>
at intervals, a now and then: *Stir the mixture at intervals.* **b** here and there: *We saw many lakes at intervals along the way.*

in·ter·vene (in′tər vēn′) *v* **in·ter·vened, in·ter·ven·ing** **1** exist or come between: *A week intervenes between Canada Day and my birthday.* **2** come in to help settle a dispute: *The prime minister intervened in the garbage strike.* <Latin *inter-* between + *venire* come>
in′ter·ven′er *n.*

SYNONYMS

Intervene involves stepping in to solve or settle something: *Mom intervened to stop the conflict.*

Arbitrate means "making a decision in a dispute": *The referee had to arbitrate when the coaches argued.*

Mediate involves acting as a go-between in a dispute: *The retired judge mediated the strike.*

in·ter·ven·tion (in′tər ven′shən) *n* **1** the act of intervening: *The strike was settled by the intervention of the Federal Government.* **2** interference, especially by one nation in the affairs of another. **3** an action taken to improve a situation, especially the course of an illness or disease.

in·ter·ven·tion·ist (in′tər ven′shən ist) *n* **1** a person who supports interference in the affairs of another country. **2** a person who is quick to recommend medical treatment rather than let an illness or disease take its natural course.
adj to do with such a person or such an attitude. **in′ter·ven′tion·ism** *n.*

in·ter·view (in′tər vyū′) *n* **1** a meeting of people face to face, to talk over something specific: *My father had an interview with the teacher about my work.* **2** a meeting between a reporter or radio or TV presenter and a person from whom information is sought.
v meet and talk with, especially to obtain information: *Reporters interviewed the returning explorers.* <French *s'entrevoir* to see each other> **in′ter·view′er** *n.*

in·ter·weave (in′tər wēv′) *v* **in·ter·wove** or **in·ter·weaved, in·ter·wov·en, in·ter·weav·ing** **1** weave together. **2** blend or connect closely: *In his book, the author has interwoven the stories of two families.*

in·tes·tate (in tes′tāt) *adj* of a person, having made no valid will. The opposite is TESTATE. <Latin *in-* not + *testare* make a will>

in·tes·ti·nal (in tes′tə nəl) *adj* to do with the intestines. **in·tes′ti·nal·ly** *adv.*

in·tes·tine (in tes′tən) *n* **1** either of the two parts, the **small intestine** and the **large intestine**, of the alimentary canal that extends from the stomach to the anus. **2 intestines** *pl* the bowels. <Latin *intestina,* from *intus* within> **in·tes′ti·nal·ly** *adv.*

in·ti·fa·da (in ti fa′da) *n* the Palestinian resistance to the Israeli occupation of the West Bank and Gaza Strip since 1987. <Arabic = revolt>

in·ti·ma·cy (in′tə mə sē) *n, pl* **in·ti·ma·cies** **1** deep friendship. **2** a private or intimate act.

in·ti·mate[1] (in′tə mit) *adj* **1** known very well: *an intimate friend.* **2** resulting from deep familiarity: *an intimate knowledge.* **3** personal or private: *A diary is a very intimate book.*
n a close friend: *He invited his intimates to a special dinner.* <Latin *intimus* inmost> **in′ti·mate·ly** *adv.*

in·ti·mate[2] (in′tə māt′) *v* **in·ti·mat·ed, in·ti·mat·ing** **1** state or make known: *In a statement, the police officer intimated that an arrest would be made soon.* **2** suggest indirectly; hint: *She didn't say so, but she intimated that she intended to quit school.* <Latin *intimus* inmost>

in·tim·i·date (in tim′ə dāt′) *v* **in·tim·i·dated, in·tim·i·dat·ing** frighten, especially in order to influence or force: *The banker told police that the men had tried to intimidate him by telling him they were holding his wife as hostage.* <Latin *in-* in + *timidus* fearful>
in·tim′i·da′tion *n.* **in·tim′i·da′tor** *n.*

in·to (in′tū) *prep* **1** to or toward the inside of: *to go into the house. I will look into the matter.* **2** to the condition or form of: *to get into mischief, a house divided into ten rooms. Cold weather turns water into ice.* **3** to a further time in: *She worked on into the night.* **4** against: *He wasn't watching and ran into the wall.* **5** *Informal* involved with or deeply interested in: *She's really into science fiction these days.* <Old English>

in·tol·er·a·ble (in tol′ə rə bəl) *adj* unable to be endured: *The headache was almost intolerable.* **in·tol′er·a·bil′i·ty** *n.* **in·tol′er·a·ble·ness** *n.* **in·tol′er·a·bly** *adv.*

in·tol·er·ance (in tol′ə rəns) *n* **1** unwillingness to let others do and think as they choose, especially in matters of religion: *Religious intolerance has been the cause of many wars.* **2** inability or unwillingness to endure: *intolerance to penicillin, intolerance of popular music.*

in·tol·er·ant (in tol′ə rənt) *adj* **1** unwilling to let others do and think as they choose, especially in matters of religion. **2** unwilling to accept people of different backgrounds as equals. **in·tol′er·ant·ly** *adv.*

in·to·na·tion (in′tō nā′shən) *n* **1** a manner of producing speech: *She has a monotonous intonation. British intonation is different from standard Canadian intonation.* **2** the accuracy of musical pitch: *Intonation is a problem for cellists.*

in·tone (in tōn′) *v* **in·toned, in·ton·ing** read or recite in a singing voice: *A priest intones part of the service.* <Latin *in-* in + *tonus* tone>

in to·to (in′ tō′tō) *adv* entirely; completely; altogether. <Latin = as a whole>

in·tox·i·cant (in tok′sə kənt) *n* something that intoxicates, especially alcoholic liquor.
adj intoxicating: *an intoxicant drug.*

in·tox·i·cate (in tok′sə kāt′) *v* **in·tox·i·cat·ed, in·tox·i·cat·ing** 1 make drunk: *Too much wine intoxicates people.* 2 excite greatly: *The early election returns intoxicated her supporters with thoughts of victory.* <Latin *in-* in + *toxicum* poison> **in·tox′i·cat′ing** *adj.* **in·tox′i·cat′ing·ly** *adv.*

in·tox·i·cat·ed (in tok′sə kā′tid) *adj* 1 drunk. 2 greatly excited.

in·tox·i·ca·tion (in tok′sə kā′shən) *n* 1 drunkenness. 2 great excitement. 3 poisoning by a drug or toxic substance.

intra– *prefix* within, inside, or on the inside: *intravenous.* <Latin>

in·trac·ta·ble (in trak′tə bəl) *adj* stubborn or hard to manage. **in·trac′ta·bil′i·ty** *n.* **in·trac′ta·bly** *adv.*

in·tra·mu·ral (in′trə myu̇′rəl) *adj* taking place within the same school, college, or university. <*intra-* within + Latin *murus* wall>

in·tra·net (in′trə net) *Computers n* a network linking computers inside one organization.

in·tran·si·gence (in tran′sə jəns) *n* unwillingness to agree or compromise.

in·tran·si·gent (in tran′sə jənt) *adj* unwilling to agree or compromise.
n a person who is unwilling to agree or compromise. <Latin *in-* not + *transigere* agree> **in·tran′si·gence** *n.* **in·tran′si·gent·ly** *adv.*

in·tran·si·tive (in tran′sə tiv) *Grammar adj* of a verb, not taking a direct object. Some verbs, like *go*, are always intransitive; many verbs can be either intransitive or transitive. **in·tran′si·tive·ly** *adv.*

intrauterine device (in′trə yū′tər in) *or* (in′trə yū′tər īn′) IUD.

in·tra·ve·nous (in′trə vē′nəs) *adj* 1 within a vein or the veins. 2 into a vein: *an intravenous injection.* <Latin *intra-* inside + *vena* vein> **in′tra·ve′nous·ly** *adv.*

in–tray (in′trā) *n* a tray in a person's office for incoming mail, memos, or anything else that must be dealt with.

in·trep·id (in trep′id) *adj* fearless and adventurous: *an intrepid explorer.* <Latin *in-* not + *trepidus* alarmed> **in′tre·pid′i·ty** *n.* **in·trep′id·ly** *adv.*

in·tri·ca·cy (in′trə kə sē) *n, pl* **in·tri·ca·cies** 1 the state or quality of being intricate: *They admired the delicacy and intricacy of the design.* 2 something intricate: *the intricacies of international diplomacy.*

in·tri·cate (in′trə kit) *adj* 1 entangled or complicated: *an intricate knot, an intricate maze, an intricate plot.* 2 very hard to understand; puzzling: *an intricate problem.* <Latin *in-* into + *tricare* entangle> **in′tri·cate·ly** *adv.* **in′tri·cate·ness** *n.*

in·trigue (in trēg′) *or* (in′trēg) *for n,* (in trēg′) *for v. n* secret scheming or plotting: *The royal palace was filled with intrigue.*
v **in·trigued, in·tri·guing** 1 carry on a secret plot. 2 excite the curiosity and interest of: *The book's unusual title intrigued me.* <French, from Latin *intricare* entangle> **in·tri′guing** *adj.* **in·tri′guing·ly** *adv.*

in·trin·sic (in trin′sik) *or* (in trin′zik) *adj* belonging to a thing by its very nature: *The intrinsic value of a fifty-dollar bill is only that of a piece of paper.* <French, from Latin *intrinsecus* internal> **in·trin′si·cal·ly** *adv.*

in·tro (in′trō) *Informal n, adj* introduction or introductory: *Can you play a short intro to this song?* (*n*). *an intro course in psychology* (*adj*).

intro– *combining form* into: *introduction.*

in·tro·duce (in′trə dyūs′) *or* (in′trə dūs′) *v* **in·tro·duced, in·tro·duc·ing** 1 bring in: *She introduced a new subject into the conversation.* 2 put in or insert: *The doctor introduced a long tube into the man's throat.* 3 bring into use, notice, or knowledge: *to introduce a new word.* 4 a make known: *The chairman introduced the speaker to the audience.* b acquaint someone with something: *I introduced my cousin to the city by showing her the sights.* 5 begin with something: *He introduced his speech with a joke.* <*intro-* + *ducere* lead> **in′tro·duc′er** *n.*

in·tro·duc·tion (in′trə duk′shən) *n* 1 the act of introducing or being introduced: *The introduction of steel made skyscrapers easy to build. She gave me an introduction to her aunt.* 2 something that introduces, especially the first part of a book, speech, or piece of music leading up to the main part. 3 a first book for beginners. 4 something brought into use: *Radios are a later introduction than telephones.*

in·tro·duc·to·ry (in′trə duk′tə rē) *or* (in′trə duk′trē) *adj* used to introduce: *introductory remarks, an introductory offer.*

in·tro·spec·tion (in′trə spek′shən) *n* an examination and analysis of one's own thoughts and feelings.

in·tro·spec·tive (in′trə spek′tiv) *adj* inclined to examine one's own thoughts and feelings. <*intro-* + *specere* look> **in′tro·spec′tive·ly** *adv.*

in·tro·ver·sion (in′trə vər′zhən) *n* a tendency to be more interested in one's own thoughts and feelings than in other people or in what is going on around one.

in·tro·vert (in′trə vərt′) *n* a person more interested in his or her own thoughts and feelings than in other people or in what is going on around him or her. <*intro-* + *vertere* to turn>

in·trude (in trūd′) *v* **in·trud·ed, in·trud·ing** enter or put oneself where one is not invited or wanted: *If you are busy, I will not intrude.* <Latin *in-* in + *trudere* thrust> **in·trud′er** *n.*

in·tru·sion (in trū′zhən) *n* the act of entering or putting oneself where one is not invited or wanted.

in·tru·sive (in trū′siv) *adj* entering or putting oneself where one is not invited or wanted. **in·tru′sive·ly** *adv.*

a bat	e bed	i bid	o pot	u cup	th **thin**
ā cake	ē me	ī bite	ō go	ū rude	TH **then**
à bar	ə about	ər over	ȯ for	u̇ put	zh measure

in·tu·it (in tyū′ət) *or* (in tū′ət) *v* know or learn by intuition.

in·tu·i·tion (in′tyū ish′ən) *or* (in′tū ish′ən) *n* **1** immediate understanding of facts without reasoning: *His intuition told him that the strangers were not what they appeared to be.* **2** something understood in this way. <French, from Latin *intueri* contemplate>

in·tu·i·tive (in tyū′ə tiv) *or* (in tū′ə tiv) *adj* acquired by intuition: *intuitive knowledge.* **in·tu′i·tive·ly** *adv.*

I·nu·it (in′ū it), (in′yū it), *or* (in′yə wit) *pl n, sing* **I·nuk** an Aboriginal people living mainly in the Canadian Arctic and along the northwestern coasts of Alaska.
adj to do with these people: *Inuit games.* <Inuktitut *inuk* person>

GRAMMAR AND USAGE

In Canada, the word **Inuit**, which means "the people," should be used instead of *Eskimo*. The word Eskimo, which probably comes from a word in an Algonquian language, is considered insulting and is not used by the Inuit. The Inuit use their own Inuktitut names for their many different communities.

I·nuk (in′ůk) See INUIT.

i·nuk·shuk (i nůk′shůk) *n, pl* **i·nuk·shuks** or **i·nuk·shu·it** a stone cairn that has the rough outline of a human figure: *Inukshuks were traditionally built by the Inuit to serve as landmarks, or to drive caribou toward waiting hunters.* Also, **inuksuk**, **inukshook**.

ETYMOLOGY

Inukshuk means "the shape of a person" in Inuktitut. It comes from *inuk*, meaning "a person." The term **Inuit** comes from *inuk* as well.

In 1999, the inukshuk was chosen to symbolize the people of the north on the official flag for the territory of Nunavut.

I·nuk·ti·tuk (i nůk′tə tůk′) INUKTITUT.

I·nuk·ti·tut (i nůk′tə tůt′) *n* a language of the Inuit, also called **Inuinnaqtun** in the western Arctic and **Inuvialuktun** in the region of the Mackenzie River delta. Also, **Inuktituk**. <Inuktitut *inuk* person + *titut* speech>

in·un·date (in′ən dāt′) *v* **in·un·dat·ed, in·un·dat·ing** **1** overflow or flood: *The water from the swollen river inundated the valley.* **2** overwhelm, as if by a flood: *The contest winner was inundated by requests for interviews.* <Latin *in-* onto + *undare* flow> **in′un·da′tion** *n.*

I·nu·pi·at (i nū′pē at′) a language of the Inuit, understandable by speakers of Inuktitut. Also, **Inupiaq**.

in·ure (i nyůr′) *v* **in·ured, in·ur·ing** toughen or harden: *Many years in the wilderness had inured them to hardships.* <*en-* in + Old French *euvre* work> **in·ure′ment** *n.*

in·vade (in vād′) *v* **in·vad·ed, in·vad·ing** **1** enter with force or as an enemy: *Soldiers invaded the country. Grasshoppers invade fields and eat the crops. Disease invades the body.* **2** enter as if to take possession: *Tourists invaded the city.* **3** interfere with: *The law punishes people who invade the rights of others.* <Latin *in-* in + *vadere* go> **in·vad′er** *n.* **in·vas′ion** *n.*

in·va·lid[1] (in′və lid) *n* a person who is weak because of sickness or injury: *An invalid cannot get about and do things.*
adj **1** ill or weakened. **2** to do with an invalid: *an invalid diet.*
v remove from active service because of sickness or injury: *The wounded soldier was invalided home.* <Latin *invalidus* not strong>

in·val·id[2] (in val′id) *adj* not true because based on faulty information or reasoning: *an invalid statement. If a will is not signed, it is invalid.* **in·va·lid′·i·ty** *n.* **in·val′id·ly** *adv.*

in·val·i·date (in val′ə dāt′) *v* **in·val·i·dat·ed, in·val·i·dat·ing** deprive of force or effect: *Breaking this seal will invalidate the warranty.* **in·val′i·da′tion** *n.*

in·val·u·a·ble (in val′yə bəl) *or* (in val′yū ə bəl) *adj* extremely useful: *her invaluable assistance, without which they would never have succeeded.* **in·val′u·a·bil′i·ty** *n.* **in·val′u·a·ble·ness** *n.* **in·val′u·a·bly** *adv.*

in·var·i·a·ble (in ver′ē ə bəl) *adj* always the same; unchangeable: *After dinner it was her invariable habit to take a walk.* **in·var′i·a·bil′i·ty** *n.* **in·var′i·a·ble·ness** *n.* **in·var′i·a·bly** *adv.*

in·va·sion (in vā′zhən) *n* **1** the act of invading: *There has been no attempted invasion of Canada since 1812.* **2** an interference or encroachment: *She objected to the invasion of her privacy.* <Latin *in-* in + *vadere* go>

in·va·sive (in vā′ziv) *adj* **1** with the nature of an invasion, especially of one's privacy: *invasive questioning.* **2** tending to spread rapidly and harmfully, especially as a disease or a plant. **3** involving the use of instruments introduced into the body as part of a medical procedure. **in·va′sive·ly** *adv.* **in·va′sive·ness** *n.*

in·vec·tive (in vek′tiv) *n* a violent attack in words. <Latin *invectivus* abusive, from *invehi* to attack with words>

in·veigh (in vā′) *v* (*with* **against**) protest with great hostility: *She inveighed against the poor working conditions in the factory.* <Latin *in-* against + *vehere* carry>

in·vei·gle (in vā′gəl) *or* (in vē′gəl) *v* **in·vei·gled, in·vei·gling** win over by trickery: *The saleswoman inveigled the poor girl into buying four pairs of shoes.* <Old French *aveugle* blind, from Latin *ab-* without + *oculus* sight> **in·vei′gler** *n.*

in·vent (in vent′) *v* **1** design or create something that has not existed before: *Alexander Graham Bell invented the telephone.* **2** make up something, especially as a way to deceive: *to invent an excuse.* <Latin *invenire* discover>

in·ven·tion (in ven′shən) *n* **1** the act or process of inventing: *the invention of the wheel.* **2** the thing invented: *The airplane is an invention of the 1900s.* **3** the power of inventing: *To be a good novelist, a person needs invention.* **4** a made-up story, especially a falsehood: *Her account of the robbery was pure invention.*

in·ven·tive (in ven′tiv) *adj* good at inventing or quick to invent things: *An inventive person thinks up ways to save time, money, and effort.* **in·ven′tive·ly** *adv.* **in·ven′tive·ness** *n.*

in·ven·tor (in ven′tər) *n* a person who invents: *Abraham Gesner was the inventor of kerosene.*

in·ven·to·ry (in′vən tȯ′rē) *n, pl* **in·ven·to·ries** **1** a detailed list of articles with their estimated value. **2** a collection of articles that are so listed: *The storekeeper had a sale to reduce his inventory.*
v **in·ven·to·ried, in·ven·to·ry·ing** make a detailed list of: *Some stores inventory their stock once a month.* <Latin *inventorium*>

in·verse (in vərs′) *or* (in′vərs) *adj* reversed in position or direction: *DCBA is the inverse order of ABCD.*
n **1** *Mathematics* something reversed: *The inverse of 3/4 is 4/3.* **2** the direct opposite: *Evil is the inverse of good.* <Latin *in-* over + *vertere* turn> **in·verse′ly** *adv.*

inverse operation *Mathematics n* an operation that undoes another operation. Multiplication and division are inverse operations.

in·ver·sion (in vər′zhən) *n* **1** an inverting or being inverted. **2** something inverted.

in·vert (in vərt′) *v* **1** turn upside down: *to invert a glass.* **2** reverse in position, direction, or order: *If you invert "I can," you have "Can I?"* <Latin *in-* over + *vertere* turn>

in·ver·te·brate (in vər′tə brāt′) *or* (in vər′tə brit) *adj* **1** without a backbone. **2** to do with invertebrates: *invertebrate zoology.*
n an animal without a backbone. Shellfish are invertebrates. <Latin *in-* not + *vertebratus* jointed>

in·vest (in vest′) *v* **1** use money to buy something that is expected to produce a profit, or income, or both: *She invested money in stocks, bonds, and land. Learn to invest wisely.* **2** spend time or energy for later benefit: *A lot of time has been invested in our science project, so we hope it wins a prize.* **3** give power, authority, or right to: *He invested his lawyer with complete power to act for him.* **4** install in office with a ceremony: *A queen is invested by being crowned.* **5** surround with an armed force: *The enemy invested the city and cut it off from our army.* <Latin *in-* in + *vestis* clothing. *Invest* originally meant to clothe in the insignia of an office.>

in·ves·ti·gate (in ves′tə gāt′) *v* **in·ves·ti·gat·ed, in·ves·ti·gat·ing** search into carefully or examine closely: *to investigate a complaint. Detectives investigate crimes.* <Latin *investigare* to search into, from *in-* in + *vestigare* track> **in·ves′ti·ga′tion** *n.* **in·ves′ti·ga′tor** *n.*

in·ves·ti·ga·tive (in ves′tə gā′tiv) *adj* based on in-depth research: *investigative journalism.*

in·ves·ti·ture (in ves′tə chər′) *n* a formal ceremony conferring a person with honours or an office. <See INVEST.>

in·vest·ment (in vest′mənt) *n* **1** the use of money to buy something that is expected to produce a profit, or income, or both: *Getting an education is a wise investment of time and money.* **2** the amount of money invested: *Her investments amount to thousands of dollars.* **3** something that is expected to yield money as income or profit or both: *Canada Savings Bonds are a safe investment.* **4** the act of surrounding with an armed force. **5** investiture.

investment bank *n* a company that buys large holdings of newly issued securities and resells them to investors.

in·ves·tor (in ves′tər) *n* one who invests money.

in·vet·er·ate (in vet′ə rit) *adj* **1** confirmed in a habit, practice, or feeling: *an inveterate gambler.* **2** long and firmly established: *Cats have an inveterate dislike of dogs.* <Latin *inveterare* become old, from *in-* into + *veteris* old> **in·vet′er·ate·ly** *adv.*

in·vig·i·late (in vij′ə lāt′) *v* **in·vig·i·lat·ed, in·vig·i·lat·ing** supervise the writing of an exam. <Latin *in-* on + *vigilare* keep watch> **in·vig′i·la′tion** *n.* **in·vig′i·la′tor** *n.*

in·vig·or·ate (in vig′ə rāt′) *v* **in·vig·or·at·ed, in·vig·or·at·ing** fill with life and energy: *The brisk weather was invigorating.* <Latin *in-* in + *vigere* thrive> **in·vig′or·at′ing** *adj.* **in·vig′or·at′ing·ly** *adv.*

in·vin·ci·ble (in vin′sə bəl) *adj* too powerful to be overcome: *The champion wrestler seemed invincible.* <Old French, from Latin *in-* not + *vincere* conquer> **in·vin′ci·bil′i·ty** *n.* **in·vin′ci·bly** *adv.*

in·vi·o·la·ble (in vī′ə lə bəl) *adj* that must not be violated or injured: *an inviolable vow, an inviolable sanctuary.* **in·vi′o·la·bil′i·ty** *n.* **in·vi′o·la·bly** *adv.*

in·vi·o·late (in vī′ə lit) *or* (in vī′ə lāt′) *adj* free or safe from violation or injury. **in·vi′o·late·ly** *adv.* **in·vi′o·late·ness** *n.*

in·vis·i·ble (in viz′ə bəl) *adj* **1** not capable of being seen: *Thought is invisible.* **2** not in sight: *The queen kept herself invisible in her palace.* **3** too small to be perceived: *Germs are invisible to the naked eye.* **in·vis′i·bil′i·ty** *n.* **in·vis′i·bly** *adv.*

invisible ink *n* ink that is colourless, and thus invisible, until treated with a chemical, heat, or light.

in·vi·ta·tion (in′və tā′shən) *n* **1** a request to be at some place or to do something: *Formal invitations are written or printed.* **2** the act of inviting. **3** temptation or inducement: *Leaving the keys in the car was an open invitation to theft.*

invitational *adj* open only to those specifically invited to participate: *an invitational tournament.*
n Sports a tournament by invitation.

in·vite (in vīt′) *for v,* (in′vīt) *for n. v* **in·vit·ed, in·vit·ing** **1** ask someone politely to be at some place or to do something: *We invited her to join us.* **2** make a polite request for: *to invite an opinion.* **3** tend to cause: *Carelessness invites trouble.* **4** attract or encourage: *The calm water invited swimming.*
n Informal an INVITATION (def. 1). <Latin *invitare*>

in·vit·ee (in vī′tē) *n* one who has been invited.

in·vit·ing (in vī′ting) *adj* attractive or tempting: *A cold drink is inviting on a hot day.* **in·vit′ing·ly** *adv.*

in vit·ro (vē′trō) *Biology adj, adv* taking place as a process or reaction within an artificial environment, such as a test tube: *in vitro fertilization* (*adj*), *to cultivate plant cells in vitro* (*adv*). <Latin = in glass>

in vitro fertilization *n* the artificial process of fertilizing eggs with sperm in a laboratory.

a bat	e bed	i bid	o pot	u cup	th **thin**
ā cake	ē me	ī bite	ō go	ū rude	TH **then**
ȧ bar	ə about	ər over	ȯ for	u̇ put	zh measure

I

in·vo·ca·tion (in′və kā′shən) *n* **1** an appeal for help or protection through prayer. **2** a calling forth of spirits or a god by magic. <See INVOKE.>

in·voice (in′vois) *n* a form listing goods sent to a purchaser showing prices, amounts owing, and other information.
v **in·voiced, in·voic·ing** make an invoice. <Old French *envoi* send goods, from *envoyer* to send>

in·voke (in vōk′) *v* **in·voked, in·vok·ing 1** appeal to an authority to perform an action or support an argument. **2** ask earnestly for: *The condemned criminal invoked the judge's mercy.* **3** summon a spirit or call forth by magic: *In the story of Aladdin, the hero invoked the genie of the magic lamp.* <Latin *in-* in + *vocare* call>

in·vol·un·tar·y (in vol′ən ter′ē) *adj* **1** not done of one's own free will: *She was threatened until she gave involuntary consent to the plan.* **2** not done on purpose: *An accident is involuntary.* **3** concerned with bodily processes that are not controlled by the will: *Breathing is mainly involuntary.* **in·vol′un·tar′i·ly** *adv.* **in·vol′un·tar′i·ness** *n.*

in·volve (in volv′) *v* **in·volved, in·volv·ing 1** have as a necessary part, condition, or result: *Housekeeping involves cooking and cleaning.* **2** have an effect on: *These changes to the environment involve all of us.* **3** cause to be unpleasantly concerned: *One foolish mistake can involve you in a lot of trouble.* **4** complicate: *A sentence that is involved is often hard to understand.* **5** take up the attention of: *She was involved in working out a puzzle.* <Latin *involvere* surround> **in·volve′ment** *n.*

in·volved (in volvd′) *adj* **1** complicated or intricate: *The situation is too involved for me to explain it to you.* **2** (*with* **with**) having a romantic relationship: *Is she involved with anyone right now?*

in·vul·ner·a·bil·i·ty (in vul′nə rə bil′ə tē) *n* being invulnerable.

in·vul·ner·a·ble (in vul′nə rə bəl) *adj* impossible to harm or injure: *Achilles was invulnerable except for his heel.* **in·vul′ner·a·bil′i·ty** *n.* **in·vul′ner·a·bly** *adv.*

in–wait·ing (in wā′ting) (*in compounds*) **1** about to happen or to take form: *government-in-waiting.* **2** to do with the position of a royal attendant: *lady-in-waiting.*

in·ward (in′wərd) *adv* **1** toward the inside or centre: *a passage leading inward.* **2** into the mind or soul: *Turn your thoughts inward.* Also, **inwards.**
adj **1** placed within: *the inward parts of the body.* **2** directed toward the inside: *The hallway had an inward slant.* **3** within the mind or soul: *inward happiness.* <Old English *inweard*>

in·ward·ly (in′wər dlē) *adv* existing within the mind but not expressed: *She was inwardly pleased but said nothing.*

in–your–face (in′yūr fās′) *Informal adj* explicit and aggressive: *I don't mind discussing the problem; it's her in-your-face manner I don't like.*

i·o·dine (ī′ə dīn′) *n* **1** a non-metallic element, usually in the form of greyish crystals that give off a dense, purple vapour. Iodine is used in medicine, in making dyes, in photography, etc. *Symbol* **I 2** a brown liquid, sometimes called **tincture of iodine,** used as an antiseptic. <French, from Greek *ioeides* violet-coloured>

i·o·dize (ī′ə dīz′) *v* **i·o·dized, i·o·diz·ing** combine with iodine: *iodized salt.* **i′o·diz′er** *n.*

i·on (ī′on) *or* (ī′ən) *n* **1** an atom or group of atoms with a negative (**negative ion**) or positive (**positive ion**) electric charge as a result of having lost or gained one or more electrons. **2** an electrically charged particle formed in a gas. <Greek *ienai* go, so called because ions move toward electrodes that have an opposite charge>

–ion *suffix* **1** with a particular effect: *attraction.* **2** the condition or state of something: *adoption.* **3** the result of something having happened: *abbreviation.* <Latin>

i·on·ic (ī on′ik) *adj* to do with ions.

I·on·ic (ī on′ik) *adj* to do with one of the three types of classical Greek architecture, characterized by a column with scroll shapes at its top. See COLUMN for picture.

i·o·ni·um (ī ō′nē əm) *n* a naturally occurring radioactive isotope of thorium. *Symbol* **Io**

i·on·ize (ī′ə nīz′) *v* **i·on·ized, i·on·iz·ing** separate into ions: *Acids, bases, and salts ionize in solution.* **i′on·iz′er** *n.*

i·on·o·sphere (ī on′ə sfēr′) *n* a region of low-pressure ionized layers above the stratosphere that help to reflect radio waves so that they travel over long distances.

i·o·ta (ī ō′tə) *n* **1** a very small quantity: *There is not an iota of truth in the prisoner's story.* **2** the ninth letter of the Greek alphabet.

IOU or **I.O.U.** *n* an informal note showing a debt: *Write me an IOU for ten dollars.* <pronunciation of "*I owe you*">

IP in full, **Internet Protocol** the technology that enables data to be sent from one network to another over the Internet. IP divides up the data into units which then travel over the Internet and arrive at their destination in a scrambled order. A second protocol, **TCP** (**transmission control protocol**) rearranges the units back into their original order.

IPA or **I.P.A.** International Phonetic Alphabet.

IP address *Computers n* a numeric address, usually four sets of numbers separated by periods, that is given to servers and users connected to the Internet. For servers, it is translated into a domain name (URL). For users, it is assigned by the Internet Service Provider (ISP) when the user goes online.

ip·e·cac (ip′ə kak′) *n* a medicine made from the dried roots of a S American vine, used as an emetic or purgative. <Tupi (a language of S America) *ipe* small + *kaa* leaves + *guene* vomit>

ip·so fac·to (ip′sō fak′tō) *adv* by that fact or act: *If you resign as Class Representative, then that position is ipso facto vacant.* <Latin = by the fact itself>

IQ or **I.Q.** in full, **intelligence quotient** a number used to describe a person's relative intelligence in terms of certain kinds of thinking skills, measured in a standardized test.

ir–[1] *prefix* a form of IN-[1] occurring before the letter *r*: *irrational.*

ir–[2] *prefix* IN-[2] occurring before *r*: *irradiate.*

IRA Irish Republican Army.

I·ran (i ran′) *n* a country in southwest Asia. See the APPENDIX. **I·ra′ni·an** (i rā′nē ən) *adj, n.*

I·raq (i rȧk′) *n* a country in southwest Asia. See the APPENDIX. **I·ra′qi** (i rā′kē) *adj, n.*

i·ras·ci·ble (i ras′ə bəl) *adj* easily made angry or irritable. <Latin *ira* anger> **i·ras′ci·bil′i·ty** *n.* **i·ras′ci·bly** *adv.*

i·rate (ī′rāt) *or* (ī rāt′) *adj* angry. <Latin *ira* anger> **i′rate·ly** *adv.*

ire (īr) *n* anger. <Old French, from Latin *ira*>

Ire·land (īr′lənd) *n* an island of western Europe, most of it forming the **Republic of Ireland**, with the remainder being **Northern Ireland**, a part of the UNITED KINGDOM. See the APPENDIX.

i·ren·ic (ī ren′ik) *adj* promoting peace; conciliatory. <Greek *eirene* peace>

ir·i·des·cent (ir′ə des′ənt) *adj* displaying luminous colours that seem to change when seen from different positions. <Latin *iris* rainbow> **ir′i·des′cence** *n.* **ir′i·des′cent·ly** *adv.*

i·rid·i·um (i rid′ē əm) *n* a heavy, white metallic element that resembles platinum. *Symbol* **Ir** <*iridescent,* which it is in solution>

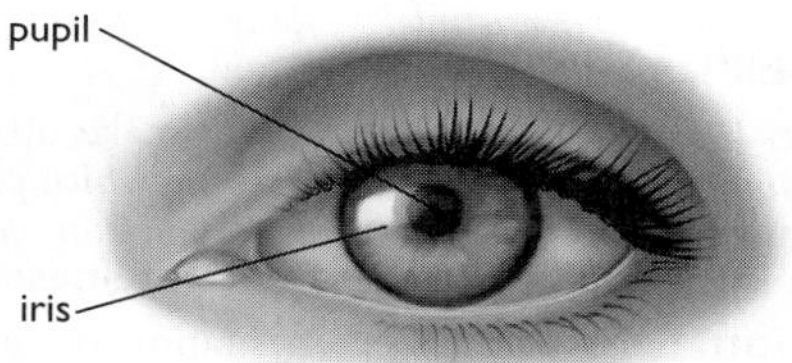

i·ris (ī′ris) *n* **1** a perennial plant found in temperate regions of the northern hemisphere, with sword-shaped leaves and large flowers. **2** the coloured part of the eye: *The iris controls the amount of light entering the eye.* <Latin, from Greek *iris* rainbow>

I·rish (ī′rish) *adj* to do with Ireland, its people, or their language.

Irish coffee *n* coffee with Irish whisky and whipped cream in it.

Irish stew *n* stew made of meat, potatoes, and onions.

irk (ərk) *v* irritate or annoy: *It irks me to wait for people who are always late.* <Middle English>

irk·some (ərk′səm) *adj* irritating or annoying: *Writing an essay by hand is an irksome task.* **irk′some·ly** *adv.* **irk′some·ness** *n.*

i·ron (ī′ərn) *n* **1** a strong, hard, metallic element, much used in industry and construction, especially in the form of steel. *Symbol* **Fe** **2** a tool, instrument, or weapon made from this metal: *A tire iron is used to remove automobile tires.* **3** a tool with a flat surface that is heated for smoothing cloth or pressing clothes. **4** a golf club with an iron or steel head. **5 irons** *pl* chains or bands of iron; handcuffs; shackles.
adj **1** made with iron: *an iron fence.* **2** hard, strong, or unyielding: *an iron determination, an iron will.*
v smooth or press something with a heated IRON (def. 3). <Old English *iren*>
a will of iron, a very stubborn will.
have (too) many irons in the fire, try to do (too) many things at once.
iron out, straighten out or smooth away: *A tactful person can iron out many problems between people.*
strike while the iron is hot, act while conditions are favourable.

Iron Age *n* a period of human culture characterized by the use of tools and weapons made of iron that in Europe began about 1000 BCE.

i·ron·clad (ī′ərn klad′) *adj* very hard to change or get out of: *An ironclad agreement can't be broken.*
n in the 1800s, a warship protected with iron plates.

Iron Curtain *n* an imaginary line thought of as separating the former Soviet Union and the nations under its control or influence from the rest of the world from about 1945 to 1989.

iron hand *n* a firm, strict manner.

i·ron·ic (ī ron′ik) *adj* **1** expressing one thing and meaning the opposite: *"Speedy" would be an ironic name for a pet turtle.* **2** contrary to what would naturally be expected: *It was ironic that the woman was run over by her own car.* **3** using or showing irony: *an ironic person, an ironic statement.* <See IRONY.>

ironing board *n* a board covered with a smooth cloth, used for ironing clothes on: *An ironing board usually has folding legs.*

i·ron·stone (ī′ərn stōn′) *n* a hard variety of white ceramic ware.

i·ron·weed (ī′ərn wēd′) *n* a plant of the same family as the aster, with clusters of small flowers.

i·ron–willed (ī′ərn wild′) *adj* with an exceptionally firm will.

i·ron·wood (ī′ərn wu̇d′) *n* a tree with very hard, heavy wood.

i·ro·ny (ī′rə nē) *n, pl* **i·ro·nies** **1** a method of expression in which the meaning intended is the opposite of that expressed: *Naming the thin dog "Fatty" was irony.* **2** an event or outcome contrary to what would naturally be expected: *It was the irony of fate that the great cancer doctor himself died of cancer.* <Latin, from Greek *eiron* pretender, i.e., pretending to be the opposite of what someone or something is>

GRAMMAR AND USAGE

Irony involves deliberately saying the opposite of what you mean, using tone of voice to show the real meaning: *"Nice weather!" she said glumly, during the thunderstorm.*

Sarcasm applies only to insulting remarks that, although perhaps stated ironically, are always intended to hurt: *"I didn't need those toes today, anyway," he snarled to the man who had stepped on his foot.*

a bat	e bed	i bid	o pot	u cup	th **thin**
ā cake	ē me	ī bite	ō go	ū rude	TH **then**
ȧ bar	ə about	ər over	ȯ for	u̇ put	zh measure

I

Ir·o·quoi·an (ir′ə kwo′yən) *n* **1** a group of N American Aboriginal languages, including Huron, Mohawk, Oneida, Onondaga, Cayuga, Seneca, Tuscarora, and Cherokee. **2** a member of any of the peoples that speak these languages. *adj* to do with any of these languages or the peoples that speak them.

Ir·o·quois (ir′ə kwo′) *or* (ir′ə kwoi′) *n, pl* **Ir·o·quois** in former times, a member of a confederacy of First Nations and Native American peoples called the Five Nations (Cayuga, Mohawk, Oneida, Onondaga, and Seneca) and later, with the addition of the Tuscarora, the Six Nations. These peoples lived mostly in Québec, Ontario, and northern New York State. See also HAUDENOSAUNEE.
adj to do with these people.

ir·ra·di·ate (i rā′dē āt′) *v* **ir·ra·di·at·ed, ir·ra·di·at·ing** **1** expose with radiation, especially expose food to gamma rays to kill micro-organisms. **2** make something shine by or as if by putting light on it. <Latin *irradiare,* from *in-* upon + *radius* ray> **ir·ra′di·a′tion** *n.*

ir·ra·tion·al (i rash′ə nəl) *adj* **1** not rational or reasonable: *It is irrational to be afraid of a harmless spider.* **2** unable to think and reason clearly. **ir·ra′tion·al·ly** *adv.*

ir·ra·tion·al·i·ty (i rash′ə nal′ə tē) *n, pl* **ir·ra·tion·al·i·ties** **1** the state of being irrational. **2** something irrational.

irrational number *Mathematics n* a number that cannot be expressed as a whole number or fraction. Its decimal expansion neither terminates nor repeats. Examples: π, $\sqrt{2}$

ir·rec·on·cil·a·ble (i rek′ən sī′lə bəl) *or* (i′rek′ən sī lə bəl) *adj* that cannot be made to agree or reconcile: *irreconcilable enemies.*
n an idea, fact, or statement that cannot be made compatible with another. **ir·rec′on·cil′a·bil′i·ty** *n.* **ir·rec′on·cil′a·bly** *adv.*

ir·re·cov·er·a·ble (ir′i kuv′ə rə bəl) *adj* that cannot be regained or remedied: *Wasted time is irrecoverable.* **ir′re·cov′er·a·ble·ness** *n.* **ir′re·cov′er·a·bly** *adv.*

ir·ref·u·ta·ble (i ref′yə tə bəl) *or* (ir′i fyū′tə bəl) *adj* that cannot be refuted or disproved: *an irrefutable statement.* **ir·ref′u·ta·bil′i·ty** *n.* **ir·ref′u·ta·ble·ness** *n.* **ir·ref′u·ta·bly** *adv.*

ir·reg·u·lar (i reg′yə lər) *adj* **1** out of the usual order or natural way: *irregular breathing.* **2** not even, smooth, or straight: *irregular features, an irregular coastline.* **3** not according to law or morals: *irregular behaviour.* **4** not inflected as a word in the usual way: *"Be" is an irregular verb.*
n a soldier not in a regular army unit. **ir·reg′u·lar·ly** *adv.*

ir·reg·u·lar·i·ty (i reg′yə lar′ə tē) *or* (i reg′yə ler′ə tē) *n, pl* **ir·reg·u·lar·i·ties** **1** a lack of regularity: *the irregularity of the coastline.* **2** something irregular: *There were a number of irregularities in the evidence.* **3** lack of regularity of bowel movements: *Do you suffer from irregularity?*

ir·rel·e·vance (i rel′ə vəns) *n* **1** the state or quality of being irrelevant. **2** something irrelevant.

ir·rel·e·vant (i rel′ə vənt) *adj* not connected or relevant to a subject: *A question about economics is irrelevant in a music lesson.* **ir·rel′e·vant·ly** *adv.*

ir·re·li·gious (ir′i lij′əs) *adj* indifferent or hostile to religion. **ir′re·li′gious·ly** *adv.*

ir·re·me·di·a·ble (ir′i mēd′i ə bəl) *adj* impossible to cure or repair. <Latin *in-* not + *remedium* remedy> **in′re·me′di·a·bil′i·ty** *n.* **ir′re·me′di·ab·ly** *adv.*

ir·rep·a·ra·ble (i rep′ə rə bəl) *adj* that cannot be repaired or made good: *The burnt money is an irreparable loss.* <Latin *in-* not + *reparare* repair> **ir·rep′a·ra·bil′i·ty** *n.* **ir·rep′a·ra·ble·ness** *n.* **ir·rep′a·ra·bly** *adv.*

ir·re·place·a·ble (ir′i plā′sə bəl) *adj* impossible to replace with another person or thing: *The photograph of my grandmother as a child was irreplaceable.* **ir′re·plac′a·bil′i·ty** *n.* **ir′re·place′·a·ble·ness** *n.* **ir′re·place′a·bly** *adv.*

ir·re·press·i·ble (ir′i pres′ə bəl) *adj* that cannot be repressed or restrained. **ir′re·press′i·bil′i·ty** *n.* **ir′re·press′i·bly** *adv.*

ir·re·proach·a·ble (ir′i prō′chə bəl) *adj* free from blame: *She had led an irreproachable life.* **ir′re·proach′a·bil′i·ty** *n.* **ir′re·proach′a·ble·ness** *n.* **ir′re·proach′a·bly** *adv.*

ir·re·sist·i·ble (ir′i zis′tə bəl) *adj* that cannot be resisted or withstood: *an irresistible desire to laugh.* **ir′re·sist′i·bil′i·ty** *n.* **ir′re·sist′i·bly** *adv.*

ir·res·o·lute (i rez′ə lūt′) *adj* **1** unable to make up one's mind: *He stood there irresolute, not knowing which path to try.* **2** lacking in resoluteness: *An irresolute person makes a poor leader.* **ir·res′o·lute·ly** *adv.* **ir·res′o·lute·ness** *n.*

ir·res·o·lu·tion (i rez′ə lū′shən) *n* hesitation or lack of resolution.

ir·re·spec·tive (ir′i spek′tiv) *adj* regardless: *Any person, irrespective of age, may join the club.*

ir·re·spon·si·ble (ir′i spon′sə bəl) *adj* **1** without or not showing a proper sense of responsibility: *It was irresponsible to leave the broken glass on the sidewalk.* **2** not responsible to any authority: *A dictator is an irresponsible ruler.* **ir′re·spon′si·bil′i·ty** *n.* **ir′re·spon′si·bly** *adv.*

ir·re·triev·a·ble (ir′i trē′və bəl) *adj* that cannot be retrieved or recovered. **ir′re·triev′a·bil′i·ty** *n.* **ir′re·triev′a·bly** *adv.*

ir·rev·er·ent (i rev′ə rənt) *adj* not reverent or respectful to something or someone usually taken seriously. **ir·rev′er·ence** *n.* **ir·rev′er·ent·ly** *adv.*

ir·re·vers·i·ble (ir′i vər′sə bəl) *adj* not capable of being undone or altered. **ir′re·vers′i·bil′i·ty** *n.* **ir′re·vers′i·bly** *adv.*

ir·rev·o·ca·ble (i rev′ə kə bəl) *or* (i′ re vōk′ə bəl) *adj* not to be recalled, withdrawn, or annulled: *an irrevocable decision.* <Latin *in-* not + *re-* back + *vocare* call> **ir·rev′o·ca·bil′i·ty** *n.* **ir·rev′o·ca·bly** *adv.*

ir·ri·gate (ir′ə gāt′) *v* **ir·ri·gat·ed, ir·ri·gat·ing** **1** supply land with water by means of ditches or sprinklers: *Farmers irrigate dry land to make crops grow better.* **2** wash out a wound or cavity in the body with a continuous flow of some liquid as part of medical treatment: *to irrigate the nose and throat with warm water.* <Latin *in-* in + *rigare* wet> **ir′ri·ga′tion** *n.*

ir·ri·ta·ble (ir′ə tə bəl) *adj* **1** easily made angry or impatient: *When the rain spoiled her plans, she was irritable for the rest of the day.* **2** unnaturally sensitive or

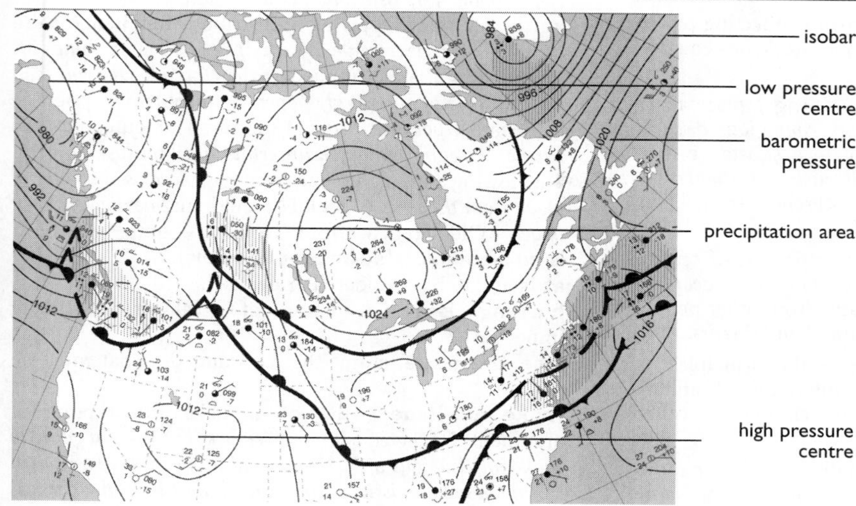

The numbers on the isobars shown on this map indicate the barometric pressure of the places the isobar connects. The map also shows centres of high and low atmospheric pressure; warm, cold, and stationary fronts; different types of air masses; and wind direction and speed.

Daily weather reports are based on the information shown on this type of map.

sore in a bodily part or organ: *A baby's skin is often quite irritable.* <Latin *irritare* enrage> **ir′ri·ta·bil′i·ty** *n.* **ir′ri·ta·ble·ness** *n.* **ir′ri·ta·bly** *adv.*

ir·ri·tant (ir′ə tənt) *n* a thing that causes irritation: *A mustard plaster is an irritant.*
adj causing slight inflammation or discomfort to the body.

ir·ri·tate (ir′ə tāt′) *v* **ir·ri·tat·ed, ir·ri·tat·ing** 1 make impatient or upset: *The boy's foolish questions irritated his father. Flies irritate horses.* 2 make unnaturally sensitive or sore: *Too much sun irritates the skin.* <Latin *irritare* enrage> **ir′ri·tat′ing** *adj.* **ir′ri·tat′ing·ly** *adv.*

ir·ri·ta·tion (ir′ə tā′shən) *n* 1 the act or process of feeling angry or impatient. 2 an irritated condition of the body: *An irritation in my nose made me sneeze.*

is (iz) *v* third person singular, present tense of BE: *The earth is round. He is at school.*
as is, in its present condition.

ISBN *n* in full, **International Standard Book Number** a ten-digit identification number that is assigned to a book before publication.

–ish *suffix* 1 somewhat: *sweetish.* 2 resembling or like: *a childish person.* 3 with the characteristics of: *a childish idea.* 4 to do with: *Spanish.* 5 near, but usually past: *fortyish.* <Old English *-isc*>

i·sin·glass (ī′zing glas′) *n* 1 a kind of gelatin obtained from fish, used for making glue and clarifying liquid. 2 thin, semi-transparent sheets of mica. <Dutch *huysenblass* fish bladder>

I·sis (ī′sis) *n* the ancient Egyptian goddess of fertility.

Is·lam (is′ləm) *or* (i slám′) *n* 1 the religion of Muslims, following the teachings of Muhammad as the prophet of the one God, Allah. 2 Muslims as a group. 3 the civilization of Muslim peoples. 4 all the countries in which Islam is the main religion. <Arabic = submission> **Is·lam′ic** (i slam′ik) *or* (i slá′mik) *adj.*

is·land (ī′lənd) *n* 1 **a** a body of land smaller than a continent and completely surrounded by water: *To reach the island, you go on a boat.* **b** 🍁 **the Island** Prince Edward Island or Vancouver Island. 2 something resembling this, especially in being isolated, detached, or surrounded in some way: *The city built a safety island at the busy intersection.* 3 a unit with a counter in a kitchen, allowing access from all sides. <Old English *igland*> **is′land·like′** *adj.*

is·land·er (ī′lən dər) *n* 1 a native or inhabitant of an island. 2 🍁 **Islander** a native or inhabitant of Prince Edward Island or Vancouver Island.

isle (īl) *n* an island, especially a small one.

is·let (ī′lit) *n* a tiny island.

ism (iz′əm) *n* a distinctive doctrine, theory, system, or practice: *Capitalism and communism are competing isms.*

–ism *suffix* 1 an action or practice: *criticism.* 2 a doctrine, system, or principle: *socialism.* 3 a quality, characteristic, or condition: *heroism.* 4 an example or illustration: *witticism.* 5 unfair discrimination on the basis of something: *ageism.* <Greek *ismos*>

Is·mae·li (is mā′li) *or* (is mī′li) *n* a Muslim of the Shia sect.
adj to do with this sect.

is·n't (iz′ənt) *contraction* is not.

iso– *prefix* equal: *isobar.* <Greek>

ISO *n* in full, **International Standards Organization** an organization that promotes universal standards for measurement, the meanings of technical terms, and workplace environments for various products and services.

i·so·bar (ī′sə bár′) *n* a line on a map connecting places with the same average atmospheric pressure. <Greek *iso-* equal + *baros* weight> **i′so·bar′ic** *adj.*

a bat	e bed	i bid	o pot	u cup	th **thin**
ā cake	ē me	ī bite	ō go	ü rude	ᴛʜ **then**
á bar	ə about	ər over	ȯ for	ú put	zh measure

i·so·hy·et (ī′sō hī′ət) *n* a line on a map connecting places with the same average precipitation. <Greek *iso-* equal + *hyetos* rain> **i′so·hy′e·tal** *adj.*

i·so·late (ī′sə lāt′) *v* **i·so·lat·ed, i·so·lat·ing 1** place apart or separate from others: *People with contagious diseases should be isolated.* **2** *Chemistry* obtain a substance in a pure or uncombined form: *A chemist can isolate the oxygen from the hydrogen in water.* <French, from Latin *insula* island>

i·so·la·tion (ī′sə lā′shən) *n* **1** the act or process of setting apart or being set apart: *The isolation of infectious people is essential.* **2** the state of being separated from other people or things: *Robinson Crusoe lived in isolation for years.*

i·so·la·tion·ism (ī′sə lā′shə niz′əm) *n* the principles or practice of not participating in international affairs, especially in wars or the political activities of other countries. **i′so·la′tion·ist** *n.*

i·so·mer (ī′sə mər) *n* **1** *Chemistry* either of two or more compounds that contain the same atoms in the same proportions, but that have different properties because their atoms are arranged differently. **2** *Physics* a nucleus of an atom that has the same atomic number and the same mass number as another, but has a different energy state. <Greek *iso-* equal + *meros* part> **i′so·mer′ic** *adj.* **i·som′er·ism′** *n.*

i·so·met·ric (ī′sə met′rik) *adj* to do with an exercise in which muscles are tensed then relaxed, without noticeable movement of body parts.

i·so·pro·pyl alcohol (ī′sə prō′pəl) *n* a colourless, flammable, poisonous liquid, used as rubbing alcohol, as a solvent, in cosmetics, and in antifreeze.

i·sos·ce·les (ī sos′ə lēz′) *Mathematics adj* **1** of a triangle, with two sides equal. **2** of a trapezoid, with the non-parallel sides equal. <Greek *isosceles* with equal sides, from *iso-* equal + *skelos* leg>

i·so·therm (ī′sə thərm′) *n* a line on a map connecting places with the same average temperature. <Greek *iso-* equal + *therme* heat>

i·so·tope (ī′sə tōp′) *Chemistry n* an atom of an element with the same number of protons and almost the same chemical properties, but with a different number of neutrons and different physical properties. For example, one of the isotopes of hydrogen is deuterium, sometimes called heavy hydrogen. <Greek *iso-* equal + *topos* place>

ISP *n* in full, **Internet Service Provider** a company that provides users with access to the Internet. For a monthly fee, the ISP provides a software package, a user name, a password, and an access number.

Is·ra·el (iz′ri əl) *or* (iz′rā əl) *n* a country in the Middle East, on the Mediterranean Sea. See the APPENDIX.
Is·rae′li (iz rā′lē) *adj, n.*

Is·sei (ēs′sā′) *n, pl* **Is·sei** a first-generation Japanese living in Canada or the US. Compare NISEI, SANSEI. <Japanese *ichi* one + *sei* generation>

is·sue (ish′ū) *v* **is·sued, is·su·ing 1** send out or come out from: *The government issues money and stamps. Smoke was issuing from the chimney.* **2** publish or put into public circulation: *to issue a new edition of a book, to issue a statement to the press.* **3** distribute to a person or people: *Heavy boots were issued to all the troops.*
n **1** the action of supplying or distributing an item for use or sale: *The next issue of stamps will be on June 11.* **2** something that is supplied or distributed: *Did you read the last issue of our weekly paper?* **3** a problem or point to be debated: *political issues.* **4** the result or outcome: *The issue of the game remained uncertain until the last moment.* **5** a flowing out or discharge: *A nosebleed is an issue of blood from the nose.* **6** a child or children: *She died without issue.* <Old French, from Latin *ex-* out + *ire* go> **is′su·a·ble** *adj.* **is′su·ance** *n.* **is′su·er** *n.*
at issue, to be considered or decided.
burning issue, a matter of great or immediate importance.
face the issue, admit the facts and do what must be done.
make an issue (out) of, a make into a point of argument: *I disagree with that remark, but I'm not going to make an issue out of it.* **b** *Informal* force others to notice: *He made such an issue of standing up that I asked what was wrong.*
take issue, disagree: *I take issue with you on that point.*

–ist *suffix* **1** a person who does or makes: *tourist.* **2** one who knows about or has skill with something: *biologist.* **3** one who believes in: *idealist.* **4** one who practises unfair discrimination on the basis of something: *sexist.* <Middle English *-iste*>

isth·mus (is′məs) *n, pl* **isth·mus·es** a narrow strip of land with water on either side, connecting two larger bodies of land: *The Isthmus of Panama connects North America and South America.* <Latin, from Greek *isthmos*>

it (it) *pron* **1** a thing or animal already referred to and identified: *I closed the door and locked it. The dog raised its paw. She washed the towels and folded them.* **2** the subject of an impersonal verb: *It is raining.* **3** an apparent subject of a clause when the real subject appears later. Example: In *It is hard to believe that she just left*, the real subject is the clause *that she just left.* You could say *That she just left is hard to believe.* **4** the antecedent to any relative pronoun when separated by the predicate: *It was a blue car that passed.*
n in certain children's games, the player who must catch, find, or guess someone or something. <Old English *hit*>

IT *n* in full, **information technology** all the technology involved in generating, storing, processing, retrieving, and transferring information electronically.

i·tal·ic (i tal′ik) *or* (ī tal′ik) *adj* to do with type in which the letters slant to the right: *These words are in italic type.*
n **1** an italic type, letter, or number. Also, **italics**. **2 Italic** a style of handwriting or calligraphy.

ETYMOLOGY

Italic type was introduced in the 1600s by an Italian printer of Venice, who gave the style this name to distinguish it from the upright letters of roman type. The term *italic* had been used earlier for a plain, sloping style of handwriting.

i·tal·i·cize (i tal′ə sīz′) *v* **i·tal·i·cized, i·tal·i·ciz·ing 1** print in type in which the letters slant to the right: *This sentence is italicized.* **2** underline with a single line to indicate italics: *We italicize words or expressions that are to be emphasized.* **i·tal′i·ci·za′tion** *n.*

It·al·y (it′əl ē) *n* a country in southern Europe. See the APPENDIX. **I·tal′i·an** (i tal′yən) *adj, n.*

itch (ich) *n* **1** a tickly feeling in the skin that makes one want to scratch. **2** a restless feeling or desire for something: *an itch to get away and explore.*
v feel a strong or restless desire to do something: *Mosquito bites itch. Wool makes me itch. She itched to know our secret.* <Old English *gyccan*> **itch′i·ness** *n.* **itch′y** *adj.*

CONFUSABLES

Itch is a noun that means "a sensation on the skin that creates the desire to scratch the area."

Scratch is a verb that means "rub or scrape the skin to relieve an itch."

I can't reach the itch on my back. Please scratch it for me.

it'd (it′əd) *contraction* **1** it had: *It'd been a hot day.* **2** it would: *It'd be a pleasure.*

–ite *suffix* a native or inhabitant of: *Vancouverite.* <Latin, from Greek *–ites* connected with>

i·tem (ī′təm) *n* **1** a separate thing or article: *The list contains twelve items. There were several interesting items in today's paper.* **2** *Informal* a couple recognized as romantically involved: *You and I are an item.*
adv (*used in introducing each item of a list*) also; likewise. <Latin = likewise>

i·tem·ize (ī′tə mīz′) *v* **i·tem·ized, i·tem·iz·ing** list by items: *to itemize the cost of a trip.*

it·er·ate (it′ə rāt′) *v* **it·er·at·ed, it·er·at·ing** produce or state repeatedly, often with slight modifications. <Latin *iterum* again> **it′er·a′tion** *n.*

i·tin·er·ant (ī tin′ə rənt) *adj* travelling from place to place, especially on a regular route: *an itinerant salesperson.*
n a person who travels from place to place. <Latin *itinerari* travel> **i·tin′er·ant·ly** *adv.*

i·tin·er·ar·y (ī tin′ə rer′ē) *n, pl* **i·tin·er·ar·ies** the route or plan of a journey. <Latin *itineris* journey>

–itis *suffix* inflammation of or inflammatory disease of: *appendicitis.* <Greek>

it'll (it′əl) *contraction* it will.

it's (its) *contraction* **1** it is: *It's my turn.* **2** it has: *It's been a beautiful day.*

its (its) *adj* a possessive form of IT: *The cat licked its paw.*
pron a possessive form of IT; that which belongs to it: *The dog's food bowl is its and its alone.* <Old English>

CONFUSABLES

It's means "it is" or "it has": *It's almost time to leave. It's been snowing all day.*

Its indicates possession: *The satisfied cat licked its paws.*

it·self (it self′) *reflexive pron* **1** the object of a reflexive verb with *it* as subject: *The dog came out of the lake and then it shook itself.* **2** an intensive pronoun, used to emphasize the noun or pronoun it follows: *The land itself is worth more than the price of the farm.* **3** its usual self: *After repairs, my bike is itself again.*

–ity *suffix* **1** a condition or quality: *sincerity.* **2** an example of this: *a monstrosity.* <French, from Latin *-itatis*>

IU or **I.U.** *n* in full, **international unit** an internationally agreed amount of a biologically active substance, such as a vitamin or hormone, that will produce a specific response when taken.

IUD *n* in full, **intrauterine device** a contraceptive device that is inserted and left in the uterus, preventing fertilized eggs from becoming implanted.

IV intravenous.

I've (īv) *contraction* I have.

i·vo·ry (ī′və rē) *or* (ī′vrē) *n, pl* **i·vo·ries** a hard, white substance. The tusks of an elephant, walrus, or narwhal are made of ivory: *The mass slaughter of wild animals caused some countries to ban trading in ivory.*
adj **1** made of ivory. **2** creamy white: *The room has ivory walls and a white ceiling.* <Old French, from Latin *ebur*>

ivory tower *n* a condition of withdrawal from the world of action into a world of ideas and dreams.

i·vy (ī′vē) *n, pl* **i·vies** a climbing plant with smooth, shiny leaves: *Poison ivy is not ivy at all; it is a type of cashew.* <Old English *ifig*>

Ivy League *n* a group of long-established, prestigious universities of the eastern US, including Harvard, Yale, and Princeton. <Many of the university buildings are ivy-covered.>

–ize *suffix* **1** make: *legalize.* **2** become: *crystallize.* **3** engage in, be busy with, or use: *apologize.* **4** treat with or combine with: *oxidize.* <French, from Greek *-izein*>

Jj

j or **J** (jā) *n, pl* **j's** or **J's** **1** the tenth letter of the English alphabet, or any speech sound represented by it. **2** the tenth thing in a list or series: *Do parts (a) to (j) in question 2.*

J joule(s).

jab (jab) *v* **jabbed, jab·bing** **1** thrust with something sharp or pointed: *He jabbed his fork into the potato.* **2** poke roughly or quickly: *Don't jab your finger at me!.* **3** pierce or stab: *I just jabbed myself with a pin.*
n a quick, sharp blow, especially with a fist or something pointed: *She gave him a jab with her elbow. The first boxer had a very fast left jab.* <Middle English *jobben*>

jab·ber (jab′ər) *v* talk very fast in a confused or senseless way.
n very fast, confused, or senseless talk. <imitative> **jab′ber·er** *n.*

jac·a·ran·da (ja′ kə ran′də) *n* a flowering tropical tree of the Americas. <Tupi-Guarani (a language of S America) *yacaranda*>

ja·cinth (jā′sinth) *n* a reddish orange gem, a variety of zircon. <Old French *jacinte,* from Latin *hyacinthos*>

jack (jak) *n* **1** a device for lifting or pushing up heavy weights a short distance: *Jacks are sometimes used to raise a house so that a basement may be added.* **2** an electrical device to receive a plug: *a telephone jack.* **3** a playing card with a picture of a royal servant on it. **4** a small ball for players to aim at in some forms of bowling. **5** a flag used on a ship to show nationality or as a signal. **6** (*in compounds*) the male of some animals: *jackrabbit.* **7** (*in compounds*) a person in a specialized job: *lumberjack.* **8** usually, **Jack a** an ordinary man, especially a manual labourer. **b** a sailor. **9** **jacks** *pl* pebbles or small bits of metal that are tossed and caught or picked up in various ways, or the children's game in which they are used. Also, **jackstones**.
v **1** lift or push up with a jack. **2** hunt or fish, especially illegally, by means of a jacklight. <Middle English *Jack,* variant of *John.* Common proper names were sometimes extended to tools or appliances. See also JIMMY.>
every man jack, *Informal* everyone.
jack up, a lift up with a jack. **b** *Informal* raise prices or wages by a considerable amount: *Stores jacked up many prices this month.*

jack·al (jak′əl) *or* (jak′ol) *n* a slender, long-legged wild animal of Africa and southern Asia, closely related to the dog: *Jackals hunt in packs at night and feed on small animals and carrion left by large animals.* <Persian *sagal*>

jack·a·napes (jak′ə nāps′) *n* an insolent, conceited person.

jack·ass (jack′as′) *n* **1** a male donkey. **2** a fool or very stupid person.

jack·boot (jak′būt′) *n* a heavy, leather, military boot reaching up to or above the knee.

jack·daw (jak′do′) *n* a small, grey-headed European crow that nests in tall buildings and chimneys.

jack·et (jak′it) *n* **1** an outer garment for the upper part of the body, with a front opening, sleeves, and, usually, a collar with lapels. **2** an outer covering, such as the skin of a potato or the casing around a pipe. **3** dust jacket. <Old French *jacque*> **jack′et·less** *adj.*

jack·fish (jak′fish′) *n, pl* **jack·fish** or **jack·fish·es** a fish of the pike family with a long, slender body and large head, found in most parts of Canada.

Jack Frost *n* frost or freezing cold weather, thought of as a person.

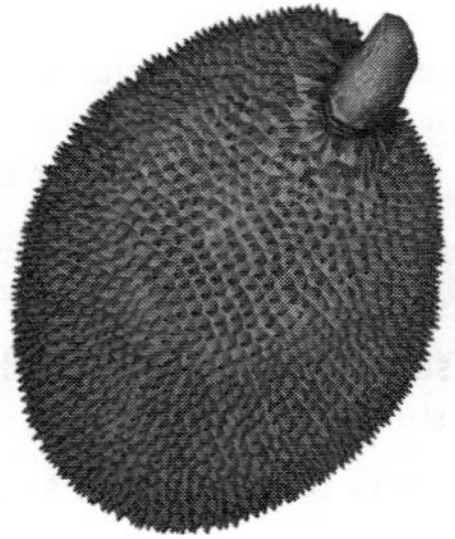

The **jackfruit** is the largest tree-borne fruit in the world, growing to 1 m long, 50 cm in diameter, and weighing up to 36 kg. It is yellow or green outside and tastes and smells somewhat like a banana.

jack·fruit (jak′frūt′) *n* the large, edible fruit of a tropical tree of Asia and America.

jack·ham·mer (jak′ham′mər) *n* a large, noisy power tool for drilling or breaking up rock or concrete, driven by compressed air.

jack–in–the–box (jak′ in ᴛʜə boks′) *n, pl* **jack-in-the-box·es** a toy figure that springs up from a box when the lid is unfastened.

jack–in–the–pul·pit (jak′ in ᴛʜə pu̇l′pit) *n, pl* **jack-in-the-pul·pits** a plant with a greenish hood arched up over a spike of tiny flowers: *The jack-in-the-pulpit is found from Nova Scotia to Ontario.*

jack·knife (jak′nīf′) *n, pl* **jack·knives** **1** a large, strong pocketknife. **2** a headfirst dive in which the diver touches the feet with the hands while keeping the legs straight, and then straightens out again before touching the water.
v **jack·knifed, jack·knif·ing** **1** double up like a jackknife. **2** perform a jackknife dive. **3** double up at the connecting hitch when a trailer or railway car is suddenly stopped or thrown off course.

🍁 **jack·light** (jak′līt′) *n* a light used for hunting or fishing at night: *Fish or game are attracted by the jacklight so that they may be easily caught.*
v hunt or fish, especially illegally, by means of a jacklight. **jack′light′er** *n.*

🍁 **jack·light·ing** (jak′lī′ting) *n* the act or practice, often illegal, of hunting or fishing with a jacklight.

jack of all trades *n* a person who can do many different kinds of work adequately.

jack–o'–lan·tern (jak′ə lan′tərn) *n* a pumpkin hollowed out and cut to look like a face, used at Halloween.

jack pine *n* a pine tree of Ontario, Québec, and the Prairie Provinces, with stiff, sharp needles and cones that are often curved.

jack·pot (jak′pot′) *n* **1** a large fund of money that is competed for regularly and that increases as contestants fail to win it. **2** in poker, the stakes that accumulate until some player wins with a pair of jacks or something better.

hit the jackpot, *Informal* **a** win a jackpot. **b** have sudden great success, such as making a lot of money quickly.

jack·rab·bit (jak′rab′it) *n* a large hare of western N America with very long ears and long back legs.

jack·stones (jak′stōnz′) JACK (*n* def. 9).

jack·straws (jak′stro′) *n* a game played with a set of straws or strips of wood thrown down in a pile. These have to be picked up one at a time without any of the rest of the pile being moved.

Jac·o·be·an (jak′ə bē′ən) *adj* to do with the architecture or furniture styles of the reign of King James I of England, from 1603 to 1625. <Latin *Jacobus* James>

Jac·o·bite (jak′ə bīt) *n* in England, a supporter of James II (1633–1701) and his descendants in their claims to the throne. <Latin *Jacobus* James> **Jac′o·bite′** *adj.*

Ja·cob's–lad·der (jā′kəbz lad′ər) *n* a flowering garden plant with rows of ladderlike leaves.

jac·quard (jə kard′) *adj* to do with a fabric woven on a **jacquard loom**, which produces elaborate figured designs. <J. *Jacquard*, 19c weaver>

Ja·cuz·zi (ja kū′zē) *Trademark n* a whirlpool bath or hot tub.

jade (jād) *n* a hard stone, usually green, used for jewellery and ornaments. <Spanish *piedra de ijada* stone for colic, which it was thought to cure>

jad·ed (jā′did) *adj* tired, bored, or without enthusiasm after having had too much of something: *a jaded appetite.* <origin uncertain>

jag[1] (jag) *n* a sharp point sticking out: *a jag of rock.*
v **jagged, jag·ging 1** make notches or indentations in. **2** cut or tear unevenly. <Middle English *jagge* a cut>

jag[2] *Informal n* a period of uncontrolled behaviour or indulgence: *a crying jag, a shopping jag.* <origin uncertain>

jag·ged (jag′id) *adj* with sharp points sticking out caused by an uneven cut or tear: *We cut our bare feet on the jagged rocks.* **jag′ged·ly** *adv.*

Most cats dislike water, but the **jaguar** is an excellent swimmer that feeds on aquatic animals as well as terrestrial ones. It rarely attacks humans.

jag·uar (jag′wȧr) *or* (jag′yū ȧr′) *n* a large cat of Central and South America that usually has a yellowish brown coat with black spots.
<Tupi-Guarani (a language of S America) *yaguara*>

jag·ua·run·di (jag′wər undi) *n* a small, wild cat with a red or grey coat found from Arizona to S America. <Tupi-Guarani (a language of S America) *yaguara* + *undi* dark>

jai a·lai (hī′ lī′), (hī′ə lī′), *or* (hī′ə lī′) *n* a game played by two to four players on a walled court with a small, hard ball and racquets. <Basque *jai* festival + *alai* merry>

jail (jāl) *n* **1** a prison, especially one for people awaiting trial or being punished for minor offences. **2** imprisonment.
v put or keep in jail. <Old French *jaiole*, from Latin *cavea* cage> **jail′-like′** *adj.*

jail·bird (jāl′bərd′) *Informal n* **1** a prisoner in jail. **2** a person who has been in jail many times.

jail·break (jāl′brāk′) *n* an escape from jail or prison.

jail·er or **jail·or** (jā′lər) *n* **1** the keeper of a jail. **2** a person who keeps someone or something confined.

Jain (jān) *or* (jīn) *n* a member or adherent of **Jainism**, a religion founded about 500 BCE whose teachings include the practice of not injuring living creatures.
adj to do with the Jains or their religion.
<Sanskrit *jya* = overcome>

J

ja·la·pe·ño (ha′lə pān′yo) *n* a Mexican hot green pepper. <Mexican Spanish> See CHILI for picture.

ja·lop·y (ja lo′pē) *Informal n, pl* **ja·lop·ies** an old, rundown car. <origin uncertain>

jal·ou·sie (jal′ů zē′) *n* a window blind made of horizontal slats of wood, metal, etc., that can be adjusted to regulate the light or air entering a room. <Old French *gelosie* latticework screen>

jam[1] (jam) *v* **jammed, jam·ming 1** squeeze or pack into a space: *to jam one more book into my backpack. The whole school was jammed into the gym for the assembly. The river was jammed with logs.* **2** crush or bruise: *to jam your fingers in the door.* **3** stick fast or get caught so as not to work properly: *The window has jammed. The key broke off and jammed the lock.* **4** cause telephone lines to be continuously busy with a large number of calls. **5** make radio signals unintelligible by sending out others of approximately the same frequency. **6** *Music* improvise with other musicians, especially in playing jazz or blues.
n **1** a mass of people or things crowded together so that they cannot move freely: *a traffic jam.* **2** *Informal* a difficult or awkward situation. <perhaps imitative>
jam on the brakes, *Informal* apply quick, hard pressure to brakes.

jam[2] (jam) *n* a preserve made by boiling fruit with sugar until thick. <perhaps *jam*[1]> **jam′like′** *adj.*

Ja·mai·ca (jə mā′kə) *n* an island country in the Caribbean. See the APPENDIX. **Ja·mai′can** *adj, n.*

jamb (jam) *n* the upright piece forming the side of a doorway, window, or fireplace. <Old French *jambe* leg>

a bat	e bed	i bid	o pot	u cup	th thin
ā cake	ē me	ī bite	ō go	ū rude	ᴛʜ then
ȧ bar	ə about	ər over	ȯ for	ů put	zh measure

jam·ba·la·ya (jam′bə lī′ə) *n* a Cajun dish consisting of rice, tomatoes, shrimp, and herbs. <Provençal (a language of S France) *jambalaia*>

jam·bo·ree (jam′bə rē′) *n* **1** *Informal* a noisy party or lively entertainment. **2** a large rally or gathering. <origin uncertain>

jam–packed (jam′pakt′) *Informal adj* extremely crowded or packed tightly: *The arena was jam-packed for the final game.*

jam session *Informal n* an informal gathering of musicians who improvise together, especially in playing jazz or blues.

Jane Doe (jān dō) *n* a fictitious name used in legal forms or proceedings for the name of an unspecified female. Compare JOHN DOE.

jan·gle (jang′gəl) *v* **jan·gled, jan·gling** **1** make or cause to make a ringing metallic sound: *The bell on my cat's collar jangles when the cat moves.* **2** make tense or strained: *Their continual complaints jangled her nerves.*
n **1** a ringing metallic sound: *The jangle of the telephone woke him up.* <Old French *jangler*> **jan′gler** *n.*

jan·i·tor (jan′ə tər) *n* a person hired to take care of a building or office. <Latin *janua* door>

jan·na (jȧ′nə) *Islam n* heaven or paradise. <Arabic>

jan·na·nam (jȧ′nə nam) *Islam n* hell. <Arabic>

Jan·u·ar·y (jan′yə wer′ē) *or* (jan′yū er′ē) *n, pl* **Jan·u·ar·ies** the first month of the year, with 31 days. *Abbrev.* **Jan**

ETYMOLOGY

January can be traced back to Latin *Januarius,* for *Janus,* the Roman god of doors and beginnings. He had two faces: one looked forward, one backward.

ja·pan (jə pan′) *n* **1** a hard, glossy varnish: *Black japan is used on wood or metal.* **2** articles varnished and decorated in the Japanese manner.
v **ja·panned, ja·pan·ning** put japan on. <*Japan*>

Japan *n* a country of several islands off the east coast of Asia. See the APPENDIX. **Jap′a·nese′** *adj, n.*

Jap·an·i·ma·tion (jap′ə ni mā′ shən) ANIME. <*Japan* + *animation*>

jape (jāp) *n* a joke.
v **japed, jap·ing** say something as a joke. <Middle English> **jap′er** *n.*

ja·pon·i·ca (jə pon′ə kə) *n* any of several closely related flowering shrubs of the rose family. <Latin *japonicus* Japanese>

jar[1] (jȧr) *n* **1** a wide-mouthed container made of glass or earthenware, often with a removable lid. **2** the amount that it holds: *My brother claims he can eat a whole jar of peanut butter at breakfast.* <Arabic *jarra*>

jar[2] (jȧr) *v* **jarred, jar·ring** **1** cause to shake or rattle: *The heavy footsteps jarred my desk so that I had trouble writing.* **2** have a harsh, unpleasant effect on: *The sound of the alarm bell jarred his nerves.* **3** send a painful or damaging shock through something, especially a part of the body: *I jarred my knee during the game.* **4** clash: *Our opinions jar.*
n **1** a shake or rattle. **2** a harsh, grating noise. **3** a harsh, unpleasant effect or shock. **4** a clash or quarrel. <probably imitative>

jar·di·niere (jȧr′də nēr′) *n* an ornamental pot or stand for flowers or plants. <French = female gardener>

jar·gon (jȧr′gən) *n* **1** special words and expressions peculiar to members of a profession or group, especially when difficult to understand by outsiders. **2** a form of speech made up of features from two or more languages, used for communication between peoples whose native languages differ: *Chinook jargon.* <Old French *jargoun*>

GRAMMAR AND USAGE

Using **jargon** (definition 1) can confuse an audience. It is better either to use simple English words to replace the jargon, or explain what the technical words mean.

Jargon (definition 2) is a technical term that linguists use and implies no criticism of the kinds of language it describes.

jas·mine or **jas·min** (jas′mən) *n* a shrub or climbing plant with clusters of fragrant flowers. Also, **jessamine.** <Persian *yasamin*>

jas·per (jas′pər) *n* a coloured quartz, usually red, yellow, or brown. <Old French, from Greek *iaspis*>

jaun·dice (jon′dis) *n* **1** a disease that causes yellowness of the skin, eyes, and body fluids. **2** a bitter, resentful, or envious mental outlook.
v **jaun·diced, jaun·dic·ing** **1** cause jaundice in. **2** cause bitterness, resentment, or envy. <Old French, from Latin *galbinus* yellow>

jaunt (jont) *n* a short pleasure trip or excursion.
v take a short pleasure trip or excursion. <origin uncertain>

jaun·ty (jon′tē) *adj* **jaun·ti·er, jaun·ti·est** **1** carefree and lively: *The happy child walked with jaunty steps.* **2** dapper and stylish: *a jaunty little hat.* <French *gentil* nice> **jaun′ti·ly** *adv.* **jaun′ti·ness** *n.*

Ja·va (ja′va) *n* **1** an island that is part of Indonesia. **2** a kind of coffee obtained from this island. **3 java** *Slang* coffee. **Jav′a·nese′** *adj, n.*

Java man *n* an early form of human being whose fossil remains were found in Java.

jave·lin (jav′lən) *n* **1** a light spear thrown by hand. **2** a wooden or metal spear, thrown for distance in field contests. See TRACK AND FIELD for picture. <Old French *javeline*>

jaw (jo) *n* **1** either of the two bones, or sets of bones, that hold the teeth and together form the framework of the mouth in most vertebrates. The lower jaw is usually movable, while the upper jaw is fixed. **2** the lower part of the face, especially the lower jaw: *She has a square jaw.* **3 jaws** *pl* **a** the mouth with its jawbones and teeth. **b** the parts in a tool that grip and hold: *A vise has jaws.*
v talk, especially chatter at length. <Old French *joe*> **jaw′less** *adj.*

jaw·bone (jo′bōn′) *n* **1** the bone of either jaw. **2** the bone of the lower jaw.

jaw·break·er (jo′brā′kər) *n* **1** a big, round piece of hard candy or bubble gum. **2** *Informal* a word that is hard to pronounce. **3** a machine for crushing ore.

Jaws of Life *Trademark n* a large tool driven by compressed air, used to pry accident victims out of wrecked vehicles.

jay (jā) *n* a bird of N America and Eurasia, related to the crow, often with a crest and a long tail. Two kinds of jay in Canada are the **Canada jay** and the **blue jay**. See BLUE JAY for picture. <Old French, from Latin *Gaius* masculine name, from the practice of giving birds proper names, as in *robin*>

jay·walk (jā′wok′) *v* walk across a street at a place other than a regular crossing or without paying attention to traffic. **jay′walk′er** *n.*

jazz (jaz) *n* a style of music characterized by strong rhythms and improvisation of a basic melody. Jazz originated among black musicians in New Orleans in the rhythmic traditions of African music. <origin uncertain>
all that jazz, *Informal* all that sort of thing.
jazz up, *Informal* make more lively, exciting, or decorative: *I got some brightly coloured curtains to jazz up my room a bit.*

jaz·zy (jaz′ē) *Informal adj* loud, flashy, or unrestrained: *jazzy clothes.*

jeal·ous (jel′əs) *adj* **1** fearful that a person one loves may love or prefer someone else: *He gets jealous if I talk to other boys.* **2** full of envy or resentment: *She is jealous of me and of my high marks.* **3** watchful in keeping or guarding something: *Each province is jealous of its rights within Confederation. The dog was a jealous guardian of the child.* <Old French, from Greek *zelos*> **jeal′ous·ly** *adv.* **jeal′ous·ness** *n.* **jeal′ous·y** *n.*

CONFUSABLES

Jealous (definition 1) means "fearful that a loved one may love or prefer another."

Envious means "full of discontent" or "resentment toward another's good fortune, wishing it for oneself."

jeans (jēnz) *pln* pants made of a strong, twilled cotton cloth, usually blue denim: *The cowboy wore blue jeans under his chaps.*
adj **jean** made of this material: *a jean jacket.* <French *Genes* Genoa, Italy, where the material was originally produced>

jeep (jēp) *n* a small, powerful general-purpose vehicle in which power is transmitted to all four wheels. <*Jeep,* a trademark, from the sound of the initial letters of *general purpose*>

jeer (jēr) *v* make fun of someone rudely or unkindly: *Do not jeer at the mistakes or misfortunes of others.*
n a rude or unkind remark. <origin uncertain> **jeer′er** *n.* **jeer′ing** *adj.* **jeer′ing·ly** *adv.*

Je·ho·vah (ji hō′və) *n* in the Old Testament of the Bible, a form of the Hebrew name for God. <Latin, from Hebrew *Yahweh*>

Jehovah's Witnesses *pln* a Christian sect, more formally called the Watch Tower Bible and Tract Society, that believes a person's own faith and conscience are more important than the rules of government or of organized religion.

je·june (ji jūn′) *adj* **1** dull and uninteresting: *jejune comments.* **2** immature and superficial: *jejune opinions.* <Old French, from Latin *jejunus* meagre>

je·ju·num (ji jū′nəm) *n* the middle portion of the small intestine, between the duodenum and the ileum. <Latin *jejunus* empty, from the belief that the *jejunum* is empty after death>

Jek·yll and Hyde (je′kəl′ ən hīd) *n* a person with a dual personality, part good and part evil.
adj **Jekyll-and-Hyde** to do with such a person: *a Jekyll-and-Hyde personality.*

ETYMOLOGY

Jekyll and Hyde comes from Robert Louis Stevenson's late-1800s novel, *The Strange Case of Dr. Jekyll and Mr. Hyde.*

In the story, a doctor develops a potion that transforms him from a respectable man into an evil person called Mr. Hyde.

J

jell (jel) *v* **1** become jelly. **2** take definite form or become fixed: *Our plans have jelled.*

jel·lied (jel′ēd) *adj* turned into, made with, or with the consistency of jelly: *jellied salad.*

jel·ly (jel′ē) *n, pl* **jel·lies** **1** a food that is liquid when hot but somewhat firm when cold. Jelly can be made by boiling fruit juice and sugar together, or by cooking bones and meat in water, or by using some stiffening preparation like gelatin. **2** a jellylike substance: *petroleum jelly.*
v **jel·lied, jel·ly·ing** become or turn into jelly. <Old French *gelée* jelly, frost, from Latin *gelu* frost>
jel′lylike′ *adj.*

jel·ly·bean (jel′ē bēn′) *n* a small bean-shaped candy made of jellied sugar, coated in different colours.

jel·ly·fish (jel′ē fish′) *n, pl* **jel·ly·fish** or **jel·ly·fish·es** an invertebrate sea animal with a body formed of a mass of jellylike tissue that is almost transparent. Most jellyfish have long trailing tentacles that may sting.

jelly roll *n* a thin layer of sponge cake spread with fruit jelly or jam and rolled up while still warm.

jelly sandals *n* casual sandals whose tops are made of semi-transparent coloured plastic openwork.

je ne sais quoi (zhən se kwa′) *n* an indefinable quality or thing. <French = I don't know what>

jen·ny (jen′ē) *n, pl* **jen·nies** **1** a spinning jenny. **2** the female of some animals: *a jenny wren.* <variant of female name *Janet*>

a **bat**	e **bed**	i **bid**	o **pot**	u **cup**	th **thin**
ā **cake**	ē **me**	ī **bite**	ō **go**	ū **rude**	ᴛʜ **then**
ȧ **bar**	ə **about**	ər **over**	ȯ **for**	u̇ **put**	zh **measure**

jeop·ard·ize (jep′ər dīz′) *v* **jeop·ard·ized, jeop·ard·iz·ing** put in danger; risk: *Soldiers jeopardize their lives in war.*

jeop·ard·y (jep′ər dē) *n* risk, danger, or peril: *The firefighters put their lives in jeopardy when they entered the burning building.* <Old French *jeu parti* game in which the chances of winning or losing were evenly divided>

The **jerboa** is an amazing little jumper. It can leap 1 m from a standing position and up to 3 m when moving quickly. Although a jerboa's body might be only 20 cm long, its tail can be as long as 30 cm, which helps this rodent keep its balance when jumping.

jer·bo·a (jər bō′ə) *n* a small, jumping, mouselike mammal found from N Africa to Central Asia. <Arabic *yarbu*>

jer·e·mi·ad (jer′ə mī′ad) *n* a mournful complaint. <*Jeremiah*, a Hebrew prophet who denounced the evils of his time>

jerk[1] (jərk) *n* **1** a sudden, sharp pull, twist, or start: *The old lawn mower started with a jerk.* **2** a pull or twist of the muscles that one cannot control. **3** *Informal* a contemptible and foolish person.
v **1** pull or twist suddenly: *If the water is unexpectedly hot, you jerk your hand out.* **2** throw with a movement that stops suddenly. **3** move with a jerk: *the old wagon jerked along.* **4** speak or say abruptly. <probably imitative>

jerk[2] (jərk) *v* **1** preserve meat by cutting it into long thin slices and drying it in the sun: *The Indians taught the early settlers in America how to jerk beef.* **2** marinate chicken or pork in spices and grill it, especially over an open fire.
adj prepare meat or poultry in this way: *We had jerk chicken at our favourite Jamaican restaurant.* <Quechua (a language of S America) *echarqui* dried flesh>

jer·kin (jər′kən) *n* a short, close-fitting coat or jacket without sleeves. <origin uncertain>

jerk·y[1] (jər′kē) *adj* **jerk·i·er, jerk·i·est** with sudden starts and stops: *The jerky motion of the old locomotive made father sick.* <probably imitative> **jerk′i·ly** *adv.* **jerk′i·ness** *n.*

jerk·y[2] (jər′kē) *n* dried beef. <Quechua (a language of S America) *echarqui* dried flesh.>

jer·ry–built (jer′ē bilt′) *adj* built quickly and cheaply of poor materials. <origin uncertain>

jer·sey (jər′zē) *n, pl* **jer·seys** **1** a close-fitting sweater that is pulled on over the head. **2** a woman's close-fitting knitted undergarment. **3** a machine-knitted cloth. **4 Jersey** a breed of fawn-coloured dairy cattle whose milk is rich in butterfat. <*Jersey*, an island in the English Channel, from which these cattle originally came. The knitted fabric and garments are named for the woollen sweaters traditionally worn by the fishermen of Jersey.>

Je·ru·sa·lem artichoke (je rū′sə ləm) *n* **1** the tuber of a kind of sunflower, eaten as a vegetable.

jess (jes) *n* a short strap fastened around a trained falcon's leg and attached to a leash. <Old French, from Latin *jacere* throw. The falconer releases the bird by "throwing" it up into the air.>

jes·sa·mine (jes′ə min) JASMIN.

jest (jest) *n* **1** joke. **2** the act of making fun of. **3** something intended to be mocked or laughed at.
v **1** to make a joke. **2** make fun of. <Latin *gesta* deeds, from *gerere* perform> **jest′ing** *adj.* **jest′ing·ly** *adv.*
in jest, not seriously: *Her words were spoken in jest.*

jest·er (jes′tər) *n* a person who jests: *In the Middle Ages, kings often had jesters to amuse them.*

Jes·u·it (je′zyū′it) *or* (je′zū′it) *Catholicism n* a member of a religious teaching order called the **Society of Jesus**, founded by Saint Ignatius Loyola in 1534.
adj to do with this order. <Latin *Jesus*> **Jes′u·i′tic** *adj.*

Je·sus (jē′zəs) *n* in full, **Jesus Christ** a teacher and prophet who was the founder of the Christian religion, considered by his followers to be the son of God and saviour of the world. <Hebrew *Yeshoshua* Joshua>

jet[1] (jet) *n* **1** a stream of gas or liquid, sent with force, especially from a small opening: *A fountain sends up a jet of water.* **2** a spout or nozzle for sending out a jet. **3** a jet-propelled aircraft.
adj to do with the use of jet-propelled aircraft or jet propulsion: *jet travel.*
v **jet·ted, jet·ting** **1** gush out; shoot forth in a jet or forceful stream. **2** travel or carry by jet aircraft. <French, from Latin *jacere* to throw>

jet[2] (jet) *n* a hard, black variety of lignite that can be carved and polished to a high sheen: *Her hair is the colour of jet.* <Old French, from Greek *gagates* Gagai, a town in Asia Minor where this was found>

jet–black (jet′blak′) *adj* very black.

jet engine *n* an engine that produces motion by using a backward ejection of a high-speed jet of gas or liquid.

jet lag *n* a delayed effect of fatigue and sleepiness after a long flight in a jet aircraft, especially when several time zones have been crossed.

jet·lin·er (jet′lī′nər) *n* a large jet aircraft used for carrying passengers on commercial flights.

jet plane *n* an aircraft that is driven by one or more jet engines.

jet–pro·pelled (jet′prə peld′) *adj* driven by **jet propulsion**, in a backward ejection of a high-speed jet of gas or liquid.

jet·sam (jet′səm) *n* **1** goods thrown overboard to lighten a ship in distress and often afterwards washed ashore. Compare FLOTSAM. **2** anything that is thrown out because it is considered useless. <variant of *jettison*>

jet set *n* a wealthy social group, especially one whose members frequently visit fashionable resorts in various countries.

Jet Ski *Trademark n* a motorized watercraft for a driver and one or two passengers, with a seat, handlebars, and a ski on the bottom for skimming over the water.

jet stream *n* a current of air travelling at very high speed from west to east at high altitudes.

jet·ti·son (jet′ə sən) *v* **1** throw goods overboard to lighten a ship in distress. **2** throw away or discard. <Old French, from Latin *jacere* throw>

jet·ty (jet′ē) *n, pl* **jet·ties 1** a landing place, pier, or dock. **2** a structure built out into the water to protect a harbour or to control the current or tide. <Old French *jeter* to throw outward>

Jew (jū) *n* **1** a member of a people and cultural community descended from the Hebrew people of ancient Israel. **2** a person whose religion is Judaism. <Hebrew *yehudah* Judah> **Jew′ish** *adj.*

jew·el (jū′əl) *n* **1** a precious stone or gem. **2** a valuable ornament to be worn, set with precious stones. **3** a person who or thing that is very precious. **4** a gem or other piece of hard material used as a bearing in a watch.
v **jew·elled** or **jew·eled, jew·el·ling** or **jew·el·ing** set or adorn with jewels or with things like jewels: *a jewelled bracelet. The sky was jewelled with stars.* <Old French> **jew′el-like′** *adj.*

jewel case *n* **1** a box or case to hold jewellery. **2** a plastic case that holds a CD or DVD.

jew·el·ler or **jew·el·er** (jū′ə lər) *or* (jū′lər) *n* a person who makes, sells, or repairs jewels or jewellery.

jew·el·ler·y or **jew·el·ry** (jū′əl rē) *or* (jūl′rē) *n* jewels and ornaments set with gems.

Jew·ry (jū′rē) *n* the Jewish people.

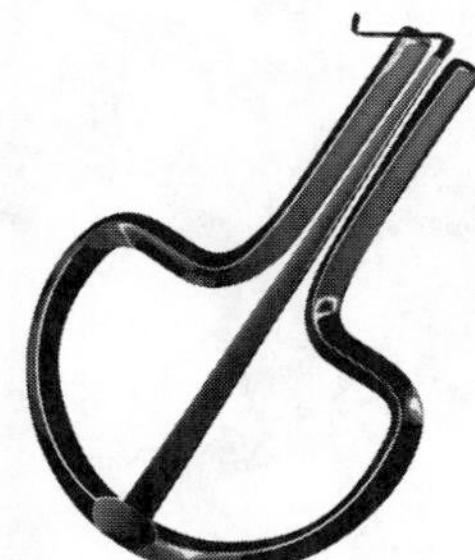

The **jews' harp** isn't a harp and it isn't a traditional Jewish musical instrument.

When played well, it produces a rhythmic droning or buzzing sound.

jews'–harp or **jew's–harp** (jūz′hȧrp′) *n* a musical instrument that is held between the teeth and played by striking the free end of a flexible piece of metal with a finger. <origin uncertain>

jib[1] (jib) *n* **1** a triangular sail in front of the foremast of a boat or ship. **2** the projecting arm of a crane. <origin uncertain>
the cut of someone's jib, *Informal* a person's outward appearance: *You wear such great clothes that everyone admires the cut of your jib.*

jib[2] (jib) *v* **jibbed, jib·bing** move sideways or backwards instead of forward. <origin uncertain>
jib at, refuse to face or deal with: *The horse jibbed at the high fence. I jibbed at having to babysit my brother for the whole weekend.*

jibe[1] (jīb) *v* **jibed, jib·ing 1** shift a sail from one side of a ship to the other when sailing before the wind. **2** shift itself in this way: *Be careful or your mainsail will jibe.* <Dutch *gijben*>

jibe[2] (jīb) *v* **jibed, jib·ing** be in harmony; agree. Also called **jive.** <origin uncertain>

jibe[3] (jīb) GIBE.

jif·fy (jif′ē) *Informal n, pl* **jif·fies** a very short time: *I'll be there in a jiffy.* <origin uncertain>

jig (jig) *n* **1** a lively dance with leaping movements, or the music for this dance. **2** a fishing lure made of one or more fish-hooks for bobbing up and down or drawing through the water. **3** a device that guides a drill, file, or other tool.
v **jigged, jig·ging 1** dance a jig. **2** move jerkily; jerk up and down or back and forth. **3** fish with a jig. <origin uncertain>
in jig time, *Informal* quickly.
the jig is up, *Slang* it's all over; there's no way out: *The teacher saw me passing the note, so I knew the jig was up.*

jig·ger (jig′ər) *n* **1** a machine or vehicle with a part that moves back and forth, such as a jigsaw. **2** a small nonmetric measure for liquor, less than 50 mL. **3** a small sail set at the stern of a boat or ship. **4** 🍁 **a** a device upon which a gill net is hung below ice. **b** a fish-shaped weight with two hooks at the end of a fishing line. **5** 🍁 a small vehicle used by railway workers, motorized or operated by hand.
I'll be jiggered, *Informal* an expression of surprise: *Well, I'll be jiggered! It was here all along!*

jig·gle (jig′əl) *v* **jig·gled, jig·gling** shake or jerk slightly: *Please don't jiggle the desk when I'm trying to write.*
n a slight shake or light jerk. <origin uncertain>

jig·saw (jig′so′) *n* a saw with a narrow blade mounted in a frame and worked with an up-and-down motion, used to cut curves or irregular lines.

jigsaw puzzle *n* a picture cut into irregular pieces that can be fitted together again.

ji·had (ji hȧd′) *Islam n* a holy war undertaken against the enemies of the Islam religion. <Arabic = struggle>

jil·lion (jil′yən) *Slang n* a huge number or too many to count. <invented, on the analogy of *million, billion,* etc.>

jilt (jilt) *v* suddenly reject or abandon someone with whom one is romantically involved.
n a person who suddenly rejects or abandons someone with whom he or she is romantically involved. <origin uncertain> **jilt′er** *n.*

jim–dan·dy (jim dan′dē) *Slang adj* excellent or fine. <*Jim,* a personal name + *dandy*>

jim·jams (jim′jamz) *Slang pln* (*with* **the**) a fit of nervousness. <imitative>

jim·my (jim′ē) *n, pl* **jim·mies** a short crowbar used by a burglar to force windows or doors open.
v **jim·mied, jim·my·ing** force open with or as if with a jimmy: *to jimmy a window.* <*Jimmy,* variant of James. See JACK.>

a bat	e bed	i bid	o pot	u cup	th thin
ā cake	ē me	ī bite	ō go	ū rude	ᴛʜ then
ȧ bar	ə about	ər over	ȯ for	u̇ put	zh measure

jim·son weed or **Jim·son weed** (jim′sən) *n* a tall, coarse, bad-smelling weed with poisonous leaves.

jin·gle (jing′gəl) *n* **1** a light, ringing sound like that made by little bells, or of coins or keys being shaken. **2** a verse or song that repeats sounds or has a catchy rhythm, especially one used in advertising: *Please stop humming that shampoo jingle.*
v **jin·gled, jin·gling 1** make a jingling sound: *The sleigh bells jingle as we ride.* **2** cause to jingle: *He jingled the coins in his pocket.* <imitative>

jin·gly (jing′glē) *adj* like a jingle.

jin·go (jing′gō) *n, pl* **jin·goes** a patriotic person who favours an aggressive foreign policy that might lead to war. <from a phrase in a British popular song of the 1800s that supported the sending of a British fleet into Turkish waters to resist Russia> **jin′go·ism** *n.* **jin′go·ist′ic** *adj.*
by jingo, *Informal* an expression used for emphasis or surprise: *If you want to do such a silly thing, then by jingo, you go right ahead.*

jinn (jin) GENIE.

jinx (jingks) *Informal n* a person who or thing that is believed to bring bad luck: *I must be a jinx, because we've lost every game since I joined the team.*
v bring bad luck to. <Latin, from Greek *iynx* bird used in magic>

jit·ney (jit′nē) *n, pl* **jit·neys** an automobile that carries passengers for a small fare: *A jitney usually travels along a regular route.* <*Jitney,* former slang for a nickel. The vehicle was so named because original jitney buses charged a five-cent fare.>

jit·ter·bug (jit′ər bug′) *Informal n* a fast dance of the 1940s, done to swing music.
v **jit·ter·bugged, jit·ter·bug·ging** dance in such a way. <*jitter(y) + bug*>

jit·ters (jit′ərz) *pln* (*with* **the**) extreme nervousness. <origin uncertain>

jit·ter·y (jit′ə rē) *adj* nervous.

jiu·jit·su (jū jit′sū) JUJITSU.

jive[1] (jīv) *n* **1 a** a style of dancing popular from the 1940s to the early 1960s, done to swing music and later to rock and roll. **b** the music for this. **2** *Informal* worthless or deceptive talk: *That salesman just gave me a lot of jive.*
v **jived, jiv·ing 1** dance to jive music. **2** play jive. **3** *Informal* deceive or mislead: *Go on, you're jiving me!* <origin uncertain>

jive[2] (jīv) JIBE[2].

job (job) *n* **1 a** a piece of work: *I had the job of painting the boat.* **b** anything a person has to do: *It's my brother's job to wash the dishes.* 2 **a** a definite piece of work undertaken for a fixed price: *If you want your computer fixed, I will do the job for $50.* **b** regular work or employment: *My brother is hunting for a job.* **3** *Informal* a crime, especially a robbery: *a bank job, an inside job.* **4** *Computers* an operation or series of operations that is considered as a single unit. **5** *Informal* something done to improve the appearance of a person or thing: *a nose job, a paint job.*
v **jobbed, job·bing 1** work at odd jobs. **2** buy goods from manufacturers in large quantities and sell to dealers in smaller lots. **3** let out work to different contractors or workers. <origin uncertain>
a good job, good work: *You did a good job on that flowerbed.*
on the job, a at the workplace: *safety on the job.* **b** engaged in doing one's duties: *I can't make phone calls when I'm on the job.*

job·ber (job′ər) *n* **1** a person who buys goods from manufacturers in large quantities and sells to retailers in smaller quantities. **2** a person who works and is paid by the job or by the piece of work done.

job·hold·er (job′hōl′dər) *n* a person regularly employed.

job·less (job′ləs) *adj* unemployed.
n **the jobless** *pl* all the people who are unemployed. **job′less·ness** *n.*

job lot *n* a quantity of goods bought or sold together, usually containing several different kinds of things.

job–shad·ow·ing (job′shad′ ōw ing) *n* observation of an experienced person at work in order to learn what the job involves, especially such observation by a student at the workplace of a family member as part of a special program. **job′-shad′ow·er** *n.*

job–shar·ing (job′shā ring) *n* the policy of dividing a full-time job between two or more part-time workers who do the same duties at different times.

jock (jok) *Slang n* an athlete or sports enthusiast. <*jockstrap,* slang for male genitals>

Many **jockeys** first learn to handle horses when they are young girls and boys by exercising them in early morning workouts. Their career starts when they become apprentice jockeys.

Jockeys are paid a fee for each race they ride in and receive a percentage of the purse (the prize money) if their horse wins.

jock·ey (jok′ē) *n, pl* **jock·eys** a person whose work is riding horses in races.
v **jock·eyed, jock·ey·ing 1** ride a horse in a race. **2** manoeuvre to get an advantage: *The crews were jockeying their boats to get into the best position for the race.* <variant of the masculine name *Jock*>
jockey for, try to achieve something by every possible means: *Several entrants were jockeying for first place in the music competition.*

jockey shorts *pln* underpants for men and boys that fit snugly at the crotch.

jock·strap (jok′strap) *Informal n* an elastic support worn by male athletes to support the genitals. Its formal name is **athletic support**.

jo·cose (jə kōs′) *adj* joking, playful, or humorous: *He was in a jocose mood.* <Latin *jocus* joke> **jocosely** *adv.* **jocosity** (jə kos′it ē) *n.*

joc·u·lar (jok′yə lər) *adj* joking: *She spoke in a jocular way about her experiences as a babysitter.* <Latin *jocus* joke> **joc′u·lar·ly** *adv.*

joc·u·lar·i·ty (jok′yə lar′ə tē) *or* (jok′yə ler′ə tē) *n, pl* **joc·u·lar·i·ties** **1** a jocular quality. **2** jocular talk or behaviour. **3** a jocular remark or act.

joc·und (jok′ənd) *adj* cheerful or merry: *a jocund manner.* <Latin *jocus* joke> **jo·cun′di·ty** *n.*

jodh·purs (jod′pərz) *pl n* breeches for horseback riding, loose above the knees and fitting closely below. <*Jodhpur*, a city in India, where similar garments were and are worn by men as a part of everyday dress.>

joe or **Joe** (jō) *Slang n* a man, especially an ordinary one: *Ask some joe for directions.* <variant of masculine personal name *Joseph*>

Joe Blow *Informal n* a name representing an average or anonymous person. Also called **Joe Public**.

joe job *Slang n* a dull, routine, or low-paying job.

jo·ey (jō′ē) *Australian n* a young kangaroo, wallaby, or possum. <Australian Aboriginal *joe*>

jog[1] (jog) *v* **jogged, jog·ging** **1** shake with a push or jerk: *You may jog a person's elbow to get her attention.* **2** stir up with a hint or reminder: *to jog your memory.* **3** move up or down with a jerk or a shaking motion: *The old horse jogged along, and jogged me up and down on his back.* **4** run at a steady gentle rate: *My sister goes jogging every day for exercise.* **5** go forward heavily and slowly.
n **1** a slow walk or trot: *The riders went at a jog along the path.* **2** a shake, push, or nudge. **3** a hint or reminder: *This should give your memory a jog.* <Middle English>
jog′ger *n.*

jog[2] (jog) *n* **1** a part that sticks out or in, or an unevenness in a line or surface: *a jog in a wall.* **2** an abrupt, temporary change in direction: *There's a jog in the road where it goes around the poplar bluff.*
v make or form a jog: *The road jogs to the left just before you get to our place.* <variant of *jag*[1]>

jog·gle[1] (jog′əl) *v* **jog·gled, jog·gling** shake or jolt slightly: *The milk spilled because you joggled my elbow.*
n a slight shake or jolt. <*jog*[1]>

jog trot *n* **1** a slow, regular trot. **2** a routine or humdrum way of doing things.

john (jon) *Informal n* **1** a toilet. **2** the client of a prostitute. <*John*, masculine name>

John Bull *n* a supposedly typical Englishman represented as stout and red-faced, in top hat and high boots. It is often used as a name for the English nation. <Created in 1712 by writer J. Arbuthnot after a character in *Law is a Bottomless Pit*>

John Doe (dō) *n* a fictitious name used in legal forms or proceedings for the name of an unspecified male. Compare JANE DOE.

John Do·ry (dô′rē) *n, pl* **John Do·rys** an edible sea fish that has a flat body and spiny fins.

john·ny·cake (jon′ē kāk′) *n* cornbread in the form of a flat cake. <origin uncertain>

🍁 **Johnny Can·uck** ((jon′ē kan uk′) *n, pl* **Johnny Can·ucks** **1** a supposedly typical Canadian. **2** a name for Canada: *Johnny Canuck can do a lot more than play hockey.*

John·ny–come–late·ly (jon′ē kum lāt′lē) *Informal n, pl* **John·ny-come-late·lies** or **John·nies-come-late·ly** a person who is late to arrive at a place, activity, or point of view and thus is considered to be a newcomer.

John·ny–jump–up (jon′ē jum′pup′) *n* a wild pansy or violet.

joie de vi·vre (zhwad vē vr′) *n* the joy of living. <French>

join (join) *v* **1 a** bring or put together: *to join hands, to join an island to the mainland by a bridge.* **b** come together or meet: *The two roads join here.* **2** make or become one: *to join in marriage.* **3** become a member of: *to join a club.* **4** come into the company of: *Go now, and I'll join you later.* **5** take or return to one's place in: *After a few days on shore, the sailor joined his ship.*
n a place of joining. <Old French, from Latin *jungere*>
join battle, begin to fight.
join forces, combine effort.
join hands, a shake or clasp hands. **b** agree to work together.
join in, take part.
join up, a enlist in the armed forces. **b** (*with* ***with***) meet or join: *I'll drop by the store and join up with you later.*

J

join·er (joi′nər) *n* **1** a person who or thing that joins. **2** a skilled worker who makes woodwork and furniture.

joint (joint) *n* **1 a** the place at which two things or parts are joined together. **b** the joining of two bones in a person or animal in such a way as to allow movement. See ARTICULATE for picture. **2 a** the way parts are joined: *a perfect joint in a picture frame.* **b** one of the parts of which a jointed thing is made up: *the middle joint of the finger.* **3** the part of the stem from which a leaf or branch grows. **4** *Informal* a place where people gather, especially to dine, drink, or be entertained: *a burger joint.* **5** a marijuana cigarette.
v divide meat or poultry at the joints: *Joint the chicken before frying it.*
adj **1** shared or done by two or more people: *By our joint efforts we managed to push the car back on the road.* **2** regarded together: *My sister and I are joint owners of this dog.* <Old French, from Latin *jungere* join>
out of joint, a out of place at the joint. **b** out of order.

joint committee *n* **1** a parliamentary committee with members from the House of Commons and the Senate. **2** a committee with members from different groups.

joint·ly (join′tlē) *adv* together or in common: *The two girls owned the canoe jointly.*

a bat	e bed	i bid	o pot	u cup	th **thin**
ā cake	ē me	ī bite	ō go	ū rude	ᴛʜ **then**
ä bar	ə about	ər over	ô for	ů put	zh measure

joist (joist) *n* a parallel horizontal piece of timber extending from wall to wall across a building, to which the boards of a floor or ceiling are fastened. <Old French, from Latin *jacere* lie horizontally>

jo·jo·ba (hō ho′bə) *n* a shrub of the southwestern US and Mexico with leathery leaves and edible seeds whose oil is used in shampoos and cosmetics. <Spanish>

joke (jōk) *n* **1** something deliberately said or done to cause laughter: *This was a good joke on me.* **2** a person or thing laughed at: *This haircut of mine is a joke.* **3** something that is not actually meant.
v **joked, jok·ing** say or do something as a joke. <Latin *jocus*> **jok′ing** *adj.* **jok′ing·ly** *adv.*
no joke, a serious matter: *That snowstorm was no joke.*

jok·er (jō′kər) *n* **1** a person who tells funny stories or plays tricks on others. **2** *Informal* a foolish or inept person: *Who does that joker think he is?* **3** a playing card with a figure of a jester on it.

jol·li·fi·ca·tion (jol′ə fə kā′shən) *n* a lively celebration.

jol·li·ty (jol′ə tē) *n, pl* **jol·li·ties** a lively and cheerful activity or celebration.

jol·ly (jol′ē) *adj* **jol·li·er, jol·li·est** full of fun and good humour.
v **jol·lied, jol·ly·ing** *Informal* (*with* ***along***) flatter a person to make him or her feel good or agreeable: *We jollied him along a bit.* <Old French *joli* festive> **jol′li·ly** *adv.* **jol′li·ness** *n.*
get your jollies, *Slang* get pleasure or excitement: *She gets her jollies by criticizing other people.*

🍁 **Jolly Jumper** *Trademark n* an exerciser for a baby, consisting of a snug body harness suspended by a long spring and elastic cable, in which a baby can bounce up and down in an upright position.

Jolly Roger *n* a pirate's flag, with a white skull and crossbones on a black background.

jolt (jōlt) *v* **1** jar or shake up: *The wagon jolted us when the wheel went over a rock.* **2** move with a shock or jerk: *The car jolted across the rough road.* **3** shock or surprise: *I was jolted by my poor marks and decided I'd better do something.*
n **1** a jarring or jerking movement: *She put her brakes on suddenly and the car stopped with a jolt.* **2** a sudden surprise or shock: *The loss of the money was a severe jolt.* <origin uncertain>

jon·quil (jong′kwəl) *n* a plant much like a daffodil.

Jor·dan (jor′dən) *n* a country in the Middle East. **Jor·dan′ian** (jor′dān′i ən) *adj, n.*

josh (josh) *v* make good-natured fun of. <origin uncertain>

Jo·shu·a tree (josh′wə) *n* a tree of the agave family, with clusters of spiny leaves. It grows in southwest N America.

joss (jos) *n* a statue or image of a Chinese god. <Chinese pidgin English, from Latin *deus* god>

joss stick *n* a slender stick of a fragrant, slow-burning substance used as incense.

jos·tle (jos′əl) *v* **jos·tled, jos·tling** crowd, shove, or push against: *We were jostled by the big crowd at the stadium entrance.*
n a jostling or pushing. <Middle English *jousten*> **jos′tler** *n.*

jot (jot) *n* a very small amount: *I do not care a jot.*
v **jot·ted, jot·ting** (*often with* ***down***) write briefly or in haste: *He jotted notes on the back of an envelope. The waiter jotted down the order.* <Latin, from Greek *iota*, the smallest letter in the Greek alphabet> **jot′ter** *n.*

jot·ting (jot′ ing) *n* a short, informal note: *collected jottings of a writer.*

🍁 **joual** (zhal), (zhū ál′), *or* (zhū al′) *n* a form of Canadian French. <from a pronunciation of *cheval* horse>

joule (jūl) *n* the SI unit for measuring work done or energy used. One joule is the amount of work done (or energy used) in applying one newton of force to move a body one metre in the direction of the force. *Symbol* **J** <J.P. *Joule*, 19c physicist>

jounce (jouns) *v* **jounced, jounc·ing,** jolt or bump.
n a jolt or bump.

jour·nal (jər′nəl) *n* **1** a daily record of events, or a book for keeping such a record. A diary and a ship's log are journals. **2** a personal record of experiences, ideas, and thoughts, kept on a regular basis. **3** a newspaper or magazine dealing with a specific subject or activity. **4** *Accounting* a book in which every item of business is written down so that it can be entered under the proper account. <Old French, from Latin *diurnalis* daily>

jour·nal·ese (jər′nə lēz′) *n* a loose style of writing using many clichés, such as is sometimes used in newspapers and magazines.

jour·nal·ism (jər′nə liz′əm) *n* the work of writing for, editing, managing, or publishing a newspaper or magazine or of broadcasting news on radio, television, and the Internet. **jour′nal·ist** *n.* **jour′nal·is′tic** *adj.*

jour·ney (jər′nē) *n, pl* **jour·neys** a trip, especially a long one: *a journey around the world.*
v **jour·neyed, jour·ney·ing** take a trip or travel: *to journey to New Brunswick.* <Old French, from Latin *diurnus* of one day>

jour·ney·man (jər′nē mən) *n, pl* **jour·ney·men** (-mən) **1** a worker who knows a trade. **2** a worker who has completed an apprenticeship or is otherwise qualified to practise a trade, but is not an employer or master. <Latin *diurnus* of one day. A *journeyman* was originally one who had finished an apprenticeship in his trade and was qualified to work for daily wages.>

joust (joust) *n* **1** a combat between two knights on horseback, armed with lances. **2 jousts** *pl* a tournament.
v fight with lances on horseback: *Knights used to joust with each other for sport.* <Old French, from Latin *juxta* beside> **joust′er** *n.*

Jove (jōv) *Roman myth n* the god Jupiter. <Latin *Jovis* Jupiter>

jo·vi·al (jō′vē əl) *adj* good-humoured and full of fun. <Latin *Jovialis* of Jupiter. People born under that planet's sign were thought to have those characteristics.> **jo′vi·al′i·ty** *n.* **jo′vi·al·ly** *adv.* **jo′vi·al·ness** *n.*

jowl (joul) *n* **1** the lower, sometimes loose or drooping, part of the cheek under the jaw. <Old English *ceole*>

joy (joi) *n* **1** a strong feeling of pleasure or happiness: *She jumped for joy when she saw the notice announcing the concert.* **2** something that causes pleasure or happiness: *It was a joy to see him skate.* **3** success or satisfaction: *The bad exam results gave us no joy.* <Old French, from Latin *gaudere* rejoice>

joy·ful (joi′fəl) *adj* **1** feeling gladness, happiness, or great pleasure: *a joyful heart.* **2** causing joy: *joyful news.* **3** showing joy: *a joyful look on her face.* **joy′ful·ly** *adv.* **joy′ful·ness** *n.*

joy·less (joi′lis) *adj* **1** sad or dismal. **2** not causing joy: *A rainy weather forecast is a joyless prospect.* **joy′less·ly** *adv.* **joy′less·ness** *n.*

joy·ous (joi′əs) *adj* joyful or very happy: *a joyous song.* **joy′ous·ly** *adv.* **joy′ous·ness** *n.*

joy·ride (joi′rīd) *Informal n* a ride in an automobile for pleasure, especially when the car is driven recklessly and used without the owner's permission. **joy′ride** *v.* **joy′rid′er** *n.*

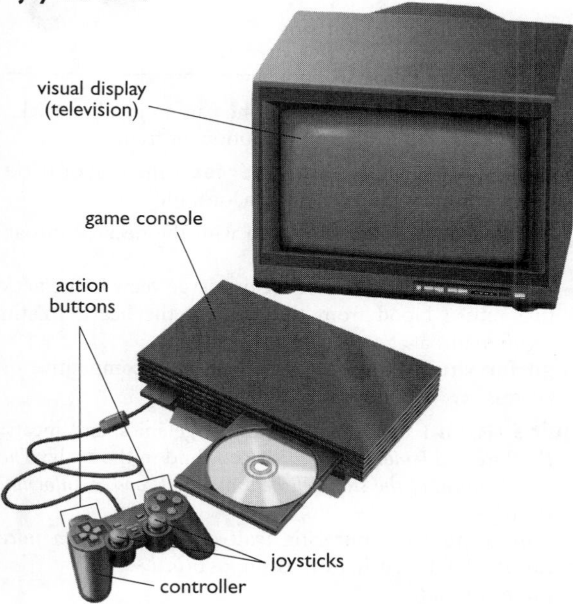

The first **joysticks** were control mechanisms used by pilots to guide the movement of aircraft. The design proved useful for computer-based flight simulators, and then was adapted for video game controllers.

joy·stick (joi′stik′) *n* a small handle used as the control mechanism for some computer and video games.

jpeg or **JPEG** (jā′peg) *Computers* in full, **Joint Photographic Experts Group** the name of the committee that designed this image compression standard, used to store images and to transfer them over the Internet.

ju·bi·lant (jū′bə lənt) *adj* expressing or showing joy: *The crowd was jubilant when we scored the winning goal.* <Latin *jubilare* shout with joy> **ju′bi·lant·ly** *adv.*

ju·bi·la·tion (jū′bə lā′shən) *n* great happiness or rejoicing.

ju·bi·lee (jū′bə lē′) *n* **1** an anniversary thought of as a time of rejoicing: *a fiftieth wedding jubilee.* **2** a time of rejoicing: *to have a jubilee in celebration of a victory.*

ETYMOLOGY

Jubilee comes from Hebrew *yobel,* meaning "ram" or "ram's horn." In the Old Testament, a year of celebration was proclaimed by the Jews every fifty years (when mortgaged lands were made free of mortgage) by the blowing of a ram's horn.

Ju·dae·o–Chris·tian (jū dā′ō kris′ chən) *adj* to do with the beliefs and traditions shared by Jews and Christians.

Ju·da·i·ca (jū dā′i ka) *n* literature and objects relating to Judaism or Jewish history and traditions: *a store selling Judaica.*

Ju·da·ism (jū′dā iz′əm) *n* the religion of the Jews, based on the Biblical covenant between God and Abraham, and the teaching of Moses and the prophets as revealed to them by God. <Greek *Ioudaios* Jew> **Ju·da′ic** (jū dā′ik) *adj.*

judge (juj) *n* **1** an official appointed to hear and decide cases in a law court. **2** a person chosen to settle a dispute or decide who wins. **3** a person who can decide how good a thing is: *a good judge of cattle, a poor judge of poetry.* **4** in ancient Israel, a ruler before the time of the kings.
v **judged, judg·ing 1** hear and decide cases as a judge in a law court. **2** settle a dispute or decide who wins a race or contest. **3** form an opinion or estimate of: *to judge the merits of a book.* **4** think, suppose, or conclude: *I judged that you had forgotten to come.* <Old French, from Latin *jus* law + *dicere* say> **judg′er** *n.*

judge·ship (juj′ship) *n* the position, duties, or term of office of a judge.

judg·ment or **judge·ment** (juj′mənt) *n* **1** the act of judging. **2 a** a decision, decree, or sentence given by a judge or court. **b** a decision made by anyone who judges. **3** a debt arising from a judge's decision. **4** an opinion or estimate: *It was a bad plan, in my judgment.* **5** the ability to form sound opinions: *My grandmother was a woman of judgment.* **6** criticism or condemnation: *Do not pass judgment on your neighbours.*

judg·men·tal (juj men′təl) *adj* quick to judge or condemn.

Judgment Day *n* in some systems of religious belief, the day of God's final judgment of humankind at the end of the world.

ju·di·cial (jū dish′əl) *adj* **1** to do with courts, judges, or the administration of justice. **2** ordered, permitted, or enforced by a judge or a court: *My aunt got a judicial separation from her husband.* **3** impartial and fair: *A judicial mind considers both sides of a dispute before making a decision.* <Latin *jus* law + *dicere* say> **ju·di′cial·ly** *adv.*

a bat	e bed	i bid	o pot	u cup	th thin
ā cake	ē me	ī bite	ō go	ū rude	ᴛʜ then
à bar	ə about	ər over	ȯ for	ů put	zh measure

ju·di·ci·ar·y (jū dish′ē er′ē) *or* (jū dish′ə rē) *n, pl* **ju·di·ci·ar·ies** **1** the branch of government that administers justice. **2** the system of courts of justice of a country. **3** judges as a group.
adj to do with courts, judges, or the administration of justice.

ju·di·cious (jū dish′əs) *adj* with, using, or showing good judgment: *a judicious use of natural resources.* **ju·di′cious·ly** *adv.*

ju·do (jū′dō) *n* a martial art that derives from jujitsu and uses holds and leverage to put an opponent off balance. <Japanese *ju* gentle + *do* way>

jug (jug) *n* a container for liquids, usually with a handle and either a spout or a narrow neck.
v **jugged, jug·ging** **1** put in a jug. **2** stew in a covered container: *jugged hare.* <perhaps alteration of *Joan, Joanna,* or *Jenny,* feminine names>

jug·ger·naut (jug′ər not′) *n* a huge, powerful, and overwhelming force, movement, or organization.

ETYMOLOGY

Juggernaut comes from Hindi *Jagannath*, the name of a huge idol of the god Krishna, which every year is wheeled through the streets of Puri in India.

jug·gle (jug′əl) *v* **jug·gled, jug·gling** **1** do tricks that require skill of hand or eye. **2** keep several objects in motion in the air at the same time by rapidly tossing them up in turn and catching them as they fall: *She can juggle three balls, keeping them all in the air at one time.* **3** change so as to deceive or cheat: *The bookkeeper juggled the club's accounts to hide her thefts.*
n the act of juggling. <Old French, from Latin *joculari* entertain, amuse>

jug·gler (jug′lər) *n* **1** a person who can do juggling tricks. **2** a person who uses tricks, deception, or fraud.

jug·gler·y (jug′lə rē) *n, pl* **jug·gler·ies** **1** the skill or tricks of a juggler. **2** trickery, deception, or fraud.

jug·u·lar (jug′yə lər) *adj* **1** to do with the neck or throat. **2** to do with the jugular vein.
n the **jugular vein**, one of the two large veins in the neck that return blood from the head to the heart. <Latin *jugulum* throat>
go for the jugular, *Slang* be ruthlessly competitive or aggressive.

juice (jūs) *n* **1** the liquid in fruits, vegetables, and meats: *the juice of a lemon, meat juices.* **2** a fluid in the body: *The gastric juices of the stomach help to digest food.* **3** *Informal* electricity.
v make juice by squeezing fruit or vegetables: *to juice carrots.* <Old French, from Latin *jus* broth>
juice′less *adj.*

juic·er (jū′sər) *n* an apparatus for squeezing juice out of fruits or vegetables.

juic·y (jū′sē) *adj* **juic·i·er, juic·i·est** **1** full of juice. **2** full of interest: *a juicy piece of gossip.*
juic′i·ly *adv.*

ju·jit·su (jū jit′sū) *n* a Japanese martial art that uses the strength and weight of an opponent to his or her disadvantage. Also, **jiujitsu**.

ETYMOLOGY

Jujitsu comes from Japanese *jujutsu*, made up of *ju*, meaning "soft and yielding" + *jutsu*, meaning "art."

ju·jube (jū′jūb) *n* **1** a lozenge or small tablet of gummy candy. **2** an edible datelike fruit of a shrub or tree, used to flavour this candy. <French *jujube,* from Greek *zizyphos*>

juke·box (jūk′boks) *n* a machine that plays a record when a coin is deposited in the slot. <Gullah (dialect spoken on the southeast US coast) *juke* disorderly house + *box*>

ju·lep (jū′ləp) *n* a drink made of whisky or brandy, sugar, crushed ice, and fresh mint.

Jul·ian calendar (jūl′yən) *n* a calendar of former times, in which the average length of a year was 365.25 days. It was introduced by Julius Caesar in 46 BCE, and revised in 1582 to become the GREGORIAN CALENDAR.

ju·li·enne (jū′lē en′) *adj, v* of food, cut in thin strips or small pieces: *Julienne potatoes are cut in thin strips and fried* (*adj*), *to julienne carrots* (*v*). <French>

Ju·ly (jū lī′) *n, pl* **Ju·lies** the seventh month of the year, with 31 days. *Abbrev.* **Jul**

ETYMOLOGY

July comes through Old French from Latin *Julius,* named after *Julius Caesar,* because he was born at this time of year.

jum·ble (jum′bəl) *v* **jum·bled, jum·bling** mix or confuse: *She jumbled up everything in the drawer when she was hunting for her gloves.*
n a confused mixture: *After I had studied history for two hours, my mind was a jumble of events.* <perhaps imitative>

jum·bo (jum′bō) *Informal n, pl* **jum·bos** something unusually large of its kind.
adj very big: *a jumbo ice-cream cone.* <*Jumbo,* a famous elephant in a 19c circus>

jumbo jet *n* a large airliner for several hundred passengers.

Jum·bo·Tron (jum′bō tron′) *Trademark n* a large screen or set of screens in a stadium on which the live action is displayed so that all spectators can see everything regardless of where they are sitting. <*jumbo* + (*elec*)*tron*(*ic*)>

jump (jump) *v* **1** spring from a horizontal surface such as the ground: *to jump up and down.* **2** leap over or cause to leap: *to jump a stream, to jump a horse over a fence.* **3** give a sudden jerk: *You made me jump.* **4** rise suddenly: *Prices jumped.* **5** in checkers, pass over and capture an opponent's piece. **6** start a motor vehicle using jumper cables.
n **1** a spring from a horizontal surface such as the ground. **2** the thing to be jumped over. **3** the distance jumped. **4** a contest in jumping: *Who won the broad jump?* **5** a sudden nervous jerk. **6** a sudden rise: *a jump in the cost of living.* **7** in the game of checkers, a move made to capture an opponent's piece. **8** a start of a motor vehicle by using jumper cables: *My battery is dead. Can you give me a jump?* <probably imitative>
get (or **have**) **the jump on,** *Informal* get (or have) an advantage over.
jump a claim, seize a piece of land claimed by another.
jump at, accept eagerly and quickly: *jump at an offer.*
jump bail, avoid a trial by running away.
jump on, *Informal* criticize with sudden violence.
jump out of your skin, *Informal* be very startled or frightened.
jump the gun, *Informal* start doing something too soon.
jump the rails (or **track**)**,** leave the train rails suddenly.
jump to conclusions, make an unfair assumption.
jump to it! *Informal* be quick!

jump ball *Basketball n* the putting of the ball into play by the referee, who tosses it between two opposing players.

jump·er[1] (jum′pər) *n* **1** a person who or thing that jumps. **2** a short length of wire used to make a temporary electrical connection. **3** a simply constructed sleigh on low wooden runners.

jump·er[2] (jum′pər) *n* **1** a sleeveless dress, usually worn over a blouse. **2** a loose jacket, such as that by workmen to protect their clothes and by sailors as part of their uniform. <Arabic *jubba* coat>

jumper cables BOOSTER CABLES.

jump·ing bean (jum′ping) *n* a seed of a Mexican plant that contains a small moth larva whose movements cause the seed to jump.

jumping jack *n* a toy man or animal that can be made to jump by pulling a string.

jump rope *especially US n* skipping rope.

jump·shot (jump′shot) *Basketball n* a shot in which a player throws the ball while at the height of his or her jump.

jump–start (jump′start′) *v* **1** start a vehicle by using jumper cables. **2** give an impetus to something that has stopped or is moving slowly: *The Bank of Canada has lowered interest rates to jump-start the economy.*
n the fact of being jump-started: *This ought to give his tired campaign a jump-start.*

jump·suit (jump′sūt′) *n* a one-piece garment consisting of a shirtlike top and long or short pants. <originally applied to a suit worn by parachutists>

jump·y (jum′pē) *adj* **jump·i·er, jump·i·est** **1** making sudden, sharp jerks. **2** easily excited, frightened, or made nervous. **jump′i·ly** *adv.* **jump′i·ness** *n.*

jun·co (jung′kō) *n, pl* **jun·cos** a small, mainly grey bird, a type of N American finch often seen in flocks during the winter.

junc·tion (jungk′shən) *n* **1** a joining or being joined: *the junction of two rivers.* **2** a place where things join or meet: *A railway junction is a place where railway lines meet or cross.* <Latin *jungere* join>

junction box *n* a device for connecting or branching electric circuits without splicing the wires.

junc·ture (jungk′chər) *n* **1** a particular point in events or time: *At this juncture, the surgeon decided to operate.* **2** a place where things join. **3** a joining or being joined. <Latin *jungere* join>

a bat	e bed	i bid	o pot	u cup	th **thin**
ā cake	ē me	ī bite	ō go	ū rude	TH **then**
ȧ bar	ə about	ər over	ȯ for	ů put	zh measure

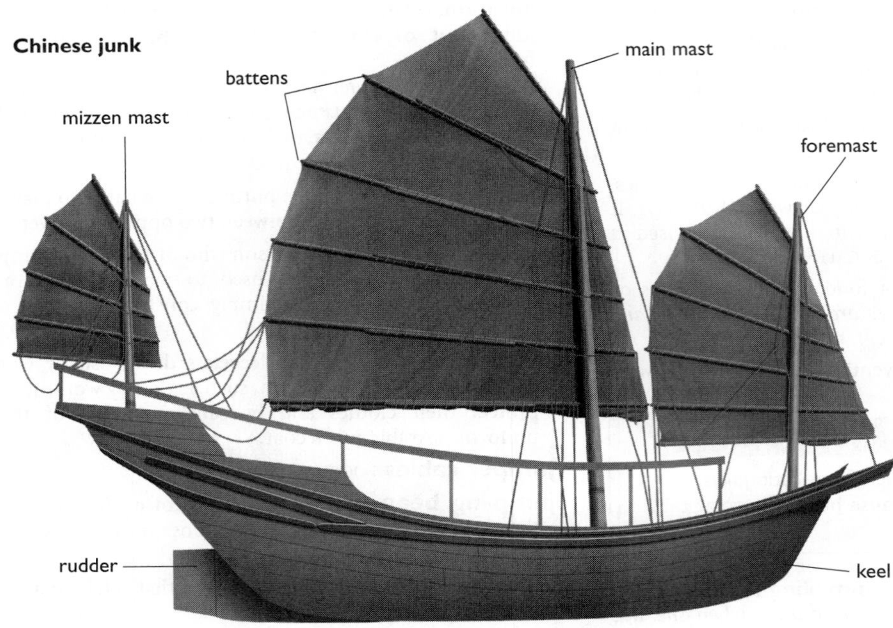

A **junk** is made of wood and usually has either a flat bottom or a small keel and a long rudder. The front, or *prow*, of the junk is broad and flat. The three sails are covered with coarse cotton and braced flat by bamboo strips, or *battens*.

The Chinese, Japanese, and Javanese people use junks for fishing and for transportation. Some junks also serve as living quarters.

June (jūn) *n* the sixth month of the year, with 30 days. *Abbrev.* **Jun** <Latin *Junius* the goddess Juno>

June·ber·ry (jūn′ber′ē) *n* a serviceberry.

June bug *n* a large, brown beetle that appears in June. Also called **June beetle**.

Jung·i·an (yung′ē ən) *adj* to do with Carl Gustav Jung, a 20th century psychologist, or his theories of how the mind works.
n a follower of Jung's theories.

jun·gle (jung′gəl) *n* **1** wild land thickly overgrown with bushes, vines, and trees. **2** a tangled mass. **3** a place characterized by vicious competition or struggle for survival: *She says the city is a jungle.* <Sanskrit *jangala* forest>
law of the jungle, the principle that only the strong and ruthless will succeed.

jungle fever *n* a severe form of malaria.

jungle fowl *n* a wild bird of southern Asia that is related to domestic fowl.

jungle gym *n* a climbing structure for children to play or exercise on, including ladders, ropes, bars, and suspension bridges.

jun·ior (jū′nyər) *adj* **1** the younger, used of a son with the same name as his father. **2** of a lower position, rank, or standing: *a junior officer, a junior partner.* **3** of or for students in grades 4–6: *junior school.* **4** of or for young people: *a junior tennis match, junior hockey.*
n **1** a younger person: *He is his sister's junior by two years.* **2** a person of lower rank or shorter service. <Latin *juvenis* young>

junior college *n* a college giving only the first year or the first two years of a regular university degree program.

junior high school *n* a school consisting of grades 7, 8, and 9.

ju·ni·per (jū′nə pər) *n* an evergreen shrub or tree of the northern hemisphere with small blue cones. <Latin *juniperus*>

junk[1] (jungk) *n* **1** *Informal* old, useless, or discarded items. **2** *Informal* worthless ideas, talk, or writings. **3** *Slang* heroin.
v Informal throw away or discard as junk: *I junked my old calculator and got a new one.* <Middle English>

junk[2] (jungk) *n* a Chinese sailing ship. <probably Javanese *jong*>

Jun·ker or **jun·ker** (yủng′kər) *n* a member of the aristocratic, formerly privileged class in Prussia.

jun·ket (jung′kit) *n* **1** curdled milk, sweetened and flavoured. **2** a pleasure trip. **3** an unnecessary trip taken by an official at the expense of the government or the firm he or she works for.
v go on a pleasure trip. <Old French *jonquette* basket, from Latin *juncus* basket in which food is served, extended to a feast or other such pleasure> **jun′ket·er** *n.*

junk food *n* prepackaged snack food with a high carbohydrate content and little nutritive value.

junk·ie (jung′kē) *Slang n* **1** a drug addict. **2** an addict of any kind: *a video junkie.*

junk mail *n* mail consisting of unwanted advertisements or promotional material.

junk·yard (jungk'yard') *n* a yard for the collection and resale of junk, especially scrap metal.

Ju·no (jū'nō) *n* **1** 🍁 an award presented annually to the best Canadian recording artists. **2** *Roman myth* the queen of the gods.

jun·ta (jun'tə) *or* (hùn'tə) *n* a group of people forming a government, especially as the result of a revolution: *The country was ruled by a military junta.* <Spanish, from Latin *jungere* join>

Ju·pi·ter (jū'pə tər) *n* the largest planet in the solar system. See EARTH for picture. <*Jupiter,* the supreme god of the Romans>

Ju·ras·sic (jə ras'ik) *Geology n* the middle period of the Mesozoic era, beginning about 205 million years ago, when birds first appeared on the earth.
adj to do with this period or the rocks formed then. <after the *Jura* Mountains in France and Switzerland>

ju·rid·i·cal (jə rid'ə kəl) *adj* to do with the administration of justice. **ju·rid'i·cal·ly** *adv.*

ju·ris·dic·tion (jù'ris dik'shən) *n* **1** the right or power of administering law or justice. **2** authority, power, or control. **3** the extent of authority: *The judge ruled that the case was not within her jurisdiction.* **4** the territory over which authority extends. <Latin *juris* law + *dicere* say>

ju·ris·pru·dence (jù'ris prū'dəns) *n* the theory or philosophy of law. <Latin *juris* law + *prudentia* knowledge>

ju·rist (jù'rist) *n* **1** a judge or lawyer. **2** an expert in law.

ju·ris·tic (jù ris'tik) *adj* to do with jurists or jurisprudence.

ju·ror (jù'rər) *n* a member of a jury.

ju·ry[1] (jù'rē) *n, pl* **ju·ries** **1** a group of people selected to hear evidence in a law court and sworn to give a decision in accordance with the evidence presented to it. **2** a group of people chosen to give a judgment or to decide who is the winner in a contest: *The jury gave her poem the first prize.* <Old French, from Latin *jurare* swear>

just (just) *adj* **1** morally correct: *a just life.* **2** proper; fair: *a just price.* **3** deserved: *a just reward.* **4** lawful: *a just claim.* **5** true or correct; exact: *a just description, just weights.*
adv **1** exactly: *The distance is just a metre.* **2** very close in space or time: *There is a picture just above the fireplace. She has just gone. I just managed to catch the school bus.* **3** only or merely: *They are just ordinary people, the same as us.* **4** *Informal* truly: *The weather is just glorious.* <Latin *jus* law> **just'ness** *n.*
just about, almost: *Careful! You just about knocked me over!*
just now, **a** exactly at this moment: *I don't know where she is just now.* **b** only a very short time ago: *I saw him just now.*

jus·tice (jus'tis) *n* **1** just conduct or fair dealing: *to have a sense of justice.* **2** fairness, rightness, or correctness: *to uphold the justice of our cause.* **3** well-founded reason: *She complained with justice of the bad treatment she had received.* **4** *Law* **a** the administration of law: *a court of justice.* **b** a judge. **c** a justice of the peace. <Old French, from Latin *jus* law>
bring someone to justice, do what is necessary in order that a person shall be legally punished for his or her crime or crimes.
do justice to, **a** treat fairly. **b** see the good points of. **c** show proper appreciation for: *The crowd's applause did not do justice to his performance.*
do yourself justice, do as well as you really can do: *She did not do herself justice on the test.*

justice of the peace *n* a local magistrate who tries minor cases and administers oaths. *Abbrev.* **JP** or **J.P.**

jus·tice·ship (jus'tis ship') *n* the position, duties, or term of office of a justice.

jus·ti·fi·a·ble (jus'tə fī'ə bəl) *adj* capable of being justified; that can be shown to be just and proper: *Their bad behaviour was not justifiable, even though they were provoked.* **jus'ti·fi'a·bil'i·ty** *n.* **jus'ti·fi'a·bly** *adv.*

jus·ti·fy (jus'tə fī') *v* **jus·ti·fied, jus·ti·fy·ing** **1** show to be just or proper: *The fine quality of the cloth justifies its high price.* **2** clear of blame or guilt: *It is impossible to justify the actions of a bully.* **3** *Printing* adjust the spacing between words so that the lines are of even length, aligned both on the left and on the right. The lines in this dictionary are justified. <French, from Latin *jus* law>
jus·ti·fi·ca·tion (jus'tə fə kā'shən) *n.* **jus'ti·fi'er** *n.*

just·ly (just'lē) *adv* **1** in a just manner: *The accused woman was tried justly.* **2** rightly: *You were justly angered by that insult.*

jut (jut) *v* **jut·ted, jut·ting** stick out or project: *The pier juts out from the shore into the water.*
n a part that sticks out. <variant of *jet* gush out>

jute (jūt) *n* a strong fibre made from the stems of a tropical plant, used for making coarse sacks, burlap, and rope. <Sanskrit *jutah* twisted hair>

ju·ve·nile (jū'və nīl') *or* (jū'və nəl) *adj* **1** youthful or immature: *juvenile behaviour.* **2** of or for young people: *juvenile crime.*
n a young person. <Latin *juvenis* young>

juvenile court YOUTH COURT.

juvenile delinquent *n* an earlier term for an adolescent who engages in crime. **juvenile delinquency** *n.*

jux·ta·pose (juk'stə pōz') *v* **jux·ta·posed, jux·ta·pos·ing** place side by side for contrasting effect. <French, from Latin *juxta* near + French *poser* place>
jux'ta·po·si'tion (juk'stə pə zish'ən) *n.*

Kk

k or **K** (kā) *n, pl* **k's** or **K's 1** the eleventh letter of the English alphabet, or any speech sound represented by it. **2** the eleventh thing in a list or series: *Can you help me with part (k) of this math question?*

k 1 kilo- (an SI prefix) **2** karat(s).

K 1 *Computers* a unit of computer memory, 1024 bytes: *This home computer is old and has a storage capacity of only 64 K.* **2** *Informal* a thousand dollars: *Would you pay 90 K for a car?* **3** potassium. **4** kelvin(s).

Ka (kȧ) *n* in the religion of ancient Egypt, the soul that is said to dwell in a person's body, and, after death, in his or her tomb or statue. Also, **ka**. <Egyptian>

Kaa·ba (kȧ'bə) *Islam n* the holiest shrine of Islam, located at Mecca in Saudi Arabia, toward which Muslims face when praying. <Arabic *kabah* square building>

Kab·loo·na or **kab·loo·na** (kab lū'nə) *n* among the Inuit, a white person. <Inuktitut *kablunak* one with big eyebrows>

ka·bob (kə bob') KEBAB.

ka·bu·ki (kə bū'kē) *n* a popular Japanese musical drama with elaborate costumes and highly stylized acting. <Japanese *ka* song + *bu* dance + *ki* art>

kad·dish (kȧ'dish) *or* (kȧ dish') *Judaism n, pl* **kad·dish·im** a portion of the daily prayer said in the synagogue, also used as a public or official prayer of mourning for a dead relative. <Aramaic *qaddis* holy>

kaf·tan (kaf'tan) CAFTAN.

ka·fuf·fle (kə fu'fəl) KERFUFFLE.

Kah·na·wa·ke (gȧ'nə wȧ'gē) *n, pl* **Kah·na·wa·ke** a member of a First Nations people living near Montréal.
adj to do with these people.
Also called **Caughnawaugha**.

Kai·la (kī'lə) *n* the supreme god of an Inuit religion. <Inuktitut>

Kai·nai (kī'nī) *n, pl* **Kai·nai 1** a member of a First Nations people living in southern Alberta. **2** the language of these people.
adj to do with these people or their language.
Also called **Blood**.

kai·ser (kī'zər) *n* **1** the title of the rulers of Germany, Austria, and the Holy Roman Empire at various stages in their history. **2** a large, round, crusty bun. <Latin *Caesar*>

kale (kāl) *n* a kind of cabbage that has large, loose leaves instead of a compact head. <Latin *caulis* cabbage>

ka·lei·do·scope (kə lī'də skop') *n* **1** a tube containing bits of coloured glass and two or more mirrors that, when turned, reflects continually changing patterns. **2** anything that changes continually: *the kaleidoscope of current events.* <Greek *kalos* pretty + *eidos* shape>
ka·lei'do·scop'ic (kə lī'də skop'ik) *adj.*

Ka·li (kȧ'lē) *Hinduism n* the goddess of life and death. <Sanskrit = black>

ka·mi (kȧ'mē) *Shintoism n, pl* **ka·mi** a divine being. <Japanese>

ka·mik (kȧ'mik) *n* a soft, knee-length boot of sealskin or caribou hide, worn in eastern Arctic regions. <Inuktitut>

ka·mi·ka·ze (kȧ'mi kȧ'zē) *n* in World War II, a Japanese aircraft pilot who carried out a suicide mission in which a plane loaded with explosives was deliberately crashed on a target.
adj **1** to do with such a pilot or aircraft. **2** reckless and self-destructive: *a kamikaze mission.* <Japanese = divine wind>

Kam·loops trout (kam'lūps) *n* a subspecies of the steelhead trout found in the British Columbian interior.

Kangaroos are one kind of several marsupials found in Australia, Tasmania, and New Guinea. Wallabies, koalas, and Tasmanian devils are other marsupials that are native to the area. The opossum is the only marsupial found in the western hemisphere.

kan·ga·roo (kang'gə rū') *n, pl* **kan·ga·roos** or (*especially collectively*) **kan·ga·roo** a marsupial of Australia and New Guinea with small forelegs and large, strong hind legs. The female has a pouch in front in which she carries her young. <origin uncertain>

karate

Speed, strength, and technique are the three important elements of **karate**. From the starting position, focused blows with the hands and feet are accompanied by special breathing and shouts.

The study of **karate** emphasizes a positive attitude, self-discipline, and a high moral purpose.

Karate originated in eastern Asia over 1000 years ago. Chinese monks were the first to use the techniques, incorporating them into their religious training. Later, peasants used the techniques for self-defence. In the 1600s, the Japanese developed karate into an art.

Karate achievements are acknowledged by belts of different colours, and each colour signifies the degree of skill a person has reached. A novice is acknowledged with a white belt, while a black belt indicates the highest level of achievement.

K

kangaroo court *n* an unauthorized court in which the law is disregarded or misinterpreted.

kangaroo rat *n* a mouselike N American desert rodent with long, strong hind legs adapted for leaping.

Kan·i·en'·ke·ha (kan yən'kā'ha') *n, pl* **Kan·i·en'·ke·ha·ka** (kan yən' kā ha'ka) **1** a member of a First Nations people now living mainly in southern Ontario and Québec. **2** the language of these people.
adj to do with these people or their language. Also called **Mohawk**.

kan·ji (kȧn'jē) *n, pl* **kan·ji** or **kan·jis** **1** Japanese script using symbols from Chinese, representing whole words or ideas rather than sounds. **2** any such symbol. <Japanese *kan* Chinese + *ji* ideograph>

ka·o·lin or **ka·o·line** (kā'ə lin) *n* a fine white clay, used in making porcelain. <*Gaoling* mountain in China, where the clay is found>

ka·pok (kā'pok) *n* the silky fibres around the seeds of a tropical tree, used for stuffing cushions, toys, and life preservers. <Malay>

Ka·po·si's sar·co·ma (kə pō'zēz sȧr kō'ma) *n* a skin cancer caused by a deficiency in the immune system. <M.K. *Kaposi*, 19c dermatologist>

ka·put (kȧ pu̇t') *or* (kə pu̇t') *Informal adj* (*never before a noun*) ruined, broken, or useless: *This computer is kaput.* <German, from French *être capot* be defeated>

kar·a (kȧr'ə) *Sikhism n* the steel bracelet worn by all baptized Sikhs. <Sanskrit>

kar·a·kul (kar'ə kəl) *or* (ker'ə kəl) *n* **1** a variety of Russian or Asiatic sheep with a dark, curled fleece. **2** the fleece of this sheep. <Russian>

ka·ra·o·ke (ker'ē ō'kē) *n* a form of entertainment in bars and clubs that allows a person to sing, with amplification, to recorded music. <Japanese>

kar·at (kar'ət) *or* (ker'ət) *n* a unit used to specify the proportion of gold in an alloy; one of 24 equal parts. For example, an 18-karat gold ring is 18 parts pure gold and 6 parts alloy. *Symbol* **k** or **kt** <French, from Greek *keration* a small bean used as a weight>

ka·ra·te (kə rȧ'tē) *n* a Japanese martial art, using hands and feet to deliver and block blows. <Japanese = empty hand>

kar·ma (kȧr'mə) *n* **1** in Buddhism and Hinduism, the totality of a person's actions in this and previous lives that affect or determine his or her fate. **2** destiny; fate. <Sanskrit = fate>

kart (kȧrt) *n* GO-KART.
v take part in a go-kart race.

a bat	e bed	i bid	o pot	u cup	th thin
ā cake	ē me	ī bite	ō go	ū rude	ᴛʜ then
ȧ bar	ə about	ər over	ȯ for	u̇ put	zh measure

kar·y·o·tin (kar′ē ō tin) *or* (ker′ē ō tīn) *n* chromatin.

ka·ry·o·type (kar′ē ō tīp′) *or* (ker′ē ō tīp′) *n* the appearance (size, shape, number, etc.) of the chromosomes in a somatic cell of an individual or a species. <Latin, from Greek *karyon* kernel i.e., nucleus>

Kash·mir (kash′mēr) *n* a region on the border of northeast Pakistan and northern India and claimed by both countries. **Kash·mir′i** *n, adj.*

kash·rut (kash rūt′) *or* (kash′rūt) *Judaism n* Jewish dietary law. <Hebrew = fitness>

Kas·ka (kus′kə) *n, pl* **Kas·ka** or **Kas·kas** **1** a member of a First Nations people living in northern British Columbia and Yukon Territory. **2** their Athapascan language.

ka·ty·did (kā′tē did′) *n* a large grasshopper. The male makes a shrill noise by rubbing its front wings together. <imitative>

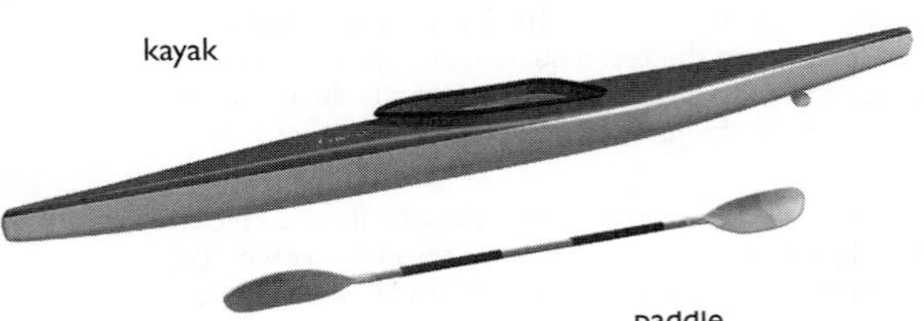

kay·ak (kī′ak) *n* a light, narrow boat with pointed ends, originally made by the Inuit, that has a small opening in the middle for the user: *Kayaks were traditionally used by the Inuit for hunting.* <Inuktitut *qayaq*>

Ka·yon·kwe'·ha·ka (ka yon kwā′ ha ka′) CAYUGA.

Ka·zakh·stan (ka′zək stan′) a country in central Asia. See the APPENDIX. **Ka′zakh·stan′i** *adj, n.*

ka·zoo (kə zū′) *n* a toy musical instrument made of a tube sealed off at one end with a membrane or paper that produces a buzzing sound when one hums into the tube. <imitative>

KB kilobyte(s).

ke·a (kā′ə) *or* (kē′ə) *n* a large, greenish parrot of New Zealand. <Maori (a language of New Zealand)>

ke·bab (kə bob′) *n* pieces of meat or vegetables cooked on a skewer. Also, **kabob**. <Arabic *kabab*>

keek·wil·lie or **keek·wil·lie house** (kēk′wi lē) *British Columbia n* a large underground winter dwelling formerly used by some First Nations peoples, covered with split logs and a layer of mud. <Chinook *gigwalix*>

keel (kēl) *n* **1** the main timber or steel piece that extends the whole length of the bottom of a ship or boat. **2** a part, as on an aircraft, that is like a ship's keel.
v turn over on its side. <Old Norse *kjolr*>
keel over, a turn over or upside down: *The sailboat keeled over in the storm.* **b** *Informal* faint or fall over suddenly.
on an even keel, a horizontal. **b** steady and properly balanced: *His emotions are on an even keel again.*

keel·haul (kēl′hol′) *v* in former times, haul a person from side to side under the keel of a ship as a punishment.

keen[1] (kēn) *adj* **1** sharp enough to cut well: *a keen blade.* **2** sharp or piercing in quality: *a keen wind, keen hunger, a keen wit, keen pain.* **3** strong or vivid: *keen competition.* **4** able to do its work quickly and accurately: *a keen mind, a keen sense of smell.* **5** full of enthusiasm: *a keen player, keen about sailing.* <Old English *cene*> **keen′ly** *adv.* **keen′ness** *n.*
be keen on, be very much in favour of: *I'm not keen on going alone.*

keen[2] (kēn) *v* to wail in grief for a dead person. <Irish *caoinim* I wail>

keen·er (kēn′ər) *Informal n* a person who tries hard to show how enthusiastic and hard-working he or she is.

keep (kēp) *v* **kept, keep·ing** **1** possess permanently: *You may keep this book.* **2** have and not let go: *The accused was kept in custody until the trial.* **3** not reveal: *Will you promise to keep my secret?* **4** retain: *Keep this in mind.* **5** hold back or prevent: *What is keeping her from being on time?* **6** maintain or remain in good condition: *to keep a garden. Butter will keep in a refrigerator. My uncle keeps chickens.* **7 a** stay the same or cause to continue in some stated place or condition: *Keep awake. Keep going along this road for two kilometres, to keep a student after school, to keep a light burning.* **8** make regular entries in: *to keep score, to keep a diary.* **9** be faithful to: *to keep a promise.* **10** provide for or support: *He is not able to keep himself, much less a family.*
n **1** food and a place to sleep: *She earns her keep.* **2** the strongest part of a castle or fort. <Old English *cepan*>
be keeping, in a question regarding health: *How is your grandmother keeping? I hope she's well.*
for keeps, a for an indefinitely long period: *She gave me the bracelet for keeps.* **b** seriously and permanently: *I've finished with him for keeps.*
keep in with, *Informal* keep friendship with.
keep on, continue or go on: *We kept on swimming in spite of the rain.*
keep time, give the correct time in a clock or watch.
keep to yourself, a not mix with others: *He keeps to himself because he is shy.* **b** not tell others: *If you know the answer already, keep it to yourself!*
keep up, a continue or prevent from ending: *We kept up a small fire.* **b** maintain in good condition. **c** remain close or alongside.
keep up with, a go or move as fast as. **b** live or do as well as: *She tried hard to keep up with her wealthy friends.* **c** stay up to date with: *I like to keep up with the news. Try to keep up with your reading.*

keep·er (kē′pər) *n* **1** a person who or thing that keeps. **2** a guard. **3** a guardian or protector: *The custodian of animals in a zoo is called a keeper.* **4** *Informal* anything worth keeping: *That photograph of you is a keeper.*

keep·ing (kē′ping) *n* **1** care or maintenance: *The keeping of the orphaned children was paid for by their uncle.* **2** celebration or observance: *The keeping of Thanksgiving Day is an old North American custom.* **3** the fact or condition of being kept for future use.
in keeping, in agreement: *Their ideas are not in keeping with ours.*

keep·sake (kēp′sāk′) *n* something kept in memory of the giver: *My friend gave me her picture as a keepsake before going away.*

keg (keg) *n* a small barrel. <Old Norse *kaggi*>

kelp (kelp) *n* a large, tough, brown seaweed. <Middle English *culpe*>

kel·vin (kel′vin) *n* **1** the SI unit of temperature on the Kelvin scale. One kelvin equals one degree Celsius. **2 Kelvin** to do with the scale of temperature on which 0 represents absolute zero, or –273°C. *Symbol* **K**

ETYMOLOGY

Kelvin is named after William Thomson, Lord *Kelvin* (1824–1907), the physicist who developed the Kelvin scale.

He also invented the first ship's compass that was not affected by the iron in the ship.

ken (ken) *n* a person's range of sight or knowledge: *What happens on Jupiter is beyond our ken.* <Old English *cennan* make known>

ken·nel (ken′əl) *n* **1** a house for a dog or dogs: *We built a kennel for our dog.* **2** a place where dogs are bred, lodged, or cared for: *Our puppy came from a well-known kennel near Ottawa.*
v **ken·nelled** or **ken·neled, ken·nel·ling** or **ken·nel·ing** put, keep, or lodge in a kennel. <Old French, from Latin *canis* dog>

ke·no (kē′nō) *n* a gambling game resembling bingo.

Ken·ya (ken′yə) *or* (kēn′yə) *n* a country in east Africa. See the APPENDIX. **Ken′yan** *adj, n.*

kep·i (kep′ē) *n, pl* **kep·is** a cap with a round, flat top, worn by some French soldiers. <French *képi*>

kept (kept) *v* past tense and past participle of KEEP.

ker·a·tin (ker′ə tin) *n* a complex protein, the chief constituent of horn, nails, hair, and feathers. <Greek *keratos* horn>

ker·chief (kər′chif) *n* a piece of cloth worn over the head or around the neck. <Old French *couvrir* cover + *chief* head>

ker·fuf·fle (kər fu′fəl) *n* a commotion or uproar. Also, **kafuffle**. <probably Scottish Gaelic>

ker·mes (kər′mēz) *n* a red dye once made from scale insects. <Arabic *qirmiz*>

kern (kərn) *Computers, Printing v* cause letters to be positioned, in print or on a computer screen, as closely together as their shapes will allow.
n the part of a letter that projects beyond the body of the piece of type. <French *carne* corner of type, from Latin *cardinis* hinge>

ker·nel (kər′nəl) *n* **1** the softer part inside the hard shell of a nut, seed, or the stone of a fruit. **2** a grain or seed, especially of wheat or corn. **3** the central or most important part: *the kernel of an argument.* <Old English *cyrnel*>

ker·o·sene (ker′ə sēn′) *n* a thin oil, a mixture of hydrocarbons, usually produced by distilling petroleum, and used as a fuel. <Greek *keros* wax>

kes·trel (kes′trəl) *n* a small falcon. <Middle English>

ket·a (kā′tə) *or* (kē′tə) CHUM³. <origin uncertain>

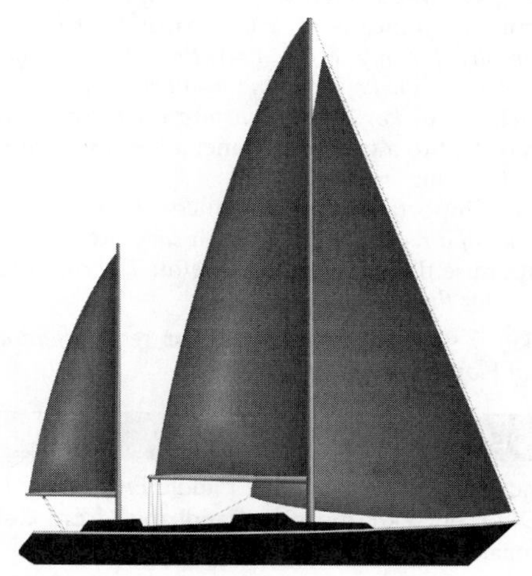

ketch (kech) *n* a fore-and-aft-rigged sailing ship with a large mainmast toward the bow and a smaller mast toward the stern. <perhaps from *catch*>

ketch·up (kech′əp) *n* a sauce made from tomato, vinegar, and spices and eaten cold. Also called **catsup**. <perhaps Cantonese *ke chap* tomato juice>

ket·tle (ket′əl) *n* **1** a metal pot for boiling or stewing food. **2** a teakettle. **3** *Geology* a depression in glacial drift remaining after the melting of an isolated mass of buried ice. <Latin *catinus* vessel>
a (fine) kettle of fish, *Informal* a mess or muddle: *We were in a fine kettle of fish when I lost the compass.*

ket·tle·drum (ket′əl drum′) *n* a drum shaped like a large brass or copper hemisphere. See PERCUSSION INSTRUMENT for picture.

Kev·lar (kev′lar) *Trademark n* a strong synthetic fibre used in making tires, bulletproof vests, canoes, etc.

key¹ (kē) *n, pl* **keys 1 a** a small, shaped metal instrument that locks and unlocks: *I lost the key to the padlock on my bicycle.* **b** anything like this in shape or use: *a key to wind an old clock, a key to open and close a valve.* **2** something that explains or answers: *the key to a puzzle. The key in a math book gives answers to the problems.* **3** an important or essential person or thing: *Exercising regularly is the key to fitness.* **4** one of a set of parts pressed down by the fingers, on a computer keyboard, in playing a piano and other instruments, etc. **5** *Music* a scale or system of related musical tones based on a particular tone: *a song written in the key of C.* **6** *Basketball* the space (including the foul line) in front of each basket, usually painted a different colour from the rest of the court. Also called **keyhole**. **7** an explanation of abbreviations or symbols used in a map, dictionary, or other text: *There is a pronunciation key on the right-hand pages of this dictionary.*

a bat	e bed	i bid	o pot	u cup	th **thin**
ā cake	ē me	ī bite	ō go	ū rude	ᴛʜ **then**
ä bar	ə about	ər over	ô for	ů put	zh measure

v **keyed, key·ing** 1 often, **key in** *Computers* enter data in a computer by means of a keyboard: *I have to key the bibliography for my essay, and then I'm finished. The computer operator keyed in the numbers.* 2 *Music* regulate the pitch of: *to key a piano before a concert.* 3 adjust a speech or text to a particular tone: *a greeting card keyed to a tone of sorrow.*
adj very important: *a key witness in a trial, the key industries of a region.* <Old English *cæg*> **key′less** *adj.*
key up, raise the courage or nerve of: *The coach keyed up the team for the big game.*

key[2] (kē) *n, pl* **keys** a low island or reef: *There are keys south of Florida.*

> **ETYMOLOGY**
>
> **Key** and **quay** come from late Middle English *key, keye* from Old French *kai,* meaning "sandbank," from Celtic *kagio*, meaning "to encompass or enclose."

🍁 **key block** *n* a large conical block of snow, dropped into place at the centre of an igloo dome, serving to lock the structure firmly together.

key·board (kē′bôrd′) *n* the set of keys in a computer, piano, or calculator. See ELECTRONIC INSTRUMENTS for picture.
v 1 *Computers* KEY (*v* def. 1). 2 *Music* play (a composition) on a piano or keyboard. **key′board′ing** *n.*
key′board′ist *n.*

key·chain (kē′chān′) *n* a small chain or ring to which keys may be attached.

key grip *n* the chief GRIP (*n* def. 8) on a movie set.

key·hole (kē′hōl′) *n* 1 an opening in a lock through which a key is inserted to turn the lock. 2 KEY (*n* def. 7).

Key·nes·i·an (kā′nēz ī ən) *adj* to do with the theory of 20th century economist J. M. Keynes, that in a depression a government should spend money on public works and set lower interest rates to promote recovery.

key·note (kē′nōt′) *n* 1 *Music* the note on which a scale or system of tones is based. 2 the main idea or guiding principle: *World peace was the keynote of his speech.*

keynote speech *n* a speech that presents the main issues of interest to the audience.

key·pad (kē′pad′) *Computers n* that part of a computer or other keyboard that contains numbers and special keys.

key signature *Music n* the sharps or flats placed after the clef at the beginning of a staff of music to indicate the key.

key·stone (kē′stōn′) *n* 1 the middle stone at the top of an arch, holding the other stones or pieces in place. 2 the principle on which other associated parts depend: *Freedom of choice is the keystone of our society.*

key·stroke (kē′strōk′) *n* a stroke of a key on a keyboard.

key·word (kē′wərd′) *n* 1 a word or phrase that is much used or of great significance. 2 *Computers* a word used as a reference point for finding information, such as one keyed in to search for and retrieve a document on the Internet, or one mentioned in an index. 3 a word that is needed to decipher a code.

kg kilogram(s).

KGB *n* the secret police of the former Soviet Union. <Russian *Komitet Gosudarstvennoi Bezopasnosti* State Security Committee>

khak·i (kar′kē), (kä′kē), *or* (kak′ē) *adj* dull yellowish brown.
n, pl **khak·is** 1 a strong cloth of this colour, often used for soldiers' uniforms. 2 a uniform or uniforms made of this cloth: *Khakis will be worn for drill.*

> **ETYMOLOGY**
>
> **Khaki** comes from Urdu *khaki*, meaning "dusty," which came from Persian *khak*, meaning "dust." It was first introduced for uniforms of the British cavalry in India in 1846.

kha·lif (kā′lif) *or* (kal′if) CALIPH.

Khal·sa (kal′sə) *Sikhism n* the worldwide community of members who have been ritually admitted to the religion. <Arabic *kalis* pure>

khan (kän) *n* 1 a title given to rulers and high officials in some Muslim countries. 2 the former title of a supreme ruler among Tartar, Mongol, or Turkish peoples, or of the emperor of China during the Middle Ages. <Turkish>

kha·tib (kə tēb′) *Islam n* the preacher, usually a mullah, who delivers the **khutba**, or sermon, in a mosque. <Arabic *khataba* preach>

kHz kilohertz.

kib·ble (ki′bəl) *n* a substance consisting of coarse particles, especially dog food. <origin uncertain>

kib·butz (ki bůts′) *Hebrew n, pl* **kib·butz·im** (ki bůt sēm′) a communal settlement or farm co-operative in Israel. <Hebrew *qibbus* gathering>

kib·butz·nik (ki bůts′nik) *Hebrew n* a member of a kibbutz.

kibi– *prefix* about a thousand (2^{10}). A **kibibyte** (ki′bi bīt) is 1024 bytes. *Symbol* **Ki** <*ki*(*lo*-) *bi*(*nary*)>

kib·itz (kib′its) *Informal v* look on as an outsider and offer unwanted advice. <Yiddish> **kib′itz·er** *n.*

ki·bosh (kī′bosh) *or* (ki bosh′) *n* <origin uncertain>
put the kibosh on, *Informal* put an end to: *My mother put the kibosh on my Internet access.*

kick (kik) *v* 1 strike out or strike with the foot: *That horse kicks when anyone comes near it. The horse kicked the girl.* 2 drive, force, or move by kicking: *to kick a ball.* 3 win by a kick: *to kick a goal in football.* 4 of a gun, spring back when fired: 5 *Informal* complain, object, or grumble.
n 1 the act of kicking. 2 the recoil of a gun when it is fired. 3 *Informal* a complaint or objection. 4 *Informal* a thrill: *She gets a kick out of snowboarding.* 5 *Informal* the power of a drink or drug to intoxicate. <Middle English>
kick around, *Informal* **a** lie around: *These magazines have been kicking around for ages. Do you still want them?* **b** go around aimlessly: *After lunch we spent some time kicking around downtown.* **c** consider casually: *We kicked around a few ideas but didn't decide anything.* **d** treat without respect: *Don't let anyone kick you around.*

kick back, *Informal* **a** spring back suddenly and unexpectedly. **b** return a portion of money from an illegal payment.
kick in, *Informal* **a** begin taking effect: *The cough medicine is starting to kick in.* **b** contribute a share: *If everyone kicks in a toonie, we can order a large pizza.*
kick off, a put a football in play with a kick. **b** *Informal* begin.
kick out, *Informal* expel in a humiliating way: *She should be kicked out of our club.*
kick up, *Informal* make, cause, or raise: *to kick up trouble, to kick up a fuss, to kick up a cloud of dust.*

kick·back (kik′bak′) *Informal n* **1** the amount or portion returned, especially as an illicit fee: *He will expect a kickback for finding the money for you.* **2** the recoil of a gun.

kick·box·ing (kik′bok′sing) *n* a martial art that incorporates boxing and karate moves, especially kicking. **kick′box′er** *n.*

kick·er (kik′ər) *n* **1** a person who or animal or thing that kicks. **2** *Informal* an unexpected or unpleasant discovery or turn of events. **3** a small outboard motor.

kick·off (kik′of′) *n* **1** the start of a football game: *The kickoff is scheduled for 2 p.m.* **2** the start of any activity.

kick·stand (kik′stand′) *n* a lever attached to the rear wheel of a bicycle or motorcycle that can be used to support the vehicle when it is not in use.

kick–start (kik′stȧrt′) *v* **1** start a motorcycle engine by kicking downward against a pedal at the side. **2** start or, sometimes, revive something by a sudden powerful injection of energy or resources: *The government kick-started the project with a million-dollar grant.*

kid[1] (kid) *n* **1** a young goat. **2** its flesh, used as food. **3** its skin, used as fur. **4** the leather made from the skin of young goats. **5** *Informal* a child or young person: *The kids like the playground.* <Old Norse *kith*>
handle with kid gloves, treat very carefully or cautiously.

kid[2] (kid) *Informal v* **kid·ded, kid·ding 1** talk jokingly. **2** deceive or fool someone. <perhaps *kid*[1], i.e., treat as a child> **kid′der** *n.*
kid around, joke or tease.
no kidding, a an expression of surprise or disbelief. **b** I mean this; I am not joking.

kid·die (ki′dē) *Informal n* a young child.
adj for or involving young children.

kid·dush (ki dūsh′) *or* (ki′dəsh) *Judaism n* the prayer or blessing recited over wine on the Sabbath eve. <Hebrew *qiddus* blessing>

kid·nap (kid′nap′) *v* **kid·napped** or **kid·naped, kid·nap·ping** or **kid·nap·ing** abduct and hold a person against his or her will by force: *The banker's child was kidnapped and held for ransom. The gang planned to kidnap the movie star.* <*kid*[1] + *nap*, slang for nab or seize>

kid·nap·per or **kid·nap·er** (kid′nap′ər) *n* a person who abducts and holds another by force: *The kidnappers demanded a ransom.*

kid·ney (kid′nē) *n, pl* **kid·neys** one of the pair of organs in vertebrates that separate waste matter and water from the blood and pass them out through the bladder as urine. <Middle English> **kid′ney·like′** *adj.*

kidney bean *n* the kidney-shaped, usually dark red seed of several varieties of bean, dried for use in cooking.

kidney stone *n* an abnormal hard mass in a kidney, formed from the salts of various acids.

kiel·ba·sa (kēl bȧ′sə) *n* a lightly spiced sausage flavoured with garlic that is usually eaten cold. <Polish = sausage>

kill (kil) *v* **1** cause the death of a living thing: *The explosion killed several people.* **2** put an end to or get rid of: *to kill odours, to kill a rumour.* **3** defeat or veto a legislative bill. **4** destroy or neutralize the active qualities of: *to kill land with pesticides.* **5** spoil the effect of: *One colour may kill another near it.* **6** use up time: *We killed an hour at the zoo.* **7** *Informal* overcome completely: *My sore foot is killing me. Her jokes really kill me.*
n **1** the act of killing. **2** the animal or animals killed. <Middle English *kyllen*>
kill off, wipe out or kill all of: *A disease killed off his entire herd of cows.*
kill a penalty, *Hockey* overcome the disadvantage of a penalty by preventing the opposing team from scoring.
move in for the kill, a swiftly approach a hunted animal to kill it: *The lion moved in for the kill.* **b** *Informal* prepare a final and decisive attack: *After a very aggressive campaign, the premier's rival moved in for the kill.*

kill·deer (kil′dēr′) *n, pl* **kill·deers** or (*especially collectively*) **kill·deer** a N American wading bird that has a loud, shrill cry. <imitative>

kill·er (kil′ər) *n* **1** a person who or animal or thing that kills. **2** a criminal who is hired to kill others. **3** *Informal* anything that is very difficult: *That assignment was a killer.*

killer bee *n* a honeybee native to Africa that is quick to attack when provoked.

Killer whales can be found in every ocean, and they move about according to the migration habits of their food, such as herring, other types of fish, and seals.

killer whale *n* a small whale with black-and-white markings that hunts in groups for fish, seals, and penguins. Also called **orca**.

a bat	e bed	i bid	o pot	u cup	th thin
ā cake	ē me	ī bite	ō go	ū rude	ᴛʜ then
ȧ bar	ə about	ər over	ȯ for	u̇ put	zh measure

kil·lick (kil′ik) *n* an anchor made of wooden poles or sticks bound around one or more rocks, used especially in the Atlantic Provinces and New England. <origin uncertain>

kill·ing (kil′ing) *adj* **1** deadly or destructive: *a killing frost.* **2** overpowering or exhausting: *She rode her horse at a killing pace.* **3** *Informal* extremely funny.
n Informal a sudden great financial success: *to make a killing in the stock market.* **kill′ing·ly** *adv.*

kill·joy (kil′joi′) *n* a person who spoils other people's fun.

kiln (kiln) *or* (kil) *n* a furnace or oven for burning, baking, or drying something: *Limestone is burned in a kiln to make lime. Bricks are baked in a kiln.*
v burn, bake, or dry in a kiln. <Old English, from Latin *culina* kitchen>

ki·lo (kē′lō) *or* (kil′ō) *n, pl* **ki·los** a kilogram.

kilo– *combining form* thousand: *kilometre.* <French, from Greek *chilioi*>

kil·o·bit (kil′ə bit′) *Computers n* a unit of digital information roughly equal to 1000 bits (actually 1024, which is 2^{10}).

kil·o·byte (kil′ə bīt′) *Computers n* a unit of digital information roughly equal to 1000 bytes (actually 1024, which is 2^{10}). *Symbol* **KB**

kil·o·gram (kil′ə gram′) *n* the SI unit for measuring mass, equal to 1000 grams. Also, **kilogramme**. *Symbol* **kg**

kil·o·hertz (kil′ə hərts′) *n, pl* **kil·o·hertz** a unit of frequency of waves and vibrations, equal to 1000 hertz. *Symbol* **kHz**

kil·o·joule (kil′ə jūl′) *n* a unit of energy, equal to 1000 joules. *Symbol* **kJ**

kil·o·met·rage (kil′ə mē′trij) *or* (kə lom′ə trij) *n* **1** the total number of kilometres travelled: *The kilometrage on a new car should be zero.* **2** the distance in kilometres that a motor vehicle can go on a given amount of fuel: *Slower speeds give better kilometrage.* **3** an allowance for travelling expenses at a fixed rate per kilometre: *My aunt gets kilometrage at the company she works for.* Compare MILEAGE.

kil·o·me·tre (kil′ə mē′tər) *or* (kə lom′ə tər) *n* a unit of length or distance, equal to 1000 metres. It takes about twelve minutes to walk one kilometre. Also, **kilometer**. *Symbol* **km**

kil·o·pas·cal (kil′ə pas′kəl) *n* a unit of air pressure, equal to 1000 pascals. *Symbol* **kPa**

kil·o·ton (kil′ə tun′) *n* a unit of explosive force, equal to 1000 tons (about 907 tonnes) of TNT.

kil·o·volt (kil′ə vōlt′) *n* a unit of electric pressure, equal to 1000 volts. *Symbol* **kV**

kil·o·watt (kil′ə wot′) *n* a unit of power, equal to 1000 watts. *Symbol* **kW**

kil·o·watt–hour (kil′ə wot′our′) *n* a unit of electrical energy, equal to the number of kilowatts of electrical power used per hour. *Symbol* **kWh**

kilt (kilt) *n* a pleated, knee-length skirt worn by men in the Scottish Highlands, by soldiers in Scottish regiments, and in Scottish Highland formal wear.
v gather fabric or a garment in vertical folds. <Scandinavian> **kilt′like′** *adj.*

kil·ter (kil′tər) *Informal n* (*especially negatively, preceded by* ***out of***) good condition or order: *Our radio is out of kilter.* <origin uncertain>

ki·mo·no (kə mō′nə) *n, pl* **ki·mo·nos** **1** a loose outer garment held in place by a sash, worn by Japanese men and women. **2** a loose dressing gown. <Japanese *ki* wear + *mono* thing>

kin (kin) *n* **1** a person's family or relatives: *All our kin came to the family reunion.* **2** connection by birth or marriage: *What kin is she to you?*
adj related: *My cousins are kin to me.* <Old English *cynn*>
kin′less *adj.*
next of kin, nearest living relative: *His next of kin is his mother.*
of kin, related.

kind[1] (kīnd) *adj* **1** friendly, generous, or considerate: *kind words. Be kind to animals.* **2** showing or characterized by kindness: *The dog had a kind owner.* <Old English *gecynde* nature, natural>

kind[2] (kīnd) *n* a group of people or things with similar characteristics: *all kinds of candy. A kilt is a kind of skirt.* <Old English *gecynde* nature, natural>
all kinds of, plenty or a lot of: *all kinds of good wishes.*
in kind, a in goods or produce, not in money. **b** in something of the same sort. **c** in characteristic quality: *There is difference in kind, not merely in size, between a bloodhound and a terrier.*
kind of, *Informal* somewhat or rather: *The room was kind of dark.*
of a kind, a of the same kind: *The cakes were all of a kind—chocolate!* **b** of a poor or mediocre quality: *Two boxes and a plank make a table of a kind.*

GRAMMAR AND USAGE

Kind in its singular form takes a singular adjective before it: *I like that kind of fruit.*

Kinds in the plural takes a plural adjective: *I like those kinds of fruit.*

Do not use a plural determiner with a singular noun:
Incorrect: *these kind of shoes.*
Correct: *this kind of shoes.*

kin·der·gar·ten (kin′dər gär′tən) *n* an introduction to school for children of preschool age, in preparation for the first grade. In Canada, a **junior kindergarten** class may be offered for four-year-olds, and a **senior kindergarten** for five-year-olds. **kin′der·gart′ner** *n.*

ETYMOLOGY

Kindergarten comes from German *Kindergarten,* literally meaning "children's garden." The word was coined to suggest that this type of school is a garden in which children are cultivated, just as flowers are cultivated in a flower garden. The first kindergarten was started in Germany in 1840.

kind–heart·ed (kīnd′hȧr′tid) *adj* with or showing kindness or sympathy: *A kind-hearted girl helped me pick up my books.* **kind′-heart′ed·ly** *adv.* **kind′-heart′ed·ness** *n.*

kin·dle (kin′dəl) *v* **kin·dled, kin·dling 1** set on fire: *Light the paper with a match to kindle the wood.* **2** begin to burn: *This damp wood will never kindle.* **3** arouse or stir up: *His cruelty to the cat kindled our anger.* **4** light up or brighten: *Her face kindled as she talked about her family.* <Old Norse *kindill* candle>

kind·li·ness (kīn′dlē nis) *n* **1** a kindly feeling or quality. **2** a kindly act.

kin·dling (kin′dling) *n* material, such as small pieces of wood, for starting a fire. <Old Norse *kindill* candle>

kind·ly (kīn′dlē) *adj* **kind·li·er, kind·li·est 1** kind or friendly: *kindly faces.* **2** pleasant or agreeable: *a kindly summer breeze.*
adv **1** in a kind or friendly way: *The children liked the school bus driver because she always treated them kindly.* **2** please: *Kindly pay the rent at the end of the month.*
take kindly to, like or accept: *He does not take kindly to criticism.*

kind·ness (kīnd′nis) *n, pl* **kind·ness·es 1** a kind nature: *We admire her kindness.* **2** kind treatment: *Thank you for your kindness.* **3** a kind act: *He showed me many kindnesses.*

kin·dred (kin′drid) *adj* **1** like or similar: *We are studying about dew, frost, and kindred facts of nature.* **2** related: *kindred tribes.*
n **1** one's family or relatives. **2** connection by birth or marriage: *Does he claim kindred with you?* **3** a likeness or resemblance. <Old English *cynn* kin>

kin·es·the·sia (kin′əs thē′zhə) *n* the sensation of movement in the muscles and joints. <Latin, from Greek *kinein* move + *aisthesis* sensation> **kin′es·thet′ic** *adj.*

ki·net·ic (ki net′ik) *adj* related to, or caused by motion.
n **kinetics** (*with singular verb*) the branch of mechanics that studies how forces cause or change the motion of bodies. <Greek *kinein* move>

kinetic energy *n* the energy of a body due to its motion.

kin·folk (kin′fōk′) KINSFOLK.

king (king) *n* **1** the male ruler of a country: *Richard the Lion-hearted was King of England.* **2** a person who or animal or thing that is best or most important in a certain sphere or class: *The lion is called the king of the beasts. Babe Ruth was a king of baseball.* **3** in chess, the chief piece. **4** in checkers, a piece that has moved entirely across the board. **5** a playing card bearing a picture of a king. <Old English *cyning*> **king′like′** *adj.*

King Ar·thur (ar′thər) *n* the central figure in a group of legends about the knights of the Round Table.

king·bird (king′bərd′) *n* a N American bird of the flycatcher family with a grey head and back, known for its aggressiveness.

king cobra *n* a large, poisonous snake of tropical Asia that feeds mainly on other snakes.

king crab HORSESHOE CRAB.

king·dom (king′dəm) *n* **1** a country that is governed by a king or a queen. **2** one of the three traditional broad divisions of the natural world as animals, plants, and minerals: *Humans are part of the animal kingdom.* **3** *Biology* one of the major categories into which living things are classified. In a five-kingdom system, the kingdoms are animals, plants, fungi, protists, and monera; in a six-kingdom system the kingdoms are animals, plants, fungi, protists, archaea, and bacteria. See also DIVISION, PHYLUM, CLASS, ORDER, FAMILY, GENUS, and SPECIES. <Old English *cyningdom* kingship>

king·fish (king′fish′) *n, pl* **king·fish** or **king·fish·es** a large food fish of the Atlantic or Pacific coast.

king·fish·er (king′fish′ər) *n* a bright-coloured diving bird with a large head and a strong beak.

king·let (king′lit) *n* **1** a minor king. **2** a small warbler with a yellowish crown of feathers.

king·ly (king′lē) *adj* **king·li·er, king·li·est** like, or fit for a king or kings: *a kingly crown, kingly pride.*
adv as a king does. **king′li·ness** *n.*

king·mak·er (king′mā′kər) *n* a powerful person who can influence or dictate the political careers of others.

king·pin (king′pin′) *n* **1** *Bowling* the pin in front or in the centre. **2** *Informal* the most important person or thing.

king salmon CHINOOK (def. 2).

K

king·ship (king′ship) *n* the position, rank, or rule of a king.

king–size (king′sīz′) *adj* **1** unusually large: *I made myself a king-size sandwich.* **2** longest or largest in a standard range of sizes: *a king-size bed.* **3** designed for use with a king-size bed: *king-size sheets.*

king's ransom *n* a very large amount of money.

kink (kingk) *n* **1** a twist or curl in rope, hair, or a thread. **2** a pain or stiffness in the muscles of the neck or back. **3** *Informal* a mental twist or odd idea: *Some inventors have many kinks.*
v form a kink or kinks: *The rope kinked as she rolled it up. Don't kink the clothesline.* <probably Dutch *kink* twist>

kin·ka·jou (king′kə jū′) *n* a yellowish-brown mammal of Central and South America with a long, prehensile tail. <Tupi-Guarani (a language of S America)>

kink·y (king′kē) *adj* **kink·i·er, kink·i·est 1** twisted or in small, tight curls: *kinky hair.* **2** *Informal* to do with unusual sexual behaviour. **kink′i·ness** *n.*

🍁 **kin·ni·kin·ik** or **kin·ni·kin·nik** (kin′ə kə nik′) *n* **1** a smoking mixture made from the leaves or bark of various plants. **2** a shrub from which the smoking mixture is made. <Algonquian *kinikinic* mixture>

kins·folk (kinz′fōk′) *pl n* family, relatives, or kin. Also, **kinfolk**.

kin·ship (kin′ship) *n* **1** a family relationship: *Her kinship with the owner of the factory helped her to get a summer job.* **2** a relationship or resemblance: *Tennis and badminton have a kinship.*

a bat	e bed	i bid	o pot	u cup	th thin
ā cake	ē me	ī bite	ō go	ū rude	ᴛʜ then
ȧ bar	ə about	ər over	ȯ for	u̇ put	zh measure

kins·man (kin′zmən) *n, pl* **kins·men** (-zmən) a male relative. Uncles are kinsmen.

kins·wom·an (kin′zwu̇m′ən) *n, pl* **kins·wom·en** (-zwim′ən) a female relative. Aunts are kinswomen.

ki·osk (kē′osk) *or* (kē osk′) *n* **1** a small building, usually with one or more sides open, such as a newsstand, bus shelter, or information booth. **2** *Computers* an information booth where the information is provided by a computer. Data may be stored on CD-ROM or accessed via a network such as the Internet. <Turkish *kosk* pavilion>

kip·per (kip′ər) *n* **1** a split, salted, and dried fish, especially a herring. **2** the male salmon or sea trout during or after the spawning season.
v split, salt, and dry fish, especially herring. <Old English *cypera* salmon>

Ki·ri·ba·ti (ki′ri bat′i) *n* a country of several islands in the S Pacific.

kirk (kərk) *Scottish n* a church.

kir·pan (kēr′pan) *Sikhism n* a ceremonial dagger worn by Sikhs. <Sanskrit>

kis·met (kiz′met) *or* (kis′met) *n* fate or destiny. <Turkish, from Arabic *qismat* fate>

kiss (kis) *v* **1** touch with the lips as a sign of love, greeting, respect, or comfort. **2** touch gently: *A soft wind kissed the treetops.*
n **1** a touch with the lips. **2** a gentle touch. **3** a small piece of candy wrapped in a twist of paper: *a chocolate kiss.* <Old English *cyssan*> **kiss′a·ble** *adj.*
kiss of death, an event or fact that leads to ruin: *The televised debate was the kiss of death for his campaign.*
kiss of life, mouth-to-mouth resuscitation.
kiss something goodbye, *Informal* resign yourself to losing or giving up something: *One more loss and we can kiss the hockey championship goodbye.*

kiss·er (kis′ər) *n* **1** a person who kisses someone: *a good kisser, a lousy kisser.* **2** *Slang* the face or mouth.

kit[1] (kit) *n* **1** a set of materials, supplies, or tools required for a particular job or purpose: *a first-aid kit, a sewing kit, a shaving kit.* **2** a set of parts intended to be put together to make a particular thing: *a radio kit, a model airplane kit.* **3** a set of printed materials issued for instruction and information: *a sales kit, a museum visitor's kit.* **4** the uniform or other clothing and personal equipment required for a certain activity: *a soldier's kit, soccer kit.* <Dutch *kitte* wooden container>
(**the whole**) **kit and caboodle,** *Informal* the complete thing or group: *My aunt met the children and their friends at the theatre and took the whole kit and caboodle out to eat.*

kit[2] (kit) *n* the young of some fur-bearing wild animals.

kit–bag (kit′bag′) *n* a tall, rounded bag, usually made of canvas and closed at the top by a drawstring, for carrying personal belongings.

kitch·en (kich′ən) *n* a room where food is cooked or prepared. <Old English *cycene*>

kitch·en·ette (kich′ə net′) *n* a small, compactly arranged kitchen.

kitchen garden *n* a garden where vegetables, herbs, and fruit are grown for household use.

kitchen midden *n* a mound of shells, bones, and other refuse at a place where prehistoric people lived.

kitch·en·ware (kich′ən wer′) *n* kitchen utensils such as pots, kettles, and pans.

kite (kīt) *n* **1** a light frame covered with paper, cloth, or plastic and flown in the air at the end of a long string. **2** a large bird of prey with pointed wings and a forked tail.
v **kit·ed, kit·ing** *Informal* **1** fly swiftly and easily like a kite. **2** fly a kite. **3** write or use a document fraudulently, especially a cheque. <Old English *cyta*>
go fly a kite, *Slang* a command to go away.

kit fox the SWIFT FOX.

kith (kith) *n* friends and acquaintances. <Old English *cyth*th>
kith and kin, friends and relatives.

Kit·i·mat (kit′ə mat′) HAISLA.

kitsch (kich) *n* art or decoration considered gaudy, garish, or overly cute. <German> **kitsch′y** *adj.*

kit·ten (kit′ən) *n* **1** a young cat. **2** the young of some other animals, like rabbits. <Latin *cattus*>

kit·ten·ish (kit′ə nish) *adj* **1** like a kitten. **2** playful and flirtatious.

kit·ti·wake (kit′ē wāk′) *n* a medium-sized gull that has mainly white plumage with black-tipped grey wings. <imitative>

kit·ty[1] (kit′ē) *n, pl* **kit·ties** a pet name for a cat or kitten.

kit·ty[2] (kit′ē) *n, pl* **kit·ties** **1** a fund of money for the use of a group, made up of contributions from its members. **2** the money pooled by the players in poker and other card games: *The kitty goes to the winner.* **3** in some card games, a number of cards that may be used by the person making the highest bid. <origin uncertain>

kit·ty–cor·ner (kit′ē kȯr′nər) *adj* diagonally opposite: *There is a small drugstore kitty-corner from the garage.*
adv diagonally: *She walked kitty-corner across the field.* <French *quatre* four + *corner*>

ki·wi (kē′wē) *n, pl* **ki·wis** **1** a flightless bird of New Zealand with shaggy feathers and a long, slender bill. **2** in full, **kiwi fruit** the edible fruit of a climbing plant. Kiwi fruit have thin hairy skins and greenish flesh. <Maori (a language of New Zealand)>

kJ kilojoule(s).

KKK Ku Klux Klan.

kL kilolitre(s).

Klan KU KLUX KLAN.

klee·nex (klē′neks) *n* **1** a small piece of soft, absorbent paper tissue, often used as a handkerchief or to remove something: *She put two kleenexes in her pocket.* **2** a box or supply of such tissues: *We need more kleenex.* <*Kleenex*, a trademark>

klep·to·ma·ni·a (klep′tə mā′nē ə) *n* an uncontrollable impulse to steal. <Greek *kleptes* thief + *mania*> **klep′to·ma′ni·ac′** *n.*

klick (klik) *Slang n* a kilometre: *How many klicks does this car have on it?* <*kilometre* + *click* from the turning over of an odometer>

🍁 **Klon·dike** (klon′dīk) *n* a region of the Yukon where gold was discovered in 1897.

klutz (kluts) *Informal n* a clumsy or inept person. <Yiddish *klots* clumsy, from German *Klotz* clod, blockhead>

km kilometre(s).

km/h kilometres per hour: *The top speed of this car is 120 km/h.*

kn KNOT(s)[1] (*n* def. 6).

knack (nak) *n* **1** a power to do something easily: *The clown has the knack of making funny faces.* **2** a trick; a habit. <origin uncertain>

knap·sack (nap′sak′) *n* a sturdy bag for carrying clothes, food, and other items on the back. <German *knappen* to eat + *Sack* bag>

knave (nāv) *n* **1** a tricky or dishonest person; a rogue; a rascal. **2** the jack, a playing card with a picture of a royal servant. <Old English *cnafa* boy>

knav·er·y (nā′və rē) *n, pl* **knav·er·ies** **1** behaviour typical of a knave. **2** a tricky, dishonest act.

knav·ish (nā′vish) *adj* tricky or dishonest.
knav′ish·ly *adv.* **knav′ish·ness** *n.*

knead (nēd) *v* **1** mix a moist flour mixture or clay into a dough or paste by pressing and stretching, usually with the hands: *A baker kneads dough.* **2** press and squeeze with the hands: *Kneading the muscles in a stiff shoulder will sometimes take away the stiffness.* **3** make or shape by kneading. See NEED for confusable. <Old English *cnedan*>

knee (nē) *n* **1** the joint between the thigh and the lower leg. **2** any joint of an animal corresponding to the human knee or elbow. **3** anything like a bent knee in shape or position. **4** the part of pants or stockings covering the knee: *My jeans have a tear in the knee.*
v **kneed, knee·ing** strike with the knee. <Old English *cneo*>

knee breeches *pl n* breeches reaching to or just below the knees.

knee·cap (nē′kap′) *n* **1** the flat, movable bone at the front of the knee. **2** a covering to protect the knee.

knee–deep (nē′dēp′) *adj* deep enough to reach just to the knees.

knee–high (nē′hī′) *adj* reaching up to the knees.
n usually, **knee-highs** *pl* women's nylon stockings reaching to the knee.
knee-high to a grasshopper, *Informal* very young: *My grandfather said that that when he was knee-high to a grasshopper, bread was five cents a loaf.*

knee–jerk (nē′jərk′) *Informal adj* responding in an automatic way, without reflection: *a knee-jerk reaction.*

kneel (nēl) *v* **knelt** or **kneeled, kneel·ing** **1** go down on one's knee or knees: *She knelt down to pull a weed from the flower bed.* **2** remain in this position: *They knelt for several minutes.* **kneel′er** *n.*

knee·pad (nē′pad′) *n* a pad worn around the knee for protection.

knell (nel) *n* **1** the sound of a bell rung slowly after a death or at a funeral. **2** a sign or warning of death, failure, or defeat: *Their refusal rang the knell of our hopes.*
v **1** ring slowly and solemnly. **2** make such a slow and solemn sound. <Old English *cnyllan*>

knelt (nelt) *v* a past tense and past participle of KNEEL.

knew (nyū) *or* (nū) past tense of KNOW. See NEW for confusable.

knick·er·bock·ers (nik′ər bok′ərz) *pl n* short, loose-fitting trousers gathered in at, or just below, the knee. Also, **knickers.** <from the costume illustrations in the book *Knickerbocker's History of New York*>

knick–knack (nik′nak′) *n* a small decorative object, especially a household ornament. <varied reduplication of *knack*>

knife (nīf) *n, pl* **knives** **1** a thin, flat blade, usually of metal, fastened in a handle so that it can be used to cut or spread. See SOUP SPOON for picture. **2** a weapon with a short blade and a sharp edge and point. **3** a cutting blade in a tool or machine: *The knives of a lawn mower cut grass.*
v **knifed, knif·ing** **1** cut or stab with a knife. **2** pierce or cut as a knife does: *The wind knifed through her thin jacket.* <Old English *cnif*> **knife′like′** *adj.*
knife in the back, an act of betrayal.

knife–edge (nīf′ej′) *n* **1** the edge of the blade of a knife. **2** a sharp, straight edge: *She pressed her pants to give them a knife-edge.* **knife-edge** *adj.*

knife·point (nīf′point′) *n* the pointed end of a knife.
at knifepoint, under the threat of stabbing or other violence: *He was robbed at knifepoint.*

knight (nīt) *n* **1** in the Middle Ages, a man raised to a military rank by a sovereign after serving as a page and squire. See ARMOUR for picture. **2** in modern times, a man given a special title by the sovereign because of personal achievement or because he has won distinction in some way: *A knight has the title Sir before his name.* Compare DAME. **3** *Poetic* a man devoted to the service or protection of a lady. **4** a piece in the game of chess.
v raise to the rank of knight: *He was knighted by the queen.* <Old English *cniht* boy>
knight in shining armour, **a** someone who rescues another in a dramatic or heroic way. **b** an idealized romantic partner: *When you meet your knight in shining armour, you'll know it.*

knight–er·rant (nī′ter′ənt) *n, pl* **knights-er·rant** in the Middle Ages, a knight travelling in search of adventure.

knight–er·rant·ry (nī′ter′ən trē) *n* in the Middle Ages, the deeds of knights travelling in search of adventures.

knight·hood (nīt′hůd′) *n* **1** the title, rank, or status of a knight. **2** knights as a group or class: *All the knighthood of France came to the aid of the king.*

a bat	e bed	i bid	o pot	u cup	th thin
ā cake	ē me	ī bite	ō go	ū rude	ᴛʜ then
à bar	ə about	ər over	ȯ for	ů put	zh measure

K

knots

figure eight

overhand

bowline

running bowline

reef knot

granny knot

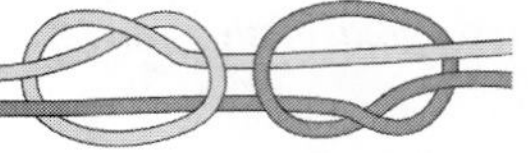
fisherman's knot

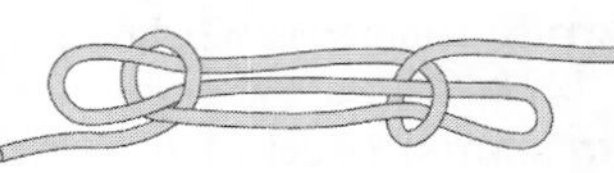
sheepshank

knight·ly (nī′tlē) *adj* like a knight, especially in being brave, generous, and courteous.
adv behaving in this way. **knight′li·ness** *n.*

knish (kə nish′) *n* in Jewish cookery, dough stuffed with a filling and baked or fried. <Yiddish, from Russian *knysh*>

knit (nit) *v* **knit·ted** or **knit, knit·ting** 1 make by looping yarn or thread together with long needles or on a machine: *She knitted all afternoon. He succeeded in knitting a sweater.* 2 join closely and firmly together. 3 grow or be joined together: *It takes time for a broken bone to knit.* <Old English *cnyttan*> **knit′ter** *n.*

knit·ting (nit′ing) *n* knitted work.

knitting needle *n* one of a pair of long needles used in knitting.

knives (nīvz) plural of KNIFE.

knob (nob) *n* 1 a rounded lump, especially at the end or on the surface of something: *She turned the knob of the radio clockwise.* 2 a handle of a door or drawer shaped like a ball or lump. 3 a rounded hill or mountain. <German *knobbe*>

knob·by (nob′ē) *adj* **knob·bi·er, knob·bi·est** 1 covered with knobs: *Some kinds of squash have a knobby rind.* 2 rounded like a knob. **knob′bi·ness** *n.*

knock (nok) *v* 1 strike a blow with the fist, knuckles, or anything hard: *She knocked him on the head.* 2 hit and cause to fall: *She ran into another girl and knocked her down.* 3 make a noise by hitting: *to knock on a door.* 4 make a noise, especially a rattling or pounding noise: *The engine is knocking.* 5 *Informal* criticize or find fault: *A good friend doesn't knock you all the time.*
n 1 a hit: *The hard knock made him cry.* 2 the act or sound of knocking: *She did not hear the knock at the door.* 3 a pounding or rattling sound in an engine. <Old English *cnocian*>
knock about, *Informal* **a** wander from place to place. **b** hit repeatedly.
knock back, *Slang* eat or drink (something) quickly: *She knocked back three milkshakes in a row.*
knock down, a sell an article to the highest bidder at an auction. **b** take apart: *We knocked down the bookcase and packed it in the car.*
knock it off, *Slang* a command to stop what you are doing: *I'm tired of your complaining. Knock it off!*
knock off, *Informal* **a** take off (from a price): *to knock fifty percent off the price.* **b** stop (work or other activity): *We knock off at noon for lunch.* **c** do quickly: *She knocked off a poem in just a few minutes.* **d** illegally make an imitation of: *to knock off a piece of software.*
knock out, a hit so hard as to make helpless or unconscious. **b** decisively defeat.
knock together, make or put together hastily.

knock–down (nok′doun′) *adj* 1 made to be taken apart or put together easily: *knock-down furniture.* 2 to do with a big reduction in price: *You can have this for the knock-down price of one dollar.*

knock–down, drag–out (drag′out′) *Informal adj* fierce and violent: *a knock-down, drag-out argument between my brothers.*

knock·er (nok′ər) *n* 1 a person who or thing that knocks. 2 a knob or ring fastened on a door for use in knocking.

knock–kneed (nok′nēd′) *adj* with legs curved inward so that the knees tend to touch when walking. Compare BOWLEGGED.

knock–off (nok′of′) *Informal n* a copy or imitation: *Those are just a knock-off of designer jeans.*

knock·out (nok′out′) *n* 1 the act of rendering unconscious or helpless by a punch: *He won the fight by a knockout. Abbrev.* **KO** or **K.O.** 2 a blow that knocks out. 3 *Informal* a person or thing considered outstanding: *The party was a knockout.*
adj Informal that knocks out: *a knockout blow.*

knoll (nōl) *n* a small, rounded hill: *The house stood on a wooded knoll.* <Old English *cnoll*>

knot[1] (not) *n* 1 a fastening made by tying or twining together pieces of rope, string, etc.: *a square knot, a slip-knot.* 2 an accidental twisting of something, such as hair or string. 3 a small group or cluster: *A knot of people stood talking outside the door.* 4 **a** a hard mass of wood formed where a branch grows out from a tree, which shows as a roundish, cross-grained piece in a board. **b** a joint where leaves grow out on the stem of a plant. 5 a hard lump: *A knot sometimes forms in a tired muscle.* 6 a unit for measuring the speed of a ship, an aircraft, or the wind, equal to about 1850 m/h. *Symbol* **kn**
v **knot·ted, knot·ting** 1 tie or twine together in a knot. 2 tangle in knots. 3 make knots for a fringe, or make a fringe by tying knots. 4 form into a hard lump. <Old English *cnotta*> **knot′less** *adj.*
tie the knot, *Informal* get married.

knot[2] (not) *n* a small sandpiper that breeds in the Canadian Arctic.

knot·hole (not′hōl′) *n* a hole in a board where a knot in the wood has fallen out.

knot·ty (not′ē) *adj* **knot·ti·er, knot·ti·est** 1 full of knots: *knotty wood.* 2 difficult or puzzling: *a knotty problem.* **knot′ti·ness** *n.*

knot·weed (not′wēd′) *n* a plant whose stems have large joints. Also called **knotgrass**.

know (nō) *v* **knew, known, know·ing** 1 have true information about: *She knows the cause of the accident because she witnessed it.* 2 have firmly in the mind or memory: *to know a part in a play.* 3 remember having seen or heard: *to know a person's name.* 4 be sure or certain because of experience or knowledge: *I don't have to guess, because I know the answer.* 5 be acquainted or familiar with: *Do you know his brother?* 6 have an understanding of or experience with: *She knows Canadian literature.* 7 recognize or identify: *You would hardly know him since his illness. You will know their house by the blue roof.* <Old English *cnawan*> **know′er** *n.*
don't I know it! *Informal* used to show strong agreement with a statement.
in the know, *Informal* be aware of information few people have.
know no bounds, have no limits.
know the ropes, understand what to do.
know what's what, *Informal* be well informed.
what do you know? *Informal* used to show surprise: *What do you know? I won!*

SYNONYMS

Know implies being well-informed about something: *I know a lot about video games.*

Realize means "become fully aware": *I realize how hard you have worked on your project.*

Understand suggests acquiring knowledge of a particular thing: *I now understand the math problem.*

know·a·ble (nō′ə bəl) *adj* capable of being known.

know–how (nō′hou′) *Informal n* the knowledge or ability required to get something done.

know·ing (nō′ing) *adj* 1 suggesting a shrewd or secret understanding: *Her only answer was a knowing look.* 2 well-informed. 3 clever or shrewd.

know·ing·ly (nō′ing lē) *adv* 1 in a knowing way. 2 with knowledge or on purpose: *You would not knowingly hurt anyone, would you?*

know–it–all (nō′it ol′) *Informal n* an annoying person who pretends to know more than everybody else or has all the answers. Also, **know-all** (nō′ol′).

knowl·edge (nol′ij) *n* 1 what one knows: *Her knowledge of the subject is limited.* 2 all that is known or can be learned: *Science is a part of knowledge.* 3 the act or fact of knowing: *a knowledge of the surrounding countryside. The knowledge of our victory caused great joy.*
to the best of my knowledge, going by my own understanding, though I could be wrong: *To the best of my knowledge, she has always lived in Regina.*

knowl·edge·a·ble (nol′i jə bəl) *adj* well-informed, especially about a particular subject. **knowl′edge·a·bly** *adj.*

known (nōn) *adj* widely recognized: *a known fact, a known artist.*
v past participle of KNOW.

know–noth·ing (nō′nuth′ing) *n* an ignorant person.

knuck·le (nuk′əl) *n* 1 a finger joint, especially one of the joints between a finger and the rest of the hand. 2 the knee or hock joint of an animal used as food: *boiled pigs' knuckles.*
v **knuck·led, knuck·ling** press or rub with the knuckles. <German *knoke* bone>
knuckle down, *Informal* work hard.
knuckle under, *Informal* submit or yield: *She would not knuckle down under their attack. She refused to knuckle under to her enemies.*

knuck·le·ball (nuk′əl bol′) *Baseball n* a slow pitch made by holding the ball with the thumb and the knuckles of the first two or three fingers.

knuck·le·bone (nuk′əl bōn′) *n* a bone forming or like part of a knuckle.

knuck·le·dust·er (nuk′əl dus′tər) *n* a piece of metal worn over the knuckles as a weapon.

knuck·le·head (nuk′əl hed′) *Slang n* a thoughtless or inept person.

knurl (nərl) *n* a small knob or ridge, such as one of a series on the edge of a coin. <Middle English *knorre* knot>

KO or **K.O.** (kā′ō′) *Slang v* **KO'd** or **K.O.'d, KO'ing** or **K.O.'ing** knock out: *He was KO'd in the first round.*
n, pl **KO's** or **K.O.'s** a knockout.

ko·a·la (kō á′lə) *n* a furry, grey marsupial of Australia that lives in trees, eats eucalyptus leaves, and carries its young in a pouch. Koalas belong to the same order as kangaroos. See KANGAROO for picture. <Australian Aboriginal name>

ko·an (kō′án) *Zen Buddhism n, pl* **ko·ans** or **ko·an** a short statement or riddle without an obvious answer, used to show the limits of logic, or to promote enlightenment. Example: *What is the sound of one hand clapping?* <Japanese = material for public thought>

Ko·di·ak bear (kō′dē ak′) *n* a subspecies of the brown bear, found on islands to the north of Alaska. It is the largest living carnivore. Also called **Alaskan brown bear**.

Kog·mo·lik (kog′mō lik) *n, pl* **Kog·mo·lik** or **Kog·mo·liks** 1 a member of an Inuit people living to the east of the Mackenzie River delta. 2 the variety of Inuktitut spoken by these people.
adj to do with these people or their language.

kohl (kōl) *n* a black powder used for eye makeup, especially by women and girls in the Middle East and Asia. <Arabic *kohl* metallic powder>

a bat	e bed	i bid	o pot	u cup	th thin
ā cake	ē me	ī bite	ō go	ū rude	TH then
á bar	ə about	ər over	ó for	ú put	zh measure

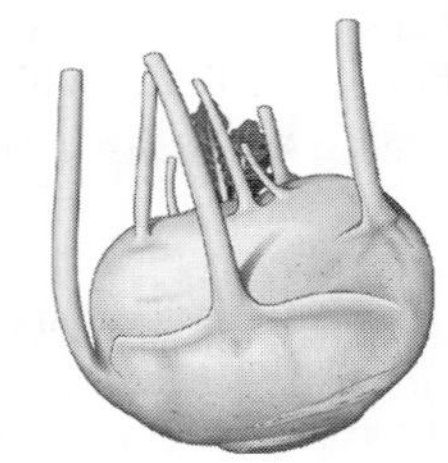

kohlrabi

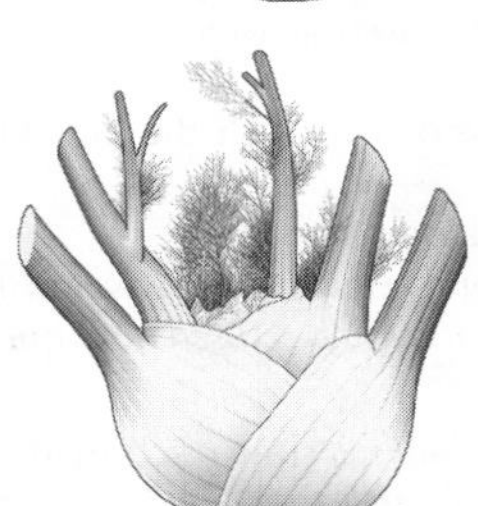

fennel

Although **kohlrabi** and fennel are similar in appearance, their flavours are quite different. Kohlrabi, a member of the cabbage family, tastes something like a turnip, while fennel, a member of the parsley family, has a strong licorice flavour.

kohl·ra·bi (kōl′rȧ′bē) *or* (kōl′rȧ′bē) *n, pl* **kohl·ra·bies** a plant related to the cabbage that has a crisp, turnip-shaped stem, eaten as a vegetable. <German, from Italian *cavolo* cabbage + *rapa* turnip>

ko·ka·nee (kō′kə nē′) *n* a freshwater form of the sockeye salmon, found in British Columbia lakes and rivers. Compare OUANANICHE. <perhaps from *Kokanee* Creek, B.C.>

ko·la (kō′lə) *n* cola.

kol·khoz (kol′koz′) *n* in the former Soviet Union, a collective farm. <Russian *kol(lektivno) khoz(yaistvo)*>

kom·a·tik (kom′ə tik′) *n* a large wooden dogsled used in the North, made of closely-spaced crossbars lashed to two broad runners.

ETYMOLOGY

Komatik comes from Inuktitut *qamutik*, from *qamut*, meaning "sled runner." (Putting the *ik* on the end makes the word mean "two sled runners."

ko·mo·do dragon (kə mō′dō) *n* the largest living lizard, found in Indonesia. <*Komodo* Island, Indonesia>

kook (kūk) *Slang n* an eccentric or crazy person. <perhaps from *cuckoo*> **kook′y** *adj.*

kook·a·bur·ra (kůk′ə bər′ə) *n* a large Australian kingfisher with a cry that resembles loud, harsh laughter. <Wiradjuri (a language of Australia) *gugubarra*>

Koo·te·nay (ků′tə nā) KTUNAXA.

Ko·ran (kȯ rȧn′) *or* (kȯ ran′) QUR'AN.

Ko·re·a (kə rē′ə) a country in east Asia, since 1948 divided into **North Korea** and **South Korea.** See the APPENDIX. **Ko·re′an** *adj, n.*

ko·sher (kō′shər) *adj* **1** proper or clean according to Jewish ritual law: *kosher meat.* **2** dealing in products that meet the requirements of Jewish ritual law: *a kosher butcher.* <Hebrew *kasher* proper>

kow·tow (kou′tou′) *or* (kō′tou′) *v* **1** show slavish respect or obedience. **2** in former Chinese custom, to kneel and touch the ground with the forehead to show deep respect, submission, or worship.
n the act of kowtowing. <Mandarin *ko-tou* knock the head> **kow′tow′er** *n.*

K.P. *US Military n* work in the kitchen assisting the cook, sometimes as a punishment for slight offences. <*kitchen police*>

kPa kilopascal(s).

kraft paper (krȧft) *n* tough brown wrapping paper. <German *Kraft* strength>

kra·ken (krȧ′kən) *n* a mythical monster supposed to live in Norwegian waters. <Norwegian>

Krem·lin (krem′lən) *n* **1** the citadel of Moscow. **2** the government offices of Russia, housed within this citadel. <Russian *kreml* citadel>

krill (kril) *n* the tiny, shrimplike, planktonic crustaceans that occur in periodic swarms, especially in polar seas and is the chief food of baleen whales. <Norwegian *kril* young fry>

kris (krēs) *n* a dagger with a wavy blade, used by Malays. <Malay *kiris*>

Krish·na (krish′nə) *Hinduism n* a human form of the god Vishnu, often shown playing the flute. <Sanskrit>

Kris Krin·gle (kris′kring′gəl) SANTA CLAUS.

krul·ler (krul′ər) CRULLER.

kryp·ton (krip′ton) *n* an element that is an inert gas distilled from liquid air. *Symbol* **Kr** <Latin, from Greek = hidden, so called because it is a rare gas>

kt karat(s).

Ktu·na·xa (ktů nak′sə) *n, pl* **Ktu·na·xa** **1** a member of a First Nations people living near Kootenay Lake in southeastern British Columbia, and in the state of Washington. **2** the language of these people.
adj to do with these people or their language. Also called **Kootenay**, **Kutenai**.

kud·lik (kūd′lik) *n* a dishlike soapstone lamp that burns caribou or seal oil, traditionally used by Inuit. <Inuktitut *gudlik*>

ku·dos (kū′dōz) *or* (kū′dos); (kyū′dōz) *or* (kyū′dos) *Informal n* praise and honour received for some achievement. <Greek *kydos*>

ku·du (kū′dū) *n* a large, greyish brown African antelope with white vertical stripes. <Nama (a language of South Africa)>

Ku Klux Klan (kū′kluks′klan) *n* a secret society formed in the southern US after the Civil War to regain and maintain control by white people, and later to oppose blacks, Jews, Catholics, and foreigners. *Abbrev.* **Klan, KKK** <probably Greek *kyklos* circle + *clan*>
Klans′man *n.*

ku·le·tuk (kū′lə tuk′) *n* a hooded, close-fitting jacket made of skins, often trimmed with fur. <Inuktitut>

kum·quat (kum′kwot) *n* an orange-yellow fruit resembling a small orange with a sour pulp and a sweet rind. <Cantonese>

traditional kung fu costume

Kung fu is similar to karate, but it involves additional techniques and is executed in a more acrobatic form. Many of the body movements are inspired by the way animals move.

The traditional kung fu costume has an officer's collar and is fastened with buttons. Although combatants can wear red, yellow, or white, they most often choose black. A coloured sash indicates the level of skill the combatant has achieved.

Hung-gar-Kuen is a kung fu style characterized by low positions in which strikes with the feet are never higher than the opponent's waist.

The **tong-long** style is inspired by the praying mantis, which hooks its forelegs and jumps as it attacks. Hand movements and fast footwork imitate the insect.

The **wing-chun** style uses techniques selected as the most basic and effective. It is said to have been developed by a woman.

K

kung fu (kůng′fů′) *n* a Chinese martial art similar to karate. <Mandarin *chuan-fa* = boxing principles>

Kurd (kərd) *n* a member of a nomadic people living chiefly in **Kurdistan**, a mountainous region extending from Turkey through Iraq and into Iran.
Kurd′ish *adj, n.*

Kut·chin (kůch′in) GWICH'IN.

Ku·te·nai (ků′tə nā) KTUNAXA.

Ku·wait (kū wāt′) a country in west Asia. See the APPENDIX. **Ku·wai′ti** (kū wā′tē) *adj, n.*

kV kilovolt(s).

kvetch (kvech) *Slang v* complain or grumble.
n a habitual complainer. <Yiddish>

kW kilowatt(s).

Kwa·kwa·ka'·wakw (kwȧ kwȧ′ki wȧk′) *n, pl* **Kwa·kwa·ka'·wakw** a member of a First Nations people living in southwestern British Columbia.
adj to do with these people.
Also called **Kwakiutl** (kwȧ′kē ů′təl).

Kwak'·wa·la (kwȧk wȧ′la) *n* the language of the Kwakwaka'wakw.

Kwan·zaa or **Kwan·za** (kwan′zə) *n* a festival held from December 26 to January 1 to celebrate black culture and the history of Africa.

ETYMOLOGY

Kwanzaa is a short form of *matunda ya kwanza*, meaning "first fruits of the harvest" in Swahili, an African language. Kwanzaa was first celebrated in 1966.

Today, millions of people in African communities throughout the world celebrate this festival.

kWh kilowatt-hour(s).

🍁 **kwu·nu·se·la** (kwů′nů sə lə) *Pacific Coast n* the thunderbird. <Kwakiutl>

Kyr·gyz·stan (kir′gə stan′) *n* a country in central Asia.

l or **L** (el) *n, pl* **l's** or **L's** 1 the twelfth letter of the English alphabet, or any speech sound represented by it. 2 the twelfth thing in a list or series: *Answer the first twelve questions, from* (*a*) *to* (*l*). 3 the Roman numeral for 50.

L litre(s).

la (lä) *Music n* 1 the sixth tone of an eight-tone major scale, especially as sung to sol-fa syllables: *do, re, mi, fa, so, la, ti, do.* 2 the tone A. Also, **lah**.

L.A. Legislative Assembly.

lab (lab) *Informal n* a laboratory.

la·bel (lā′bəl) *n* 1 a slip of paper or other material attached to anything and marked to show what or whose it is, or where it is to go: *Can you read the label on the box?* 2 a short phrase that is used to describe some person, thing, or idea in a restrictive way: *"Land of Opportunity" is a label often given to Canada.* 3 a company that produces recorded music: *an independent label.*
v **la·belled** or **la·beled, la·bel·ling** or **la·bel·ing** 1 put or write a label on: *The bottle is labelled "Poison."* 2 describe in a restrictive way: *He labelled the boastful man a liar.* <Old French = ribbon> **la′bel·ler** or **la′bel·er** *n.*

la·bor (lā′bər) LABOUR.

lab·o·ra·to·ry (lab′rə tô′rē) *or* (lə bô′rə tô′rē) *n, pl* **lab·o·ra·to·ries** 1 a room or building fitted with apparatus for conducting scientific tests, experiments, research, or teaching. 2 a place fitted up for manufacturing drugs or chemicals. <Latin *laborare* to work>

la·bo·ri·ous (lə bô′rē əs) *adj* 1 requiring hard work: *Climbing a mountain is laborious.* 2 showing signs of effort: *laborious breathing.* **la·bo′ri·ous·ly** *adv.*

la·bour or **la·bor** (lā′bər) *n* 1 the effort in doing or making something: *He was well paid for his labour.* 2 a task or piece of work: *A myth tells how Hercules performed twelve labours.* 3 work done by skilled and unskilled workers who are not clerks, managers, professional workers, or owners. 4 skilled and unskilled workers as a group: *Labour favours safe working conditions.* 5 childbirth.
v 1 do work; work hard: *She laboured all day on her essay.* 2 elaborate with effort or in detail: *The speaker laboured the point so that we lost interest.* 3 move slowly and heavily: *The ship laboured in the high waves. The old car laboured as it climbed the steep hill.* 4 (*with* ***under***) be burdened with or troubled by: *to labour under a mistake.* 5 be in childbirth. <Old French, from Latin *labor*>

Labour Day or **Labor Day** *n* the first Monday in September, a legal holiday in Canada and the US in honour of labour and labourers.

la·boured or **la·bored** (lā′bərd) *adj* done with effort.

la·bour·er or **la·bor·er** (lā′bə rər) *n* 1 a worker. 2 a person who does manual work requiring strength and endurance for wages.

la·bour–in·ten·sive (lā′bər in ten′siv) *adj* requiring a large labour force or a large amount of work in relation to output.

la·bour·ite or **la·bor·ite** (lā′bər ȳt) *n* a member of a labour party.

Labour Party or **Labor Party** *n* a political party organized to protect and promote the interests of workers, especially the Labour Party of Great Britain.

la·bour–sav·ing or **la·bor–sav·ing** (lā′bər sā′ving) *adj* that takes the place of or lessens labour: *a labour-saving device.*

labour union or **labor union** *n* an association of workers to protect and promote their interests, and for dealing collectively with employers.

Lab·ra·dor (lab′rə dôr′) *or* (lab′rə dôr′) *n* a region on the northeast coast of Canada, forming the mainland part of the province of Newfoundland and Labrador.
adj to do with Labrador: *Labrador mineral resources.* **Lab′ra·dor′i·an** *n.*

Labrador Current *n* the cold arctic current that flows southward past Labrador and Newfoundland, where it joins the Gulf Stream.

Labrador Inuit *n* the Inuit living in N Labrador.

lab·ra·dor·ite (lab′rə dôr′īt) *n* a brilliantly coloured feldspar, a piece of this stone, or a gem made from it.

Labrador retriever *n* a breed of medium-sized retriever dog originating in Newfoundland and Labrador, with a thick, short coat.

Labrador tea *n* a drink made by steeping the leaves of a small evergreen shrub of the heath family.

la·bur·num (lə bər′nəm) *n* a small tree or shrub with hanging clusters of yellow flowers and poisonous seeds.

lab·y·rinth (lab′ə rinth′) *n* 1 a complicated, irregular network of paths through which it is hard to find the way out. 2 a confusing, complicated arrangement or situation. 3 the internal ear.

ETYMOLOGY

Labyrinth comes from Latin *labyrinthus*, from Greek *labyrinthos*, meaning "maze" or "large building with intricate passages." In Greek mythology, King Minos had a labyrinth built to hold a monster called the Minotaur.

lab·y·rin·thine (lab′ə rin′thən) *or* (lab′ə rin′thēn) *adj* 1 to do with a labyrinth. 2 intricate and confusing.

lace (lās) *n* 1 a delicate fabric woven in an open or netlike ornamental pattern. 2 a cord for pulling or holding something together: *These shoes need new laces.* 3 gold or silver braid used for trimming: *Some uniforms have lace on them.*
v **laced, lac·ing** 1 hold or be held together with a lace or laces. *These ice skates take a long time to lace.* 2 trim with lace or braid: *His uniform was laced with gold.* 3 entwine or tangle: *to lace your fingers together.* 4 mark with streaks: *a white flower laced with pink.* 5 add alcoholic liquor to a drink or food to strengthen it or enhance its flavour. <Old French *laz* string, from Latin *laqueus* noose>
lace′like′ *adj.*
lace into, *Informal* **a** attack. **b** criticize severely.

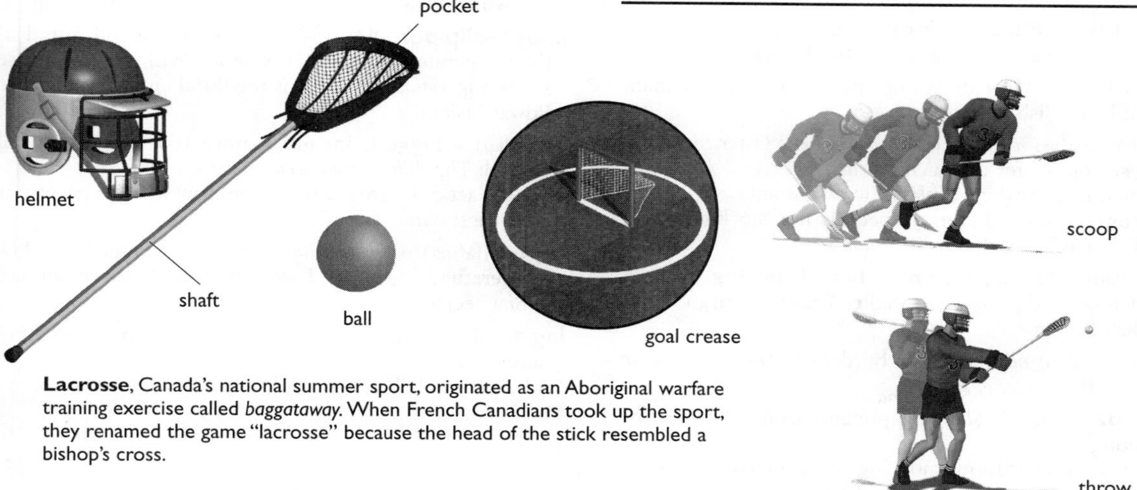

Lacrosse, Canada's national summer sport, originated as an Aboriginal warfare training exercise called *baggataway*. When French Canadians took up the sport, they renamed the game "lacrosse" because the head of the stick resembled a bishop's cross.

lac·er·ate (las′ə rāt′) *v* **lac·er·at·ed, lac·er·at·ing 1** tear roughly: *The bear's claws lacerated the side of the tent.* **2** cause pain or suffering to: *The coach's sharp words lacerated the team's morale.* <Latin *lacer* mangled>

lac·er·a·tion (las′ə rā′shən) *n* **1** the act of tearing roughly. **2** a rough tear or wound.

lace·wing (lā′swing′) *n* a slender insect that has four lacelike wings and often eats aphids.

lach·ry·mal (lak′rə məl) *adj* of or producing tears: *lachrymal glands.* <Latin *lacrima* tear>

lach·ry·mose (lak′rə mōs′) *adj* tearful. **lach′ry·mose·ly** *adv.*

lac·ing (lā′sing) *n* **1** a cord or string, etc., for pulling or holding something together. **2** gold or silver braid used for trimming. **3** *Informal* a lashing or beating.

lack (lak) *v* **1** have not enough: *A desert lacks water.* **2** be without: *The cabin lacks indoor plumbing.*
n a shortage or absence of something: *Lack of rest made her tired. The campers' main lack was wood for a fire.* <perhaps Dutch *lac*>
supply the lack, supply what is needed.

lack·a·dai·si·cal (lak′ə dā′zə kəl) *adj* listlessly or carelessly lazy. **lack′a·dai′si·cal·ly** *adv.*

lack·ey (lak′ē) *n, pl* **lack·eys 1** a male servant or footman. **2** a slavish follower. <French *laquais*>

lack·ing (lak′ing) *adj* **1** without enough: *A weak person is lacking in strength.* **2** missing or absent: *The puzzle is lacking a few pieces.*
prep without: *Lacking anything better, use what you have.*

lack·lus·tre (lak′lus′tər) *adj* **1** not shining or bright. **2** lacking vitality or interest: *a lacklustre production of a play.* Also, **lackluster**.

la·con·ic (lə kon′ik) *adj* using few words. <Latin, from Greek *Lakon* Laconian. Laconians came from the ancient district of Laconia in S Greece and were noted for speaking briefly.> **la·con′i·cal·ly** *adv.*

lac·quer (lak′ər) *n* **1** a varnish consisting of shellac dissolved in a solvent, used to give a protective coating or a shiny appearance to metals, wood, or other materials. **2** a varnish made from the resin of a sumac tree of southeastern Asia: *Lacquer gives a high polish on wood.* **3** wooden articles coated with such varnish. **4** a nail polish.
v coat with lacquer. <French *lacre* sealing wax, from Portuguese *laca* resin secreted by an insect>
lac′quer·er *n.*

🍁 **la·crosse** (lə kros′) *n* a game played either indoors (**box lacrosse**) or outdoors (**field lacrosse**) in which long-handled sticks with webbed pouches are used by players to carry and pass a ball in an attempt to score a goal. <Cdn French *la crosse* the stick used in the game>

lac·tase (lak′tās) *n* a digestive enzyme in the intestinal glands that helps to break down carbohydrates into glucose.

lac·tate (lak′tāt) *n* a salt of lactic acid.
v **lac·tat·ed, lac·tat·ing** secrete milk. <Latin *lactis* milk>

lac·ta·tion (lak tā′shən) *n* **1** the act of suckling a baby. **2** the time during which a mother gives milk. **3** the secretion or formation of milk.

lac·tic (lak′tik) *adj* to do with milk.

lactic acid *n* a colourless, odourless acid formed in sour milk, and produced in muscle tissues during vigorous exercise.

lac·tose (lak′tōs) *n* a crystalline sugar present in milk.

la·cu·na (lə kyū′nə) *n, pl* **la·cu·nas** or **la·cu·nae** (-nē) *or* (-nī) **1** an empty space, gap, or blank: *There were several lacunas in her test paper where words had been erased.* **2** a tiny cavity in bones or tissues. <Latin = hole>

a bat	e bed	i bid	o pot	u cup	th **thin**
ā cake	ē me	ī bite	ō go	ū rude	ᴛʜ **then**
ä bar	ə about	ər over	ô for	ù put	zh measure

lac·y (lā′sē) *adj* **lac·i·er, lac·i·est** of or like lace: *a lacy tablecloth, the lacy leaves of a fern.* **lac′i·ness** *n.*

lad (lad) *n* **1** a boy or young man. **2** *Informal* a man. <Middle English *ladde*>

lad·der (lad′ər) *n* **1** a set of rungs or steps fastened to two long sidepieces, for use in climbing. See EXTENSION LADDER for picture. **2** a means of: *Hard work is a ladder to success.* **3** a run in a knitted fabric, especially in a stocking. <Old English *hlæder*> **lad′der·like′** *adj.*

lade (lād) *v* **lad·ed, lad·en** or **lad·ed, lad·ing** **1** put a burden on. **2** dip, scoop, or ladle. **3** take on cargo. <Old English *hladan*>

lad·en (lā′dən) *adj* loaded or burdened: *The camels were laden with bundles of silk.*

la–di–da (la′di da′) *Slang adj* pretentious in behaviour or speaking.
interj an exclamation mocking such behaviour: *Well, la-di-da! Too good for us, are you?* <imitative>

lad·ing (lā′ding) *n* **1** the act of loading. **2** freight or cargo.

la·dle (lā′dəl) *n* a large, cup-shaped spoon with a long handle, for dipping out liquids.
v **la·dled, la·dling** dip out and carry or serve in a ladle or other utensil: *The cook is ladling the soup.* <Old English *hladan* to draw out> **la′dler** *n.*
ladle out, *Informal* give freely: *That teacher ladles out compliments to students who work hard.*

la·dy (lā′dē) *n, pl* **la·dies** **1** a woman of refinement and courtesy. **2** a woman of high social position. **3** a woman: *The librarian is a nice lady.* **4** **Lady** *UK* **a** a title used in referring to a female member of the nobility. **b** a title given by courtesy to the wife of a nobleman of a certain rank. <Old English *hlafdige* mistress of a household, from *hlaf* loaf + *dige* knead>

GRAMMAR AND USAGE

In formal English, **lady** is used to refer to a woman of high social position, or a woman of refinement. Though *lady* is sometimes used in everyday speech to refer to any woman (*lady cab driver, lady clerk*), the word can be interpreted as affected or condescending. **Woman** is the preferred general term.

la·dy·bird (lā′dē bərd′) *n* a ladybug.

la·dy·bug (lā′dē bug′) *n* a small beetle with a rounded back, usually red or orange with black spots: *Ladybugs eat harmful insects.* See BEETLE for picture.

la·dy·fin·ger (lā′dē fing′gər) *n* a small, finger-shaped sponge cake with a crunchy sugar crust.

la·dy–in–wait·ing (lā′dē in wā′ting) *n, pl* **la·dies-in-wait·ing** a lady who is an attendant of a queen or princess.

la·dy–kil·ler (lā′dē kil′ər) *Informal n* a man who is supposed to be dangerously fascinating to women.

la·dy·like (lā′dē līk′) *adj* **1** like a lady. **2** suitable for a lady: *Her behaviour is invariably ladylike.*

La·dy·ship (lā′dē ship′) *UK n* a title used in speaking to or of a woman with the rank of Lady: *"Yes, your Ladyship."*

la·dy's–slip·per (lā′dēz slip′ər) *n* a wild orchid found in the temperate regions of N America, with flowers whose shape suggests a slipper. It is the floral emblem of Prince Edward Island.

lag (lag) *v* **lagged, lag·ging** move too slowly and fall behind: *The child lagged because she was tired.*
n **1** the act of lagging. **2** the amount by which a person or thing lags: *a time lag.* <Scandinavian>

la·ger (lä′gər) *n* a beer that is slowly fermented at a low temperature. <German *Lagerbier,* from *Lager* storehouse + *Bier* beer>

lag·gard (lag′ərd) *n* a person who moves too slowly and falls behind.
adj slow and falling behind. **lag′gard·ly** *adv.*

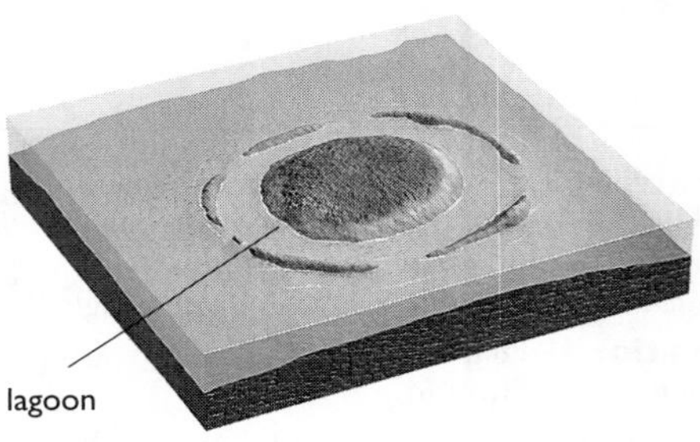

Lagoons contain sea water that is transferred either by natural or artificial means. They also have various levels of fresh water introduced through precipitation and ground runoff. Consequently, the degree of salinity varies from lagoon to lagoon.

la·goon (lə gūn′) *n* **1** a pond or small lake connected with a larger body of water. **2** shallow water separated from the sea by low sandbanks. <Italian, from Latin *lacuna* pool>

lah (la) LA.

laid (lād) past tense and past participle of LAY[1].
laid up, **a** put away for future use. **b** *Informal* forced by illness or injury to stay indoors or in bed. **c** of ships, dismantled and put in dock.

laid–back (lād′bak′) *adj* **1** placed in a backward position or direction: *The horse's laid-back ears were a sign that it was nervous.* **2** *Informal* very relaxed in manner.

lain (lān) past participle of LIE[2].

lair (ler) *n* the den or resting place of a wild animal. <Old English *leger* resting place>

lais·sez–faire or **lais·ser–faire** (les′ā fer′) *n* **1** the principle of letting people do as they please. **2** the government policy of avoiding regulation or interference in the workings of a free market. <French = allow to do> **lais′sez–faire′** *adj.*

la·i·ty (lā′ə tē) *n, pl* **la·i·ties** people as distinguished from the clergy or from a professional class: *Doctors use many words that the laity do not understand.*

lakes

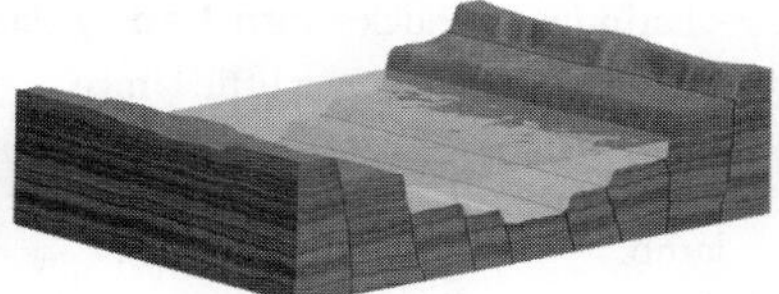

Volcanic lakes form when water collects in the basinlike craters (called *calderas*) of dormant or extinct volcanoes.

Glacial lakes were created when giant glaciers gouged the earth's surface during the Ice Age to create lake basins. These filled with meltwater from the glaciers.

Tectonic lakes are formed when water collects in natural fissures. One example is Lake Tanganyika in Africa's Great Rift Valley.

Oxbow lakes are formed during periods of flooding. When flood water recedes, a loop of a meandering river may be cut off, creating a crescent-shaped lake.

An **oasis** is formed from a depression in a fertile spot in the desert where the water table approaches the surface.

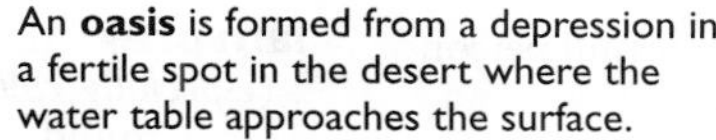

Humans form **artificial lakes** by creating a depression where water can collect for uses such as irrigation or the production of hydro-electricity.

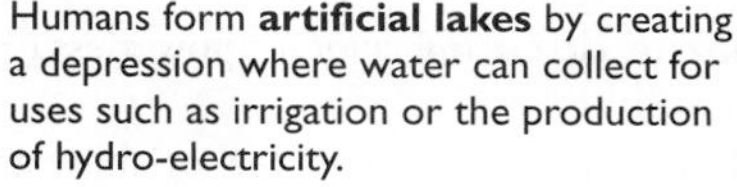

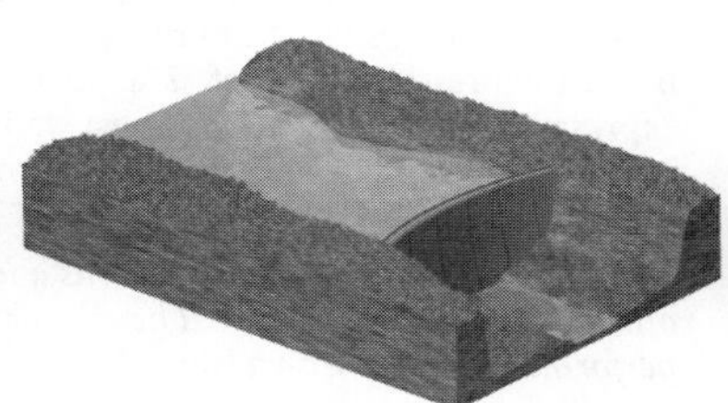

L

lake (lāk) *n* **1** a large body of fresh water entirely, or almost entirely, surrounded by land. **2** a large pool of liquid. <Latin *lacus*>

lake dweller *n* in prehistoric times, a person who lived in a **lake dwelling**, a house built on piles over a lake.

lake·front (lāk′frunt′) *n* land or land with buildings at the edge of a lake.
adj of or on a lakefront: *We have a lakefront cottage in Muskoka.*

🍁 **Lake·head** (lāk′hed′) *n* the city of Thunder Bay, Ontario, and the surrounding region, on the northwest shore of Lake Superior.

laker *n* **1** 🍁 a lake boat, especially one operating on the Great Lakes. **2** 🍁 a lake fish, especially a trout.

lake·side (lāk′sīd′) *adj* beside a lake: *a lakeside cottage.*

lake trout *n* a large, grey trout of the lakes of N America. It is an important food and game fish.

La·ko·ta (lā kō′tə) DAKOTA.

Lak·shmi (luk′shmē) *Hinduism n* the goddess of good fortune to whom DIWALI is dedicated.

la–la land (lä′lä′) *n* **1** a place whose lifestyle or attitudes are regarded as unrealistic. **2** a state of mind characterized by unrealistic ideas or a lack of seriousness. <from *L*(*os*) *A*(*ngeles*) i.e., Hollywood>

lam (lam) *n* <origin uncertain>
on the lam, *Slang* escaping or hiding, especially from the law.

la·ma (lä′mə) *n* a Buddhist priest or monk in Tibet and Mongolia. <Tibetan *blama*>

La·ma·ism (lä′mə iz′əm) *n* the Buddhist religious system of the lamas in Tibet and Mongolia.

La·marck·ism (la mark′izəm) *n* the evolutionary theory of Jean de Lamarck, an eighteenth-century French naturalist, who held that acquired characteristics can become hereditary. **La·marck′i·an** *adj, n.*

la·ma·ser·y (lä′mə ser′ē) *n, pl* **la·ma·ser·ies** a building, or group of buildings, where lamas live, work, and worship.

lamb (lam) *n* **1** a very young sheep. **2** lambskin. **3** a young, dear, or innocent person.
v give birth to a lamb or lambs. <Old English>
lamb′like′ *adj.*
like a lamb, meekly or timidly.

lam·baste (lam bāst′) *Informal v* **lam·bast·ed, lam·bast·ing** scold severely. <perhaps Scandinavian *lam* + Old Norse *beysta* beat>

a bat	e bed	i bid	o pot	u cup	th **thin**
ā cake	ē me	ī bite	ō go	ū rude	ᴛʜ **then**
ä bar	ə about	ər over	ȯ for	ů put	zh measure

lam·bent (lam′bənt) *adj* **1** moving lightly over a surface: *a lambent flame.* **2** softly bright: *Moonlight is lambent.* <Latin *lambere* lick> **lam′ben·cy** (lam′bən sē) *n.*

lamb·kin (lam′kin) *n* a little lamb.

lamb·skin (lam′skin′) *n* **1** the skin of a lamb, especially with the wool on it. **2** leather made from the skin of a lamb.

lame (lām) *adj* **lam·er, lam·est** **1** unable to walk easily. **2** stiff and sore: *Her arm is lame from playing ball.* **3** poor, weak, or unsatisfactory: *Forgetting to set the alarm is a lame excuse for being late.*
v **lamed, lam·ing** make or become lame: *The accident lamed the horse for life.* <Old English *lama*> **lame′ly** *adv.* **lame′ness** *n.*

la·mé (la mā′) *n* a rich fabric made with metallic threads. <French, from Latin *lamina* thin piece of metal>

lame duck *Informal n* a powerless or unsuccessful person or thing.

la·ment (lə ment′) *v* **1** feel or show grief for: *to lament the dead.* **2** feel or show grief: *to lament bitterly.* **3** regret: *We lamented your absence from the celebrations.*
n **1** an expression of grief. **2** a poem, song, or tune that expresses grief. <Latin *lamentum* a wailing>
la·ment′er *n.* **la·ment′ing** *adj.* **la·ment′ing·ly** *adv.*

lam·en·ta·ble (lam′ən tə bəl) *adj* **1** to be regretted or pitied: *a lamentable accident. It was a lamentable day when our dog died.* **2** inferior: *The singer gave a lamentable performance.* **lam′en·ta·bly** *adv.*

lam·en·ta·tion (lam′ən tā′shən) *n* mourning or wailing.

lam·i·na (lam′ə nə) *n* a thin plate, scale, or layer of sedimentary rock, organic tissue, or other material. <See LAMINATE. > **lam′i·nar** *adj.*

lam·i·nate (lam′ə nāt′) *for v,* (lam′ə nāt′) *or* (lam′ə nit) *for adj or n.* *v* **lam·i·nat·ed, lam·i·nat·ing** **1** split into thin layers. **2** make by putting layer on layer: *Plywood is made by laminating thin sheets of wood.* **3** beat or roll metal into a thin plate. **4** cover with thin plates.
adj laminated.
n a laminated plastic: *a bookcase of walnut-finished, high-pressure laminate on a core of hardwood.* <Latin *lamina* thin piece of metal> **lam′i·na′tion** *n.*

lamp (lamp) *n* **1** a device that provides artificial light and, sometimes, heat: *a street lamp, a floor lamp. An oil lamp holds oil and a wick by which the oil is burned.* **2** a device for providing ultraviolet rays: *a sun lamp.* <Old French, from Greek *lampein* shine>

lamp·black (lamp′blak′) *n* a fine black soot consisting of almost pure carbon that is deposited when oil or gas burns incompletely: *Lampblack is used as a colouring matter in paint and ink.*

lamp·light (lam′plīt′) *n* the light from a lamp.

lamp·light·er (lam′plī′tər) *n* a person formerly employed to light street lamps.

lam·poon (lam pūn′) *n* a piece of writing that ridicules a person.
v attack in a lampoon. <French *lampon*>
lam·poon′er *n.* **lam·poon′ist** *n.*

lamp·post (lamp′pōst′) *n* a post used to support a street lamp.

Although the **lamprey** and the eel have many similarities, their breeding habitats are different. Lamprey spawn in fresh water, swimming upstream much like salmon, while freshwater eels return to the ocean to spawn.

lam·prey (lam′prē) *or* (lam′prā) *n, pl* **lam·preys** or (*especially collectively*) **lam·prey** an eel-like fish with a large round mouth and rasping teeth. Some species of lamprey attach themselves by their mouths to fish from which they suck body fluids. <Old French, probably from Latin *lambere* to lick + *petra* stone, from their habit of attaching themselves to rocks>

lamp·shade (lamp′shād) *n* a cover fitted over a lamp to soften or direct the light.

LAN (lan) local area network.

lance (lans) *n* a long wooden spear with a sharp iron or steel head: *Knights used to carry lances.*
v **lanced, lanc·ing** **1** pierce with a lance. **2** cut open with a lancet: *The dentist lanced the gum so that the new tooth could come through.* <Old French, from Latin *lancea* spear>

Lan·ce·lot (lan′sə lot′) *n* in the legends about King Arthur, the bravest of the knights of the Round Table: *Sir Lancelot was the father of Galahad.*

lan·cet (lan′sit) *n* a small, sharp-pointed surgical knife, usually with two edges: *Doctors use lancets for opening boils, abscesses, etc.*

land (land) *n* **1** the solid part of the earth's surface: *dry land.* **2** ground or soil: *This is good land for wheat.* **3** ground used as property: *The farmer invested in land and machinery.* **4** a country or region: *throughout the land, mountainous land.*
v **1** come or bring to land: *The ship landed at the pier. The pilot landed the airplane in a field.* **2** put or go on land: *The ship landed its passengers. The passengers landed safely.* **3** come to a stop, arrive, or cause to arrive: *The car landed in the ditch. The thief landed in jail. This boat will land you in St. Johns.* **4** *Informal* catch or get: *to land a job, to land a fish.* <Old English> **land′less** *adj.*
how the land lies, what the situation is.

–land *combining form* a place, region, sphere of activity, or community, characterized by a specific thing: *woodland, Toryland, sportsland, a winter wonderland. Good morning all you listeners out there in radioland!* <Old English>

❋ **land claim** *n* a claim made by an Aboriginal group with regard to the possession or use of a certain piece of land, usually based on a treaty.

land·ed (lan′did) *adj* 1 owning land: *landed nobles.* 2 consisting of land: *Landed property is real estate.*

✱ **landed immigrant** *n* a person admitted to Canada as a settler and potential Canadian citizen, officially termed a **permanent resident**.

land·fall (land′fol′) *n* 1 a sighting of land, or approach to land from the sea or air. 2 the land sighted or reached after a voyage or flight: *The explorer's landfall was near the mouth of the St. Lawrence.*

land·fill (land′fil′) *n* 1 the disposal of waste by burying it under a shallow layer of earth. 2 a place where waste is disposed of in this way.

land·form (land′fôrm′) *n* the natural physical features of the land.

land·hold·er (land′hōl′dər) *n* a person who owns or occupies land.

land·hold·ing (land′hōl′ding) *adj* that owns or occupies land.
n an owning or occupying of land.

land·ing (lan′ding) *n* 1 a coming or bringing to land: *The Canadian Armed Forces made a landing in France during World War II. The pilot made a bumpy landing.* 2 a place where people or goods are landed from a boat, ship, or helicopter: *A wharf, dock, or pier is a landing for boats.* 3 a level area at the top of a flight of stairs.

landing field *n* a field large enough and smooth enough for aircraft to land on and take off from safely.

landing gear *n* the wheels and parts under an aircraft that enable it to land: *When on land or water, an aircraft rests on its landing gear.*

landing strip *n* a runway, often unpaved or temporary, for aircraft to take off from and land on.

land·la·dy (lan′dlā′dē) *n, pl* **land·la·dies** 1 a woman who owns buildings or land that she rents to others. 2 a woman who keeps a boarding house, lodging house, or inn.

land·locked (lan′dlokt′) *adj* 1 shut in, or nearly shut in, by land: *a landlocked harbour.* 2 living in waters shut off from the sea: *landlocked salmon.*

land·lord (lan′dlôrd′) *n* 1 a person who owns buildings or land that he or she rents to others. 2 the keeper of a boarding house, lodging house, or inn.

land·lub·ber (lan′dlub′ər) *n* a person not used to being on ships. <*land* + *lubber*>

land·mark (land′märk′) *n* 1 something familiar or easily seen, used as a guide: *That tall tower makes a good landmark.* 2 an important fact or event: *The inventions of the printing press, telephone, telegraph, and radio are landmarks in the history of communications.* 3 a stone or other object that marks the boundary of a piece of land.

land mass *n* a very large, unbroken area of land.

land mine *n* a container filled with explosives or chemicals, placed on the ground or lightly covered, and usually set off by the weight of vehicles or people passing over it.

land office *n* a government office that takes care of the business connected with public lands, and records sales and transfers.

✱ **Land of the Little Sticks** *n* a region of stunted trees at the southern end of the Barren Ground in northern Canada.

✱ **Land of the Midnight Sun** *n* the Far North.

land·own·er (lan′dō′nər) *n* one who owns land.

land–poor (land′pūr′) *adj* owning land but lacking money to maintain or improve it.

land·scape (land′skāp′) *or* (lan′skāp) *n* 1 a view of scenery on land: *The two hills with the valley between formed a beautiful landscape.* 2 a painting or other work of art showing such a view. 3 a page or illustration displayed or printed wider than it is high. Compare PORTRAIT.
v **land·scaped, land·scap·ing** make land more pleasing to look at by arranging trees, shrubs, and flowers: *The builder agreed to landscape the lot around the new house.*

landscape gardening *n* an arrangement of trees, shrubs, flowers, etc., to give a pleasing appearance to grounds, parks, or gardens. Also called **landscaping**. **landscape gardener** *n.*

land·slide (land′slīd′) *n* 1 a sliding down of a mass of soil or rock on a steep slope. 2 a mass that slides down. 3 an overwhelming majority of votes for one political party or candidate.

lands·man (land′zmən) *n, pl* **lands·men** (-zmən) 1 a man who lives or works on land. 2 an inexperienced seaman.

land·ward (lan′dwərd) *adj, adv* toward the land: *to steer a landward course* (*adj*), *to steer a ship landward* (*adv*). Also (*adv*), **landwards**.

lane (lān) *n* 1 a narrow road or path, especially one between buildings, walls, hedges, or fences. 2 a narrow way: *The couple walked down a lane formed by two lines of wedding guests.* 3 a course or route used by vehicles, ships, or aircraft going in the same direction: *an express lane on a highway, shipping lanes, air lanes.* 4 one of the strips into which a running track or swimming pool is divided for races. 5 one of the long strips of wooden flooring in a bowling alley. 6 *Basketball* **a** the rectangular area marked on a court from the end line to the foul line. **b** a free area through which a player can move toward the hoop. 7 *Sports* a lengthwise area of a playing field, ice rink, etc., considered to be the main playing area for a particular position, such as a left wing in hockey. <Old English>

lan·guage (lang′gwij) *n* 1 human speech, spoken or written. 2 the distinct form of speech common to a people, nation, or group of peoples: *the French language.* 3 a form, style, or kind of speech or writing: *bad language, the language of chemistry.* 4 the wording or words: *The language of the contract had to be explained by a lawyer.* 5 the expression of thoughts or feelings otherwise than by words: *sign language, a computer language. A dog's language is made up of barks, looks, and actions.* <Old French, from Latin *lingua* tongue>

a bat	e bed	i bid	o pot	u cup	th thin
ā cake	ē me	ī bite	ō go	ū rude	ᴛʜ then
ä bar	ə about	ər over	ô for	u̇ put	zh measure

language arts *n* a group of school subjects directly concerned with the study of language, especially speaking, listening, reading, and writing.

language laboratory *n* a room in a school, college, or university equipped with machines, often tape recorders. Students can practise speaking and listening to a language they are studying.

❋ **language police** *Derogatory n* the officials of the *Commission de protection de le langue française*, who enforce Québec's language laws.

lan·guid (lang′gwid) *adj* **1** slow, relaxed, and disinclined to make a physical effort: *A hot, sticky day makes a person feel languid.* **2** weak or sluggish, especially from disease or fatigue: *She made a languid response to my suggestion.* <French, from Latin *languere* be faint> **lan′guid·ly** *adv.* **lan′guid·ness** *n.*

lan·guish (lang′gwish) *v* **1** become weak or weary: *The flowers languished from lack of water.* **2** suffer for a long period under unfavourable conditions: *languish in poverty. Wild animals often languish in captivity.* **3** grow dull, slack, or less intense: *His vigilance never languished.* **4** long or pine for: *to languish for home. He gave a languishing look at the girl he loved.* **lan′guish·er** *n.* **lan′guish·ing** *adj.* **lan′guish·ing·ly** *adv.* **lan′guish·ment** *n.*

lan·guor (lang′gər) *n* a listless feeling, sometimes pleasant, or a lack of energy or willingness to make an effort. **2** an oppressive stillness of the air: *the languor of a hot summer afternoon.* **lan′guor·ous** *adj.* **lan′guor·ous·ly** *adv.*

lan·gur (lung gůr′) *n* a large, long-tailed, slender monkey of S Asia.

La Ni·ña (la nēn′yə) *n* a cooling of the ocean surface off the western coast of South America, occurring every four to twelve years. It affects weather patterns all over the world. Compare EL NIÑO. <Spanish = the girl, in comparison to *El Niño* = the boy>

lank (langk) *adj* limp and straight in how hair grows. <Old English *hlanc*> **lank′ly** *adv.* **lank′ness** *n.*

lank·y (lang′kē) *adj* **lank·i·er, lank·i·est** awkwardly tall and thin. **lank′i·ly** *adv.* **lank′i·ness** *n.*

lan·o·lin (lan′ə lin) *n* fat or grease obtained from wool, used in ointments. Also, **lanoline**. <Latin *lana* wool + *oleum* oil>

lan·tern (lan′tərn) *n* a lamp with a case to protect a light, often with a handle so it can be carried. A lantern has sides of glass or some other material through which the light can shine. <Old French, from Greek *lampein* shine>

lantern fish *n* a deep-sea fish with phosphorescent organs that glow on the sides and head.

lan·tha·num (lan′thə nəm) *n* a silver-white rare metallic element. *Symbol* **La** <Greek *lanthanein* to lie hidden. Lanthanum was found concealed in oxide of cerium.>

la·nu·go (lə nyū′gō) *or* (lə nū′gō) *n* the downy hair covering a leaf, insect, or especially the body of a newborn baby. <Latin *lana* wool>

lan·yard (lan′yərd) *n* a short rope or cord used on ships to fasten rigging. <Old French *laniere* strap + *yard*[2]>

La·os (la′os) *or* (lā′os) *n* a country in southeast Asia. **La·o′ti·an** (la o′shən) or **La′o** (la′o) *or* (lā′o) *adj, n.*

Lao Tzu (lou′dzū′) *n* a Chinese philosopher traditionally regarded as the founder of Taoism and the author of the **Tao Te Ching**, its scripture.

lap[1] (lap) *n* the front part from the waist to the knees of a person sitting down: *I held my baby sister on my lap.* <Old English *læppa*>
drop in someone's lap, give someone the responsibility for.
in the lap of luxury, in luxurious circumstances.
in the lap of the gods, beyond human control.

lap[2] (lap) *v* **lapped, lap·ping 1** place or be placed together, one partly over another: *We lapped shingles on the roof.* **2** get a lap or more ahead of other competitors in a race. **3** extend out beyond a limit: *The reign of Queen Elizabeth I (from 1558 to 1603) lapped over into the 17th century.* **4** wrap around; wrap up in: *He lapped himself in a warm, dry blanket.* **5** surround or envelop: *The movie star was lapped in comfort.*
n **1** the part that laps over, or the amount of overlap. **2** one time around a racetrack. **3** a part of a course travelled: *The last lap of our mountain hike was the toughest.* <Middle English *lappen* fold, wrap>

lap[3] (lap) *v* **lapped, lap·ping 1** drink by lifting up with the tongue: *Cats and dogs lap water.* **2** move gently with a soft splashing sound: *Little waves lapped against the boat.*
n **1** the act of lapping: *The cat took one lap of the sour milk and turned away.* **2** the sound of lapping: *the lap of the waves against the shore.* <Old English *lapian*> **lap′per** *n.*
lap up, a drink by lapping. **b** *Informal* consume or absorb eagerly: *The students lapped up the new math course.*

lap·dog (lap′dog) *n* a small pet dog.

la·pel (lə pel′) *n* the part of the front of a coat that is folded back just below the collar. <*lap*[1] + diminutive suffix *-el*>

lap·ful (lap′fůl) *n, pl* **lap·fuls** as much as a LAP[1] can hold.

lap·i·dar·y (lap′ə der′ē) *n, pl* **lap·i·dar·ies** a person who cuts, polishes, or engraves precious stones.
adj **1** to do with cutting or engraving precious stones. **2** engraved on stone, or with a elegant writing style suitable for engraving on stone. <Latin *lapidis* stone>

lap·is laz·u·li (lap′is laz′yū lē′) *or* (laz′yū lī′) *n* a deep blue, opaque, semiprecious stone used for ornaments and jewellery.

Lapp (lap) *n* a member of an indigenous people living in **Lapland**, a region in northern Norway, Sweden, Finland, and northwestern Russia. Also, **Laplander**. **2** the language of the Lapps.

lap robe *n* a blanket or robe, used to keep the lap and legs warm when riding in a motor vehicle, horse-drawn carriage, or sleigh.

lapse (laps) *n* **1** a slight mistake or error: *A slip of the tongue, pen, or memory is a lapse.* **2** a slipping or falling away from what is proper: *a moral lapse.* **3** a slipping back: *a lapse into my old habit of biting my nails.* **4** a slipping by: *A minute is a short lapse of time.* **5** the ending of a right or privilege because it was not renewed, not used, or otherwise neglected: *the lapse of a lease.*

v **lapsed, laps·ing 1** make a slight mistake or error. **2** slip or fall away from what is proper. **3** slip back or sink down: *The house lapsed into ruin.* **4** slip by: *The boy's interest in the story soon lapsed.* **5** end in this way: *She allowed her driver's licence to lapse.* <Latin *lapsare* to slip>

lapse rate *n* the rate at which temperature goes down as altitude increases.

lap·top (lap′top′) *Computers n* in full, **laptop computer** a computer small enough to fit on a person's lap.

lap·wing (lap′wing′) *n* a crested plover of Europe, Asia, and N Africa that has a slow, irregular flight.

lar·board (lȧr′bərd) *or* (lȧr′bȯrd) *n* the side of a ship to the left of a person looking from the stern toward the bow.
adj on this side of a ship. <Middle English *laddeborde* loading side, from *laden* to load + *bord* ship's side>

lar·ce·nous (lȧr′sə nəs) *adj* **1** to do with larceny. **2** guilty of larceny.

lar·ce·ny (lȧr′sə nē) *n, pl* **lar·ce·nies** theft of personal property. <Old French, from Latin *latrocinium* robbery>

larch (lȧrch) *n* a tree of the pine family found in the northern hemisphere, with soft, needlelike leaves that are shed in the fall. The three species of larch native to Canada are the **tamarack**, **alpine larch**, and **western larch**. <German, from Latin *larix*>

lard (lȧrd) *n* the fat of pigs, melted down and made clear: *Lard is used in cooking.*
v **1** insert strips of bacon or salt pork in meat or poultry before cooking. **2** put lard on or in: *Lard the pan well.* **3** give variety to or enrich: *to lard a long speech with jokes.* <Old French, from Latin *lardum*>

lar·der (lȧr′dər) *n* **1** a room or large cupboard where food is kept. **2** a supply of food.

lar·es and pe·na·tes (lȧ′rēz ən pə nȧ′tēz) *n* treasured household possessions. <the household gods of the ancient Romans>

large (lȧrj) *adj* **larg·er, larg·est 1** of more than the usual size, amount, or number: *Canada is a large country, a large animal, a large sum of money, a large crowd.* **2** of great scope or range: *an individual of large experience.* **3** on a great scale: *a large employer of labour.* <Old French, from Latin *largus* generous> **large′ness** *n.*
at large, a escaped from confinement and not yet captured: *Is the escaped prisoner still at large?* **b** in detail. **c** as a whole; altogether: *The people at large want peace.* **d** representing a whole area, business, or group: *the firm's representative at large.*
in large or **in the large,** on a big scale.

SYNONYMS

Large is a neutral word meaning "of more than ordinary size or amount": *Our large family has seven children.*

Abundant suggests an amount that is more than enough: *The strawberries are abundant this year, so there are lots left to pick.*

Grand suggests not only large, but also of fine appearance: *The grand staircase was a showpiece in the mansion.*

Massive suggests being bulky as well as large: *That massive oak tree is probably over one hundred years old.*

large intestine *n* the lower part of the intestines, between the small intestine and the anus.

large·ly (lȧrj′lē) *adv* **1** to a great extent: *This region consists largely of desert.* **2** in great quantity.

large·mouth bass (larj′mouth′) *n* a N American freshwater fish with a large upper jaw. Compare SMALLMOUTH BASS.

large–scale (lȧrj′skāl′) *adj* **1** involving many people or things: *Hurricanes can cause large-scale disaster.* **2** made or drawn to a large SCALE[3] (def. 4): *a large-scale map.*

lar·gesse or **lar·gess** (lȧr′jis) *or* (lȧr jes′) *n* **1** generous giving. **2** a generous gift or gifts. <Old French, from Latin *largus* generous>

larg·ish (lȧr′jish) *adj* rather large.

lar·go (lȧr′gō) *Music adj* slow and dignified. <Italian>

lar·i·at (lar′ē ət) *or* (ler′ē ət) *n* **1** a lasso. **2** a rope for fastening horses or mules to a stake while they are grazing. <Spanish *la reata* the rope>

lark[1] (lȧrk) *n* a small songbird with brown feathers and long hind claws. One kind of lark, the **skylark**, sings while soaring in the air. The **meadowlark** is a similar N American songbird. <Old English *læwerce*>

lark[2] (lȧrk) *Informal n* a merry or amusing time, especially something done for fun as a result of daring or mischief: *What a lark we had at the picnic.*
v enjoy or play in a daring or mischievous way: *The boy was always larking.* <origin uncertain>

lark·spur (lȧrk′spər′) DELPHINIUM.

❋ **lar·ri·gan** (lar′ə gən) *or* (ler′ə gən) *n* an oiled leather moccasin. <origin uncertain>

lar·va (lȧr′və) *n, pl* **lar·vae** (lȧr′vā) **1** the early form of an insect from the time it leaves the egg until it becomes a pupa. A caterpillar is the larva of a butterfly or moth. Maggots are the larvae of flies. **2** a young form of certain animals that is different in structure from the adult form. A tadpole is the larva of a frog or toad. <Latin = mask. This term was applied to larva because the adult form is masked or hidden in the larval stage of development.> **lar′val** *adj.*

la·ryn·ge·al (lə rin′jē əl) *adj* to do with the larynx.

lar·yn·gi·tis (lar′ən jī′tis) *or* (ler′ən jī′tis) *n* inflammation of the larynx, usually resulting in a temporary huskiness or loss of the voice: *A person with laryngitis finds it difficult and even painful to talk.*

lar·ynx (lar′ingks) *or* (ler′ingks) *n, pl* **lar·ynx·es** or **lar·yng·es** (lə rin′jēz) **1** the cavity at the upper end of the human windpipe, containing the vocal cords and acting as a speech organ. **2** a corresponding structure in other animals. <Latin, from Greek>

a bat	e bed	i bid	o pot	u cup	th thin
ā cake	ē me	ī bite	ō go	ū rude	ᴛʜ then
ȧ bar	ə about	ər over	ȯ for	u̇ put	zh measure

L

la·sa·gna (lə zä′nyə) *n* a dish consisting of broad, flat, pre-cooked noodles baked in layers with a sauce of ground meat or vegetables, cheese, and tomatoes. Also, **lasagne.** <Italian>

las·civ·i·ous (lə siv′ē əs) *adj* feeling, showing, or causing lust. <Latin *lascivus* lustful> **las·civ′i·ous·ly** *adv.* **las·civ′i·ous·ness** *n.*

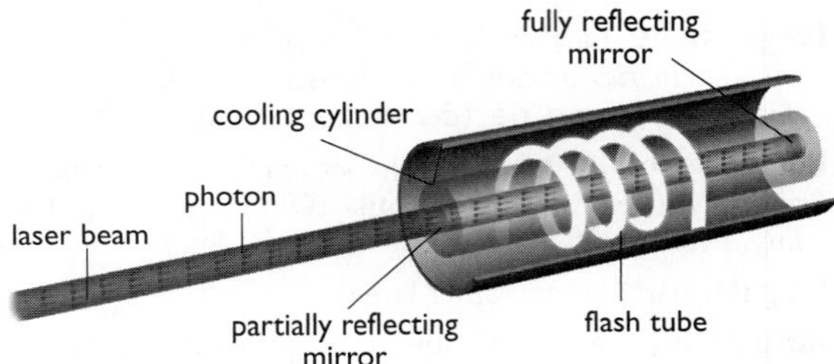

Apollo astronauts placed corner reflectors on the surface of the moon to measure the distance from Earth. From Texas, a **laser** pulse was sent to the reflector from a ruby laser like this one, and the time of the reflection was measured to determine the distance.

la·ser (lā′zər) *n* a device for amplifying light waves, producing an intense, narrow beam of light that can create holograms and cut through metal. Lasers have many potential uses in surgery, communications, etc. <*l(ight) a(mplification) by s(timulated) e(mission) of r(adiation)*>

laser disc *n* a disc on which images and sounds are digitally stored, to be read by a special machine using a laser beam. CDs, CD-ROMs, and DVDs are all laser discs. Also called **optical disc**.

laser printer *Computers n* a printer that uses a laser beam to give the paper an electric charge in an area that is the exact shape of the letter or other image.

laser surgery *n* delicate surgery using laser beams to cut tissue.

laser tag *n* an indoor game played in the dark, in which players wear vests with laser-sensing targets on them and try to hit one another's targets with gunlike devices that emit laser beams.

lash[1] (lash) *n* **1** a whip, especially the rope or thong that is attached to the handle. **2** a stroke or blow with a whip or thong. **3** a sudden, swift movement: *The cat lashed its tail in annoyance.* **4** something that hurts as a blow from a whip does. **5** the hair on the edge of an eyelid.
v **1** beat or drive with a whip: *The driver of the team lashed her horses on.* **2** wave or beat back and forth: *The wind lashes the sails.* **3** beat against something: *The rain lashed against the windows.* **4** kick or strike violently: *The horse lashed at him with its hoofs.* **5** attack severely with words: *The captain lashed the crew with his tongue.* <origin uncertain> **lash′er** *n.*
lash out, a attack or strike. **b** attack severely in words.

lash[2] (lash) *v* tie or fasten with a rope or cord: *We lashed logs together to make a raft.* <Old French, from Latin *laqueare* to ensnare>

lash·ing (lash′ing) *n* **1** a whipping, especially as a punishment. **2** a severe attack in words.

lass (las) *n* a girl or young woman. <Old Norse *laskura* unmarried>

las·si·tude (las′ə tyūd′) *or* (las′ə tūd′) *n* weariness, weakness, or lack of energy. <Latin *lassus* tired>

las·so (la sū′) *or* (las′ū) *n, pl* **las·sos** or **las·soes** a long rope with a running noose at one end: *The cowboy threw a lasso over the steer's head and pulled the animal to the ground.*
v **las·soed, las·so·ing** catch with a lasso. <Spanish, from Latin *laqueus* noose>

last[1] (last) *adj* **1** being after all others: *the last page of the book.* **2** next before a specified point of time; previous: *last year. The last movie we saw was better than this one.* **3** most unlikely or least suitable: *That is the last thing I would expect.* **4** that remains: *I used my last quarter to make a phone call.*
adv **1** after all others: *He arrived last.* **2** on the latest or most recent occasion: *When did you last see him?*
n **1** a person who or thing that is after all others: *She was the last in the line.* **2** the end: *You have not heard the last of this.* <Old English *latost* after others in a series>
at last, after a long or seemingly long time: *So you have arrived at last.*
breathe your last, die.
see the last of, not see again.

last[2] (last) *v* **1** go on or continue to be: *The storm lasted three days.* **2** continue in good condition, force, or effectiveness: *I hope this old pen lasts until I finish writing the test.* <Old English *læstan*>

last[3] (last) *n* a block shaped like a person's foot, on which shoes and boots are made or repaired. <Old English *læste*>
stick to your last, pay attention to your own work.

last–ditch (las′dich′) *adj* **1** being the last resort or the last line of defence: *a last-ditch effort.* **2** resisting to the very end: *last-ditch survivors of the attack.*

last gasp *n* the final stages or efforts of something, just before it ends or fails: *Tonight will be the last gasp of studying for the final exam.* **last-′gasp′** *adj.*

last·ing (las′ting) *adj* that lasts a long time: *The experience had a lasting effect on her.* **last′ing·ly** *adv.*

last·ly (las′tlē) *adv* in conclusion: *Lastly, I want to thank all of you for your help.*

last name *n* a surname or family name.

last post *n* in the armed forces, the bugle call that gives the hour of retiring and is sounded also at military funerals and Remembrance Day ceremonies.

last quarter *n* the period between the second half moon and new moon.

last resort *n* the solution chosen only when a person is most desperate: *I will only complain to the police as a last resort.*

last rites *pln* religious ceremonies performed for a dying person or at a funeral.

last sleep *n* death.

last straw *n* the last of a series of troublesome things that finally causes a collapse or outburst.

last word *n* **1** the last thing said. **2** *Informal* the most up-to-date style. **3** *Informal* something that cannot be improved.

latch (lach) *n* a catch for fastening a door, gate, or window: *A latch consists of a movable piece of metal or wood that fits into a notch, opening, etc.*
v fasten with a latch: *Latch the door.* <Old English *læccan* to grasp>
latch on, *Informal* understand.
latch onto, *Informal* **a** seize. **b** get. **c** understand. **d** stick closely to a person or group of people.

latch·key (lach′kē′) *n* a key used to unfasten the latch on a door from the outside.

latchkey child *n* a child who must routinely let himself or herself in on coming home from school because no adult is home.

late (lāt) *adj* **lat·er** or **lat·ter, lat·est** or **last** **1** happening or coming after the usual or proper time: *We had a late dinner last night.* **2** happening or coming at an advanced time: *success late in life.* **3** recent: *The late storm did much harm.* **4** recently dead: *Her late husband was a kind man.* **5** gone out of or retired from office: *The late prime minister is still working actively.*
adv **lat·er, lat·est** or **last** **1** after the usual or proper time: *She worked late.* **2** at an advanced time: *It rained late in the afternoon.* **3** recently. **4** recently but no longer: *Our new teacher, late of Charlottetown, misses the sound of the sea.* <Old English *læt*> **late′ness** *n.*
of late, lately or recently: *I haven't seen her of late.*

late·com·er (lāt′kum′ər) *n* someone who arrives late, or after most others.

la·teen or **la·teen–rigged** (la tēn′rigd) *adj* with a **lateen sail**, which is a triangular sail held up by a long pole on a short mast.

❦ **Late Loyalist** *n* an American settler who moved into Canada between 1790 and 1800, after the true refugees loyal to the British monarch had arrived.

late·ly (lāt′lē) *adv* a short time ago: *He has not been looking well lately.*

la·tent (lā′tənt) *adj* **1** present or available but not used or seen: *a latent talent. The power of a seed to grow into a plant remains latent if it is not planted.* **2** not present as symptoms in a disease. <Latin *latentis* lie hidden> **la′ten·cy** (lā′tən sē) *n.* **la′tent·ly** *adv.*

latent heat *Physics n* the amount of heat absorbed or released when a substance changes its state from liquid to gas, to solid from liquid, etc.

lat·er·al (lat′ə rəl) *adj* **1** of, at, or from the side: *A lateral branch of a family is a branch not in the direct line of descent.* **2** *Mathematics* to do with the edges or sides or faces of a shape or solid, not its base.
n a lateral part or outgrowth. <Latin *lateralis* side> **lat′er·al·ly** *adv.*

lateral thinking *n* a method of solving problems unconventionally or indirectly, rather than logically. **lateral thinker** *n*

la·tex (lā′teks) *n, pl* **la·tex·es** (lā′tek siz) **1** a milky liquid in certain plants, such as milkweed, poppies, and plants yielding rubber. **2** an emulsion of rubber or a plastic and water, used in paint and adhesives. <Latin = liquid>

lath (lath) *n, pl* **laths** (laths) *or* (laᴛʜz) **1** a thin, narrow strip of wood used with others to form a support for the plaster of a wall or ceiling, or to make a lattice. **2** a sheet of metal mesh, used as a support for plaster. <Old English *lætt*>

lathe (lāᴛʜ) *n* a machine for holding pieces of wood or metal, etc., and turning them against a cutting tool that shapes them. <Old Norse>

lath·er (laᴛʜ′ər) *n* **1** the foam made from soap or detergent mixed in water. **2** foam formed in sweating: *the lather on a horse after a race.*
v **1** put lather on: *My dad lathers his face before shaving.* **2** form a lather: *This soap lathers well.* **3** *Informal* beat or flog. <Old English *læthor*>

Lat·in (lat′ən) *n* **1** the language of the ancient Romans. **2** a member of the peoples whose languages came from Latin. Italians, French, Spanish, Portuguese, and Romanians are Latins.
adj **1** to do with the Latin language: *Latin poetry, Latin grammar, a Latin scholar.* **2** to do with Latin peoples or their languages. <Latin *Latinus* of Latium, an ancient territory in Italy>

Latin America *n* S America, Central America, Mexico, and some of the Caribbean islands.
Lat′in-A·mer′i·can *adj, n.*

La·ti·no (la tē′nō) *n* a person of Latin-American descent living in N America. A female may be called a **Latina**.

lat·ish (lā′tish) *adj, adv* rather late.

lat·i·tude (lat′ə tyūd′) *or* (lat′ə tūd′) *n* **1** the distance north or south of the equator, measured in degrees from the equator. On maps, lines running parallel to the equator represent latitudes. Compare LONGITUDE. **2** a place or region with a certain latitude: *Polar bears live in the cold latitudes.* **3** room to act or think: *An artist has more latitude than a bricklayer.* <Latin, from *latus* wide> **lat′i·tu′di·nal** *adj.*

lat·ke (lat′kə) *n* a potato pancake. <Yiddish>

la·trine (lə trēn′) *n* a toilet in a camp or barracks. <Latin *latrina* washroom, from *lavare* to wash>

lat·te (la′tā) *n* espresso made with hot milk. <Italian *caffe latte* coffee milk>

lat·ter (lat′ər) *adj* more recent: *Friday is in the latter part of the week.*
n **the latter** the second of two: *Canada and the US are in North America; the former lies north of the latter.*

GRAMMAR AND USAGE

Latter refers to the second of two items: *We have apple pie and vanilla cake for dessert; the latter is my favourite.*

To refer to the last of three or more items, use "last-named": *The server described all the dishes on the menu, and I chose the last-named item.*

a bat	e bed	i bid	o pot	u cup	th **thin**
ā cake	ē me	ī bite	ō go	ū rude	ᴛʜ **then**
à bar	ə about	ər over	ȯ for	ů put	zh measure

L

lat·ter·ly (lat′ər lē) *adv* lately or recently.

lat·tice (lat′is) *n* **1** a structure of crossed wooden or metal strips with open spaces between them. **2** an interlaced structure or pattern resembling this. **3** *Physics* a repeated three-dimensional arrangement of atoms, ions, or molecules in a metal or other crystalline solid.
v **lat·ticed, lat·tic·ing 1** form into or like a lattice. **2** furnish with a lattice. <Old French *latte* lath> **lat′tice·like′** *adj.*

lat·tice·work (lat′i swərk′) *n* a LATTICE (def. 1) or lattices.

Lat·vi·a (lat′vē ə) *n* a country in Europe, on the Baltic Sea. **Lat′vi·an** *adj, n.*

laud (lod) *v* highly praise a person or achievement.
n a song or hymn of praise. <Old French, from Latin *laudis* praise>

laud·a·ble (lod′ə bəl) *adj* worthy of praise: *Unselfishness is laudable.* **laud′a·bil′i·ty** *n.* **laud′a·ble·ness** *n.* **laud′a·bly** *adv.*

lau·da·num (lo′də nəm) *n* a solution of opium in alcohol, formerly used to lessen pain.

laud·a·to·ry (lod′ə tò′rē) *adj* expressing praise.

laugh (laf) *v* **1** make the sounds and movements of the face and body that show amusement or pleasure at humour or nonsense: *We all laughed at the joke.* **2** express with laughter: *to laugh a reply.* **3** drive, put, or bring by or with laughing: *to laugh your tears away.*
n the act or sound of laughing: *a hearty laugh.* <Old English *hliehhan*> **laugh′er** *n.*
have the last laugh, be proved correct after being treated with disbelief or scorn: *When his old car won the race, he had the last laugh.*
laugh at, a make fun of: *They laughed at me for being scared of spiders.* **b** disregard or make light of: *She laughed at danger.*
laugh off, dismiss with a laugh: *She laughed off my warning that the ice was not safe and walked to the middle of the pond.*
laugh on (or **out of**) **the other side of your mouth,** *Informal* be annoyed or sorry after feeling satisfaction or confidence about something.
laugh up your sleeve, *Informal* laugh secretly or to yourself.

SYNONYMS

Laugh is a neutral word that does not suggest the level of intensity: *I couldn't help but laugh when I realized the foolish mistake I had made.*

Chortle emphasizes chuckling and snorting at the same time, usually with glee: *The toddler chortled as her older brother played chase with her.*

Giggle suggests a soft kind of laugh, often from nervousness or silliness: *We giggled when the principal mispronounced the new teacher's name.*

Guffaw suggests laughing noisily and coarsely: *My uncle guffawed when my father fell into the pool with all his clothes on.*

laugh·a·ble (laf′ə bəl) *adj* such as to cause laughter: *a laughable mistake.* **laugh′a·ble·ness** *n.* **laugh′a·bly** *adv.*

laughing gas *Informal n* nitrous oxide, a colourless gas that lessens pain and may make some people laugh or become exhilarated.

laughing jackass *n* a kookaburra.

laugh·ing·stock (laf′ing stok′) *n* an object of ridicule.

laugh·ter (laf′tər) *n* **1** the action of laughing. **2** a sound of laughing: *Laughter filled the room.*

laugh track *n* a recording of audience laughter, played at appropriate moments during a television comedy show.

launch[1] (lonch) *v* **1** cause to slide into the water: *A new ship is launched from the supports on which it has been built.* **2** push out or put forth on the water or into the air: *to launch a plane from an aircraft carrier.* **3** start or set out: *His friends launched him in business by lending him money. He used the money to launch into a new hobby.* **4** throw or send out: *launch a rocket or missile.* **5** begin suddenly: *The rebel launched into a violent attack on the government.*
n **1** the movement of a boat or ship from the land into the water. **2** the act of launching a rocket, ship, or aircraft: *We watched the space launch on TV.* <Old French *lancer*> **launch′er** *n.*
launch out, begin or start.

launch[2] (lonch) *n* **1** a large motorboat used for short trips. **2** in former times, the largest boat carried by a warship. <Spanish, from Malay *lancharan* boat, from *lancha* speed>

laun·der (lon′dər) *v* **1** wash and iron clothes or linens. **2** be able to be washed: *Cotton materials usually launder well.* <Old French, from Latin *lavare* to wash> **laun′der·er** *n.*

laun·dro·mat (lon′drə mat′) *n* a self-service laundry with automatic washing machines and dryers, especially one with coin-operated machines.

laun·dry (lon′drē) *n, pl* **laun·dries 1** a room or building where clothes and linens are washed and ironed, especially a business that does this. **2** clothes and linens washed or to be washed. **3** the washing and ironing of clothes and linens.

lau·re·ate (lò′rē it) *adj* crowned with a laurel wreath as a mark of honour.
n a poet laureate.

lau·rel (lò′rəl) *n* **1** BAY[4]. **2 laurels** *pl* honour, fame, or victory: *The laurels went to a young athlete who had not competed before.* <Old French, from Latin *laurus.* The ancient Greeks wove laurel leaves into wreaths to crown heroes and champion athletes.>
look to your laurels, guard your reputation or record from rivals.
rest on your laurels, be satisfied with the honours that you have already won.

lau·relled or **lau·reled** (lò′rəld) *adj* **1** crowned with a laurel wreath. **2** honoured.

✱ **Lau·ren·tian** (lò ren′shən) *adj* to do with the St. Lawrence River and neighbouring lands.

✱ **Laurentian Shield** *n* the Canadian Shield.

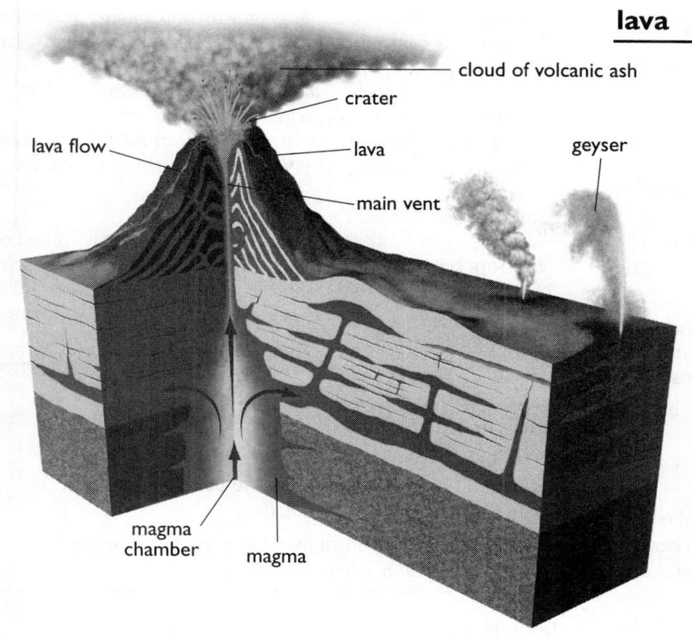

A volcano begins as a fissure in the earth's crust, through which molten rock called *magma* and other fragmented volcanic materials are ejected. As the materials cool, **lava** accumulates to form a cone. The top of the cone has a bowl-shaped vent called a *crater*. As new eruptions occur, lava flows away from the vent, increasing the size of the cone. When volcanic activity happens on the ocean floor, the accumulation eventually creates a volcanic island.

la·va (lav′ə) *or* (lä′və) *n* **1** the molten rock flowing from a volcano or fissure in the earth. **2** the rock formed by the cooling of this molten rock. Some lavas, such as obsidian, are hard and glassy; others are light and porous. <Italian *lava* stream, from Latin *lavare* to wash>

lav·a·to·ry (lav′ə trē) *or* (lav′ə tô′rē) *n, pl* **lav·a·to·ries** **1** a room where a person can wash his or her hands and face. **2** a bowl or basin to wash in. **3** a toilet or washroom. <Latin *lavare* to wash>

lav·en·der (lav′ən dər) *n* a small shrub with spikes of fragrant purple flowers yielding an oil used in perfumes and soaps. The dried flowers, leaves, and stalks are used to perfume linens or clothes, etc.
adj pale purple. <Old French, from Latin *lavendula*>

lav·ish (lav′ish) *adj* **1** very free or too free in giving or spending: *A very rich person can be lavish with money.* **2** abundant, rich, or elaborate: *many lavish gifts.*
v give or spend very freely or too freely: *It is a mistake to lavish kindness on ungrateful people.* <Old French *lavasse* flood, from Latin *lavare* to wash> **lav′ish·er** *n.* **lav′ish·ly** *adv.* **lav′ish·ness** *n.*

law (lo) *n* **1 a** a body of rules recognized by a country, state, province, etc., as binding on its members: *English law is different from French law.* **b** one of these rules: *a law against discrimination.* **c** a body of such rules concerned with a particular subject: *criminal law.* **2** the legal profession: *to enter the law.* **3** *Informal* a police officer or detective, or the police in general. **4** a rule or principle that must be obeyed: *the laws of the game.* **5** a statement describing an observable and predictable set of events in science, philosophy, etc.: *the law of gravity.* <Old Norse *lag* something fixed>
go to law, take legal action.
law and order, the condition of society brought about by observing the law: *to maintain law and order.*
lay down the law, a give orders that must be obeyed. **b** give a scolding.
read law, study to be a lawyer.
take the law into your own hands, take steps to gain your rights or avenge a wrong without going to court.

law–a·bid·ing (lo′ə bī′ding) *adj* obedient to the law: *Law-abiding citizens obey traffic signals.*

law·break·ing (lo′brā′king) *n* a breaking of the law. **law′break·er** *n.*

law court *n* a place where justice is administered.

law·ful (lo′fəl) *adj* according to or allowed by law: *lawful arrest, lawful demands.* **law′ful·ly** *adv.* **law′ful·ness** *n.*

law·giv·er (lo′giv′ər) *n* a person who prepares and puts into effect a system of laws for a people.

law·less (lo′lis) *adj* **1** paying no attention to the law: *A thief leads a lawless life.* **2** hard to control or unruly: *a lawless mob.* **3** with no laws: *a lawless frontier town.* **law′less·ly** *adv.* **law′less·ness** *n.*

law·mak·ing (lo′mā′king) *adj* with the duty and power of making laws.
n the making of laws. **law′mak·er** *n.*

lawn (lon) *n* land covered with grass kept closely cut, especially near or around a house or for recreational purposes. <Old French, from Celtic>

lawn bowling *n* a game played on a lawn called a **bowling green**, with a lopsided or unsymmetrically weighted wooden ball that is rolled toward a small, white target ball (the **jack**).

a bat	e bed	i bid	o pot	u cup	th thin
ā cake	ē me	ī bite	ō go	ū rude	ᴛʜ then
ä bar	ə about	ər over	ô for	ů put	zh measure

lawn mower *n* a machine with revolving blades for cutting the grass on a lawn.

law·ren·ci·um (lȯ ren′sē əm) *n* an artificial radioactive element. *Symbol* **Lr** <E.O. *Lawrence*, 20c physicist>

law·suit (los′ūt′) *n* a case in a civil law court: *Injustices are often remedied by lawsuits.*

law·yer (lo′yər) *or* (loi′ər) *n* a person whose profession is giving advice about the laws or acting for others in a law court.

lax (laks) *adj* careless or not strict enough: *lax behaviour. Don't let yourself become lax about doing your homework.* <Latin *laxus* loose> **lax′i·ty** *n.* **lax′ly** *adv.* **lax′ness** *n.*

lax·a·tive (lak′sə tiv) *n* a medicine that makes the bowels move.
adj making the bowels move. <Old French, from Latin *laxus* loose>

lay[1] (lā) *v* **laid, lay·ing 1** bring or beat down: *A storm laid the crops low. The rain has laid the dust.* **2** place in a certain position, or in a lying-down position: *Lay your books over there. Lay the baby down gently.* **3** locate in a certain place: *The scene of the story is laid in Montréal.* **4** place in proper position: *to lay bricks.* **5** devise or arrange: *to lay plans.* **6** put down as a bet: *I'll lay five dollars that he won't show up.* **7** make quiet or make disappear: *to lay a fear of water, to lay a ghost.* **8** impose a task or penalty: *to lay a burden on someone, to lay a tax on property.* **9** present or bring forward: *to lay a claim on an estate, to lay claim to an inheritance.* **10** produce an egg or eggs from the body: *Birds, fish, and reptiles lay eggs.* **11** (*with* **to**) apply oneself vigorously: *The rowing crew laid to their oars.*
n the position in which a thing is laid or lies: *to check the lay of the ground before a battle.* <Old English *lecgan*>
lay about, hit out on all sides.
lay away (or **aside** or **by**), **a** put away for future use: *I laid away some money every week toward buying skates.* **b** put away; put on one side: *Lay aside your problems for now.*
lay down, a declare or state: *The umpire laid down the conditions for settling the argument.* **b** sacrifice: *to lay down your life for another.* **c** begin building (on the ground): *We must lay down a new patio.*
lay for, *Informal* lie in wait for.
lay in, put aside for the future: *The trapper laid in enough supplies for the winter.*
lay into, *Informal* beat or thrash: *She laid into the vicious dog with a stick.*
lay it on thick, *Informal* flatter or exaggerate.
lay off, a give up: *He laid off junk food.* **b** *Informal* tell someone to stop doing something: *Lay off—I'm tired of your complaints.* **c** dismiss a worker temporarily or permanently because of a shortage of work or a cutting of costs: *She was laid off from her job yesterday.*
lay on, supply with something: *to lay on a big meal for the whole family.*
lay open, a expose or make vulnerable to: *He lays himself open to ridicule by wearing those silly clothes.* **b** make a wound in: *With one stroke of his knife the villain laid open the hero's cheek.*
lay out, a spread out: *Supper was laid out on the table.* **b** prepare a dead body for burial. **c** arrange or plan: *to lay out a program of study.* **d** mark off: *They laid out a tennis court.* **e** spend: *They laid out two thousand dollars in repairs.* **f** *Informal* make someone lose consciousness.
lay something on someone, *Informal* tell or show someone something: *If you've got something to say, lay it on me.*
lay to rest, See REST.
lay up, a put away for future use. **b** cause to stay in bed or indoors because of illness or injury: *She was laid up with flu for a week.*
lay yourself out, *Informal* make a big effort: *I laid myself out to be agreeable.*

CONFUSABLES

Lay and **lie** both mean "rest flat on a surface." Their forms are *lay, laid, laid*; and *lie, lay, lain.*

Lay always has an object: *Lay the book on the table. We laid a new floor in the kitchen.*

Lie does not take an object: *I'm going to lie on the bed. The village lay in a valley.*

lay[2] (lā) past tense of LIE[2].

lay[3] (lā) *adj* **1** not belonging to the clergy: *A lay sermon is one preached by a person who is not a member of the clergy.* **2** not belonging to a professional group or with expert knowledge: *The lay mind understands little of the causes of disease.* <Old French, from Greek *laos* people>

lay[4] (lā) *n* a short poem to be sung. <Old French>

lay·a·bout (lā′ə bout′) *n* a lazy or unproductive person.

lay·a·way (lā′ə wā′) *n* a system allowing goods to be put away for a specific customer, who pays for them in instalments.

lay·er (lā′ər) *n* **1** one thickness or fold: *A cake is often made of two or more layers put together.* **2** one that lays: *That hen is a champion layer.*

lay·ette (lā et′) *n* a set of clothes and bedding for a newborn baby.

lay·man (lā′mən) *n, pl* **lay·men** (-mən) **1** a member of the church who is not a clergyman: *The priest and several laymen planned the church budget.* **2** a person who is not a member of a particular profession: *It is hard for most laymen to read doctors' prescriptions.*

lay·off (lā′of′) *n* **1** a temporary dismissal of workers: *Because of a shortage of steel, there was a layoff at the plant.* **2** the time during which such a dismissal lasts.

lay of the land *n* **1** the physical features of a place: *A scouting party was sent ahead to find out the lay of the land.* **2** the existing situation or condition: *Find out the lay of the land before asking for a bigger allowance.* Also, **lie of the land.**

lay·out (lā′out′) *n* **1** the act of laying out. **2** an arrangement or plan: *This map shows the layout of the camp.* **3** a visual plan or design, especially for a book, magazine, or advertisement. **4** a thing laid or spread out. **5** an outfit, supply, or set.

lay·o·ver (lā′ō′vər) *n* a stopping for a time in a place.

lay·up or **lay–up** (lā′up′) *Basketball n* a shot on the basket at close range, often deliberately bounced off the backboard.

laze (lāz) *v* **lazed, laz·ing** be lazy or idle.

la·zy (lā′zē) *adj* **la·zi·er, la·zi·est 1** not willing to work or be active: *She was too lazy to get up to turn off the TV.* **2** moving slowly: *a lazy stream.* <origin uncertain> **la′zi·ly** *adv.* **la′zi·ness** *n.*

la·zy·bones (lā′zē bōnz′) *Informal n* a lazy person.

lazy Susan *n* a revolving tray for holding different kinds of food, placed on a table or used for storage in a cupboard.

LCD *Computers n* **1** in full, **liquid crystal display** a means of displaying characters by using a liquid with crystalline properties, sandwiched between plastic or glass. The liquid darkens in an electric field, allowing characters to be read. It is often used on calculators, digital clocks, TV screens, etc. Compare LED, PLASMA. **2** lowest (or least) common denominator.

LCM lowest (or least) common multiple.

LDL *n* in full, **low-density lipoprotein** a fat and protein molecule complex found in the blood. It holds a large amount of cholesterol. Excess LDL is associated with increased risk of heart disease and strokes. This is the so-called "bad cholesterol." Compare HDL. <Greek *lipos* fat + *protein*>

lea (lē) *n* a grassy field, meadow, or pasture. <Old English *leath*>

leach (lēch) *v* **1** run water or other liquid through slowly. **2 a** dissolve out by running water through slowly: *Potash is leached from wood ashes.* **b** lose soluble parts when water passes through. <Old English *leccan* to water>

lead[1] (lēd) *v* **led** (led)**, lead·ing 1** show the way by going along with or in front of: *He led the horses to the water.* **2** be first among: *She leads the class in spelling.* **3** guide or direct in action, policy, or opinion: *Such actions lead us to distrust them.* **4** be a way or road: *Hard work can lead to success.* **5** pass or spend time in some special way: *He leads a quiet life in the country.* **6** begin a game or other activity: *You may lead this time.* **7** be chief of: *A general leads an army. A woman led the singing.*
n **1** guidance or direction: *Many scientists followed the lead of her research.* **2** the place of leader: *She always takes the lead when we plan to do anything.* **3** the right to go first or begin: *It is your lead this time.* **4** the extent or degree that one is ahead: *He had a lead of three metres at the halfway mark.* **5** the principal part in a play, film, or broadcast program, or the actor who plays this part. **6** a guiding indication: *I was not sure where to look for the information, but the librarian gave me some good leads.* **7 a** the introductory section of a news story. **b** the most important news story. **8** the opening sentence that catches the reader's attention. <Old English *lædan*>
lead astray, a give false information to. **b** encourage to do wrong.
lead nowhere, have no effect.
lead off, begin or start.
lead on, a influence: *It's not my fault! The others led me on!* **b** deceive.
lead up to, prepare the way for; act as an introduction to: *He admitted he was wrong, as a way of leading up to an apology.*

> **GRAMMAR AND USAGE**
>
> Unlike the verb *read*, whose past tense is *read* (pronounced *red*), the past tense of **lead** is spelled *led*, not *lead*: *We led the horse home* (past tense). *My parents lead a quiet life* (present tense).

lead[2] (led) *n* **1** a soft, heavy, grey metallic element with a low melting point. *Symbol* **Pb 2** a weight on a line used to find out the depth of water. **3** bullets or pellets: *a hail of lead.* **4** a long, thin piece of graphite or other substance in or for a pencil. **5 leads** *pl* **a** strips of lead used to cover roofs. **b** the frames of lead in which panes of glass are set. <Old English>

❦ **lead dog** (lēd) *n* the dog that leads a dogsled team.

lead·en (led′ən) *adj* **1** made of lead: *a leaden coffin.* **2** heavy and hard to lift or move: *The tired runner could hardly lift his leaden legs.* **3** oppressive: *leaden air.* **4** dull or gloomy: *We had become a bit leaden by the time our team scored.* **5** grey: *leaden clouds.*

lead·er (lē′dər) *n* **1** a person who or thing that leads: *an orchestra leader. The leader of the dogsled team was a powerful husky.* **2** a person who is well qualified to lead. **3** an editorial or commentary in a newspaper or magazine. **4** a short length of wire used to attach the lure to a fishing line. **5** an article offered at a low price to attract customers. **6 leaders** *pl* a row of dots or dashes to guide the eye across a printed page. **lead′er·less** *adj.*

❦ **Leader of the Opposition** *n* the leader of the political party with the second highest number of seats in the House of Commons or a legislative assembly, and not a part of a coalition of parties forming the government.

lead·er·ship (lē′dər ship′) *n* **1** the state or position of being a leader. **2** the ability to lead: *Leadership is a great asset to a politician.*

❦ **leadership convention** *n* a convention held by a political party for the purpose of electing a new leader.

lead–in (lē′din′) *n* **1** a wire that runs from an antenna to a radio or television receiver or transmitter. **2** an introduction: *a lengthy lead-in.*

lead·ing[1] (lē′ding) *adj* **1** in first place; first in popularity: *The race is nearly over, but I can't tell who's leading. Is this the leading brand of soft drink?* **2** most important; chief; principal: *the leading lady in the play.*

leading[2] (le′ding) *n* **1** in older printing systems, metal strips for creating space between lines of type. **2** in editing software, the space between lines of text, adjustable by the user.

a bat	e bed	i bid	o pot	u cup	th thin
ā cake	ē me	ī bite	ō go	ū rude	TH then
à bar	ə about	ər over	ȯ for	u̇ put	zh measure

L

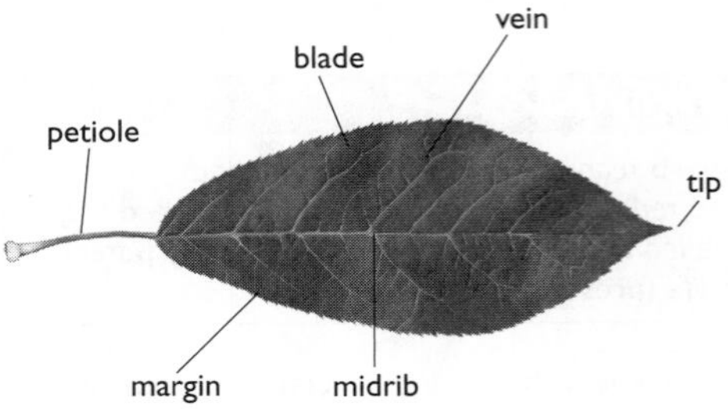

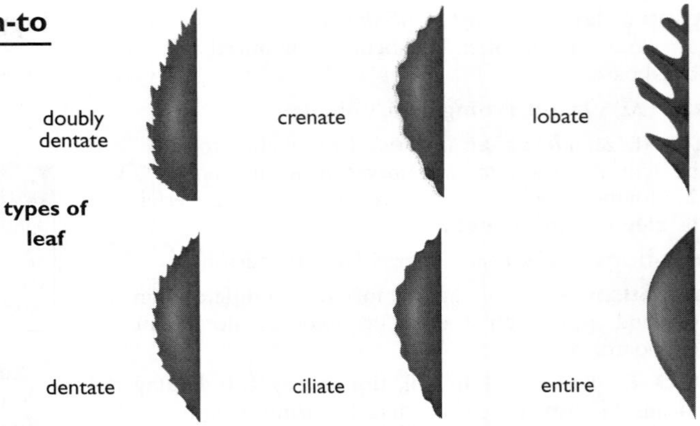

leading lady (lē′ding) *n* an actor who plays the main female role in a play or film.

leading man (lē′ding) *n* an actor who plays the main male role in a play or film.

leading question (lē′ding) *n* a question so worded that it suggests the answer desired.

lead pencil (led) *n* an ordinary pencil with a graphite lead.

lead time (lēd) *n* **1** time needed to prepare something: *Next time you want me to write an article for the yearbook, give me a bit more lead time so that I don't have to rush.* **2** the time needed to develop and manufacture a product.

leaf (lēf) *n, pl* **leaves** (lēvz) **1** one of the thin, flat, green parts that grow on the stem of a plant. **2** a sheet of paper: *Each side of a leaf of a book is a page.* **3** a very thin piece of metal or other material: *gold leaf.* **4** a movable piece of a table top.
v **1** put forth leaves: *The trees along the river leaf earlier than those on the hill.* **2** turn the pages: *to leaf quickly through a book.* <Old English> **leaf′less** *n.* **leaf′like′** *adj.*
in leaf, with fully developed leaves on: *The trees were already in leaf in Victoria.*
take a leaf from someone's book, follow someone's example.
turn over a new leaf, try to do or be better in the future: *I promised to turn over a new leaf and study harder.*

leaf·let (lē′flit) *n* **1** a small, flat or folded sheet of printed matter: *advertising leaflets.* **2** a small or young leaf. **3** a separate blade or division of a compound leaf.

leaf miner *n* a larva that feeds on leaves.

leaf spring *n* a spring on a vehicle, made up of several layers of metal strips.

leaf·stalk (lēf′stok′) *n* the stalk by which a leaf is attached to a stem.

leaf·y (lē′fē) *adj* **leaf·i·er, leaf·i·est** **1** with many leaves. **2** resembling a leaf: *We chose a fabric with a leafy design.* **leaf′i·ness** *n.*

league[1] (lēg) *n* **1 a** an association of people, parties, or countries formed to help one another. **b** the people, parties, or countries associated in a league. **2** a group of teams that play a schedule of games against each other: *a baseball league, a bowling league.*
v **leagued, lea·guing** associate in or form a league. <French, from Latin *ligare* to bind>
in league, united or in association: *They were in league against us. The suspected spies were thought to be in league with the enemy.*

league[2] (lēg) *n* an old measure of distance, usually equal to about five kilometres.

League of Arab States ARAB LEAGUE.

League of Nations *n* an association of many countries for the purpose of peace and security, formed in 1919 and replaced by the United Nations in 1945.

lea·guer (lē′gər) *n* a member of a league.

leak (lēk) *n* **1** a hole or crack, caused either by accident or by wear and tear, that lets something in or out: *a leak in a pipe.* **2** the means by which something is let in or out, or the escape or loss itself.
v **1** go in or out through a hole or crack. **2** let something in that should be kept out; let something out that should be kept in: *The boat leaks.* **3** let something pass in or out: *That pipe leaks gas.* **4** make or become known: *The secret leaked out.* **5** come in or go out in a secret or stealthy way: *Spies somehow leaked into the city.* <Middle English>

leak·age (lē′kij) *n* **1** an entering or escaping through a leak. **2** that which leaks in or out. **3** the amount of leaking: *The leakage was estimated at 40 L an hour.*

leak·y (lē′kē) *adj* **leak·i·er, leak·i·est** with a leak or leaks. **leak′i·ness** *n.*

lean[1] (lēn) *v* **leaned** or **leant** (lent)**, lean·ing** **1** stand slanting: *A small tree leans over in the wind.* **2** rest in a sloping or slanting position: *Lean against me.* **3** set or put in a leaning position. **4** depend or rely on: *to lean on a friend's advice.* **5** (*with* **to** *or* **toward**) show a preference or inclination: *to lean toward mercy. Her favourite sport was tennis, but now she leans more to swimming.*
n the act of leaning: *The old barn has more of a lean this year.* <Old English *hlinian*>

lean[2] (lēn) *adj* **1** with little or no fat: *a lean horse.* **2** producing little: *a lean harvest.*
n with little fat. <Old English *hlæne*> **lean′ly** *adv.* **lean′ness** *n.*

lean·ing (lē′ning) *n* a tendency or inclination.

lean–to (lēn′tū′) *n, pl* **lean-tos** **1** a building attached to another, toward which its roof or supports slant. **2** a crude

shelter built or leaning against posts, trees, or rock: *We built a lean-to to protect the firewood from the rain.*
adj with supports pitched against or leaning on an adjoining wall or building: *a lean-to roof.*

leap (lēp) *n* **1** a jump or spring. **2** something to be jumped. **3** the distance covered by a jump.
v **leaped** or **leapt** (lept)**, leap·ing 1** jump: *A frog leaps.* **2** pass, arrive, or rise as if with a leap or bound: *An idea leaped to her mind. A sudden breeze made the leaves leap.* **3** jump over: *to leap a fence.* <Old English *hleapan*>
by leaps and bounds, very fast and very much.
leap at, *Informal* take or accept with eagerness: *You should leap at such a chance.*
leap in the dark, an action taken without knowing what its results will be.

leap·frog (lēp′frog′) *n* a game in which one player jumps over the bent back of another.
v **leap·frogged, leap·frog·ging** leap or jump as in this game.

leap year *n* a year with 366 days, the extra day being February 29. A year is a leap year if its number can be divided exactly by four except years at the end of a century, which must be exactly divisible by 400.

learn (lərn) *v* **learned** or **learnt, learn·ing 1** gain knowledge by study, instruction, or experience: *to learn French, to learn a new game, to learn to fly a plane. He learns easily.* **2** memorize: *I must learn the poem before Monday.* **3** find out or become informed: *He tried to learn the details of the accident. I first learned of his illness from your phone call.* <Old English *leornian*> **learn′a·ble** *adj.* **learn′er** *n.*

CONFUSABLES

Learn means "come to know": *I learned how to skate.*

Teach means "instruct": *She taught me how to skate.*

The usage *She learned me how to skate* is considered to be incorrect.

learn·ed (lər′nid) *adj* with, showing, or requiring much knowledge: *a learned man, a learned book.*
learn′ed·ly *adv.*

learn·ing (lər′ning) *n* **1** the gaining of knowledge or skill. **2** the possession of knowledge gained by study. **3** knowledge.

learning curve *n* the rate of progress in gaining knowledge or skill, sometimes shown as a graph.

learnt (lərnt) a past tense and a past participle of LEARN.

lease (lēs) *n* **1** a contract, usually in the form of a written agreement, giving the right to use property for a certain length of time, usually by paying rent: *He read the lease carefully before signing it.* **2** the length of time for which such an agreement is made: *They have a long lease on the property.*
v **leased, leas·ing 1** give a lease on: *The dealer on the corner leases cars.* **2** rent: *They have leased an apartment for one year.* **3** be leased. <Old French *lesser* let go>
new lease on life, a chance to live longer, better, or more happily.

lease·hold (lēs′hōld′) *Law n* real estate held by a LEASE (def. 1). Compare FREEHOLD. **lease′hold·er** *n.*

leash (lēsh) *n* a strap or chain for holding or leading a dog or other animal in check.
v fasten, hold, or control with a leash. <Old French *laissier* loosen>
hold in leash, control.

least (lēst) *adj* less than any other: *The least bit of dirt in a watch may make it stop.*
n the smallest amount or degree: *It's the least you can do.*
adv to the least extent, amount, or degree: *She liked that book least of all.* <Old English *læst*>
at least or **at the least, a** at the lowest estimate: *The temperature was at least 35°C.* **b** at any rate or in any case: *He may have been late, but at least he got here.*
not in the least, not at all.

least common denominator LOWEST COMMON DENOMINATOR.

least common multiple LOWEST COMMON MULTIPLE.

least·ways (lē′stwāz′) *Informal adv* at least; rather. Also, **leastwise**.

leath·er (leᴛʜ′ər) *n* animal skin that has been prepared for use by removing all the flesh and hair from the skin and then tanning it. <Old English *lether*>

leath·er·ette (leᴛʜ′ə ret′) *n* imitation leather.

leath·er·y (leᴛʜ′ə rē) *adj* tough and like leather: *Exposure to harsh weather had made his face leathery.* **leath′er·i·ness** *n.*

leave[1] (lēv) *v* **left** (left)**, leav·ing 1** go away, or go away from: *We leave tonight. She left the house.* **2** stop living in, belonging to, or working at or for: *to leave the country, to leave a club.* **3** go without taking something with you: *I left a book on the table. Don't leave the dog outside the store while you're shopping.* **4** go away and let remain in a particular condition: *to leave a window open.* **5** let remain when one dies: *He left a large fortune.* **6** let a person do something: *Leave me to settle the matter. I left the planning to my sister.* **7** let remain uneaten, unused, or unremoved: *There is some pizza left.* **8** not attend to: *I will leave my homework till tomorrow.* <Old English *læfan* to remain>
leave off, stop: *Continue the story from where I left off.*
leave out, not do, say, or put in: *She left out two words when she read the sentence.*

leave[2] (lēv) *n* **1** permission or consent: *My teacher gave me leave to go.* **2 a** permission to be absent from duty. **b** the length of time that such permission lasts: *Their annual leave is thirty days.* <Old English *leaf* permission>
by your leave, *Formal or Humorous* with your permission.
leave of absence, a permission to stay away. **b** the length of time that this lasts.
on leave, absent from duty with permission.
take leave of, say goodbye to.
take your leave, say goodbye and depart.

a bat	e bed	i bid	o pot	u cup	th **thin**
ā cake	ē me	ī bite	ō go	ü rude	ᴛʜ **then**
ä bar	ə about	ər over	ô for	ů put	zh measure

L

leave[3] (lēv) *v* **leaved, leav·ing** put forth leaves: *Trees leave in the spring.*

leav·en (lev′ən) *n* **1** a substance, such as yeast, that will cause fermentation and make dough rise. **2** a modifying influence, often spreading silently and strongly: *The solemn speech had a leaven of humour. A leaven of hope brightened our despair.*
v **1** make dough light or lighter. **2** spread through and transform. <Old French, from Latin *levare* to lift>

leav·en·ing (lev′ə ning) *n* a thing that leavens.

leaves (lēvz) **1** plural of LEAF. **2** plural of LEAVE[2].

leave–tak·ing (lēv′tā′king) *n* the act of saying goodbye.

leav·ings (lē′vingz) *pln* leftovers or remnants.

Leb·a·non (leb′ə non) *n* a country at the eastern end of the Mediterranean. See the APPENDIX. **Leb′a·nese′** *n.*

Le·bens·raum or **le·bens·raum** (lā′benz rom) *n* the territory that a nation supposedly needs in order to be self-sufficient. <German = living space>

lech·er·y (lech′ə rē) *n* indulgence of lust. <Old French *lecheor* glutton, lecher> **lech′er** *n.* **lech′er·ous** *adj.*

lec·i·thin (les′ə thin) *n* a fatty substance found in egg yolks and animal tissues. It can be used as an emulsifier in food products. <Greek *lekithos* egg yolk>

lec·tern (lek′tərn) *n* a tall stand with a sloping top to hold a book or notes from which one can read while standing up in a hall or church. <Old French, from Latin *legere* read>

lec·ture (lek′chər) *n* **1 a** a speech on a chosen subject, usually for the purpose of instruction. **b** such a speech written down or printed. **2** a scolding: *My mother gives me a lecture when I get home late.*
v **lec·tured, lec·tur·ing 1** give a lecture. **2** scold. <Latin *legere* to read>

SYNONYMS

Lecture suggests a formal talk given to teach or inform a group: *The professor gave a lecture on Canadian literature.*

Address suggests a formal speech, usually not one that teaches: *The mayor gave an address to the city council.*

Oration emphasizes a formal public speech delivered on a special occasion: *The baseball commissioner delivered an oration at the opening of the new stadium.*

lec·tur·er (lek′chə rər) *n* **1** a person who gives a lecture or lectures. **2** a teacher of junior rank at some universities.

led (led) past tense and past participle of LEAD[1].

LED or **L.E.D.** *n* in full, **light-emitting diode** a device that gives off light when electricity is applied. It is used especially for displays of numerals in calculators and digital clocks. Compare LCD.

ledge (lej) *n* **1** a narrow shelf: *a window ledge.* **2** a shelf or ridge of rock. **3** a layer or mass of metal-bearing rock. <Middle English>

ledg·er (lej′ər) *n* a book of accounts in which a business keeps a record of all money transactions. <Middle English *legger* Bible or prayer book, i.e., a big book that lies in a permanent place. Ledgers traditionally were big books.>

ledger line *Music n* a line added above or below the staff for notes too high or low to be written on the staff.

lee (lē) *n* **1** shelter. **2** the side or part sheltered or away from the wind: *The wind was so fierce that we ran to the lee of the house.* **3** the side away from the wind. **4** the direction toward which the wind is blowing.
adj **1** sheltered or away from the wind: *the lee side of a ship.* **2** on the side away from the wind. **3** in the direction toward which the wind is blowing. <Old English *hleow* shelter>

leech (lēch) *n* **1** a worm that lives in ponds and streams, and sucks the blood of animals: *Doctors formerly used leeches to suck blood from sick people.* **2** a person who persistently tries to get what he or she can out of others. <Old English *læce*>

leek (lēk) *n* a vegetable resembling an onion but with larger leaves, a smaller, cylindrical bulb, and a milder flavour: *The leek is the emblem of Wales.* See ONION for picture. <Old English *leac*>

leer (lēr) *n* a sly, sidelong, unpleasant look.
v give a sly, sidelong, unpleasant look. <perhaps Old English *hleor* cheek, from the idea of looking sideways, over one's cheek> **leer′ing** *adj.* **leer′ing·ly** *adv.*

leer·y (lē′rē) *Informal adj* wary or suspicious: *We are leery of his advice.*

lees (lēz) *pln* dregs or sediment. <Old French *lies*>

lee·ward (lē′wərd) *or* (lü′ərd) *adj, adv* **1** on the side away from the wind. **2** in the direction toward which the wind is blowing.
n the side away from the wind.

lee·way (lē′wā′) *n* **1** the side movement of a ship to leeward. **2** more time, space, or money than is needed as a margin of safety: *If you have $100 more than you need on a trip, you are allowing yourself a leeway of $100.* **3** convenient room or scope for action.

left[1] (left) *adj* **1** to do with the side that is toward the west when the main side faces north: *the left wing of an army. Make a left turn at the next light.* **2** when looking to the front, situated nearer the observer's or speaker's left hand than his or her right. **3** favouring social and economic reform, especially in the redistribution of wealth.
adv on or to the left side: *to turn left.*
n **1** the left side or hand: *She sat at my left.* **2 the Left** the groups or political parties who favour social and economic reform, especially in the redistribution of wealth. <Old English *lyft* weak. The left hand was generally considered weaker than the right.>

left[2] (left) past tense and past participle of LEAVE[1].

left brain *n* the left hemisphere of the brain, which controls the right side of the body and such mental functions as logic, language, and calculation.
left′-brain′ or **left′-brained′** *adj.*

left–click (left′klik′) *Computers v* position the cursor and click the left button of the mouse: *Left-click on the paintbrush icon.*

left face *v* turn to the left.

left field *n* **1** *Baseball* the part of the outfield beyond third base. **2** *Informal* the source of ideas that are extremely unusual or completely wrong: *His interpretation of the poem seemed to come from left field.*

left–hand (left′hand′) *adj* **1** on or to the left. **2** of, for, or with the left hand.

left–hand·ed (left′han′did) *adj* **1** using the left hand more easily and readily than the right. **2** done or made to be used with the left hand. **3** turning from right to left: *a left-handed screw.* **4** ambiguous or insincere: *a left-handed compliment.* **left′-hand′ed·ly** *adv.* **left′-hand′ed·ness** *n.*

left·ist (lef′tist) *n* a person who supports the left wing in politics.
adj Informal tending to support social and economic reform, especially in the redistribution of wealth.

left·o·ver (lef′tō′vər) *n* anything that is left: *Scraps of food from a meal are leftovers.*
adj remaining.

left wing *n* **1** the people supporting or favouring reform, especially the radical members of a political organization. **2** in hockey, lacrosse, and some other sports, the playing position to the left of centre on a forward line, or the player in this position. **left winger** *n.*

left·y (lef′ti) *n, pl* **left·ies** *Informal* a left-handed person.

leg (leg) *n* **1** one of the limbs on which humans and animals stand or walk. **2** anything shaped or used like a leg: *a table leg.* **3** a distinct part of a route or journey: *the last leg of a trip.* <Old Norse *leggr*> **leg′less** *adj.*
not have a leg to stand on, *Informal* not have any defence or reason.
give a leg up, *Informal* help.
leg it, *Informal* walk or run.
on your last legs, about to fall, collapse, or die: *I feel as if I am on my last legs but a shower will revive me.*
pull someone's leg, *Informal* fool, trick, or make fun of someone: *I didn't know he was pulling my leg until I heard you laugh.*
shake a leg, *Slang* hurry up.
stretch your legs, *Informal* take a walk.

leg·a·cy (leg′ə sē) *n, pl* **leg·a·cies** **1** the money or other property left to a person by a will. **2** something that has been handed down from an ancestor or predecessor. <Old French, from Latin *legare* hand down to>

le·gal (lē′gəl) *adj* **1** of law or lawyers: *legal knowledge, legal advice.* **2** according to law: *Hunting is legal only during certain seasons.* <French, from Latin *legis* law>

legal aid *n* a program providing free or low-cost services from lawyers to people of low income, or the services provided in this way.

le·gal·ese (lē′gə lēz′) *n* the formal and technical language of lawyers and judges, especially when thought of as overly complicated.

le·gal·ism (lē′gə liz′əm) *n* strict adherence to law or a rule. **le′gal·ist** *n.* **le′gal·is′tic** *adj.*

le·gal·i·ty (li gal′ə tē) *n, pl* **le·gal·i·ties** accordance with law.

le·gal·ize (lē′gə līz′) *v* **le·gal·ized, le·gal·iz·ing** make legal or authorize by law. **le′gal·i·za′tion** *n.*

le·gal·ly (lē′gə lē) *adv* in a legal manner or according to law: *Are parents legally responsible for their children's debts?*

le·gal–size (lē′gəl sīz′) *adj* **1** measuring 22 cm x 36 cm as a size of paper. **2** designed to hold or fit such paper, such as an envelope or filing cabinet.

legal tender *n* money that must, by law, be accepted in payment of debts.

leg·ate (leg′it) *n* **1** a representative of the Pope. **2** an ambassador or messenger. <Latin *legare* send as a deputy, from *legis* law>

le·ga·tion (li gā′shən) *n* **1** a diplomatic representative of a country and his or her staff of assistants: *A legation ranks next below an embassy.* **2** the official residence and offices of such a representative in a foreign country. **3** the office, position, or status of a legate.

le·ga·to (li gȧ′tō) *Music adj, adv* smooth and connected. <Italian, from Latin *ligare* to tie together>

leg·end (lej′ənd) *n* **1** a traditional story or group of stories that are widely accepted as fact: *The stories about King Arthur and his Knights of the Round Table are legends, not history.* **2** the wording that accompanies a picture, map, or diagram, often giving the meaning of symbols. **3** the inscription on a coin or medal. <Latin *legenda* passages to be read, from *legere* read>

GRAMMAR AND USAGE

A **legend** tells a story that glorifies a hero, saint, or some great event from a people's past. It may contain an element of fact, or it may be wholly untrue.

A **myth** relates to a people's religion and is usually about a god, gods, or other superhuman beings. Its original purpose was to explain a religious belief or some aspect of life or nature.

leg·end·ar·y (lej′ən der′ē) *adj* of or like a legend or legends: *Robin Hood is a legendary person.*

leg·er·de·main (lej′ər də mān′) *n* **1** sleight of hand or conjuring tricks: *A common trick of legerdemain is to take rabbits from an apparently empty hat.* **2** deception or trickery. <French *léger de main* light of hand>

leg·gings (leg′ingz) *pln* extra outer coverings of cloth or leather for the legs, for use out-of-doors.

leg·gy (leg′ē) *adj* **1** with long legs. **2** with a long or straggling stem in a plant.

leg·horn (leg′hȯrn) *or* (leg′ərn) *n* **1** a hat made of flat, yellow, braided straw. **2** the braided straw from which such a hat is made.

leg·i·ble (lej′ə bəl) *adj* **1** that can be read. **2** easy to read: *legible handwriting.* <Latin *legere* read> **leg′i·bil′i·ty** *n.* **leg′ib·ly** *adv.*

a bat	e bed	i bid	o pot	u cup	th **thin**
ā cake	ē me	ī bite	ō go	ū rude	TH **then**
ȧ bar	ə about	ər over	ȯ for	u̇ put	zh measure

L

le·gion (lē′jən) *n* **1** a great many: *a legion of difficulties, a legion of supporters.* **2** in the ancient Roman army, a body of soldiers consisting of 3000 to 6000 foot soldiers and 300 to 700 cavalrymen. **3 Legion** an organization of former military personnel, especially war veterans. <Old French, from Latin *legionem* those gathered together>

le·gion·ar·y (lē′jə ner′ē) *adj* to do with a legion.
n, pl **le·gion·ar·ies** a soldier of a legion.

le·gion·naire (lē′jə ner′) *n* **1** a member of the Royal Canadian Legion. **2** a soldier of a legion.

Legionnaires' disease *n* a form of bacterial pneumonia characterized by fever, coughing, muscle aches, and chest pains. <from a convention of the American *Legion,* Philadelphia, 1976, where it was first reported>

Legion of Honour or **Honor** *n* an honorary society founded by Napoleon in 1802, in which membership is given as a reward for services to France.

leg·is·late (lej′i slāt′) *v* **leg·is·lat·ed, leg·is·lat·ing 1** make laws: *Parliament legislates for Canada.* **2** force by legislation: *The council legislated her out of office.* <Latin *legis lator* proposer of a law>

leg·is·la·tion (lej′i slā′shən) *n* **1** the making of laws: *Parliament has the power of legislation.* **2** the laws made: *Important legislation is reported in today's newspaper.*

leg·is·la·tive (lej′i slə tiv) *or* (lej′i slā′tiv) *adj* **1** to do with making laws: *legislative reforms.* **2** with the duty and power of making laws: *Parliament is a legislative body.* **3** ordered by law: *a legislative decree.* **leg′is·la′tive·ly** *adv.*

❦ **legislative assembly** *n* the group of representatives elected to the legislature of a province or territory.

❦ **Legislative Council** *n* formerly, in Québec, the upper chamber of the legislature, composed of 24 members appointed for life by the Lieutenant-Governor in Council. It was abolished in 1968.

leg·is·la·tor (lej′i slā′tər) *n* a lawmaker: *MP's and MLA's are legislators.*

leg·is·la·ture (lej′i slā′chər) *n* **1** a group of people with the duty and the power to make laws for a country, province, or state: *Each Canadian province has a legislature.* **2** the place where the legislators meet.

le·git (lə jit′) *Informal adj* legitimate.

le·git·i·mate (lə jit′ə mit) *for adj,* (lə jit′ə māt′) *for v.*
adj **1** rightful or lawful: *The Prince of Wales is the legitimate heir to the throne of England.* **2** allowed or acceptable: *Illness is a legitimate reason for absence from school.* **3** to do with drama acted on stage, as opposed to films, broadcast media, and other stage entertainment: *the legitimate theatre.* **4** born of parents who are married. **5** logical or valid: *a legitimate conclusion.*
v **le·git·i·mat·ed, le·git·i·mat·ing** make or declare lawful. <Latin *legitimus* lawful, from *legis* law> **le·git′i·ma·cy** *n.* **le·git′i·mate·ly** *adv.*

le·git·i·mize (lə jit′ə mīz′) *v* **le·git·i·mized, le·git·i·miz·ing** make or declare to be legitimate. **le·git′i·mi·za′tion** *n.*

leg·room (leg′rüm) *n* space in which to comfortably rest or stretch one's legs while seated: *These theatre seats don't have enough legroom.*

leg·ume (leg′yūm) *or* (li gyūm′) *n* a plant with a number of seeds in a pod, such as beans or peas. The roots of legumes hold nitrogen-fixing bacteria. <Latin *legumen* bean, from *legere* to pick (a crop)>
le·gu′mi·nous (li gyū′mə nəs) *adj.*

leg warmers *pl n* coverings for the legs reaching from knee to ankle, used especially by dancers in preliminary or practice exercises. See EXERCISE for picture.

legwork *n* the part of a project that involves walking or travelling around, especially to find people, information, or resources: *Planning this arts day involved a lot of legwork.*

lei (lā) *n, pl* **leis** a garland of fresh flowers and leaves worn around the neck in Hawaii. <Hawaiian>

leis·ure (lezh′ər) *or* (lē′zhər) *n* the time free from required work in which a person may rest, amuse himself or herself, and do the things he or she likes to do: *Busy people don't have much leisure for reading.*
adj free to enjoy rest or recreation: *leisure hours.* <Old French *leisir,* from Latin *licere* be free to do something>
at leisure, a not busy with work. **b** without hurry.
at your leisure, whenever it is convenient for you.

leis·ured (lezh′ərd) *or* (lē′zhərd) *adj* **1** having leisure. **2** leisurely.

leis·ure·ly (lezh′ər lē) *or* (lē′zhər lē) *adj* without hurry: *He was a man of leisurely habits.*
adv in a leisurely manner: *We walked leisurely across the street.* **leis′ure·li·ness** *n.*

leit·mo·tif or **leit·mo·tiv** (līt′mō tēf′) *n* a short theme or passage in a musical or literary composition, repeated throughout the work and associated with a certain person, situation, or idea. <German = leading motive, i.e., recurring theme>

lem·ming (lem′ing) *n* a small, mouselike Arctic rodent with greyish or brownish fur, a short tail, and furry feet. <Norwegian>

lem·on (lem′ən) *n* **1** the acid-tasting, pale yellow fruit of a citrus tree that grows in warm climates. **2** *Informal* a thing or person that is considered inferior or disagreeable: *After its third breakdown in a month, she admitted that the car was a lemon.*
adj pale yellow. <Old French, from Arabic *limun*>
lem′on·like′ *adj.*

lem·on·ade (lem′ə nād′) *n* a drink made of lemon juice, sugar, and water.

lemon grass *n* a tropical grass used as a flavouring in cooking. Its leaves produce a lemon-scented oil.

le·mur (lē′mər) *n* an animal related to the monkey, but with a foxlike face and woolly fur, found mainly in Madagascar. <Latin *lemures* ghosts, from their being active at night>

lend (lend) *v* **lent, lend·ing 1** let another have or use for a time: *Will you lend me your bicycle for an hour?* **2** give the use of money for a fixed or specified amount of payment: *Banks lend money and charge interest.* **3** make a loan or loans: *A person who borrows should be willing to lend.*

4 give, contribute, or add: *A lace curtain lends charm to a window. Canadians are quick to lend aid in time of disaster.* See BORROW for confusable. <Old English *læn* loan> **lend′er** *n.*

lend a hand, help: *She lent a hand with the dishes.*

lend itself to, be suitable for: *The old engine lent itself to our purposes.*

lend yourself to, make yourself available for: *Don't lend yourself to foolish schemes.*

CONFUSABLES

Lend and **loan** are verbs that mean "give something temporarily": *I'd like you to lend me some money. I'll be happy to loan you the money.*

Loan is also a noun: *Thanks for the loan!*

length (length) *or* (lengkth) *n* **1** the extent of something in space or time: *the length of your arm, the length of a race, the length of a visit, the length of an hour.* **2** a long stretch or extent: *There will be quite a length of time before the show starts.* **3** a piece or portion of a substance, often cut from a larger piece or meant to be joined to another piece: *a length of rope, three lengths of pipe.* <Old English *lengthu*>

at full length, with the body stretched out flat.

at length, a at last or finally: *At length, after many delays, the meeting started.* **b** with all the details: *She told of her adventures at length.*

go to any length, do everything possible.

keep at arm's length, discourage from being too familiar.

length·en (leng′thən) *or* (lengk′thən) *v* **1** make longer: *A tailor can lengthen your pants.* **2** become or grow longer: *Your legs have lengthened a great deal since you were five years old.*

length·wise (leng′thwīz′) *adv, adj* in the direction of the length: *a lengthwise measurement* (*adj*). *She cut the cloth lengthwise* (*adv*).

length·y (leng′thē) *adj* **length·i·er, length·i·est** long or too long: *His directions were so lengthy that everybody got confused.*

le·ni·en·cy (lē′nē ən sē) *or* (lē′nyən sē) *n* gentleness and mercy.

le·ni·ent (lē′nē ənt) *or* (lē′nyənt) *adj* gentle and merciful: *a lenient punishment.* <Latin *lenis* mild> **le′ni·en·cy** *n.* **len′ient·ly** *adv.*

lens (lenz) *n, pl* **lens·es 1** a piece of glass, or something like glass, that brings closer together or sends wider apart the rays of light passing through it: *The lenses of a telescope make things look larger and nearer.* **2** a clear, oval structure in the eye directly behind the iris, that directs light rays upon the retina. <Latin = lentil, from its shape>

lent (lent) past tense and past participle of LEND.

Lent (lent) *Christianity n* the six-and-a-half weeks (forty days excluding Sundays) before Easter, observed in many churches as a time for fasting and repentance. <Old English *lencten* spring, in reference to the lengthening of the days at this time of year> **Lent′en** *adj.*

len·til (len′təl) *n* the dried seed of a plant of the pea family native to the Mediterranean and Africa, whose pods contain two seeds. <Old French, from Latin *lentis*>

len·to (len′tō) *Music adj* slow. <Italian>

Le·o (lē′ō) *n* **1** *Astronomy* a northern constellation shaped somewhat like a lion. **2** *Astrology* **a** the fifth sign of the zodiac. The sun enters Leo about July 22. **b** a person born under this sign.

Le·o·nids (lē′ə nidz′) *pl n* a shower of meteors appearing to come from the constellation Leo, occurring every year about mid November.

le·o·nine (lē′ə nīn′) *adj* to do with lions. <Old French, from Latin *leo* lion>

leop·ard (lep′ərd) *n* a large wild cat of Africa and Asia with dull yellowish fur spotted with black. The female may be called a **leopardess**. <Old French, from Greek *leon* lion + *pardos* leopard>

A **leotard** allows unrestricted movement, which is essential in gymnastics. A routine on the balance beam consists of tumbling moves, turns, jumps, and leaps. The balance beam is 10 cm wide, 5 m long, and stands 1.2 m off the floor.

le·o·tard (lē′ə tärd′) *n* **1** a one-piece, close-fitting garment worn by dancers or acrobats. **2 leotards** *pl* tights. <J. *Léotard*, 19c gymnast>

lep·er (lep′ər) *n* a person who has leprosy.

lep·i·dop·ter·ist (lep′ə dop′tə rist) a person who studies or collects butterflies and moths, that is, insects belonging to the order **Lepidoptera**. These have four broad wings covered with tiny coloured scales. <Latin, from Greek *lepidos* scale + *pteron* wing>

a bat	e bed	i bid	o pot	u cup	th thin
ā cake	ē me	ī bite	ō go	ū rude	ᴛʜ then
ä bar	ə about	ər over	ô for	ů put	zh measure

lep·re·chaun (lep′rə kon′) *n* in Irish folklore, a sprite or goblin resembling a little old man. <Irish *lu* small + *corp* body>

lep·ro·sy (lep′rə sē) *n* a contagious disease that affects the skin, mucous membranes, and nerves, causing discoloration and lumps on the skin, and sometimes other deformities. Also called **Hansen's Disease**, named after G. Hansen, a 19th-century physician. **lep′rous** *adj.* <Old French, from Greek *lepros* scaly>

lep·ton (lep′ton) *Physics n* a subatomic particle that is believed to have no mass. The leptons include the electron, the muon, the neutrino, and their antiparticles. <Greek *leptos* small>

Les·bi·an or **les·bi·an** (lez′bē ən) *n* a homosexual woman. *adj* to do with homosexuality in women. <*Lesbos,* home of the Greek poet Sappho, supposedly homosexual>

le·sion (lē′zhən) *n* a part of tissue or an organ that has suffered damage through injury or disease. <Old French, from Latin *laedere* injure>

Le·so·tho (lə sü′tü) *or* (lə so′to) *n* a country in southern Africa, bordered on all sides by South Africa.

less (les) *adj* **1** smaller in amount: *of less width, of less importance.* **2** not so much: *to have less rain, to put on less butter.* **3** fewer in number: *Five is less than seven.* **4** lower in age, rank, or importance: *I am no less a citizen than the prime minister is.*
n a smaller amount or quantity: *She refused to take less than minimum wage.*
adv to a smaller extent or degree: *less known.*
prep lacking or without: *a year less two days.* <Old English *læssa*>
more or less, a somewhat: *We are all more or less impatient.* **b** approximately: *The cost is fifty dollars, more or less.*

CONFUSABLES

Less means "not so much," and refers only to amount: *I have less spare time now that I'm in the chess club.*

Fewer means "not so many," and usually refers to countable things: *I made fewer errors this time.*

–less *suffix* **1** without or lacking: *homeless, flavourless.* **2** not able to do or not able to be: *ceaseless, countless.* <Old English *leas* free from>

les·see (le sē′) *n* a person who is granted a LEASE (def. 1).

less·en (les′ən) *v* make or become less.

less·er (les′ər) *adj* **1** less or smaller. **2** the less important of two.

CONFUSABLES

Less and **lesser** are comparatives of **little**.

Less usually refers to size or quantity: *less expensive; less space.*

Lesser refers to value or importance: *a lesser amount of money; a lesser problem.*

lesser panda PANDA (def. 2).

les·son (les′ən) *n* **1** something learned or studied: *Children study many different lessons in school.* **2** a unit of learning or teaching: *Our math text is divided into 20 lessons.* **3** a meeting of a student or class with a teacher to study a given subject: *She has gone for a piano lesson. There will be no lesson today.* **4** an instructive experience, serving to encourage or warn: *The accident was a lesson to me.* **5** a selection from the Bible or other sacred writings, read as part of a religious service. <Old French, from Latin *lectionis* a reading>

les·sor (les′ôr) *n* a person who grants a LEASE (def. 1).

lest (lest) *conj* **1** for fear that: *Be careful lest you fall from that tree.* **2** that: *They were afraid lest she should arrive too late to save them.* <Middle English *leste*>

let (let) *v* **let, let·ting 1** allow, or allow to do: *to let the dog have a bone, to let passengers get off a plane.* **2** rent or be rented: *to let rooms in a house. That boat lets for an hourly rate.* **3** used to make or respond to a suggestion, or give an instruction: *Let us eat supper early today. Let's get out of here. Shall we go? Yes, let's.* **4** used to defy or challenge something: *If he wants to leave, let him!* **5** used when offering to help: *"Here, let me carry that," he offered.* **6** used to suppose or assume: *Let x be the unknown number.* <Old English *lætan* to permit>
let down, a lower. **b** disappoint: *Don't let us down, because we're depending on you.* **c** make clothes longer: *I shall have to let that coat down; it's too short.*
let go, a stop holding. **b** dismiss from a job.
let in, admit or permit to enter.
let off, a allow to go free or release: *let off with a warning.* **b** free from: *The teacher would not let us off homework.* **c** fire or explode: *let off a firework.*
let off steam, *Informal* give way to feelings: *He let off steam by shouting.*
let on, *Informal* **a** allow to be known: *He didn't let on his surprise at the news.* **b** pretend: *She let on that she didn't see me.*
let out, a permit to go out. **b** make a garment larger. **c** rent: *Has the room been let out yet?* **d** make known: *to let out details of the plan.*
let someone in for, *Informal* involve someone in something unpleasant: *With such high expectations, you're letting yourself in for a big disappointment.*
let up, *Informal* stop or pause: *They refused to let up in the fight.*
let yourself go, a cease to restrain yourself. **b** cease to take care of your appearance.

–let *suffix* **1** little: *booklet.* **2** a small thing worn as a band on: *anklet.* <Old French *–elet,* from Latin *-ellus* diminutive suffix>

let·down (let′doun′) *n* **1** a slowing up. **2** a disappointment. **3** humiliation.

le·thal (lē′thəl) *adj* causing death: *lethal weapons, a lethal dose.* <Latin *letum* death>

le·thar·gic (lə thär′jik) *adj* producing a lack of energy and enthusiasm.

leth·ar·gy (leth′ər jē) *n, pl* **leth·ar·gies** a lack of energy or enthusiasm. <Latin, from Greek *lethe* forgetfulness + *argos* lazy> **le·thar′gic** *adj.*

let's (lets) *contraction* let us.

let·ter (let′ər) *n* **1** a symbol of an alphabet: *There are twenty-six letters in English.* **2** a written or printed message, usually with several paragraphs. **3** a badge representing the initial letter of a school or college, given as an award for achievement, especially in athletics. **4 letters** *pl* a knowledge of literature or literary culture: *a man of letters.*
v mark, inscribe, or make alphabet letters. <Old French, from Latin *littera*> **let′ter·er** *n.*
the letter of the law, the exact wording or actual terms: *He kept the letter of the law but not the spirit.*
to the letter, very exactly: *A soldier is trained to carry out orders to the letter.*

let·ter·box (let′ər boks′) *n* a video format that adapts the image from a wide-screen movie to fit a TV screen, leaving a black band on the top and bottom.
v adapt a film to letterbox format. <from the shape of a mail slot, called a *letter box* in the UK>

letter carrier *n* a person who collects or delivers mail: *My aunt was a letter carrier in Whitehorse.* Also called **mail carrier**.

let·tered (let′ərd) *adj* **1** marked with letters. **2** able to read and write. **3** knowing literature or with literary culture.

let·ter·head (let′ər hed′) *n* **1** words printed at the top of a sheet of paper, usually a name and address. **2** a sheet of paper so printed.

let·ter·ing (let′ə ring) *n* **1** letters drawn, painted, or stamped. **2** the making of letters.

let·ter–per·fect (let′ər pər′fikt) *adj* **1** knowing one's part or lesson perfectly: *He worked hard to learn his part in the play and was soon letter-perfect.* **2** correct in every detail: *Your lab procedure must be letter-perfect, or the results will be useless.*

let·ter–size (let′ər sīz′) *adj* **1** measuring 22 cm by 28 cm as a size of paper. **2** of other things, made to fit or hold such paper: *a letter-size envelope.* Also, **letter-sized**.

letters patent (pat′ənt) *or* (pā′tənt) *n* an official document giving a person or a corporation authority from a government to do some act or to have some right.

let·tuce (let′is) *n* a garden vegetable grown in several varieties, all with leaves that grow out from a very short central stalk. Lettuce is usually eaten raw, in salads. See ICEBERG LETTUCE for picture. <Old French, from Latin *lactis* milk, from the milky juice of the plant>

let·up (let′up′) *Informal n* a lessening or stopping: *They've been working since morning, without letup. After a slight letup, the rain started again, harder than ever.*

leu·co·cyte or **leu·ko·cyte** (lū′kə sīt′) *n* a white or colourless cell that occurs in the blood and helps the body fight infection. Compare ERYTHROCYTE. <Greek *leukos* white + *-cyte* cell>

leu·ke·mi·a (lū kē′mē ə) *n* a cancer characterized by the abnormal growth of leucocytes in the bone marrow, lymphatic tissue, or spleen, usually resulting in an excess of these cells in the blood.

lev·ee[1] (lev′ē) *n* **1** an embankment built along a river to prevent flooding. **2** a landing place for boats on the bank of a river. <French, from Latin *levare* to raise>

🍁 **lev·ee**[2] (lev′ē) *n* a usually formal reception, especially one held during the day: *She received an invitation to the Governor General's levee.* <French *levé* a getting up, from Latin *levare* to raise. Levees were held by French kings as they got dressed in the morning.>

lev·el (lev′əl) *adj* **1** with the same height everywhere; horizontal: *The floor is not quite level.* **2** at the same height: *The table is level with the window sill.* **3** steady, calm, or sensible: *She's got a level head. He answered in a level voice.* **4** equal or balanced in rank, degree, or quality: *These two jobs are level in responsibility, but not in salary.* **5** (*only in compounds*) to do with a particular rank or degree: *High-level talks have begun between the major powers.*
n **1** an instrument for showing whether a surface is horizontal. **2** a measuring of differences in height or altitude between two points by means of such an instrument: *to take a level.* **3** height, degree, rate, or style: *We hung the picture at eye level. The flood waters have risen to a level of three metres. The noise level in the library makes it hard to concentrate. His work is not up to a professional level.*
v **levelled** or **leveled, lev·el·ling** or **lev·el·ing, 1** make level: *They used a bulldozer to level the ground.* **2** (*usually with* ***off***) come to a level position or condition: *The path climbs for about 200 metres and then levels off.* **3** bring to the level of the ground: *The tornado levelled every house in the village.* **4** raise and hold level: *The soldier levelled his rifle.* **5** aim words or intentions: *She levelled a sharp rebuke at the speaker.* **6** *Informal* (*with* ***with***) be honest: *You can level with me; what really happened?* **7** bring to a common level: *Death levels all.* <Old French, from Latin *libella* balance scale> **lev′el·ler** or **lev′el·er** *n.* **lev′el·ly** *adv.* **lev′el·ness** *n.*
find your (or **its**) **level,** arrive at the most appropriate position: *After failing as a painter, he found his level as a successful cartoonist.*
on the level, *Informal* **a** honest and straightforward: *Is that offer on the level?* **b** honestly and straightforwardly: *He always works on the level.*
your level best, *Informal* as well or as much as you can do: *He tried his level best but couldn't persuade them.*

GRAMMAR AND USAGE

Levels of usage are different styles of language that are appropriate for different occasions. Two basic levels are **standard English** and **non-standard**.

Standard usage may be **formal** or **informal**, and other levels may be distinguished within these two.
See also the notes at INFORMAL and STANDARD.

level crossing *n* a place where a railway track crosses a road or another railway track at the same level.

a bat	e bed	i bid	o pot	u cup	th thin
ā cake	ē me	ī bite	ō go	ū rude	ᴛʜ then
ȧ bar	ə about	ər over	ȯ for	u̇ put	zh measure

L

lev·el–head·ed (lev′əl hed′id) *adj* with good common sense or good judgment.

level playing field *n* a situation in which people's advantages and disadvantages are compensated for so that everyone has the same chances of success.

le·ver (lē′vər) *or* (lev′ər) *n* **1** a bar used for moving or prying something: *A crowbar is a lever.* **2** anything used as a tool to influence or force: *He used his family's name as a social lever.* **3** a simple machine consisting of a rigid bar supported and turning on a fixed point called the fulcrum, using force, or effort, at a second point to move or lift a mass situated at a third point: *A wheelbarrow is one kind of a lever.*
v **1** pry, raise, or move with or as if with a lever: *She levered the rock out of the ground.* **2** use a lever or levers: *He levered for weeks and finally got the job.* <Old French, from Latin *levare* to raise>

lev·er·age (lē′və rij) *or* (lev′ə rij) *n* **1 a** the action of a lever. **b** the advantage or power gained by using a lever. **2** increased power of action.
v use borrowed money for an investment, hoping that the profits will be greater than the interest that has to be paid.

leveraged buyout *n* the purchase of a company by its management, using borrowed funds.

le·vi·a·than (lə vī′ə thən) *n* **1** in the Bible, a huge sea animal. **2** a huge ship. **3** a great and powerful person or thing. <Latin, from Hebrew *livyathan* dragon>

lev·i·tate (lev′ə tāt′) *v* **lev·i·tat·ed, lev·i·tat·ing 1** rise or float in the air. **2** cause to rise or float in the air. <Latin *levis* light> **lev′i·ta′tion** *n.*

lev·i·ty (lev′ə tē) *n, pl* **lev·i·ties** lack of seriousness, especially in a humorous or disrespectful way: *The issue is a serious one and should not be treated with levity.* <Latin *levis* light>

lev·y (lev′ē) *v* **lev·ied, lev·y·ing 1** order to be paid: *The government levies taxes to pay its expenses.* **2** draft or enlist for an army: *to levy troops in time of war.* **3** seize by law for unpaid debts: *They levied on his property for unpaid rent.*
n, pl **lev·ies 1** money collected by authority or force. **2** the troops drafted or enlisted for an army. **3** an act of levying. <French, from Latin *lever* raise, in reference to an obsolete sense of raising taxes>

lewd (lūd) *adj* showing or designed to arouse sexual desire, especially in a coarse or offensive way: *a lewd glance, lewd pictures.* <Old English *læwede* ignorant> **lewd′ly** *adv.* **lewd′ness** *n.*

lex·i·cal (lek′sə kəl) *adj* **1** to do with words as separate units, rather than as parts of phrases, sentences, etc. **2** to do with lexicography or a lexicon.

lex·i·cog·ra·phy (lek′sə kog′rə fē) *n* the science or practice of compiling dictionaries. **lex′i·co′graph·er** *n.* **lex′i·co·graph′i·cal** *adj.* **lex′i·co·graph′i·cal·ly** *adv.*

lex·i·con (lek′sə kən) *n* **1** a dictionary, especially of Greek, Latin, or Hebrew. **2** the total vocabulary of a person, language, or branch of knowledge. <Greek *lexis* word, from *legein* speak>

Ley·den jar (lī′dən) *n* in former times, a device for collecting and storing an electric charge, consisting of a glass jar coated inside and outside with layers of metal foil. <*Leyden*, Netherlands, where it was invented>

li·a·bil·i·ty (lī′ə bil′ə tē) *n, pl* **li·a·bil·i·ties 1** the state of being susceptible: *Insufficient rest can increase your liability to disease.* **2** the state of being under obligation: *liability for damage. He refused to acknowledge any liability for his brother's debt.* **3** a person who or thing that acts as a disadvantage: *Her short temper is a liability in dealing with people.* **4** usually, **liabilities** *pl* debts: *The monthly statement shows the company's assets and liabilities.*

li·a·ble (lī′ə bəl) *adj* **1** likely, especially unpleasantly likely: *Glass is liable to break. People are liable to slip on ice.* **2** in danger of having or doing: *We are all liable to diseases.* **3** responsible or bound by law to pay: *Canada Post is not liable for damage to a parcel sent by mail unless it is insured.* **4** under obligation: *Citizens are liable to jury duty.* <Old French, from Latin *ligare* be obliged to>

CONFUSABLES

Liable (definition 1) is best used when referring to something happening to someone or something: *He is liable to be blamed for the accident.*

Likely is the better word when the reference is to somebody doing something: *The police are likely to charge him for causing the accident.*

li·aise (lē āz′) *v* **li·aised, li·ais·ing** act as a liaison or contact person: *One teacher is assigned to the student council to liaise with staff.*

li·ai·son (lē ā′zən) *n* **1** communication in order to co-ordinate activities between parts of a whole, such as parts of a military unit, schools in a system, or departments within a government. **2** a close bond or connection. **3** an illicit love affair. <French, from Latin *ligare* tie together>

li·a·na (lē ä′nə) *n* a climbing vine with a woody stem. Giant lianas wind around the trunks and climb from tree to tree in jungles. <French *liane*>

li·ar (lī′ər) *n* a person who tells lies.

li·ba·tion (lī bā′shən) *n* **1** a pouring out of wine or other liquid as an offering to a god, or the liquid offered in this way. **2** *Humorous* a drink: *Would you care for a libation?* <Latin *libare* pour out>

li·bel (lī′bəl) *n* **1** *Law* a false written statement tending to damage a person's reputation. Compare SLANDER. **2** any false or damaging statement about a person.
v **li·belled** or **li·beled, li·bel·ling** or **li·bel·ing 1** write or publish a libel about. **2** make false or damaging statements about. <Latin *libellus* a written note, from *liber* book> **li′bel·ler** or **li′bel·er** *n.*
li′bel·lous or **li′bel·ous** *adj.*

lib·er·al (lib′ə rəl) *or* (lib′rəl) *adj* **1** generous or plentiful: *a liberal donation. He cut a liberal supply of wood for the winter.* **2** willing to respect or accept different ideas and behaviour: *a liberal thinker.* **3 Liberal** in Canada, to do with the Liberal Party. **4** favouring the principles of LIBERALISM (def. 1). **5** giving the general thought, not a word-for-word rendering: *a liberal interpretation of the speaker's ideas.*

n **1** a person who favours liberal principles. **2 Liberal** in Canada, a supporter of the Liberal Party. <Old French, from Latin *liber* free> **lib′er·al·ly** *adv.* **lib′er·al·ness** *n.*

liberal arts *pl n* subjects such as literature, languages, history, and philosophy as distinct from technical or professional subjects.

liberal education *n* an education in the liberal arts, especially as distinct from a technical or professional education.

lib·er·al·ism (lib′ə rə liz′əm) *or* (lib′rə liz′əm) *n* **1** a political philosophy that emphasizes belief in progress, individual freedom, and a democratic form of government. **2** the quality or state of being liberal. **lib′er·al·ist** *n.*

lib·er·al·i·ty (lib′ə ral′ə tē) *n, pl* **lib·er·al·i·ties 1** generosity: *We were allowed to use the pool because of the liberality of the club members.* **2** broad-mindedness.

lib·er·al·ize (lib′ə rə līz′) *or* (lib′rə līz′) *v* **lib·er·al·ized, lib·er·al·iz·ing** make or become liberal. **lib′er·al·i·za′tion** *n.*

Liberal Party *n* one of the registered political parties of Canada.

lib·er·ate (lib′ə rāt′) *v* **lib·er·at·ed, lib·er·at·ing 1** set free: *to liberate a country, to liberate a slave.* **2** release from rigid social conventions: *to liberate women and give them equal status with men.* **3** *Chemistry, Physics* release as a result of a chemical reaction or physical decomposition: *to liberate a gas.* <Latin *liber* free> **lib′er·a′tion** (lib′ə rā′shən) *n.* **lib′er·a′tor** *n.*

Li·be·ri·a (lī bē′rē ə) *n* a country in West Africa. **Li·be′ri·an** *adj, n.*

lib·er·tar·i·an (lib′ər tā′ri ən) *n* **1** a person who believes in full civil liberty in thought and action, unrestricted by rules. **2 Libertarian** a supporter of a political party advocating maximum individual freedom and minimum governmental control. **3** a person who believes in the freedom of the human will. See also DETERMINISM.
adj **1** to do with libertarians or their beliefs. **2 Libertarian** to do with Libertarians or their party.

Libertarian Party *n* one of the registered political parties of Canada.

lib·er·tine (lib′ər tēn′) *n* a person who lives without regard to convention or accepted moral standards.
adj to do with a libertine. <Latin *liber* free>

lib·er·ty (lib′ər tē) *n, pl* **lib·er·ties 1** freedom or independence: *The prisoner yearned for liberty. The colony finally won its liberty.* **2** the right or power to do as one pleases: *liberty of speech and action.* **3** the leave granted to a sailor to go ashore. **4** the right of being in, using, etc.: *We give our dog the liberty of the yard.* <Old French, from Latin *liber* free>
at liberty, a free: *The escaped lion is still at liberty.* **b** allowed or permitted: *You are at liberty to make any choice you please.* **c** not busy: *The principal will see you as soon as she is at liberty.*
take liberties, a be too familiar: *to take liberties with a person.* **b** treat too freely: *The author took liberties with the facts to make the story more interesting.*

li·bi·do (lə bē′dō) *n* **1** sexual desire or instinct. **2** emotional or mental drive or energy. <Latin = desire>

Li·bra (lē′brə) *n* **1** *Astronomy* a southern constellation shaped somewhat like a pair of scales. **2** *Astrology* **a** the seventh sign of the zodiac. The sun enters Libra about September 23. **b** a person born under this sign.

li·brar·i·an (lī brer′ē ən) *n* **1** a person trained in library science, especially one who makes it his or her work. **2** a person in charge of a library.

li·brar·y (lī′brer′ē) *n, pl* **li·brar·ies 1** a room or building where a collection of books, periodicals, or audio-visual materials is kept to be used, rented, or borrowed, but not sold: *Our town has a very good public library.* **2** a collection of books, periodicals, or other materials, especially a large collection that is systematically arranged: *They have an extensive library of rare books.* <Old French, from Latin *liber* book>

library science *n* the principles and practice of library organization and management.

li·bret·to (lə bret′ō) *n, pl* **li·bret·tos** the text of an opera or other long vocal work, written by a **librettist**. <Italian, from Latin *liber* book>

Lib·ya (lib′ē ə) *n* a country in northern Africa. See the APPENDIX. **Lib′yan** *adj, n.*

lice (līs) plural of LOUSE.

li·cence or **li·cense** (lī′səns) *n* **1 a** permission given by law or other authority to do something. **b** the document, card, etc. showing such permission: *The dentist hung her licence on the wall.* **2** freedom of action, speech, or thought that is permitted or conceded: *Poetic licence is the freedom from rules that is permitted in poetry and art.* **3** disregard of what is proper: *The dogs were given licence to invade the neighbours' gardens.* <Old French, from Latin *licere* be allowed>

CONFUSABLES

In Canada, **licence** is the spelling we use for the noun, while **license** is our spelling for the verb.

He found his driver's licence in his coat pocket.
She is now licensed as a doctor.

licence plate *n* a metal plate attached to a motor vehicle, bearing the **licence number** of a vehicle and an indication that the registration fee has been paid.

li·cense or **li·cence** (lī′səns) *v* **li·censed** or **li·cenced, li·cens·ing** or **li·cenc·ing 1** give a LICENCE (def. 1) to: *to license a new driver.* **2** permit or authorize, especially by law: *A doctor is licensed to practise medicine.* **li′cen·ser** *n.*

li·censed or **li·cenced** (lī′sənst) *adj* **1** holding a government LICENCE (def. 1) to sell alcoholic liquors for drinking on the premises: *a licensed restaurant.* **2** holding another kind of licence: *I am a licensed driver. He is a licensed mechanic.*

a bat	e bed	i bid	o pot	u cup	th **thin**
ā cake	ē me	ī bite	ō go	ū rude	TH **then**
ä bar	ə about	ər over	ô for	ů put	zh measure

L

li·cen·see (lī′sən sē′) *n* a person to whom a LICENCE (def. 1) is given.

li·cen·tious (lī sen′shəs) *adj* disregarding commonly accepted moral principles, especially in sexual behaviour. **li·cen′tious·ly** *adv.* **li·cen′tious·ness** *n.*

li·chee (lī′chē) *or* (lē′chē) LYCHEE.

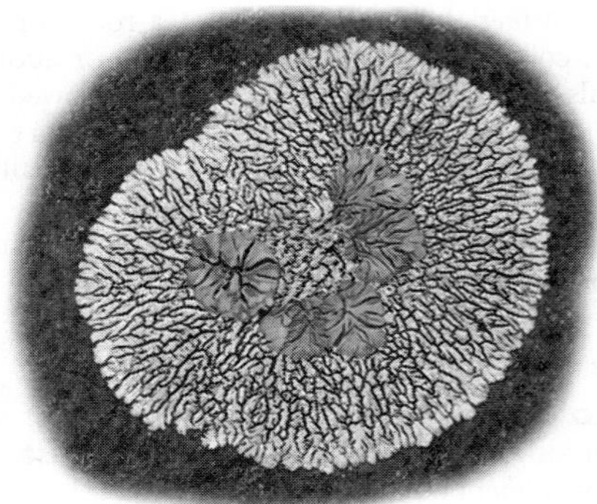

A crustose **lichen** is flat and crusty like a flaky pie shell. This kind of lichen grows on rocks, tree bark, and even soil, and can be very colourful.

li·chen (lī′kən) *n* a flowerless, slow-growing plant that forms a branching growth on rocks, trees, and walls. A lichen consists of a fungus and an alga growing together so that they look like one plant. <Latin, from Greek *leichen* what eats around itself, from *leichein* to lick>

lic·it (lis′it) *adj* permitted by law or regulations. <Latin *licere* be allowed>

lick (lik) *v* **1** pass the tongue over; make or bring by using the tongue: *to lick a stamp. The cat licked the plate clean.* **2** move lightly over or around like a tongue: *The flames were licking the roof.* **3** *Informal* overcome or defeat: *So far we've licked every problem without help. I could lick him with one hand tied behind my back.*
n **1** a stroke of the tongue over something: *She gave the ice-cream cone a big lick.* **2** a place where salt is found and where animals go to lick it up. **3** *Informal* a blow: *I lost the fight, but I got in a few good licks.* **4** *Informal* a small quantity: *She didn't do a lick of work.* **5** *Slang* speed: *She ran down the road at a great lick.* **6** a short musical phrase, played solo: *He showed me several good guitar licks.* **7 licks** *pl Informal* opportunity or chance: *I'm sure you'll get your licks in later.* <Old English *liccian*>
lick into shape, *Informal* make presentable or usable.

lick·e·ty–split (lik′ə tē split′) *Informal adv* at a great speed: *She was off down the sidewalk lickety-split before they could stop her.* <probably *lick* (def. 5)>

lick·ing (lik′ing) *Informal n* **1** a thrashing or spanking. **2** a defeat or setback.

lic·o·rice (lik′ə rish), (lik′rish), *or* (lik′ə ris) *n* **1** a sweet, black, gummy extract obtained from the roots of a European plant, used as a flavouring. **2** candy flavoured with this extract. **3** the plant that yields licorice. Also, **liquorice**. <Old French *lycorys*, from Greek *glykus* sweet + *rhiza* root>

lid (lid) *n* **1** a movable cover or top: *the lid of a box.* **2** the cover of skin that is moved in opening and shutting the eye. <Old English *hlid*>
blow the lid off, *Slang* reveal publicly: *The report blew the lid off government waste of public funds.*
keep a lid on it, *Slang* be quiet.
keep a lid on something, *Informal* keep something secret.

lid·less (lid′lis) *adj* **1** with no lid. **2** with no eyelids.

lie[1] (lī) *n* a false statement, known to be false by the person who makes it: *The child told a lie to avoid punishment.*
v **lied, ly·ing** **1** tell a lie or lies. **2** get, bring, or put by lying: *to lie oneself out of a difficulty.* <Old English *lyge*>
give the lie to, a accuse of lying. **b** show to be false.

lie[2] (lī) *v* **lay, lain, ly·ing** **1** have or put one's body in a flat position along the ground or other surface: *to lie on the grass, to lie down on a couch.* **2** be in a horizontal or flat position: *The book was lying on the table.* **3** be kept or stay in a given position or condition: *The machinery lay idle while the workers were on strike.* **4** be or be placed: *Most of the US lies to the south of Canada.* **5** exist, have its place, or belong: *The cure lies in education.* **6** be in the grave: *His body lies in his hometown, Halifax.* <Old English *licgan*>
lie about (or **around**), **a** be lazy: *We just lay about the house all day yesterday.* **b** be left: *Please don't leave your clothes lying around.*
lie behind, be the reason for.
lie down on the job, neglect your duties.
lie in, a in former times, be confined in childbirth. **b** stay in bed later than usual.
lie off, of a ship, be not far from shore or another ship.
lie over, be left waiting until a later time.

CONFUSABLES

Lie and **lay** both mean *rest flat on a surface.* Their forms are *lie, lay, lain*; and *lay, laid, laid.*

Lie does not take an object:
I'm going to lie down to rest.
How long has that cat lain in the sun?

Lay always has an object:
Lay your coat down and stay for a while.
She laid careful plans for the party.

Liech·ten·stein (lik′tən stīn) *n* a small country in central Europe.

liege (lēj) *n* in the Middle Ages, **1** a lord with a right to the homage and loyal service of his vassals. Also called **liege lord**. **2** a vassal obliged to give homage and loyal service to his lord. Also called **liegeman**. <Old French, from Latin *laetus* serf> **liege** *adj.*

lien (lēn) *Law n* a claim placed on the property of another as a safeguard for payment of a debt in connection with that property. <French, from Latin *ligare* to bind>

lie of the land LAY OF THE LAND.

lieu (lū) *adj* 🍁 to do with time off in exchange for overtime: *lieu day.* <French, from Latin *locum* place>
in lieu of, instead of: *During hard times, they gave the landlord produce in lieu of money for rent.*

lieu·ten·an·cy (lef ten′ən sē) *or* (lū ten′ən sē) *n, pl* **lieu·ten·an·cies** the rank, commission, or authority of a LIEUTENANT (def. 2).

lieu·ten·ant (lef ten′ənt) *or* (lū ten′ənt) *n* **1** a person who acts for someone senior to him or her in authority: *The coach used the two boys as his lieutenants.* **2** a junior commissioned officer in the armed forces. <Old French, from Latin *locus* place + *tenere* to hold. A lieutenant held the place of a captain who was absent.>

✱ **Lieu·ten·ant–Gov·er·nor** (lef ten′ənt guv′ər nər) *or* (lū ten′ənt guv′ər nər) *n* the appointed representative of the Crown in a province.

life (līf) *n, pl* **lives** (līvz) **1** the condition of living or being alive in an animal or plant, including the capacity for growth, reproduction, functional activity, and continual change up until the point of death. **2** the time of being alive: *She enjoyed a long life.* **3** the period of existence or action: *The life of that government was very short. This computer's life is about five years.* **4** a person: *Five lives were saved by the firefighters' bravery.* **5** living things considered together: *The desert island had almost no animal or vegetable life.* **6** a way of living: *a dull life.* **7** an account of a person's life: *a life of Pierre Elliot Trudeau.* **8** vigour or vitality: *Put more life into your work.* <Old English *līf*>

as large (or **as big**) **as life,** in person.

for dear life, to save or as if to save your life: *He ran for dear life.*

for life, for the rest of your life.

for the life of me, *Informal* (*used only in negative expressions*) even if my life depended on it: *I couldn't for the life of me remember where I put the key.*

from life, using a living model: *The drawing was made from life.*

get a life, *Slang* find something more worthwhile to do with your time.

not on your life, *Informal* under no circumstances.

see life, get experience, especially of the exciting features of human activities.

take life, kill.

take your own life, kill yourself.

to save your life, *Informal* even if your life depended on it: *He can't carry a tune to save his life.*

to the life, exactly like the model.

true to life, as in actual life: *Good novels are true to life.*

life and limb *n* physical safety and survival: *The old bridge is a danger to life and limb.*

life·blood (līf′blud′) *n* **1** blood necessary to life. **2** a source of strength and energy: *The young people became the lifeblood of the organization.*

life·boat (līf′bōt′) *n* **1** a strong boat specially built for saving lives at sea or along a coast. **2** a boat carried on a ship for use by the passengers in an emergency.

life·buoy (līf′boi′) *n* a life preserver in the form of a thick hoop.

life cycle *n* **1** the various stages through which an organism goes in the course of its life, from fertilization to reproduction to death: *the life cycle of the frog.* **2** the stages of development and eventual fading or failure of an organization, industry, trend, or product: *the life cycle of steamboats.*

life expectancy *n* the number of years one can reasonably expect to live, based on average statistics: *The life expectancy of women is greater than that of men.* Compare LIFESPAN.

life·guard (līf′gärd′) *n* a person who is responsible for the safety of swimmers and bathers at a public pool or beach.

life insurance *n* insurance that provides for the payment of a specified amount of money to a person or to persons on the death of the insured, or to the insured on reaching a certain age.

life jacket *n* a life preserver in the form of a vest.

life·less (līf′lis) *adj* **1** without life: *Statues are lifeless.* **2** dead: *lifeless bodies on the battlefield.* **3** with no living things: *a lifeless planet.* **4** dull: *a lifeless performance.* **life′less·ly** *adv.* **life′less·ness** *n.*

life·like (līf′līk′) *adj* looking as if alive: *a lifelike portrait.* **life′like′ness** *n.*

life·line (līf′līn′) **1** a rope for saving life, such as one thrown to a ship from shore. **2** a line used to raise or lower a deep-sea diver. **3** whatever helps to maintain something that cannot survive by itself: *Food parcels were a lifeline to the flooded town.* **4** an emergency telephone response service.

life·long (līf′long′) *adj* lasting all one's life: *a lifelong friendship.*

life of Ri·ley (rī′lē) *Informal n* an easy, luxurious life. <origin unknown>

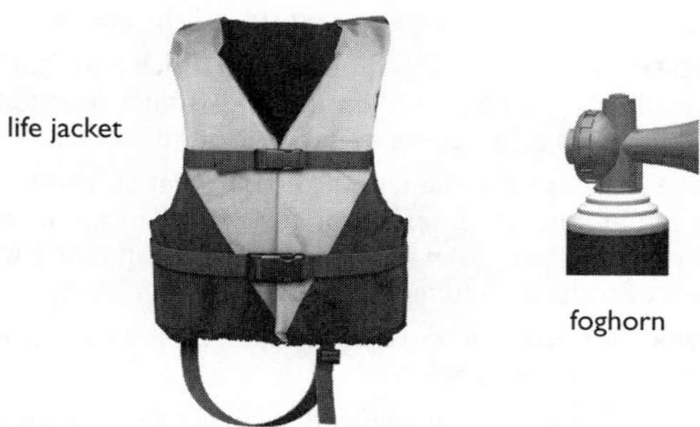

Failure to wear a **life preserver** is the most common contributor to boating fatalities. Foghorns and other signalling devices are also helpful in a boating emergency.

life preserver *n* a device made of buoyant or inflatable material, designed to keep a person afloat in water to prevent drowning. It may be in the form of a vest, a wide belt, or a thick hoop.

lif·er (līf′er) *Informal n* **1** a person serving a prison sentence for life. **2** someone with a lifelong contract or commitment, such as to a military career.

life raft *n* a raft for saving lives in a shipwreck or the wreck of an aircraft at sea.

a bat	e bed	i bid	o pot	u cup	th **thin**
ā cake	ē me	ī bite	ō go	ū rude	ᴛʜ **then**
ä bar	ə about	ər over	ô for	ů put	zh measure

L

life·sav·er (līf′sā′vər) *n* **1** a person who or thing that saves people from drowning, especially a lifeguard. **2** *Informal* a person who or thing that saves one from trouble, discomfort, or embarrassment: *The interruption was a lifesaver, because I didn't know what to say next.*

life·sav·ing (līf′sā′ving) *n* the skill, act, or practice of saving people's lives, especially by preventing drowning.
adj to do with saving people's lives: *lifesaving classes, lifesaving equipment.*

life science *n* the study of living organisms. Biology is a life science. Compare SOCIAL SCIENCE, PHYSICAL SCIENCE.

life–size (līf′sīz′) *adj* with the same size as the living person or animal: *a life-size statue.*

life·span (līf′span′) *n* the length of time that a person, animal or plant, machine, or institution exists or functions, or can be expected to exist or function: *Human lifespan is increasing. Proper care will extend the lifespan of these leather hiking boots.* Compare LIFE EXPECTANCY.

life·style (līf′stīl′) *n* the typical habits, pastimes, consumer preferences, and attitudes of a person or group: *a casual lifestyle. Their downtown apartment suits their lifestyle.*

life–sup·port (līf′sə port′) *n* equipment to which a patient is connected, designed to carry on the body's vital functions while the person is in a coma or has a serious disability.

life·time (līf′tīm′) *n* **1** the length of time that someone is alive or that something exists or functions: *In his whole lifetime he had never been in an airplane.* **2** lasting for such a length of time: *a lifetime commitment.*

life·work (līf′wərk′) *n* work that takes or lasts a whole lifetime. Also, **life's work**.

lift (lift) *v* **1** move or be moved into a higher position, or a different position: *to lift a chair. This window will not lift. Lift the box down from the shelf.* **2** move upward and away; disappear: *The fog lifted at dawn. The rain lifted by evening.* **3** raise morale or confidence: *The sun lifted our spirits. Her heart lifted.* **4** formally remove a ban or restriction: *The sanctions were lifted two years after the war ended.* **5** transport by air: *The helicopter lifted the injured climber to hospital.* **6 a** remove root crops such as potatoes from the ground. **b** remove plants or bulbs from the ground for transplanting. **7** send up loudly: *Lift your voice and shout.* **8** *Informal* steal or use without acknowledgment: *to lift things from a store. He lifted the idea from his sister.*
n **1** something that is used for lifting: *Why is it called a ski lift when it lifts skiers?* **2** the act of lifting, or the distance through which a thing is lifted: *The skaters performed a difficult lift.* **3** an act of help in lifting: *I gave him a lift with the heavy box.* **4** a free ride by someone in a vehicle: *She often gave the neighbour's boy a lift to school.* **5** an improvement in morale or confidence: *Winning a tough game always gives a team a lift.* **6** the component of the aerodynamic forces acting upward on a wing, etc. See AIRPLANE for picture. **7** perform cosmetic surgery in order to remove wrinkles or sagging skin. See also FACELIFT. **8** *especially UK* an elevator. <Old Norse *lypta* to raise>
lift′er *n.*
lift off, rise from the ground: *The space shuttle will lift off in two hours.*

lift lock *n* a canal or river lock in which each water-filled compartment itself is raised and lowered while the water level within the compartment remains the same.

lift·off (lif′tof′) *n* the vertical takeoff of an aircraft, rocket, or spaceship.

lig·a·ment (lig′ə mənt) *n* **1** in anatomy, a band of strong tissue that connects bones or holds organs in place. **2** a tie or bond. <Latin *ligare* tie up>

lig·a·ture (lig′ə chər) *or* (lig′ə chůr′) *n* **1** something used to tie up, especially a thread used to tie up a bleeding artery. **2** something that unites or connects. **3** *Music* a slur or a group of notes connected by a slur. **4** *Printing* two or three letters joined, as the *æ* in some old spellings like *encyclopædia.* <Latin *ligare* tie up>

light[1] (līt) *n* **1** the form of radiant energy that acts on the retina of the eye and permits vision: *The sun gives light to the earth, a dim light.* **2** something that gives light, such as the sun, a lamp, or a lighthouse. **3** daytime or dawn: *The worker got up before light.* **4** something with which to set wood, tobacco, etc. on fire. **5** knowledge or information: *We need some light on this subject.* **6** the way in which something is looked at: *He put the matter in the proper light.* **7** a model or example: *That actor was a leading light in the theatre.* **8** *Informal* a traffic light.
adj **1** with light or much light: *a light room.* **2** bright or clear: *It is as light as day.* **3** pale in colour: *light hair, light blue.*
v **light·ed** or **lit, light·ing** **1** cause to give light or give light to: *She lit the lamp. The room is lighted by six windows.* **2** (*often with* ***up***) make bright or become bright: *Her face was lit by a smile. The sky lights up at sunset.* **3** show the way by giving light: *Her flashlight lighted us through the tunnel.* **4** set fire to: *She lit the fire.* <Old English *leoht*>
according to your lights, following your own ideas in the best way that you know.
bring to light, reveal or expose: *Many facts were brought to light during the investigation.*
come to light, be revealed or exposed.
in (**the**) **light of,** by considering.
see the light (**of day**), **a** come into existence. **b** be made public. **c** get the correct idea.
shed (or **throw**) **light on,** explain or make clear.

light[2] (līt) *adj* **1** easy to carry: *a light load.* **2** less than usual or average in mass, amount, force, strength, etc.: *light clothes, a light meal, a light rain, a light sleep, a light metal, a light wine.* **3** easy to do or bear: *a light task.* **4** cheerfully careless: *a light laugh.* **5** not serious or important: *a light mind, light reading.*
adv **1** lightly. **2** with as little luggage as possible: *I like to travel light.* <Old English *liht*>
light in the head, a dizzy. **b** silly or foolish.
light on your feet, moving easily and gracefully: *For such a big man, he's very light on his feet.*
make light of, treat as of little importance.

SYNONYMS

Light suggests something that is of little mass for its size: *The snow was surprisingly light to shovel.*

Weightless suggests something that appears to have no weight at all: *The feather felt weightless in my hand.*

light[3] (līt) *v* **light·ed** or **lit, light·ing 1** land on the ground or something solid: *He lighted from his horse. The bird lighted on a branch.* **2** happen on by chance: *Her eye lit on the missing contact lens.* <Old English *lihtan* to lighten a load>
light into, *Informal* scold or attack verbally: *She lit into me with such force that I could only stand there staring at her.*
light out, *Informal* leave suddenly and swiftly: *He hated parties, and would always light out for home.*

light bulb *n* a glass bulb containing a filament of very fine wire that becomes white hot and gives off light when an electric current flows through it.

light–e·mit·ting di·ode (līt′ē mit′ing dī′ōd) LED.

light·en[1] (lī′tən) *v* **1** make or become bright or brighter: *Dawn lightens the sky. The sky gradually lightened.* **2** make or become pale or paler in colour: *The summer sun lightened my hair.* **3** flash with lightning: *I just saw it lighten in the west.*

light·en[2] (lī′tən) *v* **1** reduce the load of something, such as a ship. **2** make or become less of a burden: *to lighten taxes.* **3** make or become more cheerful: *The good news lightened their hearts. His face lightened when he saw her.*
lighten up, *Informal* take things less seriously: *She's a good teacher, but I wish she'd lighten up.*

light·er (lī′tər) *n* a device used to light such things as pipes, candles, or fires.

light–fin·gered (līt′fing′gərd) *adj* prone to steal.

light–foot·ed (līt′fu̇t′id) *adj* stepping lightly.

light–head·ed (līt′hed′id) *adj* **1** dizzy or giddy: *The fever was gone, but she still felt a little light-headed.* **2** silly or frivolous: *My friend is much too light-headed to take on a responsible job.*

light–heart·ed (līt′hȧr′tid) *adj* carefree or cheerful. **light′-heart′ed·ly** *adv.* **light′-heart′ed·ness** *n.*

light heavyweight *n* a boxer who weighs between 76 and 81 kilograms.

light·house (līt′hous′) *n* a tower with a bright light that shines far over the water. Lighthouses are usually located at dangerous places to warn and guide ships.

light industry *n* the manufacture of small articles, usually consumer goods. Compare HEAVY INDUSTRY.

light·ing (lī′ting) *n* **1** the giving or providing of light. **2** the way in which lights are arranged. **3** light, and lighting equipment.

light·ly (lī′tlē) *adv* **1** with little pressure or force: *Her hand rested lightly on his arm. He held the bird lightly in his hand.* **2** to a small degree or extent: *lightly clad.* **3** quickly or easily: *She jumped lightly aside.* **4** cheerfully: *to take bad news lightly.* **5** indifferently or carelessly: *The issue is too important to be passed over lightly.*

light meter *n* a device for measuring the intensity of light, especially an exposure meter. It is commonly part of a camera, and works automatically.

light–mind·ed (līt′mīn′did) *adj* thoughtless and frivolous. **light′-mind′ed·ly** *adv.* **light′-mind′ed·ness** *n.*

light·ness[1] (līt′nis) *n* **1** the quality or state of being bright or clear: *The lightness of the sky showed that the rain was over.* **2** the quality or state of being light in colour or pale: *He has to be extremely careful in the sun because of the lightness of his skin.*

light·ness[2] (līt′nis) *n* **1** the quality or state of having little mass, force, strength, etc.: *The lightness of the second load was a relief after the first one he had carried, the lightness of a gentle touch.* **2** lack of severity: *The lightness of the sentence surprised the defendant.* **3** cheerfulness or gaiety: *lightness of spirits.* **4** lack of proper seriousness: *Such lightness of conduct is not permitted in a courtroom.*

light·ning (līt′ning) *n* a flash of light in the sky caused by a discharge of electricity between clouds, or between a cloud and the earth's surface.
adj very fast or sudden: *a lightning decision, a lightning change of mood.*

lightning bug a firefly.

lightning rod *n* a metal rod fixed on a building or ship to conduct lightning into the earth or water to prevent fire.

light pen *Computers n* an electronic device to allow a user to control data on a computer terminal by pointing to it.

light·proof (līt′prüf′) *adj* sealed so that no light can enter: *A camera must be lightproof.*

light rapid transit LRT.

light·weight (lī′twāt′) *n* **1** a person or thing of less than average mass. **2** a boxer who weighs between 59 and 61 kilograms. **3** a person of little importance or influence: *She is regarded as a lightweight in the literary world.*
adj **1** with less than the average or usual mass: *a lightweight portable sewing machine.* **2** to do with lightweights: *the lightweight boxing championship, a lightweight intellect.*

light–year (lī′tyēr′) *Astronomy n* a unit of distance equal to the distance that light travels in one year in a vacuum, about 9 460 500 000 000 km: *The nearest star is more than four light-years away.*

a bat	e bed	i bid	o pot	u cup	th thin
ā cake	ē me	ī bite	ō go	ü rude	ᴛʜ then
ȧ bar	ə about	ər over	ȯ for	u̇ put	zh measure

L

lig·ne·ous (lig′nē əs) *adj* to do with wood.

lig·nin (lig′nin) *Botany n* an organic substance that, together with cellulose, makes up the woody tissue of plants. <Latin *lignum* wood>

lig·nite (lig′nīt) *n* a very soft, brownish coal, often with a woody texture.

lig·num vi·tae (lig′nəm vī′tē) *or* (vē′tī) *n* a tropical evergreen tree whose wood is very resinous, and so dense that it will not float in water. <Latin = wood of life. Originally, the resin obtained from this wood was thought to have medicinal value.>

lik·a·ble (lī′kə bəl) LIKEABLE.

like[1] (līk) *prep* **1** similar to: *I'm like my sister. I never saw anything like it.* **2** in the same way as: *She can run like a deer. He acted like a tyrant.* **3** typical of: *Isn't that just like him?* **4** in the proper frame of mind for doing or having something: *She felt like working. I feel like a cup of coffee.* **5** giving promise of: *It looks like rain.* **6** such as: *They offer technical courses like mechanics and plumbing.*
adj of the same or nearly the same form, kind, appearance, or amount: *Her uncle promised her $50 if she could save a like sum.*
conj Informal **1** as: *He reacted just like I did.* **2** as if: *It looks like we'll have to do it ourselves.*
n a person or thing like another: *We will not see her like again. They had never seen the like before.*
adv Informal probably: *Like enough it will rain.* <Old Norse *likr*>
and the like, and similar things: *She studied music, painting, and the like.*
I'm (or **he's** or **she's**) **like,** *Slang* I (or he, or she) said: *So I'm like, "When?" and she's like, "Right now!"*
like crazy (**mad**, etc.)**,** *Informal* with great speed, effort, or intensity: *She works like crazy.*
nothing like, not nearly: *It's nothing like as cold as it was yesterday.*
something like, about or almost like: *The tune goes something like this.*
the likes (or **like**) **of,** *Informal* someone or something like: *These thousand-dollar bikes are not for the likes of you and me.*

GRAMMAR AND USAGE

Like is often used informally instead of **as** in comparisons: *He tells it like it is.*
In more formal language, use **as** when a clause follows: *She looks as her mother did at that age.*

Use **like** if just a noun follows, with or without adjectives: *He acts like a baby.*

like[2] (līk) *v* **liked, lik·ing 1** enjoy, or be pleased or satisfied with: *Do you like milk? She likes the job but not the salary.* **2** have a friendly feeling toward: *They like their new math teacher.* **3** (*with* **would**) wish for: *I would like a glass of milk, please. I'd like to get my hands on the person who took my bike.* **4** choose: *Call whenever you like.*
n **likes** *pl* preferences: *My mother knows most of my likes and dislikes.* <Old English *lician* be pleasing>

–like *combining form* **1** like: *wolflike.* **2** characteristic of: *childlike.* **3** suited to: *businesslike.*

like·a·ble (lī′kə bəl) *adj* easy to like: *a likeable person.* Also, **likable. like′a·bil′i·ty** *n.* **like′a·ble·ness** *n.*
like′a·bly *adv.*

like·li·hood (lī′klē hůd′) *n* probability: *Is there any likelihood of rain this afternoon?*

like·ly (lī′klē) *adj* **like·li·er, like·li·est 1** probable: *One likely result of the heavy rains is a flood.* **2** to be expected: *It is likely to be hot in August.* **3** suitable: *Is there a likely place to fish?* **4** promising: *a likely boy.*
adv probably: *I'll likely be home today.* <Old Norse *likligr*>

CONFUSABLES

Likely is used when someone is doing something:
The criminal is likely to escape.

Liable (definition 1) is best used when something is happening to someone:
He is liable to be caught.

like–mind·ed (līk′mīnd′əd) *adj* sharing the same tastes and ideas. **like′-mind′ed·ness** *n.*

lik·en (lī′kən) *v* represent or describe as like something: *The poet likens life to a dream.*

like·ness (līk′nis) *n* **1** a resemblance: *There is a strong likeness between the girl and her mother.* **2** a copy or representation, especially a painting, drawing, or photograph: *The portrait is a good likeness of her.* **3** the appearance or shape: *I wrote a story in which a wizard assumed the likeness of a very old man.*

like·wise (lī′kwīz′) *adv* **1** in the same way: *Watch what I do, and do likewise.* **2** also: *He was a painter, a sculptor, and likewise a writer.*

lik·ing (lī′king) *n* **1** a preference or taste: *She had a great liking for apples. The entertainment was not to his liking.* **2** a fondness or kindly feeling: *She had a liking for children.*

li·lac (lī′lək) *or* (lī′lok) *n* a shrub with clusters of tiny, fragrant flowers.
adj pale purple. <French, from Persian *lilak*>

Lil·li·pu·tian (lil′ə pyū′shən) *adj* very small.
n a very small person or thing. <after *Lilliput*, an imaginary country in J. Swift's 18c novel *Gulliver's Travels*, whose inhabitants were tiny>

lilt (lilt) *v* sing or play a tune in a light, tripping manner.
n **1** a lively song or tune. **2** a way of speaking in which the pitch of the voice varies in a pleasing manner: *She talks with an Irish lilt.* **3** a lively, springy movement. <Middle English *lulte*>

lil·y (lil′ē) *n, pl* **lil·ies, 1** a plant that grows from bulbs, with a tall, slender stem and large, usually trumpet-shaped flowers. The **prairie lily** (sometimes called the **western red lily**) is the floral emblem of Saskatchewan. The **white lily** is the floral emblem of Québec. **2** a plant of a different family with similar flowers, such as the **calla lily** and **water lily**. **3** a family of plants that includes the trilliums, hyacinths, and tulips. <Latin *lilium*>
lil′y·like′ *adj.*
gild the lily, try to improve on something that is already excellent or satisfactory.

lil·y–liv·ered (lil′ē liv′ərd) *adj* cowardly.

lily of the valley *n, pl* **lilies of the valley** a low-growing perennial plant of the lily family with small, bell-shaped, fragrant flowers.

lily pad *n* one of the large, round, floating leaves of a water lily.

lily–white (li′lē wīt′) *adj* **1** pure white. **2** (*often ironic*) uncorrupted or blameless: *a lily-white politician.*

lima bean (lī′mə) *n* a bean with broad, flat seeds that are eaten as a vegetable. <*Lima*, Peru, where it was first introduced>

limb (lim) *n* **1** a leg, arm, or wing. **2** a large branch of a tree: *They sawed off the dead limb.* **3** the part that projects: *the four limbs of a cross.* **4** a person or thing thought of as a part, branch, or representative: *A police officer is a limb of the law.* <Old English *lim*> **limb′less** *adj.* **limb′less·ness** *n.*
out on a limb, in or into a dangerous or exposed position: *The producer of the play was left out on a limb when his backers suddenly withdrew their support.*
tear (rip) limb from limb, tear a body violently apart.

lim·ber[1] (lim′bər) *adj* flexible and supple: *A pianist has to have limber fingers.*
v (*with* ***up***) make or become supple or more easily flexed: *We did some exercises to limber up before the game.* <Middle English> **lim′ber·ness** *n.*

lim·bic system (lim′bik) *n* a part of the brain below the cortex, thought to be responsible for basic emotions and drives. <French, from Latin *limbus* edge>

lim·bo[1] (lim′bō) *n* **1** a condition or place of disregard: *The belief that the earth is flat belongs to the limbo of outworn ideas.* **2** an indefinite condition or place: *He was left in limbo for some time before he was told he definitely had the job.* **3** in some Christian beliefs, the home of unbaptized souls and of good people who died before Christ's arrival. <Latin *in limbo* on the edge>

lim·bo[2] (lim′bō) *n* a Caribbean dance in which dancers bend over backwards from the knees and pass under a low bar with only the feet touching the ground. The bar is brought lower for each pass a dancer makes. <*limber*>

Lim·burg·er (lim′bər gər) *n* a soft white cheese with a strong smell.

lime[1] (līm) *n* calcium oxide, a white substance obtained by burning limestone, shells, or bones. Lime is used to make mortar and to improve soil.
v **limed, lim·ing** put lime on: *He drained the land and limed it.* <Old English *lim*>

lime[2] (līm) *n* a green citrus fruit that resembles a lemon, but is smaller and sweeter.
adj yellowish green. <French, from Arabic *lima*>

lime[3] (līm) *n* the linden, especially the European linden.

lime·ade (lī′mād′) *n* a drink made of lime juice, sugar, and water.

lime·light (līm′līt′) *n* **1** an intense white light produced by heating LIME[1], formerly used as a stage spotlight in theatres. **2** the centre of public attention and interest: *Some actors try to avoid the limelight.*

lim·er·ick (lim′ə rik′) *n* a humorous poem consisting of five lines, with the first two lines rhyming with the last, and the third and fourth rhyming with each other. Example: *There were two young people called Bright/ Whose speed was much faster than light/ They set out one day/ In a relative way/ And returned on the previous night.* <apparently from a song about the city of *Limerick*, Irish Republic>

lime·stone (līm′stōn′) *n* rock formed mainly from organic remains, such as shells or coral, and consisting mostly of calcium carbonate, used for building and for making lime.

lim·it (lim′it) *n* **1** the furthest point or edge: *the limit of your vision. I have reached the limit of my patience.* **2** the largest amount or quantity allowed or accepted: *One helping of dessert is my limit. Yesterday they caught their limit of fish.* **3 limits** *pl* boundary: *Keep within the limits of the school grounds.*
v set a limit to: *We must limit our spending to $60.* <Old French, from Latin *limitis* boundary> **lim′it·a·ble** *adj.* **lim′it·er** *n.* **lim′it·less** *adj.*
off limits, outside an area where you are permitted to be.

lim·i·ta·tion (lim′ə tā′shən) *n* **1** limiting or being limited. **2** something that limits: *The new government imposed limitations on the freedom of the press.* **3** *Law* a period of time after which a claim or suit cannot be brought in court. A **statute of limitations** fixes such a period of time.

lim·it·ed (lim′ə tid) *adj* **1** kept within limits: *a limited edition, a limited number of seats. He's having only limited success in raising funds for the class trip.* **2** of a business organization, restricted to the amount of debt that a individual member is liable for. **3** travelling rapidly and making only a few stops: *a limited bus.*

limited edition *n* a special edition of a book, print, or other object limited to a certain number of copies.

limited monarchy CONSTITUTIONAL MONARCHY.

lim·o (lim′ō) *Informal n, pl* **lim·os** a limousine.

lim·ou·sine (lim′ə zēn′) *or* (lim′ə zēn′) *n* **1** a large, luxurious automobile, especially one driven by a chauffeur: *A limousine sometimes has a glass partition separating the passenger compartment from the driver's seat.* **2** a large automobile or small bus used to carry passengers to and from an airport.

ETYMOLOGY

Limousine comes from French *limousine*, from *Limousin*, an adjective referring to the city of Limoges in central France. The word was applied to an early automobile in which the driver was in the open but the passengers were not. In profile, this car looked like the hoods worn in Limoges.

a bat	e bed	i bid	o pot	u cup	th thin
ā cake	ē me	ī bite	ō go	ū rude	TH then
à bar	ə about	ər over	ȯ for	ů put	zh measure

L

limp[1] (limp) *n* a lame step or walk.
v walk with a limp: *After falling down the stairs, she limped for several days.* <Middle English> **limp′er** *n.*

limp[2] (limp) *adj* tending to bend or droop: *The lettuce had lost its crispness and was quite limp. I am so tired I feel as limp as a rag.* <origin uncertain> **limp′ly** *adv.* **limp′ness** *n.*

Like **limpets**, mussels also cling to rocks on the shoreline, but they are easier to remove. Mussels are found in both salt water and fresh water.

lim·pet (lim′pet) *n* **1** a marine mollusc that lives on shoreline rocks, and clings very tightly when disturbed. **2** anything that clings tightly to someone or something: *a limpet mine placed on a ship's hull.* <Middle English *lempet*>

lim·pid (lim′pid) *adj* **1** clear or transparent: *limpid water, limpid eyes.* **2** clear and accessible, especially as writing or music: *a limpid style.* <Latin *limpidus* clear>
lim·pid′i·ty *n.* **lim′pid·ly** *adv.*

lin·age (lī′nij) *n* **1** the number of lines of printed or written matter on a page. **2** payment according to the number of lines. Also, **lineage** (lī′nij).

linch·pin (linch′pin′) *n* a locking pin inserted through a hole in the end of an axle to keep the wheel on. <Old English *lynis* linchpin + *pin*>

lin·dane (lin′dān) *n* a benzene compound used as an insecticide.

lin·den (lin′dən) *n* a tree native to the temperate regions of the northern hemisphere, with heart-shaped leaves and fragrant flowers.

line[1] (līn) *n* **1** a long, thin mark: *Draw a line across the page.* **2** a limit or boundary: *a property line, the poverty line, to skate across the centre line.* **3** a number of people, things, or events coming one after another in space or time: *a line of people buying movie tickets, a plot line, a line of English monarchs.* **4** a horizontal row of written or printed words: *a poem of ten lines.* **5 a** a piece of rope, cord, or wire used for a particular purpose: *a fishing line, telephone lines.* **b** a telephone number: *Can you hold? I'm on the other line.* **6** a wrinkle or crease in the skin of the hands, face, etc. **7** *Mathematics* a straight or curved path that a moving point would make. Such a line is considered to have length, but no thickness. **8 a** one branch of a system of transportation: *the main line of a railway.* **b** a whole system of transportation: *a shipping line.* **9** a kind or brand of commercial goods: *an expensive line of sportswear.* **10** the outline as a design feature in artistic compositions: *The artist's use of line gave depth to the painting.* **11** a course of action, conduct, or thought: *a dangerous line of policy. Don't take that line with me, thinking along the same lines.* **12** a branch of business or kind of activity: *What line of work would you prefer?* **13** *Informal* an exaggerated story: *She gave me some line about why she was late.* **14** *Military* **a** a connected series of defences or fortified positions facing an enemy. **b** an arrangement of an army or fleet for battle. **15** 🍁 **a** *especially Ontario* a CONCESSION ROAD. **b** *Newfoundland* a road cut through rough country that links coastal settlements. **16** a short letter: *Send me a line to say when you'll arrive.* **17 lines** *pl* an actor's words in a play or movie: *I forgot my lines and had to be prompted.*
v **lined, lin·ing 1** cover or mark with lines: *a face lined by age.* **2** arrange or be arranged in a line or row: *Line your books on the shelf. Parked cars lined the street.* <Old English *line* and French *ligne*, both from Latin *linea* linen thread, string>
all along the line, at every stage of something.
bring into line, cause to agree or conform: *If she can bring the other members into line, then her plan will be accepted.*
come into line, agree or conform.
cross the line, do something unacceptable.
down the line, at some future time: *If you get it wrong now, you'll have trouble down the line.*
get (or **have**) **a line on,** get (or have) information about.
hold the line, a wait on the phone. **b** stand firm against an attack or challenge.
in line, a in alignment: *Get in line and walk quickly down the hall.* **b** in agreement: *My opinions are in line with yours.* **c** under control: *Keep your temper in line.*
in line for, due for or about to get: *He's in line for a promotion.*
in the line of duty, while doing your job.
lay it on the line, state things firmly and clearly: *If you must lay it on the line, just say that your decision is final.*
line up, a form or wait in a line of people. **b** organize: *The student council has lined up a great band for the dance.*
on the line, at risk. *A politician's job is on the line at election time.*
out of line, not agreeing, suitable, or proper: *Her last remark was out of line. He is always out of line with the rest of the group.*
read between the lines, find a hidden meaning.
string (or **feed**) **someone a line,** *Informal* tell someone a false story.

line[2] (līn) *v* **lined, lin·ing** put a covering inside, or serve as an inside covering for: *I want to line this jacket with red cloth. This piece of satin would line the coat very nicely.* <Old English *lin* linen cloth>
line your pocket(**s**), *Informal* make a lot of money, usually by illegal means.

lin·e·age[1] (lin′ē ij) *n* descent in a direct line from an ancestor.

line·age[2] (lī′nij) LINAGE.

lin·e·al (lin′ē əl) *adj* **1** in the direct line of descent: *A granddaughter is a lineal descendant of her grandfather.* **2** to do with ancestors: *The lands were his by lineal right.*
lin′e·al·ly *adv.*

lin·e·a·ment (lin′ē ə mənt) *n* a part or feature of a face with attention to its outline.

lin·e·ar (lin′ē ər) *adj* **1** to do with a line or lines: *linear symmetry.* **2** made of lines: *a linear drawing, a linear arrangement of trees.* **3** *Mathematics, Physics* involving measurement in one dimension only: *linear measure.* **4** *Botany* long, narrow, and even in width: *Grass has linear leaves.* **5** to do with length: *the linear dimensions of the building.*

Linear A *n* a system of writing, not yet deciphered, found in Minos on Crete. Compare LINEAR B.

Linear B *n* a syllabic script used in Greek tablets of Crete from the 1400s to the 1200s BCE. Compare LINEAR A.

linear equation *Mathematics n* an equation whose graph is a straight line.

linear measure *n* **1** the measurement of length. **2** a unit or system of units for measuring length.

line·back·er (līn′bak′ər) *Football n* a defensive player whose position is just behind the line of scrimmage.

line dancing *n* a popular form of dancing, often to country music, in which dancers perform steps in rows, all facing the same way.

line drive *Baseball n* a ball hit with great force in a straight line.

line graph *Mathematics n* a graph in which points representing different values are connected by a straight line, or a series of straight lines.

line·man (līn′mən) *n, pl* **line·men** (-mən) **1** a person who sets up or repairs telephone or electric wires. **2** *Football* a centre, guard, tackle, or end. **3** a person who inspects railway tracks. **4** *Surveying* the person who carries the line or chain.

lin·en (lin′ən) *n* **1** thread or yarn spun from flax, or the cloth made from this: *Linen is very strong and is cool in summer.* **2** (*often plural*) articles made of linen or of cotton, synthetics, or blends: *Tablecloths and serviettes are called table linen, and sheets, blankets, etc. are called bed linen.* <Old English = made of flax>

line of best fit *Mathematics n* a line drawn through or very close to as many points on a graph as possible. Such a line may pass through some of the points, none of the points, or all of the points.

line of credit *n* credit allowed by a bank to a borrower up to a stated limit, with terms of repayment like those of a credit card but at an interest rate similar to that of a regular loan.

line of fire *n* **1** the path of a bullet or shell: *He threw himself on the ground to get out of the line of fire.* **2** a dangerous or vulnerable position.

line of force *n* the line that indicates the direction in which the force is acting in a field of electrical or magnetic force.

line of scrimmage *especially Football n* the line along which opposing teams face one another for a scrimmage.

lin·er[1] (lī′nər) *n* **1** a ship or airplane belonging to a transportation system. **2** (*usually in compounds*) a device that makes lines: *eyeliner.* **3** a baseball hit so that it travels not far above the ground.

lin·er[2] (lī′nər) *n* something that serves as a lining: *a hat liner.*

lines·man (līn′zmən) *n, pl* **lines·men** (-zmən) **1** a lineman. **2** *Sports* a person who watches the lines that mark out the field, rink, or court, and assists the umpire or referee.

line·up or **line–up** (lī′nup′) *n* **1 a** a number of people arranged in a line: *There was a long lineup for tickets.* **b** a group including a suspected offender, lined up for identification. **2** in some sports, the list of players on a team arranged according to position of play, or the players on such a list.

ling (ling) *n, pl* **lings** or (*especially collectively*) **ling** a large food fish of the eastern Atlantic. <Old English>

–ling *suffix* **1** little, young, or unimportant: *duckling.* **2** one that is, belongs to, or is concerned with: *underling.* <Old English>

ling cod *n* a large food fish found along the Pacific coast of N America.

lin·ger (ling′gər) *v* **1** stay on, especially because of reluctance to leave: *Several fans lingered at the stage door for some time after the actor had gone in.* **2** continue to stay or live, although gradually becoming less: *Daylight lingers long in the summertime.* **3** spend time slowly: *They lingered over their meal.* <Middle English *leng* delay>

lin·ge·rie (lan′zhə rē′) *or* (lon′zhə rā′) *n* women's undergarments and nightclothes. <French *linge* linen>

lin·go (ling′gō) *Informal n, pl* **lin·goes** language, especially a dialect or jargon regarded as incomprehensible to the general public: *the lingo of sports writers, the lingo of medical people.* <probably Provençal (a language of S France), from Latin *lingua* tongue>

lin·gon·ber·ry (ling′gon ber′ē) *n, pl* **lin·gon·ber·ries** a dark red edible berry related to the blueberry, common in Scandinavian cuisine. <Swedish *lingon* mountain cranberry + *berry*>

lin·gua fran·ca (ling′gwə frang′kə) *n, pl* **lin·gua fran·cas** or **lin·guae fran·cae** (ling′gwē frang′kə) *or* (ling′gwī frang′kī) **1** a language or dialect used as a common means of communication between groups whose native languages are different: *Chinook Jargon was the lingua franca of Canada's Pacific coast, used by Europeans and First Nations.* **2** a code or system used as a common means of communication between people of different languages or backgrounds: *Pop music is the new lingua franca.*

ETYMOLOGY

Lingua franca is Italian, meaning "Frankish language." The original Lingua Franca was a hybrid language based on Italian, with elements of other languages, and used for trade in Mediterranean ports.

lin·gual (ling′gwəl) *adj* **1** to do with the tongue: *a lingual defect.* **2** formed as a sound with the aid of the tongue. **3** to do with speech or languages. <Latin *lingua* tongue>

a bat	e bed	i bid	o pot	u cup	th **thin**
ā cake	ē me	ī bite	ō go	ū rude	ᴛʜ **then**
à bar	ə about	ər over	ȯ for	ů put	zh measure

L

lin·gui·ne (ling gwē′nē) *n* flat, narrow strips of pasta. <Italian *lingua* tongue>

lin·guist (ling′gwist) *n* **1** a person skilled in a number of languages besides his or her own. **2** a person trained in linguistics, especially one who makes it his or her work. **3** a philologist. <Italian *lingua* tongue>

lin·guis·tic (ling gwis′tik) *adj* to do with language or the study of languages.
n **linguistics** (*with singular verb*) the study of human speech. Linguistics also includes the historical development of language and languages. Compare PHILOLOGY. <Italian *lingua* tongue> **lin·guis′ti·cal·ly** *adv.*

lin·i·ment (lin′ə mənt) *n* a liquid for rubbing on the skin to relieve soreness, sprains, or bruises. <Latin *linere* to smear>

lin·ing (lī′ning) *n* **1** a layer of material covering the inner surface of something: *the lining of a coat, the lining of a stove.* **2** the material used for lining: *I bought satin lining for the coat.*

link (lingk) *n* **1** one ring or loop of a chain. **2** something that joins as a link joins: *a cuff link, a link in a chain of evidence.* **3** *Computers* text or images on a web page that a user can click on to access another web page or website. **4** a nonmetric unit of length used in surveying, about 20 cm.
v **1** unite or connect. **2** *Computers* by clicking on text or images on a web page, access a different page or another place on the same web page, link to a file that will download, launch an application, etc. See also HYPERLINK, HOTLINK. <Old Norse *hlekkr*>

link·age (ling′kij) *n* **1** a linking or being linked. **2** an arrangement of links.

linking verb *n* a verb (such as *be, become,* or *seem*) that does not express action. It links a subject with an adjective, or with a noun or pronoun that stands for the same person or thing as the subject: Examples: *I am sleepy. He turned pale. She is a doctor. They became friends.*

GRAMMAR AND USAGE

Linking verbs are useful and necessary, but try to include as many strong action verbs as you can in your writing. *It was raining hard* is not as strong as *A storm raged.*

links (lingks) *pln* (*with singular or plural verb*) a golf course.

lin·net (lin′it) *n* a small brown or grey songbird of Europe, Asia, and Africa. <Old French *lin* flax. The *linnet* feeds on flaxseeds.>

li·no·le·um (lə nō′lē əm) *n* a durable, washable floor covering, originally made by putting a hard surface of ground cork mixed with linseed oil onto a canvas base. Often shortened to **lino** (lī′nō). <*Linoleum*, a trademark, from Latin *linum* flax + *oleum* oil>

lin·seed (lin′sēd′) *n* the seed of flax. **Linseed oil** is a yellowish oil pressed from linseed, used especially in making paints, printing inks, and varnishes. <Old English *lin* flax + *sæd* seed>

lint (lint) *n* **1** a soft down or fleecy material obtained by scraping linen. **2** fuzz or fluff consisting of tiny bits of fibre from yarn or cloth. <probably Latin *linteus* made of linen, from *linum* flax>

lin·tel (lin′təl) *n* a horizontal beam or stone over a door or window that carries the weight of the wall above it. <Old French, from Latin *limen* threshold>

li·on (lī′ən) *n* **1** a large wild cat, with a dull yellow coat, and, in the adult male, a heavy, shaggy, brown mane around the neck and shoulders. Lions are native to Africa and southwestern Asia. The female is usually called a **lioness**. **2** a very brave or strong person. **3** a famous or important person: *a literary lion.* <Old French, from Greek *leon*>
lion′like′ *adj.*
beard the lion in its den, defy a person in his or her own home or workplace.
put your head in the lion's mouth, put yourself in a dangerous position.

li·on–heart·ed (lī′ən hȧr′tid) *adj* brave.

li·on·ize (lī′ə nīz′) *v* **li·on·ized, li·on·iz·ing** treat as very important: *The visiting artist was lionized by the press.* **li′on·i·za′tion** *n.*

lion's share *v* the biggest or best part: *She managed to get the lion's share of the cake before the rest of us got there.*

lip (lip) *n* **1** either of the two fleshy, movable edges of the mouth. **2** a folding or bent-out edge of an opening: *the lip of a pitcher.* **3** the mouthpiece of a musical instrument. **4** *Informal* impudent talk. **5 lips** *pl* the mouth.
v **lipped, lip·ping 1** touch with the lips. **2** use the lips in playing a wind instrument. <Old English *lippa*>
lip′like′ *adj.*
button (or **zip**) **your lip,** *Informal* keep quiet or stop talking, especially to keep a secret.
hang on the lips of, listen to with great attentiveness and admiration.
keep a stiff upper lip, show no fear or discouragement.
pay lip service to something or someone, support or praise outwardly without really meaning it or acting upon it.
smack your lips, enjoy something, especially food, in anticipation.

li·pase (lī′pās) *n* an enzyme occurring in the pancreatic juice and in certain seeds, capable of changing fats into fatty acids and glycerin.

lip·id (lip′əd) *n* any of a group of organic compounds that are the main components of a living cell. Fats, oils, and waxes are lipids. <French, from Greek *lipos* fat>

lip·o·pro·tein (lip′o prō′tēn) *or* (līp′o prō′tēn) *n* any of a group of proteins that contain a lipid. Cholesterol is a lipoprotein. <Greek *lipos* fat + *suction*>

lip·o·suc·tion (lip′o suk′shən) *or* (līp′o suk′shən) *n* the surgical removal of fatty tissue by suction through a small hole. <Greek *lipos* fat + *suction*>

lip·py (lip′ē) *Informal adj* **lip·pi·er, lip·pi·est** disrespectful.

lip–read (lip′rēd′) *v* interpret speech without hearing it by watching the lip movements and facial expressions of the speaker. **lip′-read′er** *n.* **lip′-read′ing** *n.*

lip·stick (lip′stik′) *n* **1** a smooth cosmetic paste for the lips, usually coloured and often in the form of a stick in a case. **2** a case containing this cosmetic.

lip–sync (lip′sink′) *v* mouth the words of a song or speech while a recording of it is being played, to make it seem that one is singing or speaking. <*lip* + *synchronize*> **lip′-sync·er** *n.*

liq·ue·fy (lik′wə fī′) *v* **liq·ue·fied, liq·ue·fy·ing** change into a liquid: *Liquefied air is extremely cold.* **liq′ue·fac′tion** *n.* **liq′ue·fi′a·ble** *adj.* **liq′ue·fi′er** *n.*

li·queur (li kyůr′) *or* (li kər′) *n* a strong, sweet, highly flavoured alcoholic drink.

liq·uid (lik′wid) *n* a substance that is neither a solid nor a gas, flowing freely and with a constant volume.
adj **1** in the form of a liquid: *liquid soap.* **2** clear and bright like water. **3** of sound, clear and smooth: *the liquid notes of a bird.* **4** easily turned into cash: *Canada Savings Bonds are a liquid investment.* <Latin *liquere* be fluid>

liquid air *n* the intensely cold, transparent liquid formed when air is very greatly compressed and then cooled. It is used mainly as a refrigerant.

liquid assets *pln* things easily converted into cash. Savings Bonds are liquid assets.

liq·ui·date (lik′wə dāt′) *v* **liq·ui·dat·ed, liq·ui·dat·ing** **1** pay a debt. **2** settle the accounts of a business when it has ended. **3** get rid of an undesirable person or thing, especially by killing: *The Russian revolution liquidated the nobility.* **liq′ui·da′tion** *n.*

liquid crystal display LCD.

li·quid·i·ty (li kwid′ə tē) *n* **1** the state of being a liquid. **2** the state of having liquid assets.

liquid measure *n* **1** the measurement of liquids. **2** a unit or system of units for measuring liquids.

liq·uor (lik′ər) *n* **1** an alcoholic drink, such as brandy, gin, rum, or whisky. **2** a liquid in which food is packaged, canned, or cooked: *Pickles are bottled in a salty liquor.* <Old French, from Latin>

🍁 **liquor control board** *n* a provincial government board regulating the distribution and sale of alcohol.

liq·uor·ice (lik′ə rish), (lik′rish) *or* (lik′ər is) LICORICE.

lisp (lisp) *v* **1** use the sound of *th* instead of the sound of *s* or *z* in speaking: *A person who lisps might say "thing a thong" for "sing a song."* **2** speak imperfectly: *Babies are said to lisp.*
n the act, habit, or sound of speaking in this way: *She speaks with a lisp.* <Old English *wlisp* lisping> **lisp′er** *n.*

lis·some or **lis·som** (lis′əm) *adj* thin, supple, and graceful. <*lithe*>

list[1] (list) *n* a series of numbers or words, written typically one below the other: *a shopping list.*
v make into a list: *I'm listing the things I have to do today.* <French *liste*>

list[2] (list) *n* a tilt to one side: *the list of a ship.*
v tilt to one side: *The sinking ship was listing so that water ran over her decks.* <origin uncertain>

lis·ten (lis′ən) *v* **1** pay attention so as to hear: *She listened for the sound of the car. I like to listen to music.* **2** give heed or pay attention: *I don't know how to do these math problems because I did not listen in class.*
n an act of listening: *Give a listen to what I have to say.* <Old English *hlyst* hearing> **lis′ten·er** *n.*
listen in, a listen to others talking on a telephone: *I listened in on the extension.* **b** listen to the radio: *Listen in next week for another drama.*
listen up, *Informal* pay attention.

list·ing (list′ing) *n* **1** a document that lists, in some order, items in a collection or category. Often, the document is a computer-generated and lists entries in a database. **2** an entry or item in such a document: *a real-estate listing.*

list·less (list′lis) *adj* seeming too tired or unenthusiastic to care about something: *a dull and listless mood.* <Middle English *list* desire + *-less*> **list′less·ly** *adv.* **list′less·ness** *n.*

list price *n* the price given in a catalogue or list.

lists (lists) *pln* **1** in the Middle Ages, a field where knights fought in tournaments. **2** the barriers enclosing such a field. <Old English *liste* border>
enter the lists, join in a competition, fight, or argument.

List·serv (list′sərv) *Trademark n* **1** a computer application that runs an e-mail list shared by a group, so that a subscribing member can automatically post messages to all the others. **2** the list of group members using this service. <*list* + *server*>

lit[1] (lit) **1** a past tense and a past participle of LIGHT[1]. **2** a past tense and a past participle of LIGHT[3].

lit[2] *Informal n* (*often in compounds*) literature: *CanLit.*

lit·a·ny (lit′ə nē) *n* **1** a form of prayer for use in church services, consisting of a series of petitions recited by the clergy, alternating with fixed responses from the congregation. **2** a recital or account involving much repetition: *a litany of complaints.* <Old French, from Greek *litaneia* prayer>

li·tchi (lī′chē) *or* (lē′chē) LYCHEE.

lite (līt) *adj* (*often follows the noun*) **1** *Commercial* low in fat, cholesterol, calories, or alcohol: *lite beer, cream cheese lite.* **2** *Informal* simplistic, superficial, or less challenging in some way: *That is not punk rock, it's punk rock lite.* <variant of *light*>

li·ter (lē′tər) LITRE.

lit·er·a·cy (lit′ə rə sē) *n* the ability to read and write. Compare ORACY.

lit·er·al (lit′ə rəl) *or* (lit′rəl) *adj* **1** following the exact words of the original: *a literal translation.* **2** taking words in their usual or basic meaning: *a literal interpretation. When we say "He flew down the stairs to meet them," we do not mean "fly" in the literal sense of the word.* **3** concerned mainly with facts: *a literal type of mind.* **4** true to fact: *a literal account. The literal truth of the matter is that he was terrified.* **5** to do with letters of the alphabet. <Old French, from Latin *littera* letter>

a bat	e bed	i bid	o pot	u cup	th **thin**
ā cake	ē me	ī bite	ō go	ū rude	ᴛʜ **then**
ȧ bar	ə about	ər over	ȯ for	ů put	zh measure

L

lit·er·al·ism (lit′ə rə liz′əm) *or* (lit′rə liz′əm) *n* a keeping to the literal meaning in translation or interpretation.

lit·er·al·ly (lit′ə rə lē) *or* (lit′rə lē) *adv* **1** word for word: *to translate a passage literally.* **2** without exaggeration: *I was literally penniless; I couldn't even buy a cup of coffee.*

GRAMMAR AND USAGE

Literally is sometimes used informally to add force to a comment: *I was literally starving to death before I had some breakfast.*

This usage gives **literally** the exact opposite of its real meaning of *actually*, and should be avoided in formal written or spoken English.

lit·er·ar·y (lit′ə rer′ē) *adj* **1** to do with literature or books: *a literary journal, a literary agent.* **2** knowing much about and enjoying literature: *They are a very literary family.*

lit·er·ate (lit′ə rit) *adj* **1** able to read and write. Compare NUMERATE. **2** acquainted with literature. **3** familiar with literature or some other subject: *computer literate.*
n a person who can read and write.

CONFUSABLES

Literate means "able to read and write": *One of the goals of our country's school system is to make sure that all students become literate.*

Literary has to do with literature: *The literary critic reviews new books each week in the newspaper.*

lit·e·ra·ti (lit′ə rȧ′tē) *pln* scholarly or literary people.

lit·er·a·ture (lit′ə rə chůr), (lit′rə chər), *or* (lit′ə rə chər) *n* **1** the writings of a period or of a country, especially those kept alive by the excellence of style or thought: *Stephen Leacock is a famous name in Canadian literature.* **2** all the books and articles on a subject: *the literature of stamp collecting.* **3** the profession of a writer. **4** the study of literature: *I am going to take literature and mathematics this spring.* **5** *Informal* printed matter of any kind: *Do you have any literature describing the programs offered at your school?*

lithe (līᴛʜ) *adj* supple or bending easily: *lithe of body, a lithe willow.* <Middle English> **lithe′ly** *adv.* **lithe′ness** *n.*

lith·i·um (lith′ē əm) *n* **1** a soft, silver-white metallic element similar to sodium. Lithium is the lightest of all metals. *Symbol* **Li** **2** a salt of lithium used as a mood-stabilizing drug. <Greek *lithos* stone, from the mineral or "stone" origin of this alkali metal. Previously known alkalis were of vegetable origin.>

lith·o·graph (lith′ə graf′) *n* a picture, print, etc. made by lithography.

li·thog·ra·phy (li thog′rə fē) *n* the art or process of transferring an image onto paper from a flat surface such as a stone or metal plate, by preparing the surface so that certain parts receive ink while other parts repel it. <German *Lithographie*, from Greek *lithos* stone>

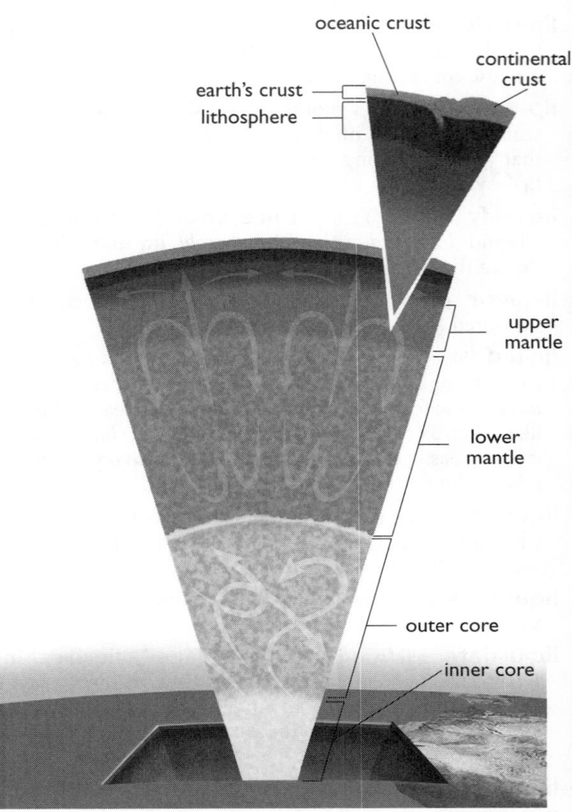

lith·o·sphere (lith′ə sfēr′) *n* the solid outer shell of the earth, including the crust and upper mantle, thought to be from about 70 to 150 kilometres thick. Many scientists believe the lithosphere to consist of separate rigid plates that move on the softer rock of the lower mantle. Compare ATMOSPHERE, HYDROSPHERE. <Greek *lithos* stone + *sphere*>

Lith·u·a·ni·a (lith′yū ā′ nē ə) *or* (lith′ū ā′nē ə) *n* a country in Europe, on the Baltic Sea. See the APPENDIX. **Lith′·u·a′ni·an** *adj, n.*

lit·i·gant (lit′ə gənt) *n* a person engaged in a lawsuit.
adj engaging in a lawsuit.

lit·i·gate (lit′ə gāt′) *v* **lit·i·gat·ed, lit·i·gat·ing** engage in a lawsuit. <Latin *litis* lawsuit + *agere* drive> **lit′i·ga′tion** *n.*

lit·i·ga·tor (lit′ə gāt′ər) *especially US n* a trial lawyer.

li·ti·gious (lə tij′əs) *adj* **1** with the habit of going to law to settle disputes, often unreasonably. **2** to do with lawsuits or litigation.

lit·mus (lit′məs) *n* a blue colouring matter obtained from lichens that turns red in an acid solution and remains blue in an alkali solution. It is used to indicate whether a particular chemical solution is an acid or a base. Litmus is often used in the form of **litmus paper**, that is, paper treated with litmus. <Old Norse *litr* dye + *mosi* moss>

li·to·tes (lī′tə tēz) *or* (lī tō′tēz) *n, pl* **li·to·tes** a form of understatement in which something is said by denying its opposite. Example: *an actor of no small talent.* Compare HYPERBOLE. <Greek *litos* simple>

li·tre (lē′tər) *n* a unit of volume or capacity, equal to one cubic decimetre. One litre of water has a mass of one kilogram. *Symbol* **L.** Also, **liter**. <French, from Greek *litra* a unit of mass>

> **GRAMMAR AND USAGE**
>
> The international symbol for **litre** is *l*. However, the capital letter *L* has been adopted as the official symbol in Canada because the lower-case letter can be confused in printing with the numeral 1.

lit·ter (lit′ər) *n* **1** things scattered about: *You should pick up your own litter.* **2** the young animals born at the same time from one mother: *a litter of puppies.* **3** in former times, **a** stretcher for carrying a sick or wounded person. **b** a framework to be carried on men's shoulders or by horses, containing a couch for a passenger.
v **1** leave odds and ends lying around; make untidy: *He littered his room with books and papers, and the yard with bottles and cans.* **2** give birth to young animals. <Old French, from Latin *lectus* bed>

lit·ter·bug (lit′ər bug′) *n* a person who leaves litter lying about in public places.

lit·tle (lit′əl) *adj* **less** or **less·er, least**; or **lit·tler, lit·tlest** **1** small in size: *A grain of sand is little.* **2** small in number, amount, degree, or importance: *little money, little hope, a little army.* **3** short or brief: *She took a little walk.* **4** mean and narrow in thought or feeling: *Only a little person would refuse to help someone in need. That little sneak stole my sweater.*
adv **less, least** **1** in a small amount or degree: *They lived in a little-known town. She travels little.* **2** hardly at all: *He little knows what will happen.*
n **1** a small amount, quantity, or degree: *to add a little.* **2** a short time or distance: *to move a little to the left.* <Old English *lytel*> **lit′tle·ness** *n.*
in little, on a small scale.
little by little, by a small amount at a time.
make little of, treat or represent as of little importance: *She made little of her troubles.*
not a little, much or very: *He was not a little upset by the accident.*
think little of, a not value much. **b** not hesitate about.

little finger *n* the finger that is smallest and farthest from the thumb: *He wears a ring on his little finger.*

little league *n* a league for children in a sport, especially baseball. **lit′tle-league′** *adj.*

little theatre *n* **1** a small theatre, usually amateur, that presents plays. **2** the drama produced by a little theatre.

lit·to·ral (lit′ə rəl) *adj* **1** to do with a shore, especially of the sea. **2** found or growing on or near the shore.
n the region along a shore, especially the zone between the marks of high and low tide. <Latin *litoris* shore>

lit·ur·gy (lit′ər jē) *n, pl* **lit·ur·gies** **1** a form or ritual for public worship: *Different churches use different liturgies.* **2 Liturgy** the Communion service, especially in the Eastern Orthodox Church. <Latin, from Greek *leitourgia* public worship> **li·tur′gi·cal** *adj.* **li·tur′gi·cal·ly** *adv.*

liv·a·ble (liv′ə bəl) *adj* **1** fit to live in: *a livable house.* **2** easy to live with: *a livable person.* **3** worth living or endurable. Also, **liveable**.

live[1] (liv) *v* **lived, liv·ing** **1** be alive or remain alive: *All creatures have a right to live. She lived through the war.* **2** keep up life or support oneself: *Rabbits live mainly on grass, to live on your income.* **3** have a particular kind of life: *to live well, to live a life of misery.* **4** (*often with* ***in***) reside: *My aunt lives in Victoria. Who lives here?* **5** have a rich and full life: *Those people know how to live!* <Old English *lifian*>
know where someone lives, *Slang* know enough about a person to have power over her or him.
live and let live, exercise your freedom without interfering with the freedom of others.
live down, live so worthily that some fault or sin of the past is overlooked: *He is determined to live down that disgrace.*
live for, take great interest in.
live in, live at the place where you work.
live it up, *Informal* enjoy life to the full.
live on, a support oneself by. **b** use someone as a source of income or supplies. **c** continue to exist.
live out, a live away from where you work. **b** spend the rest of (your life): *to live out your life in peace.* **c** to do what had previously only been imagined: *to live out a dream of being a professional athlete.*
live up to, act according to: *The software has not lived up to its claims.*
live with, a accept or tolerate: *I don't like that solution but I can live with it.* **b** be in a common-law relationship with.

live[2] (līv) *adj* **1** alive or with life: *a live dog, live action.* **2** broadcast as performed and not from a tape or film made beforehand: *a live TV show.* **3** full of energy or activity: *She's a live one, always on the go.* **4** *Informal* up to date or of current interest: *live ideas, a live question.* **5** carrying an electric current: *That wire is live.* **6** charged with explosive: *live ammunition.*
adv recorded or broadcast as performed before an audience: *The concert was recorded live.*

live·li·hood (lī′vlē hůd′) *n* a means of obtaining the money necessary to support oneself: *She writes for a livelihood. He earns his livelihood as a farmer.*

live load (līv) *n* a moving, variable weight (such as traffic on a bridge) to which a structure is subjected in addition to its own weight.

live·long (liv′long′) *Poetic adj* whole length of: *She is busy the livelong day.*

live·ly (lī′vlē) *adj* **live·li·er, live·li·est** **1** full of life: *A good night's sleep made us all lively again.* **2** exciting: *We had a lively time at the class picnic.* **3** bright or vivid: *lively colours.* **4** cheerful: *a lively conversation.*
adv in a vigorous manner: *step lively.* **live′li·ness** *n.*

a bat	e bed	i bid	o pot	u cup	th **thin**
ā cake	ē me	ī bite	ō go	ū rude	ᴛʜ **then**
ä bar	ə about	ər over	ô for	ů put	zh measure

liv·en (lī′vən) *v* (*often with* ***up***) make or become more lively or interesting: *The show isn't bad, but they could liven it up a little.*

liv·er (liv′ər) *n* **1** a large organ in vertebrates that secretes bile, helps to absorb food, frees the blood of its waste matter, and has other metabolic functions. **2** the liver of an animal used as food. Liver is a good dietary source of iron and vitamins. <Old English *lifer*>

liv·er·ied (liv′ə rēd) *adj* dressed in livery: *They had liveried attendants.*

liver spot *n* a brownish spot on the skin that many people associate with age and that was once thought to be caused by a malfunctioning liver.

liv·er·wort (liv′ər wərt′) *n* a small, flowerless, green plant that grows mostly on damp ground or the moist trunks of trees. Liverworts are a bit like mosses.

liv·er·wurst (liv′ər wərst′) *n* a sausage consisting largely of ground liver.

liv·er·y (liv′ə rē) *or* (liv′rē) *n, pl* **liv·er·ies** **1** a special uniform provided for the servants of a household. **2** the feeding, stabling, and care of horses for pay. <Old French *liverée* food allowance, from Latin *liberare* make free>

lives (līvz) plural of LIFE.

live·stock (līv′stok′) *pln* farm animals: *Cows, horses, sheep, and pigs are livestock.*

live wire (līv) *n* **1** a wire through which an electric current is flowing: *It is dangerous to touch an unprotected live wire.* **2** *Informal* an energetic person: *He is such a live wire that he's busy all day long.*

✱ **live·yere** (liv′yər) *Newfoundland n* a permanent resident of Newfoundland and Labrador. Also, **livyer**.

liv·id (liv′id) *adj* **1** with a dull bluish colour, as from a bruise: *livid marks on an arm.* **2** *Informal* furiously angry: *He was livid about being sent home. The insults made her livid.* <Latin *livere* be bluish>

liv·ing (liv′ing) *adj* **1** with life or being alive: *a living plant.* **2** in actual existence or still in use: *a living language.* **3** for living in: *good living conditions.* **4** lifelike or vivid: *a living picture.*
n **1** the act or condition of being alive: *to be full of the joy of living.* **2** a means of obtaining what is needed to support life: *to earn a living as a salesperson.* **3** a manner of life: *healthy living.* **4** **the living** *pl* all the people who are alive.
in living memory, within the lifetime of people currently alive: *the mildest winter in living memory.*

living hell *n* an unbearable experience or existence: *Working deep in the gold mine was a living hell.*

living room *n* a room in a house or apartment, used for the general leisure activities of the occupants, or for entertaining guests.

living wage *n* a wage sufficient to enable a person or family to live in reasonable comfort and security.

living will *n* a document in which a person states what medical treatment they wish to receive, especially a connection to a life-support system, if he or she is unable to give consent at the time.

liz·ard (liz′ərd) *n* **1** a reptile belonging to the same order as snakes. Lizards have external ears, eyes with movable lids, dry, scaly skin, and, in most species, a long, slender body with a long tail and four short legs. Geckos and chameleons are lizards. Compare AMPHIBIAN. **2** an animal with a relatively long body, short legs, and a tail, such as the salamander, alligator, or dinosaur. <Old French, from Latin *lacertus*> **liz′ard·like′** *adj.*

lla·ma (lä′mə) *or* (lam′ə) *n, pl* **lla·mas** or (*especially collectively*) **lla·ma** a domesticated animal of South America related to the camel, but smaller and with soft woolly fleece. Llamas are raised for their wool, milk, and meat, and are also used as beasts of burden. <Spanish, probably from Quechua (a language of S America)>

lm lumen(s).

load (lōd) *n* **1** whatever is being carried: *The cart has a load of hay.* **2** (*often in compounds*) the amount usually carried at one time: *a planeload of tourists. Send us four loads of sand.* **3** *Informal* something that weighs down or oppresses: *That's a load off my mind!* **4** the weight supported by a structure or part. **5** **loads** *pl Informal* a great quantity or number: *Don't worry; we have loads of food.*
v **1** place in or on a carrier, or take on (a load): *to load a basket with groceries, to load grain on a ship. The ship is still loading.* **2** (*often with* ***down***) oppress or burden: *loaded down with debt. Don't load your mind with useless worry.* **3** (*often with* ***down***) supply amply or in excess: *They loaded her with compliments.* **4** put a charge in a gun. **5** place something needed to begin operation into a device: *to load a cassette into a VCR, to load a camera.* <Old English *lad* a journey, a carrying> **load′er** *n.*

load·ed (lō′did) *adj* **1** carrying a load: *a loaded truck.* **2** with a charge in it: *a loaded gun.* **3** weighted unfairly: *loaded dice.* **4** *Informal* with plenty of money. **5** *Informal* full of half-hidden and unexpected meanings and suggestions: *Loaded questions are often intended to trap a person into saying more than she wants to say.* **6** *Informal* equipped: *This new car is loaded with options.*

loaf[1] (lōf) *n, pl* **loaves** (lōvz) **1** a quantity of bread baked as one piece in a more or less oblong or round shape: *Bread is usually sold by the loaf.* **2** a mass of food shaped like a loaf and baked: *a salmon loaf.* **3** in former times, a cone-shaped mass of sugar. <Old English *hlaf*>

loaf[2] (lōf) *v* spend time idly: *I can loaf all day Saturday.* <probably *loafer*>

loaf·er (lō′fər) *n* **1** a person who loafs. **2** a shoe resembling a moccasin, but with sole and heel stitched to the upper. <perhaps German *Landlaüfer* vagabond>

loam (lōm) *n* **1** rich, fertile earth in which decaying and decayed plant matter is mixed with clay and sand. **2** a mixture of clay, sand, and straw, used to make moulds for large metal castings and to plaster walls.
v cover or fill with loam. <Old English *lam* clay>
loam′y *adj.*

loan (lōn) *n* **1** the act of lending for temporary use: *She asked for the loan of his pen.* **2** a thing that is lent, especially money: *He asked his sister for a loan.*
v make a loan: *His sister loaned him the money.* <Old Norse *lan*>
on loan, lent for temporary use or service: *This artwork is on loan from the National Gallery of Canada. The book was out on loan so I had to wait.*

GRAMMAR AND USAGE

Although some people object to the use of **loan** as a verb, its use as both a verb and a noun is standard English: *Would you loan [lend] me your silver bracelet? I could use a loan of twenty dollars.*

loan·er (lōn′ər) *n* **1** an item lent to someone for a limited time, especially as a replacement for something that is being repaired, such as a car. **2** someone who loans something to another.

loan shark *Informal n* a person who lends money at an extremely high or unlawful rate of interest.

loan·word (lōn′wərd′) *n* a word taken into a language from another language and adopted as part of that language, often being slightly changed in the process: *"Degree" is a very old loanword that came into English from French.*

loath (lōth) *adj* unwilling or reluctant: *The little girl was loath to leave her mother.* Also, **loth**. <Old English *lath* hostile>
nothing loath, willing or willingly: *They invited him to stay for dinner, and he was nothing loath.*

CONFUSABLES

Loath is an adjective that means "unenthusiastic" or "opposed": *She was loath to lend me money because I was slow to repay her last time.*

Loathe means "feel strong disgust for": *I loathe people who treat animals unkindly.*

loathe (lōᴛʜ) *v* **loathed, loath·ing** feel strong dislike and disgust for: *I loathe the smell of roasting meat.*

loath·ing (lō′ᴛʜing) *n* strong dislike and disgust: *an intense loathing for spiders.*

loath·some (lōᴛʜ′səm) *adj* disgusting or sickening: *a loathsome odour.* **loath′some·ly** *adv.*
loath′some·ness *n.*

loaves (lōvz) plural of LOAF[1].

lob (lob) *n* **1** a tennis ball hit high to the back of the opponent's court. **2** a slow, underarm throw.
v **lobbed, lob·bing 1** hit a tennis ball high to the back of an opponent's court. **2** throw with a slow, underarm movement. <probably German>

lo·bar (lō′bər) *adj* to do with a lobe or lobes.

lob·by (lob′ē) *n, pl* **lob·bies 1** a large entrance hall or vestibule in a building: *A lobby often has chairs or couches to sit on.* **2** a room or hall outside a legislative chamber: *the lobby of the House of Commons.* **3** a person who or group that tries to influence legislators or public officials.
v **lob·bied, lob·by·ing** try to persuade or influence legislators or public officials: *The textile manufacturers are lobbying for a tax on imported fabrics.* <Latin *lobia* covered walk>

lob·by·ist (lob′ē ist) *n* a person who tries to influence legislators or public officials.

lobe (lōb) *n* a rounded, flattish projecting part of something: *The lobe of the ear is the rounded lower end. The leaves of the white oak have deeply cut, narrow lobes.* <Latin, from Greek *lobos*> **lobed** *adj.*

lo·bel·ia (lō bē′lē ə) *n* a flowering plant of the bellflower family. <M. de *Lobel*, 17c botanist>

lo·bot·o·my (lə bot′ə mē) *n, pl* **lo·bot·o·mies** the cutting into the frontal lobe of the brain, formerly used as a treatment for mental disorders that were thought to be otherwise incurable. <Greek *lobos* lobe + *tome* a cutting>

lob shot *Hockey n* a deceptively slow-moving shot.

lob·ster (lob′stər) *n* **1** an edible sea CRUSTACEAN with eyes on stalks, a long body, and ten legs. The front pair of legs end in large pincerlike claws. **2** a similar crustacean, the **spiny lobster**, which has thin claws. <Old English *loppe* spider>

lobster pot *n* a trap for lobsters.

🍁 **lob·stick** (lob′stik′) *n* in the North, a spruce or pine tree trimmed of all but the top branches: *Travellers often use lobsticks as landmarks.* Also, **lopstick**. <*lopped stick*>

lo·cal (lō′kəl) *adj* **1** to do with a certain place: *our local park, local politics, local news.* **2** of just one part of the body: *a local anesthetic.* **3** making all, or almost all, stops: *a local train.*
n **1** a branch or chapter of a labour union or fraternity. **2** a train or bus that stops at all of the stations on its route. <Latin *locus* place> **lo′cal·ly** *adv.*

local area network *Computers n* a network of computers able to share and exchange programs.
Abbrev. **LAN**

local colour or **color** *n* the customs, peculiarities, etc., of a certain place or period, used in stories, films, and plays to make them seem more real.

lo·cale (lō kal′) *n* a location, site, or place, especially with reference to events or circumstances connected with it: *The locale of "Don Quixote" is Spain in the 1500s.*

a bat	e bed	i bid	o pot	u cup	th **thin**
ā cake	ē me	ī bite	ō go	ū rude	ᴛʜ **then**
ä bar	ə about	ər over	ô for	ů put	zh measure

local government *n* **1** the system of administration of local affairs in a township, city, etc., by its own people. **2** the group elected for this purpose.

local improvement district *n* in some provinces, a district administered by provincial officials because it is too thinly populated to have a municipal government of its own. Also called **local government district**.

lo·cal·ism (lō′kə liz′əm) *n* **1** a local practice or custom. **2** a word or expression peculiar to a certain area: *"Outport," meaning an outlying fishing village, is a Newfoundland localism.* **3** a preference for a particular place.

lo·cal·i·ty (lō kal′ə tē) *n, pl* **lo·cal·i·ties** **1** a particular place, location, or neighbourhood: *Are there any stores in this locality?* **2** a situation or position: *What is the locality of the gold mine?*

lo·cal·ize (lō′kə līz′) *v* **lo·cal·ized, lo·cal·iz·ing** locate, assign, or limit to a particular place or locality: *The infection seemed to be localized in the foot.*
lo′cal·i·za′tion *n.*

lo·cate (lō′kāt) *or* (lō kāt′) *v* **lo·cat·ed, lo·cat·ing** **1** establish something in a place: *My uncle located his new store in Yellowknife.* **2** establish oneself in a place: *Early settlers located where there was water.* **3** find out the exact position of: *The general tried to locate the enemy's camp.* **4** state or show the position of: *Locate Regina on the map.*
lo′ca·tor *n.*
be located, be situated: *Ottawa is located on a river.*

lo·ca·tion (lō kā′shən) *n* **1** a locating or being located: *We argued about the best place for the location of the camp.* **2** a position or place: *The cottage was in a sheltered location.* **3** a plot of ground marked out by boundaries: *a mining location.* **4** **a** in full, **absolute location** an area or place defined by lines of latitude and longitude: *Find the location of Toronto on the map.* **b** in full, **relative location** an area or place described by landmarks, time, direction or distance from one place to another: *According to the map he drew, the location of the camping site was two kilometres north of the entrance to the park.*
on location, at a place outside a film studio: *All the outdoor scenes were shot on location.*

lo·ci (lō′sī), (lō′sē), (lō′kī), *or* (lō′kē) plural of LOCUS.

lock[1] (lok) *n* **1** a means of fastening doors, lids, containers, etc., usually needing a key of special shape to open it. **2** an enclosed section of a canal or dock, in which the level of the water can be changed by letting water in or out, to raise or lower boats. See LIFT LOCK for picture. **3** a device to keep something from turning: *a steering lock on a vehicle.* **4** a bubble that stops air or liquid from circulating in a pipe. **5** an airtight chamber admitting to a compartment in which there is compressed air. **6** a hold in wrestling.
v **1** fasten or become fastened with a lock: *I forgot to lock the door.* **2** shut something in or out or up: *We lock up jewels in a safe.* **3** become or cause to become immovable: *The ship was locked in ice. Sudden braking may lock a car's wheels.* **4** join, or become joined, securely: *The girls locked arms. The two fighters were locked in combat.* <Old English *loc*>
lock and load, *Slang* get prepared for an imminent event.
lock in, invest money so that it cannot be taken out before a specified time.
lock out, refuse to give work to workers until they accept the employer's terms.
lock, stock, and barrel, *Informal* completely.
lock up, lock a building for the night: *Be sure to lock up as you leave.*
under lock and key, locked up.

lock[2] (lok) *n* **1** a curl or ringlet of hair. **2** **locks** *pl* the hair of the head: *The child has curly locks.* <Old English *locc*>

lock·down (lok′down′) *n* the confining of people in rooms until some problem or potential crisis has been dealt with.

lock·er (lok′ər) *n* **1** a chest, drawer, closet, or cupboard that can be locked. **2** a large refrigerated compartment for storing frozen food for a long time: *Lockers are usually rented from cold-storage plants.*

locker room *n* a room in a sports or exercise facility where players can shower, change their clothes, and store gear in lockers. **locker-room** *adj.*

lock·et (lok′it) *n* a small ornamental case of gold, silver, or other metal. for holding a picture or a lock of hair: *A locket is usually worn on a necklace.*

lock·jaw (lok′jo′) TETANUS.

lock·out (lok′out′) *n* a refusal to give work to workers until they accept the employer's terms in a dispute.

lock·smith (lok′smith′) *n* a person who makes or repairs locks and keys.

lock·step (lok′step′) *n* a way of marching in step very close together.

lock·up (lok′up′) *Informal n* a jail.

lo·co (lō′kō) *n, pl* **lo·cos** **1** in full, **locoweed** a plant of western N America that poisons the brains of livestock that eat it. **2** the disease of livestock caused by eating this weed.
adj Slang crazy. <Spanish = insane>

lo·co·mo·tion (lō′kə mō′shən) *n* the act or power of moving from place to place: *Walking and flying are common forms of locomotion.* <Latin *locus* a place + *motion*> **lo′co·mo′tor** *adj.*

lo·co·mo·tive (lō′kə mō′tiv) *n* an engine that runs on rails on its own power, used to move railway cars.
adj to do with the power to move from place to place: *locomotive bacteria.*

lo·cus (lō′kəs) *n, pl* **lo·ci** (lō′sī), (lō′sē), (lō′kī), *or* (lō′kē) a place. <Latin>

lo·cust (lō′kəst) *n* **1** a grasshopper with short antennae, especially of a species that migrates in great swarms, often destroying all vegetation in the areas they pass through. **2** *especially US* a cicada. **3** a hardwood tree of the pea family, such as the **black locust** and the **honey locust**, both N American trees. <Old French, from Latin *locusta*>

lo·cu·tion (lō kyū′shən) *n* **1** style of speech. **2** a form of expression or phrasing, especially a word or expression characteristic of a particular region or group of people. <Latin *loqui* speak>

lode (lōd) *n* a vein of metal ore: *The miners struck a rich lode of copper.* <Old English *lad* carrying. *Lode* is the first element of LODESTAR and LODESTONE.>

lode·star (lōd′stär′) *n* **1** a star that shows the way, especially the North Star. **2** a guiding principle.

lode·stone (lōd′stōn′) *n* **1** an oxide of iron that is highly magnetic. **2** a thing that attracts strongly: *Gold was the lodestone that drew adventurers to the Yukon.*

lodge (loj) *v* **lodged, lodg·ing 1** live in a place or provide a place to live in for a time: *We lodged with friends for the weekend. Can you lodge us for the weekend?* **2** live in a rented room or rooms: *We are lodging at present.* **3** get caught in a place or send into a place: *My kite lodged in the top of a tree. The archer lodged an arrow in the target.* **4** put for safekeeping. **5** put before some authority: *We lodged a complaint with the police.*
n **1** an inn, hotel, or motel. **2** a small or temporary house: *My aunt rents a lodge in the mountains every summer.* **3 a** a branch of a club or society **b** the place where such a group meets. **4** the den of an animal such as a beaver or otter. **5** a First Nations house. <Old French *loge* covered walk>

✱ **lodge·pole pine** (loj′pōl′) *n* a pine tree found in British Columbia and western Alberta, occurring as a short, often crooked tree on the coast (a **shore pine**) and a tall, straight, slender tree growing inland.

ETYMOLOGY

The **lodgepole pine** is so called because it was used in building First Nations LODGES (definition 5). Its very flexible wood made it ideal as a building material.

lodg·er (loj′ər) *n* a person who lives in a rented room or rooms.

lodg·ing (loj′ing) *n* **1** a place to live in for a time: *a lodging for the night.* **2 lodgings** *pl* a rented room or rooms in a house, not in a hotel.

lodging house *n* a house in which rooms are rented.

lo·ess (lō′is) *n* a deposit of fine, yellowish brown LOAM (def. 1) found in river valleys in N America, Europe, and Asia, believed to have been deposited by the wind. Loess is very fertile when irrigated. <German>

loft (loft) *n* **1** a room or rooms just under the roof of a house, barn, or stable. **2** an upper floor of a business building or warehouse, especially when used as living space: *a studio loft.* **3** a gallery in a church or hall: *a choir loft.* **4** *Golf* **a** the backward slope of the face of a golf club. **b** a stroke that drives a golf ball upward. **c** the elevation given by such a stroke.
v hit a ball high in the air. <Old Norse *lopt* sky>

loft·y (lof′tē) *adj* **loft·i·er, loft·i·est 1** very high: *lofty mountains.* **2** high in character or spirit: *lofty aims, lofty ideals.* **3** proud and haughty: *a lofty contempt for others.* **loft′i·ly** *adv.* **loft′i·ness** *n.*

log (log) *n* **1** a length of wood just as it comes from the tree. **2** an official record of events during a trip taken by a ship or aircraft. **3** any careful record of events. For example, a **reading log** is a record of the books, stories, etc. that a person has read, often with details like the number of pages read per week, the number of hours spent reading, and so on. **4** a float for measuring the speed of a ship.
adj made of logs: *a log house.*
v **logged, log·ging 1** cut down trees, cut them into logs, and get them out of the forest. **2** enter in a ship's log. <Middle English> **log′like′** *adj.*
log in (or **on**), be able to begin a session of work on a computer by entering a password or other identification.
log off (or **out**), end a session of work on a computer by signing off.
log out, mark your departure in a book.

✱ **lo·gan**[1] (lō′gən) *n* a pokelogan.

✱ **lo·gan**[2] (lō′gən) *Newfoundland n* a boot made of leather, with a rubber foot, reaching to the knee.

lo·gan·ber·ry (lō′gən ber′ē) *n, pl* **lo·gan·ber·ries** a large, purplish red berry, a variety of blackberry, that grows mainly along the Pacific coast of N America. <J.H. *Logan*, 19c horticulturalist>

log·a·rithm (log′ə riᴛʜ′əm) *n* **1** the EXPONENT (def. 3) of the power to which a base, usually 10, must be raised in order to produce a given number. If the base is 10, the logarithm of 1000 is 3; the logarithm of 10 000 is 4; the logarithm of 100 000 is 5, and so on. **2** one of a system of such exponents formerly used to shorten calculations in mathematics. <Latin, from Greek *logos* ratio + *arithmos* number> **log′a·rith′mic** *adj.*

log·book (log′bůk′) *n* **1** LOG (def. 2). **2** a traveller's diary. **3** a book containing a record of progress or performance over a period of time.

log·ger (log′ər) *n* **1** a person whose work is felling trees and getting them to a mill. **2** a machine for loading or hauling logs.

log·ger·head (log′ər hed′) *n* **1** a large-headed, meat-eating turtle of the western Atlantic. **2** an iron instrument with a long handle with a ball at the end that is heated for melting tar. <earlier *logger* block of wood for hobbling a horse + *head*>
at loggerheads, in great disagreement: *The council members are still at loggerheads over the housing issue.*

log·gia (loj′ə) *n* a gallery arcade open to the air on at least one side. <Italian = lodge>

log·ging (log′ing) *n* the work of cutting down trees, cutting them into logs, and removing them from the forest.

log·ic (loj′ik) *n* **1** reasoning done or assessed according to strict principles. **2** use of clear and convincing argument: *The lawyer won her case because her logic was sound. There's a lot of logic in what you say.* **3** *Computers* a system that determines how elements in a computer or electronic device are arranged to perform a task. <Old French, from Greek *logos* reason>

log·i·cal (loj′ə kəl) *adj* **1** to do with the principles of logic: *logical reasoning.* **2** reasonably expected: *Fatigue is a logical result of poor nutrition.* **3** reasoning correctly: *a clear and logical mind.* **log′i·cal·ly** *adv.*

a bat	e bed	i bid	o pot	u cup	th thin
ā cake	ē me	ī bite	ō go	ū rude	ᴛʜ then
ä bar	ə about	ər over	ô for	ů put	zh measure

L

logic bomb *Computers n* a set of instructions in a program that can cause it to fail in certain circumstances, especially when the instructions have been written with that purpose in mind.

lo·gi·cian (lō jish′ən) *n* a person trained in logic.

log·in (log′in) *Computers n* the act of connecting to a remote computer system, network, server, or website, usually by providing a user name and a password. Also, **logon** or **log-on**.

lo·gis·tics (lō jis′tiks) *pln* the co-ordination of a complex operation involving many people and things, especially a military operation. <French *loger* lodge> **log·is′tic** *adj.* **log·is′ti·cal** *adj.* **log·is′ti·cal·ly** *adv.*

log·jam (log′jam′) *n* **1** an accumulation of floating logs jammed together in the water. **2** a deadlock or blockage.
v **log·jammed, log·jam·ming** delay, block, or obstruct.

lo·go (lō′gō) *or* (log′ō) *n* an identifying symbol or small design used as a trademark..

log·roll·ing (log′rō′ling) *n* the act of rolling logs in water, especially by treading on them as part of a contest. **log′roll** *v.* **log′roll·er** *n.*

lo·gy (lō′gē) *adj* **lo·gi·er, lo·gi·est** heavy, sluggish, or dull. <origin uncertain>

–logy *combining form* **1** account, doctrine, or science of: *biology.* **2** writing or discussion: *anthology.* <Greek *legein* speak of>

loin (loin) *n* **1** a piece of meat from the part of an animal between the ribs and the back end: *a loin of pork.* **2** usually, **loins** *pl* the part of the body between the ribs and the hips: *The loins are on both sides of the backbone.* <Old French, from Latin *lumbus*>
gird up your loins, get ready for action.

loin·cloth (loin′kloth′) *n* a piece of cloth fastened around the waist to cover the lower parts of the body, sometimes worn by people in hot countries.

loi·ter (loi′tər) *v* **1** walk idly and with frequent pauses: *He loitered along the path, daydreaming.* **2** stand or wait around idly: *to loiter the whole afternoon away.* <perhaps Dutch *loteren* wobble> **loi′ter·er** *n.*

loll (lol) *v* **1** recline or lean in a lazy manner: *to loll on a couch.* **2** hang out or allow to hang out loosely or droop: *A dog's tongue lolls out in hot weather. A dog lolls out its tongue.* <Middle English *lollen*>

lol·li·pop or **lol·ly·pop** (lol′ē pop′) *n* a piece of hard candy on the end of a small stick. <perhaps earlier *lolly* tongue>

lone (lōn) *adj* **1** with no company or companion: *We met a lone traveller on our way.* **2** lonely: *a lone life.* **3** standing apart or isolated: *a lone house on a hill.* <shortening of *alone*>

lone·ly (lōn′lē) *adj* **lone·li·er, lone·li·est 1** feeling oneself alone and longing for the company of friends: *He was lonely while his sister was away.* **2** without many people: *a lonely road.* **3** alone: *a lonely tree.* **lone′li·ness** *n.*

lon·er (lō′nər) *Informal n* a person who prefers to live or be alone.

lone·some (lōn′səm) *adj* **lone·som·er, lone·som·est 1** feeling lonely. **2** making one feel lonely: *a lonesome journey.*

lone wolf *n* a person who prefers to work or live alone.

long[1] (long) *adj* **1** measuring much, or more than usual, from end to end in space or time: *a long distance, a long speech.* **2** with a specified length in space or time: *five metres long, two hours long.* **3** thin and narrow: *a long pole.* **4** extending to a great distance in space or time: *long sight, a long memory.* **5** in some languages, of vowels or syllables, taking a comparatively long time to speak.
adv **1** throughout the whole length of: *all night long.* **2** for a long time: *a day long awaited.* **3** at a point of time far distant from the time indicated: *long before, long since.* <Old English *lang*>
a long face, a sad expression.
as long as or **so long as,** provided that.
before long, soon.
for long, for a long time: *You won't have to wait for long.*
in the long run, over a long period of time.
the long and short of it, the sum total of something: *He says he will never forgive you, and that is the long and short of it.*

long[2] (long) *v* wish very much or have a strong desire: *He longed for his mother. She longed to see him.* <Old English *langian* grow long>

long·boat (long′bōt′) *n* the largest and strongest boat carried by a sailing ship.

long·bow (long′bō′) *n* a bow drawn by hand and shooting a long feathered arrow. Compare CROSSBOW.

long–dis·tance (long′dis′təns) *adj* **1** to do with telephone service outside one's local area. **2** for or over great distances: *a long-distance moving van.*
n an operator or exchange that takes care of long-distance calls.

long division *Mathematics n* division involving numbers containing usually two or more digits, and in which the steps of the process are written down in full.

long–drawn (long′dron′) *adj* lasting a long time or prolonged to great length: *the long-drawn howl of a coyote, a long-drawn speech.*

lon·gev·i·ty (lon jev′ə tē) *n* long life: *The woman said she attributed her longevity to an active life.* <Latin *longus* long + *aevum* age>

long·hand (long′hand′) *n* ordinary writing, not shorthand or typewriting.

long·horn (long′hôrn′) *n* an animal of a breed of cattle with very long horns, especially one common in the southwestern US in former times.

long·house (long′hous′) *n* a large dwelling of certain First Nations peoples, especially the Iroquois, in which several families of a community lived together.

long·ing (long′ing) *n* an earnest desire: *a longing for home.*
adj with or showing earnest desire: *a child's longing look at a store window full of toys.* **long′ing·ly** *adv.*

long·ish (long′ish) *adj* somewhat long.

longitude and latitude

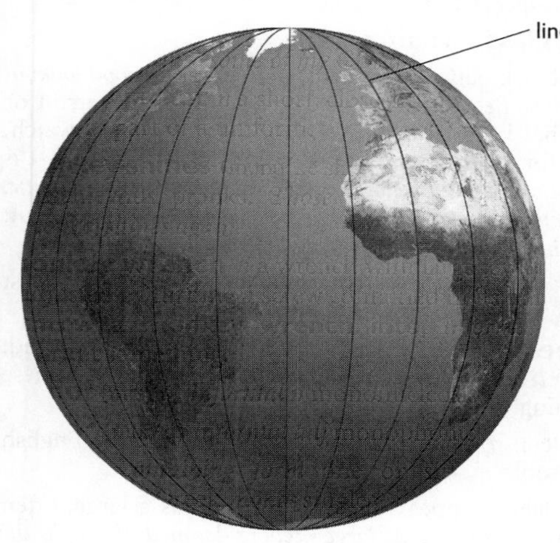

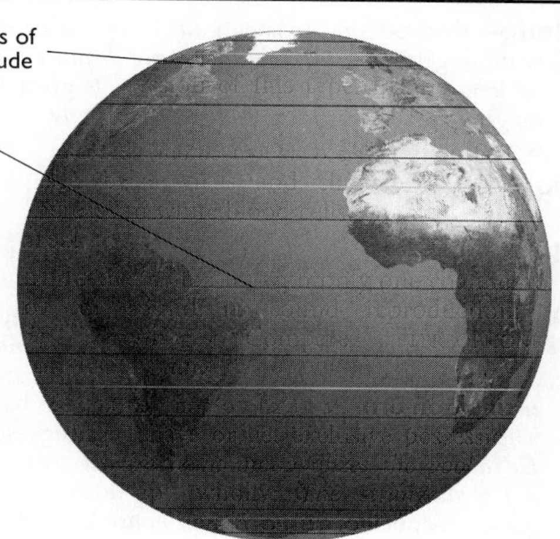

Intersecting lines of **latitude** and **longitude** are used to help locate and describe specific places in the world. The equator, which divides the world into the northern and southern hemispheres, is located at 0° latitude.

lon·gi·tude (lon′jə tyūd′), (lon′jə tūd′), (long′gə tyūd), *or* (lon′gə tūd′) *n* a distance east or west on the earth's surface, measured in degrees from the PRIME MERIDIAN, the line of longitude which passes through Greenwich, England. On maps, lines running between the North and South Poles represent longitudes. Compare LATITUDE. <Latin *longitudino* length>

lon·gi·tu·di·nal (lon′jə tyū′də nəl) *or* (lon′jə tū′də nəl) *adj* **1** to do with length or the lengthwise dimension: *longitudinal measurements. The drapes have longitudinal stripes.* **2** to do with longitude. **lon′gi·tu′di·nal·ly** *adv.*

long·johns or **long–johns** (long′jonz) *Informal n* long underwear.

long jump *n* **1** an athletic event or contest in which contestants try to jump over as much ground as possible. The long jump from a running start is one of the Olympic TRACK AND FIELD events. **2** a jump of this kind. **3 standing long jump** a long jump from a standing start. The standing long jump is often included in school meets.

long·line (long′līn) *n* a fishing line with many baited hooks, used for deep-sea fishing.

✱ **long·lin·er** (long′līn ər) *n* a fishing vessel that uses longlines.

long–lived (long′livd′) *adj* living or lasting a long time.

long–range (long′rānj′) *adj* **1** looking far into future: *long-range plans.* **2** capable of covering a great distance: *long-range missiles.*

long·shore·man (long′shȯr′mən) *n, pl* **long·shore·men** (-mən) a person whose work is loading and unloading ships at a seaport. <from the phrase *along shore*>

long shot *n* **1** *Informal* a bet, or wager, against great odds, but which therefore carries great possible winnings. **2** *Informal* a venture or undertaking involving great risk or only slight chance of success, but offering great rewards if successful. **3** in films, videos, and TV, a scene photographed from a distance.
not by a long shot, certainly not.

long–sight·ed (long′sī′tid) *adj* **1** far-sighted. **2** with wise foresight. **long′-sight′ed·ness** *n.*

long–stand·ing (long′stan′ding) *adj* having lasted for a long time: *a long-standing feud.*

long–suf·fer·ing (long′suf′ə ring) *adj* enduring trouble, pain, or injury long and patiently.
n long and patient endurance of trouble, pain, or injury.

long suit *n* **1** in card games, the suit in which one has the most cards. **2** something in which a person excels: *Patience is not her long suit.*

long–term (long′tərm′) *adj* **1** lasting or intended for a long time: *our long-term plans and ambitions.* **2** falling due in several years: *a long-term loan.*

long–term memory *n* memory for events that happened when the person was very much younger. Compare SHORT-TERM MEMORY.

long·time (long′tīm′) *adj* that has been for a long time: *a longtime friend, a longtime dream of mine.*

long ton TON (def. 2b)

long underwear *n* **1** underpants with long legs. **2** such underpants together with a long-sleeved undershirt, often in one piece.

long–waist·ed (long′wā′stid) *adj* with a relatively long upper body. Compare SHORT-WAISTED.

long·wave (long′wāv′) *n* a radio wave with a wavelength above one kilometre and a frequency below 300 kiloherz. **long′wave** *adj.*

long·ways (long′wāz′) *adv* lengthwise.

a bat	e bed	i bid	o pot	u cup	th **thin**
ā cake	ē me	ī bite	ō go	ū rude	ᴛʜ **then**
à bar	ə about	ər over	ȯ for	ů put	zh measure

L

long–wind·ed (long′win′did) *adj* **1** capable of long effort without getting out of breath: *A long-distance runner must be long-winded.* **2** talking or writing at great lengths: *a long-winded speaker.* **long′-wind′ed·ly** *adv.* **long′-wind′ed·ness** *n.*

loo (lū) *especially UK, Informal n* a toilet. <origin uncertain>

loo·fah (lū′fa) *n* the dried fibres from a tropical gourd, used as a bath sponge. <Latin, from Arabic *luf*>

look (lůk) *v* **1** see or try to see: *He looked this way.* **2** search: *I looked through the drawer to see if I could find my keys.* **3** (*with* ***at***) examine or pay attention: *You must look at all the facts.* **4** seem or appear: *She looks pale.* **5** have a view: *The cottage looks over a lake.* **6** express or suggest by looks: *He said nothing, but looked his disappointment.*
n **1** a glance: *She took a quick look at the magazine.* **2** a search. **3** appearance: *A deserted house has a desolate look.* **4** general appearance: *the look of a situation.* **5** **looks** *pl* personal appearance: *Good looks means a good appearance.* <Old English *locian*>
look after, take care of.
look alive, *Informal* hurry.
look around (or **round**)**,** consider many possibilities.
look back, think about the past.
look bad, appear improper or unsuitable: *Chewing gum while giving a speech looks bad.*
look black, seem hopeless: *With several enemies blocking the exit, things looked black for the hero.*
look daggers at, look at with hatred or anger.
look down on, despise or scorn.
look for, a seek or search for. **b** expect: *We'll look for you tonight.* **c** act so as to cause: *You're just looking for trouble.*
look forward to, expect, usually hopefully: *We look forward to seeing you. When the crops failed, they knew they had to look forward to a bad winter.*
look in, make a short visit: *She said she'd look in on her way back.*
look into, investigate: *She promised to look into the matter.*
look on, a watch without taking part: *The teacher conducted the experiment while we looked on.* **b** regard or consider: *I look on her as a very able person.*
look out, be careful: *Look out for cars as you cross the street.*
look out for, take care of; protect: *He always looked out for his little sister.*
look over, examine or inspect: *The police officer looked over the man's driver's licence.*
look sharp (or **snappy**)**,** *Informal* be quick.
look through, examine.
look to, a attend to or take care of. **b** turn to for help.
look up, a find or refer to: *She looked up the word in the dictionary.* **b** *Informal* call on or visit: *Look me up when you're in town.* **c** *Informal* get better or improve.
look up to, respect or admire.
look yourself, look well: *She has been quite ill and still doesn't look herself.*

look–a·like (lůk′ə līk′) *n* a person or thing closely resembling one that is famous: *They used a Jim Carrey look-alike for that commercial.*
adj being such a person or thing: *The look-alike watch is much cheaper than the original.*

looking glass *n* a mirror.

look·out (lůk′out′) *n* **1** a careful watch: *Keep a good lookout for Mother. Be on the lookout for trouble.* **2** the person or group that keeps watch. **3** a place from which to watch, such as for forest fires: *A crow's nest is a lookout.* **4** what is seen ahead: *See those clouds! A poor lookout for our picnic.* **5** *Informal* something to be cared for or worried about: *That is his lookout.*

lookout tower *n* a high tower from which a forest ranger watches for fires.

look–see (lůk′sē′) *Slang n* a quick search or look around: *She went to the book sale to have a look-see.* <Chinese pidgin English>

loom[1] (lūm) *n* a machine for weaving cloth. <Old English *geloma* tool>

loom[2] (lūm) *v* appear dimly or vaguely as a large, often threatening, shape: *A large iceberg loomed through the thick, grey fog.* <probably German>
loom large, seem important.

loon[1] (lūn) *n* a large, web-footed diving bird that has a loud, wild cry. It is the provincial bird of Ontario. <Old Norse *lomr*>

loon[2] (lūn) *Informal n* a crazy or stupid person. <*loon*[1], after the bird's actions in escaping from danger>

loon·ie (lū′nē) *Informal n, pl* **loon·ies** a Canadian one-dollar coin. Also, **loony**. <from the picture of a *loon* on the reverse>

loon·y (lū′nē) *Slang adj* **loon·i·er, loon·i·est** crazy.
n, pl **loon·ies** a crazy person. **loon′i·ness** *n.*

loop (lūp) *n* **1** the shape of a curved string, thread, ribbon, or bent wire, that crosses itself. **2** a thing, bend, course, or motion shaped somewhat like this: *In handwriting, the letters b, g, h, and l often have loops. The road makes a wide loop around the lake.* **3** a fastening or ornament of something bent and crossed. **4** a turn like the handwritten letter *l*, especially one made by an airplane. **5 a** *Computers* a program or instruction that repeats continuously. **b** a taped audio or video recording that repeats continuously.
v make a loop or loops in. <Middle English>
in (or **out of**) **the loop,** *Informal* in (or out of) regular communication with others, especially decision makers.
loop the loop, *Informal* turn over and over in the air.
throw (or **knock**) **for a loop,** *Informal* surprise and confuse.

loop·hole (lūp′hōl′) *n* **1** a small opening in a wall to shoot through, look through, or let in light and air. **2** a means of escape, especially something in a law or contract that is unclear and so makes it possible to avoid its consequences. <Middle English *loupe* opening in a wall>

loose (lūs) *adj* **loos·er, loos·est** **1** not firmly set or fastened: *a loose tooth, a loose thread.* **2** not tight: *loose clothing.* **3** not bound together: *loose papers.* **4** not shut in or up: *Don't leave the cat loose at night.* **5** not solid or close: *loose earth, cloth with a loose weave.* **6** not strict or exact: *a loose translation.* **7** to do with too little control or restraint: *loose conduct, a loose tongue.*
v **loosed, loos·ing** set free or let go: *They loosed the dogs.*

adv in a loose manner. <Old Norse *lauss*> **loose′ly** *adv.* **loose′ness** *n.*
break (or **cut**) **loose, a** separate from something. **b** run away or free oneself.
cast loose, unfasten or separate.
let (or **set** or **turn**) **loose,** set free or release.
on the loose, free and without restraint.

> **CONFUSABLES**
>
> **Loose** means "not tight": *These pants have been loose since I lost some weight.*
>
> **Lose** can mean "misplace": *Try not to lose your gloves when you go tobogganing.*
>
> **Loss** can mean "not winning": *Our team has only one loss this season, and that was against a more experienced team.*

loose end *n* **1** something left hanging loose: *There's a loose end hanging from your sleeve.* **2** an unfinished detail or relatively minor thing that remains to be done: *We've finished the main job, but there are still a few loose ends to tie up.*
at loose ends, unsettled or with nothing specific to do: *He's finished university, but is still at loose ends about what he wants to do.*

loose–leaf (lūs′lēf′) *adj* with pages or sheets in a notebook that can be taken out and replaced.

loos·en (lū′sən) *v* **1** make loose or looser: *The doctor loosened the stricken man's collar.* **2** become loose or looser: *Your ring will loosen when your fingers are cold.* **loos′en·er** *n.*
loosen up, a warm up one's muscles with exercise. **b** be more tolerant or relaxed.

loose·strife (lūs′strīf′) *n* **1** a tall plant with upright spikes of flowers. One plant, the **purple loosestrife**, is considered a weed in N America. **2** a plant of the primrose family with leafy stems and spikes of flowers. <Greek *Lysimachos*, the supposed discoverer of the plant>

loot (lūt) *n* plunder or booty: *loot taken by soldiers from a captured town, burglar's loot.*
v plunder or rob: *The jewellery store was looted by burglars.* <Hindi, from Sanskrit *lunth-* rob> **loot′er** *n.*

loot bag *n* a small bag of treats or small toys taken home from a children's party by each guest.

lop[1] (lop) *v* **lopped, lop·ping 1** (*usually with* ***off***) cut: *I lopped off a big chunk of cheese.* **2** trim a tree by cutting off branches and twigs. <Middle English>

lop[2] (lop) *v* **lopped, lop·ping** hang loosely or droop.

lope (lōp) *v* **loped, lop·ing** run with a long, bounding stride: *The coyote loped along the trail.*
n a long, easy stride. <Old Norse *hlaupa* to leap>
lop′er *n.*

lop–eared (lop′ērd′) *adj* with ears that hang loosely or droop.

lop·sid·ed (lop′sī′did) *adj* larger or heavier on one side than the other. **lop′sid′ed·ly** *adv.* **lop′sid′ed·ness** *n.*

❋ **lop·stick** (lop′stik′) LOBSTICK.

lo·qua·cious (lō kwā′shəs) *adj* talking much. <Latin *loqui* to talk> **lo·quac′i·ty** (lō kwas′ə tē) *n.*

lo·quat (lō′kwot) *n* the yellow, edible, plumlike fruit of a small evergreen East Asian tree. <Cantonese *lo kwat* rush orange>

lo·ran (lô′rən) *n* a device by which a ship or aircraft can determine its geographical position by comparing the times of arrival of signals sent out from two radio stations. <*lo*(*ng*) *ra*(*nge*) *n*(*avigation*)>

lord (lôrd) *n* **1** a ruler, master, or chief. **2** a feudal superior. **3 Lord** *UK* **a** a title used in referring to noblemen of certain ranks: *Lord Beaverbrook was born in Ontario.* **b** a title given by courtesy to men holding certain positions: *Lord Chief Justice.* **4 the Lord** *Christianity* **a** God. **b** Christ.
lord it over, act in a vain, proud way toward someone: *When my older brother tries to lord it over me, I ignore him.*

> **ETYMOLOGY**
>
> **Lord** comes from Middle English *laverd, loverd*, from Old English *hlaford*, meaning "master of a household," "ruler," and "superior."

lord·ly (lôr′dlē) *adj* **lord·li·er, lord·li·est 1** like or suitable for a lord. **2** insolent or scornful: *His lordly airs annoyed many people.*
adv in a lordly manner. **lord′li·ness** *n.*

lord·ship (lôrd′ship) *UK n* **1** the rank of a lord. **2** rule or ownership: *His lordship over these lands is not questioned.* **3 Lordship** a title used in speaking to or of a lord: *your Lordship, his Lordship.*

Lord's Prayer *Christianity n* a prayer taught by Jesus to his disciples and often used in public worship.

lore (lôr) *n* **1** the facts and stories about a certain subject: *fairy lore, bird lore, Irish lore.* **2** learning or knowledge. <Old English *lar*>

lor·gnette (lôr nyet′) *n* eyeglasses or opera glasses mounted on a handle.

lor·ry (lô′rē) *n, pl* **lor·ries 1** a long, flat wagon without sides. **2** *UK* a motor truck.

lose (lūz) *v* **lost, los·ing 1** not have any longer; fail to keep: *to lose your life, to lose patience, to lose a leg in an accident, to lose a job.* **2** be unable to find: *to lose your way, to lose a sock in the dryer.* **3** fail to get, catch, see, hear, or understand: *to lose a sale, to lose a train, to lose sight of someone, to lose a few words of what was said, to lose the sense of a speech.* **4** fail to win: *to lose a bet, to lose a baseball game.* **5** waste: *to lose money gambling, to lose time.* **6** bring to destruction: *The ship and crew were lost.* **7** run slow in a watch or clock: *That clock loses five minutes a day.* <Old English *los*>
lose it, *Informal* lose control of your emotions.
lose out, fail.
lose yourself, a let yourself go astray or become bewildered. **b** become absorbed in something.

a bat	e bed	i bid	o pot	u cup	th **thin**
ā cake	ē me	ī bite	ō go	ū rude	ᴛʜ **then**
à bar	ə about	ər over	ȯ for	ů put	zh measure

los·er (lū′zər) *n* **1** one who loses: *The loser deals the next round.* **2** a person who, through lack of skills and all-round weak character, is habitually unsuccessful. **3** one who takes defeat in a particular way: *a poor loser.*

los·ing (lū′zing) *adj* that cannot win: *My friends told me I was playing a losing game, but I wouldn't listen.*

loss (los) *n* **1** losing or being lost: *The loss of your health is serious, but the loss of a pencil is not.* **2** the person or thing lost: *The fire was finally put out, but the house was a complete loss.* **3** the harm or disadvantage caused by losing something: *Your leaving us will be a great loss to the team.* **4** a defeat: *Our team had two losses and one tie out of ten games played.*
at a loss, puzzled or uncertain: *She was at a loss for words.*
at a loss to, unable to.
cut your losses, *Informal* keep unavoidable losses or bad consequences to a minimum.

CONFUSABLES

Loss can mean "not winning": *The players took the loss like the good sports they were, despite having lost four games in a row.*

Lose can mean "misplace": *You might lose your keys if you don't put them all on a keychain.*

Loose means "not tight": *These shoes are too loose; I need to try on a smaller size.*

loss leader *n* an item sold at a loss in order to attract customers into a store.

lost (lost) *v* past tense and past participle of LOSE.
adj **1** no longer had or kept: *lost friends.* **2** no longer to be found: *lost gloves.* **3** no longer visible: *She was soon lost in the crowd.* **4** attended with defeat: *a lost battle.* **5** not used to good purpose: *lost time.* **6** having gone astray: *a lost kitten.* **7** destroyed or ruined: *a lost ship, a lost soul.* **8** bewildered: *She looked completely lost.* **9** (*with* ***in***) absorbed in or engrossed: *lost in thought, lost in a book.*
get lost, *Slang* a rude way to tell someone to go away.
lost on, wasted on: *Sarcasm is lost on her.*
lost to, a no longer possible or open to. **b** no longer belonging to. **c** insensible to: *The deserters were lost to all sense of duty to their country.*

lost cause *n* an undertaking already defeated or one certain to be defeated.

lost sheep *n* a person who has strayed from the correct sort of conduct or religious belief.

lot (lot) *Informal n* **1** a large number or amount: *a lot of books, a lot of money. There's a lot of truth in what you say.* **2** a number of people or things considered as a group: *This lot of ballots still has to be counted.* **3** a plot of ground, especially one with fixed boundaries, such as in a town or city: *Our house is on a corner lot.* **4 a** an object used to decide something by chance: *We drew lots to decide who should be team captain.* **b** a choice made in this way: *The lot fell to me.* **c** this method of deciding: *to win prizes by lot.* **5** what one gets as one's share, often by fate or fortune: *Her lot was to carry the boxes, and his was to unpack them, a happy lot.* **6** an item for sale at an auction: *This lot is number 34.* **7 lots** *Informal* (*with singular or plural verb*) a large number or amount: *There are lots of people. There is lots of money.*
adv **lots** *Informal* much: *This table is lots nicer than that one.* <Old English *hlot*>
a lot, much: *I feel a lot better. She skis a lot.*
cast (or **draw**) **lots,** use LOTS (*n* def. 4a) to decide something.
cast (or **throw in**) **your lot with,** share the fate of or become a partner with.

GRAMMAR AND USAGE

Lots, meaning "a lot," is informal and is generally avoided in written English. In informal English, you might write *She tried lots of different shots, but lost the game anyway.* In more formal English, you might write *She tried a lot of different* (or *many different*) *shots, but lost the game anyway.*

loth (lōth) LOATH.

lo·tion (lō′shən) *n* a liquid medicine or cosmetic that is applied to the skin: *Lotions are used to relieve pain, to heal, to cleanse, or to beautify the skin.* <Latin *lavere* to wash>

lot·ter·y (lot′ə rē) *n, pl* **lot·ter·ies** a scheme for distributing prizes by lot or chance: *In a lottery, many tickets are sold, only some of which win prizes.*

lot·to (lot′ō) *n* a game played by drawing numbered discs from a bag or box and covering the corresponding numbers on cards.

lo·tus (lō′təs) *n* a water lily that grows in Egypt and Asia. <Greek *lotos* the lotus plant>

lo·tus–eat·er (lō′təs ē′tər) *n* a person who leads a life of dreamy, lazy ease. <In Greek myth, eating the lotus plant caused a feeling of great relaxation.>

🍁 **Lotus Land** *Informal n* southwest British Columbia, especially Vancouver. <with reference to the presumably relaxed lifestyle of a *lotus-eater*>

loud (loud) *adj* **1** noisy or high in volume: *The music is too loud.* **2** producing a loud sound: *She has a very loud voice.* **3** clamorous or insistent: *They were loud in their demands for higher pay.* **4** *Informal* showy, flashy, or vulgar: *loud clothes.*
adv in a loud or noisy way: *She blew the bugle loud and long. Don't talk so loud.* <Old English *hlud*> **loud′ly** *adv.* **loud′ness** *n.*
out loud, loud enough to be heard: *She repeated her lines out loud to herself.*

loud·mouth (loud′mouth) *Informal n* a person who talks too much and too loudly or rudely. **loud′mouthed** *adj.*

loud·speak·er (loud′spēk′ər) *n* a device for amplifying sound, especially in a public place.

Lou Geh·rig's disease (lū gā′rigz) ALS.

lounge (lounj) *v* **lounged, loung·ing** stand, stroll, sit, or lie at ease and lazily: *He lounged in an old chair.*
n **1** the act or state of lounging. **2** a comfortable, informal room in which one can lounge and be at ease: *a theatre lounge.* **3** a couch. <origin uncertain> **loung′er** *n.*

lour (lour) LOWER[2].

louse (lous) *n, pl* **lice** **1** a small, wingless insect that infests the hair or skin of people and animals, causing great irritation. See FLEA for picture. **2** an insect that is parasitic on aquatic animals or plants such as the **fish louse** or **plant louse**. **3** *Informal* a person considered to be contemptible or unpleasant. <Old English *lus*>
louse up, *Slang* make a mess of: *We loused up the science report so badly, we had to do it over.*

lous·y (lou′zē) *adj* **lous·i·er, lous·i·est** **1** infested with lice. **2** *Informal* disgusting or bad: *lousy weather, lousy luck.* **3** in poor health or depressed: *He felt lousy.*

lout (lout) *n* an awkward, stupid fellow: *The lout didn't even wipe his muddy boots when he came in.* <Old English *lutan* to stoop, bend down>

lout·ish (lou′tish) *adj* awkward and stupid.

lou·vre or **lou·ver** (lū′vər) *n* **1** a strip of wood, glass, etc., set slanting in a frame, window, or other opening. **2** an opening covered with such strips so as to keep out rain or light but provide ventilation. <Old French *lovier*>

lov·a·ble (luv′ə bəl) *adj* endearing or very likeable. Also, **loveable**. **lov′a·ble·ness** *n*. **lov′a·bly** *adv.*

love (luv) *n* **1** a deep and intense feeling of attachment and affection: *love of your family, love of country.* **2** a powerful romantic or sexual attraction: *He was surprised to find himself in love.* **3** a person who or thing that is loved: *the love of my life.* **4** a strong liking: *a love of books.* **5** no score in tennis and certain other games.
v **loved, lov·ing** **1** have a deep and intense feeling of attachment and affection: *She loves her mother. I love my city.* **2** feel a powerful romantic or sexual attraction. **3** like very much or take great pleasure in: *She loves music. He loved ice cream.* <Old English *lufu*>
fall in love, begin to feel romantic love.
for love, for pleasure, and not for money.
for the love of, because of.
make love to, become sexually intimate with.
no love lost, a definite dislike between people.
not for love or money, not on any terms.

love affair *n* **1** a romantic relationship between two people who are not married to each other. **2** an intense interest in or enthusiasm about something: *a love affair with science fiction.*

love·bird (luv′bərd′) *n* **1** a small parrot with mainly green plumage that is often kept as a caged bird and behaves affectionately to its mate. **2 lovebirds** *pl Informal* two people who appear to be much in love with each other.

love child *n* in former times, a child born to parents who had an affair together but are not married.

love handles *Informal pln* a roll of flesh around a person's middle, just below the waist.

love·less (luv′lis) *adj* **1** not loving. **2** not loved.

love–lies–bleed·ing (luv′līz′blē′ding) *n* a plant of the amaranth family that has long, drooping, tassel-like spikes of dark red flowers.

love·li·ness (luv′lē nis) *n* the quality or condition of being lovely.

love·lorn (luv′lôrn′) *adj* unhappy because a loved one does not respond with love.

love·ly (luv′lē) *adj* **love·li·er, love·li·est** **1** with beauty, harmony, or grace: *a lovely woman. She is a lovely person.* **2** delightful: *We had a lovely holiday.*

love·mak·ing (luv′mā′king) *n* sexual intimacy.

lov·er (luv′ər) *n* **1** a person who is in love with another. **2** a person with a strong liking for something: *a lover of books.* **3 lovers** *pl* two people who are in love with each other. **lov′er·like′** *adj.*

love·seat (luv′sēt′) *n* a small couch seating two people.

love·sick (luv′sik′) *adj* unable to behave normally because one is in love.

love triangle *n* a man or woman and two rival lovers.

lov·ing (luv′ing) *adj* feeling or showing love; affectionate; fond. **lov′ing·ly** *adv.*

lov·ing–kind·ness (luv′ing kīnd′nis) *n* deep affection and tenderness.

low[1] (lō) *adj* **1** not high or tall: *A low wall enclosed the garden. This stool is too low.* **2** of less than average or usual height, amount, force, degree, etc.: *low ground. The river is low this year, a low voice, a low price.* **3** near the ground or base: *a low shelf, a low jump.* **4** almost used up: *The furnace oil is low.* **5** not advanced in development, organization, or complexity: *Bacteria are low organisms.* **6** humble in rank or status: *She rose from a low position to president of the company.* **7** lacking health, or depressed: *Her mother is very low, in low spirits.* **8** unfavourable or poor: *He had a low opinion of their abilities.* **9** mean or coarse: *a low trick, low language.* **10** not high in a musical scale: *a low note.*
adv **1** to do with a low position, amount, rank, strength, degree, etc.: *The lamp hangs too low. The sun sank low. Supplies are running low. She spoke low so as not to disturb her sleeping brother.* **2** low in musical pitch: *She sang very low.*
n **1** a low point, level, or figure: *an all-time low.* **2** an area of low barometric pressure. <Old Norse *lagr*>
low′ness *n.*
lay low, knock down; overcome: *The first blow laid him low.*
lie low, *Informal* stay hidden or keep still: *The robbers will lie low for a time.*

low[2] (lō) *n* the deep sound or mooing that a cow makes. *v* make this sound. <Old English *hlowan*>

low beams *pln* headlights on a motor vehicle on their normal low setting: *When another car approaches, switch back to your low beams.* Compare HIGH BEAMS.

low blow *n* **1** in boxing, an illegal hit below the belt. **2** an unfair or dishonourable action.

low·born (lō′bôrn′) *adj* born into a family of low social rank.

low·boy (lō′boi′) *n* a chest or side table with drawers, about the height of a table and with fairly short legs.

low·bred (lō′bred′) *adj* coarse, rude, or vulgar.

a bat	e bed	i bid	o pot	u cup	th **thin**
ā cake	ē me	ī bite	ō go	ū rude	TH **then**
â bar	ə about	ər over	ô for	ú put	zh measure

L

low·brow (lō′brou′) *Informal n* a person who does not like or understand intellectual or artistic things.
adj not intellectual or cultured.

low–cal (lō′kal′) *Informal adj* low-calorie.

Low Coun·tries (lō′kun′trēz) *pl n* the European region consisting of the Netherlands, Belgium, and Luxembourg.

low–cut (lō′kut′) *adj* with a low neckline: *a low-cut dress.*

low–down (lō′doun′) *Informal adj* mean or nasty: *a low-down trick.*

low·down (lō′doun′) *Informal n* usually, **the lowdown** the full report or account: *Give me the lowdown on what happened at lunchtime.*

low·er[1] (lō′ər) *v* **1** let down or haul down: *to lower the flag.* **2** make lower: *to lower the volume of a radio.* **3** sink or become lower: *The sun lowered slowly.*
adj, adv the comparative of LOW. <*low*[1]>

low·er[2] (lou′ər) *v* **1** become or appear dark and threatening: *a lowering sky.* **2** frown or scowl: *She sat there lowering at them.*
n a frowning or threatening appearance or look. Also, **lour**. <Middle English *louren* frown>

✱ **Lower Canada** *n* the name of the present province of Québec before 1841, when UPPER CANADA and Lower Canada were united as the Province of Canada. Lower Canada was lower down the St. Lawrence River than Upper Canada.

lower case *adj* formed with small letters as opposed to capital letters.
n small letters. Compare UPPER CASE. Also, **lowercase**.

> **ETYMOLOGY**
>
> **Lower case** comes from the old days of printing, when metal type was kept in two trays or cases, the lower one for small letters and the upper one for capital letters.

lower class *n* the social group that is mostly poor, including many manual workers and their families. Compare MIDDLE CLASS, UPPER CLASS.

Lower House or **lower house** *n* the larger branch, usually elected, of a legislature that has two branches: *In Canada, the Lower House is the House of Commons.* Compare UPPER HOUSE.

✱ **Lower Lakes** *n* the most southerly of the Great Lakes, Lakes Erie and Ontario.

✱ **Lower Mainland** *n* the southwest part of the mainland of British Columbia.

low·er·most (lō′ər mōst′) *adj* lowest.

lower regions *Archaic or Poetic pl n* hell.

lowest common denominator *n* **1** *Mathematics* the lowest number by which all the denominators of a set of fractions can be evenly divided. The lowest common denominator for the fractions 2/3, 7/8, and 5/6 is 24. Also, **least common denominator**. **2** the level of the tastes, attitudes, or opinions supposedly shared by the majority of people: *Does a movie have to be aimed at the lowest common denominator in order to make a lot of money?*

lowest common multiple *Mathematics n* the lowest quantity that is a multiple of two or more quantities. The lowest common multiple of 6 and 4 is 12. Also, **least common multiple**.

lowest terms fraction *Mathematics n* a fraction whose numerator and denominator have no factor in common. Also called **simplest terms fraction**.

low frequency *n* the range of radio frequencies between 30 and 300 kilohertz: *Low frequency is the range next above very low frequency. Symbol* **LF**. **low′-fre′quen·cy** *adj.*

low–grade (lō′grād′) *adj* **1** of poor quality: *low-grade lumber.* **2** of or at a low level: *a low-grade fever.*

low–key (lō′kē′) *adj* subdued or restrained: *a low-key attack on government policy.*

low·land (lō′lənd) *n* land that is lower and flatter than the surrounding land.

low·life (lō′life′) *Informal n, pl* **low·lifes** a debased, crude, or contemptible person. **low′life** *adj.*

low·ly (lō′lē) *adj* **low·li·er, low·li·est** **1** low in rank, status, or position: *a lowly servant, a lowly occupation.* **2** modest in feeling, behaviour, or condition: *He held a lowly opinion of himself.*
adv humbly or meekly. **low′li·ness** *n.*

low–mind·ed (lō′mīn′did) *adj* with or showing a low or vulgar mind.

low–necked (lō′nekt′) *adj* cut low in clothing so as to show the neck, part of the bosom, and shoulders or back.

low–pitched (lō′picht′) *adj* **1** with a deep tone: *a low-pitched musical instrument.* **2** with little slope: *a low-pitched roof.*

low–pres·sure (lō′presh′ər) *adj* **1** with or using relatively little pressure: *a low-pressure laminate.* **2** with a low barometric pressure: *There is a low-pressure region to the south.* **3** not forceful: *a low-pressure sales pitch.*

low profile *n* a policy of keeping quiet about oneself, or one's work or reputation, and not attracting attention.

low relief BAS-RELIEF.

low–rise (lō′rīz′) *adj* **1** with only a few storeys in a building: *Only low-rise apartments are permitted in this area of the city.* **2** of pants, especially jeans, with a waistband low on the hips.
n a building with only a few storeys. Compare HIGH-RISE.

low spirits *n* sadness or depression. **low-′spir′it·ed** *adj.* **low-′spir′it·ed·ness** *n.*

low tech *n* technology that is not very advanced or complex: *He prefers to stick to low tech and uses pen and paper instead of a computer.* **low-′tech′** *adj.*

low tide *n* **1** the lowest level of the tide, or the time when the tide is lowest: *At low tide there is a very wide beach. The boat must have left sometime after low tide.* **2** the lowest point of something: *The low tide of summer tourism was in early June.*

low water *n* **1** the lowest level of water in a lake or river. **2** LOW TIDE (def. 1).

low–wat·er mark (lō wo′tər) **1** a mark showing low water. **2** the lowest point of anything: *Critics say that book was the low-water mark of his career.*

lox (loks) *n* thinly sliced smoked salmon. <Yiddish, from German *lahs* salmon>

loy·al (loi′əl) *adj* **1** faithful to love, a promise, or duty. **2** faithful to one's sovereign, government, or country: *a loyal citizen.* <French, from Latin *legis* law> **loy′al·ly** *adv.*

loy·al·ist (loi′ə list) *n* **1** a person who supports the existing government or sovereign, especially in time of revolt. **2 Loyalist** 🍁 in full, **United Empire Loyalist** an American who favoured Britain at the time of the American Revolution.

loy·al·ty (loi′əl tē) *n, pl* **loy·al·ties** loyal feeling or behaviour.

loz·enge (loz′inj) *n* **1** a small tablet of medicine or a piece of candy: *Cough drops are sometimes called lozenges.* **2** a design or figure shaped like a diamond or rhombus. <Old French, from Latin *lausa* four-sided slab>

LRT *n* in full, **light rapid transit** or **light rail transit** public high-speed transportation by rail, usually raised above the ground, within a city.

LSD *n* in full, **lysergic acid diethylamide** a drug that can produce hallucinations and schizophrenic symptoms.

LSI *n* in full, **large-scale integration** an electronic circuit on a small semiconductor chip, with very many microcircuits.

lu·au (lū′ow) *n* a Hawaiian-style feast, usually with entertainment. <Hawaiian *lu'au*>

Lu·ba·vitch (lū′bə vich) *Judaism n* a form of Hasidic Judaism emphasizing the unity and community of Jews, strict observance of Jewish tradition and ritual, and personal piety. Also called **Chabad** (ha bod′). **Lu′ba·vitch′er** *adj, n.*

lube (lūb) *Informal n* an oiling of the parts of a car engine or other machine, usually as part of regular maintenance.
v **lubed, lub·ing** apply oil or grease to. <*lubrication*>

lu·bri·cant (lū′brə kənt) *n* the oil or grease used for putting on surfaces that slide or move against one another, such as parts of machines, in order to reduce friction and make the surfaces move smoothly and easily.
adj lubricating. <Latin *lubricus* slippery>

lu·bri·cate (lū′brə kāt′) *v* **lu·bri·cat·ed, lu·bri·cat·ing** **1** put oil or grease on surfaces that slide or move against one another, such as parts of machines. **2** make slippery or smooth. **lu′bri·ca′tion** *n.* **lu′bri·ca′tor** *n.*

lu·cid (lū′sid) *adj* **1** easy to understand: *a lucid explanation.* **2** shining bright. **3** sane: *Insane people sometimes have lucid intervals.* **4** clear or transparent: *a lucid stream.* <Latin *lucis* light> **lu·cid′i·ty** *n.* **lu′cid·ly** *adv.* **lu′cid·ness** *n.*

Lu·ci·fer (lū′sə fər) *n* Satan. <Latin = morning star. A passage in the Bible about Lucifer, a name for the king of Babylon, was interpreted as a reference to Satan because of the mention of a fall from Heaven.>

Lu·cite (lū′sīt) *Trademark n* a solid, clear, plastic compound made of the same material as Plexiglas. <Latin *lucis* light>

luck (luk) *n* **1** that which seems to happen by chance: *Luck was against the losers.* **2** chance considered as a force that brings good or bad fortune: *bad luck.* **3** good fortune: *Lots of luck to you.* <perhaps German *lucke*>
down on your luck, *Informal* with bad luck.
in luck, with good luck: *I must be in luck today, because I just found a dollar.*
luck out, *Informal* be lucky.
out of luck, with bad luck.
push (or **crowd**) **your luck,** take unnecessary chances when things are going favourably: *You've won every game so far, but don't push your luck.*
try your luck, see what you can do: *Try your luck with this puzzle.*
worse luck, unfortunately.

luck·less (luk′lis) *adj* with or bringing bad luck. **luck′less·ness** *n.*

luck·y (luk′ē) *adj* **luck·i·er, luck·i·est** **1** with good luck: *She was lucky to win the card game yesterday.* **2** bringing good luck: *a lucky day, a lucky charm.* **3** happening by good fortune: *a lucky coincidence.* **luck′i·ly** *adv.* **luck′i·ness** *n.*

SYNONYMS

Lucky emphasizes good luck: *I was lucky to find some money in the pocket of a second-hand coat that I bought.*

Auspicious suggests fortunate or favourable: *The journey got off to an auspicious start when everyone showed up early and in a good mood.*

Serendipitous suggests something fortunate happening unexpectedly: *It was a serendipitous encounter, because he gave me some free tickets for the game I want to see tonight.*

lu·cra·tive (lū′krə tiv) *adj* bringing in good profits: *a lucrative business.* <Latin *lucrum* gain>
lu′cra·tive·ly *adv.* **lu′cra·tive·ness** *n.*

lu·cre (lū′kər) *Archaic or Humorous n* money: *filthy lucre.*

Lud·dite (lůd′īt) *n* **1** an English worker who belonged to a group who smashed machinery (1811–1816) as a protest against mechanization and the resulting lowered wages. **2** someone who is opposed to technological progress. <perhaps after N. *Ludd*, a worker who smashed machinery>

lu·di·crous (lū′də krəs) *adj* amusingly absurd. <Latin *ludicrum* source of amusement, from *ludus* game> **lu′di·crous·ly** *adv.* **lu′di·crous·ness** *n.*

luff (luf) *v* turn the bow of a ship toward the wind.
n **1** the act of turning the bow of a ship toward the wind. **2** the forward edge of a fore-and-aft sail.

lug[1] (lug) *v* **lugged, lug·ging** pull along or carry with effort: *The children lugged home a big Christmas tree.* <probably Scandinavian>

lug[2] (lug) *n* a projecting part used to hold or grip something. <probably Scandinavian>

a bat	e bed	i bid	o pot	u cup	th thin
ā cake	ē me	ī bite	ō go	ū rude	ᴛʜ then
ä bar	ə about	ər over	ȯ for	ů put	zh measure

luge

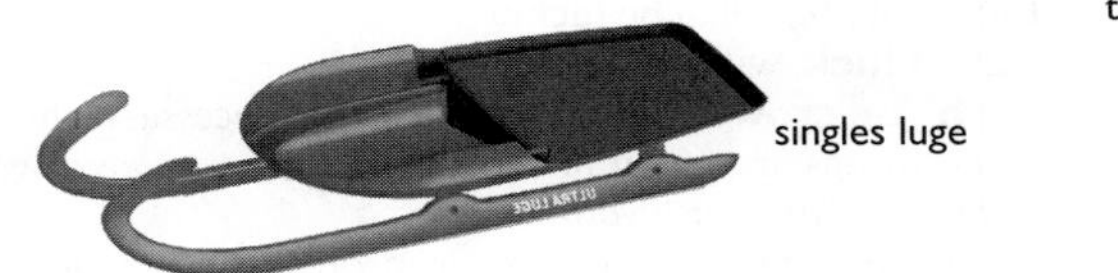

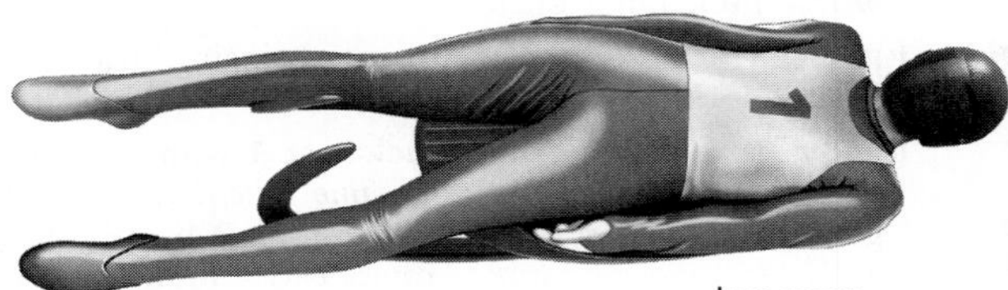

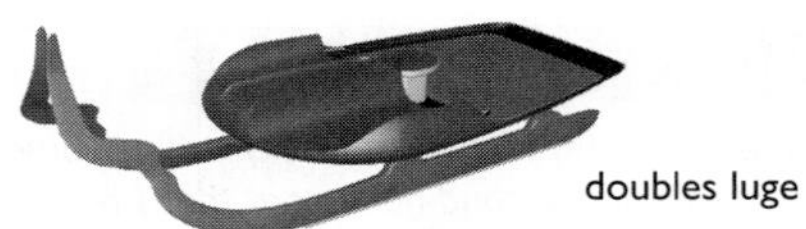

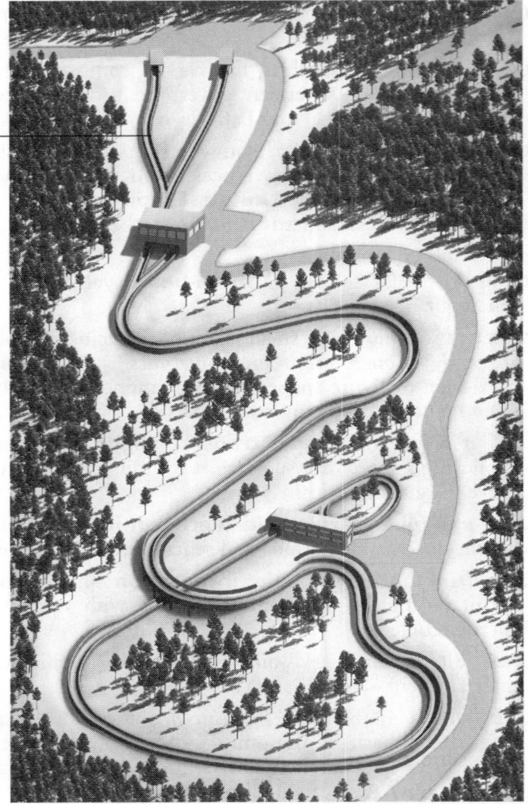

Luge racing at the Olympic level involves rocketing down a winding, icy chute on a 23 kg sled at speeds of up to 150 km/hr. Not a sport for the faint of heart!

luge (lūzh) *n* a small sled that a person rides lying on his or her back, used in downhill races over snow or ice, often on a specially designed course. <French>

lug·gage (lug′ij) *n* suitcases or other bags used by a traveller for personal belongings.

lugs (lugz) *pln* cloth flaps in some caps, pulled down as protection for the ears in cold weather. <*lug*[2]>

lu·gu·bri·ous (lə gū′brē əs) *adj* sad or mournful, especially in an exaggerated or affected way. <Latin *lugere* mourn>
lu·gu′bri·ous·ly *adv.*

lug·worm (lug′wərm′) *n* a worm that burrows in sand along the seashore, used as bait in fishing. <obsolete *lug*>

luke·warm (lū′kwôrm′) *adj* **1** of a liquid, neither hot nor cold when tasted or felt. **2** showing little enthusiasm: *a lukewarm greeting.* <probably Old English *hleow* warm>
luke′warm′ness *n.*

lull (lul) *v* **1** calm someone to sleep: *The mother lulled the crying baby.* **2** make or become calm or more nearly calm: *The wind lulled.* **3** set at rest: *to lull your suspicions, to lull people into a false sense of security.*
n a temporary period of less noise or activity; brief calm: *a lull in a storm.* <imitative of quieting a child>

lul·la·by (lul′ə bī′) *n, pl* **lul·la·bies 1** a quiet, gentle song to lull a baby or child to sleep. **2** a soothing song or piece of music.

lum·ba·go (lum bā′gō) *n* an injury of the muscles in the lower back producing pain. <Latin *lumbus* loin>

lum·bar (lum′bər) *adj* to do with the lower part of the back. <Latin *lumbus* loin>

lum·ber[1] (lum′bər) *n* **1** timber, logs, beams, or boards, cut and prepared for use. **2** household articles no longer in use that take up space.
v **1** cut and prepare lumber. **2** fill up or obstruct by taking space that is wanted for something else. <perhaps *lumber*[2]>
lumber with, *Informal* burden with.

lum·ber[2] (lum′bər) *v* move along slowly and heavily: *The old stagecoach lumbered down the dusty road.* <Middle English>

lum·ber·ing[1] (lum′bə ring) *n* the business of cutting and preparing timber for use.

lum·ber·ing[2] (lum′bə ring) *adj* to do with moving slowly and heavily: *a lumbering old elephant.*
lum′ber·ing·ly *adv.*

lum·ber·jack (lum′bər jak′) *n* a person whose work is cutting down trees and transporting them to a mill.

lum·ber·man (lum′bər mən) *n, pl* **lum·ber·men** (-mən) **1** a LOGGER (def. 1). **2** a person whose business is buying and selling timber or lumber.

lum·ber·yard (lum′bər yärd′) *n* a place where lumber is stored and sold.

lu·men (lū′mən) *n* the SI unit for measuring the rate of emission of light rays. *Symbol* **lm** <Latin = opening>

lu·mi·nar·y (lū′mə ner′ē) *n, pl* **lu·mi·nar·ies** **1** the sun, moon, or other light-giving body. **2** a distinguished person, especially one who enlightens.

lu·mi·nes·cence (lū′mə nes′əns) *n* an emission of light by a process other than incandescence, such as by fluorescence or phosphorescence. **lu′mi·nes′cent** *adj.*

lu·min·ous (lū′mə nəs) *adj* **1** shining by its own light: *The sun and stars are luminous.* **2** full of light: *a luminous sunset.* **3** treated with some substance that glows in the dark: *luminous paint.* **4** easily understood: *She explained the method in a luminous way.* **lu′mi·nos′i·ty** *n.* **lu′mi·nous·ly** *adv.* **lu′mi·nous·ness** *n.*

lum·mox (lum′əks) *Informal n* an awkward, stupid person. <origin uncertain>

lump[1] (lump) *n* **1** a solid mass of no particular shape: *a lump of rock.* **2** a swelling: *a lump on the head.* **3** a small cube or oblong piece of sugar. **4** *Informal* a dull or stupid person. **5** a heavy, sturdy person.
v **1** form into a lump or lumps: *The pudding lumped because it was not stirred.* **2** put together: *We will lump all our expenses.* <Middle English>
a lump in your throat, *Informal* difficulty swallowing because you are holding back tears.
a lump sum, an amount of money that covers the entire cost of something, or the cost of a number of items: *He paid for the car in a lump sum rather than by instalments.*
in a lump, as a whole or in one amount.

lump[2] (lump) *v* suffer in silence; sulk. <origin uncertain>
lump it, *Informal* accept or endure a situation: *If you don't like it, you can lump it.*

lump·ec·to·my (lum pek′tə mē) *n, pl* **lump·ec·to·mies** surgery to remove a lump or tumour in an organ without removing the whole organ. <*lump*[1] + Greek *ek-* out + *tomia* a cutting>

lump·ish (lum′pish) *adj* **1** heavy and clumsy. **2** stolid or stupid.

lump sugar *n* small blocks of sugar shaped like cubes.

lump·y (lum′pē) *adj* **lump·i·er, lump·i·est** **1** full of lumps: *lumpy gravy.* **2** covered with lumps: *lumpy ground.* **3** heavy and clumsy: *a lumpy animal.* **4** with choppy waves in a body of water. **lump′i·ly** *adv.* **lump′i·ness** *n.*

lu·na·cy (lū′nə sē) *n, pl* **lu·na·cies** **1** insanity. **2** extreme folly.

lu·nar (lū′nər) *adj* **1** to do with the moon: *a lunar eclipse, a lunar vehicle.* **2** measured by the revolutions of the moon: *a lunar month.* <Latin *luna* moon>

lunar module *n* a small spacecraft used for travel between the moon's surface and an orbiting spacecraft.

lunar month *n* the period of one complete revolution of the moon around the earth, about 29.5 days.

lu·na·tic (lū′nə tik′) *n* **1** an insane person. **2** an extremely foolish person.
adj **1** insane. **2** for insane people. **3** extremely foolish: *a lunatic search for buried treasure.* <Old French, from Latin *luna* moon. Insanity was once thought to be caused by the changes of the moon.>

lunatic fringe *n* members on the radical edge of a group, whose zeal for some cause or movement goes far beyond the views or activities of most members.

lunch (lunch) *n* a light meal between breakfast and dinner, or breakfast and supper: *We have lunch at noon.*
v eat lunch. <*luncheon*> **lunch′er** *n.*
out to lunch, *Slang* crazy.

lunch·eon (lun′chən) *n* a formal meal taken around noon. <perhaps *nuncheon*, from Middle English *none* noon + *schench* drink>

lunch·eon·ette (lun′chə net′) *n* a small informal restaurant that serves lunches.

lunch·room (lunch′rům′) *n* **1** a luncheonette. **2** a room in a workplace or school where people may eat the lunches they have brought.

lunch·time (lunch′tīm′) *n* the time when lunch is served or eaten, usually around the middle of the day.

lune (lūn) *n* a thing shaped like a crescent or a half moon.

lung (lung) *n* **1** one of the pair of breathing organs in vertebrates by means of which the blood receives oxygen and is relieved of carbon dioxide. **2** a similar organ in invertebrates. <Old English *lungen*> **lunged** (lungd) *adj.* **lung′ful** *n.* **lung′less** *adj.*

lunge[1] (lunj) *n* a sudden forward movement or thrust: *The catcher made a lunge toward the ball.*
v **lunged, lung·ing** move suddenly toward: *The dog lunged at the stranger.* <French, from Latin *ad-* toward + *longus* long> **lung′er** *n.*

lunge[2] (lunj) *Informal n* a muskellunge.

lung·fish (lung′fish′) *n, pl* **lung·fish·es** or (*especially collectively*) **lung·fish** a fish that can obtain oxygen by gulping air through the mouth as well as by passing water through its gills. Lungfish are found in Australia, Africa, and S America.

lup·in or **lu·pine**[1] (lū′pən) *n* a plant of the pea family that has long spikes of flowers, radiating clusters of greyish, hairy leaflets, and flat pods with bean-shaped seeds. <Latin *lupinus*>

lu·pine[2] (lū′pīn) *adj* to do with wolves. <Latin *lupus* wolf>

lu·pus (lū′pəs) *n* a chronic, non-contagious disorder of the immune system. The most serious form is called **systemic lupus erythematosus** or **SLE**, which can affect any organ in the body, most usually the skin, joints, kidneys, heart, and lymph nodes. <Latin = wolf. The characteristic rash over the nose and cheeks is supposed to look like the bite of a wolf.>

lurch[1] (lərch) *n* a sudden leaning or roll to one side: *The car gave a lurch and overturned.*
v stagger or make a lurch: *The wounded deer lurched forward.* <origin uncertain>

lurch[2] (lərch) *n* in the card game called cribbage, the losing position of a player who scores 30 or less.
leave in the lurch, leave in a helpless condition or in a difficult situation.

a bat	e bed	i bid	o pot	u cup	th **thin**
ā cake	ē me	ī bite	ō go	ū rude	TH **then**
à bar	ə about	ər over	ò for	ů put	zh measure

lure (lūr) *n* **1** attraction: *the lure of the sea.* **2** a decoy or bait.
v **lured, lur·ing 1** lead away or into something by awakening desire or attraction: *Bees are lured by the scent of flowers.* **2** attract with a bait. <Old French> **lur′er** *n.*

lu·rid (lū′rid) *adj* **1** lighted up with a red or fiery glare: *The sky was lurid with the flames of the burning city.* **2** sensational or causing horror: *a lurid crime. The newspaper carried a lurid account of the kidnapping.* **3** glaring in brightness or colour: *Her dress was a lurid yellow.* <Latin *luridus*>

lurk (lərk) *v* **1** stay around without arousing attention: *A tiger was lurking in the jungle.* **2** be hidden or only just visible. <perhaps *lower*[2]>

lus·cious (lush′əs) *adj* **1** deliciously rich and sweet: *a luscious peach.* **2** pleasing to the senses, especially those of taste and smell. <Middle English, perhaps variant of *delicious*> **lus′cious·ly** *adv.* **lus′cious·ness** *n.*

lush[1] (lush) *adj* **1** growing thick and green, or rich in vegetation: *Lush grass grew along the river banks.* **2** rich in giving sensory pleasure: *lush upholstery.* **3** flowery or ornamental: *lush description.* <Middle English>
lush′ly *adv.* **lush′ness** *n.*

lush[2] *Slang n* a person who drinks too much alcohol or is frequently drunk; an alcoholic. <perhaps from *lush*[1]>

lust (lust) *n* **1** sexual desire, especially when intense. **2** excessively strong desire: *a lust for power, a lust for revenge.*
v (*usually with* ***after*** *or* ***for***) feel a very strong desire: *A miser lusts after gold.* <Old English = pleasure>
lust′ful *adj.* **lust′ful·ly** *adv.* **lust′ful·ness** *n.*

lus·tre (lus′tər) *n* **1** a bright, even shine on the surface, without sparkle or glitter: *the lustre of pearls.* **2** brightness: *Her eyes lost their lustre.* **3** fame or glory. **4** china or pottery that has a lustrous metallic, often iridescent, surface. Also, **luster**. <French, from Latin *lustrare* light up>

lus·trous (lus′trəs) *adj* shining and glossy: *lustrous satin.* **lus′trous·ly** *adv.*

lus·ty (lus′tē) *adj* **lust·i·er, lust·i·est** strong, healthy, and full of vigour: *a lusty boy.* **lust′i·ly** *adv.* **lust′i·ness** *n.*

lute (lūt) *n* a stringed musical instrument like a large mandolin and shaped like a halved pear. <Old French, from Arabic *al ud*>

lu·te·ti·um (lū tē′shē əm) *n* a rare metallic element. Also, **lutecium**. *Symbol* **Lu**

lux (luks) *n, pl* **lux** the SI unit for measuring illumination of a source of light per unit area on a surface. One lux is the illumination of one lumen over an area of one square metre. *Symbol* **lx** <Latin = light>

Lux·em·bourg (luks′əm berg) *n* a small country in west Europe.

lux·u·ri·ant (lug zhu̇′rē ənt) *adj* **1** growing in a vigorous and healthy way: *In spring the grass on our lawn is luxuriant. She has a luxuriant head of hair.* **2** producing abundantly. **3** rich in ornament. See LUXURIOUS for confusable. **lux·u′ri·ance** *n.* **lux·u′ri·ant·ly** *adv.*

lux·u·ri·ate (lug zhu̇′rē āt′) *v* **lux·u·ri·at·ed, lux·u·ri·at·ing** indulge oneself luxuriously (in): *luxuriating in a hot bath.*

lux·u·ri·ous (lug zhu̇′rē əs) *adj* **1** fond of or tending toward luxury. **2** giving luxury. **lux·u′ri·ous·ly** *adv.* **lux·u′ri·ous·ness** *n.*

CONFUSABLES

Luxurious means "fond of luxury": *She is enjoying her luxurious penthouse apartment.*

Luxuriant means "growing thickly and abundantly": *The jungle has luxuriant vegetation.*

lux·u·ry (luk′shə rē) *or* (lug′zhə rē) *n, pl* **lux·u·ries 1** an abundance of comforts: *After two weeks of hiking through the wilderness, we thought of home as luxury.* **2** the use of the best and most costly food, clothes, houses, furniture, and amusements: *The movie star soon became accustomed to luxury.* **3** a thing that one enjoys, usually something choice and costly: *She saves some money for luxuries such as fine paintings.* **4** something pleasant but not necessary: *Candy is a luxury.* <Old French, from Latin *luxus* excess>

lx lux.

–ly[1] *suffix* **1** in a specified manner, or to a specified degree or extent: *cheerfully, greatly.* **2** with regard to a specified way: *financially.* **3** to do with a specified direction: *northerly.* **4** in a specified rank: *thirdly.* <Old English *-lice*>

GRAMMAR AND USAGE

The suffix **–ly** usually forms adverbs, but also can form adjectives. Sometimes a word ending in **–ly** can be either an adverb or an adjective: *He came in the early morning* (adjective). *We rose early* (adverb).

–ly[2] *suffix* **1** like something, or characteristic of something: *a ghostly appearance, a brotherly kiss, friendly behaviour.* **2** occurring once during a specified period: *daily routine, yearly progress.* <Old English *lic* = *like*[1]>

ly·chee (lī′chē) *or* (lē′chē) *n, pl* **ly·chees** a nut-shaped, sweet fruit with a hard, rough skin. Also, **lichee, litchi.** <Mandarin *lizhi*>

Ly·cra (lī′krə) *Trademark n* a light, elastic fabric used to make tight-fitting garments, often sportswear.

lye (lī) *n* a strong alkaline substance, especially sodium hydroxide or potassium hydroxide: *Lye is used in making soap and in cleaning.* <Old English *leag*>

ly·ing[1] (lī′ing) *n* the telling of a lie or habit of telling lies.
adj false: *a lying report.*

ly·ing[2] (lī′ing) present participle of LIE[2].

Lyme disease (līm) *n* a form of arthritis caused by bacteria transmitted by ticks. <*Lyme*, Connecticut, where it was first diagnosed>

lymph (limf) *n* a colourless liquid in the tissues of the body, resembling blood plasma and containing only white blood cells. <Latin *lympha* clear water> **lymph′oid** *adj.*

lym·phat·ic (lim fat′ik) *adj* to do with lymph.
n a veinlike vessel that contains or carries lymph.

lymph node *n* a rounded mass of tissue lying along the course of the lymphatic vessels, in which the lymph is purified and lymphocytes are formed. Also called **lymph gland**.

lym·pho·cyte (lim′fə sīt′) *n* a colourless cell of lymph produced in the lymph nodes.

lynch (linch) *v* kill, usually by hanging, through mob action and without a lawful trial. <W. *Lynch*, an 18c magistrate> **lynch′er** *n*. **lynch′ing** *n*.

lynch law *n* the punishment of an accused person without a lawful trial, usually by putting him or her to death.

The **lynx** is a solitary animal that loves to hunt at night. In North America, its favourite prey is the snowshoe hare, but it also eats other animals, including ducks, foxes, and occasionally deer. It has wide, padded feet for travelling on snow, and is also an excellent climber.

lynx (lingks) *n, pl* **lynx·es** or (*especially collectively*) **lynx** a medium-sized wild cat with a very short tail, ear tufts, and thick, silky fur with dark spots. The two species of lynx found in N America are the **Canada lynx** and the **bobcat**. <Latin, from Greek *lynx*> **lynx′like′** *adj*.

Different kinds of **lyres** were played throughout Europe, Africa, and the Middle East for thousands of years. Ordinary lyres often were made of tortoise shells, horn, and animal hide, but could also be made of wood. Musicians would pluck the strings of the lyre as they sang their poetry.

lyre (līr) *n* an ancient stringed musical instrument resembling a small harp. <Old French, from Greek *lyra*>

lyr·ic (lir′ik) *n* **1** a short poem expressing personal emotion: *A love poem, a patriotic song, a lament, and a hymn are lyrics.* **2 lyrics** *pl* the words for a song.
adj **1** to do with lyric poems: *a lyric poet.* **2** characterized by a spontaneous expression of feeling. **3** of or suitable for singing. <Latin, from Greek *lyra* lyre>

lyr·i·cal (lir′ə kəl) *adj* showing or expressing great enthusiasm and emotion: *She was lyrical in her praise of the new auditorium.* **lyr′i·cal·ly** *adv*.

ly·sin (lī′sən) *n* any antibody or enzyme that can destroy bacteria, blood corpuscles, and other cellular elements.

ly·so·some (lī′sə sōm′) *n* a part of a cell which contains digestive enzymes capable of digesting living organisms such as bacteria, and that also helps to decompose the cell after death.

Mm

m or **M** (em) *n, pl* **m's** or **M's** **1** the thirteenth letter of the English alphabet, or any speech sound represented by it. **2** the thirteenth thing in a list or series. **3** the Roman numeral for 1000.

m **1** male. **2** *Grammar* female. **3** metre(s).

ma (mo), (mȧ) *or* (ma) *Informal n* mama; mother.

ma'am (mam) *n* madam.

ma·ca·bre (mə kȧ′brə) *or* (mə kȧ′bər) *adj* gruesome, horrible, or ghastly. <French>

ma·cad·am (mə kad′əm) *n* **1** material for making roads, consisting of small, broken stones of nearly uniform size that are mixed with a binding agent such as tar or asphalt: *Several layers of macadam are put down to make a road, each layer rolled until solid and smooth before the next layer is laid down.* **2** a road made with layers of macadam. <J.L. *McAdam*, 19c engineer, who invented this process of road making> **mac·ad′am·ize** *v.*

mac·a·da·mi·a (mak′ə dā′mē ə) *n* in full, **macadamia nut** the edible seed of an Australian evergreen tree. <J. *Macadam*, 19c chemist>

ma·caque (mə kȧk′) *n* a medium-sized monkey of Asia and Africa that has a long face and cheek pouches for holding food. See MONKEY for picture. <French and Portuguese, from Bantu (a group of languages of Africa) *kaku* monkey>

ma·ca·re·na (mȧ′kȧ rā′nȧ) *n* **1** a line dance involving hand and arm movements. **2** the song that goes with it. <*Macarena*, Venezuelan flamenco dancer>

mac·a·ro·ni (mak′ə rō′nē) *n, pl* **mac·a·ro·nis** or **mac·a·ro·nies** pasta in the form of short, hollow tubes. <Italian, from Greek *makaria* food made from barley>

mac·a·roon (mak′ə rün′) *n* a sweet, chewy cookie, usually made of egg whites, sugar, and ground almonds or coconut. <French, from Italian *maccarone*>

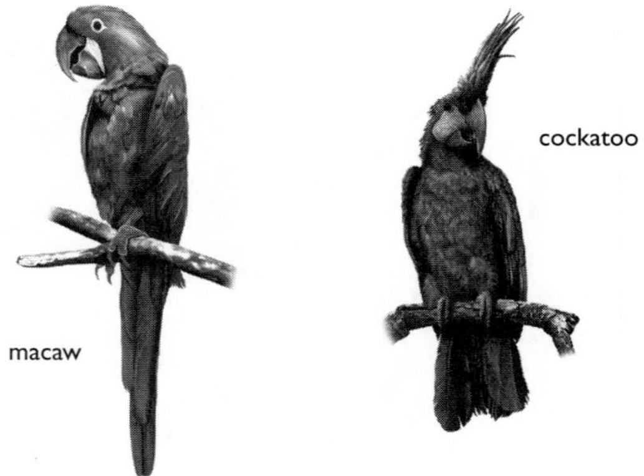

Both the **macaw** and the cockatoo come from the tropics and are often kept as pets. Some cockatoos are capable of mimicking human speech.

ma·caw (mə ko′) *n* a large parrot of South and Central America, characterized by a long tail, brilliant feathers, and a harsh voice. <Portuguese *macao*>

mace[1] (mās) *n* **1** a war club used in the Middle Ages. **2** a staff used as a symbol of authority. <Old French, from Latin *matteola* hammer>

mace[2] (mās) *n* a spice made from the dried outer covering of a nutmeg. <Old French, from Latin *macir*>

Mace (mās) *Trademark n* a liquid chemical that produces tears, temporary blindness, and dizziness when sprayed on a person. <probably *mace*[1]>

mace·bear·er (mās′bãr′ər) *n* an official who carries a staff of authority in a procession.

mac·é·doine (mas′ə dwȧn′) *or* (mas′ā dwȧn′) *n* a mixture of vegetables or fruits, sometimes in jelly. <French = Macedonia, in reference to the mixture of nationalities in the Macedonian Empire>

Ma·ce·do·nia (ma sə dō′nē ə) *n* a country in southeast Europe. **Ma·ce·do′ni·an** *adj, n.*

ma·chet·e (mə chet′ē) *or* (mə shet′ē) *n* a large, heavy knife, used as a tool and weapon in South America, Central America, and the Caribbean. <Spanish, from Latin *mactare* kill>

Mach·i·a·vel·li·an (mak′ē ə vel′ē ən) *adj* using subtle or unscrupulous cunning. <*Machiavelli* 15c politician and writer, famous for his theory of expediency>

ma·chic·o·la·tion (mə chik′ə lā′shən) *n* an opening in the floor of a projecting gallery or parapet, or in the roof of an entrance, through which objects or hot liquids might be dropped on attackers in medieval times. <Provençal (a language of S France) *macacol* = neck crusher>

mach·i·nate (mak′ə nāt′) *v* **mach·i·nat·ed, mach·i·nat·ing** plan or plot, especially with an evil purpose. <French, from Greek *mekhos*>
mach′i·na′tor *n.*

mach·i·na·tion (mak′ə nā′shən) *n* (*usually plural*) a secret or cunning scheme, especially one with an evil purpose: *He could not have been overthrown without the machinations of his enemies.*

ma·chine (mə shēn′) *n* **1** a device that uses energy to do a particular kind of work: *a sewing machine. Levers and pulleys are simple machines.* **2** produced by or with a machine, not by hand: *machine printing.* **3** a dispenser operated by inserting a coin or a card: *a coffee machine.* **4** a highly organized group of people, especially a group controlling a political organization: *the party machine.*
v **ma·chined, ma·chin·ing** make or finish by machine. <French, from Greek *mekhos*>

machine gun *n* a gun that fires bullets automatically and rapidly.

ma·chine–gun (mə shēn′gun′) *v* **ma·chine-gunned, ma·chine-gun·ning** fire at with a machine gun.

machine language *Computers n* a coding system that assigns storage locations in a computer and that allows the computer to operate immediately with no translation of characters or numbers.

machine readable *Computers adj* readable and usable as text or data by a computer.

ma·chin·er·y (mə shē′nə rē) *n, pl* **ma·chin·er·ies** **1** machines: *There is a lot of machinery in a shoe factory.*

2 the parts or works of a machine: *She examined the machinery of her watch.* **3** a combination of people or things by which something is kept going or something is done: *Police officers, judges, courts, and prisons are the machinery of the law.*

machine shop *n* a workshop where machines or parts of machines are made or repaired.

ma·chin·ist (mə shē′nist) *n* a person skilled in using machine tools or in running machines, or who makes and repairs machinery.

ma·chis·mo (mo kēz′mō) *n* an exaggerated or aggressive effort to appear masculine. <Spanish, from Latin *masculus* male>

Mach number (mák) *n* a number for the ratio of the speed of an object to the speed of sound in the same medium. Mach 1 is the speed of sound, Mach 2 is twice the speed of sound, and Mach 0.5 is half the speed of sound.

ma·cho (má′chō) *adj* masculine in an exaggerated way: *a macho swagger.*
n a man who is proudly or aggressively masculine. <Spanish, from Latin *masculus* male>

mack·er·el (mak′ə rəl) *n, pl* **mack·er·els** or (*especially collectively*) **mack·er·el** a saltwater fish of the N Atlantic Ocean, much used for food. <Old French *maquerel*>

mackerel sky *n* a sky spotted with small, white, fleecy clouds like the scales on a mackerel.

mack·i·naw (mak′ə no′) *n* **1** a short coat made of heavy woollen cloth. **2** a thick woollen blanket that often has wide bands of colour. **3** a large, heavy, flat-bottomed boat, formerly used in the region of the Upper Lakes.

ETYMOLOGY

Mackinaw comes from the original name of Mackinac Island in Lake Huron: *Michilimackinac.* That name came from an Ojibwa word meaning "large turtle" because the centre of the island resembled a turtle's back.

mack·in·tosh (mak′ən tosh′) *n* a full-length waterproof coat, or the cloth from which this coat is made. Also, **macintosh**. <after C. *MacIntosh*, 19c chemist who invented a method of waterproofing cloth>

mac·ra·mé (mak′rə mā′) *or* (mak′rə mā′) *n* **1** a heavy, coarse lace or fringe made by knotting twine or cord in decorative patterns: *She liked to make macramé wall hangings.* **2** the art of making such lace or fringes: *a course in macramé.* <French, from Arabic *migramah* striped cloth>

mac·ro (ma′krō) *Computers n* a set of detailed instructions that can be activated by a single instruction such as a keystroke.

macro– *combining form* large: *macrocosm.* Compare MICRO-. <Greek *makros*>

mac·ro·cosm (mak′rə koz′əm) *n* the universe or cosmos.

mac·ro·e·co·nom·ics (mak′rō ek′ə nom′iks) *or* (mak′rō ēk′ə nom′iks) *n* (*with singular verb*) the study of general economic factors in a country as a whole. Compare MICROECONOMICS.

ma·cron (mak′ron) *or* (mā′kron) *n* a short, horizontal line placed over a vowel letter to identify a sound that is a long vowel, or a stressed vowel in verse. Example: ā <Greek *macros* long>

mac·u·lar degeneration (mak′yə lər) *n* deterioration of the central part of the retina of the eye, causing lack of clear vision. <Latin *macula* spot>

mad (mad) *adj* **mad·der, mad·dest 1** insane: *He must be mad to hurt himself on purpose.* **2** *Informal* very angry: *The insult made her mad.* **3** much excited or wild: *The dog made mad efforts to catch up with the automobile.* **4** foolish or very unwise: *a mad undertaking.* **5** blindly and unreasonably fond: *Some people are mad about video games.* <Old English *gemad*>
like mad, *Informal* very hard or fast: *I ran like mad to catch the school bus.*
mad as a hatter, completely crazy.

GRAMMAR AND USAGE

Mad, **crazy**, and **insane** have been used as labels for people with mental illness. These words are increasingly perceived as insulting; phrasings such as *a person with schizophrenia* are preferred.

Mad·a·gas·car (mad ə gas′kər) *n* an island country in the Indian Ocean, near the coast of Africa.
Mad·a·gas′can *adj, n.*

mad·am (mad′əm) *n, pl* **mad·ams** or **mes·dames** (mā dam′) **1** (*used alone, not with a name*) a polite or formal title used in speaking to a woman: *The line is busy, madam. Would you care to hold?* **2** a formal title for a woman used before the name of her rank or office: *Madam Chair, Madam Prime Minister.* **3** a woman who runs a brothel. <Old French *ma dame* my lady>

Mad·ame (mad′əm) *n, pl* **Mes·dames** (mā dám′) **1** a French title for a married woman. **2** a title sometimes used by women in the arts. *Abbrev.* **Mme**

mad·cap (mad′kap′) *adj* impulsive, wild, or foolish: *a madcap escapade.*
n a person who habitually does impulsive, wild, or foolish things. <*mad* + *cap* head>

mad cow disease *n* a fatal viral disease of cattle that affects the nervous system and can be transmitted to humans through animal products. Its scientific name is **bovine spongiform encephalopathy**, usually abbreviated to **BSE**.

mad·den (mad′ən) *v* **1** make insane. **2** make very angry or excited.

made (mād) *adj* **1** built or formed: *a strongly made swing.* **2** specially prepared: *made gravy, a made dish.* **3** *Informal* certain of success: *When he won the lottery, he thought he had it made.*
v past tense of MAKE.

M

a bat	e bed	i bid	o pot	u cup	th thin
ā cake	ē me	ī bite	ō go	ū rude	TH then
á bar	ə about	ər over	ò for	ù put	zh measure

Mad·e·moi·selle (mad′ə mə zel′) *n, pl* **Mes·de·moi·selles** (mād mwȧ zel′) a French title for an unmarried woman. *Abbrev.* **Mlle.**

made–to–meas·ure (mād′tū me′zhər) *adj* made to a buyer's own measurements or exact requirements: *a made-to-measure suit.*

made–to–or·der (mād′tū or′dər) *adj* 1 made-to-measure. 2 **made to order** ideally suited for some purpose: *The weather seemed made to order for our pool party.*

made–up (mā′dup′) *adj* 1 invented, not true: *a made-up story.* 2 wearing cosmetics: *made-up lips.* 3 put together or arranged.

mad·house (mad′hous′) *n* 1 in former times, a hospital for the insane. 2 a place of uproar and confusion: *The arena was a madhouse after the home team won the championship game.*

Mad·i·son Avenue (mad′i sən) *n* the American advertising industry, including its techniques, language, influence, and images. <after the name of a street in New York City where many advertising agencies are located>

mad·ly (mad′lē) *adv* 1 suggesting insanity: *Her only response was to glare madly at me.* 2 in an uncontrolled way: *My heart beat madly when I heard the news.*

mad·man (mad′man′) *or* (mad′mən) *n, pl* **mad·men** (-men′) *or* (-mən) a man who is insane or behaves like someone who is insane.

mad·ness (mad′nis) *n* 1 the condition of being insane: *In his madness, he struck his best friend.* 2 extreme foolishness: *It was madness to take a sailboat out in that storm.*

Ma·don·na (mə do′nə) *Christianity n* 1 **the Madonna** Mary, the mother of Jesus. 2 a picture or statue of her. <Italian *ma* my + *donna* my lady>

Madonna lily *n* a garden lily with large, white, trumpet-shaped flowers.

mad·ras (məd ras′) *n* lightweight cotton or silk fabric in a plain weave, usually with brightly coloured woven stripes, checks, or plaids: *a madras shirt.* <*Madras,* city in S India where this type of cloth was made>

ma·dra·sa (mə dras′ə) *Islam n* a school or college for instruction in Islamic subjects. <Arabic *darasa* to study>

mad·ri·gal (mad′rə gəl) *n* a song with parts for several voices, sung without instrumental accompaniment. <Italian>

mad·wo·man (mad′wu̇m′ən) *n, pl* **mad·wo·men** (-wim′ən) a woman who is insane or behaves like someone who is insane.

mael·strom (māl′strəm) *n* 1 a powerful whirlpool in a sea or river. 2 a violent confusion of feelings, ideas, or events. <Dutch *maalen* whirl around + *stroom* stream>

maes·tro (mī′strō) *n, pl* **maes·tros** 1 a great musician, especially a conductor or performer of classical music. 2 a great or distinguished figure in any art. <Italian, from Latin *magister* master>

Ma·fi·a (mȧ′fē ə) *n* 1 an international secret organization of criminals, chiefly active in Italy, the US, and Canada. 2 **mafia** a similar organization of criminals operating in a specific country: *the Russian mafia.* <Italian = boldness>

ma·fi·o·so (mȧ′fē ō′sō) *n, pl* **ma·fi·o·si** (mȧ′fē ō′sē) a member of a mafia or the Mafia.

mag·a·zine (mag′ə zēn′) *or* (mag′ə zēn′) *n* 1 a publication issued at regular intervals, especially weekly or monthly, that contains a variety of texts and illustrations by various contributors. 2 a room in a fort or warship for keeping gunpowder and other explosives. 3 a place for storing goods or supplies, such as a warehouse or military supply depot. 4 a holder for cartridges to be fed into a gun. <French, from Arabic *kazana* store up>

Ma·gen Da·vid (mō′gən dā′vid) *Judaism n* Star of David.

ma·gen·ta (mə jen′tə) *n* a light purplish red dye.
adj light purplish red. <Battle of *Magenta,* Italy. The dye was discovered soon after the battle was fought.>

mag·got (mag′ət) *n* a soft-bodied fly or other insect in the earliest, legless stage, found in decaying matter. <Old Norse *mathkr*>

Ma·gi (ma′jī) *pln, sing* **Ma·gus** (mā′gəs) the wise men, later called kings, who travelled from the East to bring gifts to the baby Jesus, as told in the Bible. <Latin, from Persian *magus*>

mag·ic (maj′ik) *n* 1 **a** the apparent power to change the course of events or create supernatural effects by the use of mysterious charms, spells, and actions. **b** the use of tricks of this kind, such as making things disappear, as a form of entertainment. 2 something that produces results as if by some unexplained power: *the magic of music.*
adj 1 made or done as if by magic: *A magic palace stood in place of their hut.* 2 with supernatural powers: *a magic wand.* 3 producing a feeling of rapture or enchantment: *magic moments.* <Old French, from Persian *magus*>

mag·i·cal (maj′ə kəl) *adj* 1 used in, or done apparently by magic. 2 mysterious and unexplained. 3 romantic; wonderful. **mag′i·cal·ly** *adv.*

ma·gi·cian (mə jish′ən) *n* 1 a person who has supposedly magical powers. 2 a person skilled in the use of magic tricks to entertain: *The magician pulled three rabbits out of his hat.*

magic square *n* a square array of numbers such that the sum of each row, column, or diagonal is the same

mag·is·te·ri·al (maj′i stē′rē əl) *adj* 1 of or suited to a magistrate: *A judge has magisterial rank.* 2 showing authority: *The captain spoke with a magisterial voice.* 3 domineering or overbearing. **mag′is·te′ri·al·ly** *adv.*

mag·is·tra·cy (maj′i strə sē) *n, pl* **mag·is·tra·cies** 1 the position, rank, or duties of a magistrate. 2 magistrates as a group.

mag·is·trate (maj′i strāt′) *n* a government official appointed to hear and decide cases in a magistrate's court or similar lower court. <Latin *magister* master>

mag·ma (mag′mə) *n, pl* **magmas** the very hot, fluid substance that is found below the earth's crust and from which lava and igneous rocks are formed. <Latin, from Greek *magma* an ointment>

Mag·na Car·ta or **Mag·na Char·ta** (mag′nə kår′tə) *n* the document guaranteeing the liberties of the people of England, forcibly secured from King John by the English barons at Runnymede in 1215. <Latin = great charter>

mag·na cum lau·de (mag′nə ku̇m′lou′dā) with high honours. <Latin = with great praise>

mag·nan·i·mous (mag nan′ə məs) *adj* generous and forgiving. <Latin *magnus* great + *animus* spirit> **mag′na·nim′i·ty** *n.* **mag·nan′i·mous·ly** *adv.*

mag·nate (mag′nāt) *n* an important or powerful person, especially in business or industry: *an oil magnate.* <Latin *magnus* great>

mag·ne·sia (mag nē′zhə), (mag nē′zē ə), *or* (mag nē′shə) *n* magnesium oxide, used as an antacid and laxative. <Latin, from Greek *Magnesia* a mineral from Magnesia, ancient city in Asia Minor>

mag·ne·si·um (mag nē′zē əm) *or* (mag nē′zhē əm) *n* a light, silver-white metallic element that burns with a dazzling white light. *Symbol* **Mg** <See MAGNESIA.>

mag·net (mag′nit) *n* **1** a piece, ore, or alloy of iron that attracts another such material to it or aligns itself in a magnetic field. **2** something that strongly attracts: *The rabbits in our backyard were a magnet that attracted all the children in the neighbourhood.* <Old French, from Greek *magnes lithos* magnet>

mag·net·ic (mag net′ik) *adj* **1** with the properties of a magnet: *the magnetic needle of a compass.* **2** to do with the earth's magnetism: *the magnetic meridian.* **3** attractive: *a magnetic personality.* **mag·net′i·cal·ly** *adv.*

magnetic declination *n* the deviation of a compass needle from true north or south. Also called **magnetic deviation**, **magnetic variation**.

magnetic disk DISK (def. 1).

magnetic field *n* the region of magnetic influence or force around a magnet, a magnetic body such as the earth, or a body carrying an electric current.

magnetic north *n* the direction in which the north end of a compass needle or other freely suspended magnet points in response to the earth's magnetic field.

magnetic pole *n* **1** one of the two slightly shifting points on the earth where the lines of the earth's magnetic field converge and toward which a magnetic needle points. The **north magnetic pole** is about at 71°N 95°W. The **south magnetic pole** is about at 72°S 154°E. **2** one of the two poles of a magnet.

magnetic resonance imaging MRI.

magnetic tape *n* a plastic ribbon coated on one side with a substance that magnetizes easily, used for recording sounds, pictures, or computer data by electromagnetic means.

mag·net·ism (mag′nə tiz′əm) *n* **1** the physical property by which one object is attracted or repelled by another. **2** the power to strongly attract or charm: *The hero's magnetism won him many friends and admirers.*

mag·net·ize (mag′nə tīz′) *v* **mag·net·ized, mag·net·iz·ing 1** give the properties of a magnet to: *The electric current in the coil around the iron bar magnetized the bar.* **2** attract or influence like a magnet: *Her beautiful voice magnetized the audience.* <Old French, from Greek *magnes lithos* magnet> **mag′net·iz′a·ble** *adj.* **mag′net·i·za′tion** *n.* **mag′net·iz′er** *n.*

mag·ne·to (mag nē′tō) *n, pl* **mag·ne·tos** a small electric generator that uses a magnetic field to produce an electric current. In some engines, a magneto supplies an electric spark to explode the gasoline vapour.

mag·ne·tom·e·ter (mag′nə tom′ə tər) *n* an instrument used to measure magnetic forces, especially the earth's magnetic field. **mag′ne·tom′e·try** *n.*

mag·ne·to·sphere (mag nē′tə sfēr′) *n* the region surrounding the earth in which ionized particles are controlled by the earth's magnetic field.

mag·ni·fi·ca·tion (mag′nə fi kā′shən) *n* **1** the act of magnifying. **2** a magnified condition. **3** the degree to which something is magnified.

mag·nif·i·cent (mag nif′ə sənt) *adj* **1** richly coloured or decorated: *a magnificent palace.* **2** impressive, noble, or exalted: *magnificent words, magnificent ideas.* **3** extraordinarily fine: *a magnificent view of the mountains.* <Old French, from Latin *magnus* great> **mag·nif′i·cence** *n.* **mag·nif′i·cent·ly** *adv.*

SYNONYMS

Magnificent means "splendid" or "very fine": *She wore a magnificent diamond necklace.*

Grand suggests having a fine appearance and being large: *The grand oak table could seat twelve.*

Majestic means "grand, noble, and dignified": *All eyes watched the majestic prince make his entrance.*

mag·ni·fi·er (mag′nə fī′ər) *n* a person or thing that magnifies, especially a lens or combination of lenses that makes things appear larger than they really are.

mag·ni·fy (mag′nə fī′) *v* **mag·ni·fied, mag·ni·fy·ing 1** cause to look larger than the actual size: *A microscope magnifies things to many times their real size.* **2** exaggerate: *She not only tells tales on him, but she magnifies them.* <Old French, from Latin *magnus* great + *facere* make>

magnifying glass *n* a lens or combination of lenses that makes things look larger than they really are.

mag·ni·tude (mag′nə tyüd′) *or* (mag′nə tüd′) *n* **1** the great size or extent of something: *The magnitude of the flood was not as great as they had feared.* **2** great importance or effect: *You don't understand the magnitude of what you've done.* **3** a measure of the brightness of a star: *Stars of the first magnitude are the brightest.* <Latin *magnus* large>

mag·no·lia (mag nō′lē ə) *or* (mag nō′lyə) *n* a shrub or tree with simple leaves and large flowers that bloom in early spring. <P. *Magnol*, 17c botanist>

mag·num o·pus (mag′nəm ō′pəs) *n* a great work of literature, music, or art, especially the greatest work of a particular artist or writer. <Latin = great work>

a bat	e bed	i bid	o pot	u cup	th **thin**
ā cake	ē me	ī bite	ō go	ü rude	TH **then**
å bar	ə about	ər over	ȯ for	u̇ put	zh measure

mag·pie (mag′pī) *n* a noisy, black-and-white crow with a long tail, supposedly fond of collecting bright objects. <probably Middle English>

Mag·yar (mag′yȧr); *Hungarian,* (mod′yor) *n* **1** a member of a people that make up most of the population of Hungary. **2** the Hungarian language.
adj to do with the Magyars or their language.

ma·ha·ra·jah or **ma·ha·ra·ja** (mȧ′hə rȧ′jə) *n* in former times, the title of certain ruling princes in India, or a man holding this title. <Hindi, from Sanskrit *maha* great + *rajan* king>

ma·ha·ra·ni or **ma·ha·ra·nee** (mȧ′hə rȧ′nē) *n* the wife or widow of a maharajah. <Hindi, from Sanskrit *maha* great + *rajni* queen>

ma·ha·ri·shi or **Ma·ha·ri·shi** (mȧ′hə rē′shi) *Hinduism n* a wise spiritual leader, or a title given to such a person. <Hindi, from Sanskrit *maha* great + *rsi* wise person>

ma·hat·ma (mə hat′mə) *n* in the Indian subcontinent, a person who is regarded as exceptionally wise or holy. <Sanskrit *maha* great + *atman* soul>

Ma·ha·vi·ra (mə hȧ′vē′rə) *n* the chief founder of the Jain religion, a contemporary of Buddha.

Ma·ha·ya·na (mȧ′hə yȧ′nə) *n* one of two major branches of Buddhism, practised in various forms. Compare THERAVADA.

Mah·di (mȧ′dē) *n, pl* **Mah·dis** **1** a leader expected by some Muslims to rule before the end of the world and restore religion and justice. **2** a person claiming to be this leader. <Arabic *hada* to guide>

Ma·hi·can (mə hē′kən) *n, pl* **Ma·hi·can** or **Ma·hi·cans** **1** in former times, a member of a confederacy of Aboriginal peoples living in the northeastern US. **2** their Algonquian language.
adj to do with these people or their language. Also, **Mohican**.

mah–jong or **mah–jongg** (mȧ′jong′) *n* a game of Chinese origin usually played by four people and using rectangular pieces called tiles. <Cantonese *ma-tsiang,* sparrows, from the image on one tile>

ma·hog·a·ny (mə hog′ə nē) *n, pl* **ma·hog·a·nies** the hard, reddish brown wood of a large tropical evergreen tree.
adj dark reddish brown. <origin uncertain>

maid (mād) *n* **1** a woman servant: *a kitchen maid.* **2** *Archaic or Poetic* a young unmarried woman. **3 the Maid** Joan of Arc (1412–1431), a French heroine who led armies against the invading English. <*maiden*>

maid·en (mā′dən) *Archaic or Poetic n* a young unmarried woman.
adj **1** *Archaic or Poetic* to do with a maiden: *maiden blushes.* **2** unmarried: *a maiden aunt.* **3** first as an attempt or act of its kind: *a ship's maiden voyage.* <Old English *mægden*> **maid′en·li·ness** *n.* **maid′en·ly** *adj.*

maid·en·hair (mā′dən her′) *n* a chiefly tropical fern with very slender stalks and delicate, finely divided fronds. Also, **maidenhair fern**.

maid·en·hood (mā′dən hu̇d′) *n* the condition or time of being a maiden.

maiden name *n* a woman's surname before her marriage. The term **birth name** is often preferred.

maid of honour or **honor** *n* **1** an unmarried woman who is the main bridesmaid at a wedding. **2** an unmarried woman who attends a queen or a princess.

maid·serv·ant (mād′sər′vənt) *n* in former times, a female servant.

mail[1] (māl) *n* **1** letters, postcards, papers, parcels, or messages sent or to be sent by post or electronic means. **2** a system by which such items are sent or received. **3** all that arrives by one post or delivery: *He opened the box to look for the mail.*
v send by mail: *I mailed your birthday card yesterday.* <Old French *male* traveling bag>

mail[2] (māl) *n* **1** flexible armour made of metal rings, loops of chain, or small plates linked together. **2** the hard, protective covering of some animals, such as turtles. <Old French, from Latin *macula* mesh>

mail·box (māl′boks′) *n* **1** a public box for depositing outgoing mail that is to be collected by the post office. **2** a private box from which a holder can collect mail. **3** the part of an e-mail program where incoming messages are stored.

mail carrier LETTER CARRIER.

mailed (māld) *adj* covered or protected with MAIL[2].

mail·er (mā′lər) *n* **1** a person who mails a letter or package. **2** a container in which something may be mailed: *Cylindrical mailers are often used for maps and posters.* **3** an advertising pamphlet or flyer mailed inside an envelope.

mailing list *n* a list of names and addresses of people to whom newsletters, advertising, or catalogues are sent regularly, either by mail or e-mail: *Please forward this e-mail to everyone on your mailing list.*

mail order *n* an order for goods sent by mail.
adj **mail-order** to do with mail orders or a business that operates by mail.

maim (mām) *v* cause permanent damage to or loss of a part of the body: *He lost two toes in the accident, but we were glad that he was not more seriously maimed.* <Old French *mahaignier*>

main (mān) *adj* most important or largest: *the main street of a town.*
n a large pipe for sending water or gas to buildings, or taking sewage from them. <Old English *mægen* strength>
by main force (or **strength**)**,** by using full strength.
in the main, chiefly or mostly: *Her grades were excellent in the main.*
with might and main, with all your force: *They argued with might and main.*

main clause *Grammar n* a unit made up of a subject and predicate and able to stand alone as a sentence. Example: *I am going home.* Compare SUBORDINATE CLAUSE. Also called **independent clause, principal clause**.

main drag *Informal n* the main street of a town or city.

main·frame (mān′frām′) *Computers adj* to do with a central computer of large capacity, serving numerous workstations or peripheral devices.
n a mainframe computer.

main·land (mān′land′) *or* (mān′lənd) *n* **1** the main part of a continent or land mass, excluding offshore islands. **2** 🍁 **the Mainland** *Newfoundland* **a** the provinces and territories of Canada other than Newfoundland. **b** Labrador. **3** 🍁 **the Mainland** *Cape Breton Island* the Nova Scotian peninsula. **4** 🍁 *British Columbia* LOWER MAINLAND.

main·line (mān′līn) *adj* **1** dominant or established: *the mainline churches.* **2** to do with the most important route or system of a railway or bus company.
v **main·lined, main·lin·ing** *Informal* inject a drug such as heroin directly into a major vein. **main′lin·er** *n.*

main·ly (mān′lē) *adv* chiefly or mostly: *He is interested mainly in sports and neglects his schoolwork.*

main·mast (mān′mast′) *or* (mān′məst) *n* the principal mast of a sailing ship, usually the second one from the bow.

main·sail (mān′sāl′) *or* (mān′səl) *n* the largest sail on the mainmast of a sailing ship.

main·spring (mān′spring′) *n* **1** the principal spring in a clock or watch. **2** the main cause, motive, or influence.

main·stay (mān′stā′) *n* **1** a supporting rope or wire extending from the top of the mainmast of a sailing ship to the foot of the foremast. **2** the main support: *His friends were his mainstay through his time of trouble.*

main·stream (mān′strēm′) *n* **1** the main current of a river. **2** the main trend or direction of a fashion, body of opinion, or activity: *She is not well known to the critics because her painting is outside the mainstream of modern art.*
v integrate a child or children with special needs into a regular class.
adj to do with the mainstream.

🍁 **main·street·ing** (mān′strēt′ing) *n* the practice, by a politician, of walking around the main streets of a town or city in order to meet and greet potential supporters.

main·tain (mān tān′) *v* **1** keep up or carry on: *to maintain a business, to maintain your composure.* **2** keep from failing or declining in quality: *He employs a mechanic to maintain his fleet of trucks.* **3** pay the expenses of or provide for: *She maintains a family of four.* **4** uphold or argue for: *to maintain an opinion. She maintains her innocence.* **main·tain′er** *n.*

ETYMOLOGY

Maintain comes through Old French *maintenir* from a Latin phrase *manu tenere*, meaning "hold by the hand."

main·te·nance (mān′tə nəns) *n* **1** maintaining or being maintained: *the maintenance of good government.* **2** keeping in good repair: *The army devotes much time to the maintenance of its equipment.* **3** the regular payment of money by one spouse to another after divorce or separation as a means of support, or to provide for children from the marriage. Compare ALIMONY.

mai·tre d′ (mā′tər dē′) *Informal n, pl* **mai·tre d′s** (mā′tər dēz′) a head waiter. <French *maître d'hôtel* master of the house>

maize (māz) *n* CORN[1].
adj bright yellow.

ma·jes·tic (mə jes′tik) *adj* grand, noble, and stately. **ma·jes′ti·cal·ly** *adv.*

maj·es·ty (maj′i stē) *n, pl* **maj·es·ties** **1** grandeur, nobility, and stateliness: *We were much impressed by the majesty of the coronation ceremony.* **2** the supreme power or authority: *Police officers and judges uphold the majesty of the law.* **3** **Majesty** a title used in speaking to or of a sovereign: *Your Majesty, His Majesty, Her Majesty.* <Old French, from Latin *magnus* great>

ma·jol·i·ca (mə jol′ə kə) *n* an enamelled Italian pottery richly decorated in colours. <Italian *Maiolica* Majorca>

ma·jor (mā′jər) *adj* **1** larger, greater, or more important: *Take the major share.* **2** of the first rank or order. **3** very serious or important: *a major disaster.* **4** *Music* **a** to do with a musical scale or mode with half steps between the third and fourth and between the seventh and eighth degree. **b** a major interval, key, scale, or chord: *The scale of C major has neither sharps nor flats.*
n **1** a commissioned officer in the armed forces, senior to a captain and junior to a lieutenant-colonel. **2** a person of the legal age of responsibility. **3** the subject or course of study to which a student gives most of his or her time and attention. **4** *Music* **a** a major scale, key, interval, or mode. **b** a chord containing a major third between the first and second notes and a minor third between the second and third notes. <Latin, comparative of *magnus* great>
major in, specialize in a subject or course of study: *to major in mathematics.*

ma·jor–do·mo (mā′jər dō′mō) *n, pl* **ma·jor-do·mos** a steward or butler in charge of a large household.

ma·jor·ette (mā jə ret′) in full, **drum majorette** one of a group of female baton twirlers, usually marching as part of a parade.

ma·jor·i·ty (mə jȯ′rə tē) *n, pl* **ma·jor·i·ties** **1** the larger number or greater part: *A majority of the students passed the test.* **2** in a contest involving two or more candidates, the number of votes cast for one candidate when that number is more than half the total number of votes for all candidates. Compare PLURALITY. **3** the legal age of responsibility.

GRAMMAR AND USAGE

Majority is used to talk about what can be counted: *The majority of students work hard.*

Most is used to talk about an amount that cannot be counted: *The twins shovelled most of the snow.*

major league *n* the highest ranking league in a professional sport.

major penalty *Hockey n* a five-minute penalty for breaking certain rules, such as fighting.

M

a bat	e bed	i bid	o pot	u cup	th thin
ā cake	ē me	ī bite	ō go	ū rude	TH then
ä bar	ə about	ər over	ȯ for	u̇ put	zh measure

make (māk) *v* **made, mak·ing** 1 bring into being, put together, or build: *to make a dessert, to make a poem, to make a boat.* 2 have the qualities needed for: *Wood makes a good fire. She will make a good doctor.* 3 cause or cause to be: *to make trouble, to make a room warm, to make a fool of yourself.* 4 force to: *He made me go.* 5 get ready for use or arrange: *to make a bed.* 6 obtain, acquire, or earn: *to make a fortune.* 7 do or perform: *to make an attempt, to make a mistake.* 8 amount to: *Two and two make four.* 9 think of as or estimate: *I make the distance across about five metres.* 10 cause the success of: *That one big deal made the young businesswoman.* 11 get on or get a place on: *I made the hockey team.* 12 win a trick or hand in card games.
n 1 the way in which a thing is made: *Do you like the make of that coat?* 2 a kind or brand: *What make of car is this?* <Old English *macian*>
make after, chase or run off after: *She checked to see that I was OK and then made after the thief.*
make away with, a get rid of. b kill. c steal: *The treasurer made away with the club's funds.*
make believe, pretend: *The little girl liked to make believe she was a princess.*
make fast, attach firmly.
make for, a go toward: *Make for the hills!* b rush at and attack. c help bring about: *Careful driving makes for fewer accidents.*
make fun of, mock or ridicule.
make good, a succeed. b prove: *Can you make good your claim?*
make good time, travel faster than might have been expected.
make it, *Informal* succeed.
make like, *Informal* a imitate: *to make like a dog.* b pretend or act as if: *She made like she was sorry, but she wasn't really.*
make off, run away.
make off with, steal or take without permission: *He made off with some apples.*
make or break, cause to succeed or fail.
make out, a write out: *I must make out an application for camp.* b show (to be) or try to prove: *That makes me out to be very selfish.* c understand: *I had a hard time making out the problem.* d see: *I can barely make out three ships near the horizon.* e *Informal* engage in sexual activity.
make over, a alter or make different: *to make over a room.* b hand over or transfer ownership of: *Grandfather made over his farm to my mother.*
make something of, a *Informal* start an argument or dispute: *So I'm a few minutes late; you want to make something of it?* b make something worthwhile out of: *Get a proper education and make something of yourself.*
make time, go fast.
make up, a put together: *to make up cloth into a dress.* b invent: *to make up a story.* c make satisfactory. d become friends again after a quarrel. e put cosmetics on the face. f complete, comprise, or fill out: *The committee is made up of students and teachers.*
make up for, give or do in place of: *make up for lost time.*
make up to, try to get the friendship of or flatter.
make up your mind, decide.
on the make, *Informal* ambitiously trying for success.

make–be·lieve (māk′bi lēv′) *n* imagination, especially that things are better than they actually are: *Goblins live in the land of make-believe.*
adj pretended or imagined: *Children often have make-believe playmates.*

make·ov·er (māk′ōv ər) *n* a transformation: *My bedroom had a complete makeover—new bed, new carpet, the works!*

mak·er (mā′kər) *n* 1 a person who or thing that makes. 2 **Maker** God.

make·shift (māk′shift′) *n* something used for a time in place of the proper thing: *When the power went off, we used candles as a makeshift.*
adj used for a time instead of the proper thing: *a makeshift tent made from a blanket.*

make·up (mā′kup′) *n* 1 the cosmetics put on the face, or that especially used by actors or other performers: *His makeup was so effective that we didn't recognize him.* 2 the way of being put together or the contents of something: *the makeup of a magazine.* 3 a person's nature or disposition: *a nervous makeup.* 4 a test or assignment given to a student who has missed or failed the original one.

make–work (māk′wərk′) *adj* 1 planned so as to provide jobs and so stimulate the economy: *The new highway was a government make-work project.* 2 to do with unnecessary work done or assigned in order to look or keep busy.
n work that serves either of these purposes.

mak·ing (mā′king) *n* 1 the cause of a person's success: *Early hardships were the making of him.* 2 the process of making or producing something. 3 **makings** *pl* ingredients or contributory factors.
in the making, in the process of being made.

mal– *combining form* bad or badly: *malnutrition, maltreat.* <Old French, from Latin *malus* bad>

mal·a·chite (mal′ə kīt′) *n* copper carbonate, used for making ornamental objects. <Latin, from Greek *malakhe* mallow, possibly from the similarity in colour between the mineral and the leaves of the mallow plant>

mal·ad·just·ed (mal′ə jus′tid) *adj* badly adjusted, especially not in harmony with the environment and conditions of life. **mal′ad·just′ment** *n.*

mal·a·droit (mal′ə droit′) *adj* unskilful or awkward. <French *mal* bad + *à droit* to the right> **mal′a·droit′ness** *n.*

mal·a·dy (mal′ə dē) *n, pl* **mal·a·dies** a sickness or disease: *an incurable malady.* <Old French, from Latin *male* ill + *habitus* having as a condition>

ma·laise (ma lāz′) *n* a vague discomfort or uneasiness: *a spiritual malaise.* <Old French *mal* bad + *aise* ease>

🍁 **mal·a·mute** (mal′ə myūt′) *n* a large, powerful dog with a heavy grey, black, and white coat, erect ears, and a tail that curls over the back. Also, **malemute.** <Inupiaq *Malimiut.* The breed was developed by a Yupik people of W Alaska.>

mal·a·prop·ism (mal′ə pro piz′əm) *n* a ridiculous example of a misuse of words, especially of words that sound alike. Example: The word *pineapple* in *He is the pineapple of politeness* should be the word *pinnacle.* <Mrs. *Malaprop,* a character in an 18c play, *The Rivals,* often used the wrong word.>

ma·lar·i·a (mə ler′ē ə) *n* a disease characterized by intermittent chills and fevers, caused by minute parasites in the red blood cells, often transmitted by the bite of mosquitoes in tropical or subtropical regions.

ETYMOLOGY

Malaria comes from Italian *mal'aria,* a shortening of *mala aria,* meaning "bad air," since the disease was once thought to be caused by bad air coming from swamps.

ma·lar·i·al (mə ler′ē əl) *adj* with, causing, or like malaria.

ma·lar·key (mə lar′kē) *Informal n* nonsense. <origin uncertain>

ma·la·thi·on (mal′ə thī′ən) *n* a powerful synthetic insecticide, recognizable by its pungent smell.

Ma·la·wi (mə la′wē) *n* a country in south central Africa. **Ma·la′wi·an** *adj, n.*

Ma·lay·sia (mə lā′zhə) *n* a country in southeast Asia. See the APPENDIX. **Ma·lay′sian** *adj, n.*

mal·con·tent (mal′kən tent′) *adj* discontented or rebellious.
n a discontented or rebellious person.

Mal·dives (mal′dīvz) *or* (mol′dīvz) *n* a country of several islands in the Indian Ocean. **Mal·div′i·an** (mal dīv′i ən) *or* (mol dīv′i ən) *adj, n.*

male (māl) *adj* **1** belonging to the sex that fertilizes the eggs of a female to produce young. **2** to do with men and boys: *a male contraceptive.* **3** *Botany* with stamens and no pistils. **4** with a part or connection in a machine that projects into a corresponding cavity or hollow part.
n a male person, animal, or plant. <Old French, from Latin *mas* male>

male chauvinist *n* a man who believes women are inferior and treats them as if they were.
male chauvinism *n.*

mal·e·dic·tion (mal′ə dik′shən) *n* a curse, especially a magical word or phrase intended to bring harm to the person being cursed. <Latin *male* ill + *dicere* speak>

mal·e·fac·tor (mal′ə fak′tər) *n* a criminal or evildoer. <Latin *male* ill + *facere* do>

mal·e·mute (mal′ə myūt′) MALAMUTE.

ma·lev·o·lent (mə lev′ə lənt) *adj* with or showing a wish to do harm to others: *a malevolent smile.* <Latin *male* ill + *velle* to wish> **ma·lev′o·lence** *n.* **ma·lev′o·lent·ly** *adv.*

mal·fea·sance (mal fē′zəns) *n* misconduct, especially by a public official. <Old French *mal-* evil + *faisance* activity>

mal·for·ma·tion (mal′fȯr mā′shən) *n* an irregular, faulty, or abnormal shape or structure: *a congenital malformation.* **mal·formed′** *adj.*

mal·func·tion (mal′fungk′shən) *n* a failure in functioning properly: *a body malfunction, a malfunction in a machine.*
v function poorly.

Ma·li (ma′lē) *n* a country in west Africa. **Mal′i·an** *adj, n.*

mal·ic acid (mal′ik) *n* an acid found in unripe apples and other fruits.

mal·ice (mal′is) *n* **1** a wish to do harm to others. **2** *Law* an intent to commit an act that will result in harm to another person. <Old French, from Latin *malus* bad>

ma·li·cious (mə lish′əs) *adj* wishing to do harm to others: *a malicious telltale, malicious gossip.* **ma·li′cious·ly** *adv.*

ma·lign (mə līn′) *v* speak about someone critically and spitefully.
adj evil or injurious: *He said that gambling often has a malign influence.* <Old French, from Latin *malus* bad> **ma·lign′er** *n.*

ma·lig·nan·cy (mə lig′nən sē) *n* **1** the condition or presence of a malignant tumour, or the tumour itself. **2** the quality of being malign or malevolent.

ma·lig·nant (mə lig′nənt) *adj* **1** tending to grow and spread as a tumour or cyst, causing harm to healthy tissues around it. Compare BENIGN (def. 1). **2** infectious and dangerous: *malignant cholera.* **3** malevolent. **ma·lig′nan·cy** *n.* **ma·lig′nant·ly** *adv.*

ma·lin·ger (mə ling′gər) *v* pretend to be sick in order to escape work or duty. <French *malingrer* to suffer, from *malingre* sickly> **ma·lin′ger·er** *n.*

Mal·i·seet (mal′ə sēt′) *n, pl* **Mal·i·seet** or **Mal·i·seets** **1** a member of a First Nations people living in New Brunswick and eastern Québec. **2** their Algonquian language.
adj to do with these people or their language.

mall (mol) *n* in full, **shopping mall** a concentration of retail stores, usually in a suburban residential district, built as a single unit and with ample parking. Also called **shopping centre**. <*The Mall,* a street full of stores, in London, England>

The **mallard** is a hardy duck that is able to thrive in urban areas as well as wetlands. Despite its adaptability, its numbers are shrinking because of loss of habitat.

mal·lard (mal′ərd) *n, pl* **mal·lards** or (*especially collectively*) **mal·lard** a wild duck of the northern hemisphere, the male of which has a greenish black head and a white band around its neck. <Old French *masle* male>

mal·le·a·ble (mal′ē ə bəl) *adj* **1** capable of being hammered or pressed into various shapes without being broken. **2** adaptable or easily influenced: *a malleable person.* <Old French, from Latin *malleus* hammer> **mal′le·a·bil′i·ty** *n.*

a bat	e bed	i bid	o pot	u cup	th **thin**
ā cake	ē me	ī bite	ō go	ū rude	TH **then**
à bar	ə about	ər over	ȯ for	u̇ put	zh measure

mal·let (mal′it) *n* **1** a hammer with a head of wood, rubber, or plastic. **2** a long-handled wooden mallet used to play croquet or polo. <Old French, from Latin *malleus* hammer>

mal·le·us (mal′ē əs) See HAMMER (def. 3). <Latin = hammer>

mal·low (mal′ō) *n* a flowering plant with lobed leaves, hairy stems, and disc-shaped fruit. <Old English, from Latin *malva*>

mall rat *Slang n* a person, especially a young person, who spends a lot of time loitering in malls.

mal·nu·tri·tion (mal′nyə trish′ən) *or* (mal′nə trish′ən) *n* poor nourishment, such as from eating the wrong kinds of foods or from eating too little.

mal·o·dor·ous (mal′ō′də rəs) *adj* smelling bad. **mal·o′dor·ous·ly** *adv.*

mal·peque (mal pēk′) *n* a variety of oyster found in Malpeque Bay, Prince Edward Island.

mal·prac·tice (mal′prak′tis) *n* criminal neglect or unethical conduct by a doctor, lawyer, or public official.

malt (molt) *n* **1** barley or other grain that is soaked in water until it sprouts and is then dried and aged, used in brewing beer, distilling whisky, or making vinegar. **2** in full, **malted milk** a sweet, cold drink made from milk, powdered malted cereal and sometimes ice cream and flavouring. **3** whisky made from malted barley and not blended with other spirits.
v change or be changed into malt. <Old English *mealt*>

Mal·ta (mol′ tə) *n* an island country in the Mediterranean. **Mal·tese′** (mol tēz′) *adj, n.*

mal·tase (mol′tās) *n* a digestive enzyme in saliva and pancreatic juice that catalyzes maltose into sugar.

Maltese cross a cross with triangular arms that taper toward the centre.

malt extract *n* a sugary substance obtained by soaking malt in water.

malt·ose (mol′tōs) *n* a sugar made by the action of breaking down starch, for example, in malt or saliva.

mal·treat (mal trēt′) *v* treat roughly or cruelly: *to maltreat an animal.* **mal·treat′ment** *n.*

ma·ma or **mam·ma** (mom′ə) *or* (mä′mə) *n* a mother. <imitative of an infant's first syllables>

mam·ba (mäm′ba) *n* a long, slender, poisonous snake of central and S Africa that belongs to the same family as the cobras and coral snakes. <Zulu *inamba*>

mam·bo (mäm′bō) *or* (mam′bō) *n* a Latin American ballroom dance, or the music for such a dance. <Haitian Creole, from Yoruba = to talk>

mam·mal (mam′əl) *n* a warm-blooded vertebrate animal, the females of which typically give birth to live young and have glands that produce milk for feeding them. <Latin *mamma* breast> **mam·ma′li·an** (ma mā′lē ən) *adj.*

mam·ma·ry (mam′ə rē) *adj* to do with a milk-giving gland in female mammals. <Latin *mamma* breast>

mam·mo·gram (mam′ə gram′) *n* an X-ray of the breasts, used for early detection of tumours. <Latin *mamma* breast + *gram* something recorded>

Mam·mon or **mam·mon** (mam′ən) *n* material wealth or possessions thought of as an evil influence or false object of worship. <Latin, from Aramaic *mamon* riches>

mam·moth (mam′əth) *n* a large extinct elephant that had a hairy hide and long, curved tusks.
adj gigantic: *a mammoth undertaking.* <Russian *mamont*>

man (man) *n, pl* **men** (men) **1** an adult male human. **2** (*The use of "man" to represent "human being" is generally considered sexist.*) human beings, or an individual human being: *the history of man. All men share certain qualities.* **3** male adults in general: *The man of today likes to travel.* **4** a male person associated with a particular place, activity, or occupation: *the furnace man.* **5** a male follower, servant, or employee: *the story of Robin Hood and his merry men.* **6** one of the playing pieces used in games such as chess and checkers.
v **manned, man·ning** (*The use of "man" as a verb may be considered sexist.*) provide someone for a job or task, or supply with personnel or a crew: *We can man ten ships.* <Old English *mann*>

GRAMMAR AND USAGE

Man used to be used generically to mean "all people" (both men and women). Today, many people consider this generic use of *man,* and similar words such as *mankind* and *man-made*, to be offensive. Non-sexist words like *person*, *people*, and *humankind* are preferred.

man·a·cle (man′ə kəl) *n* a handcuff or other restraint.
v **man·a·cled, man·a·cling** put handcuffs or other restraints on: *The pirates manacled their prisoners.* <Old French, from Latin *manus* hand>

man·age (man′ij) *v* **man·aged, man·ag·ing** **1** control or direct: *to manage a horse.* **2** be in charge and run a business, organization, or project. **3** succeed in accomplishing: *I finally managed to get the job done.* **4** make the most of your resources: *to manage on your income.* <Italian, from Latin *manus*>

man·age·a·ble (man′i jə bəl) *adj* able to be managed. **man′age·a·bil′i·ty** *n.* **man′age·a·bly** *adv.*

man·age·ment (man′ij mənt) *n* **1** control, handling, or direction: *The new store failed because of bad management.* **2** the people that manage a business, organization, or project: *The management of the store decided to keep it open every evening.* **3** *Medicine* the treatment or control of diseases, injuries, or disorders.

management consultant *n* an expert who can be hired to examine the operations of a company and advise on planning, organization, and the use of resources.

management information system MIS.

man·ag·er (man′i jər) *n* **1** a person who manages activity, time, or money: *My sister is a good manager of her time, and always finishes her homework before I do.* **2** a person in an executive position in a business or organization: *the manager of the theatre.* **3** a person who directs the activities of a sports team, athlete, or entertainer.

man·a·ge·ri·al (man′ə jē′rē əl) *adj* to do with management or a manager.

ma·ña·na (mon yo′nə) *n, adv* some indefinite time in the future. <Spanish = tomorrow>

man–at–arms (man′ət ȧrmz′) *n, pl* **men-at-arms** (men′) in former times, a soldier, especially one who was heavily armed and mounted on horseback.

man·a·tee (man′ə tē′) *n* a large sea mammal with two flippers and a flat, oval tail, living in warm, shallow water near the tropical coasts of the Atlantic. Manatees are often referred to informally as **sea cows**. <Spanish, from Carib (a group of languages of the Caribbean) *manati*>

Man·chu (man′chū) *n, pl* **Man·chu** or **Man·chus** a member of an Asiatic people, originally living in Manchuria, who ruled China from 644 CE to 1912.
adj to do with the Manchu.

man·da·rin[1] (man′də rin) *n* a small, sweet orange with a thin, very loose peel. <French *mandarine*>

man·da·rin[2] (man′də rin) *n* **1** in former times, an official of high rank in the Chinese Empire. **2** a person of high position whose work is not publicized but who has, or is thought to have, considerable influence. **3 Mandarin** the standard literary and official language of modern China. <Portuguese, from Hindi *mantri* counsellor>

man·date (man′dāt) *or* (man′dit) *n* **1** a command or official order. **2** an order from a higher court or official to a lower one. **3** a direction or authority given to a government by the votes of the people in an election: *The prime minister said he had a mandate to increase taxes.* **4** in former times, a commission given to one nation by a group of nations to administer a territory.
v **man·dat·ed, man·dat·ing 1** give a person, group, or nation authority to act in a certain way. **2** require something to be done: *Regulations mandated helmets for all cyclists.* <Latin *manus* hand + *dare* give>

man·da·to·ry (man′də tȯ′rē) *adj* required by or conveying a law, command, or order.

man·di·ble (man′də bəl) *n* **1** a member of the foremost pair of mouth parts of an insect, spider, or lobster, adapted for seizing and biting. **2** the upper or lower part of the beak of a bird or of a beaked animal such as an octopus. **3** the jaw of a vertebrate, especially the lower jaw. <Old French, from Latin *mandere* chew>

man·do·lin (man′də lin′) *or* (man′də lin′) *n* a musical instrument with a pear-shaped body and metal strings, played with a plectrum. <French, from Greek *pandoura* three-stringed instrument>

man·drake (man′drāk) *n* a Mediterranean plant of the nightshade family with a very short stem and a thick root, formerly used in medicine and in magic spells. <possibly Dutch, from Greek *mandragoras*>

man·drill (man′drəl) *n* a large African baboon that has a brightly coloured red and blue face. The male has a blue rump. <*man* + *drill* W African baboon>

mane (mān) *n* the long, heavy hair growing on the back or around the neck of a horse, lion, or other animal. <Old English *manu*>

man–eat·ing (man′ēt ing) *adj* in a wild animal, acquiring a taste for human flesh.

ma·neu·ver (mə nū′vər) MANOEUVRE.

man·ful (man′fəl) *adj* with or showing courage and determination. **man′ful·ly** *adv.*

man·ga·nese (mang′gə nēz′) *n* a hard, brittle, greyish metallic element, used in making special steels and magnetic alloys. *Symbol* **Mn** <French, from Latin *magnesia*>

mange (mānj) *n* an itchy skin disease of mammals caused by parasitic mites, in which tiny scabs form and hair falls off in patches. <Old French, from Latin *mandere* to chew>

man·ger (mān′jər) *n* a box or trough in which hay or other food can be placed for horses or cattle to eat. <Old French, from Latin *mandere* to chew>

man·gle[1] (mang′gəl) *v* **man·gled, man·gling 1** damage by cutting or tearing roughly: *His arm was badly mangled in the accident.* **2** do very badly: *The music was too difficult for her, and she mangled it.* <Old French *mahaignier* injure>

man·gle[2] (mang′gəl) *n* a machine for pressing and smoothing cloth by passing it between rollers.
v **man·gled, man·gling** press with or put through a mangle. <Dutch, from Greek *manganon* engine>

man·go (mang′gō) *n, pl* **man·goes** or **man·gos** a juicy tropical fruit with a thick rind. <Portuguese, from Tamil *mankay*>

man·grove (man′grōv) *or* (mang′grōv) *n* a tropical tree with branches that send down many roots that look like new trunks or stems but twine together to make dense thickets, often in tidal swamps. <Spanish, from Arawak (a language of S America)>

man·gy (mān′jē) *adj* **man·gi·er, man·gi·est 1** with the mange and the hair falling out: *a mangy dog.* **2** shabby and dirty: *a mangy house.* **man′gi·ness** *n.*

man·han·dle (man′han′dəl) *v* **man·han·dled, man·han·dling 1** treat roughly. **2** move a heavy object by human strength: *The movers manhandled the piano down the steps and into the truck.*

man·hole (man′hōl′) *n* a hole, especially in a street or a metal floor, through which a worker may enter a sewer or location of machinery in order to maintain or repair something.

man·hood (man′hu̇d) *n* **1** the condition or time of being a man. **2** the qualities traditionally associated with being a man, such as strength. **3** men as a group, especially of a country: *Canadian manhood.*

man–hour (man′our′) *n* an hour of work by one person, used as a unit of time in industry.

man·hunt (man′hunt) *n* a systematic search for a criminal or fugitive.

a bat	e bed	i bid	o pot	u cup	th **thin**
ā cake	ē me	ī bite	ō go	ū rude	TH **then**
ȧ bar	ə about	ər over	ȯ for	u̇ put	zh measure

M

ma·ni·a (mā′nē ə) *n* **1** a mental illness characterized by great excitement, delusions, and overactivity. **2** an excessive enthusiasm or desire: *a mania for dancing.* <Latin, from Greek = madness>

ma·ni·ac (mā′nē ak′) *n* **1** a person affected by mania, especially when violent or dangerous. **2** *Informal* a person with a great interest in or enthusiasm for something: *a sports maniac.*

ma·ni·a·cal (mə nī′ə kəl) *adj* insane or seemingly insane: *maniacal laughter.* **ma·ni′a·cal·ly** *adv.*

man·ic (man′ik) *or* (mā′nik) *adj* to do with MANIA (def. 1).

man·ic–de·pres·sive (man′ik di pres′iv) *adj* with BIPOLAR (AFFECTIVE) DISORDER.
n a person who has such attacks.

man·i·cure (man′ə kyůr′) *v* **man·i·cured, man·i·cur·ing** **1** to care for the fingernails and hands, especially, to trim, clean, and polish the fingernails. **2** trim something closely and evenly: *a manicured lawn.*
n a cosmetic treatment for the hands and fingernails: *She made an appointment for a manicure at the salon.* <French, from Latin *manus* hand + *cura* care> **man′i·cur′ist** *n.*

man·i·fest[1] (man′ə fest′) *adj* clear to see or understand: *The thief left so many clues that his guilt was manifest.*
v **1** show plainly. **2** be evidence of: *His neatness was manifested in a beautifully arranged stamp collection.* <Latin *manufestus* caught in the act, from *manus* hand + *festus* able to be seized> **man′i·fest′ly** *adv.*

man·i·fest[2] (man′ə fest′) *n* a list of passengers or cargo in a ship or aircraft. <French, from Latin *manifestare* to make plain>

man·i·fes·ta·tion (man′ə fə stā′shən) *n* an event, action, or object that clearly shows or embodies something: *a characteristic manifestation.*

man·i·fes·to (man′ə fes′tō) *n, pl* **man·i·fes·toes** a public declaration of intentions, purposes, or motives, especially of a political nature. <See MANIFEST[1].>

man·i·fold (man′ə fōld′) *adj* **1** many and various: *manifold duties.* **2** with many parts or forms: *The hero was praised for his manifold goodness.*
n a pipe or chamber with several openings for connection with other pipes, such as in an automobile. <Old English *manig* many + *feald* fold>

Ma·nil·a (mə nil′ə) *n* **1** in full, **Manila hemp** a strong fibre of a Philippine plant, used to make rope, matting, and paper. **2** Manila paper: *a Manila envelope.* <after *Manila*, a major port in the Philippines>

man in the street *n* an average person.

man·i·oc (man′ē ok′) *n* a cassava.

ma·nip·u·late (mə nip′yə lāt′) *v* **ma·nip·u·lat·ed, ma·nip·u·lat·ing** **1** handle or treat, especially in a skilful way: *manipulate a dial.* **2** manage by clever use of personal influence, especially unfair influence: *He manipulated the team cleverly enough to be elected captain.* **3** mislead for your own purpose or advantage: *The secretary manipulated the club's accounts to cover up her error.* <Latin *manus* hand> **ma·nip′u·la′tion** *n.*
ma·nip′u·la′tor *n.*

ma·nip·u·la·tive (mə nip′yə lə tiv) *or* (mə nip′yə lā′tiv) *adj* to do with manipulating or being manipulated.
n (*usually plural*) a small item, such as a plastic block, that children can use to develop their reasoning skills.

Man·i·to·ba (man′ə tō′bə) *n* a western Canadian province, between Saskatchewan and Ontario. Manitoba is one of the PRAIRIE PROVINCES. *Abbrev.* **Man.**; postal symbol **MB**; URL **www.gov.mb.ca**
adj to do with Manitoba: *Manitoba wheat.*
Man′i·to′ban *adj, n.*

✱ **Manitoba maple** (man′ə tō′bə) *n* a fast-growing, medium-sized maple with compound leaves.

man·i·tou or **man·i·tu** (man′ə tū′) *n* in the traditional religion of the Algonquian peoples, a spirit representing a good or evil power in nature. The chief manitou or great spirit is called **gitchi** (or **kitshi**) **manitou**. <French, from Algonquian>

man·kind (man′kīnd′) *n* all human beings. This usage is generally considered unacceptable today; the preferred terms are **human race** or **humankind**.

man·like (man′līk′) *adj* resembling a human being. This usage is generally considered unacceptable today; the preferred term is **humanlike**.

man·ly (man′lē) *adj* **man·li·er, man·li·est** to do with the supposed characteristics of men. **man′li·ness** *n.*

man–made (man′mād′) *adj* made by humans artificially. This usage is is generally considered unacceptable today; the preferred terms are **synthetic**, **artificial**, or **human-made**.

man·na (man′ə) *n* **1** a substance mentioned in the Bible that miraculously supplied food to the Israelites in the wilderness. **2** a much-needed thing that is unexpectedly supplied: *Winning the lottery was like manna from heaven for her.* <Hebrew *man*>

manned (mand) *adj* containing or attended by an operator or crew, not automatic or remote-controlled: *manned spacecraft, a manned tollbooth.*

GRAMMAR AND USAGE

Some people object to **manned** as sexist, but there is no single, general alternative that applies. Some possible substitutes: *staffed, crewed, operated, run.*

man·ne·quin (man′ə kin) *n* a model of a human figure used to display clothes in a store window: *Many clothing stores use mannequins for their window displays.* <Dutch *man* man>

man·ner (man′ər) *n* **1** the way something happens or is done: *The trouble arose in a curious manner.* **2** a way of acting, behaving, or dressing: *She has a kind manner. He dresses in a strange manner.* **3 manners** *pl* **a** ways or customs: *Books and movies show us the manners of other times and places.* **b** ways of behaving toward others: *bad manners.* **c** polite behaviour: *It is nice to see a child with manners.* <Old French, from Latin *manus* hand>
all manner of, all kinds of: *all manner of birds.*
in a manner of speaking, as you might say.
to the manner born, accustomed since birth to some way or condition.

man·nered (man′ərd) *adj* **1** with manners of a certain kind: *a well-mannered child.* **2** affected or artificial: *She has a very mannered style of writing.*

man·ner·ism (man′ə riz′əm) *n* **1** too much use of some manner in speaking, writing, or behaving. **2** too much or too self-conscious use of a distinctive style in art, literature, or music.

man·ner·ly (man′ər lē) *adj* with or showing good manners. **man′ner·li·ness** *n.*

man·nish (man′ish) *adj* traditionally associated with a man rather than a woman: *She has a mannish haircut.* **man′nish·ly** *adv.*

ma·noeu·vre (mə nū′vər) *n* **1** a planned movement of troops or warships: *The army practises warfare by holding manoeuvres.* **2** a skilful or deceptive plan or movement: *Her superior manoeuvres won the game.*
v **ma·noeu·vred, ma·noeu·vring** **1** perform or cause to perform something skilfully: *She manoeuvred the car into the parking spot. One trolley was carefully manoeuvred behind another.* **2** plan or contrive skilfully: *She manoeuvred her mother into letting her have a party.* Also, **maneuver**. <French, from Latin *manus* hand + *operari* work> **ma·noeuv′ra·bil′i·ty** *n.* **ma·noeuv′ra·ble** *adj.*

man–of–war (man′ə wor′) *n, pl* **man-of-wars** or **men-of-war** **1** a warship. **2 Portuguese man-of-war** a stinging jellyfish.

man·or (man′ər) *n* a feudal estate, part of which was set aside for the lord and the rest divided among his peasants. <Old French *maneir* to dwell, from Latin *manere* stay> **ma·no′ri·al** (mə nȯ′rē əl) *adj.*

man·pow·er (man′pou′ər) *n* **1** strength thought of in terms of the number of people needed or available. **2** 🍁 **Manpower** in former times, a federal government service that offered job referrals to the unemployed. The current equivalent service is called **Human Resources Development**.

man·sard (man′särd) *n* a four-sided roof with two slopes on each side, with the lower slope much steeper than the upper one. <F. *Mansart*, 17c architect>

manse (mans) *n* a Presbyterian minister's residence. <See MANSION.>

man·serv·ant (man′sər′vənt) *n, pl* **men·serv·ants** in former times, a male servant.

man·sion (man′shən) *n* a large, impressive house. <Latin *mansus* dwelling, from *manere* to stay>

man·slaugh·ter (man′slot′ər) *n* the unlawful killing of another human being without malice or premeditation.

man·ta (man′tə) *n* in full, **manta ray** a large tropical fish with winglike pectoral fins, a whiplike tail, and two hornlike fins projecting from the head. Mantas are informally called **devilfish.**

man·tel (man′təl) *n* a shelf or other structure built above, or above and around, a fireplace. <variant of *mantle*>

man·tel·piece (man′təl pēs′) *n* a shelf above a fireplace.

man·tis (man′tis) *n* a slender insect related to the cockroach that holds its forelegs doubled up as if praying. See INSECT for picture. <Latin, from Greek = prophet, from its praying posture>

man·tle (man′təl) *n* **1** a loose, sleeveless cloak or shawl. **2** a thing that covers or conceals like a mantle: *The ground had a mantle of snow.* **3** an important role or responsibility that passes from one person to another: *mantle of power.* **4** the part of the earth's interior between the crust and the core, composed of hot, dense, silicate rock. **5** a netlike sheath fixed around the flame of a gas lamp, made of a substance that glows with an intense white light when it becomes hot.
v **man·tled, man·tling** *Poetic* clothe, cover, or conceal with or as if with a mantle: *mountaintops mantled with snow.* <Old English, from Latin *mantum* cloak>

man·tra (man′trə) *n* a word or formula used as an aid to meditation, especially in Hinduism and Buddhism. <Sanskrit = instrument of thought>

man·u·al (man′yū əl) *adj* **1** to do with the hands: *manual labour. He has great manual dexterity.* **2** done or operated by hand, not automatically: *a manual gearshift.*
n **1** a small book that helps its readers to understand or use something. **2** an organ keyboard played with the hands. <Old French, from Latin *manus* hand> **man′u·al·ly** *adv.*

GRAMMAR AND USAGE

Manual, manacle, manage, mandate, manipulate, manoeuvre, manufacture, and **manuscript** all come from the Latin *manus*, meaning "hand," rather than having anything to do with *man* as meaning "all people."

They are non-sexist terms and do not need to be replaced.

manual transmission *n* a gear system in a motor vehicle over which the driver has control, changing the gears by hand using a lever.

man·u·fac·ture (man′yə fak′chər) *v* **man·u·fac·tured, man·u·fac·tur·ing** **1** make by hand or by machine, especially on a large scale. **2** make into something useful. **3** invent or fabricate: *The dishonest lawyer manufactured evidence.* <French, from Italian> **man′u·fac′tur·ing** *n.*

man·u·fac·tur·er (man′yə fak′chə rər) *n* a person whose business is manufacturing: *an aircraft manufacturer.*

ma·nure (mə nyůr′) *or* (mə nůr′) *n* a compost, especially animal waste, put in or on the soil as fertilizer.
v **ma·nured, ma·nur·ing** put manure in or on. <Latin *manuoperas* manual work>

man·u·script (man′yə skript′) *n* a book or other text written by hand or with a typewriter or computer.
adj written by hand or with a typewriter or computer. <Latin *manu* + by hand *scribere* write>

Manx (mangks) *adj* to do with the Isle of Man, an island off the west coast of England, its people, or their language.
n **1** the people of the Isle of Man. **2** their language, a Celtic tongue, now almost extinct.

M

a bat	e bed	i bid	o pot	u cup	th **thin**
ā cake	ē me	ī bite	ō go	ū rude	TH **then**
ä bar	ə about	ər over	ȯ for	ů put	zh measure

Manx cat *n* a breed of cat that is tailless.

man·y (men′ē) *adj* **more, most** with a large number of: *many people, many years ago.*
n, pron **1** a large number of people or things: *There were many at the fair.* **2 the many a** most people. **b** people. <Old English *manig*>
a good many, a fairly large number of people or things.
a great many, a very large number of people or things.
one too many for, more than a match for.

man·y–sid·ed (men′ē sī′did) *adj* with many aspects, interests, or abilities.

Mao·ism (mou′iz əm) *n* communism as interpreted and put into effect by Mao Zedong (mou′dzə dong′), leader of the People's Republic of China from 1949 to 1976. **Mao′ist** *adj, n.*

Mao·ri (mou′rē) *or* (mȧ′ō rē) *n, pl* **Ma·o·ris** or **Ma·o·ri** **1** a member of a Polynesian people of New Zealand. **2** the language of these people.
adj to do with the Maoris or their language.

map (map) *n* **1** a drawing representing the earth's surface or part of it, usually showing its political boundaries and/or geographical features, cities, roads, etc. **2** a drawing representing part of the sky, showing the position of the stars. **3** *Mathematics* a diagram showing the correspondence between two sets of items. **4** any diagram showing the relationships among ideas, people, events: *a concept map, a mind map, a character map, a story map.*
v **mapped, map·ping** **1** make a map of or show on a map. **2** plan or arrange in detail: *to map out the week's work.* <Latin *mappa* sheet + *mundus* world>
off the map, unknown or of no importance.
on the map, notable: *Hosting the Olympics would put this town on the map.*

SYNONYMS

Map can refer to a plan of roads or other routes on land.

Chart is used especially for plans showing air or sea routes.

Atlas refers to a book of maps covering a large area or the whole world.

ma·ple (mā′pəl) *n* a tree or shrub with usually lobed leaves that grow in opposite pairs and dry fruits with normally two winglike extensions, each containing a seed, or the light-coloured, hard, close-grained wood of certain maples.
adj made of or flavoured with maple sugar or syrup: *maple ice cream, maple candy.* <Old English *mapel*>

🍁 **maple bush** *n* a small wooded area, especially on someone's property, containing many sugar maple trees.

maple candy *n* candy made from maple sugar.

🍁 **maple leaf** *n* **1** a leaf of the maple tree, or this leaf coloured red, as a symbol of Canada. **2 Maple Leaf** the Canadian flag.

maple sugar *n* sugar made from the sap of the sugar maple.

maple syrup *n* syrup made from the sap of the sugar maple.

mar (mär) *v* **marred, mar·ring** spoil the appearance of: *The nails in the workers' boots have marred the newly finished floors.* <Old English *merran* waste>

mar·a·bou (mar′ə bū′) *or* (mer′ə bū′) *n* a large African stork with a huge bill and a large neck pouch. Its soft feathers are made into a furlike trimming. <French, from Arabic *marabit* holy man, because the stork is considered a holy bird>

ma·ra·ca (mə rȧ′kə) *or* (mə rak′ə) *n* a percussion instrument resembling a rattle, made of a gourd or a gourd-shaped object containing seeds or pebbles. Maracas are usually played in pairs. <Portuguese, from Tupi-Garani (a language of S America)>

mar·a·schi·no cherry (mar′ə skē′nō) *or* (mer′ə skē′nō); (mar′ə shē′nō) *or* (mer′ə shē′nō) *n* a cherry preserved in a syrup flavoured with **maraschino**, a strong, sweet liqueur made from a kind of small black cherry.

Legend tells that the Greek messenger who ran from Marathon to Athens in 490 BCE had just enough energy to deliver his news before he died of exhaustion. Today's fastest **marathon** runners seem to have plenty of energy. The fastest women finish in about 2 hours 15 minutes; the fastest men in about 2 hours 5 minutes. That means they're running 19 km/hr or faster.

mar·a·thon (mar′ə thon′) *or* (mer′ə thon′) *n*
1 a long-distance foot race, officially measured at 42.195 km. **2** a long-distance race or endurance contest: *a marathon swim, a dance marathon.*

ETYMOLOGY

Marathon is named after *Marathon,* the site where the Greeks defeated the Persians in 490 BCE. A Greek messenger ran 37 km from Marathon to Athens to bring news of the victory. The run was introduced as an athletic event in the 1896 revival of the Olympics.

ma·raud (mə rod′) *v* go about in search of things to steal or people to attack. <French = rogue> **ma·raud′er** *n.*

mar·ble (mär′bəl) *n* **1** a hard limestone, white or coloured, capable of taking a polish. **2** a small ball of clay, glass, or stone, used in games. **3 marbles** *pl* **a** (*with singular verb*) a game played with marbles. **b** (*with plural verb*) a collection of marble sculptures.
adj **1** made of marble. **2** like marble, especially in seeming cold or unfeeling.
v **mar·bled, mar·bling** colour in imitation of the patterns in marble: *a marbled countertop.* <Old French, from Greek *marmaros* gleaming stone>

marble cake *n* a cake made by mixing dark and light batters in streaks or swirls, giving it a marblelike appearance when baked.

mar·ca·site (mär′kə sīt′) *n* a semiprecious stone consisting of iron pyrites.

march[1] (märch) *v* **1** walk as soldiers do, taking rhythmic steps of the same length. **2** walk or proceed quickly and steadily: *The students marched out of the room in protest.* **3** cause to march or go: *The police officers marched the thief off to jail.*
n **1** the movement of troops: *The army is prepared for the march.* **2** the act or fact of marching, especially as a protest or in aid of a cause: *The march was a great success and earned hundreds of dollars for charity.* **3** music for marching. **4** the distance marched: *It was a long march to the next town.* **5** a period of time, especially as an advance or progress: *History records the march of events.* <French *marchier* to walk> **march′er** *n.*
on the march, moving forward, especially as a military force.
steal a march on, gain an advantage over someone without being noticed.

march[2] (märch) *n* **1** the land along the border of a country. **2 the Marches** *pl* in former times, the districts along the border between England and Scotland, or between England and Wales. <Old French>

March (märch) *n* the third month of the year, with 31 days. *Abbrev.* **Mar** <Old French, from Latin *Martius* of Mars, the Roman god of war>

🍁 **March break** *n* a school holiday of one or two weeks, held sometime in March.

marching orders *n* a command to leave or move on.

mar·chion·ess (mär′shə nis) *or* (mär′shə nes′) *n* **1** the wife or widow of a marquis. **2** a woman equal in rank to a marquis. See also MARQUISE (def. 1).

Mar·di Gras (mor′dē gro′) *Christianity n* **1** the last day before Lent. **2** a traditional public carnival celebrating this day, especially in New Orleans.

ETYMOLOGY

Since Lent is a time when many Christians give up meat or other foods or luxuries, **Mardi Gras** takes place just before Lent begins, and has traditionally been a time of much feasting and celebration. The name is French, and literally means "fat Tuesday."

mare[1] (mer) *n* a female horse, donkey, or pony. <Old English *mere*>

mare[2] (ma′rā) *or* (me′rā) *Astronomy n, pl* **ma·ri·a** (mar′ē ə) *or* (mer′ē ə) a large plain on the moon. <Latin = sea. Galileo thought the dark areas he saw on the moon and Mars were seas.>

mare's–nest (merz′nest′) *Informal n* a situation that is complex and confused.

mar·ga·rine (mär′jə rin) *or* (mär′jə rēn′) *n* a substitute for butter, usually made from vegetable oils. <French, from Greek *margaron* pearl, from the pearly appearance of the fatty acids from which it was originally made>

mar·gin (mär′jən) *n* **1** an edge or border: *the margin of a lake.* **2** the blank space around the writing or printing on a page: *Do not write in the margin.* **3** an amount beyond what is necessary: *a margin of 15 minutes in catching a train, a margin of error.* **4** the difference between what something is bought and sold for: *profit margin.* **5** the money pledged by a purchaser to protect a broker against loss on an account or transaction. <Latin *margo* edge>

mar·gin·al (mär′jə nəl) *adj* **1** written or printed in a MARGIN (def. 2): *marginal notes.* **2** of a MARGIN (def. 1), edge, or border: *marginal forests.* **3** barely useful, acceptable, or profitable: *marginal knowledge, marginal land.*

mar·gin·a·li·a (mär′jə nā′lē ə) *pln* notes written in the margin or margins of a manuscript, book, or other text.

mar·gin·al·ize (mär′jə nə līz′) *v* **mar·gin·al·ized, mar·gin·al·iz·ing** deprive of power or the opportunity to be involved: *Minorities are marginalized in some countries.*

mar·gin·al·ly (mär′jə nə lē) *adv* slightly or to a limited extent: *She is marginally better today.*

mar·grave (mär′grāv) *n* the title of certain princes of the Holy Roman Empire.

mar·gue·rite (mär′gə rēt′) *n* a daisy with white or pale yellow petals and a yellow centre. Also called **ox-eye daisy**. <French = Margaret>

ma·ri·a·chi (mor′ē och′ē) *n* a type of traditional Mexican folk music, usually performed by a band of strolling musicians. <Spanish. Such musicians often play at weddings, in a wedding procession or moving among the guests.>

mar·i·gold (mar′ə gōld′) *or* (mer′ə gōld′) *n* a plant of the daisy family with yellowish flowers. <Middle English>

mar·i·jua·na (mar′ə won′ə) *n* CANNABIS (def. 1). <Middle English>

🍁 **Marijuana Party** *n* one of the registered political parties of Canada.

ma·rim·ba (mə rim′bə) *n* a musical instrument resembling a xylophone. <Portuguese, from Bantu (a group of languages of Africa)>

a bat	e bed	i bid	o pot	u cup	th **thin**
ā cake	ē me	ī bite	ō go	ū rude	ᴛʜ **then**
ä bar	ə about	ər over	ö for	u̇ put	zh measure

M

ma·ri·na (mə rē′nə) *n* a place along a waterfront where boats may be moored and where fuel and equipment may be bought.

> **ETYMOLOGY**
>
> **Marina, marine, mariner,** and **maritime** all come originally through Italian, French, or Latin forms, from Latin *mare*, meaning "sea."
>
> **Marinade** (noun) and **marinate** (verb) also come from this root, since the mixtures used for marinating often contain a lot of salt, like sea water.

mar·i·nade (mar′ə nād′) *or* (mer′ə nād′) *for n,* (mar′ə nād′) *or* (mer′ə nād′) *for v.*
n a sauce in which meat, fish, or other food is immersed for some time before cooking in order to flavour or tenderize it.
v **mar·i·nad·ed, mar·i·nad·ing** marinate. <French *mariner* to pickle (in sea brine), from Latin *mare* sea>

ma·ri·na·ra (mar′ə nar′ə) *n* an Italian sauce made from tomatoes and herbs. <Italian *alla marinara* = sailor-style>

mar·i·nate (mar′ə nāt′) *or* (mer′ə nāt′) *v* **mar·i·nat·ed, mar·i·nat·ing** immerse for a time in a marinade. <See MARINADE.>

ma·rine (mə rēn′) *adj* **1** of, found in, or produced by the sea: *marine animals.* **2** to do with shipping or naval matters: *marine law, marine power.* **3** for use at sea or on a ship: *marine supplies, a marine engine.*
n **1** a soldier trained to serve on land or at sea. **2** a fleet of ships: *our merchant marine.* **3** a picture showing a sea scene. <Old French, from Latin *mare* sea>

mar·i·ner (mar′ə nər) *or* (mer′ə nər) *n* a sailor. <Old French, from Latin *mare* sea>

mar·i·o·nette (mar′ē ə net′) *or* (mer′ē ə net′) *n* a small doll or puppet made to imitate a person or an animal and moved by strings. <French, from *Marie* Mary, a common name for female characters in Old French plays>

mar·i·tal (mar′ə təl) *or* (mer′ə təl) *adj* to do with marriage: *marital vows.* <Latin *maritus* husband>
mar′i·tal·ly *adv.*

> **CONFUSABLES**
>
> **Marital** means "to do with marriage": *Couples who have marital problems sometimes consult a counsellor.*
>
> **Martial** means "of or suitable for war": *The citizens complained that their political rights were at risk when martial law was declared.*

mar·i·time (mar′ə tīm′) *or* (mer′ə tīm′) *adj* **1** on or near the sea: *a maritime city.* **2** living near the sea: *maritime peoples.* **3** to do with shipping and sailing: *maritime law.* **4 Maritime** to do with the Maritime Provinces. <Latin *mare* sea>

🍁 **Maritime Command** *n* the naval branch of the Canadian Forces, formerly known as the Royal Canadian Navy.

🍁 **Maritime Provinces** *pln* the provinces of New Brunswick, Nova Scotia, and Prince Edward Island. See also ATLANTIC PROVINCES. Also, **the Maritimes. Mar′i·tim′er** *n.*

> **GRAMMAR AND USAGE**
>
> The terms **Maritime Provinces** and **Maritimes** do not include Newfoundland and Labrador.
>
> The term **Atlantic Provinces** includes all the Maritime Provinces and Newfoundland and Labrador.

mar·jo·ram (mår′jə rəm) *n* a plant of the mint family, especially **sweet marjoram**, whose fragrant leaves are used for flavouring in cooking. <Old French, from Latin *majorana*>

mark (mårk) *n* **1** a trace or impression made by some object on the surface of another. **2** an object, line, dot, etc. put as a guide or sign: *a mark for pilots, a question mark.* **3** a thing that indicates a quality or characteristic: *a mark of courtesy, a distinguishing mark.* **4** a letter or number to show how well a person has done: *My mark in arithmetic was a B.* **5** a thing that or person who is a target: *an easy mark.* **6** influence or impression: *A great woman leaves her mark on whatever she does.*
v **1** make a mark on by stamping, cutting, writing, etc.: *Be careful not to mark the table.* **2** show by means of a sign: *Mark all the large cities on this map. This post marks the city limits.* **3** put a tag, label, brand, etc. on an article, to show the price, quality, maker, or owner. **4** show clearly or make plain: *A tall pine marks the beginning of the trail. A frown marked her displeasure.* **5** give interest or importance to: *Many important inventions mark the last 150 years.* **6** give grades to: *The teacher marked our examination papers.* **7** *Formal* give attention to: *Mark how carefully she moves. Mark well my words.* **8** *Soccer, Hockey, Lacrosse, etc.* guard an opponent closely. **9** select as if by a mark: *marked for promotion.* <Old English *mearc*>
beside the mark, not relevant.
hit the mark, a succeed in doing what you tried to do. **b** be exactly correct or proper.
make your mark, succeed or achieve recognition.
mark down, mark for sale at a lower price.
mark off (or **out**)**,** make lines or other marks to show the position of or to separate.
mark time, a move the feet as in marching, but remaining in the same spot. **b** go through motions without accomplishing anything.
mark up, a spoil the look of by making marks on: *Don't mark up the desks.* **b** mark for sale at a higher price. **c** prepare a manuscript for printing.
miss the mark, fail to do what you tried to do.
up to the mark, meeting a certain standard: *I'm afraid this piece of work is not up to the mark.*
wide of the mark, a missing the thing aimed at by a considerable margin. **b** irrelevant.

mark·down (mårk′doun′) *n* a reduction in price: *There's a markdown of 50 percent on Valentine's Day candy after February 14.*

marked (mårkt) *adj* **1** with a mark or marks: *This shirt is marked with oil.* **2** very noticeable, clear, or easily recognized: *a marked difference.*

mark·ed·ly (mår′ki dlē) *adv* in a conspicuous manner or degree.

mar·ker (mår′kər) *n* **1** an object used to indicate a position, place, or route: *They placed markers to show the limits of the property.* **2** a person who assesses the quality of a written test or examination. **3** a felt-tip pen with a broad nib.

mar·ket (mår′kit) *n* **1** a meeting of people for the purpose of buying and selling: *There is a fruit and vegetable market here every Saturday.* **2** a space or building in which things, especially food or livestock, are shown for sale: *a fruit market, a cattle market.* **3** trade, especially involving a particular item: *the wheat market. Several countries became a new market for wheat.* **4** the opportunity to buy or sell: *to lose your market.* **5** the demand for goods or services: *There was not enough cheese to supply the market.* *v* **1** sell in a market. **2** advertise or promote something: *The new product was marketed in unusual ways.* <Old French, from Latin *mercari* to buy> **mar′ket·er** *n.*
be in the market for, be a possible buyer of: *She is in the market for a new bike.*
on the market, for sale: *Several properties were on the market.*
play the market, speculate on the stock exchange.
price out of the market, lose business by asking too high a price for something.

mar·ket·a·ble (mår′ki tə bəl) *adj* **1** able or fit to be sold: *a marketable commodity.* **2** in demand: *marketable skills.*

market economy *n* an economy where prices and wages are determined by supply and demand, and are not controlled by the government.

market garden *mainly UK n* a farm where vegetables are grown for market. **market gardener** *n.* **market gardening** *n.*

mar·ket·ing (mår′ki ting) *n* the business or process of planning and carrying out ways to advertise and promote goods or services.

mar·ket·place (mår′kit plās′) *n* **1** a place where a market is held. **2** the world of business and commerce.

market research *n* research, such as interviewing consumers and gathering statistics about buying habits, carried out in order to give a company guidance on how to sell its goods or services.

market value *n* the price that an article brings if sold.

mark·ing (mår′king) *n* **1** a mark or marks, especially as an identification. **2** the arrangement of marks: *I like the marking on your cat's coat.*

mark–re·cap·ture (mårk′rē kap′chər) *n* capture-recapture.

marks·man (mårk′smən) *n, pl* **marks·men** (-smən) a person who shoots with a weapon, especially one who shoots well: *an army marksman.*

marks·man·ship (mårk′smən ship′) *n* skill in shooting.

mark·up (mår′kup′) *n* the difference between the cost and the selling price of an item.

marl (mårl) *n* soil containing clay and calcium carbonate, formerly used as a fertilizer.

mar·lin (mår′lən) *n* a large, heavy, edible fish of warm seas that has a spearlike upper jaw <*marlinespike.* The fish's snout resembles this pointed metal tool used by sailors.>

mar·ma·lade (mår′mə lād′) *n* a preserve like jam, made of oranges or other fruit. <Portuguese, from Greek *meli* honey + *melon* apple>

mar·mo·set (mår′mə set′) *or* (mår′mə zet′) *n* a small monkey with soft, thick fur that lives in Central and S America. <Old French *marmouset* monkey>

mar·mot (mår′mət) *n* a burrowing rodent of N America and Eurasia that has a thick body and a bushy tail, typically living in mountainous country. <French, from Latin *mus* mouse + *montanus* mountain>

ma·roon[1] (mə rūn′) *adj* dark brownish red. <French, from Greek *maraon* chestnut>

ma·roon[2] (mə rūn′) *v* put a person ashore in a lonely place or in a lonely, helpless position. <French, from Spanish *cimarrón* wild>

mar·quee (mår kē′) *n* **1** a rooflike shelter over an entrance. **2** a large tent, often one put up for some outdoor entertainment. <French *marquise* a canopy over an army officer's tent>

mar·quis (mår′kwis) *or* (mår kē′) *n* a nobleman ranking below a duke and above an earl or count. Also, **marquess.** <Old French = ruler of a border area>

mar·quise (mår kēz′) *n* **1** a woman equal in rank to a marquis, or the wife or widow of a marquis. **2** a gem of a pointed oval shape, or a ring set with such a stone. <French>

M

mar·riage (mar′ij) *or* (mer′ij) *n* **1** the ongoing relationship between spouses: *We wished them a happy marriage.* **2** the ceremony of becoming married. **3** a close union: *the marriage of words and melody.*

mar·riage·a·ble (mar′i jə bəl) *or* (mer′i jə bəl) *adj* fit for marriage or old enough to marry: *of marriageable age.* **mar′riage·a·bil′i·ty** *n.*

marriage of convenience *n* a marriage for the sake of some advantage and not because of mutual attraction.

mar·row (mar′ō) *or* (mer′ō) *n* **1** the soft fatty substance that fills the cavities of most bones, in which blood cells are produced. **2** the inmost or essential part: *The icy wind chilled me to the marrow.* <Old English *mearg*>

mar·row·fat (mar′ō fat′) *or* (mer′ō fat′) *n* a pea that has large seeds, often processed and canned.

mar·ry (mar′ē) *or* (mer′ē) *v* **mar·ried, mar·ry·ing** **1** join two people as spouses: *The minister married them.* **2** become married: *She married late in life.* **3** (*often with* ***off***) give in marriage: *They married their daughter off to a wealthy nobleman.* **4** unite closely: *the marriage of oil and vinegar in salad dressing.* <Old French, from Latin *maritus* husband>

a bat	e bed	i bid	o pot	u cup	th thin
ā cake	ē me	ī bite	ō go	ū rude	TH then
å bar	ə about	ər over	ô for	ů put	zh measure

Mars (mȧrz) *n* the planet nearest to the earth and the fourth in order from the sun. See EARTH for picture. <*Mars,* Roman god of war>

Mar·seill·aise (mȧr′sā yāz′) *n* the national anthem of France, written in 1792 during the French Revolution. <*Marseilles,* France, because it was first sung by people from there>

marsh (mȧrsh) *n* an area of wet, low-lying, muddy land that is flooded in wet seasons or at high tide and has a variety of plant life. <Old English *mersc*>

mar·shal (mȧr′shəl) *n* **1** the head of a fire department or, in the US, a federal or municipal law officer: *a fire marshal.* **2** the officer of the highest rank in certain armed forces: *a field marshal.* **3** a person who arranges or is in charge of public events, especially parades or sports events.
v **mar·shalled** or **mar·shaled, mar·shal·ling** or **mar·shal·ing 1** arrange or order properly or effectively: *She spent a lot of time marshalling her arguments for the debate.* **2** conduct with ceremony: *We were marshalled before the queen.* <Old French *mareschal*>

Mar·shall Islands (mar′shal) *n* a country of several islands in the Pacific Ocean. **Mar′shall Islander** *n.*

marsh gas *Informal n* methane.

marsh·land (marsh′land′) *n* marshy land.

marsh mallow *n* a tall, pink-flowered European plant found in marshy areas, and with a root that secretes a gummy substance originally used to make marshmallow.

marsh·mal·low (mȧrsh′mal′ō) *or* (mȧrsh′mel′ō) *n* a soft, spongy confection originally made from the root of the marsh mallow, now made from corn syrup, sugar, gelatin, and flavouring: *a bag of marshmallows.*

marsh marigold *n* a plant of the buttercup family with yellow flowers and round leaves. Also called **cowslip.**

marsh·y (mȧr′shē) *adj* **marsh·i·er, marsh·i·est 1** soft and wet like a marsh: *a marshy field.* **2** of or with many marshes. **marsh′i·ness** *n.*

mar·su·pi·al (mȧr sū′pē əl) *n* a mammal whose young are born incompletely developed and then carried and suckled in a pouch on the mother's belly, such as the kangaroo and opossum. See KANGAROO for picture. <Latin, from Greek *marsupion* pouch>

mart (mȧrt) *n* a store or market. <Dutch of *marct* market>

Mar·tel·lo tower (mȧr′te′lō) *n* a fort like a round tower, formerly built on coasts for defence against invasion. Also, **martello tower.** <alteration of Cape *Martella,* Corsica, where such a tower was built>

mar·ten (mȧr′tən) *n, pl* **mar·tens** or (*especially collectively*) **mar·ten** a small flesh-eating mammal related to the weasel, but larger. <Old French *martre*>

mar·tial (mȧr′shəl) *adj* **1** of or suitable for war: *martial music.* **2** fond of fighting in wars: *a man of martial spirit.* <Latin *Mars* god of war> **mar′tial·ly** *adv.*

martial art *n* a sport or skill of self-defence or attack, especially one from east Asia. The **martial arts** include AIKIDO, KARATE, JUDO, and TAE KWON DO.

martial law *n* rule by the army or militia with special military courts instead of by the usual civil authorities. Compare MILITARY LAW.

Mar·tian (mȧr′shən) *adj* to do with the planet Mars.
n a supposed inhabitant of the planet Mars.

mar·tin (mȧr′tən) *n* a swallow with a forked tail and stout bill. The adult male has glossy, dark purple plumage. <French, probably from the November feast of St. *Martin,* because the birds were believed to migrate around the same time>

mar·ti·net (mȧr′tə net′) *n* a person who enforces severe discipline. <J. *Martinet,* 17c army drillmaster>

mar·tyr (mȧr′tər) *n* **1** a person who chooses to die or suffer rather than renounce religious faith or some great cause. **2** (*with* ***to***) a person who suffers constant pain or anguish: *a martyr to migraine headaches.* **3** a person who puts on a false appearance of suffering in order to attract sympathy or attention.
v **1** put a person to death or torture because of religious or other beliefs. **2** cause to suffer greatly. <Greek = witness> **mar′tyr·like′** *adj.*

mar·tyr·dom (mȧr′tər dəm) *n* the death or suffering of a MARTYR (def. 1).

mar·vel (mȧr′vəl) *n* something or someone wonderful or astonishing: *Television and the airplane are among the marvels of invention.*
v **mar·velled** or **mar·veled, mar·vel·ling** or **mar·vel·ing** be filled with wonder or astonishment: *She marvelled at the beautiful sunset.* <Old French, from Latin *mirari* wonder at>

mar·vel·lous or **mar·vel·ous** (mȧr′və ləs) *adj* **1** causing wonder or astonishment. **2** excellent or extremely pleasing: *a marvellous time.* **mar′vel·lous·ly** or **mar′vel·ous·ly** *adv.* **mar′vel·lous·ness** or **mar′vel·ous·ness** *n.*

Marx·ism (mȧrk′siz əm) *n* the political and economic theories of Karl Marx that were developed to become the basis for the theories and practice of communism. **Marx′ist** *n.*

🍁 **Marx·ist–Len·in·ist Party** (mȧrk′sist len′in ist) *n* one of the registered political parties of Canada.

mar·zi·pan (mȧr′zə pan′) *n* a paste of ground almonds and sugar, often moulded into various forms. <Italian, perhaps from Arabic>

mas·car·a (mas kar′ə) *or* (mas ker′ə) *n* a cosmetic used for darkening and thickening the eyelashes. <Italian, from Arabic *maskara* clown>

mas·cot (mas′kot) *n* an animal, person, or thing supposed to bring good luck or to symbolize a particular organization or event: *The girls kept the stray dog as a mascot, a team mascot.* <French, from Provençal (a language of S France) *mascotto* lucky charm>

mas·cu·line (mas′kyə lin) *adj* **1** to do with men and boys: *a masculine name, a masculine voice, masculine features.* **2** *Grammar* to do with a class of noun that includes nouns for male people and animals. Examples: *king, bull*
n Grammar the masculine gender, or a word or form in this gender: *"Emperor" is the masculine of "empress."* <Old French, from Latin *mas* male> **mas′cu·lin′i·ty** *n.*

ma·ser (mā′zər) *n* a device for amplifying microwaves to produce a very narrow, intense beam of radiation. <*m*(icrowave) *a*(mplification) by *s*(timulated) *e*(mission) of *r*(adiation)>

mash (mash) *n* **1** a soft mixture or mass. **2** a warm mixture of bran or meal and water for horses and other livestock. **3** crushed malt or grain soaked in hot water for making beer. **4** a similar preparation of grain used to make whisky.
v **1** crush and mix into a soft mass: *Please mash the potatoes.* **2** mix crushed malt with hot water in brewing. <Old English *masc-*> **mash′er** *n.*

mas·jid (mus′jid) *Islam n* a mosque. <Arabic>

mask (mask) *n* **1** a covering for the face, worn for disguise or in fun. **2** a thing that hides or disguises: *a mask of friendship.* **3** a covering or device for the face, worn for protection from cold or against infection, or to aid breathing: *a ski mask, a surgical mask, a gas mask, an oxygen mask.* **4** a clay, wax, or plaster likeness of a person's face.
v **1** cover the face with a mask. **2** hide or disguise: *A smile masked her disappointment.* <Latin *masca*> **mask′er** *n.*

masked (maskt) *adj* **1** wearing a mask: *a masked dancer.* **2** hidden or disguised: *masked jealousy.*

masked ball *n* a formal dance at which masks are worn.

mask·ing tape (mas′king) *n* sticky paper tape, often used to cover areas that are not to be painted.

✱ **mas·kin·onge** (mas′kə nonj′) *n* a muskellunge. <Cdn French, from Algonquian>

GRAMMAR AND USAGE

Maskinonge is the official Canadian name for this fish, although **muskellunge** is now the more common term.

mas·och·ism (mas′ə kiz′əm) *or* (maz′ə kiz′əm) *n* the psychological tendency to experience pleasure from being hurt or humiliated. <L. von Sacher-*Masoch* 19c novelist who described it>

ma·son (mā′sən) *n* **1** a person whose work is building with stone, brick, or similar materials. **2** in full, **Freemason** a member of an international association dedicated to mutual help. <Old French *masson*>

Ma·son·ite (mā′sən īt) *Trademark n* a building material in the form of smooth, dense sheets of fine wood fibres pressed together.

Mason jar *n* a wide-mouthed glass jar with a top that screws on, used especially for home canning and preserving. <J.L. *Mason,* a 19c inventor who patented such a jar>

ma·son·ry (mā′sən rē) *n, pl* **ma·son·ries** **1** the work done by a mason. **2** something constructed of stone, brick, or similar materials, such as a chimney or wall.

masque (mask) *n* an amateur entertainment among the nobility in England in the 1500s and 1600s that featured masked actors and dancers.

mas·quer·ade (mas′kə rād′) *n* **1** a party or dance at which masks and fancy costumes are worn. **2** a false pretence or disguise.
v **mas·quer·ad·ed, mas·quer·ad·ing** disguise yourself or pretend to be something you are not: *The king masqueraded as a beggar to find out if his people really liked him.* **mas′quer·ad′er** *n.*

ETYMOLOGY

Masquerade comes from Spanish *mascarada, mascara,* meaning "mask." Masquerades became popular in England in the 1700s.

mass[1] (mas) *n* **1** a lump of matter with no definite shape: *a mass of dough.* **2** a large quantity of individual parts together: *a mass of flowers.* **3** the majority or greater part: *The mass of people consider themselves sensible.* **4** on a large scale: *mass buying.* **5** bulk or size: *the huge mass of an iceberg.* **6** *Physics* a measure of the amount of matter a body contains. **7 the masses** the people or general population: *Most TV programs are entertainment for the masses.*
v assemble or be assembled in large numbers or amounts: *Refugees are massing on the border.*
adj to do with many people or things: *a mass assembly.* <Old French, from Greek *maza* barley bread>

mass[2] (mas) *Christianity n* **1 Mass** Holy Communion in a service of worship in the Catholic Church and in some other Christian churches. **2** a piece of music written for or suggested by parts of the Mass. <possibly from the last words of the service in latin: *Ite, missa est* Go, it is the dismissal>

mas·sa·cre (mas′ə kər) *n* a wholesale, brutal slaughter of people or animals.
v **mas·sa·cred, mas·sa·cring** kill many people or animals needlessly or brutally. <Old French *macecle* slaughterhouse>

mas·sage (mə sȧzh′) *or* (mə sȧj′) *n* a rubbing and kneading of the body to stimulate the circulation of blood and make the muscles and joints more supple: *A thorough massage relaxes tired muscles.*
v **mas·saged, mas·sag·ing** give a massage to. <French, from Portuguese *massa* knead>

massage parlour *n* a place of business that offers body massage and may offer sexual services.

mas·sa·sau·ga (mas′ə sog′ə) *n* a small rattlesnake found in southern Ontario and the eastern US. <*Mississauga* River, Ontario, from Ojibwa *misi* great + *sauk* river mouth>

mas·seur (ma sər′) *n* a man whose work is massaging.

mas·seuse (ma səz′) *n* a woman whose work is massaging.

a bat	e bed	i bid	o pot	u cup	th **thin**
ā cake	ē me	ī bite	ō go	ū rude	ᴛʜ **then**
ȧ bar	ə about	ər over	ȯ for	u̇ put	zh measure

mas·sif (ma sēf′) *Geology n* a compact group of mountains, especially one separated from other mountains: *Mount Logan in Yukon Territory is the highest point of the world's largest massif.* <French = massive>

mas·sive (mas′iv) *adj* **1** big, heavy, broad, and solid: *a massive wrestler, massive arms.* **2** very intense or severe: *a massive thunderstorm, a massive heart attack.* **3** exceptionally large: *massive crowds.* **mas′sive·ly** *adv.* **mas′sive·ness** *n.*

mass market *n* the general population considered as a market for a product or service, as opposed to smaller parts of the population that represent specialized markets. **mass-market** *adj.*

mass marketing *n* the marketing of goods to be sold to large numbers of people.

mass media MEDIA (def. 1).

mass noun *Grammar n* a noun that stands for something that cannot be counted, like milk.

GRAMMAR AND USAGE

A **mass noun** cannot be used with an indefinite article (*a, one*) or in the plural. *Some* and *much* can be used with mass nouns: *some sand, much honesty.*

mass number *Physics, Chemistry n* the whole number that most closely indicates the mass of an isotope, equal to the sum of the protons and neutrons in the nucleus.

mass–pro·duce (mas′prə dyūs′) *or* (mas′prə dūs′) *v* **mass-pro·duced, mass-pro·duc·ing** make or manufacture an item in very large numbers, especially using an assembly line. **mass production** *n.*

mass transit *n* public transportation within an urban area that may include buses, commuter trains, and subways.

mast[1] (mast) *n* **1** a long pole of wood or metal set upright on a ship to support the sails and rigging. **2** an upright pole: *a flag mast, a television mast.* <Old English *mæst*> **mast′less** *adj.* **mast′like′** *adj.*

mast[2] (mast) *n* the fruit of forest trees fallen to the ground, used as food by pigs and wild animals. <Old English *mæst*>

mas·tec·to·my (ma stek′tə mē) *n, pl* **mas·tec·to·mies** a surgical operation to remove a breast. <Greek *mastos* breast + *-ectomy* surgical removal>

mas·ter (mas′tər) *n* **1** a person who has power, authority, or control in an organization or group. **2** a great artist, or a picture by a great artist: *an old master.* **3 a** a person who is an expert in some work or subject. **b** a skilled worker, or craftsperson, qualified to teach apprentices. **4** the captain of a merchant ship. **5** a male teacher, especially in a private school, or the head of a college or school. **6** an initial recording, film, object, or document from which duplicates are made.
adj main or controlling: *a master switch, a master plan.*
v **1** acquire thorough knowledge or skill in something: *to master another language.* **2** gain control of or overcome: *Learn to master your temper.* <Latin *magister* chief>

master builder *n* a person skilled in planning or constructing buildings.

mas·ter·ful (mas′tər fəl) *adj* **1** powerful and able to control others. **2** expert or very skilful: *The actor gave a masterful performance.* **mas′ter·ful·ly** *adv.*

master key *n* a key that opens all the different locks in a building.

mas·ter·ly (mas′tər lē) *adj* expert or skilful: *a masterly painter.* **mas′ter·li·ness** *n.*

mas·ter·mind (mas′tər mīnd′) *n* a person with a remarkable intellect, especially one who plans and directs a complex project.
v plan and direct a complex project.

master of ceremonies *n* a person in charge of a ceremony or entertainment who announces the successive events and makes sure that they take place in the proper order.

mas·ter·piece (mas′tər pēs′) *n* **1** a thing done or made with wonderful skill. **2** an artist's greatest piece of work.

master stroke *n* a very skilful act or achievement.

mas·ter·y (mas′tə rē) *n, pl* **mas·ter·ies** **1** great knowledge or skill: *mastery of foreign languages.* **2** control or victory over something: *mastery over nature. Two teams competed for mastery.*

mast·head (mast′hed′) *n* **1** the top of a ship's mast. **2** the part of a newspaper or magazine that gives the title, the names of the publisher and editors, and the publication address.

mas·tic (mas′tik) *n* **1** a yellowish resin from the bark of a Mediterranean tree, used in making varnish, chewing gum, and as a flavouring, or the tree itself. **2** a puttylike waterproof filler and sealant used in building. <Old French, from Greek *mastiche*>

mas·ti·cate (mas′tə kāt′) *v* **mas·ti·cat·ed, mas·ti·cat·ing** CHEW (def. 1). **mas′ti·ca′ble** (mas′tə kə bəl) *adj.* **mas′ti·ca′tion** *n.* **mas′ti·ca′tor** *n.*

mas·tiff (mas′tif) *n* a large, strong dog with drooping ears and hanging jowls.

mas·to·don (mas′tə don′) *n* a large, extinct mammal that resembled an elephant. <Latin, from Greek *mastos* breast + *odontos* tooth, from the breastlike projections on its molars>

mas·tur·bate *v* **mas·tur·bat·ed, mas·tur·bat·ing** fondle or stimulate one's own genitals to achieve sexual satisfaction. <Latin *masturbari*> **mas·tur·ba′tion** *n.*

mat[1] (mat) *n* **1** a piece of protective material placed on a floor, especially a piece of coarse fabric like a woven rug. **2** a small piece of material to put under a dish, glass, etc. **3** a layer of something packed or tangled thickly together: *a mat of weeds, a mat of chest hair.*
v **mat·ted, mat·ting** **1** cover with a mat. **2** pack or tangle together like a mat: *The swimmer's wet hair was matted.* <Latin *matta*>

mat[2] (mat) *n* **1** a dull, flat colour, paint, or surface. Also, **matte**. **2** a sheet of cardboard placed on the back of a picture or photograph as a mounting or to form a border.
adj with a dull finish in a colour, paint, or surface. Also, **matte**.

mat·a·dor (mat′ə dôr′) *n* the chief performer in a bullfight, who kills the bull. <Spanish, from Persian *mat* dead>

match[1] (mach) *n* **1** a person or thing equal to another in quality or strength: *The poorly trained team was no match for their opponents.* **2** a person or thing like another: *The identical twins were a perfect match.* **3** two people or things that are alike and go well together: *Those two horses make a good match.* **4** a game or contest: *a tennis match.* **5 a** a marriage. **b** a person considered as a possible spouse: *That young man was considered a good match.*
v **1** be equal to: *No one could match the unknown archer.* **2** be alike or go well together: *The rugs and the wallpaper match.* **3** be the same as: *The two documents matched exactly.* **4** find one like: *They were able to match the ornament with another.* <Old English *gemæcca* companion> **match′er** *n.*
meet your match, be faced with a person or thing you cannot defeat or overcome: *She was unbeatable at chess, but she finally met her match.*

match[2] (mach) *n* a short, slender piece of wood or pasteboard tipped with a mixture that catches fire when rubbed on a specially prepared surface. <Old French, from Greek *muxa* lamp wick>

match·book (mach′bu̇k) *n* a small cardboard folder with cardboard matches fastened into it and a striking surface on the cover.

match·box (mach′boks) *n* a small box for matches, often with a striking surface on one side.

match·less (mach′lis) *adj* so great or wonderful that it cannot be equalled. **match′less·ly** *adv.* **match′less·ness** *n.*

match·mak·er (mach′mā′kər) *n* **1** a person who arranges, or tries to arrange, marriages or relationships for others. **2** a person who arranges contests, competitions, or commercial transactions. **match′mak·ing** *n.*

match point *n* the final point needed to win a sports match, especially in tennis.

match·stick (mach′stik′) *n* a small, thin stick of wood made into a MATCH[2].

match·wood (mach′wu̇d′) *n* splinters or tiny pieces of wood.

mate[1] (māt) *n* **1** one of a pair: *Where is the mate to this glove?* **2** either of two animals or birds, one male and one female, who become a pair to produce young: *The bird called to its mate.* **3** a spouse. **4** an assistant or deputy, especially an assistant to a skilled worker or to the captain of a ship: *cook's mate.* **5** *UK, Informal* a companion or fellow worker: *The two men were mates in the army.*
v **mat·ed, mat·ing 1** put, bring, or become a pair to be bred or to produce young: *Birds mate in the spring.* **2** marry. **3** join together mechanically, as one part to another. <German = comrade>

mate[2] (māt) *n, v* **mat·ed, mat·ing** checkmate in chess. <Old French>

ma·te·ri·al (mə tē′rē əl) *n* **1** the matter or collection of items that is used to make or do something: *dress material, building materials, writing materials.* **2** written or printed information or ideas.
adj **1** of physical matter or things: *the material world.* **2** concerned with physical needs or desires, such as food and shelter, sometimes to the neglect of spiritual values. **3** important, relevant, or significant: *Hard work was a material factor in her success.* <Latin *materia* substance>

ma·te·ri·al·ism (mə tē′rē ə liz′əm) *n* **1** a tendency to care too much for personal possessions and physical comforts rather than spiritual values. **2** the belief that nothing exists except matter and that all action, thought, and feeling can be explained by the movements and changes of matter. **ma·te′ri·al′ist** *n.* **ma·te′ri·al·is′ti·c** *adj.* **ma·te′ri·al·is′ti·cal·ly** *adv.*

ma·te·ri·al·ize (mə tē′rē ə līz′) *v* **ma·te·ri·al·ized, ma·te·ri·al·iz·ing 1** become an actual fact: *Our plan for the party did not materialize.* **2** appear or cause to appear in material or bodily form: *A spirit materialized from the smoke of the magician's fire.* **ma·te′ri·al·i·za′tion** *n.*

ma·te·ri·al·ly (mə tē′rē ə lē) *adv* **1** with regard to material things or physically: *She improved materially and morally.* **2** considerably or greatly: *The tide helped the progress of the boat materially.*

ma·té·ri·el (mə tē rē el′) *n* the equipment and supplies of a group, especially an army. <French = material>

ma·ter·nal (mə tər′nəl) *adj* **1** to do with a mother: *maternal care, maternal instincts.* **2** related on the mother's side of the family: *maternal grandparents.* Compare PATERNAL. <French, from Latin *mater* mother> **ma·ter′nal·ly** *adv.*

ma·ter·ni·ty (mə tər′nə tē) *n* the fact or condition of being a mother; motherhood.

maternity hospital *n* a hospital for women giving birth.

maternity leave *n* paid time off work for a mother for a period of time before she bears or adopts a baby.

math (math) *Informal n* mathematics.

math·e·mat·i·cal (math′ə mat′ə kəl) *adj* **1** to do with mathematics: *mathematical problems.* **2** exact or accurate: *mathematical precision.* **math′e·mat′i·cal·ly** *adv.*

math·e·mat·ics (math′ə mat′iks) *n* (*with singular verb*) the science that studies the abstract properties and relationships of numbers, quantities, and spatial arrangements. <Old French, from Greek *methematos* mathematical learning>
math′e·ma·ti′cian (math′ə mə tish′ən) *n.*

mat·i·née or **mat·i·nee** (mat′ə nā′) *or* (mat′ə nā′) *n* a performance held in the afternoon, especially a dramatic or musical one. <French *matin* morning, i.e., during the day>

ma·tri·arch (mā′trē ärk′) *n* **1** a mother who is the ruler of a family or tribe. **2** a usually older woman who is powerful within a family. <Latin *mater* mother + Greek *arches* ruler> **ma′tri·ar′chal** *adj.*

a **bat**	e **bed**	i **bid**	o **pot**	u **cup**	th **thin**
ā **cake**	ē **me**	ī **bite**	ō **go**	ū **rude**	TH **then**
ä **bar**	ə **about**	ər **over**	ô **for**	u̇ **put**	zh **measure**

M

ma·tri·ar·chy (mā′trē är′kē) *n, pl* **ma·tri·ar·chies** a form of social organization in which a woman is the ruler of a family or tribe, descent being traced through her. Compare PATRIARCHY.

ma·tri·ces (mā′trə sēz′) *or* (mat′rə sēz′) a plural of MATRIX.

ma·tric·u·late (mə trik′yə lāt′) *v* **ma·tric·u·lat·ed, ma·tric·u·lat·ing** be enrolled or admitted as a student in a college or university. <Latin *matrix* register> **ma·tric′u·la′tion** *n.*

ma·tri·lin·e·al (mat′rə lin′ē əl) *adj* to do with descent or kinship through the maternal line. Compare PATRILINEAL. **ma′tri·lin′e·al·ly** *adv.*

mat·ri·mo·ny (mat′rə mō′nē) *n, pl* **mat·ri·mo·nies** the act or ceremony of marrying, or the condition of being married. <Latin *matrimonium* marriage, from *mater* mother> **ma′tri·mo′ni·al** *adj.*

ma·trix (mā′triks) *or* (mat′riks) *n, pl* **ma·tri·ces** or **ma·trix·es 1** an environment or material within which something develops or is structured, such as a mould for a casting or the rock in which gems are embedded. **2** a rectangular array of quantities or things arranged in rows and columns that is treated as one thing and manipulated according to certain rules. <Latin *mater* mother>

ma·tron (mā′trən) *n* **1** an older married woman or widow. **2** a woman who manages the household affairs or supervises the inmates of a school, hospital, or other institution. <Latin *mater* mother>

ma·tron·ly (mā′trən lē) *adj* like or suitable for a MATRON (def. 1). **ma′tron·li·ness** *n.*

matron of honour or **honor** *n* a married woman who is the chief attendant of the bride at a wedding.

matte (mat) MAT[2].

mat·ted (mat′id) *adj* formed or entangled into a mat or thick mass: *a matted growth of shrubs.*

mat·ter (mat′ər) *n* **1** the physical material of which a thing is made. Matter has mass and occupies space. **2** a situation being considered or dealt with: *a matter of life and death.* **3** the content of what is said or written, apart from the way in which it is said or written: *There was very little matter in her speech.* **4** (*used with* **the**) the basis or cause of distress or a problem: *What is the matter with her?* **5** a thing with a specified quality: *a matter of fact.* **6** things written or printed: *reading matter.* **7** importance or significance: *Let it go since it is of no matter.* **8** a substance in or discharged from the body: *waste matter.*
v **1** be important or significant: *Nothing seems to matter when you are very sick.* **2** be influential as a person: *the people who matter.* <Latin *materia* substance>
for that matter, so far as that is concerned: *He doesn't belong here or, for that matter, anywhere.*
matter of course, something that is to be expected: *She'll make the high-school basketball team next year as a matter of course.*
no matter, a it is not important: *We don't have paper; oh well, no matter.* **b** regardless of: *She wants a bicycle, no matter what it costs.*

mat·ter–of–fact (mat′ər əv fakt′) *adj* dealing with facts, and not imaginative or fanciful: *a matter-of-fact report.*

mat·tock (mat′ək) *n* a tool like a pickaxe but with a flat blade on one side or flat blades on both sides, used for loosening soil and cutting roots. <Old English *mattuc*>

mat·tress (mat′ris) *n* a long, thick pad made of a material encased in a covering of strong cloth, and used on a bed or as a bed. <Old French, from Arabic *matrah* cushion>

ma·ture (mə chůr′) *adj* **1** ripe or full-grown: *Grain is harvested when it is mature.* **2** with or showing full development of the body or mind: *a mature face, mature thinking.* **3** fully worked out; carefully and completely thought out: *By next year, there will be a mature plan for the subway.* **4** due or payable: *a mature loan.*
v **ma·tured, ma·tur·ing 1** come or bring to full growth: *The apples are maturing rapidly. More sun is needed to mature the crops.* **2** come or bring to full development of the mind or body: *The experience has matured her understanding.* **3** make or become ready or complete: *to mature a plan.* **4** fall due or become payable: *The note to the bank matured yesterday.* <Latin *maturus* ripe> **mat′u·ra′tion** *n.* **ma·ture′ly** *adv.*

ma·tu·ri·ty (mə chůr′rə tē) *n* **1** a condition of full growth or development: *She had reached maturity by the time she was twenty.* **2** the condition of being completed or ready: *When their preparations reached maturity, they were able to begin.* **3** the time when a debt is payable.

matz·o (mȧ′tsō) *n pl* **matz·os** a thin piece of unleavened bread, traditionally eaten by Jews, especially during the Passover. <Hebrew *matsah*>

maud·lin (mod′lən) *adj* sentimental in a weak or tearful way, sometimes because of drunkenness or excitement. <Old French, from Latin *Magdalena,* since Mary Magdalene is often portrayed as weeping>

maul (mol) *v* wound by scratching, tearing, or other rough treatment: *The lion mauled its keeper badly.*
n a very heavy hammer or mallet. <Old French, from Latin *malleus* mallet>

maun·der (mon′dər) *v* **1** talk in a rambling, foolish way: *People who maunder talk much but say little.* **2** move or act in an aimless or vague manner. <origin uncertain>

Mau·ri·ta·nia (mō ri tā′nya) *n* a country in northwest Africa. **Mau·ri·ta′ni·an** *adj, n.*

Mau·ri·tius (mō ri′shəs) *n* an island country in the Indian Ocean. **Mau·ri′tian** *adj, n.*

mau·so·le·um (mos′ə lē′əm) *or* (moz′ə lē′əm) *n, pl* **mau·so·le·ums** or **mau·so·le·a** (-lē′ə) a large, stately tomb.

ETYMOLOGY

Mausoleum comes through Latin from Greek *Mausoleion,* the tomb of King Mausolos of Caria in Asia Minor. This magnificent tomb was erected in 353 BCE and was considered one of the seven wonders of the ancient world.

It was elaborately decorated, with statues by the best sculptors of the day. The tomb stood for 16 centuries, but in 1304 BCE an earthquake destroyed it. Though it was looted, some of the statues still survive.

mauve (mōv) *or* (mov) *adj* pale purple. <French, from Latin *malva* mallow, from the colour of the mallow plant>

ma·ven or **ma·vin** (mā′vən) *Informal n* a person who knows much about a particular subject: *a railway maven.* <Yiddish>

mav·er·ick (mav′ə rik) *n* **1** a person who is unconventional or unwilling to conform, especially to a group or party. **2** a calf or other animal not marked with an owner's brand. <S. *Maverick,* 19c rancher who did not brand his cattle>

maw (mȯ) *n* the mouth and throat of a fierce or greedy animal or person. <Old English *maga*>

mawk·ish (mȯk′ish) *adj* sickly sentimental or weakly emotional. <Old Norse *mathkr*> **mawk′ish·ly** *adv.* **mawk′ish·ness** *n.*

max (maks) *Slang adv, adj, n* maximum: *It'll take me two hours, max (adv). This song sounds best at max volume (adj). Fifty bucks is the max I can give you for it (n).*
v raise to the maximum: *It's a good way to max your profits.*
max out, reach the upper limit of capacity or ability: *He can't buy anything because his credit card's maxed out.*
to the max, as far, as much, or as high as possible: *Enjoy yourself to the max.*

maxi– *combining form* large for its kind: *maxiburger.*
n **maxi** *Informal* something large for its kind. <*maximum*>

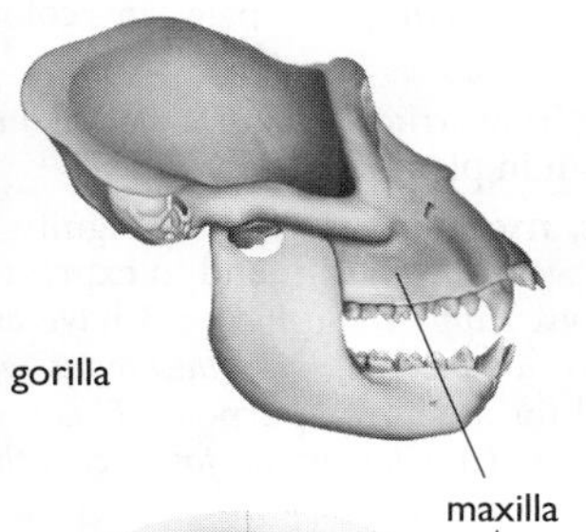
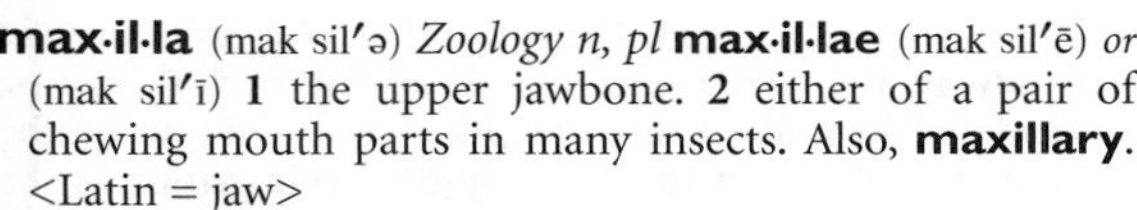

The **maxilla** consists of two irregularly shaped bones that are fused in the middle to form the upper jaw and support the upper teeth. The maxilla is hollow and contains an air cavity called a *maxillary sinus* that leads to the main sinus opening.

max·il·la (mak sil′ə) *Zoology n, pl* **max·il·lae** (mak sil′ē) *or* (mak sil′ī) **1** the upper jawbone. **2** either of a pair of chewing mouth parts in many insects. Also, **maxillary.** <Latin = jaw>
max′il·lar′y (mak′sə ler′ē) *adj.*

max·im (mak′səm) *n* a short rule of conduct, proverb, or statement of a general truth. "Look before you leap" is a maxim. <French, from Latin *maxima propositio* greatest proposition>

max·i·mize (mak′sə mīz′) *v* **max·i·mized, max·i·miz·ing** **1** make as great as possible: *Maximize your expectation of getting good grades by working extra hard.* **2** treat or cause to seem as great or important: *Her review maximized the positive aspects of the program.*

max·i·mum (mak′sə məm) *n, pl* **max·i·mums** or **max·i·ma** the largest or highest amount: *Drivers must not exceed the maximum of 60 km/h.*
adj largest, highest, or greatest: *The maximum score on this test is 100.* <Latin *magnus* great>

may (mā) *v, past tense* **might** an auxiliary verb used to express **1** permission, opportunity, or possibility: *You may go now. You may if you can. She may have been the one.* **2** a wish or prayer: *May you be very happy.* **3** contingency, especially in clauses expressing condition, concession, purpose, or result: *I write that you may know my plans.* <Old English *mæg*>

GRAMMAR AND USAGE

May, in formal English, means "being allowed" or "permitted": *May I close the door?*

Can means "physically able to do something": *I can close the door.*

However, in informal language, people use *can* for both meanings: *Can I close the door?*

May (mā) *n* the fifth month of the year, with 31 days. <Latin *Maius*>

Ma·ya (mȧ′yə) *n, pl* **Ma·ya** or **Ma·yas** **1** a member of an Indian people mainly of Mexico, Belize, and Guatemala, descendants of an ancient civilization that reached its height between about 300 and 900 CE. **2** the language of the Maya. **Ma′yan** *adj, n.*

May apple *n* a N American plant with a large white flower, or its edible, yellowish, egg-shaped fruit.

may·be (mā′bē) *adv* possibly or perhaps.

CONFUSABLES

Maybe as an adverb is one word, meaning "perhaps": *Maybe I should take my umbrella. Maybe you should come with me.*

May be is a two-word verb phrase and suggests something that will likely happen: *She may be home soon.*

May Day *n* May 1, often celebrated as a festival in honour of springtime or of working people.

May·day (mā′dā′) *n* an international signal of distress used in emergencies by ships and aircraft. <French *m'aider* help me>

may·flow·er (mā′flou′ər) *n* **1** a plant or tree that flowers in May, especially the **trailing arbutus**. It is the floral emblem of Nova Scotia. **2** **Mayflower** the ship on which the Pilgrims sailed to America in 1620.

may·fly (mā′flī) *n* a slender insect, with the forewings much larger than the hind wings, that dies soon after reaching the adult stage.

a bat	e bed	i bid	o pot	u cup	th **thin**
ā cake	ē me	ī bite	ō go	ū rude	ᴛʜ **then**
ȧ bar	ə about	ər over	ȯ for	ů put	zh measure

may·hem (mā′hem) *n* violent or destructive disorder. <Old French>

may·n't (mā′ənt) *or* (mānt) *contraction* may not.

ma·yo (mā′ō) *Informal n* mayonnaise.

may·on·naise (mā′ə nāz′) *n* a thick dressing for salads, made of egg yolks, vegetable oil, vinegar or lemon juice, and seasoning. <French, probably from Port *Mahon* seaport in Minorca, where it was thought to have been introduced>

may·or (mā′ər) *n* the person at the head of the government of a city, town, or village. <Old French, from Latin *major*>

may·or·al·ty (mā′ə rəl tē) *or* (mer′əl tē) *n, pl* **may·or·al·ties 1** the position of mayor. **2** a mayor's term of office.

May·pole or **may·pole** (mā′pōl′) *n* a high pole decorated with flowers or ribbons, around which merrymakers traditionally dance on MAY DAY.

May queen *n* a girl traditionally crowned with flowers and honoured as queen on May Day.

maze (māz) *n* **1** a network of paths through which it is hard to find the way: *A guide led us through a maze of caves.* **2** a complicated arrangement, such as of offices, streets, or buildings. <variant of *amaze*>

ma·zel tov (ma′zəl tov′) *Hebrew interj* Congratulations! Best Wishes! <Hebrew *mazzal tob* = good star>

ma·zur·ka or **ma·zour·ka** (mə zər′kə) *or* (mə zůr′kə) *n* a lively Polish dance, or the music for it. <German, from Polish>

M.C. EMCEE.

Mc·Car·thy·ism (mə kar′thē iz′əm) *n* the practice of holding public investigations or making public accusations against political figures or public servants, especially on slight evidence. <J. *McCarthy*, chairman of the US Senate Permanent Investigations Committee in the 1950s during the Cold War. He was noted for his somewhat paranoid and heavy-handed approach to ferreting out and dealing with suspected Communist sympathizers.>

Mc·Coy (mə koi′) *n* <origin uncertain>
the real McCoy, *Slang* a genuine person or thing: *This is not a fake diamond; it's the real McCoy.*

Mc·In·tosh (mak′ən tosh′) *n* a bright red eating apple with crisp, white flesh. <J. *McIntosh*, 18c Ontario farmer who found such an apple tree while clearing his farm.>

me (mē) *pron* the objective form of I: *The dog bit me. Give me a bandage.*
n MI. <Old English>

GRAMMAR AND USAGE

Me is always the correct form to use as the object of a verb or of a preposition: *Between you and me, I like the oval table best. The ball hit me on the head.*

Some people use *It is I* in very formal writing or speech. However, it is entirely acceptable to say *It is me* or *It's me* in speech and in most writing.

mead (mēd) *n* an alcoholic drink made from fermented honey and water. <Old English *medu*>

mead·ow (med′ō) *n* **1** a piece of grassy land, especially one where hay is grown. **2** low, grassy land near a stream. <Old English *mædwe*>

mead·ow·lark (med′ō lark′) *n* a N American songbird of the blackbird family, with a brown, streaky back and yellow and black underparts.

mea·gre (mē′gər) *adj* **1** poor or scanty: *a meagre meal.* **2** thin or lean: *a meagre face.* Also, **meager**. <Old French, from Latin *macer* thin> **mea′gre·ness** *n.*

meal[1] (mēl) *n* the food served or eaten at any one time. <Old English *mæl*>

meal[2] (mēl) *n* **1** ground grain, especially cornmeal. **2** a thing ground to a powder. <Old English *melu*>

meal ticket *n* **1** a ticket giving the holder the right to a meal. **2** *Informal* someone or something that provides a living, especially for little or no effort: *He stays with her because she's his meal ticket.*

meal·time (mēl′tīm′) *n* the usual time for eating a meal.

meal·worm (mēl′wərm′) *n* the larva of various beetles that feeds on flour and other grain products.

meal·y (mē′lē) *adj* **meal·i·er, meal·i·est 1** dry and powdery: *mealy potatoes.* **2** of or covered with ground grain: *the miller's mealy hands.* **3** pale in colour. **meal′i·ness** *n.*

meal·y–mouthed (mē′lē mouᴛʜd′) *or* (mē′lē moutht′) *adj* unwilling to tell the truth in plain words.

mean[1] (mēn) *v* **meant, mean·ing 1** refer to, signify, or denote: *What does this word mean?* **2** intend to express or convey: *What is that look supposed to mean?* **3** have as a purpose or intent: *I do not mean to go. She means well.* **4** design or be destined for a definite purpose: *This toy is meant for young children. Fate meant us for each other.* <Old English *mænan*>
mean well by, have kindly feelings toward.

mean[2] (mēn) *adj* **1** of poor appearance or quality: *a mean little house.* **2** unkind or unfair: *mean thoughts.* **3** unwilling to give or share: *mean about money.* **4** aggressive, vicious, and bad-tempered: *a mean horse.* **5** *Informal* excellent: *She still plays a mean guitar.* **6** *Archaic* low in social position or rank: *She was of mean birth.* <Old English *gemæne*> **mean′ly** *adv.* **mean′ness** *n.*
no mean, very good: *He is no mean swimmer.*

mean[3] (mēn) *n* **1** *Mathematics* the quotient of the sum of several quantities and their number. An **arithmetic mean** is the average of a set of numerical values, calculated by adding them together and dividing by the number of terms in the set. A **geometric mean** is the central number in a geometric sequence, such as 8 in 2, 4, 8, 16, 32. **2** a condition, quality, or course of action halfway between two extremes or opposites: *the golden mean.* **3** **means** *pl* (*with singular or plural verb*) an action or system by which something is brought about: *A car is a means of transportation. The means to be successful in life are within our own hands.* **4** **means** *pl* money or resources: *to live within your means, a woman of means. His means allow him to be generous.*
adj **1** halfway between the two extremes of several quantities and their numbers: *The mean temperature for*

July in Yarmouth is 16°C. **2** intermediate in kind, quality, or degree: *She is trying to discover a mean course between the two extremes of telling nothing and telling everything.* <Old French, from Latin *medianus* middle>

by all (**no**) **means,** certainly (not): *By all means stay for dinner. This work is by no means easy.*

by any means, certainly not (*with a negative*): *I'm not finished by any means.*

by means of, by the use of: *I found my dog by means of a notice in the paper.*

means to an end, a way of getting or doing something: *She said that education was an end in itself, not just a means to an end.*

GRAMMAR AND USAGE

Means, meaning "how something is done," is plural in form, and singular or plural in use:
What is your means of transportation?
These are effective means for dealing with the problem.

me·an·der (mē an′dər) *v* **1** of a road or a river, follow a winding course: *A brook meandered through the meadow.* **2** wander aimlessly: *We meandered through the park.*
n **1** a winding curve or bend of a road or a river. **2** an aimless wandering. <Latin, from Greek *Maiandros* winding river in Asia Minor>

mean·ie (mē′nē) *Informal n* an unkind or cruel person.

mean·ing (mē′ning) *n* what is meant, intended, or signified: *The meaning of the sentence is clear.*
adj intended to communicate something significant: *a meaning look.* **mean′ing·ful** *adj.* **mean′ing·ful·ly** *adv.* **mean′ing·ful·ness** *n.* **mean′ing·less** *adj.* **mean′ing·less·ly** *adv.* **mean′ing·less·ness** *n.* **mean′ing·ly** *adv.*

means test *n* an inquiry into the income and assets of a person applying for financial help of some kind, to see whether it is really needed.

meant (ment) past tense and past participle of MEAN[1].

mean·time (mēn′tīm′) *n* the time between: *The carnival doesn't start until Friday, so in the meantime we will make our costumes.*
adv in the time between: *Classes finish at 12 noon and begin again at 2 p.m.; meantime we can have lunch.*

mean·while (mēn′wīl′) *adv* **1** in the time or period between: *Classes finish at 12 and start again at 2; meanwhile we can swim and have lunch.* **2** at the same time, especially in a different place: *We hiked to the top of the ridge; meanwhile, burglars were robbing our house.*
n meantime.

mea·sles (mē′zəlz) *n* an infectious viral disease characterized by fever and a breaking out of small red spots on the skin. <probably Dutch *masel* spot>

mea·sly (mē′zlē) *adj* **mea·sli·er, mea·sli·est** contemptibly small or few: *He only gave me a few measly jellybeans.*

meas·ur·a·ble (mezh′ə rə bəl) *adj* capable of being measured.

meas·ure (mezh′ər) *v* **meas·ured, meas·ur·ing 1** find out the size, extent, etc. of something by using a device marked in standard units, or by comparing it with an object of known size: *to measure a room.* **2** be of a certain size or amount: *This brick measures 5 cm by 10 cm by 20 cm.* **3** (*usually with **off** or **out***) get or take by measuring: *Measure out a kilogram of potatoes.* **4** compare in order to judge something: *The soldier measured his strength with that of his enemy in a hand-to-hand-fight.*
n **1** the size, extent, etc. of something, especially by comparison with a standard: *Her waist measure is 60 cm.* **2** a system of measuring: *dry measure, square measure.* **3** a unit or standard of measuring, such as a centimetre, kilogram, litre, or hour. **4** a definite quantity measured out: *a measure of corn.* **5** a standard of comparison, estimation, or judgment: *By any measure he's an excellent musician.* **6** quantity, extent, degree, or proportion: *The measure of his courage was remarkable.* **7** a course of action or procedure: *to take measures to relieve suffering.* **8** rhythm in poetry or music: *the stately measure of blank verse.* **9** *Music* a bar of music, or the time of a piece of music. <Old French, from Latin *metiri* to measure>
meas′ur·er *n.*

beyond measure, greatly or exceedingly.

for good measure, as something extra or not necessarily expected.

in full (or **some**) **measure,** completely (partly or to some extent).

made to measure, made to the buyer's own measurements or exact requirements.

measure out, a distribute by measuring. **b** distribute carefully.

measure up, have the necessary features or meet a required standard: *The party did not measure up to her expectations.*

take someone's measure, judge someone's character or abilities.

SYNONYMS

Measure involves accurate measurement: *My dad measures my height each year.*

Calculate requires the use of mathematics to measure: *Calculate the area of the soccer field.*

Determine suggests a less accurate way of measuring: *We determined that we had picked about 10 kg of apples.*

Weigh involves finding the mass of someone or something: *The cashier weighed the bag of candy.*

meas·ured (mezh′ərd) *adj* **1** slow, regular, or uniform in rhythm: *the measured march of soldiers.* **2** restrained and carefully considered: *a measured answer.*

meas·ure·less (mezh′ər lis) *adj* too great to be measured: *the measureless ocean.*

meas·ure·ment (mezh′ər mənt) *n* **1** the action of measuring or finding the size, quantity, or amount. **2** the size found by measuring: *The measurements of the room are 6 m by 4 m.*

a bat	e bed	i bid	o pot	u cup	th **thin**
ā cake	ē me	ī bite	ō go	ū rude	ᴛʜ **then**
ȧ bar	ə about	ər over	ȯ for	u̇ put	zh measure

measures of central tendency *Statistics pln* the mean, median, and mode of a set of data.

measures of distribution *Statistics pln* the range, quartiles, extremes, clusters, and gaps in a set of data.

measuring cup *n* a cup marked with a scale of amounts for measuring pourable substances, especially cooking ingredients.

meat (mēt) *n* **1** animal flesh used as food: *Fish is not usually called meat.* **2** food of any kind: *meat and drink.* **3** the edible part of fruits, nuts, or eggs. **4** the essential part or parts: *the meat of an argument, the meat of a book.* <Old English *mete*> **meat′less** *adj.* **meat′like′** *adj.*
meat and potatoes, a basic but important thing: *I was OK in other subjects, but math was my meat and potatoes.*

meat·ball (mēt′bol′) *n* ground meat shaped into a small ball for cooking.

meat·loaf (mēt′lōf′) *n* ground meat mixed with breadcrumbs, beaten egg, and seasoning, baked in a loaf pan and sliced for eating.

meat·y (mē′tē) *adj* **meat·i·er, meat·i·est** **1** to do with the flavour of meat. **2** full of substance: *The speech was very meaty; it contained many valuable ideas.*

mebi– *Computers prefix* about a million (2^{20}). A mebibyte (me′bi bīt) is 1 048 576 bytes. *Symbol* **Mi** <*me*(*ga*) + *bi*(*nary*)>

Mec·ca or **mec·ca** (mek′ə) *n* a place that many people visit for a particular reason: *a tourist mecca.*

GRAMMAR AND USAGE

Mecca was the birthplace of Mohammed and is a place of pilgrimage for Muslims. It comes from Arabic *Makkah*. Most Muslims dislike the form *Mecca* and use the traditional *Makkah* instead.

The pilgrimage to Mecca is known as the *hajj*, and is one of the five requirements of Islam. Pilgrims fulfill a number of rituals in the course of their journey.

me·chan·ic (mə kan′ik) *n* a skilled worker who works with tools and maintains and repairs machines. <Old French, from Greek *mechane* machine>

me·chan·i·cal (mə kan′ə kəl) *adj* **1** to do with machinery or mechanisms: *a mechanical engineer.* **2** made or caused by machinery: *a mechanical failure.* **3** like a machine: *Her reading is very mechanical.* **4** to do with physical forces or motion. **me·chan′i·cal·ly** *adv.*

mechanical advantage *n* the measure of how much a machine converts a force. It is calculated as the ratio of the force produced by a machine to the force needed to make it work.

mechanical device *n* a DEVICE (def. 1) made up of two or more simple machines.

mechanical engineering *n* the branch of engineering that studies the design, production, and use of machines.

mechanical mixture *n* a mixture whose components can be separated by mechanical means.

me·chan·ics (mə kan′iks) *n* **1** (*with singular verb*) **a** the branch of physics dealing with motion and the effect of forces on bodies to produce motion or a state of balance. **b** the application of the principles of mechanics to the design, construction, and operation of machinery. **2** (*with plural verb*) the mechanical or technical aspects of something: *the mechanics of playing the piano. The mechanics of writing include a knowledge of the rules of punctuation.*

mech·a·nism (mek′ə niz′əm) *n* **1** a machine or its working parts: *Something must be wrong with the mechanism of our refrigerator.* **2** a system of parts working together as the parts of a machine do: *The bones and muscles are parts of the mechanism of the body.* **3** the means or way by which something is done: *Committees are a useful mechanism for getting things done.*

mech·a·nis·tic (mek′ə nis′tik) *adj* to do with mechanism, mechanics, or mechanical theories.

mech·a·nize (mek′ə nīz′) *v* **mech·a·nized, mech·a·niz·ing** **1** make use of machines or automatic devices in a process, activity, or place, especially to replace people or animals: *Much housework can be mechanized.* **2** modernize a military unit with armoured vehicles and tanks. **mech′a·ni·za′tion** (mek′ə nə zā′shən) *or* (mek′ə nī zā′shən) *n.*

med·al (med′əl) *n* a small, flat piece of metal stamped with a figure and an inscription to commemorate some event or as a mark of honour: *The captain won a medal for bravery. She won the gold medal for having the highest marks. A medal was struck to commemorate the moon landing.* <French *médaille*>

me·dal·lion (mə dal′yən) *n* **1** a large medal-shaped piece of jewellery, often worn as a pendant. **2** a round or oval design or ornament, such as on a book or as a pattern.

med·al·list (med′ə list) *n* a person who has won a medal: *a gold medallist at the Olympics.* Also, especially *US,* **medalist.**

med·dle (med′əl) *v* **med·dled, med·dling** interfere with other people's things or activities without being asked or needed: *Don't meddle with my books or my toys. That busybody has been meddling in my business.* <Old French, from Latin *miscere* to mix> **med′dler** *n.*

med·dle·some (med′əl səm) *adj* fond of meddling in other people's activities.

med·e·vac (med′ə vak) *n* an air ambulance. Also, **medivac.** <*med*(*ical*) + *evac*(*uate*)>

me·di·a (mē′dē ə) *pln* **1** (*with singular verb or, more formally, plural verb*) all the forms of communication that reach a huge audience, such as newspapers, radio, TV, magazines, film, and the Internet: *The media has a powerful influence on people's opinions* (*sing*). *The media believe that people prefer sensational news items* (*pl*). Also called **mass media.** **2** a plural of MEDIUM (defs. 1–4).
adj to do with the mass media: *media studies, a media event.*

GRAMMAR AND USAGE

Media is the plural of **medium**, and takes a plural verb: *The news media are interested in the story.*

Careful writers and speakers avoid using **media** as a singular noun or **medias** as a plural.

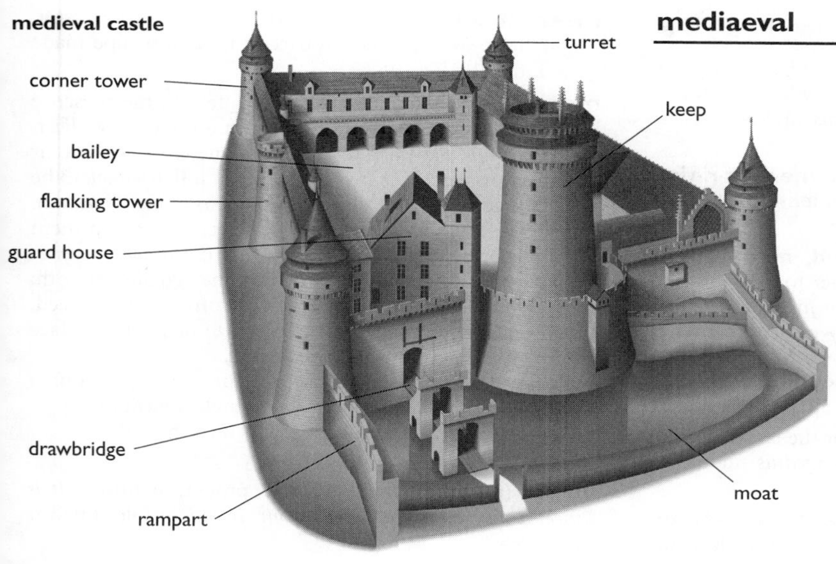

A **medieval** castle owned by a wealthy lord in the Middle Ages was essentially a fortress built to withstand lengthy attacks. It was protected with corner towers, flanking towers, ramparts, a moat, and a drawbridge.

The lord and his family lived in the keep, which was also heavily fortified and often had its own water supply. Even the animals lived inside the castle in an enclosure called a bailey.

me·di·ae·val (mē′dē ē′vəl) *or* (med′ē ē′vəl) MEDIEVAL.

me·di·al (mē′dē əl) *adj* in the middle. <Latin *medius* middle> **me′di·al·ly** *adv.*

media literacy *n* the understanding of the nature of media communications, particularly in regard to the structural features of the media, and how these may influence the content of the communications.
media literate *adj.*

me·di·an (mē′dē ən) *adj* in the middle of a distribution of values or quantities.
n **1** *Statistics* the middle number or point of a series. The median of 1, 3, 4, 8, 9 is 4. The median of 1, 3, 4, 8, 9, 10 is 6, that is, the average of the two middle numbers 4 and 8. **2** a central strip of grass or pavement on a highway separating the lanes used by traffic proceeding in opposite directions. <Latin *medius* middle>

me·di·ate (mē′dē āt′) *for v,* (mē′dē it) *for adj. v* **me·di·at·ed, me·di·at·ing 1** act in order to bring about an agreement between people or sides: *The mayor tried to mediate between the bus company and its employees.* **2** be the medium for bringing about a result, creating a link, or for communicating knowledge: *The book sought to mediate the connections between money and power.* <Latin *medius* middle> **me′di·a′tion** *n.* **me′di·a′tor** *n.*

med·ic (med′ik) *Informal n* a physician, medical student, or member of the medical branch of the armed forces. <*medical*>

med·i·ca·ble (med′ə kə bəl) *adj* capable of being cured or relieved by medical treatment.

med·i·cal (med′ə kəl) *adj* to do with healing or with the science and art of medicine: *medical advice, medical schools, medical treatment.*
n a medical examination. **med′ical·ly** *adv.*

med·i·care (med′ə ker′) *n* a government-sponsored program of health insurance, usually covering hospital costs, doctors' fees, and other medical expenses.

med·i·cate (med′ə kāt′) *v* **med·i·cat·ed, med·i·cat·ing** treat with medicine or a medical drug. **med′i·cat′ed** *adj.* **med′i·ca′tion** *adj.*

me·dic·i·nal (mə dis′ə nəl) *adj* with value as medicine or for healing. **me·dic′i·nal·ly** *adv.*

med·i·cine (med′ə sən) *or* (med′sən) *n* **1** a substance such as a drug, especially one taken by mouth, used to cure disease or improve health. **2** the art and science of curing disease or improving health: *The young woman decided to study medicine.* **3** among some Aboriginal peoples, a spell or charm believed to have healing, protective, or other power: *good medicine, bad medicine.* <Old French, from Latin *medicus* doctor>
give someone a taste of his or her own medicine, treat someone as that person has treated others.
take your medicine, submit to something unpleasant, such as punishment.

medicine ball *n* a large, heavy, leather ball tossed from one person to another for exercise.

medicine lodge *n* a sweat lodge.

medicine man or **woman** *n* a person traditionally believed by some Aboriginal peoples to have supernatural power over diseases and evil spirits.

🍁 **medicine wheel** *n* a circle of stones found at old Aboriginal encampments on the Prairies. These stones are believed to be associated with the religious life of the people who constructed them.

me·di·e·val or **me·di·ae·val** (mē′dē ē′vəl) *or* (med′ē ē′vəl) *adj* **1** to do with the Middle Ages, the period from about 500 CE to about 1450 CE: *medieval customs.* **2** *Informal* old-fashioned or primitive: *to laugh at medieval ideas about women's rights.* <Latin *medium* middle + *aevum* age>

a bat	e bed	i bid	o pot	u cup	th thin
ā cake	ē me	ī bite	ō go	ū rude	ᴛʜ then
ä bar	ə about	ər over	ô for	ů put	zh measure

M

me·di·o·cre (mē′dē ō′kər) *or* (mē′dē ō′kər) *adj* neither good nor bad: *a mediocre cake, a mediocre student.* <Latin = halfway up the mountain, from *medius* middle + *ocris* rugged mountain>

me·di·oc·ri·ty (mē′dē ok′rə tē) *n, pl* **me·di·oc·ri·ties** 1 mediocre quality, ability, or accomplishment. 2 a mediocre person.

med·i·tate (med′ə tāt′) *v* **med·i·tat·ed, med·i·tat·ing** 1 think quietly or focus the mind, either to relax or as a spiritual or religious act: *She meditated for half an hour.* 2 think about, consider, or plan deeply or carefully: *Our general was meditating an attack.* <Latin *meditari*> **med′i·ta′tion** *n.* **med′i·ta′tive** *adj.* **med′i·ta′tive·ly** *adv.*

Med·i·ter·ra·ne·an (med′ə tə rā′nē ən) *or* (med′ə tə rā′nyən) *adj* to do with the Mediterranean Sea or the lands around it. <Latin *mediterraneus* inland, from *medius* middle + *terra* land>

me·di·um (mē′dē əm) *n, pl* **me·di·a** (defs. 1–4) or **me·di·ums** (defs. 5, 6) 1 a means of doing something or through which a thing acts: *Cellphones are a medium of communication.* 2 a means of artistic expression: *The sculptor does some carving in stone, but her favourite medium is wood.* 3 a substance in which an organism lives or can be cultured: *a nutrient-rich medium.* 4 a liquid with which paints are mixed. 5 a person through whom spirits of the dead can supposedly communicate with the living. 6 a middle quality, condition, or balance between two extremes: *He thought that life in a small town was a happy medium between city and country life.* 7 **the media** MEDIA (def. 1).
adj about midway between two extremes of size or another quality: *Eggs can be cooked hard, soft, or medium.* <Latin = middle>

medium frequency *n* the range of radio frequencies between 300 and 3000 kilohertz, ranking next above low frequency.

me·di·um–sized (mē′dē əm sīzd′) *adj* neither large nor small of its kind.

med·ley (med′lē) *n, pl* **med·leys** 1 a mixture of things that ordinarily do not belong together. 2 a piece of music made up of tunes or extracts from other pieces. 3 a swimming race in which contestants swim sections in different strokes. <Old French, from Latin *misculare* to mix>

me·dul·la (mə dul′ə) *n, pl* **me·dul·lae** (mə dul′ē) *or* (mə dul′ī) 1 in full, **medulla oblongata** (ob′long gá′tə) the lowest part of the brain, at the top end of the spinal cord. 2 the inner substance of an organ or tissue such as a kidney. 3 the pith of plants. <Latin = marrow>

med·ul·lar·y (med′ə ler′ē) *adj* to do with the medulla or the medulla oblongata.

me·du·sa (mə dyū′sə) *or* (mə dū′sə) *n, pl* **me·du·sas** or **me·du·sae** (-sē) *or* (-sī) a jellyfish. <from its resemblance to *Medusa*, a monster in Greek legend with snakes for hair>

meek (mēk) *adj* quiet, gentle, and mild, especially in submitting to the authority or discipline of others: *The girl was meek as a lamb when she was scolded.* <Old Norse *meoc*> **meek′ly** *adv.* **meek′ness** *n.*

meer·schaum (mēr′shəm) *or* (mēr′shom) *n* a very soft, light stone used to make tobacco pipes, or a pipe made from it.

meet[1] (mēt) *v* **met, meet·ing** 1 come into the presence or company of another, especially in a direct way: *Their cars met on the narrow road.* 2 come into contact or connection with: *The two streets met at a sharp angle.* 3 be or get together: *The hosts met their guests at the restaurant. Parliament will meet next month.* 4 keep an appointment with; be present at the arrival of: *Meet me at noon, to meet a plane.* 5 be introduced to or become acquainted with: *Have you met my sister?* 6 satisfy or comply with a need, requirement, or condition: *to meet an obligation.* 7 face directly: *He met her stare with a smile.*
n an organized event, especially for a competition: *a racing meet, an athletic meet.* <Old English *metan*>
meet the eye (or **the ear**)**,** be seen (or heard).
meet up with, meet or join.

meet[2] (mēt) *Archaic adj* suitable, proper, or fitting: *It is meet that you should help your friends.* <Old English *gemæte*>

meet·ing (mē′ting) *n* 1 the gathering of two or more people for some purpose, such as for business, religious worship, or a social engagement: *He looked forward to the meeting with his friend's sister.* 2 a junction or place where two or more things meet: *a meeting of roads.*

meeting house *n* a place of Protestant, especially Quaker, worship.

meg (meg) *Informal n* megabyte(s).

meg·a (meg′a) *Informal adj, adv* extreme or extremely: *You'll get yourself in mega trouble doing that* (*adj*). *Everything they sell is mega expensive* (*adv*). <*mega-*>

mega– *combining form* 1 million: *megavolt.* See also the APPENDIX. 2 great or large: *megalith.* <Greek *megas* great>

> **GRAMMAR AND USAGE**
>
> The combining form **mega–** comes from Greek *megas*, meaning "great." It is found in *megabyte, megacity,* and *megaphone*. In slang English, it is added to words for emphasis: *megabucks, megarich, megastar*.

meg·a·buck (meg′a buk) *Slang n, pl* **megabucks** a million dollars, or any huge sum of money.

meg·a·byte (meg′a bīt) *Computers n* a unit of digital information about equal to one million bytes. *Abbrev.* **MB**

meg·a·cit·y (meg′a sit′ē) *n, pl* **meg·a·cit·ies** 1 a large metropolitan area under one central municipal government. 2 a city with a population of over ten million.

meg·a·death (meg′ə deth′) *n* the death of at least a million people.

meg·a·dose (meg′ə dōs′) *n* a dose of a vitamin or drug many times the normal size: *Some people say megadoses of vitamin C help you get over a cold faster.*

meg·a·flop (meg′ə flop′) *Computers n* a unit of computing speed equal to one million floating-point operations per second.

meg·a·hertz (meg′ə hərts′) *n, pl* **meg·a·hertz** a unit of frequency, equal to 1 000 000 hertz. *Symbol* **MHz**

meg·a·lith (meg′ə lith′) *n* a stone of great size, especially in ancient construction work or in monuments left by people of prehistoric times. <Greek *mega-* great + *lithos* stone>

meg·a·lo·ma·ni·a (meg′ə lō mā′nē ə) *n* obsession marked by delusions of fame, wealth, or power. <French *mégalonmanie,* from Greek *mega-* great + *mania* madness> **meg′a·lo·ma′ni·ac** *n.*

meg·a·lop·o·lis (meg′ə lop′ə lis) *n* a heavily populated urban and industrial area made up of several cities. <Greek *mega-* great + *polis* city>

meg·a·phone (meg′ə fōn′) *n* a large, funnel-shaped horn used to increase the loudness of the voice and direct it over a distance. <Greek *mega-* great + *-phone* sound>

meg·a·pro·ject (meg′ə pro′jekt) *n* a huge, expensive building project, such as a major highway, large power dam, or airport.

meg·a·ton (meg′ə tun′) *n* a measure of atomic power equivalent to the energy released by one million tons of high explosive.

meg·a·volt (meg′ə vōlt′) *n* one million volts of electricity. *Symbol* **MV**

meg·a·watt (meg′ə wot′) *n* one million watts of electrical power. *Symbol* **MW**

mei·o·sis (mī ō′sis) *n* the division of the reproductive cells in organisms that results in two daughter cells, each with half the chromosome number of the parent cell. Compare MITOSIS. <Greek *meion* less>

mel·a·mine (mel′ə mēn′) *n* a hard, strong plastic made from a synthetic resin, used for moulded articles, such as kitchen dishes, and protective surfaces, such as countertops.

mel·an·chol·y (mel′ən kol′ē) *n, pl* **mel·an·chol·ies** deep and long-lasting sadness.
adj **1** sad, gloomy, or depressed. **2** causing sadness or depression: *a melancholy scene.* <Latin, from Greek *melas* black + *chole* bile. In medieval times, black bile, one of the four bodily humours, was thought to cause depression.> **mel′an·chol′ic** *adj.* **mel′an·chol′i·cal·ly** *adv.*

Mel·a·ne·sia (mel′ə nē′zhə) *n* a group of islands in the Pacific, south of Micronesia. **Mel·a·ne′sian** *adj, n.*

mel·a·nin (mel′ə nən) *n* a dark brown or black pigment present in the skin, hair, and eyes of humans and some animals. <Greek *melas* black>

mel·a·no·ma (mel′ə nō′ma) *Medicine n, pl* **mel·a·no·mas** or **mel·a·no·ma·ta** a skin tumour developed from cells that form melanin and typically associated with skin cancer.

Mel·ba toast (mel′bə) *n* very thin, crisp toast.

meld (meld) *v* merge, blend, or combine, or become merged, blended, or combined: *Her art melded the old and the new.*
n a blend or combination. <perhaps blend of *melt* + *weld*>

me·lee or **mê·lée** (me′lā) *or* (mā′lā) *n* **1** a confused fight or scuffle among a number of people: *Some people were injured in the melee.* **2** a confused mass of people: *I lost my friend in the melee outside the concert.* <French>

mel·lif·lu·ous (mə lif′lū əs) *adj* sweetly or smoothly flowing: *a mellifluous speech.* <Latin *mel* honey + *fluere* to flow> **mel·lif′lu·ous·ly** *adv.*

mel·low (mel′ō) *adj* **1** soft, smooth, and full-flavoured when ripe or matured: *a mellow apple, mellow wine.* **2** soft and rich: *a violin with a mellow tone, a mellow light, a mellow colour.* **3** made gentler and wiser by age and experience. **4** *Informal* relaxed and good-humoured.
v **1** make or become mellow: *The apples mellowed after we picked them.* **2** make gentler and wiser by age and experience: *Time had mellowed her youthful temper.* <Middle English> **mel′low·ly** *adv.* **mel′low·ness** *n.*

me·lod·ic (mə lod′ik) *adj* **1** to do with melody. **2** melodious. **me·lod′i·cal·ly** *adv.*

me·lo·di·ous (mə lō′dē əs) *adj* **1** sweet-sounding or pleasing to the ear: *a melodious voice.* **2** producing melody: *a melodious bird.* **me·lo′di·ous·ly** *adv.* **me·lo′di·ous·ness** *n.*

mel·o·dra·ma (mel′ə dram′ə) *or* (mel′ə drȧ′mə) *n* **1** a sensational drama with exaggerated appeal to the emotions. **2** a sensational piece of writing, speech, or action that appeals to the emotions. <French, from Greek *melos* song + *drama*> **mel′o·dra·mat′ic** *adj.* **mel′o·dra·mat′i·cal·ly** *adv.*

mel·o·dy (mel′ə dē) *n, pl* **mel·o·dies** **1** a satisfying sequence of single musical notes, or a quality of sound resembling this: *the melody of birdsong.* **2** the main tune in harmonized music. <Old French, from Greek *melos* song>

mel·on (mel′ən) *n* a large, juicy fruit of the gourd family that grows on a vine. Cantaloupes are melons. <Old French, from Greek *melon* apple + *pepon* gourd>

melt (melt) *v* **melt·ed, melt·ed** or **mol·ten, melt·ing** **1** change or be changed from solid to liquid by the action of heat: *Ice becomes water when it melts.* Compare FREEZE. **2** disappear or cause to disappear gradually: *As the sun came out, the clouds melted away.* **3** blend or merge gradually: *In a rainbow, the green melts into blue, the blue into violet.* **4** soften emotionally or cause to become sympathetic: *Pity for his wounded enemy melted his heart.* <Old English *meltan*> **melt′er** *n.*

melt·down (melt′doun′) *n* **1** a situation in a nuclear reactor resulting from a failure of the cooling system so that the fuel overheats and melts the reactor core or shield. **2** any situation that becomes uncontrollable and has disastrous consequences. **3** *Informal* an emotional breakdown.

melting point *n* the temperature at which a solid substance melts.

melting pot *n* **1** a pot or other vessel to melt metals or other materials in. **2** a place in which different peoples, styles, or theories are mixed together: *America is often called a melting pot.*

a bat	e bed	i bid	o pot	u cup	th **thin**
ā cake	ē me	ī bite	ō go	ū rude	ᴛʜ **then**
ȧ bar	ə about	ər over	ȯ for	u̇ put	zh measure

M

mel·ton (melt′ən) *n* a smooth, heavy woollen cloth used for overcoats. <*Melton* Mowbray, a town in England where it was manufactured>

melt·wa·ter (melt′wot′ər) *n* water from melting glaciers or snows.

mem·ber (mem′bər) *n* **1** a person belonging to a group or organization: *a member of our club.* **2** a person elected to a legislative body: *a Member of Parliament, a Member of the Legislative Assembly.* **3** a constituent part of a whole: *a member of an equation.* **4** a limb or a part of a human or animal body or of a plant, especially a leg, arm, wing, or branch. <Old French, from Latin *membrum* limb>

🍁 **Member of Parliament** *n* in Canada, a title given to each of the representatives elected to the Parliament in Ottawa. *Abbrev.* **MP** or **M.P.**

🍁 **Member of the House of Assembly** *n* in Newfoundland, a member of the Legislative Assembly. *Abbrev.* **MHA** or **M.H.A.**

🍁 **Member of the Legislative Assembly** *n* a title given to each of the representatives elected to the legislatures of most Canadian provinces.
Abbrev. **MLA** or **M.L.A.**

🍁 **Member of the National Assembly** *n* in Québec, a title given to each of the representatives elected to the provincial legislature. *Abbrev.* **MNA** or **M.N.A.**

🍁 **Member of the Provincial Parliament** in Ontario, a title given to each of the representatives elected to the provincial legislature. *Abbrev.* **MPP** or **M.P.P.**

mem·ber·ship (mem′bər ship′) *n* **1** the fact or condition of being a member. **2** all the members of a group or organization, or the number of members: *The whole membership of the club was present. The membership of our club is over 30.*

mem·brane (mem′brān) *n* **1** a thin, soft, pliable sheet or layer of tissue lining or covering some part of the body or of a plant. **2** a thin pliable sheet or skin used to line or cover something. <Latin *membrum* limb>
mem′bra·nous (mem′brə nəs) *adj.*

me·men·to (mə men′tō) *n, pl* **me·men·tos** or **me·men·toes** something serving as a reminder, warning, or remembrance: *These postcards are mementos of our trip to Labrador.* <Latin = remember>

memento mo·ri (mô′rē) *n* an object that reminds one that death is inevitable. <Latin = remember that you have to die>

mem·o (mem′ō) *Informal n, pl* **mem·os** memorandum.

mem·oirs (mem′wärz) *pln* **1** a record of facts and events written from personal knowledge or special information. **2** a record of a person's own experiences, especially encounters with other people: *The retired judge wrote her memoirs.* <French, from Latin *memoria* memory>

mem·o·ra·bil·i·a (mem′ə rə bil′ē ə) *pln* objects kept or collected because of their historical or personal interest.

mem·o·ra·ble (mem′ə rə bəl) *adj* worth remembering or not to be forgotten. **mem′o·ra·bly** *adv.*

mem·o·ran·dum (mem′ə ran′dəm) *n, pl* **mem·o·ran·dums** or **mem·o·ran·da** (-ran′də) **1** a short written statement as a note to aid the memory, or to be a record: *She made a memorandum of what happened at the meeting.* **2** a written letter, note, or report, especially in business or diplomacy.

me·mo·ri·al (mə mô′rē əl) *n* a thing that is a reminder of some event or person, such as a statue, arch or column, book, or public holiday.
adj helping people to remember some person, thing, or event: *We have memorial services on Remembrance Day.*

me·mo·ri·al·ize (mə mô′rē ə līz′) *v* **me·mo·ri·al·ized, me·mo·ri·al·iz·ing** commemorate or preserve the memory of.

mem·o·rize (mem′ə rīz′) *v* **mem·o·rized, mem·o·riz·ing** commit to memory in every detail: *memorize the alphabet.* **mem′o·ri·za′tion** *n.*
mem′o·riz′er *n.*

mem·o·ry (mem′ə rē) *n, pl* **mem·ories** **1** the ability to remember. **2** remembrance or remembering: *That vacation lives in her memory.* **3** a person, thing, or event that is remembered: *His mother died when he was small, and she is only a memory to him now.* **4** the mind considered as a place in which things are remembered: *This is the hottest summer within my memory.* **5** the remembering by the living of people after they have died: *The song was dedicated to the memory of his wife.* **6** *Computers* the part of a computer that stores data. A **memory card** is a plug-in chip encased in plastic, for extra storage and retrieval of data; a **memory board** is a detachable storage device which can be installed to give additonal capacity to the computer's memory. <Old French, from Latin *memor* remembering>
in memory of, as a remembrance of: *On November 11, we observe a two-minute silence in memory of those who died for our country.*

SYNONYMS

Memory suggests the ability to keep in the mind: *I have fond memories of my grandmother, who died last year.*

Recollection emphasizes something not thought of for a long time: *My recollection of the accident was hazy.*

Reminiscence suggests a looking back on past, usually enjoyable, experiences: *The old friends shared their reminiscences with the others.*

mem·sa·hib (mem′so′ib) *n* in former times, a title of respect used in the Indian subcontinent when speaking to or of a married European woman, especially the wife of a British colonial official. <*mem* (local pronunciation of English *ma'am*) + Arabic *sahib* sir>

men (men) plural of MAN.

men·ace (men′is) *n* a threat of harm: *In dry weather, forest fires are a great menace.*
v **men·aced, men·ac·ing** threaten with harm: *Floods menaced the valley towns with destruction.* <Old French, from Latin *minae* threats> **men′ac·ing** *adj.*
men′ac·ing·ly *adv.*

mé·nage or **me·nage** (mā näzh′) *n* the members of a household. <French = household>

me·nag·er·ie (mə naj′ə rē) *n* **1** a collection of wild animals kept for exhibition. **2** a strange or diverse collection of people or things. <French>

mend (mend) *v* **1** make whole or repair: *She mended the broken cup with cement.* **2** correct or improve: *He should mend his manners.* **3** get back one's health: *The child will soon mend if she has enough to eat.*
n **1** a place that has been mended: *The mend in your dress hardly shows.* **2** a mending or improvement. <*amend*>
on the mend, improving in health.

men·da·cious (men dā′shəs) *adj* not telling the truth: *a mendacious child, a mendacious rumour.* <Latin *mendax* lying> **men·da′cious·ly** *adv.*

men·dac·i·ty (men das′ə tē) *n, pl* **men·dac·i·ties** the habit of telling lies.

Men·de·li·an (men dē′lē ən) *adj* to do with G. J. Mendel, a 19c botanist, who discovered the principles of genetics. **Mendel's Law** describes how many characteristics in animals and plants are inherited.

men·di·cant (men′də kənt) *adj* given to begging, or part of a religious order that originally relied solely on charity.
n a beggar or a member of a mendicant order. <Latin *mendicus* beggar> **men′di·can·cy** *n.*

men·folk (men′fōk′) *pln* men of a particular family or community, considered as a group.

men·hir (men′hir′) *n* a single block of stone serving as a monument or holy place, especially in ancient Celtic religion. <Breton (a language of France) *men* stone + *hir* long>

me·ni·al (mē′nē əl) *adj* not requiring much skill and lacking prestige: *Cinderella had to do menial tasks.*
n a person with a menial job. <Old French *mesnee* household> **me′ni·al·ly** *adv.*

men·in·gi·tis (men′in jī′tis) *n* an inflammation of the **meninges** (men in′jēz), the membranes that surround the brain and spinal cord, caused by bacteria or a virus that causes intense headache and fever and in severe cases can be fatal.

me·nis·cus (mə nis′kəs) *n, pl* **me·nis·cus·es** or **me·nis·ci** (-nis′ī) *or* (-nis′ē) **1** the curved upper surface of a column of liquid. **2** a lens that is concave on one side and convex on the other. <Latin, from Greek *meniskos* crescent>

Men·non·ite (men′ə nīt′) *n* a member of a Protestant group that adopts a simple way of life, rejects church organization, and refuses to take part in military service or public office. <after *Menno* Simons, 16c founder of this group>

men·o·pause (men′ə poz′) *n* the period in a woman's life during which menstruation ceases permanently, usually between the ages of 45 and 55. Also called **change of life**. <French, from Greek *men* month + *pausis* pause>

men·o·rah or **Men·o·rah** (mə nó′rə) *Judaism n* a candelabrum used in Jewish worship. <Hebrew>

men·stru·a·tion (men′strū ā′shən) *or* (men strā′shən) *n* the regular discharge of blood and other material from the lining of the uterus about every month from puberty to menopause, except during pregnancy. Also called **menstrual period**, **period**. <Latin *mensis* month> **men′stru·al** *adj.* **men′stru·ate** *v.*

–ment *suffix* **1** expressing the means, product, or result of an action: *management, enjoyment, pavement.* **2** expressing the result of an experience or mental state: *amazement, merriment.* <French, from Latin *–mentum*>

men·tal (men′təl) *adj* **1** to do with the mind: *a mental disease.* **2** for or done by the mind: *mental arithmetic.* **3** *Informal* with a mental disease or weakness. **4** for people who are mentally ill: *a mental hospital.* <Latin *mens* mind> **men′tal·ly** *adv.*

mental age *Psychology n* an estimate of the level of a person's mental development by reference to the age at which the average person reaches the same stage.

men·tal·i·ty (men tal′ə tē) *n, pl* **men·tal·i·ties** **1** mental capacity. **2** characteristic attitude: *the teen mentality.*

mental telepathy ESP.

men·thol (men′thol) *n* a white crystalline substance with a cooling minty taste and smell, found in peppermint and other natural oils and used as a flavouring. <German, from Latin *mentha* mint + *oleum* oil>

men·tho·lat·ed (men′thə lā′tid) *adj* containing menthol.

men·tion (men′shən) *v* speak about or refer to without giving details: *I mentioned the party, but did not say who was there.*
n a short statement about or reference to: *There was mention of the school party in the newspaper.* <Latin *mentio*>
make mention of, speak of or refer to: *She made mention of her most famous student.*
not to mention, not even considering.

men·tor (men′tər) *n* a wise and trusted adviser.

ETYMOLOGY

Mentor comes from *Mentor,* a figure from Greek legend. He was a friend of the hero Ulysses, and the teacher of Ulysses' son Telemachus.

men·u (men′yū) *n* **1** a list of the food that may be chosen as parts of a meal, especially in a restaurant. **2** the food served. **3** *Computers* in software programs, a list of choices that allows the user to select a topic. **Menu-driven** software relies on menus to guide users. <French, from Latin *minutus* detailed list>

me·ow (mē ou′) *n* the crying sound made by a cat.
v make this sound or one like it. Also, **miaow**, **miaou**. <imitative>

mer·can·tile (mər′kən tīl′) *adj* to do with trade or commerce: *a mercantile firm, mercantile law.* <French, from Italian *mercante* merchant>

mer·can·til·ism (mər′kən tī liz′əm) *n* in former times, an economic theory that stressed the holding of gold and other precious metals, a greater volume of exports than imports, and the exploitation of colonies.

a bat	e bed	i bid	o pot	u cup	th thin
ā cake	ē me	ī bite	ō go	ū rude	ᴛʜ then
à bar	ə about	ər over	ó for	ú put	zh measure

M

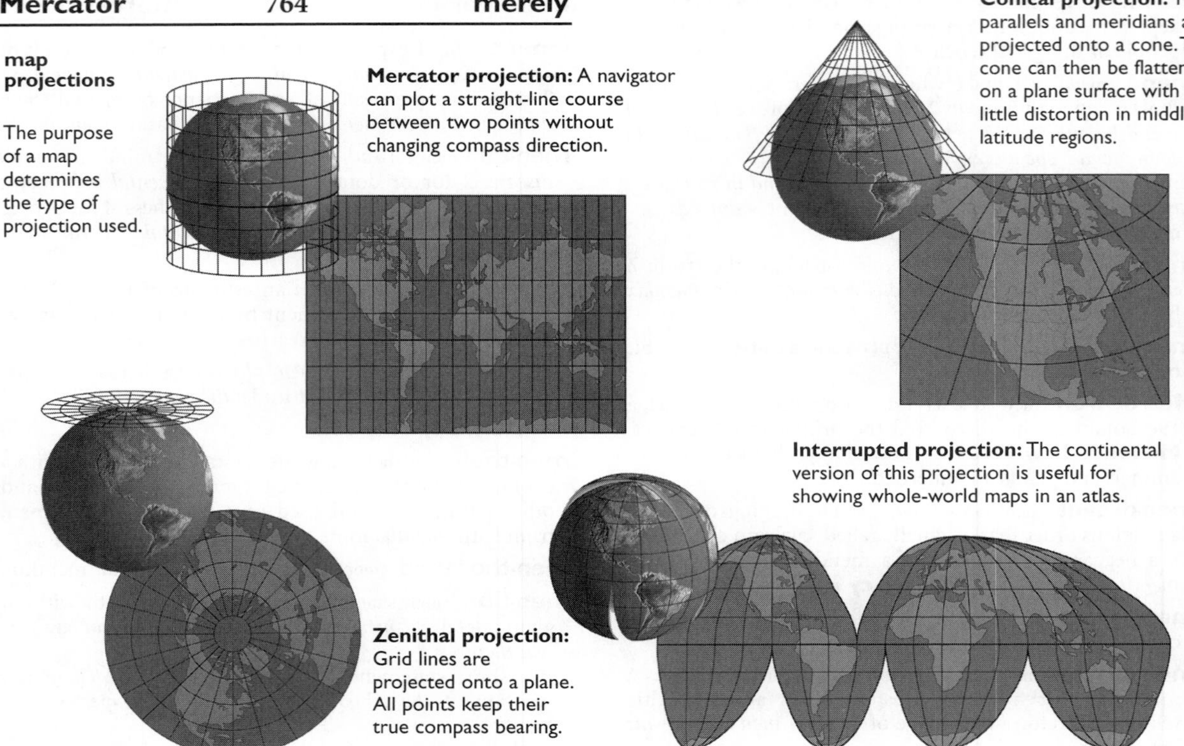

map projections
The purpose of a map determines the type of projection used.
Mercator projection: A navigator can plot a straight-line course between two points without changing compass direction.
Conical projection: The parallels and meridians are projected onto a cone. The cone can then be flattened on a plane surface with little distortion in middle latitude regions.
Interrupted projection: The continental version of this projection is useful for showing whole-world maps in an atlas.
Zenithal projection: Grid lines are projected onto a plane. All points keep their true compass bearing.

Mer·ca·tor projection (mər kā′tər) *n* a method of drawing maps with straight instead of curved lines for latitude and longitude. <G. *Mercator,*16c mapmaker>

mer·ce·nar·y (mər′sə ner′ē) *adj* working for money as the only motive, especially in an unethical way.
n, pl **mer·ce·nar·ies** 1 a soldier serving for pay in a foreign army. 2 a person who works only for money, especially in an unethical way. <Latin *merces* reward>

mer·cer·ize (mər′sə rīz′) *v* **mer·cer·ized, mer·cer·iz·ing** treat cotton thread or cloth with a chemical solution that strengthens it and makes it hold dyes better. <J. *Mercer,* 19c textile printer>

mer·chan·dise (mər′chən dīs′) *for n,* (m ər′chən dīz′) *for v.*
n goods or items that are bought and sold.
v **mer·chan·dised, mer·chan·dis·ing** market or sell goods or items. **mer′chan·dis′er** *n.*

mer·chant (mər′chənt) *n* 1 a person who or company that buys and sells goods. 2 a retail storekeeper.
adj to do with trade: *merchant ships.* <Old French, from Latin *mercis* merchandise>

merchant marine *n* ships and shipping used in commerce and trade.

merchant vessel *n* a ship used in commerce or trade.

mer·ci·ful (mər′si fəl) *adj* showing, feeling, or full of mercy. **mer′ci·ful·ly** *adv.* **mer′ci·ful·ness** *n.*

mer·ci·less (mər′si lis) *adj* without mercy: *The invader's attack on the town was merciless.* **mer′ci·less·ly** *adv.* **mer′ci·less·ness** *n.*

mer·cu·ri·al (mər kyu̇′rē əl) *adj* 1 highly changeable in mood. 2 caused by or containing mercury: *mercurial poisoning.* **mer·cu′ri·al·ly** *adv.*

mer·cu·ry (mər′kyə rē) *n, pl* **mer·cu·ries** 1 a heavy, silver-white metallic element that is liquid at ordinary temperatures. *Symbol* **Hg** 2 the column of mercury in a thermometer or barometer: *The mercury's rising.* <See MERCURY.>

Mer·cu·ry (mər′kyə rē) *n* the planet nearest the sun. See EARTH for picture. <*Mercury,* Roman god of commerce, travel, and thievery>

mer·cy (mər′sē) *n, pl* **mer·cies** 1 more kindness than what can be claimed or expected: *The judge showed mercy to the young offender.* 2 motivated by compassion or pity. 3 an event to be thankful for: *It's a mercy that they arrived safely through the storm.* <Old French, from Latin *mercedum* reward>
at the mercy of, in the power of: *Without friends we were at the mercy of strangers.*

🍁 **mercy flight** *n* an unscheduled aircraft flight, especially in the North, to fetch a seriously ill or injured person to the hospital.

mercy killing *n* euthanasia.

mere (mēr) *adj, superlative* **mer·est** solely and nothing else than: *The cut was a mere scratch.* <Old French, from Latin *merus* pure>

mere·ly (mēr′lē) *adv* simply or only.

mer·e·tri·cious (mer′ə trish′əs) *adj* apparently attractive but with little or no value: *meretricious gimmicks for tourists.* <Latin *mereri* to earn money> **mer′e·tri′cious·ly** *adv.* **mer′e·tri′cious·ness** *n.*

mer·gan·ser (mər gan′sər) *n, pl* **mer·gan·sers** or (*especially collectively*) **mer·gan·ser** a duck that dives for fish and has a long, slender bill. The male has a crested head. <Latin *mergere* to dive + *anser* goose>

merge (mərj) *v* **merged, merg·ing 1** combine or blend, especially as a business: *The sisters decided to merge their two stores.* **2** combine or blend gradually: *Traffic on this road merges with eastbound traffic on the highway. The jogger merged into the darkness.* <Latin *mergere* to dive, i.e., to immerse in an activity>

merg·er (mər′jər) *n* the act of merging: *One big company was formed by the merger of four small ones.*

me·rid·i·an (mə rid′ē ən) *n* **1** an imaginary circle passing through any place on the earth's surface and through the North and South Poles. **2** the half of such a circle from pole to pole. All the places on the same meridian have the same LONGITUDE. **3** the highest point that the sun or a star reaches in the sky. **4** the highest point or time of greatest success and happiness: *The meridian of life is the prime of life.* **5** in acupuncture and Chinese medicine, each of a set of twelve pathways in the body along which vital energy is said to flow.
adj to do with or located at a meridian. <Old French, from Latin *medius* middle + *dies* day>

me·ringue (mə rang′) *n* **1** a mixture of egg white and sugar, beaten until stiff, often spread on pies or puddings, and lightly browned in the oven. **2** a small pastry or confection made of this mixture. <French>

me·ri·no (mə rē′nō) *n, pl* **me·ri·nos** a sheep of a breed with long, fine wool, or a soft yarn or cloth made from this wool. <Spanish>

mer·it (mer′it) *n* **1** goodness, worth, or value: *The council agreed that our plan for a community playground had merit.* **2 merits** *pl* actual facts or qualities: *The judge will consider the case on its merits.*
v deserve: *A hard-working student merits praise.* <Old French, from Latin *mereri* deserve>

mer·i·toc·ra·cy (mer′ə tok′rə sē) *n, pl* **mer·i·toc·ra·cies 1** a government or the holding of power by people on the basis of their ability rather than inheritance or wealth. **2** a social system in which members of such a group have the most status and power.

mer·i·to·ri·ous (mer′ə tȯ′rē əs) *adj* deserving reward or praise. **mer′i·to′ri·ous·ly** *adv.* **mer′i·to′ri·ous·ness** *n.*

mer·lin (mər′lin) *n* a small, dark falcon. <Old French *esmeril*>

Mer·lin (mər′lin) *n* in Arthurian legend, the wizard who was adviser to King Arthur.

mer·maid (mər′mād′) *n* an imaginary sea maiden with the form of a fish from the waist down. <Old English *mere* sea + *maid*>

mer·man (mər′man′) *or* (mər′mən) *n, pl* **mer·men** (-men′) *or* (-mən) an imaginary man of the sea with the form of a fish from the waist down.

mer·ri·ment (mer′ē mənt) *n* laughter and fun.

mer·ry (mer′ē) *adj* **mer·ri·er, mer·ri·est 1** full of or loving fun. **2** happy or joyful: *a merry holiday.* <Old English *myrge*> **mer′ri·ly** *adv.*
make merry, laugh and have fun.

mer·ry–go–round (mer′ē gō round′) *n* **1** a set of animal figures and seats on a platform that is driven round by machinery and that people ride for fun. **2** a whirl or rapid round of activity: *a merry-go-round of parties.*

mer·ry·mak·ing (mer′ē mā′king) *n* laughter and fun. **mer′ry·mak′er** *n.*

me·sa (mā′sə) *n* a wide, isolated, flat-topped hill or upland with steep sides. <Spanish = table, from Latin *mensa*>

mes·cal (mes kal′) *n* **1** an agave plant, used as a source of food and liquor. **2** PEYOTE (def. 2). <Spanish, from Nahuatl (a language of Central and S America) *mexcalli*>

Mes·dames (mā dȧm′) plural of MADAME.

Mes·de·moi·selles (mād mwȧ zel′) plural of MADEMOISELLE.

mesh (mesh) *n* **1** one of the open spaces of a net, sieve, or screen: *This net has one-centimetre meshes.* **2** cord, wire, or thread used in a net, sieve, or screen: *We found an old fly swatter made of wire mesh.* **3** an interlaced structure: *Seaweed was caught in the meshes of the net.*
v **1** make or become entangled or entwined. **2** engage or become engaged in the teeth of gears. **3** agree or harmonize: *Their ideas do not mesh.* <Old English>

mes·mer·ize (mes′mə rīz′) *v* **mes·mer·ized, mes·mer·iz·ing** hypnotize. <F. *Mesmer*, 18c doctor who made hypnotism popular> **mes′mer·ism** *n.* **mes′mer·iz′er** *n.*

M

Mes·o·lith·ic (mez′ə lith′ik) *or* (mes′ə lith′ik) *adj* to do with the middle period in the Stone Age, between the PALEOLITHIC and NEOLITHIC periods.

mes·on (mes′on) *n* a subatomic particle that has a mass between an electron and a proton and transmits the strong interactions that bind together the atomic nucleus. <Greek *mesos* middle>

mes·o·sphere (mes′ə sfēr′) *n* the layer of the earth's atmosphere lying above the stratosphere, extending from about 50 km to about 80 km above the earth's surface. See OZONE LAYER for picture.

Mes·o·zo·ic (mez′ə zō′ik) *or* (mes′ə zō′ik) *Geology n* the era extending from the appearance of the first dinosaurs, about 250 million years ago, to their extinction, about 70 million years ago. It covers the TRIASSIC, JURASSIC, and CRETACEOUS periods. Compare CENOZOIC, PALEOZOIC.
adj to do with this era or the rocks formed then. <Greek *mesos* middle + *zoion* animal>

mes·quite (mes kēt′) *or* (mes′kēt) *n* a spiny tree or shrub of the pea family found in the southwestern US and Mexico, bearing pods of seeds used as fodder. <Spanish, from Nahuatl (a language of Central and S America) *mizquitl*>

a bat	e bed	i bid	o pot	u cup	th **thin**
ā cake	ē me	ī bite	ō go	ū rude	ᴛʜ **then**
ȧ bar	ə about	ər over	ȯ for	ů put	zh measure

mess (mes) *n* **1** a dirty or untidy mass or group of things: *There was a mess of dirty dishes in the sink.* **2** a confused, difficult, or unpleasant situation or condition: *He made a mess of his final examinations.* **3** a person whose life or activities are confused or troubled: *She's been a mess ever since she was turned down for the squad.* **4** a building or room for people who eat together regularly, especially such a group in the armed forces. **5** a large mixed portion of food: *a mess of fish.*
v **1** make dirty or untidy: *She messed up her book by scribbling on the pages.* **2** eat meals with others in a particular place, especially in the armed forces. <Old French *mes* dish of food, from Latin *missus* course at dinner> **mess′i·ly** *adv.* **mess′y** *adj.*
mess about (or **mess around**), busy oneself without seeming to accomplish a thing.
mess up, *Informal* **a** spoil or botch: *I messed up my speech because I was so nervous.* **b** cause to be poorly adjusted socially or emotionally: *The poor kid was totally messed up by the experience.* **c** do wrong or commit an offence: *She forgives me when I mess up.*
mess with, *Informal* **a** interfere or tamper with: *I don't believe you; you're just messing with my mind.* **b** defy or provoke: *Don't mess with strangers.*

mes·sage (mes′ij) *n* **1** information or instructions sent from one person to another. **2** a lesson, significant point, or central theme, especially one of political, social, or moral importance: *The message of the candidate's campaign was his reliability.* **3** inspired words: *the message of a prophet.* <Old French, from Latin *mittere* send>
get the message, understand, especially something hinted at.

SYNONYMS

Message suggests information sent from one person or group to another, either oral or written: *My friend passed me a folded-up message during class.*

Directive suggests any detailed instruction or command, either oral or written: *The soldier received a directive from his commanding officer.*

Missive is a more formal word for a letter or written message: *She wrote a missive to the diplomat.*

mes·sen·ger (mes′ən jər) *n* **1** a person who carries a message or goes on an errand. **2** an animal or thing thought of as carrying a message: *Frost on the window is a messenger of winter.*

messenger RNA *n* the form of RNA in which genetic information is transferred from DNA to the ribosomes. *Abbrev.* **mRNA**

mess hall *n* in the armed forces, a place where a group of people eat together regularly.

Mes·si·ah (mes′ī ə) *n* **1 a** *Judaism* the promised deliverer of the Jewish people prophesized in the Hebrew Bible. **b** *Christianity* Jesus Christ as the fulfilment of these prophecies. **2 messiah** a person regarded as coming to the rescue of a group, nation, or people: *The party leader was portrayed as a messiah to the downtrodden.* <Latin, from Hebrew *mashiah* anointed>

Mes·sieurs (mes′ərz) plural of MONSIEUR.

Messrs. (mes′ərz) plural of MR.

mess·y (mes′ē) *adj* **mess·i·er, mess·i·est 1** untidy or dirty, or involving mess or untidiness: *a messy kitchen.* **2** confused and difficult to handle: *a messy divorce.* **mess′i·ness** *n.*

mes·ti·zo (mes tē′zō) *n* a person, one of whose parents is of Spanish ancestry and the other is a member of an Aboriginal people of the Americas. A girl or woman may be called a **mestiza** (mes tē′za). <Spanish, from Latin *mixtus* mixed>

met (met) past tense and past participle of MEET[1].

me·tab·o·lism (mə tab′ə liz′əm) *n* the chemical process by which a living organism maintains life. <Greek *metabolikos* changeable, from *metaballein* to change> **met′a·bol′ic** (met′ə bol′ik) *adj.*

met·a·car·pus (met′ə kȧr′pəs) *n, pl* **met·a·car·pi** (-pī) *or* (-pē) **1** the part of the hand between the wrist and the fingers, containing five long bones. See CARPAL for picture. **2** the corresponding part in the foreleg of an animal or the long bone or bones between the knee and the paw or hoof. <Greek *meta-* after + *karpos* wrist> **met′a·car′pal** *adj.*

me·ta·cog·ni·tion (me′tə kog ni′shən) *n* the process of considering and revising your own thoughts and mental processes. <Greek *meta-* with + Latin *cognoscere* know>

met·al (met′əl) *n* **1** a solid substance that is a good conductor of heat and electricity, and can be made into wire or hammered into sheets. Gold, iron, brass, tin, and steel are metals. **2** an element that can form a salt by replacing the hydrogen of an acid, or a mixture of such elements. **3** broken stone, cinders, or other materials used for roads and roadbeds. **4** material or substance: *Cowards are not made of the same metal as heroes.*
adj made of metal or a mixture of metals: *a metal container, a metal trophy.* <Old French, from Greek *matallon* mine>

me·tal·lic (mə tal′ik) *adj* **1** to do with metal: *a metallic substance.* **2** like or suggesting metal: *a shiny metallic fabric, a metallic voice.*

met·al·lif·er·ous (met′ə lif′ə rəs) *adj* containing or yielding metal: *metalliferous rocks.*

met·al·lur·gy (met′ə lər′jē) *n* the science or art of working with metals, including the separating of them from their ores and refining them for use. **met′al·lur′gi·cal** *adj.* **met′al·lur′gist** *n.*

met·al·work (met′əl wərk′) *n* **1** things made out of metal. **2** the act of making things out of metal. **met′al·work′er** *n.*

met·a·mor·phic (met′ə mȯr′fik) *adj* **1** to do with physical change of form. **2** derived from igneous or sedimentary rock that has undergone changes through the action of pressure, heat, and moisture. Slate is a metamorphic rock formed from shale.

met·a·mor·phism (met′ə mȯr′fiz əm) *n* **1** a change of form. **2** a change in the structure of a rock caused by pressure, heat, or moisture.

met·a·mor·pho·sis (met′ə mȯr′fə sis) *or* (met′ə mȯr fō′sis) *n, pl* **met·a·mor·pho·ses** (-sēz′) **1** a change of physical form, or the changed form itself: *Tadpoles become frogs by metamorphosis; they lose their tails and grow legs. A butterfly is the metamorphosis of a caterpillar.* 2 a noticeable or complete change of character, appearance, or condition. <Greek *meta-* change + *morphe* form> **met′a·mor′phose** *v.*

met·a·phase (met′ə fāz′) *n* the second stage of MITOSIS, in which the nuclear membrane disintegrates, and the split chromosomes form a straight line.

met·a·phor (met′ə fər) *or* (met′ə fȯr′) *n* an implied identification or association of two different things. Examples: *a copper sky, a heart of stone.* Compare SIMILE. <Greek *meta-* across + *pherein* carry>
mix metaphors, confuse two or more metaphors in the same expression: *If you put your back into it, you will rise to the top.*

GRAMMAR AND USAGE

Metaphors and **similes** both make comparisons.

A **metaphor** talks about one thing as if it were another: *Her eyes were diamonds.*

A **simile** uses *like* or *as* to compare two things: *Her eyes shone like diamonds. Her eyes were as bright as diamonds.*

met·a·phor·i·cal (met′ə fȯ′rə kəl) *adj* using metaphors or figurative expressions. **met′a·phor′i·cal·ly** *adv.*

met·a·phys·ics (met′ə fiz′iks) *n* (*with singular verb*) the branch of philosophy that studies the first principles of things and the nature of reality, including abstract concepts like being, knowing, substance, cause, identity, time, and space. **met′a·phys′i·cal** *adj.*
met′a·phys′i·cal·ly *adv.*

me·tas·ta·sis (mə tas′tə sis) *n, pl* **me·tas·ta·ses** (-sēz) the growth or spread of cells, especially of the diseased cells of a tumour or cancer, from one organ or part of the body to another. <Greek = transition> **me·tas′ta·size′** *v.*

met·a·tar·sus (met′ə tȧr′səs) *n, pl* **met·a·tar·si** (-sī) *or* (-sē) 1 the part of the foot between the heel and ankle and the toes, containing five long bones. The metatarsus includes the instep and arch of the foot. 2 the corresponding part in the hind leg of an animal. <*Greek* meta- *with, across* + *tarsos* flat of the foot>
met′a·tar′sal *adj.*

mete (mēt) *v* **met·ed, met·ing** give to each a share of something: *The judges will mete out praise and blame.* <Old English *metan*>

me·te·or (mē′tē ər) *n* a mass of stone or metal that comes toward the earth from outer space at enormous speed and heat and that usually burns while travelling. <Latin, from Greek *meteoros* raised above the ground>

me·te·or·ic (mē′tē ȯ′rik) *adj* 1 to do with meteors: *a meteoric shower.* 2 brilliant and rapid in development: *a singer's meteoric rise to fame.* 3 to do with water from the earth's atmosphere that precipitates or condenses.

me·te·or·ite (mē′tē ə rīt′) *n* a mass of stone or metal that has fallen to the earth as a meteor from outer space.

me·te·or·oid (mē′tē ə roid′) *n* a small body in outer space that is seen as a meteor on entering the earth's atmosphere.

me·te·or·ol·o·gy (mē′tē ə rol′ə jē) *n* the science that studies the atmosphere, especially as a means of forecasting the weather. **me′te·or·o·log′i·cal** *adj.* **me′te·or·ol′o·gist** *n.*

meteor shower *n* all the meteors seen when the earth passes through a group of them.

me·ter[1] (mē′tər) METRE.

me·ter[2] (mē′tər) *n* a device that measures and sometimes records: *a parking meter, a water meter.*
v measure with a meter. <Greek *metron* measure>

–meter *combining form* 1 as a device for measuring: *speedometer.* 2 in poetry, with metrical feet: *pentameter.* <Greek *metron* measure>

meth·a·done (meth′ə dōn′) *n* a synthetic narcotic drug similar to morphine that is used to relieve pain and as a substitute for heroin in the treatment of addicts.

meth·am·phet·a·mine (meth′am fet′ə mēn) *n* a powerful mood-elevating drug derived from amphetamine.

meth·ane (meth′ān) *n* a colourless, odourless, flammable gas, the simplest of the hydrocarbons and the main constituent of natural gas.

meth·a·nol (meth′ə nol′) *n* a colourless, poisonous, volatile, flammable liquid obtained from the destructive distillation of wood and used as a fuel, antifreeze, or solvent. <*methane*>

me·thinks (mē thinks′) *Archaic or Humorous v, past tense* **me·thought** it seems to me: *Methinks I hear a footstep outside.* <Old English *me* to me + *thyncan* seem>

meth·od (meth′əd) *n* 1 a way of doing something: *a method of teaching music. Roasting is one method of cooking meat.* 2 order or system in getting things done or in thinking: *If you used more method, you wouldn't waste so much time.* <Latin, from Greek *methodos* going after>
method in your madness, system and sense in what appears to be foolishness.

me·thod·i·cal (mə thod′ə kəl) *adj* 1 done or arranged according to a method or order: *a methodical procedure.* 2 tending to act according to a method: *a methodical thinker.* **me·thod′i·cal·ly** *adv.* **me·thod′i·cal·ness** *n.*

Me·thod·ist (mə′thod ist) *n* a member of any of the churches that grew out of a reform movement in the Church of England in the 1700s, led by John and Charles Wesley.

meth·od·ol·o·gy (meth′ə dol′ə jē) *n* a system or body of procedures, methods, and rules used in a particular field of study or activity.

meth·yl alcohol (meth′əl) *n* wood alcohol.

meth·yl·at·ed spirits (meth′ə lā′tid) *n* alcohol that has been made unfit for drinking by mixing it with a small amount of wood alcohol. It is used as a solvent.

a bat	e bed	i bid	o pot	u cup	th **thin**
ā cake	ē me	ī bite	ō go	ū rude	ᴛʜ **then**
ȧ bar	ə about	ər over	ȯ for	u̇ put	zh measure

me·tic·u·lous (mə tik′yə ləs) *adj* extremely careful about small details. <Latin *metus* fear, in reference to the original meaning of the word> **me·tic′u·lous·ly** *adv.*

mé·tier (mā tyā′) *n* **1** a trade or profession. **2** the kind of work for which a person has special ability. <French, from Latin *ministerium* service>

🍁 **Mé·tis** or **Me·tis** (mā′tē) *or* (mā tē′) *n, pl* **Mé·tis** or **Me·tis** a person descended from mixed European and First Nations people who lived in the Canadian West during the early 1800s, forming a distinct cultural group.
adj to do with the Métis. <Cdn French, from Latin *mixtus* mixed>

me·ton·y·my (mə ton′ə mē) *n* the use of the name of one thing for that of another that it logically suggests. Example: *The pen* (power of literature) *is mightier than the sword* (violence). <Greek *meta-* change + *onyma* name>

me·tre[1] (mē′tər) *n* **1** the arrangement of beats or accents in a line of poetry: *The metre of "Jack and Jill went up the hill" is different from that of "Hiawatha."* **2** an arrangement of beats in music: *Three-four metre is waltz time.* Also, **meter**. <Greek *metron* measure>

me·tre[2] (mē′tər) *n* the SI unit for measuring length, equal to 100 centimetres. *Symbol* **m** Also, **meter**. <French, from Greek *metron* measure>

met·ric (met′rik) *adj* **1** to do with the METRE[2] or the system of measurement based on it. **2** METRICAL.

met·ri·cal (met′rə kəl) *adj* **1** in verse, not prose. **2** based on the metre as a standard of measurement: *There is a list of metrical equivalents in the Appendix.* **met′ri·cal·ly** *adv.*

met·ri·cate (met′rə kāt′) *v* **met·ri·cat·ed, met·ri·cat·ing** change into or express in a metric system of measurement. **met′ri·ca′tion** *n.*

metric system *n* a system of measurement based on tens, traditionally using the metre as the basic unit of length, the kilogram as the basic unit of mass, and the litre as the basic unit of volume or capacity.

metric ton TONNE.

met·ro (met′rō) *Informal n* **1** a metropolitan government or area. **2** a subway system, such as that of Montréal or Paris.

met·ro·nome (met′rə nōm′) *n* a device with a pendulum that can be adjusted to tick at different speeds, used to help keep time while practising a musical instrument. <Greek *metron* measure + *-nemein* regulate>

me·trop·o·lis (mə trop′ə lis) *n* **1** the most important city of a country or region: *London is the metropolis of England.* **2** a large city or important centre: *Montréal is a busy metropolis.* **3** the chief diocese of a Christian church province, especially in the Orthodox Church. <Latin, from Greek *meter* mother + *polis* city>

met·ro·pol·i·tan (met′rə pol′ə tən) *adj* **1** of a large city: *metropolitan newspapers.* **2** forming a government combining those of several municipalities: *a metropolitan area.*
n **1** a person who lives in a large city and knows it well. **2** the chief bishop who has authority over the bishops of a church province, especially in the Orthodox Church.

met·tle (met′əl) *n* the courageous ability of a person to cope with difficulties or pressing demands. <variant of *metal,* def. 4>
on your mettle, ready to do your best in a demanding situation or circumstance.

mew (myū) *n* the high-pitched crying sound made by a cat or kitten.
v make this sound. See also MEOW. <imitative>

mewl (myūl) *v* cry feebly, especially as a baby. <imitative>

mews (myūz) *especially UK n* dwellings built around a court or alley that have been converted from stables or built to look like former stables.

Mex·i·co (mek′sə kō) *n* a country in southern N America. See the APPENDIX. **Mex′i·can** *adj, n.*

me·zu·zah (mə zū′zə) *Judaism n* a piece of parchment with religious texts written on it, kept in a small case or tube fixed to the doorpost of some Jewish homes as a sign of faith. <Hebrew = doorpost>

mez·za·nine (mez′ə nēn′) *n* **1** a partial storey between two main floors of a building: *Many hotels have a mezzanine between the ground floor and the next main floor up.* **2** the lowest balcony of a theatre: *Tickets are more expensive for seats in the mezzanine than for the second balcony.* <French, from Latin *medianus* middle>

mez·zo·for·te (met′sō fȯr′tā) *or* (mez′ō fȯr′tā) *adj, adv* in music, moderately loud, or half as loud as forte.

mez·zo–so·pran·o (met′sō sə pran′ō) *or* (mez′ō sə pran′ō) *n, pl* **mez·zo-so·pran·os** an adult female singing voice with an intermediate range between SOPRANO and CONTRALTO, or a singer with such a range.
adj to do with a mezzo-soprano. <Italian *mezzo* half + *soprano*>

mez·zo·tint (met′sō tint′) *or* (mez′ō tint′) *n* **1** an engraving on copper or steel made by polishing and scraping away parts of a roughened surface, or a print made from such an engraving. **2** this method of engraving.
v engrave in mezzotint. <Italian *mezzo* half + *tinto* tint>

MFD *Computers n* in full, **multifunction device** a machine that combines the functions of a fax machine, a copier, and a printer.

mg milligram(s).

Mgr. **1** Monseigneur. **2** Monsignor.

🍁 **MHA** or **M.H.A.** Member of the House of Assembly (in Newfoundland).

MHz megahertz.

mi (mē) *Music n* **1** the third tone of an eight-tone major scale, especially as sung to sol-fa syllables: *do, re, mi, fa, so, la, ti, do.* **2** the tone E. Also, **me**.

MIA in full, **missing in action** to do with a member of an armed force not known to be alive, but not confirmed dead.

mi·aow or **mi·aou** (mē ou′) MEOW.

mi·as·ma (mī az′mə) *or* (mē az′mə) *n, pl* **mi·as·mas** or **mi·as·ma·ta** (-mə tə) **1** an unpleasant or unhealthy smell or vapour: *A miasma rose from the sewage pipe.* **2** an unpleasant atmosphere or influence that infects or corrupts: *a miasma of evil thoughts.* <Greek = pollution>
mi·as′mic *adj.*

mi·ca (mī′kə) *n* a shiny silicate mineral, found as scales in granite or other rocks, that divides into thin layers. <Latin = grain, because it separates into tiny pieces>

mice (mīs) plural of MOUSE.

mick·ey (mik′ē) *Slang n* a half bottle (about 375 mL) of liquor or wine. <origin uncertain>

Mickey Mouse *Informal adj* not worthwhile or serious: *Mickey Mouse college courses.* <Name of cartoon character by W. Disney, producer of animation films. Alludes to the simple and trivial nature of these cartoons.>

Mic·mac (mig′mok′) MI'KMAW.

micro– *combining form* **1** one-millionth: *microsecond.* See also the APPENDIX. **2** very small: *micro-organism, microfilm.* Compare MACRO-. **3** to do with the use of a microscope: *microbiology.* <Greek *mikros* small>

mi·crobe (mī′krōb) *n* a micro-organism, especially a bacterium that causes disease or fermentation. <French, from Greek *mikros* small + *bios* life> **mi·cro′bi·al** *adj.* **mi·cro′bic** *adj.*

mi·cro·bi·ol·o·gy (mī′krō bī ol′ə jē) *n* the branch of biology that studies micro-organisms.

mi·cro·brew·e·ry (mī′krō brū′ə rē) *n, pl* **microbreweries** a small brewery producing a specialty beer in small amounts, usually for a local market.

mi·cro·chip (mī′krō chip′) *Computers n* a very small piece of semiconducting material containing the information for a computer circuit.

mi·cro·cir·cuit (mī′krō sər′kit) *Computers n* an electronic circuit consisting of miniature components, especially an integrated circuit in a computer.

mi·cro·com·put·er (mī′krō kəm pyū′tər) *n* a small computer that contains a microprocessor as its central processor.

mi·cro·cosm (mī′krə koz′əm) *n* a community, place, or situation that is regarded as representing in miniature something much larger. <Old French, from Greek *mikros* small + *kosmos* world> **mi′cro·cos′mic** *adj.* **mi′cro·cos′mi·cal·ly** *adv.*

mic·ro·e·co·nom·ics (mīk′rō ek′ə nom′iks) *or* (mīk′rō ēk′ə nom′iks) *n* (*with singular verb*) economics at a detailed and restricted level, such as one dealing with a particular product, a narrow category of consumers, a single corporation, or a small community. Compare MACROECONOMICS.

mi·cro·e·lec·tron·ics (mī′krō i lek tron′iks) *n* (*with singular verb*) the design, manufacture, and use of electronic components of miniature size.

mi·cro·fi·bre (mī′krō fī′bər) *n* a soft, warm, wrinkle-resistant synthetic yarn made of fine fibres.

mi·cro·fiche (mī′krō fēsh′) *n, pl* **mi·cro·fiche** a single sheet of microfilm carrying tiny copies of numerous pages of printed matter: *Back issues of the newspaper are available on microfiche.* <micro- + French *fiche* card>

mi·cro·film (mī′krō film′) *n* a length of film that contains miniature photographs of pages of printed matter to preserve them in a compact form.
v photograph on microfilm.

mi·crom·e·ter (mī krom′ə tər) *n* an instrument for measuring very small distances, angles, or diameters, especially one used on a telescope, microscope, or calliper.

mi·cro·me·tre (mī′krō mē′tər) *n* a unit of length, equal to one-millionth of a metre. Also, **micrometer**, **micron**.

Mi·cro·ne·sia (mī′krō nē′zhə) *n* a country of islands in the Pacific, north of Australia. **Mi·cro·ne′sian** *adj, n.*

mi·cro–or·gan·ism (mī′krō ȯr′gə niz′əm) *n* a one-celled organism too small to be seen with the unaided eye. Bacteria and viruses are micro-organisms. Most contain no chlorophyll.

mi·cro·phone (mī′krə fōn′) *n* an instrument for increasing the loudness of sounds or for transmitting sounds.

mi·cro·pro·ces·sor (mī′krō prō′se sər) *or* (mī′krō pros′e sər) *Computers n* a single chip of semiconductor material that carries an integrated circuit responsible for many functions.

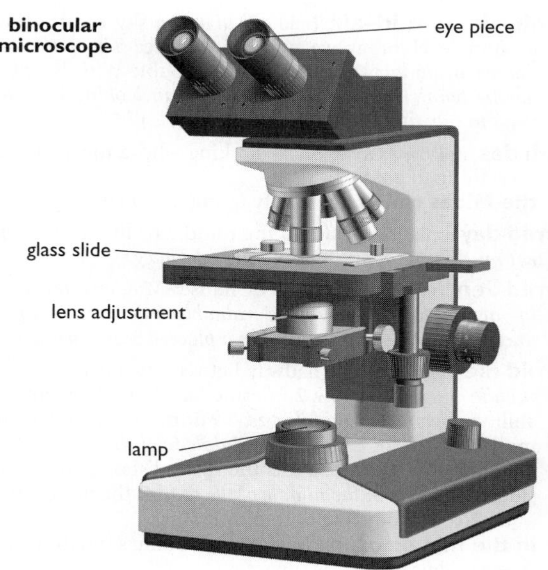

mi·cro·scope (mī′krə skōp′) *n* an instrument with one lens (a **simple microscope**) or with a combination of lenses (a **compound microscope**) for magnifying objects so that you can see things not visible to the unaided eye. See also ELECTRON MICROSCOPE.

mi·cro·scop·ic (mī′krə skop′ik) *adj* **1** unable to be seen without using a microscope: *a microscopic grain of pollen.* **2** like or suggesting a microscope: *a microscopic eye for mistakes.* **3** of or with a microscope: *She made a microscopic examination of a fly's wing.*

mi·cros·co·py (mī kros′kə pē) *n* the use of or investigation with a microscope. **mi·cros′co·pist** *n.*

a bat	e bed	i bid	o pot	u cup	th **thin**
ā cake	ē me	ī bite	ō go	ū rude	ᴛʜ **then**
ä bar	ə about	ər over	ȯ for	u̇ put	zh measure

mi·cro·sec·ond (mī′kro sek′ənd) *n* a unit of time equal to one-millionth of a second.

mi·cro·sur·ger·y (mī′kro sər′jə rē) *n, pl* **mi·cro·sur·ger·ies** very delicate surgery performed on a small area with the help of microscopes and finely calibrated instruments.

mi·cro·tech·nol·o·gy (mī′kro tek nol′ə jē) *n, pl* **mi·cro·tech·nol·o·gies** technology involving microelectronics and devices that are very small and fast. **mi·cro·tech′no·log′i·cal** *adj.*

mi·cro·wave (mī′krō wāv′) *n* **1** a very short electromagnetic wave, especially one with a wavelength shorter than a normal radio wave but longer than infrared radiation. **2** in full, **microwave oven** a small oven in which food is cooked by means of the heat produced by microwaves

mid (mid) *adj* in the middle of. <Old English *midd*>

mid– *prefix* to do with the middle: *midday, midsentence.* <Old English>

mid·air or **mid–air** (mid′er′) *n* **1** the sky or air above ground level or above another surface: *The parachute floated in midair.* **2** uncertainty or doubt: *With her place on the tennis team in midair, she began looking for other ways to stay fit.*

Mi·das (mī′dəs) *Greek myth n* a king whose touch turned everything to gold.
the Midas touch, the ability to make money easily.

mid·day (mid′dā′) *n* noon; the middle of the day: *I don't eat much at midday.* <Old English *middæg*>

mid·den (mid′ən) *n* a heap of refuse: *Middens uncovered by archaeologists may give valuable information about ancient people who once lived in a place.* <Scandinavian>

mid·dle (mid′əl) *adj* **1** halfway between two extremes: *the middle house in the row.* **2** intermediate in rank, quality, or ability: *a woman of middle size.* **3 Middle** between old and modern forms of a language: *Middle English.*
n **1** the point or part that is the same distance from each side, edge, or end: *the middle of the road.* **2** the middle part of a person's body. <Old English *middel*>
in the middle of, in the process of doing something: *I'm in the middle of making supper.*

mid·dle–aged (mid′əl ājd′) *adj* between youth and old age, from about 40 to about 60 years of age.
middle age *n.*

Middle Ages *n* (*with singular verb*) the period of European history between ancient and modern times, from about 500 CE to about 1450 CE.

middle C *n* the musical note on the first added line below the treble staff.

middle class *n* the social group that is neither wealthy nor poor, including many professional, business, and industrial workers and their families. Compare LOWER CLASS, UPPER CLASS.

middle ear *n* a cavity between the eardrum and the inner ear. See AURICLE for picture.

Middle East *n* the region in southwest Asia and northern Africa between the eastern Mediterranean and Pakistan, including the Arabian peninsula.

Middle English *n* the English language as it developed between Old English and Modern English, lasting from about 1100 CE to about 1450 CE.

mid·dle·man (mid′əl man′) *n, pl* **mid·dle·men** (-men′) **1** a trader or merchant who buys goods from the producer and sells them to a retailer or directly to the consumer. **2** a go-between or person who arranges deals between others.

middle management *n* supervisors and managers in a company at a level between executives and ordinary employees.

mid·dle–of–the–road (mid′əl əv thə rōd′) *adj* moderate and avoiding extremes, sometimes to the point of being bland or characterless.

middle school *n* a school at a level between elementary school and high school.

mid·dle·weight (mid′əl wāt′) *n* a boxer who weighs between 70 and 73 kilograms.

mid·dling (mid′ling) *adj* medium in size, quality, or rank. *adv* moderately or fairly.

mid·dy blouse (mid′ē) *n* a loose blouse like a sailor's, with a collar with a broad flap at the back.

Mid·east (mid′ēst′) *n* the Middle East.

midge (mij) *n* a tiny insect often found in swarms near water or swampy areas. <Old English *mycg*>

midg·et (mij′it) *n* **1** a person much smaller than normal. **2** a thing much smaller than the usual size for its kind. **3** 🍁 in amateur sports, a player aged 16 or 17.

MIDI (mid′ē) *Computers n* a piece of equipment that connects electronic musical instruments with a computer. <*m*(*usical*) *i*(*nstrument*) *d*(*igital*) *i*(*nterface*)>

mid·life crisis (mid′līf′) *n* an emotional questioning of oneself and one's choices that may occur around middle age.

mid·night (mid′nīt′) *n* twelve o'clock at night or the middle of the night.
burn the midnight oil, work or study far into the night: *I'll have to burn the midnight oil again tonight if I want to get my project done.*

mid·point (mid′point′) *n* a point at or near the centre or middle: *the midpoint of a line, the midpoint of a career.*

mid·riff (mid′rif) *n* the muscular wall separating the chest cavity from the abdomen or diaphragm. <Old English *midd* mid + *hrif* belly>

mid·sen·tence (mid′sen′tens) *n* the middle of a sentence: *He interrupted me in midsentence.*
adv in the middle of a sentence: *She stopped midsentence and gasped in fear.*

mid·ship·man (mid′ship′mən) *n, pl* **mid·ship·men** (-mən) **1** a student training for a commission in a navy. **2** in former times, a boy who assisted the officers of a ship.

midst (midst) *Archaic or Poetic n* middle.
prep amid. <Old English *middes* middle>
in our (or **your** or **their**) **midst,** among us (you, them).
in the midst of, a among or surrounded by: *The bomb fell in the midst of the crowd.* **b** during: *The announcement was made in the midst of the program.*

mid·stream (mid′strēm′) *n* the middle of a stream.

mid·stride (mid′strīd′) *n* the middle of a step or stride: *She changed her mind in midstride.*
adv in the middle of taking a step or stride: *He turned midstride and came back.*

mid·sum·mer (mid′sum′ər) *n* **1** the middle of summer. **2** the time around June 21, the summer solstice.
adj in the middle of summer.

mid·term (mid′tərm) *n* **1** the middle of a term at a school or university. **2** a major test or exam held in the middle of the term.
adj to do with the middle of a term or a test held then.

mid·way (mid′wā′) *adv, adj* halfway or in the middle: *lying midway between the two towns* (*adv*), *a midway point on the chart* (*adj*).
n **1** a middle way or course. **2** the place for games, rides, and other amusements at a fair or exhibition. <Old English *midweg*>

mid·week (mid′wēk′) *n* the middle of the week.
adj in the middle of the week.

Mid·west (mid′west′) *n* the northern states of the US, from Ohio west to the Rocky Mountains.
Mid·west′ern *adj.*

mid·wife (mid′wīf′) *n, pl* **mid·wives** (-wīvz′) a person trained to assist women in childbirth. <Old English *mid* with + *wif* woman>

mid·wife·ry (mid′wī′fə rē) *or* (mid′wif′ə rē) *n* the work or profession of assisting women in childbirth.

mid·win·ter (mid′win′tər) *n* **1** the middle of winter. **2** the time around December 21, the winter solstice.
adj in the middle of winter.

mien (mēn) *n* a manner of holding the head and body: *The colonel had the mien of a soldier.* <probably French *mine* facial expression>

miff (mif) *Informal n* a petty quarrel or feeling of pique.
v be annoyed: *I was miffed at not getting an invitation to the party.* <origin uncertain>

might[1] (mīt) past tense of MAY.

GRAMMAR AND USAGE

Might, the past tense of **may**, is now used mainly to express doubt or slight possibility: *It looks as if it might rain this afternoon.*

might[2] (mīt) *n* great power or strength: *Work with all your might.* <Old English *miht*>
with might and main, with all your strength.

might·y (mī′tē) *adj* **might·i·er, might·i·est** **1** showing strength or power: *a mighty ruler, a mighty force.* **2** very great: *a mighty famine.*
adv Informal very or extremely: *a mighty cold day.*
might′i·ly *adv.*

mi·graine (mī′grān) *n* a recurring severe headache, usually on one side of the head. <French, from Greek *hemi-* half + *kranion* skull>

mi·grant (mī′grənt) *n* a person who or animal, bird, or plant that migrates.
adj migrating: *The apple crops were picked by migrant workers.*

mi·grate (mī′grāt) *or* (mī grāt′) *v* **mi·grat·ed, mi·grat·ing** **1** go as a bird or fish from one region to another with the change in the seasons: *Most birds migrate to warmer countries in the winter.* **2** move from one place to settle in another, especially in search of work: *Many rural dwellers migrated to the big cities.* **3** move from one specific part of something, especially of the body, to another: *The pain migrated from her back to her neck.* <Latin *migrare*>
mi·gra′tion *n.* **mi′gra·to′ry** *adj.*

mi·ka·do (mə kȧ′dō) *n,* **mi·ka·dos** the ancient title of the emperor of Japan. <Japanese>

mike (mīk) *Informal n* microphone.

Mi'k·maw (mig′mo) *n* **Mi'k·maq** (mig′mok) **1** a member of a First Nations people living in the Maritimes. **2** their Algonquian language.
adj to do with these people or their language.

mil (mil) *n* a nonmetric unit for measuring length, equal to 0.001 inch (about 25 micrometres).

mi·la·dy (mi lā′dē) *n, pl* **mi·la·dies** formerly used to address or refer to a woman of the nobility.

milch (milch) *adj* giving milk or kept for the milk it gives: *a milch cow.* <Old English *melcan* to milk>

mild (mīld) *adj* **1** gentle and kind: *a mild response.* **2** temperate or moderate: *a mild climate, a mild winter.* **3** soft or sweet to the senses; not strong or sharp: *mild cheese.* <Old English *milde* gracious> **mild′ly** *adv.* **mild′ness** *n.*

mil·dew (mil′dyū) *or* (mil′dū) *n* a whitish coating or discolouring caused by a fungus that grows on plants or on such organic materials as paper, clothes, or leather.
v cover or become covered with mildew. <Old English *mildeaw* honeydew, in reference to the honeylike appearance of some mildew>

mile (mīl) *n* **1** a nonmetric unit for measuring distance on land, equal to about 1.6 km. **2** a nautical mile. **3** **miles** *pl* a relatively great distance: *The sun went down, but we were still miles from home. From here you can see for miles.* <Latin *mille* thousand>

mile·age (mī′lij) *n* **1** **a** the total distance travelled. **b** the distance that a motor vehicle can go on a given amount of fuel. **c** an allowance for travelling expenses at a fixed rate per mile. Compare KILOMETRAGE. **2** the profit or benefit a person is getting or can get out of something: *He's getting a lot of mileage out of that one joke.*

GRAMMAR AND USAGE

Although metric is standard in Canada, and distances are officially measured in kilometres, the nonmetric term *mile* still comes up in words like **mileage** and **milestone**.

a bat	e bed	i bid	o pot	u cup	th **thin**
ā cake	ē me	ī bite	ō go	ū rude	ᴛʜ **then**
ȧ bar	ə about	ər over	ȯ for	u̇ put	zh measure

M

mile·stone (mīl′stōn′) *n* **1** a stone set up to show the distance in miles to a certain place. **2** an important event in history: *The invention of printing was a milestone in the progress of education.*

mi·lieu (mē lyū′) *n* surroundings or environment. <French *mi* mid + *lieu* place>

mil·i·tant (mil′ə tənt) *adj* combative, aggressive, or warlike: *a militant environmentalist.*
n a person aggressively active in serving a cause or in spreading a belief. **mil′i·tan·cy** *n.* **mil′i·tant·ly** *adv.*

mil·i·ta·rism (mil′ə tə riz′əm) *n* the tendency, belief, or policy that a country should maintain a strong military force, and be prepared to use it to advance national interests. **mil′i·ta·rist** *n.* **mil′i·ta·rist′ic** *adj.*

mil·i·ta·rize (mil′ə tə rīz′) *v* **mil·i·ta·rized, mil·i·ta·riz·ing** make the military of a country powerful, or fill with military spirit and ideals. **mil′i·ta·ri·za′tion** *n.*

mil·i·tar·y (mil′ə ter′ē) *adj* of soldiers or armed forces: *military training, military history, military manoeuvres.*
n **the military** the armed forces or soldiers: *The military did rescue work during the flood.* <Latin *militis* soldier> **mil′i·tar′i·ly** *adv.*

military law *n* a system of regulations governing the armed forces and others in military service. Compare MARTIAL LAW.

CONFUSABLES

Military law applies to soldiers or armed forces.

Martial law replaces civil law in times of emergency, and applies to civilians as well as military personnel.

military police *pl n* soldiers who act as police for an army. *Abbrev.* **MP** or **M.P.**

🍁 **Military Regime** *n* in Canada, the period of military rule between 1759 and 1764.

mil·i·tate (mil′ə tāt′) *v* **mil·i·tat·ed, mil·i·tat·ing** act or work or operate, usually negatively: *Bad weather militated against the success of the picnic.* <Latin *militis* soldier>

CONFUSABLES

Militate means "operate" or "have an effect": *The poor weather militated against our plans to go swimming.*

Mitigate means "make less intense or severe": *The sale will mitigate the impact of the unexpected price increases.*

mi·li·tia (mə lish′ə) *n* a military force made up of citizens who undergo special training and supplement the regular armed forces.

mil·i·um (mi′lē əm) *n, pl* **mil·i·a** a small white nodule on the skin, usually the result of a plugged sebaceous gland. <Latin = millet grain>

milk (milk) *n* **1** the white liquid secreted by female mammals for the nourishment of their young, especially that from cows. **2** a liquid resembling this, such as the white juice of a plant, tree, or nut: *coconut milk.*
v **1** draw the milk from: *He used to milk twenty cows a day.* **2** yield or produce milk. **3** drain contents, strength, information, or wealth from something: *The dishonest treasurer milked the club treasury.* **4** draw juice or poison from: *to milk a snake.* <Old English *milc*> **milk′er** *n.*
cry over spilt milk, waste sorrow or regret on what has happened and cannot be remedied.

milk·maid (milk′mād′) *n* in former times, a woman whose job was to milk cows.

milk·man (milk′mən′) *n, pl* **milk·men** (-mən′) a person who sells or delivers milk.

milk of human kindness *n* natural sympathy and affection.

milk of magnesia *n* a medicine made of magnesium carbonate in water, used to counteract acidity.

milk·shake (milk′shāk′) *n* a drink consisting of milk, flavouring, and often ice cream, shaken or beaten until frothy.

milk snake *n* a small, harmless snake of N America, often with red, black, yellow, or white bands.

milk sugar *n* lactose.

milk tooth *n* one of the first set of teeth.

milkweed (mil′kwēd′) *n* a plant whose stem contains white sap that looks like milk. Some milkweeds attract butterflies and others are grown as ornamentals.

milk·y (mil′kē) *adj* **milk·i·er, milk·i·est 1** of, like, or containing milk. **2** of a liquid, gemstone, etc., not clear; clouded. **milk′i·ness** *n.*

Milky Way *n* a broad band of faint light that stretches across the sky at night, made up of countless stars too far away to see separately without a telescope.

mill[1] (mil) *n* **1** a machine for grinding or crushing, such as a flour mill that grinds wheat into flour, or a coffee mill that grinds coffee beans. **2** a building containing a machine for grinding grain. **3** a building where manufacturing is done: *a pulp mill, a paper mill.*
v **1** grind or crush something in a mill: *Some wheat will be milled before it is exported.* **2** cut or shape with a rotating tool, especially in manufacturing. **3** cut a series of fine notches or ridges on the edge of a coin. **4** move around in a confused way: *There were many people milling around after the parade.* <Latin *molere* to grind>
go through the mill, *Informal* learn by hard or painful experience.
put through the mill, *Informal* teach or test by hard or painful experience.

mill[2] (mil) *n* $0.001, or one-tenth of a cent, used only in calculations. <Latin *mille* thousand>

mil·len·ni·um (mə len′ē əm) *n, pl* **mil·len·ni·ums** or **mil·len·ni·a** (mə len′ē ə) **1** a period of a thousand years: *The world is many millenniums old.* **2** *Christianity* according to the Bible, the period of a thousand years at the end of time that Christ will reign on earth. **3** a period of good government, happiness, and prosperity. <Latin *mille* thousand + *annus* year> **mil·le′ni·al** *adj.*

millennium bug *Computers n* a problem involving two-digit coding of dates in computer programs that was expected to cause system failures at the start of the year 2000, but did not. See also Y2K.

mill·er (mil′ər) *n* **1** a person who owns or runs a mill, especially a flour mill. **2** a moth whose wings look as if they were powdered with flour.

mil·let (mil′it) *n* a fast-growing cereal, mainly cultivated in warm countries. Its small whitish seeds are eaten by themselves, and are also used to make flour and alcoholic drinks. See GRAIN for picture. <French, from Latin *milium*>

milli– *combining form* one-thousandth: *milligram.* See also the APPENDIX. <Latin *mille* thousand>

mil·li·am·pere (mil′ē am′pēr) *n* a unit of electric current, equal to one-thousandth of an ampere.

mil·li·bar (mil′ə bȧr′) *n* a unit of pressure, equal to 0.1 kilopascals. Atmospheric pressure readings are sometimes given in millibars.

mil·li·gram (mil′ə gram′) *n* a unit for measuring weight, equal to one-thousandth of a gram. *Symbol* **mg**
Also, **milligramme**.

mil·li·li·tre (mil′ə lē′tər) *n* a unit of volume or capacity, equal to one-thousandth of a litre. *Symbol* **mL**
Also, **milliliter**.

mil·li·me·tre (mil′ə mē′tər) *n* a unit of length, equal to one-thousandth of a metre. *Symbol* **mm**
Also, **millimeter**.

mil·li·ner (mil′ə nər) *n* a person who makes or sells women's hats. <*Milaner* native of Milan, Italy, a city famous for fine straw work and fancy goods>

mil·li·ner·y (mil′ə ner′ē) *n* **1** women's hats. **2** the business of making or selling women's hats.

mill·ing (mil′ing) *n* **1** the business or process of grinding grain in a mill. **2** cutting metal with a rotating tool, especially in manufacturing. **3 a** the business or process of cutting notches or ridges on an edge. **b** such notches or ridges.

mil·lion (mil′yən) *n, pl* **mil·lions** or (*after a number*) **mil·lion** **1** one thousand thousand (1 000 000). **2** a very large number: *He can always think of a million reasons for not helping with the dishes.*
adj one thousand thousand: *a million dollars.* <Old French, from Latin *mille* thousand> **mil′lionth** *adj, adv.*

mil·lion·aire (mil′yə ner′) *n* **1** a person who has a million or more dollars or owns property worth that amount. **2** a very wealthy person.

mil·lionth (mil′yənth) *n* **1** last in a series of a million. **2** one of a million equal parts.
adj, adv See MILLION.

mil·li·pede (mil′ə pēd′) *n* a small, wormlike arthropod that has two pairs of legs apiece for most of its segments. Also, **millepede**. <Latin *mille* thousand + *pedis* foot>

mil·li·sec·ond (mil′ə sek′ənd) *n* a unit of time equal to one-thousandth of a second.

mill·pond (mil′pond′) *n* a pond supplying water to drive a mill wheel.

mill·race (mil′rās′) *n* a current or channel of water that drives a mill wheel.

mill rate *n* a rate used for calculating municipal taxes. A mill rate of 45.6 means that a property owner pays a tax of 45.6 mills ($0.0456) for every dollar of the property value.

mill·stone (mil′stōn′) *n* **1** either of a pair of round, flat stones used for grinding grain. **2** a heavy burden: *Doing housework became a millstone around her neck.*

mill wheel *n* a wheel that is turned by water and supplies power for a mill.

mill·wright (mil′rīt′) *n* a person whose work is designing, building, setting up, or maintaining mill machinery.

milque·toast (milk′tōst′) *n* an extremely timid person. <C. *Milquetoast*, a character from an early 20c comic strip called "The Timid Soul">

milt (milt) *n* **1** the sperm cells of male fish with the milky fluid containing them. **2** the reproductive gland in male fish. <Old English *milte* spleen>

mime (mīm) *n* **1** a form of drama in which the actors use movement and gestures but no words. **2** communicating through gestures but without the use of words: *He told his story in mime.* **3** an actor who performs mime. **4** in ancient Greece and Rome, a simple farce using funny actions and gestures.
v **mimed, mim·ing** communicate in this way: *He mimed the story of his first date.* <Latin, from Greek *mimos*> **mim′er** *n.*

mi·met·ic (mi met′ik) *adj* **1** imitative: *mimetic gestures.* **2** to do with or exhibiting protective mimicry in a plant or animal.

M

mim·ic (mim′ik) *v* **mim·icked, mim·ick·ing** **1** make fun of by imitating: *We like to get him to mimic our old music teacher.* **2** copy closely or imitate: *A parrot can mimic a person's voice.* **3** resemble closely, especially as camouflage: *Some insects mimic leaves.*
n a person who or thing that imitates.
adj imitated or pretended for some purpose: *The soldiers staged a mimic battle for the visiting general.* <Latin, from Greek *mimos* mime> **mim′ic·ry** *n.*

SYNONYMS

Mimic means "imitate speech or manner," perhaps making fun of a person: *The comedian made the audience laugh by mimicking the singer.*

Parody involves a humorous imitation of a piece of writing or work of art: *She wrote a parody of the horror film.*

mi·mo·sa (mi mō′sə) *n* a tree, shrub, or plant of tropical or warm regions, usually with fernlike leaves and heads or spikes of small flowers.

min·a·ret (min′ə ret′) *or* (min′ə ret′) *n* a slender, high tower of a Moslem mosque, with one or more balconies from which a crier calls the people to prayer. <Spanish, from Arabic *manaret* lighthouse>

mince (mins) *v* **minced, minc·ing 1** grind into very small pieces. **2** speak or move in a delicate, affected way. **3** soften or moderate words, as when stating unpleasant facts: *The judge addressed the jury bluntly, without mincing words.*
n **1** meat ground into very small pieces or ground beef, pork, or lamb. **2** mincemeat, or made with mincemeat: *mince pie.* <Old French, from Latin *minutus* small>
not to mince matters, to speak plainly and frankly.

mince·meat (min′smēt′) *n* a mixture of chopped apples, raisins, currants, candied fruits, and sometimes suet and meat, used as a filling for pies.
make mincemeat (out) of, *Informal* defeat overwhelmingly: *Don't play chess with my dad or he'll make mincemeat of you!*

minc·ing (min′sing) *adj* overly polite, elegant, or delicate: *a mincing courtier.* **minc′ing·ly** *adv.*

mind (mīnd) *n* **1** the part of a person that knows, thinks, remembers, feels, and wills: *He set his mind on going to the show. Keep the rules in mind.* **2** a person's intellect: *Her good mind made it easy for her to learn languages.* **3** a person identified with his or her intelligence: *He was one of the great minds of his day.* **4** sanity: *to be out of one's mind.* **5** a way of thinking or feeling: *I changed my mind.*
v **1** remember or pay attention to: *Mind my words!* **2** regard as important: *Never mind the rain; you'll soon be home.* **3** be careful concerning: *Mind the step.* **4** look after: *Mind the baby.* **5** obey: *Be sure to mind your grandmother when you are out with her.* <Old English *gemynd*>
bear in mind, keep your attention on or remember.
be of one mind, agree: *They were both of one mind.*
come to mind, recall or remember.
give someone a piece of your mind, speak to angrily.
have a mind of your own, have definite and personal intentions or opinions.
have a mind to, intend to: *I have a mind to watch the hockey game tonight.*
have half a mind, be somewhat inclined.
have in mind, consider, intend; plan: *I need to exercise more, but kickboxing was not what I had in mind.*
in (or **of**) **two minds,** wavering between two opinions.
keep in mind, remember.
know your own mind, know what you really think, wish, or intend.
make up your mind, decide or resolve.
mind you, *Informal* **a** however: *This car uses a lot of gas. Mind you, I haven't had to spend much on repairs.* **b** moreover: *They paid me in full—and on time, mind you!*
never mind, pay no attention (to): *Never mind what they say. If you're too tired, never mind. We'll do it later.*
on your mind, much in your thoughts.
out of your mind, crazy.
put in mind, remind.
set your mind on, want very much.
speak your mind, give your frank opinion.
take someone's mind off, distract someone from something unpleasant.

mind–blow·ing (mīnd′blō′ing) *Informal adj* amazing or beyond comprehension.

mind–bog·gling (mīnd′bog′ling) *adj* too huge, amazing, or terrible to be understood or believed.

mind·ful (mīnd′fəl) *adj* being aware or careful: *Mindful of your advice, I went slowly.* **mind′ful·ly** *adv.* **mind′ful·ness** *n.*

mind·less (mīn′dlis) *adj* **1** acting without concern for the consequences: *mindless drunken driving.* **2** done for no particular reason, especially in a careless or harmful way: *mindless enthusiasm.* **mind′less·ly** *adv.*

mind reader *n* a person who supposedly knows the thoughts of others.

mind·set (mīnd′set′) *n* a habitual mental attitude or set way of understanding and responding to things.

mind's eye *n* imagination.

mine[1] (mīn) *pron* a possessive form of I: *The dog is mine. These must be your shoes, because mine are over there.* <Old English *min*>

mine[2] (mīn) *n* **1** a large hole or space dug in the earth to get out valuable minerals: *a coal mine, a gold mine.* **2** a rich or plentiful source: *a mine of information.* **3** a container holding an explosive charge that is put on or just below the surface of the ground or water and explodes when a person, vehicle, or ship causes vibrations, produces magnetic attraction, or comes in contact with it. **4** in former times, an underground passage in which an explosive is placed to blow up an enemy fort.
v **mined, min·ing 1** dig into the earth for minerals, or get minerals from a mine. **2** make a hole, space, or passage in and below the earth. **3** extract something valuable from a rich or plentiful source: *We mined the reference section of the library for what we needed.* **4** put explosive mines in or under something. <Old French>

mine·field (mīn′fēld′) *n* **1** an area throughout which explosive mines have been laid, or the pattern of mines in such an area. **2** a situation or subject of discussion that has hidden dangers or problems and is best avoided or treated very carefully.

min·er (mī′nər) *n* **1** a person who works in a mine: *a coal miner.* **2** in former times, a soldier who laid explosive mines.

min·er·al (min′ə rəl) *n* a solid, inorganic substance that occurs naturally in the earth's crust, and can be obtained by quarrying or mining.
adj of or containing minerals: *mineral water.*

min·er·al·o·gy (min′ə rol′ə jē) *or* (min′ə ral′ə jē) *n* the science that studies the physical and chemical properties of minerals, their classification, and the form and structure of their crystals. **min′er·a·log′i·cal** *adj.* **min′er·a·log′i·cal·ly** *adv.* **min′er·al′o·gist** *n.*

mineral oil *n* an oil derived from a mineral substance, especially a colourless, odourless, tasteless oil obtained from petroleum, used as a laxative, lubricant, or moisturizer.

mineral water *n* water containing mineral salts or gases, sometimes drunk as a beverage.

min·e·stro·ne (min′ə strō′nē) *n* a thick soup containing vegetables and pasta. <Italian>

mine·sweep·er (mīn′swēp′ər) *n* a warship equipped for dragging a harbour or the sea in order to remove enemy mines or make them harmless.

Ming (ming) *n* **1** in China, the ruling dynasty from 1368 to 1644. **2** fine china made during this period. <Mandarin = clear, bright>

min·gle (ming′gəl) *v* **min·gled, min·gling 1** mix or cause to mix together. **2** move freely around a place or social gathering in order to associate with others: *to mingle with important people.* <Old English *mengan* mix>
min′gler *n.*

mini– *combining form* small for its kind: *miniskirt, mini-lesson.*
n **mini** *Informal* something small for its kind. <*miniature*>

min·i·a·ture (min′ē ə chər) *or* (min′ə chər) *n* **1** a thing that is much smaller than normal, such as a small model or copy: *In the museum there is a miniature of the* Bluenose. **2** a very small painting, usually a portrait.
adj done or made on a very small scale: *She collected miniature furniture for her dollhouse.* <Italian *miniatura* small picture>
in miniature, on a small scale.

min·i·bus (min′ē bus′) *n* a small bus used for short runs, as between an airport and a hotel.

min·i·golf (min′ē golf′) *n* an amusement-park version of golf in which people try to hit the ball through, over, and under obstacles into the hole on a very small course with separate greens for each hole.

min·i·mal (min′ə məl) *adj* the least possible amount, quantity, or degree: *The article claimed that the side effects of the drug were minimal.*

min·i·mize (min′ə mīz′) *v* **min·i·mized, min·i·miz·ing 1** reduce to the least possible amount or degree: *The polar explorers took every precaution to minimize the dangers of their trip.* **2** state at the lowest possible estimate: *An ungrateful person minimizes the help others have given her.*
min′i·mi·za′tion *n.* **min′i·mi·zer** *n.*

min·i·mum (min′ə məm) *n, pl* **min·i·mums** or **min·i·ma** the least amount or smallest quantity possible or permitted: *I need a minimum of eight hours sleep a night.*
adj smallest or lowest: *a minimum rate.* <Latin = smallest>

minimum wage *n* the lowest wage paid or allowed, especially the wage fixed by law as the lowest that can be paid to an employed person or in certain categories of employment.

min·ing (mī′ning) *n* **1** the act, process, or business of digging minerals: **2** the act or process of laying explosive mines.

min·ion (min′yən) *n* a person who is willing to do whatever he or she is ordered by a powerful person. <French *mignon*>

min·i·ser·ies (min′i sē′rēz) *n* a TV program, especially a drama, in a series of episodes, but not lasting an entire season.

min·i·skirt (min′ē skərt′) *n* a very short skirt ending well above the knees.

min·is·ter (min′i stər) *n* **1** a member of the clergy in charge of a Protestant church. **2** a member of a cabinet who is in charge of a government department: *the Minister of Finance.*
v attend to someone's needs: *She ministers to the sick.* <Old French, from Latin = servant> **min′is·te′ri·al** *adj.* **min′is·te′ri·al·ly** *adv.*

minister without portfolio *n* a CABINET MINISTER who is not connected with a particular cabinet post or department.

min·is·tra·tion (min′i strā′shən) *n* the act or process of ministering: *ministration to the sick.*

min·is·try (min′i strē) *n, pl* **min·is·tries 1** the office, duties, or time of service of a minister of religion. **2** the ministers of a church. **3** the ministers of a government. **4** in Canada and some other countries, a government department under a minister. **5** ministering or serving.

mi·ni·van (min′ē van) *n* a vehicle shaped like a very small bus, able to carry more passengers and cargo than the average car. The rear seats can usually be removed or folded down.

mink (mingk) *n* a small animal, related to the weasel, that lives in water part of the time. <Swedish *mank*>
mink′like′ *adj.*

min·now (min′ō) *n* a very small freshwater fish, often used as live bait. <Old English *myne*>

mi·nor (mī′nər) *adj* **1** smaller or lesser: *a minor fault, a minor poet.* **2** under the legal age of being responsible for your actions. **3** *Music* **a** to do with an interval less by a half step than a corresponding major interval. **b** to do with a scale, mode, or key whose third tone is minor in relation to the fundamental tone.
n **1** a person who is not considered to be legally responsible for an action. **2** *Music* a minor musical interval, key, scale, or chord: *the scale of A minor.* **3** a subject or course of study to which a student gives time and attention, but less than to a major subject. <Latin = lesser>
minor in, take as a minor subject of study.

mi·nor·i·ty (mə nȯ′rə tē) *or* (mī nȯ′rə tē) *n, pl* **mi·nor·i·ties 1** the smaller number or part, especially less than half the total: *The minority must often do what the majority decides to do.* **2** a group within a country or place that differs in race, religion, or national origin from the larger part of the population. **3** of, constituting, or belonging to a minority: *a minority vote, a minority group, a minority opinion.* **4** the condition or time of being under the age of legal responsibility.

a bat	e bed	i bid	o pot	u cup	th **thin**
ā cake	ē me	ī bite	ō go	ū rude	TH **then**
ȧ bar	ə about	ər over	ȯ for	u̇ put	zh measure

minor league *n* a professional sports league or association, especially in baseball or hockey, other than the major leagues.

minor penalty *Hockey n* a two-minute penalty awarded for breaking certain rules.

min·ster (min′stər) *especially UK n* a large or important church, typically one that was built as part of a monastery. <Old English *mynster*>

min·strel (min′strəl) *n* **1** a medieval singer or musician who sang or recited poetry to a musical accompaniment. **2** a musician or poet. <Old French, from Latin *ministerium* ministry>

min·strel·sy (min′strəl sē) *n, pl* **min·strel·sies** the art or practice of being a minstrel.

mint[1] (mint) *n* **1** a scented herb, especially one of several species used for seasoning or flavouring food, such as peppermint or spearmint. See HERB for picture. **2** a piece of candy flavoured with mint, especially peppermint or spearmint. <Latin, from Greek *minthe*> **mint′y** *adj.*

mint[2] (mint) *n* **1** a place where money is made by government authority. **2** *Informal* a large sum of money: *She made a mint when she sold her house.*
v **1** make coins or medals: *This quarter was minted in 1938.* **2** produce for the first time: *newly minted software.* <Latin *moneta* money>
in mint condition, without a blemish and as good as new: *an old car in mint condition.*

min·u·end (min′yū end′) *n* a number or quantity from which another is to be subtracted.
Example: In 100 – 23 = 77, the minuend is 100.

min·u·et (min′yū et′) *n* a slow, stately ballroom dance, popular in the 1700s, or the music for it. <Old French *menuet* small, delicate, from the tiny steps that are a feature of the dance>

mi·nus (mī′nəs) *prep* **1** decreased or reduced by: *Five minus two is three.* **2** *Informal* without or lacking: *a book minus its cover.*
n the sign (–) meaning that the quantity following it is to be subtracted.
adj **1** showing subtraction: *The minus sign is –.* **2** (*never used before a noun*) less than: *A mark of B minus is not as high as B.* **3** negative or less than zero: *a minus quantity. The temperature this morning was minus thirteen degrees.* <Latin = less>

min·us·cule (min′ə skyūl′) *adj* tiny: *The dollhouse came with a lot of minuscule furniture.* <French, from Latin *minus* less> **mi·nus′cu·lar** *adj.*

min·ute[1] (min′it) *n* **1** a unit for measuring time, equal to sixty seconds or one-sixtieth of an hour. *Symbol* **min** **2** a short period of time: *It will only take me a minute to put the dishes away. She paused for a minute to listen.* **3** a point in time: *Get over here this minute.* **4** a unit for measuring plane angles, equal to sixty seconds or one-sixtieth of a degree, used mainly by geographers. *Symbol* **′**
5 minutes *pl* a written summary or official record of the proceedings of a group, such as a board or committee. <Latin *minutus* small, from *minuere* lessen>
up to the minute, up-to-date.

mi·nute[2] (mī nyūt′) *or* (mī nūt′) *adj* **1** tiny: *a minute speck of dust.* **2** going into or concerned with very small details: *a minute observer, minute instructions.* <Latin *minuere* lessen> **mi·nute′ly** *adv.* **mi·nute′ness** *n.*

minute hand (min′it) *n* the longer of the two hands on a watch or clock, indicating the minutes: *The minute hand moves around the dial once every hour.*

mi·nu·ti·ae (mi nyū′shē ē′) *or* (mi nū′shē ē′), (mi nyū′shē ī′) *or* (mi nū′shē ī′) *pl n* very small matters or details.

minx (mingks) *n* a bold or impudent girl. <origin uncertain>

min·yan (min′yən) *or* (mēn yan′) *Judaism n* a quorum of ten men needed for traditional Jewish public worship. <Hebrew = reckoning>

Mi·o·cene (mī′ə sēn) *n* the geological epoch lasting from about 20 million to 10 million years ago, when the climate was mild and apes first appeared. See also CENOZOIC, TERTIARY.
adj to do with this epoch. <Greek *meion* less + *kainos* new>

mir·a·cle (mir′ə kəl) *n* **1** a wonderful happening that is contrary to or independent of the known laws of nature: *It would be a miracle if the earth stood still in space for an hour.* **2** something marvellous or extremely unexpected. <Old French, from Latin *mirus* wonderful>

miracle drug *n* a new drug that treats or cures conditions previously thought to be untreatable.

miracle play *n* a medieval religious drama dealing with Biblical stories or the lives of the saints.

mi·rac·u·lous (mə rak′yə ləs) *adj* **1** contrary to or independent of the known laws of nature. **2** wonderful or marvellous: *Meeting you here is a piece of miraculous good luck!* **mi·rac′u·lous·ly** *adv.* **mi·rac′u·lous·ness** *n.*

mi·rage (mə räzh′) *n* **1** a misleading appearance caused by the refraction of light from the sky by heated air, as for example, the appearance of a sheet of water in a desert. **2** an illusion. <French *se mirer* to be reflected, from Latin *mirar* look at>

Mi·ran·da (mi rand′ə) *US adj* to do with the legal right of an arrested person to remain silent and have access to a lawyer. Police must inform the person of these rights at the time of arrest: *a person's Miranda rights.* <*Miranda*, defendant's surname in the case that gave rise to this ruling> **Mi·ran′dize** *Slang v.*

mire (mīr) *n* **1** soft, deep mud, especially in a bog or swamp. **2** a situation in which it is hard to extricate oneself.
v **mired, mir·ing** **1** stick or cause to get stuck. **2** get hampered by or involved in difficulties: *She got mired in a traffic jam.* <Old Norse *myrr*>

mir·ror (mir′ər) *n* **1** a surface that reflects light, especially of a clear image. **2** whatever reflects or gives a true description: *This book is a mirror of the author's life.* **3** a model or example: *That knight was a mirror of chivalry.*
v **1** reflect as a mirror does: *The still water mirrored the trees along the bank.* **2** give a true description or picture of: *The book mirrored colonial life in Canada.* <Old French, from Latin *mirare* look at> **mir′ror·like′** *adj.*

mirth (mərth) *n* merriment accompanied by laughter: *Her sides shook with mirth.* <Old English *myrgth*>
mirth′ful *adj.* **mirth′ful·ly** *adv.* **mirth′ful·ness** *n.*

mirth·less (mərth′lis) *adj* joyless or gloomy. **mirth′less·ly** *adv.* **mirth′less·ness** *n.*

mir·y (mī′rē) *adj* **mir·i·er, mir·i·est 1** muddy or boggy. **2** dirty or filthy. **mir′i·ness** *n.*

mis– *prefix* **1** bad or badly: *mismanagement, misbehave.* **2** wrong or wrongly: *mispronunciation, misunderstand.* <Old English>

MIS *Computers n* in full, **Management Information System** an organization's computer systems, especially as used to store and process data needed by managers to make decisions or keep track of operations.

mis·ad·ven·ture (mis′əd ven′chər) *n* **1** an unfortunate incident or occasion: *We had several misadventures on our vacation.* **2** bad luck: *By some misadventure, the file got lost.*

mis·al·li·ance (mis′ə lī′əns) *n* an unsuitable alliance or association, especially in marriage.

mis·an·thro·py (mi san′thrə pē) *n* a hatred, dislike, or distrust of human beings. <Greek *misein* to hate + *anthropos* man> **mis′an·thrope′** (mis′ən thrōp′) *n.* **mis′an·throp′ic** (mis′ən throp′ik) *adj.*

mis·ap·pro·pri·ate (mis′ə prō′prē āt′) *v* **mis·ap·pro·pri·at·ed, mis·ap·pro·pri·at·ing** make use of for oneself without authority or right: *The treasurer had misappropriated the club funds.*
mis′ap·pro·pri·a′tion *n.*

mis·be·got·ten (mis′bi got′ən) *adj* poorly conceived, designed, or done: *a misbegotten plan.*

mis·be·have (mis′bi hāv′) *v* **mis·be·haved, mis·be·hav·ing** behave badly: *The child was punished for misbehaving at the party.* **mis′be·hav′iour** or **mis′be·hav′ior** (mis′bi hā′vyər) *n.*

misc. miscellaneous.

mis·cal·cu·late (mis kal′kyə lāt′) *v* **mis·cal·cu·lat·ed, mis·cal·cu·lat·ing** calculate wrongly: *His arrow fell short because he had miscalculated the distance.* **mis′cal·cu·la′tion** *n.*

mis·call (mis kol′) *v* call by a wrong name.

mis·car·riage (mis kar′ij) *or* (mis ker′ij) *n* **1** the involuntary expulsion of a fetus from the womb before it has developed enough to survive. **2** an unsuccessful outcome of something planned or intended: *a miscarriage of justice.* **mis·car′ry** *v.*

mis·cast (mis kast′) *v* **mis·cast, mis·cast·ing** cast in an unsuitable role: *The young actress was badly miscast as a bank manager.*

mis·ce·ge·na·tion (mis′ə jə nā′shən) *n* marriage or sexual relations between two people considered to be of different races. <Latin *miscere* mix + *genus* race>

mis·cel·la·ne·ous (mis′ə lā′nē əs) *adj* **1** formed or consisting of different things or parts, and not arranged in a pattern or system: *a miscellaneous collection of stamps. She writes a newspaper column of miscellaneous comments.* **2** with or showing various qualities or interests: *a miscellaneous writer.* <Latin *miscere* to mix> **mis′cel·la′ne·ous·ly** *adv.* **mis′cel·la′ne·ous·ness** *n.*

mis·cel·la·ny (mis′ə lā′nē) *or* (mi sel′ə nē) *n, pl* **mis·cel·la·nies 1** a collection or mixture of various things. **2 miscellanies** *pl* a collection of texts by different authors in one book.

mis·chance (mis chans′) *n* bad luck: *By some mischance, he didn't receive my e-mail.*

mis·chief (mis′chif) *n* **1** action or conduct that causes trouble or harm, often not intentionally: *Mischief with matches may cause a serious fire. I'm always getting into mischief.* **2** playful mocking or fooling: *Her eyes were full of mischief.* **3** harm or injury, especially when done by a person: *He'll try to do you a mischief if you meddle.* **4** a person who causes annoyance, irritation, or harm: *He's a little mischief.* <Old French *mes-* badly + *chever* come to an end>

mis·chie·vous (mis′chə vəs) *adj* **1** causing or tending to cause harm or annoyance: *mischievous gossip, mischievous behaviour.* **2** full of pranks and teasing fun: *mischievous children, a mischievous look.* **mis′chie·vous·ly** *adv.* **mis′chie·vous·ness** *n.*

mis·ci·ble (mis′ə bəl) *adj* capable of being mixed to form a liquid that has the same composition throughout: *Water and alcohol are miscible, but water and oil are not.* <Latin *miscere* mix>

mis·con·ceive (mis′kən sēv′) *v* **mis·con·ceived, mis·con·ceiv·ing** have wrong ideas about or misunderstand: *The reporter misconceived the speaker's meaning.*

mis·con·cep·tion (mis′kən sep′shən) *n* a mistaken idea.

mis·con·duct (mis kon′dukt) *for n,* (mis′kən dukt′) *for v.*
n **1** bad behaviour or improper conduct. **2** bad or dishonest management, especially by a public official or a member of the military. **3** *Hockey* a penalty to any player except the goalkeeper that results in removal from the game for a ten-minute period or longer.
v **1** behave badly. **2** manage duties badly.

mis·con·struc·tion (mis′kən struk′shən) *n* the act or process of taking something in the wrong sense, or an example of this: *Such vague and ambiguous statements are open to misconstruction.*

mis·con·strue (mis′kən strū′) *v* **mis·con·strued, mis·con·stru·ing** take in a wrong sense: *Shyness is sometimes misconstrued as rudeness.*

mis·count (mis kount′) *for v,* (mis′kount′) *for n.*
v count wrongly.
n a wrong count.

mis·cue (mis kyū′) *n* **1** a bad stroke in billiards and snooker in which the cue slips and does not hit the ball squarely. **2** a mistake or miscalculated action.
v **mis·cued, mis·cu·ing** make a miscue.

mis·deal (mis dēl′) *for v,* (mis′dēl′) *for n.*
v **mis·dealt** (mis delt), **mis·deal·ing** deal wrongly at cards.
n a wrong deal at cards.

a bat	e bed	i bid	o pot	u cup	th **thin**
ā cake	ē me	ī bite	ō go	ū rude	TH **then**
ä bar	ə about	ər over	ò for	ů put	zh measure

mis·deed (mis dēd′) *n* a bad or immoral act.

mis·de·mean·our or **mis·de·mean·or** (mis′di mē′nər) *n* **1** a minor wrongdoing. **2** *especially US Law* a minor criminal offence, less serious than a felony. It is similar to a SUMMARY OFFENCE in Canada.

mis·di·ag·nose (mis′di ag nōs′) *v* **mis·di·ag·nosed, mis·di·ag·nos·ing** diagnose incorrectly: *His allergy was misdiagnosed as an ulcer at first.* **mis·di·ag·no′sis** *n.*

mis·di·rect (mis′də rekt′) *v* direct wrongly: *The thief left false clues to misdirect the police.* **mis′di·rec′tion** *n.*

mise en scène (mēs on sen′) *n* the arrangement of scenery and stage properties on a stage. <French = putting on stage>

mi·ser (mī′zər) *n* a person who loves money for its own sake, especially one who lives poorly in order to save money and keep it: *A miser dislikes spending money.* <Latin = wretched> **mi′ser·li·ness** *n.* **mi′ser·ly** *adv.*

mis·er·a·ble (miz′ə rə bəl) *or* (miz′rə bəl) *adj* **1** very unhappy or uncomfortable: *A sick child is often miserable.* **2** causing trouble or unhappiness: *a miserable cold.* **3** poor or pitiful: *They live in a cold, miserable house.* <French, from Latin *miser* wretched> **mis′er·a·ble·ness** *n.* **mis′er·a·bly** *adv.*

SYNONYMS

Miserable can mean "gloomy" or "sad": *She was miserable after she broke her leg.*

Disconsolate means "grief-stricken": *He was disconsolate when his grandfather died.*

Distressed can mean "troubled" or "anxious": *I was distressed when I misplaced my homework.*

mis·er·y (miz′ə rē) *or* (miz′rē) *n, pl* **mis·er·ies** **1** a very unhappy, distressed, or uncomfortable state of mind: *Think of the misery of having no home or friends.* **2** extremely poor and uncomfortable living conditions: *Some very poor people live in misery, without beauty or comfort around them.*

mis·file (mis fīl′) *v* **mis·filed, mis·fil·ing** file in the wrong place.

mis·fire (mis fīr′) *v* **mis·fired, mis·fir·ing** **1** fail to discharge or go off as a gun or missile. **2** fail to ignite properly, or at the proper moment, in an internal combustion engine. **3** fail to have an intended effect: *The robber's scheme misfired.*
n a failure to discharge or explode properly.

mis·fit (mis′fit′) *n* a person who is not suited to an environment or does not get along well with other people.

mis·for·tune (mis fôr′chən) *n* **1** bad luck: *She had the misfortune to break her arm.* **2** a piece of bad luck or unlucky accident.

mis·give (mis giv′) *v* **mis·gave, mis·giv·en, mis·giv·ing** cause to feel doubt, suspicion, or anxiety: *His heart misgave him when he realized how far he still had to go.*

mis·giv·ing (mis giv′ing) *n* a feeling of doubt, suspicion, or anxiety: *We started off through the storm with misgivings.*

mis·gov·ern (mis guv′ərn) *v* govern or manage badly. **mis·gov′ern·ment** *n.*

mis·guid·ed (mis gī′did) *adj* erring or misled in thought or action: *He mixed everything up in a well-meaning but misguided attempt to help.*

mis·han·dle (mis han′dəl) *v* **mis·han·dled, mis·han·dling** **1** handle roughly or harshly: *to mishandle a horse.* **2** manage badly or ignorantly: *to mishandle the club's money.*

mis·hap (mis′hap) *n* an unlucky accident. <Middle English *mis-* + *hap* luck>

mis·hear (mis hēr′) *v* **mis·heard** (mis hərd′), **mis·hear·ing** fail to identify sounds or speech correctly: *Sorry, I misheard you; when you said "writing" I thought you said "riding."*

mish·mash (mish′mash′) *n* a confused, random mixture. <probably reduplication of *mash*>

Mish·nah or **Mish·na** (mish′nə) *Judaism n* the collection of the traditional oral interpretations of the law of Moses, forming the first part of the Talmud. <Hebrew *misnah* teaching by repetition>

mis·in·form (mis′in fôrm′) *v* give wrong or misleading information to. **mis′in·for·ma′tion** *n.*

mis·in·ter·pret (mis′in tər′prit) *v* interpret wrongly: *She misinterpreted their signal to wait, and drove off before they were ready.* **mis′in·ter·pre·ta′tion** *n.*

mis·judge (mis juj′) *v* **mis·judged, mis·judg·ing** judge or estimate wrongly or unfairly: *The archer misjudged the distance to the target, and her arrow fell short. The teacher soon discovered that he had misjudged the girl's capabilities.* **mis·judg′ment** or **mis·judge′ment** *n.*

mis·la·bel (mis lā′bəl) *v* **mis·la·belled, mis·la·bel·ling** attach the wrong label to or call by the wrong name.

mis·lay (mis lā′) *v* **mis·laid, mis·lay·ing** put in a place and then forget where it is: *My mother is always mislaying her glasses.*

mis·lead (mis lēd′) *v* **mis·led** (mis led′), **mis·lead·ing** cause someone to have the wrong idea or impression: *Her cheerfulness misled us into believing that everything was fine. He was accused of misleading his followers.* **mis·lead′er** *n.* **mis·lead′ing** *adj.*

mis·man·age·ment (mis man′ij mənt) *n* bad management: *The collapse of the firm was due to years of mismanagement.* **mis·man′age** *v.*

mis·match (mis mach′) *for v,* (mis′mach) *for n.* *v* match incorrectly or unsuitably, or fail to match: *He was wearing a mismatched pair of socks.*
n a poor or unsuitable match: *That marriage is definitely a mismatch.*

mis·name (mis nām′) *v* **mis·named, mis·nam·ing** call by a wrong or unsuitable name: *The slow horse was misnamed "Lightning."*

mis·no·mer (mis nō′mər) *n* a wrong or unsuitable name or term: *"Speedy" is a misnomer for a pet turtle.* <Old French *mesnommer* to misname, from Latin *nominare* to call by name>

mi·sog·a·my (mi sog′ə mē) *n* hatred of marriage. <Greek *misos* hatred + *gamos* marriage> **mi·sog′a·mist** *n.*

mi·sog·y·ny (mi soj′ə nē) *n* hatred of women. <Greek *misos* hatred + *gyne* woman> **mi·sog′y·nist** *n.*

mis·place (mis plās′) *v* **mis·placed, mis·plac·ing 1** put in the wrong place: *a misplaced adjective.* **2** put in a place and then forget where it is. **3** place affection or trust on an unworthy or unsuitable object. **mis·place′ment** *n.*

misplaced modifier *Grammar n* a participle, past or present, that is not logically or grammatically attached to the noun or pronoun it is intended to modify. Example: *Swimming in the pond, the car was out of sight.* Also called **dangling modifier, dangling participle.**

mis·print (mis′print′) *for n,* (mis print′) *for v. n* a mistake in printing.
v print wrongly.

mis·pro·nounce (mis′prə nouns′) *v* **mis·pro·nounced, mis·pro·nounc·ing** pronounce in a way considered incorrect. **mis′pro·nun·ci·a′tion** *n.*

mis·quote (mis kwōt′) *v* **mis·quot·ed, mis·quot·ing** quote incorrectly. **mis′quo·ta′tion** *n.*

mis·read (mis rēd′) *v* **mis·read** (mis red′), **mis·read·ing 1** read wrongly: *I misread "tapering" as "papering" and got the whole sentence wrong.* **2** misinterpret or misunderstand: *She misread his silence as agreement.*

mis·rep·re·sent (mis′rep ri zent′) *v* **1** give a wrong or untrue idea of, especially in order to deceive: *The salesman misrepresented the car when he said it was in perfect condition.* **2** be a bad or inadequate representative of: *His new novel misrepresents his status as a writer.* **mis′rep·re·sen·ta′tion** *n.*

miss[1] (mis) *v* **1** fail to hit or catch something: *She shot two arrows, but both missed the target. He reached out, but just missed the ball.* **2** be too late to catch a passenger vehicle: *I missed my bus by five minutes.* **3** fail to attend or participate in an activity: *I missed this morning's assembly.* **4** fail to hear something: *Sorry, I missed what you said.* **5** fail to take advantage of: *I missed my chance.* **6** escape or avoid: *I barely missed being hit.* **7** notice the absence of: *I did not miss my wallet till I got home.* **8** feel keenly the absence of: *He missed his mother when she went away.* **9** fail to include: *to miss a word in reading.*
n **1** a failure to hit, catch, or reach something. **2** a failure, especially an unsuccessful recording or film. <Old English *missan*>
give something a miss, *Informal* not go to an event on purpose.

miss[2] (mis) *n, pl* **miss·es 1 Miss** a title put before a girl's or unmarried woman's name: *Miss Lee, the Misses Lee, the Miss Lees.* **2** a form of address used without a name, in speaking to a girl, or a woman assumed to be unmarried: *I beg your pardon, miss.* <*Mistress*>

mis·sal (mis′əl) *Catholicism n* a book containing the liturgy and prayers for celebrating the MASS throughout the year. <Latin *missa* Mass>

mis·shape (mis shāp′) *v* **mis·shaped, mis·shaped** or **mis·shap·en, mis·shap·ing** shape badly or deform. **mis·shap′en** *adj.*

mis·sile (mis′īl) *or* (mis′əl) *n* **1** an object that is thrown or shot at a target, such as a stone, arrow, or bullet. **2** a self-propelled rocket containing explosives that can be launched from land, air, or water. <Latin *mittere* send>

miss·ing (mis′ing) *adj* **1** out of the usual or a known place: *The missing ring was found under the dresser.* **2** absent: *Only two students were missing from class today.* **3** lacking: *It was quite a good dinner, but there was something missing.*

missing link *n* **1** the one piece of information or evidence that, when found, will explain some mystery. **2** evidence for an intermediate species between apes and humans that will explain how this transition or evolution is supposed to have happened.

mis·sion (mish′ən) *n* **1** the act of sending or being sent on some special task for political, religious, or commercial purposes. **2** a group of people sent on some special business: *She was one of a mission sent by our government to France.* **3** the business on which a person or group is sent: *Their mission was to blow up the bridge.* **4** the station or headquarters of a religious mission. **5** a place where people may go for aid, such as food, clothing, shelter, or counsel. **6** a person's purpose in life: *It seemed to be her mission to care for her brother's children.* <Latin *mittere* send>

mis·sion·ar·y (mish′ə ner′ē) *n, pl* **mis·sion·ar·ies 1** a person sent on a religious, especially Christian, mission. **2** a person who works to advance some cause or idea: *a missionary for science.*
adj to do with, or characteristic of, missions or missionaries: *He spoke with missionary zeal of a new social order.*

mission statement *n* a document issued by an organization, such as a university or corporation, setting out its reason for existence, and its fundamental values and goals.

mis·sive (mis′iv) *n* a written message. <Latin *mittere* send>

mis·spell (mis spel′) *v* **mis·spelled** or **mis·spelt, mis·spell·ing** spell incorrectly. **mis′spell′ing** *n.*

mis·spend (mis spend′) *v* **mis·spent, mis·spend·ing** spend foolishly or wrongly: *The old man regretted that he had misspent his youth.*

mis·state·ment (mis stāt′mənt) *n* a wrong or misleading statement: *The newspaper account of the game was full of misstatements.* **mis·state′** *v.*

mis·step (mis step′) *n* **1** a wrong step: *a single misstep would have plunged her into the abyss.* **2** an error in judgment: *A misstep now could ruin his career.*

mist (mist) *n* **1** a cloud of tiny water droplets in the air. **2** a thing that dims, blurs, or obscures: *The ideas were lost in a mist of long words.* **3** a haze before the eyes due to illness or tears.
v **1** come down in mist. **2** become covered with a mist: *The windows are misting.* **3** make the eyes film over with tears, obscuring vision: *Her eyes misted as she watched the movie's sad ending.* <Old English>
mist over (or **up**), become covered with mist.

a bat	e bed	i bid	o pot	u cup	th thin
ā cake	ē me	ī bite	ō go	ū rude	ᴛʜ then
ä bar	ə about	ər over	ô for	ů put	zh measure

M

mis·take (mi stāk′) *n* a misunderstanding of the meaning or use of something: *I used your towel by mistake.*
v **mis·took, mis·tak·en, mis·tak·ing** 1 misunderstand what is seen or heard: *I was mistaken when I said she would be here on time.* 2 take to be some other person or thing: *I mistook that stick for a snake.* <Old Norse *mistaka*>
and no mistake, without a doubt.

SYNONYMS

Mistake suggests a wrong idea or action: *I made a mistake by turning right instead of left on the street.*

Blunder suggests a stupid mistake: *I made a blunder when I forgot my friend's birthday.*

Typo is used for an error in typing or in setting type: *Her essay was full of typos.*

mis·tak·en (mi stā′kən) *adj* 1 having made a mistake: *A mistaken person should admit his error.* 2 wrong or wrongly judged: *It was a mistaken kindness to give that boy more candy; it will make him sick.*
v past participle of MISTAKE. **mis·tak′en·ly** *adv.*

mis·ter (mis′tər) *n* 1 **Mister** the spoken form of **Mr.**, used before a man's last name or the name of his rank or office. 2 *Informal* a form of address used without a name, in speaking to a man: *Hey, mister! You dropped your wallet.* <variant of *master*>

GRAMMAR AND USAGE

When used as a title before a name or office, the word **mister** is generally written in its abbreviated form: **Mr.**

mis·time (mis tīm′) *v* **mis·timed, mis·tim·ing** say or do at the wrong time.

mis·tle·toe (mis′əl tō′) *n* 1 an evergreen plant that grows as a parasite on trees. It has small white berries. <Old English *mistel* mistletoe + *tan* twig>

mis·took (mi stu̇k′) past tense of MISTAKE.

mis·tral (mis′trəl) *or* (mi stràl′) *n* a strong, cold, northwesterly wind of southern France that blows mainly in winter. <French, from Latin *magistralis* (*ventus*) = master wind>

mis·trans·late (mis′tran slāt′) *or* (mis′tran zlāt′), (mis tran′slāt) *or* (mis tran′zlāt) *v* **mis·trans·lat·ed, mis·trans·lat·ing** translate incorrectly.
mis′trans·la′tion (mis′tran slā′shən) *or* (mis′tran zlā′shən) *n.*

mis·treat (mis trēt′) *v* treat badly or abuse: *That man mistreats his horses.* **mis′treat′ment** *n.*

mis·tress (mis′tris) *n* 1 a woman who has power or authority, such as a female head of a household or institution. 2 a woman or girl as owner or possessor: *The dog was sitting outside the door, waiting for its mistress.* 3 a woman with thorough knowledge or skill: *mistress of the difficult art of fencing. She is mistress of the situation.* 4 a woman who has a continuing sexual relationship with a man without being legally married to him. 5 *especially UK* a female teacher: *the dancing mistress.* <Old French, from Latin *magister* master>

mis·tri·al (mis trī′əl) *n* 1 a trial declared to have no effect in law because of some error or serious misconduct in the proceedings. 2 a trial that is inconclusive because the jury has failed to reach a verdict.

mis·trust (mis trust′) *v* have no confidence or trust in: *She mistrusted her ability to learn to swim.*
n lack of trust or confidence. **mis·trust′ful** *adj.*
mis·trust′ful·ly *adv.*

mis·trust·ful (mis trust′fəl) *adj* lacking confidence in something or someone.

mist·y (mis′tē) *adj* **mist·i·er, mist·i·est** 1 full of or covered with mist: *misty hills, misty air.* 2 not clearly seen or outlined: *The children imagined they saw a misty shape in the graveyard.* 3 vague and indistinct: *a misty idea.*
mist′i·ly *adv.* **mist′i·ness** *n.*

mis·un·der·stand (mis′un dər stand′) *v*
mis·un·der·stood, mis·un·der·stand·ing understand wrongly, take in a wrong sense, or give the wrong meaning to: *We misunderstood the directions and made a wrong turn. Don't misunderstand me; I said I liked her, but that doesn't mean I trust her.*

mis·un·der·stand·ing (mis′un dər stan′ding) *n* 1 a failure to understand: *a misunderstanding of the facts.* 2 a disagreement: *After their misunderstanding, they scarcely spoke to each other for months.*

mis·un·der·stood (mis′un dər stu̇d′) *adj* not understood or properly appreciated: *As a child, he had always felt misunderstood.*
v past tense and past participle of MISUNDERSTAND.

mis·use (mis yüz′) *for v,* (mis yüs′) *for n. v* **mis·used, mis·us·ing** 1 use for the wrong purpose: *He misuses his knife at the table by lifting food with it.* 2 abuse or ill-treat: *She misuses her sled dogs by driving them too hard.*
n wrong or improper use: *the misuse of public funds, a misuse of words.*

mite (mīt) *n* 1 a tiny animal related to the ticks that are often parasites on plants or animals, and some of which carry diseases. See ARACHNID for picture. 2 a very small object or creature: *Our cat was just a mite when we got her.*
adv Informal a tiny bit or very little: *I think she's a mite tired.* <Old English>

mi·ter (mī′tər) MITRE.

Mith·ras (mith′ràs) *n* a god of light, truth, and honour, probably of Persian origin and associated with merchants and the protection of warriors. The cult of **Mithraism** (mith′rà izm) was popular among Roman soldiers.

mit·i·gate (mit′ə gāt′) *v* **mit·i·gat·ed, mit·i·gat·ing** make or become less severe, painful, or harsh: *to mitigate a person's anger by apologizing. Medicine will mitigate the pain. Aid from friendly countries can mitigate the effects of war.* See MILITATE for confusable. <Latin *mitis* gentle>
mit′i·ga′tion *n.*

mi·to·chon·dri·on (mī′tō kon′drē ən) *n,*
pl **mi·to·chon·dri·a** (-drē ə) an organelle that provides the cell with energy through chemical reaction.

mi·to·sis (mi tō′sis) *or* (mī tō′sis) *n* the biological process by which a plant or animal cell divides to produce two daughter cells that are identical to the parent. Compare MEIOSIS. <Greek *mitos* thread. During the first stage of

mitosis, the chromatin in the cell nucleus resembles long threads.>

mi·tre (mī′tər) *n* **1** a tall, pointed cap worn by Christian bishops and abbots during certain ceremonies as a symbol of office. **2** a joint or corner where two pieces of wood or other material are fitted together at right angles, with the ends cut slanting, as at the corners of a picture frame.
v join in a mitre joint. Also, **miter**. <Greek *mitra* headband>

mitre box *n* a box designed to guide a saw in making a diagonal cut in order to make a mitre joint.

mi·tred (mī′tərd) *adj* **1** with a mitre joint. **2** wearing or entitled to wear a bishop's mitre.

mitt (mit) *n* **1** a mitten. **2** *Baseball* a padded, oversized mitten used for catching the ball: *a catcher's mitt.* **3** a knitted or lace hand covering that resembles a glove but does not cover the fingers. **4** a covering or pad worn over the hand, designed for a particular use: *a bath mitt, oven mitts.* <*mitten*>

mit·ten (mit′ən) *n* a winter glove covering the four fingers together and the thumb separately.

mix (miks) *v* **mixed, mix·ing 1** put or stir well together: *to mix ingredients to make cookies.* **2** prepare by putting together or blending different things: *to mix a salad.* **3** join or combine: *to mix business and pleasure. Milk and water mix.* **4** get along together or make friends easily: *She found it difficult to mix with strangers.*
n **1** an already mixed preparation: *a cake mix.* **2** a mixture of different people, elements, or ingredients. <back formation from *mixed*>
be (or **get**) **mixed up, a** (*with* ***in***) be (or get) involved in something, especially something bad or risky: *He was mixed up in a plot to overthrow the government.* **b** (*with* ***with***) be (or get) involved with someone dishonest or immoral: *Don't get mixed up with him, because he'll tell you lies.*
mix and match, choose from a selection of items that are co-ordinated and interchangeable.
mixed up, confused.
mix it up, argue or fight, or cause others to do so.
mix up, confuse: *Don't mix me up while I'm counting.*

mixed (mikst) *adj* **1** put together or formed by mixing: *mixed candies, mixed emotions.* **2** of different classes or kinds: *a mixed company.* **3** of or for people of both sexes: *She sings in the mixed chorus.*

mixed bag *Informal n* a collection of very different people or things: *The people at the party were really a mixed bag.*

mixed blessing *n* an advantage that also has some negative aspects.

mixed doubles *n* a match in tennis or badminton, each side consisting of a man and a woman.

mixed drink *n* a drink of alcohol mixed with fruit juice, club soda, pop, etc.

mixed economy *n* an economy in which both government-owned businesses and privately owned businesses can operate.

mixed farming *n* raising crops and livestock on the same farm.

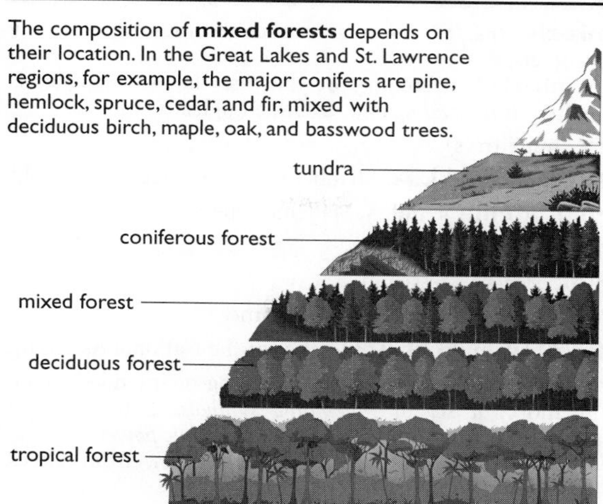

The composition of **mixed forests** depends on their location. In the Great Lakes and St. Lawrence regions, for example, the major conifers are pine, hemlock, spruce, cedar, and fir, mixed with deciduous birch, maple, oak, and basswood trees.

mixed forest *n* a forest composed of several tree species.

mixed marriage *n* a marriage between people of different ethnic groups or religions.

mixed media *n* **1** the integrated use of different artistic media, such as oil paint and collage, in a single piece of artwork. **2** the combined use of mass media, such as TV, radio, print, and the Internet, in advertising or publicity.
mixed′-me′di·a *adj.*

mixed metaphor *n* a metaphor in which two or more different images or ideas get confused. Example: *The horse sailed around the track at full throttle.*

mixed number *Mathematics n* a number consisting of a whole number and a fraction, such as 2 1/2.

mixed–up (mikst′up′) *adj* confused, often emotionally or psychologically: *a mixed-up youth.*

mix·er (mik′sər) *n* **1** an apparatus or appliance for mixing foods or other substances. **2** a device that merges input signals in sound recording and making films to produce a combined output in the form of sound or pictures. **3** a person who gets along well with others, making friends easily: *She is a good mixer.* **4** a soft drink that can be mixed with alcohol.

mix·ture (miks′chər) *n* **1** something made by mixing: *The mixture is put into a greased dish and baked. Green is a mixture of blue and yellow.* **2** a chemical substance consisting of a combination of two or more ingredients that keep their individual chemical properties and can be separated by non-chemical means: *A sugar-and-water mixture can be separated by boiling off the water.* Compare COMPOUND[1] (*n* def. 2). **3** a person regarded as having contrasting qualities: *She was a mixture of good and evil.*

mix–up (miks′up′) *n* confusion or mess: *A misprint in the notice caused a mix-up over the date of the meeting.*

M

a **bat**	e **bed**	i **bid**	o **pot**	u **cup**	th **thin**
ā **cake**	ē **me**	ī **bite**	ō **go**	ū **rude**	ᴛʜ **then**
ä **bar**	ə **about**	ər **over**	ô **for**	ů **put**	zh **measure**

miz·zle (miz′əl) *Informal n* a continuous rain of tiny droplets.
v **miz·zled, miz·zling** be the case that such a rain is falling: *It is mizzling out.* <Middle English>

mL millilitre(s).

✱ **MLA** or **M.L.A.** Member of the Legislative Assembly.

Mlle. or **Mlle** *pl* **Mlles.** Mademoiselle.

mm millimetre(s).

MM. or **MM** Messieurs.

Mme. or **Mme** *pl* **Mmes.** Madame.

✱ **MNA** or **M.N.A.** Member of the National Assembly.

mne·mon·ic (ni mon′ik) *adj* **1** aiding or intended to aid memory: *a set of mnemonic symbols.* **2** to do with memory: *He was a man of great mnemonic power.*
n a device to aid the memory. <Latin, from Greek *mnemon* remember>

moan (mōn) *n* **1** a long, low sound of suffering. **2** a similar sound, especially one made by the wind.
v **1** make moans or utter with a moan: *They heard the sick woman moan. "I can't hang on any longer," he moaned.* **2** complain without much cause: *He was always moaning about his luck.* <Middle English> **moan′ing** *adj.* **moan′ing·ly** *adv.*

moat (mōt) *n* a deep, wide ditch, usually filled with water and dug around part or all of a castle or town as a protection against enemies. See MEDIEVAL for picture.
v surround with a moat. <Old French *mote* mound>

mob (mob) *n* **1** a crowd of people, especially one that can become destructive or violent: *There was a great mob at the gate, waiting to get in. The crowd had turned into an ugly mob.* **2 a the mob** MASS[1] (def. 7). **b the Mob** the Mafia or a similar organization.
v **mobbed, mob·bing 1** attack with violence, as a mob might. **2** crowd around too closely in excessive eagerness or curiosity: *Autograph hunters mobbed the singer outside her hotel.* <Latin *mobile vulgus* fickle crowd>

mo·bile[1] (mō′bīl) *or* (mō′bəl) *adj* **1** capable of moving or being moved easily: *The emergency force was highly mobile.* **2** quick to change from one position or expression to another: *Actors often have mobile features.* <French, from Latin *movere* to move>

mo·bile[2] (mō′bīl) *or* (mō′bēl) *n* a decorative or artistic construction of small shapes suspended from a balanced arrangement of horizontal bars so that the shapes will move in a current of air.

–mobile *combining form* a vehicle suitable for a particular person, terrain, or environment: *snowmobile.* <Latin *mobilis* movable>

✱ **Mobile Command** (mō′bīl) *or* (mō′bəl) *n* the combat-ready land forces of the Canadian Forces.

mobile home (mō′bīl) *or* (mō′bəl) *n* a large trailer that is used as a permanent dwelling.

mobile phone (mō′bīl) *or* (mō′bəl) *n* a cellphone.

mo·bi·lize (mō′bə līz′) *v* **mo·bi·lized, mo·bi·liz·ing 1** prepare and organize military forces for active service, especially for war: *The troops mobilized quickly.* **2** put into motion or active use: *to mobilize the wealth of a country.* **mo′bi·liz′a·ble** *adj.*

Mö·bi·us strip (mō′bē əs) *Mathematics n* a one-sided, continuous surface, made by twisting one end of a long, narrow, rectangular strip through 180° and joining it to the other end. Also, **Moebius strip**. <A.F. *Möbius,* 19c mathematician>

mob·ster (mob′stər) *Informal n* a member of an organized criminal group.

moc·ca·sin (mok′ə sən) *n* a soft, heel-less leather shoe or boot with the bottom and sides made of a single piece of leather. <Algonquian>

moccasin flower *n* a LADY'S-SLIPPER, especially a species with pink or white flowers.

mo·cha (mō′kə) *n* **1** a variety of coffee originally grown in the Arabian Peninsula. **2** a flavouring made from strong coffee or a mixture of coffee and cocoa or chocolate.
adj dark brown. <*Mocha,* a port in Yemen, where this coffee was originally grown.>

mock (mok) *v* **1** laugh at or make fun of scornfully, especially by imitating: *The thoughtless kids mocked the boy's unfashionable clothes.* **2** not take seriously.
adj not authentic or actual, but with no intention to deceive: *a mock trial.* <Old French *mocquer*> **mock′er** *n.*
make mock of, ridicule.

mock·er·y (mok′ə rē) *n, pl* **mock·er·ies 1** derision or ridicule: *Their mockery of her hat hurt her feelings.* **2** a person or thing to be made fun of: *Through his foolishness he became a mockery in the village.* **3** an absurd misrepresentation or imitation: *The unfair trial was a mockery of justice.*
make a mockery of something, make something seem foolish or ridiculous.

mock–he·ro·ic (mok′hi rō′ik) *adj* imitating what is heroic for the purposes of satire.
n a satirical imitation of what is heroic.

mock·ing (mok′ing) *adj* ridiculing or making fun of: *mocking laughter.* **mock′ing·ly** *adv.*

mock·ing·bird (mok′ing bərd′) *n* a long-tailed N American songbird with greyish feathers, famous for being able to imitate the songs and calls of other birds.

mock orange (mok′ô′rinj) *n* a bushy shrub with white flowers whose scent resembles that of orange blossoms.

mock–up (mok′up′) *n* a full-sized model of a machine or structure, built accurately to scale and used for display or for teaching or experimental purposes.

mo·dal (mō′dəl) *adj* **1** to do with a verb that expresses a fact, command, question, possibility, or wish. Examples: *can, may, will, should, ought.* **2** to do with melodies or harmonies based on modes other than major and minor scales. **3** *Statistics* with the value that occurs most frequently in a given set of data.
n a modal verb.

mo·dal·i·ty (mō dal′i tē) *n, pl* **mo·dal·i·ties 1** a particular way in which something exists or is experienced, especially as a particular method or procedure. **2** a modal musical quality.

mode (mōd) *n* **1** the manner in which a thing occurs, is experienced, or is done: *Riding on a donkey is a slow mode of travel.* **2** the style, fashion, or custom that prevails: *Bobbed hair was the mode about 1920.* **3** a set of musical notes forming a scale and from which melodies and harmonies are made. **4** *Statistics* the value that occurs most frequently in a given set of data. <Latin *modus* manner>

mod·el (mod′əl) *n* **1** a small copy of an item, or of an item designed but not yet made: *a model of an old sailing ship, a model of what the new stadium will look like.* **2** a particular style or design of a thing: *Some car manufacturers produce a new model every year.* **3** a thing or person to be imitated: *The teacher used my essay as a model for the class.* **4** a person who poses for artists or photographers. **5** a person employed to help sell clothing by wearing it for customers to see.

v **mod·elled** or **mod·eled, mod·el·ling** or **mod·el·ing** **1** fashion or shape something, especially out of clay or wax: *to model a bird's nest in clay.* **2** show the effects of light and shade on objects or figures to make them appear three-dimensional in a drawing or painting. **3** follow as a model: *He modelled himself on his mother.* **4** be a model for clothing. **5** pose as a model for artists or photographers.

adj proper or perfect, especially in conduct: *a model child.* <French, from Latin *modulus* standard>

on the model of, in imitation of.

mo·dem (mō′dem′) *Computers n* a device that enables a computer to receive and send data over telephone lines. <*mo(dulator)* + *dem(odulator)*>

mod·er·ate (mod′ə rit) *for adj or n,* (mod′ə rāt′) *for v.* *adj* **1** kept or keeping within proper bounds: *moderate expenses.* **2** average in amount, intensity, quality, or degree: *a moderate profit, a moderate pace.*

n a person who holds moderate opinions, especially in politics.

v **mod·er·at·ed, mod·er·at·ing** **1** make or become less extreme or violent: *The wind is moderating.* **2** preside over a discussion or debate: *Our hockey coach will moderate a panel discussion on the plans for a sports program.* <Latin *moderare* regulate> **mod′er·ate·ly** *adv.*

mod·er·a·tion (mod′ə rā′shən) *n* **1** avoidance of excesses or extremes: *He still has to learn the value of moderation.* **2** a moderating or moving away from an extreme: *We all welcomed the moderation of the uncomfortably hot weather.*
in moderation, within limits: *She eats sweets in moderation.*

mod·e·ra·to (mod′ə ro′tō) *Music adj, adv* in a moderate tempo. <Italian>

mod·er·a·tor (mod′ə rā′tər) *n* **1** a presiding officer or chairperson: *the moderator of a town meeting.* **2** an arbitrator or mediator. **3** *Computers* a person who volunteers to screen messages sent to a NEWSGROUP, FORUM, or MAILING LIST. **4** the chief elected officer in some churches. **5** a material used in a REACTOR to slow down nuclear FISSION.

mod·ern (mod′ərn) *adj* **1** of the present time or times not long past: *Television is a modern invention.* **2** using or involving recent techniques, ideas, or technology: *They bought the most modern style of kitchen range available.*

n a person of the present time or of times not long past: *She is studying English dramatists, specializing in the moderns.* <Latin *modo* just now> **mod′ern·ness** *n.*

Modern English *n* the English language from about 1450 to the present.

mod·ern·ism (mod′ər niz′əm) *n* **1** modern attitudes, ideas, methods, or styles. **2** sympathy with what is modern. **mod′ern·ist** *n.* **mod′ern·is′tic** *adj.*

mo·der·ni·ty (mə dər′nə tē) *n* the period of time in which modern attitudes, ideas, etc. occur or are expressed.

mod·ern·ize (mod′ər nīz′) *v* **mod·ern·ized, mod·ern·iz·ing** make modern. **mod′ern·i·za′tion** (mod′ər nə zā′shən) *or* (mod′ər nī zā′shən) *n.*

mod·est (mod′ist) *adj* **1** not thinking too highly of oneself: *In spite of the honours he received, the scientist remained a modest man.* **2** not sexually revealing or suggestive, such as in the kind of clothes worn. **3** with or showing a sense of what is fit and proper: *People liked the modest behaviour of the children.* **4** not asking too much: *a modest request.* **5** humble and unassuming in appearance: *a modest little house.* <Latin *modestus*> **mod′est·ly** *adv.* **mod′es·ty** *n.*

mod·i·cum (mod′ə kəm) *n* a small or moderate quantity of something: *He is so bright that even with a modicum of effort he does excellent work.* <Latin = moderate>

mod·i·fi·er (mod′ə fi′ər) *n* a word or group of words that limits the meaning of another word or group of words. Example: The adjective *tight* in *a very tight coat* is a modifier of *coat,* and the adverb *very* is a modifier of *tight.*

M

GRAMMAR AND USAGE

A misplaced **modifier** appears to modify the wrong word or words because it is too far from what it modifies: *An apple lay on the table that she had partially eaten* is more clearly written as *The apple that she had partially eaten lay on the table.*

mod·i·fy (mod′ə fī′) *v* **mod·i·fied, mod·i·fy·ing** **1** change somewhat, typically to make minor changes for the sake of improvement or to make it less extreme: *to modify the terms of a lease, to modify your demands.* **2** limit or qualify the meaning of a word, especially a noun. **3** make structural changes in a part of an organism, usually resulting in a different function or orientation of the part: *A narwhal's tusk is a modified tooth.* <Latin *modificare* to limit, from *modus* measure> **mod′i·fi′a·ble** *adj.* **mod′i·fi′a·bly** *adv.* **mod′i·fi·ca′tion** *n.*

mod·ish (mō′dish) *adj* fashionable or stylish: *a modish hat.* **mod′ish·ly** *adv.* **mod′ish·ness** *n.*

mod·u·lar (moj′ə lər) *adj* **1** to do with a module. **2** designed or constructed in standardized sizes or units that can be interchanged and fitted together in a variety of ways: *modular storage units, modular furniture.*

a bat	e bed	i bid	o pot	u cup	th thin
ā cake	ē me	ī bite	ō go	ū rude	ᴛʜ then
à bar	ə about	ər over	ȯ for	ů put	zh measure

mod·u·late (moj′ə lāt′) *v* **mod·u·lat·ed, mod·u·lat·ing** 1 regulate or adjust. 2 alter the voice for expression: *Her speech is always beautifully modulated.* 3 change from one musical key to another. 4 vary the frequency of electrical waves. 5 change a radio current by adding sound waves to it. <Latin *modus* measure>

mod·u·la·tor (moj′ə lā′tər) *n* a person who or thing that modulates, especially a device for varying the range of frequency of a signal or wave in broadcasting.

mod·ule (moj′ūl) *n* 1 a standardized piece or component of a larger structure. 2 a distinct but interrelated unit that forms part of a larger, complex structure: *The command module of a spacecraft can function independently.* <Latin *modulus* small measure>

mo·dus o·pe·ran·di (mō′dəs op′ə ran′dī) *or* (op′ə ran′dē) *n* a method or manner of working. <Latin = way of operating>

mo·gul[1] (mō′gul) *n* 1 an important or powerful person. 2 **Mogul** a member of a Muslim dynasty that ruled much of India from the 1500s to the 1800s. <Arabic, from Persian *Mugul* Mongol>

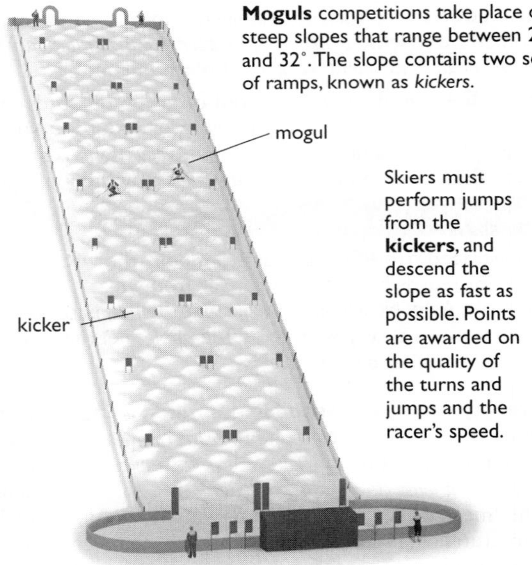

Moguls competitions take place on steep slopes that range between 28° and 32°. The slope contains two sets of ramps, known as *kickers*.

Skiers must perform jumps from the **kickers**, and descend the slope as fast as possible. Points are awarded on the quality of the turns and jumps and the racer's speed.

mo·gul[2] (mō′gul) *n* a mound or bump of hard snow on a ski run. <probably Scandinavian>

mo·hair (mō′her) *n* cloth or yarn made from the long, silky hair of the Angora goat, or the hair of this goat. <Arabic *mukayyarr*>

Mo·ham·med (mō ham′id) MUHAMMAD.

Mo·hawk (mō′hok) *n* 1 KANIEN'KEHA. 2 a haircut in which the head is partly shaved, leaving a strip of hair standing upright over the head from the forehead to the neck. It is supposed to be the style formerly worn by men of the Mohawk peoples.

Mo·hi·can (mə hē′kən) MAHICAN.

Mohs scale (mōz) *Geology n* a scale that categorizes minerals by their hardness. Diamond is the hardest (10) and talc is the softest (1). <after F. *Mohs*, 18c mineralogist who invented it>

moi·ré or **moire** (mwä rā′), (mwär), *or* (mò rā′) *n* an irregular wavy finish.
adj with such a finish: *moiré effect.* <French *moire* mohair>

moist (moist) *adj* 1 slightly wet, damp, or humid: *a moist towel, a moist climate.* 2 filled with tears: *His eyes were moist, but he did not cry.* <Old French, from Latin *mucus* mucus> **moist′en** *v.* **moist′ly** *adv.* **moist′ness** *n.*

mois·ture (mois′chər) *n* water or other liquid spread in very small drops in the air or on a surface.

mois·tur·ize (mois′chər īz′) *v* **mois·tur·ized, mois·tur·iz·ing** restore natural moisture to something, especially the skin or hair. **mois′tur·iz′er** *n.*

mo·jo (mō′jō) *Slang n* a magic charm.

mok·sha (mōk′shə) *Hinduism, Jainism n* spiritual release and freedom from the ongoing cycle of death and rebirth. <Sanskrit>

mo·lar (mō′lər) *n* a tooth with a broad surface for grinding: *A person's back teeth are molars.*
adj to do with the molar teeth. <Latin *molaris dens* grinding tooth, from *mola* millstone>

mo·las·ses (mə las′iz) *n* a sweet syrup obtained in making sugar from sugar cane. <Portuguese, from Latin *mel* honey>

mold (mōld) MOULD.

mold·er (mōl′dər) MOULDER.

mold·ing (mōl′ding) MOULDING.

Mol·do·va (mol dō′və) *n* a country in eastern Europe. **Mol·do′van** *adj, n.*

mold·y (mōl′dē) MOULDY.

mole[1] (mōl) *n* a small, permanent spot on the skin, usually brown and slightly raised. <Old English *mal*>

mole[2] (mōl) *n* 1 a small burrowing mammal that has soft fur, front feet modified for digging, and weak eyes. 2 a spy within an organization. <Dutch and German *mol*> **mole′like′** *adj.*

mole[3] (mōl) *n* a barrier built of stone to break the force of the waves, or a harbour formed by such a barrier. <French, from Latin *moles* mass>

mol·e·cule (mol′ə kyūl′) *n* 1 the smallest particle into which a substance can be divided without chemical change. A molecule of an element consists of one or more atoms. 2 a very small bit or particle. <French, from Latin *moles* mass> **mo·lec′u·lar** (mə lek′yə lər) *adj.*

mole·hill (mōl′hil′) *n* a small mound or ridge of earth raised up by moles burrowing under the ground.

mo·lest (mə lest′) *v* 1 annoy, meddle with, or persecute, especially so as to injure: *It is cruel to molest animals.* 2 sexually assault or abuse someone, especially a woman or child. <Old French, from Latin *molestus* troublesome> **mo′les·ta′tion** *n.* **mo·lest′er** *n.*

moll (mol) *Informal n* a female companion of a criminal. <*Molly*, a form of *Mary*>

mol·li·fy (mol′ə fī′) *v* **mol·li·fied, mol·li·fy·ing** 1 soothe or appease: *The angry child refused all our attempts to mollify him.* 2 soften or mitigate: *Her anger was finally mollified.* <French, from Latin *mollis* soft + *facere* make> **mol′li·fi·ca′tion** *n.*

mol·lusc or **mol·lusk** (mol′əsk) *n* any of a large group of invertebrate animals with soft, unsegmented bodies covered with a hard shell. Abalones, clams, cockles, limpets, mussels, octopuses, oysters, scallops, snails, and whelks are molluscs. <Latin *mollis* soft>

mol·ly·cod·dle (mol′ē kod′əl) *n* a person, especially a boy or man, accustomed to being fussed over and pampered. *v* **mol·ly·cod·dled, mol·ly·cod·dling** coddle or pamper. <*molly* effeminate man or boy+ *coddle*>

Mol·o·tov cocktail (mol′ə tof′) *n* a crude hand grenade consisting of a gasoline-filled bottle with a short fuse or wick that is ignited just before being thrown. <V.M. *Molotov*, 20c revolutionary who became an official in the Soviet Union>

molt (mōlt) MOULT.

mol·ten (mōl′tən) *adj* made liquid in a material with a high melting point, such as metal or glass: *molten steel, molten lava.*
v a past participle of MELT.

mo·lyb·de·num (mə lib′də nəm) *n* a brittle, silver-white metallic element of the chromium group. *Symbol* **Mo** <Latin, from Greek *molybdos* lead>

mom (mom) *or* (mum) *Informal n* a mother.

mom–and–pop (mom′ən pop′) *Informal adj* to do with a small business owned and operated by a family: *a mom-and-pop grocery store.*

mo·ment (mō′mənt) *n* 1 a very short period of time: *In a moment, all was changed.* 2 a particular point of time: *We both arrived at the same moment.* 3 importance or significance: *a matter of moment.* 4 the tendency to cause rotation around a point or axis. <Latin *movere* to move> **moment of truth,** the moment when a critical decision or action must be taken.

> **GRAMMAR AND USAGE**
>
> **Moment** suggests a short space of time: *Wait a moment so I can catch up.*
>
> **Jiffy** is an informal word meaning "a very short time": *I'll be there in a jiffy.*
>
> **Second** is an actual measurement of time: *There are 60 seconds in a minute.* However, **second** is also used informally: *It took just a second to change the light bulb.*

mo·men·tar·i·ly (mō′mən ter′ə lē) *or* (mō′mən ter′ə lē) *adv* 1 for a moment: *to hesitate momentarily.* 2 at any moment: *We expect her to arrive momentarily.*

mo·men·tar·y (mō′mən ter′ē) *adj* lasting only a moment: *momentary hesitation.*

mo·men·tous (mō men′təs) *adj* very important: *a momentous decision. His graduation was a momentous occasion.* **mo·men′tous·ly** *adv.* **mo·men′tous·ness** *n.*

mo·men·tum (mō men′təm) *n, pl* **mo·men·tums** or **mo·men·ta** (-tə) 1 the force with which a body moves, the product of its mass and its velocity. 2 the impetus resulting from movement: *The runner's momentum carried her far beyond the finish line.* 3 the impetus acquired by the development of a process or sequence of events: *The investigation gathered momentum after the vital clue was discovered.* <Latin *movere* to move>

mom·my (mo′mē) *Informal n* a child's word for mother. <*mom*>

mommy track *Informal n* a work schedule for female employees with young children that offers flexible hours but may provide little opportunity for advancement.

Mo·na·co (mon′ə kō′) *n* a small country on the Mediterranean coast, between France and Italy. **Mo·ne·gasque′** (mo nā gask′) *adj, n.*

mon·arch (mon′ərk) *n* 1 a king, queen, emperor, or empress. 2 a person or thing like a monarch: *The lion has been called the monarch of the beasts.* 3 a large orange-and-black butterfly. See BUTTERFLY for picture. <Latin, from Greek *monos* alone + *archein* rule>

mo·nar·chic (mə nȧr′kik) *adj* to do with a monarch. Also, **monarchical, monarchal. mo·nar′chic·al·ly** *adv.*

mon·ar·chism (mon′ər kiz′əm) *n* support for the principles of monarchy. **mon′ar·chist** *adj, n.*

mon·ar·chy (mon′ər kē) *n, pl* **mon·ar·chies** 1 government by or under a monarch. 2 a nation or other political unit governed or headed by a monarch.

mon·as·ter·y (mon′ə ster′ē) *n, pl* **mon·as·ter·ies** a building or buildings where monks or nuns live and work in a religious community. <Latin, from Greek *monos* alone>

mo·nas·tic (mə nas′tik) *adj* 1 of monks or nuns, or the community in which they live: *monastic vows.* 2 like that of monks or nuns or their way of life in being simple, solitary, and celibate: *He lives an almost monastic life.*
n a monk or other follower of a religious rule.

mo·nas·ti·cism (mə nas′tə siz′əm) *n* the system or condition of living according to fixed rules and under religious vows, usually in a monastery or convent.

mon·au·ral (mo nȯ′rəl) *adj* 1 monophonic. 2 having or involving one ear only.

Mon·day (mun′dā′) *n* the day of the week after Sunday and before Tuesday. *Abbrev.* **Mon** <Old English *monandæg* moon's day>

Mo·né·gasque See MONACO.

mon·er·a (mo ni′rə) *pln* one of the KINGDOMS (def. 3) into which organisms can be classified, in a five-kingdom system. Monera are divided into two kingdoms, ARCHAEA and BACTERIA, in a six-kingdom system. See also PROKARYOTE.

mon·e·tar·y (mon′ə ter′ē) *adj* 1 to do with the currency of a country: *The monetary unit in Canada is the dollar.* 2 to do with money: *a monetary reward.*

a bat	e bed	i bid	o pot	u cup	th **thin**
ā cake	ē me	ī bite	ō go	ū rude	TH **then**
ȧ bar	ə about	ər over	ȯ for	u̇ put	zh measure

M

mon·ey (mun′ē) *n* **1** officially issued coins and paper notes used as a standard medium of exchange: *I have five dollars left in Canadian money.* **2** a particular form or denomination of money. **3** wealth or financial gain: *She has a lot of money.* **4 moneys** or **monies** *pl* sums of money: *The treasurer was responsible for the moneys entrusted to her.* <Old French, from Latin *Moneto*, title of the goddess Juno. Roman money was made in her temple.> **mon′ey·less** *adj.*
for my money, *Informal* in my opinion.
in the money, doing well financially.
make money, a earn or receive money. **b** become rich.
money in the bank, a gain or asset that you can be sure of.
on the money, correct; exact: *Weather forecasts from Environment Canada weather forecast are on the money almost every time.*

GRAMMAR AND USAGE

Exact sums of **money** that are not round figures are usually written in numerals: *66 cents, $3.99, $184.* Approximate amounts are more likely to be written in words: *about two hundred dollars.*

mon·ey·bags (mun′ē bagz′) *Slang n* a rich person.

mon·ey·chang·er (mun′ē chān′jər) *n* a person whose business is to exchange money, usually that of one country for that of another.

mon·eyed (mun′ēd) *adj* wealthy: *a moneyed family, moneyed interests.*

mon·ey·grub·ber (mun′ē grub′ər) *Informal n* a person whose main or only concern is making or saving money. **mon′ey·grub′bing** *adj, n.*

mon·ey·lend·er (mun′ē len′dər) *n* a person whose business is lending money at interest. **mon′ey·lend′ing** *adj, n.*

mon·ey·mak·er (mun′ē māk′ər) *n* **1** a person who is clever at making money. **2** a very profitable product, investment, or idea. **mon′ey·mak′ing** *adj, n.*

money order *n* an order issued by a post office or bank for the payment of a particular amount of money by a post office or bank in another place.

–monger *combining form* **1** a person who sells: *fishmonger.* **2** a person who promotes something bad: *warmonger, scandalmonger.* <Old English>

Mon·go·lia (mong gō′lē ə) *n* a country in east Asia. **Mon·go′li·an** *adj, n.*

mon·goose (mong′gūs) *n, pl* **mon·goos·es** a small meat-eating mammal of Africa and Asia, especially a slender, ferretlike animal of India that is able to kill poisonous snakes without being harmed. <Marathi (a language of India) *mangus*>

mon·grel (mung′grəl) *or* (mong′grəl) *n* an animal or plant of mixed breed, especially a dog.
adj of mixed breed or origin: *He habitually used a mongrel speech that was half English and half French.* <Old English *gemong* mixture>

mon·ies (mun′ēz) a plural of MONEY.

mon·i·tor (mon′ə tər) *n* **1** a person who or thing that is used to observe, check, or keep a continuous record of a process or quantity: *a heart monitor.* **2** a student in school with special duties, such as helping to keep order and taking attendance. **3** a device used for checking and listening to broadcast or telephone transmissions or recordings. **4** *Computers* a device that provides a video display of a computer's output. **5** a large tropical lizard of Africa, Australia, and southern Asia.
v observe and systematically review the progress or quality of something over a period of time: *All the new equipment was carefully monitored for a week. They monitored the patient's condition for several days.* <Latin = one who warns, from *monere* warn>

monk (mungk) *n* a man who has taken certain vows to live his life in a way prescribed by a religious community. <Greek *monos* alone> **monk′ish** *adj.* **monk′like′** *adj.*

The golden lion tamarin is a **New World monkey** native to Brazil. Like the other tamarins and marmosets, it is small (.5 kg and 25 cm long without tail). New World monkeys have flattened noses and many have long, prehensile tails. They are superb climbers and live in the forest canopy.

The rhesus monkey is one of the **Old World monkeys** (monkeys that live in Africa and Asia). Baboons, mandrills, and other macaques are also in this group. Although rhesus monkeys are comfortable climbers, they spend much of their time on the ground.

mon·key (mung′kē) *n, pl* **mon·keys** **1** a usually long-tailed member of the primate order. New World monkeys grasp things with their tails, Old World monkeys cannot. **2** a member of the primate order of animals. **3** a person, especially a child, who is full of mischief.
v **mon·keyed, mon·key·ing** *Informal* behave in a silly or playful way: *Don't monkey with the TV.* <origin uncertain> **mon′key·like′** *adj.*

monkey bars *n* **1** an open structure of vertical and horizontal pipes or bars, designed for children to climb and play on, especially on playgrounds. **2** a structure of horizontal bars built against a wall, as in a gymnasium, used for climbing exercises.

monkey business *Informal n* **1** silly or mischievous acts: *Those kids are always full of monkey business.* **2** deceitful or treacherous acts: *There must have been some monkey business, because some of my CDs are missing.*

monkey jacket *n* a short, close-fitting jacket, sometimes worn as part of a uniform.

mon·key·shines (mung′kē shīnz′) *Informal pln* mischievous pranks: *Those kids have been up to their monkeyshines again.*

monkey wrench *n* a wrench with large jaws that can be adjusted by turning a screw contained in its handle.
throw a monkey wrench into, *Informal* hinder or disrupt something.

mono[1] (mon′ō) *Informal n* mononucleosis.

mono[2] (mon′ō) *Informal adj* monophonic.

mono– *combining form* one or single: *monochrome, monotone.* <Greek *monos* single>

mon·o·chrome (mon′ə krōm′) *n* a painting, drawing, engraving, or photograph in a single colour or in shades of a single colour. <*mono-* + Greek *chroma* colour> **mon′o·chro·mat′ic** *adj.*

mon·o·cle (mon′ə kəl) *n* an eyeglass for one eye. <French, from Greek *monos* single + Latin *oculus* eye> **mon′o·cled** *adj.*

mo·no·coque (mon′ə kok) *n* an aircraft or vehicle structure in which the body and chassis are formed from one piece. <French *mono-* single + *coque* shell>

mon·o·cot·y·le·don (mon′ə kot′ə lē′dən) *n* a seed plant with an embryo with only one COTYLEDON, such as a grass.

mo·nog·a·my (mə nog′ə mē) *n* **1** the practice or condition of being married to, or having a sexual relationship with, one person at a time. **2** *Zoology* the habit of having only one mate at a time. <French, from Greek *monos* single + *gamos* marriage> **mo·nog′a·mist** *n.* **mo·nog′a·mous** *adj.*

mon·o·gram (mon′ə gram′) *n* a design made by combining letters, usually the initials of a person's name.

mon·o·graph (mon′ə graf′) *n* a scholarly book or article on a single specialized subject or aspect of it.

mon·o·lin·gual (mon′ə ling′gwal) *or* (mon′ə ling′gyə wəl) *adj* knowing or using only one language: *a monolingual person, a monolingual conversation.*

mon·o·lith (mon′ə lith′) *n* **1** a large block of stone. **2** a monument, column, or statue formed from a single large block of stone. **3** a structure, system, or organization that is massive, impersonal, rigid, and unyielding in its attitudes and policies. <French, from Greek *monos* single + *lithos* stone> **mon′o·lith′ic** *adj.*

mon·o·logue (mon′ə log′) *n* **1** a part in a film, play, or broadcast in which one person speaks alone. **2** a long, often tedious speech by one person in the course of a conversation. **3** a spoken entertainment by one performer. Also, **monolog**. <French, from Greek *monos* single + *logos* discourse> **mon′·o·logu′·ist** *n.*

mon·o·ma·ni·a (mon′ə mā′nē ə) *n* an exaggerated or obsessive interest in or preoccupation with something, so as to almost seem insane. **mon′o·ma′ni·ac** *n.*

mo·no·mi·al (mo nō′mē əl) *adj* consisting of a single term in an algebraic expression.
n an algebraic expression of this type. Examples: x; $3x$; abc; a^3b^4

mon·o·nu·cle·o·sis (mo′nə nyū′kli ō′sis) *n* an infectious disease caused by a virus and characterized by an abnormal increase in white blood cells, often with a fever and sore throat.

mon·o·phon·ic (mo′nȯ fon′ik) with only one channel for transmission of sound in sound reproduction: *a monophonic recording.* Compare STEREOPHONIC. **mon′o·phon′ic·al·ly** *adv.*

mo·nop·o·lize (mə nop′ə līz′) *v* **mo·nop·o·lized, mo·nop·o·liz·ing** **1** have or get exclusive possession or control of: *The swim team monopolizes the pool during lunch hour.* **2** occupy wholly: *The stranger tried to monopolize our conversation.* **mo·nop′o·liz′er** *n.*

mo·nop·o·ly (mə nop′ə lē) *n, pl* **mo·nop·o·lies** **1** control of a commodity or service for a particular market, with little or no competition: *The new dairy bought out the other two dairies in town and now has a monopoly on milk.* **2** such control granted by a government. **3** a commodity or service that one company or group has a monopoly on. **4** a company with a monopoly. **5** the exclusive possession or control of something: *No one person has a monopoly on virtue.* <Latin, from Greek *monos* single + *polein* sell>

mon·o·rail (mon′ə rāl′) *n* **1** a single rail serving as a complete track for a wheeled vehicle. **2** a railway in which cars run on a single rail.

M

mo·no·so·di·um glu·ta·mate (mon′ə sō′di əm glū′tə māt′) MSG.

mon·o·syl·lab·ic (mon′ə sə lab′ik) *adj* **1** with only one syllable. **2** consisting of a word or words of one syllable each: *"No, not now" was his monosyllabic reply.*

mon·o·syl·la·ble (mon′ə sil′ə bəl) *n* a word of one syllable, such as "yes" or "no."

mon·o·the·ism (mon′ə thē′iz əm) *n* the doctrine or belief that there is only one God. **mon′o·the·ist** *n.* **mon′o·the·ist′ic** *adj.*

mon·o·tone (mon′ə tōn′) *n* an unchanging and ongoing sameness of tone and pitch, especially in a person's voice: *He reads in a monotone, which makes every story boring.*
adj unchanging in pitch and tone: *a monotone reading.*

mo·not·o·nous (mə not′ə nəs) *adj* **1** continuing in the same tone of voice: *She spoke in a monotonous voice.* **2** tedious or wearing because of lack of variety: *monotonous food, monotonous work.*
mo·not′o·nous·ly *adv.* **mo·not′o·ny** *n.*

mon·ox·ide (mon ok′sīd) *n* an oxide containing one oxygen atom in each molecule.

mo·no·zy·got·ic (mon′ō zī got′ik) *Biology adj* arising from a single fertilized egg: *Monozygotic twins are identical.*

a bat	e bed	i bid	o pot	u cup	th **thin**
ā cake	ē me	ī bite	ō go	ū rude	ᴛʜ **then**
à bar	ə about	ər over	ȯ for	ù put	zh measure

Mon·sei·gneur or **mon·sei·gneur** (mòn′sen yůr′) *n, pl* **Mes·sei·gneurs** or **mes·sei·gneurs** (mòn′sen yůr′) a title of honour given to princes, bishops, and other people of importance, usually used in front of a title of office. <French *mon* my + *seigneur* lord>

Mon·sieur (mə syů′) *n, pl* **Mes·sieurs** (mā syů′) a title or form of address given to or used of a French-speaking man, corresponding to "Mr." or "sir." <French = my lord>

Mon·sign·or (mon sēn′yər) *Catholicism n, pl* **Mon·si·gnors** or **Mon·si·gno·ri** (mon sēn′yo′rē) a title given to certain senior dignitaries, such an officer of a papal court. <Italian, on pattern of French *Monseigneur*>

mon·soon (mon sūn′) *n* **1** a seasonal wind of the Indian subcontinent and southeast Asia, blowing from the southwest from May to September, bringing heavy rains, or from the northeast during the rest of the year. **2** the rainy season during which this wind blows from the southwest. <Portuguese, from Arabic *mawsim* season>

mon·ster (mon′stər) *n* **1** an imaginary creature of strange or grotesque appearance, especially one who is large and frightening: *The movie was about monsters from Mars.* **2** something that is huge: *a monster of a book.* **3** a person who is extremely immoral or cruel: *The man in charge of the slaves was a monster.*
adj huge in size or extent: *a monster tuna.* <Latin *monstrum*>

monster home *n* a very large house occupying most of a city or rural lot.

mon·stros·i·ty (mon stros′ə tē) *n, pl* **mon·stros·i·ties** something that is very large and unattractive.

mon·strous (mon′strəs) *adj* **1** huge, ugly, and frightening. **2** extremely wrong or immoral. **mon′strous·ly** *adv.* **mon′strous·ness** *n.*

mon·tage (mon tȧzh′) *n* **1** the combination of several distinct pictures to make a composite picture, or the composite picture so made. **2** in motion pictures or TV, the use of a sequence of rapidly changing pictures to suggest an emotional reaction, or quality of mind, etc. <Old French *monter* to mount>

Mon·ta·gnais (mon tən yā′) See INNU.

mon·te (mon′tē) *n* a Latin American gambling game of cards. <Spanish = mountain>

Monte Car·lo method (kar′lō) *Mathematics n* a method of using probability tools like dice and coins in order to solve problems dealing with random events. <*Monte Carlo* a place famous for gambling>

Mon·ter·ey Jack (mon′tə rā′) *n* a mild, light yellow cheese. <*Monterey* County, California, where it was first made>

Mon·tes·so·ri (mon′tə so′rē) *n* an educational system for the primary grades that emphasizes child-directed, individualized, hands-on learning in an unstructured environment. <M. *Montessori,* 20c educator>

Mon·te·zu·ma's revenge (mon′tə zū′ma) *Informal n* diarrhea experienced by tourists as a result of food eaten, especially in Mexico. <*Montezuma* II, 16c Aztec emperor of Mexico. The suggestion is that the malady is revenge for the loss of Montezuma's empire to the Spanish.>

month (munth) *n* **1** one of the twelve parts into which the year is divided. **2 a** four weeks. **b** thirty days. **3** the period of time from any day of one month to the corresponding day of the next month: *It will take us about a month to finish the project.* <Old English *monath*>

GRAMMAR AND USAGE

In informal writing, the names of **months** with more than four letters are abbreviated in dates: *Oct 16, 2007.* When only the month and year are given, abbreviations are not normally used: *October 2007.*

month·ly (mun′thlē) *adj* **1** of, for, or lasting a month: *a monthly supply.* **2** done, happening, or payable once a month: *a monthly salary.*
adv once a month.
n, pl **month·lies** a magazine published once a month.

🍁 **Montréal canoe** *n* in former times, the largest canoe of the fur trade, used especially on the Great Lakes and the St. Lawrence River.

mon·u·ment (mon′yə mənt) *n* **1** something set up to keep a person or an event from being forgotten, such as a building, pillar, arch, statue, tomb, or stone. **2** a thing that keeps alive the memory of a person or an event. **3** an enduring or prominent instance or example: *The professor's writings were monuments of learning.* **4** something set up to mark a boundary. <French, from Latin *monere* remind>

mon·u·men·tal (mon′yə men′təl) *adj* **1** to do with a monument. **2** like a monument in being weighty, lasting, and important: *monumental works of art.* **3** very great: *monumental ignorance, a monumental achievement.* **mon′u·men′tal·ly** *adv.*

moo (mū) *n, pl* **moos** (mūz) the deep resonant sound made by a cow.
v **mooed, moo·ing** make this sound. <imitative>

mooch (mūch) *Informal v* **1** get something at another person's expense: *He's always mooching cookies off me at lunch.* **2** sneak or skulk around.
n a person who gets things by mooching. <origin uncertain> **mooch′er** *n.*

mood[1] (mūd) *n* **1** a temporary state of mind or feeling: *I'm not in the mood to play a video game just now; I'd rather read.* **2** the atmosphere or prevailing tone of something: *the mood of the period.* <Old English *mod*>

mood[2] (mūd) *n* the form of a verb that shows whether the act or state expressed is thought of as fact, or as a command, question, possibility, or wish. The indicative mood is used for statements of facts; the imperative mood is used for commands. <*mode,* influenced by *mood*[1]>

mood·y (mū′dē) *adj* **mood·i·er, mood·i·est** **1** likely to have changes of mood: *He's a very moody person, so it's hard to say how he'll react.* **2** often in a gloomy or sullen mood: *She has been moody ever since she lost her place on the softball team.* **3** sunk in sadness; gloomy: *They sat in moody silence.* **mood′i·ly** *adv.* **mood′i·ness** *n.*

moo·lah (mū′la) *Slang n* money. <origin unknown>

phases of the moon

new moon

new crescent

first quarter

waxing gibbous

full moon

waning gibbous

last quarter

old crescent

In the northern hemisphere, it is easy to tell whether the moon is coming (waxing) or going (waning) by using the natural curve of a hand, from the first finger to the thumb. If the moon's crescent fits the curve of the right hand, it is increasing (coming); if it fits the curve of the left hand, then it is decreasing (going). In the southern hemisphere, the reverse is true.

---

moon (mūn) *n* **1** a celestial body that revolves around the earth from west to east once in approximately 29.5 days. **2** the moon at a certain period of time. The **new moon** and the **old moon** are visible as slender crescents, the **half moon** as a half circle, and the **full moon** as a circle. **3** a lunar month of about 29 days. **4** moonlight. **5** a natural or artificial satellite: *the moons of Jupiter.*
v wander about or gaze idly or listlessly: *Don't moon when you have work to do.* <Old English *mona*>
moon′like′ *adj.*

moon·beam (mūn′bēm′) *n* a ray of moonlight.

moon·less (mūn′lis) *adj* **1** lacking the light of the moon: *a moonless night.* **2** with no natural satellite: *a moonless planet.*

moon·light (mūn′līt′) *n* the light of the moon: *It is sometimes possible to read by moonlight.*
adj with or by the light of the moon: *a moonlight swim.*
v Informal work at a second job, usually at night, in order to supplement the wages earned at a regular job.

moon·lit (mūn′lit′) *adj* lighted by the moon.

moon·rise (mūn′rīz′) *n* **1** the rising of the moon above the horizon. **2** the time when the moon rises above the horizon.

moon·scape (mūn′skāp′) *n* **1** a view of the surface of the moon. **2** a barren and desolate area on earth, thought of as resembling the surface of the moon.

moon·set (mūn′set′) *n* the disappearance of the moon below the horizon, or the time of night when this happens.

moon·shine (mūn′shīn′) *n* **1** moonlight. **2** empty talk or nonsense. **3** *Informal* intoxicating liquor made unlawfully, or smuggled.

moon·stone (mūn′stōn′) *n* a translucent whitish gem with a pearly lustre, a variety of feldspar.

moon·struck (mūn′struk′) *adj* dazed or crazed.

moon·walk (mūn′wok′) *n* a series of weightless steps taken by an astronaut on the moon, or a walk that suggests this.
v walk in this way.

moor[1] (mūr) *v* **1** put or keep a ship or boat in place by means of ropes or chains fastened to the shore or to anchors. <probably Dutch *moren*>

moor[2] (mūr) *UK n* open wasteland, usually hilly or high up and with low plant growth. <Old English *mor*>

Moor (mūr) *n* a member of a Muslim people in northwest Africa who conquered Spain in the 700s. **Moor′ish** *adj.*

moor·age (mūr′ij) *n* a place for mooring a boat, or the charge for using this place.

moor·ing (mū′ring) *n* **1** a place where a ship, boat, or aircraft is made fast. **2 moorings** *pl* the ropes, cables, or anchors by which a ship or boat is made fast.

moose (mūs) *n, pl* **moose** a large DEER with a sloping back, a pendulous muzzle, and broad, branching antlers in the male, native to forests of northern North America and northern Eurasia. <Abenaki *mos*>

moose·bird (mūs′bərd′) CANADA JAY.

moose·fly (mūs′flī) *n, pl* **moose·flies** a kind of horsefly.

moose pasture *Slang n* land considered worthless for mining or farming.

moot (mūt) *adj* debatable: *a moot point.*
v bring forward a question or topic for discussion.
n in full, **moot court** a mock trial set up in a law school as practice for students. <Old English *gemot* meeting>

mop (mop) *n* **1** a bundle of coarse strings or a sponge fastened at the end of a stick, for cleaning floors and other surfaces. **2** something resembling a mop: *He is going to have his mop of hair cut before he goes for his interview.*
v **mopped, mop·ping 1** wash or wipe up: *to mop the floor.* **2** remove liquid or moisture by wiping: *He mopped his brow with his handkerchief.* <Old French, from Latin *mappa* napkin>

mope (mōp) *v* **moped, mop·ing** be listless, silent, and sad.
n a person who tends to mope. <perhaps Scandinavian>

mo·ped (mō′ped) *n* a motorized bicycle. See SCOOTER for picture. <*mo*(*tor*) + *ped*(*al*)>

mop·pet (mop′it) *n* a child. <Middle Englis *moppe*>

mop–up (mop′up) *Informal n* a finishing off or cleanup.

a bat	e bed	i bid	o pot	u cup	th **thin**
ā cake	ē me	ī bite	ō go	ū rude	ᴛʜ then
à bar	ə about	ər over	ȯ for	ů put	zh measure

M

mo·raine (mə rān′) *n* a mass or ridge of rocks and sediment deposited at the sides or end of a GLACIER after being carried down or pushed aside by the pressure of the ice. <French, from Latin *murrum* round object>

mor·al (mȯ′rəl) *adj* **1** good, according to standards of right and wrong: *a moral act, a moral person.* **2** capable of understanding right and wrong: *a moral being.* **3** to do with the difference between right and wrong: *a moral question.* **4** with a good influence: *a moral book.* **5** encouraging and giving confidence: *We gave moral support to the team by cheering loudly.*
n **1** the lesson, inner meaning, or teaching of a fable, story, or event: *The moral of the story was "Look before you leap."* **2 morals** *pl* character or behaviour in matters of right and wrong. <Latin *mores* morals>

CONFUSABLES

Moral means "lesson": *She understood the moral of the story, which was "don't be greedy."*

Morale means "mental condition" regarding courage, confidence, enthusiasm, etc.: *The coach was pleased with the high morale of the team.*

moral certainty *n* a probability so great that it might just as well be a certainty.

mo·rale (mə ral′) *or* (mə räl′) *n* the confidence and enthusiasm of a person or group at a particular time: *The morale of the team was low after its defeat.* <French *moral*>

mo·ral·i·ty (mə ral′ə tē) *n, pl* **mo·ral·i·ties 1** the rightness or wrongness of an action: *They argued about the morality of using animals for medical research.* **2** the doing of correct or proper actions: *She ranks very high in both intelligence and morality.* **3** a set or system of rules or principles of conduct. **4** a moral instruction or a moral lesson.

morality play *n* a form of drama popular during the 1400s and 1500s, in which vices and virtues appear as real people.

🍁 **morality squad** *n* members of a police force who specialize in investigating illegal gambling, pornography, or prostitution.

mor·al·ize (mȯ′rə līz′) *v* **mor·al·ized, mor·al·iz·ing 1** comment on questions of right and wrong, especially in a superior or self-satisfied way. **2** point out the lesson or inner meaning of something. **mor′al·ist** *n.* **mor′al·is′tic** *adj.* **mor′al·iz·a′tion** *n.* **mor′al·iz·er** *n.*

mor·al·ly (mȯ′rə lē) *adv* **1** from a moral point of view: *What he did was morally wrong.* **2** in a moral manner. **3** on the basis of strong evidence, especially about a person's character: *I am morally certain that he could not have committed the crime.*

moral support *n* approval, but not active help.

moral victory *n* a defeat that has the effect on the mind that a victory would have.

mo·rass (mə ras′) *n* **1** a piece of low, soft, wet ground. **2** a difficult or confused situation. <Dutch, from Latin *mariscus* marsh>

mor·a·to·ri·um (mȯ′rə tȯ′rē əm) *n, pl* **mor·a·to·ri·ums** or **mor·a·to·ri·a** (-rē ə) **1** a legal authorization to delay payments of money due, or the period during which such authorization is in effect. **2** a temporary prohibition of an activity: *a moratorium on bringing skateboards to school.* <Latin *mora* delay>

mo·ray (mȯ′rā) *n* an eel-like fish of warm seas, with a heavy body, a large mouth, and strong, sharp teeth. <Portuguese, from Greek *muraina*>

mor·bid (mȯr′bid) *adj* **1** appealing to an unhealthy or abnormal interest in something disturbing and unpleasant: *His mother thinks his liking of horror movies is morbid.* **2** caused by disease: *a morbid growth.* <Latin *morbus* disease> **mor′bid·ly** *adv.* **mor′bid·ness** *n.*

mor·bid·i·ty (mȯr bid′ə tē) *n* **1** the quality or condition of being morbid. **2** the proportion of sickness in a certain population: *morbidity statistics.*

mor·dant (mȯr′dənt) *adj* sharp, bitter, or biting in quality: *mordant wit, mordant humour.*
n **1** a substance that fixes colours in dyeing. **2** an acid that eats into the metal of a printing plate. <French, from Latin *mordere* to bite>

more (mȯr) *adj* **1** further or additional: *If you need to, you can take more time to finish the test.* **2** (*as the comparative of* ***much*** *or* ***many****, the superlative being* ***most***) greater in number, quantity, amount, degree, or importance: *More people prefer brand A to Brand B.*
n **1** a greater number, quantity, amount, or degree: *The more they have, the more they want.* **2** an additional amount: *Tell me more.*
adv **1** in or to a greater extent or degree: *That hurts more.* **2** in addition, further, or again: *Take one step more. Sing once more.* <Old English *mara*>
be no more, be dead.
more or less, a somewhat: *We were more or less satisfied about the result.* **b** nearly or about: *The distance is five kilometres, more or less.*

GRAMMAR AND USAGE

Use **more** and **most** to form comparatives and superlatives of adjectives and adverbs of three syllables and more: *more beautiful*. Some two-syllable adjectives and adverbs follow the same rule: *most dreadful*. Most other adjectives and adverbs use *-er* and *-est*.

more·ish (mō′rish) *Slang adj* so delicious as to make you want to eat more: *These brownies are very moreish.* <*more* + *-ish*>

mo·rel (mə rel′) *n* an edible fungus with a fleshy, pitted head on a stalk. <French, from Dutch *morilje*>

more·o·ver (mȯ rō′vər) *adv* also, besides, or furthermore: *His power is absolute and, moreover, hereditary.*

mo·res (mȯ′rēz) *pln* the essential or characteristic customs and rules of a community. <Latin = customs>

morgue (mȯrg) *n* **1** a place in which unclaimed bodies of dead people are kept until they can be identified and removed. **2** that part of a hospital where autopsies are performed. **3** a reference library in a newspaper office. <French *le Morgue*, a mortuary in Paris>

mor·i·bund (mo̍′rə bund′) *adj* **1** dying. **2** lacking vitality or vigour: *The moribund restaurant made no profit last month.* <Latin *mori* to die>

Mor·mon (mo̍r′mən′) *n* a member of the Church of Jesus Christ of Latter-day Saints, a religion founded in the US in 1830 by Joseph Smith and whose scripture is *The Book of Mormon.*
adj to do with this religion or its followers. <narrator of *The Book of Mormon*> **Mor′mon·ism′** *n.*

morn (mo̍rn) *Poetic n* morning. <Old English *morgen*>

morn·ing (mo̍r′ning) *n* **1** the early part of the day, ending at noon. **2** the first or early part of anything: *the morning of life.*
adj of or in the morning. <Old English *morgen* + *-ing* as in *evening*>

morn·ing–af·ter pill (mo̍r′ning af′tər) *n* a pill used as a contraceptive within about 36 hours after sexual intercourse.

morn·ing–glo·ry (mo̍r′ning glo̍′rē) *n, pl* **morn·ing-glo·ries** a twining plant with trumpet-shaped flowers and heart-shaped leaves.

morning sickness *n* a feeling of nausea, often accompanied by vomiting, that occurs in the morning, especially during the early months of pregnancy.

morning star *n* a planet, especially Venus, seen in the eastern sky before sunrise. Compare EVENING STAR.

mo·roc·co (mə rok′ō) *n, pl* **mo·roc·cos** a fine leather made from goatskin, used in binding books. <*Morocco,* where it was first made>

Mo·roc·co (mə rok′ō) *n* a country in northwest Africa. See the APPENDIX. **Mo·roc′can** *adj, n.*

mo·ron (mo̍′ron) *Informal n* a stupid or annoyingly ignorant person. <Greek *moros* foolish>

mo·rose (mə rōs′) *adj* gloomy and sullen: *a morose expression.* <Latin *mos* manner> **mo·rose′ly** *adv.* **mo·rose′ness** *n.*

morph (mo̍rf) *n* **1** *Biology* a variant form of an animal or plant. **2** a radically changed form of something. **3** *Computers* an image that is changed to another by small gradual steps in computer animation.
v **1** change radically in form: *The movie was about an alien who could morph into a human.* **2** *Computers* change or cause to change an image by small gradual steps in computer animation: *This program creates a graphic and then morphs it continuously.* <Greek *morphe* form>

mor·pheme (mo̍r′fēm′) *n* the smallest meaningful element of a language that cannot be further divided. Examples: *make, snow, un-, -ing.* <French, from Greek *morphe* form>

mor·phine (mo̍r′fēn) *n* an addictive drug made from opium, used to dull pain and to cause sleep. <German, from *Morpheus* Roman god of dreams>

mor·phol·o·gy (mo̍r fol′ə jē) *n* **1** the branch of biology that studies the forms and structure of animals and plants. **2** the branch of linguistics that studies the forms of words, especially inflected forms. **3** the system of word-forming elements and processes of a language: *The morphology of English is very different from that of Japanese.* <Greek *morphe* form> **mor′pho·log′i·cal** *adj.*

mor·row (mo′rō) *Archaic or Poetic n* the following day: *They decided to dine together on the morrow.* <Old English *morgen* morn>

Morse code (mo̍rs) *n* a signalling system by which an alphabet or code is represented by dots, dashes, and spaces or by long and short sounds or flashes of light. <S.F.B. *Morse,* 19c inventor>

mor·sel (mo̍r′səl) *n* a piece or fragment, especially of food. <Old French, from Latin *mordere* to bite>

mor·ta·del·la (mo̍r′tə del′ə) *n* an Italian sausage containing pieces of fat, usually eaten cold and thinly sliced. <Italian>

mor·tal (mo̍r′təl) *adj* **1** sure to die sometime. **2** to do with humanity as subject to death: *Mortal flesh has many pains and diseases.* **3** causing or liable to cause death: *a mortal wound, a mortal illness.* **4** in some Christian beliefs, to do with a serious sin that causes spiritual death. **5** lasting until death: *a mortal enemy, a mortal battle.* **6** very great or intense: *mortal terror.*
n **1** a being that is sure to die sometime: *All living creatures are mortals.* **2** a person or human being: *No mortal could survive that storm.* <Latin *mortalis* subject to death, from *mortis* death>

mor·tal·i·ty (mo̍r tal′ə tē) *n* **1** the condition of being sure to die sometime. **2** a loss of life on a large scale: *The mortality from automobile accidents is very serious.* **3** the number of deaths in a given area or period, or from a particular cause: *The mortality from typhoid fever is decreasing.*

mor·tal·ly (mo̍r′tə lē) *adv* **1** so as to cause death: *mortally wounded.* **2** very greatly or intensely: *mortally offended.*

mor·tar[1] (mo̍r′tər) *n* a mixture of lime, cement, sand, and water, used for holding bricks or stones together.
v join or fix with mortar. <Old French, from Latin *mortarium*>

mor·tar[2] (mo̍r′tər) *n* **1** a bowl made of very hard material, in which substances may be crushed or ground. See PESTLE for picture. **2** a very short artillery piece for shooting shells at high angles. <Latin *mortarium*>

mor·tar·board (mo̍r′tər bo̍rd′) *n* **1** a board with a handle used by masons to hold mortar. **2** an academic cap with a close-fitting crown topped by a stiff, flat, cloth-covered square piece, sometimes worn by teachers and students on special occasions.

mort·gage (mo̍r′gij) *n* **1** a claim on property, given to a person, bank, or firm that has lent money in case the money is not repaid when due. **2** a document that gives such a claim.
v **mort·gaged, mort·gag·ing** give a lender a claim to your property in case a debt is not paid when due. <Old French = dead pledge, because the debt becomes "dead," i.e., void when paid>

a bat	e bed	i bid	o pot	u cup	th **thin**
ā cake	ē me	ī bite	ō go	ū rude	ꟻH **then**
ȧ bar	ə about	ər over	ȯ for	u̇ put	zh measure

M

mort·ga·gee (mȯr′gi jē′) *n* the person, bank, or company to whom property is mortgaged.

mort·gag·er or **mort·ga·gor** (mȯr′gi jər) *n* a person who mortgages his or her property.

mor·ti·cian (mȯr tish′ən) *n* an undertaker.

mor·ti·fy (mȯr′tə fī′) *v* **mor·ti·fied, mor·ti·fy·ing 1** make ashamed or embarrassed: *They were mortified by their cousin's rudeness to their friend.* **2** control or overcome physical desires and feelings through self-denial or the endurance of pain. **3** become affected with or cause GANGRENE. <Old French, from Latin *mortis* death + *facere* make> **mor′ti·fi·ca′tion** *n.* **mor′ti·fi′er** *n.*

mor·tise (mȯr′tis) *n* a hole in one piece of wood cut to receive a projection on another piece, called the tenon, so as to form a joint (**mortise and tenon joint**).
v **mor·tised, mor·tis·ing** fasten by a mortise. <Old French, perhaps from Arabic *murtazz* fastened>

mor·tu·a·ry (mȯr′chū er′ē) *n, pl* **mor·tu·a·ries** the part of a building in which bodies of dead people are hygienically stored or examined prior to burial or cremation.
adj to do with burial or tombs. <Latin *mortuus* dead>

mo·sa·ic (mō zā′ik) *n* **1** a picture or design made of small pieces of variously coloured hard material, such as stone, glass, wood, or tile, set together or inlaid. **2** something made up of varied parts or elements, like a mosaic: *Canada is often called a cultural mosaic.* <French, from Latin *musium* decoration with small square stones> **mo·sa′i·cist** (mō zā′i sist) *n.*

Moses (mō′zəz) *Judaism n* a Hebrew prophet who, according to the Bible, led the people of Israel out of slavery in Egypt and recorded the ten commandments given by God. **Mo·sa′ic** *n.*

mo·sey (mō′zē) *Informal v* **mo·seyed, mo·sey·ing** move in an aimless or leisurely way: *We had lots of time, so after lunch we decided to mosey on over to the park.* <origin uncertain>

mosh (mosh) *v* at a rock concert, dance wildly so as to deliberately collide with other dancers, usually in a **mosh pit**, the area nearest the stage. <origin unknown> **mosh′er** *n.*

Mos·lem (moz′ləm) MUSLIM.

mosque (mosk) *n* a Muslim place of worship. <French, from Arabic *masgid*>

mos·qui·to (mə skē′tō) *n, pl* **mosqui·toes** or **mos·qui·tos** a small fly, the female of which can pierce the skin of people and animals and suck blood, causing a sting that itches. See DIPTEROUS for picture. <Spanish and Portuguese, from Latin *musca* fly>

mosquito net *n* **1** a floor-length canopy made of **mosquito netting**, a very fine, light mesh. **2** a similar piece of protective mesh, such as that attached to a hat for protecting the face and neck.

moss (mos) *n* **1** a soft, green or brown flowerless plant that grows in damp places and reproduces by means of spores. **2** ✱ *Prince Edward Island* in full, **Irish moss** carrageen. Gathering this seaweed at the shore is called **mossing**. <Old English *mos* bog> **moss′like′** *adj.*

✱ **moss–bag** (mos′bag′) *n* a bag of leather or cloth formerly used by some First Nations peoples to carry a baby. The moss-bag was usually strapped to a cradleboard.

moss·y (mos′ē) *adj* **moss·i·er, moss·i·est 1** covered with moss: *a mossy bank.* **2** like moss: *mossy green.* **moss′i·ness** *n.*

most (mōst) *adj* **1** (*as the superlative of* **much** *or* **many**, *the comparative being* **more**) greatest in number, quantity, amount, degree, or importance: *The winner gets the most money.* **2** the majority of: *Most children like candy.*
n the greatest quantity, amount, degree, or number: *She did most of the work.*
adv **1** in or to the greatest extent or degree: *Which movie did you like most?* **2** to a very great degree: *a most persuasive argument.* **3** *Informal* almost or nearly: *We go to Charlottetown most every summer.* <Old English *mast*>
at most or **at the most,** not more than.
for the most part, mainly or usually.
make the most of, make the best use of.

–most *suffix* greatest in quantity or degree: *topmost, innermost.* <Middle English>

most favoured nation *n* a nation given privileged status by another as an important trading partner, gaining lower tariffs and other advantages.

most·ly (mō′stlē) *adv* almost all or chiefly.

mote (mōt) *n* a speck of dust. <Old English *mot*>

mo·tel (mō tel′) *n* a hotel by a highway consisting of a building or group of buildings with rooms that can be reached directly from an outdoor parking area. <*mo*(*tor*) + (*ho*)*tel*>

mo·tet (mō tet′) *n* a musical composition with a sacred theme, usually sung unaccompanied. <Old French *mot* word>

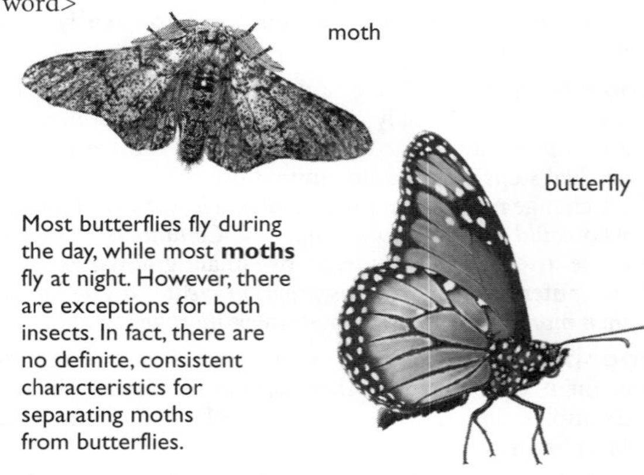

Most butterflies fly during the day, while most **moths** fly at night. However, there are exceptions for both insects. In fact, there are no definite, consistent characteristics for separating moths from butterflies.

moth (moth) *n, pl* **moths** (moᴛʜz) *or* (moths) an insect with two pairs of broad wings, typically held flat when at rest. <Old English *moththe*>

moth·ball (moth′bol′) *n* a small ball made of naphthalene or some other strong-smelling substance, used for putting in garments or in clothes closets to keep moths away.
in mothballs, a in protective storage. **b** in an inactive state or condition: *It seems the plans for the new arena are in mothballs.*

moth–eaten (moth′ē′tən) *adj* **1** with many holes made by moths. **2** worn-out or out of date.

moth·er (muᴛʜ′ər) *n* **1** a female parent, or a female who has the responsibilities of a parent. **2** a female ancestor: *the dreams and hopes of our mothers.* **3** the cause or source: *He liked to say that necessity is the mother of invention.* **4** Mother Superior.
v be mother of or act as mother to: *She mothers her baby sister.*
adj **1** being or resembling a mother: *the mother church.* **2** belonging to a person because of birth: *Scotland is my mother country and English is my mother tongue.* <Old English *modor*> **moth′er·hood** *n.* **moth′er·less** *adj.* **moth′er·li·ness** *n.* **moth′er·ly** *adj.*

moth·er·board (muᴛʜ′ər bȯrd′) *Computers n* the main circuit board in a computer, containing the major electronic components and usually expansion slots for additional cards.

🍁 **Mother Carey's chicken** (kā′rēz′) *n* the storm petrel. <origin unknown>

mother country *n* **1** the country where a person was born. **2** a country in relation to its colonies.

Mother Goose *n* the imaginary author of English nursery rhymes, which were actually of folk origin and first published in a book form in the 1700s.

mother hen *n* **1** a hen with chicks. **2** *Informal* a person who likes to protect and take care of others, fussing over them and worrying about them: *Don't be such a mother hen; I can take care of myself!*

moth·er–in–law (muᴛʜ′ər in lo′) *n, pl* **moth·ers-in-law** the mother of one's spouse.

moth·er·land (muᴛʜ′ər land′) *n* **1** one's native country. **2** the land of one's ancestors.

mother lode *n* the main vein of ore in a mine.

Mother Nature *n* (*used poetically or as a euphemism*) the natural environment and natural forces or instincts.

moth·er–of–pearl (muᴛʜ′ər əv pərl′) *n* the hard, smooth, pearly lining of certain marine shells, such as that of the pearl oyster and abalone, often used to make buttons and ornaments.

Mother's Day *n* the second Sunday in May, an unofficial day to honour mothers.

mother ship *n* a ship or spacecraft that serves as a base or supply point for one or more smaller craft.

Mother Superior *n* a woman who is the head of a community of nuns.

mother tongue *n* one's first or native language.

mother wit *n* natural intelligence or common sense.

moth·proof (moth′prūf′) *adj* treated chemically so as to keep moths away: *The carpet is mothproof.*
v make mothproof: *a mothproofed fibre.*

mo·tif (mō tēf′) *n* **1** a subject for development or treatment in art or literature; a theme: *The chivalry motif appears in the literature of many countries.* **2** a short, prominent sequence of notes that is repeated in different parts of a longer piece of music. **3** a distinctive recurring figure in a design or pattern. Also, **motive.** <French *motif* main idea>

mo·tile (mō′tīl) *or* (mō′təl) *adj* capable of motion as a living organism: *Barnacles are motile for the first two stages of their life.* **mo·til′i·ty** (mō ti′lə tē) *n.*

mo·tion (mō′shən) *n* **1** a movement or a change of position or place: *She swayed with the motion of the moving train. Everything is either in motion or at rest.* **2** a formal suggestion made in a meeting or court of law: *The motion to adjourn was carried.*
v **1** make a movement, as of the hand or head, to show your meaning: *She motioned to show us the way.* **2** show a person what to do by such a motion: *He motioned me out.* <Old French, from Latin *movere* move>
go through the motions, act mechanically, with no real commitment to what you are doing: *For the last few years he hasn't really cared about his job and seems to be just going through the motions.*
in motion, moving or going.

mo·tion·less (mō′shən lis) *adj* not moving: *She stood perfectly motionless, watching the deer with its young.* **mo′tion·less·ly** *adv.*

motion picture *n* a series of pictures on a continuous strip of film, projected on a screen in such rapid succession that the viewer gets the impression that the people and things pictured are moving, or a story or drama told by means of this process.

motion sickness *n* nausea and dizziness caused by motion, such as the pitching and rolling of a ship or boat, or the swaying of a train or car.

mo·ti·vate (mō′tə vāt′) *v* **mo·ti·vat·ed, mo·ti·vat·ing** make someone want to take action: *Pride motivated the boy to do well at school.* <*motive*> **mo′ti·va′tion** *n.*

mo·tive (mō′tiv) *n* **1** the thought or feeling that makes you take action: *His motive in going away was a wish to travel.* **2** MOTIF.
adj producing physical or mechanical motion: *a motive force.* <Latin *motivus* moving>

motive power *n* power used to impart motion to machinery: *The motive power of some trains is electricity.*

mot juste (mō zhūst′) *n* a word or phrase that exactly fits the situation. <French = the precise word>

mot·ley (mot′lē) *adj* of a widely varying character or appearance: *a motley collection of old books and toys.*
n, pl **mot·leys** an oddly assorted mixture. <Middle English>

mo·to·cross (mō′tō kros′) *n* a cross-country obstacle race on trail bikes or light motorcycles, or the sport of participating in such races. <*moto*(*rcycle*) + *cross*(*-country*)>

mo·tor (mō′tər) *n* **1** an engine that makes a machine go: *an electric motor.* **2** an internal combustion engine.
adj **1** to do with motor vehicles: *a motor tour.* **2** to do with motion or action: *Motor nerves arouse muscles to action.* <Latin = mover>

a bat	e bed	i bid	o pot	u cup	th **thin**
ā cake	ē me	ī bite	ō go	ū rude	ᴛʜ **then**
ä bar	ə about	ər over	ȯ for	u̇ put	zh measure

M

motorcycles

Motorcycles used for grand prix races are built for speed. Aerodynamic mouldings reduce the amount of drag, and lightweight aluminum or titanium alloys ensure better acceleration and handling.

Motocross motorcycles are designed for the rugged conditions of dirt tracks and rough terrain. They are light and sturdy, with a low centre of gravity. The nubby tires provide traction on dirt and obstacles.

mo·tor·bike (mō′tər bīk′) *Informal n* a motorcycle, especially a small, lightweight one.

mo·tor·boat (mō′tər bōt′) *n* a boat propelled by a motor.

mo·tor·cade (mō′tər kād′) *n* a procession or long line of automobiles.

mo·tor·cy·cle (mō′tər sī′kəl) *n* a narrow, two-wheeled motor vehicle on which the driver sits, sometimes with a sidecar that has a third supporting wheel.
v **mo·tor·cy·cled, mo·tor·cy·cling** travel by motorcycle. **mo′tor·cy′clist** *n.*

mo·tor·home (mō′tər hōm′) *n* a large motor vehicle with a completely enclosed body that is equipped for use as a travelling home. Compare MOBILE HOME.

motor hotel or **inn** *n* a hotel for accommodating motorists, somewhat more elaborate than a motel and usually consisting of several floors of rooms and suites.

mo·tor·ist (mō′tə rist) *n* a person who drives or travels by automobile.

mo·tor·ize (mō′tə rīz′) *v* **mo·tor·ized, mo·tor·iz·ing** **1** furnish with a motor or a motor-driven vehicle. **2** equip infantry with motor-driven transport vehicles, especially trucks. **mo′tor·i·za′tion** *n.*

mo·tor·mouth (mō′tər mouth′) *Informal n* a person who talks a great deal or very fast.

motor scooter *n* a light, two-wheeled motor vehicle steered by handlebars attached to the front wheel and having a broad footboard for the driver.

motor vehicle *n* a vehicle that travels under its own power and designed for use on roads and highways. Automobiles, buses, and trucks are motor vehicles.

Mo·town (mō′toun′) *Music n* a style of rhythm and blues popular in the 1960s, incorporating features of black gospel music. <From *Motown Records*, a recording company in Detroit. *Motown* comes from *Motor Town*, a nickname for Detroit because it was the centre of the American auto industry.>

mot·tle (mot′əl) *v* **mot·tled, mot·tling** mark with spots or streaks of different colours.
n a mottled colouring and pattern. <probably back-formation from *motley*> **mot′tled** *adj.*

mot·to (mot′ō) *n, pl* **mot·toes** or **mot·tos** a brief sentence or phrase adopted as a rule of conduct: *"Think before you speak" is a good motto.* <Italian = word>

mouf·lon or **mouf·flon** (mū′flon) *n* a wild mountain sheep native to Corsica and Sardinia. See SHEEP for picture. <French, from Italian *muflone*>

mould[1] or **mold** (mōld) *n* **1** a hollow shape in which anything is formed or cast: *Molten metal is poured into a mould to harden into shape.* **2** the shape or form which is given by a mould: *The moulds of ice cream were bells and bows.* **3** the model according to which anything is shaped: *The son was formed in his father's mould.* **4** something shaped in a mould: *a mould of pudding.* **5** the nature or character of anything.
v **1** form; shape: *to mould statues.* **2** make or form into shape: *We are moulding clay to make model animals. Her character was moulded by suffering.*

mould[2] or **mold** (mōld) *n* **1** a woolly or furry growth of fungus that appears on food and other animal or vegetable substances when they are left too long in a warm, moist place. **2** any fungus that produces mould.
v make or become covered with mould: *The boots moulded in the cellar.*

mould[3] or **mold** (mōld) *n* soft, rich, crumbly soil; earth mixed with decaying leaves, manure, etc.: *Many wild flowers grow in the forest mould.*

mould·er or **mold·er** (mōl′dər) *v* turn into dust by natural decay; crumble; waste away.

mould·ing or **mold·ing** (mōl′ding) *n* **1** something produced by shaping or casting. **2** a decorative shaping or contour along the top of a wall, or around a door or window.

mould·y or **mold·y** (mōl′dē) *adj* **mould·i·er** or **mold·i·er, mould·i·est** or **mold·i·est** **1** covered with mould: *a mouldy crust of bread, mouldy cheese.* **2** musty or stale: *There was a mouldy smell in the deserted house.* **mould′i·ness** or **mold′i·ness** *n.*

moult or **molt** (mōlt) *v* shed the feathers, fur, skin, shell, or horns periodically before a new growth.
n the act or process of moulting. <Old English, from Latin *mutare* to change>

mound (mound) *n* **1** a bank or heap of earth or stones. **2** a small hill. **3** *Baseball* the slightly elevated ground from which the pitcher throws the ball. **4** a heap or pile of anything: *I gave myself a big mound of ice cream.*
v heap up: *The gardener mounded the earth around a hill of corn.* <origin uncertain>

mount[1] (mount) *v* **1** go up or move up: *to mount stairs. A blush mounts to the forehead.* **2** increase; become stronger or more intense: *The cost of living mounted steadily. His anger mounted as time passed.* **3** get up on something: *to mount a platform, to mount a motorcycle and drive off.* **4** put in proper position or order for use; fix in a setting: *to mount a drawing on cardboard. The scientist mounted the sample on a microscope slide.* **5** produce a play, exhibition, or other artistic event: *to mount a production of a musical.* **6** plan and begin to carry out: *to mount a campaign to get elected.*
n **1** a horse provided for riding. **2** something on which an object is fixed: *the mount for a photograph.* <Old French, from Latin *montis* mountain>

mount[2] (mount) *n* (*usually used only in place names*) a mountain or high hill: *Mount Logan is in Yukon Territory.* <Old English, from Latin *montis* mountain>

moun·tain (moun′tən) *n* **1** a very high and large hill rising abruptly from level ground: *the Rocky Mountains.* **2** to do with, or resembling a mountain or mountains: *mountain air.* **3** living, growing, or found on mountains: *mountain plants.* **4** a large amount, heap, or pile of anything: *a mountain of rubbish, a mountain of difficulties.* <Old French, from Latin *montis* mountain>
make a mountain (out) of a molehill, give great importance to something that is really insignificant, especially a minor hindrance or obstacle.

mountain ash *n* a tree of the rose family with white flowers and bright red berries.

mountain a·vens (av′ənz) *n* a woody, evergreen plant of the rose family found especially in northern and mountainous regions. It is the floral emblem of the Northwest Territories.

mountain bike *n* a bicycle designed for rough, rocky terrain, with wide, deep-tread tires, a sturdy frame, and many gears. **mountain biker** *n.* **mountain biking** *n.*

mountain dew *Informal n* homemade whisky.

moun·tain·eer (moun′tə nēr′) *n* one skilled in mountain climbing.
v climb mountains.

mountain goat *n* an antelope of the Rocky Mountains with shaggy white hair and backward curving horns.

mountain lion COUGAR.

moun·tain·ous (moun′tə nəs) *adj* **1** covered with mountain ranges: *mountainous country.* **2** huge: *a mountainous wave.*

mountain range *n* a series of connected mountains.

moun·tain·side (moun′tən sīd′) *n* the side or face of a mountain: *The whole mountainside was covered with trees.*

moun·tain·top (moun′tən top′) *n* the very top of a mountain.

moun·te·bank (moun′tə bangk′) *n* a person who tries to deceive people, especially to trick them out of their money. <Italian *monta in banco* climb on the bench, from the tradition of standing on a wagon or platform to sell goods or entertain an audience>

mount·ed (moun′tid) *adj* **1** on horseback. **2** in a position for use: *a mounted telescope.* **3** with a proper support or setting: *a mounted photograph.*

✱ **Mount·ie** or **mount·ie** (moun′tē) *Informal n, pl* **Mount·ies** or **mount·ies** a member of the ROYAL CANADIAN MOUNTED POLICE.

mount·ing (moun′ting) *n* a backing, support, or setting for something, such as a gem or a photograph.

mourn (mȯrn) *v* feel or show deep sorrow or regret: *She mourned her lost cat.* <Old English *murnan*> **mourn′er** *n.*

mourn·ful (mȯrn′fəl) *adj* **1** full of grief or sorrow. **2** gloomy or dreary: *a mournful occasion, a mournful voice.* **mourn′ful·ly** *adv.* **mourn′ful·ness** *n.*

mourn·ing (mȯr′ning) *n* **1** the act of sorrowing or grieving. **2 a** the outward signs of sorrow, such as the wearing of black, the draping of buildings, or the flying of flags at half-mast, or the period during which such signs are shown. **b** clothes, decorations, or draperies worn or displayed to show such sorrow: *dressed in mourning.*
adj of or used in mourning.

mourning dove *n* a wild dove of N America that makes a mournful sound.

mouse (mous) *n, pl* **mice** (mīs) **1** a small rodent with a pointed snout, large ears, and a long, scaly tail. **2** a shy, timid person. **3** *Computers* an electronic handheld device that is dragged across a flat surface, enabling the user to move the cursor on a computer screen, or select various computing functions. The user can **point** (place the pointer over an item on the screen), **click** (press and release a mouse button), **double-click** (press and release twice, rapidly), **right-click** (press and release the button on the right side of the mouse), and **drag** (hold down the (or the left) mouse button while moving the mouse).
v **moused, mous·ing** hunt for mice. <Old English *mys*> **mouse′like′** *adj.*

mouse pad *Computers n* a firm, small pad with a smooth covering layer, used as a surface on which to move a mouse for a computer.

mous·er (mou′sər) *or* (mou′zər) *n* an animal that catches mice: *Our cat is a good mouser.*

a bat	e bed	i bid	o pot	u cup	th thin
ā cake	ē me	ī bite	ō go	ū rude	ᴛʜ then
ȧ bar	ə about	ər over	ȯ for	u̇ put	zh measure

M

mouse·trap (mous′trap′) *n* a trap for catching mice.

mous·sa·ka (mū so′kə) or (mū′sə ka) *n* a Greek dish consisting of layers of ground beef and eggplant, covered with a sauce and baked. <Turkish, from Arabic>

mousse (mūs) *n* **1** a chilled or frozen dessert made with sweetened whipped cream or gelatin: *chocolate mousse.* **2** finely ground cooked meat or fish mixed with cream and other ingredients and poached, steamed, or set with gelatin. **3** a substance with a foamy texture, such as hair setting lotion. <French = froth>

mous·tache (mus′tash) *or* (mə stash′) MUSTACHE.

mous·y (mou′sē) *adj* **mous·i·er, mous·i·est** resembling or suggesting a mouse in being timid, drab in colour, or quiet: *My hair is mousy.* Also, **mousey**.

mouth (mouth) *for n,* (mouᴛʜ) *for v. n, pl* **mouths** (mouᴛʜz) **1** the opening in the lower part of the face through which a person or animal takes in food, and from which speech or other sounds are made. See PALATE for picture. **2** the part of the face around the mouth, especially the lips. **3** an opening suggesting a mouth: *the mouth of a cave.* **4** a part of a river or creek where its waters are emptied into some other body of water: *the mouth of the St. Lawrence River.*
v **1** utter words in an affected, pompous, or insincere way: *I dislike actors who mouth their lines.* **2** speak clearly and distinctly. **3** take in or touch with the mouth. **4** form words with the lips without speaking. <Old English *muth*>
down in the mouth, *Informal* discouraged.
have a big mouth, *Informal* have a tendency to talk too much or to reveal secrets.
mouth off, *Informal* speak disrespectfully.
put your money where your mouth is, *Informal* back up what you say with concrete action or financial support.
shoot off your mouth, *Informal* talk freely and in an unwise, disrespectful, or arrogant way.
the horse's mouth, *Informal* the original source: *The news came straight from the horse's mouth.*

mouth·ful (mouth′fu̇l′) *n, pl* **mouth·fuls** **1** the amount the mouth can easily hold. **2** *Informal* a long or complicated word, phrase, or statement.

mouth organ HARMONICA.

mouth·piece (mouth′pēs′) *n* **1** the part of a musical instrument that is placed against or in the mouth of the player. **2** a piece placed at or forming the mouth of something: *the mouthpiece of a telephone.* **3** a person, group, or organization used by other people or groups to express their views: *The school newspaper is just a mouthpiece for the student government.*

mouth–to–mouth (mouth′tə mouth′) *adj* to do with a method of artificial respiration in which one person breathes air into an unconscious person's lungs.

mouth·wash (mouth′wosh′) *n* an antiseptic liquid for rinsing the inside of the mouth or gargling.

mouth–wa·ter·ing (mouth′wot′ə ring) *adj* very appealing, especially to the appetite: *a mouth-watering menu, a mouth-watering bowl of fruit.*

mouth·y (mou′ᴛʜē) *or* (mou′thē) *adj* **mouth·i·er, mouth·i·est** loud-mouthed or overly assertive.

mov·a·ble (mū′və bəl) *adj* **1** able to be moved: *Our fingers are movable.* **2** able to be carried from place to place as personal possessions can. **3** changing from one date to another in different years: *Easter is a movable holy day.*
n **1** a thing that can be carried from place to place: *All the furniture and other movables had been taken away, leaving the house bare.* **2** **movables** *pl* personal property, not including land or buildings. Also, **moveable**.

move (mūv) *v* **moved, mov·ing** **1** change position or change the position of: *The child moved in his sleep. I'm going to move that chair nearer the window. The train moved slowly.* **2** change your place of living or working: *We move to the East Coast next week.* **3** put or keep in motion: *The wind moves the leaves.* **4** take action: *The committee moved very slowly.* **5** impel; rouse; excite; affect with emotion: *Whatever moved you to do that? The sad story moved her to tears.* **6** make a formal request or proposal: *Madam Chair, I move that we adjourn.* **7** sell or be sold: *These pink sneakers are moving slowly.* **8** exist or be active: *She moves in a small group of friends and relations.*
n **1** the moving of a piece in board games: *That was a good move. It's your move.* **2** movement or the act of moving: *If you make a move, the dog will bark, a move to the other side of the town.* **3** an action taken to bring about some result: *a move to reduce traffic jams on the highway.* <Old French, from Latin *movere*>
get a move on, *Slang* hurry up.
make your move, take decisive action.
move heaven and earth, do everything possible.
move in, move into a new place to live or work.
move out, move from where you have lived or worked.
movers and shakers, people with power and influence.
on the move, moving about: *They are restless and always on the move.*

move·ment (mūv′mənt) *n* **1** the act or fact of moving: *We run by movements of the legs.* **2** the moving parts of a machine: *The movement of a watch consists of many little wheels.* **3** the kind of rhythm or speed a musical piece has: *The movement of a waltz is very different from the movement of a march.* **4** one section of a long piece of music: *The program included only the first movement of the symphony.* **5** an initiative by a group of people to bring about something: *the movement for peace.*

mov·er (mū′vər) *n* a person who or thing that moves, especially a person whose work is moving furniture and other belongings from one residence or place of work to another: *The movers will be here tomorrow.*

mov·ie (mū′vē) *n* a motion picture.

mo·vie·go·er (mū′vē gō′ər) *n* a person who regularly goes to see movies. **mo′vie·go′ing** *adj, n.*

mo·vie·mak·er (mū′vē māk′ər) *n* **1** a company that owns or runs a movie studio: *One of the big moviemakers was interested in the script.* **2** a movie producer or director. **mo′vie·mak′ing** *adj, n.*

mov·ing (mū′ving) *adj* **1** capable of or characterized by movement. **2** to do with changing a place of residence or work: *a moving company, moving expenses.* **3** causing a strong emotional response, especially sadness or sympathy: *a moving story.* **mov′ing·ly** *adv.*

moving sidewalk *n* a path for people to walk on, which moves forward mechanically and fairly slowly on an endless belt, such as in an airport or subway.

mow[1] (mō) *v* **mowed, mowed** or **mown, mow·ing** 1 cut down grass or hay with a machine or a scythe: *to mow grass, to mow a field.* 2 destroy rapidly or in large numbers, as if by mowing: *The houses were mowed down by the strength of the wind.* <Old English *mawan*>

mow[2] (mou) *or* (mō) *n* 1 the place in a barn where hay, grain, straw, or some other crop is piled or stored. 2 a pile of hay, grain, or other crop in a barn. <Old English *muga*>

mow·er (mō′ər) *n* a person who or thing that mows: *a lawn mower.*

mox·ie (mok′sē) *Informal n* courage and determination. <*Moxie* a soft drink (no longer available) believed to give a person courage>

Mo·zam·bique (mo′zəm bēk′) *n* a country in S Africa. See the APPENDIX. **Mo′zam·bi′can** or **Mo′zam·bi′qan** *adj, n.*

moz·za·rel·la (mot′sə rel′ə) *n* a mild, soft Italian cheese, often used on pizza. <Italian>

MP or **M.P.** 1 Member of Parliament. 2 Military Police.

MP3 *Computers n* in full, **MPEG-1 layer 3** a file format for compressing a computerized sound recording for downloading. <MPEG is an acronym for *m(otion) p(icture) e(xpert) g(roup)*, the group that originally developed the format>

✱ **MPP** or **M.P.P.** Member of the (Ontario) Provincial Parliament.

Mr. or **Mr** (mis′tər) *pl* **Messrs.** a title for a man, used before his last name or the name of his rank or office. The plural is mostly found in a mailing address: *Mr. Martinez, Mr. Speaker, Messrs. Lee and Bartleby, Chartered Accountants.* <abbreviation of *mister*>

MRI *n* in full, **magnetic resonance imaging** a technique that produces an image of an object in cross-section that is used in medicine to make diagnoses.

Mrs. or **Mrs** (mis′iz) a title for a married woman, used before her last name. <*Mistress*>

ms millisecond(s).

Ms. or **Ms** (miz) a title used in front of the name of a woman or girl. <combination of *Miss* and *Mrs.*>

GRAMMAR AND USAGE

Ms. is a form made up in the early 1950s to parallel Mr. and Mrs. Unlike them, it is not an abbreviation, but it imitates them in usually being followed by a period. Like Mr., Ms. does not identify a woman as being married or unmarried.

MS multiple sclerosis.

MS., MS, ms., or **ms** manuscript(s).

MSG *n* in full, **monosodium glutamate** a white, crystalline powder made from vegetable proteins and used to season foods and enhance their colour.

Mt. 1 Mount: *Mt. Robson.* 2 **Mts.** Mountains: (*as a label on maps rather than in writing*) *Laurentian Mts.*

much (much) *adj* **more, most** in a great quantity, amount, or degree: *much money, much time.*
adv **more, most** 1 to a great extent or degree: *much pleased, much better.* 2 nearly or about: *This is much the same as the others.*
n 1 a great deal: *Much of this is not true.* 2 a great, important, or notable thing or matter: *The rain did not amount to much.* <Old English *micel*>
a bit much, far-fetched, presumptuous, or exaggerated.
as much, exactly that: *Leaving early, eh? I thought as much.*
as much as, in effect: *She as much as told him to get lost.*
make much of, treat, represent, or consider as of great importance.
much as, although: *Much as I like her, her constant chatter gets on my nerves.*
much less, not to mention (something greater): *He won't even call, much less write.*
much of a muchness, much alike.
not much of a ——, not a very good ——: *This is not much of a game.*
too much for, more than you can cope with: *The work is too much for her. Their team was too much for ours.*

mu·ci·lage (myū′sə lij) *n* 1 a sticky, gummy substance used to make things stick together. 2 a substance like glue or gelatin found in plants. <Latin *mucus*>
mu′ci·lag′i·nous (myū′sə laj′ə nəs) *adj.*

muck (muk) *n* 1 dirt or filth. 2 something filthy, dirty, or disgusting. 3 moist farmyard manure. <Scandinavian>
muck about (or **around**)**,** putter or go about aimlessly: *She's mucking about in the basement.*
muck out, clean out something, such as a stable.
muck up, *Informal* ruin or spoil.

✱ **muck·a·muck** (muk′ə muk′) See HIGH MUCKAMUCK.

muck·rake (muk′rāk′) *v* **muck·raked, muck·rak·ing** hunt out and expose real or imagined corruption or misconduct, especially of prominent people or public officials. **muck′rak′er** *n.*

mu·cous (myū′kəs) *adj* to do with mucus. The **mucous membrane** is the lining tissue of the nose, throat, and other inner cavities of the body.

mu·cus (myū′kəs) *n* a slimy substance that is secreted by mucous membranes and glands, and is used by the body for lubrication and protection: *A cold in the head causes a discharge of mucus.* <Latin>

mud (mud) *n* soft, sticky, wet earth: *mud on the ground after rain, mud at the bottom of a pond.* <German *mudde*>
clear as mud, incomprehensible or obscure.
drag in the mud, bring great dishonour to: *They dragged his good name in the mud.*
here's mud in your eye, *Informal* used to make a friendly toast or expression of congratulation.
your name is mud, you are in disgrace.

a bat	e bed	i bid	o pot	u cup	th thin
ā cake	ē me	ī bite	ō go	ū rude	ᴛʜ then
à bar	ə about	ər over	ȯ for	u̇ put	zh measure

mud·dle (mud′əl) *v* **mud·dled, mud·dling 1** mix or mess up: *to muddle a piece of work. She was trying to help, but she only muddled it up.* **2** make confused or stupid: *a mind muddled by alcohol. The more you talk the more you muddle me.* **3** think or act in a confused, blundering way: *He is still muddling along, without accomplishing much.*
n a mess or confusion: *Everything is in a muddle.* <Dutch *modden* make muddy, i.e., confuse> **mud′dler** *n.*
muddle through, succeed in spite of lack of skill or foresight: *Don't worry; I'll muddle through.*

mud·dy (mud′ē) *adj* **mud·di·er, mud·di·est 1** full of or covered with mud: *a muddy sidewalk, muddy water.* **2** to do with mud: *The dog left muddy footprints on the floor.* **3** suggesting or resembling mud: *a muddy colour, a muddy flavour.* **4** confused: *muddy thinking.*
v **mud·died, mud·dy·ing** make or become muddy: *Don't muddy the floor.*
muddy the water, confuse matters.

mud flat *n* level, low-lying land bordering a river, especially one that regularly overflows and deposits alluvial soil.

mud·guard (mud′gärd′) *n* a guard or shield so placed as to protect riders from the mud thrown up by the moving wheels of a vehicle: *My bicycle has two mudguards.*

mud hen *n* the N American coot.

mud·pie (mud′pȳ′) *n* a round shape made of mud, usually by means of a small pail or other container used as a mould.

mud puppy *n* a large N American salamander that has fluffy, red gills on either side of the head and lives in mud under water.

mud room *n* a room near the entrance to a home or other building, in which boots or other footwear are left before entering.

mud·slide (mud′slīd′) *n* a mass of mud that has slid down the side of a hill or the face of a cliff: *buried under a mudslide.*

mud·sling·ing (mud′sling′ing) *n* public name calling and accusations intended to destroy a competitor's reputation. **mud′sling′er** *n.*

mud trout BROOK TROUT.

mues·li (myüz′li) *n* a breakfast cereal made of rolled oats, dried fruit and nuts, usually eaten with milk for breakfast. <German>

mu·ez·zin (myü ez′ən) *Islam n* a man who, at certain hours, calls Muslims to prayer from the minaret of a mosque. <Arabic *addana* proclaim>

muff[1] (muf) *n* a cylindrical covering of fur or other material into which the hands are thrust from both ends to keep them warm. <Dutch *mof,* from Latin *muffla*>

muff[2] (muf) *n* **1** a clumsy failure to catch and hold a ball that comes into your hands: *The catcher's muff allowed the runner to score.* **2** an awkward handling or bungling.
v **1** fail to catch and hold a ball when it comes into your hands. **2** handle awkwardly or bungle: *My brother muffed his chance to get that job.* <origin unknown>

muf·fin (muf′ən) *n* **1** a small, round cake made of flour, bran, or cornmeal, egg, and baking powder, often eaten with butter: *bran muffin, blueberry muffin.* **2** an English muffin. <possibly German *muffen* small cakes>

muf·fle (muf′əl) *v* **muf·fled, muf·fling 1** wrap or cover up in order to keep warm and dry: *She muffled her throat in a warm scarf.* **2** wrap or cover in order to soften or stop the sound: *A bell can be muffled with cloth.* **3** dull or deaden a sound.
n something that muffles. <Old French *mouffle* thick glove>

muf·fler (muf′lər) *n* **1** a scarf worn around the neck for warmth. **2** a device attached to an automobile or similar engine in order to reduce the noise of the exhaust. **3** a thing used to deaden sound.

muf·ti (muf′tē) *n* ordinary clothes, not the uniform worn at work, such as that of a soldier or police officer: *The general appeared in mufti.* <origin uncertain>

mug (mug) *n* **1** a usually large and heavy earthenware or metal drinking cup with a handle, used without a saucer. **2** the amount a mug holds: *to drink a mug of warm milk before bed.* **3** *Informal* a person's face. **4** *Informal* a stupid or gullible person.
v **mugged, mug·ging 1** attack and rob a person. **2** make faces, especially in a silly or exaggerated way. <probably Scandinavian>

mug·ger (mug′ər) *n* a person who attacks another person with the intent to rob.

mug·gy (mug′ē) *adj* **mug·gi·er, mug·gi·est** warm and humid: *The weather was muggy.* **mug′gi·ness** *n.*

mug shot *Informal n* **1** a police photograph of a suspect. **2** any photograph of a person's face.

Mu·ham·mad (mů ham′əd) *n* a religious teacher and military leader who founded Islam in the 600s. Muslims believe that Muhammad as a prophet received God's final revelation, recorded in the QUR'AN. Also, **Mohammed**.

muk·luk (muk′luk) *n* **1** a high, waterproof boot, often made of sealskin, worn by Inuit and others in the Arctic. **2** a similar boot, made of leather, canvas, or other material. <Inuktituk *muklok* bearded seal>

muk·tuk (muk′tuk) *n* the thin outer skin of the BELUGA, used as food in the Arctic. <Inuktituk>

mul·ber·ry (mul′ber′ē) *n, pl* **mul·ber·ries** a tree or shrub with broad leaves and edible, berrylike fruit, or the fruit itself.
adj dark reddish purple. <Latin, from Greek *moron*>

mulch (mulch) *n* straw, leaves, or loose earth spread on the ground around trees or plants and used to enrich or insulate the soil.
v apply a mulch. <Old English *mylsc* mellow, moist>

mulct (mulkt) *v* **1** deprive of something by fraud or deceit: *He was mulcted of his money by a shrewd trick.* **2** fine or tax.
n a fine or compulsory penalty.

mule[1] (myül) *n* **1** the offspring of a donkey and a horse, especially of a male donkey and a mare. **2** *Informal* a stubborn person. <Latin *mulus*>

mule[2] (myül) *n* a slipper or light shoe that leaves the heel uncovered. <French = slipper>

mule deer *n* a deer of western N America that has long ears and a white tail with a black tip.

mul·ish (myū′lish) *adj* resembling a mule in being stubborn. **mul′ish·ly** *adv.* **mul′ish·ness** *n.*

mull[1] (mul) *v* think about something deeply and at length: *She mulled over her problems.* <origin uncertain>

mull[2] (mul) *v* make wine, beer, or cider into a hot drink, with sugar and spices. <origin uncertain>

mul·lah (mul′ə) *Islam n* a Muslim who is learned in Islamic theology and sacred law. <Arabic *mawla*>

mul·lein or **mul·len** (mul′ən) *n* a plant with coarse, woolly leaves and spikes of flowers.

mul·let (mul′it) *n, pl* **mul·lets** or (*especially collectively*) **mul·let** a food fish of small or medium size, with soft fins and a streamlined, rounded body, such as the **grey mullet** and the **red mullet**. <Old French, from Greek *mullos*>

mul·li·gan (mul′i gən) *n* a stew of mixed odds and ends of meat and vegetables. <origin uncertain>

mul·li·ga·taw·ny (mul′i gə ton′ē) *n, pl* **mul·li·ga·taw·nies** a soup made of chicken or meat stock, flavoured with curry powder. <Tamil *milaku-tanni* pepper water>

mul·lion (mul′yən) *n* a vertical bar between the panes of glass in a window. <Old French *moinel* middle> **mul′lioned** *adj.*

multi– *combining form* **1** with or consisting of several or many: *multicoloured.* **2** involving or affecting many: *multinational.* **3** several or many times more than: *multimillionaire.* <Latin>

GRAMMAR AND USAGE

Words beginning with **multi–** may be spelled with or without a hyphen.

In this dictionary a hyphen is not used: *multicoloured, multiculturalism, multimedia, multinational, multipurpose, multistorey, multitasking.*

mul·ti·cel·lu·lar (mul′tē sel′yə lər) *adj* with many cells.

mul·ti·col·oured or **mul·ti·col·ored** (mul′tē kul′ərd) *adj* with many colours: *a multicoloured cotton print.*

mul·ti·cul·tur·al (mul′tē kul′chə rəl) *adj* **1** of or with several distinct cultures existing within a society: *Canada is a multicultural country.* **2** designed for a society with several distinct cultures existing side by side: *multicultural programs.*

🍁 **mul·ti·cul·tur·al·ism** (mul′tē kul′chə rə liz′əm) *n* **1** the fact or condition of being multicultural: *She wrote a report on multiculturalism in the schools.* **2** a policy supporting or promoting the independent identities of several distinct cultural groups side by side within a society.

mul·ti·eth·nic (mul′tē eth′nik′) *adj* involving persons of many nationalities or peoples.

mul·ti·fac·et·ed (mul′tē fas′ət əd) *adj* with many different aspects, sides, or parts: *a multifaceted personality.*

mul·ti·far·i·ous (mul′tə fer′ē əs) *adj* with many different kinds: *multifarious talents.* <*multi-* + Latin *fariam* parts> **mul′ti·far′i·ous·ly** *adv.* **mul′ti·far′i·ous·ness** *n.*

mul·ti·lat·er·al (mul′tē lat′ə rəl) *adj* involving three or more groups, especially governments of different countries: *a multilateral trade agreement.*

mul·ti·lin·gual (mul′tē ling′gwəl) *or* (mul′tē ling′gyə wəl) *adj* **1** able to speak several languages well: *The company needs several multilingual sales representatives.* **2** expressed in or containing several languages: *a multilingual conversation, a multilingual dictionary.* **mul′ti·lin′gual·ism** *n.* **mul′ti·lin′gual·ly** *adv.*

mul·ti·me·di·a (mul′tē mē′dē ə) *adj* **1** to do with combining several media, such as slides with videos and posters, especially in education: *a multimedia presentation.* **2** *Computers* making use of audio, video, and textual material within a single piece of software.

mul·ti·mil·lion·aire (mul′tē mil′yə ner′) *n* a person whose wealth amounts to many millions of dollars.

mul·ti·na·tion·al (mul′tē nash′ə nəl) *or* (mul′tē nash′nəl) *adj* **1** to do with, or involving several nations: *a multinational empire, a multinational agreement.* **2** to do with divisions of a business operating in several nations: *a multinational food corporation.*
n a multinational company: *Several multinationals have already located in this area.*

mul·ti·play·er (mul′tē plā′ər) *Computers adj* designed for or involving several players of a game using different computers over the Internet or other network.
n **1** *Computers* a system or setting designed for or involving several players of such a game. **2** a compact disc player that can play several discs in succession.

mul·ti·ple (mul′tə pəl) *adj* of or involving many parts, causes, elements, or relations: *a woman of multiple interests.*
n a number or quantity that contains another number or quantity a certain number of times without a remainder: *Twelve is a multiple of three. The kilometre is a multiple of the metre.* <French, from Latin *multi-* + *plus* fold> **mul′ti·ply** (mul′tə plī) *adv.*

multiple choice *n* a style of test or questionnaire in which one of several possible answers must be chosen. **mul′ti·ple-′choice** *adj.*

multiple personality disorder *Psychiatry n* a rare form of mental illness in which a patient displays two or more different personalities that function separately, with different memories and perceptions.

multiple scle·ro·sis (sklə rō′sis) *adj* a disease of the nerve cells in the brain and spinal cord, which can eventually result in paralysis. *Abbrev.* **MS**

mul·ti·plex (mul′tə pleks′) *adj* **1** consisting of many elements in a complex relationship. **2** involving several messages sent along a single communications channel at the same time.
n a movie theatre that has several different screens. See also CINEPLEX.

M

a bat	e bed	i bid	o pot	u cup	th thin
ā cake	ē me	ī bite	ō go	ū rude	ᴛʜ then
à bar	ə about	ər over	ȯ for	ů put	zh measure

mul·ti·plic·i·ty (mul′tə plis′ə tē) *n, pl* **mul·ti·plic·i·ties** a great many: *a multiplicity of interests.*

mul·ti·ply (mul′tə plī′) *v* **mul·ti·plied, mul·ti·ply·ing** **1** increase in number or amount: *As we climbed up the mountain, the difficulties multiplied.* **2** take a number or quantity a given number of times. The number or quantity to be multiplied is called the **multiplicand**, and the number of times it is to be multiplied is the **multiplier**. Example: To multiply 16 by 3 means to take 16 three times, making 48. *Symbol* **x**. **mul′ti·pli·ca′tion** *n.*

mul·ti·pur·pose (mul′tē pər′pəs) *adj* with several different functions or uses.

mul·ti·ra·cial (mul′tē rā′shəl) *adj* involving several different peoples.

mul·ti·stage (mul′tē stāj′) *adj* **1** with several sections of a rocket or missile, each of which lifts it to a greater height before burning out and dropping off. **2** with a number of stages for the completion of a process: *a multistage investigation.*

mul·ti·sto·rey (mul′tē stōr′ē) *adj* with many storeys: *Multistorey buildings are not allowed on this street.*

mul·ti·task·ing (mul′tē task′ing) *n* **1** the act or practice of handling a number of different tasks at the same time: *An efficient employee must be good at multitasking.* **2** *Computers* a feature of a computer operating system allowing it to run more than one application simultaneously. **mul′ti·task′** *v.* **mul′ti·task′er** *n.*

mul·ti·tude (mul′tə tyūd′) *or* (mul′tə tūd′) *n* **1** a great many. **2 the multitude** a large group of ordinary people. <Old French, from Latin *multus* many>

mul·ti·tu·di·nous (mul′tə tyū′də nəs) *or* (mul′tə tū′də nəs) *adj* **1** very numerous. **2** including many parts, elements, items, or features. **mul′ti·tu′di·nous·ly** *adv.*

mul·ti·vi·ta·min (mul′tē vī′tə min′) *n* a pill containing a daily dose of several different vitamins and, sometimes, minerals.

mum[1] (mum) *adj* saying nothing: *I must keep mum about this and tell no one.* <Middle English>
mum's the word, keep silent.

mum[2] (mum) *especially UK, Informal n* mother.

mum[3] (mum) *Informal n* a chrysanthemum.

mum·ble (mum′bəl) *v* **mum·bled, mum·bling** **1** speak indistinctly, as a person does when the lips are partly closed. **2** chew with toothless gums or without making much use of the teeth.
n a mumbling. <Middle English *momelen*>
mum′bler *n.*

mum·bo–jum·bo (mum′bō jum′bō) *n* a foolish or meaningless ritual or form of language. <origin uncertain>

mum·mer (mum′ər) *n* a person who wears a mask, fancy costume, or disguise for fun, sometimes visiting from home to home. <Old French *momer* act in a mime>

mum·mer·y (mum′ə rē) *n, pl* **mum·mer·ies** **1** a performance of mummers. **2** a useless or silly show or ceremony.

mum·mi·fy (mum′ə fī′) *v* **mum·mi·fied, mum·mi·fy·ing** **1** preserve a dead body by embalming and wrapping it in cloth. **2** dry or shrivel up.

mum·my[1] (mum′ē) *n, pl* **mum·mies** a dead body preserved by embalming it and wrapping it in cloth, as practised by the ancient Egyptians: *Egyptian mummies have lasted more than 3000 years.*

ETYMOLOGY

Mummy comes through French and Latin from Old French *mum*, meaning "wax." Wax was used in embalming.

mum·my[2] (mum′ē) *especially UK, Informal* mommy.

mumps (mumps) *n* (*with singular verb*) a contagious disease caused by a virus, characterized especially by inflammation and swelling of the saliva glands below the ears and by difficulty in swallowing. <*mump* to grimace, because the disease causes the face to swell, making it difficult and painful to swallow or speak>

munch (munch) *v* chew vigorously and steadily: *A horse munches its oats.* <imitative>

munch·ies (mun′shēz) *Informal pln* **1** snacks or small items of food: *Everybody brought some munchies to the party.* **2 the munchies** an appetite, especially for snack food: *I've got the munchies because I didn't eat breakfast.*

munch·kin (munch′kin) *Informal n* a child or other small, endearing creature. <one of a race of small, childlike characters in L.F. Baum's *The Wizard of Oz*>

mun·dane (mun′dān) *adj* **1** ordinary and humdrum: *mundane matters of business.* **2** of this world, not of a spiritual one. <French, from Latin *mundus* world>

mung bean (mung) *n* an annual bean grown for forage or as a source of bean sprouts and other foods.

mu·nic·i·pal (myū nis′ə pəl) *adj* **1** to do with the activities of a city, town, or other municipality: *The provincial police assisted the municipal police.* **2** run by a municipality: *municipal affairs.* <Latin *munia* official duties + *capere* take on> **mu·nic′i·pal·ly** *adv.*

🍁 **municipal district** *Prairies and North n* a large municipality.

mu·nic·i·pal·i·ty (myū nis′ə pal′ə tē) *n, pl* **mu·nic·i·pal·i·ties** a city, town, county, district, township, or other area with local self-government.

mu·nif·i·cent (myū nif′ə sənt) *adj* extremely generous. <Latin *munus* gift + *facere* make> **mu·nif′i·cence** *n.* **mu·nif′i·cent·ly** *adv.*

mu·ni·tion (myū nish′ən) *n* **1** to do with military supplies: *A munition plant is a factory for making munitions.* **2 munitions** *pl* material used in war, such as weapons, ammunition, equipment, and supplies.
v provide with military supplies: *to munition a fort.* <French, from Latin *munire* fortify>

mu·on (myū′on) *Physics n* an unstable elementary particle with a positive or negative charge and a mass about 200 times that of an electron. <*mu meson,* from *mu* twelfth letter of the Greek alphabet + *meson,* its former classification>

mu·ral (myu̇′rəl) *adj* to do with a wall: *A mural painting covers one whole wall of that building.*
n a picture painted on a wall. <Latin *murus* wall>

mur·der (mər′dər) *n* **1** the intentional and unlawful killing of a human being by another: *There has never been a murder in this town.* **2** *Informal* something very hard, disagreeable, or dangerous: *The traffic was murder last night. The last part of the climb is murder.*
v kill a human being intentionally: *Is it possible that he murdered his brother?* <Old English *morthor*>
murder will out, a murder cannot be hidden. **b** a great wrong will be found out.
scream bloody (or **blue**) **murder,** *Slang* **1** scream or yell very loudly. **2** make a huge fuss.

mur·der·er (mər′də rər) *n* a person who is guilty of MURDER (def. 1).

mur·der·ous (mər′də rəs) *adj* **1** able or likely to kill: *a murderous blow.* **2** ready or intending to murder: *a murderous villain.* **3** causing murder: *a murderous plot.* **mur′der·ous·ly** *adv.*

murk (mərk) *n* darkness or thick mist, making it difficult to see. <Old English *mirce*>

murk·y (mər′kē) *adj* **murk·i·er, murk·i·est 1** dark and gloomy. **2** dark and dirty in a liquid: *a murky pond.* **murk′i·ly** *adv.* **murk′i·ness** *n.*

mur·mur (mər′mər) *n* **1** a soft, low, indistinct sound that rises and falls a little but goes on without breaks: *the murmur of a stream, the murmur of voices.* **2** a sound in the heart or lungs, especially an abnormal sound due to a leaky valve in the heart. **3** a softly spoken word or sentence.
v **1** make a soft, low, indistinct sound. **2** utter in a murmur: *The girl murmured her thanks.* <Latin> **mur′mur·ing** *adj.* **mur′mur·ing·ly** *adv.*

Mur·phy bed (mər′fē) *n* a bed that may be folded or swung up into a wall cabinet when not in use.

Murphy's Law *Humorous n* the supposed principle that everything that can go wrong will go wrong. <20c engineer E.A. *Murphy*>

murre (mur) *n* a black-and-white seabird related to the auk. <origin uncertain>

mus·cat (mus′kat) *n* a light-coloured grape with the flavour or odour of musk, or a wine made from this grape. Also, **muscatel**.

mus·cle (mus′əl) *n* **1** a band or bundle of human or animal tissue consisting of long cells that contract and relax to produce movement. **2** strength: *It takes muscle to move a piano.* **3** *Informal* power or influence, especially when based on force or the threat of force: *The organization has enough muscle to get its way with the city council.*
v **mus·cled, mus·cling** *Informal* move or gain by using force or the threat of force: *He muscled his way past the doorman.* <Latin *mus* mouse. A moving muscle was thought to look like a running mouse.>
muscle in, *Informal* force yourself in where you are not wanted: *She tried to muscle in on our meeting.*
not move a muscle, keep perfectly still.

mus·cle–bound (mus′əl bound′) *adj* with well-developed or overdeveloped muscles.

muscle car *Informal n* a car with much speed and power, often with flashy styling.

muscle shirt *n* a men's sleeveless, low-cut knit shirt with large armholes.

mus·cu·lar (mus′kyə lər) *adj* **1** to do with a muscle or muscles: *a muscular strain, muscular activity.* **2** with well-developed muscles: *a muscular arm.*

muscular dys·tro·phy (dis′trə fē) *n* a hereditary disease in which the muscles weaken over a period of time.

mus·cu·lar·i·ty (mus′kyə lar′ə tē) *n* muscular development or strength.

mus·cu·la·ture (mus′kyə lə chər) *n* a system or arrangement of muscles.

muse[1] (myūz) *v* **mused, mus·ing 1** be absorbed in thought: *The boy spent the afternoon in musing about being an astronaut.* **2** gaze thoughtfully. **3** say thoughtfully. <Old French *muser* to ponder> **mus′er** *n.*

muse[2] (myūz) *n* a spirit or force, especially one considered to be feminine, that inspires a writer or artist. <Old French, from Greek *mousa* Muse, one of the nine goddesses of the arts and sciences>

mu·se·um (myū zē′əm) *n* the building or rooms where objects of historical, artistic, scientific, or cultural interest are kept and displayed. <Latin, from Greek *mouseion*>

mush[1] (mush) *n* **1** *especially US* cornmeal boiled in water. **2** a soft, thick mass: *The heavy rain made mush of the old dirt road.* **3** *Informal* weak sentiment. <variant of *mash*>

mush[2] (mush) *n* **1** a command to advance, given to sled dogs. **2** a journey made by dogsled, especially while driving the team from behind the sled.
v journey across snow by dogsled. **mush′er** *n.*

ETYMOLOGY

Mush comes from Canadian French *marchons* from *marcher*, meaning "go" or "walk," used as a command to horses, sled dogs, and other animals.

mush·room (mush′ru̇m) *n* **1** the fruiting body of a fungus, often with a domed cap on a stalk and with gills on the underside of the cap, especially of a species that is edible. See CHANTERELLE, EDIBLE for picture. **2** a thing shaped or growing like a mushroom. **3** a person who or thing that appears or develops suddenly.
v **1** grow very fast: *Her business mushroomed when she opened the new store.* **2** flatten at the end of a bullet on impact. <Old French, from Latin *mussirio*>

mushroom cloud *n* a rapidly rising mushroom-shaped cloud of dust and debris that is formed after a nuclear explosion.

mush·y (mush′ē) *adj* **mush·i·er, mush·i·est 1** soft and pulpy: *a mushy apple.* **2** *Informal* weakly sentimental: *The children thought it was a mushy story.* **mush′i·ness** *n.*

a bat	e bed	i bid	o pot	u cup	th **thin**
ā cake	ē me	ī bite	ō go	ū rude	TH **then**
ä bar	ə about	ər over	ȯ for	u̇ put	zh measure

mu·sic (myū′zik) *n* **1** the art of putting sounds together in beautiful, expressive, or interesting arrangements. **2** such arrangements of sounds: *I like listening to music.* **3** a succession of pleasant sounds: *the music of streams, the music of the breeze.* **4** written or printed signs for musical tones: *This book has the words and music for the song.* <Old French, from Greek *mousike techne* art of the Muses. Originally referring to any or all of the arts, but later applied to music.>
face the music, *Informal* meet trouble boldly or bravely.
set to music, provide the words of a text with music.

mu·si·cal (myū′zə kəl) *adj* **1** to do with music: *musical knowledge, musical instruments.* **2** melodious and pleasant: *a musical voice.* **3** set to music or accompanied by music: *a musical comedy.* **4** fond of or skilled in making music.
n a stage entertainment or film in which a story is told through music, singing, and dancing as well as dialogue. **mu′si·cal·ly** *adv.*

musical chairs *n* (*with singular verb*) a party game in which players march to music around chairs, with one chair fewer than the players. When the music stops, all rush to sit down and the one left standing is out of the game.

🍁 **musical ride** *n* a performance in which mounted police or other riders do manoeuvres to music.

music box *n* a box or case containing an apparatus for producing music mechanically.

music hall *especially UK n* a theatre for singing, dancing, and comic routines.

mu·si·cian (myū zish′ən) *n* a person trained in music, especially one who earns a living by playing, conducting, composing, or singing.

mu·si·cian·ship (myū zish′ən ship′) *n* skill in playing, conducting, composing, or singing music.

mu·si·col·o·gy (myū′zə kol′ə jē) *n* the study of the forms, principles, literature, and history of music. **mu′si·col′o·gist** *n.*

music theatre *n* a modern type of stage performance incorporating singing and acting, on a smaller scale than OPERA: *Did you see* Phantom of the Opera? *No, I don't like music theatre.*

music video *n* a short videotape of an interpretation of a piece of music, especially for showing on TV. Music videos usually feature the musicians performing the song.

musk (musk) *n* a substance with a strong and lasting odour secreted by a male musk deer, used in making perfumes. <Latin, perhaps from Sanskrit *mushka* scrotum, from the appearance of the musk deer's musk bag>

musk deer *n* a small hornless deer of central Asia, the male of which has a gland containing musk.

🍁 **mus·keg** (mus′keg) *n* a bog, swamp, or marsh of northern N America. <Algonquian, probably from Cree *muskak* swamp>

🍁 **mus·kel·lunge** (mus′kə lunj′) *n, pl* **mus·kel·lunge** a large freshwater fish of the pike family. Also called **maskinonge, muskie** (mus′kē).
<Algonquian *mashkinonge* great pike>

mus·ket (mus′kit) *n* in former times, a light gun with a long barrel that was fired from the shoulder. <French *mousquette* a kind of hawk that looks speckled with flies. Weapons were often named after animals.>

mus·ket·eer (mus′kə tēr′) *n* a soldier armed with a musket.

musk·mel·on (musk′mel′ən) CANTALOUPE.

musk·ox (mus′koks′) *n, pl* **musk·ox·en** or (*especially collectively*) **musk·ox** a large, shaggy-haired mammal with massive horns, native to the tundra of northern N America and Greenland.

musk·rat (mus′krat′) *n, pl* **musk·rats** or (*especially collectively*) **musk·rat** a water rodent of N America with a musky smell and webbed hind feet. <Algonquian *muscascus*>

musk·y (mus′kē) *adj* **musk·i·er, musk·i·est** with an odour of musk: *a musky perfume.*

Mus·lim (muz′ləm) *n* a believer in Islam.
adj to do with Islam, its teachings, or its followers. Also, **Moslem**. <Arabic *aslama* one who submits>

mus·lin (muz′lən) *n* a cotton cloth in a plain weave, made in a variety of weights ranging from sheer to coarse, and used for dresses, sheets, or curtains.
adj made of muslin. <French, from Italian *mussolina* from Mosul, Iraq, where this cloth was first made>

muss (mus) *Informal v* rumple: *The child's dress was mussed.*
n disorder or untidiness. <variant of *mess*>

mus·sel (mus′əl) *n* a saltwater MOLLUSC, usually with a hinged shell that is often dark blue on the outside and pearly inside. See LIMPET for picture.<Old English *musle*>

muss·y (mus′ē) *Informal adj* **muss·i·er, muss·i·est** untidy or rumpled: *Your hair is mussy.*

must[1] (must) *v, past tense* **must** **1** an auxiliary or helping verb meaning: **1** be obliged to: *We must eat to live. I must go home soon.* **2** be certain to seem: *I must seem very rude.* **3** be supposed or expected to: *You must have that book.*
n something necessary: *This rule is a must.*
adj Informal necessary: *a must item, must legislation.* <Old English *motan* have to>

> **GRAMMAR AND USAGE**
>
> **Must have**, **could have**, or **may have** are often mistakenly written as *must of*, *could of*, or *may of*. The correct usage: *I must have forgotten my book.*

must[2] (must) *n* grape juice before or during fermentation into wine. <Latin *vinum mustum* fresh wine, from *mustus* new>

mus·tache or **mous·tache** (mus′tash) *or* (mə stash′) *n* **1** the hair that grows on the upper lip, especially when groomed by a man and not shaved smooth. **2** the hairs or bristles growing near the mouth of an animal. <French, from Greek *mustakis*>

mus·tach·i·o (mus tash′ō) *or* (mə stash′ē ō) *n* a large or fancy mustache. <Spanish, from Italian *mostaccio*> **mus′ta·chioed** (mus tash′ōd) *or* (mə stash′ē ōd) *adj.*

mus·tang (mus′tang) *n* a small, wild or half-wild horse of the N American plains. <Spanish, from Latin *miscere* to mix>

mus·tard (mus′tərd) *n* a yellow or brown powder or paste used as seasoning to give food a pungent taste, or the yellow-flowered plant whose seeds are ground for this seasoning.
adj dark yellow. <Old French, from Latin *mustum*>

mustard gas *n* a colourless, oily, poisonous liquid whose vapour is used in chemical weapons. <An impure form of the gas has an odour similar to *mustard*.>

mus·ter (mus′tər) *v* **1** assemble or gather together. **2** summon up a particular feeling, attitude, or response: *to muster up courage.*
n **1** an assembly or collection, especially a bringing together of people or troops for review or service. **2** the list of those mustered, or the number mustered. <Old French, from Latin *monstrare* to show>
muster in, enlist.
muster out, discharge.
pass muster, be inspected and approved.

must·n′t (mus′ənt) *contraction* must not.

mus·ty (mus′tē) *adj* **mus·ti·er, mus·ti·est 1** with a smell or taste suggesting mould or damp: *a musty room, musty crackers.* **2** stale or out-of-date: *musty laws.* <perhaps *moist* + *-y*> **mus′ti·ness** *n.*

mu·ta·ble (myū′tə bəl) *adj* liable to change: *mutable customs.* <Latin *mutare* to change> **mu′ta·bil′i·ty** *n.*

mu·ta·gen (myū′tə jen) *n* a thing that causes mutation in an organism by changing the DNA. **mu·ta·gen′ic** *adj.*

mu·tant (myū′tənt) *adj* to do with mutation.
n a new variety of plant or animal resulting from mutation.

mu·tate (myū′tāt) *or* (myū tāt′) *v* **mu·tat·ed, mu·tat·ing 1** change in form or nature. **2** produce a mutation (def. 2).

mu·ta·tion (myū tā′shən) *n* **1** a change. **2** a sudden change in the genetic structure of an animal or plant that produces a new feature or characteristic. **3** a new variety of animal or plant resulting from such a change. <Latin *mutare* to change> **mu′tate** or **mu·tate′** *v.*

mute (myūt) *adj* **1** not making a sound: *The little girl stood mute.* **2** unable to speak. **3** not pronounced. Example: The *e* in *mute* is mute.
n **1** a person who cannot speak. **2** a clip or some other device put on a musical instrument to soften the sound. **3** in full, **mute button** the device that turns off the sound from a TV, stereo, etc.
v soften the sound of a musical instrument: *He muted the strings of his violin.* <Old French, from Latin *mutus*>

mu·ti·late (myū′tə lāt′) *v* **mu·ti·lat·ed, mu·ti·lat·ing 1** cut, tear off, or destroy a part of a body: *Many of the victims of the accident had been badly mutilated.* **2** tear, break, cut off, or remove some part of something so as to damage or ruin it: *The book had been mutilated by someone who had torn some pages and written on others. The story had been mutilated by an editor.* <Latin *mutilus* maimed> **mu′ti·la′tion** *n.* **mu′ti·la′tor** *n.*

mu·ti·neer (myū′tə nēr′) *n* a person who takes part in a mutiny.

mu·ti·nous (myū′tə nəs) *adj* **1** rebelling against authority, especially the authority of a superior officer or officers on a ship or in the armed forces: *a mutinous crew.* **2** to do with mutiny: *mutinous talk.* **3** wilful or disobedient. **mu′ti·nous·ly** *adv.*

mu·ti·ny (myū′tə nē) *n, pl* **mu·ti·nies** an open rebellion against lawful authority, especially by sailors or soldiers against their officers.
v **mu·ti·nied, mu·ti·ny·ing** take part in a mutiny. <Old French *mutin* rebellious, from Latin *movere* move (against)>

mutt (mut) *Informal n* **1** a dog, especially a mongrel. **2** a stupid person. <from *muttonhead* stupid person>

mut·ter (mut′ər) *v* speak softly and indistinctly with lips partly closed, especially when expressing secret anger or discontent: *He was muttering the numbers to himself as he counted. "I'll get even with him," she muttered.*
n muttered words. <imitative> **mut′ter·er** *n.*

mut·ton (mut′ən) *n* the meat from a mature sheep. <Old French, from Latin *multon*>

mutton chop *n* **1** a slice of mutton, usually from the ribs or loin, for broiling or frying. **2 mutton chops** *pl* side whiskers shaped somewhat like mutton chops, extending from the ears to the side of the chin.

mu·tu·al (myū′chū əl) *adj* **1** done, said, or felt by each toward the other: *mutual promises, mutual dislike.* **2** each to the other: *mutual enemies.* **3** belonging to each of several: *our mutual friend.* <Old French, from Latin *mutuus* reciprocal> **mu′tu·al·ly** *adv.*

mutual fund *n* a financial fund that pools all the capital of its members and invests it in a variety of securities.

mu·tu·al·ism (myū′chū əl izm) *Biology n* a relationship between two species in which both benefit from the association. Compare PARASITISM.

muu·muu (mū′mū′) *n* a woman's long, loose, flowing gown that is gathered at the neckline. <Hawaiian>

Mu·zak (myū′zak′) *Trademark n* recorded background music played in public places or over the telephone. <alteration of *music*>

muz·zle (muz′əl) *n* **1** the nose and mouth of a four-footed animal, especially a dog or horse. **2** a cover of straps or wires for putting over an animal's head and mouth to keep it from biting or eating. **3** the open front end of a firearm's barrel.
v **muz·zled, muz·zling 1** put a muzzle on. **2** compel to keep silent about something; prevent from expressing views: *The government muzzled the newspapers during the revolt.* <Old French, from Latin *musum*> **muz′zler** *n.*
put a muzzle on, *Informal* prevent someone or something from expressing free opinions.

a bat	e bed	i bid	o pot	u cup	th thin
ā cake	ē me	ī bite	ō go	ū rude	TH then
ä bar	ə about	ər over	ȯ for	u̇ put	zh measure

M

muz·zle·load·ing (muz′əl lō′ding) *adj* loaded in a firearm by putting gunpowder in through the open front end and ramming it down.

MVP *Sports n* most valuable player.

my (mī) *adj* **1** a possessive form of I: *I hurt my arm.* **2** a word used as part of certain formal titles: *The horses are ready, my lord.* **3** *Informal* a word used before certain other words in addressing a person: *How are you, my boy?*
interj **1** *Informal* a word used as an exclamation of surprise, often together with another word: *My, what a big cat! My word!* **2** *Informal* a word used together with the name of some part of the body as an exclamation of disbelief or doubt: *Accident, my eye! It was plain carelessness.* <Old English *min*>

GRAMMAR AND USAGE

My and **mine** are possessive forms of **I**.

My is a determiner and is always followed by a noun: *This is my hat.*

Mine is a pronoun and stands alone: *This hat is mine.*

My·an·mar (mī′ən mar) *n* a country in southeast Asia, formerly called Burma. **My′an·mar′i·an** *adj, n.*

my·ce·li·um (mī sē′lē əm) *n, pl* **my·ce·li·a** (-lē ə) the main part of a fungus, consisting of interwoven fibres. <Latin, from Greek *mykes* fungus>

my·col·o·gy (mī kol′ə jē) *n* the branch of botany that deals with FUNGI. <Greek *mykes* fungus + *-ology*>
my·col′o·gist *n.*

my·e·lin (mī′ə lən) *n* a soft, white substance consisting of fats and protein that forms a protective sheath around nerve fibres. <Greek *myelos* marrow>

my·e·lit·is (mī′ə lī′tis) *n* inflammation of the spinal cord or of the bone marrow. <Greek *myelos* marrow>

my·na or **my·nah** (mī′nə) *n* a starling of Asia and Australasia that has a loud call and can sometimes imitate human speech sounds. <Hindi *maina*>

my·o·car·di·um (mī′ō kor′dē əm) *n, pl* **my·o·car·di·a** the muscular middle layer of the wall of the heart. <Greek *mys* muscle + *kardia* heart> **my′o·car′di·al** *adj.*

my·o·pi·a (mī ō′pē ə) *n* near-sightedness. Compare HYPEROPIA. See VISION for picture. <Latin, from Greek *myein* shut + *ops* eye> **my·op′ic** (mī op′ik) *adj.*

myr·i·ad (mir′ē əd) *n* a very great number: *There are myriads of stars.*
adj countless: *We saw myriad stars that summer night.* <French, from Greek *myrioi* ten thousand>

myrrh (mər) *n* a fragrant, gummy substance obtained from a shrub in the Middle East and Africa, used in medicines, perfumes, and incense. <Greek *myrra*>

myr·tle (mər′təl) *n* **1** an evergreen shrub with shiny leaves, fragrant white flowers, and black berries. **2** a low, creeping evergreen vine with blue flowers. <Greek *myrtos*>

my·self (mī self′) *pron* **1** the object of a reflexive verb with *I* as the subject: *I told myself that it didn't really matter.* **2** an intensive pronoun, used to emphasize the noun or pronoun it follows: *I will go myself.* **3** my usual self: *I'm sorry I shouted; I'm not myself today.*

mys·te·ri·ous (mis tē′rē əs) *adj* **1** hard to explain or understand. **2** suggesting mystery: *a mysterious look.* **mys·te′ri·ous·ly** *adv.* **mys·te′ri·ous·ness** *n.*

mys·ter·y (mis′tə rē) *or* (mis′trē) *n, pl* **mys·ter·ies** **1** something that is difficult or impossible to understand or explain. **2** a story, novel, or play of suspense, telling of the development and solution of a crime or crimes, or about strange or secret events: *a writer of mysteries.* **3** a religious idea or doctrine that human reason cannot understand. <Latin, from Greek *musterion* secret rites>

mys·tic (mis′tik) *adj* mystical.
n a person who seeks union with God or the absolute. <Latin, from Greek *mystes* one who has been initiated>
my′sti·cism *n.*

mys·ti·cal (mis′tə kəl) *adj* **1** with a spiritual meaning or reality that is beyond human understanding: *the mystical food of the sacrament.* **2** spiritually symbolic: *Many religions have mystical symbols.* **3** to do with with mystics or mysticism: *a mystical experience.* **mys′ti·cal·ly** *adv.* **mys′ti·cal·ness** *n.*

mys·ti·fy (mis′tə fī′) *v* **mys·ti·fied, mys·ti·fy·ing** **1** bewilder or perplex: *The magician's tricks mystified the audience.* **2** make mysterious or obscure.
mys′ti·fi·ca′tion *n.*

mys·tique (mis tēk′) *n* **1** a mystical or peculiar way of interpreting reality. **2** an atmosphere of mystery associated with a particular person, institution, or profession.

myth (mith) *n* **1** a legend or story, especially about the early history of a people or explaining some aspect of nature, often making use of supernatural beings or events. **2** an invented story, or imaginary person or thing: *Her wealthy uncle was a myth invented to impress others.* <Latin, from Greek *mythos*> **myth′i·cal** *adj.*
myth′i·cal·ly *adv.*

SYNONYMS

A **myth** relates to a people's religion or beliefs and is usually about a god, gods, or other superhuman beings. The original aim was to explain a religious belief or some aspect of life or nature.

A **legend** relates to a people's past and usually glorifies a hero, saint, great event, etc. It may contain an element of fact, or it may be wholly untrue.

my·thol·o·gy (mi thol′ə jē) *n, pl* **my·thol·o·gies** a body of myths relating to a particular religious or cultural tradition: *Greek mythology.* **myth′o·log′i·cal** *adj.*
myth′o·log′i·cal·ly *adv.*

Nn

n or **N** (en) *n, pl* **n's** or **N's** 1 the fourteenth letter of the English alphabet, or any speech sound represented by it. 2 the fourteenth thing in a list or series: *Part N of this guide gives information about the school dress code.*

n 1 in algebra, an indefinite number. 2 nano-.

N 1 nitrogen. 2 north; northern. 3 newton(s).

n/a not applicable.

naan (nan) NAN.

nab (nab) *Informal v* **nabbed, nab·bing** catch or seize suddenly someone who is doing wrong: *He was nabbed while robbing a convenience store.* <origin uncertain>

na·bob (nā′bob) *n* 1 a provincial governor under the Mogul empire in India. 2 a conspicuously wealthy person, originally one who had returned to Europe after making a fortune in India. <Hindi, from Arabic *nuwwab*>

na·cho (ná′chō) *n, pl* **na·chos** a small piece of tortilla chip, often topped with melted cheese. <Spanish>

na·cre (nā′kər) *n* mother-of-pearl. <French, from Arabic *naqqarah* shell>

na·dir (nā′dər) *n* the point in the sky directly below an observer, opposite the zenith. <French, from Arabic *nazir* opposite>

NAFTA (naf′ta) *n* in full, **North American Free Trade Agreement** an agreement to remove trade barriers, signed between Canada and the US in 1989, and extended to include Mexico in 1994.

nag[1] (nag) *v* **nagged, nag·ging** 1 find fault or annoy by peevish complaints: *If you nag her too much she won't do anything.* 2 continue to cause annoyance, irritation, or pain: *a nagging headache.* <perhaps Scandinavian>

nag[2] (nag) *n* a horse, especially one that is old and worn out. <Middle English>

Na·hua·tl (na′wat′l) *n, pl* **Na·hua·tl** or **Na·hua·tls** a member of a group of Aboriginal peoples native to S Mexico and Central America, or a language spoken by one of these peoples.
adj to do with these peoples or their languages.

nail (nāl) *n* 1 a slender piece of metal to be hammered into or through pieces of wood or other material to hold them together. 2 the hard, hornlike substance covering the upper side of the end of a finger or toe.
v 1 fasten with a nail or nails. 2 *Informal* be easily successful at: *I nailed the math test.* 3 *Informal* expose or catch a wrongdoer: *It took three weeks to nail the thief.* <Old English *nægel*> **nail′er** *n.*
hard as nails, *Informal* **a** tough and physically fit. **b** without pity or mercy.
hit the nail on the head, *Informal* guess or understand correctly.
nail down, *Informal* win, settle, or get with certainty: *He nailed down first place in the singing competition.*
on the nail, *Informal* at once: *to pay cash on the nail.*

na·ive (nī ēv) *adj* 1 simple and innocent. 2 showing a lack of informed judgment: *a child's naive ignorance.* <French, from Latin *nativus* natural> **na·ive′ly** *adv.*

na·ive·te (nī ēv′tā) *or* (nī ēv′ə tā′) *n* 1 the quality of innocence and simplicity. 2 lack of experience and judgment: *In her naivete, she thought she could go backstage at the concert.*

na·ked (nā′kid) *adj* 1 with no clothes on: *a naked mannequin in a store.* 2 stripped of the usual cover or protection: *The trees stood naked in the snow.* 3 plain and without the addition of anything else: *the naked truth.* <Old English *nacod*> **na′ked·ly** *adv.* **na′ked·ness** *n.*
to the naked eye, with the unaided eye alone.

Na·ko·da (nə kō′də) *n, pl* **Na·ko·da** or **Na·ko·das** 1 a member of a First Nations people living mainly in Alberta and Saskatchewan. 2 the Siouan language of these people.
adj to do with these people or their language. Also called **Stoney**.

Na·ko·ta (nə kō′tə) *n, pl* **Na·ko·ta** or **Na·ko·tas** 1 a member of a First Nations or Native American people living on the northern Great Plains, in Canada mainly in Alberta and Saskatchewan. 2 the Siouan language of these people.
adj to do with these people or their language. Also called **Assiniboine**.

nam·by–pam·by (nam′bē pam′bē) *adj* weakly simple or sentimental: *That poem is too namby-pamby.*
n, pl **nam·by-pam·bies** a namby-pamby person. <*Nam* short for *Am*brose Philips, 18c poet ridiculed by another poet, A. Pope>

name (nām) *n* 1 the word or words by which a person, animal, place, or thing is known: *Our dog's name is Chippy. The name of our country is Canada.* 2 a famous person: *He was a big name in the movie business.* 3 fame or reputation: *She made a name for herself as a writer.*
v **named, nam·ing** 1 give a name to: *They named the baby Mary.* 2 call, mention, or identify by name: *Three persons were named in the report. Can you name these flowers?* 3 mention or speak of: *She named several reasons for her decision.* 4 specify: *to name a price. They named the day for their wedding.* 5 nominate or appoint: *My sister was named captain of the softball team.*
adj with a reputation that is known by a name: *The plumber buys all his supplies from name manufacturers.* <Old English *nama*> **name′a·ble** *adj.*
call names, insult by swearing at.
in name only, supposed to be, but not really so.
in the name of, a on the authority of or acting for: *He bought the car in the name of his father.* **b** for the sake of: *We did it in the name of charity.*
know only by name, know only by hearing about.
name after (or **for**), give someone or something the same name as.
name of the game, *Informal* the main objective.

name brand *n* a product identified by the name of a well-known manufacturer: *I rarely buy name brands.* **name-brand** *adj.*

a bat	e bed	i bid	o pot	u cup	th thin
ā cake	ē me	ī bite	ō go	ū rude	TH then
á bar	ə about	ər over	ȯ for	ů put	zh measure

name–cal·ling (nām′kol′ing) *n* the act of calling a person by an insulting name or by making a damaging accusation. **name′-cal′ler** *n.*

name day *n* the day on which a child is given a name, the feast day of a saint for which he or she is named.

name–drop·ping (nām′drop′ing) *n* the habit of trying to impress someone by mentioning famous people's names in casual conversation in such a way as to imply that one has met them or knows them. **name′-drop′per** *n.*

name·less (nām′lis) *adj* **1** with no name: *a nameless baby.* **2** not marked with a name: *a nameless grave.* **3** not named or known: *a book by a nameless writer.* **4** unable to be named or described: *a strange, nameless longing.* **name′less·ly** *adv.* **name′less·ness** *n.*

name·ly (nām′lē) *adv* that is to say: *We had two pets, namely, a dog and a cat.*

name·sake (nām′sāk′) *n* a person or thing with the same name as another, especially one named after another: *I was proud to be the namesake of my uncle.*

Na·mib·i·a (nə mib′ē ə) *n* a country in southwest Africa. See the APPENDIX. **Na·mib′i·an** *adj, n.*

nan or **naan** (nan) *n* a flat, unleavened bread, usually cooked in a clay oven, common in Indian cooking. <Urdu *nan*>

Na·na·bo·zho (nan′ə bō′zhō) *n* a trickster hero of Algonquian mythology. Also, **Nanabush** (nan′ə bōzh′).

🍁 **Na·nai·mo bar** (nan′ī′mō) *n* a layered dessert of chocolate, nuts, butter, and sugar.

nan·ny (nan′ē) *n, pl* **nan·nies** **1** a woman hired to look after the children of a family. **2** a female goat. <*Nan* variant of *Ann*>

nano– *combining form* **1** one-billionth: *nanosecond.* **2** extremely small, or involving extremely small quantities or objects: *nanotechnology.* <Latin, from Greek *nanos* dwarf>

na·no·sec·ond (nan′ə sek′ənd) *n* a unit of time equal to one-billionth of a second.

na·no·tech·nol·o·gy (nan′ə tek′no′lə jē) *n, pl* **na·no·tech·nol·o·gies** the technology of electronic devices or circuits built from single atoms or molecules. **na′no·tech′no·log′i·cal** *adj.* **na′no·tech′nol′o·gist** *n.*

nap[1] (nap) *n* a short sleep: *to have a nap in the afternoon.*
v **napped, nap·ping** take a short sleep: *Grandfather often naps in his chair.* <Old English *hnappian* sleep lightly>
catch someone napping, find someone unprepared: *The test caught me napping.*

nap[2] (nap) *n* the soft, short, woolly threads or hairs on the surface of a cloth such as velvet and flannelette. <Dutch *noppe*> **nap′less** *adj.*

na·palm (nā′pom′) *or* (nā′pȧm′) *n* a highly flammable jelly made from fatty acids that, combined with gasoline, is used in certain bombs and flame-throwers.
v attack or destroy with napalm. <*na*(*phthenic*) and *palm*(*itic*) acids>

nape (nāp) *n* the back of the neck. <Middle English>

naph·tha (naf′thə) *or* (nap′thə) *n* a colourless, often highly flammable oil used as a fuel and in solvents. <Greek>

naph·tha·lene (naf′thə lēn′) *or* (nap′thə lēn′) *n* a white crystalline compound prepared from coal tar, used in mothballs and in making dyes.

nap·kin (nap′kin) *n* **1** a piece of cloth or paper used at meals for protecting the clothing or for wiping the lips or fingers. **2** a sanitary napkin. <Old French *nape* cloth>

Na·po·le·on·ic code (nə pō′lē on′ik) *n* the basis of civil law in France, Québec, and some other places, first established by Napoleon I.

nap·pie or **nap·py** (nap′ē) *especially UK n, pl* **nap·pies** a baby's diaper. <alteration of *napkin*>

narc (nark) *Informal n* a law-enforcement officer who investigates drug-related offences. <*narcotics*>

nar·cis·sism (nȧr′sis iz′əm) *n* obsession with one's own feelings, experiences, and needs. <Latin, from Greek *Narkissos*, a character in myth who fell in love with his own reflection> **nar′cis·sist** *n.* **nar′cis·sis′tic** *adj.* **nar′cis·sis′tic·al·ly** *adv.*

nar·cis·sus (nȧr sis′əs) *n, pl* **nar·cis·sus·es** or **nar·cis·si** (-ī) *or* (-ē) a spring plant with yellow or white flowers and growing from a bulb. <Latin, perhaps from Greek *narke* numbness. Some plants were thought to have narcotic properties.>

nar·co·lep·sy (nȧr′kə lep′sē) *n* a condition in which a person is overtaken by sudden, deep sleep at random moments. <Greek *narke* numbness + *lepsis* seizure> **nar′co·lep′tic** *adj, n.*

nar·co·sis (nȧr kō′sis) *n* a stupor, drowsiness, or unconsciousness brought about by a drug.

nar·cot·ic (nȧr kot′ik) *n* a strong drug, especially an illegal one, that affects mood or behaviour and is not used as a medicine.
adj with the properties and effects of a narcotic. <Old French, from Greek *narke* numbness>

nar·rate (na rāt′) *or* (nar′āt) *v* **nar·rat·ed, nar·rat·ing** **1** tell a story. **2** provide a spoken commentary to accompany a film, broadcast, or piece of music. <Latin *gnarus* knowing> **nar·ra′tion** *n.* **nar·ra′tor** *n.*

nar·ra·tive (nar′ə tiv) *or* (ner′ə tiv) *n* **1** a story: *His trip through the Rockies made an interesting narrative.* **2** the art of telling a story.
adj telling a story: *a narrative poem.*

nar·row (nar′ō) *or* (ner′ō) *adj* **1** of less than the average or usual width: *a narrow hallway.* **2** limited in extent, space, amount, range, or scope: *She had only a narrow circle of friends.* **3** with only a small margin: *a narrow escape.* **4** lacking sympathy or tolerance: *A person who says that all modern music is rubbish has a narrow point of view about music.*
v **1** make or become narrow: *The road narrows here.* **2** (*often with* **down**) fix the limits of: *At last we could narrow our search to three places. I've narrowed down the pizza toppings I want to mushrooms and extra cheese.*
n **narrows** *pl* the narrow channel connecting two larger bodies of water. <Old English *nearu*> **nar·row·ly** *adv.* **nar′row·ness** *n.*

nar·row·cast (nar′ō kast′) *v* broadcast a program, especially by cable, to a specialized audience.
n this form of broadcasting, or a program broadcast in this way. **nar′row·cast′ing** *n.*

Toothed whales vary greatly in size and appearance. The male **narwhal** can grow to be 3 m long, the beluga is slightly larger at 4.5 m, the killer whale (or orca) reaches about 10 m, while the sperm whale can be 18 m. Colouration also varies.

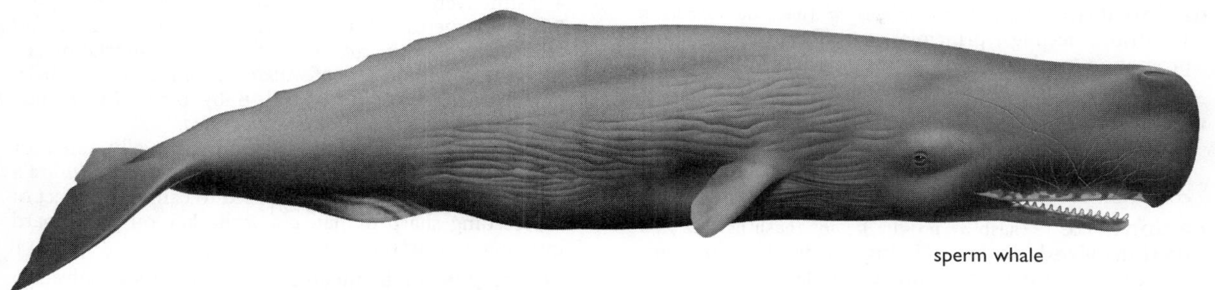

nar·row–gauge (nar′ō gāj′) *or* (ner′ō gāj′) *adj* with railway tracks less than the usual width.

nar·row–mind·ed (nar′ō mīn′did) *or* (ner′ō mīn′did) *adj* intolerant to other points of view. **nar′row-mind′ed·ly** *adv.* **nar′row-mind′ed·ness** *n.*

nar·whal (nȧr′wəl) *n* a small, toothed whale of the Arctic seas. The male has a long tusk extending forward from a tooth in the upper jaw. <Dutch and Danish, from Old Norse *nar* corpse + *hval* whale. The narwal's whitish skin colour resembles that of a corpse.>

nar·y (nā rē′) *Archaic or Humorous adj* (*before indefinite article*) not any: *We were out in the boat all morning, but nary a fish did we catch.* <*ne'er a* never a>

NASA (na′sa) *n* in full, **National Aeronautics and Space Administration** a US government agency responsible for space exploration.

na·sal (nā′zəl) *adj* **1** of, in, or from the nose: *nasal bones, a nasal discharge, nasal passages.* **2** expressed as or characterized as sound by the breath resonating in the nose: *a nasal voice.*
n a speech sound produced in this way. <Latin *nasus* nose> **na·sal′i·ty** *n.* **na′sal·ly** *adv.*

na·sal·ize (nā′zə līz′) *v* **na·sal·ized, na·sal·iz·ing** utter or speak with a nasal sound.

nas·cent (nas′ənt) *or* (nā′sənt) *adj* in the process of coming into existence: *a nascent tumour, nascent ideas of liberty.* <Latin *nasci* be born>

Nas·ka·pi (nas′kə pē) *or* (nə skap′ē) INNU.

Nass–Git·xsan (nas′git′ksan) *n* the language of the Gitxsan and Nisga'a.

na·stur·tium (nə stər′shəm) *n* a flowering plant with sharp-tasting seeds and leaves. <Latin, perhaps *nasus* nose + of *torquere* to twist, because of the sharpness of the flower's odour>

nas·ty (nas′tē) *adj* **nas·ti·er, nas·ti·est 1** highly unpleasant to the senses or to the mind: *a nasty smell, a nasty story.* **2** unpleasantly cold or wet: *nasty weather.* **3** ill-natured: *a nasty temper.* **4** harmful: *a nasty accident.*
n, pl **nas·ties** *Informal* an unpleasant or harmful person: *The nasties were captured at the end of the movie.* <Middle English *nasti*> **nas′ti·ly** *adv.* **nas′ti·ness** *n.*

na·tal (nā′təl) *adj* to do with birth: *a natal star, a natal day.* <Latin *nascii* be born>

na·ta·to·ri·al (nā′tə tȯ′rē əl) *adj* to do with swimming: *Ducks are natatorial birds.* Also, **natatory**. <Latin *natare* swim>

na·tion (nā′shən) *n* **1** a community of people occupying and possessing a defined territory, united under one government. **2** a people with the same descent and social and political history and, usually, sharing a common language: *The Scottish nation, the Québécois nation.* **3** a group of Aboriginal people sharing a culture, language, and heritage, especially one recognized as a band by the Federal Government. <Latin *nasci* be born>

GRAMMAR AND USAGE

Definition 1 for **nation** refers to people who have an independent government. This is its primary meaning in English. The secondary meaning, shown in definition 2, refers to people with common ties of birth, language, and culture. The frequency of the secondary meaning is increasing, and has been reinforced in Canada by similar uses of the word *nation* in Canadian French.

a bat	e bed	i bid	o pot	u cup	th **thin**
ā cake	ē me	ī bite	ō go	ū rude	TH **then**
ȧ bar	ə about	ər over	ȯ for	u̇ put	zh measure

na·tion·al (nash′ə nəl) *or* (nash′nəl) *adj* affecting or belonging to a whole nation: *national laws, a national disaster.*
n a citizen of a nation: *Each year many nationals of Canada visit the United States.* **na·tion·al·ly** *adv.*

National Aboriginal Day *n* June 21, proclaimed in 1996 as an annual day to recognize the contributions of the First Nations, Inuit, and Métis peoples to Canada.

National Assembly *n* in Québec, the group of representatives elected to the legislature.

na·tion·al·ism (nash′ə nə liz′əm) *or* (nash′nə liz′əm) *n* **1** patriotic feelings, principles, or efforts. **2** the desire, promotion, and plans of political independence for a particular country. **na′tion·al·ist** *n.* **na′tion·al·is′tic** *adj.*

na·tion·al·i·ty (nash′ə nal′ə tē) *or* (nash′nal′ə tē) *n, pl* **na·tion·al·i·ties** **1** the fact of belonging to a nation: *His passport showed that his nationality was Canadian.* **2** the condition of being a distinctive or independent nation.

na·tion·al·ize (nash′ə nə līz′) *or* (nash′nə līz′) *v* **na·tion·al·ized, na·tion·al·iz·ing** **1** bring land, or some branch of industry or commerce, under the control or ownership of a national government. **2** make distinctly national. **na′tion·al·i·za′tion** *n.*

national park *n* land owned by the Federal Government and kept for people to enjoy, or to preserve the wildlife in it.

na·tion·hood (nā′shən hůd′) *n* the condition of being a nation.

na·tion–wide (nā′shən wīd′) *adj* extending throughout the nation: *a nation-wide election.*

na·tive (nā′tiv) *n* **1** a person born in a certain place or country: *She is a native of Montréal.* **2** **Native** a member of a people who are descended from the original inhabitants of a region or country. In Canada, this name may be offensive to a First Nations, Métis, or Inuit person, and should be replaced by the name *Aboriginal.* **3** an animal or plant living in the place where it originated.
adj **1** born in a certain place or country: *My native land is Canada.* **2** associated with one's country or the nation to which one belongs: *Her native language is Italian.* **3** natural, as having been born in a person: *native ability.* **4** to do with the original inhabitants of a region or country: *native customs, native rights.* See also *n* (def. 2). Also, **Native**. **5** originating, grown, or produced in a certain place: *The Manitoba maple is native to Canada.* <Latin *nasci* be born> **na′tive·ly** *adv.* **na′tive·ness** *n.*

Native American *n* an Aboriginal person living in the US.
adj to do with the Aboriginal peoples living in the US.

na·tive–born (nā′tiv bôrn′) *adj* born in a particular place: *My father is a native-born Canadian, but my mother was born in Iceland.*

na·tiv·i·ty (nə tiv′ə tē) *n, pl* **na·tiv·i·ties** birth.

NATO (nā′tō) *n* in full, **North Atlantic Treaty Organization** an association of North American and European countries, formed in 1949 in opposition to the USSR.

nat·ter (nat′ər) *v* chatter at length on some unimportant topic: *We could hear her in the other room nattering away on the phone.*
n a lengthy casual conversation. <imitative>

nat·ty (nat′ē) *adj* **nat·ti·er, nat·ti·est** trim, tidy, and smart in dress or appearance: *a natty uniform, a natty young officer.* <origin uncertain> **nat′ti·ly** *adv.*

nat·u·ral (nach′ə rəl) *or* (nach′rəl) *adj* **1** in or caused by nature, not by human beings: *She preferred natural, not synthetic, products.* **2** instinctive or inborn: *It is natural for ducks to know how to swim.* **3** occurring in the ordinary course of events or circumstances: *a natural death.* **4** instinctively felt to be proper and fair: *natural rights.* **5** like or true to nature; not treated or disguised: *Is that your natural hair colour?* **6** free from affectation or restraint: *a natural way of walking.* **7** *Music* neither sharp nor flat in music: *C natural.* **8** by birth: *My mother adopted me after my natural mother died.*
n **1** a person who or thing that seems especially suited for something: *He's a natural for the football team.* **2** *Music* **a** a natural tone or note. **b** a sign ♮ used to cancel the effect of a preceding sharp or flat. **c** a white key on a keyboard instrument. **nat′u·ral·ness** *n.*

natural gas *n* a flammable gas that occurs dissolved in petroleum and is also found in separate natural deposits in the earth. It is used as a fuel.

natural history *n* **1** the study of nature, especially animals and plants, that is based on observation, not experiment, and recorded in popular, not academic, form. **2** a book or article on some aspect of nature.

nat·u·ral·ism (nach′ə rə liz′əm) *or* (nach′rə liz′əm) *n* a literary or artistic style characterized by accurate details and a highly realistic portrayal of life.

nat·u·ral·ist (nach′ə rə list) *or* (nach′rə list) *n* **1** a person who studies nature, especially animals and plants. **2** a person who uses naturalism in a literary or artistic work.
adj to do with naturalism. **nat′u·ral·is′tic** *adj.*

nat·u·ral·ize (nach′ə rə līz′) *or* (nach′rə līz′) *v* **nat·u·ral·ized, nat·u·ral·iz·ing** **1** grant the rights of citizenship to persons native to other countries: *My father is a naturalized Canadian, but my mother was born here.* **2** adopt a foreign word or custom: *"Chauffeur" is a French word that has been naturalized in English.* **3** introduce and make at home in another country: *The English sparrow has become naturalized in parts of Canada.* **4** regard or explain as natural rather than supernatural. **nat′u·ral·i·za′tion** *n.*

nat·u·ral·ly (nach′ə rə lē) *or* (nach′rə lē) *adv* **1** in a natural way: *to speak naturally.* **2** by nature: *a naturally obedient child.* **3** as might be expected: *Naturally, I accepted her gift.*

natural number *n* a positive whole number. Example: The numbers 1 and 2 are natural numbers; 0, –1, and –2 are not.

natural resource *n* a material such as water, that is supplied by nature and is useful or necessary to people.

natural science *n* a science that studies nature and the physical world, including biology, chemistry, physics, and geology.

natural selection *n* the process by which animals and plants best adapted to their environment tend to survive.

na·ture (nā′chər) *n* **1** the physical world, excluding things made by human beings. **2** the sum total of the forces at work throughout the universe: *the laws of nature.* **3** the instincts or inherent tendencies directing conduct: *It is the nature of children to be trusting.* **4** the qualities or abilities with which a person or animal is born: *It is the nature of birds to fly.* **5** the basic features of something: *Books of a scientific nature do not interest him.* **6 Nature** the personification of all natural facts and forces. <Old French, from Latin *nasci* be born>
by nature, because of the essential character of the person or thing.
of (or **in**) **the nature of,** with the essential features of something: *This essay is more in the nature of a speech.*

na·tur·ism (nā′chər iz′əm) *n* nudism. **na′tur·ist** *n, adj.*

na·tur·o·path (nā′chər ə path′) *n* a person who seeks to prevent or treat disease through nutrition, herbal medicines, exercise, or massage, rather than by surgery and drugs. **na′tur·o·path′ic** *adj.* **na′tur·op′ath·y** *n.*

naught (not) *n* nothing: *All his work went for naught.* <Old English *na* no + *wiht* thing>

naugh·ty (not′ē) *adj* **naugh·ti·er, naugh·ti·est** **1** disobedient or badly behaved, especially in children. **2** mildly rude or improper: *a naughty story.* <Middle English *naught* wickedness> **naugh′ti·ly** *adv.* **naugh′ti·ness** *n.*

Na·u·ru (na ū′rū) *n* an island country in the Pacific Ocean. **Na·u′ru·an** *adj, n.*

nau·se·a (noz′ē ə) *or* (nosh′ə) *n* **1** the feeling of sickness that one has when about to vomit. **2** extreme loathing or disgust. <Latin *nausea* seasickness, from Greek *naus* ship>

nau·se·ate (noz′ē āt′) *or* (nos′ē āt′) *v* **nau·se·at·ed, nau·se·at·ing** **1** cause a feeling that one is going to vomit. **2** fill with a feeling of disgust or loathing.

nau·se·ous (noz′e əs) *or* (nosh′əs) *adj* **1** feeling about to vomit. **2** disgusting or offensive. **nau′se·ous·ly** *adv.*

nau·ti·cal (not′ə kəl) *adj* to do with ships, sailors, or navigation. <Greek *naus* ship> **nau′ti·cal·ly** *adv.*

nautical mile *n* a nonmetric unit for measuring distance in sea navigation, equal to about 1850 metres. See also KNOT (def. 6).

nau·ti·lus (not′ə ləs) *n, pl* **nau·tilus·es** or (*especially collectively*) **nau·ti·li** (-lī′) *or* (lē) a marine animal related to squids and octopuses. The **pearly nautilus** has a spiral shell with a pearly lining. As it grows, the nautilus adds a new chamber to its shell. Each new chamber is closed off at the back, so the nautilus always lives in the outermost chamber.

Nav·a·ho or **Nav·a·jo** (nav′ə ho′) *n, pl* **Nav·a·ho** or **Nav·a·hos, Nav·a·jo** or **Nav·a·jos** a member of a Native American people living in New Mexico, Arizona, and Utah.

na·val (nā′vəl) *adj* of, for, or with warships or the navy: *a naval officer, naval supplies, the naval powers.* **nav′al·ly** *adv.*

nave (nāv) *n* the main part of a church or cathedral between the side aisles. <Latin *navis* ship>

na·vel (nā′vəl) *n* a place, usually a small rounded hollow in the middle of the abdomen, that marks where the umbilical cord was attached before and at birth. <Old English *nafela*>

navel orange *n* a seedless orange with a small depression at the top that resembles a navel in shape and contains a small secondary fruit.

nav·i·ga·ble (nav′ə gə bəl) *adj* capable of being travelled on, especially by ships or boats: *a navigable river, a road navigable by car in dry weather.* **nav′i·ga·bil′i·ty** *n.*

nav·i·gate (nav′ə gāt′) *v* **nav·i·gat·ed, nav·i·gat·ing** **1** sail, manage, or steer a ship, aircraft, or other form of transport: *navigate the seaway.* **2** plot the position and course of a ship, aircraft, or other form of transport. **3** move or find your way: *It was difficult to navigate along the icy streets.* <Latin *navis* ship + *agere* drive>

nav·i·ga·tion (nav′ə gā′shən) *n* **1** the act or process of navigating. **2** the science of determining the position, course, and distance travelled of a ship, aircraft, or spacecraft.

nav·i·ga·tor (nav′ə gā′tər) *n* **1** a person who is qualified to navigate: *The captain took on a special navigator to guide the ship through the dangerous waters. He served as a navigator in the air force.* **2** a person who sails the seas as an explorer: *a story of one of the early navigators.*

nav·jo·te (nȧv′jō tē′) *Zoroastrianism n* the initiation ceremony in which boys and girls are received into full membership.

nav·vy (nav′ē) *UK n, pl* **nav·vies** in former times, an unskilled labourer who worked on the construction of railways, canals, or roads.

na·vy (nā′vē) *n, pl* **na·vies** all the warships of a country, with their personnel. In Canada, the function of a navy is served by the Maritime Command of the Canadian Forces.
adj dark blue. <Old French, from Latin *navis* ship>

navy bean *n* the common white bean, dried for use.

Naw Ruz (nȧ rūz′) *Bahaism, Zoroastrianism n* the New Year festival celebrated at the vernal equinox.

nay (nā) *adv* not only that, but also: *We are willing, nay, eager to go.*
n a negative answer: *The nays outnumbered the yeas.* <Old Norse *ne* not + *ei* ever>

nay·say·er (nā′sā′ər) *n* a person who usually expresses a negative or pessimistic view.

Na·zi (nat′sē) *n* **1** a member or supporter of the **National Socialist German Workers' Party** led by Adolf Hitler, which governed Germany from 1933 to 1945. **2** a person who supports similar doctrines or policies, such as the idea of racial superiority and total obedience to a leader.
adj to do with the Nazis or their ideas. <German *Nationalsozialist* National Socialist> **Na′zi·ism** or **Naz′ism** *n.*

N.B. used in a written text to precede a note, showing that special attention must be paid to it. <abbreviation of Latin *nota bene* = note well>

a bat	e bed	i bid	o pot	u cup	th thin
ā cake	ē me	ī bite	ō go	ū rude	ᴛʜ then
ȧ bar	ə about	ər over	ȯ for	ů put	zh measure

The first **NBA** game took place November 1, 1946, in Toronto. (At that time, the league was called the BAA—the Basketball Association of America.) The New York Knickerbockers defeated the hometown Toronto Huskies 68–66. The most expensive regular tickets were $2.50.

NBA *n* in full, the **National Basketball Association** the major basketball league in the US and Canada.

NCO or **N.C.O.** *n* a non-commissioned officer.

🍁 **NDP** or **N.D.P.** New Democratic Party.

NE northeast; northeastern.

Ne·an·der·thal (nē an′dər tål′) *or* (nē an′dər thol′) *n* to do with an extinct human species that, up to 35 000 years ago, lived during the Ice Age in Europe.

Ne·a·pol·i·tan (nē ə pol′i tən) *n* **1** ice cream with layers of chocolate, strawberry, and vanilla. **2** a native or inhabitant of Naples, a city in Italy.
adj to do with this kind of ice cream or with Naples. <Latin, from Greek *neos* new + *polis* city>

neap tide (nēp) *n* the lowest level of high tide, occurring twice a month, just after the first or third quarters of the moon. Compare SPRING TIDE. <Old English *nepflod*>

near (nēr) *adj* **1** close by in time or space: *the near future. The library is quite near.* **2** closely resembling or similar: *a sadness near despair.* **3** short or direct: *Go by the nearest route.* **4** by a small margin: *a near escape.* **5** closer, especially on the left side of a vehicle or animal: *the near back wheel, the dog's near front paw.* Compare OFF (def. 6).
prep close to in space, time, or condition: *Our house is near the river. It's near time to go. He was near to collapse.*
adv **1** at or to a short distance or time away: *The car drew near. Evening was drawing near.* **2** almost: *He was near crazy with fright.*
v come near to: *The ship neared the land.* <Old Norse *na*>
near′ness *n.*
come near to (doing something), almost do: *I came near to forgetting my glasses.*
near at hand, a within easy reach: *My pen is always near at hand.* **b** not far in the future.

near·by (nēr′bī′) *for adv,* (nēr′bī′) *for adj. adv* close by: *They live nearby.*
adj near: *They live in a nearby house.*

Near East *n* the countries of southwest Asia, between the Mediterranean Sea and India. The term Middle East, which often refers to a broader area, is now more commonly used than Near East.

near·ly (nēr′lē) *adv* **1** almost: *I nearly missed the school bus.* **2** closely: *Anyone who isn't even nearly related has a claim on the estate.*

near miss *n* a narrow escape from danger.

near–sight·ed (nēr′sī′tid) *adj* with a condition of the eyes in which the visual images of distant objects come to a focus before they reach the retina, so that they are not clear. Compare FAR-SIGHTED. See vision for PICTURE. **near′-sight′ed·ly** *adv.* **near′-sight′ed·ness** *n.*

neat (nēt) *adj* **1** clean and in order: *a neat desk, a neat room, a neat school uniform.* **2** able and willing to keep things in order: *She's a very neat person.* **3** well-formed or in proportion: *a neat design.* **4** skilful or clever: *a neat trick.* **5** not diluted or mixed with anything, especially alcoholic liquor. <French, from Latin *nitere* to shine> **neat′ly** *adv.* **neat′ness** *n.*

neat·en (nē′tən) *v* make neat or tidy up.

neb·u·la (neb′yə lə) *n, pl* **neb·u·las** or **neb·u·lae** (-lē′) *or* (-lī′) a cloudlike cluster of gas, dust, or stars in outer space visible in the sky at night. <Latin = mist> **neb′u·lar** *adj.*

nebular hypothesis *n* the hypothesis, now largely rejected, that the sun and planets developed from a luminous, rotating mass of gas.

neb·u·lous (neb′yə ləs) *adj* **1** hazy, vague, or indistinct: *Our holiday plans are still somewhat nebulous.* **2** to do with a nebula. **neb′u·los′i·ty** *n.* **neb′u·lous·ly** *adv.*

nec·es·sar·i·ly (nes′ə ser′ə lē) *or* (nes′ə ser′ə lē) *adv* invariably or inevitably: *Leaves are not necessarily green. Wealth does not necessarily bring happiness.*

nec·es·sar·y (nes′ə ser′ē) *adj* required to be present, done, or achieved: *You won't be able to completethe lab without the necessary equipment.*
n, pl **nec·es·sar·ies** something essential, for example, food, clothing, and shelter. <Latin *necesse*>

SYNONYMS

Necessary applies to whatever is generally required: *Homework is a necessary part of school.*

Crucial can mean "vital" or "important": *It is crucial that we have enough volunteers for the dance.*

Essential means "indispensable" or "absolutely necessary": *Water and sunshine are essential to plants.*

ne·ces·si·tate (nə ses′ə tāt′) *v* **ne·ces·si·tat·ed, ne·ces·si·tat·ing** make necessary: *Her broken leg necessitated a surgical operation.*

ne·ces·si·ty (nə ses′ə tē) *n, pl* **ne·ces·si·ties** **1** the fact or quality of being necessary: *the necessity of eating.* **2** a basic requirement; something indispensable: *Water is a necessity.* **3** a condition or circumstance that forces one to act or accept something in a certain way: *a matter of necessity.*
of necessity, because it must be: *Of necessity, we left in the afternoon, since there is no bus service at night.*

neck (nek) *n* **1** the narrow part of the body that connects the head with the shoulders. **2** the narrow part of a garment that fits around the neck. **3** a narrow part like a neck: *A narrow neck of land joins the two islands, the neck of a bottle.* **4** the length of the neck of a horse or other animal, used to measure distance in a race: *The grey horse won by a neck.*
v Informal kiss and caress someone. <Old English *hnecca* back of the neck>
get it in the neck, *Informal* receive a verbal or physical defeat or punishment.
neck and neck, equal or even in a race or contest: *The two horses ran neck and neck for a kilometre.*
neck of the woods, *Informal* district or neighbourhood: *What are you doing up in this neck of the woods?*
risk your neck, put yourself in a dangerous position.
stick your neck out, *Informal* put yourself in a dangerous or vulnerable position, especially through a statement or action.
up to the (or **your**) **neck in,** *Informal* almost overwhelmed by: *I'm up to my neck in work.*

neck·er·chief (nek′ər chif) *n* a square of cloth worn around the neck.

neck·lace (nek′lis) *n* a string of beads, jewels, or links worn around the neck as an ornament.

neck·line (nek′līn′) *n* the line formed by the neck opening of a garment: *a plain neckline, a low neckline.*

neck·tie (nek′tī′) *n* a TIE (def. 7).

nec·ro·man·cy (nek′rə man′sē) *n* **1** a supposed foretelling of the future by communicating with the dead. **2** magic or sorcery. **nec′ro·man′cer** *n.*

ne·crop·o·lis (ne krop′ə lis) *n, pl* **ne·crop·o·lis·es** a cemetery.

ne·cro·sis (ni krō′sis) *n, pl* **ne·cro·ses** (-sēz) the death or decay of cells in body tissues or organs. <Latin, from Greek *nekros* dead>

nec·ro·tiz·ing fas·ci·i·tis (nek′rə tī′zing fash′ī′təs) FLESH-EATING DISEASE.

nec·tar (nek′tər) *n* **1** the drink of the gods in Greek and Roman mythology. **2** a delicious drink. **3** a sweet liquid secreted by plants, often within flowers, in order to encourage pollination by insects and other animals. Bees gather nectar and make it into honey. <Greek *nektar*> **nec′tar·like′** *adj.*

nec·tar·ine (nek′tə rēn′) *or* (nek′tə rēn′) *n* a peach with a smooth skin. See APRICOT for picture.

née or **nee** (nā) *adj* born. **Née** may be placed after the name of a married woman to indicate her birth name: *Mrs. Chris Lee, née Adams.* <French = born>

need (nēd) *n* **1 a** the lack of a useful or desired thing: *The loss by our team showed the need of practice.* **b** the thing itself: *In the desert, their need was water.* **2** a necessity or requirement: *There is no need to hurry.* **3** a situation or time of difficulty: *a friend in need.* **4** extreme poverty: *This family's need was so great that the children were underfed.*
v **1** have need of: *to need money.* **2** be necessary: *Something needs to be done to save it. He need not go. Need she go?* **3** be lacking something important: *Give to those that need.* <Old English *ned*>
if need be, if it has to be: *If need be, I'll go to the dance by myself.*

> **CONFUSABLES**
>
> **Need** means "must have": *I need some money if we're going to see a movie.*
>
> **Knead** means "press with your hands": *Kneading the dough is an important step in making bread.*

need·ful (nēd′fəl) *adj* needed or necessary: *a needful change.* **need′ful·ly** *adv.*

nee·dle (nē′dəl) *n* **1** a slender tool, pointed at one end with a hole at the other to pass a thread through, used in sewing. **2** a slender rod used in knitting. **3** a thin steel pointer on a compass or on an electrical device. **4** a slender tube with a sharp point, used for injecting or extracting something: *The doctor jabbed the needle into my arm.* **5** a needle-shaped rod that controls the opening of a valve. **6** the needle-shaped leaf of the fir, pine, spruce, or larch.
v **nee·dled, nee·dling** tease or incite: *The boys needled him into losing his temper.* <Old English *nedl*>
a needle in a haystack, something almost impossible to find.

nee·dle·fish (nē′dəl fish′) *n* a sea fish with a long, thin body and many sharp teeth.

nee·dle·point (nē′dəl point′) *n* embroidery in even stitches made on coarse, stiff cloth and used as a partial covering on furniture.
adj to do with such embroidery.

need·less (nē′dlis) *adj* unnecessary: *needless worry.* **need′less·ly** *adv.* **need′less·ness** *n.*

needle valve *n* a valve whose very small opening is controlled by a slender, needle-shaped rod.

nee·dle·work (nē′dəl wərk′) *n* work done with a needle, especially handwork such as embroidery, needlepoint, or fine hand sewing.

need·n't (nē′dənt) *contraction* need not.

needs (nēdz) *Archaic adv* because of necessity: *A soldier needs must go where duty calls.*

need·y (nē′dē) *adj* **need·i·er, need·i·est** lacking some of the necessities of life: *a needy family.* **need′i·ness** *n.*

ne'er–do–well (ner′dū wel′) *n* a person who is lazy and irresponsible.
adj lazy and irresponsible.

ne·far·i·ous (ni fer′ē əs) *adj* wicked or criminal: *a nefarious crime.* <Latin *nefarius* wicked, from *nefas* crime> **ne·far′i·ous·ly** *adv.*

a bat	e bed	i bid	o pot	u cup	th thin
ā cake	ē me	ī bite	ō go	ū rude	TH then
à bar	ə about	ər over	ȯ for	u̇ put	zh measure

N

ne·gate (ni gāt′) *v* **ne·gat·ed, ne·gat·ing** deny, contradict, or make ineffective: *His blunder negated all his previous success* <Latin *negare* say no>

ne·ga·tion (ni gā′shən) *n* **1** a denial or contradiction: *When she shook her head, we took it as a sign of negation.* **2** the absence or opposite of some positive thing or quality: *He said that darkness was the negation of light.*

neg·a·tive (neg′ə tiv) *adj* **1** saying no: *Her answer was negative.* **2** not positive or helpful: *a negative attitude.* **3** minus: *a negative quantity.* **4** with more electrons than protons: *a negative particle.* **5** showing the lights and shade or colour reversed from the original in a photographic image. **6** showing an absence of something, such as a substance or condition related to a disease: *The hospital tests were all negative.*
n **1** a word or statement that says no or denies: *"I won't" is a negative.* **2** the side that says no or argues against a question being debated. **3** a negative quality or characteristic. **4** a minus quantity or sign. **5** the negative element in an electric cell. **6** a photographic image in which the lights and shade or colour are reversed. **neg′a·tive·ly** *adv.* **neg′a·tive·ness** *n.* **neg′a·tiv′i·ty** *n.*
in the negative, expressing disagreement by saying no: *Most of the replies were in the negative.*

GRAMMAR AND USAGE

Two **negatives** should not be used together in a sentence: *I don't know nothing* should be corrected to *I know nothing* or *I don't know anything.*

Double negatives were used in and before Shakespeare's time, but they are no longer accepted in standard English.

neg·a·tiv·ism (neg′ə ti viz′əm) *n* a tendency to be negative or skeptical without offering an alternative.
neg′a·tiv′ist *n.* **neg′a·tiv·ist′·ic** *adj.*

neg·lect (ni glekt′) *v* **1** give little care, respect, or attention to: *Don't neglect your health. He neglected his lawyer's advice.* **2** leave undone or not attend to: *The maid neglected her work.* **3** omit or fail: *Don't neglect to water the plants.*
n **1** the act or fact of neglecting or disregarding: *His neglect of the truth was astonishing.* **2** a want of attention to what should be done: *That car has been ruined by neglect.* **3** the condition or situation of being neglected: *The dog suffered from neglect.* <Latin *neg-* not + *leger* pick up> **neg·lect′er** *n.* **neg·lect′ful** *adj.* **neg·lect′ful·ly** *adv.*

neg·li·gee (neg′lə zhā′) *n* a woman's loose, often sheer, dressing gown. <French>

neg·li·gent (neg′lə jənt) *adj* **1** given to or showing neglect. **2** careless or indifferent: *His negligent behaviour resulted in an accident.* **neg′li·gence** *n.* **neg′li·gent·ly** *adv.*

neg·li·gi·ble (neg′lə jə bəl) *adj* of little importance: *The difference in size between the two pieces of cake was negligible, so I chose the one closer to me.* **neg′li·gib·ly** *adv.*

ne·go·ti·a·ble (ni gō′shə bəl) *adj* able to be negotiated: *a negotiable price, a negotiable cheque.* **ne·go′ti·a·bil′i·ty** *n.*

ne·go·ti·ate (ni gō′shē āt′) *v* **ne·go·ti·at·ed, ne·go·ti·at·ing** **1** discuss and try to arrange terms, or bring something about in this way: *The rebels negotiated for peace with the government. An agent negotiated the sale of our house.* **2** find a way through, past, or over: *The driver negotiated the sharp curve by slowing down.* <Latin *negotiari* to do business, from *neg-* not + *otium* leisure> **ne·go′ti·a′tion** *n.* **ne·go′ti·a′tor** *n.*

Ne·hi·yaw (ne′hē yȧw′) CREE.

neigh (nā) *n* the sound that a horse makes.
v make this sound or one like it. <Old English *hnægan*>

neigh·bour or **neigh·bor** (nā′bər) *n* **1** a person who lives near another: *Their nearest neighbours are five kilometres away.* **2** a person who or thing that is near another: *The big tree brought down several of its smaller neighbours as it fell.* **3** a fellow human being.
v be near or next to. <Old English *neah* nigh + *gebur* farmer>

neigh·bour·hood or **neigh·bor·hood** (nā′bər hu̇d′) *n* **1** a district, especially one forming a community within a town or city: *an attractive neighbourhood.* **2** a district near some place or thing: *She lives in the neighbourhood of the mall.* **3** the people of a district: *The whole neighbourhood went to the party.*
in the neighbourhood of, about: *It will take me in the neighbourhood of five hours to complete this project.*

neigh·bour·ing or **neigh·bor·ing** (nā′bə ring) *adj* living or being near someone or something: *We heard the bird in the neighbouring woods.*

neigh·bour·ly or **neigh·bor·ly** (nā′bər lē) *adj* to do with neighbours who get along with each other, especially in a sociable or kindly way: *a neighbourly chat, a neighbourly atmosphere.* **neigh′bour·li·ness** *or* **neigh′bor·li·ness** *n.*

nei·ther (nē′ᴛʜər) *or* (nī′ᴛʜər) *conj* **1** (*with* ***nor***) indicating before the first of two or more possibilities that none is true or has happened: *neither a friend nor an enemy.* **2** not the one or the other of two people or things: *They did not go, so neither did we.*
adj, pron not the one or the other of two people or things: *Neither statement is true (adj). Neither of the statements is true (pron).* <Old English *ne* no + *hwæther* whether>

GRAMMAR AND USAGE

When **neither** is followed by a *plural noun*, the verb can be *plural*: *Neither of these CDs are new.*

When **neither** precedes two singular subjects, the verb is singular: *Neither the cat nor the dog is being quiet.*

nem·a·tode (nem′ə tōd′) *n* a worm with a long, unsegmented, round body, such as the hookworm or pinworm. <Greek *nematis* thread>

nem·e·sis (nem′ə sis) *n, pl* **nem·e·ses** (-sēz′) **1** a downfall resulting from immoral actions, or the inescapable punishment for them. **2** a person by whom or means by which someone receives a downfall or punishment: *When he saw his opponent, he knew he had met his nemesis, and could not win the contest.* <Greek *Nemesis*, the goddess of vengeance and punisher of excessive pride, from *nemein* give what is deserved>

neo– *combining form* new or recent: *neophyte.* <Greek *neos* new>

ne·o·con·serv·a·tive (nē′ō kən′sər′və tiv) *adj* to do with a version of conservativism in politics and society that arose in reaction to the liberalism considered to be prevalent in the 1960s.
n a person with neoconservative views.
ne′o·con·serv′a·tiv·ism′ *n.*

ne·o·dym·i·um (nē′ō dim′ē əm) *n* a rare metallic element. *Symbol* **Nd** <*neo-* + (*di*)*dymium*>

ne·o·fas·cism (nē′ō fash′iz əm) *n* a movement to restore the beliefs or principles of fascism.

ne·o·lith·ic (nē′ə lith′ik) *adj* of the later Stone Age, when polished stone weapons and tools were made and used: *neolithic man.* <*neo-* + Greek *lithos* stone>

ne·ol·o·gism (nē ol′ə jiz′əm) *n* a new word. <Greek *neos* new + *logos* word>

ne·on (nē′on) *n* an element that is a colourless, odourless gas, found in very small quantities in the atmosphere. Neon is often used in electric lighting because it gives off a glow when electricity is passed through it. *Symbol* **Ne** <Greek *neos* new>

ne·o·nat·al (nē′ō nā′təl) *adj* to do with newborn children or mammals (**neonates**): *a neonatal hospital unit.* <*neo-* + Latin *natus* born>

neo–Na·zi (nē′ō nat′sē) *n* a member of a party or movement seeking to restore Nazi doctrines and policies.
adj to do with such a party or movement or its members.
ne·o-Na′zi·ism or **ne·o-Naz′ism** *n.*

ne·o·phyte (nē′ə fīt′) *n* **1** a beginner or novice in a subject, activity, or belief. **2** a new convert, especially one recently admitted to a religious body. <Greek *neos* new + *phyton* plant>

ne·o·prene (nē′ə prēn′) *n* a synthetic rubber used to make water-resistant materials, paints, adhesives, etc.

Ne·pal (nə pol′) *n* a country in central Asia, north of India.
Nep′a·lese′ (ne′pol ēz′) *adj, n.*

neph·ew (nef′yū) *n* **1** a son of one's brother or sister. **2** a son of a brother or sister of one's spouse. <Old French, from Latin *nepos*>

ne plus ul·tra (nē plus′ ul′trə) *n* the highest or furthest point attainable, such as of excellence or achievement. <Latin = no more beyond>

nep·o·tism (nep′ə tiz′əm) *n* the showing of favour to relatives by someone with power or influence, especially by getting them jobs. <French, from Latin *nepos* nephew>

Nep·tune (nep′tyūn) *or* (nep′tūn) *n* a planet of the solar system, the fourth largest planet and eighth in order from the sun. See EARTH for picture. <*Neptune,* Roman god of the sea>

nep·tu·ni·um (nep tyū′nē əm) *or* (nep tū′nē əm) *n* a radioactive element similar to uranium, obtained as a by-product in the production of plutonium. *Symbol* **Np**

nerd (nərd) *Slang n* a socially incompetent, unfashionable person who is intelligent and obsessed with some intellectual or highly technical pursuit: *a computer nerd, a science nerd.* <origin uncertain> **nerd′y** *adj.*

nerve (nərv) *n* **1** a fibre or bundle of fibres that connects the brain or spinal cord to the muscles and organs of the body, and transmits impulses of sensation. **2** mental strength or courage: *The diver lost her nerve and wouldn't go off the high board.* **3** *Informal* rude boldness or impudence: *You've got a lot of nerve to ask me that!* **4** a prominent, unbranched rib of a leaf, especially in the leaf of a moss. **5 nerves** *pl* nervousness or anxiety.
v **nerved, nerv·ing** take on strength or courage in order to face a demanding situation: *The soldiers nerved themselves for the battle.* <Latin *nervus* sinew>
get on someone's nerves, *Informal* annoy or irritate someone.
strain every nerve, exert yourself to the utmost.

nerve cell *Informal n* a neuron.

nerve centre *n* **1** a group of neurons closely connected with one another and with a common function. **2** a source of leadership or energy, such as a control centre or headquarters: *Ottawa is the political nerve centre of the nation.*

nerve fibre *n* a long, threadlike fibre of a neuron that conducts impulses toward or away from the body of the neuron. A neuron contains many such fibres.

nerve gas *n* a gas used as a weapon, containing invisible particles that penetrate the skin and rapidly disables or kills by disrupting the transmission of nerve impulses.

nerve·less (nərv′lis) *adj* **1** without strength or vigour: *The cup dropped from his nerveless hand.* **2** without NERVES (def. 5). **nerve′less·ly** *adv.*

nerve–rack·ing or **nerve–wrack·ing** (nərv′rak′ing) *adj* causing great stress or anxiety: *a nerve-racking experience.*

nerv·ous (nər′vəs) *adj* **1** easily anxious, apprehensive, or alarmed: *a nervous patient, a nervous tapping of the fingers.* **2** resulting from anxiety or anticipation as a feeling or reaction: *nervous energy.* **3** to do with the nerves: *The brain is a part of the nervous system.* **4** related to or affecting the nerves: *a nervous disorder.* **ner′vous·ly** *adv.* **nerv′ous·ness** *n.*

SYNONYMS

Nervous suggests being uneasy or afraid of something: *He felt nervous just before the play.*

Apprehensive suggests being fearful about something that may happen: *The woman was apprehensive driving in the freezing rain.*

Tense can mean "stressed out": *He was so tense before the final game that he wasn't able to relax.*

nervous breakdown *n* a period of mental illness or instability resulting from severe depression, stress, or anxiety.

a bat	e bed	i bid	o pot	u cup	th thin
ā cake	ē me	ī bite	ō go	ū rude	ᴛʜ then
à bar	ə about	ər over	ȯ for	u̇ put	zh measure

N

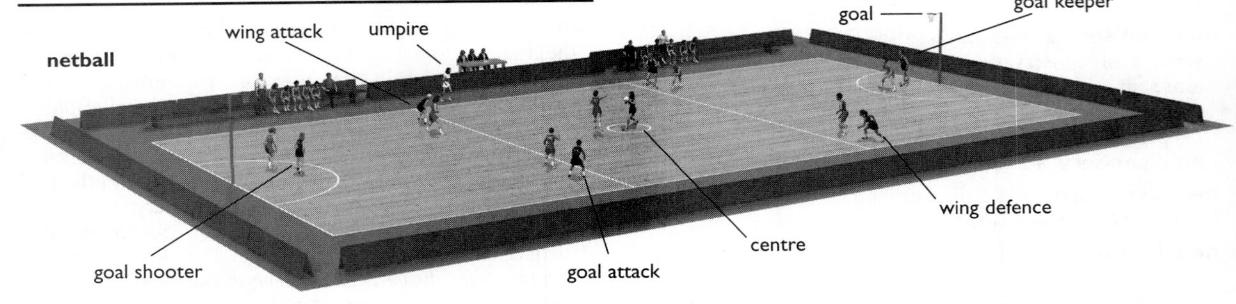

In **netball**, there is an emphasis on quick passes. A player can tip or hit the ball with one or two hands, but she cannot use a closed fist.

When shooting at the ring, a player holds the ball high with open hands and then throws, extending her knees. The netball ring is higher and smaller than a basketball hoop.

nervous system *n* the system of neurons and fibres that transmits nerve impulses to different parts of the body in a human being or animal.

nerv·y (nər′vē) *adj* **nerv·i·er, nerv·i·est 1** rude and bold: *It was nervy of her to tell me how I should behave.* **2** showing courage or firmness: *Climbing the rock face was a nervy thing to do.*

–ness *suffix* a quality, state, or condition: *kindness, sadness, wildness.* <Old English>

GRAMMAR AND USAGE

The suffix **–ness** is called a productive suffix and can be freely added to any adjective to form a new word.

nest (nest) *n* **1** a structure or place used by birds for laying eggs and sheltering young. **2** a place used by a mammal, reptile, fish, or insect to breed or shelter. **3** a snug retreat or resting place: *The little girl cuddled down in a nest among the sofa cushions.* **4** a place where undesirable or harmful people gather: *a nest of thieves.* **5** a set or series, often from large to small, such that each fits within another: *a nest of drinking cups.*
v **1** build and use a nest. **2** place or fit together in a nest: *The chairs were nested and placed along the wall.* **3** *Computers* place an object or element in a certain position in a hierarchy, especially in a lower position. <Old English>

nest egg *n* **1** a thing, usually a sum of money, set aside as a reserve to be drawn on in the future: *When he got married, he had already saved quite a nest egg.* **2** a natural or artificial egg left in a nest to induce a hen to lay eggs there.

nes·tle (nes′əl) *v* **nes·tled, nes·tling** (nes′ling.) **1** settle oneself, or be situated comfortably and cozily: *nestle down in a big chair, a house nestling among trees.* **2** press close in love or for comfort: *The mother nestled her baby in her arms.* <Old English *nestlian*> **nes′tler** *n.*

nest·ling (nes′tling) *n* a bird too young to leave the nest.

net[1] (net) *n* **1** an open fabric made of string, wire, etc., knotted together so as to leave holes regularly arranged, and made for a special purpose: *a fishing net, a tennis net.* **2 a** *Hockey, Soccer, Lacrosse* a piece of net supported by a frame, used as part of a goal. **b** *Volleyball, Tennis, Badminton, etc.* a piece of net supported by a cord between posts that divides the playing area. **3** a lacelike cloth, such as that for curtains or veils. **4 a** a communications network. **b the Net** the Internet. **5** *Mathematics* a two-dimensional shape that can be folded into a three-dimensional object.
v **net·ted, net·ting 1** catch in a net: *to net a fish.* **2** cover, confine, or protect with a net. **3** construct a net. **4** *Tennis, Volleyball, etc.* hit a ball into the net. <Old English *nett*> **net′like′** *adj.*

net[2] (net) *adj* after all reductions or additions have been made: *a net gain, the net weight, the net result.*
n a net amount of something, such as profit or weight.
v **net·ted, net·ting** gain as a clear profit: *The sale netted me a good gain.* <French>

net·ball (net′bol′) *n* a game similar to basketball, traditionally played by women. Players may not walk or run with the ball, but must throw it or hand it to a teammate.

neth·er (neᴛʜ′ər) *adj* lower in position: *nether garments, nether regions.* <Old English *neothera*>

Neth·er·lands (neᴛʜ′ər ləndz) *n* a country in northwest Europe on the North Sea. This country was formerly called Holland. See the APPENDIX, and see DUTCH.

neth·er·most (neᴛʜ′ər mōst′) *adj* lowest in position.

net·i·quette (net′ē ket′) *Informal n* good manners in communicating over the Internet. <*(Inter)net* + *(et)iquette*>

net·i·zen or **Net·i·zen** (net′ə zen) *Informal n* a person who is familiar with the Internet and uses it frequently. <*(Inter)net* + *(cit)izen*>

Net·sil·ik (net sil′ik) *n, pl* **Net·sil·ik** a member of an Inuit people living in the central Arctic west of Hudson Bay, mostly on the northern coast.

net·ting (net′ing) *n* **1** a netted or meshed material: *mosquito netting, wire netting.* **2** the process of making a net or netting.
v present participle of NET.

net·tle (net′əl) *n* a plant with jagged leaves and hairs that sting the skin when touched.
v **net·tled, net·tling** irritate or annoy: *She was nettled by her friend's frequent interruptions.* <Old English *netele*>

net·work (net′wərk′) *n* **1 a** an arrangement of intersecting vertical and horizontal lines; a grid. **b** a combination or system of lines or channels that resembles this: *a network of vines, a network of highways.* **2** a group of radio or TV stations, so connected that the same schedule of programs may be broadcast by all. **3** *Computers* a system of communication links interconnecting a set of computers and peripheral devices.
v **1** connect into a network. **2** interact with other people to exchange ideas or further one's own interests.

neu·ral (nyů′rəl) *or* (nů′rəl) *adj* to do with a nerve or the nervous system. <Greek *neuron* nerve>

neu·ral·gia (nyů ral′jə) *or* (nů ral′jə) *n* a sharp, usually intermittent pain along the course of a nerve, especially in the head or face. **neu·ral′gic** *adj.*

neu·ri·tis (nyů rī′tis) *or* (nů rī′tis) *n* inflammation of a nerve or nerves, usually causing pain or loss of function.

neu·rol·o·gy (nyů rol′ə jē) *or* (nů rol′ə jē) *n* the study of the nervous system and its disorders. **neu·ro·log′ic·al** *adj.* **neu·rol′o·gist** *n.*

neu·ron (nyů′ron) *or* (nů′ron) *n* a specialized cell of the body that transmits nerve impulses. Also informally called **nerve cell**. <Greek = nerve>

neu·ro·sis (nyů rō′sis) *or* (nů rō′sis) *n, pl* **neu·ro·ses** (-sēz) a usually mild mental disorder caused, not by disease, but by stress, fear, or anxiety. <Greek *neuron* nerve>

neu·ro·sur·ger·y (nyů′rō′sər jə rē) *or* (nů′rō′sər jə rē) *n* surgery directly involving the nervous system, especially the brain and spinal cord. **neu′ro·sur′geon** *n.* **neu′ro·sur′gi·cal** *adj.*

neu·rot·ic (nyů rot′ik) *or* (nů rot′ik) *adj* **1** to do with a neurosis. **2** *Informal* with or showing a tendency to be obsessive, tense, anxious, or overly sensitive.
n a neurotic person. **neu·rot′i·cal·ly** *adv.* **neu·rot′i·cism** *n.*

neu·ro·trans·mit·ter (nyů′ro trans′mit tər) *or* (nů′ro trans′mit tər); (nyů′ro tranz′mit tər) *or* (nů′ro tranzs′mit tər) *n* a chemical substance that helps impulses to be transmitted and transferred at the end of a nerve fibre.

neu·ter (nyū′tər) *or* (nū′tər) *adj* **1** of a word in some languages, neither masculine nor feminine. **2 a** of an animal, with no sex organs, or with sex organs that are not fully developed. **b** of a plant, without stamens or pistils.
n **1** a neuter word. **2** the neuter gender. **3** an animal or plant that is neuter. <Latin *ne-* not + *uter* either>

neu·tral (nyū′trəl) *or* (nū′trəl) *adj* **1 a** not taking part in a quarrel, contest, or war: *Ireland was neutral in World War II.* **b** of or belonging to a neutral country or neutral zone: *a neutral port.* **2** being neither one thing nor the other. **3** without positive features or characteristics: *I prefer neutral colours.* **4** neither acid nor alkaline. **5** neither positive nor negative as electricity.
n **1** a neutral person or country. **2** the position of gears when they do not transmit motion from the engine to the wheels or other working parts: *Never leave a car in neutral.* <Latin *ne-* not + *uter* either>

neu·tral·ism (nyū′trə liz′əm) *or* (nū′trə liz′əm) *n* a policy, or the support of a policy, of remaining NEUTRAL (def. 1), especially in international conflicts. **neu′tra·list** *adj, n.*

neu·tral·i·ty (nyū tral′ə tē) *or* (nū tral′ə tē) *n* the policy of not taking part in a quarrel, contest, or war.

neu·tral·ize (nyū′trə līz′) *or* (nū′trə līz′) *v* **neu·tral·ized, neu·tral·iz·ing** take away the power or effect of something by using an opposite power or force: *The dim light neutralized the bright colours in this room.* **neu′tral·i·za′tion** *n.* **neu′tral·i·zer** *n.*

neu·tri·no (nyū trē′nō) *or* (nū trē′nō) *n* a subatomic particle that has no electric charge and almost no mass, and that interacts rarely with matter. <Italian *neutro* neutral>

neu·tron (nyū′tron) *or* (nū′tron) *n* a subatomic particle of about the same mass as a proton but with no electric charge, found in the nucleus of every kind of atom except that of ordinary hydrogen. See ATOM for picture. <*neutral* + *-on*>

neutron bomb *n* a nuclear bomb designed to produce a large number of neutrons that cause intense radiation resulting in loss of life but relatively little destruction of property.

neutron star *n* a dense celestial object with a very small radius, thought to be composed of the remains of a collapsed supernova.

nev·er (nev′ər) *adv* **1** not ever: *He never had to work for a living.* **2** in no case: *She was never the better for her experience. If we're careful, they'll be never the wiser.* <Old English *ne* not + *æfre* ever>
never mind, pay no attention to: *Never mind the noise. Never mind your coats; it's warm outside.*

GRAMMAR AND USAGE

Although in informal speech **never** is sometimes used to mean "not," you should avoid this usage in formal writing. It is preferable to write *I'm sure I didn't see her standing there,* rather than *I'm sure I never saw her standing there.*

a bat	e bed	i bid	o pot	u cup	th thin
ā cake	ē me	ī bite	ō go	ū rude	ᴛʜ then
à bar	ə about	ər over	ȯ for	ů put	zh measure

N

nev·er·more (nev′ər mȯr′) *adv* never again.

nev·er·the·less (nev′ər ᴛʜə les′) *adv* however: *She was very tired; nevertheless, she kept on working.*

new (nyū) *or* (nū) *adj* **1** having been produced only a short time ago: *a new invention, a new idea.* **2** now first used: *I've found a new way to get to school.* **3** beginning again or renewed: *the new moon, to resume running with new strength.* **4** different or changed: *After taking a shower, he felt like a new person.* **5** not familiar: *It was a new situation for me.* **6** having just reached a position: *a new arrival.* **7 New** being the later or latest of two or more things of the same kind: *New France.* **8** having been known only a short time, though existing before: *a new galaxy. The detective uncovered several new facts.* **9** recently acquired: *a new T-shirt, a new video.*
adv (*usually in compounds*) recently or lately: *new-mown hay, a new-found friend.* <Old English *neowe*>
new′ness *n.*
the new ——, referring to a fashion that has recently replaced another fashion: *Grey is the new black.*

> **CONFUSABLES**
>
> **New** means "unused": *She bought a new computer to replace her old one.*
>
> **Knew** means "understood": *He knew how to solve the problem.*

New Age *n* **1** a cultural movement of the late 1900s, characterized by sensitivity to spiritual forces, holistic beliefs, and a mystical approach to nature. **2** a style of popular instrumental music, often incorporating nature sounds, designed to produce a serene mood.
New Ager *n.*

new·born (nyū′bȯrn′) *or* (nū′bȯrn′) *adj* **1** recently or only just born: *a newborn baby.* **2** ready to start a new existence: *a newborn neighbourhood.*

New Bruns·wick (brun′zwik) *n* an eastern Canadian province, between Québec and Nova Scotia. New Brunswick is one of the ATLANTIC PROVINCES.
Abbrev. **N.B.**; postal symbol **NB**; URL **www.gov.nb.ca**
See also MARITIME PROVINCES.
adj to do with New Brunswick: *New Brunswick clams.*
New Bruns′wick·er *n.*

New Cal·e·do·ni·a (kal′ə dō′nē ə) *n* an early name for that part of British Columbia lying between the Rocky Mountains and the Coast Range.

🍁 **New Canadian** *n* a person who has recently arrived in Canada from another country and has become a Canadian citizen or plans to become one.

new·com·er (nyū′kum′ər) *or* (nū′kum′ər) *n* a person who has just arrived or who arrived not long ago.

🍁 **New Democratic Party** *n* one of the registered political parties of Canada. *Abbrev.* **NDP**

new·el (nyū′əl) *or* (nū′əl) *n* **1** the post at the top or bottom of a staircase that supports the railing. **2** the central post of a winding staircase.

New England *n* the northeast part of the US, consisting of Vermont, Maine, New Hampshire, Massachusetts, Rhode Island, and Connecticut. **New Eng′land·er** *n.*

new·fan·gled (nyū′fang′gəld) *or* (nū′fang′gəld) *adj* lately come into fashion: *He's always coming up with newfangled ideas.*

🍁 **New·fie** (nyū′fē) *or* (nū′fē) *Informal n* a Newfoundlander.
adj to do with Newfoundland or Newfoundlanders.
Also, **Newfy**.

New·found·land (nyū′fənd land′) *or* (nū′fənd land′); (nyū′fənd lənd) *or* (nū′fənd lənd) *n* a large island off the northeast coast of Canada, forming part of the province of Newfoundland and Labrador.
adj to do with Newfoundland: *Newfoundland fish stocks.*
New′found·land′er *n.*

Newfoundland and Labrador *n* the easternmost province of Canada. It is one of the ATLANTIC PROVINCES.
Abbrev. **N.L.**; postal symbol **NL**; URL **www.gov.nl.ca**
See also MARITIME PROVINCES.

🍁 **Newfoundland dog** *n* a large dog with a coarse, shaggy, usually black coat. This powerful swimming dog originated in Newfoundland, where it was trained to rescue people from drowning.

New France *n* the name of the territory in N America belonging to France from 1609 to 1763. Among other regions, it included Québec, Acadia, and the Louisiana Territory.

new·ly (nyū′lē) *or* (nū′lē) *adv* **1** lately or recently: *newly discovered.* **2** once again: *newly painted walls.*

new·ly·wed (nyū′lē wed′) *or* (nū′lē wed′) *n* a newly married person.

new moon *n* **1** the phase of the moon when it is between the earth and the sun, and the moon is invisible or visible only as a slender crescent. **2** the moon in this phase, or the time during which it is.

news (nyūz) *or* (nūz) *n* **1** (*with singular verb*) information about something that has just happened or will soon happen: *The news that our teacher was leaving made us sad. The news from the various districts is sent to a central office.* **2** a report of a current happening or happenings in a newspaper, or on radio, TV, or the Internet: *I turned off the radio when the news was finished.*
break the news, make something known for the first time.

news·boy (nyūz′boi′) *or* (nūz′boi′) *n* especially in former times, a boy who sells or delivers newspapers.

news·cast (nyūz′kast′) *or* (nūz′kast′) *n* a radio or TV program devoted to news reports. <*news* + (*broad*)*cast*>
news′cast′er *n.*

news·group (nyūz′grūp′) *or* (nūz′grūp′) *n* a group of Internet users who can view and exchange e-mail messages at one site on a topic of shared interest: *a stop-smoking newsgroup.*

news·let·ter (nyūz′let′ər) *or* (nūz′let′ər) *n* a bulletin of topical news issued periodically to the members of a family, organization, or business.

news·man (nyū′zmən′) *or* (nū′zmən′) *n, pl* **news·men** (-men′) a male reporter, journalist, or broadcaster.

news·pa·per (nyūz′pā′pər) *or* (nūz′pā′pər); (nyū′spā′pər)*or* (nū′spā′pər) *n* **1** a publication consisting of folded, unstapled sheets of paper, usually printed daily or weekly and containing news, features, correspondence, advertisements, and other reading matter. **2** the company or organization that publishes a newspaper: *She wants to work for a newspaper when she graduates.* **3** the printed sheets making up a newspaper: *The plants were wrapped in newspaper.*

news·pa·per·man (nyū′zpā′pər mən′) *or* (nū′zpā′pər mən′) *n, pl* **news·pa·per·men** (-men′) a male reporter or journalist.

news·pa·per·wo·man (nyū′zpā′pər wu̇ mən′) *or* (nū′zpā′pər wu̇ mən′) *n, pl* **news·pa·per·wo·men** (-wim′ən) a female reporter or journalist.

news·print (nyūz′print′) *or* (nūz′print′); (nyū′sprint′) *or* (nū′sprint′) *n* a soft, cheap, coarse paper made from wood pulp on which newspapers are usually printed.

news·reel (nyūz′rēl′) *or* (nūz′rēl′) *n* a short film depicting news and current events, formerly made for showing as part of the program in a movie theatre.

news release PRESS RELEASE.

news·room (nyūz′rūm′) *or* (nūz′rūm′) *n* a room or section of a newspaper office or broadcasting station where news is collected and edited for publication or broadcast.

news·stand (nyūz′stand′) *or* (nūz′stand′) *n* a stall or store where newspapers and magazines are sold.

news·wo·man (nyū′z wə man′) *or* (nū′z wə man′) *n, pl* **news·wo·men** (-wim′ən) a female reporter, journalist, or broadcaster.

news·wor·thy (nyū′zwər′ᴛʜē) *or* (nū′zwər′ᴛʜē) *adj* **news·wor·thi·er, news·wor·thi·est** interesting or important enough to the general public to be included in a newspaper or newscast: *The reporter tried to think of an angle that would make the story newsworthy.*

news·y (nyū′zē) *or* (nū′zē) *Informal adj* **news·i·er, news·i·est** full of news.

newt (nyūt) *or* (nūt) *n* a small, slender-bodied salamander that mostly lives on land but returns to the water to breed. See AMPHIBIAN for picture. <Old English *efeta*>

New Testament *Christianity n* the second division of the Bible, containing stories and teachings of Jesus and the apostles, letters from St. Paul to the early churches, and the Revelation of St. John.

new·ton (nyū′tən) *or* (nū′tən) *n* the SI unit for measuring the force required to give an acceleration of one metre per second per second to a mass of one kilogram. *Symbol* **N** <I. *Newton*, 18c physicist>

New·to·ni·an (nyū tō′nē ən) *or* (nū tō′nē ən) *adj* to do with Sir Isaac Newton or his theories: *Newtonian physics.*

New World *n* the Americas, including the Caribbean, considered in relation to Europe.
adj to do with the New World: *New World monkeys have tails adapted for grasping and holding on.*

New Year or **New Year's** *n* the first day or days of the year. **New Year's Day**, January 1, is usually observed as a legal holiday.

New Zea·land (zē′lənd) *n* a country of islands in the S Pacific. See the APPENDIX. **New Zea′land·er** *n.*

next (nekst) *adj* **1** following immediately: *We'll catch the next train.* **2** the first time after this one: *On your next visit, bring your guitar.*
prep nearest to: *We live in the house next the church.*
adv in the place, time, or position that is nearest: *I am going to do my arithmetic problems next.* <Old English *neah* near>
next door to, almost or very close to: *Cheating is an act next door to a crime.*
next to, a immediately following or adjacent to: *Who was the girl next to you?* **b** almost: *Chairs like these cost next to nothing. It was next to impossible to move in the crowd.*

next–door (nekst′dȯr′) *adj* in or at the next house or apartment: *We get along well with our next-door neighbours.*

next of kin *n* the nearest close relative.

nex·us (nek′səs) *n, pl* **nex·us·es** or **nex·us** **1** a connection or series of connections between two or more things. **2** a connected group or series. **3** the central and most important point or place. <Latin *nectere* to bind>

✱ **NFB** or **N.F.B.** *n* in full, the **National Film Board of Canada** a public agency that produces films and other audiovisual material that represent Canada.

NGO non-government organization, or non-governmental organization.

✱ **NHL** or **N.H.L.** *n* in full, the **National Hockey League** an organization of professional hockey teams from Canada and the US.

ni·a·cin (nī′ə sin) *n* a vitamin found in foods such as milk, wheat germ, and meats. Also called **nicotinic acid.** <*ni*(*cotinic*) *ac*(*id*) + *-in*>

nib (nib) *n* **1** the point of a pen. **2** the point or tip of an object. <Old English *nebbe* tip>

nib·ble (nib′əl) *v* **nib·bled, nib·bling** **1** eat away with quick, small bites, as a rabbit or a mouse does. **2** bite gently or lightly: *A fish nibbled at the bait.*
n **1** an act of nibbling: *We've been fishing all morning and haven't had a nibble.* **2** a small piece, especially of food: *I just want a nibble of the cake.* <probably German or Dutch> **nib′bler** *n.*
nibble at, *Informal* be interested in: *I'm nibbling at the idea of learning to dance.*

Nic·a·ra·gua (nik′ə rȧ′gwə) *n* a country in Central America. See the APPENDIX. **Nic′a·ra′guan** *adj, n.*

nice (nīs) *adj* **nic·er, nic·est** **1** pleasing, agreeable, or satisfactory: *a nice day, a nice ride.* **2** thoughtful or kind: *She was nice to us.* **3** fine, subtle, or precise: *a nice distinction, a nice shade of meaning.* **4** requiring care, skill, or tact: *a nice problem.* **5** refined or cultured: *nice manners.* <Middle English, from Old French *nice* silly. The current popular meanings developed later.> **nice′ly** *adv.* **nice′ness** *n.*

a bat	e bed	i bid	o pot	u cup	th thin
ā cake	ē me	ī bite	ō go	ū rude	ᴛʜ then
ȧ bar	ə about	ər over	ȯ for	u̇ put	zh measure

ni·ce·ty (nī′sə tē) *n, pl* **ni·ce·ties** **1** a fine point, small distinction, or detail: *I can paint, but I have not yet learned all the little niceties of composition.* **2** accuracy or precision.

niche (nich) *n* **1** a recess or hollow in a wall for a statue, vase, or ornament. **2** a place for which a person is suited: *She found her niche in the company.* **3** the space or role occupied by an organism or species in its specific habitat. The organism's way of life includes its food and its interactions with abiotic and other biotic factors in its habitat. <French = recess>

nick (nik) *n* a place where a small bit has been cut or broken out: *He cut nicks in a stick to keep count of his score.*
v **1** make a nick or nicks in: *I nicked the edge of the plate while washing it.* **2** cut into or wound slightly: *I nicked my finger on the cupboard door.* **3** *Informal* arrest or apprehend someone. <origin uncertain>
in the nick of time, just in time.

nick·el (nik′əl) *n* **1** a silver-white metallic element that is resistant to rust, used mainly in alloys. *Symbol* **Ni** **2** five cents, or a five-cent piece: *This paper used to cost a nickel a sheet.* <German *Kupfernickel* copper devil, from nickel's resemblance to copper>

nick·el–and–dime (nik′əl ən dīm′) *v* **nick·el-and-dimed, nick·el-and-dim·ing** *Informal* **1 a** get into money difficulties by dealing in many small amounts: *The price increases in the cafeteria are nickel-and-diming me out of my whole allowance.* **b** accumulate in many small amounts: *I've nickel-and-dimed enough money to buy Mom a great birthday gift.* **2** harass someone with trivial matters: *My kid sister whines and nickel-and-dimes till she gets what she wants.*
adj of little importance: *nickel-and-dime stuff.*

nick·el·o·de·on (nik′ə lō′dē ən) *n* **1** in former times, a juke box. **2** in the early days of movies, a cinema to which the price of admission was five cents.

nickel plate *n* a thin coating of NICKEL (def. 1) deposited on a metal object to prevent rust or improve the appearance. **nick′el-plate′** *v.*

nick·name (nik′nām′) *n* a short or playful form of a proper name, such as "The Great One" for the hockey player Wayne Gretzky.
v **nick·named, nick·nam·ing** give a nickname to: *They nicknamed the short boy "Shorty."*

ETYMOLOGY

Nickname comes from Middle English *ekename*, meaning "another name," but when people heard the words *an ekename*, it sounded like *a nekename*. Over time, *nekename* became "nickname."

nic·o·tine (nik′ə tēn′) *n* a toxic liquid in tobacco that is a stimulant in small amounts. <J. *Nicot,* 16c diplomat, who introduced tobacco into France about 1560>

nic·o·tin·ic acid (nik′ə tin′ik) NIACIN.

niece (nēs) *n* **1** a daughter of one's brother or sister. **2** a daughter of a brother or sister of one's spouse. <Old French, from Latin *neptis*>

nif·ty (nif′tē) *Slang adj* **nif·ti·er, nif·ti·est** clever, convenient, stylish, or impressive. <origin unknown>

Ni·ger (nī′jər) *or* (nē′zhār) *n* a country in west central Africa.

Ni·ge·ri·a (nī jē′rē ə) *n* a country in west Africa. See the APPENDIX. **Ni·ge′ri·an** *adj, n.*

nig·gard·ly (nig′ər dlē) *adj* **1** stingy: *a niggardly gift.* **2** meagre or scanty: *a niggardly meal.*
adv stingily. <Middle English> **nig′gard·li·ness** *n.*

nigh (nī) *Archaic or Poetic adv, adj* near or nearly: *Dawn was nigh (adj). He was nigh starving (adv).* <Old English *neah*>

night (nīt) *n* **1** the time between sunset and sunrise. **2** the darkness of night: *She went out into the night.* **3** an evening reserved for some special activity, or spent or regarded in a particular way: *a girls' night out.* **4** nightfall: *We expect to get back before night.*
adj **1** to do with night: *cold night winds.* **2** working or for use at night: *a night light.* **3** **nights** *pl* regularly or habitually in the nighttime: *He works nights.* <Old English *niht*>
make a night of it, celebrate until very late at night.

night·cap (nīt′kap′) *n* **1** in former times, a cap for wearing in bed. **2** *Informal* a drink taken just before going to bed.

night·club (nīt′klub′) *n* a place for dancing, drinking, eating, and entertainment, open only at night.

night·fall (nīt′fol′) *n* the coming of night.

night·gown (nīt′goun′) *n* **1** a light, loose garment worn in bed by girls and women. **2** a nightshirt.

night·hawk (nīt′hok′) *n* **1** an insect-eating bird that flies at night and has sharply pointed wings. **2** *Informal* a person who often stays up late at night.

night·in·gale (nī′tən gāl′) *or* (nī′ting gāl′) *n* a thrush of Europe and Asia with brownish feathers, noted for the rich, melodious song of the male.

night light *n* a small lamp that provides a dim light, used especially by the bed of a child or of a sick person at night.

night·long (nī′tlong′) *adj* lasting all night: *a nightlong vigil, a nightlong celebration.*

night·ly (nī′tlē) *adj* **1** done, happening, or appearing every night: *a nightly performance.* **2** done, happening, or appearing in the night: *nightly dew.*
adv **1** every night: *Performances are given nightly except on Sunday.* **2** at or by night: *Many animals come out nightly.*

night·mare (nīt′mer′) *n* **1** a frightening dream: *He had nightmares about falling from a high roof.* **2** a very unpleasant or frightening experience: *The dust storm was a nightmare.*

night·mar·ish (nīt′mer′ish) *adj* strange and horrifying, as in a nightmare.

night owl *Informal n* a person who often stays up late.

night school *n* a school held in the evening for people who work during the day.

night·shade (nīt′shād′) *n* a plant related to the potato, with black or red berries that are typically poisonous, such as the **deadly nightshade**.

night·shirt (nīt′shərt′) *n* a loose garment worn in bed by boys and men.

night table or **stand** *n* a small table at the side of a bed, often with drawers or shelves.

night·time (nīt′tīm′) *n* the time between evening and morning.

night watch *n* a watch or guard kept during the night, or the person or persons keeping such a watch.

night watch·man *n, pl* **night watch·men** a person who guards a building at night.

ni·hil·ism (nī′ə liz′əm) *n* the rejection of all religious and moral principles in the belief that life is meaningless. <Latin *nihil* nothing> **ni′hil·ist** *n.* **ni′hil·is′tic** *adj.*

Ni·hon Sho·ki (nē′hon shō′kē) *Shintoism n* an account of Japan's history and imperial ancestry from mythic origins to the 800s CE. It is one of the highly revered texts of the Shinto religion.

nil (nil) *n* nothing, used especially as a score in some games: *seven to nil.* <Latin *nihil* nothing>

nim·ble (nim′bəl) *adj* **nim·bler, nim·blest** 1 able to move lightly and quickly: *Her nimble fingers flew over the piano keys.* 2 quick to understand: *a nimble mind.* <Old English *næmel* clever> **nim′ble·ness** *n.* **nim′bly** *adv.*

nim·bo·stra·tus (nim′bō strā′təs) *or* (nim′bō strat′əs) *n, pl* **nim·bo·stra·ti** (-tī) *or* (-tē) a low, dark grey layer of rain or snow cloud. See ALTOCUMULUS for picture.

nim·bus (nim′bəs) *n, pl* **nim·bus·es** or **nim·bi** (-bī) *or* (bē) 1 a light disc or other radiance about the head of a saint or divine being. 2 a large, dark rain cloud. <Latin = cloud>

NIMBY or **Nimby** (nim′bē) *n, pl* **NIMBYs** or **Nimbys** someone who opposes locating something considered unpleasant or dangerous near his or her home. <from *n*(*ot*) *i*(*n*) *m*(*y*) *b*(*ack*) *y*(*ard*)> **nim′by·ism** *n.*

nin·com·poop (nin′kəm pūp′) *or* (ning′kəm pūp′) *n* a foolish or stupid person. <origin uncertain>

nine (nīn) *n* 1 a cardinal number that is one more than eight. 2 the numeral 9. 3 a playing card with nine spots: *the nine of clubs.*
adj 1 one more than eight. *My little brother is nine years old.* 2 (*after the noun*) ninth in a series: *Chapter Nine was very exciting.* <Old English *nigon*> **ninth** *adj, adv.*
dressed to the nines, *Informal* very formally or elaborately dressed: *I showed up in my jeans and found out that everyone else was dressed to the nines.*
the whole nine yards, *Informal* everything; as much (great, etc.) as possible.

nine·fold (nīn′fōld′) *adj, adv.* 1 nine times as much or as many. 2 consisting of nine parts.

nine·pins (nīn′pinz′) *n* (*with singular verb*) a game in which nine large wooden pins are set up to be bowled down with a ball: *She said ninepins was popular in the UK.*

nine·teen (nīn′tēn′) *n* 1 nine more than ten. 2 the numeral 19.
adj 1 nine more than ten: *He lived there for nineteen years.* 2 (*after the noun*) nineteenth in a set or series: *Chapter Nineteen.* **nine′teenth′** *adj, adv.*

nine·teenth (nīn′tēnth′) *n* 1 next after the eighteenth: *He was nineteenth in line at the movies.* 2 one of nineteen equal parts: *One-nineteenth of thirty-eight is two.*
adj, adv See NINETEEN.

nine·ti·eth (nīn′tē ith) *n* 1 next after the eighty-ninth. 2 one of ninety equal parts.
adj, adv See NINETY.

nine·ty (nīn′tē) *n, pl* **nine·ties** 1 nine times ten. 2 **nineties** *pl* the years from ninety through ninety-nine, especially of a century or of a person's life: *She was in her nineties when she died.*
adj 1 nine times ten: *ninety paperclips in a pack.* 2 (*after the noun*) ninetieth in a set or series: *page ninety.* **nine′ti·eth** *adj, adv.*

nin·ja (nin′jə) *n* in medieval Japan, a person highly skilled in stealth tactics and the martial arts, or someone who imitates such a person. <Japanese = spy>

nin·ny (nin′ē) *n, pl* **nin·nies** a weak and foolish person. <perhaps *innocent*>

ninth (nīnth) *adj, n* 1 next after the eighth: *in the ninth day* (*adj*). *I'm ninth in line* (*n*). 2 one, or being one, of nine equal parts: *We took a ninth part of the cash* (*adj*). *I wanted a ninth of the cash, but they gave me only a tenth* (*n*). **ninth′ly′** *adv.*

ni·o·bi·um (nī ō′bē əm) *n* a rare metallic element. *Symbol* **Nb** <in Greek myth, named after *Niobe* the daughter of *Tantulus,* because the element *niobium* occurs in nature with the element *tantulum*>

nip[1] (nip) *v* **nipped, nip·ping** 1 squeeze tight and suddenly: *The crab nipped my toe.* 2 take off by biting, pinching, or snipping: *She nipped off a bit of metal with the shears.* 3 stop or spoil growth, progress, or fulfilment: *nip inflation.* 4 injure or make numb with cold: *The cold wind nipped our ears. The flowers were all nipped by frost.*
n 1 a tight squeeze or pinch. 2 stinging cold: *There was a nip in the air.* <probably German or Dutch>
nip and tuck, *Informal* so evenly matched in a race or contest that the issue remains in doubt till the end.
nip in the bud, stop or spoil at the beginning: *All his plans were nipped in the bud by the accident.*

nip[2] (nip) *n* a small drink: *a nip of brandy.* <origin uncertain>

nip·per (nip′ər) *n* 1 a thing that or person who nips, especially a big claw of a lobster or crab. 2 *Informal* a small boy. 3 **nippers** *pl* pincers, forceps, pliers, or other tool that nips.

nip·ple (nip′əl) *n* 1 the small projection on a female breast, through which a baby or young animal gets its mother's milk. 2 the mouthpiece of a baby's bottle. 3 a thing shaped or used like a nipple. <perhaps Old English *nebb* projecting part>

nip·py (nip′ē) *adj* **nip·pi·er, nip·pi·est** 1 bitingly cold: *nippy weather.* 2 sharp and pungent: *nippy cheese.* 3 quick and nimble: *a nippy car.*

a bat	e bed	i bid	o pot	u cup	th **thin**
ā cake	ē me	ī bite	ō go	ū rude	TH **then**
ȧ bar	ə about	ər over	ȯ for	u̇ put	zh measure

nir·va·na or **Nir·va·na** (nir vä′nə) *n* **1** *Buddhism* the enlightened level of being in which there is no death, suffering, desire, or sense of self. **2** an ideally happy place or state of mind. <Sanskrit = disappearance, extinction>

Ni·sei (nē′sā′) *n, pl* **Ni·sei** a native-born Canadian or US citizen whose parents were Japanese immigrants. Compare ISSEI, SANSEI. <Japanese *ni* two + *sei* generation>

Nis·ga'a or **Nish·ga** (nis′gä) *or* (nish′gä) *n, pl* **Nis·ga'a, Nish·ga,** or **Nish·gas 1** a member of a First Nations people living in the Skeena River area of British Columbia. **2** their Tsimshian language.
adj to do with these people or their language.

nit (nit) *n* the egg or the young of a louse or similar insect. <Old English *hnitu*>

ni·ter (nī′tər) NITRE.

nit–pick·ing (nit′pik′ing) *n, adj* criticizing and complaining about small or unimportant errors or faults: *A little nit-picking can be a good thing* (*n*). *You're being more than a little nit-picking in your criticism* (*adj*). **nit′-pick** *v.* **nit′-pick′er** *n.*

ni·trate (nī′trāt) *n* a salt or ester of nitric acid.
v **ni·trat·ed, ni·trat·ing** treat with nitric acid or a nitrate. **ni·tra′tion** *n.*

ni·tre (nī′tər) POTASSIUM NITRATE. Also, **niter**.

ni·tric (nī′trik) *adj* of or containing nitrogen, especially with a higher valence than in corresponding nitrous compounds.

nitric acid *n* a clear, colourless or pale yellow acid that is poisonous and corrosive.

ni·trite (nī′trīt) *n* a salt or ester of nitrous acid.

ni·tro·gen (nī′trə jən) *n* an element that is a colourless, tasteless, odourless inert gas. Nitrogen makes up about four-fifths of the air by volume. Liquid nitrogen is used as a coolant and preservative. *Symbol* **N** <French, from Greek *nitron* + *-gen*>

nitrogen cycle *n* the cycle of chemical changes that returns nitrogen to its original form after it has been used by plants and bacteria.

nitrogen dioxide *n* a brown poisonous gas found in car exhaust fumes.

ni·tro·glyc·er·in or **ni·tro·glyc·er·ine** (nī′trə glis′ə rin) *n* an explosive liquid mainly used to make explosives such as dynamite. In tiny amounts it can be used as a medicine for treating some heart ailments.

ni·trous (nī′trəs) *adj* of or containing nitrogen, especially with a lower valence than in corresponding nitric compounds.

nitrous oxide *n* a colourless gas with a sweetish odour that causes exhilaration and inability to feel pain.

nit·ty–grit·ty (nit′ē grit′ē) *Informal n* the most important details or practical aspects of a subject or situation: *Let's get down to the nitty-gritty of who is going to pay for the broken window.* <*nit* + *grit*>

nit·wit (nit′wit′) *Informal n* a stupid or scatterbrained person. <*nit* + *wit*>

nix (niks) *Informal pron, interj* **1** used to deny or refuse something. **2** nothing.
v reject or veto: *The student council nixed the proposal.* <German *nichts* nothing>

Nla·ka'·pa·mux (əng′hlo ko′pə mə) *n* **1** a member of a First Nations people living in southern British Columbia. **2** their Salishan language.
adj to do with these people or their language. Also called **Thompson**.

NNE north-northeast.

NNW north-northwest.

no (nō) *n, pl* **noes 1** a denial or refusal. **2** a negative vote or voter: *The noes won.*
adv not at all or to no extent: *No, I will not go. She is no better.*
adj **1** not any: *He has no friends.* **2** opposite to what is specified: *He's no fool.* **3** forbidding or rejecting something: *No Smoking.* <Old English *ne* not + *a* ever>

No. or **no.** *n, pl* **Nos.** or **nos.** number.

> **GRAMMAR AND USAGE**
>
> The abbreviation **No.** for number is usually written with a capital. It is appropriate chiefly in business and technical English, and is often replaced by the symbol #.

no–ac·count (nō′ə kount′) *Informal adj* no good or worthless.
n a good-for-nothing or insignificant person.

No·bel prize (nō bel′) *n* an annual international prize awarded for outstanding work in physics, chemistry, physiology or medicine, literature, economics, or the promotion of peace, first awarded in 1901.

no·bil·i·ty (nō bil′ə tē) *n, pl* **no·bil·i·ties 1** the quality of being noble in character, mind, or rank. **2** people who are nobles.

no·ble (nō′bəl) *adj* **no·bler, no·blest 1** belonging by birth to the class of people who have inherited their rank and position in society: *a noble family.* **2** with or showing high moral principles: *a noble person, a noble deed.* **3** splendid and impressive: *Niagara Falls is a noble sight.*
n a person who has inherited a rank and position in society: *The king summoned all the nobles to court.* <Old French, from Latin *nobilis* renowned> **no′ble·ness** *n.* **no′bly** *adv.*

noble gas *n* any of the gases helium, neon, argon, krypton, xenon, and radon. These gases are very resistant to chemical reaction with other elements.

no·ble·man (nō′bəl mən) *n, pl* **no·ble·men** (-men) a man who belongs to the nobility.

noble metal *n* any of the metals silver, gold, and platinum. These metals are very resistant to chemical reaction with oxygen.

no·blesse o·blige (nò bles ò blēzh′) *n* charitable or honourable behaviour expected from a person of high rank. <French = nobility is an obligation>

no·ble·wom·an (nō′bəl wům′ən) *n, pl* **no·ble·wom·en** (-wim′ən) a woman who belongs to the nobility.

no·bod·y (nō′bud′ē) *or* (nō′bod′ē) *pron* no person.
n, pl **no·bod·ies** a person of no importance.

no–brain·er (nō′brā′nər) *Informal n* something very easy to figure out or decide: *The first question was a no-brainer.*

nock (nok) *n* a notch on a bow or arrow for the bowstring.
v fit an arrow to the bowstring for shooting. <perhaps Dutch *nocke* tip>

The great horned owl is a **nocturnal** bird of prey. Thanks to excellent night vision and sensitive hearing, owls hunt in the darkness and rest when the sun is bright.

The golden eagle hunts by day, and its sharp eyes are adapted to that purpose. Studies show that an eagle can see a rabbit from 3 km away.

noc·tur·nal (nok tər′nəl) *adj* **1** of, belonging to, or occurring at night: *a nocturnal journey.* **2** active during the night instead of the day: *The owl is a nocturnal bird.* **3** with flowers in a plant that open only at night: *Some cactus plants are nocturnal.* <Latin *noctis* night>
noc·tur′nal·ly *adv.*

noc·turne (nok′tərn) *n* **1** a short, dreamy or romantic musical piece. **2** a painting of a night scene.

nod (nod) *v* **nod·ded, nod·ding 1** bow the head slightly and raise it again quickly. **2** show agreement by nodding: *I asked him if the baby was asleep and he nodded.* **3** express agreement or understanding by bowing the head: *to nod consent.* **4** let the head fall forward and slowly bob about when sleepy or falling asleep: *She was beginning to nod before the meeting was halfway through.* **5** droop, bend, or sway back and forth: *The trees nodded in the wind.*
n a nodding of the head: *She gave us a nod as she passed.* <perhaps German>
give someone the nod, express consent.
nodding acquaintance, slight or casual acquaintance.
nod off, fall asleep.

node (nōd) *n* **1** a central point in a network, system, or diagram at which lines or paths intersect or branch. **2** a joint in a stem from which leaves grow. **3** a natural knob, knot, or swelling, especially in the body: *a lymph node.* <Latin *nodus* knot> **nod′al** *adj.*

nod·ule (noj′ūl) *n* **1** a small knot, knob, or swelling, especially in the body. **2** a small, rounded mass or lump of some material, especially a mineral. **nod′u·lar** *adj.*

Noël (nō el′) *n* Christmas. <French>

no–fault (nō′folt) *adj* to do with a vehicle insurance program under which a person is paid by an insurance company for injury or damage due to an accident, no matter whose fault it was.

no–fly zone (nō′flī′) *n* a part of a country's airspace in which foreign military aircraft are not allowed to enter.

no–hit·ter (nō′hit′ər) *Baseball n* a game in which a pitcher allows the opposing team no hits.

no–holds–barred (nō′hōldz′bȧrd) *adj* unrestrained by rules or other restrictions: *a no-holds-barred fight.*

noise (noiz) *n* **1** a loud, harsh, or unpleasant sound or sound that causes a disturbance: *The noise kept me awake.* **2** irregular fluctuations that accompany a transmitted electrical signal and tend to interfere with it.
noise′less *adj.* **noise′less·ly** *adv.* **noise′less·ness** *n.*

ETYMOLOGY

Noise comes through Old French *noise*, meaning "din" or "loud disturbance" from Latin *nausea*, meaning "seasickness," because of the unpleasant din made by a shipful of seasick passengers!

noise·mak·er (noi′zmā′kər) *n* a person who or thing that makes noise, especially a horn or rattle used to make noise at a party or sports event.

noi·some (noi′səm) *adj* offensive or disgusting, especially in smelling bad: *a noisome slum, a noisome sewer.* <Old French *enui* annoyance> **noi′some·ly** *adv.*
noi′some·ness *n.*

nois·y (noi′zē) *adj* **nois·i·er, nois·i·est 1** making much noise: *a noisy crowd, a noisy little bus.* **2** full of or characterized by noise: *a noisy street, a noisy quarrel.*
nois′i·ly *adv.* **nois′i·ness** *n.*

no·mad (nō′mad) *n* **1** a member of a people who move from place to place so as to have pasture for livestock or to be near food or a water supply. **2** a wanderer.
adj to do with being a nomad: *the nomad way of life.* <French, from Greek *nemein* to pasture> **no·mad′ic** *adj.*

no·mad·ism (nō′ma diz′əm) *n* the way that nomads live.

no–man's–land or **no man's land** (nō′manz′land′) *n* **1** in war, the disputed land or area between two entrenched opposing armies. **2** a tract of land to which no one has a recognized or established claim, or an area of involvement or operation that is not clearly defined: *a legal no-man's-land.*

nom de plume (nom′ də plūm′) *n* a name used by an author instead of his or her real name. <French = pen name>

no·men·cla·ture (nō′mən klā′chər) *or* (nō men′klə chər) *n* a system of names or terms used in a particular science or other discipline, or the devising and choosing of such names. <French, from Latin *nomen* name + *calare* to call>

a bat	e bed	i bid	o pot	u cup	th **thin**
ā cake	ē me	ī bite	ō go	ū rude	ᴛʜ **then**
ȧ bar	ə about	ər over	ȯ for	u̇ put	zh measure

nom·i·nal (nom′ə nəl) *adj* **1** existing in name only: *The president is the nominal head of the club, but the secretary is the one who really runs its affairs.* **2** so small that it is not worth considering: *My dad pays his friend a nominal rent for the cottage each summer.* **3** to do with a name. **4** to do with a noun.
n a word or group of words used as a noun. <Latin *nomen* name>

nom·i·nal·ly (nom′ə nə lē) *adv* in name only.

nom·i·nate (nom′ə nāt′) *v* **nom·i·nat·ed, nom·i·nat·ing** **1** propose or formally enter as a candidate for an office or for an honour or award: *She has been nominated as Liberal candidate in our riding.* **2** specify something formally, typically a date or place for an event: *to nominate a day for an election.* **nom′i·na′tor** *n.*

nom·i·na·tion (nom′ə nā′shən) *n* **1** the proposal of someone as a candidate for an office, honour, or prize: *The nominations for president of the club were written on the chalkboard.* **2** a person who or thing that is nominated: *He was hopeful, but his friend got the nomination.*

nom·i·na·tive (nom′ə nə tiv) *or* (nom′nə tiv) *adj* to do with the grammatical case that in many languages shows that a noun, pronoun, or adjective is part of the subject of a sentence. The English personal pronouns *I, he, she, we,* and *they* are in the nominative case.
n the nominative case.

nom·i·nee (nom′ə nē′) *n* a person nominated for an office, prize, or honour.

non– *prefix* not, the opposite of, or lack of: *non-combatant, nonconformity, non-circulating.* <Latin = not>

nona– *combining form* nine: *nonagon.* <Latin>

non–ac·cept·ance (non′ak sep′təns) *n* a failure or refusal to accept.

non·age (non′ij) *n* the period of being immature or under the legal age of responsibility.

non·a·ge·nar·i·an (non′ə jə ner′ē ən) *n* a person who is between 90 and 100 years old.
adj between 90 and 100 years old. <Latin *nonaginta* ninety>

non–ag·gres·sion (non′ə gresh′ən) *n* an absence of aggressiveness, especially in a nation or government.

non·a·gon (non′ə gon′) *Mathematics n* a closed plane figure with nine interior angles and nine sides. <Latin *nonus* nine + Greek *gonia* angle>

non–al·co·hol·ic (non′al kə hol′ik) *adj* containing no alcohol: *a non-alcoholic drink.*

non–at·tend·ance (non′ə ten′dəns) *n* failure to be present.

nonce (nons) *adj* coined on only one occasion as a word or phrase: *a nonce word.* <Middle English *then anes* the one purpose>
for the nonce, for the present time or occasion.

non·cha·lant (non′shə lont′) *or* (non′shə lənt) *adj* casual, calm, and relaxed: *She remained nonchalant during all the excitement.* <French *non-* not + *chaloir* be warm> **non′cha·lance** *n.* **non′cha·lant·ly** *adv.*

non–cir·cu·la·ting (non′sər′kyə lā′ting) *adj* containing library items only for use on the premises and are not to be borrowed.

non–com (non′kom′) *Informal n* a non-commissioned officer.

non–com·bat·ant (non′kəm bat′ənt) *or* (non′kom′bə tənt) *n* a person in the armed forces who is not engaged in fighting during a war, such as a surgeon, nurse, or chaplain, or any civilian in wartime.
adj not fighting.

non–com·mis·sioned (non′kə mish′ənd) *adj* without a commission in the armed forces, as in the rank of a sergeant or corporal.

non·com·mit·tal (non′kə mit′əl) *adj* not committing oneself to an opinion or course of action: *"I will think it over" is a noncommittal answer.* **non′com·mit′tal·ly** *adv.*

non–com·pli·ance (non′kəm plī′əns) *n* the act or fact of not complying with a wish or command.
non′-com·pli′ant *adv.*

non com·pos men·tis (non′ kom′pəs men′tis) *adj* not sane. <Latin = not having control of one's mind>

non–con·duct·ing (non′kən duk′ting) *adj* not conducting heat or electricity. **non-con·duc′tor** *n.*

non·con·form·ist (non′kən fôr′mist) *n* a person who does not conform to accepted ideas or practices.

non·con·form·i·ty (non′kən fôr′mə tē) *n* a failure or refusal to conform.

non–dair·y (non′dā′rē) *adj* containing no milk or milk products, especially in a product used as a substitute for milk or cream.

non·de·script (non′də skript′) *adj* lacking interesting or distinctive features: *an apartment in a nondescript highrise.*
n a nondescript person or thing. <*non-* + Latin *descriptus* described>

none (nun) *pron* **1** not any: *We have none of that paper left.* **2** no or not one: *None of these is a typical case.* **3** no people or things: *None have arrived.* **4** no part or nothing: *This is a silly idea, and I will have none of it.*
adv to no extent or in no way: *Our supply is none too great.* <Old English *ne* not + *an* one>

GRAMMAR AND USAGE

None may be either singular or plural:

I looked at a lot of different topics for my essay, but none is interesting enough to research.

She phoned three friends, but none were home.

It is more common to use it with a plural verb.

non·en·ti·ty (non en′tə tē) *n, pl* **non·en·ti·ties** **1** a person or thing of little or no importance. **2** a thing that does not exist.

non–es·sen·tial (non′ə sen′shəl) *adj* not necessary.
n a person who or thing that is not essential.

none·the·less (nun′thə les′) *adv* nevertheless or regardless: *I told her not to, but she showed up nonetheless.*

non–e·vent (non′ē vent′) *n* a happening that is disappointing or insignificant.

non–ex·ist·ent (non′eg zis′tənt) *adj* having no existence; not being real or present. **non′-exist′ence** *n.*

non·fic·tion (non fik′shən) *n* prose literature that is not fictional, such as biographies and histories.

non·flam·ma·ble (non flam′ə bəl) *adj* not easily set on fire and not burning fast if set on fire.

GRAMMAR AND USAGE

Nonflammable is the opposite of both *flammable* and *inflammable*. Flammable and inflammable mean the same, but inflammable is sometimes misunderstood because it looks like a negative.

non–in·ter·ven·tion (non′in tər ven′shən) *n* a failure or refusal to become involved in a situation concerning others, especially such a policy practised by a country in relation to other nations.

non–in·vas·ive (non′in vā′siv) *adj* not involving the insertion of instruments during surgery or other medical treatment.

non–met·al (non met′əl) *n* an element not having the character of a metal. Carbon and nitrogen are non-metals. **non′-me·tal′lic** *adj.*

non·met·ric (non met′rik) *adj* to do with measurement on a scale that is not metric.

✱ **non–Na·tive** (non′nā′tiv) *n* a person who does not belong to one of Canada's Aboriginal groups.
adj to do with such people.

no–no (nō′nō′) *Informal n* an action that is forbidden, improper, or unwise.

no–non·sense (nō′non′sens′) *adj* practical, straightforward, and firm: *That teacher has a no–nonsense manner that students appreciate.*

non·pa·reil (non′pə rel′) *adj* with no equal or rival.
n a person or thing with no equal. <French, from Latin *non* not + *par* equal>

non–par·ti·san (non pär′tə zən) *or* (non pär′tə zan′) *adj* not controlled by or supporting any single faction or political party.

non–per·form·ance (non′pər fôr′məns) *n* a failure to perform an action.

non·plus (non plus′) *or* (non′plus) *v* **non·plussed** or **non·plused, non·plus·sing** or **non·plus·ing** surprise and puzzle so much that a person is unable to react: *We were nonplussed to see two roads leading off to the left where we had expected only one.*
n a state of being surprised and puzzled. <Latin *non plus* not more>

non–poi·son·ous (non poi′ze nəs) *adj* containing no poison.

non–po·lit·i·cal (non′pə lit′ə kəl) *adj* not concerned with politics.

non–pre·scrip·tion (non′prē skrip′shən) *adj* of medicine, able to be bought without a doctor's prescription.

non–prof·it (non prof′it) *adj* not conducted in order to make a profit: *a non-profit organization.*

non–re·new·able (non′rē nyū′ə bəl) *or* (non′rē nū′ə bəl) *adj* unable to be replaced: *non-renewable resources.*

non–res·i·dent (non rez′ə dənt) *adj* **1** not living in a particular place. **2** not living where one's work, study, or official duty is carried on.
n a person not living in a particular place.

non–re·sist·ance (non′ri zis′təns) *n* the principle or practice of not resisting authority, even when it is unjust. **non–re·sist′ant** *adj, n.*

non–re·stric·tive (non′ri strik′tiv) *adj* **1** not involving restrictions. **2** in grammar, not limiting the meaning of a noun phrase or relative clause.

GRAMMAR AND USAGE

A **non-restrictive** phrase includes some words not necessary for the meaning of a sentence: *My uncle, **who likes to travel**, came to visit us.*

In a **restrictive** phrase, all the words are essential: *The singer **who calls herself "Cheri"** was in town today.*

non–sched·uled (non′skej′əld) *or* (non′shej′əld) *adj* **1** of an airline, with no fixed or published flying schedule. **2** of an airplane flight, in an aircraft that is not a private aircraft and that is not operated on a scheduled flight.

non–sec·tar·i·an (non′sek ter′ē ən) *adj* not connected with a religious denomination.

non·sense (non′səns) *n* **1** words, ideas, or acts without meaning: *The magician talks nonsense as he is doing the tricks.* **2** foolish talk or doings: *It is nonsense to say that we can walk that far in an hour.* **3** impudent or silly behaviour or conduct: *She doesn't take any nonsense from her students.* <*non-* + *sense*>

non·sen·si·cal (non sen′sə kəl) *adj* foolish or absurd.

non se·qui·tur (non sek′wə tər) *n* a statement or reply that has no relationship to what has just been said. <Latin = it does not follow>

non–skid (non skid′) *adj* made so as to prevent skidding or slipping: *non-skid tires, boots with non-skid soles.*

non–smok·ing (non′smō′king) *adj* **1** not using cigarettes or other tobacco products: *my non-smoking relatives.* **2** not permitting smoking: *All Federal Government buildings are non-smoking.* **non–smok′er** *n.*

non–stand·ard (non′stan′dərd) *adj* not average, normal, or usual.

GRAMMAR AND USAGE

Non-standard English includes *slang* and *non-standard forms*. It is separate from informal **English**. See notes at INFORMAL and STANDARD.

a **bat**	e **bed**	i **bid**	o **pot**	u **cup**	th **thin**
ā **cake**	ē **me**	ī **bite**	ō **go**	ū **rude**	ᴛʜ **then**
ä **bar**	ə **about**	ər **over**	ô **for**	ů **put**	zh **measure**

Nordic ski jumping

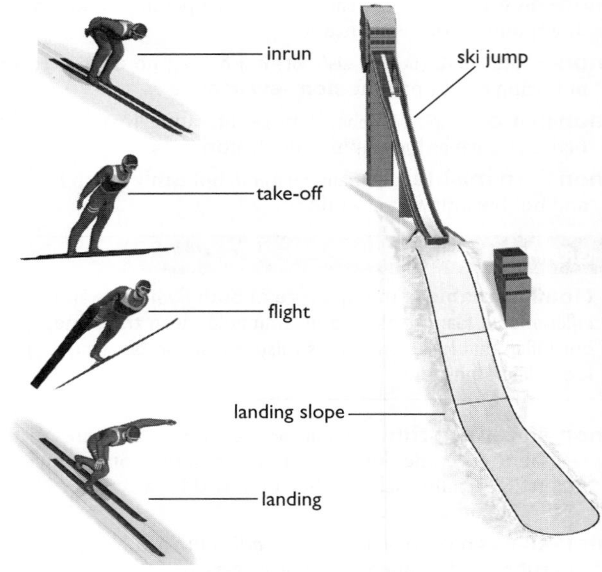

In **Nordic** ski jumping competition, jumpers use their skis and bodies like wings. Assuming an aerodynamic position, jumpers try to minimize resistance and achieve great distance. Points are awarded for both distance jumped and technique.

🍁 **non–sta·tus** (non′stat′əs) *or* (non′stā′təs) *adj* not registered as a First Nations person with the Federal Government.

non–stick (non′stik′) *adj* designed to keep food from sticking to cookware: *a non-stick frying pan.*

non–stop (non′stop′) *for adj,* (non′stop′) *for adv.*
adj without stopping: *We took a non-stop flight from Toronto to Rome.*
adv without a stop: *We flew non-stop from Regina to Montréal.*

non–sup·port (non′sə pȯrt′) *n* failure to support someone financially, especially the failure to provide for someone for whom one is legally responsible.

🍁 **non–trea·ty** (non′trē′tē) *adj* not under the terms of a treaty between a First Nations people and the Federal Government.

non–un·ion (non yū′nyən) *adj* **1** not with or belonging to a trade union. **2** not made with union labour.

non·ver·bal (non vėr′bəl) *adj* not involving language. Actions and facial expressions that show meaning or emotion are nonverbal: *Smiling is nonverbal communication.* **non·ver′bal·ly** *adv.*

non–violent (non vī′ə lənt) *adj* **1** free from violence: *a non-violent demonstration.* **2** supporting or using peaceful means to resist authority. **non-vi′o·lence** *n.*

noo·dle (nū′dəl) *n* a thin, long strip of pasta or a similar paste of flour and water, left whole or cut into pieces: *egg noodles, Chinese noodles.*
adj made with noodles: *noodle soup.* <origin uncertain>

nook (nu̇k) *n* a corner or recess, especially one that is cosy and sheltered: *There is a wonderful nook in the woods behind our house.* <Middle English *noke*>
every nook and cranny, everywhere, especially the least obvious places: *I searched every nook and cranny for the lost kitten.*

noon (nūn) *n* twelve o'clock in the daytime, the middle of the day.
adj to do with twelve o'clock in the daytime: *noon hour, a noon-hour concert.* <Latin *nona* (*hora*) ninth (hour), the ninth hour of daylight (3 p.m.) when church prayers originally took place. Eventually, prayers were said at the sixth hour (12 p.m.) but the use of the Old English term *non* to denote the ninth hour, came to mean noon.>

noon·day (nūn′dā′) *n* noon: *Lunch is our noonday meal.*

no one or **no–one** (nō′wun′) *pron* nobody: *No one was hurt in the car accident.*

noose (nūs) *n* **1** a loop with a slip-knot that tightens as the string or rope is pulled: *Nooses are used especially in lassos and snares.* **2** a thing that restricts or snares like a noose.
v **noosed, noos·ing 1** catch in a noose or as if in a noose. **2** make a noose with or in. <Old French, from Latin *nodus* knot>

Noot·ka (nu̇t′kə) NUU-CHAH-NULTH.

nope (nōp) *Informal adv* no.

nor (nȯr) *conj* **1** (*preceded by* **not** *or* **neither**) indicating that each of two or more possibilities are each untrue or will not happen: *Not a boy nor a girl moved. There was neither river nor stream in that desert.* **2** introducing a further negative statement: *We didn't go shopping, nor did we see a show. I have neither been there, nor am I planning to go.* <Old English *nother* neither>

NORAD (nȯr′ad) *n* in full, **North American Aerospace Defence Command** a joint Canadian and US organization that watches for unidentified craft in the air or in space in order to warn of possible attack.

Nor·dic (nȯr′dik) *n* in full, **Nordic skiing** forms of skiing that developed primarily in Scandinavian countries. Nordic ski events include cross-country skiing and ski jumping.

no·ri·a (nô′rē ə) *or* (nō′rē ə) PERSIAN WHEEL.

norm (nôrm) *n* **1 the norm** a thing that is usual, typical, or standard: *High prices were the norm during that decade.* **2 norms** *pl* a typical standard or pattern of behaviour in a group: *the norms of politeness.* <Latin *norma* a rule>

nor·mal (nôr′məl) *adj* of the usual standard or type: *The normal temperature of the human body is 37°C.*
n **1** the usual condition or level of something: *Bus service will be back to normal next week.* **2** *Mathematics, Science* a line drawn at right angles to another. **nor·mal′i·ty** *n.* **nor′mal·ly** *adv.*

nor·mal·cy (nôr′məl sē) *n, pl* **nor·mal·cies** the normal condition of something.

normal distribution *Statistics n* a theoretical distribution of a set of data, where the mean, median, and mode have the same value. Its graph is a symmetrical bell-shaped curve.

nor·mal·ize (nôr′mə līz′) *v* **nor·mal·ized, nor·mal·iz·ing** make normal. **nor′mal·i·za′tion** *n.*

Nor·man (nôr′mən) *n* **1** a native or inhabitant of Normandy in France. **2** a member of the Scandinavian people who conquered Normandy in the 900s. **3** a member of the Norman-French people who conquered England in 1066.
adj to do with the Normans or Normandy.

Norman French *n* **1** the northern form of Old French spoken by the medieval Normans. A variety of this language was used in law courts in England from the 1000s to the 1200s. **2** the form of French spoken by modern inhabitants of Normandy.

Norse (nôrs) *adj* to do with ancient or medieval Scandinavia, especially Norway, or its people or language.
n the Norwegian language, especially in its ancient or medieval form. <Dutch *noord* north>

Norse·man (nôr′smən) *n, pl* **Norse·men** (-smen) a Norwegian who lived in ancient or medieval Scandinavia.

north (nôrth) *n* **1** the direction to which a compass needle normally points, to the right as one faces the setting sun. **2 the North** the part of any country, especially Canada, toward the north: *Nunavut is in the North.*
adj **1** toward, in, or facing the north. **2** (*especially of the wind*) from the north: *a north wind.*
adv toward the north: *Go north two blocks.* Also, **northerly**. <Old English>

North America *n* the continent that is the northern part of the American land mass, bordered by the Pacific to the west and the Atlantic to the east, the Arctic to the north, and Central America to the south. All of North America is north of the equator.
North American *adj, n.*

North American Free Trade Agreement NAFTA.

north·bound (nôrth′bound′) *adj* going north.

north·east (nôr′thēst′) *n* **1** the direction midway between north and east. **2** a place that is in the northeast part or direction.
adj **1** toward, in, or facing the northeast. **2** (*especially of the wind*) from the northeast: *a northeast wind.*
adv toward the northeast: *They travelled northeast.* Also, **northeasterly**.

north·east·er (nôr′thē′stər) *n* a wind or storm from the northeast.

north·east·er·ly (nôr′thē′stər lē) *adj* northeast.
adv from the northeast: *The wind blew northeasterly.*

north·east·ern (nôr′thē′stərn) *adj* to do with the northeast.

north·east·ward (nôr′thē′stwərd) *adj, adv* toward the northeast: *to set a northeastward course* (*adj*). *The road turns northeastward* (*adv*). Also (*adv*), **northeastwards**. **north′east′ward·ly** *adj, adv.*

north·er (nôr′ᴛʜər) *n* a wind or storm from the north. Also, **northerly**.

north·er·ly (nôr′ᴛʜər lē) *adj* north.
adv from the north: *The wind blew northerly.*
n, pl **north·er·lies** NORTHER.

north·ern (nôr′ᴛʜərn) *adj* **1** to do with the north: *the northern side of a building.* **2** 🍁 **Northern** to do with the North of Canada: *Churchill is a Northern port.*

north·ern·er (nôr′ᴛʜər nər) *n* a person born in or living in the northern part of the country.

northern lights AURORA BOREALIS.

north·ern·most (nôr′ᴛʜərn mōst′) *adj* farthest north.

northern pike PIKE[2].

north·ing (nôr′thing) *or* (nôr′ᴛʜing) *n* **1** the distance northward of a point from a certain parallel, given by the second part of a map grid reference. **2** a latitudinal grid line. Compare EASTING.

north·land (nôr′thland′) *n* the northern part of a region or country.

north–north·east (nôrth′nôrth′ēst′) *n* a direction midway between north and northeast.
adj, adv in, toward, or from this direction. *Abbrev.* **NNE**

north–north·west (nôrth′nôrth′west′) *n* a direction midway between north and northwest.
adj, adv in, toward, or from this direction. *Abbrev.* **NNW**

North Pole *n* the northern end of the earth's axis.

🍁 **North Shore** *n* **1** the northern shore of the St. Lawrence River. **2** the northern coast of Nova Scotia.

north·ward (nôr′thwərd) *adj, adv* toward the north: *The orchard is on the northward slope of the hill* (*adj*). *Rocks lay northward of the ship's course* (*adv*). Also (*adv*), **northwards**. **north′ward·ly** *adj, adv.*

north·west (nôr′thwest′) *n* **1** the direction or compass point midway between north and west. **2** a place that is in the northwest part or direction. **3** 🍁 **the Northwest** the region of Canada north and west of the Great Lakes.
adv to or toward the northwest: *They travelled northwest.*
adj to do with the northwest: *a northwest wind.*

🍁 **North West Company** *n* a group of fur-trading companies and partners formed in Montréal during the late 1700s.

a bat	e bed	i bid	o pot	u cup	th **thin**
ā cake	ē me	ī bite	ō go	ū rude	ᴛʜ **then**
à bar	ə about	ər over	ô for	ů put	zh measure

N

north·west·er (nòr′thwes′tər) *n* **1** a wind or storm from the northwest. **2** ✱ **Northwester** in former times, a wintering partner or employee of the North West Company.

north·west·er·ly (nòr′thwes′tər lē) *adj* northwest.
adv from the northwest: *The wind blew northwesterly.*

north·west·ern (nòr′thwes′tərn) *adj* to do with the northwest.

✱ **North West Mounted Police** *n* a former name of the Royal Canadian Mounted Police.

Northwest Passage *n* a passage for ships from the Atlantic to the Pacific along the northern coast of N America.

✱ **Northwest Rebellion** *n* an armed uprising of Métis, European settlers, and Native Peoples in Saskatchewan in 1885, led by Louis Riel.

Northwest Territories *n* a large area in northern Canada between Yukon Territory and Nunavut, administered by a territorial government.
Abbrev. **N.W.T.**; postal symbol **NT**; URL **www.gov.nt.ca**

north·west·ward (nòr′thwes′twərd) *adj, adv* toward the northwest: *to set a northwestward course* (*adj*). *The road turns northwestward here* (*adv*). Also (*adv*), **northwestwards**. **north′west′ward·ly** *adj, adv.*

Nor·way (nòr′wā) *n* a country in northern Europe. See the APPENDIX. **Nor·we′gian** (nòr wē′jən) *adj, n.*

nor′west·er (nòr wes′tər) *n* **1** a NORTHWESTER (def. 1). **2** a heavy, waterproof oilskin hat. See also SOU'WESTER.

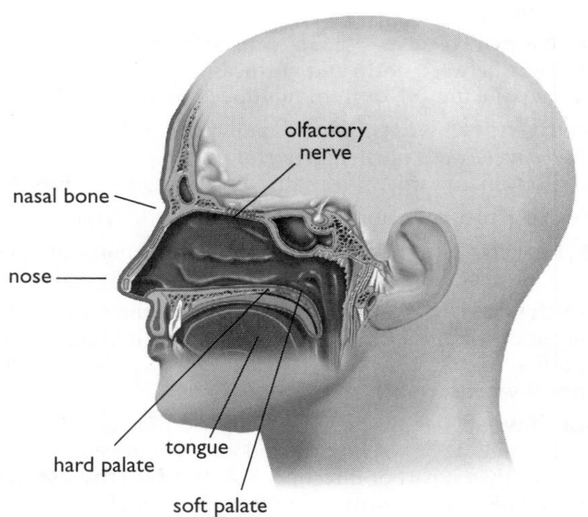

nose (nōz) *n* **1** the part of the face or head that projects above the mouth in the face of a human being or animal, containing the nostrils and used for breathing and smelling. **2** the sense of smell: *A mouse has a good nose for cheese.* **3** an ability to perceive or detect something: *A successful reporter must have a nose for news.* **4** a forward end that stands out, especially the front of a ship, boat, or aircraft: *We saw the steamer's nose poking around the cliff.*
v **nosed, nos·ing 1** discover by smelling. **2** rub or thrust with the nose: *The cat nosed her kittens.* **3** push with the forward end or push one's way carefully: *The bulldozer nosed the great rock off the road. The boat nosed along between the rocks.* **4** (*often with* **around**) search or pry into: *The detective nosed around in the suspect's backyard.* <Old English *nosu*>
count noses, *Informal* find out how many people are present.
follow your nose, a go straight ahead. **b** be guided by your instinct.
lead (lēd) **by the nose,** *Informal* have complete control over.
look down your nose at, feel contempt for.
nose out, a find out by looking quietly or secretly: *The private detective nosed out the facts.* **b** defeat by a narrow margin in a contest or competition.
on the nose, exactly correct: *Your guess was right on the nose.*
pay through the nose, *Informal* pay a great deal too much.
poke your nose into, *Informal* pry into or meddle in.
put someone's nose out of joint, *Informal* upset or annoy someone.
turn up your nose at, treat with contempt or scorn.
under your (**very**) **nose,** in plain sight.

nose·bleed (nōz′blēd′) *n* a flow of blood from the nose.

nose cone *n* the front section of a missile, made to carry the payload and to withstand the intense heat met with in re-entering the earth's atmosphere.

nose·dive (nōz′dīv′) *n* **1** a swift plunge straight downward by an aircraft. **2** a sudden, sharp drop: *The thermometer took a nosedive the day before New Year's.*
v **nose·dived, nose·div·ing 1** plunge swiftly downward. **2** take a sharp, sudden drop: *The price of beef nosedived.*

nos·ey (nō′zē) NOSY.

no–show (nō′shō′) *n* a person who has made an appointment, reservation, or booking and neither cancels nor keeps it.

nos·tal·gia (nos tal′jə) *or* (nos tal′jē ə) *n* a sentimental affection for something in the past: *She thought with nostalgia of how they used to go hiking in the hills.* <Latin, from Greek *nostos* return home + *algos* pain>
nos·tal′gic *adj.* **nos·tal′gi·cal·ly** *adv.*

nos·tril (nos′trəl) *n* either of the two openings in the nose that admits air to the lungs and smells to the olfactory nerves. <Old English *nosu* nose + *thyril* hole>

nos·trum (nos′trəm) *n* a medicine prepared and recommended by someone, usually without scientific evidence of its effectiveness. <Latin *nostrum* (*remedium*) our (remedy), from *noster* ours>

nos·y (nō′zē) *adj* **nos·i·er, nos·i·est** too curious about other people's business. Also, **nosey**. **nos′i·ly** *adv.* **nos′i·ness** *n.*

not (not) *adv* used to make a negative statement, or to exclude something or someone: *Six and two do not make ten. He has not been here. We expect to visit you in the not too distant future.* <*nought*>

no·ta be·ne (nō′tə bē′nē) *or* (ben′ē) used to draw attention to what follows. *Abbrev.* **N.B.** <Latin = note well>

no·ta·ble (nō′tə bəl) *adj* worthy of notice: *a notable event, a notable book, a notable painter.*
n an important or famous person: *Many notables attended the Governor General's levee.* **no′ta·bil′i·ty** *n.* **no′ta·bly** *adv.*

no·ta·rize (nō′tə rīz′) *v* **no·ta·rized, no·ta·riz·ing** certify a legal document.

no·ta·ry (nō′tə rē) *n, pl* **no·ta·ries 1** a notary public. **2** 🍁 in Québec, a lawyer who can draft legal documents but is not permitted to plead in court. <Latin *nota* mark>

notary public *n, pl* **notaries public** a person authorized to certify deeds and contracts, take oaths, and attend to certain other legal matters.

no·ta·tion (nō tā′shən) *n* **1** a set of signs or symbols used to represent numbers, quantities, or other values. **2** the representing of numbers, quantities, or other values by symbols or signs: *Music has a special system of notation, and so has chemistry.* **3** a note to assist memory: *She made a notation on the margin of the page.* **no·tate′** *v.* **no·tat′or** *n.*

notch (noch) *n* **1** a V-shaped nick or cut made in an edge or on a curving surface: **2** a deep, narrow pass or gap between mountains. **3** a grade, step, or degree: *In this hot weather, many people set their air conditioners several notches higher.*
v **1** make a notch or notches in. **2** record by notches. <probably Old French *osche*>

note (nōt) *n* **1** a brief written record of facts or thoughts, used as a reminder. **2** a brief personal e-mail or letter: *a thank-you note.* **3** a formal letter from one government to another: *France sent a note of protest to the US.* **4** *Music* **a** a single sound of definite pitch made by a musical instrument or voice: *Let me hear that note again.* **b** a symbol for such a sound, to show its pitch and length. **5** a bird's song or call, or a single tone of it. **6** a quality or tone that shows a mood or attitude: *There was a note of anxiety in her voice.* **7** importance: *of great note, of little note.* **8** *especially UK* a banknote.
v **not·ed, not·ing 1** briefly record as a thing to be remembered: *I noted the date of the party in my diary.* **2** notice or pay particular attention to something: *Please note what I do next. I noted that she had missed class for several days. The teacher noted the difference between "may" and "can."* <Old French, from Latin *nota*> **note′less** *adj.* **not′er** *n.*
compare notes, exchange ideas or opinions.
make a note of, write down as something to be remembered.
of note, important, great, or notable: *Louis Riel was a person of note.*
strike the right note, say or do something suitable.
take note of, give attention to or notice: *She took note of what her mother said.*
take notes, write down things to be remembered.

note·book (nōt′bu̇k′) *n* **1** a book in which to write notes of things to be learned or remembered. **2** *Computers* a portable computer smaller than a desktop computer; a laptop.

not·ed (nō′tid) *adj* well-known or celebrated: *Margaret Atwood is a noted Canadian author.*
v past tense and past participle of NOTE.

note–mak·ing (nōt′mā′king) *n* making a brief record of things to be remembered. Also called **note-taking**.

note·pad (nōt′pad′) *n* a small pad of paper for taking notes.

note·pa·per (nōt′pā′pər) *n* paper used for writing letters.

note·wor·thy (nōt′wər′ᴛʜē) *adj* worthy of notice: *The first flight across the Atlantic was a noteworthy achievement.* **note′wor′thi·ness** *n.*

not–for–pro·fit (not′fər prof′it) *adj* not operated for the purpose of making a profit: *schools, hospitals, and other not-for-profit organizations.*

noth·ing (nuth′ing) *n* **1** no thing: *Nothing was said.* **2** something that does not exist: *to create a world out of nothing.* **3** a thing or person of no importance or value: *People regard him as a nothing.* **4** zero.
adv not at all: *She cares nothing for appearances.*
adj Informal of little or no value or significance: *He had a series of nothing jobs.* <*no* + *thing*>
make nothing of, a be unable to understand. **b** fail to use or do. **c** treat as unimportant or worthless.
nothing less than, just the same as.
think nothing of, a consider as easy to do. **b** treat as unimportant or worthless.

GRAMMAR AND USAGE

Nothing and **nobody** are singular:
Nothing is bothering me.
Nobody wants his or her parent to be disappointed.
Informally, **nobody** is sometimes followed by a plural pronoun: *Nobody wants their parent to be disappointed.*

noth·ing·ness (nuth′ing nis) *n* **1** the absence of life or existence: *He thought that death was simply nothingness.* **2** worthlessness, insignificance, or unimportance.

no·tice (nō′tis) *n* **1** attention or observation: *No, that did not escape my notice. A sudden movement caught her notice.* **2** advance information or warning: *The whistle blew to give notice that the boat was about to leave.* **3** a written or printed sign posted in a public place: *A notice about band practice was taped to the classroom door.* **4** a warning that one is leaving rented premises or leaving a job by a certain date: *The carpenter gave his boss notice.* **5** a review or article about something: *The new book got a favourable notice.*
v **no·ticed, no·tic·ing 1** take notice of: *I noticed a big difference in my grades once I decided to work harder.* **2** mention or refer to. <Old French, from Latin *noscere* come to know>
serve notice, give warning.
take notice, observe.

no·tice·a·ble (nō′ti sə bəl) *adj* easily seen or noticed: *The class has made noticeable improvement.* **no′tice·a·bly** *adv.*

a bat	e bed	i bid	o pot	u cup	th **thin**
ā cake	ē me	ī bite	ō go	ü rude	ᴛʜ **then**
à bar	ə about	ər over	ȯ for	u̇ put	zh measure

N

no·ti·fy (nō′tə fī′) *v* **no·ti·fied, no·ti·fy·ing** give formal or official notice to: *Our teacher notified us that there would be a test on Monday.* <Old French, from Latin *notus* known + *facere* to make> **no′ti·fi·ca′tion** *n.*

no·tion (nō′shən) *n* **1** an idea or understanding of something: *He has no notion of what I mean.* **2** an opinion or belief: *One common notion is that red hair goes with a quick temper.* **3** intention: *He has no notion of risking his money.* **4** an impulse or desire, especially a whimsical one: *She had a notion to visit her grandmother.* **5 notions** *pl* small items used in sewing. Pins, needles, thread, and tape are notions. <Latin *noscere* to know>

no·to·ri·ous (nō tȯ′rē əs) *adj* famous, especially because of a bad quality or action: *The notorious criminal has been sent to prison.* <Latin *notus* known> **no′to·ri′e·ty** *n.* **no·to′ri·ous·ly** *adv.* **no·to′ri·ous·ness** *n.*

SYNONYMS

Notorious means "widely known," mostly in a negative way: *The actor was notorious for his temper.*

Dishonourable suggests behaving in an improper way: *The dishonourable lawyer stole from clients.*

Disreputable suggests having a bad reputation: *Don't wander into that disreputable part of the city!*

not·with·stand·ing (not′with stan′ding) *or* (not′wiᴛʜ stan′ding) *prep* in spite of: *She bought it notwithstanding the high price.*
conj in spite of the fact that: *Notwithstanding there was need for haste, he still delayed.*
adv nevertheless: *It is raining but I shall go shopping, notwithstanding.*

🍁 **notwithstanding clause** *n* in the Canadian Charter of Rights and Freedoms, a clause that may be used by the federal or provincial parliaments to override other charter provisions.

nou·gat (nū′gət) *or* (nū′gȧ) *n* a soft candy containing honey, egg white, and sometimes nuts. <French, from Latin *nucis* nut>

nought (not) *n* **1** zero: *Two noughts after a six make six hundred.* **2** naught.

noun (noun) *n* a word other than a pronoun used to identify a person, place, or thing. Words like *John* and *Halifax* that identify particular people or things are **proper nouns**. Words like *table, school, kindness, skill* and *party* are **common nouns**. <Old French, from Latin *nomen* name>

GRAMMAR AND USAGE

Concrete nouns are things you can touch: *book, broccoli, cow.*

Abstract nouns are things that you cannot touch: *confidence, vanity, wisdom.*

Collective nouns refer to a group or collection of things: *bunch, committee, team.*

A well-chosen noun can replace a whole phrase. *Pitchfork* is more precise than *large fork with a long handle.*

nour·ish (nər′ish) *v* **1** make grow, or keep alive and well, by providing with food: *Milk nourishes a baby.* **2** foster or encourage: *to nourish a hope.* <Old French, from Latin *nutrire* to feed>

nour·ish·ment (nər′i shmənt) *n* **1** the substances needed to provide growth and health: *The nurse said that vitamins and minerals were essential for good nourishment.* **2** food. **3** the action of nourishing or being nourished.

nou·veau riche (nū vō rēsh′) *n, pl* **nou·veaux riches** (nū vō rēsh′) a person who has recently become rich, especially someone who makes a vulgar display of wealth. <French = new rich>

no·va (nō′və) *n, pl* **no·vas** or **no·vae** (nō′vē) *or* (nō′vī) a star that suddenly becomes brighter and then gradually fades away. <Latin *novus* new>

Nova Sco·tia (skō′shə) *n* an eastern Canadian province, south of Newfoundland and Labrador, and east of New Brunswick. Nova Scotia is one of the Atlantic Provinces. *Abbrev.* **N.S.**; postal symbol **NS**; URL **www.gov.ns.ca** See also Maritime Provinces.
adj to do with Nova Scotia: *Nova Scotia timber.*
Nova Sco′tian (skō′shən) *n.*

nov·el[1] (nov′əl) *adj* of a new or unusual kind or quality: *a novel idea.* <Old French, from Latin *novus* new>

nov·el[2] (nov′əl) *n* a fictitious book-length story with characters and action. <Italian, from Latin *novus* new>

nov·el·ette (nov′ə let′) *n* a short novel, especially one that is considered trite or sentimental.

nov·el·ist (nov′ə list) *n* a writer of novels.

nov·el·la (nov′el′ə) *n* a story that is longer than a short story but shorter than a novel.

nov·el·ty (nov′əl tē) *n, pl* **nov·el·ties** **1** the quality of being new or unusual: *After the novelty of the video game wore off, she lost interest in it.* **2** a new or unusual thing: *Staying up late was a novelty to the children.* **3 novelties** *pl* small, inexpensive items such as toys, ornaments, and jewellery.

No·vem·ber (nō vem′bər) *n* the eleventh month of the year, with 30 days. *Abbrev.* **Nov** <Latin *novem* nine, the ninth month of the Roman calendar>

nov·ice (nov′is) *n* **1** someone who is new to an activity or situation: *Novices are likely to make some mistakes.* **2** a person who has been received into a religious group but has not yet taken final vows. <Old French, from Latin *novus* new>

no·vi·ti·ate or **no·vi·ci·ate** (nō vish′ē it) *n* **1** in a religious order, a period of preparation before taking final vows. **2** a novice (def. 2). **3** a house or rooms occupied by religious novices.

now (nou) *adv* **1** at or by the present time or moment: *She is here now. He must have arrived at school by now.* **2** at once: *Do it now!* **3** as the next thing to happen: *We have signed the petition and it now goes to the school principal.* **4** used to introduce, emphasize, or lessen the severity of a sentence: *Now what do you mean by that?*
n the present time or moment: *until now, from now on.*
conj since: *Now I'm older, I'm less noisy.* <Old English *nu*>
just now, only a few moments ago.
now and again, from time to time.
now and then, once in a while.

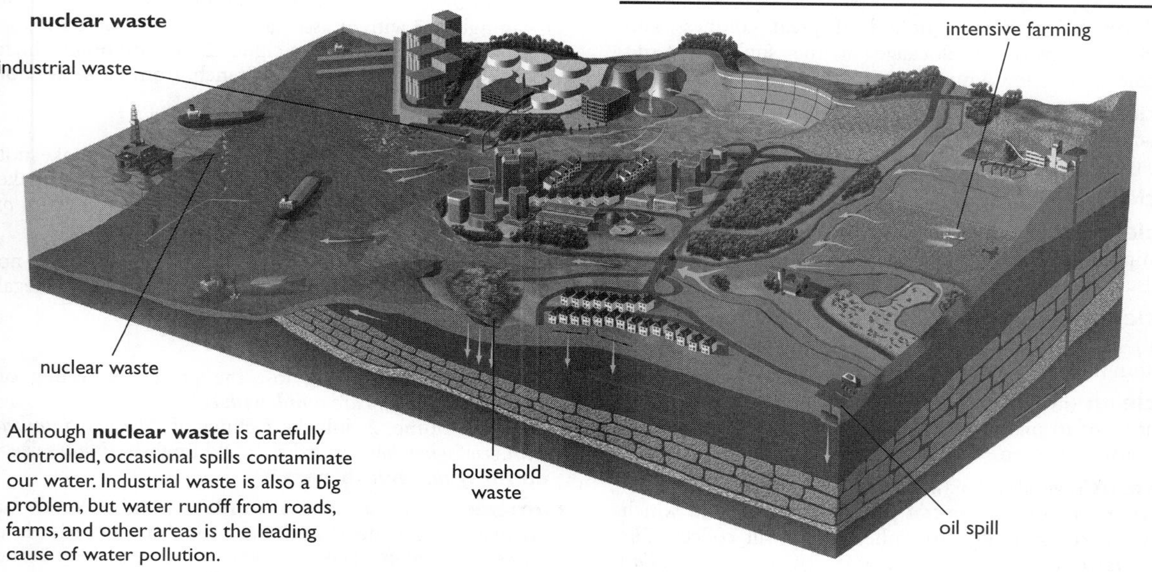

Although **nuclear waste** is carefully controlled, occasional spills contaminate our water. Industrial waste is also a big problem, but water runoff from roads, farms, and other areas is the leading cause of water pollution.

now·a·days (nou′ə dāz′) *adv* in the present time: *Nowadays, e-mail is a common form of correspondence.*
n the present time.

no·where (nō′wer′) *adv* in, at, or to no place: *The supervisor was nowhere to be seen.*
pron no place: *There was nowhere for me to sit.* <Old English *nahwær*>
get nowhere, have no success at all; make no progress.
nowhere near, not even close to: *nowhere near enough food for six people.*

no–win (nō′win′) *adj* in which nobody gains anything, and success or a good outcome is impossible: *a no-win solution.*

nox·ious (nok′shəs) *adv* harmful, poisonous, or unpleasant: *noxious fumes.* <Latin *noxa* to harm> **nox′ious·ly** *adv.* **nox′ious·ness** *n.*

noz·zle (noz′əl) *n* a tip or spout put on a hose, pipe, or tube to control the outward flow of liquid or gas, often made so that the user can adjust its force: *I adjusted the nozzle so that the water came out in a fine spray.* <*nose*>

NSF or **nsf** not sufficient funds.

nth (enth) *Informal adj* denoting an unspecified member of a series, especially of numbers or numbered items: *She was ejected from the game for the nth time.*
to the nth degree, *Informal* to the utmost: *He was dressed to the nth degree for the occasion.*

nu·ance (nyū ȧns′) *or* (nū ȧns′), (nyū′ȧns) *or* (nū′ȧns) *n* a subtle difference of expression, meaning, or feeling.
v give nuance to: *The speech was nuanced by quiet asides.* <French *nuance* slight difference, from Latin *nubes* cloud>

nub (nub) *n* **1** the point or gist of something: *the nub of the question, the nub of the matter.* **2** a small knob or protuberance. **3** a lump or small piece. <German *knubbe* knob>

nu·bile (nyū′bīl) *or* (nū′bīl), (nyū′bəl) *or* (nū′bəl) *adj* **1** old enough as a girl or woman to be married. **2** sexually attractive as a girl or woman. <Latin *nubere* put on a wedding veil>

nu·cle·ar (nyū′klē ər) *or* (nū′klē ər) *adj* **1** to do with a nucleus or the nuclei of atoms: *nuclear physics.* **2** to do with atomic energy: *nuclear submarine.* **3** forming a nucleus of a cell.

nuclear energy *n* the energy contained in the nucleus of an atom, released as a result of a fission or fusion reaction.

nuclear family *n* a parent or parents and their child or children living together, without people from other generations or other branches of the family.

nuclear fission *n* FISSION (def. 2).

nuclear fuel *n* a fissile substance that will sustain a chain reaction.

nuclear fusion *n* FUSION (def. 4).

nuclear medicine *n* the use of radioactive substances and X-rays to diagnose and treat disease.

nuclear physics *n* (*with singular verb*) the branch of physics that studies atoms and their nuclear structure.

nuclear power *n* electrical or motive power from nuclear energy produced in a nuclear reactor.

nuclear reactor *n* a device or structure in which fissile material is made to undergo a controlled, self-sustaining nuclear reaction, producing energy.

nuclear waste *n* harmful or useless radioactive material produced in the course of using or generating nuclear energy.

a bat	e bed	i bid	o pot	u cup	th **thin**
ā cake	ē me	ī bite	ō go	ū rude	ᴛʜ **then**
ȧ bar	ə about	ər over	ȯ for	u̇ put	zh measure

N

nuclear winter *n* a period of great coldness and darkness caused by blockage of the sun's rays and predicted to follow a nuclear war.

nu·cle·ate (nyū′klē āt′) *or* (nū′klē āt′) *v* **nu·cle·a·ted, nu·cle·a·ting** form a nucleus.
adj with a nucleus. **nu·cle·a′tion** *n.*

nu·cle·i (nyū′klē ī′) *or* (nū′klē ī′) plural of NUCLEUS.

nu·cle·ic acid (nyū klā′ik) *n* a group of complex compounds, especially DNA and RNA, found in all living cells and viruses. Nucleic acid controls heredity.

nu·cle·o·lus (nyū klē′ə ləs) *or* (nū klē′ə ləs) *n, pl* **nu·cle·o·li** (-lī′) *or* (-lē′) a small structure, usually round, found within the nucleus in most cells.

nu·cle·on (nyū′klē on′) *or* (nū′klē on′) *n* an atomic particle that helps to make up the nucleus of an atom, such as a neutron or proton.

nu·cle·us (nyū′klē əs) *or* (nū′klē əs) *n, pl* **nu·cle·i** (nyū ′klē ī) or **nu·cle·us·es** 1 a central part or thing around which other parts or things are collected or will collect: *The downtown area is the nucleus of a city. A rare Canadian penny formed the nucleus of her coin collection.* 2 *Physics* a group of protons and neutrons forming the central part of an atom and carrying a positive electric charge. See ATOM for picture. 3 *Biology* a mass of protoplasm found in most plant and animal cells, containing genetic material without which a cell cannot grow and divide. 4 *Astronomy* the dense, central part of a comet's head. 5 *Meteorology* a particle on which molecules of water vapour accumulate to form a raindrop or ice crystal. <Latin *nucis* nut>

nude (nyūd) *or* (nūd) *adj* wearing no clothes.
n a naked human figure in a painting, drawing, sculpture, or photograph. <Latin *nudus*> **nude′ness** *n.*
in the nude, without clothes on: *The boys went swimming in the nude.*

nudge (nuj) *v* **nudged, nudg·ing** 1 push slightly with the elbow to draw attention to someone: *Nudge me when you see the man we are looking for.* 2 gently coax someone to do something: *nudge into action.*
n a slight push or jog: *When he gave me a nudge, I spilled the milk.* <origin uncertain>

nud·ism (nyū′diz əm) *or* (nū′diz əm) *n* the practice of going naked whenever possible. Also called **naturism.**
nu′dist *n.*

nu·di·ty (nyū′də tē) *or* (nū′də tē) *n, pl* **nu·di·ties** nakedness.

nug·get (nug′it) *n* 1 a lump of metal in its natural state, especially of gold. 2 something valuable: *nuggets of wisdom.* <origin uncertain>

nui·sance (nyū′səns) *or* (nū′səns) *n* a thing that or person who annoys, troubles, offends, or is disagreeable: *He found that flies were a nuisance.* <Old French, from Latin *nocere* to harm>

nuke (nyūk) *or* (nūk) *Slang v* **nuked, nuk·ing** 1 destroy with or as if with nuclear bombs. 2 *Informal* cook or heat in a microwave oven.
n a nuclear weapon or reactor. <*nuclear*>

null (nul) *adj* 1 not binding or of no effect: *A promise obtained by force is legally null.* 2 unimportant, useless, or meaningless. 3 with or associated with the value zero.
n 1 a meaningless letter in a cipher. 2 a condition in which there is no electronic signal. <French, from Latin *ne-* not + *ullus* any>
null and void, without legal force or effect.

nul·li·fy (nul′ə fī′) *v* **nul·li·fied, nul·li·fy·ing** 1 make not binding or with no legal effect: *to nullify a law.* 2 make unimportant, useless, or meaningless: *The difficulties of the plan nullify its advantages.* **nul′li·fi·ca′tion** *n.*

nul·li·ty (nul′ə tē) *n, pl* **nul·li·ties** 1 a thing of no importance or worth. 2 the condition of being of no legal effect, or something that is legally invalid

null set EMPTY SET.

numb (num) *adj* having lost the power of feeling or moving: *My fingers are numb with cold.*
v 1 make numb. 2 dull the feelings of: *She was numbed with grief when her turtle died.* <Old English *niman* seize>
numb′ly *adv.* **numb′ness** *n.*

num·ber (num′bər) *n* 1 a word or symbol used for calculations, for identification, or for showing order in a series. *Symbol* **#**. See NUMERAL for confusable. 2 the amount, sum, or total of units: *The number of toes you have is ten.* 3 a large quantity: *a number of birds.* 4 one of a numbered series, often a particular set of numerals identifying a person or thing: *a telephone number, an apartment number.* 5 a single item on a program of events: *The program consisted of four musical numbers.* 6 a song or other piece of music: *She can sing many old numbers.* 7 a single issue of a magazine: *I'm looking for a back number of* Canadian Geographic. 8 a select class or set of people: *I want to become one of their number.* 9 *Grammar* the property of words that indicates whether they refer to one person or thing, or more than one. In an English sentence, the subject and the verb must agree in number.
v 1 assign a number to: *The pages of this book are numbered.* 2 have or include: *This city numbers a million inhabitants.* 3 include as one of a class or set: *I number you among my best friends.* 4 fix or limit the number of: *His days as president of our club are numbered.* Also, **numbers**. <Old French, from Latin *numerus*>
num′ber·er *n.*
a number of, several or many.
beyond number, too many to count.
do a number on someone, *Slang* to treat someone unfairly or harshly.
have someone's number, know someone's motives or character, and so have power over him or her: *I've got your number.*
someone's number is up, *Informal* someone is doomed.
without number, too many to be counted: *stars without number.*

GRAMMAR AND USAGE

Number is a collective noun, requiring a singular or plural verb, according to whether the total or the individual units are meant:

A number of students are waiting in line.
The number of stars in a galaxy is enormous.

number cruncher *Informal n* **1** *Computers* a computer or piece of software that can make rapid calculations of large amounts of numerical data. **2** an accountant or other person whose job is to deal with large amounts of numerical data. **number crunching** *n.*

num·ber·less (num′bər lis) *adj* **1** very numerous: *There are numberless fish in the sea.* **2** without a number.

number line *Mathematics n* a line which shows the real numbers as a series of points in which the magnitude of any number is represented by its distance from zero.

number one *n* **1** *Informal* oneself: *He worries too much about number one.* **2** the first or best.

numb·skull (num′skul′) *n* a stupid or foolish person. Also, **numskull**.

nu·mer·a·cy (nyū′mə rə sē) *or* (nū′mə rə sē) *n* the ability to deal confidently with arithmetic or with using numbers in ordinary life.

nu·mer·al (nyū′mə rəl) *or* (nū′mə rəl) *n* a word, figure, or a group of figures standing for a number. The numerals we use today, like 2, 15, 100, etc. are Arabic numerals. In the Roman system, II, XV, and C were numerals for 2, 15, and 100. <Latin *numerus* number>

CONFUSABLES

Numeral means "a figure that represents a number": *The numeral 10 stands for ten.*

Number means "an amount": *The number of friends I can invite to my party is six.*

nu·mer·ate (nyū′mə rət) *or* (nū′mə rət) *adj* able to deal confidently with arithmetic or with using numbers in ordinary life. Compare LITERATE.

nu·mer·a·tion (nyū′mə rā′shən) *or* (nū′mə rā′shən) *n* the action or process of calculating with numbers or assigning numbers.

nu·mer·a·tor (nyū′mə rā′tər) *or* (nū ′mə rā′tər) *n* **1** the number above the line in a fraction. Example: In 3/8, 3 is the numerator and 8 is the denominator. **2** a person who or thing that makes a count or takes a census.

nu·mer·i·cal (nyū mer′ə kəl) *or* (nū mer′ə kəl) *adj* **1** to do with number or numbers. **2** shown by numbers, not by letters. **nu·mer′i·cal·ly** *adv.*

num·er·ol·o·gy (nyū′mər ol′o jē) *or* (nū′mər ol′o jē) *n* a system of interpreting events or texts by attaching meaning to specific numbers, associating a numerical value with each letter, or looking for numerical patterns. **num·er·o·log′i·cal** *adj.* **num·er·ol′o·gist** *n.*

nu·mer·ous (nyū′mə rəs) *or* (nū′mə rəs) *adj* very many or in great numbers: *The child asked numerous questions. She has a numerous acquaintance among musicians.* **nu′mer·ous·ly** *adv.* **nu′mer·ous·ness** *n.*

nu·mis·mat·ic (nyū′miz mat′ik) *or* (nū′miz mat′ik) *adj* to do with coins and medals.
n **numismatics** (*with singular verb*) the study or collection of coins and medals. <French, from Greek = current coin, from *nomizein* in current use> **nu·mis′ma·tist** (nyū′miz mət′ist) *or* (nū′miz mət′ist) *n.*

num·skull (num′skul′) NUMBSKULL.

nun (nun) *n* a woman who has taken certain vows to live her life in a way prescribed by a religious community. <Latin *nonmus* monk>

Nu·na·vut (nu̇′na vut′) *n* a large area in northern Canada east of the Northwest Territories, and administered by a territorial government. *Abbrev.* **Nvt.**; postal symbol **NU**; URL **www.gov.nu.ca**

nun·cio (nun′shē ō′) *n, pl* **nun·ci·os** an ambassador from the Pope to a government.

nun·ner·y (nun′ə rē) *n, pl* **nun·ner·ies** a convent.

nup·tial (nup′shəl) *or* (nup′chəl) *adj* to do with marriage or weddings.
n **nuptials** *pl* a wedding or the wedding ceremony. <Old French, from Latin *nubere* to marry>

nurse (nərs) *n* **1** a person trained to take care of people who are sick, injured, very young, or very old, especially in a hospital or clinic under the supervision of doctors. **2** in former times, a woman hired to care for the young children or babies of another person.
v **nursed, nurs·ing 1** be or act as a nurse. **2** treat or use with special care: *She nursed a bad cold by going to bed. He nursed his sore arm by using it very little.* **3** feed milk to a baby at the breast, or be fed this way: *She nursed all her children. The baby nursed badly at first.* **4** nourish, guide, or supervise something, so that it will grow: *to nurse a plant, to nurse a hatred in your mind.* <Old French, from Latin *nutrire* nourish>

SYNONYMS

Nurse means "care for" or "look after": *She nursed the patient until he was well.*

Minister means "give aid or help": *The volunteers ministered to the victims of the flood by providing food and shelter.*

Treat can mean "give medical attention": *The doctor gave me medicine to treat my cold.*

nurse·maid (nər′smād′) *n* a woman employed to care for children.

nurs·er·y (nər′sə rē) *n, pl* **nurs·er·ies 1** a room set apart for the use of babies and children. **2** a daycare centre. **3** a nursery school. **4** a piece of ground or place where young plants are grown for transplanting or sale.

nursery rhyme *n* a short piece of verse for young children.

nursery school *n* a school for children more than three years old and, usually, under five.

nurs·ing (nər′sing) *n* the occupation of being a nurse, or the training required for it.

nursing home *n* a residence providing personal or nursing care for people who are elderly, chronically ill, or have a disability.

a bat	e bed	i bid	o pot	u cup	th **thin**
ā cake	ē me	ī bite	ō go	ū rude	ᴛʜ **then**
ȧ bar	ə about	ər over	ȯ for	u̇ put	zh measure

N

nursing station *n* **1** a place serving as a base and office area in a hospital for the nurses working on a certain floor or in a certain ward. **2** 🍁 a small hospital for emergency treatment in the North, staffed by nurses and visited periodically by a doctor.

nurs·ling (nər′sling) *n* **1** a baby who is being NURSED (def. 3). **2** a person who or thing that receives tender care.

nur·ture (nər′chər) *v* **nur·tured, nur·tur·ing 1** bring up and care for: *She nurtured the child as if he had been her own.* **2** nourish: *Minerals in the soil nurture the plants.*
n **1** the act or process of bringing up and caring for. **2** food or nourishment. <Old French, from Latin *nutrire*>
nur′tur·er *n.*

nut (nut) *n* **1** a dry fruit or seed with a hard, woody or leathery shell and a kernel inside, or the kernel itself. **2** a small block, usually of metal, that screws onto a bolt to hold the bolt in place. **3** a piece at the upper end of a stringed instrument over which the strings pass. **4** *Informal* a crazy or very eccentric person.
v **nut·ted, nut·ting** gather nuts. <Old English *hnutu*>
hard nut to crack, *Informal* a difficult question, problem, or undertaking.
nuts and bolts, practical details.

nut·crack·er (nut′krak′ər) *n* **1** a device for cracking the shells of nuts. **2** a small bird of the crow family that feeds on the seeds of conifers.

nut·hatch (nut′hach′) *n* a small, sharp-beaked songbird with a stiffened tail that climbs up and down tree trunks and feeds on small nuts, seeds, and insects.

nut·meat (nut′mēt′) *n* the kernel of a nut.

nut·meg (nut′meg′) *n* an aromatic seed obtained from the fruit of a tropical tree. It is used in grated form as a spice. <Old French, from Latin *nux* nut + *muscus* musk>

nu·tri·a (nyū′trē ə) *or* (nū′trē ə) *n* the skin or fur of the coypu, an aquatic rodent of S America. <Spanish = otter>

nu·tri·ent (nyū′trē ənt) *or* (nū ′trē ənt) *n* a nourishing substance.
adj nourishing.

nu·tri·tion (nyū trish′ən) *or* (nū trish′ən) *n* **1** nourishment: *A balanced diet gives good nutrition.* **2** the series of processes by which food is changed to living tissue. **nu·tri′tion·al** *adj.* **nu·tri′tion·al·ly** *adv.*

nu·tri·tious (nyū trish′əs) *or* (nū trish′əs) *adj* nourishing. <Latin *nutrire* nourish> **nu·tri′tious·ly** *adv.*
nu·tri′tious·ness *n.*

nu·tri·tive (nyū′trə tiv) *or* (nū ′trə tiv) *adj* **1** to do with foods and the use of foods: *Digestion is part of the nutritive process.* **2** nutritious. **nu′tri·tive·ness** *n.*

nut·shell (nut′shel′) *n* the shell of a nut.
in a nutshell, in a very brief form or in a few words.

nut·ty (nut′ē) *adj* **nut·ti·er, nut·ti·est 1** containing many nuts: *nutty cake.* **2** like nuts or tasting like nuts: *Some cereals have a nutty flavour.* **3** *Informal* mildly crazy or eccentric: *nutty jokes.* **nut′ti·ness** *n.*

Nuu–chah–nulth (nù′chə nulth) *n, pl* **Nuu–chah–nulth 1** a member of a First Nations people living mainly on Vancouver Island. **2** their Salishan language.
adj to do with these people or their language. Also called **Nootka**.

Nux·alk (nūks′əlk) *n, pl* **Nux·alk 1** a member of a First Nations people living mainly on the central coast of British Columbia. **2** the Salishan language of these people.
adj to do with these people or their language. Also called **Bella Coola**.

nuz·zle (nuz′əl) *v* **nuz·zled, nuz·zling 1** poke or rub with the nose: *The calf nuzzled its mother.* **2** nestle, snuggle, or cuddle. <Old English *nosu*>

NW northwest; northwestern.

NWMP or **N.W.M.P.** North West Mounted Police.

ny·lon (nī′lon) *n* **1** a strong, durable, plastic substance, used to make filaments, material, and moulded objects used for many purposes. **2 nylons** *pl* stockings made of nylon.
adj made of nylon: *nylon rope.* <*Nylon*, a trademark>

nymph (nimf) *n* **1** a beautiful or graceful young woman. **2** an insect such as the dragonfly, mayfly, or locust in the stage of development between larva and adult. <Old French, from Greek *nymphe*> **nymph′like** *adj.*

Oo

o or **O** (ō) *n, pl* **o's** or **O's** **1** the fifteenth letter of the English alphabet, or any speech sound represented by it. **2** the fifteenth thing in a list or series: *The items are labelled from (a) to (o).*

o' (ə) *or* (ō) *prep* on; of: *o'clock, will-o'-the-wisp.*

O[1] **1** one of the four main blood groups. The others are A, B, and AB. **2** oxygen.

O[2] *interj* used formally to address someone or something: *O Canada, our home and native land.*

GRAMMAR AND USAGE

The spelling O is usually used only before a name or other proper noun: *O Canada*. In other cases, the spelling is usually Oh: *Oh my goodness!*

oaf (ōf) *n, pl* **oafs** a stupid, ignorant, or clumsy person. *I felt like an oaf when I dropped my glass.* <Old Norse *alfr* silly person> **oaf'ish** *adj.*

oak (ōk) *n* **1** a large hardwood tree with nuts called acorns, or the hard, durable wood of this tree. **2** a tree or shrub resembling or suggesting an oak.
adj to do with oak: *oak leaves, an oak table and chairs.* <Old English *ac*>

oak·en (ō'kən) *adj* made of oak wood: *the old oaken bucket.*

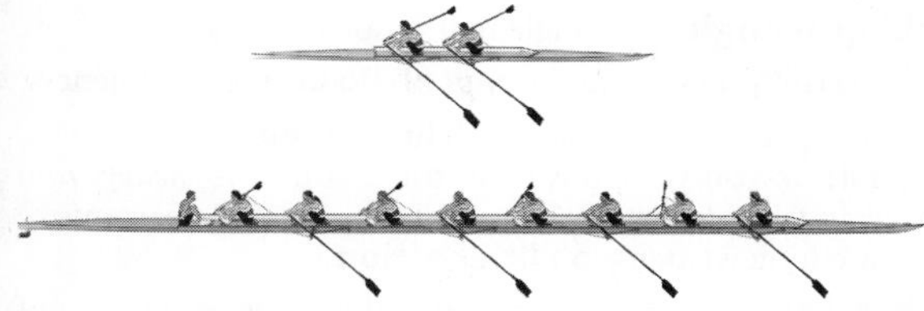

In sculling or scull racing, two or four rowers use one pair of **oars** each. In crew or sweep oar racing, each of the eight crew uses only one oar.

oar (ȯr) *n* **1** a long pole with a broad, flat blade at one end, used for rowing or steering a boat. **2** a person who rows: *She is the best oar in our crew.*
v row. <Old English *ar*>
put your oar in, *Informal* meddle or interfere.
rest on your oars, stop working or trying and take a rest.

oar·lock (ȯr'lok') *n* a notch or U-shaped support for holding an oar in place while rowing.

oars·man (ȯr'zmən) *n, pl* **oars·men** (-zmən) a person who rows.

OAS or **O.A.S.** *n* **1** 🍁 in full, **Old Age Security** a modest government pension provided at age 65 to those who have lived in Canada for at least 10 years. Low-income seniors may be eligible for other benefits as early as age 60. **2** in full, **Organization of American States** an association of Latin American countries and the US, created in 1948 to promote military, economic, social, and cultural co-operation.

o·a·sis (ō ā'sis) *n, pl* **o·a·ses** (ō ā'sēs) **1** a fertile spot in the desert where water is found. See LAKE for picture. **2** a pleasant or peaceful place or situation in the midst of difficulty or unfriendliness. <Latin, from Greek>

oat (ōt) *n* **1** a tall cereal grass grown in cool climates, whose seeds are used in making oatmeal and as a food for livestock. See GRAIN for picture. **2 oats** the seeds of the oat plant used as food. <Old English *ate*>
feel your oats, *Informal* be lively or energetic.
sow your wild oats, behave irresponsibly when young.

oat·cake (ōt'kāk') *n* a thin cake made of oatmeal.

oath (ōth) *n, pl* **oaths** (ōᴛʜz) *or* (ōths) **1** a solemn promise or statement that something is true, especially such a promise made in a law court. **2** a curse or swear word. <Old English *ath*>
take an oath (or **oaths**), certify or attest an oath: *A notary public is authorized to take oaths.*
under oath, bound by an oath: *She gave her evidence under oath.*

oat·meal (ōt'mēl') *n* oats ground or rolled, or porridge made from rolled oats or oatmeal.

ob·du·rate (ob'dyə rit) *or* (ob'də rit) *adj* stubborn or unyielding: *an obdurate refusal.* <Latin *ob-* against + *durare* harden> **ob'du·ra·cy** *n.* **ob'du·rate·ly** *adv.*

o·be·di·ence (ō bē'dē əns) *n* the act or habit of doing what one is told: *Our puppy is learning obedience.* **o·be'di·ent** *adj.* **o·be'di·ent·ly** *adv.*

obedience school *n* a school where dogs are trained to obey commands.

o·bei·sance (ō bā'səns) *or* (ō bē'səns) *n* a movement of the body or form of words expressing deep respect: *The men made obeisance to the king.* <Old French, from Latin>

ob·e·lisk (ob'ə lisk') *n* a tapering, four-sided shaft of stone with a top shaped like a pyramid, set up as a monument or landmark. <Latin, from Greek *obelos*>

o·bese (ō bēs') *adj* extremely fat. <Latin *ob-* completely + *edere* eat> **o·bes'i·ty** *n.*

o·bey (ō bā') *v* **1** follow or carry out a demand, request, or command: *The dog obeyed and went home. We obeyed our mother.* **2** act in accordance with: *obey a law, obey a rule.* <Old French, from Latin *ob-* to + *audire* hear>

ob·fus·cate (ob'fə skāt') *or* (ob fus'kāt) *v* **ob·fus·cat·ed, ob·fus·cat·ing** confuse or make unclear: *He was accused of obfuscating the facts.* <Latin *ob-* over + *fuscus* dark> **ob'fus·ca'tion** *n.* **ob'fus·ca'tor** *n.*

o·bi (ō'bē) *n* a long, broad sash worn around the waist of a Japanese kimono. <Japanese = belt>

o·bit (ō bit') *Informal n* an obituary.

o·bit·u·ary (ō bich'ū er'ē) *n, pl* **o·bit·u·ar·ies** a notice of death, often with a brief account of the person's life.
adj recording a death: *an obituary notice.* <Latin *obire* to die>

a bat	e bed	i bid	o pot	u cup	th thin
ā cake	ē me	ī bite	ō go	ū rude	ᴛʜ then
ȧ bar	ə about	ər over	ȯ for	u̇ put	zh measure

O

ob·ject (ob′jikt) *for n*, (əb jekt′) *for v*. *n* **1** a thing that can be seen or touched: *What is that object by the fence?* **2** a person or thing toward which feeling, thought, or action is directed: *an object of charity, an object of study.* **3** a purpose or goal: *My object in coming here was to give you a gift.* **4** a noun, pronoun, or noun phrase that is affected by a verb or a preposition. Example: In *He threw the ball to his brother*, the object of *threw* is *ball*, and the object of *to* is *brother.*
v **1** be opposed to or feel dislike for: *I made my suggestion, but my friend objected. Many people object to loud noise.* **2** give as a reason against something: *Mother objected that the weather was too wet to play outdoors.* <Latin *ob-* against + *jacere* to throw> **ob·jec′tor** *n.*

ob·jec·ti·fy (əb jek′tə fī′) *v* **ob·jec·ti·fied, ob·jec·ti·fy·ing** make into a fact or object instead of being abstract: *Experiments in chemistry objectify theories.*

ob·jec·tion (əb jek′shən) *n* **1** a reason or argument against something: *One of her objections to the plan was that it would cost too much.* **2** a feeling of disapproval or dislike: *He raised strong objections to cleaning his room.*

ob·jec·tion·a·ble (əb jek′shə nə bəl) *adj* likely to be objected to, especially to something unpleasant or disagreeable. **ob·jec′tion·a·bly** *adv.*

ob·jec·tive (əb jek′tiv) *adj* **1** dealing with facts or objects, not with thoughts or feelings; not biased: *Your family can't give you an objective opinion of your looks.* Compare SUBJECTIVE. **2** *Grammar* to do with the object of a verb or preposition.
n **1** a goal or purpose: *My objective this summer will be learning to play tennis better.* **2** *Grammar* the form used for the object of a verb or preposition. Example: *Him* is the objective of *he*. Other objectives are *me, us, her, them,* and *whom.* **3** the lens or set of lenses in a microscope or telescope that is nearest to the object being viewed and that forms the image of the object. **ob·jec′tive·ly** *adv.*

GRAMMAR AND USAGE

Objective and **subjective** are grammar terms that describe different parts of a sentence: the *subject* and the *object.*

Objective also means "dealing with information in a factual, impersonal way," while **subjective** also means "reacting to information according to personal ideas and feelings." Most kinds of formal writing demand an objective point of view, in which the writer presents information fairly.

ob·jec·tiv·i·ty (ob′jek tiv′ə tē) *n* the act or fact of dealing with something actual and observable, not with thoughts and feelings.

object lesson (ob′jikt) *n* a practical illustration of a principle: *Many street accidents are object lessons in the dangers of carelessness.*

ob·jet d'art (ob zhe dàr′) *n, pl* **ob·jets d'art** (ob zhā dàr′) a small decoration or object of some artistic value. <French = object of art>

ob·late (ob′lāt) *adj* flattened at the poles of a spheroid. <Latin *ob-* inversely + *-latus* carried> **ob′late·ness** *n.*

ob·la·tion (o blā′shən) *n* an offering to God or a god. <Old French, from Latin *offere* to offer>

ob·li·gate (ob′lə gāt′) *v* **ob·li·gat·ed, ob·li·gat·ing** bind morally or legally: *A witness in court is obligated to tell the truth.* <Latin *ob-* to + *ligare* bind>

ob·li·ga·tion (ob′lə gā′shən) *n* **1** a duty to which a person is bound due to a promise or contract: *The man is under obligation to paint our house first.* **2** the binding power of a law, promise, or sense of duty: *The one who did the damage is under obligation to pay for it.* **3** a debt or something owed: *The firm was not able to meet its obligations.*

ob·lig·a·to·ry (əb lig′ə tô′rē) *or* (ob′lə gə tô′rē) *adj* binding morally or legally: *obligatory attendance.*

o·blige (ə blīj′) *v* **o·bliged, o·blig·ing** **1** bind by a promise, contract, or duty: *The law obliges parents to send their children to school.* **2** do a favour to: *Kindly oblige me by closing the door.* **o·blig′er** *n.*
be obliged, be grateful to someone for a service: *I am obliged to you for letting me stay so long at your house.*

o·blig·ing (ə blī′jing) *adj* willing to do favours: *Her obliging good nature won her friends.* **o·blig′ing·ly** *adv.* **o·blig′ing·ness** *n.*

ob·lique (ə blēk′) *adj* **1** slanting, and not parallel or at right angles to another line. **2** not straightforward or direct: *an oblique glance. She made an oblique reference to her illness, but did not mention it directly.* <Latin *obliquus*> **ob·lique′ly** *adv.* **ob·lique′ness** *n.*

oblique angle *n* an angle that is not a right angle.

ob·liq·ui·ty (ə blik′wə tē) *n, pl* **ob·liq·ui·ties** obliqueness.

ob·lit·er·ate (ə blit′ə rāt′) *v* **ob·lit·er·at·ed, ob·lit·er·at·ing** remove all traces of: *The heavy rain obliterated her footprints.* <Latin *obliterare* remove something written> **ob·lit′er·a′tion** *n.*

ob·liv·i·on (ə bliv′ē ən) *n* **1** the condition of being unaware of what is going on: *He was so exhausted, he just dropped into oblivion.* **2** the condition of being entirely forgotten, especially by the public: *Many ancient cities have long since passed into oblivion.* <Old French, from Latin *oblivisci* forget>

ob·liv·i·ous (ə bliv′ē əs) *adj* not aware of what is going on: *The book was so interesting that I was oblivious of my surroundings.* **ob·liv′i·ous·ly** *adv.* **ob·liv′i·ous·ness** *n.*

ob·long (ob′long) *adj* longer than broad or round: *an oblong loaf of bread.*
n an object or flat figure in this shape. <Latin *ob-* thoroughly + *longus* long>

ob·nox·ious (əb nok′shəs) *adj* extremely disagreeable or unpleasant: *His disgusting table manners made him obnoxious.* **ob·nox′ious·ly** *adv.* **ob·nox′ious·ness** *n.*

obo or **o.b.o.** (*in advertisements for private sales*) or best offer: *Electric guitar, good condition, $175 obo.*

o·boe (ō′bō) *n* a woodwind instrument in which a tone is produced by a double reed. <French *haut* high + *bois* wood>

ob·scene (əb sēn′) *or* (ob sēn′) *adj* offending ordinary standards of decency or morality: *We were annoyed by the man's obscene swearing.* <Latin *obscenus*> **ob·scene′ly** *adv.*

Observatories are not a modern concept. The first ones, probably just tall platforms, were built by the Chinese and the Babylonians around 2300 BCE.

The first European observatory was built in 1471 in what is now Germany. Other European countries soon followed suit.

After the invention of the telescope in 1609, the French and the British established observatories, but it was not until the 1800s that observatories were built in North America.

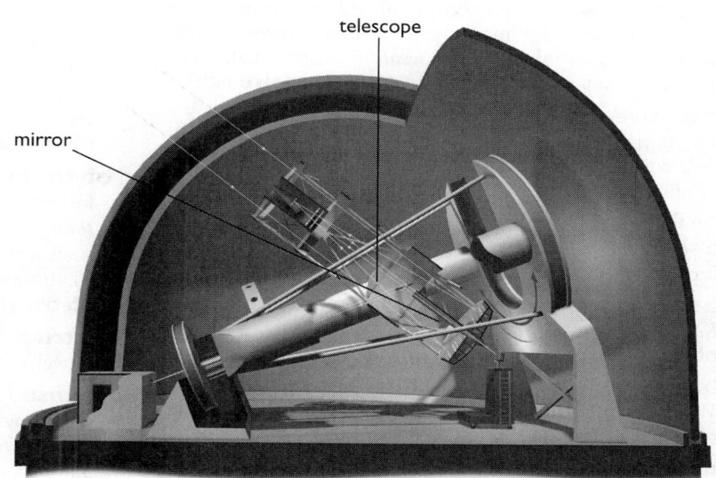

ob·scen·i·ty (əb sen′ə tē) *or* (əb sē′nə tē) *n, pl* **ob·scen·i·ties** **1** the condition or quality of being obscene. **2** an obscene word or act.

ob·scur·ant·ism (əb skyů′rən tiz′əm) *or* (ob′skyə ran′tiz əm) *n* opposition to the spread of knowledge among the public, or the prevention of facts or the full details of something from becoming known. **ob·scu′rant·ist′** or **ob′scu·rant′ist** *n.*

ob·scure (əb skyůr′) *adj* **ob·scur·er, ob·scur·est** **1** not clearly expressed or easily understood: *an obscure passage in a book.* **2** not well-known: *an obscure little village, an obscure poet, obscure origins.* **3** not sharply defined in shape, sound, or colour: *an obscure form.*
v **ob·scured, ob·scur·ing** **1** hide from view or keep from being seen: *Clouds obscured the sun.* **2** make unclear and difficult to understand: *His emotional language tended to obscure his ideas.* <Old French, from Latin *ob-* over + *scurus* covered> **ob·scure′ly** *adv.* **ob·scure′ness** *n.* **ob·scur′er** *n.*

ob·scu·ri·ty (əb skyů′rə tē) *n, pl* **ob·scu·ri·ties** **1** a lack of clearness, or difficulty in being understood: *The obscurity of the passage makes several interpretations possible.* **2** something obscure or hard to understand: *The movie had so many obscurities that we didn't enjoy it.* **3** the state or condition of being unknown: *The actor rose from obscurity to fame with her first movie.*

ob·se·qui·ous (əb sē′kwē əs) *adj* polite or obedient from a hope of gaining something or out of fear: *Obsequious courtiers greeted the queen.* <Latin *ex-* out + *sequi* follow> **ob·se′qui·ous·ly** *adv.* **ob·se′qui·ous·ness** *n.*

ob·serv·a·ble (əb zər′və bəl) *adj* **1** able to be noticed or seen. **2** able to be followed as a rule or custom. **ob·serv′a·bly** *adv.*

ob·serv·ance (əb zər′vəns) *n* **1** the act or process of fulfilling or respecting a law or custom: *the observance of polite behaviour.* **2** an act performed as part of a ritual, rule, or custom.

ob·serv·ant (əb zər′vənt) *adj* **1** quick to notice things: *If you are observant in the fields and woods, you will find many flowers that others fail to notice.* **2** careful in observing a law, rule, or custom, especially of a religion: *observant of sacraments.* **ob·serv′ant·ly** *adv.*

ob·ser·va·tion (ob′zər vā′shən) *n* **1** the act, habit, or power of seeing and noting: *Her keen observation helped her to become a good scientist.* **2** the act or fact of being seen: *The thief escaped observation.* **3** something seen and noted: *The student of bird life kept a record of his observations.* **4** a remark or comment.

ob·ser·va·tion·al (ob′zər vā′shə nəl) *adj* to do with observation, especially as contrasted with experiment.

ob·serv·a·to·ry (əb zər′və tô′rē) *n, pl* **ob·serv·a·to·ries** a place or building equipped with a telescope or other scientific equipment for observing nature, especially stars and other celestial bodies.

ob·serve (əb zərv′) *v* **ob·served, ob·serv·ing** **1** see and note, especially as being significant: *I observed nothing strange in her behaviour.* **2** watch for some special purpose: *The astronomer observed the stars.* **3** make a remark or comment: *"Bad weather," the captain observed.* **4** follow a rule or custom: *to observe silence, to observe a rule.* **5** show regard for or celebrate an anniversary: *We observed her 80th birthday.*

ob·serv·er (əb zər′vər) *n* **1** a person who watches or notices something: *a casual observer, a close observer.* **2** a person who follows events or situations closely, and comments on them: *Some observers thought the party would lose the next election.* **3** a person who attends a meeting, conference, or enquiry but takes no official part in it, or who watches and makes notes of some public event.

a bat	e bed	i bid	o pot	u cup	th **thin**
ā cake	ē me	ī bite	ō go	ū rude	ᴛʜ **then**
ä bar	ə about	ər over	ô for	ů put	zh measure

ob·sess (əb ses′) *v* preoccupy or fill the mind in a continual and troubling way: *Fear that someone might steal his money obsessed the wealthy miser.* <Latin *ob-* opposite + *sidere* sit> **ob·ses′sion** *n.* **ob·ses′sive** *adj.*

ob·ses·sive–com·pul·sive (əb ses′iv cəm pul′siv) *Psychiatry adj* to do with a disorder in which a person feels compelled to perform certain repeated acts as a way of relieving intense anxiety about something.
n a person with this disorder.

ob·sid·i·an (ob sid′ē ən) *n* a hard, dark, glassy rock that is formed when lava cools.

ob·so·les·cent (ob′sə les′ənt) *adj* passing out of use: *Kerosene lamps have become obsolescent.*
ob′so·les′cence *n.*

ob·so·lete (ob′sə lēt′) *adj* out-of-date or no longer in use: *We still use this machine even though it is obsolete.* <Latin *ob-* off + *solere* be customary>

ob·sta·cle (ob′stə kəl) *n* a thing that stands in the way or stops progress in an activity: *A tree fallen across the road was an obstacle to the cyclists.* <Old French, from Latin *ob-* against + *stare* stand>

obstacle course *n* **1** a course used for a race or exercise that includes several obstacles such as walls, fences, or ditches. **2** a process or course of events that is full of difficulties.

ob·stet·ric (ob stet′rik) *adj* to do with the care of women in childbirth: *the obstetric wing of the hospital.*
n **obstetrics** (*with singular verb*) the branch of medicine and surgery concerned with caring for and treating women in, before, and after childbirth. <Latin *ob-* by + *stare* present> **ob′ste·tri′cian** (ob′stə trish′ən) *n.*

ob·sti·nate (ob′stə nit) *adj* **1** stubborn: *The obstinate girl would go her own way, in spite of all warnings.* **2** hard to control or treat: *an obstinate cough.* <Latin *ob-* against + *stare* persist> **ob′sti·na·cy** *n.* **ob′sti·nate·ly** *adv.*

SYNONYMS

Obstinate (definition 1) and **stubborn** both mean "fixed in purpose or opinion."

Obstinate often suggests being unreasonable or wilful: *The obstinate musician wouldn't perform.*

Stubborn suggests being firm enough not to yield. When used of animals, the word suggests being hard to handle: *The stubborn horse refused to jump.*

ob·strep·er·ous (əb strep′ə rəs) *adj* noisy, boisterous, and unruly. <Latin *ob-* against + *strepere* make noise> **ob·strep′er·ous·ly** *adv.* **ob·strep′er·ous·ness** *n.*

ob·struct (əb strukt′) *v* **1** block or make hard to pass through: *Fallen trees obstructed the road.* **2** be in the way of or hinder: *A strike obstructed the work of the factory.* <Latin *ob-* against + *struere* build> **ob·struc′tive** *adj.*

ob·struc·tion (əb struk′shən) *n* **1** the act or fact of obstructing or being obstructed: *the obstruction of progress by prejudices.* **2** a thing that obstructs: *The soldiers had to get over such obstructions as ditches and barbed wire.* **3** an action that deliberately hinders the police in their duties.

ob·struc·tion·ism (əb struk′shə niz′əm) *n* the practice or policy of hindering the progress of legal, legislative, or other procedures. **ob·struc′tion·ist** *n.*

ob·tain (əb tān′) *v* **1** get, acquire, or secure something: *She worked hard to obtain first prize.* **2** be in use, prevail, or be customary: *Different rules obtain in different schools.* <Old French, from Latin *ob-* to + *tenere* hold>
ob·tain′a·ble *adj.*

ob·trude (əb trūd′) *v* **ob·trud·ed, ob·trud·ing** **1** put forward unasked and unwanted: *Noise obtruded into his thoughts.* **2** impose or force something on someone in such a way: *I don't want to obtrude my worries on you.* <Latin *ob-* toward + *trudere* to push>
ob·tru′sion (əb trū′zhən) *n.*

ob·tru·sive (əb trū′siv) *adj* noticeable or prominent in an unwelcome way. **ob·tru′sive·ly** *adv.* **ob·tru′sive·ness** *n.*

ob·tuse (əb tyūs′) *or* (əb tūs′) *adj* **1** slow in understanding or annoyingly insensitive: *She was too obtuse to take the hint.* **2** with an angle more than 90° but less than 180°. **3** not sharply pointed or sharply edged. <Latin *ob-* against + *tundere* beat> **ob·tuse′ly** *adv.*

ob·verse (ob′vərs) *for n,* (ob vərs′) *or* (ob′vərs) *for adj.* *n* **1** the side of a coin or medal that has the principal design or head. **2** the opposite or counterpart of something. *adj* **1** turned toward the observer. **2** being the opposite or counterpart to something else. <Latin *ob-* to + *vertere* to turn> **ob·verse′ly** *adv.*

ob·vi·ate (ob′vē āt′) *v* **ob·vi·at·ed, ob·vi·at·ing** remove a need or difficulty: *to obviate objections.* <Latin *ob-* in + *via* way> **ob′vi·a′tion** *n.*

ob·vi·ous (ob′vē əs) *adj* **1** easily seen or understood: *It is obvious that two and two make four.* **2** predictable and not subtle: *an obvious remark.* <Latin *ob-* in + *via* way> **ob′vi·ous·ly** *adv.* **ob′vi·ous·ness** *n.*

oc·a·ri·na (ok′ə rē′nə) *n* an egg-shaped musical instrument, with finger holes and a mouthpiece.

oc·ca·sion (ə kā′zhən) *or* (ō kā′zhən) *n* **1** a particular time when something occurs: *We have met her on several occasions.* **2** a special event: *The jewels were worn only on great occasions.* **3** a good chance to do something: *The trip gave us an occasion to get better acquainted.* **4** a cause or reason: *The dog that was the occasion of the quarrel had run away.*
v cause or bring about: *Her strange behaviour occasioned talk.* <Latin *ob-* toward + *cadere* to fall>
on occasion, now and then.

oc·ca·sion·al (ə kā′zhə nəl) *adj* **1** happening, appearing, or done now and then: *We had fine weather except for an occasional thunderstorm.* **2** produced for or intended to be for some special time or event: *She composed a piece of occasional music to be played at the opening concert in the new auditorium.* **3** made or adapted for use as furniture on a certain occasion or for use only now and then: *an occasional table.*

oc·ca·sion·al·ly (ə kā′zhə nə lē) *adv* now and then.

Oc·ci·dent (ok′sə dənt) *n* the countries of Europe and the Americas. <Old French, from Latin *ob-* toward + *cadere* to fall>

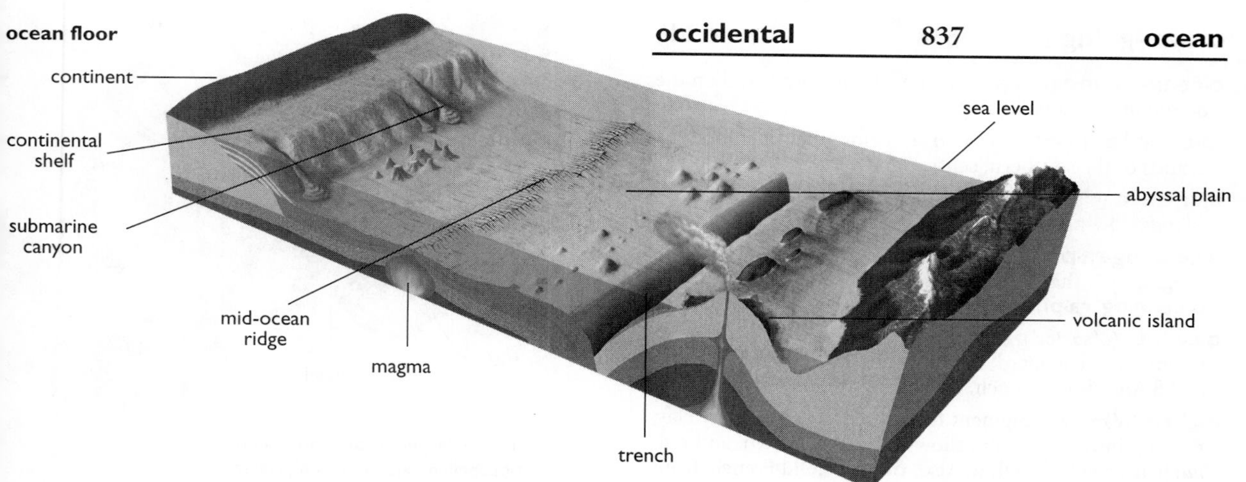

oc·ci·den·tal or **Oc·ci·den·tal** (ok′sə den′təl) *adj* to do with the countries of Europe and the Americas or Western civilizations in general: *occidental music.*
n Offensive a native or inhabitant of Europe and the Americas.

oc·cip·i·tal (ok sip′ə təl) *adj* to do with the back part of the head or skull.
n the occipital bone. <Old French, from Latin *ob-* behind + *caput* head>

oc·clude (o klūd′) *v* **oc·clud·ed, oc·clud·ing 1** close up or obstruct an opening or passage. **2** shut in, out, or off. **3** absorb and retain a gas or impurity. **4** of a tooth, come into contact with another tooth in the opposite jaw. **5** force air to rise, such as when a cold front overtakes and pushes under a warm front. <Latin *ob-* up + *claudere* shut> **oc·clu′sion** *n.*

occluded front *n* the front created when a cold front overtakes a warm front, forcing warm air up between two layers of cold air.

oc·cult (ə kult′) *or* (ok′ult) *adj* **1** beyond the bounds of ordinary knowledge or the laws of the natural world, as in something magical, mystical, or supernatural. **2** not accompanied by easily detectable signs or symptoms in a disease or physiological process.
n occult studies or beliefs. <Latin *occulare* cover over>

oc·cult·ism (o kul′tiz əm) *or* (ok′əl tiz′əm) *n* **1** a belief in occult powers. **2** the study or use of occult principles.

oc·cu·pan·cy (ok′yə pən sē) *n* the act or fact of occupying something: *The occupancy of the land by cattlemen was disputed by the farmers.*

oc·cu·pant (ok′yə pənt) *n* **1** a person who occupies something: *the occupant of the chair. The occupant of the apartment was not at home.* **2** the person in actual possession of something at a given time.

oc·cu·pa·tion (ok′yə pā′shən) *n* **1** a person's business or employment: *a professional occupation.* **2** the action, condition, or period of occupying or being occupied, especially by a military force: *the occupation of a town by the enemy.* **3** the act or fact of entering, taking control, living in, or using a building or other place: *The strikers remained in occupation of the factory for several days. Mom and I took occupation of our home in June.*

oc·cu·pa·tion·al (ok′yə pā′shə nəl) *adj* to do with work or an occupation: *occupational safety.*

occupational hazard *n* a risk or danger that goes with a particular job: *Backache is an occupational hazard for piano movers.*

occupational therapy *n* the treatment of people with physical or mental disabilities to improve their capabilities, independence, or recovery from illness or injury.

oc·cu·py (ok′yə pī′) *v* **oc·cu·pied, oc·cu·py·ing 1** fill or take up a space: *The building occupies an entire block.* **2** live in or have work in a building: *The owner and her son occupy the house.* **3 a** fill or preoccupy the mind or thoughts: *My mind was occupied with all sorts of problems.* **b** keep busy at some activity: *While I waited for you to call, I occupied myself by doing my homework.* **4** take possession of, especially by force or military conquest: *The soldiers occupied the town.* **5** keep possession of, have, or hold: *He occupied the position of Student Council President for two years.* <Old French, from Latin *ob-* up + *caperè* grasp> **oc′cu·pi′er** *n.*

oc·cur (ə kər′) *v* **oc·curred, oc·cur·ring 1** take place or happen: *Storms often occur in winter.* **2** be found in or exist: *In English, the letter "e" occurs in print more than any other letter.* **3** come to mind: *Did it occur to you to close the window?* <Latin *ob-* across + *currere* to run>

oc·cur·rence (ə kər′əns) *n* **1** the act or fact of occurring: *The occurrence of storms delayed our trip.* **2** an event or happening: *an unexpected occurrence.*

o·cean (ō′shən) *n* **1** a huge expanse of salt water that covers much of the earth, especially each of the main areas into which it is divided, such as the Atlantic, Pacific, Indian, and Arctic. **2** a vast expanse or quantity: *oceans of trouble.* <Old French, from Greek *okeanos* great stream>

a bat	e bed	i bid	o pot	u cup	th thin
ā cake	ē me	ī bite	ō go	ū rude	ᴛʜ then
à bar	ə about	ər over	ȯ for	u̇ put	zh measure

o·cean–go·ing (ō′shən gō′ing) *adj* to do with travel on the ocean: *an ocean-going ship.*

O·ce·an·i·a (ō′shē ā′nē ə) *n* a region that includes the islands of the southern, central, and western Pacific.

o·ce·an·ic (ō′shē an′ik) *adj* **1** to do with the ocean: *oceanic islands.* **2** living in the ocean: *oceanic fish.*

o·cean·og·ra·phy (ō′shə nog′rə fē) *n* a branch of physical geography that studies oceans and ocean life. **o′cean·og′ra·pher** *n.*

o·ce·lot (ō′sə lot′) *or* (os′ə lot′) *n* a spotted, wild cat resembling a leopard that is native to Central America and S America. <French, from Nahuatl *tlatlocelotl*>

o·chre (ō′kər) *n* a pigment found in earth, especially clay, ranging in colour from yellow to orange, brown, and red. *adj* pale brownish yellow. Also, **ocher**. <Old French, from Greek *ochra* yellow ochre>

Ock·ham's razor (o′ kəmz) *n* the principle that using the simpler of two theories is the better way to explain something. Also, **Occam's razor**. <William of *Ockham*, 14c philosopher>

o'clock (ə klok′) *adv* used to express time in units of one hour: *The clock struck three o'clock.* <*of the clock*>

OCR *n* in full, **optical character recognition** the ability to convert letters, numbers, and images into digital codes. A photoelectric machine called an **optical scanner** uses light to recognize characters, bar codes, etc., and converts them into digital codes. Optical scanners at supermarket checkouts convert bar codes to prices.

octa– *combining form* eight: *octagon.* Also, **oct-**, **octo-**. <Greek>

oc·ta·gon (ok′tə gon′) *n* a closed plane figure with eight interior angles and eight sides. <Latin, from Greek *okt-* eight + *gonia* angle> **oc·tag′on·al** *adj.*

oc·ta·he·dron (ok′tə hē′drən) *n, pl* **oc·ta·he·drons** or **oc·ta·he·dra** (-drə) a solid figure with eight plane faces or sides. <Greek *okta-* eight + *hedros* faced>
oc′ta·hed′ral *adj.*

oc·tane (ok′tān) *n* a colourless, liquid hydrocarbon that occurs in petroleum. <*oct-* eight + *–ane*, chemical suffix>

oc·tave (ok′tiv) *or* (ok′tāv) *n* **1** *Music* the interval between a musical tone and another tone with twice or half as many vibrations per second, or a series of tones or of keys of an instrument, filling the interval between a tone and its octave. **2** a group or stanza of eight lines of poetry.

oc·tet or **oc·tette** (ok tet′) *n* **1** *Music* a musical composition for eight voices or instruments, or the singers or players themselves. **2** the first eight lines of a sonnet.

Oc·to·ber (ok tō′bər) *n* the tenth month of the year, with 31 days. *Abbrev.* **Oct** <Old English, from Latin *octo* eight. October was the eighth month of the ancient Roman calendar.>

oc·to·ge·nar·i·an (ok′tə jə ner′ē ən) *n* a person who is between 80 and 90 years old.
adj between 80 and 90 years old. <Latin *octoginta* eighty>

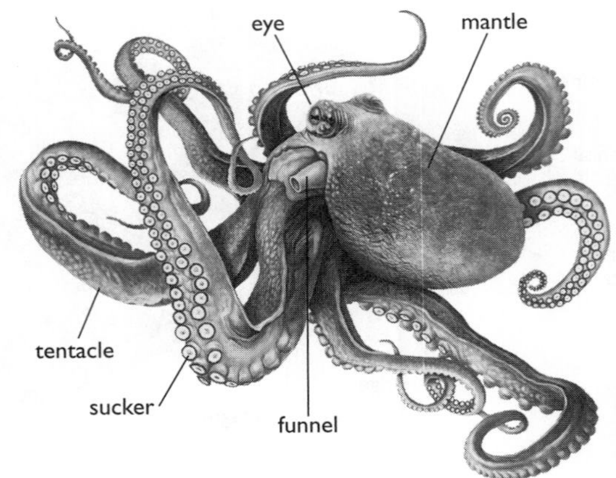

When in danger, an **octopus** can make a jet-propelled exit by drawing water into its mantle cavity and ejecting it with great force through a funnel.

oc·to·pus (ok′tə pəs) *n, pl* **oc·to·pus·es** or **oc·to·pi** (-pī) a sea MOLLUSC with a soft, saclike body, and eight arms with suckers on them. <Greek *okto* eight + *pous* foot>

oc·u·lar (ok′yə lər) *adj* to do with the eye or vision: *an ocular muscle.*
n an eyepiece. <Latin *oculus* eye>

oc·u·list (ok′yə list) *n* **1** an ophthalmologist. **2** an optometrist.

OD *Informal v* **OD'd, OD'ing** overdose: *He OD'd on cocaine.*

O·da·wa (o da′wə) OTTAWA.

odd (od) *adj* **1** strange or peculiar: *It is odd that I cannot remember her name.* **2** leaving a remainder of 1 in a whole number when divided by 2. **3** being one of a pair or set of which the rest is missing: *an odd sock.* **4** extra, occasional, or casual: *odd jobs, odd moments.* **5** about; approximately: *The crowd of people numbered six hundred odd.* <Old Norse *oddi* angle> **odd′ness** *n.*
odd man (or **one**) **out,** *Informal* someone who does not fit into a group or is left out.

odd·ball (od′bol) *Informal n* an eccentric or unconventional person.
adj eccentric or unconventional: *an oddball idea.*

odd·i·ty (od′ə tē) *n, pl* **odd·i·ties** **1** the quality of being strange or peculiar: *We noticed the oddity of her wearing a fur coat over a bathing suit.* **2** a strange or peculiar person or thing.

odd·ly (od′lē) *adv* strangely or peculiarly.

odd·ment (od′mənt) *n* a thing left over or extra bit.

odd number *n* a number that has a remainder of 1 when divided by 2. The numbers 3, 5, 7, etc. are odd numbers.

odds (odz) *pl n* **1** a difference in favour of one event and against another. In gambling, odds of 3 to 2 means that a gambler will be paid 3 on a winning bet, and must pay 2 if he or she loses: *The grey-white horse ran at 5–1 odds.* **2** the chances or likelihood of something happening or being true: *The odds are that it will snow today. The odds are in our favour.*

at odds, quarrelling or disagreeing: *The two boys had been at odds for months.*
odds and ends, miscellaneous things.

odds–on (od′zon′) *adj* with a good chance to win in a contest.

ode (ōd) *n* a lyric poem full of dignified feeling, often, addressed to some person or thing: *Ode to a Nightingale.* <French, from Greek *aeidein* sing>

o·di·ous (ō′dē əs) *adj* extremely displeasing or offensive: *odious behaviour.* **o′di·ous·ly** *adv.* **o′di·ous·ness** *n.*

o·di·um (ō′dē əm) *n* widespread hatred or disgust.

o·dom·e·ter (ō dom′ə tər) *n* an instrument for measuring the distance a vehicle travels by counting how many times the wheel turns.

o·dor·if·er·ous (ō′də rif′ə rəs) *adj* giving forth a smell, especially an unpleasant one.

o·dour or **o·dor** (ō′dər) *n* **1** a smell or scent: *the odour of roses, the odour of garbage.* **2** a lingering impression or feeling, especially concerning a reputation: *They were in bad odour because of a suspected theft.* <Latin *odor*> **o′dour·less** or **o′dor·less** *adj.* **o′dour·less·ly** or **o′dor·less·ly** *adv.* **o′dour·less·ness** or **o′dor·less·ness** *n.* **o′dor·ous** *adj.* **o′dor·ous·ly** *adv.* **o′dor·ous·ness** *n.*

Od·ys·sey (od′ə sē) *n, pl* **Od·ys·seys** **1** a Greek epic poem by Homer, describing the ten years of wandering of Ulysses after the Trojan War and his final return home. **2 odyssey** a long series of wanderings and adventures.

Oed·i·pus complex (ē′də pəs) *Psychiatry n* the theory that a son tends to be attracted to his mother and to compete with his father. <*Oedipus*, a character in Greek myth who unwittingly killed his father and married his mother>

o'er *Poetic adv, prep* over.

oe·soph·a·gus (i sof′ə gəs) ESOPHAGUS.

of (uv) *or* (ov) *prep* **1** belonging to, associated with, or forming a part of: *the cause of the quarrel.* **2** made from or composed of: *boots of Spanish leather.* **3** with or containing: *a village of 500 people.* **4** with a particular quality: *a shout of joy.* **5** named or called: *the city of Vancouver.* **6** away from: *north of Brandon.* **7** concerning or about: *to be fond of someone.* **8** with a special purpose: *a minute of silence.* **9** by: *the writings of Shakespeare.* **10** as a result of: *to die of grief.* **11** out of or arising from: *We expect much of a new medicine.* <Old English>

off (of) *adv* **1** away from the usual or correct position or condition: *He took off his tuque.* **2** begin a journey or race: *to go off on a trip. They're off!* **3** distant in time: *My holiday is only five weeks off.* **4** so as to stop or be stopped: *Turn the water off.*
prep **1** not in the usual or correct position or condition: *There's a button off your shirt.* **2** away from: *The ship anchored just off the shore.* **3** supported by: *He lived off his relatives.* **4** with a dislike of something, usually temporary: *Our dog is off its food.*
adj **1** no longer due to take place: *Our field trip is off.* **2** stopped or not connected: *The electricity is off.* **3** without work: *Are you working on Saturday, or are you off?* **4** unsatisfactory, worse than usual: *Bad weather made last summer an off season for fruit. Her piano playing was a bit off yesterday.* **5** in error: *Your figures are way off.* **6** more distant, especially on the right side of a vehicle or animal: *the off front wheel, the horse's off back leg.* **7** *Informal* slightly unwell: *I feel off today.*
n (*in combination*) a competition: *a bake-off.*
v Slang kill: *The gang leader threatened to off anyone who talked to the police.* <Old English *of*>
off and on, now and then: *She has lived in Edmonton off and on for ten years.*
off limits, See LIMIT.
off with, a remove: *Off with her head!* **b** go away: *Off with you!*
the off chance, possible but not likely: *I went on the off chance that I would find you.*

GRAMMAR AND USAGE

Although used informally in speech, it is not usually acceptable in formal English to use **of** after **off**: *She stepped off the bus* is preferable to *She stepped off of the bus*.

off–air (of′er) *adj* relating to a radio or TV program but not broadcast: *Her off-air remarks were very rude.* Compare ON-AIR.

of·fal (of′əl) *n* **1** the entrails and internal organs of an animal used for food. **2** refuse or waste material. <probably Middle Dutch *af* off + *vallen* to fall>

off–and–on (of′ən on′) *adj* stopping and starting again at intervals: *off-and-on rain, an off-and-on relationship.*

off–bal·ance (of bal′əns) *adj* unsteady or poorly balanced.

off·beat (of′bēt′) *n* a musical beat that has relatively little stress.
adj **1** not coinciding with a musical beat. **2** *Informal* unconventional or eccentric.

off–ca·me·ra (of ka′me ra) *adj, adv* outside the area photographed by a camera, especially in making a movie, video, or TV show: *an off-camera explosion* (*adj*). *In this scene he's talking to his wife, who is washing dishes off-camera* (*adv*).

off–col·our or **off–col·or** (of′kul′ər) *adj* **1** sexually suggestive: *an off-colour joke.* **2** slightly unwell: *She was feeling off-colour yesterday.*

of·fence or **of·fense** (ə fens′) *or* (ō fens′) *n* **1** the act or fact of breaking the law: *Offences against the law are punished by fines or imprisonment.* **2** an act or thing that offends or causes displeasure: *an offence against good taste.* **3** the condition of offending or being offended: *to cause offence. No offence was intended.* **4** the action of attacking, or an attacking force: *Our football team has a good offence.* <Old French, from Latin *ob-* against + *fendere* strike>
give offence, offend.
take offence, be offended.

a bat	e bed	i bid	o pot	u cup	th **thin**
ā cake	ē me	ī bite	ō go	ū rude	ᴛʜ **then**
á bar	ə about	ər over	ò for	ù put	zh measure

O

of·fend (ə fend′) *v* **1** cause to feel upset, annoyed, or resentful: *My friend was offended.* **2** commit an offence or illegal act: *In what way have I offended?* **of·fend′er** *n.*

of·fense (ə fens′) *or* (ō fens′) OFFENCE.

of·fen·sive (ə fen′siv) *adj* **1** causing someone to feel upset or angry. **2** unpleasant or disgusting: *Bad eggs have an offensive odour.* **3** to do with attacking: *offensive weapons.*
n **1** a position or attitude of attack: *The army took the offensive.* **2** an attack: *An offensive against polio began when the proper vaccine was developed.* **of·fen′sive·ly** *adv.* **of·fen′sive·ness** *n.*

of·fer (of′ər) *v* **1** hold out to be taken or refused: *to offer a suggestion, to be offered a choice of mushrooms or olives.* **2** present for sale: *to offer sports equipment at reduced prices.* **3** be willing or volunteer: *She offered to help us.* **4** bid as a price: *He offered twenty dollars for the old stove.* **5** give or show: *to offer no resistance when attacked.* **6** occur: *I will call if the opportunity offers.*
n **1** the act of offering: *an offer of money, an offer of help.* **2** a thing that is offered: *There's a bid of ten dollars. What's your offer?* <Old English, from Latin *ob-* to + *ferre* bring>

of·fer·ing (of′ə ring) *or* (of′ring) *n* **1** a contribution or gift: *They gave us some offerings for the rummage sale.* **2** the giving of money as part of an act of worship: *to take up an offering in church.* **3** a thing produced or made for entertainment or sale: *The summer movie offerings were amazing.*

of·fer·to·ry (of′ər tô′rē) *Christianity n, pl* **of·fer·to·ries** **1** the offering of bread and wine as part of the Eucharist. **2** an offering or collection at a religious service. **3** the music sung or played while an offering is received.

off·hand (of′hand′) *for adv,* (of′hand′) *for adj. adv* without previous thought or preparation: *The carpenter could not tell offhand how much the work would cost.*
adj **1** done or made without previous thought or planning: *Her offhand remarks were often very funny.* **2** casual or informal.

of·fice (of′is) *n* **1 a** the place in which the work of a business or profession is done: *The executive offices were on the second floor.* **b** the people carrying on work in an office: *Half the office is on vacation.* **2** a position of authority or trust, or the time during which the duties involved in this are carried out: *The MP was appointed to the office of the Minister of Defence. The government was in office four years.* **3 offices** *pl* an act of kindness or service: *Through the good offices of a friend, she was able to get a job.* **4 offices** *pl* a religious ceremony or prayer: *the last offices.* <Old French, from Latin *opus* work + *facere* do>

of·fice·hold·er (of′is hōl′dər) *n* a person who holds a public office.

of·fi·cer (of′ə sər) *n* **1** a person who commands others and, especially, holds a commission in the armed forces, the merchant marine, or on a passenger ship. **2** a person who holds an office in a church or in the public service: *a health officer, a police officer.* **3** a holder of a post in a society, company, or other organization, especially at a senior level of management.
v **1** provide with military officers. **2** direct, conduct, or manage, especially a military unit.

of·fi·cial (ə fish′əl) *or* (ō fish′əl) *n* **1** a person who holds a public position or who is in charge of some public work or duty: *a government official.* **2** a person holding office in an organization: *a bank official.*
adj **1** to do with an office or officers: *an official uniform.* **2** with authority: *An official record is kept of the proceedings of our club.* **3** being an official: *an official representative.* **4** suitable for or characteristic of a person in office: *an official attitude.* See OFFICIOUS for confusable. **of·fi′cial·ly** *adv.*

of·fi·cial·dom (ə fish′əl dəm) *or* (ō fish′əl dəm) *n* officials considered as a group.

of·fi·cial·ese (ə fish′əl ēz) *n* pompous, complicated, or obscure language thought of as being typical of officials.

🍁 **Official Languages Act** *n* the law passed in 1969 making French and English the official languages of Canada and requiring the Federal Government to provide services in both.

of·fi·ci·ate (ə fish′ē āt′) *or* (ō fish′ē āt′) *v* **of·fi·ci·at·ed, of·fi·ci·at·ing** **1** perform the duties of an office or position: *The president officiates as chairman at meetings.* **2** perform the duties of a priest, minister, or rabbi: *The bishop officiated at the cathedral.* **3** serve as a referee or umpire in a sport.

of·fi·cious (ə fish′əs) *adj* too ready to offer services or advice, or in asserting authority: *An officious attendant ticketed our car while my dad was paying for parking.* **of·fi′cious·ly** *adv.* **of·fi′cious·ness** *n.*

CONFUSABLES

Officious suggests a sense of self-importance: *The officious salesclerk wouldn't stop giving us advice.*

Official means "authorized": *The prime minister has official powers.*

off·ing (of′ing) *n* the more distant part of the sea in view. **in the offing,** likely to happen or appear soon: *There is a general election in the offing.*

off–key (of′kē′) *adj* **1** not in the correct musical key. **2** *Informal* inappropriate or ill-timed.

off·line or **off–line** (of′līn′) *Computers adj* not controlled by or connected to a computer or computer network: *The old printer was always offline for a minute after being opened up.*
adv **1** while not connected to a computer or computer network: *Wait a minute till I get offline.* **2** out of operation: *The system went offline and may be down for about an hour.*

off·load (of′lōd′) *v* **1** unload: *The ferry will offload cars at the terminal.* **2** delegate or pass responsibility to another: *The club president offloaded most of the work to the vice-president.*

off·print (of′print′) *n* a separate reprint or reproduction of a text from a book or periodical.
v print separately as an excerpt.

off–put·ting (of′put′ing) *adj* unpleasant or disconcerting: *I'd like to get to know him, but his manner is a little off-putting.*

An **off-road** motorcycle has heavy-duty shock absorbers in the front forks to protect bike and rider from jolts.

An all-terrain vehicle is built for rough ground, with four large tires and a powerful engine.

off–road (of′rōd′) *adj* involving or designed for travel over rough ground that is not a road or highway: *an off-road vehicle.*
adv over rough ground not a road or highway: *Can this thing be driven off-road?*

off·screen (of′skrēn′) *adj, adv* **1** not seen on a movie or TV screen: *an offscreen commentary. Someone can be heard yelling offscreen.* **2** outside of one's work in movies or TV: *her offscreen activities. He only ever plays villains, but he's very nice offscreen.*

off–sea·son (of′sē′zən) *n* the season of low activity in a business, recreation, or sport.
adj in or for the off-season: *off-season rates.*

off·set (of′set′ *for v,* (of′set′) *for n. v* **off·set, off·set·ting** counterbalance or compensate for: *The greater distance was offset by the better roads.*
n **1** a thing that compensates for something else: *In football, his weight and strength were an offset to his slowness.* **2** a short side shoot from a main stem or root that starts a new plant. **3** *Printing* a process in which the inked impression is first made on a roller and then on the paper, instead of directly on the paper.

off·shoot (of′shūt′) *n* **1** a shoot or branch growing out from the main stem of a plant or tree. **2** a thing coming, or thought of as coming, from a main part or group: *an offshoot of a mountain range.*

off·shore (of′shor′) *for adv,* (of′shȯr) *for adj. adv* toward the water from the land: *The wind was blowing offshore.*
adj **1** in water some distance away from the shore: *offshore fisheries.* **2** (*of wind*) going from the land toward the water: *an offshore breeze.*

off·side or **off–side** (of′sīd′) *Sports adj* in some team sports, being in or moving into an illegal position, when play usually stops.

off–site (of′sīt′) *adj, adv* away from the main location or property: *Off-site parking is available nearby* (*adj*). *A lot of the work for this client can be done off-site* (*adv*).

off·spring (of′spring′) *n* the young of a person, animal, or plant: *Every one of my aunt's offspring had red hair.*

off·stage (of′stāj′) *adj, adv* away from the part of the stage that the audience can see: *offstage whispers* (*adj*). *She led the actors offstage* (*adv*).

off–street (of′strēt′) *adj* away from the street: *He said we need more off-street parking downtown.*

off–the–cuff (of′ᴛʜə kuf′) *adj* casual and not prepared beforehand: *off-the-cuff remarks.*

off–the–rec·ord (of′ᴛʜə rek′ərd) *adj, adv* **1** not to be written in the minutes or proceedings of a meeting, trial, or conference: *The judge said the remarks were off the record.* **2** not for publication or release: *an off-the-record interview.*

off–the–wall (of′ᴛʜə wol′) *Informal adj* unusual, strange, or eccentric: *an off-the-wall idea.*

off–white (of′wīt′) *adj* very pale beige or light grey, almost white.

off year *n* a year of unusually poor performance or conditions in a business, occupation, or sport.

oft (oft) *Archaic or Poetic adv* often.

of·ten (of′ən) *or* (of′tən) *adv* frequently: *She comes here often.* <Old English *oft*>

of·ten·times (of′ən tīmz′) *or* (of′tən tīmz′) *adv* often.

o·give (ō′gīv) *n* **1** *Architecture* a pointed arch. See TREFOIL for picture. **2** *Statistics* a cumulative frequency graph. <origin uncertain>

o·gle (ō′gəl) *v* **o·gled, o·gling** stare at someone because of sexual or romantic attraction.
n an ogling look. <probably German or Dutch>
o′gler *n.*

✱ **O·go·po·go** (ō′gō pō′gō) *n* a monster supposedly sighted from time to time in Okanagan Lake, B.C. <name in a English music hall song>

o·gre (ō′gər) *n* **1** in folklore and fairy tales, a giant or monster that supposedly eats people. **2** a dreaded or cruel person. <French>

oh or **Oh** (ō) *interj* used to express surprise, joy, grief, pain, or another strong emotion: *Oh, dear me! Oh, look!*

O–Ha·rai (ō′ha rī′) *Shinto n* the purification ceremony observed in June and December, during which believers receive absolution from the sun goddess, Amaterasu. <Japanese>

a bat	e bed	i bid	o pot	u cup	th **thin**
ā cake	ē me	ī bite	ō go	ū rude	ᴛʜ **then**
ä bar	ə about	ər over	ȯ for	u̇ put	zh measure

ohm (ōm) *n* the SI unit for measuring the resistance of a conductor to an electric current sent through it. <G.S. *Ohm*, 19c physicist>

ohm·met·er (ōm′mē tər) *Electricity n* a device for measuring the resistance of a conductor in ohms.

Ohm's law *Electricity n* the law that states that the electric current (*I*) in a circuit is directly proportional to the voltage (*V*) and inversely proportional to the resistance (*R*), that is, $V = IR$.

–oid *suffix* resembling or like: *asteroid, humanoid.* <Latin, from Greek *eidos* form>

oil (oil) *n* **1** a fatty or greasy liquid that floats on water, burns easily, and dissolves in alcohol. **2** petroleum. **3** oil used in cooking: *vegetable oil.* **4** a substance that resembles oil, such as a liquid used on the hair or skin as a cosmetic: *suntan oil.* **5 a** paint made by grinding colouring matter in oil: *The art class is now painting with oils.* **b** a painting in oils: *We like the oils of that artist better than her charcoal sketches.*
v put oil on or in for use in cooking or as a lubricant: *He oiled the baking sheet. The repairman oiled the wheels.* <Old French, from Greek *elaion*>
burn the midnight oil, See MIDNIGHT.
pour oil on troubled waters, make things calm and peaceful.
strike oil, *Informal* find something very profitable.

oil·cloth (oil′kloth′) *n* a cloth made waterproof and shiny on one side by coating it with a mixture of oil, clay, and colouring.

oil·er (oi′lər) *n* **1** a person who or thing that oils. **2** a can with a long spout used in oiling machinery. **3** an oil tanker. **4 oilers** *pl* oilskin or other waterproof clothing.

oil·field (oil′fēld′) *n* an area where petroleum has been found.

oil paint *n* a mixture of colour pigment and oil. Also called **oil colour**.

oil painting *n* **1** a picture painted with oil colours. **2** the art of painting with oil colours.

oil rig *n* an installation of machinery used to extract petroleum from the earth.

❧ **oil sands** *n* sand or sandstone that contains large deposits of hydrocarbons, from which petroleum can be distilled.

oil·skin (oil′skin′) *n* **1** cloth treated with oil to make it waterproof. **2 oilskins** *pl* a coat and trousers made of this cloth.

oil slick *n* a film of oil on water, especially one covering a large area, or a similar film on the surface of a road.

oil well *n* a well drilled in the earth to draw up petroleum.

oil·y (oi′lē) *adj* **oil·i·er, oil·i·est** **1** to do with oil: *an oily smell.* **2** containing, covered, or soaked with oil: *oily salad dressing, oily rags.* **3** like oil in being smooth and slippery: *The calm sea had an oily look.* **4** suspiciously or disagreeably smooth: *an oily smile.* **oil′i·ness** *n.*

oint·ment (oint′mənt) *n* a substance made with oil or fat, often containing medicine, used on the skin to heal or to make it soft. <Old French, from Latin *unguere* anoint>

O·jib·way or **O·jib·wa** (ō jib′wā) ANISHINABE.

OK or **O.K.** (ō′kā′) *Informal adj, adv* all right: *The new schedule was OK (adj). He said he was ill, but he looked OK to me (adv).*
v **OK'd** or **O.K.'d, OK'ing** or **O.K.'ing** endorse or approve: *After my teacher had OK'd the outline, I began to write the report.*
n, pl **OK's** or **O.K.'s** approval: *The principal gave us her OK.* Also, **okay**. <perhaps *oll* k*orrect*, humorous misspelling of *all correct*>

GRAMMAR AND USAGE

OK, O.K., and **okay** are all acceptable in informal speech and writing. **All right** is the preferred term for more formal speech or writing.

❧ **O·ka** *n* a cheese, cured with brine, originally made by Trappist monks in Oka, Québec.

O·kan·a·gan (ō′kə na′gən) *n* **1** a member of a First Nations people living in S British Columbia. **2** their Salishan language.
adj to do with these people or their language.

o·kra (ō′krə) *n* a herb of the mallow family with long, tapering seed pods, which are eaten as a vegetable. <West African>

❧ **o·lal·lie** (ō la′lē) *n* a berry of the Pacific Northwest, especially the salmonberry. <Chinook Jargon = berry>

old (ōld) *adj* **old·er** or **eld·er, old·est** or **eld·est** **1 a** having lived for many years: *an old man.* **b** having existed for a long time: *an old wall, an old grudge.* **2** of a specified age: *a year old.* **3** long-established or known: *old friends.* **4** much worn by age or use: *old clothes.* **5** former: *an old boyfriend.* **6** familiar or dear: *This is a good old chair.* **7** *Informal* to intensify some preceding adjective: *I can't move that big old desk. We had a high old time at the party.*
n **1** the time long ago: *the heroes of old.* **2 the old** elderly people. <Old English *ald*> **old′ness** *n.*

GRAMMAR AND USAGE

Old, when used to describe people or animals, usually means "near the end of life."

Old, when used to describe things, means "having existed a long time."

Elderly is used only to describe people, and means "past middle age and getting old."

old age *n* the last part of life when a person is very old.

❧ **Old Age Security** OAS (def. 1).

old–boy network (ōld′boi) *n* a loose but exclusive group of men sharing a high educational and social background, and expected to help one another in their careers or other activities.

Old Country *n* the native land of people living elsewhere.

old·en (ōld′ən) *Poetic adj* old: *in olden times.*

Old English *n* the language of the English people up to about 1100 CE.

old–fash·ioned (ōld′fash′ənd) *adj* to do with a style no longer current or common: *an old-fashioned hairstyle.*

old guard *n* the original or long-serving members of a group or party, especially those unwilling to accept change.

old hand *n* a very skilled or experienced person.

old hat *Informal n* already familiar: *Of course, all this information is probably old hat to you.*

✱ **old home week** *n* a festival during which former residents of a town, village, etc. return for the celebrations.

old·ish (ōl′dish) *adj* somewhat old.

old maid *n* **1 a** *Offensive* a woman who has not married and seems unlikely to do so. **b** a prim, fussy person: *What an old maid he is!* **2** a very simple card game.

old master *n* **1** any great European painter who lived between the 1200s and the 1600s. **2** a painting by such an artist.

old school *n* a group of people who have old-fashioned or conservative ideas.

old school tie *n* **1** a tie bearing the crest of one of the British private schools. **2** the attitudes and social relationships shared by graduates of these schools. **old-school-tie** *adj.*

old·ster (ōld′stər) *Informal n* an old person.

Old Testament *Christianity n* the first division of the Bible, containing the main texts concerning the law, history, poetry, and prophecy of the ancient people of Israel.

old–time (ōld′tīm′) *adj* of or like former times: *old-time music.*

old–tim·er (ōld′tī′mər) *Informal n* a person who has long been a resident, member, or worker in a place, group, or community.

old wives' tale *n* a foolish story or silly belief.

old–world (ōld′wərld′) *adj* to do with former times, especially when considered quaint or attractive: *old-world courtesy.*

Old World *n* Europe, Asia, and Africa. Compare NEW WORLD.
adj **old-world** belonging to or associated with former times or the ancient world: *old-world charm.*

o·le·ag·i·nous (ō′lē aj′ə nəs) *adj* oily. <French, from Latin *olea, oliva* olive>

o·le·an·der (ō′lē an′dər) *n* a poisonous evergreen shrub with fragrant flowers.

ol·fac·tion (ol fak′shən) *n* the sense of smell. <Lation *olere* to smell + *facere* make>

ol·fac·to·ry (ol fak′tə rē) *adj* to do with smelling: *an olfactory organ.*

ol·i·garch (ol′ə gärk′) *n* a person who belongs to a small group that controls a country, organization, or institution.

ol·i·gar·chy (ol′ə gär′kē) *n, pl* **ol·i·gar·chies** **1** a form of government in which a few people have power and control, or the people who have this control. **2** a country, organization, or institution with such a government. **ol′i·gar′chic** *adj.*

Ol·i·go·cene (ol′i gō sēn′) *n* the geological epoch lasting from about 40 million to 20 million years ago, when the climate was mild and the Hawaiian Islands began to form. See also CENOZOIC, TERTIARY.
adj to do with this epoch. <Greek *oligos* small + *kainos* new>

ol·i·go·troph·ic (o′lə go trō′fik) *or* (o′lə go tro′fik) *Biology adj* with reference to the deeper parts of a lake or river, low in plant nutrients and plant life but rich in oxygen. <Greek *oligos* little + *trophe* food> **ol′i·got′roph·y** *n.*

ol·ive (ol′iv) *n* the small, oval, edible fruit of a tree that grows in warm climates. Olives can be eaten unripe or ripe, and can be pressed to give olive oil.
adj **1** greyish green in colour. **2** yellowish brown in skin colour. <Latin, from Greek *elaion* oil>

olive branch *n* **1** a branch of an olive tree, symbolizing peace. **2** a thing offered as a sign of peace.

olive drab *adj* dark greenish yellow, sometimes the colour of military uniforms.

olive oil *n* oil pressed from olives, mainly used in cooking.

O·lym·pi·ad or **o·lym·pi·ad** (ō lim′pē ad′) *n* **1** a celebration of the ancient or modern Olympic Games, held every four years. **2** an international contest in chess, science projects, etc., held regularly. <Latin, from Greek *Olympikos*, site of games in honour of the god Zeus>

O·lym·pi·an (ō lim′pē ən) *adj* **1** to do with Olympia in Greece or with Mount Olympus. **2** like a god, especially in seeming aloof and superior: *Olympian calm.*
n **1** one of the major Greek gods. **2** a person of high position or great achievements. **3** a competitor in the Olympic Games.

Olympic Games (ō lim′pik) *n* **1** a group of athletic contests held once every four years in a different country, in which athletes from many nations compete. **2** a group of contests in athletics, poetry, and music, held every four years at Olympia by the ancient Greeks, in honour of the god Zeus. Also called **the Olympics**.

O·man (ō man′) *n* a country in the east of the Arabian peninsula. **O·man′i** (ō man′ē) *adj, n.*

o·ma·sum (ō mā′səm) *n, pl* **o·ma·sa** (-sə) the third stomach of a cow or other ruminant. The omasum receives the food when it is swallowed the second time. <Latin = bullock's tripe>

om·buds·man (om′bəd zmən) *or* (om bud′zmən) *n, pl* **om·buds·men** (-mən) an official appointed to receive and investigate citizens' grievances against a government, organization, or institution. <Swedish *ombud* commission>

o·me·ga (ō meg′ə), (ō mē′gə), *or* (ō′mi gə) *n* **1** the last letter of the Greek alphabet (Ω or ω). **2** the last of a series or a final development. <Greek>

a bat	e bed	i bid	o pot	u cup	th **thin**
ā cake	ē me	ī bite	ō go	ū rude	TH **then**
ä bar	ə about	ər over	ô for	ů put	zh measure

om·e·lette or **om·e·let** (om′ə lit) *or* (om′lit) *n* eggs beaten with milk or water, cooked, and folded over, sometimes including a filling: *a mushroom omelette.* <French, from Latin *lamella* knife blade, from its flatness>

o·men (ō′mən) *n* an event, object, or animal regarded as a sign of what is to happen, or the prophetic meaning given to it: *a bird of ill omen, an omen of recovery.*
v be a sign of what is to happen. <Latin>

om·i·nous (om′ə nəs) *adj* unfavourable or threatening: *The watchdog gave an ominous growl.* **om′i·nous·ly** *adv.* **om′i·nous·ness** *n.*

SYNONYMS

Ominous suggests something of an unpleasant nature: *We knew from the ominous thunder that the storm was getting closer.*

Menacing suggests intimidation or a sense of fear: *There was a menacing look on the bully's face as he walked toward us.*

Prophetic emphasizes giving an indication of what is going to happen: *She hoped that her dream about the party would turn out to be prophetic.*

o·mis·sion (ō mish′ən) *n* **1** the act or fact of omitting or being omitted: *omission of a paragraph.* **2** something omitted: *Her song was the only omission from the program.*

o·mit (ō mit′) *v* **o·mit·ted, o·mit·ting 1** leave out: *to omit a letter in a word.* **2** fail to do or neglect: *He omitted to mention he'd received several awards.* <Latin *ob-* down + *mittere* let go>

omni– *combining form* all or everything: *omnidirectional, omnivorous.* <Latin *omnis* all>

om·ni·bus (om′nə bus′) *n, pl* **om·ni·bus·es 1** a large motor vehicle with seats for passengers inside and sometimes also on an upper level. **2** a collection in one volume of many texts by the same author or on the same subject.
adj comprising many items: *an omnibus law.* <French, from Latin *omnis* all>

om·ni·di·rec·tion·al (om′nə də rek′shən əl′) *adj* receiving or sending signals in all directions.

om·nip·o·tent (om nip′ə tənt) *adj* **1** with complete or unlimited power: *an omnipotent ruler.* **2 the Omnipotent** God. **om·nip′o·tence** *n.* **om·nip′o·tent·ly** *adv.*

om·ni·pres·ent (om′nə prez′ənt) *adj* present everywhere at the same time. **om·ni′pres′ence** *n.*

om·nis·cient (om nis′ē ənt) *or* (om nish′ənt) *adj* with knowledge of everything. **om·nis′cience** *n.* **om·nis′cient·ly** *adv.*

om·ni·vore (om′ni vȯr′) *n* an animal that or person who eats every kind of food.

om·niv·o·rous (om niv′ə rəs) *adj* **1** eating every kind of food. **2** taking in or using whatever is available: *She had omnivorous tastes in reading.* <*omni-* + Latin *vorare* eat> **om·niv′o·rous·ly** *adv.* **om·niv′o·rous·ness** *n.*

on (on) *prep* **1** physically in contact with and supported by: *The book is on the table.* **2** close to or along the edge of: *She lives on the next street.* **3** in the direction of: *The soldiers marched on the capital.* **4** against or upon: *The picture is on the wall.* **5** among or included in: *I am on the committee.* **6** by means of: *We heard it on the radio.* **7** engaged in doing or in the process of: *on purpose, on duty.* **8** at the time of: *They greeted us on our arrival.* **9** not early or late in: *on time, on schedule.* **10** concerning: *a book on Canadian mammals.*
adv **1** physically in contact with and supported by: *Put your jacket on.* **2** continuing a movement, action, or process: *Why do you keep on doing that?* **3** performing, or taking place as a performance: *You will be going on in five minutes. They're putting a good play on.* **4** functioning as an electrical appliance or power supply: *Turn the gas on.* **5** from a time forward: *later on, from that day on.*
adj in action or operation: *The race is on. The TV is on.* <Old English>
and so on, and more of the same.
be on about, *Informal* talk a lot about: *They're always on about how clever they are.*
on and off, at some times and not others.
on and on, without stopping.
you're on, *Informal* **a** it's your turn: *"Okay, you're on. Let's see how you do."* **b** agreed: *"I'll bet you he'll be late." "You're on."*

GRAMMAR AND USAGE

When **on** is an adverb and **to** is a preposition (when **on** is not part of the prepositional phrase), they are written as two words: *We left the city and drove on to the country.*

Onto is a compound preposition and is one word: *The team members waved as they skated onto the ice.*

on–air (on′er) *adj* relating to a radio or TV program being broadcast: *to prepare some on-air replies.* Compare OFF-AIR.

on·board (on′bȯrd′) *adj* situated inside a boat, car, plane, or any similar means of transportation: *an onboard computer.*

once (wuns) *adv* **1** one time only: *She calls once a day.* **2** at some one time in the past: *a once powerful nation.* **3** even a single time: *If the facts once became known, everybody would laugh at her.*
n a single occasion: *Once is enough.*
conj as soon as: *Once you cross the river, you are safe.* <Old English *an* one>
at once or **all at once, a** immediately: *Leave at once.* **b** at the same time: *Everyone shouted at once.*
for once, for one time at least.
just this once, for this time only.
once and again, repeatedly.
once and for all, finally.
once in a while, at one time or another.
once or twice, a few times.
once upon a time, long ago.

once–o·ver (wun′sō′vər) *Informal n* a quick look of appraisal: *He gave the stranger the once-over.*

on·col·o·gy (on kol′ə jē) *n* the branch of medicine that deals with the diagnosis and treatment of tumours. <Greek *onkos* mass> **on·co·log′i·cal** *adj.* **on·col′o·gist** *n.*

on·com·ing (on′kum′ing) *adj* **1** approaching from the front: *an oncoming car.* **2** due to happen soon: *an oncoming storm.*
n the fact of happening soon: *the oncoming of puberty.*

one (wun) *n* **1** the first and lowest cardinal number. **2** the numeral 1: *What does the 1 in the margin mean?* **3** a playing card or side of a die with one spot. **4** a single person or thing: *I gave him the one he wanted.*
adj **1** being a single unit or individual: *one apple.* **2** (*after the noun*) first in a series: *We'll start with Chapter One.* **3** at some unspecified time: *One day she will be sorry.* **4** shared, joined together, or united: *They held one opinion. They replied in one voice.* **5** being a certain person or thing: *After the vote, one Chris Peterson was elected.*
pron **1** a single person or thing: *One of her poems was selected for the anthology.* **2** an unspecified person or people in general: *One must work hard to achieve success.* **3** the same person or thing: *Dr. Jekyll and Mr. Hyde were one and the same.* <Old English *an*>
all one, exactly the same or making no difference: *They are all one in their love of hockey. It is all one to me whether you stay or go.*
at one, in agreement: *The two judges were at one about the winner.*
one and all, everyone.
one and the same, the very same.
one by one, one after another.
one or two, a few.
one up on, with an advantage over: *He always has to be one up on the next guy.*

GRAMMAR AND USAGE

The use of the impersonal pronoun **one**, as used to mean "people in general," is formal, especially if it must be repeated.

Formal: *One can't be too careful, can one?*

Informal: *You can't be too careful, can you?*

one another *n* each of several people or things in an action or relation that is common to all: *They were in one another's way.*

one–celled (wun′seld′) *adj* with only one cell.

one–horse (wun′hôrs′) *adj* **1** drawn or worked by a single horse: *a one-horse sleigh.* **2** of little scope, capacity, or importance: *a one-horse town.*

O·nei·da (ō nā′də) *n, pl* **O·nei·da** or **O·nei·das** **1** a member of a Native American or First Nations people, originally living in New York State and later in southwest Ontario. **2** their Iroquoian language.
adj to do with these people or their language. Also called **Onyota'aka.**

one–liner (wun′lī′nər) *n* a joke that is just one short sentence.

one·ness (wun′nis) *n* **1** the quality of being one in number or the same in kind. **2** the fact of forming a unity. **3** agreement in mind, feeling, or purpose.

one–night stand (wun′nīt′) *n* **1** a single performance in one place, as by a touring theatrical company or band. **2** a single sexual encounter.

one–off (wun′of′) *Informal n* something that happens only once.

one–on–one (wun′on wun′) *adj, adv* with interaction between just two individuals: *a one-on-one confrontation* (*adj*). *The teacher worked one-on-one with her students* (*adv*).
n a casual form of basketball in which just two people play against each other.

one–piece (wun′pēs′) *adj* consisting of one single piece: *a one-piece swimsuit.*
n a garment consisting of a single piece.

on·er·ous (on′ə rəs) *or* (ō′nə rəs) *adj* burdensome or oppressive: *an onerous task.* **on′er·ous·ly** *adv.* **on′er·ous·ness** *n.*

one·self (wun self′) *pron* **1** the object of a reflexive verb with *one* as subject: *One might ask oneself if it is worth the trouble.* **2** an intensive pronoun, used to emphasize the noun or pronoun it follows: *One has to do the real work oneself.* **3** one's usual self: *It's nice to be oneself again after an illness.*

one–shot (wun′shot′) *adj* being the only one, not part of a series: *a one-shot deal.*

one–sid·ed (wun′sī′did) *adj* **1** seeing only one side of a question: *The umpire seemed one-sided in her decisions.* **2** uneven or unequal: *If one team is much better than the other, a game is one-sided.* **3** with but one side, or on only one side: *one-sided page.* **4** with one side larger or more developed than the other: *one-sided lump.*

one–time (wun′tīm′) *adj* of the past: *the one-time mayor of the city.*

one–to–one (wun′tū wun′) *adj* **1** with proportional amounts on both sides. **2** *Mathematics* allowing for one member of a class or set to pair with only one of another class or set.

one–track (wun′trak′) *Informal adj* understanding or preoccupied with only one thing at a time: *a one-track mind.*

one–two (wun′tū′) *n* a pair of punches in rapid succession, especially with alternate hands.

one–up·man·ship (wun′up′mən ship′) *Informal n* the technique or act of gaining a sense of superiority over someone else.

one–way (wun′wā′) *adj* moving or allowing movement in only one direction: *one-way traffic, a one-way ticket.*

on·go·ing (on′gō′ing) *adj* in process or continuing: *This is not an isolated crime, but part of an ongoing social problem.*

a bat	e bed	i bid	o pot	u cup	th **thin**
ā cake	ē me	ī bite	ō go	ū rude	ᴛʜ **then**
à bar	ə about	ər over	ô for	ů put	zh measure

O

yellow onion

red onion

white onion

pickling onions

scallion

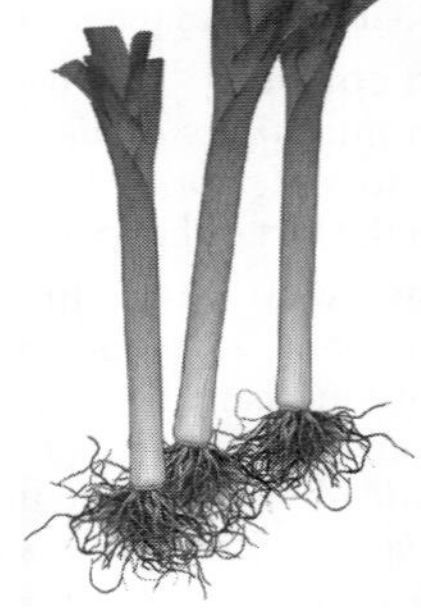
leeks

shallot

garlic

When you cut an onion, a gas rises and mixes with the water in your eyes to form sulphuric acid. Your eyes respond by making tears to flush out the irritant.

chives

on·ion (un′yən) *n* the bulb of a plant of the lily family that has a sharp, strong taste and smell and is used in cooking as a vegetable or for flavouring. <Old French, from Latin *unio*> **on′ion·y** *adj.*

onion ring *n* (*usually plural*) a slice of onion dipped in batter and deep-fried: *Are you eating onion rings?*

on·ion·skin (un′yən skin′) *n* **1** the thin, papery outer skin of an onion. **2** a thin, translucent paper.

on·line or **on–line** (on′līn′) *Computers adj* controlled by or connected to a computer or computer network: *Her flight was booked through the online reservation system.*
adv **1** while connected to a computer or computer network: *to search for something online.* **2** in or into operation: *The new power plant went online last month.*

online learning E-LEARNING.

on·look·er (on′lůk′ər) *n* a person who watches without taking part.

on·ly (ōn′lē) *adv* **1** with no one or nothing more: *Only he remained. I did it only through friendship.* **2** merely or just: *He sold only two. She was in Rimouski for one week only.* **3** no longer ago or not until: *The discovery was made only last year. The news reached me only this morning.*
adj **1** alone by itself or themselves: *an only son. Those were the only clothes she owned. This is the only road along the shore.* **2** the best or finest: *You're the only one for me.*
conj **1** except that: *I would have gone only I didn't have the money.* **2** but it must be added that: *We had camped right beside a stream, only the water was not fit to drink.* <Old English *anlic*>
if only, I wish: *If only wars would cease!*
only too, very: *She was only too glad to help us.*

GRAMMAR AND USAGE

To avoid uncertainty, **only** as an adverb should be placed as close as possible to the word or words it modifies. The following three sentences have different meanings:

Only she went shopping last night. (That is, she and nobody else went shopping.)

She only went shopping last night. (That is, she went shopping and did nothing else.)

She went shopping last night only. (That is, it was the one night she went shopping.)

on·o·mast·ic (on′ə mas′tic) *adj* to do with the study of proper names or of words used in specialized fields.
n **onomastics** (*with singular verb*) the study of proper names or of words used in specialized fields. <French, from Greek *onoma* name>

on·o·mat·o·poe·ia (on′ə mat′ə pē′ə) *n* the formation of a word by imitating the sound associated with a thing or action, as in *buzz, hum, cuckoo, slap*, and *splash*, or the use of such words to create an effect. <Latin, from Greek *onoma* name + *-poios* making>

On·on·da·ga (on′on da′gə) *n, pl* **On·on·da·ga** or **On·on·da·gas** **1** a member of a Native American or First Nations people now living mainly in Ontario. **2** their Iroquoian language.
adj to do with these people or their language.

on·rush (on′rush′) *n* a violent forward movement: *She was knocked down by the onrush of water.*

on·screen (on′skrēn′) *adj, adv* on a computer, TV, video, or movie screen: *Follow the onscreen instructions* (*adj*). *You hear the narrator's voice but she never appears onscreen* (*adv*).

on·set (on′set′) *n* the beginning of something, especially something undesirable: *the onset of a disease. The onset of winter was marked by a severe snowstorm.*

on·shore (on′shȯr′) *for adv,* (on′shȯr′) *for adj. adv* toward the land: *The wind veered onshore.*
adj on the land: *an onshore patrol.*

on·side (on′sīd′) *adj, adv* in a position allowed by the rules of a sport or game.

on–site (on′site′) *adj* at the actual location: *Resort guests are invited to use the on-site hairdressing salon.*

on·slaught (on′slot′) *n* **1** a vigorous or fierce attack: *The attackers were driven back by a sudden onslaught from within the city.* **2** a large number of people who or things that are difficult to cope with: *An onslaught of shoppers overwhelmed the store's staff.*

on·stage (on′stāj′) *adj, adv* on or onto a stage in a theatre: *onstage characters* (*adj*). *He carried the sword onstage* (*adv*).

On·tar·i·o (on ter′i ō) *n* a central Canadian province, between Manitoba and Québec. Ontario is one of the CENTRAL PROVINCES. *Abbrev.* **Ont.**; postal symbol **ON**; URL **www.gov.on.ca**
adj to do with Ontario: *Ontario farmland.* **On·tar′i·an** *n.*

on·to (on′tū) *prep* **1** a position on: *to throw a ball onto the roof, to get onto a horse.* **2** *Informal* familiar with or aware of: *Are you onto your new job yet? We're onto his tricks.*

on·tog·e·ny (on toj′ə nē) *n* the development of an individual organism. Compare PHYLOGENY. <Greek *on* being + *geneia* origin>

on·tol·o·gy (on tol′ə jē) *n, pl* **on·tol·o·gies** the branch of philosophy that studies the nature of being. <Greek *on* being> **on·to·log′i·cal** *adj.*

o·nus (ō′nəs) *n* a burden or responsibility: *Since she made the accusation, the onus is on her to prove it.* <Latin = load>

on·ward (on′wərd) *adv, adj* on or farther on in space or time; forward: *The army marched onward* (*adv*). *From tomorrow onward, classes will begin at 9:30* (*adv*). *She continued her onward course* (*adj*). Also (*adv*), **onwards**.

On·yo·ta'·a·ka (on′yō tə ak′a) ONEIDA.

on·yx (on′iks) *n* a translucent variety of QUARTZ in coloured layers. <Old French, from Greek *onyx* fingernail>

oo·dles (ū′dəlz) *Informal pl n* large or unlimited quantities: *oodles of money.* <origin unknown>

🍁 **Ook·pik** (ūk′pik) *Trademark n* an Inuit doll resembling an owl, invented in 1963, and adopted as a symbol of Canadian handicraft exhibits abroad.

🍁 **oo·li·chan** (ū′lə kən) *n, pl* **oo·li·chans** or (*especially collectively*) **oo·li·chan** a small, oily fish of the smelt family, found on the Pacific coast. Also, **eulachon**. <Chinook Jargon>

🍁 **oo·loo** (ū′lū) ULU.

🍁 **oo·mi·ak** (ū′mē ak′) UMIAK.

oomph (ūmf) *Informal n* vigour or energy. < imitative>

oops (ūps) *interj* used when one has made or witnessed a minor mistake: *Oops, I spelled "February" incorrectly.*

ooze[1] (ūz) *v* **oozed, ooz·ing 1** pass slowly through small openings: *Blood oozed from her scraped knee. The mud oozed into his boots.* **2** slowly disappear or drain away: *Her courage oozed away as she waited.*
n a very slow flow of a liquid. <Old English *wase* juice>

ooze[2] (ūz) *n* soft mud or slime, especially that at the bottom of a body of water. <Old English *wase* mud>

oo·zy (ū′zē) *adj* **1** containing ooze. **2** leaking out: *an oozy wound.* **oo′zi·ly** *adv.*

op (op) *Informal n* **1** opportunity: *a photo op.* **2** *Medicine, Military* an operation.

o·pac·i·ty (ō pas′ə tē) *n, pl* **o·pac·i·ties** the quality or condition of being opaque: *Plain glass has less opacity than frosted glass.*

o·pal (ō′pəl) *n* a gemstone that is a form of SILICA. A **black opal** is green and blue, some so dark as to seem almost black. A **milk opal** is milky white. A **fire opal** is red and yellow. <French, from Sanskrit *upala* precious stone>

o·pal·es·cence (ō′pə les′əns) *n* a play of colours like that of an opal. **o′pal·es′cent** *adj.*

o·paque (ō pāk′) *adj* **1** not letting light through: *Muddy water is opaque.* **2** hard to understand.
n something opaque. <Latin *opacus* dark, shady> **o·paque′ness** or **o·pac′it·y** *n.*

op art *n* a style of drawing and painting that creates optical illusions of motion and depth by means of complex geometrical designs. <*optical art*>

OPEC (ō′pek) *n* in full, the **Organization of Petroleum Exporting Countries** an international organization of countries whose main source of income is oil revenues. The current members are Algeria, Indonesia, Iran, Iraq, Kuwait, Libya, Nigeria, Qatar, Saudi Arabia, the United Arab Emirates, and Venezuela.

o·pen (ō′pən) *adj* **1** allowing access, a view, or passage in or out: *Open windows let in fresh air.* **2** not having a lid, roof, cover, gate, etc.: *an open box.* **3** able to be entered, used, shared, etc. by all: *an open house.* **4** ready for business or for admission of the public: *The store stayed open late. The exhibition is now open.* **5** without restriction or prohibition: *open season for salmon fishing.* **6** undecided or not settled: *an open question.* **7** exposed and unprotected: *open to temptation.* **8** ready to consider new ideas: *an open mind.* **9** able to be seen or noticed: *open disregard of rules.* **10** uttered with relatively wide opening between the tongue and the roof of the mouth: *an open vowel.* **11** unreserved, candid, or frank: *an open face.* **12** spread out or expanded: *an open flower, an open newspaper.* **13** generous: *to give with an open hand.* **14** free from obstruction, especially from ice: *open water. The harbour is now open.*
v **1** cause to become open: *Open the door. I can't open the vent.* **2** remove or undo the lid, cover, roof, gate, etc. of something: *to open a parcel.* **3** establish or get going; start: *She has opened a new store. School opens tomorrow.* **4** begin the proceedings of: *to open negotiations. The Governor General opened Parliament.* **5** allow entry: *This hall opens into the bedrooms.* **6** cause to make accessible or free of obstructions: *Use your elbows to open a path through a crowd.* **7** make or become accessible to knowledge or sympathy: *to open your eyes to the poverty in the world.* **8** expand, extend, or spread out: *Open the book at page 55.*
n **1** public view or knowledge: *Bring the problem out into the open.* **2 Open** a championship or competition with few restrictions who may enter: *the Canadian Open.* **3 the open** the open country, air, or sea: *I spent the afternoon out in the open and got badly sunburned.* <Old English> **o′pen·ly** *adv.*
be open with, speak candidly.
in (or **into**) **the open, a** out of doors. **b** not concealed: *Our relationship was forced into the open.*
open up, a make or become open: *He opened up the trunk.* **b** begin shooting: *They opened up with heavy fire.* **c** open a way to and develop, especially an area or territory: *The settlers opened up what had been uninhabited land.* **d** fully reveal or make known: *She finally opened up and told me the truth.*
with your eyes open or **with open eyes,** fully aware of the implications: *I volunteered for the job with my eyes open.*

a bat	e bed	i bid	o pot	u cup	th **thin**
ā cake	ē me	ī bite	ō go	ū rude	TH **then**
à bar	ə about	ər over	ô for	ù put	zh measure

open air *n* the outdoors. **o′pen–air′** *adj.*

o·pen–and–shut (ō′pən ən shut′) *Informal adj* simple, direct, and obvious: *The Crown Attorney was sure they had an open-and-shut case against the accused.*

open book *n* someone who or something that is clear for all to see and understand: *I have no secrets; my life is an open book.*

open–book (ō′pən bu̇k′) *adj* done with one's textbook or other resource available during a test.

open concept *n* a design for the interior of a building that leaves the space open instead of dividing it up into separate rooms with walls. **open-concept** *adj.*

open door *n* **1** freedom of access or admission: *an open door policy.*

o·pen–end·ed (ō′pən en′did) *adj* with no set boundary, limit, or definition: *an open-ended agreement. The audience participated in an open-ended discussion after the speech.*

o·pen·er (ō′pə nər) *or* (ōp′nər) *n* **1** a person who or thing that opens, especially a device for opening bottles, cans, or letters. **2** *Informal* the first game of a scheduled series, or the first goal in a sporting event.
for openers, *Informal* as a beginning.

o·pen–face (ō′pən fās′) *adj* made as a sandwich without the top slice of bread.

o·pen–hand·ed (ō′pən han′did) *adj* generous. **op′en-hand′ed·ly** *adv.* **op′en-hand′ed·ness** *n.*

o·pen–heart (ō′pən hart′) *adj* to do with an operation in which the heart is opened while the blood is diverted through a bypass.

o·pen–heart·ed (ō′pən hȧr′tid) *adj* kindly or generous. **o′pen-heart′ed·ly** *adv.* **o′pen-heart′ed·ness** *n.*

open house *n* **1** an informal social event that is open to all: *My family dropped in at our neighbour's open house.* **2** an occasion when a school, university, factory, or other place is opened to be seen by the public: *The art college has an open house every spring to display the students' work.* **3** a time when a house for sale is open to inspection by buyers and agents.

o·pen·ing (ō′pə ning) *or* (ōp′ning) *n* **1** an open or clear space: *an opening in a wall, an opening in the forest.* **2** the first part of something: *the opening of a lecture.* **3** an official ceremony to mark a beginning of something: *The opening of the new city hall was last week. Were you there for the opening?* **4** a job, place, or position that is open or vacant: *an opening for a teller in a bank.* **5** a favourable chance or opportunity: *He waited for an opening before asking to borrow the car.*
adj first or beginning: *the opening words of her speech.*

open letter *n* a letter addressed to a particular person but publicly available.

o·pen–line (ō′pən līn′) *adj* giving listeners or viewers of a broadcast the chance to call in and ask questions or express opinions: *an open-line talk show.*

open mike *Informal n* an opportunity at a public gathering for anyone to use the microphone and address the group.

open mind *n* a mind ready to consider new arguments or ideas: *A politician ought to keep an open mind.*

o·pen–mind·ed (ō′pən mīn′did) *adj* with or showing a mind open to new arguments or ideas.
o′pen-mind′ed·ly *adv.* **o′pen-mind′ed·ness** *n.*

o·pen–mouthed (ō′pən mouᴛʜd′) *or* (ō′pən moutht′) *adj* with the mouth open or open wide, especially gaping with surprise or astonishment.

o·pen·ness (ō′pen nis) *n* the quality or condition of being open: *They like the new location because of its openness to the sea. Her openness to different opinions and ideas makes her a very popular politician.*

o·pen–pit (ō′pən pit′) *adj* to do with mining done from the exposed surface of the earth, or slightly below the surface.

open question *n* a matter that has not been decided and on which differences of opinion are accepted.

open season *n* a period during which it is legal to hunt and kill fish or game that is protected by law at other times.

open secret *n* a matter that is supposed to be secret but that everyone knows about: *It's an open secret that she will be made team captain this term.*

open shop *n* a factory, shop, or other establishment that will employ both union and non-union workers. Compare CLOSED SHOP.

open syllable *n* a syllable that ends with a vowel sound. Examples: *free* in *freedom*, or *o* in *open*. Compare CLOSED SYLLABLE.

Open University *n* an organization offering university level courses by broadcasting, the Internet, or correspondence, often with no admission requirements.

o·pen·work (ō′pən wərk′) *n* ornamental work in cloth or metal that has openings in the material.

op·er·a[1] (op′ə rə) *or* (op′rə) *n* **1** a drama set to music, performed by a group of singers usually to an orchestral accompaniment. In an opera, the words are usually sung, rather than spoken. **2** the art of creating or performing operas: *the history of opera.* **3** a theatre where operas are performed. <Italian, from Latin *opus* work>
op′er·at′ic *adj.* **op′er·at′i·cal·ly** *adv.*

op·er·a[2] (op′ə rə) plural of OPUS.

op·er·a·ble (op′ə rə bəl) *or* (op′rə bəl) *adj* **1** fit or suitable for a surgical operation. **2** able to be used: *an operable machine.*

opera glasses *n* small binoculars for use at the opera and in theatres.

opera house *n* a theatre where operas or other entertainments are presented.

op·er·ate (op′ə rāt′) *v* **op·er·at·ed, op·er·at·ing 1** control how a machine, process, or system functions: *Who operates this ski lift?* **2** function as a machine, process, or system in a specified way: *The machinery must operate 24/7.* **3** go into action or become effective: *The medicine operated quickly.* **4** perform a surgical operation: *The doctor operated on the injured child.* **5** carry on military activities in a certain area or from a certain base: *The army operated mainly in the northeast.* <Latin *opus* work>

operating system OS.

op·er·a·tion (op′ə rā′shən) *n* **1** the fact or condition of working or functioning: *The operation of an airline requires many people.* **2** an active process: *the operation of brushing your teeth.* **3** a medical treatment in which instruments are used to cut into the body in order to remove, replace, or repair an organ or part: *She had her operation yesterday and is doing well.* **4** movements of soldiers, ships, or military supplies: *naval operations.* **5** a business organization, or an activity in which such an organization is involved: *a commercial operation. They moved their operations to a different city.* **6** something done to a number or mathematical quantity, such as addition, subtraction, multiplication, and division in arithmetic.
in operation, in use or effect.

op·er·a·tion·al (op′ə rā′shə nəl) *or* (op′ə rā′shnəl) *adj* **1** to do with an operation. **2** of equipment, in working order. **3** ready or equipped to perform a certain part of a military operation. **op′er·a′tion·al·ly** *adv.*

op·er·a·tive (op′ə rə tiv) *or* (op′ə rā′tiv) *adj* **1** operating or effective: *the laws operative in a community.* **2** of, concerned with, or resulting from a surgical operation. **3** relevant or significant: *the operative word in a sentence.*
n **1** a person who operates a machine. **2** a private detective or secret agent.

op·er·a·tor (op′ə rā′tər) *n* **1** a person who operates something, especially a skilled worker. **2** *Informal* a person who is skilled in avoiding problems or restrictions or manipulating people for his or her own ends.

op·er·et·ta (op′ə ret′ə) *n, pl* **op·er·et·tas** a short, amusing opera with some words spoken rather than sung.

oph·thal·mic (of thal′mik) *adj* to do with the eye and its diseases.

oph·thal·mol·o·gy (of′thal mol′ə jē) *n* a branch of medical science that deals with the structure, functions, and diseases of the eye. <Greek *ophthalmos* eye> **oph′thal·mol′o·gist** *n.*

GRAMMAR AND USAGE

Ophthalmology is a medical science dealing with the eye. An **ophthalmologist** is a physician who can treat diseases of the eye as well as recommend eyeglasses. An **optometrist** is trained to examine eyes and recommend eyeglasses.

o·pi·ate (ō′pē it) *or* (ō′pē āt′) *n* **1** a drug derived from or containing opium. **2** a thing that soothes or quiets.
adj containing opium or a derivative of it.

o·pine (ō pīn′) *v* **o·pined, o·pin·ing** have or express an opinion: *He opined that the weather would improve by evening.*

o·pin·ion (ə pin′yən) *or* (ō pin′yən) *n* **1** a view or belief based on judgment rather than knowledge: *I try to learn the facts and form my own opinions.* **2** an impression or estimate: *Everyone has a poor opinion of a coward.* **3** a formal judgment made by an expert: *a legal opinion.* <Old French, from Latin *opinari* think, believe>

o·pin·ion·at·ed (ə pin′yə nā′tid) *or* (ō pin′yə nā′tid) *adj* obstinate or conceited with regard to one's opinions: *He is too opinionated to listen to anybody else.*

o·pi·um (ō′pē əm) *n* **1** a powerful, addictive drug prepared from the juice of a Eurasian poppy. **2** a thing that has a dulling or tranquillizing effect. <Greek *opion*, from *opos* vegetable juice>

o·pos·sum (ə pos′əm) *n* a small N American marsupial that is nocturnal and lives mainly in trees. It has a long tail that can grasp things. See KANGAROO for picture. <Algonquian *op* white + *assom* dog>

op·po·nent (ə pō′nənt) *n* a person who is on the other side in a competition or argument: *She defeated her three opponents in the election.*
adj opposing. <Latin *ob-* against + *ponere* put>

op·por·tune (op′ər tyūn′) *or* (op′ər tūn′) *adj* convenient, favourable, or at the proper moment: *You have arrived at an opportune moment, because I need your help.* <Old French, from Latin *ob-* in the direction of + *portus* harbour, i.e., with a favourable wind>
op′por·tune′ly *adv.* **op′por·tune′ness** *n.*

op·por·tun·ism (op′ər tyū′niz əm) *or* (op′ər tū′niz əm) *n* the policy or practice of taking advantage of opportunities and adapting thought and action to particular circumstances, especially with little regard for principles.
op′por·tun′ist *n.*

op·por·tu·ni·ty (op′ər tyū′nə tē) *or* (op′ər tū′nə tē) *n, pl* **op·por·tu·ni·ties** a good chance or convenient occasion: *I had an opportunity travel across Canada by rail. I have had no opportunity to give him your message, because I haven't seen him.*

op·pos·a·ble (ə pō′zə bəl) *adj* **1** capable of being opposed or resisted. **2** capable of being placed opposite something else, such as the thumb to the fingers.

op·pose (ə pōz′) *v* **op·posed, op·pos·ing 1** act, fight, or struggle against: *The residents opposed the widening of the street. The army's advance was fiercely opposed.* **2** put in contrast or against as a defence or reply: *Let us oppose good nature to anger.* **3** compete with someone in a contest or competition. <Old French, from Latin *ob-* against + *ponere* put> **op·pos′er** *n.*

op·posed (ə pōzd′) *adj* placed in opposition: *The two brothers had strongly opposed characters.*
v past tense and past participle of OPPOSE.
as opposed to, compared with: *We talked of the merits of train travel as opposed to air travel.*

op·po·site (op′ə zit) *adj* **1** placed face to face, back to back, or at the other end or side: *the opposite side of the street.* **2** as different as can be: *North and South are opposite directions.*
n a thing who or person that is opposite: *Black is the opposite of white.*
prep **1** on the other side or facing: *the building opposite the school. The map is opposite page 37.* **2** in a complementary role in a movie or play: *She played opposite a famous actor in her first starring role.* **op′po·site·ly** *adv.* **op′po·site·ness** *n.*

a bat	e bed	i bid	o pot	u cup	th thin
ā cake	ē me	ī bite	ō go	ū rude	ᴛʜ then
ä bar	ə about	ər over	ȯ for	u̇ put	zh measure

op·po·si·tion (op′ə zish′ən) *n* **1** action against or resistance in action or argument: *The mob offered opposition to the police. His views were in opposition to mine.* **2** the political party or parties not in power: *the official opposition.* **3** an opponent or group of opponents: *Our team easily defeated the opposition.* **4** a position opposite: *the opposition of the thumb to the fingers.* **5** in astrology and astronomy, the apparent position of two celestial bodies when they are directly opposite each other.

op·press (ə pres′) *or* (ō pres′) *v* **1** use authority harshly, unjustly, or to create hardship: *The tyrant oppressed the poor.* **2** weigh down or burden: *A fear of trouble ahead oppressed my spirits.* <Old French, from Latin *ob-* against + *premere* to press> **op·pres′sion** *n.*

op·pres·sive (ə pres′iv) *or* (ō pres′iv) *adj* **1** harsh, severe, or unjust: *Oppressive measures were taken to crush the rebellion.* **2** burdensome: *The great heat was oppressive.* **op·pres′sive·ly** *adv.* **op·pres′sive·ness** *n.*

op·pres·sor (ə pres′ər) *or* (ō pres′ər) *n* a person who is harsh or unjust to people over whom he or she has authority or power.

op·pro·bri·ous (ə prō′brē əs) *adj* expressing scorn, reproach, or abuse: *"Coward" and "liar" were just two of the opprobrious names he called me.* **op·pro′bri·ous·ly** *adv.*

op·pro·bri·um (ə prō′brē əm) *n* **1** harsh criticism of conduct considered shameful. **2** the public disgrace arising from someone's shameful conduct. <Latin *ob-* against + *probrum* disgraceful act>

opt (opt) *v* (*usually with* **for**) make a choice, especially in favour of something: *The class opted for a field trip.* <French, from Latin *optare*>
opt in, choose to join.
opt out (of), choose to drop out of some activity or organization: *Which nation wanted to opt out of the alliance?*

op·tic (op′tik) *adj* of the eye or the sense of sight.
n **1** a lens or other component of an optical instrument. **2 optics** (*with singular verb*) the science that studies light and vision. <French, from Greek *optos* seen>

op·ti·cal (op′tə kəl) *adj* **1** to do with the eye or the sense of sight: *an optical illusion.* **2** made to assist sight or according to the principles of optics: *an optical instrument.* **3** to do with optics. **op′ti·cal·ly** *adv.*

optical character recognition OCR.

optical disc LASER DISC.

optical fibre *n* a very thin fibre made of glass or plastic, through which light is transmitted. These fibres can transmit information in the form of pulses of light, and are much used in telecommunications.

optical illusion *n* an image made in such a way as to trick the eye into a wrong interpretation.

optical microscope *n* a microscope using visible light, viewed directly by the eye. See MICROSCOPE for picture. Compare ELECTRON MICROSCOPE.

op·ti·cian (op tish′ən) *n* a maker or seller of eyeglasses and other optical instruments.

optic nerve *n* a nerve that goes from the eye to the brain, conducting visual stimuli. See EYEBALL for picture.

op·ti·mal (op′tə məl) *adj* most favourable or desirable. **op′ti·mal·ly** *adv.*

op·ti·mism (op′tə miz′əm) *n* a tendency to be hopeful and confident about the outcome of a situation or event, or the belief that everything will turn out for the best. Compare PESSIMISM. <French, from Latin *optimus* best> **op′ti·mist** *n.* **op′ti·mis′tic** *adj.* **op′ti·mis′ti·cal·ly** *adv.*

op·ti·mize (op′tə mīz′) *v* **op·ti·mized, op·ti·miz·ing** make as satisfactory or effective as possible: *She checked every detail of design to optimize the effect of the poster.*

op·ti·mum (op′tə məm) *n, pl* **op·ti·mums** or **op·ti·ma** (-mə) the best or most favourable point, degree, or amount for a particular purpose.
adj most favourable, desirable, or satisfactory: *an optimum temperature for growth.*

op·tion (op′shən) *n* **1** the freedom, right, or power to choose: *We have the option of rejecting this offer and waiting for a better one.* **2** something chosen or that may be chosen: *One of the options open to her was to accept a grant to study abroad. One option offered with this car model is air conditioning.* **3** a right to buy something at a certain price within a certain time: *to hold an option on land.*

op·tion·al (op′shə nəl) *adj* not required or standard: *optional equipment on a car.* **op′tion·al·ly** *adv.*

op·tom·e·try (op tom′ə trē) *n* the profession of examining the eyes for defects in vision and prescribing lenses or exercises to correct such defects. <Greek *optos* seen + *metron* measure> **op·tom′e·trist** *adv.*

op·u·lent (op′yə lənt) *adj* rich, luxurious, or lavish: *the opulent furniture of the hotel lobby, an opulent musical style.* <Latin *opes* wealth> **op′u·lence** *n.*

o·pus (ō′pəs) *n, pl* **op·er·a** (op′ə rə) or **o·pus·es** a musical or literary composition: *The violinist played his own opus, No. 16.* <Latin = work>

or (ȯr) *conj* **1** used to express a choice, alternative, or difference, or to connect words or groups of words in a sentence: *You can go or stay. Is it sweet or sour?* **2** otherwise: *Either eat this or go hungry. Hurry, or you will be late.* **3** being the same as: *This is the end or last part.* <Old English *a* ever + *hwæther* either>

–or *suffix* **1** the person who or thing that performs an action: *survivor, accelerator.* **2** showing a state or condition: *error, terror.* **3** making an implied comparison: *minor, senior.* <Latin>

GRAMMAR AND USAGE

The suffix **–or** entered English from Latin: *horror, terror.* With a few words, the spelling **–our** was introduced from French: *colour, labour.* American English prefers **–or**. In Canada, both spellings are acceptable, but **–our** is the more frequent and is the variant given first in this dictionary.

OR or **O.R.** *n* in full, **operating room** the area in a hospital or other health facility where surgery is performed.

or·a·cle (ȯ′rə kəl) *n* **1** in ancient times, a priest or priestess through whom an answer was given by a god. **2** the place where the god gave answers: *A famous oracle was at Delphi.* **3** an answer given by a god. **4** a person who or thing that is regarded as a sure authority or guide. <Latin *oraculum*, from *orare* pray>

or·ac·u·lar (ȯ rak′yə lər) *adj* **1** to do with an oracle. **2** with a hidden meaning that is difficult to understand. **o·rac′u·lar·ly** *adv.*

or·ac·y (ȯ′rə sē) *adj* the ability to speak fluently and with skill, and to understand and respond to what others say. Compare LITERACY. <from *oral*, modelled on *literacy*>

o·ral (ȯ′rəl) *adj* **1** spoken: *An oral promise is enough for now, but we must have a written agreement by tomorrow.* **2** of the mouth: *The oral opening in an earthworm is small.* **3** taken by mouth: *oral medicine.* <Latin *oris* mouth> **o′ral·ly** *adv.*

oral tradition *n* the spoken preservation of a people's cultural and historical background, passed on from one generation to the next in spoken stories and song, as distinct from being written down.

or·ange (ȯ′rinj) *n* the round, edible fruit of a citrus tree that grows in warm climates. Oranges are reddish yellow when ripe and have a sweet or tangy, juicy pulp.
adj reddish yellow. <Old French, from Persian *narang*>

or·ange·ade (ȯ′rin jād′) *n* a drink made of orange juice, sugar, and water.

Or·ange·man (ȯ′rinj mən) *n, pl* **Or·ange·men** (-mən) a member of an Irish fraternal society formed in 1795 to uphold the Protestant religion. The Orange Order had branches in Canada.

orange pekoe (pē′kō) *n* a black tea, usually from India or Sri Lanka, made from young leaves.

Orangutans live mostly in trees, swinging from limb to limb with their long powerful arms. They sleep in platform nests made of sticks. Orangutans even drink in the trees, from water that collects in the holes.

Poaching and the destruction of its natural habitat threaten the survival of the orangutan, which is now an endangered species.

o·rang·u·tan or **o·rang–u·tan** (ȯ rang′ů tan′) *or* (ȯ rang′ ə tan′) *n* a large ape of the forests of Borneo and Sumatra, with long arms, long, reddish hair, and hooked hands and feet. <Malay *orang* man + *huan* forest>

o·ra·tion (ȯ rā′shən) *n* a formal public speech, especially one that is eloquent, delivered on a special occasion. <Latin *orare* pray, plead> **o·rate′** *v.* **or′a·tor** *n.* **or′a·tor′i·cal** *adj.* **or′a·tor′i·cal·ly** *adv.*

or·a·to·ri·o (ȯ′rə tȯ′rē ō′) *n, pl* **or·a·to·ri·os** a musical drama performed without action, costumes, or scenery, for solo voices, chorus, and orchestra, usually based on Biblical or historical themes. <Italian, from Latin *orare* pray, plead>

or·a·to·ry[1] (ȯ′rə tȯ′rē) *n* **1** the art or practice of public speaking. **2** eloquent language used in public speaking.

or·a·to·ry[2] (ȯ′rə tȯ′rē) *n, pl* **or·a·to·ries** a small chapel, especially for private prayer.

orb (ȯrb) *n* **1** *Poetic* **a** a globe, especially a celestial object: *the sun's orb.* **b** the eyeball or eye. **2** a jewelled sphere, especially a symbol of royal power. <Latin *orbis* ring>

or·bit (ȯr′bit) *n* **1** the path of a celestial object, spacecraft, or satellite around a star or planet. **2** a sphere of activity or interest: *Her studies in math were outside my orbit.* **3** the bony cavity or socket in which the eyeball is set.
v **1** travel in an orbit: *The moon orbits the earth, and the earth orbits the sun.* **2** put into an orbit: *They plan to orbit a new weather satellite.* <Latin *orbis* ring>
or′bit·al *adj.*

orca KILLER WHALE. <Latin>

or·chard (ȯr′chərd) *n* a piece of ground on which fruit trees are grown, or the trees that grow on it. <Old English *ort-* from Latin *hortus* garden + *geard* yard>

or·ches·tra (ȯr′ki strə) *n* **1** a large group of musicians who play instruments for public performances, especially one combining the string, woodwind, brass, and percussion sections. Compare BAND. See STRINGED INSTRUMENT for picture. **2** the part of a theatre just in front of the stage, where musicians sit to play. **3** the main floor of a theatre, especially the part near the front. <Latin, from Greek *orcheisthai* to dance>

or·ches·tral (ȯr kes′trəl) *adj* of, composed for, or performed by an orchestra.

or·ches·trate (ȯr′ki strāt′) *v* **or·ches·trat·ed, or·ches·trat·ing** compose or arrange music for performance by an orchestra. **or′ches·tra′tion** *n.*

or·chid (ȯr′kid) *n* a perennial plant that often has brilliantly coloured flowers with unusual shapes. <Latin, from Greek *orchis* testicle, from the shape of its tuber>

or·dain (ȯr dān′) *v* **1** *Law, Formal* order or establish by law or by decree: *The law ordains that such persons shall be imprisoned.* **2** *Christianity* officially appoint as a member of the clergy. <Old French, from Latin *ordinis* rank>

or·deal (ȯr dēl′) *n* a severe test or experience: *Written examinations were always an ordeal for her. The newspaper story described the ordeal of the survivors of the plane crash.* <Old English *ordæl*>

a bat	e bed	i bid	o pot	u cup	th **thin**
ā cake	ē me	ī bite	ō go	ū rude	ᴛʜ **then**
ä bar	ə about	ər over	ȯ for	ů put	zh measure

or·der (ȯr′dər) *n* **1** the arrangement by which one person or thing follows another: *in order of size, in alphabetical order.* **2** a condition in which every part is in its correct place: *to put a room in order.* **3** an overall condition: *His restaurant business is in good order.* **4** the way things inevitably occur, or in which they exist: *the order of nature.* **5** a situation in which the law is obeyed and there is no trouble: *The police officer tried hard to keep order.* **6** the principles and rules by which a meeting is run: *a point of order.* **7** a command or instruction, especially by someone or something in authority: *a court order. The orders of the captain must be obeyed.* **8 a** a spoken or written request for goods that one wants to buy or receive: *a grocery order.* **b** the goods so requested: *Mother asked when they would deliver our order.* **9** a document saying that money is to be given or paid, or something handed over: *a money order.* **10** a kind or sort: *to have ability of a high order.* **11** *Biology* a category in the classification of living things. An order is more specific than a CLASS, and more general than a FAMILY. See also KINGDOM, DIVISION, PHYLUM, GENUS, and SPECIES. **12** a group of people banded together for some purpose, united by something they share, or to which they are admitted as an honour: *the Franciscan order, the Order of Freemasons.* **13** a type of column and decoration forming the basis of the five classical styles of architecture. The five orders are *Doric, Ionic, Corinthian, Tuscan,* and *Composite.* **14** a portion or serving in a restaurant or other place that sells food: *"I'd like one order of fish and chips, please."*

v **1** arrange or put in order: *to order your thoughts.* **2** command or instruct: *The judge ordered the people in the courtroom to be quiet.* **3** give a request for: *Please order dinner for me.* **4** decide or determine: *The authorities ordered it otherwise.* <Old French, from Latin *ordo, ordin-* row, series, rank>

by order, according to an order given by the proper person: *by order of the premier.*

call to order, ask to be quiet and start work: *She called the meeting to order.*

in holy orders, being a member of the Christian clergy.

in order, a in the correct arrangement or condition: *Are all the pages in order?* **b** working properly. **c** allowed by the rules of a meeting.

in order that, with the purpose that.

in order to, as a means to or for the purpose of: *She worked hard in order to win the prize.*

in short order, quickly: *They got the broken window replaced in short order.*

on order, having been ordered but not yet received.

on the order of, resembling: *a house on the order of ours.*

order about (or **around**)**,** constantly command, direct, or instruct: *Stop ordering me around.*

out of order, a in the wrong arrangement or condition: *These pages are out of order.* **b** not working properly: *The radio is out of order.* **c** against the rules of a meeting: *Your motion is out of order.*

take holy orders, become a member of the Christian clergy.

to order, according to the buyer's specifications: *They had the furniture made to order.*

or·dered (ȯr′dərd) *adj* **1** characterized by regular arrangement or order: *They led a quiet, ordered existence. The window gave a wide view of ordered lawns and gardens.* **2** with elements arranged in a specific order, especially in an algebraic expression.

ordered pair *Mathematics n* two numbers in order, especially two numbers that identify a point on a coordinate plane.

Or·der–in–Coun·cil (ȯr′dər in coun′səl) *n* a regulation made by a federal or provincial cabinet under the authority of the Governor General or a Lieutenant-Governor.

or·der·ly (ȯr′dər lē) *adj* **1** with a regular arrangement, method, or system: *an orderly mind.* **2** well-behaved or regulated: *an orderly class.* **3** concerned with carrying out orders in the armed forces: *orderly sergeant.*

n, pl **or·der·lies 1** a non-medical hospital attendant who keeps things clean and in order. **2** a soldier who carries out orders or performs minor tasks: *The general's orderly delivered the message.* **or′der·li·ness** *n.*

Order of Canada *n* an order established in 1967 to honour Canadians for outstanding achievement or service. There are three categories: Companion (CC), Officer (OC), and Member (CM).

order of magnitude *n* **1** the category to which a thing belongs on the basis of its relative size or importance: *This project uses similar skills, but it's of a completely different order of magnitude from the first one.* **2** an arrangement of a number of objects, each one being greater or smaller than the other, usually by a factor of ten.

or·di·nal (ȯr′də nəl) *adj* showing order or position in a series.

n **1** an ordinal number. **2** *Christianity* a book of special forms for certain Christian church ceremonies.

ordinal number *n* a number that shows order or position in a series. *First, second, third,* and so on are ordinal numbers. Compare CARDINAL NUMBER.

or·di·nance (ȯr′də nəns) *n* **1** a rule or law made by an authority, especially a bylaw: *Many cities have ordinances against burning leaves or garbage.* **2** an established religious ceremony. <Old French, from Latin *ordinis* rank>

or·di·nar·i·ly (ȯr′də ner′ə lē) *or* (ȯr′də ner′ə lē) *adv* **1** usually: *We ordinarily go to the movies on Saturday.* **2** in a normal way: *dressed ordinarily.*

or·di·nar·y (ȯr′də ner′ē) *adj* **1** usual or customary: *His ordinary supper was a hamburger and fries.* **2** everyday or average: *an ordinary person, an ordinary situation.* **3** uninteresting or mediocre: *The speech was ordinary and tiresome.*

n, pl **or·di·nar·ies 1** a person who has authority in his or her own right, especially a bishop or a judge. **2** *Catholicism* a form of saying Mass that does not vary from day to day. <Old French, from Latin *ordinis* rank>

out of the ordinary, unusual: *It wasn't anything out of the ordinary for her to jog 15 km.*

or·di·nate (ȯr′də nāt′) *or* (ȯr′də nət′) *Mathematics n* the y-value or vertical coordinate in a system of coordinates. Compare ABSCISSA. <Old French, from Latin *ordinis* rank>

or·di·na·tion (ȯr′də nā′shən) *n* the act or ceremony of admitting a person to the Christian ministry.

ord·nance (ȯrd′nəns) *n* **1** artillery. **2** missiles and bombs. <variant of *ordinance*>

Or·do·vi·cian (or′də vi′chən) *n* the geological period lasting from about 500 million to 440 million years ago, when the first amphibians appeared. See also PALEOZOIC. *adj* to do with this period or the rocks formed then. <Latin *Ordovices* a Celtic tribe living where such rocks were plentiful>

ore (ȯr) *n* a naturally occurring solid material containing a valuable substance such as a metal or a mineral. <Old English *ar* unwrought metal>

o·reg·a·no (ə reg′ə nō) *n* a plant related to marjoram, whose leaves and small purple flowers when dried are used as a seasoning, especially in Mediterranean dishes. See HERB for picture. <Spanish, from Greek *oros* mountain + *ganos* brightness>

✱ **Or·e·gon territory** (o′rə gon) *n* in former times, the region stretching from northern California to Alaska on the Pacific coast. The part south of the forty-ninth parallel was ceded to the US by the UK in 1846.

or·gan (ȯr′gən) *n* **1 a** a large musical wind instrument consisting of sets of pipes that are sounded by forcing air through them by means of keys and pedals. **b** a smaller instrument in which a similar sound is produced by electronic means. **2** a structure in an animal or plant, such as an eye or a stamen, that is composed of different cells and tissues organized to perform a particular function. **3** a group or organization that performs a particular function within a larger group or organization: *an organ of administration.* **4** a means of giving information or expressing opinions, such as a newspaper or magazine, that represents the views of an organization or political party. <Old English, from Greek *ergon* work>

organ donor *n* a person who donates an organ while living or gives permission for it to be used for transplant after death.

or·gan·dy or **or·gan·die** (ȯr′gən dē) *n, pl* **or·gan·dies** a thin, sheer cotton cloth with a crisp finish, woven in a plain weave with tightly twisted yarns.

or·gan·elle (ȯr′gə nel′) *n* a separate organized or specialized structure within a cell, such as a cilium.

organ grinder *n* a person who plays a hand organ by turning a crank.

or·gan·ic (ȯr gan′ik) *adj* **1** to do with an organ of the body: *an organic disease.* **2** made up of related and co-ordinated parts: *Every part of an organic whole depends on every other part.* **3** forming part of the basic structure of something fundamental: *The music is not just background but an organic part of the movie.* **4** to do with compounds of carbon that have a biological origin: *organic chemistry.* **5** to do with raising plants or animals without using chemical substances such as pesticides or growth hormones, or with fruit, vegetables, or meat produced in this way: *organic gardening, organic beef.*
or·gan′i·cal·ly *adv.*

organic chemistry *n* the branch of chemistry that studies compounds of carbon.

or·gan·ism (ȯr′gə niz′əm) *n* **1** a living body with organs or an organized structure in which each part has a particular function but all depend on each other. **2** a very tiny living thing or one-celled life form **3** a complex structure made of related parts that work together and are dependent on each other and on the whole structure: *A community may be spoken of as a social organism.*

or·gan·ist (ȯr′gə nist) *n* a person who plays the organ, especially a skilled player.

or·gan·i·za·tion (ȯr′gə nə zā′shən) *or* (ȯr′gə nī zā′shən) *n* **1** a group of people united for some purpose, such as a business, church, club, or political party. **2** the grouping and arranging of parts to form the whole: *The organization of a big picnic takes time and thought.* **3** the way in which a thing's parts are arranged to work together: *The organization of the human body is very complicated.* **4** a thing made up of related parts, each with a special task. **or′ga·ni·za′tion·al** *adj.*
or′ga·ni·za′tion·al·ly *adv.*

Organization of American States OAS (def. 2).

or·gan·ize (ȯr′gə nīz′) *v* **or·gan·ized, or·gan·iz·ing** **1** arrange to work or form a whole: *The general organized his soldiers into a powerful fighting force.* **2** plan and lead, get started, or carry out: *The explorer organized an expedition to the North Pole.* **3** arrange in a system: *She organized her thoughts. He organized his stamp collection.* **4** *Informal* make oneself ready to do what is required: *Please wait—I'm not organized yet.* **5** bring into or form a labour union. **or′gan·iz′er** *n.*

organized labour *n* the workers who belong to labour unions.

or·gan·za (ȯr gan′zə) *n* a thin, stiff dress fabric that is made out of silk or a synthetic yarn.

or·gasm (ȯr′gaz′əm) *n* the climax of sexual excitement. <French, from Greek *organ* to swell> **or′gas′mic** *adj.*

or·gy (ȯr′jē) *n, pl* **or·gies** **1** a wild party, especially one involving drunkenness and indiscriminate sexual activity. **2** something resembling an orgy in lack of control: *an orgy of destruction, an orgy of bloodshed.* **3 orgies** *pl* secret rites or ceremonies in the worship of certain Greek and Roman gods, especially Bacchus and Dionysus, celebrated with drinking, wild dancing, and singing. <French, from Greek *orgia* secret rites> **or′gi·as′tic** *adj.*

o·ri·ent (ȯ′rē ənt) *for n or adj;* (ȯ′rē ent′) *for v.* *v* **1** place or face in a certain position: *The building is oriented north and south.* **2** adjust to or adapt to specific circumstances or needs: *She is oriented toward a career in business.*
n **the Orient** *Poetic* the regions lying to the east of Europe and the Mediterranean Sea, especially the Far East. <Old French, from Latin *oriri* to rise>
orient yourself, bring into the proper relationship with your surroundings: *It takes a while to orient yourself in a strange city.*

o·ri·en·tal or **O·ri·en·tal** (ȯ′rē en′təl) *adj* to do with east Asia or Eastern civilizations in general: *oriental music.*
n Offensive a native or inhabitant of eastern Asia.

a bat	e bed	i bid	o pot	u cup	th thin
ā cake	ē me	ī bite	ō go	ū rude	ᴛʜ then
ȧ bar	ə about	ər over	ȯ for	ů put	zh measure

O

o·ri·en·ta·tion (ô′rē en tā′shən) *or* (ô′rē ən tā′shən) *n* **1** the act or process of orienting or the condition of being oriented. **2** a general tendency or direction of interest or thought: *Her orientation toward the dramatic shows clearly in her dress designs.*

or·i·en·teer·ing (ô′rē ən tē′ring) *n* the sport of finding one's way through unfamiliar territory by means of a map and compass, usually involving a given starting and finishing point with a series of checkpoints in between. **or′i·en·teer′** *n, v.*

or·i·fice (ô′rə fis) *n* an opening, such as a mouth, hole, or vent, through which something may pass. <French, from Latin *os, or-* mouth + *facere* to make>

or·i·gam·i (ô′ri gä′mē) *n* a paper sculpture developed by the Japanese, in which paper is folded in a variety of ways to make shapes and figures such as birds and flowers. <Japanese *oru, ori-* fold + *kami* paper>

or·i·gin (ô′rə jin) *n* **1** the beginning of something's existence: *the origin of a quarrel, the origin of a disease.* **2** parentage or ancestry: *The professor was a man of humble origin. The word "beef" is of French origin.* **3** the place or point on the body where a muscle, nerve, or other part arises. **4** *Mathematics* a fixed point from which coordinates are measured; the point where the x-axis and the y-axis meet. <French, from Latin *oriri* to rise>

o·rig·i·nal (ə rij′ə nəl) *adj* **1** used or created at the beginning or earliest stage of something: *the original settlers, a skirt marked down from its original price.* **2** fresh and unusual: *She has written a very original story. They thought up several original games for the party.* **3** able to do, make, or think something new: *The inventor had an original mind.* **4** not copied, imitated, or translated from something else: *This is the original manuscript.*
n **1** the first version or actual thing from which something is copied, imitated, or translated: *This sculpture is a plaster copy of the original.* **2** the language in which a book was first written: *She has read* War and Peace *in the original.* **3** an unusual or eccentric person.

o·rig·i·nal·i·ty (ə rij′ə nal′ə tē) *n* **1** the quality or condition of being original: *Several experts questioned the originality of the manuscript.* **2** freshness or novelty of style: *The furniture has a striking originality of design.* **3** the ability to do, make, or think up something new: *He is known for his originality in thinking up plots.*

o·rig·i·nal·ly (ə rij′ə nə lē) *adv* **1** by origin: *His family was originally Irish.* **2** at first: *a house originally small.* **3** in a creatively original manner: *The room was very originally decorated.*

original sin *n* in some Christian belief, the tendency to evil that all human beings inherit from Adam as a consequence of his disobeying God.

o·rig·i·nate (ə rij′ə nāt′) *v* **o·rig·i·nat·ed, o·rig·i·nat·ing** **1** cause to be or invent: *to originate a new style of painting.* **2** come into being: *Where did that story originate?* **o·rig′i·na′tion** *n.* **o·rig′i·na′tor** *n.*

o·ri·ole (ô′rē əl) *or* (ô′rē ōl′) *n* a songbird. The adult males have black and orange or yellow plumage; the females are mainly yellowish.

or·na·ment (ôr′nə mənt) *for n,* (ôr′nə ment′ *for v.*
n **1** something used to add beauty, especially a beautiful object or part that has no particular function in itself. **2** the use of ornaments or ornamentation: *Ornament played an important part in rococo architecture.* **3** a person who, or act or quality that, adds beauty, grace, or distinction: *He was an ornament to his time.*
v make more pleasing or attractive: *A single brooch ornamented her dress.* <Old French, from Latin *ornare* adorn> **or′na·men′tal** *adj.* **or′na·men′tal·ly** *adv.*

or·na·men·ta·tion (ôr′nə men tā′shən) *n* **1** the act or fact of ornamenting or being ornamental. **2** decorations or ornaments: *The room was simple, with no ornamentation.*

or·nate (ôr nāt′) *adj* much adorned or ornamented: *She liked ornate furniture.* **or·nate′ly** *adv.* **or·nate′ness** *n.*

SYNONYMS

Ornate suggests elaborately decorated: *She wore an ornate necklace made with many different kinds of beads.*

Encrusted emphasizes decorated with a layer of costly materials: *The wedding gown was encrusted with pearls.*

Gilded means "decorated with a thin layer of gold": *The gilded frame made the mirror very expensive.*

or·ner·y (ôr′nə rē) *Informal adj* irritable or bad-tempered: *an ornery horse.* <variant of *ordinary*> **or′ner·i·ness** *n.*

or·ni·thol·o·gy (ôr′nə thol′ə jē) *n* a branch of zoology that makes a study of birds. <Latin, from Greek *ornithos* bird> **or′ni·tho·log′i·cal** *adj.* **or′ni·thol′o·gist** *n.*

or·o·tund (ôr′ə tund′) *or* (ōr′ə tund′) *n* **1** full and rich in voice: *orotund speech.* **2** pompous; wordy: *an orotund writing style.* <Latin *ore rotundo* = with round mouth>

or·phan (ôr′fən) *n* **1** a child whose parents are dead. **2** a word or line left alone at the top of a page.
v make an orphan of: *The war orphaned my grandfather at an early age.* <Greek *orphanos* bereaved>

or·phan·age (ôr′fə nij) *n* a residential institution in which orphans are cared for and educated.

or·tho·don·tic (ôr′thə don′tik) *n* **orthodontics** (*with singular verb*) the branch of dentistry that treats irregular or crooked teeth by straightening or adjusting them.
adj to do with orthodontics. <Greek *orthos* straight + *odontos* tooth> **or′tho·don′tist** *n.*

or·tho·dox (ôr′thə doks′) *adj* **1** conforming to established doctrine and customs, especially in religion: *an orthodox Jew.* **2** conforming to custom: *Our new teacher doesn't use orthodox methods of teaching mathematics.* <Greek *orthos* straight + *doxa* opinion>

Orthodox Church *Christianity n* in full, **Orthodox Eastern Church** the family of churches that separated from the Catholic Church in the 1000s, and includes the national churches of Russia and Greece, among others.

Orthodox Judaism *n* a branch of Judaism involving the observance of strict rules relating to dietary laws, the keeping of the Sabbath, study of the Torah, daily prayer, and the keeping of holy days.

or·tho·dox·y (ȯr′thə dok′sē) *n, pl* **or·tho·dox·ies** the holding of correct or generally accepted beliefs.

or·thog·o·nal projection (ȯr thog′ə nəl) *n* the two-dimensional representation of a three-dimensional object, using parallel lines to project the object's outline onto a flat surface. Maps of the world are often made using orthogonal projection. Also called **orthographic projection**. <Old French, from Greek *orthos* right + *gonia* angle>

or·thog·ra·phy (ȯr thog′rə fē) *n, pl* **or·thog·ra·phies** **1** the spelling system of a language. **2** the study of spelling and how letters combine to represent sounds and form words. <Old French, from Greek *orthos* right + *gonia* angle> **or·tho′graph·er** *n.* **or′tho·graph′i·cal** *adj.* **or′tho·graph′i·cal·ly** *adv.*

or·tho·pe·dic (ȯr′thə pē′dik) *n* **orthopedics** (*with singular verb*) the branch of surgery that treats deformities, diseases, and injuries of bones and joints.
adj to do with orthopedics: *orthopedic shoes.* <French, from Greek *orthos* correct + *paideia* nurture> **or′tho·pe′dist** *n.*

orthotic *n* **1** a device used to straighten or support a foot or other body part that has an orthopedic problem. **2** **orthotics** (*with singular verb*) the branch of medicine that uses special devices to support or straighten weakened or abnormal joints and limbs.
adj to do with orthotics. <Greek *orthos* straight> **or′tho′tist** *n.*

–ory *suffix* **1** of, relating, or characterized by: *auditory, compensatory, conciliatory.* **2** a place used for or connected with something: *conservatory.* <Latin *-orium*>

o·ryx (ȯ′riks) *n, pl* **o·ryx·es** or (*especially collectively*) **o·ryx** a large African or Arabian antelope with dark markings on the face and long, nearly straight horns. <Latin, from Greek *oryx* pickaxe, because of its horns>

OS *Computers n* in full, **operating system** a collection of programs that control the basic functions of a computer.

Os·car (os′kər′) *Trademark n* a statuette awarded annually by the American Academy of Motion Picture Arts and Sciences for the best achievements in filmmaking during the year. Also called **Academy Award**.

os·cil·late (os′ə lāt′) *v* **os·cil·lat·ed, os·cil·lat·ing** **1** swing back and forth at a regular speed. **2** vary between extreme or opposing opinions, purposes, beliefs, or theories. **3** *Physics* vary in magnitude or position in a regular way around a central point. <Latin *oscillare* to swing>

os·cil·la·tion (os′ə lā′shən) *n* **1** the fact or process of oscillating. **2** a single swing of an oscillating body.

os·cil·lo·scope (ə sil′ə skōp′) *n* an electronic instrument for representing waves or vibrations on a screen. <*oscillation* + *-scope*>

o·sier (ō′zhər) *n* a small Eurasian willow that grows in wet habitats and has long, flexible shoots that are used in basketwork.

O·si·ris (ō sī′ris) *n* a god of ancient Egypt, associated with fertility and taken to be ruler of the afterlife.

–osis *suffix* **1** an act, process, or state: *hypnosis, osmosis.* **2** a diseased condition: *neurosis.* <Latin, from Greek>

os·mi·um (oz′mē əm) *n* a hard, dense, metallic element of the platinum group, used for electric light filaments. *Symbol* **Os** <Latin, from Greek *osme* odour, from the pungent smell of its oxide>

os·mo·sis (oz mō′sis) *n* **1** *Biology, Chemistry* a process by which a fluid tends to pass through a membrane from a less concentrated solution to a more concentrated one. **2** a process of gradual, often unconscious, absorption of ideas or knowledge: *He thought he could learn French by osmosis, without doing any work.* <Latin, from Greek *osmos* a push>

os·prey (os′prē) *or* (os′prā) *n, pl* **os·preys** or (*especially collectively*) **os·prey** a large, long-winged, brown-and-white hawk that feeds on fish. It is the provincial bird of Nova Scotia. <Old French, from Latin *os* bone + *frangere* to break>

os·se·ous (os′ē əs) *adj* consisting of or resembling bone.

os·si·fy (os′ə fī′) *v* **os·si·fied, os·si·fy·ing** **1** change into bone: *The soft parts of a baby's skull ossify as the baby grows older.* **2** make or become fixed, rigid, or hardened: *The once free and spontaneous exchange of ideas among the group members had ossified into mere ritual.* <French, from Latin *os* bone> **os′si·fi·ca′tion** *n.*

os·ten·si·ble (os ten′sə bəl) *adj* apparent or pretended: *The ostensible reason for her resignation was ill health, but we think she was fired.* <French, from Latin *ob-* in view of + *tendere* to stretch> **os·ten′si·bly** *adv.*

os·ten·ta·tious (os′tən tā′shəs) *or* (os′ten tā′shəs) *adj* done for display or to attract notice: *He rode his new bicycle up and down in an ostentatious way.* **os′ten·ta′tion** *n.* **os′ten·ta′tious·ly** *adv.*

os·te·o·ar·thri·tis (os′tē o ar thrī′tis) *n* arthritis caused by the degeneration of joints and cartilage. <Greek *osteon* bone + *arthritis*> **os′te·o·ar·thri′tic** (os′tē o ar thri′tik) *adj.*

os·te·o·path (os′tē ə path′) *n* a person who practises a system of medical practice that treats disorders through the manipulation of bones and massage of muscles. <Greek *osteon* bone + *pathein* suffer>
os′te·o·path′ic *adj.* **os′te·o′path·y** (os′tē o′path ē) *n.*

os·te·o·po·ro·sis (os′tē o pə rō′sis) *n* a bone condition common especially in older women, characterized by loss of bone mass and brittleness of bones, due to a lack of calcium. <Greek *osteon* bone + *poros* pore>

os·tra·cize (os′trə sīz′) *v* **os·tra·cized, os·tra·ciz·ing** exclude someone from society or a group: *The group finally ostracized her completely because of her inability to get along with people.* <Greek *ostrakon* broken piece of ceramics. This was used as a ballot in voting to banish an unpopular or too powerful citizen.>
os′tra·cism (os′trə siz′əm) *n.*

os·trich (os′trich) *n* a large African bird that can run swiftly but cannot fly. It is the largest living bird. See BIRD for picture. <Old French, from Greek *strouthos*>

a bat	e bed	i bid	o pot	u cup	th thin
ā cake	ē me	ī bite	ō go	ū rude	ᴛʜ then
à bar	ə about	ər over	ȯ for	u̇ put	zh measure

ostrich fern *n* a tall fern with long, green fronds that form a crown. The young, curled fronds are called **fiddleheads** or **fiddlehead greens**.

oth·er (uTH′ər) *adj, pron* **1** different or distinct from something or someone already mentioned or known about: *She's here, but the other girls are at school.* **2** additional or further: *I have no other books with me.* **3** the alternative of two: *Turn back to the other page.*
adv otherwise: *I can't do other than go.* <Old English *other*>
every other, every second; alternating: *She buys cream every other day.*
none other than, no one else but: *The presentation was made by none other than the prime minister.*
no other than, no one less than.
other than, apart from: *Other than your sister, nobody knew about it.*
something (or **someone**) **other,** some indefinite thing (or person): *He said something or other about a meal, but I forget what.*
the other day (**night**, etc.)**,** recently.

other half *Informal n* **1** a spouse, or domestic partner. Also called **better half**. **2** a different group in society: *seeing how the other half lives.*

oth·er·ness (uTH′ər nes) *n* the quality of being separate or different in a fundamental way.

oth·er·wise (uTH′ər wīz′) *adv* **1** in a different way: *I could not do otherwise.* **2** in other respects: *He is noisy, but otherwise a very nice boy.* **3** under other circumstances: *She reminded me of what I should otherwise have forgotten.*
adj in a different condition or situation: *Go at once, otherwise you will be too late.*

other world *n* **the other world** the supernatural or spirit world.

oth·er·world·ly (uTH′ər wərl′dlē) *adj* of or devoted to an imaginary or spiritual world: *She was a very withdrawn and otherworldly person.* **oth′er·world′li·ness** *n.*

o·ti·ose (ō′shē ōs′) *or* (ō′tē ōs′) *adj* with no practical purpose or result: *The article was wordy and full of otiose comments and digressions.* <Latin *otium* leisure>

o·ti·tis (ō tī′tis) *n* inflammation of the ear, especially the middle ear. <Greek *otos* ear + *-itis*>

Ot·ta·wa (ot′ə wo′) *or* (ot′ə wə) **1 a** *pl* **Ottawa** or **Ottawas** a member of a First Nations or Native American people living mainly in southern Ontario. **b** the language of these people. Also called **Odawa**. **2** 🍁 the capital city of Canada.
adj to do with the Ottawa people or their language.

ot·ter (ot′ər) *n, pl* **ot·ters** or (*especially collectively*) **ot·ter** a fish-eating water mammal of the weasel family with webbed feet and short, thick, glossy brown fur. <Old English *otr, ottor*>

ot·to·man (ot′ə man) *or* (ot′ə mən) *n, pl* **ot·to·mans** **1** a low, cushioned seat without back or arms. **2 Ottoman** a Turk living under the rule or belonging to the dynasty that ruled the **Ottoman Empire**, a former empire of the Turks in Europe, Asia, and Africa. <French, from *Ottoman* Turk>

🍁 **oua·na·niche** (wä′nə nish′) *n, pl* **oua·na·niche** a freshwater form of the Atlantic salmon, found in Newfoundland and Labrador, Québec, and Ontario. Compare KOKANEE. <Cdn French, from Montagnais *wananish* little salmon>

ou·bli·ette (ū′blē et′) *n* a secret dungeon with a trapdoor in the ceiling as its only entrance. <French *oublier* forget about. Someone in such a place could certainly be forgotten!>

ouch (ouch) *interj* used to express sudden pain. <imitative>

ought (ot) *v* **1** have a duty: *You ought to obey your parents.* **2** be proper or suitable: *The theatre ought to allow children in free. I ought to go before it rains.* **3** be expected or desirable: *At your age you ought to know better.* **4** be very likely: *He left here an hour ago, so he ought to be home by now.* <Old English *agan* owe>

ought·n't (ot′ənt) *contraction* ought not.

Oui·ja board (wē jə) *or* (wē jē) *Trademark n* a board with letters, numbers, or other signs around its edge. To get an answer to a question, users rest the fingers lightly on an object that seems to move, by itself, toward the signs so as to spell out a message. <French *oui* yes + German *ja* yes. Most users probably want a positive answer.>

ounce (ouns) *n* **1** a nonmetric unit for measuring mass, one-sixteenth of a pound (about 28 g) in avoirdupois, and one-twelfth of a pound (about 31 g) in troy weight. **2** a nonmetric unit for measuring liquids, equal to one-twentieth of a pint (about 28 mL). **3** a very small amount of something: *She hadn't an ounce of pity left.* <Old French, from Latin *uncia* twelfth part>

our (our) *or* (är) *adj* a possessive form of WE: *We went to get our coats.* <Old English *ure*>

CONFUSABLES

Our and **ours** are possessive forms of *we*.

Our is a determiner and is always followed by a noun: *This is our apartment.*

Ours is a pronoun and stands alone: *This apartment is ours.*

ours (ourz) *or* (ärz) *pron* a possessive form of WE; that which belongs to us: *They got their tickets yesterday, but ours aren't here yet.*

our·selves (our selvz′) *or* (är selvz′) *pron* **1** the object of a reflexive verb with *we* as subject: *We cannot see ourselves as others see us.* **2** an intensive pronoun, used to emphasize the noun or pronoun it follows: *We ourselves are responsible for what happened.* **3** our usual selves: *We weren't ourselves when we let them get away with that.*

–ous *suffix* characterized by: *dangerous, joyous, zealous.* <Old French, from Latin *–osus*>

oust (oust) *v* force or drive out: *The sparrows have ousted the bluebirds from our birdhouse.* <Old French, from Latin *obstare* oppose, hinder>

oust·er (ou′stər) *n* **1** a dismissal or expulsion from a position: *the ouster of the chief executive.* **2** a forced removal, especially an illegal forcing of a person out of his or her property.

out (out) *adv* **1** away from inside a particular place: *Come out of there! Drain out the oil from the engine.* **2** not in or at a place, position, or situation: *out of fashion. Is it snowing out?* **3 a** to or at an end: *I threw my back out. The anesthetic put him out for hours. Put the light out. Will the people vote the government out? The fire has gone out. Hand in your essay before the day is out.* **b** completely or effectively: *tired out. The money has run out.* **4 a** in or into existence or view: *An epidemic broke out. Her new book has come out. Cherry blossoms popped out. The sun came out.* **b** in or into activity or competition: *She went out for hockey.* **5** aloud; boldly: *Speak out.* **6** from among others: *She picked out a new jacket.* **7** into the possession of others: *to share out the pizza, to hand out prizes.* **8** showing a loss: *to be out ten dollars.*
adj **1** not at home or in a workplace: *I phoned her but she was out.* **2** revealed, especially as a declaration that someone is homosexual or lesbian: *The secret is out. I've been out for two years.* **3** no more in fashion: *Short skirts were out that year.* **4** no longer in operation or operational: *The fire is out. The power is out.* **5** at an end: *School's out at the end of June. "Have you any candy left?" "No, I'm out."* **6** not possible or doable: *The weather was awful, so a picnic was out.* **7** incorrect: *to be out in your calculations.* **8 a** *Baseball, Cricket* having your team's at bat, or innings, ended by the fielding side: *We were soon out and the other team was at bat.* **b** *Tennis, Volleyball, etc.* with the ball outside the designated playing area.
n **1** a defence or excuse: *Having homework gave me an out for doing laundry.* **2** *Baseball* the act of putting a player out: *three outs per inning.*
v be revealed: *The truth will out.* <Old English *ut*>
on the outs or **at outs,** *Informal* quarrelling; no longer being friends: *I'm on the outs with him. We're at outs.*
out and about, doing what you usually do, especially after illness or injury: *I had a bad asthma attack, but now I'm out and about again.*
out and away, by far: *She is out and away the best player.*
out for, looking for or trying to achieve: *It's vacation time and we're out for some fun.*
out of, a without or lacking: *We are out of coffee.* **b** because of: *I went out of curiosity.*
out of hand, See HAND.
out of it or **right out of it,** *Informal* **a** dazed: *I banged my head and was out of it for several minutes.* **b** out of touch; unaware: *My older brothers are right out of it.*
out of line, See LINE.
out to, eagerly trying to: *Their team is out to make the finals.*
out with it, say what you are thinking; tell the truth: *I really do want your opinion, so out with it!*

out– *prefix* **1** more than or longer than: *outnumber, outlive.* **2** external or separate: *outfield, outbuilding.* **3** away from: *outspread.*

out·age (out′əj) *n* a time of interrupted service, especially a suspension of hydro, gas, or water supply: *We got through the power outage with flashlights and candles.*

out–and–out (out′ən out′) *adj* thorough or complete: *an out-and-out defeat, an out-and-out scoundrel.*

out·back (out′bak′) *n* the sparsely populated part of the interior of Australia.

out·bid (out′bid′) *v* **out·bid, out·bid** or **out·bid·den, out·bid·ding** bid higher than someone else.

out·board (out′bȯrd′) *adj, adv* outside the hull of a ship or boat.
n a boat equipped with an outboard motor, or the motor itself.

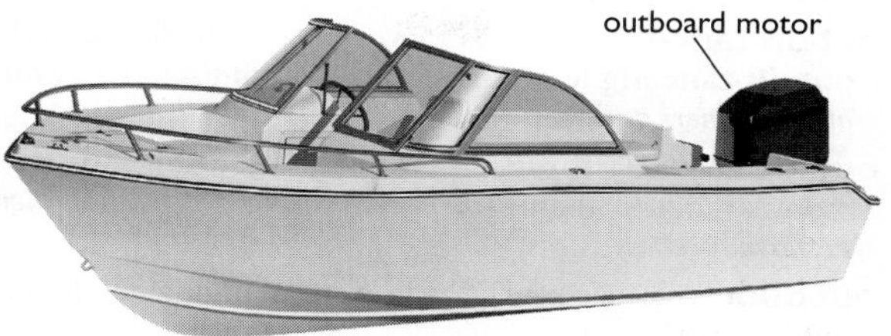

outboard motor *n* a portable INTERNAL COMBUSTION ENGINE with an attached propeller, that is mounted on the outside of the stern of a small boat or canoe.

out·bound (out′bound′) *adj* outward bound: *an outbound ship.*

out·break (out′brāk′) *n* **1** a sudden or violent start of something unwelcome: *an outbreak of flu, an outbreak of rioting.*

out·build·ing (out′bil′ding) *n* a shed or building built near a main building.

out·burst (out′bərst′) *n* a sudden, strong release of an emotion or activity: *an outburst of applause, an outburst of laughter.*

out·cast (out′kast′) *n* a person or animal rejected by society or a social group.
adj homeless or friendless.

O

SYNONYMS

An **outcast** is someone who has been excluded from a society or system: *She was an outcast from the club because she refused to follow the rules.*

An **exile** is one who has been banished: *Napoleon Bonaparte was an exile on the island of Elba.*

A **pariah** is a person who is rejected by society: *The man became a pariah because of his criminal activities.*

out·class (out′klas′) *v* be superior to: *He is a good runner, but his younger brother definitely outclasses him.*

out·come (out′kum′) *n* a result or consequence: *The outcome of the election was in doubt until the very end.*

out·crop (out′krop′) *for n,* (out′krop′) *for v.* *n* a rock formation that appears on the surface of the earth: *The outcrop proved to be very rich in gold.*
v **out·crop·ped, out·crop·ping** appear as an outcrop.

a bat	e bed	i bid	o pot	u cup	th **thin**
ā cake	ē me	ī bite	ō go	ū rude	ᴛʜ **then**
à bar	ə about	ər over	ȯ for	u̇ put	zh measure

out·cry (out′krī′) *n, pl* **out·cries** 1 a sudden cry or clamour. 2 a strong protest: *There was a public outcry against the proposal to widen the street into a four-lane highway.*

out·dat·ed (out′dā′tid) *adj* out-of-date.

out·did (out′did′) past tense of OUTDO.

out·dis·tance (out′dis′tәns) *v* **out·dis·tanced, out·dis·tanc·ing** leave far behind: *She outdistanced all the other runners and won the race.*

out·do (out′dū′) *v* **out·did, out·done, out·do·ing** do more or better than: *You'll find it hard to outdo her performance.*

out·door (out′dôr′) *adj* done, used, or living outdoors: *outdoor games.*

out·doors (out′dôrz′) *adv* out in the open air: *The minute it stopped raining, we all went outdoors.*
n **the outdoors** (*with singular verb*) the world outside of buildings or the open air: *We spend most of the summer in the outdoors, which is great.*

out·doors·man (out′dôr′zmәn) *n, pl* **out·doors·men** (-zmәn) a person who enjoys the outdoors and spends much time in outdoor activities or sports.

out·door·sy (out′dôr′zē) *Informal adj* to do with, or fond of the outdoors or outdoor activities: *She's an outdoorsy person, always going off on hikes.*

out·er (ou′tәr) *adj* 1 of or on the outside: *The outer door is locked.* 2 farther out: *the outer suburbs of Montréal.*

outer ear *n* the outer, visible part of the ear that directs sound waves toward the eardrum. See AURICLE (the formal name) for picture.

out·er·most (ou′tәr mōst′) *adj* farthest out.

outer planet *n* a planet in the solar system that is farther from the sun than Mars is. Saturn, Jupiter, Neptune, Uranus, and Pluto are the outer planets. See EARTH for picture.

outer space *n* space beyond the earth's atmosphere.

out·er·wear (ou′tәr wār′) *n* clothing worn over other clothes.

out·face (out′fās′) *v* **out·faced, out·fac·ing** confront boldly.

out·field (out′fēld′) *n* the part of a baseball field beyond the diamond or infield, or the three players in the outfield. **out′field′er** *n.*

out·fit (out′fit) *for n,* (out′fit) *or* (out fit′) *for v. n* 1 all the items needed for an undertaking or purpose: *a sailor's outfit, the outfit for a camping trip.* 2 a group of people working together: *They were in the same outfit during the war. He worked for the same outfit for five years.* 3 a set of clothes to be worn together: *a bride's outfit, a summer outfit.*
v **out·fit·ted, out·fit·ting** 1 furnish with everything necessary for a purpose: *She outfitted herself for camp.* 2 supply: *The whole family was outfitted with new coats last winter.*

out·fit·ter (out′fit әr) *n* a person or company that deals in supplies for camping and wilderness expeditions.

out·flank (out′flangk′) *v* 1 go or extend beyond the flank of an opposing army. 2 get the better of or outmanoeuvre: *They outflanked us and won the debate.*

out·flow (out′flō′) *n* a large amount of money, liquid, or people that moves or is moved out of a place: *a cash outflow, the outflow from a water pipe, an outflow of sympathy.*

out·fox (out′fox′) *v* get the better of or outsmart: *The escaped convict outfoxed his pursuers.*

out·go·ing (out′gō′ing) *adj* 1 departing or outward bound: *outgoing ships, the outgoing mail.* 2 retiring or withdrawing from office: *A dinner was held for the outgoing president.* 3 friendly and sociable: *She is very outgoing and enjoys giving parties.*

out·grow (out′grō′) *v* **out·grew, out·grown, out·grow·ing** 1 grow too large for: *to outgrow your clothes.* 2 grow beyond or away from: *to outgrow childhood friends.* 3 grow or increase faster than: *She outgrew her twin sister. The population is outgrowing the food supply.*

out·growth (out′grōth′) *n* 1 a natural development, product, or result: *This big store is an outgrowth of the little shop she started ten years ago.* 2 a thing that has grown out of something else: *an outgrowth on a toe.* 3 the process of growing out or forth: *the outgrowth of leaves.*

out·house (out′hous′) *n* 1 an outdoor toilet. 2 a separate building used in connection with a main building, especially on a farm.

out·ing (ou′ting) *n* a short pleasure trip: *On Sunday the family went on an outing to Grand Bend.*

out·land·ish (ou′tlan′dish) *adj* strange or ridiculous: *an outlandish hairstyle.*

out·last (ou′tlast′) *v* last longer than: *His stamina outlasted mine.*

out·law (ou′tlo′) *n* 1 a person who has broken the law, especially one who has not been caught. 2 an unbroken horse.
v 1 make or declare a person an outlaw. 2 make or declare illegal: *A group of nations agreed to outlaw war.*

out·lay (ou′tlā′) *for n,* (ou′tlā′) *for v. n* an amount of money spent on something: *a large outlay for school supplies.*

out·let (ou′tlet′) *or* (ou′tlit) *n* 1 a means or place of letting out or getting out: *the outlet of a lake, an outlet for your energies.* 2 a market for a product: *an outlet for manufactured goods.* 3 a point from which goods are sold or distributed: *The company had several retail outlets.* 4 a place in a surface for inserting an electric plug to make connection with an electric circuit.

out·li·er (ou′tlī′әr) *Statistics n* in a set of data, any value that is above the upper quartile (or below the lower quartile) by more than 1.5 times the interquartile range.

out·line (ou′tlīn′) *n* 1 the line that shows the shape of an object: *We saw the outlines of the mountains against the evening sky.* 2 a drawing or style of drawing that gives only outer lines: *an outline of Canada.* 3 a general plan or draft: *Make an outline before trying to write a composition.*
v **out·lined, out·lin·ing** 1 draw the outer line of: *Outline a map of Canada.* 2 give a plan of: *to outline the day's events.*
in outline, a with only the outline shown. b with only the main features.

out·live (ou′tliv′) *v* **out·lived, out·liv·ing** live or last longer than: *She outlived her older sister. The idea was good once, but it has outlived its usefulness.*

out·look (ou′tlůk′) *n* **1** a general attitude to life: *a gloomy outlook.* **2** a view of what one sees on looking out: *The room has a pleasant outlook.* **3** the prospect of what seems likely to happen: *Because of the black clouds, the outlook for our picnic is not very good.* **4** a weather report for the near future: *The outlook for tomorrow is cool, cloudy, with a chance of showers.*

out·ly·ing (ou′tlī′ing) *adj* far from the centre: *the outlying houses in the settlement.*

out·ma·noeu·vre (out′mə nū′vər) *v* **out·ma·noeu·vred, out·ma·noeu·vring** **1** get the better of by skill and cunning: *I was outmanoeuvred by my opponent, and lost the chess game.* **2** move faster and with more agility than a competitor: *This car can outmanoeuvre any other car of its size on the market.* Also, **outmaneuver**.

out·mod·ed (out′mō′did) *adj* out-of-date.

out·most (out′mōst′) *adj* farthest out.

out·num·ber (out′num′bər) *v* be more numerous than: *The bullies outnumbered us three to one.*

out–of–bounds (ou′təv boundz′) *adj, adv* **1** in sports, outside the boundary line. **2** outside the established limits of use or entry: *The front yard was out-of-bounds to the dog.*

out of date *adj* old-fashioned and not used much at present; obsolete: *That schedule is out of date. A horse and buggy is an out-of-date means of travelling.*

out–of–the–way (ou′təv ᴛʜə wā′) *adj* **1** remote or secluded: *an out-of-the-way cottage.* **2** seldom encountered: *out-of-the-way bits of information.*

out·pace (out′pās′) *v* **out·paced, out·pac·ing** run or progress faster than: *I outpaced the others and won the race.*

out·pa·tient (out′pā′shənt) *n* a patient receiving treatment at a hospital but not staying there.

out·per·form (out′pər form′) *v* perform better or longer than.

✱ **out·port** (out′pôrt′) *n* a small settlement with a harbour, especially a fishing village on a coast of Newfoundland.

out·post (out′pōst′) *n* **1** a guard, or small group of soldiers, placed at some distance from an army or camp to prevent a surprise attack, or the place where these people are stationed. **2** a settlement or village in an outlying place.

out·pour·ing (out′pô′ring) *n* **1** an uncontrolled expression of thoughts or feelings. **2** a thing that pours out rapidly.

out·put (out′půt′) *n* **1** the amount produced: *the daily output of automobiles. Last year's output surpassed anything she had written before.* **2** an action or process of producing something: *With a sudden output of effort, she moved the rock.* **3** power, energy, or information supplied by a device or system.

out·rage (ou′trāj′) *for n,* (ou′trāj′) *or* (ou′trāj′) *for v.* *n* **1** an act or event that causes anger, shock, or indignation: *The thug was guilty of many outrages.* **2** the angry, shocked, or indignant feelings aroused by such an act or event.
v **out·raged, out·rag·ing** **1** arouse anger, shock, or indignation: *His callous attitude outraged me.* **2** violate a principle, custom, or law: *She outraged all rules of behaviour.* <Old French, from Latin *ultra* beyond>

out·ra·geous (ou trā′jəs) *adj* shockingly bad or excessive: *an outrageous disregard for the rights of others, outrageous behaviour.* **out·ra′geous·ly** *adv.* **out·ra′geous·ness** *n.*

out·ran (ou′tran′) past tense of OUTRUN.

out·rank (ou′trangk′) *v* rank higher than: *A captain outranks a lieutenant.*

ou·tré (ū′trā) *adj* overstepping the limits of what is considered proper or acceptable: *an outré remark about her figure.* <French = exceeded>

out·reach (ou′trēch′) *for v,* (ou′trēch′) *for n.* *v* exceed or reach beyond: *Her accomplishments far outreached those of her predecessors.*
n **1** the act or fact of reaching out: *The social aid program has too little outreach into the community.* **2** the extent or limit of reach: *the outreach of the flood.*

out·ride (ou′trīd′) *v* **out·rode, out·rid·den, out·rid·ing** **1** ride faster or better than. **2** come safely through a storm as a ship.

out·rid·er (ou′trī′dər) *n* an escort or guide who goes on a horse or motor vehicle in front of or beside a vehicle.

out·rig·ger (ou′trig′ər) *n* **1** a beam, spar, or framework projecting from or over the side of a boat or aircraft. **2** a float or secondary hull fixed parallel to a boat in order to keep it stable. **3** a boat equipped with such a structure. See DUGOUT for picture.

out·right (out′rīt′) *adv* **1** altogether; at once: *Dad has to decide whether to pay for a flat-screen TV over two years, or buy it outright.* **2** openly and without restraint: *I laughed outright.*
adj **1** complete or thorough: *an outright loss.* **2** straightforward and direct: *an outright refusal.*

out·rode (ou′trōd′) past tense of OUTRIDE.

out·run (ou′trun′) *v* **out·ran, out·run, out·run·ning** **1** run or travel faster than: *She outran me in the last lap.* **2** go beyond: *His story outruns the facts.*

out·sell (out′sel′) *v* **out·sold, out·sell·ing** **1** outdo in selling or salesmanship: *She can easily outsell any of the other sales reps.* **2** sell in greater amounts than: *His second novel outsold his first by a wide margin.*

out·set (out′set′) *n* the start or beginning: *At the outset, it looked like a nice day.*

out·shine (out′shīn′) *v* **out·shone, out·shin·ing** **1** shine more brightly than. **2** be more brilliant or excellent than: *She outshone me in playing the piano.*

a bat	e bed	i bid	o pot	u cup	th thin
ā cake	ē me	ī bite	ō go	ū rude	ᴛʜ then
à bar	ə about	ər over	ô for	ů put	zh measure

O

out·shoot (out′shūt′) *v* **out·shot, out·shoot·ing 1** shoot better or farther than. **2** score more shots on goal than another player or team.

out·side (out′sīd′); *also,* (out′sīd′) *for prep.*
n **1** the side or surface that faces outward: *The outside of the coat is stained.* **2** the external appearance of something: *From the outside, the situation looked bad.* **3** 🍁 the southerly or settled parts of Canada, as considered by residents of the Far North.
adj **1** on or near the side or surface that faces outward: *the outside leaves.* **2** not belonging to or coming from a certain group: *Outside people tried to get control of the business.* **3** being, acting, done, or originating without or beyond an area: *Outside noises disturbed the class.* **4** highest or reaching the utmost limit: *an outside estimate of the cost.* **5** slight or small: *He had only an outside chance of winning the race.*
adv outdoors: *Run outside and look.*
prep beyond the limits of: *Stay outside the house.*
at the outside, *Informal* at the most: *I can do it in a week, at the outside.*
outside of, *Informal* with the exception of: *Outside of a few, none of us liked the play.*

out·sid·er (out′sī′dər) *n* **1** a person who does not belong to a particular group. **2** a competitor who or thing that is not expected to win.

out·size (out′sīz′) *adj* larger than the usual size.
n a thing, such as an article of clothing, larger than the usual size.

out·skirts (out′skərts′) *pl n* the outer parts or edges of an urban or geographical area: *There is a ravine on the northern outskirts of town. We live on the outskirts of Hamilton, very close to Lake Ontario.*

out·smart (out′smårt′) *Informal v* outdo in cleverness: *By clever questioning, the lawyer outsmarted the suspect.*

out·sold (out′sōld′) past tense and past participle of OUTSELL.

out·source (out′sôrs′) *v* **out·sourced, out·sourc·ing** obtain goods or services by means of a contract with an outside supplier: *They used to do the packaging in the warehouse, but they're outsourcing it now.*
out·sourc′ing *n.*

out·spo·ken (out′spō′kən) *adj* frank with opinions, however candid or controversial: *an outspoken person, outspoken criticism.* **out′spo′ken·ly** *adv.*
out′spo′ken·ness *n.*

out·spread (out′spred′) *for adj,* (out′spred′) *for v. adj* spread out or extended: *an eagle with outspread wings.*
v **out·spread, out·spread·ing** spread out or extend.

out·stand·ing (out stan′ding) *adj* **1** exceptionally good in quality or skill: *She is an outstanding basketball player.* **2** unpaid: *outstanding debts.* **3** needing attention: *outstanding letters.* **out·stand′ing·ly** *adv.*

out·stare (out′stār′) *v* **out·stared, out·star·ing** stare at someone until that person looks away or blinks.

out·stay (out′stā′) *v* **1** stay beyond the limit of: *He outstayed his welcome.* **2** stay longer than: *She outstayed all the other buyers. He outstayed the other guests.*

out·stretched (out′strecht′) *adj* stretched out or extended: *He welcomed his old friend with outstretched arms.*

out·strip (out′strip′) *v* **out·stripped, out·strip·ping 1** go faster than: *A horse can outstrip a man.* **2** do better than: *He outstrips his friends in both sports and studies.*

out·take (out′tāk) *n* part of a film or broadcast that is edited out.

out·talk (out′tok′) *v* talk better, faster, longer, or louder than someone else.

out–tray (out′trā) *n* a container for outgoing mail or memos, or for things that have been dealt with and can be filed.

out·vote (out′vōt′) *v* **out·vot·ed, out·vot·ing** defeat in voting: *The radical faction was outvoted on the issue.*

out·ward (ou′twərd) *adv* toward the outside: *Porches extend outward from the house. She folded the coat with the lining outward.* Also, **outwards.**
adj **1** going or turned toward the outside: *an outward motion.* **2** on the surface: *to all outward appearances.*

out·ward·ly (ou′twər dlē) *adv* on the surface, especially as it appears to an onlooker: *Though frightened, the boy remained outwardly calm.*

out·wash (ou′twosh′) *n* rock fragments or other glacial debris carried beyond a glacier by meltwater. Compare TILL[4].

out·weigh (ou′twā′) *v* **1** weigh more than: *My older brother outweighs me by five kilograms.* **2** exceed in value, importance, or influence: *The advantages of the plan outweigh its disadvantages.*

out·wit (ou′twit′) *v* **out·wit·ted, out·wit·ting** get the better of by being more intelligent: *The prisoner outwitted his guards and escaped.*

out·worn (ou′twôrn′) *for adj,* (ou′twôrn′) *for v. adj* **1** worn out: *outworn clothes.* **2** out-of-date: *outworn opinions, outworn habits.*
v past participle of OUTWEAR.

ou·zel (ū′zəl) *n* **1** in full, **ring ouzel** a large European thrush with a white ring or bar on the neck. **2** in full, **water ouzel** a diving bird.

ou·zo (ū′zō) *n* a strong, colourless, Greek liquor flavoured with aniseed that turns milky when diluted. <Greek *ouzon*>

o·va (ō′və) plural of OVUM.

o·val (ō′vəl) *adj* with a rounded and slightly elongated shape like that of an egg.
n a thing with this shape. <Latin *ovum*> **o′val·ly** *adj.*
o′val·ness *n.*

o·va·ry (ō′və rē) *n, pl* **o·va·ries 1** in female animals, the reproductive organ that produces the egg cells and, in vertebrates, female sex hormones. **2** the part of the pistil in a seed-bearing plant that contains the young seeds, called ovules. **o·var′i·an** (ō ver′ē ən) *adj.*

o·vate (ō′vāt) *adj* egg-shaped: *an ovate leaf.*

o·va·tion (ō vā′shən) *n* an enthusiastic and sustained show of appreciation, such as a prolonged burst of applause, often with cheering: *The dancer received a great ovation.* <Latin *ovare* rejoice>

ov·en (uv′ən) *n* **1** a space, usually part of a stove, for baking or roasting food. **2** a small furnace for heating or drying. <Old English *ofen*>

ov·en·proof (uv′ən prūf′) *adj* able to withstand the heat of an oven.

ov·en·ware (uv′ən wãr′) *n* dishes made to be ovenproof.

o·ver (ō′vər) *prep* **1** at a higher level or layer than: *There were clouds over the city.* **2** more than: *It costs over a thousand dollars. Are you over 16?* **3 a** in preference to: *I chose that card over all the others.* **b** in superiority to: *to have an advantage over the other team.* **4** so as to cover: *Put the coat over your shoulders. The water is so deep it would have been over your head.* **5** to or on the other side of: *We drove over the bridge, distant lands over the sea. The horse jumped over the fence.* **6 a** out and down from: *She fell over the edge of the cliff.* **b** on top of or down on: *I tripped over the dog.* **7** all through: *She shopped all over town to find your gift.* **8** during: *These things happened over many years. Let's look at it over lunch.* **9 a** concerning: *I am upset over my exam results.* **b** while engaged in or concerned with: *to fall asleep over your homework.* **10** by means of: *I can't tell you over the phone.* **11** being recovered from; at the end of: *to get over an illness, to get over a bad mood.*
adv **1** above in place or position: *Climb the wall and look over.* **2** so as to cover or affect a surface: *There was a mark, but I painted it over.* **3** across or through some space: *Go over to the store for me. Hand the money over.* **4** beyond and falling: *The ball went too near the edge and rolled over. When he lost his balance, he fell over.* **5** so as to bring the upper side or end down or under: *Turn the page over and start writing, please.* **6** again, repeated, or from beginning to end: *ten times over. I'll have to do that assignment over.* **7** throughout or beyond a period of time: *Please stay over until Monday.* **8** more or besides: *She spent seventy dollars and had thirty dollars over.*
adj at an end: *The play is over.*
n Cricket the sequence of six balls delivered between successive changes of bowlers. <Old English *ofer*>
over again, once more: *Let's do that over again.*
over against, a in contrast to: *Over against darkness is light.* **b** adjacent to: *over against the car.*
over and above, besides.
over and over, again and again: *She keeps telling the same story over and over.*
over with or **over and done with,** finished or completed: *I have to get this homework over with today.*

over– *prefix* **1** too much or excessively: *overcrowded, oversleep.* **2** completely: *overjoyed.* **3** beyond: *overtime.* **4** over or above: *overhang.*

o·ver·a·chieve (ō′vər ə chēv′) *v* **o·ver·a·chieved, o·ver·a·chiev·ing** perform better than required, sometimes to satisfy the unreasonable expectations of another or to compensate for feeling insecure. **o′ver·a·chiev′er** *n.*

o·ver·act (ō′və rakt′) *v* act a part in an exaggerated way.

o·ver·ac·tive (ō′və rak′tiv) *adj* too active: *an overactive thyroid gland, an overactive imagination.*
o′ver·ac′tive·ly *adv.*

o·ver·age[1] (ō′vər āj′) *adj* over a specified age limit: *Overage children are not allowed in this play facility.*

o·ver·age[2] (ō′vər əj) *n* a surplus or extra amount.

o·ver·all (ō′və rol′) *for adj or n,* (o′və rol′) *for adv. adj* **1** from one end to the other: *The overall length of the house is ten metres.* **2** including everything: *an overall estimate.*
adv generally: *Overall, it was a successful meeting.*
n **1** *especially UK* a loose-fitting smock or outer garment worn over other clothes to protect them. **2 overalls** *pl* loose trousers of strong, usually cotton, cloth worn over clothes to keep them clean, usually with a part that covers the chest.

o·ver·anx·ious (ō′və rangk′shəs) *or* (ō′və rang′shəs) *adj* too anxious.

o·ver·arch (ō′və rärch′) *v* curve like an arch: *The street was overarched by elm trees.*

o·ver·arm (ō′və rärm′) *adj, adv* with the arm raised above the shoulder: *to throw overarm.*

o·ver·ate (ō′və rāt′) past tense of OVEREAT.

o·ver·awe (ō′və ro′) *v* **o·ver·awed, o·ver·aw·ing** be silent or inhibited because one is deeply impressed: *She was overawed by the grandeur of the estate.*

o·ver·bal·ance (ō′vər bal′əns) *v* **o·ver·bal·anced, o·ver·bal·anc·ing** **1** be greater in weight, importance, or value: *The gains overbalanced the losses.* **2** lose or cause to lose balance: *As he leaned over, his weight overbalanced the canoe and it tipped. He overbalanced and fell.*

o·ver·bear (ō′vər ber′) *v* **o·ver·bore, o·ver·borne, o·ver·bear·ing** overcome by weight or force: *His mother overbore his objections.*

o·ver·bear·ing (ō′vər ber′ing) *adj* domineering: *He was too overbearing to be a good leader.* **o′ver·bear′ing·ly** *adv.*

o·ver·bite (ō′vər bīt′) *Dentistry n* a condition in which the top front teeth project over the bottom ones.

o·ver·blown (ō′vər blōn′) *adj* **1** past the peak of beauty of a flower. **2** inflated, pompous, or pretentious: *His acceptance speech was filled with flowery, overblown sentiments.*

o·ver·board (ō′vər bȯrd′) *adv* from a ship or boat into the water: *She fell overboard. They were fined for throwing garbage overboard.*
go overboard, go too far in an effort because of extreme enthusiasm: *She went overboard and bought more than she needed.*
throw overboard, abandon or discard: *We had to throw all our plans overboard and start again from scratch.*

o·ver·book (ō′vər bu̇k′) *v* issue tickets or reservations to more people than there is room for: *The airline had overbooked the flight and we had to wait for the next one.*

o·ver·bore (ō′vər bȯr′) past tense of OVERBEAR.

o·ver·borne (ō′vər bȯrn′) past participle of OVERBEAR.

o·ver·bur·den (ō′vər bər′dən) *v* load with too great a burden: *The overburdened donkey collapsed. She was overburdened with debts.*

o·ver·came (ō′vər kām′) past tense of OVERCOME.

a bat	e bed	i bid	o pot	u cup	th thin
ā cake	ē me	ī bite	ō go	ū rude	ᴛʜ then
ä bar	ə about	ər over	ȯ for	u̇ put	zh measure

O

o·ver·cast (ō′vər kast′) *adj* **1** cloudy, dark, or gloomy: *The sky was overcast all day, but it did not rain.* **2** sewn with overcast stitches.
v **o·ver·cast, o·ver·cast·ing 1** cover or be covered with clouds. **2** sew over and through the edges of a seam with long stitches to prevent ravelling.

o·ver·charge (ō′vər chärj′) *for v,* (ō′vər chärj′) *for n.*
v **o·ver·charged, o·ver·charg·ing 1** charge too high a price or beyond the correct amount: *The grocer overcharged you for the eggs.* **2** put too much electrical charge into a battery.
n a charge that is too great.

o·ver·coat (ō′vər kōt′) *n* **1** a long coat worn for warmth over regular clothing. **2** the top coat of paint or other covering.

o·ver·come (ō′vər kum′) *v* **o·ver·came, o·ver·come, o·ver·com·ing 1** win a victory over: *to overcome an enemy, to overcome difficulties.* **2** make weak or helpless: *Weariness overcame her, and she fell asleep.* **3** confuse or overwhelm: *The girl was so overcome by the noise and the lights that she couldn't speak.*

SYNONYMS

Overcome means "triumph over": *Before I could go skydiving, I had to overcome my fear of heights.*

Conquer means "defeat" or "subdue," especially by force: *To conquer the enemy forces, we will need to strike quickly.*

Overpower means "have more strength than": *Our basketball team overpowered the competition.*

o·ver·com·pen·sate (ō′vər kom′pən sāt′) *v*
o·ver·com·pen·sat·ed, o·ver·com·pen·sat·ing 1 go too far in trying to make up for or get rid of a feeling of not being good or worthy enough: *She overcompensated for her shyness at the party by insulting half the guests.* **2** receive too much payment: *He thought his boss was overcompensated.* **o′ver·com′pen·sa′tion** *n.*

o·ver·con·fi·dent (ō′vər kon′fə dənt) *adj* too confident. **o′ver·con′fi·dence** *n.* **o′ver·con′fi·dent·ly** *adv.*

o·ver·cook (ō′vər kủk′) *v* cook a dish or meal for too long: *Meat loses its flavour when it is overcooked.*

o·ver·cor·rect (ō′vər kȯr rekt′) *v* **1** make a correction going beyond what is needed, as in steering a car. **2** make an error due to trying too hard to avoid a different error. Example: Saying *between you and I,* instead of the correct form *between you and me.* **o′ver·cor·rec′tion** *adv.*

o·ver·crowd (ō′vər kroud′) *v* crowd too much: *The boat sank because it was overcrowded.*

o·ver·de·vel·op (ō′vər di vel′əp) *v* develop too much or too long: *If a photograph is overdeveloped, it will be too dark.*

o·ver·do (ō′vər dū′) *v* **o·ver·did, o·ver·done, o·ver·do·ing 1** do or attempt too much: *She overdoes exercise. He overdid it and became tired.* **2** exaggerate: *The funny scenes in the play were overdone.*

o·ver·dose (ō′vər dōs′) *for n,* (ō′vər dōs′) *for v. n* too big a dose.
v **o·ver·dosed, o·ver·dos·ing** give too large a dose to.

o·ver·draft (ō′vər draft′) *n* a deficit in a bank account caused by withdrawing more money than it holds.

o·ver·draw (ō′vər dro′) *v* **o·ver·drew, o·ver·drawn, o·ver·draw·ing 1** draw from a bank account more money than it holds: *He overdrew his account by $24.00.* **2** exaggerate: *The characters in the book were greatly overdrawn.*

o·ver·dress (ō′vər dres′) *v* dress or decorate too formally or elaborately: *He decided not to wear his tuxedo because he did not want to risk being overdressed.*

o·ver·drive (ō′vər drīv′) *n* **1** an arrangement of gears whereby less power produces more speed than in high gear. **2** high or intense activity: *Her preparation for the exams went into overdrive.*

o·ver·due (ō′vər dyū′) *or* (ō′vər dū′) *adj* **1** not yet having arrived, happened, or been done: *The plane is overdue.* **2** due but not yet paid: *This bill is overdue.*

o·ver·eat (ō′və rēt′) *v* **o·ver·ate, o·ver·eat·en, o·ver·eat·ing** eat too much.

o·ver·em·pha·size (ō′vər em′fə sīz′) *v*
o·ver·em·pha·sized, o·ver·em·pha·siz·ing put too much emphasis on: *I think he overemphasizes the importance of talent.*
o′ver·em′pha·sis (ō′vər em′ fə sis′) *n.*

o·ver·es·ti·mate (ō′vər es′tə māt′) *for v,* (ō′vər es′tə mət) *for n. v* **o·ver·es·ti·mat·ed, o·ver·es·ti·mat·ing** estimate at too high a value, amount, or rate.
n an estimate that is too high. **o′ver·es′ti·ma′tion** *n.*

o·ver·ex·cite (ō′və rek sīt′) *v* **o·ver·ex·cit·ed, o·ver·ex·cit·ing** excite or be excited too much. **o′ver·ex·cit′able** *adj.* **o′ver·ex·cite′ment** *n.*

o·ver·ex·ert (ō′və reg zərt′) *v* put forth too much effort: *He hurt his back when he overexerted himself in gymnastics.* **o′ver·ex·er′tion** *n.*

o·ver·ex·pose (ō′və rek spōz′) *v* **o·ver·ex·posed, o·ver·ex·pos·ing 1** expose to too much light or radiation: *Be careful not to overexpose yourself to the sun. If you overexpose a film, the photographs will be too pale.* **2** expose too much or for too long: *Don't overexpose small children to TV. Every time I listen to a radio, I hear that song; it has definitely been overexposed.* **o′ver·ex·po′sure** *n.*

o·ver·ex·tend (ō′və rek stend′) *v* extend too far, especially, commit oneself financially beyond what one can pay: *She overextended herself in her business and went bankrupt.*

o·ver·feed (ō′vər fēd′) *v* **o·ver·fed, o·ver·feed·ing** feed too much: *Their puppy is so fat because they overfeed it.*

o·ver·fill (ō′vər fil′) *v* fill too full.

o·ver·fish (ō′vər fish′) *v* deplete the stock of fish in a body of water by fishing too much.

o·ver·flow (ō′vər flō′) *for v,* (ō′vər flō′) *for n.*
v **o·ver·flowed, o·ver·flown, o·ver·flow·ing 1** flow over the bounds: *The river overflowed its banks.* **2** be so full that the contents go over the sides: *He filled my glass so quickly that the juice overflowed.* **3** extend out beyond: *The crowd overflowed the little room and filled the hall.* **4** be very full or abundant: *an overflowing harvest, overflowing kindness.*

n **1** an overflowing: *The overflow from the glass ran into the sink.* **2** an excess: *We caught the overflow in a pail.*

o·ver·gar·ment (ō′vər gȧr′ mənt) *n* an outer garment.

o·ver·graze (ō′vər grāz′) *v* **o·ver·grazed, o·ver·graz·ing** harm the ecology of an area by allowing too much grazing by livestock, so that the grass does not have a chance to renew itself.

o·ver·grow (ō′vər grō′) *v* **o·ver·grew, o·ver·grown, o·ver·grow·ing** **1** grow or spread over something, especially so as to stifle other vegetation: *The wall is overgrown with vines.* **2** grow too fast or big.

o·ver·growth (ō′vər grōth′) *n* too great or rapid growth.

o·ver·hand (ō′vər hand′) *adv, adj* **1** with the hand raised above the shoulder: *an overhand throw* (*adj*), *to pitch overhand* (*adv*). **2** with the knuckles upward. **3** with sewing stitches passing successively over an edge.
n an overhand stroke or throw: *He's practising his overhand.*

o·ver·hang (ō′vər hang′) *for v,* (ō′vər hang′) *for n.*
v **o·ver·hung, o·ver·hang·ing** **1** hang or project over: *Trees overhang the street to form an arch of branches.* **2** hang over so as to sadden or threaten: *The threat of an invasion overhung the city.*
n a thing that sticks out, or the amount it projects: *The overhang of the roof shaded the flower bed beneath.*

o·ver·haul (ō′vər hol′) *for v,* (ō′vər hol′) *for n.* *v* examine thoroughly and make any repairs or changes that are needed: *to overhaul a boat, to overhaul a course of study.*
n a thorough examination to find and make necessary repairs: *The engine needs an overhaul.*

o·ver·head (ō′vər hed′) *for adv,* (ō′vər hed′) *for adj or n.*
adv over the head: *The plane flew overhead.*
adj **1** being, working, or passing overhead: *overhead wires.* **2** incurred as general expenses in running a business, such as rent, lighting, and heating.
n usually, **overheads** *pl* the general expenses of running a business.

overhead projector *n* a projecting device in which transparencies are placed on a glass surface that is lit from below. The image is focused and reflected onto a wall or screen by means of an overhead lens and mirror.

o·ver·hear (ō′vər hēr′) *v* **o·ver·heard, o·ver·hear·ing** hear what one is not meant to hear: *They spoke so loudly that I could not help overhearing what they said.*

SYNONYMS

Overhear involves hearing something spoken to another, often unintentionally: *I couldn't help but overhear your conversation.*

Bug is an informal word meaning "record secretly using a hidden microphone": *The RCMP bugged the suspect's room.*

Eavesdrop means "listen secretly to a conversation": *He eavesdropped on his brother's phone conversation.*

o·ver·heat (ō′vər hēt′) *v* heat too much: *They always overheat their house in winter.*

o·ver·hung (ō′vər hung′) *for adj,* (ō′vər hung′) *for v.* *adj* hung from above: *an overhung door.*
v past tense and past participle of OVERHANG.

o·ver·in·dulge (ō′və rin dulj′) *v* **o·ver·in·dulged, o·ver·in·dulg·ing** indulge too much.

o·ver·joyed (ō′vər joid′) *adj* filled with great joy: *She was overjoyed at finding the pup safe and sound.*

o·ver·kill (ō′vər kil′) *n* **1** a capacity for destruction greater than that required to destroy a target or enemy. **2** too much use, treatment, or action for the intended purpose: *Ten pages of critical comments was overkill!*

o·ver·laid (ō′vər lād′) past tense and past participle of OVERLAY[1].

o·ver·lain (ō′vər lān′) past participle of OVERLIE.

o·ver·land (ō′vər land′) *or* (ō′vər lənd) *adj, adv* on or by land: *an overland route* (*adj*), *to travel overland* (*adv*).

o·ver·lap (ō′vər lap′) *for v,* (ō′vər lap′) *for n.* *v* **o·ver·lapped, o·ver·lap·ping** place or be placed so that one piece or common area covers part of the next: *Shingles are laid to overlap each other.*
n the part, amount, or common area that overlaps: *Allow for an overlap of ten centimetres. Some of her duties overlapped mine.*

o·ver·lay[1] (ō′vər lā′) *for v,* (ō′vər lā′) *for n.* *v* **o·ver·laid, o·ver·lay·ing** **1** lay or place one thing over or upon another. **2** cover, overspread, or surmount with something, especially, finish with a layer or applied decoration of something: *The dome is overlaid with gold.* **3** become more prominent than something previous: *My joy at being rescued was overlaid by embarrassment for having fallen out of the boat.*
n **1** a thing laid over something else, such as a covering or a transparent sheet. **2** an ornamental layer: *The lid of the box had a gold overlay.*

o·ver·leaf (ō′vər lēf′) *adv, adj* on the other side of the page: *The photo overleaf shows a lioness and cub* (*adj*). *Check overleaf for the answers* (*adv*).

o·ver·lie (ō′vər lī′) *v* **o·ver·lay, o·ver·lain, o·ver·ly·ing** lie over or upon.

o·ver·load (ō′vər lōd′) *for v,* (ō′vər lōd′) *for n.*
v load too heavily: *to overload a boat.*
n too great a load: *The overload of electric current broke the circuit.*

o·ver·look (ō′vər lu̇k′) *v* **1** fail to see: *Here are the letters you overlooked.* **2** pay no attention to: *His boss said he would overlook the mistake.* **3** have a view of from above: *This window overlooks half the city.*

o·ver·lord (ō′vər lôrd′) *n* a supreme ruler, especially a person who is lord over another lord or other lords: *The duke was the overlord of barons and knights who held land from him.*

a bat	e bed	i bid	o pot	u cup	th thin
ā cake	ē me	ī bite	ō go	ū rude	ᴛʜ then
ȧ bar	ə about	ər over	ȯ for	u̇ put	zh measure

o·ver·ly (ō′vər lē) *adv* too much: *She's overly sensitive to criticism.*

o·ver·much (ō′vər much′) *adj, adv, n* too much.

o·ver·nice (ō′vər nīs′) *adj* too fussy or FASTIDIOUS.

o·ver·night (ō′vər nīt′) *for adv,* (ō′vər nīt′) *for adj. adv* **1** for one night: *to stay overnight.* **2** on the night before: *Preparations were made overnight for an early start.* **3** at once or in a very short time: *Change will not happen overnight.*
adj **1** done or occurring from one day to the next: *an overnight stop.* **2** for use for one night: *an overnight bag.*
n a stop or stay for one night.

overnight bag *n* a small piece of hand luggage to hold articles needed for a night's stay.

o·ver·pass (ō′vər pas′) *n* a bridge over a road, railway, or canal: *An overpass was built to replace the level crossing.*

o·ver·pay (ō′vər pā′) *v* **o·ver·paid, o·ver·pay·ing** pay too much. **o′ver·pay′ment** *n.*

o·ver·play (ō′vər plā′) *v* **1** play a part or role in an exaggerated way. **2** give undue importance to.

o·ver·pop·u·late (ō′vər pop′ū lāt′) *v* **o·ver·pop·u·lat·ed, o·ver·pop·u·lat·ing** allow or cause an area to become too densely populated, resulting in social, economic, or ecological problems. **o′ver·pop′u·la′tion** *n.*

o·ver·pow·er (ō′vər pou′ər) *v* **1** overcome or overwhelm: *to overpower your enemies. I was overpowered by the heat.* **2** be so much greater than that nothing else is felt: *Sudden anger overpowered every other feeling.*
o′ver·pow′er·ing·ly *adv.*

o·ver·price (ō′vər prīs′) *v* **o·ver·priced, o·ver·pric·ing** price too high: *His paintings aren't selling well because they're overpriced.*

o·ver·pro·duce (ō′vər prə dyūs′) *or* (ō′vər prə dūs′) **o·ver·pro·duced, o·ver·pro·duc·ing** *v* produce more than there is a need or demand for. **o′ver·pro·duc′tion** *n.*

o·ver·pro·tect (ō′vər prə tekt′) *v* protect more than is necessary or desirable: *He had a hard time when he first left home because he had been overprotected as a child.* **o′ver·pro·tec′tion** *n.* **o′ver·pro·tec′tive** *adj.*

o·ver·qual·i·fied (ō′vər kwol′i fīd′) *adj* with more education, training, or experience than a job calls for.

o·ver·ran past tense of OVERRUN.

o·ver·rate (ō′vər rāt′) *v* **o·ver·rat·ed, o·ver·rat·ing** rate or estimate too highly: *The movie was overrated, and none of us enjoyed it.*

o·ver·reach (ō′vər rēch′) *v* **1** reach over or beyond, especially, reach too far. **2** get the better of by cunning: *to overreach another in a bargain.*
overreach yourself, a fail or miss by trying for too much. **b** fail by being too crafty or tricky.

o·ver·re·act (ō′vər rē akt′) *v* react too strongly or unreasonably: *He overreacted to the joke and stormed out of the room.* **o′ver·re·ac′tion** *n.*

o·ver·rep·re·sent (ō′vər rep′rə zent′) *v* include too many of, so that a single group may have unfair influence: *Few of the boys volunteered, so girls are overrepresented on the student council.* **o′ver·rep′re·sen·ta′tion** *n.*

o·ver·ride (ō′vər rīd′) *v* **o·ver·rode, o·ver·rid·den, o·ver·rid·ing** **1** use authority to reject or cancel something: *to override advice or objections. The new rule overrides all previous ones.* **2** interrupt the action of an automatic device, typically in order to take manual control: *override the power steering.* **3** travel or move over a place or thing. **4** tire out by riding: *to override a horse.*
n **1** an action, process, or device for suspending an automatic function: *a manual override.* **2** an increase or excess on a budget, salary, or cost: *commission overrides, cost overrides.*

o·ver·ripe (ō′vər rīp′) *adj* past the best stage of ripeness.

o·ver·rule (ō′vər rūl′) *v* **o·ver·ruled, o·ver·rul·ing** **1** decide against an argument or objection: *The president overruled my plan.* **2** be stronger than or prevail over: *The majority overruled me.*

o·ver·run (ō′vər run′) *v* **o·ver·ran, o·ver·run, o·ver·run·ning** **1** spread over rapidly or in great numbers: *Weeds had overrun the old garden. The barn was overrun with rats.* **2** invade and conquer, occupy, or destroy: *Enemy troops overran most of the country.* **3** run or go beyond: *The speaker overran the time set for her.*

o·ver·saw (ō′vər so′) past tense of OVERSEE.

o·ver·seas (ō′vər sēz′) *for adv,* (ō′vər sēz′) *for adj.*
adv **1** across or beyond the sea: *to travel overseas.* **2** serving across the sea as part of a military force: *My grandfather was overseas during the war.*
adj **1** foreign: *overseas trade.* **2** done, used, or serving overseas: *overseas service.* Also, **oversea**.

o·ver·see (ō′vər sē′) *v* **o·ver·saw, o·ver·seen, o·ver·see·ing** manage and direct work or workers: *to oversee a factory.* **o′ver·se′er** *n.*

o·ver·sell (ō′vər sel′) *v* **o·ver·sold, o·ver·sell·ing** sell or promise more than can be delivered.

o·ver·sexed (ō′vər sekst′) *adj* with an abnormally strong sex drive.

o·ver·shad·ow (ō′vər shad′ō) *v* **1** be or appear more important than: *The boy overshadowed his older brother as a hockey player.* **2** cast a shadow over.

o·ver·shoe (ō′vər shū′) *n* a waterproof shoe or boot, often made of rubber, worn over another shoe to keep the foot dry and warm.

o·ver·shoot (ō′vər shūt′) *v* **o·ver·shot, o·ver·shoot·ing** **1** pass as an aircraft beyond the limit of the runway or landing field when trying to land. **2** shoot or go beyond the target, mark, or limit.

o·ver·sight (ō′vər sīt′) *n* **1** an unintentional mistake or omission: *Through an oversight, the kitten had no supper last night.* **2** watchful care or supervision: *While children are at school, they are under their teacher's oversight.*

o·ver·sim·pli·fy (ō′vər sim′plə fī′) *v* **o·ver·sim·pli·fied, o·ver·sim·pli·fy·ing** make so simple that it distorts or overlooks important facts: *She has oversimplified the problem, since there are several important factors she did not consider.* **o′ver·sim′pli·fi·ca′tion** *n.*

o·ver·size (ō′vər sīz′) *adj* larger than the usual size. Also, **oversized**.

o·ver·sleep (ō′vər slēp′) *v* **o·ver·slept, o·ver·sleep·ing** sleep beyond the time set for waking: *I was late for school this morning because I overslept.*

o·ver·spend (ō′vər spend′) *v* **o·ver·spent, o·ver·spend·ing** spend more than one should.

o·ver·spread (ō′vər spred′) *v* **o·ver·spread, o·ver·spread·ing** spread over: *Some bushes had overspread the path.*

o·ver·state (ō′vər stāt′) *v* **o·ver·stat·ed, o·ver·stat·ing** state too strongly or exaggerate. **o′ver·state′ment** *n.*

o·ver·stay (ō′vər stā′) *v* stay beyond the time or limits of: *to overstay your welcome.*

o·ver·step (ō′vər step′) *v* **o·ver·stepped, o·ver·step·ping** go beyond a limit: *He overstepped the limits of politeness by asking such personal questions.*

o·ver·stim·u·late (ō′vər stim′ ū lāt′) *v* **o·ver·stim·u·lat·ed, o·ver·stim·u·lat·ing** tire or bewilder with too many interesting experiences, especially sensory ones: *The baby gets cranky when he's overstimulated.* **o′ver·stim′u·la′tion** *n.*

o·ver·stock (ō′vər stok′) *for v,* (ō′vər stok′) *for n. v* stock or supply with more than is needed or can readily be used: *Stores often have sales when they're overstocked.*
n too great a stock or supply.

o·ver·stuffed (ō′vər stuft′) *adj* with a very thick stuffing or filling: *a large, comfortable, overstuffed armchair, an overstuffed sandwich.*

o·ver·sup·ply (ō′vər sə plī′) *for v,* (ō′vər sə plī′) *for n. v* **o·ver·sup·plied, o·ver·sup·ply·ing** supply with more than is needed.
n too great a supply.

o·vert (ō′vərt) *or* (ō vərt′) *adj* done or shown openly: *an overt act.* <Old French, from Latin *aperire* to open> **o·vert′ly** *adv.* **o′vert·ness** *n.*

o·ver·take (ō′vər tāk′) *v* **o·ver·took, o·ver·tak·en, o·ver·tak·ing 1** catch up to: *If you hurry, you might be able to overtake her before she reaches her car.* **2** catch up with and pass: *They overtook us and arrived before we did.* **3** catch up with suddenly, especially as an unfortunate event: *A storm overtook the children.*

o·ver·tax (ō′vər taks′) *v* **1** tax too heavily. **2** put on too heavy a burden: *The boss overtaxed us with work.* **o′ver·tax·a′tion** *n.*

o·ver–the–count·er (ō′vər ᴛʜə koun′tər) *adj* sold as medicines without a prescription.

o·ver–the–top (ō′vər ᴛʜə top′) *Informal adj* excessive; exaggerated; extravagant: *an over-the-top graduation outfit. Thank you, but this present is over-the-top.*

o·ver·throw (ō′vər thrō′) *for v,* (ō′vər thrō′) *for n. v* **o·ver·threw, o·ver·thrown, o·ver·throw·ing 1** forcibly take away the power of: *to overthrow a government.* **2** put an end to or destroy: *to overthrow slavery.* **3** throw a ball over or past the player or place aimed for.
n **1** a defeat, especially a removal from power: *overthrow of a government.* **2** a ball thrown over or past the player or place aimed for.

o·ver·time (ō′vər tīm′) *n* **1** time beyond the regular hours of work, or the wages for this period. **2** *Sports* a period or periods beyond the normal game time.
adv beyond the regular hours: *She worked overtime. The teams played overtime.*
adj to do with overtime: *overtime work.*

o·ver·tone (ō′vər tōn′) *n* **1** a musical tone heard along with the main or fundamental tone and whose rate of vibration is a multiple of the main tone. **2** a hint or suggestion of something felt or believed: *an overtone of anger in her voice.*

o·ver·took (ō′vər tu̇k′) past tense of OVERTAKE.

o·ver·top (ō′vər top′) *v* **o·ver·topped, o·ver·top·ping** be higher than: *The new building will overtop our apartment.*

o·ver·ture (ō′vər chu̇r′) *or* (ō′vər chər) *n* **1** (*often plural*) an initial formal proposal or offer: *peace overtures.* **2** a musical composition played by the orchestra as an introduction to an extended work, such as an opera, oratorio, or concert. <Old French, from Latin *apertura* opening>

o·ver·turn (ō′vər tərn′) *for v,* (ō′vər tərn′) *for n. v* **1** turn something on its side or upside down: *The boat overturned.* **2** overthrow or abolish: *The rebels overturned the government.*
n an act or fact of overturning.

o·ver·use (ō′vər yūz′) *v* **o·ver·used, o·ver·us·ing** use too much: *The phrase "in the wake of" is overused.*

o·ver·view (ō′vər vyū′) *n* a brief, general survey or summary of a subject.

o·ver·ween·ing (ō′vər wē′ning) *adj* showing too much confidence or pride.

o·ver·weight (ō′vər wāt′) *adj* **1** with a weight that is too great in proportion to height and build: *He is overweight because he eats too many sweet things.* **2** totalling a greater weight than allowed by regulations: *overweight baggage.*
n more weight than is needed, desired, or specified: *The butcher gave us overweight on this roast.*

o·ver·whelm (ō′vər welm′) *v* **1** overcome completely: *to overwhelm with grief.* **2** cover completely as a flood might: *A great wave overwhelmed the boat.*

o·ver·whelm·ing (ō′vər wel′ming) *adj* too many, too great, or too much to be resisted: *an overwhelming majority of votes.*

o·ver·wind (ō′vər wīnd′) *v* **o·ver·wound, o·ver·wind·ing** wind a clock, toy, or device too far or too tightly so that it will not run.

o·ver·win·ter (ō′vər win′tər) *v* spend the winter: *Some birds overwinter in Canada, but many fly south.*

o·ver·work (ō′vər wərk′) *for n,* (ō′vər wərk′) *for v. n* too much or too hard work: *A lazy person is not likely to die of overwork.*
v work too hard or too long.

a bat	e bed	i bid	o pot	u cup	th **thin**
ā cake	ē me	ī bite	ō go	ū rude	ᴛʜ **then**
à bar	ə about	ər over	ȯ for	u̇ put	zh measure

o·ver·write (ō′vər rīt′) *v* **o·ver·wrote, o·ver·writ·ten, o·ver·writ·ing** **1** *Computers* destroy data in a computer file by recording new data in its place: *I must have accidentally overwritten my final version with an earlier draft!* **2** use a writing style that is too wordy or elaborate: *She badly overwrote her essay by using too many adverbs. You have a tendency to overwrite.* **3** write on top of another piece of writing.

o·ver·wrought (ō′vər rot′) *adj* **1** wearied or exhausted by too much excitement: *overwrought nerves.* **2** too elaborate or overly decorated.

o·ver·zeal·ous (ō′vər zel′əs) *adj* too zealous in attitude or behaviour: *An overzealous police officer put a parking ticket on our car.*

o·vi·duct (ō′və dukt′) *n* the tube through which ova (eggs) pass from the ovary to the uterus or to an outside opening. <Latin *ovum* egg + *duct*>

o·vi·form (ō′və fȯrm′) *adj* egg-shaped.

o·vip·a·rous (ō vip′ə rəs) *Zoology adj* producing eggs that are hatched after leaving the body. Compare VIVIPAROUS, OVOVIVIPAROUS.

o·vi·pos·i·tor (ō′və poz′ə tər) *n* a tubular organ in insects and fish at the end of the abdomen, by which eggs are deposited. <Latin *ovum* egg + *ponere* to place>

o·void (ō′void) *adj* egg-shaped.
n an egg-shaped object. <French, from Latin *ovum* egg>

o·vo·vi·vip·a·rous (ō′və və vip′ə rəs) *Zoology adj* producing eggs that hatch inside the mother's body. Compare VIVIPAROUS, OVIPAROUS. <Latin *ovum* egg + *vivus* alive + *parere* bring forth>

o·vu·lar (ō′vyə lər) *adj* of or being an ovule.

o·vu·late (ō′vyə lāt′) *v* **o·vu·lat·ed, o·vu·lat·ing** **1** produce an ovum. **2** discharge the ovum from an ovary. <French, from Latin *ovum* = egg>

o·vu·la·tion (ō′vyə lā′shən) *n* **1** the period when an ovum or female germ cell is produced or formed. **2** the discharge of an ovum from an ovary.

o·vule (ō′vyūl) *n* **1** a small ovum, especially one in an early stage of growth. **2** the part of a plant that develops into a seed. See ANTHER for picture.<Latin *ovum* egg>

o·vum (ō′vəm) *n, pl* **o·va** (ō′və) a mature female reproductive cell, especially of a human or other animal, that can divide to produce an embryo usually after fertilization by a male cell. <Latin = egg>

ow (ou) *interj* an exclamation of pain: *Ow! I stubbed my toe.*

owe (ō) *v* **owed, ow·ing** **1** have to pay or repay: *I owe my brother $20.* **2** be in debt: *He is always owing for something.* **3** be obliged or indebted for: *She owes her success to her own determination.* **4** be obliged to give or offer: *We owe friends our trust.* <Old English *agan*>

ow·ing (ō′ing) *adj* due or owed: *to pay what is owing.*
owing to, because of or due to: *The ball game was called off owing to rain.*

owl (oul) *n* a bird of prey, active at night, that has a large head in proportion to the body, big eyes, a hooked beak, and a flexible neck. The **great grey owl** is the provincial bird of Manitoba; the **great horned owl** is the provincial bird of Alberta (see NOCTURNAL for picture); and the **snowy owl** is the provincial bird of Québec. <Old English *ule*>

owl·et (ou′lit) *n* a young owl.

owl·ish (ou′lish) *adj* like or characteristic of an owl, especially in having large, unblinking eyes or seemingly wise or solemn: *He gave me an owlish look.*

own (ōn) *adj* **1** of oneself or itself: *We have our own troubles. The house is her own.* **2** particular to the person or thing mentioned: *The painting has its own charm.*
n the one or ones belonging to oneself or itself: *They demanded their own and not a substitute.*
v **1** have or possess: *She owns much land.* **2** acknowledge or admit: *She owns to many faults.* <English *agan* owe>
come into your own, a get what belongs to you. **b** get the success or credit that you deserve.
get your own back, get revenge.
hold your own, keep your position of strength.
of your own, belonging to yourself.
on your own, alone or unaided.
own up (to), confess or admit: *The prisoner owned up to the crime.*

own·er (ō′nər) *n* a person who owns something: *Owners of dogs have to buy licences for them. Will the owner please stand up?* **own′er·less** *adj.*

own·er·ship (ō′nər ship′) *n* the possessing or right to possess something.

ox (oks) *n, pl* **ox·en** **1** a full-grown, castrated male of cattle, usually at least three or four years old, typically used as a draft animal. **2** a member of a subfamily of animals that includes cattle, the yak, and buffalo. <Old English *oxa*>

ox·bow (oks′bō′) *n* **1** a U-shaped frame of wood or iron that forms the lower part of a yoke for an ox. **2** a U-shaped bend in a river, or the land contained within such a bend. See LAKE and RIVER for pictures.

ox·cart (ok′skärt′) *n* a cart drawn by oxen.

ox–eye daisy (ok′sī′) MARGUERITE.

ox·ford (ok′sfərd) *n* a low-heeled shoe, laced over the instep.

ox·i·da·tion (ok′sə dā′shən) *n* the combining of oxygen with another element to form one or more new substances. Burning is one kind of oxidation.

ox·ide (ok′sīd) *n* a compound of oxygen with another element or a radical.

ox·i·dize (ok′sə dīz′) *v* **ox·i·dized, ox·i·diz·ing 1** combine or become combined with oxygen. **2** become covered with rust. **ox′i·diz′er** *n.*

ox·tail (oks tāl′) *n* the tail of a cow or steer, skinned and cut up for food.

oxy– *combining form* oxygen or containing oxygen: *oxyacetylene.*

ox·y·a·cet·y·lene (ok′sē ə set′ə lēn′) *adj* to do with a mixture of oxygen and acetylene. An **oxyacetylene torch** uses a mixture of oxygen and acetylene to produce a very hot flame for welding or cutting metals. See ACETYLENE for picture.

ox·y·gen (ok′sə jən) *n* a colourless, odourless, tasteless gas that forms one fifth of the air and is also combined in water and most mineral and organic substances. It is the most abundant of all elements. *Symbol* **O** <French, from Greek *oxys* sharp (i.e., acidic) + *-gen*>

ox·y·gen·ate (ok′sə jə nāt′) *v* **ox·y·gen·at·ed, ox·y·gen·at·ing** treat, combine, or supply with oxygen: *to oxygenate the blood.* **ox′y·gen·a′tion** *n.*

oxygen mask *n* a device worn over the nose and mouth through which oxygen is supplied from a storage tank.

oxygen tent *n* a small, clear plastic tent or canopy that can be placed over the head of a patient lying in bed and supplies a measured flow of oxygen.

ox·y·mo·ron (ōk′sə mō′ron) *n* an expression combining words or ideas that seem to contradict each other. Examples: *make haste slowly, tough love.* <Greek pointedly stupid, from *oxys* sharp + *moros* stupid>

O·yez or **O·yes** (ō′yes) *interj* a call uttered, usually three times, such as by a public crier, to command silence and attention before an announcement is made.

oys·ter (oi′stər) *n* **1** a MOLLUSC used as food, with a rough, irregular shell in two halves, found in shallow water along seacoasts. Some oysters yield pearls. See PEARL for picture. **2** one of the two oyster-shaped bits of dark meat found on each side of the backbone in poultry. <Old French, from Greek *ostreon*>

oyster bed *n* a place where oysters breed or are cultivated.

o·zone (ō′zōn) *n* **1** a poisonous form of oxygen whose molecules have three atoms instead of the usual two. It is produced mainly by electricity and is present in the air, especially after a thunderstorm. *Symbol* O_3 **2** *Informal* air that is refreshing and invigorating, due to its chlorine-like scent. <German, from Greek *ozein* to smell>
o·zo′nic (ō zō′nik) *or* (ō zon′ik) *adj.*

ozone layer *n* a region of the upper stratosphere containing a relatively high concentration of ozone that protects earth from excessive ultraviolet radiation from the sun. The ozone layer has been damaged by atmospheric pollutants such as CFCs.

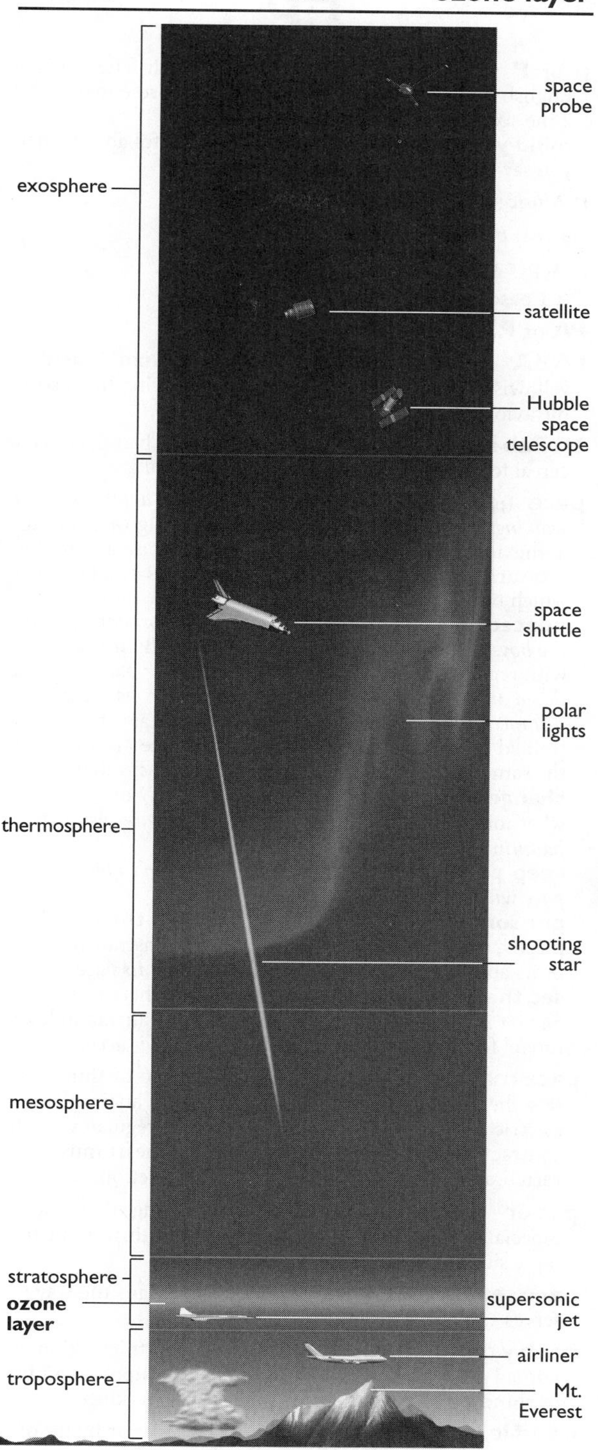

Pp

p or **P** (pē) *n, pl* **p's** or **P's** **1** the sixteenth letter of the English alphabet, or any speech sound represented by it. **2** the sixteenth thing in a list or series.
mind your P's and Q's, *Informal* be careful about what you say or do.

p *Music* PIANO[2].

pa (pa) *Informal n* papa or father.

p.a. per annum.

Pa **1** pascal(s). **2** protactinium.

PA or **P.A.** public address system.

PABA (pa′bə) *n* in full, **para-aminobenzoic acid** a yellowish crystalline acid with the capacity to absorb ultraviolet rays. It is used in sunscreen lotions.

🍁 **Pab·lum** (pab′lum) *Trademark n* a soft, bland, cooked cereal food for infants. <Latin *pabulum* food>

pace (pās) *n* **1** a rate of speed: *She sets a fast pace in walking.* **2** a single step taken when walking or running. **3** the length of a step in walking, used as a unit for measuring length. **4** one of the trained gaits of a horse, in which both legs on one side are raised at the same time.
v **paced, pac·ing** **1** set the pace for: *A motorboat will pace the boys training for the rowing match.* **2** walk or walk over with regular steps: *to pace the floor. The tiger paced up and down in its cage.* **3** measure by paces: *We paced off the distance and found it to be 69 steps.* **4** move as a horse at a trained gait in which both legs on one side are raised at the same time. <Old French, from Latin *passus* step>
change of pace, a switch to a new activity or role from what one is used to: *As a change of pace we played badminton instead of tennis.*
keep pace with, keep up with: *We weren't able to keep pace with all the assignments.*
put someone (or **something**) **through their** (or **its**) **paces,** make someone or something demonstrate his, her, or its abilities: *They put the new car through its paces.*
set the pace, a set a rate of speed for others to follow: *She set the pace for the other sprinters.* **b** be an example or model for others to follow: *He set the pace for accuracy.*

pace·mak·er (pā′smā′kər) *n* **1** a person who or thing that sets the pace for another, as in a race. **2** an implanted electrical device that stimulates and regulates each contraction of the heart. **3** the part of the heart muscle in vertebrates that normally performs this function.

pac·er (pā′sər) *n* a person who or thing that paces, especially a horse that runs by raising both legs on the same side at the same time.

pace·set·ter (pās′set′ər) *n* a person who leads the way or serves as a model or example for others.

pach·y·derm (pak′ə dərm′) *n* a large, thick-skinned, hoofed mammal, especially the elephant, hippopotamus, or rhinoceros. <Greek *pachys* thick + *derma* skin>

pa·cif·ic (pə sif′ik) *adj* **1** peaceful in character or intention: *a pacific nature.* **2** **Pacific** to do with the Pacific Ocean, the ocean west of North, Central, and South America: *a Pacific time zone.* <Latin *pacis* peace + *facere* to make>
pa·cif′i·cal·ly *adv.*

🍁 **Pacific Coast** *n* the part of Canada that borders the Pacific; British Columbia.

Pacific Rim *n* the coastal areas and countries bordering the Pacific, especially with reference to trade, cultural, and diplomatic relations.

Pacific salmon *n* a member of a salmon family found in the Pacific, such as the sockeye, chum, coho, pink, and spring salmon.

pac·i·fi·er (pas′ə fi′ər) *n* a person who or thing that pacifies, especially a rubber nipple or ring given to a baby to suck.

pac·i·fism (pas′ə fiz′əm) *n* the refusal, usually for religious or ethical reasons, to make war or use violence.
pac′i·fist *adj, n.*

pac·i·fy (pas′ə fī′) *v* **pac·i·fied, pac·i·fy·ing** **1** calm or make quiet: *I managed to pacify the crying baby.* **2** bring order to a place, especially by the use or threat of military force: *Soldiers were sent to pacify the country.*

pack[1] (pak) *n* **1** a small paper container and the items it contains: *a pack of gum.* **2** a group of related documents, often carried in a folder: *an information pack.* **3** a group or set of similar things or people, especially those considered objectionable: *a pack of thieves, a pack of lies.* **4** a number of animals hunting together: *Wolves hunt in packs, but foxes hunt alone.* **5** a complete set of playing cards, usually 52. **6** a large area of floating pieces of ice pushed together: *A ship forced its way through the pack.* **7** something put on the body or skin as a treatment: *A cloth soaked in hot or cold water is often used as a pack.*
v **1** put together together in a bag, suitcase, or other container: *to pack a suitcase. Pack your clothes in this bag. Are you going to pack?* **2** be able to be folded up for transport or storage: *These goods pack well.* **3** press or crowd closely together: *A hundred people were packed into one small room. The theatre was packed.* **4** put into a container to be sold or stored. **5** make tight so that something cannot leak through: *The plumber packed the joint between two sections of pipe.* **6** *Informal* carry: *He's packing plenty of cash.* **7** carry in a pack: *She packed a month's supplies for the journey into the bush.* **8** *Informal* possess as a characteristic or power: *That guy packs quite a punch.* <origin uncertain>
pack it in, *Informal* quit what you are doing.
pack off, send away: *The child was packed off to bed.*
pack up, *Informal* stop working or cease operating; fail: *One of the aircraft's engines packed up.*
send packing, *Informal* send away abruptly.

pack[2] (pak) *v* fill a group, such as a jury or committee, with people likely to support a desired decision or policy.

pack·age (pak′ij) *n* **1** a bundle of items packed or wrapped together. **2** a box or other container in which items are packed, or such a container with its contents.
v **pack·aged, pack·ag·ing** put in a package.

package deal *n* a bargain, sale, or business deal in which a number of items are presented as a single offer.

package tour *n* an arrangement for a holiday including airfare, accommodations, ground transport, and, sometimes, leisure activities.

pack·ag·ing (pak′ə jing) *n* **1** materials that are used to wrap or protect goods: *Half of the weight of these groceries must be packaging!* **2** the business or process of putting goods into packages. **3** the presentation of a person, service, or activity in a particular way: *Good packaging will make this movie into a blockbuster.*

pack animal *n* an animal used for carrying loads or packs.

pack·er (pak′ər) *n* a person who or thing that packs, especially a person who or company that packs food to be sold at wholesale: *a meat packer.*

pack·et (pak′it) *n* a small package or parcel.

pack horse *n* a horse used to carry packs.

pack ice *n* ice pushed by wind or current into a solid mass.

pack·ing (pak′ing) *n* **1** the act or process of packing something: *He finished his packing just before he left.* **2** material used to protect goods, especially in transit. **3** material used to prevent leakage, especially around a pipe join.

packing house *n* a place where food is prepared and packed for sale.

pack rat *n* **1** a large, bushy-tailed wood rat found in the Rocky Mountains, with well-developed cheek pouches. Pack rats gather small objects in or around their nests. **2** *Informal* a person who has a tendency to hoard objects, especially useless ones.

pack·saddle (pak′sad′əl) *n* a saddle specially adapted for supporting the load on a pack animal.

pact (pakt) *n* an agreement between individuals, groups, or countries: *The two nations signed a peace pact.* <Old French, from Latin *paciscere* to agree>

pad[1] (pad) *n* **1** something soft used for comfort, protection, or stuffing: *I put a foam pad on top of the old mattress to make it more comfortable.* **2** a fleshy part on the bottom side of an animal foot or human finger. **3** a number of sheets of paper fastened or glued along an edge or edges: *a writing pad.* **4** a cloth soaked with ink to use with a rubber stamp. **5** a flat structure used for helicopter takeoff, or as the launching platform for a rocket or missile: *The rocket rose from the pad at midday.*
v **pad·ded, pad·ding 1** fill with something soft: *to pad a chair.* **2** make a text or speech longer by using unnecessary words: *Don't pad your compositions.* <origin uncertain>

pad[2] (pad) *v* **pad·ded, pad·ding** walk with soft, steady steps: *a wolf padding through the bush.*
n a dull or muffled sound, as of steady footsteps. <origin uncertain>

padded cell *n* a room in a psychiatric hospital with padded walls to prevent violent patients from injuring themselves.

pad·ding (pad′ing) *n* **1** material used to pad with, such as foam rubber, cotton, or synthetic fibre. **2** unnecessary words used to make a speech or a written text longer.

pad·dle[1] (pad′əl) *n* **1** a short oar with a broad blade at one end or both ends, used without resting it against the boat. See CANOE for picture. **2** the act of using a paddle. **3** a short-handled bat used in some games, such as table tennis. **4** a broad board fixed around a mill wheel to push, or be pushed by, the water. **5** a paddle-shaped piece of wood used for stirring, mixing, or beating.
v **pad·dled, pad·dling 1** move a boat or canoe with a paddle or paddles. **2** swim with short, fast strokes, especially as a bird or animal. <Middle English> **pad′dler** *n.*
paddle your own canoe, *Informal* act independently.

pad·dle[2] (pad′əl) *v* **pad·dled, pad·dling 1** dabble the hands or feet in water: *The children were paddling in the creek.* **2** wade barefoot in shallow water: *Children love to paddle at the beach.* <origin uncertain> **pad′dler** *n.*

pad·dle·wheel (pad′əl wēl′) *n* a wheel that propels a boat through the water by means of an arrangement of paddles.

pad·dock (pad′ək) *n* **1** a small field near a stable or house, used for exercising animals or as a pasture. **2** a pen for horses at a racetrack. <Old English *pearroc*>

pad·dy (pad′ē) *n, pl* **pad·dies 1** a field of rice. **2** rice in the husk or before threshing. <Malay *padi*>

paddy wagon *Informal n* a police van.

pad·lock (pad′lok′) *n* a removable lock with a hinged bar that is passed through a loop or eye on a door, gate, or lid.
v fasten with such a lock: *The gate is padlocked at night.*

pa·dre (pod′rā′) *n* a Christian priest or chaplain. <Italian, from Latin *pater* father>

pae·an (pē′ən) *n* a song of praise, joy, or triumph.

pa·el·la (pī′el′ə) *n* a Spanish dish made of rice flavoured with saffron, and usually seafood, sausage, and chicken. <Catalan (a language of Spain), from Latin *patella* pan>

pa·gan (pā′gən) *n* a person who holds religious views other than those of such world religions as Christianity, Islam, or Judaism.
adj to do with pagans: *pagan customs.* <Latin *paganus* peasant>

GRAMMAR AND USAGE

Both **pagan** and **heathen** have an implied meaning of "unenlightened" or "unbelieving." Many people regard these terms as offensive, so it is best to use them in historical contexts only: *Julius Caesar was a pagan. The Goths were heathen.*

pa·gan·ism (pā′gə niz′əm) *n* pagan beliefs and practices.

page[1] (pāj) *n* **1** one side of a leaf or sheet of paper: *The book has 350 pages.* **2** a leaf or sheet of paper, especially in a book or periodical: *Turn to page 34.* **3** what is printed, written, or pictured on one side of a leaf: *This page is hard to read.* **4** an event or period worth recording: *a glorious page in the history of the country.* **5** *Computers* a part of a computer document that can be displayed, usually one screen at a time.
v **paged, pag·ing 1** number pages: *Make sure you page your essay.* **2** quickly turn the pages of a book or periodical: *Bored, I paged through an old magazine.* <Old French, from Latin *pangina*>

a bat	e bed	i bid	o pot	u cup	th thin
ā cake	ē me	ī bite	ō go	ū rude	TH then
à bar	ə about	ər over	ȯ for	u̇ put	zh measure

page[2] (pāj) *n* **1** a person, usually uniformed, who runs errands and does other tasks for guests at a hotel or club. **2** a messenger for members of the House of Commons, the Senate, or a legislative assembly. **3** in former times, a young man who was preparing to be a knight.
v **paged, pag·ing** summon a person by name by means of an announcement, either on a public address system, or by means of a PAGER. <Old French, from Greek *pais* boy>

pag·eant (paj′ənt) *n* an elaborate public entertainment, such as a procession in costume, or a performance of a historical scene: *The coronation of the new king was a splendid pageant.* <Middle English *pagyn*>

pag·eant·ry (paj′ən trē) *n, pl* **pag·eant·ries** an elaborate display or ceremony.

page·boy (pāj′boi′) *n* a girl's or woman's hair style in which the hair, usually about shoulder length, is curled smoothly under at the ends.

pag·er (pā′jər) *n* a small, portable radio device carried on the body, used to page the wearer by means of a sound or vibration.

pag·i·na·tion (paj′ə nā′shən) *n* the act of numbering the pages of a book, magazine, etc., or the figures with which pages are numbered. **pag′i·nate** *v.*

pa·go·da (pə gō′də) *n* a Hindu or Buddhist temple or sacred building, typically with many tiers and a roof curving upward from each tier. <Portuguese, from Sanskrit *bhagavati* divine>

paid (pād) *adj* **1** receiving money: *a paid vacation.* **2** no longer owed: *a paid loan.*
v a past tense and past participle of PAY[1].
put paid to, put a stop or end to: *The principal put paid to bringing cellphones to school.*

pail (pāl) *n* a fairly large, usually round container, with a wide top and a handle that is attached at each side and arches over the top, or the amount this container holds. <origin uncertain>

pail·ful (pāl′fu̇l′) *n, pl* **pail·fuls** the amount that fills a pail.

pain (pān) *n* **1** suffering or discomfort in the body or a particular part of it, due to stimulus of the nerve endings caused by injury or disease: *He felt a sharp pain in his back.* **2** mental suffering: *The memory of that horrible day still gave her pain.* **3 pains** *pl* careful effort or trouble to do something: *He said he would not interfere, because he would get nothing but trouble for his pains.*
v cause to suffer: *My tooth was paining me a great deal.* <Old French, from Greek poine> **pain′ful** *adj.* **pain′ful·ly** *adv.* **pain′ful·ness** *n.* **pain′less** *adj.* **pain′less·ly** *adv.* **pain′less·ness** *n.*
be at pains, make a conscientious effort: *She was at great pains to make them understand.*
on (or **under**) **pain of,** as a way of avoiding the punishment or penalty of: *The traitor was ordered to leave the country on pain of death.*
pain in the neck, *Informal* a cause of frustration or annoyance.
take pains, be careful: *She took pains to do a good job.*

pained (pānd) *adj* affected with pain, especially mental pain: *a pained expression on his face.*

pain·kil·ler (pān′kil ər) *n* a medicine that relieves pain.

pains·tak·ing (pānz′tā′king) *adj* very careful and thorough: *a painstaking painter.* **pains′tak′ing·ly** *adv.*

paint (pānt) *n* **1** a mixture of a solid colouring matter and liquid that can be put on a surface to dry as a coloured coating. **2** the solid colouring matter alone: *a box of paints.* **3** cosmetics or colouring matter put on the face or body.
v **1** cover or decorate with paint: *to paint a house.* **2** represent a person, object, or scene in colours: *The artist painted the lights of the city.* **3** make pictures in oils or watercolours: *She spends her weekends painting.* **4** picture vividly in words: *The traveller painted an exciting picture of her trip to Baffin Island.* **5** cover like paint: *The doctor painted iodine on the cut.* <Old French, from Latin *pingere*>

paint·ball (pānt′bol) *n* a game where people shoot at each other with little paint-filled balls that burst on impact.

paint·brush (pānt′brush′) *n* **1** a brush for putting on paint. **2** a N American plant with spikes of small flowers surrounded by large, brightly coloured bracts.

paint·er[1] (pān′tər) *n* **1** an artist who paints pictures. **2** a person who paints walls, window frames, doors, and other parts of a building.

paint·er[2] (pān′tər) *n* a rope, usually fastened to the bow of a boat for tying it. <origin uncertain>

paint·ing (pān′ting) *n* **1** a picture that has been painted. **2** the act or process of one who paints a picture or for decoration.

pair (per) *n, pl* **pairs** or (*sometimes after a numeral*) **pair** **1** a set of two things: *a pair of shoes.* **2** a single thing consisting of two parts that cannot be used separately: *a pair of jeans.* **3** two people considered together: *What a pair those two are!* **4** either or both of two members on opposite sides of a legislative assembly who arrange not to vote on a certain question.
v arrange or be arranged in sets of two: *to pair socks, to be paired for swimming.* <Latin *paria* equals>
pair off, arrange in pairs: *The boys and girls paired off to learn the new dance.*

GRAMMAR AND USAGE

Pair referring to a unit takes a singular verb: *That pair of glasses is attractive on you.*

Pair referring to two individual items takes a plural verb: *The pair of students were honoured for bravery.*

pais·ley (pāz′lē) *n, pl* **pais·leys** an elaborate, colourful fabric design of curving, feather-shaped lines and figures, or something made of fabric with such a design.
adj made of fabric with a paisley design: *a paisley scarf.*

pa·ja·mas (pə jam′əz) *or* (pə jä′məz) PYJAMAS.

Pak·i·stan (pak′i stan) *n* a country in S Asia. See the APPENDIX. **Pak′i·stan′i** (pak′i stan′ē) *adj, n.*

pal (pal) *n* a close friend.
v **palled, pal·ling** form a close friendship. <Romany, from Sanskrit *bhratr* brother>
pal around, *Informal* spend time with a good friend: *Not long after I met him we began to pal around.*

pal·ace (pal′is) *n* **1** the official home of a monarch, bishop, or other important person. **2** a large, impressive house. <Old French, from Latin *Palatium* Palatine Hill in Rome>

pal·at·a·ble (pal′ə tə bəl) *adj* pleasant to the taste: *The lunch was not very palatable.* **pal′at·a·bly** *adv.*

pal·a·tal (pal′ə təl) *adj* **1** to do with the palate. **2** uttered with the tongue near or touching the hard palate. The *y* in *yet* is a palatal sound.

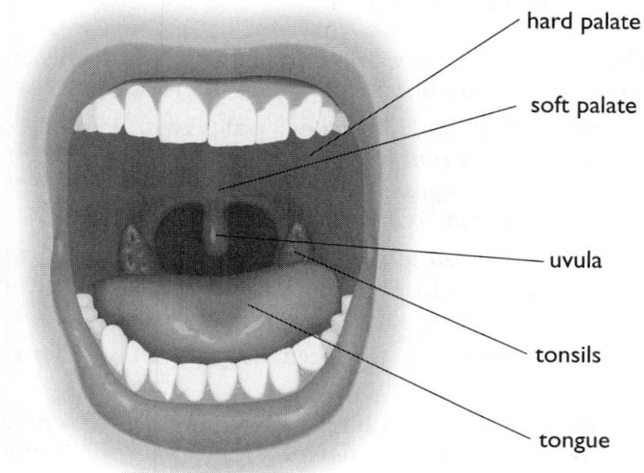

pal·ate (pal′it) *n* **1** the roof of the mouth. The bony part in front is the **hard palate**; the fleshy part at the back is the **soft palate**. **2** the sense of taste: *The new flavour pleased his palate.* **3** a liking or preference. <Latin *palatum*>

pa·la·tial (pə lā′shəl) *adj* like or fit for a palace: *a palatial apartment.* **pa·la′tial·ly** *adv.*

Pa·lau (pə lou′) *n* a country of several islands in the west Pacific.

pa·lav·er (pə lav′ər) *n* **1** a long, purposeless discussion or explanation. **2** fluent, flattering talk.
v **1** chatter idly. **2** talk fluently and flatteringly. <Portuguese *palavra* talk, from Latin *parabola* speech>

pa·laz·zo (pə lot′sō) *n, pl* **pa·laz·zi** (pə lot′sē) a palace or mansion. <Italian>

pale[1] (pāl) *adj* **pal·er, pal·est** without much colour or brightness: *pale blue, a pale complexion.*
v **paled, pal·ing** lose or cause to lose colour or brightness: *Her face paled at the bad news.* <Old French, from Latin *pallere* be pale> **pale′ly** *adv.* **pale′ness** *n.*

pale[2] (pāl) *n* **1** a long, narrow board, pointed at the top, used for fences. **2** a boundary: *Murder is an act outside the pale of society.*
v **paled, pal·ing** enclose with pales. <Old French, from Latin *palus* stake>

paleo– *combining form* old or ancient: *paleolithic.* <Greek *palaios* ancient>

Pa·le·o·cene (pā′lē ə sēn′) *n* the geological epoch lasting from about 70 million to 60 million years ago, when dinosaurs became extinct and the first mammals appeared. See also CENOZOIC, TERTIARY.
adj to do with this epoch.

pa·le·o·lith·ic (pā′lē ə lith′ik) *adj* to do with the earlier part of the Stone Age, when tools were made from stone.

pal·e·on·tol·o·gy (pā′lē on tol′ə jē) *n* the science that studies the forms of life existing long ago in other geological periods, as known from fossil remains of animals and plants. **pa′le·on·tol′o·gist** *n.*

Pa·le·o·zo·ic (pā′lē ə zō′ik) *Geology n* the era when hard-shelled fossils were formed, extending from about 600 million to 250 million years ago. It covers the CAMBRIAN, ORDOVICIAN, DEVONIAN, CARBONIFEROUS, and PERMIAN periods. Compare CENOZOIC, MESOZOIC.
adj to do with this era or the rocks formed then.

Pal·es·tine (pal′i stīn′) *n* **1** in former times, the kingdoms of Israel and Judah on the east coast of the Mediterranean. **2** a territory in the Middle East, roughly co-extensive with modern Israel and the West Bank of the Jordan river, where the **PLO** (Palestine Liberation Organization) has declared its intention of forming the Arab state of Palestine. As of 1994, they have achieved limited self-rule in the Gaza Strip and the West Bank. **Pal′es·tin′i·an** (pal′i stin′ ē ən) *adj, n.*

pal·ette (pal′it) *n* **1** a thin board, usually oval or oblong, with a thumb hole at one end, used by painters to lay and mix colours on, or the range of colours on this board. **2** a range of colours, shapes, or tones from which one may be selected. <French, from Latin *pala* spade, from its shape>

palette knife *n* a thin blade with a handle for mixing paints or applying or removing them.

pal·frey (pol′frē) *Archaic n, pl* **pal·freys** a gentle riding horse, especially one used by women.

pal·i·mo·ny (pal′ə mō′nē) *n Informal* money paid to one member of an unmarried couple to the other on the breakup of the relationship. <*pal* + (*al*)*imony*>

pal·in·drome (pal′in drōm′) *n* a word, phrase, or sentence that reads the same backwards or forward. Examples: *kayak; never odd or even.* <Greek *palin* back + *dramein* to run>

pal·ing (pā′ling) *n* a fence of pointed stakes, or one of the stakes in such a fence.

pal·i·sade (pal′ə sād′) *n* **1** a fence of wooden stakes or iron railings set firmly in the ground to enclose or defend a settlement. **2** **palisades** *pl* a line of high, steep cliffs.
v **pal·i·sad·ed, pal·i·sad·ing** furnish or surround with a palisade. <French, from Latin *palus* stake>

pall[1] (pol) *n* **1** a heavy cloth, often made of velvet, spread over a coffin, a hearse, or a tomb. **2** a dark, gloomy covering of smoke, dust, or fog. <Old English, from Latin *pallium* cloak>

pall[2] (pol) *v* **1** become distasteful or tiresome because there has been too much of something: *Even the tastiest food palls if it is served day after day.* <*appall*>

pal·la·di·um (pə lā′dē əm) *n* a rare, silver-white metallic element resembling platinum. *Symbol* **Pd** <*Pallas*, asteroid named after the Greek goddess *Pallas*>

a bat	e bed	i bid	o pot	u cup	th thin
ā cake	ē me	ī bite	ō go	ū rude	ᴛʜ then
ä bar	ə about	ər over	ȯ for	u̇ put	zh measure

pall·bear·er (pol′ber′ər) *n* a person who accompanies or helps to carry the coffin at a funeral.

pal·let[1] (pal′it) *n* **1** a straw bed. **2** a small, hard, or crude bed. <Old French, from Latin *palea* straw>

pal·let[2] (pal′it) *n* **1** a flat wooden blade with a handle, used to shape clay or plaster. **2** a portable platform on which goods can be stacked and transported from place to place. <French, from Latin *pala* spade>

pal·li·a·tive (pal′ē ə tiv) *or* (pal′ē ā′tiv) *adj* relieve pain or lessen a problem without dealing with the underlying cause: *palliative care.*
n something that lessens or relieves, such as a treatment or medicine. **pal′li·ate** *v.*

pal·lid (pal′id) *adj* with less colour than normal or usual: *a face pallid from lack of sleep.* <Latin *pallere* be pale>

pal·lor (pal′ər) *n* an unhealthy lack of colour.

palm[1] (pom) *or* (päm) *n* **1** the inside of the hand between the wrist and the fingers. **2** the part of a glove or mitten that covers this.
v conceal in the hand: *The conjurer palmed a loonie.* <Old French, from Latin *palma*>
grease the palm of, *Informal* bribe.
have an itching palm, *Informal* be greedy for money.
have (or **hold**) **someone in the palm of your hand,** fully control or influence someone: *The singer had the audience in the palm of his hand.*
palm off, pass off or get accepted by fraud or deceit: *The book she palmed off on me had some pages missing.*

palm[2] (pom) *or* (päm) *n* **1** a tropical or subtropical tree that has a tall, pillarlike trunk crowned by large, fan-shaped or feather-shaped leaves. **2** a leaf of a palm tree used as a symbol of victory or triumph. <Old English, from Latin *palma* palm of hand, from the shape of the leaves>

pal·mate (pal′māt) *adj* shaped like a hand with the fingers spread out: *a palmate leaf.*

pal·met·to (pal met′ō) *n, pl* **pal·met·tos** or **pal·met·toes** a palm with fan-shaped leaves found from the southern US to northern S America.

palm·is·try (pom′i strē) *or* (pä′mi strē) *n* the art or practice of telling a person's future or reading his or her character from the lines and marks in the palm of the hand. **palm′ist** *n.*

palm oil *n* an edible fat obtained from the fruit of several species of palm tree, used in cooking and to make soap and candles.

Palm Sunday *Christianity n* the Sunday before Easter, used to celebrate the entry of Jesus into Jerusalem.

palm·top (pom′top′) *Computers n* a handheld computer, for use especially as a personal organizer.

pal·o·mi·no (pal′ə mē′nō) *n, pl* **pal·o·mi·nos** a horse of mainly Arabian stock, with a cream, golden, or tan coat and a white or ivory mane and tail. <Spanish, from Latin *palumbinus* resembling a dove>

pal·pa·ble (pal′pə bəl) *adj* **1** readily seen or heard and recognized: *a palpable error.* **2** able to be touched or felt. **pal′pa·bil′i·ty** *n.* **pal′pa·bly** *adv.*

pal·pate (pal′pāt′) *v* **pal·pat·ed, pal·pat·ing** examine or feel with the hands in order to make a medical diagnosis. <Latin *palpare* touch gently> **pal·pa′tion** *n.*

pal·pi·tate (pal′pə tāt′) *v* **pal·pi·tat·ed, pal·pi·tat·ing** **1** beat rapidly: *He was so fearful that his heart began to palpitate.* **2** tremble. <Latin *palpare* touch gently> **pal′pi·ta′tion** *n.*

pal·sy (pol′zē) *n, pl* **pal·sies** complete or partial paralysis of the muscles, especially when accompanied by involuntary tremors. <Old French, from Latin *paralysis*> **pal′sied** *adj.*

pal·sy–wal·sy (pal′zē walzē) *Informal adj* very friendly and intimate. <variant of *pal*>

pal·try (pol′trē) *adj* **pal·tri·er, pal·tri·est** **1** small or meagre: *a paltry sum of money.* **2** petty or trivial: *Pay no attention to paltry gossip.* <origin uncertain>
pal′tri·ly *adv.* **pal′tri·ness** *n.*

pam·pas (pam′pəs) *pln* the vast, almost treeless plains of S America, especially in central Argentina. <Spanish, from Quechua (a language of S America) *pampa* plain>

pampas grass *n* a tall, reedlike grass of southern S America with silvery plumes.

pam·per (pam′per) *v* indulge with attention and comfort: *to pamper a child, to pamper your appetite.* <origin uncertain> **pam′per·er** *n.*

SYNONYMS

Pamper suggests treating indulgently: *She pampered her cat with delicacies and attention.*

Coddle suggests overprotecting: *He was coddled so much by his parents that he couldn't look after himself.*

Indulge suggests satisfying or yielding to simple desires: *She often indulged in her liking for chocolate.*

Spoil emphasizes excessive indulgence: *Her grandparents spoil her with too many treats.*

pam·phlet (pam′flit) *n* a short printed work, usually with no binding or with a stapled paper cover. <from a Latin love poem *Pamphilus*>

pam·phlet·eer (pam′fli tēr′) *n* a writer of pamphlets.

pan[1] (pan) *n* **1** a dish for cooking or other uses, usually broad, shallow, and with no cover. **2** hard subsoil. **3** in full, **ice pan** a flat cake of drifting ice, often with upturned edges.
v **panned, pan·ning** **1** cook in a pan. **2** wash in a pan to separate gold from gravel. **3** *Informal* criticize severely: *The drama critic panned the new play.* <Old English *panne*>
pan out, *Informal* turn out: *His scheme panned out well.*

pan[2] (pan) *v* **panned, pan·ning** swing a film, video, or TV camera so as to take in a whole scene or to follow a subject. <*pan(orama)*>

pan·a·ce·a (pan′ə sē′ə) *n* a remedy for all diseases or difficulties. <Latin, from Greek *pan* all + *akos* remedy>

pa·nache (pə nash′) *or* (pə nosh′) *n* **1** showy confidence of style or manner: *She showed great panache as a fashion model.* **2** in former times, an ornamental feather or bunch of feathers, especially on a helmet or headdress. <French, from Latin *pinna* feather>

pan·a·ma (pan′ə mȧ′) *n* a wide-brimmed hat originally woven from the young leaves of a palmlike plant of Central and S America. <after the country of *Panama*>

Pan·a·ma (pan′ə ma) *n* a country in Central America. See the APPENDIX. **Pan′a·man′i·an** *adj, n.*

Pan–A·mer·i·can (pan′ə mer′ə kən) *adj* to do with all the countries of North, Central, and South America.

Pan–A·mer·i·can·ism (pan′ə mer′ə kə niz′əm) *n* the principle or policy that all the countries in South America, Central America, and North America should co-operate for shared progress and improvement.

pan·cake (pan′kāk′) *n* **1** a thin, flat cake of batter, cooked in a pan or on a griddle. **2** makeup consisting of a flat, solid layer of compressed, powdered cosmetics.
v **pan·caked, pan·cak·ing 1** make a pancake landing. **2** flatten or become flattened.

pancake landing *n* an emergency landing in which an aircraft is levelled out close to the ground and drops vertically with its undercarriage still retracted.

pan·cre·as (pan′krē əs) *or* (pang′krē əs) *n* a large gland near the stomach that secretes digestive enzymes into the duodenum and the hormone insulin into the blood. <Latin, from Greek *pan* all + *kreas* flesh>
pan′cre·at′ic *adj.*

pan·da (pan′də) *n* **1** a large black-and-white, bearlike mammal found in the bamboo forests of China. Also called **giant panda**. **2** a small, reddish brown, raccoonlike mammal with a bushy tail, found in bamboo forests from the Himalayas to southern China. Also called **lesser panda** or **red panda**. <Nepali (a language of Nepal)>

pan·dem·ic (pan dem′ik) *adj* of a disease, affecting a large proportion of the population.
n an outbreak of such a disease. <Greek *pan* all + *demos* people>

pan·de·mo·ni·um (pan′də mō′nē əm) *n* wild disorder and confusion. <Greek *pan* all + *daimon* demon>

pan·der (pan′dər) *n* a person who caters to or exploits an immoral or distasteful desire, need, or habit.
v (*with* **to**) supply material or opportunity for vices: *The newspaper pandered to people's liking for sensational stories.* <*Pandarus* character in a poem by Chaucer>

Pandora's box (pān do′ rə) *n* a potential source of many problems or evils: *the Pandora's box of modern technology.* **open a Pandora's box,** do or attempt something that gives rise to a variety of problems or evils.

ETYMOLOGY

In Greek myth, the god Zeus gave **Pandora** a box that contained all human evils. She foolishly opened the box and all the contents escaped.

pane (pān) *n* a single sheet of glass in a window or door. <Old French, from Latin *pannus* piece of cloth>

pan·e·gyr·ic (pan′ə jir′ik) *or* (pan′ə jī′rik) *n* something written or spoken in praise of a person or thing. <Greek *pan* all + *agyris* assembly>

pan·el (pan′əl) *n* **1** a separate strip or surface that is usually set off from what is around it, such as in a door or other woodwork, on large pieces of furniture, or made as parts of a dress. **2** a long, narrow picture, hanging, or design. **3** a list of people called to be available as jurors for a trial. **4** a small group of people selected for a special purpose, such as holding a discussion, judging a contest, or participating in a quiz. **5** a board containing the instruments, controls, or indicators used in operating an automobile, aircraft, computer, or other mechanism.
v **pan·elled** or **pan·eled, pan·el·ling** or **pan·el·ing** arrange or decorate with panels: *The room was panelled with oak.* <Old French, Latin *pannus* piece of cloth>

panel discussion *n* the discussion of a particular issue by a selected group of people, usually experts.

pan·el·ling or **pan·el·ing** (pan′ə ling) *n* panels joined together to make a single surface, especially wooden panels forming a decorative wall surface: *We have pine panelling in the rec room.*

pan·el·list or **pan·el·ist** (pan′ə list) *n* one of a group of people making up a PANEL (def. 4).

pan–fry (pan′frī′) *v* **pan-fried, pan-fry·ing** fry in a frying pan or skillet: *pan-fried fish.*

pang (pang) *n* **1** a sudden, short, sharp pain: *the pangs of a toothache.* **2** a sudden feeling of distress or anguish: *a pang of remorse.* <origin uncertain>

pan·gae·a or **Pan·ge·a** (pan jē′ə) *n* a hypothetical single continent, of about 245 million years ago, that included all the land masses of the earth.

pan·go·lin (pang gō′lən) *n* an Asian and African mammal with a body covered with an armour of overlapping brownish scales, a long, toothless snout, and a long, sticky tongue used for catching ants and termites for food.

pan·han·dle[1] (pan′han′dəl) *n* **1** the handle of a pan. **2** a narrow strip of land projecting like a handle: *the Alaska Panhandle.*

pan·han·dle[2] (pan′han′dəl) *Informal v* **pan·han·dled, pan·han·dling** beg, especially in the streets.
pan′han′dler *n.*

pan·ic (pan′ik) *n* a sudden fear that causes an individual or entire group to lose self-control: *When the theatre caught fire, there was a panic. When the stock market crashed, there was panic among investors.*
adj caused by or showing panic: *panic haste.*
v **pan·icked, pan·ick·ing 1** lose control of oneself through fear: *I thought the younger children would panic at the thunder, but they just squealed with excitement.* **2** cause panic in: *Talk of snakes panicked her.*

ETYMOLOGY

Panic comes originally from Greek *panikos*, meaning "of or like Pan." Pan, a god of woods, fields, and flocks, was also thought to cause terror.

a bat	e bed	i bid	o pot	u cup	th thin
ā cake	ē me	ī bite	ō go	ū rude	ᴛʜ then
ȧ bar	ə about	ər over	ȯ for	u̇ put	zh measure

panic attack ANXIETY ATTACK.

panic button *n* a button that can be pressed in a crisis to summon help.
push (or **press**, or **hit**) **the panic button,** *Informal* react with panic to what may or may not be an emergency.

pan·ick·y (pan′i kē) *adj* affected with or liable to panic: *She began to get panicky as the deadline approached.*

pan·ic–strick·en (pan′ik strik′ən) *adj* affected with panic.

pan·jan·drum (pan jan′drum) *n* a mock title for an official of imaginary or exaggerated importance: *To get a new blue box, we had to speak to the local panjandrum in charge of public works.* <coined by S. Foote, 18c dramatist>

pan·ni·er (pan′ē ər) *n* a basket, especially one of a pair of considerable size, to be slung across the shoulders or across the back of a pack animal. <Old French, from Latin *panarium* bread basket (from *panis* bread)>

pan·o·ply (pan′ə plē) *n, pl* **pan·o·plies** a complete or impressive collection of things: *a panoply of compliments.* <French, from Greek *panoplia* complete suit of armour>

pan·o·rama (pan′ə ram′ə) *n* **1** a wide, unbroken view of a surrounding region: *a panorama of beach and sea.* **2** a survey or view of some subject, scene, or sequence of events: *a panorama of the development of the snowmobile, the panorama of city life.* **3** a picture or presentation of a wide view of something, such as a landscape. <Greek *pan* all + *horan* see> **pan′o·ram′ic** *adj.* **pan′o·ram′i·cal·ly** *adv.*

pan·pipes (pan′pīps′) *n* a musical instrument made from a row of pipes of different lengths, fastened together in the order of their length and played by blowing across their tops. <*Pan*, Greek god of flocks>

pan·sy (pan′zē) *n, pl* **pan·sies** a flowering plant of the violet family with velvety petals of several colours. <French, from Latin *pendere* think. Pansies were considered to represent thought or remembrance.>

pant[1] (pant) *v* **1** breathe hard and quickly: *The dog panted in the heat.* **2** speak with short, quick breaths: *"I've been running," she panted.* **3** long for eagerly: *I am just panting for my turn.*
n a short, quick breath. <Old French, from Latin *pantasiare* struggle for breath during a nightmare>

pan·ta·loons (pan′tə lūnz′) *pln* **1** in former times, **a** men's wide pants gathered at the knee or ankle. **b** tight pants with straps that go under the instep. **2** baggy pants gathered at the ankles, usually worn by women. <French *pantalon*>

pan·the·ism (pan′thē iz′əm) *n* the belief that the universe is God or a manifestation of God. **pan′the·ist** *n.* **pan′the·is′tic** *adj.* **pan′the·is′ti·cal·ly** *adv.*

pan·the·on (pan′thē on′) *or* (pan′thē ən) *n* **1** an ancient Greek temple dedicated to all the gods. **2** all the gods of a people or religion, especially those that are officially recognized. **3** a public building containing tombs or memorials of the illustrious dead of a nation. **4** a group of famous or illustrious people. <Latin, from Greek *pan* all + *theos* god>

pan·ther (pan′thər) *n, pl* **pan·thers** or (*especially collectively*) **pan·ther** a large, wild member of the cat family, such as the puma, jaguar, or black leopard. <Old French, from Greek>

pan·ties (pan′tēz) *pln* short undergarments worn below the waist by women and girls.

pan·to·mime (pan′tə mīm′) *n* **1** a play without words, in which the actors express themselves by gestures. **2** a series of gestures without words that tell a story or make a point. **3** *especially UK* a theatrical entertainment, mainly for children at Christmas, that includes music, jokes, and comedy based on a fairy tale or nursery story.
v **pan·to·mimed, pan·to·mim·ing** express by gestures. <Latin, from Greek *pantos* all + *mimos* mimic>
pan′to·mim′ic (pan′tə mim′ik) *adj.*

pan·try (pan′trē) *n, pl* **pan·tries** a small room or cupboard used for storing food, dishes, etc. <Old French, from Latin *panis* bread>

pants (pants) *pln* **1** trousers. **2** panties. <*pantaloon*>

pant·suit (pant′sūt′) *n* a suit for women, consisting of a jacket and long pants.

pant·y·hose (pan′tē hōse)*n* an undergarment for women, consisting of sheer stockings knitted in one piece with a pantylike top of the same or slightly heavier material.

pap (pap) *n* **1** soft, bland food for infants or invalids. **2** ideas or entertainment that lacks substance. <German, from Latin *pappare* eat>

pa·pa (pop′ə) *or* (pȧ′pə) *n* father. <French, from Greek *papas*>

pa·pa·cy (pā′pə sē) *n, pl* **pa·pa·cies** **1** the position, rank, or authority of the Pope. **2** the time during which a pope rules.

pa·pal (pā′pəl) *adj* to do with the Pope or the papacy: *a papal visit to Canada.*

pa·pa·raz·zi (pop′ə rot′sē) *pln, sing* **pa·pa·raz·zo** (pop′ə rot′sō) a group of freelance photographers who pursue celebrities to take photos of them. <Italian>

pa·pa·ya (pə pȧ′yə) *n* the melonlike fruit of a palmlike tropical tree. It has orange flesh and small black seeds. Also called **pawpaw**. <Spanish, from Carib (a group of languages of the Caribbean)>

pa·per (pā′pər) *n* **1** a thin sheet made from wood pulp or other fibrous substances and used for writing, printing, wrapping packages, etc. **2** a newspaper. **3** an article or essay, especially one to be read publicly: *At the conference there were several papers given on the teaching of English.* **4 papers** *pl* **a** official documents that tell who or what one is. **b** important documents: *He kept his papers in a safety deposit box at the bank.*
v cover with paper, especially wallpaper: *to paper a room.*
adj **1** made of paper: *paper serviettes.* **2** like paper: *almonds with paper skins.* **3** existing only on paper, not as a fact: *When she tried to sell, her paper profits disappeared.* <Old French, from Greek *papyros*> **pa′per·er** *n.*
pa′per·like′ *adj.*
on paper, a in writing or in print. **b** in theory: *The plan looks fine on paper but it may not work.*

pa·per·back (pā′pər bak′) *n* a book with a flexible paper binding and cover, especially one that is smaller and less expensive than a hardcover edition.

a par 5 golf hole

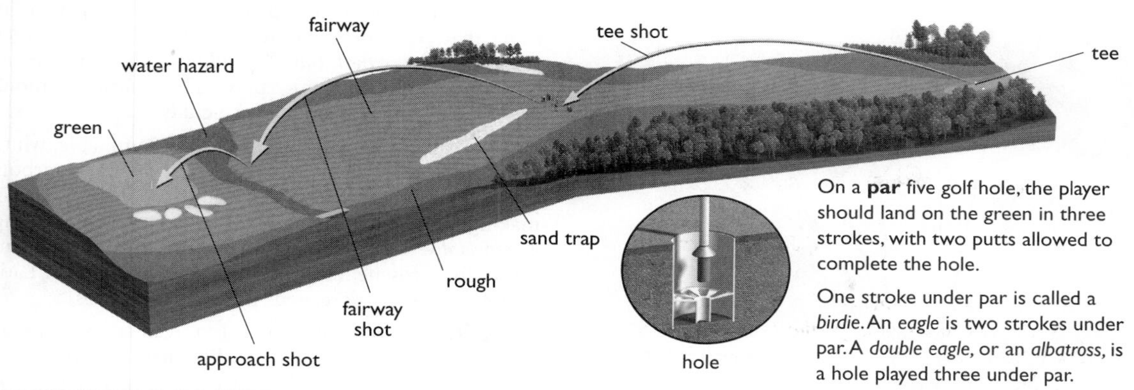

On a **par** five golf hole, the player should land on the green in three strokes, with two putts allowed to complete the hole.

One stroke under par is called a *birdie.* An *eagle* is two strokes under par. A *double eagle,* or an *albatross,* is a hole played three under par.

paper birch WHITE BIRCH.

pa·per·boy (pā′pər boi′) *n* a boy who delivers newspapers.

paper clip *n* a flat clip of flexible bent wire, used to slip over the edge of a small bundle of papers to hold them together.

pa·per·girl (pā′pər gərl′) *n* a girl who delivers newspapers.

pa·per·hang·er (pā′pər hang′ər) *n* a person whose work is applying wallpaper.

paper money *n* money made of paper, not metal.

paper tiger *n* a person, group, country, or organization who or that appears very threatening but is actually weak.

pa·per·weight (pā′pər wāt′) *n* a small, heavy object put on papers to keep them from being scattered.

pa·per·work (pā′pər wərk′) *n* work done on or with paper, such as writing, filing, or other clerical work: *She hates all the paperwork involved in her job.*

pa·per·y (pā′pə rē) *adj* thin like paper.

pa·pier–mâ·ché (pā′pər ma shā′) *n* a paper pulp mixed with a stiffener and used for modelling. It becomes hard and strong when dry. <French = chewed paper>

pa·pil·la (pə pil′ə) *n, pl* **pap·il·lae** (-lē) *or* (-lī) a small, nipplelike projection on a part or organ of the body, such as one of the protuberances concerned with the senses of touch, taste, or smell. <Latin = nipple> **pa·pil′lar·y** *adj.*

pa·poose (pa pūs′) *or* (pə pūs′) *n* a small child or baby of First Nations or Native American parents. <Algonquian>

GRAMMAR AND USAGE

The use of **papoose** by non-Aboriginal people may be seen as offensive because it has been associated with an attitude that stereotyped Aboriginal people.

pap·ri·ka (pap′rə kə) *or* (pa prē′kə) *n* a red-coloured pepper made of the dried, ground-up pods of various sweet-pepper plants. <Hungarian>

Pap smear or **test** (pap) *n* a test for detecting early stages of cancer of the uterus or cervix, consisting of a microscopic examination of castoff cells found in vaginal fluid. <G. *Papanicolaou,* 20c scientist>

Pap·u·a New Gui·nea (pap′wə nyū gin′ē) *n* a country of islands in the western Pacific.

pa·py·rus (pə pī′rəs) *n, pl* **pa·py·ri** (-rī) *or* (-rē) **1** a tall water plant of the Nile valley from which the ancient Egyptians, Greeks, and Romans made paper, or the writing or other material made from its pith. **2** an ancient record written on papyrus. <Latin, from Greek *papyros*>

par (pȧr) *n* **1** equality or an equal level: *The gains and losses are about on a par. She is quite on a par with her sister in intelligence.* **2** an average or normal amount, degree, or condition: *to feel below par.* **3** the value of a share of stock or other security that is printed on it: *That stock is selling at par, but they predict it will be above par tomorrow.* **4** the established normal value of the money of one country in terms of the money of another country. **5** *Golf* the number of strokes set as an expert score for a course or for any one hole.
adj average or normal. <Latin = equal>
par for the course, *Informal* to be expected.

para–[1] *prefix* **1** beside or adjacent: *parallel.* **2** beyond or distinct from: *paranormal, paralegal.* Also, **par-**. <Greek = beside>

para–[2] *combining form* protecting against or warding off: *parasol.*

par·a·ble (par′ə bəl) *or* (per′ə bəl) *n* a short, simple story used to teach a truth or moral lesson. <Old French, from Greek *para-* beside + *ballein* to throw>

pa·rab·o·la (pə rab′ə lə) *n* a curve formed by the intersection of a cone with a plane parallel to one side of the cone: *If there is no wind resistance, an arrow will travel in a parabola.* <See PARABLE.> **par′a·bol′ic** (par′ə bol′ik) *or* (per′ə bol′ik) *adj.*

a bat	e bed	i bid	o pot	u cup	th thin
ā cake	ē me	ī bite	ō go	ū rude	ᴛʜ then
ȧ bar	ə about	ər over	ȯ for	u̇ put	zh measure

P

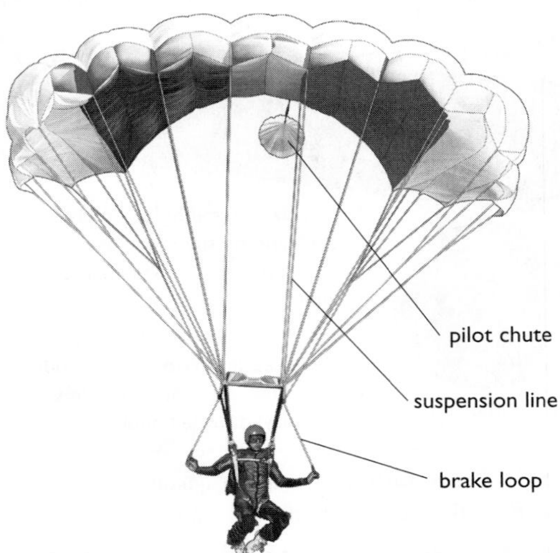

Leonardo da Vinci (1452–1519) was the first person to envision the **parachute**. However, it wasn't until 1793 that the first successful human parachute jump occurred, when Jean Pierre Blanchard jumped from a balloon.

par·a·chute (par′ə shüt′) *or* (per′ə shüt′) *n* **1** a fabric canopy that fills with air and allows someone or something attached to it to descend slowly when dropped from an aircraft. **2** a fabric canopy that can be released from the rear of a vehicle or a landing aircraft to act as a brake.

v **par·a·chut·ed, par·a·chut·ing 1** move or send down by a parachute: *The pilot of the burning plane parachuted to the ground.* **2** ✱ bring an outsider into a political campaign: *Campaign workers from all over the province were parachuted in to help at the by-election.* <French *para-* guard against + *chute* fall> **par′a·chut′ist** *n.*

pa·rade (pə rād′) *n* **1** a public procession, especially one celebrating a special day or event: *The circus had a parade.* **2** a military display or review of troops. **3** a series of people or things on display one after the other: *a parade of celebrities on the red carpet.* **4** a distasteful show or display of something: *She made a parade of her wealth.*

v **pa·rad·ed, pa·rad·ing 1** walk or march in a public procession: *The performers and animals paraded the streets.* **2** walk proudly as if in a parade. **3** display something publicly in order to impress or attract attention. **4** assemble and publicly display a military formation of troops. <French, from Latin *parare* prepare> **pa·rad′er** *n.*

par·a·digm (par′ə dīm′) *or* (per′ə dīm′) *n* a typical and important pattern, model, or example. <Latin, from Greek *para-* beside + *deiknynai* to show>

pa′ra·dig·mat′ic (par′ə dig ma′tik) *or* (per′ə dig ma′tik) *adj.*

par·a·dise (par′ə dīs′) *or* (per′ə dīs′) *n* **1** *Religion* heaven, considered by some religions as the ultimate dwelling place of the virtuous. **2** a place or condition of great happiness or beauty. <Old French, from Persian *pairidaeza* park>

par·a·dox (par′ə doks′) *or* (per′ə doks′) *n* **1** a statement that may be true but seems to say two opposite things. Example: *More haste, less speed.* **2** a situation, person, or thing that combines contradictory features or qualities: *It was a paradox that, though wealthy, he had little money to spend.* <Greek *para-* beyond + *doxa* opinion> **par′a·dox′i·cal** *adj.* **par′a·dox′i·cal·ly** *adv.*

par·af·fin (par′ə fin) *or* (per′ə fin) *n* **1** a flammable, white, waxy substance that is a mixture of hydrocarbons obtained especially from petroleum or shale, used for making candles and cosmetics, or for coating or sealing. **2** *especially UK* a similar substance in liquid form, especially kerosene, used as a fuel. <German, from Latin *parum* little + *affinis* related (to other substances)>

par·a·glid·er (pa′ra glī′dər) *n* **1** a recreational aircraft consisting of a large parachute-like airfoil of ribbed or cellular construction, with a harness from which a rider hangs while gliding from a height. See AIRCRAFT for picture. **2** a person who flies with one of these. Compare HANG-GLIDER. **par′a·glide′** *v.* **par′a·glid′ing** *n.*

par·a·gon (par′ə gon′) *or* (per′ə gon′) *n* a model of excellence or perfection. <French, from Italian *paragonare* compare, test on a touchstone, from Greek *parakonan* to sharpen against>

par·a·graph (par′ə graf′) *or* (per′ə graf′) *n* a group of sentences relating to the same idea or topic and forming a distinct part of a chapter, letter, or other piece of writing. *v* divide into paragraphs. <French, from Greek *para-* beside + *graphein* write>

GRAMMAR AND USAGE

A **paragraph** should deal with only one main idea. It should have a *topic sentence* that states the idea being developed. All other sentences in the paragraph should explain and support the topic sentence, and should be arranged in a clear and logical order.

Par·a·guay (par′ə gwī) *n* a country in S America. See the APPENDIX. **Par′a·guay′an** *adj, n.*

par·a·keet (par′ə kēt′) *or* (per′ə kēt′) *n* a small parrot with green plumage, a slender body, and a long tail. <Old French>

par·a·le·gal (par′ə lē′gəl) *n* a trained assistant to a lawyer. *adj* to do with such an assistant or his or her duties.

par·al·lax (par′ə laks′) *or* (per′ə laks′) *n* the apparent change in the direction or position of an object as seen from two different points, such as first through a camera viewfinder and then through the camera lens. <French, from Greek *para-* beside + *allos* other>

par·al·lel (par′ə lel′) *or* (per′ə lel′) *adj* **1** at or being the same distance apart everywhere, like the two rails of a railway track. **2** corresponding in time or occurring in the same way: *There were parallel points in the characters of the two men.*

n **1** a parallel line or surface. **2** an imaginary circle around the earth parallel to the equator, marking degrees of latitude: *Much of the boundary between Canada and the US lies along the forty-ninth parallel.* **3** something similar

to another thing: *Her experience was an interesting parallel to ours.* **4** *Electricity* an arrangement of circuits or components in which the current can run along two or more possible paths. Compare SERIES (def. 3).
v **par·al·lelled** or **par·al·leled, par·al·lel·ling** or **par·al·lel·ing 1** be or cause to be at the same distance apart throughout the length: *The street parallels the railway.* **2** be similar or parallel to: *Your story closely parallels what she told me.* <French, from Greek *para-* beside + *allelos* one another>

parallel bars *pl n* two parallel wooden bars mounted horizontally on upright posts, used for gymnastic exercises.

par·al·lel·e·pi·ped (par′ə lel′ə pīp′id) *Mathematics n* a solid whose faces are all parallelograms. <Greek *parallelos* parallel + *epipedon* a plane surface>

par·al·lel·ism (par′ə le liz′əm) *or* (per′ə le liz′əm) *n* **1** the quality or condition of being parallel. **2** in writing, a balance between parts of a sentence or paragraph, obtained by deliberately repeating sentence structure or words. **3** *Biology* the development of similar characteristics in groups of plants or animals as a result of being in similar environments.

par·al·lel·o·gram (par′ə lel′ə gram′) *or* (per′ə lel′ə gram′) *n* a four-sided plane figure with opposite sides parallel and equal. Squares, rhombuses, and rhomboids are parallelograms.

parallel parking *n* parking so that the side of the vehicle is next to a curb or other edge.

parallel port *Computers n* a connector for a device that sends or receives bits of a data byte simultaneously by using more than one wire. Computer printers typically use parallel ports. Compare SERIAL PORT.

pa·ral·y·sis (pə ral′ə sis) *n, pl* **pa·ral·y·ses** (-sēz′)
1 a lessening or loss of the power of motion or sensation in part of the body: *The accident left her with paralysis of the legs.* **2** a condition of powerlessness or helpless inactivity: *The ice storm caused a paralysis in Ottawa.*

par·a·lyt·ic (par′ə lit′ik) *or* (per′ə lit′ik) *adj* to do with paralysis: *a paralytic limb.*
n a person who has paralysis.

par·a·lyze or **par·a·lyse** (par′ə līz′) *or* (per′ə līz′) *v* **par·a·lyzed** or **par·a·lysed, par·a·lyz·ing** or **par·a·lys·ing 1** affect with a lessening or loss of the power of motion or feeling in a part of the body: *Her left arm was paralyzed after the accident.* **2** make powerless or ineffective: *The whole project was paralyzed when the funds were cut off.* **3** make unable to think or act normally, especially through panic or fear. <Latin *paralysis*>

par·a·me·ci·um (par′ə mē′sē əm) *or* (per′ə mē′sē əm) *n, pl* **par·a·me·ci·a** (-sē ə) *or* (-shē ə) a free-swimming, one-celled animal with a groove along one side leading into the mouth cavity. <Latin, from Greek *para-* beside + *mekos* length>

par·a·med·ic (par′ə med′ik) *or* (per′ə med′ik) *n* a person trained in auxiliary medicine, such as emergency first aid or medical technology. **par′a·med′i·cal** *adj.*

pa·ram·e·ter (pə ram′ə tər) *n* **1** a mathematical quantity that is constant in a particular calculation or case but varies in other cases. **2** a set of measurable features or properties that determine the characteristics or behaviour of something: *parameters of space and time.* **3** a limiting or defining element or feature: *She found the parameters of her life too restricting.* <Latin, from Greek *para-* beside + *metron* meter>

par·a·mil·i·tar·y (par′ə mil′i ter′ē) *adj* to do with an unofficial group or unit organized along military lines: *A paramilitary unit was used for crowd control at the protest.*
n, pl **par·a·mil·i·tar·ies** a member of this group or unit: *Some of the paramilitaries were accused of threatening unarmed civilians.*

par·a·mount (par′ə mount′) *or* (per′ə mount′) *adj* chief in importance: *Truth is of paramount importance.* <Old French, from Latin *a mont* upward>

par·a·noi·a (par′ə noi′ə) *or* (per′ə noi′ə) *n* a mental condition characterized by the strong belief that one is being persecuted, or by exaggerated self-importance. <Latin, from Greek *para-* beside + *nous* mind>

par·a·noid (par′ə noid′ *or* per′ə noid′) *adj* to do with paranoia, especially a tendency to mistrust people and suspect them of ill will or bad intentions.
n a person affected by paranoia.
Also, **paranoiac** (par′ə noi′ak) *or* (per′ə noi′ak).

par·a·nor·mal (par′ə nor′məl) *adj* not explainable by science: *a paranormal experience.*
n events and forces of this kind: *He is very interested in the paranormal and has written a book on ghost sightings.*

par·a·pet (par′ə pet′) *or* (per′ə pet′) *n* a low protective wall at the edge of a balcony, roof, bridge, or trench. See ABUTMENT for picture. <Italian *parapetto* chest-high wall, from Latin *para-* beside + *pectus* breast>

par·a·pher·nal·ia (par′ə fə nā′lē ə) *or* (per′ə fə nā′lē) *n, sing or pl* miscellaneous items, especially the equipment needed for a particular activity. <Latin, from Greek *parapherna* a woman's property besides her dowry>

par·a·phrase (par′ə frāz′) *or* (per′ə frāz′) *v*
par·a·phrased, par·a·phras·ing state the meaning of a passage in different words.
n an expression of the meaning of a passage in different words.

par·a·ple·gi·a (par′ə plē′jē ə) *or* (per′ə plē′jē ə) *n* paralysis of the legs and the lower part of the trunk. <Latin, from Greek *para-* beside + *plessein* to strike>
par′a·ple′gic (par′ə plē′jik) *or* (per′ə plē′jik), (par′ə plej′ik) *or* (per′ə plej′ik) *adj, n.*

par·a·pro·fes·sion·al (par′ə prə fesh′ə nəl) *n* a trained assistant to a professional such as a doctor or lawyer.
adj to do with such a trained assistant.

par·a·psy·chol·o·gy (par′ə sī kol′ə jē) *or* (per′ə sī kol′ə jē) *n* the study of mental phenomena such as telepathy, not explainable in terms of known physical laws. **par′a·psy·chol′o·gist** *n.*

par·a·site (par′ə sīt′) *or* (per′ə sīt′) *n* **1** an animal or plant that lives on or in another, from which it gets its food: *Mistletoe is a parasite on oak trees.* **2** a person who lives on others without making any useful or suitable repayment: *The lazy woman was a parasite on her family.* <Latin, from Greek *para-* beside + *sitos* food> **par′a·sit′ic** *adj.* **par′a·sit′i·cal·ly** *adv.*

par·a·sit·ism (par′ə si tiz′əm) *or* (per′ə si tiz′əm) *n* a form of SYMBIOSIS in which one species benefits from the association, and the other is damaged. Compare MUTUALISM.

par·a·sol (par′ə sol′) *or* (per′ə sol′) *n* a light umbrella used as a protection from the sun. <French, from Italian *para-* beyond+ Latin *sol* sun>

par·a·troop·er (par′ə trū′pər) *or* (per′ə trū′pər) *n* a soldier trained to use a parachute for descent from an aircraft into a battle area.

par·a·troops (par′ə trūps′) *or* (per′ə trūps′) *pln* troops moved by air and landed by parachutes in a battle area.

par·boil (pȧr′boil′) *v* boil till partly cooked: *parboil beans.* <Old French, from Latin *per-* completely + *bullire* to boil>

par·cel (pȧr′səl) *n* **1** a bundle of things wrapped or packed together: *The lady had her arms filled with parcels.* **2** a quantity or amount of things or people: *a parcel of liars.* **3** a piece of land, considered as part of a property.
v **par·celled** or **par·celed, par·cel·ling** or **par·cel·ing** make a parcel of. <Old French, from Latin *partis* part>
parcel out, divide into portions or distribute in portions.

parch (pȧrch) *v* **1** make or become hot and dry or thirsty: *The fever parched her. I was parched with the heat.* **2** lightly roast corn, grains, or peas and beans. <Middle English>

parch·ment (pȧrch′mənt) *n* **1** the skin of sheep or goats, prepared in former times for use as writing material, or a manuscript or document written on parchment. **2** a stiff paper that looks like this material. <Old French, from Greek *Pergamon*>

par·don (pȧr′dən) *n* **1** the action of forgiveness or being forgiven: *I beg your pardon but I'm afraid I am late.* **2** a setting free from punishment, or the legal document setting a person free.
v **1** forgive or excuse: *She pardoned his bad manners.* **2** set free from punishment. <Old French, from Latin *per-* completely + *donare* give> **par′don·a·ble** *adj.* **par′don·a·bly** *adv.*
pardon me or **I beg your pardon, a** please excuse me. **b** please repeat what you have just said.

pare (per) *v* **pared, par·ing 1** trim by cutting away excess or irregular bits: *to pare your nails.* **2** cut or shave off the outer skin or layer of: *to pare an apple.* **3** cut away or lessen little by little: *We're trying to pare expenses.* <Old French, from Latin *parare* prepare>

pa·ren·chy·ma (pə reng′kə mə) *Biology n* **1** the functional tissue that makes up much of the substance of the softer parts of leaves, the pulp of fruits, bark, and the pith of stems. **2** the functional tissue of an animal organ, as distinguished from its connective or supporting tissue.

par·ent (per′ənt) *n* **1** a father or mother. **2** a living thing that produces offspring or seed.
v take care of a child or children: *Parenting classes are often given in high school.* <Old French, from Latin *parere* bring forth> **pa·ren′tal** *adj.* **pa·ren′tal·ly** *adv.*

par·ent·age (per′ən tij) *n* the identity and origins of parents: *a child of unknown parentage.*

parental leave *n* paid leave from a job for either a mother or father to look after a new baby.

pa·ren·the·sis (pə ren′thə sis) *n, pl* **pa·ren·the·ses** (pə ren′thə sēz) **1** a word, phrase, or sentence, inserted in a sentence to explain or qualify something, and usually set off by brackets, commas, or dashes. **2** either or both of two curved lines () used to set off such an expression. <Latin *para-* beside + Greek *en-* in + *thesis* a placing>

GRAMMAR AND USAGE

Use **parentheses** to set off non-essential comments in a sentence: *The boy limped (because he had just twisted his ankle) as he slowly walked home.*

You can also place whole sentences in parentheses.

par·en·thet·i·cal (par′ən thet′ə kəl) *or* (per′ən thet′ə kəl) qualifying or explanatory. Also, **parenthetic**. **par′en·thet′i·cal·ly** *adv.*

pa·rent·hood (per′ənt hu̇d′) *n* the condition of being a parent.

Par·ent–Teach·er Association (per′ənt tē′chər) *n* an organization made up of parents and teachers who meet from time to time in the interests of schoolchildren. *Abbrev.* **PTA** or **P.T.A.**

pa·re·sis (pə rē′sis) *n, pl* **pa·re·ses** (pə rē′sēs) **1** an incomplete paralysis caused by nerve damage or disease that affects the ability to move, but not the ability to feel. **2** an inflammation of the brain that causes general paralysis. <Latin, from Greek *para-* beside + *hienai* let go> **pa·ret′ic** (pə ret′ik) *or* (pə rē′tik) *adj, n.*

par ex·cel·lence (pȧr ek sə lȧns′) *adj* better than others of the same kind. <French = by excellence>

par·fait (pȧr fā′) *n* **1** ice cream with syrup or crushed fruit and whipped cream, served in a tall glass. **2** a rich ice cream, containing eggs and whipped cream, frozen unstirred. <French = perfect>

par·he·li·on (pȧr hē′lē ən) *n, pl* **par·he·li·a** (-hē′lē ə) a bright, circular spot on a solar halo. Also called **sundog**.

pa·ri·ah (pə rī′ə) *n* **1** an outcast. **2** traditionally, a member of a lowly ranked caste in southern India. <Tamil *parai* a drum. This caste provided drummers at festivals.>

pa·ri·e·tal (pə rī′ə təl) *adj* a wall of the body or of a body cavity or hollow structure, especially two bones that form part of the sides and top of the skull. See MAXILLA for picture.
n a parietal structure. <Latin *parietis* wall>

par·i–mu·tu·el (par′ē myū′chū əl) *or* (per′ē myū′chū əl) *n* a system of betting on horse races in which those who have bet on the winning horses divide the money lost by the losers. <French = mutual stake>

par·ing (per′ing) *n* a part pared off, such as a skin or rind: *apple parings, nail parings.*

par·ish (par′ish) *or* (per′ish) *n* **1 a** a district that has its own Christian church and minister or priest. **b** the people of a parish. **2** 🍁 *Québec and New Brunswick* an administrative subdivision of a county. **b** *US Louisiana* an administrative division corresponding to a county. **c** *UK* a civil district. <Old French, from Greek *para-* beside + *oikos* dwelling>

pa·rish·ion·er (pə rish′ə nər) *n* a member of a church parish.

Pa·ri·sian (pə rizh′ən) *adj* to do with Paris, the capital of France, or its people.
n a native or resident of Paris.

par·i·ty (par′ə tē) *or* (per′ə tē) *n* **1** equality or close similarity, especially with regard to status or pay. **2** the value of a currency in terms of another at a fixed exchange rate. <Latin *par* equal>

park (pårk) *n* **1** a piece of land in or near an urban area, set apart for public recreation: *Let's have a picnic in the park.* **2** an area of land kept in a natural state as a place for outdoor recreation and as a refuge for wildlife: *Elk Island National Park is in Alberta.* **3** an area devoted to a specified purpose: *an industrial park, an amusement park.* **4** a place to leave an automobile for a time: *a car park.* **5** the position of a gear selector in a motor vehicle with automatic transmission in which the gears are locked: *Put the car in park.*
v **1** leave a motor vehicle for a time in a certain place. **2** *Informal* place, put, or leave something: *Just park your books on the table.* <Old French, from Latin *parricus* enclosure>

🍁 **par·ka** (pår′kə) *n* **1** a knee-length fur pullover with a hood, traditionally worn by Inuit in the North. **2** a warm, hip-length or knee-length coat with a hood, worn in cold weather. <Yupik *purka* skin>

🍁 **park·ade** (pår′kād) *especially British Columbia and the Prairie Provinces n* an above-ground structure with several storeys for parking a large number of vehicles. <*park* + (*arc*)*ade*>

🍁 **park·ette** (pår′ket) *n* a small public park in a town or city.

park·ing lot (pår′king) *n* an unenclosed area used for parking motor vehicles.

parking meter *n* a device containing a coin-operated clock mechanism for indicating the amount of parking time that has been bought for a vehicle.

Par·kin·son's disease (pår′kin sənz′) *n* a progressive disorder of the nervous system occurring especially in men over the age of fifty. It is characterized by trembling, muscular rigidity, and poor muscular co-ordination. <J. *Parkinson*, 19c surgeon>

park·land (pår′kland′) *n* **1** open land consisting of fields and scattered groups of trees. **2** 🍁 **a** the grassy region between the foothills of the Rockies and the prairie. **b** the lightly wooded region between the Barrens and the prairie. **3** land maintained as a public park.

park·way (pår′kwā′) *n* a highway landscaped with grass, trees, or flowers.

par·lance (pår′ləns) *n* a way of speaking or using words: *The will was written in legal parlance.* <Old French, from Latin *parlare* speak>

par·lay (pår′lā) *or* (pår′lē) *v* turn the amount of an original bet or stake into a larger amount by gambling or taking a risk: *She parlayed a few hundred dollars into a fortune.*
n a series of bets or stakes made by parlaying each one in turn. <French, from Latin *par* equal>

par·ley (pår′lē) *n, pl* **par·leys** a conference with an enemy or opposing side to discuss the terms of something.
v **par·leyed, par·ley·ing** discuss the terms of something, especially with an enemy. <Old French, from Latin *parlare* speak>

par·lia·ment (pår′lə mənt) *n* **1** the highest lawmaking body in certain countries. **2 Parliament a** 🍁 the national lawmaking body of Canada, consisting of the House of Commons and Senate. **b** the national lawmaking body of the UK, consisting of the House of Commons and House of Lords. <Old French, from Latin *parlare* speak>

par·lia·men·tar·i·an (pår′lə men ter′ē ən) *n* a person skilled in parliamentary procedure or debate.

par·lia·men·ta·ry (pår′lə men′tə rē) *adj* **1** to do with a parliament: *parliamentary authority, parliamentary democracy.* **2** according to the rules and customs of a parliament or other lawmaking body: *Our debating society is run by the rules of parliamentary procedure.*

🍁 **parliamentary secretary** *n* a member of the House of Commons in Canada, appointed to assist a cabinet minister in his or her work.

🍁 **Parliament Hill** *n* the location of the federal parliament buildings in Ottawa.

par·lour or **par·lor** (pår′lər) *n* **1** a room for receiving or entertaining guests in a house. **2** a room or rooms specially furnished or equipped for a certain kind of business: *a beauty parlour, a tanning parlour.* **3** a place where refreshments of various kinds are sold: *an ice-cream parlour, a beer parlour.* <Old French, from Latin *parlare* speak>

Par·me·san (pår′mə zan′) *n* a hard Italian cheese with a sharp flavour, usually used in grated form. <French, from Italian *parmigiano* of Parma, where it was originally made>

par·mi·gia·na (por mi zhon′ə) *adj* containing or prepared with Parmesan cheese. <Italian = of Parma>

pa·ro·chi·al (pə rō′kē əl) *adj* **1** *Christianity* to do with a parish: *a parochial school.* **2** narrow or limited in outlook: *a parochial viewpoint.*

pa·ro·chi·al·ism (pə rō′kē ə liz′əm) *n* narrow or limited character, interests, or views.

parochial school *n* a school maintained by a church.

a bat	e bed	i bid	o pot	u cup	th thin
ā cake	ē me	ī bite	ō go	ū rude	ᴛʜ then
å bar	ə about	ər over	ȯ for	u̇ put	zh measure

P

par·o·dy (par′ə dē) *or* (per′ə dē) *n, pl* **par·o·dies** 1 a humorously exaggerated imitation of a piece of writing or work of art. 2 a poor imitation: *His design was so bad it looked like a parody of what it should be.*
v **par·o·died, par·o·dy·ing** 1 make fun of by imitating. 2 imitate poorly. <Latin, from Greek *para-* beside + *oide* song> **par′o·dist** *n.*

SYNONYMS

Parody involves a humorous imitation of something written or a work of art.

Caricature is a humorous form of drawing or description that usually exaggerates a notable feature of its subject.

Satire uses biting humour—especially irony and sarcasm—to criticize someone or something.

pa·role (pə rōl′) *n* a conditional release from prison or jail before the full term is served: *The prisoner was released on parole.* <Old French = word, from Latin *parabola* speech>
v **pa·roled, pa·rol·ing** give a parole.

pa·rot·id (pə rot′id) *adj* to do with the ear. The **parotid glands**, one in front of each ear, supply saliva to the mouth.

par·ox·ysm (par′ək siz′əm) *or* (per′ək siz′əm) *n* 1 a sudden attack or increase of symptoms of a disease: *a paroxysm of coughing.* 2 a sudden, violent expression of an emotion or activity: *a paroxysm of rage.* <French, from Greek *para-* beyond + *oxys* sharp> **par′ox·ys′mal** *adj.*

par·quet (pȧr kā′) *or* (pȧr ket′) *n* 1 a flooring made of inlaid pieces of wood, often of different kinds, fitted together to form a pattern. 2 the main floor of a theatre or auditorium, especially from the orchestra pit to the part under the balconies.
v **par·quetted** or **par·queted, par·quet·ting** or **par·quet·ing** furnish with a parquet floor: *to parquet a room.* <French = small park>

parr (pȧr) *n, pl* **parrs** or (*especially collectively*) **parr** a young salmon, larger than a fry. <origin unknown>

par·rot (par′ət) *or* (per′ət) *n* 1 a tropical or subtropical bird with a stout, hooked bill, grasping feet, often bright plumage, and a raucous voice. Some parrots can imitate human speech. 2 a person who repeats words or acts without understanding them.
v repeat without understanding: *The small child parroted the words of the song.* <origin uncertain>
par′rot·like′ *adj.*

par·ry (par′ē) *or* (per′ē) *v* **par·ried, par·ry·ing** 1 ward off a weapon or attack, especially by making a countermove: *He parried the sword with his dagger.* 2 answer evasively: *She parried the question by asking one.*
n, pl **par·ries** the act of warding off or avoiding. <probably French, from Italian *pararer* ward off>

parse (pȧrs) *v* **parsed, pars·ing** 1 analyze a sentence grammatically, telling its parts of speech and their uses in the sentence. 2 systematically analyze something by breaking it up into components. <Old French, from Latin *pars* part>

par·sec (por′sek) *Astronomy n* the unit used with the SI for measuring distance in outer space, equal to about 3.26 light years. *Symbol* **ps** <*par*(*allax*) + *sec*(*ond*)[2]>

Par·see or **Par·si** (pȧr′sē) *n* a member of a Zoroastrian sect in India, descended from Persians.

par·si·mo·ni·ous (pȧr′sə mō′nē əs) *adj* unwilling to spend money or use resources. <Latin *parcere* be sparing> **par′si·mo′ni·ous·ly** *adv.* **par′si·mo′ny** *n.*

pars·ley (pȧr′slē) *n, pl* **pars·leys** a plant with finely divided, fragrant leaves, used to flavour or garnish food. See HERB for picture. <Old English, from Greek *petra* rock + *selinon* parsley>

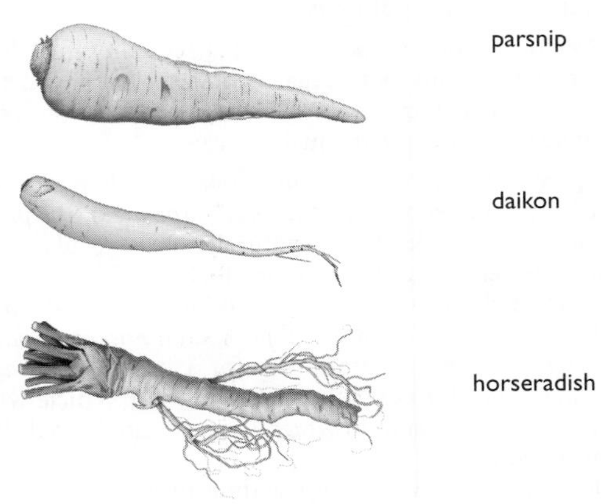

These root vegetables look similar, but their flavours are quite different. **Parsnips** have a sweet, but slightly bitter flavour. Daikon is sweet and zesty with a mild bite, and horseradish is quite sharp and hot-tasting.

pars·nip (pȧr′snip) *n* a plant with a long, tapering, whitish root that is eaten as a vegetable. <Old French, from Latin *pastinaca*>

par·son (pȧr′sən) *n* a Christian minister in charge of a parish or congregation. <Old French, from Latin *persona* person>

par·son·age (pȧr′sə nij) *n* the house provided for a Christian minister by his or her church.

part (pȧrt) *n* 1 something less than the whole: *What part of the chicken do you like best?* 2 each of several equal quantities into which a whole may be divided: *A dime is a tenth part of a dollar.* 3 a thing that helps to make up a whole: *A computer has many parts.* 4 a share of some activity: *We will all do our part.* 5 a side in a dispute or contest: *You always take your sister's part.* 6 **a** a character in a drama: *She acted the part of Juliet in the school play.* **b** the words spoken by a character: *An actor has to learn his part quickly.* 7 a dividing line left in combing one's hair. 8 a melody or other element in harmony assigned to a voice or instrument, such as the soprano, alto, tenor, or bass. 9 **parts** *pl* a region or place: *She has travelled much in foreign parts.*
v 1 move away from each other: *Her lips parted in a smile.* 2 force apart or divide: *The police officer on horseback parted the crowd.* 3 go apart or separate: *The friends parted in anger.* 4 comb the hair away from a dividing line.

adj less than the whole: *a part owner in a business.*
adv in some measure or degree: *She only went part way to meet me.* <Old English, from Latin *pars* part>
for my part, as far as I am concerned.
for the most part, mostly: *The attempts were for the most part unsuccessful.*
in good part, in a friendly or gracious way: *She took the teasing in good part.*
in part, to some extent.
on the part of someone or **on someone's part,** as someone's responsibility: *That was an error on my part.*
part and parcel, a necessary or essential part: *Practising is part and parcel of learning to play the piano.*
part from, go away from.
part with, give up or let go.
play a part, **a** be a contributing factor: *Alcohol plays a part in many traffic accidents.* **b** behave so as to impress or deceive others: *She seems to be sorry, but really she's just playing a part.*
take part, take or have a share.

par·take (pȧr tāk′) *v* **par·took, par·tak·en, par·tak·ing** join in an activity: *We were invited to partake in the celebrations.* <*part-taker*> **par·tak′er** *n.*
partake of, a have to some extent the nature or character of: *His hospitality partakes of condescension.* **b** eat or drink something.

par·terre (por tãr′) *n* **1** the part of the main floor of a theatre under the balcony. **2** an ornamental arrangement of flower beds and paths in a garden. <French *par terre* on the ground>

par·the·no·gen·e·sis (por′thə nō jen′i sis) *Biology n* reproduction by the development of an unfertilized ovum, especially among the lower plants and invertebrate animals. <Latin, from Greek *parthenos* virgin + *genesis* creation>

par·tial (pȧr′shəl) *adj* **1** not complete: *Mother has made a partial payment on our new car.* **2** inclined to favour one side or thing more than another: *He was partial to his youngest child.* **3** (*with* ***to***) with a liking for: *She is partial to sports.* <Old French, from Latin *pars* part>
par′tial·ly *adv.*

par·ti·al·i·ty (pȧr′shē al′ə tē) *n, pl* **par·ti·al·i·ties** **1** a favouring of one more than another or others. **2** a particular liking or fondness for: *He had a partiality for chocolate bars.*

❋ **Par·ti·ci·pac·tion** (pȧr tis′ə pak′shən) *n* formerly, a non-profit organization, partially funded by the Federal Government, whose purpose was to encourage and motivate the general public to become physically fit through regular exercise.

par·tic·i·pant (pȧr tis′ə pənt) *n* a person who shares or participates in an activity.

par·tic·i·pate (pȧr tis′ə pāt′) *v* **par·tic·i·pat·ed, par·tic·i·pat·ing** have a share or take part in: *The teacher participated in the children's games.* <Latin *pars* part + *capere* take> **par·tic′i·pa′tion** *n.* **par·tic′i·pa′tor** *n.* **par·tic′i·pa·to·ry** *adj.*

par·ti·cip·i·al (pȧr′tə sip′ē əl) *Grammar adj* to do with a participle. Examples: *a masked man, a becoming outfit* (participial adjectives); *good at dog training, the fatigue of marching* (participial nouns). **par′ti·cip′i·al·ly** *adv.*

par·ti·ci·ple (pȧr′tə sip′əl) *Grammar n* a verb form that can be used with an AUXILIARY VERB to form various tenses. A **present participle** indicates that an action is continuing. A **past participle** indicates time gone by, or a former situation. Examples: In *They are reading,* the present participle is *reading.* In *She has played all day* and *The ball should have been thrown to me,* the past participles are *played* and *thrown.* <Old French, from Latin *participare* be part of>

> **GRAMMAR AND USAGE**
>
> **Participles** can stand alone as adjectives. When used in this way, the participle modifies a noun or a pronoun:
>
> In *running water,* the word *running* is the **present participle** and modifies *water.*
>
> In *ironed shirts,* the word *ironed* is the **past participle** and modifies *shirts.*

par·ti·cle (pȧr′tə kəl) *n* **1** a tiny bit: *I have a particle of dust in my eye.* **2** a word that performs a grammatical function rather than conveys a meaning. Example: *to* in *to sing.* **3** an elementary or subatomic particle. <Latin *partis* part>

particle accelerator *n* a machine to accelerate subatomic particles to high speeds, usually to collide with other particles.

par·ti·cle·board (par′tik əl bōrd′) *n* a building material in the form of large, rigid sheets made of wood chips and fibres pressed together using a synthetic resin. Also called **chipboard.**

par·tic·u·lar (pər tik′yə lər) *adj* **1** apart from others and considered separately: *That particular chair is already sold.* **2** specific or special: *A particular characteristic of a skunk is its smell.* **3** great or intense: *take particular care.* **4** insisting that everything is correct or suitable: *She is very particular, in that nothing but the best will do.*
n an individual part or item: *The work is complete in every particular.* <Old French, from Latin *particularis* concerning a part>
in particular, especially: *We drove around, going nowhere in particular.*

par·tic·u·lar·i·ty (pər tik′yə lar′ə tē) *or* (par tik′yə ler′ə tē) *n, pl* **par·tic·u·lar·i·ties** **1** special carefulness and attentiveness to details. **2** a particular characteristic, feature, or trait. **3** the quality or fact of being a particular thing.

par·tic·u·lar·ize (pər tik′yə lə rīz′) *v* **par·tic·u·lar·ized, par·tic·u·lar·iz·ing** mention particularly, specifically, or individually. **par·tic′u·lar·i·za′tion** *n.*

par·tic·u·lar·ly (pər tik′yə lər lē) *adv* **1** especially: *The teacher praised the new student particularly.* **2** in detail or to a higher degree than is usual: *The inspector examined the machine particularly.*

a bat	e bed	i bid	o pot	u cup	th **thin**
ā cake	ē me	ī bite	ō go	ū rude	ᴛʜ **then**
ȧ bar	ə about	ər over	ȯ for	u̇ put	zh measure

P

par·ti·cul·ate (pår′tik′yū lāt) *n* matter in the form of particles: *Much air pollution is in the form of particulates.*
adj to do with particles.

part·ing (pår′ting) *n* **1** a departure or taking leave. **2** the action of separating: *the parting of the ways.* **3** a division or separation, or a place of division or separation.
adj said or done when going away: *a parting gift.*

Par·ti Québécois (pår tē′kā bek wå′) *n* a political party in Québec, formed in 1968.

par·ti·san (pår′tə zan′) *or* (pår′tə zən) *n* **1** a strong supporter of a person, party, or cause, especially one whose support is based on feeling rather than on reason. **2** a member of a party of light, irregular troops, often working behind enemy lines.
adj of or like a partisan. Also, **partizan**. <French, from Latin *pars* part>

par·ti·san·ship (pår′tə zən ship′) *n* strong loyalty to a party or cause.

par·ti·tion (pår tish′ən) *n* **1** the act or fact of dividing or being divided into parts, especially as separate areas of government in a country. **2** something that separates, especially a thin interior wall: *an office partition.*
v **1** divide into parts: *The empire was partitioned after the emperor's death.* **2** (*with* ***off***) separate by a partition: *A corner of the basement was partitioned off for a washroom.*

par·ti·tive (pår′tə tiv) *Grammar adj* expressing a part of a collective whole in a grammatical construction. Example: *some of the milk.*
n a word or phrase that is the first term in such a construction, such as *some* or *any*. **par′ti·tive·ly** *adv.*

part·ly (pårt′lē) *adv* in some measure or degree: *She is partly to blame.*

part·ner (pårt′nər) *n* **1** a member of a partnership. **2** an associate or colleague: *The thief climbed through the window while his partner watched the street.* **3** a spouse or domestic partner. **4** either person of a couple dancing together. **5** in games such as cards or tennis, either of two players playing together against another pair. **6** one who shares in an activity: *I'm looking for a new dance partner.*
v be a partner of. <Old French, from Latin *partitio* partition>

part·ner·ship (pårt′nər ship′) *n* **1** a legal association of two or more people in a business enterprise, or the people associated in a partnership: *The members of a partnership share the risks and profits of their business.* **2** the condition of being a partner.

part of speech *Grammar n* a class of words that have a function in a sentence, such as the noun, pronoun, adjective, verb, adverb, preposition, conjunction, and interjection.

GRAMMAR AND USAGE

Many words in English can function as more than one **part of speech**:

In *I can run fast*, the word *run* is a verb.

In *I am going for a run*, the same word is a noun.

par·took (pår tůk′) *v* past tense of PARTAKE.

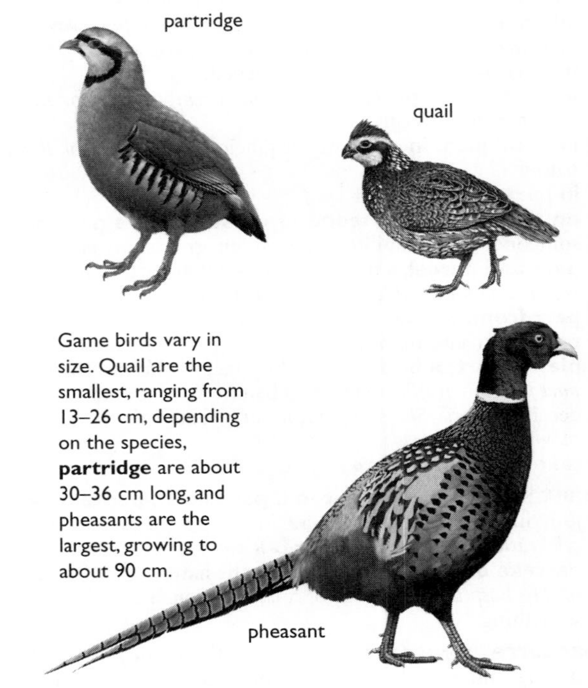

Game birds vary in size. Quail are the smallest, ranging from 13–26 cm, depending on the species, **partridge** are about 30–36 cm long, and pheasants are the largest, growing to about 90 cm.

par·tridge (pår′trij) *n, pl* **par·tridg·es** or (*especially collectively*) **par·tridge** **1** a medium-sized, short-tailed game bird native to Europe and Asia. **2** a N American game bird resembling the partridge, such as the quail. <Old French, from Latin *perdix*>

part–song (part′song′) *n* a song consisting of parts for two or more voices in harmony, with one voice carrying the melody, usually sung without accompaniment.

part–time (pårt′tīm′) *adj* using or working only part of the standard or usual number of hours: *a part-time job, part-time employees.*
adv for only part of the usual number of hours: *She's working part-time this year.*

part·way (pårt′wā) *adv* part of the way: *Partway through the book, I lost interest. We travelled together partway.*

par·ty (pår′tē) *n, pl* **par·ties** **1** a social gathering for the purpose of pleasure: *On her birthday she had a party and invited her friends.* **2** a group of people doing something together: *a dinner party.* **3** a group of people with similar political aims, organized together to gain influence and control. **4** a person who takes part in, aids, or knows about: *She was a party to our plot.* **5** each of the people or sides in or affected by a contract or dispute: *There were several parties to the lawsuit.* **6** a person: *A third party helped the two of them settle their dispute.*
adj to do with a party, or fond of parties: *He was a party guy.* <Old French, from Latin *partiri* divide into parts>

party line *n* **1** the official policy or policies of a political party: *The members of parliament were not expected to vote along party lines on the issue.* **2** a telephone line by which two or more subscribers are connected with the exchange by one circuit.

par·ty–lin·er (pȧr′tē lī′nər) *n* a person who follows closely the officially adopted policies of his or her political party.

party politics *n* (*with singular verb*) politics based on the interests of political parties, regardless of the public good.

party–pooper (pȧr′tē pū′pər) *Informal n* someone who spoils a party by refusing to take part in its activities or join in its mood.

party whip *n* a political official whose job is to organize party members to vote on a certain issue or attend important debates in the legislature.

par value *n* the value of a stock, bond, or other security. It is printed on the document.

par·ve·nu (pȧr′və nyū′) *or* (pȧr′və nū′) *n* a person who has risen quickly to a position of wealth or power, but is not yet socially accepted in this new position.
adj like or characteristic of a parvenu. <French = arrived>

pas·cal (pas′kəl) *n* the SI unit for measuring pressure or stress, equal to the pressure produced by the force of one newton applied to an area of one square metre. *Symbol* **Pa** <B. *Pascal,* 17c mathematician>

PASCAL (pas′kəl) *Computers n* a high-level computer language. <B. *Pascal,* 17c mathematician, who built the first mechanical calculator>

pas·chal (pas′kəl) *adj* **1** to do with Easter. **2** to do with Passover.

pas de deux (po′də dyū′) *n* **1** in ballet, a dance for two people. **2** in classical ballet, a set of five dances for a ballerina and her partner. <French = step for two>

pasque·flow·er (pask′flou′ər) *n* an anemone with mauve or white flowers, especially the PRAIRIE CROCUS. <French *passé-fleur*>

pass (pas) *v* **passed, pass·ing 1** move or cause to move in a stated way: *to pass through a heavily wooded area, to pass a dangerous section of the road successfully. He passed a rope around his waist for support.* **2** go by or move past: *The parade passed. We passed the big truck.* **3** go or cause to go from one to another: *Her estate passed to her children. Please pass the butter.* **4** be successful in an examination or course: *He passed arithmetic.* **5** approve as complete or accurate: *to pass accounts as correct.* **6** legalize or be authorized (by): *to pass a law. The new law passed the city council.* **7** come to an end: *The pain will pass.* **8** go beyond or exceed; surpass: *Her strange story passes belief.* **9** use, spend, or occupy: *We passed the days pleasantly.* **10** change: *Water passes from a liquid to a solid state when it freezes.* **11** happen: *Tell me all that passed.* **12** issue judgment on: *A judge passes sentence on guilty people.* **13** go without notice or action: *She was rude, but let that pass.* **14** leave out, omit, or refuse to do: *I'll pass on that question.* **15** *Sports* transfer the puck or ball from one player to another in hockey, football, etc. **16** in card playing, give up a chance to bid or to play a hand.
n **1** an act or fact of moving past or through something: *The invading army made a swift pass through the country.* **2** success in an examination or course. **3** permission to do something: *He needed a pass to enter the workout room.* **4** a free ticket: *a movie pass.* **5** a state or condition: *How could we have arrived at such a sorry pass?* **6** a motion of the hands, as in performing a magic trick. **7** a narrow route through mountains. **8 a** *Sports* a transfer of a puck or ball in hockey, football, etc. **b** a thrust in fencing. **9** an attempt to kiss someone or otherwise flirt. <Old French, from Latin *passus* pace> **pass′er** *n.*
bring to pass, accomplish or cause to be.
come to pass, take place.
pass as (or **for**), be accepted as: *Use silk, or a material that will pass as silk.*
pass away, die.
pass by, a move past. **b** fail to notice.
pass off, a go away. **b** take place. **c** get accepted or pretend to be.
pass on, a move or move something on from one person to another. **b** die.
pass out, a faint; lose consciousness. **b** hand out or circulate: *The teacher passed out the report cards.*
pass over, fail to notice: *She passed over my mistake.*
pass up, a give up or renounce: *to pass up a chance to go to college.* **b** fail to take advantage of.

CONFUSABLES

Passed is the past tense of the verb **pass** and means "went by": *I passed the park on the way home.*

Past means "beyond": *I went past the gate into the field.*

Past also means "time before": *In the past, there was no TV.*

pass·a·ble (pas′ə bəl) *adj* **1** fairly good: *a passable performance. Her French is only passable.* **2** able to be crossed or travelled on: *The roads are just barely passable.*

pass·a·bly (pas′ə blē) *adv* fairly or moderately: *a passably good time.*

pas·sage (pas′ij) *n* **1** a hall or way through a building. **2** a means of passing: *passage through a crowd.* **3** the right, liberty, or permission to pass: *The guard refused us passage.* **4** a transition or passing of something: *the passage of time.* **5** a section or part of a speech, text, or musical composition: *a passage from the first symphony of Beethoven.* **6** a journey, especially by sea: *We had a rough passage across Hudson Bay.* **7** the action of making into law by vote of a legislature: *the passage of a bill.*

pas·sage·way (pas′ij wā′) *n* a way along which one can pass, such as a hall or alley.

pass·book (pas′bůk) *n* a small book used to keep a record of a person's bank account transactions.

pas·sé (pa sā′) *adj* no longer useful or fashionable: *That expression is very passé.* <French = passed>

pas·sen·ger (pas′ən jər) *n* a traveller in a train, motor vehicle, boat, or airplane who has nothing to do with its operation: *None of the passengers was hurt in the accident.*

passenger pigeon *n* in former times, a wild pigeon of N America. It was abundant in the early 1800s, but a century later humans had hunted it to extinction.

pass·er·by (pas′ər bī′) *n, pl* **pass·ers·by** a person who passes by: *The robbery was seen by a passerby who called the police.*

a bat	e bed	i bid	o pot	u cup	th **thin**
ā cake	ē me	ī bite	ō go	ū rude	TH **then**
ȧ bar	ə about	ər over	ȯ for	ů put	zh measure

pas·ser·ine (pas′ə rīn′) *or* (pas′ə rin) *adj* to do with an order of birds, including all songbirds, whose feet are adapted for perching. See CLAW for picture.
n a bird belonging to this order. <Latin *passer* sparrow>

pass·ing (pas′ing) *adj* **1** going past: *passing traffic.* **2** carried out or occurring over a brief period: *a passing idea, a passing fashion.* **3** showing that one has passed an examination or test: *a passing mark.*
n **1** the passage of something, especially time: *the passing of summer.* **2** the action of kicking, hitting, or throwing a ball or puck from one team member to another while playing a game. **3** the death of someone.
in passing, a as one proceeds or passes. **b** incidentally: *In passing, I'd like to compliment you on your excellent work.*

pas·sion (pash′ən) *n* **1** very strong feeling, such as love and hate. **2** a violent anger: *She flew into a passion.* **3** intense love or sexual desire. **4** a very strong liking or devotion: *a passion for music.* **5** the object of a passion: *Music is my passion.* <Latin *pati* suffer>

pas·sion·ate (pash′ə nit) *adj* **1** affected with or easily moved to strong emotion, especially anger or indignation: *a passionate believer in freedom, a passionate person.* **2** caused by or showing strong emotion: *a passionate defence of the accused man.* **3** affected with or influenced by sexual desire. **pas′sion·ate·ly** *adv.*

passion fruit *n* the edible purple fruit of the **passionflower**, a mainly tropical evergreen vine.

Passion play *n* a play representing the sufferings and death of Christ.

pas·sive (pas′iv) *adj* **1** being acted on without itself acting: *a passive disposition.* **2** not resisting: *His passive nature made him a target for bullies.* **3** *Grammar* to do with the verb form that shows the subject of a verb is being acted on, rather than performing the action. Compare ACTIVE. <Latin *pati* suffer> **pas′sive·ly** *adv.* **pas·siv′i·ty** *n.*

GRAMMAR AND USAGE

In *The window was broken by my sister*, the verb *was broken* is in the **passive voice**. In *My sister broke the window,* the verb *broke* is in the **active voice**.

When a sentence is in the passive voice, the subject of the verb is affected by the action, rather than performing the action. This is useful when the doer of the action is unknown, unimportant, or obvious: *The travel restrictions were lifted after several months.*

passive resistance *n* resistance to authority, especially by non-violent refusal to co-operate.

passive smoking *n* the act of breathing smoke from another person's cigarette, cigar, or pipe.

pass·key (pas′kē′) *n* **1** a key for opening several locks. **2** a private key to a restricted area.

Pass·o·ver (pas′ō′vər) *n* an annual Jewish holiday in memory of the escape of the Hebrews from Egypt, where they had been slaves. Also called **Pesach**. <*pass over.* In the Book of Exodus in the Bible, a destroying angel passes over the houses of the Israelites when it kills the first-born males of their enemies.>

pass·port (pas′pôrt′) *n* **1** an official document showing the holder's identity and citizenship of the holder, and giving the holder permission to leave and return to the country issuing the document. **2** a thing that gives one admission or acceptance: *An interest in gardening was a passport to my aunt's favour.*

pass·word (pas′wərd′) *n* **1** a secret word or phrase that identifies a person speaking it and allows him or her to pass. **2** *Computers* a private code or word that enables its possessor to use a computer by keying in the code.

past (past) *adj* **1** ended: *Summer is past. Our troubles are past.* **2** just gone by: *The past year was full of trouble.* **3** having served a term in office: *a past president.* **4** *Grammar* the past tense or a verb form in it.
n **1** time gone by: *Life began far back in the past.* **2** a past life or history: *Our country has a glorious past.* **3** a person's past life, especially if hidden or unknown: *He always refused to answer when anyone asked him about his past.*
prep **1** beyond or farther on than: *The arrow went past the mark.* **2** later than: *half past two. It is past noon.* **3** beyond in number, amount, or degree. **4** beyond the ability, range, or scope of: *absurd fancies that are past belief.*
adv so as to pass by or beyond: *The bus goes past once an hour.* <Middle English, past tense of *pass*>
See PASS for confusables.
not put it past someone, believe someone capable of doing something (bad): *I wouldn't put it past him to cheat on a test.*

pas·ta (pas′tə) *or* (pä′stə) *n* food or foods made from a flour paste and cut in various shapes, such as spaghetti, macaroni, and ravioli. <Italian = paste>

paste (pāst) *n* **1** a soft, thick, moist mixture of dry and wet ingredients, used to stick paper or other light materials together, or for putting on wallpaper. **2** a mixture of flour and water, used as dough for pastry. **3** a mixture of clay and water, used in making pottery. **4** a hard, glassy material used in making imitations of precious stones. **5** a mixture of ground meat, seafood, or vegetables used for spreading on bread.
v **past·ed, past·ing** stick with paste or cover by pasting: *paste a label on a box, paste a door over with notices.* <Old French, from Greek *passein* sprinkle> **past′er** *n.*

paste·board (pāst′bôrd′) *n* a stiff material made of sheets of paper pasted together or of paper pulp pressed and dried.

pas·tel (pas tel′) *n* **1** a crayon made of ground colouring matter and gum or resin, used in drawing. **2** a drawing made with such crayons. **3** a soft, pale shade of a colour.
adj pale: *pastel pink.* <French, from Greek *pasta* paste>

pas·tern (pas′tərn) *n* the part of a horse's foot between the fetlock and the hoof, or a corresponding part in other domestic animals. See HORSE for picture.

pas·teur·ize (pas′chə rīz′) *v* **pas·teur·ized, pas·teur·iz·ing** heat a liquid, such as milk or beer, to a prescribed temperature and chill it quickly to destroy harmful bacteria without causing a major chemical change to the substance itself. <L. *Pasteur,* 19c chemist who discovered this way of destroying bacteria> **pas′teur·i·za′tion** (pas′chə rə zā′shən) *or* (pas′chə rī zā′shən) *n.*

pas·tiche (pos tēsh′) *n* **1** a piece of writing, music, or other artistic work consisting mainly of bits borrowed from various sources, or intended to caricature a certain artist's style. **2** an unlikely mixture of materials or styles. <French, from Latin *pasta* paste>

pas·tille (pas tēl′) *n* **1** a flavoured or medicated lozenge. **2** a small roll or cone of aromatic paste, burnt as incense or a deodorizer. <French, from Latin *pastillus* round lozenge>

pas·time (pas′tīm′) *n* a game or other thing that causes the time to pass pleasantly.

past master *n* **1** a person who has much experience in a profession or art. **2** one who has filled the office of master in an organization.

pas·tor (pas′tər) *n* a member of the Christian clergy in charge of a church or congregation. <Latin *pastor* shepherd, from *pascere* to feed>

pas·tor·al (pas′tə rəl) *adj* **1** to do with shepherds or country life. **2** portraying or suggesting country life: *a pastoral scene.* **3** to do with a pastor.
n a pastoral play, poem, music, or picture.

pas·to·rale (pas′tə rol′) *Music n* a piece of music in a simple style intended to suggest rural life and scenes.

pas·tor·ate (pas′tər it) *n* **1** the position or term of service of a pastor. **2** pastors as a group.

past participle *Grammar n* See PARTICIPLE.

past perfect *Grammar n* See PERFECT TENSE.

pas·tra·mi (pə strȧ′mē) *n* smoked and highly seasoned beef, usually served in thin slices. <Yiddish>

pas·try (pā′strē) *n, pl* **pas·tries** **1** a paste or dough of flour and lard, butter, or shortening, used to make pie crusts, tarts, and other baked foods, or food made wholly or partly from it: *I don't like tough pastry.* **2** a piece of pastry, such as a tart or turnover. <*paste*>

past tense *Grammar n* a verb tense that expresses occurrence in time gone by, or a former action or situation. Example: In the sentence *I went to bed early last night,* the verb *went* is in the past tense.

GRAMMAR AND USAGE

To make the **simple past tense** of most verbs, add *-ed* to the root word:
talk becomes *talked*
research becomes *researched*

Irregular verbs form the simple past tense in other ways:
run becomes *ran*
take becomes *took*

pas·ture (pas′chər) *n* a grassy field or hillside on which livestock can feed, or the grass and other plants on it: *These lands afford good pasture.*
v **pas·tured, pas·tur·ing** put livestock to graze on a pasture or graze on a pasture: *He pastured his herd on a back field. The cattle pastured happily all summer.* <Old French, from Latin *pascere* to feed>
put out to pasture, *Informal* persuade or force older employees or members to retire or be less active: *They put him out to pasture as soon as he turned 65.*

past·y[1] (pā′stē) *adj,* **past·i·er, past·i·est** of or like paste in appearance or texture, especially pale and unhealthy looking. **past′i·ness** *n.*

pas·ty[2] (pas′tē) *n, pl* **pas·ties** a folded turnover filled with seasoned meat and vegetables: *a Cornish pasty.*

pat (pat) *v* **pat·ted, pat·ting** **1** strike or tap lightly with something flat: *She patted the dough into a flat cake.* **2** tap lightly with the hand as a sign of sympathy, approval, or affection: *to pat a dog.*
n **1** a light stroke or tap with the hand or with something flat. **2** the sound made by patting. **3** a very small compact mass, especially of butter.
adj simple and glib or unconvincing: *a pat reply.*
adv convenient or timely, especially too much so. <Middle English *patte*>
have down (or **know**) **pat,** *Informal* know perfectly or thoroughly: *She has the history lesson down pat.*
pat on the back, praise or compliment.
stand pat, *Informal* keep to the same position or decision: *The principal stood pat on her decision to ban cellphones in the classroom.*

patch (pach) *n* **1** a piece of some material put on to mend a hole or a tear, or to strengthen a weak place. **2** a protective pad for placing over an injured eye: *The doctor ordered him to wear a patch over his right eye.* **3 a** a small piece of material worn next to the skin so that a drug in it can be absorbed gradually. **b the patch** such a patch delivering nicotine to someone trying to quit smoking. **4** a small piece of cloth, especially one used for patchwork. **5** a tiny bit of black cloth that people used to stick on their bodies to hide a blemish or to contrast with their powdered skin. **6** a small area different from that around it: *a patch of brown on the skin.* **7** a small piece of ground: *a garden patch.* **8** a temporary electrical or telephone connection. **9** *Computers* a small piece of software code inserted into a program to enhance it or to correct a flaw.
v **1** put on a patch: *to patch a sleeve.* **2** put pieces together: *to patch a quilt.* **3** modify software code to improve it. **4** make an electrical or telephone patch. <origin uncertain> **patch′er** *n.*
patch someone up, apply first aid to someone after an injury.
patch up, a put an end to or settle: *to patch up a quarrel.* **b** fix hastily or for a time: *to patch up a leaking tap.* **c** put together hastily or poorly: *to patch up a costume for the masquerade party.*

patch·work (pach′wərk′) *n* **1** pieces of cloth of various colours or shapes sewn together: *a piece of patchwork.* **2** the craft of sewing things in this way: *I enjoy patchwork.* **3** a thing resembling cloth patchwork: *From the airplane, we saw a patchwork of fields and woods.*
adj made in this way: *a patchwork quilt.*

patch·y (pach′ē) *adj* **patch·i·er, patch·i·est** **1** with many patches: *a patchy lawn.* **2** not consistent or regular: *a patchy performance.* **patch′i·ness** *n.*

a bat	e bed	i bid	o pot	u cup	th **thin**
ā cake	ē me	ī bite	ō go	ū rude	ᴛʜ **then**
ȧ bar	ə about	ər over	ȯ for	u̇ put	zh measure

P

pate (pāt) *n* the top of the head: *a bald pate.* <origin uncertain>

pâ·té or **pa·te** (pȧ tā′) *n* a baked mixture of minced and seasoned meat, fish, or vegetables. <Old French *paste*>

pâté de foie gras (pȧ′tā də fwȧ′grȧ′) *n* a rich paste made with livers of specially fattened geese or duck. <French>

pa·tel·la (pə tel′ə) *n, pl* **pa·tel·las** or **pa·tel·lae** (-tel′ē) *or* (-tel′ī) the kneecap. <Latin *patina* shallow pan, from its shape> **pa·tel′lar** *adj.*

pat·ent (pat′ənt) *or* (pā′tənt) *for n or v;* (pā′tənt) *for adj.* *n* a registered right given by a government to a person by which he or she is the only one allowed to make, use, or sell a new invention for a certain period.
adj obvious: *the patent nervousness of the actors at the audition.*
v get a patent for: *The inventor patented many inventions.* <Old French, from Latin *patere* lie open>
pat′ent·a·ble *adj.*

pat·ent·ee (pat′ən tē′) *n* a person to whom a patent is granted.

patent leather *n* leather with a very glossy, smooth surface, usually black.

pa·tent·ly (pā′tən tlē) *or* (pat′ən tlē) *adv* clearly or obviously.

patent medicine *n* a medicine not requiring a doctor's prescription.

pa·ter·fa·mil·i·as (pat′ər fə mil′ē əs) *or* (pā′tər fə mil′ē əs) *n* a father or head of a family.

pa·ter·nal (pə tər′nəl) *adj* **1** to do with a father: *He took great paternal pride in his children's achievements.* **2** related on the father's side of the family: *paternal grandparent.* Compare MATERNAL. <Latin *pater* father>
pa·ter′nal·ly *adv.*

pa·ter·nal·ism (pə tər′nə liz′əm) *n* the principle or practice of people with authority to treat others as if those others lacked responsibility for their own actions. **pa·ter′nal·ist′** *n.* **pa·ter′nal·is′tic** *adj.*

pa·ter·ni·ty (pə tər′nə tē) *n* **1** the fact or condition of being a father. **2** paternal origin: *King Arthur's paternity was unknown.* Compare MATERNITY.

path (path) *n, pl* **paths** (paᴛʜz) **1** a track, usually narrow, made by people or animals walking. **2** a way made to walk upon or to ride upon: *She laid stone for a garden path.* **3** a line or route along which a person or thing moves: *The moon has a regular path through the sky.* **4** a way of acting or behaving: *Some people choose the hard path.* <Old English *pæth*> **path′less** *adj.*

pa·thet·ic (pə thet′ik) *adj* **1** arousing pity and compassion: *A lost child is a pathetic sight.* **2** pitifully inadequate or unsuccessful: *a pathetic attempt to be funny.* <Latin, from Greek *pathos* suffering>
pa·thet′i·cal·ly (pə thet′i klē) *adv.*

pathetic fallacy *n* the giving of human feelings to natural or inanimate things in a literary text.

path·find·er (path′fin′dər) *n* a person who finds a path or way, especially through a wilderness.

path·o·gen (path′ə jen′) *n* a disease-causing agent, such as a virus or bacterium <Greek *pathos* disease + *gen-* produce> **path′o·gen′ic** *adj.*

path·o·log·i·cal (path′ə loj′ə kəl) *adj* **1** dealing with or concerned with diseases. **2** due to disease or accompanying disease: *a pathological condition of the blood cells.* **3** caused or controlled by an obsession: *a pathological hatred of cats. He's a pathological liar.* **path′o·log′i·cal·ly** *adv.*

pa·thol·o·gy (pə thol′ə jē) *n, pl* **pa·thol·o·gies** **1** the study of the nature and causes of disease and of the changes in the body caused by them. **2** unhealthy conditions and processes caused by a disease. **pa·thol′o·gist** *n.*

pa·thos (pā′thos) *n* a quality in experience or events, or in literature, art, or music, that arouses a feeling of pity or sadness. <Greek = suffering>

path·way (path′wā′) *n* a path.

–pathy *combining form* **1** a feeling: *antipathy.* **2** the treatment of disease: *osteopathy.* <Greek *pathos* suffering>

pa·tience (pā′shəns) *n* **1** the ability to accept calmly things that trouble or annoy, or that require long waiting or effort: *The cat showed patience in watching the mousehole.* **2** steady, painstaking effort: *This carving shows the skill and patience of the artist.* **3** a card game played by one person. <Old French, from Latin *pati* suffer>

pa·tient (pā′shənt) *adj* **1** with or showing patience: *patient suffering.* **2** with steady, painstaking effort: *patient research.*
n a person who is being treated by a doctor, dentist, or other medical professional. <Latin *pati* suffer>
pa′tient·ly *adv.*

pat·i·na (pat′ə nə) *n* **1** a film, usually green, formed naturally over time on the surface of copper or bronze. **2** a smooth appearance produced by age and exposure on wood or stone: *The old table had a beautiful patina.* <Italian, from Latin = shallow pan, in reference to the encrustations found on ancient dishes>

pat·i·o (pat′ē ō) *n, pl* **pat·i·os** **1** a paved outdoor area adjoining a house. **2** an inner court or yard open to the sky. <Spanish>

pa·tis·se·rie (pə tis′ə rē) *n* **1** a bakery that sells fancy or French pastries and cakes. **2** a single pastry of this kind, or such pastries as a group. <French>

pat·ois (pat′wȧ) *n, pl* **pat·ois** (pat′wȧz) **1** a dialect different from the standard language of a country or district, especially one spoken in rural areas. **2** the informal or specialized language characteristic of a particular group. <French = rough speech>

pa·tri·arch (pā′trē ȧrk′) *n* **1** a father who is the ruler of a family or tribe. **2** a man thought of as the father or founder of something. **3** *Christianity* a high-ranking bishop in certain churches, especially the Roman Catholic Church and the Orthodox Church. <Old French, from Greek *patria* family + *archos* ruler> **pa′tri·ar′chal** *adj.*

pa·tri·ar·chy (pā′trē ȧr′kē) *n, pl* **pa·tri·ar·chies** a form of social organization in which a man is the ruler of a family or tribe, descent being traced through him. Compare MATRIARCHY.

✱ **pa·tri·ate** (pā′trē āt′) *or* (pat′rē āt′) *v* **pat·ri·a·ted, pa·tri·a·ting** bring under the direct political control of the people of a given nation: *to patriate the Canadian constitution.* <*repatriate*> **pa′tri·a′tion** *n.*

pa·tri·cian (pə trish′ən) *n* **1** in ancient Rome, a member of the nobility. Compare PLEBEIAN (def. 1). **2** a person from the nobility or of high social rank.
adj **1** to do with the patricians. **2** to do with the nobility. <Old French, from Latin *pater* father>

pat·ri·li·ne·al (pat′rə li′nē əl) *adj* to do with descent or kinship through the paternal line. Compare MATRILINEAL. **pa′tri·lin′e·al·ly** *adv.*

pat·ri·mo·ny (pat′rə mō′nē) *n, pl* **pat·ri·mo·nies** **1** property inherited from one's father or ancestors. **2** heritage: *cultural patrimony.* **pat′ri·mo′ni·al** *adj.*

pa·tri·ot (pā′trē ət) *or* (pat′rē ət) *n* a person who avidly supports the interests and rights of his or her country. <French, from Greek *patris* fatherland> **pa′tri·ot′ic** *adj.* **pa′tri·ot′i·cal·ly** *adv.* **pa′tri·ot′ism** *n.*

pa·trol (pə trōl′) *n* **1** the people or group who keep watch over an area by regularly travelling around it, as a watchman or a police officer does: *The patrol was changed at midnight.* **2** the process of making rounds to watch or guard: *She was on hallway patrol during the lunch hour.* **3** a group of soldiers, ships, or airplanes, sent out to find out all they can about the enemy.
v **pa·trolled, pa·trol·ling** keep watch over an area by regularly travelling around it. <German, from French *patte* paw + *rouille* mud> **pa·troll′er** *n.*

patrol car *n* a police car used for patrolling roads or districts: *The patrol car caught him speeding.*

pa·tron (pā′trən) *n* **1** a person who buys regularly at a certain store or goes regularly to a certain restaurant or other place of business. **2** a person, especially one with social or political influence, who sponsors or supports another person or a cause, institution, or organization: *a patron of the arts.* **3** a guardian saint or god.
adj guarding or protecting: *a patron saint.* <Old French, from Latin *pater* father>

pa·tron·age (pā′trə nij) *or* (pat′rə nij) *n* **1** the regular business given to a store or other place of business by customers. **2** the favour, encouragement, or support given by a patron. **3** favour or kindness given in a condescending way: *an air of patronage.* **4** the power to give jobs or favours, or the jobs or favours themselves.

pa·tron·ize (pā′trə nīz′) *or* (pat′rə nīz′) *v* **pa·tron·ized, pa·tron·iz·ing** **1** be a regular customer of: *We patronize our neighbourhood stores.* **2** act as a patron toward: *to patronize the ballet.* **3** treat in a condescending way: *Children do not like being patronized by adults.* **pa′tron·iz′ing** *adj.* **pa′tron·iz′ing·ly** *adv.*

patron saint *n* a saint regarded as the special guardian of a particular place, group of people, or activity: *St. Apollonia is a patron saint of dentists.*

pat·ro·nym·ic (pat′rə nim′ik) *n* a name derived from the name of a father or ancestor. Example: *Johnson = son of John.* <Greek *pater* father + *onyma* name>

pat·sy (pat′sē) *Informal n, pl* **pat·sies** a person who is easily victimized or deceived, especially by becoming a scapegoat. <origin uncertain>

pat·ter[1] (pat′ər) *v* **1** make rapid taps: *The rain pattered against the window.* **2** move with light, rapid steps: *She pattered down the stairs.*
n a series of quick taps or the sound they make: *the patter of hail on the roof.* <*pat*[1]>

pat·ter[2] (pat′ər) *n* **1** rapid and easy talk, such as that of a magician or comedian. **2** the specialized vocabulary of a certain group. **3** rapid speech, usually for comic effect, introduced into a song.
v talk or say rapidly and easily, without much thought. <*pater* in *paternoster* = our father, from the Christian Lord's prayer in Latin>

pat·tern (pat′ərn) *n* **1** an arrangement of forms and colours, as in wallpaper, rugs, cloth, and jewellery. **2** a model or guide for something to be made: *I made this birdhouse from a pattern I found on the Internet.* **3** a fine example or model to be followed: *The captain was a pattern of courage and resolve.* **4** an arrangement of characteristics or actions that does not normally change: *behaviour patterns, speech patterns.*
v **1** make according to a pattern. **2** work or decorate with a pattern. **3** use as an example: *He patterned himself after his older brother.* <Latin *patronus* example, from *pater* father>

pat·ty (pat′ē) *n, pl* **pat·ties** **1** a small hollow shell of pastry with a smooth filling. **2** a small, flat, usually round cake of chopped food: *hamburger patties.* **3** a small, round, flat piece of candy: *a peppermint patty.* <French *pâté*>

pau·ci·ty (pos′ə tē) *n* a small or insufficient number or amount. <Old French, from Latin *paucus* few>

paunch (ponch) *n* a large belly that sticks out. <Old French from Latin *panticem* belly> **paunch′i·ness** *n.* **paunch′y** *adj.*

pau·per (pop′ər) *n* a very poor person; in former times, a person supported by charity. <Latin = poor>

pau·per·ize (pop′ə rīz′) *v* **pau·per·ized, pau·per·iz·ing** make a pauper of. **pau′per·i·za′tion** *n.*

pause (poz) *v* **paused, paus·ing** **1** stop for a brief period: *The dog paused when she heard me.* **2** dwell or linger: *to pause upon a word.*
n **1** a moment of silence. **2** a brief stop in speaking or reading: *She made a short pause and then went on reading.* **3** a punctuation mark used to indicate such a stop. **4** *Music* a sign (𝄐) above or below a note or rest, meaning that it is to be held for a longer time. <Old French, from Greek *pausein* to stop>
give you pause, cause you to reconsider or question.

pave (pāv) *v* **paved, pav·ing** cover a street, highway, or sidewalk with PAVEMENT (def. 1). <Old French, from Latin *pavire* tread down>
pave the way, make something smooth or easy: *She paved the way for me by doing careful work.*

a bat	e bed	i bid	o pot	u cup	th **thin**
ā cake	ē me	ī bite	ō go	ū rude	ᴛʜ **then**
à bar	ə about	ər over	ȯ for	u̇ put	zh measure

pave·ment (pāv′mənt) *n* **1** a covering, or surface, for streets, sidewalks, and highways made of stones, gravel, concrete, or asphalt, or the surface so formed. **2** *UK* a sidewalk.

pa·vil·ion (pə vil′yən) *n* **1** a building, usually open-sided, used for a special purpose: *a park pavilion, the cricket pavilion.* **2** a large tent, often luxurious, for entertainment or shelter. **3** a building that houses an exhibition at a fair, or a temporary building or stand in a trade fair. **4** a part of a building higher or more decorated than the rest. **5** one of a group of buildings forming a hospital or complex.
v enclose or shelter in a pavilion. <Old French, Latin *papilio* tent>

pav·ing (pā′ving) *n* the material used for a pavement.

paw (po) *n* **1** the foot of an animal with a claw and pad, such as that of a cat or dog. **2** *Informal* a hand, especially when large or clumsy.
v **1** strike at or touch with a paw: *The kitten pawed the ball of yarn.* **2** scrape or strike with or as if with a hoof: *The horse was pawing the ground, eager to go.* **3** handle, touch, or grab for awkwardly, rudely, or too intimately. <Old French *poue*>

pawn[1] (pon) *v* give something as security for money borrowed: *She pawned her watch to buy food until she could get work.*
n something left as security. <Old French *pan*>
in pawn, in another's possession as security: *Her guitar is in pawn to the man who lent her money.*

pawn[2] (pon) *n* **1** in chess, one of the pieces of lowest value. **2** a person or thing used by someone to further his or her own purposes: *She used her friends and colleagues as pawns in her race for political power.* <Old French, from Latin *pes* foot>

pawn·bro·ker (pon′brō′kər) *n* a person who lends money on articles that are left with him or her as security for the loan.

pawn·shop (pon′shop′) *n* a pawnbroker's shop.

paw·paw (pop′o) PAPAYA.

pay[1] (pā) *v* **paid,** or (for def. 8) **payed, pay·ing 1** give a person money for goods, services, or work: *I paid the sales clerk.* **2** give money for: *Pay your way.* **3** hand over money owed: *to pay a debt.* **4** give, make, or offer: *to pay attention, to pay compliments, to pay a visit.* **5** be profitable or worthwhile to: *It wouldn't pay anyone to take that job. Being patient doesn't always pay.* **6** reward or punish: *She paid them for their insults by causing them trouble.* **7** suffer or undergo: *to pay a penalty.* **8** let out (a rope, line, etc.) gradually.
n money or an equivalent given for goods, services, or work: *He gets his pay every Saturday.*
adj requiring a cash payment or the insertion of coins or tokens: *pay TV, a pay phone.* <Old French *paiier* satisfy, appease, from Latin *pacis* peace>
in the pay of, paid by and working for.
pay as you go, pay for something at the same time as it is used.
pay back, a return borrowed money. **b** give the same treatment as received: *I'll pay her back for her hospitality by inviting her for dinner.* **c** take revenge on: *I'll pay you back yet!*
pay down, a reduce or get rid of a debt by making payments: *I'll use my allowance to pay down the money I owe you.* **b** pay a part of the full price at the time of purchase, with the rest to be paid later: *She paid half down on the car and took out a loan for the rest.*
pay off, give all the money that is owed.
pay up, pay in full.
pay your way, a pay your fare or travel expenses. **b** contribute your share.

SYNONYMS

Pay is the word most often used when giving someone money due for goods, work, or services: *We paid for the groceries.*

Compensate suggests paying for such things as time spent or things lost or damaged: *They compensated the woman after they broke her window.*

Remunerate suggests giving a reward or payment for services: *The boy was remunerated for finding the lost kitten.*

pay·a·ble (pā′ə bəl) *adj* **1** required to be paid: *accounts payable.* **2** able to be paid.

pay·back (pā′bak′) *n* the act or fact of returning a favour or harm done: *It's time for payback.*

pay·cheque (pā′chek′) *n* a cheque issued regularly to an employee in payment of wages or salary.

pay·day (pā′dā′) *n* a day on which wages are paid.

pay dirt *n* **1** *Informal* something that yields a profit or beneficial result. **2** earth or ore containing enough metal to be worth mining.
hit (or **strike**) **pay dirt,** find a source of wealth or success.

pay·ee (pā ē′) *n* a person to whom money is paid or is to be paid.

pay·er (pā′ər) *n* a person who pays or is to pay.

pay·load (pā′lōd′) *n* **1** the part of a vehicle's load that produces revenue, such as passengers or cargo. **2** the explosive warhead of a missile, or the equipment, personnel, or satellites carried by a spacecraft.

pay·ment (pā′mənt) *n* **1** the act or fact of paying. **2** the amount paid: *a monthly payment of ninety dollars.* **3** reward or punishment: *The girl who rescued the little boy said that his smile was payment enough.*

pay·off (pā′of′) *n* **1** a payment made to someone, such as a bribe or reward: *He received a payoff for playing the song on his radio program.* **2** income from an investment or a bet. **3** *Informal* **a** a final outcome or conclusion. **b** the climax of a narrative or sequence of events.

pay–per–view (pā′pər vyū′) *n* a television service in which extra money is paid in advance to be able to receive a movie or program for viewing.

pay phone *n* a telephone that is operated by coins or some kind of credit card.

pay·roll (pā′rōl′) *n* a list of people to be paid for work and the amount that each one is to receive, or the total amount to be paid to them.

pay TV *n* a TV service for which extra payment is made.

PC or **P.C.** 1 personal computer. 2 Police Constable. 3 politically correct.

PCB *n* in full, **polychlorinated biphenyl** a highly toxic chemical compound.

PDF *Computers n* in full, **portable document format** a standardized format for documents used and transferred on the Internet.

pea (pē) *n, pl* **peas** 1 a vine producing edible, round seeds in pods. The seeds and sometimes the pods are eaten as a vegetable. 2 (*usually in compounds*) a plant like the pea vine: *chick pea, sweet pea.* 3 especially in the Caribbean, the fresh or dried seed of a bean plant: *rice and peas.* <Old English *pise*>
as like as two peas in a pod, exactly alike.

peace (pēs) *n* 1 freedom from war or strife of any kind: *to work for world peace.* 2 public quiet, order, and security. 3 an agreement between contending parties to end a war: *to sign the peace.* 4 quiet or calm: *peace of mind.* <Old French, from Latin *pacis*> **peace′ful** *adj.*
peace′ful·ly *adv.* **peace′ful·ness** *n.*
at peace, a not in a state of war or quarrelling. **b** quiet and calm. **c** dead.
hold (or **keep**) **your peace,** be silent or keep still.
keep the peace, a avoid conflict: *I did not want to eat out, but I gave in to keep the peace.* **b** make sure that public order is not disturbed: *The police help to keep the peace.*
make peace, be reconciled after a conflict.
make your peace with, gradually accept an unpleasant fact or situation: *She has made her peace with her difficult past.*

peace·a·ble (pē′sə bəl) *adj* 1 liking or keeping peace: *Peaceable people keep out of quarrels.* 2 peaceful: *a peaceable reign.* **peace′a·ble·ness** *n.* **peace′a·bly** *adv.*

peace·keep·ing (pē′skē′ping) *n* the preserving of peace, especially the enforcement of peace between hostile nations or groups by means of an international body: *a peacekeeping force.* **peace′keep′er** *n.*

peace·mak·er (pē′smā′kər) *n* a person who makes peace, especially by reconciling conflicts or quarrels between individuals or groups.

peace offering *n* 1 an offering made to obtain peace. 2 *Christianity* an offering of thanksgiving to God.

peace pipe *n* a pipe smoked by First Nations or Native American peoples as a token or pledge of peace.

🍁 **Peace River Block** *n* a settled region in northern British Columbia and Alberta, lying in the fertile valley of the Peace River: *The Peace River Block is often called the Peace River Country.*

peace·time (pē′stīm′) *n* a time of peace: *in peacetime or in war.*

peach (pēch) *n* a juicy fruit with a pinkish yellow, fuzzy skin and a rough stone. See APRICOT for picture.
adj yellowish pink. <Old French, from Latin *Persicum malum* Persian apple>

peach·y (pē′chē) *adj* **peach·i·er, peach·i·est** 1 like a peach in colour or texture. 2 (*often used ironically*) attractive; marvellous: *It's raining—well, isn't that just peachy!* **peach′i·ness** *n.*

A **peacock's** diet includes worms, insects, small snakes, and seeds. A peacock will trick a venomous snake into striking repeatedly, and will then kill and eat it when it tires.

pea·cock (pē′kok′) *n, pl* **pea·cocks** or (*especially collectively*) **pea·cock** an adult male peafowl with brilliant green and blue tail feathers with eyelike spots. The tail can be spread out and held upright like a fan.
adj bright blue-green. <Latin *pavo* + *cock*[1]>

pea·fowl (pē′foul′) *n, pl* **pea·fowl** a peacock or peahen.

pea·hen (pē′hen′) *n* an adult female peafowl.

pea jacket *n* a short coat of thick woollen cloth, worn especially by sailors.

peak (pēk) *n* 1 the pointed top of a mountain or hill: *snowy peaks.* 2 a mountain that stands alone, especially one with a pointed top. 3 the highest point: *to reach the peak of one's profession.* 4 a pointed end or top: *the peak of a roof.* 5 the front part or the brim of a cap.
v reach the highest point: *Sales were expected to peak in December.* <Middle English> **peak′less** *adj.*

peaked[1] (pēkt) *or* (pē′kid) *adj* with a peak: *a peaked hat.*

peak·ed[2] (pē′kid) *adj* sickly in appearance. <obsolete *peak* get pale and sickly>

peal (pēl) *n* 1 a loud, long, repeated sound: *a peal of thunder, peals of laughter.* 2 the loud ringing of bells.
v ring out: *The bells pealed their message of joy.* <*appeal*>

pea·nut (pē′nut′) *n* 1 a pod of the pea family. The pods ripen underground and contain usually two large seeds that are used as nuts when roasted, and that also yield an oil used in cooking. 2 **peanuts** (*with singular verb*) *Informal* something of little value, especially a small amount of money: *It costs peanuts to run this car.*

peanut brittle *n* hard, thin, crunchy butterscotch candy containing peanuts.

peanut butter *n* a spread made from ground peanuts, used as a filling.

pear (per) *n* 1 the sweet, juicy, edible fruit of a tree that grows in temperate climates. It is rounded at one end and smaller toward the stem end. 2 *especially Caribbean, Informal* an avocado. <Latin *pirum*>

a bat	e bed	i bid	o pot	u cup	th **thin**
ā cake	ē me	ī bite	ō go	ū rude	ᴛʜ **then**
ä bar	ə about	ər over	ô for	ů put	zh measure

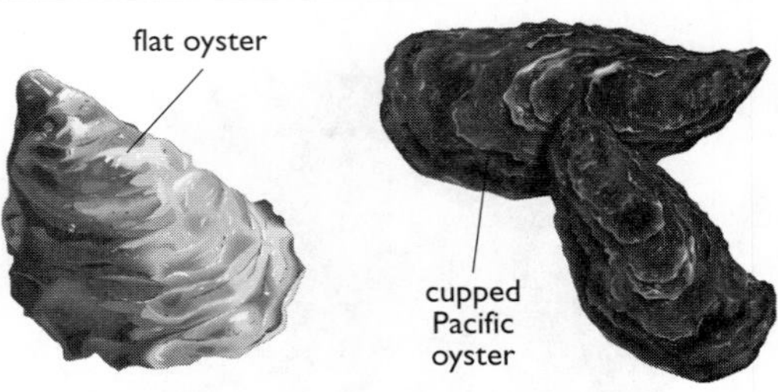

When a grain of sand or other tiny particle of matter invades its body, the oyster produces a smooth material, layer on layer, to protect itself from the irritant. This process eventually produces a **pearl**.

pearl (pərl) *n* **1** a white or nearly white gem that has a soft shine like satin, formed inside the shell of a kind of oyster, or in other similar shellfish. **2** a similar gem made artificially. **3** a thing that looks like a pearl, such as a dewdrop or a tear. **4** a very fine one of its kind: *She is a pearl among women.*
adj **1** very pale, clear bluish grey. **2** formed into something resembling a pearl: *pearl tapioca.*
v hunt or dive for pearls. <Latin *perla*>
cast pearls before swine, give something very fine to a person who cannot appreciate it.

pearl onion *n* a small, sweet onion, often pickled.

pearl·y (pər′lē) *adj* **pearl·i·er, pearl·i·est** with the colour or lustre of pearls: *pearly teeth.* **pearl′i·ness** *n.*

pear–shaped (pār′shāpd) *adj* **1** with a rounded shape, smaller at the top and bulging at the bottom. **2** full, clear, and resonant in sung tones or spoken vowels.

peas·ant (pez′ənt) *n* a person who works on the land, especially a farm labourer or tenant farmer.
adj to do with peasants: *peasant labour.* <Old French, from Latin *pagus* country district>

peas·ant·ry (pez′ən trē) *n* peasants as a group.

pea·shoot·er (pē′shū′tər) *n* a toy blowgun through which to blow dried peas and other small objects.

peat (pēt) *n* vegetable matter consisting of mosses and other plants that have decomposed in water and become partly carbonized, used as fertilizer and as a fuel when dried. <Latin>

peat moss *n* a moss that grows only in wet, acid areas. It forms peat when it dies and decomposes together with other plants.

pea·vey (pē′vē) *n, pl* **pea·veys** a pole tipped with a pointed metal spike, and with a hinged hook near the end, used to turn and move logs. The logger can use a stabbing motion to dig the spike and hook into the log. Compare CANT-HOOK. Also **peavy, peevee.** <said to be named after J. *Peavey*, its supposed inventor>

peb·ble (peb′əl) *n* **1** a small stone, usually worn smooth and round by being rolled about by water. **2** a rough, uneven surface on leather, paper, or other surface.
v **peb·bled, peb·bling** prepare leather so that it has a grained surface. <Old English> **peb′ble·like′** *adj.*

peb·bly (peb′lē) *adj* with many, or covered with, pebbles.

pe·can (pē′kan) *or* (pi kan′) *n* an edible nut similar to the walnut with a smooth, thin shell. <French, from Algonquian *pakan* hard-shelled nut>

pec·ca·dil·lo (pek′ə dil′ō) *n, pl* **pec·ca·dil·loes** or **pec·ca·dil·los** a slight offence or fault. <Spanish, from Latin *peccare*>

pec·ca·ry (pek′ə rē) *n, pl* **pec·ca·ries** or (*especially collectively*) **pec·ca·ry** a small, piglike mammal of N and S America with sharp tusks, erect ears, and a short tail. See UNGULATE for picture.

peck[1] (pek) *n* **1** a nonmetric unit of measure for volume, equal to eight quarts or a quarter of a bushel (about nine litres). **2** a great deal: *a peck of trouble.*

peck[2] (pek) *v* **1** strike and pick with the beak or with something like a beak. **2** make by striking with the beak or with something pointed: *Woodpeckers peck holes in trees.* **3** strike at and pick up with the beak: *A hen pecks corn.*
n **1** a stroke made with the beak: *The hen gave me a peck.* **2** a hole or mark made by pecking: *The bark of the tree was riddled with pecks.* **3** a hurried or casual kiss: *She gave him a peck on the cheek as she hurried out the door.* <origin uncertain>
peck at, a try to peck. **b** *Informal* eat only a little, bit by bit: *She just pecked at her food.*

peck·er (pek′ər) *n* a person who or thing that pecks, especially a bird such as a woodpecker.

pecking order *n* a hierarchy established among people or animals, originally observed in flocks of chickens, in which each individual dominates the one ranking below it.

peck·ish (pek′ish) *Informal adj* somewhat hungry.

pecs (peks) *Informal pln* the pectoral or chest muscles, especially if well developed by strenuous exercise.

pec·tin (pek′tən) *n* a substance that is found in ripe fruits and is used to thicken jams and jellies. <Greek *pegnuein* stiffen>

pec·to·ral (pek′tə rəl) *adj* to do with the breast or chest. <Latin *pectoris* chest>

pectoral fin *n* one of the two fins behind the head of a fish.

pe·cul·iar (pi kyū′lyər) *adj* **1** strange, odd, or unusual: *It was peculiar that the fish market had no fish yesterday.* **2** belonging to one person or thing and not to another: *peculiar to that place.* <Latin *peculiaris* of one's own property, from *pecu* cattle, i.e., property>
pe·cu′li·ar′i·ty (pi kyū′lē ar′ə tē) *or* (pi kyū′lē er′ə tē) *n.* **pe·cul′iar·ly** *adv.*

pe·cu·ni·ar·y (pi kyū′nē er′ē) *adj* to do with money. <Latin *pecunia* money>

ped·a·gogue (ped′ə gog′) *n* a teacher, often a strict one.

ped·a·go·gy (ped′ə goj′ē) *n* the profession, science, or art of teaching. <Latin, from Greek *paidis* boy + *agogos* guide> **ped′a·gog′ic** or **ped′a·gog′i·cal** *adj.* **ped′a·gog′i·cal·ly** *adv.*

ped·al (ped′əl) *n* a lever worked by the foot.
v **ped·alled** or **ped·aled, ped·al·ling** or **ped·al·ing** work or use pedals: *She pedalled her bicycle slowly up the hill.* <French, from Latin *pes* foot>

ped·ant (ped′ənt) *n* a person who displays detailed knowledge in an unnecessary or tiresome way. <Old French, from Italian *pedante* teacher>
pe·dan′tic (pə dan′tik) *adj.* **pe·dan′ti·cal·ly** *adv.*

ped·ant·ry (ped′ən trē) *n, pl* **ped·ant·ries** a pedantic way of presenting or applying knowledge, or an example of this: *The author's many pedantries make the book difficult to read.*

ped·dle (ped′əl) *v* **ped·dled, ped·dling 1** go from place to place to sell something, especially in small quantities: *to peddle newspapers.* **2** promote an idea, opinion, or story persistently or widely: *to peddle gossip.* <*pedlar*>

ped·dler (ped′lər) *n* a person who travels about selling things, especially in small quantities. Also, **pedlar**.

ped·es·tal (ped′i stəl) *n* **1** the base supporting a column or pillar. **2** a base on which a statue, vase, or lamp stands. **3** a position of prominence due to uncritical admiration: *to knock someone off their pedestal.* <French, from Latin *ped* foot + *di* of + *stallo* stall>
put (or **set**) **on a pedestal,** regard as extremely admirable or important.

pe·des·tri·an (pə des′trē ən) *n* a person who walks in an urban area or along a road.
adj **1** walking: *Pedestrian traffic is not permitted on this bridge.* **2** without imagination: *a pedestrian style in writing.* <French, from Latin *pes* foot>

pe·di·at·rics (pē′dē at′riks) *n* (*with singular verb*) the branch of medicine that treats children's diseases and deals with the care and development of babies and children. <Greek *paidos* child + *iatros* physician>
pe′di·a′tric *adj.* **pe′di·a·tri′cian** *n.*

ped·i·cel (ped′ə səl) *n* a stalk on a plant that supports a single flower. <Latin *pes* foot>

ped·i·cure (ped′ə kyūr′) *n* a cosmetic treatment for the feet, toes, and toenails. <Latin *pedis* foot + *cura* care>

ped·i·gree (ped′ə grē′) *n* **1** the list of the ancestors of a purebred animal. **2** a recorded ancestry or distinctive background. <Old French *pé de grue* foot of a crane, from a mark used in genealogies> **ped′i·greed′** *adj.*

ped·i·ment (ped′ə mənt) *n* a low, triangular part forming the front of a building, or as a decoration on a door or window.

pe·dom·e·ter (pi dom′ə tər) *n* an instrument for recording the number of steps taken and thus measuring the distance travelled.

ped·o·phile (ped′ə fīl) *or* (pēd′ə fīl) *n* an adult who is sexually attracted to children. <Greek *pais* child + *philos* loving> **ped·o·phil·i·a** (ped′ə fil′ē ə) *or* (pēd′ə fil′ē ə) *n.*

pe·dun·cle (pi dung′kəl) *n* a stalk on a plant that bears a flower, flower cluster, or fruit. <Latin *pes* foot>

peek (pēk) *v* **1** look quickly or secretively: *He pretended to have his eyes covered, but I could see he was peeking between his fingers. She peeked around the corner.* **2** look through a small narrow hole or crack: *I peeked through the hole in the fence.*
n **1** a quick, secretive look: *I took a peek at my sister's diary.* **2** a look through a hole or crack: *to take a peek into the refrigerator.* <Middle English *pike*>

peek·a·boo (pē′kə bū′) *n* a game played with a young child in which either person hides the face or eyes and then reveals them again.
interj the cry of either player on completing a round of this game, or the playful cry of anyone who sees someone supposed to be hiding.

peel (pēl) *n* the rind or outer covering of fruit or vegetables.
v **1** strip the skin, shell, rind, or bark from: *to peel an orange, to peel an egg.* **2** remove or come off in strips: *You can peel this kind of wallpaper. When I was sunburnt, my skin peeled.* <Latin *pilare* strip away hair>
peel′a·ble *adj.*
keep your eyes peeled, *Informal* be on the alert: *Keep your eyes peeled for cars turning off the highway here.*

peel·ing (pē′ling) *n* a piece or strip, as of rind or skin, peeled or pared off: *potato peelings.*

peep[1] (pēp) *v* **1** look through a small or narrow hole or crack. **2** look quickly and secretively. **3** show slightly: *Violets peeped among the leaves. Her toe peeped through the hole in her sock.*
n **1** a look through a hole or crack. **2** a quick, secret look: *Take a peep into the pantry and see if there are any cookies.* <Middle English *piken*>

peep[2] (pēp) *n* **1** a short, high sound such as that made by a baby bird: *the peeps of newly hatched chicks.* **2** a slight, feeble utterance, especially of protest: *I don't want to hear another peep out of you.*
v **1** make such a sound. **2** speak in a small, weak voice. <imitative>

peep·er (pē′pər) *n* **1** a person who or thing that peeps. **2** a small N American tree frog, the male of which makes peeping noises in the spring. **3 peepers** *pl Informal* eyes.

peep·hole (pēp′hōl′) *n* a hole through which one may peep.

P

Peep·ing Tom (pēp′ing tom) *n* a man who finds pleasure in secretly watching women undressing or taking part in sexual activity.

ETYMOLOGY

According to legend, Lady Godiva rode naked through the city of Coventry in England in order to persuade her husband not to tax the people so heavily. The only person to look at her was a man named Tom.

peer[1] (pēr) *n* **1** a person of the same status, ability, or age as another: *a jury of one's peers.* **2** *UK* a nobleman. <Old French, from Latin *par* equal>

peer[2] (pēr) *v* **1** look closely to see clearly, as a near-sighted person does: *She peered at the tag to read the price.* **2** be barely visible or come out slightly: *The sun was peering from behind a cloud.* <origin uncertain>

a bat	e bed	i bid	o pot	u cup	th **thin**
ā cake	ē me	ī bite	ō go	ū rude	ᴛʜ **then**
ä bar	ə about	ər over	ô for	ů put	zh measure

peer·age (pē′rij) *n* **1** all the titled peers of a country. **2** a book giving a list of titled peers with their genealogy.

peer·ess (pē′ris) *n* a female peer, or the wife or widow of a peer.

peer evaluation *n* a review or assessment by people of about the same age or status: *Part of your final score will come from peer evaluation.* Also called **peer assessment, peer review**.

peer group *n* the people of about the same age or status within a culture or community: *As a boy, he was heavily influenced by his peer group at school.*

peer·less (pēr′lis) *adj* without an equal: *She was a peerless leader of our country.*

peer pressure *n* pressure to conform, exerted by those of the same age or status.

peer–to–peer (pēr′tə pēr′) *Computers adj* to do with a computer network in which each computer has access to all the files, software, and peripheral devices of all the others. *Abbrev.* **P2P** Compare CLIENT-SERVER NETWORK.

peeve (pēv) *Informal v* **peeved, peev·ing** annoy or irritate.
n an annoyance or irritation. <*peevish*>

pee·vee (pē′vē) PEAVEY.

pee·vish (pē′vish) *adj* cross, fretful, or complaining. <Middle English> **pee′vish·ly** *adv.* **pee′vish·ness** *n.*

pee·wee (pē′wē) *n* **1** a very small person or thing. **2** in amateur sports, a player aged 12 or 13. <*pewee* a small bird>

peg (peg) *n* **1** a pin or small bolt of wood, metal, or plastic used to fasten parts together, to hang things on, to stop a hole, to make fast a rope or string, or to mark the score in a game. **2** a clothespeg.
v **pegged, peg·ging** **1** fasten, mark, or hold with pegs: *to peg down a tent.* **2** fix a price, rate, or amount at a certain level: *to peg wages.* **3** work hard and steadily: *She pegged away at her studies and earned high marks.* <origin uncertain>
square peg in a round hole, a person or thing in a totally unsuitable position.
take someone down a peg, make someone realize that they are less important than they think they are.

peg·board (peg′bȯrd′) *n* a board with evenly spaced holes in which pegs or hooks are inserted to hold things.

peg leg *n* **1** *Informal* an artificial leg. **2** *Offensive* a person who has an artificial leg.

peg·ma·tite (peg′mə tīt) *n* a type of granite, sometimes rich in rare minerals like uranium.

Pei·gan (pē′gan) PIIKANI.

pei·gnoir (pān wor′) *n* a woman's light dressing gown. <French, from Latin *pectinare* to comb. In the past this garment was worn when the hair was being combed.>

pe·jor·a·tive (pi jor′ə tiv), (pe jor′ə tiv), *or* (pē jor′ə tiv) *adj* contemptuous or disapproving: *a pejorative account, a pejorative name.*
n a pejorative word or expression. <French, from Latin *pejor* worse>

Pe·king·ese (pē′ki nēz′) *for n,* (pē′king ēz′) *for adj. n, pl* **Pe·king·ese** a small dog with long, soft hair and a flat nose whose breed was originally developed in China.
adj to do with Beijing, its people, or their culture or cuisine. Beijing was formerly spelled Peking.

pe·koe (pē′kō) *n* a black tea made from young leaves.

pelf (pelf) *Archaic n* money or riches, especially when gained in a dishonest or dishonourable way. <Old French *pelfre* spoils>

pel·i·can (pel′ə kən) *n* a large water bird with a huge bill. This has a pouch on the underside for scooping up and holding fish. <Greek *pelekan*>

pe·lisse (pə lēs′) *n* in former times, a coat or long cloak, often lined or trimmed with fur.

pel·let (pel′it) *n* **1** a little compressed ball of a substance, such as paper, mud, medicine, or compressed food for animals. **2** a small piece of shot or lightweight bullet. <Old French, from Latin *pila* ball>

pell–mell (pel′mel′) *adv* in a rushing, tumbling mass or crowd: *The children dashed pell-mell down the beach and into the waves.*
adj recklessly hasty or disorganized.
n hasty disorder or confusion. <French reduplication *pêle-mêle*, from *mêler* mix>

pel·lu·cid (pə lū′sid) *adj* **1** transparent: *a pellucid stream.* **2** clearly expressed: *pellucid language.* <Latin *per-* through + *lucere* to shine>

Pel·o·pon·ne·sian (pel′ə pə nē′shən) *adj* to do with the Peloponnesus, a mountainous peninsula in southern Greece, or its people.

pelt[1] (pelt) *v* **1** attack by repeatedly throwing things at: *The boys were pelting the dog with stones.* **2** fall quickly and heavily as snow, rain, or hail. **3** run quickly: *He pelted after me.* <origin unknown>
at full pelt, as fast as possible: *She ran at full pelt across the parking lot.*

pelt[2] (pelt) *n* the skin of a fur-bearing animal with the fur, wool, or hair still on. <Old French, from Latin *pellis* skin>

pel·vis (pel′vis) *n* the basin-shaped structure in many vertebrates formed by the hipbones and the end of the backbone. <Latin = basin> **pel′vic** *adj.*

🍁 **pem·mi·can** (pem′ə kən) *n* dried, lean meat pounded into a paste with melted fat, formerly used by Aboriginal peoples and explorers.

ETYMOLOGY

Pemmican comes from the Cree words *pimii*, meaning "fat" + *-kan*, meaning "prepared."

Pemmican was often used in trade.

pen[1] (pen) *n* **1** a writing instrument supplying a continuous flow of ink, such as a fountain pen, ballpoint, or felt-tip pen. **2** *Computers* an electronic penlike device used to enter commands or data. **3** writing as an occupation: *She makes her living with her pen.*
v **penned, pen·ning** write: *He penned a few lines to his mother.* <Old French, from Latin *penna* feather, since the first pens were made from feathers, or quills>
pen′like′ *adj.*

pen² (pen) *n* **1** a small, closed yard for keeping livestock or domestic animals in. **2** the animals in a pen. **3** a small place of confinement. **4** *Slang* a penitentiary.
v **penned** or **pent, pen·ning 1** shut in a pen. **2** confine closely: *I kept the dog penned in a corner while they hunted for the leash.* <Old English *penn*> **pen′like′** *adj.*

pen³ (pen) *n* a female swan. <origin unknown>

pe·nal (pē′nəl) *adj* **1** to do with punishment: *penal laws, penal labour.* **2** liable to be punished: *Robbery is a penal offence.* **3** used as a prison or place of punishment: *a penal colony.* <Latin *poena* penalty>

penal code *n* a collection of laws and the penalties for breaking them.

pe·nal·ize (pē′nə līz′) *or* (pen′ə līz′) *v* **pe·nal·ized, pe·nal·iz·ing 1** declare punishable by law or by a rule: *Fouls are penalized in many games.* **2** inflict a penalty on: *Our team was penalized five yards.*

pen·al·ty (pen′əl tē) *n, pl* **pen·al·ties 1** a punishment for breaking a law or rule: *The penalty for speeding was a fine.* **2** a disadvantage imposed on a side or player for breaking the rules of a sport or game. **3** a disadvantage attached to some act or condition: *the penalties of old age.*

❋ **penalty box** *n* a special bench in hockey or lacrosse where players awarded penalties spend their time off the ice or field.

In soccer tournament competition, if the score remains tied after an overtime has been played, the game is decided by having individual players from each team alternate **penalty kicks,** 11 m away from the goal, defended only by the goalkeeper.

If a player kicks, holds, or trips an opponent, the opponent is awarded a **free kick** from the point where the violation occurred.

penalty kick *Soccer n* a free kick on the goal defended only by the goalkeeper, awarded when a defensive player has committed a foul in the penalty area.

pen·al·ty–kil·ler (pen′əl tē kil′ər) *Hockey n* a player put on the ice when the team is shorthanded because of a penalty. The penalty-killer controls the puck as much as possible to prevent scoring by the other side.

penalty shot *Hockey n* a shot on goal, with only the goaltender defending. Once the shot is taken, the play is over, so a goal cannot be scored on a rebound.

pen·ance (pen′əns) *n* **1** a voluntary punishment to show regret for having done wrong. **2** *Catholicism* the sacrament in which a member of the church confesses sins to a priest and is given absolution, or the duty or observance required of the person as part of this sacrament. <Old French, from Latin *paenitere* be sorry>
do penance, perform some duty or observance as an act of regret for having done wrong.

pence (pens) plural of PENNY (def. 2b).

pen·chant (pen′chənt) *n* a strong taste or liking for something: *a penchant for taking long walks.* <French, from Latin *pendere* to hang>

pen·cil (pen′səl) *n* **1** a pointed tool for writing or drawing, with a long, thin piece of black or coloured material in the centre. **2** an object of a similar shape. **3** a stick of colouring matter, such as a cosmetic: *eyebrow pencil.*
v **pen·cilled** or **pen·ciled, pen·cil·ling** or **pen·cil·ing** mark, write, or draw with a pencil. <Old French, from Latin *penicillus* paintbrush>
pencil someone in, make a tentative arrangement with or for someone, as by writing on a calendar: *When can I pencil you in for an interview?*
pencil something in, a fill in an area or shape with pencil strokes. **b** arrange or note down something tentatively: *September 30 was pencilled in as the appointment date.*

pend·ant (pen′dənt) *n* **1** a hanging ornament, especially one attached to an earring, necklace, or bracelet. **2** an ornament hanging down from a ceiling or roof. <Old French, from Latin *pendere* to hang>

pend·ing (pen′ding) *adj* waiting to be decided or settled: *while the agreement was pending.*
prep **1** while waiting for: *Pending his return, let us get everything ready.* **2** about to happen: *An election was pending.* <French, from Latin *pendere* hang>

pen·du·lous (pen′jə ləs) *or* (pen′dyə ləs) *adj* **1** hanging down loosely: *pendulous jowls.* **2** suspended so as to swing freely. <Latin *pendere* hang> **pen′du·lous·ly** *adv.* **pen′du·lous·ness** *n.*

pen·du·lum (pen′jə ləm) *or* (pen′dyə ləm) *n* a weight hung from a fixed point so as to swing freely to and fro under the forces of gravity and momentum.

pe·ne·plain (pēn′ə plān) *n* a formerly mountainous or hilly area reduced nearly to a plain by erosion. The Canadian Shield is a peneplain. <Latin *paene* almost>

pen·e·trate (pen′ə trāt′) *v* **pen·e·trat·ed, pen·e·trat·ing 1** pass into or through: *The iceberg penetrated the ship's hull.* **2** force through: *Our eyes could not penetrate the darkness. Even where the trees were thickest, the sunshine penetrated.* **3** soak or spread through: *The damp penetrated the whole house.* **4** see into or understand: *I could not penetrate the mystery.* <Latin *penitus* inner> **pen′e·tra·bil′i·ty** *n.* **pen′e·tra·ble** (pen′ə trə bəl) *adj.*

a bat	e bed	i bid	o pot	u cup	th **thin**
ā cake	ē me	ī bite	ō go	ū rude	TH **then**
à bar	ə about	ər over	ȯ for	u̇ put	zh measure

P

pen·e·trat·ing (pen′ə trā′ting) *adj* **1** sharp and piercing as a sound: *a penetrating scream.* **2** acute or keen: *a penetrating insight.* **3** able to penetrate: *penetrating oil.* **pen′e·trat′ing·ly** *adv.*

pen·e·tra·tion (pen′ə trā′shən) *n* **1** the act or power of penetrating something. **2** the act of entering a country and gaining influence there. **3** the depth to which something penetrates. **4** the ability to understand deeply: *a mind of great acuteness and penetration.*

pen·guin (pen′gwin) *or* (peng′gwin) *n* a flightless seabird of the southern hemisphere, with wings modified into flippers, which are used for diving and swimming. <origin unknown>

pen·hold·er (pen′hōl′dər) *n* a stand or rack for a pen or pens.

pen·i·cil·lin (pen′ə sil′ən) *n* an antibiotic acid that is produced by moulds or synthetically. <Latin *penicillum* paintbrush, because the penicillium cells resemble small brushes>

pen·in·su·la (pə nin′sə lə) *or* (pə nin′syə lə) *n* a piece of land almost surrounded by water. <Latin *paene* almost + *insula* island> **pen·in′su·lar** *adj.*

pe·nis (pē′nis) *n* the male sex organ, that, in mammals, is also the organ through which urine is excreted. <Latin = tail> **pen′ile** (pē′nīl) *adj.*

pen·i·tence (pen′ə təns) *n* regret for having done wrong. <Old French, from Latin *paenitere* repent>

pen·i·tent (pen′ə tənt) *adj* sorry for having done wrong.
n **1** a person who is sorry for having done wrong. **2** *Catholicism* a church member who confesses and does penance for having done wrong.
pen′i·tent·ly *adv.*

pen·i·ten·tial (pen′ə ten′shəl) *adj* to do with penitence: *The penitential psalms express remorse for sin.*

pen·i·ten·tia·ry (pen′ə ten′shə rē) *n, pl* **pen·i·ten·tia·ries** a prison, especially a federal prison for people convicted of serious crimes.
adj making one liable to imprisonment: *a penitentiary offence.* <Latin *paenitere* repent>

pen·knife (pen′nīf′) *n, pl* **pen·knives** (pen′nīvz′) a small folding pocketknife.

pen·man·ship (pen′mən ship′) *n* **1** skill in writing with a pen or pencil. **2** a style of handwriting.

pen name *n* a name used by a writer instead of his or her real name. The French version of this is **nom de plume** (nom də plūm).

pen·nant (pen′ənt) *n* a flag, usually narrow and tapering, used on ships for signalling, or as a school or athletics banner: *Our team won the baseball pennant.* <origin uncertain>

pen·ni·less (pen′i lis) *adj* with no money.

Penn·syl·van·ia Dutch (pen′səl vā′nē ə) *adj* to do with the descendants of immigrants to Pennsylvania from southern Germany and Switzerland, some of whom settled in Upper Canada after the American Revolution, or the form of German spoken by these people.

pen·ny (pen′ē) *n, pl* **pen·nies 1** a piece or sum of money: *I wouldn't give him a penny.* **2** *Canada, US* one cent. **3 pence**, *pl* **pence** *UK* a coin and monetary unit equal to one-hundredth of a pound. <Old English *pening*>
a penny for your thoughts, what are you thinking about?
a pretty penny, *Informal* a large sum of money.
in for a penny, in for a pound, do everything possible, if it's to be done at all.
turn an honest penny, earn money honestly.

pen·ny–pinch·ing (pen′ē pinch′ing) *adj* stingy or miserly.
n habitual stinginess.

pen·ny–wise (pen′ē wīz′) *adj* thrifty in regard to small sums.
penny-wise and pound-foolish, thrifty in small expenses and wasteful in big ones.

pen·ny·worth (pen′ē wərth′) *n* as much as can be bought for a penny.

pe·nol·o·gy (pē nol′ə jē) *n* the study of the treatment of criminals and the management of prisons. <Greek *poena* penalty>

pen pal *n* a person with whom one develops a friendship by correspondence.

pen·sion (pen′shən) *n* money other than wages paid regularly to a person after a resignation or retirement from regular work, or sometimes as compensation.
v give a pension to. <Old French, from Latin *pendere* to pay>
pension off, retire someone from service, with a pension.

pen·sion·er (pen′shə nər) *n* a person who receives or lives on a pension.

pen·sive (pen′siv) *adj* thoughtful in a serious or sad way: *She was in a pensive mood, and sat staring out of the window.* <Old French, from Latin *pendere* weigh> **pen′sive·ly** *adv.* **pen′sive·ness** *n.*

pent (pent) PENT-UP.

penta– *combining form* five: *pentagon.* Also, **pent-**. <Greek *pente*>

pen·ta·gon (pen′tə gon′) *n* **1** *Mathematics* a plane figure with five sides and five interior angles. **2 the Pentagon** in the US, a building that is the headquarters of the Department of Defense, just outside Washington, D.C., or the department itself.

pen·tag·o·nal (pen tag′ə nəl) *adj* with five sides and five interior angles.

pen·ta·gram (pen′tə gram) *n* a five-pointed star, sometimes used as a magical symbol.

pen·ta·he·dron (pen′tə hē′drən) *n, pl* **pen·ta·he·drons** or **pen·ta·he·dra** (-drə) a solid figure with five plane faces.

pen·tam·e·ter (pen tam′ə tər) *n* a line of verse consisting of five metrical feet. Example: *A lit′tle learn′ing is′ a dan′g'rous thing′.* <penta- five + *meter*>

pen·tath·lete (pen tath′lēt) *n* an athlete who competes in the **pentathlon**, an athletic contest consisting of five different events, in which the person with the highest total score wins. The **modern pentathlon** includes fencing, riding, shooting, cross-country running, and swimming.

pen·ta·ton·ic scale (pen′tə ton′ik) *Music n* a scale with only five tones, consisting of the tonic and the second, third, fifth, and sixth intervals.

Pen·te·cost (pen′tə kost′) *n* **1** *Christianity* the seventh Sunday after Easter, a festival in memory of the descent of the Holy Ghost on the Apostles. Also called **Whitsunday**. **2** *Judaism* the festival of SHAVUOTH. <Greek *pentekoste* fiftieth (day)>

Pen·te·cost·al (pen′tə kost′əl) *Christianity n* **1** to do with the Pentecost. **2** to do with the Protestant churches that emphasize baptism by the Holy Spirit.

pent·house (pent′hous′) *n* an apartment or house built on the top of a building, usually luxurious and with a fine view. <Old French, from Latin *appendere* hang on>

pent–up (pen′tup′) *adj* shut up or closely confined: *Her pent-up feelings could no longer be restrained, and she burst into tears.* Also, **pent**.

pe·nul·ti·mate (pi nul′tə mit) *adj* next to the last in a series. <Latin *paene* almost + *ultimus* last>

pe·num·bra (pi num′brə) *n, pl* **pe·num·bras** or **pe·num·brae** (-brē) *or* (brī) the shadow formed by the sun or moon during a partial eclipse. See ECLIPSE for picture. <Latin *paene* almost + *umbra* shadow>

pe·nu·ri·ous (pi nyü′rē əs) *or* (pi nü′rē əs) *adj* characteristic of or suffering from poverty: *penurious surroundings.* **pe·nu′ri·ous·ly** *adv.* **pe·nu′ri·ous·ness** *n.*

pen·u·ry (pen′yə rē) *n* very great poverty. <Latin *penuria*>

pe·on (pē′on) *n* **1** in Spanish America, a labourer or unskilled farm worker. **2** a person with little power who does hard work for low wages. <Portuguese, from Latin *pedonem* foot soldier>

pe·o·ny (pē′ə nē) *n, pl* **pe·o·nies** a perennial garden plant with large, usually fragrant, flowers. <Greek *Paion* physician of the gods, so named because the plant was used in medicine>

peo·ple (pē′pəl) *n, pl* **peo·ple** or (for def. 2) **peo·ples** **1** human beings: *There were ten people present.* **2** the men, women, and children of a particular nation, culture, community, or ethnic group: *the Canadian people, the peoples of Asia.* **3** the people of a place, class, or social group: *city people, prairie people.* **4 the people** those without special status, power, or authority: *The politician claimed to be a man of the people.* **5** people in relation to a superior: *A queen rules over her people.* **6** family or relatives.

v **peo·pled, peo·pling** fill or provide with people: *Newcomers peopled the wilderness.* <Latin *populus*>

peo·ple–watch·ing (pē′pəl wotch′ing) *n* the pastime of observing people in public places. **peo′ple-watch′er** *n.*

pep (pep) *Informal n* energy or enthusiasm.

v **pepped, pep·ping** (*with* ***up***) fill or inspire with energy or enthusiasm: *to pep up a party.* <*pepper*>

pep·lum (pep′ləm) *n* **1** a short flared, gathered, or pleated piece of material attached to the waistline of a jacket, blouse, or dress and extending to the hips. **2** a loose outer garment worn by women in ancient Greece.

pep·per (pep′ər) *n* **1** a seasoning with a hot taste, made from the ground-up berries of a tropical woody vine. See BLACK PEPPER, WHITE PEPPER. **2** the hollow fruit of a capsicum plant, eaten raw, cooked, or pickled. **3** the small, hot-tasting fruit of other capsicums, such as cayenne or chili. See CHILI for picture.

v **1** season or sprinkle with black or white pepper. **2** sprinkle thickly: *Her face is peppered with freckles.* **3** hit with small objects sent thick and fast: *We peppered the others with snowballs.* <Latin, from Greek *peperi*>

pep·per·corn (pep′ər kôrn′) *n* a dried berry of the pepper plant that is ground up to make black or white pepper.

pep·per·mint (pep′ər mint′) *n* **1** a plant of the mint family that yields a sweet-smelling oil used in medicine and as a flavouring. **2** candy flavoured with peppermint oil.

pep·per·o·ni (pep′ə rō′nē) *n* a spicy Italian sausage, often put on pizza.

pep·per·y (pep′ə rē) *adj* **1** of, like, or full of pepper: *a peppery stew.* **2** sharp or pungent. **3** easily made angry. **pep′per·i·ness** *n.*

pep·py (pep′ē) *Informal adj* **pep·pi·er, pep·pi·est** energetic. **pep′pi·ness** *n.*

pep rally *Informal n* a meeting organized to stimulate support and enthusiasm for a team, cause, or campaign.

pep·sin (pep′sən) *n* **1** an enzyme in the gastric juice of the stomach that helps to digest meat, eggs, cheese, and other proteins. **2** a medicine to help digestion, containing this enzyme. <Greek *pepsis* digestion>

pep talk *Informal n* a short, emotional talk intended to encourage a person or group in some activity: *The coach gave us a pep talk before the game.*

pep·tic (pep′tik) *adj* **1** promoting digestion, especially with the aid of pepsin. **2** to do with the action of digestive juices: *a peptic ulcer.*

pep·tide (pep′tīd′) *Biochemistry n* a compound made up of two or more amino acids chemically bonded together. <German *Peptid*, back-formation from *polypeptide*>

Pé·quiste (pā kēst′) *n* a member or supporter of the Parti Québécois. <French>

per (pər) *prep* **1** for each: *The recipe calls for 125 grams of ground beef per person.* **2** by, through, or by means of: *The letter was sent per messenger.* **3** according to: *a payment calculated per number of children in the family. The order was sent out as per instructions.* <Latin = through, by means of>

per·am·bu·late (pə ram′byə lāt′) *v* **per·am·bu·lat·ed, per·am·bu·lat·ing** walk through or about a place or area: *perambulating the street.* **per·am′bu·la′tion** *n.*

per·am·bu·la·tor (pə ram′byə lā′tər) *UK n* a baby carriage.

per an·num (pər an′əm) *adv* yearly: *Her salary was $34 000 per annum.*

per·cale (pər kāl′) *n* a smooth, firm, cotton cloth in a close weave and in different thicknesses.

a bat	e bed	i bid	o pot	u cup	th **thin**
ā cake	ē me	ī bite	ō go	ū rude	ᴛʜ **then**
ä bar	ə about	ər over	ô for	ü put	zh measure

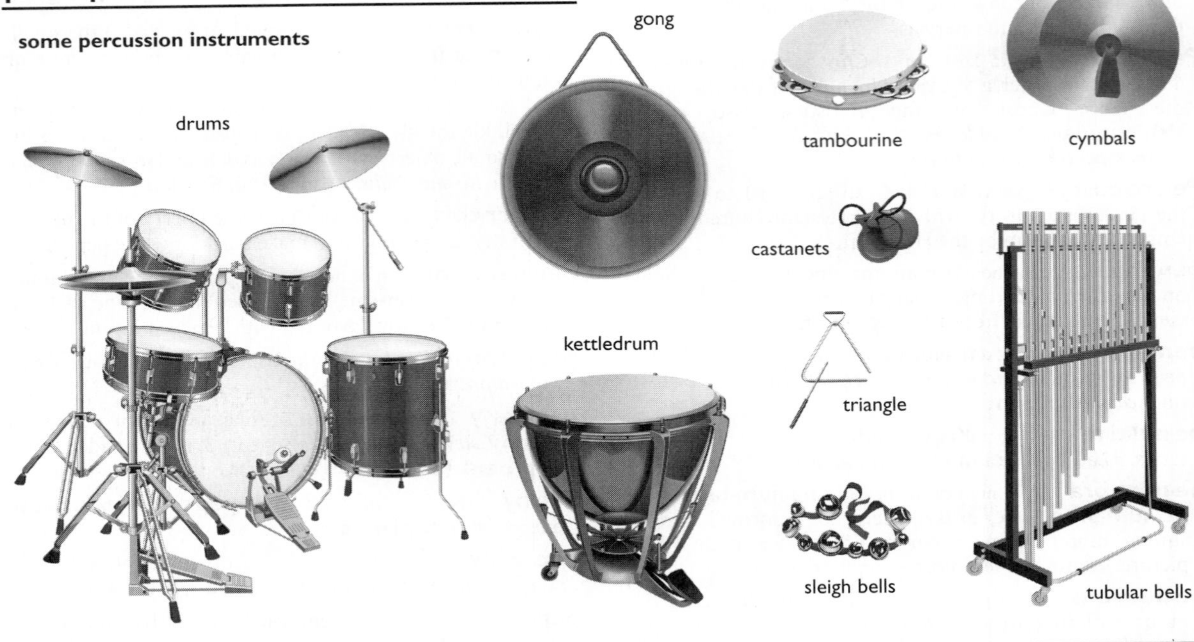

per cap·i·ta (pər kap′ə tə) *adj, adv* for each person: *$40 for eight people amounts to $5 per capita.*

per·ceive (pər sēv′) *v* **per·ceived, per·ceiv·ing** **1** be aware of through one of the senses: *Did you perceive the drop in temperature?* **2** become aware or conscious of something: *I perceived that I could not make her change her mind.* <Old French, from Latin *per-* fully + *capere* to grasp>

per·cent or **per cent** (pər sent′) *n* **1** hundredths: *Five percent is 5 out of 100. Symbol* **%** **2** for or in each hundred: *Seven percent of the children failed.* <Latin *per centum* for each hundred>

per·cent·age (pər sen′tij) *n* **1** the rate or proportion in each hundred units: *What percentage of children were absent?* **2** a part or proportion: *A large percentage of schoolbooks now have pictures.*

per·cen·tile (pər sen′tīl) *n* a value in a series of points on a scale arrived at by dividing a group into 100 equal parts. For example, a test score equal to, or more than, 90 percent is in the 90th percentile.

per·cept (pər′sept) *n* an object of perception.

per·cep·ti·ble (pər sep′tə bəl) *adj* able to be seen or noticed, especially by means of a slight movement or change: *The other ship was barely perceptible in the fog.* **per·cep′ti·bly** *adv.*

per·cep·tion (pər sep′shən) *n* **1** the ability to see, hear, or become aware of something through the senses. **2** the process of becoming aware of something through the senses: *keen perception.* **3** a strong mental impression: *Having a clear perception of what was wrong, he soon corrected it.*

per·cep·tive (pər sep′tiv) *adj* with or showing sensitive insight. **per·cep′tive·ly** *adv.* **per·cep′tive·ness** *n.*

perch[1] (pərch) *n* **1** a bar, branch, or anything else on which a bird can alight and remain. **2** a place, typically high, where someone or something rests or remains.
v **1** alight and remain: *A robin perched on our porch railing.* **2** sit, especially on something high: *She perched on a stool.* **3** be located in a high position: *The village was perched on a hill.* <Old French, from Latin *pertica* pole> **perch′er** *n.*

perch[2] (pərch) *n, pl* **perch·es** or (*especially collectively*) **perch** **1** a small freshwater food fish with a high, spiny dorsal fin and orange lower fins. **2** a member of a family of freshwater fishes including the perch and the walleye, or a freshwater or saltwater fish resembling one of this family. <Old French, from Greek *perke*>

per·chance (pər chans′) *Archaic, Poetic, or Humorous adv* perhaps. <Old French *par chance* by chance>

per·co·late (pər′kə lāt′) *v* **per·co·lat·ed, per·co·lat·ing** **1** drip or drain through small holes or spaces as a liquid or gas. **2** spread gradually as an idea, feeling, or piece of information: *News of her promotion percolated through the company.* **3** make coffee in a percolator. <Latin *per-* through + *colum* strainer>

per·co·la·tor (pər′kə lā′tər) *n* a coffee pot in which boiling water continually bubbles up through a tube and drips down through ground coffee.

per·cus·sion (pər kush′ən) *n* **1 a** the striking of one object against another with force: *Caps are exploded by percussion.* **b** the shock made by the striking of one object against another. **2** *Medicine* the technique of tapping a part of the body as part of a diagnosis. **3** *Music* a percussion instrument or group of such instruments. <Latin *per-* through + *quatere* to strike>

percussion instrument *n* a musical instrument played by striking it, such as a drum or cymbal.

per di·em (pər dē′əm) *or* (pər dī′əm) *adj, adv* per day.
n an allowance of money made each day: *a fixed salary plus travel expenses and a per diem of $50 for food.* <Latin>

per·di·tion (pər dish′ən) *n* in some Christian beliefs, a state after death in which a sinner who is not sorry for having done wrong is condemned to eternal punishment. <Latin *perdere* destroy>

per·e·gri·nate (per′ə grə nāt′) *v* **per·e·gri·nat·ed, per·e·gri·nat·ing** travel or wander from place to place. <Latin *per-* through + *ager* field> **per′e·gri·na′tion** *n.*

per·e·grine (per′ə grin) *or* (per′ə grēn) *n* a large powerful falcon, used in FALCONRY. <Latin *peregrinus* from foreign lands, because falcons were caught during migration rather than taken from their nests>

per·emp·to·ry (pə remp′tə rē) *adj* insisting on immediate attention or obedience: *a peremptory command.* <Latin *per-* completely + *emere* take> **per·emp′to·ri·ly** *adv.* **per·emp′to·ri·ness** *n.*

per·en·ni·al (pə ren′ē əl) *adj* **1** lasting for a very long or apparently infinite period of time: *the perennial beauty of the hills.* **2** with underground parts that live for several years: *perennial garden plants.* **3** continually occurring, especially as a difficulty: *a perennial problem.*
n a perennial plant: *a hardy perennial.* <Latin *per-* through + *annus* year> **per·en′ni·al·ly** *adv.*

per·e·stroi·ka (per′ i stroi′ kə) *n* a plan for economic and political reform in the 1980s in the former Soviet Union. <Russian = restructuring>

per·fect (pər′fikt) *for adj or n,* (pər fekt′) *for v. adj* **1** without any defects: *a perfect exam result.* **2** completely skilled: *a perfect golfer.* **3** with all its parts complete: *The set of dishes was perfect, with nothing missing or broken.* **4** entire or total: *a perfect stranger to us.* **5** exact: *a perfect copy.*
v remove all faults or defects from something: *to perfect an invention. The artist was perfecting her picture.* <Old French, from Latin *per-* fully + *facere* do> **perfect′er** *n.*

SYNONYMS

Perfect means "without defect": *She drew a perfect circle with the aid of a compass.*

Flawless suggests having nothing that lessens the value or beauty of something: *The gymnast gave a flawless performance and earned a perfect score.*

Impeccable suggests faultless, especially in performance: *The chef cooked an impeccable meal for the wedding reception.*

per·fect·i·ble (pər fek′tə bəl) *adj* capable of becoming or being made perfect.

per·fec·tion (pər fek′shən) *n* **1** a condition or quality without flaws or defects. **2** a perfect person or thing: *Her work is always perfection.* **3** the action or process of making complete or perfect: *The perfection of our plans will take another week.*
to perfection, perfectly: *He played the violin concerto to perfection.*

per·fec·tion·ist (pər fek′shə nist) *n* a person who is not content with anything that is not perfect or nearly perfect. **per·fec′tion·ism** *n.*

per·fect·ly (pər′fik tlē) *adv* **1** in a perfect manner or degree: *a perfectly drawn circle.* **2** to an adequate extent: *This winter coat is still perfectly good.*

perfect participle *Grammar n* a past participle preceded by a form of the verb *have,* expressing action completed before the time of speaking or acting. Example: In *Having written the letter, she e-mailed it,* the perfect participle is *having written.*

perfect pitch *Music n* absolute pitch.

perfect square SQUARE NUMBER.

perfect tense *Grammar n* the verb tense used to indicate the completion of an action.

GRAMMAR AND USAGE

The **present perfect tense** is formed by *has* or *have* and a past participle, and shows an action that has been completed at the time of speaking:
They have gone to the movies.

The **past perfect tense** is formed by *had* and a past participle, and shows an action that was completed before another action or time in the past:
He had learned to read by the time he went to school.

The **future perfect tense** is formed by *will have* or *shall have* and a past participle, and shows an action that will already have been completed at a future time:
She will have done it by tonight.

per·fid·i·ous (pər fid′ē əs) *adj* deceitful and untrustworthy. <Latin *per-* away from + *fides* faith, trust> **per·fid′i·ous·ly** *adv.* **per′fi·dy** *n.*

per·fo·rate (pər′fə rāt′) *v* **per·fo·rat·ed, per·fo·rat·ing** **1** make a hole or holes through: *Perforate the paper with this hole punch.* **2** make a series of small holes through in order to make separation easier: *Sheets of postage stamps are perforated.* <Latin *per-* through + *forare* pierce>

P

per·fo·ra·tion (pər′fə rā′shən) *n* **1** a hole or series of holes bored or punched through something: *She removed the coupon by tearing along the perforation.* **2** the action or condition of being perforated.

per·force (pər fôrs′) *adv* by necessity; inevitably. <Old French *par force* by force>

per·form (pər fôrm′) *v* **1** do or carry out: *The surgeon performed an operation.* **2** act, play, sing, or entertain in public. <Old French *par-* fully + *fournir* provide>

per·form·ance (pər fôr′məns) *n* **1** the act of carrying out or doing something: *in the performance of your duties.* **2** an act, task, or operation viewed as having been successfully or badly performed: *a disgraceful performance.* **3** the act of giving a public entertainment: *The evening performance is at eight o'clock.*

a bat	e bed	i bid	o pot	u cup	th thin
ā cake	ē me	ī bite	ō go	ū rude	TH then
ä bar	ə about	ər over	ô for	ů put	zh measure

per·form·er (pər fôr′mər) *n* a person who performs for the entertainment of others.

per·form·ing arts (pər fôr′ming) *n* drama, dance, and music performed for an audience.

per·fume (pər′fyūm) *or* (pər fyūm′) *for n,* (pər fyūm′) *for v.* *n* **1** the scent of something that smells sweet: *the perfume of flowers.* **2** a substance with a sweet smell, especially a liquid prepared from essences of flowers or from synthetic substances and applied to the skin or clothes to produce a pleasant scent.
v **per·fumed, per·fum·ing 1** fill with a sweet odour: *Flowers perfumed the air.* **2** put a sweet-smelling liquid on something. <French, from Latin *per-* through + *fumus* smoke>

per·fum·er (pər fyū′mər) *n* a maker or seller of perfumes.

per·fum·er·y (pər fyū′mə rē) *n, pl* **per·fum·er·ies 1** the products made by a perfumer. **2** a place where perfumes are sold.

per·func·to·ry (pər fungk′tə rē) *adj* done with little physical or mental effort: *The little girl gave her face a perfunctory washing.* <Latin *perfungi* get through> **per·func′to·ri·ly** *adv.* **per·func′to·ri·ness** *n.*

per·haps (pər haps′) *adv* maybe or possibly: *Perhaps she'll do it if you ask her. It would perhaps be better to wait.* <Middle English>

peri– *prefix* **1** around or about: *perimeter.* **2** at a point nearest to a celestial body: *perigee.* <Greek = around, about>

per·i·car·di·um (per′ə kär′dē əm) *n, pl* **per·i·car·di·a** (-dē ə) the membrane enclosing the heart. **per′i·car′di·al** *adj.*

per·i·carp (per′ə kärp′) *n* the walls of a fruit formed from the wall of a ripened ovary.

per·i·gee (per′ə jē′) *n* **1** the point in the orbit of an earth satellite or earth-orbiting vehicle where it is closest to the earth. Compare APOGEE, PERIHELION. **2** the nearest or lowest point. <French, from Greek *peri-* near + *ge* earth>

per·i·he·li·on (per′ə hē′lē ən) *n, pl* **per·i·he·li·a** (-lē ə) the point in the orbit of a planet, comet, etc. where it is closest to the sun. Compare APHELION, PERIGEE. <Greek *peri-* near + *helios* sun>

per·il (per′əl) *n* exposure to danger or the risk of being injured or destroyed: *This bridge is not safe, and you cross it at your peril.*
v **per·illed** or **per·iled, per·il·ling** or **per·il·ing** put in danger. <Old French, from Latin *periculum* danger>

per·il·ous (per′ə ləs) *adj* full of dangers: *a perilous journey.* **per′il·ous·ly** *adv.*

pe·rim·e·ter (pə rim′ə tər) *n* **1** the outer boundary of a plane figure or an area: *the perimeter of a circle. A fence marked the perimeter of the field.* **2** the distance around such a boundary: *The perimeter of a square equals four times the length of one side.* <Latin, from Greek *peri-* around + *metron* measure>

per·i·na·tal (per′i nā′təl) *adj* to do with the period immediately before and after birth.

pe·ri·od (pē′rē əd) *n* **1** a portion of time, with distinctive features or conditions: *the period of the Great War. She visited us for a short period.* **2** a portion of time marked off by events that recur: *the period from one new moon to another.* **3** a division of geological time, shorter than an era and longer than an epoch. **4** the portion of a game during which there is actual play: *There are three twenty-minute periods in a hockey game.* **5** a portion of time into which part of a school day is divided. **6** a flow of blood and other material from the lining of the uterus that occurs in women who are of childbearing age but not pregnant, occurring at intervals of about one month. **7** a mark [.] of punctuation, marking the end of statements or showing an abbreviation. Examples: *Ms., Dec* **8** the interval of time between repeated occurrences in a cycle such as an alternating current. <Latin, from Greek *periodos* cycle>

GRAMMAR AND USAGE

A **period** coming at the end of a quotation is generally placed inside the quotation marks: *"What you see," he said, "is what you get."*

Periods should be used for abbreviations such as *Mr., Mrs.,* or *Dr.* Abbreviations of companies or organizations are sometimes written without periods: *CBC, NHL, RCMP.*

pe·ri·od·ic (pē′rē od′ik) *adj* **1** occurring, appearing, or done again and again at regular intervals: *periodic attacks of malaria.* **2** happening every now and then: *a periodic fit of clearing up my desk.* **pe′ri·od′i·cal·ly** *adv.*

pe·ri·od·i·cal (pē′rē od′ə kəl) *n* a magazine or newspaper that appears regularly: *a Canadian periodical.*
adj **1** occurring or appearing at intervals. **2** published at regular intervals, less often than daily.

pe·ri·o·dic·i·ty (pē′rē ə dis′ə tē) *n, pl* **pe·ri·o·dic·i·ties** the character or quality of recurring at intervals.

periodic sentence *Grammar n* a complex sentence with the main clause at the end. Example: In *When he was ready, he left the room,* the main clause is *he left the room.*

periodic table *Physics, Chemistry n* a table in which the elements, arranged in the order of their atomic weights, are shown in related groups.

per·i·o·don·tics (per′ ē ə don′tiks) *n (with singular verb)* the branch of dentistry that deals with the tissues or structures around the teeth. <Greek *peri-* around + *odontis* tooth> **per′i·o·don′tal** *adj.* **per′i·o·don′tist** *n.*

period piece *n* a work of art, such as a painting, novel, play, or building, that strongly evokes a particular period of history.

per·i·pa·tet·ic (per′ə pə tet′ik) *adj* travelling from place to place, especially working or living in places for relatively short periods. <Old French, from Greek *peri-* around + *patein* to walk>

pe·riph·er·al (pə rif′ə rəl) *adj* **1** to do with an outside boundary: *The wall marks the peripheral limits of the yard. The doctor checked my peripheral vision.* **2** *Computers* to do with hardware that is connected to a computer to make up a computer system. Printers, monitors, and disk drives are peripheral devices. **pe·riph′er·al·ly** *adv.*

peripheral nervous system *n* all the nerves in the body outside the brain and spinal cord. Compare CENTRAL NERVOUS SYSTEM.

peripheral vision *n* the field of vision outside the line of direct sight.

pe·riph·er·y (pə rif′ə rē) *n, pl* **pe·riph·er·ies** **1** an outside boundary: *The periphery of a circle is called the circumference.* **2** an area outside the centre or main area: *the periphery of a city.* **3** the area surrounding a nerve ending, such as a sense organ or muscle. <Latin, from Greek *peri-* around + *pharein* to carry>

per·i·scope (per′ə skōp′) *n* a device consisting of a tube with an arrangement of mirrors or prisms that permits a person to see things that are otherwise out of sight, such as from a submerged submarine. <Greek *peri* around + *skopein* look>

per·ish (per′ish) *v* **1** die or be destroyed, especially in a violent, sudden, or untimely way: *Several ships perished in the storm.* **2** decay or become spoiled: *Fruit will perish quickly in hot weather.* <Old French, from Latin *per-* away + *ire* go>

per·ish·a·ble (per′i shə bəl) *adj* liable to spoil or decay: *Fresh fruit is perishable.*
n **perishables** *pl* things that are liable to spoil or decay, especially fresh food: *We put the perishables into the refrigerator right away, but left the canned goods in the bag.* **per′ish·a·bil′i·ty** *n.* **per′ish·a·ble·ness** *n.*

per·i·stal·sis (per′ə stal′sis) *n, pl* **per·i·stal·ses** (-sēz) the successive wavelike contractions of the muscles of the intestines by which its contents are propelled onward. <Latin, from Greek *peri-* around + *stalsis* compression> **per′i·stal′tic** *adj.*

per·i·to·ne·um (per′ə tə nē′əm) *n, pl* **per·i·to·ne·a** (-nē′ə) the smooth, transparent membrane that lines the walls of the abdomen of a mammal and covers the organs in it. <Greek *peri-* around + *tenein* stretch> **per′i·to·ne′al** *adj.*

per·i·to·ni·tis (per′ə tə nī′tis) *n* inflammation of the peritoneum.

per·i·win·kle[1] (per′ə wing′kəl) *n* a low, trailing evergreen plant with blue, five-petalled flowers and glossy leaves. <Latin *pervinca*>

per·i·win·kle[2] (per′ə wing′kəl) *n* an edible sea snail with a thick, cone-shaped, spiral shell. <origin uncertain>

per·jure (pər′jər) *v* **per·jured, per·jur·ing** (*with a pronoun ending in* **-self**) make oneself guilty of making a false statement after having taken an oath: *The witness perjured herself at the trial.* <Old French, from Latin *per-* to ill effect + *jurare* swear>

per·jured (pər′jərd) *adj* **1** guilty of perjury: *a perjured witness.* **2** characterized by or involving perjury: *perjured evidence.*

per·ju·ry (pər′jə rē) *n, pl* **per·ju·ries** the offence of telling an untruth in a court after having taken an oath or affirmation to tell the truth. **per′jur·er** *n.*

perk[1] (pərk) *v* (*used with* **up**) become more cheerful or lively: *She perked up after she had eaten.* <origin uncertain>

perk[2] (pərk) *Informal v* **1** percolate: *to perk a pot of coffee. We could hear the coffee perking.* **2** be in a state of brisk activity: *A new tax cut will get the economy perking.*

perk[3] (pərk) *Informal n* additional money, goods, or some other benefit that is received and results directly from one's job or position, especially something promised or expected: *The secretary's perk was membership in the golf club.* <*perquisite*>

perk·y (pər′kē) *adj* **perk·i·er, perk·i·est** cheerful and lively: *a perky squirrel.* **perk′i·ly** *adv.* **perk′i·ness** *n.*

per·lite (pər′līt′) *n* volcanic glass with a pearl-like lustre, used for insulation and as a planting medium. <French *perle* pearl>

perm (pərm) *Informal n* a permanent wave.

per·ma·frost (pər′mə frost′) *n* ground or subsoil that is permanently frozen. <*perma(nent)* + *frost*>

per·ma·nent (pər′mə nənt) *adj* lasting or intended to last for a long period of time: *a permanent filling in a tooth. After doing odd jobs for a week, she got a permanent position as an assistant.*
n a permanent wave. <Latin *per-* through + *manere* stay> **per′ma·nence** *n.* **per′ma·nent·ly** *adv.*

permanent press *n* a chemical treatment given to fabric to make it resistant to creases and, often, to provide a garment with permanent pleats or folds. **permanent-press** *adj.*

🍁 **permanent resident** *n* a person admitted to Canada as a settler and potential Canadian citizen. Formerly called a **landed immigrant**.

permanent tooth *n* one of the second set of teeth in a mammal that follow the baby teeth.

permanent wave *n* a wave produced in the hair by chemicals or heat, that lasts even after the hair is washed many times.

per·me·a·ble (pər′mē ə bəl) *adj* allowing liquids or gases to pass through a substance. **per′me·a·bil′i·ty** *n.*

per·me·ate (pər′mē āt′) *v* **per·me·at·ed, per·me·at·ing** spread or diffuse through the whole of something: *The smell permeated the house. Anger permeated through the crowd.* <Latin *per-* through + *meare* pass> **per′me·a′tion** *n.*

Per·mi·an (pər′mi ən) *n* the geological period lasting from about 280 million to 250 million years ago, when there was major glaciation. See also PALEOZOIC.
adj to do with this period or the rocks formed then.

per·mis·si·ble (pər mis′ə bəl) *adj* able to be permitted. **per·mis′si·bly** *adv.*

per·mis·sion (pər mish′ən) *n* consent or authorization: *She asked the teacher's permission to go early.*

per·mis·sive (pər mis′iv) *adj* **1** allowing a great deal of freedom: *a permissive society, permissive grandparents.* **2** allowed in law but not obligatory: *a permissive statute.* **per·mis′sive·ly** *adv.* **per·mis′sive·ness** *n.*

a bat	e bed	i bid	o pot	u cup	th thin
ā cake	ē me	ī bite	ō go	ū rude	TH then
ȧ bar	ə about	ər over	ȯ for	ů put	zh measure

P

per·mit (pər mit′) *for v,* (pər′mit) *or* (pər mit′) *for n.* *v* **per·mit·ted, per·mit·ting** 1 allow or authorize a person to do something: *His mother permitted him to borrow her car when he was nineteen.* 2 let something be done or occur: *The law does not permit smoking here.*
n a formal written order giving permission to do something: *a permit to hunt.* <Latin *per-* through + *mittere* let go>

per·mu·ta·tion (pər′myə tā′shən) *n* 1 a changing of the order or arrangement of every element in a set of things. 2 such an arrangement or group. The permutations of *a, b,* and *c* are *abc, acb, bac, bca, cab, cba.* <Latin *per-* across + *mutare* change> **per′mu·tate** or **per·mute′** *v.*

per·ni·cious (pər nish′əs) *adj* with a harmful effect, especially in a gradual or subtle way: *pernicious habits.* <Latin *per-* completely + *nex* death> **per·ni′cious·ly** *adv.*

per·nick·e·ty or **per·snick·e·ty** (pər nik′ə tē), (pər snik′ə tē) *Informal adj* too concerned with minor or trivial details. <origin uncertain>

per·o·gy (pə rog′ē) *n, pl* **per·o·gies** pastries with a meat, cheese, or vegetable filling. <Ukrainian>

per·o·rate (per′ə rāt′) *v* **per·o·rat·ed, per·o·rat·ing** speak at length.

per·o·ra·tion (per′ə rā′shən) *n* the last part of an oration, summing up what has been said and intended to arouse enthusiasm. <Latin *per-* to an end + *orare* orate>

per·ox·ide (pə rok′sīd) *n* hydrogen peroxide.
v **per·ox·id·ed, per·ox·id·ing** bleach hair by applying hydrogen peroxide.
adj bleached with hydrogen peroxide: *a peroxide blonde.* <Latin *per-* fully + *oxide*>

per·pen·dic·u·lar (pər′pən dik′yə lər) *adj* at right angles to a given line, plane, or surface. A line is perpendicular to another when it makes a square corner with it: *a perpendicular cliff.*
n a perpendicular line, plane, or position. <Old French, from Latin *per-* through + *pendere* hang>

per·pe·trate (pər′pə trāt′) *v* **per·pe·trat·ed, per·pe·trat·ing** do or commit crime, fraud, or a bad or foolish act: *to perpetrate a robbery, to perpetrate a hoax.* <Latin *per-* fully + *patrare* carry out> **per′pe·tra′tion** *n.* **per′pe·tra′tor** *n.*

per·pet·u·al (pər pech′ū əl) *adj* 1 never ending or changing: *the perpetual hills.* 2 lasting throughout life: *a perpetual income.* 3 continuous: *a perpetual stream of visitors, perpetual motion.* <Latin *perpetis* continuous> **per·pet′u·al·ly** *adv.*

perpetual calendar *n* a calendar or table that allows one to find out the day of the week for any given date over a wide range of years.

per·pet·u·ate (pər pech′ū āt′) *v* **per·pet·u·at·ed, per·pet·u·at·ing** cause or attempt to cause something to last indefinitely: *perpetuate a species.* **per·pet′u·a′tion** *n.* **per·pet′u·a′tor** *n.*

per·pe·tu·i·ty (pər′pə tyū′ə tē) *or* (pər′pə tū′ə tē) *n, pl* **per·pe·tu·i·ties** the condition of lasting forever or for an indefinite period.
in perpetuity, forever.

per·plex (pər pleks′) *v* be so complicated or baffling that it cannot be thought about clearly or logically: *The problem is hard enough to perplex even the teacher.* <Latin *per-* completely + *plectere* intertwine> **per·plex′ing** *adj.* **per·plex′ing·ly** *adv.*

per·plexed (pər plekst′) *adj* not knowing what to do or how to act: *She was greatly perplexed by her friend's strange manner.*

per·plex·i·ty (pər plek′sə tē) *n, pl* **per·plex·i·ties** 1 the condition of being puzzled or of not knowing what to do or how to act: *His perplexity was so great that he had to ask for advice.* 2 something that perplexes: *There are many perplexities in that job.*

per se (pər sā′) *or* (pər sē′) *adv* in itself or themselves. <Latin>

per·se·cute (pər′sə kyūt′) *v* **per·se·cut·ed, per·se·cut·ing** 1 subject someone to harm or hostility, especially for religious, ethnic, or political reasons: *The child was persecuted by other children because of her background.* 2 annoy or harass: *She was persecuted with endless questions.* See PROSECUTE for confusable. <Old French, from Latin *persequi* to take vengeance upon> **per′se·cu′tion** *n.* **per′se·cu′tor** *n.*

Per·se·ids (pər′sē idz) *pln* the brilliant and extensive meteor showers that occur each year in August and appear to come from the constellation Perseus.

per·se·vere (pər′sə vēr′) *v* **per·se·vered, per·se·ver·ing** continue steadily in doing something difficult. <Old French, Latin *per-* completely + *severus* strict> **per′se·ver′ance** *n.* **per′se·ver′ing** *adj.* **per′se·ver′ing·ly** *adv.*

Per·sian (pər′zhən) *adj* to do with Persia (nowadays called Iran), a country in southwest Asia, its people, or their language.

Persian carpet *n* a rug woven in Iran or elsewhere that has a stylized design based on a traditional Persian pattern.

Persian cat *n* a cat of a breed with a broad, round head, short thick legs, a stocky body, and long hair.

Persian wheel *n* a water wheel with buckets attached to its rim, used to raise water from a stream, especially for transfer to an irrigation channel. Also called **noria.**

per·sim·mon (pər sim′ən) *n* a N American plumlike fruit, containing one to ten seeds, that is bitter when green but sweet when ripe, or the hardwood tree that bears this fruit. <Algonquian>

per·sist (pər sist′) *v* 1 continue firmly or stubbornly in an opinion or course of action: *My kid brother persists in eating with his fingers. She persisted till she had solved the difficult problem.* 2 last, especially past a usual, normal, or expected time: *The cold weather will persist for some time.* <Latin *per-* through + *sistere* to stand> **per·sist′ence** *n.*

per·sist·ent (pər sis′tənt) *adj* 1 with lasting qualities, especially in the face of dislike, disapproval, or difficulties: *a persistent worker, a persistent beggar.* 2 lasting, going on, or continuing: *a persistent headache.* **per·sist′ent·ly** *adv.*

per·snick·e·ty (pər′snik′ə tē) PERNICKETY.

per·son (pər′sən) *n* 1 a man, woman, or child considered as an individual: *Any person who wishes may go to the fair.* 2 a human body: *The person of the king was well guarded.*

3 bodily appearance: *He kept his person neat and trim.* **4** a change in a pronoun or verb to show the person speaking (**first person**), the person spoken to (**second person**), or the person or thing spoken of (**third person**). <Old French, from Latin *persona* individual>

in person, with or by one's own action or presence: *Don't just phone, go there in person.*

GRAMMAR AND USAGE

Person is the ordinary word for a human being of either sex: *A well-known person came into the room.*

Individual emphasizes the person's uniqueness: *A strange individual came into the room.*
This term can also be applied to animals and objects.

The phrase *a person* is sometimes used instead of the impersonal pronoun *one*, which can sound awkward and pretentious:

Exercise makes a person hungry. (preferred)

Exercise makes one hungry. (awkward)

–person *combining form* filling a certain duty, function, or relationship, often as a gender-neutral substitute for *-man* or *-woman*: *spokesperson, chairperson.*

per·so·na (pər sō′nə) *n, pl* **per·so·nas** or **per·so·nae** (-nē) *or* (-nī) a character or personality that a person adopts and presents to the public: *In private life, the premier drops his public persona.* <Latin = character>

per·son·a·ble (pər′sə nə bəl) *adj* with a pleasing appearance and personality: *a personable young man.*

per·son·age (pər′sə nij) *n* a person of importance or high status.

per·son·al (pər′sə nəl) *adj* **1** individual or private: *a personal letter.* **2** done in person: *a personal visit.* **3** to do with the body or bodily appearance: *personal beauty.* **4** about or against a person or people: *personal abuse.* **5** inclined to make remarks to or ask questions of others about their private affairs: *Don't be too personal.* **6** *Grammar* indicating one of the three persons: *personal pronoun.* **7** to do with possessions that can be moved, not land or buildings: *personal belongings.*
n a short advertisement or message in a newspaper about a particular person or people.

personal computer *n* a desktop computer designed for use by individuals at home or in an office, as opposed to a mainframe.

personal effects *pln* personal belongings normally worn or carried, such as clothing or cosmetics.

per·son·al·i·ty (pər′sə nal′ə tē) *n, pl* **per·son·al·i·ties** **1** the personal or individual quality that makes one person be different or act differently from another: *Her personality makes her a lady to be admired.* **2** a remark made about or against one particular person: *Tactful people avoid personalities.* **3** a person who is regularly faces the public in the course of work: *a TV personality.*

per·son·al·ize (pər′sə nə līz′) *v* **per·son·al·ized, per·son·al·iz·ing** make personal or individual.

per·son·al·ly (pər′sə nə lē) *adv* **1** in person: *The hostess personally greeted her guests.* **2** as far as oneself is concerned: *Personally, I like fruit better than nuts.* **3** as a person: *We like him personally, but we dislike his way of living.* **4** as being meant for oneself: *He intended no insult to you, so please do not take what he said personally.*

personal organizer *n* a loose-leaf notebook or a handheld, preprogrammed computer that is designed to keep track of appointments, addresses, and tasks.

personal pronoun *Grammar n* the person(s) speaking (*I, we*); the person(s) being spoken about (*he, she, it, they*); the person(s) addressed (*you*).

GRAMMAR AND USAGE

Remember to ensure that a **personal pronoun** fits the number (singular or plural) and gender (male or female) of the noun it replaces.

Singular pronouns: *I, me, you, he, she, him, her, it.*

Plural pronouns: *we, us, you, they, them.*

personal property *n* property that is temporary or movable.

A **personal watercraft** is powered by a jet of water that is forced through a nozzle at the rear of the boat. The handlebars turn the nozzle to provide steering.

personal watercraft *n* a small, motorized, recreational watercraft with a seat and handlebars.

P

per·so·na non gra·ta (pər sō′nə non′ grà′tə) *n* a person who is not acceptable or welcome. <Latin *persona* individual + *non* not + *gratus* pleasing>

per·son·i·fi·ca·tion (pər son′ə fə kā′shən) *n* **1** the representation of a thing or idea as a person or as having human qualities: *For fans, the football game personified a contest between good and evil.* **2** a person, creature, or divinity representing a thing or idea, such as a heart signifying love, or a lion, courage. **3** a person or thing seen as a striking example or embodiment of a quality or characteristic: *He was the personification of greed.*

per·son·i·fy (pər son′ə fī′) *v* **per·son·i·fied, per·son·i·fy·ing** **1** regard or represent as a person or as having human qualities: *The sea is often personified in poetry.* **2** be a representative of: *A lion personifies bravery.*

per·son·nel (pər′sə nel′) *n* people employed in work, business, or service: *All personnel must attend this meeting.*

a bat	e bed	i bid	o pot	u cup	th **thin**
ā cake	ē me	ī bite	ō go	ū rude	ᴛʜ **then**
à bar	ə about	ər over	ȯ for	ů put	zh measure

per·spec·tive (pər spek′tiv) *n* **1** the art of picturing objects on a flat surface so as to give the appearance of distance. **2** the effect of distance on the appearance of objects: *Railway tracks seem to meet at the horizon because of perspective.* **3** the effect that the distance of events has on the mind: *Many happenings of last year seem less important when viewed in perspective.* **4** a view of things or facts in which they are correct related to each other: *to have a good perspective on life.* <Latin *per-* through + *specere* look>
in (or **out of**) **perspective,** properly regarded (or not regarded) in terms of importance.

per·spi·ca·cious (pər′spə kā′shəs) *adj* keen in observing and understanding. <Latin *perspicere* look at closely> **per′spi·ca′ci·ty** *n.* **per′spi·ca′cious·ly** *adv.*

per·spire (pər spīr′) *v* **per·spired, per·spir·ing** sweat: *We perspire when we work hard on a hot day.* <French, from Latin *per-* through + *spirare* breathe>
per′spi·ra′tion (pər′spə rā′shən) *n.*

per·suade (pər swād′) *v* **per·suad·ed, per·suad·ing** cause a person to do or believe something by reasoning or argument: *I knew that I should have studied, but he persuaded me to go to the movies. They finally persuaded her of the truth of the rumour.* <Latin *per-* completely + *suadere* advise>

per·sua·sion (pər swā′zhən) *n* **1** the process of persuading someone to believe or do something: *Despite all our persuasion, she would not go.* **2** the power of persuading: *a man of great persuasion.* **3** a firm belief or conviction: *He and his brother were of different political persuasions.*

per·sua·sive (pər swā′siv) *or* (pər swā′ziv) *adj* effective in persuading: *The salesman had a very persuasive way of talking.* **per·sua′sive·ly** *adv.* **per·sua′sive·ness** *n.*

pert (pərt) *adj* **1** lively and mildly rude in an attractive way: *a pert answer.* **2** neat and jaunty in appearance: *a pert nose.* <Old French, from Latin *aperire* to open, i.e., be frank> **pert′ly** *adv.* **pert′ness** *n.*

per·tain (pər tān′) *v* **1** be appropriate, related to, or applicable: *She spoke of home and everything pertaining to it.* **2** belong or be connected as a part or possession: *We own the house and the land pertaining to it.* <Old French, from Latin *per-* through + *tenere* hold>

per·ti·nent (pər′tə nənt) *adj* to do with what is being considered: *If your question is pertinent, I will answer it.* **per′ti·nence** *n.* **per′ti·nent·ly** *adv.*

per·turb (pər tərb′) *v* make uneasy or troubled: *The management was perturbed at the possibility of another strike.* <Old French, from Latin *per-* completely + *turbare* confuse> **per′tur·ba′tion** *n.*

Pe·ru (pə rū′) *n* a country in western S America. See the APPENDIX. **Per·u′vi·an** (pə rū′vi ən) *adj, n.*

pe·ruke (pə rūk′) *n* a wig, especially a style of wig commonly worn by European men in the 1600s and 1700s.

pe·rus·al (pə rū′zəl) *n* the action of reading or examining something: *the perusal of a letter.*

pe·ruse (pə rūz′) *v* **pe·rused, pe·rus·ing** read or consider thoroughly and carefully. <Latin *per-* completely + *use*>

per·vade (pər vād′) *v* **per·vad·ed, per·vad·ing** spread and be perceived throughout, especially as a smell: *The odour of pines pervades the air.* <Latin *per-* throughout + *vadere* go> **per·va′sion** *n.*

per·va·sive (pər vā′siv) *or* (pər vā′ziv) *adj* spreading widely, especially as something physical or unwelcome: *a pervasive smell, a pervasive tendency to fear the worst.* **per·va′sive·ness** *n.*

per·verse (pər vərs′) *adj* contrary and wilful, especially in persistently doing wrong: *He was perverse and did just what we told him not to do.* <Old French, from Latin *perversus* turned the wrong way> **per·verse′ly** *adv.* **per·verse′ness** *n.*

per·ver·sion (pər vər′zhən) *n* a change to what is distorted, unnatural, abnormal, or wrong: *a perversion of the law.*

per·ver·si·ty (pər vər′sə tē) *n, pl* **per·ver·si·ties** **1** the quality of being perverse. **2** a perverse character or perverse behaviour.

per·vert (pər vərt′) *for v,* (pər′vərt) *for n. v* **1** lead or turn from the correct way or from the truth: *He said that reading comic books often perverts our taste for good books.* **2** give a wrong meaning to: *His enemies perverted his friendly remark and made it into an insult.* **3** change from what is natural or normal.
n a person whose sexual behaviour is considered abnormal or unacceptable. **per·vert′er** *n.*

Pe·sach (pā′säH) PASSOVER.

pes·ky (pes′kē) *Informal adj* **pes·ki·er, pes·ki·est** troublesome or annoying: *a pesky cold, pesky mosquitoes.* <origin uncertain>

pes·si·mism (pes′ə miz′əm) *n* a tendency to see the worst aspects of things, or to foresee difficulties and disadvantages: *His outlook on life was one of pessimism. I had a feeling of pessimism about the whole trip because so many things were going wrong.* Compare OPTIMISM. <Latin *pessimus* worst> **pes′si·mist** *n.* **pes′si·mis′tic** *adj.* **pes′si·mis′ti·cal·ly** *adv.*

pest (pest) *n* **1** a thing or person that causes injury, disease, or destruction, especially an insect or animal: *a common garden pest.* **2** a nuisance or an annoying person or thing: *By constantly interrupting, he became a real pest.* <French, from Latin *pestis* plague>

pes·ter (pes′tər) *v* **1** annoy or trouble: *If we sit outside, we'll be pestered by flies.* **2** bother with repeated requests or demands: *He kept pestering his older sister till she gave in and took him along.* <French *empestrer* encumber, influenced by *pest*>

pes·ti·cide (pes′tə sīd′) *n* a chemical agent or other substance used to destroy plant or animal pests.

pes·ti·lence (pes′tə ləns) *n* **1** a fatal infectious or contagious epidemic disease, especially bubonic plague. **2** a thing that is extremely destructive or deadly in its effect.

pes·ti·lent (pes′tə lənt) *adj* **1** often causing death: *Bubonic plague was a pestilent disease.* **2** troublesome or annoying.

pes·ti·len·tial (pes′tə len′shəl) *adj* **1** to do with pestilence. **2** morally or socially harmful. **3** irritating or annoying.

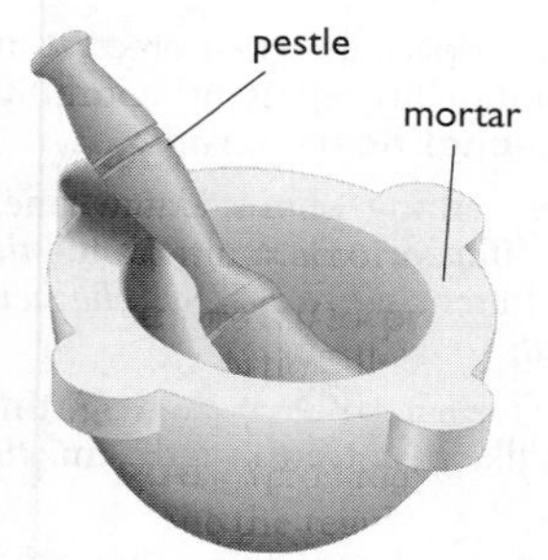

In the Middle Ages, the mortar and **pestle** was used to crush various ingredients into powder to make medicines. Today, the primary use for these tools is to grind spices for food preparation.

pes·tle (pes′əl) *n* a heavy, rounded tool for pounding or crushing substances into a powder. See also MORTAR.
v **pes·tled, pes·tling** pound or crush with a pestle. <Old French, from Latin *pinsere* to pound>

pes·to (pes′tō) *n* a sauce prepared by grinding together garlic, pine or other nuts, fresh basil, olive oil, and Parmesan cheese, usually served with pasta or other foods. <Italian *pestara* grind>

pet (pet) *n* **1** a domestic or tamed animal or bird that is cared for and treated with affection. **2** a person treated with special favour: *teacher's pet.*
adj **1** treated as a pet: *a pet rabbit.* **2** showing affection: *a pet name.* **3** *Informal* particular or special: *a pet aversion, a pet theory.*
v **pet·ted, pet·ting 1** treat as a pet. **2** stroke or pat gently and affectionately: *Be gentle when petting the new kitten.* <origin unknown>

pet·al (pet′əl) *n* a segment of the corolla of a flower that is a modified leaf and usually coloured: *A daisy has many petals.* See ANTHER for picture. <Latin, from Greek *petalon* leaf> **pet′al-like′** *adj.*

pe·tard (pi tärd′) *n* a small bomb formerly used to break down a door or gate or to breach a wall: *The petard was fastened to the gate or wall and ignited.* <French *péter* break wind>
hoist with (or **by**) **your own petard,** have a plan or attempt to harm others backfire on you.

pe·ter (pē′tər) *v* (*with* **out**) gradually fail or be at an end: *We were forced to ration our food as supplies began to peter out.* <origin unknown>

❋ **Pe·ter·bor·ough canoe** (pē′tər bər′ə) *n* a wooden canoe formerly manufactured at Lakefield, Ontario, by the Peterborough Canoe Company.

❋ **Pe·ter·head** or **pe·ter·head** (pē′tər hed′) *n* a launch or large whaleboat with a deck, a single sail, and a small motor, much used by Inuit and others in the eastern Arctic. Also called **Peterhead boat**, **Peterhead launch**, **Peterhead schooner**. <*Peterhead*, Scotland, where early boats of this type were made>

pet·i·ole (pet′ē ōl′) *n* the slender stalk by which a leaf is attached to the stem. <French, from Latin of *petiolus* stalk>

pe·tite (pə tēt′) *adj* of a small size, especially with reference to a woman or girl. <French = little>

pe·ti·tion (pə tish′ən) *n* **1** a formal request to a superior or to one in authority for some privilege, right, or benefit: *The people signed a petition asking the city council for a new sidewalk.* **2** a prayer or an appeal to a deity or some higher authority.
v **1** make a petition to: *They petitioned the mayor to use his influence with the city council.* **2** pray or appeal to a deity or higher authority. <Latin *petitionem* a request, from *petere* seek> **pe·ti′tion·er** *n.*

pet·it mal (pet′ē mol′) *n* a type of epilepsy with only brief attacks of unconsciousnes and without convulsions. <French = small illness>

pet·it point (pet′ē point′) *n* fine embroidery on canvas. <French = little stitch>

pet·rel (pet′rəl) *n* a small, black-and-white seabird with long, pointed wings that flies far from land. <From the name of St. *Peter*. St. Peter walked on the water and petrels were named after him because they appear to walk on the sea as they feed on sea organisms and refuse.>

Pe·tri dish or **pe·tri dish** (pā′trē) *or* (pē′trē) *n* a round, shallow, glass container with a loose cover, used in laboratories to hold micro-organism cultures. See TEST TUBE for picture. <J. Petri, 20c bacteriologist>

pet·ri·fy (pet′rə fī′) *v* **pet·ri·fied, pet·ri·fy·ing 1** turn animal or vegetable cells into a stony substance: *The girls found a piece of petrified wood.* **2** paralyze with fear, horror, or surprise: *They heard a footstep upstairs and stopped, petrified.* <French, from Greek *petra* rock> **pet′ri·fac′tion** or **pet′ri·fi·ca′tion** *n.*

pet·ro·chem·i·cal (pet′rō kem′ə kəl) *n* a chemical made from petroleum or natural gas, used in the manufacture of plastics, synthetic fibres, paints, and other products.
adj to do with petrochemicals.

pet·ro·dol·lar (pet′rō dol′ər) *n* usually, **petrodollars** *pl* money got from the sale of petroleum, especially when thought of as a source of economic or political power.

pet·ro·glyph (pet′rə glif′) *n* a prehistoric carving or inscription on rock. <Greek *petra* rock + *glyphe* carving>

pet·rol (pet′rəl) *especially UK n* gasoline.

pe·tro·le·um (pə trō′lē əm) *n* a usually dark liquid that consists of a mixture of hydrocarbons, and can be extracted from rock strata and refined to become fuels and lubricants <Latin, from Greek *petra* rock + *oleum* oil>

petroleum jelly *n* a smooth, greasy substance obtained from petroleum, used as an ointment and as a lubricant.

pet·ti·coat (pet′ē kōt′) *n* a light, loose undergarment worn beneath a dress or outer skirt. <Middle English *petty coat* little coat>

pet·ti·fog·ger (pet′ē fog′ər) *n* **1** a lawyer who uses petty, underhanded, or dishonest methods, or someone who uses similar methods. **2** a person who quibbles over small details. <origin uncertain> **pet′ti·fog′ging** *adj.*

pet·ty (pet′ē) *adj* **pet·ti·er, pet·ti·est 1** with little importance or value: *She insisted on telling me all her petty troubles.* **2** ungenerous, especially in small matters. **3** lower in rank or importance: *a petty official behind a counter.* <Old French *petit* little> **pet′ti·ness** *n.*

a bat	e bed	i bid	o pot	u cup	th **thin**
ā cake	ē me	ī bite	ō go	ū rude	TH **then**
ä bar	ə about	ər over	ô for	ů put	zh measure

petty cash *n* a fund of cash kept on hand to pay small expenses, especially in an office.

petty officer *n* a non-commissioned officer in the navy.

pet·u·lant (pech′ə lənt) *adj* sulky and bad-tempered, especially about small matters. <Latin *petulant* bold> **pet′u·lance** *n.* **pet′u·lant·ly** *adv.*

Pe·tun (pə tūn′) *n, pl* **Pe·tun 1** in former times, a member of a First Nations people who lived between Lakes Huron and Ontario, noted for raising and trading tobacco. **2** the language or culture of this people.

pe·tu·ni·a (pə tyū′nē ə) *or* (pə tū′nē ə) *n* a plant with funnel-shaped flowers. <Latin, from Tupi-Guarani (a language of S America) *pety* tobacco, a related plant>

pew (pyū′) *n* a bench in a church for people to sit on, with a back and often fastened to the floor. <Old French, from Latin *podium* elevated place>

pew·ter (pyū′tər) *n* an ALLOY composed mainly of tin, or dishes or other utensils made of this. <Old French *peutre*>

pe·yo·te (pā ō′tē) *n* **1** a spineless cactus of Central America and the southwestern US, with buttonlike tops when dried. **2** a drug containing the hallucinogen **mescaline** made from these dried buttons. Also called **mescal.** <Old French *peutre*>

PG *n* in full, **Parental Guidance** a movie rating informing parents that children of all ages may attend but that some scenes or language may be unsuitable for young children.

pH a symbol, on a scale of 0 to 14, used to express acid or alkaline content of a substance. High alkaline content will be indicated by a pH of 14, high acidity by a pH of 0, and neutral by a pH of 7. <*p*(*otential of*) *h*(*ydrogen*)>

phag·o·cyte (fag′ə sīt′) *n* a white blood cell capable of absorbing and destroying waste or harmful material, such as bacteria causing disease. <Greek *phagein* eat + *-cyte*>

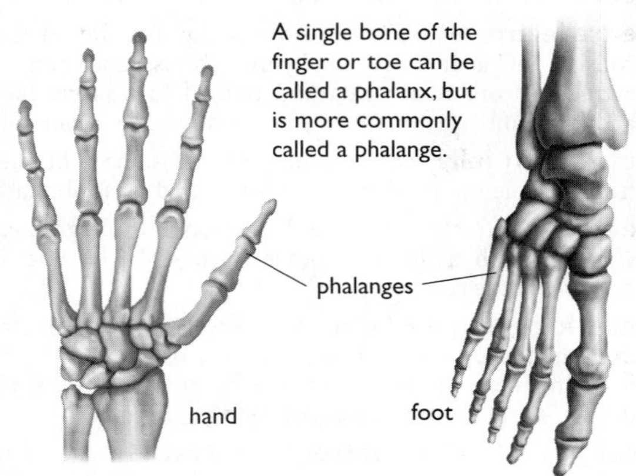
A single bone of the finger or toe can be called a phalanx, but is more commonly called a phalange.
phalanges
hand
foot

phal·anx (fal′angks) *or* (fā′langks) *n, pl* **phal·anx·es** or (for def. 3) **phal·ang·es** (fa lan′jēz) **1** in ancient Greece, a special battle formation of infantry fighting in close ranks with their shields joined and long spears overlapping each other. **2** a compact or closely massed or united body of people, animals, or things: *They were opposed in the debate by a phalanx of opposition MPs.* **3 phalanges** *pl* bones of the finger or toe. <Latin, from Greek>

phal·lus (fal′əs) *n* **1** a penis, especially when erect. **2** an image of an erect penis, traditionally representing fertility or potency. <Greek *phallos*> **phal′lic** (fal′ik) *adj.*

phan·tasm (fan′taz əm) *n* a thing seen only in one's imagination, such as an illusion or apparition: *the phantasms of a dream.* <Old French, from Greek *phainein* to show> **phan·tas′mal** *adj.*

phan·tas·ma·go·ri·a (fan taz′mə gȯ′rē ə) *n* a shifting scene of imaginary images like that seen in a dream: *the phantasmagoria of a dream.*

phan·tom (fan′təm) *n* **1** a ghost. **2** something that exists only in the imagination: *phantoms of a dream.*
adj like a ghost: *a phantom ship.* <Old French, from Greek *phantasma* image>

Phar·aoh (fer′ō) *n* a title given to the kings of ancient Egypt.

phar·i·see (far′ə sē′) *or* (fer′ə sē′) *n* a person who makes an outward show of religious or moral conduct without behaving according to its real spirit. <*Pharisee,* member of an ancient Jewish sect mentioned in the New Testament> **phar′i·sa′ic** (far′ə sā′ik) *or* (fer′ə sā′ik) *adv.* **phar′i·sa′i·cal·ly** *adv.*

phar·ma·ceu·ti·cal (fȧr′mə sū′tə kəl) *adj* to do with pharmacy or pharmacists.
n a medicinal drug.

phar·ma·ceu·tics (fȧr′mə sū′tiks) PHARMACY (def. 1).

phar·ma·col·o·gy (fȧr′mə kol′ə jē) *n* the branch of medicine that studies drugs, their sources and properties, and their preparation, uses, and effects. **phar′ma·col′o·gist** *n.*

phar·ma·co·poe·ia (fȧr′mə kə pē′ə) *n* **1** a book containing an official list and description of drugs and medicines. **2** a stock or collection of drugs.

phar·ma·cy (fȧr′mə sē) *n* **1** the practice of preparing and dispensing drugs and medicines. Also called **pharmaceutics** (fȧr′mə sū′tiks). **2 phar·ma·cies** *pl* a drugstore or department of a hospital where drugs, medicine, etc. are prepared. <Old French, from Greek *pharmakon* drug> **phar′ma·cist** *n.*

phar·ynx (far′ingks) *or* (fer′ingks) *n, pl* **phar·ynx·es** or **pha·ryn·ges** (fə rin′jēz) the muscular tube connecting the mouth cavity with the esophagus. <Latin, from Greek *pharynx* throat> **pha′ryn·ge′al** (far′in jē′əl) *adj.*

phase (fāz) *n* **1** a distinct stage in the changing conditions or stages of development of a person or thing: *The pupa is a phase in the life cycle of the moth.* **2** the shape of the moon or of a planet as it is seen at a given time. <Latin, from Greek *phasis* appearance>
phase in (or **out**)**,** introduce (or get rid of) gradually in distinct stages: *The new curriculum is to be phased in over three years.*

phase·out (fāz′out) *n* the process by which some practice or system is gradually ended in ordered stages.

phat (fat) *Slang adj* excellent. <origin uncertain>

pheas·ant (fez′ənt) *n, pl* **pheas·ants** or (*especially collectively*) **pheas·ant** a game bird or domestic fowl, with a long tail and, in the male, brilliant feathers. See PARTRIDGE for picture. <Old French, from Greek *phasianos* of the river Phasis>

phe·nol (fē′nol) *or* (fē′nōl) CARBOLIC ACID.

phe·nom (fə nom′) *Informal n* a person showing extraordinary talent or skill in some field, especially sports or entertainment: *The young acting phenom has already starred in three hit movies.* <*phenomenon*>

phe·nom·e·nal (fə nom′ə nəl) *adj* **1** to do with a phenomenon or phenomena. **2** extraordinary: *a phenomenal memory.* **phe·nom′e·nal·ly** *adv.*

phe·nom·e·non (fə nom′ə non′) *n, pl* **phe·nom·e·na** or (especially for def. 2) **phe·nom·e·nons 1** a fact, event, or circumstance that can be observed, especially one whose cause or explanation can be questioned: *Lightning is an electrical phenomenon. Fever and inflammation are phenomena of disease.* **2** something or someone extraordinary or remarkable: *An eclipse is an interesting phenomenon.* <Latin, from Greek *phainein* to show>

phe·no·type (fē′nə tīp′) *n* the set of characteristics of an organism as determined by the interaction of its genetic inheritance (**genotype**) and its environment. <German, from Greek *phainein* to show + *type*>

pher·o·mone (fer′ə mōn) *n* a chemical substance released by an animal and serving to send messages to others of the same species. <Greek *pherein* convey + *hormone*>

phew (fyū′) *interj* used to make an exclamation of relief: *Phew! I'm glad that test is over!*

phi·al (fī′əl) *n* a small glass bottle, especially for medicines or medical samples. <Old French, from Greek *phiale* a broad, flat container>

phi·lan·der (fə lan′dər) *v* have frequent and casual sexual relationships. <Greek *philein* to love + *aner* man> **phi·lan′der·er** *n.*

phil·an·thro·pist (fə lan′thrə pist) *n* a person who practises philanthropy, especially a wealthy person who supports charities.

ETYMOLOGY

Phil- comes from Greek *philos*, meaning "loving." *Anthropos* means "mankind." Thus, a **philanthropist** is a "lover of people."

phi·lan·thro·py (fə lan′thrə pē) *n, pl* **phi·lan·thro·pies** a desire to improve the welfare of others, especially as shown by practical kindness: *Charitable institutions appeal to our philanthropy.* <Latin, from Greek *philein* to love + *anthropos* human being> **phil·an·thro′pic** *adj.* **phil′an·throp′i·cal·ly** *adv.*

phi·lat·e·ly (fə lat′ə lē) *n* the collection and study of postage stamps and related items. **phil′a·tel′ic** *adj.* **phi·lat′e·list** *n.*

ETYMOLOGY

Philately comes from Greek *philos*, meaning "loving" + *ateleia*, meaning "freedom from tax." A stamp shows that a letter has been paid for and is tax free; philately is thus the love of stamps.

–phile *combining form* love or fondness: *bibliophile, Francophile.* <Greek *philos* loving>

phil·har·mon·ic (fil′här mon′ik) *adj* (*chiefly in the names of orchestras*) devoted to music. <French, from Greek *philos* loving + *harmonikos* musical>

Phil·ip·pines (fil′ə pēnz) *n* a country of many islands in the S Pacific. See the APPENDIX. **Fil·i·pi′na** *n* (*female*). **Fil·i·pi′no** *n* (*male*), *adj.*

phi·lis·tine (fə lis′tən), (fil′ə stīn′), *or* (fil′ə stēn′) *n* a person who is ignorant of and hostile to culture and the arts. *adj* ignorant of and hostile to culture and the arts. <*Philistine*, a member of an ancient people in conflict with the Israelites> **phi·lis′tin·ism′** (fə lis′tə niz′əm) or **phil′is·tin·ism′** (fil′ə sti niz′əm) *n.*

Phil·lips *Trademark n* a screwdriver with a cross-shaped tapered tip designed to fit into a **Phillips screw**, which has two slots crossed at right angles at the centre of the head. <N.F. *Phillips*, its 20c inventor>

phil·o·den·dron (fil′ə den′drən) *n* a tropical plant that is cultivated for its thick, glossy leaves. <Greek *philos* loving + *dendron* tree>

phi·lol·o·gy (fə lol′ə jē) *n* the historical and comparative study of languages, especially through literature and written documents. Compare LINGUISTICS. <French, from Greek *philos* loving + *logos* word> **phil′o·log′i·cal** *adj.* **phi·lol′o·gist** *n.*

phi·los·o·pher (fə los′ə fər) *n* **1** a person who studies or has a system of philosophy. **2** a person who shows the calmness of philosophy under hard conditions, accepting life and making the best of it.

philosophers' stone *n* an imaginary stone, substance, or chemical preparation sought by alchemists in the belief that it had the power to change any metal into gold or silver.

phil·o·soph·ic·al (fil′ə sof′ik əl) *adj* **1** to do with philosophers or philosophy. **2** like a philosopher, especially in being wise or in taking a calm, patient attitude in the face of trouble: *to take a philosophical attitude to being ill.* Also, **philosophic**. **phil′o·soph′i·cal·ly** *adv.*

phi·los·o·phize (fə los′ə fīz′) *v* **phi·los·o·phized, phi·los·o·phiz·ing** think, reason, or explain as a philosopher does: *to philosophize about life and death.* **phi·los′o·phiz′er** *n.*

phi·los·o·phy (fə los′ə fē) *n, pl* **phi·los·o·phies 1** the study of the truth or principles underlying knowledge, reality, and existence. **2** a set of views and theories of a particular philosopher. **3** an overall set of guiding principles: *a philosophy of life.* **4** the broad general principles of a particular subject: *the philosophy of history.* <Old French, from Greek *philos* loving + *sophia* wisdom>

phle·bi·tis (fli bī′tis) *n* the inflammation of the walls of a vein. <Latin, from Greek *phlebis* vein>

a bat	e bed	i bid	o pot	u cup	th **thin**
ā cake	ē me	ī bite	ō go	ū rude	ᴛʜ **then**
ä bar	ə about	ər over	ô for	ů put	zh measure

P

phlegm (flem) *n* **1** the thick discharge from the nose and throat during a cold or other respiratory disease. **2 a** in former times, a fluid of the body thought to be associated with a calm or apathetic personality. See also HUMOUR (def. 6). **b** coolness or calmness. <Old French, from Latin *phlegma* a bodily fluid, from Greek *phlegein* to burn>

phleg·mat·ic (fleg mat′ik) *adj* unemotional and stolid. **phleg·mat′i·cal·ly** *adv.*

phlo·em or **phlo·ëm** (flō′əm) *n* the soft tissue in plants that transports and stores food materials. Compare XYLEM. <Greek *phloos* bark>

phlox (floks) *n* a garden plant with dense clusters of colourful flowers, or the flower of this plant. <Latin, from Greek = flame, in reference to its bright flowers>

–phobe *combining form* with an extreme or irrational fear: *technophobe.* <French, from Greek *phobos* fear>

pho·bi·a (fō′bē ə) *n* an irrational, exaggerated fear of or aversion to a particular thing or situation. Example: *Arachnophobia* is a fear of spiders. <Latin, from Greek *phobos* fear>

–phobia *combining form* irrational or extreme fear: *claustrophobia.*

phoe·be (fē′bē) *n* a small N American bird with a greyish brown back and a low crest on the head. <imitative of its song, influenced by *Phoebe*, the name of a Greek goddess>

Phoe·ni·cian (fə nish′ən) *adj* to do with Phoenicia, an ancient country in Syria, its people, or their language.

phoe·nix (fē′niks) *n* a mythical bird, the only one of its kind, said to burn itself to ashes on a funeral pyre, and to rise again from the ashes, fresh and beautiful, for another long life. <Old French, from Greek *phoinix*>

phone[1] (fōn) *Informal n, v* **phoned, phon·ing** telephone.

phone[2] (fōn) *n* a speech sound.

–phone *combining form* **1** sound: *telephone, xylophone.* **2** a speaker of a language: *Francophone.*

phone booth *n* a small structure containing a wall-mounted public telephone operated by coins, credit card, etc.

phone card *n* a prepaid card for use in pay phones, representing a limited amount of phone time. Units of time are subtracted each time the card is used.

pho·neme (fō′nēm) *n* a sound used to distinguish the meaning of a word from that of another word. Example: In *fat, bat,* and *sat, f, b,* and *s* are phonemes. <French, from Greek *phonein* speak> **pho·nem′ic** *adj.*

pho·nem·ics (fə nēm′iks) *n* (*with singular verb*) the description of the sounds of a language that are used to distinguish word meanings. Compare PHONETICS.

phone sex *n* sexually explicit conversation by telephone, often with a stranger for pay.

pho·net·ic (fə net′ik) *adj* **1** to do with sounds of speech: *phonetic spelling.* **2** representing the sounds of speech in writing. Example: In this dictionary, the phonetic symbol (ə) stands for the vowel sound in the second syllable of *taken, pencil, lemon,* and *circus.* <Latin, from Greek *phonein* speak> **pho·net′i·cal·ly** *adv.*

pho·net·ics (fə net′iks) *n* (*with singular verb*) the description of the production of speech sounds. Compare PHONEMICS. **pho′ne·ti′cian** (fō′nə tish′ən) *n.*

pho·ney (fō′nē) PHONY.

phon·ic (fon′ik) *or* (fō′nik) *adj* to do with speech sounds. <Greek *phone* voice> **phon′i·cal·ly** *adv.*

phon·ics (fon′iks) *or* (fō′niks) *n* (*with singular verb*) a method of learning to read or pronounce words by relating the sounds of a language to the letters or groups of letters used to represent them.

phono– *combining form* sound or sounds: *phonology.* <Greek *phonos* sound, voice>

pho·no·graph (fō′nə graf′) *n* a record player.

pho·nol·o·gy (fō nol′ə jē) *or* (fə nol′ə jē) *n* **1** the study of human speech sounds, especially of their systems and historical changes in particular languages. **2** the sounds and systems of sounds used in a language. **pho·nol′o·gist** *n.*

pho·ny (fō′nē) *adj* **pho·ni·er, pho·ni·est** not genuine: *a phony smile, a phony $20 bill.*
n, pl **pho·nies** a fake or pretender: *I think he's a phony who never did any of the things he talked about.*
Also, **phoney**. **pho′ni·ness** *n.*

ETYMOLOGY

Phony perhaps comes from *fawny,* a thief's name for a cheap ring sold as genuine gold.

phoo·ey (fū′ē) *Informal interj* used to make an exclamation of contempt or distaste. <origin uncertain>

phos·gene (fos′jēn) *n* a colourless, poisonous gas, a compound of carbon monoxide and chlorine. <Greek *phos* light + *-gen*>

phos·phate (fos′fāt) *n* a salt or ester of an acid containing phosphorus, or a fertilizer containing such salts. <French, from Greek *phosphore* phosphorus>

phos·phor (fos′fər) *n* a synthetic phosphorescent substance, especially one that emits light when subjected to radiation. <Latin, from Greek *phos* light + *pherein* bring>

phos·pho·res·cence (fos′fə res′əns) *n* the act or process of giving out light without burning or by very slow burning that seems not to give out heat, or the light itself: *the phosphorescence of fireflies.* **phos′pho·res′cent** *adj.*

phos·phor·ic acid (fos′fər ik) *n* a colourless, odourless acid containing phosphorus, used in making fertilizers and soaps, and in food processing.

phos·pho·rous (fos′fə rəs) *adj* to do with phosphorus.

phos·pho·rus (fos′fə rəs) *n* a solid, non-metallic element. *Symbol* **P** <Latin, from Greek *phos* light + *-phorein* bring, from its flammability>

pho·tic (fō′tik) *adj* **1** to do with light. **2** to do with the layer of a lake, ocean, etc. that receives sufficient sunlight for plant growth. <Greek *photos* light>

pho·to (fō′tō) *Informal n, pl* **pho·tos** a photograph.

photo– *combining form* **1** light: *photometer.* **2** photographic or photograph: *photocopy.* <Greek *photos* light>

Photo CD *Trademark n* a compact disc for digitally storing photographs and displaying them on a TV screen.

pho·to·chem·i·cal (fō′tō kem′ə kəl) *adj* to do with the chemical action of light or other radiant energy, especially the action of sunlight on pollutants, which produces smog.

pho·to·cop·i·er (fō′tō kop′ē ər) *n* a machine that makes photocopies.

pho·to·cop·y (fō′tō kop′ē) *n, pl* **pho·to·cop·ies** a photographic reproduction of a document or other printed matter.
v **pho·to·cop·ied, pho·to·cop·y·ing** make a photocopy.

pho·to·e·lec·tric (fō′tō i lek′trik) *adj* to do with the electrical effects produced by light. A **photoelectric cell** uses light to generate current, which can then be used to open doors automatically, set off alarms, etc.

pho·to–en·grav·ing (fō′tō en grā′ving) *n* a process by which plates to print from are produced with the aid of photography, or a plate or picture so produced.

photo finish *n* a finish in a race so close that a photograph is required to decide the winner.

pho·to·fin·ish·ing (fo′to fin′i shing) *n* the process of developing exposed photographic film into prints.

pho·to·gen·ic (fō′tō jen′ik) *adj* **1** looking or likely to look attractive in photographs, TV broadcasts, or films: *a photogenic face.* **2** emitting a light in an organism, through phosphorescence.

pho·to·graph (fō′tə graf′) *n* a picture made with a camera by the action of light on a sensitive surface, such as photographic film or a computer chip.
v **1** take a photograph. **2** appear in a particular way in a photograph: *She does not photograph well.*

pho·to·graph·ic (fō′tə graf′ik) *adj* **1** of or like photography: *photographic accuracy.* **2** used in or produced by photography: *photographic plates, a photographic record of a trip.* **pho′to·graph′i·cal·ly** *adv.*

pho·tog·ra·phy (fə tog′rə fē) *n* the art or process of making photographs. **pho·tog′ra·pher** *n.*

pho·to·gra·vure (fō′tō grə vyůr′) *n* a picture printed from a metal plate on which a photograph has been engraved.

pho·to·jour·nal·ism (fo′to jər′nal iz′əm) *n* journalism in which photographs, rather than written material, are used to convey most of the information. **pho·to·jour·nal·ist** *n.* **pho·to·journ·al·ist·ic** *adj.*

pho·tom·e·ter (fō tom′ə tər) *n* an instrument for measuring the intensity of light or the relative illuminating power of different lights.

pho·to·mon·tage (fo′to mon tozh′) *n* a composite picture made up of photographs or parts of photographs.

pho·ton (fō′ton) *n* a particle made up of light or other radiant energy, with a momentum equal to its energy. <*phot(o) (electr)on*>

photo radar *n* a device used by police to detect speeding vehicles and to photograph the offender's licence plate.

pho·to·sen·si·tive (fō′tō sen′sə tiv) *adj* easily stimulated by light or other radiant energy.

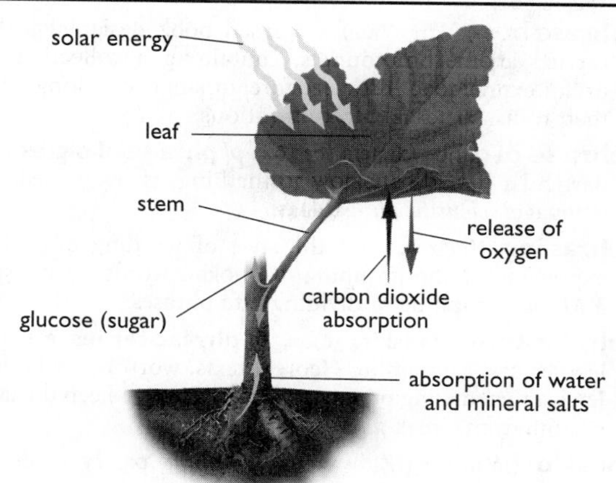

pho·to·syn·the·sis (fō′tə sin′thə sis) *n* the process by which plant cells make sugar from carbon dioxide and water in the presence of chlorophyl and light.

pho·tot·rop·ism (fō tot′rə piz′əm) *or* (fō′tō trō′piz əm) *n* the tendency of plants to orient themselves toward or away from a source of light.

pho·to·vol·ta·ic (fō′tō′vol tā′ik) *or* (fō′tō′vōl tā′ik) *adj* to do with electric current produced by means of light or other radiant energy at the junction where two substances, such as a metal and a semiconductor, are exposed to it. A solar calculator, for example, is powered by a photovoltaic cell.

phras·al verb (frāz′əl) *Grammar n* a verb used in combination with an adverb or preposition, or both, whose meaning cannot be obtained from the meanings of the separate words. Example: In *She looked up the word, looked up* is a phrasal verb. In *She looked up the stair, looked up* is not a phrasal verb.

phrase (frāz) *n* **1** a combination of words in a clause or sentence that has no subject or predicate but is used to convey meaning. In *He went to the house,* the words *to the house* form a phrase. **2** a short, frequently used expression. *His favourite phrase is "So it goes."* **3** *Music* a distinct group of notes in a longer passage of music.
v **phrased, phras·ing 1** express in a particular way: *She phrased her excuse politely.* **2** *Music* mark off or bring out the phrases of a piece of music. <Latin, from Greek *phrazein* tell>

GRAMMAR AND USAGE

A **phrase** is a group of words combined together. It cannot stand on its own to describe an idea or situation, but requires additional words to form a meaningful sentence:
eating a peach (phrase)
I was eating a peach. (sentence)

P

a bat	e bed	i bid	o pot	u cup	th thin
ā cake	ē me	ī bite	ō go	ū rude	ᴛʜ then
ä bar	ə about	ər over	ô for	ů put	zh measure

phrase·book (frāz′bu̇k) *n* a small book designed to be carried around by tourists, containing a collection of useful expressions used in a foreign language, along with their translations and pronunciations.

phra·se·ol·o·gy (frā′zē ol′ə jē) *n, pl* **phra·se·ol·o·gies** the particular way in which something is expressed in language: *scientific phraseology.*

phras·ing (frā′zing) *n* **1** the style of wording or verbal expression. **2** the grouping of spoken words by pauses. **3** *Music* a grouping or dividing into phrases.

phy·lac·ter·y (fə lak′tə rē) *n, pl* **phy·lac·ter·ies** a small leather case containing Hebrew texts, worn by orthodox Jewish men during prayer to remind them to keep the law. <Latin, from Greek *phylassein* to guard>

phyl·lo (fē′lō) *or* (fī′lō) *n* a flaky Greek pastry made in layers with butter. <Greek *phyllon* leaf>

phy·lum (fī′ləm) *Biology n, pl* **phy·la** (-lə) a category in the classification of animals, corresponding to a DIVISION for plants. A phylum is more specific than a KINGDOM and more general than a CLASS. See also ORDER, FAMILY, GENUS and SPECIES. <Latin, from Greek *phylon* race>

phys·i·cal (fiz′ə kəl) *adj* **1** of the body, as distinct from the mind: *physical exercise.* **2** involving bodily contact or activity: *physical sports.* **3** to do with physics or natural forces: *physical laws.*
n Informal a medical examination: *my annual physical.* <Latin, from Greek *physis* nature> **phys′i·cal·ly** *adv.*

physical education *n* instruction in how to exercise and take care of the body, especially as a course at school or college.

physical geography *n* the study of land forms, climate, winds, and other physical features of the earth.

physical science *n* the study of inanimate matter. Chemistry is a physical science. Compare LIFE SCIENCE, SOCIAL SCIENCE.

phy·si·cian (fə zish′ən) *n* a doctor of medicine.

phys·ics (fiz′iks) *n* (*with singular verb*) the science that studies matter and energy and their relationships, excluding chemical and biological change. **phys′i·cist** *n.*

phys·i·cal (fiz′ə kəl) *adj* **1** of the body, as distinct from the mind: *physical exercise.* **2** involving bodily contact or activity: *physical sports.* **3** to do with physics or natural forces: *physical laws.*

phys·i·o (fiz′ē o) *Informal n* physiotherapy.

phys·i·ol·o·gy (fiz′ē ol′ə jē) *n* **1** the science that studies the normal functions of living things or their parts: *animal physiology, plant physiology.* **2** the functions and activities of a living thing or of one of its parts. <Greek *physis* nature + *-logos* treating of> **phys′i·o·log′i·cal** *adj.* **phys′i·o·log′i·cal·ly** *adv.* **phys′i·ol′og·ist** *n.*

phys·i·o·ther·a·py (fiz′ē ō ther′ə pē) *n* the treatment of sprained muscles and broken bones by physical remedies, such as massage, heat treatment, or exercise rather than by drugs or surgery. **phys′i·o·ther′a·pist** *n.*

phy·sique (fə zēk′) *n* the form, size, and development of a person's body: *a strong physique.* <French = physical>

pi (pī) *n* the numerical ratio of the circumference of a circle to its diameter, equal to about 3.1412. *Symbol* π <Greek first letter of *periphereia* periphery>

pi·a·nis·si·mo (pē′ə nis′ə mō′) *adj, adv* played or to be played very softly in music.

pi·an·o[1] (pē an′ō) *n, pl* **pi·an·os** a large musical instrument with strings that sound when struck by hammers operated by the keys on a keyboard. See UPRIGHT for picture. <*pianoforte,* from Italian *piano* soft + *forte* loud> **pi′an·ist** *n.*

pi·an·o[2] (pē an′ō) *Music adj, adv* soft or softly. *Symbol* **p** <Italian = soft>

pi·an·o·for·te (pē an′ə fȯr′tē) *n* a piano.

pi·az·za (pē at′sə) *n* an open public square in a town, especially in Italy. <Italian>

pi·ca (pī′kə) *n* a measure of type size and line length equal to twelve POINTS (def. 12), about 4.2 mm. <Latin, from Greek = magpie>

pic·a·dor (pik′ə dȯr′) *n* one of the horsemen who begin a bullfight by irritating the bull with pricks of their lances.

pic·a·resque (pik′ə resk′) *adj* to do with a style of fiction that tells the adventures of a rough and dishonest but intereresting or appealing hero: *a picaresque novel.* <French, from Spanish *picaro* rogue>

pic·a·yune (pik′ə yūn′) *adj* small, petty, or worthless. <French, from Provençal (a language of S France) *picaioun* coin>

pic·co·lo (pik′ə lō′) *n, pl* **pic·co·los** a small flute, sounding an octave higher than the ordinary flute. <Italian = small>

pick[1] (pik) *v* **1** choose from several persons or things, usually after some thought: *I picked a funny card for your birthday.* **2** pull away a flower, fruit, or vegetable with the fingers: *to pick grapes.* **3** use something pointed to remove things from: *to pick your teeth.* **4** (*with* ***up***) take hold of and lift or move: *Pick up the towel from the bathroom floor.* **5** use the fingers or a small tool with a plucking motion, such as while playing a guitar or banjo. **6** seek and find occasion for: *to pick a quarrel.* **7** repeatedly pull at something with the fingers: *Stop picking at your sweater!*
n **1** a choice, or the act of making it: *This red rose is my pick.* **2** the best or most desirable part: *We got a high price for the pick of our peaches.* **3** the amount of a crop gathered at one time: *a heavy strawberry pick.* **4** a small tool held in the fingers and used to pluck the strings of a musical instrument. <origin uncertain>
pick a lock, open a lock with a pointed instrument or wire.
pick and choose, be very fussy or arbitrary about choosing: *When the supplies are being donated, you can't very well pick and choose.*
pick apart, find many flaws in: *I don't want my essay picked apart in front of the class.*
pick a pocket, steal from a person's pocket.
pick at, a pull on with the fingers: *The sick woman picked at the blankets.* **b** eat only a little at a time. **c** *Informal* find fault with or nag.
pick off, shoot one at a time.
pick on, *Informal* **a** find fault with: *The teacher picked on him for always being late.* **b** annoy or tease: *The bigger boys picked on the new boy during recess.* **c** bully or take advantage of.

pick out, a choose: *Pick out a shirt you would like to wear.* **b** distinguish a thing from its surroundings: *Can you pick me out in this group picture?* **c** make out the sense or meaning.

pick someone's brain(**s**), ask for opinions, information, or advice from a knowledgeable person: *I'm going to ask my aunt if I can pick her brains for my science fair project.*

pick up, **a** get by chance: *to pick up a bargain.* **b** learn without being taught: *She picks up games easily.* **c** take up into a vehicle, boat, or ship: *The bus picked up passengers at every other corner.* **d** *Informal* improve or recover: *He seemed to pick up quickly after his fever.* **e** regain, find, or begin again: *to pick up where you left off.* **f** increase in speed: *to pick up the tempo.* **g** become acquainted with without being introduced. **h** pay for: *Dad picked up the bill for the meal.*

pick up on, notice and understand: *I didn't pick up on that line the first time I saw the movie.*

pick your way, move with great caution: *We picked our way down the icy driveway.*

SYNONYMS

Pick is a general word that means "choose" or "select": *I want to pick the most beautiful card for my mother.*

Cull can mean "select specifically for elimination": *The herd of cows had to be culled to avoid the spread of disease.*

Winnow means "separate" or "sift": *The jury must winnow the truth from all the evidence.*

pick[2] (pik) *v* **1** a sharp-pointed tool, usually with a long handle, used for breaking up something hard or embedded. **2** a pickaxe. <*pike*[1]>

pick·axe (pik′aks′) *n* a heavy metal tool that is pointed at one or both ends and has a long wooden handle, used for breaking up dirt, rocks, or other hard substances. Also, **pickax**.

pick·er (pik′ər) *n* a person who or thing that gathers, picks, or collects.

pick·er·el (pik′ə rəl) *n, pl* **pick·er·els** or (*especially collectively*) **pick·er·el** a small N American pike. <*pike*[2]>

pick·et (pik′it) *n* **1** a pointed stake or peg driven into the ground, such as to form part of a **picket fence**, or to tie a horse to. **2** a small body of troops, or one person, posted at some place to watch for the enemy and guard against surprise attacks. **3** a person or group of people forming a **picket line** near a place of work where there is a strike in order to protest or to prevent others from entering the workplace.
v act as a picket at a workplace: *to picket a factory.* <French *pic*>

pick·ings (pik′ingz) *pln* **1** leftovers or remaining scraps. **2** profits or rewards that are gained dishonestly or acquired with little effort.

pick·le (pik′əl) *n* **1** a vegetable or fruit preserved in vinegar, brine, salt, or mustard, especially a cucumber preserved in this way. **2** *Informal* trouble or difficulty: *I got in a bad pickle today.*
v **pick·led, pick·ling** preserve in a pickling solution: *to pickle beets.* <Dutch *pekel*>

pick–me–up (pik′mē up′) *n* something that makes one more energetic or cheerful.

pick·pock·et (pik′pok′it) *n* a person who steals from people's pockets.

pick·up (pik′up′) *n* **1** an act of collecting things or people, especially in a vehicle: *free pickup and delivery, garbage pickup.* **2** an acceleration or increase in speed: *a car with great pickup.* **3** *Informal* a person met casually, usually for sexual relations. **4** *Sports* the act of catching a ball very soon after it has bounced on the ground. **5** a small truck with an open back, and a tailgate for loading and unloading. **6** a small electromagnetic device attached to a musical instrument to amplify its sounds.
adj to do with using available material, people, etc., without any organizing beforehand: *a pickup game of basketball.*

pick·y (pik′ē) *adj* **pick·i·er, pick·i·est** tending to find fault with trivial things. **pick′i·ness** *n.*

pic·nic (pik′nik) *n* an outing or occasion that involves taking along and eating a packed meal in the open air.
v **pic·nicked, pic·nick·ing** go on a picnic, or eat in picnic style: *Our family often picnics at the beach.* <French *pique-nique*> **pic′nick·er** *n.*

Pict (pikt) *n* a member of a people of disputed origin, formerly living in Scotland, especially northern Scotland.

pic·to·graph (pik′tə graf′) *n* **1** a picture or symbol used to represent a word or idea. **2** a chart or graph on which symbols are used to represent quantities such as population or production of goods. **pic′to·graph′ic** *adj.*

pic·to·ri·al (pik tô′rē əl) *adj* **1** to do with pictures. **2** making a picture for the mind: *a pictorial way of writing.* **3** illustrated by pictures: *a pictorial history.*
n a periodical in which pictures are an important feature. **pic·to′ri·al·ly** *adv.*

pic·ture (pik′chər) *n* **1** a drawing, a painting, a photograph, or an image on a screen. **2** a scene: *The trees and brook make a lovely picture.* **3** something beautiful: *My mother was a picture in her new dress.* **4** an image of or likeness: *He is the picture of his grandfather.* **5** a mental image or idea: *I have a clear picture of the problem.* **6** *Informal* a general situation: *the employment picture.*
v **pic·tured, pic·tur·ing** **1** form a picture of in the mind: *It is hard to picture life a hundred years ago.* **2** show or describe by words: *The speaker pictured the suffering of the poor.* <Latin *pingere* paint>

get the picture, *Informal* understand, without further explanation.

in (or **out**) **of the picture,** part (or not part) of a certain situation.

picture perfect, very neat and attractive, as if preserved in a picture.

a bat	e bed	i bid	o pot	u cup	th thin
ā cake	ē me	ī bite	ō go	ū rude	ᴛʜ then
ä bar	ə about	ər over	ô for	ů put	zh measure

pic·tur·esque (pik′chə resk′) *adj* 1 quaint or interesting enough to be used as the subject of a picture: *a picturesque old mill.* 2 making a vivid picture for the mind: *picturesque language.* **pic′tur·esque′ly** *adv.* **pic′tur·esque′ly** *n.*

picture tube *n* a cathode ray tube that produces the transmitted picture on a TV screen.

picture window *n* a large window that seems to frame the view seen through it.

pid·dle (pid′əl) *Informal v* **pid·dled, pid·dling** 1 (*with **about** or **around***) do something in a trifling or ineffective way. 2 urinate. <origin uncertain> **pid′dler** *n.*

pid·dling (pid′ling) *Informal adj* trifling or petty. Also, **piddly**.

pid·gin (pij′ən) *n* a simplified form of a language with limited grammar and vocabulary from two or more different languages, used for trade or communication between different peoples or groups. <Cantonese pronunciation of *business*>

pidgin English *n* one of several forms of English, with reduced grammatical structure and vocabulary, used as a medium of communications where English is not the first language: *Chinese pidgin English.*

pie (pī) *n* a baked or chilled dish consisting of fruit, meat, or other foods set in a shell and sometimes with a top of pastry: *apple pie, chicken pot pie.* <Middle English *pye*>
(**as**) **easy as pie,** very easy.
pie in the sky, something desirable but very unrealistic or unlikely: *Most of the candidate's promises are only pie in the sky.*

pie·bald (pī′bold′) *adj* spotted in two colours, especially black and white.
n a spotted animal, especially a horse. <(*mag*)*pie* (from its dark colour) + obsolete *bald* streaked with white>

piece (pēs) *n* 1 one of the parts into which a thing is divided or broken: *a piece of pie. The cup broke in pieces.* 2 a limited or small quantity: *a piece of land containing two hectares, a piece of bread.* 3 a single thing of a set: *This set of china has 144 pieces.* 4 an example: *What you said is a piece of nonsense.* 5 a single work of art: *a piece of music.* 6 a gun or cannon. 7 a figure, disc, or block, used in playing board games. 8 *Informal* a share, especially in financial matters: *a piece of the profits.*
v **pieced, piec·ing** 1 make or repair by adding or joining pieces: *to piece a quilt.* 2 (*with **together***) put something together, often slowly; join the pieces of: *I pieced together what happened by listening to everyone who had been at the meeting.* <Old French, from Latin *pettia*>
go to pieces, a fall apart or break up: *Another ship had gone to pieces on the rocks.* **b** break down or collapse: *When he failed to make the team, he went completely to pieces.*
of a piece, of the same kind: *The plan is of a piece with the rest of his silly suggestions.*
piece of cake, *Informal* a very easy task; easily done.
piece of my mind, *Informal* a scolding: *I gave her a piece of my mind for being late.*
piece of work, *Informal* a difficult person to deal with.
speak (or **say**) **your piece,** express your opinion.

pièce de ré·sis·tance (pyez də rā zē stäns′) *n* 1 the most important or remarkable item or feature. 2 the most impressive part of a meal. <French = piece (means) of resistance>

piece·meal (pē′smēl′) *adv, adj* done or as if piece by piece or a little at a time: *work done piecemeal, piecemeal assembly.*

piece of eight *n* in former times, a Spanish dollar.

piece·work (pē′swərk′) *n* work paid for by the amount done, not by the time it takes: *Employees in shoe factories are usually on piecework.* **piece′work·er** *n.*

pie chart *Mathematics n* a graph in which the parts of a whole are shown as sectors of a circle, like slices of a pie. Also called **circle graph**.

pied (pīd) *adj* with patches of two or more colours.

pied–à–terre (pyā′də ter′) *n, pl* **pieds-à-terre** (pyā′də ter′) a house or apartment kept for occasional use. <French = foot to earth>

Pie·gan (pē′gan) PIIKANI.

pier (pēr) *n* 1 a structure supported on columns extending into the water, used as a walk or a landing place for ships. 2 a breakwater. 3 a solid support on which the arches of a bridge rest. See ABUTMENT for picture. 4 the solid part of a wall between windows and doors. <Latin *pera*>

pierce (pērs) *v* **pierced, pierc·ing** 1 make a hole in or bore into or through: *A nail pierced the tire of my bike.* 2 go into or through, such as a tunnel: *A tunnel pierces the mountain.* 3 force a way through or into: *A sharp cry pierced the air.* 4 make a way through with the eye or mind: *to pierce a disguise, to pierce a mystery.* 5 affect sharply with some feeling: *Her heart was pierced with grief.* <Old French, from Latin *pertundere* pierce>

pierc·ing (pēr′sing) *adj* penetrating, sharp, or keen: *piercing cold, a piercing look.* **pierc′ing·ly** *adv.*

pi·e·ty (pī′ə tē) *n, pl* **pi·e·ties** 1 reverence for or devotion to God. 2 a reverential act, remark, or belief about someone or something. <See PIOUS.>

pif·fle (pif′əl) *Informal n* silly talk or nonsense. <origin uncertain>

pig (pig) *n* 1 a cloven-hoofed mammal with a long snout and a stout, heavy body, especially one that is raised for its meat. 2 *Informal* a person who is regarded as greedy, dirty, or stubborn. 3 an oblong mass of metal that has been run into a mould while hot. <origin uncertain>
pig out, *Informal* overindulge in food: *We pigged out on barbecued chicken wings.*

pi·geon (pij′ən) *n* 1 a wild or domesticated bird with a stout body, small head, and a cooing voice. 2 a clay pigeon. <Old French, from Latin *pipio* young cheeping bird>

pigeon hawk *n* a merlin.

pi·geon·hole (pij′ən hōl′) *n* 1 a small place, built, usually as one of a series, for a pigeon to nest in. 2 a boxlike compartment for holding papers and other items.
v **pi·geon·holed, pi·geon·hol·ing** 1 put in a pigeonhole. 2 classify, especially in a way that is too rigid or restrictive. 3 put aside for later consideration: *to pigeonhole a request.*

pi·geon–toed (pij′ən tōd′) *adj* with the feet turned inward.

pig·gish (pig′ish) *adj* like a pig.

pig·gy (pig′ē) *Informal n, pl* **pig·gies** a little pig.

pig·gy·back (pig′ē bak′) *adv* **1** on the back or shoulders: *to ride piggyback.* **2** on top of something else, such as truck trailers on railway flatcars: *The goods will be sent piggyback to Edmonton.*
n a carrying or being carried on the back or shoulders: *She gave the child a piggyback.*
v carry by piggyback.

piggy bank *n* a small container in the shape of a pig, with a slot in the top for coins.

pig·head·ed (pig′hed′id) *adj* stupidly stubborn.

pig iron *n* crude iron as it first comes from the blast furnace or smelter, usually cast into oblong masses called pigs.

pig Latin *n* a children's jargon in which the syllable *-ay* (ā) is added to the end of a word, any initial consonant being placed immediately before this ending. Examples: *oodgay = good, orfay = for, ordway = word.*

pig·let (pig′lət) *n* a young pig.

pig·ment (pig′mənt) *n* **1** a natural colouring matter of animal or plant tissue. **2** a substance used for colouring or painting, such as that mixed with oil, water, or another medium. <Latin *pingere* paint>

pig·men·ta·tion (pig′mən tā′shən) *n* **1** a deposit of pigment in the tissue of a living animal or plant, causing colouration or discolouration. **2** the colouring of a person's skin.

pig·my (pig′mē) PYGMY.

pig·pen (pig′pen′) *n* **1** a pen where pigs are kept. **2** a filthy or very untidy place: *My bedroom's a pigpen.* Also called **pigsty** (pig′stī′).

pig·skin (pig′skin′) *n* **1** the skin of a pig, or leather made from it. **2** *Informal* a football.

pig·tail (pig′tāl′) *n* a braid of hair hanging from the back of the head.

Pii·kan·i (pē′kan i) *n, pl* **Pii·kan·i** **1** a member of a First Nations or Native American people, part of the Blackfoot confederacy, living mainly in southern Alberta and the state of Montana. **2** their Algonquian language.
adj to do with these people or their language. Also called **Peigan, Piegan**.

Hares are generally larger than rabbits, which, in turn, are larger than **pikas**. They all have two sets of incisors, unlike rodents, which have one set.

pi·ka (pī′kə) *n* a small, rabbitlike mammal found in mountains and deserts of Asia and N America. <Tungus (a language of Siberia) *piika*>

pike[1] (pīk) *n* a weapon with a long wooden handle and a pointed metal head, once carried by foot soldiers. <French *pic* pick[2]>

pike[2] (pīk) *n* a large freshwater food and game fish with a narrow, pointed head and many sharp teeth. Also called **northern pike**. <*pike*[1], from the shape of its snout>

pike[3] (pīk) *n* a turnpike.

pike[4] (pīk) *Swimming, Gymnastics n* a jackknife position.

pike·staff (pīk′staf′) *n, pl* **pike·staves** (-stāvz′) the wooden shaft of a PIKE[1].

pi·laf or **pi·laff** (pi läf′) *n* a rice or wheat dish originally from the Middle East and India, typically baked with spices, meat, fish, or other foods. Also **pilau** (pi lo′). <Turkish *pilav*>

pi·las·ter (pə las′tər) *n* a rectangular pillar, especially when it forms part of a wall from which it projects. <French, from Latin *pila* pillar>

pile[1] (pīl) *n* **1** many things lying one upon another; a heap of something: *a pile of wood, a huge pile of dirt.* **2** a large amount: *a pile of work, a pile of dishes.* **3** *Informal* a large amount of money. **4** 🍁 *Newfoundland and Labrador* a stack of salted cod being dried. **5** a nuclear reactor.
v **piled, pil·ing** make into a pile, or rise into a pile: *Pile the blankets in a corner. Snow piled against the fences.* <Old French, from Latin *pila* pillar>
pile in (or **out**)**,** go in (or out) in a confused rush: *Everyone piled in the car, to pile out into the street.*
pile something on, use in great amounts or too much: *Some journalists like to pile on the sensational details. It's nice to be complimented, but she really piles it on.*
pile up, heap up or collect together.

SYNONYMS

Pile suggests things lying on top of each other: *She had a pile of dirty clothes on her bedroom floor.*

Accumulation suggests a buildup or mass of something: *There was an accumulation of snow on the roof of the cottage.*

Collection suggests items that are together in one place: *The album contained a superb collection of stamps.*

pile[2] (pīl) *n* a heavy beam driven upright into the earth, often under water, to support a bridge, wharf, or building.
v **piled, pil·ing** furnish with piles or drive piles into. <Old English *pīl*>

pile[3] (pīl) *n* the soft surface of certain fabrics woven with loops of yarn which may be uncut, as towelling, or cut, as in velvet or carpeting. <Latin *pilus* hair>

pi·le·at·ed woodpecker (pī′lē ā′tid) *n* a large black-and-white woodpecker with a prominent red crest on the head. <Latin *pileus* felt cap>

a bat	e bed	i bid	o pot	u cup	th **thin**
ā cake	ē me	ī bite	ō go	ū rude	TH **then**
ä bar	ə about	ər over	ô for	ů put	zh measure

pile·driv·er (pīl′drī′vər) *n* a machine for driving down piles or stakes, usually a tall framework in which a heavy weight is raised and then allowed to fall upon the pile.

piles (pīlz) *Informal pln* hemorrhoids. <origin uncertain>

pile–up (pī′lup′) *n* a crash involving several vehicles.

pil·fer (pil′fər) *v* steal things of little value and in small amounts: *Someone pilfered an orange from the fruit display.* <Old French *pelfrer* rob>

pil·grim (pil′grəm) *n* **1** a person who goes on a journey to a sacred or holy place as an act of religious devotion: *In the Middle Ages, many people went as pilgrims to Jerusalem.* **2** a person whose life is considered as a journey. <Provençal (a language of S. France), from Latin *peregrinus* foreign>

pil·grim·age (pil′grə mij) *n* **1** a journey to a sacred place as an act of religious devotion. **2** a journey to a place associated with a special person or historical event. **3** life thought of as a journey.

pil·ing (pī′ling) *n* piles or heavy beams driven into soft ground or a riverbed, forming a structure for a foundation.

Pil·i·pi·no (pī′li pē′nō) *n* an official language of the Philippines.

pill (pil) *n* **1** medicine made up into a tiny ball, tablet, or capsule, to be swallowed whole. **2** something unpleasant that has to be endured: *Our defeat was a bitter pill.* **3** a very small ball of a substance. **4 the pill** or **the Pill** an oral contraceptive.
v of a knitted or woven fabric, become matted into small balls: *This sweater is pilling badly.* <Latin *pila* ball>

pil·lage (pil′ij) *v* **pil·laged, pil·lag·ing** rob using violence, especially in wartime: *Pirates pillaged the towns all along the coast.*
n a robbery using violence. <Old French *piller* plunder>
pil′lag·er *n.*

pil·lar (pil′ər) *n* **1** a slender, upright column, usually made of stone, wood, or metal and used as a support or ornament for a building. **2** anything slender and upright like a pillar: *a pillar of smoke.* **3** a person who is an important supporter: *She is a pillar of the community.* <Old French, from Latin *pila* pillar>
from pillar to post, from one thing or place to another without a definite purpose.

pill·box (pil′boks′) *n* **1** a box, usually shallow and often round, for holding pills. **2** a small, partly underground fort with thick walls and roof, used as an outpost in a battle. **3** a round, brimless hat with a flat crown.

pil·lion (pil′yən) *n* a pad attached behind a saddle on a horse or motorcycle for a passenger to sit on. <Gaelic>

pil·lo·ry (pil′ə rē) *n, pl* **pil·lo·ries** a frame of wood and set up in a public place, with holes through which a person's head and hands were put in former times as a punishment.
v **pil·lo·ried, pil·lo·ry·ing** **1** put in a pillory. **2** expose to public ridicule, contempt, or abuse: *Is it fair to pillory politicians for every mistake they have made?* <Old French *pellori*>

pil·low (pil′ō) *n* a bag or case filled with feathers, down, or other soft material, usually used to support the head when resting or sleeping.
v **1** rest on or as if on a pillow: *She pillowed her head on a pile of leaves.* **2** be a pillow for. <Latin *pulvinus* cushion>
pil′low·like′ *adj.*

pil·low·case (pil′ō kās′) *n* a removable cover for a pillow. Also called **pillowslip**.

pi·lot (pī′lət) *n* **1** a person who operates the controls of an aircraft in flight. **2** a person whose business is steering ships in or out of a harbour or through dangerous waters. **3** a guide or leader. **4** a device that controls the action of one part of a machine, motor, or device. **5** an advance version or sample of an action, operation, device, or program.
v **1** act as the pilot of: *The businesswoman piloted her own plane.* **2** guide or lead: *The tour guide piloted us through the museum.*
adj serving as an advance or experimental version or sample of a plan, action, operation, or device: *a pilot program, a pilot film.* <French, from Greek *pedon* oar>

pilot fish *n* a small, bluish fish found in warm seas, often accompanying sharks.

pi·lot·house (pī′lət hous′) *n* an enclosed place on the deck of a ship, sheltering the person at the wheel.

pilot light *n* a small flame kept burning all the time and used to light a main burner whenever desired. Gas stoves and gas water heaters have pilot lights.

pilot whale *n* a small, black, toothed whale, with a low dorsal fin and a square, bulbous head.

pi·men·to (pə men′tō) *n, pl* **pi·men·tos** a sweet red pepper used in salads, cooked dishes, and as stuffing for olives. <Spanish, from Latin *pigmentum* spice>

pimp (pimp) *n* a man who manages a group of prostitutes, finds clients for them, and takes part or most of their earnings.
v act as or like a pimp. <origin uncertain>

pim·per·nel (pim′pər nel′) *n* a small plant of the primrose family with flowers that close in bad weather. <Old French, from Latin *piper* pepper, because its fruit resembles peppercorns>

pim·ple (pim′pəl) *n* a small, inflamed swelling in the skin, sometimes containing pus. <Middle English *pymple*>

pim·pled (pim′pəld) *adj* with pimples.

pim·ply (pim′plē) *adj* **pim·pli·er, pim·pli·est** with pimples.

pin (pin) *n* **1** a short, slender piece of wire with a point at one end and a head at the other, used for fastening things together. **2** a brooch or badge with a pin or clasp to fasten it to clothing: *She wore her class pin.* **3** a peg used to fasten things together, hold something, or hang things on: *a safety pin.* **4** a metal rod used to join the ends of fractured bones while they heal. **5** one of the bottle-shaped pieces of wood toward which a bowling ball is rolled. See BOWLING for picture. **6** a metal projection from a plug or an integrated circuit used as an electrical connection. **7** *Golf* the stick for the flag marking a hole on a golf course. **8 pins** *pl Informal* legs: *After the accident, he was shaky on his pins.*

v **pinned, pin·ning** 1 fasten with a pin or pins: *to pin a medal on someone's chest.* 2 hold someone or something rigidly or without escape: *She pinned her wrestling partner to the mat.* <Old English *pinn* peg>

on pins and needles, anxious or uneasy.

pin down, a hold or bind to an undertaking or pledge. **b** prevent someone from escaping from a position or location.

pin on, *Informal* fix blame or responsibility: *The police could not pin the crime on him.*

pin your hopes on, rely heavily on.

PIN (pin) *n* in full, **personal identification number** a number unique to a customer, that gives access to banking services.

pin·a·fore (pin′ə fôr′) *n* 1 a collarless, sleeveless garment worn over a blouse. 2 *especially UK* a loose sleeveless garment, usually full-length, and worn over clothes to keep them clean. <*pin* + *afore* before, because it was originally pinned over clothes>

pi·ña·ta (pēn yä′tə) *n* a Mexican papier-mâché or clay figure, usually of an animal, filled with candies. Blindfolded children hit the piñata with sticks to release the candy. <Spanish, from Latin *pinea* pine cone, because of its shape>

pin·ball (pin′bol′) *n* a game in which the player scores points by releasing a small metal ball that rolls down a sloping board, which is studded with pins or pegs, so that it drops into a numbered compartment.

pince–nez (pans′nā′) *or* (pins′nā′) *n* eyeglasses kept in place by a clip across the bridge of the nose. See CONTACT LENS for picture. <French = pinches nose>

pin·cer (pin′sər) *n* 1 a claw of a crab, lobster, or other crustacean, used to pinch or nip. 2 a military operation in which the enemy is surrounded by the meeting of converging bodies of troops. 3 **pincers** *pl* a tool for gripping and holding tight, made like scissors but with jaws instead of blades. <Old French *pincier* to pinch>

pinch (pinch) *v* 1 squeeze or press so as to hurt: *I pinched my finger in the door. The new shoes pinched her feet.* 2 cause to shrink or become thin: *a face pinched by hunger.* 3 limit closely: *to be pinched for space.* 4 live frugally: *to pinch and scrape.* 5 (*usually with* **back**) remove a bud or leaf in order to encourage growth in a plant: *Pinch back the buds in June, and there will be more flowers in September.* 6 *Informal* arrest someone.

n 1 a squeeze between two hard edges: *He gave his arm a pinch to keep awake.* 2 sharp pressure that hurts: *the pinch of tight shoes.* 3 as much as can be taken up with the tips of finger and thumb: *a pinch of salt.* 4 discomfort, need, or distress, or the time when this is experienced: *the pinch of hunger. We will ask for help in a pinch.* 5 *Informal* arrest by the police. <Old French *pincier* to pinch> **pinch′er** *n.*

feel the pinch, feel hardship or the effects of a difficult situation: *By the third month of drought they were beginning to feel the pinch.*

pinched (pinchd) *adj* showing the effects of cold, worry, or hunger by looking tense and pale.

pinch–hit (pinch′hit′) *v* **pinch-hit, pinch-hit·ting** 1 *Baseball* bat for another player, especially when a hit is badly needed. 2 take another's place in an emergency: *The pianist is ill and our teacher will pinch-hit for her at the concert tonight.* **pinch′-hit′ter** *n.*

pin·cush·ion (pin′ku̇sh′ən) *n* a small cushion to stick pins in until they are needed.

pine[1] (pīn) *n* an evergreen tree with long, needlelike leaves growing in tufts from the stems or the wood of this tree. <Latin *pinus*>

pine[2] (pīn) *v* **pined, pin·ing** 1 miss and long for the return of someone or something: *The mother was pining to see her son.* 2 waste away with pain, hunger, grief, or desire. <Latin *peona* pain>

pine·ap·ple (pī′nap′əl) *n* a large tropical fruit with a tough, segmented skin topped by a tuft of spiny leaves, and with juicy yellow flesh.

pine cone *n* a cone of a pine tree.

pine needle *n* the needlelike leaf of a pine tree.

pine cone

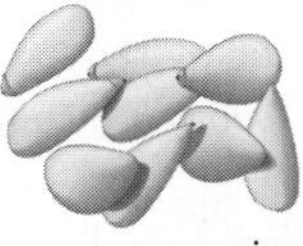
pine nuts

pine nut *n* the edible seed of a pine tree found in the southwest US and Mexico.

pine tar *n* a brownish black, semisolid tar obtained by distilling pine wood and used especially in roofing materials, paints, and varnishes, and as an antiseptic.

pine·y (pīn′ē) PINY.

ping (ping) *n* a short, ringing sound like that of the sound produced when a metal object is struck.

v Computers using a program called *Packet Internet Groper*, send a message to a computer to check that it is reachable: *I pinged you at home, but got no reply.*

✱ **pin·go** (ping′gō) *n* a dome-shaped mound of soil with a core of ice, found in permafrost regions. <Inuktitut *pinguq*>

Ping–Pong (ping′pong′) *Trademark n* table tennis.

pin·head (pin′hed′) *n* 1 the head of a pin. 2 *Informal* a stupid person.

pin·head·ed (pin′hed′əd) *Informal adj* stupid or foolish: *That was a pinheaded thing to do.*

pin·hole (pin′hōl′) *n* a tiny hole made by or as if by a pin.

pin·ion[1] (pin′yən) *n* the outermost part of a bird's wing, including the stiff flight feathers.

v 1 cut off or tie the pinions of a bird to prevent its flying. 2 tie or hold the arms or legs of someone: *His arms were pinioned behind his back.* <Old French, from Latin *pinna* feather>

pin·ion[2] (pin′yən) *n* a small gear with teeth that fit into those of a larger gear or RACK[1] (def. 4). <French, from Latin *pinus* pine>

a bat	e bed	i bid	o pot	u cup	th **thin**
ā cake	ē me	ī bite	ō go	ū rude	TH **then**
ä bar	ə about	ər over	ô for	u̇ put	zh measure

P

pink[1] (pingk) *n* **1** a plant with long, slender leaves, stems with swollen joints, and fragrant flowers. **2** the highest degree or condition of excellence: *An athlete needs to be in the pink of health.*
adj very pale red: *a pink pig with black spots.* <origin uncertain>

pink[2] (pingk) *v* cut the edge of cloth in small scallops or notches, such as to prevent fraying. <Old English *pynca* point>

pink·eye (ping′kī′) *n* a contagious disease characterized by inflammation and soreness of the membrane that lines the eyelids and covers the eyeball.

pink·ie (ping′kē) *Informal n* the smallest finger.

pink·ing shears (ping′king) *pln* shears with a serrated blade, used to cut a zigzag edge in fabric.

pink salmon *n* a Pacific salmon with pale pink flesh that is found along the coast of British Columbia and neighbouring coastal areas of the US.

pink slip *Informal n* notice of being fired or dismissed from one's job.

pin money *n* **1** money set aside for buying extra or minor things. **2** in former times, an allowance of money given to a wife for her personal expenses.

pin·na·cle (pin′ə kəl) *n* **1** a slender turret or spire built as an ornament to a roof. **2** a high peak or point of rock. **3** the highest point of development or achievement: *at the pinnacle of her fame.* <Latin *pinna* peak>

pin·nate (pin′āt) *adj* of or like a leaf that has parts arranged on either sides of a stem, typically in pairs opposite each other. <Latin *pinna* feather, so called for its resemblance to a feather> **pin′nate·ly** *adv.*

pi·noch·le or **pi·noc·le** (pē′nuk′əl) *n* a card game played with 48 cards, in which points are scored according to the value of certain combinations of cards, or the combination of the jack of diamonds and the queen of spades in this game. <origin uncertain>

pin·point (pin′point′) *n* **1** the point of a pin. **2** something very small or sharp: *We could see a pinpoint of light through a hole in the blind.*
v aim at or locate precisely: *to pinpoint the heart of the problem.*
adj extremely accurate or precise: *pinpoint bombing.*

pin·prick (pin′prik′) *n* a tiny mark, hole, or pain from a pin or something like a pin.

pin·stripe (pin′strīp′) *n* a fabric with narrow stripes, or a garment, especially a business suit, made with such cloth.

pint (pīnt) *n* a nonmetric unit for measuring liquids, equal to about 0.57 L. <Old French *pinte*>

pin·tail (pin′tāl′) *n* a slender duck with grey, white, and brown plumage, and pointed tail feathers.

pin·to (pin′tō) *adj* spotted in two or more colours.
n, pl **pin·tos** a horse with this colouring.

pinto bean *n* a medium-size speckled variety of kidney bean.

pint–sized (pīnt′sīzd′) *Informal adj* small.

pin–up (pin′up′) *n* a picture or poster of a famous or attractive person, pinned up on a wall, or the person who is so displayed.
adj very attractive.

pin·wheel (pin′wēl′) *n* a toy made of a wheel fastened to a stick by a pin so that it revolves in the wind, or something that spins or rotates like this, decorated with a flat spiral design.
adj to do with a flat spiral design: *pinwheel sandwiches.*

pin·worm (pin′wərm′) *n* a small, threadlike worm that is an intestinal parasite in vertebrates, especially a worm that infests the rectum and large intestine of human beings.

pin·y (pī′nē) *adj* **pin·i·er, pin·i·est 1** abounding in or covered with pine trees: *piny mountains.* **2** to do with pine trees: *a piny fragrance.* Also, **piney**.

Pin·yin (pin′yin′) *n* the system for transcribing Chinese words into roman letters. <Mandarin = spell-sound>

pi·on (pī′on) *Physics n* a meson with a positive, negative, or no electric charge and a mass many times that of an electron. <*pi*, Greek letter p, + *meson*>

pi·o·neer (pī′ə nēr′) *n* **1** a person who settles in a region that has not been settled before. **2** a person who goes first or does something and so prepares a way for others. **3** one of a group of soldiers whose job it is to go in advance of other troops, preparing roads or terrain for the main body of troops.
v prepare or open up for others: *Astronauts pioneered outer space.*

ETYMOLOGY

Pioneer, originally *pionner*, came (in the 1500s) from French *pionnier*, meaning "soldier who goes ahead of an army to prepare the route." Pioneers, similarly, are those who go ahead of others.

pioneer organism *Ecology n* any of the first species to establish itself in a recently destroyed habitat or biome.

pi·ous (pī′əs) *adj* **1** with or showing reverence for God: *a pious person, a pious act.* **2** showing scruples in a smug or self-righteous way, especially when not sincere: *pious platitudes about work and duty.* <Latin *pius*>
pi′ous·ly *adv.* **pi′ous·ness** *n.*

pip[1] (pip) *n* a small hard seed of a fruit, such as of an apple or orange. <*pippin*, a type of apple>

pip[2] (pip) *n* **1** a spot on a playing card, domino, or die. **2** a small shape or symbol, especially, in the British army, a star of rank worn on the shoulder of an officer. <origin uncertain>

pipe (pīp) *n* **1** a tube through which a liquid or gas flows. **2** a tube with a bowl at one end, for smoking tobacco or some other substance. **3** a musical instrument with a single tube into which the player blows. **4** one of the tubes in a pipe organ.
v **piped, pip·ing 1** carry by means of a pipe or pipes: *water piped from a well.* **2** (*with* ***in***) transmit music, speech, or sounds by means of an electronic system: *The background music for the reception will be piped in.* **3** play music on a pipe. **4** sing or speak in a shrill voice. **5** give

orders or signals by whistle or pipe: *All hands were piped on deck.* **6** decorate with a cordlike fold: *a red cushion piped with gold.* <Old English = musical tube>
pipe down, *Slang* be quiet or quieter.
pipe up, *Informal* begin to speak, especially in a high voice.
put that in your pipe and smoke it, *Informal* see if you can accept that.

pipe cleaner *n* a short length of fine twisted wire covered with small tufts of yarn, used to clean the inside of a smoker's pipe.

pipe dream *Informal n* an impractical idea.

pipe·ful (pīp′fůl) *n, pl* **pipe·fuls** the amount needed to fill the bowl of a smoker's pipe.

pipe·line (pī′plīn′) *n* **1** a line of pipes for carrying gas, oil, or other liquids: *Some pipelines were hundreds of kilometres long.* **2** a direct channel for supplying information: *The student council acts as a pipeline between the students and the school administration.*
v **pipe·lined, pipe·lin·ing** carry by a pipeline.
in the pipeline, about to appear or happen: *New antipollution legislation is in the pipeline.*

pipe organ *Music n* a large wind instrument consisting of sets of pipes of different diameters and lengths which are sounded by forcing air through them by means of keys and pedals.

pip·er (pī′pər) *n* a person who plays on a pipe or bagpipe, especially one who goes from place to place to do it.
pay the piper, bear the consequences of an action.

pi·pette (pi pet′) *or* (pī pet′) *n* a slender pipe or tube for transferring or measuring liquids, especially in chemical laboratories.

pipe wrench *n* an adjustable wrench for gripping and turning pipes.

pip·ing (pī′ping) *n* **1** a quantity or system of pipes: *copper piping.* **2** the music of a pipe or pipes. **3** shrill sounds or calls: *the piping of frogs in the spring.* **4** a narrow band of material, sometimes containing a cord, used for trimming along edges and seams of clothing, curtains, or upholstery. **5** ornamental lines of icing or meringue on a cake or pastry.
adj shrill.
piping hot, very hot.

✱ **pip·sis·se·wa** (pip sis′ə wə) *n* a small plant with evergreen leaves and waxy flowers. <Abenaki *kpi-pskwahsawe* flower of the woods>

pip·squeak (pip′skwēk′) *Informal n* a person considered to be unimportant, either because of youth or small size. <imitative>

pi·quant (pē′kənt) *adj* **1** sharp or pungent in a pleasing way: *a piquant sauce.* **2** pleasantly stimulating to the mind: *a piquant bit of news.* **pi′quan·cy** *n.* **pi′quant·ly** *adv.*

pique (pēk) *n* a feeling of irritation or resentment at being slighted: *She left the party in a pique.*
v **piqued, pi·quing** **1** cause a feeling of irritation or resentment in: *It piqued her that they had gone ahead with their plans without consulting her.* **2** stimulate interest or curiosity: *Our curiosity was piqued by the locked trunk.* <French = irritate>

pi·ra·cy (pī′rə sē) *n, pl* **pi·ra·cies** **1** the act of attacking and robbing ships at sea. **2** an act of violent seizure resembling this, especially hijacking: *air piracy.* **3** the use or reproduction of someone else's work without permission.

pi·ra·nha (pi rå′nyə) *or* (pi ran′ə) *n* a small freshwater fish of tropical America with very sharp teeth. Some piranhas tear flesh from their prey and groups of them can attack human beings or large animals. <Portuguese, from Tupi (a language of S America) *pira* fish + *sainha* tooth>

pi·rate (pī′rit) *n* **1** one who attacks and robs ships at sea. **2** a person who uses or reproduces another's work without permission and usually to make a profit.
v **pi·rat·ed, pi·rat·ing** **1** use or reproduce another's work without permission. <Latin, from Greek *peira* attack>
pi·rat′i·cal *adj.* **pi·rat′i·cal·ly** *adv.*

pi·rosh·ki or **pi·rozh·ki** (pir′əsh kē′) *pln* small pastry turnovers filled usually with a beef mixture. <Russian>

pir·ou·ette (pir′ū et′) *n* the act of whirling about on one foot or on the toes, especially in ballet, usually with the raised foot touching the knee of the supporting leg.
v **pir·ou·et·ted, pir·ou·et·ting** whirl in this way. <French = spinning top>

pis·ca·to·ri·al (pis′kə tȯ′rē əl) *adj* to do with fishing.

Pis·ces (pī′sēz) *n* **1** *Astronomy* a northern constellation thought of as having the shape of two fishes with a ribbon connecting their tails. **2** *Astrology* **a** the twelfth sign of the zodiac. The sun enters Pisces about February 21. **b** a person born under this sign. <Latin *piscis* fish>

pis·ta·chi·o (pis tash′ē ō′) *or* (pis tå′shē ō′) *n,*
pl **pis·ta·chi·os** the greenish, edible seed of a small tree of the cashew family that grows in warm climates.
adj light yellowish green. <Old French, from Greek *pistakion*>

pis·til (pis′təl) *n* the part of a flower that produces seeds, consisting of a base section called the ovary, a thinner middle section, the style, and, at the top, the stigma. See ANTHER for picture. <French, from Latin *pistilllum* pestle>

pis·til·late (pis′tə lāt) *Botany adj* with a pistil or pistils, but with no stamens.

pis·tol (pis′təl) *n* a small, short gun capable of being held and fired with one hand. <French, from Czech *pist'ala*>

pis·ton (pis′tən) *n* **1** a short cylinder or disc in an engine or pump that closely fits inside a tube in which it is moved back and forth by the force of exploding vapour or steam. **2** a sliding valve in a wind musical instrument that, when pressed by the fingers, lowers the pitch. <French, from Latin *pinsere* pound>

piston ring *n* a metal ring split so it can expand, put around a piston to ensure a tight fit.

piston rod *n* a rod that moves or is moved by a piston.

a bat	e bed	i bid	o pot	u cup	th **thin**
ā cake	ē me	ī bite	ō go	ū rude	TH **then**
å bar	ə about	ər over	ȯ for	ů put	zh measure

P

pitching softball

fast pitch

In a **fast-pitch** game (a form of softball), the pitches are thrown underhand. The ball, which is larger than a regulation baseball, is thrown as fast as possible.

slow pitch

In **slow-pitch** (also called slo-pitch), the softball is thrown underhand, but the pitch must be thrown at a moderate speed in an arc that reaches between 1.6 m and 3.7 m from the ground.

---

pit[1] (pit) *n* **1 a** a large hole in the ground: *Deep pits are used to trap wild animals.* **b** a large hole in the ground containing a certain material: *a tar pit, a gravel pit.* **2** a small hollow on a surface: *pits on a copper pot, pits on the face as a result of acne.* **3 a** the area directly in front of and below the stage of a theatre, where the orchestra sits. **b** *UK* the rear part of the main floor of a theatre, or the people who sit there. **4** the part of a casino where gambling takes place: *The people in charge of the pit are looking for cheaters.* **5** an enclosed place where animals or birds are made to fight each other: *a pit for bearbaiting.* **6** an area in a service station, often below floor level, used in repairing and servicing vehicles. **7** an area alongside a car racetrack where the cars are serviced or repaired during a race.
v **pit·ted, pit·ting 1** mark with small hollows or indentations: *a puddle pitted by raindrops.* **2** set to fight or compete: *The sisters were pitted against each other in the tennis tournament.* <Old English *pytt*>
be the pits, *Informal* be very unpleasant or of bad quality: *That exam was the pits.*

pit[2] (pit) *n* the hard seed or stone of a fruit.
v **pit·ted, pit·ting** remove pits from fruit. <Dutch>

pi·ta (pē′tə) *n* a flat, hollow bread that can be split open to hold a filling. <Greek *pitta* cake>

pit·a·pat (pit′ə pat′) *adv* with a quick succession of beats or taps: *My heart was going pitapat.*
n the movement or sound of something going pitapat.

pit bull *n* in full, **pit bull terrier** a small, powerful dog with strong jaws, originally trained to fight other dogs.

pitch[1] (pich) *v* **1** throw or fling, especially roughly or casually: *She pitched the paper cup into the garbage can.* **2** throw a baseball toward a batter. **3** erect or set up a temporary structure: *to pitch a tent, to pitch camp.* **4** make an attempt to persuade someone, especially to buy something or to grant a contract: *He pitched the virtues of the new product.* **5** fall or plunge forward: *The man lost his balance and pitched down the cliff.* **6** of a ship or boat, plunge with the bow rising and then falling: *The ship pitched about in the storm.* **7** set the voice or a piece of music at a certain level or a particular key: *Pitch your voice a little higher at the end of this phrase.* **8** express at a particular level of ease or difficulty: *Her talk was pitched perfectly for a young audience.*
n **1** a level of intensity: *The poor woman has reached the lowest pitch of bad fortune.* **2** the highness or lowness of a sound. **3** a form of words used when trying to persuade someone to buy or accept something: *a sales pitch.* **4** a swaying of a ship, aircraft, or motor vehicle around a horizontal axis at right angles to the direction of motion. **5** *Baseball* the delivery of a ball by a pitcher. **6** the steepness of a slope. **7 a** the place where certain games are played: *a horseshoe pitch.* **b** the place where an activity is carried on, such as where a street vendor or a performer works: *Our class had the best pitch at the school Bake Sale.* <Middle English>
pitch in, *Informal* work or begin to work vigorously, usually with others: *All the girls pitched in to get the job done.*
pitch into, *Informal* attack verbally or physically.

pitch[2] (pich) *n* **1** a black, sticky substance obtained from distilling tar or turpentine, used for waterproofing. **2** a similar substance, such as asphalt or bitumen. <Old English *pic*>

pitch–black (pich′blak′) *adj* very dark or black.

pitch·blende (pich′blend′) *n* a mineral consisting largely of uranium oxide, occurring in black or brown pitchlike masses. <German *Pech* pitch, because of its black colour + *blenden* deceive, because it often resembles a different mineral>

pitch–dark (pich′därk′) *adj* with no light at all: *It was pitch-dark in the room when the curtains were pulled shut.*

pitched battle *n* an intense battle involving close combat.

pitch·er[1] (pich′ər) *n* a container for holding and pouring liquids, with a lip on one side and a handle on the other, or the the amount that a pitcher holds. <Old French, from Latin *picarium*>

pitch·er[2] (pich′ər) *n* the player on a baseball team who throws the ball to the batter.

pitch·er·ful (pich′ər fůl′) *n, pl* **pitch·er·fuls** the amount needed to fill a pitcher.

pitcher plant *n* a plant that grows in bogs, with a deep, pitcherlike pouch in which insects are trapped, to be digested by the plant. It is the floral emblem of Newfoundland and Labrador.

pitch·fork (pich′fôrk′) *n* a large fork with a long handle and two or three slightly curved prongs, used for lifting and throwing hay or straw.
v lift and throw with a pitchfork.

pitch pine *n* a pine whose resin is used to make pitch or turpentine, especially a N American pine with yellowish green needles.

pitch pipe *n* a small musical pipe with one or more fixed tones, used to give the desired musical pitch for singing or for tuning an instrument.

pit·e·ous (pit′ē əs) *adj* to be pitied: *The abandoned kitten was a piteous sight.* **pit′e·ous·ly** *adv.* **pit′e·ous·ness** *n.*

pit·fall (pit′fol′) *n* an unsuspected danger or difficulty.

pith (pith) *n* **1** the central, spongy tissue in the stems of some plants. **2** a similar tissue found in other parts of plants, such as that lining the skin of an orange. **3** an important or essential part: *the pith of a speech.* **4** strong and vigorous expression: *Her talk had a lot of pith to it.* <Old English *pitha*>

pith helmet *n* a sun hat with a rounded top, originally made from the dried pith of a tropical plant.

pith·y (pith′ē) *adj* **pith·i·er, pith·i·est** **1** full of substance, meaning, force, or vigour: *pithy phrases, a pithy speaker.* **2** to do with plant pith. **pith′i·ly** *adv.* **pith′i·ness** *n.*

pit·i·a·ble (pit′ē ə bəl) *adj* **1** to be pitied. **2** deserving contempt: *His half-hearted attempts to help were pitiable.* **pit′i·a·bly** *adv.*

pit·i·ful (pit′ē fəl) *adj* **1** to be pitied: *The deserted animals were a pitiful sight.* **2** deserving contempt: *a pitiful performance.* **pit′i·ful·ly** *adv.* **pit′i·ful·ness** *n.*

CONFUSABLES

Pitiful means "arousing pity" and emphasizes the effect on others: *The homeless kittens were pitiful.*

Piteous emphasizes that quality that makes an appeal for pity: *The lost child had a piteous cry.*

pit·i·less (pit′ē lis) *adj* showing no pity or mercy: *a pitiless tyrant, a pitiless act.* **pit′i·less·ly** *adv.* **pit′i·less·ness** *n.*

🍁 **pit·lamp·ing** (pit′lamp ing) *especially British Columbia* *n* fishing or hunting wearing a lamp; jacklighting. **pit′lamp** *v.* **pit′lamp·er** *n.*

pi·ton (pē′ton) *or* (pē ton′) *n* an iron spike with a ring at one end, used in mountain climbing. It can be driven into a crack in rock or ice and used as a foothold or as an anchor for a rope. <French = eye bolt>

pit stop *n* **1** a stop for repairs or refuelling during an auto race. **2** *Informal* a short break, especially one made during a journey. **3** a place where such a stop is made.

pit·tance *n* an inadequate payment, share, allowance, or wage. <Old French, from Latin *pietas* pity>

pit·ted[1] (pit′əd) *adj* marked with pits: *pitted asphalt. His face was badly pitted with acne scars.* <*pit*[1]>

pit·ted[2] (pit′əd) *adj* with the pits removed: *pitted olives, pitted cherries.* <*pit*[2]>

pit·ter–pat·ter (pit′ər pat′ər) *n* a rapid series of light beats or taps, as of raindrops, or the sound this creates.
adv with a rapid series of light beats or taps: *steps that go pitter-patter.*
v move or fall with a pitter-patter: *Rain pitter-pattered on the roof.* <*patter*[1]>

ETYMOLOGY

Pitter-patter is an example of a frequent pattern of word formation in English in which syllables are repeated, either with a change of vowel as in *mishmash, dilly-dally,* and *teeter-totter*, or a change of initial consonant as in *hodgepodge, claptrap,* and *helter-skelter.* This process, called reduplication, produces words that have an informal or playful effect.

pi·tu·i·tar·y gland (pi tū′i ter′ē) *or* (pi tyū′i ter′ē) *n* a small, oval endocrine gland situated at the base of the brain. It secretes hormones that promote growth, stimulate other glands, and regulate basic bodily functions. <Latin *pituita* phlegm>

pit viper *n* a poisonous snake, such as the rattlesnake, which has heat-sensitive pits on the head that allows it to sense the presence of warm-blooded animals.

pit·y (pit′ē) *n, pl* **pit·ies** **1** sympathy, feeling, or sorrow for another's suffering or distress. **2** a cause for pity or regret: *It is a pity to be kept in the house in good weather.*
v **pit·ied, pit·y·ing** feel pity for. <Old French, from Latin *pietas*> **pit′y·ing·ly** *adv.*
have (or **take**) **pity on,** show pity for.

piv·ot (piv′ət) *n* a shaft, pin, or point on which something turns.
v turn on a pivot or something like a pivot: *to pivot on your heel.* <origin uncertain> **piv′ot·al** *adj.*

pix·el (pik′səl) *n* a tiny illuminated dot, one of many that make up an image on a computer or TV screen. <*pict*(*ure*) + *el*(*ement*)>

pix·ie or **pix·y** (pik′sē) *n, pl* **pix·ies** a fairy or elf. <origin uncertain>

a bat	e bed	i bid	o pot	u cup	th **thin**
ā cake	ē me	ī bite	ō go	ū rude	ᴛʜ **then**
ä bar	ə about	ər over	ô for	ů put	zh measure

P

piz·za (pē′tsə) *n* a thin layer of bread dough covered with one or more toppings of cheese, sausage, vegetables, etc., and quickly baked at high heat. <Italian = pie>

pizza parlour *n* a pizzeria.

piz·zazz (pi′zaz) *Informal n* glamour and vitality: *Accessories add pizzazz to a basic suit. His ideas are no better, but he's got more pizzazz as a leader.* Also, **pizazz.** <origin uncertain> **piz·zaz·zy** *adj.*

piz·ze·ri·a (pē′tsə rē′ə) *n* a place where pizzas are made and sold for taking out, to be delivered, or for eating on the premises.

piz·zi·ca·to (pit′sə kȧ′tō) *Music adv* the act of plucking the strings of a musical instrument with the finger instead of using the bow.
adj played in this way.
n, pl **piz·zi·ca·ti** (-tē) the technique of playing in this way. <Italian *pizzicare* to twang>

pj's or **p.j.'s** *Informal pln* pyjamas.

plac·ard (plak′ȧrd) *for n,* (plə kȧrd′) *or* (plak′ȧrd) *for v.*
n a notice to be posted in a public place.
v put placards on or in: *The circus placarded the city with advertisements.* <Old French, from Dutch *placken*>

pla·cate (plak′āt), (plā′kāt), *or* (plə kāt′) *v* **pla·cat·ed, pla·cat·ing** soothe or satisfy the anger of: *to placate a person you have offended.* <Latin *placare*>

place (plās) *n* **1** a particular part of an area or a surface: *This would be a good place for a picnic.* **2** a geographical location: *faraway places with strange names.* **3** a building or spot used for a certain purpose: *a place of business.* **4** a home or dwelling: *We all went to my place for supper after skating.* **5** a part of or spot in something: *There's a place at the table for you. There's a sore place on my leg where I bumped into the table.* **6 a** the proper or natural position: *This is neither the time nor the place for a private conversation. Put the books in place on the shelf.* **b** the appropriate right or duty: *It is not my place to tell you how to live your life.* **7 a** a position in time or space: *The performance went too slowly in several places. I've lost my place in the book.* **b** a particular situation or set of circumstances: *How would you feel if you put yourself in my place?* **8** a space or seat for a person: *Keep a place for me if you reach the boat first.* **9** official employment or position: *to get a place in a department store.* **10** a step in the order of proceeding: *In the first place, the room is too small, and in the second place, it is too dirty.* **11** in arithmetic, the position of a figure in a number or series: *correct to the first decimal place.* **12** a position at the finish of a race or contest: *She won first place.*
v **placed, plac·ing 1** put in a spot, position, condition, or relation: *Place the golf ball on the tee. The kitten was placed in a good home. The people placed confidence in their leader. Do you place health before wealth?* **2** give the place, position, or condition of: *I remember his name, but I cannot place him.* **3** appoint a person to a position or office: *to be placed in an important position in the government.* **4** be among the leaders at the finish of a race or competition: *He failed to place in the first race and was eliminated.* <Old French, from Greek *platus* broad>
all over the place, *Informal* **a** everywhere. **b** disorderly, imprecise, or inconsistent, etc.: *Their strategy was all over the place.*
give place, a make room. **b** yield or give in: *His anger gave place to remorse.*
go places, *Informal* achieve success.
in place, a in the proper or usual place: *Make sure all the tools are in place on the shelf.* **b** ready for action or use: *New policies are in place to deal with the situation.*
in place of, instead of: *Use water in place of milk in that recipe.*
know your place, act according to your position in life.
out of place, a not in the proper or usual place. **b** inappropriate or ill-timed.
place in the sun, a favourable position.
put someone in his or **her place,** tell or show that a person is unduly conceited.
take place, happen or occur.

pla·ce·bo (plə sē′bō) *n, pl* **pla·ce·bos** or **pla·ce·boes** a pill or other substance that, although containing no medicine, has satisfying or satisfactory effects, or is used as a control in an experiment to test a new drug. <Latin = I shall please>

place card *n* a small card with a person's name on it, to indicate where one is to sit at the table.

place·mat (plās′mat) *n* a small, usually oblong, mat of cloth, paper, or plastic that serves as an individual table cover for a person at a meal.

place·ment (plās′mənt) *n* **1** a location or arrangement. **2** the process of finding work or a job for a person.

placement kick *n* a kick given a football after it has been put on the ground.

pla·cen·ta (plə sen′tə) *n, pl* **pla·cen·tas** the organ by which a mammal's fetus is attached to the wall of the womb and is nourished. <Latin, from Greek *plakos* flat cake> **pla·cen′tal** *adj.*

plac·er[1] (plā′sər) *n* a person who or thing that places.

plac·er[2] (plas′ər) *n* a deposit of sand or gravel containing particles of gold or other valuable minerals that can be washed out. <Spanish = deposit>

placer mining (plas′ər) *n* the process of washing loose sand or gravel for gold or other minerals.

place setting *n* the dishes and cutlery required to set one person's place at a table.

place value *n* the value of a digit according to its position in a number. Example: In 582, the place values are 5 x 100, 8 x 10, 2 x 1.

plac·id (plas′id) *adj* calm, peaceful, and quiet: *a placid lake, a placid face.* <Latin *placidus* peaceful> **pla·cid′i·ty** *n.* **plac′id·ly** *adv.* **plac′id·ness** *n.*

SYNONYMS

Placid is one of several words that can suggest an untroubled state for people or things: *She looked placid in spite of her troubles. It was a placid meeting.*

Serene suggests calm: *He felt serene as he watched the beautiful sunset.*

Tranquil suggests free from agitation or disturbance: *The lake became tranquil after the storm.*

plack·et (plak′it) *n* an opening or slit at the top of a garment to make it easy to put on.

pla·gia·rism (plā′jə riz′əm) *n* **1** the act or practice of using someone else's work or ideas without permission or acknowledgment. **2** a work or idea taken from another and used as one's own. **pla′gia·rist** *n.* **pla′gia·rize′** *v.* **pla′gia·riz′er** *n.*

plague (plāg) *n* **1** a contagious disease that spreads rapidly and kills many people: *bubonic plague.* **2** an unusually large number of troublesome insects, birds, or animals.
v **plagued, pla·guing 1** cause to suffer from a disease or calamity. **2** annoy or bother: *Stop plaguing me for money.* <Latin *plaga* wound>

pla·guy (plā′gē) *Informal adj* troublesome or annoying.

plaice (plās) *n, pl* **plaice** or **plaic·es** a N Atlantic or European flatfish used as food. <Old French, from Greek *platus* broad>

plaid (plad) *n* a pattern consisting of a repeated design of broad and narrow unevenly spaced stripes crossing each other at right angles. <Gaelic *plaide* blanket>

plain (plān) *adj* **1** easy to understand: *The meaning is plain.* **2 a** without ornament or decoration: *a plain cake.* **b** without a pattern or variegated colour: *a plain blue fabric.* **3** not rich or highly seasoned: *plain food.* **4 a** simple in manner: *They're plain people.* **b** frank and honest: *plain speech.* **5** without special attractiveness: *a plain face.*
adv in a plain manner: *Speak it plain.*
n often, **plains** *pl* a large, more or less flat and treeless stretch of land: *The rain in Spain stays mainly in the plain. Buffalo used to roam the North American plains.* <Old French, from Latin *planus* flat> **plain′ly** *adv.* **plain′ness** *n.*

SYNONYMS

Plain is a general word meaning "easy to understand": *The intense emotions crossing her face were plain for all to see.*

Evident means "being clearly seen or understood": *It was evident that the teacher did not appreciate the disruption to the class.*

Lucid is a more formal word meaning "easy to understand": *The lawyer provided a lucid definition of the bylaw.*

plain·clothes (plān′klōz) *adj* wearing ordinary clothes, not a uniform, when on duty: *a plainclothes police officer.*

Plain People *n* the Mennonites, Amish, and other groups who have a plain, simple way of life and style of wearing clothes.

plain sailing *n* a clear, simple course of action with easy, unobstructed progress: *We had some problems at first but after that it was plain sailing.*

plains buffalo *n* a buffalo native to the great plains, smaller than the wood buffalo.

Plains Cree *n* See CREE.

Plains Indians *pln* in former times, a First Nations or Native American people who inhabited the Great Plains of western N America.

Plains of A·bra·ham (ā′brə ham′) *n* a field outside and just west of Québec City, the site of the battle of 1759 that gave the British military supremacy in N America.

plain·song (plān′song′) *n* vocal music used in the Christian church, sung in unison and unaccompanied, and with a limited musical scale and free rhythm corresponding to the words of the liturgy. See also GREGORIAN CHANT. <translation of Latin *cantus planus*>

plain–spo·ken (plān′spō′kən) *adj* plain or frank in speech.

plaint (plānt) *Poetic n* complaint. <Old French *plainte,* from Latin *planctus* lamenting>

plain·tiff (plān′tif) *n* a person who begins a lawsuit against another.

plain·tive (plān′tiv) *adj* mournful and sad: *a plaintive song.* **plain′tive·ly** *adv.* **plain′tive·ness** *n.*

plait (plāt) *or* (plat) *n* a single length of braided hair, straw, rope, or other material: *I sometimes wear my hair in a plait.*
v braid: *She plaits her own hair.* <Old French, from Latin *plicare* to fold>

plan (plan) *n* **1** a way of making or doing something that has been worked out in advance: *He explained his plan for attracting more tourists to the area.* **2** a goal, purpose, or aim: *Her plan is to have a black belt in karate by the end of the year.* **3** a detailed diagram, drawing, or map, especially one showing how floors of a building are arranged and the relative size of its rooms, or a large-scale, detailed map of a small area.
v **planned, plan·ning 1** think out in advance how something is to be made or done: *to plan a program.* **2** have in mind as a purpose: *We are planning to take a long vacation this year.* **3** make a drawing, diagram, or map of something. <French, from Latin *planus* flat surface>
plan on, a intend or have plans for: *I plan on going. They plan on an early start.* **b** base one's plans on: *If we plan on 200 guests, we'll need a lot of food.*

plane[1] (plān) *n* **1** a flat or level surface. **2** a level of existence, thought, conduct, or achievement: *the intellectual plane. He keeps his work on a high plane.* **3** an airplane. **4** *Mathematics* a geometrical surface such that if two points on it are joined by a straight line, the line will be contained wholly in the surface.
adj **1** flat or level. **2** *Mathematics* to do with a geometrical plane: *A circle is a plane figure, but a sphere is a solid.*
v **planed, plan·ing 1** glide as a bird, airborne object, or aircraft does. **2** skim over the surface of the water, as a speedboat or surfboard does. <Latin *planus* flat surface>

plane[2] (plān) *n* a carpenter's tool with a blade for smoothing or shaping wood.
v **planed, plan·ing** make smooth or level by means of a plane. <French, from Latin *planus* flat surface>

plane[3] (plān) *n* a tree with large, lobed leaves and spreading branches.

a bat	e bed	i bid	o pot	u cup	th **thin**
ā cake	ē me	ī bite	ō go	ū rude	ᴛʜ **then**
à bar	ə about	ər over	ȯ for	u̇ put	zh measure

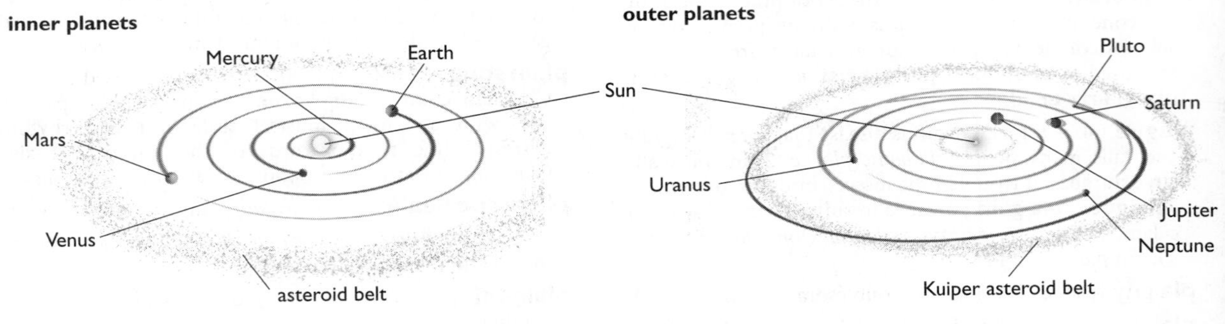

plane figure *n* a figure that lies in one geometrical plane.

plane geometry *n* a branch of geometry dealing with plane figures.

plane·load (plān′lōd′) *n* a load that fills an airplane: *a planeload of supplies.*

plan·er (plā′nər) *n* a person who or thing that planes, especially a machine for planing wood or for finishing flat surfaces on metal.

plan·et (plan′it) *Astronomy n* a celestial body that moves around a star in an elliptical orbit. In our solar system, that star is the Sun. The planets Mercury, Venus, Earth, and Mars are called the **inner planets**; Jupiter, Saturn, Uranus, Neptune, and Pluto are the **outer planets.** <Old French, from Greek *planan* wander> **plan′e·tar′y** *adj.*

plan·e·tar·i·um (plan′ə ter′ē əm) *n, pl* **plan·e·tar·i·ums** or **plan·e·tar·i·a** (-ē ə) a domed building in which images of the sun, moon, planets, and stars are projected for public entertainment or education.

plan·gent (plan′jənt) *adj* with a deep, loud, sombre or melancholy sound. <Latin *plangere* lament>

plank (plangk) *n* **1** a long, narrow, flat piece of sawed timber. **2** a feature of a political party's PLATFORM (def. 2): *The main plank of the party's election platform was a proposal to stimulate economic growth.*
v cook and serve on a wooden board: *planked salmon.* <Old French, from Latin *planca* board>
walk the plank, a in former times, be forced by pirates to walk off a plank extending from a ship's side over the water. **b** *Informal* undergo something unpleasant, such as the loss of a job or position.

🍁 **plank house** *n* among First Nations peoples of the Pacific Northwest, a long, rectangular communal building made of cedar, and capable of housing several families. Now used mainly for ceremonial events. Compare LONGHOUSE.

plank·ing (plang′king) *n* **1** the act of laying or covering with planks. **2** a quantity of planks together: *They bought planking for the floor of the shed.*

plank·ton (plangk′tən) *n* the mass of very small or microscopic animal or plant life that floats or drifts near the surface of bodies of salt and fresh water, providing food for fish and other water animals. <German, from Greek *plazein* wander>

plan·ner (plan′ər) *n* a person who plans, especially one whose job is planning things, such as a **city planner** who is employed to oversee urban development.

plant (plant) *n* **1 a** any of a KINGDOM (def. 3) of living things that typically grow in one place, absorb water and inorganic substances through roots, and synthesize nutrients in their leaves by photosynthesis. See also EUKARYOTE. **b** a small organism of this kind that has a soft stem, in contrast to a tree or shrub: *a tomato plant.* See VENATION for picture. **2** a place where industry, manufacturing, or maintenance is carried out: *an automotive plant, a school plant.* **3 a** a thing placed so as to trap: *She claimed that the money found in her room was a plant.* **b** a person placed within a group to act as a spy or informer.
v **1 a** put or set in the ground to grow: *to plant seeds.* **b** provide with seed or plants: *We planted our garden last weekend.* **2** set or place firmly: *She planted her feet firmly apart and pulled hard on the rope.* **3** by careful means, make someone absorb ideas: *Who planted that notion in your head?* **4** place a person or thing so as to deceive: *The evidence was planted.* <Old English, from Latin *planta* sprout>

Plan·tag·e·net (plan taj′ə nit) *n* the royal family that ruled England from 1154 to 1485, from Henry II through Richard III.

plan·tain[1] (plan′tān) *n* a large banana with much starch and little sugar. <Spanish *platano*>

plan·tain[2] (plan′tān) *n* a plant with spikes of tiny, greenish flowers and broad leaves that flatten out from the base of the stem, often growing as a weed on lawns. <Old French, from Latin *planta* sole of the foot, because of the appearance of its leaves>

plantain lily HOSTA.

plan·tar (plan′tər) *adj* to do with the sole of the foot: *a plantar wart.* <Latin *planta* sole of the foot>

plan·ta·tion (plan tā′shən) *n* **1** a large farm or estate, especially in a tropical or semitropical country, on which crops such as cotton, tobacco, or sugar are grown. **2** a large group of trees or other plants that have been planted: *a rubber plantation.* **3** 🍁 a colony or settlement, such as that established in Newfoundland in the early 1600s.

plant·er (plan′tər) *n* **1** a person who owns or runs a plantation: *a cotton planter.* **2** a machine that or person who plants: *a corn planter.* **3** a decorative container in which flowers are planted. **4** 🍁 *Newfoundland* in former times, a person who hired others to fish, advancing their supplies and taking a share of the catch.

plaque (plak) *n* **1** an ornamental tablet of metal, plastic, porcelain, or wood that is fixed to a wall or other surface and is inscribed to commemorate a person or event. **2** a sticky deposit on teeth in which bacteria grow. **3** a small, raised, potentially harmful patch or area within the body, such as a fatty deposit on the wall of an artery. <French, from Dutch *plakken* to stick>

plas·ma (plaz′mə) *n* **1** the liquid, colourless part of blood or lymph, in which corpuscles are suspended. **2** the liquid, colourless part of milk, in which globules of fat are suspended. **3** *Physics* a gas heated to become a state of matter distinct from solids, liquids, and normal gases. A **plasma TV screen** holds many thousands of tiny glass bubbles filled with a neon-xenon mix. When an electrical current is applied, these gases heat up and form plasma, which in turn produces UV light. Compare LCD. <Latin, from Greek = something moulded>

plas·ter (plas′tər) *n* **1** a mixture of lime, sand, and water, that dries to a smooth surface. It is used for covering walls or ceilings. **2** plaster of Paris. **3** a medical substance spread on cloth that will stick to the body and protect cuts, relieve pain, or lessen congestion. **4** *UK* an adhesive bandage.
v **1** cover a surface with plaster. **2** spread with anything thickly: *My shoes were plastered with mud.* **3** make smooth and flat: *He plastered his wet hair down.* **4** apply a plaster to, or apply like a plaster. <Greek *en-* on + *plassein* mould>

plas·ter·board (plas′tər bȯrd′) *n* a thin board made of a layer of plaster between fibreboard or paper sheets, used for walls and partitions.

plas·tered (plas′tərd) *Informal adj* very drunk.

plas·ter·er (plas′tə rər) *n* a person who plasters walls, ceilings, or other surfaces.

plaster of Par·is (par′is) *n* a mixture of powdered gypsum and water that hardens quickly and is used for making moulds, statuary, or casts.

plas·tic (plas′tik) *n* **1** a material produced from organic polymers. After being moulded under heat or pressure, plastics harden and keep their shape. **2** *Informal* a credit card, or credit cards in general.
adj **1** made of plastic: *plastic cups.* **2** concerned with moulding or modelling: *Sculpture is a plastic art.* **3 a** easily moulded or shaped as a material, such as clay, wax, and plaster. **b** easily influenced or impressionable. **4** looking or tasting artificial: *plastic food.* <French, from Greek *plassein* to mould>

Plas·ti·cine (plas′ti sēn) *Trademark n* an oil-based modelling material, made in different colours, that is used especially by children.

plas·tic·i·ty (plas tis′ə tē) *n* the quality of being easily shaped or moulded.

plas·ti·cize (plas′tə sīz′) *v* **plas·ti·cized, plas·ti·ciz·ing** **1** make or become plastic. **2** treat with a plastic: *a plasticized fabric.*

plastic surgery *n* the repair or reconstruction of parts of the body, especially the face, by the transfer of tissue. Plastic surgery may be used to correct injuries or birth defects, or for cosmetic reasons. **plastic surgeon** *n.*

plastic wrap *n* a thin, stretchable, clinging film of plastic on a roll, used especially to wrap food.

plate (plāt) *n* **1 a** a china, plastic, paper, or metal dish, usually round and almost flat. **b** the contents of such a dish: *a plate of potatoes.* **2** the food served to one person at a formal meal: *The dinner will cost $30 a plate.* **3** a container similar to a plate, such as that passed in a church to receive a collection. **4** dishes or utensils made of or covered with silver or gold. **5 a** a thin, flat piece of metal, or armour made of such pieces of metal: *The warship was covered with steel plate.* **b** a body part resembling such metal plates: *Armadillos have a shell of overlapping bony plates.* **6** an enormous rigid segment of the earth's crust, several of which make up the earth's surface, slowly floating and moving on the softer mantle below. **7** the place where the batter in baseball stands to receive a pitched ball. **8** the part of a set of false teeth that fits to the gums, and in which the teeth are fixed: *an upper plate.* **9** a thin sheet of glass coated with chemicals that are sensitive to light: *Plates are sometimes used in taking photographs.* **10** a thin strip of metal that acts as an electrode in a storage battery, or the anode of an electron tube.
v **plat·ed, plat·ing** **1** cover with a thin layer of silver, gold, or other metal. **2** arrange food on a plate or plates prior to serving it. <Old French, from Greek *platus* flat>
on a plate, *Informal* with no effort required: *She plans to become a concert pianist, but she wants it on a plate.*
on your plate, requiring your time, effort, and attention: *You have too much on your plate to sign up for another activity.*

P

pla·teau (plat ō′) *n, pl* **pla·teaus** or **pla·teaux** (-tōz′) **1** a large level or mainly level area of land in the mountains or rising sharply from the sea or a lowland area. See SUMMIT for picture. **2** a level of progress or achievement at which something is stabilized for a time: *Our volleyball team improved rapidly and then reached a plateau.*
v **plat·eaued, plat·eau·ing** reach a level of progress or achievement, especially the level at which something is stabilized for a time. <French, from Greek *platus* flat>

plate·ful (plāt′fu̇l) *n, pl* **plate·fuls** as much or as many as a plate will hold: *a plateful of cookies.*

plate glass *n* thick, polished glass that is often used for mirrors and the windows or doors of stores and other business establishments.

plate·let (plā′tlət) *n* a tiny, colourless, disc-shaped cell fragment found in blood that assists in blood clotting.

a bat	e bed	i bid	o pot	u cup	th **thin**
ā cake	ē me	ī bite	ō go	ū rude	TH **then**
ä bar	ə about	ər over	ȯ for	u̇ put	zh measure

tectonic plates

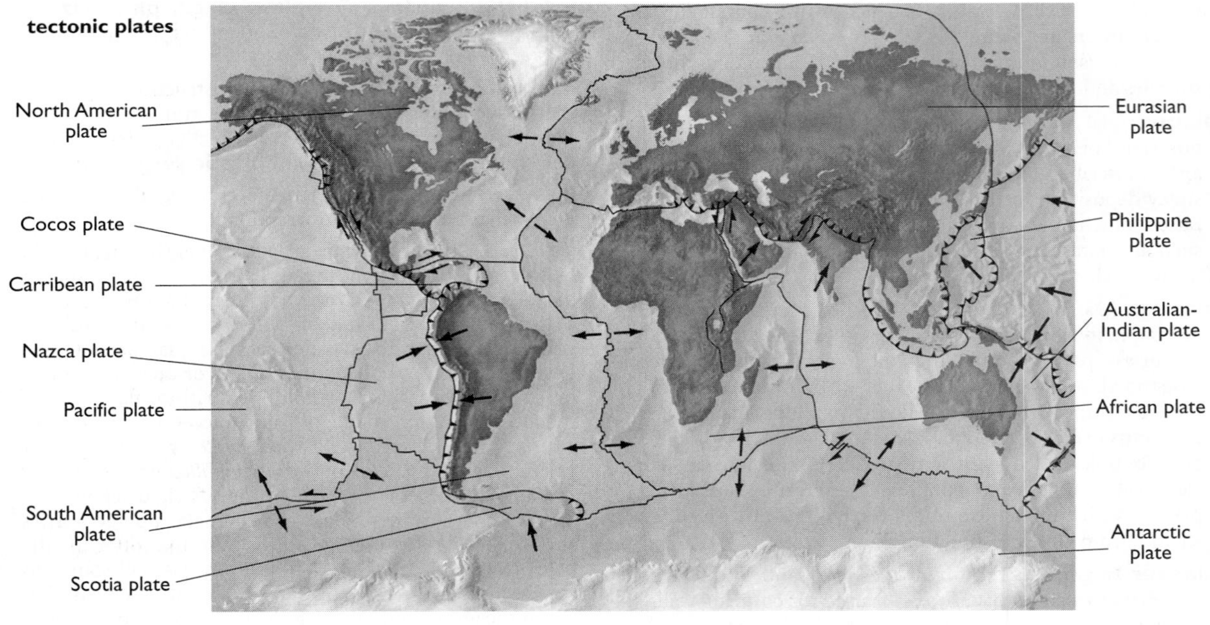

plate tectonics *n* (*with singular verb*) the study of the earth's crust and the enormous rigid segments of it that slowly float and move on the softer mantle below, causing the drift of continents and the rise of mountains.

plat·form (plat′fôrm) *n* **1** a raised, level surface on which people and things can stand, such as one beside a subway track or at the front of an auditorium. **2** a plan of action or statement of principles of a group, especially a political party. **3** *Computers* the type of operating system used by a computer or software application: *This machine has a Macintosh platform.* <French *plateforme* ground plan>

plat·ing (plā′ting) *n* a thin layer of silver, gold, or other metal.

plat·i·num (plat′ə nəm) *n* **1** a heavy, precious, metallic element that looks like silver or white gold and does not tarnish or melt easily. *Symbol* **Pt** **2** greyish or silvery white <Spanish *plata* silver>

platinum blonde *n* a woman with silvery blonde hair, or the colour of such hair.

plat·i·tude (plat′ə tyūd′) *or* (plat′ə tūd′) *n* a dull or commonplace remark, especially given out solemnly as if it were fresh and important. <French, from Greek *platus* flat> **plat′i·tu′di·nous** *adj.*

Pla·ton·ic (plə ton′ik) *adj* **1** to do with the fourth century BCE Greek philospher Plato, or his philosophy. **2 platonic** to do with love or friendship that is free from sexual desire or activity. **pla·ton′i·cal·ly** *adv.*

pla·toon (plə tūn′) *n* **1** a formation of soldiers, several of which makes up a company. **2** a small group of people sharing an activity or interest. <French *pelote* ball>

plat·ter (plat′ər) *n* **1** a large, often oval or oblong plate, used especially for holding or serving a main dish such as meat or fish. **2** an object that has this or a similar shape. **on a silver platter,** *Informal* involving no effort: *The position was practically handed to her on a platter.*

plat·y·pus (plat′ə pəs) *n, pl* **plat·y·pus·es** or **plat·y·pi** (-pī′) *or* (-pē′) a small, egg-laying water mammal of eastern Australia with a broad, flat, rubbery snout resembling a duck's bill, thick fur, four webbed feet, and a broad, flat tail. <Latin, from Greek *platus* flat + *pous* foot. The animal's webbed feet are broad and flat.>

plau·dit (plod′it) *n* an enthusiastic expression of approval or praise: *to enjoy the plaudits of the critics.* <Latin *plaudite* applaud>

plau·si·ble (ploz′ə bəl) *adj* **1** appearing true, reasonable, or fair: *The story sounded plausible to us.* **2** apparently worthy of confidence but often not really so: *a plausible liar.* <Latin *plausibilis* worthy of applause, from *plaudere* applaud> **plau′si·bil′i·ty** *n.* **plau′si·bly** *adv.*

play (plā) *v* **1** do something for fun or recreation: *The puppy plays with its tail.* **2** do for amusement or to deceive or mock: *to play a joke on someone.* **3** take part in a game, especially against an opponent: *Our team played the Grade 9 team.* **4** put in or cause to play in a game or sports contest: *Play your ten of hearts. Each coach played his best goalie.* **5 a** act in a dramatic performance: *to play the hero in a tragedy.* **b** pretend, in order to fool someone: *to play sick. Don't play the innocent with me.* **c** make believe or pretend in fun: *Don't get upset; we're just playing.* **6** make or produce music on an instrument or a machine: *to play a tune, to play a CD. We could hear the piano playing in the* *next apartment.* **7 a** move lightly or quickly: *A breeze played on the water.* **b** move or work, or cause to move or work, especially as a quick, repeated action: *to play a hose on a burning building.* **8** gamble or bet: *She plays the horses.* **9** make a certain impression on someone: *Being late doesn't play well with my teachers.* **10** allow a hooked fish to exhaust itself by pulling on the line: *to play a salmon.*

n **1** activity intended as fun or recreation: *Her children were happy at play.* **2 a** a turn in a game: *It is your play next.* **b** the action of carrying on a game or sports contest: *Play was slow in the first half of the game.* **3** a story written for or presented as a dramatic performance: *They chose a comedy as their next play.* **4** a pretence made to fool someone: *His tears are just a play for sympathy.* **5** a process or series of actions: *fair play.* **6** a light, quick movement: *the play of sunlight on leaves.* **7** freedom for action or movement: *The girl gave her imagination full play in telling what she could do with a million dollars.* **8** movement in operation: *There is too much play in the front wheel.* <Old English *plegan* exercise>

in (or **out of**) **play,** in a position or condition to be (or not be) legally played in a game.

play at, do something in a superficial, uncommitted way: *If you want to excel at something, you can't just play at it.*

play down, make unimportant or less important: *The government tried to play down the unfavourable results of the opinion poll.*

played out, a exhausted. **b** finished or done with.

play fair, play or act according to the rules or according to basic principles of honour.

play for time, delay in order to gain an advantage or avoid loss.

play into someone's hands, act so as to give a person the advantage.

play it safe (or **smart**, or **cool**, etc.)**,** act in a safe (or smart, etc.) way to achieve a certain result.

play off, a hold a competition in which players or teams are pitted against each other to decide a championship. **b** play an extra game or round to settle a tie.

play on or **upon,** take advantage or make use of: *She played on her mother's good nature.*

play out, bring to an end.

play up, make the most of: *The singer's agent played up her extensive background in classical music.*

play up to, *Informal* try to get favour or some benefit through attention or flattery.

play·a·ble (plā′ə bəl) *adj* able to be played or fit to be played on.

play–act (plā′akt′) *v* **1** pretend, especially in an exaggerated way: *We used to enjoy play-acting when we were little.* **2** perform in a play.

play·back (plā′bak′) *n* a replaying of a tape recording or videotape, especially when it has just been made: *We noticed several weak spots when we listened to the playback.*

play·bill (plā′bil′) *n* **1** a poster announcing a play. **2** the printed program of a play.

play·boy (plā′boi′) *n* a man, usually rich, who devotes his time to having fun.

play–by–play (plā′bī plā′) *adj* to do with a commentary describing each event or action as it happens or happened: *a play-by-play broadcast of a hockey game.*

n such a commentary: *She gave us a play-by-play of the whole silly misunderstanding.*

play·dough (plā′dō′) *n* a soft, doughlike material used by children to make shapes, models, etc.

play·er (plā′ər) *n* **1** a person who plays a game: *a baseball player.* **2** an actor. **3** a person who plays a musical instrument. **4** a device that plays pre-recorded sounds or films: *a DVD player.* **5** *Informal* a person who or group that is important or has influence in an area or activity: *He was a big player in municipal politics.*

player piano *n* a piano played by machinery.

play·fel·low (plā′fel′ō) *n* a playmate.

play·ful (plā′fəl) *adj* **1** full of fun or fond of playing: *a playful kitten.* **2** joking in a light or easy way: *a playful remark.* **play′ful·ly** *adv.* **play′ful·ness** *n.*

play·go·er (plā′gō′ər) *n* a person who goes often to the theatre.

play·ground (plā′ground′) *n* **1** a place for outdoor play by children, especially one provided with equipment they can use. **2** a popular place for leisure activity, such as a resort area: *a playground of the wealthy.*

play·house (plā′hous′) *n* **1** a small house for children to play in. **2** a theatre.

playing card *n* a rectangular plastic or paper card used in games, with one side marked with numbers and symbols for rank and group, or suit, and forming part of a set: *They used a regular deck of fifty-two playing cards.*

playing field *n* a piece of level ground for athletic events or sports, often marked with lines for particular games.

play·mate (plā′māt′) *n* a person who plays with another in games and other activities.

play·off (plā′of′) *n* **1** an extra game or round played to settle a tie. **2** a series of games played by the top teams in a league to determine the winner of the championship or a special trophy.

play on words *n* a pun.

play·pen (plā′pen′) *n* a small portable enclosure for very young children to play in.

play·room (plā′rūm′) *n* a room for children to play in.

play therapy *n* play as a means of expressing emotions or hidden problems and exploring possible solutions, especially as a form of therapy for children.

play·thing (plā′thing′) *n* **1** a thing to play with: *The dog's favourite plaything was an old sock.* **2** a person considered to be amusing but unimportant.

play·time (plā′tīm′) *n* a time for playing.

play·wright (plā′rīt′) *n* a writer of plays.

pla·za (plaz′ə) *or* (plȧ′zə) *n* **1** a public square in a city or town. **2** a shopping centre. <Spanish = place>

a bat	e bed	i bid	o pot	u cup	th thin
ā cake	ē me	ī bite	ō go	ū rude	ᴛʜ then
ȧ bar	ə about	ər over	ȯ for	u̇ put	zh measure

P

plea (plē) *n* **1** a request or appeal: *a plea for pity.* **2** an excuse: *The man's plea was that he had not seen the signal.* **3** the answer made by a defendant to a charge against him or her in a law court: *The defendant entered a plea of not guilty.* <Old French, from Latin *placere* please>

plea bargain *n* an arrangement between a prosecutor and a defendant before the trial in which the defendant pleads guilty to a lesser charge in return for having more serious charges dropped. **plea bargain** *v.*

plead (plēd) *v* **plead·ed** or **pled** (pled), **plead·ing** **1** offer reasons for or against: *She pleaded the cause of the evicted tenants.* **2** make a serious appeal: *He pleaded for more time to finish his paper.* **3** offer as an excuse: *The woman who stole pleaded poverty.* **4** act as a lawyer for someone, or conduct a case in a court of law: *They will need a good lawyer to plead the case. Who is pleading for the defence?* **5** answer to a charge in a court of law: *Do you plead guilty or not guilty?* **plead′ing·ly** *adv.*

plead with, ask someone earnestly or repeatedly: *He pleaded with her not to throw out his old comics.*

pleas·ant (plez′ənt) *adj* **1** pleasing, agreeable, or giving pleasure: *a pleasant swim on a hot day, pleasant weather.* **2** friendly or easy to get along with. **pleas′ant·ly** *adv.* **pleas′ant·ness** *n.*

CONFUSABLES

Pleasant emphasizes that the person or thing described has qualities that give pleasure.

Pleasing emphasizes the good feeling that an experience creates in someone.

pleas·ant·ry (plez′ən trē) *n, pl* **pleas·ant·ries** a mild joke or good-humoured remark: *After some pleasantries, we started to have a serious conversation.* <Old French *plaisant* pleasing>

please (plēz) *v* **pleased, pleas·ing** **1** cause to be happy or satisfied: *The presents pleased us. Such a fine meal cannot fail to please.* **2** wish or think fit: *Do what you please.* **3** be the will of: *It pleased her to remain anonymous.*

adv **1** (*in polite requests*) if it pleases: *Sit down, please. Will you please sit down? Please sit down.* **2** (*to politely reply to an offer*) yes: "*Would you like some water?*" "*Please.*" <Old French, from Latin *placere*>

if you please, if you like or with your permission: *Leave your boots here, if you please.*

please yourself, do what you like, since it makes no difference to me: *You don't want to eat? Please yourself.*

pleas·ing (plē′zing) *adj* giving pleasure: *a pleasing manner.* See PLEASANT for confusable. **pleas′ing·ly** *adv.*

pleas·ur·a·ble (plezh′ə rə bəl) *adj* giving pleasure. **pleas′ur·a·bly** *adv.*

pleas·ure (plezh′ər) *n* **1** a feeling of being pleased: *The girl's pleasure in the gift was good to see.* **2** something that pleases: *It would be a pleasure to see you again.* **3** a thing that provides enjoyment: *He takes much pleasure in biking.* **4** *Formal* a will, desire, or choice: *What is your pleasure in the matter?*

pleat (plēt) *n* a flat, usually narrow, fold made by doubling material on itself.

v fold or arrange in pleats: *to pleat curtains.* <variant of *plait*>

ple·be·ian (pli bē′ən) *n* **1** in ancient Rome, a person with no official rank or high status. Compare PATRICIAN (def. 1). **2** an ordinary person.

adj **1** to do with the plebeians. **2** to do with ordinary people.

pleb·i·scite (pleb′ə sīt′) *or* (pleb′ə sit) *n* a direct vote by the qualified voters in a country, province, or other place in answer to a particular question. <French, from Latin *plebs* the common people + *siscere* vote for>

plec·trum (plek′trəm) *n, pl* **plec·trums** or **plec·tra** (-trə) a small piece of plastic or other material used for plucking the strings of a musical instrument such as a guitar. <Latin, from Greek *plessein* strike>

pled (pled) a past tense and a past participle of PLEAD.

pledge (plej) *n* **1** a solemn promise or agreement: *He signed a pledge never to drink again.* **2** a thing that is given as security to ensure that a contract is fulfilled, or that a debt is repaid: *I left my watch as a pledge for the money I borrowed.* **3** a person who has promised to join an organization but is serving a period of probation before being granted membership. **4** something given to show favour or love or as a promise of something to come: *He gave her a brooch as a pledge of his friendship.* **5** the drinking of a health or toast.

v **pledged, pledg·ing** **1** promise formally or solemnly: *to pledge money to the United Way.* **2** cause to promise solemnly: *The conspirators were pledged to secrecy.* **3** give as security. **4** drink a toast to someone and wish him or her well: *The knights rose from the banquet table to pledge the king.* <Old French, from Latin *pleblum*> **pledg′er** *n.*

take the pledge, *Informal* promise not to drink alcoholic liquor.

Pleis·to·cene (plī′stə sēn′) *n* the geological epoch lasting from about 2 million to 10 thousand years ago, when ice sheets covered most of the northern hemisphere. See also CENOZOIC, QUATERNARY.

adj to do with this epoch. <Greek *pleistos* most + *kainos* new>

ple·na·ry (plē′nə rē) *or* (plen′ə rē) *adj* **1** full or complete. **2** attended or to be attended by all qualified members at a meeting: *a plenary session at the end of the conference.* <Latin *plenus* full>

plen·i·po·ten·ti·ar·y (plen′ə pə ten′shē er′ē) *n, pl* **plen·i·po·ten·ti·ar·ies** a diplomatic agent with full power or authority to act independently.

adj with or giving full power and authority. <Latin *plenus* full + *potentia* power>

plen·i·tude (plen′ə tyūd′) *or* (plen′ə tūd′) *n* **1** fullness or completeness: *in the plenitude of health and vigour.* **2** abundance: *They consumed a plenitude of food and drink in the course of the evening.* <Old French, from Latin *plenus* full>

plen·ti·ful (plen′ti fəl) *adj* more than enough: *a plentiful supply of gasoline for the trip, a plentiful harvest.* **plen′ti·ful·ly** *adv.* **plen′ti·ful·ness** *n.*

plen·ty (plen′tē) *n* **1** a full supply: *You have plenty of time to catch the bus.* **2** the quality or condition of being plentiful: *years of peace and plenty.*
adj enough: *Six potatoes will be plenty.*
adv Informal quite enough or fully: *plenty good enough.* <Old French, from Latin *plenus* full>

SYNONYMS

Plenty emphasizes a full supply: *We have plenty of food for our picnic.*

Abundance suggests having more than enough: *An abundance of rain made the river overflow.*

Enough refers to having as much or as many as is needed: *I have enough money to buy the ticket.*

ple·o·nasm (plē′ə naz′əm) *n* the use of more words than are needed to express an idea. Example: The *two twins* arrived together (twins are always two). The *realization of* his dream *came true.* (*His dream came true* is sufficient.) <Latin, from Greek *pleon* more>
ple·o·nas·tic (plē′ə nas′tik) *adj.*

pleth·o·ra (pleth′ə rə) *n* too much of something: *a plethora of forms to fill out.* <Latin, from Greek *plethein* be full>

pleu·ra (plů′rə) *n, pl* **pleu·rae** (plů′rē) *or* (plů′rī) a thin membrane, a pair of which line the thorax and cover the surface of the lungs of humans and other mammals. <Latin, from Greek *pleura* side of the body> **pleu′ral** *adj.*

pleu·ri·sy (plů′rə sē) *n* inflammation of the pleura, in which varying amounts of fluid from the inflamed membrane enter the chest cavity.

Plex·i·glas (plek′si glas′) *Trademark n* a light, transparent, flexible but firm acrylic plastic, sometimes used in place of glass. <*pl*(*astic*) + (*f*)*lexi*(*ble*) + *glas*(*s*)>

plex·us (plek′səs) *n, pl* **plex·us·es** or **plex·us** **1** a network of nerves or blood vessels. The **solar plexus** is a collection of nerves behind the stomach. **2** an interwoven combination of parts in a system. <Latin *plectere* to braid>

pli·a·ble (plī′ə bəl) *adj* **1** easily bent or flexible. **2** easily influenced: *She is too pliable to be a good leader.* <French *plier* to bend> **pli′a·bil′i·ty** *n.*

pli·ant (plī′ənt) *adj* **1** easily bent or flexible. **2** easily influenced. **pli′an·cy** (plī′ən sē) *n.* **pli′ant·ly** *adv.*

pli·ers (plī′ərz) *pln* small pincers with long jaws used for bending or cutting wire, or for holding small objects. <*ply*[1]>

plight (plīt) *n* a difficult, dangerous, or undesirable condition or state: *He was in a sad plight, ill and penniless.* <Old French *pleit* condition>

Plim·soll mark or **line** (plim′səl) *n* a mark or line painted on a ship's hull to show how heavily it may safely be loaded.

plink (plink) *v* make a clinking or metallic ringing sound, especially on a musical instrument: *plinking away on the banjo. He plinked out the tune on the piano.*
n a clinking, metallic, or ringing sound. <imitative>

plinth (plinth) *n* the lowest, square part of the base of a column, statue, or vase. <Latin, from Greek *plinthos*>

Pli·o·cene (plī′ə sēn′) *n* the geological epoch lasting from about 10 million to 2 million years ago, when the climate cooled and grasslands replaced the earlier forests. See also CENOZOIC, TERTIARY.
adj to do with this period. Also, **Pleiocene**. <Greek *pleion* more + *kainos* new>

PLO or **P.L.O.** *n* in full, **Palestine Liberation Organization** a political body working to create a state for Palestinian Arabs in some or all of PALESTINE.

plod (plod) *v* **plod·ded, plod·ding** **1** walk slowly and heavily: *The old man plods wearily along the road. We plodded the mountain path.* **2** proceed in a slow, careful, and unexciting way: *My brother plods away at his homework until it's done.* <perhaps imitative> **plod′der** *n.* **plod′ding** *adj.* **plod′ding·ly** *adv.*

plonk (plongk) *Informal n* wine, especially cheap or inferior wine. <origin uncertain>

plop (plop) *n* a sound like that of a flat object striking water without a splash.
v **plopped, plop·ping** **1** fall or drop with such a sound: *The stone plopped into the water.* **2** allow oneself to fall heavily: *She plopped into the first soft chair she saw.*
adv with a plop: *My lunch fell plop into the puddle.* <imitative>

plot (plot) *n* **1** the plan or main story of a play, novel, film, or other work: *The story has a very exciting plot.* **2** a secret plan, especially to do something wrong: *Two men formed a plot to rob the bank.* **3** a small piece of ground: *a garden plot.* **4** a graph or diagram.
v **plot·ted, plot·ting** **1** plan secretly with others: *The rebels plotted against the government.* **2** plan the main story of a play, novel, film, or other work. **3** divide land into plots: *The farm was plotted into house lots.* **4** make a graph or diagram, or mark something on it: *The nurse plotted the patient's temperature over several days.* <Old English> **plot′less** *adj.*

plot·ter (plot′ər) *n* **1** a person who plots. **2** *Computers* a computer-controlled device to produce diagrams and pictures on paper.

plough or **plow** (plou) *n* **1** a farm implement used for cutting the soil and turning it over. **2** usually, **plow** a similar machine for moving snow.
v **1** turn over soil with a plough: *to plough a field.* **2** use a plough: *He was ploughing yesterday.* **3** move as a plough does, slowly and with effort: *The ship ploughed through the waves. The girl ploughed through two books to get material for her essay.* <Old English *ploh*> **plough′er** or **plow′er** *n.*
plough back, reinvest profits in the same business.
plough into, *Informal* **a** hit hard and slam into: *The car went out of control and ploughed into the building.* **b** undertake a job or project with energy and determination.
plough under, **a** plough into the ground to enrich the soil. **b** defeat, destroy, or overwhelm.

a bat	e bed	i bid	o pot	u cup	th **thin**
ā cake	ē me	ī bite	ō go	ū rude	ᴛʜ **then**
à bar	ə about	ər over	ô for	ů put	zh measure

ploughing match *n* a competition among farmers to determine who is the most skilful at ploughing.

plough·man or **plow·man** (plou′mən) *n, pl* **plough·men** or **plow·men** (-mən) a person who guides a plough.

plough·share or **plow·share** (plou′sher′) *n* the part of a plough that cuts the soil.

plov·er (pluv′ər) *or* (plō′vər) *n* a shorebird with a plump body, greyish plumage, long wings, and, usually, no hind toes. <Old French, from Latin *pluvia* rain. The bird was believed to call before rain.>

ploy *n* a tactic or strategy, especially a sly or crafty one: *Don't try to use that clever ploy on me.* <origin uncertain>

pluck (pluk) *v* **1** pull off or pick: *to pluck flowers. She plucked a bit of lint from the blanket.* **2** pull or pull at: *The little girl plucked at her sleeve.* **3** pick or pull at the strings of a musical instrument: *to pluck a banjo, to pluck the strings of a violin for a pizzicato passage.* **4** pull off the feathers or hair from: *to pluck a chicken, to pluck your eyebrows.*
n **1** the act of picking or pulling. **2** courage; boldness and spirit: *It took pluck to stand up to that bully.* **3** the heart, liver, and lungs of an animal used as food. <Old English *pluccian*>
pluck up your spirits (**courage**, etc.) take courage: *She plucked up her spirits and carried on.*

pluck·y (pluk′ē) *adj* **pluck·i·er, pluck·i·est** with or showing courage: *a plucky fellow.* **pluck′i·ly** *adv.* **pluck′i·ness** *n.*

SYNONYMS

Plucky emphasizes courage: *The plucky child climbed all the way up the tree to rescue the cat.*

Fearless means "a lack of any fear": *The fearless firefighter ran into the burning townhouse.*

Spunky is an informal word that suggests either courage or spirit: *I liked the spunky way you jumped in to help us when the storm hit.*

plug (plug) *n* **1** a piece of wood or other material used to block a hole. **2** a disc of rubber or metal for blocking the drain of a sink, basin, or bathtub. **3** a device used to make an electrical connection. **4** *Informal* an advertisement or recommendation: *The interview was mainly a plug for her latest book. I'll put in a plug for you when I talk to her.* **5** a piece of pressed tobacco for chewing.
v **plugged, plug·ging 1** block with a plug. **2** (*with* ***in*** *or* ***into***) insert the plug of an electrical appliance or device into an outlet: *Where can I plug in the hair dryer?* **3** (*with* ***into***) connect to a certain type of electrical outlet: *a coffee maker that plugs into the cigarette lighter of the car.* **4** *Informal* work steadily: *She plugged away at her homework.* **5** *Informal* recommend or advertise, especially on a radio or TV program: *to plug a new product.* <Dutch *plugge*> **plug′ger** *n.*
pull the plug, *Informal* **a** put an end to something, often by discontinuing support: *The government pulled the plug on that research project.* **b** disconnect the life-support systems to which a terminally ill patient is attached.

plug–in (plug′in′) *n* **1** *Computers* a module or software that can be added to a computer system to give extra features or functions: **2** 🍁 an electric socket in a parking lot or garage into which a BLOCK HEATER can be connected to a vehicle.
adj designed to operate by being plugged into an electric outlet: *a plug-in light fixture.*

plug–ug·ly (plug′ ug′lē) *Slang adj* very ugly.
n, pl **plug-ug·lies** a thug or hoodlum.

plum (plum) *n* **1** a roundish fruit with a smooth skin, juicy flesh, and a somewhat flat stone. **2** something very good or desirable: *His new job is a fine plum.*
adj dark reddish purple. <Greek *proumnon*>
plum′like′ *adj.*

plum·age (plū′mij) *n* the feathers of a bird.

plumb (plum) *n* a small weight used on the end of a line to find the depth of water or to see if a wall is vertical.
adj vertical: *The wall is not quite plumb.*
adv **1** vertically. **2** *Informal* completely or thoroughly: *My horse is plumb worn out.*
v **1** test or adjust by a plumb line: *Our line was not long enough to plumb the depths of the lake.* **2** get to the bottom of: *No one could plumb the mystery.* <Old French, from Latin *plumbum* lead (the metal)>
out of plumb or **off plumb,** not vertical.

plumb·er (plum′ər) *n* a person whose work is putting in, maintaining, and repairing water pipes and fixtures in buildings.

plumb·ing (plum′ing) *n* **1** the work or trade of a plumber. **2** the water pipes and fixtures in a building: *the bathroom plumbing.*

plumb line *n* a line with a weight called a **plumb bob** at the end, used to find the depth of water or to see if a wall is vertical.

plume (plūm) *n* **1** a large, long, soft feather, such as that on a bird. **2** a feather, bunch of feathers, or tuft of hair worn as an ornament. **3** a thing resembling a plume, such as a moving column of something such as smoke or snow: *Snow rose in a plume from the snowblower.* **4** a narrow, jetlike flow of hot material from deep in the earth's mantle.
v **plumed, plum·ing 1** furnish with plumes. **2** smooth or arrange the feathers of: *The eagle plumed its wing.* <Old French, from Latin *pluma* down of a bird>

plum·met (plum′it) *v* plunge or drop straight down at high speed.
n **1** a steep or rapid plunge or drop. **2** a plumb or plumb line. <Old French, from Latin *plumbum* lead (the metal)>

plum·my (plum′ē) *adj* **1** like or full of plums: *a plummy flavour.* **2** *Informal* good or desirable: *She got herself a plummy part in the new play.* **3** rich and full in vocal tone.

plump[1] (plump) *adj* rounded out and attractively fat.
v make or become plump: *He plumped the pillows on the bed.* <Dutch *plomp* blunt> **plump′ness** *n.*

plump[2] (plump) *v* fall or drop heavily or suddenly: *All out of breath, she plumped down on a chair.*
adv heavily or suddenly: *She ran plump into me.* <probably imitative>
plump for, *Informal* give one's complete support to or champion vigorously: *to plump for no homework on Fridays.*

plum pudding *n* a rich, cooked pudding containing raisins, currants, and spices, made originally with plums.

plum tomato *n* a small, thick-skinned, egg-shaped or pear-shaped tomato, low in acid, and often used for cooking.

plun·der (plun′dər) *v* rob by force, especially during war or some other form of disorder: *The raiders plundered the town.*
n **1** things taken in plundering: *They carried off the plunder in their ships.* **2** the act of plundering: *The invading army abstained from plunder.* <German = household goods> **plun′der·er** *n.*

plunge (plunj) *v* **plunged, plung·ing 1** forcefully throw or thrust into something, especially a liquid: *She plunged her hand into the water to rescue the watch. The police officer plunged into the river and saved the drowning boy.* **2** throw suddenly or violently into an undesirable condition: *to plunge the world into war, to plunge the room into darkness.* **3** fall suddenly: *Prices plunged on the stock exchange. The mountain path plunged into a narrow valley.* **4** throw oneself into an activity: *He plunged into his homework.* **5** act recklessly or in great haste: *She plunged into the crowd.* **6** *Informal* gamble heavily.
n **1** the act of plunging. **2** a dive or jump into the water. **3** a swift and drastic fall in value or amount. **4** a sudden rush. <Old French *plongier* thrust down, from Latin *plumbum* plummet>
take the plunge, a *Informal* dare to do something that requires courage. **b** *Humorous* get married.

plung·er (plun′jər) *n* **1** a rubber suction cup on a long stick, used for unplugging blocked drains or toilets. **2** *Informal* a reckless gambler or speculator. **3** a person who or thing that plunges.

plunk (plungk) *v* **1** hit or pluck so as to produce a short hollow metallic sound: *to plunk a banjo string.* **2** put down or drop heavily or suddenly: *She plunked her books on the table.*
n the act or sound of plunking.
adv with a thud or twang: *He sat down plunk on the ground.* <imitative>

plu·ral (plů′rəl) *adj* more than one: *plural citizenship.*
n a form of a word to show that it means or refers to more than one. Examples: *Books* is the plural of *book. These* is the plural of *this.* <Old French, from Latin *pluralis* more>

GRAMMAR AND USAGE

Plural nouns are usually formed by adding *-s* to a singular noun: *barn* becomes *barns*; *mountain* becomes *mountains*; *boat* becomes *boats*.

However, there are many exceptions to this rule. Some plurals are formed with *-es*, some are formed with *-ies*, and some words do not change.

Words that came into English from Italian sometimes have plurals ending in *-i*: *graffito* becomes *graffiti*; *paparazzo* becomes *papparazzi*.

Some words that came into English from Hebrew have plurals ending in *-im*: *cherub* becomes *cherubim*; *kibbutz* becomes *kibbutzim*.

plu·ral·ism (plů′rə liz′əm) *n* **1** a condition or system in which two or more concepts, principles, or groups are considered to be important or have authority. **2** a social policy by which members of minority groups are encouraged to maintain their independent cultural traditions, or a society in which this is a fact. **3** a theory or philosophy in which there is more than one ultimate principle. **plu′ral·ist** *n, adj.* **plu′ral·is′tic** *adj.*

plu·ral·i·ty (plů ral′ə tē) *n, pl* **plu·ral·i·ties 1 a** the number of votes cast for a winning candidate in an election when that number is more than for any other candidate, but not more than half the total number of votes. Compare MAJORITY. **b** a greater number of votes cast for a candidate than for an opposing candidate. **2** a large number of people or things. **3** the condition of being plural.

plus (plus) *prep* **1** added to: *Three plus two equals five.* **2** and also: *This work requires intelligence plus experience.*
conj also: *I read the whole thing; plus, I had to check all the other reports.*
adj **1** showing addition: *the plus sign.* **2** *Informal* additional or extra: *a plus value.* **3** larger than average: *This jacket is available in plus sizes.* **4** with a positive electrical charge.
n **1** the plus sign (+). **2** an added mathematical quantity. **3** an advantage: *Her ability to speak languages was a great plus.* <Latin = more>

plus–fours (plus′fōrz′) *pln* loose knickerbockers that overhang the knee. <Plus fours are four inches (10 cm) longer than regular knickers, to allow for the overhang.>

plush (plush) *n* a rich fabric that has a deep, soft surface.
adj **1** to do with plush: *plush toys, plush upholstery.* **2** luxurious and expensive: *plush surroundings.* <Old French, from Latin *pilus* hair>

Plu·to (plū′tō) *n* the planet farthest from the sun. See EARTH for picture. <*Pluto*, Roman god of the underworld>

plu·toc·ra·cy (plū tok′rə sē) *n, pl* **plu·toc·ra·cies** **1** a system of government in which the rich rule. **2** a ruling class of wealthy people.

plu·to·crat (plū′tə krat′) *n* a person who has power or influence because of having wealth. <Greek *ploutos* wealth + *kratos* power> **plu′to·crat′ic** *adj.*

plu·to·ni·um (plū tō′nē əm) *n* a dense, silvery radioactive metallic element that is only found in trace amounts but is manufactured from a uranium isotope for use in nuclear weapons and reactors. *Symbol* **Pu**

plu·vi·al (plū′vē əl) *adj* to do with rainfall. <French, from Latin *pluvia* rain>

ply[1] (plī) *v* **plied, ply·ing 1** work with or use, especially in steady, rhythmic movements: *The dressmaker plied her needle.* **2** work steadily or busily at or on something: *The carpenter plied his trade.* **3** supply with in a pressing manner: *to ply a person with food or drink.* **4** go back and forth regularly between certain places: *Boats ply the river.* <variant of *apply*>

a **bat**	e **bed**	i **bid**	o **pot**	u **cup**	th **thin**
ā **cake**	ē **me**	ī **bite**	ō **go**	ū **rude**	TH **then**
ä **bar**	ə **about**	ər **over**	ȯ **for**	ů **put**	zh **measure**

ply[2] (plī) *n, pl* **plies** a thickness or layer of a folded or laminated material: *three-ply rope.* <French, from Latin *plicare* to fold>

ply·wood (plī′wůd′) *n* a large, thin board or sheet made of several thin layers of wood glued together, with the grain in adjacent layers running at right angles to each other.

p.m. or **P.M.** (*with a particular time*) after noon and before midnight: *The store closes at 6 p.m.*

ETYMOLOGY

p.m. is an abbreviation of Latin *post meridiem*, meaning "after noon."

PMS *n* in full, **premenstrual syndrome** a set of symptoms experienced by some women in the days before a menstruation period, and that may include emotional tension and physical retention of fluids.

pneu·mat·ic (nyū mat′ik) *or* (nū mat′ik) *adj* **1** worked by air pressure: *a pneumatic drill.* **2** filled with air: *a pneumatic tire.* <French, from Greek *pnein* breathe>
pneu·mat′i·cal·ly *adv.*

pneu·mo·nia (nyū mō′nyə) *or* (nū mō′nyə) *n* a bacterial or viral infection in which the lungs become inflamed. <Latin, from Greek *pneumon* lung>

poach[1] (pōch) *v* **1** trespass on another's land, especially to hunt or fish illegally. **2** take or acquire something in an unfair way. <perhaps French *pocher* enclose in a bag>

poach[2] (pōch) *v* **1** cook an egg by breaking it and simmering the egg in or over shallow boiling water. **2** cook another food by simmering in a small amount of liquid. <Old French *poche* pocket, because the cooked white of the egg forms a pocket around the yolk>

poach·er (pō′chər) *n* a person who hunts or fishes on another's land without any right.

pock (pok) *n* a pockmark.
v mark or pit with pocks. <Old English *pocc*>

pock·et (pok′it) *n* **1** a small, flat bag sewn to clothing for carrying small items. **2 a** a pouch attached to the inside of a surface, such as that of a suitcase or car door. **b** *Billiards, Pool* a bag at each corner and on each side of a pool or billiard table. **c** *Baseball* the hollow in the centre of the glove. **3 a** a hollow place or area separated from surrounding areas: *a pocket of air in a snowbank, a pocket of resistance in enemy territory.* **b** a cavity in the earth containing ore, oil, water, or gas. **c** a small deposit of ore: *The miner struck a pocket of silver.* **4 a** *Sports* a position in a race where one competitor is blocked by others. **b** *Football* an area behind the offensive line where a quarterback can stand to throw the ball. **c** *Bowling* the space between two pins.
v **1 a** put in one's pocket: *She pocketed her change.* **b** *Billiards, Pool* hit a ball into a pocket. **2** enclose, as in a pocket: *The horse was pocketed by three others, and lost the race.* **3** hold back or hide: *He pocketed his pride and said nothing.* **4** take secretly or dishonestly: *The crook pocketed all the profits.* <Old French *poche*>
be out of pocket, spend or lose money.
have deep pockets, *Informal* have a lot of money or financial resources.
in pocket, having gained money in a transaction.
in someone's pocket, *Informal* controlled or paid by someone: *His enemies said the politician was in the gangster's pocket.*
out of pocket, a having lost money in a transaction. **b** paid in cash: *out-of-pocket expenses.*
own pocket, personal money: *He paid for the damage out of his own pocket.*
pick someone's pocket, steal from someone's pocket without being noticed.

pock·et·book (pok′it bůk′) *n* **1** a small case for carrying money or papers in a pocket. **2** financial resources: *The jeans were just too expensive for my pocketbook.* **3 pocket book** an inexpensive, paper-covered edition of a book.

pock·et·ful (pok′it fůl′) *n, pl* **pock·et·fuls** as much as a pocket will hold.

pock·et·knife (pok′it nīf′) *n, pl* **pock·et·knives** a small knife with one or more blades that fold into the handle.

pocket money *n* money for occasional or minor personal expenses.

pock·et–size (pok′it sīz′) *adj* **1** small enough to go in a pocket: *a pocket-size radio.* **2** *Informal* small for its kind: *a pocket-size country.*

pock·mark (pok′märk′) *n* **1** a scar or pit in the skin such as that left by a disease or injury. **2** a small hollow suggesting such a scar.
v cover or scar with pockmarks. **pock′marked′** *adj.*

pod[1] (pod) *n* **1** the shell or case in which plants like beans and peas grow their seeds. **2** a self-contained or detachable unit on an aircraft, spacecraft, motor vehicle, boat, or ship that has a specific function: *a missile pod.*
v **pod·ded, pod·ding 1** produce pods or fill out into a pod. **2** remove peas, beans, etc. from their pods. <origin uncertain>

pod[2] (pod) *n* a small herd of whales or other marine animals. <origin unknown>

pod·cast (pod′kast) *Computers n* a pre-recorded audio file posted online and available for downloading to a computer or MP3 player.
v post a podcast. <(*I*)*Pod* + (*broad*)*cast*> **pod′cast·ing** *n.*

po·di·a·try (pə dī′ə trē) CHIROPODY.

po·di·um (pō′dē əm) *n, pl* **po·di·a** (-dē ə) a small raised platform, especially a platform used by an orchestra conductor or someone making a speech. <Latin, from Greek *podos* foot>

pod·zol (pod′zŏl) *n* a greyish, infertile type of soil, usually found under coniferous forests in moist subpolar climates. Also, **podsol**. <Russian *pod* under + *zola* ashes>
pod·zol′ic *adj.*

po·em (pō′əm) *n* **1** a piece of writing that uses language with special intensity by controlling rhythm and the choice of words, usually arranged in lines to produce a pattern of sounds and images. **2** something very beautiful: *The dancer was a poem in motion.* <French, from Greek *poiein* create>

po·et (pō′it) *n* **1** a person who writes poetry. **2** a person, especially a creative artist, who has great ability to feel and express beauty or emotion: *She is a poet with her paintbrush.*

po·et·as·ter (pō′i tas′tər) *n* a writer of poor poetry.

po·et·ic (pō et′ik) *adj* **1** to do with poets or poetry: *poetic imagery.* **2** written as poems: *Her poetic compositions are all very short.* **3** showing beautiful or noble language, imagery, or thought: *a poetic description of a scene.* **po·et′i·cal** *adj.* **po·et′i·cal·ly** *adv.*

poetic justice *n* justice in which the punishment is especially fitting.

poetic licence *n* a freedom traditionally granted to poets to violate certain grammatical rules or to alter fact or history for effect within a poetic work.

poet laureate *n, pl* **poets laureate** in some countries, an eminent poet officially recognized by the government.

po·et·ry (pō′i trē) *n* **1** poems or poetical works: *a book of poetry.* **2** the art or theory of writing poems. **3** an emotionally intense or imaginative style of expression: *His skating is pure poetry.*

🍁 **po·gey** or **po·gy** (pō′gē) *Slang n* financial assistance provided by the government to individuals, especially as welfare payments. <origin uncertain>

po·go stick (pō′gō) *n* a stick used in playing to hop from place to place by jumping up and down on the spring-supported footrests.

po·grom (pō grom′) *or* (pō′grəm) *n* an organized massacre of a minority group, especially of Jews in Russia or eastern Europe. <Russian = devastation>

poign·ant (poi′nyənt) *or* (poi′nənt) *adj* evoking a keen sense of sadness or pity: *a poignant cry, a poignant story.* <Old French, from Latin *pungere* to grieve>
poign′an·cy (poi′nyən sē) *or* (poi′nən sē) *n.*
poign′ant·ly *adv.*

poin·set·ti·a (poin set′ē ə) *or* (poin set′ə) *n* a plant with a small flower surrounded by large leaves resembling petals. <J.R. *Poinsett*, its 19c discoverer>

point (point) *n* **1** a sharp, tapered end of a tool, weapon, or other object: *the point of a needle.* **2** a tiny, round mark used in punctuation: *A period is a point. Use a point to set off decimals.* **3** *Mathematics* something that has position but no length or width: *Two lines meet or cross at a point.* **4 a** a particular place or time: *This is the point where we turned around and went back. At this point, he lost interest in the game.* **b** a particular condition or degree: *boiling point.* **5 a** an item or detail: *She answered my questions point by point.* **b** the most important or essential thing: *I missed the point of his talk.* **6** a distinguishing mark or quality: *my good points.* **7** force or effectiveness: *The story gave point to her advice.* **8** a particular aim, end, or purpose: *What's the point of going on when we don't know where we are?* **9** each of the thirty-two positions indicating direction marked at the circumference of the card of a compass, or the interval between two adjacent points of a compass. **10** a piece of land whose end sticks out into a body of water. **11** a unit of scoring or measuring: *We're three points ahead.* **12** in printing, a unit for measuring type. There are tweleve points in a PICA. **13** *Hockey* a position at the opponents' blue line, taken by an offensive player when the puck is within their defensive zone, especially during a power play. **14** *Lacrosse* one of the defencemen playing out in front of the goalie.
v **1** indicate position or direction, or direct attention with, or as if with, the finger: *Point in the direction of your home.* **2** direct or aim a finger or weapon: *It's rude to point your finger. The cannon were pointing in the wrong direction.* **3** have or face a specified direction: *The signboard points north.* **4** *Computers* place the pointer over an item on the screen: *point and click.* **5** aim or tend toward: *Everything seems to point to our having a good day today.* **6** of a dog, show the presence of game by standing rigid and looking toward it. **7** fill joints of brickwork with mortar or cement. <Old French, from Latin *pungere* to prick>
at the point of, very near to or on the verge of: *at the point of death.*
beside the point, with little or nothing to do with the subject.
in point, apt or relevant: *the case in point.*
in point of fact, as a matter of fact: *In point of fact, she never left the house at all.*
make a point of, be particular about: *She always makes a point of being on time.*
make your point, convince a person that an idea or argument is reasonable or correct: *He is not a very good speaker, but he made his point.*
on the point of, just about or on the verge of: *I was on the point of starting my homework when my friend called.*
point off, mark off with points or dots.
point out, show or call attention to: *Please point out my mistakes.*
point up, show clearly: *Synonym boxes in this dictionary point up the differences between similar words.*
strain (or **stretch**) **a point, a** exceed the reasonable limit. **b** make a special exception.
to the point, apt or appropriate: *Her speech was brief and to the point.*

point–and–click (point′ən clik′) *Computers adj* to do with an interface that allows users to access data and activate programs by clicking on a mouse or other input device.

point–blank (point′blangk′) *for adj,* (point′blangk′) *for adv. adj, adv* **1** fired with a weapon or as a shot or bullet straight at and very close to a target: *to shoot at point-blank range (adj), to shoot point-blank (adv).* **2** plain, blunt, and direct: *a point-blank question (adj). One boy gave excuses, but the other refused point-blank (adv).* <*point* + *blank*, in the sense of the white spot in the centre of a target>

🍁 **point blanket** *n* a Hudson's Bay Company blanket.

pointe (point) *n* the toe in ballet, especially the reinforced toe of a ballet shoe. <French = tip>

a bat	e bed	i bid	o pot	u cup	th thin
ā cake	ē me	ī bite	ō go	ū rude	TH then
ä bar	ə about	ər over	ô for	ü put	zh measure

P

warning symbols

poison

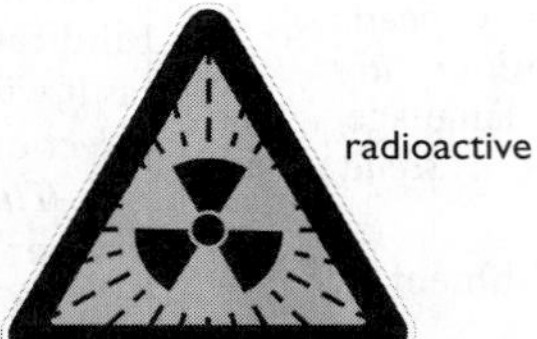
radioactive

corrosive

flammable

explosive

electrical hazard

point·ed (poin′tid) *adj* **1** with or as if sharpened to a point or points: *a pointed pencil, a pointed arch.* **2** sharp or direct, especially in expressing or implying criticism: *a pointed wit, a pointed remark, a pointed refusal.* **point′ed·ly** *adv.* **point′ed·ness** *n.*

point·er (poin′tər) *n* **1** a person who or thing that points. **2** a long, tapering stick used in pointing things out. **3** a thin piece of metal or other material on a scale or dial to indicate a figure or position. **4** a hunting dog trained to show where game is by standing rigid and looking toward it. **5** a useful hint or suggestion: *She gave him some pointers on improving his tennis.* **6** an indication of what might happen in future: *I have heard that an extremely cold autumn is a pointer that winter will be very long.*

point form *n* a short, quick way of writing things down, listing main ideas in simple phrases or key words.

poin·til·lism (pwan′tē iz′əm) *n* a painting technique that uses tiny dots of colour placed close together on a white background so that the dots blend together when seen from a distance. <French *point* dot> **poin′til·list** *n, adj.*

point·less (poin′tlis) *adj* **1** without sense, meaning, or relevance: *a pointless question.* **2** without having scored in a game or competition.

point man *n* **1** *Hockey* a player on offence assigned to play a position at the opponents' blue line. **2** a person who leads the advance of a movement, such as the leader of a patrol, or a person at the forefront of an activity or enterprise.

point of departure *n* a starting point of a line of thought or course of action.

point of honour or **honor** *n* a matter that seriously affects a person's honour or principles: *It is a point of honour with our teacher to give equal time to every student.*

point of no return *n* a stage in an action or event after which there is no turning back, so that one is obliged to continue.

point of order *n* in a debate or meeting, a question raised as to whether proceedings are according to the rules.

point of sale *n* the checkout area of a store, regarded as a stage in a retail transaction. **point-of-sale** *adj.*

point of view *n* **1** a particular attitude or way of considering something: *Farmers and campers sometimes have different points of view about rain.* **2** the position of a storyteller in relation to the story being told: *a novel told from a first-person point of view.* **3** a physical position from which someone or something is considered.

poise (poiz) *n* **1** mental balance, composure, or self-possession: *She has perfect poise and never seems embarrassed.* **2** a graceful or elegant way in which the body and head are held.
v **poised, pois·ing 1** be or cause to be balanced or suspended: *Poise yourself on your toes.* **2** be ready and prepared to take action: *The government was poised to call an election.* <Old French, from Latin *pendere* weigh>

poi·son (poi′zən) *n* **1** a drug or other substance that is dangerous to health and capable of causing death. **2** something dangerous, destructive, or deadly: *Hate had become a poison in her mind.*
v kill or harm by poison, or put poison in or on: *to poison arrows. He poisoned his friend's mind against the girl.* <Old French, from Latin *potio* potion> **poi′son·er** *n.*

poison ivy *n* a N American woody vine or shrub whose leaves, flowers, fruit, and bark secrete an oil that causes a severe rash on contact with the skin.

poison oak *n* a shrub with leaflets shaped like oak leaves that is related to poison ivy, and has similar harmful effects when the skin comes in contact with it.

poi·son·ous (poi′zə nəs) *adj* **1** containing poison: *The snake's bite was poisonous.* **2** with a harmful effect: *a poisonous lie.* **poi′son·ous·ly** *adv.* **poi′son·ous·ness** *n.*

poison pill *n* a tactic used by a business to discourage another company from taking it over, usually by making it very expensive to do so.

poison sumac *n* a shrub growing in swamps that bears white berrylike fruit and causes a severe rash on most people if they touch it.

poke[1] (pōk) *v* **poked, pok·ing 1** push against with something pointed: *He poked me in the ribs with his elbow.* **2** thrust or push so as to become seen: *She poked her head in the kitchen window.* **3** stir a fire with a poker or other object. **4** *Informal* punch someone: *He threatened to poke his brother in the nose.* **5 a** (*usually with* ***around***) search aimlessly: *Why are you poking around in the basement?* **b** usually, **poke one's nose** pry or interfere: *Stop poking your nose into other people's business.* **6** make a hole by jabbing or prodding: *He accidentally poked a hole in the tablecloth with his pencil.* **7** proceed in a slow or lazy way: *Quit poking along or you'll make us late.*
n **1** a thrust or push. **2** *Informal* a punch at someone. <origin uncertain>

poke[2] (pōk) *n* <Old French *poche* pocket>
buy a pig in a poke, buy something without seeing it first.

poke check *Hockey n* a quick thrust or jab with the stick at the puck in order to get it away from an opponent. **poke′–check′** *v.*

🍁 **poke·lo·gan** (pō′klō′gən) *n* a small, stagnant backwater in a stream. <Algonquian>

pok·er[1] (pō′kər) *n* a person who or thing that pokes, especially a metal rod for stirring a fire.

pok·er[2] (pō′kər) *n* a card game in which a player bets that the sequence of the cards held is greater than that of the cards held by the other players. <origin uncertain>

poker face *Informal n* a face or facial expression that does not show one's thoughts or feelings, or a person with such a face or facial expression. **pok′er-faced′** *adj.*

pok·ey[1] or **pok·y** (pō′kē) *adj* **pok·i·er, pok·i·est 1** annoyingly slow to move or act. **2** of a room or building, uncomfortably small.

pok·ey[2] (pō′kē) *Informal n* a jail. <origin unknown>

Po·land (pō lənd) *n* a country in central Europe. See the APPENDIX. **Pole** *n.* **Pol′ish** *adj.*

po·lar (pō′lər) *adj* **1** to do with the North or South Pole: *the polar wastes, a polar wind. We flew the polar route to Europe last year.* **2** to do with the poles of a magnet or battery. **3** directly opposite in character or tendency: *Good and evil are polar elements.*

polar bear *n* a large, white bear living in the arctic regions.

po·lar·i·ty (pō lar′ə tē) *or* (pō ler′ə tē) *n* **1** the possession of two opposed poles, such as in a magnet or battery. **2** the possession or exhibition of two opposite or contrasted principles or tendencies.

po·lar·ize (pō′lə rīz′) *v* **po·lar·ized, po·lar·iz·ing 1** produce or acquire polarity. **2** restrict light waves so that they move in only one direction: *polarized sunglasses.* **3** divide into two opposite extremes of opinion or belief: *The proposed charge for health services polarized the voters.* **po′lar·i·za′tion** (pō′lə rə zā′shən) *or* (pō′lə rī zā′shən) *n.*

Po·la·roid (pō′lə roid′) *Trademark n* a camera that develops and prints the photo immediately.

pol·der (pōl′dər) *n* an area of low, marshy land reclaimed from the sea or some other body of water and protected by dikes, as in the Netherlands. <Dutch>

pole[1] (pōl) *n* a long, slender, usually round piece of wood, metal, plastic, or other material: *a telephone pole, a ski pole.*
v **poled, pol·ing** *Boating, Skiing* push or make something go with a pole: *to pole a raft. We poled down the slope through the deep, powdery snow.* <Latin *palus* stake>

pole[2] (pōl) *n* **1** either end of the axis of the earth or of a celestial object. **2** either of two parts or points where opposite forces are strongest, such as in a magnet or battery. **3** either end of the axis of a sphere. **4** either of two opinions, forces, principles, or ideas considered as being opposed or contradictory. <Latin, from Greek *polos*>
poles apart, very much different or in strong disagreement: *The bargaining parties are still poles apart and there is no sign of a settlement.*

pole·axe (pōl′aks′) *n* an axe with a long handle and a hook or spike opposite the blade.
v **pole·axed, pole·ax·ing** (*usually figurative*) **1** cause great shock, as if brought down with a poleaxe: *The poor guy was completely poleaxed by the news.* **2** hit or bring down with or as if with a poleaxe. <Middle English *polle* head + *ax* axe>

pole·cat (pōl′kat′) *n* **1** a small, dark brown, carnivorous European mammal of the weasel family. **2** *especially US* the N American skunk. <Old French *pole* chicken + *cat,* because it sometimes preys on poultry>

po·lem·ic (pə lem′ik) *n* **1** a strong argument against or attack on an idea, belief, or opinion: *The book is nothing but a long polemic against communism.* **2 polemics** *pl* (*with singular or plural verb*) the art or practice of argument or controversy: *This is not the time to indulge in polemics.*
adj to do with controversy or disagreement: *a polemic writer.* <Latin, from Greek *polemos* war>
po·lem′i·cal·ly *adv.*

pole position *n* the inside lane or the inside starting position on a racetrack.

Pole·star (pōl′stär′) *n* **1** *Astronomy* the North Star, **Polaris**, formerly used as a guide by sailors. **2 polestar** a guiding principle or centre of attraction, interest, or attention.

pole vault *n* **1** an athletic event or contest in which contestants jump over a high, horizontal bar with the aid of a long, flexible pole. **2** a vault performed in this way. **pole vault** *v.* **pole vault′er** *n.*

po·lice (pə lēs′) *n* the civil force of a community or nation, whose duty is to guard lives and property, to preserve order, and to arrest those who commit crimes: *The police arrived within ten minutes.*
v **policed, po·lic·ing 1** guard to keep order in: *to police the streets.* **2** enforce regulations or an agreement: *A special force was formed to police the treaty.* <French, from Greek *polis* city>

police dog *n* a dog trained for use in police work.

a bat	e bed	i bid	o pot	u cup	th **thin**
ā cake	ē me	ī bite	ō go	ū rude	TH **then**
ä bar	ə about	ər over	ô for	ů put	zh measure

P

police force *n* the law-enforcing body of a community.

po·lice·man (pə lēs′mən) *n, pl* **police·men** (-mən) a male police officer.

police officer *n* a member of a police force.

police state *n* a nation strictly controlled by governmental authority, especially with the aid of a secret police organization.

police station *n* the headquarters of the police of an area or district in a city, or of the local police force of a small community.

po·lice·wom·an (pə lēs′wu̇m′ən) *n, pl* **po·lice·wom·en** (-wim′ən) a female police officer.

pol·i·cy[1] (pol′ə sē) *n, pl* **pol·i·cies** a plan or method of action that has been deliberately chosen and that guides or influences future decisions: *The candidate explained her party's policy.* <Old French, from Greek *polis* city>

pol·i·cy[2] (pol′ə sē) *n, pl* **pol·i·cies** a written contract for insurance coverage: *The fire-insurance policy expires in October.* <French, from Greek *apodeixis* proof>

pol·i·cy·hold·er (pol′ə sē hōl′dər) *n* the owner of an insurance policy.

po·li·o (pō′lē ō) *n* in full, **poliomyelitis** (pō′lē ō mī′ə lī′tis) an acute infectious disease caused by a virus that affects the central nervous system and can lead to temporary or permanent paralysis of muscles. <Latin, from Greek *polios* grey + *myelos* marrow, because the disease causes inflamation of the grey matter in the spinal cord>

pol·ish (pol′ish) *v* **1** make or become smooth and shiny: *to polish shoes. This leather polishes well.* **2** (*with* ***off*** *or* ***away***) remove by smoothing. **3** (*often with* ***up***) put into a better condition or improve: *to polish a manuscript, to polish up your French.*
n **1** a substance used to give smoothness or shine: *silver polish.* **2** a condition of shininess and smoothness: *The table has a high polish.* **3** culture, elegance, or refinement: **4** the act or process of polishing: *I gave the table a quick polish.* <Old French, from Latin *polire*> **pol′ish·er** *n.*
polish off, *Informal* finish or complete: *polish off a pizza.*

Po·lit·bu·ro (pə lit′byu̇′rō) *or* (pol′it byu̇′rō) *n* an executive committee of a Communist Party that controlled policy, especially in the former Soviet Union.

po·lite (pə līt′) *adj* **1** with or showing good manners: *The polite man gave the lady his seat on the bus.* **2** refined and elegant: *She wished to learn all the customs of polite society.* <Latin *polire* to polish> **po·lite′ly** *adv.* **po·lite′ness** *n.*

pol·i·tic (pol′ə tik′) *adj* seeming sensible and prudent: *It was not politic to arouse his irritation.* <Old French, from Greek *polis* city> **pol′i·tic·ly** *adv.*

po·lit·i·cal (pə lit′ə kəl) *adj* **1** of or concerned with politics or politicians. **2** to do with public affairs or government: *political office.* **3** concerned with seeking status or power rather than acting according to principles.
po·lit′i·cal·ly *adv.*

political economy *n* in former times, a social science dealing with the ways in which political and economic processes are related to each other.

politically correct *adj* avoiding anything that could be interpreted as racism, sexism, or another form of discrimination. *Abbrev.* **PC. political correctness** *n.*

political party *n* a group of people that has a common set of ideas by which it attempts to influence public policy, especially through the election of its members and the formation of a governnment.

political science *n* a social science dealing with political institutions and processes, especially with the principles and conduct of government.

pol·i·ti·cian (pol′ə tish′ən) *n* a person holding or seeking to hold a political office.

po·lit·i·cize (pə lit′i sīz′) *v* **po·lit·i·cized, po·lit·i·ciz·ing** **1** make politically aware: *a politicized society.* **2** give a political character or tone to: *to politicize an issue.*
po·lit′i·ci·za′tion *n.*

pol·i·tick (pol′ə tik′) *v* take part in political activity, especially in order to directly or indirectly solicit votes: *She's politicking in the Maritimes this week.*
pol′i·tick′er *n.*

pol·i·tics (pol′ə tiks′) *n* **1** (*with singular verb*) **a** the process of governing a community or of forming and enforcing public policy: *She was engaged in politics for many years.* **b** the science and art of government, or its academic study. **2** (*with plural verb*) political ideas or opinions: *My father's politics were strongly against rule by any one person.*

pol·i·ty (pol′ə tē) *n, pl* **pol·i·ties** **1** a form or process of forming a government or constitution. **2** a politically organized society or community.

pol·ka (pōl′kə) *or* (pō′kə) *n* a lively dance of eastern European origin, or the music for this dance.
v **pol·kaed, pol·ka·ing** dance a polka. <Czech *pulka* half-step>

polka dot *n* a dot or round spot repeated to form a regular pattern on a fabric, or a pattern or fabric with such dots. **pol′ka-dot** or **pol·ka-dot′ted** *adj.*

poll (pōl) *n* **1** **a** the process of voting in an election: *The class took a poll to decide where the picnic would be held.* **b** the number of votes cast: *If it rains on election day, there is often a light poll.* **c** a list of voters. **d** the place where votes are cast or counted: *The polls will be open till eight o'clock tonight.* **2** a survey of public opinion concerning a particular subject. **3** the head, especially the part of it on which the hair grows.
v **1** **a** receive as votes: *The mayor polled a record vote.* **b** vote. **c** take or register the votes of. **2** cut off or cut short the horns of an animal, especially a young animal. <Middle English *pol* head>

🍁 **poll captain** *n* on an election day, a person responsible for reminding or persuading voters in a given area to cast their ballots for a particular party.

pol·len (pol′ən) *n* a fine, yellowish powder formed in the anthers of flowers, consisting of tiny grains that are the male sex cells which fertilize the ovules. <Latin = mill dust>

pollen count *n* a count of pollen particles in the air, for the information of people with allergies.

pol·li·nate (pol′ə nāt′) *v* **pol·li·nat·ed, pol·li·nat·ing** carry pollen from stamens to pistils of flowers, such as bees do. **pol′li·na′tion** *n.*

pol·ling booth (pōl′ing) *n* a screened or otherwise enclosed space at a polling station where voters can marks their ballots in privacy.

polling station *n* a room or building set up for the voters of a constituency to mark their ballots.

pol·li·wog (pol′ē wog′) *n* a tadpole. Also, **pollywog**.

pol·lock (pol′ək) *n, pl* **pollocks** or (*especially collectively*) **pollock** a fish of the cod family found in the N Atlantic, with a small barbel under the jaw. <perhaps Celtic>

poll·ster (pōl′stər) *n* a person who takes public opinion polls.

poll tax *n* a tax levied on each individual, rather than on income or property.

pol·lu·tant (pə lū′tənt) *n* something that pollutes.

pol·lute (pə lūt′) *v* **pol·lut·ed, pol·lut·ing 1** make physically impure or unclean, especially, contaminate the air, water, or soil: *the polluted air of cities. The lake has been polluted with waste from a large factory.* **2** make morally impure or corrupt. <Latin *lutum* mud> **pol·lut′er** *n.* **pol·lu′tion** *n.*

Pol·ly·an·na (pol′ē an′ə) *n* one who is overly cheerful or optimistic. <character in 20c stories by E.H. Porter>

pol·ly·wog (pol′ē wog′) POLLIWOG.

Outdoor **polo** is played with four players on each team and the game is divided into six or eight periods called *chukkers* of seven minutes each. In the event of a tie, additional sudden-death periods are played until the winning goal is scored.

po·lo (pō′lō) *n* a game played by two teams of players on horseback, who use long-handled mallets to drive a wooden ball through the opposing team's goal. <Balti (a language of Pakistan) = ball>

pol·o·naise (pol′ə nāz′) *or* (pō′lə nāz′) *n* a slow, stately dance in three-four time, or the music for this dance. <French, from Latin *Polonia* Poland, where it originated>

po·lo·ni·um (pə lō′nē əm) *n* an element that occurs as a product of the radioactive decay of uranium. *Symbol* **Po** <Latin *Polonia* Poland, homeland of M. Curie, 20c scientist who discovered the element>

polo shirt *n* a man's casual pullover-style knit shirt with a collar and a buttoned neck opening.

pol·ter·geist (pol′tər gīst′) *n* a ghost or spirit supposedly responsible for unexplained disturbances and noises such as door slamming, chain rattling, or rapping sounds on walls or tables. <German *poltern* noisy + *Geist* ghost>

pol·troon (pol trūn′) *Archaic n* a complete coward. <French, perhaps from Italian *poltro* sluggard>

poly– *combining form* **1** many or much: *polychrome.* **2** with many atoms or groups of a specified kind in a molecule: *polyethylene.* <Greek *polloi* many>

pol·y·an·dry (pol′ē an′drē) *n* **1** the practice or condition of a wife having more than one husband at the same time. Compare POLYGAMY. **2** *Botany* the state of having numerous stamens. <*poly-* many + Greek *andros* male> **pol′y·an′drist** *n.* **pol′y·an′drous** *adj.*

po·ly·chro·mat·ic (pol′i krō ma′tik) *adj* many-coloured.

po·ly·chrome (pol′i krōm′) *adj* painted, decorated, or printed in many colours.
n a work of art in many colours, especially a painted statue.

pol·y·clin·ic (pol′i klin′ik) *n* a clinic or hospital treating many different diseases and injuries.

pol·y·es·ter (pol′ē es′tər) *n* a group of synthetic polymers, chiefly used to make textile fibres. <*poly-* many + *ester*>

pol·y·eth·y·lene (pol′ē eth′ə lēn′) *n* a strong, lightweight, synthetic polymer of ethylene that is chiefly used to make insulation, moulded containers, and thin films or sheets for packaging.

po·lyg·a·my (pə lig′ə mē) *n* the practice or condition of having more than one spouse or mate at one time. Compare POLYANDRY. <*poly-* many + Greek *gamos* marriage> **po·lyg′a·mist** *n.* **po·lyg′a·mous** *adj.*

pol·y·glot (pol′i glot′) *adj* knowing or using several languages.
n a person who knows or uses several languages. <*poly-* many + Greek *glotta* tongue>

pol·y·gon (pol′i gon′) *n* a closed plane figure with three or more interior angles and straight sides. <*poly-* many + Greek *gonia* angle> **po·lyg′o·nal** *adj.*

pol·y·graph (pol′i graf′) *n* **1** a device for recording various physiological responses, such as changes in blood pressure, body temperature, or breathing rate, and often used as a lie detector. **2** a lie-detector test carried out with this device.

a bat	e bed	i bid	o pot	u cup	th **thin**
ā cake	ē me	ī bite	ō go	ū rude	TH **then**
à bar	ə about	ər over	ȯ for	ů put	zh measure

pol·y·he·dron (pol′i hē′drən) *n, pl* **pol·y·he·drons** or **pol·y·he·dra** (-drə) a solid figure formed by four or more faces. <*poly-* many + Greek *hedra* base>
pol·y·he′dral *adj.*

pol·y·math (pol′i math′) *n* a person of great learning in a variety of fields. <*poly-* many + Greek *manthanein* learn>

pol·y·mer (pol′i mər) *n* a compound composed of very large molecules that are made up of many simple molecules chemically linked together. <*poly-* many + Greek *meros* a share> **pol′y·mer′ic** (pol′i mer′ik) *adj.*

pol·y·mer·i·za·tion (pol′i mə rə zā′shən) *or* (pol′i mə rī zā′shən) *n* the chemical union of many simple molecules into very large molecules to form a polymer.

pol·y·morph (pol′i mȯrf′) *n* an organism, object, or material that takes various forms. <*poly-* many + Greek *morphe* form> **pol′y·mor′phic** or **pol′y·mor′phous** *adj.*

pol·y·mor·phism (pol′i mȯr′fiz əm) *n* **1** the occurrence of different forms or colour types in an individual organism or in different individuals of one species. **2** the property of a chemical compound of crystallizing in at least two distinct forms.

Pol·y·ne·sia (pol′ə nē′zhə) *n* islands of the central and eastern Pacific, including Hawaii. **Pol′y·ne′sian** *adj, n.*

pol·y·no·mi·al (pol′i nō′mē əl) *n* an algebraic expression of one or more terms. Examples: *ab* (a monomial); *ab* + *cd* (a binomial); *ab* + *cd* – *ef* (a trinomial).
adj consisting of two or more algebraic terms: *polynomial equations.* <*poly-* many + (*bi*)*nomial*>

pol·yp (pol′ip) *n* **1** a small water animal that has a mouthlike opening surrounded by tentacles for gathering in food. Sea anemones are polyps. **2** a small growth protruding from a mucous membrane in the body. It is usually not malignant. <Old French, from Greek *polus* many + *podos* foot>

pol·y·pro·pyl·ene (pol′i prō′pə lēn′) *n* a lightweight thermoplastic, similar to polyethylene but harder, used to make moulded items and insulating materials.

pol·y·sac·cha·ride (pol′i sak′ə rīd′) *n* a natural carbohydrate, such as starch, whose molecules consist of two or more molecules of simple sugars linked together.

pol·y·sty·rene (pol′i stī′rēn) *n* a synthetic organic polymer that is rigid, colourless, and resistant to other chemicals, often used as an insulator and for moulded products such as dishes or toys.

pol·y·syl·la·ble (pol′i sil′ə bəl) *n* a word of more than three syllables. **pol′y·syl·lab′ic** *adj.*

pol·y·tech·nic (pol′i tek′nik) *adj* to do with instruction in many technical arts or applied sciences.
n a polytechnic school.

pol·y·the·ism (pol′i thē′iz əm) *n* belief in or worship of more than one god. **pol′y·the·ist′ic** *adj.*

pol·y·un·sat·u·rat·ed (pol′i un sat′yū rā təd) *Chemistry adj* to do with a class of vegetable and animal fats whose molecules consist of long carbon chains with many double bonds.

pol·y·ur·e·thane (pol′ē yu̇′rə thān′) *n* a synthetic organic polymer that may be rubbery, resinous, or fibrous, and is often made in the form of flexible or rigid foams used in mattresses, cushions, and insulation.

pol·y·vi·nyl chloride (pol′i vī′nəl) *n* a colourless, synthetic thermoplastic produced by the polymerization of vinyl chloride that is used to make moulded articles, tubing, or electrical insulation. *Abbrev.* **PVC**

po·made (pom ād′) *or* (pom ȧd′) *n* a perfumed ointment for the scalp and hair. <French, from Latin *pomum* apple, because it originally contained apples>

pome (pōm) *n* a fruit consisting of firm, juicy flesh surrounding a core that contains several seeds. Apples are pomes. <Old French, from Latin *pomum* apple>

pome·gran·ate (pom′gran′it) *or* (pom′ə gran′it) *n* a fruit with a leathery, reddish skin, juicy red pulp, and many seeds. <Old French, from Latin *pomus* apple + *granum* seed>

pom·mel (pom′əl) *or* (pum′əl) *for n,* (pum′əl) *for v. n* **1** an upward curving knob on a saddle in front of a rider. **2** a rounded knob on the hilt of a sword, dagger, or old-fashioned gun.
v PUMMEL. <Old French *pomel* knob, from Latin *pomus* apple>

pommel horse *Gymnastics n* a padded structure on legs, about waist height, with removable U-shaped handles called **pommels.**

pomp (pomp) *n* a stately or splendid display or ceremony: *The queen was crowned with great pomp.* <Old French, from Greek *pompein* send>

pom·pa·dour (pom′pə dȯr′) *n* **1** a woman's hairstyle in which the hair is puffed high over the forehead and turned under in a roll. **2** a man's hairstyle in which the hair is brushed straight up and back from the forehead. <Marquise de *Pompadour,* 18c noblewoman who is pictured with her hair/wig styled in this way>

pom·pa·no (pom′pə nō′) *n* a saltwater food fish of the Caribbean and neighbouring coasts of N America with a deep body, no teeth, and a forked tail. <Spanish *pampano*>

pom·pom (pom′pom) *n* **1** an ornamental ball or tuft of yarn or feathers, used especially on clothing, hats, or shoes. **2** a chrysanthemum, dahlia, or aster with a small, rounded flower head. <French *pompon*>

pom·pous (pom′pəs) *adj* with or showing a tendency to display oneself in an overly grand or self-important way: *a pompous speech.* **pom·pos′i·ty** (pom pos′ə tē) *n.* **pom′pous·ly** *adv.* **pom′pous·ness** *n.*

pon·cho (pon′chō) *n, pl* **pon·chos** **1** a cloak consisting basically of a large piece of cloth with a slit in the middle for the head to go through, worn especially in Latin America. **2** a similar garment, especially one that is waterproof, and worn as a raincoat. <Spanish *pontho*>

pond (pond) *n* a body of still water, smaller than a lake: *a duck pond.* <Middle English *ponde* enclosure>

pon·der (pon′dər) *v* consider carefully: *to ponder a problem.* <Old French, from Latin *pondus* weight>

pon·de·ro·sa pine (pon′də rō′sə) *n* a large pine tree found in western N America with very long needles and large cones with prickles.

pon·der·ous (pon′də rəs) *adj* **1** slow and clumsy because of being very heavy: *Slowly he lifted his ponderous bulk from the chair.* **2** overly dull, solemn, and laboured: *a ponderous way of speaking.* <French, from Latin *pondus* weight> **pon′der·ous·ly** *adv.* **pon′der·ous·ness** *n.*

🍁 **pond hockey** *n* informal or unorganized hockey played on a frozen body of water.

pond scum *n* **1** a mass of algae forming a green film on still, fresh water. **2** *Slang* a contemptible person or people.

pond·weed (pon′dwēd′) *n* a water plant that grows in quiet water, typically with oval leaves that grow on the surface of the water and grasslike leaves under the surface.

pon·iard (pon′yərd) *n* a dagger.

pon·tiff (pon′tif) *n* the Pope. <Latin *pontifex* pathmaker, in reference to the Pope's role as a leader>

pon·tif·i·cal (pon tif′ə kəl) *adj* **1** to do with the Pope. **2** so pompous as to pretend to be infallible: *a pontifical comment.* **pon·tif′i·cal·ly** *adv.*

pon·tif·i·cate (pon tif′ə kit) *or* (pon tif′ə kāt′) *for n,* (pon tif′ə kāt′) *for v. n* the office or term of office of a pope. *v* **pon·tif·i·cat·ed, pon·tif·i·cat·ing** **1** officiate as the Pope, especially at Mass. **2** speak dogmatically and pompously: *He loved to pontificate on the virtues of thrift.*

pon·toon (pon tūn′) *n* **1** a low, flat-bottomed boat or some other floating structure, used with others to form the supports of a temporary **pontoon bridge**. **2** a boat-shaped float on an aircraft, used for coming down on or taking off from water. <French, from Latin *pons* bridge>

po·ny (pō′nē) *n, pl* **po·nies** **1** a small horse, especially of a gentle, stocky breed, usually less than 150 cm high. **2** *Informal* a small drinking glass or the amount it will hold. <Scottish, from Latin *pullus* young of a horse>
pony up, *Informal* pay or contribute money for something.

pony·tail (pō′nē tāl′) *n* a hairstyle in which the main length is pulled back tightly and held together at the head by a fastener, flowing free below this point like a pony's tail.

pooch (pūch) *Informal n* a dog. <origin uncertain>

poo·dle (pū′dəl) *n* an intelligent, active dog with thick, wool-like hair, often clipped in a pattern. Poodles have three sizes: toy, miniature, and standard.
poo′dle·like′ *adj.*

ETYMOLOGY

Poodle comes from German *Pudelhund*, from *pudeln* (to splash in water) + *Hund* (dog). Poodles were used by hunters to bring game from water.

poof (pūf) *n* a sound like the puff of breath in blowing out a candle, or like a small, muffled explosion.
interj an exclamation suggesting a sudden or magical appearance, disappearance, or transformation: *He said the magic words, and poof! a basket of flowers appeared on the table.* <imitative>

pooh (pū) *interj* used to express disgust, scorn, or impatience.

pooh–bah (pū′ba′) *Informal n* a pompous and self-important official. <*Pooh-Bah*, name of a character in Gilbert and Sullivan's operetta *The Mikado*>

pooh–pooh (pū′pū′) *Informal v* dimiss an idea as being foolish or unrealistic: *She pooh-poohed my plans for the day, and made me go biking instead.*

pool[1] (pūl) *n* **1** a small body of still water. **2** a deep place in a river. **3** a puddle of water or any other liquid: *There was a pool of oil under the car. The water stood in pools in the garden after the rain.* **4** a swimming pool.
v form a puddle on the ground or another surface. <Old English *pol*>

pool[2] (pūl) *n* **1** the things or money put together by different people for their common advantage: *Our apartment building has a pool of sports equipment.* **2** 🍁 *Prairie Provinces* a co-operative grain-marketing organization among farmers. **3** a group of people, usually with the same skills, who are drawn upon as needed: *a secretarial pool.* **4** a carpool. **5 a** a fund of money bet by members of a group, often a group of employees, on the outcome of a sports event: *a hockey pool.* **b** the people who form such a pool. **6** a version of BILLIARDS played with 15 coloured, numbered balls and a white cue ball. Compare SNOOKER.
v put things, ideas, or money together for common advantage: *The three girls pooled their money and went home in a cab.* <French *poule* stake>

pool hall *n* a building that holds a **pool room** where people play the game of pool.

pool table *n* a table specially designed for playing pool, covered with fabric and with a bank around the edge with six pockets. See BILLIARDS for picture.

poop[1] (pūp) *n* a deck at the stern above the ordinary deck, often forming the roof of a cabin.
v break as a wave over the stern of a ship. <Old French, from Latin *puppis* stern>

poop[2] (pūp) *Informal v* make or become exhausted: *All of us were pooped after the climb.* <origin uncertain>

poop[3] (pūp) *Informal n* information, especially the most recent or current inside information. <origin uncertain>

poop[4] (pūp) *Informal n* excrement. <origin uncertain>

poor (pūr) *adj* **1** not having enough income to maintain a standard of living regarded as normal or comfortable: *They were poor, but never hungry.* **2** not favourable: *a poor chance for recovery.* **3** worse than usual and not good in quality: *poor soil, a poor cook, poor health.* **4** deserving pity or sympathy: *The poor man had a broken hip.*
n **the poor** *pl* people who have not enough income to maintain a standard of living regarded as normal or comfortable. <Old French, from Latin *pauper*> **poor′ness** *n.*

poor·house (pūr′hous′) *n* in former times, a place in which impoverished people lived at public expense.

a **bat**	e **bed**	i **bid**	o **pot**	u **cup**	th **thin**
ā **cake**	ē **me**	ī **bite**	ō **go**	ū **rude**	ᴛʜ **then**
ä **bar**	ə **about**	ər **over**	ô **for**	ů **put**	zh **measure**

P

poor·ly (pūr′lē) *adv* badly or in a poor manner: *A desert is poorly supplied with water. I did poorly on the test.*
adj Informal somewhat ill: *I feel poorly today.*

pop[1] (pop) *v* **popped, pop·ping 1** make a short, quick, explosive sound: *The firecrackers popped in bunches.* **2** move, go, or arrive suddenly or unexpectedly: *Our neighbour popped in for a short call.* **3** thrust or put suddenly: *She popped her head out of the car window.* **4** burst or cause to burst open with a pop: *The chestnuts were popping in the fire. Heat popcorn until it bursts with a pop.* **5** bulge: *The surprise made her eyes pop out.* **6** hit a pop fly in baseball.
n **1** a short, quick, explosive sound: *the pop of a cork.* **2** a non-alcoholic carbonated drink: *strawberry pop.*
adv suddenly making a popping sound: *The bottle went pop.* <imitative>
a pop, *Informal* for each person or thing: *Admission is $5 a pop.*
pop the question, *Informal* propose marriage.

pop[2] (pop) *adj* popular or commercial, especially in music.

pop[3] (pop) *Informal n* father.

pop art *n* an art style, especially in painting and sculpture, that is based on the styles in popular culture or the mass media, and sometimes uses common manufactured items as subject matter.

pop·corn (pop′kôrn′) *n* a variety of corn whose hard kernels burst open and puff out in a white mass when heated, or the white, puffed-out kernels, usually eaten salted and buttered.

Pope or **pope** (pōp) *n* the supreme head of the Roman Catholic Church: *the Pope, the last three popes.* <Greek *papas* father>

pop fly *Baseball n* a ball hit high into the air and easily caught by the pitcher or a fielder.

pop·gun (pop′gun′) *n* a toy gun that shoots with a popping sound.

pop·lar (pop′lər) *n* a slender, fast-growing tree found mainly in north temperate regions, with flowers in drooping catkins. Its wood is soft and light. <Old French, from Latin *populus*>

pop·lin (pop′lən) *n* a strong, lightweight, usually cotton fabric with a crosswise rib. <French, from Italian *papalina* papal, perhaps from the former papal seat Avignon, where the fabric was first made>

pop·o·ver (pop′ō′vər) *n* a very light and hollow muffin made from a thin batter.

pop·per (pop′ər) *n* a metal pan or other utensil used for popping popcorn.

pop·pet (pop′it) *n* a small, cute person, especially a pretty child. <variant of *puppet*>

pop·py (pop′ē) *n, pl* **pop·pies 1** a plant with a milky sap, colourful flowers, and seeds in a capsule. Some poppies are sources of morphine and codeine; others are cultivated as garden plants. **2** the bright red flower of a poppy, often used as a symbol on Remembrance Day to commemorate those who died in wars. <Latin *papaver*>

pop·py·cock (pop′ē kok′) *Informal n, interj* nonsense. <Dutch *pap* soft + *kak* dung>

pop·py·seed (pop′ē sēd′) *n* the tiny black seed of the poppy plant, used in cooking as a topping or flavouring, often for baked goods.

Pop·si·cle (pop′si kəl) *Trademark n* sweet, fruit-flavoured ice on a small stick. <*pop*[1] + *icicle*>

pop·u·lace (pop′yə ləs) *n* the people living in a particular country or area.

pop·u·lar (pop′yə lər) *adj* **1** liked by a great many people, or by a particular person or group: *The song quickly became popular. She was always popular with her co-workers.* **2** intended to appeal to the current tastes of the general public: *popular music, popular science.* **3** within the means of the average person: *popular prices.* **4** to do with representing the people: *He led the struggle to gain popular government.* **5** widespread among many people: *It is a popular belief that chicken soup helps cure a cold.* <Latin *populus* people>

SYNONYMS

Popular suggests having widespread approval, favour, or appreciation: *He listened only to whatever music was popular at the time.*

Celebrated suggests well-known and much talked about: *The celebrated actor had her picture taken everywhere that she went.*

Fashionable suggests conforming to what is in style: *Those colours are fashionable now, but that won't last.*

pop·u·lar·i·ty (pop′yə lar′ə tē) *or* (pop′yə ler′ə tē) *n* the quality or condition of being liked by most people.

pop·u·lar·ize (pop′yə lə rīz′) *v* **pop·u·lar·ized, pop·u·lar·iz·ing 1** change, especially by simplifying and presenting in an interesting form, so as to appeal to a great number of people instead of a special group: *He wrote history in a popularized form.* **2** cause to be generally liked: *popularize a tune.* **pop′u·lar·i·za′tion** *n.* **pop′u·lar·i·zer** *n.*

pop·u·lar·ly (pop′yə lər lē) *adv* by people in general or commonly known: *The defendant was popularly believed to have been guilty, though she was acquitted.*

popular vote *n* the number of votes cast for a party or candidate in an election as distinct from the seats won.

pop·u·late (pop′yə lāt′) *v* **pop·u·lat·ed, pop·u·lat·ing** inhabit or provide with inhabitants: *This city is densely populated. They populated the area about the middle of the nineteenth century.*

pop·u·la·tion (pop′yə lā′shən) *n* **1** the people of a place: *The population was outraged at the new law.* **2** the total number of such people in a place, or some other political or geographical unit: *The world's population increased greatly in the last century.* **3** a part of the inhabitants distinguished in some way from the rest: *the urban population, the Inuit population.* **4** the total number of members of a species (animals, birds, or other organisms) living in a defined area: *the deer population of North America.* **5** *Statistics* the total number people or things being measured, estimated, studied, etc.

pop·u·list (pop′yu list) *adj* appealing to the interests of ordinary people rather than the best educated, or most wealthy or powerful.
n a person who approves of appealing to the interests of ordinary people. <Latin *populus* people> **pop′u·lism** *n.*

pop·u·lous (pop′yə ləs) *adj* inhabited by many people: *a populous region.*

pop–up (pop′up′) *n* **1** a folding picture with parts that stand up or out when it is unfolded. **2** *Baseball* a pop fly. **3** *Computers* a small window that suddenly appears on the screen.
adj **1** to do with pop-ups: *a pop-up book, a pop-up menu.* **2** with a mechanical feature that automatically raises something at the proper time: *a pop-up toaster.*

por·ce·lain (pȯr′sə lin) *or* (pȯr′sə lən) *n* very fine, hard, translucent earthenware. <French *porcelaine* cowrie shell, from Latin *porcus* pig, from the shape of a cowrie shell>

porch (pȯrch) *n* **1** a covered shelter projecting in front of an entrance to a building. **2** a veranda. <Old French, from Latin *porta* passage>

por·cine (pȯr′sīn) *adj* to do with pigs. <French, from Latin *porcus* pig>

por·cu·pine (pȯr′kyə pīn′) *n* a heavyset, short-legged rodent with long, sharp, barbed spines that are used for defence. <Old French, from Latin *porcus* pig + *spina* thorn>

pore[1] (pȯr) *v* **pored, por·ing** (*with* ***over***) study or read long and steadily: *She pored over the magnificent old book for hours.* <origin uncertain> **por′er** *n.*

CONFUSABLES

Pore means "study": *He pored over his notes in preparation for the quiz.*

Pour means "flow": *She poured maple syrup on the pancakes.*

pore[2] (pȯr) *n* a tiny opening through which fluids may pass, especially an opening in the skin of people or animals, or in the leaves of plants, through which fluids, gases, or microscopic particles are passed: *sweat pores.* <Old French, from Greek *poros* passage>

por·gy (pȯr′gē) *n, pl* **por·gies** or (*especially collectively*) **por·gy** a deep-bodied marine fish found mainly in tropical and subtropical coastal waters. It has strong teeth. <Spanish, from Greek *phagros* sea bream>

pork (pȯrk) *n* the flesh of a pig used for food. <Old French, from Latin *porcus* pig>

pork barrel *Informal n* spending by a government on projects that may not be needed but should win votes.

pork·er (pȯr′kər) *n* a pig, especially one fattened for meat.

porn (pȯrn) *Informal n, adj* pornography or pornographic.

por·nog·ra·pher (pȯr nog′rə fər) *n* a person who produces pornography.

por·nog·ra·phy (pȯr nog′rə fē) *n* written or visual material that describes or displays sexual organs or sexual activity chiefly as a way to arouse erotic feelings. **por′no·graph′ic** *adj.*

po·rous (pȯ′rəs) *adj* full of pores or tiny holes through which liquids or air may pass. **po′rous·ness** or **po·ros′i·ty** (pȯ ros′ə tē) *n.*

por·phy·ry (pȯr′fə rē) *n, pl* **por·phy·ries** a hard rock consisting of white or red crystals embedded in a dark red or purplish mass. <Latin, from Greek *porphyra* purple>

por·poise (pȯr′pəs) *n, pl* **por·pois·es** or (*especially collectively*) **por·poise** a small whale found especially in the northern Atlantic and Pacific, with a blunt snout and flattened, spade-shaped teeth. <Old French, from Latin *porcus* pig + *piscis* fish>

por·ridge (pȯ′rij) *n* a food made of oatmeal or other cereal boiled in water or milk until it thickens. <Old French *pottage* soup>

por·rin·ger (pȯ′rən jər) *n* in former times, a small dish, usually with a handle, from which porridge, etc. was eaten.

port[1] (pȯrt) *n* **1** a harbour where ships load and unload, especially one where customs officers are located. **2** a city or town with such a harbour. <Old English, from Latin *portus*>

port[2] (pȯrt) *n* **1 a** an opening in the side of a ship for letting in light and air. **b** an opening in the side of a wall, ship, aircraft, or armoured vehicle through which guns may be fired. **2** an opening in machinery for steam, liquid, or gas to pass through. **3** *Computers* a device for connecting a computer to other hardware or to a network.
v Computers transfer software from one computer or computer system to another. <Latin *porta* gate>

port[3] (pȯrt) *adj* on the left side of a ship or aircraft. Compare STARBOARD.
n **1** the left side of a ship or aircraft when facing forward. **2** the position of a weapon held diagonally, with the upper part close to the left shoulder.
v **1** (*used mainly as a command*) turn or shift to the left side. **2** carry a weapon diagonally, with the upper part close to the left shoulder. <origin uncertain>

port[4] (pȯrt) *n* a strong, often sweet wine that is usually dark red. <*Oporto*, city in Portugal, where it originated>

por·ta·bel·la or **por·ta·bel·lo** (pȯrt ə bel′ə) PORTOBELLO.

port·a·ble (pȯr′tə bəl) *adj* able to be carried or easily carried: *a portable radio.*
n **1** a portable radio, TV, or other electronics device. **2** a temporary, transportable building on the grounds of a school, used as an extra classroom. <Old French, from Latin *portare* carry>

por·tage (pȯr täzh′) *n* **1** the process of carrying boats, canoes, or supplies overland from one stretch of water to another: *They made the canoe trip without a single portage.* **2** a place where such carrying takes place: *The hunters pitched camp at the portage.*
v **por·taged, por·tag·ing** carry canoes or other objects from one stretch of water to another: *He had to portage five times during the trip.* <French, from Latin *portare* carry>

a bat	e bed	i bid	o pot	u cup	th **thin**
ā cake	ē me	ī bite	ō go	ū rude	TH **then**
ä bar	ə about	ər over	ȯ for	u̇ put	zh measure

P

por·tal (pȯr′təl) *n* **1** a door, gate, or entrance, especially a large, elaborate one. **2** *Computers* a website used as an entry point to other sites, especially one with a search engine. <Old French, from Latin *porta* gate>

port authority *n* a commission appointed to manage a port.

port·cul·lis (pȯrt kul′is) *n* a strong gate or grating of iron sliding up and down in grooves, used to close the gateway of an ancient castle or fortress. <Old French, from Latin *porta* gate + *colare* to filter>

por·tend (pȯr tend′) *v* be a sign or warning that something will happen, especially something important: *Black clouds portended a storm.* <Latin *por-* before + *tendere* extend>

por·tent (pȯr′tent) *n* **1** a significant sign of something to come: *The scandal was regarded as a portent of worse things to come.* **2** future significance: *an event of great portent.* <See PORTEND.>

por·ten·tous (pȯr ten′təs) *adj* **1** to do with a portent: *a portentous occurrence.* **2** done in a self-important or pompous way: *With a portentous clearing of the throat, she began to speak.* **por·ten′tous·ly** *adv.* **por·ten′tous·ness** *n.*

por·ter[1] (pȯr′tər) *n* **1** a person employed to carry objects, especially one who carries luggage or other items for people in a railway station, airport, hotel, or market. **2** an attendant in a sleeping car of a railway train. <Old French, from Latin *portare* carry>

por·ter[2] (pȯr′tər) *n* **1** a person who guards a door or entrance to a large building. **2** a janitor. <Old French, from Latin *porta* gate>

por·ter[3] (pȯr′tər) *n* a heavy, dark brown beer made from browned or charred malt. <*porter's ale*, i.e., ale for a *porter*[1]>

por·ter·house (pȯr′tər hous′) *n* a thick beefsteak containing the tenderloin.

port·fo·li·o (pȯrt fō′lē ō′) *n, pl* **port·fo·li·os** **1** a large, thin, flat case used to hold loose papers, drawings, or maps. **2 a** a set of pieces of creative work, gathered by someone to display work to a potential employer or exhibitor: *a photography portfolio.* **b** a collection of pieces of work done in class. Selections are usually made by both teacher and student. **3** the position and duties of a cabinet member or a minister of state: *The minister of labour resigned her portfolio.* **4** a range of investments held by a person or group. <Italian, from Latin *portare* carry + *foglio* paper>

port·hole (pȯrt′hōl′) *n* an opening in the side of a ship or aircraft to let in light and air.

por·ti·co (pȯr′tə kō′) *n, pl* **por·ti·coes** or **por·ti·cos** a porch or covered walk with the roof supported by columns. <Italian, from Latin *porta* passage>

por·tion (pȯr′shən) *n* **1** a part or share: *A portion of each school day is devoted to arithmetic.* **2** the quantity of food served for one person: *The restaurant serves large portions.* **3** the part of an estate that goes to an heir. **4** *Archaic* one's fate or destiny.
v divide into parts or shares, or give a thing to a person as a share: *Portion the food equally.* <Old French, from Latin *portio* proportion>

Port·land cement (pȯr′tlənd) *n* a cement made by burning limestone and clay in a kiln.

port·ly (pȯr′tlē) *adj* **port·li·er, port·li·est** with a stout body. <Latin *portare* carry> **port′li·ness** *n.*

port·man·teau (pȯrt man′tō) *especially UK n, pl* **port·man·teaus** or **port·man·teaux** (-tōz) a travelling bag, especially a stiff, oblong bag with two compartments opening like a book.

por·to·bel·lo (pȯrt ə bel′ə) *n* a large cultivated mushroom. Also, **portabella, portabello**. <origin uncertain>

port of entry *n* a harbour, airport, highway, or town that has customs officers to deal with goods and travellers.

por·trait (pȯr′trit) *or* (pȯr′trāt) *n* **1** a picture, especially a painting, drawing, photograph, or engraving of a person. **2** a picture in words or depiction in a film, play, or TV program. **3** a page or illustration displayed or printed narrower than it is high. Compare LANDSCAPE. <Old French *portraire* portray>

por·trait·ist (pȯr′trə tist) *n* a person who paints portraits.

por·trai·ture (pȯr′trə chər) *or* (pȯr′trə chůr′) *n* **1** the act or art of making a portrait. **2** a detailed description.

por·tray (pȯr trā′) *v* **1** describe or depict in words or pictures: *The book* Black Beauty *portrays the life of a horse.* **2** represent someone or something in a stage, film, or TV production. <Old French *portraire* portray> **por·tray′er** *n.*

por·tray·al (pȯr trā′əl) *n* a portrait in pictures or words.

Por·tu·gal (pōr′tyū gəl) *n* a country in western Europe. See the APPENDIX. **Por′tu·guese′** (pōr′tyū gēz′) *adj, n.*

Portuguese man–of–war (man′əv wor′) *n* an invertebrate water animal of warm seas that has a large sac with a sail-like structure on top which enables it to float, and long, dangling tentacles with stinging cells.

pose[1] (pōz) *v* **posed, pos·ing** **1** hold a position while standing or sitting: *She posed an hour for her portrait.* **2** put or place in a certain position: *The artist posed him before painting his picture.* **3** pretend, especially for effect: *He posed as a rich man, though he owed more than he owned.* **4** put forward or state for consideration: *to pose a question.* **5** present or be made up of a problem, danger, or difficulty: *The discharge from the factory posed a threat to the river's fish.*
n **1** a position of the body while standing or sitting: *That snapshot shows her in an attractive pose.* **2** an attitude assumed for effect: *She takes the pose of being a snob when really she is just shy.* <Old French, from Latin *ponere* to place>

pos·er[1] (pō′zər) *n* a person who poses for an artist. <*pose*>

pos·er[2] (pō′zər) *n* a puzzling problem: *The last question on the test was a real poser.* <obsolete *pose* puzzle completely, from *oppose*>

po·seur (pō zər′) *n* an affected person who tries to impress others. <French>

posh (posh) *Informal adj* elegant or luxurious: *They have a very posh apartment in a new high-rise downtown.* <origin uncertain>

pos·it (poz′it) *v* lay down or assume as a fact or principle. <Latin *ponere* to place>

po·si·tion (pə zish′ən) *n* **1** a place where a thing or person is located: *The house is in a sheltered position.* **2** a way of being placed: *Sit in a more comfortable position.* **3** the proper place for a person or thing: *Is everyone in position?* **4 a** a job: *He has a position in a bank.* **b** a rank or status, especially of high status: *She was raised to the position of captain.* **5** an opinion: *What is your position on this question?* **6** the place held by a player on a team: *My position on the hockey team was defence.* **7** a relationship with other people: *Your careless remark put me in an awkward position.*
v put or arrange someone or something in a particular place or way: *The riders positioned their horses at the starting gate.* <Old French, from Latin *ponere* to place>

po·si·tion·al (pə zish′ə nəl) *adj* especially in sports, to do with position or context: *The coach kept the same players on the field, but made some positional changes.*

pos·i·tive (poz′ə tiv) *adj* **1** without doubt: *We have positive knowledge that the earth moves around the sun.* **2** definite and emphatic: *a positive refusal.* **3** affirmative or approving: *Do you think we can expect a positive answer?* **4** confident and optimistic: *You should take a more positive attitude.* **5** doing or adding something: *Don't just make criticisms; give us some positive help.* **6** to do with any direction considered to be progressive: *Clockwise motion is positive.* **7** greater than zero in quantity. **8** with an electrical charge in which electrons are lost or lacking. **9** with the basic form of an adjective or adverb, not comparative or superlative.
n **1** a good or affirmative degree or quantity: *She turned her weakness into a positive.* **2** a number greater than zero. **3** the basic form of an adjective or adverb. Example: *bad* is the positive, *worse* is the comparative, *worst* is the superlative. <Old French, from Latin *ponere* to place>
pos′i·tive·ly *adv.* **pos′i·tive·ness** *n.*

GRAMMAR AND USAGE

A **positive** adjective or adverb is used for a description but not a comparison: *quick, quickly; dry, dryly; successful, successfully.*

Comparative and **superlative** adjectives and adverbs are used for comparisons: *sweeter, closest.*

pos·i·tiv·ism (poz′i ti viz′əm) *n* a system of philosophy that maintains that, in order to be true, every statement must be verified scientifically, or be capable of being proved logically or mathematically. **pos′i·tiv·ist** *adj, n.*

pos·i·tron (poz′ə tron) *n* a subatomic particle with the same mass as an electron and a numerically equal but positive charge. <*posit(ive)* + *(elect)ron*>

pos·se (pos′ē) *n* **1** *especially US* in former times, a group of people summoned by a law officer to help, as in an emergency: *The sheriff formed a posse to capture the bank robbers.* **2** a search party. **3** a small group of people that have an interest or activity in common, sometimes a criminal one. <Latin = be able>

pos·sess (pə zes′) *v* **1** own or have: *The general possessed great wisdom.* **2** hold or occupy as property. **3** control or influence strongly: *She was possessed by the desire to be rich.* **4** control by a supernatural or unconscious force: *She fought like one possessed.* <Old French, from Latin *possidere*>

pos·ses·sion (pə zesh′ən) *n* **1** a condition of having, owning, or controlling something: *Our soldiers fought hard for possession of the hilltop. At his mother's death, he came into possession of a million dollars.* **2** something owned as property: *She put most of her possessions in storage before she left.* **3** a territory or country under the rule of another. **4** domination by a particular feeling, idea, opinion, or attitude. **5** control by a supernatural force: *a state of possession.*

pos·ses·sive (pə zes′iv) *adj* **1** to do with possession: *the possessive instinct.* **2** to do with a strong desire to own or dominate: *a possessive manner, a possessive nature.* **3** to do with the form of a noun or pronoun that shows it refers to the possessor or source of something, or to a part of a larger whole. Examples: *My* is the possessive form of *I* in *my books* and *bird's* is the possessive form of *bird* in *a bird's wing.*
n the possessive form of a word. Examples: *their, woman's.*
pos·ses′sive·ly *adv.* **pos·ses′sive·ness** *n.*

GRAMMAR AND USAGE

The **possessive** case is formed by adding an apostrophe and the letter -*s* to the dictionary form of a word: *friend's, brother's.*

For plural nouns ending in -*s*, add only an apostrophe: *students' bicycles, neighbours' fences.*

possessive adjective *n* the possessive pronoun used with a noun. Example: In *my friend was late,* the word *my* is a possessive adjective.

possessive pronoun *n* a pronoun in the possessive form. Example: In *the book is hers, hers* is a possessive pronoun.

P

pos·ses·sor (pə zes′ər) *n* a person who or thing that occupies, owns, or controls: *the possessor of a lease. She is the proud possessor of a grand piano.*

pos·si·bil·i·ty (pos′ə bil′ə tē) *n, pl* **pos·si·bil·i·ties** **1** the condition of being possible: *There is a possibility that the train may be late.* **2** a person who or thing that is considered possible: *He would be a good possibility for captain. A whole week of rain is a possibility.*

pos·si·ble (pos′ə bəl) *adj* **1** able to happen or be done: *If it's at all possible, I'll be there.* **2** able to be true or a fact: *It is possible that he left by the rear exit.* **3** able to be done properly: *the only possible candidate.* <Latin *posse* be able>

pos·si·bly (pos′ə blē) *adv* **1** in a way that is likely to happen or able to be achieved: *I cannot possibly go.* **2** perhaps: *Possibly you are correct.*

pos·sum (pos′əm) *Informal n* an opossum.
play possum, *Informal* pretend to be dead or asleep.

a bat	e bed	i bid	o pot	u cup	th thin
ā cake	ē me	ī bite	ō go	ü rude	TH then
ä bar	ə about	ər over	ô for	ů put	zh measure

post[1] (pōst) *n* **1** a length of timber, metal, or plastic, set upright, usually as a support or a marker: *fence post, hitching post.* **2** the point at which a race starts or ends. **3** a goalpost.
v **1** fasten a notice up in a place where it can easily be seen: *The list of winners will be posted soon.* **2** make known by, or as if by, a posted notice: *Signs were posted around the area. The police posted a reward for information.* **3** record or achieve a score or result by a player or team: *They posted three wins in their first five games.* **4** *Computers* send a message or information to a newsgroup, chat room, bulletin-board service, or e-mail list. <Latin *postis* doorpost>
keep someone posted, keep someone fully informed: *They kept us posted on new developments.*

post[2] (pōst) *n* **1** a place where a soldier, guard, or police officer is stationed when on duty. **2** a place where a military force is stationed at a permanent position or camp. **3** a paid job or position: *My grandmother has a new post as district manager.* **4** a place where a particular activity is carried on: *a fur-trading post.* **5** *especially US* a local branch of a war veterans' organization.
v **1** send someone to a particular place, or to take up an appointment: *Some of the employees were posted to another city.* **2** station a soldier, guard, or police officer in a particular place: *We posted guards at the door.* <French, from Latin *ponere* put>

post[3] (pōst) *n* **1** *especially UK* an official service or system for delivering letters, papers, and parcels: *to send by post.* **2** in former times, one of a series of fixed stations along a route for providing relays of people and horses for carrying mail or passengers.
v **1** *especially UK* send by mail: *to post a letter.* **2** in former times, travel by means of a series of relays of horses and stations. **3** record or supply with up-to-date information: *Please keep me posted on your plans for the summer.* **4** transfer a bookkeeping entry in a ledger. <French, from Latin *ponere* put>

post– *prefix* after: *postdate.* <Latin = after, behind>

post·age (pō′stij) *n* the amount paid on a thing sent by mail.

postage stamp *n* a stamp placed on mail to show that postage has been paid.

post·al (pō′stəl) *adj* to do with mail or the post office: *postal regulations.*

✱ **postal code** *n* a part of an address that uses a system of alternating letters and numerals to identify a particular postal delivery route or point.

postal station *n* one of several branch post offices in a large community.

post·card (pōst′kärd′) *n* a card used without an envelope for sending a short message by mail, often with a picture on one side.

post·date (pōst′dāt′) *v* **post·dat·ed, post·dat·ing 1** give a letter, cheque, or other document a later date than the actual date of writing it. **2** occur or arrive at a later date.

post·er (pō′stər) *n* **1** a large printed advertisement, or notice, often illustrated, put up in some public place or as a decoration. **2** a person who sends a message or information to a newsgroup, chat room, bulletin-board service, or e-mail list.

poster child *Informal n* a person thought of as the ideal representative of something: *My brother is the poster child for sleep deprivation.* Also called **poster boy**, **poster girl**. <from the practice of using a child's photo in advertisements>

pos·te·ri·or (pos tē′rē ər) *adj* **1** farther back in position. **2** later or coming after.
n Informal the buttocks. <Latin *post* after>

pos·ter·i·ty (pos ter′ə tē) *n* **1** the generations of the future: *Posterity may travel to distant planets.* **2** all of a person's descendants. <Old French, from Latin *post* after>

poster paint *n* watercolour mixed with other ingredients that make it less transparent.

post·grad·u·ate (pōst′graj′ū it) *n* a student who continues university studies at a level beyond that of a bachelor's degree.
adj to do with postgraduates or with taking a course of study at such a level.

post·haste (pōst′hāst′) *adv* very speedily or in great haste.

post·hu·mous (pos′chə məs) *adj* **1** happening after death: *posthumous fame, a posthumous book.* **2** born after the death of the father: *a posthumous son.* <Latin *post* after + *humus* ground, i.e., after burial> **post′hu·mous·ly** *adv.*

post–im·press·ion·ism (pōst′im presh′on izm) *n* a movement in painting, begun in France in the late 1800s, that developed out of impressionism and explored colour and line. **post′-im·press′ion·ist** *n, adj.*
post′-im·press′ion·is′tic *adj.*

post·ing (pōst′ing) *n* **1** a position to which a person has been assigned, especially in military or diplomatic service. **2** *Computers* a message or information contributed to a newsgroup, chat room, bulletin-board service, or e-mail list: *In your last posting you mentioned a novel you were reading, but I've forgotten the title.*

Post–it (pōst′it) *Trademark n* a small piece of paper for writing notes on, with a slightly adhesive strip across one end that allows it to be easily removed or repositioned.

post·lude (pōs′tlūd) *n* **1** a closing piece of music, especially a composition played at the end of a church service. **2** a final or concluding phase: *the postlude of an era.* Compare PRELUDE. <*post-* after + (*pre*)*lude*>

post·mark (pōst′märk′) *n* an official mark stamped on mail to cancel the postage stamp and record the place and date of mailing.
v stamp with a postmark.

post·me·rid·i·an (pōst′mə rid′ē ən) P.M.

post–mor·tem (pōst′môr′təm) *adj* of or relating to an examination of a dead body to determine the cause of death: *A post-mortem examination showed that the woman had been poisoned.*
n an examination of a dead body to determine the cause of death. <Latin = after death>

post·na·tal (pōst′nā′təl) *adj* to do with the period immediately following childbirth: *postnatal care, postnatal depression.*

post office *n* a local office where mail is received and sorted for delivery or placement in individual boxes, and where other postal services are provided.

post–op·er·a·tive (pōst op′ər ə tiv) *or* (pōst op′ə rā′tiv) *adj* of or occurring in the period immediately following a surgical operation: *a post-operative infection.*

post·paid (pōst′pād′) *adj* with the postage paid for.

post·par·tum (pōst por′təm) *adj, adv* to do with the period immediately following childbirth. <*post-* after + Latin *parere* to bear>

post·pone (pō spōn′) *or* (pōst pōn′) *v* **post·poned, post·pon·ing** put off to a later time: *The ball game was postponed because of rain.* <*post-* after + Latin *ponere* put> **post·pone′ment** *n.*

post·pran·di·al (pōst′pran′dē əl) *adj* to do with the period after dinner or lunch: *postprandial speeches.* <*post-* after + Latin *prandium* meal>

post·script (pōst′skript) *n* **1** an addition to a letter, written after the writer's name has been signed. **2** an additional statement or action that provides further information, such as a supplement to a composition or literary work.

post–sec·ond·ar·y (pōst sek′ən də′rē) *adj* to do with education beyond the high school level.

post–trau·mat·ic stress disorder or **syndrome** (pōst′trou mat′ik) *n* a condition of mental and physical stress resulting from a severe injury or psychological shock.

pos·tu·lant (pos′chə lənt) *n* a candidate, especially for admission to a religious order. <French, from Latin *postulare* ask>

pos·tu·late (pos′chə lit) *for n,* (pos′chə lāt′) *for v.* *n* something taken for granted or assumed as a basis for reasoning, discussion, or belief: *One postulate of geometry is that a straight line may be drawn between any two points.* *v* **pos·tu·lat·ed, pos·tu·lat·ing** take for granted or assume as a basis for reasoning, discussion, or belief. <Latin *postulare* ask>

pos·ture (pos′chər) *n* **1** the position of the body when standing or sitting. **2** a particular way of dealing with or considering something: *The prime minister took a defensive posture in answering the questions put to him.* *v* **pos·tured, pos·tur·ing** behave so as to impress or mislead others: *She thought the way he postured had a lot of macho in it.* <French, from *ponere* to place> **pos′tur·al** *adj.*

post·war (pō′stwȯr′) *adj* to do with the period immediately following a war: *a postwar construction boom.*

po·sy (pō′zē) *n, pl* **po·sies** a small bunch of flowers. <Middle English>

pot[1] (pot) *n* **1** a deep, rounded or cylindrical container used to hold, store, or cook something: *a soup pot, a plant pot.* **2** a basket used to catch fish, crab, or lobsters. **3** all the money bet at one time, or contributed for a particular purpose: *Everybody put money into the pot.* **4** a pot-belly. *v* **pot·ted, pot·ting 1** plant in a flowerpot: *We potted young tomato plants.* **2** preserve food, especially meat or fish, in a sealed jar or pot. **3** take a potshot. <Old English> **go to pot,** *Informal* go to ruin: *I quit practising, and my piano playing went to pot.*

pot[2] (pot) *Informal n* marijuana. <perhaps Spanish *potiguaya* cannabis leaves>

po·ta·ble (pō′tə bəl) *adj* safe to drink. <French, from Latin *potare* to drink>

pot·ash (pot′ash′) *n* an alkaline potassium compound, especially potassium carbonate or potassium hydroxide, used in fertilizers. <Obsolete Dutch *potaschen* = pot ashes. Potash was originally obtained by evaporating a wood ash solution in an iron pot.>

po·tas·si·um (pə tas′ē əm) *n* a soft, silver-white metallic element, occurring in nature only in compounds. *Symbol* **K** <Latin, from French *potasse* potash>

potassium chloride *n* a crystalline compound that occurs naturally as a mineral. It is used in fertilizers and as a salt substitute.

potassium hy·drox·ide (hī drok′sīd′) *n* a strong alkali used especially in making soap.

potassium nitrate *n* a crystalline salt that occurs naturally in nitre. It is used in preserving meats and in explosives. Also called **nitre, saltpetre**.

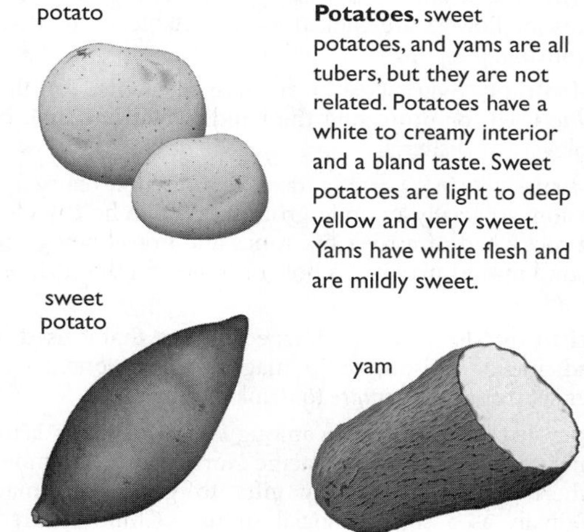

Potatoes, sweet potatoes, and yams are all tubers, but they are not related. Potatoes have a white to creamy interior and a bland taste. Sweet potatoes are light to deep yellow and very sweet. Yams have white flesh and are mildly sweet.

po·ta·to (pə tā′tō) *n, pl* **po·ta·toes** a hard, starchy tuber of a cultivated plant, cooked and eaten as a vegetable. <Spanish, from Arawak (a language of S America) *batata*>

potato beetle *n* a beetle with black and yellow stripes that damages potato plants. Also called **potato bug**.

potato chip *n* a crisp, thin, dry slice of potato that has been fried in deep fat: *We each took a soft drink and a bag of potato chips.*

pot–bel·lied (pot′bel′ēd) *adj* shaped like a pot-belly: *a pot-bellied stove.*

pot·bel·ly (pot′bel′ē) *n* a large, protruding belly.

a bat	e bed	i bid	o pot	u cup	th **thin**
ā cake	ē me	ī bite	ō go	ū rude	ᴛʜ **then**
ä bar	ə about	ər over	ȯ for	ů put	zh measure

pot·boil·er (pot′boi′lər) *Informal n* a work of literature or art produced to make a living by catering to popular taste.

po·tent (pō′tənt) *adj* **1** with power or effectiveness in action: *a potent remedy for a disease.* **2** able as a male to achieve an erection or to reach orgasm. <Latin *potentis* having power> **po′ten·cy** *n.* **po′tent·ly** *adv.*

po·ten·tate (pō′tən tāt′) *n* a ruler with great power, especially in former times.

po·ten·tial (pə ten′shəl) *adj* capable of coming into being or action: *a potential danger.*
n **1** a thing capable of coming into being or action. **2** *Physics* the quantity determining the energy of mass in a gravitational field or of charge in an electric field. <See POTENT.> **po·ten′ti·al′i·ty** (pə ten′shē al′ə tē) *n.* **po·ten′tial·ly** *adv.*

potential energy *Physics n* the energy that something has that is due to its position or its structure, not to motion.

pot·head (pot′hed) *n* **1** a pilot whale. **2** *Slang* a person who habitually smokes marijuana.

pot·herb (pot′ərb′) *or* (pot′hərb′) *n* a plant whose leaves, stems, or flowers are cooked as a vegetable, or used as a flavouring.

pot·hold·er (pot′hōl′dər) *n* a piece of quilted or thick fabric used for protecting the hands when handling hot cookware or dishes.

pot·hole (pot′hōl′) *n* **1** a deep, round hole caused by erosion, especially an underground cave or a hole made in the rocky bed of a river by stones and gravel being spun around in the current. **2** a hole or hollow in the surface of a road.

po·tion (pō′shən) *n* a liquid, especially one that is used as a medicine or poison, or in magic: *a love potion.* <Old French, from Latin *potare* to drink>

pot·latch (pot′lach′) *n* among First Nations or Native American peoples of the Pacific Northwest, a ceremonial gathering at which costly gifts to guests are made, originally as a sign of social status. <Chinook Jargon, from Nootka *p'acitl* gift>

pot·luck (pot′luk′) *n* whatever food happens to be ready or on hand for a meal: *Come into the house and take potluck with us.*
adj contributed to a meal by everyone present: *a potluck lunch.*

pot pie *n* a baked meat or poultry and vegetable pie, baked in a dish and usually with only a top crust: *chicken pot pie.*

pot·pour·ri (pō′pu̇ rē′) *n* **1** a fragrant mixture of dried flower petals and spices. **2** a mixture of things, especially musical or literary medley. <French = rotten pot>

pot roast *n* a large piece of meat, usually beef, cooked slowly with a little water in a deep, heavy, tightly covered dish.

pot·sherd (pot′shərd′) *n* a broken piece of earthenware.

pot·shot (pot′shot) *n* **1** a shot fired unexpectedly or at random at someone or something. **2** a random or undeserved criticism.

pot·ted (pot′id) *adj* **1** planted or grown in a flowerpot. **2** preserved as food, especially meat or fish, in a sealed jar or pot. **3** made into short and readable form as a literary work or description: *a potted history, a potted biography.*

pot·ter[1] (pot′ər) *n* a person who makes pottery.

pot·ter[2] (pot′ər) PUTTER[1].

potter's wheel *n* a rotating horizontal disc upon which clay is moulded into pots and other earthenware.

pot·ter·y (pot′ə rē) *n, pl* **pot·ter·ies** **1** pots, dishes, vases, or other earthenware, especially as distinct from porcelain or stoneware. **2** the art or craft of making pottery. **3** a place where pottery is made. <Old French *potier* a potter>

pot·ty[1] (pot′ē) *n, pl* **pot·ties** a small, low container or structure designed for a young child to sit on and use as a toilet while being toilet-trained.

pot·ty[2] (pot′ē) *Informal adj* slightly crazy or eccentric.

pouch (pouch) *n* **1** a small bag or flexible container, typically attached to a belt or carried in a pocket: *a letter carrier's pouch.* **2** a baglike cavity or receptacle in the body of a marsupial, such as the kangaroo, in which the young are carried while receiving milk from their mother. **3** a loose fold of skin: *pouches under the eyes.* **4** a large bag that can be locked, used for transporting mail or government dispatches: *a diplomatic pouch.*
v form a pouch or form into a pouch. <Old French *poche* bag> **pouch′like′** *adj.*

pouf (pūf) *n* **1** a woman's hairstyle that is made up of high rolls or puffs of hair, or one of these rolls or puffs. **2** a puffed or gathered part of a dress. **3** a small, soft ottoman. Also, **pouff**, **pouffe**. <French>

poul·tice (pōl′tis) *n* a soft, moist mass of a substance, such as flour or mustard, applied to the body as a medicine and held in place by a cloth.
v **poul·ticed, poul·tic·ing** put a poultice on. <Latin *puls* mush>

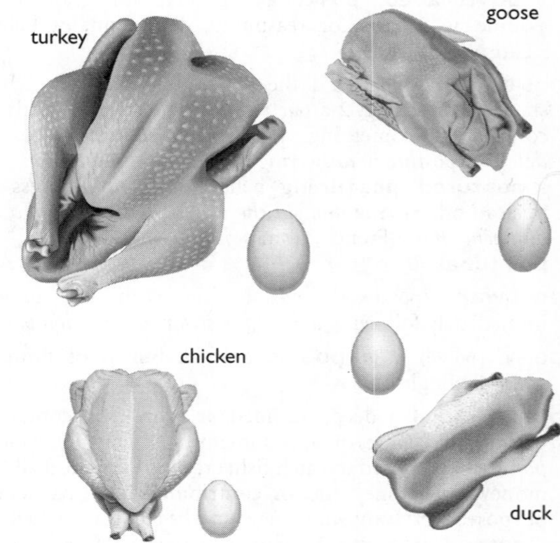

poul·try (pōl′trē) *n* birds raised for their meat or eggs, such as chickens, turkeys, geese, or ducks. <Old French, from Latin *pullus* young fowl>

pounce (pouns) *v* **pounced, pounc·ing 1** spring or swoop suddenly so as to attack or seize: *The cat pounced upon the mouse.* **2** take sudden decisive action or advantage of an opportunity: *The shoppers pounced on the specials being offered.*
n a sudden swoop or spring. <origin uncertain>

pound[1] (pound) *n* **1** a nonmetric measure of mass equalling 16 ounces (about 454 g). **2** a unit of money in the UK. *Symbol* **£** <Old English, from Latin (*libra*) *pondo*>

pound[2] (pound) *v* **1** hit hard and heavily again and again: *I pounded the door with my fist.* **2** beat, throb, or vibrate hard: *After running fast, you can feel your heart pound.* **3** crush to powder or pulp by beating: *He pounded walnuts for the cake.* **4** run with heavy steps: *She pounded down the hill to catch the bus.* **5** severely defeat an opponent: *Our team pounded the opposition 7–1.* <Old English *punian*>

pound[3] (pound) *n* **1** an enclosed place for keeping stray or unlicensed animals, especially dogs and cats, until claimed by the owners, adopted, or disposed of. **2** a place for keeping automobiles or other personal property until redeemed by the owners. <Old English *pund-*>

pound·age (poun′dij) *n* a weight in POUNDS[1] (def. 1).

pound cake *n* a rich butter cake containing equal amounts of the principal ingredients, such as sugar, flour, and butter.

pound key *n* the button on a telephone marked with the symbol #.

pour (pȯr) *v* **1** cause to flow in a steady stream: *I poured the milk from the bottle.* **2** flow in a steady stream: *The crowd poured out of the cinema. The rain poured down.*
n the act or fact of pouring. See PORE for confusable. <Middle English *pouren*> **pour′er** *n.*
it never rains but it pours, events of the same kind, especially misfortunes, that happen all at the same time: *I missed my bus, forgot my report, and failed my history test—it never rains but it pours!*
pour it on, *Informal* do or express something with great, or too much, energy, speed, or enthusiasm.

pour·quoi tale (pȯr kwa′) *n* a legend or story that gives an imaginative explanation of natural phenomena. Such stories usually feature animals, and end when the so-called explanation is revealed. <French = why>

pout (pout) *v* thrust or push out the lips, as a displeased or sulky child may do.
n a pushing out of the lips when displeased or sulky. <Middle English, perhaps from Swedish *puta* be inflamed>

✱ **pou·tine** (pū tēn′) *n* French fries topped with gravy and cheese curds. <Cdn French>

pout·y (pou′tē) *adj* inclined to pout.

pov·er·ty (pov′ər tē) *n* **1** the condition of not having enough income to maintain a standard of living regarded as normal in a community: *She died in poverty.* **2** the renunciation of the right to own property as an individual: *When he joined the religious order, he took a vow of poverty.* **3** a lack of what is needed: *The poverty of the soil here makes farming difficult, a poverty of ideas.*

pov·er·ty–strick·en (pov′ər tē strik′ən) *adj* extremely poor.

POW prisoner of war.

pow·der (pou′dər) *n* **1** a solid substance reduced to dust by pounding, crushing, or grinding. **2** something made or prepared as powder: *talcum powder.*
v **1** make into powder, or become powder: *powdered sugar.* **2** sprinkle or apply powder or anything like powder: *to powder a cake with sugar. The ground was powdered with snow.* <Old French, from Latin *pulveris* dust>
pow′der·y *adj.*
keep your powder dry, remain cautiously ready to take action.
take a powder, *Informal* leave quickly, especially in order to avoid a conflict or difficulty.

powder blue *adj* pale blue.

powder burn *n* a burn on the skin resulting from the explosion of gunpowder at close range.

powder horn *n* an animal's horn used to hold gunpowder.

powder keg *n* **1** a small cask for holding gunpowder or blasting powder. **2** a thing that is liable to explode: *The whole country was a powder keg after the death of the dictator.*

powder puff *n* a soft puff or pad for applying cosmetic powder to the skin.

powder room *n* **1** a small bathroom in a home, with only a toilet, sink, and mirror. **2** a public washroom for women, especially one with seats for resting and a long vanity or counter for applying makeup, usually in a room separate from the toilets and sinks.

pow·er (pou′ər) *n* **1 a** energy or force that can do work: *Running water can produce power to turn a wheel.* **b** electricity: *Turn on the power.* **2** strength, force, or effectiveness: *a medicine of great power.* **3** the ability to do or act: *I will give you all the help in my power. She has great powers of concentration.* **4** a person, thing, body, or nation with authority or influence: *He's quite a power in the fashion industry. Parliament has power to declare war. Five powers held a peace conference.* **5** the product of a number multiplied by itself a certain number of times. Sixteen, for example, is the fourth power of 2. **6** of a telescope or microscope, the capacity to magnify an image.
v provide with power or energy: *a boat powered by an outboard motor.*
adj **1** operated by or equipped with a motor: *power steering.* **2** showing or with the appearance of power or importance: *a power lunch.* <Old French, from Latin *potere* be able>
in power, with control or authority: *the government in power.*
the powers that be, those who have control or authority.

power brakes *n* a braking system in a motor vehicle that uses power produced by the engine to increase the effect of pressure on the brake pedal.

a bat	e bed	i bid	o pot	u cup	th thin
ā cake	ē me	ī bite	ō go	ū rude	ᴛʜ then
ȧ bar	ə about	ər over	ȯ for	u̇ put	zh measure

P

pow·er–dive (pou′ər dīv′) *v* **-dived** or **-dove, -dived, -div·ing** of an aircraft, make a dive speeded up by the power of the engine. **power dive** *n.*

pow·er·ful (pou′ər fəl) *adj* with great power, force, or effectiveness: *a powerful speech, a powerful nation, a powerful emotion.* **pow′er·ful·ly** *adv.* **pow′er·ful·ness** *n.*

power grid *n* a network of wires distributing hydroelectric power from a central station.

pow·er·house (pou′ər hous′) *n* **1** a building containing boilers, engines, or dynamos for generating electric power. **2** *Informal* a person or group with great power, energy, or drive: *That new teacher is a real powerhouse.*

pow·er·less (pou′ər lis) *adj* without power: *The mouse was powerless in the cat's claws.* **pow′er·less·ly** *adv.* **pow′er·less·ness** *n.*

power nap *n* a short sleep to renew energy. **power-nap** *v.*

power of attorney *n* a written statement giving one person legal power to act for another.

power pack *n* a device that converts the voltage from a power line or battery to the voltage required by the elements of an electronic circuit, as in a radio or TV.

power plant *n* **1** a building with machinery for generating power. **2** a motor or engine.

power play *Hockey n* a special combination of players put on the ice when the opposition is short-handed.

Pow·er·Point (pou′ər point′) *Trademark n* a software tool used for presenting information in a SLIDE SHOW.

power politics *n* (*with singular verb*) international political strategy that uses the threat of superior military or economic power to advance national interests.

power station *n* POWERHOUSE (def. 1).

power steering *n* a steering mechanism that uses power from an engine to increase the effect of the force used in turning the steering wheel.

power surge *n* a sharp increase in current in an electric circuit, sometimes damaging machines connected to it.

power tool *n* a tool provided with power from an electric or gasoline motor.

pow·wow (pou′wou′) *n* **1** among First Nations and Native American peoples, a celebration or ceremony, usually featuring feasting, dancing and certain rites. **2** *Informal* a conference or meeting.
v hold a powwow.

ETYMOLOGY

Powwow is an Algonquian word meaning "he dreams," originally referring to a medicine man who was thought to learn the craft from dreams.

pox (poks) *n* (*especially in compounds*) a viral disease that is characterized by pus-filled pimples or pocks when healed: *chicken pox.* <variant of *pock*>

ppb parts per billion.

ppm parts per million.

PR public relations.

prac·ti·ca·ble (prak′tə kə bəl) *adj* capable of being put into practice or use: *a practicable idea, a practicable road.* **prac′ti·ca·bil′i·ty** *n.* **prac′ti·ca·bly** *adv.*

CONFUSABLES

Practicable means "doable" or "capable of being accomplished": *She delivered a practicable proposal.*

Practical means "efficient" or "functional": *A wrench is a practical tool.*

prac·ti·cal (prak′tə kəl) *adj* **1** to do with action or practice rather than thought or theory: *Earning a living is a practical matter.* **2** able to be put into practice or use: *a practical plan. His legal knowledge was not very practical when he became a chemist.* **3** good sense: *a practical person.* **4** engaged in actual practice or work. <Old French, from Greek *prattein* to do> **prac′ti·cal·ness** *n.*

prac·ti·cal·i·ty (prak′tə kal′ə tē) *n, pl* **prac·ti·cal·i·ties** **1** the quality of being practical. **2** the aspects of a situation that involve action or experience: *She finds it hard to face the practicalities of earning a living.*

practical joke *n* a kind of trick that depends for its effect or humour on a person being put at a disadvantage or embarrassed in some way.

prac·ti·cal·ly (prak′ti klē) *adv* **1** almost or nearly: *We are practically home. They practically ran the show.* **2** in a practical way: *He reacted very practically to the emergency.*

practical nurse *n* a nurse whose occupation is to care for the sick, but who has not the training required of a registered nurse.

prac·tice (prak′tis) *n* **1** an action done many times over in order to gain skill: *Practice makes perfect.* **2** the skill gained by experience or exercise: *He was out of practice at batting.* **3** the action or process of doing or being something: *Her plan is good in theory, but not in actual practice.* **4** the usual way or custom: *It is the practice at school to ring a bell at the end of a period.* **5** the occupation or business of a doctor, dentist, or lawyer: *He has sold his practice to a younger doctor.* **6** a period set aside for practising: *She went to hockey practice last night.* <Old French, from Greek *prattein* do>

prac·tise or **prac·tice** (prak′tis) *v* **prac·tised** or **prac·ticed, prac·tis·ing** or **prac·tic·ing** **1** do something again and again so as to learn to do it well: *to practise playing the piano.* **2** do as a rule or make a custom of: *to practise moderation.* **3** work at or follow as a profession, art, or occupation: *to practise law.* **4** observe the teachings and rules of a religion: *They were encouraged to practise their faith.*

CONFUSABLES

Practise is a verb: *I need to practise lacrosse so that I will improve my skills.*

Practice is a noun: *I have lacrosse practice twice a week, on Tuesday and Friday.*

prac·tised or **prac·ticed** (prak′tist) *adj* experienced and skilled: *a practised musician.*

prac·tis·ing or **prac·tic·ing** (prak′tə sing) *adj* actively engaged in a particular profession or career: *a practising lawyer.*

prac·ti·tion·er (prak tish′ə nər) *n* a person engaged in the practice of a profession: *a medical practitioner.*

prae·to·ri·an (prē tȯ′rē ən) *adj* **1** to do with a **praetor**, a magistrate in ancient Rome, ranking next below a consul. **2** to do with the bodyguard of a Roman commander or emperor.

prag·ma·tism (prag′mə tiz′əm) *n* **1** the quality or condition of being practical and matter-of-fact. **2** a philosophy that tests the value and truth of ideas by their practical consequences. <Latin, from Greek *prattein* do> **prag·mat′ic** *adj.* **prag·mat′i·cal·ly** *adv.* **prag′ma·tist** *n.*

prai·rie (prer′ē) *n* **1** a large area of level or rolling land with grass but very few or no trees. **2 the Prairies** *pl* the great, almost treeless plain of central N America, such as that covering much of central and southern Manitoba, Saskatchewan, and Alberta. <French, from Latin *pratum* meadow>

prairie chicken *n* a large, deep-bodied grouse found on the Prairies.

prairie crocus *n* a small wildflower of the central N American plains. It is the floral emblem of Manitoba.

prairie dog *n* a N American rodent that lives in a large system of interconnected burrows.

prairie lily *n* a N American wild lily found in dry or wet places on the Prairies and in open woods. It is the floral emblem of Saskatchewan. Also called **Western Red Lily**.

prairie oyster *n* **1** a raw egg seasoned with Worcestershire sauce, swallowed whole. **2** a testicle of a bull calf, cooked and served as food.

🍁 **Prairie Provinces** *pln* Manitoba, Saskatchewan, and Alberta.

prairie schooner *n* a large covered wagon formerly used on the plains of N America, especially by settlers.

prairie wolf *n* a coyote.

praise (prāz) *n* **1** the expression of approval or admiration for someone or something: *When he won the race, his friends heaped praise upon him.* **2** the expression of respect for and gratitude to God, especially in song.
v **praised, prais·ing 1** express approval or admiration: *Everyone praised the winning team for its fine play.* **2** worship in words or song: *to praise God.* <Old French, from Latin *pretium* prize> **prais′er** *n.*
damn with faint praise, praise with so little enthusiasm as to condemn.
sing the praise (or **praises**) **of,** praise with enthusiasm.

praise·wor·thy (prā′zwər′ᴛʜē) *adj* worthy of praise or deserving approval: *a praiseworthy act.*
praise′wor′thi·ly *adv.* **praise′wor′thi·ness** *n.*

pra·line (prȧ′lēn) *n* a brown candy made of sugar and nuts, sometimes used as a filling for chocolates.
<M. de Duplessis-*Praslin*, 17c, whose cook invented it>

pram *especially UK n* a baby carriage. <*perambulator*>

prance (prans) *v* **pranced, pranc·ing 1** spring about with high steps, such as a horse may do. **2** walk with proud, exaggerated movements: *The children pranced about in their party clothes.*
n the act or fact of prancing. <Middle English *prancen*>

prank (prangk) *n* a piece of mischief or playful trick. <origin uncertain>

prank·ish (prang′kish) *adj* full or fond of pranks. **prank′ish·ness** *n.*

prank·ster (prangk′stər) *n* a person who plays pranks.

pra·se·o·dym·i·um (prā′zē ō dim′ē əm) *n* a rare metallic element of the same group as cerium. *Symbol* **Pr** <Latin, from Greek *prasios* bluish green + German *Didym* didymium>

prate (prāt) *v* **prat·ed, prat·ing** talk a great deal in a foolish way.
n empty or foolish talk. <German *praten*>

prat·tle (prat′əl) *v* **prat·tled, prat·tling** talk freely and carelessly.
n foolish or childish talk. <*prate*> **prat′tler** *n.*

prawn (pron) *n* an edible shellfish resembling shrimp. <Middle English *prane*>

pray (prā) *v* **1** *Religion* speak to God or a god, especially to express gratitude or make a request: *to pray for help, to pray for your family.* **2** wish or hope strongly for a particular outcome: *She prayed that her friend wouldn't notice the mistake.* **3** *Formal* politely request or instruct: *Pray be seated.* <Old French, from Latin *prex* prayer>

CONFUSABLES

Pray means "speak to God": *Many religious people pray in a house of worship.*

Prey means "victim": *The falcon swooped down to capture its prey.*

prayer (prer) *n* **1** *Religion* **a** words or thoughts addressed to God or a god, especially to express gratitude or make a request. **b** the act of praying or form of worship: *She was at prayer. They always have morning prayers.* **2** a strong hope or wish: *The warm weather was the answer to our prayers.*

prayer·ful (prer′fəl) *adj* **1** with the custom of praying often. **2** like a prayer. **prayer′ful·ly** *adv.* **prayer′ful·ness** *n.*

prayer rug *n* a small rug used by Muslims to kneel on when praying.

prayer shawl *n* a shawl with a fringe traditionally worn over the head and shoulders by Jewish men for morning prayers.

prayer wheel *n* among the Buddhists of Tibet, a wheel or cylinder inscribed with prayers, each rotation counting as an uttered prayer.

a bat	e bed	i bid	o pot	u cup	th thin
ā cake	ē me	ī bite	ō go	ū rude	ᴛʜ then
ȧ bar	ə about	ər over	ȯ for	ů put	zh measure

praying mantis *n* a mantis. See INSECT for picture.

pre– *prefix* before, in time or order: *preheat, pre-eminent.* <Latin *prae-* before>

preach (prēch) *v* **1** deliver a sermon or speak publicly on a religious subject. **2** make known by preaching: *to preach the Gospel.* **3** advise or recommend strongly: *The coach was always preaching exercise and fresh air. My older sister is forever preaching about good table manners.* <Old French, from Latin *prae-* before + *dicare* proclaim>

preach·er (prē′chər) *n* a person who preaches, especially a member of the clergy.

preach·i·fy (prē′chə fī′) *Informal v* **preach·i·fied, preach·i·fy·ing** preach or moralize too much.

preach·y (prē′chē) *Informal adj* **preach·i·er, preach·i·est** with or showing too great a desire to preach or moralize: *Don't be so preachy; I know it was a stupid thing to do.*

pre·am·ble (prē′am′bəl) *n* a preliminary or introductory statement. <Old French, from Latin *prae-* before + *ambulum* walk>

pre·ar·range (prē′ə rānj′) *v* **pre·ar·ranged, pre·ar·rang·ing** arrange beforehand: *a prearranged meeting place, a prearranged signal.* **pre′ar·range′ment** *n.*

pre·as·signed (prē′ə sīnd′) *adj* assigned beforehand: *The seats at the conference table were preassigned.*

Pre·cam·bri·an or **Pre–Cam·bri·an** (prē′kam′brē ən) *adj* to do with the earliest eon of geological time, lasting from perhaps 4.5 billion to 600 million years ago, or the rocks formed during this time.

pre·can·cer·ous (prē kan′sər əs) *adj* showing abnormal changes likely to lead to malignancy.

pre·car·i·ous (pri ker′ē əs) *or* (pri kar′ē əs) *adj* not safe or secure: *Her hold on the branch was precarious.* <Latin *prex* prayer> **pre·car′i·ous·ly** *adv.* **pre·car′i·ous·ness** *n.*

pre·cau·tion (pri kosh′ən) *n* an act done beforehand to prevent harm or to secure good results: *Locking the door of a house is taking a precaution against theft.*
pre·cau′tion·ar′y *adj.*

pre·cede (prē sēd′) *v* **pre·ced·ed, pre·ced·ing 1** go or be before: *The rain was preceded by a violent windstorm. A band preceded the first float in the parade.* **2** be higher than in rank or importance: *A major precedes a captain.* <Old French, from Latin *prae* - before + *cedere go*>

CONFUSABLES

Precede means "go or come before": *Friday precedes Saturday. The bridesmaids preceded the bride up the aisle.*

Proceed means "move forward": *Please proceed with caution when merging with traffic. Proceed directly to the auditorium for the assembly.*

prec·e·dence (pres′ə dəns) *or* (prē′sə dəns) *n* **1** the condition of being considered more important in position or rank: *This work takes precedence over all other work.* **2** the right to precede others in ceremonies or social affairs: *A duchess takes precedence over a countess.*

prec·e·dent (pres′ə dənt) *or* (prē′sə dənt) *n* a case that may serve as an example or reason for a later case: *He refused his assistant's request for time off because he didn't want to set a precedent.*

pre·ced·ing (prē sē′ding) *adj* going or coming before: *the preceding page, the preceding year.*

pre·cept (prē′sept) *n* a general rule of action or behaviour: *"If at first you don't succeed, try, try again" is a familiar precept.* <Latin *praecipere* give rules to>

pre·cinct (prē′singkt) *n* **1** usually, **precincts** *pl* an area within walls, or a boundary of a particular building or place: *the school precincts.* **2** *US* a district within certain boundaries, for administrative or other purposes: *a police precinct.* <Latin *prae-* before + *cingere* surround>

pre·ci·os·i·ty (presh′ē os′ə tē) *n, pl* **pre·ci·os·i·ties** too much refinement in language, music, or art.

pre·cious (presh′əs) *adj* **1** of great value. **2** much loved or treasured: *a precious child.* **3** too elegant or refined. **4** *Informal* supposed to be greatly valued but actually contemptible: *a precious mess.*
n someone greatly valued or treasured, especially a child: *OK, precious, let's watch that video.* <Old French, from Latin *pretium* price> **pre′cious·ness** *n.*

SYNONYMS

Precious emphasizes extreme value: *a precious metal.*

Costly means "expensive": *The watch was so costly she was afraid to wear it.*

Priceless suggests something that cannot have a price put on it: *The week I spent at my uncle and aunt's place was priceless to me.*

precious metal *n* gold, silver, or platinum.

precious stone *n* a gemstone, such as a diamond.

prec·i·pice (pres′ə pis) *n* a steep rock face or cliff, especially a tall one. <French, from Latin *praeciptitium* steep place, from *praecipitis* headlong>

pre·cip·i·tant (pri sip′ə tənt) *n* a substance that causes another substance in solution to be deposited in solid form.
adj precipitate. **pre·cip′i·tant·ly** *adv.*

pre·cip·i·tate (pri sip′ə tāt′) *for v,* (pri sip′ə tit′) *for adj,* (pri sip′ə tāt′) *or* (pri sip′ə tit′) *for n.*
v **pre·cip·i·tat·ed, pre·cip·i·tat·ing 1** cause to happen suddenly: *a disagreement that precipitated a war.* **2** cause to move suddenly and forcefully: *He precipitated himself into the crowd and pushed toward the door.* **3** separate a substance out from a solution as a solid. **4** condense moisture or be condensed from vapour in the form of rain, hail, snow, or dew.
adj **1** very hurried or sudden: *A cool breeze caused a precipitate drop in the temperature.* **2** with great haste and force: *a precipitate rush to the door.* **3** with haste and insufficient consideration: *You'll regret making a precipitate decision.*
n a solid substance, usually crystalline, separated out from a solution as a result of a chemical change. <Latin *praecipitare* fall, from *praecipitis* headlong>
pre·cip′i·tate·ly *adv.*

winter precipitation

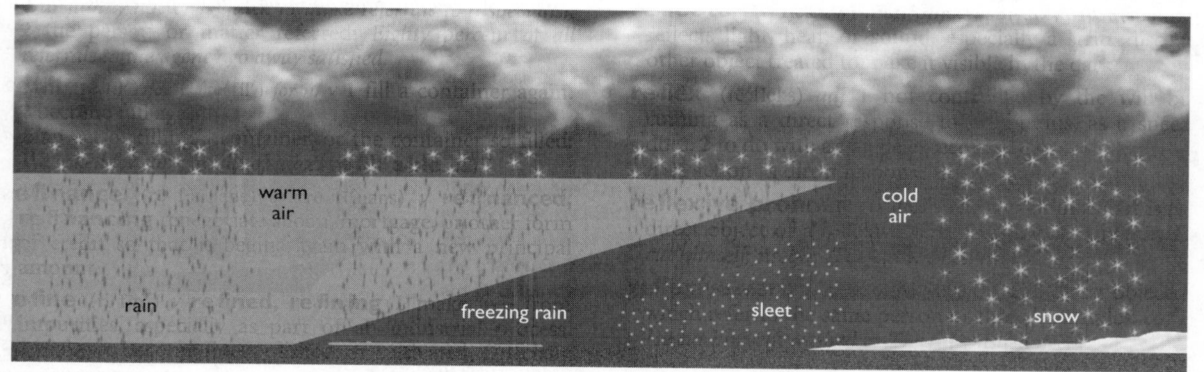

pre·cip·i·ta·tion (pri sip′ə tā′shən) *n* **1 a** the action or process by which moisture is deposited in the form of rain, dew, or snow. **b** the moisture itself. **2** a thing that is precipitated, such as a solid from a solution.

pre·cip·i·tous (pri sip′ə təs) *adj* **1** dangerously high and steep: *precipitous cliffs.* **2** hasty and rash: *Running away was a precipitous action.* **pre·cip′i·tous·ness** *n.*

pré·cis (prā′sē) *n, pl* **pré·cis** (-sēz) a summary. <French= precise>

pre·cise (pri sīs′) *adj* **1** exact or accurate: *The precise sum was $31.28. I got a phone call at that precise moment.* **2** careful and exact: *precise handwriting. She is precise in her manners.* <Old French, from Latin *praecidere* to shorten> **pre·cise′ly** *adv.* **pre·cise′ness** *n.*

pre·ci·sion (pri sizh′ən) *n* **1** the quality or condition of being precise or exact: *the precision of a machine. The precision of her calculations was amazing.* **2** the degree of refinement or exactness obtained.
adj designed for or marked by precision: *precision instruments, precision drawing.*

pre·clin·i·cal (prē klin′i kəl) *adj* **1** to do with the first, chiefly theoretical, stage of a medical education. **2** to do with the stage in a disease prior to the appearance of symptoms.

pre·clude (pri klūd′) *v* **pre·clud·ed, pre·clud·ing** prevent from happening or make impossible: *Buying a house now would preclude any possibility of a holiday trip for the next few years.* <Latin *prae-* before + *claudere* shut> **pre·clu′sion** *n.*

pre·co·cious (pri kō′shəs) *adj* developed much earlier than normal in knowledge or skill: *She was so precocious that she was composing music at the age of six.* **pre·co′cious·ly** *adv.* **pre·co′cious·ness** *n.* **pre·coc′i·ty** (pri kos′ə tē) *adv.*

pre·con·ceive (prē′kən sēv′) *v* **pre·con·ceived, pre·con·ceiv·ing** form an idea or opinion of before having any actual experience or knowledge: *Her first sea voyage didn't fit any of her preconceived notions of what it would be like.*

pre·con·cep·tion (prē′kən sep′shən) *n* an idea or opinion formed beforehand.

pre·con·di·tion (prē′kən dish′ən) *n* a condition that must be fulfilled before something else can happen.
v prepare or condition an action to happen in a certain way.

🍁 **pre–Con·fed·e·ra·tion** (prē′kən fed′ə rā′shən) *adj* to do with the period in Canada before 1867, when Confederation was established.

pre·cook (prē ku̇k′) *v* cook food partly or completely ahead of time in order to shorten or simplify the final preparation.

pre·cur·sor (pri kər′sər) *n* a person who or thing that comes before another: *A severe cold may be the precursor of pneumonia.* <Latin *prae-* beforehand + *currere* to run>

pre·date (prē′dāt′) *v* **pre·dat·ed, pre·dat·ing 1** happen before in time: *Her teaching career predated her entry into politics.* **2** assign something to a date before its actual date: *He predated the cheque to make it look as if he had written it a week earlier.*

pred·a·tor (pred′ə tər) *n* **1** an animal that lives by killing and eating other animals. **2** a person who lives by exploiting or preying on others. <Latin *praedaro*> **pred′a·to·ry** *adj.*

pre·de·cease (prē də sēs′) *v* **pre·de·ceased, pre·de·ceas·ing** die before someone else: *Parents usually predecease their offspring.*

pred·e·ces·sor (prē′də ses′ər) *or* (pred′ə ses′ər) *n* **1** a person holding a position or office before another: *She was the present manager's predecessor.* **2** a thing that has been followed or replaced by another. <Latin *prae-* before + from *de-* away + *cedere* go>

pre·des·ti·na·tion (prē′des tə nā′shən) *n* a Christian doctrine holding that before the beginning of time God determined all that would happen in the future.

pre·des·tine (prē des′tən) *v* **pre·des·tined, pre·des·tin·ing** determine or settle beforehand, especially by predestination: *predestined to failure and disappointment, predestined to rule.*

a bat	e bed	i bid	o pot	u cup	th **thin**
ā cake	ē me	ī bite	ō go	ū rude	ᴛʜ then
à bar	ə about	ər over	ȯ for	u̇ put	zh measure

pre·de·ter·mine (prē′di tər′mən) *v* **pre·de·ter·mined, pre·de·ter·min·ing** determine or decide beforehand: *The time for the meeting was predetermined.*

pre·dic·a·ment (pri dik′ə mənt) *n* an unpleasant, difficult, or dangerous situation: *She was in a predicament when she missed the last train home.* <Latin *prae-* before + *praedicare* make known>

pred·i·cate (pred′ə kit) *for n or adj,* (pred′ə kāt′) *for v.*
n a word or words in a sentence that expresses what is said about the subject and that contains the verb. Example: Women *work.* The committee *has organized a fund-raising drive.* The men *are musicians.*
v **pred·i·cat·ed, pred·i·cat·ing** base a statement, argument, or action on something: *Most religions predicate life after death. Our trip was predicated on getting enough money for it.* <Latin *prae-* before + *dicare* make known>

pred·i·ca·tion (pred′ə kā′shən) *n* the basis of a statement, argument, or action.

pred·i·ca·tive (pred′ə kā′tiv) *or* (pri dik′ə tiv) *adj* forming or contained in a predicate. **pre·dic′a·tive·ly** *adv.*

pre·dict (pri dikt′) *v* say what will happen in future, or what will be the consequence of an action: *The weather bureau predicts rain for tomorrow. She predicted that the novel would be a bestseller.* <Latin *prae-* before + *dicere* say> **pre·dic′tion** *n.* **pre·dic′tor** *n.*

pre·dict·a·ble (pri dik′tə bəl) *adj* able to be predicted reliably. **pre·dict′a·bly** *adv.*

pre·di·gest (prē′dī jest′) *or* (prē′di jest′) *v* **1** cause food to be partly digested beforehand by a natural or artificial process. **2** simplify to make easier to use: *I preferred the original book, not the predigested version.*
pre′di·ges′tion *n.*

pre·di·lec·tion (prē′də lek′shən) *or* (pred′ə lek′shən) *n* a special liking or preference: *She had always had a predilection for ornate furniture.* <Latin *prae-* before + *diligere* choose>

pre·dis·pose (prē′di spōz′) *v* **pre·dis·posed, pre·dis·pos·ing** (*with* ***to***) give an inclination or tendency to: *A cold predisposes a person to other diseases.*

pre·dis·po·si·tion (prē′di spə zish′ən) *n* an inclination or tendency: *She has a predisposition to look on the dark side of things.*

pre·dom·i·nant (pri dom′ə nənt) *adj* **1** with more power, authority, or influence than others: *Which will be the predominant nation in Europe in fifty years?* **2** most noticeable or frequent: *Green was the predominant colour in the room.* **pre·dom′i·nance** *n.* **pre·dom′i·nant·ly** *adv.*

pre·dom·i·nate (pri dom′ə nāt′) *v* **pre·dom·i·nat·ed, pre·dom·i·nat·ing** be greater in power, strength, influence, or numbers: *Kindness finally predominated in their decision.*

pree·mie (prē′mē) *Informal n* a baby born prematurely. <*premature*>

pre–em·i·nent (prē em′ə nənt) *adj* superior to others in some quality: *a pre-eminent scientist.* **pre-em′i·nence** *n.* **pre-em′i·nent·ly** *adv.*

pre–empt (prē empt′) *v* **1** secure before someone else can: *The cat had pre-empted the comfortable chair.* **2** take the place of: *Regular programming will be pre-empted by the election results telecast.* <Latin *prae-* before + *emere* to buy>
pre-emp′tion (prē emp′shən) *n.*

pre–emp·tive (prē emp′tiv) *adj* serving or intended to pre-empt or prevent something from happening, especially by disabling an enemy before it can attack: *a pre-emptive strike.* <Latin *prae-* before + *emere* to buy>

preen (prēn) *v* **1** smooth or arrange feathers, as a bird does with its beak. **2** make efforts to make oneself look attractive and then admire the result: *She preened in front of the mirror for fifteen minutes. He's always preening himself.* <origin uncertain>
preen yourself on, show pride and self-satisfaction in an achievement or skill: *My brother preens himself on his dancing skill.*

pre–ex·ist (prē′eg zist′) *v* exist beforehand, or before something else: *Dinosaurs pre-existed elephants.*
pre′-ex·ist′ence *n.* **pre′-ex·ist′ent** *adj.*

pre·fab (prē fab′) *or* (prē′fab) *Informal n* a prefabricated structure, especially a building.

pre·fab·ri·cate (prē fab′rə kāt′) *v* **pre·fab·ri·cat·ed, pre·fab·ri·cat·ing** **1** make all the standardized parts of something at a factory, so that construction at a site consists mainly of assembling the various parts: *a prefabricated house.* **2** put together or prepare in advance, especially in an artificial way: *a prefabricated excuse.*
pre′fab·ri·ca′tion *n.*

pref·ace (pref′is) *n* an introduction to a book, writing, or speech: *A preface sometimes explains how a book came to be written.*
v **pref·aced, pref·ac·ing** **1** introduce by written or spoken remarks. **2** be a preface to. <Old French, from Latin *prae-* before + *fari* speak>

pref·a·to·ry (pref′ə tô′rē) *adj* to do with a preface.

pre·fect (prē′fekt) *n* **1** in ancient Rome, a senior magistrate or governor. **2** the chief administrative official of a region or department of some countries, for example, France. **3** in some schools, a senior student who has some authority over other students. <Old French, from Latin *praeficere* to place in authority over>

pre·fec·ture (prē′fek chər) *n* the office, jurisdiction, territory, or official residence of a PREFECT (defs. 1, 2).

pre·fer (pri fər′) *v* **pre·ferred, pre·fer·ring** **1** like or choose: *I will arrive later, if you prefer. She prefers reading to sewing. I would prefer to go home.* **2** put forward or present: *They decided not to prefer charges against the boy because he had returned the car. She preferred her claim to the inheritance.* <Old French, from Latin *prae-* before + *ferre* carry>

pref·er·a·ble (pref′ə rə bəl) *or* (pref′rə bəl) *adj* more desirable: *She decided that going along was preferable to staying home alone.* **pref′er·a·bly** *adv.*

pref·er·ence (pref′ə rəns) *or* (pref′rəns) *n* **1** the act or fact of favouring one person or thing over another: *A teacher should not show preference for any one student.* **2** something preferred: *My preference in reading is historical novels.*

P

pref·er·en·tial (pref′ə ren′shəl) *adj* to do with preference: *She was given preferential treatment at the hotel because her father had once been the manager.* **pref′er·en′tial·ly** *adv.*

pre·fer·ment (pri fər′mənt) *n* advancement or promotion: *a sought-after preferment.*

preferred stock *n* STOCK (def. 9) that is guaranteed priority over COMMON STOCK in the payment of dividends and, usually, in the distribution of assets.

pre·fig·ure (prē fig′ər) *or* (prē fig′yər) *v* **pre·fig·ured, pre·fig·ur·ing** show or suggest a model or an early version of something: *The abacus prefigured the electronic calculator.* **pre′fig·ur·a′tion** *n.* **pre′fig′ur·a·tive** *adj.* **pre′fig′ur·a·tive′ly** *adv.*

pre·fix (prē′fiks) *for n,* (prē′fiks) *or* (prē fiks′) *for v.* *n* a syllable, syllables, or word put at the beginning of a word to change its meaning or to form a new word. Examples: *pre*paid, *pre*-industrial, *under*line, *un*like. *v* put before: *Prefix your speech by giving your name.*

GRAMMAR AND USAGE

Knowing what a **prefix** means can help you determine the meaning of a new word. Some common prefixes and their meanings:
bi– (two)
dis– (not)
mis– (wrong)
non– (not)

preg·nan·cy (preg′nən sē) *n, pl* **preg·nan·cies** the state or condition of being PREGNANT (def. 1).

preg·nant (preg′nənt) *adj* **1** with an embryo or embryos developing in the uterus of a woman or female animal. **2** full of meanings or suggestions: *a mind pregnant with ideas, a scheme pregnant with possibilities, a pregnant pause.* <Latin *prae-* before + *gnasci* be born>

pre·heat (prē hēt′) *v* heat beforehand, especially in an oven to a particular temperature before placing something in it to cook.

pre·hen·sile (pri hen′sīl) *or* (pri hen′səl) *adj* adapted for seizing, grasping, or holding on: *New World monkeys have prehensile tails, but Old World monkeys do not.* <French, from Latin *prae-* before + *hendere* grasp>

pre·his·tor·ic (prē′hi stó′rik) *adj* to do with periods before recorded history: *Fossils and artifacts provide us with information about prehistoric people and animals.* **pre′his·tor′i·cal·ly** *adv.*

pre·his·to·ry (prē his′tə rē) *n* **1** the time before history began to be written down. **2** all that happened during this period.

pre–in·dus·tri·al (prē′in dus′trē əl) *adj* to do with a society that does not yet have a developed, established manufacturing base as part of its economy.

pre·judge (prē juj′) *v* **pre·judged, pre·judging** judge without knowing all the facts.

prej·u·dice (prej′ə dis) *n* **1** an opinion or judgment based on irrelevant considerations or inadequate knowledge, especially an unfavourable opinion or judgment: *a prejudice against doctors.* **2** unreasonable hostility toward a particular person, group, or nation. **3** injury or disadvantage resulting from another's action or judgment that ignores one's rights: *They feel that the new bylaw works to the prejudice of apartment dwellers.*
v **prej·u·diced, prej·u·dic·ing** **1** cause prejudice in: *The unpleasant experience prejudiced her against lawyers.* **2** injure or damage: *She was careful to say nothing that might prejudice their interests.* <Old French, from Latin *prae-* before + *judicium* judgment>

prej·u·diced (prej′ə dist) *adj* to do with showing a prejudice for or (more usually) against someone or something: *a prejudiced report.*

prej·u·di·cial (prej′ə dish′əl) *adj* causing prejudice or disadvantage. **prej·u·di′cial·ly** *adv.*

pre·lim (prē′lim) *Informal n* (*often plural*) a preliminary: *Our team lost in the prelims.*

pre·lim·i·nar·y (pri lim′ə ner′ē) *adj* leading to something more important: *After preliminary remarks by the principal, the school play began.*
n, pl **pre·lim·i·nar·ies** a preliminary or preparatory step: *A physical examination is a preliminary to joining the armed forces.* <Latin *prae-* before + *limen, limin-* threshold>

pre·lit·er·ate (prē lit′ə rit) *adj* to do with a society or culture that has not yet developed a written language.

prel·ude (prel′yüd) *or* (prē′lüd) *n* **1 a** a piece of music that introduces another piece. **b** a short instrumental composition especially for the piano. Compare POSTLUDE. **2** a thing serving as an introduction: *Their meeting was a prelude to a long friendship.* Compare POSTLUDE. **3** an introductory part of a poem or literary work.
v **prel·ud·ed, prel·ud·ing** **1** be a prelude or introduction to. **2** introduce with a prelude. <French, from Latin *prae-* before + *ludere* to play>

pre·mar·i·tal (prē mar′ə təl) *or* (prē mer′ə təl) *adj* existing or happening before marriage.

pre·ma·ture (prē′mə chůr′) *or* (prem′ə chůr′) *adj* **1** born before the full term of gestation is completed, especially three or more weeks before the end: *premature baby.* **2** before the usual or proper time: *His premature arrival spoiled our plan to surprise him.* **pre′ma·ture·ly** *adv.*

pre·med·i·cal (prē med′ə kəl) *adj* preparing for the study of medicine: *a premedical student.*

pre·med·i·tat·ed (prē med′ə tā′təd) *adj* thought out or planned beforehand: *It looked more like accidental death than premeditated murder.* **pre′med·i·ta′tion** *n.*

pre·men·stru·al syndrome (prē men′strü əl) PMS.

pre·mier (prē′mēr), (prē′myər), *or* (pri mēr′) *n* **1** 🍁 the chief executive officer and leader of the cabinet of a provincial government in Canada: *The premiers are attending a conference with the prime minister.* **2** the chief officer of a national government.
adj **1** first in rank or quality: *a novel of premier importance.* **2** earliest. <Old French, from Latin *primaries* first> **pre′mier·ship** *n.*

a bat	e bed	i bid	o pot	u cup	th **thin**
ā cake	ē me	ī bite	ō go	ü rude	ᴛʜ **then**
à bar	ə about	ər over	ó for	ů put	zh measure

pre·miere (pri mēr′) *or* (prə myer′) *n* the first public performance or showing of an entertainment: *Many dignitaries attended the premiere of the latest play.*
v **pre·miered, pre·mier·ing 1** give a first public performance or showing of an entertainment: *The theatre group is premiering a new play.* **2** have or give a first public performance: *The film is premiering at the Toronto Film Festival.*

prem·ise (prem′əs) *for n,* (pri mīz′) *or* (prem′əs) *for v.*
n **1** a statement in logic assumed to be true, and from which a conclusion can be drawn. **2 premises** *pl* a house or building with its grounds and outbuildings, occupied by a business or considered in an official way: *He was not allowed on the premises.*
v **pre·mised, pre·mis·ing** give as an introduction or explanation beforehand. <Old French, from Latin *prae-* before + *mittere* send>

pre·mi·um (prē′mē əm) *n* **1** a reward, prize, or incentive: *Some magazines give premiums for obtaining new subscriptions.* **2** something added to the ordinary price, charge, or wage: *Her contract allows for premiums such as overtime pay. They had to pay a considerable premium to get first-quality goods.* **3** money paid regularly for an insurance policy: *He pays his life insurance premium in two instalments.* **4** an unusually high value: *The company puts a premium on accuracy of work.* <Latin *prae-* before + *emere* buy>
at a premium, much valued and in demand: *Good housing is at a premium these days.*

pre·mo·lar (prē mō′lər) *n* a permanent tooth in front of a molar.

pre·mo·ni·tion (prē′mə nish′ən) *or* (prem′ə nish′ən) *n* a strong feeling that something bad is about to happen. <Latin *prae-* before + *monere* warn>

pre·mon·i·to·ry (pri mon′ə tô′rē) *adj* giving warning beforehand.

pre·na·tal (prē nā′təl) *adj* to do with pregnancy: *prenatal classes, prenatal care.*

pre·nup·tial (prē nup′chəl) *or* (prē nup′shəl) *adj* **1** before marriage or before a wedding: *a prenuptial contract, a prenuptial celebration.* **2** *Zoology* before mating.
n **pre·nup** (prē′nup′) *Informal* a prenuptial agreement.

pre·oc·cu·py (prē ok′yə pī′) *v* **pre·oc·cu·pied, pre·oc·cu·pying** take up all one's attention: *The question of getting home preoccupied her mind.*
pre·oc′cu·pa′tion *n.* **pre·oc′cu·pied′** *adj.*

pre·or·dain (prē′ôr dān′) *v* decide or settle beforehand. **pre′or·dained′** *adj.* **pre′or·di·na′tion** *n.*

pre–owned (prē ōnd′) *adj* previously used or owned; used; second-hand.

pre·pack·age (prē pak′əj) *v* **pre·pack·aged, pre·pack·ag·ing** package before sale in a certain standard amount, packaging, or format.

pre·paid (prē pād′) *v* past tense and past participle of PREPAY.

prep·a·ra·tion (prep′ə rā′shən) *n* **1** the action or process of preparing or making ready: *I'm studying in preparation for a test.* **2 preparations** *pl* anything done to get ready: *She made careful preparations for her vacation.* **3** a medicine, food, or other substance made by a special process: *The preparation included honey.*

pre·par·a·to·ry (pri par′ə tô′rē) *or* (pri per′ə tô′rē) *adj* to do with preparation: *a preparatory test as practice for the final exam.*
preparatory to, as a preparation for: *Preparatory to taking a trip, plan your route.*

pre·pare (pri per′) *v* **pre·pared, pre·par·ing 1** put together or make from ingredients or parts: *They prepared a delicious meal for us. The pharmacist prepared a prescription.* **2** make or get ready for some purpose: *to prepare for school, to prepare someone for bad news.* **3** work out the details of a plan: *to prepare an adequate defence.* <French, from Latin *prae-* before + *parare* make ready>
pre·par′er *n.*

pre·par·ed·ness (pri per′id nis) *n* a condition of being prepared or in readiness, especially for war.

pre·pay (prē pā′) *v* **pre·paid, pre·pay·ing** pay in advance: *They prepaid the charges.* **pre·pay′ment** *n.*

pre·pon·der·ant (pri pon′də rənt) *adj* with a greater power, importance, amount, or influence: *Greed is a miser's preponderant characteristic. Mixed farms are preponderant in the region.* **pre·pon′der·ance** *n.* **pre·pon′der·ant·ly** *adv.*

pre·pon·der·ate (pri pon′də rāt′) *v* **pre·pon·der·at·ed, pre·pon·der·at·ing** be the chief, most important, or most numerous element: *Oak and maple preponderate in our eastern woods.* <Latin *prae-* before + *ponderare* consider>

prep·o·si·tion (prep′ə zish′ən) *n* a word that shows relationships of time, direction, or position between other words. Example: *With, for,* and *by* are prepositions in *A man with rugs for sale walked by our house.* <Latin *prae-* before + *ponere* put> **prep′o·si′tion·al** *adj.* **prep′o·si′tion·al·ly** *adv.*

> **GRAMMAR AND USAGE**
>
> **Prepositions** may tell you the place of something in relation to another thing: *above, at, in, under.*
>
> They may also indicate movement (*into, through*) or time (*at, on, for*).

pre·pos·sess·ing (prē′pə zes′ing) *adj* attractive or appealing in appearance or manners.

pre·pos·ter·ous (pri pos′tə rəs) *adj* contrary to nature, reason, or common sense: *It would be preposterous to shovel snow with a teaspoon.* <Latin *praeposterus* absurd>
pre·pos′ter·ous·ly *adv.*

prep·py (prep′ē) *Informal n, pl* **prep·pies** a student or graduate of an expensive American preparatory school.
adj **prep·pi·er, prep·pi·est** of or like such a student or graduate, especially in dress or appearance.

prequel *n* a novel or film that follows an earlier one but tells a part of the story that happened before the events in the original work. <*pre-* + (*se*)*quel*>

pre–re·cord (prē′re kord′) *v* **1** record for later broadcast on radio or TV, or record sound as part of a film to be

released: *The interview was pre-recorded.* **2** load a tape, CD, DVD, etc. with music or images for sale: *Blank CDs are much cheaper than pre-recorded ones.*
pre′-re·cord′ed *adj.* **pre′-re·cord′ing** *n.*

pre·req·ui·site (prē rek′wə zit) *n* a thing that is necessary to achieve an end or as a condition before something else can be considered: *A high-school course is the usual prerequisite to college work.*
adj required beforehand.

pre·rog·a·tive (pri rog′ə tiv) *n* a right or privilege that nobody else has: *The government has the prerogative of coining money.*
adj with or exercising a prerogative. <Old French, from Latin *prae-* before + *rogare* ask>

pres·age (pres′ij) *for n,* (pri sāj′) *for v. n* a sign or warning that something, usually bad, will happen: *a sure presage of evil.*
v **pre·saged, pre·sag·ing 1** give warning of something bad that will happen: *Some people think that a circle around the moon presages a storm.* <French, from Latin *prae-* before + *sagire* perceive keenly>

Pres·by·te·ri·an (prēz′bi tēr′ē ən) *Christianity adj* to do with any of several Protestant churches which are administered locally by ministers together with groups of elected elders.
n a member of such a church. <Old French, from Greek *presbyteros* elder>

pre·school (prē′skūl′) *adj* to do with the period in a child's life after infancy and before the child begins elementary school.

pre·school·er (prē′skū′lər) *n* a child who is too young to go to elementary school, especially one between the ages of two and five.

pre·sci·ent (prē′shē ənt) *or* (presh′ē ənt) *adj* to do with knowing something before it exists or happens. <Latin *prae-* before + *scire* know> **pre′sci·ence** (prē′shē əns) *or* (presh′ē əns) *n.*

pre·scribe (pri skrīb′) *v* **pre·scribed, pre·scrib·ing 1** state or order as a rule or guide: *to do what the law prescribes. There are two prescribed texts for this course.* **2** order as a medical remedy or treatment: *The doctor prescribed quinine.* **3** recommend as something beneficial. <Latin *prae-* before + *scribere* write>

CONFUSABLES

Prescribe means "lay down as a rule or guide": *The coach prescribed running four laps before games.*

Proscribe means "condemn" or "forbid": *Our parents have proscribed any smoking in our house.*

pre·scrip·tion (pri skrip′shən) *n* **1** a written direction or order for preparing and using a medicine: *a prescription for a cough.* *Symbol* **Rx** **2** medicine that has been prescribed: *Did you use up the whole prescription?*

pre·scrip·tive (pri skrip′tiv) *adj* **1** to do with a prescribed rule or method. **2** attempting to impose rules of correct usage on the writers or speakers of a language. **3** established by long use or custom.

pre–sel·ect (prē sə lekt′) *v* select in advance.
pre′sel·ec′tion *n.*

pres·ence (prez′əns) *n* **1** the fact or condition of being present in a place: *I knew of her presence in the other room.* **2** the place where a person is: *The messenger was admitted to the leader's presence.* **3** an impressive manner or appearance: *a man of noble presence.* **4** influence and recognition in a certain area: *The new company has no market presence yet.* **5** something that seems to be present, especially a ghost or spirit. <Old French, from Latin *prae-* before + *esse* be>
in the presence of, in the sight or company of: *You must sign your name in the presence of two witnesses.*

presence of mind *n* the ability to think calmly and quickly when taken by surprise.

pres·ent[1] (prez′ənt) *adj* **1** the act or fact of being in a proper or expected place: *Every member of the class was present.* **2** being or occurring now: *the present ruler, present prices.* **3** *Grammar* to do with a verb form indicating action now going on or a condition now existing. Example: The present tense of the verb *sing* is *sing,* and the present participle is *singing.*
n the present time: *At present, people need courage.*

pre·sent[2] (pri zent′) *for v,* (prez′ənt) *for n. v* **1** give, usually formally: *They presented flowers to the singer after the performance. The plumber presented his bill.* **2** (*with* ***with***) make a formal gift to: *The retiring principal was presented with a silver tray.* **3** bring before the public or perform: *Our school presented a play.* **4** set forth in words: *The speaker presented arguments for her side.* **5** introduce formally: *I'd like to present a new teacher to you.* **6** bring before a person of high rank: *She was presented to the Governor General.* **7** direct, point, or turn in a particular direction: *The actor presented his profile to the camera.*
n a gift: *I got the DVD player as a birthday present.*
present (pri zent′) **arms,** bring a rifle to a vertical position in front of the body as a salute.

pre·sent·a·ble (pri zen′tə bəl) *adj* fit to be introduced or to be seen in public: *It took him an hour to make himself presentable again after cleaning the basement.*
pre·sent′a·bly *adv.*

pres·en·ta·tion (prez′ən tā′shən) *n* **1** the act of giving or delivering, usually formally: *the presentation of a gift, the presentation of a speech.* **2** a talk made to a group of people, often with diagrams or other visual aids: *The class agreed that our group's presentation was the most informative.* **3** an offering, exhibition, or entertainment: *the presentation of a play.* **4** a formal introduction, especially to somebody of high rank: *the presentation of a lady to the queen.* **pre·sent′er** *n.*

pres·ent–day (prez′ənt dā′) *adj* of the present time: *present-day living standards, present-day attitudes.*

pre·sen·ti·ment (pri zen′tə mənt) *n* a feeling or impression that something is about to happen.

a bat	e bed	i bid	o pot	u cup	th **thin**
ā cake	ē me	ī bite	ō go	ū rude	ᴛʜ **then**
ä bar	ə about	ər over	ô for	ů put	zh measure

pres·ent·ly (prez′ən tlē) *adv* **1** soon: *The clock will strike presently.* **2** at present: *The prime minister is presently in Ottawa.*

present tense *Grammar n* a verb tense used to express an action taking place now, or as if it were now. Examples: *I am walking to school. I walk to school.*

> **GRAMMAR AND USAGE**
>
> **Present tense** can be expressed in two main ways:
>
> Use *simple present tense* if something happens regularly: *I think. He jogs.*
>
> Use *present progressive tense* if something is happening right now: *I am thinking. He is jogging.*
>
> The present can also be indicated by using a form of the verb *to do* before a verb to add emphasis: *She does work hard.*

pres·er·va·tion (prez′ər vā′shən) *n* the act or process of preserving or being preserved: *the preservation of your health. The artifacts were in an excellent state of preservation.*

pre·serv·a·tive (pri zər′və tiv) *n* a substance that will prevent decay or injury: *Paint is a preservative for wood surfaces. Salt is a preservative for meat.*
adj acting to preserve something.

pre·serve (pri zərv′) *v* **pre·served, pre·serv·ing** **1** keep from harm or change. **2** keep up or maintain. **3** prepare food to keep it from spoiling, such as by boiling with sugar, salting, smoking, freezing, or pickling.
n **1** an area or region where wild animals, fish, or trees and plants are protected. **2** fruit cooked with sugar and sealed from the air: *plum preserve.* <Old French, from Latin *prae-* before + *servare* keep> **pre·serv′a·ble** *adj.* **pre·ser′ver** *n.*

pre·set (prē set′) *for v,* (prē′set) *for n. v* **pre·set, pre·set·ting** set or arrange beforehand.
n a control that allows one to set some function beforehand.

pre·shrink (prē′shringk′) *v* **pre·shrank, pre·shrunk** shrink a fabric or a garment before sale so that it will not shrink when it is washed.

pre·side (pri zīd′) *v* **pre·sid·ed, pre·sid·ing** **1** have charge of a meeting or gathering: *Our principal will preside at our election of school officers.* **2** have authority over a place or situation: *The manager presides over the business of the store.* <French, from Latin *prae-* before + *sedere* sit>

pres·i·den·cy (prez′ə dən sē) *n, pl* **pres·i·den·cies** **1** the office or position of president: *Who was elected to the presidency of the Athletic Club?* **2** the time during which a president is in office: *Her presidency of the club lasted two years.*

pres·i·dent (prez′ə dənt) *n* **1** the chief officer of a company, organization, or institution. **2** the highest executive officer of a republic. **pres′i·den′tial** *adj.* **pres′i·den′tial·ly** *adv.*

pres·i·dent–e·lect (prez′ə dənt i lekt′) *n, pl* **pres·i·dents–e·lect** a president who has been elected but has not yet taken office.

press[1] (pres) *v* **1** move something by pushing steadily up, down, or against something: *Press the button to ring the bell.* **2** squeeze or squeeze out: *Press all the juice from the oranges.* **3** clasp or hug: *Mother pressed the baby to her.* **4** make smooth or flatten: *to press clothes with an iron.* **5** push forward or keep pushing: *The boy pressed on in spite of the wind.* **6** strongly urge a person to do something: *It was stormy, so we pressed our guest to stay all night. I can't answer, so please don't press me.* **7** constrain, compel, or force: *The government pressed people into its service.* **8** in weightlifting, raise a weight by first lifting it to shoulder height and then above the head.
n **1** an emotional pressure or push: *the press of ambition. The press of many duties keeps me busy.* **2** a machine for exerting pressure, such as a machine for ironing clothes. **3** a publisher, or an establishment for printing books. **4** newspapers, magazines, and the people who work for them: *Our school's fundraising drive was reported by the press.* **5** a crowd or throng: *The little boy was lost in the press of people.* **6** *Weightlifting* the action of raising a weight by first lifting it to shoulder height and then above the head. <Old French, from Latin *premere* to press>
be pressed for, be challenged by a shortage of something: *We are really pressed for time here, so let's not waste a moment.*
go to press, begin to be printed: *The newspaper goes to press at midnight.*

press[2] (pres) *v* **1** in former times, force to serve in the armed forces, especially in the navy. **2** put someone or something to use, usually a temporary or improvised measure: *To move the stove, we pressed an old skateboard into service.*
n in former times, a forcible enlistment into military service. <Old French, from Latin *praestare* make available (for service)>

press agent *n* a person in charge of publicity for an individual or for an organization.

press box *n* an enclosed space set aside for reporters at a sports stadium, arena, or racetrack.

press conference *n* a meeting for the purpose of giving information to reporters.

press corps *n* all the newspaper reporters covering an event or area of activity: *the parliamentary press corps.*

press gang *n* in former times, a group of men whose job it was to forcibly obtain men for service in the navy or army.

press·ing (pres′ing) *adj* requiring immediate action or attention.
n the act of creasing or pressing with an iron: *That dress needs a good pressing.* **press′ing·ly** *adv.*

press release *n* a story or statement officially prepared and given to the press. Also called **news release**.

press secretary *n* a person responsible for communication with the media on behalf of an elected official, organization, or prominent person.

pres·sure (presh′ər) *n* **1** the continued action of a weight or force: *The pressure of the wind filled the sails of the boat.* **2** the force per unit of area: *Bicycle tires need a pressure of about 300 kilopascals.* **3** a compelling force or influence:

Pressure was brought to bear on the premier. **4** constant demand on one's time, attention, and energy: *The pressure of being captain of the hockey team and Student Council president was difficult to handle.* **5** atmospheric pressure.
v **pres·sured, pres·sur·ing** force or urge strongly: *The salesman tried to pressure my mother into buying the car.* <Old French, from Latin *premere* to press>

pressure cooker *n* an airtight pot that cooks with steam under pressure.

pressure group *n* a business, professional, or labour group that attempts to advance its interests by influencing government.

pressure point *n* **1** a point on the body where an artery passes close under the skin and in front of a bony structure, so that pressure applied at that point will check bleeding. **2** a point on the skin that is highly sensitive to pressure. **3** an area, issue, or aspect of a situation that is sensitive to political or other pressure.

pres·sur·ize (presh′ə rīz′) *v* **pres·sur·ized, pres·sur·iz·ing** keep the ATMOSPHERIC PRESSURE inside the cabin of an aircraft at a normal level in spite of the altitude.

pres·tige (pres tēzh′) *or* (pres tēj′) *n* reputation based on what is known of one's abilities, achievements, or associations: *His success in the courts gave him great prestige as a lawyer.* <French = illusion, from Latin *praestigiae* magic tricks>

pres·to (pres′tō) *adv* quickly.
adj quick.
n, pl **pres·tos** a quick part in a piece of music. <Italian, from Latin *praestus* ready to hand>

pre–stressed concrete (prē′strest′) *n* concrete that has been cast around steel cables or rods inserted under tension before the concrete is set in order to give it added strength.

pre·sum·a·bly (pri zū′mə blē) *or* (pri zyū′mə blē) *adv* very likely, though not known for certain: *Presumably they'll get here by noon.*

pre·sume (pri zūm′) *or* (pri zyūm′) *v* **pre·sumed, pre·sum·ing 1** take for granted without proving: *The law presumes innocence until guilt is proved.* **2** take upon oneself to say or do: *May I presume to tell you what to do?* **3** (*with* ***on*** *or* ***upon***) take an unfair advantage: *Don't presume on her good nature by borrowing from her every week.* <Old French, from Latin *prae-* before + *sumere* take> **pre·sum′a·ble** *adj.*

CONFUSABLES

Presume implies that something is true because there is no evidence against it.

Assume implies that something is accepted without evidence for or against.

pre·sump·tion (pri zump′shən) *n* **1** the act or fact of taking for granted without proving. **2** a conclusion based on evidence: *Since he had the stolen jewels, the presumption was that he was the thief.* **3** a cause or reason for presuming. **4** behaviour considered to be arrogant, disrespectful, or going beyond what is permitted or appropriate: *It is presumption to go to a party when you haven't been invited.*
presumption of innocence, *Law* the presumption that an accused person is innocent until proven guilty.

pre·sump·tive (pri zump′tiv) *adj* based on likelihood.

pre·sump·tu·ous (pri zump′chū əs) *adj* acting without permission or right. **pre·sump′tu·ous·ly** *adv.* **pre·sump′tu·ous·ness** *n.*

pre·sup·pose (prē′sə pōz′) *v* **pre·sup·posed, pre·sup·pos·ing 1** take for granted in advance: *Let us presuppose that she wants more money.* **2** require as a necessary condition in an action, process, or argument: *A fight presupposes fighters.*
pre′sup·po·si′tion (prē′sup ə zish′ən) *n.*

pre·teen or **pre–teen** (prē′tēn′) *n* a young person before adolescence, usually eleven or twelve years old.

pre·tence (pri tens′) *or* (prē′tens) *n* **1** a false appearance: *Under pretence of picking up the handkerchief, she took the money.* **2** a false claim or display: *The girl made a pretence of knowing the answer. His anger was all pretence.* Also, **pretense**.

pre·tend (pri tend′) *v* **1** make believe, as in a game or fantasy. **2** claim falsely: *She pretended to like the meal so she wouldn't offend the hostess.* **3** claim falsely to have: *He pretended illness to avoid his chores.* **4** claim: *I don't pretend to be a musician.*
adj not really what it seems, as in a game or fantasy: *The kids were playing pretend school.* <Latin *praetendre*>

pre·tend·ed (pri ten′did) *adj* claimed or asserted falsely: *She would sometimes show a pretended interest in my life.* **pre·tend′ed·ly** *adv.*

pre·tend·er (pri ten′dər) *n* **1** a person who pretends. **2** a person who makes claims to a throne.

pre·ten·sion (pri ten′shən) *n* **1** a claim: *The young prince has pretensions to the throne.* **2** the practice of doing things for show or to make a fine impression: *People were often amused by her pretensions.*

pre·ten·tious (pri ten′shəs) *adj* **1** making claims to excellence or importance: *a pretentious book.* **2** done for show or to make a fine appearance: *a pretentious style of entertaining guests.* **pre·ten′tious·ly** *adv.* **pre·ten′tious·ness** *n.*

pre·ter·nat·u·ral (prē′tər nach′ə rəl) *or* (prē′tər nach′rəl) *adj* beyond what is normal or natural. <Latin *praeter-* beyond + *natural*> **pre′ter·nat′u·ral·ly** *adv.*

pre·test (prē′test) *for n,* (prē test′) *for v. n* a test taken before instruction, to determine the existing level of knowledge.
v give such a test.

pre·text (prē′tekst) *n* a false reason concealing the real reason: *He used his sore finger as a pretext for not going to school.* <Latin *praetexere* to disguise>

a **bat**	e **bed**	i **bid**	o **pot**	u **cup**	th **thin**
ā **cake**	ē **me**	ī **bite**	ō **go**	ū **rude**	ŦH **then**
ȧ **bar**	ə **about**	ər **over**	ȯ **for**	u̇ **put**	zh **measure**

prey

The cheetah takes its **prey** on the run, at an average speed of 72 km/h. Over short distances, it is the fastest land animal and can reach speeds of up to 110 km/h. Unlike other cats, cheetahs hunt during the day, killing small animals with a single bite to the skull. Their chief prey is small antelope.

pret·ti·fy (prit′ə fī′) *v* **pret·ti·fied, pret·ti·fy·ing** make pretty or attractive, especially in a superficial way.

pret·ty (prit′ē) *adj* **pret·ti·er, pret·ti·est 1** attractive or pleasing: *a pretty face, a pretty tune.* **2** not at all pleasing: *a pretty mess.*
n, pl **pret·ties** a pretty person or thing.
adv fairly or rather: *It is pretty late.* <Old English *prættig*>
pret′ti·ly *adv.* **pret·ti·ness** *n.*
pretty as a picture, very pretty.
sitting pretty, *Informal* be in a good position or situation.

pret·zel (pret′səl) *n* a hard biscuit, usually made in the shape of a loose knot and salted on the outside. <German *Brezel*, from Latin *brachium* arm, because the biscuit was baked in the shape of a pair of folded arms>

pre·vail (pri vāl′) *v* **1** exist in many places or be in general use: *That custom still prevails.* **2** be stronger or more powerful than an opposing force: *Sadness prevailed in our minds. The knights prevailed against their foe.* <Latin *praevaricari* deviate>
prevail on (or **upon**) persuade: *Can't I prevail on you to stay for dinner?*

pre·vail·ing (pri vā′ling) *adj* **1** with superior force, influence, or frequency: *prevailing winds.* **2** in general use or most common: *a prevailing style.* **pre·vail′ing·ly** *adv.*

prev·a·lent (prev′ə lənt) *adj* widespread in area or time: *Colds are prevalent in the winter.* **prev′a·lence** *n.*

pre·var·i·cate (pri var′ə kāt′) *or* (pri ver′ə kāt′) *v* **pre·var·i·cat·ed, pre·var·i·cat·ing** speak or behave in an evasive way; tell a lie. <Latin *pravaricari* deviate>

pre·var·i·ca·tor (pri var′ə kā′tər *or* pri ver′ə kā′tər) *n* a person who evades the truth.

pre·vent (pri vent′) *v* **1** (*with* ***from***) keep or restrain: *Illness prevented him from doing his work.* **2** keep from happening or hinder: *Rain prevented the start of the game. I'll meet you if nothing prevents it.* <Latin *prae-* before + *venire* come> **pre·vent′a·ble** or **pre·vent′i·ble** *adj.* **pre·vent′er** *n.* **pre·ven′tion** *n.*

pre·ven·tive (pri ven′tiv) *adj* able to prevent: *preventive measures against disease.*
n something that prevents: *Vaccination is a preventive against polio.* Also, **preventative.**

pre·view (prē′vyū′) *n* **1** a previous viewing or inspection of something before it is bought or becomes generally available. **2** an advance showing of scenes from a motion picture, play, or TV program.
v view beforehand.

pre·vi·ous (prē′vē əs) *adj* coming or going on earlier: *She did better in the previous lesson than in this one.* <Latin *prae-* before + *via* way>
previous to, before: *Previous to her departure she gave a party for all her friends.*

pre·vi·ous·ly (prē′vē ə slē) *adv* at a previous time: *I had not met him previously.*

pre·war (prē′wôr′) *adj* before a war: *Prewar prices seem incredibly low today.*

prey (prā) *n* **1** an animal hunted or killed for food, especially by another animal: *Mice and birds are the prey of cats.* **2** a person or thing injured, taken advantage of, or vulnerable in some other way: *to be a prey to fear or disease.* See PRAY for confusable. <Old French, from Latin *praeda* booty>
bird (**beast**) **of prey** a bird (or animal), such as a hawk or lion, that hunts and kills other animals for food.
prey on (or **upon**), **a** hunt or kill for food: *Cats prey on mice.* **b** cause emotional stress: *Worry about her many debts preys upon her mind.* **c** rob or plunder.

price (prīs) *n* **1** the amount for which a thing is sold or can be bought. **2** a reward offered for the capture of a person alive or dead: *Every outlaw had a price on his head.* **3** what must be given, done, or undergone to obtain a thing: *The price of good grades is loss of some leisure time.* **4** *Archaic* value or worth: *a pearl of great price.*
v **priced, pric·ing 1** put or set a price on. **2** ask or find out the price of: *to price a rug.* <Old French, from Latin *pretium*>
at any price, at any cost, no matter how great: *She wanted to win at any price.*
beyond (or **without**) **price,** so valuable that it cannot be bought or be given a value in money.

price fixing *n* the practice of conspiring to illegally set prices at a predetermined level: *The major fuel companies were accused of price fixing.*

price·less (prī′slis) *adj* beyond price or extremely valuable: *a priceless painting.* **price′less·ness** *n.*

price point *n* a retail price of a product when considered as one of a scale of possible marketing prices: *They cannot market this kind of software below the $50 price point.*

price support *n* a system of subsidies by which the government guarantees a given price to producers of goods, especially farmers.

price tag *n* **1** a ticket or label on merchandise, showing its price. **2** *Informal* an estimated value, price, or cost: *What's the price tag on a system like the one you've got?*

price war *n* a situation in which competitors try to capture the market by repeatedly undercutting one another's prices: *The two gas stations on the corner are having a price war.*

price·y (prī′sē) *Informal adj* **pric·i·er, pric·i·est** expensive. Also, **pricy**.

prick (prik) *n* **1** a sharp point. **2** a little hole or mark made by a sharp point. **3** the act of pricking. **4** a sharp pain.
v **1** make a little hole in with a sharp point: *I pricked the map with a pin to show our route.* **2** mark with a sharp point. **3** cause or feel sharp pain: *The cat pricked me with its claws.* <Old English *prica* point> **prick′er** *n.*
prick up, point upward.
prick up the ears, a point the ears upward: *The dog pricked up its ears.* **b** give sudden attention to: *We pricked up our ears when the teacher started talking about a trip.*

prick·le (prik′əl) *n* **1** a small, sharp point, especially a short, slender, sharp-pointed outgrowth on the bark of a plant or skin of an animal. **2** a tingling sensation on someone's skin, especially caused by a strong emotion.
v **prick·led, prick·ling 1** feel a tingling or prickly sensation: *Her skin prickled when she saw the big snake.* **2** cause such a sensation. <Old English *pricel* instrument for prickling>

prick·ly (prik′lē) *adj* **prick·li·er, prick·li·est 1** with many sharp points like thorns: *a prickly rosebush.* **2** tingling and itchy: *Heat sometimes causes a prickly rash on the skin.* **3** hard to deal with or likely to raise problems or controversy: *a prickly question.* **4** quick to take offence or easily angered: *He is a prickly individual.* **prick′li·ness** *n.*

prickly heat *n* an itching rash on the skin caused by inflammation of the sweat glands.

prickly pear *n* a pear-shaped, edible fruit of a cactus that has jointed stems, oval flattened segments, and barbed bristles.

pric·y (prī′sē) PRICEY.

pride (prīd) *n* **1** a high opinion of one's own worth or possessions: *Pride in our city should force us to keep it clean.* **2** pleasure or satisfaction in something or someone concerned with oneself: *take pride in a hard job well done. Her youngest child is her great pride.* **3** the best part or most flourishing period: *in the pride of manhood.* **4** a group of lions forming a social unit. <Old English *prud* proud>
pride yourself on, be proud about: *He prides himself on his mathematical ability.*

pride of place *n* the highest or most important position: *His mother holds pride of place in his affections.*

prie–dieu (prē′dyū′) *n, pl* **prie–dieux** a small desk for a prayer book or the elbows to rest on, with a lower piece on which to kneel. <French = pray God>

priest (prēst) *n* **1** an ordained minister of the Roman Catholic, Orthodox, or Anglican church. **2** a person who performed or performs religious duties or ceremonies in a non-Christian religion: *a priest of Apollo, a Buddhist priest.* <Greek *presbyteros* elder> **priest′ly** *adj.*

priest·ess (prē′stis) *n* a female priest of a non-Christian religion: *a priestess of the goddess Diana.*

priest·hood (prēst′hủd) *n* **1** the position or rank of priest: *He was admitted to the priesthood.* **2** priests as a group: *the priesthood of Spain.*

prig (prig) *n* someone who is smug and thinks he or she is more moral than others. <origin uncertain>

prig·gish (prig′ish) *adj* smug and priding oneself on being more moral than others. **prig′gish·ness** *n.*

prim (prim) *adj* **prim·mer, prim·mest** stiffly precise, neat, proper, or formal: *a prim appearance.* <origin unknown> **prim′ly** *adv.* **prim′ness** *n.*

pri·ma·cy (prī′mə sē) *n, pl* **pri·ma·cies 1** the condition of being first in order or rank. **2** the position or rank of a church primate. <Old French, from Latin *primus* first>

pri·ma don·na (prē′mə don′ə) *n, pl* **pri·ma don·nas 1** the principal woman singer in an opera. **2** a woman who is temperamental and has an exaggerated opinion of her own talent or importance. <Italian = first lady>

pri·ma fa·cie (prī′mə fā′shē ē) *or* (prī′mə fā′shē) at first view or prior to investigation. <Latin *primus* first + *facies* face>

pri·mal (prī′məl) *adj* **1** fundamental or essential. **2** early in the history of human development. <Latin *primus* first> **pri′mal·ly** *adv.*

pri·ma·ri·ly (prī′mer′ə lē) *or* (prī mer′ə lē) *adv* chiefly or principally.

pri·ma·ry (prī′mer′ē) *or* (prī′mə rē) *adj* **1** first in time or chronological order: *the primary stage of development.* **2** first in importance: *The primary reason for the party is to celebrate her birthday.* **3** to do with a level of education for children between the ages of about five and eleven: *a primary teacher.* **4** *Biology, Medicine* to do with the first stage of development or growth: *primary tumour.*
n, pl **pri·mar·ies** *US* in full, **primary election** a meeting of the voters of a political party in a district to choose candidates for office. <Latin *primus* first>

primary colour or **color** *n* one of three colours that can be mixed together to make any other colour. Red, green, and blue are the primary colours in the spectrum; magenta (red), yellow, and cyan (blue) are the primary colours in pigment. See also ADDITIVE THEORY, SUBTRACTIVE THEORY.

a bat	e bed	i bid	o pot	u cup	th **thin**
ā cake	ē me	ī bite	ō go	ū rude	ᴛʜ **then**
ä bar	ə about	ər over	ȯ for	ủ put	zh measure

primary school *n* the first three or four grades of elementary school.

primary source *n* **1** information from which conclusions are drawn directly in research, as opposed to the results of research by other people. **2** a main or important source: *Tourism is this region's primary source of income.*

primary stress *n* the strongest stress or accent in the pronunciation of a word. Example: In *tel′e·phone′* there is primary stress on the first syllable and secondary stress on the last syllable.

pri·mate (prī′mit) *or* (prī′māt) *n* **1** the highest order of mammals, including human beings, apes, and monkeys. **2** an archbishop or bishop ranking above all other bishops. <Latin *primus* first>

prime[1] (prīm) *adj* **1** first in rank or importance: *Her prime object was to lower the tax rate.* **2** first in time or chronological order: *the prime causes of war.* **3** first in quality: *prime ribs of beef.*
n **1** the best period or condition of strength, success, or vitality. **2** a prime number. **3** a prime rate. **4** a mark ′ written after a letter or symbol as a distinguishing mark. <Latin *primus* first> **prime′ness** *n.*

prime[2] (prīm) *v* **primed, prim·ing** **1** prepare by putting something in or on. **2** prepare a gun or explosive device for firing. **3** cover a surface with a first coat of paint or oil so that other coats of paint will not soak in. **4** equip a person with information or words. **5** pour water into a pump to start its action. <origin uncertain>

prime factor *Mathematics n* a FACTOR (def. 2) that is also a prime number. Writing a COMPOSITE NUMBER as a product of its prime factors is called **prime factorization**.

prime meridian *n* the meridian whose longitude is 0° and from which longitude east and west is measured. The prime meridian passes through Greenwich, England.

prime minister *n* the chief minister in certain governments, such as the federal government of Canada.

prime number *n* a number not exactly divisible by any whole number other than itself and 1. The numbers 3, 5, and 7 are prime numbers, but the number 9 is not, since it is exactly divisible by another number, 3. Zero is not considered to be a prime number, nor is the number 1 itself. Compare COMPOSITE NUMBER.

prim·er[1] (prim′ər) *n* a first book, especially a textbook, in reading or some other subject: *a chemistry primer.*

prim·er[2] (prī′mər) *n* **1** a person who or thing that primes. **2** a cap or cylinder containing a substance that ignites the charge in a gun cartridge or explosive. **3** a first coat of paint or oil as a prepared surface for other coats.

prime rate *n* in full, **prime lending rate** or **prime interest rate** the lowest rate of interest charged by a bank on commercial loans to its most preferred customers.

prime time *n* the period of the day when the largest audience for radio and TV broadcasts can be expected, usually the early evening hours.

pri·me·val (prī mē′vəl) *adj* to do with great age or the earliest time: *primeval forests.* <Latin *primus* first + *aevum* age> **pri·me′val·ly** *adv.*

prim·i·tive (prim′ə tiv) *adj* **1** of early times or long ago: *Primitive people often lived in caves.* **2** not developed from anything else. **3** in the first or earliest stage of formation or development. **4** very simple or basic: *A primitive way of making fire is by rubbing two sticks together.*
n **1** an artist belonging to an early period, especially before the Renaissance. **2** an artist who imitates early painters, or who paints with directness and simplicity. **3** a picture by such an artist. <Old French, from Latin *primus* first> **prim′i·tive·ly** *adv.*

prim·i·tiv·ism (prim′ə tiv iz′əm) *n* **1** the condition of being primitive. **2** the belief that simple and unsophisticated things, ideas, or culture are superior to more technologically advanced ones. **prim′i·tiv·ist** *n, adj.* **prim′i·tiv·ist′ic** *adj.*

pri·mo·gen·i·tor (prī′mə jen′ə tər) *n* an ancestor, especially the earliest one.

pri·mo·gen·i·ture (prī′mə jen′ə chər) *n* the right or principle of inheritance or succession by the first-born, especially the inheritance of a family estate by the eldest son. <Latin *primo* at first + *genitura* a birth>

pri·mor·di·al (prī môr′dē əl) *adj* **1** existing at the very beginning of time. **2** basic and fundamental. <Latin *primus* first + *ordiri* begin>

primp (primp) *v* dress oneself or arrange one's hair or clothing in a fussy or careful way, to make oneself look smart or showy. <*prim*>

prim·rose (prim′rōz′) *n* a perennial plant with large leaves and showy flowers of many different colours. European primroses are pale yellow. <Latin *prima rosa* first rose>

primrose path *n* the pursuit of pleasure, especially when it brings bad consequences.

Pri·mus stove (prīm′əs) *Trademark n* a portable stove that burns vaporized oil.

prince (prins) *n* **1** the son of a monarch, or a close male relative of a monarch, such as a grandson. **2** a high-ranking member of the nobility in certain countries. **3** the greatest or best of a group: *a merchant prince, a prince among artists.* <Old French, from Latin *princeps* ruler>

Prince Charming *Informal n* the handsome, chivalrous, glamorous ideal of a male romantic partner.

prince consort *n* a prince who is the spouse of a queen or empress.

prince·dom (prins′dəm) *n* **1** the territory ruled by a prince. **2** the position, rank, or authority of a prince.

Prince Edward Island *n* an eastern Canadian province, just north of New Brunswick and Nova Scotia. Prince Edward Island is one of the ATLANTIC PROVINCES.
Abbrev. **P.E.I.**; postal symbol **PE**; URL **www.gov.pe.ca** See also MARITIME PROVINCES.
adj to do with Prince Edward Island: *Prince Edward Island potatoes.* **Prince Edward Islander** *n.*

prince·ling (prin′sling) *n* **1** a young prince. **2** the ruler of a very small principality.

prince·ly (prin′slē) *adj* **prince·li·er, prince·li·est** 1 to do with a prince. 2 splendid and luxurious. 3 large and generous as a sum of money: *a princely salary.* **prince′li·ness** *n.*

prince of the blood *n* a prince of a royal family.

Prince of Wales *n* a title given to the heir apparent to the British throne.

prince royal *n* the oldest son of a king or queen.

prin·cess (prin′sis) *or* (prin′ses) *n* 1 a daughter of a monarch, or a close female relative of the monarch, especially a granddaughter. 2 the wife or widow of a prince. 3 *Informal* a spoiled or arrogant young woman.

princess royal *n* the oldest daughter of a king or queen.

prin·ci·pal (prin′sə pəl) *adj* most important or chief: *a principal city.*
n 1 a person with the highest rank or authority. 2 the head of a school or college. 3 a sum of money on which interest is paid, or the money or property from which income is received. 4 a person who hires another person to act as an agent or representative. 5 a person directly responsible for a crime. See PRINCIPLE for confusable. <Old French, from Latin *primus* first + *capere* take >

principal clause MAIN CLAUSE.

prin·ci·pal·i·ty (prin′sə pal′ə tē) *n, pl* **prin·ci·pal·i·ties** a small state or country ruled by a prince.

prin·ci·pal·ly (prin′sə plē) *or* (prin′sə pə lē) *adv* for the most part or chiefly.

principal parts *pln* the main parts of a verb, from which the rest can be derived. These are: the present tense, the past tense, the present participle, and the past participle. Examples: *go, went, going, gone.*

prin·ci·pal·ship (prin′sə pəl ship′) *n* the position or office of a PRINCIPAL (def. 2).

prin·ci·ple (prin′sə pəl) *n* 1 a rule of conduct: *I make it a principle to save some money each week.* 2 morally correct behaviour: *a woman of principle.* 3 a fact or belief on which other ideas are based: *Science is based on the principle that events can be explained.* 4 a rule of science explaining how things act, or a natural law explaining a method of operation: *the principle of the lever.* <Latin *principium* first part, from principis first>
in principle, as regards the general truth or rule, although the details have not been worked out: *to approve something in principle.*
on principle, a according to a certain principle. b for good moral reasons.

CONFUSABLES

Principle means "a basic fact, rule, or method" and is a noun: *Follow the principle of "honesty first."*

Principal means "chief person" or "chief" and is a noun (*school principal*) or an adjective (*principal reason*).

prin·ci·pled (prin′sə pəld) *adj* guided by or based on reasonable or moral principles.

prink (pringk) *v* primp.

print (print) *v* 1 produce texts, especially in large quantities, by a process in which words or designs are transferred to paper or some other surface: *Who prints this newspaper?* 2 make words or letters the way they look in print instead of in writing: *Print your name clearly.* 3 stamp something with designs, patterns, or pictures: *printed cotton.* 4 make permanent in someone's mind: *The scene is printed on my memory.* 5 produce a photograph by transmission of light through a NEGATIVE (def. 5).
n 1 printed words or letters: *This book has clear print.* 2 a picture or design printed from an engraved block or plate. *a framed print.* 3 cloth with a pattern printed on it: *a batik print.* 4 a mark made by pressing or stamping: *the print of a raccoon's paw in the mud.* 5 a photograph produced from a negative. <Old French, from Latin *premere* press>
in (or **out of**) **print,** still (or no longer) available for purchase as a book from its publisher.

print·a·ble (prin′tə bəl) *adj* 1 able to be printed. 2 suitable or fit to be printed or published.

printed circuit *n* an electrical circuit in which some of the components and the conductors have been printed or etched in fine lines using electrically conductive ink on an insulating board.

print·er (prin′tər) *n* 1 a person whose business or work is printing or setting type. 2 a machine or device used for printing, such as the part of a computer system that produces printouts.

print·ing (prin′ting) *n* 1 the production of publications or other printed material. 2 printed texts, words, or letters. 3 all the copies of a book or other publication printed at one time. 4 handwritten letters made like those in printed material.

printing press *n* a machine for printing from movable type or plates.

print·out (prin′tout′) *Computers n* a page or group of pages of printed material generated by a computer.

pri·on (prē′ən) *n* a protein particle similar to a virus that is believed to be the cause of some brain diseases. <*pro*(*teinaceous*) *in*(*fectious particle*)>

pri·or[1] (prī′ər) *adj* coming earlier: *I can't go with you because I have a prior engagement.*
n Slang a previous criminal conviction. <Latin = previous>
prior to, coming before in time, order, or importance.

pri·or[2] (prī′ər) *n* the head of a priory or monastery for men, usually ranking below an abbot.

pri·or·ess (prī′ə ris) *n* the head of a convent or priory for women, usually ranking below an abbess.

pri·or·i·tize (prī ȯ′rə tīz) *v* **pri·or·i·tized, pri·or·i·tiz·ing** rank in order of priority. **pri·or′i·ti·za′tion** *n.*

pri·or·i·ty (prī ȯ′rə tē) *n, pl* **pri·or·i·ties** 1 a thing that is regarded as more important than others: *Being on time was a priority for her.* 2 the fact or condition of being more important: *He gave his homework top priority.*

pri·o·ry (prī′ə rē) *n, pl* **pri·o·ries** a monastery or convent governed by a prior or prioress.

a bat	e bed	i bid	o pot	u cup	th thin
ā cake	ē me	ī bite	ō go	ū rude	ᴛʜ then
ȧ bar	ə about	ər over	ȯ for	u̇ put	zh measure

prism (priz′əm) *n* **1** *Mathematics* a solid whose ends are congruent polygons, and each of whose sides are rectangles. A cardboard box is a prism. **2** a transparent block of glass or plastic, usually with triangular ends, that separates white light passing through it into the colours of the spectrum. <Latin, from Greek *prisma* something sawed off, from its shape>

pris·mat·ic (priz mat′ik) *adj* **1** to do with a prism. **2** varied and brilliant in colour. **pris·mat′i·cal·ly** *adv.*

prismatic colours or **colors** *n* the colours formed when white light passes through a prism: red, orange, yellow, green, blue, indigo, and violet.

pris·on (priz′ən) *n* **1** a public building in which criminals are confined. **2** confinement in such a place.
v Poetic confine in a prison. <Latin *prehendere* seize>

pris·on·er (priz′ə nər) *or* (priz′nər) *n* **1** a person who is under arrest or held in a jail or prison. **2** a person who is kept confined by an enemy, opponent, or criminal.
prisoner of war, a person taken by the enemy in war.

pris·sy (pris′ē) *adj* **pris·si·er, pris·si·est** seeming too fussy, respectable, and easily shocked. <blend of *prim* and *sissy*>

pris·tine (pris′tēn) *adj* **1** as fresh as in the original condition. **2** spotlessly clean and fresh. <Latin *pristinus* former>

pri·va·cy (prī′və sē) *n, pl* **pri·va·cies** **1** the condition of being free from being observed or disturbed: *in the privacy of your home.* **2** free from public attention.

pri·vate (prī′vit) *adj* **1** for just a few special people or for one: *a private airplane.* **2** not public: *the private life of a movie star.* **3** secret or confidential: *I can't tell you what he said, because it's private.* **4** secluded: *a private corner in the library.* **5** with no public or official role or position: *a private citizen.* **6** provided or owned by an independent commercial firm rather than a government: *a private company.*
n 🍁 a person holding the lowest rank in the Canadian Forces. <Latin *privus* individual> **pri′vate·ly** *adv.* **pri′vate·ness** *n.*
in private, **a** not publicly: *My mother spoke to the principal in private.* **b** secretly: *We met in private to plan her surprise birthday party.*

SYNONYMS

Private suggests that something is not seen, used, or shared by others: *The leaders held a private conversation behind closed doors.*

Exclusive emphasizes purposely shutting out certain things or people: *The court ruled that the exclusive club had to admit both men and women.*

private enterprise *n* the production, sale, or hire of goods and services by industries that are owned by individuals or companies rather than a government.

pri·va·teer (prī′və tēr′) *n* **1** in former times, an armed ship owned by private persons and holding a government commission to attack and capture enemy ships. **2** a commander or one of the crew of a privateer.

private investigator *n* a person who is not a member of a public police force but engages in investigative work on behalf of private clients for a fee. Often informally called **private eye**. *Abbrev.* **PI**

private member *n* a member of a legislature who is not a cabinet member or a leading member of an opposition party.

private parts *n* the genitals.

private school *n* a school that is under private management and is not part of the public school system. Also called **independent school**.

private sector *n* business and industry that is not owned or controlled by a government.

pri·va·tion (prī vā′shən) *n* the lack of the comforts or necessities of life: *Many children were hungry or homeless because of privation during the war.* <Latin *privatio* deprivation>

pri·va·tize (prī′və tīz) *v* **pri·va·tized pri·va·tiz·ing** transfer from public or government control to ownership by individuals or companies: *She was against privatizing the crown corporation.* **pri′va·ti·za′tion** *n.*

priv·et (priv′it) *n* a shrub of the olive family with small white flowers, often used for hedges. <origin uncertain>

priv·i·lege (priv′ə lij) *or* (priv′lij) *n* a special right, advantage, or favour.
v **priv·i·leged, priv·i·leg·ing** give a privilege to: *He said we were privileged to belong to this university.* <Latin *privilegium* law applying to one individual>

priv·i·leged (priv′ə lijd) *adj* **1** with a privilege or privileges: *the privileged classes of society.* **2** not to be revealed in a court of law: *Communication between a lawyer and client is privileged.*

priv·y (priv′ē) *adj* knowing something secret or private: *I wasn't privy to what she was thinking.*
n, pl **priv·ies** a small outhouse used as a toilet. <Old French, from Latin *privus* individual>

🍁 **Privy Council** *n* the body of advisers to the Governor General, chiefly honorary. **Privy Councillor** *n.*

prix fixe (prē fēks′) *n* a set price for a complete meal. <French = fixed price>

prize[1] (prīz) *n* **1** a reward won or offered in a contest or competition: *Prizes will be given for the three best stories.* **2** a reward worth working for. **3** in former times, a thing or person captured in war, especially an enemy's ship taken at sea.
adj **1** given or awarded as a prize. **2** worthy of a prize: *prize vegetables.*
v **prized, priz·ing** value highly: *She prizes her best china.* <Old French, from Latin *pretium* reward>

prize[2] (prīz) *v* **prized, priz·ing** PRY[2].

prize·fight (prīz′fīt′) *n* a boxing match fought for money. **prize·fight·er** *n.*

pro[1] (prō) *adv* in favour of: *They were strongly pro the change to the law.*
n, pl **pros** an advantage of something or a reason in favour of: *The pros and cons of a question are the arguments for and against it.* <Latin = in favour of>

pro[2] (prō) *Informal n, pl* **pros** *adj* a professional, such as a professional athlete or actor.

pro– *prefix* **1** forward: *proceed.* **2** forth or out: *prolong, proclaim.* **3** in favour of: *pro-American.* **4** in place of or acting as: *pronoun.* <Latin, from Greek *pro*>

pro·ac·tive (prō ak′tiv) *adj* taking the initiative in a situation rather than responding to something when it happens: *If you want a better relationship with your friend, you're going to have to be proactive about it.*
pro·ac′tive·ly *adv.*

prob·a·bil·i·ty (prob′ə bil′ə tē) *n, pl* **prob·a·bil·i·ties** **1** the quality or fact of being likely or probable: *There is a probability that school will close a week earlier than usual.* **2** a probable event. **3** *Mathematics* of an event, the ratio of the number of favourable (that is, wanted) outcomes to the number of possible outcomes.
in all probability, probably.

prob·a·ble (prob′ə bəl) *adj* **1** likely to happen: *Cooler weather is probable after rain.* **2** likely to be true: *Something she ate is the probable cause of her pain.* <Old French, from Latin *probabilis* something that may be proved> **prob′a·bly** *adv.*

pro·bate (prō′bāt) *n* **1** *Law* the official proving of a will as genuine. **2** a true copy of a will with a certificate that it has been proved genuine.
adj of or concerned with the probating of wills: *a probate court.*
v **pro·bat·ed, pro·bat·ing** prove by legal process the genuineness of a will. <Latin *probare* to test>

pro·ba·tion (prō bā′shən) *n* **1** a trial or testing of conduct, character, or qualifications, or the time during which it goes on: *She was admitted to the sixth grade on probation.* **2 a** the system of freeing someone imprisoned for a crime, subject to a period of good behaviour while supervised by a **probation officer** appointed by a court of law: *on probation.* **b** the period during which the person is supervised. <Latin *probare* to test> **pro·ba′tion·ar′y** *adj.*

probe (prōb) *v* **probed, prob·ing** **1** seek to acquire information about something or someone: *She probed her thoughts and feelings to find out why she acted as she did.* **2** physically examine or explore something with the hands or an instrument: *The doctor probed the wound to find the pieces of glass.*
n **1** a thorough examination or investigation. **2** a slender instrument with a rounded end for exploring a wound or part of the body. **3** an instrument, often electronic, used to test or explore. **4** an unmanned spacecraft carrying scientific instruments to record and transmit information about outer space and the objects in it: *a lunar probe.* <Latin *probare* to test> **prob′er** *n.* **prob′ing·ly** *adv.*

pro·bi·ty (prō′bə tē) *n* the quality of having strong moral principles. <Latin *probus* good>

prob·lem (prob′ləm) *n* **1** a matter or situation that causes doubt or difficulty. **2** a question or task for which the method of solution is not immediately apparent: *a math problem.*
adj causing difficulty: *a problem child.* <Old French, from Greek *pro* forward + *ballein* to throw>

prob·lem·at·ic (prob′lə mat′ik) *adj* made up of or presenting a problem or difficulty: *What the weather will be is often problematic.* **prob′lem·at′i·cal·ly** *adv.*

pro bo·no pu·bli·co (prō′ bō′nō pub′lə kō′) for the public welfare. <Latin = for the public good>

pro·bos·cis (prō bos′is) *n, pl* **pro·bos·ci·des** (-ki dēz) **1** the nose of a mammal, especially a long and flexible one, such as an elephant's trunk. **2** the mouth parts of some insects, such as a fly or mosquito, that are developed to great length for sucking. **3** *Informal* a person's nose. <Latin, from Greek from *pro* before + *boskein* to feed>

pro·ca·ry·ote (prō kar′ē ət) *or* (prō ker′ē ət) PROKARYOTE.

pro·ce·dure (prə sē′jər) *n* **1** a way of proceeding or method for doing things: *What is the procedure for nominating a candidate?* **2** the customary manner or ways of conducting business: *parliamentary procedure, legal procedure.* **3** a surgical operation: *a cardiac procedure.*

pro·ceed (prə sēd′) *or* (prō sēd′) *v* **1** begin or continue: *The trial may proceed. Please proceed with your story. He proceeded to polish his shoes.* **2** come from or come out from: *Heat proceeds from fire.* **3** *Law* start a lawsuit against someone. **4** move forward, especially after reaching a certain point: *Turn left and proceed two blocks.* See PRECEDE for confusable. <Old French, from Latin *pro* forward + *cedere* move> **pro·ceed′er** *n.*

pro·ceed·ing (prə sē′ding) *or* (prō sē′ding) *n* **1** action or conduct: *What a strange and unheard-of proceeding!* **2 proceedings** *pl* **a** an action in a case in a law court. **b** a record of what was done at a meetings of an organization.

pro·ceeds (prō′sēdz) *pln* the money obtained from an event or activity: *the proceeds from the school play.*

pro·cess[1] (prō′ses) *or* (pros′es) *n* **1** a set of actions or changes arranged in a particular order: *By what process is cloth made from wool?* **2** a part that grows out or sticks out from a body: *the process of a bone.* **3** a written order or summons to appear in a law court.
v **1** treat or prepare by some special method: *This cloth has been processed to make it waterproof.* **2 a** start legal action against someone. **b** issue a writ or summons to appear in court. <Old French, from Latin *pro* forward + *cedere* move>

pro·cess[2] (prō ses′) *v* move in a procession: *The graduands will process toward the front of the hall.* <*procession*>

processed cheese *n* a blend of various cheeses, milk products, and other ingredients.

pro·ces·sion (prə sesh′ən) *n* **1** a group of people or vehicles moving forward in an orderly way, especially as part of a ceremony or festival: *A funeral procession filled the street.* **2** the action of moving forward in an orderly way: *We formed lines to march in procession onto the platform.* <Latin *pro* forward + *cedere* move>

pro·ces·sion·al (prə sesh′ə nəl) *adj* to do with a religious or ceremonial procession.
n **1** processional music: *The choir and clergy marched into the church singing the processional.* **2** a book containing hymns and other texts for use in religious processions.

a bat	e bed	i bid	o pot	u cup	th thin
ā cake	ē me	ī bite	ō go	ū rude	TH then
à bar	ə about	ər over	ȯ for	u̇ put	zh measure

pro·ces·sor (prō′se sər) *or* (pros′e sər) *n* **1** a machine that processes something, such as a kitchen appliance that chops, mixes, and blends foods. **2** *Computers* a central processing unit in a computer. **3** a person who or thing that processes.

pro–choice (prō′chois′) *adj* supporting the right of a woman to choose whether or not she will have an abortion. Compare PRO-LIFE. **pro-choic′er** *n.*

pro·claim (prə klām′) *v* make known publicly and officially: *War was proclaimed. The people proclaimed her queen.* <Latin *pro-* forth + *clamare* shout>

proc·la·ma·tion (prok′lə mā′shən) *n* an official announcement or a public declaration: *A proclamation was issued to announce the forthcoming election.*

pro·cliv·i·ty (prō kliv′ə tē) *n, pl* **pro·cliv·i·ties** a tendency or inclination to do something regularly. <Latin *proclivis* prone to>

pro·con·sul (prō kon′səl) *n* the governor or military commander of a province in the ancient Roman empire.

pro·cras·ti·nate (prō kras′tə nāt′) *v* **pro·cras·ti·nat·ed, pro·cras·ti·nat·ing** repeatedly delay or postpone doing something: *Lazy people tend to procrastinate.* <Latin *pro-* forward + *cras* tomorrow> **pro·cras′ti·na′tion** *n.* **pro·cras′ti·na′tor** *n.*

pro·cre·ate (prō′krē āt′) *v* **pro·cre·at·ed, pro·cre·at·ing** produce offspring. <Latin *pro-* forth + *creare* create> **pro′cre·a′tion** *n.*

proc·tor (prok′tər) *n* a person who supervises examinations at a college or university. <*procurator*>

proc·u·ra·tor (prok′yə rā′tər) *n* **1** a person employed to represent others in a court of law in some countries. **2** a financial agent or administrator of a province in the ancient Roman empire. <Old French, from Latin *pro-* on behalf of + *cura* care>

pro·cure (prə kyůr′) *v* **pro·cured, pro·cur·ing** obtain by using care or effort: *A friend procured a position in the bank for my daughter.* <Latin *procurare* manage, from *pro-* on behalf of + *cura* care> **pro·cur′a·ble** *adj.* **pro·cur′ment** *n.*

prod (prod) *v* **prod·ded, prod·ding 1** poke or jab with a finger, foot, or a pointed object: *to prod an animal with a stick.* **2** stimulate, persuade, or remind someone: *We've been trying to prod our councillor into doing something about the noise on our street.*
n **1** a poke or thrust with the finger, foot, or pointed object: *That prod in the ribs hurt.* **2** an act of stimulating, persuading, or reminding a person to do something. **3** a pointed tool used to make an animal move, especially one that discharges electricity: *a cattle prod.* <origin uncertain> **prod′der** *n.*

prod·i·gal (prod′ə gəl) *adj* **1** spending money or resources recklessly: *prodigal habits.* **2** abundant or lavish: *prodigal hospitality.*
n a person who is wasteful or extravagant. <Latin *prodigere* squander> **prod′i·gal·ly** *adv.*

prod·i·gal·i·ty (prod′ə gal′ə tē) *n, pl* **prod·i·gal·i·ties 1** wasteful or reckless extravagance. **2** rich abundance or lavishness.

pro·di·gious (prə dij′əs) *adj* remarkably or impressively great in extent, size, or degree: *The ocean contains a prodigious amount of water, a prodigious achievement.* **pro·di′gious·ly** *adv.* **pro·di′gious·ness** *n.*

prod·i·gy (prod′ə jē) *n, pl* **prod·i·gies 1** a person, especially a child, who has exceptional qualities or abilities. **2** an impressive, amazing, or unusual example of something: *a prodigy of single-mindedness.* <Latin *prodigium* omen>

pro·duce (prə dyūs′) *or* (prə dūs′) *for v,* (prod′yūs) *or* (prō′dūs) *for n. v* **pro·duced, pro·duc·ing 1** make or manufacture: *This factory produces stoves.* **2** bring about or cause: *Hard work produces success.* **3** bring forth or yield things or results:. *Hens produce eggs. The tree produced only a few apples this year.* **4** show or present: *Produce your proof.* **5** bring a play, film, or other entertainment before the public.
n things that have been produced or grown: *garden produce.* <Latin *pro-* forth + *ducere* to lead> **pro·duc′i·ble** *adj.*

pro·duc·er (prə dyū′sər) *or* (prə dū′sər) *n* **1** a person who or thing that produces. **2** a person who grows or makes things that are to be used or consumed by others. **3** a person in charge of financing and organizing the production of a play, movie, or TV program. **4** *Biology* an organism that makes its own food from inorganic compounds. Green plants are producers.

prod·uct (prod′əkt) *n* **1** the result of work or of growth: *factory products, farm products.* **2** a number or quantity resulting from multiplying: *The product of 5 and 8 is 40.*

pro·duc·tion (prə duk′shən) *n* **1** the act of making or manufacturing: *the production of automobiles.* **2** a thing that is produced: *The school play was a fine production.* **3** the total amount produced.
make a production of, draw much attention to or treat as something big or complicated: *Every time he helps out he makes such a production of it, it's embarrassing.*

production line *n* a row of machines and equipment in a factory, with workers standing or sitting alongside and overseeing the various stages of manufacturing something.

production values *pln* the standard or quality of production in a recording, film, or play with regard to such technical aspects as sound, costume and set design, and special effects.

pro·duc·tive (prə duk′tiv) *adj* **1** be able to produce or bring forth: *fields now productive only of weeds, hasty words that are productive of quarrels.* **2** producing food or other articles of commerce: *Farming is productive labour.* **3** producing abundantly. **pro·duc′tive·ly** *adv.* **pro·duc′tive·ness** *n.* **pro′duc·tiv′i·ty** *n.*

prof (prof) *Informal n* professor.

prof·a·na·tion (prof′ə nā′shən) *n* the act of showing contempt or disregard toward something sacred.

pro·fane (prə fān′) *or* (prō fān′) *adj* **1** not concerning or devoted to the sacred or biblical: *Mozart wrote both*

religious and profane music. 2 using rude and coarse language.
v **pro·faned, pro·fan·ing** treat holy things with contempt or disregard: *Rebels profaned the church by stabling horses there.* <Latin *profanus* not consecrated> **pro·fane′ly** *adv.* **pro·fane′ness** *n.*

pro·fan·i·ty (prə fan′ə tē) *n, pl* **pro·fan·i·ties** 1 the use of profane language. 2 a swear word.

pro·fess (prə fes′) *v* 1 claim as being true: *She professed the greatest respect for the law. I don't profess to be an expert.* 2 declare openly: *He professed his loyalty to his country.* <Latin *pro-* before + *fateri* confess>

pro·fessed (prə fest′) *adj* 1 alleged or pretended. 2 openly declared to be. 3 having taken the vows of, or been received into, a religious order.

pro·fess·ed·ly (prə fes′i dlē) *adv* apparently or ostensibly: *The new law was professedly made to stop littering.*

pro·fes·sion (prə fesh′ən) *n* 1 an occupation requiring special education and training, such as law, medicine, teaching, or nursing. 2 the people engaged in such an occupation: *The medical profession favours this law.* 3 an open declaration: *I welcomed her profession of friendship.* 4 a declaration of belief in a religion.

pro·fes·sion·al (prə fesh′ə nəl) *adj* 1 to do with a profession: *professional skill, a professional manner.* 2 making a business or trade of something that others do for pleasure: *a professional ballplayer.* 3 making a business of something not properly to be regarded as a business: *a professional politician.*
n a person who is or acts as a professional. **pro·fes′sion·al·ly** *adv.*

SYNONYMS

A **professional** is someone who has appropriate standards: *The lawyer is a professional of great stature.*

An **expert** is someone who is very skilled at what he or she does: *She is an expert in the field of economics and is often interviewed on TV.*

A **specialist** is an expert in one area of his or her work: *The doctor is a specialist in heart surgery.*

pro·fes·sion·al·ism (prə fesh′ə nə liz′əm) *n* 1 professional character, spirit, or methods. 2 the practice or methods of a professional, as distinguished from those of an amateur.

pro·fes·sor (prə fes′ər) *n* a teacher of the highest rank in a college or university. **prof′es·so′ri·al** *adj.* **prof′es·so′ri·al·ly** *adv.*

pro·fes·sor·ship (prə fes′ər ship′) *n* the position, rank or term of office of an academic professor.

prof·fer (pro′fər) *v* offer for acceptance or present courteously: *She rejected the proffered apology.*
n an offer made: *The counsellor's proffer of advice was gratefully accepted.* <Old French, from Latin *pro-* on behalf of + *facere* do>

pro·fi·cient (prə fish′ənt) *adj* competent or skilled in an art, science, or subject: *She was very proficient in music.* <Latin *proficere* to make progress> **pro·fi′cien·cy** *n.* **pro·fi′cient·ly** *adv.*

pro·file (prō′fīl) *n* 1 an outline of something, especially of the human face, as seen from one side, or a drawing of such an outline. 2 a drawing of a transverse vertical section of a building, bridge, or other structure. 3 a concise description of a person's abilities, character, or career: *The magazine carried an interesting profile of the mayor.* 4 the extent to which a person or thing is known or recognized publicly: *She has a very high profile in the movie industry.*
v **pro·filed, pro·fil·ing** 1 draw a profile of. 2 describe or show the main aspects of a person or organization. <Italian *profilare* to draw in outline, from Latin *pro-* forth + *filum* thread>
keep a low profile, try to avoid drawing attention to yourself.

prof·it (prof′it) *n* 1 the financial gain after all expenses from conducting a business are subtracted from the money earned: *The profit from the Charity Car Wash was enormous.* 2 advantage or benefit: *What profit is there in worrying?*
v 1 make such a financial gain. 2 obtain an advantage or benefit: *A wise person profits by mistakes.* <Latin *proficere* to make progress> **prof′it·less** *adj.*

prof·it·a·ble (prof′ə tə bəl) *adj* 1 providing a financial profit: *a profitable sale.* 2 giving an advantage or benefit: *We spent a profitable afternoon in the library.* **prof′it·a·bil′i·ty** *n.* **prof′it·a·ble·ness** *n.* **prof′it·a·bly** *adv.*

prof·it·eer (prof′ə tēr′) *n* a person who makes an unfair profit, especially illegally.
v seek to make unfair profits, especially illegally.

profit margin *n* the amount by which revenue from sales in a business exceeds costs.

profit sharing *n* the sharing of profits in a business between employer and employees.

prof·li·gate (prof′lə git) *adj* 1 indulging too much in sensual pleasures. 2 recklessly extravagant.
n a person who indulges too much in sensual pleasures. <Latin *profligatus* immoral, from *profligare* ruin> **prof′li·ga·cy** *n.* **prof′li·gate·ly** *adv.*

pro for·ma (prō for′mə) *adj* 1 done merely for the sake of form: *It was just a pro forma interview, since he knew they would hire him.* 2 providing or prescribing a set form or method: *a pro forma invoice.*
n a document setting out the rules, method, or format by which something is to be done: *To have this independent study course approved, you have to submit a pro forma.* <Latin = as a matter of form>

pro·found (prə found′) *adj* 1 great, intense, or deeply felt: *a profound sigh, a profound sleep, profound despair.* 2 with or showing great depth of knowledge or understanding: *a profound book, a profound thinker.* <Old French, from Latin *pro-* before + *fundus* bottom> **pro·found′ly** *adv.* **pro·found′ness** *n.*

a bat	e bed	i bid	o pot	u cup	th thin
ā cake	ē me	ī bite	ō go	ū rude	TH then
à bar	ə about	ər over	ô for	ů put	zh measure

pro·fun·di·ty (prə fun′də tē) *n, pl* **pro·fun·di·ties** **1** great depth or intensity of a quality or emotion. **2** deep insight or knowledge.

pro·fuse (prə fyūs′) *adj* very plentiful: *profuse thanks.* <Latin *pro-* forth + *fundere* pour> **pro·fuse′ly** *adv.* **pro·fuse′ness** *n.*

pro·fu·sion (prə fyū′zhən) *n* a great many: *a profusion of flowers in spring.*

pro·gen·i·tor (prō jen′ə tər) *n* an ancestor from whom or which a person, animal, or plant descends in a direct line. <Old French, from Latin *pro-* forth + *gignere* produce>

prog·e·ny (proj′ə nē) *n* a descendant or the descendants of a person, animal, or plant.

pro·ges·ter·one (prō jes′tə rōn′) *n* **1** a natural steroid hormone that prepares the uterus for pregnancy. **2** a drug prepared from natural or synthetic progesterone that is used to treat various conditions of the female reproductive system or in forms of birth control. <*gestation*>

prog·no·sis (prog nō′sis) *n, pl* **prog·no·ses** (-sēz) **1** a forecast of the probable course of a disease. **2** an estimate of what will probably happen. <Latin, from Greek *pro-* before + *gignoskein* recognize>

prog·nos·ti·cate (prog nos′tə kāt′) *v* **prog·nos·ti·cat·ed, prog·nos·ti·cat·ing** predict an event. **prog·nos′ti·ca′tion** *n.* **prog·nos′ti·ca′tor** *n.*

pro·gram or **pro·gramme** (prō′gram) *n* **1** a plan of what is to be done: *a government program.* **2** a radio or TV show: *We watched a TV program about sea otters.* **3** a list of items or events, especially for an entertainment, or the items themselves: *a theatre program. The entire program was very well performed.* **4** a set of educational courses: *an undergraduate program.* **5** *Computers* a set of instructions outlining the steps to be performed in a specific operation.
v **pro·grammed, pro·gram·ming** **1** arrange a program for: *to program the fall TV series.* **2** *Computers* prepare a set of instructions for a computer operation. <Latin, from Greek *pro-* before + *graphein* write>

pro·gram·ma·tic (prō′gra ma′ tik) *adj* **1** to do with a program, schedule, or method. **2** seeming to follow a program in being predictable or mechanical.

programmed learning *n* a method of study by which a person works step by step through a series of problems, checking the correctness of his or her response to each step before proceeding to the next.

pro·gram·mer (prō′gram ər) *Computers n* a person who prepares a program or programs, especially for a computer or other machine.

pro·gram·ming (prō′gram ing) *n* **1** the shows offered by a TV or radio station, or the planning of such shows. **2** *Computers* the action or process of writing computer software.

programming language *Computers n* a system of words and codes that allows a person to put instructions into a computer in a form that the computer can recognize and process.

prog·ress (prō′gres) *or* (prog′res) *for n,* (prə gres′) *for v.* *n* **1** an ongoing advance, growth, development, or improvement: *the progress of science.* **2** a forward or onward movement toward a destination: *It was sunny and mild, so we made rapid progress on our hike.*
v **1** advance toward a more complete or improved condition: *Research techniques progressed a great deal in the first part of the century.* **2** move forward in space or time: *The building of the city hall has progressed a great deal this week.* <Latin *pro-* forward + *gradi* step>
in progress, in the course of being done or conducted: *The meeting was in progress.*

pro·gres·sion (prə gresh′ən) *n* **1** a moving forward or development toward a more advanced condition, especially gradually or in stages: *He made a steady progression toward getting a spot on the national swim team.* **2** *Mathematics* a series of quantities in which there is always the same relation between each quantity and the one after it. In an **arithmetical progression**, each quantity is the result of adding the same thing each time: 1, 4, 7, 10. In a **geometrical progression**, each quantity is the result of multiplying by the same thing each time: 1, 3, 9, 27.

pro·gres·sive (prə gres′iv) *adj* **1** favouring or putting into effect social reform or new, liberal ideas. **2** developing steadily in stages: *a progressive disease, a progressive decline.* **3** going from one to the next in a game or dance, involving shifts of people from one location to another: *progressive bridge.* **4** *Grammar* showing the action of a verb as ongoing. Example: *Is reading, was reading,* and *has been reading* are progressive forms of the verb *read.*
n a person who favours or puts into effect social reform or new, liberal ideas. **pro·gres′sive·ly** *adv.* **pro·gres′sive·ness** *n.*

🍁 **Progressive Canadian Party** *n* one of the registered political parties of Canada.

🍁 **Progressive Conservative Party** *n* **1** in former times, a federal political party. See CONSERVATIVE PARTY. **2** a provincial political party.

pro·hib·it (prō hib′it) *v* **1** forbid by a law, rule, or other authority: *Picking flowers in this park is prohibited.* **2** prevent: *The high price prohibits my buying the bicycle.* <Latin *pro-* in front + *habere* to hold>

pro·hi·bi·tion (prō′ə bish′ən) *n* **1** the act of prohibiting or forbidding: *The prohibition of swimming in the city's reservoirs is sensible.* **2** a law or order that prohibits. **3 Prohibition** a law or laws against making or selling alcoholic liquors, especially such a law in the US from 1920 to 1933.

pro·hi·bi·tion·ist (prō′ə bish′ə nist) *n* a person who favours laws against the manufacture and sale of alcoholic liquors.

pro·hib·i·tive (prō hib′ə tiv) *adj* prohibiting or restricting something, especially because of its high cost or price: *The price of a new car was prohibitive.*

pro·ject (prō′jekt) *or* (proj′ekt) *for n,* (prə jekt′) *for v.* *n* **1** a carefully planned and designed undertaking: *a research project.* **2** a piece of school or college work that a student researches and submits to be marked: *a science project.* **3** *US* a government-subsidized housing complex for people who have low incomes.

v **1** forecast or estimate something: *The profit he projected didn't make sense.* **2** stick out or cause to stick out: *The rocky point projects far into the water.* **3** (*usually in the passive*) throw: *The missile was projected into space.* **4** cause to fall on a surface: *to project an image onto a screen.* **5** present or promote an idea or impression: *She wanted to project an image of youthfulness.* **6** make one's voice be heard clearly at a distance: *You must project so that people at the back can hear every word.* <Latin *pro-* forth + *jacere* to throw>

pro·jec·tile (prə jek′tīl) *or* (prə jek′təl) *n* an object that is thrown, hurled, or shot, such as a rocket, stone, or bullet. *adj* capable of being thrown, hurled, or shot: *a projectile weapon, projectile vomiting.*

pro·jec·tion (prə jek′shən) *n* **1** an estimate or forecast of a future situation based on a study of present situations: *Weather projections are unreliable.* **2** a part that projects or sticks out: *rocky projections on the face of a cliff.* **3** the condition or quality of sticking out: *The projection of these nails is dangerous.* **4** an act of throwing or casting forward: *the projection of a missile.* **5** a representation on a flat surface of all or part of the (curved) surface of the earth. See also MERCATOR PROJECTION.

pro·jec·tion·ist (prə jek′shə nist) *n* a person who operates a movie projector.

pro·jec·tor (prə jek′tər) *n* an apparatus for projecting a picture or a movie onto a screen. See also OVERHEAD PROJECTOR.

pro·kar·y·ote (prō′kar′ē ət) *or* (prō ker′ē ət) *n* a single-celled organism, such as a bacterium, that has no distinct nucleus. Compare EUKARYOTE. Also, **procaryote**. <Greek *pro-* before + *karyote* cell nucleus, from Greek *karyon* kernel> **pro·ka·ry·o·tic** *adj.*

pro·lapse (prō′laps) *for n,* (prō′laps) *or* (prō laps′) *for v. Medicine n* a forward or downward slippage of a part or organ of the body.
v slip forward or downward. <Latin *prolapsus* falling out of place>

pro·le·tar·i·an (prō′lə ter′ē ən) *Economics adj* to do with the **proletariat**, people who make their living by working for others to earn wages.
n a person belonging to the proletariat.

pro–life (prō′līf′) *adj* opposing abortion and euthanasia. Also called **right-to-life. pro-lifer** *n.*

pro·lif·er·ate (prə lif′ə rāt′) *v* **pro·lif·er·at·ed, pro·lif·er·at·ing 1** increase rapidly by reproduction. **2** produce or be produced rapidly and in great numbers: *Pirated copies of that videotape have been proliferating over the last two weeks. New cases of the disease are proliferating worldwide.* <French, from Latin *proles* offspring + *ferre* bear> **pro·lif′er·a′tion** *n.*

pro·lif·ic (prə lif′ik) *adj* **1** producing fruit, foliage, or offspring abundantly: *prolific animals.* **2** producing much or many: *a prolific writer.* **pro·lif′i·cal·ly** *adv.*

pro·lix (prō liks′) *or* (prō′liks) *adj* using or containing too many words. <Old French, from Latin *pro-* outward + *liquere* to flow> **pro·lix′i·ty** *n.* **pro·lix′ly** *adv.*

pro·logue (prō′log) *n* **1** a speech or poem addressed to the audience of a theatrical, literary, or musical work. **2** an introductory act or event. Also, **prolog**. <Old French, from Greek *pro-* before + *logos* speech>

pro·long (prə long′) *v* make long in time: *Good care may prolong life. The lonesome dog uttered prolonged howls.* <Old French, from Latin *pro-* forward + *longus* long> **pro′lon·ga′tion** *n.*

prom (prom) *Informal n* a dance or ball given by a college or high-school class. <*promenade*>

PROM (prom) *Computers n* a read-only memory chip whose contents can be programmed to suit specific needs. <*Programmable Read-Only Memory*>

prom·e·nade (prom′ə nād′) *or* (prom′ə nȧd′) *n*
1 a a leisurely walk in a public place so as to meet or be seen by others. **b** a public place for taking such a walk: **2** a formal dance.
v **prom·e·nad·ed, prom·e·nad·ing** take a leisurely walk in a public place so as to meet or be seen by others: *She promenaded back and forth on the ship's deck.* <French *promener* take for a walk> **prom′e·nad′er** *n.*

pro·me·thi·um (prə mē′thē əm) *n* a rare, radioactive metallic element. *Symbol* **Pm**

ETYMOLOGY

In Greek myth, Prometheus stole fire from the gods, for humans to use. The element **promethium** was associated with the energy from nuclear fission, which humans could use.

prom·i·nence (prom′ə nəns) *n* **1** the quality or fact of being prominent, distinguished, or conspicuous: *the prominence of athletics in some schools.* **2** the fact or condition of jutting out or projecting, especially upward. **3** a thing that juts out or projects, such as a hill.

prom·i·nent (prom′ə nənt) *adj* **1** well-known or important: *a prominent citizen.* **2** easy to see, such as a single tree in a field. **3** standing out or projecting: *Some insects have prominent eyes.* <Latin *pro-* forward + *minere* jut> **prom′i·nent·ly** *adv.*

pro·mis·cu·ous (prə mis′kyū əs) *adj* **1** unselective, especially in having many casual sexual contacts: *promiscuous friendships.* **2** mixed and in disorder: *a promiscuous heap of clothing on your closet floor.* <Latin *pro-* thoroughly + *miscere* mix> **pro′mis·cu′i·ty** *n.* **pro·mis′cu·ous·ly** *adv.* **pro·mis′cu·ous·ness** *n.*

prom·ise (prom′is) *n* **1** a statement made by a person that he or she will do or not do something: *keep a promise.* **2** an indication of what may be expected: *The clouds give promise of rain.* **3** an indication of future excellence or success: *a young scholar who shows promise.*
v **prom·ised, prom·is·ing 1** make a statement that something will or will not be done: *to promise help. She promised to stay till we got there.* **2** give a good indication that something will happen: *The rainbow promises fair weather.* <Latin *promittere*>

a bat	e bed	i bid	o pot	u cup	th **thin**
ā cake	ē me	ī bite	ō go	ū rude	ᴛʜ then
ȧ bar	ə about	ər over	ȯ for	ů put	zh measure

Promised Land *n* **1** in the Bible, the country promised by God to Abraham and his descendants. **2 promised land** a place or condition of expected happiness: *For some immigrants, Canada was a promised land.*

prom·is·ing (prom′i sing) *adj* likely to turn out well: *a promising violinist.* **prom′is·ing·ly** *adv.*

prom·is·so·ry note (prom′i sər′ē) *n* a written promise to pay a stated sum of money to a certain person at a certain time.

pro·mo (prō′mō) *Informal n, pl* **pro·mos** a piece of publicity or advertising, such as a free sample or sponsored event. <*promotion*>

prom·on·to·ry (prom′ən tô′rē) *n, pl* **prom·on·to·ries** a high point of land extending from the shore into the water. <Latin *pro-* forward + *mons* mountain>

pro·mote (prə mōt′) *v* **pro·mot·ed, pro·mot·ing 1** raise in rank, condition, or importance: *Those who pass the test will be promoted to the next higher grade.* **2** help to grow or develop: *The United Nations has done much to promote peace.* **3** help to organize: *Several bankers promoted the new company.* **4** further the sale of an article by advertising or publicity: *to promote a new product.* <Latin *pro-* forward + *movere* move>

pro·mot·er (prə mō′tər) *n* **1** a person who or thing that promotes: *a rock-concert promoter. Good humour is a promoter of friendship.* **2** a person who organizes new companies and secures capital for them.

pro·mo·tion (prə mō′shən) *n* **1** an advance in rank or importance: *The clerk was given a promotion and an increase in salary.* **2** the act or process of helping to grow, develop, or succeed: *The doctors were busy in the promotion of a health campaign.* **3** publicity or advertising.

pro·mo·tion·al (prə mō′shən əl) *adj* to do with the PROMOTION (def. 3) of a person, product, or organization: *a promotional campaign. This article is not to be used for promotional purposes.*

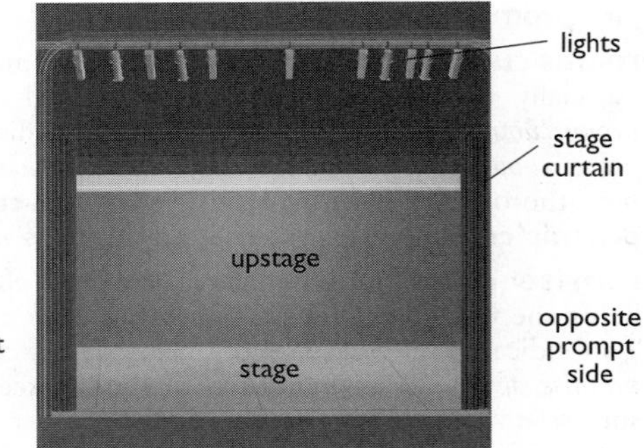

prompt (prompt) *adj* on time, quickly, or without delay: *Be prompt to obey. I expect a prompt answer.*
v **1** cause someone to do something: *Her curiosity prompted her to ask questions. A kind thought prompted the gift.* **2** remind a speaker or actor of the words or actions needed: *She will prompt you if you forget your lines in the play.* **3** *Computers* request input from a user through a message on a computer screen.
n **1** an act of assisting or encouraging a speaker who hesitates. **2** *Computers* a message on a computer screen requesting input. <Old French, from Latin *promptus* at hand, ready> **prompt′ly** *adv.* **prompt′ness** *n.*

prompt·er (promp′tər) *n* a person who is out of sight and tells actors what to say when they forget their lines.

pro·mul·gate (prom′əl gāt′) *or* (prō mul′gāt) *v* **pro·mul·gat·ed, pro·mul·gat·ing 1** proclaim formally or announce officially: *The queen promulgated a decree.* **2** promote or make widely known an idea, habit, or policy. <Latin *promulgare* to bring to public knowledge> **pro′mul·ga′tion** *n.*

prone (prōn) *adj* **1** (*with* ***to***) inclined or liable: *He was prone to believe the worst of everyone.* **2** (*in compounds*) very likely to have: *She is accident-prone.* **3** lying face downward. Compare SUPINE. <Latin *pronus* bent forward>

prone·ness (prōn′nis) *n* a tendency or preference: *Because of a proneness to pneumonia, she tries to avoid colds.*

prong (prong) *n* **1** one of the pointed ends of a fork, device, or antler. **2** a separate part of an attack or procedure: *The union's two prongs were preserving jobs and raising wages.*
v pierce or stab with a fork. <Middle English *prange*> **pronged** *adj.*

prong·horn (prong′hôrn′) *n, pl* **prong·horns** or (*especially collectively*) **prong·horn** a deerlike mammal with short, curved horns, found on the plains of western N America.

pro·nom·i·nal (prō nom′ə nəl) *adj* to do with pronouns.

pro·noun (prō′noun) *n* a word used instead of a noun that can refer to the people involved or to someone or something mentioned elsewhere. Examples: *I, we, you, he, it, they, who, whose, which, this, mine, whatever.* <Latin *pro-* in place of + *nomen* noun>

GRAMMAR AND USAGE

Personal pronouns replace the subject or object of a sentence: *He milked the cow. The police found her.*

Reflexive pronouns replace the object when it is the same person or thing as the subject: *Dad cut himself shaving.*

Interrogative pronouns ask questions: *Where is the book that was on the table? Who is going to the party?*

pro·nounce (prə nouns′) *v* **pro·nounced, pro·nounc·ing 1** make the sound of a word or part of a word: *He pronounces your name differently than I do.* **2** give an opinion or decision: *Only an expert should pronounce on this case.* **3** declare or announce a person or thing to be as described: *The doctor pronounced her cured.* **4** declare formally or solemnly: *The judge pronounced sentence on the criminal.* <Old French, from Latin *pro-* forth + *nuntius* messenger> **pro·nounce′a·bil′i·ty** *n.* **pro·nounce′a·ble** *adj.*

pro·nounced (prə nounsd′) *adj* strongly marked or noticeable: *She held pronounced opinions on gambling.* **pro·nounc′ed·ly** (prə noun′sid lē) *adv.*

pro·nounce·ment (prə noun′smənt) *n* a formal statement, declaration, or opinion.

CONFUSABLES

Pronouncement means "formal statement": *The coroner issued a pronouncement of death at the scene of the accident.*

Pronunciation refers to the manner of pronouncing words: *When I have trouble with the pronunciation of certain words, I try to sound them out.*

pron·to (pron′tō) *Informal adv* promptly or quickly. <Spanish = quick, from Latin *promptus* prompt>

pro·nun·ci·a·tion (prə nun′sē ā′shən) *n* the way of pronouncing a word or part of a word: *Many dictionaries give the pronunciation of each entry word.*

proof (prūf) *n* **1** a way or means of showing beyond doubt the truth of something: *Is what you say a guess or have you proof?* **2** establishment of the truth of anything. **3** the act of testing the truth or facts about something: *That box looks big enough, but let us put it to the proof.* **4** the condition of having been tested and approved. **5** a trial print of a graphic work, such as a photographic negative.
adj of tested value against something: *Now we know that we are proof against being taken by surprise.*
v proofread. <Old French, from Latin *probare* prove>

–proof *combining form* protected against or safe from: *fireproof, waterproof, bombproof.* <See PROOF.>

proof·read (prū′frēd′) *v* **proof·read** (prū′fred′) **proof·read·ing** read printed text and mark errors to be corrected. **proof′read′er** *n.*

proof spirit *n* liquor, or a mix of alcohol and water, containing a standard proportion of ethyl alcohol. In Canada and the UK, proof is 57.1 percent by volume, and in the US, 50 percent.

prop[1] (prop) *v* **propped, prop·ping 1** (*usually with* ***up***) hold up by placing a support under or against: *When reading in bed I prop up my back with two pillows.* **2** support or sustain: *to prop a failing cause.*
n a thing or person used to support another: *That branch is heavy with apples and needs a prop. She was my prop when I had problems.* <origin uncertain>

prop[2] (prop) *Informal n* an item, such as a table or a weapon, used in staging a play. See PROPERTY (def. 4). <*(stage) property*>

prop[3] (prop) *Informal n* a propeller.

prop·a·gan·da (prop′ə gan′də) *n* **1** systematic efforts to spread opinions or beliefs, especially by distortion and deception: *The Nazis were experts in propaganda.* **2** the opinions or beliefs thus spread. **prop′a·gan′dist** *adj, n.* **prop′a·gan′dize** *v.*

ETYMOLOGY

Though **propaganda** is still used sometimes in a neutral way to describe the systematic spreading of any opinions or beliefs, it more often has a negative connotation and refers to the unscrupulous spreading of misleading information.

prop·a·gate (prop′ə gāt′) *v* **prop·a·gat·ed, prop·a·gat·ing 1** produce offspring of plants or animals through a natural process from parent stock: *Trees propagate themselves by seeds.* **2** cause to increase in number or amount. **3** spread and promote ideas, theories, news, or knowledge: *Don't propagate unkind reports.* **4** transmit motion, light, or sound in a particular direction or through a particular medium: *Sound is propagated by vibrations.* <Latin *propaginis* offspring> **prop′a·ga′tion** *n.*

pro·pane (prō′pān) *n* a heavy, colourless, hydrocarbon gas used for fuel and refrigeration. <*prop(yl)* + *(meth)ane*>

pro·pel (prə pel′) *v* **pro·pelled, pro·pel·ling** drive forward or force ahead: *to propel a boat by oars, a person propelled by ambition.* <Latin *pro-* forward + *pellere* to drive>

pro·pel·lant (prə pel′ənt) *n* a thing or substance that causes something to move or be driven forward or outward, such as the fuel of a missile or the explosive charge of a shell.

pro·pel·ler (prə pel′ər) *n* **1** a device with revolving blades, for propelling boats and aircraft. **2** a person who or thing that propels.

pro·pen·si·ty (prə pen′sə tē) *n, pl* **pro·pen·si·ties** a natural inclination or tendency: *The dog had a propensity for playing with water.* <Latin *propendere* incline to>

prop·er (prop′ər) *adj* **1** suitable or appropriate: *the proper time to sleep. Put the book back in its proper place on the shelf.* **2** socially correct or respectable: *proper conduct.* **3** identifying a particular person, place, or organization: *It's customary to capitalize a proper name.* **4** (*after the noun*) what something is strictly regarded to be: *The population of the city proper does not include people living in the suburbs.* **5** *Informal* complete or thorough: *a proper mess.* <Old French, from Latin *proprius* one's own>

SYNONYMS

Proper emphasizes suitable or appropriate: *He chose the proper drill bit for the job.*

Befitting is a more formal word for "suitable": *The politician's joking remarks were not befitting on such a solemn occasion.*

Correct suggests in accordance with accepted standards of good taste: *His behaviour was correct.*

Just suggests what is legally or ethically right or fitting: *The just law protects children's rights.*

proper adjective *Grammar n* an adjective formed from a proper noun and always capitalized. Examples: *Canadian, Shakespearean.*

proper fraction *Mathematics n* a fraction less than 1. Examples: 2/3, 125/200.

a bat	e bed	i bid	o pot	u cup	th **thin**
ā cake	ē me	ī bite	ō go	ū rude	TH **then**
à bar	ə about	ər over	ò for	ù put	zh measure

prop·er·ly (prop′ər lē) *adv* **1** in a suitable, correct, or appropriate manner: *This job must be done properly.* **2** rightly or justly: *The police officer was properly indignant at the offer of a bribe.* **3** strictly: *Properly speaking, a whale is not a fish.*

proper noun *Grammar n* a noun that identifies a particular person, place, time, group, or organization. Examples: *Sarah, Calgary, New Year, Parliament.* Compare COMMON NOUN.

prop·er·tied (prop′ər tēd) *adj* owning valuable things, especially land.

prop·er·ty (prop′ər tē) *n, pl* **prop·er·ties** **1** a thing or things owned: *This house is her property.* **2** a piece of land or real estate: *They own some property out West.* **3** a quality or power belonging specially to something: *Soap has the property of removing dirt.* **4** **properties** *pl* the items, such as furniture, used in staging a play, film, or broadcast scene. <Old French, from Latin *proprius* one's own>

pro·phase (prō′fāz) *n* the first stage of MITOSIS, in which changes take place in the nucleus of a cell.

proph·e·sy (prof′ə sī′) *v* **proph·e·sied, proph·e·sy·ing** **1** tell what will happen: *The sailor prophesied a severe storm.* **2** speak when or as if divinely inspired. **proph′e·cy** (prof′ə sē) *n.*

proph·et (prof′it) *n* **1** a person who tells what will happen. **2** a person who is regarded as teaching or preaching what is inspired by God. **3 the Prophet** among Muslims, Muhammad. **4 the Prophets** *pl* books of the Old Testament attributed to the major and minor prophets.

proph·et·ess (prof′i tis) *n* a female prophet.

pro·phet·ic (prə fet′ik) *adj* **1** belonging or attributed to a prophet: *prophetic books.* **2** telling what is to happen: *His warnings proved to be prophetic.* **pro·phet′i·cal·ly** *adv.*

pro·phy·lac·tic (prō′fə lak′tik) *or* (prof′ə lak′tik) *adj* protecting from disease.
n **1** a medicine or treatment that protects against disease. **2** a condom. <French, from Greek *pro-* before + *phylakos* act of guarding>

pro·phy·lax·is (prō′fə lak′sis) *or* (prof′ə lak′sis) *n* action taken to prevent or protect against disease.

pro·pin·qui·ty (prō ping′kwə tē) *n* nearness to someone or something. <Old French, from Latin *prope* near to>

pro·pi·ti·ate (prə pish′ē āt′) *v* **pro·pi·ti·at·ed, pro·pi·ti·at·ing** win or regain favour by doing something that pleases a person, spirit, or god. <Latin *propitius* gracious> **pro·pi′ti·a′tion** *n.* **pro·pi′ti·a′tor** *n.* **pro·pi′ti·a′tory** *adj.*

pro·pi·tious (prə pish′əs) *adj* favourable or indicating a good chance of success: *It seemed propitious weather for our trip.* <Latin> **pro·pi′tious·ly** *adv.* **pro·pi′tious·ness** *n.*

pro·po·nent (prə pō′nənt) *n* a person who supports or promotes a theory, proposal, or project.

pro·por·tion (prə pôr′shən) *n* **1** the relation of one thing compared or in ratio to another: *Your grade will be in proportion to your contribution to the class discussion.* **2** a relationship between parts of a whole: *His short legs were out of proportion to his long body.* **3** a part or share: *A large proportion of the country was mountainous.* **4 proportions** *pl* **a** size, extent, or dimension: *Canada has forests of huge proportions.* **b** comparative measurements or size of different parts: *The proportions of the furniture are wrong for this small room.* **c** *Mathematics* equations that show two ratios are equivalent.
v adjust or regulate something so that it is in a particular or suitable relationship to another: *The designs in that rug are well-proportioned.* <Old French, from Latin *pro portione* in relation to the part>

pro·por·tion·al (prə pôr′shə nəl) *adj* corresponding in size or amount to another thing: *The increase in price is proportional to the increase in production costs.* **pro·por′tion·al·ly** *adv.*

proportional representation *n* an electoral system in which the number of seats that each party is given is proportional to its share of the total number of votes cast.

pro·por·tion·ate (prə pôr′shə nit) *adj* corresponding in size or amount to another thing. **pro·por′tion·ate·ly** *adj.*

pro·pos·al (prə pō′zəl) *n* **1** a plan or suggestion to others, especially a formal or written one: *The club welcomed the member's proposal.* **2** the act of proposing something. **3** an offer of marriage.

pro·pose (prə pōz′) *v* **pro·posed, pro·pos·ing** **1** put forward for consideration or discussion: *I propose that we take turns at the swing.* **2** present the name of someone for membership or an elected office. **3** present as a toast to be drunk. **4** intend or plan: *She proposes to save half of all she earns.* **5** make an offer of marriage. <Old French, from Latin *pro-* forward + *ponere* to put>

prop·o·si·tion (prop′ə zish′ən) *n* **1** an offer to be considered: *The tailor made a proposition to buy out his rival's business.* **2** a statement that expresses a judgment or opinion: *He disagreed with the proposition that rich people pay too much tax.* **3** a suggestion or enterprise considered in terms of whether it is pleasing or likely to be successful: *an attractive proposition, a paying proposition.* **4** *Informal* an offer of sexual intercourse, especially an unwelcome one.
v Informal propose a scheme to someone, especially an unwelcome offer of sexual intercourse.

pro·pound (prə pound′) *v* put forward an idea, theory, or point of view for consideration. <Latin *pro-* forward + *ponere* put> **pro·pound′er** *n.*

pro·pri·e·tar·y (prə prī′ə ter′ē) *adj* **1** to do with an owner or ownership. **2** behaving as if one owns something: *My little brother has a proprietary attitude toward our baby sister.* **3** marketed as a product that is protected by a registered trademark: *a proprietary drug.* <Old French, from Latin *proprius* one's own>

pro·pri·e·tor (prə prī′ə tər) *n* an owner, especially of a business.

pro·pri·e·tor·ship (prə prī′ə tər ship′) *n* ownership.

pro·pri·e·ty (prə prī′ə tē) *n, pl* **pro·pri·e·ties** **1** the quality or condition of conforming to accepted standards of behaviour. **2 proprieties** *pl* the accepted standards or requirements of behaviour: *She insisted on obeying all the proprieties.* <Old French, from Latin *proprius* one's own>

pro·pul·sion (prə pul′shən) *n* the action of driving forward or onward: *the propulsion of jet engines.* <See PROPEL.>

P

pro·pyl·ene (prō′pə lēn′) *Chemistry n* a colourless hydrocarbon gas obtained from propane.

pro ra·ta (prō rȧ′ta) *or* (prō rā′tə) *adj, adv* in proportion: *Test marks are usually pro rata with the amount of work done.* <Latin = according to the rate>

pro·rate (prō rāt′) *v* **pro·rat·ed, pro·rat·ing** distribute or assess proportionally: *The money was prorated according to the number of days each had worked.*

pro·rogue (prō rōg′) *v* **pro·rogued, pro·rogu·ing** discontinue the regular meetings of a lawmaking body for a time. <Latin *prorogare* defer>
pro′ro·ga′tion (prō′rə gā′shən) *n.*

pro·sa·ic (prō zā′ik) *adj* matter-of-fact or unexciting: *The new play was rather prosaic.* **pro·sa′i·cal·ly** *adv.*

pro·sce·ni·um (prō sē′nē əm) *n, pl* **pro·sce·ni·a** (-nē ə) the part of the stage in front of the curtain. <Latin, from Greek *pro-* in front of + *skene* stage>

pro·sciut·to (prō shū′tō) *n* a raw, dried Italian ham, served finely sliced. <Italian *prosciugare* dry out>

pro·scribe (prō skrīb′) *v* **pro·scribed, pro·scrib·ing** forbid as wrong or dangerous, especially by law: *They proscribed drinking on the premises.* See PRESCRIBE for confusable. <Latin *pro-* in front of + *scribere* write>
pro·scrip′tion (prō skrip′shən) *n.*

prose (prōz) *n* the ordinary form of spoken or written language that is not arranged in a poetic metre: *This writer's prose is better than her poetry.* <Old French, from Latin *prosa oratio* plain speech>

pros·e·cute (pros′ə kyūt′) *v* **pros·e·cut·ed, pros·e·cut·ing** 1 bring a case before a court of criminal law: *Reckless drivers will be prosecuted.* 2 continue with a course of action with the intention of carrying it out: *to prosecute a war.* <Latin *pro-* onward + *sequi* follow>

CONFUSABLES

Prosecute can mean "take legal action against": *The police plan to prosecute the man they caught.*

Persecute means "harass" with the idea of doing harm. *Jewish people were persecuted by the Nazis.*

pros·e·cu·tion (pros′ə kyū′shən) *n* 1 the action or process of bringing a case before a court dealing with criminal law: *The next court case was a prosecution of a robbery charge.* 2 (*with* **the**) the side that starts action against another in a court dealing with criminal law: *a witness for the prosecution.* 3 a continuation of a course of action with the intention of carrying it out: *She was intent on the prosecution of her own plan, and would not listen to me.*

pros·e·cu·tor (pros′ə kyū′tər) *n* a person, especially a public official, who conducts proceedings in a law court against people accused of crimes.

pros·e·lyte (pros′ə līt′) *n* a person who has been converted from one opinion, religion, or political party to another. <Latin, from Greek *pros-* over + *elytos* one who has arrived>

pros·e·lyt·ize (pros′ə lə tīz′) *v* **pros·e·lyt·ized, pros·e·lyt·iz·ing** convert or attempt to convert someone from one opinion, religion, or political party to another. **pros′e·lyt·iz′er** *n.*

pros·o·dy (pros′ə dē) *n* the rules and patterns of rhythm and sound used in poetry, or the theory or study of them. <Latin, from Greek *pros-* toward + *oide* song>

pros·pect (pros′pekt) *n* 1 the possibility or likelihood of something occurring: *good prospects in business.* 2 the act of looking forward or expecting: *The prospect of a vacation is pleasant.* 3 a person who is regarded as a potential customer, subscriber, or candidate: *The saleswoman had several prospects in mind.* 4 an extensive view of a landscape: *The prospect from the mountain was grand.*
v search for mineral deposits in a place, especially by means of small experimental drillings: *to prospect for gold.* <Latin *pro-* forward + *specere* to look>
in prospect, expected.

pro·spec·tive (prə spek′tiv) *adj* 1 expected or expecting to be something specific in the future: *a prospective client.* 2 likely to happen in the future: *prospective changes.* **pro·spec′tive·ly** *adv.*

pros·pec·tor (pros′pek tər) *n* a person who explores or examines a place for mineral deposits.

pro·spec·tus (prə spek′təs) *n* a printed statement describing and advertising something: *a company prospectus.* <Latin *pro-* forward + *specere* to look>

pros·per (pros′pər) *v* 1 be successful financially: *That man prospers in everything he attempts.* 2 achieve success, especially in health or strength. <Old French, from Latin *prosperus* doing well> **pros·per′i·ty** *n.* **pros′per·ous** *adj.* **pros′per·ous·ly** *adv.* **pros′per·ous·ness** *n.*

pros·tate (pros′tāt) *n* a gland surrounding the neck of the bladder in male mammals and releasing the fluid component of semen. <French, from Greek *pro-* in front + *stenai* to stand, in reference to the prostates position in front of the bladder>

pros·the·sis (pros′thə sis) *or* (pros thē′sis) *n, pl* **pros·the·ses** (-sēz′) an artificial body part, such as a leg, heart, tooth, or breast implant. <Latin, from Greek *pros-* in addition to + *tithenai* to place>

pros·ti·tute (pros′tə tyūt′) *or* (pros′tə tūt′) *n* 1 a person who accepts money to engage in sexual acts. 2 a person who misuses his or her talents in exchange for money or other rewards.
v **pros·ti·tut·ed, pros·ti·tut·ing** 1 offer oneself or another person for hire to engage in sexual acts. 2 misuse talents in exchange for money or other rewards: *He has prostituted his art by selling paintings that he knows are not well done.* <Latin *prostituere* to offer for sale>
pros′ti·tu′tion *n.*

pros·trate (pros′trāt) *v* **pros·trat·ed, pros·trat·ing** 1 throw oneself flat with the face downward: *The captives prostrated themselves before the conqueror.* 2 make very weak or helpless: *Sickness can prostrate people.*
adj 1 lying flat, with the face downward. 2 helpless or powerless: *a prostrate enemy.* <Latin *pro-* before + *sternere* lay flat> **pros·tra′tion** *n.*

a bat	e bed	i bid	o pot	u cup	th **thin**
ā cake	ē me	ī bite	ō go	ū rude	TH **then**
ȧ bar	ə about	ər over	ȯ for	u̇ put	zh measure

pros·y (prō′zē) *adj* **pros·i·er, pros·i·est** commonplace or dull. **pros′i·ness** *n.*

prot·ac·tin·i·um (prō′tak tin′ē əm) *n* a rare radioactive metallic element. *Symbol* **Pa** <*proto-* + *actinium*>

pro·tag·o·nist (prō tag′ə nist) *n* **1** the main character in a play, story, or novel. **2** someone who is the main or most prominent person in a situation. <Greek *protos* first + *agonistes* actor>

pro·tect (prə tekt′) *v* **1** shield from harm or injury: *Protect the baby's eyes from the sun.* **2** aim to preserve a plant, animal, or area of land through legislation: *protected marshland.* **3** be covered by an insurance policy. **4** shield domestic industry against competition from foreign goods by taxing those that are imported into the country. <Old French, from Latin *pro-* in front + *tegere* to cover>

pro·tec·tion (prə tek′shən) *n* **1** the action of protecting someone or something: *The police officers were there for our protection.* **2** a thing that or person who prevents harm, damage, or injury: *This apron is my protection against paint splatters.* **3** coverage by an insurance policy. **4** money that businesspeople pay to criminals in exchange for a guarantee that the criminals will not use violence against those people or their property.

pro·tec·tion·ism (prə tek′shə niz′əm) *n* the economic system or theory of taxing foreign goods so that people are more likely to buy goods made in their own country. Compare FREE TRADE. **pro·tec′tion·ist** *adj, n.*

pro·tec·tive (prə tek′tiv) *adj* **1** capable of or intended to shield someone or something from harm or injury: *a protective helmet.* **2** feeling a strong desire to keep someone or something safe from harm: *He was protective about his little daughter.* **3** guarding against foreign-made goods by putting a high tax or duty on them: *a protective tariff.* **pro·tec′tive·ly** *adv.* **pro·tec′tive·ness** *n.*

pro·tec·tor (prə tek′tər) *n* **1** a person who or thing that protects. **2** in former times, a person who was in charge of a country when a king or queen could not rule.

pro·tec·tor·ate (prə tek′tə rit) *n* **1** a country under the protection and control of another, or the relationship between two such countries. **2** the position or term of a PROTECTOR (def. 2). **3** government by a PROTECTOR (def. 2).

pro·té·gé (prō′tə zhā′) *n* a male person who is guided and advised by someone older and more experienced. A female protégé is called a **protégée** (prō′tə zhā′). <French = protected>

pro·tein (prō′tēn) *or* (prō′tē in) *n* a complex organic compound that contains nitrogen and is an essential part of the cells of animals and plants. <French, from Greek *protos* first, because it is a primary component of all living organisms>

pro tem (prō′tem′) for the time being: *While he was away, I became Class Representative pro tem.* <Latin *pro tempore*>

Pro·ter·o·zo·ic (prō′ter ə zō′ik) *Geology n* the era extending from about 2500 million to 570 million years ago, during which time life (in the form of bacteria) first appeared. See also PRECAMBRIAN.
adj to do with this era or the rocks formed then. <Greek *proteros* prior + *zoe* life>

pro·test (prō′test) *for n,* (prə test′) *for v. n* **1** a statement or action that expresses strong disapproval of or objection to something: *They yielded only after much protest.* **2** an organized public demonstration against some policy or action of an authority: *There were large protests against the war.* **3** a written statement by a notary public that a bill, note, or cheque has been presented to someone who has refused to pay it or accept it.
v **1** express strong disapproval of or objection to something. **2** take part in an organized public demonstration against some policy or action of an authority: *They protested by marching with signs around the entrance.* **3** declare firmly and vigorously despite doubts or accusations from others: *The accused man protested his innocence.* <Latin *protestari*>
under protest, having stated an unwillingness: *The prisoner obeyed under protest.*

Prot·es·tant (prot′i stənt) *n* a member or follower of certain Christian churches that developed after the break with the Roman Catholic Church in the 1500s. Baptist and Presbyterian churches are Protestant churches.
adj to do with Protestants or their religion. <Latin *protestare* protest> **Prot′es·tant·ism′** *n.*

prot·es·ta·tion (prot′i stā′shən) *n* **1** a strong and vigorous declaration that something is or is not the case: *a protestation of innocence.* **2** an objection or protest.

pro·tist (prō′tist) *n* any of a KINGDOM (def. 3) of one-celled micro-organisms that live in water or moist habitats. Protozoa, algae, and slime moulds are protists. See also EUKARYOTE.

proto– *combining form* **1** first in time or importance; being the original from which others were developed or derived: *prototype.* **2** *Chemistry* being the parent form of a substance: *protoplasm.* <Greek *protos* first>

pro·to·col (prō′tə kol′) *n* **1** a first draft or record from which a document, especially a treaty, is prepared. **2** the rules of etiquette for diplomats. **3** a formal or official record of observations made during a scientific experiment. **4** *Computers* a set of standards that allow different computers or systems to communicate with each other. See also HTTP. <Old French, from Greek *protokollon* first page of a document, i.e., table of contents>

pro·ton (prō′ton) *n* a subatomic particle carrying one unit of positive electric charge, found in the nucleus of an atom. See ATOM for picture. <Greek *protos* first>

pro·to·plasm (prō′tə plaz′əm) *n* a colourless substance that makes up the living substance of a plant and animal cell. <*proto-* + Greek *plassein* mould>
pro′to·plas′mic *adj.*

pro·to·type (prō′tə tīp′) *n* the first or preliminary model of anything, especially a machine, from which other forms are developed or copied.

pro·to·zo·an (prō′tə zō′ən) *n, pl* **pro·to·zo·a** a member of a grouping of microscopic animals that consist of a single cell. Amoebas are protozoans. <Latin, from *proto-* + Greek *zoion* animal>

pro·tract (prō trakt′) *v* prolong: *to protract a visit from one week to two weeks.* <Latin *pro-* out + *trahere* draw>

pro·tract·ed (prō trak′tid) *adj* lasting for a long time or longer than expected: *a protracted argument.*

pro·trac·tile (prō trak′tīl) *or* (prō trak′təl) *adj* of a part of the body, capable of being lengthened or thrust outward: *The turtle has a protractile head.*

pro·trac·tion (prō trak′shən) *n* **1** the action of prolonging something, or the condition of being prolonged. **2** the action of extending a part of the body.

pro·trac·tor (prō trak′tər) *n* **1** an instrument in the form of a semicircle, for drawing or measuring angles. **2** a muscle serving to extend a part of the body.

pro·trude (prō trūd′) *or* (prə trūd′) *v* **pro·trud·ed, pro·trud·ing** thrust forth or stick out: *When she wasn't looking, he protruded his tongue. Her teeth protrude too far.* <Latin *pro-* forward + *trudere* thrust>
pro·tru′sion (prō trū′zhən) *or* (prə trū′zhən) *n.*

pro·tu·ber·ant (prō tyū′bə rənt) *or* (prō tū′bə rənt) *adj* bulging or sticking out. <Latin *pro-* forward + *tuber* lump> **pro·tu′ber·ance** *n.* **pro·tu′ber·ant·ly** *adv.*

proud (proud) *adj* **1 a** feeling pleasure or great satisfaction as a result of an achievement, quality, or possession: *a proud parent.* **b** to do with such a feeling: *a proud moment.* **2** being conscious of one's dignity: *She was too proud to cry when in pain.* **3** feeling or showing too much pleasure or satisfaction about oneself: *The man was proud and arrogant. She was too proud to share a taxi with a stranger.* **4** impressive or majestic: *the proud peak of Mount Assiniboine.* <Latin *prodesse* be useful> **proud′ly** *adv.* **proud′ness** *n.*
do someone (or **yourself**) **proud,** bring honour or credit to by one's performance or behaviour: *He did his mother proud at the recital.*

SYNONYMS

Proud often suggests being excessively pleased with oneself: *She was so proud of her paintings that she was always bragging about them.*

Egotistic means "self-centred": *Don't be so egotistic—let someone else speak for a change!*

Smug can mean "having a gloating manner": *The winner of the spelling bee had a smug look on his face.*

prove (prūv) *v* **proved, proved** or **proven, prov·ing** **1** establish as true or certain: *Can you prove his guilt in court?* **2** establish the genuineness or validity of something, especially of a will. **3** be found to be the actual fact: *This book proved interesting.* **4** try out or subject to a test: *The test pilot spent months proving the new plane.* **prov′a·ble** *adj.* **prov′a·bly** *adv.*
prove yourself, show yourself to be: *He proved himself honest.*

prov·en (prū′vən) a past participle of PROVE.

prov·e·nance (prov′ə nəns′) *n* the place of origin or earliest history of something, especially of a piece of art. <French, from Latin *pro-* forth + *venire* come>

prov·en·der (prov′ən dər) *n* food. <Old French, from Latin *prae* before + *habere* have>

prov·erb (prov′ərb) *n* a short, wise saying used for a long time by many people: *"Haste makes waste" is a well-known proverb.* <Latin *pro-* (put) forth + *verbum* word>

pro·ver·bi·al (prə vər′bē əl) *adj* **1** of, like, or expressed in a proverb: *proverbial wisdom, a proverbial saying.* **2** having become a proverb: *the proverbial stitch in time.* **3** well-known: *the proverbial loyalty of dogs.* **pro·ver′bi·al·ly** *adv.*

pro·vide (prə vīd′) *v* **pro·vid·ed, pro·vid·ing** **1** supply or make available for use: *Sheep provide us with wool.* **2** supply or arrange to supply a means of support: *to provide for old age. Parents provide for their children. Her will provided that her pets would be given every comfort.* **3** state as a condition beforehand: *Our club's rules provide that dues must be paid monthly.* **4** make adequate preparation for a possible event: *The software designers failed to provide for human error.* <Latin *providere* to provide for, from *pro-* ahead + *videre* see> **pro·vid′er** *n.*

pro·vid·ed (prə vī′did) *conj* on the condition that: *She will go provided her friends can go also.*

prov·i·dence (prov′ə dəns) *n* God's or nature's protective care.

prov·i·dent (prov′ə dənt) *adj* with or showing timely preparations for the future: *Some provident parents put aside money for their families.* **prov′i·dent·ly** *adv.*

prov·i·den·tial (prov′ə den′shəl) *adj* **1** occurring at exactly the correct time: *Your arrival is providential, since I need someone to help me move this table.* **2** to do with divine power or influence.

pro·vid·ing (prə vī′ding) *conj* provided.

prov·ince (prov′əns) *n* **1** 🍁 one of the ten main political and administrative divisions in Canada. **2** in certain other countries, a main political or administrative division. **3** an area of special knowledge, skill, interest, or responsibility: *Teaching spelling is not within the province of a college.* **4** an ancient Roman territory outside Italy, ruled by a Roman governor. **5 provinces** *pl UK* (*with* ***the***) the parts of a country at a distance from the capital or the largest cities, and generally considered to be unsophisticated: *She was accustomed to city life and did not like living in the provinces.* <Old French, from Latin *provincia*>

pro·vin·cial (prə vin′shəl) *adj* **1** 🍁 to do with a province: *provincial sales tax.* **2** *UK* (*with the*) lacking sophistication or open-mindedness: *a provincial point of view.*
n 🍁 **provincials** a contest or competition between representatives of the provinces. **pro·vin′cial·ly** *adv.*

pro·vin·cial·ism (prə vin′shə liz′əm) *n* **1** a word, expression, or way of pronunciation peculiar to a district of a country. **2** *UK* narrow-mindedness or lack of sophistication.

🍁 **provincial park** *n* a tract of land established by a provincial government as a preserve for wildlife and as a recreational area.

a bat	e bed	i bid	o pot	u cup	th **thin**
ā cake	ē me	ī bite	ō go	ū rude	ᴛʜ **then**
ä bar	ə about	ər over	ô for	ů put	zh measure

provincial parliament *n* the legislative assembly of a province.

pro·vi·sion (prə vizh′ən) *n* **1** a statement making a condition, especially in a legal document: *A provision of the lease is that the rent must be paid promptly.* **2** the action of providing or supplying something for use: *provision of essential services.* **3** care taken for the future or an arrangement made beforehand: *There is a provision for making the building larger if necessary.* **4** a supply or stock of something. **5 provisions** *pl* a supply of food and drink.
v supply with provisions.
make provision, take care for the future or make arrangements beforehand.

pro·vi·sion·al (prə vizh′ə nəl) *adj* arranged or existing for the time being: *a provisional agreement, a provisional government.* **pro·vi′sion·al·ly** *adv.*

pro·vi·so (prə vī′zō) *n, pl* **pro·vi·sos** or **pro·vi·soes** a part of a contract or other agreement that states a condition: *He was allowed back into the club with the proviso that he paid the dues he owed.*

pro·voc·a·tive (prə vok′ə tiv) *adj* causing anger, indignation, or another strong emotion: *a provocative remark.* **prov′o·ca′tion** *n.* **pro·voc′a·tive·ly** *adv.* **pro·voc′a·tive·ness** *n.*

pro·voke (prə vōk′) *v* **pro·voked, pro·vok·ing 1** make angry, indignant, or with some other strong emotion: *She provoked him by her teasing.* **2** stimulate to do something: *The speech provoked much discussion.* <Old French, from Latin *pro-* forth + *vocare* to call>

pro·vok·ing (prə vō′king) *adj* causing anger or annoyance: *The habit of being late for meals was provoking to the cook.* **provok′ing·ly** *adv.*

pro·vo·lo·ne (prō′və lō′nē) *n* a hard, sharp cheese with a smoky flavour. <Italian>

prov·ost (prov′əst) *n* a senior administrative officer, such as the head of certain colleges or churches.

The stern of a canoe is much the same shape as the **prow**, allowing easy movement forward or backwards.

prow (prou) *n* **1** the front, pointed part of a ship or boat. **2** the projecting front part of something, such as a car or building. <Old French, from Latin *pro-* in front>

prow·ess (prou′is) *n* **1** unusual skill or ability. *Her prowess as a skater was widely recognized.* **2** brave or daring acts. <Old French *prou* valiant>

prowl (proul) *v* **1** go about in a slow and stealthy way to hunt or as if to hunt for something to eat: *Wild animals prowled outside our cabin.* **2** move in a slow, stealthy way: *He got up and prowled around his room.*
n the act of prowling. <Middle English *prollen*>
on the prowl, prowling about.

prowl·er (prou′lər) *n* a person who moves in a secret and stealthy way near a place in order to commit a crime.

prox·i·mate (prok′sə mit) *adj* closest in relationship, especially as a cause of something.

prox·im·i·ty (prok sim′ə tē) *n* nearness in space, time, or relationship: *She and her cat enjoy proximity to the fire.* <French, from Latin *proximus* nearest>

prox·y (prok′sē) *n, pl* **prox·ies 1** the authority to act as a representative of another person. **2** a person authorized to act for another: *I acted as proxy for the child's godmother at the christening.* <Middle English *procuracy*>

prude (prūd) *n* a person who appears to be too easily shocked by matters relating to sex or nudity. <French, from Old French *prode femme* respectable woman> **prud′ish** *adj.* **prud′ish·ness** *n.*

pru·dent (prū′dənt) *adj* showing or acting with care concerning what may happen in the future: *The prudent worker saved part of his wages.* <Latin *providentem* having foresight> **pru′dence** *n.* **pru′dent·ly** *adv.*

prud·er·y (prū′də rē) *n, pl* **prud·er·ies 1** a condition or quality of appearing to be too easily shocked by matters relating to sex or nudity. **2** a prudish act or remark.

prune[1] (prūn) *n* a dried, sweet plum. <Old French, from Greek *proumnon*>

prune[2] (prūn) *v* **pruned, prun·ing 1** cut out useless or undesirable parts from: *The editor pruned the needless words from the writer's manuscript.* **2** cut superfluous or undesirable twigs or branches from a bush, shrub, or tree. <Old French *proignier* to clip, from Latin *propago* a cutting>

pruning hook *n* an implement with a hooked blade, used for pruning.

pru·ri·ent (prū′rē ənt) *adj* with too much interest in sexual matters. <Latin *prurire* be lustful> **pru′ri·ence** *n.* **pru′ri·ent·ly** *adv.*

pry[1] (prī) *v* **pried, pry·ing** enquire too much into others' activities: *She likes to pry into her friend's business.* <Middle English *prien*>

pry[2] (prī) *v* **pried, pry·ing 1** move or separate one thing from another by using force: *Pry up that stone with your pickaxe.* **2** obtain with much effort: *We finally pried the secret out of him.* <origin unknown>

pry·ing (prī′ing) *adj* too inquisitive about others' activities.

ps parsec(s)

PS postscript.

psalm (som) *or* (säm) *n* a sacred song or hymn. <Latin *psalmus,* from Greek *psalm* a song accompanied on the harp>

psalm·ist (som′ist) *or* (sä′mist) *n* the author of a psalm or psalms.

pseu·do (sū′dō) *Informal adj* false or pretended. <Greek *pseudos* falsehood>

pseudo– *combining form* false or pretended: *pseudonym.*

pseu·do·nym (sū′də nim′) *n* a name used by an author instead of his or her real name: *Mark Twain is a pseudonym for Samuel Langhorne Clemens.* <*pseudo-* false + Greek *onyma* name>

pshaw (sho) *Archaic or Humorous interj* an exclamation of scorn or impatience.

psit·ta·co·sis (sit′ə kō′sis) *n* a contagious disease of parrots and other birds, communicable to people. <Latin, from Greek *psittakos* parrot>

psych (sīk) *Informal v* mentally prepare for a demanding task or situation: *Are you psyched for the interview?*
n psychology as an academic subject: *She majored in clinical psych.* <*psych*(*oanalyze*)>
psych out, *Informal* lose or cause to lose one's nerve or calmness: *He was psyched out by his opponent's fixed stare.*
psych up, *Informal* mentally prepare for a demanding task or occasion: *I like when they visit, but I have to psych myself up for it.*

psy·che (sī′kē) *n* the human soul, mind, or spirit. <Latin, from Greek *psyche* mind>

psy·che·del·ic (sī′kə del′ik) *adj* **1** to do with drugs that produce hallucinations, heightened awareness, or other changes of consciousness. **2** suggesting or imitating the intense colours, patterns, or sounds experienced with psychedelic drugs: *psychedelic pink, psychedelic music.* <*psyche* mind + Greek *delos* clear>

psy·chi·at·ric (sī′kē at′rik) *adj* to do with the treatment of mental diseases.

psy·chi·a·try (sī kī′ə trē) *n* the study and treatment of mental disorders. <*psyche* mind + Greek *iatreia* healer> **psy′chi·at′ric** *adj.* **psy·chi′a·trist** *n.*

psy·chic (sī′kik) *adj* **1** to do with the soul or mind: *psychic distress.* **2** outside the known laws of nature: *psychic gifts.*
n a person supposed to be specially sensitive or responsive to psychic forces: *The psychic we consulted used a crystal ball.* <Greek *psyche* mind>

psy·cho (sī′kō) *Informal n, adj* psychopath(ic) or psychotic.

psycho– *combining form* to do with the mind or with psychology: *psychobabble.* <Greek *psyche* mind>

psy·cho·a·nal·y·sis (sī′kō ə nal′ə sis) *n* a system of psychological theory and therapy that aims to treat mental disorders by determining how unconscious and conscious forces in the mind interact. **psy′cho·an′a·lyst** *n.* **psy′cho·an′a·lyze** or **psy′cho·an′a·lyse** *v.*

psy·cho·bab·ble (sī′kō ba bəl) *n* talk or writing that uses the jargon from psychology or psychiatry in a loose or superficial way.

psy·cho·log·i·cal (sī′kə loj′ə kəl) *adj* **1** to do with the mind. **2** to do with psychology or psychologists. **psy′cho·log′i·cal·ly** *adv.*

psychological warfare *n* systematic efforts to reduce the morale or loyalty of an opponent, especially in war.

psy·chol·o·gy (sī kol′ə jē) *n, pl* **psy·chol·o·gies** **1** the study of the mind and its functions, especially as they affect human behaviour. **2** the mental characteristics or factors of a person, group, or activity: *crowd psychology.* <Latin, from Greek *psyche* mind> **psy·chol′o·gist** *n.*

psy·chom·e·try (sī kom′ə trē) *n* the supposed ability to deduce facts about the history of an object or about its owner by touching or being near the object.

psy·cho·mo·tor (sī ko mō′tər) *adj* to do with the mental processes that control muscular activity.

psy·cho·path (sī′kə path′) *n* a person who is affected by a severe mental disorder that leads to extremely abnormal or violent behaviour. **psy′cho·path′ic** *adj.*

psy·cho·sis (sī kō′sis) *n, pl* **psy·cho·ses** (-sēz) a severe mental disorder in which thought and emotions are so impaired that contact is lost with people and events. <Greek *psyche* mind> **psy·chot′ic** (sī kot′ik) *adj, n.*

psy·cho·so·mat·ic (sī′kō sə mat′ik) *adj* to do with physical disorders caused or worsened by a mental factor such as conflict or stress.

psy·cho·ther·a·py (sī′kō ther′ə pē) *n* the treatment of mental disorders by psychological therapy. **psy′cho·ther′a·pist** *n.*

psy·cho·tro·pic (sī kō trop′ik) *adj* acting on a mental state by means of a drug. <*psycho-* + Greek *trope* change>

PTA or **P.T.A.** Parent-Teacher Association.

ptar·mi·gan (tär′mə gən) *n, pl* **ptar·mi·gans** or (*especially collectively*) **ptar·mi·gan** a grouse that has feathered feet and is found in mountainous and cold regions. <Gaelic *tarmachan*>

pter·o·dac·tyl (ter′ə dak′təl) *n* an extinct flying reptile that had wings resembling those of a bat. <Latin, from Greek *pteron* wing + *daktylos* finger>

PTO please turn (the page) over.

Ptol·e·ma·ic (tol′ə mā′ik) *adj* **1** to do with the astronomer Ptolemy, who lived in the second century CE. The **Ptolemaic system** claimed that the earth was the fixed centre of the universe, around which the stars and planets moved. **2** to do with the Ptolemies, who were rulers of ancient Egypt.

pto·maine (tō′mān) *n* a compound of unpleasant taste and smell produced in decaying animal and vegetable matter. <French, from Greek *ptoma* corpse>

pub (pub) *n* a tavern. <*public house*>

pu·ber·ty (pyū′bər tē) *n* the period during which human beings become sexually mature, usually in the early teenage years. <Latin *puber* adult>

pu·be·scent (pyū be′sənt) *adj* approaching or experiencing puberty. <Latin *pubescere* reaching puberty>

pu·bic (pyū′bik) *adj* to do with the **pubes**, the lower part of the abdomen: *pubic hair.*

pub·lic (pub′lik) *adj* **1** to do with people as a group: *public affairs, public buildings.* **2** open to or serving all people: *a public park, public meetings.* **3** to do with serving or dealing with people: *a public official.* **4** known to many or all: *The fact became public.*
n **1** people in general: *The building is open to the public. The public is not likely to accept more restraints.* **2** a particular group of people sharing an interest or connection: *the reading public.* <Old French, from Latin *populus* people and *pubes* adult>
go public, **a** let people know information that was previously private or secret. **b** issue shares for sale to the public, so as to become a public company.
in public, not in private or secretly.

a bat	e bed	i bid	o pot	u cup	th **thin**
ā cake	ē me	ī bite	ō go	ū rude	ᴛʜ **then**
ä bar	ə about	ər over	ȯ for	ů put	zh measure

public address system *n* an arrangement of microphones, amplifiers, and loudspeakers used to spread music or messages in a building or at an outdoor gathering. *Abbrev.* **PA**

pub·li·ca·tion (pub′lə kā′shən) *n* **1** a book, newspaper, or magazine: *This magazine is a weekly publication.* **2** the preparation and issuing of books, newspapers, magazines, and sheet music. **3** the action of making something generally known: *This information is top secret and is not for publication.*

public company *n* a company owned by shareholders whose shares can be freely traded on a stock exchange.

public domain *n* the state of being available for use with no COPYRIGHT or other legal restrictions, especially as applied to written and musical works: *She could quote as much as she wanted from that book because it was now in the public domain.*

public enemy *n* one who is a menace to the public.

public health *n* a government department that deals with health issues affecting the general population or large numbers of people.

public housing *n* housing subsidized and maintained by a government, for people of low income.

pub·li·cist (pub′lə sist) *n* a person responsible for publicizing a product, service, person, or company.

pub·lic·i·ty (pub lis′ə tē) *n* **1** the act or fact of being brought to public notice through advertising. **2** the advertising methods used for getting public notice: *a publicity campaign.* **pub′li·cize′** (pub′lə sīz′) *v.*

pub·lic·ly (pub′li klē) *adv* **1** in a public manner: *to apologize publicly.* **2** by the public: *This statue was publicly funded.*

public opinion *n* the prevalent opinion of the people in a country or community: *a survey of public opinion.*

public relations *n* the professional management and maintenance of a favourable public image by a company, organization, or famous person, or by a firm hired to do so. *Abbrev.* **PR** or **P.R.**

public school *n* **1** *Canada, US* a school maintained by taxes paid by the public. **2** *UK* a private school, especially a boarding school.

public sector *n* business and industry under direct control of the government.

public servant *n* a person who works in a department or branch of the government.

public service *n* **1** civil service. **2** a service done for the benefit of the community: *The local library runs a drop-in centre as a public service.*

public speaking *n* the art of making a speech in front of an audience.

pub·lic–spir·it·ed (pub′lik spir′ə tid) *adj* with or showing an unselfish desire for the public good.

public television *n* a TV channel whose programming is paid for by donations and public funds rather than advertising, featuring educational programs and quality entertainment.

public utility *n* a company formed or chartered to render services to the public, such as a company furnishing electricity or gas, a railway, or a streetcar or bus line.

public works *n* things built by the government at public expense and for public use, such as roads, bridges, docks, canals, and waterworks, or the government department that oversees this activity.

pub·lish (pub′lish) *v* **1** prepare, issue, and distribute a printed or electronic work. **2** formally read or announce something. <Old French, from Latin *publicus* public> **pub′lish·a·ble** *adj.*

pub·lish·er (pub′lish ər) *n* a person or company whose business is to publish printed or electronic works.

puce (pyūs) *adj* purplish brown. <French *couleur puce* flea colour, from Latin *pulex* flea>

puck (puk) *n* a hard, black, rubber disc used in the game of hockey. <origin uncertain>

puck–car·ri·er (puk′kar′ē ər) *or* (puk′ker′ē ər) *n* the hockey player in possession of the puck.

puck·er (puk′ər) *v* draw into wrinkles or irregular folds: *to pucker your brow. The baby's lips puckered just before he began to cry.*
n an irregular fold or wrinkle: *There are puckers at the back of this ill-fitting coat.* <probably *poke*[2] and *pocket*>

pud·ding (pu̇d′ing) *n* **1** a soft, cooked food, usually sweet: *Rice pudding is nourishing.* **2** a cakelike dessert, usually steamed or baked: *plum pudding.* <origin uncertain>

pud·dle (pud′əl) *n* **1** a small pool of water, especially dirty water: *a puddle of rainwater.* **2** a small pool of any liquid: *a puddle of ink.*
v **pud·dled, pud·dling** **1** make wet or muddy. **2** form a small pool. <Old English *pudd* ditch>

pud·dly (pud′lē) *adj* full of puddles or like a puddle.

pudg·y (puj′ē) *adj* **pudg·i·er, pudg·i·est** short and fat or thick: *a pudgy hand, a pudgy puppy.* <origin uncertain> **pudg′i·ness** *n.*

pueb·lo (pweb′lō) *n* **1** a communal dwelling of some Native American peoples of the southwest US, consisting of joined, flat-roofed houses of adobe or stone, or an individual house built in this style. **2** a town or village in Spain, Latin America, or the southwest US. <Spanish = people, from Latin *populus*>

pu·er·ile (pyū′rīl) *or* (pyu̇′rəl) *adj* foolish for a grown person to say or do: *Hiding one of my sneakers was a puerile trick.* <Latin *puer* child>

puff (puf) *v* **1** move with short, quick bursts: *The bellows puffed on the fire. The engine puffed out of the station. Smoke puffed out of the chimney.* **2** breathe with repeated short gasps: *She puffed as she climbed the stairs.* **3** smoke: *to puff a cigar.* **4** cause to swell or become swollen: *He puffed out his cheeks.* **5** praise in an exaggerated way: *They puffed him to the skies.*
n **1** a short, quick burst: *a puff of wind, to blow out the candles in one puff.* **2** a small pad for putting cosmetics on the skin. **3** a light pastry with a filling such as whipped cream or jam: *a cream puff.* **4** exaggerated praise, for promotional purposes: *several puffs on the back cover of a book.* <perhaps Old English *pyf*>

puff adder *n* a large, poisonous African snake that puffs up the upper part of its body when excited.

puff·ball (puf′bol′) *n* a ball-shaped FUNGUS resembling a mushroom that, when ripe and suddenly broken, gives off a cloud of tiny spores.

puff·er (puf′ər) *n* **1** a person who or thing that puffs. **2** an INHALER (def. 1). **3** a fish capable of inflating its body for defence against predators.

puf·fin (puf′ən) *n* a seabird of the N Atlantic, with a massive, brightly coloured triangular bill. It is the provincial bird of Newfoundland and Labrador. <Middle English *poffin*>

puff pastry *n* a light, flaky, rich pastry used in making pie crusts and filled pastries.

puff·y (puf′ē) *adj* **puff·i·er, puff·i·est 1** puffed out or swollen: *Her eyes are puffy from crying.* **2** soft, rounded, and light. **3** blowing or breathing in puffs. **puff′i·ness** *n.*

pug (pug) *n* a small dog with a short, turned-up nose. <origin uncertain>

pu·gi·list (pyū′jə list) *n* a person who fights with the fists, especially a professional boxer. <Latin *pugil* boxer>

pug·na·cious (pug nā′shəs) *adj* eager or looking eager to quarrel, argue, or fight: *a pugnacious young man.* <Latin *pugnus* fist> **pug·na′cious·ly** *adv.* **pug·na′cious·ness** *n.* **pug·nac′i·ty** (pug na′sə tē) *n.*

pug nose *n* a short, turned-up nose. **pug′–nosed′** *adj.*

pu·ja (pū′jə) *Hinduism n* a ceremonial offering. <Sanskrit = worship>

puke (pyūk) *Informal v* **puked, puk·ing** vomit.
n vomit. <probably imitative>

puk·ka (puk′ə) *Informal adj* genuine; good. <Hindi, from Sanskrit *pakva*>

pul·chri·tude (pul′krə tyūd′) *or* (pul′krə tūd′) *n* physical beauty. <Latin *pulchris* beautiful>

Pu·lit·zer Prize (pủl′it sər) *or* (pyủl′it sər) *n* an annual award in the US for an outstanding achievement in American journalism, literature, or music. <J. *Pulitzer,* 19c newspaper publisher who established them>

pull (pủl) *v* **1** apply force so as to move something or someone toward oneself or the source of the force: *Pull the door open; don't push it.* **2** take hold of and tug: *He pulled at the laces, but that made the knot even tighter.* **3** move a thing or person steadily in one direction or to reach a specified point: *to pull a toboggan uphill. I pulled ahead of the others in the race.* **4** stretch or strain so as to cause an injury to a muscle or ligament: *to pull a muscle in your shoulder.* **5** cause an interest or attraction: *The free concert pulled in thousands of visitors.* **6** cancel or withdraw something or someone: *The company pulled the offensive ad. The pitcher was pulled in the seventh inning.* **7** *Informal* perform or carry through: *Don't pull any tricks.* **8** *Baseball, Golf, Cricket* strike a ball in a certain manner or direction: *He pulled the ball to the left.*
n **1** the act or effort of applying force so as to move something or someone toward oneself or the source of the force: *The girl gave a pull on the rope.* **2** a difficult climb or other effort: *It was a hard pull to get up the hill.* **3** a handle or other thing to pull by: *a curtain pull.* **4** a force that attracts or influences: *magnetic pull.* **5** a strain or injury to a muscle or ligament. **6** *Informal* influence or advantage: *He had a lot of pull in the mayor's office.* <Old English *pullian*> **pull′er** *n.*
pull down, *Informal* receive as a salary: *How much does she pull down in a year?*
pull for, *Informal* give help to: *to pull for the underdog.*
pull in, a stop; check. **b** *Informal* arrest: *She was pulled in for speeding.* **c** arrive: *He pulled in this morning.*
pull off, successfully complete.
pull out, a withdraw from a venture or undertaking. **b** leave: *The train pulled out of the station.*
pull over, steer or cause to steer a vehicle toward the curb and stop: *Pull over, I want to get something out of the trunk. The officer pulled her over for speeding.*
pull through, get through a difficult or dangerous situation.
pull together, work in harmony.
pull to pieces or **pull apart, a** separate into pieces by pulling: *to pull a toy to pieces.* **b** be severely critical of: *to pull apart an essay.*
pull up, a tear up or uproot. **b** bring or come to a halt.
pull your punches, See PUNCH.
pull yourself together, recover control of your emotions.

pull–down menu (pủl′doun′) *Computers n* a list of options that appears only when the user clicks on a word or icon. A selection is made by moving the cursor down the list with the mouse. Compare DROP-DOWN MENU.

pul·let (pủl′it) *n* a young hen, usually less than a year old. <Old French, from Latin *pullus* chicken>

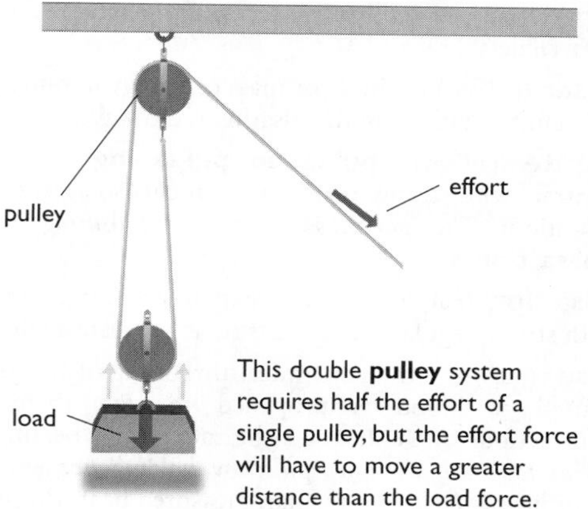

This double **pulley** system requires half the effort of a single pulley, but the effort force will have to move a greater distance than the load force.

pul·ley (pủl′ē) *n, pl* **pul·leys 1** a wheel with a grooved rim in which a rope, belt, or wire can run, making it possible to change the direction of the pull. **2** a wheel used to transfer power by driving or being driven by a belt that moves some other part of the machine. <Old French, from Greek *polos* axle>

a bat	e bed	i bid	o pot	u cup	th **thin**
ā cake	ē me	ī bite	ō go	ū rude	ᴛʜ **then**
ȧ bar	ə about	ər over	ȯ for	ủ put	zh measure

Pull·man car (pu̇l′mən) *n* a comfortable railway car with meals offered to seated passengers, and areas in which they may sleep. <G. *Pullman*, 19c inventor>

pull·out (pu̇l′out) *adj* designed to be pulled out, or opened out by pulling: *a pullout sofa, a pullout section of a magazine.*
n **1** something designed to be pulled out. **2** the act of withdrawing from some place, organization, or activity: *the pullout of troops from the war zone. With the pullout of two corporate sponsors, the event fell through.*

pull·o·ver (pu̇l′ō′vər) *n* a sweater put on by pulling it over the head.

pul·mo·nar·y (pul′mə ner′ē) *adj* to do with the lungs. <Latin *pulmo* lung>

pulp (pulp) *n* **1** the soft inner part of a fruit or vegetable. **2** a soft, moist mixture of fibrous material, such as ground-up wood, from which paper is made. **3** any soft, wet, shapeless mass of material. **4** in full, **pulp fiction** popular or sensational writing found in cheaply-produced books or magazines.
v **1** crush or reduce to a soft, shapeless mass **2** remove pulp from a fruit or vegetable. <Latin *pulpa*>

pul·pit (pu̇l′pit) *n* **1** a platform or raised structure in a church from which the priest or minister preaches. **2** (*with* ***the***) religious teaching as expressed in sermons, or by preachers as a group: *the influence of the pulpit.* <Latin *pulpitum* platform>

pulp·wood (pulp′wu̇d′) *n* wood suitable for or reduced to pulp for making paper.

pulp·y (pul′pē) *adj* **pulp·i·er, pulp·i·est** to do with PULP (*n* defs. 1, 2, and 3).

pul·sar (pul′sär) *n* a body or mass of energy in outer space that emits regular, rapid, pulsating radio waves.

pul·sate (pul′sāt) *v* **pul·sat·ed, pul·sat·ing** expand and contract with strong, regular movements so as to create a vibration: *The patient's heart was pulsating rapidly.* **pul·sa′tion** *n.*

pul·sa·tion (pul sā′shən) *n* an expansion and contraction with strong regular movements so as to create a vibration.

pulse[1] (puls) *n* **1** the rhythmical throbbing of the arteries caused as blood is propelled through them after contractions of the heart. **2** the rate of this beating: *The nurse took the woman's pulse by holding her wrist and counting the beats.* **3** a regular, measured beat: *the pulse in music, the pulse of an engine.* **4** a general attitude, feeling, or sentiment: *the pulse of the nation.*
v **pulsed, puls·ing** throb rhythmically: *Her heart pulsed with excitement.* <Latin *pellere* beat>

pulse[2] (puls) *n* the edible seeds of leguminous plants such as peas and beans. <Old French, from Latin *puls* porridge>

pul·ver·ize (pul′və rīz′) *v* **pul·ver·ized, pul·ver·iz·ing** **1** reduce to powder, dust, or fine pieces. **2** defeat completely: *We pulverized the opposition.* <Latin *pulvis* dust>

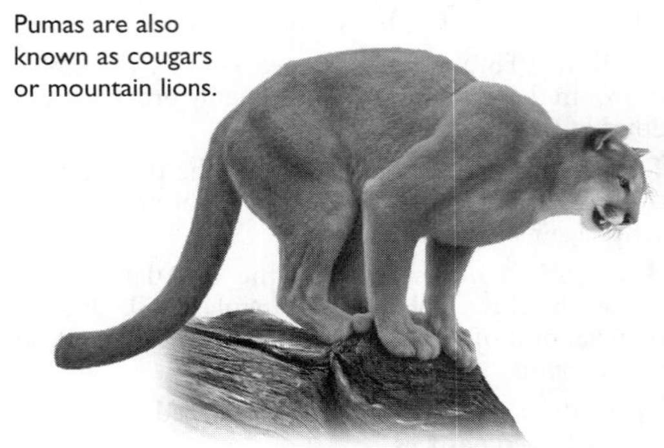
Pumas are also known as cougars or mountain lions.

pu·ma (pyū′mə) *n* a large, wild cat of the Americas with a sandy-coloured coat. <Spanish, from Quechua (a language of S America)>

pum·ice (pum′is) *n* a light, spongy rock from a volcano, formed when froth from lava solidifies quickly. It is used for cleaning, smoothing, and polishing.
v **pum·iced, pum·ic·ing** clean, smooth, or polish with pumice. <Old French, from Latin *pumex*>

pum·mel (pum′əl) *v* **pum·melled** or **pum·meled, pum·mel·ling** or **pum·mel·ing** beat repeatedly with the fists. Also, **pommel**. <Old French, from Latin *pomum* fruit>

pump[1] (pump) *n* an apparatus or machine for forcing liquids or gases into or out of things: *a water pump, an oil pump.*
v **1** (*often with* ***up*** *or* ***into***) force a liquid or gas in a specified direction by a pump: *Pump water from the well into a pail. Pump up the car's tires. Pump the well dry.* **2** move vigorously up and down or to and fro: *pumping legs.* **3** move something vigorously up and down as a pump handle does: *She pumped my hand.* **4** *Informal* get or try to get information out of: *Don't let him pump you.* <Middle English>
pump iron, *Informal* do weightlifting exercises.
pump up, a intensify or strengthen: *The party decided they needed to pump up their campaign.* **b** rouse to enthusiasm: *Her little pep talk really pumped up the team.*

pump[2] (pump) *n* a low-cut shoe with no laces, straps, or other fastenings. <origin uncertain>

pumped (pumpt) *Informal adj* stimulated or filled with excitement or enthusiasm.

pump·er (pump′ər) *n* a firetruck equipped with hoses and a water tank to pump water at the site of a fire.

pum·per·nick·el (pum′pər nik′əl) *n* a slightly sour bread made of coarsely ground rye flour. <origin uncertain>

pump·kin (pump′kin) *n* a large, roundish, orange-yellow fruit of a trailing vine, used for making pies, as a vegetable, and as a carved decoration for Halloween. Its seeds are edible, and are often eaten roasted. <French, from Greek *pepon* large melon>

pun (pun) *n* a use of language in which different possible meanings of the same-sounding word are employed for a humorous or witty effect. Example: *Humpty Dumpty had a great fall, but his winter was rough.*
v **punned, pun·ning** make puns. <origin uncertain>

punch[1] (punch) *v* **1** hit with the fist: *They punched each other like boxers.* **2** herd or drive cattle: *He punched cows for a living.*
n **1** a blow with the fist. **2** *Informal* vigorous force or effectiveness: *This story lacks punch.* <variant of *pounce*> **punch′er** *n.*
beat to the punch, *Informal* be quicker than someone in doing something.
pack a punch, *Informal* be forcefully effective.
pull your punches, *Informal* hold back, especially to spare your opponent.
punch in (or **out**), **a** in some workplaces, record your time of arrival (or departure) by means of a time clock. **b** input (or output) data using a keyboard: *What do I do after I've punched in the price code?*
punch up, a use a keyboard to bring up data on a computer screen: *He punched up the latest sales figures. Informal* **b** make more lively, exciting, or intense: *The plot of your story is good, but you need to punch up the dialogue.*

punch[2] (punch) *n* a tool or device for piercing, perforating, or stamping material, especially making a hole.
v pierce, cut, stamp, force, or drive with a punch, especially to make a hole: *The train conductor punched our tickets.* <Old French, from Latin *pungere* to prick> **punch′er** *n.*

punch[3] (punch) *n* a drink made of different liquors and juices mixed together. <Hindi, from Sanskrit *pana* five, from the number of ingredients>

Punch (punch) *n* a hook-nosed doll who quarrels violently with his wife Judy in the puppet show *Punch and Judy.*
pleased (or **proud**) **as Punch,** very much pleased.

punch–drunk (punch′drunk′) *adj* bewildered or dazed as a result of repeated blows to the head, or behaving in this way.

punching bag *n* a leather bag filled with air or stuffed, to be hung up and punched with the fists for exercise, especially by a boxer.

punch·line (punch′līn′) *n* a final phrase or sentence that gives the point of a joke or story.

punch·y (punch′ē) *Informal adj* **punch·i·er, punch·i·est** **1** attention-getting or making a strong impression: *That's a punchy title.* **2** punch-drunk.

punc·til·i·ous (pungk til′ē əs) *adj* **1** very careful and exact about details: *The nurse was punctilious in obeying the doctor's orders.* **2** paying strict attention to details of conduct and ceremony. <Italian *punctilio* a small detail, from Latin *punctus* point> **punc·til′i·ous·ly** *adv.*

punc·tu·al (pungk′chū əl) *adj* happening or doing something at the agreed or proper time: *She is punctual to the minute.* <Latin *punctum* a point> **punc′tu·al′i·ty** *n.* **punc′tu·al·ly** *adv.*

punc·tu·ate (pungk′chů āt′) *v* **punc·tu·at·ed, punc·tu·at·ing** **1** use periods, commas, and other marks in writing or printing to help make the meaning clear. **2** occur at intervals throughout a continuing event or a place: *a speech punctuated with cheers. She punctuated her remarks with gestures.* <Latin *punctum* a point>

punc·tu·a·tion (pungk′chů ā′shən) *n* **1** the use of periods, commas, etc. to help make the meaning clear. **2** a punctuation mark.

punctuation mark *n* a symbol used in writing or printing to help make the meaning clear. Periods, commas, question marks, colons, semicolons, quotation marks, and exclamation marks are punctuation marks.

punc·ture (pungk′chər) *n* a hole, especially a small one, made by something pointed.
v **punc·tured, punc·tur·ing** **1** make such a hole in. **2** have or get a puncture. **3** reduce, collapse, or deflate as if by a puncture: *A sharp voice punctured my dreams.* <Latin *pungere* to prick>

pun·dit (pun′dit) *n* a learned person, expert, or authority on something. <Sanskrit *pandita* learned>

pun·gent (pun′jənt) *adj* **1** sharply and strongly affecting the organs of taste or smell: *a pungent pickle, the pungent smell of burning leaves.* **2** sharp and biting in quality: *pungent criticism, a pungent wit.* <Latin *pungere* to prick> **pun′gen·cy** *n.* **pun′gent·ly** *adv.*

Pu·nic (pyů′nik) *adj* to do with ancient Carthage.

pun·ish (pun′ish) *v* **1** cause a person pain, loss, or discomfort for some fault or offence: *He was punished with a heavy fine for being cruel to animals.* **2** cause pain, loss, or discomfort for: *The law punishes crimes.* **3** *Informal* deal with severely or harshly. <Old French, from Latin *poena* penalty> **pun′ish·a·ble** *adj.* **pun′ish·er** *n.*

pun·ish·ment (pun′i shmənt) *n* **1** the act or fact of punishing. **2** pain, suffering, or loss. **3** *Informal* severe or rough treatment.

pu·ni·tive (pyů′nə tiv) *adj* **1** concerned with, intending, or inflicting, punishment: *a punitive military expedition.* **2** extremely high in amount of money: *the punitive cost of housing in big cities.*

punk[1] (pungk) *n* a substance, especially soft, crumbly wood, that burns very slowly and is used for lighting fires or fireworks. <origin uncertain>

punk[2] (pungk) *Informal n* **1** a worthless person. **2** a criminal or a petty gangster. **3** in full, **punk rock** a form of rock music originating in the 1970s and often expressing anger and discontent, or the styles of clothing, makeup, and hair associated with it.
adj **1** poor or bad in quality. **2** to do with punk rock. <perhaps *punk*[1] = something rotten>

pun·ster (pun′stər) *n* a person fond of making puns.

punt[1] (punt) *v* kick a football before it touches the ground after being dropped from a holder's hands.
n such a kick: *The punt went over the goal line.* <origin uncertain> **punt′er** *n.*

punt[2] (punt) *n* a shallow, flat-bottomed boat with square ends, usually moved by pushing with a pole against the bottom of a body of water.
v **1** propel a boat by pushing with a pole against the bottom of a body of water. **2** use or travel by a punt: *We loved to punt on the river.* <Latin *ponto*> **punt′er** *n.*

a bat	e bed	i bid	o pot	u cup	th **thin**
ā cake	ē me	ī bite	ō go	ū rude	ᴛʜ **then**
ä bar	ə about	ər over	ȯ for	ů put	zh measure

pu·ny (pyū′nē) *adj* **pu·ni·er, pu·ni·est** of less than usual size, strength, amount, or quality. <Old French, from Latin *postea* born later, younger> **pu′ni·ness** *n.*

pup (pup) *n* **1** a young dog or puppy. **2** a young fox, wolf, or seal. **3** a silly, conceited or arrogant young man. <*puppy*>

pu·pa (pyū′pə) *n, pl* **pu·pas** or **pu·pae** (pyū′pē) a stage between the larva and the adult in the development of many insects. **2** the form of an insect in this stage. <Latin = doll> **pu′pal** *adj.*

pu·pate (pyū pāt′) *Zoology v* **pu·pat·ed, pu·pat·ing** pass through the pupal stage: *Some moths pupate underground.*

pu·pil[1] (pyū′pəl) *n* a person who is learning in school or being taught by someone. <Old French, from Latin *pupus* boy and *pupa* girl>

pu·pil[2] (pyū′pəl) *n* the opening in the centre of the iris of the eye where the light enters. The pupil expands and contracts, thus controlling the amount of light that strikes the retina. See EYEBALL for picture.

ETYMOLOGY

Pupil comes from Latin *pupilla*, meaning "little doll," from the tiny reflection of oneself as seen when looking in another person's eyes.

pup·pet (pup′it) *n* **1** a figure made to look like a person or animal and moved by wires, strings, or the hands. **2** a person who, or a group or country, that is told what do and how to behave by another. <Old French, from Latin *pupa* doll> **pup′pet·like′** *adj.*

pup·pe·teer (pup′ə tēr′) *n* a person who designs or makes puppets or who manipulates puppets in puppet shows.

pup·pet·ry (pup′i trē) *n* the art of making and manipulating puppets.

pup·py (pup′ē) *n, pl* **pup·pies** a pup.

puppy love *n* sentimental love that may exist briefly between young people.

pup tent *n* a small, light, two-person tent, especially one in an A-shape.

pur·blind (pər′blīnd′) *adj* **1** nearly blind. **2** slow to discern or understand. <Middle English *pur blind* totally blind> **pur′blind′ness** *n.*

pur·chase (pər′chəs) *v* **pur·chased, pur·chas·ing** **1** obtain by paying a price: *We purchased a new car.* **2** get in return for something: *to purchase safety at the cost of happiness.*
n **1** the act of buying: *the purchase of a new car.* **2** the thing bought: *That coat was a good purchase.* **3** a firm hold to help move something or to keep from slipping: *Wind the rope twice around the tree to get a better purchase.* <Old French, from Latin *pro-* forth + *capere* take> **pur′chas·a·ble** *adj.* **pur′chas·er** *n.*

pur·dah (pər′də) *n* among some Hindus and Muslims, the practice of placing women in separate living quarters or behind a curtain, or wearing clothes covering the body, in order to remain out of the sight of men or strangers. <Hindi, from Persian *parda* curtain>

pure (pyūr) *adj* **pur·er, pur·est** **1** not mixed with another substance or material: *pure gold.* **2** without defects or contaminants: *a pure singing voice, pure water.* **3** nothing else than: *pure accident.* **4** with no evil or sin: *a pure mind.* **5** abstract or theoretical: *pure mathematics.* Compare APPLIED. **6** keeping the same qualities or characteristics from one generation to another: *The pure wolf travels in packs.* <Old French, from Latin *purus*> **pure′ness** *n.*
pure and simple, plainly; without doubt or question.
pure as the driven snow, totally innocent; uncontaminated.

pure·bred (pyůr′bred′) *adj* being an animal or plant whose ancestors are known to have belonged to one breed and that will itself breed true to type: *purebred cows.*

pu·rée (pyů rā′) *or* (pyů′rā) *n* **1** food boiled soft and put through a sieve or blender. **2** a thick, creamy soup.
v **pu·réed, pu·rée·ing** make into a purée. <French = purified>

🍁 **pure laine** (pūr′len) *adj* to do with a Québécois whose ancestors can all be traced back to the original settlement of New France. <French = pure wool>

pure·ly (pyůr′lē) *adv* **1** in a pure manner. **2** exclusively or entirely: *She scored the goal purely by chance.*

pur·ga·tive (pər′gə tiv) *n* a medicine or other substance that empties the bowels.

pur·ga·to·ry (pər′gə tô′rē) *n, pl* **pur·ga·to·ries** **1** *Catholicism* a temporary condition or place in which, after death, the souls of sinners suffer and atone for their sins before being admitted to heaven. **2** a condition or place of temporary suffering or punishment: *Spending August with my leg in a cast was purgatory.*

purge (pərj) *v* **purged, purg·ing** **1** rid or remove an unwanted feeling, memory, or condition, typically providing a sense of relief: *By helping others, she purged her sense of guilt.* **2** remove an unwanted person or group of unwanted people: *The prime minister purged half his cabinet.* **3** clear of something undesired, such as air in a water pipe. **4** empty the bowels.
n **1** the act of removing someone or something unwanted. **2** a medicine that purges. <Old French, from Latin *purus* pure>

pu·ri·fy (pyů′rə fī′) *v* **pu·ri·fied, pu·ri·fy·ing** make or become pure: *Filters are used to purify water.* **pu′ri·fi·ca′tion** *n.* **pu′ri·fi′er** *n.*

Pu·rim (pūr′im) *Judaism n* a religious festival celebrated each year in the spring in memory of how the Jews were delivered from being massacred. <Hebrew *pur* lot>

pur·ism (pyů′riz əm) *n* an insistence on purity and correctness, especially in language and art. **pur′ist** *n.*

Pu·ri·tan (pyů′rə tən) *n* **1** a member of a group of Protestants during the 1500s and 1600s who wanted simpler forms of worship and stricter morals: *Many Puritans settled in New England.* **2** **puritan** a person who is very strict in morals and religious practice.
adj **1** to do with the Puritans. **2** **puritan** very strict in morals and religion. <Latin *purus* pure>

pu·ri·tan·i·cal (pyů′rə tan′ə kəl) *adj* very strict or too strict in morals or religious practice.

pu·ri·ty (pyů′rə tē) *n* **1** freedom from dirt or other contaminating substance: *the purity of drinking water.* **2** freedom from immorality, especially sexual immorality: *The colour white is often associated with purity.* **3** freedom from unsuitable elements: *purity of style.* <See PURE.>

purl[1] (pərl) *v* flow with rippling motions and a murmuring sound.
n a purling motion or sound. <probably imitative>

purl[2] (pərl) *v* knit with inverted stitches: *knit one, purl one.* <origin uncertain>

pur·lieu (pər′lū) *n* **1** an area near or surrounding a place. **2** one's own area or surroundings. **3** in former times, a tract of land on the border of a forest. <Old French>

pur·loin (pər loin′) *v* steal: *The stealthy thief purloined a chicken.* <Old French *purloigner* to put at a distance>

pur·ple (pər′pəl) *n* **1** purple clothing, especially as worn by emperors or monarchs to indicate high rank. **2** the scarlet official robes of a cardinal.
adj to do with the colour midway between red and blue. <Old English, from Greek *porphyra* shellfish yielding purple dye>
born to the purple, born in a royal or imperial family: *The prince was born to the purple.*

pur·plish (pər′plish) *adj* somewhat purple.

pur·port (pər pȯrt′) *for v,* (pər′pȯrt) *for n. v* appear to do or be something, especially falsely: *The document purported to be official.*
n the meaning or main idea: *The purport of her e-mail was that she had to cancel the date.* <Old French, from Latin *pro-* forth + *portare* carry>

pur·pose (pər′pəs) *n* **1** a reason for which a thing is made, done, or used: *What is the purpose of this machine? His purpose was to pass his exams.* **2** a feeling of personal resolve or determination: *a sense of purpose.* **3 purposes** a particular requirement or fact: *You can deduct those expenses for tax purposes.*
v **pur·posed, pur·pos·ing** plan, aim, or intend. <Old French *propose,* from Latin *pro-* forward + *ponere* put>
pur′pose·ful *adj.* **pur′pose·ful·ly** *adv.*
pur′pose·ful·ness *n.* **pur′pose·less** *adj.*
pur′pose·less·ly *adv.* **pur′pose·less·ness** *n.*
on purpose, with a purpose and not by accident: *He tripped me on purpose.*
to good purpose, with good results.
to little (or **no**) **purpose,** with few or no results.

pur·pose·ly (pər′pə slē) *adv* intentionally.

purr (pər) *n* a low, murmuring sound such as a cat makes when contented.
v make this sound. <imitative>

purse (pərs) *n* **1** a bag or case for carrying money, usually carried in a handbag or pocket. **2** a handbag: *She put her keys and gloves in her purse.* **3** money or resources: *The family purse cannot afford a vacation.* **4** a sum of money offered as a prize, especially in a sporting event such as boxing.
v **pursed, purs·ing** pucker or contract the lips, especially in disapproval or irritation: *She pursed her lips and frowned.* <Latin *bursa* bag, from Greek *bursa* leather>

purs·er (pər′sər) *n* an officer who keeps the accounts of a ship or aircraft, pays wages, and attends to other matters of business.

purse seine *n* a large fishing net held by two boats, one on each side of a school of fish, so that the ends can be pulled like a drawstring purse to enclose the fish.

purse strings *pln* control of expenses.

purs·lane (pər′slān) *n* a plant that has small flowers and leaves, and grows in damp or marshy places. <Old French, from Latin *portulaca*>

pur·su·ant (pər sū′ənt) *adv* (*with* ***to***) in accordance with a law, legal document, or resolution at a meeting: *pursuant to section 2 of the Charter.*

pur·sue (pər sū′) *v* **pur·sued, pur·su·ing 1** follow to catch or attack. **2** continue or proceed along a path or route: *She pursued a wise course by taking no chances.* **3** strive for or try to get: *to pursue pleasure.* **4** keep on with an activity: *She pursued the study of French for four years.* **5** continue to investigate, discuss, or explore a topic: *She decided to pursue the matter by asking questions.* <Old French, from Latin *prosequi* prosecute> **pur·su′a·ble** *adj.* **pur·su′er** *n.*

SYNONYMS

Pursue can mean "chase": *She pursued her brother in a game of tag.*

Hunt can mean "look for carefully": *He hunted everywhere for his lost keys.*

Seek means "look for": *I'm going to seek a summer job this year.*

Stalk means "pursue without being seen or heard": *The cat stalked the mouse.*

Shadow means "follow secretly" and implies following a person: *The detective shadowed the suspect for days.*

pur·suit (pər sūt′) *n* **1** the act of following or pursuing someone or something: *The dog was in hot pursuit of the cat. The pursuit of the escaped convict continued all night.* **2** an occupation or pastime: *Fishing is his favourite pursuit.*

pur·vey (pər vā′) *v* supply food or provisions, especially as a business: *The shop purveyed cold cuts and salads.* <Old French, from Latin *providere* attend to>

pur·vey·ance (pər vā′əns) *n* the action of purveying something.

pur·vey·or (pər vā′ər) *n* a person whose business is the supplying of provisions.

pur·view (pər′vyů) *n* the scope or extent of influence, concerns, thought, or experience: *Modern poetry was outside my purview.* <Old French *purvue* forseen>

pus (pus) *n* a thick, yellowish or greenish liquid formed in infected tissue of the body, containing dead white blood cells, bacteria, tissue debris, and blood serum. <Latin>

a bat	e bed	i bid	o pot	u cup	th **thin**
ā cake	ē me	ī bite	ō go	ū rude	ᴛʜ **then**
à bar	ə about	ər over	ȯ for	ů put	zh measure

push (pu̇sh) *v* **1** apply force so as to move something or someone away from oneself or away the source of the force: *Push the door; don't pull it. Push him outdoors.* **2** move forward by using force to pass people or make them move aside: *He pushed his way through the crowd.* **3** hold and apply force on something to cause it to go in front of one: *to push a shopping cart.* **4** press a part of a machine or device: *Push the button of the elevator.* **5** strive to attain something or achieve a goal: *to push a claim to a piece of land.* **6** *Informal* urge the use or sale of something: *The salespeople pushed the old merchandise to get rid of it.*
n **1** *Informal* force; energy; the power to succeed: *She has plenty of push.* **2** the act of pushing: *Give it a push.* **3** a hard effort; determined advance: *one last push.* <Old French, from Latin *pulsare*>
push around, *Informal* treat roughly or with contempt: *Don't let him push you around.*
pushed for, challenged or limited by a lack or shortage: *We're pushed for time, so I think we'll go now.*
push for, promote or advocate strongly: *to push for better working conditions.*
push it, overdo it or take an unwise risk.
push off, a move from shore: *We pushed off in the boat.* **b** *Informal* go away or depart.
push on, keep going despite difficulty or fatigue.
when push comes to shove, when the crisis comes or a problem must be faced.

push–but·ton (pu̇sh′but′ən) *adj* pushed with a small button or knob to close or open an electric circuit in a device: *a push-button telephone.*

push·cart (pu̇sh′kärt′) *n* a light cart pushed by hand.

push·er (pu̇sh′ər) *n* **1** a person who or thing that pushes. **2** *Informal* a dealer in illegal drugs.

push·o·ver (pu̇sh′ō′vər) *Informal n* **1** something very easy to do. **2** a person very easy to influence or to beat in a contest.

push–up or **push·up** (pu̇sh′up′) *n* an exercise performed in a prone position facing the floor, in which one raises then lowers the body by straightening and bending the arms while keeping the body and legs straight.

push·y (pu̇sh′ē) *adj* offensively forceful and aggressive. **push′i·ness** *n.*

pu·sil·lan·i·mous (pyū′sə lan′ə məs) *adj* showing a lack of courage or determination: *The pusillanimous bully avoided the fight.* <Latin *pusillus* little + *animus* spirit> **pu′sil·la·nim′i·ty** *n.* **pu′sil·lan′i·mous·ly** *adv.*

puss·y (pu̇s′ē) *Informal n, pl* **puss·ies** a cat. Also, **puss**.

puss·y·foot (pu̇s′ē fu̇t′) *v* **1** *Informal* move softly and cautiously to avoid being seen or heard. **2** be cautious about revealing one's opinions or committing oneself.

pussy willow *n* a small willow with silky catkins that appear before the leaves.

pus·tule (pus′chu̇l) *n* a pimple, blister, or other swelling containing pus. <Latin *pus* pus>

put (pu̇t) *v* **put, put·ting 1** cause to be in some place or location: *I put sugar in my tea. Put away your clothes.* **2** cause to be in some condition, position, or relation: *Traitors were put to death. Put your room in order.* **3** express or write: *The teacher puts things clearly.* **4** propose or submit for consideration: *I put several suggestions to him.* **5** proceed in a ship, often in a specified direction: *The ship put to sea. The ship put in to harbour.* **6** throw or cast with an overhand motion from the shoulder: *to put a shot.* **7** set or estimate a particular value: *She puts the distance at five kilometres.* **8** apply: *The doctor put her skill to good use.* **9** impose; add: *to put a tax on gasoline.*
n a throw or cast. <Old English *putung*>
put about, put a ship on the opposite tack.
put across, *Informal* **a** carry out successfully. **b** get accepted.
put aside (or **by**)**,** save for future use.
put away, a lay aside for future use: *I've always put my winter clothes away during the summer.* **b** *Informal* commit to a prison or psychiatric hospital: *The judge put him away for ten years.*
put down, a put an end to or suppress. **b** write down. **c** pay as a down payment. **d** *Informal* have a pet or other domestic animal put to death, especially to prevent excessive suffering: *We had to put our dog down after she was hit by a car.* **e** *Informal* insult or belittle.
put forth, a grow, sprout, or issue: *to put forth buds.* **b** use fully or exert: *to put forth effort.*
put forward, suggest or present for others to consider.
put in, a spend time doing: *She always puts in a good day's work.* **b** make a claim, plea, or offer: *She put in for a loan.*
put in at ——, enter the port of ——.
put off, a lay aside or postpone: *Don't put off going to the dentist.* **b** go away or start out: *The ship put off for England.* **c** *Informal* annoy or irritate: *Her bad manners put me off.*
put on, a clothe or adorn oneself with: *She put on her new hat.* **b** assume or take on, especially as a pretence: *She put on an air of innocence.* **c** add to or increase: *The driver put on speed.* **d** apply or exert: *to put on pressure.* **e** advance; move ahead: *to put the clock on.* **f** present on a stage: *The class put on a play.*
put out, a extinguish; turn off: *Put out the light.* **b** confuse, annoy, or embarrass. *I am quite put out by your rudeness.* **c** distract, disturb, or interrupt: *Am I putting you out by calling so late?* **d** *Baseball* cause a player to be out. **e** dislocate: *I put out my shoulder when I fell.* **f** publish: *to put out a magazine.*
put over, *Informal* carry out successfully.
put someone on to, tell someone about: *Who put them on to our plan?*
put someone up to something, *Informal* encourage or influence someone to do something: *Who put you up to this?*
put through, carry out successfully.
put to it, put in difficulty: *I don't want to put you to any trouble.*
put up, a offer or show: *to put up a house for sale.* **b** make or build: *to put up a monument.* **c** prepare or preserve for later use: *to put up jams and jellies.* **d** give lodging or food to: *Can you put them up for one night?* **e** make available: *He put up the money for the car.*
put up with, tolerate.
stay put, stay in the same position or place.

pu·ta·tive (pyü′tə tiv) *adj* supposed: *the putative author of a book.* <Latin *putativis* supposed, from *putare* to consider>

put–down (pu̇t′doun′) *Informal n* a comment or reply that slights, snubs, or belittles a person or thing.

put–on (pu̇t′on) *adj* pretended or insincere.
n a pretence or hoax: *Her interest in classical music is just a put-on.*

pu·tre·fy (pyü′trə fī′) *v* **pu·tre·fied, pu·tre·fy·ing** rot or decay: *The putrefying meat has a bad smell.* **pu′tre·fac′tion** *n.*

pu·tres·cent (pyü tres′ənt) *adj* becoming rotten or decayed. **pu·tres′cence** *n.*

pu·trid (pyü′trid) *adj* **1** rotting or decaying, and giving off a foul odour: *putrid meat.* **2** very unpleasant. <Latin *puter* rotten> **pu′trid·ly** *adv.* **pu′trid·ness** *n.*

putt (put) *v* strike a golf ball gently and carefully in an effort to make it roll into the hole.
n the stroke itself. <Scottish>

put·tee (put′ē) *or* (pu tē′) *n* **1** a long, narrow strip of cloth wound round the leg from ankle to knee. **2** a legging of cloth or leather reaching from ankle to knee.

put·ter[1] (put′ər) *v* keep busy in a pleasantly aimless way: *She spent the day puttering in the garden.* Also, **potter**. <variant of *potter*[2]> **put′ter·er** *n.*

putt·er[2] (put′ər) *n* **1** a person who putts. **2** a golf club used in putting.

putt·ing green (put′ing) *n* the smooth turf of a golf course outside the hazards but near the hole, where the ball may be putted.

put·ty (put′ē) *n, pl* **put·ties** a soft paste that hardens quickly and is used mainly for fastening panes of glass into window frames.
v **put·tied, put·ty·ing** stop up or cover with putty: *She puttied up the holes in the woodwork before painting it.* <French *potée* paste (originally used for polishing)>

put–up (pu̇t′up′) *Informal adj* planned beforehand or deliberately in a secret or crafty manner: *A put-up attempt to get rid of him failed.*

put–up·on (pu̇t′ə pon′) *adj* exploited unfairly or taken advantage of: *If I ask him again, he might feel put-upon.*

puz·zle (puz′əl) *n* **1** a person who or thing that is difficult to understand or explain: *How to get all my things into one trunk is a puzzle.* **2** a game, toy, or problem that gives pleasure in trying to solve: *This puzzle has seventy pieces of wood to fit together.*
v **puz·zled, puz·zling** **1** make difficult to answer, solve, or understand something: *How the cat got out puzzled us.* **2** (*with* ***over***) exercise one's mind on something difficult: *I puzzle over arithmetic every night.* <origin uncertain>
puz·zler *n.*
puzzle out, find out by thinking or trying hard: *to puzzle out the meaning of a sentence.*

puz·zled (puz′əld) *adj* unable or hard pressed to find an answer or solve a problem: *He frowned in a puzzled way.* **puz′zled·ly** *adv.* **puz′zle·ment** *n.*

PVC polyvinyl chloride.

pyg·my (pig′mē) *n, pl* **pyg·mies** **1** a very short person, animal, or thing. **2** an insignificant person, especially one who lacks a particular thing. **3** **Pygmy** a member of a short people of equatorial Africa.
adj very small. Also, **pigmy**. <Latin, from Greek *pygme* length from elbow to knuckle>

py·ja·mas or **pa·ja·mas** (pə jam′əz) *or* (pə jȧ′məz) *pl n* **1** garments for sleeping or lounging in, consisting of a loose jacket and a pair of loose pants fastened at the waist. **2** loose trousers worn in some Asian countries, tied with a drawstring around the waist. <Persian *pay* leg + *jama* garment>

py·lon (pī′lon) *n* **1** an orange plastic cone used on roads to mark an area to be avoided, or to separate lines of traffic during road construction. Also called **traffic cone**. **2** a post or tower for guiding aircraft pilots. **3** *UK* a tall steel framework used to carry high-tension wires across country. **4** either of a pair of high supporting structures marking an entrance at either end of a bridge. **5** a gateway, especially of an ancient Egyptian temple. <Greek *pyle* gate>

pyr·a·mid (pir′ə mid′) *n* **1** a solid geometrical figure with a polygonal base and triangular sides meeting at a point. **2** a thing or things with the form of a pyramid. **3** **Pyramids** *pl* the huge stone pyramids, serving as royal tombs, built by the ancient Egyptians.
v **1** be or put in the form of a pyramid. **2** achieve a substantial return based on only a small investment or speculation. <Latin, from Greek *pyramidos*>
py·ram′i·dal *adj.*

pyre (pīr) *n* a pile of combustible material such as wood on which a dead body is burned as part of a funeral rite. <Latin, from Greek *pyr* fire>

Py·rex (pī′reks′) *Trademark n* a hard, heat-resistant form of glassware.

py·ro·ma·ni·a (pī′rə mā′nē ə) *n* an uncontrollable desire to set things on fire. <Greek *pyr* fire + *-mania*>
py′ro·ma′ni·ac *n.*

py·ro·tech·nics (pī′rə tek′niks) *n* **1** (*with singular verb*) the art of making fireworks. **2** (*with plural verb*) **a** a display of fireworks. **b** any brilliant or sensational display. <Greek *pyr* fire + *-technical*> **py′ro·tech′nic** *adj.*

Pyr·rhic victory (pir′ik) *n* a victory won at too great a cost. <*Pyrrhus*, an ancient Greek king, who won a battle, but with great loss of life for his troops>

pys·chol·o·gist (sī kol′ə jist) *n* a person trained in PSYCHOLOGY (def. 1), especially one who makes it his or her work.

Py·thag·o·re·an theorem (pī thag′ə rē′ən) *or* (pə thag′ə rē′ən) *n* the geometry theorem that the square of the hypotenuse of a right triangle is equal to the sum of the squares of the other two sides. A **Pythagorean triple** is a set of three numbers such as 3, 4, 5 that result from this theorem. That is, $5^2 = 3^2 + 4^2$. <*Pythagoras*, 6c BCE Greek philosopher and mathematician>

py·thon (pī′thon) *n* a large, heavy-bodied snake that kills its prey by squeezing. <Latin, from Greek *Python* name of huge serpent killed by Apollo>

P

Qq

q or **Q** (kyū) *n, pl* **q's** or **Q's** **1** the seventeenth letter of the English alphabet, or any speech sound represented by it. **2** the seventeenth thing in a list or series: *The question had seventeen parts, going from (a) to (q).*

qag·giq (ka′gik) *n* **1** an Inuit festival marking the first sunrise of the new year and the beginning of hunting season. Traditionally, elders light soapstone lamps fuelled by seal fat, which are then extinguished and relit by children. **2** the place, which may be a structure specially built, for this festival. <Inuktitut = celebration>

Q and A or **Q & A** questions and answers.

Qa·tar (ka tar′) *n* a country on the west coast of the Persian Gulf. **Qua·tar′i** (ka tar′ē) *adj, n.*

Q.C. Queen's Counsel.

q.t. or **Q.T.** *Informal* <from abbreviation for quiet>
on the q.t., secretly.

qua (kwa) *prep* in the role of: *Qua father, he pitied the boy; qua judge, he condemned him.* <Latin, form of *qui* who>

quack[1] (kwak) *n* the sound a duck makes, or a sound similar to it.
v make the sound of a duck or one like it. <imitative>

quack[2] (kwak) *n* a person who falsely claims to have special knowledge or skill, especially a fraudulent medical doctor: *Don't pay a quack for medicine.*
adj not genuine. <obsolete *quacksalver,* from Dutch *quacken* to hawk + *salf* ointment> **quack′er·y** *n.*

quack grass COUCH GRASS.

quad[1] (kwod) *Informal n* in full, **quadriceps** the large extensor muscle at the front of the thigh.

quad[2] (kwod) *Informal n* a quadruplet.

quadr– *combining form* four; fourth: *quadruped.* <Latin *quadri* four>

quad·ran·gle (kwod′rang′gəl) *n* a four-sided space or courtyard wholly or nearly surrounded by buildings. <Latin *quadri-* four + Latin *angulus* angle>

quad·ran·gu·lar (kwod rang′gyə lər) *adj* with four corners or angles.

quad·rant (kwod′rənt) *n* **1** *Mathematics* **a** a quarter of a circle or of its circumference. **b** one of the four regions of a plane formed by two lines at right angles: *the lower left quadrant.* **2** an instrument used in former times for taking angular measurements of altitude in astronomy and navigation. <Latin *quattuor* four>

quad·ra·phon·ic (kwod′rə fon′ik) *adj* using four transmission channels to feed four separate speakers for sound reproduction. <Latin *quadri-* four + Greek *phone* sound>

quad·rat (kwod′rət) *Ecology n* a small, usually rectangular plot of land set up for a study of the distribution of plants or animals in an area. <French, from Latin *quattuor* four>

quad·rat·ic (kwod rat′ik) *Mathematics adj* involving the second and no higher power of an unknown quantity or variable. Here is an example of a **quadratic equation**: $x^2 + 3x + 2 = 12$. <French, from Latin *quattuor* four>

quad·ren·ni·al (kwod ren′ē əl) *adj* **1** occurring every four years: *a quadrennial election.* **2** of or lasting four years. <Latin *quadri-* four + *annus* year>

quad·ren·ni·al·ly (kwod ren′ē ə lē) *adv* once in four years.

quad·ri·lat·er·al (kwod′rə lat′ə rəl) *adj* with four sides and four interior angles.
n such a plane figure.

> **ETYMOLOGY**
>
> **Quadrilateral** comes from two Latin words: *quadri-*, which means "four," and *lateris*, meaning "side." Squares and trapezoids are quadrilateral figures.

qua·drille (kwə dril′) *n* a square dance for four couples that has five parts or movements, or the music for such a dance. <French, from Latin *quadrus* square>

quad·ri·ple·gia (kwod′rə plē′jə) *n* paralysis of all four limbs. <Latin *quadri-* four + Greek *plege* stroke (from *plessein* to strike)> **quad′ri·ple′gic** *adj, n.*

quad·ru·ped (kwod′rə ped′) *n* an animal, especially a cud-chewing mammal, that has four feet.
adj with four feet. <Latin *quadru-* four + *pes* foot>

quad·ru·ple (kwod′rə pəl) *or* (kwo drū′pəl) *adj* consisting of four parts.
adv four times as great.
n a thing, number, or amount four times as great as another: *The quadruple of 20 is 80.*
v **quad·ru·pled, quad·ru·pling** make or become four times as great. <French, from Latin *quadru-* four + *duo* two>

quad·ru·plet (kwo drū′plit) *or* (kwod′rə plit) *n* **1** one of four children born at the same time from the same mother. **2** a group of four musical notes to be performed in the time of three.

quad·ru·pli·cate (kwo drū′plə kit) *or* (kwod′rə plə kit) *adj, n* one, or being one, of four copies. <Latin *quadru-* four + *plicare* to fold>
in quadruplicate, in four copies: *The application must be submitted in quadruplicate.*

quaff (kwof) *or* (kwaf) *v* drink deeply and freely.
n an act of quaffing. <origin uncertain>

quag·mire (kwag′mīr′) *n* soft, muddy ground on which it is difficult to walk. <obsolete *quag* to shake + *mire*>

qua·hog (kwo′hog) *or* (kwə hog′) *n* an edible clam of the Atlantic coast of N America, with a hard, thick, rounded shell. Also, **quahaug**. <Algonquian>

quail[1] (kwāl) *n, pl* **quails** or (*especially collectively*) **quail** a small game bird resembling a partridge. See PARTRIDGE for picture. <Old French, from Latin *coacula*>

quail[2] (kwāl) *v* feel or show fear: *They quailed in face of danger.* <Middle English>

quaint (kwānt) *adj* strange or odd in an interesting, pleasing, or amusing way: *quaint customs.* <Old French cointe *pretty, pleasing,* from Latin *cognoscere* to know well> **quaint′ly** *adv.* **quaint′ness** *n.*

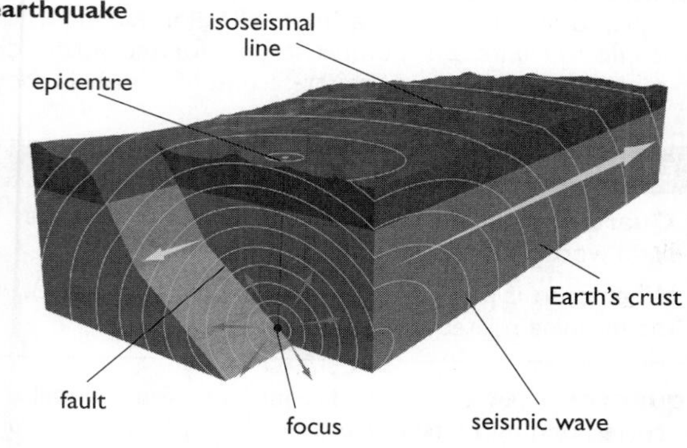

quake (kwāk) *v* **quaked, quak·ing** shake or tremble: *He quaked with fear.*
n **1** the act or fact of shaking or trembling. **2** an earthquake. <Old English *cwacian*>

Quak·er (kwā′kər) *n* a member of a Christian group, officially called the Religious Society of Friends, that rejects set forms of worship, and whose non-violent principles forbids taking part in wars. <*quake*> **Quak′er·ism** *n.*

qual·i·fi·ca·tion (kwol′ə fə kā′shən) *n* **1** a quality or accomplishment that makes a person fit or eligible for a job, task, or office: *Good eyesight is a necessary qualification for a pilot.* **2** a condition that limits, modifies, or restricts: *I enjoyed the movie with one qualification—you weren't there to enjoy it, too.* **3** a modification, limitation, or restriction: *The statement was made without any qualification.* **4** the act or fact of qualifying or being eligible for something.

qual·i·fied (kwol′ə fid′) *adj* **1** with the desirable or required qualifications: *He is fully qualified for his job.* **2** modified, limited, or restricted: *Her qualified answer was "I will go, but only if you will go with me."*

qual·i·fi·er (kwol′ə fi′ər) *n* **1** a person who or thing that qualifies. **2** a word that qualifies another word, such as an adjective or adverb.

qual·i·fy (kwol′ə fi′) *v* **qual·i·fied, qual·i·fy·ing** **1** make fit or competent, especially for a profession or activity: *to qualify herself for a job.* **2** be entitled to a benefit or privilege by fulfilling a required condition: *When my grandfather retired he qualified for a pension.* **3** be or make entitled to be classed or thought of in a particular way: *His pranks qualified him as a first-class pest.* **4** gain the right to compete in a race, contest, or tournament: *She qualified for the tennis tournament.* **5** add reservations to a statement, making it less absolute: *Qualify your statement that dogs are loyal by adding "usually."* <French, from Latin *qualificare* attribute a quality to>

qual·i·ta·tive (kwol′ə tə tiv) *or* (kwol′ə tā′tiv) *adj* concerned with quality or qualities. **qual′i·ta′tive·ly** *adv.*

qualitative analysis *n* the process of determining the chemical components in a sample of a substance.

qual·i·ty (kwol′ə tē) *n, pl* **qual·i·ties** **1** something special about an object that makes it what it is: *One quality of iron is hardness; one quality of sugar is sweetness.* **2** a distinctive characteristic: *She has excellent leadership qualities.* **3** a grade or degree of worth: *That is a poor quality of cloth.* **4** general excellence: *Look for quality rather than quantity.* **5** the distinguishing character of a speech sound.
adj excellent: *quality goods.* <Old French, from Latin *qualis* of what sort>

quality control *n* the process or system of ensuring that a manufactured product is of consistently high quality.

quality of life *n* the amount of pleasure and satisfaction experienced in everyday life, as opposed to material success.

quality time *n* time spent with another person in a direct, personal, and meaningful way.

qualm (kwom) *or* (kwåm) *n* **1** a sudden feeling of doubt, worry, or fear: *I tried the test with some qualms. She felt some qualms at missing school two days in a row.* **2** a momentary feeling of faintness or nausea. <Old English *cwealm* torment>

quan·da·ry (kwon′də rē) *or* (kwon′drē) *n, pl* **quan·da·ries** **1** a condition of being perplexed or uncertain about something: *She was in a quandary about whether to stay in school or take the job offer.* **2** a difficult situation or dilemma: *He found himself in a legal quandary.* <origin uncertain>

quan·ti·fy (kwon′tə fī) *v* **quan·ti·fied, quan·ti·fy·ing** express as a number or amount of: *to quantify the results of a survey.* <Latin *quantus* how much + *facere* make> **quan′ti·fi′a·ble** *adj.*

quan·ti·ta·tive (kwon′tə tə tiv) *or* (kwon′tə tā′tiv) *adj* concerned with measuring, or measured by a quantity. **quan′ti·ta′tive·ly** *adv.*

quantitative analysis *n* the measurement of the amounts of chemical components making up a sample of a substance.

quan·ti·ty (kwon′tə tē) *n, pl* **quan·ti·ties** **1** the amount or number of something: *Equal quantities of nuts and raisins were used in the cake.* **2** a large amount or number: *The baker buys flour in quantity. She owns quantities of books.* **3** a certain, usually specified, number or amount of something: *a large quantity of CDs.* **4** a value or component in mathematics or physics that can be expressed in numbers. **5** in speech, the length of a vowel sound or a syllable. <Latin *quantus* how much>

quan·tum (kwon′təm) *Physics n, pl* **quan·ta** (-tə) the smallest amount of energy that can exist independently, especially of electromagnetic radiation, or a unit representing it. <Latin = how much>

quantum jump *n* **1** a sudden transition of an electron, atom, or molecule from one quantum state to another, with the absorption or emission of a quantum. **2** QUANTUM LEAP.

quantum leap *n* a sudden major increase or advance: *a quantum leap in information technology.* Also called **quantum jump**.

a bat	e bed	i bid	o pot	u cup	th **thin**
ā cake	ē me	ī bite	ō go	ū rude	TH **then**
å bar	ə about	ər over	ô for	ů put	zh measure

Q

quantum mechanics *n* (*with singular verb*) the branch of physics that studies the behaviour of atoms and elementary particles, such as electrons, on the basis of **quantum theory**, which states that energy and matter can have the characteristics of both a wave and a particle.

quantum number *n* any of a set of numbers that indicate the magnitude of various quantities, such as electric charge, of a particle or system.

quar·an·tine (kwȯ′rən tēn′) *v* **quar·an·tined, quar·an·tin·ing** isolate from others, especially to prevent the spread of an infectious disease: *The people with yellow fever were quarantined.*
n the condition, period, or place of being quarantined: *Our house was in quarantine when I had scarlet fever.* <Italian, from Latin *quadraginta* forty, from the period in days of quarantine>

quark (kwȯrk) *or* (kwärk) *n* a subatomic particle that is considered to be a building block for larger particles such as protons and neutrons. <coined by M. Gell-Mann, 20c physicist>

quar·rel (kwȯ′rəl) *n* **1** an angry dispute or disagreement: *The children had a quarrel over the division of the candy.* **2** (*usually with* ***no***) a cause for a dispute or disagreement: *He said he had no quarrel with the way he was treated while in custody.*
v **quar·relled** or **quar·reled, quar·rel·ling** or **quar·rel·ing** **1** dispute or disagree angrily: *They quarrelled about whether the puck actually went in the net.* **2** disagree with something: *She quarrelled with the conclusions of the report.* <Old French, from Latin *queri* complain> **quar′rel·ler** or **quar′rel·er** *n.*

SYNONYMS

Quarrel means "brief, angry disagreement": *They had a quarrel over who should do the dishes.*

Row means "noisy quarrel": *The row in the upstairs apartment disturbed the neighbours.*

Feud means "long, often deadly, hostility": *The two gangs have carried on a feud for the last ten years.*

Argument often means "reasoned discussion between persons who have different points of view": *Each team presented its argument in the debate.*

Conflict is a general word for "fight," "struggle," or "disagreement": *The conflict between them is over.*

quar·rel·some (kwȯ′rəl səm) *adj* too ready to quarrel. **quar′rel·some·ness** *n.*

quar·ry[1] (kwȯ′rē) *n, pl* **quar·ries** a place, such as a deep pit, where stone is dug, cut, or blasted out.
v **quar·ried, quar·ry·ing** obtain from a quarry: *We watched the workers quarry a huge block of stone.* <Old French, from Latin *quadrum* square, in reference to square building stones> **quar′ri·er** *n.*

quar·ry[2] (kwȯ′rē) *n, pl* **quar·ries** **1** an animal or group of animals pursued by a hunter, dog, predatory animal, or bird of prey. **2** a thing that or person who is chased or pursued. <Old French, from Latin *coruim* leather>

quart (kwȯrt) *n* **1** a nonmetric unit for measuring liquid, equal to one quarter of an Imperial gallon (about 1.1 L): *a quart of milk.* **2** a nonmetric unit for measuring dry substances, equal to one thirty-second of a bushel (about 1.1 L): *a quart of blueberries.*

ETYMOLOGY

Quart can be traced back through Old French to the Latin word *quattuor*, which means "fourth."

When *quart* is part of a longer word (*quarter, quartet*), the meaning relates to the number four.

quar·ter (kwȯr′tər) *n* **1** one of four equal or corresponding parts: *a quarter of an apple, a quarter of a tonne.* **2** *Canada, US* a coin worth twenty-five cents. **3 a** one-fourth of an hour, fifteen minutes. **b** one-fourth of a year, three months. **4** one of the four phases of the moon: *The quarters of the moon are four periods of about seven days each.* **5** a part of a town or city with a distinctive characteristic or use: *The French quarter is on the south side of the town.* **6** a particular part of a community or group: *The theory was not accepted in other quarters.* **7** a direction of a point of the compass: *In what quarter is the wind?* **8** mercy shown to a defeated enemy who is in one's power: *The victorious knights gave no quarter.* **9** in heraldry, one of four or more parts into which a shield is divided by lines at right angles. **10** *Football, Basketball* one of four equal periods of play in a game. **11** **quarters** *pl* a place to live or stay: *servants' quarters, officers' quarters.*
v **1** divide into quarters: *She quartered the apple.* **2** give a place to live in: *Soldiers were quartered in all the houses of the town.*
adj (*usually in compounds*) being one of four equal parts: *a quarter-cup.* <Old French, from Latin *quattuor* four>
at close quarters, close together: *The two families lived at close quarters until a second apartment was found.*

quar·ter·back (kwȯr′tər bak′) *n* the player on offence in football whose position is immediately behind the centre of the line of scrimmage, and who directs the team's play in the field. See FOOTBALL for picture.

quar·ter·deck (kwȯr′tər dek′) *n* the part of the upper deck between the mainmast and the stern, used especially by the officers of a ship.

quar·ter·fi·nal (kwȯr′tər fī′ nəl) *n* the games at a late stage in a sports tournament in which eight players or teams compete, all others having been eliminated earlier: *Our team made it to the quarterfinals.*

quarter horse *n* a small, stocky horse originally bred for racing over short distances.

quar·ter–hour (kwȯr′tər our′) *n* **1** fifteen minutes. **2** the point one fourth of the way through an hour, or a point of time fifteen minutes before or after any hour.

quar·ter·ly (kwȯr′tər lē) *adj* happening, produced, or done four times a year: *to make quarterly payments on a tax bill.*
adv once each quarter of a year: *to pay membership fees quarterly.*
n, pl **quar·ter·lies** a magazine published four times a year.

quar·ter·round (kwȯr′tər round′) *n* a convex moulding, or piece of wood trim, whose cross-section is a quarter of a circle.

quarter section *n* a piece of land, usually square, containing 160 acres (about 65 hectares).

quar·ter·staff (kwȯr′tər staf′) *n, pl* **quar·ter·staves** (kwor′tər stāvz) an old English weapon consisting of a stout pole two to three metres long, tipped with iron.

quar·tet or **quar·tette** (kwȯr tet′) *n* **1** a group of four singers or instrumental players. **2** a piece of music for four voices or instruments. **3** a set of four people or things. <Italian, from Latin *quattuor* four>

quar·tile (kwor′tīl) *Statistics n* **1** any of the four equal groups into which a statistical sample can be divided. **2** any of the three values that divide a sample into four parts, each containing a quarter of the sample population.

quar·to (kwȯr′tō) *n, pl* **quar·tos** **1** the page size of a book in which each leaf is one quarter of a whole sheet of paper. **2** a book with this size, about 20 cm by 25 cm.

quartz (kwȯrts) *n* a hard mineral composed of silica that is usually colourless or white, but may be coloured by impurities, as in amethyst or jasper. <German *Quarz*>

qua·sar (kwā′sȧr) *or* (kwā′zȧr) *n* a massive celestial body, resembling a star when viewed in a telescope, that is very distant from the earth and gives off extremely large amounts of energy. <*quas*(*i*)- + (*stell*)*ar*>

quash (kwosh) *v* **1** reject as invalid: *The appeals court quashed the earlier verdict.* **2** crush or suppress: *to quash a rumour.* <Old French, from Latin *cassus* void>

quasi– *combining form* seemingly or apparently: *quasi-official.* <Latin *quasi* as if>

Qua·ter·na·ry (kwə tər′nə rē) *n* the geological period lasting from about two million years ago to the present, when the great ice shields formed, then melted, and humans appeared. See also CENOZOIC.
adj to do with this period or the rocks formed then. <Latin *quattuor* four>

quat·rain (kwot′rān) *n* a four-line stanza or poem. <French, from Latin *quattuor* four>

quat·re·foil (kat′ər foil′) *or* (kat′rə foil′) *n* **1** a leaf or flower composed of four leaflets or petals: *The four-leaf clover is a quatrefoil.* **2** an architectural ornament with four lobes or leaves. <Old French, from Latin *quattuor* four + *folium* leaf>

qua·ver (kwā′vər) *v* shake or tremble in speaking or singing: *The man's voice quavered from nervousness.*
n a shaking or trembling of the voice. <Middle English *quave* shake> **qua′ver·ing·ly** *adv.* **qua′ver·y** *adj.*

quay (kē) *n* a solid landing place built of stone or metal where ships load and unload.

ETYMOLOGY

Quay and *key*[2] have different spellings, but they sound the same and share the same history. Both come from Celtic through Old French *kai* and Middle English *key* or *keye*. The Florida Keys is a familiar example of the *key* spelling.

quea·sy (kwē′zē) *adj* **quea·si·er, quea·si·est** **1** inclined to nausea: *a queasy stomach.* **2** uneasy or nervous about something. <Middle English> **quea′si·ly** *adv.* **quea′si·ness** *n.*

Qué·bec (kwi bek′) *or* (kā bek′) *n* a central Canadian province, just east of Ontario. Québec is one of the CENTRAL PROVINCES. *Abbrev.* **Que.**; postal symbol **QC**; URL **www.gov.qc.ca**
adj to do with Québec: *Québec tourism.*

Qué·beck·er (kwi bek′ər) *or* (kā bek′ər) *n* a person living in or from the province of Québec.

Qué·béc·ois (kā bā kwȧ′) *n, pl* **Qué·béc·ois** a male person living in or from the province of Québec, especially a French-speaking one. <French>

Qué·béc·oise (kā bā kwȧz′) *n, pl* **Qué·béc·oises** a female person living in or from the province of Québec, especially a French-speaking one. <French>

Quech·ua (kech′wə) *n, pl* **Quech·ua** or **Quech·uas** **1** a member of a group of Aboriginal peoples of the Andes. **2** the language of these peoples. **Quech′uan** *adj.*

queen (kwēn) *n* **1 a** the female ruler of a country: *Elizabeth the First was Queen of England.* **b** the wife of a king. **2** a woman, or some object considered to be feminine, judged to be first or best in importance or another quality: *a beauty queen. The rose is the queen of flowers.* **3** a female animal that lays eggs, such as in a colony of bees, ants, or termites. **4** in chess, the piece that can move in any straight or diagonal row. **5** a playing card bearing a picture of a queen. <Old English *cwen*>
queen′like′ *adj.*

queen bee *n* **1** a fertile female bee, usually the only one in a hive. See BEE for picture. **2** a woman in a prominent or controlling position.

queen consort *n* the wife of a reigning king.

GRAMMAR AND USAGE

The husband of a reigning queen is given the title Prince or Prince Consort, never King or King Consort.

queen·ly (kwēn′lē) *adj* **queen·li·er, queen·li·est** to do with a queen.
adv in a queenly manner or as a queen behaves. **queen′li·ness** *n.*

queen mother *n* the widow of a former king and mother of a reigning king or queen.

✱ **Queen's Counsel** *n* a lawyer appointed by the Attorney General to an honorary position in recognition of experience.

Queen's English *n* the English that is recognized as correct and standard in the UK.

Queen's evidence *n* testimony given in court by a criminal against his or her associates in a crime.

Q

a bat	e bed	i bid	o pot	u cup	th **thin**
ā cake	ē me	ī bite	ō go	ū rude	ᴛʜ **then**
ȧ bar	ə about	ər over	ȯ for	u̇ put	zh measure

Queen's Highway *n* a main road that is the responsibility of a provincial government.

queen–size (kwēn′sīz′) *adj* **1** to do with a bed or mattress larger than double but smaller than king-size. **2** to do with the second-largest size in a series of some commercial product.

Queen's Printer *n* the printer of all government documents, federal and provincial.

queer (kwēr) *adj* **1** different from what is conventional or usual: *a queer remark, a queer noise.* **2** *Offensive* homosexual. <origin uncertain> **queer′ly** *adv.* **queer′ness** *n.*

quell (kwel) *v* **1** put down disorder or a rebellion: *quell an uprising.* **2** suppress or subdue: *to quell my fears.* <Old English *cwellan* to kill>

quench (kwench) *v* **1** satisfy thirst by drinking a liquid. **2** extinguish a fire: *Fire hoses quenched the flames.* **3** cool suddenly red-hot metal or other material by plunging into water or other liquid. **4** stifle or suppress a feeling: *He quenched his anger at the remark.* <Old English *acwencean* extinguish>

quer·u·lous (kwer′ə ləs) *or* (kwer′yə ləs) *adj* complaining in a whining or peevish way: *a querulous voice.* <Latin *queri* complain> **quer′u·lous·ly** *adv.*

que·ry (kwē′rē) *n, pl* **que·ries** **1** a question or inquiry, such as one addressed to an official, authority, or organization. **2** *Computers* a request for a particular file, website, etc. in a search engine or database.
v **que·ried, que·ry·ing** **1** put as a question: *"How long will that be?" she queried.* **2** ask questions of: *They queried him about his future plans.* **3** ask about, especially to express doubt: *She queried the wisdom of accepting the first offer.* <Latin *quaerere* seek>

que·sa·dil·la (kā′sə dē′yə) *n* a Mexican dish consisting of a crust covered with cheese and other items. <Spanish *queso* cheese>

quest (kwest) *n* **1** a long or difficult search: *I went to the library in quest of something to read.* **2** an expedition or journey in search of something noble, ideal, or holy: *There are many stories about the quest for the Holy Grail.*
v search for or seek. <Old French, from Latin *quaerere* seek>

ques·tion (kwes′chən) *n* **1** a sentence in interrogative form, addressed to someone to get information. **2** a matter of doubt or dispute; a controversy: *A question arose about the ownership of the property.* **3** a matter to be discussed, investigated, or considered: *the question of prohibition.* **4** the act of taking a vote on a proposal: *The president asked if the club members were ready for the question.*
v **1** ask in order to get information: *The police questioned the witness to the accident.* **2** express doubt: *I question the truth of his story.* <Old French, from Latin *quaerere* seek>
ques′tion·er *n.* **ques′tion·ing·ly** *adv.*
beside the question, not the topic discussed.
beyond (or **without**) **question,** without doubt: *The statements in that book are true beyond question. She is without question the brightest student in the school.*
call in (or **into**) **question,** dispute or challenge.
in question, a under consideration or discussion. **b** in dispute.
out of the question, not to be considered.

SYNONYMS

Ask is a general word for inquiring about something: *He asked me what the time was.*

Question often means "ask a series of questions": *The teacher questioned the student for fifteen minutes about the incident in the schoolyard.*

Interrogate is a formal word meaning "question formally and methodically": *The police interrogated the suspects about the crime.*

ques·tion·a·ble (kwes′chə nə bəl) *adj* **1** open to question or dispute: *a questionable statement, calculations of questionable accuracy.* **2** of doubtful honesty, morality, or respectability: *questionable motives.*

question mark *n* a mark [?] put after a question or used to express doubt about something written or printed.

GRAMMAR AND USAGE

Use a question mark at the end of a direct question: *What movie are you going to see?*

Use a period after an indirect question: *Our parents want to know what movie we are going to see.*

Use a period after a polite request: *Will you please tell them to be quiet.*

ques·tion·naire (kwes′chə ner′) *n* a set of questions designed for obtaining information, or a form containing such questions, with spaces for answers: *to fill out a questionnaire. I thought the questionnaire was quite straightforward.*

question period *n* in the House of Commons, a short period several times a week in which ministers answer questions submitted in advance by Members of Parliament, or a similar period in a provincial legislative assembly.

quet·zal (ket säl′) *n* a Central American bird with brilliant plumage. The male has long, flowing tail feathers. <Spanish, from Nahuatl (a language of Central and S America) *quetzalli* brilliantly coloured tail feathers>

queue (kyū) *n* **1** a line of people or vehicles awaiting some service or the order to proceed: *There was a long queue in front of the movie theatre.* **2** *Computers* a list of data or commands stored in a computer so as to be retrievable in a definite order. **3** a braid of hair hanging down the back.
v **queued, queu·ing** (*usually with* **up**) form or stand in a line while waiting for service or an order to proceed: *We had to queue up to get tickets.* <French = tail, from Latin *cauda*>

quib·ble (kwib′əl) *n* **1** an evasion of the main point, especially a petty one, or one that depends on words that are vague or have a double meaning: *a legal quibble.* **2** a minor criticism or objection: *The meeting was delayed for several minutes because of a quibble about procedure.*

v **quib·bled, quib·bling** resort to petty objections or evasions: *This is no time to quibble about a few cents in change.* <origin uncertain>

quiche (kēsh) *n* a pie usually served as a main dish, consisting of a pastry shell filled with an egg and cream mixture together with other ingredients. <French, from German *Kuchen* cake>

quick (kwik) *adj* **1** fast and sudden: *a quick turn.* **2** begun and ended in a very short time: *a quick visit.* **3** prompt or acting quickly: *a quick reply, a quick wit.* **4** hasty and impatient: *a quick temper.* **5** understanding or learning quickly: *a child who is quick in school.*
n **1** tender, sensitive flesh, especially the flesh under a fingernail or toenail: *The child bit his nails down to the quick.* **2** the tender, sensitive part of one's feelings: *Their insults cut her to the quick.* **3** *Archaic* living people: *the quick and the dead.*
adv quickly: *Come quick!* <Old English *cwic* alive, i.e., lively> **quick′ness** *n.*

quick bread *n* bread made with a leavening agent that does not require the dough to be left to rise and can be baked quickly.

quick·en (kwik′ən) *v* **1** make or become more rapid: *He quickened his pace. Her pulse quickened.* **2** make or become stimulated or animated: *My interest quickened when the discussion turned to travel.*

quick–freeze (kwik′frēz′) *v* **quick-froze, quick-fro·zen, quick-freez·ing** freeze food quickly in preparation for storage, so that the ice crystals formed during the freezing process are too small to rupture the cells, thus preserving natural juices and flavour.

❋ **quick·hatch** (kwik′hach′) *n* a wolverine.

quick·ie (kwik′ē) *Informal n* something made or done very quickly or superficially: *His last film was just a quickie.*

quick·lime (kwik′līm′) *n* a white alkaline substance usually obtained by burning limestone and used for making mortar and cement.

quick·ly (kwik′lē) *adv* with haste or speed: *They walked quickly. The wound healed quickly.*

quick march in the armed forces, an order to begin marching in **quick time**, a marching rate of 120 paces per minute.

quick·sand (kwik′sand′) *n* deep, soft, wet sand that yields easily to pressure and sucks in anything resting or falling into it, or an expanse of such sand: *The horse was swallowed by the quicksand.*

quick·sil·ver (kwik′sil′vər) *n* mercury.

quick·step (kwik′step′) *n* a lively dance step, or the music for this dance.

quick study *n* someone who learns or memorizes material quickly.

quick–tem·pered (kwik′tem′pərd) *adj* easily angered.

quick–wit·ted (kwik′wit′id) *adj* able to think or respond quickly.

quid (kwid) *n* **1** a lump of chewing tobacco. **2** *UK, Informal* a POUND[1] (def. 2). <Old English *cwidu* cud>

quid pro quo (kwid′prō kwō′) *n* one thing in return for another. <Latin = something for something>

qui·et (kwī′ət) *adj* **1** with no or little noise: *quiet footsteps, a quiet room.* **2** with little disturbance or activity: *a quiet evening at home.* **3** peaceful, gentle, or unobtrusive: *a quiet mind, quiet manners.*
n the absence of noise, disturbance, or activity: *to read in quiet.*
v make or become silent, calm, or still: *The father quieted his frightened child. The wind quieted down.*
adv in a quiet manner. <Old French, from Latin *quies* rest> **qui′et·ly** *adv.* **qui′et·ness** *n.*

qui·et·en (kwī′ə tən) *v* (*often with* **down**) cause to or become quiet: *She asked the class to quieten down. The wind finally quietened.*

❋ **Quiet Revolution** *n* the important social and political changes that happened in Québec in the 1960s.

qui·e·tude (kwī′ə tyūd′) *or* (kwī′ə tūd′) *n* quietness, stillness, or calmness.

qui·e·tus (kwī ē′təs) *n* death or something that causes death, considered as a release. <Latin *quietus est* = he is at rest>

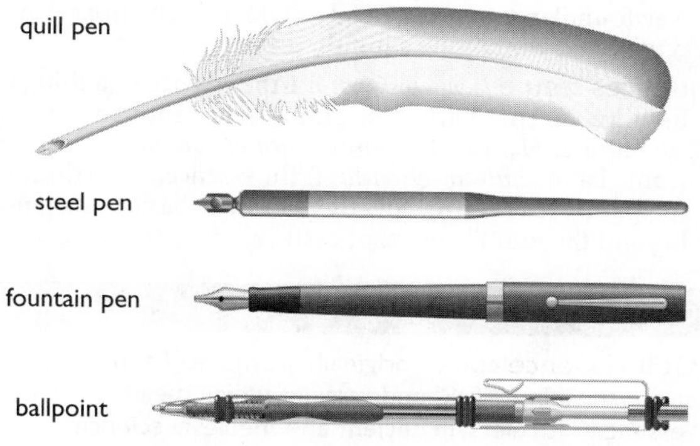

The **quill** pen was the main writing implement for nearly 1300 years. It was replaced in the early 1800s by the first patented steel pen. The fountain pen followed about 80 years later. In 1938, the first ballpoint pen was invented, and the ballpoint design is still in widespread use.

quill (kwil) *n* **1** a large, stiff feather from the wing or tail of a bird, or the hollow stem of a feather. **2** a thing made from the hollow stem of a feather, such as a pen or toothpick. **3** one of the spines of a porcupine or hedgehog. <origin uncertain>

quilt (kwilt) *n* a bed covering made of two layers of cloth with a filling between them that is held in place by lines of stitching, often in decorative patterns, or a bedspread resembling this.
v join together layers of fabric or padding with lines of stitching to form a decorative bed covering or warm garment: *My mother and her friends quilted a bedspread for me.* <Old French, from Latin *culcita* cushion> **quilt′er** *n.*

Q

a bat	e bed	i bid	o pot	u cup	th thin
ā cake	ē me	ī bite	ō go	ū rude	ᴛʜ then
à bar	ə about	ər over	ȯ for	ů put	zh measure

quilt·ing (kwil′ting) *n* **1** the process of making quilts. **2** material that is quilted or used for making quilts.

quince (kwins) *n* a hard, yellowish, acid fruit, used for preserves and jelly. <Old French, from Latin *cotoneum*>

quin·cunx (kwin′kungks′) *n* an arrangement or group of five objects with four forming the corners of a square or rectangle and the fifth in the centre, like the five on a die or playing card. <Latin = five-twelfths, from *quinque* five + *uncia* twelfth>

qui·nine (kwī′nīn) *or* (kwi nēn′) *n* a bitter, colourless, crystalline compound made from the bark of the cinchona, a S American tree. Quinine is used in medicine, and also to flavour tonic water. <Spanish, from Quechua (a language of S America) *kina* bark>

quin·quen·ni·al (kwing kwen′ē əl) *adj* **1** occurring every five years. **2** of or for five years. <Latin *quinque* five + *annus* year> **quin·quen′nial·ly** *adv.*

quint (kwint) *Informal n* a quintuplet.

quin·tal (kan′təl) *n* a nonmetric unit of weight equal to 112 pounds (about 51 kg), formerly used in Newfoundland to weigh cod. <Old French, from Latin *centenarius* containing a hundred>

quin·tes·sence (kwin tes′əns) *n* **1** the essence of a thing in its purest form. **2** the best example or representative of something: *He was the quintessence of goodness.* <French, from Latin *quinta essentia* fifth essence, referring in medieval science to an unidentified basic substance beyond the four elements of earth, air, fire, and water>

GRAMMAR AND USAGE

Quintessence comes originally from two Latin words: *quinta*, meaning "fifth," and *essentia*, which means "essence." It refers, in ancient and medieval science, to an unidentified basic substance other than the four elements of earth, air, fire, and water.

quin·tes·sen·tial (kwin′tə sen′shəl) *adj* of the purest or most perfect kind: *a quintessential homemaker.* **quin′te·sen′tial·ly** *adv.*

quin·tet or **quin·tette** (kwin tet′) *n* **1** a group of five musicians who perform or sing together. **2** a piece of music for five voices or instruments. **3** any group of five people or things. <French or Italian, from Latin *quintus* fifth>

quin·tu·ple (kwin tyū′pəl), (kwin tū′pəl), *or* (kwin tup′əl) *adj* **1** consisting of five parts. **2** five times as great or as many.
v **quin·tu·pled, quin·tu·pling** make or become five times as great or as many: *He quintupled his investment. His investment quintupled.*
n a number or amount five times as great as another. <French, from Latin *quintus* fifth + (*quadr*)*uple*>

quin·tu·plet (kwin tyū′plit), (kwin tū′plit), (kwin tup′lit), *or* (kwin′tə plit) *n* one of five offspring born at one birth from the same mother.

quip (kwip) *n* a clever or witty remark.
v **quip·ped, quip·ping** make a clever or witty remark. <origin uncertain>

quire (kwīr) *n* **1** four sheets of paper, folded to form eight leaves, as in medieval manuscripts. **2** a set of 24 or 25 sheets of paper of the same size and kind. See also REAM[1]. <Old French, from Latin *quaterni* set of four>

quirk (kwərk) *n* **1** an odd mannerism or way of behaving: *She has some irritating quirks.* **2** an unexpected or sudden happening or action: *a quirk of fate.* **3** a sudden turn, twist, or curve, for example, of the mouth. <origin uncertain>

quis·ling (kwiz′ling) *n* a person who collaborates with an enemy occupying his or her country. <V. *Quisling*, a Norwegian army officer and politician, who co-operated with the Germans when they invaded Norway during World War II>

quit (kwit) *v* **quit** or **quit·ted, quit·ting 1** stop or discontinue: *The miners quit work when the whistle blew.* **2** leave, especially permanently: *They quit their camp to go further into the wilderness.* **3** resign from a job: *Angry at her boss, she suddenly quit.*
adj rid of: *I gave him money to be quit of him.* <Old French, from Latin *quies* rest>

quite (kwīt) *adv* **1** completely: *That's not quite true. I'm afraid it's quite impossible for me to go.* **2** really or positively: *It's quite the thing these days.* **3** to a considerable degree: *This pattern is quite nice, but I like the other one better. He plays the piano quite well.*

quits (kwits) *adj* (*never before a noun*) on even terms between two people, especially after a debt or score has been settled: *After the book was returned undamaged, the boys were quits.*
call it quits, *Informal* stop doing something: *The mosquitoes got so bad that we finally had to call it quits and go home.*

quit·ter (kwit′ər) *n* a person who gives up too easily.

quiv·er[1] (kwiv′ər) *v* shake or tremble: *His voice quivered. The dog quivered with excitement.*
n a slight shaking or trembling movement or sound: *A quiver of his mouth showed that he was about to cry.* <Old English *cwifer* nimble, quick>

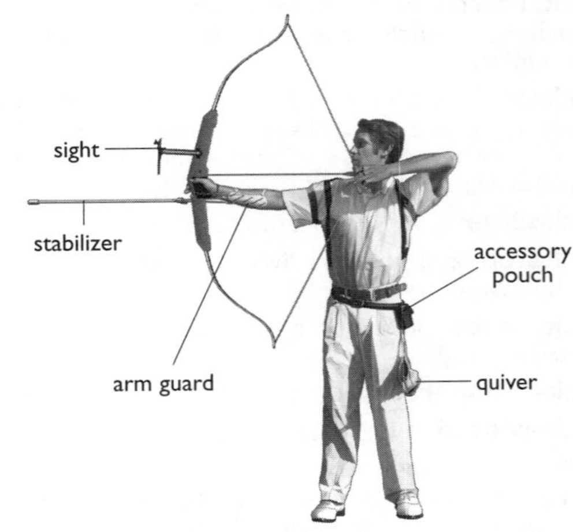

quiv·er[2] (kwiv′ər) *n* a portable case to hold arrows. <Old French *quivre*>

quix·ot·ic (kwik sot′ik) *adj* with high but impractical ideals or extravagant chivalry. <*Don Quixote*>
quix·ot′i·cal·ly *adv.*

quiz (kwiz) *n, pl* **quiz·zes** a short or informal test: *a quiz in geography.*
v **quizzed, quiz·zing** 1 give such a test: *to quiz a class in history.* 2 question or interrogate: *The lawyer quizzed the witness.* <origin uncertain>

quiz show *n* a radio or TV program in which contestants are given prizes for answering questions correctly.

quiz·zi·cal (kwiz′ə kəl) *adj* showing mild amusement or puzzlement: *a quizzical smile.* **quiz′zi·cal·ly** *adv.*

quoit (kwoit) *n* 1 a heavy, flattish ring of iron, rope, or rubber used in a game. A quoit is thrown at a peg stuck in the ground to encircle it or come as close to it as possible. 2 **quoits** *pln* (*with singular verb*) the game in which quoits are thrown at a peg. <origin unknown>

quon·dam (kwon′dəm) *adj* former: *The quondam servant is now master.* <Latin = formerly>

Quon·set hut (kwon′sit) *Trademark n* a prefabricated, semicircular metal hut. <*Quonset* Point, Rhode Island, where such huts were first made>

quo·rum (kwô′rəm) *n* the number of members of a society or assembly that must be present if the business done is to be legal or binding: *In our club, twenty-five people make a quorum.* <Latin = of whom>

quo·ta (kwō′tə) *n* 1 a share or proportion that is required of or due to a person or group: *Each club member was given his or her quota of tickets to sell for the dance.* 2 a quantity or proportion that is allowed: *a government quota on imports.* <Latin *quot* how many>

quot·a·ble (kwō′tə bəl) *adj* suitable for or worth quoting: *The politician made some quotable comments in her speech.*

quo·ta·tion (kwō tā′shən) *n* 1 somebody's words repeated exactly by another: *From what author does this quotation come?* 2 the act or process of repeating someone else's words: *Quotation is a habit of some teachers.* 3 a short musical passage or visual image repeated in another piece of music or art. 4 the stated current price of a stock, bond, or commodity. 5 a statement setting out the estimated cost of a particular job or service: *It's best to get at least three quotations on the cost of replacing a roof.*

quotation mark *n* one of a pair of punctuation marks used to indicate dialogue, or the beginning and end of a quotation. The usual marks are [“ ”] for a single quotation and [‘ ’] for a quotation within a quotation.

quote (kwōt) *v* **quot·ed, quot·ing** 1 repeat the exact words of another person or text: *to quote Shakespeare. He often quotes his grandchildren.* 2 bring forward as an example or authority: *The judge quoted various cases in support of his opinion.* 3 give a formal estimate of a cost for a job or service.
n 1 a QUOTATION (def. 1). 2 a QUOTATION MARK.
adv 1 an expression used orally to introduce a quotation being read aloud: *According to the manual, the system is quote “foolproof.”* 2 a an expression used orally to introduce a euphemism, or a word or words considered doubtful: *She was absent yesterday because she was quote “not feeling well.”* b **quote unquote** an expression used orally to introduce a word or words considered doubtful or pretentious: *He says he's not a programmer, he's a quote unquote “software architect.”* <Latin *quot* how many>
quot′a·bil′i·ty *n.* **quot′a·ble** *adj.* **quot′er** *n.*

GRAMMAR AND USAGE

Always use **quotation marks** at the beginning and at the end of someone's exact words: *She said, “It's the first time I've run a marathon.”*

Do not use quotation marks when you are quoting someone indirectly: *She said that it was the first time she had run a marathon.*

Use quotation marks for the titles of short stories, newspaper articles, magazine articles, and episodes of television shows: *You should read his latest article in the school newspaper called “Healthier food needed in the cafeteria.”*

quoth *Archaic v* (*always precedes the subject, first and third person singular only*) said: *“Verily, the hour has come,” quoth he.* <Middle English>

quo·tid·i·an (kwō tid′ē ən) *adj* 1 happening or appearing each day. 2 ordinary or commonplace. <Old French, from Latin *cotidie* daily>

quo·tient (kwō′shənt) *n* the number obtained by dividing one number by another. Example: If 12 is divided by 3, the quotient is 4. <Latin *quot* how many>

Qur'an (ku̇ rän′) or (kə rän′) *Islam n* the sacred book of Islam, containing the revelations believed to have been made to the prophet Mohammed by Allah through the angel Gabriel. Also **Quran**, **Koran**.

q.v. used to direct a reader to another part of a text for further information. <Latin *quod vide* = which see>

QWERTY keyboard (kwər′tē) *n* a keyboard for a typewriter or computer with the alphabetical and numerical keys in the traditional order. <from the letters of the first six alphabetical keys>

Rr

r or **R** (är) *n, pl* **r's** or **R's** 1 the eighteenth letter of the English alphabet, or any speech sound represented by it. 2 the eighteenth thing in a list or series.
the three R's, *Informal* reading, writing, and arithmetic.

r radius.

R Restricted, a movie rating indicating that only those of specified age or older will be admitted.

R. 1 River. 2 Rex (King) or Regina (Queen).

rab·bet (rab′it) *n* a groove made on a wooden surface to receive the end of another piece of wood shaped to fit it, or a joint made in this way. Also, **rabbet joint**.
v **rab·bet·ed, rab·bet·ing** cut and join with a rabbet.

rab·bi (rab′ī) *n, pl* **rab·bis** 1 a teacher or scholar of the Jewish law. 2 a Jewish religious leader, especially the spiritual head of a congregation. <Latin, from Hebrew *rab* master> **rab·bin′i·cal** (rə bin′ə kəl) *adj.*

rab·bit (rab′it) *n* a burrowing mammal with soft fur, long ears, and long hind legs. See PIKA for picture. <Middle English *rabet*> **rab′bit·like′** *adj.*

rabbit ears *Informal pln* an indoor TV antenna consisting of two rods of adjustable length attached to a small base. The rods can be swivelled apart to form a wide or narrow V.

rabbit punch *n* a quick, hard blow to the base of the skull or the nape of the neck.

rab·ble (rab′əl) *n* 1 a disorderly crowd: *The noisy rabble protesting outside the building disturbed the meeting.* 2 **the rabble** ordinary people, especially when considered socially inferior. <Middle English *rablen* jabber>

rab·ble–rous·er (rab′əl rou′zər) *n* a person who tries to emotionally rouse groups of people, especially for political reasons.

rab·id (rab′id) *adj* 1 unreasonably extreme in a belief: *The rebels are rabid idealists.* 2 to do with rabies: *a rabid dog.* <Latin *rabere* to rave> **rab′id·ly** *adv.* **rab′id·ness** *n.*

ra·bies (rā′bēz) *n* a fatal viral disease of dogs and other mammals that can be transmitted to other animals and humans through saliva.

rac·coon (ra kūn′) *n* a small, greyish mammal with a bushy, ringed tail and a dark patch around each eye. Also, **racoon**. <Algonquian>

race[1] (rās) *n* 1 a competition between humans, animals, vehicles, or boats to see which is the fastest in covering a set course. 2 a series of such competitions for horses or dogs. 3 a contest that suggests or resembles such a competition: *a political race.* 4 a strong or fast current of water flowing through a narrow channel. 5 a groove, channel, or passage, especially a channel leading water to or from a place where its energy is used, or a track or groove for a sliding or rolling part of a machine.
v **raced, rac·ing** 1 engage in a contest of speed: *We plan to race in the regatta. I'll race you to the corner.* 2 cause to run in a race. 3 run, move, or go swiftly, or cause to do so: *The fire engine raced to the scene of the fire. He raced his favourite horse.* 4 of a wheel or motor, run too fast when the resistance lessens without a corresponding lessening of power. <Old Norse *ras* running>
off to the races, *Informal* making a good start or real progress: *Now that I've finished the research for this project, it's off to the races!*

race[2] (rās) *n* 1 **a** a subdivision of human beings based on distinct inherited characteristics, such as blood type, resistance to particular diseases, skin colour, or body proportions. **b** the fact or condition of belonging to such a group: *Intelligence does not depend on race.* 2 a variety, especially a subspecies, of animals or plants: *a race of hunting dogs, a race of flowering shrubs.* 3 a group of people sharing the same history, culture, or language: *Her speech reveals her to be of the Irish race.* <French, from Italian *razza*>
the human race, all the people of the world.

GRAMMAR AND USAGE

Race can be an imprecise word when referring to human beings. As a result, many people now prefer to use *ethnic group* or *ethnic background.*

race·course (rā′skôrs′) *n* a course or track for racing horses or dogs.

race·horse (rās′hôrs′) *n* a horse bred or kept for racing.

ra·ceme (rā sēm′) *or* (rə sēm′) *n* a simple flower cluster with its flowers on short stalks along a stem, the lower flowers blooming first, such as in the lily of the valley, the currant, or the chokecherry. <Latin *racemus* bunch of grapes>

rac·er (rā′sər) *n* 1 a person who races or an animal, vehicle, boat, or aircraft that is used for racing. 2 a harmless, slender-bodied snake that can move very fast.

race riot *n* an outbreak of violence resulting from racial hostility or hatred.

race·track (rā′strak′) *n* a track or course, usually oval in shape, on which races with horses, dogs, or vehicles are run.

ra·cial (rā′shəl) *adj* 1 to do with a RACE[2] (def. 1): *racial traits.* 2 involving more than one RACE[2] (def. 1): *racial tensions, racial harmony.* **ra′cial·ly** *adv.*

ra·cial·ize (rā′shəl īz) *adj* categorize according to RACE[2] (def. 1). **ra′cial·i·za′tion** *n.*

racial profiling *n* the practice, among police or security officials, of treating members of an ethnic group as potential suspects because it is supposed that they are more likely to commit crimes.

rac·i·ness (rā′sē nis) *n* the quality of being racy.

rac·ism (rā′siz əm) *n* 1 the belief that all members of a particular race share characteristics, qualities, or abilities, especially in considering the race superior or inferior. 2 prejudice or discrimination against a person or group because of these supposed differences.

rack[1] (rak) *n* 1 a frame with bars, shelves, or pegs to hold, arrange, or keep things in or on: *a towel rack, a hat rack, a luggage rack.* 2 a frame of bars to hold hay and other food for livestock. 3 in former times, an instrument used for torturing people by stretching their arms and legs. 4 a bar with pegs or teeth on one edge, into which teeth on the

rim of a wheel can fit: *a steering rack.* **5** a triangular frame for positioning balls in the game of pool.
v **1** cause great physical or mental pain: *racked with grief. A toothache racked her jaw.* **2** place in or on a rack. <origin uncertain>
off the rack, sold as ready-made clothes.
on the rack, in great pain.
rack my brains, *Informal* think as hard as I can.
rack up, score or gain points or a victory.

rack[2] (rak) *n* a wreck; destruction. <*wreck*>
go to rack and ruin, fall into great disrepair.

rack·et[1] (rak′it) *n* **1** a loud, unpleasant noise: *Stop that racket!* **2** a dishonest scheme for getting money. **3** *Informal* a line of business or way of life: *My friend's mom is in the landscaping racket.* <origin uncertain>

rack·et[2] (rak′it) RACQUET.

rack·et·eer (rak′ə tēr′) *n* a person who operates an illegal business, especially someone who extorts money by threats of violence or blackmail.
v obtain money by such means. **rack′et·eer′ing** *adj.*

rac·on·teur (rak′on tər′) *n* a person who is skilful at telling stories or anecdotes. <French *raconter* tell>

rac·quet (rak′it) *n* a light, wide bat used in games like tennis, badminton, and squash, consisting of a network of strings stretched in an oval or round frame attached to a handle. Also, **racket**. See TENNIS for picture. <French, from Arabic *rahat* palm of the hand>

rac·quet·ball (rak′it bol′) *n* an indoor game played by two or four players in a walled court, using short racquets and a hollow rubber ball. Also called **racquets.**

rac·y (rā′sē) *adj* **rac·i·er, rac·i·est** **1** lively and entertaining, especially in a sexually suggestive way: *a racy novel.* **2** with a distinctive quality characteristic of something in its best or original form: *racy flavour.*

rad[1] (rad) *Informal n* a radiator.

rad[2] (rad) *n* a unit of nuclear radiation equal to 100 ergs of energy per gram, for measuring absorbed doses of radiation. <*rad(iation)*>

rad[3] (rad) radian(s).

ra·dar (rā′dàr) *n* the process of determining, by means of a special instrument, the presence, distance, direction, or speed of unseen aircraft, ships, or vehicles by the reflection of high-frequency radio waves.

ETYMOLOGY

Radar is an acronym, coming from the first letters of *radio detection and ranging.*

radar trap *n* an apparatus, usually located in a hidden or unexpected place, that uses radar to detect road vehicles travelling faster than the speed limit.

ra·di·al (rā′dē əl) *adj* **1** arranged like or in radii or rays from a centre, like the petals of a daisy or the spokes of a bicycle wheel. **2** to do with the bone called the radius.
n a radial tire.

ra·di·al·ly (rā′dē ə lē) *adv* arranged like or in radii or rays from a centre.

radial symmetry *n* symmetry with the parts arranged like rays from a centre.

radial tire *n* a tire for a motor vehicle in which the plies of cord extending to the edges of the tire are at right angles to the centre line of the tread.

ra·di·an (rā′dē ən) *n* an SI unit for measuring plane angles, equal to the angle formed between two radii of a circle that cuts off an arc on the circumference equal in length to the radius. *Symbol* **rad**

ra·di·ant (rā′dē ənt) *adj* **1** shining or glowing: *a radiant glow from the fire.* **2** sending out rays of light or heat: *radiant energy.* **3** clearly showing joy, love, or health: *a radiant smile.* **ra′di·ance** *n.* **ra′di·ant·ly** *adv.*

radiant heating *n* a method of heating a building or room without a fan by means of pipes or radiators, wires concealed in walls or floors, or electrical elements in a baseboard heater.

ra·di·ate (rā′dē āt′) *v* **ra·di·at·ed, ra·di·at·ing** **1** give out rays of: *The sun radiates light and heat.* **2** show or send forth: *Her face radiates joy.* **3** spread out from or as if from a centre: *Roads radiate from the city in every direction.*
adj with rays or radiating from a centre: *A daisy is a radiate flower.* <Latin *radiare* to shine>

ra·di·a·tion (rā′dē ā′shən) *n* **1** the act or process of giving out light, heat, or other radiant energy, or the energy transmitted in this way. **2** a radioactive ray or rays. **3** the process of treating disease by radiation from a radioactive material such as radium.

radiation sickness *n* a disease resulting from an overdose of radiation from radioactive materials, usually marked by nausea, hair loss, and internal bleeding.

radiation therapy *n* the treatment of disease, especially cancer, using X-rays and other forms of radiation.

ra·di·a·tor (rā′dē ā′tər) *n* **1** a heating device consisting of a set of pipes through which steam or hot water passes. **2** a device for circulating water as a way of cooling the engine of a motor vehicle or aircraft.

rad·i·cal (rad′ə kəl) *adj* **1** to do with or affecting the fundamental nature of something: *My teacher says that I have to make a radical change in my study habits if I want to improve my grades.* **2** favouring extreme and thorough changes or reforms. **3** of or from the root or roots, especially of a number, word, musical chord, or plant.
n **1** a person who favours extreme and thorough changes or reforms, especially in politics. **2** a group of atoms acting as a unit in a number of chemical compounds. **3** a quantity forming or expressed as the root of another. The mathematical sign ($\sqrt{\ }$) put before an expression shows that some root of it is to be extracted. **4** the root or base form of a word. **5** a Chinese character that is a basic element in composing other characters. <Latin *radicis* root> **rad′i·cal·ly** *adv.* **rad′i·cal·ness** *n.*

a bat	e bed	i bid	o pot	u cup	th thin
ā cake	ē me	ī bite	ō go	ū rude	TH then
à bar	ə about	ər over	ȯ for	u̇ put	zh measure

rad·i·cal·ism (rad′ə kə liz′əm) *n* the principles or practices of radical persons, especially in politics.

ra·dic·chi·o (rə dē′ kē ō) *n* a chicory that has a small oval head of purplish red, white-streaked leaves with a bitter taste, often used raw in salads. <Italian>

rad·i·ces (rad′i sēz′) a plural of RADIX.

rad·i·cle (rad′ə kəl) *n* the part of a seed that develops into the main root. See COTYLEDON for picture.

ra·di·i (rā′dē ī′) a plural of RADIUS.

ra·di·o (rā′dē ō′) *n, pl* **ra·di·os** **1** the process of sending and receiving sound in the form of electromagnetic waves of a specific frequency and without connecting wires. **2** a device for receiving and making audible such sound. **3** the activity or industry of broadcasting programs to be received by such a device.
adj **1** to do with radio: *a radio set, a radio announcer.* **2** to do with electromagnetic frequencies for radio transmission.
v **ra·di·oed, ra·di·o·ing** transmit or send out by radio: *The ship radioed a call for help.* <*radio-telephony*>

radio– *combining form* **1** to do with radio: *radio-controlled.* **2** to do with rays or radiation: *radiograph.* **3** to do with radioactivity: *radioisotope.*

ra·di·o·ac·tive (rā′dē ō ak′tiv) *adj* giving off radiant energy in the form of alpha, beta, or gamma rays as a result of the breaking up of atoms, such as in the elements radium, uranium, and thorium. **ra′di·o·ac·tiv′i·ty** *n.*

radioactive dating *n* a method of determining the age of an earth material or artifact of organic origin by measuring the rate of decay of radioactive carbon isotopes.

radioactive series *n* a series of isotopes of certain elements, each of which disintegrates into the next until a stable element (usually lead) is reached. This disintegration is called **radioactive decay**.

radio astronomy *n* the branch of astronomy that studies objects in space by analyzing radio waves given off by or reflected from them.

ra·di·o·car·bon (rā′dē ō kär′bən) *n* radioactive carbon, especially CARBON-14, used in finding out the age of organic materials. See CARBON DATING.

radio control *n* control by means of radio signals: *This model truck is operated by radio control.* **ra′di·o-con·trolled′** *adj.*

radio frequency *n* a frequency of electromagnetic waves between about 3 kilohertz and 300 000 megahertz, used especially in transmitting radio and TV signals.

ra·di·o·graph (rā′dē ō graf′) *n* a picture produced by X-rays or gamma rays on a photographic plate.
v make such a picture.

ra·di·o·iso·tope (rā′dē ō ī′sə tōp′) *n* a radioactive isotope.

ra·di·ol·o·gy (rā′dē ol′ə jē) *n* the science that deals with radioactive rays or other high-energy radiation, especially their use in medical diagnoses and treatment. **ra′di·ol′o·gist** *n.*

ra·di·o·me·ter (rā′dē o′mə tər) *n* an instrument that detects or measures radiant energy or the conversion of radiant energy into mechanical force.

ra·di·o·paque (rā′dē o pāk′) *adj* blocking the passage of X-rays or other forms of radiant energy, hence, visible in X-ray photographs.

radio source *Astronomy n* a supernova, quasar, or other celestial source of radio waves.

radio telescope *n* an apparatus for making observations of bodies in outer space by detecting and recording radio waves coming from or reflected by them.

ra·di·o·ther·a·py (rā′dē ō ther′ə pē) *n* the treatment of disease by means of radiation.

radio wave *n* an electromagnetic wave of radio frequency.

Radishes come in a variety of shapes and sizes. This small, round radish is red with a white interior. It tastes mildly bitter and hot.

Beets have a deep red skin and interior. They are cooked and peeled before they are eaten, and are quite sweet.

rad·ish (rad′ish) *n* a small, red-skinned, pungent root used as a relish and in salads. <Latin *radicis* root>

ra·di·um (rā′dē əm) *n* a radioactive, silver-white metallic element found in very small amounts in uranium ores. *Symbol* **Ra** <Latin *radius* ray>

ra·di·us (rā′dē əs) *n, pl* **ra·di·i** (rā′dē ī) or **ra·di·us·es** **1** a line segment going straight from the centre to any point on the outside of a circle or a sphere. See DIAMETER for picture. **2** a circular area measured by the length of its radius: *The explosion could be heard within a radius of ten kilometres.* **3 a** one of the two bones of the human forearm that is on the thumb side. **b** a corresponding bone in the forelimb of other vertebrates. <Latin>

ra·dix (rā′diks) *n, pl* **ra·dix·es** or **ra·dic·es** (rad′ə sēz′) *or* (rā′də sēz′) **1** a source of something hidden. **2** a number taken as the base of a system of numbers, for example, ten in the decimal system.

ra·don (rā′don) *n* a heavy, radioactive gas that is a rare element given off by radium. *Symbol* **Rn** <*radium*>

raf·fi·a (raf′ē ə) *n* a fibre from the leaves of a palm tree native to tropical Africa and Madagascar, used in making baskets, mats, and hats. <Malagasy *rafia*>

raf·fish (raf′ish) *adj* attractively unconventional and slightly disreputable. <*riffraff*> **raf′fish·ly** *adv.* **raf′fish·ness** *n.*

raf·fle (raf′əl) *n* a lottery, often held for charity, in which many people each pay a small sum for a chance to win a prize.
v **raf·fled, raf·fling** (*often with* ***off***) sell an article by such a lottery: *to raffle off a quilt.* <Old French *rafle* dice game>

raft[1] (raft) *n* **1** a structure or platform made of timber or other materials fastened together and used for transportation or support on water. **2** pieces of timber lashed together for floating downstream, such as to a mill.
v **1** send by or carry on such a structure. **2** make such a structure. <Old Norse *raptr* rafter>

raft[2] (raft) *Informal n* a large number or amount: *My teacher has a whole raft of essays to mark.* <origin uncertain>

raft·er (raf′tər) *n* a supporting beam, often slanting, of a roof. <Old English *ræfter*>

🍁 **raftered ice** (raf′tərd) *n* ice that has been caused to be piled high, layer upon layer, as a result of pressure. Also, **rafted ice, rafting ice.**

rag[1] (rag) *n* **1** an old or torn piece of cloth: *Use clean rags to polish this mirror.* **2** a remnant that is a small piece of a thing of no value: *The meat was boiled to rags.* **3** *Informal* a newspaper, considered to be of low quality: *You mean you're actually reading that rag?* **4 rags** *pl* tattered or worn-out clothes.
adj made from rags: *a rag doll, a rag rug.* <Middle English> **rag′like′** *adj.*
in rags, torn or worn out: *His clothing was in rags.*

rag[2] (rag) *Informal v* **ragged, rag·ging** tease, especially in a loud, boisterous way.
n a boisterous prank or practical joke. <origin uncertain>
rag the puck, keep control of a hockey puck by skilful stickhandling and elusive skating, usually as a means of killing time when one's team is shorthanded.

rag[3] (rag) *n* a piece of music in ragtime. <*ragtime*>

ra·ga (ra′ga) *Music n* a pattern of notes in music from India that is used as a basis for improvisation. <Sanskrit = musical tone>

rag·a·muf·fin (rag′ə muf′ən) *n* a ragged, dirty person, especially a child. <Middle English>

rag doll *n* a doll made of cloth, especially scraps, stuffed with some soft material.

rage (rāj) *n* **1** violent, uncontrollable anger: *to quiver with rage, to be in a rage.* **2** a movement, idea, or fashion that is popular for a short time: *Hula hoops were all the rage in the fifties.* **3** a very strong desire or passion: *a rage for order.*
v **raged, rag·ing 1** feel or express violent, uncontrollable anger. **2** of an illness, spread rapidly or uncontrollably: *The flu epidemic raged for at least a month.* **3** move, proceed, or continue with great violence: *A storm was raging.* <Old French, from Latin *rabere* to rave>

rag·ga (rag′ə) *n* a style of music incorporating elements of reggae and hip hop. <*ragamuffin*, from the style of clothes worn by some dancers>

rag·ged (rag′id) *adj* **1** worn or torn into rags: *a ragged pair of jeans.* **2** wearing torn or badly worn-out clothing: *a ragged refugee.* **3** with a rough or uneven surface or appearance: *a dog's ragged coat.* **4** lacking finish or uniformity: *ragged organization.* **5** rough or uneven in sound: *a ragged voice.* <Scandinavian> **rag′ged·ly** *adv.* **rag′ged·ness** *n.*
run ragged, wear out or exhaust because of too much demanding activity.

rag·lan sleeve (rag′lən) *n* a sleeve that is cut to continue up to the neckline instead of ending at the shoulder. <Lord *Raglan*, who invented such a style of sleeve>

ra·gout (ra gū′) *n* a highly seasoned stew of meat and vegetables. <French *ragoûter* revive the taste of>

rag·tag (rag′tag′) *adj* untidy, disorganized, or with an odd mixture of elements. <*rag* and *tag*>

rag·time (rag′tīm′) *n* an early style of jazz characterized by a strong, regular rhythm. <origin uncertain>

rag·weed (rag′wēd′) *n* a N American plant of the daisy family whose tiny green flowers produce pollen, a common cause of hay fever.

rah (rȧ) *interj* hurrah.

raid (rād) *n* **1** a sudden surprise attack on an enemy during a war: *a bombing raid.* **2** a sudden surprise visit by a police force to arrest suspects or to seize illegal goods. **3** a rapid surprise attack to commit a crime, or to enter and seize something: *The hungry girls made a raid on the refrigerator.*
v **1** attack suddenly: *The enemy raided the unguarded camp.* **2** engage in a raid. <Old English *rad* military expedition> **raid′er** *n.*

rail[1] (rāl) *n* **1** a horizontal or slanting bar of wood or metal extending between supports or posts and used as a barrier, guard, to hang things on, or form part of a fence: *a stair rail. She leaned against the top rail of the fence.* **2** a steel bar or series of bars forming a continuous railway track, or the railway itself: *We travelled to Halifax by rail.* See RAILWAY for picture.
v supply or enclose with rails or a railing. <Old French, from Latin *regula* straight stick>
off the rails, *Informal* off the proper course or not functioning properly: *The committee is a little off the rails at the moment.*

rail[2] (rāl) *v* (*usually with* ***at***) complain or protest strongly and persistently: *He railed at his hard luck.* <French, from Latin *rugire* bellow> **rail′er** *n.*

rail[3] (rāl) *n, pl* **rails** or (*especially collectively*) **rail** a small or medium-sized wading bird with short wings and tail, a narrow body, and strong legs with very long toes. <French, from Latin *rascla*>

rail fence *n* a fence made by hand out of rails split from logs.

rail·head (rāl′hed) *n* **1** the point of a railway from where roads and other transport routes begin. **2** 🍁 the farthest point to which a railway under construction has been built.

rail·ing (rā′ling) *n* a barrier made of rails, especially along the edge of a balcony, or such rails collectively: *A pile of railing lay by the barn.*

a bat	e bed	i bid	o pot	u cup	th thin
ā cake	ē me	ī bite	ō go	ū rude	ᴛʜ then
ȧ bar	ə about	ər over	ȯ for	u̇ put	zh measure

R

rail·ler·y (rā′lə rē) *n, pl* **rail·ler·ies** good-humoured and high-spirited teasing. <French *railler* to tease>

rail·road (rāl′rōd′) *n* a railway.
v **1** send or carry on a railway. **2** work on a railway: *He has been railroading all his life.* **3** *Informal* rush through or too hastily, especially so as to prevent fair and careful consideration: *They railroaded the bill through a committee.* **rail′road′ing** *n.*

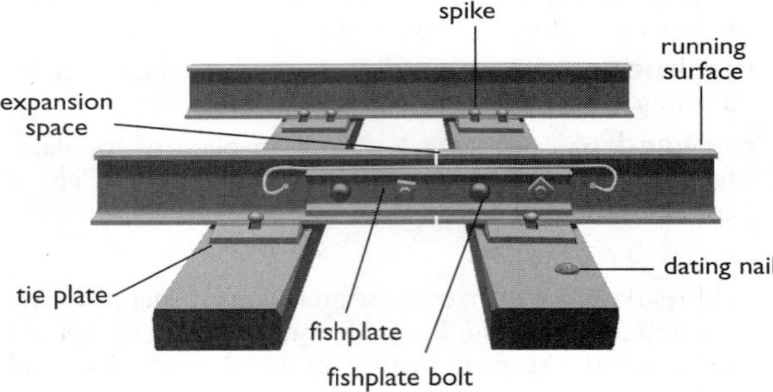

rail·way (rāl′wā′) *n* **1** a road or track for trains, consisting of parallel steel rails along which the wheels of the locomotives and cars go. **2** tracks, stations, trains, and other property of a system of transportation that uses rails, together with the people who manage them.

rai·ment (rā′mənt) *Archaic or Poetic n* clothing or garments. <Middle English *arrayment* clothing>

rain (rān) *n* **1** condensed moisture falling in drops from clouds. **2** the fall of such drops: *There was a light rain this morning.* **3** a thick, fast fall of anything: *a rain of ash from a volcano.* **4 the rains** *pl* the rainy season, as in a tropical climate.
v **1** fall in drops of condensed moisture: *It rained all day.* **2** fall like rain: *Tears rained down his cheeks. Sparks rained down from the fire.* **3** send or give like rain: *The crowds rained praises on the victorious legions. The angry child rained blows with her fists on the door.* <Old English *regn*>
rain cats and dogs, *Informal* rain very hard.
rained out, cancelled as an event because of rain: *The first game of the season was rained out.*

rain·bow (rān′bō′) *n* an arch of coloured light, showing the different colours of the spectrum, that is seen in the sky when the sun's rays are seen through rain, mist, or spray.

rainbow trout *n* a trout with black spots and a pinkish or reddish band along its sides.

rain check *n* **1** a ticket for future use, given to the spectators at a baseball game or other outdoor performance that has been stopped because of rain. **2** an understanding that an invitation that cannot be accepted will be given another time: *May I take a rain check on your invitation to dinner?* **3** a promise by a store to honour a special price for goods even after they have run out.

rain·coat (rān′kōt′) *n* a waterproof or water-repellent coat worn for protection from rain.

rain date *n* an alternative date for an outdoor event in case of rain on the date of first choice.

rain·drop (rān′drop′) *n* a single drop of rain.

rain·fall (rān′fol′) *n* **1** a shower of rain: *There was a light rainfall during the night.* **2** the amount of rain that falls in a particular area over a certain period of time.

rain·for·est (rān′for′ist) *n* a large, densely wooded region where there is very heavy rainfall throughout the year, usually in tropical climates.

rain gauge *n* an instrument for measuring rainfall.

rain·mak·er (rān′mā′kər) *n* **1** a person who tries to make rain fall. **2** *Informal* a person who is highly successful, especially in business or politics.

rain·proof (rān′prūf′) *adj* preventing rain from getting through: *The roof of our cottage isn't rainproof anymore.*

rain·storm (rān′stórm′) *n* a storm with much rain.

rain·wa·ter (rān′wot′ər) *n* water that has been collected from rain.

rain·wear (rān′wer′) *n* clothing to be worn in the rain, such as overshoes and raincoats.

rain·y (rā′nē) *adj* **rain·i·er, rain·i·est** **1** with rain, especially much rain: *rainy weather, the rainy season.* **2** wet with rain: *rainy streets.*
a rainy day *Informal* a time of need in the future: *to save for a rainy day.*

raise (rāz) *v* **raised, rais·ing** **1** lift or move to a higher position or level: *to raise your hand.* **2** cause to rise or form: *to raise a cloud of dust, to raise a monument.* **3** promote someone to a higher rank or office: *to raise a salesperson to manager.* **4** increase in degree or amount: *to raise the rent.* **5** make louder or pitch higher: *I cannot hear you, so would you please raise your voice?* **6** bet or make a higher bid more than an opponent in a card game, especially in poker. **7** gather together or collect a group of people: *The leader raised a band of firefighters.* **8** breed or grow: *The farmer raised cattle and feed corn.* **9** cause or bring about: *A funny remark raised a laugh.* **10** bring forward for discussion: *The speaker raised an interesting point.* **11** bring up or rear: *They raised a large family.* **12** cause to become leavened: *Yeast raises bread.* **13** abandon or force an enemy to abandon something: *Our soldiers raised the siege of the fort by driving away the surrounding enemy army.*
n **1** an increase in degree or amount, especially of wages or salary: *She's happy because she just got a big raise.* **2** an increase of a bet in a card game. See RISE for confusable. <Old Norse *reisa*>
raise Cain (or **hell**, or **a stink**, or **the devil**), *Informal* create an uproar.

SYNONYMS

Raise means "bring something to a higher level": *The teacher said he would raise my mark if I made the corrections.*

Lift means "pick up something, often heavy, from a lower level": *Please ask someone to help you lift that box.*

Elevate mainly means "raise in quality or rank": *She was elevated to the position of captain.*

rais·er (rā′zər) *n* a person who grows or raises things: *a cattle raiser.*

rai·sin (rā′zən) *n* a sweet, partially dried grape. <Old French, from Latin *racemus* grape cluster>

rai·son d'être (re zôn detr′) the most important reason for someone's or something's existence. <French = reason for being>

raj or **Raj** (råj) *n* in former times in India, British sovereignty.

ra·ja (rå′jə) *n* in former times, a member of a hereditary class of kings and princes in India, Malaysia, and Indonesia. Also, **rajah**.

rake[1] (rāk) *n* **1** a long-handled tool with a bar at one end with teeth in it, used for smoothing the soil or gathering together loose leaves, hay, straw, or other dry materials. **2** a similar, usually smaller tool used for other purposes, such as to draw in money on a gaming table.
v **raked, rak·ing 1** move with a rake: *Rake the leaves off the grass.* **2** make clear, clean, or smooth a surface with or as if with a rake: *Rake the yard.* **3** make a long sweeping movement, such as with fingers, or a comb: *She raked her fingernails across the chalkboard. He raked a comb through his hair.* **4** (*with **up** or **together***) gather together: *She raked up enough money to rent a canoe.* **5** search or rummage through something: *He raked the closet for something to wear to the party.* <Old English *raca*>
rake in, *Informal* gather something, especially money, in great amounts very quickly.
rake up, expose unpleasant facts about someone or something.

rake[2] (rāk) *n* a fashionable or wealthy man with immoral habits. <obsolete *rakehell*>

rake[3] (rāk) *n* a slant or slope of something.
v **raked, rak·ing** have a slant or slope: *The masts raked backwards.* <origin uncertain>

rak·ish (rā′kish) *adj* with a jaunty, dashing, or slightly disreputable quality or appearance: *a cap set at a rakish angle.* **rak′ish·ly** *adv.* **rak′ish·ness** *n.*

ral·ly (ral′ē) *v* **ral·lied, ral·ly·ing 1** reassemble as a force, especially a military force, in order to continue action after having been scattered or temporarily defeated: *The commander was able to rally the fleeing troops.* **2** gather all available energy or initiative to do something: *The runner rallied all her energy for one last effort.* **3** assemble as a group for a common purpose: *The children rallied to help clean up the school after the fun fair.* **4** come to help a person, party, or cause: *She rallied to the side of her injured friend.* **5** recover health or strength: *The sick woman may rally now. The dollar rallied after being down all day.* **6** take part in a competition for motor vehicles in which they are driven a long distance over public roads or rough terrain.
n, pl **ral·lies 1** the act or fact of recovering from a setback or a period of weakness. **2** a mass meeting for some common purpose: *a political rally.* **3** a competition for motor vehicles in which they are driven a long distance over public roads or rough terrain: *a sports-car rally.* **4** *Sports* an extended series of strokes between players in tennis or other racquet games. <French *re-* again + *allier* to ally>

ram (ram) *n* **1** an adult, uncastrated, male sheep. **2** a machine or part of a machine that strikes heavy blows, for example, to drive piles into the ground. **3** a battering ram. **4** a water-raising machine or part of a machine, such as a piston or plunger.
v **rammed, ram·ming 1** violently butt, strike, or crash against: *One ship rammed the other.* **2** drive down or in by heavy force: *He rammed the bolt into the wall.* <Old English *ramm*>

RAM *Computers n* in full, **random access memory** the part of a computer's memory in which information can be changed or erased. <*r(andom) a(ccess) m(emory)*>

Ram·a·dan (ram′ə dån′) *Islam n* the ninth month of the Islamic calendar, during which fasting is done from sunrise to sunset. <Arabic *ramada* be hot, since it was originally supposed to take place during a hot month>

ram·ble (ram′bəl) *v* **ram·bled, ram·bling 1** wander about for pleasure: *We rambled here and there through the woods.* **2** talk or write about first one thing and then another, with no clear connection between them. **3** grow or spread irregularly in various directions: *Vines rambled over the wall.*
n a walk for pleasure, not to go to a special place. <Middle English *romen* roam>

ram·bler (ram′blər) *n* **1** a person who rambles. **2** a type of climbing rose.

ram·bling (ram′bling) *adj* **1** wandering about from place to place: *a rambling man.* **2** writing or speaking without clear connections between topics: *a rambling speech.* **3** climbing or straggling upward: *rambling roses.* **4** extending irregularly in various directions or without being planned: *a rambling old farmhouse.*

ram·bunc·tious (ram bungk′shəs) *adj* boisterous and unruly: *My young cousins were very rambunctious after travelling all day.* <origin uncertain>

ram·ie (ram′ē) *or* (rām′ē) *n* a plant native to tropical Asia, with stalks that yield a strong, glossy fibre used in making fabric. <Malay *rami* plant>

ram·i·fi·ca·tion (ram′ə fə kā′shən) *n* **1** the process of dividing or spreading out into branches or parts. **2** a branch or part. **3** a consequence of an action, idea, or event, especially when complex or unwelcome: *the ramifications of a decision.* <Old French, from Latin *ramus* branch + *facere* make> **ram′i·fy′** (ram′ə fī′) *v.*

ram·jet (ram′jet′) *n* a jet engine in which the fuel is fed into air that is compressed by forward motion instead of by means of a compressor.

ram·mer (ram′ər) *n* a person who or thing that rams, especially a device for driving or compacting something.

ramp (ramp) *n* **1** a sloping walk or roadway connecting two different levels of a building, structure, or road. **2** a staircase for going into or out of aircraft. <Old French *ramper* to climb>

a bat	e bed	i bid	o pot	u cup	th thin
ā cake	ē me	ī bite	ō go	ū rude	ᴛʜ then
å bar	ə about	ər over	ȯ for	u̇ put	zh measure

ram·page (ram′pāj) *for n,* (ram pāj′) *or* (ram′pāj) *for v.* *n* a spell of violent or uncontrollable behaviour, accompanied by rushing around wildly: *The sick elephant went on a rampage and injured its keeper.*
v **ram·paged, ram·pag·ing** rush around in a wild and uncontrollable way. <origin uncertain>
on the rampage, acting in an uncontrolled or destructive way: *She's been on the rampage ever since she was falsely accused of stealing.*

ramp·ant (ram′pənt) *adj* **1** growing or spreading in an uncontrolled way: *The vines ran rampant over the fence.* **2** violent and unrestrained: *Anarchy was rampant after the dictator died.* **3** in heraldry, standing up on the hind legs: *a lion rampant.* <Old French *ramper* to climb> **ramp′ant·ly** *adv.*

ram·part (ram′pårt) *n* **1** a wide bank of earth, often with a wall on top, built around a fort or walled city to help defend it. **2** 🍁 **ramparts** *pl especially North and Western Provinces* steep rock walls on either side of a river gorge. <Middle French *remparer* to fortify>

ram·rod (ram′rod′) *n* a rod for ramming down the charge in old firearms that were loaded from the muzzle.
adv rigid and upright: *She held herself ramrod straight.*

ram·shack·le (ram′shak′əl) *adj* loosely held, shaky, and likely to come apart: *ramshackle old buildings.* <obsolete *ransackled* ransacked>

ran (ran) past tense of RUN.

ranch (ranch) *n* **1** a large farm with grazing land, for raising livestock in large numbers. **2** the persons working or living on a ranch: *The entire ranch was at the party.*
v work on or operate a ranch. <Spanish *rancho* group of people eating together> **ranch′er** *n.*

ran·che·ro (ran chā′rō) *n* a ranch owner or ranch worker in Mexico or the southwestern US. The feminine is **ranchera**.
adj **rancheros** baked with a spicy tomato and onion sauce: *chicken rancheros.* <Spanish *rancho* group of people eating together>

ranch hand *n* a person employed on a ranch, especially a cattle ranch.

ranch house *n* **1** the main residential building on a ranch. **2** a long, low, spacious, one-storey house.

ran·cid (ran′sid) *adj* **1** stale or spoiled, especially in foods containing fat or oil: *rancid butter.* **2** tasting or smelling like stale fat or oil: *a rancid odour.* <Latin *rancere* be rank> **ran·cid′i·ty** *n.*

ran·cour or **ran·cor** (rang′kər) *n* long-lasting bitter resentment or ill will. <Old French, from Latin *rancere* be rank> **ran′cor·ous** *adj.* **ran′cor·ous·ly** *adv.* **ran′cor·ous·ness** *n.*

R & B *n* in full, **rhythm and blues** a style of popular music that developed in black urban areas in the US from blues, with the addition of rhythms taken from jazz.

R & D research and development

ran·dom (ran′dəm) *adj* **1** made, done, chosen, or happening without a method or plan: *a random sample.* **2** in statistics, governed by or involving equal chances for each item. <Old French> **ran′dom·ly** *adv.*
ran′dom·ness *n.*
at random, with no plan or method: *She took a book at random from the shelf.*

> **SYNONYMS**
>
> **Random** suggests the absence of a plan or purpose: *I made a random choice from the magazine rack.*
>
> **Chance** means "unforeseeable" or "accidental": *Their chance meeting that day was the beginning of a close friendship.*
>
> **Haphazard** suggests carelessness in thinking or action: *Haphazard driving causes accidents.*

random access *Computers n* the process by which a computer transfers information to or from memory, and in which each memory location can be accessed directly.

R & R rest and relaxation; rest and recuperation.
<US army slang for *rest and recuperation leave*>

ran·dy (ran′dē) *adj* **ran·di·er, ran·di·est** lustful or sexually aroused. **ran′di·ly** *adv.* **ran′di·ness** *n.*

rang (rang) past tense of RING².

range (rānj) *n* **1 a** the area of variation between the upper and lower limits on a scale: *a range of prices from twenty-five up to a hundred dollars.* **b** *Statistics* the difference between the upper and lower extremes in a set of data. **2** the distance a weapon can shoot. **3** a place to practise shooting or other skills, or to test equipment: *a driving range, a missile range.* **4** the distance within which a person can see or hear, or within which broadcast transmissions can be made: *He wasn't in her range of vision. The radio station had a huge range.* **5** the scope of a human voice or a musical instrument: *Her singing had a great range.* **6** a row or line of mountains or hills. **7** a large area of open land for grazing livestock: *He rode the range.* **8** a set of different things of the same type: *a wide range of opportunities.* **9** an area in which certain plants or animals live or travel. **10** a stove for cooking: *At our summer cottage, we cook on a wood range.*
v **ranged, rang·ing** **1** vary within certain limits: *temperatures ranging from 12° to 20°.* **2** wander over a large area: *Buffalo once ranged these plains.* **3** put in a row or rows, or in a specified order, manner, group, or class: *Range the books by size.* **4** run in a line or extend: *a boundary ranging east and west.* **5** extend over a wide variety of topics in speaking or writing: *Our talk ranged over all that had happened on our holidays.* **6** be found or occur in: *a plant ranging from Canada to Mexico.* <Old French *rang* rank>

range finder *n* an instrument for determining the distance between an object or target, especially for a camera or weapon.

🍁 **range lily** *n* the wild orange-red lily.

range of tolerance *n* the range within which an organism can tolerate abiotic factors (heat, light, etc.) in its ecosystem. Some species of fish, for example, can only survive within a small range of oxygen levels.

rang·er (rān′jər) *n* **1** a person employed to guard or maintain a park, forest, or area of countryside. **2** a person who or thing that ranges. **3** a soldier of certain regiments or special forces.

rang·y (rān′jē) *adj* **rang·i·er, rang·i·est** slender and long limbed: *a rangy horse, a rangy youth.* <*range*> **rang′i·ness** *n.*

ra·ni (rȧ′nē) *n* in former times, a Hindu queen, either by marriage to a raja or in her own right.

rank[1] (rangk) *n* **1** a row or line of people or things, especially soldiers. **2** a position, grade, or class in a hierarchy, especially the armed forces: *the rank of colonel.* **3** a high position in society or an organization: *A duchess is a woman of rank.* **4 ranks** *pl* private soldiers and junior non-commissioned officers: *She came up through the ranks to become an officer in the armed forces.*
v **1** give someone or something a place within a graded system: *Rank the provinces in order of population.* **2** have a certain place or position in relation to other persons or things: *She ranked low in the test.* **3** arrange in a line or row. <Old French *renc*>
pull rank, use a superior position to take advantage of someone or get your own way.

rank[2] (rangk) *adj* **1** thick and coarse: *rank grass.* **2** with a strong, unpleasant smell or taste: *rank meat, rank tobacco.* **3** strongly marked or extreme: *rank ingratitude, rank nonsense.* <Old English *ranc* overbearing> **rank′ly** *adv.* **rank′ness** *n.*

rank and file *n* **1** the members of an armed force, excluding its officers. **2** the members of an organization, society, or other group, excluding the leaders: *The union leaders were in favour of the offer, but it was rejected by the rank and file.*

rank·ing (rang′king) *adj* **1** with the highest rank: *Who's the ranking officer on the base?* **2** recognized as being of high calibre: *They are all ranking artists.*
n **1** a list, especially an official one, of people or things in order of their position relative to some standard: *She's at the top of the tennis ranking this year.* **2** one's position in such a list: *Winning this tournament improves his ranking.*

ran·kle (rang′kəl) *v* **ran·kled, ran·kling** cause persistent annoyance or resentment: *Even after all those years, the memory of the insult still rankled.* <Old French *draoncle* festering sore, from Latin *dracunculus* little snake>

ran·sack (ran′sak) *or* (ran sak′) *v* **1** search so thoroughly that it causes disorder or damage: *I ransacked the whole closet, but couldn't find the belt.* **2** cause damage and disorder in the course of a robbery: *When I returned to my locker after lunch, I found that it had been ransacked and my CD player was gone.* <Old Norse *rann* house + *sæja* search>

ran·som (ran′səm) *n* **1** the price paid or demanded before a captive or prisoner is set free: *The robbers held the travellers as prisoners for ransom.* **2** the act or fact of holding or freeing a captive or prisoner in return for payment.
v obtain the release of a captive or prisoner by paying a price. <Old French, from Latin *redimere* to redeem>

rant (rant) *v* speak wildly or noisily.
n a wild or noisy speech. <Dutch *ranten* rave> **rant′er** *n.*
rant and rave, *Informal* speak wildly and noisily.

rap[1] (rap) *n* a quick, light knock or blow: *a rap at the door, a rap across the knuckles.*
v **rapped, rap·ping 1** knock sharply and lightly: *The chairman rapped on the table for order.* **2** criticize sharply: *She rapped me for arriving late.* **3** say sharply or suddenly: *to rap out an answer.* <imitative>
beat the rap, *Informal* escape punishment.
rap on the knuckles, *Informal* **a** too light a punishment: *All he got was a rap on the knuckles.* **b** punish too lightly: *They rapped that con artist on the knuckles and let her go.*
take the rap, *Informal* pay the penalty or take the blame.

CONFUSABLES

Rap means "knock": *The chairperson rapped on the table to bring the meeting to order.*

Wrap means "cover by winding or folding around": *Please wrap the present with this paper.*

rap[2] (rap) *Informal n* the least bit: *I don't care a rap.* <origin uncertain>

rap[3] (rap) *n* **1** a type of popular music consisting of rhyming verse, chanted or shouted to a strong, repetitive beat. **2** *Informal* a talk or discussion, especially an informal one.
v **rapped, rap·ping 1** perform rap music. **2** *Informal* talk freely and informally. <*rap*[1]> **rap′per** *n.*

ra·pa·cious (rə pā′shəs) *adj* aggressively greedy: *rapacious pirates, a rapacious miser.* <Latin *rapere* to snatch> **ra·pa′cious·ly** *adv.* **ra·pa′cious·ness** *n.* **ra·pac′i·ty** *n.*

rape[1] (rāp) *n* **1** the crime of an individual who violently inflicts sexual contact on another person without consent. **2** a forcible or outrageous interference or violation: *the rape of natural resources.*
v **raped, rap·ing** inflict sexual contact without consent. <Old French, from Latin *rapere* to snatch>

rape[2] (rāp) *n* a plant of the cabbage family whose leaves are used as food for livestock and whose seeds are a source of cooking oil. <Latin *rapa* turnip>

rap·ee pie or **rap·pé pie** (ro′pē) *or* (ro′pā) *n* a traditional Acadian dish of baked chicken, pork, or rabbit with grated potatoes and onions. <French *râper* to grate>

rape·seed (rāp′sēd′) *n* the seed of the rape plant, used as a source of cooking oil.

rap·id (rap′id) *adj* **1** moving, acting, or doing quickly: *a rapid worker.* **2** going on or forward at a fast rate: *rapid growth.*
n **rapids** *pl* a part of a river's course where the water rushes quickly, often over rocks near the surface: *The boat overturned in the rapids.* <Latin *rapere* hurry away> **rap′id·i·ty** *n.* **rap′id·ly** *adv.* **rap′id·ness** *n.*

rapid eye movement REM.

a bat	e bed	i bid	o pot	u cup	th thin
ā cake	ē me	ī bite	ō go	ū rude	TH then
ȧ bar	ə about	ər over	ȯ for	u̇ put	zh measure

rap·id–fire (rap′id fīr′) *adj* **1** firing or adapted for firing shots in quick succession. **2** done or carried on quickly or sharply: *rapid-fire speech.*

rapid transit *n* a system of fast public transportation by railway in urban areas, often elevated or underground.

ra·pi·er (rā′pē ər) *n* a light, straight, two-edged sword used for thrusting.
adj quick and sharp, especially in speech or intelligence: *a rapier wit.* <origin uncertain> **ra′pi·er·like′** *adj.*

rap·ist (rāp′ist) *n* a person who commits the crime of rape.

rap·pel (ra pel′) *v* **rap·pelled, rap·pel·ling** descend a vertical surface of rock by means of a double rope that is secured above and passed around the body in such a way that the rate of descent is controlled.
n an act of descending in this way. <French *rappeler* bring back to oneself>

rap·port (rȧ pôr′) *n* a connection or relationship, especially a harmonious or agreeable one: *He has no rapport with his students. My twin brother and I have always had a good rapport.* <French *rapporter* bring back>

rap·proche·ment (rȧ prôsh mäɴ′) *n* the establishment or renewal of friendly relations. <French *re-* again + *approcher* to approach>

rap·scal·lion (rap skal′yən) *n* a mischievous person. <origin uncertain>

rap sheet *Informal n* a person's police record, listing arrests and convictions.

rapt (rapt) *adj* **1** completely entranced or fascinated: *We listened to the story with rapt attention.* **2** caused by or showing great pleasure or delight: *a rapt smile.* <Latin *rapere* to seize> **rapt′ly** *adv.*

rap·tor (rap′tər) *n* a bird of prey, such as an eagle, hawk, or owl. <Latin *rapere* to take by force>

rap·to·ri·al (rap tô′rē əl) *adj* with a hooked beak and sharp claws suited for seizing prey.

rap·ture (rap′chər) *n* **1** intense pleasure or joy: *The mother gazed with rapture at her newborn baby.* **2 raptures** *pl* expressions of great joy: *She went into raptures about the new CD.* **rap′tur·ous** *adj.* **rap′tur·ous·ly** *adv.*

rare[1] (rer) *adj* **rar·er, rar·est 1** seldom seen, occurring, or found: *The whooping crane has become very rare. For him, going to a party was a rare event.* **2** unusually good or great: *He had rare powers as an inventor.* <Latin *rarus*>

SYNONYMS

Rare can suggest "uncommon" or "unusual": *It was rare for the children to play on the busy street.*

Scarce suggests "once commonly plentiful, but no longer so": *Water is becoming a scarce resource in some parts of the world.*

Sparse means "thinly scattered" or "occurring here and there": *The vegetation on the mountain had become sparse because of the drought.*

rare[2] (rer) *adj* **rar·er, rar·est** cooked so that the inside of meat is still red: *rare steak.* <Old English *hrer*>

rare–earth element or **metal** (rer′ərth′) *n* a metallic element, one of a group whose members are chemically similar, tend to occur together in nature, and are difficult to separate from one another.

rar·e·fac·tion (rer′ə fak′shən) *n* a decrease in density or pressure in something, especially air or a gas.

ra·re·fied (rā′rə fīd) *adj* **1** of air, containing less oxygen than is usual: *the rarefied air high up in the Rockies.* **2** far removed from the lives and interests of ordinary people: *a rarefied discussion of theatre in ancient Greece.*

rar·e·fy (rer′ə fī′) *v* **rar·e·fied, rar·e·fy·ing 1** cause or be made to have a decrease in density or pressure in something, especially air or a gas. **2** refine or purify.

rare·ly (rer′lē) *adv* **1** seldom. **2** *Archaic* unusually well: *a rarely carved panel.*

rar·ing (rer′ing) *Informal adj* enthusiastic and eager: *raring to go, raring for a fight.* <*rare*, variation of *roar* or *rear*[2]>

rar·i·ty (rer′ə tē) *n, pl* **rar·i·ties 1** something rare: *A thirty-year-old car is a rarity.* **2** the quality or condition of being rare or scarce: *The value of diamonds is partly due to their rarity.*

ras·cal (ras′kəl) *n* **1** a mischievous person or animal: *Come back here with my slipper, you rascal!* **2** a rogue or dishonest person. <Old French *rascaille* rabble> **ras′cal·ly** *adj.*

SYNONYMS

Rascal is often used playfully, especially with reference to children: *Turn off the TV, you rascals.*

Scoundrel means "person without principles": *The scoundrel lied to his sister about the stolen money.*

Villain also means "scoundrel," often referring to a fictional character: *She played a scary villain in that movie.*

rash[1] (rash) *adj* too hasty, reckless, or bold: *He was rash to cross the street without looking both ways.* <origin uncertain> **rash′ly** *adv.* **rash′ness** *n.*

rash[2] (rash) *n* **1** an area of reddening of a person's skin, sometimes with small raised spots: *Perfumed soaps give me a rash.* **2** a sudden appearance of many things of the same type, especially when unpleasant or undesirable: *There was a rash of angry letters following the publication of the article.* <French *rach* a sore, from Latin *radere* to scrape>

rash·er (rash′ər) *n* a thin slice of bacon or ham for frying or broiling.

rasp (rasp) *v* **1** make or utter a harsh, grating sound: *The file rasped on the scythe blade, to rasp out a command.* **2** use a coarse metal file or similar tool with a roughened surface to scrape, file, or rub a hard surface or material.
n **1** a harsh, grating sound: *the rasp of crickets, a rasp in a person's voice.* **2** a coarse file with a roughened surface. See CHISEL for picture. <Old French>

rasp·ber·ry (raz′ber′ē) *n, pl* **rasp·ber·ries 1** a small, soft fruit that grows on prickly stems. **2** *Informal* a sound of disapproval or contempt made with the tongue and lips.
adj made of or flavoured with raspberry: *raspberry pie.* <origin uncertain>

rasp·y (rasp′ē) *adj* of a voice, hoarse or grating.

Ras·ta·far·i·an (ras′tə fā′ri ən) *n* a follower of a Jamaican religious movement believing that blacks are the chosen people, that Emperor Haile Selassie (hī′li sə la′ sā) was the Messiah, and that all black people one day will return to Africa, their homeland.
adj to do with Rastafarians or their beliefs. <*Ras Tafari* Prince Tafari, original name and title of Haile Selassie> **Ras′ta·far′i·an·ism′** *n.*

ras·ter (ras′tər) *n* a pattern of horizontal scanning lines traced by an electron beam on a TV screen or computer monitor when no picture is being transmitted. <German, from Latin *radere* to rake> **ras′ter·ize** *v.*

rat (rat) *n* **1** a long-tailed rodent with a pointed snout resembling a large mouse. See FIELD MOUSE for picture. **2** a treacherous or disloyal person.
v **rat·ted, rat·ting** hunt for or catch rats. <Old English *rætt*>
smell a rat, *Informal* suspect a trick or scheme: *I smelled a rat when none of the others showed up.*

ra·ta·tou·ille (rat′ə tū′ē) *n* a dish made from eggplant, tomatoes, zucchini, onion, and green peppers, stewed in oil. <French *touiller* stir>

ratch·et (rach′it) *n* a wheel or bar with teeth that strike against a catch so that motion is permitted in one direction but not in the other. <French *rochet*>

rate (rāt) *n* **1** a comparison of two quantities measured in different units, often distance, money, etc. compared to time: *The car was moving at the rate of thirty kilometres per hour. The rental rate is four dollars a day.* Compare RATIO. **2** a fixed price for something: *We pay the regular rate.* **3** the speed with which something moves, happens, or changes: *a heart rate.* **4** a local tax, often on property.
v **rat·ed, rat·ing** **1** assign a standard or value to something according to a scale. **2** consider or classify as of a certain quality, standard, or rank: *She was rated as one of the richest women in town. As a mechanic, he simply doesn't rate.* **3** assess the value of something, especially property: *We rated the house at $250 000.* <Old French, from Latin *reri* reckon> **rat′er** *n.*
at any rate, under any circumstances: *Even if they don't win, at any rate they'll enjoy playing.*
at this (or **that**) **rate,** under such circumstances: *If we keep going at this rate we'll never get home.*

rate·pay·er (rāt′pā′ər) *n* a person who pays municipal taxes.

rath·er (raтн′ər) *or* (rȧ′тнər) *adv* **1** more readily or more willingly: *I would rather go than stay.* **2** more properly or justly: *This is rather for your mother to decide than for you.* **3** more accurately or precisely: *It was last Monday night, or, rather, early Tuesday morning.* **4** (*with a verb*) in some degree: *She rather felt that this was unwise.* **5** to some extent: *This pie is rather good.* **6** on the contrary: *The sick man is no better today; rather, he is worse.* <Old English *hrathor*>
had rather, would prefer to: *I'd rather not go, thanks.*

rat·i·fy (rat′ə fī′) *v* **rat·i·fied, rat·i·fy·ing** approve formally and consent to a treaty, contract, or agreement: *The two countries will ratify the agreement made by their representatives.* <Old French, from Latin *ratus* fixed + *facere* make> **rat′i·fi·ca′tion** *n.* **rat′i·fi′er** *n.*

rat·ing (rā′ting) *n* **1** a classification or grade: *a high rating, a rating of "Satisfactory" in English.* **2** a level of popularity as established by a survey, especially of TV programs.

ra·ti·o (rā′shē ō′) *or* (rā′shō) *n, pl* **ra·ti·os** a comparison of quantities given as a proportion. This can also be expressed as a fraction or as a percent. Example: In a group with 5 boys and 8 girls, the ratio of boys to girls is 5 : 8. The ratio of girls to boys is 8 : 5. Compare RATE (def. 1). <Latin *reri* reckon>

ra·tion (rash′ən) *n* **1** a fixed allowance of food, fuel, or other commodity, especially during a time of shortage. **2 rations** *pl* an amount of food supplied on a regular basis: *army rations, emergency rations.*
v allow each person to have a fixed allowance of food, fuel, or other commodity: *Food was rationed to the public in wartime.* <French, from Latin *reri* reckon>

ra·tion·al (rash′ə nəl) *or* (rash′nəl) *adj* **1** based on reason and logic: *When very angry, people seldom act in a rational way.* **2** able to think and reason clearly: *As children grow older, they become more rational.* <Latin *reri* reckon> **ra′tion·al·ly** *adv.*

ra·tion·ale (rash′ə nal′) *n* a set of reasons or a logical basis for an action or belief.

ra·tion·al·ism (rash′ə nə liz′əm) *or* (rash′nə liz′əm) *n* **1** the principle or practice of accepting reason as the supreme authority in matters of opinion, belief, or conduct. **2** the theory in philosophy that reason rather than experience accounts for knowing that something is true. **ra′tion·al·ist** *n.* **ra′tion·al·is′tic** *adj.*

ra·tion·al·i·ty (rash′ə nal′ə tē) *or* (rash′nal′ə tē) *n* the possession of reason: *He is somewhat strange, but no one doubts his rationality.*

ra·tion·al·ize (rash′ə nə līz′) *or* (rash′nə līz′) *v* **ra·tion·al·ized, ra·tion·al·iz·ing** **1** attempt to explain or justify one's own or another's conduct or attitude with logical or plausible reasons, even if they are not true or appropriate: *I rationalize my greediness by thinking, "I must eat to keep up my strength."* **2** attempt to make a process, system, company, or industry more efficient by making it more logical or consistent, especially by reducing unneeded workers or equipment. **ra′tion·al·i·za′tion** *n.*

rational number *Mathematics n* a number that can be expressed as a ratio of two integers, excluding zero as a denominator. That is, the number 5 is rational because it can be expressed as the ratio 5 : 1. Examples: 0, –2, 2000, 0.25, 1/2

rat race *Informal n* a way of life in which people scramble or struggle to achieve wealth or power.

a bat	e bed	i bid	o pot	u cup	th thin
ā cake	ē me	ī bite	ō go	ū rude	тн then
ȧ bar	ə about	ər over	ȯ for	u̇ put	zh measure

R

rat–tail (rat′tāl′) *n* a long, thin, taperless tail that is hairless like a rat's, or something resembling it.

rat·tan (ra tan′) *n* a climbing palm with very long, jointed, pliable stems used to make furniture. <Malay *rotan*>

rat·ter (rat′ər) *n* a dog or other animal that catches rats: *Our terrier is a good ratter.*

rat·tle (rat′əl) *v* **rat·tled, rat·tling 1** make, cause, or move with a rapid succession of short knocking sounds: *The window rattled in the wind. The earthquake rattled the dishes on the shelves. The cart rattled down the street.* **2** talk quickly, on and on. **3** cause someone to be confused or upset: *I was so rattled by the applause that I forgot my speech.*
n **1** a rapid succession of short knocking sounds: *the rattle of empty bottles.* **2** a thing used to make a rapid succession of short knocking sounds, such as a toy or instrument that makes a noise when it is shaken: *The baby shook her rattle.* **3** the hornlike pieces at the end of a rattlesnake's tail that are shaken with a dry buzzing sound as a warning. **4** a gurgling sound in the throat of a dying person. <Middle English *ratelen*>
rattle around in, live or work in a place that is much larger than one needs.

The **rattler** shakes its rattle vigorously as a warning to intruders. Each time the rattler sheds its skin, a new section is added to the rattle.

rat·tler (rat′lər) *Informal n* a rattlesnake.

rat·tle·snake (rat′əl snāk′) *n* a poisonous snake with a thick body and a broad, triangular head that makes a rattling noise with its tail.

rat·tle·trap (rat′əl trap′) *n* something shaky, rickety, or rattling, especially an old, worn-out car.

rat–trap (rat′trap′) *n* **1** a trap to catch rats. **2** a dirty, rundown building. **3** a situation that allows no escape or chance of improvement.

rat·ty (rat′ē) *adj* **rat·ti·er, rat·ti·est 1** of, like, or full of rats. **2** *Informal* shabby or ramshackle.

rau·cous (rok′əs) *adj* hoarse, harsh, and loud: *the raucous caw of a crow.* <Latin *raucus* hoarse> **rau′cous·ly** *adv.*

raun·chy (ron′chē) *adj* **raun·chi·er, raun·chi·est** energetic and sexually explicit: *That video is a bit raunchy.* <origin uncertain> **raunch′i·ly** *adv* **raunch′i·ness** *n.*

rav·age (rav′ij) *v* **rav·aged, rav·ag·ing** damage greatly: *The fire ravaged huge areas of forest.*
n the damaging or destructive effects of something: *the ravages of a hard life.* <Old French = destruction, from *ravir* to take away hastily> **rav′ag·er** *n.*

rave (rāv) *v* **raved, rav·ing 1** talk wildly, as if one were delirious or insane. **2** talk or write about something with great enthusiasm or admiration: *She raved about her food.*
n **1** *Informal* unrestrained praise, especially a highly enthusiastic review of a piece of entertainment: *The play got raves in the local press.* **2** a large, informal gathering of young people with dancing to fast, electronic music. <origin uncertain>

rav·el (rav′əl) *v* **rav·elled** or **rav·eled, rav·el·ling** or **rav·el·ing 1** separate into threads or strands: *The sweater has ravelled at the wrist.* **2** become involved or confused. <Dutch *rafel* frayed thread>

ra·ven (rā′vən) *n* **1** a large member of the crow family with mainly black feathers. It is the provincial bird of Yukon Territory. **2** 🍁 **Raven** *Pacific Northwest* a trickster spirit in the form of a giant raven.
adj deep, glossy black: *She has raven hair.* <Old English *hræfn*>

rav·en·ing (rav′ə ning) *adj* extremely hungry and hunting for prey: *ravening wolves.*

rav·en·ous (rav′ə nəs) *adj* **1** very hungry: *The hikers were all ravenous by the time they stopped to eat.* **2** very great in degree: *ravenous hunger. He was ravenous for praise.* <Old French *ravinos* violent> **rav′en·ous·ly** *adv.*

ra·vine (rə vēn′) *n* a long, deep, narrow gorge worn by running water or by the action of glaciers. <Old French>

rav·ing (rā′ving) *adj* **1** delirious or frenzied. **2** *Informal* remarkable or extraordinary: *Our school music night was a raving success.*
n delirious or frenzied talk. **rav′ing·ly** *adv.*

rav·i·o·li (rav′ē ō′lē) *n* small, thin envelopes of pasta filled with ground meat, cheese, or vegetables, boiled in water and usually served with a sauce. <Italian>

rav·ish (rav′ish) *v* **1** fill with delight: *ravished by the beauty of the scene.* **2** *Archaic* rape someone. <Old French, from Latin *rapere* seize>

rav·ish·ing (rav′i shing) *adj* very delightful or enchanting: *jewels of ravishing beauty.* **rav′ish·ing·ly** *adv.* **rav′ish·ment** *n.*

raw (ro) *adj* **1** not cooked as food: *raw oysters.* **2** natural and not manufactured, processed, treated, or prepared: *raw materials.* **3** new to an activity or job, and hence not skilled: *a raw recruit.* **4** unpleasantly damp or cold: *raw weather.* **5** red and painful in a part of the body, especially with the skin rubbed or torn off: *a raw spot.* **6** frank, strong, and undisguised: *raw emotions.* **7** cruel and unfair: *a raw deal.* <Old English *hreaw*> **raw′ly** *adv.* **raw′ness** *n.*
in the raw, a *Informal* naked: *to sleep in the raw.* **b** in an unrefined or very realistic way: *experiencing life in the raw.*

raw–boned (rob′ōnd′) *adj* bony or gaunt, especially with a large, somewhat bony frame.

raw·hide (ro′hīd′) *n* the untanned skin of cattle, or a rope or whip made of it.
v **raw·hid·ed, raw·hid·ing** whip or drive with a rawhide.

raw material *n* a basic material before it has been manufactured, treated, or prepared.

ray[1] (rā) *n* **1** a line or beam of light: *rays of the sun.* **2** a line or stream of radiant energy: *X-rays.* **3** something like a ray, coming out from a centre, such as the petals of a daisy.

4 a slight trace, especially of a positive or welcome quality: *Not a ray of hope pierced our gloom.* 5 *Mathematics* a straight line passing through a point. <Old French, from Latin *radius*>

ray[2] (rā) *n* a fish with a broad, flat body, winglike pectoral fins, and a long, slender tail. Some rays have poisonous spines or organs that shock its prey with electricity. <Latin *raia*>

ray flower *n* one of the petal-like flowers forming the outside of the flower head of a composite plant: *The flower head of a daisy consists of central disc flowers surrounded by ray flowers.* See DISC FLOWER for picture.

ray·on (rā′on) *n* a fibre or fabric made from cellulose treated with chemicals. <origin uncertain>

raze (rāz) *v* **razed, raz·ing** tear down or destroy: *The old school was razed and a new one was built in the same place.* <Old French, from Latin *radere*>

ra·zor (rā′zər) *n* a small instrument with a sharp blade or blades, used for shaving or cutting hair: *an electric razor, a safety razor.* <Old French, from Latin *radere*>

ra·zor·back (rā′zər bak′) *n* 1 a narrow-bodied, half-wild hog of the southeastern US that has a high, narrow, ridged back. 2 a steep-sided, narrow ridge of land.

ra·zor·bill (rā′zər bil′) *n* a black-and-white bird of the N Atlantic that has a curved bill with a white line down the sides.

razor blade *n* a thin, flexible, extremely sharp, two-edged blade of a manual razor, now often put to other uses.

razz (raz) *Slang v* tease or heckle playfully. <*raspberry*>

raz·zle–daz·zle (ra′zəl da′zəl) *Informal n* noisy and exciting activity and display, especially when colourful and spectacular.
adj noisy, exciting, and flashy.
v **raz·zle-daz·zled, raz·zle-daz·zling** impress with something flashy or spectacular. <*dazzle*>

razz·ma·tazz (raz′mə taz′) *Informal n* razzle-dazzle.

RBI *Baseball n, pl* **RBIs, RBI's,** or **RBI** run batted in.

✱ **RCMP** or **R.C.M.P.** Royal Canadian Mounted Police.

RDA *n* in full, the **recommended daily allowance** of a vitamin or other nutrient.

GRAMMAR AND USAGE

Most words beginning with **re–** have no hyphen: *reassure, refresh*. However, a hyphen is often used if the *re-* is followed by an *e*: *re-entry, re-examine*.

A hyphen is always used to distinguish between a word in which *re-* means "again" (*re-cover*: "cover again") and a word that looks the same but has no hyphen (*recover*: "get back" or "get better").

re[1] (rā) *Music n* 1 the second tone of an eight-tone scale, especially as sung to sol-fa syllables: *do, re, mi, fa, so, la, ti, do.* 2 the tone D.

re[2] (rē) *prep* with reference to: *re your letter of June 15.* <Latin *res* thing>

re– *prefix* 1 again, anew, or once more: *reappear, rebuild, reheat.* 2 back; in return or mutually: *react.* <Latin>

reach (rēch) *v* 1 arrive at: *He reached the top of a hill. She reached the end of the book.* 2 stretch out an arm in order to grasp or touch something: *to reach toward a book.* 3 a (*with* ***to***) extend in space, time, operation, or effect: *The power of Rome reached to the ends of the known world.* b extend to: *TV reaches millions.* c amount to: *The cost of the war reached billions.* 4 get at or influence: *Some people are reached by flattery.* 5 succeed in achieving: *to reach an agreement.* 6 make contact or get in communication with someone: *I tried to reach you this morning.* 7 hand something to someone: *Reach me the sugar.*
n 1 a the act or fact of stretching out a hand or arm: *By a long reach, the drowning woman grasped the rope.* b the extent or distance of this stretching: *out of your reach.* 2 range, power, or capacity: *the reach of the mind.* 3 a continuous stretch or extent, such as a part of a river between bends. <Old English *rǣcan*>

re–act (rē akt′) *v* act over again: *to re-act a scene in a play.*

re·act (rē akt′) *v* 1 behave in a particular way in response to something: *Some people react against fads.* 2 interact and undergo a chemical or physical change: *Acids react on metals.*

re·act·ant (rē ak′tənt) *n* a substance participating in or undergoing a chemical reaction.

re·ac·tion (rē ak′shən) *n* 1 an action in response to some influence or force: *Our reaction to the joke was to laugh. The doctor carefully observed her patient's reactions to certain tests.* 2 an adverse physical response to something that is breathed, ingested, or touched: *an allergic reaction.* 3 an opposition to a belief or situation: *They formed a movement in reaction to the way the political system worked.* 4 the chemical action of two substances on each other that results in the formation of one or more additional substances: *The reaction between nitrogen and hydrogen produces ammonia.*

re·ac·tion·ar·y (rē ak′shə ner′ē) *adj* to do with or favouring a return to a previous condition, especially in politics: *The bad results of the revolution brought about a reactionary feeling.*
n, pl **re·ac·tion·ar·ies** a person who favours such a return.

reaction time *n* the time between applying a stimulus and noting a response.

re·ac·ti·vate (rē ak′tə vāt′) *v* **re·ac·ti·vat·ed, re·ac·ti·vat·ing** make active or effective again. **re′ac·ti·va′tion** *n.*

re·ac·tor (rē ak′tər) *n* 1 a person or animal that reacts, especially one that reacts positively to a medical test for a disease or allergy. 2 a nuclear reactor.

a bat	e bed	i bid	o pot	u cup	th thin
ā cake	ē me	ī bite	ō go	ū rude	TH then
ä bar	ə about	ər over	ô for	ů put	zh measure

read (rēd) *v* **read** (red), **read·ing 1 a** understand the meaning of symbols, especially those used in writing or printing: *to read a book. Braille is read with the fingers.* **b** speak printed or written words: *Read this story to me.* **2** show by letters, figures, signs, or symbols: *The thermometer reads 30°.* **3** give as the word or words in a particular passage: *For "fail," which is a misprint, read "fall."* **4** get the meaning of, understand, or interpret: *As I read her intention, she means to resign. He read a hostile intent in a friendly letter.* **5** produce a certain impression when understood as written or printed symbols: *This does not read like a child's essay. A rule that reads two ways.* **6** hear and understand someone speaking on a radio transmitter: *Do you read me?* **7** *Computers* copy or transfer data on a computer.
n Informal a book or other text: *That novel is a good read.*
adj (*in compounds*) with knowledge gained by reading: *a well-read woman.* <Old English *rædan*>
read between the lines, find a meaning not actually expressed in a text.
read into, interpret in a certain way, often attributing more than intended: *to read an insult into a silly remark.*
read out, read aloud: *She read out her answer to the class.*
read up on, research or learn about by reading.

read·a·bil·i·ty (rē′də bil′ə tē) *n* the quality or condition of being difficult to read: *Short words improve the readability of a piece of writing.*

read·a·ble (rē′də bəl) *adj* interesting or enjoyable to read: *His novels are very readable.*

read·er (rē′dər) *n* **1** a person who reads: *She is an avid reader. They are both poor readers.* **2** a person employed to read manuscripts and estimate their fitness for publication. **3** a book for learning and practising reading.

read·er·ship (rēd′ər ship) *n* the audience of a particular publication or author, or the number of people it includes: *a readership of 5000. This kind of ad will appeal to the readership of our school newspaper.*

readers' theatre *n* a performance in which a story, poem, etc. is used as a script and read to an audience.

read·i·ly (red′ə lē) *adv* **1** without hesitation or reluctance: *She answered me readily. I don't readily accept advice.* **2** without difficulty: *The parts fitted together readily.*

read·i·ness (red′ē nis) *n* **1** being ready or prepared for something: *readiness for action.* **2** willingness to do something: *readiness to accept a proposal.* **3** quickness or promptness: *readiness of speech.*

read·ing (rē′ding) *n* **1** the act or process of reading written or printed matter silently or aloud. **2** written or printed matter read or to be read: *There's good reading in this magazine.* **3** the information shown by letters, figures, or signs on the scale of an instrument: *The reading on the thermometer was 38°.* **4** an interpretation of a text, message, or situation: *Her reading of his words was that he wasn't angry at all. Each actor gave the lines a different reading.* **5** a stage of debate in a parliament through which a piece of legislation must pass before it can become law: *the third reading.* **6** the formal reading aloud of a legal document: *the reading of a will.*
adj used for reading: *reading glasses.*

reading response *n* thoughts and reactions to a text, written down to show understanding of the text.

reading room *n* a special room for reading in a library, organization, or club.

re·ad·just (rē′ə just′) *v* adjust or arrange again. **re′ad·just′ment** *n.*

read–only memory ROM.

read·out (rē′dout′) *Computers n* the process of retrieving information from a computer storage or memory device and displaying it in understandable form, such as in words or numerals, or the information so displayed.

read·y (red′ē) *adj* **read·i·er, read·i·est 1** prepared for immediate action or use: *ready for the exam.* **2** willing: *The knights were ready to die for their lords.* **3** quick or prompt in thought or action: *a ready welcome, a ready wit.* **4** apt or likely: *She is too ready to find fault.* **5** immediately available: *ready money.*
v **read·ied, read·y·ing** prepare something or someone for an activity or purpose. <Old English *ræde*>
at the ready, prepared or available for instant action: *The goalie crouched with her hockey stick at the ready.*
make ready, prepare.

read·y–made (red′ē mād′) *adj* **1** made beforehand in standard sizes and specifications: *ready-made clothes.* **2** ready to be served without further preparation: *a ready-made cake.* **3** conveniently established and available: *The postal strike provided her with a ready-made excuse for not writing.*

read·y–mix (red′ē miks′) *adj* ready to cook or use after adding liquid to dry ingredients: *ready-mix muffins, ready-mix cement.*

re·a·gent (rē ā′jənt) *n* a substance used to detect the presence of other substances by the chemical reactions it causes.

re·al (rē′əl) *or* (rēl) *adj* **1** existing as a fact or thing: *a real experience.* **2** genuine; not fake: *a real diamond.* **3** to do with immovable property, such as land and houses. **4** *Mathematics* either rational or irrational, not imaginary. **5** adjusted for changes in the value of money as purchasing power: *Real income fell last year.* **6** complete: *a real mess.*
adv Informal really or very: *He talked real loud.* <Old French, from Latin *res* thing>
for real, *Informal* **a** truly or in fact: *I'm apologizing for real this time.* **b** as remarkable as it (or one) seems: *Are you for real?*
get real, *Informal* **a** don't be ridiculous: *Sixty bucks for that piece of junk? Get real!* **b** become serious and sincere: *Sometimes we have a conversation where she gets real.*
in real life, in reality: *He plays a gangster in the TV series, but in real life he's a very gentle man.*

GRAMMAR AND USAGE

Real is an adjective meaning "true": *He's a real friend who is always willing to help.*

Really is an adverb meaning "very" and is often used to stress an adjective: *That's really good.*

Note that the word *real* is often used as an adverb in familiar speech *(That's real good)*, but that use should be avoided in writing.

real estate *n* property consisting of land or buildings.

real estate agent *n* a person who sells, rents, or leases real estate.

real image *Physics n* an optical image of something that is produced by reflection or refraction and can be transferred onto a surface such as the film inside a camera.

re·al·ism (rē′ə liz′əm) *n* **1** the attitude and practice of accepting and dealing with facts and situations as they are: *His realism made him dislike far-fetched schemes.* **2** the quality or fact of showing people and things as they actually are in life, especially when they are depicted in art or literature.

re·al·ist (rē′ə list) *n* **1** a person who accepts and deals with facts and conditions as they are. **2** a person who shows people and things as they actually are in life, especially an artist or writer.

re·al·is·tic (rē′ə lis′tik) *adj* **1** with or showing a sensible or practical idea of what can be achieved or expected. **2** representing life as it actually is, especially in art or literature. **re′al·is′ti·cal·ly** *adv.*

re·al·i·ty (rē al′ə tē) *n, pl* **re·al·i·ties 1** the quality or state of actually existing, as opposed to being imagined: *He was convinced of the reality of what he had seen. Her blog entries are an attempt to escape from reality.* **2** an actual thing, fact, or event: *the terrible realities of war. My dream became a reality.*
in reality, in actual fact: *We thought she was joking, but in reality she was serious.*

reality TV *n* TV programs that record how ordinary people react and behave after they have been placed in situations that make unusual demands on them.

re·al·i·za·tion (rē′ə lə zā′shən) *or* (rē′ə lī zā′shən) *n* **1** the act or fact of being realized: *The explorers had a full realization of the dangers they might face. For years they saved, waiting for the realization of their hopes.* **2** a thing that is realized: *Owning a farm would be the realization of all her dreams.*

re·al·ize (rē′ə līz′) *v* **re·al·ized, re·al·iz·ing 1** understand clearly or become fully aware of something as a fact: *Does your teacher realize how hard you worked?* **2** cause something desired or anticipated to become actual: *Her uncle's present made it possible for her to realize her dream of going to college.* **3** give actual or physical form to something: *The stage set was beautifully realized.* **4** bring or obtain as a price, return, or profit: *He realized thousands of dollars from his investment.*

re·al·ly (rē′ə lē) *or* (rē′lē) *adv* **1** in actual fact: *things as they really are. She really didn't know who it was.* **2** very, truly, or thoroughly: *a really magnificent house.*
interj used to express surprise, disbelief, or disapproval: *Really? I don't believe it!*

realm (relm) *n* **1** a monarchy. **2** a range or domain of activity or interest: *the realm of science. Such an occurrence is outside the realm of possibility.* <Old French, from Latin *regere* to rule>

real number *n* a member of the mathematical set of numbers that includes all the rational numbers and all the irrational numbers.

re·al·po·li·tik (rā al′po′lə tēk′) *n* a system of politics or policy based on power, convenience, or other practical considerations rather than morals or ideals. <German = practical politics>

real time *Computers n* the time for input data in a computer system to be processed so quickly that it is available as feedback almost instantaneously. **real-time** *adj.*

re·al·tor (rē′əl tər) *or* (rēl′tər) *n* **1** a person or company whose business is buying and selling real estate or helping others to do so. **2 Realtor** a real estate agent who belongs to a professional organization of real estate firms.

re·al·ty (rē′əl tē) *or* (rēl′tē) real estate.

ream[1] (rēm) *n* **1** about 500 sheets of paper of the same stock and size. **2 reams** *pl* a large quantity: *He took reams of notes.* <Old French, from Arabic *rizma* bundle>

ream[2] (rēm) *v* enlarge or shape a hole with a reamer. <origin uncertain>

ream·er (rē′mər) *n* **1** a tool for enlarging or shaping a drilled hole. **2** a utensil for squeezing the juice out of citrus fruits.

reap (rēp) *v* **1** cut or gather a crop or harvest, especially of grain: *to reap a field.* **2** get as a return or reward: *Kind acts often reap happy smiles.* <Old English *reopan*>

reap·er (rē′pər) *n* a person who or machine that cuts grain or gathers a crop.

re·ap·pear (rē′ə pēr′) *v* appear again. **re′ap·pear′ance** *n.*

rear[1] (rēr) *n* **1** the back part of something, especially a vehicle or building: *the rear of the house.* **2** the space or position at the back: *He moved toward the rear.*
adj at or in the back: *the rear door of the car.* <Old French, from Latin *retro* back>
at (or **in**) **the rear of,** behind.
bring up the rear, be last: *We filed through the woods, with me bringing up the rear.*

rear[2] (rēr) *v* **1** bring up and care for offspring: *Our mother was careful in rearing us.* **2** set up or build: *to rear a temple.* **3** raise or lift up: *to rear your head.* **4** rise on the hind legs, especially of a horse: *The horse reared as the fire engine dashed past.* **5** extend to a great height: *Mountain peaks reared up behind the valley.* <Old English *rǣran* raise>

rear–end (rēr′end′) *v* hit another vehicle from behind.

rear·guard (rēr′gard) *n* that part of an army that protects the rear.
adj defensive: *a rearguard action.*

re·arm (rē ärm′) *v* arm again with new or better weapons, especially in a nation or a military force. **re·ar′ma·ment** *n.*

rear·most (rēr′mōst) *adj* farthest in the rear.

re·ar·range (rē′ə rānj′) *v* **re·ar·ranged, re·ar·rang·ing** arrange or order in a new or different way: *to rearrange furniture.* **re′ar·range′ment** *n.*

rear·view mirror (rēr′vyü′) *n* a mirror on a motor vehicle attached so as to give a view of the area to the rear.

rear·ward (rēr′wərd) *adj, adv* toward or in the rear.

a bat	e bed	i bid	o pot	u cup	th thin
ā cake	ē me	ī bite	ō go	ū rude	ᴛʜ then
ä bar	ə about	ər over	ȯ for	ů put	zh measure

R

rea·son (rē′zən) *n* **1** a cause, motive, or justification for a thought, feeling, action, or event: *I have my own reasons for doing this. What is your reason for doing such poor work?* **2** the ability or power to think and draw conclusions: *That man has lost his reason.* **3** good sense: *The stubborn woman was at last brought to reason.*
v **1** think and draw conclusions: *He reasoned that his friend would be back soon.* **2** persuade someone by argument: *Reason with him to do things differently.* <Old French, from Latin *reri* consider> **rea′son·er** *n.*
beyond all reason, completely unreasonable or unreasonably.
bring to reason, cause to be reasonable.
by reason of, because of.
in reason, within reasonable and sensible limits.
it stands to reason, be reasonable and sensible: *It stands to reason that he would resent your insults.*
reason away, get rid of by rational argument: *She reasoned away our fears.*
reason out, figure out by logic; think through and come to a conclusion.

GRAMMAR AND USAGE

Avoid using **reason** followed by *because*:
Her reason for being late is because she slept in.
Replace *because* with *that*:
Her reason for being late is that she slept in.

rea·son·a·ble (rē′zə nə bəl) *adj* **1** according to reason and making sense: *a reasonable explanation, a reasonable theory.* **2** fair or moderate: *a reasonable request.* **3** fairly priced: *I expected the dress to be expensive, but it was really very reasonable.* **4** sensible and ready to listen to reason: *She's a reasonable person. Be reasonable and you'll see it can't possibly work that way.* **5** with the ability to reason: *Any reasonable person would turn down the offer.* **rea′son·a·ble·ness** *n.* **rea′son·a·bly** *adv.*

rea·soned (rē′sənd) *adj* based on logic or good sense: *a reasoned conclusion.*

rea·son·ing (rē′zə ning) *n* **1** the process of drawing conclusions from facts or ideas. **2** the reasons or arguments resulting from or used in this process: *I didn't understand her reasoning.*

re·as·sem·ble (rē′ə sem′bəl) *v* **re·as·sem·bled, re·as·sem·bling** **1** bring or be brought together again: *We shall reassemble here after recess.* **2** assemble something that has been taken apart: *My dad and I reassembled the old clock piece by piece.*

re·as·sure (rē′ə shůr′) *v* **re·as·sured, re·as·sur·ing** remove any doubts or fears a person may have: *The captain's confidence during the storm reassured the passengers. We reassured her that we would get there on time.* **re′as·sur′ance** *n.* **re′as·sur′ing** *adj.* **re′as·sur′ing·ly** *adv.*

Reb (reb) *n* a Jewish traditional title of respect or form of address for a man. <Yiddish, from Hebrew *rabbi* my master>

re·bate (rē′bāt) *n* the return of part of the money paid for something.
v **re·bat·ed, re·bat·ing** give as a rebate. <Old French *rebattre* to beat down, i.e., reduce>

reb·be (reb′ə) *Judaism n* **1** a rabbi, especially a respected spiritual leader among the Hasid. **2 Rebbe** a title of respect for this person. <Yiddish, from Hebrew *rabbi* my master>

reb·el (reb′əl) *for n,* (ri bel′) *for v. n* **1** a person who opposes or uses force against a government or ruler. **2** a person who resists authority, control, or convention: *She was always a rebel, and was never understood by her family.*
adj to do with persons who use force against a government or ruler: *a rebel stronghold, a rebel army.*
v **re·belled, re·bel·ling** **1** use force to oppose a government or an authority: *The people rebelled when the new tax was imposed. The troops rebelled against their commander.* **2** resist authority, control, or convention: *He rebelled against his family's wishes.* **3** feel or express a great dislike: *We rebelled at the thought of having to stay home all weekend.* <Old French, from Latin *re-* in return + *bellum* war>

re·bel·lion (ri bel′yən) *n* **1** organized resistance against the authority of a government: *The army put down the rebellion with great cruelty.* **2** an act of resistance against authority, control, or convention.

re·bel·lious (ri bel′yəs) *adj* defying authority, convention, or control: *rebellious troops.* **re·bel′lious·ly** *adv.* **re·bel′lious·ness** *n.*

re·birth (rē′bərth′) *or* (rē bərth′) *n* **1** the act or fact of being born again or reincarnated. **2** a revival after a period of decline: *the rebirth of nationalism, the rebirth of hope.*

re·boot (rē büt′) *Computers v* restart a computer or its operating system: *After installing the antiviral software, you must reboot.*

re·born (rē bôrn′) *adj* born again, renewed, or revived: *Our hopes for a win were reborn when we heard she would be playing after all.*

re·bound (ri bound′) *for v,* (rē′bound′) *for n. v* **1** spring back through the air after hitting a hard surface. **2** recover in value, amount, or strength: *After a brief sharp decline in the market, the dollar rebounded strongly.*
n **1** a ball or shot that springs back through the air after hitting a hard surface: *He hit the ball on the rebound.* **2** *Basketball* a ball that bounces off the backboard when a scoring attempt has been missed. <*re-* back + *bound*[2]>
on the rebound, while still affected by emotions caused by the ending of a love affair.

re·broad·cast (rē brod′kast′) *v* **re·broad·cast** or **re·broad·cast·ed, re·broad·cast·ing** **1** broadcast again at a later time or date: *The interview with the prime minister will be rebroadcast after the evening news.* **2** relay a TV or radio program as it is being received from another station.
n a relayed or repeated TV or radio broadcast.

re·buff (ri buf′) *n* a blunt or abrupt rejection of something: *Her offer to help him met with the rebuff "Leave me alone."*
v reject bluntly or abruptly: *The friendly dog was rebuffed by a kick.* <French, from Italian *ribuffo* a snub>

re·build (rē′bild′) *v* **re·built, re·build·ing** build again: *The snowman fell down and the children are trying to rebuild it.*

re·buke (ri byūk′) *v* **re·buked, re·buk·ing** express sharp disapproval or criticism of someone.
n an expression of sharp disapproval or criticism: *We got a rebuke for turning up late.* <Old French *re-* back + *buchier* hack down> **re·buk′er** *n.* **re·buk′ing** *adj.* **re·buk′ing·ly** *adv.*

re·bus (rē′bəs) *n* a representation of a word or phrase by pictures suggesting syllables or words. Example: a picture of a cat and a log = catalogue. <French, from Latin *res* thing>

re·but (ri but′) *v* **re·but·ted, re·but·ting** claim or prove that evidence or an accusation is false: *Each team in the debate was given two minutes to rebut the other's arguments.* <Old French *re-* opposing + *boter* butt[3]> **re·but′tal** *n.*

re·cal·ci·trant (ri kal′sə trənt) *adj* stubbornly resisting authority or control. <Latin *recalcitrare* to kick back> **re·cal′ci·trance** *n.*

re·call (ri kol′); *usually* (rē′kol′) *for n. v* **1** bring back into one's mind a fact, event, or situation, especially so as to tell others about it. **2** officially order someone to return to a place: *The ambassador was recalled.* **3** take back or withdraw: *The company recalled all its new cars.*
n **1** the act or fact of bringing back into one's mind a fact, event, or situation. **2** the action or ability to remember something learned or experienced: *She had extraordinary recall of the facts.* **3** the act or process of taking back or withdrawing something. **4** the removal of a public official from office by vote of the people.

re·cant (ri kant′) *v* formally withdraw an opinion or belief: *Though he was tortured to make him change his religion, the prisoner would not recant.* <Latin *re-* back + *cantare* chant> **re′can·ta′tion** *n.*

re·cap (rē′kap′) *or* (rē′kap′) *for v,* (rē′kap′) *for n.*
v **re·capped, re·cap·ping** *Informal* recapitulate.
n a recapitulation.

re·ca·pit·u·late (rē′kə pich′ə lāt′) *v* **re·ca·pit·u·lat·ed, re·ca·pit·u·lat·ing** summarize and repeat the main points of a speech or text. <Latin *re-* again + *caput* head> **re′ca·pit′u·la′tion** *n.*

re·cap·ture (rē kap′chər) *v* **re·cap·tured, re·cap·tur·ing** **1** capture a person who or animal that has escaped. **2** regain or recreate something that has been lost or forgotten: *The painting recaptured the days of the horse and buggy.*
n a taking or being taken again.

re·cast (rē kast′) *for v,* (rē′kast′) *for n. v* **re·cast, re·cast·ing** **1** give a metal object a new form by melting it down and reshaping it: *to recast a bell.* **2** present or organize in a different form or style: *to recast a sentence.* **3** distribute the parts to different actors in a movie, play, or other entertainment.
n a recasting.

re·cede (ri sēd′) *v* **re·ced·ed, re·ced·ing** **1** move back or away from a previous position: *Houses and trees seemed to recede as we rode past.* **2** gradually diminish as a quality, feeling, or possibility: *Our hopes receded after we learned she'd be late arriving.* **3** have hair on the head cease to grow at the temples and above the forehead: *a receding hairline.* **4** slope backward as a facial feature: *He has a chin that recedes.* <Latin *re-* back + *cedere* go>

re·ceipt (ri sēt′) *n* **1** a written or printed statement that money or goods have been paid for or have arrived. **2** the act or fact of receiving or being received: *The goods will be sent on receipt of payment. She wrote to acknowledge receipt of the package.* **3** *pl* the amount of money that has been received by a business or organization during a certain period: *The expenses were greater than the receipts.*
v write on or stamp a bill to indicate that something has been received or paid for: *Pay the bill and ask the grocer to receipt it.*

re·ceiv·a·ble (ri sē′və bəl) *adj* **1** able to be received. **2** on which payment is to be received. **Accounts receivable** is the opposite of **accounts payable**.
n **receivables** *pl* the amounts owed to a business or organization.

re·ceive (ri sēv′) *v* **re·ceived, re·ceiv·ing** **1** take something offered, presented, or sent: *to receive gifts. We received your greetings.* **2** take or let into the mind, especially accept as true or valid: *to receive new ideas, a theory widely received.* **3** experience, suffer, or endure: *to receive a blow.* **4** let into one's home, company, or surroundings: *The people of the neighbourhood were glad to receive the new couple, to receive strangers, to receive a person into the club.* **5** *Formal* be at home to friends and visitors: *She receives on Tuesdays.* **6** *Radio, Television* change electromagnetic waves into sound or picture signals. **7** be admitted as a member: *to be received into the church.* <Old French, from Latin *re-* back + *capere* take>
be on (or **at**) **the receiving end,** *Informal* be subjected to something unpleasant.

SYNONYMS

Both **receive** and **accept** mean "take something given or offered."

Receive suggests nothing more than take in or get: *She received several e-mails today.*

Accept always suggests a definite wish or decision to take what is offered: *The group accepted the proposal that he made.*

re·ceived (ri sēvd′) *adj* accepted as standard or conventional: *received pronunciation.*

re·ceiv·er (ri sē′vər) *n* **1** a person who gets or accepts something that has been sent or given. **2** the part of a telephone held to the ear, in which electrical signals are converted into sounds. **3** a device that changes electromagnetic waves into sound or picture signals: *a radio receiver.* **4** a person appointed by law to take charge of the property of others after a bankruptcy: *A receiver for the firm's assets will be appointed tomorrow.*

a bat	e bed	i bid	o pot	u cup	th thin
ā cake	ē me	ī bite	ō go	ū rude	ᴛʜ then
ȧ bar	ə about	ər over	ȯ for	ů put	zh measure

R

re·ceiv·er·ship (ri sē′vər ship′) *n* **1** the position of a RECEIVER (def. 4) in charge of the property of others. **2** the process of being controlled by a RECEIVER (def. 4).

receiving blanket *n* a small, lightweight blanket for wrapping a very young baby.

receiving line *n* a group of people who stand in a row at a wedding reception or other formal occasion in order to welcome each guest individually.

re·cent (rē′sənt) *adj* done, made, or happening not long ago: *recent events, a recent period in history.* <Latin *recentis*> **re′cent·ly** *n.* **re′cent·ness** *n.*

re·cep·ta·cle (ri sep′tə kəl) *n* a container or place used to contain things, such as a bag, basket, or vault. <Old French, from Latin *recipere* to hold>

re·cep·tion (ri sep′shən) *n* **1** the action or process of receiving something sent, given, or inflicted: *reception of news.* **2** the act or fact of being admitted to a place, group, or organization: *Her reception as a club member pleased her.* **3** the way in which a person or group reacts to someone or something: *a warm reception.* **4** a gathering to receive and welcome people: *Our school gave a reception to our new principal.* **5** the quality of the sound in a radio or of the sound and picture signals in a TV set. **6** an area of a hotel, office, or other place where guests and visitors are greeted and dealt with: *She turned up at reception ahead of time.* <Latin *receptionem* a receiving, from *recipere* to hold>

re·cep·tion·ist (ri sep′shə nist) *n* a person employed in an office or other place to welcome and deal with visitors.

re·cep·tive (ri sep′tiv) *adj* able, quick, or willing to receive ideas, suggestions, or impressions: *a receptive mind, a receptive audience.* **re·cep′tive·ly** *adv.* **re·cep′tive·ness** *n.* **re′cep·ti′vi·ty** *n.*

re·cep·tor (ri sep′tər) *n* a body cell or group of cells sensitive to stimuli.

re·cess (rē′ses) *or* (ri ses′) *for n,* (ri ses′) *for v. n* **1** a period of time during which work, study, or a proceeding is halted: *There will be a short recess before the next meeting. The committee resumed its work after a month's recess. Recess between classes was five minutes.* **2** a part in a wall or other surface set back from the rest. **3 recesses** *pl* remote, secluded, or inner places: *the recesses of a cave, the recesses of your secret thoughts.*
v **1** take a recess: *The court recessed until after lunch.* **2** make a recess in a wall or other surface. <Latin *re-* back + *cedere* go>

re·ces·sion (ri sesh′ən) *n* **1** a period of temporary economic decline in which trade and industrial activity lessens, but shorter and less extreme than a depression. **2** the action of moving away from the observer.

re·ces·sion·al (ri se′shən əl) *n* a piece of music sung or played while the main participants in a church service or other ceremony exit.
adj to do with such an exit or the music that accompanies it: *a recessional hymn.*

re·ces·sive (ri ses′iv) *adj* **1** tending to go back or recede. **2** *Biology* of an inherited genetic characteristic, appearing only when there is no dominant characteristic inherited from one parent. Compare DOMINANT.

re·charge (ri charj′) *v* **re·charged, re·charg·ing 1** restore the electric charge to a battery or a battery-operated device. **2** refill something: *recharge a glass.* **3** regain vitality or strength: *Our good vacation recharged us.* **re·charge′able** *adj.* **re·charg′er** *n.*
recharge your batteries, *Informal* refresh yourself or regain your energy.

re·cher·ché (rə sher′shā) *adj* rare, exotic, or obscure: *recherché works of art.* <French = carefully sought after>

re·cid·i·vism (ri sid′i vizm′) *n* the tendency of a criminal offender to relapse into crime or antisocial behaviour, especially if done repeatedly: *There is a lower rate of recidivism for convicts who go through rehabilitation.* <Latin *re-* back + *cadere* to fall> **re·cid′i·vist** *adj, n.*

rec·i·pe (res′ə pē) *n* **1** a set of directions for preparing something to eat: *I'd like to try this recipe for oatmeal cookies.* **2** a set of directions for preparing a thing by combining various ingredients: *Grandmother's recipe for making soap was highly prized.* **3** a means of reaching some state or condition: *There is no single recipe for happiness.* <Latin = Take! It was first used as an instruction in medical prescriptions.>

re·cip·i·ent (ri sip′ē ənt) *n* a person who or thing that receives something: *The recipients of the prizes had their names printed in the paper.*
adj receiving or able to receive something.

re·cip·ro·cal (re sip′rə kəl) *adj* **1** in return: *Although I gave her many presents, I had no reciprocal gifts from her.* **2** including or involving each of two persons or groups equally: *reciprocal liking, reciprocal distrust.* **3** expressing a mutual action or relation in a pronoun or verb. Example: In *The two children like each other, each other* is a reciprocal pronoun. **4** related as a mathematical quantity or function to another so that their product is unity. **5** differing from a given course or bearing by 180°.
n **1** a number so related to another that when multiplied together they give 1. Example: The reciprocal of 3 is 1/3, and the reciprocal of 1/3 is 3. **2** a pronoun or verb that expresses a mutual action or relation. <Latin *reciprocus* alternating> **re·cip′ro·cal·ly** (ri sip′rə kə lē) *or* (ri sip′rə klē) *adv.*

re·cip·ro·cate (ri sip′rə kāt′) *v* **re·cip·ro·cat·ed, re·cip·ro·cat·ing 1** give, do, feel, or show in return: *She likes me, and I reciprocate her liking. He said he appreciated what they had done for him and wanted to reciprocate.* **2** move or cause to move with an alternating backward and forward motion: *a reciprocating valve.* <Latin *reciprocus* alternating> **re·cip′ro·ca′tion** *n.*

rec·i·proc·i·ty (res′ə pros′ə tē) *n* a mutual exchange, especially an exchange of special privileges in regard to trade between two countries or organizations.

re·cit·al (ri sī′təl) *n* **1** the act of giving a list of connected names, facts, or elements. **2** a lengthy story or account: *Her recital of her experiences in the hospital bored her friends.* **3** a program of music or dance given by a single performer or several individual performers, or by a small ensemble.

rec·i·ta·tion (res′ə tā′shən) *n* **1** a list of connected names, facts, or elements. **2** a process of repeating something from memory, or the piece so repeated.

rec·i·ta·tive (res′ə tə tēv′) *n* a style of musical speech halfway between speaking and singing, often to give narrative and dialogue in an opera.

re·cite (ri sīt′) *v* **re·cit·ed, re·cit·ing** 1 tell in order, especially names and facts: *They recited a long list of grievances.* 2 repeat from memory a poem or other piece before an audience. <Old French, from Latin *re-* again + *citare* cite> **rec′i·ta′tion** *n.*

reck·less (rek′lis) *adj* done without thinking or caring about the consequences of an action: *He was reckless in having several drinks before driving away from the party.* <Old English *recceleas*> **reck′less·ly** *adv* **reck′less·ness** *n.*

reck·on (rek′ən) *v* 1 find the number or value of by counting or calculation: *Reckon the cost before you decide.* 2 be of the opinion, think, or suppose: *She is reckoned the best speller in the class.* <Old English *gerecenian* to recount> **reck′on·er** *n.*
reckon on, a take into account: *He didn't reckon on breaking his leg when he decided to try skiing.* **b** depend on or rely: *You can reckon on our help.*
to be reckoned with, be taken seriously: *The new party was a force to be reckoned with.*
to reckon with, take into account: *We are going to have to reckon with higher prices for school supplies.*

reck·on·ing (rek′ə ning) *n* 1 the act or fact of counting or calculating: *By my reckoning, we still have about seven kilometres to go.* 2 the avenging or punishing of past mistakes or misdeeds: *a day of reckoning.* 3 a bill or amount owed. 4 the calculation of the position of a ship, or the position so calculated.
day of reckoning, a time when one must account for or be punished for one's actions: *There will be a day of reckoning for your foolish behaviour.*

re·claim (ri klām′) *v* 1 retrieve or recover something previously lost, given, or paid: *She reclaimed her purse at the manager's office.* 2 retrieve or recover something discarded or neglected, such as land: *to reclaim a swamp, to reclaim tin cans.* <Old French, from Latin *reclamare* cry out against> **re·claim′a·ble** *adj* **re·claim′er** *n.* **re′cla·ma′tion** (rek′lə mā′shən) *n.*

re·cline (ri klīn′) *v* **re·clined, re·clin·ing** 1 lean back or lie back in a relaxed position with the back supported: *to recline on a couch.* 2 move or be able to move the back of something into a sloping position: *The seat reclines.* <Latin *re-* back + *-clinare* to bend>

re·clin·er (ri klīn′ər) *n* an armchair with a movable back and seat that can be adjusted by body motion or by a lever.

rec·luse (rek′lūs) *or* (ri klūs′) *for n,* (ri klūs′) *for adj. n* a person who lives a solitary life and tends not to mingle with other people. <Old French, from Latin *re-* back + *claudere* to shut> **re·clu′sive** *adj.* **re·clu′sive·ness** *n.*

re·clu·sion (ri klū′zhən) *adj* 1 the condition of being a recluse. 2 the state of being in solitary confinement.

rec·og·ni·tion (rek′əg nish′ən) *n* 1 the action or process of recognizing or being recognized: *By a good disguise, he escaped recognition.* 2 an acknowledgment: *We insisted on complete recognition of our rights.* 3 favourable notice: *The actor soon won recognition from the public.* 4 formal approval or acceptance: *to seek recognition by the court.*

re·cog·ni·zance (ri kog′nə zəns) *Law n* a bond that requires a person to do some particular act or follow some condition, especially to appear when summoned.

rec·og·nize (rek′əg nīz′) *v* **rec·og·nized, rec·og·niz·ing** 1 identify someone or something from having known them or their description before: *I could scarcely recognize my old friend.* 2 acknowledge that something exists, is valid, or is legal: *He recognized his duty to defend his country.* 3 take formal or official notice or acknowledgment of: *Those who wish to speak in a public meeting should stand up and wait till the chair recognizes them. For some years certain nations did not recognize the new government.* 4 show approval or appreciation of: *She was finally recognized for her good deeds.* <Old French, from Latin *re-* again + *cognoscere* know> **rec′og·niz′a·ble** *adj.* **rec′og·niz′a·bly** *adv.*

re·coil (ri koil′) *for v,* (ri koil′) *or* (rē′koil) *for n. v* 1 suddenly spring or flinch back because of fear, horror, or disgust, or feel like doing this because of a thought or prospect: *Most people would recoil at seeing a snake in their path. She recoiled at the idea of taking the exam again.* 2 move abruptly back, as a gun being fired.
n the act or fact of recoiling. <Old French *reculer* move back, from Latin *culus* buttocks>

rec·ol·lect (rek′ə lekt′) *v* remember something. <Latin *re-* back + *colligere* to collect>

rec·ol·lec·tion (rek′ə lek′shən) *n* 1 the act or power of remembering something. 2 the thing that is remembered: *This is the hottest summer within my recollection. His recollections of his youth were of great interest to us.* <Latin *re-* back + *colligere* to collect> **rec′ol·lect′** (rek′ə lekt′) *v.*

re·com·bi·nant DNA (rē kom′bə nənt) *Genetics n* DNA segments from different organisms that have been artificially linked.

rec·om·mend (rek′ə mend′) *v* 1 speak or write in favour of someone or something: *They recommended me for the babysitting job.* 2 advise or suggest something as a course of action: *The doctor recommended that she stay in bed.* 3 make pleasing or attractive: *The location of the camp recommends it as a summer home.* <Latin *re-* again + *commendare* commit to the care of>

rec·om·men·da·tion (rek′ə men dā′shən) *n* 1 the act or fact of recommending someone or something. 2 something that recommends a person by expressing praise: *She got a very good recommendation from her former boss.* 3 something recommended: *The doctor's recommendation was that I stay in bed for a few days.*

rec·om·pense (rek′əm pens′) *v* **rec·om·pensed, rec·om·pens·ing** 1 pay or reward someone for effort or work. 2 pay or make amends to someone for loss or harm suffered: *The insurance company recompensed him for the loss of his car.*
n a payment to someone for loss or harm suffered. <Latin *re-* again + *compensare* balance out>

a bat	e bed	i bid	o pot	u cup	th thin
ā cake	ē me	ī bite	ō go	ū rude	ᴛʜ then
ä bar	ə about	ər over	ȯ for	ů put	zh measure

R

rec·on·cile (rek′ən sīl′) *v* **rec·on·ciled, rec·on·cil·ing** 1 restore friendly relations between: *The children had quarrelled but were soon reconciled.* 2 settle a quarrel or disagreement. 3 make, show, or bring into harmony or compatibility: *It is impossible to reconcile his story with the facts.* 4 make satisfied or content with: *It is hard to reconcile oneself to being sick for a long time.* <Old French, from Latin *re-* back + *conciliare* bring together>
rec′on·cil′a·ble *adj.*
rec′on·cil′i·a′tion (rek′ən sil′ē ā′shən) *n.*

rec·on·dite (rek′ən dīt′) *adj* little known or obscure. <Latin *reconditus* hidden away>

re·con·di·tion (rē′kən dish′ən) *v* restore to a good or satisfactory condition by repairing or replacing parts: *The motor has been completely reconditioned.*

re·con·fig·ure (rē′kən fig′ər) *v* **re·con·fig·ured, re·con·fig·ur·ing** rearrange the parts or settings of something: *to reconfigure a computer to accept a different printer.* **re′con·fig′ur·a′tion** *n.*

re·con·nais·sance (ri kon′ə səns) *n* observation or a survey, especially for military purposes. <French *reconnaître* recognize>

rec·on·noi·tre (rek′ə noi′tər) *or* (rē′kə noi′tər) *v* **rec·on·noi·tred, rec·on·noi·tring** make an observation of an area for military purposes. Also, **reconnoiter.** <Middle French, from Latin *recognoscere* to examine>

re·con·sid·er (rē′kən sid′ər) *v* consider again with a view to changing or reversing a position or decision: *The assembly voted to reconsider the proposal. My dad said I couldn't go, but I'm hoping he will reconsider.* **re′con·sid′er·a′tion** *n.*

re·con·sti·tute (rē kon′stə tyūt′) *or* (rē kon′stə tūt′) *v* **re·con·sti·tut·ed, re·con·sti·tut·ing** build again from parts or elements, such as to restore a condensed or dehydrated substance to its original liquid state by adding water: *reconstituted orange juice.* **re·con′sti·tu′tion** *n.*

re·con·struct (rē′kən strukt′) *v* 1 build or form something again after it has been damaged or destroyed. 2 go back over and form a model or re-enactment of a past event or thing: *When the police reconstructed the crime, they realized who the murderer must be.* **re′con·struc′tion** *n.*

re·cord (ri kòrd′) *for v,* (rek′ərd) *for n. v* 1 set down in writing or in some other permanent form so as to keep for future use: *Listen to the speaker and record what she says. History is recorded in books.* 2 put onto a magnetic tape, videotape, CD, etc. 3 show or register by an instrument or observer: *The thermometer records temperatures.*
n 1 a piece of evidence about the past, especially an account kept in permanent form. 2 an official written account: *The secretary kept a record of what was done at the meeting.* 3 a thin, flat, plastic disc with narrow spiral grooves on its surface that reproduces sounds when played on a record player. 4 the known facts about what a person or thing has done or performed: *I have a fine record at school. She has a criminal record.* 5 a remarkable performance or event, going beyond others of the same kind, especially the best achievement in a sport: *to hold the Canadian record for the high jump.* 6 an act of recording or of being recorded: *What happened is a matter of record.*
adj greater, higher, or better than ever before: *a record wheat crop.*
break a record, improve on a record previously set in some event, usually sports.
go on record, state publicly.
off the record, not to be recorded or quoted: *The prime minister was speaking off the record.*
on record, written down or otherwise made permanently available: *The facts of the crime are now on record.*
set the record straight, correct a faulty view or report of what was said or done: *Just to set the record straight: I did NOT say you were clumsy!*

ETYMOLOGY

Record comes from Old French *record,* meaning "remembrance" and *recorder,* meaning "remember," from *Latin recordare,* which means "have in mind" or "bring back to mind."

re·cord·er (ri kòr′dər) *n* 1 a person who keeps records. 2 a machine that records, especially a tape recorder. 3 a wooden or plastic woodwind instrument with a tone similar to that of a flute.

re·cord·ing (ri kòr′ding) *n* 1 a sound record made on a disc or tape: *I bought their new recording yesterday.* 2 the original transcription of a sound or combination of sounds: *to make a recording of birdsong.*

record player (rek′ərd) *n* an instrument that plays back sounds that have been recorded on phonograph discs.

re·count[1] (ri kount′) *v* tell someone about an event or experience: *He recounted all the happenings of the day.* <Old French *re-* again + *conter* tell (the story of)>

re·count[2] (rē′kount′) *n* a second count, as of votes: *The vote was so close that we asked for a recount.*
v count something a second time.

re·coup (ri kūp′) *v* 1 regain something lost, especially money: *He recouped his losses.* 2 repay someone for money spent or lost: *I will recoup you for any money you spend.* <French from *re-* back + *couper* cut>

re·course (rē′kòrs) *or* (ri kòrs′) *n* 1 an appeal to somebody or something for help or protection: *I think my best recourse is to ask the teacher for help.* 2 a person or thing appealed to or turned to for help or protection: *He was our reliable recourse in times of trouble.* <Latin *recursus* retreat>
have recourse to, appeal or turn to for help: *When we do not know what a word means, we have recourse to a dictionary.*

re·cov·er (ri kuv′ər) *v* 1 get back something lost, taken away, or stolen: *to recover your temper or health, to recover a lost wallet, to recover lost time.* 2 bring back to life, health, one's senses, or a normal condition. 3 restore to physical or mental balance: *He started to fall but recovered himself.* 4 obtain compensation by judgment in a law court or through subsequent profits. 5 remove or extract something, such as an energy source or industrial chemical, for use, reuse, or waste treatment. <Old French, from Latin *recuperare* get again> **re·cov′er·er** *n.*

re·cov·er·y (ri kuv′ə rē) *n, pl* **re·cov·er·ies** **1** a return to health, strength, or a normal condition. **2** the action or process of regaining possession or control of something stolen or lost. **3** an act of regaining a proper position or condition: *The skater started to fall, but made a quick recovery.* **4** the process of removing or extracting something, such as an energy source or industrial chemical, for use, reuse, or waste treatment.

recovery room *n* a room in a hospital where patients are taken immediately after surgery, in order to recover from the effects of the anesthetic.

re·cre·ate (rē′krē āt′) *v* **re·cre·at·ed, re·cre·at·ing** create anew. **re′cre·a′tion** (rē′krē ā′shən) *n.*

rec·re·a·tion (rek′rē ā′shən) *n* **1** the process of refreshing the body and spirit after working, through play or amusement: *rest and recreation.* **2** a form of play or amusement that serves as recreation: *Her favourite recreation is tennis.* <Old French, from Latin *re-* again + *creare* create> **rec′re·a′tion·al** *adj.*

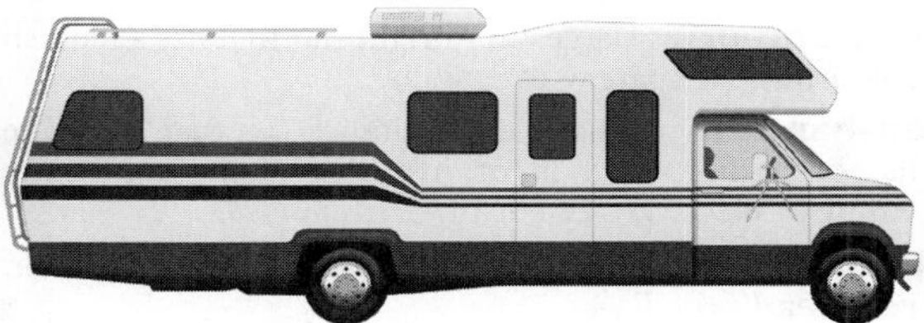

Recreational vehicles, also known as RVs, allow people to tour the countryside without the expense of accommodation. Many RVs have TV, air conditioning, and other modern conveniences.

recreational vehicle *n* a large motor vehicle fitted out as temporary living quarters and used for camping or recreational travel.

recreation room (rek′rē ā′shən) *n* **1** a room in an institution or workplace in which people can relax and engage in recreational activities **2** REC ROOM.

re·crim·i·na·tion (ri krim′ə nā′shən) *n* an accusation in response to one from another person: *The quarrelling children indulged in many recriminations.* <Latin *re-* back + *crimen* charge> **re·crim′i·na·to′ry** *adj.*

rec room (rek) *Informal n* in full, **recreation room** a room in a house, often in the basement, used for recreation and relaxation.

re·cruit (ri krūt′) *n* **1** a newly enlisted member of the armed forces. **2** a new member of an organization or cause.
v **1** enlist someone in the armed forces, especially to strengthen or supply it with new members. **2** persuade someone to help or join in an activity: *to recruit volunteers, to recruit teachers.* <Old French, from Latin *re-* again + *crescere* grow> **re·cruit′er** *n.* **re·cruit′ment** *n.*

rec·tal (rek′təl) *adj* to do with the rectum.

rec·tan·gle (rek′tang′gəl) *n* a PARALLELOGRAM with four right angles, especially one with unequal adjacent sides. <Latin *rectus* right + *angulus* angle> **rec·tan′gu·lar** *adj.* **rec·tan′gu·lar·ly** *adv.*

rec·ti·fi·er (rek′tə fi′ər) *n* **1** a person who or thing that corrects or adjusts. **2** a device for changing alternating current into direct current.

rec·ti·fy (rek′tə fi′) *v* **rec·ti·fied, rec·ti·fy·ing** **1** adjust or correct: *The storekeeper was willing to rectify his error.* **2** change an alternating electrical current into a direct current. <Old French, from Latin *rectus* right + *facere* make> **rec′ti·fi·ca′tion** *n.*

rec·ti·lin·e·ar (rek′tə lin′ē ər) *adj* in, moving in, or forming a straight line or lines. <Latin *rectus* straight + *linea* line>

rec·ti·tude (rek′tə tyūd′) *or* (rek′tə tūd′) *n* morally correct conduct or character. <Latin *rectus* right>

rec·to (rek′tō) *n* the front of a sheet of printed paper, or the right-hand page of an open book or periodical. Compare VERSO. <Latin *rectus* right>

rec·tor (rek′tər) *n* **1** a member of the clergy in the Anglican church, in charge of a parish. **2** the head of certain universities, colleges, or schools. <Latin *regere* to rule>

rec·to·ry (rek′tə rē) *n, pl* **rec·tor·ies** the residence of a rector.

rec·tum (rek′təm) *n* the final section of the large intestine, ending at the anus. <Latin *rectum intestinium* the straight intestine>

re·cum·bent (ri kum′bənt) *adj* lying down. <Latin *re-* back + *cumbere* lie down>

re·cu·per·ate (ri kū′pə rāt′) *or* (ri kyū′pə rāt′) *v* **re·cu·per·at·ed, re·cu·per·at·ing** **1** recover from illness, injury, or exhaustion: *She is at home, recuperating from surgery.* **2** regain or recover something: *He worked hard to recuperate his losses after the fire.* <Latin *re-* back + *capere* take> **re·cu′per·a′tion** *n.* **re·cu′per·a·tive** *adj.*

re·cur (ri kər′) *v* **re·curred, re·cur·ring** **1** occur again, periodically, or repeatedly. **2** return in thought or speech: *The image kept recurring to him.* <Latin *recurrere* to return> **re·cur′rence** *n.*

re·cur·rent (ri kər′ənt) *adj* occurring often or repeatedly: *recurrent attacks of hay fever.* **re·cur′rent·ly** *adv.*

re·cy·cle (rē sī′kəl) *v* **re·cy·cled, re·cy·cling** process or convert waste material so that it can be used again. **re·cyc′lable** *adj, n.* **re·cyc′ler** *n.* **re·cyc′ling** *n.*

red (red) *adj* **red·der, red·dest** **1** with the colour of the spectrum with the longest light waves, such as the colour of blood: *red ink, red hair.* **2** of eyes, bloodshot or inflamed. **3** flushed, rosy, or blushing. **4 Red** *Informal* to do with communism or socialism. **red′ness** *n.* <Old English *read*>
in the red, operating at a loss or in debt: *The company was in the red for some time before it closed.*
see red, *Informal* become very angry: *She sees red as soon as you mention the new bylaw.*

red alert *n* the final stage of alert, when an attack by an enemy is expected at any moment.

a bat	e bed	i bid	o pot	u cup	th **thin**
ā cake	ē me	ī bite	ō go	ū rude	ᴛʜ **then**
à bar	ə about	ər over	ȯ for	ů put	zh measure

red blood cell See BLOOD CELL.

red–blood·ed (red′blud′id) *adj* vigorous and virile.

At about 14 cm, the redbreast is much smaller than the North American robin, which is about 25 cm long.

red·breast (red′brest′) *Poetic n* the European robin.

red·cap (red′kap′) *n* a porter at a railway or bus station.

red carpet *n* a carpet, traditionally red, laid out for distinguished visitors to walk on.
roll out the red carpet, welcome and treat with special consideration.

red–car·pet (red′kȧr′pət) *Informal adj* showing special courtesy and consideration: *They got the red-carpet treatment.*

red cent *Informal n* the smallest amount of money: *That thing is not worth a red cent.*

🍁 **Red Chamber** *n* the Canadian Senate.

red·coat (red′kōt′) *n* **1** in former times, a British soldier. **2** 🍁 a member of the Royal Northwest Mounted Police.

red corpuscle *n* one of many blood cells in vertebrates that carry oxygen to the tissues of the body. Compare WHITE CORPUSCLE. See BLOOD COUNT for picture.

Red Cross *n* an international humanitarian organization that seeks to relieve human suffering during wars or natural disasters.

red deer *n* a deer of N America, Eurasia, and N Africa that has a smooth, reddish coat and a buff-coloured patch on the rump. The male has large, branched antlers.

red·den (red′ən) *v* **1** make or become red: *The sky was just beginning to redden when we left home.* **2** blush: *She reddened with embarrassment.*

red·dish (red′ish) *adj* somewhat red.

re·de·co·rate (rē dek′ə rāt) *v* **re·de·co·rat·ed, re·de·co·rat·ing** apply new or different paint, wallpaper, curtains, or carpeting in a room or building: *We're busy redecorating. They've redecorated the main floor.*

re·deem (ri dēm′) *v* **1** gain or regain possession of something by making a payment: *We redeemed the mortgage.* **2** do something that makes up for the faults or bad aspects of something, especially bad behaviour: *He redeemed his bad attendance record by writing a brilliant exam.* **3** repay a bond or other security at the maturity date. **4** exchange a coupon or voucher for goods, a discount, or money. **5** fulfill a pledge or promise. <Old French, from Latin *re-* back + *emere* buy>

re·deem·er (ri dē′mər) *n* a person who redeems.

re·demp·tion (ri demp′shən) *n* **1 a** the action of saving or being saved, especially in religious belief, from sin, error, or evil. **b** the thing that or person who is redeemed. **2** the action of gaining or regaining possession of something in exchange for payment.

Red Ensign *n* any of several mainly red flags that show a small national flag of the UK in an upper corner. A variant of the Red Ensign was, until 1965, the national flag of Canada.

re·de·ploy (rē′di ploi′) *v* assign troops, employees, or resources to a new place or task. **re′de·ploy′ment** *n.*

re·de·sign (rē′di zīn′) *v* revise the appearance or function of.

red·eye or **red–eye** (red′ī) *n* **1** an undesired effect of flash photography in which the pupils of a person's eyes appear red because of reflection from the retina. **2** *Slang* **a** 🍁 a drink made of beer and tomato juice. Also called **Calgary redeye**. **b** a cheap liquor, especially whisky. **3** *Informal* in full, **redeye flight** an overnight airplane flight.

red-faced (red′fāsd) *adj* embarassed; ashamed.

red flag *n* **1** a symbol of socialist revolution. **2** a symbol of danger. **3** a thing that arouses anger: *Talking about politics at mealtimes is a red flag to my father.*

red giant *n* a very large, very bright star that has a reddish colouring. Compare WHITE DWARF.

red–hand·ed (red′han′did) *adj* indicating that someone has been discovered in or just after doing something wrong or illegal: *a robber caught red-handed.*

red·head (red′hed′) *n* a person with red hair. **red′head′ed** *adj.*

red·head·ed (red′hed′id) *adj* **1** with red hair. **2** with a red head in a bird, insect, or other animal.

red herring *n* **1** a smoked herring, turned red by the smoke. **2** a thing, especially a clue, that is intended to be misleading or distracting. <from the practice of using the scent of dried herrings in the training of hounds>

red–hot (red′hot′) *adj* **1** red with heat: *a red-hot iron.* **2** very enthusiastic, exciting, or popular: *red-hot rumours.*

re·di·al (rē′dī′əl) or (rē′dīl′) *v* **re·dialled** or **re·dialed, re·dial·ling** or **re·dial·ing** dial a telephone number again. *n* a telephone feature that automatically re-enters a whole telephone number at the push of one button by the user.

red ink *n* a business loss, debt, or deficit.

re·di·rect (rē′də rekt′) *or* (rē′dī rekt′) *v* direct again, anew, or for a new purpose: *to redirect a letter, to redirect the activities of an organization.* **re′di·rec′tion** *n.*

re·dis·trib·ute (rē′dis trib′yūt) *v* **re·dis·trib·uted, re·dis·trib·ut·ing** distribute something differently or again, especially to make it fairer or more equitable: *I think our group should redistribute the tasks for this project.* **re′dis·tri·bu′tion** *n.*

red–let·ter (red′let′ər) *adj* **1** marked by red letters. **2** memorable or especially happy: *The day we won the cup for hockey was a red-letter day.*

red light *Informal n* a warning signal or instruction to stop.

red–light district (red′līt) *n* an area of a town or city in which prostitution and illegal activity is common.

red line *Hockey n* the red line drawn across the centre of the ice, midway between the two blue lines.

red meat *n* beef or other meat that is red when raw.

re·do (rē dü′) *v* do something again or differently.

red·o·lent (red′ə lənt) *adj* **1** strongly suggesting something, especially in the past: *redolent of romance.* **2** with a strong odour of something, especially something fragrant: *redolent with incense, a house redolent of fresh paint.* <Latin *re-* again + *olere* to smell> **red′o·lence** *n.*

re·dou·ble (rē dub′əl) *v* **re·dou·bled, re·dou·bling 1** make or become much greater, more intense, or more numerous: *When he saw land ahead, the swimmer redoubled his speed.* **2** double back: *The fox redoubled on its trail to escape the hunters.*

re·doubt (ri dout′) *n* a small, temporary or supplementary fort standing alone.

re·doubt·a·ble (ri dou′tə bəl) *adj* formidable, especially in deserving to be feared or dreaded: *a redoubtable warrior, a redoubtable debater.* <Old French *redouter* to dread> **re·doubt′a·bly** *adv.*

re·dound (ri dound′) *v* (*with* ***to***) contribute greatly to a person's credit or honour: *The number of scholarships we gained redound to the honour of our school.*

red panda PANDA (def. 2).

red pepper *n* the red, hollow fruit of a sweet pepper, eaten as a vegetable.

re·draft (rē draft′) *for v,* (rē′draft′) *for n. v* draft a text or map again or anew.
n a new draft of a text or map.

re·dress (ri dres′) *for v,* (rē′dres) *or* (ri dres′) *for n.*
v correct an undesirable or unfair situation: *to redress wrongs.*
n a remedy or compensation for a wrong or grievance: *Any person who has been treated unfairly deserves redress.* <Old French *re-* again + *dresser* straighten, i.e, to correct>

🍁 **Red River cart** *n* a strong, two-wheeled cart pulled by oxen or horses during pioneer times on the Prairies.

🍁 **Red River Rebellion** *n* the uprising in 1869–70 of mainly Métis settlers in the Red River region against the takeover of their territory by the government of Canada.

🍁 **red salmon** SOCKEYE.

red shift *n* a movement of light from distant galaxies to the red end of the spectrum, which has longer wavelengths.

red squirrel *n* a small Eurasian or N American tree squirrel, with reddish fur.

red tape *n* the strict attention to form and detail, especially in the bureaucracy of a government or organization, that causes delay and irritation.

ETYMOLOGY

The term **red tape** came into use because many British official documents, especially legal ones, used to be tied in red (or pink) cloth tape. This helped to indicate their importance.

red tide *n* an area of sea water caused by numerous micro-organisms that are constituents of plankton and are toxic to many forms of marine life, or a population of such micro-organisms.

🍁 **Red Tory** *n* a member of a Conservative party who has conservative economic principles but liberal views on social issues.

re·duce (ri dyüs′) *or* (ri düs′) *v* **re·duced, re·duc·ing 1** make or become smaller or less in amount, degree, or size: *to reduce expenses, to reduce your intake of carbohydrates.* **2** bring someone or something to a lower, weaker, or other undesirable condition: *Misfortune reduced the poor woman to begging. I was reduced to tears by your cruel words.* **3** boil a sauce or other liquid in cooking so that it becomes thicker and more concentrated. <Latin *re-* back + *ducere* bring>

re·duc·i·ble (ri dyü′sə bəl) *or* (ri dü′sə bəl) *adj* able to be simplified in presentation or analysis, especially as a subject, problem, or mathematical fraction.

re·duc·tion (ri duk′shən) *n* **1** the act or fact of reducing or being reduced. **2** the amount by which a thing is reduced. **3** a form of something produced by reducing.

re·dun·dan·cy (ri dun′dən sē) *n, pl* **re·dun·dan·cies 1** a situation in which something is no longer needed, efficient, or useful: *workforce redundancy.* **2** a thing, part, amount, or element that is no longer needed, efficient, or useful. **3** the use of unnecessary words. **4** the inclusion of components in engineering that are not strictly necessary but can perform a function if others fail.

re·dun·dant (ri dun′dənt) *adj* **1** no longer needed or useful. **2** able to be omitted as words without a loss of meaning or function. Example: In *We two both had an apple each*, the sentence could read *We both had an apple* or *We two had an apple each.* <Latin *redundare* to overflow> **re·dun′dant·ly** *adv.*

re·du·pli·cate (ri dyü′plə kāt′) *or* (ri dü′plə kāt′) *v* **re·du·pli·cat·ed, re·du·pli·cat·ing** repeat or copy so as to form another of the same kind. **re·du′pli·ca′tion** *n.*

re·dux (rē duks′) *adj* (*after the noun*) brought back or revived. <Latin *reducere* bring back>

red·wing (red′wing′) *n* in full, **red-winged blackbird** a N American blackbird, the male of which has a scarlet patch on each wing.

red·wood (red′wu̇d′) *n* a very large evergreen tree of California and the northwestern US. Redwoods are the tallest known trees.

ree·bok (rē′bok) *n* a deerlike South African antelope with slender horns, and a bushy tail. <Afrikaans>

re–ech·o (rē ek′ō) *v* **re·ech·oed, re·ech·o·ing** echo again and again.
n, pl **re-ech·oes** the echo of an echo.

reed (rēd) *n* **1** a tall plant that grows in wet places and has a hollow, jointed stalk, or the stalk itself. **2** a thin piece of wood, metal, or plastic in a musical instrument that produces sound when a current of air moves it.
adj producing tones by means of reeds: *a reed organ.* <Old English *hreod*>

a bat	e bed	i bid	o pot	u cup	th thin
ā cake	ē me	ī bite	ō go	ü rude	ᴛʜ then
ä bar	ə about	ər over	ȯ for	u̇ put	zh measure

R

reed instrument *n* a musical instrument that produces sound by means of a vibrating reed or reeds, such as the oboe, clarinet, or saxophone.

re–ed·u·cate (rē ej′ə kāt′) *v* **re-ed·u·cat·ed, re-ed·u·cat·ing** teach new attitudes, habits, values, or behaviour to someone: *The government set aside funds to re-educate workers for the changing labour market.* **re′-ed·u·ca′tion** *n.*

reed·y (rē′dē) *adj* **reed·i·er, reed·i·est 1** full of or edged with reeds. **2** made of or like a reed or reeds. **3** high and thin in tone like a reed instrument: *a thin, reedy voice.*

reef[1] (rēf) *n* **1** a narrow ridge of rocks, coral, or sand at or near the surface of the water: *The ship was wrecked on a hidden reef.* **2** a vein or lode in a mine, especially of gold. <Old Norse *rif* ridge>

reef[2] (rēf) *n* the part of a sail that can be rolled or folded up to reduce its size.
v reduce the size of a sail by rolling or folding up a part of it. <Old Norse *rif*>

reef·er[1] (rē′fər) *n* a cannabis cigarette. <origin uncertain>

reef·er[2] (rē′fər) *n* **1** a person who reefs a sail. **2** a thick, close-fitting, double-breasted jacket. <*reef*>

reef knot *n* a knot firmly joining two loose ends of rope or cord. Each end is formed into a loop that both encloses and passes through the other. Also called **square knot**.

reek (rēk) *n* a strong, unpleasant odour: *We noticed the reek of rotting vegetables as we entered the cottage.*
v **1** send out a strong, unpleasant odour: *She reeked of cheap perfume.* **2** suggest something unpleasant or undesirable: *His newspaper column reeked of racism.* <Old English *rec* smoke>

reel (rēl) *n* **1 a** a device consisting of a frame turning on an axis, such as for winding thread, fishing line, rope, etc. **b** a thing wound on such a device: *two reels of motion-picture film.* **2** a lively dance of Scottish or Irish origin, or the music for it. **3** a loss of balance resulting in a violent stagger or lurch.
v **1** wind on a reel by turning it. **2** move with swaying or staggering movements: *to reel in a fish. The drunkard reeled down the street.* **3** be disoriented or bewildered, especially by an unexpected setback: *She reeled from all the abuse she took.* <Old English *hreol*>
reel off, say, write, or make in a quick, easy way: *My grandfather can reel off stories by the hour.*

re–e·lect (rē′i lekt′) *v* elect again. **re′-e·lec′tion** *n.*

reel–to–reel (rēl′ tə rēl′) *adj* to do with a tape recorder or film projection system using two separate reels on which the tape or film must be threaded to run from one to another.

re–en·ter (rē en′tər) *v* enter something again.

re–en·try (rē en′trē) *n, pl* **re-en·tries** the action or process of entering again or returning, especially of a rocket or spacecraft into the earth's atmosphere after flight in outer space.

re–es·tab·lish (rē′is tab′lish) *v* establish something again or anew: *They have re-established the extracurricular program.* **re′-es·tab′lish·ment** *n.*

re–e·val·u·ate (rē′i val′yū āt) *v* **re-e·val·u·a·ted, re-e·val·u·a·ting** evaluate again or differently. **re′-e·val·u·a′tion** *n.*

reeve (rēv) *n* **1** 🍁 *Ontario, Western Provinces* the elected head of a village or rural municipal council. **2** in ancient times, the chief magistrate of a town or district. <Old English *refa*>

re–ex·a·mine (rē′eg za′mən) *v* **re-ex·a·mined, re-ex·a·min·ing** examine again or further, with the possibility of coming to a different conclusion: *We must re-examine the evidence.* **re′-ex·a·min·a′tion** *n.*

ref (ref) *Informal n* a referee: *The ref blew his whistle.*
v **reffed, ref·fing** referee: *She refs intramurals in the gym at noon.*

re·face (rē fās′) *v* **re·faced, re·fac·ing** repair or replace the surface of a wall or building.

re·fec·to·ry (ri fek′tə rē) *n, pl* **re·fec·to·ries** a room for meals, especially in a monastery, convent, or school. <Latin *refectus* refreshed>

re·fer (ri fər′) *v* **re·ferred, re·fer·ring 1** direct attention to or speak about: *May I refer to the minutes of the last meeting?* **2** regard as belonging to a certain period, place, or class of thing: *The rule refers only to special cases.* **3** send or direct for information, help, judgment, or action: *We referred him to the boss.* **4** turn for information or help: *Writers often refer to a dictionary.* **5** describe or denote: *The book refers to animals several times in the first chapter.* <Latin *re-* back + *ferre* bring>

> **GRAMMAR AND USAGE**
>
> Since the meaning "back" is already contained in the first two letters of the word **refer** (Latin *re-* meaning "back"), *back* should not be used after *refer:*
>
> *Please refer back to the notes from the last class.* (incorrect)
>
> *Please refer to the notes from the last class.* (correct)

ref·er·ee (ref′ə rē′) *n* **1** a judge of play in certain games and sports, including hockey and soccer. **2** a person to whom something is referred for decision or settlement.
v **ref·er·eed, ref·er·ee·ing** act as a referee.

ref·er·ence (ref′ə rəns) *n* **1** the action of mentioning or referring to something. **2** in a text, a mention or citation of a source of information: *This history contains many references to larger histories.* **3** something used as a source of information or help: *A dictionary is a book of reference.* **4** a person who can give information about another person's character or ability, or a statement by such a person: *I gave our principal as a reference. She had excellent references from previous employers.* **5** the act or fact of being related or referred to: *This test is to be taken by all students without reference to age or grade.*
adj used for information or help: *a reference library.* **re·fer·en′tial** (ref′ə rən′shəl) *adj.*
in (or **with**) **reference to,** about or concerning.
make reference to, mention.

ref·er·en·dum (ref′ə ren′dəm) *n, pl* **ref·er·en·dums** or **ref·er·en·da** (-də) the process of submitting a law or measure to a direct vote of the citizens for approval or rejection.

re·fer·ral (rē fər′əl) *n* **1** the act of referring or directing a person or matter to some place, official, or professional: *Our family doctor is quick to make referrals to a specialist.* **2** the person or matter referred: *Eighty percent of all referrals to the agency go away satisfied.*

re·fill (rē fil′) *for v,* (rē′fil′) *for n.* *v* **1** fill a container again. **2** become full again.
n an act of filling a container, or the container so filled: *We asked for some refills of juice.* **re·fill′a·ble** *adj.*

re·fi·nance (rē fə nans) *or* (rē fī′nans) *v* **re·fi·nanced, re·fi·nanc·ing** renegotiate a loan, mortgage, or other form of credit so that it begins again with a new principal amount.

re·fine (ri fīn′) *v* **re·fined, re·fin·ing** **1** make free from impurities, especially as part of an industrial process. **2** make or become fine, polished, or cultivated, especially by small changes: *Reading good books helped to refine her speech.* <*re-* again + *fine* make fine>
refine on (or **upon**), improve.

re·fined (ri fīnd′) *adj* **1** freed from impurities: *refined sugar.* **2** freed or free from coarseness, crudeness, or vulgarity: *refined tastes, a refined voice, refined manners.*

re·fine·ment (ri fīn′mənt) *n* **1** fineness of feeling, taste, manners, or language: *She said that good manners is a mark of refinement.* **2** the act or result of refining: *Gasoline is produced by the refinement of petroleum.* **3** improvement or clarification, especially by making small changes. **4** a thing that is improved, clarified, or made more subtle.

re·fin·er·y (ri fī′nə rē) *n, pl* **re·fin·er·ies** a building and machinery for purifying a substance, such as metal, sugar, or petroleum.

re·fin·ish (rē fin′ish) *v* give a new surface to an object, especially furniture: *Mom refinished the old rolltop desk for me.* **re·fin′ish·er** *n.*

re·fit (rē fit′) *for v,* (rē′fit) *for n.* *v* **re·fit·ted, re·fit·ting** fit, prepare, or equip for use again: *to refit an old ship.*
n a fitting, preparing, or equipping for use again: *The ship went to the dry dock for a refit.*

re·flect (ri flekt′) *v* **1** turn back or throw back light, heat, or sound without absorbing it: *The sidewalks reflect heat on a hot day.* **2** show an image or likeness of: *A mirror reflects your face and body.* **3** reproduce or show in a faithful or appropriate way: *The poor turnout at the pep rally reflects student apathy.* **4** think deeply or carefully: *Take time to reflect before doing important things.* **5** bring a good or bad impression of: *The brave act reflected well on the young boy* <Latin *re-* back + *flectere* to bend>

reflecting telescope *n* a type of optical telescope in which the light rays entering it are brought to a focus by means of a concave mirror. Compare REFRACTING TELESCOPE.

re·flec·tion (ri flek′shən) *n* **1** **a** the throwing back by a body or surface of light, heat, or sound. **b** an amount of light, heat, or sound that is so thrown back. **2** a likeness or image seen in a mirror, glass, or shiny surface. **3** serious thought or consideration: *On reflection, the plan seemed too dangerous.* **4** a thing that is a consequence of something else: *Her laziness was a reflection of her upbringing.*

re·flec·tive (ri flek′tiv) *adj* **1** able to reflect heat, light, or sound: *the reflective surface of polished metal.* **2** thoughtful: *a reflective look.*

re·flec·tor (ri flek′tər) *n* an object, surface, or device that reflects light, heat, or sound, especially a strip, disc, or other object treated to make it visible in the dark.

re·flex (rē′fleks) *adj* **1** not controlled by the will but coming as a direct response to a stimulus, as a sneeze does. **2** to do with an angle exceeding 180°.
n an action in direct response to a stimulus.

re·flex·ive pronoun (ri′flek′siv) *n* a pronoun that is the direct object of a reflexive verb. Examples: *himself* in *He cut himself; itself* in *The cat washed itself.*

reflexive verb *n* a verb, the subject and direct object of which refer to the same person or thing. Examples: *cut* in *He cut himself; washed* in *The cat washed itself.*

re·for·est (rē fô′rist) *v* replant with trees or cover with a forest. **re′for·est·a′tion** *n.*

re–form (rē fôrm′) *v* form or cause to form again.

re·form (ri fôrm′) *v* **1** make changes in something, especially a social, political, or economic system or situation, in order to improve it: *He was a leader in reforming the justice system.* **2** correct one's own faults or improve one's behaviour: *The girl promised to reform if given another chance.*
n the action or process of making changes for the sake of improvement: *The new government put through many reforms.* <Latin *re-* again + *forma* form>
re·form′a·ble *adj.* **re·form′er** *n.*

ref·or·ma·tion (ref′ər mā′shən) *n* **1** the action or process of reforming or being reformed. **2** **Reformation** the religious movement in Europe in the 1500s that began with the aim of reforms in the Catholic Church and ended with the establishment of Protestantism.

re·form·a·to·ry (ri fôr′mə tô′rē) *adj* serving or intended to reform. Also called **reform school**.
n, pl **re·form·a·to·ries** an institution for reforming young offenders.

re·form·ism (ri fôrm′iz əm) *n* a policy in favour of gradual, not violent, reform. **re·form′ist** *adj, n.*

❦ **Reform Party** *n* in former times, a federal political party. See ALLLIANCE (def. 2).

re·fract (ri frakt′) *v* **1** make a ray of light change direction when it enters water, air, glass, etc. **2** measure the focusing characteristic of an eye or eyes. <Latin refractus, from *refringere* to break up> **re·frac′tion** *n.* **re·frac′tive** *adj.*

refracting telescope *n* an optical telescope with one lens that bends light rays to a focus and a second lens that acts as an eyepiece. Compare REFLECTING TELESCOPE.

re·frac·to·ry (ri frak′tə rē) *adj* **1** stubborn or hard to manage. **2** not yielding readily to a treatment, process, or stimulus: *She had a refractory cough.* **3** resistant to heat and hard to melt, reduce, or work. <Latin *refractarius* stubborn> **re·frac′to·ri·ly** *adv.* **re·frac′to·ri·ness** *n.*

a bat	e bed	i bid	o pot	u cup	th thin
ā cake	ē me	ī bite	ō go	ū rude	TH then
ä bar	ə about	ər over	ô for	ů put	zh measure

re·frain[1] (ri frān′) *v* hold oneself back from doing something: *refrain from drinking.* <Old French, from Latin *re-* back + *frenum* to restrain>

re·frain[2] (ri frān′) *n* a repeated line of verse or groups of lines repeated regularly in a song or poem, or the music for such a line or lines. <Old French, from Latin *refringere* to break, because the refrain breaks the flow in a song>

re·fran·gi·ble (ri fran′jə bəl) *adj* able to be refracted.

re·fresh (ri fresh′) *v* **1** give new strength or energy to: *He refreshed his memory by a glance at the book. She refreshed herself with a cup of tea.* **2** revise or update skills or knowledge. **3** *Computers* update the display on a computer screen. **4** pour a new drink for someone or refill a container with a drink: *to refresh a glass.* **5** place or keep food in cold water so as to cool or maintain freshness.

re·fresh·er (ri fresh′ər) *adj* helping to renew or give new knowledge or abilities: *a refresher course.*
n a thing that refreshes.

re·fresh·ing (ri fresh′ing) *adj* **1** serving to give new strength and energy. **2** welcome as a pleasing change. **re·fresh′ing·ly** *adv.*

re·fresh·ment (ri fresh′mənt) *n* **1** the process of giving fresh strength and energy. **2** a thing that refreshes. **3 refreshments** *pl* light food or beverages: *We served refreshments at the party.*

re·fried beans (rē′frīd′) *n* a Mexican dish consisting of beans cooked in water and then fried and eaten with a main dish.

re·frig·er·ant (ri frij′ə rənt) *adj* causing cooling or refrigeration.
n a substance used for cooling.

re·frig·er·ate (ri frij′ə rāt′) *v* **re·frig·er·at·ed, re·frig·er·at·ing** make or keep cold or cool. <Latin *re-* again + *frigoris* cold> **re·frig′er·a′tion** *n.*

re·frig·er·a·tor (ri frij′ə rā′tər) *n* an appliance or compartment used to store and keep things cool, especially food and beverages.

re·fu·el (rē fyū′əl) *v* **1** supply a motor vehicle or aircraft with fuel again. **2** take on a fresh supply of fuel.

ref·uge (ref′yūj) *n* **1** a condition of being safe from pursuit, danger, or trouble: *The cat took refuge in a tree.* **2** a person who or thing that gives such safety, security, or comfort. <Old French, from Latin *re-* back + *fugere* flee>

ref·u·gee (ref′yə jē) *or* (ref′yə jē′) *n* a person who flees for refuge or safety, especially to a foreign country, in time of persecution, war, or natural disaster.

re·ful·gent (ri ful′jənt) *Poetic adj* shining brightly; radiant; splendid: *a refulgent sunrise.* <Latin *re-* back + *fulgere* shine> **re·ful′gence** *n.*

re·fund[1] (ri fund′) *for v,* (rē′fund) *for n. v* pay back money, especially to a customer who is not satisfied with purchased goods or services: *If these shoes do not wear well, the shop will refund your money.*
n **1** the return of money paid. **2** the money paid back: *a full refund.* <Latin *re-* back + *fundere* pour>

re·fur·bish (rē fər′bish) *v* renovate or redecorate a building. **re·fur′bish·ment** *n.*

re·fus·al (ri fyū′zəl) *n* **1** the act of refusing to do or give something: *Her refusal to play provoked the others.* **2** the right to refuse or take a thing before it is offered to others: *I had first refusal on the bicycle.*

re·fuse[1] (ri fyūz′) *v* **re·fused, re·fus·ing 1** decline to do or accept something: *to refuse an offer.* **2** deny a request, demand, or invitation: *to refuse admittance.* <Old French, from Latin *refundere* give back>

ref·use[2] (ref′yūs) *n* waste or worthless matter that is thrown away: *The street-cleaning department took away all refuse from the streets.* <Old French *refus* waste product, from Latin *refundere* give back>

ref·u·ta·tion (ref′yə tā′shən) *n* disproof of a claim, opinion, or argument.

re·fute (ri fyūt′) *v* **re·fut·ed, re·fut·ing** prove a claim, opinion, or argument to be false or incorrect: *How would you refute the statement that the cow jumped over the moon?* <Latin *re-* back + *futare* make fall>
ref′u·ta·ble (ref′yə tə bəl) or **re·fu′ta·ble** (ri fyū′tə bəl) *adj.* **ref′u·ta′tion** *n.* **re·fut′er** *n.*

re·gain (ri gān′) *v* **1** get or use something again after losing it: *to regain health.* **2** get back to or reach again: *to regain the shore.*

re·gal (rē′gəl) *adj* of, like, owned by, or fit for a king or queen, especially in being magnificent or dignified: *He had a regal bearing. It was a regal banquet.* <Latin *regis* king>

re·gale (ri gāl′) *v* **re·galed, re·gal·ing 1** entertain or amuse someone with talk: *My grandmother regaled us with stories of her childhood.* **2** give plenty of pleasing food or drinks: *The children were regaled with ice cream and candy.* <Old French *re-* thoroughly + *gale* make merry>

re·ga·li·a (ri gā′lē ə) *or* (ri gā′lyə) *pln* **1** the emblems of royalty, especially crowns, sceptres, and other items used at a coronation **2** distinctive clothing, emblems, or decorations worn on formal occasions, especially by members of an organization.

re·gard (ri gärd′) *v* **1** gaze at steadily in a specific way: *He regarded me sternly.* **2** consider or think of someone in a specified way: *She is regarded as the best doctor in town.* **3** concern or be connected to: *My comments only regarded myself.*
n **1** attention to or concern for something: *He had little regard for the feelings of others.* **2** a steady gaze: *Her regard seemed fixed upon some distant object.* **3** a high or good opinion of someone or something: *The coach has high regard for your ability.* **4 regards** *pl* used to express good wishes, especially at the end of a message. <Old French *regarder* take notice of>
as regards, as for or concerning: *As regards money, I have enough.*
in (or **with**) **regard to,** concerning.
without regard to, not considering.

re·gard·ful (ri gärd′fəl) *adj* paying attention to, or mindful of.

re·gard·ing (ri gär′ding) *prep* with regard to or concerning: *I got a phone call regarding the offer.*

re·gard·less (ri gär′dlis) *adv* without paying attention to a situation or circumstances: *We plan to leave on Monday, regardless.*

re·gat·ta (ri gat′ə) *n* a series of yacht or boat races held as a special event. <Italian = contest>

re·gen·cy (rē′jən sē) *n, pl* **re·gen·cies 1** the position or period of government of a regent. **2 Regency** the period in the UK from 1811 to 1820 during which George, Prince of Wales, acted as regent for King George III.
adj **Regency** to do with British architecture, clothing, and furniture of the late 1700s and early 1800s. <Latin *regere* to rule>

re·gen·er·ate (ri jen′ə rāt′) *for v,* (ri jen′ə rit) *for adj. v* **re·gen·er·at·ed, re·gen·er·at·ing 1** regrow new tissue in an organism, organ, or tissue to replace what was lost or injured: *If a young crab loses a claw, it can regenerate a new one.* **2** bring into renewed existence or into a new and more vigorous life: *to regenerate a neighbourhood.* **3** give a new or higher spiritual nature, especially in Christian belief.
adj reformed or reborn, especially in a moral or spiritual way. <Latin *re-* again + *generis* birth>
re·gen′er·a′tion *n.* **re·gen′er·a′tive** *adj.*

re·gent (rē′jənt) *n* **1** a person who rules in the name of a sick or absent sovereign, or for a sovereign who is not yet grown up: *The regent ruled for seven years until the boy king came of age.* **2** a member of a governing board of a university or other academic body.
adj (*after the noun*) acting as a regent: *a queen regent.* <Latin *regere* rule>

reg·gae (reg′ā) *n* a style of music, developed in Jamaica in the late 1960s, that blends rock rhythms and traditional Caribbean melodies and whose lyrics often express Rastafarian ideas. <origin uncertain>

reg·i·cide (rej′ə sīd′) *n* **1** the action of killing a king or queen. **2** a person who kills a king or queen. <Latin *regis* king + -CIDE[1]> **reg·i·cid′al** *adj.*

re·gime or **ré·gime** (ri zhēm′) *or* (rā zhēm′) *n* **1** a system of government or rule, especially an authoritarian one: *a dictatorial regime.* **2** a system or planned way of doing things: *Under the old regime, women could not vote.* **3** a set of rules or habits for promoting or restoring health: *The baby's regime includes two naps a day.* <French, from Latin *regere* to rule>

reg·i·men (rej′ə mən) *n* a set of rules or habits intended to improve or restore health. <Latin *regere* to rule>

reg·i·ment (rej′ə mənt) *for n,* (rej′ə ment′) *for v.*
n **1** a permanent unit of an army, often divided into two battalions. **2** a large number of people or things.
v organize in a strict or uniform system, pattern, or manner: *A totalitarian state regiments its citizens.* <Old French, from Latin *regere* to rule> **reg′i·men′tal** *adj.* **reg′i·men′tal·ly** *adv.*

reg·i·men·ta·tion (rej′ə men tā′shən) *n* organization in a strict or uniform system, pattern, or manner.

re·gion (rē′jən) *n* **1** a division of an area, especially part of a country or of the world, that has certain characteristics but may not have a fixed boundary: *the equatorial region.* **2 a** the parts of a country or other political unit outside the capital. In Canada, the regions are often taken to be Atlantic Canada, Québec, Ontario, the Prairies, British Columbia, and the Far North. **3** 🍁 *Ontario* a geographical division for purposes of government, with wider powers than those of a county. **4** part of the body, especially around or near an organ: *the region of the liver.* **5** an area of interest or activity: *Her skill at carving takes it into the region of art.* <Old French, from Latin *regere* to rule (a large piece of land)>
in the region of, approximately.

re·gion·al (rē′je nəl) *adj* of or in a particular region: *a regional storm.* **re′gion·al·ly** *adv.*

re·gion·al·ism (rē′je nəl iz′əm) *n* **1** the theory or practice of emphasizing a region's political, economic, or cultural importance rather than that of a country of which it is part, or the world as a whole. **2** a word, phrase, or expression specific to a certain region.

🍁 **regional municipality** *Ontario, Québec n* a municipal unit that administers more than one municipality within a regional area.

reg·is·ter (rej′i stər) *n* **1** an official list or record: *A register of attendance is kept in our school.* **2** a book in which a list or record is kept, or a device that records: *a hotel register, a cash register.* **3** a particular part of the range of a voice or musical instrument: *Her voice has a low register.* **4** an opening in a wall or floor with an arrangement to regulate the amount of cooled or heated air that passes through. **5** *Computers* a location in a store of data in computers and other electronic devices, used for a specific purpose and to give quick access time.
v **1** enter or record in an official list: *to register the names of the new members.* **2** have one's name put in a list or record: *You must register if you want to attend the conference.* **3** detect, show, or give rise to a reading automatically in a device: *The thermometer registered 25°.* **4** show or make an impression in or on a person's mind, especially by the expression on one's face or gestures: *His angry words did not register with her. Nothing registered on his face.* **5** have a letter or parcel recorded in a post office, paying extra for it to be sent by REGISTERED MAIL. <Latin *regerere* to record>

registered mail *n* a postal service that provides proof that a letter or parcel has been sent and delivered.

registered nurse *n* a nurse who is licensed to practice and who belongs to a nurses' association.

reg·is·trant (rej′i strant′) *n* a person who has registered himself or herself for something.

reg·is·trar (rej′i strär′) *n* **1** a person who keeps official records. **2** the official in charge of administering admissions, examinations, and general regulations in some colleges and universities.

reg·is·tra·tion (rej′i strā′shən) *n* **1** the action or process of registering or being registered. **2** an entry in a register, especially a number, or series of letters and numbers. **3** the number of people registered: *Registration for camp is higher this year than last.*

a bat	e bed	i bid	o pot	u cup	th **thin**
ā cake	ē me	ī bite	ō go	ū rude	ᴛʜ **then**
ä bar	ə about	ər over	ô for	ů put	zh measure

reg·is·try (rej′i strē) *n, pl* **reg·is·tries** **1** the action or process of registering or being registered. **2** a place where a registration is done. **3** a book or place in computer storage in which a list or record is kept.

re·gress (ri gres′) *for v,* (rē′gres) *for n. v* return or be returned to an earlier or less advanced condition.
n a return to an earlier or less advanced condition. <Latin *re-* back + *gradi* walk> **re·gres′sion** *n.*

re·gret (ri gret′) *v* **re·gret·ted, re·gret·ting** feel sadness, regret, or disappointment about: *We regretted her absence. He e-mailed me, regretting that he could not visit me this weekend.*
n **1** a feeing of sadness, regret, or disappointment about something. **2** **regrets** *pl* a polite reply declining an invitation: *I could not go to the party, so I sent regrets.* <Old French *regreter* lament> **re·gret′ful** *adj.* **re·gret′ful·ly** *adv.* **re·gret′ful·ness** *n.*

re·gret·ta·ble (ri gret′ə bəl) *adj* causing regret in being undesirable or unwelcome as conduct or an event: *His rudeness was highly regrettable.* **re·gret′ta·bly** *adv.*

CONFUSABLES

Regrettable means "unfortunate," "deplorable," or "unwelcome": *It's regrettable that she went to the movies instead of going to see her cousins.*

Regretful means "sorry" or "disappointed": *We were regretful that we were not able to visit our friend when he was sick.*

re·group (rē′grūp′) *v* form again or be formed again into organized groups, especially after being attacked or defeated: *to regroup military forces.*

reg·u·lar (reg′yə lər) *adj* **1** fixed by custom or rule as a pattern, especially with the same amount of space or time between each occurrence: *Eat at regular intervals. Six o'clock was her regular hour of rising.* **2** following some rule or principle: *A period is the regular ending for a sentence.* **3** happening again and again at the same time: *a regular two-week holiday in July.* **4** steady, habitual, or usual: *a regular customer, a regular worshipper, our regular suppliers.* **5** arranged or structured in a symmetrical or harmonious way: *regular features.* **6** normal, ordinary, or conventional: *He ordered a regular breakfast. How do you want your coffee? Regular?* **7** done or happening frequently: *You are being suspended for regular violations of school rules.* **8** orderly or methodical: *The movie star claimed he led a regular life.* **9** with the normal patterns of inflection, especially in verbs. **10** *Informal* rightly called, complete, or absolute: *a regular bore.* **11** agreeable or compatible: *He's a regular fellow.* **12** permanently organized: *The regular army was under the direct control of the government.* **13** *Mathematics* **a** in a polygon, with all sides and angles equal. **b** in a polyhedron, with all faces identical regular polygons.
n **1** a full-time member of a group, especially a member or customer: *The fire department was made up of regulars and volunteers. Some regulars went to the pub every week.* **2** a person who is a permanent member of the armed forces. **3** a person belonging to a religious order bound by certain rules. **4** a player who plays in all or most of a team's games in a sport. <Old French, from Latin *regula* rule> **reg′u·lar′i·ty** *n.* **reg′u·lar·ly** *adv.*

reg·u·late (reg′yə lāt′) *v* **reg·u·lat·ed, reg·u·lat·ing** **1** control or maintain the rate or speed of a machine or process so that it works properly: *A thermostat regulates temperature.* **2** control or supervise something by means of rules and regulations: *The new rules regulated how companies could acquire one another.*

reg·u·la·tion (reg′yə lā′shən) *n* **1** a rule, principle, or system enforced by an authority: *traffic regulations.* **2** the action or process of regulating or being regulated.
adj according to or as if required by a regulation: *She wore a regulation uniform. All of them wore regulation teenage jeans.*

reg·u·la·tor (reg′yə lā′tər) *n* **1** a person who or thing that regulates. **2** a person or group that supervises a particular industry or business activity: *an insurance regulator.* **3** a device that regulates the rate at which a machine works, such as a device that controls the flow of a fluid or one in a clock or watch that regulates its speed.

reg·u·la·to·ry (reg′yə lə tô′rē) *adj* serving to or intended to regulate something.

re·gur·gi·tate (rē gər′jə tāt′) *v* **re·gur·gi·tat·ed, re·gur·gi·tat·ing** **1** bring swallowed food or liquid up again to the mouth. **2** repeat information without analyzing or understanding it. <Latin *regurgitare* to overflow> **re·gur′gi·ta′tion** *n.*

re·hab (rē′hab) *Informal n* rehabilitation.

re·ha·bil·i·tate (rē′hə bil′ə tāt′) *v* **re·ha·bil·i·tat·ed, re·ha·bil·i·tat·ing** **1** restore someone to health or normal life by training and therapy after imprisonment, addiction, illness, or injury. **2** restore something, especially part of the environment, to its former good condition. **3** restore to former privileges or reputation after a period of disfavour. <Latin *re-* again + *habilis* fit> **re′ha·bil′i·ta′tion** *n.*

re·hash (rē hash′) *for v,* (rē′hash) *for n. v* put, consider, or discuss old ideas or material in a new form without significant change or improvement: *The question had been rehashed again and again.*
n a reuse of old ideas or material without significant change or improvement: *That essay is simply a rehash of an article in the encyclopedia.*

re·hears·al (ri hər′səl) *n* **1** the action or process of rehearsing. **2** a practice or trial performance of a play, piece of music, or other work for later public performance.

re·hearse (ri hərs′) *v* **re·hearsed, re·hears·ing** **1** practise or supervise a play, piece of music, or other work for later public performance: *We rehearsed our parts for the school play. The director rehearsed us thoroughly for the concert.* **2** mentally prepare words to be said later. **3** inwardly repeat at length what has happened before: *She rehearsed all the events of the day.* <Old French *rehercier* to rake over>

re·heat (rē hēt′) *v* heat cooked food that has gone cold.

reign (rān) *n* **1** the period of power of a monarch: *Queen Victoria's reign lasted sixty-four years.* **2** the period during which a person or group holds power or a title, especially

a sports player or team: *The team's long reign in the league ended during the playoffs, a reign of terror.*
v **1** hold power or a title, especially by a sports player or team: *The king reigned briefly and unhappily. The champion reigned for five years.* **2** prevail: *Silence reigned.* <Old French, from Latin *regis* king>

re·im·burse (rē′im bərs′) *v* **re·im·bursed, re·im·burs·ing** repay a person who has spent or lost money: *Most employers reimburse staff for travelling expenses.* <*re-* back + Latin *in-* into + *bursa* purse> **re′im·burse′ment** *n.*

rein (rān) *n* **1** a long, narrow strap or line fastened to the bit of a bridle, by which to guide and control an animal, especially a horse. See BRIDLE for picture. **2** a means of control: *to seize the reins of government.*
v **1** check or pull with reins. **2** guide, control, or restrain: *Rein your expenses.* <Old French, from Latin *retinere* retain>
give rein to, let move or act freely, without guidance or control: *give rein to your feelings.*
keep a tight rein on, keep under close supervision and control.
rein in, cause to stop or to go slower.

re·in·car·nate (rē′in kår′nāt) *v* **re·in·car·nat·ed, re·in·car·nat·ing** give a new body to a soul, or be reborn in this way.

re·in·car·na·tion (rē′in kår nā′shən) *n* **1** a rebirth of the soul in a new body. **2** a person or animal in whom a new soul is reborn. **3** a new or similar version of something in the past: *The new design was a reincarnation of one popular twenty years earlier.*

rein·deer (rān′dēr′) *n, pl* **rein·deer** a large deer of northern regions of Eurasia and N America, with big branching antlers. <Old Norse *hreinn* reindeer + *dyr* deer>

reindeer moss *n* a grey lichen found in arctic and subarctic regions, providing the major food for reindeer and muskox.

re·in·force (rē′in fȯrs′) *v* **re·in·forced, re·in·forc·ing** **1** strengthen or support with new people or materials: *to reinforce an army or a fleet, to reinforce a garment with an extra thickness of cloth, to reinforce a wall.* **2** strengthen an existing feeling, idea, or habit: *to reinforce an argument.*

reinforced concrete *n* concrete with metal embedded in it to make the structure stronger.

re·in·force·ment (rē′in fȯr′smənt) *n* **1** the action or process of reinforcing. **2** the process of encouraging or establishing a belief or pattern of behaviour, especially by giving a reward. **3** a thing that reinforces.
4 reinforcements *pl* extra personnel sent to strengthen a military or other force.

re·in·state (rē′in stāt′) *v* **re·in·stat·ed, re·in·stat·ing** restore to a former position or condition. **re′in·state′ment** *n.*

re·in·te·grate (rē in′tə grāt′) *v* **re·in·te·grat·ed, re·in·te·grat·ing** restore or have restored separate parts to make something whole again, or as a functioning part of a system: *reintegrate offenders into society.*
re·in′te·gra′tion *n.*

re·in·ter·pret (rē′in tər′prit) *v* interpret again in a different way. **re′in·ter·pre·ta′tion** *n.*

re·in·vent (rē′in vent′) *v* invent again or anew. **re′in·ven′tion** *n.*
reinvent the wheel, *Informal* unwittingly duplicate what has been done, such as solving a problem that has already been solved.

re·in·vest (rē′in vest′) *v* invest the interest earned on a previous investment. **re′in·vest′ment** *n.*

re·it·er·ate (rē it′ə rāt′) *v* **re·it·er·at·ed, re·it·er·at·ing** say again or several times, especially to emphasize or clarify something: *The boy did not move, though the teacher reiterated her command.* <Latin *re-* again + *iterare* do a second time> **re·it′er·a′tion** *n.*

re·ject (ri jekt′) *for v,* (rē′jekt) *for n. v* **1** dismiss, disregard, or ignore something or someone as inadequate, unwelcome, or undesired: *She rejected our help. He tried out for the choir but was rejected.* **2** throw away as useless or unsatisfactory: *She rejected all the apples with soft spots.* **3** produce an immune response in the body to a transplanted organ or tissue that as a result fails to survive.
n a thing or person dismissed or put aside as inadequate, unwelcome, or undesired: *The rejects were sold at a lower price.* <Latin *re-* back + *jacere* to throw> **re·ject′er** *n.* **re·ject′ion** *n.*

re·joice (ri jois′) *v* **re·joiced, re·joic·ing** feel or show great joy or delight. <Old French, from Latin *re-* again + *gaudere* be glad> **re·joic′ing** *n.*

re·join[1] (rē join′) *v* **1** join together again: *The bricks were painstakingly rejoined.* **2** return to a companion, organization, or route after an absence: *After a few years as a freelancer, my aunt rejoined her old company.*

re·join[2] (ri join′) *v* answer or reply, especially in a rude, discouraging, or aggressive way: *"Not on your life," she rejoined.* <French *re-* back + *joindre* to join>

re·join·der (ri join′dər) *n* a reply, especially one that is sharp or witty.

re·ju·ve·nate (ri jū′və nāt′) *v* **re·ju·ve·nat·ed, re·ju·ve·nat·ing** make someone feel young or vigorous again: *The long rest and new clothes have rejuvenated her.* <*re-* again + Latin *juvenis* young> **re·ju′ve·na′tion** *n.* **re·ju′ve·na′tor** *n.*

re·kin·dle (rē kin′dəl) *v* **re·kin·dled, re·kin·dling** relight a fire.

re–laid (rē lād′) past tense and past participle of RE-LAY.

re·lapse (ri laps′); *usually* (rē′laps) *for n. v* **re·lapsed, re·laps·ing** **1** return to a former poor condition after a period of improvement: *He felt better after the surgery but then relapsed badly.* **2** return to a less active condition: *After a cry of surprise, she relapsed into silence.*
n a return to a former poor condition after a period of improvement: *He seemed to be getting over his illness but had a relapse.* <Latin *re-* back + *labi* slip>

a bat	e bed	i bid	o pot	u cup	th **thin**
ā cake	ē me	ī bite	ō go	ū rude	ᴛʜ **then**
å bar	ə about	ər over	ȯ for	ů put	zh measure

re·late (ri lāt′) *v* **re·lat·ed, re·lat·ing 1** give an account of a series of events: *The traveller related her adventures.* **2** connect in thought or meaning: *"Better" and "best" are related to "good."* **3** discuss something in order to indicate a connection with another thing: *He related increasing crime to rising unemployment.* **4** be connected by blood or marriage: *She was distantly related to my family.* <Latin *re-* back + *ferre* bring>

re·lat·ed (ri lā′tid) *adj* **1** (*sometimes in compounds*) belonging to the same group or type: *related factors, income-related.* **2** belonging to the same family. **re·lat′ed·ness** *n.*

re·la·tion (ri lā′shən) *n* **1** a connection in thought or meaning between two or more concepts, objects, or people: *Your answer has no relation to the question.* **2** connections or dealings between people, groups, organizations, or countries: *The relation of mother and child is a very close one.* **3** a person who belongs to the same family as another, such as a father, sister, or aunt. **4** the action of telling a story: *We were amused by his relation of his adventures.* **5 relations** *pl* the way in which two or more people, countries, or organizations consider or deal with one another: *diplomatic relations.*
in (or **with**) **relation to,** about or to do with: *We must plan in relation to next year.*

re·la·tion·ship (ri lā′shən ship′) *n* **1** the way in which two or more concepts, objects, or people are connected, or the fact that they are connected: *What is the relationship of clouds to rain?* **2** the condition of belonging to the same family. **3** the way in which two or more people or organizations regard or deal with one another: *a landlord-tenant relationship.* **4** an emotional or romantic tie between two people: *Theirs was a serious relationship.*

rel·a·tive (rel′ə tiv) *n* **1** a person who belongs to the same family as another, such as a mother, brother, or uncle. **2** a relative pronoun or adverb.
adj **1** related or compared to each other: *Before ordering our meal, we considered the relative merits of chicken and tofu.* **2** depending for meaning on a relation to something else: *"East" is a relative term, since it depends where you live.* **3** introducing a subordinate clause in referring to another person or thing. Example: In *The girl who arrived was a stranger*, the relative pronoun is *who*, and the subordinate clause is *who arrived.*
relative to, a about or concerning: *a letter relative to my proposal.* **b** in proportion to: *This subject is little understood relative to its importance.*

GRAMMAR AND USAGE

Relative clauses limit or add to the meaning of a noun. They can begin with a pronoun (*that, which, who*) or an adverb (*where, when, why*):

Only people ***who have tickets*** *will be admitted.*

This is the spot ***where it happened.***

relative density *n* the ratio of the density of a substance to the density of a particular substance used as a standard. For solids and liquids, the usual standard is water and for gases, it is air.

relative frequency *n* the ratio of the number of times something has happened to the number of times it could happen. This is often expressed as a fraction or a percent. Example: If it rained on two days in one week, the relative frequency of rainy days was 2 to 7, or about 29 percent.

relative humidity *n* the ratio between the amount of water vapour actually present in the air and the amount it would take to saturate the air at the same temperature, expressed as a percentage.

rel·a·tive·ly (rel′ə ti vlē) *adv* in relation to something else: *a relatively small difference.*

rel·a·tiv·ism (rel′ə ti vizm′) *n* the doctrine or belief that knowledge, truth, and morality depend on a cultural, social, or historical context. **rel′a·tiv·ist′** *adj, n.* **rel′a·tiv·ist′ic** *adj.*

rel·a·tiv·i·ty (rel′ə tiv′ə tē) *n* **1** the absence of standards that are universal or absolute. **2** *Physics* a doctrine in physics that light, space, time, and gravity are affected by such factors as the relative motion of the observer and the observed object, as well as the speed of light in a vacuum.

re·lax (ri laks′) *v* **1** make or become less tense or stiff: *She relaxed her muscles to rest them.* **2** make or become less strict or strenuous: *The army relaxed some of its restrictions. Don't relax your efforts until the game is over.* **3** rest or enjoy an activity so as to become less tired or anxious: *He relaxed and began to enjoy his vacation.* <Latin *re-* back + *laxus* loose> **re′lax·a′tion** *n.*

re–lay (rē lā′) *v* **re-laid, re-lay·ing** lay something again or anew.

re·lay (rē′lā) *for n,* (ri lā′) *or* (rē′lā) *for v. n* **1** a group of people who or animals that work or are active for a period of time and then are replaced by a similar group: *New relays of volunteers were sent to the disaster area.* **2** a relay race. **3** a device to receive, reinforce, and retransmit a broadcast or program.
v **1** receive and pass on information or a message. **2** transmit by an electrical or broadcast relay. <Old French *re-* back + *laier* to leave>

re·lay race (rē′lā) *Sports n* in running, skiing, swimming, etc., a race in which each member of a team competes only a certain part of the distance, one taking over from the other.

re·lease (ri lēs′) *v* **re·leased, re·leas·ing 1** allow or enable someone to escape from confinement or something unpleasant: *The prisoner was released.* **2** allow a person or thing to stop one activity so that he, she, or it is available to do something else: *The nurse was released from duty at seven o'clock.* **3** give up a legal right or claim. **4** make a movie, recording, or other product available to the public. **5** allow information to become generally available.
n **1** the action or process of allowing or enabling someone to escape from confinement or something unpleasant: *They took up a petition to have the prisoner released.* **2** a device for releasing a part or parts of a mechanism. **3** the surrender of a legal right or claim, or a document that does this. **4** authorization to make a movie, recording, or other product available to the public. **5** information made generally available: *a press release.* <Old French, from Latin *re-* thoroughly + *laxus* loose>

rel·e·gate (rel′ə gāt′) *v* **rel·e·gat·ed, rel·e·gat·ing** consign or dismiss, usually to an inferior position or condition: *to* *relegate a dress to the rag bag.* <Latin *relegare* dismiss> **rel′e·ga′tion** *n.*

re·lent (ri lent′) *v* become less harsh, cruel, or severe: *After hours of questioning the suspect, the police relented and allowed him to rest.* <Latin *re-* again + *lentus* flexible>

re·lent·less (ri len′tlis) *adj* never ending and oppressive: *The storm raged with relentless fury.* **re·lent′less·ly** *adv.* **re·lent′less·ness** *n.*

rel·e·vant (rel′ə vənt) *adj* closely connected or appropriate to what is being considered or done: *relevant questions.* <Latin *re-* back + *levis* light> **rel′e·vance** *n.*

re·li·a·ble (ri lī′ə bəl) *adj* consistently good in quality or action: *reliable sources of news.* **re·li′a·bil′i·ty** *n.* **re·li′a·bly** *adv.*

> **SYNONYMS**
>
> **Reliable** can mean "dependable" or "predictable": *This computer is a reliable brand.*
>
> **Faithful** can mean "accurate" or "precise": *The witness gave a faithful account of the accident.*
>
> **Trustworthy** means "deserving of trust": *She's always been a trustworthy friend.*

re·li·ant (ri lī′ənt) *adj* trusting or depending on someone or something. **re·li′ance** *n.*

rel·ic (rel′ik) *n* **1** an object, custom, or belief that has survived from an earlier time: *This ruined bridge is a relic of pioneer days.* **2** something belonging to a holy person that is kept as a sacred memorial. **3** an object of interest because of its age or its associations with the past. **4 relics** *pl* all that is left of something. <Old French, from Latin *reliquere* to leave>

rel·ict (rel′ikt) *n* a thing, animal, or plant that has survived from an earlier period or in a more primitive form. <Old French, from Latin *relinquere* to leave>

re·lief (ri lēf′) *n* **1 a** a feeling of having been released from anxiety, pain, or distress. **b** something that lessens or frees from anxiety, pain, or distress, such as help given to the poor or to those affected by a natural disaster: *Relief was quickly sent to the survivors of the flood.* **2** a thing that makes a pleasing change or lessens strain: *It was a relief to see sunshine after days of rain.* **3 a** a release from a post of duty, often by the arrival of a substitute: *This nurse is on duty from seven in the morning until seven at night, with only two hours' relief.* **b** a person or persons replacing others from duty: *The sentry was waiting for his relief.* **4** the condition of being visible and clearly set apart from a background, such as projection of figures and designs from a surface. See LOW RELIEF, HIGH RELIEF.
in relief, standing out from a surface or background.
on relief, receiving money to live on from public funds.

relief map *n* a map that shows the different heights of a surface by using shading, colours, or solid materials.

relief pitcher *Baseball n* a pitcher who replaces another in a game.

re·lieve (ri lēv′) *v* **re·lieved, re·liev·ing 1** cause pain, distress, or difficulty to become less or easier: *This pill will relieve a headache.* **2** release someone from duty or burden by assuming it, or taking it over. **3** bring military aid to a place that is attacked and surrounded: *Soldiers were sent to relieve the fort.* **4** give variety or a pleasing change to: *The black dress was relieved by red trimming.* **5** make less boring or monotonous. <Old French, from Latin *relevare* alleviate>

re·li·gion (ri lij′ən) *n* **1** belief in or worship of a higher power, especially God or gods. **2** a matter of supreme importance: *She makes a religion of keeping her house neat.* **3** a particular system of religious belief and worship: *the Christian religion, the Islamic religon.* <Latin *religio-* obligation>
get religion, *Informal* be converted to religious belief or practice, or something equivalent to it.

re·li·gi·ose (ri lij′ē ōs′) *adj* excessively religious. **re·li·gi·os·i·ty** (ri lij′ē os′ə tē) *n.*

re·li·gious (ri lij′əs) *adj* **1** believing in and worshipping a higher power, especially God or gods: *She is very religious and goes to church every day.* **2** to do with such a system of belief and worship: *a religious meeting, religious books, religious differences.* **3** belonging or to do with a **religious order** such as that of monks or nuns. **4** treated or regarded with devotion and great seriousness: *We paid religious attention to the doctor's orders.*
n, pl **re·li·gious** a person who belongs to a religious order. **re·li′gious·ly** *adv.* **re·li′gious·ness** *n.*

re·lin·quish (ri ling′kwish) *v* give up or let go: *She has relinquished all hope of going abroad this year.* <French, from Latin *re-* back + *linquere* leave> **re·lin′quish·ment** *n.*

rel·ish (rel′ish) *n* **1** much enjoyment of something: *Hunger gives relish to food.* **2** a condiment to add flavour to food, such as a spicy sauce or pickle. **3** a liking for or pleasurable anticipation of something: *I had no relish for the new job.*
v like, enjoy, or be pleased about: *The cat relished cream. He did not relish the prospect of staying after school.* <Old French *relesser* stretch out again>

re·live (re liv′) *v* **re·lived, re·liv·ing** experience all over again, whether through memory, re-enactment, or reconstruction: *Photographs can help you relive happy moments in your life.*

re·lo·cate (re′lo kāt′) *v* **re·lo·cat·ed, re·lo·cat·ing** move or be moved to a new location, especially as a business or organization: *The music store has relocated and is now on main street.* **re′lo·ca′tion** *n.*

re·luc·tant (ri luk′tənt) *adj* unwilling or disinclined to do something: *I was reluctant to spend that much on a DVD.* <Latin *reluctari* to struggle against> **re·luc′tance** *n.* **re·luc′tant·ly** *adv.*

re·ly (ri lī′) *v* **re·lied, re·ly·ing** depend on with trust or confidence: *He relied on his own efforts.* <Old French *relier* attach, from Latin *re-* thoroughly + *ligare* to bind>

rem (rem) *n* a unit for measuring the harm caused by radiation on human tissue. It is equal to one roentgen of X-rays. <*r*(*oentgen*) + *e*(*quivalent*) + *m*(*an*)>

a bat	e bed	i bid	o pot	u cup	th **thin**
ā cake	ē me	ī bite	ō go	ū rude	ᴛʜ **then**
ȧ bar	ə about	ər over	ȯ for	u̇ put	zh measure

REM (rem) *n* in full, **rapid eye movement**. The dream stage of sleep that occurs at intervals during the night, marked by rapid eye movements, more body movements, and faster pulse and breathing is called **REM sleep**.

re·main (ri mān′) *v* **1** continue to stay in a place: *We remained at Gander Lake until September.* **2** continue to have a particular need or fulfill a particular function: *The town remains the same year after year.* **3** continue to exist, especially after other similar or related people or things have not: *A few apples remain on the trees.*
n **1 remains** *pl* the parts that are left over after other parts have been removed, used, or destroyed: *the remains of dinner.* **2** ancient or historical relics. **3** a person's body after death. <Old French, from Latin *re-* back + *manere* to stay>

re·main·der (ri mān′dər) *n* **1** a part, number, or quantity that is left over or is still to come: *After studying for an hour, she spent the remainder of the afternoon in play.* **2** the number that is left over after subtracting one number from another, or after dividing a number by another number which is not one of its factors. Example: In 14 ÷ 3, the quotient is 4 with a remainder of 2.

re·make (rē māk′) *for v,* (rē′māk) *for n.* *v* **re·made, re·mak·ing** make something again or differently.
n something that is made new or differently: *The movie was a remake of an earlier one.*

re·mand (ri mand′) *v* put a prisoner or accused person back in custody, especially to await a trial or while an investigation goes on.
n the act or process of remanding or being remanded. <Latin *re-* back + *mandare* commit>

re·mark (ri mȧrk′) *v* **1** make a comment: *Mother remarked that my hands would be better for a wash.* **2** observe or notice: *Did you remark that oddly shaped cloud?*
n **1** a short written or spoken comment: *The student council president made a few remarks.* **2** the act or process of observing or noticing. <French *re-* thoroughly + *marquer* mark>

re·mark·a·ble (ri mȧr′kə bəl) *adj* worthy of special notice. **re·mark′a·bly** *adv.*

re·mar·ry (rē mar′ē) *or* (rē mer′ē) *v* **re·mar·ried, re·mar·ry·ing** marry again.

re·match (rē′mach) *n* a second match or game involving the same players or teams.

re·me·di·a·ble (ri mē′dē ə bəl) *adj* able to be remedied or cured. **re·me′di·a·bly** *adv.*

re·me·di·al (ri mē′dē əl) *adj* intended as a remedy or cure. **re·me′di·al·ly** *adv.*

rem·e·dy (rem′ə dē) *n, pl* **rem·e·dies** **1** a medicine or treatment for an illness or injury: *Honey and chicken broth are two traditional cold remedies.* **2** a means of counteracting or removing something undesirable, harmful, or wrong: *The chance to play for an hour or two was a remedy for the children's bad spirits.*
v **rem·e·died, rem·e·dy·ing** correct something undesirable: *to remedy a bad situation.* <Old French, from Latin *re-* again + *mederi* heal>

re·mem·ber (ri mem′bər) *v* **1** have an awareness of something come into the mind from the past: *Then I remembered where I was.* **2** take care not to forget: *Remember my birthday.* **3** keep someone in mind by making a gift: *My aunt remembered us in her will.* **4** mention a person as sending friendly greetings: *Please remember me to your brother.* <Old French, from Latin *re-* again + *memor* mindful>

re·mem·brance (ri mem′brəns) *n* **1** the action of or power to remember. **2** the action of remembering the dead, especially as a ceremony. **3** a thing or action that makes one remember a person, place, or event. **4** a memory or recollection.

Remembrance Day *n* November 11, the day set aside to honour the memory of those killed in wars.

re·mind (ri mīnd′) *v* **1** make a person think of something or someone. **2** cause someone to think of someone because of a similarity or likeness: *He was so big and burly he reminded me of a bear.* **3** bring something to the attention of another person: *Let me remind you that you can't smoke here.*

re·mind·er (ri mīn′dər) *n* a thing that causes someone to remember something.

rem·i·nisce (rem′ə nis′) *v* **rem·i·nisced, rem·i·nisc·ing** indulge in talk about past experiences or events.

rem·i·nis·cence (rem′ə nis′əns) *n* an account of incidents and experiences remembered: *reminiscences of the war.* <Latin *reminisci* remember>

rem·i·nis·cent (rem′ə nis′ənt) *adj* tending to remind one of something or to awaken memories: *She had a manner reminiscent of a statelier age.* **rem′i·nis′cent·ly** *adv.*

re·miss (ri mis′) *adj* without care or attention to duty: *I was remiss in not locking the door.* <Latin *re-* back + *mittere* let go> **re·miss′ness** *n.*

re·mis·sion (ri mish′ən) *n* **1** the cancellation of a debt, charge, or penalty: *remission of tuition fees.* **2** a lessening, usually temporary, of the seriousness or intensity of disease or pain: *For some months, her cancer was in remission.* **3** forgiveness or pardon: *remission of sins.*

re·mit (ri mit′) *v* **re·mit·ted, re·mit·ting** **1** send money to a person or place as payment: *Please remit the amount shown on this invoice.* **2** cancel or refrain from collecting a debt or inflicting a punishment: *The judge remitted part of the prisoner's sentence.* **3** pardon a sin. **4** refer a legal case to a different court. <Latin *re-* back + *mittere* send> **re·mit′ter** *n.*

re·mit·tance (ri mit′əns) *n* **1** the action of sending money for goods or services. **2** the money that is sent.

rem·nant (rem′nənt) *n* **1** a small part of something that remains: *This town has only a remnant of its former population.* **2** a piece of cloth or fabric left after the rest has been used or sold: *She bought a remnant of silk at a bargain.* <Old French, from Latin *re-* back + *manere* to stay>

re·mod·el (rē mod′əl) *v* **re·mod·elled** or **re·mod·eled, re·mod·el·ling** or **re·mod·el·ing** change the structure or form of something, especially a building: *The old barn was remodelled into a house.*

re·mon·strance (ri mon′strəns) *n* a forceful and reproachful protest, in speech or writing.

re·mon·strate (ri mon′strāt) *or* (rem′ən strāt′) *v* **re·mon·strat·ed, re·mon·strat·ing** make a forceful and reproachful protest: *The lawyer remonstrated with the judge against the sentence.* <Latin *remonstrare* point out> **re′mon·stra′tion** *n.*

rem·o·ra (rem′ə rə) *n* a fish that attaches itself to a larger fish by means of a sucker on top of its head, feeding on the host's external parasites. <Latin = hindrance, because it was thought that the *remora* slowed down ships>

re·morse (ri mȯrs′) *n* deep, painful regret or guilt for having done wrong: *Because he felt remorse for his crime, the thief confessed.* <Old French, from Latin *remordere* to disturb> **re·morse′ful** *adj.* **re·morse′ful·ly** *adv.* **re·morse′ful·ness** *n.*

re·morse·less (ri mȯr′slis) *adj* **1** without regret or guilt: *a remorseless killer.* **2** of something unpleasant, never getting better or ending: *remorseless poverty.*
re·morse′less·ly *adv.* **re·morse′less·ness** *n.*

re·mote (ri mōt′) *adj* **re·mot·er, re·mot·est** **1** far away from a given place or time: *Dinosaurs lived in the remote past.* **2** far from the main centres of population: *a remote village.* **3** distantly related or connected: *a remote relative.* **4** slight or faint: *I haven't the remotest idea what you mean.* *n Informal* the remote control device for a TV, VCR, DVD player, etc.: *Pass me the remote, please.* <Latin *re-* away + *movere* to move> **re·mote′ly** *adv.*

remote control *n* **1** control from a distance, usually by electronic impulses or radio signals: *Some model airplanes can be flown by remote control.* **2** the device used for operating a remote control system. **remote-controlled** *adj.*

re·mount (rē mount′) *for v,* (rē′mount) *for n.* *v* **1** get on the back of an animal again: *The fallen rider remounted his horse.* **2** attach to a new frame or setting. **3** produce a play or other entertainment again.
n a fresh horse, or a supply of fresh horses, for a rider.

re·mov·al (ri mü′vəl) *n* **1** the action of removing someone or something, especially taking away something unwanted or undesirable: *garbage removal, the removal of a tumour.* **2** a change of location of a business or residence: *The store announced its removal to larger quarters.* **3** a dismissal from an office or position.

re·move (ri müv′) *v* **re·moved, re·mov·ing** **1** take away something unwanted or unnecessary from a place or position: *Remove your hat.* **2** get rid of something or someone: *to remove all doubt.* **3** dismiss from an office or position: *to remove an official for taking bribes.*
n a degree of distance or separation: *His cruelty was only one remove from crime.* <Old French, from Latin *re-* back + *movere* move> **re·mov′a·ble** *adj.* **re·mov′er** *n.*

re·moved (ri müvd′) *adj* **1** separated in space, time, or nature. **2** separated in a family by a specified degree of descent. For example, one's first cousin once removed is the child of one's first cousin.

re·mu·ner·a·tion (ri myü′nə rā′shən) *n* a payment made for services provided or work done: *Do you get a remuneration for babysitting your sister?* **re·mu′ner·ate** *v.*

re·mu·ner·a·tive (ri myü′nə rə tiv) *or* (ri myü′nə rā′tiv) *adj* paying well; profitable.

Ren·ais·sance (ren′ə säns′) *or* (ren′ə säns′) *n* **1** the revival of interest in classical art, architecture, learning, and literature that took place in Europe between the 1200s and the 1500s. A **Renaissance man** or **woman** is any person who has a wide range of interests, knowledge, talents, or skills. **2** **renaissance** a revival of something that has been dormant. <French from Latin *re-* again + *nasci* be born>

GRAMMAR AND USAGE

Capitalize **Renaissance** when referring to this period of history: *I love the art of the Renaissance.*

Use lower case to refer something revived from a former time: *There's been a renaissance of music from the sixties.*

re·nal (rē′nəl) *adj* to do with the kidneys: *the renal arteries.* <French, from Latin *ren* kidney>

re·name (rē nām′) *v* **re·named, re·nam·ing** give a new name to.

re·nas·cence (ri nas′əns) *or* (ri nā′səns) *n* a rebirth or revival, especially of culture.

re·nas·cent (ri nas′ənt) *or* (ri nā′sənt) *adj* becoming active or popular again. <Latin *re-* again + *nasci* be born>

rend (rend) *v* **rent, rend·ing** **1** tear or wrench something violently apart: *to rend flesh. Lightning rent the tree.* **2** cause great mental pain: *Her mind was rent by doubt.* <Old English *rendan*>

ren·der (ren′dər) *v* **1** cause to be or to make: *An accident has rendered him helpless.* **2** provide a service: *She rendered us a great service by her help.* **3** submit or present for inspection: *The treasurer rendered an account of all the money spent.* **4** represent artistically: *The actor rendered the part of Hamlet well.* **5** play or sing music. **6** deliver a verdict or judgment. **7** process parts of the carcass of an animal, especially by melting fat, in order to extract usable food. <Old French, from Latin *re-* back + *dare* give>

ren·der·ing (ren′də ring) *n* **1** a performance or interpretation, especially in performing or making a piece of music or art. **2** a translation from another language.

ren·dez·vous (ron′də vü′) *n, pl* **ren·dez·vous** (-vüz′) **1** a meeting at an agreed time and place, especially between two people. **2** a place and time agreed on for a meeting, such as a popular public spot for friends to get together, or a fixed location for troops, ships, aircraft, or spacecraft to assemble or meet.
v **ren·dez·voused** (-vüd) **ren·dez·vous·ing** (-vü′ing) meet at an agreed time and place. <French *rendez-vous* present yourself>

R

ren·di·tion (ren dish′ən) *n* **1** a performance or interpretation, especially of a dramatic role or piece of music. **2** a visual representation or reproduction. **3** a translation from another language.

ren·e·gade (ren′ə gād′) *n* **1** a person who deserts and betrays an organization, society, or set of principles. **2** a person who is rebellious and unconventional. <Spanish, from Latin *re-* completely + *negare* deny>

a bat	e bed	i bid	o pot	u cup	th **thin**
ā cake	ē me	ī bite	ō go	ü rude	ᴛʜ **then**
ä bar	ə about	ər over	ȯ for	ů put	zh measure

re·nege (ri neg′) *or* (ri nāg′) *v* **re·neged, re·neg·ing** 1 fail to keep a promise. 2 fail to play a card of the suit that is led in a card game, although being able to do so. <*re-* completely + *negare* deny>

re·new (ri nyū′) *or* (ri nū′) *v* 1 begin again: *to renew an attack, to renew a vow.* 2 give fresh life or strength to. 3 extend for a further period: *I renewed my gym membership for another year.* **re·new′al** *n.*

re·new·a·ble (ri nyū′əb əl) *or* (ri nū′əb əl) *adj* 1 able to be renewed. 2 not depleted as a source of energy when used: *Wood is a renewable resource.*

ren·net (ren′it) *n* a substance containing **rennin**, an enzyme that coagulates milk, used for curdling milk to make cheese and other foods.

re·nounce (ri nouns′) *v* **re·nounced, re·nounc·ing** 1 formally declare that a claim, right, or possession is being given up: *He renounced his claim to the money.* 2 refuse to accept, recognize, support, or engage in something: *to renounce an agreement, to renounce an armed struggle.* 3 reject and stop using or consuming: *She renounced dairy products.* <Old French, from Latin *re-* reverse + *nuntiare* announce> **re·nounce′ment** *n.*

ren·o·va·tion (ren′ə vā′shən) *n* 1 the restoring of an old building, or part of it, to a good or improved condition. 2 the restored building, or the restored part.
ren′o·vate *v.* **ren′o·va′tor** *n.*

re·nown (ri noun′) *n* the condition of being widely known: *He was a speaker of great renown.* <Old French *re-* repeatedly + *nomer* to name, i.e., make famous, from Latin *nominare* to name> **re·nowned′** *adj.*

rent[1] (rent) *n* a regular payment to an owner for the use of property or land.
v 1 pay at regular times for the use of property or land. 2 receive regular payments for the use of property or land: *She rents several other houses.* 3 be leased or let for rent: *This house rents for $1200 a month.* <Old French *rente* revenue, from Latin *re-* back + *dare* give> **ren′ter** *n.*
for rent, available in return for rent paid: *That vacant apartment is for rent.*

rent[2] (rent) *n* a torn place in a piece of fabric.
adj torn or split.
v past tense and past participle of REND.

rent·al (ren′təl) *n* 1 an amount received or paid as rent: *The hourly rental for a bicycle is twenty dollars.* 2 something rented or able to be rented.
adj available for rent: *a rental car.*

rent–to–own (rent′tū ōn′) *n* an arrangement in which a renter may become owner of something rented after payments have reached a specified amount.
adj to do with such an arrangement.

re·nun·ci·a·tion (ri nun′sē ā′shən) *n* the formal rejection of something, typically a belief, claim, or course of action.

re·o·pen (rē ō′pən) *v* 1 open again: *After the damage was repaired, the store reopened.* 2 bring up again for consideration or discussion: *The matter is settled and cannot be reopened.*

re·or·der (rē ȯr′dər) *v* 1 put in good order again. 2 give a second or repeated order for something to be made, supplied, or served again.
n a second or repeated order for goods.

re·or·gan·ize (rē ȯr′gə nīz′) *v* **re·or·gan·ized, re·or·gan·iz·ing** change the way in which something is organized: *I reorganized the things in my room, and now there's more space.* **re′or·gan·i·za′tion** *n.*
re·or′gan·iz′er *n.*

rep (rep) *Informal n* a representative.

re·paid (ri pād′) past tense and past participle of REPAY.

re·pair[1] (ri per′) *v* 1 put something in a good condition again after it has suffered from damage or a flaw. 2 correct a damaged relationship or unwelcome situation: *How can I repair the harm done?*
n 1 the act or work of mending or correcting: *Repairs on the school building are made during the summer.* 2 a result of such mending or improvement. 3 the relative physical condition of something: *in good repair, in bad repair.* <Old French, from Latin *reparare* renew>
re·pair′a·ble *adj.* **re·pair′er** *n.*

re·pair[2] (ri per′) *v* go to a place, especially with other people: *After dinner we repaired to the porch.* <Old French *repairier* to frequent, from Latin *re-* back + *patria* one's own country>

re·pair·man (ri per′man′) *or* (ri per′mən) *n,*
pl **re·pair·men** (-men′) *or* (-mən) a person whose work is repairing machines, vehicles, or appliances.

rep·a·ra·ble (rep′ə rə bəl) *adj* possible to be repaired or remedied.

> **CONFUSABLES**
>
> **Reparable** usually describes abstract things like personal relationships: *Their friendship is reparable.*
>
> **Repairable** more often describes physical objects: *The skateboard is broken but repairable.*

rep·a·ra·tion (rep′ə rā′shən) *n* 1 the process of giving satisfaction or compensation for wrong or injury done. 2 a compensation for a wrong or injury. 3 **reparations** *pl* compensation demanded from a defeated enemy for damage done during a war.

rep·ar·tee (rep′ər tē′) *n* a witty reply or replies, or cleverness and wit in making replies. <Old French *repartir* reply promptly>

re·past (ri past′) *n* a meal. <Old French, from Latin *re-* again + *pascere* feed>

re·pa·tri·ate (rē pā′trē āt′) *or* (rē pat′rē āt′) *for v,*
(rē pā′trē it′) *or* (rē pat′rē it′) *for n.*
v **re·pa·tri·at·ed, re·pa·tri·at·ing** send someone back to his or her own country: *After peace was declared, refugees and prisoners of war were repatriated.*
n a person who is sent back to his or her own country. <Latin *re-* back + *patria* homeland> **re·pa′tri·a′tion** *n.*

re·pay (ri pā′) *v* **re·paid, re·pay·ing** 1 pay back a loan or debt: *She repaid the money she had borrowed.* 2 do or give something in return for a favour or kindness. 3 be worth doing: *The boy's success repaid all the time he'd spent in training.* **re·pay′ment** *n.*

re·peal (ri pēl′) *v* revoke or cancel a law or act of parliament.
n the action of removing or cancelling. <Old French *re-* back + *apeler* to call>

re·peat (ri pēt′) *v* **1** do or make again, especially a number of times: *to repeat an error.* **2 a** say again: *to repeat a word for emphasis.* **b** say after another says: *Repeat the oath after me.* **3** broadcast a radio or TV program again. **4** tell to another or others: *I promised not to repeat the secret.* **5** occur again in the same way or form: *History repeats itself.*
n **1** an action, event, or thing that occurs or is done again. **2** a broadcast that is transmitted again: *We saw the repeat last night.* **3** *Music* a musical passage to be repeated, usually indicated by a series of dots. **4** an order of goods sent or received again.
adj occurring, dispensed, or used more than once: *a repeat prescription.* <Old French, from Latin *re-* back + *petere* seek>
repeat oneself, say what one has already said.

re·peat·ed (ri pē′tid) *adj* said, done, made, or happening a number of times: *Her repeated efforts at last won success.* **re·peat′ed·ly** *adv.*

re·peat·er (ri pē′tər) *n* **1** a person who or thing that repeats. **2** a gun that fires several shots without needing to be reloaded.

repeating decimal *Mathematics n* a decimal that shows an indefinite repetition of the same digit or series of digits. Examples: 0.3333…, 1.43666…, 1.2323…

re·pel (ri pel′) *v* **re·pelled, re·pel·ling 1** drive or force back an attack or attacker: *They repelled the enemy.* **2** resist mixing with or fail to absorb another substance: *Oil and water repel each other. This tent repels moisture.* **3** force a magnetized or charged object apart or away by a similarly charged magnetic pole or electrical fields. **4** cause displeasure or disgust in someone: *Spiders and worms repel me.* **5** reject something, especially an argument or theory. <Latin *re-* back + *pellere* drive>

re·pel·lent (ri pel′ənt) *adj* **1** (*often in combination*) able to repel something: *a water-repellent coat.* **2** causing displeasure or disgust.
n a thing, especially a substance, that repels: *We sprayed an insect repellent on our arms and legs to keep the mosquitoes away.*

re·pent (ri pent′) *v* feel or express a great regret for having made a bad decision or having done a wrong. <Old French, from Latin *paenitere* make sorry>
re·pent′ance *n.* **re·pent′er** *n.*

re·pent·ant (ri pen′tənt) *adj* feeling or expressing regret for having done wrong. **re·pent′ant·ly** *adv.*

re·per·cus·sion (rē′pər kush′ən) *n* an indirect influence or reaction from an event or action. <Old French, from Latin *re-* back + *percutere* to strike>

rep·er·toire (rep′ər twär′) *n* **1** the stock of plays, parts, dances, or pieces of music that a performer or group is able to perform. **2** a group of skills or types of behaviour that a person regularly uses: *The long jump isn't in my athletic repertoire.* <French, from Latin *repertorium* inventory>

rep·er·to·ry (rep′ər tô′rē) *n, pl* **rep·er·to·ries 1** the performance of various plays or dances by a theatre company at regular short intervals. **2** a store or stock of things ready for use, especially items of information. **3** a repertoire. <Latin *repertoruim* inventory, from *reperire* to invent>

repertory theatre *n* a theatre in which a company of actors or dancers presents a repertoire of productions at regular intervals.

rep·e·ti·tion (rep′e tish′ən) *n* **1** the action of repeating something that has already been said, written, or done. **2** the thing repeated. **re·pet′i·tive** (ri pet′ə tiv) *adj.* **re·pet′i·tive·ly** *adv.*

GRAMMAR AND USAGE

Avoid **repetition** in writing by using synonyms.

For example, instead of *The new captain of the team works well with the team,* say *The new captain of the team works well with the players.*

A dictionary and thesaurus are handy tools for finding synonyms, but make sure any new words fit the context of the sentence.

rep·e·ti·tious (rep′ə tish′əs) *adj* full of or characterized by repetitions, especially in a tiresome way.
rep′e·ti′tious·ly *adv.* **rep′e·ti′tious·ness** *n.*

repetitive strain injury damage to tendons and muscles caused by making the same movement over and over again for a prolonged period. *Abbrev.* **RSI**

re·phrase (rē frāz′) *v* **re·phrased, re·phras·ing** phrase in a new or different way: *to rephrase a speech, to rephrase a melody.*

re·place (ri plās′) *v* **re·placed, re·plac·ing 1** fill or take the place of. **2** get another in place of: *I will replace the cup I broke.* **3** put back in place again: *Replace the books on the shelf.* **re·place′able** *adj.*

re·place·ment (ri plā′smənt) *n* **1** the action of replacing or being replaced. **2** a person who or thing that takes the place of another.

replacement therapy *n* medical treatment aimed at making up for a deficiency of a substance in the body by replacing the substance with a different one or by delivering the substance in a different way.

re·play (rē′plā) *for n,* (rē′plā′) *for v. n* **1** the playing again of a section of a recording or transmission, such as part of a sportscast or a sequence of film or tape: *slow-motion replay.* **2** a repeat of a series of actions or events: *This year's conversation at the family reunion was a replay of last year's.* **3** an action of redoing a play in a game, or of playing a game over again.
v **1** play again. **2** play a match or competition again after the original contest ended in a draw or had a disputed result.

a bat	e bed	i bid	o pot	u cup	th **thin**
ā cake	ē me	ī bite	ō go	ū rude	ᴛʜ **then**
ä bar	ə about	ər over	ô for	ů put	zh measure

re·plen·ish (ri plen′ish) *v* fill again or provide a new supply for: *The bird feeder needs replenishing. You had better replenish the fire.* <Old French, from Latin *re-* again + *plenus* full> **re·plen′ish·er** *n.* **re·plen′ish·ment** *n.*

re·plete (ri plēt′) *adj* filled or abundantly supplied. <Old French, from Latin *replere* to fill>

rep·li·ca (rep′lə kə) *n* an exact copy or model of something, especially in smaller form: *The artist made a replica of her picture.* <Italian, from Latin *replicare* to repeat>

rep·li·cate (rep′lə kāt′) *v* **rep·li·cat·ed, rep·li·cat·ing** duplicate or repeat as exactly as possible: *to replicate an experiment.* <Latin *replicare* to repeat> **rep·li·ca′tion** *n.*

re·ply (ri plī′) *v* **re·plied, re·ply·ing 1** answer by words or action: *Has she replied to your e-mail? The mutineers replied with a burst of gunfire.* **2** give as an answer: *He replied, "I have no intention of going."*
n, pl **re·plies** a response or answer. <Old French, from Latin *replicare* to repeat>

> **SYNONYMS**
>
> **Reply** means "answer": *I replied to her e-mail on the same day that I received it.*
>
> **Respond** can mean "acknowledge": *We responded quickly to the invitation to the wedding.*
>
> **Retort** means "reply quickly and sharply to a remark or accusation": *"I think your complaint is ridiculous," he retorted.*

re·po (rē′pō) *Informal n* repossession of property, because of failure to pay a loan or mortgage. <*repossession*>

re·port (ri pórt′) *n* **1** an account or statement of something that has been observed, heard, done, or investigated: *a news report.* **2** an account officially presented after a thorough investigation or consideration: *an annual report.* **3** the sound of a shot or an explosion: *the report of a gun.* **4** a rumour or piece of information that may not be factually true: *Report has it that our neighbours are leaving town.*
v **1** make an account or statement of something that has been observed, done, etc.: *Report on your findings, please.* **2** give a formal or official account of: *Our treasurer reports that all dues are paid up.* **3** record or report something, especially as a journalist. **4** make a formal statement or complaint about a wrong done: *She reported him to the police.* **5** indicate that something has occurred, though the action cannot be confirmed: *It was reported that he owed a lot of money.* **6** present oneself: *Report for duty at 9 a.m.* <Old French, from Latin *re-* back + *portare* carry>

re·port·a·ble (ri pór′tə bəl) *adj* capable of or worth being reported.

re·port·age (ri pór′tij) *n* the process or manner of reporting news or other factual information, especially in a journalistic style.

report card *n* a report sent regularly by a school to parents or guardians, showing the quality of a student's work.

re·port·ed (ri pór′tid) *adj* **1** according to a report: *The reported cause of the accident was speeding.* **2** made known to authorities: *sixty reported cases of vandalism.* **re·port′ed·ly** *adv.*

reported speech INDIRECT SPEECH.

re·port·er (ri pór′tər) *n* a person who reports, especially one who gathers news for a newspaper, magazine, radio or TV station.

re·pose[1] (ri pōz′) *n* **1** rest or sleep: *Do not disturb her repose.* **2** a condition of peace or rest: *the repose of a soul.*
v **re·posed, re·pos·ing 1** be lying, situated, or kept in a particular place: *The cat reposed upon the cushion.* **2** lie down to rest. **3** lay something to rest in or on. <Old French, from Latin *repausare* cause to rest>

re·pose[2] (ri pōz′) *v* **re·posed, re·pos·ing** place something, especially confidence or trust, in: *You reposed a lot of trust in us.* <Latin *re-* back + *ponere* place>

re·pose·ful (ri pōz′fəl) *adj* calm or peaceful.

re·pos·i·to·ry (ri poz′ə tó′rē) *n, pl* **re·pos·i·to·ries** a place, container, or building where things are stored or kept: *The box was the repository for old magazines.*

re·pos·sess (rē′pə zes′) *v* get possession of again, especially of something on which a buyer has failed to keep up payments. **re′pos·ses′sion** *n.*

rep·re·hen·si·ble (rep′ri hen′sə bəl) *adj* deserving reproof, rebuke, or blame: *a reprehensible act.* <Latin *reprehendere* to blame> **rep′re·hen′si·bly** *adv.*

rep·re·sent (rep′ri zent′) *v* **1** stand for or be a sign or symbol of: *The stars on this map represent cities.* **2** speak or act for another: *People are elected to represent us in the government.* **3** act the part of: *In the play, each child will represent a farm animal.* **4** show a subject in a picture or other work of art: *This painting represents a group of victorious warriors.* **5** be an example of: *A hollowed log represents a very simple kind of boat.* **6** state or point out something clearly: *She represented the plan as safe.*

rep·re·sen·ta·tion (rep′ri zen tā′shən) *n* **1** an action of speaking or acting on behalf of another. **2** representatives considered as a group: *Farmers had a large representation at the convention.* **3** a description or portrayal of someone or something in a particular way or as being of a certain nature. **4** a statement or allegation about something: *a false representation.* **5** **representations** formal statements made to an authority, especially as to convey an opinion, protest, or complaint.

rep·re·sen·ta·tion·al (rep′ri zen tā′shən əl) *Art adj* to do with a style that aims to depict the physical appearance of things rather than symbolically or abstractly. **rep′re·sen·ta′tion·al·ism′** *n.*

rep·re·sent·a·tive (rep′ri zen′tə tiv) *n* **1** a person appointed or elected to act or speak for others: *She is the club's representative at the convention.* **2** a typical example: *The tiger is a representative of the cat family.* **3** **Representative** *US* a member of the House of Representatives.
adj **1** with its citizens represented by chosen persons: *a representative government.* **2** representing: *Images representative of animals were made by the children.* **3** serving as a typical example of: *Oak, birch, and maple are representative North American hardwoods.*

re·press (ri pres′) *v* restrain or prevent something or someone from an action, feeling, or thought: *She repressed her desire to laugh. The dictator repressed the revolt.* <Latin *re-* back + *premere* to press> **re·press′er** *n.* **re·pres′sible** *adj.* **re·pres′sion** *n.*

re·pressed (ri prest′) *adj* restrained or inhibited, especially in expressing thoughts, feelings, or desires.

re·pres·sive (ri pres′iv) *adj* tending to or with power to repress freedom, especially in a social or political system.

re·prieve (ri prēv′) *v* **re·prieved, re·priev·ing 1** cancel or postpone the punishment of someone, especially the execution of a person condemned to death. **2** give relief from a hardship or trouble.
n **1 a** a delay in carrying out a punishment, especially of the death penalty. **b** the order giving authority for such delay. **2** a temporary relief from a hardship or trouble: *We had a reprieve of two days, and then the rain started again.* <Old French, from Latin *reprehendere* recover>

rep·ri·mand (rep′rə mand′) *n* an official or formal rebuke.
v rebuke officially or formally. <French, from Latin *re-* back + *premere* to press>

re·print (rē print′) *for v,* (rē′print′) *for n. v* print again or in a different form.
n a new or different printing.

re·pris·al (ri prī′zəl) *n* **1** a measure, economic or military, taken in retaliation by one nation against another. **2** an act of retaliation by one person against another. <Old French, from Latin *reprehendere* to take back>

re·prise (rə prēz′) *n* a repetition, return, or re-enactment.
v **re·prised, re·pris·ing** repeat, perform, or produce again. <French>

re·proach (ri prōch′) *n* **1** an expression of blame, disappointment, or disapproval. **2** a object of blame, disappointment, or disapproval: *The criminal was a reproach to his family.*
v address someone in such a way as to express blame, disappointment, or disapproval. <Old French *reproche* blame> **re·proach′ful** *adj.* **re·proach′ful·ly** *adv.* **re·proach′ful·ness** *n.*

rep·ro·bate (rep′rə bāt′) *n* (*often used humorously or affectionately*) an unprincipled person.
adj without principles. <Latin *re-* opposite + *probare* approve>

re·pro·duce (rē′prə dyūs′) *or* (rē′prə dūs′) *v* **re·pro·duced, re·pro·duc·ing 1** produce again: *The new CD reproduced the band's sound perfectly.* **2** make a copy of: *She took the picture to the printer to be reproduced.* **3** produce offspring: *Most plants reproduce by seeds.* **re′pro·duc′i·ble** *adj.*

re·pro·duc·tion (rē′prə duk′shən) *n* **1** the action or process of reproducing or being reproduced. **2** a copy of a print, photograph, or visual work. **3** the process by which offspring are produced. **re′pro·duc′tive** *adj.* **re′pro·duc′tive·ly** *adv.* **re′pro·duc′tive·ness** *n.*

reproductive technology *n* the design or use of *in vitro* fertilization, the transfer of embryos, surrogate motherhood, fertility drugs, and other ways of increasing the success of natural reproduction.

re·proof (ri prūf′) *n* words of blame or disapproval.

re·prove (ri prūv′) *v* **re·proved, re·prov·ing** find fault with someone: *He was reproved for teasing the cat.* <Old French, from Latin *re-* reversing + *probare* approve>

The poisonous coral snake is a brightly marked **reptile** with red, yellow, and black rings. It injects a lethal venom, which acts on the nervous system, through two short fangs in the front of its mouth.

rep·tile (rep′tīl) *n* **1** a cold-blooded vertebrate animal that has a dry, scaly skin and typically lays soft-shelled eggs on land. Snakes, lizards, turtles, alligators, and crocodiles are reptiles. **2** *Informal* a person considered to be loathsome or contemptible.
adj of or like a reptile. <Latin *repere* to crawl>

rep·til·i·an (rep til′ē ən) *adj* **1** to do with reptiles. **2** considered to be loathsome or contemptible: *reptilian features.*

re·pub·lic (ri pub′lik) *n* a nation or state in which the citizens elect representatives to manage the government, which is usually headed by a president rather than by a monarch or prime minister. <French, from Latin *res* + concern *publicus* of the people>

re·pub·li·can (ri pub′lə kən) *adj* **1** of, belonging to, or characteristic of a republic. **2** favouring or supporting a republic. **3 Republican** *US* to do with the Republican Party.
n **1** a person who favours or supports a republic. **2 Republican** *US* a member of the Republican Party.

re·pub·li·can·ism (ri pub′lə kə niz′əm) *n* the theory or practice of the republican system of government.

Republican Party *n* one of the two main political parties in the US.

re·pu·di·ate (ri pyū′dē āt′) *v* **re·pu·di·at·ed, re·pu·di·at·ing 1** refuse to accept or be associated with someone or something: *to repudiate a doctrine, to repudiate a child.* **2** refuse to acknowledge or pay: *to repudiate a debt.* **3** deny the truth or validity of something. <Latin *repudium* rejection> **re·pu′di·a′tion** *n.*

re·pug·nant (ri pug′nənt) *adj* disgusting or distasteful: *Snakes are repugnant to her.* <Latin *repugnare* to resist> **re·pug′nance** *n.*

a bat	e bed	i bid	o pot	u cup	th **thin**
ā cake	ē me	ī bite	ō go	ū rude	ᴛʜ **then**
à bar	ə about	ər over	ȯ for	ů put	zh measure

R

re·pulse (ri puls′) *v* **re·pulsed, re·puls·ing 1** drive back an attack. **2** cause someone to feel intense dislike or distaste: *She was repulsed by his behaviour.*
n **1** the action of driving back an attack: *After the second repulse, the enemy surrendered.* **2** a discouraging response to a friendly gesture: *She saw his silence as a repulse to her friendly greeting.* <Latin *re-* back + *pellere* to drive>

re·pul·sion (ri pul′shən) *n* **1** a strong dislike or aversion. **2** a physical force under the influence of which objects tend to move away from each other, as objects with the same magnetic polarity do.

re·pul·sive (ri pul′siv) *adj* **1** causing strong dislike or aversion: *Snakes are repulsive to some people.* **2** to do with the physical repulsion of objects. **re·pul′sive·ness** *n.*

re·pur·pose (ri pər′pəs) *Computers v* **re·pur·posed, re·pur·pos·ing** convert for use in another format: *to repurpose a book as a CD.*

rep·u·ta·ble (rep′yə tə bəl) *adj* with a good reputation. **rep′u·ta·bly** *adv.*

rep·u·ta·tion (rep′yə tā′shən) *n* **1** the beliefs or opinions that are generally held about someone or something: *He had a reputation for honesty. She has an international reputation.* **2** a widespread belief that someone or something has a particular quality: *a good reputation.* <Latin *reputationem* credit>

re·pute (ri pyūt′) *n* reputation: *This is a district of bad repute on account of many robberies.*
v **re·put·ed, re·put·ing** generally suppose (to be): *He is reputed to be the richest man in Regina.*

re·put·ed (ri pyū′tid) *adj* generally supposed to be such: *the reputed author of a book.* **re·put′ed·ly** *adv.*

re·quest (ri kwest′) *v* ask for politely or formally: *She requested a copy of her high school transcript.*
n **1** the act of asking for something politely or formally: *She did it at our request.* **2** a thing that is asked for: *He granted my request.* <Old French, from Latin *requaerere* to seek>
by request, in response to a request: *The library remained open all evening by request of the students.*

SYNONYMS

Request means "ask for" or "ask," usually in a rather formal way: *Sorry to trouble you, but I'd like to request a favour.*

Demand means "ask for with authority": *The judge demanded that the witness answer the question.*

Entreat means "ask earnestly": *They entreated their teacher to give them more time to complete the project.*

Req·ui·em or **req·ui·em** (rek′wē əm) *or* (rē′kwē əm) *especially Catholicism n* a church service for the dead, or the music for this service. <Latin *requies* rest>

re·quire (ri kwīr′) *v* **re·quired, re·quir·ing 1** have need for: *If I have to buy lunch for everyone, I will require more money.* **2** command, order, or demand: *The rules require us all to be present.* <Old French, from Latin *re-* repeatedly + *quaerere* seek>

re·quire·ment (ri kwīr′mənt) *n* **1** a thing that is needed: *Patience is a requirement in teaching.* **2** a demand or something demanded: *She has filled all requirements for graduation.*

req·ui·site (rek′wə zit) *adj* required by circumstances or regulations: *the qualities requisite for a leader.*
n the thing needed for a purpose: *Food and air are requisites for life.* <See REQUIRE.> **req′ui·site·ly** *adv.* **req′ui·site·ness** *n.*

req·ui·si·tion (rek′wə zish′ən) *n* a formal demand made for the use of property, materials, or services: *the requisition of supplies for troops.*
v formally demand the use of property, materials, or services: *to requisition supplies or labour.*

re·quit·al (ri kwī′təl) *n* make an appropriate return or reward for a favour or service: *What requital can we make for all her kindness to us?*

re·quite (ri kwīt′) *v* **re·quit·ed, re·quit·ing** make an appropriate return or reward for a favour or service: *To his great sadness, she did not requite his love.* <Middle English *re-* back + *quite* pay up>

re·read (rē′rēd′) *v* **re·read,** (-red′) **re·read·ing** read a text or message again: *She reread the letter several times.*

rere·dos (rēr′dos) *n* a screen or a decorated part of the wall behind an altar in a Christian church. <Old French *arere* behind + *dos* back>

re·route (rē rūt′) *or* (rē rout′) *v* **re·rout·ed, re·rout·ing** send by a new or different route: *Buses will be rerouted while the parade is on.*

re·run (rē run′) *for v,* (rē′run′) *for n. v* **re·ran, re·run·ning 1** run again or in a different form. **2** show or perform a play, TV program, or movie again.
n a play, TV program, or movie that is shown or performed again.

re·sale (rē′sāl′) *or* (rē sāl′) *n* the action of selling something that was previously bought. **re′sell′** *v.*

re·scind (ri sind′) *v* revoke, cancel, or repeal a law, order, or agreement. <Latin *re-* back + *scindere* cut>

res·cue (res′kyū) *v* **res·cued, res·cuing 1** save from danger or distress: *Searchers rescued the boy lost in the Misty Mountains.* **2** keep from being lost or destroyed: *He rescued the sandwich he dropped before the dog could get it.*
n the action of saving or freeing from danger or distress: *The firefighter was praised for his brave rescue of the children in the burning house.* <Old French, from Latin *re-* thoroughly + *excutere* shake out> **res′cu·er** *n.*

re·search (ri sərch′) *or* (rē′sərch′) *n* the systematic investigation into and study of materials and sources in order to establish facts and reach new conclusions: *Medical research has done much to lessen disease.*
v investigate systematically.
adj to do with such an investigation: *a research paper.*
re·search′er *n.*

re·sem·ble (ri zem′bəl) *v* **re·sem·bled, re·sem·bling** be like or similar, especially in appearance: *Twins usually resemble each other.* <Old French, from Latin *re-* again + *similis* similar> **re·sem′blance** *n.*

re·sent (ri zent′) *v* feel bitter or indignant at a circumstance, action, or person: *Our cat seems to resent having anyone sit in its chair.* <French, from Latin *sentire* feel> **re·sent′ful** *adj.* **re·sent′ful·ly** *adv.* **re·sent′ful·ness** *n.* **re·sent′ment** *n.*

res·er·va·tion (rez′ər vā′shən) *n* **1** a limiting condition, especially a qualification to an expression of agreement: *The committee accepted the plan with reservations plainly stated.* **2** land set aside for a special purpose: *a forest reservation.* **3** an arrangement to book or reserve something, especially a seat or room, for a particular person: *We made reservations for the end of the month.* **4** 🍁 the provision made for the withholding of royal assent to a bill, federal or provincial, until it has been re-examined. **5** land set apart for the exclusive use of Native Americans in the US, and for Aboriginals in Australia. Compare RESERVE (*n* def. 2).

re·serve (ri zərv′) *v* **re·served, re·serv·ing 1** refrain from using or disposing of something with a view to using it later: *I'll reserve criticism until I've read the whole book.* **2** use or engage in something only in particular circumstances: *time reserved for recreation.* **3** save for use later: *Reserve enough money for your fare home.* **4** set aside for the use of a particular person or people: *Reserve a table.*
n **1** a supply of money or goods available if required: *natural gas reserves.* **2** 🍁 a tract of land set aside by the Federal Government for the exclusive use of a First Nations band, usually by treaty. Compare RESERVATION (def. 5). **3** land set apart by the government to protect a natural habitat: *a forest reserve.* **4** *Sports* a person kept in reserve or available as a substitute on a sports team. **5** the stated minimum price at which an item may be sold at an auction. **6 reserves** *pl* members of the armed forces not in active service but ready to serve if needed: *You may speak here without reserve.*
adj forming a reserve. <Latin *re-* back + *servare* keep>
in reserve, available if required.

re·served (ri zərvd′) *adj* **1** kept in reserve or by special arrangement: *reserved seats.* **2** self-restrained in action or speech: *a reserved manner.* **3** disposed to keep to oneself: *A reserved person does not make friends easily.*

re·serv·ist (ri zər′vist) *n* a member of the armed forces not in active service but available if needed.

res·er·voir (rez′ər vwȧr′) *n* **1** a large natural or artificial lake that is used as a water supply for a city or community. **2** a container or part of a machine designed to hold a fluid, such as that in a fountain pen. **3** a place where a fluid collects, such as in rock strata or in the body. **4** a supply of something. <French *réserver* to reserve>

re·set (rē set′) *for v*, (rē′set′) *for n. v* **re·set, re·set·ting** set again or differently: *The diamonds were reset in platinum.*

re·shape (rē shāp′) *v* **re·shaped, re·shap·ing** form into a new or different shape.

re·side (ri zīd′) *v* **re·sid·ed, re·sid·ing 1** live in or at a particular place for a long time. **2** be present or located in: *Her charm resides in her happy smile.* <Latin *re-* back + *sedere* sit> **re·sid′er** *n.*

res·i·dence (rez′i dəns) *n* **1** a house where a person lives, especially a large or impressive one. **2** the act or fact of living in a particular place: *Long residence in Québec made him very fond of French food.* **3** a building in which university or college students live. Often shortened to **res.**
in residence, living in an institution while on duty or doing active work: *an artist in residence.*

res·i·den·cy (rez′i dən sē) *n, pl* **res·i·den·cies 1** a period of advanced training as a specialist after receiving a medical degree, usually by working in a hospital under supervision, or the doctor's position during this period. **2** a position held by someone, especially a writer, musician, or artist, that requires the person to live in a certain place. **3** the act or fact of living in a place: *Residency in Canada was one of the scholarship's requirements.*

res·i·dent (rez′i dənt) *n* **1** a person dwelling in a place, such as a city, for an extended period or for a briefer period in a boarding school or hotel as a boarder or guest. **2** a medical graduate engaged in specialized practice under supervision in a hospital. **3** a bird, butterfly, or other animal of a species that does not migrate.
adj **1** dwelling somewhere for an extended period: *a resident owner.* **2** living in a place while on duty or doing active work: *a resident physician at the hospital.* **3** not migratory: *resident birds.*

res·i·den·tial (rez′i den′shəl) *adj* **1** to do with homes or residences: *a residential district.* **2** to do with residence.

🍁 **residential school** *North n* a boarding school operated or subsidized by a religious body or the Federal Government for Inuit and First Nations students to be educated away from their own communities.

re·sid·u·al (ri zij′ū əl) *adj* remaining after the greater part or quantity has gone.
n a quantity remaining after other things have been subtracted or allowed for, such as a royalty paid to a performer or writer for a repeat of a play, TV show, or other entertainment.

res·i·due (rez′ə dyū′) *or* (rez′ə dū′) *n* **1** a small amount of something that remains after the main part has been removed or used: *The syrup had dried up, leaving a sticky residue.* **2** the part of a legal estate that is left after the payment of charges, debts, and bequests. <Old French, from Latin *residere* stay behind>

re·sign (ri zīn′) *v* **1** (*often with* **from**) give up a job or other position: *He resigned his seat in Parliament. She has resigned from the club.* **2** (*with a reflexive pronoun*) give in or yield, often unwillingly, but without complaint: *He had to resign himself to a week in bed when he hurt his back.* <Old French, from Latin *resignare* give up>

res·ig·na·tion (rez′ig nā′shən) *n* **1 a** an act of giving up a job or other position. **b** a written statement giving notice that a person has resigned. **2** patient acceptance of something undesirable but inevitable: *She bore the pain with resignation.*

a bat	e bed	i bid	o pot	u cup	th **thin**
ā cake	ē me	ī bite	ō go	ū rude	ᴛʜ **then**
ȧ bar	ə about	ər over	ȯ for	u̇ put	zh measure

R

re·signed (ri zīnd′) *adj* showing or feeling patient acceptance of something undesirable but inevitable: *resigned to an unhappy fate.* **re·sign′ed·ly** *adv.*

re·sil·i·ent (ri zil′ē ənt) *adj* **1** able to recoil or spring back to an original form or position after being bent, compressed, or stretched. **2** able to withstand or recover quickly from trouble or difficulty. <Latin *re-* back + *salire* to jump> **re·sil′i·ence** *n.*

res·in (rez′ən) *n* **1** a sticky, yellow or brown insoluble substance that flows from certain plants and trees, especially the pine and fir. **2** a similar substance that is made synthetically, used to make plastics, adhesives, and other products. <Latin *resina*> **res′in·ous** *adj.*

re·sist (ri zist′) *v* **1** withstand the action or effect of: *The window resisted his efforts to open it. A healthy body resists disease.* **2** struggle against something or someone: *Do not resist.* **3** succeed in ignoring the attraction of something wrong or unwise: *I could not resist laughing.* <Old French, from Latin *re-* opposing + *sistere* stop> **re·sist′er** *n.*

SYNONYMS

Resist suggests striving to fend off someone or something: *We resisted the temptation to laugh.*

Fight can mean "oppose strongly": *The citizens were determined to fight the plan to cut down the trees.*

Withstand suggests successfully warding off someone or something: *It's difficult to withstand today's high-pressure marketing of cellphones.*

re·sist·ance (ri zis′təns) *n* **1** the act or fact of refusing to accept or comply with something: *The bank clerk made no resistance to the robbers.* **2** the power not to be affected by something, especially adversely: *She has little resistance to germs and so is often ill.* **3** armed or violent opposition: *The invaders met with little resistance.* **4** the impeding, slowing, or stopping effect that one physical thing exerts on another: *air resistance.* **5** the property of a conductor that opposes the passage of an electric current and changes electric energy into heat or light. **6 Resistance** the people in a country occupied or controlled by another country who secretly organize and fight against it.

re·sist·ant (ri zis′tənt) *adj* offering resistance.

re·sis·tor (ri zis′tər) *n* a device that resists the passage of an electric current in a circuit.

re·sole (rē sōl′) *v* **re·soled, re·sol·ing** put a new sole on a shoe or other footwear.

res·o·lute (rez′ə lūt′) *adj* admirably determined and unwavering: *She was resolute in her attempt to climb to the top of Barbeau Peak.* <Latin *resolvere* break into parts, i.e., final, absolute> **res′o·lute·ly** *adv.*

res·o·lu·tion (rez′ə lū′shən) *n* **1** a firm decision to do or not to do something: *He made a resolution to get up early.* **2** the action of solving a problem, dispute, or conflict. **3** the quality of being determined and unwavering: *The man's firm resolution overcame the handicap of poverty.* **4** a formal expression of opinion or intention agreed on by a legislative body, committee, or other formal meeting, typically after taking a vote: *The club passed a resolution thanking him for his help throughout the year.* **5** the sharpness of a photographic or television image. **6** *Computers* **a** the number of pixels (horizontally) and lines (vertically) on a screen. **b** a measurement expressed in DPI that describes the sharpness of a printed image.

re·solve (ri zolv′) *v* **re·solved, re·solv·ing 1** decide firmly on what to do: *She resolved to do better work in the future.* **2** settle or find a solution to a problem, dispute, or conflict: *His letter resolved all our doubts.* **3** decide by vote of a legislative body, committee, or formal meeting: *It was resolved that our school have a uniform.* **4** separate or cause to be separated into parts or components, especially in a chemical process. **5** reduce a subject, statement, or group into separate elements or a simpler form: *The assembly resolved itself into committees.*
n a determination to do something: *She kept her resolve to do better.* <Latin *resolvere* break into parts, dissolve>

re·solved (ri zolvd′) *adj* determined to do something.

res·o·nance (rez′ə nəns) *n* **1** the quality in a sound of being deep, full, and reverberating. **2** the reinforcing and prolonging of sound by reflection or by vibration of other objects: *The sounding board of a piano gives it resonance.* **3** the condition of an electrical circuit or device adjusted to allow the greatest flow of current at a certain frequency. **4** the ability to bring to mind images, memories, or emotions: *The old movie had a lot of resonance for her.* <Old French, from Latin *re-* back + *sonus* sound>

res·o·nate (rez′ə nāt′) *v* **res·o·nat·ed, res·o·nat·ing 1** produce or be filled with a deep, full, reverberating sound. **2** bring to mind images, memories, or emotions: *The song lyrics resonated with thoughts of last summer.* <Old French, from Latin *re-* back + *sonus* sound> **res′o·nant** *adj.* **res′o·nant·ly** *adv.*

res·o·na·tor (rez′ə nā′tər) *n* a device that increases the resistance of a sound, especially the hollow part of a musical instrument.

re·sort (ri zòrt′) *n* **1** a place that is popular for people to go to for relaxation or recreation: *a holiday resort.* **2** the action of pursuing a tactic, strategy, or action so as to resolve a difficult situation: *Must we resort to violence in settling a dispute?* **3** a person or thing turned to as a source of support or help.
v pursue a tactic, strategy, or action so as to resolve a difficult situation: *In the hot weather, many people resorted to taking cold showers.* <Old French *re-* again+ *sortir* go out>

re·sound (ri zound′) *v* **1** fill a place with sound, especially with a particular sound such as an echo: *The hills resounded when we shouted.* **2** be much talked of, especially in giving praise: *The news of the first space flight resounded all over the world.* **3** be clear and emphatic: *Her liking for adventure resounded throughout her essay.* <*re-* + *sound*> **re·sound′ing** *adj.* **re·sound′ing·ly** *adv.*

re·source (ri zòrs′), (ri sòrs′), *or* (rē′zòrs′) *n* **1** a stock or supply that will meet a need: *We have resources of money, of quick wit, and of strength.* **2** a means of getting success or getting out of trouble: *Climbing a tree is a cat's resource when chased by a dog.* **3 resources** *pl* **a** the actual and potential wealth of a country, especially its reserves of minerals, land, and water. **b** available money and assets.

c the qualities a person or animal has that may provide help in difficult circumstances: *You cannot abandon a pet and leave it to its own resources.* <Old French, from Latin *re-* again + *surgere* to rise>

re·source·ful (ri zôr′sfəl) *or* (ri sôr′sfəl) *adj* good at finding ways to overcome difficulties. **re·source′ful·ly** *adv.* **re·source′ful·ness** *n.*

re·spect (ri spekt′) *n* **1** a feeling of honour or admiration because of the abilities, qualities, or achievements of someone or something: *Children should show respect to those who are older and wiser.* **2** consideration or regard for the feelings, wishes, rights, traditions, or belongings of others: *Show respect for other people's property.* **3** a particular point, aspect, or detail: *The plan is unwise in many respects.* **4 respects** *pl* public greetings: *We must pay our respects to the mayor.*
v **1** feel or show honour or admiration: *We respected him for his honesty.* **2** show consideration or regard for. <Latin *re-* back + *specere* look at, i.e. to consider> **re·spect′er** *n.*
in respect of, with reference or comparison to.
in respect that, because.
with respect to, with relation, reference, or regard to something: *We must plan with respect to the future.*

re·spect·a·ble (ri spek′tə bəl) *adj* **1** regarded by others as being good, proper, or correct. **2** satisfactory and acceptable in appearance, especially in the way a person dresses or behaves: *a respectable suit.* **3** of some merit, importance, or significance: *His school record was respectable but not brilliant. The economy had respectable growth in the last quarter.* **re·spect′a·bil′i·ty** *adv.* **re·spect′a·bly** *adv.*

re·spect·ful (ri spekt′fəl) *adj* feeling or showing respect. **re·spect′ful·ly** *adv.* **re·spect′ful·ness** *n.*

re·spect·ing (ri spek′ting) *prep* regarding or about: *A discussion arose respecting the merits of different writers.*

re·spec·tive (ri spek′tiv) *adj* belonging separately to each: *The classes went to their respective rooms.*

re·spec·tive·ly (ri spek′ti vlē) *adv* as regards each one in turn or in the order mentioned: *They are 16, 18, and 20 years old respectively.*

res·pi·ra·tion (res′pə rā′shən) *n* **1** the action of inhaling and exhaling: *Her bad cold hinders respiration.* **2** the process by which an animal, plant, or cell obtains oxygen from the air or water, distributes it, combines it with substances in the tissues, and gives off carbon dioxide. <Old French, from Latin *re-* regularly + *spirare* breathe>

res·pi·ra·tor (res′pə rā′tər) *n* **1** a device worn over the nose and mouth to prevent inhaling harmful substances. **2** a device used to help a person to breathe, such as to induce artificial respiration.

res·pi·ra·to·ry (res′pə rə tô′rē) *adj* to do with breathing.

res·pite (res′pit) *or* (res′pīt) *n* a short time of relief or rest, especially a short delay before an unpleasant obligation is met or a punishment carried out: *A thick cloud brought a respite from the glare of the sun. We had a short respite from our hard work.* <Old French, from Latin *respectus* refuge>

re·splend·ent (ri splen′dənt) *adj* attractive and impressive in being richly colourful: *The queen was resplendent with jewels.* <Latin *re-* thoroughly + *splendere* to glitter> **re·splend′ence** *n.* **re·splend′ent·ly** *adv.*

re·spond (ri spond′) *v* **1** answer or reply. **2** react to the action of someone or something: *The dog responded to my pat by giving me a lick.* <Old French, from Latin *re-* in return + *spondere* to pledge>

re·spond·ent (ri spon′dənt) *adj* **1** as a defendant in a lawsuit. **2** replying to something, especially to a questionnaire.
n **1** a person who replies to something. **2** a defendant in a lawsuit, especially one in an appeal or a divorce case.

re·sponse (ri spons′) *n* **1** a reaction to something: *Her response to my phone call was prompt. Her last song got a great response from the crowd.* **2** a set of words said or sung by the congregation or choir in answer to a minister or cantor. **3** the reaction of mind or body to a stimulus.

response time *n* the time required to respond to a request, command, or event, especially the time between the sending of an emergency call and the arrival of ambulance, fire, or police services.

re·spon·si·bil·i·ty (ri spon′sə bil′ə tē) *n, pl* **re·spon·si·bil·i·ties** **1** the act or fact of having a duty to deal with or have control over: *A little child does not feel much responsibility.* **2** something for which one has a duty to deal with or control: *Keeping accounts and preparing reports are her responsibilities.* **3** the opportunity or ability to decide and act independently.

re·spon·si·ble (ri spon′sə bəl) *adj* **1** obliged or expected to deal with something or to have control over: *As treasurer, I am responsible for the club's finances.* **2** deserving credit or blame because it is the primary cause: *The bad weather is responsible for the small attendance.* **3** trustworthy or reliable: *A responsible person should take care of the money.* **4** able to tell right from wrong. **re·spon′si·ble·ness** *n.* **re·spon′si·bly** *adv.*

SYNONYMS

Responsible often implies the expectation that someone will successfully perform an action or duty: *She's responsible for interviewing the winner.*

Answerable suggests being accountable to an authority: *He's answerable to the manager for the cleanliness of the restaurant kitchen.*

Conscientious often means "careful" or "hardworking": *She's a conscientious employee.*

✱ **responsible government** *n* a form of government in which a cabinet is chosen from the elected members of a legislature, makes decisions on behalf of the legislature, and is held accountable to it.

re·spon·sive (ri spon′siv) *adj* **1** reacting quickly and with interest or enthusiasm: *a responsive glance, responsive to kindness.* **2** answering or responding to a statement or stimulus: *a responsive tug of the safety rope.* **3** using or containing responses in a church. **re·spon′sive·ly** *adv.* **re·spon′sive·ness** *n.*

R

a bat	e bed	i bid	o pot	u cup	th **thin**
ā cake	ē me	ī bite	ō go	ū rude	TH **then**
ä bar	ə about	ər over	ô for	ů put	zh measure

rest[1] (rest) *n* **1** a period of relaxation after work or effort: *We only had a little rest before we had to start again.* **2** refreshment through sleep: *a good night's rest.* **3** the absence of motion: *The driver brought the car to rest.* **4** an object that is used to support something, such as one for a telephone receiver. **5** *Music* an interval of silence in a musical passage that has a specified duration, or a mark to show this period.
v **1** cease work or effort in order to relax or sleep: *He was able to rest during his holidays. Lie down and rest.* **2** stop or cause to stop moving: *The golfball rested very close to a tree. My eyes rested on the open book.* **3** be supported by an object: *The ladder rests against the wall.* **4** become or let remain inactive: *Let the matter rest.* **5** cause to rely or depend on: *All our hopes rest on you.* **6** lie dead in a grave: *Rest in peace.* **7** conclude a case for the prosecution or defence in a court of law: *The crown prosecutor rested her case.* <Old English *restan*>
at rest, a not moving or in motion: *The lake was at rest.* **b** tranquil and free from stress or trouble. **c** dead.
lay (or **put**) **to rest, 1** bury a dead body: *Lay his bones to rest.* **2** settle something, such as a topic, especially so as to be free of it: *They decided to put the matter to rest.*
rests with, belongs to: *The responsibility rests with you.*

rest[2] (rest) *n* the remaining part of something: *The sun was out in the morning, but it rained for the rest of the day.*
v remain or be left in a specified way: *You may rest assured that I will keep my promise.* <Old French, from Latin *re-* back + *stare* to stand>

GRAMMAR AND USAGE

When **rest** means "what is left" or "those that are left," always use *the*: *Take these two and leave the rest.*

When **rest** refers to more than one, always use the plural verb: *Three of the ten go today and the rest are leaving tomorrow.*

re·state (rē stāt′) *v* **re·stat·ed, re·stat·ing** repeat, or state again in a slightly different way. **re·state′ment** *n.*

res·tau·rant (res′tə ront) *or* (res′tront) *n* a place to buy and eat a meal. <French *restaurer* restore (with food)>

res·tau·ra·teur (res′tə rə tər′) *n* the owner or manager of a restaurant.

rest·ful (rest′fəl) *adj* quiet and soothing: *She had a restful nap. From this window, you have a restful view of the lake.* **rest′ful·ly** *adv.* **rest′ful·ness** *n.*

rest home *n* an institution for people who are recovering from serious mental or physical illness, injury, or surgery, or who are elderly and need daily care.

res·ti·tu·tion (res′tə tyū′shən) *or* (res′tə tū′shən) *n* **1** the giving back of what has been lost or taken away. **2** compensation for loss, damage, or injury. <Latin *re-* again + *statuere* establish>

res·tive (res′tiv) *adj* **1** increasingly difficult to control: *a restive horse.* **2** unable to keep silent or still: *The boring meeting made him restive.* <Old French, from Latin *restare* remain, i.e., refuse to go forward> **res′tive·ly** *adv.* **res′tive·ness** *n.*

rest·less (res′tlis) *adj* **1** unable to rest or relax: *The dog seemed restless as if it sensed some danger.* **2** involving constant activity or motion, therefore giving no physical or emotional rest: *The sick child passed a restless night.* **rest′less·ly** *adv.* **rest′less·ness** *n.*

res·to·ra·tion (res′tə rā′shən) *n* **1** the act of returning something to a former owner, place, or condition: *restoration of health.* **2** the process of repairing or renovating a building, work of art, or vehicle so as to restore it to its original condition. **3** the return to a previous practice, right, custom, or situation. **4** the return of a hereditary monarch to a throne, or a regime or head of government to power. **5 Restoration** in the UK, the re-establishment of the monarchy in 1660 under Charles II, or the period that followed it until 1688.

re·stor·a·tive (ri stó′rə tiv) *adj* with the ability to restore health, strength, or energy.
n a thing, such as a medicine or drink, that restores health, strength, or energy.

re·store (ri stór′) *v* **re·stored, re·stor·ing 1** bring back a previous right, practice, custom, or situation: *to restore order.* **2** give back something previously stolen, taken away, or lost to the original owner: *The old house has been restored.* <Old French, from Latin *restaurare* rebuild> **re·stor′er** *n.*

re·strain (ri strān′) *v* **1** prevent someone or something from doing an action: *She could not restrain her curiosity. He restrained the excited dog when guests arrived.* **2** deprive someone from freedom of movement or personal liberty. <Old French, from Latin *re-* back + *stringere* tie> **re·strain′a·ble** *adj.* **re·strain′er** *n.*

restraining order *n* an order issued by a court that someone shall not do a certain thing or go to a particular place.

re·straint (ri strānt′) *n* **1** a measure or condition that keeps someone or something under control or within limits. **2** self-control and unemotional expression or behaviour: *Please exercise some restraint.* **3** the action of keeping someone or something under control.

re·strict (ri strikt′) *v* **1** put a limit on or keep under control: *Our club membership is restricted to twelve artists.* **2** deprive someone of freedom of movement or action. <Latin *re-* back + *stringere* draw tight>

re·strict·ed (ri strik′tid) *adj* **1** limited or kept within limits: *I am on a very restricted diet, and cannot eat dairy foods.* **2** with restrictions or limiting rules about access: *restricted documents.*

re·stric·tion (ri strik′shən) *n* **1** a limiting condition or rule, especially a legal one: *The restrictions on the use of room include no smoking or drinking.* **2** the limiting or control of someone or something: *This park is open to the public without restriction.*

re·stric·tive (ri strik′tiv) *adj* imposing restrictions or limitations on activities or freedom. **re·stric′tive·ly** *adv.*

restrictive clause *Grammar n* a clause that modifies or identifies a noun and is an essential part of the whole sentence. Example: In *The movie that we saw last night was better than this one,* the restrictive clause is *that we saw last night.*

re·string (rē string′) *v* **re·strung, re·string·ing** put a new string or new strings on or in a musical instrument, tennis racquet, necklace, etc.

rest·room (rest′rūm′) *n* a room providing toilet facilities for the public in a building.

re·sult (ri zult′) *n* **1** a consequence, effect, or outcome of something: *The result of the fall was a broken leg.* **2** a good, favourable, or useful end or outcome: *We want results, not talk.* **3** a final score, mark, or placing in a sports event or examination: *We waited for our math test results.* **4** an item of information obtained by a scientific experiment or calculation.
v be or follow as a consequence. <Latin *resultare* spring back, rebound>

re·sult·ant (ri zul′tənt) *adj* occurring or produced as a result of something.
n a force or velocity that has the same effect as two or more forces acting together at the same point.

re·sume (ri zūm′) *or* (ri zyūm′) *v* **re·sumed, re·sum·ing** **1** begin to do or say something again after a pause or interruption: *Resume reading where you left off.* **2** return to the use of: *Those standing may resume their seats.* <Old French, from Latin *re-* again + *sumere* take>
re·sum′a·ble *adj.*

res·u·mé (rez′ə mā′) *n* **1** a short account of a person's education, employment history, and interests prepared for submission with a job application. **2** a summary: *a brief resumé of the news.* Also, **résumé**, **resume**. <French *résumer* resume>

re·sump·tion (ri zump′shən) *n* the action of doing something again after a pause or interruption: *the resumption of duties after absence.*

re·sur·face (rē sər′fis) *v* **re·sur·faced, re·sur·fac·ing** **1** provide with a new or different surface, such as a coating on a road, a floor, or ice. **2** come back to the surface: *The diver resurfaced a few minutes later.* **3** become evident or visible: *After he'd said nothing for a while, his objections to the plan resurfaced.*

re·sur·gent (ri sər′jənt) *adj* increasing or reviving after a period of little activity or popularity. **re·surg′ence** *n.*

res·ur·rect (rez′ə rekt′) *v* **1** restore a dead person to life. **2** bring back a practice, use, or memory: *to resurrect an old custom.*

res·ur·rec·tion (rez′ə rek′shən) *n* **1** the act or fact of bringing a dead person to life. **2** the action of bringing back a practice, use, or memory: *the resurrection of an old plan for rebuilding the city.* **3 Resurrection a** in Christian belief, the rising again of Christ after death. **b** in some Christian beliefs, the rising of the dead after the end of the world. <Old French, from Latin *re-* again + *surgere* rise>

re·sus·ci·tate (ri sus′ə tāt′) *v* **re·sus·ci·tat·ed, re·sus·ci·tat·ing** bring or come back from unconsciousness or apparent death: *The lifeguard pulled the drowning man onto the beach and resuscitated him.* <Latin *re-* again + *sub-* up + *citare* rouse>
re·sus′ci·ta′tion *n.* **re·sus′ci·ta′tive** *adj.*
re·sus′ci·ta′tor *n.*

re·tail (rē′tāl); (ri tāl′) *for v def. 2.* *n* the sale of goods to consumers, for use rather than for resale.
adj to do with selling to the consumer: *the retail trade. The retail price of this jewellery is twice as much as the wholesale price.*
v **1** sell to a consumer. **2** tell details of a story or event to others: *She retails everything she hears about her acquaintances.*
adv sold by a retail merchant: *He has to buy his supplies retail.* <Old French *rettaille* a piece cut off>

re·tail·er (rē′tā lər) *n* a retail merchant or dealer.

re·tain (ri tān′) *v* **1** continue to have or hold something: *China dishes retain heat longer than metal pans do.* **2** keep in one's memory: *She retained the tune but not the words of the song.* **3** employ by payment of a preliminary fee: *He retained the best lawyer in the city.* <Old French, from Latin *re-* back + *tenere* hold>

re·tain·er (ri tā′nər) *n* **1** a thing that holds something in place, such as a device for keeping a loose tooth in place. **2** a fee paid to secure services: *This lawyer receives a retainer before beginning to work on a case.* **3** a servant or follower of a wealthy person or member of the nobility.

retaining wall *n* a wall built to hold back a bank of earth, stones, or water on one side of it.

re·take (rē tāk′) *for v,* (rē′tāk′) *for n.* *v* **re·took, re·tak·en, re·tak·ing** **1** take again, such as a test or examination. **2** regain something left or lost: *After a fierce battle, the fort was retaken.*
n a thing that is retaken: *a retake of a scene in a movie.*

re·tal·i·ate (ri tal′ē āt′) *v* **re·tal·i·at·ed, re·tal·i·at·ing** make an attack or assault as revenge for an earlier attack: *If we insult them, they will retaliate.* <Latin *retaliare* pay back in kind, from *re-* back + *talis* such> **re·tal′i·a·to′ry** (ri tal′yə tə′rē) *adj.*

re·tard (ri tàrd′) *v* delay or hinder: *Our progress was retarded by a heavy snowfall.*
n Offensive a person who is mentally handicapped. <Latin *re-* back + *tardus* slow> **re′tar·da′tion** *n.*

re·tard·ant (ri′tàr′dənt) *n* a thing, such as a chemical, that slows or delays an effect or process such as fire.
adj tending to delay or make something slower.

re·tard·ed (ri tàr′dəd) *adj* limited in development.

retch (rech) *v* make the sound and movement of vomiting. <Old English *hroecan* to cough up>

re·tell (rē tel′) *v* **re·told, re·tell·ing** tell a story again or differently.

re·ten·tion (ri ten′shən) *n* **1** the continued possession, use, or control of something. **2** the action of absorbing and continuing to hold a substance. **3** a failure to eliminate something from the body. **4** the ability to remember.

a bat	e bed	i bid	o pot	u cup	th **thin**
ā cake	ē me	ī bite	ō go	ū rude	ᴛʜ **then**
à bar	ə about	ər over	ȯ for	ů put	zh measure

R

re·ten·tive (ri ten′tiv) *adj* **1** able to hold or keep moisture. **2** able to remember. **re·tentively** *adv.* **re·ten′tive·ness** *n.*

re·think (ri thingk′) *v* **re·thought, re·think·ing** think over again with a view to changing one's ideas, policies, or plans: *The principal has decided to rethink her position on cellphones in school.*

ret·i·cent (ret′ə sənt) *adj* tending to keep silent or say little about one's thoughts or feelings. <Latin *re-* completely + *tacere* be silent> **ret′i·cence** *n.* **ret′i·cent·ly** *adv.*

re·tic·u·lum (ri tik′yə ləm) *n, pl* **re·tic·u·la** (-lə) the second stomach of cud-chewing mammals.

ret·i·na (ret′ə nə) *n* the layer of cells at the back of the eyeball that is sensitive to light and triggers nerve impulses that pass by the optic nerve to the brain, where a visual image is formed. See BLIND SPOT for picture. <Latin *rete* net, because the blood vessels resemble a fine net> **ret′i·nal** *adj.*

ret·i·nue (ret′ə nyū′) *n* a group of advisers, assistants, or attendants accompanying an important person. <Old French *retenir* to employ, from Latin *re-* back + *tenere* hold>

re·tire (ri tīr′) *v* **re·tired, re·tir·ing** **1** give up one's job and cease to work at it, or be so removed: *My father expects to retire at sixty-five. His company retired him early.* **2** withdraw to or from a particular place: *We retired to bed.* **3** order or cause a military force to retreat from an enemy or an attacking position. **4** withdraw a bill or note from circulation or currency: *The government retired many worn or torn five-dollar bills.* **5** *Sports* withdraw from active competition in a sport, perhaps only temporarily because of an accident or injury. **6** *Baseball, Cricket* put out a batter or batsman: *The pitcher retired three batters in a row.* **7** of a jury, leave a courtroom to consider the evidence in a trial and reach a verdict: <French *re-* back + *tirer* draw>

re·tired (ri tīrd′) *adj* **1** having withdrawn from one's job and no longer working at it: *a retired sea captain.* **2** quiet and involving little contact with other people: *a shy, retired nature.* **3** quiet and secluded: *a retired spot.*

re·tir·ee (rə tīr ē′) *or* (rə tīr′ē) *n* a retired person.

re·tire·ment (ri tīr′mənt) *n* **1 a** the act or fact of leaving one's job and no longer working at it: *He retired after many years' active service.* **b** the period of time after this: *My grandfather is enjoying his retirement.* **2** the act or fact of withdrawing from active participation in a sport. **3** a quiet way of living, or the place where this is carried on: *She lives in retirement, neither making nor receiving visits.*

re·tir·ing (ri tī′ring) *adj* quiet and involving little contact with other people: *a retiring nature.*

re·told (rē tōld′) past tense and past participle of RETELL.

re·tool (rē tūl′) *v* **1** adapt or replace the equipment in a factory. **2** reorganize or redesign something in order to update it or make it more suitable. **re·tool′ing** *n.*

re·tort[1] (ri tôrt′) *v* reply quickly and sharply to a remark or accusation.
n a sharp, angry, or witty reply. <Latin *re-* back + *torquere* to twist>

re·tort[2] (ri tôrt′) *n* a container or furnace used for distilling or decomposing substances by heat. <French *retorte* a vessel with a curved neck, from Latin *re-* back + *torquere* to twist>

re·touch (rē tuch′) *v* improve or repair a painting, photograph, or other image by making slight changes or additions.

re·trace (ri trās′) *v* **re·traced, re·trac·ing** **1** go back over the same route that was just taken, or one that was taken by another: *We retraced our steps to where we started. They painstakingly retraced the explorer's journey up the Red River.* **2** trace something back to its source or beginning: *Let's retrace the first stages of modern chemistry.* **re·tract′a·ble** *adj.* **re·trace′a·ble** *adj.*

re·tract (ri trakt′) *v* **1** draw or pull something back or back in: *The kitten retracted its claws and purred when I petted it. The aircraft retracted its wheels soon after takeoff.* See CAT for picture. **2** withdraw a statement, accusation, or promise: *to retract an offer or an opinion.* <Latin *re-* back + *trahere* to drag> **re·tract′a·ble** *adj.* **re·trac′tion** *n.*

re·trac·tile (ri trak′tīl) *or* (ri trak′təl) *adj* able to be drawn back or in.

re·trac·tor (ri trak′tər) *n* **1** a device for retracting something. **2** a muscle that retracts a part of the body.

re·tread (rē tred′) *for v,* (rē′tred′) *for n.* *v* **re·tread·ed, re·tread·ing** **1** put a new tread on. **2** go back over a path or one's steps.
n **1** a tire that is given a new tread. **2** *Informal* a superficially altered version of an original.

re·treat (ri trēt′) *v* **1** withdraw part of a military force as a result of an enemy's superior power or after a defeat: *After losing half his men, the general retreated.* **2** move back or withdraw, especially to avoid a difficult or uncomfortable situation: *He retreated to his cottage on Lake Simcoe for the weekends.* **3** become smaller in size, extent, or degree: *The ice retreated from the lake.* **4** change one's decisions, plans, or attitudes, especially as a result of criticism: *He retreated from his original position on Sunday shopping.*
n **1** the action of going back or withdrawing: *The army's retreat was orderly.* **2** a signal for a military force to withdraw: *The drums beat a retreat.* **3** the action of changing one's decisions, plans, or attitude. **4** a signal on a bugle or drum, given in the army at sunset. **5** a safe, quiet place in which to rest or relax: *My room is my favourite retreat.* <Old French, from Latin *re-* back + *trahere* to drag>

re·trench (ri trench′) *v* reduce costs or spending by a person, company, or government: *In hard times, we must retrench.* <French *re-* back + *trancher* to cut> **re·trench′ment** *n.*

re·tri·al (rē trī′əl) *n* a second trial or further trial.

ret·ri·bu·tion (ret′rə byū′shən) *n* punishment that is considered to be morally correct and deserved in view of some wrong that was done: *Some people thought the disastrous fire was retribution for their sins.* <Latin *re-* back + *tribuere* assign> **re·trib′u·tive** *adj.*

re·trieve (ri trēv′) *v* **re·trieved, re·triev·ing** **1** recover possession of: *to retrieve a lost pocketbook, to retrieve your good humour.* **2** pick something up: *She retrieved her purse from the back seat.* **3** find and bring to a person: *The dog was trained to retrieve game.* **4** correct or improve an unwelcome situation. **5** *Computers* find or extract information stored in a computer. <Old French *re-* back + *trouver* find> **re·triev′al** *n.*

re·triev·er (ri trē′vər) *n* a dog trained to find killed or wounded game and bring it to a hunter.

re·tro (ret′rō) *adj* imitating a style, fashion, or design of an earlier period: *retro clothing.* <Latin *retro-* backward>

retro– *combining form* backward or reciprocal: *retroflex, retrorocket, retrospect.* <Latin *retro-* backward>

ret·ro·ac·tive (ret′rō ak′tiv) *adj* taking effect, especially as a law, from a date in the past: *The new rules were retroactive to June 15.*

ret·ro·fit (ret′rō fit′) *v* **ret·ro·fit·ted, ret·ro·fit·ting** add or provide with a new component or accessory to something that did not have it when it was manufactured: *The house is being retrofitted with more modern, more efficient insulation.*
n an action of adding or providing with a new component or accessory.

ret·ro·flex (ret′rə fleks′) *adj* turned backward. **ret·ro·flex′ion** *n.*

ret·ro·grade (ret′rə grād′) *adj* **1** directing or moving backwards: *retrograde flow.* **2** becoming worse: *To reverse the decision would be a retrograde step.*

ret·ro·gress (ret′rə gres′) *or* (ret′rə gres′) *v* return to an earlier condition, especially a worse one. **ret′ro·gres′sion** *n.* **ret′ro·gres′sive** *adj.* **ret′ro·gres′sive·ly** *adv.*

ret·ro·rock·et (ret′rō rok′it) *n* a rocket on a spacecraft or missile that fires in a direction opposite to that of the motion of the craft or missile, thus acting as a brake.

ret·ro·spect (ret′rə spekt′) *n* a survey of a past course of events or period of time.
in retrospect, when looking back on a past course of events or period of time.

ret·ro·spec·tion (ret′rə spek′shən) *n* the process of looking back on a past course of events or period of time, especially in one's own life.

ret·ro·spec·tive (ret′rə spek′tiv) *adj* **1** looking back on a past course of events or period of time **2** showing the development of an artist's work over a period of time.
n an art exhibition showing the development of an artist's work over a period of time. **ret′ro·spec′tive·ly** *adv.*

ret·rous·sé (ret′rū sā′) *adj* of a nose, attractively turned up at the tip. <French = tucked up>

ret·ro·vi·rus (ret′rə vī′rus) *n* a single-stranded RNA virus that inserts a DNA copy of its genome into a host cell in order to replicate. One retrovirus is HIV, the cause of AIDS.

re·try (rē trī′) *v* **re·tried, re·try·ing** try a defendant or case again in a court of law.

ret·si·na (ret sē′nə) *n* a resin-flavoured Greek wine. <Greek>

re·turn (ri tərn′) *v* **1** go or come back to a place: *My sister will return from Europe this summer.* **2** bring, give, send, hit, put, or pay back to a place or person: *Return that book to the library. When I play tennis, I just concentrate on returning the ball.* **3** say, feel, or do the same feeling or action in response to: *He returned her kiss.* **4** yield or make a profit: *The bake sale returned enough to fund the class picnic.* **5** report or announce officially: *The jury returned a verdict of guilty.* **6** elect to a legislature.
n **1** the action of going or coming to a place or activity: *I look forward all spring to my return to summer camp.* **2** a thing that returns or is returned. **3** the action of giving, sending, or putting something back: *a poor return for kindness.* **4** an act of going back to an earlier condition or situation: *Their move to the country marked a return to a simpler way of life.* **5** *Sports* a stroke in tennis and other games, played in response to a serve or other stroke by an opponent. **6 returns** *pl* **a** a profit or amount received: *The returns from the school play were more than enough to cover expenses.* **b** an official report or result, especially of an election.
adj **1** to do with going to or coming back: *a return ticket.* **2** sent, given, or done in exchange: *a return invitation.* **3** presented or performed again: *a return match.* <Old French, from Latin *re-* back + *tornare* to turn>
in return, as a return: *If you lend me your skates now, I'll lend you my tennis racquet next summer in return.*
many happy returns (of the day), used as a friendly greeting on a birthday.

re·turn·a·ble (ri tər′nə bəl) *adj* able to be returned: *a returnable bottle.*

re·turn·ee (ri tər′nē′) *n* a person who has returned, especially one who has returned home after capture in a war or after service abroad.

returning officer *n* in Canada and some other countries, the official who conducts the election in a particular constituency and announces the result.

return trip *n* a trip to a place and back again.

re·u·ni·fy (rē yū′nə fī′) *v* **re·u·ni·fied, re·u·ni·fy·ing** restore unity, especially political unity, to a place or group of people. **re·u′ni·fi·ca′tion** *n.*

re·un·ion (rē yū′nyən) *n* **1** the act or fact of two or more people coming together again after a period of separation: *a joyous reunion.* **2** a social gathering of people who have been separated or who have interests in common: *a family reunion.*

re·u·nite (rē′yū nīt′) *v* **re·u·nit·ed, re·u·nit·ing** bring or be brought together again: *Mother and child were reunited after years of separation.*

re·use (rē yūz′) *v* **re·used, re·us·ing** use again or more than once: *Don't keep reusing the same example.*
n a second or further use: *He said that plastic had many reuses.*

rev (rev) *Informal n* a revolution of an engine or motor per minute.
v **revved, rev·ving** increase the running speed of an engine or motor by pressing the accelerator, especially while the car is idling. <*revolution*>

a bat	e bed	i bid	o pot	u cup	th thin
ā cake	ē me	ī bite	ō go	ū rude	ᴛʜ then
à bar	ə about	ər over	ò for	ù put	zh measure

re·vamp (rē vamp′) *v* give a new and improved form, structure, or appearance to: *to revamp a magazine design.*

re·veal (ri vēl′) *v* **1** make known something hidden, secret, or mysterious: *Never reveal my secret.* **2** cause or allow something to be seen or known: *Her smile revealed her even teeth.* <Old French, from Latin *re-* opposite of + *velum* veil> **re·veal′er** *n.*

rev·eil·le (rəv′ə lē) *n* a signal on a bugle or drum to waken military personnel in the morning. <French, from Latin *vigillare*>

rev·el (rev′əl) *v* **rev·elled** or **rev·eled, rev·el·ling** or **rev·el·ing 1** (*with* ***in***) take great pleasure: *The children revel in country life.* **2** have lively and noisy fun.
n (*often plural*) a noisy good time. <Old French, from Latin *rebellare* rebel> **rev′el·ler** or **rev′el·er** *n.*

rev·e·la·tion (rev′ə lā′shən) *n* **1** the act of making known something hidden, secret, or mysterious, especially one that is made known in a dramatic way: *The revelation of the thieves' hiding place resulted in their capture.* **2** a divine or supernatural disclosure to humans of something greatly significant about human existence or the world.

rev·el·ry (rev′əl rē) *n, pl* **rev·el·ries** loud and lively fun at a party or other festivity: *the sound of revelry.*

re·venge (ri venj′) *n* **1** the action of inflicting hurt or harm in return for an injury or wrong: *a blow struck in revenge.* **2** a desire for vengeance: *She said nothing, but there was revenge in her heart.* **3** the defeat of a person or team in a sporting contest who had earlier won: *Badly beaten in the first match, he got his revenge in the second.*
v **re·venged, re·veng·ing** do harm in return for an injury or wrong done: *The knight vowed to revenge the death of his squire.* <Old French, from Latin *re-* back + *vindicare* avenge> **re·venge′ful** *adj.* **re·venge′ful·ly** *adv.*
be revenged, get revenge: *The captain swore to be revenged on the pirates for burning his ship.*
revenge oneself on, take revenge: *I'll revenge myself on her for that insult.*

rev·e·nue (rev′ə nyū′) *n* income, especially in large amounts, of a company, organization, or government. <Old French, from Latin *re-* back + *venire* come>

Revenue Canada *n* the Federal Government department that collects taxes.

re·ver·ber·ate (ri vər′bə rāt′) *v* **re·ver·ber·at·ed, re·ver·ber·at·ing 1** be repeated as a loud echo: *Her voice reverberated from the high ceiling.* **2** appear to vibrate or be disturbed because of a loud noise. **3** have continuing and serious effects: *Her comments reverberated in the association over the next few days.* <Latin *re-* back + *verberare* to beat> **re·ver′ber·a′tion** *n.*

re·vere (ri vēr′) *v* **re·vered, re·ver·ing** feel deep respect and admiration for: *People revered the great diplomat.* <Latin *re-* thoroughly + *vereri* stand in awe of>

rev·er·ence (rev′ə rəns) *n* **1** a feeling of deep respect and admiration for someone or something. **2 Reverence** a title used for some members of the Christian clergy.
v **rev·er·enced, rev·er·enc·ing** regard or treat with deep respect and admiration. <See REVERE.>

rev·er·end (rev′ə rənd) *adj* worthy of great respect.
n **1** *Informal* a member of the Christian clergy. **2 Reverend** a title used for some members of the Christian clergy.

rev·er·ent (rev′ə rənt) *adj* feeling or showing deep and solemn respect. **rev′er·ent·ly** *adv.*

rev·er·en·tial (rev′ə ren′shəl) *adj* reverent. **rev′er·en′tial·ly** *adv.*

rev·er·ie (rev′ə rē) *n* a condition of having dreamy thoughts of pleasant things: *She loved to indulge in reveries about the future.* Also, **revery**. <French *rêver* to dream>

re·ver·sal (ri vər′səl) *n* a change to the opposite.

re·verse (ri vərs′) *n* **1** the opposite or contrary: *She did the reverse of what was asked of her.* **2 a** the gear or gears that cause a machine to go in the contrary direction: *an automobile in reverse.* **b** the position of such a gear or gears: *Put the car in reverse to drive out of the garage.* **3 reverses** *pl* a change to bad fortune: *He used to be rich, but he met with reverses.* **4** the opposite side or face to the observer: *Her name is on the reverse of the medal.*
adj **1** going in or turned toward the opposite direction. **2** acting in a manner opposite or contrary to that which is usual. **3** causing an opposite or backward movement.
v **re·versed, re·vers·ing 1** move or cause to move backwards: *The car suddenly reversed and hit the truck behind it.* **2** turn something around or inside out: *Your sweatshirt is reversed.* **3** make something the opposite of what it was: *Decisive action reversed the trend.* **4** exchange the position or function of two people or things: *It was funny to see the principal and the caretaker reverse jobs.* **5** cancel an earlier decision, decree, or legal sentence. <Old French, from Latin *re-* back + *vertere* to turn>
reverse the charges, charge a long-distance telephone call to the party receiving it.

SYNONYMS

Reverse means "change to an opposite direction, position, or order": *The columnist often reverses his views and confuses his readers.*

Invert means "turn upside down" or "switch the order or position of": *If you invert the statement "She will" to "Will she?" it becomes a question.*

Revert means "return to a previous condition, practice, or topic": *We reverted to our original plan.*

re·verse–en·gin·eer (ri vərs′en jin ēr′) *v* analyze the design and construction of an existing product in order to make a similar or matching product.
re·verse-en·gin·eer′ing *n.*

reverse video *Computers n* an attribute of a field on a screen whereby the foreground and background colours are reversed, usually for the purpose of highlighting.

re·vers·i·ble (ri vər′sə bəl) *adj* **1** able to be reversed. **2** finished on both sides of a fabric or garment so that either can be used or worn on the outside. **re·vers′i·bly** *adv.*

re·vert (ri vərt′) *v* **1** return to a previous condition, practice, topic, or belief: *New evidence made her revert to her original opinion.* **2** return or have returned property to an original owner or heir. <Old French, from Latin *re-* back + *vertere* turn> **re·ver′sion** (ri vər′zhən) *n.*

re·view (ri vyū′) *v* **1** study or examine again: *She reviewed her history notes.* **2** look back on: *Before falling asleep, I reviewed the day's happenings.* **3** formally assess or examine something with the intention of making a change if necessary: *The Supreme Court of Canada may review decisions of a lower court.* **4** write a critical appraisal of something, especially a book, play, or movie. **5** make a ceremonial and formal inspection of military or naval forces.
n **1** the action or process of studying or examining again: *Before the examinations, we have a review of the term's work.* **2** the action or process of looking back on something: *A review of the trip was pleasant.* **3** a formal assessment or examination of something with the intention of making a change if necessary. **4** a critical appraisal of something, especially a book, play, or movie. **5** a ceremonial and formal inspection of military or naval forces. **6** a magazine with critical appraisals of current events or of material, such as books or art, that has recently appeared: *a law review.* <obsolete French, from Latin *re-* again + *videre* see>

re·view·er (ri vyū′ər) *n* a person who writes short critical appraisals of material, such as a book, play, or movie, that has recently appeared.

re·vile (ri vīl′) *v* **re·viled, re·vil·ing** criticize in an angry or insulting way: *The politician now reviled his old friend and ally.* <Old French *reviler* despise> **re·vile′ment** *n.*

re·vise (ri vīz′) *v* **re·vised, re·vis·ing** **1** reconsider and alter something so as to correct or improve it, such as a written or printed work: *She has revised the poem she wrote. In the light of new evidence, he had to revise his earlier opinion.* **2** change or alter: *to revise an earlier decision.* <French, from Latin *re-* again + *videre* see> **re·vis′er** *n.* **re·vis′ion** *n.*

re·vi·sion·ism (ri vizh′ən izm) *n* the practice of reinterpreting history or beliefs as a way of contradicting a body of accepted facts. **re·vi′sion·ist′** *adj, n.*

re·vis·it (ri viz′ət) *v* **1** visit or study again, noticing what has changed: *The article, titled "Canada Revisited," compares Canada before and after Confederation.* **2** consider or examine again with a view to making changes or changing one's mind: *My parents have decided to revisit the idea of going abroad.*

re·vit·a·lize (ri vīt′ə līz′) *v* **re·vit·a·lized, re·vit·a·liz·ing** bring life or vigour back into: *A thriving economy will revitalize the tourist industry in Canada.*
re·vit′a·liz·a′tion *n.*

re·viv·al (ri vī′vəl) *n* **1** an improvement in the condition or strength of something, especially a restoration to vigour or health. **2** an example of something that has become popular, active, or important again: *a revival of stamp collecting, a revival of democracy.* **3** a new production of a play or entertainment. **4** the process of restoring vigour in the mind or body: *a revival of interest in books, a revival of energy.*

re·vive (ri vīv′) *v* **re·vived, re·viv·ing** **1** bring back or come back to life or consciousness: *to revive a half-drowned person.* **2** bring or come back to a fresh, lively condition: *The flowers revived in water.* **3** restore vigour or energy: *Hot coffee revived the cold, tired man.* **4** bring back or come back to notice, use, fashion, memory, or activity: *to revive an old song.* <Old French, from Latin *re-* again + *vivere* live>

re·voke (ri vōk′) *v* **re·voked, re·vok·ing** **1** repeal, cancel, or withdraw a decree, decision, or promise: *The judge revoked the earlier sentence.* **2** in some card games, fail to follow suit despite being able to.
n a failure to follow suit in some card games despite being able to. <Old French, from Latin *re-* back + *vocare* call>

re·volt (ri vōlt′) *n* the action or process of rebelling against someone or something: *The town is in revolt.*
v **1** rebel against someone or something: *The people revolted against the dictator.* **2** cause to feel disgust: *to revolt at a bad smell.* <French, from Latin *revolvitare* overturn> **re·volt′er** *n.*

re·volt·ing (ri vōl′ting) *adj* disgusting.

rev·o·lu·tion (rev′ə lū′shən) *n* **1** a complete, often violent, overthrow of an established government or political system: *The French Revolution from 1789 to 1799 changed France from a kingdom to a republic.* **2** a complete and dramatic change: *Plastics have brought about a revolution in the packaging industry.* **3** movement in a circle or curve around some point: *One revolution of the earth around the sun takes a year.* **4** the act or fact of turning round a centre or axis: *The revolution of the earth causes day and night.* **5** a single complete turn around a centre: *The wheel of the motor turns at a rate of more than one thousand revolutions a minute.* <Old French, from Latin *revolvere* turn>

rev·o·lu·tion·ar·y (rev′ə lū′shə ner′ē) *adj* **1** engaged in or promoting political revolution: *a revolutionary army.* **2** bringing or causing great and dramatic changes.
n, pl **rev·o·lu·tion·ar·ies** a person engaged in promoting political revolution or any great dramatic change.

rev·o·lu·tion·ize (rev′ə lū′shə nīz′) *v* **rev·o·lu·tion·ized, rev·o·lu·tion·iz·ing** change completely and dramatically: *Mechanization revolutionized farm life.*

re·volve (ri volv′) *v* **re·volved, re·volv·ing** **1** move in a circle around a point: *The moon revolves around the earth.* **2** turn or cause to move round a centre or axis, such as with the wheels of a moving car. **3** treat as the most important point or element: *Her life entirely revolves around work.* **4** move in a complete cycle or series of events. <Latin *re-* back + *volvere* roll>

re·volv·er (ri vol′vər) *n* a pistol with a revolving cylinder in which the cartridges are contained. It can be fired several times without reloading.

revolving door *n* **1** a door to a large building formed from four upright sections that turn on a central pivot. A person moves the door by entering one section and pushing it forward. **2** a situation in which the same events or problems recur in a continuous cycle: *the revolving door of crime, poverty, and more crime.*

a bat	e bed	i bid	o pot	u cup	th **thin**
ā cake	ē me	ī bite	ō go	ū rude	ᴛʜ **then**
à bar	ə about	ər over	ȯ for	ů put	zh measure

re·vue (ri vyū′) *n* a theatrical entertainment consisting of a series of short sketches, songs, and dances, often dealing satirically or humorously with popular trends and current events. <French = review>

re·vul·sion (ri vul′shən) *n* a feeling of disgust and loathing: *The increased violence in the streets filled us with revulsion.* <Latin *re-* back + *vellere* tear away>

re·ward (ri wȯrd′) *n* **1** a thing given or received in recognition of effort, achievement, or other good behaviour: *She said that virtue was its own reward.* **2** a payment given or offered for information leading to the capture of criminals, or the return of lost property.
v give something in recognition of effort, achievement, or other good behaviour: *Their hard work was rewarded with a medal.* <Old French *reguard* regard, pay attention to>

re·ward·ing (ri wȯr′ding) *adj* **1** satisfying or fulfilling: *He said he found teaching students with special needs very rewarding.* **2** financially profitable: *a rewarding investment.*

re·wind (rē wīnd′) *v* **re·wound, re·wind·ing** on an audio or video tape recorder, wind the tape backwards.

re·wire (rē wīr′) *v* **re·wired, re·wir·ing** put new wires on or in an appliance, building, or motor vehicle.

re·word (rē wərd′) *v* put into other words.

re·work (rē wərk′) *v* make changes to something, especially to improve or bring it up to date.

re·writ·ab·le (rē rīt′əb əl) *Computers adj* of a CD, DVD, etc., able to have new data recorded over what is already on it. See also CD-ROM.

re·write (rē rīt′) *for v,* (rē′rīt) *for n. v* **re·wrote, re·writ·ten, re·writ·ing** write an essay, play, book, etc. in a different form so as to alter or improve it.
n something written differently in an attempt to improve it.

Rh See RH FACTOR.

rhap·so·dize (rap′sə dīz′) *v* **rhap·so·dized, rhap·so·diz·ing** talk or write with extravagant enthusiasm.

rhap·so·dy (rap′sə dē) *n, pl* **rhap·so·dies** **1** an utterance or writing marked by extravagant enthusiasm: *She went into rhapsodies over the garden.* **2** an instrumental composition irregular in form, usually highly emotional and in a fast tempo. <Latin, from Greek *rhaptein* to sew together + *olde* song>

rhe·a (rē′ə) *n* a large, flightless bird of the S American grasslands that resembles a small ostrich. <Latin genus name, from Greek goddess *Rhea*>

rhe·ni·um (rē′nē əm) *n* a rare, hard, silver-white element that occurs in trace amounts in ores of molybdenum and other metals. *Symbol* **Re** <Latin *Rhenus* the Rhine (River)>

rhe·o·stat (rē′ə stat′) *n* an instrument for regulating the strength of an electric current by introducing different amounts of resistance into the circuit. <Greek *rheos* current + *statos* standing still>

Rhe·sus factor (rē′səs) RH FACTOR.

rhe·sus monkey (rē′səs) *n* a small monkey native to southern Asia. It is often kept for use in medical research.

rhet·o·ric (ret′ə rik) *n* **1** the art of using words effectively or persuasively in speaking or writing. **2** language designed to be effective or persuasive, especially when regarded as lacking sincerity or meaningful content. <Old French, from Greek *rhetor* teacher of rhetoric> **rhe·tor′i·cal** *adj.* **rhe·tor′i·cal·ly** *adv.*

rhetorical question *n* a question asked only for effect or to make a statement, rather than to obtain information. Example: *Must you slam the door?*

rhet·o·ri·cian (ret′ə rish′ən) *n* **1** a person skilled in the art of rhetoric. **2** a person who uses language intended to impress or persuade.

rheum (rūm) *n* a watery discharge from the eyes or nose. **rheum′y** *adj.*

rheu·mat·ic (rū mat′ik) *adj* **1** to do with or caused by rheumatism. **2** affected by rheumatism in a person or a part of the body.
n a person who has rheumatism.

rheumatic fever *n* a high fever caused by a streptococcal infection, usually in young people, and marked by inflammation and pain in the joints.

rheu·ma·tism (rū′mə tiz′əm) *n* a painful disease of the joints, muscles, or connective tissue. <Latin, from Greek *rheuma* a flowing. The disease was thought to have been caused by the flow of bodily humours to the joints.>

rheu·ma·toid arthritis (rū′mə toid′) *n* a chronic disease that causes painful swelling and inflammation of the joints, tending to get worse over time.

Rh factor *n* in full, **Rhesus factor** an antigen often found in the red blood cells of many human beings and some primates. Blood containing this substance (**Rh positive**) is incompatible with blood lacking it (**Rh negative**).

rhine·stone (rīn′stōn′) *n* an imitation diamond, made of glass and used to decorate clothes and in inexpensive jewellery. <French *caillou du Rhin* pebble of the Rhine>

rhi·no (rī′nō) *Informal n, pl* **rhi·nos** a rhinoceros.

rhi·noc·er·os (rī nos′ə rəs) *n, pl* **rhi·noc·er·os·es** or (*especially collectively*) **rhi·noc·er·os** a large, heavily built, thick-skinned mammal of Africa and S Asia, with one or two upright horns on the snout. <Latin, from Greek *rhinos* nose + *keras* horn>

rhi·no·plas·ty (rī′nə plas′tē) *n, pl* **rhi·no·plas·ties** plastic surgery on the nose. <Greek *rhinos* nose + *plassein* form>

rhi·zome (rī′zōm) *n* a continuously growing horizontal underground stem that puts out lateral shoots and roots from its nodes. <Greek *rhiza* root>

rhi·zo·pod (rī′zə pod′) *n* a one-celled animal that forms temporary projections of protoplasm for moving about and taking in food. The amoeba is one kind of rhizopod.

Rhodes Scholar (rōdz) *n* a holder of a scholarship awarded annually to outstanding students from certain Commonwealth countries, South Africa, the US, and Germany for study at Oxford University in England.

ETYMOLOGY

Rhodes Scholars are named after Cecil Rhodes (1853–1902), a British imperialist and diamond-mine owner, who provided for these scholarships in his will. Rhodesia (now Zimbabwe) was also named after him.

rhythmic gymnastics

spin

balance

jump

layback

Rhythmic gymnastics is open only to women. The athletes perform choreographed routines using different types of hand devices. Judges score each event separately to determine the winner in a competition.

rho·di·um (rō′dē əm) *n* **1** a hard silver-white metallic element, often occurring with platinum. **2** *Symbol* **Rh** <Greek *rhodon* rose>

rho·do·den·dron (rō′də den′drən) *n* a shrub or small tree that has large clusters of bell-shaped flowers and, often, large evergreen leaves. Some rhododendrons are grown as garden plants. <Latin, from Greek *rhodon* rose + *dendron* tree>

rhom·boid (rom′boid) *n* a quadrilateral of which only the opposite sides and angles are equal.
adj shaped like a rhomboid or rhombus.

rhom·bus (rom′bəs) *n, pl* **rhom·bus·es** or **rhom·bi** (-bī) *or* (bē) a parallelogram with four equal sides. <Latin, from Greek *rhombos*>

rhu·barb (rū′bȧrb) *n* a garden plant with thick reddish or green leaf stalks that are cooked with sugar as a pie filling or a dessert by itself. <Old French, from Greek *rha* rhubarb + *barbaros* foreign>

rhyme (rīm) *v* **rhymed, rhym·ing 1** of a word, have or end with a sound that corresponds to another word. Example: *long* rhymes with *song.* **2** be made of lines of verse that end in words or syllables with sounds that correspond to those at the end of other lines: *The shorter poems all rhymed.* **3** make rhymes: *She enjoys rhyming.* **4** use a word with another that rhymes with it: *It's so boring to rhyme* love *with* dove.
n **1** an agreement in the final sounds of words. **2** a word or syllable at the end of a line of verse that corresponds in sound to one at the end of another line. **3** poetry or poems marked by such correspondences of sound. Also, **rime** (*Archaic*). <Old French, from Greek *rhuthmos* rhythm> **rhym′er** *n.*
without (or **with no**) **rhyme or reason,** with no system or sense.

rhyme scheme *n* the pattern of rhymes used at the ends of lines of verse, usually indicated by letters in a kind of formula. Example: A rhyme scheme represented by *abba* has one rhyme for the first and fourth lines of a verse, and a different one for the second and third lines.

rhyme·ster (rīm′stər) *n* a maker of rhymes, especially simple or common ones.

rhyming slang *n* a form of slang in which a rhyming phrase is substituted for the intended word. Example: *climbing the apples and pears* means *climbing the stairs.*

rhythm (riŦH′əm) *n* **1** a strong, regular, repeated pattern of movement or sound: *the rhythm of skating, the rhythm of your heartbeat.* **2** the systematic arrangement of musical notes according to duration and stress: *triple rhythm.* **3** the measured flow of words and phrases in prose or poetry, especially that marked by patterns of stresses. **4** a sequence of regularly recurring events, actions, or processes: *the rhythm of the seasons.* **5** a harmonious sequence of colours or elements in a work of art: *visual rhythm.* <Greek *rhein* to flow>

rhythm and blues R & B

rhyth·mic (riŦH′mik) *adj* to do with rhythm: *rhythmic gymnastics.* Also, **rhythmical. rhyth′mi·cal·ly** *adv.*

rhythm method *n* a form of birth control involving abstaining from sexual intercourse during the time of the woman's ovulation.

rib (rib) *n* **1** a slender curved bone found in pairs, extending from the backbone and enclosing the upper part of the body. **2** a long piece of material across a surface or through a structure, and typically serving to support or strengthen it. The thin rods in an umbrella are ribs. **3** a cut of meat containing a rib used for food: *ribs of beef.* **4** a vein of a leaf or an insect's wing. **5** a narrow ridge of rock, land, or cloth.
v **ribbed, rib·bing 1** mark with or form into ridges. **2** *Informal* tease in a good-natured way. <Old English>

rib·ald (rib′əld) *adj* referring to sexual matters in a humorously rude or irreverent way. <Old French>

rib·ald·ry (rib′əl drē) *n* ribald talk or behaviour.

ribbed (ribd) *adj* with a pattern of ribs or ridges, especially on a fabric or garment.

rib·bing (rib′ing) *n* **1** a pattern or structure of ribs. **2** *Informal* good-natured teasing.

rib·bon (rib′ən) *n* **1** a strip or band of fabric, used especially for tying something or for decoration. **2** a thing resembling such a strip or band: *A ribbon of moonlight stretched over the lake.* **3** a small strip of fabric worn as a sign of membership in an order, or as a military decoration. <Old French *riban*> **rib′bon·like′** *adj.*

a bat	e bed	i bid	o pot	u cup	th **thin**
ā cake	ē me	ī bite	ō go	ū rude	ŦH **then**
ȧ bar	ə about	ər over	ȯ for	u̇ put	zh measure

rib cage *n* the framework formed by the ribs of the body.

rib–eye (rib′ī′) *n* a steak cut from the outer side of the ribs of beef.

ri·bo·fla·vin (rī′bō flā′vən) *n* a vitamin that is essential for producing energy in the metabolism. It is present in milk, liver, eggs, and green vegetables. <*ribose* a sugar + Latin *flavus* yellow, because of its colour>

ri·bo·nu·cle·ic acid (rī′bō nyū klē′ik) *or* (rī′bō nū klē′ik) RNA.

ri·bo·some (rī′bə sōm′) *n* a particle consisting of RNA and associated proteins found in a living cell. Ribosomes help to synthesize proteins. <(*ribo*)*nucleic acid* + *-some*>

rib–tick·ler (rib′tik′lər) *Informal n* a joke or funny story. **rib′-tick′ling** *adj.*

rice (rīs) *n* the starchy grains of a plant grown in warm climates, especially in Asia, usually grown in flooded fields or paddies. See GRAIN, WILD RICE for pictures.
v **riced, ric·ing** reduce to a form like rice: *to rice potatoes.* <Old French, from Greek *oruza*>

rice cake *n* a round, flat cake, made of puffed rice grains.

rice paper *n* **1** a thin paper for painting or writing on, made from the straw of rice. **2** a thin, translucent, edible paper used in candies and pastries, and made from the pith of a shrub called the **rice-paper plant.**

ric·er (rīs′ər) *n* a utensil with small holes for pressing cooked potatoes or other soft foods through so that they look like grains of rice.

rich (rich) *adj* **1** with much money or property. **2** plentiful or well supplied: *Canada is rich in oil and nickel.* **3** producing abundantly: *rich soil, a rich mine.* **4** valuable or generating much wealth: *rich rewards.* **5** *Computers* enhanced with extra features: *rich e-mail.* **6** strongly flavoured as a food and containing a large amount of fat, eggs, or sugar. **7** pleasantly deep and strong in a colour or sound: *a rich brown, a rich tone.* **8** containing a high proportion of fuel to air in vehicle fuel. **9** *Informal* causing amusement or indignation: *Considering how hard I've worked, it's a bit rich for you to say I never help you.*
n **1 the rich** rich people. **2 riches** *pl* wealth in money or property. <Old English *rice*> **rich′ly** *adv.* **rich′ness** *n.*

Rich·ter scale (rik′tər) *n* a numerical scale for gauging the energy of an earthquake by the vibrations it produces. Earthquakes of magnitude 1 cannot be felt; earthquakes of more than 5.5 are hugely destructive. <Charles F. *Richter*, 20c seismologist>

rick (rik) *n* a stack of hay, straw, or grain, especially one formed or covered so as to be protected from bad weather. <Old English *hreac*>

rick·ets (rik′its) *n* a disease of children caused by a lack of vitamins that results in softening and, sometimes, bending of the bones. <origin uncertain>

rick·et·y (rik′ə tē) *adj* **1** liable to fall or break down as a structure or piece of equipment: *a rickety old chair.* **2** affected by rickets. **rick′et·i·ness** *n.*

rick·shaw (rik′sho) *n* a small, two-wheeled, hooded carriage pulled by one or more persons, especially in Asia. <*jinrikishaw*, from Japanese *jin* person + *riki* power + *sha* vehicle>

ric·o·chet (rik′ə shā′) *n* the skipping or jumping motion of an object as it rebounds one or more times off a surface, or a shot or hit that rebounds in such a way.
v **ric·o·chet·ted** or **ric·o·chet·ed** (-shād′), **ric·o·chet·ting** or **ric·o·chet·ing** (-shā′ing) rebound one or more times off a surface with a skipping or jumping motion, especially as a bullet. <French>

ri·cot·ta (ri ko′tə) *n* a soft, white, unsalted mild-tasting Italian cheese often used in lasagna. <Italian = recooked>

rid[1] (rid) *v* **rid** or **rid·ded, rid·ding** make someone or something free of a troublesome person or thing: *What will rid a house of rats?* <Old Norse *rythja*>
get rid of, a get free from: *I can't get rid of this cold.* **b** take action so as to be free of a troublesome or unwanted person or thing: *The two cats got rid of the rats in the barn.*

rid·dance (rid′əns) *n* the action of getting rid of a troublesome or unwanted person or thing.
good riddance, used to express relief that something or somebody is gone.

rid·den (rid′ən) *v* past participle of RIDE.
adj (*often in compounds*) dominated, harassed, or obsessed by: *debt-ridden, guilt-ridden.*

rid·dle[1] (rid′əl) *n* **1** a question or statement intentionally phrased so as to require ingenuity to get its answer or meaning, typically presented as a puzzle. Example: *When is a door not a door?* Answer: *When it's ajar.* **2** a person, event, or thing that is hard to understand or explain.
v **rid·dled, rid·dling** *Archaic* speak in riddles. <Old English *rædels* opinion>

rid·dle[2] (rid′əl) *v* **rid·dled, rid·dling 1** make many holes in someone or something: *Woodpeckers had riddled the tree with holes.* **2** pass a substance through a large coarse sieve: *to riddle gravel.*
n a coarse sieve, especially one for separating ashes from cinders or sand from gravel. <Old English *hriddel* sieve>

ride (rīd) *v* **rode, rid·den, rid·ing 1 a** sit on and control an animal, especially a horse, and make use of it for transport. **b** sit on and control a bicycle or motorcycle as it travels. **2** travel in or on a motor or public transit vehicle as a passenger. **3** ride over, along, or through: *He likes to ride the mountain trail.* **4** be carried along by anything with much momentum: *The surfers rode the waves.* **5** compete or perform in a race on horseback, on a bicycle, or on a motorcycle. **6** travel in or on an elevator or escalator. **7** float or seem to float along: *The ship rode the waves.* **8** *Informal* annoy, pester, or tease. **9** cause to ride or be carried: *to ride a toddler on your shoulders.*
n **1** a trip on horseback, on a bicycle or motorcycle, or in a motor vehicle: *On Sundays, we take a ride into the country.* **2** a path or road made for riding. **3** 🍁 a demonstration of horse riding performed as an entertainment. **4** a series of events or circumstances that have a particular quality: *His first days on the job were a rough ride.* **5** the quality of comfort offered by a motor vehicle while in motion: *a smooth ride.* **6** a mechanical amusement, such as a merry-go-round, roller coaster, or Ferris wheel, or a turn on one of them. <Old English *ridan*>
let ride, leave undisturbed or inactive: *Let the matter ride until the next meeting.*
ride high, be successful.

ride out, **a** withstand adverse weather: *ride out the storm.* **b** endure successfully.
ride roughshod over, show no consideration for, or treat roughly.
ride someone down, trample or overtake someone by horseback.
ride up, slide up out of place as a garment: *That coat rides up at the back.*
take for a ride, *Informal* cheat or swindle someone.

🍁 **Ri·deau Hall** (rē′dō) *n* the official residence of the Governor General of Canada, situated in Ottawa.

rid·er (rī′dər) *n* **1** a person who rides or can ride a horse, bicycle, or motor vehicle. **2** a condition added to a record, document, legislative bill, or statement after it was considered to be completed. **rid′er·less** *adj.*

rid·er·ship (rī′dər ship′) *n* the number of people who regularly use a certain transit system.

ridge (rij) *n* **1** a long, narrow hilltop, mountain range, or watershed. See SUMMIT for picture. **2** the line where two upward sloping surfaces meet: *the ridge of a roof.* **3** a narrow raised band running along or across a surface, as on cloth or the ground: *ridges in a ploughed field.* **4** an elongated region of high barometric pressure.
v **ridged, ridg·ing** **1** form or make into narrow raised bands. **2** cover or mark with such bands. <Old English *hrycg* crest>

ridge·pole (rij′pōl′) *n* the horizontal pole along the top of a roof or tent.

rid·i·cule (rid′ə kyūl′) *v* **rid·i·culed, rid·i·cul·ing** laugh at or mock: *He liked to ridicule his sisters' friends.*
n words or actions that mock somebody or something: *His silly mistakes invited ridicule.* <Latin *ridere* to laugh>

SYNONYMS

Ridicule means "make fun of someone or something": *The comedian ridiculed the new show about surviving on a desert island.*

Mock can mean "make fun of by copying or imitating": *He mocked the way she danced.*

Deride can mean "make fun of in a scornful way": *Everyone derided the latest plan to balance the budget.*

ri·dic·u·lous (ri dik′yə ləs) *adj* deserving or inviting mockery: *His attempts to be the life of the party were ridiculous.* **ri·dic′u·lous·ly** *adv.* **ri·dic′u·lous·ness** *n.*

rid·ing (rī′ding) *n* **1** 🍁 a political division represented by a member of a legislative assembly. **2** *UK* in former times, one of three administrative divisions in Yorkshire, England. <Old Norse *thrithi* third>

riding crop *n* a short, flexible whip with a loop for the hand, used in riding horses.

riding habit *n* a formal outfit worn by a woman while riding a horse.

Rid·van (riz′wan′) *Bahaism n* a major twelve-day festival taking place in the spring.

Ri·el Rebellions (rē el′) *pln* the Red River Rebellion and the Northwest Rebellion.

rife (rīf) *adj* **1** happening often, especially as something undesirable or harmful. **2** full of: *The land was rife with rumours of war.* <Old English *rife*>

riff (rif) *n* **1** a continuously repeated instrumental phrase in jazz or popular music, supporting a solo improvisation or played over changing chords and harmonies. **2** a clever or inventive commentary.
v make or play a riff. <*riffile*>

rif·fle (rif′əl) *n* **1** a quick or casual leaf or search through something. **2** the act of shuffling cards in this way. **3** a sandbar or shoal lying just below the surface of a waterway, or the ripple of water over it.
v **rif·fled, rif·fling** **1** shuffle cards by bending the edges slightly so that the two divisions of the deck slide into each other. **2** leaf through the pages of a book quickly. <perhaps *ruffle*>

riff·raff (rif′raf′) *n* people considered to be undesirable or worthless. <Old French>

ri·fle[1] (rī′fəl) *n* a gun with spiral grooves in its long barrel to spin the bullet as it is fired from the shoulder.
v **ri·fled, ri·fling** **1** cut spiral grooves in a gun's barrel or bore to make a bullet spin and thereby have more accuracy over long distances. **2** hit or kick a ball hard and straight: *The quarterback rifled a pass into the end zone.* <French *rifler* groove>

ri·fle[2] (rī′fəl) *v* **ri·fled, ri·fling** search through something hurriedly in order to find or steal something. <Old French> **ri′fler** *n.*

ri·fle·man (rī′fəl mən) *n, pl* **ri·fle·men** (-mən) a soldier armed with a rifle.

ri·fling (rī′fling) *n* the spiral grooves in a rifle.

rift (rift) *n* **1** a split, crack, or break in something: *a rift in the clouds.* **2** a breach in relations between individuals, groups, or nations. **3** a major fault separating blocks of the earth's geological surface.
v form fissures, cracks, or breaks so as to move blocks of the earth's geological surface. <Scandinavian>

rift valley *n* a long valley with steep walls formed by the sinking of a part of the earth's crust between two faults.

rig[1] (rig) *v* **rigged, rig·ging** **1** equip a boat for sailing by providing it with sails and rigging. **2** assemble and adjust the equipment of a sailing boat or aircraft to make it ready for operation. **3** set up equipment, or a device or structure, typically in a hurried and temporary way. **4** *Informal* (*usually with* **out** *or* **up**) clothe or dress: *We rigged ourselves out for the costume party.*
n **1** the arrangement of sails and rigging in a sailboat or sailing ship. **2** clothing or a costume: *His rig consisted of a silk hat and overalls.* **3** an outfit or equipment: *a drilling rig.* **4** a carriage, with its horse or horses. <origin uncertain>

rig[2] (rig) *v* **rigged, rig·ging** arrange dishonestly for one's own advantage: *to rig a race.* <origin uncertain>

a bat	e bed	i bid	o pot	u cup	th **thin**
ā cake	ē me	ī bite	ō go	ū rude	ᴛʜ **then**
à bar	ə **about**	ər **over**	ȯ **for**	ů **put**	zh **measure**

R

rig·a·to·ni (rig′ə tō′nē) *n* pasta in the shape of wide, short, ribbed tubes. <Italian *riga* line, from the ribbed pattern>

rig·ger (rig′ər) *n* **1 a** a person whose job is to rig a sailboat or sailing ship. **b** a person whose job is to erect and maintain scaffolding and lifting equipment. **c** a person who works on an oil rig or gas rig. **2** (*in compounds*) a ship with a specific kind of rigging: *a square-rigger.*

rig·ging (rig′ing) *n* **1** the system of ropes or chains used to support and work the masts, yards, and sails on a sailboat or sailing ship. **2** the ropes or wires supporting the structure of an airship, biplane, hang-glider, or parachute.

right (rīt) *adj* **1** to do with the side that is toward the east when the main side faces north: *I wear my watch on my right wrist.* **2** morally good, just, or lawful: *She did the right thing when she told the truth.* **3 a** correct or true: *the right answer.* **b** correct in one's opinion: *He was right when he said I was lazy.* **4** appropriate for a particular person or thing: *That outfit isn't right for you.* **5** healthy, satisfactory, or normal: *My head doesn't feel right.* **6** fashionable or socially important: *to be seen in all the right places.* **7** tending to oppose social and economic reform.
adv **1** on or to the right side: *Turn right.* **2** in a way that is good, just, or lawful: *He acted right when he told the truth.* **3** correctly or truly: *She guessed right.* **4** properly or well: *It's faster to do a job right the first time.* **5** favourably: *to turn out right.* **6** exactly or precisely: *Put it right here.* **7** immediately: *Stop playing right now.* **8** in a straight line or directly: *Look me right in the eye.* **9** to the furthest or most complete extent: *Her hat was knocked right off.*
interj used to indicate yes or all right: *"It's time to go to school," his mother called. "Right," he replied.*
n **1** the right side or hand: *The school is on the right.* **2** that which is morally correct or just: *Do right, not wrong.* **3** a just claim, title, or privilege: *the right to vote.* **4** a blow struck with the right hand. **5 the Right** the groups or political parties who oppose social and economic reform.
v **1** make correct: *to right errors.* **2** restore to a normal or upright position: *The ship righted as the wave passed.* <Old English *riht*> **right′ness** *n.*
by right or **by rights,** if things had happened or been done correctly.
in the right, morally correct.
in your own right, independently.
right away, at once: *She promised to do it right away.*
right now, immediately: *Stop that right now!*
right off, immediately.

right angle *n* an angle of 90°, as in the corner of a square. **right′-ang′led** *adj.*

right brain *n* the right hemisphere of the brain, which controls the left side of the body and such mental functions as creative thought and some emotions.

right–click (rīt′klik′) *v* See CLICK.

right·eous (rī′chəs) *adj* morally right or justifiable: *righteous indignation.* <Old English *riht* right + *wis* manner> **right′eous·ness** *n.*

right face *v* turn to the right.

right field *n* the part of the outfield in baseball beyond first base and to the right side of the batter. **right fielder** *n.*

right·ful (rīt′fəl) *adj* **1** according to law: *the rightful owner of this dog.* **2** legitimately or appropriately claimed: *a rightful place in society.* **right′ful·ly** *adv.* **right′ful·ness** *n.*

right–hand (rīt′hand′) *adj* **1** on or to the right side of a person. **2** to do with the right hand. **3** most helpful or useful: *He was her right-hand man.*

right–hand·ed (rīt′han′did) *adj* **1** using the right hand more easily and readily than the left. **2** made to be used with the right hand. **3** turning from left to right: *a right-handed twist.*

🍁 **Right Honourable** *n* a title given for life to the Governor General, the prime minister, and the chief justice of the Supreme Court. *Abbrev.* **Rt. Hon.**

right·ist (rī′tist) *n* a person who has conservative views in politics.
adj with conservative views in politics.

right·ly (rī′tlē) *adv* **1** justly or fairly. **2** correctly: *She rightly guessed that I wasn't telling the whole truth.* **3** properly or suitably.

right–mind·ed (rīt′mīn′did) *adj* with morally sound opinions or principles.

right–of–way (rīt′əv wā′) *n* **1** the legal right of a pedestrian, rider, or driver to have priority in going first at a particular point. **2** the right to pass over property belonging to someone else. **3** the right to build and operate a railway line, road, or utility on privately owned land, or the land on which one of these things is built.

right·siz·ing (rīt′sīz′ing) *n* the process of reducing a company to its most efficient, most profitable size. **right′size′** *v.*

right–to–life (rīt′tū līf′) PRO-LIFE.

right triangle *n* a triangle with one right angle.

right whale *n* a whale with a large head, a deeply curved jaw, and toothlike whalebones on the sides of the mouth.

right wing *n* **1** the people opposing reform, especially the conservative or reactionary members of a political party or system. **2** the playing position to the right of centre on a forward line in hockey, lacrosse, soccer, or rugby. **3** a player who occupies this position. **right winger** *n.*

rig·id (rij′id) *adj* **1** stiff or firm and unable to bend or be forced out of shape: *a rigid support.* **2** not able to be changed or adapted: *Our club has a few rigid rules.* **3** not able to be adaptable in outlook, belief, or response: *a rigid supervisor.* <Latin *rigere* be stiff> **ri·gid′i·ty** *n.* **rig′id·ly** *adv.* **rig′id·ness** *n.*

rig·ma·role (rig′mə rōl′) *n* **1** a long and needlessly complicated procedure. **2** a long, rambling story or statement. <obsolete *ragman roll* legal document recording a list of offences>

rig·or mor·tis (rig′ər mòr′tis) *n* the stiffening of the muscles after death. <Latin = stiffness of death>

rig·our or **rig·or** (rig′ər) *n* **1** the quality of being very strict or severe. **2** harshness in weather or climate. **3** the quality of being extremely thorough, painstaking, and accurate. <Old French, from Latin *rigor* stiffness> **rig′or·ous** *adj.* **rig′or·ous·ly** *adv.*

Rig–Ve·da (rig′vā′də) *Hinduism n* the oldest and most important of the ancient sacred writings of Hinduism, containing a collection of hymns in early Sanskrit.

rile (rīl) *v* **riled, ril·ing 1** make someone annoyed or irritated. **2** make water muddy or turbulent. <*roil*>

rill (ril) *n* a tiny stream. <German *rille*>

rim (rim) *n* an upper or outer edge, border, or margin on or around anything, typically something circular: *the rim of a wheel, the rim of a cup.*
v **rimmed, rim·ming** form or put a rim around: *Wildflowers and grasses rimmed the little pool.* <Old English *rima* border>

✱ **rim·rock** (rim′rok′) *especially Western Provinces n* an outcropping or ridge of rock, especially one forming a cliff at the end of a plateau.

rind (rīnd) *n* the hard or firm outer layer of something, such as the skin of citrus fruit, or the hard outer edge of cheese or bacon. <Old English = bark>

ring[1] (ring) *n* **1** a circle: *Sometimes you can see a ring around the moon on frosty nights. They danced in a ring.* **2** a thin circular band of metal or other material: *a wedding ring.* **3** a circular or oval enclosed space in which races, games, performances, shows, and demonstrations take place: *the circus ring.* **4 the ring a** the square enclosure in which boxing matches are fought. **b** the profession or sport of boxing. **5** a group of people combined for a selfish or immoral purpose: *A ring of gangsters controlled the smuggling operation.*
v **ringed, ring·ing 1** enclose or surround, especially for protection or containment. **2** draw a circle around something or form an edge around something circular. **3** toss a horseshoe ring or other object around a certain mark or post. **4** cut away the bark in a circle around a tree or branch. <Old English *hring*>

ring[2] (ring) *v* **rang, rung, ring·ing 1** produce or cause to produce a clear vibrating sound, as a bell does: *The phone rang. Ring the doorbell.* **2** call for service or attention: *Did you ring?* **3** proclaim or repeat loudly everywhere: *to ring a person's praises.* **4** resound loudly or widely: *The room rang with shouts of laughter. The mountains rang with the roll of thunder.* **5** sound or seem: *Her words rang true.* **6** have a sensation that fills the ears like the sounds of bells: *My ears are ringing.* **7** call on the telephone: *He rang me yesterday.*
n **1** the act of causing a bell to sound, or the sound caused by this: *Did you hear a ring?* **2** a sound like that of a bell: *the ring of one glass against another.* **3** a characteristic sound or quality: *a ring of sincerity.* **4** a telephone call: *Give me a ring later.* <Old English *hringan*>
ring up, a record a specified amount on a cash register. **b** call on the telephone.

ringed (ringd) *adj* **1** wearing a ring or rings. **2** decorated with a ring or rings. **3** surrounded by a ring or rings.

ring·er (ring′ər) *n* **1** a person who or thing that encircles or surrounds. **2** a person who rings a bell. **3** a horseshoe or other object thrown so as to fall over a post or mark. **4** *Informal* a person or thing very like another.

✱ **ring·ette** (ring et′) *n* an ice game similar to hockey, played by two teams of six players each, using straight sticks to try to shoot a rubber ring into the opposing team's goal.

ring finger *n* the finger next to the little finger of either hand, where an engagement or wedding ring is customarily worn.

ring·lead·er (ring′lē′dər) *n* a person who leads others, especially doing something illegal or rebellious: *the ringleaders of the mutiny.*

ring·let (ring′lit) *n* a lock of hair hanging in a corkscrew-shaped curl: *She wears her hair in ringlets.*

ring·mas·ter (ring′mas′tər) *n* a person who directs the performances in the ring of a circus.

ring·side (ring′sīd′) *n* **1** a place just outside the ring at a circus performance or boxing match. **2** a place giving a close view of some action or event.

ring tone *n* the sound made by a cellphone when a call is received.

ring·worm (ring′wərm′) *n* a contagious, itching skin disease of the scalp or feet, caused by fungi and characterized by ring-shaped patches.

rink (ringk) *n* **1 a** a sheet of ice or smooth floor for playing hockey, or for curling, roller-skating, or ice-skating. **b** a building in which there is such a sheet or floor: *This rink has 800 seats.* **2** a curling team of four players: *Some of Canada's best rinks curled in the bonspiel.* <Middle English>

✱ **rink rat** *Informal n* a young person who hangs around a hockey rink, either just for fun or to help with chores in return for free skating or admission to games.

rink·y–dink (rink′ē dink) *Informal adj* cheap, tacky, shabby, or otherwise unimpressive: *We ended up in this little rinky-dink hotel.*

rinse (rins) *v* **rinsed, rins·ing 1** wash with clean water to remove soap, detergent, or dirt. **2** clean one's mouth by swishing water or mouthwash round and round and then spitting it out.
n **1** the act of washing in clean water. **2** an act of cleaning one's mouth by swishing water or mouthwash around in it. **3** a preparation to condition or tint the hair. <Old French *rincier*>

ri·ot (rī′ət) *n* **1** a wild, violent public disturbance caused by a crowd or mob: *The guards stopped several riots in the prison.* **2** an outburst of uncontrolled feelings: *a riot of emotions.* **3** a large, bright display of something: *The autumn leaves produced a riot of colour.* **4** *Informal* a highly amusing person or performance: *She was a riot at the party.*
v **1** cause or take part in a violent public disturbance. **2** behave in an uninhibited way. <Old French *rioter* to quarrel> **ri′ot·er** *n.*
run riot, a act, function, or be expressed without restraint: *Her imagination ran riot.* **b** grow wildly or luxuriantly as plants: *The weeds have run riot in our garden.*

ri·ot·ous (rī′ə təs) *adj* **1** taking part in a violent public disturbance. **2** wild and uncontrolled: *riotous conduct.* **ri′ot·ous·ly** *adv.*

a bat	e bed	i bid	o pot	u cup	th thin
ā cake	ē me	ī bite	ō go	ū rude	ᴛʜ then
à bar	ə about	ər over	ȯ for	u̇ put	zh measure

rip[1] (rip) *v* **ripped, rip·ping** 1 tear or pull something forcibly away: *Rip the cover off this box.* 2 become torn apart: *My sleeve ripped on a nail.* 3 *Informal* move fast or forcibly: *Fire ripped through an entire city block.* 4 *Computer slang* use software to copy data from a CD, DVD, etc. This can be considered as breaking copyright: *to rip a DVD to the CD drive on a computer.*
n 1 a long tear or cut: *Please sew up this rip in my sleeve.* 2 the act of tearing something. <Middle English *rippen*>
let rip, *Informal* utter or be uttered violently: *She let rip a torrent of abuse. He let rip with his objections for several minutes.*
rip into, *Informal* attack violently, especially in words.
rip off, *Slang* **a** cheat: *That clerk ripped me off.* **b** steal: *Who ripped off my math set?*

rip[2] (rip) *n* a swift current or stretch of rough water made by cross currents meeting. <perhaps related to *rip*[1]>

R.I.P. rest in peace, used as a statement on graves. <Latin *requiescat in pace*>

ri·par·i·an (rə per′ē ən) *or* (rī per′ē ən) *adj* to do with the banks of a river: *riparian rights.* <Latin *ripa* bank>

rip cord *n* a cord that, when pulled, opens a parachute.

ripe (rīp) *adj* **rip·er, rip·est** 1 full-grown and ready to be gathered and eaten as fruit or grain. 2 resembling ripe fruit in colour and fullness: *ripe beauty.* 3 fully developed or mature as a cheese or wine, or rich, intense, and pungent as a smell or flavour. 4 ready to break or be lanced: *a ripe boil.* 5 ready or suitable for a particular action or purpose: *ripe for mischief.* <Old English>
rip′en *v.* **ripe′ness** *n.*

rip–off (rip′of) *Slang n* 1 an act of cheating or fraud. 2 an inferior imitation of something.

ri·poste (rə pōst′) *n* 1 a quick, clever reply to an insult or criticism. 2 a quick return thrust in the sport of fencing.
v **ri·post·ed, ri·post·ing** make a quick, clever reply to an insult or criticism. <French, from Latin *respondere* respond>

rip·per (rip′ər) *n* 1 a person who rips, especially a murderer who mutilates a victim's body. 2 a tool that is used to tear or break something.

rip·ple (rip′əl) *n* 1 a little wave or series of waves on the surface of water: *Throw a stone into still water and watch the ripples spread in rings.* 2 a thing that resembles a little wave: *ripples in cardboard.* 3 a sound that reminds one of little waves: *a ripple of laughter in the crowd.* 4 a particular feeling or effect that spreads through or to someone or something: *When people heard the news, there was a ripple of discontent.* 5 a type of ice cream with small waves of flavoured syrup running through it: *butterscotch ripple.*
v **rip·pled, rip·pling** 1 form or flow with little waves: *A breeze rippled the quiet water.* 2 move or cause to move in a way resembling such little waves. <origin uncertain>

ripple effect *n* the spread of the results of an event, in stages and with gradually lessening force.

rip·ply (rip′lē) *adj* characterized by ripples; rippling.

rip·saw (rip′so′) *n* a saw for cutting wood along the grain, not across the grain.

rip·tide (rip′tīd′) *n* a strong current of churning water caused by one tide meeting another.

rise (rīz) *v* **rose, ris·en, ris·ing** 1 move from a lower position to a higher one: *The balloon is rising in the air.* 2 advance to a higher level of action, thought, feeling, expression, rank, or position: *He rose from salesperson to CEO. Her spirits have risen since yesterday.* 3 get up from lying, sitting, or kneeling: *to rise at dawn, to rise from a chair.* 4 of land, incline upward or become higher: *Hills rose in the distance.* 5 increase in number, size, amount or quality: *The tower rises to a height of thirty metres. Prices are rising. His anger rose as he waited.* 6 become louder or of a higher pitch: *The singer's voice rose at the end of the song.* 7 appear above the horizon: *It was so dark it seemed the sun didn't rise that morning.* 8 start or begin: *The river rose from a spring. Quarrels often rise from small annoyances.* 9 come into being or action: *The wind rose rapidly.* 10 be built up, erected, or constructed: *Houses are rising on the edge of town.* 11 revolt or rebel: *The peasants rose against the landowners.* 12 grow larger and lighter: *The yeast failed to make the dough rise.* 13 end a meeting or session of a legislative body: *The House usually rises in July.*
n 1 an upward movement: *the rise of a kite.* 2 the action of a fish coming to the surface of the water to seize a fly or bait. 3 an increase in amount, extent, size, or number: *the gradual rise of the hill, a price rise.* 4 a source, origin, or period of initial growth: *the rise of capitalism.* 5 a piece of high ground. 6 the vertical height of a slope, arch, or step. 7 a higher rank or position: *Her rise in the company was rapid.* 8 an increase in loudness or pitch. <Old English *risan*>
get a rise out of somebody, cause a person to react to verbal teasing: *We can always get a rise out of him with an attack on hockey.*
give rise to, bring about: *The lack of details in her story gave rise to my belief that she was lying.*
rise to, be able to deal with: *They rose to the occasion.*

CONFUSABLES

Rise means "get up" or "go up": *The sun rises in the east and sets in the west.*

Raise means "lift up": *Raise your hand if you wish to go on the school skiing trip.*

Note in the above example sentences, that *rise* does not take a direct object, but *raise* does.

ris·er (rī′zər) *n* 1 a person who or thing that rises: *an early riser.* 2 the vertical part of a step. Compare TREAD.

ris·i·ble (riz′ə bəl) *adj* able to cause laughter because of something's absurdity. <Latin *ridere* to laugh>
ris′i·bil′i·ty *n.*

ris·ing (rī′zing) *n* 1 the act of ascending: *the rising of the sun.* 2 the act of getting up from sleep: *Seven o'clock is my hour for rising.* 3 a fight or revolt against a government.
adj advancing or growing in power, influence, or status.

rising action *n* the part of a play, story, etc. where the plot becomes more complicated, leading up to the climax.

risk (risk) *n* 1 a chance of harm or loss: *the risk of a heart attack. She rescued the dog at the risk of her own life.* 2 a person who or thing that is regarded as likely to turn out

river

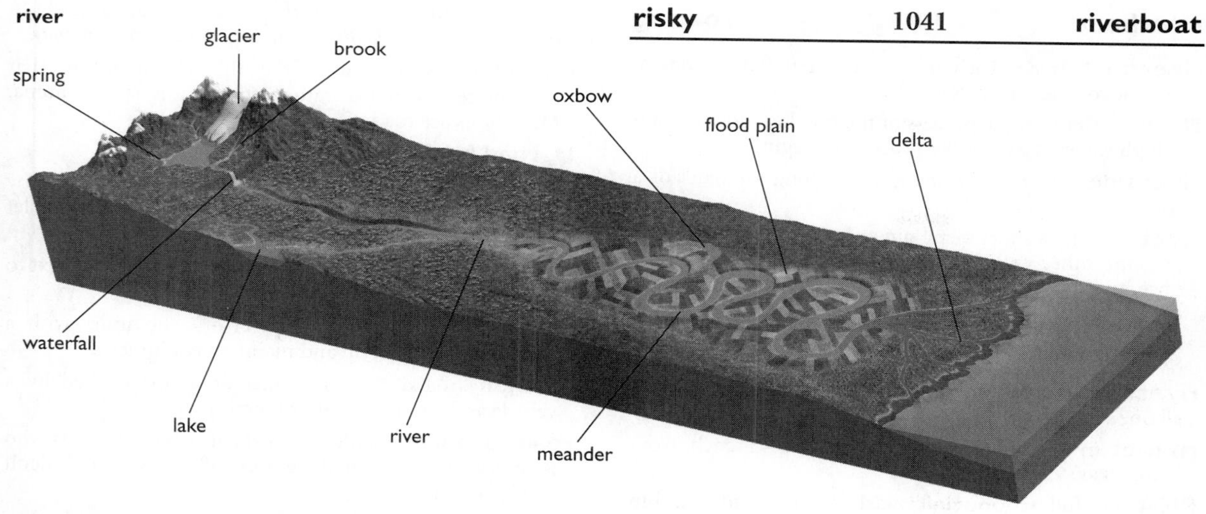

well or badly in a specified context or respect: *He gained so much weight he was not a good health risk.* **3** a possibility of harm or damage against which something is insured.
v **1** expose to the chance of harm or loss: *A climber risks his or her life.* **2** take the risk of: *They risked getting wet.* <French, from Italian *risciare* dare>
at risk, in danger of being lost or hurt: *Don't put your children at risk.*
run (or **take**) **a risk,** expose oneself to the chance of harm or loss.

risk·y (ris′kē) *adj* **risk·i·er, risk·i·est** full of the possibility of danger, failure, or loss. **risk′i·ly** *adv.* **risk′i·ness** *n.*

ri·sot·to (ri zo′tō) *n* an Italian dish consisting of rice slowly cooked in stock with meat, fish, or vegetables added. <Italian *riso* rice>

ris·qué (ris kā′) *adj* slightly shocking or sexually suggestive: *a risqué glance.* <French *risquer* to risk>

rite (rīt) *n* a religious or other solemn ceremony, such as one characteristic of a church or secret society. <Latin *ritus* custom>

rite of passage *n* a ceremony or event marking an important stage in a life, especially birth, initiation, marriage, and death.

rit·u·al (rich′ū əl) *n* **1** a religious or solemn ceremony consisting of a series of actions performed according to a fixed system. **2** a series of actions or habitual type of behaviour followed by someone: *Making the bed every morning was a ritual for him.*
adj to do with rites or behaviour like a rite: *a ritual dance.* <Latin *ritus* custom> **rit′u·al·ly** *n.*

rit·u·al·ism (rich′ū ə liz′əm) *n* a fondness for or insistence upon ritual. **rit′u·al·ist′ic** *adj.*

rit·u·al·ize (rich′ū ə līz′) *v* **rit·u·al·ized, rit·u·al·iz·ing** make into a ritual or set of rituals: *He thought they ritualized Sunday dinner.* **rit′u·al·iz·a′tion** *n.*

ritz·y (rit′sē) **ritz·i·er, ritz·i·est** *Informal adj* elegant or luxurious: *a ritzy nightclub.* <*Ritz* hotels, from C. *Ritz,* 19c hotelier>

ri·val (rī′vəl) *n* **1** a person who or thing that competes with another for the same objective or for superiority in the same area as another. **2** a thing that will bear comparison with something else: *The beauty of the Prairies has no rival.*
adj wanting or competing for the same thing as another: *The rival store tried to get the other's trade.*
v **ri·valled** or **ri·valed, ri·val·ling** or **ri·val·ing** **1** try to equal or outdo: *The stores rival each other in beautiful window displays.* **2** equal or match: *The sunset rivalled the sunrise in beauty.*

ETYMOLOGY

Rival comes from Latin *rivalis,* which originally meant "one who uses the same stream as another," which came from *rivus* meaning "stream."

ri·val·ry (rī′vəl rē) *n, pl* **ri·val·ries** the competitive action, position, or relation of a rival or rivals: *The two local teams had a fierce rivalry.*

riv·er (riv′ər) *n* **1** a large, natural stream of water that flows into a lake, ocean, or other body of water. **2** an abundant stream or flow of a substance: *Rivers of sweat poured down his face.* <Old French, from Latin *ripa* bank of a river>
sell down the river, *Informal* betray, especially by a compromise.
up the river, *Informal* in or to prison: *He was sent up the river for twenty years.*

riv·er·bank (riv′ər bank′) *n* the raised ground at the side of a river.

river basin *n* land that is drained by a river and its tributaries.

riv·er·bed (riv′ər bed′) *n* the ground over which a river flows or used to flow.

a bat	e bed	i bid	o pot	u cup	th **thin**
ā cake	ē me	ī bite	ō go	ū rude	TH **then**
à bar	ə about	ər over	ȯ for	u̇ put	zh measure

R

riv·er·boat (riv′ər bōt′) *n* a boat, often flat-bottomed, suitable for use on rivers.

🍁 **river drive** *n* the process of floating logs downstream at high water as part of the process of logging.

riv·er·side (riv′ər sīd′) *n* the ground along the bank of a river.

riv·et (riv′it) *n* a short metal pin or bolt with a head at one end, the other end made to be hammered into a head once it is in position to hold together two plates of metal. *v* **1** join or fasten with a rivet or rivets. **2** be attracted and pay total attention to: *Their eyes were riveted on the speaker.* <Old French *river* to fasten> **riv′et·er** *n.*

riv·et·ing (riv′it ing) *adj* extremely interesting and holding all one's attention.

riv·u·let (riv′yə lit) *n* a very small stream. <French, from Latin *rivus* stream>

RNA *n* in full, **ribonucleic acid** a nucleic acid found in all living cells. It mainly acts as a messenger carrying instructions from DNA for controlling the synthesis of proteins.

roach[1] (rōch) *n* **1** a cockroach. **2** *Informal* the butt of a marijuana cigarette.

roach[2] (rōch) *n, pl* **roach·es** or (*especially collectively*) **roach** a European freshwater fish of the carp family, or a similar fish, such as the N American sunfish. <Old French *roche*>

road (rōd) *n* **1** a wide path or way leading from one place to another, usually with a prepared surface on which vehicles can travel: *The road from here to the city is being paved.* **2** a way or route: *Our road to the lake went through the woods.* **3** a series of events or a course of action that will lead to a particular outcome: *the road to ruin, a road to peace.* **4** a partly sheltered stretch of water near the shore where ships can anchor. Also, **roads**. <Old English *rad* journey on horseback>
hit the road, *Informal* begin a journey or start on one's way.
hold the road, have good traction as a motor vehicle.
on the road, a travelling widely, especially as a salesperson or performer in entertainments. **b** without a permanent home and moving from place to place.
take to the road, set out on a journey or set of journeys.

CONFUSABLES

Road usually refers to a paved surface that vehicles travel on: *We took the main road to town.*

Rode is the past tense of *ride*, which means "use for transport": *They rode their bikes to the park.*

road allowance *n* land reserved by the government as public property to be used for roads.

road·bed (rōd′bed′) *n* the foundation of a road or of a railway.

road·block (rōd′blok′) *n* **1** an obstacle placed across a road so traffic may be stopped and examined: *The police set up a roadblock to stop the car thief.* **2** an obstacle to progress: *We hit a roadblock in our efforts to raise money.*

road event *Sports n* any of the athletic competitions that take place on roads rather than in a sports arena. Marathons are road events

🍁 **road hockey** STREET HOCKEY.

road hog *Informal n* a motorist who obstructs traffic by keeping a vehicle in the middle of the road, refusing to let other vehicles pass.

road·house (rōd′hous′) *n* a rural restaurant or one next to a minor highway, often with entertainment.

road·ie (rōd′ē) *Informal n* a person who tours with a musical band to set up and maintain equipment.

road·kill (rōd′kil′) *n* an animal or animals killed by a vehicle and left on a road or highway.

road rage *n* an assault or verbal abuse by a motorist who is angry and frustrated because of stress and difficult traffic conditions.

road·run·ner (rōd′run′ər) *n* a slender, long-tailed bird of the deserts of the southwestern US. It can run fast and usually does so instead of flying.

road show *n* a touring show by performers, a campaign tour by a politician, or a radio or TV program broadcast from different locations. Also, **roadshow**.

road·side (rōd′sīd′) *n* the side of a road.
adj beside a road: *a roadside inn.*

road·ster (rōd′stər) *n* an open automobile with two seats.

road test *n* **1** a test of a motor vehicle by driving it under normal operating conditions. **2** the part of the test for a driver's licence that involves driving a motor vehicle. **road-test** *v.*

road·way (rō′dwā′) *n* the part of a road, bridge, or railway intended for traffic: *Walk on the path, not in the roadway.*

road·wor·thy (rōd′wər′ᴛʜē) *adj* **road·wor·thi·er, road·wor·thi·est** fit for use or travel on the road: *This truck isn't roadworthy anymore.* **road′wor′thi·ness** *n.*

roam (rōm) *v* **1** go about with no special plan or aim: *to roam through fields.* **2** pass the hands or eyes lightly over something without stopping. **3** let one's mind drift without thinking of anything in particular.
n a walk or trip with no special plan or aim. <Middle English> **roam′er** *n.*

roan (rōn) *adj* with one main colour, especially bay or chestnut, thickly sprinkled with grey or white, especially as the colour of a horse or cow.
n an animal, especially a horse, of this colour. <Old French>

roar (rôr) *n* **1** a loud, deep, prolonged cry, such as that of a lion or other large wild animal. **2** a sound like this, such as that made by a person, a crowd, a fire, the wind, etc.
v **1** make a loud, deep, prolonged cry or sound. **2** laugh loudly. **3** move with a roar: *The express train roared past us.* <Old English *rarian*> **roar′er** *n.*

roar·ing (rôr′ing) *adj* **1** making the loud, deep, prolonged sound of a roar: *the roaring waterfall.* **2** very noisy and rowdy. **3** very successful: *a roaring business, a roaring success.*

Roaring Twenties *n* the decade of the 1920s, thought of as being filled with a spirit of energy and buoyancy.

roast (rōst) *v* **1** cook by dry heat in an oven, or before or over an open fire. **2** prepare or process a substance by subjecting it to intense heat: *to roast nuts, to roast ore.* **3** make or become very hot. **4** *Informal* make fun of someone in a good-humoured way, especially at a public event arranged for this purpose. **5** criticize severely.
n **1** a piece of meat roasted or intended for roasting. **2** an informal outdoor meal, at which some food is cooked over an open fire: *a wiener roast.* **3** a special dinner for a well-known person who is good-humouredly made fun of by guests.
adj roasted as food: *roast beef.* <Old French *rostir*>

roast·er (rō′stər) *n* **1** a pan, oven, furnace, or apparatus used in roasting. **2** a food suitable for roasting, such as beef, pork, or poultry. **3** a person who or thing that roasts.

rob (rob) *v* **robbed, rob·bing 1** take property away from a person or place by force or threats: *The old lady was robbed of all her money. Bandits robbed the bank.* **2** greatly overcharge or be overcharged: *You paid $100 for that? You were robbed!* **3** deprive someone or something of something needed, deserved, or important: *The disease has robbed him of his strength.* <Old French *rober*> **rob′ber** *n.* **rob′ber·y** *n.*
rob Peter to pay Paul, take something away from one to satisfy or help another: *She said that cutting health care to fund education is just robbing Peter to pay Paul.*

robe (rōb) *n* **1** a long, loose outer garment. **2 robes** *pl* a formal or ceremonial garment that shows a rank, office, or profession: *a judge's robe, the queen's robes of state.* **3** a covering or wrap: *Put a robe over you when you go on the sleigh ride.* **4** a bathrobe or dressing gown.
v **robed, rob·ing** put a robe or robes on. <Old French *robe*>

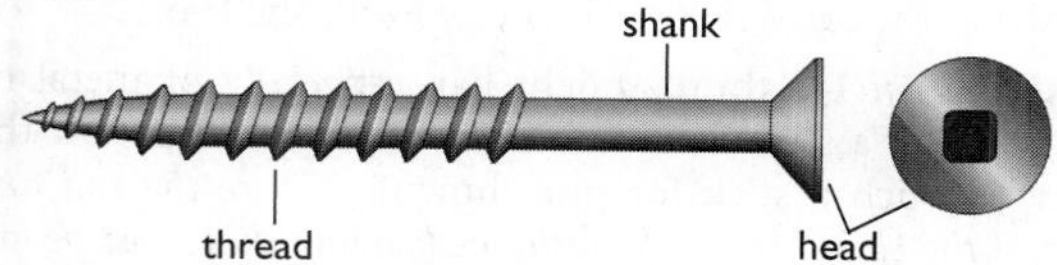

✱ Rob·ert·son screw (rob′ərt sən) *n* a screw with a square slot, used with a screwdriver that has a square point. <P. *Robertson*, 20c inventor>

rob·in (rob′ən) *n* **1** a N American thrush with a reddish breast. **2** a small European bird with a yellowish red breast. See REDBREAST for picture. <Old French *Robin*, pet name for *Robert*. Animals were sometimes given the names of people, like Jay.>

Robin Hood *n* **1** the semi-legendary leader of an outlaw band in medieval England who robbed the rich to help the poor. **2** a person considered to help the poor by taking from the wealthy.

robin run *n* the first run of maple syrup.

ro·bot (rō′bot) *or* (rō′bət) *n* **1** a machine or device, especially one that can be programmed by a computer, that can carry out automatically a series of complex actions that might normally be done by people. **2** a person who acts or works in a dull, mechanical way. <Czech *robota* forced labour, used by K. Capek, 20c playwright> **ro·bot′ic** (rō bot′ik) *adj.*

ro·bot·ics (rō bot′iks) *n* (*with singular verb*) the development and use of robots to perform tasks normally done by people.

ro·bust (rō bust′) *or* (rō′bust) *adj* **1** strong and healthy: *a robust person, a robust mind.* **2** suited to or requiring bodily strength: *robust exercises.* **3** sturdy, durable, or reliable. <Latin *robur* hard timber> **ro·bust′ly** *adv.* **ro·bust′ness** *n.*

rock[1] (rok) *n* **1** the mass of solid mineral matter forming part of the earth's crust, exposed on the surface or underlying the soil. **2** a large mass or grouping of such matter: *The ship was wrecked on the rocks.* **3** a piece of stone of any size, from a pebble to a boulder. **4** someone who or something that is strong, reliable, or hard: *My grandmother was a rock when I most needed support.* **5 ✱ the Rock** the island of Newfoundland. **6** a curling stone. <origin uncertain>
on the rocks, *Informal* **a** in a failed or failing relationship. **b** bankrupt. **c** of an alcoholic drink, with ice but without water or a mix: *whisky on the rocks.*

rock[2] (rok) *v* **1** move backwards and forward, or from side to side: *The waves rocked the ship.* **2** move or shake violently: *The earthquake rocked the houses.* **3** put to sleep or rest with swaying movements. **4** cause shock or distress: *The family was rocked by the news.* **5** dance or play rock'n'roll.
n **1** a gentle movement to and fro or from side to side. **2** rock'n'roll.
adj **1** to do with rock, the mineral: *a rock crystal.* **2** of or to do with rock'n'roll: *rock music, a rock band.* <Old English *roccian*>
rock the boat, disturb an otherwise stable or peaceful situation: *She thought the policy was unfair, but she didn't want to rock the boat.*

rock·a·billy (rok′a bi′lē) *n* a style of popular music combining features of rock'n'roll and hillbilly or bluegrass music.

rock–and–roll (rok′ən rōl′) ROCK'N'ROLL.

rock–bot·tom (rok′bot′əm′) *adj* at the lowest possible level: *rock-bottom prices.*
n **rock bottom** the lowest level: *Sometimes you have to reach rock bottom before you realize you need help.*

rock–bound (rok′bound′) *adj* rocky and inaccessible on a shore or coast.

rock candy *n* candy in the form of large, hard crystals of sugar.

rock climbing *n* the sport of going up and down sheer rock faces using special mountaineering equipment. **rock climber** *n.*

rock crystal *n* a colourless, transparent quartz that is often used for jewellery or decorative objects.

a bat	e bed	i bid	o pot	u cup	th thin
ā cake	ē me	ī bite	ō go	ū rude	ᴛʜ then
ȧ bar	ə about	ər over	ȯ for	u̇ put	zh measure

R

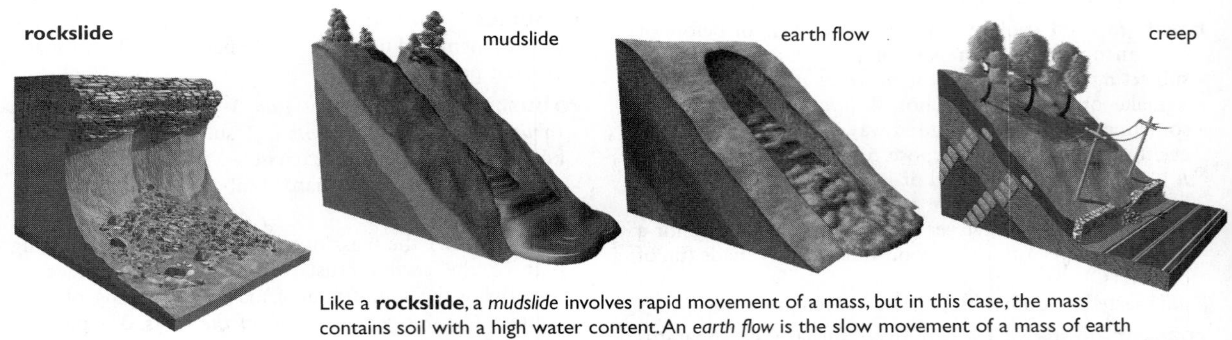

Like a **rockslide**, a *mudslide* involves rapid movement of a mass, but in this case, the mass contains soil with a high water content. An *earth flow* is the slow movement of a mass of earth caused by saturation during heavy rain or spring thaw. A *creep* is the slow, downhill movement of loose particles. It normally occurs too slowly to be perceived.

rock·er (rok′ər) *n* **1** a curved bar or support on which a rocking chair or cradle can rock. **2** a rocking chair. **3** a person who performs, dances to, or enjoys rock'n'roll.
off your rocker, *Slang* crazy.

rock·er·y (rok′ə rē) *n, pl* **rock·er·ies** an ornamental garden consisting of an arrangement of rocks and earth for growing plants. Also called **rock garden**.

rock·et[1] (rok′it) *n* **1** a cylindrical projectile that can be propelled with great speed to a great height or distance by a rapidly-burning substance that creates expanding gases, often used as a signal or firework. **2** a rocket-propelled spacecraft or missile. See BOOSTER for picture.
v rise or move extremely fast. <Italian *rocca* bobin for spinning, from the shape>

rocket[2] *n* a plant of the mustard family with fragrant flowers. The Mediterranean variety is eaten as a salad green. <French, from Latin *eruca* herb>

rock·et·ry (rok′i trē) *n* the branch of science that studies rockets and rocket propulsion.

rocket science *Informal n* (*usually in the negative*) a thing that is very complicated or hard to understand: *For twice as many people, just double the recipe; it's not rocket science!* **rocket scientist** *n.*

rock garden ROCKERY.

rock·hound (rok′hound′) *Informal n* a geologist or person who collects rocks as a hobby.

Rock·ies (rok′ēz) ROCKY MOUNTAINS.

rocking chair *n* a chair mounted on rockers, or on springs, so that it can rock back and forth.

rocking horse *n* a toy horse on rockers or springs for children to ride.

rock'n'roll (rok′ən rōl′) *n* a style of popular music with a heavy, regular beat and repetition of phrases, usually played with electronically amplified instruments, or the dancing done to this music. Often shortened to **rock**.

rock salt *n* common salt as it occurs in the earth in large mineral crystals.

rock·slide (rok′slīd′) *n* the sudden movement of a mass of loose rock down a cliff or mountainside, or the mass of rock itself.

rock·wool (rok′wu̇l′) *n* wool-like fibres made from cooled molten glass or similar materials and used for insulation and soundproofing. Also called **mineral wool**.

rock·y[1] (rok′ē) *adj* **rock·i·er, rock·i·est** full of, consisting of, or formed from rocks: *a rocky shore.*

rock·y[2] (rok′ē) *adj* **rock·i·er, rock·i·est** **1** tending to rock or shake: *That table is a bit rocky, so you may want to put a piece of wood under the short leg.* **2** unstable and full of problems: *a rocky relationship.* **3** *Informal* weak or dizzy. **rock′i·ly** *adv.* **rock′i·ness** *n.*

Rocky Mountains *pln* a range of mountains lying in Alberta and British Columbia, and the western US. Also, **the Rockies**.

ro·co·co (rō kō′kō) *n* a European style of art, decoration, and architecture with elaborate ornamentation, much used in the early 1700s. <French *rocaille* shellwork>

rod (rod) *n* **1** a thin, straight bar, especially of metal or wood. **2 a** a stick used to beat or punish. **b the rod** the use of such a stick for punishment: *"Spare the rod and spoil the child" is an old-fashioned saying that most people no longer believe.* **3** a thin, springy piece of wood, metal, etc. to which a reel may be attached, used for fishing: *Her dad gave her a rod and reel for her birthday.* **4** a nonmetric unit for measuring length, equal to about five metres. **5** a staff or wand carried as a symbol of one's position. **6** a rod-shaped cell, one of many in the retina of the eye, that is sensitive to light. <Old English *rodd*>

rode (rōd) past tense of RIDE. See ROAD for confusable.

ro·dent (rō′dənt) *n* a mammal with teeth especially adapted for gnawing, such as the rat, mouse, porcupine, or squirrel.
adj of or like this mammal. <Latin *rodere* gnaw>

ro·de·o (rō′dē ō) *or* (rō dā′ō) *n, pl* **ro·de·os** an outdoor contest or exhibition of skill in activities associated with cowboys, such as roping cattle, riding horses, and wrestling steers. <Spanish = a cattle pen>

roe[1] (rō) *n* the mass of eggs contained in the ovaries of female fish and shellfish, especially when used as food. <Middle English *rowe*>

roe[2] (rō) *n, pl* **roes** or (*especially collectively*) **roe** a small deer of Europe and Asia, with forked antlers, no visible tail, and a reddish summer coat that turns greyish in winter. <Old English *ra*>

roe·buck (rō′buk′) *n* a male roe deer.

roent·gen (rent′gən) *n* a unit of ionizing radiation, used for measuring the effect of X-rays or gamma rays. <W.K. *Roentgen*, 20c physicist>

rog·er (roj′ər) *Informal interj* used to indicate that a message is received and understood. <radio signaller's code for the letter *r*, for "received">

rogue (rōg) *n* **1** a dishonest or immoral person. **2** a mischievous person: *The little rogue has his grandma's glasses on.* **3** an animal with a dangerous or unpredictable temperament that lives apart from a herd: *a rogue elephant.* **4** a person who or animal that behaves in a dangerous, destructive, or unpredictable way. <origin uncertain>

ro·guer·y (rō′gə rē) *n, pl* **ro·guer·ies** the characteristic conduct of a rogue, especially acts of dishonesty or playful mischief.

rogues' gallery *Informal n* **1** a collection of photographs of known criminals, used for police to identify suspects. **2** a collection of people or their photographs that share some quality, especially a disreputable one.

ro·guish (rō′gish) *adj* **1** dishonest or immoral. **2** playfully mischievous: *She had a roguish twinkle in her eyes.* **ro′guish·ly** *adv.* **ro′guish·ness** *n.*

rois·ter (rois′tər) *v* enjoy oneself or celebrate in a noisy or boisterous way. <French *ruste* an uncivilized person, from Latin *rus* the countryside>

role (rōl) *n* **1** a performer's part in a play, movie, opera, or other entertainment: *the leading role.* **2** the function assumed or part played by a person or thing in a particular situation: *Nellie McClung played an important role in Canadian history.* <French *rôle* roll (of paper) on which an actor's part is written>

CONFUSABLES

Role means "a part played": *His role in the movie was to play the strongman in the circus.*

Roll means "turn over and over": *We rolled the heavy barrel up the hill.*

role model *n* someone who is an inspiration by setting a good example for others to imitate.

role–play (rōl′plā′) *v* act as oneself or another in an imaginary situation for therapeutic or other purposes: *to role-play an interview.* **role′-play·ing** *n.* **role player** *n.*

roll (rōl) *v* **1** move or cause to move along by turning over and over: *The ball rolled down the stairs. The gambler rolled the dice.* **2** turn something flexible over and over on itself to form a cylinder, tube, or ball: *Roll the string into a ball. He began to roll up his sleeping bag.* **3** move or be moved on wheels: *The shopping cart was rolling along all by itself.* **4** flow, or seem to flow: *the river rolls down to the sea. Fog will roll in later tonight.* **5** turn one's eyes upward, especially to indicate surprise or disapproval. **6** move from side to side: *The ship rolled in the waves.* **7** turn over, or over and over, especially while remaining in the same place: *The horse rolled in the dust. He rolled over in bed.* **8** make something, such as a car window or a window blind, move up or down: *Roll down the window for some air.* **9** make flat or smooth, or apply a substance, with a roller or rolling pin: *to roll paint on a wall. I like to roll the dough for cookies.* **10** issue a product from a machine or assembly line: *The first of the new models rolled off the line in March.* **11** make deep, loud sounds such as that of thunder or drums: *The organ rolled out the tune, and we all began to sing.* **12** beat a drum with rapid continuous strokes. **13** say with a trill: *to roll your R's.* **14** *Slang* rob someone, especially when the person is drunk or asleep.

n **1** a cylinder of something formed by turning it over and over on itself without folding: *rolls of paper.* **2** a somewhat rounded or rolled-up mass: *a roll of mints.* **3** continued motion from side to side. **4** a rapid, continuous beating on a drum. **5** a deep, loud sound, like that made by thunder or a drum. **6** a movement in which someone or something turns or is turned over on itself: *a roll of the dice.* **7** an official register or list of names: *Call the roll.* **8** a very small loaf of bread or pastry, eaten by itself, with something spread on it, or with a filling: *a sweet roll.* <Old French, from Latin *rota* wheel>

on a roll, *Informal* enjoying a period of success or good luck: *We're really on a roll; we've won every game so far!*

roll around, happen as a regular part of a cycle: *Our hockey league playoffs have rolled around again.*

roll back, cause to return to a lower level: *to roll back prices.*

rolled into one, combined: *It's a TV and a DVD player rolled into one!*

roll in, arrive in large amounts: *The pledges are rolling in.*

rolling in, *Informal* with plenty of: *They appear to be rolling in money.*

roll over, renew or continue an investment.

roll up, pile up or become piled up: *Bills roll up fast.*

roll with the punches, *Informal* calmly deal with things as they happen.

strike off the rolls, expel from membership.

roll·a·way (rōl′ə wā′) *adj* equipped with wheels so it can be easily moved into storage when not in use: *a rollaway cot.* *n* a folding bed with rollers or wheels so it can be easily stored.

roll bar *n* a strong metal bar in the shape of an upside-down U that sits over and across the seating compartment of a motor vehicle, to prevent crushing and reduce injuries if the vehicle rolls over.

roll call *n* the process of calling out a list of names to find out those who are present.

rolled oats *n* oats that are crushed and with the hulls removed, used as a food.

R

a bat	e bed	i bid	o pot	u cup	th thin
ā cake	ē me	ī bite	ō go	ū rude	TH then
ä bar	ə about	ər over	ô for	ů put	zh measure

roll·er (rō′lər) *n* **1** a cylinder on which something is rolled along or rolled up. **2** a cylinder of metal, stone, wood, or other material used for smoothing, pressing, or crushing, or to apply a substance: *A heavy roller was used to smooth the tennis court.* **3** a long, swelling wave: *Huge rollers broke on the sandy beach.* **4** a person who rolls something.

roller bearing *n* a bearing in which the shaft turns on rollers to lessen friction.

Rol·ler·blade (rō′lər blād′) *Trademark n* a brand of inline skates.

roller coaster *n* **1** a railway built for amusement, on which small cars roll rapidly up and down steep inclines, and round sharp corners. **2** anything characterized by sudden changes, especially up and down: *Exchange rates have been on a roller coaster this year.*

roller hockey *n* hockey played on roller skates or inline skates.

This **roller skate** is used for rink hockey. It is slower than an inline hockey skate, but the toe stop allows a player to make faster starts and stops. The wheels are made from polyurethane and measure at least 3 cm in diameter.

roller skate *n* a skate equipped with four small wheels, two at the front and two at the back, instead of a blade. **roll′er skate′** *v.* **roll′er skat′er** *n.* **roll′er-skat′ing** *n.*

rol·lick·ing (rol′i king) *adj* lively and enthusiastically jolly: *I had a rollicking time at the picnic.* <perhaps *romp* and *frolic*>

roll·ing (rō′ling) *n* the action, motion, or sound of a thing that rolls or is being rolled: *the rolling of thunder.*
adj rising and falling in gentle motions or shapes: *rolling countryside.*

rolling pin *n* a cylinder of wood, porcelain, or plastic for rolling out dough.

rolling stock *n* the locomotives and cars of a railway.

roll·top (rōl′top′) *adj* with a top that rolls back: *a rolltop desk.*

ro·ly–po·ly (rō′lē pō′lē) *adj* short and plump.

ROM *Computers n* in full, **read-only memory** the part of a computer's memory that can be read at high speed and cannot be erased. <*r*(ead)-*o*(nly) *m*(emory)>

ro·maine (rō mān′) *n* a lettuce with long, green leaves with crinkly edges that are joined loosely at the base.

ETYMOLOGY

Romaine comes from French *romain*, meaning "Roman." The lettuce was possibly introduced into France by the Romans in the 1300s.

Ro·man (rō′mən) *adj* **1** to do with ancient or modern Rome or its people. **2** **roman** in a typeface whose characters are plain and upright, and not boldface or italic. This is the style of type most used in print and on a display screen.
n **1** a native or inhabitant of Rome. **2** a typeface whose characters are plain and upright, and not boldface or italic. Example: *Most of this dictionary is in roman, but this sentence is in italic.* <Old French, from Latin *Roma* Rome>

Roman alphabet *n* the alphabet used by the Romans to write Latin, now forming the English and many other alphabets after the addition of J, U, and W.

Roman candle *n* a firework consisting of a tube that shoots out a series of flaming balls and sparks.

Roman Catholicism (ke thol′ə siz′əm) See CATHOLIC.

ro·mance (rō mans′) *or* (rō′mans) *for n,* (rō mans′) *for v.*
n **1 a** a strong feeling of excitement and mystery associated with love. **b** a relationship that involves this feeling: *Their great romance only lasted one summer.* **c** a book or movie dealing with people who are caught up in this feeling: *Romances were her favourite reading.* **2 a** a quality or feeling of mystery, adventure, and remoteness from everyday life: *The explorer's life was filled with romance.* **b** a book, poem, or story dealing with events and places that have such qualities. **3** a medieval tale dealing with a hero of chivalry, especially one written in one of the Romance languages, or the genre of fiction that such tales belong to: *an Arthurian romance.* **4** a short, informal musical work.
v **ro·manced, ro·manc·ing** *Informal* seek someone's attention or business, especially by using flattery. <Old French, from Latin *romanice* in a Romance language>

Romance languages *n* French, Italian, Spanish, Portuguese, Romanian, Provençal, and Catalan.

Ro·man·esque (rō′mən esk′) *adj* to do with a style of architecture in Europe between the 900s and the 1200s, marked by round arches, heavy columns and walls, and small windows.

Ro·ma·ni·a (rō mā′nē ə) *n* a country in central Europe. See the APPENDIX. **Ro·ma′ni·an** *adj, n.*

Roman numerals *n* a system of numerals used by the ancient Romans. Examples: XXIII, LVI, and MDCCLX, in which I = 1, V = 5, X = 10, L = 50, C = 100, D = 500, and M = 1000.

ro·man·tic (rō man′tik) *adj* **1** feeling the excitement and mystery associated with love. **2** with ideas or feelings suited to romance, especially an idealized view of reality: *She liked to read of a romantic world of handsome heroes who did daring deeds.* **3** **Romantic** appealing to the emotions and the imagination as a subject or style of literature, art, and music. **ro·man′ti·cal·ly** *adv.*

Ro·man·ti·cism (rō man′tə siz′əm) *n* a style or movement in art, music, and literature that prevailed in western Europe in the late 1700s and early 1800s (the **Romantic period**), emphasizing individual inspiration and imagination. **ro·man′ti·cist** *n.*

ro·man·ti·cize (rō man′tə sīz′) *v* **ro·man·ti·cized, ro·man·ti·ciz·ing** make something seem better or more attractive than it really is: *He romanticized about his father's early life.*

Rom·a·ny (rom′ə nē) *n, pl* **Rom·a·nies** **1** a member of a nomadic people of Europe and N America, of Hindi origin. **2** the Hindi language of these people.

adj to do with the Gypsies, their customs, or their language.

Ro·me·o (rō′mē ō′) *n* a young, attractive man who is or appears to be passionately in love. <hero of Shakespeare's *Romeo and Juliet*>

romp (romp) *v* **1** play in a rough, boisterous way, especially as a child or animal. **2** proceed without much effort to achieve something: *romp to a 6–0 win.*
n **1** a short period of rough, lively play. **2** a swift and effortless victory: *win in a romp.* <Old French *romper* to climb> **romp′er** *n.*

romp·ers (romp′ərz) *pl n* a loose outer garment, worn by young children.

ron·do (ron′dō) *or* (ron dō′) *n, pl* **ron·dos** a musical composition or movement with one recurring principal theme. <Old French *rond* round>

roof (rūf) *n, pl* **roofs** or **rooves** **1** the structure that forms the upper covering of a building. **2** a thing that in form or position resembles this structure, such that of a cave, a motor vehicle, or the mouth.
v cover or form over with such a structure. <Old English *hrof*>
go through (or **hit**) **the roof,** *Informal* **a** be very angry or shocked: *She went through the roof when she learned I was leaving early.* **b** increase to an extremely high level: *Prices went through the roof.*
raise the roof, *Informal* create a disturbance, uproar, or confusion: *He raised the roof at not being selected for the volleyball team.*

roof·er (rū′fər) *n* a person who makes or repairs roofs.

roof·ing (rū′fing) *n* material used for roofs.

roof·less (rū′flis) *adj* **1** with no roof. **2** with no home or shelter.

roof·top (rūf′top′) *n* the top outer surface of a building's roof.

rook[1] (ru̇k) *n* a European crow that often nests in trees near buildings. <Old English *hroc*>

rook[2] (ru̇k) *n* a piece, shaped like a battlement, that is used in the game of chess. <Old French, from Arabic *rukk*>

rook·ie (ru̇k′ē) *Informal n* a beginner or new recruit, especially in the army, the police, or a sports team. <origin uncertain>

room (rūm) *n* **1** a part or division of a building, separated from other parts by a ceiling, floor, and walls. **2** the people present in a room: *The entire room burst into applause.* **3** the space occupied by, or available for, something: *There is little room to move in a crowd.* **4** scope or opportunity for something to happen or be done: *room for improvement, room for advancement.*
v **1** rent or occupy a room as accommodations in a house, apartment, or college residence: *The two girls roomed together.* **2** provide accommodations by renting a room. <Old English *rum*>

room·er (rū′mər) *n* a person who lives in a rented room or rooms in another's house.

room·ette (rū met′) *n* a small, single bedroom compartment in a railway car.

room·ful (rūm′fu̇l) *n, pl* **room·fuls** **1** enough to fill a room. **2** the people or things in a room.

room·ie (rūm′ē) *Informal n* a roommate.

rooming house *n* a house with rooms to rent as accommodations.

room·mate (rūm′māt′) *n* a person who shares a room with another or others.

room service *n* a service offered by a hotel by which one may order food or drink to be brought to one's room.

room·y (rū′mē) *adj* **room·i·er, room·i·est** with plenty of room, especially as accommodations. **room′i·ness** *n.*

roost (rūst) *n* a bar, pole, perch, or other surface on which birds rest or sleep, or where bats gather to rest during the day.
v settle or gather for rest or sleep, as birds and bats do. <Old English *hrost*>
come home to roost, have bad and unexpected consequences for the doer: *She has no close friends, so I guess her selfish habits have come home to roost.*
rule the roost, *Informal* have full power or control: *He ruled the roost in that household.*

roost·er (rū′stər) *n* a male CHICKEN.

root[1] (rūt) *n* **1 a** the part of a plant that grows downward to hold the plant in place, absorb water and mineral foods from the soil, and often to store food material. **b** this part of a plant when eaten as a vegetable. Carrots are roots. **2** the embedded part of a body organ or structure such as a hair, tooth, or nail. **3** the basic cause, source, or origin of something: *Lack of affection was the root of her unhappiness.* **4 roots** family, ethnic, or cultural origins, especially as the reason for one's devotion to a place or community: *Her roots were in the Maritimes and she often returned there.* **5** *Mathematics* **a** the quantity that produces another quantity when multiplied by itself a certain number of times. Example: $3 \times 3 = 9$, so the square root of 9 is 3. **b** the quantity that satisfies an equation when substituted for an unknown quantity. Example: In the equation $x^2 + 4x + 3 = 0$, $x = -1$ or $x = -3$, so -1 and -3 are the roots. **6** a word or word element from which others are derived. Example: *room* is the root of *roominess, roomie, and roomy.*
v **1** cause a plant or plant cutting to grow roots: *Some plants root more quickly than others.* **2** fix or be fixed firmly in one place: *She was rooted to the spot by surprise.* **3** establish or be established deeply and firmly: *He was rooted to his birthplace. My dislike of the town was rooted in bad experiences I'd had there.* <Old Norse *rot*>
root′like′ *adj.* **root′less** *adj.*
root out (or **up**), get rid of completely: *root out corruption in government.*
take root, a send out roots and begin to grow. **b** become firmly established.

root[2] (rūt) *v* **1** dig with the snout in search of food, as a pig does. **2** search carelessly or rummage through an untidy mass or area: *He rooted in the crammed drawer for a pair of socks.* <Old English *wrotan*>

a bat	e bed	i bid	o pot	u cup	th thin
ā cake	ē me	ī bite	ō go	ū rude	ᴛʜ then
ä bar	ə about	ər over	ȯ for	u̇ put	zh measure

R

root[3] (rūt) *Informal v* cheer for the success of a person or group engaged in a contest. <Old Norse *rauta* to roar>

root beer *n* a carbonated soft drink flavoured with the juice of the roots and bark of certain plants, such as sarsaparilla and sassafras.

root canal *n* **1** the central, pulp-filled cavity in the root of a tooth, containing blood vessels and nerves. **2** a dental treatment for an infected or damaged root canal.

root cellar *n* the part of a house or barn below ground level, used for storing root vegetables such as carrots by keeping them cool.

root crop *n* a crop grown for its edible underground parts, such as of beets, turnips, and carrots.

root hair *n* a hairlike outgrowth from a plant root that absorbs water and dissolved minerals from the soil.

root·let (rū′tlit) *n* a small branch of a root.

root·stock (rūt′stok′) a rhizome.

rooves (rūvz) a plural of ROOF.

rope (rōp) *n* **1** a strong, thick line or cord made by twisting smaller strands of material together. **2** a thing that resembles this, such as a number of things twisted or strung together: *a rope of pearls, a rope of onions.* **3 the rope** the legal sentence for someone to be put to death by hanging. **4 the ropes** *pl* the established ways of doing things in an organization or area of activity: *to know the ropes. She showed him the ropes on the first day of his job.*
v **roped, rop·ing 1** tie, bind, or fasten with a rope. **2** enclose or mark off with a rope or tape: *The police roped off the scene of the crime.* **3** catch a horse, steer, or other animal with a lasso. <Old English *rap*>
at the end of your rope (or **tether**), in a difficult situation in which you do not know what to do next. **rope in,** *Informal* persuade someone to take part in an activity.

rop·y (rō′pē) *adj* **rop·i·er, rop·i·est** like a rope or ropes in being long, strong, and fibrous, or in forming clinging threads or strands: *ropy chewing gum.* **rop′i·ness** *n.*

ror·qual (rȯr′kwəl) *n* a baleen whale with pleated skin on the underside. <French, from Old Norse *reythr*>

Ror·schach test (rȯr′shak) *Psychology n* a test that indicates personality traits, based on the subject's interpretation of a standard set of inkblot designs. Also called **inkblot test**. <H. *Rorschach*, 20c psychiatrist>

ro·sa·ceous (rō zā′shəs) *adj* to do with the rose family.

ro·sa·ry (rō′zə rē) *Catholicism n, pl* **ro·sa·ries 1** a series of linked and repeated short prayers. The praying person keeps count of them by means of a string of beads. **2** the string of beads used for this. <Latin *rosarium* rose garden, from *rosa* rose[1]. The rose garden is meant to convey the image of a garden of prayers.>

rose[1] (rōz) *n* **1** the usually fragrant flower of a thorny plant of northern temperate areas. The **wild rose** is the floral emblem of Alberta. **2** a thing shaped like or suggesting a rose, such as a card showing the points on a compass.
adj pinkish red. <Latin *rosa*> **rose′like′** *adj.*
come up roses, *Informal* go or turn out extremely well: *Everything came up roses after she passed all her exams.*

rose[2] (rōz) past tense of RISE.

ro·sé (rō zā′) *n* a light pink wine. <French = pink>

ro·se·ate (rō′zē it) *or* (rō′zē āt′) *adj* partly pink in colour.

rose·bud (rōz′bud′) *n* the bud of a rose.

rose·bush (rōz′bu̇sh′) *n* a shrub or bush that bears roses.

rose–col·oured or **rose–col·ored** (rōz′kul′ərd) *adj* **1** pinkish red. **2** naively optimistic: *At first she viewed her job through rose-coloured glasses.*

rose·hip (rōz′hip) *n* the pod containing the ripe seed of a rosebush. Rosehips are used to make herbal tea.

rose·mary (rōz′mer′ē) *n, pl* **rose·mar·ies** an evergreen shrub whose fragrant leaves are used as a herb in cooking and in making perfume. See HERB for picture.

rose of Sharon (shar′ən) *or* (sher′ən) *n* a shrub with dense foliage and large, bell-shaped flowers.

Ro·set·ta stone (rō zet′ə) *n* an inscribed stone found in 1799 on the Nile River in Egypt. Its hieroglyphic script was deciphered and compared to its two other scripts, helping scholars interpret other ancient texts.

ro·sette (rō zet′) *n* an ornament, object, or arrangement shaped like a rose, such as a ribbon given as a prize, or a carved or moulded ornament of a building.

rose·water (rōz′wo′tər) *n* water made fragrant with oil from rose petals, used in making perfumes and sometimes in cooking.

rose window *n* a circular window with a pattern of small sections that radiate from a centre.

rose·wood (rō′zwu̇d′) *n* a reddish wood used in making furniture and musical instruments.

Rosh Ha·sha·na (rosh′hə shä′nə) *Judaism n* the Jewish New Year festival, falling usually in late September. <Hebrew = head of the year>

ro·shi (rō′shē) *Buddhism n* the spiritual leader of a group of Zen Buddhists.

ros·i·ly (rō′zə lē) *adv* **1** with a rosy tinge or colour. **2** hopefully and optimistically.

ros·in (roz′ən) *n* a hard, yellow substance extracted from pine resin that in powdered form is used for rubbing on the bows of musical instruments and to keep acrobats' and boxers' shoes from slipping.
v cover or rub with rosin. <Latin *resina*>

ros·ter (ros′tər) *n* **1** a list or plan that shows the names of individuals or groups in an organization and the times of duties assigned to them. **2** a list of members of a team or organization, especially a sports team: *He did badly in the first two games and was cut from the roster.* <Dutch *rooster* grating, because the lined paper that a list was written on resembled a grid>

ros·trum (ros′trəm) *n, pl* **ros·trums** or **ros·tra** (-trə) **1** a raised platform on which a person stands to make a public speech, receive an award or medal, play music, or conduct an orchestra or band. **2** a beaklike projection on an animal, especially a stiff snout or forward extension of the head. <Latin = beak. The speaker's platform in a Roman forum was decorated with the beaks of captured war galleys.>

ros·y (rō′zē) *adj* **ros·i·er, ros·i·est** 1 pinkish red, often considered to indicate health, youth, or embarrassment. 2 hopeful and optimistic: *She had a rosy view of her prospects.* 3 easy and pleasant: *a rosy future.* **ros′i·ness** *n.*

rot (rot) *v* **rot·ted, rot·ting** 1 decay or spoil through the action of bacteria and fungi. 2 cause to decay. 3 gradually lose vigour due to neglect or mismanagement: *At the board meeting, some parents argued that the education system had been allowed to rot.*
n 1 the process of decaying. 2 rotten or decayed matter. 3 a fungal or bacterial disease that causes tissue deterioration in plants and animals. 4 *Informal* nonsense or foolish talk. <Old English *rotian*>

ro·ta·ry (rō′tə rē) *adj* 1 turning around a centre or axis. 2 acting, especially as a machine, through the rotation of some part: *a rotary engine.*

ro·tate (rō′tāt) *or* (rō tāt′) *v* **ro·tat·ed, ro·tat·ing** 1 move or cause to move around a centre or axis, such as a wheel, a top, or the earth does. 2 change or cause to change in a regularly recurring order: *The farmer rotated crops of corn and field peas.* <Latin *rota* wheel>

ro·ta·tion (rō tā′shən) *n* 1 the act or process of moving around a centre or axis: *The earth's rotation causes night and day.* 2 a change in a regular recurring order. 3 a system of changing in regular succession: *The job of classroom roll call is done in rotation.* **ro·ta′tion·al** *adj.*

ro·ta·tor (rō′tā tər) *n* 1 a person who or thing that rotates. 2 a muscle whose contraction turns a part of the body.

rotator cuff *n* the group of tendons that supports the arm at the shoulder joint.

ro·ta·vi·rus (rō′ta vī′rəs) *Biology n* any of a group of wheel-shaped RNA viruses, some of which cause gastroenteritis. <Latin *rota* wheel + virus>

rote (rōt) *adj, n* a set, mechanical way of doing things: *rote learning.* <Middle English>
by rote, by memory without thought of the meaning: *to learn a lesson by rote.*

ro·ti (rō′tē) *n* a pancake of unleavened bread, rolled around a spicy filling of meat or vegetables and chick peas. <Hindi *roti* bread>

ro·ti·fer (rō′tə fər) *n* a tiny water animal that has one or more rings of CILIA on a disc at one end of the body by which it swims and feeds. <Latin *rota* wheel + *ferre* carry>

ro·ti·ni (rō tē′nē) *n* pasta in the shape of spirals. <Italian>

ro·tis·se·rie (rō tis′ə rē) *n* a rotating spit used in an oven, under a broiler, or over an open fire, for roasting meat or poultry. <French *rôtir* to roast>

ro·tor (rō′tər) *n* 1 the rotating part of a machine or motor vehicle. 2 a system of rotating blades by which a helicopter is enabled to fly. <*rotator*>

ro·to·till·er (rō′tō til′ər) *n* a garden tool with motorized rotating blades for breaking up the soil. **ro′to·till** *v.*

rot·ten (rot′ən) *adj* 1 decayed or spoiled: *a rotten egg.* 2 foul or disgusting: *rotten air.* 3 corrupt or dishonest: *rotten government.* 4 *Informal* bad or highly unsatisfactory: *rotten luck, to feel rotten.* **rot′ten·ly** *adv.* **rot′ten·ness** *n.*

Rott·wei·ler (rot′wī lər) *n* a large, powerful dog of a breed with a short tail and a coat of coarse black hair with tan markings. <*Rottweil*, a town in southwest Germany where the dog was originally bred>

ro·tund (rō tund′) *adj* 1 large and plump. 2 sounding or seeming rich and full: *a rotund voice.* <Latin *rota* wheel> **ro·tund′i·ty** *n.* **ro·tund′ly** *adv.*

ro·tun·da (rō tun′də) *n* a circular building or room in a building, especially one with a dome. <Italian, from Latin *rota* wheel>

rouge (rūzh) *n* 1 a reddish powder, paste, or liquid for colouring the cheeks or lips. 2 a red powder, chiefly ferric oxide, used for polishing metal or jewels. 3 🍁 *Football* a point scored when a ball kicked into the end zone is not run back into the playing area by the defending team.
v **rouged, roug·ing** colour with rouge. <French = red>

rough (ruf) *adj* 1 with an uneven or irregular surface: *a tree with rough bark.* 2 without luxury and ease: *a rough life in the bush.* 3 not completed or perfected, and only as a preliminary draft or try: *a rough sketch, a rough idea.* 4 coarse or tangled: *a dog with a rough coat of hair.* 5 rude and likely to offend others: *rough manners.* 6 disorderly or prone to violence: *a rough crowd.* 7 unpleasant or severe: *She was in for a rough time.* 8 stormy or violently disturbed or agitated: *rough weather, a rough sea.* 9 sharp and harsh to the taste: *rough cider.*
n 1 a preliminary sketch or design: *First, make a quick rough of your drawing.* 2 *Golf* ground where there is long grass around the fairway and the green: *The ball landed in the rough.*
adv Informal in a harsh or violent manner: *Those kids play too rough for me.* <Old English *ruh*> **rough′ness** *n.*
(a diamond) in the rough, not polished or refined: *He's a diamond in the rough, but kind-hearted.*
rough in, shape or sketch roughly, or do the first part of: *rough in the outlines of a face. The work crew have roughed in the plumbing for a bathroom in the basement.*
rough it, live without comforts and conveniences.
rough out, make a preliminary sketch or version of something.
rough up, beat or assault someone.

SYNONYMS

Rough can mean "bumpy" or "uneven": *The back roads are rough, so get ready for a bouncy ride.*

Coarse can mean "rough in texture": *The coarse scrubber was perfect for cleaning the barbecue.*

Jagged means "with sharp points": *The bread knife had a jagged blade.*

Turbulent can mean "rough," but usually refers to the movement of water: *The river was turbulent where the banks narrowed and the rapids began.*

a bat	e bed	i bid	o pot	u cup	th thin
ā cake	ē me	ī bite	ō go	ū rude	ᴛʜ then
ȧ bar	ə about	ər over	ȯ for	ů put	zh measure

rough·age (ruf′ij) *n* the coarse, fibrous parts or kinds of food that aid the movement of food and waste products through the intestines.

rough–and–read·y (ruf′ən red′ē) *adj* rough and crude, but good enough for the purpose.

rough–and–tum·ble (ruf′ən tum′bəl) *n* a situation without rules or organization, typically showing boisterousness or violence.

rough·en (ruf′ən) *v* make or become rough.

rough–hewn (ruf′hyūn′) *adj* shaped with a tool such as an axe without smoothing afterwards.

rough·house (ruf′hous′) *Informal n* rough play or rowdy conduct.
v **rough·housed, rough·hous·ing** act or treat someone in a rough or rowdy way.

rough·ing (ruf′ing) *Hockey, Football, etc. n* the unnecessary or excessive use of force on another player: *He got a penalty for roughing.*

rough·ly (ruf′lē) *adv* **1** in a harsh or violent manner. **2** lacking refinement or precision: *a roughly built chimney.* **3** approximately: *It's roughly a hundred kilometres from Calgary to Drumheller..*

rough·neck (ruf′nek′) *Informal n* **1** a rough, bad-mannered person. **2** a member of an oil-drilling crew.

rough·rid·er (ruf′rī′dər) *n* **1** a person used to rough, hard riding of horses. **2** a person who breaks in and rides wild horses.

rough·shod (ruf′shod′) *adj* **1** with horseshoes that have nail heads to prevent slipping. **1** to do with brutal force.
ride roughshod over someone, treat someone with disrespect or brutality.

rou·lette (rū let′) *n* **1** a gambling game in which a turn of a wheel drops a ball into a numbered compartment. Players bet on the number on which the ball comes to rest. **2** a small wheel with sharp teeth for making lines of marks, dots, or perforations. <French = little wheel>

round (round) *adj* **1** shaped like a ball, ring, sphere, or cylinder, with a circular or curved outline or surface: *a round table. The picture made her look short and round.* **2** full or complete: *a round dozen.* **3** altered to express or calculate a number conveniently. Example: 3974 in round numbers would be 4000. **4** plainly expressed or frank: *The boy's mother scolded him in good round terms.* **5** with a full, mellow tone: *to speak with round vowels.*
n **1** a thing shaped like a ball, circle, or cylinder, especially a circular piece of something: *He cut the pastry into rounds, a round of beef.* **2 a** a fixed course ending where it begins: *The security guard makes rounds of the building every hour.* **b** the action of visiting each of a number of people or places: *The doctor made his rounds of the hospital ward.* **3** a sequence of related or regularly recurring actions or events: *a round of duties, a round of drinks.* **4** a measured quantity, division, or number of something: *a round of a boxing match, a round of cards.* **5** an action that a number of people do together: *a round of applause, a round of cheers.* **6** a dance in which the dancers move in a circle. **7** a short song, sung by several people or groups beginning one after the other.
v **1** make or become round: *The carpenter rounded the corners of the table.* **2** go wholly or partly around, especially to move in a changed direction: *The car rounded the corner. The bear rounded and faced the hunters.* **3** (*often with* ***up, down,*** *or* ***off***) alter a number to a number more convenient to express or to calculate. Example: rounding 87 to the nearest ten gives 90. **4** speak a vowel with a narrowed, circular opening of the lips: *She rounds all her vowels.*
adv **1** with a circular motion: *The wheels went round.* **2** from one to another: *A rumour is going round that the school will close early today.* **3** through a set period of time: *Summer will soon come round again.* **4** without any particular purpose: *I am just looking round.* **5** for all: *There is just enough cake to go round.*
prep **1** on all sides of: *Bullets whistled round him, but he was not hit.* **2** so as to surround: *They built a fence round the yard.* **3** following a somewhat circular route past a corner or obstacle: *She walked round the corner.* **4** to or in all or various parts of: *We took our cousins round the town. There are Canada Post mailboxes all round the city.* **5** about or around: *Stand still and look round you.* <Latin *rotundus* round> **round′ness** *n.*
get (or **come**) **round someone,** persuade or outwit a person, especially through begging or flattery: *He got round my bad temper by praising my cooking.*
go the rounds, be passed, told, or shown by many people from one to another.
round and about, in various places.
round off, finish or complete: *to round off a meal with dessert.*
round on, turn so as to attack, either physically or verbally: *The dog rounded on the cat. He rounded on me for not doing enough work.*
round out, complete: *round out a paragraph, round out a career.*
round up, draw or drive together: *round up the cattle.*

GRAMMAR AND USAGE

In Canada, especially in speech and written dialogue, there is a preference for **around** rather than **round** as an adverb and a preposition:

Let's take a look around. (adverb)
They went around the block a few times. (adjective)

Round in such cases can have a more formal or literary flavour.

round·a·bout (round′ə bout′) *adj* indirect: *a roundabout route. I heard about it in a roundabout way.*
n UK a merry-go-round.

round·house (round′hous′) *n* **1** a circular building for storing or repairing locomotives, that is built about a huge turntable. **2** a cabin on the after part of a ship's deck.
adj with a wide, sweeping motion of the arm: *a roundhouse swing.*

round·ish (roun′dish) *adj* somewhat round.

round·ly (roun′dlē) *adv* **1** plainly or bluntly: *to scold roundly.* **2** thoroughly: *to refuse roundly.* **3** in a circular or roughly circular shape: *a roundly built snow fort.*

round number *n* a number in even tens or multiples of tens.

round robin *n* a petition with the signatures written in a circle, so that one cannot tell who signed first.

round–shoul·dered (round′shōl′dərd) *adj* with the shoulders bent forward so that the back is rounded.

round table *n* a small group of people gathered for an informal discussion.

Round Table *n* the legendary table around which King Arthur and his knights sat.

round–the–clock (round′ᴛʜə klok′) *adj* happening twenty-four hours a day: *round-the-clock nursing care.*

round trip *n* a trip to a place and back again.

round·up (roun′dup′) *n* **1** the act of driving or bringing cattle or horses together from long distances. **2** the people and livestock that take part in a roundup. **3** a systematic gathering together of people or things: *a roundup of criminals, a roundup of late news.*

round·worm (roun′dwərm′) *n* a unsegmented worm that has a long, round body, especially a parasitic one that lives in the intestines of mammals.

rouse (rouz) *v* **roused, rous·ing** **1** wake from sleep: *I was roused by the telephone.* **2** stir up or excite: *She was roused to anger by the insult.* <Middle English> **rous′er** *n.*

rous·ing (rou′zing) *adj* filling people with enthusiasm and energy: *a rousing speech, a rousing game.*

roust·a·bout (rou′stə bout′) *n* an unskilled or casual labourer. <*roust + about*>

rout[1] (rout) *n* **1** a disorderly retreat of defeated troops: *The enemy's retreat soon became a rout.* **2** a complete defeat.
v **1** defeat and cause to retreat in disorder: *The knights on horseback routed the foot soldiers.* **2** defeat completely: *The team routed its opponents by a score of 10 to 1.* <Old French, from Latin *rumpere* to break>

rout[2] (rout) *v* **1** cut grooves in or gouge out wood or metal. **2** ROOT[2]. <*root*[2]>

route (rüt) *or* (rout) *n* **1** a way taken or set to get from one place to another: *a bus route. Will you go to the coast by the northern route?* **2** a fixed, regular course or area assigned to a person in performing a task: *a newspaper route.* **3** a method or process leading to a specified result: *She described what she called the route to health.*
v **rout·ed, rout·ing** arrange or send by a specified route: *The bus was routed by way of the detour.* <Old French, from Latin *rumpere* to break, suggesting something (a path for example) that has been broken in through use>

rout·er (rou′tər) *n* a tool or machine for cutting grooves in or gouging out wood or metal.

rou·tine (rü tēn′) *n* **1** a fixed, regular series of actions or method of doing things: *Getting up and going to bed are parts of our daily routine.* **2** a set sequence in a performance, such as a dance or comedy act. **3** a sequence of instructions for performing a task in a software program.
adj **1** performing actions as part of a regular procedure or process: *routine methods, a routine operation.* **2** average or ordinary: *a routine show with routine performances.* <See ROUTE.> **rou·tine′ly** *adv.*

rove (rōv) *v* **roved, rov·ing** wander, or wander through or over something: *She loved to rove over the fields and woods. He roved the streets late at night.* <origin uncertain>

rov·er (rō′vər) *n* **1** a wanderer or roamer. **2** *Sports* a player who holds no special position but who may rove over the entire field. **3** a vehicle for driving over rough terrain, especially terrain on another planet, often operated by remote control.

row[1] (rō) *n* **1** a number of people or things in a straight or horizontal line: *The children stood in a row. We sat in the middle of the front row.* **2** a street with a continuous line of buildings on either side. <Old English *raw*>
hard (or **tough**) **row to hoe,** *Informal* a series of difficult tasks to do or problems to endure.
in a row, one right after another: *I made six calls in a row.*

row[2] (rō) *v* **1** move or move a boat by the use of oars: *They rowed back and forth. They rowed the dinghy across to the island.* **2** carry in a rowboat: *We were rowed to the shore.*
n **1** the act of using oars. **2** a trip in a rowboat: *We went for a row at sunset.* <Old English *rowan*> **row′er** *n.* **row′ing** *n.*

row[3] (rou) *n* **1** a noisy quarrel or disturbance: *The three children had a row over the bicycle.* **2** a loud noise or uproar.
v have a quarrel. <origin uncertain>

row·an (rou′ən) *or* (rō′ən) *n* the mountain ash, or its orange-red berries.

row·boat (rō′bōt′) *n* a small boat moved by oars.

row·dy (rou′dē) *n, pl* **row·dies** a noisy and disorderly person.
adj **row·di·er, row·di·est** noisy and disorderly. **row′di·ness** *n.*

row·dy·ism (rou′dē iz′əm) *n* noisy, disorderly conduct.

row house *n* one of several houses built together in a row and making up one frontage.

rowing machine *n* an exercise machine with a sliding seat, two handles like oars, and a place to brace the feet, on which a person can carry out the movements of rowing so as to exercise the arms and abdomen.

roy·al (roi′əl) *adj* **1** with the status of a king or queen, or a member of his or her family. **2** belonging to or exercised by a king or queen: *royal power, a royal command.* **3** favoured or encouraged by a king or queen: *a royal academy.* **4** suitable for a king or queen: *a royal welcome.*
n Informal a member of a royal family: *She liked to read about the royals.* <Old French, from Latin *regis* king> **roy′al·ly** *adv.*

🍁 **royal assent** *n* the signature of the Governor General or a lieutenant-governor, giving approval to a bill that has been passed by Parliament or by a legislative assembly, making it officially a law.

royal blue *adj* deep, rich, bright blue.

🍁 **Royal Canadian Legion** *n* an organization of Canadian former military personnel, especially war veterans.

🍁 **Royal Canadian Mounted Police** *n* the federal police force of Canada. *Abbrev.* **RCMP** or **R.C.M.P.**

a bat	e bed	i bid	o pot	u cup	th **thin**
ā cake	ē me	ī bite	ō go	ü rude	ᴛʜ **then**
ä bar	ə about	ər over	ô for	u̇ put	zh measure

R

🍁 **royal commission** *n* an investigation by a person or persons commissioned by the Crown to inquire into some matter on behalf of the Federal Government or a provincial government, and to make a report on it.

royal flush *n* a straight flush in poker, consisting of the ace, king, queen, jack, and ten of the same suit.

roy·al·ist (roi′ə list) *n* a supporter of a king or queen, or of a royal government.

royal jelly *n* a sticky, highly nutritious substance secreted by worker honey bees, fed to larvae that are being raised as potential queen bees.

roy·al·ty (roi′əl tē) *n, pl* **roy·al·ties** **1** people who belong to a royal family and have royal rank or status. **2** the status or power of a king or queen. **3** a share of receipts or profits paid to an owner of a patent or copyright, or of a property that produces minerals, oil, or natural gas.

🍁 **RRSP** *n* in full, **Registered Retirement Savings Plan** a savings plan that has certain income tax benefits.

RSI repetitive strain injury.

RSVP or **R.S.V.P.** please reply. <French *répondez s'il vous plaît*>

rub (rub) *v* **rubbed, rub·bing** **1** move one thing back and forth against another or together: *Rub your hands to warm them.* **2** move one's hand or an object over a surface: *The nurse rubbed my sore back.* **3** press or grind while moving back and forth: *That door rubs on the floor.* **4** make or bring to some condition by pressure from a hand, cloth, or other object: *to rub silver bright, to rub your skin off. The new shoes rubbed her heels.* **5** keep going with difficulty: *Money is scarce, but we shall rub along.*
n **1** the action or process of rubbing: *Give the silver a rub with this cloth.* **2** an ointment designed to be rubbed on the skin to ease pain. **3 the rub** a difficulty, especially the most important one in a situation: *I didn't have money to go to the game. That was the rub.* <Middle English>
rub down, rub or massage the body.
rub it in, *Informal* keep on mentioning something unpleasant.
rub off, remove or be removed by rubbing.
rub off on, a be transferred to another surface by rubbing against it: *A bit of paint from the wall rubbed off on my sleeve.* **b** become part of one's character through contact with another person: *Maybe some of his cheerful optimism will rub off on my mom.*
rub out, a erase or be erased. **b** *Slang* kill.
rub someone's face (or **nose**) **in it,** *Informal* remind someone of his or her failure, loss, or offence: *OK, so I'm lousy at volleyball; you don't have to rub my face in it.*
rub the right (or **wrong**) **way,** please (or irritate).

SYNONYMS

Rub means "move back and forth with pressure or friction": *He rubbed the stain on his shirt with soap.*

Massage means "knead the body's muscles and joints": *She massaged her calves before starting to run.*

Wipe means "rub with paper, cloth, etc. to make clean or dry": *Please wipe the dishes after washing them.*

rub·ber[1] (rub′ər) *n* **1** a tough elastic substance obtained from the milky juice of a tropical plant, or by a chemical process. **2** a thing made from this or a similar substance, such as that used to erase pencil marks. **3** a person who or thing that rubs. **4 rubbers** *pl* rubber boots or overshoes.
adj made of rubber: *a rubber tire.* <*rub*> **rub′ber·like′** *adj.*

rub·ber[2] (rub′ər) *n* in card games, a series of two games out of three, or three games out of five, won by the same side. <origin uncertain>

rubber band *n* an ELASTIC (def. 1).

rubber cement *n* a quick-drying adhesive consisting of rubber dissolved in a solvent.

rub·ber–chick·en circuit (rub′ər chi′kən) *Informal n* a series of events at which an after-dinner speaker is typically booked to speak.

rub·ber·ize (rub′ə rīz′) *v* **rub·ber·ized, rub·ber·iz·ing** cover or coat with RUBBER[1] (def. 1).

rub·ber·neck (rub′ər nek′) *Informal n* a person who turns or pauses to stare at something: *The traffic is being held up by all the rubbernecks gaping at the accident.*
v turn or pause and stare.

rubber plant *n* **1** a plant that yields RUBBER[1] (def. 1). **2** an evergreen tree of the fig family that has shiny, leathery leaves and is used as an ornamental house plant.

rubber stamp *n* **1** a handheld device that inks or imprints a message or design on a surface. **2** *Informal* a person who or group that approves or endorses something without thought or without power to refuse. **rubber-stamp** *v.*

rubber tree *n* a tropical tree that yields a milky liquid (latex) that is a source of rubber.

rub·ber·y (rub′ə rē) *adj* like rubber in being tough and elastic.

rub·bing (rub′ing) *n* **1** the action of rubbing something. **2** an image of an engraved or textured surface, such as a brass inscription or rock carving, made by rubbing a pencil, coloured wax, or chalk over a piece of paper placed over the surface.

rub·bish (rub′ish) *n* **1** waste or discarded material: *After the picnic we gathered up the rubbish.* **2** absurd or nonsensical words or thoughts. <origin uncertain>

rub·ble (rub′əl) *n* rough, broken stones, bricks, plaster, and cement, especially from collapsed or demolished buildings. <origin uncertain>

🍁 **rub·by** (rub′ē) *Slang n, pl* **rub·bies** an alcoholic derelict who often drinks rubbing alcohol. <*rubbing alcohol*>

rub·down (rub′doun′) *n* a massage or rubbing of the body.

ru·bel·la (rū be′lə) *n* a mild, contagious viral infection that causes low fever, headache, and a red rash. It is dangerous to women in pregnancy as it may cause serious damage to the fetus. Also called **German measles.** <Latin>

ru·bi·cund (rū′bə kund′) *adj* reddish or ruddy: *a rubicund face.*

ru·bid·i·um (rū bid′ē əm) *n* a soft, silver-white metallic element resembling potassium. *Symbol* **Rb**

ru·bric (rū′brik) *n* **1** a subtitle or heading on a document. **2** a written direction on how to follow a religious service.

3 a statement of purpose or function. **4** a scoring guide for evaluating student work. Rubrics give definitions of quality work, criteria for measuring quality work, and a scoring method (using numbers or language) to indicate level of performance. <Old French, from Latin *rubeus* red. Titles on documents used to be printed or underlined in red ink.>

ru·by (rü′bē) *n, pl* **ru·bies** a clear, hard, precious stone of a colour from deep red to pale pink.
adj deep, glowing red: *ruby lips, ruby wine.* <Old French, from Latin *rubeus* red> **ru′bylike′** *adj.*

ruck (ruk) *n* **1** a tightly packed crowd of people **2 the ruck** a great mass of ordinary people or things. <Middle English>

ruck·sack (ruk′sak′) *n* a backpack made of a strong, waterproof material and often used by hikers. <German *Rücken* back + *Sack* bag>

ruck·us (ruk′əs) *Informal n* a noisy disturbance or uproar. <*ruc(tion)* + *(rump)us*>

ruc·tion (ruk′shən) *Informal n* a disturbance or quarrel. <origin uncertain>

rud·der (rud′ər) *n* **1** a hinged, flat piece of wood or metal at the stern of a boat or ship, by which it is steered. **2** a similar piece in an aircraft or dirigible. See AILERON for picture. <Old English *rothor* paddle> **rud′der·less** *adj.*

rud·dy (rud′ē) *adj* **rud·di·er, rud·di·est** with a healthy red or reddish colour: *a ruddy glow, ruddy cheeks.* <Old English *rudig*> **rud′di·ness** *n.*

rude (rüd) *adj* **rud·er, rud·est 1** impolite or ill-mannered: *She said it was rude to stare at people.* **2** roughly made or done: *rude tools.* **3** startling and abrupt: *a rude awakening.* **4** vigorous and hearty: *rude good health.* <Latin *rudis* unlearned> **rude′ly** *adv.* **rude′ness** *n.*

ru·di·ment (rü′də mənt) *n* **1** the basic principle of a subject or part to be learned first: *the rudiments of music.* **2** a thing in a simple or primitive form: *rudiments of a furnace.* **3** an organ or part incompletely developed in size or structure, especially of an animal. <Latin *rudis* unlearned>

ru·di·men·ta·ry (rü′də men′tə rē) *or* (rü′də men′trē) *adj* **1** basic and to be learned or studied first: *rudimentary facts.* **2** in an early stage of development: *The wings on a baby chick are only rudimentary.*

rue[1] (rü) *v* **rued, ru·ing** bitterly regret: *She will rue the day she insulted her friend.* <Old English *hreow* repentance>

rue[2] (rü) *n* an evergreen shrub with leaves that have a strong smell and a bitter taste. <Old French, from Greek *rhute*>

rue·ful (rü′fəl) *adj* expressing sorrow or regret in a slightly humorous way: *a rueful expression.* **rue′ful·ly** *adv.* **rue′ful·ness** *n.*

ruff (ruf) *n* **1** a deep, stiff, starched frill, worn around the neck by men and women in the 1500s. **2** a collarlike growth of long or specially marked feathers or hairs on the neck of a bird or animal. <*ruffle*>

ruffed grouse (ruft) *n* a N American game bird with a tuft of black feathers on each side of the neck.

ruf·fi·an (ruf′ē ən) *n* a rough, brutal, or violent person. <Old French, from Italian> **ruf′fi·an·ism** *n.* **ruf′fi·an·ly** *adj.*

ruf·fle[1] (ruf′əl) *v* **ruf·fled, ruf·fling 1** make or become rough, uneven, or disarranged: *The hen ruffled her feathers at the sight of the dog. She ruffled his hair affectionately.* **2** disturb the surface of something: *A breeze ruffled the lake.* **3** disconcert or upset someone: *Nothing can ruffle her calm temper.*
n **1** a roughness or unevenness in some surface. **2** a strip of cloth, ribbon, or lace gathered along one edge and used for trimming clothes. <Middle English>

rug (rug) *n* **1** a small carpet: *scatter rugs.* **2** a thick, heavy cloth used for warmth as a covering: *We wrapped a woollen rug around ourselves when we went riding in the horse and sleigh.* <Scandinavian>

Rucks are used in the game of **rugby** to put the ball back into play after a tackle. When a player is tackled to the ground, he or she must release the ball, which must not be handled by any of the players. Instead they use their feet to heel the ball backward. If a player fails to release the ball when tackled to the ground, a penalty is awarded to the opposing team.

A player must join a ruck from behind the back foot of the last player and bind properly with the whole arm around a teammate. Joining from a side position is penalized.

a ruck

rug·by (rug′bē) *n* a game played by teams of thirteen or fifteen players who kick or pass an oval ball toward the opposing team's goal. <*Rugby*, a school for boys in Rugby, England, where the game was first played>

rug·ged (rug′id) *adj* **1** broken, rocky, and uneven as ground or terrain. **2** strong, vigorous, and sturdy: *The pioneers were rugged people.* **3** strong and irregular as facial features: *rugged good looks.* **4** designed as a machine or device to withstand rough handling: *a rugged car.* **5** requiring toughness and determination: *a rugged adventure.* <Old Norse> **rug′ged·ly** *adv.* **rug′ged·ness** *n.*

a bat	e bed	i bid	o pot	u cup	th **thin**
ā cake	ē me	ī bite	ō go	ü rude	ᴛʜ **then**
ä bar	ə about	ər over	ȯ for	ů put	zh measure

ru·in (rūʹən) *n* **1** a building, wall, or other structure that has fallen to pieces: *That ruin was once a famous castle.* **2** the severe damage or destruction of a person's assets, life, or reputation: *His enemies plotted his ruin.* **3** a condition of destruction, decay, or downfall: *The house had gone to ruin.* **4** the cause of destruction, decay, or downfall: *Heavy drinking was his ruin.*
v **1** make a place, structure, or building fall to pieces. **2** have a disastrous effect on. **3** cause to severely damage or destroy a person's assets, life, or reputation. <Old French, from Latin *ruere* to fall> **ru'in·a'tion** *n.*

SYNONYMS

Ruin means "severely damage or destroy": *The carpet was ruined when the workers knocked over the can of paint.*

Destroy suggests complete obliteration: *The storm destroyed everything in its path.*

Shatter means "break into pieces": *The glass shattered when it fell to the floor.*

ru·in·ous (rūʹə nəs) *adj* **1** bringing ruin or causing destruction. **2** fallen into ruins: *a building in ruinous condition.* **3** costing far more than can be afforded: *a ruinous expense.* **ru'in·ous·ly** *adv.*

rule (rūl) *n* **1** a statement, law, or principle of what to do and not to do within a particular field: *We understood the rules of the game.* **2** control or government of an area or people. **3** a period of power of a ruler: *The Act was passed during the rule of Queen Victoria.* **4** a regular or customary way something happens or is done: *Fair weather is the rule in summer.* **5** a strip of wood, metal, or plastic used for measuring length or marking straight lines. **6** a printed line. **7** a set of regulations, especially in a religious community: *monastic rule.*
v **ruled, rul·ing** **1** make a formal decision: *The judge ruled against them.* **2** exercise a dominant authority, control, or influence: *She tries to rule her family as a dictator rules a nation.* **3** have a powerful and restricting influence: *Her entire life was ruled by her emotions.* **4** make parallel lines across paper or other surface. <Old French, from Latin *regere* guide> **rul'a·ble** *adj.*
as a rule, usually, but not always.
rule of thumb, a rule based on experience or practice rather than on scientific knowledge.
rule out, decide against or exclude.
work to rule, perform only the duties required by a contract, with no overtime or extra effort, as a form of labour protest: *The teachers were working to rule, so there were no extracurricular activities.*

rul·er (rūʹlər) *n* **1** a person who has authority or control, especially as the head of a government. **2** a straight strip of wood, metal, or plastic marked in units, such as centimetres, and used in drawing lines or in measuring.

rul·ing (rūʹling) *n* a decision or pronouncement of a judge, court, or other authority.
adj governing or controlling.

rum (rum) *n* an alcoholic liquor made from sugar cane or molasses. <origin uncertain>

rum·ba (rumʹbə) *n* a rhythmic dance in quadruple time that originated in Cuba, or the music for such a dance. <Spanish>

rum·ble (rumʹbəl) *v* **rum·bled, rum·bling** **1** make a deep, heavy, continuous sound, like that of thunder. **2** move with such a sound, especially by a large vehicle. **3** utter in a deep, resonant way. **4** *Informal* take part in a street fight between gangs or groups.
n **1** a deep, heavy, continuous sound. **2** *Informal* a street fight between gangs or groups. <Middle English>

rumble seat an uncovered passenger seat that opens out of the rear of an automobile.

rum·bling (rumʹbling) *n* **1** a deep, loud, continuous sound. **2 rumblings** *pl* early signs or rumours of dissatisfaction or impending changes: *There were rumblings of the general strike earlier in the year.*
adj making or consisting of a deep, loud, continuous sound: *a rumbling train.*

ru·men (rūʹmən) *n, pl* **ru·mi·na** (rūʹmə nə) the first stomach of an animal that chews its cud. <Latin = throat>

ru·mi·nant (rūʹmə nənt) *n* an animal that chews its cud, such as a cow, sheep, or camel.
adj to do with such an animal.

ru·mi·nate (rūʹmə nātʹ) *v* **ru·mi·nat·ed, ru·mi·nat·ing** **1** think long and deeply about something: *She ruminated on the strange events of the past week.* **2** chew the cud. <Latin *ruminare* chew again, from *rumen* throat> **ru'min·a'tion** *n.*

ru·mi·na·tive (rūʹmə nə tiv) *or* (rūʹmə nāʹtiv) *adj* deeply thoughtful.

rum·mage (rumʹij) *v* **rum·maged, rum·mag·ing** search untidily or unsystematically in something, or find something in this way: *I rummaged in my drawer for a pair of socks.*
n an untidy or unsystematic search in something. <Old French *arumer* stow in a ship's hold>

rummage sale *n* a sale of odds and ends, usually held to raise money for charity.

rum·my (rumʹē) *n* a card game in which points are scored by forming sets of three or four cards of the same rank, or sequences of three or more of the same suit. <origin uncertain>

ru·mour or **ru·mor** (rūʹmər) *n* a story or statement talked of as news without any proof that it is true: *The rumour spread that a new mall would be built here.*
v **be rumoured** tell or spread by rumour: *It's rumoured that she's moving to a new school.* <Old French, from Latin *rumor* noise>

rump (rump) *n* **1** the hind part of the body of an animal, where the legs join the back. **2** the buttocks. <Old Norse>

rum·ple (rumʹpəl) *v* **rum·pled, rum·pling** give a creased, ruffled, or untidy appearance to: *to rumple a bed.*
n a creased, ruffled, or untidy appearance. <Dutch>

rum·pus (rumʹpəs) *Informal n* a noisy disturbance or uproar. <origin uncertain>

rumpus room REC ROOM.

rum–run·ner (rumʹrunʹər) *n* a person who or a ship that smuggles alcohol to a place. **rum'-run'ning** *n.*

run (run) *v* **ran, run, run·ning 1 a** move the legs quickly, faster than walking and never having both feet on the ground at the same time: *She ran to the gate to greet him.* **b** cause to move like this: *to run a horse up and down.* **c** move in a way that suggests this, or in a hurried or hectic manner: *to run errands. We ran around all day looking for the perfect gift.* **2** pass or cause to pass quickly: *A thought ran through my mind.* **3** move or cause to move somewhere forcefully or with a particular result: *The ship ran aground.* **4** grow or extend in a particular way: *Vines ran along the sides of the road. Shelves ran along the walls.* **5** flow as a liquid: *running water. The colours ran when the blanket was washed.* **6** make a regular trip on a particular route: *The buses are running on time.* **7** function or cause to function or be in operation: *to run a washing machine. The engine is running smoothly.* **8** manage or be in charge of: *to run a business.* **9** continue to be valid or operative for a particular period of time: *My travel pass still has a few weeks to run.* **10** become a candidate in a political election: *She decided to run in the next election.* **11** publish or be published in a newspaper or magazine: *She ran an ad in the evening paper.* **12** bring goods into a country illegally and secretly, or get past some obstacle placed by an authority: *Enemy ships tried to run the blockade.* **13** cost a specified amount: *Tickets for the concert run as high as $200.* **14** discharge fluid, mucus, or pus: *My nose is running.* **15** drive, force, or thrust into something: *She ran a splinter into her hand.* **16** have a specified character, quality, form, price, or size: *These potatoes run large.* **17** expose oneself to: *to run a risk.*
n **1** the action or period of running: *to set out at a run.* **2** a trip, especially a journey over a certain route: *The ship reached St. John's after a record-breaking Atlantic run.* **3** a succession of performances: *This play has had a two-year run.* **4** a continuous period of something: *a run of bad luck.* **5** a period of causing something to operate, or the amount of a thing produced in such a period: *During a run of eight hours the factory produced a run of 100 cars.* **6** *Baseball, Cricket* a unit for scoring in a baseball game or cricket match. **7** *Music* a rapid succession of tones. **8** freedom to go over or through, or to use: *We were given the run of the house.* **9** a number of fish moving together, especially to spawning grounds: *a run of salmon.* **10** a way, track, or route: *a ski run.* **11** an enclosed space for animals: *a chicken run.* **12** a place where stitches have slipped out or become undone: *a run in a stocking.* <Old English *rinnan*>
give someone (or **something**) **a** (**good**) **run for his** (or **her**) **money,** create strong competition or opposition.
in the long run, on the whole or in the end.
on the run, a hurrying or while running: *The baker had so many orders that he was on the run all day.* **b** in retreat or trying to evade capture: *Victory is ours; the enemy is on the run.*
run across, meet by chance.
run a fever, have a body temperature higher than normal.
run away, avoid trouble or defeat by withdrawing or leaving as fast as possible: *to run away from responsibility. His response to every argument is to run away.*
run down, a cease to go or stop working: *The clock ran down.* **b** pursue till caught or killed: *to run down a fugitive.* **c** knock down by running against: *The dog was run down by a truck.* **d** speak against or deride: *She's my friend and I would never run her down.* **e** fall off, diminish, or decrease in quality or condition. **f** put a base runner out in baseball after a tag between bases.
run into, a meet by chance. **b** crash into or collide with.
run off, a cause to be run or played: *to run off a tennis tournament.* **b** print or duplicate. **c** run away or flee.
run on, a continue indefinitely. **b** add at the end of a piece of text, without a break.
run out, come to an end.
run out of, use up or have no more: *I can't bake a cake because we have run out of sugar.*
run out on, desert someone.
run over, a ride or drive over: *The car ran over some glass.* **b** overflow: *Coffee ran over into the saucer.* **c** go through quickly: *Please run over these figures to check my addition.* **d** exceed a limit: *Our expenses ran over our budget.*
run through something, a consume or spend rapidly or recklessly: *The spendthrift ran through his inheritance in a year.* **b** pierce. **c** review or rehearse: *The teacher ran through the homework assignment a second time.*
run something up, *Informal* **a** achieve a particular result: *They ran up six wins against one loss.* **b** allow a debt or bill to accumulate quickly: *She ran up a big bill.* **c** raise a flag.
run up against, face a problem or difficulty: *We ran up against this same problem last winter.*
run with, go ahead confidently and creatively with an idea or plan: *If you have a great idea, then run with it.*

run·a·round (run′ə round′) *n* evasive conduct or refusal to answer a question directly: *She gave us the runaround by making excuses and sidestepping our questions.*

run·a·way (run′ə wā′) *n* **1** a person who has run away, especially from a family or institution. **2** an animal or vehicle that has run out of control.
adj **1** running with nobody to guide or stop it: *a runaway horse, a runaway car.* **2** easily won or achieved: *a runaway victory.*

run·down (run′doun′) *adj* **1** tired and somewhat sick. **2** in a poor or neglected condition: *a rundown building.*
n **1** an analysis or summary of something: *She gave us a rundown on the costs so far. Give me a rundown on what happened.* **2** a reduction in activity or productivity of a company or institution: *a rundown in sales.* **3** the act of putting a base runner out in baseball after a tag between bases.

rune (rūn) *n* a letter of an ancient Germanic alphabet, or a mark that looks like a rune and has some mysterious, magic meaning. <Old English *run* mystery>

rung[1] (rung) past participle of RING[2].

rung[2] (rung) *n* **1** a round rod or bar used as a step of a ladder. **2** a crosspiece set between the legs of a chair or as part of the back or arm of a chair. **3** a level in an organization or structure of a social class or career: *She had several rungs to go before she could become president.* <Old English *hrung*>

a bat	e bed	i bid	o pot	u cup	th thin
ā cake	ē me	ī bite	ō go	ū rude	ᴛʜ then
à bar	ə about	ər over	ô for	ů put	zh measure

ru·nic (rū′nik) *adj* written in runes.

run–in (run′in′) *Informal n* **1** a sharp disagreement or argument. **2** the approach to an action or event: *a run-in to a championship game.*

run·nel (run′əl) *n* a small stream. <Old English *rinelle*>

run·ner (run′ər) *n* **1** a person who or animal that runs, especially in a specified way or who does so as a sport or recreation: *a long-distance runner.* **2** a messenger, collector, or agent: *a runner for a bank.* **3** a rod, groove, or blade on which something slides. Skate blades are runners. **4** a long, narrow strip of carpet or other material. **5** (*often in compounds*) a smuggler or person or ship that tries to evade somebody: *a blockade runner, a rum-runner.* **6** a slender shoot that grows from the base of a plant along the ground and takes root at points along its length. Strawberry plants have runners. **7** *Prairie Provinces* RUNNING SHOE. See also SNEAKER.

run·ner–up (run′ə rup′) *n, pl* **run·ners–up** the person, player, or team that takes second place in a contest.

run·ning (run′ing) *n* **1** the action or movement of a person who or thing that runs, especially the sport or recreation of racing on foot. **2** the action of managing or operating something: *the running of a clothing store.*
adj **1** flowing naturally or supplied to a building: *running hot water.* **2** discharging liquid or pus in the body: *a running sore.* **3** done while running: *a running jump.* **4** going or carried on continuously: *a running commentary, a running joke.* **5** consecutive or in succession: *for three nights running.* **6** moving or sliding when pulled or hauled: *a running knot.* **7** in the normal schedule or period of operation: *The running time of the movie is two hours.*
be in (or **out of**) **the running,** have a chance (no chance) to win.

running board *n* in former times, a metal step along the side of an automobile.

running lights *pln* **1** lights on a vehicle that go on automatically if the vehicle is running. **2** lights required by law to be displayed on an aircraft or watercraft between sunset and sunrise.

running mate *n* a candidate running jointly with another, but for a less important office, such as a candidate for vice-president.

running shoe *n* a light shoe with a cloth, leather, or synthetic upper and a rubber sole with treads, used for sports or for casual wear. See also RUNNER, SNEAKER.

run·ny (run′ē) *adj* with a tendency to flow: *a runny nose. The pie filling is a bit runny.*

run·off (run′of′) *n* **1** water that spreads across the surface of the ground rather than soaking into it, as during the spring thaw or after a heavy rain. **2** a final deciding race or contest.

run–of–the–mill (run′əv ŧʜə mil′) *adj* average or commonplace: *a run-of-the-mill design.*

run–on entry (run′on) *n* a word or phrase in a dictionary that is given at the end of the entry word from which it is derived.

run–on sentence (run′on) *n* a sentence containing too many clauses strung loosely together, sometimes without the proper punctuation or connecting words.

GRAMMAR AND USAGE

A **run-on-sentence** can be fixed by rewriting it and inserting the correct punctuation.

Run-on sentence: *You can do one of two things, one is to talk with her directly the other is to phone her friend.*
Correct punctuation: *You can do one of two things: one is to talk with her directly, and the other is to phone her friend.*

runt (runt) *n* an animal or plant that is smaller than the usual size. <origin uncertain> **runt·y** *adj.*

run·way (run′wā′) *n* **1** a strip of ground with a level surface on which aircraft land and take off. **2** a channel, track, groove, or trough along which something moves or slides. **3** a raised gangway extending into the audience in a theatre or auditorium, especially for fashion shows. **4** an enclosed place for animals to run in.

Ru·pert's Land (rū′pərts) *n* the name given to the Canadian northern and western territories granted to the Hudson's Bay Company by Charles II in 1670.

rup·ture (rup′chər) *n* **1** a breakage or bursting of something, especially a pipe, vessel, or body part. **2** a hernia. **3** a breaking off of friendly relations, especially a break between nations that threatens to lead to war.
v **rup·tured, rup·tur·ing 1** burst or break: *She ruptured her spleen.* **2** suffer or cause to suffer a breaking apart of friendly relations: *Their friendship has ruptured.* <Old French, from Latin *rumpere* to break>

ru·ral (rů′rəl) *adj* to do with the country or the people who live in the country: *a rural upbringing.* <Old French, from Latin *rus* country>

🍁 **rural municipality** *n* in certain provinces, a municipal district in a sparsely populated area, administered by an elected council or by a provincial government.

rural route *n* a postal service or route by which mail is delivered by car or truck to the mailboxes of individuals or businesses from a local post office. *Abbrev.* **R.R.**

ruse (rūz) *or* (rūs) *n* an action intended to deceive someone. <Old French *ruser* use trickery>

rush[1] (rush) *v* **1** move with speed or force: *We rushed along.* **2** attack with speed and force: *On the second play, they rushed the quarterback.* **3** act with speed and haste: *She rushes into things without knowing anything about them.* **4** force with speed or haste: *Rush this order, please.*
n **1** the act of making a sudden movement, especially as a liquid: *the rush of the flood.* **2** a great or sudden effort of many people to go somewhere or get something: *the holiday rush.* **3** a sudden intense feeling: *a rush of energy.* **4** an eager demand or pressure: *The lunchtime rush kept the cafeteria staff working hard.* **5** an attempt in football to carry the ball through the opposing line. **6 rushes** *pl* the first prints made of film shot for a motion picture.
adj requiring haste: *a rush order.* <Old French *ruser* to dodge about> **rush′er** *n.*
with a rush, suddenly or quickly.

rush[2] (rush) *n* **1** a marsh plant with round, pithy stems, used as a material for chair bottoms, mats, baskets, and for wicks in candles. **2** a similar plant of wet habitats. <Old English *risc*> **rush′like′** *adj.*

rush hour *n* a time of day when traffic is heaviest. **rush–hour** *adj.*

rusk (rusk) *n* a light, dry piece of bread or cake toasted in the oven. <Spanish *rosca* roll of bread>

rus·set (rus′it) *adj* reddish brown.
n **1** a coarse, russet-coloured cloth: *Peasants used to make and wear russet.* **2** a variety of apple with a rough, brownish skin. <Old French, from Latin *russus* red>

Rus·sia (ru′shə) *n* a country in eastern Europe. Its official name is the **Russian Federation**. See the APPENDIX. **Rus′sian** *adj, n.*

Russian roulette *n* **1** a game in which someone spins the cylinder of a revolver loaded with only one bullet, points the muzzle at his or her head, and pulls the trigger. **2** a potentially deadly or extremely risky activity.

rust (rust) *n* **1** the reddish brown coating formed by oxidation on iron or steel exposed to air or moisture. **2** a condition of disrepair or deterioration resulting from neglect. **3** a plant fungal disease that leaves reddish or brownish patches on leaves and stems.
v **1** coat or become covered with rust. **2** deteriorate through neglect or lack of use.
adj reddish brown or orange. <Old English>

rust·buck·et (rust′buk ət) *Informal n* an old or rusty motor vehicle, boat, or ship.

rus·tic (rus′tik) *adj* **1** characteristic of the countryside or of people living there. **2** plain and charming, in a way considered typical of the countryside: *My uncle collects old cooking pots to decorate his rustic kitchen.* **3** made of rough timber or of branches with the bark still on them: *rustic furniture.*
n an unsophisticated person from a rural area. <Latin *rus* country> **rus′ti·cal·ly** *adv.*

rus·tic·i·ty (rus tis′ə tē) *n, pl* **rus·tic·i·ties** a rustic quality or characteristic.

rus·tle (rus′əl) *n* a light, soft sound of things gently rubbing together, such as leaves make when moved by the wind.
v **rus·tled, rus·tling** **1** make this sound: *Leaves rustled in the breeze.* **2** move or stir something so that it makes such a sound: *We could hear her rustling papers in the next room.* **3** steal cattle. **4** *Informal* act, do, or get with energy or speed: *We'll have to rustle if we want to finish in time.* <Middle English>
rustle up, *Informal* gather, find, or prepare something quickly: *The cook rustled up some food.*

rus·tler (rus′lər) *n* a cattle thief.

rust·proof (rust′prūf′) *adj* resisting rust on metal.
v treat with a preparation that resists rust: *to rustproof a car.*

rust·y (rus′tē) *adj* **rust·i·er, rust·i·est** **1** covered with or affected by rust: *a rusty knife.* **2** coloured like rust: *a rusty black.* **3** weakened from lack of use or practice: *My mother says her algebra is rusty.* **rust′i·ness** *n.*

rut[1] (rut) *n* **1** a deep track made in the ground, especially by the repeated passage of wheels of vehicles. **2** a habit or established way of acting, especially a dull routine: *She decided to change jobs because she felt she was getting into a rut.* <origin uncertain>

rut[2] (rut) *n* an annual period of sexual excitement and activity in deer and some other mammals.
v **rut·ted, rut·ting** to engage in such activity. <Old French, from Latin *rugire* to bellow>

ru·ta·ba·ga (rū′tə bā gə) *or* (rū′tə bag′ə) *n* a turnip with a large, round, yellow-fleshed root. <Swedish *rotabagge* root bag>

ru·the·ni·um (rū thē′nē əm) *n* a hard, brittle, silver-white metallic element. *Symbol* **Ru** <Latin *Ruthenia* Russia, where it was found>

ruth·less (rū′thlis) *adj* with no pity or mercy. <Middle English> **ruth′less·ly** *adv.* **ruth′less·ness** *n.*

rut·ted (rut′əd) *adj* with ruts: *The road to the cottage was deeply rutted.*

RV recreational vehicle.

Rwan·da (rū an′də) *n* a country in central Africa. See the APPENDIX. **Rwan′dan** *adj, n.*

Rx a medical prescription. <Latin *recipere* to take>

rye (rī) *n* **1 a** a cereal grass that can be grown in poor soils and in cold climates. See GRAIN for picture. **b** the seeds or grain of this plant, used for making bread and whisky, and as fodder. **c** flour made from this grain, or bread made from it: *He ordered a corned beef on rye.* **2 a** whisky made from rye. **b** 🍁 a blended whisky made from rye and other grains. <Old English *ryge*>

rye·grass (rī′gras′) *n* a Eurasian grass that is cultivated for fodder and as lawn grass.

Ss

s or **S** (es) *n, pl* **s's** or **S's** 1 the nineteenth letter of the English alphabet, or any speech sound represented by it. 2 the nineteenth thing in a list or series.

s second(s).

S south; southern.

Sab·bath (sab′əth) *n* a day of religious observance and rest, kept by Jews from Friday evening until Saturday evening, and by most Christians on Sunday. <Hebrew *sabat* to rest>

sab·bat·i·cal (sə bat′ə kəl) *n* a year's leave of absence given usually to teachers for study or travel, and originally offered only once every seven years.

sa·ber (sā′bər) SABRE.

sa·ble (sā′bəl) *n* a small, flesh-eating mammal of the forests of northern Asia, with glossy, dark brown or black fur. <French, from Hungarian *szablya*>

sable antelope *n* a large African antelope with large scimitar-shaped horns and, in the male, a black coat.

sab·ot (sa bō′) *n* a shoe hollowed out of a single piece of wood, traditionally worn by French peasants. <French>

sab·o·tage (sab′ə täzh′) *n* the destruction, damage, or obstruction of something to gain military advantage or for political reasons.
v **sab·o·taged, sab·o·tag·ing** commit sabotage on: *The rebels made no attempt to sabotage the peace negotiations.* <French *saboter* to spoil through clumsiness>

sab·o·teur (sab′ə tər′) *n* a person who practises sabotage.

sa·bre (sā′bər) *n* 1 a heavy, curved sword with a sharp point and cutting edge. 2 a light sword used in fencing or duelling, with a tapering, flexible blade with a full cutting edge along one side. Also, **saber**. <French, from Hungarian *szabni* to cut>

sa·bre–rat·tling (sā′bər rat′ling) *n* a show of military strength in order to intimidate.

sa·bre–toothed tiger (sā′bər tütht′ ti′gər) *n* an extinct tigerlike mammal of the cat family with very long, curved upper canine teeth.

sac (sak) *n* a baglike part in an animal or plant, often containing liquids: *the sac of a honeybee.* <Latin, from Greek *sakkos* sack[1]> **sac′like′** *adj.*

sac·cha·rin (sak′ə rin) *n* a sweet synthetic substance, used as a calorie-free substitute for sugar. <Latin, from Greek *sakkharon* sugar>

sac·cha·rine (sak′ə rin) *adj* too sweet or sentimental: *a saccharine smile.*

sa·chem (sā′chəm) *n* among First Nations or Native Americans, especially Algonquian peoples, a ruler or chief, especially the chief of a confederacy. <Algonquian>

sa·chet (sa shā′) *or* (sash′ā) *n* 1 a small bag or pad containing perfumed powder, used especially for scenting linens and clothes. 2 a small packet containing shampoo or cosmetics. <French, from Latin *sac* bag>

sack[1] (sak) *Informal n* 1 a large bag, usually made of coarse cloth, paper, or plastic. 2 the contents of such a bag: *She bought two sacks of potatoes.* 3 a woman's loose-fitting or shapeless dress. 4 **the sack** dismissal from a job. *He got the sack for always coming to work late.*
v 1 put into a sack or sacks: *to sack corn.* 2 *Informal* discharge from employment. <Greek *sakkos*>

sack[2] (sak) *v* plunder or pillage: *The invaders sacked the town.*
n a plundering of a captured city: *the sack of Rome.* <French, from Latin *saccare* take by force> **sack′er** *n.*

sack·cloth (sak′kloth′) *n* coarse fabric for making sacks, or a garment made from it traditionally worn as a sign of mourning or penance.

sack·ful (sak′fůl) *n, pl* **sack·fuls** enough to fill a sack: *a sackful of potatoes.*

sack·ing (sak′ing) *n* coarse cloth, such as burlap, used for making sacks.

sac·ra·ment (sak′rə mənt) *n* 1 in Christian churches, a sacred ceremony or act that is considered to be an outward sign of the inward grace that is given by God. 2 something considered especially sacred, such as a sign, token, or symbol. 3 **the Blessed** (or **Holy**) **Sacrament** the consecrated elements of the Eucharist, especially the bread. <Old French, from Latin *sacer* sacred> **sac′ra·men′tal** *adj.* **sac′ra·men′tal·ly** *adv.*

sa·cred (sā′krid) *adj* 1 belonging to or dedicated to God or a god: *a sacred building, a sacred oath.* 2 connected with religion: *sacred writings, sacred music.* 3 worthy of great respect or reverence: *There is a monument in Ottawa built to the memory of the Unknown Soldier.* <Old French, from Latin *sacer* holy> **sa′cred·ly** *adv.* **sa′cred·ness** *n.*

sacred cow *n* a person or thing unreasonably regarded to be beyond criticism.

🍁 **sacred pipe** *n* a pipe smoked by many First Nations people when praying, as part of certain ceremonies.

sac·ri·fice (sak′rə fīs′) *n* 1 **a** the act of offering something valuable to God or a god as a means of making homage or giving satisfaction. **b** the thing or person offered. 2 **a** the act of giving up or destroying one thing for the sake of something else: *She sacrificed her spare time in the interests of getting better grades.* **b** the thing given up or destroyed. 3 in chess, a tactic by a player that, in allowing an opponent to win a piece, creates a greater advantage. 4 *Baseball* a bunt or fly that helps the runner to advance although the batter is put out.
v **sac·ri·ficed, sac·ri·fic·ing** 1 give or offer to God or a god. 2 give up, suffer the loss of, or injure or destroy for a particular belief or purpose: *We decided to sacrifice part of our vacation to help at the animal shelter.* <Old French, from Latin *sacer* holy> **sac′ri·fi′cial** (sak′rə fish′əl) *adj.* **sac′ri·fi′cial·ly** *adv.*

sac·ri·lege (sak′rə lij) *n* an intentional injury or insulting treatment of a sacred person or thing: *Robbing the temple was a sacrilege.* <Old French, from Latin *sacra* sacred things>

sac·ri·le·gious (sak′rə lij′əs) *adj* injurious or insulting to sacred persons or things. **sac′ri·le′gious·ly** *adv.*

sac·ro·sanct (sak′rō sangkt′) *adj* most holy, sacred, or revered and not to be violated: *A person's right to education is sacrosanct.* <Latin *os sacrum* holy bone (because it was used in sacrifices), from *sacer* holy>

sa·crum (sā′krəm) *or* (sak′rəm) *n, pl* **sa·cra** (-krə) or **sa·crums** the triangular bone at the lower end of the spine, formed by the joining of several vertebrae and which makes up the back of the pelvis. <Latin, from Greek *hieron osteon* sacred bone>

sad (sad) *adj* **sad·der, sad·dest** 1 feeling or showing sorrow or grief: *a sad look.* 2 causing or suggesting sorrow or regret: *a sad disappointment.* <Old English *sæd* weary>

SAD (sad) *n* in full, **seasonal affective disorder** a tendency toward depression in the winter months thought to be caused by lack of light.

sad·den (sad′ən) *v* make or become sad: *It saddened him to think that he might never see them again.*

sad·dle (sad′əl) *n* 1 **a** a seat, usually padded and leather-covered, for a rider on an animal such as a horse. **b** a seat for a rider on a bicycle. 2 a ridge between two mountain peaks. 3 a cut of meat consisting of the upper back portion of an animal, including both loins: *a saddle of venison.*
v **sad·dled, sad·dling** 1 put a saddle on: *to saddle a horse.* 2 burden: *My grandfather is saddled with a big house that he does not need or want.* <Old English *sadol*>
in the saddle, *Informal* in a position of control.

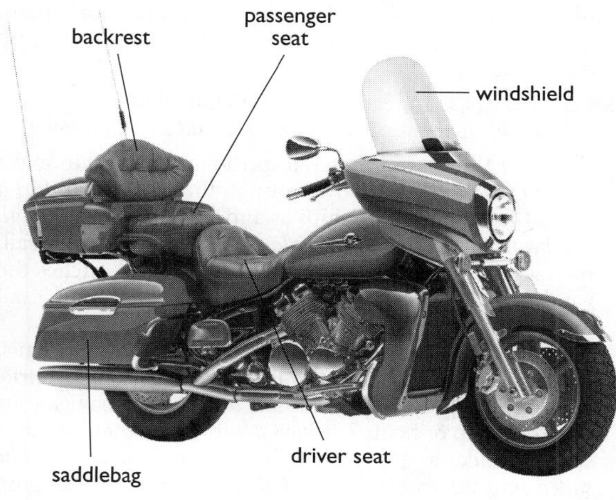

sad·dle·bag (sad′əl bag′) *n* each of a pair of bags laid over an animal's back behind the saddle, or a similar bag hanging over the rear wheel of a bicycle or motorcycle.

sad·dle·cloth (sad′əl kloth′) *n* a cloth put between an animal's back and the saddle.

sad·dler (sad′lər) *n* a person who makes or sells saddles and harness.

sad·dler·y (sad′lə rē) *n, pl* **sad·dler·ies** 1 the work of a saddler. 2 the shop of a saddler. 3 saddles, harness, and other equipment for horses.

saddle soap *n* a mild soap used for cleaning and preserving leather items.

sa·dhu (sȧ′dü) *n* a Hindu holy man. <Sanskrit>

sa·dism (sā′diz əm) *n* the tendency to take pleasure from inflicting physical or mental pain on others. <Marquis de *Sade,* 18c writer who described it> **sa′dist** *n.*
sa·dist′ic (sə dis′tik) *adj.* **sa·dist′ic·al·ly** (sə dis′ti klē) *adv.*

sad·ly (sad′lē) *adv* 1 showing or feeling sadness: *He smiled sadly.* 2 unfortunately: *Sadly, I am unable to accept the invitation.* 3 to a regrettable extent: *The runner was sadly lacking in stamina.*

sad·ness (sad′nis) *n* a feeling of sorrow or grief.

sa·do·mas·o·chism (sā′dō mas′ə kiz′əm) *n* a tendency to get pleasure from inflicting or receiving pain. **sa′do·mas′o·chist** *n.* **sa′do·mas′o·chis′tic** *adj.*

sa·fa·ri (sə fȧ′rē) *n, pl* **sa·fa·ris** a long journey or hunting expedition, especially in eastern Africa. <Swahili (a language of Africa), from Arabic *safara* to travel>

safe (sāf) *adj* **saf·er, saf·est** 1 free from or not likely to cause harm or danger: *He felt safe with her. We feel safe with the dog in the house.* 2 in a secure or protected place: *Your money is safe with me.* 3 based on good reason or evidence and thus dependable: *a safe guess, a safe move, a safe guide.*
n a strong, fireproof box or place that can be locked, used for keeping valuable things safe. <Old French, from Latin *salvus*> **safe′ly** *adv.* **safe′ness** *n.*
safe and sound, not harmed or injured: *He returned from war safe and sound.*

SYNONYMS

Safe means "out of harm's way": *The basement is a safe place to be during a hurricane.*

Secure can mean "free from care, fear, or anxiety": *He felt more secure after he got a good mark on the test.*

Protected means "shielded from harm or danger": *The rap star was protected by a bodyguard.*

Harmless means "causing no harm": *The grass snake is harmless.*

safe conduct (sāf′kon′dukt) *n* the privilege of passing safely through a region, especially in time of war, or a paper granting this privilege: *The messenger was promised safe conduct through the enemy camp.*

safe·crack·ing (sāf′krak′ing) *n* the act or practice of breaking open safes and stealing the contents. **safe′crack·er** *n.*

safe·guard (sāf′gȧrd′) *v* guard against hurt or danger: *She said that proper labels on food safeguarded our health.*
n a protection or defence, especially a law or procedure: *He said that keeping clean was one safeguard against disease.*

safe·keep·ing (sāf′kē′ping) *n* protection through being kept in a safe place: *She put her money in the bank for safekeeping.*

safe sex *n* sexual intercourse using a condom and other precautions to guard against pregnancy and disease.

a bat	e bed	i bid	o pot	u cup	th thin
ā cake	ē me	ī bite	ō go	ü rude	ᴛʜ then
ȧ bar	ə about	ər over	ȯ for	u̇ put	zh measure

S

safe·ty (sāf′tē) *n, pl* **safe·ties** **1** the quality or condition of being free from harm or danger: *They did not stop running until they had reached safety.* **2** a device on a firearm or machine, designed to prevent injury through accidental or careless operation. **3** designed to protect against harm through accident or misuse: *a safety lamp, safety glass, a safety belt.* **4** 🍁 a safety touch. <Old French, from Latin *salvus* safe>

safety belt *n* a belt or strap used by window cleaners, loggers, etc. to prevent falling.

safety deposit box *n* a box in the vault of a bank, for the storage of valuables, such as original documents, bonds, or jewellery.

safety glass *n* glass that resists shattering, made of two or more layers of glass joined together by a layer of transparent plastic.

safety island *n* a marked area or a platform built in a street to help pedestrians safely board and get off buses or streetcars: *The city built safety islands at all busy intersections.*

safety net *n* **1** a net to catch a person who falls from a tightrope or other high place. **2** a thing that protects against failure, loss, or extreme poverty, such as social insurance or a community that supports its members.

safety pin *n* a pin bent back on itself to form a spring and with a guard that covers the point in order to prevent injury or accidental unfastening.

🍁 **safety touch** *Football n* the act of putting a ball down behind one's own goal line after a player on one's own team has sent it there. It counts two points for the other team.

safety valve *n* **1** a valve in a steam boiler that opens and lets steam or fluid escape when the pressure becomes too great. **2** a thing that helps a person get rid of anger, nervousness, in a harmless way.

saf·flow·er (saf′lou′ər) *n* an annual herb with large flower heads yielding a red dye and seeds that are rich in oil. <origin uncertain>

saf·fron (saf′rən) *n* the dried orange-coloured stigmas of the purple-flowered autumn crocus, used to flavour and colour foods.
adj medium orange or orange-yellow. <Old French, from Arabic *za'faran*>

sag (sag) *v* **sagged, sag·ging** **1** sink under weight or pressure so that the middle is bent down. **2** hang down unevenly: *I think my jacket sags in the back.* **3** become less firm or elastic through weakness, weariness, or lack of effort: *Our courage sagged.* **4** decline in price.
n **1** the act, condition, or degree of sagging. **2** the place where a thing sags. <origin uncertain>

sa·ga (sȧ′gə) *or* (sag′ə) *n* an extended story of adventure or heroic deeds, especially a type of prose story of heroic deeds written in Old Norse or Old Icelandic. <Old Norse = narrative>

sa·ga·cious (sə gā′shəs) *adj* wise in a shrewd, practical, and farsighted way: *a sagacious decision.* <Latin *sagax* wise> **sa·ga′cious·ly** *adv.* **sa·ga′ci·ty** (sə gas′ə tē) *n.*

sag·a·more (sag′ə mȯr′) *n* a sachem. <Algonquian>

sage[1] (sāj) *adj* **sag·er, sag·est** showing wisdom or good judgment: *a sage reply, a sage adviser.*
n a very wise person: *The sage gave advice to the young man.* <Old French, from Latin *sapere* be wise>
sage′ly *adv.* **sage′ness** *n.*

sage[2] (sāj) *n* a plant of the mint family, grown especially for its aromatic leaves that are used in cooking. See HERB for picture. <Old French, from Latin *salvus* healthy, because of the plant's healing properties>

sage·brush (sāj′brush′) *n* a shrub of the daisy family with greyish green leaves and a smell like sage. It is native to the dry plains of western N America.

sage grouse *n* a large grouse of the plains of western N America.

Sag·it·tar·i·us (saj′ə ter′ē əs) *n* **1** *Astronomy* a southern constellation shaped somewhat like a centaur drawing a bow. **2** *Astrology* **a** the ninth sign of the zodiac. The sun enters Sagittarius about November 23. **b** a person born under this sign.

sa·go (sā′gō) *n, pl* **sa·gos** a starch obtained from the pith of a tropical palm, or the flour made from it and used as food. <Malay *sagu*>

sa·hib (so′ib) *n* a polite title or form of address for a man. It is used mainly on the Indian subcontinent. <Urdu, from Arabic>

said (sed) *v* past tense and past participle of SAY.
adj named or mentioned before: *the said sum of money.*

sail (sāl) *n* **1** a piece of material spread to the wind to make a ship or other vessel move through the water: *to unfurl a sail.* **2** the use of sailing ships as a means of transport: *Sail has been replaced by the airplane.* **3** **a** a thing like a sail, such as the part of an arm of a windmill that catches the wind. **b** *US* CONNING TOWER. **4** a trip on a boat with a sail or sails: *Let's go for a sail.*
v **1** travel on water by the action of wind on sails. **2** **a** travel on a ship of any kind: *to sail across Lake Ontario.* **b** begin a trip by water: *We sail at 2 p.m.* **3** navigate or control a ship or boat: *The boys are learning to sail.* **4** move smoothly like a ship with sails: *The eagle sailed by. She sailed into the room. The football sailed over the goal post.* <Old English *segel*>
make sail, a spread out the sails of a ship. **b** begin a trip by water.
sail into, *Informal* attack verbally.
set sail, begin a trip by water.
take in sail, lower or lessen the sails of a ship.
under sail, moving with the sails spread out.

CONFUSABLES

Sail means "travel on water": *The ship sails at noon, so all passengers must board at ten o'clock.*

Sale means "the act of selling" or "an event in which goods are sold at lower prices than usual": *They completed the sale when she gave him the money for the bike.*

sail·board (sāl′bȯrd′) *n* a long, narrow board, usually of plastic, with provision for a sail, used in windsurfing.

sail·boat (sāl′bōt′) *n* a boat that is moved by a sail or sails.

sail·cloth (sāl′kloth′) *n* **1** canvas or other material used for making sails. **2** a similar stiff, durable material used in making clothes.

sail·er (sā′lər) *n* a sailing boat or ship: *the best sailer in the fleet, a fast sailer.*

sail·fish (sāl′fish′) *n, pl* **sail·fish·es** or (*especially collectively*) **sail·fish** a large saltwater fish that has a long, high, sail-like fin on its back.

sail·ing (sā′ling) *n* the practice or sport of sailing: *I took up sailing last summer.*
adj to do with sailing or sailors: *a sailing lesson.*

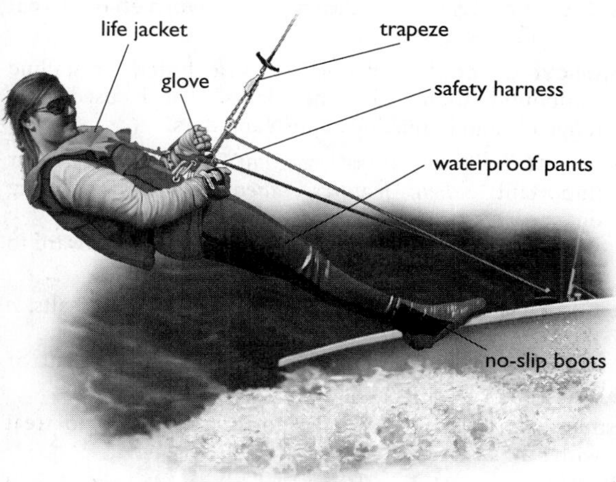

In the trapeze position, a **sailor** has feet planted firmly on the gunwale and is leaning away from the boat as far as possible. The harness and trapeze keep the sailor safely anchored to the craft. In this position, the sailor's body mass counteracts the force of the wind and helps to keep the boat from tipping over.

sail·or (sā′lər) *n* **1** a person who handles or does tasks on a sailboat or other vessel as a job or for recreation. **2** a member of a ship's crew who is not an officer. <Middle English *sailer*> **sail′or·like′** *adj.*
a good sailor, a person who does not get seasick.

sail·plane (sāl′plān′) *n* a light glider that can stay aloft for a long time supported by air currents.
v **sail·planed, sail·plan·ing** fly such a glider.

saint (sānt) *n* **1** *Christianity* a person who is regarded as being extremely holy or good, especially one so declared or regarded by a Christian church. **2** a person who is deeply respected because of his or her virtue. **3 Saint** (*as a title before the name of a canonized person or an archangel*) holy or sacred: *Saint Teresa, Saint Michael. Abbrev.* **St.** <Old French, from Latin *sanctus* holy> **saint′like′** *adj.* **saint′li·ness** *n.* **saint′ly** *adj.*

GRAMMAR AND USAGE

Most names beginning with **Saint** are written with the abbreviation **St.**

Saint Ber·nard (bər nárd′) *or* (bər′nərd) *n* a big, powerful dog of a working breed, sometimes used for rescue work in mountainous areas.

saint·ed (sān′tid) *adj* declared to be or worthy of being a saint: *my sainted mother.*

Saint El·mo's fire (sānt′el′mōz) *n* light due to a discharge of atmospheric electricity that appears on a ship or aircraft during a storm.

saint·hood (sānt′hůd) *n* the character or status of a saint.

🍁 **Saint–Jean–Bap·tiste Day** (san zhán bá tēst′) *n* the former name of the Québec holiday of June 24, celebrating French-Canadian culture and identity, now officially called **Fête nationale**.

🍁 **Saint–Jean–Baptiste Society** *n* an organization in the province of Québec that is dedicated to preserving and fostering French culture.

🍁 **Saint John's Day** (jonz) *n* June 24, the anniversary holiday of Newfoundland, held to commemorate the landing of John Cabot on the same day in 1497.

Saint–John's–wort (sānt jonz′wərt′) *n* a shrub or plant that has paired oval leaves and many clusters of yellow flowers.

Saint Kitts and Nev·is (kits) (nev′is) *n* a country of two islands in the Caribbean.

Saint Lu·cia (lū′shə) *n* an island country in the Caribbean. **Saint Lu′cian** *adj, n.*

Saint Nich·o·las (nik′ə ləs) SANTA CLAUS.

Saint Pat·rick's Day (pat′rikz) *n* March 17, the feast of St. Patrick, celebrated in honour of the patron saint of Ireland.

Saint Vin·cent and the Gren·ad·ines (vin′sənt) (gren′ə dēnz′) *n* a country of several islands in the Caribbean.

Saint Vi·tus dance (vī′təs) CHOREA.

saj·ja·da (sə já′də) *Islam n* the prayer rug upon which worshippers kneel and bow during daily prayers.

sake[1] (sāk) *n* **1** for the purpose or in the interest of: *She closed her bedroom door for the sake of peace and quiet. For the sake of argument, let us suppose that the other party wins the election.* **2** out of consideration for: *Don't go to any trouble just for my sake. For your own sake, drive carefully.* <Old English *sacu* cause at law>
for goodness (or **Pete's**, **heaven's**, **gosh**) **sake,** *Informal* used to express impatience, annoyance, or surprise: *For goodness sake, don't wear that dirty shirt.*
for old times' sake, in memory of former days: *Let's get together for old times' sake.*

sa·ke[2] (sá′kē) *n* a Japanese fermented alcoholic drink made from rice. <Japanese>

a bat	e bed	i bid	o pot	u cup	th thin
ā cake	ē me	ī bite	ō go	ū rude	ᴛʜ then
á bar	ə about	ər over	ȯ for	ů put	zh measure

sa·laam (sə läm′) *n* a salutation or greeting used especially among Muslims or speakers of Arabic, or a low bow used as a greeting, made with the palm of the right hand placed on the forehead.
v greet with or make a salaam. <Arabic *al-salam* peace>

sal·a·bil·i·ty (sā′lə bil′ə tē) *n* a saleable condition or quality.

sal·a·ble (sā′lə bəl) SALEABLE.

sa·la·cious (sə lā′shəs) *adj* **1** treating sexual matters in writings, pictures, or talk in a way that tends to arouse desire: *a salacious story.* **2** lustful or lewd: *a salacious smile.* <Latin *salire* to leap> **sa·la′cious·ly** *adv.* **sa·la′cious·ness** *n.*

sal·ad (sal′əd) *n* **1** a cold dish of raw or cooked vegetables served with a liquid dressing and sometimes including other ingredients, such as meat, fish, cheese, or eggs. **2** a cold mixture mainly containing one ingredient and dressed with mayonnaise: *egg salad.* **3** any leafy green vegetable eaten raw, especially lettuce. <Old French, from Latin *sal* salt>

salad bar *n* a number of different salad ingredients, arranged as a buffet from which a diner can choose.

salad days *pl n* **1** the days of youthful inexperience. **2** the peak or heyday of something.

salad dressing *n* a sauce used in or on a salad.

🍁 **sal·al** (sə lal′) *n* an evergreen shrub native to the Pacific coast. <Chinook Jargon *shala*>

sal·a·man·der (sal′ə man′dər) *n* **1** an amphibian that has a moist, smooth, scaleless skin and bright markings. See AMPHIBIAN for picture. **2** in myths and legends, a lizardlike reptile able to live in fire or withstand its effects. <Old French, from Greek *salamandra*>

sa·la·mi (sə lä′mē) *n* a highly seasoned meat sausage, usually thinly sliced and often flavoured with garlic. <Italian, from Latin *salare* to salt>

sal·a·ried (sal′ə rēd) *or* (sal′rēd) *adj* receiving a salary.

sal·a·ry (sal′ə rē) *or* (sal′rē) *n, pl* **sal·a·ries** a regular fixed payment for work, especially to a professional or white-collar worker, often paid monthly but usually expressed as an annual sum. Compare WAGE. <Old French, from Latin *salarium*>

sa·lat (sə lät′) *Islam n* ritual prayer offered five times daily to Allah. <Arabic *salah* prayer>

sale (sāl) *n* **1** the action or process by which goods are exchanged for money: *Did she make the sale? That was the last sale of the day.* **2** an event in which goods are sold at lower prices than usual: *This store is having a sale on shoes.* **3** an auction. **4 sales** *pl* **a** the quantity or amount sold: *Today's sales were larger than yesterday's.* **b** (*with singular verb*) the work involved in selling: *Her first job was in sales.* See SAIL for confusable. <Old Norse *sala*>
on sale, a offered at a reduced price: *All the winter boots are on sale now.* **b** for sale: *Tickets for the concert will be on sale here on Monday.*
(up) for sale, to be sold or available for buying: *There are several nice houses for sale in this area.*

sale·a·ble (sā′lə bəl) *adj* able or fit to be sold: *This shirt is not saleable because it is torn.* Also, **salable**.

sales·clerk (sālz′klərk′) *n* a person whose work is selling items in a store.

sales·la·dy (sāl′zlā′dē) *n, pl* **sales·la·dies** a saleswoman.

sales·man (sāl′zmən) *n, pl* **sales·men** (-zmən) a male salesperson.

sales·per·son (sālz′pər′sən) *n* a person who sells goods in a store, etc. or who visits places to sell goods or services on behalf of a company.

sales representative *n* a salesperson.

sales tax *n* a tax based on the amount received for articles sold.

sales·wom·an (sāl′zwům′ən) *n, pl* **sales·wom·en** (-zwim′ən) a female salesperson.

sal·i·cyl·ic acid (sal′ə sil′ik) *n* a bitter, crystalline compound, found in some plants, that is used as a fungicide and in making Aspirin and dyes.

sa·li·ent (sā′lē ənt) *or* (sā′lyənt) *adj* **1** most noticeable or important: *salient features, salient points.* **2** pointing outward: *a salient angle.*
n a part of an area or of a fortification that juts outward to form an angle. <Latin *salire* to leap>

sa·line (sā′lēn) *or* (sā′līn) *adj* to do with a salt or salts: *a saline solution.*
n a solution or substance containing common salt or another salt. <Latin *sal* salt> **sa·lin′i·ty** (sə lin′ə tē) *n.*

sa·lin·ize (sal′ə nīz) *v* **sa·lin·ized, sa·lin·iz·ing** to treat with salt. **sa′li·ni·za′tion** *n.*

Salis·bur·y steak (solz′ber′ē) *n* chopped beef shaped before cooking into a patty about twice the size of a hamburger, usually served with gravy.

Sa·lish (sā′lish) *n, pl* **Sa·lish** See COAST SALISH.
adj to do with Salish people or their languages. Also (*adj*), **Salishan**.

sa·li·va (sə lī′və) *n* the liquid that the **salivary glands** secrete into the mouth to keep it moist, to aid in chewing, and to start digestion. <Latin>

sal·i·vate (sal′ə vāt′) *v* **sal·i·vat·ed, sal·i·vat·ing 1** secrete saliva, especially in anticipating food: *The dog started to salivate as we filled his bowl.* **2** take delight in seeing or anticipating something: *I was salivating at the prospect of the summer vacation.* **sal′i·va′tion** *n.*

sal·low (sal′ō) *adj* of or with a pallid, yellowish complexion: *a sallow face.*
v make or become yellow. <Old English *salh*>
sal′low·ness *n.*

sal·ly (sal′ē) *n, pl* **sal·lies 1** a sudden attack on an enemy made from a defensive position: *The men in the fort made a brave sally and returned with many prisoners.* **2** a brief journey or sudden start into activity. **3** a witty remark, attack, or retort: *She continued her story undisturbed by the merry sallies of her audience.*
v **sal·lied, sal·ly·ing 1** go suddenly from a defensive position to attack an enemy. **2** set out from a place to do something: *We sallied forth to shop.* <French, from Latin *salire* to leap>

Sally Ann (an) *Informal n* the Salvation Army.

salm·on (sam′ən) *n, pl* **salm·on** a saltwater or freshwater fish that is farmed or caught in the wild, especially the **Atlantic salmon** of the N Atlantic or the **Pacific salmon** of the N Pacific.
adj pale yellowish pink. <Old French, from Latin *salmo*>

salm·on·ber·ry (sam′ən ber′ē) *n* a shrub of the Pacific coast that has edible, salmon-coloured fruit somewhat like raspberries.

sal·mo·nel·la (sal′mə nel′ə) *n* a bacterium that occurs in the stomach, or the food poisoning that is caused by an infection from it: *an attack of salmonella.* <D.E. *Salmon,* 20c pathologist>

sa·lon (sə lon′) *or* (sal′on) *n* **1** a business establishment that provides services such as hairdressing and manicuring. **2** a large room for receiving or entertaining guests. **3** a regular social gathering of people, especially writers and artists, held at someone's home. <French, from Italian *sala* hall>

sa·loon (sə lūn′) *n* **1** a place where alcoholic drinks are sold and drunk, especially a disreputable one. **2** a room for general or public use, such as on a passenger ship: *a dining saloon.* <See SALON.>

sal·sa (sol′sə) *n* **1** a spicy Latin American sauce based on tomatoes, often used as a dip. **2** a style of lively Latin American music, or the dance performed to this music. <Spanish = sauce>

sal·si·fy (sal′sə fē′) *n* a European plant of the daisy family, with a fleshy root eaten as a vegetable.

salt (solt) *n* **1** a white crystalline substance, sodium chloride, that is found in the earth and in sea water and is used for seasoning and preserving food. **2** something that provides liveliness, piquancy, or pungency. **3** *Chemistry* a compound derived from an acid by replacing the hydrogen wholly or partly by a metal or an electropositive radical. **4** *Informal* a sailor: *an old salt.*
adj **1** containing or tasting like salt. **2** overflowed with or growing in salt water: *salt marshes, salt grass.* **3** cured or preserved with salt: *salt pork.*
v **1** season or preserve with salt. **2** make something piquant or interesting: *Her conversation was salted with wit.* **3** sprinkle a road or path with salt in order to melt snow or ice. <Old English *sealt*>
salt a mine, create a false impression of value to a mine by adding rich ore to it.
salt away (or **down**), **a** pack with salt to preserve: *The fish were salted down in a barrel.* **b** store away: *The miser salted a lot of money away.*
salt of the earth, a person, or group of people, considered to be kind, reliable, or honest.
take with a grain of salt, regard something as exaggerated, or believe only part of a story: *The police officer took their story with a grain of salt.*
worth your salt, good or competent at a task or job.

salt cellar *n* a container or dish for holding salt for seasoning, now usually a closed container with small holes in the lid for sprinkling.

🍁 **salt·chuck** (solt′chuk) CHUCK[3].

Sal·teaux (sal′tō) *or* (sol′tō) SAULTEAUX.

salt·er (sol′tər) *n* **1** a truck that spreads salt on snowy or icy roads. **2** a person who makes or sells salt or who uses it to preserve food.

salt flat *n* flat land covered with salt deposited by sea water that has since evaporated.

salt·ine (sol tēn′) *n* a thin, crisp, salted cracker.

salt lick *n* **1** a place where salt occurs naturally on the surface of the ground and where animals go to lick it up. **2** a block of salt placed in a pasture for cattle to lick.

salt·pe·tre (solt′pē′tər) *n* **1** POTASSIUM NITRATE. **2** SODIUM NITRATE. Also, **saltpeter**. <Latin *sal petrae* salt of rock, from Greek *petra* rock>

salt pork *n* fatty pork that has been cured in salt.

salt·shak·er (solt′shā′kər) *n* a container for salt, with a perforated top for sprinkling the salt.

salt·wa·ter (solt′wot′ər) *adj* **1** to do with salt water or the sea: *a saltwater solution, saltwater fishing.* **2** living or found in the sea: *saltwater fish.*

salt·y (sol′tē) *adj* **salt·i·er, salt·i·est** **1** containing or tasting of salt: *Sweat and tears are salty. The soup is too salty.* **2** witty, pungent, or earthy: *a salty remark.* **3** suggesting the sea or nautical life: *a salty breeze.*

sa·lu·bri·ous (sə lū′brē əs) *adj* healthy or healthful.

sal·u·tar·y (sal′yə ter′ē) *adj* beneficial or producing a good effect: *My friend gave me some salutary advice.*

sal·u·ta·tion (sal′yə tā′shən) *n* **1** a gesture or form of words used as a greeting or to acknowledge that someone has arrived or departed: *The man raised his hat in salutation.* **2** a standard form of words used in a letter to address a person. Examples: *Dear Sir; Dear Ms Lee.*

GRAMMAR AND USAGE

Use a comma after the **salutation** in a friendly letter or an e-mail:
Dear Dad,
Hi Mum,

For formal letters or e-mails, use a colon after the salutation, even when using a person's first name:
Dear Editor:
Dear Janice:

a bat	e bed	i bid	o pot	u cup	th thin
ā cake	ē me	ī bite	ō go	ū rude	ᴛʜ then
ȧ bar	ə about	ər over	ȯ for	u̇ put	zh measure

S

sa·lute (sə lūt′) *v* **sa·lut·ed, sa·lut·ing 1** honour or show respect in a formal way by raising the hand to the head, by firing guns, by dipping flags, etc.: *The soldier saluted the officer.* **2** greet: *She saluted her cousin with a kiss.*
n **1** the act or fact of saluting. **2** a sign of greeting or welcome. <Latin *salutare* greet, from *salus* good health>

sal·vage (sal′vij) *v* **sal·vaged, sal·vag·ing 1** save or rescue a wrecked or disabled ship or its cargo from loss at sea. **2** save or rescue from destruction or waste: *to salvage a reputation. We salvaged quite a few parts from the old bicycle.*
n **1 a** the act or process of saving or rescuing a wrecked or disabled ship. **b** payment made or due for such saving or rescuing. **2** something saved from being destroyed or wasted. <Latin *salvus* safe>

sal·va·tion (sal vā′shən) *n* **1 a** the process of being preserved or delivered from harm. **b** a source or means of being saved in this way. **2** *Christianity* the act of being delivered from sin and its consequences. <Latin *salvare* to save, from *salvus* safe>

Salvation Army *n* an international Christian organization that has military-style ranks for its members, set up to help the poor and homeless.

salve[1] (sav) *n* **1** an ointment that heals or soothes wounds and sores. **2** a thing that soothes or consoles: *The kind words were a salve to her hurt feelings.*
v **salved, salv·ing 1** put salve on. **2** soothe or console: *He salved his conscience by the thought that his lie harmed no one.* <Old English *sealf*>

sal·ver (sal′vər) *n* a large tray, typically made of silver and used on formal occasions.

sal·vi·a (sal′vē ə) *n* a herb or shrub of the mint family, especially a garden plant with spikes of scarlet flowers.

sal·vo (sal′vō) *n, pl* **sal·vos** or **sal·voes 1** the discharge of artillery or guns at the same time. **2** a load of bombs or missiles released at the same time from an aircraft. <French, from Latin *salve* be in good health>

sal vo·la·ti·le (sal′və lat′ə lē) *n* a strong-smelling solution of ammonium carbonate in alcohol, used to revive someone who is feeling faint. <Latin = volatile salt>

sam·a·ra (sam′ə rə) *n* a small fruit that has one seed and a winglike extension, such as that of the ash and maple. <Latin *samara* elm seed>

Sa·mar·i·tan (sə mar′ə tən) *or* (sə mer′ə tən) *n* in full, **Good Samaritan** a person who helps another in trouble or distress. <from the Bible story of a man from Samaria who helped a stranger in distress>

sa·mar·i·um (sə mer′ē əm) *n* a rare, lustrous, grey metallic element. *Symbol* **Sm** <Colonel *Samarski*, 19c government official>

sam·ba (sam′bə) *n* a lively Brazilian dance of African origin, or the music for it.
v dance the samba. <Portuguese>

same (sām) *adj* **1** identical: *We came back the same way we went.* **2** of an identical type: *I have the same coat as you do.* **3** referring to a person or thing just mentioned: *The boys were talking about a man they saw at the mall; this same man wore his hair very long and always dressed in white.*
pron **1 the same** the same person or thing: *The situation is the same as before. "Sea" and "see" are pronounced the same.* **2** the person or thing just mentioned: *Make a stiff dough and roll out same.*
adv in the same way: *He frowned at me, same as usual.* <Old English>
all (or **just**) **the same, a** in spite of or nevertheless: *I knew I had to leave the cat behind, but I was sorry just the same.* **b** in any case: *Thanks all the same, but I already ate.*
same old same old, *Slang* a tiresome routine, excuse, etc. that is repeated many times: *It's the same old same old—he lost track of time and now he's late.*

same·ness (sām′nis) *n* **1** the condition of being identical. **2** a lack of variety.

Sa·mo·a (sə mō′ə) *n* a country of several islands in the S Pacific. **Sa·mo′an** *adj, n.*

sa·mo·sa (sə mō′sə) *n* a triangular deep-fried snack consisting of spicy meat or vegetables in pastry. <Hindi>

sam·o·var (sam′ə vär′) *n* a metal urn with a tap, used in Russia for heating water for tea. <Russian = self-boiler>

sam·pan (sam′pan) *n* a small boat used in the Far East and sculled by one or more oars at the stern, usually with a single sail. <Mandarin *san* three + *ban* board, from the small size of the boat>

sam·ple (sam′pəl) *n* **1** a part or single item taken to represent a larger whole or a group: *a blood sample. The display sample is not for sale. We sent a sample of the soil to the university for testing.* **2** *Statistics* a randomly selected group taken to represent an entire population: *Do you think our class could be considered a sample of the teenage population?*
v **sam·pled, sam·pling 1** take a sample of, especially in order to test quality: *We sampled the cake and found it very good.* **2** *Music* **a** convert sound into digital form in order to store or manipulate it electronically. **b** take a sample of recorded music, especially in order to digitize it for use in another recording. <Old French *essample* example>

sam·pler (sam′plər) *n* **1** a piece of cloth embroidered with various stitches to show skill in needlework. **2** a selection of something that serves as an example. **3** a person who samples. **4** *Music* an electronic device that converts analogue signals into digital form.

sam·pling (sam′pling) *n* **1** the act or process of taking a sample or samples. **2** a representative set of samples: *a sampling of cheeses from Québec.* **3** *Music* the act or process of taking a piece of music from one recording and using it in another recording, usually in an adapted form.

sam·sa·ra (səm sä′rə) *Hinduism, Sikhism n* the material world, especially the ongoing cycle of death and rebirth in the world.

sam·u·rai (sam′ə rī′) *n, pl* **sam·u·rai** in feudal Japan, a member of a powerful military class. <Japanese>

san·a·to·ri·um (san′ə tô′rē əm) *n, pl* **san·a·to·ri·ums** or **san·a·to·ri·a** (-ē ə) an establishment for medical treatment, especially of people who are convalescing or who have a chronic illness such as tuberculosis. <Latin *sanare* heal>

sanc·ti·fy (sangk′tə fī′) *v* **sanc·ti·fied, sanc·ti·fy·ing 1** set apart or declare as holy: *The shrine was considered sanctified.* **2** (*in the passive*) make legitimate, pure, or free from sin: *They almost seemed to be sanctified by their good deeds.* <Old French, from Latin *sanctus* holy> **sanc′ti·fi·ca′tion** *n.*

sanc·ti·mo·ni·ous (sangk′tə mō′nē əs) *adj* making a show of seeming to be morally superior to other people: *sanctimonious talk.* **sanc′ti·mo′ni·ous·ly** *adv.* **sanc′ti·mo′ni·ous·ness** *n.* **sanc′ti·mo′ny** *n.*

sanc·tion (sangk′shən) *n* **1** a threatened penalty for disobeying a law or rule. **2 sanctions** *pl* actions taken by a nation to make another conform to an international agreement or agreed conduct, such as restrictions on trade or official exchanges of participants in sporting or cultural events. **3** official permission or approval for an action: *We got sanction to finish the project.* **4** official confirmation of a law or decree.
v **1** give permission or approval for an action: *Her conscience does not sanction stealing.* **2** impose a penalty on: *The village was sanctioned for selling arms to the rebels.* <Latin *sancire* make sacred>

sanc·ti·ty (sangk′tə tē) *n, pl* **sanc·ti·ties** the quality or condition of being holy, sacred, or something so important it must not be violated: *the sanctity of human life.* <Old French, from Latin *sanctus* holy>

sanc·tu·ar·y (sangk′chū er′ē) *n, pl* **sanc·tu·ar·ies 1** a place of refuge or protection: *a bird sanctuary.* **2** a sacred or holy place. <Old French, from Latin *sanctus* holy>

sanc·tum (sangk′təm) *n* **1** a sacred place, especially a shrine within a temple or church. **2** a private room or office where a person can be undisturbed. <Latin = holy>

sanctum sanc·to·rum (sangk tȯ′rəm) *n* **1** the holy of holies in a Jewish temple. **2** an especially private place. <Latin, from Hebrew>

sand (sand) *n* **1** a loose, granular substance made up of grains of rock that is the main part of beaches, riverbeds, the seabed, and deserts. **2 sands** *pl* a tract or region composed mainly of sand: *the sands of the desert.*
v **1** clean, smooth, or polish by rubbing with an abrasive such as sandpaper: *to sand a table.* **2** sprinkle or overlay with sand: *The front walk is icy and should be sanded.*
adj light greyish brown. <Old English>

san·dal (san′dəl) *n* an open shoe consisting of a sole kept on the foot by means of straps over the toes or instep and often around the heel and ankle. <Latin, from Greek *sandalon* wooden shoe>

san·dalled or **san·daled** (san′dəld) *adj* wearing sandals.

san·dal·wood (san′dəl wu̇d′) *n* a fragrant tropical wood used for making boxes, fans, and burned as incense. <Latin, from Sanskrit *candana*>

sand·bag (sand′bag′) *n* a large bag filled with sand, mainly used to form temporary dams or as protective walls for military trenches.
v **sand·bagged, sand·bag·ging 1** equip with sandbags. **2** *Informal* deliberately underperform in order to deceive an opponent or competitor.

sand·bank (sand′bangk′) *n* a ridge of sand.

sand·bar (sand′bar) *n* a ridge of sand in a river or along a shore formed by the action of tides or currents.

sand·blast (sand′blast′) *v* blast a jet of sand with compressed air or steam so as to roughen or clean a surface: *to sandblast a wall.*

sand·box (sand′boks′) *n* a box for holding sand, especially for children to play in.

sand·cher·ry (sand′cher′ē) *n* a dwarf N American wild cherry shrub.

sand dollar *n* a small, flat, round sea urchin that lives on sandy parts of the ocean floor.

sand·er (san′dər) *n* **1** a power tool or machine for cleaning, smoothing, or polishing by means of sandpaper or some similar material. See ABRASIVE for picture. **2** a truck with a device for spreading sand on icy roads, or the device itself. **3** a person who or thing that sands.

sand flea *n* a flea found in sandy places.

sand·fly (sand′flī′) *n, pl* **sand·flies** a small tropical or subtropical fly, the female of which bites and sucks blood. Sandflies sometimes transmit disease.

sand·hill crane (sand′hil′) *n* a migratory crane of central and eastern N America, mainly bluish grey with a reddish crown.

sand·man (sand′man′) *n* a legendary man said to make children sleepy by sprinkling sand on their eyes.

sand·pa·per (sand′pā′pər) *n* a strong paper with a layer of sand or some other rough material glued on it, used for smoothing, cleaning, or polishing.
v smooth, clean, or polish with sandpaper.

sand·pip·er (sand′pī′pər) *n* a small shorebird with long toes and brownish or greyish plumage.

sand·stone (sand′stōn′) *n* a sedimentary rock consisting of grains of sand cemented naturally, usually red, yellow, or brown.

sand·storm (sand′stȯrm′) *n* a storm of wind that carries clouds of sand.

sand trap *n* a pit or depression filled with sand and serving as a hazard in the game of golf.

sand·wich (san′dwich) *n* **1** two or more slices of bread with a filling between them. **2** a thing, such as cake or ice cream, formed in a similar way.
v (*with* ***between***) insert or squeeze: *I was sandwiched between my sisters in the back seat of the car.*

ETYMOLOGY

The Earl of Sandwich (1717–1792) is said to have devised putting meat between slices of bread so that he could keep playing cards while he ate.

sandwich board *n* a pair of signboards, usually hinged at the top, designed to be hung from a person's shoulders with one board in front and the other behind, used for advertising or picketing.

a bat	e bed	i bid	o pot	u cup
ā cake	ē me	ī bite	ō go	ū rude
ȧ bar	ə about	ər over	ȯ for	u̇ put

sandwich generation *n* the people who have reached the stage of life where their parents and their children need care at the same time.

sand·y (san′dē) *adj* **sand·i·er, sand·i·est 1** containing, consisting of, or covered with sand: *Most of the shore is rocky, but there is a sandy beach.* **2** of the colour of sand: *sandy hair.* **3** like sand in texture. **sand′i·ness** *n.*

sane (sān) *adj* **san·er, san·est 1** not insane or mentally ill; able to make rational judgments and to appreciate the effects of one's actions. **2** reasonable or sensible: *a sane attitude toward eating.* <Latin *sanus* healthy> **sane′ly** *adv.* **sane′ness** *n.* **san′i·ty** *n.*

sang (sang) past tense of SING.

San·gat (sung′gət) *Sikhism n* a congregation, community, or assembly of worshippers: *The Sangat assembles each Sunday for worship.*

sang–froid (song fwȧ′) *n* calmness of mind, especially in dangerous or difficult circumstances. <French = cold blood>

san·gha (sang′gə) *n* a Buddhist religious community or monastic order.

san·gri·a (sang grē′ə) *n* a drink made from red wine, soda water, and bits of fruit.

san·guine (sang′gwin) *adj* **1** cheerful and hopeful: *a sanguine disposition. They were sanguine of success.* **2** in the Middle Ages, with a temperament in which blood predominates over other humours, resulting in a ruddy complexion and cheerful temperament. <Old French, from Latin *sanguis* blood>

san·i·tar·y (san′ə ter′ē) *adj* **1** to do with health and the conditions that affect health: *The city is looking for a more sanitary method of waste disposal.* **2** free from dirt or anything bad for health: *The top of the picnic table was not very sanitary.* <French, from Latin *sanus* healthy> **san′i·tar′i·ness** *n.* **san′i·tize′** *v.*

sanitary napkin or **pad** *n* a disposable absorbent pad worn by women on the outside of the body to absorb the discharge from menstruation.

san·i·ta·tion (san′ə tā′shən) *n* conditions relating to public health, especially the provision of safe drinking water and disposal of sewage.

san·i·ty (san′ə tē) *n* **1** soundness of mind, especially, the ability to make rational judgments and appreciate the effects of one's actions. **2** reasonable and rational behaviour.

sank (sangk) a past tense of SINK.

San Ma·ri·no (san mə rē′nō) *n* a small country surrounded by Italy, in Europe.

sans (sans) *prep* without: *We could spend an evening together—sans TV!* <Old French, from Latin *sine* without>

San·sei (san′sā′) *n, pl* **San·sei** or **San·seis** a native-born Canadian or American citizen whose grandparents were Japanese immigrants. Compare ISSEI, NISEI. <Japanese *san* third + *sei* generation>

San·skrit (san′skrit) *n* the ancient Indo-European literary and religious language of India. <Sanskrit *sam* together + *kr* make>

sans–ser·if (sanz′ser′if) *n, adj* in printing, type with no serifs.

San·ta Claus (san′tə kloz′) *n* the spirit or saint of Christmas gift giving, usually depicted as a jolly old man with a white beard, dressed in a fur-trimmed red suit. Often shortened to **Santa**. Also called **Saint Nicholas**, **Kris Kringle**. <Dutch *Sante Klaas* St. Nicholas>

Sao To·me and Prin·ci·pe (sou′ tō mā′) (prin′sə pə) *n* an island country off the coast of west Africa.

sap[1] (sap) *n* **1** the fluid, chiefly water with dissolved sugars and mineral salts, that circulates through a plant as blood does in animals. **2** vigour or energy: *the sap of youth.* **3** *Informal* a foolish or gullible person. <Old English *sæp*>

sap[2] (sap) *v* **sapped, sap·ping 1** weaken, undermine, or use up: *The extreme heat sapped their strength.* **2** undercut by water or glacial action. **3** dig a tunnel or trench in order to approach an enemy position in a battle.
n such a tunnel or trench. <origin uncertain>

sa·pi·ent (sā′pē ənt) *or* (sap′ē ənt) *adj* wise. **sa′pi·ence** *n.* **sa′pi·ent·ly** *adv.*

sap·ling (sap′ling) *n* a young tree, especially one with a slender trunk.

sap·o·dil·la (sap′ə dil′ə) *n* the edible fruit of an evergreen tree of tropical America. The milky latex of the tree yields chicle, used to make chewing gum. <Spanish, from Nahuatl (a language of Central and S America) *tzapotl*>

sap·per (sap′ər) *n* a military engineer who lays or detects and disarms mines.

sap·phire (saf′īr) *n* a typically bright blue gemstone.
adj bright blue. <Old French, from Greek *sappheiros*>

sap·py (sap′ē) *adj* **sap·pi·er, sap·pi·est 1** *Informal* overly sentimental. **2** full of sap. **sap′pi·ness** *n.*

sap·suck·er (sap′suk′ər) *n* a N American woodpecker that drills holes in trees to feed on sap and insects.

sap·wood (sap′wu̇d′) *n* the soft, sap-carrying tissue between the bark and the heartwood of trees.

Sar·a·cen (sar′ə sən) *or* (ser′ə sən) *n* an Arab or Muslim at the time of the Crusades in the Middle Ages.

sar·casm (sȧr′kaz əm) *n* the use of irony to mock or show contempt: *With obvious sarcasm, she called the scared boy a hero.* <Greek sarkazein = to strip off the flesh, from *sarkos* flesh> **sar·cas′tic** *adj.* **sar·cas′ti·cal·ly** *adv.*

Sar·cee (sȧr′sē) *n, pl* **Sar·cee** or **Sar·cees 1** a member of a First Nations people living mainly near Calgary. **2** their Athapascan language.
adj to do with these people or their language. Also called **Tsuu-t'in**.

sar·co·ma (sȧr kō′mə) *n* a cancerous tumour. <Latin, from Greek *sarkos* flesh>

sar·coph·a·gus (sȧr kof′ə gəs) *n, pl* **sar·coph·a·gus·es** or **sar·coph·a·gi** (-jī′) *or* (-jē′) a stone coffin, especially one ornamented with sculpture or inscriptions and used in the ancient civilizations of Egypt, Rome, and Greece. <Latin, from Greek *sarkos* flesh + *phagos-* eating, in reference to the effect of the limestone coffin on the body>

sar·dine (sȧr dēn′) *n, pl* **sar·dines** or (*especially collectively*) **sar·dine** a young or small food fish of the herring family, often preserved and canned in oil or other liquid. <Latin, from Greek *Sardo* Sardinia, where this fish was caught>
packed like sardines, very much crowded.

sar·don·ic (sȧr don′ik) *adj* grimly mocking or cynical: *She listened to their chatter with a sardonic smile.* <French, from Greek *sardonios* bitter or scornful laughter> **sar·don′i·cal·ly** *adv.*

sa·ri (sȧ′rē) *n, pl* **sa·ris** a garment worn by women especially in the Indian subcontinent, consisting of a long piece of light fabric, usually cotton or silk, draped around the body. <Hindi>

sa·rong (sə rong′) *n* a garment consisting of a long piece of cloth wrapped around the body and tucked at the waist or under the armpits, traditionally worn in southeast Asia. <Malay = sheath>

sar·sa·pa·ril·la (sas′pə ril′ə) *or* (sȧr′sə pə ril′ə) *n* a tropical American climbing or trailing plant, its root, or a medicine or drink made from the root. <Spanish *zara* bramble + *parra* vine>

sar·to·ri·al (sȧr tȯ′rē əl) *adj* to do with tailors, tailoring, or tailored clothes: *The costumes for the play were a sartorial triumph.* <Latin *sarcire* to patch>

SASE self-addressed stamped envelope.

sash[1] (sash) *n* a long, broad strip of cloth or ribbon, worn as an ornament round the waist or over one shoulder. <Arabic *shash*>

sash[2] (sash) *n* a frame that holds the glass in a window, often sliding: *She raised the sash to let in the spring air.* <*chassis*>

sa·shay (sa shā′) *Informal v* move or walk casually in a bold or swaggering manner: *He sashayed up to the front door as if he owned the place.* <French *chassé* a gliding dance step>

sa·shi·mi (sȧ shē′mē) *pln* a Japanese dish of bite-sized slices of raw fish. <Japanese>

Sas·katch·e·wan (sə skach′ə won′) *n* a western Canadian province, between Alberta and Ontario. Saskatchewan is one of the PRAIRIE PROVINCES. *Abbrev.* **Sask.**; postal symbol **SK**; URL **www.gov.sk.ca**
adj to do with Saskatchewan: *Saskatchewan wheat.* **Sas·katch′e·wan′ian** *n.*

🍁 **sas·ka·toon** (sas′kə tūn′) *n* a N American shrub of the rose family, or its edible purple berry.

ETYMOLOGY

Saskatoon comes from two Cree words: *misaskwat*, which means "tree of many branches," and *min*, which means "fruit."

Sas·quatch (sas′kwoch) *n* a wild, hairy, legendary monster of subhuman appearance, supposed to inhabit mountain regions of western N America. Also called **Bigfoot**. <Salish *sesxac*>

sass (sas) *Informal n* **1** backtalk or disrespectful replies. **2** liveliness or stylishness.
v reply disrespectfully: *Don't sass me, please.* <*saucy*> **sas′si·ly** *adv.* **sas′sy** *adj.*

sas·sa·fras (sas′ə fras′) *n* a N American hardwood tree that has fragrant, yellow flowers, or its aromatic, dried bark or root, used in medicine and as a flavouring. <Spanish, from Latin *saxifraga* saxifrage>

sat (sat) past tense and past participle of SIT.

SAT *n* in full, **Scholastic Aptitude Test** a standardized university entrance exam.

Sa·tan (sā′tən) DEVIL (def. 1b). <Hebrew = plot against>

sa·tan·ic (sā tan′ik) *adj* **1** to do with Satan: *satanic magic.* **2** showing extreme viciousness or cruelty: *a satanic act.*

Sa·tan·ism (sā′tə niz′əm) *n* the worship of Satan, typically involving the inverted or distorted use of Christian symbols and practices. **Sa′tan·ist** *adj, n.*

satch·el (sach′əl) *n* a small bag, often with a shoulder strap, for carrying books or other items.

sate (sāt) *v* **sat·ed, sat·ing 1** satisfy fully an appetite or desire: *A long drink sated her thirst.* **2** supply with more than enough, so as to disgust or weary. <Old English *sadian* become weary>

sa·teen (sa tēn′) *n* a fabric, usually cotton, with a glossy surface.

sat·el·lite (sat′ə līt′) *n* **1** a small planet that revolves around a larger planet, especially around one of the nine planets of the solar system. **2** an artificial object or vehicle sent into an orbit around the earth or other celestial body. See ANIK for picture. **3** something that is separate from but depends on or is controlled by a thing at the centre, such as a country that is nominally independent but is dominated by a more powerful one. <French, from Latin *satelles* attendant>

satellite dish *n* an antenna shaped like a dish or with a dish-shaped reflector, designed to receive communication signals transmitted by satellites.

sa·ti·ate (sā′shē āt′) *v* **sa·ti·at·ed, sa·ti·at·ing 1** satisfy fully an appetite or desire. **2** supply with more than enough, so as to disgust or weary: *He was so satiated with bananas that he couldn't look at one.* <Latin *satis* enough>

SYNONYMS

Satiate is used when a desire or bodily need has been met: *The food was abundant and they satiated their hunger.*

Satisfy can be used more broadly: *You have now satisfied the terms of the contract.*

Slake often refers to the satisfaction of thirst: *She drank two glasses of cold water to slake her thirst.*

sa·ti·e·ty (sə tī′ə tē) *n* the feeling or condition of being sated or satiated. <Old French, from Latin *satis* enough>

S

a bat	e bed	i bid	o pot	u cup	th thin
ā cake	ē me	ī bite	ō go	ū rude	ᴛʜ then
ȧ bar	ə about	ər over	ȯ for	u̇ put	zh measure

sat·in (sat′ən) *n* 1 a soft fabric, usually of silk, with a smooth, lustrous face. 2 a smoothness or glossiness like that of satin.
adj of or like satin. <Old French, from Arabic *zaytuni*>

sat·in·wood (sat′ən wůd′) *n* a smooth, glossy wood used to ornament furniture.

sat·in·y (sat′ə nē) *adj* like satin in being smooth and glossy.

sat·ire (sat′īr) *n* 1 the use of humour, irony, exaggeration, or ridicule to reveal undesirable aspects of people or their society. 2 a poem, novel, movie, or other work that uses satire. <French, from Latin *satira*>
sat′i·rize′ (sat′ə rīz′) *v.* **sat′i·rist′** (sat′ə rīst) *n.*

sa·tir·i·cal (sə tir′ə kəl) *adj* containing, showing, reflecting, or fond of using satire: *a satirical smile, a satirical novel, a satirical columnist.* Also, **satiric**. **sa·tir′i·cal·ly** *adv.*

sat·is·fac·tion (sat′is fak′shən) *n* 1 a fulfillment of a person's wishes, hopes, or needs, or the pleasure or contentment derived from this: *She got great satisfaction from her good grades. It is a great satisfaction to have things turn out just the way you want.* 2 the payment of a debt or fulfillment of an obligation or claim: *He demanded satisfaction for the damage done to his bike.*

sat·is·fac·to·ry (sat′is fak′tə rē) *or* (sat′is fak′trē) *adj* acceptable and fulfilling expectations, though not exceptional or perfect. **sat′is·fac′to·ri·ly** *adv.* **sat′is·fac′to·ri·ness** *n.*

sat·is·fy (sat′is fī′) *v* **sat·is·fied, sat·is·fy·ing** 1 meet the hopes, needs, or desires of someone: *We satisfy hunger by eating. Are you satisfied now?* 2 fully meet an objection, question, or demand: *She was able to satisfy all my doubts.* 3 adequately deal with a condition or demand: *The company was able to satisfy the market demand.* <Old French, from Latin *satis* enough + *facere* do> **sat′is·fy′ing** *adj.* **sat′is·fy′ing·ly** *adv.*

sa·to·ri (sə tȯ′rē) *Buddhism n* a sudden enlightenment.

sa·trap (sā′trap′) *n* 1 a ruler, often a tyrant, who is subordinate to a higher ruler. 2 in ancient Persia, the governor of a province. <Old French, from Persian *ksathra-pavan* country-protector>

sat·u·rate (sach′ə rāt′) *v* **sat·u·rat·ed, sat·u·rat·ing** 1 become so soaked with water or other liquid that no more can be absorbed: *to saturate soil.* 2 cause a substance to unite with the greatest possible amount of another substance: *a saturated solution of sugar.* 3 load or fill a thing to capacity: *The market was saturated with new products.* 4 fill something or someone with something so that no more can be held or absorbed: *We were saturated with information.* <Latin *satur* full>

saturated fat *n* a type of animal or vegetable fat, found in butter, meat, egg yolks, and some nut oils. It increases the cholesterol level in the blood and is considered less healthy than unsaturated fat.

saturated solution *n* a solution that contains all the solute it can hold at a given temperature.

sat·u·ra·tion (sach′ə rā′shən) *n* 1 the act or process of saturating. 2 the intensity of a colour, expressed in the degree in which it differs from white.

saturation point *Chemistry n* the point at which a substance can be absorbed into a vapour or dissolved in a solution.

Sat·ur·day (sat′ər dā′) *n* the day of the week after Friday and before Sunday. *Abbrev.* **Sat** <Latin *Saturni dies* day of Saturn>

Sat·urn (sat′ərn) *n* the second largest planet and the sixth in distance from the sun, circled by a system of rings. See EARTH for picture. <*Saturn*, Roman god of agriculture>

Sat·ur·na·li·a (sat′ər nā′lē ə) *n* 1 the ancient Roman festival of Saturn, celebrated in December with much feasting and merrymaking. 2 **saturnalia** a period of wild merrymaking.

sat·ur·nine (sat′ər nīn′) *adj* gloomy and slow: *a saturnine temperament.* **sat′ur·nine·ly** *adv.*

sat·yr (sat′ər) *or* (sā′tər) *Greek myth n* a god of the woods, often pictured with the head, arms, and body of a man and the legs and tail of a goat. <Old French, from Greek *saturos*>

sauce (sos) *n* 1 a thick or thin liquid served with food to make it taste better: *mint sauce, applesauce.* 2 *UK, Informal* sauciness.
v **sauced, sauc·ing** 1 provide or season with a sauce. 2 make more interesting. 3 *UK Informal* be saucy to. <Old French, from Latin *salis* salt>

sauce·pan (sos′pan′) *n* a deep, round utensil, usually with a lid and a long handle at the side, used for cooking on top of the stove.

sau·cer (sos′ər) *n* 1 a small, round, shallow dish with a dent in the middle used to set something on, such as a cup. 2 anything round and shallow like a saucer.

sau·cy (sos′ē) *adj* **sau·ci·er, sau·ci·est** 1 showing lack of respect; rude. 2 pert; smart: *a saucy hat.* **sau′ci·ly** *adv.* **sau′ci·ness** *n.*

Sa·u·di A·ra·bi·a (sou′dē ə rā′bē ə) *n* a country in southwest Asia. See the APPENDIX.
Sa·u′di A·ra′bi·an *adj, n.*

sauer·kraut (sour′krout′) *n* cabbage cut fine, salted, and allowed to ferment. <German *sauer* sour + *Kraut* cabbage>

Saul·teaux (sal′tō) *or* (sol′tō) *n, pl* **Saul·teaux**
1 a member of a First Nations people who are a western branch of the Anishinabe. 2 their Anishinabe dialect.
adj to do with these people or their language. Also, **Salteaux**.

sau·na (son′ə) *or* (sou′nə) *n* a small room or building used as a hot-air or steam bath for refreshing the body, or the bath itself. <Finnish>

saun·ter (son′tər) *v* walk along in a slow, relaxed way: *People sauntered through the park.*
n a slow, relaxed walk: *They went for a saunter along the Humber River.* <origin uncertain> **saun′ter·er** *n.*

–saur or **–saurus** *combining form* reptile, especially an extinct one: *dinosaur.* <Greek *sauros* lizard>

sau·sage (sos′ij) *n* chopped or ground meat, seasoned and stuffed into a thin casing. <Old French, from Latin *salsis* salted>

sau·té (sō tā′) *or* (sot ā′) *v* **sau·téed, sau·tée·ing** fry quickly in a little fat. <French *sauter* jump, as fat does in a hot frying pan>

sav·age (sav′ij) *adj* **1** fierce, violent, or uncontrolled, especially in animals or a force of nature: *savage beasts, a savage storm.* **2** wild-looking and rugged: *savage mountains.* **3** brutal and vicious: *She was the victim of a savage attack by a mugger.* **4** regarded as uncivilized or primitive in culture: *a savage people.*
n **1** a brutal and vicious person. **2** a person regarded as uncivilized or primitive in culture.
v **sav·aged, sav·ag·ing** attack brutally and viciously: *The squirrel was savaged by a dog.* <Old French, from Latin *silva* a forest> **sav′age·ly** *adv.* **sav′age·ness** *n.*

GRAMMAR AND USAGE

It is not acceptable to use **savage** to refer to people from a culture different from your own.

sav·age·ry (sav′ij rē) *n, pl* **sav·age·ries 1** the quality or condition of being savage: *The savagery of their attack took the enemy by surprise.* **2** an act of cruelty or brutality.

sa·van·na or **sa·van·nah** (sə van′ə) *n* a grassy plain with few trees in a tropical or subtropical region. <Spanish, from Arawak (a language of S America) *zavana*>

sa·vant (sə vänt′) *or* (sav′ənt) *n* a person of great learning. <French from Latin *sapere* be wise>

save[1] (sāv) *v* **saved, sav·ing 1** make safe from harm, danger, or loss: *to save a drowning person.* **2** (*often with* ***up***) keep and store something for some future purpose, especially money: *He saved enough money to pay for new skates, to save up for a holiday. She saves grocery bags. Save your questions until the presentation is over.* **3** keep from or avoid spending, wasting, or weakening: *She saved a lot of money at the discount sale, to save work. The large print saved my eyes.* **4** *Christianity* set free from sin and its results. **5** *Computers* keep data by moving a copy to a storage location: *She saved the file to a disk.*
n Sports the act of saving, especially by preventing an opponent from scoring: *The goalie made five saves in the first period.* <Old French, from Latin *salvus* safe>
sav′er *n.*

save[2] (sāv) *prep, conj* except: *She works every day of the week save Sunday.* <Old French, from Latin *salvus* safe>

sav·ing (sā′ving) *n* **1** an act or way of saving money or time: *It will be a saving to buy in bulk.* **2 savings** *pl* money that is saved.
adj (*in compounds*) preventing waste: *money-saving.*
prep except for: *Saving a piece of toast, I've eaten nothing all day.*

saving grace *n* a redeeming quality or feature.

savings account *n* an account in a bank, trust company, or credit union on which interest is paid.

sav·iour or **sav·ior** (sā′vyər) *n* **1** a person who saves or rescues. **2 the Saviour** or **the Savior** *Christianity* Jesus Christ.

sa·voir–faire (sav′wär fer′) *n* the knowledge of just the proper thing to do or say, especially in social situations. <French = know how to do>

sa·vor·y (sā′və rē) *n, pl* **sa·vor·ies** a fragrant herb of the mint family. See HERB for picture. <Latin *satureia*>

sa·vour or **sa·vor** (sā′vər) *n* **1** a flavour or smell: *The soup has a savour of onion.* **2** a distinctive quality: *There is a savour of conceit in everything he says.*
v **1** (*with* ***of***) taste or smell: *That sauce savours of lemon.* **2** perceive or appreciate by taste or smell: *She savoured the soup with pleasure.* **3** (*with* ***of***) have the quality or nature: *a request that savours of a command.* <Old French, from Latin *sapor* taste> **sa′vour·less** *adj.*

sa·vour·y or **sa·vor·y** (sā′və rē) *adj* **1** pleasing in taste or smell: *The savoury smell of roasting turkey greeted us as we entered the house.* **2** with a salty or piquant flavour and not a sweet one: *There were both sweet and savoury relishes on the table.* **3** morally acceptable: *His reputation was not particularly savoury.*
n, pl **sa·vour·ies** or **sa·vor·ies** *UK* a small portion of highly seasoned food.

sa·voy (sə voi′) *n* a cabbage with a compact head and densely wrinkled leaves.

sav·vy (sav′ē) *Informal adj* aware of and understanding how the world works: *She was a savvy manager of time.*
n shrewdness and practical knowledge: *He was known for his savvy with computers.*
v **sav·vied, sav·vy·ing** know or understand: *We've got to be on time, you savvy?* <Spanish, from Latin *sapere* be wise>

saw[1] (so) *n* a tool for cutting hard material such as wood. It consists of a blade or disc that moves back and forth, with sharp teeth on the edge.
v **sawed, sawed** or **sawn, saw·ing** use, cut, or make with a saw. <Old English *saga*>

saw[2] (so) past tense of SEE[1].

GRAMMAR AND USAGE

Saw and **seen** are both forms of the verb see.

Saw is the simple past tense and can therefore stand on its own: *I saw them just yesterday when they were coming out of the mall.*

Seen is the past participle and needs an auxiliary verb like *have, has, is, are, was,* or *were*: *I have seen them only once in the last year.*

saw[3] (so) *n* a wise saying or proverb: *"A stitch in time saves nine" is a familiar saw.* <Old English *sagu*>

saw·dust (sod′ust′) *n* tiny particles of wood produced through sawing.

sawed–off (sod′of′) *adj* **1** with the end of a gun barrel cut off: *a sawed-off shotgun.* **2** *Informal* short in height.

saw·horse (so′hörs′) *n* a frame on which wood is placed for sawing.

saw·mill (som′il′) *n* a workplace where timber is sawed into planks or boards by power-driven machines.

a bat	e bed	i bid	o pot	u cup	th **thin**
ā cake	ē me	ī bite	ō go	ū rude	ᴛʜ **then**
ä bar	ə about	ər over	ö for	ů put	zh measure

sawn (son) a past participle of SAW[1].

saw–off (so′of′) *n* **1** an arrangement, especially in politics, in which two opposing groups make concessions that balance each other. **2** a tie in a sport or game.

saw·yer (soi′yər) *or* (so′yər) *n* a person whose work is sawing timber.

sax (saks) *Informal n* a saxophone.

sax·i·frage (sak′sə frij) *n* **1** a low-growing plant with fleshy leaves growing from near the base. **2** a member of a family of herbs, shrubs, or small trees found mainly in northern temperate and subarctic regions. Currants and gooseberries are saxifrages.

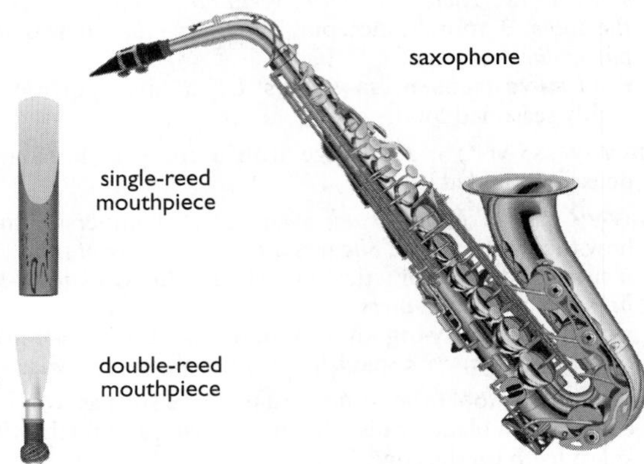

A **saxophone** has one reed, which vibrates with a buzzing sound in response to the player's breath. The oboe and bassoon have double-reed mouthpieces. The different reeds and shapes determine the sound each instrument makes.

sax·o·phone (sak′sə fōn′) *n* a musical wind instrument with a curved metal body, keys for the fingers, and a single-reed mouthpiece. <A. *Sax*, 19c inventor>
sax′o·phon′ist *n.*

say (sā) *v* **said, say·ing 1** speak: *What did you say?* **2** put into words: *Say what you think. What does that sign say?* **3** recite or repeat: *Say the poem.* **4** suppose or take as an estimate: *You can learn the basics in, say, ten lessons.* **5** express an opinion: *It is hard to say which design is better.*
n **1** what a person says or has to say: *I have had my say.* **2** the chance to say something: *We will all have our say before the meeting ends.* **3** power or authority: *Who has the say in this matter?* <Old English *secgan*> **say′a·ble** *adj.* **say′er** *n.*
go without saying, be extremely obvious: *It goes without saying that she will be furious when she sees him again.*
that is to say, in other words: *I'm going to bed, that is to say, I'm tired.*
to say nothing of, without mentioning: *The hotel itself cost a lot, to say nothing of the meals.*

say·ing (sā′ing) *n* a short, popular expression that usually offers advice or wisdom: *I remembered the saying "Haste makes waste."*

sa·yo·na·ra (sī′ə nor′ə) *interj* goodbye. <Japanese>

say–so (sā′sō′) *Informal n* **1** an unsupported statement: *He may be wrong, so don't do it just on his say-so.* **2** the authority or power to decide: *She has no say-so in the matter.*

scab (skab) *n* **1** the crust that forms over a sore or wound during healing: *A scab formed on the spot where he was vaccinated.* **2** a skin disease in animals, especially sheep. **3** a fungal disease of plants, especially on apples and potatoes, usually producing crustlike spots. **4** BLACKLEG.
v **scabbed, scab·bing 1** become covered with a scab: *The scrape on your knee will scab by tomorrow.* **2** *Informal* become a scab in a workplace. <Scandinavian>

scab·bard (skab′ərd) *n* a sheath or case for the blade of a sword or dagger. <Old Norse *skabb*>

scab·by (skab′ē) *adj* **scab·bi·er, scab·bi·est 1** covered with scabs: *scabby skin.* **2** with the disease scab: *scabby potatoes.* **3** *Informal* low or mean: *a scabby trick.*
scab′bi·ness *n.*

sca·bies (skā′bēz) *n* a contagious skin disease caused by mites that live as parasites under the skin and cause itching. <Latin *scabere* scratch>

sca·brous (skā′brəs) *adj* **1** rough and covered with, or as if with, scabs: *a scabrous leaf.* **2** unattractive or unpleasant. **3** indecent: *scabrous details of the star's private life.*

scads (skadz) *Informal pln* a large quantity. <origin uncertain>

scaf·fold (skaf′əld) *n* **1** a temporary structure for holding workers when working at a height above the ground or floor during the construction, cleaning, or repair of a building. Also, **scaffolding**. **2** a raised platform used as a base for a gallows or guillotine.
v equip or support with a scaffold.
<Old French *eschaffault*>

sca·lar (skā′lər) *Mathematics adj* of a number or quantity, having magnitude but not direction. <See SCALE[3].>

scald (skold) *v* **1** injure with very hot liquid or steam. **2** heat or be heated almost to boiling, but not quite: *to scald milk.*
n a burn caused by hot liquid or steam: *The scald on her hand came from lifting a pot cover carelessly.* <Old French, from Latin *ex-* very + *calidus* hot>

scale[1] (skāl) *n* **1** a thin, flat, hard plate, one of many forming the outer covering of some fish, snakes, and lizards. **2** a thick, dry flake of skin or other material. **3** a coating of iron oxide formed on heated metal, or a white chemical deposit formed in a container after water has evaporated.
v **scaled, scal·ing 1** remove scales from: *He scaled the fish with a sharp knife.* **2** remove tartar from: *She had her teeth scaled by the dentist.* **3** come off in thin pieces or a thin layer: *The paint is starting to scale.* <Old French *escale*>
scale′less *adj.* **scal′er** *n.*

scale[2] (skāl) *n* **1** an instrument used for weighing, in which two dishes or pans are balanced. **2 scales** *pl* any instrument for weighing. <Old Norse *skal* bowl>
tip (or **turn**) **the scale** (or **scales**), be the deciding factor: *His year of experience on the team tipped the scales in his favour and he was made captain.*
tip the scales at, have as one's weight: *She tips the scales at forty-five kilograms.*

scale[3] (skāl) *n* **1** a series of steps for measuring or grading something: *a wage scale.* **2 a** a series of marks made along a line at regular intervals, used for measuring. **b** a measuring instrument marked in this way. **3** the size of a plan, map, or model compared with what it represents: *a map drawn to the scale of one centimetre for each hundred kilometres.* **4** the relative amount, size, or extent of something: *to entertain on a large scale.* **5** a system of numbering: *the decimal scale.* **6** *Music* a specific series of musical tones ascending or descending in pitch.
v **scaled, scal·ing 1** climb up or over: *They scaled the wall by ladders.* **2** change according to a certain proportion: *All marks were scaled down ten percent.* <Latin *scala* ladder>
to scale, following a set of measurements that is used as the equivalent of another, usually larger, set: *This subway map cannot be to scale, because the stations are not really the same distance apart.*

scale drawing *n* a drawing used to accurately represent a person, animal, building, etc. too large or too small to be drawn actual size.

scale factor *Mathematics n* the ratio of any two corresponding lengths in two similar geometric figures.

scale insect *n* a small bug, the female of which mostly has the body and eggs covered by a shieldlike scale. Such insects attach to and feed on a single plant.

scale leaf *n* a leaf part that unites with others to cover a bud.

scale model *n* a model of a building, ship, or other thing that uses a set of proportionally small measurements to represent larger ones.

sca·lene (skā lēn′) *or* (skā′lēn) *adj* **1** with three unequal sides in a triangle. **2** with the axis of a cone or cylinder not perpendicular to the base. <Latin, from Greek *skalenos* uneven>

scal·lion (skal′yən) *n* **1** a young, long-necked green onion with a small, undeveloped bulb. **2** a shallot. <Old French *scalon*>

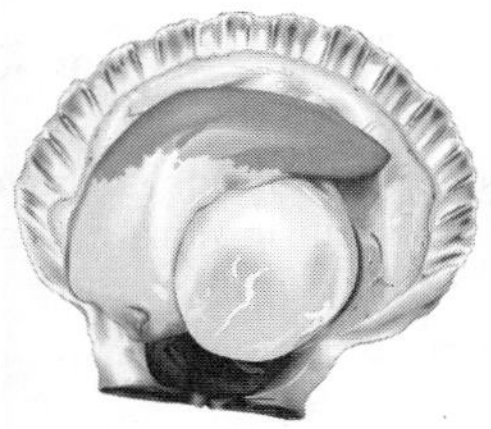

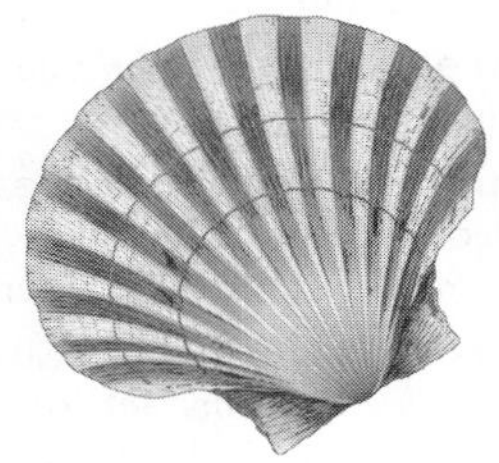

Unlike mussels, **scallops** rarely attach themselves to rocks. Instead, they rest on the ocean floor. To change locations, scallops swim by rapidly opening and closing their shells.

scal·lop (skol′əp) *or* (skal′əp) *n* **1** an edible shellfish with a ridged, fan-shaped shell. **2** one of a series of semicircular curves on an edge of a dress, resembling the edge of a scallop shell.
v **1** bake with milk or a sauce: *scalloped oysters.* **2** make with a series of semicircular curves on a dress: *She scalloped the hems of the pillowcases.* **3** gather or dredge for scallops in the sea. <Old French *escalope* shell>

scal·ly·wag (skal′ə wag′) *Informal n* a person who behaves badly but in an amusing way. Also, **scalawag.** <origin uncertain>

sca·lop·pi·ne (skal′ə pē′nē) *pln* thin boneless slices of veal for quick frying. Also, **scaloppini.** <Italian *scaloppa* envelope>

scalp (skalp) *n* **1** the skin on the top and back of the head. **2** part of this skin with the hair attached, taken in former times from a conquered enemy and kept as a token of victory.
v **1** cut or tear the scalp from. **2** *Informal* resell tickets to popular sports and entertainment events to make a quick profit. <probably Scandinavian>

scal·pel (skal′pəl) *n* a small, sharp, straight knife used in surgery. <French, from Latin *scalpere* to scratch>

scalp·er (skal′pər) *Informal n* one who scalps tickets or stocks.

🍁 **scalp lock** *n* a long lock or a tuft of hair left on the top of the shaved head of some First Nations men.

scal·y (skā′lē) *adj* **scal·i·er, scal·i·est 1** with scales like a fish. **2** covered or encrusted with a layer of a thing like scales: *This iron pipe is scaly with rust.* **3** like or suggesting scales.

scam (skam) *n* a fraud or swindle, especially a con game, intended to make a quick profit.
v **scammed, scam·ming** defraud or swindle. <origin uncertain>

scamp (skamp) *n* someone, especially a child, who is mischievous in a likeable or amusing way. <origin uncertain>

scam·per (skam′pər) *v* run or move quickly with light steps: *The mice scampered when the cat showed up.*
n an act of scampering. <See SCAMP.>

scam·pi (skam′pē) *or* (skȧm′pē) *pln* large shrimp or prawns, especially when used in Italian dishes. <Italian>

scan (skan) *v* **scanned, scan·ning 1** look at all parts of something closely: *His mother scanned his face to see if he was telling the truth.* **2** glance at quickly: *I took a few minutes to scan the newspaper headlines.* **3** find the metre of a poem by marking the lines off into feet, or fit a particular metrical pattern. Example: *Tiger!/Tiger!/ burning/bright/.* **4** use an electronic beam to pass over a surface of the body for the purpose of diagnosis. **5** *Computers* convert a document or picture into digital form for storage or processing. <Latin *scandere* climb>

scan·dal (skan′dəl) *n* **1** an action, condition, or event considered to bring disgrace or offend public opinion: *It was a scandal for the city official to take tax money for his own use.* **2** the disapproval or notoriety caused by such an action or event: *This behaviour is cause for scandal.* **3** a circumstance or situation regarded as wrong and causing great public disapproval: *It's a scandal that no one spoke up to defend him.* <Old French, from Greek *skandalon* trap>

a **bat**	e **bed**	i **bid**	o **pot**	u **cup**	th **thin**
ā **cake**	ē **me**	ī **bite**	ō **go**	ū **rude**	ᴛʜ **then**
ȧ **bar**	ə **about**	ər **over**	ȯ **for**	u̇ **put**	zh **measure**

scan·dal·ize (skan′də līz′) *v* **scan·dal·ized, scan·dal·iz·ing** offend by doing a thing thought to be wrong or improper: *She scandalized the neighbours by neglecting her children.*

scan·dal·mon·ger (skan′dəl mung′gər) *or* (skan′dəl mong′gər) *n* a person who spreads scandal and gossip.

scan·dal·ous (skan′də ləs) *adj* **1** causing public disapproval by being immoral or shocking: *scandalous behaviour.* **2** consisting of or spreading scandal or slander; slandering: *a scandalous piece of gossip.*
scan′dal·ous·ly *adv.*

scandal sheet *n* a newspaper or periodical that features sensational stories and malicious gossip.

Scan·di·na·vi·an (skan′də nā′vē ən) *adj* to do with Scandinavia, a region including Denmark, Norway, Sweden, and, often, Iceland, or its peoples, or their languages.
n **1** a native or inhabitant of Scandinavia, or one of Scandinavian descent. **2** the group of northern Germanic languages spoken in Scandinavia, descended from Old Norse.

GRAMMAR AND USAGE

The terms **Scandinavian** and **Scandinavia** are often used to include Finland, but Finland is historically distinct from the Scandinavian countries, with a very different language and different cultural traditions.

scan·di·um (skan′dē əm) *n* a rare metallic element. *Symbol* **Sc** <Latin *Scandia* Scandinavia>

scanner (skan′ər) *Computers n* **1** a device that scans the body as an aid to medical diagnosis. **2** a device that scans documents and converts texts or images into digital data: *The cashier rang up my purchase using a scanner to read the price on the label.*

scan·sion (skan′shən) *n* the analysis of the metre of a poem or poetry.

scant (skant) *adj* **1** not enough in size, amount, or quantity: *scant provisions.* **2** barely full or complete: *He takes a scant teaspoon of sugar in his tea. You have a scant hour in which to pack.*
v provide grudgingly or inadequately: *Don't scant the butter if you want a rich cake.* <Old Norse *skammr* short>
scant′ness *n.*
scant of, with not enough: *scant of breath.*

scant·y (skan′tē) *adj* **scant·i·er, scant·i·est 1** not enough: *Her scanty clothing did not keep out the cold.* **2** barely enough: *a scanty harvest.* **scant′i·ly** *adv.* **scant′i·ness** *n.*

–scape *combining form* a scene of a particular kind: *seascape.* <(*land*)*scape*>

scape·goat (skāp′gōt′) *n* a person or thing made to bear the blame for the mistakes or sins of others.
v make a scapegoat of. <(*e*)*scape* + *goat*>

scap·u·la (skap′yə lə) *n, pl* **scap·u·las** or **scap·u·lae** (-lē′) *or* (-lī′) the shoulder blade.

scar (skȧr) *n* **1** a mark left on the skin by a healed cut, wound, burn, or sore. **2** a mark like this: *A fallen leaf leaves a scar where it joined the stem. There is a small scar from a cigarette burn on the tabletop.* **3** a lasting effect caused by grief, fear, or another emotion: *War leaves deep scars on the minds of those who endure it.*
v **scarred, scar·ring** mark or be formed with a scar or scars: *The door was badly scarred by the fire.* <Old French, from Greek *esckara* scab>

scar·ab (skar′əb) *or* (sker′əb) *n* **1** a large dung beetle of the eastern Mediterranean, especially the sacred beetle of the ancient Egyptians. **2** an ancient Egyptian gem cut in the form of this beetle. <Latin, from Greek *skarabeios*>

scarce (skers) *adj* **scarc·er, scarc·est** hard to get or insufficient to meet demand: *Good cooks are always scarce.* *adv* scarcely. <Old French *escars,* from Latin *ex-* out + *carpere* gather> **scarce′ness** *n.*
make yourself scarce, *Informal* **a** go away. **b** stay away.
scarce as hen's teeth, *Informal* very scarce.

scarce·ly (sker′slē) *adv* **1** only just or barely: *scarcely old enough for school. We could scarcely see through the fog.* **2** decidedly not: *He could scarcely have said that. I will scarcely pay that much.*

scar·ci·ty (sker′sə tē) *n, pl* **scar·ci·ties** too small a supply: *There is often a scarcity of nurses.*

scare (sker) *v* **scared, scar·ing** make or become frightened: *The dog's barking scared the children. She doesn't scare easily.*
n **1** a fright: *I got a real scare when the lights went out.* **2** a condition of alarm or panic: *There was a polio scare last summer. The flight was delayed because of a bomb scare.* <Old Norse *skjarr* timid> **scared** *adj.*
scare up, *Informal* get or get something together quickly: *We made camp and then tried to scare up some food.*

scare·crow (sker′krō′) *n* **1** an object, usually a figure of a man dressed in old clothes, set in a field to frighten birds away from crops. **2** a person who is thin and gaunt or who dresses like a scarecrow.

scare·dy–cat (sker′dē kat′) *Informal n* a person who is too easily frightened.

scare·mon·ger (sker′mun′gər) *n* a person who spreads frightening rumours.

scarf[1] (skȧrf) *n, pl* **scarves** (skȧrvz) or **scarfs** a square piece of cotton, silk, wool, or other fabric worn around the neck or head. <Old French *escarpe* pilgrim's shrift>

scarf[2] (skȧrf) *Informal v* eat in large quantities: *We scarfed a whole bag of chocolate chip cookies.* <*scoff*>

scar·let (skȧr′lit) *adj* light, brilliant red with a slight tinge of orange. <origin unknown>

scarlet fever *n* a contagious disease, especially in children, characterized by a red rash, sore throat, and fever.

scarp (skȧrp) *n* **1** a steep slope or bank. **2** the inner slope or side of a ditch surrounding a fortification.
v cut or erode a slope or hillside so it becomes steep. <Italian *scarpa*>

scarves (skȧrvz) a plural of SCARF[1].

scar·y (sker′ē) *Informal adj* **scar·i·er, scar·i·est 1** causing fright or alarm: *a scary movie.* **2** uncannily impressive or surprising: *It was scary how fast he could run.*
scar′i·ly *adv.* **scar′i·ness** *n.*

scat[1] (skat) *Informal v* **scat·ted, scat·ting** (*usually in the imperative*) go away quickly: *Scat! she told the boys.* <origin uncertain>

scat[2] (skat) *n* jazz singing with meaningless syllables instead of words so that the voice is used like a musical instrument.
v **scat·ted, scat·ting** sing in the style of scat. <origin uncertain>

scat[3] *n* the feces of a wild animal. <Greek *skatos* dung>

scathe (skāᴛʜ) *n, v* hurt or harm. <Old English *sceatha*> **scathe′less** *adj.*

scath·ing (skā′ᴛʜing) *adj* severely critical or scornful: *scathing comments.* <See SCATHE.> **scath′ing·ly** *adv.*

sca·to·log·i·cal (ska′to loj′i kəl) *adj* interested in or obsessed with excrement or urine. <Greek *skatos* dung> **sca·tol′o·gy** (ska′tol′ə jē) *n.*

scat·ter (skat′ər) *v* **1** throw or sprinkle in various random directions: *He scattered sand on the icy sidewalk.* **2** separate and drive off in different directions: *The police scattered the mob.* **3** separate and go in different directions: *The hens scattered.* **4** (*in the passive*) occur or be found irregularly rather than in a group: *Several hamlets were scattered across the countryside.*
n **1** the act or fact of scattering. **2** a small dispersed amount of something: *a scatter of pebbles.* <Middle English> **scat′ter·er** *n.*

scat·ter·brain (skat′ər brān′) *n* a thoughtless, frivolous person. **scat′ter·brained′** *adj.*

scat·tered (skat′ərd) *adj* not occurring together or in large amounts: *There were scattered instances of violence. We heard scattered shouts in the distance.*

scat·ter·ing (skat′ə ring) *n* **1** the act or fact of scattering. **2** a small, dispersed amount of something.

scatter plot *n* a graph that shows the relationship between two variables by the position of a series of points on a grid. Also called **scatter diagram**.

scatter rug *n* a small, decorative rug that can be easily moved to different places.

scav·enge (skav′ənj) *v* **scav·enged, scav·eng·ing** **1** salvage something usable from discarded materials: *He makes sculptures from materials he has scavenged.* **2** feed as an animal on dead animals, garbage, or decaying matter. <Old French, from Flemish *scauwen* to show> **scav′en·ger** *n.*

scavenger hunt *n* a game in which individuals or teams race to find and collect all the items on a prepared list.

sce·nar·i·o (si ner′ē ō′) *n, pl* **sce·nar·i·os** **1** an outline of a movie, novel, or play, giving the main facts about the scenes, characters, and action. **2** an outline of action or sequence of events, proposed as a possible outcome of a real or imagined situation: *In our worst-case scenario, tests will have to be taken again.* <Italian, from Latin *scena* scene>

sce·nar·ist (si ner′ist) *n* a person who writes scenarios.

scene (sēn) *n* **1** the place where an incident or series of events occurred, or is shown as having occurred: *the scene of an accident. The scene of the novel is laid in Québec City in the year 1759.* **2 a** a subdivision of an act of a play: *Act 2, Scene 1.* **b** a sequence of continuous action in a book, movie, etc.: *The star of the movie didn't appear in the opening scenes.* **3** a view of a place, especially one presented in a painting or photograph: *a rural scene.* **4** *Informal* **a** a set of circumstances: *a bad scene.* **b** a social environment or setting: *That party just wasn't my scene.* **5** a show of strong feeling in front of others: *The child kicked and screamed and made a scene.* <Latin from Greek *skene* tent, originally where the actors changed their costumes>
behind the scenes, a out of sight of the audience. **b** not publicly: *A lot of planning for the festival was done behind the scenes.*
on the scene, part of a certain activity or group: *He was the vice-principal six years ago, which was before we arrived on the scene.*
set the scene, describe the setting of an event, and give background information.

scen·er·y (sē′nə rē) *or* (sēn′rē) *n, pl* **scen·er·ies** **1** the general appearance of the natural features of a place: *mountain scenery.* **2** the painted background used to represent natural or other features on a theatre stage or movie set. <Italian, from Latin *scena* scene>

sce·nic (sē′nik) *or* (sen′ik) *adj* **1** to do with impressive or beautiful natural scenery: *a scenic highway.* **2** to do with theatrical scenery: *The production of the musical comedy was a scenic triumph.* **3** representing an action, incident, or situation in a work of art: *a scenic painting.* **sce′nic·al·ly** *adv.*

scent (sent) *n* **1** a smell, especially a pleasant one: *the scent of new-mown hay, the scent of roses.* **2** the sense of smell: *Bloodhounds have a keen scent.* **3** a trail indicated by the particular smell of an animal that has passed: *The dogs followed the scent of the fox.* **4** a means by which a person or thing can be traced: *The police picked up the thief's scent again where he had stopped for gas.* **5** perfume: *She uses too much scent.*
v **1** become aware of through smell: *The dog immediately scented the rabbit and dashed off after it.* **2** give a pleasant smell to: *The tea was scented with jasmine. Lilacs scented the air.* **3** apply perfume to: *She scented her handkerchief.* **4** get or have a suspicion or inkling, of: *They scented trouble and left quickly.* <Old French, from Latin *sentire* to sense> **scent′less** *adj.*

CONFUSABLES

Scent means "smell": *A wonderful scent came from the perfume bottle when it was opened.*

Sent means "caused to go": *I've sent them the money.*

Cent means "penny": *They spent every cent that their mother had given them.*

scep·tic (skep′tik) SKEPTIC.

scep·tre (sep′tər) *n* the ornamental rod or staff carried by a ruler as a symbol of royal power or authority. Also, **scepter**. <Old French, from Greek *skeptron* staff>

a bat	e bed	i bid	o pot	u cup	th thin
ā cake	ē me	ī bite	ō go	ū rude	ᴛʜ then
à bar	ə about	ər over	ȯ for	ů put	zh measure

S

sched·ule (skej′ūl) *or* (shej′ūl) *n* **1** a list of planned events and times in carrying out a process or procedure: *a bus schedule.* **2** a listing of the games to be played by the teams in a league: *a hockey schedule.* **3** the time or times fixed for doing something: *The bus was an hour behind schedule.*
v **sched·uled, sched·ul·ing 1** make or enter in a schedule of. **2** plan or arrange something for a definite time or date: *I must schedule a dentist appointment for next week.* <Old French, from Greek *schida*> **sched′ul·er** *n.*
sched′uled *adj.*

sche·ma (skē′mə) *n, pl* **sche·ma·ta** (skē ma′tə) an outline or model representing a plan or theory. <Latin, from Greek *skhema*>

sche·mat·ic (skē mat′ik) *adj* shown in a diagram or drawing in symbolic and simplified form. **sche·mat′i·cal·ly** *adv.*

sche·ma·tize (skē′mə tīz′) *v* **sche·ma·tized, sche·ma·tiz·ing** arrange or show in a schematic form. **sche′ma·tiz·a′tion** *n.*

scheme (skēm) *n* **1** a systematic plan of action: *She has a scheme for extracting gold from sea water.* **2** a secret or underhanded plot: *a scheme to cheat the government.* **3** a system of connected things, parts, or thoughts: *The colour scheme of the room is blue and gold.*
v **schemed, schem·ing** plan or plot: *Those men were scheming to bring the jewels into the country without paying duty.* <See SCHEMA.>

schem·ing (skē′ming) *adj* given to forming sly or secret plans.

scher·zo (sker′tsō) *n, pl* **scher·zos** or **scher·zi** (-tsē) a light and playful musical composition, often as a part of a sonata or symphony.

schism (siz′əm), (shiz′əm), *or* (skiz′əm) *n* **1** a division between two strongly opposed sections or parties because of some difference of opinion or belief. **2** a separation of one church into two or more churches because of internal differences, especially concerning beliefs. <Old French, from Greek *skhizein* to split>

schis·mat·ic (siz mat′ik), (shiz mat′ik), *or* (skiz mat′ik) *adj* causing or likely to cause schism, especially in a church.
n a person who tries to cause or takes part in a schism.

schist (shist) *n* a coarse-grained metamorphic rock that splits easily into layers of different minerals. <Greek *schizein* split>

schiz·oid (skit′soid) *adj* characterized by, tending toward, or resulting from schizophrenia: *schizoid tendencies.*
n a schizoid person.

schiz·o·phre·ni·a (skit′sə frē′nē ə) *n* a mental disorder that may involve inappropriate actions and feelings, a tendency toward delusion, and withdrawal from everyday reality and personal relationships. <Latin, from Greek *skhizein* to split + *phren* mind>
schiz′o·phren′ic (skit′sə fren′ik) *adj, n.*

schle·miel (shlə mēl′) *Informal n* a stupid, awkward, or inept person. Also, **shlemiel**. <Yiddish, from Hebrew *Shelumiel*, a biblical character>

schlep (shlep) *Informal v* **schlepped, schlep·ping 1** haul or lug something heavy or awkward: *I don't want to schlep my hockey bag around all day.* **2** go or move awkwardly or with effort: *I spent the afternoon schlepping all over town in search of a decent bookstore.*
n **1** an inconvenient or tiresome trip. **2** a stupid or inept person. Also, **shlep**. <Yiddish, from German *sleppen* to drag>

schlock (shlok) *Informal n* shoddy, cheap, or poor quality goods or materials: *That store sells nothing but schlock.*
adj shoddy, cheap, or of poor quality: *a schlock movie.* Also, **shlock**. <Yiddish, from German *slahan* to strike>

schmaltz (shmolts) *Informal n* extreme sentimentalism, especially in music, literature, or art: *I can't stand the schmaltz in some greeting cards.* Also, **shmaltz**. <Yiddish, from German *Schmalz* melted fat> **schmaltz′y** *adj.*

schmooze (shmūz) *Informal v* **schmoozed, schmooz·ing** gossip or chat cozily, sometimes in order to manipulate another person.
n a conversation of this kind. Also, **shmooze**. <Yiddish *shmues* chat, gossip> **schmooz′er** *n.*

schmuck (shmuk) *Informal n* a foolish or contemptible person. Also, **shmuck**. <Yiddish *shmok* penis> **schmuck′y** *adj.*

schnapps (shnáps) *n* a strong alcoholic drink resembling gin. <German>

schnau·zer (shnou′zər) *or* (shnou′tsər) *n* a dog with a short, wiry coat, bushy eyebrows, and whiskers around the muzzle. <German *Schnauze* snout>

schnit·zel (shnit′səl) *n* a thin slice of breaded or floured veal or pork, quickly fried. <German *Schnitzel* slice>

schnozz (shnoz) *Slang n* the nose. Also, **schnoz**, **schnozzle**. <Yiddish>

schol·ar (skol′ər) *n* **1** a person with much knowledge in a particular branch of study, especially in the humanities: *He was a famous Latin scholar.* **2** a student who holds a scholarship: *a Rhodes scholar.* <Latin *schola*>

schol·ar·ly (skol′ər lē) *adj* **1** of, like, or fit for a scholar: *scholarly habits.* **2** with much knowledge or devotion to academic study. **schol′ar·li·ness** *n.*

schol·ar·ship (skol′ər ship′) *n* **1** academic achievement or study: *Good scholarship is more important than athletics.* **2** money or other aid to help a student continue to study. **scholarship fund,** a fund to provide this money.

scho·las·tic (skə las′tik) *adj* to do with schools or education: *scholastic achievements, to choose a scholastic life.* <Latin, from Greek *skhole* school>
scho·las′ti·cal·ly *adv.*

Scholastic Aptitude Test *n* a standardized university entrance examination made up of multiple-choice questions designed to test verbal, mathematical, and written English skills. *Abbrev.* **SAT**

school[1] (skūl) *n* **1** a place where children are taught subjects, or the building in which subjects are taught: *He was late getting to school. A new school will open in the fall.* **2** a place where instruction is given in some special subject, or a session of it: *ballet school, summer school.* **3** a particular department in a university, or the buildings set apart for the use of one department: *medical school, law school.* **4** a place of training or discipline: *a reform school.*
v train or discipline someone: *My cousins were schooled to control their tempers.* <Greek *skhole* lecture>

schooner and brig

In the past, **schooners** and **brigs** (short for brigantine) were both used commercially for coastal trading; however, the schooner required a smaller crew.

Today, schooners are used primarily for recreation. For extra speed in racing, the triangular masts, called jibs, are placed before the foremast.

school[2] (skūl) *n* a large group of the same kind of fish or water animals swimming together: *a school of herring.* <Dutch *schole* crowd>

school board *n* a group of people, usually elected, who manage the schools in a certain area.

school·book (skūl′bu̇k′) *n* a book for study in schools.

school·boy (skūl′boi′) *n* a boy attending school.

school·child (skūl′chīld′) *n, pl* **school·child·ren** a child who goes to school.

school·fel·low (skūl′fel′ō) SCHOOLMATE.

school·girl (skūl′gərl′) *n* a girl attending school.

school·house (skūl′hous′) *n* a small building used as a school, especially in a village or small community.

school·ing (skū′ling) *n* instruction in school.

school·mas·ter (skūl′mas′tər) *n* a man who teaches in or manages a school.

school·mate (skūl′māt′) *n* a companion at school. Also, **schoolfellow**.

school·mis·tress (skūl′mis′tris) *n* a woman who teaches in or manages a school.

school patrol *n* a group of older school children who escort younger ones across busy streets.

school·room (skūl′ru̇m′) *n* a room in which students are taught.

school·teach·er (skūl′tē′chər) *n* a person who teaches in a school.

school·work (skūl′wərk′) *n* assignments or lessons for school, worked on in class or at home.

school·yard (skūl′yȧrd′) *n* a piece of ground around or near a school, used for play or games.

school year *n* that part of the year during which school is in session.

schoon·er (skū′nər) *n* **1** a ship with two or more masts and fore-and-aft sails. **2** a tall glass for beer. <origin uncertain>

schuss (shu̇s) *n* a straight, downhill run on skis. *v* make such a run.

schwa (shwȧ) *n* **1** an unstressed vowel sound. Examples: the *a* in *about,* the *u* in *circus,* the *o* in *lemon.* **2** the symbol [ə] used to represent this sound. <German, from Hebrew *sewa*>

sci·at·i·ca (sī at′ə kə) *n* pain along the path of the **sciatic nerve** that begins in the lower end of the spinal cord and runs down the back of the thigh, caused by compression of a nerve in the lower back.

sci·ence (sī′əns) *n* **1** the systematic study of the structures and relationships of the physical and natural world, obtained through observation and experiment: *natural science.* **2** a branch of such study: *veterinary science.* **3** an organized branch of knowledge considered as an object of study: *a social science.* <Old French, from Latin *scire* know> **sci′en·tif′ic** *adj.* **sci′en·tif′i·cal·ly** *adv.* **sci′en·tist** *n.*

science fair *n* an event at which students display science projects they have done, often with competition for a prize.

science fiction *n* a type of fiction based on actual or imagined elements of science.

scientific method *n* the principles and procedures of scientific investigation, consisting of systematic observation, measurement, and experiment, and the forming, testing, and revision of hypotheses.

scientific notation *n* a way of writing numbers of many digits by reducing them to a decimal greater than one and less than ten, combined with a power of ten. Examples: $36\ 700\ 000 = 3.67 \times 10^7$; $0.00089 = 8.9 \times 10^{-4}$

sci–fi (sī′fī′) *Informal n* science fiction.

scim·i·tar (sim′ə tər) *or* (sim′ə tȧr′) *n* a short, curved sword with a cutting edge on the convex side, originally used in Middle Eastern countries. <French, from Italian *scimitarra*>

scin·til·la (sin til′ə) *n* a tiny trace of something: *There is not a scintilla of evidence against him.* <Latin = spark>

scin·til·late (sin′tə lāt′) *v* **scin·til·lat·ed, scin·til·lat·ing** sparkle or flash: *The snow scintillated in the sun like diamonds. Her brilliant wit scintillated us.* **scin′til·la′tion** *n.*

sci·on (sī′ən) *n* **1** a young shoot or twig of a plant, especially for grafting or rooting. **2** a descendant of a notable family. <Old French *cion*>

a bat	e bed	i bid	o pot	u cup	th thin
ā cake	ē me	ī bite	ō go	ū rude	TH then
ȧ bar	ə about	ər over	ȯ for	u̇ put	zh measure

scis·sor (siz′ər) *v* **1** cut, cut off, or cut out with scissors. **2** move the legs back and forth in the way that scissors do. <See SCISSORS.>

scis·sors (siz′ərz) *n* **1** (*with plural verb*) a tool or instrument for cutting that has two sharp blades fastened so that their edges slide against each other: *My nail scissors are very sharp.* **2** *Gymnastics* (*with singular or plural verb*) a forward and backward movement of the legs suggesting the action of scissors. **3** *Wrestling* (*with singular verb*) a hold in which the opponent's body or head is held with the legs. <Old French, from Latin *caedere* to cut>

scler·a (skler′ə) *n* the tough, fibrous, white outer membrane covering all of the eyeball, continuous with the cornea. <Latin, from Greek *skleros* hard>

scle·ro·sis (sklə rō′sis) *n, pl* **scle·ro·ses** (-sēz) an abnormal hardening of tissue in the body. See also MULTIPLE SCLEROSIS. <Latin, from Greek *skleros* hard>
scle·rot′ic (sklə rot′ik) *adj.*

scoff[1] (skof) *v* make fun of in a scornful or mocking way: *We scoffed at the idea of drowning in ten centimetres of water.*
n mocking words or acts. <origin uncertain> **scoff′er** *n.* **scoff′ing** *adj.* **scoff′ing·ly** *adv.*

scoff[2] (skof) *Slang v* eat something quickly and greedily: *to scoff your lunch.*
n 🍁 *Atlantic Provinces* a big meal, especially of seafood. <obsolete *scaff* food>

scoff·law (skof′lo′) *n* a person who has no respect for the law, especially in failing to obey a law that is hard to enforce.

scold (skōld) *v* find fault with and criticize severely or angrily: *His mother scolded him for tearing his jacket.*
n a person who makes a habit of scolding. <origin unknown> **scold′er** *n.* **scold′ing** *n.* **scold′ing·ly** *adv.*

SYNONYMS

Scold emphasizes severe or angry criticism: *The coach scolded the team for its lack of discipline.*

Reprimand means "scold formally or officially": *The teacher reprimanded the student for being late.*

Reproach means "express blame, disappointment, or disapproval": *My friend reproached me for not supporting him during the discussion.*

sconce (skons) *n* a bracket projecting from a wall, used to hold a candle or other light. <Old French, from Latin *absconsa* dark lantern>

scone (skon) *or* (skōn) *n* a thick, flat cake cooked on a griddle or in an oven. <origin uncertain>

scoop (skūp) *n* **1 a** a kitchen utensil like a deep spoon, for dipping out things from a container: *an ice-cream scoop.* **b** the amount taken up at one time by such a utensil: *two scoops of sugar.* **2** the part of a digging machine that is used for excavating. **3** a place hollowed out by an animal or by a digging machine: *a shallow scoop in the ground.* **4 a** a piece of news published or broadcast in advance of others. **b** *Informal* a piece of gossip: *Give me latest scoop on why they split up.*
v **1** take up or out with a scoop, or as a scoop does: *Scoop out a kilogram of sugar. We scooped up the snow with our hands to make a snow fort.* **2** hollow out by scooping: *They scooped holes in the sand.* **3** publish a piece of news before another does. <Dutch *schope* waterwheel bucket>

scoop·ful (skūp′fu̇l) *n, pl* **scoop·fuls** enough to fill a scoop.

scoot (skūt) *Informal v* go or leave somewhere quickly: *She scooted out of the side door just as I arrived.* <origin uncertain>

Motor scooters are less powerful than motorcycles and their wheels are much smaller, usually 20–35 cm in diameter.

Mopeds have two large motorcycle-type wheels. The vehicles are slower than scooters, and most areas restrict their speed to 50 km/h.

scoot·er (skū′tər) *n* **1** a child's vehicle consisting of a long footboard with a wheel at the front and the back, steered by raised handlebars and moved by pushing against the ground with one foot. **2** a light, two-wheeled motor vehicle with a footboard and handlebars and equipped with a seat. **3** a sailboat or other light vehicle with runners, for use on either water or ice.
v go or travel by scooter.

scope (skōp) *n* **1** the extent to which the mind can take in a subject or topic: *The words were outside the scope of my understanding.* **2** the area over which an activity extends: *This topic is not within the scope of the assignment.* **3** an opportunity or possibility to do or deal with something: *The coach said that football gives scope for courage and quick thinking.* **4** a device for viewing something.
v Informal look at carefully. <Italian, from Greek *skeptesthai* look out>
scope out, *Informal* check or examine for possibilities: *Let's scope out the area for a good campsite.*

–scope *combining form* forming names for instruments for viewing or examining: *stethoscope, telescope.* <Latin, from Greek *skopein* look at>

scorch (skôrch) *v* **1** burn the surface of something by flame or heat, or be burned in this way: *The cake tastes scorched. I scorched the shirt when I ironed it, grass scorched by the sun.* **2** criticize with harsh or sarcastic words.
n a burn on the surface of something. <origin uncertain>

scorched–earth policy (skôrch′tərth′) *n* a military policy of destroying all crops and other resources so as to leave nothing useful for the enemy.

scorch·er (skôr′chər) *n* **1** *Informal* a very hot day. **2** a scathing criticism.

score (skôr) *n* **1** the record of points made in a game, contest, or test: *The score was 7 to 2 in our favour. Her highest score was 95.* **2 a** a group or set of twenty: *A score or more were present at the party.* **b scores** *pl* a large number or amount: *Scores died in the epidemic.* **3** *Music* a written or printed piece of music arranged for different instruments or voices: *a piano score.* **4** the actual situation or circumstances, especially one involving a grievance or grudge: *Don't worry on that score, to settle an old score.* **5 the score** the truth about a thing or things in general: *The new man doesn't know what the score is yet.* **6** *Informal* a result or achievement: *a big score.* **7** a cut, line, or stroke made on a surface.
v **scored, scor·ing 1 a** make points in a game, contest, or test. **b** keep a record of the number of points made. **2** make as an addition to a score or result: *He scored a touchdown early in the game.* **3** *Music* arrange a piece of music for different instruments or voices. **4** *Informal* achieve a success: *to score big.* **5** make a cut or line in a surface, or make a stroke through: *Score the cardboard with a knife before bending. Mistakes are scored in red ink.* <Old English *scora*> **score′less** *adj.* **scor′er** *n.*
on this (or **that**) **score of,** as far as this (or that) is concerned.
pay off (or **settle**) **a score,** get even for an injury or wrong.

score·board (skôr′bôrd′) *n* a large board for posting the score and, sometimes, details of a game or other sporting event.

score·card (skôr′kärd′) *n* a card for keeping the score of a game or match.

score·keep·er (skôr′kē′pər) *n* a person who officially keeps track of the points or goals each side wins at a sporting event. **score′keep·ing** *n.*

scorn (skôrn) *n* a feeling or belief that someone or something is worthless or worthy of contempt: *an object of scorn. His betrayal made him the scorn of his friends.*
v **1** regard someone or something as worthless or worthy of contempt: *He scorned their attempts at reconciliation. She scorns her critics as being out of date and incompetent.* **2** reject or refuse contemptuously: *The judge scorned to take a bribe.* <Old French *escarnir*> **scorn′er** *n.* **scorn′ful** *adj.* **scorn′ful·ly** *adv.* **scorn′ful·ness** *n.*

Scor·pi·o (skôr′pē ō′) *n* **1** *Astronomy* a southern constellation shaped somewhat like a scorpion. **2** *Astrology* **a** the eighth sign of the zodiac. The sun enters Scorpio about October 24. **b** a person born under this sign.

scor·pi·on (skôr′pē ən) *n* a small land arachnid with pincers and a poisonous stinger at the end of its jointed tail. See ARACHNID for picture. <Old French, from Greek *skorpios*>

Scot (skot) *n* a native of Scotland or a person of Scottish descent. <Latin *Scottus*>

scotch (skoch) *v* put an end to something in a definitive way: *to scotch a rumour.*

Scotch (skoch) *n* a whisky made in Scotland.
adj to do with goods made in, or associated with, Scotland. See also SCOTTISH.

Scotch broth *n* a thick soup containing beef or mutton, vegetables, and barley.

Scotch pine *n* a pine tree with spreading branches and short, twisted, bluish green needles.

Scotch tape *Trademark n* a transparent sticky tape made of plastic, especially for use on paper.

sco·ter (skō′tər) *n* a diving sea duck of N America and Europe, the adult male with mostly black plumage, the female mostly brown.

scot–free (skot′frē′) *adv* without suffering any injury, punishment, or penalty: *His partner was convicted of fraud but he got off scot-free.* <Middle English *scot* a tax>

Scot·land (skot′lənd) *n* a country occupying, along with England and Wales, the largest island in the UK.

Scotland Yard (skot′lənd) *n* the headquarters of the London Metropolitan Police in the UK.

ETYMOLOGY

Scotland Yard is named for the building in which the London police headquarters were located in the 1800s. The building backed onto a courtyard and street called Great Scotland Yard.

Scotland Yard was relocated in 1890 and again in 1967, and so the building is now known as New Scotland Yard.

Scot·tish (skot′ish) *adj* to do with Scotland or its people. Also, **Scots**.

scoun·drel (skoun′drəl) *n* a dishonest or unprincipled person: *A scoundrel defrauded him of his money.* <origin uncertain> **scoun′drel·ly** *adj.*

scour[1] (skour) *v* **1** clean, brighten, or polish by vigorous rubbing: *Scour the frying pan with cleanser.* **2** make a channel or pool by flowing quickly over something and removing soil or rocks: *The current scoured mud and sand from the riverbed.*
n the act or process of scouring. <Dutch, from Latin *ex-* away + *curare* to clean> **scour′er** *n.*

S

scour[2] (skour) *v* thoroughly search in order to locate something: *We scoured the area for the lost puppy.* <origin uncertain>

scourge (skərj) *n* **1** a whip formerly used as a means of punishment. **2** a thing or person that causes trouble or misfortune: *Chores after school are the scourge of my life.*
v **scourged, scourg·ing 1** whip severely. **2** put hardship or suffering on: *War scourged the country for eight years.* <Old French, from Latin *ex-* out + *corriga* whip>

scour·ings (skou′ringz) *pln* dirt or other material removed by scouring or cleaning.

a bat	e bed	i bid	o pot	u cup	th **thin**
ā cake	ē me	ī bite	ō go	ū rude	TH **then**
ä bar	ə about	ər over	ô for	ů put	zh measure

scout (skout) *n* **1** a soldier or other person sent to find out what the enemy is doing, or a ship or aircraft that does this. **2** a person who looks for promising recruits in entertainment or sports. **3 Scout** a member of the **Scouting** organization, set up for young people to develop character and physical fitness, often through community and outdoor activities.
v **1** search for someone or something in various places: *Go and scout for firewood for the picnic.* **2** observe or examine to get information. **3** look for promising recruits in entertainment or sports. <Old French, from Latin *auscultare*>

scow (skou) *n* a large, flat-bottomed boat used to carry freight: *The scow was loaded with crates.*

scowl (skoul) *v* draw the eyebrows down and together and tighten the mouth, especially as an expression of anger or sullenness: *She scowled at us and asked what we were doing there. He scowled his displeasure.*
n an angry or sullen look. <origin uncertain> **scowl′er** *n.*

SYNONYMS

Scrape means "rub with something sharp or rough": *Please scrape the snow off the windshield.*

Scratch means "cut slightly with something sharp or rough" or "rub to relieve itching": *The skates scratched the fresh surface of the ice. Don't scratch mosquito bites.*

Scuff means "scrape or brush an object against a surface": *She scuffed her shoes on the low railing.*

scrab·ble (skrab′əl) *v* **scrab·bled, scrab·bling 1** scratch or scrape around with one's fingers to find, collect, or hold on to something. **2** scratch at something as an animal: *The dog scrabbled at the door.* **3** struggle or make great efforts to get somewhere or achieve something: *to scrabble for a living.*
n **1** an act of scratching or scrambling for something. **2 Scrabble** *Trademark* a game in which players create words on a board by selecting from letters printed on small tiles. <Dutch *schrabben* to scratch>

scrag·gly (skrag′lē) *adj* **scrag·gli·er, scrag·gli·est** rough, irregular, or ragged: *a scraggly garden. The child's hair was scraggly and matted.* **scrag′gli·ness** *n.*

scram (skram) *Informal v* **scrammed, scram·ming** go away quickly: *Scram! You're in the way here. She told the kids to scram.* <*scramble*>

scram·ble (skram′bəl) *v* **scram·bled, scram·bling 1** make one's way quickly or awkwardly up a steep slope or over rough ground: *It took us half an hour to scramble up the rocky hill.* **2** move hurriedly or clumsily from or into a particular place or position: *The boys scrambled to get out of the way.* **3** mix together in a confused way: *All the information scrambled my brain.* **4** cook eggs with the whites and yolks mixed together. **5** break up or mix a broadcast signal or telephone message so that it cannot be received and understood without special equipment.
n **1** a difficult climb or walk up or over something: *It was a long scramble through bushes to the top of the hill.* **2** an eager or undignified struggle with others to obtain or achieve something: *the scramble for wealth.* **3** a disordered mixture of things or activities: *a scramble for success.* <origin uncertain>

scrap[1] (skrap) *n* **1** a small detached or separated bit or piece, especially a discarded or leftover piece of food: *scraps of paper, fabric scraps. The cook gave the scraps to the dog.* **2** a small portion of something written or printed: *He read out scraps from the letter. She saves pictures and other scraps from the local newspaper.* **3** material or articles discarded as useless and fit only to be broken down, melted, and reprocessed: *a yard full of iron scrap.* **4** in the form of scrap or scraps: *scrap metal.*
v **scrapped, scrap·ping 1** throw aside as worn out or useless: *I decided to scrap my old jeans. The army scrapped the old tanks.* **2** condemn or abandon as useless, and not worth the effort: *The student council scrapped a plan to ban cellphones on school property.* <Old Norse *skrapa* scrape>

scrap[2] (skrap) *Informal n* a fight or quarrel, especially a minor or sudden one: *Our dog got into a scrap with the neighbour's cat again.*
v **scrapped, scrap·ping** have such a fight or quarrel: *Those kids are always scrapping.* <origin uncertain>

scrap·book (skrap′bu̇k′) *n* a book in which pictures or clippings are pasted and kept.

scrape (skrāp) *v* **scraped, scrap·ing 1 a** drag, pull, or rub with something sharp or rough: *Scrape your muddy shoes with this piece of wood.* **b** remove by rubbing with or against something sharp or rough: *I scraped some paint off the table as I pushed it through the doorway.* **2** scratch or graze by rubbing against something rough: *She fell and scraped her knee on the sidewalk.* **3** rub with or make a harsh, grating sound: *Don't scrape your nails on the board.* **4** (*with* ***together***) just manage to achieve or accomplish, using much effort: *He has scraped together enough money for his first year at college.*
n **1** the act or sound of scraping. **2** a scraped place. **3** a harsh, grating sound: *the scrape of a saw.* **4** an embarrassing or difficult situation caused by unwise behaviour: *She is always getting her friends into scrapes.* <Old English *scrapian* scratch with the fingernails >
scrape acquaintance, take the trouble to get acquainted.
scrape along (or **through** or **by**)**,** barely get through or manage with difficulty: *That family just scrapes along but never asks for charity. She scraped through the examination.*

scrap·er (skrā′pər) *n* an instrument or tool for scraping: *We removed the loose paint with a scraper.*

scrap·ing (skrā′ping) *n* **1** the act of a person who or thing that scrapes, or the sound produced by this: *We could hear the scraping of the shovel against the sidewalk.* **2 scrapings** *pl* a small amount of something that has been scraped off: *Put the scrapings into this box.*

scrap iron or **metal** *n* broken or waste pieces of old iron or other metal collected for recycling.

scrap·per (skrap′ər) *Informal n* a person who or animal that fights readily or effectively: *The way she took on that bully showed that she was a scrapper.*

scrap·py[1] (skrap′ē) *adj* **scrap·pi·er, scrap·pi·est** made up of disorganized, untidy, or incomplete parts.

scrap·py[2] (skrap′ē) *Informal adj* **scrap·pi·er, scrap·pi·est** fond of fighting or argument.

scratch (skrach) *v* **1** mark or cut slightly with something sharp or rough: *Your shoes have scratched the chair.* **2 a** tear or dig with the nails or claws: *The cat scratched her.* **b** rub or scrape to relieve itching: *He scratched his head.* See ITCH for confusable. **3** rub with a harsh sound: *She scratched the board with her nails to get everyone's attention.* **4** write in a hurry or carelessly: *I scratched a few notes on a scrap of paper.* **5 a** strike out, cancel, or draw a line through. **b** withdraw or be withdrawn from a race or contest. **6** use much effort to achieve or obtain: *At first, the pioneers had to scratch out a living.*
n **1** a mark or slight cut made by scratching. **2** the sound made by scratching: *the scratch of a branch against a window.* **3** a rub or scrape to relieve itching: *Dogs love a good scratch.* **4** a competitor who has been withdrawn from a race or contest.
adj made up from whatever is on hand: *a scratch meal, a scratch football team.* <origin uncertain>
from scratch, from the beginning: *She lost her notes and so had to start her project again from scratch.*
scratch the surface, do, experience, or study something in a superficial way.
up to scratch, up to standard.

scratch pad *n* a pad of paper used for drafts or casual writing.

scratch paper *n* paper used for drafts or casual writing.

scratch test *Medicine n* a medical test for allergies, done by scratching or puncturing the skin and applying an allergen to the site. Resulting redness indicates an allergy.

scratch·y (skrach′ē) *adj* **scratch·i·er, scratch·i·est 1** with a prickly, uncomfortable texture and liable to cause itchiness: *This woollen sweater is scratchy.* **2** making a scratching noise: *a scratchy pen.* **3** consisting of or made with scratches: *a scratchy drawing.* **scratch′i·ly** *adv.* **scratch′i·ness** *n.*

scrawl (skrol) *v* write or draw poorly, carelessly, or hastily: *She scrawled a note on the back of an envelope.*
n **1** poor, careless, or hasty handwriting: *I could hardly read her scrawl.* **2** something scrawled, such as a hastily or badly written letter or note. <origin uncertain>
scrawl′y *adj.*

scraw·ny (skron′ē) *adj* **scraw·ni·er, scraw·ni·est** unattractively thin and bony: *a scrawny neck.* <origin uncertain>

scream (skrēm) *v* **1** make a loud, sharp, piercing cry or in a high-pitched, frenzied way: *She screamed when she saw the mess we had made. "That's wet paint!" he screamed. We had to scream to hear each other above the music.* **2** laugh loudly or uncontrollably: *The audience screamed at his antics.* **3** produce an extremely startling effect: *"Disaster at Sea!" the headlines screamed.*
n **1** a loud, sharp, piercing cry or noise: *a scream of rage, screams of laughter, the scream of a siren.* **2** *Informal* something or somebody extremely funny: *She was a scream at the party.* <origin uncertain>

scream·er (skrē′mər) *n* **1** a person who or thing that screams. **2** a large S American marsh bird with a short bill, a sharp bony spur on each wing, and a harsh honking call.

scream·ing (skrē′ming) *adj* **1** able to scream. **2** evoking screams of laughter: *a screaming farce.* **3** startling: *screaming headlines, screaming colours.*

scream·ing·ly (skrē′ming lē) *Informal adv* to an extreme degree: *screamingly funny.*

scree (skrē) *n* a steep slope of loose, fragmented rock lying below a cliff or bluff. <Old English *scrithan* to slip>

screech (skrēch) *v* make or give a loud, harsh, piercing cry.
n **1** such a loud cry. **2** 🍁 *especially Newfoundland* a dark rum originating in Newfoundland. <obsolete *scritch,* imitative> **screech′er** *n.*

screech owl *n* a N American owl with hornlike tufts of feathers on the head and a mournful, whistling call.

screech·y (skrē′chē) *adj* **screech·i·er, screech·i·est** screeching.

screed (skrēd) *n* **1** a long speech or piece of writing. **2** a levelled layer of material, such as cement, plaster, or wood applied to a surface. <Old English *screade* shred>

screen (skrēn) *n* **1** an upright partition that is used to enclose a space, to protect against or to conceal something, or to give privacy. **2** a frame with wire woven together with small openings in between the strands: *We have screens at our windows to keep out flies.* **3** a sieve for sifting or filtering something. **4** a thing that protects, conceals, or filters like a screen: *A screen of trees hides the house from the road.* **5** a surface on which movie, video, television, or computer-generated images are shown. **6 the screen** movies or the movie industry: *a star of stage and screen.* **7** *Basketball, Hockey* an offensive player who stands between a teammate and a defender to give his teammate the chance to take an open shot.
v **1** protect, conceal, or provide privacy with a screen, or as if with a screen: *She screened her face from the fire with her hand.* **2** watch movie, video, or television images on a screen: *Critics usually screen movies before the public does.* **3** sift with a sieve: *to screen sand.* **4** examine or test very carefully: *Applicants for this job must be carefully screened.* <Old French *escren*> **screen′able** *adj.*

S

screen dump *Computers n* a copy or printout of the contents of a computer screen.

screen·ing (skrēn′ing) *n* a showing of a movie, program, or other item in a cinema or on TV.

screen·play (skrēn′plā) *n* a story or play written for production as a movie.

screen saver *Computers n* a pattern or design that appears on the screen after a computer has been inactive for a set time in order to prevent damage to the inside surface of the screen.

a bat	e bed	i bid	o pot	u cup	th **thin**
ā cake	ē me	ī bite	ō go	ū rude	ᴛʜ **then**
à bar	ə about	ər over	ȯ for	ů put	zh measure

screen shot *Hockey n* a shot on goal that the goalie cannot see because it is taken from behind one or more players standing in front of the net.

screen test *n* a short film sequence made to test a person's ability as an actor in movies or TV.

screen·writ·er (skrēn′rī′tər) *n* a person who writes scripts for movies or TV shows. **screen′writ·ing** *n.*

screw (skrū) *n* **1** a fastening device like a nail but with a ridge twisted evenly round its length: *Turn the screw to the right to tighten it.* **2 a** a simple machine consisting of a spiral ridge around a cylinder that acts to exert pressure in various ways. **b** anything that has a similar form, for example, a corkscrew.
v **1** turn or twist as a screw moves or is moved: *Screw the lid on the jar.* **2** twist or contort: *His face was screwed up with fear.* **3** fasten or tighten with a screw or screws: *The carpenter screwed the hinges to the door.* **4** *Slang* cheat, swindle, or wrong: *You paid ten dollars for that thing? You were screwed!* <Old French, from Latin *scroba*>
have a screw loose, *Informal* be eccentric or crazy.
put the screws on, *Informal* use pressure or force to get something.
screw up, a *Informal* botch, bungle, or make a serious error: *She tried to make a rhubarb pie but screwed it up.* **b** gather mental resources in order to make an effort: *She finally screwed up enough courage to try to dive.*

screw·ball (skrū′bol′) *n* **1** *Informal* an eccentric or crazy person. **2** *Baseball* a pitch thrown with a reverse spin opposite to that of a curve.
adj eccentric or crazy: *a screwball comedy. What a screwball thing to do!*

screw·driv·er (skrū′drī′vər) *n* a tool for putting in or taking out SCREWS (def. 1) by turning them.

screw·y (skrū′ē) *Informal adj* **screw·i·er, screw·i·est** **1** crazy or eccentric. **2** wrongly positioned or out of kilter: *It's all screwy because you put this part in the wrong way.* **screw′i·ness** *n.*

scrib·ble (skrib′əl) *v* **scrib·bled, scrib·bling** **1** write or draw carelessly or hastily. **2** make marks that do not mean anything.
n a thing scribbled. <Latin *scribere* write>

scrib·bler (skrib′lər) *n* **1** a person who scribbles. **2** a pad of paper or a book in which to make notes; a notebook. **3** an author of little or no importance.

scribe (skrīb) *n* **1** a person who copies documents, especially one who was employed to do this before the invention of printing. **2** a Jewish record keeper in ancient times, or, later, a teacher of the Jewish law. **3** *Informal* a writer or author. **4** a pointed instrument for making marks on a surface as a guide. Also, **scriber**.
v **scribed, scrib·ing** mark or cut with something sharp. <Latin *scribere* write> **scri′bal** *adj.*

scrim (skrim) *n* a coarse, strong fabric used for upholstery and heavy-duty curtains. <origin uncertain>

scrim·mage (skrim′ij) *n* **1** a confused fight or struggle. **2** *Football* the action that takes place between two teams from the time the ball is snapped until it is declared dead.
v **scrim·maged, scrim·mag·ing** **1** take part in a confused fight or struggle. **2** take part in a football scrimmage. <*skirmish*>

scrimp (skrimp) *v* be very thrifty in order to save as much as possible: *My aunts had to scrimp for several years to save enough for a down payment on a house.* <Scots = meagre>

scrip (skrip) *n* a receipt, certificate, or other document showing a right to acquire something, especially a prescription for medicine. <*prescription*>

script (skript) *n* **1** handwriting or written characters: *She wrote in a legible script.* **2** a style of type that uses a particular alphabet or that looks like handwriting: *German script.* **3** the written text of a play, movie, or broadcast.
v write a script for a play, movie, or broadcast.

ETYMOLOGY

Script comes from Latin *scribere*, which means "write." All English words ending in *-script* or *-scribe* can be traced back to *scribere*: *manuscript, transcript, describe, subscribe*, etc.

scrip·ture (skrip′chər) *n* **1** **Scripture** the sacred writings of Christianity contained in the Bible. **2** the sacred writings of another religion. <Latin *scribere* write> **scrip′tur·al** *adj.* **scrip′tur·al·ly** *adv.*

script·writ·er (skript′rī′tər) *n* a person who writes scripts for movies or for radio or TV.

scrod (skrod) *n* a young cod, haddock, or other fish, especially one prepared for cooking. <origin uncertain>

scroll (skrōl) *n* **1** a roll of parchment or paper, especially one with writing or painting on it: *He slowly unrolled the scroll as he read from it.* **2** an ornament resembling a partly unrolled sheet of paper, or with a spiral or coiled form, such as the curved head of a violin. **3** *Computers* a feature of a display that permits the user to move the image up, down, or across.
v **1** *Computers* move a display up, down, or across. **2** make something roll or unroll like paper. <Old French, from Latin *scroda*> **scroll′ab·le** *adj.*

scroll bar *Computers n* a long, narrow section at the side edge of a display, in which one can move the contents of the screen up, down, or across.

scroll saw *n* a narrow-bladed saw for cutting thin wood in curved or ornamental patterns.

scroll·work (skrōl′wərk′) *n* decoration in which SCROLLS (def. 2) are much used, especially that cut by a scroll saw.

Scrooge (skrūj) *n* a mean or stingy person resembling the embittered old miser in the book *A Christmas Carol,* by Charles Dickens

scro·tum (skrō′təm) *n* in most male mammals, a pouch of skin that contains the testicles. <Latin>

scrounge (skrounj) *v* **scrounged, scroung·ing** seek to obtain something, especially food or money and at the expense or through the generosity of others: *He was always scrounging free meals.* <origin uncertain> **scroung′er** *n.*

scrub[1] (skrub) *v* **scrubbed, scrub·bing 1** wash or clean by rubbing hard with a brush or cloth: *She scrubbed the kitchen floor. He had to scrub to get the ink off.* **2** *Informal* cancel or abandon something: *The shuttle launching was scrubbed.*
n an act of scrubbing someone or something: *She gave her hands a good scrub.* <Dutch *schrobben*>

scrub[2] (skrub) *n* **1** low, stunted trees or shrubs. **2** a thing that is small, or below the usual size.
adj **1** small, undersized, or inferior: *scrub pasture.* **2** less good or skilled. <*shrub*> **scrub′by** *adj.*

scruff (skruf) *n* the back of the neck or the skin at the back of the neck: *She picked up the kitten by the scruff of the neck.* <origin uncertain>

scruf·fy (skruf′ē) *adj* shabby and untidy or dirty: *scruffy jeans.*

scrum (skrum) *n* **1** *Rugby* a formation of players into which a ball is thrown so that play can be restarted. See RUGBY for picture. **2** a disorderly crowd of people or things, such as a crowd of reporters informally gathered around a politician and asking questions in a disorganized way. <*scrimmage*>

scrump·tious (skrump′shəs) *Informal adj* extremely delicious: *a scrumptious meal.* <origin uncertain>

scrunch (skrunch) *v* **1** crunch, crush, hunch, or crumple: *He scrunched the paper into a tiny ball. We scrunched down behind the fence and waited.* **2** make a loud crunching sound: *They scrunched across the snow.* <*crunch*>

🍁 **scrunch·eons** (skrun′shənz) *Newfoundland pln* small pieces of crisply fried pork fat.

scrunch·ie (skrun′shē) *n* a wide elastic band covered with fabric, for binding the hair.

scru·ple (skrū′pəl) *n* **1** a feeling of doubt about what one ought to do, especially from a moral or ethical viewpoint: *No scruple ever holds her back from prompt action. She had scruples about playing cards for money.* **2** in former times, a unit of weight used by druggists, equal to 20 grains (about 1.3 g).
v **scru·pled, scru·pling** hesitate or be unwilling to do something, especially for moral or ethical reasons: *A dishonest man does not scruple to deceive others.* <French, from Latin *scrupus* rough pebble>

scru·pu·lous (skrū′pyə ləs) *adj* **1** with or showing a strict regard for what is morally or ethically correct: *She was scrupulous in her dealings with customers.* **2** very careful, painstaking, or exact: *She paid scrupulous attention to detail.* **scru′pu·lous·ly** *adv.* **scru′pu·lous·ness** *n.*

scru·ti·neer (skrū′tə nēr′) *n* a person who represents the interests of a candidate or party on election day in order to ensure that the voting procedure and counting of ballots are properly carried out.
v act as a scrutineer.

scru·ti·nize (skrū′tə nīz′) *v* **scru·ti·nized, scru·ti·niz·ing** examine closely or inspect carefully: *The jeweller scrutinized the diamond for flaws.* **scru′ti·nizer** *n.* **scru′ti·ny** *n.*

SCSI (sku′zē) *Computers n* a means of linking peripherals to a computer. <*S*mall *C*omputer *S*ystem *I*nterface>

scu·ba (skū′bə) *n* a portable apparatus used for breathing while swimming underwater. <*s*(*elf*)-*c*(*ontained*) *u*(*nderwater*) *b*(*reathing*) *a*(*pparatus*)>

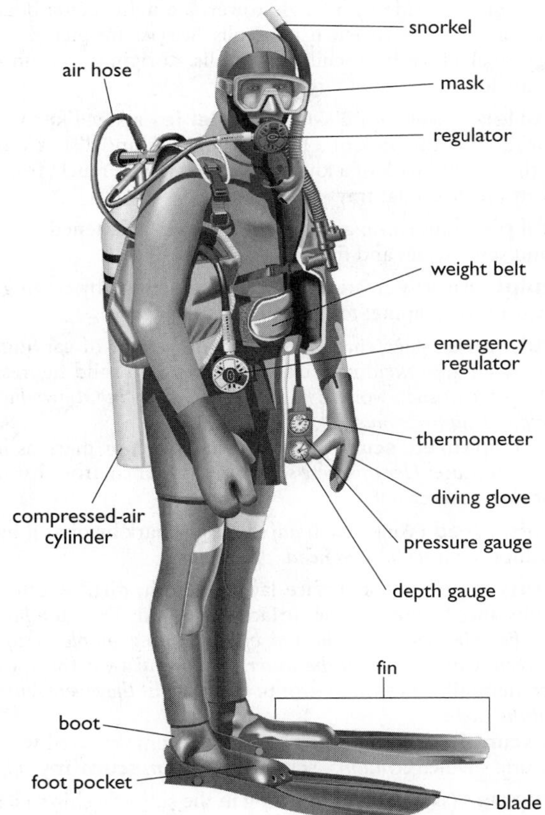

scuba diver *n* a person who uses scuba gear to breathe while swimming underwater. **scuba dive** *v.* **scuba diving** *n.*

scud (skud) *v* **scud·ded, scud·ding** run or move swiftly in a straight line because of or as if with the wind: *scudding clouds.*
n **1** the action of scudding. **2** clouds or spray driven by the wind. <origin uncertain>

scuff (skuf) *v* **1** scrape or brush a shoe or other object against a surface, or mark a surface in this way: *scuffed shoes, a scuffed floor.* **2** drag the feet or heels when walking: *He scuffed down the hall.*
n a mark made by scuffing. <origin uncertain>

scuf·fle (skuf′əl) *v* **scuf·fled, scuf·fling** engage in a brief, minor, and confused fight or struggle: *The children scuffled over who should get the prize.*
n a brief, minor, and confused fight: *The boy lost his hat in the scuffle.* <origin uncertain>

a bat	e bed	i bid	o pot	u cup	th **thin**
ā cake	ē me	ī bite	ō go	ū rude	TH **then**
à bar	ə about	ər over	ȯ for	ů put	zh measure

scull (skul) *n* **1 a** an oar worked with a side twist to make a boat go, or placed at the stern of a boat to propel it by using a side-to-side motion. **b** one of a pair of oars used one on each side by a single rower. **2** a light racing boat for one or more rowers using sculls. See OAR for picture.
v propel a boat by a scull or by sculls. <origin uncertain> **scul′ler** *n.*

scul·ler·y (skul′ə rē) *UK n, pl* **scul·ler·ies** a small kitchen or room at the back of a house where washing dishes and other rough work of a kitchen is done. <Old French, from Latin *scultra* a flat tray>

scul·pin (skul′pin) *n* a saltwater fish with a flattened head and spiny scales and fins.

sculpt (skulpt) *v* create or represent something by carving, casting, or shaping: *to sculpt clay.* **sculp′tor** *n.*

sculp·ture (skulp′chər) *n* **1** the art or process of carving, modelling, or welding hard substances into solid figures. **2** a piece of such work: *The National Gallery in Ottawa has many sculptures on show.*
v **sculp·tured, sculp·tur·ing** form, shape, or mark as if by sculpture: *Her lips were sculptured.* <French, from Latin *sculpere* carve>

sculp·tured (skulp′chərd) *adj* shape, or mark by or as if by sculpture: *a sculptured head.*

scum (skum) *n* **1** a surface layer of froth, dirt, or other substance formed on the surface of a liquid: *The scum had to be skimmed from the top of the boiling maple syrup. Green scum floated on the water.* **2** *Informal* a worthless or contemptible person or group: *She thought they were scum of the earth.*
v **scummed, scum·ming** form or become covered with scum. <Dutch *schuum*> **scum′mi·ness** *n.* **scum′my** *adj.*

scup·per (skup′ər) *n* an opening in the side of a ship to let water run off the deck. <Old French *escopir* to spit>

scurf (skərf) *n* small scales of dead skin, especially dandruff. <Old English *sceorfian* cut to shreds> **scurf′y** *adj.*

scur·ri·lous (skər′ə ləs) *adj* making or spreading a claim about someone in order to damage the person's reputation: *a scurrilous comment, a scurrilous pamphlet.* **scur·ril′i·ty** *n.* **scur′ri·lous·ly** *adv.* **scur′ri·lous·ness** *n.*

scur·ry (skər′ē) *v* **scur·ried, scur·ry·ing** hurry with short quick steps: *We could hear the mice scurrying about in the walls.*
n, pl **scur·ries** hasty and confused movement: *With much fuss and scurry, we finally got underway.* <*hurry-scurry*, reduplication of *hurry*>

scur·vy (skər′vē) *n* a disease characterized by swollen and bleeding gums and opening of previously closed wounds, mainly due to lack of nourishment, especially lack of vitamin C.
adj **scur·vi·er, scur·vi·est** worthless or contemptible: *a scurvy trick.* <*scurf*>

scut·tle[1] (skut′əl) *n* a metal container, often with a sloping hinged lid and a handle, used to carry or hold coal as fuel in a home. <Latin *scutella* bowl>

scut·tle[2] (skut′əl) *v* **scut·tled, scut·tling** run hurriedly or furtively with short steps: *The rat scuttled into its hole.* <origin uncertain> **scut′tler** *n.*

scut·tle[3] (skut′əl) *v* **scut·tled, scut·tling 1** cut a hole or holes through the bottom or sides of a ship to sink it: *After the pirates captured the ship, they scuttled it.* **2** deliberately allow something to fail: *After spending a lot of money, they then scuttled the project.*
n an opening with a lid or cover, especially in the deck or side of a ship. <Old French, from Spanish *escotilla* a small opening>

scut·tle·butt (skut′əl but′) *n* rumours or gossip: *She said that stories about her behaviour were a lot of scuttlebutt.*

ETYMOLOGY

Scuttlebutt comes from *scuttle*, meaning "opening on a ship's deck" and *butt*, meaning "large barrel." Sailors probably stood around these barrels to gossip, as office workers gather round water coolers in today's workplaces.

scu·tum (skyū′təm) *n, pl* **scu·ta** (-tə) a shieldlike part of bone, shell, etc., as on the body of certain reptiles or insects.

scuz·zy (skuz′ē) *Informal adj* **scuz·zi·er, scuz·zi·est** disgusting, sleazy, or disreputable. <origin uncertain> **scuzz** *n.* **scuzz′i·ness** *n.*

scythe (sīтн) *n* a tool used for cutting crops such as hay or grain, consisting of a long, curved blade set at an angle on the end of a long handle. See SICKLE for picture.
v **scythed, scyth·ing** cut with a scythe. <Old English *sithe*>

SE southeast; southeastern.

sea (sē) *n* **1 a** the great body of salt water that covers almost three fourths of the earth's surface and surrounds its land masses. **b** (*often in place names*) an area of this that is smaller than an ocean, partly or wholly enclosed by land: *the Beaufort Sea.* **2** (*in place names*) a large lake of fresh water: *the Caspian Sea.* **3** a large, heavy wave, or the swell of the ocean: *A high sea swept away the ship's masts.* **4** an overwhelming amount or vast expanse: *The audience was a sea of faces.* <Old English *sǣ*>
at sea, a out on the sea. **b** puzzled or confused: *Her complicated explanation left me even more at sea about the problem.*
go to sea, a become a sailor. **b** begin a voyage.
put (**out**) **to sea,** begin a voyage.

sea anemone *n* a flowerlike, often bright-coloured polyp found especially in warm seas, with a cylinder-shaped body with a mouth opening at the upper end surrounded by tentacles.

sea·bed (sē′bed′) *n* the ground under the sea.

sea·bird (sē′bərd) *n* a bird that spends most of its time on or near the open sea.

sea·board (sē′bôrd′) *n* the land bordering the sea: *the eastern seaboard.*

sea cadet *n* a person under military age who takes basic naval training in an organization subsidized by the armed forces.

sea change *n* a major transformation, especially for the better.

sea·coast (sē′kōst′) *n* the land along the sea.

sea cow *n* a manatee or similar mammal living in the sea.

sea cucumber *n* a small marine animal that has a thick, wormlike body with tentacles around the mouth and typically has rows of tube feet along the body.

sea dog *Informal n* a sailor with long experience at sea.

Sea–Doo (sē′dū) *Trademark n* a self-propelled watercraft for one person.

sea·far·ing (sē′fer′ing) *adj* going, travelling, or working on the sea: *He had been a seafaring man all his life.*
n the act or fact of travelling by sea, or of being a sailor. **sea′far′er** *n.*

sea·food (sē′fūd′) *n* edible saltwater fish and shellfish.

sea·go·ing (sē′gō′ing) *adj* suitable or designed for, or travelling on the sea: *a seagoing yacht.*

sea·gull (sē′gul′) *n* a gull, especially the herring gull.

sea horse *n* a small saltwater fish with a forward-curled tail, and a horselike head. It swims upright.

seal[1] (sēl) *n* **1** a device or substance that is used to fasten or close something tightly so that nothing can pass through. **2** the condition or fact of being fastened or closed in this way: *We found that this glue created a better seal.* **3** a design stamped on a piece of wax, lead, or other material that is attached to a document to show that it is authentic or is from the proper person: *an official seal.* **4** a thing that confirms or guarantees something: *a seal of authenticity.*
v **1** close tightly or fasten so that nothing can pass through: *Seal the letter before mailing it. She sealed the jars of fruit. His promise sealed his lips.* **2** mark or certify a document with a seal. **3** fry food quickly at high heat to prevent its losing moisture: *to seal the juices in.* **4** settle, conclude, establish, or determine: *The judge's words sealed the prisoner's fate.* **5** give a sign that something is true: *to seal a promise with a kiss. They sealed their bargain by shaking hands.* <Old French, from Latin *signum* a sign> **seal′a·ble** *adj.*
seal off, restrict access to by means of a seal or something acting as a seal: *The police sealed off the road.*
set (or **put**) **your seal to,** mark with your distinctive character: *She quickly set her seal on the company's management.*

The **eared seal** and the much larger **sea lion** are different types of seals, but both rotate their back flippers to move forward on land, while using their front flippers to prop themselves up.

seal[2] (sēl) *n, pl* **seals** or (*especially collectively*) **seal** a fish-eating saltwater mammal that breeds or rests on land, and has limbs modified into flippers.
v hunt seals. <Old English *seolh*>

seal·ant (sē′lənt) *n* a substance used for sealing pores or seams to make them airtight or watertight.

sea legs *n* legs that have become accustomed to walking steadily on a rolling or pitching ship.
get your sea legs, become accustomed to the motion of a ship, especially after an initial period of seasickness.

seal·er[1] (sē′lər) *n* **1** a thing that seals, especially a substance applied to a porous surface such as wood to prevent paint or varnish from soaking in. **2** a glass jar that can be sealed, used for home preserving of food.

seal·er[2] (sē′lər) *n* a person or ship engaged in hunting seals.

sea level *n* the level of the surface of the sea, used to record the height of geographical features such as mountains and plains, and as a standard for registering barometric pressure.

seal·ing wax (sē′ling) *n* a substance used to make seals, especially for letters and documents, consisting of a mixture of resin, shellac, turpentine, and pigment that becomes soft when heated.

sea lion *n* a large seal with external ears and hind flippers that can be turned forward for walking on land. Compare SEAL.

seal·skin (sēl′skin′) *n* the pelt or fur of a seal, especially when made into a garment.

seam (sēm) *n* **1** the line formed when two pieces of fabric or other material are sewn together. **2** a mark or line at which edges meet: *The seams of the boat must be filled in if they leak.* **3** a mark or line like a seam. **4** an underground layer of a mineral such as coal.
v join with or resemble a seam: *Years of exposure to the harsh climate had seamed her face.* <Old English *seam*> **seam′less** *adj.* **seam′less·ly** *adv.* **seam′less·ness** *n.*

CONFUSABLES

Seam means "line or mark where edges meet": *The seam on the right side of your coat has come apart.*

Seem means "appear to be": *It seems that we had the wrong date written down for the concert.*

sea·man (sē′mən) *n, pl* **sea·men** (-mən) **1** a sailor, especially one who sails the ocean. **2** a sailor in the navy who is not an officer.

sea·man·like (sē′mən līk′) *adj* like or showing the abilities of a good seaman.

sea·man·ship (sē′mən ship′) *n* the skill, techniques, or practices of handling and navigating a ship.

sea monster *n* an imaginary sea creature of terrifying size and form.

seam·stress (sēm′stris) *n* a woman who sews, especially one paid to sew.

a bat	e bed	i bid	o pot	u cup	th **thin**
ā cake	ē me	ī bite	ō go	ū rude	ᴛʜ **then**
à bar	ə about	ər over	ȯ for	ů put	zh measure

seam·y (sē′mē) *adj* **seam·i·er, seam·i·est** sordid, squalid, or disreputable: *He had a taste for the seamy side of life.*

sé·ance (sā′äns) *n* a meeting of people trying to communicate with spirits of the dead by means of a medium. <French, from Latin *sedere* sit>

sea otter *n* a large otter of northern Pacific coastal waters with large hind feet and a dense brown coat.

sea·plane (sē′plān′) *n* an aircraft with floats or skis instead of wheels, so that it that can take off from and land on water. See FLOAT for picture.

sea·port (sē′pȯrt′) *n* a city or town with a harbour that ships can reach from the sea.

sea power *n* **1** the strength of a country's navy, especially as a weapon of war. **2** a country with a large, strong, well-equipped navy.

sear (sēr) *v* **1** burn or char the surface of: *The hot iron seared his flesh.* **2** brown food quickly at high heat so that the juices are sealed in. **3** experience as a sudden burning sensation: *Her cruel words seared his heart.* <Old English *searian*>

search (sərch) *v* **1** try to find something by looking for it carefully and thoroughly: *We searched all day for the lost cat.* **2** examine a place, vehicle, or person thoroughly, especially for something concealed: *The police searched the thief to see if he had a weapon.* **3** look thoroughly at: *She searched his face for clues as to what he was thinking.*
n an act of searching for something or someone: *I found my cap after a long search.* <Old French, from Latin *circus* circle>
in search of, trying to find or looking for: *They went in search of buried treasure.*
search out, find by searching.

search and destroy *n* a military operation in which an area is systematically searched for enemy equipment and installations, which are then destroyed.

search and replace *Computers n* a word-processing operation in which a word, character, or number is found and replaced by a different one as specified by the user.

search and rescue *n* an operation of a coast guard or other rescue personnel in which an area is systematically searched for survivors of a mishap or disaster, who are then rescued.

search engine *Computers n* a program that retrieves data, files, or documents from a database or network, especially on the Internet.

search·ing (sər′ching) *adj* looking thoroughly at: *a searching gaze.* **search′er** *n.*

search·light (sərch′līt′) *n* a powerful outdoor electrical device that can throw a beam of light in any desired direction, or the beam of light itself.

search party *n* a group of people who systematically search an area for someone who or something that is lost.

search warrant *n* a legal document authorizing a police officer or other official to enter and search a house, office, or building for something.

sea room *n* space at sea free from obstruction, in which a ship can easily turn or move.

sea salt *n* salt obtained from sea water.

sea·scape (sē′skāp′) *n* a picture, often a painting, of the sea.

sea serpent *n* a huge, snakelike sea monster often reported as having been seen in the sea, but never proven to exist.

sea·shell (sē′shel′) *n* the shell of any sea mollusc such as an oyster, clam, or conch.

sea·shore (sē′shȯr′) *n* the land or beach along the sea.

sea·sick (sē′sik′) *adj* suffering from nausea and dizziness caused by the motion of a ship at sea. **sea′sick′ness** *n.*

sea·side (sē′sīd′) *n* a place by the sea, especially a beach area or vacation resort.

sea snake *n* a poisonous saltwater snake with a flattened tail, found in coastal areas of the Indian and Pacific Oceans.

sea·son (sē′zən) *n* **1** one of the four divisions of the year, being spring, summer, autumn, or winter. **2** a period of time marked by a particular climatic feature or when a thing is occurring, active, at its best, or in fashion: *the ski season, the harvest season, the baseball season.*
v **1** add flavourings such as salt, herbs, or spices to. **2** add a quality or feature to make something more interesting, exciting, or otherwise different: *to season conversation with wit.* **3** make wood suitable for use by adjusting its moisture content. **4** accustom or make used to: *The soldiers were seasoned in battle.* <Old French, from Latin *serere* to sow>
for a season, for a period of time.
in season, a at the correct or proper time. **b** in the time or condition for eating or hunting. **c** in female mammals, ready to mate.
out of season, not in season.

GRAMMAR AND USAGE

The names of the **seasons**—*spring, summer, fall* (or *autumn*), and *winter*—are not usually capitalized:
I'm really looking forward to the spring and summer after this harsh winter.

sea·son·a·ble (sē′zə nə bəl) *adj* suitable for the season: *The hot weather was seasonable for July.* **sea·son′a·bly** *adv.*

sea·son·al (sē′zə nəl) *adj* depending on or affected by the season: *seasonal rains, a seasonal worker.* **sea′son·al·ly** *adv.*

seasonal affective disorder SAD.

sea·son·ing (sē′zə ning) *n* **1** salt, herbs, or spices that are added to food to give extra flavour. **2** a thing that adds interest or variety.

season ticket *n* a ticket that gives its holder the right to attend a series of games or entertainments, or to make a certain trip on a railway for a stated period of time.

sea star *n* a starfish.

seat (sēt) *n* **1** a thing made or used for sitting on. **2** a place in which to sit, or have the right to sit: *a passenger seat. We have reserved seats in the first balcony.* **3** a right to sit as a member of a legislature, city council, etc.: *The party lost ten seats in the last election.* **4** the part of a chair, bench, or stool on which one sits or the part of the body on which one sits: *This bench has a broken seat. The seat of his*

trousers was patched. **5** a site or location of something specified: *Ottawa is the seat of the Federal Government.*
v **1** set, place, or arrange on a seat, or provide with one: *We were seated in the first row.* **2** have seats for a specified number: *Our school auditorium seats one thousand students.* <Old Norse *sæti*>
be seated, a sit down. **b** be situated.
by the seat of your pants, in a spontaneous, unsystematic way: *He had no notes but gave a speech by the seat of his pants.*

seat belt *n* a belt that helps to hold a passenger securely in the seat of a motor vehicle or aircraft.

seat·ing (sē′ting) *n* the seats with which a building or room is provided.

seat·mate (sēt′māt′) *n* a person sitting next to another on a motor vehicle, train, or aircraft.

✱ **seat sale** *n* a sale of tickets, especially airline tickets, at a reduced price.

sea turtle TURTLE (def. 1).

sea urchin *n* a round saltwater animal with a spiny shell.

sea·wall (sē′wol) *n* a wall or embankment made to act as a breakwater or to prevent waves from wearing away the shore.

sea·ward (sē′wərd) *adj, adv* toward the sea: *a seaward view* (*adj*). *Our house faces seaward* (*adv*).
Also (*adv*), **seawards**.

sea·wa·ter (sē′wo′tər) *adj* to do with the sea rather than lakes and rivers: *seawater fish.*

sea·way (sē′wā′) *n* (*often in place names*) an inland waterway that connects with the sea and is deep enough to permit ocean shipping: *the St. Lawrence Seaway.*

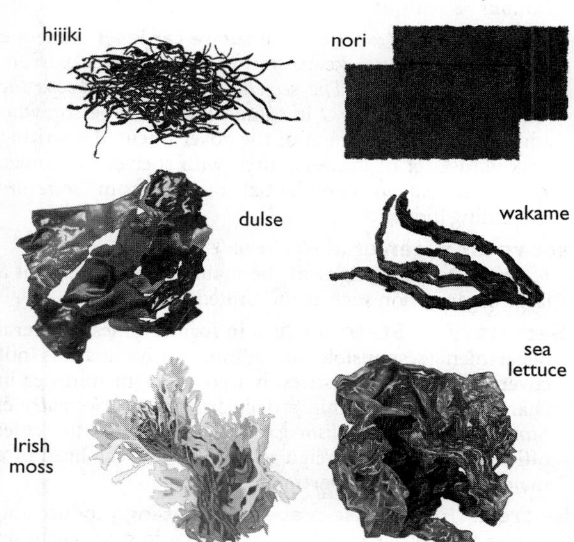

Seaweed is an important food, especially in Japan. It is also used as fertilizer, in food for livestock, and to manufacture many products.

sea·weed (sē′wēd′) *n* a plant or plants growing in the sea or on rocks below the high-water mark.

sea·wor·thy (sē′wər′ᴛʜē) *adj* fit for sailing on the sea: *a seaworthy ship.*

se·ba·ceous (si bā′shəs) *adj* **1** to do with fat or oil. **2** producing sebum: *sebaceous glands.*

se·bum (sē′bəm) *n* the oily substance produced by the sebaceous glands to lubricate the skin and hair.

se·ca·teurs (sek′ə tərz′) *or* (sek′ə tərz′) *pln* pruning shears or clippers designed to be used with one hand. <French, from Latin *secare* to cut>

se·cede (si sēd′) *v* **se·ced·ed, se·ced·ing** withdraw formally from an organization, especially from a church or a political state. <Latin *se-* apart + *cedere* go>

se·ces·sion (si sesh′ən) *n* the act of formally withdrawing from an organization or group, especially a political unit.

se·clude (si klūd′) *v* **se·clud·ed, se·clud·ing** shut off or keep apart from others: *She's secluded herself and no longer welcomes visitors.* <Latin *se-* apart + *claudere* shut>

se·clud·ed (si klū′did) *adj* little seen or visited: *a secluded cottage.*

se·clu·sion (si klū′zhən) *n* the condition of being private and away from other people: *He lives in seclusion and seldom goes out.*

sec·ond[1] (sek′ənd) *adj* **1** number two in a sequence, after the first in time, position, or importance: *the second seat from the front.* **2** *Music* **a** with the lower or lesser of two parts for the same musical instrument: *second violin.* **b** with a musical interval spanning two consecutive notes in a diatonic scale, or with the note that is higher by this interval. **3** additional to something that exists: *a second home.* **4** to do with the gear next above the lowest in a standard transmission.
adv below the first in time, position, or importance: *She finished second in the final.*
n **1** a person who or thing that is next below the first: *You're the second to arrive, to be second in a race.* **2** an assistant to a boxer or a duellist. **3** *Music* a musical interval spanning two consecutive notes in a diatonic scale, or the note that is higher by this interval. **4** *Baseball* second base. **5** the gear next above first in a standard transmission. **6 seconds** *pl* items of less than first quality.
v **1** formally support a nomination or resolution at a meeting after it has been proposed by someone else. **2** express approval or support of: *His opinion was seconded by the others present.* <Latin *secundus*, from *sequi* follow>
sec′ond·er *n.*
on second thought, after further thinking about something, leading to a change of mind: *I was going to stay home, but on second thought, I think I'll go out.*

sec·ond[2] (sek′ənd) *n* **1** the SI unit for measuring time. There are sixty seconds in one minute. *Symbol* **s** **2** a very short period of time: *I'll be with you in a second.* **3** a unit for measuring plane angles, one sixtieth of a minute, used mainly by geographers. *Symbol* ″

a bat	e bed	i bid	o pot	u cup	th **thin**
ā cake	ē me	ī bite	ō go	ū rude	ᴛʜ **then**
ȧ bar	ə about	ər over	ȯ for	ů put	zh measure

S

sec·ond·ar·y (sek′ən der′ē) *adj* **1** next after the first in order, place, time, or importance: *My teacher said that reading quickly is secondary to reading well.* **2** to do with a secondary school: *secondary education.* **3** not original; derived: *secondary sources of information.*
sec′ond·ar′i·ly *adv.*

secondary colour *n* a colour produced by mixing two or more primary colours. Compare PRIMARY COLOUR.

secondary school *n* a school attended after elementary school or junior high school.

secondary sex characteristic *n* the physical traits that distinguish male from female but are not required for reproduction, such as differences in body fat and muscularity or voice pitch.

secondary stress *n* a stress that is weaker than the strongest stress (primary stress) in a word. Example: The second syllable of *ab·bre′vi·a′tion* has a secondary stress.

sec·ond–class (sek′ənd klas′) *adj* **1** to do with a class ranking next below the first or highest. **2** of an inferior quality or grade: *Their products are definitely second-class.*

second cousin *n* the child of one's parent's first cousin.

second growth *n* a new growth of trees in an area where forest has been cut or burned, or a crop of grass or hay that comes up after the first crop has been cut.

sec·ond–guess (sek′ənd ges′) *Informal v* anticipate or predict someone's actions or thoughts by guessing them.

second hand *n* a hand on a clock or watch that moves round to indicate the seconds.

sec·ond–hand (sek′ənd hand′) *adj, adv* **1** already owned or used by someone else: *second-hand clothes, I bought the bike second-hand.* **2** accepted on the basis of someone else's knowledge or experience: *second-hand information. I learned about the theft second-hand.*

second–hand smoke *n* smoke from someone's cigarette, pipe, or cigar breathed in by others.

sec·ond·ly (sek′ən dlē) *adv* in the second place: *Firstly, he's honest; secondly, he's very competent.*

second mortgage *n* additional funding lent on the security of property such as a house. It has second claim on the property behind the first mortgage.

second nature *n* a habit, quality, or characteristic in a person that seems to be instinctive because it has appeared or occurred so often.

second person *Grammar n* **1** the category to which a pronoun or verb belongs when used to refer to the person spoken to. *You, your,* and *yours* are second person pronouns. **2** the form of a pronoun or verb indicating this. Example: *are* is the second person singular of the verb *be.*

sec·ond–rate (sek′ən drāt′) *adj* of inferior quality or value: *a second-rate diamond, a second-rate author.*

second sight *n* the supposed power to see distant objects or future events.

second thoughts *pln* doubts or a change of mind about a previous decision or course of action.

second wind *n* **1** a recovery or renewal of breath and energy following the initial feeling of exhaustion during an effort, such as in running a race. **2** a recovery or renewal of energy: *The book drive faltered after a month and then got its second wind.*

Second World War WORLD WAR II.

se·cre·cy (sē′krə sē) *n, pl* **se·cre·cies** the act or habit of keeping things secret: *They relied on her secrecy.*

se·cret (sē′krit) *adj* **1** kept from the knowledge of all others: *a secret marriage.* **2** known only to a few: *a secret society.* **3** kept from sight; hidden: *a secret drawer.* **4** working or acting in secret: *a secret agent.*
n **1** something secret or hidden. **2** a thing known only to a few. **3** a hidden cause or reason: *What's the secret of your success?* <Latin *secretus* hidden> **se′cret·ly** *adv.*
in secret, in private; not openly.

SYNONYMS

Secret means "hidden": *The answer has to be kept secret until they all arrive.*

Covert suggests the deliberate use of a cover or disguise: *The plainclothes police officers carried out a covert operation to track down the criminals.*

Confidential means "restricted to secret or private use": *The doctor's report on my health is confidential.*

secret agent *n* a spy acting for a national government.

sec·re·tar·i·al (sek′rə ter′ē əl) *adj* to do with the work of a secretary: *He learned filing and other secretarial work.*

sec·re·tar·i·at (sek′rə ter′ē it) *n* the administrative unit controlled by a secretary or secretary-general: *the United Nations Secretariat.*

sec·re·tar·y (sek′rə ter′ē) *n, pl* **sec·re·tar·ies** **1** someone who writes letters, keeps records, etc. for a person, company, club, etc.: *The secretary of our club keeps the minutes of the meeting.* **2** in some countries, a person who administers a department of the government. **3** a writing desk with a set of drawers, often with shelves for books. <Latin *secretarius* confidential officer, from *secretum* something hidden>

sec·re·tar·y–gen·er·al (sek′rə ter′ē jen′ə rəl) *n, pl* **sec·re·tar·ies-gen·er·al** the main administration of a large organization such as the United Nations.

Secretary of State *n* **1** 🍁 **a** in former times, a federal department responsible for administrative matters not covered by other ministries. **b** a government minister in charge of an area within a department: *The Secretary of State for Multiculturalism gave a speech.* **2** *US* the chief official in charge of foreign relations. **3** *UK* the head of a major government department.

se·crete[1] (si krēt′) *v* **se·cret·ed, se·cret·ing** produce and release from a cell, gland, or organ. <Latin *secernere* to set apart> **se·cre′tion** *n.*

se·crete[2] (si krēt′) *v* **se·cret·ed, se·cret·ing** hide: *The money was secreted in an abandoned car.* <See SECRET.>

se·cre·tive (sē′krə tiv) *adj* tending or appearing not to reveal feelings, intentions, or information: *secretive deals, a secretive smile.* **se′cre·tive·ly** *adv.* **se′cre·tive·ness** *n.*

secret police *n* a police force working in secret on behalf of a government.

secret service *n* the branch of a government that engages in spying.

secret society *n* an association of which some ceremonies and activities are known only to members, who are sworn to secrecy.

sect (sekt) *n* a group of people that forms part of a larger religious body but rejects some of the larger body's beliefs or customs, sometimes to the extent that it forms a new church. <Old French, from Latin *sequi* follow>

sec·tar·i·an (sek ter′ē ən) *adj* **1** to do with a sect. **2** characteristic of, prejudiced in favour of, or acting for a certain sect.
n a devoted member of a sect, especially one who rigidly follows its rules.

sec·tion (sek′shən) *n* **1** a distinct part or division of a group or thing: *He divided the cake into sections.* **2** a division of a book, periodical, statute, or other document: *Chapter 3 has seven sections.* **3** a particular part of a community or town: *The city has a business section and a residential section.* **4** a shape or cross-section of a thing as it would appear if cut straight through. **5** a district or tract of land one mile square, consisting of 640 acres (about 260 hectares): *She farms two sections.* **6** a thin slice of plant or animal tissue prepared for examination under a microscope. **7** a group of players of a family of instruments within an orchestra: *the brass section.*
v divide into sections: *to section an orange.* <French, from Latin *secare* cut>
section off, divide or mark off into a separate section or sections: *This area of the classroom has been sectioned off into a lab.*

sec·tion·al (sek′shə nəl) *adj* **1** to do with a particular SECTION (def. 3): *a sectional championship.* **2** made of or supplied in SECTIONS (def. 1): *a sectional bookcase.* **sec′tion·al·ly** *adv.*

sec·tor (sek′tər) *n* **1** an area or portion that is distinct from others, especially a particular part of a country's economy or activities: *the public sector and the private sector.* **2** *Mathematics* the part of a circle bounded by two radii and the included arc. See DIAMETER for picture. <Latin *secare* to cut>

sec·u·lar (sek′yə lər) *adj* **1** to do with things that are unconnected to religious or spiritual matters: *secular music.* **2** not living in a religious order: *the secular clergy.* <Old French, from Latin *saeculum* generation> **sec′u·lar·ly** *adv.*

sec·u·lar·ism (sek′yə lə riz′əm) *n* **1** scepticism in regard to religion. **2** opposition to the introduction of religion into public schools or other public affairs. **sec′u·lar·ist** *n.*

sec·u·lar·ize (sek′yə lə rīz′) *v* **sec·u·lar·ized, sec·u·lar·iz·ing** make secular and separate from religious connection or influence: *to secularize schools.* **sec′u·lar·i·za′tion** *n.*

se·cure (si kyůr′) *adj* **1** safe against loss, damage, or harm: *This is a secure hiding place. She said that buying land in a growing city was a secure investment.* **2** able to prevent escape from a jail or prison: *a secure cell.* **3** free from care, fear, or anxiety: *She hoped for a secure old age.* **4** firmly fixed or fastened so as not to give way, become loose, or be lost: *The boards of this bridge do not look secure.*
v **se·cured, se·cur·ing 1** make firm or fixed so that something cannot be moved or lost: *Secure the locks on the windows.* **2** protect against loss or harm: *Every loan was secured by bonds or mortgages. We must secure against the dangers of the coming storm.* **3** succeed in obtaining: *Secure your tickets early.* <Latin *se-* without + *cura* care> **se·cur′a·ble** *adj.* **se·cure′ly** *adv.*

se·cu·ri·ty (si kyů′rə tē) *n, pl* **se·cu·ri·ties 1** freedom from danger, threat, or fear: *job security.* **2** the safety of a country or group against terrorism, theft, or spying, or the measures taken to ensure such safety: *national security, tight security.* **3** a thing given as a guarantee that a person will be able to pay back a loan or fulfill some duty or promise: *The life-insurance policy was security for a loan.* **4 securities** *pl* certificates showing ownership, credit, or rights, especially the ownership of stocks or bonds. <Old French, from Latin *se-* without + *cura* care>

security blanket *n* a small blanket or other object carried around to provide comfort or reassurance, especially by a child.

Security Council *n* a permanent body in the United Nations group whose function is to maintain world peace and security. It has five permanent members (France, the UK, China, Russia, and the US) and ten elected non-permanent members.

Sec·wep·emc (shə′whep mək) *n, pl* **Sec·wep·emc 1** a member of a First Nations people living in the Thompson River area of British Columbia. **2** their Salishan language.
adj to do with these people or their language. Also called **Shuswap**.

se·dan (si dan′) *n* **1** a motor vehicle that seats four or more people. **2** in full, **sedan chair** in former times, an enclosed chair carried on two horizontal poles by two or more men. <origin uncertain>

se·date (sə dāt′) *adj* calm, dignified, and unrushed: *He moved at a sedate pace.*
v **se·dat·ed, se·dat·ing** calm a person or cause sleep with a sedative drug: *The grieving widow had to be sedated.* <Latin *sedare* to soothe> **se·date′ly** *adv.*

sed·a·tion (sə dā′shən) *n* the use of a sedative drug to produce calmness or sleep: *under sedation.*

sed·a·tive (sed′ə tiv) *n* a drug that is taken to produce calmness or sleep.
adj promoting calmness or causing sleep.

sed·en·tar·y (sed′ən ter′ē) *adj* tending to be seated and not physically active: *a sedentary job.* <French, from Latin *sedere* sit> **sed′en·tar′i·ly** *adv.* **sed′en·tar′i·ness** *n.*

Se·der (sā′dər) *n, pl* **Se·ders** or **Se·dar·im** (se dä rēm′) *or* (se də rēm′) the religious service and ceremonial dinner held in Jewish homes on the first two nights of PASSOVER. <Hebrew = order>

a bat	e bed	i bid	o pot	u cup	th **thin**
ā cake	ē me	ī bite	ō go	ū rude	TH **then**
ä bar	ə about	ər over	ô for	ů put	zh measure

S

sedge (sej) *n* a grasslike plant that grows in wet ground. <Old English *secg*> **sedg′y** *adj.*

sed·i·ment (sed′ə mənt) *n* **1** matter that settles to the bottom of a liquid. **2** particles of matter that are carried by water or wind and deposited on the land or seabed, and may eventually form rock.
v settle as a sediment or be deposited as one. <French, from Latin *sedere* sit> **sed′i·men·ta′tion** *n.*

sed·i·men·ta·ry (sed′ə men′tə rē) *adj* to do with rock that has been formed from layers of sediment deposited by water or wind.

se·di·tion (si dish′ən) *n* speech or action causing discontent or rebellion against the government. <Old French, from Latin *se-* apart + *ire* go> **se·di′tious** *adj.* **se·di′tious·ly** *adv.*

se·duce (si dyūs′) *or* (si dūs′) *v* **se·duced, se·duc·ing** **1** tempt or persuade someone to do wrong: *He was seduced into taking a bribe.* **2** entice into sexual activity. **3** subtly but powerfully attract: *The melody seduced me with its sadness.* <Latin *se-* away + *ducere* to lead, i.e., lead astray> **se·duc′er** *n.*

se·duc·tive (si duk′tiv) *adj* charming and attractive: *seductive sounds.* **se·duc′tive·ly** *adv.* **se·duc′tive·ness** *n.*

sed·u·lous (sej′ə ləs) *adj* busy and dedicated: *sedulous attention.* **sed′u·lous·ly** *adv.* **sed′u·lous·ness** *n.*

se·dum (sē′dəm) *n* a fleshy-leaved plant with small clusters of flowers. <Latin>

see[1] (sē) *v* **saw, seen, see·ing** **1** perceive with or use the eyes, or have the power of sight: *See that black cloud. That afternoon he saw a tennis match. The eye operation allowed her to see.* **2** understand: *I see what you mean.* **3** find out or learn: *I will see what needs to be done.* **4** take care or make sure: *See that you lock the back door.* **5** have experience or awareness of: *That coat has seen hard wear.* **6** escort or go with: *Her saw her home.* <Old English *seon*>
see about, a ask or find out about: *I have to see about the schedule before I sign up for the swim class.* **b** ensure something is done about: *Did you see about registering for the Science Fair?* **c** leave to be decided later in view of how things develop: *You think he can do it? We'll see about that!*
see fit, consider to be reasonable: *They saw fit to accept.*
see into, understand the real character or hidden purpose of.
see out, go through with or finish.
see someone off, go with to the starting place of a journey.
see through, a understand the real character or hidden purpose of. **b** go through with or finish. **c** watch over or help through a difficulty: *We saw her through her illness.*
see to, look after or take care of.

see[2] (sē) *n* the district under a bishop's or archbishop's authority. <Old French, from Latin *sedes* a seat>

seed (sēd) *n, pl* **seeds** or (*especially collectively*) **seed** **1** the thing from which a flower, vegetable, or other plant is reproduced, capable of growing into another such plant: *She grew the petunias from seed.* See COTYLEDON for picture. **2** the source or beginning of a thing: *seeds of trouble.* **3** semen. **4** a player of high ranking in a sports tournament.
v **1** sow land with seeds: *The farmer seeded his field with corn.* **2** produce seeds. **3** remove the seeds from: *She seeded the grapes for the salad.* **4** rank players in a sports tournament so that the best players do not meet in the early matches. **5** scatter chemicals into clouds from an airplane in an effort to produce rain artificially. <Old English *sæd*> **seed′less** *adj.* **seed′like′** *adj.*
go (or **run**) **to seed, a** come to the time of yielding seeds: *Dandelions go to seed when their heads turn white.* **b** become less strong, vigorous, or efficient: *When he lost his money he allowed himself to go to seed.*

seed·bed (sēd′bed′) *n* **1** a bed of fine soil prepared for growing plants from seed. **2** a place that fosters growth and development.

seed·case (sēd′kās′) *n* a pod, capsule, or other dry, hollow fruit that contains seeds.

seed coat *n* the outer layer protecting a seed from damage and water loss.

seed·er (sē′dər) *n* a machine or device for planting seeds.

seed·ling (sē′dling) *n* a young plant grown from a seed.

seed money *n* the first funds given to start a new business or project, often in the hope of attracting further funding.

seed pearl *n* a very small pearl.

seed·y (sē′dē) *adj* **seed·i·er, seed·i·est** **1** sordid or with a bad reputation: *a seedy bar.* **2** shabby or squalid: *seedy clothes.* **seed′i·ly** *adv.* **seed′i·ness** *n.*

see·ing (sē′ing) *conj* in view of the fact that: *Seeing it is long past ten o'clock, we will wait no longer.*

see·ing–eye dog (sē′ing ī′dog′) *n* a dog trained as a guide for blind people.

seek (sēk) *v* **sought, seek·ing** **1** try to find: *We are seeking clues to the disappearance of my bike.* **2** attempt or desire to obtain or achieve something: *Friends sought her advice.* <Old English *secan*>

seem (sēm) *v* **1** appear to be or to exist: *He seemed a very old man.* **2** appear to oneself: *I still seem to hear the music.* **3** appear to exist or to be true: *There seems no need to wait longer. It seems likely to rain.* See SEAM for confusable. <Old Norse *sæmr* fitting>

seem·ing (sē′ming) *adj* appearing to be: *a seeming advantage.*

seem·ing·ly (sē′ming lē) *adv* apparently: *This hill is seemingly the highest around here.*

seem·ly (sēm′lē) *adj* **seem·li·er, seem·li·est** suitable or proper according to usual standards: *She thought it wasn't seemly to gape at him.* **seem′li·ness** *n.*

seen (sēn) *v* past participle of SEE[1].

seep (sēp) *v* ooze, leak, or trickle: *The water seeped through the sand.* <Old English *sipian* to soak>

seep·age (sē′pij) *n* a slow escape of a liquid or gas through porous material or small holes, or the liquid or gas that escapes.

seer (sēr) *n* a person who is thought to foresee or foretell future events.

seer·suck·er (sēr′suk′ər) *n* a printed cotton or synthetic fabric with alternate stripes of plain and crinkled material: *a suit made of seersucker.*

ETYMOLOGY

Seersucker comes from Hindi *sirsakar*, from two Persian words: *shir* meaning "milk," and *shakkar* meaning "sugar." The stripes of the cloth are like the smooth surface of milk and the bumpy surface of sugar.

see·saw (sē′so′) *n* **1** a long plank, balanced and supported in the middle, that can be swung up and down by a person sitting at each end and pushing the ground alternately with the feet. Also called **teeter-totter**. **2** a situation marked by rapid, repeated changes: *In the first half of the year there was a seesaw in my grades, but later they levelled out.*
v **1** change rapidly and repeatedly. **2** move up and down or back and forth. <*saw*[1], referring to the back and forth motion of sawing wood>

seethe (sēTH) *v* **seethed, seeth·ing** **1** bubble and foam, such as a boiling liquid or the hectic movement of water in a river or the sea does: *The soup seethed in the pot. Near the waterfall, the river began to seethe.* **2** have much anger but not yet express it: *The ship's crew was seething with discontent and ready for mutiny.* <Old English *seothan* boil>

see–through (sē′thrū) *adj* transparent or nearly so, especially in clothes: *a see-through blouse.*

seg·ment (seg′mənt) *n* **1** a part marked, cut, or broken off: *She pulled the oranges apart into segments.* **2** a portion of time, especially that taken up by a broadcast item on radio or TV: *He listened to the news segment of the program.* **3** *Mathematics* a part of a circle, sphere, or other figure cut off by a line or by a plane.
v divide into segments, separate parts, or sections. <Latin *secare* to cut> **seg′men·tar′y** *adj.*

seg·men·ta·tion (seg′mən tā′shən) *n* **1** a division into segments. **2** the growth and division of a cell into two, four, eight cells, and so on.

seg·re·gate (seg′rə gāt′) *v* **seg·re·gat·ed, seg·re·gat·ing** **1** set apart from others: *The doctor segregated the child with mumps to protect the other patients.* **2** separate or divide people or activities for racial, sexual, or religious reasons: *to segregate schools.* <Latin *se-* apart + *grex* flock>

seg·re·ga·tion (seg′rə gā′shən) *n* **1** the action or process of setting someone or something apart from other people or things. **2** the enforced separation of one racial group from another or from the rest of society, especially in schools and public places. **seg′re·ga′tion·al** *adj.* **seg′re·ga′tion·ist** *n.*

se·gue (seg′wā) *or* (sāg′wā) *v* **seg·ued, se·gue·ing** **1** *Music* move without interruption from one piece of music to another. **2** make a smooth and uninterrupted transition from one thing to another: *In your essay, try to segue from one paragraph to the next.*
n a smooth and uninterrupted transition: *Dawn began its segue in the night sky.* <Italian = follows>

sei·gneur or **seign·ior** (sē nyər′) *n* a feudal lord or landowner, such as one in New France who was granted land by the king. <Old French, from Latin *senior* an elderly man>

seine (sān) *n* a fishing net that hangs straight down in the water with floats at the top and weights at the bottom edge.
v **seined, sein·ing** fish with a seine. <Greek *sagene*>

sein·er (sā′nər) *n* a fishing boat equipped with a seine, or a person who fishes with a seine.

seis·mic (sī′zmik) *adj* to do with an earthquake. <Greek *seiein* shake>

seis·mo·gram (sī′zmə gram′) *n* a record of an earthquake obtained on a seismograph.

seis·mo·graph (sī′zmə graf′) *n* an instrument for recording the direction, intensity, and duration of earthquakes. **seis′mo·graph′ic** *adj.*

seis·mol·o·gy (sī zmol′ə jē) *n* the study of earthquakes and other movements of the earth's crust. **seis′mo·log′ic·al** *adj.* **seis′mo·log′ic·al·ly** *adv.* **seis·mol′o·gist** *n.*

seize (sēz) *v* **seized, seiz·ing** **1** take hold of suddenly and forcibly: *When she lost her balance, she seized his arm.* **2** take advantage of something eagerly: *seize the initiative.* **3** capture or take over by force: *The soldiers seized the city. The army seized power in a coup.* **4** suddenly take possession of: *A fever seized her.* **5** take possession of by legal authority: *seize illegal drugs.* **6** strongly appeal to or attract: *seize the imagination.* <Old French *seisir*>
seize the day, live in the present and take whatever opportunities arise.

SYNONYMS

Seize means "grab quickly and forcefully": *The thief ran by and seized the bag.*

Grasp means "seize and hold tightly": *The monkey grasped the banana and wouldn't let it go.*

Clutch emphasizes grasping eagerly: *The baby clutched the bottle.*

sei·zure (sē′zhər) *n* **1** the action of capturing someone or something by force. **2** the action of taking possession by legal authority. **3** a sudden attack of illness, especially a stroke or an epileptic fit.

Se·ka·ni (se kä′nē) *n, pl* **Se·ka·ni** **1** a member of a First Nations people living in northern British Columbia. **2** their Athapascan language.
adj to do with these people or their language.

sel·dom (sel′dəm) *adv* not often: *She is seldom ill.* <Old English *seldan*>

se·lect (si lekt′) *v* carefully choose as being the best or most suitable: *Select the book you want.*
adj picked or provided as best or most suitable: *A few select students were allowed to try out for the spelling bee. That store carries a very select line of merchandise.* <Latin *se-* apart + *legere* choose>

a bat	e bed	i bid	o pot	u cup	th **thin**
ā cake	ē me	ī bite	ō go	ū rude	TH **then**
ä bar	ə about	ər over	ȯ for	ů put	zh measure

se·lec·tion (si lek′shən) *n* 1 the act or fact of choosing someone or something as being best or most suitable: *the selection of a jury.* 2 a person, thing, or group chosen: *The action movie was her selection, and the comedy was mine.* 3 a range of things from which one may select: *The shop offered a good selection of clothes.* 4 the process in which genetics and the environment affect which types of organisms survive, regarded as a factor in evolution.

se·lec·tive (si lek′tiv) *adj* to do with making a careful choice: *selective reading.* **se·lec′tiv·ely** *adv.* **se·lec·tiv′i·ty** *n.*

se·lec·tor (si lek′tər) *n* a person who or thing that selects.

se·le·ni·um (sə lē′nē əm) *n* a grey crystalline non-metallic element that, because its electrical resistance varies with the amount of light, is used in photoelectric cells. *Symbol* **Se** <Latin, from Greek *selene* moon>

self (self) *n, pl* **selves** 1 one's own person as distinguished from that of others: *her very self.* 2 the nature or personality of a particular person: *She does not seem like her former self.* 3 one's own interests: *a surrender of self.*
adj being the same in a trimming for clothes or for a cover as the rest of the item: *a self collar.*
pron oneself: *my good self.* <Old English>

self– *combining form* 1 of or directed toward oneself or itself: *self-control.* 2 by one's own efforts: *self-inflicted.* 3 to do with oneself or itself: *self-winding.* <*self*>

self–ab·sorbed (self′ab sȯrbd′) *adj* thinking and talking only about oneself. **self′-ab·sorp′tion** (ab sȯrp′shən) *n.*

self–ab·use (self′ab yūs′) *n* 1 behaviour that causes damage or harm to oneself. 2 masturbation. **self′-ab·use′** (self′ab yūz′) *v.*

self–act·ing (self′ak′ting) *adj* working as a machine or operation by itself without external influence or control.

self–ad·dressed (self′ə drest′) *adj* addressed to oneself: *a self-addressed envelope.*

self–ap·point·ed (self′ə point′əd) *adj* taking responsibility or authority, usually when it is not proper to do so: *She was the self-appointed judge of everybody.*

self–as·sured (self′ə shůrd′) *adj* self-confident.

self–a·ware (self′ə wār′) *adj* aware of one's own strengths and weaknesses. **self′-a·ware′ness** *n.*

self–cen·tred or **self–cen·tered** (self′sen′tərd) *adj* preoccupied with one's own interests and activities, sometimes to the extent of being selfish.

self–con·fessed (self′kon fest′) *adj* having openly admitted to being a person with certain characteristics: *a self-confessed neatness addict.*

self–con·fi·dent (self′kon′fə dənt) *adj* with a firm belief in one's own abilities, qualities, and judgment. **self′-con′fi·dence** *n.* **self′-con′fi·dent·ly** *adv.*

self–con·scious (self′kon′shəs) *adj* feeling aware or unduly aware of oneself, one's appearance, or one's actions: *He was self-conscious about his clothes.* **self′-con′scious·ly** *adv.* **self′-con′scious·ness** *n.*

self–con·tained (self′kən tānd′) *adj* 1 quiet and independent, not depending on or being influenced by others. 2 complete or with all that is needed.

self–con·trol (self′kən trōl′) *n* the ability to control one's own actions or feelings, especially in difficult situations: *She exercised a lot of self-control when others criticized her.* **self′-con·trolled′** *adj.*

self–de·feat·ing (self′di fē′ting) *adj* unable to achieve the aim for which it was intended: *Yelling at him proved to be self-defeating.*

self–de·fence or **self–de·fense** (self′di fens′) *n* a defence of one's own person or interests, especially through the use of physical force: *The judge ruled that when he attacked the thief he acted in self-defence.*

self–de·ni·al (self′di nī′əl) *n* a sacrifice of one's own needs and interests. **self′-de·ny′ing** *adj.*

self–de·struct (self′di strukt′) *v* destroy itself or oneself: *The warhead was designed to self-destruct if any part of its program failed.* **self′-de·struc′tion** *n.* **self′-de·struct′ive** *adj.* **self′-de·struct′ive·ly** *adv.*

self–de·struct·ing (self′di struk′ting) *adj* designed to destroy itself.

self–de·ter·mi·na·tion (self′di tər′mə nā′shən) *n* 1 the process by which the people of a nation decide what form of government they are to have, without reference to the wishes of others. 2 the process by which a person controls his or her own life. **self′-de·ter′mined** *adj.* **self′-de·ter′min·ing** *adj.*

self–dis·ci·pline (self′dis′ə plin) *n* the ability to control one's feelings and overcome one's weaknesses. **self′-dis′ci·plined** *adj.*

self–doubt (self′dout′) *n* lack of confidence in oneself and one's abilities. **self′-doubt′ing** *adj.*

self–ed·u·cat·ed (self′ej′ə kā′tid) *adj* educated by one's own efforts.

self–ef·fac·ing (self′ē fās′ing) *adj* modest and keeping oneself in the background. **self′-ef·face′ment** *n.* **self′-ef·fac′ing·ly** *adv.*

self–em·ployed (self′em ploid′) *adj* working for oneself rather than as an employee.

self–es·teem (self′ə stēm′) *n* confidence in one's own worth or abilities.

self–ev·i·dent (self′ev′ə dent) *adj* evident by itself and needing no proof.

self–ex·am·i·na·tion (self′eks am′ən ā′shən) *n* 1 the study of one's own behaviour and motives. 2 the action of examining one's own body to check for signs of disease. **self′-ex·am′ine** *v.*

self–ex·plan·a·to·ry (self′ek splan′ə tȯ rē) *adj* easily understood and not requiring any explanation.

self–ex·pres·sion (self′ek spresh′ən) *n* an expression of one's feelings, thoughts, or ideas, especially in the arts.

self–fer·til·iz·ing (self′fər′tə līz′ing) *adj* to do with a plant being fertilized by its own pollen or, in some invertebrate animals, being fertilized by their own sperm. **self′-fer′til·i·za′tion** *n.*

self–gov·ern·ment (self′guv′ərn ment) *or* (self′guv′ər mənt) *n* government of a group by its own members, especially of a country by its people after it has been a colony. **self′-gov′ern·ing** *adj.*

self–help (self′help′) *n* the use of one's own efforts and resources to achieve things without relying on others: *a seminar on self-help, a self-help book.*

self–help group *n* an organization of people sharing a similar problem and helping each other.

self·hood (self′hůd) *n* the quality or fact of being an individual with a distinct identity.

self–im·age (self′im′ij) *n* one's opinion or general idea of oneself, especially of how one appears to others.

self–im·por·tant (self′im pôr′tənt) *adj* having or showing too high an opinion of one's own importance. **self′-im·port′ance** *n.* **self′-im·port′ant·ly** *adv.*

self–im·posed (self′im pōzd′) *adj* imposed on oneself, not by another person or thing: *a self-imposed task.*

self–im·prove·ment (self′im prūv′mənt) *n* the improvement of one's knowledge, status, or character by one's own efforts.

self–in·duced (self′in dyūst′) *or* (self′in dūst′) *adj* brought about by oneself: *self-induced vomiting.*

self–in·dul·gent (self′in dul′jənt) *adj* to do with doing exactly what one wants, especially if this involves pleasure. **self′-in·dul′gence** *n.* **self′-in·dul′gen·tly** *adv.*

self–in·flict·ed (self′in flik′tid) *adj* inflicted as a wound or other harm on oneself.

self–in·ter·est (self′in′trist) *or* (self′in′tə rist) *n* interest in one's own welfare or personal advantage, especially when pursued with too little care for the welfare of others.

self·ish (sel′fish) *adj* concerned chiefly with one's own pleasure or profit, and lacking consideration for others: *selfish reasons.* **self′ish·ly** *adv.* **self′ish·ness** *n.*

self–know·ledge (self′nol′ij) *n* knowledge of one's own character or motives.

self·less (sel′flis) *adj* with little or no regard or thought for oneself, but concerned with the needs of others.

self–love (self′luv′) *n* regard for one's own well-being.

self–made (self′mād′) *adj* **1** successful through one's own efforts: *a self-made millionaire.* **2** made by oneself: *a self-made toy.*

self–per·pet·u·at·ing (self′pər pech′ū āt′ing) *adj* maintained or renewed indefinitely just by its own nature or structure: *self-perpetuating ignorance.*

self–pit·y (self′pit′ē) *n* too much unhappiness over one's own problems.

self–pol·li·na·ting (self′pol′in āt′ing) *adj* fertilized by the same flower or by another flower on the same plant. **self′-pol′li·na′tion** *n.*

self–por·trait (self′pôr′trit) *n* a portrait that an artist makes of himself or herself.

self–pos·sessed (self′pə zest′) *adj* with or showing control of one's feelings and acts. **self′-pos·ses′sion** *n.*

self–pres·er·va·tion (self′prez′ər vā′shən) *n* the preservation of oneself from harm or destruction.

self–pro·pelled (self′prə peld′) *adj* moving or able to move without external aid: *a self-propelled missile.*

self–reg·u·lat·ing (self′reg′yə lāt′ing) *adj* regulating oneself or itself.

self–re·li·ant (self′ri lī′ənt) *adj* relying on one's own powers and resources rather than those of others. **self′-re·li′ance** *n.* **self′-re·li′ant·ly** *adv.*

self–re·proach (self′ri prōch′) *n* blame directed at oneself.

self–re·spect (self′ri spekt′) *n* pride and confidence in oneself. **self′-re·spect′ing** *adj.*

self–re·straint (self′ri strānt′) *n* self-control.

self–right·eous (self′rī′chəs) *adj* thinking, sometimes without cause, that one is totally correct or morally superior. **self′-right′eous·ly** *adv.* **self′-right′eous·ness** *n.*

self–ris·ing flour (self′rīz′ing) *n* flour that has a leavening agent added before packaging.

self–rule (self′rūl′) *n* self-government.

self–sac·ri·fice (self′sak′rə fīs′) *n* the sacrifice of one's own interests and desires in order to help others or advance a cause. **self′-sac′ri·fic′ing** *adj.*

self·same (self′sām′) *adj* exactly the same: *We study the selfsame books that you do.*

self–sat·is·fied (self′sat′is fīd′) *adj* pleased with oneself; complacent. **self′-sat′is·fact′ion** *adj.*

self–seek·ing (self′sē′king) *adj* selfish.
n selfishness.

self–serve (self′sərv′) *adj* designed to be used by the customer without the help of an employee: *a self-serve gas station.* **self′-ser′vice** *adj, n.*

self–serv·ing (self′serv′ing) *adj* selfish.

self–start·er (self′stàr′tər) *n* a person who does or achieves something without being motivated or prompted by others.

self–styled (self′stīld′) *adj* using a description or title that one has given oneself: *a self-styled expert.*

self–suf·fi·cient (self′sə fish′ənt) *adj* **1** asking and needing no help; independent. **2** with too much confidence in one's own resources, powers, etc.; conceited. **self′-suf·fi′cien·cy** (self′sə fish′ən sē) *n.* **self′-suf·fi′cient·ly** *adv.*

self–sup·port·ing (self′sə pôr′ting) *adj* **1** able to survive or earn a living without the help of another. **2** staying up or upright without being supported by something else: *a self-supporting structure.*

self–sus·tain·ing (self′sə stā′ning) *adj* SELF-SUPPORTING (def. 1).

self–taught (self′tot′) *adj* taught by oneself without aid from others.

self–willed (self′wild′) *adj* insisting on having one's own way; objecting to doing what others ask or command. **self′-will′** *n.*

a bat	e bed	i bid	o pot	u cup	th thin
ā cake	ē me	ī bite	ō go	ū rude	ᴛʜ then
à bar	ə about	ər over	ȯ for	ů put	zh measure

S

sell (sel) *v* **sold, sell·ing 1** exchange for money or other payment: *to sell a house.* **2** deal in or have a supply of something for sale: *The butcher sells meat.* **3** be on sale or be sold: *Strawberries sell at a high price in January.* **4** betray: *The traitor sold his country for money.* **5** persuade a person or group of the merits of something or win acceptance, approval, or adoption: *He sold the idea to the public. This is a concept that will sell.* <Old English *sellan*>
sell′ab·le *adj.*
be sold on, *Informal* be convinced of something: *For a time she was sold on folk music.*
sell off, dispose of by sale.
sell out, a sell or have sold all that one has of something: *They were sold out of ice cream.* **b** *Informal* betray.
sell someone on, inspire someone with the desire to do, buy, or possess a thing: *She has sold me on going camping this summer.*

sell·er (sel′ər) *n* **1** a person who sells. **2** (*often in compounds*) a product that sells in some specified way: *That software has been a good seller for two years. This book is a bestseller.*

seller's market *n* an economic situation in which the seller has the advantage because goods are scarce and prices tend to be high. Compare BUYER'S MARKET.

sell·out (sel′out′) *n* **1** a betrayal of one's principles because it brings a personal advantage. **2** a performance of an entertainment or sports event for which all seats are sold.

selt·zer (sel′tsər) *n* a carbonated mineral water. <German (*Nieder*)*selterser,* the place in Germany where mineral water was found>

sel·vage or **sel·vedge** (sel′vij) *n* the edge of a fabric finished off to prevent ravelling. <Middle English *egge* edge>

selves (selvz) plural of SELF.

se·man·tic (sə man′tik) *adj* to do with meaning in language.
n **semantics** (*with singular verb*) the study of the meanings and the history of changes in the meanings of words and sentences. <French, from Greek *sema* sign>

sem·a·phore (sem′ə fôr′) *n* a system of signals that uses positions of the arms, flags, or the movable parts of a device with an upright structure, or the signal sent with it: *They sent a message by semaphore.*
v **sem·a·phored, sem·a·phor·ing** signal by semaphore. <French, from Greek *sema* signal + *pherein* carry>

sem·blance (sem′bləns) *n* the outward appearance or likeness of something: *His story had the semblance of truth, but was really false.* <Old French, from Latin *simulare* to imitate>

se·men (sē′mən) *n* the thick, whitish fluid produced by the male reproductive organs and containing sperm. <Latin = seed>

se·mes·ter (sə mes′tər) *n* a half of a school or university year. <German, from Latin *sex* six + *mensis* month>

sem·i (sem′ē) *or* (sem′ī) *Informal n* **1** a semitrailer. **2** a semidetached house.

semi– *prefix* **1** half: *semicircular.* **2** partly: *semi-conscious.* **3** twice in a particular period of time: *semi-annual.* <Latin *semi-* half>

sem·i–an·nu·al (sem′ē an′yū əl) *adj* occurring twice a year. **sem′i-an′nu·al·ly** *adv.*

sem·i–ar·id (sem′ē ar′id) *or* (sem′ē er′id) *adj* with very little rainfall.

sem·i–au·to·mat·ic (sem′ē ot′ə mat′ik) *adj* **1** to do with a firearm that automatically reloads itself, but does not fire continuously. **2** to do with machinery that is partly automatic and partly run by hand.

sem·i·cir·cle (sem′ē sər′kyū lər) *n* half a circle: *We sat in a semicircle around the fire.* **sem′i·cir′cu·lar** *adj.*

semicircular canal (sem′ē sər′kyū lər) *n* one of three bony, fluid-filled canals in the inner ear that help the body to maintain balance.

sem·i·co·lon (sem′ē kō′lən) *n* a mark of punctuation [;] that indicates a pause that is less than that indicated by a period.

> **GRAMMAR AND USAGE**
>
> Use a **semicolon** to separate items in a list if the items already contain commas: *My favourite foods are ham and eggs; pizza with onions, mushrooms, and cheese; and chocolate milk.*
>
> Semicolons can also separate main clauses: *You go now; I'll follow later.*

sem·i·con·duc·tor (sem′ē kən duk′tər) *n* a solid substance, such as silicon, that conducts electricity better than insulators but not as well as some other substances. Semiconductors are often used as a base for computer chips. **sem′i·con′duc′ting** *adj.*

sem·i–con·scious (sem′ē kon′shəs) *adj* only partly conscious. **sem′i-con′scious·ly** *adv.*
sem′i-con′scious·ness *n.*

sem·i·dark·ness (sem′ē dárk′nəs) *n* partial darkness.

sem·i–de·tached (sem′ē di tacht′) *adj* partly detached, used especially of a house joined to another by one common wall but separated from other buildings.

sem·i·fi·nal (sem′ē fi′nəl) *for n,* (sem′ē fi′nəl) *for adj.*
n a match or round immediately preceding the final one of a contest or sports event, the winner of which goes on to the final.
adj to do with a semifinal. **sem′i·fi′nal·ist** *n.*

sem·i·for·mal (sem′ē fôr′məl) *for adj,* (sem′ē fôr′məl) *for n.*
adj to do with a somewhat formal social occasion: *Dress will be semiformal.*
n a somewhat formal occasion, usually a dance.

sem·i·month·ly (sem′ē mun′thlē) *adj* occurring or appearing twice a month.
adv twice a month.

sem·i·nal (sem′ə nəl) *adj* **1** to do with semen or the seed of a plant: *seminal fluid.* **2** strongly influencing later developments: *a seminal theory.* <Old French, from Latin *semen* seed>

sem·i·nar (sem′ə nár′) *n* **1** a class at a college or university in which a topic is discussed by a teacher and a small group of students. **2** a conference or other meeting for discussion or training. <German, from Latin *semen* seed>

sem·i·nary (sem′ə ner′ē) *n, pl* **sem·i·nar·ies** a training college for priests or rabbis. <Latin *semen* seed>

sem·i·ot·ics (se′mi ot′iks) *n* (*with singular verb*) the study of signs and symbols. **sem′i·ot′ic** *adj.* **sem′i·ot′ic·al·ly** *adv.* **sem′i·ot′ic·i·an** (se′mi ə tish′ən) *n.*

sem·i·pre·cious (sem′ē presh′əs) *adj* to do with a gemstone not considered as valuable as a precious stone such as a diamond.

sem·i–pri·vate (sem′ē prī′vit) *adj* to do with a hospital room designed for two patients.

sem·i·skilled (sem′ē skild′) *adj* with or needing some, but not extensive, training.

sem·i·sol·id (sem′ē sol′id) *adj* midway between liquid and solid.
n a partly solid substance.

se·mi·sweet (sem′ē swēt′) *adj* slightly sweetened: *semisweet chocolate.*

Sem·ite (sem′īt) *or* (sē′mīt) *n* a member of a people who speak or spoke a Semitic language, especially the Jews and Arabs.

Se·mit·ic (sə mit′ik) *adj* to do with the Semites or their languages, a group that includes Hebrew, Arabic, and such ancient languages as Phoenician.

sem·i·tone (sem′ē tōn′) *n* a halftone.

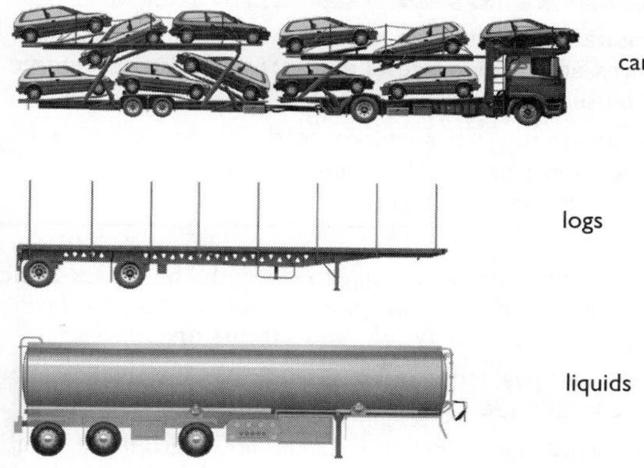

sem·i·trail·er (sem′ē trā′lər) *n* a large trailer used for carrying freight, with wheels at the back but supported in front by the truck to which it is hitched.

sem·i·trop·i·cal (sem′ē trop′ə kəl) *adj* halfway between tropical and temperate in climate.

sem·i·vow·el (sem′ē vou′əl) *n* a sound that is intermediate between a vowel and a consonant, such as in English *y* and *w.*

sem·i·week·ly (sem′ē wē′klē) *adj* occurring or appearing twice a week.
adv twice a week.

sem·o·li·na (sem′ə lē′nə) *n* the coarsely ground hard parts of wheat remaining after the fine flour has been taken away, used in making puddings and pasta. <Italian, from Latin *simila* flour>

sen·ate (sen′it) *n* **1** a governing or lawmaking assembly: *a university senate.* **2 Senate** in Canada, the upper branch of Parliament, consisting of appointed senators. <Old French, from Latin *senex* old man>

sen·a·tor (sen′ə tər) *n* a member of a senate. **sen′a·to′ri·al** *adj.*

sen·a·tor·ship (sen′ə tər ship′) *n* the position, duties, etc. of a senator.

send (send) *v* **sent, send·ing 1** cause to go or be taken from one place to another: *to send on an errand, to send an e-mail.* **2** cause to happen: *Send help at once.* **3** transmit a signal, message, or messenger: *The broadcast was sent over a wide area. They sent for a doctor.* **4** cause to move sharply or quickly: *He sent the ball sailing over the fence. The volcano sent clouds of smoke into the air.* **5** cause to be in a specified way: *I was sent crazy by her constant phone calls.* <Old English *sendan*> **send′er** *n.*
send around, have something circulate.
send away for, order or request that something be sent to one.
send packing, send away or force to leave quickly.
send up, make fun of by imitating and exaggerating.

send–off (send′of′) *n* **1** a friendly show of goodwill for a person setting out on a journey or starting a course or career. **2** a start given to a person or thing: *They gave the idea a good send-off.*

send–up (send′up′) *n* a mocking imitation of someone or something: *She did a hilarious send-up of the speech.*

Sen·e·ca (sen′ə kə) *n, pl* **Sen·e·ca** or **Sen·e·cas**
1 a member of a Native American people living mainly in New York State. **2** their Iroquoian language.
adj to do with these people or their language.

Se·ne·gal (sen′ə gol) *n* a country in west Africa. **Sen′e·gal·ese′** *adj, n.*

se·nes·cent (sə nes′ənt) *n* a person in the stage of growing old.
adj to do with this stage. <Latin *senex* old>

se·nile (sen′īl) *or* (sē′nīl) *adj* with or showing weaknesses of old age, especially the loss of memory and other mental faculties. <French, from Latin *senex* old>
se·nil′i·ty (sə nil′ə tē) *n.*

sen·ior (sē′nyər) *adj* **1** of a more advanced age: *He is five years senior to me.* **2 Senior** (*after the name*) indicating a father whose son has the same given name: *John Parker, Senior.* **3** higher in rank or longer in service: *She was the senior member of the firm* **4** to do with the final year of a high school or university.
n **1** an older or elderly person: *Seniors got a discount at the movie theatre.* **2** a person of higher rank or longer service. **3** a member of the graduating class of a high school or university. <Latin *senex* old>

senior citizen *n* a person who is 65 years of age or older.

senior high school *n* a school attended after junior high school.

sen·ior·i·ty (sē nyȯ′rə tē) *n, pl* **sen·ior·i·ties 1** the condition or fact of being older: *She felt that two years' seniority gave her the right to advise her sister.* **2** priority or higher rank in office or service: *He'd worked for the company longer and so had seniority.*

a bat	e bed	i bid	o pot	u cup	th **thin**
ā cake	ē me	ī bite	ō go	ū rude	ᴛʜ **then**
ȧ bar	ə about	ər over	ȯ for	u̇ put	zh measure

S

senior public school *n* a school for grades six to eight.

sen·na (sen′ə) *n* the dried leaves of the cassia tree, or a laxative extracted from these leaves. <Latin, from Arabic *sana*>

sen·sa·tion (sen sā′shən) *n* **1** a physical feeling or perception from something that happens to or comes into contact with the body: *a burning sensation.* **2** the ability to have such feelings or perceptions: *She'd lost sensation in her left hand.* **3** an awareness or impression that is hard to explain: *He had the eerie sensation he'd seen her before.* **4 a** a widespread reaction of interest or excitement: *Her unexpected win caused an instant sensation.* **b** a person, thing, or event that causes such a reaction: *The unexpected win made her an instant sensation.* <Latin *sentire* to feel>

sen·sa·tion·al (sen sā′shə nəl) *adj* **1** arousing great interest or excitement: *The player's sensational catch made the crowd cheer wildly.* **2** trying to arouse great interest or excitement: *a sensational newspaper story.* **3** very impressive or attractive: *Her latest story is sensational.* **sen·sa′tion·al·ly** *adv.*

sen·sa·tion·al·ism (sen sā′shə nə liz′əm) *n* the use of exciting or shocking stories or language in journalism, even if inaccurate, in order to arouse great interest or excitement. **sen·sa′tion·al·ist** *n.*

sense (sens) *n* **1** a power, either sight, hearing, touch, taste, or smell, by which the body perceives the world around it and of changes within itself, or something felt by this power: *a sense of pain.* **2** a feeling that something is the case: *The extra lock on the door gave him a sense of security.* **3 a** judgment or intelligence, especially a sane, realistic, or reasonable attitude to situations and problems: *She had the good sense to keep out of foolish quarrels.* **b senses** *pl* the normal, sound condition of the mind: *He must be out of his senses to act so.* **4** a way in which something can be interpreted or felt: *a sense of humour, a sense of direction, a sense of beauty.* **5** the general opinion: *The sense of the assembly was clear even before the vote.*
v **sensed, sens·ing** perceive by or as if by a sense or senses: *She sensed that he was tired.* <Latin *sentire* feel>
in a sense, in some respects or to some degree.
make sense, be understandable or reasonable.

sense·less (sen′slis) *adj* **1** unconscious: *A blow on the head knocked him senseless.* **2** with no or little meaning or purpose: *That senseless dog is chasing cars again.* **sense′less·ly** *adv.* **sense′less·ness** *n.*

sense organ *n* an organ of the body, such as the eye or ear, by which a person or an animal responds to sensory stimuli outside itself and conveys impulses to the sensory nervous system.

sen·si·bil·i·ty (sen′sə bil′ə tē) *n, pl* **sen·si·bil·i·ties** **1** the ability to feel and respond to the influence of art and the emotions: *She believed that reading good books enhanced her sensibility.* **2 sensibilities** a sensitivity so refined that one is easily offended or shocked: *Crude language offended his sensibilities.* <Old French, from Latin *sentire* feel>

sen·si·ble (sen′sə bəl) *adj* **1** with or showing good judgment and prudence: *You are much too sensible to do anything so foolish.* **2** practical and functional rather than decorative: *sensible shoes.* **sen′si·bly** *adv.*

sen·si·tive (sen′sə tiv) *adj* **1** able to detect or respond to slight changes, signals, or influences: *The camera was extremely sensitive to light.* **2** with or showing a quick and refined understanding of other people's feelings: *Our teacher is sensitive in dealing with the different issues that we face every day.* **3** easily damaged, injured, or distressed: *The marsh was environmentally sensitive.* **4** kept secret or with restrictions on content being disclosed: *a sensitive document.* **sen′si·tive·ly** *adv.* **sen′si·tive·ness** *n.* **sen′si·tiv′i·ty** *n.*

sen·si·tize (sen′sə tīz′) *v* **sen·si·tized, sen·si·tiz·ing** make sensitive. **sen′si·ti·za′tion** *n.* **sen′si·tiz′er** *n.*

sen·sor (sen′sər) *n* a device that detects or measures a physical stimulus and records, indicates, or otherwise responds to it: *When it was applied, the sensor could record the body's pulse and temperature.*

sen·so·ry (sen′sə rē) *adj* to do with sensation or the physical senses: *sensory organs.*

sen·su·al (sen′shū əl) *adj* of or aroused by physical pleasure in using one or more of the body's senses: *Stroking the cat's smooth fur is quite sensual.* **sen′su·al′i·ty** *n.* **sen′su·al·ly** *adv.*

CONFUSABLES

Sensual emphasizes an appeal to the bodily senses and desires, and often suggests excess: *His religion discouraged the pursuit of sensual pleasures.*

Sensuous suggests an appeal to the senses resulting in refined appreciation: *The gourmet meal provided them with many sensuous delights.*

sen·su·ous (sen′shū əs) *adj* to do with the senses rather than the intellect: *The painter had a sensuous love of colour.* **sen′su·ous·ly** *adv.* **sen′su·ous·ness** *n.*

sent (sent) past tense and past participle of SEND. See SCENT for confusables.

sen·tence (sen′təns) *n* **1** *Grammar* a group of words making a complete statement, question, request, command, or exclamation. Example: *Boys and girls* is not a sentence. *The boys and girls are here* is a sentence. **2** a decision made by a court on what punishment a convicted offender will receive.
v **sen·tenced, sen·tenc·ing** pronounce punishment on: *The judge sentenced the thief to five years in prison.* <Latin *sententia* a way of thinking>

GRAMMAR AND USAGE

All **sentences** must have a subject, which usually appears at the beginning of a sentence: ***The clouds*** *drifted across the sky.*

All sentences must also have a verb, which states what the subject is doing: *She* ***sang*** *beautifully at the school concert.*

All sentences begin with a capital letter: ***T****his is the first time they've won the debate.*

Sentences can end with a period, question mark, or exclamation mark: *There is no more room***.** *Have all the tickets been sold***?** *That's really disappointing***!**

✱ sentencing circle *n* among First Nations peoples, a group that includes offenders, victims, and other members of the community, gathered to decide the appropriate penalty for a crime.

sen·ten·tious (sen ten′shəs) *adj* given to moralizing in a pompous or affected way. **sen·ten′tious·ly** *adv.* **sen·ten′tious·ness** *n.*

sen·tient (sen′shənt) *or* (sen′shē ənt) *adj* able to feel things with the senses: *a sentient life form.* <Latin *sentire* feel> **sen′tience** *n.* **sen′tient·ly** *adv.*

sen·ti·ment (sen′tə mənt) *n* **1** an opinion or attitude toward a situation or event: *patriotic sentiments.* **2** feeling or emotion: *a loving sentiment.* <Old French, from Latin *sentire* feel>

sen·ti·men·tal (sen′tə men′təl) *adj* **1** with or showing a feeling of tenderness, sadness, or nostalgia: *sentimental reasons.* **2** dealing with or prone to such feelings in an exaggerated or overdone way: *sentimental poetry.* **sen′ti·men·tal′i·ty** *n.* **sen′ti·men′tal·ize** *v.* **sen′ti·men′tal·ly** *adv.*

sen·ti·men·tal·ism (sen′tə men′tə liz′əm) *n* a tendency to deal with feelings of tenderness, sadness, or nostalgia in an exaggerated or overdone way. **sen′ti·men′ta·list** *n.*

sen·ti·nel (sen′tə nəl) *n* a person stationed to keep watch and guard against surprise attack. <French, from Italian *sentinella*>
stand sentinel, act as a sentinel; keep watch.

sen·try (sen′trē) *n, pl* **sen·tries** a person, especially a soldier, stationed at a place to keep watch and guard against surprise attacks. <origin uncertain>
stand sentry, watch or guard: *We stood sentry over the sleeping village.*

sentry box *n* a small building for sheltering a sentry.

se·pal (sē′pəl) *n* a leaflike division of the calyx, or outer covering, of a flower, that encloses the petals. See ANTHER for picture. <French, from Greek *skepi*>

sep·a·ra·ble (sep′ə rə bəl) *or* (sep′rə bəl) *adj* able to be separated. **sep′a·ra·bil′i·ty** *n.* **sep′a·ra·bly** *adv.*

sep·a·rate (sep′ə rit) *or* (sep′rit) *for adj,* (sep′ə rāt′) *for v or n.*
adj forming or viewed as a unit apart or by itself: *These are two separate questions.*
v **sep·a·rat·ed, sep·a·rat·ing** **1** cause to move or be apart: *Families were separated during the violent storm.* **2** form a distinction or border between people, places, or things: *The two pieces of land were separated by a stream, to separate church and state.* **3** divide or cause to divide into distinct parts, elements, or groups: *She separated the eggs and beat the whites. They separated in all directions.* **4** stop living together as a couple: *They separated after five years of marriage.*
n **separates** *pl* units or items forming individual things but that may also be part of a larger group: *With these separates you can match the pants to two different jackets.* <Latin *se-* apart + *parare* prepare> **sep′a·rate·ly** *adv.* **sep′a·rate·ness** *n.*

✱ separate school *n* a publicly supported school for children that is administered by the Catholic church.

sep·a·ra·tion (sep′ə rā′shən) *n* **1** the action or condition of moving or being moved apart: *the separation of parents and children.* **2** the division of something into distinct parts: *They soon came to the separation of the path into two tracks.* **3** the condition of ceasing to live as a couple.

sep·a·ra·tism (sep′ə rə tiz′əm) *or* (sep′rə tiz′əm) *n* the principle or practice of separation for a certain group of people from a larger group, especially on the basis of ethnic background, religion, or gender. In Canada, separatism concerns support for the withdrawal of Québec or of the Western Provinces from the Canadian confederation. **sep′a·ra·tist** *n.*

sep·a·ra·tor (sep′ə rā′tər) *n* a person who or thing that separates, especially a machine or device for separating something into its distinct parts, such as to separate cream from milk.

Se·phar·di (se for′dē) *n, pl* **Se·phar·dim** (se for′dim) a Jew of Spanish or Portuguese descent. Compare ASHKENAZI. <Hebrew = Spaniard> **Se·phar′dic** *adj.*

se·pi·a (sē′pē ə) *n* a brown paint or ink prepared from the inky fluid of cuttlefish.
adj reddish brown: *a sepia print.* <Greek = cuttlefish>

se·poy (sē′poi) *n* in former times, a native of India who was a soldier in a British or other European army.

sep·sis (sep′sis) *n* the presence in body tissues of disease-producing bacteria, typically because of an infected wound. <Latin, from Greek *sepein* make rotten>

sept– *combining form* seven: *septet.* <Latin>

sep·ta·gon (sep′tə gon′) *n* a closed plane figure with seven interior angles and seven sides.

Sep·tem·ber (sep tem′bər) *n* the ninth month of the year. It has 30 days. Abbrev: **Sep** <Latin, from *septem* seven. September was the seventh month in the ancient Roman calendar.>

sep·tet or **sep·tette** (sep tet′) *n* a group of seven people singing or playing music together, or a composition for such a group. <German, from Latin *septem* seven>

sep·tic (sep′tik) *adj* causing or caused by infection with harmful bacteria. <Latin, from Greek *sepein* make rotten>

sep·ti·ce·mi·a or **sep·ti·cae·mi·a** (sep′tə sē′mē ə) *n* blood poisoning, especially that caused by bacteria. <Latin, from Greek *septikos* septic + *haima* blood>

septic system *n* a system for getting rid of sewage, consisting of an underground **septic tank** in which sewage is allowed to decompose through the action of bacteria. This tank empties into a gravel bed and drains into the earth. Buildings not connected to a town sewage system, such as those in rural areas, have septic systems.

sep·tu·a·ge·nar·i·an (sep′chū ə jə ner′ē ən) *n* a person who is in his or her seventies. <Latin *septuaginta* seventy>

sep·tum (sep′təm) *n, pl* **sep·ta** (-tə.) a partition separating two chambers, such as that between the nostrils or the chambers of the heart. <Latin *sepes* hedge>

a bat	e bed	i bid	o pot	u cup	th **thin**
ā cake	ē me	ī bite	ō go	ū rude	ᴛʜ **then**
à bar	ə about	ər over	ȯ for	ů put	zh measure

se·pul·chral (sə pul′krəl) *adj* **1** of sepulchres, tombs, or interment. **2** gloomy and dismal: *a sepulchral voice.*

sep·ul·chre or **sep·ul·cher** (sep′əl kər) *n* a small room or monument of stone or rock, in which a dead person is laid or buried. <Old French, from Latin *sepelire* bury>

se·quel (sē′kwəl) *n* **1** a published, broadcast, or recorded work that continues a story or develops the theme of an earlier one. **2** a thing that follows as a result of some earlier happening: *The sequel to the civil war was famine.* <Old French, from Latin *sequi* follow>

se·quence (sē′kwəns) *n* **1** an order in which related things follow each other: *Arrange the names in alphabetical sequence.* **2** a connected or related series of events, movements, or things: *a sequence of exercises.* **3** a part of a movie or broadcast dealing with one particular subject: *a car-chase sequence.* **4** *Mathematics* a set of numbers or pictures that follows some rule or formula. Example: Any number in the sequence 2, 4, 8, 16, … is formed by doubling the previous number. <Latin *sequi* follow>

se·quen·tial (si kwen′shəl) *adj* forming a sequence or connected series; characterized by a regular sequence of parts. **se·quen′tial·ly** *adv.*

se·ques·ter (si kwes′tər) *v* **1** remove or withdraw someone or something from use or from view: *The writer sequestered himself until his book was finished.* **2** seize by authority; take and keep: *The soldiers sequestered food from the people they conquered.* <Latin *sequestrare* to place in safekeeping, from *sequester* trustee>

se·quin (sē′kwin) *n* a small shiny disc sewn with many others on clothing as decoration. <French, from Arabic *sikka* a die for coining, because of their resemblance to gold coins>

se·quoi·a (si kwoi′ə) *n* a very tall redwood tree, especially the California redwood. <Latin, from *Sequoya*, 19c Cherokee scholar>

se·ra·pe (sə rȧ′pē) *n* a shawl or blanket, worn as a cloak in Latin American countries.

ser·aph (ser′əf) *n, pl* **ser·aphs** or **ser·aph·im** (ser′əf im) an angel. <Hebrew *serapim*> **ser·aph′ic** *adj.* **ser·aph′ic·al·ly** *adv.*

Ser·bi·a and Mon·te·ne·gro (ser′bi ə)(mon′ tə neg′rō) *n* a country in eastern Europe. See the APPENDIX. **Serb** *n.* **Ser′bi·an** *adj.* **Mon′te·neg′rin** *adj, n.*

sere (sēr) *adj* withered. <Old English *sear*>

ser·e·nade (ser′ə nād′) *n* music played or sung outdoors, typically at night, especially by someone under the window of a sweetheart, or a piece of music in this style. *v* **ser·e·nad·ed, ser·e·nad·ing** sing or play a serenade. <French, from *serenus* serene>

ser·en·dip·i·ty (ser′ən dip′ə tē) *n* the happening or development of events by chance in a good or beneficial way. <*Three Princes of Serendip*, story whose heroes make many lucky discoveries, coined by H. Walpole, 18c writer> **ser′en·dip′i·tous** *adj.* **ser′en·dip′i·tous·ly** *adv.*

se·rene (sə rēn′) *adj* peaceful and calm: *a serene smile, a serene sky.* <Latin *serenus*> **se·rene′ly** *adv.* **se·rene′ness** *adv.* **se·ren′i·ty** (sə ren′ə tē) *n.*

serf (sərf) *n* in former times, a farm labourer who had to work on a feudal estate. <Old French, from Latin *servus* slave>

serf·dom (sərf′dəm) *n* the condition of being a serf.

serge (sərj) *n* a durable fabric with slanting lines or ridges on its surface. <Old French, from Greek *serike*>

ser·geant (sȧr′jənt) *n* **1** in the Canadian Forces, a non-commissioned officer ranking next above a master corporal. *Abbrev.* **Sgt.** **2** a police officer, especially one senior to a constable. <Old French, from Latin *servire* to serve>

ser·geant–at–arms (sȧr′jənt ət ȧrmz′) *n, pl* **ser·geants-at-arms** an official of a legislative assembly who helps to maintain order and security.

se·ri·al (sē rē əl) *n* a story presented one part at a time in a magazine or newspaper or on radio or TV.
adj **1** published, broadcast, or televised one part at a time: *a serial publication.* **2** repeating the same crime or offence, typically following a set pattern of behaviour: *a serial killer.* <*series*> **se′ri·al·ly** *adv.*

CONFUSABLES

Serial means "arranged in a series": *It's a serial drama to be shown over the next six weeks.*

Cereal means "food made from grain": *Her little brother always has cereal for breakfast.*

se·ri·al·ize (sē′rē ə līz) *v* **se·ri·al·ized, se·ri·al·iz·ing** present in a series of instalments or episodes: *to serialize a novel in a magazine.* **se′ri·al·iz·a′tion** *n.*

serial number *n* an individual number given to a certain number in a series, especially one printed on a product or article as a means of identification.

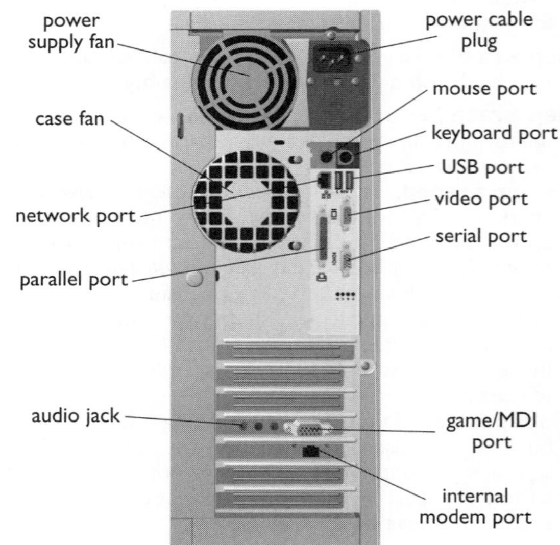

serial port *Computers n* a connector by which a device, such as a mouse or external modem, delivers data one bit at a time to a computer. Compare PARALLEL PORT.

se·ries (sē′rēz′) *n, pl* **se·ries 1** a number of similar things, events, or people that happen one after another: *A series of rooms opened off the long hall. A series of rainy days spoiled their vacation.* **2** a set of related TV or radio programs, especially of a related kind: *a drama series.* **3** an arrangement of electrical circuits or components in which the current passes through each successively. Compare PARALLEL. **4** *Mathematics* the indicated sum of a sequence. Example: 2 + 4 + 6 + 8 + 16, … <Latin = a row, from *serere* join>

ser·if (ser′if) *n* in printing, a thin or smaller line used to finish off a main stroke of a letter, as at the top and bottom of M. Compare SANS-SERIF. <origin uncertain>

se·ri·o–com·ic (sē′rē ō kom′ik) *adj* partly serious and partly comic.

se·ri·ous (sē′rē əs) *adj* **1** solemn or thoughtful in character or manner: *a serious face.* **2** acting or speaking seriously rather than jokingly: *She was serious about the subject.* **3** demanding thought and concentration: *To choose your life's work is a serious matter.* **4** significant or worrying because of danger or risk: *The injured woman was in serious condition.* **5** *Informal* impressive because of its size, number, or quality: *He offered serious money for the baseball card collection. She was a serious fan of chocolate.* <Old French, from Latin *serius*> **se′ri·ous·ly** *adv.* **se′ri·ous·ness** *n.*

ser·mon (sər′mən) *n* **1** a talk on a religious or moral subject, especially one given in church and on a passage from the Bible. **2** a long and boring talk, often giving advice or warnings: *After the guests left, the boy got a sermon on table manners from his mother.* <Old French, from Latin *sermo* a talk> **ser′mon·ize** *v.* **ser′mon·iz·er** *n.*

se·ro·to·nin (sēr′ə tō′nin) *n* a compound found in blood that acts as a neurotransmitter involved in regulating emotion, contracting muscles, and other functions. <*serum* + *ton(ic)*>

se·rous (sē′rəs) *adj* to do with serum.

ser·pent (sər′pənt) *n* **1** a snake, especially a big snake. **2** a sly, treacherous person. <Old French, from Latin *serpere* to creep>

ser·pen·tine (sər′pən tīn′) *or* (sər′pən tēn′) *adj* **1** of or like a serpent or snake. **2** winding or twisting: *a serpentine brook.* **3** complex, cunning, or treacherous.
n a dark green mineral consisting of magnesium silicate, sometimes mottled or spotted like a snake's skin. <*serpent*>

ser·rate (ser′āt) *or* (ser′it) *adj* of a leaf, with sawlike notches. <Latin *serra* a saw>

ser·rat·ed (ser′ā tid) *adj* with a jagged edge: *a serrated knife.*

ser·ra·tion (se rā′shən) *n* a tooth or point of a serrated edge or surface: *serrations of a postage stamp.*

se·rum (sē′rəm) *n, pl* **se·rums** or **se·ra** (sē′rə) **1** the clear, watery part of blood that separates from a clot when blood coagulates. **2** a liquid used to make the body immune to a disease or to diagnose a toxin. It is obtained from the blood of an animal that has been made immune to the disease.

ser·val (sər′vəl) *n* an African wild cat with long legs, large ears, and a brownish coat with black spots.

serv·ant (sər′vənt) *n* **1** a person who performs tasks for another, especially in a household. **2** a person employed by a government. See also CIVIL SERVICE.

serve (sərv) *v* **served, serv·ing 1** perform or make available duties or services for another person or for an organization: *My grandfather served his company for many years. The school served a large population.* **2** spend a period of time in a job, as a soldier, or in a prison: *The soldier served three years in the army. He served seven years for armed robbery.* **3** bring food or drink to someone, supply enough for, or give service to a customer: *The waiter served us. One pie will serve six people. How may I serve you?* **4** formally deliver a legal document to someone to whom it is addressed: *He was served with a summons to appear in court.* **5** be useful in achieving or satisfying a desire or need: *The information will serve us very well. This will serve my purpose. Boxes served as seats.* **6** *Tennis, Badminton, etc.* put the ball or shuttlecock in play by hitting it.
n the act or way of serving a ball or shuttlecock. <Old French, from Latin *servus* slave>
serve you right, be just what you deserve: *The punishment served him right.*

serv·er (sər′vər) *n* **1** a person who or thing that serves. **2** *Computers* a computer or a program that manages access to a network.

serv·ice (sər′vis) *n* **1** the action of helping or doing work for someone, or the act that is performed: *She performed many services for her country. We got good service from the waiter. He was on active service in the army.* **2** a system of supplying a public need, especially for transportation: *a bus service.* **3** a ceremony of religious worship that takes a standard form: *a funeral service.* **4** a set of matching dishes used for serving a particular meal: *a dinner service.* **5** *Tennis, Badminton, etc.* the action of serving to begin play. **6** the formal delivery of a legal document: *service of a writ.* **7 the services** the navy, army, or air force: *My great-grandfather was in the services.*
v **serv·iced, serv·ic·ing** do routine maintenance or repair on a vehicle, machine, or system: *The mechanic serviced the car.* <Latin *servus* slave>
at someone's service, ready to do what someone wants.
in service, in working order or functioning: *We'll call you as soon the telephone is in service.*
of service, helpful or useful.
out of service, not in working order or functioning: *This elevator is out of service.*

ser·vice·a·ble (sər′vi sə bəl) *adj* useful in fulfilling a function, especially for a long time: *You will find this heavy coat quite serviceable.* **serv′ice·a·bil′i·ty** *n.* **serv′ice·able·ness** *n.* **serv′ice·a·bly** *adv.*

serv·ice·ber·ry (sər′vis ber′ē) *n* a large, edible, purple berry that grows on a bush or small tree.

a bat	e bed	i bid	o pot	u cup	th **thin**
ā cake	ē me	ī bite	ō go	ū rude	ᴛʜ **then**
ä bar	ə about	ər over	ô for	ů put	zh measure

service centre *n* a stopping area adjoining a main highway, consisting of a service station, restaurant, and other facilities.

service club *n* an organization of business or professional people that aims to promote the welfare of its local community.

serv·iced (sər′vist) *adj* connected to utilities such as hydro, sewer, and water: *serviced building lots.*

serv·ice·man (sər′vis man′) *or* (sər′vis mən) *n,* *pl* **serv·ice·men** (-men′) *or* (-mən) **1** a man serving in the armed forces. **2** a person who maintains and repairs machines and appliances, especially those used in a household.

service provider *Computers n* a company that provides access to the Internet, usually for a monthly charge.

service road *n* a road, generally running parallel to a main highway, to carry local traffic and to provide access to adjoining properties.

service station *n* a place for supplying motor vehicles with gasoline, oil, and water, and where sometimes repairs and adjustments can be made or parts supplied.

serv·ice·wom·an (sər′vis wûm′ən) *n,* *pl* **serv·ice·wom·en** (-wim′ən) a woman serving in the armed forces.

ser·vi·ette (sər′vē et′) *n* a piece of cloth or paper used at meals for protecting the clothing or for wiping the lips or fingers. <Old French *servir* serve>

ser·vile (sər′vīl) *or* (sər′vəl) *adj* too willing to serve or to please others: *servile flattery.* <Latin *servus* slave> **ser′vile·ly** *adv.* **ser′vile·ness** *n.* **ser·vil′i·ty** *n.*

serv·ing (sər′ving) *n* a portion of food served to a person at one time.

ser·vi·tude (sər′və tyūd′) *or* (sər′və tūd′) *n* the condition of being a slave or totally under another's power. <Old French, from Latin *servus* slave>

ser·vo (sər′vō) *n* in full, **servomechanism** a mechanism that uses feedback to produce motion or force at a higher level of energy than that during input. It helps to automatically control a machine or vehicle.
adj to do with a servomechanism.

ses·a·me (ses′ə mē) *n* a tropical and subtropical plant whose oil-rich seeds are used whole or have their oil extracted. <Latin, from Arabic *simsim*>
open sesame a the magic words that opened the door of the robbers' den in the story of Ali Baba. **b** a thing that obtains easy admission or access: *Her education was an open sesame to the job.*

ses·qui·cen·ten·ni·al (ses′kwi sen ten′ē əl) *n* a 150th anniversary or its celebration.
adj to do with the completion of a period of a century and a half. <Latin *sesqui-* one and a half + *centennial*>

ses·qui·pe·da·li·an (ses′kwi pə dā′lē ən) *adj* **1** with many syllables in a word. **2** using long words. <Latin *sesqui* one and a half + *pes* foot>

ses·sile (ses′īl) *or* (ses′əl) *adj* **1** fixed in one place and unable to move around, such as a barnacle. **2** attached as an animal or plant structure by the base instead of by a stem: *a sessile leaf.* <Latin *sedere* sit>

ses·sion (sesh′ən) *n* **1 a** a sitting or meeting of a court, council, or legislature: *a session of Parliament.* **b** a period during which such meetings are regularly held: *This year's session of Parliament was unusually long.* **2** a period devoted to a particular activity: *a training session, a recording session, the summer session.* <Old French, from Latin *sedere* sit> **ses′sion·al** *adj.*
in session, assembled at a meeting: *The teachers were in session all Saturday morning.*

🍁 **sessional indemnity** *n* in some provinces, the remuneration paid each session to a Member of the Legislative Assembly.

set[1] (set) *v* **set, set·ting 1** put or make firm in a specified place or position: *Set the box on its end. The doctor set a broken bone. The story was set in the last century.* **2** cause something to have a specified condition or limit: *to set a clock, to set a time limit, to set a record.* **3** make something solid, semisolid, or fixed: *to set type, to set bread, to set your teeth.* **4** appear to move toward and below the earth's horizon: *The sun seemed to set more quickly in the tropics.* **5** begin to do something: *Have you set to work?* **6** arrange in musical form: *to set words to music.* <Old English *settan*>
all set, ready to go or start.
(**dead**) **set against,** (very) determined not to do or allow something.
(**dead**) **set on,** (very) determined to do or allow something.
get set, get ready to begin something, especially a race.
set about, start doing something: *to set about your homework.*
set against, a make one person unfriendly toward another. **b** balance or compare two things.
set apart, save or single out for some purpose: *We have set apart two hours for open discussion.*
set aside, a put to one side. **b** save or keep money or time for later use. **c** annul a legal decision or process: *The Supreme Court set aside the lower court's decision.*
set back, a delay or impede something or someone: *The job was set back because of the accident.* **b** *Informal* cost a person a particular amount of money: *Books and tuition set my sister back a lot.*
set down, a deposit or put down: *set down a suitcase. The bus set him down near the town.* **b** record in writing or printing. **c** consider or ascribe: *Your failure in the test can be set down to too much haste.*
set forth, a state or describe. **b** start out: *We set forth on our trip.*
set in, begin, especially something unpleasant: *Boredom set in almost at once.*
set in your ways, with stubbornly fixed habits.
set off, a detonate or ignite: *to set off fireworks.* **b** start to go: *set off for home.* **c** emphasize or enhance by contrast: *The green sweater set off her red hair. One sentence was set off from the rest by quotation marks.* **d** balance or compensate: *The poor quality of the skater's jumps were set off by his exceptional spin technique.*
set on (or **upon**)**,** cause or urge a person or animal to attack: *He set the dog on me.*
set out, a begin a journey. **b** spread out to show, sell, or use. **c** plant. **d** plan or intend to do something.

set to, begin to do something energetically: *Set to work.*
set up, a claim to be or to act like a specified kind of person: *She set herself up as a great team captain.* **b** establish someone in a particular role or activity: *His parents set him up in business.*

CONFUSABLES

Set is the simple past tense of *set*, a verb that always takes an object: *The waiters set the table for the formal dinner.*

Sit is a verb that usually does not take an object, and its simple past tense is *sat*: *We sat for hours at the airport waiting for the flight to arrive.*

set[2] (set) *n* **1** a group or collection of things that belong together, are similar, or are usually found together: *a set of dishes, a set of positive integers.* **2** the way in which something is put or positioned: *She had a determined set to her jaw, a shampoo and set.* **3** a radio or television receiver: *a TV set.* **4** a collection of scenery and stage props used for a particular scene in a play or movie, or the place in which filming takes place. **5** *Tennis, Volleyball, etc.* a group of games counting as a unit toward a match. <Old French, from Latin *secta* sect>

se·ta (sē′tə) *n, pl* **se·tae** (sē′tē) *or* (sē′tī) a slender, stiff, bristlelike structure, especially in an invertebrate such as an earthworm.

set·back (set′bak′) *n* **1** a reversal or check to progress. **2** the amount or distance by which a thing is out of line, such as part of a wall set back. **3** the distance by which a building or part of a building is set back from the property line.

set piece *n* a self-contained piece of writing, music, or drama that draws attention to itself.

set point *Tennis n* the point that, if won, enables the player to win the set.

set square *n* a flat, right-angled piece of wood, plastic, or metal used as a guide for accurately drawing straight lines and right angles.

set·tee (se tē′) *n* a sofa or long bench with a back and, usually, arms. <*settle*[2]>

set·ter (set′ər) *n* **1** a person who sets or arranges things: *wage-setter.* **2** a long-haired hunting dog, trained to stand rigid and point its nose toward the game that it scents.

set theory *n* the branch of mathematics that deals with the properties and relations of sets.

set·ting (set′ing) *n* **1** the place or type of surroundings in which something is positioned: *The jewel had a beautiful setting.* **2** the time and place at which an event, especially in a play, novel, or movie, is represented as happening: *a scenic mountain setting.* **3** the music composed to go with particular words. **4** a speed, height, or temperature at which a machine or device can be adjusted to operate: *a thermostat setting.* **5** the dishes or cutlery required to set one place at a table.

set·tle[1] (set′əl) *v* **set·tled, set·tling 1** determine or agree on something: *They settled on the time for leaving, to settle a debt, to settle a court case.* **2** sit or lie in a comfortable position, or cause this to happen: *The cat settled on the couch.* **3** take up residence in a new country or place: *to settle in Manitoba.* **4** go down or sink, or sink to the bottom: *The end of that wall has settled five centimetres.* **5** make or become quiet: *Rest will settle your nerves.* **6** establish, especially in a long-term job or household: *to lead a more settled way of life.* <Old English *setl* a place to sit>
settle down, a live a more regular life. **b** (*with* **to**) direct steady effort or attention: *Settle down to your work, please.* **c** calm down or become quiet: *Settle down!*
settle for, accept in place of what one really wants: *She was dying for a hot shower, but had to settle for a lukewarm bath.*
settle up, pay a bill.
settle upon (or **on**)**,** give money or property through a legal deed or will.
settle with, a pay a debt to. **b** come to an agreement with: *The two parties agreed to settle out of court.*

set·tle[2] (set′əl) *n* a long wooden bench with arms and a high back. <Old English *setl* a place to sit>

set·tle·ment (set′əl mənt) *n* **1** an agreement intended to resolve a dispute or conflict, such as an arrangement between individuals or groups to settle a lawsuit out of court. **2** a place where people establish a community, especially a place previously uninhabited, or the process by which this is done. **3** an arrangement whereby a person's money or property passes to others, or the money or property given: *a marriage settlement.* **4** the action or process of settling an account or paying a debt, or the payment so made: *Settlement of all claims against the firm will be made shortly.* **5** a centre providing community services in an underprivileged district.

set·tler (set′lər) *n* a person who settles, especially one who settles in a previously uninhabited place.

set–to (set′tū′) *Informal n, pl* **set–tos** a fight or dispute.

set–up (set′up′) *n* **1** the planning and arrangement of an organization or equipment, or the organization or arrangement itself: *I dislike the set-up of the committee.* **2** a pass or a play in game intended to provide a chance for another player to score. **3** a trick or situation intended to incriminate or deceive someone: *Don't take the money! It's a set-up!*

sev·en (sev′ən) *n* **1** a cardinal number that is one more than six. **2** the numeral 7. **3** a playing card with seven spots.
adj **1** one more than six: *They stayed seven days.* **2** (*after the noun*) seventh in a series: *Lesson Seven was interesting.* <Old English *seofon*> **sev′enth** *adj, adv.*

sev·en·fold (sev′ən fōld′) *adj, adv* **1** seven times as much or as many. **2** consisting of seven parts.

seven seas *pl n* all the oceans of the world, considered to be the Arctic, Antarctic, N Atlantic, S Atlantic, N Pacific, S Pacific, and Indian: *to sail the seven seas.*

a bat	e bed	i bid	o pot	u cup	th **thin**
ā cake	ē me	ī bite	ō go	ū rude	ᴛʜ **then**
à bar	ə about	ər over	ȯ for	ů put	zh measure

S

sev·en·teen (sev′ən tēn′) *n* **1** seven more than ten. **2** the numeral 17.
adj **1** seven more than ten: *It cost about seventeen dollars.* **2** (*after the noun*) seventeenth in a set or series: *Chapter Seventeen.* <Old English *seofontene*>
sev′en·teenth′ *adj, adv.*

sev·en·teenth (sev′ən tēnth′) *n* **1** next after the sixteenth. **2** one of seventeen equal parts.
adj, adv See SEVENTEEN.

sev·enth (sev′ənth) *adj, n* **1** next after the sixth: *on the seventh day* (*adj*). *I'm seventh in line* (*n*). **2** one, or being one, of seven equal parts: *She was given a seventh part of the money* (*adj*). *He donated a seventh of his savings to charity* (*n*).

seventh heaven *n* a condition of great joy.
in seventh heaven, in a state of great joy.

sev·en·ti·eth (sev′ən tē ith) *n* **1** next after the sixty-ninth. **2** one of seventy equal parts.
adj, adv See SEVENTY.

sev·en·ty (sev′ən tē) *n, pl* **sev·en·ties 1** seven times ten. **2 seventies** *pl* the years from seventy through seventy-nine, especially of a century or of a person's life: *That movie came out in the seventies.*
adj **1** seven times ten. **2** (*after the noun*) seventieth in a series: *page seventy.* <Old English *seofontig*> **sev′en·ti·eth′** *adj, adv.*

Seven Wonders of the World *pln* seven ancient structures built by human beings that are considered by many to be the most spectacular. They are the Egyptian Pyramids, the Mausoleum at Halicarnassus, the Temple of Artemis at Ephesus, the hanging gardens of Babylon, the Colossus of Rhodes, the statue of Zeus at Olympia, and the Pharos (lighthouse) at Alexandria.

Seven Years' War *n* a war fought between Britain and France and their allies from 1756 to 1763 in Europe and abroad. In N America, France was defeated by Britain in 1759, making New France a British colony.

sev·er (sev′ər) *v* **1** cut apart or cut off: *to sever a rope. The axe severed the dead branch from the tree.* **2** put an end to a relationship: *The two countries severed friendly relations.* <Old French, from Latin *separare* to divide> **sev′er·a·bil′i·ty** *n.* **sev′er·a·ble** *adj.*

sev·er·al (sev′ər əl) *or* (sev′rəl) *adj* **1** being more than two or three but not many: *to gain several kilograms.* **2** individual or different: *The boys went their several ways, each concerned with his own business.* **3** applied or regarded separately in law.
pron more than two or three but not many: *Several had given their consent.* <Old French, from Latin *separare* to divide>

sev·er·al·ly (sev′ə rə lē) *or* (sev′rə lē) *adv* separately; singly; individually: *Consider these points, first severally and then collectively.*

sev·er·ance (sev′ə rəns) *or* (sev′rəns) *n* **1** the action of ending a connection or relationship, or the condition that results from this action. **2** a dismissal or discharge from a job, or the **severance pay** made as a settlement for it. <Old French, from Latin *separare* to divide>

se·vere (sə vēr′) *adj* **se·ver·er, se·ver·est 1** very great or intense: *a severe storm.* **2** strict or harsh: *a severe criticism.* **3** demanding great ability, skill, or toughness: *a severe test.* **4** very plain or simple: *a severe style.* <French, from Latin *severus*> **se·vere′ly** *adv.* **se·vere′ness** *n.* **se·ver′i·ty** *n.*

sew (sō) *v* **sewed, sewn** or **sewed, sew·ing** make, join, fasten, or repair something with stitches using a needle and thread. <Old English *siwan*>
sew up, a close with stitches: *The doctor sewed up the wound.* **b** *Informal* bring something to a successful conclusion: *They sewed up the deal last night.*

sew·age (sū′ij) *n* the waste matter that passes through sewers. <*sewer*>

sew·er[1] (sū′ər) *n* an underground pipe or channel to carry off waste water and refuse. <Old French, from Latin *ex-* out of + *aqua* water>

sew·er[2] (sō′ər) *n* a person who or thing that sews.

sew·ing (sō′ing) *n* the action or activity of sewing, or work that is to be or is being sewn.
adj for or used in sewing: *a sewing room.*

sewing circle *n* a group of people who meet regularly to sew as a means of raising money for charity.

sewing machine *n* a machine for sewing or stitching cloth.

sewn (sōn) a past participle of SEW.

sex (seks) *n* **1** either of the two categories, male and female, into which human beings, animals, and most other living things are divided according to their function in the reproductive process: *People were admitted without regard to age or sex.* **2** sexual activity, including sexual intercourse.
v determine the sex of: *to sex fish.* <Old French, from Latin *sexus*> **sex′less** *adj.*

sex– *combining form* six: *sextet.* <Latin>

sex·a·ge·nar·i·an (sek′sə jə ner′ē ən) *n* a person who is in his or her sixties. <Latin *sexaginta* sixty>

sex appeal *n* the quality of having sexual attractiveness.

sex chromosome *n* a chromosome (X or Y) that is different in shape and function from the other chromosomes and determines an individual's sex in most animals and some plants.

sex hormone *n* a hormone, such as estrogen or testosterone, that affects sexual development or reproduction.

sex·ist (sek′sist) *adj* characterized by prejudice or discrimination on the basis of sex: *a sexist attitude, a sexist statement.*
n a person who has such an attitude. **sex′ism** *n.*

sex symbol *n* a person who is famous for his or her sex appeal.

sex·tant (sek′stənt) *n* an instrument with a sighting mechanism used by navigators and surveyors for measuring the angular distance between two objects. <Latin *sextus* six>

sex·tet or **sex·tette** (sek stet′) *n* **1** a group of six singers or players, or a musical composition for six voices or instruments. **2** a group of six persons or things. <Latin *sex* six>

sex·ton (sek′stən) *n* a person who takes care of a church and churchyard. <Old French, from Latin *sacer* holy>

sex·u·al (sek′shū əl) *adj* **1** to do with sex or the sexes: *sexual differences.* **2** to do with relations between the sexes: *sexual morality.* **sex′u·al·ly** *adv.*

sexual harassment *n* unwelcome sexual advances or comments directed toward someone, especially a woman, in the workplace, a school, or in a social situation.

sexual intercourse *n* an act between people that involves genital contact and the sexual organs.

sex·u·al·i·ty (sek′shū al′ə tē) *n* **1** the capacity to have sexual feelings. **2** a person's sexual orientation or preferences.

sex·y (sek′sē) *adj* **sex·i·er, sex·i·est 1** sexually attractive or exciting: *a sexy dress.* **2** sexually aroused. **3** *Informal* exciting or appealing: *a sexy motorbike.*

Sey·chelles (sā shels′) *n* a country of many islands in the Indian Ocean.

SF science fiction.

SGML *n* in full, **Standard Generalized Markup Language** a language for tagging electronic text with codes that contain formatting and other information.

sh (sh) *interj* in full, **hush** a word used to urge silence.

Shab·bat (sha′bət) *Judaism n* the Sabbath. Also, **Shabbos**.

shab·by (shab′ē) *adj* **shab·bi·er, shab·bi·est 1** in bad condition because of long use or lack of care: *a shabby suit.* **2** wearing old or much worn clothes. **3** mean and unfair: *It was shabby not to speak to her old friend because he was poor.* <Old English sceabb> **shab′bi·ly** *adv.* **shab′bi·ness** *n.*

shack (shak) *n* a roughly built or poorly maintained hut, cabin, or house: *The girls made a shack in the backyard.* <origin uncertain>
shack up, *Informal* move in or live with a person one is sexually involved with, but not married to.

shack·le (shak′əl) *n* **1 shackles** *pl* a pair of metal bands connected by a chain, used to fasten the wrists or ankles of a prisoner. **2** a metal link, typically U-shaped and closed by a bolt, used to secure a chain or rope to something. **3** a thing that restrains or impedes freedom of action or thought.
v **shack·led, shack·ling 1** chain with shackles. **2** restrain or impede. <Old English *scacel*>

shad (shad) *n, pl* **shads** or (*especially collectively*) **shad** a herringlike fish that spends much of its life in the sea but enters rivers to spawn. <Old English *sceadd*>

🍁 **shad·bush** (shad′bůsh′) *Maritime Provinces n* the serviceberry. Also called **shadberry**.

shade (shād) *n* **1** a relatively cool, dark place caused by shelter from direct sunlight: *He sat in the shade of a big tree.* **2** a position that is relatively inferior or obscure: *His fame tended to put his sister in the shade.* **3** a colour, especially with regard to how dark it is: *shades of green.* **4 a** a screen or blind on a window. **b** a lampshade. **5** a very small difference, amount, or degree: *These pants are a shade too long.* **6 a** a ghost. **b the shades** *pl* the world in which ghosts are supposed to live.
v **shad·ed, shad·ing 1** screen from direct light: *The big hat shaded her eyes.* **2** cover, lessen, or exclude the light: *He shaded the flashlight with his hand.* **3** darken or colour an illustration or diagram with parallel lines or a block of colour. **4** gradually change from one colour to another: *This scarf shades from deep rose to pale pink.* **5** make a slight reduction in an amount or rate: *Can't you shade the price for me?* **6** *Informal* narrowly win or gain an advantage in a contest: *Their team shaded ours 4 to 3.* <Old English *scadu*> **shade′less** *adj.*
shades of, recalling or comparing with someone or something specified: *Did you see that guy on TV last night? Shades of Elvis!*

🍁 **shad·fly** (shad′flī′) *Maritimes n, pl* **shad·flies** the mayfly, or another winged insect that appears in the spring.

shad·ing (shā′ding) *n* **1** a darkening or colouring of an illustration or diagram with parallel lines or a block of colour to give the effect of shade or depth. **2** a slight variation, usually in colour or meaning: *shadings of interpretation.* **3** a layer of paint or material used to provide a shade.

shad·ow (shad′ō) *n* **1** a dark area or shape produced by a person or thing coming between rays of light and a surface: *The tall building cast a long shadow on the street.* **2** a shaded part, such as the shaded part of a picture, or a dark area on a surface: *There were dark shadows under his eyes.* **3** a little bit or slight suggestion of something: *There's not a shadow of a doubt about his guilt.* **4** a faint image or likeness: *You look worn to a shadow.* **5 a** a person who follows another closely and secretly. **b** a constant companion or follower. **6** a relatively inferior or obscure thing or quality: *She lived in the shadow of her mother.* **7** an ominous or gloomy thing or quality: *the shadow of war.*
v **1** fill with shadows or cast a shadow over: *The grass is shadowed by huge oaks.* **2** follow closely and secretly: *The detective shadowed the suspect.* <Old English *sceadu* shade>

shadow box *n* **1** a boxlike frame for hanging on a wall, in which an arrangement of small objects, a painting, piece of stained glass, etc. may be displayed. **2** a framelike device to shade a surface so that a film may be projected on it in daylight.

shad·ow·box (shad′ō boks′) *v* box before a mirror, or with an imaginary opponent, for exercise or training. **shad′ow·box′ing** *n.*

shadow cabinet *n* the senior, policy-making members of an opposition party in a legislature, each one assigned as critic to the corresponding member of the cabinet in government.

shad·ow·er (shad′ō ər′) *n* a person or thing that shadows.

shad·ow·less (shad′ō lis) *adj* with or casting no shadow: *shadowless light.*

shad·ow·y (shad′ō ē) *adj* **1** full of shadows: *We went out of the sunshine into the cool, shadowy room.* **2** dim, faint, or slight: *She saw a shadowy outline on the window curtain.* **3** uncertain in identity or nature. **shad′ow·i·ness′** *n.*

a bat	e bed	i bid	o pot	u cup	th **thin**
ā cake	ē me	ī bite	ō go	ū rude	ᴛʜ **then**
á bar	ə about	ər over	ô for	ů put	zh measure

S

shad·y (shā′dē) *adj* **shad·i·er, shad·i·est 1** in the shade or giving shade. **2** of doubtful honesty or character: *He has engaged in rather shady occupations.* **shad′i·ness** *n.*

shaft (shaft) *n* **1** in a machine, a cylindrical bar that rotates or supports rotating parts. **2** a deep passage sunk in the earth, or a deep, narrow space: *The entrance to a mine is called a shaft, an elevator shaft.* **3** the straight stem of something such as a tool or a weapon: *the shaft of a hammer.* **4** a ray or beam of light: *a shaft of sunlight.* **5** a wooden pole by means of which a horse is harnessed to a carriage, etc. <Old English *sceaft* handle of a spear>
get (or **give someone**) **the shaft,** *Slang* get (or give someone) harsh or unfair treatment.

shag (shag) *n* **1** a carpet or rug with a long, rough pile. **2** a coarse tobacco cut into shreds. <Old English *sceacga* matted hair>

✱ **shag·a·nap·pi** (shag′ə nap′ē) *n* a thong, strap, line, or cord made from rawhide. <Cree *pisakanapiy*>

shag·bark (shag′bärk′) *n* a hickory tree whose rough bark peels off in long strips.

shag·gy (shag′ē) *adj* **shag·gi·er, shag·gi·est** rough, coarse, or unkempt, especially with a thick, rough mass of hair or fur: *a shaggy dog, shaggy eyebrows.*

shag·gy–dog story (shag′ē dog) *n* a joke or funny story that involves a long, rambling narrative before a pointless or nonsensical punchline. <from an original story of this type about a shaggy dog>

Shah (shä) *n* in former times, a title of the monarch of Iran.

shake (shāk) *v* **shook, shak·en, shak·ing 1** tremble or vibrate, or cause to do so: *Her voice shook. The explosion shook the town. He was shaking with cold.* **2** move an object or person up and down or from side to side with rapid, forceful, jerky movements: *I shook sand out of my shoes.* **3** grasp and slightly move someone's hand as a sign of greeting, parting, friendship, or congratulation. **4** upset, shock, or astonish, or cause a change of mood or attitude by shocking or disturbing someone: *His courage began to shake. The revolution shook the foundations of society. Her lie shook my faith in her honesty.* **5** *Informal* get rid of: *Can't you shake him?*
n **1** the act or fact of shaking: *a shake of the head.* **2** *Informal* an earthquake or earth tremor. **3** a milkshake. **4 the shakes** *pl Informal* a fit of trembling or shivering. <Old English *sceacan*>
no great shakes, *Informal* not unusual, extraordinary, or important.
shake down, a bring or throw down by shaking. **b** cause to settle down or function normally.
shake off, get rid of or manage to evade: *shake off a cold.*
shake out, a empty something out by shaking a container. **b** spread or open something, such as a cloth or garment, by shaking it.
shake up, a mix ingredients by shaking. **b** make big changes in an organization or structure: *The new owner shook up the company.* **c** rouse or disturb: *The poor results shook us up and we resolved to do better next time. He was somewhat shaken up by the experience.*

shake·down (shāk′doun′) *Informal n* **1** a thorough search of a person or place. **2** an act of forcing payment from someone, as in forms of blackmail or political graft. **3** a test of a new product or model, especially a vehicle or ship: *The yacht was given a shakedown by a trial voyage.* **4** a makeshift bed.

shak·er (shā′kər) *n* **1** a person who shakes a thing. **2** a machine or utensil used for mixing ingredients, or to shake out a substance, especially through a perforated top: *a salt shaker.*

Shake·spear·e·an (shāk spē′rē ən) *adj* to do with William Shakespeare or his works.

shake·up (shā′kup′) *Informal n* a sudden and complete change or rearrangement in an organization or structure: *a shakeup in the government.*

shak·o (shāk′ō) *n, pl* **shak·os** a high, stiff military hat with a plume or other ornament. <French, from German *Zacken* spike>

Shak·ti (shuk′tē) *Hinduism n* the female principle of divine energy, especially when worshipped as a god.

shak·y (shā′kē) *adj* **shak·i·er, shak·i·est 1** shaking or trembling: *a shaky voice.* **2** liable to break down because of poor construction or heavy use: *a shaky porch.* **3** uncertain and unreliable: *a shaky firm, a shaky knowledge.*
shak′i·ly *adv.* **shak′i·ness** *n.*

shale (shāl) *n* a fine-grained sedimentary rock formed from clay that has been subjected to great pressure and can be split easily into thin layers. <Old English *scealu* shell>

shall (shal) *v* **should** a word used **1** in questions to ask what one is to do: *Shall we go? Shall I wait?* **2** in statements with *you, he, she,* or *they* to show that a person has to do something: *You shall pay attention. He shall stay in his room for an hour.* **3** with *I* and *we* to indicate simple future time: *I shall go tomorrow if I can't make it today.* <Old English *sceal*>

GRAMMAR AND USAGE

Some people use both shall and will to express future time. However, the two words are used differently in more formal English:

Shall is used to express the simple future only with *I* and *we*: *I (We) shall be there tomorrow.*

Will is used to express the simple future with *he, she, you,* and *they*: *She (You) will play the guitar.*

shal·lot (shə lot′) *n* a small bulb that resembles an onion but is composed of smaller bulbs, or the plant related to the onion that produces it. See ONION for picture. <French, from Old French *eschaloigne*>

shal·low (shal′ō) *adj* **1** not deep, or located at no great depth: *shallow water, a shallow dish.* **2** lacking depth of thought, knowledge, or feeling: *a shallow mind.*
n **shallows** *pl* a shallow place: *The girls splashed in the shallows of the pond.* <Old English *sceald*>
shal′low·ly *adj.* **shal′low·ness** *n.*

sha·lom (sho lōm′) *or* (she lōm′) *interj* used by Jews to indicate peace at meeting or parting from someone. <Hebrew *salom*>

sham (sham) *n* a pretence or fraud, or a person who pretends to be something or someone he or she is not.
adj bogus or false: *a sham proposal.*
v **shammed, sham·ming** falsely pretend something as a fact: *He shammed sickness so he wouldn't have to go to school.* <*shame*> **sham′mer** *n.*

sha·man (shä′mən), (shā′mən), *or* (sham′ən) *n* a person who is believed to have the power to influence spirits for good or evil, especially among some peoples of northern Asia and N America. <Russian, from Sanskrit *sramah* religious exercise>

sha·man·ism (shä′mən izəm), (shā′mən izəm), *or* (sham′ən izəm) *n* a religion characterized by a belief in spirits, demons, and gods that inhabit physical things and that can be influenced by shamans. **sha′man·ist** *adj, n.* **sha′man·ist′ic** *adj.*

sham·ble (sham′bəl) *v* **sham·bled, sham·bling** walk in a slow, awkward, shuffling way: *The bear shambled into the bushes.*
n a shambling walk. <origin uncertain>

sham·bles (sham′bəlz) *n* (*with singular verb*) a condition of total disorder: *The room was a shambles after the party.*

shame (shām) *n* **1** a painful feeling of having done something wrong or foolish: *to blush with shame.* **2** a loss of respect or esteem: *That young man's conviction brought shame to his family.* **3** a regrettable or unfortunate situation or action: *It is a shame to be so wasteful.* **4** a person or thing to be ashamed of: *The garbage on the street was the shame of the neighbourhood.* **5** a sense of what is decent or proper.
v **shamed, sham·ing** make or cause someone to feel ashamed or inadequate: *My silly mistake shamed me.* <Old English *sceamu*> **shame′ful** *adj.* **shame′ful·ly** *adv.* **shame′ful·ness** *n.* **shame′less** *adj.* **shame′less·ly** *adv.* **shame′less·ness** *n.*
for shame! shame on you!
put to shame, a disgrace or make ashamed. **b** much surpass: *Her careful work put all the rest to shame.*
shame on ——! (someone) should be ashamed: *You kicked your little brother? Shame on you!*

shame·faced (shām′fāst′) *adj* showing shame or embarrassment.

sham·poo (sham pū′) *n* **1** a liquid substance containing soap for washing the hair, or a similar preparation for cleaning a carpet, soft furnishings, or a motor vehicle. **2** an act of cleaning or washing something, especially the hair.
v **sham·pooed, sham·poo·ing** wash something, especially the hair, with a soapy preparation. <Hindi *champna* to knead>

sham·rock (sham′rok) *n* a low-growing, bright green plant of the clover family, or a spray or leaf of this plant. One kind of shamrock is considered an emblem of Ireland. <Irish Gaelic *seamar* clover>

Shan·gri–La (shang′gri lä′) *n* an idyllic earthly paradise. <*Shangri-La*, Tibetan utopia in *Lost Horizon*, a novel by J. Hilton>

shank (shangk) *n* **1** the part of the leg between the knee and the ankle, or the corresponding part in animals. **2** the shaft or stem of a tool or instrument. **3** a part by which something is attached to another thing.
v Golf hit the ball with the heel of the club, so that it goes in the wrong direction. <Old English *sceanca*>

shan't (shant) *contraction* shall not.

🍁 **shan·ty**[1] (shan′tē) *n, pl* **shan·ties** a roughly built hut, cabin, or living quarters. <Cdn French *chantier* logging camp, from Latin cantherius frame>

shan·ty[2] (shan′tē) *n, pl* **shan·ties** a song sung by sailors in rhythm with the motions made during their work. Also, **chantey, chanty**. <probably French *chanter* sing>

shan·ty·town (shan′tē toun′) *n* a slum area of a city where people live in shacks.

shape (shāp) *n* **1** the outward contour or outline of a person or thing: *the shape of a triangle.* **2** a form or guise assumed by someone or something: *In the last chapter, the witch took the shape of a cat.* **3** something seen, or thought to be seen, though with no definite form: *A white shape stood at his bedside.* **4** a condition or state of someone or something: *Exercise keeps you in good shape.* **5** a definite and orderly arrangement: *Take time to get your thoughts into shape.*
v **shaped, shap·ing 1** form into a particular form or shape: *The child shapes clay into balls.* **2** take shape or assume form: *Her plan is shaping well.* **3** fit the form of something else: *That hat is shaped to your head.* **4** give definite form or character to, or develop in a particular way: *Several events shaped his course in life.* **5** form or produce a sound or words: *She shaped a question.* <Old English *gesceap* external form and *sceppan* create> **shaped** *adj.* **shap′er** *n.*
shape up, develop or happen in a particular way.
take shape, have or take on a definite form.

shape·less (shā′plis) *adj* lacking a distinctive or attractive shape, especially of a garment: *a shapeless dress.* **shape′less·ly** *adv.* **shape′less·ness** *n.*

shape·ly (shā′plē) *adj* **shape·li·er, shape·li·est** with a pleasing or well-proportioned shape. **shape′li·ness** *n.*

shard (shärd) *n* a sharp-edged piece of broken ceramic, metal, glass, or rock. <Old English *sceard*>

share (sher) *n* **1** a part or portion of a larger amount that is divided among a number of people, or to which several people contribute: *Do your share of the work. One of the fishermen offered to sell his share in the boat.* **2** each of the parts into which the ownership of a company or corporation is divided: *The ownership of the company was divided into several million shares.*
v **shared, shar·ing 1** have or give a portion of a thing to another or others: *He shared his candy with his sister. The sisters shared a room.* **2** use, occupy, or enjoy a thing with another or others: *Everyone shared in making the picnic a success.* **3** possess a view or quality in common with others: *He didn't share my opinion of the new teacher.* **4** tell something to another, especially something personal: *I would like to share my memories of my pet dog.* See SHEAR for confusables. <Old English *scearu* division>

a bat	e bed	i bid	o pot	u cup	th thin
ā cake	ē me	ī bite	ō go	ū rude	ᴛʜ then
ä bar	ə about	ər over	ô for	ů put	zh measure

share·crop·per (sher′krop′ər) *n* a person, especially in former times in the US, who farms land for the landowner in return for part of the crops. **share′crop** *v.*

share·hold·er (sher′hōl′dər) *n* a person owning shares of stock in a company or enterprise.

share·ware (sher′wer′) *Computers n* software that is distributed at no cost, usually with a request that a fee be paid eventually if one decides to continue it.

shark (shȧrk) *n* **1** a long-bodied, mainly marine predatory fish with a skeleton formed of cartilage and a prominent dorsal fin. Some larger sharks are dangerous to swimmers and divers. See CARTILAGE for picture. **2** *Informal* a dishonest or ruthless person who preys on others: *a loan shark.* <origin uncertain>

sharp (shȧrp) *adj* **1 a** with a thin edge or point that can cut or pierce: *a sharp knife, a sharp pencil.* **b** tapering to a point or edge: *a sharp nose.* **2** sudden and marked as an action or sensation: *a sharp turn, a sharp pain.* **3** very cold: *a sharp wind.* **4** intended or intending to criticize or hurt: *sharp words.* **5** clear and distinct: *a sharp contrast.* **6** alert or acutely aware: *a sharp eye, sharp ears, a sharp mind.* **7** shrewd and cunning: *sharp practice.* **8** *Music* above true or normal pitch, such as a halftone higher than a specified note: *F sharp.* **9** *Slang* attractive or striking in looks: *a sharp car.*
adv **1** exact in time: *Be there at one o'clock sharp.* **2** in a sudden, alert way: *Look sharp!* **3** *Music* above the true or normal pitch of musical pitch: *She was playing a bit sharp on the low notes.*
n **1** a musical note raised a semitone above natural pitch, or a sign [♮] that stands for this. **2** *Informal* a swindler or cheat: *a card sharp.* <Old English *scearp*> **sharp′ly** *adv.* **sharp′ness** *n.*

sharp·en (shȧr′pən) *v* make or become sharp: *to sharpen a pencil. Her voice sharpened as she became angry.* **sharp′en·er** *n.*

sharp·er (shȧr′pər) *n* a swindler, especially at cards.

sharp·shoot·er (shȧrp′shū′tər) *n* a person who shoots very well, especially with a rifle. **sharp′shoot·ing** *adj, n.*

sharp–tongued (shȧrp′tungd′) *adj* tending to be harsh, sarcastic, or highly critical.

sharp–wit·ted (shȧr′pwit′id) *adj* with or showing a quick, keen mind.

Shas·ta daisy (shas′tə) *n* a tall plant that bears a single large, white, daisylike flower.

shat·ter (shat′ər) *v* **1** suddenly and violently break into pieces: *A stone shattered the window.* **2** disturb greatly or destroy: *The low mark shattered his confidence.* <origin uncertain> **shat′ter·er** *n.* **shat′ter·ing** *adj.* **shat′ter·ing·ly** *adv.*

shat·ter·proof (shat′ər prūf′) *adj* designed so as not to shatter when it breaks: *a shatterproof bowl.*

shave (shāv) *v* **shaved, shaved** or **shav·en, shav·ing** **1** remove hair from the face or another part of the body with a razor: *He shaves every day. The actor shaved his head for the movie.* **2** cut a thin slice from the surface of: *shave roast beef.* **3** come very close to: *The car shaved the corner.*
n **1** the act of shaving hair from the face or part of the body. **2** a tool for shaving very thin slices or layers from wood or other material. **3** a narrow miss or escape: *The shot missed him, but it was a close shave.* <Old English *sceafan*>

shav·en (shā′vən) a past participle of SHAVE.

shav·er (shā′vər) *n* **1** a person who shaves. **2** an electric razor. **3** *Informal* a small boy.

shav·ing (shā′ving) *n* **1** a very thin piece or slice cut off a surface: *wood shavings.* **2** the act or process of cutting hair with a razor.

Sha·vu·ot (shə vū′ōt′) *Judaism n* a holiday commemorating the giving of the law on Mount Sinai, originally a spring harvest celebration. <Hebrew *sabuot* weeks, from seba seven, because the feast was held on the sixth and seventh day of the feast of Sivan>

shawl (shol′) *n* a square or oblong piece of cloth to be worn around the shoulders or head. <Persian *sal*>

she (shē) *pron* a female person already referred to and identified: *My mom has to work hard, but she enjoys it.* <Old English *sie*>

sheaf (shēf) *n, pl* **sheaves** **1** a bundle of cut grain bound in the middle for drying, loading, and stacking. **2** a bundle of things that are alike: *a sheaf of notes.* <Old English *sceaf*>

shear (shēr) *v* **sheared, sheared** or **shorn, shear·ing** **1** cut hair, wool, or grass with shears or scissors: *The farmer sheared her sheep.* **2** strip or deprive as if by cutting: *The assembly had been shorn of its legislative powers.* **3** break by a force causing two parts or pieces to slide over each other in opposite directions: *One of the wings of the plane was completely sheared off.*
n a force causing two parts or pieces to slide over each other in opposite directions and break. <Old English *sceran*> **shear′er** *n.*

CONFUSABLES

Shear means "cut with shears or scissors": *She sheared off the top of the hedge with the new electric hedge trimmer.*

Share means "give a part of something to others" or "use something with others": *He shared his lunch with his friend.*

Sheer is an adjective that means "complete": *It was sheer folly to leave the car window open when you knew it was going to rain.*

shear·ling (shēr′ling) *n* a sheep that has been shorn only once, or the wool or fleece from such a sheep.

shears (shērz) *pl n* a cutting instrument resembling large scissors: *grass shears, tin shears.*

shear·wa·ter (shēr′wot′ər) *n* a long-winged seabird related to the petrels, often flying low over the surface of the water far from land.

sheath (shēth) *n, pl* **sheaths** (shēᴛʜz) **1** a close-fitting case or covering for something elongated in shape, such as a knife or sword. **2** a structure of living tissue on an animal or plant that closely envelops another. **3** a dress with a fitted bodice and straight skirt, usually unbelted. <Old English *sceath* scabbard>

sheathe (shēTH) *v* **sheathed, sheath·ing** put into or enclose in a sheath: *Her legs were sheathed in white stockings.*

sheath·ing (shē′THing) *n* a protective casing or covering.

sheath knife *n* a short knife carried in a sheath.

sheaves (shēvz) plural of SHEAF.

she·bang (shə bang′) *Informal n* a matter, operation, or set of circumstances: *We asked who was running the whole shebang.* <origin uncertain>

shed[1] (shed) *n* a simple, usually one-storeyed, roofed structure, typically made of wood or metal, used for garden storage, to shelter animals, or as a workshop. <Old English *scead* shelter>

shed[2] (shed) *v* **shed, shed·ding 1** allow leaves or fruit of a tree or other plant to fall to the ground: *By late fall the maple had shed all its leaves.* **2** allow the skin or shell of a reptile to come off, to be replaced by another one that has grown underneath: *The snake shed its skin.* **3** lose hair as a mammal as a result of moulting, disease, or age. **4** discard or remove something unneeded or undesirable: *to shed clothes.* **5** allow or cause something to fall off, spill, or flow: *to shed blood, to shed tears.* <Old English *sceadan*>

she'd (shēd) *contraction* **1** she had: *She'd forgotten her homework.* **2** she would: *She'd always be on time.*

sheen (shēn) *n* a soft lustre on a surface: *Satin and polished silver have a sheen.* <Old English *sciene*>

Sheep were first domesticated about 11 000 years ago. It is believed that they are descendants of the mouflon, a wild animal found in western Asia.

sheep (shēp) *n, pl* **sheep 1** a cud-chewing domestic animal raised for wool, milk, meat, and skin. **2** a wild animal related to this, such as the mountain sheep. **3** a person considered to be weak, timid, or easily led. <Old English *sceap*> **sheep′like′** *adj.*
make sheep's eyes, give a foolishly amorous look.
separate the sheep from the goats, distinguish the better or superior from the rest.

sheep dip *n* liquid disinfectant and insecticide in which sheep are bathed to kill parasites and to preserve the wool, or a place where this is done.

sheep·dog (shēp′dog) *n* a collie or other dog trained to guard and herd sheep.

sheep·ish (shē′pish) *adj* awkwardly bashful or embarrassed: *a sheepish smile.* **sheep′ish·ly** *adv.* **sheep′ish·ness** *n.*

sheep·shank (shēp′shank′) *n* a kind of knot made in a rope in order to shorten it temporarily. See KNOT for picture.

sheep·skin (shēp′skin′) *n* **1** the skin of a sheep with the wool on it. **2** leather made from the skin of a sheep and used in bookbinding. **3** *Informal* a diploma.

sheer (shēr) *adj* **1** complete and unmixed with anything else: *sheer weariness.* **2** so thin as to be almost transparent: *sheer white drapes.* **3** straight up or down: *From the top, there was a sheer drop to the water below.* See SHEAR for confusables.
n **sheers** *pl* very thin, almost transparent drapes.
adv straight up or down: *The cliff rose sheer from the river's edge.* <Middle English> **sheer′ness** *n.*

sheer·ly (shēr′lē) *adv* absolutely or thoroughly.

sheet[1] (shēt) *n* **1** a large piece of cloth of cotton or other fabric, used to sleep on or under. **2** a broad, thin piece of material such as metal or glass. **3** a rectangular piece of paper for writing or printing on, especially of a standard size, or a quantity of text on such a piece of paper. **4** a broad, flat, extensive surface of something: *a sheet of water.*
v cover, wrap, or fill with a sheet. <Old English *scete*>

sheet[2] (shēt) *n* a rope that controls the angle at which a sail is set. <Old English *sceata* lower corner of a sail>

sheet anchor *n* a spare anchor used in emergencies.

sheet bend *n* a kind of knot for fastening one rope through the loop of another.

sheet·ing (shē′ting) *n* material formed into or used as a sheet, such as a protective lining or covering.

sheet lightning *n* lightning reflected from clouds in broad flashes.

sheet metal *n* metal made in thin pieces or plates, typically by rolling or hammering.

sheet music *n* music printed on sheets of paper, as distinguished from performed or recorded music.

sheik or **sheikh** (shēk) *or* (shāk) *n* **1** an Arab chief of a family or village, or ruler of a certain territory (**sheikdom**). **2** a leader in a Muslim community or organization. <Arabic *shaykh* old man>

shek·el (shek′əl) *n* **1** a silver coin and unit of weight used in ancient Israel and the Middle East. **2** the basic unit of money in Israel. <Hebrew *saqal* weigh>

shelf (shelf) *n, pl* **shelves 1** a thin, flat piece of rigid material fastened to a wall, frame, or piece of furniture to hold or display things. **2** a ledge of rock, coral, or protruding strip of land. <German *schelf*>
on the shelf, no longer useful or desirable.

shelf life *n* the length of time that an item remains usable, fit for consumption, or saleable.

a **bat**	e **bed**	i **bid**	o **pot**	u **cup**	th **thin**
ā **cake**	ē **me**	ī **bite**	ō **go**	ū **rude**	TH **then**
à **bar**	ə **about**	ər **over**	ȯ **for**	u̇ **put**	zh **measure**

shell (shel) *n* **1 a** the hard outside protective covering of an animal such as a mollusc, crustacean, or turtle. **b** the hard outside protective covering of a nut, seed, or fruit. **c** the protective outside covering of an animal's egg, such as that of a bird or reptile. **2** a thing resembling a shell, such as the frame of a house, a light racing boat, or a hollow pastry case. **3** *Mathematics* a three-dimensional model with an empty interior. See also SKELETON, SOLID. **4** a cartridge used in a rifle or shotgun, or a metal projectile filled with explosives that is fired by artillery and explodes on impact.
v **1** fire artillery shells, or in a way like this: *They shelled the enemy position.* **2** remove the shell or pod of a nut or seed: *to shell peas, shelled walnuts.* <Old English *scell*>
shel′ler *n.* **shell-less** *adj.* **shell-like** *adj.*
come out of your shell, stop being shy or reserved and become sociable.
shell out, *Informal* hand over money or pay up, especially in an unwilling way: *He shelled out $25 for roses.*

she'll (shēl) *contraction* **1** she will. **2** she shall.

shel·lac (shə lak′) *n* a liquid resinous substance used for coating wood or metal that hardens into a smooth, shiny finish.
v **shel·lacked, shel·lack·ing 1** put shellac on. **2** *Informal* defeat completely. <*shell* + *lac* insect that secretes the resinous substance>

shell·fire (shel′fir′) *n* bombardment by explosive shells.

shell·fish (shel′fish′) *n, pl* **shell·fish·es** or (*especially collectively*) **shell·fish** an edible mollusc such as a clam, or a crustacean such as a lobster, that has a shell and lives in the water.

shell game *n* **1** a game in which bets are made about which of three cups or nutshells has a small object hidden under it. **2** *Informal* a swindle or deception.

shell·proof (shel′prūf′) *adj* secure against explosive shells or bombs.

shell shock *n* mental disturbance caused by prolonged exposure to active warfare, especially in being under attack by artillery. **shell′-shocked′** *adj.*

shel·ter (shel′tər) *n* **1** a place that temporarily protects against bad weather or danger: *The trees were a shelter from the sun.* **2** a safe or protected condition: *We took shelter from the storm in a barn.*
v **1** protect or shield from something harmful: *to shelter refugees.* **2** find refuge or take cover from bad weather or danger: *The sheep sheltered from the hot sun in the shade of the haystack.* <origin uncertain> **shel′ter·er** *n.* **shel′ter·less** *adj.*

shel·tered (shel′tərd) *adj* **1** of a place, protected against bad weather: *a sheltered spot near the garden fence.* **2** kept protected from unpleasantness or hardship: *He led such a sheltered life that he didn't even watch the evening news.*

shelve (shelv) *v* **shelved, shelv·ing 1** place or arrange items on a shelf. **2** decide not to proceed with a plan, project, or discussion: *Let's shelve that argument.* **3** furnish with shelves. **4** slope gradually: *The sandy bottom of the lake shelves down to rock in the middle.*

shelves (shelvz) plural of SHELF.

shelv·ing (shel′ving) *n* shelves collectively.

she·moz·zle (shə moz′əl) *Informal n* a condition or situation of muddle or confusion: *the whole shemozzle.* Also, **shmozzle.** <Yiddish>

she·nan·i·gans (shə nan′ə gənz) *Informal pln* secretly planned mischief or trickery. <origin uncertain>

shep·herd (shep′ərd) *n* a person who tends and rears sheep.
v **1** tend sheep: *to shepherd a flock.* **2** guide in a particular direction: *They shepherded the tenants safely out of the burning building.* <Old English *sceap* sheep + *hierde* herder>

shep·herd·ess (shep′ər dis) *n* a woman who tends and rears sheep.

shepherd's pie *n* a baked dish consisting of cubed or ground beef or lamb mixed with gravy and topped with mashed potatoes.

sher·bet (shər′bət) *n* a frozen dessert made of fruit juice, sugar, water, gelatin, and, sometimes, milk or egg white. <Turkish, from Arabic *sariba* to drink>

sher·iff (sher′if) *n* **1** 🍁 an official whose job is to enforce certain court orders, such as evicting people for failure to pay rent and escorting convicted people to prison. **2** *US* the most important law-enforcing officer of a county. <Old English *scir* shire + *gerefa* chief official>

Sher·pa (shər′pa) *n* a member of a Himalayan people living on the border of Tibet and Nepal, famous as mountain climbers and guides.

sher·ry (sher′ē) *n, pl* **sher·ries** a strong sweet or dry wine originally made in southern Spain, and now made in other countries, varying in colour from pale yellow to brown. <Spanish *Xeres* a region of S Spain>

she's (shēz) *contraction* **1** she is: *She's very clever.* **2** she has: *She's been working very hard this year.*

Shet·land pony (shet′lənd) *n* a small, sturdy, rough-coated pony, originally from the Shetland Islands.

Shi·a (shē′ə) *n* one of the two major branches of Islam, that regards Ali (the fourth caliph after Muhammad) as Muhammad's true successor. Compare SUNNI. <Arabic *sia* a party of Ali> **Shi·ite** (shē′īt) *n.*

shi·at·su (shē ot′sū) *n* a form of therapy in which pressure is applied to certain parts of the body using the hands. <Japanese = finger pressure>

shib·bo·leth (shib′ə lith) *n* a peculiarity of speech, habit, or custom considered distinctive of a particular group or class, especially one considered to be outmoded or no longer important. <Hebrew *sibbolet* ear of corn, mentioned in the Bible as a test of nationality by its difficult pronunciation>

shield (shēld) *n* **1** a broad piece of metal or other hard material, held by straps or a handle attached on one side, used as a protection in a contest or battle. **2** a person who or thing that protects: *She held up a newspaper as a shield against the sun.* **3** something shaped like a shield. **4 the Shield** the Canadian Shield.
v protect someone or something from a danger, risk, or unpleasant experience: *His mother shielded him from punishment.* <Old English *scild*>

shift (shift) *v* **1** move or cause to move from one place, position, or person to another; change: *The wind has shifted to the southeast. He shifted the heavy bag from one hand to the other.* **2** change or have changed the emphasis, direction, or focus: *His opinions shifted sharply over the years.* **3** manage to get along: *When her parents went on vacation, she had to shift for herself.* **4** change the position of the gears of an automobile.
n **1** a change in direction, position, or tendency: *a shift of the wind, a shift in policy.* **2** a group of workers who work during the same period of time, or the recurring period during which they work: *He works on the night shift.* **3** a tricky or devious action: *The lazy girl tried every shift to avoid doing her work.* **4** *Football* a change in the arrangement of players before a football is put into play. **5** a key on a keyboard used to switch between two sets of characters or functions, especially between lower-case and upper-case letters. <Old English *sciftan* arrange> **shift′ab·le** *adj.* **shift′er** *n.*
make shift, do what one wants to do, or as well as one can, in spite of adverse conditions.

shift·less (shif′tlis) *adj* lazy, unambitious, and inefficient. **shift′less·ly** *adv.* **shift′less·ness** *n.*

shift·y (shif′tē) *adj* **shift·i·er, shift·i·est** appearing deceitful or evasive. **shift′i·ly** *adv.* **shift′i·ness** *n.*

Shih Tzu (shē′dzū′) *n* a breed of dog originally from China with a curved, plumelike tail, and short legs covered by long, silky fur.

Shi·ite (shē′īt) See SHIA.

shill (shil) *n* a person who acts as a decoy or accomplice of a peddler or gambler, trying to make people buy or bet.
v work as a shill. <origin uncertain>

shil·le·lagh (shə lā′lē) *Irish n* a thick wooden stick used as a weapon.

shil·ly–shal·ly (shil′ē shal′ē) *v* **shil·ly-shal·lied, shil·ly-shal·ly·ing** be unable to make a decision or take action.
n an inability to make a decision or take action.

shim (shim) *n* a thin strip of metal or wood used to align parts, make them fit, or reduce wear.
v **shimmed, shim·ming** put a shim or shims in. <origin uncertain>

shim·mer (shim′ər) *v* shine with a soft light: *The satin cloak shimmered in the moonlight.*
n a soft, gleaming light: *The pearls had a beautiful shimmer.* <Old English *scymrian*> **shim′mer·ing·ly** *adv.* **shim′mer·y** *adj.*

shim·my (shim′ē) *n, pl* **shim·mies** an unusual shaking or vibration, especially of the front wheels of a car, truck, etc.
v **shim·mied, shim·my·ing** shake or vibrate. <variant of *chemise*>

shin (shin) *n* **1** the front part of the leg from the knee to the ankle. **2** the lower part of the foreleg in beef cattle.
v **shinned, shin·ning** SHINNY[2]. <Old English *scinu*>

shin·bone (shin′bōn′) *n* the front bone of the leg below the knee.

shin·dig (shin′dig′) *Informal n* a large, lively party, especially a celebration. <origin uncertain>

shine (shīn) *v* **shone** or (*for def. 2*) **shined, shin·ing** **1** send out or reflect light from the sun or other source: *The sun shone directly down. She shone a flashlight ahead of us.* **2** do very well at something: *He shone in history, but struggled in math.* **3** make a leather, metal, or wood object bright by rubbing, especially with polish: *to shine shoes.*
n **1** a quality of brightness, especially through reflected light: *the shine of polished silver.* **2** sunshine: *rain or shine.* <Old English *scinan*>
take a shine to, *Informal* develop a liking for: *We took a shine to our new neighbours.*

shin·er (shī′nər) *n* **1** a thing that shines or reflects light. **2** a small silvery N American freshwater fish with colourful markings. **3** *Informal* a BLACK EYE (def. 1).

shin·gle[1] (shing′gəl) *n* **1** a thin piece of asphalt, wood, etc. used with others to cover roofs or walls. **2** *Informal* a small signboard, especially outside a doctor's or lawyer's office.
v **shin·gled, shin·gling** cover with shingles: *to shingle a roof.* <Latin *scindula* a split piece of wood>
hang out your shingle, *Informal* begin to practise a profession.

shin·gle[2] (shing′gəl) *n* a mass of loose stones or pebbles such as lie on the seashore, or a beach or other place covered with it. <origin uncertain>

shin·gles (shing′gəlz) *n* (*with singular or plural verb*) a disease caused by the same virus as chicken pox that causes painful irritation of a group of nerves and a rash on the body. <Latin *cingulum* girdle, from *cingere* gird, because the inflamation caused by shingles often affects the middle of the body>

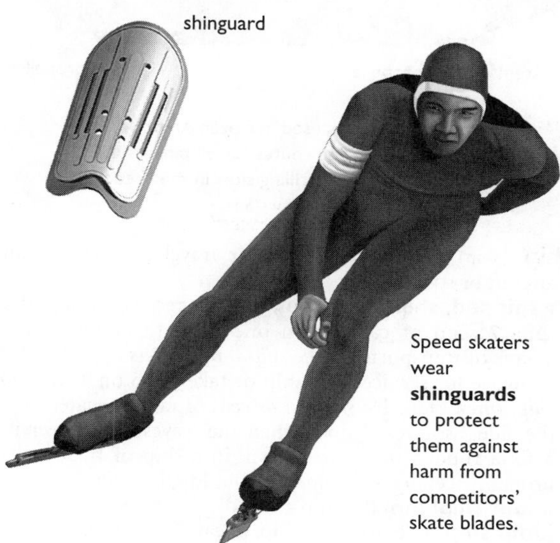

Speed skaters wear **shinguards** to protect them against harm from competitors' skate blades.

shin·guard (shin′gärd′) *n* a protective pad worn on the shins in various sports. Also called **shinpad**.

a bat	e bed	i bid	o pot	u cup	th thin
ā cake	ē me	ī bite	ō go	ū rude	ᴛʜ then
ä bar	ə about	ər over	ò for	ů put	zh measure

S

shin·ing (shī′ning) *adj* **1** bright. **2** brilliant or outstanding. **shin′ing·ly** *adv.*

🍁 **shin·ny**[1] (shin′ē) *n, pl* **shin·nies** a simple kind of hockey, played on the ice with skates, or without skates on the street or in a field, sometimes with a ball instead of a puck.
v **shin·nied, shin·ny·ing** play shinny. <origin uncertain>

shin·ny[2] (shin′ē) *v* **shin·nied, shin·ny·ing** climb up or down a rope, pole, or tree by gripping alternately with the hands and feet.

shin splints *n* a painful strain of the lower leg muscles, which can occur after prolonged running on a hard surface.

Shin·to (shin′tō) *n* a Japanese religion that includes the worship of ancestors and nature spirits and a belief in sacred power residing in living and non-living things. Also, **Shintoism**. <Japanese, from Mandarin *shin tao* way of the gods> **Shin′to·ist** *n.*

shin·y (shī′nē) *adj* **shin·i·er, shin·i·est** reflecting bright light from a smooth surface: *a shiny new nickel.*
shin′i·ly *adv.* **shin′i·ness** *n.*

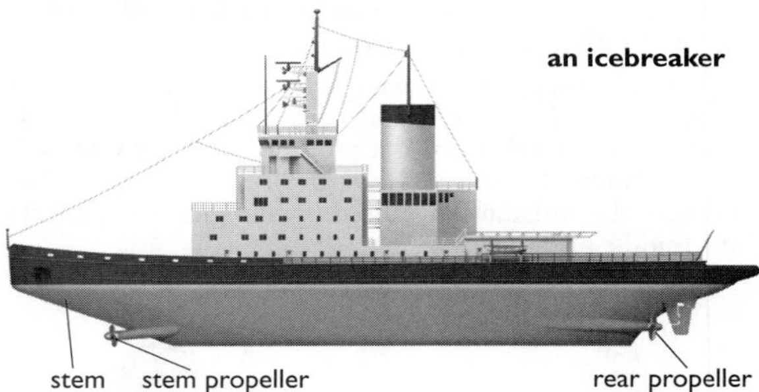

Icebreakers are **ships** used in frozen Arctic waters to clear transportation routes for oil tankers that move petroleum from drilling sites in the Arctic Archipelago and the Beaufort Sea.

ship (ship) *n* **1** a large vessel for travel on water. **2** an aircraft or spacecraft.
v **shipped, ship·ping 1** put, take, or receive on board a ship. **2** send or carry from one place to another by a means of transport: *Did he ship it by express or by freight?* **3** engage for service on a ship or take a job on a ship: *to ship a new crew. He shipped as cook.* **4** take in water over the side, as a vessel does when the waves break over it. **5** fix a rudder, mast, or oarlock in a ship or boat in its proper place: *to ship a rudder.* <Old English *scip*>
about ship! turn the ship around!
jump ship, a desert one's ship. **b** leave an organization or other group to avoid a difficult situation.
run a tight ship, manage an organization in a strict, efficient way.
ship out (or **off**), **a** go to sea. **b** send out by transport: *The container was shipped out yesterday.* **c** send away: *Her guardian shipped her off to a boarding school.*
when your ship comes home (or **in**), when you have achieved success.

–ship *suffix* **1** a quality or condition: *partnership.* **2** a status, office, or honour: *ambassadorship.* **3** a skill in a certain activity: *penmanship.* **4** all the individuals of a group: *membership.* <Old English *–scipe*>

ship·board (ship′bôrd′) *n, adj* to do with being on board a ship: *a shipboard romance.*

ship·build·er (ship′bil′dər) *n* a person who or company that designs or constructs ships. **ship′build·ing** *n.*

ship·load (ship′lōd′) *n* a full load for a ship.

ship·mas·ter (ship′mas′tər) *n* a master, commander, or captain of a ship.

ship·mate (ship′māt′) *n* a fellow sailor on a ship.

ship·ment (ship′mənt) *n* **1** the action of shipping goods. **2** goods shipped at one single time: *Two shipments were delivered yesterday.*

ship·per (ship′ər) *n* a person who or company that ships goods.

ship·ping (ship′ing) *n* **1** the act or business of sending goods by transport. **2** ships collectively: *There is a lot of shipping in the harbour.*

shipping clerk *n* a person whose work is to see to the packing and shipping of goods.

ship·shape (ship′shāp′) *adj* trim, neat, or in good order.

ship·way (ship′wā′) *n* **1** a canal or other waterway wide and deep enough for ships to use. **2** the structure supporting a ship during construction or in dry dock.

ship·wreck (ship′rek′) *n* the destruction or loss of a ship at sea, or a ship so destroyed: *Only two people were saved from the shipwreck.*
v suffer a shipwreck.

ship·wright (ship′rīt′) *n* a person who builds or repairs ships.

ship·yard (ship′yärd′) *n* an enclosed place near the water where ships are built or repaired.

shire (shīr) *n* a county, especially in England.

shirk (shərk) *v* avoid or neglect a duty or responsibility: *She lost her job because she shirked paperwork.* <origin uncertain> **shirk′er** *n.*

shirr (shər) *v* **1** draw up or gather cloth on parallel threads. **2** bake eggs in a shallow dish. <origin uncertain>

shirt (shərt) *n* **1** a garment for the upper part of the body with collar and sleeves, and usually buttons down the front. **2** a similar garment of stretchable material without full fastenings. <Old English *scyrte*> **shirt′less** *adj.*
keep your shirt on, *Informal* stay calm and not lose your temper.
lose your shirt, *Informal* lose everything you own, especially as the result of a failure.

shirt·dress (shərt′dres′) *n* a fitted dress whose upper part is styled like a shirt.

shirt·ing (shər′ting) *n* cloth for making shirts.

shirt·sleeve (shərt′slēv′) *n* the sleeve of a shirt.
in your shirtsleeves, wearing a shirt, but without a jacket or coat.

shirt·tail (shərt′tāl′) *n* the part of a shirt that extends below the waist, usually worn tucked into the pants or skirt.

shish ke·bab (shish′ kə bob′) *n* cubes of marinated meat and vegetables cooked and served on skewers. <Turkish *sis* skewer + *kepap* roast meat>

shi·va (shē′və) *Judaism n* the period of seven days' formal mourning for the dead, beginning immediately after the funeral. <Hebrew *sibah* seven>
sit shiva, mourn in this way.

Shi·va (shē′və) *Hinduism n* a god regarded as the supreme being or as one of the three principal gods. Also, **Siva**.

shi·va·ree (shi′və rē) *n* a noisy celebration.

shiv·er[1] (shiv′ər) *v* tremble as a result of being cold, frightened, or excited: *He crept shivering into bed.*
n a brief trembling movement. <Old English *ceafl*> **shiv′er·er** *n.* **shiv′er·ing·ly** *adv.* **shiv′er·y** *adj.*

SYNONYMS

Shiver is used mainly when talking of people or animals, suggesting continuous trembling: *The horses shivered when the cold wind blew across the field.*

Shudder suggests a single, sudden, and sharp shaking, especially from fear or disgust: *The child shuddered at the sight of the dead animal.*

shiv·er[2] (shiv′ər) *n* a fragment or splinter of something, especially glass, that has been shattered.
v break into such fragments. <Middle English>

shle·miel (shlə mēl′) SCHLEMIEL.

shlep (shlep) SCHLEP.

shlock (shlok) SCHLOCK.

shmaltz (shmolts) SCHMALTZ.

shmooze (shmūz) SCHMOOZE.

shmoz·zle (shə moz′əl) SHEMOZZLE.

shmuck (shmuk) SCHMUCK.

shnoz (shnoz) SCHNOZZ.

shnoz·zle (shnoz′əl) SCHNOZZ.

shoal[1] (shōl) *n* a place in a body of water where the water is shallow, or a sandbank or sandbar that makes the water shallow: *The ship was wrecked on the shoals.*
adj of water, shallow.
v become shallow. <Old English *sceald*> **shoal′y** *adj.*

shoal[2] (shōl) *n* a large number of fish swimming together.
v form into a shoal. <Old English *scola*>

shoat (shōt) *n* a young pig that is newly weaned.

shock[1] (shok) *n* **1** a sudden upsetting or surprising event or experience: *Having to switch schools was a great shock to him.* **2** a sudden, violent, shaking movement caused by an impact, explosion, or earth tremor: *The two trains collided with a terrible shock.* **3** a medical condition that can occur after a severe injury or emotional upset, involving a sudden drop in blood pressure, cold pallid skin, irregular breathing, and a rapid pulse: *The operation was successful, but the patient suffered from shock.* **4** a shock absorber.
v **1** cause to feel surprise, horror, or disgust: *His bad language shocked everyone.* **2** affect with shock as a medical condition. <French *choquer* strike against> **shock′a·bil′i·ty** *n.* **shock′able** *adj.*

shock[2] (shok) *n* a thick, bushy mass of hair. <origin uncertain>

shock absorber *n* a device used, especially on motor vehicles, to absorb or lessen jolts or vibrations.

shock·er (shok′ər) *n* **1** a startling, highly unpleasant experience, thing, or person. **2** a sensational story, play, or movie that is intended to shock people.

shock·ing (shok′ing) *adj* causing intense and painful surprise or dismay: *shocking news.* **shock′ing·ly** *adv.*

shock jock *Informal n* a radio disc jockey or show host whose main appeal is **shock talk**, talk that is intentionally offensive or controversial.

shock·proof (shok′prūf′) *adj* able to withstand sudden severe impact: *a shockproof watch.*

shock treatment *n* electroconvulsive therapy. Also called **shock therapy**.

shock wave *n* **1** a sharp change of pressure within a medium, especially air, caused by an explosion, such as from an earthquake, or from an object moving faster than the speed of sound. **2** a dramatic effect caused by some violent or sudden event: *Her death sent shock waves through the community.*

shod (shod) past tense and past participle of SHOE.

shod·dy (shod′ē) *adj* **shod·di·er, shod·di·est 1** badly made or done: *a shoddy necklace, shoddy workmanship.* **2** unethical or dishonest: *shoddy treatment, shoddy practices.*
n, pl **shod·dies** inferior yarn or fabric made from the shredded fibres of waste woollen cloth or clippings. <origin uncertain> **shod′di·ly** *adv.* **shod′di·ness** *n.*

shoe (shū) *n, pl* **shoes 1** an outer covering, usually of leather, for a foot. Shoes usually do not extend above the ankle. **2** a horseshoe. **3** the part of a brake that presses on a wheel.
v **shod, shoe·ing 1** fit a horse with a shoe or shoes: *The blacksmith shod the pony.* **2** fit with or be wearing shoes of a certain kind: *to be shod in sneakers.* <Old English *scoh*> **shoe′less** *adj.*
fill another's shoes, take another person's place.
if the shoe fits, wear it, if the statement applies to your case, bear it in mind.
in another's shoes, in another's place, situation, or circumstances: *I wouldn't like to be in your shoes right now.*
the shoe is on the other foot, the situation is reversed.
wait for the other shoe to drop, expect a certain thing to happen next.

shoe·box (shū′boks′) *n* a cardboard container with a lid, meant to hold one pair of footwear.

shoe·horn (shū′hȯrn′) *n* a curved piece of plastic or metal inserted at the heel of a shoe to make it slip on easily.
v force into too small a space: *All of us were shoehorned into a minivan.*

a bat	e bed	i bid	o pot	u cup	th **thin**
ā cake	ē me	ī bite	ō go	ū rude	ᴛʜ **then**
ȧ bar	ə about	ər over	ȯ for	u̇ put	zh measure

shoe·lace (shū′lās′) *n* a cord, braid, or leather strip for fastening a shoe.

shoe·mak·er (shū′mā′kər) *n* a person who makes or repairs shoes.

shoe·shine (shū′shīn′) *n* an act of shining or polishing of shoes, or the polished look of shined shoes.

shoe·string (shū′string′) *n* **1** a shoelace. **2** *Informal* a small or inadequate budget: *He ran the office on a shoestring.*

shoe·tree (shū′tree) *n* a block with a shaped front for keeping a shoe in shape when it is not being worn.

sho·gun (shō′gən) *n* the hereditary commander-in-chief of the Japanese army in feudal times. <Japanese, from Mandarin *jiang jun* general>

shone (shon) a past tense and a past participle of SHINE.

shoo (shū) *interj* used to scare away a person or animal.
v **shooed, shoo·ing** make a person or animal go away by saying "shoo!" at the same time as waving the arms or making discouraging movements: *Shoo those flies away from the sugar.*

shoo·fly pie (shū′flī′) *n* a one-crust pie with a filling of molasses and brown sugar. <*shoo* + *fly*, because the sweetness attracts flies>

shoo–in (shū′in′) *Informal n* a person who or thing that is certain to succeed, especially in a competition.

shook (shůk) past tense of SHAKE.

shoot (shūt) *v* **shot, shoot·ing 1 a** hit, wound, or kill with a bullet or arrow, or use a weapon in this way: *to shoot a rabbit. This rifle shoots straight.* **b** forcefully propel something: *He shot question after question at us.* **2** move suddenly and swiftly: *Flames shot out from the burning house. Pain shot up her arm. We shot several rapids.* **3** send out buds or shoots: *The corn was shooting up in the warm weather.* **4** record a picture with a movie, video, or photographic camera: *to shoot a home movie.* **5** *Sports* kick, hit, or throw a ball or puck in an attempt to score.
n **1** a young branch or sucker springing from the main part of a tree or other plant: *The rosebush was putting out new shoots.* **2** an occasion when professionals take photographs or make a movie or video: *a photo shoot, a fashion shoot.* **3** an occasion when a group of people hunt and shoot game for sport: *a pigeon shoot.* <Old English *sceotan*>
shoot at (or **for**)**,** aim at or aspire to.
shoot down, a reject or criticize harshly: *He made some suggestions, but they were all shot down.* **b** kill or bring down by shooting.
shoot (**straight**) **from the hip,** *Informal* **a** speak frankly. **b** speak without much forethought.
shoot off your mouth, *Informal* speak arrogantly, rudely, or without thinking.
shoot yourself in the foot, act without realizing that your action is against your own interests: *Can't he see that by neglecting his work he's only shooting himself in the foot?*
shoot up, a grow quickly, such as a plant, building, or young person. **b** inject with an illegal narcotic drug.

shoot·er (shūt′ər) *n* **1 a** a person who fires a rifle, etc. **b** *Slang* a firearm. **2** *Sports* a player who aims or takes a shot at the goal, basket, net, etc. **3** a small drink of alcohol.

shoot·ing (shū′ting) *n* **1** the practice or sport of shooting firearms. **2** an instance of wounding or killing by shooting firearms: *There's been a shooting, and a man has been badly injured.*
adj **1** to do with shooting firearms: *a shooting accident.* **2** of pain, sharp, sudden, and swift-moving: *a shooting pain in my arm.*

shooting gallery *n* a long room or deep booth fitted with targets for practice in shooting.

shooting star *n* a small, rapidly moving meteor that burns up on entering the earth's atmosphere.

shoot·out (shūt′out′) *n* **1** a gun battle that ends in the death or defeat of one party. **2** *Soccer* a tiebreaker in a game in which each side takes a specified number of penalty shots.

shop (shop) *n* **1** a building or part of a building where goods or services are sold. **2** a place where things are made or repaired: *a carpenter's shop.*
v **shopped, shop·ping** go to a store or stores to look at or to buy things: *She shopped all morning for a coat.* <Old French *eschoppe*>
set up shop, start work or business.
shop around, compare the price, quality, or selection of an item.
shut up shop, give up work or business.
talk shop, talk about one's work or occupation.

shop·keep·er (shop′kē′pər) *n* a person who carries on business in a shop or store.

shop·lift·ing (shop′lif′ting) *n* the act of stealing goods from a store while pretending to be a customer.
shop′lift *v.* **shop′lift·er** *n.*

shop·per (shop′ər) *n* a person who visits stores to look at or buy things.

shop·ping (shop′ing) *n* the action of buying of goods from stores: *Our family likes to do the shopping together.*

shopping centre MALL.

shop steward *n* a union worker elected by fellow workers to represent them in dealings with management.

shop·talk (shop′tok′) *n* the language of a business, occupation, or profession, especially on informal or social occasions.

GRAMMAR AND USAGE

Shoptalk is similar in meaning to *jargon*, but is less formal. It is appropriate to use shoptalk when speaking or writing informally for and about people in a particular line of work. It should be avoided, however, in more formal speaking and writing.

shop·worn (shop′wôrn′) *adj* soiled by being displayed or handled in a store.

shore[1] (shôr) *n* **1** the land at the edge of a large body of water. **2** *Law* the land between high-water and low-water marks. **3 shores** *pl* a country or other geographic area, usually bounded by a coast: *foreign shores.* <German *schore*>
in shore, in or on the water, near to the shore or nearer to the shore.
off shore, in or on the water, not far from the shore.

shore[2] (shôr) *n* a prop or beam placed against or beneath something to support it.
v **shored, shor·ing** prop up or support with such props or beams: *They shored up the shaky ceiling.* <Middle English *schorien*>

shore·bird (shôr′bərd′) *n* a bird that spends much of its time on the shores of oceans and other large bodies of water. Sandpipers are shorebirds.

shore ice *n* sea ice that is anchored to the shore and extends out into the sea like a huge shelf.

shore leave *n* leisure time spent ashore by sailors.

shore·line (shôr′līn′) *n* the line where shore and water meet.

shore·ward (shôr′wərd) *adv, adj* toward the shore. Also **shorewards**.

shorn (shôrn) a past participle of SHEAR.

short (shôrt) *adj* **1** not long in length or time; of small extent from end to end, or taking a small amount of time: *a short distance, a short talk.* **2** relatively small in extent: *a short essay, a short book.* **3** short with regard to quality and length in a vowel. Example: The *i* in *shin* is short; the *i* in *shine* is long. **4** highly probable in odds or a chance: *Many people backed the champion at short odds.* **5** crumbly as pastry because of a high proportion of fat to flour: *short crust.*
adv to do with the near side of a particular point: *The horse stopped short in front of the fence. She stopped short of actual crime.*
n **1** a short thing, especially a short film as distinguished from a feature film. **2** a short-circuit.
v short-circuit. <Old English *sceort*> **short′ness** *n.*
bring up short, make someone pause abruptly.
cut short, end suddenly.
fall short, a fail to reach. **b** be insufficient.
for short, to make shorter: *in my humble opinion or IMHO, for short.*
in short, briefly.
make short work of, deal with quickly.
run short, not have or be enough: *I ran short of time to finish my report.*
sell short, a fail to give what is due: *By working so many hours, he is selling his family short.* **b** represent as less good than it, he, or she really is: *Don't sell yourself short; you're quite capable of passing all your subjects.*
short and sweet, pleasant and brief.
short end of the stick, unfair treatment.
short of, a less than: *Nothing short of your best work will satisfy me.* **b** not reaching as far as: *His throw was short of the mark.*

short·age (shôr′tij) *n* a situation in which something needed cannot be obtained in large enough amounts: *There is a shortage of grain because of poor crops.*

short·bread (shôrt′bred′) *n* a rich, crisp type of cookie that crumbles easily.

short·cake (shôrt′kāk′) *n* a cake made of rich biscuit dough, covered or filled with berries or other fruit.

short·change (shôrt′chānj′) *v* **short·changed, short·chang·ing** deliberately give less than the correct change to or treat unfairly by withholding something of value.

short–cir·cuit (shôrt′sər′kət) *n* an electrical circuit, usually formed accidentally by the contact of components, that bypasses the main circuit: *A short circuit was the cause of the house fire.* **short-cir′cuit** *v.*

short·com·ing (shôrt′kum′ing) *n* a fault or failure to meet a certain standard, especially in a person's character, a plan, or a system: *She said his rudeness was a serious shortcoming.*

short·cut (shôrt′kut′) *n* **1** a quicker or less distant route: *We took a shortcut through the field.* **2** a way of doing or achieving something that is simpler or quicker than the standard one: *He knew some good cooking shortcuts.*
v **short·cut, short·cut·ting** use or take a shortcut.

short·en (shôr′tən) *v* make or become shorter: *The new highway shortens the trip.*

SYNONYMS

Shorten is a general word meaning "reduce the extent of": *Is there any way we can shorten the hike?*

Abbreviate implies omitting what is non-essential: *She gave an abbreviated speech because time was running short.*

Curtail is a more formal word meaning "cut short": *The climbers curtailed their efforts to reach the top.*

short·en·ing (shôr′tə ning) *n* butter, lard, or vegetable fat used in making pastry.

short·fall (shôrt′fol′) *n* an amount lacking in an attempt to meet a need or reach a goal: *The chair of the fundraising campaign has predicted a large shortfall.*

short fuse *Informal n* a quick temper.

short·hair (shôrt′hār) *n* a domestic cat with short hair.

short·hand (shôrt′hand′) *n* **1** a method of rapid writing that uses symbols or a combination of letters and symbols to represent sounds, or writing done in such symbols. **2** a short and simple way of expressing or referring to something: *"Blue collar" is shorthand for "manual workers and their attitudes."*

short–hand·ed (shôrt′han′did) *adj* **1** not having enough workers or helpers. **2** *Sports* playing without the services of one or more players as a result of penalties.

short·horn (shôrt′hôrn′) *n* a member of a breed of beef cattle with short horns, or the breed itself.

short·ie (shôr′tē) *Informal n* a piece of clothing shorter than usual: *My new raincoat is a shortie.*

short·ish (shôr′tish) *adj* rather short.

short list *n* a narrowed-down list from which a final choice is made. **short′list** *v.*

short–lived (shôr′tlivd′) *adj* living or lasting only a short time.

short·ly (shôr′tlē) *adv* **1** soon: *I will be with you shortly.* **2** in a few words. **3** abruptly, sharply, or curtly.

a bat	e bed	i bid	o pot	u cup	th thin
ā cake	ē me	ī bite	ō go	ū rude	TH then
ȧ bar	ə about	ər over	ȯ for	u̇ put	zh measure

hockey shots

slapshot

The slapshot is the most powerful—but least accurate—shot in hockey. The player swings the stick back and then slaps the puck toward the goal.

backhand shot

The backhand shot is the most difficult to execute because of the curve of the stick blade. For this reason, it is also the least powerful shot.

wrist shot

The wrist shot is much more accurate, but a little less powerful than the slapshot. It is very effective right in front of the goal.

snap shot

To execute a snap shot, the player pushes the puck forward, and then increases the pressure on the puck to pass the puck to another player or to shoot at the goal.

short notice *n* very little warning in advance: *I know it's short notice, but I'd like you to be at my birthday party tomorrow.*

short order *n* a menu item that can be prepared and served quickly in a place that sells food. **short′-or′der** *adj.*

short–range (shòr′trānj′) *adj* not extending far or not over a long period of time: *short-range missile, short-range plans.*

shorts (shòrts) *pln* short, loose-fitting pants that reach no lower than the knees: *In hot weather he wore shorts.* **2** short underpants worn by men or boys.

short shrift *n* rapid, curt, or unsympathetic treatment.

short–sight·ed (shòrt′sī′tid) *adj* **1** unable to see things clearly unless they are relatively close to the eyes. **2** lacking in foresight or imagination: *a short-sighted plan.* **short sight** *n.* **short′-sight′ed·ly** *adv.* **short′-sight′ed·ness** *n.*

short–staffed (shòrt′staft′) *adj* with too few workers.

short·stop (shòrt′stop′) *n* a baseball player positioned between second base and third base.

short story *n* a prose story with a developed theme but much shorter and simpler than a full-length novel.

short–tem·pered (shòrt′tem′pərd) a tendency to lose one's temper quickly.

short–term (shòrt′tərm′) *adj* lasting or intended for a short period of time: *a short-term loan.*

short–term memory *n* memory for very recent events. Compare LONG-TERM MEMORY.

short ton TON (def. 2a).

short–waist·ed (shòr′twā′stid) *adj* short from neck to waistline.

short·wave (shòr′twāv′) *n* a radio wave with a wavelength under 100 metres and a frequency between 3 and 30 megahertz.

shot[1] (shot) *n, pl* **shots** or (for def. 2a) **shot** **1 a** the discharge of a gun or cannon, or an attempt to hit a target by shooting: *She heard two shots.* **b** something resembling this, such the act of forcefully hitting an object, a forceful attempt at something, or a harsh or critical remark: *The right winger had an extremely hard shot. He took a good shot at the job. "Leave me alone!" was his parting shot.* **2 a** small pellets of lead or steel that make up the charge of a shotgun cartridge. **b** a heavy metal or stone ball used as a missile shot from a cannon or large gun. **c** a metal ball thrown in the athletic event of shot put. **3** a person who shoots: *My sister is a good shot.* **4** *Informal* an injection of a vaccine or drug: *a flu shot.* **5** a single picture taken with a camera. **6** *Informal* a small alcoholic drink: *a shot of whisky.* **7** *Informal* an amount due or to be paid: *Mother paid the shot at the restaurant.* <Old English *sceot*>
call the shots, *Informal* be in a position of control.
like a shot, very quickly or eagerly.
not by a long shot, not at all.
shot in the arm, something that renews interest, energy, or strength: *That new factory was a shot in the arm for the local economy.*
shot in the dark, a wild guess.

shot[2] (shot) *v* past tense and past participle of SHOOT.
adj **1** woven as cloth so as to show a play of colours: *The scarf was blue silk shot with gold.* **2** *Informal* ruined or worn out: *My nerves are shot.* <*shot*[1]>
shot through with, full of a particular colour or feature.

shot·gun (shot′gun′) *n* a large firearm that fires cartridges filled with SHOT (def. 2a).

shot put (pu̇t) *n* a contest in which a person throws a heavy metal ball as far as possible. See TRACK AND FIELD for picture.

shot rock *Curling n* the stone nearest to the centre of the target.

should (shu̇d) *v* **1** stating that one ought to do something: *Everyone should learn to swim.* **2** suggesting that the speaker is uncertain about a thing or unwilling to believe something: *I don't see why you should think that. It's strange that they should be so late.* **3** expressing a possible action in the future. Example: The statement *I will be there in an hour* is a promise; *I should be there in an hour* means that the speaker is not sure and therefore is not willing to promise. **4** expressing a belief: *She should be there by now.* **5** past tense of SHALL. <Old English *sceolde*>

shoul·der (shōl′dər) *n* **1** the part of the body to which an arm of a human being, a foreleg of an animal, or a wing of a bird is attached, or the part of a garment covering this in a human being. **2** a part of something resembling this in shape, position, or function: *the shoulder of a hill, the shoulder of a road.* **3** **shoulders** *pl* the two shoulders and the upper part of the back, imagined as bearing responsibility or hardship or providing strength: *She has a big load on her shoulders.*
v **1** take upon or support with the shoulder or shoulders: *to shoulder a tray.* **2** take on a burden or responsibility: *They shouldered the task between them.* **3** push with the shoulders: *He shouldered his way through the crowd.* <Old English *sculdor*>
cry on someone's shoulder, pour out one's problems to someone in hopes of gaining sympathy.
put your shoulder to the wheel, make a great effort.
shoulder arms, hold a rifle almost upright with the barrel resting in the hollow of the shoulder and the butt in the hand.
shoulder to shoulder, side by side, especially as a united effort.
straight from the shoulder, frankly or directly.
turn (or **give**) **a cold shoulder to,** shun or show dislike for.

shoulder blade *n* one of two flat triangular bones in the upper back behind either shoulder.

should·n't (shu̇d′ənt) *contraction* should not.

should·'ve (shu̇d′əv) *contraction* should have: *You should've been there.*

shout (shout) *v* **1** call or cry loudly and vigorously, especially as the result of a strong emotion: *Somebody shouted "Fire!"* **2** talk or laugh very loudly. **3** express by a shout or shouts: *The officer shouted his commands.*
n a loud, vigorous call or cry: *Shouts of joy rang through the halls.* <Middle English> **shout′er** *n.*
shout someone down, silence a person by very loud talk.

shove (shuv) *v* **shoved, shov·ing** **1** push someone or something roughly, or make one's way by doing this: *People shoved to get on the crowded bus.* **2** put something somewhere carelessly or roughly: *Shove your coat over there.*
n a strong push: *She gave the boat a shove that sent it far out into the water.* <Old English *scufan*> **shov′er** *n.*

shov·el (shuv′əl) *n* **1** a tool with a long handle and a broad, concave blade, used to lift and throw loose material: *a snow shovel.* **2** a machine or part of a machine with a similar use. **3** an amount of something carried or moved with a shovel.
v **shov·elled** or **shov·eled, shov·el·ling** or **shov·el·ing** **1** lift, throw, work, or make with a shovel: *They shovelled a path through the snow.* **2** put or push something, especially food, somewhere quickly and in large amounts: *The man greedily shovelled pasta into his mouth.* <Old English *scofl*>

shov·el·ful (shuv′əl fu̇l′) *n, pl* **shov·el·fuls** the amount that a shovel can hold.

shov·el·ler or **shov·el·er** (shuv′ə lər) *or* (shuv′lər) *n* **1** a person who or thing that shovels. **2** a freshwater duck with a broad, flat bill.

show (shō) *v* **showed, shown** or **showed, show·ing** **1** allow or cause to be seen or made known: *She showed us her new computer. Anger showed in his face.* **2** offer something to be examined or inspected: *We showed identification to the guard.* **3** display in an exhibition or competition: *The art gallery showed his latest paintings.* **4** display a quality, emotion, or characteristic: *He showed his honesty by promptly repaying the money he owed me.* **5** demonstrate or prove: *Show us how to do the problem.* **6** escort or accompany: *Show him out.*
n **1** a display of something, especially for effect: *The jewels made a fine show. He put on a show of learning in order to impress us.* **2** a public exhibition or display: *a horse show.* **3** a public entertainment, such as a stage play or movie. **4** an outward appearance or display, sometimes false, of a quality or feeling: *a show of affection.* <Old English *sceawian* look at>
for show, for effect or to attract attention: *Some houses are furnished for show, not comfort.*
get the show on the road, *Informal* get started or underway.
run the show, *Informal* be in charge.
show off, act or talk for effect or to attract attention: *He was showing off his new bike. That girl is always showing off.*
show up, a expose something or someone as being bad or faulty in some way: *We showed her up for the rude person she is.* **b** make someone or something conspicuous or clearly visible: *He is very tall and shows up in any crowd.* **c** put in an appearance: *They only showed up at the first concert and did not perform.*
steal the show, take attention away from the main participant or all other participants.

show and tell *n* a teaching method, especially for young

a bat	e bed	i bid	o pot	u cup	th thin
ā cake	ē me	ī bite	ō go	ū rude	ᴛʜ then
ȧ bar	ə about	ər over	ȯ for	u̇ put	zh measure

S

children, in which students are encouraged to bring items they have selected to class and talk about them.

show·biz (shō′biz′) *Informal n* show business.

show·boat (shō′bōt′) *n* a river steamboat on which plays are presented.

show business *n* the theatre, movies, TV, and pop music considered as a profession or industry.

show·case (shō′kās′) *n* **1** a glass case to display and protect items in stores or museums. **2** a place or occasion where something is publicly displayed or presented.
v publicly display or present something.

show·down (shō′doun′) *n* a final test or confrontation in which a dispute is settled.

show·er (shou′ər) *n* **1** a brief fall of rain, hail, snow, or sleet: *The sun came out right after the shower.* **2** a mass of small things falling or moving at the same time: *a shower of tears, a shower of sparks.* **3** a party for giving presents to a woman or couple about to be married, or on some other special occasion. **4** an enclosure or bath in which water is sprayed over the body from above in small jets, or the act of washing oneself in such a shower. **5** a large number of things happening or given to someone at the same time: *a shower of praise.*
v **1** fall as rain, snow, etc. for a short time. **2** wash oneself in a shower: *He showered after football practice.* **3** fall or be thrown in a shower: *Broken glass showered on them.* **4** send or pour down like a shower: *They showered gifts on her.* <Old English *scur*> **show′er·y** *adj.*

show·girl (shō′gərl′) *n* a young woman who sings and dances in musicals, variety acts, and similar shows.

show·ing (shō′ing) *n* **1** the action of making something seen or the fact of being shown. **2** a presentation of a TV program or a movie: *repeated showings of an old movie.* **3** an action or performance that has a specified quality: *a poor showing.*

show jump·ing (shō′jum′ping) *n* the competitive sport of riding horses over fences and other obstacles outdoors or in an arena, with penalty points for errors. See EQUESTRIAN for picture. **show′ jump′er** *n.*

show·man (shō′mən) *n, pl* **show·men** (-mən) **1** a person whose work is to produce or present shows, especially circuses, fairs, or variety shows. **2** a person skilled in presenting things in a dramatic and exciting way. **show′man·ship** *n.*

shown (shōn) a past participle of SHOW.

show–off (shō′of′) *n* someone who makes a public display of personal qualities, possessions, or accomplishments.

show–piece (shō′pēs′) *n* a thing displayed as an outstanding example of its kind.

show·piece (shō′pēs′) *n* a thing displayed as an outstanding example of its kind.

show·place (shō′plās′) *n* a place that attracts visitors because of its beauty or importance.

show·room (shō′rủm′) *n* a room used for the display of goods, especially appliances, cars, or furniture.

show·y (shō′ē) *adj* **show·i·er, show·i·est** with a striking appearance or style, such as being bright or colourful: *Peonies are showy flowers.* **show′i·ly** *adv.* **show′i·ness** *n.*

shrank (shrangk) a past tense of SHRINK.

shrap·nel (shrap′nəl) *n* fragments of metal inside a bomb, shell, or other object designed to be thrown out in an explosion: *He showed us the scars made when he was hit by shrapnel.* <H. *Shrapnel*, 19c army officer, its inventor>

shred (shred) *n* **1** a very small piece torn off, cut off, or scraped from something, such as paper, cloth, or food: *The wind tore the sail to shreds.* **2** a very small amount: *There's not a shred of evidence that he took the money.*
v **shred·ded** or **shred, shred·ding** tear or cut into shreds. <Old English *scread*>

shred·der (shred′ər) *n* a machine for destroying documents by tearing them into shreds.

shrew (shrū) *n* **1** a small, mouselike, insect-eating mammal with a long snout and brownish fur. **2** an aggressively bad-tempered or quarrelsome woman. <Middle English>

shrewd (shrūd) *adj* with a sharp, practical mind: *She is a shrewd businesswoman.* <Middle English *schrewe* rascal> **shrewd′ly** *adv.* **shrewd′ness** *n.*

SYNONYMS

Shrewd emphasizes cleverness in practical matters: *He was shrewd enough not to lend them the money.*

Astute emphasizes cleverness and insight: *Her astute comments made everything clear to them.*

Crafty often means "skilful in deceiving others": *The crafty salesperson told me that the ring was gold.*

shrew·ish (shrū′ish) *adj* aggressively bad-tempered or quarrelsome. **shrew′ish·ly** *adv.* **shrew′ish·ness** *n.*

shriek (shrēk) *v* make a high-pitched piercing sound or words, especially to express terror, pain, or excitement: *to shriek with terror, to shriek with laughter.*
n such a sound: *We heard the shriek of the engine's whistle.* <Old Norse *skrækja*>

SYNONYMS

Shriek means "make a high-pitched scream": *They all shrieked as the roller coaster plunged downward.*

Howl means "make a long, loud, mournful cry": *The coyotes howled all night and kept the campers awake.*

Bellow means "roar" or "shout loudly": *The coach bellowed at the players from the sidelines.*

shrike (shrīk) *n* a songbird with a strong, hooked beak that impales its prey of insects, lizards, and small birds on thorns. <Old English *scric* thrush (a songbird)>

shrill (shril) *adj* **1** with a high-pitched piercing voice or sound: *shrill laughter.* **2** loud and forceful: *a shrill complaint, a shrill demand.*
v make a shrill sound: *The whistle shrilled.*
n a shrill sound or cry.
adv with a shrill sound: *She sang shrill and loud.* <Middle English> **shrill′ness** *n.* **shril′ly** *adv.*

shrimp (shrimp) *n, pl* **shrimps** or (*especially collectively*) **shrimp 1** a small, long-tailed shellfish, used for food. See CRUSTACEAN for picture. **2** a person considered to be small or insignificant.
v fish for shrimps. <Middle English> **shrimp′like′** *adj.*

shrine (shrīn) *n* **1** a place, building, or object considered as holy because it is associated with divine acts or things; a sacred place of worship. **2** a place associated with, or containing things that belonged to, a person or thing considered especially respected: *The pop star's first home became a shrine.* **3** a casket containing sacred relics, or a niche or enclosure containing a religious statue or other object. <Latin *scrinium* chest for books>

shrink (shringk) *v* **shrank** or **shrunk, shrunk** or **shrunk·en, shrink·ing 1** become or make smaller in size or amount: *The layoffs shrank the workforce by half.* **2** become smaller as the result of being immersed in water: *The shirt shrank when I washed it.* **3** move back or away, especially because of fear or disgust: *The dog shrank from the strangers.*
n Slang a psychiatrist. <Old English *scrincan*>
shrink′a·ble *adj.* **shrink′er** *n.* **shrink′ing** *adj.*

shrink·age (shring′kij) *n* the process, fact, or amount of shrinking.

shrinking violet *Informal n* a very shy person.

shrink wrap *n* a thin, clear plastic film used to wrap food and merchandise. It shrinks closely around the contours of the article as it is sealed. **shrink′-wrap′** *v.* **shrink′-wrapped′** *adj.*

shriv·el (shriv′əl) *v* **shriv·elled** or **shriv·eled, shriv·el·ling** or **shriv·el·ing 1** wrinkle and become smaller or cause to wrinkle and become smaller, especially due to loss of moisture: *The hot sunshine shrivelled the grass.* **2** lose energy, will, or desire. <origin unknown>

shroud (shroud) *n* **1** a cloth or garment in which a dead person is wrapped for burial. **2** a thing that covers, conceals, or veils: *The fog was a shroud over the city.* **3** one of the ropes from a mast to the side of a ship.
v **1** wrap a body for burial. **2** cover or conceal: *The farm was shrouded in darkness.* <Old English *scrud* garment>

shrub (shrub) *n* a woody plant smaller than a tree, usually with separate stems starting from or near the ground. <Old English *scrybb* brush> **shrub′like′** *adj.*

shrub·ber·y (shrub′ə rē) *n, pl* **shrub·ber·ies** a group of shrubs close to each other.

shrug (shrug) *v* **shrugged, shrug·ging** raise the shoulders slightly and briefly to express doubt, ignorance, or indifference: *She shrugged and walked away.*
n a raising of the shoulders in this way. <Middle English>
shrug off, dismiss lightly as unimportant: *He merely shrugged off their insults.*

shrunk (shrungk) a past tense and a past participle of SHRINK.

shrunk·en (shrung′kən) a past participle of SHRINK.

shtetl (shtet′l) *or* (shtāt′l) *n* in former times, a small Jewish town or village in eastern Europe. <Yiddish = little town>

shtick (shtik) *n* an attention-getting routine, gimmick, or talent. <Yiddish, from German *Stück* piece>

shuck (shuk) *v* remove the outer covering from something, especially the husk of an ear of corn. <origin uncertain> **shuck′er** *n.*

shucks (shuks) *Informal interj* used to express surprise, regret, irritation, or a modest reply to praise: *Shucks, you didn't have to give me anything.* <origin uncertain>

shud·der (shud′ər) *v* **1** strongly tremble, especially from fear or disgust: *She shudders at the sight of a snake.* **2** shake or vibrate deeply, especially as a vehicle, machine, or building.
n an act of shuddering. <Dutch *schudderen*> **shud′der·ing** *adj.* **shud′der·ing·ly** *adv.*

shuf·fle (shuf′əl) *v* **shuf·fled, shuf·fling 1** walk by dragging one's feet or without lifting them fully from the ground: *The sick man shuffled down the hall.* **2** shift one's position while sitting or move one's feet while standing, especially because of boredom, nervousness, or embarrassment. **3** rearrange playing cards by sliding them over each other quickly. **4** move people or things around so as to occupy different positions or to be in a different order: *The prime minister decided to shuffle his cabinet. She shuffled her papers before speaking.* **5** put part of one's body into an item of clothing, especially in a clumsy way: *He shuffled his feet into a pair of slippers.*
n a shuffling movement, walk, or sound, or the act of shuffling. <Middle English *shovelen* to move with dragging feet> **shuf′fler** *n.*
get lost in the shuffle, *Informal* be overlooked or missed in a confused or crowded situation.

shuf·fle·board (shuf′əl bȯrd′) *n* a game played by pushing discs along a marked surface.

shul (shul) *n, pl* **shuln** a synagogue. <Yiddish, from German *Schule* school>

shun (shun) *v* **shunned, shun·ning** avoid, ignore, or reject someone or something: *She was lazy and shunned work.* <Old English *scunian* shrink back from fear>

shunt (shunt) *v* **1** push or pull a train or part of a train from the main line to a siding or from one line of rails to another. **2** move someone or something from one position to another, especially to a less important place or position. **3** provide an electrical current with a conductor joining two parts of a circuit, through which more or less of the current may be diverted.
n **1** an act of pushing or shoving something. **2** a conductor joining two points in an electric circuit and forming a path through which part of the current will pass. **3** an alternative path for the passage of the blood or other body fluid made during surgery. <origin uncertain>

shush (shush) *v* tell, signal, or cause to be silent: *I shushed the little kids so I could make a phone call.*
interj used to demand silence: *Shush! I'm trying to listen to the radio.*

Shu·swap (shů′swop) SECWEPEMC.

a bat	e bed	i bid	o pot	u cup	th thin
ā cake	ē me	ī bite	ō go	ū rude	ᴛʜ then
ä bar	ə about	ər over	ȯ for	ů put	zh measure

shut (shut) *v* **shut, shut·ting 1** move something, be moved, or have something moved into a position that blocks an opening: *to shut a window. The door shut behind her.* **2** close something by folding or bringing parts together: *Shut your eyes.* **3** close tightly; close securely; close doors or other openings of: *After Labour day, we shut our cottage up for the winter.* **4** prevent access to or along: *They shut the highway after the accident.* **5** enclose or confine: *The dog had to be shut in the basement when we had visitors.*
shut down, cease or cause something to cease, such as a business or activity: *Fewer orders caused the factory to shut down.*
shut in, keep from going out by closing something.
shut off, stop or cause something to stop: *Shut off the radio.*
shut out, a keep from coming in: *The curtains shut out the light.* **b** defeat a sports team without allowing it to score.
shut up, a shut the doors and windows of. **b** *Informal* stop or cause someone to stop talking. **c** keep someone or something from going outside.

shut·down (shut′doun′) *n* a closure of a factory, device, or system, especially a temporary closure due to a fault or for maintenance.

shut–eye (shut′ī′) *Informal n* sleep.

shut–in (shut′in′) *adj* confined.
n a person who is kept indoors, especially as a result of illness or physical weakness.

shut–off (shut′of′) *n* **1** a valve, switch, or other mechanism that stops the flow or movement of something. **2** the act of stopping a flow or movement: *There'll be a water shut-off tonight while they work on the sewers.*

shut·out (shut′out′) *n* the defeat of a sports team without allowing it to score.

shut·ter (shut′ər) *n* **1** a hinged, movable panel for a window that can be closed for security or to keep out the light: *When we shut up our cottage for the winter, we put shutters on all the windows.* **2** a device that opens and closes to expose the film in a camera. **3** a person who or thing that shuts.
v put a shutter or shutters on or over. <*shut*>

shut·ter·bug (shut′ər bug′) *Informal n* an enthusiastic photographer.

shut·tle (shut′əl) *n* **1** a form of transport that travels regularly between two places. **2** a device in weaving or in a sewing machine that carries one kind of thread back and forth between other threads.
v **shut·tled, shut·tling** travel regularly between two places, or transport in a shuttle. <Old English *scytel* dart>

shut·tle·cock (shut′əl kok′) *n* a cone of feathers or light plastic with a cork or similar base, used in the game of badminton.

shy[1] (shī) *adj* **shy·er** or **shi·er, shy·est** or **shi·est 1** nervous or timid in the company of other people: *He's shy and dislikes parties.* **2** reluctant as an animal or bird to remain near humans. **3** (*with* ***of*** *or* ***about***): slow or reluctant to do something: *He's not shy about telling us how smart he is.*
v **shied, shy·ing 1** start back or aside suddenly, especially as a horse: *The mare shied at the fence.* **2** (*with away*) avoid doing or becoming involved in something because of nervousness or a lack of confidence: *He shied away from making a commitment.*
n, pl **shies** a sudden start to one side. <Old English *sceoh*> **shy′ly** *adv.* **shy′ness** *n.*
fight shy of, keep away from or avoid.
shy of, *Informal* less than: *He found he was shy of the full price of the movie ticket.*

shy[2] (shī) *v* **shied, shy·ing** throw or fling something at a target: *The boy shied a stone at the tree.*
n, pl **shies** a throw or toss of something at a target. <origin uncertain>

shy·ster (shī′stər) *Informal n* a person who uses improper or fraudulent methods in a business or profession. <origin uncertain>

SI *n* in full, **International System of Units** an international system of standard measurements. See also METRIC SYSTEM. <French *S(ystème) I(nternational)*>

Si·a·mese (sī′ə mēz′) *n* a cat of a breed with pale fur, dark tips to the ears, tail, and feet, and slanting eyes. <*Siam* former name of Thailand>

Si·be·ri·a (sī′bē′rē ə) *n* a large region in northern Russia. **Si·be′ri·an** *adj.*

sib·i·lant (sib′ə lənt) *adj* hissing.
n a hissing sound. Examples: the sounds represented by *s* and *sh* are sibilants. <Latin *sibilare* hiss> **sib′i·lance** *n.* **sib′i·lant·ly** *adv.*

sib·ling (sib′ling) *n* a brother or sister. <Old English = related by blood + *-ling*>

sib·yl (sib′əl) *n* among the ancient Greeks and Romans, a woman supposed to utter the sayings of a god, especially about the future. <Old French, from Greek *Sibulla*>

sic (sik) *adv* used in brackets after a quoted word that appears odd or erroneous to show that the word is quoted just as it was used in the original. <Latin = so, thus>

GRAMMAR AND USAGE

In the following sentence, **sic** identifies an erroneous word: *Its [sic] now time to think seriously about the future.* Always use square brackets [ ] to indicate that *sic* is not part of the original statement.

sic·ca·tive (sik′ə tiv) *n* a drying agent used in making paint. <Latin *siccare* to dry>

Si·chuan (sech wan′) *or* (sesh wan′) *n* a province in China.
adj **Szechuan** or **Szechwan** (sech wan′), (sesh wan′) to do with the spicy style of cooking done in that province.

sick (sik) *adj* **1** to do with physical or mental illness. **2** feeling inclined to vomit or otherwise feel unwell: *a sick feeling.* **3** intensely annoyed with or bored by someone or something: *I'm sick of all these tests.* **4** with many serious problems: *a sick society.* **5** with death, illness, or misfortune as a subject and dealing with it in a cruel or morbid way: *a sick joke, sick humour.*
n **the sick** sick people. <Old English *seoc*>
be sick, vomit: *She bent over and was sick on the floor.*

sick bay *n* a room or building set aside for the treatment or housing of the sick, especially within a military base, ship, or school.

sick·bed (sik′bed′) *n* the bed of a sick person, or the condition of being sick.

sick building syndrome *n* illness due to poor ventilation or other environmental conditions in a building, especially a large office building.

sick·en (sik′ən) *v* **1** make someone feel disgusted or appalled: *The violent events shown on the news sickened her.* **2** become ill: *to sicken with flu.*

sick·en·ing (sik′ə ning) *adj* causing or liable to cause a feeling of nausea or disgust. **sick′en·ing·ly** *adv.*

sick·ish (sik′ish) *adj* **1** somewhat sick. **2** somewhat sickening. **sick′ish·ly** *adv.* **sick′ish·ness** *n.*

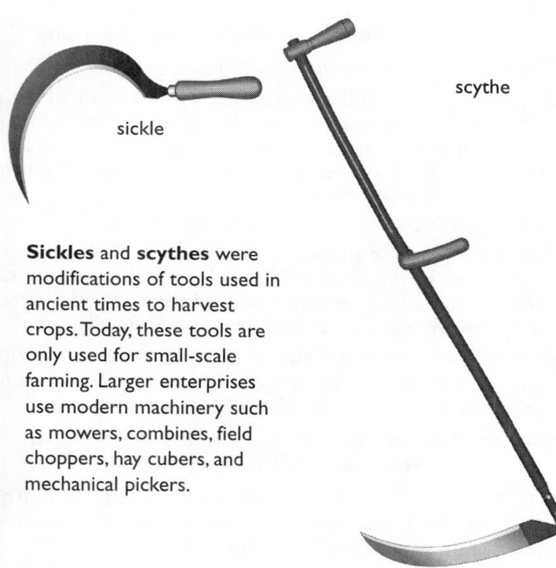

Sickles and **scythes** were modifications of tools used in ancient times to harvest crops. Today, these tools are only used for small-scale farming. Larger enterprises use modern machinery such as mowers, combines, field choppers, hay cubers, and mechanical pickers.

sick·le (sik′əl) *n* a tool consisting of a short, curved blade on a short handle, used for cutting, lopping, or trimming plants or crops.
v mow or cut with a sickle. <Latin *secare* to cut>

sick leave *n* paid time off from work, allowed for sickness or injury.

sick·le–cell anemia (sik′əl sel′) *n* a severe hereditary form of anemia in which defective hemoglobin causes numbers of red blood cells to take on a crescent shape.

sick·ly (sik′lē) *adj* **sick·li·er, sick·li·est 1** often ill. **2** to do with sickness or weakness: *Her skin is a sickly yellow. That place has a sickly climate.* **3** so unpleasant as a flavour, smell, or colour that it creates discomfort or nausea: *a sickly yellow.* **sick′li·ness** *n.*

sick·ness (sik′nis) *n* **1** the condition or fact of being ill. **2** the feeling or fact of being affected with nausea or vomiting.

sick pay *n* wages paid to an employee on sick leave.

sick·room *n* a room in a school or workplace occupied or set aside for people who are unwell.

side (sīd) *n* **1** a position to the left or right of an object, place, or central point: *the other side of town.* **2** an upright or sloping surface of a structure or object that is not the top or bottom and generally not the front or back: *She crashed into the side of my car.* **3** either of the two surfaces of something flat and thin: *Write on one side of the paper.* **4** a part near the edge and away from the middle of something: *the side of the road.* **5** either the right or the left part of the body of a person or an animal: *a pain in my side.* **6** a person or group opposing another or others in a dispute, contest, or debate: *Which side are you on?* **7** an aspect or view of someone or something: *Always look on the bright side.* **8** a part of a family or line of descent: *The man is English on his mother's side.*
adj **1** to do with one side: *a side view.* **2** less important: *a side issue.*
v **sid·ed, sid·ing** (*with* ***with*** *or* ***against***) support or oppose in a conflict, dispute, or debate. <Old English>
by your side, near one.
on the side, *Informal* in addition to ordinary duties or to a relationship.
side by side, beside one another.
split your sides, laugh very hard.
take sides, place oneself with one person or group against another.

side arm *n* a weapon such as a knife or a gun, carried at the side or in a belt.

side·arm (sīd′arm′) *adj, adv* thrown, pitched, or cast with a sweeping motion of the arm from the side of the body at or below shoulder level.
v throw a pitch or ball with this motion.

side·bar (sīd′bȧr′) *n* **1** a brief text printed next to a main article, expanding on some aspect of it, quoting from it, or dealing with a related topic. **2** a less important but related matter, comment, or piece of information.

side·board (sīd′bȯrd′) *n* a flat-topped piece of furniture with cupboards and drawers, used for storing dishes, glasses, and table linen.

side·burns (sīd′bərnz′) *pln* hair growing down the face in front of the ears, especially when the chin is shaved.

ETYMOLOGY

Sideburns are named after Ambrose Burnside, an American general in the 1800s who wore such side whiskers. They were originally called *burnsides.*

side·car (sīd′kȧr′) *n* a small, one-wheeled car for a passenger attached to the side of a motorcycle.

side dish *n* a dish served along with the main dish of a meal or course.

side effect *n* **1** a secondary result or effect of a drug or medical treatment, especially an undesirable reaction. **2** an incidental effect, especially an unpleasant one.

a bat	e bed	i bid	o pot	u cup	th **thin**
ā cake	ē me	ī bite	ō go	ū rude	ᴛʜ **then**
ȧ bar	ə about	ər over	ȯ for	u̇ put	zh measure

S

side·kick (sīd′kik′) *Informal n* a partner, assistant, or close companion.

side·light (sī′dlīt′) *n* **1** a light placed at the side of something. **2** incidental information about a subject that helps to clarify or enliven it. **3** either of two navigation lights carried by a moving ship. **4** a narrow window or pane of glass alongside a door or larger window.

side·line (sī′dlīn′) *n* **1** an activity done in addition to one's main job, especially to earn extra income. **2** a different line of goods or services offered in addition to the main one. **3 sidelines** *pl* lines that mark the limit of play on the sides of a sports field or basketball court, or the area beyond it for non-players or spectators.
v cause a person, especially a player in a sport or contest, to be unable to take part.
on the sidelines, observing a situation, but unable or unwilling to be directly involved.

side·long (sī′dlong′) *adj, adv* directed to or from one side: *a sidelong glance.*

side·out (sī′dout′) *Volleyball n* a win of a rally by the receiving team, which then becomes the serving team.

side road *n* **1** a minor road, especially one branching from a main road. **2** ✱ **sideroad** *especially Ontario and Québec* a minor road running at right angles to a CONCESSION ROAD.

side·sad·dle (sīd′sad′əl) *n* a woman's saddle so made that both of the rider's legs are on the same side of the horse.
adj sitting in a saddle in this position.

side·show (sīd′shō′) *n* **1** a small show or display in connection with the main one at an exhibition, fair, or circus. **2** an incident or issue that is less important than the main one.

side·slip (sīd′slip′) *n* **1** a sideways skip or slip, especially in an aircraft banking steeply. **2** *Skiing, Snowboarding, etc.* a sideways slide down a slope.
v **side·slipped, side·slip·ping** slip sideways in an aircraft or on skis, etc.

side–split·ting (sīd′split′ing) *adj* extremely funny.

side·step (sīd′step′) *v* **side·step·ped, side·step·ping** **1** step aside. **2** avoid by stepping aside; evade: *sidestep a responsibility.*
n a step taken sideways. **side′step·per** *n.*

side street *n* a minor or lesser street.

side·stroke (sīd′strōk′) *n* a swimming stroke done while lying on one's side in the water, the arms moving in a way similar to the breaststroke and the legs in a scissor kick.

side·swipe (sīd′swīp′) *v* **side·swiped, side·swip·ing** hit with a sweeping blow along the side.
n **1** a sweeping blow along the side. **2** a passing critical remark about someone or something.

side·track (sīd′trak′) *v* **1** cause someone to be distracted from an immediate or important issue, or divert a project or debate away from an important issue or plan: *She refused to be sidetracked by questions on other subjects.* **2** direct a train into a branch line or siding.
n a minor path or track.

side trip *n* a short, extra trip taken off the main route during a longer journey.

side·walk (sī′dwok′) *n* a path, usually paved, for walking at the side of a street.

side·ways (sī′dwāz′) *adj, adv* **1** to, toward, or from the side: *a sideways glance.* **2** with one side facing forward: *to stand sideways.*

side·wind·er (sīd′wīnd′dər) *n* a small burrowing rattlesnake of N American desert regions that moves over loose sand by forming sideways loops.

sid·ing (sī′ding) *n* **1** a short railway track, loop, or line to which cars can be switched from a main track, either for shunting or to pick up goods. **2** the boards, shingles, or insulation forming the outside walls of a building.

si·dle (sī′dəl) *v* **si·dled, si·dling** move furtively or shyly, especially sideways: *The little boy shyly sidled up to the visitor.*
n a movement in this way. <obsolete *sideling* sidelong>

SIDS sudden infant death syndrome.

siege (sēj) *n* **1** a military or police operation in which a city, town, or structure is surrounded with the aim of compelling the surrender of those inside. **2** a long or persistent effort to overcome something: *a siege of illness.* <Old French *asiegier* besiege>
lay siege to, conduct a siege: *lay siege to a city.*

si·en·na (sē en′ə) *n* an earth containing iron that is used as a pigment in painting, yellowish brown in colour (**raw sienna**) or reddish brown (**burnt sienna**) when roasted.
adj yellowish brown or reddish brown. <*Siena,* city in Italy>

si·er·ra (sē er′ə) *n* a chain of hills or mountains with jagged peaks, especially in Spanish-speaking countries or the western US. <Spanish, from Latin *serra* saw>

Si·er·ra Le·one (lē ōn′) *n* a country on the coast of west Africa. **Si·er′ra Le·o′ne·an** *adj, n.*

si·es·ta (sē es′tə) *n* a nap or rest taken during the hottest parts of the day, at noon or in the afternoon. <Spanish, from Latin *sexta* (*hora*) sixth (hour) i.e., noon>

sieve (siv) *n* a utensil with a metal or plastic mesh that lets only liquids and small pieces pass through.
v **sieved, siev·ing** put through a sieve. <Old English *sife*>

sift (sift) *v* **1** put a fine, loose, or powdery substance through a sieve so as to remove lumps or large particles: *to sift flour.* **2** cause to flow or pass as through a sieve: *The snow sifted softly down.* **3** examine very carefully and thoroughly so as to identify what is most important or useful: *The jury sifted the evidence.* <Old English *siftan*> **sift′er** *n.*

sigh (sī) *v* **1** draw in or let out a long, deep breath because one is sad, tired, bored, or relieved. **2** make a sound resembling this: *The wind sighed in the treetops.* **3** feel a deep wish for something or someone lost or distant: *She often sighed for home and friends.*
n the act or sound of sighing: *a sigh of regret, a sigh of relief.* <Old English *sican*> **sigh′ing** *adj.* **sigh′ing·ly** *adv.*

sight (sīt) *n* **1** the power of seeing: *to lose your sight.* **2** the act or fact of seeing: *love at first sight.* **3** the area or distance within which something can be seen: *Land was in sight.* **4** a thing that is seen or can be seen: *a familiar sight.* **5 sights** *pl* things worth seeing: *to see the sights of the city.*

6 sights *pl* a device on a gun or optical instrument used in taking aim or observing.

v **1** manage to see someone or something, especially to catch an initial glimpse: *At last they sighted land.* **2** take aim or make an observation by looking through the sights of a gun or optical instrument: *The hunter sighted carefully before firing.* <Old English *gesiht*>

a sight for sore eyes, *Informal* a welcome or pleasant sight.

catch (or **get**) **sight of,** see: *I caught sight of him.*

in (or **within**) **sight of, a** where one can see or be seen by: *We live in sight of the school.* **b** within reach of: *I was in sight of the answer to my question.*

know by sight, know sufficiently to recognize when seen: *I've never met him but I know him by sight.*

lower (or **raise**) **your sights,** aim for a lesser (or higher) goal.

on sight, as soon as seen.

out of sight of, a where one cannot see or be seen by: *out of sight of land, out of sight of the neighbours.*

set your sights on, aim for or try to achieve.

sight unseen, not seen beforehand: *She refused to buy my old bike sight unseen.*

CONFUSABLES

Sight means "ability to see" or "view": *At the sight of the singer, the fans broke through the barriers.*

Site means "area of ground" or "place for an activity": *Everyone agreed that the shady end of the park would be the best site for the picnic.*

sight·ed (sī′tid) *adj* of a person, able to see.

sight·less (sī′tlis) *adj* unable to see.

sight·read (sī′trēd′) *v* play a musical instrument or sing by reading music not previously seen. **sight′read·er** *n.* **sight′read·ing** *n.*

sight·see·ing (sī′tsē′ing) *n* the activity of going around to see objects or places of interest: *a weekend of sightseeing.* **sight′see** *v.* **sight′se′er** *n.*

sig·moid (sig′moid) *adj* **1** shaped like the letter S. **2** shaped like the letter C. <Greek *sigma*>

sign (sīn) *n* **1** an object, quality, or event whose presence indicates the probable occurrence of something else: *no sign of life. The campers found signs of deer.* **2** a mark used to mean, represent, or point out something. Example: The sign for addition is **+**. **3** a motion or gesture used to mean or point out something: *His slight nod was his only sign of agreement.* **4** an inscribed board or space that provides information, a command, a warning, or an advertisement: *a stop sign.* **5** an indication of a coming event: *a sign of spring.* **6** *Astrology* one of the twelve divisions of the zodiac.

v **1** write one's name or initials in order to identify oneself: *Sign this library card.* **2** hire or accept employment by a written agreement: *to sign a new player. He signed for three years.* **3** use gestures to convey information or instructions: *By a wave of her hand, she signed to me to shut the door.* **4** communicate in sign language: *Do you know how to sign?* <Old French, from Latin *signum* mark> **sign′er** *n.*

sign away (or **over**), assign one's rights or property to someone else.

sign in, indicate by signing something that one is present: *Everyone at the office had to sign in each morning.*

sign off, a conclude a letter, broadcast, or other message. **b** conclude an activity.

sign off on, agree or give one's approval: *The union leaders signed off on the new contract.*

sign on (or **up**), **a** commit oneself to a job or undertaking: *Ten people signed on with the company last week.* **b** hire or newly employ: *The company signed up twenty new men.*

sign out, indicate by signing something that one will not be present: *The worker signed out an hour ago.*

sign over, hand over by signing one's name.

sign·age (sī′nəj′) *n* signs considered as a group, especially for advertising or for public display and information.

sig·nal (sig′nəl) *n* **1** a gesture, action, or sound that is used to convey information or instructions, especially by some means agreed upon by the people concerned: *a warning signal.* **2** an electrical impulse or radio wave transmitted or received: *a TV signal.*

v **sig·nalled** or **sig·naled, sig·nal·ling** or **sig·nal·ing** transmit information or instructions by means of a gesture, action, or sound: *He signalled the class to be quiet by raising his hand. A bell signalled the end of the school day.*

adj **1** used as a signal or in signalling: *a signal flag.* **2** remarkable, striking, or notable: *a signal invention.* <Old French, from Latin *signum* mark> **sig′nal·ler** *n.* **sig′nal·ly** *adv.*

sig·nal·ize (sig′nə līz′) *v* **sig·nal·ized, sig·nal·iz·ing** mark or indicate something, especially in a conspicuous way: *to signalize a change.*

sig·nal·man (sig′nəl mən) *or* (sig′nəl man′) *n, pl* **sig·nal·men** (-mən) *or* (-men′) **1** a railway worker who operates signals. **2** a person who sends and receives military signals.

sig·na·to·ry (sig′nə tò′rē) *n, pl* **sig·na·to·ries** a signer of an agreement, especially a country that has signed a treaty.

sig·na·ture (sig′nə chər) *n* **1** a person's name given in a distinctive way as a means of identifying the writer. **2** the action of signing something. **3** a sign printed at the beginning of a staff in a piece of written music to show the key and time. **4** a sheet folded into pages, forming a section of a book. **5** a tune, song, or slogan used to identify a radio or TV program. <Latin *signare* to sign>

sign·board (sīn′bòrd′) *n* a board with a sign, notice, advertisement, or inscription on it.

sig·net (sig′nit) *n* in former times, a small seal, especially one set in a **signet ring**, used instead of (or with) a signature on an official document. <Old French, from Latin *signum* seal>

S

a bat	e bed	i bid	o pot	u cup	th **thin**
ā cake	ē me	ī bite	ō go	ū rude	ᴛʜ **then**
à bar	ə about	ər over	ò for	ů put	zh measure

sig·nif·i·cant (sig nif′ə kənt) *adj* **1** great or important enough to be noteworthy: *a significant date.* **2** with or indicating a particular meaning: *a significant look.* **3** *Statistics* to do with the extent to which a result in statistics varies from that expected to arise simply from random variation or errors in sampling. **sig·nif′i·cance** *n.* **sig·nif′i·cant·ly** *adv.*

sig·ni·fy (sig′nə fī′) *v* **sig·ni·fied, sig·ni·fy·ing 1** be a sign of or indication: *His frown signified his displeasure.* **2** be a symbol of: *The cross on the sign signified a church.* <Old French, from Latin *signum* mark + *facere* make>

sign·ing (sī′ning) *n* **1 a** the action of writing one's signature on an official document. **b** (*in compounds*) the action of writing one's autograph: *a book-signing session.* **2** the action of recruiting someone, especially to a professional sports team or record company. **3** speaking in sign language.

sign language *n* a system of communication using visual gestures and signs, as used by people whose hearing or speech is impaired.

sign·post (sīn′pōst′) *n* a sign giving information such as the direction and distance to a place.
v provide an area with a signpost or signposts.

Sikh (sēk) *n* a follower of **Sikhism**, a religion founded in the 1400s that contains elements from Hinduism and from Islam. <Hindi = disciple>

Sik·sik·a (sik′si kə) *n, pl* **Sik·sik·a 1** a member of a First Nations people living mainly in Alberta. **2** their Algonquian language.
adj to do with these people or their language. Also called **Blackfoot**.

si·lage (sī′lij) *n* green fodder for farm animals, preserved and stored in an airtight silo and used as winter feed.

si·lence (sī′ləns) *n* **1** the absence of sound. **2** the fact or condition of not speaking. **3** the avoidance or omission of mentioning something: *His silence about the hockey game was surprising.*
v **si·lenced, si·lenc·ing 1** cause to become silent: *Her angry look silenced everyone in the room.* **2** prohibit or prevent from speaking.
interj command to be silent: *Silence!* <Old French, from Latin *silere* be silent>
in silence, without saying anything: *She passed over his foolish remarks in silence.*

SYNONYMS

Silence can mean "prevent from speaking," often in a stern or abrupt manner: *His father's annoyed expression silenced him.*

Dumbfound means "cause to be speechless": *Her success in the race dumbfounded everyone.*

Quiet means "cause to become calm": *If you want to quiet the baby, why don't you take him for a walk?*

si·len·cer (sī′lən sər) *n* a device for reducing the noise caused by a mechanism, especially that of a gun or the exhaust system of a motor vehicle.

si·lent (sī′lənt) *adj* **1** not making or accompanied by any sound: *a silent house.* **2** not speaking or not speaking much: *a silent person.* **3** not said out loud: *a silent prayer, a silent letter.* **4** taking no open or active part: *a silent partner.* **5** omitting mention of something: *She was silent on the subject of her family.* **si′lent·ly** *adv.*

sil·hou·ette (sil′ū et′) *n* an outline portrait cut out of black paper or filled in with some single colour, or a dark image outlined against a lighter background.
v **sil·hou·et·ted, sil·hou·et·ting** show in outline: *The mountain was silhouetted against the sky.* <E. de *Silhouette*, 18c author and politician>
in silhouette, shown in outline, or in black against a white background.

sil·i·ca (sil′ə kə) *n* silicon dioxide, a compound salt containing silicon and oxygen that occurs in crystalline form in many rocks and as the main ingredient of sand. A highly absorbent form of silica, called **silica gel**, is used as a drying and deodorizing agent. <Latin *silex* flint> **si·li′ceous** or **si·li′cious** (sə lish′əs) *adj.*

sil·i·cate (sil′ə kit) *or* (sil′ə kāt′) *n* a compound salt of silicon, oxygen, and a metal or metals, that makes up the largest class of minerals.

sil·i·con (sil′ə kən) *n* a non-metallic, crystalline element that occurs naturally only in compounds, has semiconducting properties, and is used for making electronic circuits. *Symbol* **Si**

silicon chip *n* a microchip made of silicon.

sil·i·cone (sil′i kōn′) *n* a synthetic polymer that contains silicon and oxygen, with organic groups attached to the silicon atoms, used to make lubricants, plastics, synthetic rubber, and waterproof polishes.

Silicon Valley *Informal n* an area in the valley region southeast of San Francisco, California, where much computing and electronics industry is located. <from the silicon wafers or chips used in semiconductor devices>

sil·i·co·sis (sil′ə kō′sis) *n* a disease of the lungs caused by inhaling dust containing silica.

silk (silk) *n* **1 a** a fine fibre produced by silkworms in making cocoons and used to make thread and fabric. **b** the soft, shiny fabric made from this fibre. **2** a similar fibre produced by other insect larvae and by most spiders. **3 silks** *pl* garments made of silk or silklike material and worn by a jockey or harness race driver to identify the colours of a particular horse owner. **4** a thing that resembles silk in softness or shine: *corn silk.* <Greek *Seres* people from the Far East, from which silk first came to Europe> **silk′like′** *adj.*

silk·en (sil′kən) *adj* **1** made of silk: *silken sheets.* **2** smooth, soft, glossy, or otherwise resembling silk: *silken hair.*

silk–screen (silk′skrēn′) *n* a method of colour printing in which a screen of fine material is prepared as a stencil and the colouring matter is forced through the mesh onto the printing surface.
v produce a print by means of silk-screen.

silk·worm (sil′kwərm′) *n* the hairless, yellowish caterpillar of a large Asian moth that is bred to produce the silk used for thread and fabric.

silk·y (sil′kē) *adj* **silk·i·er, silk·i·est** 1 of or like silk: *silky fur.* 2 smooth and suave in speech or manner, especially as a way of persuading someone: *silky tones.* **silk′i·ly** *adv.* **silk′i·ness** *n.*

sill (sil) *n* 1 a shelf or slab piece of wood, stone, or metal that forms the bottom of a window, door, or other structure. 2 a mass or sheet of igneous rock that has formed between layers of other rock while molten and has solidified there. <Old English *syll*>

sil·ly (sil′ē) *adj* **sil·li·er, sil·li·est** 1 with or showing a lack of sense or reason; foolish or ridiculous; nonsensical: *The movie was just too silly to be funny. You're just being silly when you say you can swim that far.* 2 *Informal* stunned; dazed: *The blow knocked him silly. I was scared silly.*
n a foolish person. <Old English *sæl* happiness> **sil′li·ness** *n.*

SYNONYMS

Silly suggests lacking worth or importance: *The group couldn't take her silly suggestion seriously.*

Stupid strongly emphasizes a lack of intelligence or common sense: *What a stupid comment to make!*

Ridiculous means "deserving or inviting mockery": *He had a ridiculous excuse for being late.*

si·lo (sī′lō) *n, pl* **si·los** 1 an airtight tower or pit in which green fodder or grain for farm animals is stored. 2 a vertical underground shaft in which a guided missile is kept ready for launching. <Spanish, from Greek *siros* grain pit>

silt (silt) *n* fine sand, clay, or earth carried by moving water and deposited as sediment, especially in a channel or harbour: *The river mouth is being choked up with silt.*
v make or become blocked with silt. <Scandinavian> **silt′y** *adj.*

silt·stone (silt′stōn′) *n* a fine-grained sedimentary rock formed from silt that has been subjected to pressure.

Si·lur·i·an (si lū′rē ən) *or* (sī lū′rē ən) *n* the geological period lasting from about 440 million to 400 million years ago, when the first true fish and land plants appeared. See also PALEOZOIC.
adj to do with this period or the rocks formed then.

sil·van (sil′vən) SYLVAN.

sil·ver (sil′vər) *n* 1 a shiny grey-white metallic element that is used for jewellery, cutlery, coins, etc. *Symbol* **Ag** 2 eloquent: *a silver tongue.*
adj 1 to do with silver: *a silver spoon.* 2 resembling silver: *silver hair.*
v 1 cover or coat with silver or something like silver: *to silver the back of a mirror.* 2 make or become white or very light grey: *Her hair had silvered since he had last seen her.* <Old English *siolfor*>
silver lining, a good side of a sad or unfortunate situation.
the silver screen, the movie industry, or movies considered as a group.

sil·ver·back (sil′vər bak) *n* a mature male mountain gorilla with greying fur on its back.

silver birch *n* a birch tree native to Eurasia, with silvery white bark that peels off in long strips.

silver bullet *n* 1 a simple, guaranteed solution to a problem: *There is no silver bullet for pollution.* <from the old idea that silver has magical qualities, so that the bullet would work against enemies with great power>

sil·ver·fish (sil′vər fish′) *n* a small, wingless insect with silvery scales on its body and a bristly tail, often found in houses and feeding on starchy materials.

silver fox *n* a variety of N American red fox with white-tipped black fur.

silver iodide *n* a pale yellow, powdery compound that darkens on exposure to light. It is used in photography and medicine and to seed clouds in artificial rainmaking.

silver leaf *n* silver beaten into very thin sheets.

silver nitrate *n* a white crystalline salt obtained by treating silver with nitric acid, used in medicine as an antiseptic, as well as in photography and dyeing.

silver plate *n* a thin plating of silver, or the metal plates and dishes with this plating.
v **sil·ver-plate** (sil′vər plāt), **sil·ver-plat·ed, sil·ver-pla·ting** coat with silver, especially by electroplating.

sil·ver·smith (sil′vər smith′) *n* a person who makes or repairs silver objects.

silver thaw *n* a thin, glittering coat of ice encrusting trees, rocks, and other surfaces.

sil·ver·tip (sil′vər tip′) *n* a colour phase of the grizzly bear found in the Rocky Mountain region, in which the fur is dark brown with the long hairs of the back and shoulders tipped with white.

sil·ver–tongued (sil′vər tungd′) *adj* eloquent.

sil·ver·ware (sil′vər wer′) *n* objects, especially cutlery or dishes, made of or plated with silver.

silver wedding *n* the 25th anniversary of a wedding.

sil·ver·y (sil′və rē) *adj* 1 with a luster, sheen, or colour like that of silver: *silvery moonbeams, silvery hair.* 2 with a soft, clear, melodious sound: *silvery laughter.* **sil′ver·i·ness** *n.*

sil·vi·cul·ture *n* the cultivation and management of forests. <French, from Latin *silva* forest + *culture*> **sil′vi·cul′tur·al** *adj.* **sil′vi·cul′tur·ist** *n.*

sim·i·an (sim′ē ən) *adj* to do with apes or monkeys.
n an ape or monkey. <Latin, from Greek *simos* flat-nosed>

sim·i·lar (sim′ə lər) *adj* 1 much the same in appearance, character, or quality: *Your desk is similar to mine.* 2 with the same shape as a geometrical figure but not necessarily the same size: *similar triangles.* <French, from Latin *similes* like> **sim′i·lar·ly** *adv.*

sim·i·lar·i·ty (sim′ə lar′ə tē) *or* (sim′ə ler′ə tē) *n, pl* **sim·i·lar·i·ties** the condition or fact of being similar.

sim·i·le (sim′ə lē) *n* a figure of speech that compares two different things or ideas, usually by means of *like* or *as.* Examples: *a face like marble, a girl as brave as a lioness.* Compare METAPHOR. <Latin = like>

a bat	e bed	i bid	o pot	u cup	th **thin**
ā cake	ē me	ī bite	ō go	ū rude	TH **then**
ä bar	ə about	ər over	ô for	ù put	zh measu

S

sim·mer (sim′ər) *v* **1** stay or keep just below the boiling point as food or water and gently bubble: *The stew should be simmered for two hours.* **2** be in a state of suppressed anger or excitement: *She simmered with indignation, but said nothing.*
n a condition or temperature of just below the boiling point: *Keep the sauce at a simmer.* <origin uncertain>
simmer down, calm or quiet down: *She told the excited child to simmer down.*

si·mon–pure (sī′mən pyůr′) *Informal adj* completely genuine or authentic.

si·mo·ny (sī′mə nē) *or* (sim′ə nē) *n* in former times, the buying or selling of ecclesiastical privileges, such as pardons or positions.

si·moom (sə mūm′) *n* a hot, dry, dust-laden wind of deserts, especially in the Arabian peninsula.

sim·per (sim′pər) *v* smile or gesture in an affected, coy, or flirtatious way.
n a smile or gesture made in this way. <origin uncertain>

sim·ple (sim′pəl) *adj* **sim·pler, sim·plest 1** easy to do or understand: *a simple problem, simple language.* **2** composed of a single element, not divided or compound: *a simple leaf.* **3** with nothing added: *My story is the simple truth.* **4** common or ordinary: *a simple citizen.* <Old French, from Latin *simplus*> **sim′ple·ness** *n.*

simple fraction COMMON FRACTION.

sim·ple–heart·ed (sim′pəl hȧr′tid) *adj* with or showing a simple, unaffected, sincere nature.

simple interest *n* interest paid only on the principal of a loan. Compare COMPOUND INTEREST.

simple machine *n* an elementary device on which another machine is based. The lever, wedge, pulley, wheel and axle, inclined plane, and screw are the six simple machines.

sim·ple–mind·ed (sim′pəl mīn′did) *adj* with little intelligence or judgment.

simple sentence *Grammar n* a sentence made up of one main clause. Examples: *The whistle blew. We got back yesterday.*

simplest terms fraction LOWEST TERMS FRACTION.

sim·ple·ton (sim′pəl tən) *n* a silly or foolish person.

sim·plic·i·ty (sim plis′ə tē) *n, pl* **sim·plic·i·ties 1** the quality or condition of being easy to understand or do: *They appreciated the simplicity of the directions he had given them.* **2** the quality or condition of being plain or natural: *simplicity of design.* **3** a thing that is plain, natural, or easy to understand: *She enjoyed the simplicities of rural life.* <Old French, from Latin *simplex* single>

sim·pli·fy (sim′plə fī′) *v* **sim·pli·fied, sim·pli·fy·ing** make something simpler or easier to do or understand: *to simplify a design.* <French, from Latin *simplus* simple + *facere* to make> **sim′pli·fi·ca′tion** *n.* **sim′pli·fi′er** *n.*

sim·plis·tic (sim plis′tik) *adj* treating complex issues and
ns as if they were much simpler than they really
simplistic interpretation, a simplistic solution.
′ti·cal·ly *adv.*

im′plē) *adv* **1** in a simple, straightforward, or
ner: *to dress simply. She explained the procedure simply and clearly.* **2** merely, just, or only: *The baby did not simply cry; she yelled. He thinks of his car as simply a means of transportation.* **3** absolutely or completely: *simply perfect.*

sim·u·la·crum (sim′yə lā′krəm) *n, pl* **sim·u·la·crums** or **sim·u·la·cra** (sim′yə lā′krə) an imitation or representation of someone or something, especially an unsatisfactory imitation or substitute: *The dictator permitted only a simulacrum of democracy.*

sim·u·late (sim′yə lāt′) *v* **sim·u·lat·ed, sim·u·lat·ing 1** imitate the appearance or character of: *Certain insects simulate leaves.* **2** pretend to have or feel an emotion: *She simulated interest to please her friend.* **3** create a representation or model of something, often using computer software: *Our group made a computer model to simulate the process of continental drift.* <Latin *similis* like> **sim′u·la′ted** *adj.* **sim′u·la′tive** *adj.* **sim′u·la′tion** *n.* **sim′u·la′tor** *n.*

sim·ul·cast (sim′əl kast′) *or* (sī′məl kast′) *v* **sim·ul·cast** or **sim·ul·cast·ed, sim·ul·cast·ing** broadcast a program over radio and TV at the same time, or on two or more channels.
n a broadcast made in this way. <*simul*(*taneous*) + (*broad*)*cast*>

sim·ul·ta·ne·ous (sim′əl tā′nē əs) *or* (sī′məl tā′nē əs) *adj* existing, done, or happening at the same time: *We all cheered in a simultaneous expression of joy.* <Latin *simul* at the same time> **si′mul·tan·e′i·ty** (sim′əl tə nē′i tē) or (sīm′əl tə nē′i tē) *n.* **si′mul·ta′ne·ous·ly** *adv.*

sin (sin) *n* **1** an act that is considered immoral and an offence because it deliberately violates a divine law. **2** an act regarded as a serious or regrettable fault, offence, or omission: *She said it was a sin to waste food.* **sin′ner** *n.*
v **sinned, sin·ning** commit a sin. <Old English *synn*>

🍁 **SIN** (sin) Social Insurance Number.

sin bin *Hockey, Slang n* penalty box.

since (sins) *prep, conj, adv* **1** from, in, or at a past time until now: *The package has been ready since noon. He has written home only once since he left us. She got sick last Saturday and has been in bed ever since.* **2** because: *Since you feel tired, you should rest.*
adv before now or ago: *I heard that old joke long since.* <Old English *siththan*>

GRAMMAR AND USAGE

Avoid using *ago* with **since**. Say *It's been a long time since they've seen each other*, rather than *It's been a long time ago since they've seen each other.*

If you want to include *ago*, revise the sentence: *They last saw each other a long time ago.*

sin·cere (sin sēr′) *adj* **sin·cer·er, sin·cer·est** free from pretence or deceit and genuine in feeling: *sincere sympathy, a sincere person.* <Latin *sincerus* pure> **sin·cere′ly** *adv.* **sin·cer′i·ty** (sin ser′ə tē) *n.*

si·ne·cure (sī′nə kyůr′) *n* a job or position requiring little or no work but giving the holder status or a financial benefit. <Latin *sine cura* without care>

sin·e qua non (sin′ē kwȧ′nōn′) *or* (sī′nē kwā′non′) *n* an essential or indispensable condition or thing: *It was a* sine qua non *that all parties concerned should be included in the negotiations.* <Latin = without which not>

sin·ew (sin′yū) *n* a tough, strong band or cord that joins muscle to bone, such as a tendon or ligament. <Old English *sionu*>

sin·ew·y (sin′yū ē) *adj* **1** with strong or many sinews: *sinewy arms, sinewy beef.* **2** vigorous or forceful: *sinewy prose.*

sin·ful (sin′fəl) *adj* committing or characterized by sin. **sin′ful·ly** *adv.* **sin′ful·ness** *n.*

sing (sing) *v* **sang, sung, sing·ing 1** make musical sounds with the voice, especially words with a set melody: *She sings background on this CD.* **2** of birds, make characteristic whistling or twittering sounds. **3** make a high-pitched whistling or buzzing sound: *The water boiled, making the kettle sing.* **4** *Archaic or Poetic* tell or tell of in song, poetry, or praise: *The poet sang of a vanished age.* **5** *Slang* act as an informer to the police. <Old English *singan*>
sing along, sing as an accompaniment to a song or piece of music.
sing out, call loudly or shout.

> **GRAMMAR AND USAGE**
>
> **Sang** is the simple past tense of *sing*: *Can you remember who sang that song?*
>
> **Sung** is the past participle of *sing*: *We have sung that song together many times.*

sing·a·long (sing′ə long) *n* a casual gathering for group singing.

Sin·ga·pore (sing′gə pōr) *n* a country in southeast Asia. See the APPENDIX. **Sin·ga·po′re·an** *adj, n.*

singe (sinj) *v* **singed, singe·ing 1** burn a little or lightly, or be burnt in this way: *He got too close to the fire and singed his eyebrows.* **2** burn the bristles or down off the carcass of a pig or poultry to prepare it for cooking.
n a slight burn. <Old English *sengan*>

sing·er (sing′ər) *n* a person who or thing that sings, especially one who sings well or whose profession is singing: *an opera singer. Our canary is a fine singer.*

🍁 **singing house** *n* in Inuit culture, a special building where communal singing and dancing take place.

sin·gle (sing′gəl) *adj* **1** one and no more: *Please give me a single piece of paper.* **2** designed or suitable for only one person: *a single bed.* **3** separate and distinct from each other or others in a group: *They could hear every single word.* **4** not married or in a domestic relationship: *a single woman.* **5** with only one on each side: *The knights engaged in single combat.*
n **1** a single thing or person rather than part of a pair or a group. **2 a** *Baseball* a hit that allows the batter to reach first base only. **b** *Cricket* a hit for which one run is scored. **c** *Canadian football* a single point scored by kicking into or beyond the end zone. **3 singles** *pl* a game played with only one person on each side, especially in tennis or badminton. **4** an alcoholic drink containing one measure.
v **sin·gled, sin·gling 1** (*with **out***) pick from among others: *The teacher singled her out for praise.* **2** *Baseball* make a hit allowing the player to reach first base only. <Old French, from Latin *singulus* individual>

sin·gle–breast·ed (sing′gəl bres′tid) *adj* showing only one row of buttons at the front of a jacket or coat.

sin·gle–dig·it (sing′gəl dij′it) *adj* expressing a quantity or percentage between 1 and 9: *single-digit unemployment.*

single file *n* **1** a line of people or things arranged one behind another. **2** one behind the other: *We walked single file along the narrow path.*

sin·gle–hand·ed (sing′gəl han′did) *adj* **1** alone and without help from others: *It was his single-handed effort that saved the ship.* **2** using or requiring only one hand: *a single-handed sword.*
adv without help: *She built all the cupboards single-handed.* **sin′gle-hand′ed·ly** *adv.*

sin·gle–heart·ed (sing′gəl hȧr′tid) *adj* with or showing sincerity and devotion to one purpose or aim. **sin′gle-heart′ed·ly** *adv.*

sin·gle–mind·ed (sing′gəl mīn′did) *adj* with only one aim or purpose in mind: *She pursued fame in a single-minded way.* **sin′gle-mind′ed·ly** *adv.* **sin′gle-mind′ed·ness** *n.*

sin·gle·ness (sing′gəl nis) *n* the condition or quality of being single: *singleness of purpose.*

single parent *n* a parent who raises a child or children without a partner in the home.

singles bar *n* a drinking place visited mostly by unmarried men and women.

sin·gle–space (sing′gəl spās) *v* **sin·gle-spaced, sin·gle-spac·ing** write or type text on every line. Compare DOUBLE-SPACE.

sin·gly (sing′glē) *adv* **1** as a single person or thing: *She said that misfortunes never happen singly.* **2** one by one in a sequence: *Let us consider each point singly.*

sing·song (sing′song′) *n* a monotonous, repeated rising and falling rhythm.
adj with this rhythm: *a singsong recitation.*

sin·gu·lar (sing′gyə lər) *adj* **1** exceptionally good, great, or remarkable: *The lake was a sight of singular beauty.* **2** strange or peculiar: *The detectives were greatly puzzled by the singular nature of the crime.* **3** being the only one of its kind: *a singular event.* **4** *Grammar* meaning one only, as a word or form. Example: The word *girl* is singular; *girls* is plural.
n a word or form showing that only one is meant. Example: The singular of *oxen* is *ox.* <Old French, from Latin *singulus* single> **sin′gu·lar·ly** *adv.*

a bat	e bed	i bid	o pot	u cup	th **thin**
ā cake	ē me	ī bite	ō go	ū rude	ᴛʜ **then**
ȧ bar	ə about	ər over	ȯ for	ů put	zh measure

sin·gu·lar·i·ty (sing′gyə lar′ə tē) *or* (sing′gyə ler′ə tē) *n, pl* **sin·gu·lar·i·ties** **1** the condition or fact of being singular: *One of the giraffe's singularities is the length of its neck.* **2** a peculiar or odd trait: *The singularity of the stranger's appearance attracted much attention.* **3** *Mathematics, Physics* a hypothetical region in space, such as at the centre of a black hole, in which gravitational forces cause matter to be infinitely compressed and space and time to become infinitely distorted.

Sin·ha·lese (sin′hə lēz′) *n, pl* **Sin·ha·lese** **1** a member of a people originally from northern India, who make up the majority of the population of Sri Lanka. **2** the language of these people. Also, **Sinhala**.
adj to do with these people or their language.

sin·is·ter (sin′i stər) *adj* **1** showing or suggesting that something harmful or evil is happening or will happen: *a sinister look, a sinister motive.* **2** in heraldry, of or on the left-hand side of a coat of arms from the point of view of the person bearing it.

ETYMOLOGY

Sinister is from Middle English and Old French *sinistre*, meaning "unfavourable," and Latin *sinister*, meaning "on the left."

The Romans considered the left side to be unlucky.

sink (singk) *v* **sank** or **sunk, sunk, sink·ing** **1** go down or make go down below the surface of something, especially a liquid: *The boat slowly sank in the water. The submarine sank three of our ships.* **2** descend or cause to descend from a higher to a lower position: *Lack of rain sank the water level of the lake. She sank her voice to a whisper.* **3 a** *Basketball* score by putting a ball through a basket. **b** *Golf* hit the ball into a hole. **4** decrease or decline in value, amount, quality, or intensity: *Yesterday the dollar sank. His spirits sank when he heard the bad news.* **5** insert beneath a surface by digging or hollowing out: *She sank several screws into the shelf. They decided to sink a well.* **6** invest money unprofitably: *He sank thousands of dollars in a bad investment.* **7** fall in or become hollow: *The sick woman's cheeks have sunk.*
n **1** a shallow basin with a water supply and a drainpipe: *a kitchen sink.* **2** a SINKHOLE (def. 2). **3** a body or process that acts to absorb or remove energy from a system: *a heat sink.* **4** a place of vice or corruption: *the sinks of a big city.* <Old English *sincan*> **sink′a·ble** *adj.*
sink in, a be fully absorbed and understood by the mind: *That's what I keep telling him, but it doesn't seem to sink in.* **b** put money or energy into something: *They sank a lot of money in the project.*
sink into, a cause something sharp to penetrate a surface: *The dog sank his teeth into my arm.* **b** put money or energy into something.

sink·er (sing′kər) *n* a person who or thing that sinks, such a lead weight for sinking a fishing line, or a baseball pitch that drops sharply when it nears the plate.

sink·hole (singk′hōl′) *n* **1** the hole in a sink, etc. for waste to pass through. **2** a hollow or cavity in the ground, especially in limestone, through which water drains.

sinking fund *n* a fund set up by a government or company in which money is regularly set aside for the gradual repayment of a debt or replacement of a declining asset.

sin·less (sin′lis) *adj* without or free from sin. **sin′less·ly** *adv.* **sin′less·ness** *n.*

Sino– (sī′nō) *combining form* Chinese: *Sino-American.* <French, from Arabic *Sin* China>

sin·u·os·i·ty (sin′yū os′ə tē) *n, pl* **sin·u·os·i·ties** the ability to curve or bend easily or flexibly, or a bend, especially in a stream or road.

sin·u·ous (sin′yū əs) *adj* **1** with many curves or turns: *a sinuous trail.* **2** lithe and supple. <French, from Latin *sinus* curve> **sin′u·ous·ly** *adv.* **sin′u·ous·ness** *n.*

si·nus (sī′nəs) *n* **1** a cavity within a bone or tissue, especially one in the bones of the face or skull connecting with the cavities of the nose. **2** an infected channel leading from a deep-seated infection that discharges pus to the surface. **3** a rounded notch between two lobes on the margin of a leaf or petal. <Latin = curve>

si·nus·i·tis (sī′nə sī′tis) *n* the inflammation of a SINUS (def. 1) of the skull.

Siou·an (sū′ən) *n* a family of languages spoken by the Dakota and related Aboriginal peoples of central and eastern N America.
adj to do with these peoples or their languages.

Sioux (sū) DAKOTA.

sip (sip) *v* **sipped, sip·ping** drink something by taking in small amounts: *She sipped her tea.*
n a small amount of liquid taken in by the mouth: *He took a sip of his drink.* <Middle English>

si·phon (sī′fən) *n* **1** a tube through which liquid can be drawn over the edge of one container into another at a lower level by air pressure. **2** a bottle for soda water, with a tube through which the liquid is forced out by the pressure of the gas in the bottle. **3** a tube-shaped organ of some aquatic animals, especially molluscs, through which water is drawn in or expelled.
v **1** draw off or convey liquid by means of a siphon: *She siphoned water from the rain barrel onto the garden.* **2** draw off or transfer over a period of time, especially illegally or unfairly: *The treasurer was siphoning some of the club's money.* <French, from Greek = pipe>

sir (sər) *n* **1** (*used alone, never with a name*) a respectful or formal term of address used to a man: *Excuse me, sir.* **2 Sir** the title used before the given name or full name of a knight or baronet: *Sir Wilfrid Laurier.* <*sire*>

sire (sīr) *n* **1** the male parent of an animal, especially a domestic animal. **2** *Archaic* a respectful form of address for a king or a noble: *Sire, I desire to accompany you.*
v **sired, sir·ing** be the father of an animal, especially a domestic one: *The stallion sired many notable racehorses.* <Old French, from Latin *senior* older>

si·ren (sī′rən) *n* **1** a device that produces a loud, prolonged signal or warning sound, such as from an ambulance or police car, or before an air raid. **2** *Greek myth* a human or partly human female whose sweet singing lured sailors to destruction upon rocks. **3** a woman who is considered to be dangerously attractive. <Old French, from Greek *Seiren*>

sir·loin (sər′loin) *n* a choice cut of meat from the part of the loin in front of the rump. <Old French *sur* above + *longe* loin>

si·roc·co (sə rok′ō) *n, pl* **si·roc·cos** a hot, dusty or rainy wind blowing from northern Africa across the Mediterranean to southern Europe. <French, from Arabic *Saluk* east wind>

sir·ree (sər rē′) *Informal interj* used after yes or no to add emphasis: *Yes, sirree, that was one awful storm!* <sir>

sis·al (sis′əl) *or* (sī′səl) *n* a strong fibre used for making rope or matting. <*Sisal*, a town in Mexico from which the fibre was exported>

sis·sy (sis′ē) *Informal n, pl* **sis·sies** a person regarded as being effeminate or cowardly: *Don't be such a sissy; there's nothing to be afraid of.* <*sis*(*ter*)>

sis·ter (sis′tər) *n* **1** a woman or girl with the same parents or parent as another person. **2** a woman closely associated or feeling kinship with another, especially in a group. **3** a member of a religious order of women.
adj to do with something thought of as female that is closely connected with another: *a sister ship.* <Old English> **sis′ter·li·ness** *n.* **sis′ter·ly** *adj.*

sis·ter·hood (sis′tər hu̇d′) *n* **1** the relationship between sisters. **2** a feeling of kinship with and closeness to a group of women or all women. **3** an association or society of women with some common aim, characteristic, or set of beliefs.

sis·ter–in–law (sis′tə rin lo′) *n, pl* **sis·ters-in-law** **1** the sister of one's spouse. **2** the wife of one's brother or brother-in-law.

sit (sit) *v* **sat, sit·ting** **1** take or be in a position in which one's weight is supported by one's buttocks and one's back is upright, or cause to be such a position: *He sat in the biggest chair. They sat us at the front of the restaurant.* **2** rest as an animal or bird with the hind legs bent and the body close to a horizontal surface. **3** ride or keep one's seat on a horse. **4** be or remain in a certain position or condition: *The books sat in boxes for several years.* **5** be engaged in business as a legislature, committee, or court of law, or serve in such a group: *The court sits next month.* **6** (*in compounds*) look after a house, domestic animal, or small child while its owner or parent is away: *to house-sit, to babysit.* <Old English *sittan*>
sit back, a lean back and relax with one's back supported. **b** be inactive and choose not to be involved.
sit down, put oneself in a sitting position.
sit in, a take part in a meeting or discussion without taking an active part in it: *Several people sat in on our debate.* **b** take part in a sit-in.
sit on (or **upon**), **a** take part in a panel, jury, council, commission, or committee. **b** fail to deal with: *The committee sat on the request for several weeks.*
sit on your hands, take no action.
sit out, a not take part in a particular event or activity. **b** wait until an unwelcome situation or process is over: *to sit out a storm.*
sit up, a raise the body, or cause someone else to move the body, to an erect sitting position. **b** stay up instead of going to bed.
sit up and take notice, be suddenly interested: *When it starts to personally affect them, they'll sit up and take notice.*
sit well with, feel correct, proper, or appropriate: *That decision just doesn't sit well with me.*

si·tar (si tär′) *n* a lutelike instrument from India with a long neck and movable frets.

ETYMOLOGY

Sitar comes from Urdu *sitar*, from two Persian words: *si* meaning "three" and *tar* meaning "string." This is probably a reference to the number of strings on the original instrument. The modern sitar has six or seven main playing strings, as well up to thirteen additional strings for resonance.

sit·com (sit′kom′) *Informal n* a situation comedy.

sit–down strike (sit′doun′) *n* a strike in which employees stop working but stay in their place of employment until their demands are met.

site (sīt) *n* **1** an area of ground on which a structure or group of structures is, was, or will be located: *the site of a monument.* **2** a place where a particular event or activity is occurring or has occured: *a construction site, the site of a battle.* See SIGHT for confusable.
v **sit·ed, sit·ing** locate or build something in a particular place: *They sited the new building on a hill.* <Latin *situs* local position, from *sinere* to be place>

sit–in (sit′in′) *n* a form of protest in which a group of people occupy a public place and refuse to leave until their demands are met: *The college students staged a sit-in to protest the increase in fees.*

The **Sitka spruce** is a giant, but other species of spruce are similar in appearance to fir trees. A spruce has squarish needles, whereas fir needles are flattened.

Sit·ka spruce (sit′kə) *n* a tall spruce tree found along the Pacific coast of N America with stiff, sharp needles and long cones.

sit·ter (sit′ər) *n* **1** a person who looks after a house,

a bat	e bed	i bid	o pot	u cup	th thin
ā cake	ē me	ī bite	ō go	ū rude	TH then
ä bar	ə about	ər over	ȯ for	u̇ put	zh measure

domestic animal, or small child while its owner or parent is away. **2** a person who or thing that sits.

sit·ting (sit′ing) *n* **1** a continuous period of being seated, especially when engaged in a particular activity, such as time spent as a model for an artist or photographer: *She read eight chapters at one sitting. The portrait required several sittings.* **2** a meeting or session of a committee or legislature. **3** a scheduled period of time when a group of people are served a meal, especially in a restaurant: *the second sitting for dinner.*
adj **1** of or for sitting: *a sitting position.* **2** currently serving as an elected representative: *the sitting member of Parliament.* **3** settled as a bird on eggs for the purpose of incubating them: *a sitting hen.*

sitting duck *Informal n* an easy target for an attack or other source of danger.

sit·u·ate (sich′ū āt′) *v* **sit·u·at·ed, sit·u·at·ing** put, build, or locate something in a certain place or position: *They situated the new city hall in the middle of downtown.* <Latin *situs* site>

sit·u·at·ed (sich′ū ā′tid) *adj* **1** with a particular location or site: *a conveniently situated neighbourhood.* **2** with a certain financial or social position: *The doctor was quite well situated.*

sit·u·a·tion (sich′ū ā′shən) *n* **1** a set of circumstances: *the political situation.* **2** the location and surroundings of a place: *Our house has a beautiful situation on a hill.* **3** a job: *She's trying to find a situation.*

sit·u·a·tion·al (sich′ū ā′shən əl) *adj* to do with the specific situation: *situational factors.*

situation comedy *n* a radio or TV comedy series consisting of unconnected, usually weekly episodes featuring the same cast of characters.

sit–up (sit′up′) *n* a physical exercise that consists of raising the body from lying face downward to sitting upright without using the hands for support. Compare CURL-UP.

sitz bath (sits) *or* (zits) *n* a basin or tub for bathing in a sitting position, so that only the buttocks and hips are immersed, or a bath so taken, especially as part of a medical treatment. <German *sitzen* seat + *Bad* bath>

Si·va (sē′və) *or* (shē′və) SHIVA.

six (siks) *n* **1** a cardinal number that is one more than five. **2** the numeral 6. **3** a playing card or side of a die with six spots: *I need a six to win.*
adj **1** one more than five: *They asked for six copies.* **2** (*after the noun*) sixth in a series: *I've read Chapter Six.* <Old English *siex*> **sixth** *adj, adv.*
at sixes and sevens, in confusion or disagreement.
six of one, half a dozen of the other the same either way: *Whether you go or stay doesn't matter; it's six of one, half a dozen of the other.*

six·fold (siks′fōld′) *adj, adv* **1** six times as much or as many. **2** consisting of six parts.

Six Nations *n* a federation of Iroquois nations, called the FIVE NATIONS until the Tuscarora joined in about 1722.

six–pack (siks′pak′) *n* a package of six of the same things sold as a unit, especially cans or bottles of beer or soft drinks. *There's a six-pack in the cooler.*

six–shoot·er (siks′shū′tər) *n* a revolver that can fire six shots without being reloaded.

six·teen (sik′stēn′) *n* **1** six more than ten. **2** the numeral 16.
adj **1** six more than ten: *sixteen candles on the cake.* **2** (*after the noun*) sixteenth in a series: *Section Sixteen.* <Old English *sixtene*> **six′teenth′** *adj, adv.*

six·teenth (sik′stēnth′) *n* **1** next after the fifteenth: *I am sixteenth in line at the movie.* **2** one of sixteen equal parts: *The cousins each get a sixteenth of the inheritance.*
adj, adv. See SIXTEEN.

sixth (siksth) *adj, n* **1** next after the fifth: *on the sixth day* (*adj*). *I'm sixth in line* (*n*). **2** one, or being one, of six equal parts: *He was given a sixth part of the inheritance* (*adj*). *She donated a sixth of her money to charity* (*n*).

sixth sense *n* an unusual power of perception, beyond that given by the five senses.

six·ti·eth (sik′stē ith) *n* **1** next after the fifty-ninth. **2** one of sixty equal parts.
adj, adv See SIXTY.

six·ty (sik′stē) *n, pl* **six·ties 1** six times ten. **2 sixties** *pl* the years from sixty through sixty-nine, especially of a century or of a person's life: *Rock music became popular in the sixties.*
adj **1** six times ten. **2** (*after the noun*) sixtieth in a series: *page sixty.* <Old English *siextig*> **six′ti·eth′** *adj, adv.*

siz·a·ble (sī′zə bəl) *adj* fairly large: *He had a sizable income, but always seemed to be in debt.* Also, **sizeable**.
siz′a·bly *adv.*

size[1] (sīz) *n* **1** the extent of a surface or area a thing takes up: *books of all sizes.* **2** a large extent of something: *She was awed by the size of the landslide.* **3** a measure forming part of a series, especially of garments or other items, or a person or garment corresponding to such a numbered series: *His shoes are size 10. She's a size 6.* **4** *Informal* the actual condition or true description of something: *That's about the size of things.*
v **sized, siz·ing** arrange according to size or in sizes: *Will you size these nails?*
adj sized: *size 11 shoes.* <Old French, from Latin *assidere* assess>
of a size, of the same size.
size up, *Informal* form an opinion or estimate of.

size[2] (sīz) *n* a sticky preparation made from materials like glue, starch, or resin and used for glazing paper, stiffening textiles, and preparing plastered walls for decoration.
v **sized, siz·ing** coat or treat with size. <Old French *sise* a setting, from *assidere* assess>

size·a·ble (sī′zə bəl) SIZABLE.

sized (sīzd) *adj* (*only in compounds*) with a size of a specified kind: *giant-sized.*

siz·ing (sī′zing) *n* SIZE[2].

siz·zle (siz′əl) *v* **siz·zled, siz·zling 1** make a hissing sound, as fat does when it is frying. **2** be very hot: *sizzle with anger.*
n a hissing sound, as of fat frying. <imitative>

ollie

An ollie is a basic skateboard trick used to jump over obstacles. The skateboarder approaches the obstacle with legs bent. Pressure is applied to the tail of the skateboard to start the jump.

ollie kick flip

An ollie kick flip is an ollie that adds one or more rotations of the skateboard. The board is spun by hitting it with the tip of the shoe. The hardest part is returning to the board just before landing.

skate[1] (skāt) *n* **1** in full, **ice skate** a boot with a metal blade attached to the sole, designed for gliding over ice. See BLADE for picture. **2** roller skate. **3** inline skate.
v **skat·ed, skat·ing** glide or move along on, or as if on, skates. <Dutch, from Old French *eschasse* stilt> **skat′er** *n.* **skat′ing** *n.*

skate[2] (skāt) *n, pl* **skates** or (*especially collectively*) **skate** a broad, flat, marine fish of the ray family. <Old Norse *skata*>

skate·board (skāt′bȯrd′) *n* a short, narrow board of wood or plastic with small wheels, on which a person can ride in a standing or crouching position, propelled by occasionally pushing a foot on the ground.
v ride on a skateboard. **skate′board·er** *n.*

skate·guard (skāt′gard′) *n* a long piece of hard plastic with a groove in it, used as a protective covering for the blade of an ice skate.

skating rink *n* a smooth sheet of ice for skating, or a smooth floor for roller-skating.

ske·dad·dle (ski dad′əl) *Informal v* **ske·dad·dled, ske·dad·dling** run away or leave in a hurry. <origin uncertain>

skeet (skēt) *n* a sport in which people fire rifles at clay targets that are released into the air so as to imitate the flight of birds. <apparently *shoot*>

skein (skān) *n* **1** a loosely coiled and knotted length of yarn or thread. **2** a confused or complicated arrangement, condition, or situation. **3** a flock of wild geese or swans in flight. <Old French *escaigne*>

skel·e·ton (skel′ə tən) *n* **1** an internal or external framework of bones, cartilage, or other rigid material supporting the body of an animal or plant. **2** a very thin person or animal: *He was just a skeleton after his long illness.* **3** the basic framework or structure of something: *the skeleton of an office tower, the skeleton of a story.* **4** *Mathematics* a three-dimensional model showing only edges and vertices. See also SHELL, SOLID. **5** *Sports* a form of bobsled racing for individuals, using a small, simple sled. It is considered to be the first sliding sport.
adj with the basic or minimum number of people, things, or parts necessary for something: *A skeleton crew remained on board while the ship was at the dock.* <Latin, from Greek *skellein* dry up> **skel′e·tal** *adj.*
skeleton in the closet, something shameful that is kept secret, as in a family.

skeleton key *n* a key made to open many locks.

skep·tic (skep′tik) *n* a person who questions the truth of a particular theory, belief, or apparent fact. Also, **sceptic.** <French, from Greek *skepsis* doubt> **skep′ti·cal** *adj.* **skep′ti·cal·ly** *adv.* **skep′ti·cism′** (skep′tə siz′əm) *n.*

sketch (skech) *n* **1** a rough, quickly done drawing, painting, or design, often made to assist in making a more finished picture. **2** a brief written or spoken account or description of someone or something, giving only basic details. **3** a short, humorous play or performance, especially a scene in a revue or comedy program.
v **1** make a sketch or sketches: *We spent the afternoon sketching.* **2** give a brief account or general outline. <Dutch from Greek *skhedios* impromptu> **sketch′er** *n.*

sketch·book (skech′bu̇k′) *n* a book of or for rough, quick drawings: *She takes her sketchbook along wherever she goes.*

sketch·y (skech′ē) *adj* **sketch·i·er, sketch·i·est 1** with or giving only outlines or main features. **2** incomplete or inadequate: *a sketchy meal.* **sketch′i·ly** *adv.* **sketch′i·ness** *n.*

skew (skyū) *adj* twisted to one side or with a part that deviates from a straight line, right angle, etc.
v **1** suddenly change direction or position, especially as to slant or twist. **2** represent in a distorted or unfair way: *to skew data.* <Old French *eschiver* eschew>

skew·er (skyū′ər) *n* a long, thin piece of wood or metal stuck through chunks of food to hold them together while they are cooking.
v fasten together or pierce with a pin or skewer, or in a way that resembles this. <origin uncertain>

a bat	e bed	i bid	o pot	u cup	th thin
ā cake	ē me	ī bite	ō go	ū rude	ᴛʜ then
ȧ bar	ə about	ər over	ȯ for	u̇ put	zh measure

S

Weight is the speed skier's friend—the heavier the skier, the faster she will **ski**. Small lead beads are often used to add mass to helmets and poles.

ski (skē) *n, pl* **skis** or **ski** **1** each of a pair of long, narrow, pointed pieces of wood, metal, or plastic that can be fastened to boots to enable a person to glide over snow. **2** a similar device fastened beneath a vehicle or aircraft for moving on or landing in snow, sand, or water. **3** a water ski.
v **skied, ski·ing** travel over the snow on skis. <Norwegian, from Old Norse *skith* snowshoe>
ski′a·ble *adj.* **ski′er** *n.* **ski′ing** *n.*

skid (skid) *v* **skid·ded, skid·ding** **1** slip or slide sideways out of control, while moving, or cause to do so: *The car skidded on the slippery road.* **2** move a heavy object on a skid or skids. **3** decline or deteriorate.
n **1** an act of skidding or sliding: *His truck went into a skid.* **2** a runner attached to the underside of an aircraft for use in landing on snow or grass. **3** each of a set of rollers used for moving a log or some other heavy object. **4** a braking device consisting of a wooden or metal shoe preventing a wheel from turning. **5** a beam or plank of wood used to support a ship under construction or repair. <origin uncertain>
hit the skids, *Informal* suffer a serious decline or failure.
on the skids, *Informal* headed for failure or doing badly.
put the skids under, *Informal* cause the failure or downfall of.

ski·doo (ski dū′) *or* (skē′dū) *n* a type of snowmobile.
v **ski·dooed, ski·doo·ing** travel by skidoo. <*Ski-Doo*, a trademark> **ski·doo′er** *n.*

skid road *n* **1** a road formed from greased skids, over which logs were dragged. **2** skid row.

skid row *n* **1** a rundown district frequented by vagrants and alcoholics. **2** a desperate, unfortunate, or difficult situation: *He'd wasted all his money and found himself on skid row.* <*skid road*>

skiff[1] (skif) *n* a small, light rowboat with a rounded bottom and flat stern, typically for one person. <Middle English *skif*>

skiff[2] (skif) *n* a light sprinkling of snow. <perhaps Gaelic>

ski jump *n* a structure made to provide a steep slope levelling off before a sharp drop. It allows a skier to leap through the air and land some distance away. In competition, the longest correctly executed leap wins. See NORDIC for picture. **ski jumper** *n.* **ski jumping** *n.*

skil·ful or **skill·ful** (skil′fəl) *adj* with or showing skill: *a skilful surgeon. That painting was a skilful piece of work.* **skil′ful·ly** or **skill′ful·ly** *adj.* **skil′ful·ness** or **skill′ful·ness** *n.*

ski lift *n* a mechanism for carrying skiers to the top of a slope, usually by means of a chair running on a suspended cable.

skill (skil) *n* **1** the ability to do something well: *He had great skill as a carpenter* **2** a particular ability: *language skills.* <Old Norse *skil*>

skilled (skild) *adj* with or showing skill: *a skilled worker, skilled labour.*

skil·let (skil′it) *n* a heavy shallow pan with a long handle, used for frying: *He made the pancakes in a skillet.* <Old French, from Latin *scutella* serving platter>

skill·ful (skil′fəl) SKILFUL.

skim (skim) *v* **skimmed, skim·ming** **1** remove a substance from the surface of a liquid: *The cook skimmed scum from the boiling broth.* **2** *Informal* steal or embezzle money, especially in small amounts over a period of time. **3** go or move quickly and lightly over or on a surface or through the air: *The swallows were skimming by.* **4** throw a flat stone over the surface of water so that it bounces several times. **5** read, deal with, or treat a text or subject rapidly or superficially so as to cover only the important points or general sense: *It took me an hour to skim the book. He skimmed over the subject of his past.*
n **1** a thin layer of a substance on the surface of a liquid: *a skim of ice.* **2** an act of reading something quickly and superficially: *She took a quick skim through the opening chapter.* <Old French escume scum>

skim·mer (skim′ər) *n* **1** a person who or thing that skims, especially a long-handled, shallow ladle with small holes, used in skimming liquids. **2** a long-winged seabird related to the tern.

skim milk *n* milk from which all fat has been removed.

skimp (skimp) *v* expend or use less time, money, or material than is usual or necessary, especially as an attempt to economize: *Don't skimp the butter in making a cake. She had to skimp to send her son to university.* <origin uncertain>

skimp·y (skim′pē) *adj* **skimp·i·er, skimp·i·est** **1** providing or consisting of less than is needed or usual: *a skimpy meal.* **2** short and revealing as a garment: *a skimpy dress.*

skin (skin) *n* **1** the outer layer of tissue forming the natural outer covering of the body of a person or animal: *She used a lot of lotion on her skin.* See DERMIS for picture. **2** the skin of a dead animal with or without the fur, used as a material for clothing or other items. **3** a thin outer layer or covering, such as the peel of some fruits and vegetables, or the casing of a sausage. **4** a thin layer forming on the surface of a hot liquid, such as milk, when it cools.

v **skinned, skin·ning** 1 remove the skin from an animal, fruit, or vegetable: *The hunter skinned the deer.* 2 graze a part of one's body: *He skinned his knee when he fell.* <Old Norse *skinn*>

by the skin of your teeth, very narrowly or barely: *He passed the exam by the skin of his teeth.*

get under someone's skin, annoy or irritate someone.

have a thick (or **thin**) **skin,** be very insensitive (or sensitive) to criticism.

save your skin, escape without harm.

SYNONYMS

Skin is a general word for the natural outer covering of a person, animal, fruit, etc.: *The sun burned her skin. The skin of the apple is tough.*

Hide usually refers to the skin of a large animal, raw or tanned: *Buffalo hide was used to make teepees.*

Pelt refers to the skin of a fur-bearing animal: *The trapper put three fresh beaver pelts on the table.*

skin–deep (skin′dēp′) *adj* not deep or lasting as an emotion, impression, quality, or effect.

skin diving *n* the action or sport of swimming under water with flippers, a face mask, and, usually, a snorkel rather than a portable air supply. **skin diver** *n.*

skin flick *Slang n* a movie exploiting nudity and explicit sex.

skin·flint (skin′flint′) *n* a stingy person or miser.

skin graft *n* a piece of healthy skin that is transplanted to a new place on the body or to a different individual to replace damaged or lost tissue, or the surgical operation in which this is done.

skin·head (skin′hed′) *n* a young person who belongs to a group whose members have close-cropped hair and heavy boots, often considered aggressive, violent, and racist.

skink (skingk) *n* a small lizard with a long, round body, small, smooth scales, and short or absent limbs. <Latin, from Greek *skinkos*>

skin·less (skin′lis) *adj* without a skin or casing: *skinless wieners.*

skin·ny (skin′ē) *adj* **skin·ni·er, skin·ni·est** 1 unattractively thin: *She was skinny as a child.* 2 small or tight-fitting: *skinny pants.* **skin′ni·ness** *n.*

skinny dip *Informal n* a swim in the nude. **skin′ny-dip′** *v.* **skin′ny-dip′per** *n.* **skin′ny-dip′ping** *n.*

skin test *n* a test in which a substance is applied to or injected under the skin in order to detect whether there is an immune reaction to a disease or allergy.

skin–tight (skin′tīt′) *adj* fitting closely to the skin as clothes.

skip[1] (skip) *v* **skipped, skip·ping** 1 move along lightly, stepping from one foot to the other with a hop or bounce: *Lambs skipped in the fields.* 2 jump over a rope that is held at both ends by oneself or two other people and turned repeatedly over the head and under the feet, as a game or an exercise. 3 throw a stone so that it bounds over the surface of the water: *Children like to skip stones on the lake.* 4 omit something, or fail to attend or to deal properly with it: *to skip classes. She skipped the hard words.* 5 of a CD, fail to play properly by sticking or by jumping from one place to another, usually because of a defect. 6 *Informal* leave in a hurry: *In the movie, the villain skipped town to avoid meeting the hero.*

n 1 a light bouncing step or skipping movement. 2 the act of passing over or omitting something. <origin uncertain>

skip[2] (skip) *n* the captain of a curling team or a lawn bowling team. <*skipper*>

ski patrol *n* a group of expert skiers who patrol ski slopes in order to help skiers who are in trouble or to enforce rules.

ski pole *n* either of a pair of light poles held by a skier to assist in balance or to propel the skier along the surface of the snow.

skip·per (skip′ər) *n* 1 the captain of a ship or boat, especially of a small trading or fishing boat. 2 the captain of a side in a game or sport. <Dutch *schip* ship>

skipping rope *n* a length of rope, often with a handle at each end, used to SKIP (def. 2) with.

skirl (skərl) *n* a loud, shrill sound, especially that of the bagpipes.

v make such a sound. <origin uncertain>

skir·mish (skər′mish) *n* a minor or irregular fight in a battle, conflict, or argument.

v take part in a skirmish. <Old French *eskirmir* defend> **skir′mish·er** *n.* **skir′mish·ing** *n.*

skirt (skərt) *n* 1 a woman's outer garment fastened around the waist and handing freely over the legs: *She wore a skirt and jacket.* 2 the part of a coat or dress that extends from the waist down. 3 a border, edge, or rim.

v 1 extend along or form a border or edge: *The road skirts the lake.* 2 pass along a border or edge: *The boys skirted the forest because they did not want to go through it.* <Old Norse *skyrta* shirt>

ski run *n* a slope prepared for skiing.

skit (skit) *n* a short dramatic sketch that contains humour or satire. <origin uncertain>

ski tow (tō) *n* a motorized conveyor for towing skiers to the top of a slope on their skis, usually consisting of a moving rope or cable that skiers hang onto.

skit·ter (skit′ər) *v* 1 move lightly and quickly or hurriedly. 2 draw a fishing lure over the surface of the water with a skipping motion. <earlier *skite* to dart>

skit·tish (skit′ish) *adj* nervous, lively, and unpredictable: *a skittish horse.* **skit′tish·ly** *adv.* **skit′tish·ness** *n.*

skit·tle (skit′əl) *n* 1 one of the wooden pins used in the game of skittles. 2 **skittles** a game in which the players try to knock down nine wooden pins by rolling or throwing wooden discs or balls at them. <origin uncertain>

a bat	e bed	i bid	o pot	u cup	th thin
ā cake	ē me	ī bite	ō go	ū rude	ᴛʜ then
à bar	ə about	ər over	ȯ for	ů put	zh measure

skiv·vies (skiv′ēz) *Informal pln* underwear. <origin uncertain>

✱ **skoo·kum** (sků′kəm) *adj* strong, vigorous, or impressive. <Chinook Jargon>

sku·a (skyū′ə) *n* a large, brown seabird that is related to the gull.

skul·dug·ger·y (skul dug′ə rē) *n* unscrupulous, or underhanded behaviour. <Scots *sculddery*>

skulk (skulk) *v* keep out of sight, especially in a stealthy, furtive way: *The burglar skulked around the house, looking for an easy way in.* <Scandinavian> **skulk′er** *n.* **skulk′ing** *adj.* **skulk′ing·ly** *adv.*

skull (skul) *n* **1** the bones of the head, the part of the skeleton of a person or vertebrate animal that encloses and protects the brain and other organs. See MAXILLA for picture. **2** a person's brain or head: *It's impossible to get anything into his thick skull.* <Middle English *scolle*>

skull and crossbones *n* a picture of a human skull above two crossed bones, usually seen on pirates' flags as a symbol of death, or on the labels of poisonous drugs or toxic chemicals.

skull·cap (skul′kap′) *n* **1** a close-fitting cap without a brim. **2** the top part of the skull.

skunk (skungk) *n* **1** a black, bushy-tailed mammal with white-and-black striped fur that gives off a powerful, unpleasant smell when frightened or attacked. **2** *Informal* a contemptible person. <Algonquian>

skunk cabbage *n* a broad-leaved N American plant with an unpleasant smell, growing commonly in moist ground.

sky (skī) *n, pl* **skies** the region that appears high above the earth, appearing as a great arch or dome, and including the atmosphere and outer space: *a blue sky, a cloudy sky.* <Old Norse = cloud>

out of a clear (**blue**) **sky,** suddenly or unexpectedly.

to the skies, very highly; extravagantly: *The review praised him to the skies.*

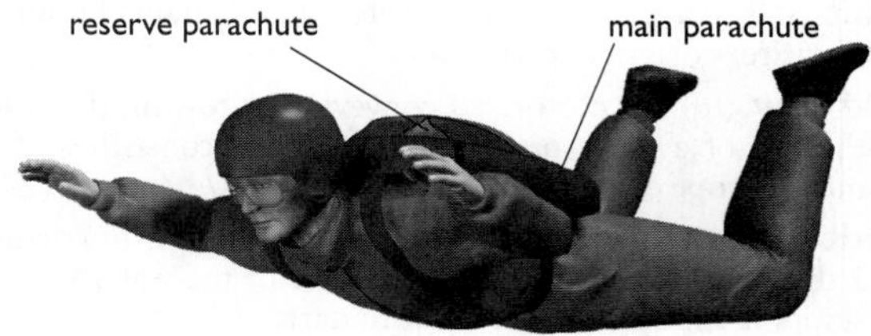

Skydiving began over 100 years before the first airplane flew. The Frenchman André Jacques Garnerin made the first successful parachute jump from a balloon in 1797.

sky·div·ing (skī′dī′ving) *n* the sport of jumping from an airplane and making certain manoeuvres while falling free before opening one's parachute. See also picture at PARACHUTE. **sky′div′er** *n.*

sky–high (skī′hī′) *adj, adv* **1** to a great height: *He threw the ball sky-high.* **2** to a high degree or level: *Prices have gone sky-high in the last month.*

sky·lark (skī′lårk′) *n* a lark of farmland and open country, with brown-streaked plumage and a prolonged song given while hovering in flight.

v pass time by indulging in pranks, jokes, or horseplay.

sky·light (skī′līt′) *n* a window in a roof or ceiling at the same angle.

sky·line (skī′līn′) *n* the outline of land and buildings as seen against the sky from a distance: *a city skyline.*

sky·rock·et (skī′rok′it) *n* a rocket used in fireworks or as a signal that bursts in a shower of sparks and stars high in the air.

v rise or increase suddenly and quickly, like a skyrocket: *Prices were skyrocketing. The actor had skyrocketed to fame with his first movie.*

sky·scrap·er (skī′skrā′pər) *n* a very tall building of many storeys.

sky·ward (skī′wərd) *adj, adv* toward the sky: *A skyward glance told him the storm was approaching fast* (*adj*). *The rocket shot skyward* (*adv*). Also (*adv*), **skywards**.

sky·way (skī′wā′) *n* **1** a route used by aircraft. **2** a stretch of elevated highway such as a bridge or overpass. **3** a covered walkway between upper storeys of two buildings or towers.

sky·writ·ing (skī′rī′ting) *n* the action of tracing of words against the sky from an airplane by means of smoke or some similar substance, or the words so traced.

slab (slab) *n* a broad, flat, thick piece of stone, cement, wood, meat, or other substance: *The hungry boy ate a slab of cheese as big as his hand.* <Middle English *slabbe*>

slack (slak) *adj* **1** loose: *The rope is too slack to hold anything.* **2** careless or negligent: *He is a slack housekeeper.* **3** slow or sluggish: *The horse was moving at a slack pace.* **4** without much activity or work in a business or trade: *Sales are slack at present.*

n **1** the part of a rope or line that hangs loose: *She wound in the slack of the fishing line.* **2** a spell of inactivity or laziness. **3** **slacks** *pl* trousers for casual wear.

adv in a slack manner.

v loosen something, especially a rope. <Old English *slæc* inclined to be lazy>

cut someone some slack, *Informal* allow someone some leeway in how the person behaves.

pick (or **take**) **up the slack,** improve the use of resources to avoid a lull or unusual demand in business or activity.

slack off, decrease in quantity or intensity.

slack up, slow down or work less hard.

slack·en (slak′ən) *v* make or become slack: *Work slackened as the temperature climbed. His business slackens in the winter. She slackened the rope.*

slack·er (slak′ər) *Informal n* a person who avoids work or evades a duty.

slack–jawed (slak′jod′) *adj* with the mouth hanging open in surprise or confusion.

slag (slag) *n* **1** the stony waste matter left after metal is separated from ore by smelting. **2** a similar material produced by a volcano. <German *slagge*>

slain (slān) past participle of SLAY.

slake (slāk) *v* **slaked, slak·ing** 1 quench or satisfy thirst: *We slaked our thirst at the spring.* 2 satisfy a desire: *The massacre seemed to slake the rebels' lust for revenge.* 3 change quicklime from calcium oxide to calcium hydroxide (**slaked lime**) by combining with water, or be changed in this way. <Old English *slæc* slack>

sla·lom (slä′ləm) *or* (slal′əm) *n* a race in which skiers zigzag downhill along a course set between a series of poles.
v ski on such a course or rapidly move in a way that suggests it. <Norwegian = sloping track>

slam[1] (slam) *v* **slammed, slam·ming** 1 shut a door, window, or lid forcefully and loudly, or be shut in this way: *He slammed the window down. She heard a car door slam.* 2 crash into or collide: *The jeep slammed into the truck.* 3 hit something or put something in action suddenly and forcefully: *She slammed on the brakes. He slammed two home runs in the last three innings.* 4 *Informal* criticize harshly.
n 1 a loud noise caused by the forceful shutting of something, such as a door or window; a bang: *He threw his books down with a slam.* 2 *Informal* a harsh criticism. 3 *Informal* a poetry competition in which contestants recite their entries and are judged by members of an audience. <origin uncertain>

slam[2] (slam) *n* the winning of twelve (**small slam**) or all thirteen (**grand slam**) tricks in the game of bridge. <origin uncertain>

slam–bang (slam′bang′) *Informal adj* exciting and energetic: *a slam-bang video.*
adv suddenly and forcefully: *I walked slam-bang into a wall.*

slam dunk *n* See DUNK (def. 3). **slam′-dunk′** *v.*

slam·mer (slam′ər) *Informal n* **the slammer** prison.

slan·der (slan′dər) *Law n* the action or crime of making a false spoken statement that damages another person's reputation, or the false, damaging statement itself.
v make false and damaging statements about someone. Compare LIBEL. <Old French, from Latin *scandalum*> **slan′der·er** *n.* **slan′der·ous** *adj.* **slan′der·ous·ly** *adv.*

slang (slang) *n* a type of language usage that consists of words and phrases that are regarded as very informal, are more common in speech than writing, and are restricted to a particular context or group of people: *drug slang.*
v attack someone by using abusive language: *He slanged me for not waiting for him.* <origin uncertain>

GRAMMAR AND USAGE

Slang can be used to make spoken and written dialogue more lively, but is not considered appropriate in formal speaking and writing.

Avoid slang even in informal situations when communicating with people outside your own group.

See also notes at *informal* and *standard.*

slang·y (slang′ē) *adj* **slang·i·er, slang·i·est** using or containing much slang: *The writing is too slangy for an essay.*

slant (slant) *v* 1 slope, lean, or fall in a particular direction: *His handwriting slants to the left.* 2 present from a particular angle to appeal to a certain group or interest, especially in an unfair or distorted way: *The newspaper slanted the story by leaving out some of the facts.*
n 1 a slanting direction or position: *The greenhouse roof has a sharp slant.* 2 a personal attitude or viewpoint: *Her memoirs provide us with an interesting slant on the political scene of the sixties.* <Scandinavian>

slant·ing (slan′ting) *adj* sloping. **slant′ing·ly** *adv.*

slant·wise (slan′twīz′) *adv, adj* in a slanting way.

slap (slap) *v* **slapped, slap·ping** 1 strike someone or something with the open hand or with a flat object, or the sound made by doing this: *She slapped his hand down hard when he reached for the hot plate.* 2 hit against or into something with the sound of such an action: *He slapped the book down.*
n a blow with the open hand or with a flat object, or the sound made by doing this.
adv Informal suddenly and directly: *The thief ran slap into a police officer.* <Middle English>
slap down, *Informal* reprimand forcefully: *She slapped him down for being late.*
slap on, a apply makeup carelessly or hastily. **b** impose a fine or other penalty on: *The government slapped on an extra tax on imports.*

slap·dash (slap′dash′) *Informal adj* hasty and careless: *She said that slapdash people do slapdash work.*
adv done hastily and carelessly: *He always went at his work slapdash.*

slap·hap·py (slap′hap′ē) *adj* **slap·hap·pier, slap·hap·pi·est** casual, flippant, or irresponsible: *slaphappy methods.* **slap·hap′pi·ly** *adv.*

slap·shot (slap′shot′) *Hockey n* a hard shot made by raising the stick just above or below the waist before striking the puck with a sharp, slapping motion.

slap·stick (slap′stik′) *n* 1 comedy full of deliberately clumsy actions and embarrassing events. 2 a device consisting of two long, narrow sticks fastened so as to slap together loudly when a clown or comic actor uses it.
adj full of clumsy actions and embarrassing events: *slapstick comedy.*

slap–up (slap′up′) *Informal adj* abundant and excellent: *a slap-up dinner.*

slash (slash) *v* 1 cut with a violent sweeping stroke, especially with a knife or sword: *to slash a tire.* 2 greatly reduce a price, quantity, or amount: *to slash prices.*
n 1 a cut made with a wide, sweeping stroke, or the wound made by such a stroke: *the slash of a sword.* 2 a sharp reduction: *a slash in salary.* 3 a slanting stroke [/] in print or writing, used between alternatives, in fractions, in ratios, or between separate elements of a word or phrase. Examples: *and/or, 2/3, kilometres/hour.* 4 a litter of chips, broken branches, and other debris in a forest resulting from the felling or destruction of trees. 5 a bright patch or flash of colour or light: *a slash of yellow.* <origin uncertain>

a bat	e bed	i bid	o pot	u cup	th thin
ā cake	ē me	ī bite	ō go	ū rude	TH then
ä bar	ə about	ər over	ô for	ů put	zh measure

slash–and–burn (slash′ən bərn′) *adj* **1** to do with a method of agriculture in which existing plants are cut down and burned off before new seeds are sown, used as a crude way of clearing forest land for farming. **2** violent and destructive: *slash-and-burn tactics.*

slash·er (slash′ər) *n* a person who or thing that slashes, especially a person who attacks another with a knife or razor.

✱ **slash fire** *n* a fire in SLASH (*n* def. 4), usually deliberately set and carefully controlled, to tidy up the area and encourage future growth.

slash·ing (slash′ing) *Hockey, Lacrosse n* the illegal act of striking or swinging at an opposing player with a stick.
adj aggressive and effective: *a slashing commentary.*

slash pocket *n* a pocket set in a garment with a slit for an opening.

slat (slat) *n* a long, thin, narrow piece of wood, plastic, or metal: *The slats of the venetian blind needed cleaning.* <Old French *esclater* to split>

slate (slāt) *n* **1** a fine-grained, usually grey rock formed from the compression of layers of shale or clay that splits easily into thin, smooth layers. **2** a thin piece of slate or material like slate, especially one formerly used for writing on in classrooms, or as a roofing tile. **3** a list of candidates for election to a post or office, especially a group sharing a set of political views: *a reform slate.*
v **slat·ed, slat·ing 1** cover with slate or slates: *to slate a roof.* **2** list as a candidate: *She is slated for the office of club president.*
adj bluish grey. <Old French *esclat* splinter, because slate splits easily into thin layers> **sla′ty** *adj.*
a clean slate, a record not marked by mistakes or wrongdoing: *to enter public office with a clean slate.*

slath·er (slaᴛʜ′ər) *Informal v* spread or smear thickly or lavishly.
n **slathers** *pl* a large amount: *slathers of bacon and eggs.* <origin uncertain>

slat·tern (slat′ərn) *n* a woman who is dirty, careless, or untidy in her dress, her ways, her housekeeping, etc. **slat′tern·ly** *adj.*

slaugh·ter (slot′ər) *n* **1** the killing of an animal or animals for food. **2** the brutal and needless killing of a large number of people or animals: *The battle resulted in a frightful slaughter.*
v **1** kill animals for food. **2** kill many people or animals in a brutal way. <Old Norse *slatr* butcher's meat> **slaugh′ter·er** *n.*

slaugh·ter·house (slot′ər hous′) *n* a place where animals are killed for food.

Slav (slav) *or* (slȧv) *n* a member of a group of central and eastern European peoples who speak Slavic languages. Russians are Slavs. <Latin *Sclavus* a captive Slav>
Slav′ic *adj.*

slave (slāv) *n* **1** a person who was the legal property of another. **2** a person who is controlled or ruled by some desire, habit, or influence: *a slave of alcohol.*
v **slaved, slav·ing** work very hard: *He slaved to make a living.*
adj to do with slaves: *slave labour.* <Old French, from Latin *sclavus* Slav. Many Slavs were captured and sold into slavery during the Middle Ages.> **slave′like′** *adj.*

Slave (slāv) DENE-THAH.

slave–driv·er (slāv′drī′vər) *n* **1** a person who supervises slaves at work. **2** an employer or manager who is too harsh or demanding.

slav·er[1] (slā′vər) *n* in former times, a dealer in slaves, or a ship used for transporting slaves.

slav·er[2] (slav′ər) *v* let saliva run from the mouth.
n saliva running from the mouth. <origin uncertain>

slav·er·y (slā′və rē) *n* **1 a** the condition of being a slave. **b** the practice or system of owning slaves. **2** a condition like that of a slave, involving very hard work and little reward: *He said the job was pure slavery.* **3** too much dependence on or devotion to something: *slavery to fashion.*

slave trade *n* the buying and selling of slaves for profit, especially the former trade in African blacks.

Slav·ey (slā′vē) DENE-THAH.

slav·ish (slā′vish) *adj* **1** to do with someone who is submissive and servile: *a slavish follower.* **2** lacking originality and independence: *a slavish translation.* **slav′ish·ly** *adv.* **slav′ish·ness** *n.*

slaw (slo) *n* coleslaw, or something shredded like coleslaw.

slay (slā) *v* **slew, slain, slay·ing** violently kill a person or animal: *Many soldiers were slain on that plain.* <Old English *slean*> **slay′er** *n.*

sleaze (slēz′) *n* **1** sleazy content or behaviour: *a magazine full of sleaze.* **2** a person who behaves in a sleazy way. Also called **sleazebag**. <origin uncertain>

slea·zy (slē′zē) *adj* **slea·zi·er, slea·zi·est 1** shabby, dirty, or vulgar: *a sleazy bar.* **2** sordid, immoral, or corrupt, especially in business or politics: *a sleazy councillor.* <origin uncertain> **slea′zi·ness** *n.*

sled (sled) *n* a small, low vehicle with runners instead of wheels, used for carrying loads over ice and snow and pushed, pulled, drawn by horses or dogs, or allowed to slide downhill.
v **sled·ded, sled·ding** ride or carry on a sled. <Dutch *sledde*>

sled·ding (sled′ing) *n* **1** the action of riding or coasting on a sled. **2** the condition of the snow or ice as a surface for a sled: *The new snow made for good sledding.* **3** an advance toward a goal; progress: *I found the new school tough sledding at first because everything was strange to me.*
hard sledding, unfavourable conditions.

sled dog *n* a dog trained and used to draw a sled, especially in the Arctic.

sledge[1] (slej) *UK n* a low, heavy vehicle mounted on runners, used for carrying loads and drawn over snow or ice or dragged over the ground by draft animals.

sledge[2] (slej) *n* a sledgehammer.

sledge·ham·mer (slej′ham′ər) *n* a large, heavy hammer, usually swung with both hands.

v hit with, or as if with, a sledgehammer. <Old English *slecg* + *hammer*>

sleek (slēk) *adj* **1** smooth and glossy in hair, fur, or skin: *a sleek coat.* **2** looking wealthy and well-groomed. **3** trim and elegant: *a sleek ship.*
v make smooth or glossy <*slick*> **sleek′ly** *adv.* **sleek′ness** *n.*

sleep (slēp) *n* **1** a naturally occurring condition in which the body and mind are inactive for a period of time, with the eyes closed, the muscles relaxed, and consciousness partly suspended: *I need more sleep than my sister does.* **2** a state or condition compared to or resembling sleep, such as death or complete silence or stillness. **3** mucus that is found in the corners of the eyes after sleep: *She rubbed sleep from her eyes.*
v **slept, sleep·ing** **1** rest the body and mind with consciousness partly suspended, or spend time in sleeping: *I was very tired and slept for ten hours. He slept the night in peace.* **2** be inactive or dormant: *The seeds slept in the ground.* **3** provide accommodations for sleeping: *This room sleeps two.* <Old English *slæpan*>
put to sleep, put an animal to death humanely, especially a pet: *We had to put our dog to sleep because she was old and sick.*
sleep in, a remain in bed later than usual: *My brother always sleeps in on a Sunday morning. He was late because he slept in.* **b** sleep by night at one's own place of work: *Some workers slept in at the factory.*
sleep like a log, sleep soundly or heavily.
sleep off, get rid of by sleeping: *She was sleeping off a headache.*
sleep on, take more time in deciding about something: *He said he would sleep on the idea.*
sleep over, spend the night at another person's home.
sleep tight! sleep well.

sleep·er (slē′pər) *n* **1** a person who or animal that sleeps: *I'm a sound sleeper.* **2** a thing used for or related to sleeping, such as a railway sleeping car. **3** a movie, book, or play that achieves sudden unexpected success after initially attracting very little attention: *Her play was the sleeper of the season.* **4 sleepers** *pl* one-piece pyjamas for children, extending from the neck and covering the feet.

sleeping bag *n* a zippered bag for sleeping in, usually waterproof and warmly lined, used especially when camping.

sleeping car *n* a railway car with berths or small rooms for passengers to sleep in.

sleeping partner *n* a partner who takes no active part in managing a business.

sleeping pill *n* a pill or capsule containing a drug that causes sleep.

sleeping sickness *n* a disease spread by the tsetse fly that causes fever, chills, pain, sleepiness, and finally death.

sleep·less (slē′plis) *adj* **1** not able to sleep: *He lay there sleepless for several hours.* **2** not providing or producing sleep: *sleepless nights.* **3** *Poetic* continually active or watchful: *a sleepless memory.* **sleep′less·ly** *adv.* **sleep′less·ness** *n.*

sleep·o·ver (slēp′ō′vər) *n* an occasion of spending the night away from home, especially by a child.

sleep·walk (slē′pwok′) *v* walk around and sometimes perform other actions while asleep: *She used to sleepwalk when she was a child.* **sleep′walk·er** *n.* **sleep′walk·ing** *n.*

sleep·y (slē′pē) *adj* **sleep·i·er, sleep·i·est** **1** needing or ready to go to sleep, or showing the effects of sleep: *She never gets enough rest and is always sleepy. He rubbed his sleepy eyes.* **2** without much activity: *a sleepy day, a sleepy town.* **sleep′i·ly** *adv.* **sleep′i·ness** *n.*

sleep·y·head (slē′pē hed′) *n* a person who is sleepy or not paying attention: *Wake up, sleepyhead!*

sleet (slēt) *n* partly frozen rain.
v come down as sleet: *It sleeted, then it snowed, and then it rained.* <Middle English> **sleet′i·ness** *n.* **sleet′y** *adj.*

sleeve (slēv) *n* **1** the tubelike part of a garment that extends from the shoulder and covers the arm or part of the arm. **2** a tube or tubelike machine part enclosing a rod or another tube. **3** a paper or plastic cover for a phonograph record. <Old English *sliefe*> **sleeve′less** *adj.*
have up your sleeve, have in reserve, concealed but ready for use when needed: *She had one more trick up her sleeve.*

sleigh (slā) *n* **1** a light carriage mounted on runners, used for carrying people over snow or ice, and usually drawn by a horse or horses. **2** a small, low vehicle consisting of a platform of boards on narrow metal runners, used as a plaything for going over snow or ice and coasting down snow-covered hills.
v travel or ride in a sleigh. <Dutch *slede* sled>

sleight of hand (slīt) *n* **1** skill and quickness in moving the hands, as in juggling or conjuring tricks, or a display of this. **2** a skilful deception resembling this display.

slen·der (slen′dər) *adj* **1** attractively or gracefully thin in a body or part of a body: *a tall, slender person, a slender hand.* **2** long and thin: *a slender sapling.* **3** barely adequate in its basis or amount: *a slender meal, a slender income.* <origin uncertain> **slen′der·ly** *adv.* **slen′der·ness** *n.*

slen·der·ize (slen′də rīz′) *v* **slen·der·ized, slen·der·iz·ing** make a person or part of the body appear more slender: *a slenderizing dress.*

slept (slept) past tense and past participle of SLEEP.

sleuth (slūth) *Informal n* a detective.
v be or act like a detective. <Old Norse *sloth* track>

slew[1] (slū) past tense of SLAY.

slew[2] (slū) *v* turn or slide violently or uncontrollably in a particular direction, or turn or slide something in this way: *The car slewed around the curve. We slewed the telescope around to the east.*
n a violent or uncontrollable sliding movement. <origin uncertain>

slew[3] (slū) *Informal n* a large number or amount of something: *A whole slew of people were waiting at the stage door.* <Irish Gaelic *sluagh* crowd>

a bat	e bed	i bid	o pot	u cup	th thin
ā cake	ē me	ī bite	ō go	ū rude	TH then
ä bar	ə about	ər over	ô for	u̇ put	zh measure

slice (slīs) *n* **1** a thin, flat, broad piece cut from something, especially food: *a slice of bread, a slice of pie.* **2** a portion or share of something: *She wanted a slice of the profits.* **3 a** *Golf, Baseball* a stroke that causes the ball to curve in the direction of the dominant hand of the player (that is, left for a left-handed golfer). Compare HOOK (def. 5). **b** *Tennis* a stroke made so that the ball spins while travelling forward. **4** a knife or spatula with a thin, broad blade used for lifting foods.
v **sliced, slic·ing 1** cut into slices or cut off as a slice: *He sliced the loaf of bread. I sliced a piece of the meatloaf for myself.* **2** cut or pass through like a knife: *A bullet sliced the air by his head. The plough sliced through the earth.* **3** *Sports* hit a ball so that it curves in the direction of the dominant hand, or spins while travelling forward. <Old French *esclice* splinter> **slice′a·ble** *adj.*
any way you slice it, no matter how you look at it.
slice of life, a realistic portrayal or view of everyday life.

slic·er (slī′sər) *n* a person who or thing that slices, especially a device for slicing food: *a meat slicer.*

slick (slik) *adj* **1** done, operating, or presented in a smooth, efficient, and clever, sometimes superficial way: *slick advertising.* **2** smooth and glossy in skin or hair: *slick hair.* **3** smooth, wet, and slippery: *The road was slick with ice.*
n a small smear or patch of a glossy or wet substance, especially one of oil.
v make one's hair flat, smooth, and glossy by applying water, oil, or cream. <origin uncertain> **slick′ly** *adv.* **slick′ness** *n.*

slick·er (slik′ər) *n* **1** a long, loose, smooth waterproof coat. **2** *Informal* a person who is convincingly deceptive.

slide (slīd) *v* **slid, slid·ing 1** move or move something smoothly over a surface: *The car slid into the ditch. Slide the key across to me.* **2** move or move something easily, quietly, or secretly: *Let's slide behind the curtain and hide. She slid the comb into her pocket.* **3** change gradually to a worse condition or lower level: *He was sliding into bad habits.*
n **1** the act of moving smoothly across a surface, or the surface on which a thing is slid: *The children each take a slide in turn.* **2** a sloping structure on which children can slide down smoothly. **3** a part of a machine or musical instrument that slides. **4** a mass of earth, snow, or mud that has slid. **5** a small, thin sheet of glass on which objects are placed for examination under a microscope. **6** a small transparent photograph placed in a projector for viewing on a screen. <Old English *slidan*> **slid′er** *n.*
let slide, neglect or not bother about: *He has been letting his grades slide lately.*

slide projector *n* a piece of equipment for projecting the image on a slide onto a screen or wall.

slide rule *n* a ruler with a sliding piece, both marked with logarithmic scales, used in former times for making rapid calculations.

slide show *n* the presentation of a sequence of photographic slides or computer-generated material, projected on a screen. Slide shows can be for informational purposes or for entertainment. See also POWERPOINT.

slid·ing (slī′ding) *adj* moving or operating on a track or groove: *a sliding door.*

sliding scale *n* a scale or standard, as for wages, taxes, or fees, that is adjusted to fit certain conditions or situations, such as the cost of living.

slight (slīt) *adj* **1** small in degree: *I have a slight headache.* **2** not sturdy or strongly built as a person: *She is a slight girl.* **3** trivial or superficial: *a slight excuse.*
v insult someone by showing a lack of respect or attention: *She felt slighted because she was not asked to the party.*
n an insult caused by showing a lack of respect or attention: *He assured her that the slight was unintentional.* <Old Norse *slettr* smooth>

SYNONYMS

Slight as a verb can mean "give offence to by ignoring": *She slights anyone that she thinks is not as smart as she is.*

Snub often means "humiliate by ignoring": *Don't try to talk to him because he'll snub you.*

Neglect means "not pay attention to": *They neglected the warnings to stay on the path.*

Shun means "avoid" or "ignore": *The grade seven students were told not to shun the grade sixes.*

slight·ing (slī′ting) *adj* that detracts; contemptuous; disrespectful: *a slighting remark.* **slight′ing·ly** *adv.*

slight·ly (slī′tlē) *adv* **1** to a slight degree: *I knew him slightly.* **2** in a slender way: *He was tall but slightly built.* **slight′ness** *n.*

slim (slim) *adj* **slim·mer, slim·mest 1** slenderly and gracefully built as a person or part of a person: *a slim waist* **2** small in width and usually long and narrow in shape: *a slim bracelet.* **3** very small in something abstract, not physical: *There is a slim chance that she will get the letter in time. His chances of escape were slim.*
v **slimmed, slim·ming** make or become slender, more slender, or less substantial: *He is trying to slim down. The exercise was designed to slim the figure. They decided to slim down the organization.* <Dutch>

slime (slīm) *n* a moist, soft, sticky substance, typically regarded as unpleasant: *His shoes were covered with slime from the swamp.*
v cover with slime: *The rock was slimed over with mud.* <Old English *slim*>

slime mould or **mold** *n* an organism that consists of jellylike protoplasm containing nuclei that later form multiple spores. It lives on dung and decaying vegetation.

slim·y (slī′mē) *adj* **slim·i·er, slim·i·est 1** covered with or like slime: *The pond is too slimy to swim in.* **2** disgustingly immoral or dishonest.

sling (sling) *n* **1** a flexible strap or belt used in the form of a loop to support or raise a hanging weight: *They lowered the crate into the cellar by a sling.* **2** a bandage or soft strap looped around the neck to support an injured arm or hand. **3** a pouch or frame for carrying a baby, supported by a strap around the neck or shoulders. **4** a simple weapon in the form of a strap or loop, used to hurl stones or other small objects.

v **slung, sling·ing** 1 suspend or arrange something, especially with a strap or straps, so that it hangs loosely in a certain position, or move something while arranged like this: *to sling a hammock.* 2 carry something casually, especially a garment or weapon: *A backpack slung over one shoulder can damage your back.* 3 throw or fling: *He slung a couple of shirts into a suitcase.* <origin uncertain>

sling·shot (sling′shot′) *n* a Y-shaped stick with a band of rubber between its prongs, used to shoot small objects.

slink (slingk) *v* **slunk, slink·ing** move smoothly and quietly with gliding steps, in a furtive or sensuous way: *When it saw us coming, the cat slunk around the corner. She slinks around everywhere, hoping to look glamorous.* <Old English *slincan* creep> **slink′ing** *adj.* **slink′ing·ly** *adv.*

slink·y (sling′kē) *adj* graceful and sinuous in movement, line, or figure: *a slinky gown.*

slip[1] (slip) *v* **slipped, slip·ping** 1 slide unintentionally for a short distance or move out of position or from someone's grasp: *to slip on an icy sidewalk. The knife slipped and cut him.* 2 go quietly or quickly, without attracting attention: *They slipped out of the room. Time slips by.* 3 put something in or away from a particular place quietly, quickly, or furtively: *She slipped the ring from her finger. He's always slipping notes into her hand.* 4 change to a worse condition, typically in a gradual way: *His marks slipped this term. Don't let this opportunity slip.* 5 escape or get loose from: *The coin slipped from her fingers.* 6 fail to be remembered: *His name slipped my mind.*
n 1 the act or fact of slipping: *His broken leg was caused by a slip on a banana peel.* 2 a fall to a lower level or standard. 3 a minor or careless mistake: *I only made one slip in the test.* 4 a space for ships in a dock, or an inclined platform alongside the water, on which vessels are built or repaired. <origin uncertain>
give someone the slip, *Informal* evade or escape from someone: *She gave her creditors the slip.*
let slip, tell without meaning to: *He let the secret slip in a careless moment.*
slip of the tongue, a remark made by mistake.
slip one over on, *Informal* get the advantage of, especially by trickery.
slip out, be unintentionally stated or revealed: *The truth about my absence just slipped out while we were talking.*
slip up, *Informal* make a mistake or error.

slip[2] (slip) *n* 1 a small piece of paper, typically for writing on or to give printed information: *a sales slip.* 2 a small stem or shoot cut from a plant, used to grow a new plant, either by rooting or grafting. 3 a small, slim person: *She was just a slip of a girl.* <origin uncertain>

slip·cov·er (slip′kuv′ər) *n* a removable cloth cover for a piece of furniture, especially a chair or sofa.

slip–knot (slip′not′) *n* a knot made to be undone by a pull.

slip–on (slip′on′) *adj* able to be put on or taken off easily or quickly, especially as shoes or clothes.
n a shoe or garment that can be easily slipped on or off.

slip·page (slip′əj) *n* 1 the act or fact of slipping. 2 a decline from a standard.

slipped disc *n* a painful condition caused when one of the discs of cartilage between vertebrae moves out of position, resulting in pressure on nearby nerves.

slip·per (slip′ər) *n* a light, soft shoe that is easily slipped on and off the foot, especially one worn indoors.
slip′pered *adj.*

slip·per·y (slip′ə rē) *adj* **slip·per·i·er, slip·per·i·est** 1 causing or likely to cause sliding and slipping because a surface or object is smooth, wet, or greasy: *a slippery street, a slippery floor.* 2 with a shifting or elusive meaning: *a slippery concept.* 3 tricky or not to be depended on: *a slippery character.* **slip′per·i·ness** *n.*

slippery elm *n* a N American elm with a slimy or slippery inner bark.

slippery slope *n* an idea or course of action that leads to something wrong or disastrous.

slip·shod (slip′shod′) *adj* careless in thought or working methods: *slipshod work, a slipshod essay.*

slip·stitch (slip′stich′) *n* 1 a loose stitch in sewing that joins layers of fabric but is not visible on the surface. 2 a stitch in knitting in which the stitches are moved from one needle to the other without being knitted.

slip·stream (slip′strēm′) *n* 1 a strong current of air or water driven back by a revolving, rapidly moving propeller, motor vehicle, or jet engine. 2 the area of decreased air pressure immediately behind such a moving object.

slip–up (slip′up′) *Informal n* a mistake: *There was a slip-up somewhere, and the message was never sent at all.*

slit (slit) *v* **slit, slit·ting** 1 make a long, straight cut or opening: *She used a paper knife to slit the envelope open.* 2 cut lengthwise into strips: *to slit leather into thongs.*
n a straight, narrow cut or opening: *His eyes were just slits.* <Old English *slitan*> **slit′like′** *adj.* **slit′ter** *n.*

slith·er (sliTH′ər) *v* 1 move smoothly over a surface with a twisting or sliding motion: *The snake slithered across our path.* 2 slip or slide unsteadily on a loose or slippery surface: *We slithered down the hillside.*
n a slithering movement. <Old English *slidrian*> **slith′er·y** *adj.*

sliv·er (sliv′ər) *n* a small, thin piece of something cut or split off: *a sliver of wood, a sliver of glass.*
v split or break into slivers. <Old English *slifan* split>

slob (slob) *n* 1 a lazy and untidy person. 2 🍁 slob ice. <probably Irish Gaelic *slab* mud>

slob·ber (slob′ər) *v* 1 let saliva drip from the mouth: *The dog slobbered all over my skirt.* 2 show too much enthusiasm for: *The fan slobbered over the star to get an autograph.*
n saliva dripping from the mouth. <origin uncertain> **slob′ber·i·ness** *n.* **slob′ber·y** *adj.*

🍁 **slob ice** *n* a dense mass of small pieces of ice, especially sea ice: *The boat pushed its way through the slob ice.*

a bat	e bed	i bid	o pot	u cup	th **thin**
ā cake	ē me	ī bite	ō go	ū rude	TH **then**
ä bar	ə about	ər over	ȯ for	u̇ put	zh measure

S

sloe (slō) *n* a small, dark purple fruit that grows on a thorny shrub. <Old English *sla*>

sloe–eyed (slō′īd′) *adj* with dark, almond-shaped eyes.

slog (slog) *v* **slogged, slog·ging 1** plod heavily and with a lot of effort: *We slogged through the snow to the cabin.* **2** work hard and steadily at something difficult: *She slogged away at the hard assignment.*
n a spell of hard, steady work at something difficult. <origin uncertain>
slog it out, fight or compete hard.

slo·gan (slō′gən) *n* a memorable word or phrase used to advertise or promote something: *"Service with a smile" was the store's slogan.* <Gaelic *sluagh* army + *gairm* cry>

slo–mo (slō′mō′) *Informal n* slow motion.

sloop (slūp) *n* a one-masted sailboat with a mainsail and jib rigged fore-and-aft. <Dutch *sloepe*>

slop (slop) *v* **slopped, slop·ping 1** spill or cause to spill over the edge of a container, typically as a result of careless handling: *The tea slopped over into the saucer. He slopped part of his drink on his trousers.* **2** splash through mud, slush, or water.
n **1** weak or sentimental language or material: *We thought the song lyrics were mostly slop.* **2 slops** *pl* waste water or refuse from a kitchen, bathroom, or chamber pot that has to be emptied by hand. <Middle English>

slope (slōp) *n* **1** a line or surface of which one end or side is at a higher level than another: *He tripped running down the slope.* **2** a difference in level or sideways position between the two ends or sides of a thing: *The floor of the theatre has a slope of one metre from back to front.* **3 slopes** *pl* a part of the side of a hill or mountain, especially as a place for skiing.
v **sloped, slop·ing 1** lie at an angle or slant as a surface or line: *The land sloped toward the sea.* **2** cause to slant: *He sloped the ground so that rainwater would run away from the basement wall.* <Old English *aslupan* to slip away, from *slupan* to slip>

slop·py (slop′ē) *adj* **slop·pi·er, slop·pi·est 1** containing too much liquid, water, or rain: *sloppy ground, sloppy weather.* **2** careless and too casual: *sloppy work.* **3** weakly or foolishly sentimental: *a sloppy romance.* **slop′pi·ly** *adv.* **slop′pi·ness** *n.*

sloppy Joe *n* a dish consisting of ground beef cooked with tomato sauce and spices, served in or on a bun.

slosh (slosh) *v* move through liquid steadily but irregularly and with a splashing sound: *Water from the flooded basement sloshed around our feet.*
n the action or sound of splashing in this way. <*slush*>

sloshed (slosht) *Informal adj* drunk.

slot[1] (slot) *n* **1** a small, narrow opening or groove: *coin slots. We have a letter slot in our front door.* **2** a place in a scheme: *The new comedy series has a good time slot.*
v **slot·ted, slot·ting 1** make a slot or slots in. **2** place in a scheme: *The new show will be slotted after the six o'clock news.* <origin uncertain>

sloth (slōth) *or* (sloth) *n* **1** unwillingness to work or exert oneself: *His sloth keeps him from taking out the garbage.* **2** a slow-moving mammal of the tropical Americas that hangs upside down from the branches of trees using its long limbs and hooked claws. <Old English *slaw* sluggish>

sloth·ful (slōth′fəl) *or* (sloth′fəl) *adj* unwilling to work or exert oneself. **sloth′ful·ly** *adv.* **sloth′ful·ness** *n.*

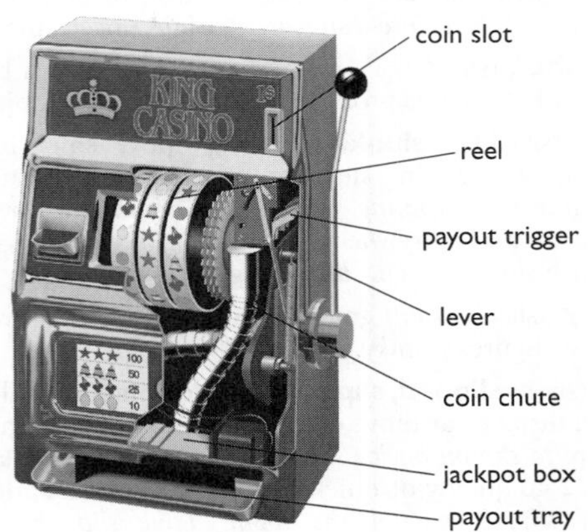

The first mechanical **slot machine** was invented in 1895. Today, most slot machines are electronic.

slot machine *n* a coin-operated machine, especially a gambling machine in which one pulls a handle, presses a button, etc., to try to match up a series of symbols.

slouch (slouch) *v* stand, sit, move, or walk in a lazy, drooping way: *He was slouched on the sofa. She slouched her shoulders.*
n **1** a lazy, drooping posture or movement. **2** (*with a negative*) an awkward, slovenly, or inefficient person: *He's no slouch at cricket.* <origin uncertain>
be no slouch, *Informal* have skill or ability: *She's no slouch at math.*

slouch·y (slou′chē) *adj* **slouch·i·er, slouch·i·est** not erect in posture or gait; slouching: *a slouchy walk.*

slough[1] (slū) *n* **1** a swamp or area of soft muddy ground. **2** 🍁 **a** *Prairie Provinces* a small marshy body of water formed in a depression in the ground by rain or melted snow: *Wild ducks nested on the prairie sloughs.* **b** *British Columbia* a backwater or side channel of a stream, or a shallow, marshy inlet of the sea. <Old English *sloh*>

slough[2] (sluf) *v* **1** cast off or shed an old skin or dead skin: *The snake sloughed its skin.* **2** (*usually with* **off**) cast off as something undesirable or tiresome: *She sloughed off a heavy backpack. He sloughed off his depression and started anew.*
n **1** the process of dropping off old or dead skin. **2** a thing that has been shed or cast off, especially the skin of a snake. <Middle English>

Slo·va·ki·a (slō vak′ē ə) *n* a country in central Europe. See the APPENDIX. **Slo′vak** or **Slo·vak′i·an** *adj, n.*

Slo·ve·ni·a (slō vē′nē ə) *n* a country in central Europe. **Slo′vene** or **Slo·ven′i·an** *adj, n.*

slov·en·ly (sluv′ən lē) *adj* **slov·en·li·er, slov·en·li·est** untidy, dirty, or careless in appearance or habits: *slovenly work.* <perhaps Flemish *sloef* dirty or Dutch *slof* careless> **slov′en·li·ness** *n.*

slow (slō) *adj* **1** moving or designed for moving at a low speed: *a slow train, a slow runner. He drove in the slow lane.* **2** showing a time earlier than the correct time: *Her watch was ten minutes slow.* **3** burning or heating slowly or gently: *a slow oven.* **4** not prompt to understand, think, or learn: *He was slow to pick up the idea.* **5** uneventful and dull, with little activity: *a slow day, slow sales.*
v (*often with* **down**) make or become slow or slower: *He slowed at the intersection. Business slowed down in the second half of the year.*
adv in a slow way: *She said to go slow.* <Old English *slaw* sluggish> **slow′ly** *adv.* **slow′ness** *n.*

GRAMMAR AND USAGE

Slow and **slowly** are both used as adverbs. In most written English, however, **slowly** is preferred as an adverb, except in certain set phrases to make them more forceful: *Go slow! Drive slow!*

slow–cook·er (slō′ku̇′kər) *n* an electric cooking pot, usually of metal with a china liner and a tight-fitting lid, used for cooking main dishes very slowly at low temperatures.

slow·down (slō′down′) *n* an act of slowing down: *There has been a slowdown in housing construction lately.*

slow motion *n* the action of showing a film or video more slowly than it was made or recorded, so that the action appears much slower than it actually was, or an action resembling this. **slow′-mo′tion** *adj.*

slow·poke (slō′pōk′) *Informal n* a person who acts or moves slowly.

slow–wit·ted (slō′wit′id) *adj* slow at thinking.

sludge (sluj) *n* **1** a thick, soft, wet mixture of liquids and solids, especially the product of an industrial or refining process, such as dirty oil or the sediment extracted from sewage after treatment. **2** a mass of small pieces of newly formed sea ice. <origin uncertain>

slug[1] (slug) *n* **1** a slow-moving mollusc resembling a snail without a shell, or with only a partly developed shell. **2** a caterpillar or larva. **3** a bullet. **4** a small disc, especially one used illegally instead of a coin in a coin-operated machine. <Middle English *slugg* sluggard>

slug[2] (slug) *Informal v* **slugged, slug·ging** hit hard with the fist, a bat, or a blunt weapon.
n a hard blow. <origin uncertain> **slug′ger** *n.*

slug·gard (slug′ərd) *n* a lazy, slow-moving person. <Middle English *slug* slow>

slug·gish (slug′ish) *adj* **1** lacking energy or vigour: *a sluggish mind.* **2** very slow in movement, growth, or flow: *a sluggish river, sluggish blood circulation. The economy has been sluggish for the past few months.* **slug′gish·ly** *adv.* **slug′gish·ness** *n.*

sluice (slūs) *n* **1** a structure with a sliding gate for holding back or controlling the water of a canal, river, or lake, the gate itself, or the water held back or controlled by the gate. **2** a long, sloping trough through which water flows, used to wash gold from sand, dirt, or gravel. **3** a channel for carrying off overflow or surplus water.
v **sluiced, sluic·ing** wash, pour, or flow freely with a stream or shower of water: *He sluiced his face in the icy water.* <Old French, from Latin *excludere* exclude>

slum (slum) *n* often, **slums** *pl* a district or area in a city characterized by overpopulation, poor housing and sanitation, and social problems.
v **slummed, slum·ming** visit slums or other places considered inferior to one's usual surroundings, especially out of curiosity. <origin uncertain>

slum·ber (slum′bər) *v* **1** sleep: *The baby slumbered peacefully through the uproar.* **2** be inactive or dormant: *The volcano had slumbered for years. The incident awakened his slumbering conscience.*
n **1** **slumbers** *pl* a sleep: *Her slumbers were interrupted by the sound of a siren.* **2** an inactive or dormant condition. <Old English *sluma*> **slum′ber·er** *n.* **slum′ber·ous** or **slum′brous** *adj.*

slum·lord (slum′lȯrd′) *n* an absentee owner of slum property, especially one who charges unreasonable rent.

slump (slump) *v* **1** sit, lean, or fall heavily and limply: *He slumped to the floor in a dead faint. The bored students slumped in their seats.* **2** go into a marked decline in price, value, or amount: *Sales have slumped.*
n **1** a great or sudden decline in price, value, or amount: *The economy was in a slump.* **2** a long period of failure or decline: *Having lost several games in a row, the team was in a bad slump.* <origin uncertain>

slung (slung) past tense and past participle of SLING.

slunk (slungk) past tense and past participle of SLINK.

slur (slər) *v* **slurred, slur·ring** **1** pronounce or be pronounced indistinctly so that the sounds run into one another: *"How're you?" he slurred.* **2** pass over a fact or aspect so as to conceal or minimize: *She slurred or ignored all his good qualities.* **3** *Music* glide over two or more notes smoothly, without a break. **4** make damaging or insulting comments about someone.
n **1** a damaging or insulting comment about someone: *His comments were a slur on the entire staff.* **2** an act of pronouncing something indistinctly so that the sounds run into one another. **3** *Music* a curved mark indicating that a group of two or more notes are to be sung or played smoothly, without a break. <origin uncertain>

slurp (slərp) *Informal v* eat or drink noisily or with a loud sucking sound.
n a slurping sound. <Dutch *slurpen*>

slur·ry (slər′ē) *n, pl* **slur·ries** a mixture of water and fine particles of an insoluble substance such as cement, mud, or clay. <origin uncertain>

slush (slush) *n* **1** partly melted snow or ice. **2** watery mud. **3** *Informal* overly sentimental talk or writing. <origin uncertain> **slush′i·ness** *n.* **slush′y** *adj.*

slush fund *n* money set aside for special projects generally, especially money collected or set aside for dishonest purposes such as bribery.

a bat	e bed	i bid	o pot	u cup	th thin
ā cake	ē me	ī bite	ō go	ū rude	ᴛʜ then
ä bar	ə about	ər over	ȯ for	u̇ put	zh measure

slut (slut) *n* **1** a woman considered to be sexually promiscuous. **2** a woman whose housework is untidy, caring little about cleanliness. <Middle English> **slut′tish** *adj.* **slut′tish·ly** *adv.* **slut′tish·ness** *n.*

sly (slī) *adj* **sly·er** or **sli·er, sly·est** or **sli·est** **1** clever in deceiving or tricking: *The sly cat stole the meat while the cook's back was turned.* **2** not straightforward or open: *Her sly questions were intended to get them to reveal more than they realized.* **3** playfully mischievous or knowing: *a sly wink.* <Old Norse *slægr* cunning> **sly′ly** *adv.* **sly′ness** *n.*
on the sly, in a way meant to avoid notice: *They got their information on the sly.*

smack[1] (smak) *n* **1** a sharp slap or blow, especially one given with the back of the hand, or the loud, sharp sound made in this way. **2** a loud kiss.
v **1** strike someone or something with a sharp slap or blow. **2** kiss loudly. **3** smash, drive, or put forcefully into or on something: *He smacked the ball into the far left corner.* **4** part one's lips noisily in anticipation or enjoyment of food, drink, or something else.
adv Informal **1** exactly or precisely: *She lived smack in the middle of downtown.* **2** in a sudden and violent way: *He fell smack on his face.* Also, **smack dab.** <origin uncertain>
smack down, sharply rebuke someone.

smack[2] (smak) *v* have a flavour of: *Her statement smacked of deceit.*
n **1** a slight taste or flavour: *The sauce had a smack of nutmeg.* **2** a trace or suggestion of: *The old sailor still had a smack of the sea about him.* <Old English *smæcc*>

smack[3] (smak) *n* a small sailboat with one mast. <Dutch>

smack·er (smak′ər) *Informal n* **1** a noisy kiss. **2** a dollar. Also, **smackeroo.**

small (smol) *adj* **1** of a size that is less than normal or usual: *The room was small and cosy.* **2** not great in amount, number, strength, or power: *a small dose, a small quantity, small hope of success.* **3** insignificant or unimportant: *a small matter.* **4** not fully grown or developed: *a small child.* **5** operating on a modest scale: *a small farmer, a small merchant.* **6** of a voice or sound, lacking strength or confidence.
adv **1** into small pieces: *Cut up the carrots small.* **2** in a small size: *He wrote very small.* <Old English *smæl*> **small′ish** *adj.* **small′ness** *n.*
feel small, be ashamed or humiliated.
small potatoes, something quite insignificant or unimportant: *The last deal was just small potatoes, compared with what she's planning now.*

small arms *n* weapons easily carried by a person, and held in the hand or hands while being fired: *Rifles and revolvers are classed as small arms.*

small capital *n* a capital letter that is only about as high as a lower-case letter. Example: In the sentence *Caesar conquered Britain in 54 CE*, the letters CE are printed in small capitals.

small change *n* **1** coins of low value. **2** a thing that is considered trivial.

small claims court *n* a court that deals quickly and inexpensively with claims for small sums of money without the use of lawyers.

small fry *n* **1** young fish, animals, or children. **2** people or things considered insignificant.

small hours *pln* the early hours of the morning after midnight.

small intestine *n* the long, narrow part of the intestine where most of the absorption of digested food takes place, extending from the stomach to the large intestine.

small letter *n* a lower-case letter, not a capital. Example: In this sentence, all the letters except the first one are small letters.

small–mind·ed (smol′mīn′did) *adj* with or showing a narrow outlook. **small′-mind′ed·ness** *n.*

small·mouth bass (smol′mouth′) *n* a N American freshwater fish with a short upper jaw. Compare LARGEMOUTH BASS.

small·pox (smol′poks′) *n* a contagious viral disease, thought to be destroyed through vaccination, characterized by fever and sores on the skin that leave scars.

small–scale (smol′skāl′) *adj* **1** limited in operation or scope: *She runs a small-scale import business.* **2** drawn to a small scale as a map or diagram.

small screen *n* television. **small-screen** *adj.*

small talk *n* polite, informal conversation that does not deal with important or controversial topics.

small–time (smol′tīm′) *Informal adj* minor, petty, or insignificant: *a small-time crook.*

small–town (smol′toun′) *adj* of or coming from a small town, sometimes considered as being narrow-minded or petty: *a small-town girl, small-town bigotry.*

smarm·y (smȧr′mē) *Informal adj* **smarm·i·er, smarm·i·est** using exaggerated or insincere flattery. <dialect *smalm* to smear> **smarm′i·ly** *adv.* **smarm′i·ness** *n.*

smart (smȧrt) *adj* **1** with or showing quick intelligence. *My sister says I'm the smart one in the family.* **2** quick or brisk: *a smart pace.* **3** clean, tidy, and well-dressed: *She looked smart in her school uniform.* **4** sarcastic or clever in an annoying way: *a smart answer.* **5** intended to boost mental powers: *This is being marketed as a smart drink.*
v **1** cause or feel a sharp, stinging pain: *My eyes smarted from the chlorine in the pool. The cut on my finger smarts.* **2** feel upset or irritated: *He smarted from the scolding.*
n **1** a sharp, stinging pain. **2 smarts** *pl Informal* practical intelligence. <Old English *smeorten*> **smart′ly** *adv.* **smart′ness** *n.*

smart al·eck or **al·ec** (al′ik) *Informal n* someone who is irritating because of giving too many clever answers or showing off intelligence.

smarten (smar′tən) *v* improve in appearance.
smarten up, *Informal* move, behave, or work more briskly or efficiently: *The boss told him to smarten up or he'd lose his job*

smash (smash) *v* **1** violently break something into pieces, or have broken in this way: *He smashed the window. The vase smashed when it fell on the floor.* **2** completely defeat or destroy something regarded as hostile or dangerous: *She smashed his argument with some hard facts.* **3** go bankrupt or fail financially. **4** move so as to hit or collide with something with great force and impact, or be severely damaged in this way: *The car smashed into a tree. The car was badly smashed up.* **5 a** *Badminton, Tennis, etc.* hit a ball or shuttlecock with a hard, overhand stroke. **b** *Baseball* hit a ball hard and far, usually for a home run or extra bases.

n **1** the act or sound of a smash or crash: *the smash of broken glass.* **2** a violent collision or impact between two vehicles. **3** a business failure or bankruptcy. **4 a** *Badminton, Tennis, etc.* a hard, fast, overhand stroke. **b** *Baseball* a hit that allows a batter to circle the bases and score a run without a fielding error, usually on a ball hit over the outfield fence. **5** a violent blow. **6** *Informal* a very successful song, movie, show, or performer. Also, **smash hit**. <probably imitative>

smash–up (smash′up′) *n* **1** a serious collision of vehicles: *She was involved in a smash-up and is still in hospital.* **2** a complete collapse or failure.

smat·ter·ing (smat′ə ring) *n* a slight or superficial knowledge of a language or a subject: *She has only a smattering of Latin.* <origin uncertain>

smear (smēr) *v* **1** cover or stain messily or carelessly with something sticky, greasy, or dirty, or receive a mark or stain in this way: *She smeared her fingers with jam. Wet paint smears easily.* **2** spread a greasy or sticky substance over something: *I smeared some suntan lotion on my face.* **3** messily blur or smudge the outline of something: *Her makeup was smeared.* **4** harm the reputation of someone by making a false accusation: *She attempted to smear her rival by suggesting that he had cheated on a test.*

n **1** a mark or stain left by smearing: *You have a smear of paint on your cheek.* **2** a sample of material spread thinly on a microscope slide for examination, typically to aid in medical diagnosis. **3** a false charge or accusation: *The smear was unsuccessful.* <Old English *smeoru* grease> **smear′i·ness** *n.* **smear′y** *adj.*

smear campaign *n* a deliberate attempt to destroy a person's reputation by spreading false accusations.

smell (smel) *v* **smelled** or **smelt, smell·ing** **1** perceive or detect the odour or scent of something. **2** detect or suspect something by means of instinct or intuition: *to smell danger.* **3** give out a scent or odour of a specified kind: *That meat smells bad.* **4** find or have a trace or suggestion of: *We smelled trouble.* **5** hunt or find by the faculty of smell: *The dog will smell out the thief.*

n **1** the faculty or power of perceiving odours or scents by means of the organs in the nose, or an act of inhaling in order to determine an odour or scent: *the sense of smell. Have a smell of that bouquet.* **2** the quality in a thing that affects the sense of smell: *the smell of burning oil.* **3** a trace or suggestion: *the smell of treachery.* <Middle English>

SYNONYMS

Smell and **odour** both refer to the quality of something that can be detected by our sense of smell: *The smell of oranges. The odour of mothballs.*

Scent and **aroma** emphasize pleasant smells: *I love that scent on you. What a memorable aroma!*

Stench means "strong, unpleasant smell": *The stench of the garbage made them sick.*

smelling salts *pl n* a pungent substance, usually containing ammonium. In former times, this was inhaled to relieve faintness or headaches.

smell·y (smel′ē) *adj* **smell·i·er, smell·i·est** giving off a strong, unpleasant odour: *The garbage can should be washed because it's getting smelly.*

smelt[1] (smelt) *v* melt ore in order to get the metal out of it, or obtain metal in this way. <Dutch *smelten*>

smelt[2] (smelt) *n, pl* **smelts** or (*especially collectively*) **smelt** a small, edible fish with silvery scales that lives in both salt water and fresh water. <Old English>

smelt[3] (smelt) a past tense and a past participle of SMELL.

smelt·er (smel′tər) *n* a place where ores or metals are smelted, or a person whose work or business is smelting ores or metals.

smid·gen (smij′ən) *Informal n* a tiny piece or amount of something. <origin uncertain>

smile (smīl) *v* **smiled, smil·ing** **1** make an upward curve of the mouth with the corners turned up to give a pleased, kind, or amused expression. **2** act favourably toward: *Luck smiled on us.* **3** give a smile of a specified kind: *She smiled a sunny smile.* **4** express by a smile: *She smiled her consent.*

n the act of smiling: *a friendly smile.* <origin uncertain> **smil′er** *n.* **smil′ing** *adj.* **smil′ing·ly** *adv.*

smirch (smərch) *v* **1** make something soiled. **2** discredit a person or a person's reputation.

n **1** a dirty mark or stain. **2** a thing that brings discredit to someone. <origin uncertain>

smirk (smərk) *v* smile in an irritatingly smug way.

n a smug smile. <Old English *smearcian* smile>

smite (smīt) *v* **smote, smit·ten** (smit′ən), **smit·ing** **1** *Poetic* strike with a firm blow: *He smote the dragon with his sword.* **2** (*always in the passive*) be strongly attracted by someone or something: *The moment I saw her I was smitten.* **3** (*usually with* ***with***) suddenly and strongly affected: *They were smitten with terror.* <Old English *smitan*>

smith (smith) *n* (*usually in compounds*) a person who makes or shapes things out of metal: *a blacksmith, a goldsmith.* <Old English>

smith·er·eens (smiŦH′ə rēnz′) *Informal pl n* small pieces: *She smashed the plate to smithereens.* <Irish *smidirin*>

smith·y (smith′ē) *or* (smiŦH′ē) *n, pl* **smith·ies** the workshop of a blacksmith.

smock (smok) *n* a loose, coatlike outer garment worn to protect clothing.

v decorate with **smocking**, decorative stitching used on clothing, made by gathering material closely with rows of stitches in a honeycomb pattern: *The little girl's dress was smocked from the neckline to the waist.* <Old English *smocc*>

a bat	e bed	i bid	o pot	u cup	th **thin**
ā cake	ē **me**	ī bite	ō **go**	ū **rude**	ŦH **then**
ä bar	ə **about**	ər **over**	ô **for**	ů **put**	zh measure

smog (smog) *n* fog or haze intensified by smoke or other pollution in the air. <*smoke* + *fog*>

smoke (smōk) *n* **1** the visible mixture of carbon and other particles in air that rises when a thing burns. **2** an act of smoking tobacco, or a cigarette or cigar that is smoked.
v **smoked, smok·ing 1** give off smoke, steam, or a vapour: *The fireplace smokes.* **2** draw the smoke from a pipe, cigar, or cigarette into the mouth or lungs and then exhale it. **3** cure or preserve meat or fish by exposing it to smoke. **4** drive someone or something out by smoke, or as if by smoke: *They smoked the groundhog from its hole.* **5** colour, darken, or stain with smoke. <Old English *smoca*>
go up in smoke, be unsuccessful: *All her dreams went up in smoke.*
smoke and mirrors, statements or activities intended to give a false impression: *All that fuss about feeling ill is smoke and mirrors; he just wants a day off school.*
smoke out, a drive out with smoke. **b** force someone to make something known.

smoke bomb *n* a bomb containing chemicals that give out dense smoke when it explodes.

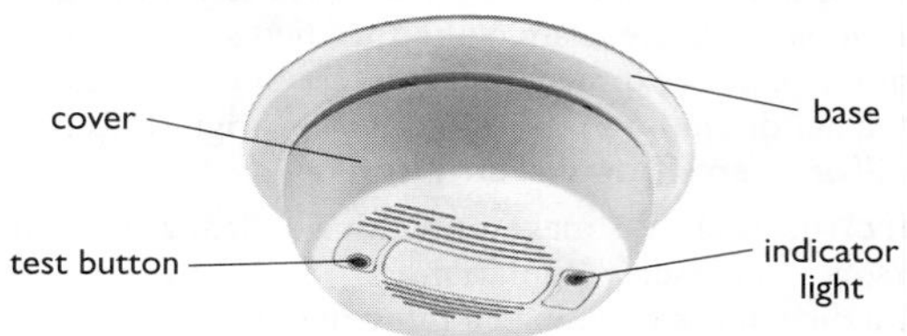

A **smoke detector** is so sensitive that an amount of smoke that is too small to see will trigger the alarm.

smoke detector *n* a device, installed in a home or other building, that warns of possible fire by making a piercing noise if smoke or abnormally high temperature is detected.

✱ **smoked meat** *n* cured beef similar to pastrami, often associated with Montréal.

smoke·house (smōk′hous′) *n* a building where meat or fish is treated with smoke to preserve and flavour it.

smoke·less (smō′klis) *adj* with or producing no smoke: *a smokeless flame.*

smok·er (smō′kər) *n* **1** a person who smokes tobacco. **2** a person or device that smokes fish or meat.

smoke·screen (smōk′skrēn′) *n* **1** a mass of thick smoke created to conceal a military operation from the enemy. **2** a thing that hides or obscures actual intentions or activities.

smoke·stack (smōk′stak′) *n* a tall chimney or funnel for discharging smoke from a locomotive, ship, or factory.

smoking gun *n* clear evidence of wrongdoing.

smok·y (smō′kē) *adj* **smok·i·er, smok·i·est 1** giving off or obscured by much smoke: *a smoky fire.* **2** full of or smelling of smoke: *a smoky room.* **3** darkened or stained with smoke. **4** with the taste and aroma of smoked food: *smoky ham.* **smok′i·ly** *adv.* **smok′i·ness** *n.*

smol·der (smōl′dər) SMOULDER.

smolt (smōlt) *n* a young salmon or trout that becomes silvery and migrates to the sea for the first time.

smooch (smüch) *Informal v* kiss.
n a kiss or spell of kissing. **smooch′er** *n.* **smooch′y** *adj.*

smooth (smüᴛʜ) *adj* **1** with an even and regular surface, like glass: *smooth stones.* **2** without heavy waves in a body of water: *a smooth voyage.* **3** without lumps in a liquid: *a smooth sauce.* **4** not wrinkled, pitted, or hairy in a person's face or skin. **5** without problems or difficulty in an action, event, or process: *a smooth course of affairs.* **6** charming and polished in manner, action, or words. **7** not harsh in sound or taste: *smooth verses, smooth wine.*
v **1** make smooth or smoother: *He smoothed out the ball of crushed paper and read it.* **2** make easy or easier: *His tact smoothed the way to an agreement.* <Old English *smoth*>
smooth′er *n.* **smooth′ly** *adv.* **smooth′ness** *n.*
smooth over, make something seem less wrong, unpleasant, or noticeable: *She tried to smooth over the argument between them.*

smooth–faced (smüᴛʜ′fāst′) *adj* **1** beardless or cleanshaven. **2** with the appearance of being agreeable and sincere: *a smooth-faced hypocrite.*

smooth·ie or **smooth·y** (smü′ᴛʜē) *Informal n*
1 a smooth, persuasive, often insincere person. **2** a thick drink of fruit blended with milk, yogurt, or ice cream.

smooth–tongued (smüᴛʜ′tungd′) *adj* speaking smoothly and agreeably but insincerely: *a smooth-tongued liar.*

smor·gas·bord (smôr′gəs bôrd′) *n* a buffet meal, featuring a large variety of foods. <Swedish *smörgås* sandwich + *bord* table>

smote (smōt) past tense of SMITE.

smoth·er (smuᴛʜ′ər) *v* **1** kill someone by covering the nose and mouth so that breathing is impossible: *The murderer smothered his victim with a pillow.* **2** put out a fire by covering it. **3** cover thickly or entirely: *In the fall the grass is smothered with leaves.* **4** suppress a feeling or action: *She smothered a sharp reply.* **5** make someone feel trapped and oppressed by being overly protective.
n a thing that smothers. <Middle English *smorther* suffocate> **smoth′er·y** *adj.*

smould·er or **smol·der** (smōl′dər) *v* **1** burn slowly and smoke but without flame: *The fire smouldered most of the night.* **2** show or feel barely suppressed anger, hatred, or other powerful emotion: *The people's discontent smouldered for years before it broke out into open rebellion. The woman's eyes smouldered with anger.*
n a slow, smoky burning without flame. <Middle English *smolderen*> **smould′er·ing** *adj.* **smould′er·ing·ly** *adv.*

smudge (smuj) *n* **1** a blurred dirty mark or smear. **2** a smoky fire made to drive away insects or to protect plants from frost.
v **smudged, smudg·ing 1** become or cause to become blurred and indistinct: *The drawing was smudged.* **2** use a smoky fire, especially in an orchard. <origin uncertain>

✱ **smudg·ing** (smuj′ing) *n* a ceremony practised by some First Nations peoples and others in which smoke from burning herbs is dispersed as a means of purifying a person or place.

smudg·y (smuj′ē) *adj* **smudg·i·er, smudg·i·est** smeared or blurred from being smudged.

smug (smug) *adj* **smug·ger, smug·gest** with or showing too much pride in oneself or one's achievements: *smug complacency.* <German *smuk* pretty> **smug′ly** *adv.* **smug′ness** *n.*

smug·gle (smug′əl) *v* **smug·gled, smug·gling 1** illegally and secretly take something into or out of a country. **2** take someone or something to a place without being seen: *The girl tried to smuggle her puppy onto the airplane with her.* <German *smuggeln*> **smug′gler** *n.*

smut (smut) *n* **1** a small flake of soot or other dirt, or the mark or smudge made by such a flake. **2** speech, written texts, or pictures that are considered indecent or obscene. **3** a plant disease in which the ears of grain are changed to a black powder, or the fungus that causes it.
v **smut·ted, smut·ting** soil or be soiled with a flake of smut. <Middle English> **smut′ti·ly** *adv.* **smut′ti·ness** *n.* **smut′ty** *adj.*

snack (snak) *n* a small amount of food eaten before meals, especially a light meal that is eaten in a hurry or in a casual way: *She ate a snack before going to bed.*
v eat a snack. <Dutch *snappen* to bite>

snack bar *n* a counter or small store where light meals are served.

snaf·fle (snaf′əl) *n* a slender, jointed bit on a bridle that is used with a single pair of reins, or a bridle with such a bit.
v **snaf·fled, snaf·fling** *Informal* take something for oneself, especially quickly and without permission. <origin uncertain>

sna·fu (sna fū′) *Informal n* a typical incident of confusion or disorder: *He missed the bus because of some snafu.*
adj in typical confusion or disorder.
v **sna·fued, sna·fu·ing** put into disorder or confusion. <military slang>

snag (snag) *n* **1** a hidden or unexpected obstacle: *She had to drop her plans because of a snag.* **2 a** a sharp or rough projecting point, such as the broken end of a branch. **b** a tear in fabric caused by such a point. **3** a tree or branch held fast in a river or lake.
v **snagged, snag·ging 1** catch or tear something on a projecting point, or become caught on it. **2** catch or obtain someone or something: *I snagged a lot of candy on my birthday.* <origin uncertain> **snag′gy** *adj.*

snag·gle–toothed (snag′əl tūtht′) *adj* with uneven, broken, or projecting teeth.

snail (snāl) *n* a small, soft-bodied mollusc that crawls very slowly and has a single spiral shell into which its whole body can be withdrawn. See GASTROPOD for picture. <Old English *snægl*>

snail mail *Informal n* the postal service, as opposed to electronic mail.

snail's pace *n* an extremely slow speed: *Traffic was moving at a snail's pace.*

snake (snāk) *n* **1** a long reptile with no legs or eyelids, a short tail, and jaws that can open wide. Snakes move by twisting their bodies over the ground or in the water. See ANACONDA, COBRA, REPTILE, RATTLER, and VIPER for pictures. **2** in full, **snake in the grass** a sly, treacherous person. **3** a long, flexible wire used to clear pipes of obstructions.
v **snaked, snak·ing** move, wind, or curve like a snake: *The road snaked through the hills.* <Old English *snaca*> **snake′like′** *adj.*

snake·bite (snāk′bīt′) *n* the bite of a snake, especially a poisonous one, or the condition resulting from the bite.

snake charmer *n* a person who entertains an audience by demonstrating an apparent power to hypnotize or charm snakes, especially by means of music.

snake dance *n* **1** an informal single-file procession of people who join hands and dance in a weaving path, especially as part of a celebration. **2** a ceremonial dance among certain peoples in which live snakes are handled.

snake oil *n* a liquid presented as a cure-all, but with no true medicinal properties.

snake·pit (snāk′pit′) *n* **1** a pit filled with snakes. **2** a scene of ruthless behaviour or ruthless competiton.

snake·root (snā′krūt′) *n* a plant whose roots have been regarded as a remedy for snakebites or are shaped like snakes.

snake·skin (snāk′skin′) *n* the skin of a snake, or the leather made from it.

snak·y (snā′kē) *adj* **snak·i·er, snak·i·est 1** of or like a snake or snakes. **2** curving, turning, or twisting, suggesting the movements of a snake: *a snaky path.* **3** showing coldness, malice, or cunning in a way regarded as typical of a snake. **snak′i·ly** *adv.* **snak′i·ness** *n.*

snap (snap) *v* **snapped, snap·ping 1** break or cause to break suddenly and completely, typically with a sudden, sharp sound: *The violin string snapped.* **2** make a sudden, sharp, cracking sound: *She snapped her fingers in time to the music.* **3** make a sudden, quick bite or snatch: *The dog snapped at my hand.* **4** move or cause to move in a specified way with a brisk movement and usually a sharp sound: *He snapped the lid shut.* **5** become suddenly unable to endure a strain: *His nerves snapped.* **6** seize eagerly: *She snapped at the chance to go to Nunavut.* **7** speak sharply or impatiently: *Don't snap at him; he doesn't understand what you want.* **8** move quickly and sharply: *The soldiers snapped to attention. Her eyes snapped with anger.* **9** take a snapshot of. **10** *Football* put the ball in play by passing it in a quick backward movement.
n **1** a sudden, sharp cracking sound or movement: *The box shut with a snap.* **2** a sharp or impatient tone or manner. **3** *Informal* an easy task: *She said the exam was a snap.* **4** DOME FASTENER. **5** a thin, crisp cookie: *ginger snaps.* **6** a snapshot. **7** *Football* a quick backward movement of the ball as it is put into play.
adj made or done quickly or unexpectedly: *a snap judgment, a snap election.* <Dutch *snappen* to seize>
snap out of it, *Informal* suddenly change one's attitude or conduct: *You're slacking off, so you'd better snap out of it!*

a bat	e bed	i bid	o pot	u cup	th thin
ā cake	ē me	ī bite	ō go	ū rude	ᴛʜ then
ä bar	ə about	ər over	ô for	ů put	zh measure

snap·drag·on (snap′drag′ən) *n* a garden plant with spikes of brightly coloured flowers that gape like a mouth when a bee lands on the curved lips.

snap fastener DOME FASTENER.

snap·per (snap′ər) *n* **1** a person who or thing that snaps. **2** a snapping turtle. **3** a reddish fish of tropical seas, especially the red snapper.

snapping turtle *n* a freshwater N American turtle with a long neck and strong jaws.

snap·pish (snap′ish) *adj* **1** quick and sharp in speech or manner; curt and irritable: *He's very snappish today.* **2** apt to bite or snap, especially as a dog.

snap·py (snap′ē) *Informal adj* **snap·pi·er, snap·pi·est** **1** brisk and vigorous: *We went at a snappy pace.* **2** sharp and cool as weather: *a snappy fall day.* **3** stylish: *a snappy sports jacket. She's a snappy dresser.*
make it snappy, *Informal* hurry when doing something: *We're waiting, so make it snappy with your phone call.*

snap·shot (snap′shot′) *n* **1** an informal photograph, such as one taken by an amateur photographer with a handheld camera: *We got some excellent snapshots of Sable Island.* **2** a brief look at or summary of something.

snare[1] (sner) *n* **1** a noose of wire or cord for catching small animals and birds. **2** a thing that is likely to lure or tempt someone into harm or making a mistake: *She said it was easy to be caught in the snare of quick profits.*
v **snared, snar·ing** catch with a snare: *One day they snared a rabbit.* <Old Norse *snara*>

snare[2] (sner) *n* a length of wire or cord stretched across the bottom of a drum, producing a rattling sound when the drum is struck. <Dutch *snaar* string>

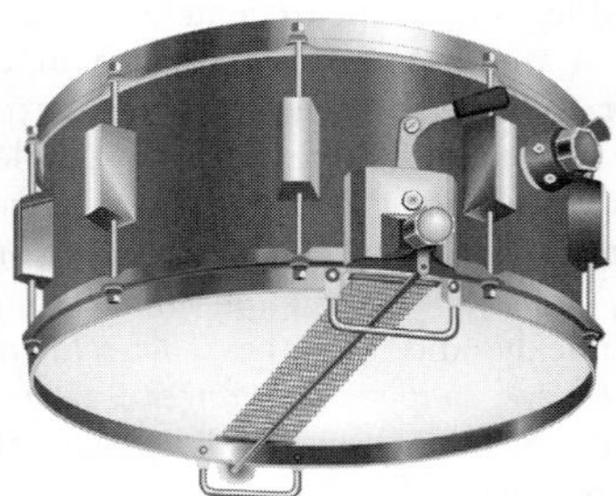

The **snare drum** began as a military instrument, used since the 1600s to set a marching pace for foot soldiers.

snare drum *n* a small drum with lengths of wire or cord stretched across the bottom of a double-headed drum to make a rattling sound when the drum is struck.

snark·y (snär′kē) *Informal adj* **snark·i·er, snark·i·est** sharply sarcastic or critical: *He made one snarky comment after another.* <Dutch *snorken* to snort> **snark′i·ly** *adv.* **snark′i·ness** *n.*

snarl[1] (snärl) *v* **1** growl aggressively while baring the teeth as a dog or similar animal: *The dog snarled at the stranger.* **2** speak harshly in a sharp, hostile tone, or say something in this way: *The kidnapper snarled at his prisoner. The bully snarled a threat.*
n the act or sound of snarling. <origin uncertain> **snarl′er** *n.* **snarl′ing** *adj.* **snarl′ing·ly** *adv.* **snarl′y** *adj.*

snarl[2] (snärl) *v* entangle or impede, or become entangled and impeded: *The knitting yarn was badly snarled. Traffic soon became snarled when the traffic lights broke down.*
n a knot or tangle: *She combed the snarls out of her hair. His legal affairs were in a snarl.* <*snare*[1]>

snatch (snach) *v* **1** quickly seize something in a rude or eager way: *She snatched her jacket and ran.* **2** *Informal* steal something or kidnap someone, typically by seizing or grabbing: *The police said the child was snatched from her own home.* **3** save or attain by quick action: *They snatched a victory from defeat.*
n **1** the act of snatching: *The boy made a snatch at the ball.* **2** a short spell of doing something: *He had a snatch of sleep sitting in his chair.* **3** a fragment of song or talk: *He could only hear snatches of conversation.* <Middle English> **snatch′er** *n.*
snatch at, a try to seize or grasp: *She snatched at the railing to keep herself from falling.* **b** eagerly take advantage of: *He snatched at the chance to travel.*

snaz·zy (snaz′ē) *Informal adj* **snazz·i·er, snazz·i·est** attractive and impressive in a stylish way: *a snazzy car, a snazzy new outfit.* <origin uncertain> **snazz′i·ly** *adv.* **snazz′i·ness** *n.*

sneak (snēk) *v* **sneaked** or **snuck, sneak·ing** **1** move or go in a stealthy, sly way: *The man sneaked past the house, looking for an open window.* **2** get, put, or pass something in a stealthy, sly way: *He sneaked a camera into the art gallery.* **3** creep up on someone without being detected.
n **1** the action of sneaking. **2** a sneaky, cowardly person, especially someone who reports the misdeeds of friends to an authority.
adj acting or done in a stealthy, underhanded, or unofficial way, or without warning: *a sneak attack.* <Old English *snican*> **sneak′i·ly** *adv.* **sneak′i·ness** *n.* **sneak′y** *adj.*

sneak·er (snē′kər) *n* **1** a shoe with a cloth upper and a pliable sole, used for playing sports or for general casual wear: *She was dressed in a sweater, blue jeans, and sneakers.* **2** a person who sneaks.

sneak·ing (snē′king) *adj* **1** present in the mind, but reluctantly held or not fully recognized: *I have a sneaking suspicion that she doesn't know what she's talking about.* **2** cowardly and underhanded: *sneaking treachery.* **sneak′ing·ly** *adv.*

sneak preview *n* a special single showing of a new movie in advance of regular distribution in order to test audience reaction.

sneak thief *n* a person who takes advantage of open doors, windows, or other easy opportunities to steal.

sneak·y (snē′kē) *adj* **sneak·i·er, sneak·i·est** sly, mean, or underhanded.

sneer (snēr) *n* a contemptuous or mocking smile, remark, or tone: *There was a sneer on her face.*
v smile or speak in a contemptuous or mocking way: *She sneers at any expression of sentiment.* <Middle English *sneren*> **sneer′er** *n.* **sneer′ing** *adj.* **sneer′ing·ly** *adv.*

sneeze (snēz) *v* **sneezed, sneez·ing** expel air suddenly and violently through the nose and mouth due to irritation of one's nostrils.
n a sudden, violent expelling of air through the nose and mouth. <Middle English>

not to be sneezed at, *Informal* not to be disregarded or despised: *A saving of twenty dollars is not to be sneezed at.*

snick (snik) *v* **1** cut or snip with small strokes. **2** make or cause something to make a sharp, clicking sound.
n **1** a small notch or cut. **2** a sharp click. <origin uncertain>

snick·er (snik′ər) *n* a half-suppressed and usually disrespectful laugh.
v laugh in this way. <imitative>

snide (snīd) *adj* spitefully or slyly sarcastic: *When he did not get the part in the play, he started making snide remarks about the director.* <origin uncertain> **snide′ly** *adj.* **snide′ness** *n.*

sniff (snif) *v* **1** draw air through the nose in short, quick breaths that can be heard in order to detect a smell, to stop it running, or to express contempt: *She sniffed the steam to clear her head. He sniffed at the cheap gift.* **2** draw in a scent, substance, or air through the nose: *The dog sniffed suspiciously at the stranger.* **3** suspect or detect: *The police sniffed a plot and broke up the meeting.*
n **1** the act or sound of sniffing: *a loud sniff.* **2** an amount of air or a substance taken up in such a way. **3** a hint or suggestion. <Middle English>
sniff out, find by following up clues: *The police soon sniffed out the gang leader.*

snif·fle (snif′əl) *Informal v* **snif·fled, snif·fling** sniff slightly and repeatedly, especially because of a cold or fit of crying: *Don't sniffle; blow your nose.*
n **1** the act or sound of sniffling. **2 the sniffles** *pl* a head cold marked by a runny nose and sniffling. <imitative> **snif′fler** *n.*

sniff·y (snif′ē) *Informal adj* **sniff·i·er, sniff·i·est** inclined to be scornful or contemptuous.

snif·ter (snif′tər) *n* a pear-shaped glass with a short stem and used especially for brandy.

snig·ger (snig′ər) *n* a snicker.

snip (snip) *v* **snipped, snip·ping** cut with a small, quick stroke or series of strokes with scissors: *She snipped the thread.*
n **1** the act of snipping: *With a few snips, she cut out a paper doll.* **2** a small piece cut off from something: *Pick up the snips of cloth and thread from the floor.* **3** *Informal* a small or unimportant person. **4 snips** *pl* hand shears for cutting metal. <German *snip* small piece>

snipe (snīp) *n, pl* **snipes** or (*especially collectively*) **snipe** a shorebird of the sandpiper family, with a long bill used in digging for worms in the mud.
v **sniped, snip·ing** **1** shoot at someone from a hiding place, especially at long range. **2** make a sly or petty verbal attack. <Old Norse *snipa*>

snip·er (snī′pər) *n* a person who shoots from a hiding place at one enemy or target at a time, especially at long range.

snip·pet (snip′it) *n* a small piece or brief extract: *snippets of information.*

snip·py (snip′ē) *Informal adj* **snip·pi·er, snip·pi·est** sharp or curt, especially in a disdainful way. **snip′pi·ly** *adv.* **snip′pi·ness** *n.*

snit (snit) *Informal n* a fit of sulks or irritation: *There's no need to get into a snit about it.* <origin uncertain>

snitch (snich) *Informal v* **1** steal. **2** inform on someone.
n an informer or tattletale. <origin uncertain>
snitch′er *n.*

sniv·el (sniv′əl) *v* **sniv·elled** or **sniv·eled, sniv·el·ling** or **sniv·el·ing** **1** cry and sniffle. **2** complain in a whining or tearful way.
n a slight sniff indicating suppressed emotion or crying. <Old English *snofl* mucus> **sniv′el·ler** or **sniv′e·ler** *n.*

snob (snob) *n* **1** a person who is too anxious to please or imitate people who are socially more powerful, and ignores those considered socially inferior. **2** a person who believes that his or her taste in something is superior to those of other people: *a wine snob.* <origin uncertain>
snob′ber·y *n.* **snob′by** *adj.*

snob·bish (snob′ish) *adj* of or like a snob.
snob′bish·ly *adv.* **snob′bish·ness** *n.*

snook·er (snůk′ər) *or* (snů′kər) *n* a game played on a special table with cues, fifteen red balls, and six other balls of different colours. Players aim the cue at a white ball to send the other balls into pockets in a set order. See also BILLIARDS, POOL. <origin uncertain>

snoop (snūp) *Informal v* investigate or look around in a stealthy way in order to find out something, especially information about private matters: *I think she snooped in my room and read my diary.*
n a person who snoops. <Dutch *snœpen* eat in secret>
snoop′er *n.*

snoot (snūt) *Informal n* a nose. <*snout*>

snoot·y (snū′tē) *Informal adj* **snoot·i·er, snoot·i·est** snobbish and conceited, showing disapproval or contempt of other people.

ETYMOLOGY

Snooty comes from *snoot*, Scottish dialect for *snout* meaning "nose." Snooty people are often thought of as walking around with their noses in the air.

snooze (snūz) *Informal v* **snoozed, snooz·ing** take a short nap, especially during the day.
n a short nap. <origin uncertain> **snooz′y** *adj.*

snooz·er (snūz′ər) *Informal n* **1** a person taking a short nap. **2** a boring movie, book, TV program, etc.

snore (snôr) *v* **snored, snor·ing** breathe during sleep with a harsh, rough sound: *The lazy man snored away the afternoon.*
n the sound made in snoring. <origin uncertain>

snor·kel (snôr′kəl) *n* a curved tube for taking in air, allowing a swimmer to breathe while under water near the surface. See SCUBA DIVER for picture. <German *Schnorchel*>

a bat	e bed	i bid	o pot	u cup	th thin
ā cake	ē me	ī bite	ō go	ū rude	TH then
à bar	ə about	ər over	ô for	ů put	zh measure

snort (snôrt) *v* **1** force the breath violently through the nose with a loud, harsh sound, especially to indicate mockery, surprise, or displeasure: *a snort of indignation.* **2** make a sound like this: *The engine snorted.* **3** *Informal* inhale an illegal drug.
n the act or sound of snorting. <Middle English *snoren*>
snort′er *n.*

snout (snout) *n* the projecting part of an animal's head that contains the nose and mouth, especially of a mammal. <Dutch *snut*>

snow (snō) *n* **1** water vapour from the air frozen into crystals that fall to earth in light, white flakes. **2** something resembling or suggesting snow in colour or texture.
v **1** fall as snow: *It snowed all day.* **2** let fall or scatter in a way resembling snow: *Petals from the apple blossoms were snowing over the garden.* **3** *Informal* arrive as an overwhelming quantity: *We were snowed with requests for the pamphlet.* **4** *Informal* mislead or charm someone with insincere statements or flattery: *He completely snowed us with all his compliments.* <Old English *snaw*>
pure as the driven snow, See PURE.
snowed in, shut in, covered, or blocked by snow: *The town was snowed in for a week.*
snow under, a cover with snow. **b** *Informal* overwhelm: *He is snowed under with work.*

snow angel *n* a shape like that of an angel figure, made in the snow by lying down and moving one's outstretched arms and legs to form the shape of wings and gown.

snow apple *n* an eating apple with white flesh.

snow·ball (snō′bol′) *n* **1** a ball made of snow pressed together, especially one that people make for throwing at each other for fun. **2** a thing that grows rapidly in strength or importance: *a snowball effect.* **3** a shrub with white flowers in large white clusters like snowballs.
v **1** throw balls of snow at. **2** increase rapidly in size or strength like a rolling snowball: *The number of signers of the petition for a swimming pool snowballed.*

snow·bank (snō′bangk′) *n* a large mass or drift of snow.

snow·belt (snō′belt′) *n* a region that has more snowfalls in winter than surrounding areas.

snow·bird (snō′bərd′) *n* **1** a snow bunting. **2** a junco. **3** *Informal* a person who spends the winter in a place with a warmer climate.

snow–blind (snō′blīnd′) *adj* blinded, usually temporarily, by being overexposed to the glare of sunlight on wide expanses of snow or ice. **snow blindness** *n.*

snow·blow·er (snō′blō′ər) *n* a machine that clears snow by drawing it in and blowing it out in another direction.

snow·board (snō′bōrd′) *n* a short board with upturned ends, for standing or crouching on while sliding down a snowy slope. See COVERALLS for picture of a snowboarder. **snow′board·er** *n.* **snow′board·ing** *n.*

snow·bound (snō′bound′) *adj* shut in by snow: *We were snowbound for two days after the blizzard and couldn't go to school.*

snow bunting *n* a small songbird that breeds in the Arctic and winters in northern temperate regions, with mostly white feathers.

snow·capped (snō′kapt′) *adj* of a mountain, with its top covered with snow. **snow′cap** *n.*

snow devil *n* a whirling column of snow sucked up into the air by the wind.

snow·drift (snō′drift′) *n* a mass or bank of snow piled up by the wind.

snow·drop (snō′drop′) *n* a small plant with drooping white flowers that blooms early in the spring.

snow·fall (snō′fol′) *n* **1** a fall of snow. **2** the amount of snow falling within a certain time and area: *The snowfall in that one storm was thirty centimetres.*

snow fence *n* a temporary fence erected in winter on the windward side to prevent snow from drifting.

snow·field (snō′fēld′) *n* a large expanse of snow, especially in mountainous or polar regions.

snow·flake (snō′flāk′) *n* a small, feathery piece of snow, usually in the form of a sixfold crystal.

snow goose *n* a wild goose that breeds in the Arctic, the adult typically white with black wing tips.

snowhouse (snō′hous′) *n* **1** an igloo or other structure made of snow blocks. **2** a hut, cave, or fort made out of snow for playing in.

snow job *Informal n* an attempt to deceive or win over with persuasive, flattering talk.

snow leopard *n* a large wild cat found in the mountains of central Asia, with a long, thick, greyish coat marked with dark spots arranged in rosettes.

snow lily *n* a glacier lily.

snow·line (snō′līn′) *n* the altitude above which there is snow all year round.

snow·man (snō′man′) *n, pl* **snow·men** (-men′) a mass of snow shaped into a figure somewhat like a person standing.

snow·melt (snō′melt′) *n* the melting of fallen slow, or the water resulting from it.

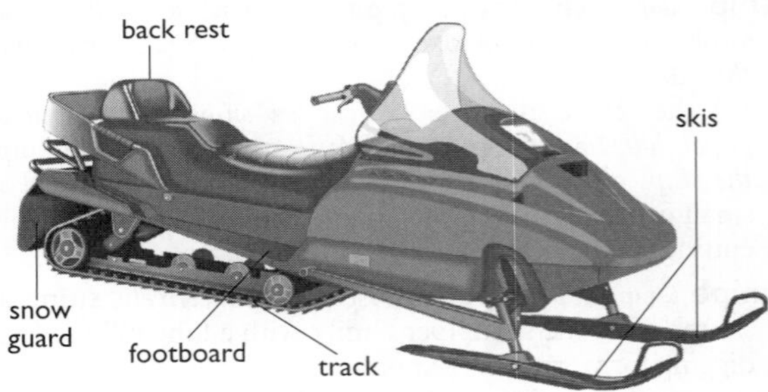

(Joseph) Armand Bombardier of Québec introduced the Ski-Doo **snowmobile** in 1959. It was a smaller version of a ski-steered, 12-passenger vehicle that Bombardier had designed for military use during World War II.

snow·mo·bile (snō′mə bēl′) *n* a small, open or closed motor vehicle for travelling over snow and ice and equipped with skis and a caterpillar track, or with two tracks.
v **snow·mo·biled, snow·mo·bil·ing** travel by snowmobile.

snow–on–the–moun·tain (snō′ən ᴛʜə moun′tən) *n* a N American plant with white-edged upper leaves and small but showy white bracts under them.

snow·pack (snō′pak′) *n* a mass of fallen snow that is compressed and hardened by its own weight.

snow·pants (snō′pants′) *pln* heavily lined, often waterproof pants worn in cold or snowy weather over regular pants, especially as part of a two-piece snowsuit.

snow pea *n* a variety of pea whose pods are sweet and crisp, eaten when the pod is young and flat.

snow·plow or **snow·plough** (snō′plou′) *n* **1** a vehicle equipped to clear away thick snow from roads by means of a large blade that pushes the snow aside. **2** *Skiing* a method of stopping by bringing the front tips of the skis together, almost touching, while keeping the back ends spread outward.

❋ **snow route** *n* a major road in a city, marked for priority snow clearing.

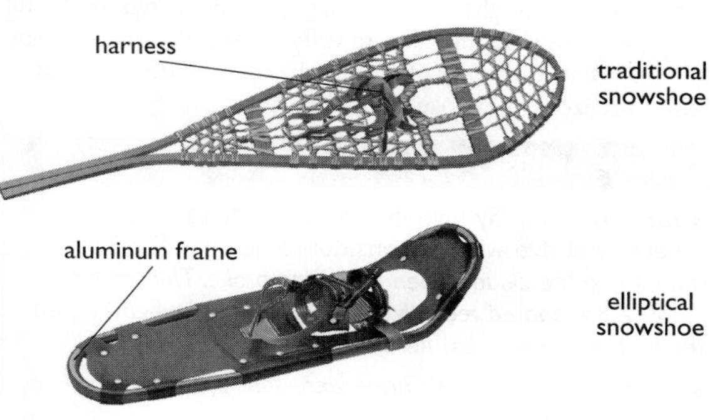

Canada's Inuit and Aboriginal peoples made **snowshoes** by binding pine branches together and adding rawhide straps to hold the foot.

snow·shoe (snō′shū′) *n* a light, flat frame that is attached to the sole of a boot and used to walk on snow.
v **snow·shoed, snow·shoe·ing** travel on snowshoes.

snowshoe hare *n* a medium-sized N American hare with large hind feet, fairly small ears, and a white winter coat. Also called **snowshoe rabbit**.

snow shovel *n* a shovel with a large square blade and slightly curved sides that is used for clearing snow.

snow·slide (snō′slīd′) *n* the action of a mass of snow sliding down a steep slope, or the mass of snow that slides.

snow·storm (snō′stôrm′) *n* a storm with much snow and, usually, a high wind.

snow·suit (snō′sūt′) *n* a one-piece or two-piece outer garment, usually with a hood, worn in cold or snowy weather, especially by children.

snow tire *n* a tire for motor vehicles that has a deeply cut tread to give extra traction when driving in snow.

snow–white (snō′wīt′) *adj* of a pure white colour.

snow·y (snō′ē) *adj* **snow·i·er, snow·i·est 1** characterized by or covered with snow: *snowy clothing.* **2** of or like snow, especially in being pure white: *snowy hair.*

snowy owl *n* a large owl with yellow eyes and feathered toes that breeds mainly in the Arctic tundra.

snub (snub) *v* **snubbed, snub·bing 1** ignore or treat scornfully: *The wealthy widow snubbed her poor cousin.* **2** check or stop a horse or a boat, especially by a rope wound round a post.
n an act of ignoring someone or showing scorn.
adj short and turned-up at the end of a person's nose: *snub-nosed, a snub nose.* <Old Norse *snubba* reprove>

snub·by (snub′ē) *adj* **snub·bi·er, snub·bi·est** short and turned up at the tip of a nose.

snuck (snuk) a past participle of SNEAK.

snuff[1] (snuf) *v* extinguish a lighted candle.
n the burned part of a candlewick. <origin uncertain>
snuff out, put an end to suddenly and brutally: *The new dictator snuffed out the people's hopes for freedom.*

snuff[2] (snuf) *n* powdered tobacco that is sniffed up the nostril rather than smoked.
v inhale or sniff at something: *He snuffed up salt and water to relieve his cold.* <Dutch *snuffen* sniffle>
up to snuff, *Informal* **a** in good order or condition. **b** in good health.

snuff·box (snuf′boks′) *n* a small box for holding SNUFF[2].

snuff·er (snuf′ər) *n* a small, hollow, metal cone or similar shape on the end of a handle, used to extinguish a lighted candle by smothering the flame.

snuf·fle (snuf′əl) *v* **snuf·fled, snuf·fling 1** breathe noisily through the nose due to a cold or crying. **2** make repeated sniffing sounds, especially as an animal.
n **1** the act or sound of snuffling. **2 the snuffles** *pl Informal* a cold or other infection that can cause snuffling. <German *snuffelen*>

snug (snug) *adj* **snug·ger, snug·gest 1** comfortable, warm, and cosy: *The cat has found a snug corner near the fireplace.* **2** neat, trim, and compact: *There were snug cabins on the boat.* **3** fitting closely or too tight as clothing: *That coat is a little too snug.* **4** safe and secure: *a snug income.*
v **snugged, snug·ging** make snug. <origin uncertain>
snug′ly *adv.* **snug′ness** *n.*

S

SYNONYMS

Snug emphasizes the comfort, warmth, and security of a small place: *All the kids were snug in their beds.*

Sheltered means "protected from unpleasantness or hardship": *The cave offered a sheltered spot for the animals during the storm.*

snug·gle (snug′əl) *v* **snug·gled, snug·gling** settle or move into a warm, comfortable position. <*snug*>

a bat	e bed	i bid	o pot	u cup	th thin
ā cake	ē me	ī bite	ō go	ū rude	ᴛʜ then
à bar	ə about	ər over	ȯ for	ů put	zh measure

snye or **sny** (snī) *n, pl* **snyes** or **snies** a side channel of a stream, especially one that rejoins the stream after forming an island.

ETYMOLOGY

Snye comes from Canadian French *chenail*, which means "channel," especially a side channel that bypasses falls or rapids. *Chenail* came through Old French *chanel* from Latin *canalem*, meaning "pipe."

so[1] (sō) *adv* **1** to such a great extent: *We were so cold we nearly died. You are so kind.* **2** to the same extent: *He was not so cold as she was.* **3** *Informal* (*with a gesture*) indicating size: *The fish was about so long.* **4** in the way shown: *Hold your pen so.* **5** referring to something previously mentioned, for example, in stating that such is the case, that things are similar, or to express agreement: *Is that really so? They say you are a painter—is that so?* **6** *Informal* (*with words that are not usually modified*) extremely: *Oh, that's so not true!*
conj **1** and for this reason or with the result that: *Go away so I can rest.* **2** with the purpose or intention that: *I did the work so she would not need to.* **3** introducing a question or statement: *So, what did you do on your vacation? So that's the way it is.* **4** in the same way: *Just as he was bored, so we were just as much.* <Old English *swa*>
and so, a likewise or also: *He is here, and so is she.* **b** accordingly: *I said I would go, and so I shall.*
and so on or **and so forth,** and other things of the same kind.
just so, exactly correct and orderly: *She insists on having everything just so.*
or so, more or less: *The card arrived a day or so ago.*
so as, with the aim or purpose: *She goes to bed early so as to get enough sleep.*
so much for, a with enough said or done about: *So much for my opinion; now let's hear yours.* **b** it is clear that something has completely failed to live up to expectations: *So much for their "sale to end all sales"!*
so what? why does that matter?

so[2] (sō) *Music n* **1** the fifth tone of an eight-tone major scale, especially as sung to sol-fa syllables: *do, re, mi, fa, so, la, ti, do.* **2** the tone G. Also, **soh**, **sol**.

soak (sōk) *v* **1** make or allow something to become thoroughly wet by immersing it in liquid, or be immersed in water or another liquid: *The rain soaked our clothes.* **2** *Informal* impose heavy charges on: *She was soaked by the long distance charges on her cellphone.*
n **1** the act or process of soaking: *Give the clothes a long soak.* **2** the condition of being soaked. <Old English *socian*>
soak up, a absorb or suck up: *to soak up sunshine.* **b** take into the mind: *to soak up knowledge.*

so–and–so (sō′ən sō′) *Informal n, pl* **so-and-sos** **1** a person or thing not named. **2** an unpleasant person.

soap (sōp) *n* a substance used with water for washing or cleaning, usually made of a fat and a strong alkali, often with perfume and colouring added.
v wash with soap: *Soap the dirty shirts well.* <Old English *sape*> **soap′less** *adj.*

soap·ber·ry (sōp′ber′ē) *n, pl* **soap·ber·ries** a tree or shrub with berries that produce a soapy froth when crushed.

soap·box (sōp′boks′) *n* **1** a box or crate used as a stand by a public speaker in the open air. **2** a box or crate formerly used to pack and transport soap.

soap opera *n* a radio or TV drama presented in serial form, often during the daytime, dealing with daily events in the lives of the same group of characters.

soap·stone (sōp′stōn′) *n* a heavy, soft stone composed mainly of talc, and often used for carving.

soap·suds (sōp′sudz′) *pl n* bubbles and foam made with soap and water.

soap·y (sō′pē) *adj* **soap·i·er, soap·i·est** **1** containing or covered with soap or soapsuds. **2** of or like soap. **3** *Informal* unpleasantly flattering.

soar (sôr) *v* **1** fly or rise high in the air, especially in maintaining height without flapping the wings or using engine power. **2** increase rapidly above the usual level: *Prices were soaring.* <Old French, from *Latin* ex- out + *aura* breeze, i.e., expose to the breezes>

CONFUSABLES

Soar can mean "fly high in the air" or "rise quickly," especially above what is considered normal: *The kite soared into the clouds when the string broke. The price of gasoline has soared recently. My spirits soared when I heard she had recovered from her illness.*

Sore refers to pain: *His arms were sore after the long swim across the channel.*

sob (sob) *v* **sobbed, sob·bing** **1** cry with short, loud breaths: *She sobbed herself to sleep.* **2** say or express with sobs: *He sobbed out his sad story.*
n an act or sound of sobbing. <Middle English *sobben*>

so·ber (sō′bər) *adj* **1** having drunk no alcohol. **2** quiet, serious, and solemn: *a sober expression.* **3** muted in colour: *dressed in sober grey.*
v make or become sober: *Seeing the car accident sobered us all.* <Old French, from Latin *sobrius*> **so′ber·ly** *adv.* **so′ber·ness** *n.*
sober down, become quiet, serious, or solemn.
sober up, recover from having drunk too much alcohol.

so·ber–mind·ed (sō′bər mīn′did) *adj* with or showing a sober mind.

so·bri·e·ty (sə brī′ə tē) *n, pl* **so·bri·e·ties** **1** the condition of being sober. **2** the quality of being quiet, serious, and solemn.

so·bri·quet (sō′brə kā′) *n* a nickname. Also, **soubriquet**.

sob story *Informal n* a story or explanation that is too sentimental.

so·ca (sō′kə) *n* a type of music, originally from Trinidad, that blends elements of soul and calypso. <*soul* + *calypso*>

so–called (sō′kold′) *adj* commonly called thus, especially inappropriately or incorrectly: *My so-called friends forgot to ask me to their party.*

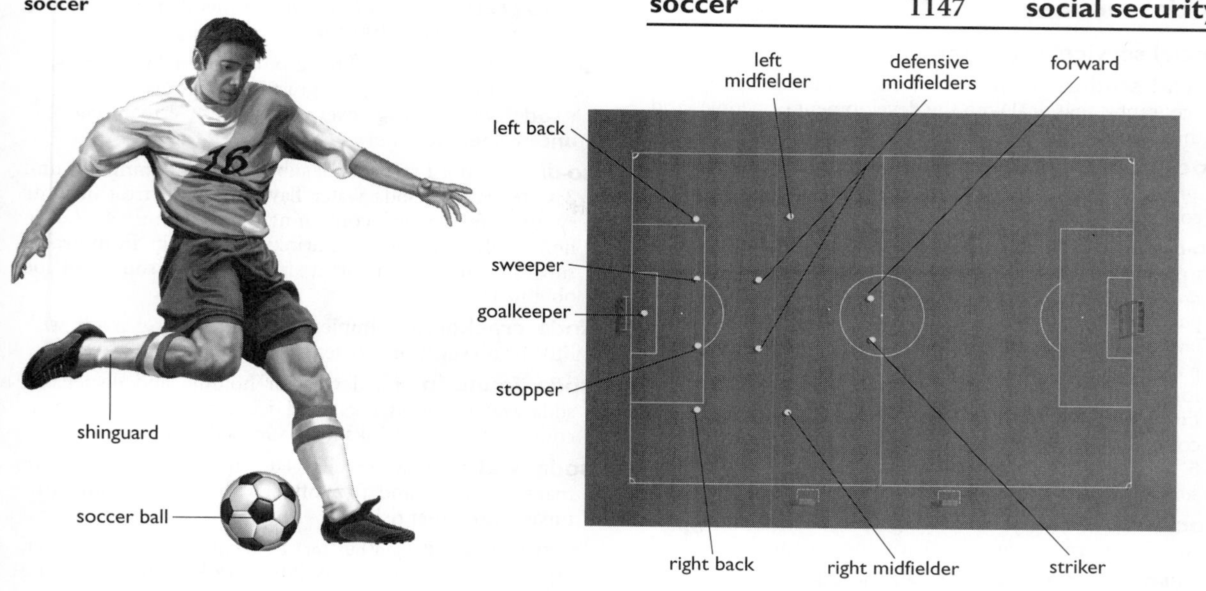

soc·cer (sok′ər) *n* a game played between two teams of eleven players each, using a round ball. Only the goalie may touch the ball with hands and arms. <(*As*)*soc*(*iation football*), the official name of the game in the UK>

so·cia·ble (sō′shə bəl) *adj* **1** willing to talk and engage in friendly activities with other people. **2** marked by friendliness: *a sociable afternoon.* <See SOCIAL.> **so′cia·bil′i·ty** *n.* **so′cia·bly** *adv.*

CONFUSABLES

Sociable means "seeking and enjoying company": *Her sociable nature won her many friends.*

Social suggests little more than interacting with others: *He's a loner, but quite social at family gatherings.*

so·cial (sō′shəl) *adj* **1** of or dealing with human beings in their relations to each other in society or in an organization: *social problems, social sciences.* **2** to do with rank in society: *social class.* **3** for the companionship involved in group activities: *a social club.* **4** of animals, living together in organized communities: *Ants are social insects.*
n an informal social gathering or party, especially one organized by a club or group: *a church social.* <Old French, from Latin *socius* friend>

❦ **social assistance** *n* money paid by the government to those in need, e.g., the elderly.

social climber *n* a person who tries hard to gain higher social status, sometimes even at the cost of personal integrity. **social climbing** *n.*

social contract or **compact** *n* the unspoken agreement, according to some philosophers, by which members of a society co-operate for social benefits, such as giving up some individual freedom for state protection.

❦ **Social Credit Party** *n* a federal and provincial political party founded in Alberta in the 1930s.

❦ **Social Insurance Number** *n* a nine-digit number by which the Federal Government identifies an individual. *Abbrev.* **SIN**

so·cial·ism (sō′shə liz′əm) *n* a political and economic system in which the means of production and distribution are owned, managed, or controlled by a central, democratically elected authority. Compare CAPITALISM, COMMUNISM. **so′cial·ist′** *adj, n.*

so·cial·ite (sō′shə līt′) *n* a person who is well-known and active in fashionable society.

so·cial·ize (sō′shə līz′) *v* **so·cial·ized, so·cial·iz·ing 1** mix socially with others: *During lunch hour, we had time to socialize.* **2** prepare someone to behave in a way that is acceptable to society: *The newcomers had no trouble becoming socialized into their new culture.* **3** organize according to the principles of socialism.

socialized medicine *n* the provision of medical care and hospital services for all people by means of government funds.

so·cial·ly (sō′shə lē) *adv* **1** in relation to other people. **2** as a member of society or of a social group: *He's a private person, but can function well socially.*

social science *n* the study of human society and social relationships. History is a social science. Compare LIFE SCIENCE, PHYSICAL SCIENCE.

social security *especially US n* money paid by the government to those in need, e.g., the elderly.

a bat	e bed	i bid	o pot	u cup	th **thin**
ā cake	ē me	ī bite	ō go	ū rude	TH **then**
ä bar	ə about	ər over	ȯ for	u̇ put	zh measure

social service *n* social work.

social studies *n* school subjects, including history and geography, that deal with the development of peoples and their societies.

social work *n* work carried out by trained personnel that aims for the betterment of social conditions in a community. **social worker** *n.*

so·ci·e·ty (sə sī′ə tē) *n, pl* **so·ci·e·ties 1** all people living together in communities: *Drug abuse is considered a danger to society.* **2 a** a community of people living in a particular country or region and with shared customs, laws, and organizations: *Canadian society.* **b** a specified part of such a community: *high society.* **3** an organization formed for a particular purpose or activity: *We formed a birdwatching society.* **4** the situation of being in the company of other people: *He avoided the society of others.* **5** a plant or animal community. <French, from Latin *socius* companion> **so·ci′e·tal** *adj.*

socio– *combining form* relating to society, sociology, or social concerns: *sociopath.* <Latin *socius* companion>

so·ci·o–e·co·nom·ic (sō′sē ō ē′kə nom′ik) *or* (sō′sē ō ek′ə nom′ik) *adj* to do with the interaction of social and economic factors: *They presented a socio-economic study on poverty in big cities.*

so·ci·o·gram (sō′sē ō gram′) *n* a chart or other graphic showing the relationships among people in a group situation: *I want to make a sociogram of the characters in* Lord of the Rings.

so·ci·ol·o·gy (sō′sē ol′ə jē) *n* the study of the development, structure, and functioning of human society. **so′ci·o·log′i·cal** *adj.* **so′ci·o·log′i·cal·ly** *adv.* **so′ci·o′log·ist** *n.*

so·ci·o·path (sō′sē ə path′) *or* (sō′shē ə path′) *n* a person with a personality disorder that leads to extreme antisocial attitudes and behaviour.

sock (sok) *n* **1** a close-fitting, knitted covering for the foot and lower leg, typically woven from wool, cotton, or nylon. **2** a white marking on the foot or lowest part of an animal's leg. **3** *Informal* a hard blow: *a sock on the jaw.*
v Informal hit forcefully: *He socked him on the chin.* <Greek *sukkhos* comic actor's shoe>
sock away, *Informal* put money aside as savings.

sock·et (sok′it) *n* **1** a hollow part or piece into which something fits or revolves: *Her eyes were set deeply in their sockets.* **2** a connecting place for an electric plug or wire. <Old French *soc* ploughshare. A socket was originally a weapon shaped like a ploughshare (the cutting blade of a plough.)>

🍁 **sock·eye** (sok′ī′) *n, pl* **sock·eyes** or (*especially collectively*) **sock·eye** in full, **sockeye salmon** a salmon found along the coasts of the N Pacific and rivers draining into it. Also called **red salmon**. <Salish *sukai* fish of fishes>

So·crat·ic (sō krat′ik) *adj* to do with Socrates (469–399 BCE), a Greek philosopher, or his philosophy.

Socratic method *n* a teaching method that uses a series of questions to lead students to think and make the logical steps needed to reach a conclusion.

🍁 **So·cred** (sō′kred′) *Informal n* a member or supporter of a SOCIAL CREDIT PARTY.

sod (sod) *n* the surface of the ground covered with grass, or a piece of it containing the grass and its roots.
v **sod·ded, sod·ding** cover with sods. <German *sode*>
under the sod, *Informal* buried.

so·da (sō′də) *n* **1** a chemical substance containing sodium. **2** soda water. **3** soda water flavoured with fruit juice or syrup, and often containing ice cream. **4** *US* a non-alcoholic carbonated drink; pop. <Latin, from Arabic *suwwad* saltwort, a plant from which soda can be obtained>

soda cracker *n* a simple, light, thin cracker made with little or no sugar or shortening.

soda fountain *n* a device for holding and dispensing soda water, soft drinks, and ice cream, or a store or counter that sells drinks from such a device.

soda water *n* water charged with carbon dioxide to make it bubble and fizz, often with a flavour added or mixed with other drinks.

🍁 **sod·bust·er** (sod′bus′tər) *Informal n* a prairie farmer, especially one of the early homesteaders, or one raising field crops instead of livestock.

sod·den (sod′ən) *adj* soaked through: *The girl's clothing was sodden with rain.* <*seethe*> **sod′den·ness** *n.*

so·di·um (sō′dē əm) *n* a soft, silver-white metallic element that occurs in nature only in compounds. *Symbol* **Na** <*soda*>

sodium bicarbonate *n* a white powder that dissolves in water. It is used in fire extinguishers and fizzy drinks as well as to help foods rise in baking. Also called **bicarbonate of soda, baking soda**.

sodium carbonate *n* a white compound that dissolves in water and is used in making soap and glass. Also called **washing soda**.

sodium chloride *n* common salt.

sodium fluoride *n* a white crystalline salt, used in the fluoridation of water, and as an insecticide and disinfectant.

sodium hydroxide *n* a white, strongly alkaline compound that is used in making soap and paper. Also called **caustic soda**.

sodium nitrate *n* a white crystalline compound used in making solid rocket propellants, explosives, enamel, and fertilizer. Also called **saltpetre**.

🍁 **sod·turn·ing** (sod′tər′ning) *n* the first breaking of ground for the construction of a building, often accompanied by a ceremony.

so·fa (sō′fə) *n* a long, upholstered seat or couch with a back and arms. <French, from Arabic *suffa*>

sofa bed *n* a couch that folds out into a bed.

sof·fit *n* the underside of an architectural structure, such as an arch, balcony, or overhanging eaves. <Italian, from Latin *sub-* under + *figere* fix>

soft (soft) *adj* **1** easy to mould, cut, or fold because it is not hard or firm to the touch: *soft ground.* **2** with a smooth surface or texture that is pleasant to the touch: *soft skin.*

3 rounded, not angular: *soft edges.* 4 with a subtle effect or contrast rather than sharp definition: *soft shadows.* 5 quiet and gentle: *a soft voice, a soft breeze.* 6 not harsh or angry: *soft words.* 7 requiring little effort: *a soft job, a soft option.* 8 foolish or silly: *soft in the head.* 9 pronounced with the sound of *c* as in *city* and not as in *corn,* or *g* as in *gem* and not as in *go.* 10 not considered likely to cause addiction: *soft drugs.* <Old English *softe* gentle> **soft′ly** *adv.* **soft′ness** *n.*

soft on, a lenient toward: *He said the mayor was too soft on crime.* **b** fond of or infatuated with.

soft·ball (soft′bol′) *n* 1 a modified kind of baseball played on a smaller field with a larger, softer ball, seven rather than nine innings, and underarm pitching. See PITCH for picture. 2 the ball used in that game.

soft–boiled (soft′boild′) *adj* boiled as an egg for a short time, so that the yolk is soft.

soft·cover (soft′ku′vər) *n* a book with a soft cover made of paper, vinyl, or other flexible material.
adj with such a cover.

soft drink *n* a non-alcoholic carbonated drink; pop.

soft·en (sof′ən) *v* 1 make or become softer: *She used hand lotion to soften her skin.* 2 make or become less severe: *He softened his harsh words.* 3 (*often with **up***) undermine the resistance of someone or something: *We can try to soften Dad up by behaving well, and then we can ask about having a party.*

soft·en·er (sof′nər) *n* a substance or device that softens something, especially fabric.

soft–heart·ed (soft′härt′tid) *adj* kind or compassionate. **soft′-heart′ed·ly** *adv.* **soft′-heart′ed·ness** *n.*

soft palate *n* the fleshy, flexible part toward the back of the roof of the mouth. See PALATE for picture.

soft–ped·al (soft′ped′əl) *v* **soft-ped·alled** or **soft-ped·aled, soft-ped·al·ling** or **soft-ped·al·ing** 1 press a pedal on a piano to make musical tones softer. 2 play down unpleasant or negative aspects of something: *The ambassador soft-pedalled the increase in his country's armed forces.*

soft return *Computers n* a word-processing operation to start a new line that is not the beginning of a new paragraph. Compare HARD RETURN.

soft sell *Informal n* a sales approach that uses indirect, persuasive tactics rather than aggressive ones. Compare HARD SELL.

soft·shell crab (soft′shel′) *n* a N American crab, especially a blue crab, that has recently moulted and has a new shell that is soft and edible.

soft shoulder *n* an unpaved strip of land at the side of a road.

soft soap *n* 1 a liquid or partly liquid soap. 2 *Informal* flattery.
v **soft-soap** flatter or cajole.

soft–spo·ken (soft′spō′kən) *adj* speaking or said with a gentle, quiet voice.

soft spot *n* 1 a feeling of tenderness or affection: *She still had a soft spot in her heart for her first boyfriend.* 2 a vulnerable spot or point: *It was a soft spot in an otherwise strong argument.*

soft touch *Informal n* a person who lends or gives money easily.

soft·ware (sof′twer′) *Computers n* the programs and other operating instructions used by a computer. Compare HARDWARE.

soft water *n* water containing few or no minerals, in which soapsuds are easily formed. Compare HARD WATER.

soft·wood (sof′twůd′) *n* any conifer. 2 the wood of such a tree. Compare HARDWOOD.

soft·y (sof′tē) *Informal n, pl* **soft·ies** a weak person, or one who is easily imposed upon.

sog·gy (sog′ē) *adj* **sog·gi·er, sog·gi·est** soft and very wet or damp: *a soggy washcloth, soggy pastry.* <origin uncertain> **sog′gi·ly** *adv.* **sog′gi·ness** *n.*

soh (sō) SO[2].

soi·gnée (swon yā′) *adj* of a female, well-groomed and elegant. <French = cared for>

soil[1] (soil) *n* 1 the upper layer of earth in which plants grow, typically consisting of a mixture of organic material, clay, and rock particles. 2 something thought of as a place for growth. 3 the territory of a particular country: *my native soil.* <Old French, from Latin *solium* seat>

soil[2] (soil) *v* 1 make or become dirty: *He soiled his clean clothes. White shirts soil easily.* 2 bring disgrace or discredit to: *His actions have soiled the family name.*
n waste matter, especially sewage containing excrement. <Old French, from Latin *sus* pig>

soi·ree or **soi·rée** (swä rā′) *n* an evening party or social gathering, especially in a private house. <French *soir* evening>

so·journ (sō′jərn′) *or* (sō jərn′) *v* stay somewhere temporarily: *We sojourned for three weeks at the cottage.*
n a temporary stay. <Old French, from Latin *sub-* under + *diurnus* day> **so·journ′er** *n.*

sol (sōl) SO[2].

sol·ace (sol′is) *n* comfort or consolation in a time of distress or sadness: *She found solace from her troubles by playing music.*
v **sol·aced, sol·ac·ing** give solace to: *He solaced himself with a book.* <Old French, from Latin *solari* console>

so·lar (sō′lər) *adj* 1 to do with the sun or its energy: *a solar eclipse, solar heat.* 2 working by means of the sun's light or heat: *a solar battery.* <Latin *sol* sun>

solar cell *n* a small device for converting sunlight into electrical energy.

solar day *n* the period of time from when the sun is at the meridian at a place on earth until the next time it reaches the same meridian.

a bat	e bed	i bid	o pot	u cup	th **thin**
ā cake	ē me	ī bite	ō go	ū rude	ᴛʜ **then**
ä bar	ə about	ər over	ȯ for	ů put	zh measure

solar energy *n* energy derived from the sun's radiation as a source of electrical power. Also called **solar power**.

solar flare *n* a sudden discharge of high-energy radiation from the sun's surface, associated with SUNSPOTS and causing radio and magnetic disturbances on the earth.

so·lar·i·um (sə ler′ē əm) *n, pl* **so·lar·i·a** (-ler′ē ə) **1** a room equipped with sunlamps that can be used to acquire an artificial suntan. **2** a room fitted with extensive areas of glass to admit sunlight.

solar panel *n* a panel designed to absorb the sun's rays as a source of energy for generating electicity or heating.

solar plex·us (plek′səs) *n* the network of nerves located at the pit of the stomach, or the place where this is located.

solar power *n* solar energy.

solar system *n* the sun and the nine planets and their moons in orbit around it, including such smaller bodies as asteroids and comets.

solar wind *n* a continuous flow of ionized gas particles from the sun into the solar system.

solar year *n* the period of time required for the earth to make one revolution around the sun, which equals about 365.25 days.

sold (sōld) past tense and past participle of SELL.

sol·der (sod′ər) *n* **1** an alloy, especially one based on lead and tin, that can be melted and used for joining or mending metal surfaces or parts. **2** a thing that unites firmly or joins closely.
v **1** fasten, mend, or join with solder. **2** unite or join closely. <Old French, from Latin *solidus* solid>
sol′der·er *n.*

soldering iron (sod′ər ing) *n* an electrical tool with a pointed or wedge-shaped tip that heats up in order to melt and apply solder.

sol·dier (sōl′jər) *n* **1** a person who serves in an army, or a person with skill or experience in war. **2** a person who serves in a cause: *soldiers in the battle against drugs.* **3** a wingless ant or termite with a large head and powerful jaws that acts to defend a colony.
v act or serve as a soldier. <Old French *soudier* one who serves in an army for pay, from Latin *solidus* Roman coin>
sol′dier·ly *adj.*
soldier on, carry on, in spite of difficulty.

soldier of fortune *n* a person serving or ready to serve for pay as a soldier for any group or country.

sole[1] (sōl) *adj* **1** one and only: *the sole heir.* **2** to do with only one person or group and not others: *the sole right to photocopy.* <Old French, from Latin *solus* alone>

sole[2] (sōl) *n* **1** the bottom or undersurface of the foot. **2** the underside of a piece of footwear.
v **soled, sol·ing** put a new sole on a piece of footwear. <Old French, from Latin *solum* bottom>

sole[3] (sōl) *n, pl* **soles** or (*especially collectively*) **sole**
a marine flatfish, used as food. See FLATFISH for picture. <Old French, from Latin *solea* a sandal, so called because of the shape of the fish>

sol·e·cism (sol′ə siz′əm) *n* **1** a mistake in grammar, in speech, or in writing. Example: *I done it.* **2** an example of bad manners or incorrect social behaviour. <French, from Greek *soloikos* speaking incorrectly>

sole·ly (sōl′lē) *adv* not involving anyone or anything else: *You will be solely responsible.*

sol·emn (sol′əm) *adj* **1** serious and unsmiling: *a solemn face.* **2** formal and dignified: *solemn music, a solemn procession.* **3** marked by deep sincerity: *a solemn promise.* <Old French, from Latin *sollemnis* formal>
sol′emn·ly *adv.* **sol′emn·ness** *n.*

so·lem·ni·ty (sə lem′nə tē) *n, pl* **so·lem·ni·ties** **1** the condition or quality of being serious and dignified: *The funeral was conducted with great solemnity.* **2** a formal, dignified rite or ceremony: *The solemnities were concluded with the singing of the national anthem.*

sol·em·nize (sol′əm nīz′) *v* **sol·em·nized, sol·em·niz·ing** **1** hold or perform a ceremony or service: *The marriage was solemnized before a large crowd.* **2** mark with a formal ceremony: *Remembrance Day was solemnized by tributes to the dead.* **sol′em·ni·za′tion** *n.*

so·le·noid (sō′lə noid′) *n* a cylindrical coil of wire that acts like a magnet when an electric current passes through it. <French, from Greek *solen* a tube>

sol·fa (sōl′fə) *n* the syllables *do, re, mi, fa, so, la, ti, do* that represent the eight tones of a scale.

so·lic·it (sə lis′it) *v* **1** ask for or try to obtain something from someone: *Someone at the door was soliciting contributions.* **2** offer one's or someone's services as a prostitute. <Old French, from Latin *sollus* entire + *ciere* set in motion> **so·lic′i·ta′tion** *n.*

so·lic·i·tor (sə lis′ə tər) *n* **1** 🍁 a lawyer. **2** *UK* a lawyer who deals with matters of civil law, such as wills and the transfer of property, and who may advise clients and work with a **barrister**, who pleads in court. **3** the chief law officer of a city, town, or government department. **4** a person who tries to obtain business orders or advertising. <Old French, from Latin *solicitare* disturb>

solicitor general *n, pl* **solicitors general** **1** 🍁 **Solicitor General** a member of a federal or provincial cabinet who oversees correctional services, law enforcement, and some forms of licensing. Compare ATTORNEY GENERAL. **2** *US* the law officer ranking below the Attorney General.

so·lic·it·ous (sə lis′ə təs) *adj* marked by or showing care or concern: *She was solicitous about the health of her neighbour.* **so·lic′it·ous·ly** *adv.* **so·lic′it·ous·ness** *n.*

so·lic·i·tude (sə lis′ə tyūd′) *or* (sə lis′ə tūd′) *n* care or concern for someone or something: *That woman shows great solicitude for her elderly mother.*

sol·id (sol′id) *adj* **1** firm and stable in shape, not liquid or gas: *Water becomes solid when it freezes.* **2** not hollow or containing gaps: *solid cement.* **3** hard; firm: *They were glad to leave the boat and put their feet on solid ground.* **4** strongly made or put together: *This is not a very solid table.* **5** consisting of the same substance or quality throughout: *The cutlery was solid silver.* **6** unanimous or undivided: *solid support.* **7** without spaces in a line or surface: *a solid outline.* **8** dependable, sound, or strong: *She is a solid citizen.* **9** uninterrupted in time: *I waited*

three solid hours. **10** *Mathematics* a three-dimensional model with the interior filled, or presumed to be filled. See also SHELL, SKELETON.
n **1** a substance or object that is not a liquid or a gas. **2** a body or geometrical figure that has length, breadth, and thickness. <Latin *solidus*> **so·lid′i·ty** *n.* **sol′id·ly** *adv.* **sol′id·ness** *n.*

sol·i·dar·i·ty (sol′ə dar′ə tē) *or* (sol′ə der′ə tē) *n, pl* **sol·i·dar·i·ties** unity or agreement of feeling and action, especially among those who have common responsibilities and interests. <French, from Latin *sollus* entire>

so·lid·i·fy (sə lid′ə fī′) *v* **so·lid·i·fied, so·lid·i·fy·ing** **1** make or become solid: *Extreme cold will solidify water.* **2** make stronger or reinforce: *Our opinions solidified during the election campaign.* **so·lid′i·fi·ca′tion** *n.*

sol·id–state (sol′id stāt′) *adj* **1** to do with the study of the properties of solid materials, in which atoms and molecules occupy fixed positions with respect to each other: *solid-state physics.* **2** in a device, making use of the electronic properties of solid semiconductors.

so·lil·o·quy (sə lil′ə kwē) *n, pl* **so·lil·o·quies** the act of speaking thoughts aloud without any hearers, especially by a character in a play, or a speech made in this way. <Latin *solus* alone + *loqui* speak> **so·lil′o·quize** *v.*

sol·i·taire (sol′ə ter′) *n* **1** a card game for one player. **2** a diamond or other gem set by itself, or a ring set with such a gem. <French, from Latin *solus* alone>

sol·i·tar·y (sol′ə ter′ē) *adj* **1** done or existing alone: *A solitary rider was seen in the distance.* **2** secluded, isolated, or away from other people: *a solitary life, a solitary spot.* **3** living as a bird, mammal, or insect alone or in pairs, especially in contrast to animals that live in groups.
n, pl **sol·i·tar·ies** a person who lives alone and away from other people. <Latin *solus* alone> **sol′i·tar′i·ness** *n.*

solitary confinement *n* the isolation of a prisoner from others as a punishment. Often shortened to **solitary**.

sol·i·tude (sol′ə tyūd′) *or* (sol′ə tūd′) *n* the condition or situation of being alone: *She likes company and hates solitude.* <Old French, from Latin *solus* alone>

SYNONYMS

Solitude emphasizes being alone: *After a busy day of school, she loved the solitude of her bedroom.*

Isolation emphasizes being away from others: *The lonely cabin in the woods provided her with the isolation she needed to finish writing her book.*

Confinement emphasizes being separated from others and often has a negative connotation: *The disobedient dog was kept in confinement in the yard.*

so·lo (sō′lō) *n, pl* **so·los** a thing done by one person alone, such as a piece of music or dance, or a part of it, done by one performer, or an unaccompanied flight by a pilot in an aircraft.
adj, adv for or done by one person alone: *a solo violin, a solo flight. He played the part solo.*
v **so·loed, so·lo·ing** do or perform something alone. <Italian, from Latin *solus* alone> **so′lo·ist** *n.*

🍁 **Sol·o·mon Gun·dy** (sol′ə mən gun′dē) *n* salted herring marinated in vinegar, with spices and onions.

ETYMOLOGY

Solomon Gundy comes from French *salmigondis* meaning "seasoned salt meat" (from *sel* salt and *condir* to season).

Solomon Islands *n* a country of islands in the southwest Pacific.

so long *Informal interj* goodbye.

sol·stice (sol′stis) *n* either of the two times in the year when the sun is at its greatest distance from the celestial equator. In the northern hemisphere, the **summer solstice** (June 21 or 22) is the longest day of the year and the **winter solstice** (December 21 or 22) is the shortest. Compare EQUINOX. See VERNAL for picture. <Old French, from Latin *sol* sun + *sistere* be stopped>
sol·sti′tial (sol sti′shəl) *adj.*

sol·u·ble (sol′yə bəl) *adj* **1** having the ability to be dissolved, especially in water: *Sugar is soluble.* **2** of a problem, able to be solved. <Old French, from Latin *solvere* dissolve> **sol′u·bil′i·ty** *n.*

sol·ute (sol′yūt) *or* (sol′ūt) *n* the minor component in a solution that is dissolved in a solvent, for example, salt in sea water. <Latin *solvere* loosen>

so·lu·tion (sə lū′shən) *n* **1** a means of solving a problem or dealing with a difficult situation: *The police are seeking the solution to the crime.* **2** the correct answer to a puzzle. **3** *Mathematics* the value of the variable that makes an equation true. **4** **a** a liquid mixture in which one component (the solute) is uniformly distributed within the major component (the solvent): *a salt solution.* **b** the process by which this is done, or the condition in which this exists. <Old French, from Latin *solvere* loosen>

solution set *Mathematics n* the set of values that satisfy a particular equation or condition.

solve (solv) *v* **solved, solv·ing** find an answer to, explanation for, or means of effectively dealing with a problem or mystery: *He found a way to solve his family's crisis.* <Latin *solvere* loosen> **solv′a·bil′i·ty** *n.*
solv′a·ble *adj.* **solv′er** *n.*

sol·ven·cy (sol′vən sē) *n, pl* **sol·ven·cies** the ability to pay all that is owed because assets are greater than liabilities.

sol·vent (sol′vənt) *adj* **1** able to pay all that is owed because one has more assets than liabilities: *a solvent company.* **2** able to dissolve other substances.
n a liquid, for example, water, that can dissolve other substances. <Latin *solvere* loosen>

a bat	e bed	i bid	o pot	u cup	th thin
ā cake	ē me	ī bite	ō go	ū rude	ᴛʜ then
à bar	ə about	ər over	ȯ for	u̇ put	zh measure

so·ma (sō′mə) *n, pl* **so·ma·ta** (sō′mə tə) the parts of an organism other than the reproductive cells. <Greek *soma* body>

So·ma·li·a (sō ma′lē ə) *n* a country in southern Africa. See the APPENDIX. **So·ma′li** *adj, n.*

so·mat·ic (sō mat′ik) *adj* to do with the body, especially as distinct from the mind. <Greek *soma* body> **so·mat′ic·al·ly** *adv.*

somatic cell *n* any cell of an animal or plant, except reproductive cells.

som·bre (som′bər) *adj* **1** dark or dull in colour or tone: *The cloudy winter day was sombre.* **2** grave and melancholy in mood: *a sombre expression.* Also, **somber**. <French, from Latin *sub-* under + *umbra* shade> **som′bre·ly** *adv.* **som′bre·ness** *n.*

som·brer·o (som brer′ō) *n, pl* **som·brer·os** a broad-brimmed hat worn by men in Mexico and the southwestern US. <Spanish, from Latin *sub-* under + *umbra* shade>

some (sum) *adj* **1** of an unspecified amount or number: *Some people sleep more than others. Drink some milk.* **2** referring to someone or something that is unknown or unspecified: *She left the city some years ago.* **3** approximately: *Some dozen items were missing.* **4** *Informal* emphasizing size, amount, or degree, or a lack of it: *That was some storm! You dropped the box on my foot. That was some help.*
pron an unspecified number of people or things: *Some think so. He ate some and threw the rest away.*
adv Informal to a great degree or extent: *That's going some!* <Old English *sum*>
and then some, *Informal* and a good deal more than that, too: *He's a top-notch cook and then some.*

CONFUSABLES

Some refers to an unspecified amount or number: *They knew that they had to accept some of the responsibility for the accident.*

Sum refers to a particular or total amount: *What's the sum of these three numbers?*

–some[1] *suffix* **1** producing or resulting in: *meddlesome.* **2** causing: *awesome.* **3** apt to: *tiresome.* <Old English *-sum*>

–some[2] *suffix* indicating a group of a specified number: *twosome.* <Old English *sum* some>

some·bod·y (sum′bud′ē) *or* (sum′bod′ē) *pron* a person not known or named: *Somebody has taken my pen.*
n, pl **some·bod·ies** a person of importance: *She acts as if she were somebody since she won the prize.*

some·day (sum′dā′) *adv* at some future time.

some·how (sum′hou′) *adv* in a way not known or not stated: *I'll finish this work somehow.*
somehow or other, in one way or another.

some·one (sum′wun′) *or* (sum′wən) *pron* a person not named or known.

some·place (sum′plās′) *adv* in or to some place: *I met you someplace in the past.*

som·er·sault (sum′ər solt′) *n* an acrobatic movement in which a person turns head over heels in the air or on the ground and lands or finishes with a complete roll of the body.
v perform such a movement either intentionally or by accident. Also, **summersault**. <Old French, from Latin *supra* over + *ambulare* walk>
turn a somersault, make a somersault.

some·thing (sum′thing′) *pron* **1** a thing that is not named or not known: *I've got something important to tell you. He has something on his mind.* **2** an inexact amount, quantity, or quality: *She felt something between doubt and regret. He's something of a violinist.* **3** *Informal* a thing or person of some value or importance: *He thinks he's something.*
adv Informal to some extent or degree: *My broken wrist hurts something awful.*

–something *Informal suffix* indicating a range of age, or a person in this range: *They were all thirty-somethings.*

some·time (sum′tīm′) *adv* at an unstated or unknown time: *It happened sometime last March.*
adj former: *a sometime editor.*

GRAMMAR AND USAGE

Sometime means "at an unspecified time": *I'd like to see you sometime.*

Sometimes means "now and then": *We go to the movies sometimes.*

Some time means "a period of time": *They've kept the DVDs for some time.*

some·times (sum′tīmz′) *adv* now and then: *She visits me sometimes.*

some·what (sum′ wut′) *adv* to some extent or degree: *somewhat round.*

some·where (sum′wer′) *adv* **1** in or to some place: *She lives somewhere in the neighbourhood.* **2** indicating an approximate amount: *It cost somewhere around ten dollars.*
get somewhere, *Informal* make progress or succeed.

som·me·lier (sum′əl yā′) or (sò mə lyā′) *n* a person whose job is to choose and serve wines in a restaurant. <French = butler, from Latin *sagma* pack saddle>

som·nam·bu·lism (som nam′byə liz′əm) *n* sleepwalking. **som·nam′bu·list** *n.*

som·nif·er·ous (som nif′ə rəs) *adj* tending to cause sleep.

som·no·lent (som′nə lənt) *adj* sleepy or drowsy. <Old French, from Latin *somnus* sleep> **som′no·lent·ly** *adv.*

son (sun) *n* **1** a male child or person, spoken of in relation to either or both of his parents. **2** a male offspring of an animal. **3** a male descendant. **4** a man considered in relation to his country, experience, or environment: *sons of liberty.* **5** a term of address to a boy or from an older person. **6 the Son** *Christianity* Christ as the second person of the Trinity. <Old English *sunu*>

so·nar (sō′når) *n* a device for detecting and locating objects under water by the reflection of sound waves. <*so*(*und*) *na*(*vigation*) and *r*(*anging*)>

so·na·ta (sə nä′tə) *n* a piece of classical music for one instrument, usually with a piano accompaniment. It is typically in several movements in contrasted rhythms but related keys. <Italian, from Latin *sonus* sound>

song (song) *n* **1** a short piece of verse or other set of words put to music or meant to be sung. **2** singing or vocal music: *They suddenly broke into song.* **3** a musical composition or other series of sounds suggesting or resembling a song: *the song of the stream.* **4** the musical phrases uttered by some birds, whales, and insects, forming a repeated sequence of sounds and used mainly to defend territory or to attract mates. **5** a poem, especially in rhymed stanzas. <Old English *sang*>
for a song, *Informal* very cheaply: *to buy things for a song.*
song and dance, *Informal* a long explanation that is pointless or evasive: *She made a great song and dance about having to do the job.*

song·bird (song′bərd′) *n* a bird, usually small, that has a musical song.

song·ster (song′stər) *n* **1** a person who sings, especially in a skilful way. **2** a writer of songs or poems.

song·stress (song′stris) *n* a female songster.

song·writ·er (song′rī′tər) *n* a person who writes popular songs or the music for them. **song′writ·ing** *n.*

son·ic (son′ik) *adj* **1** to do with sound waves. **2** to do with the speed of sound in the air (331 metres per second or about 1192 kilometres per hour at 0°C). <Latin *sonus* sound>

sonic barrier *n* the sound barrier.

sonic boom *n* a loud explosive noise caused by shock waves from an aircraft or other object travelling faster than the speed of sound.

son–in–law (sun′in lo′) *n, pl* **sons-in-law** the husband of a daughter.

son·net (son′it) *n* a poem with fourteen lines, usually one of several fixed rhyme schemes, and in English typically with ten syllables per line. <French, from Latin *sonus* sound>

son·ny (sun′ē) *Informal n, pl* **son·nies** a form of address spoken to a young boy: *Say, sonny, can you tell me how to get to the city hall from here?*

so·no·graph (son′ə graf′) *n* a device that produces **sonograms**, visual images of sound waves. Sonographs that work by ultrasound are used in medical diagnosis. <Latin *sonus* sound + *-graph* to draw> **so·no′gra·pher** *n.* **so·no′gra·phy** *n.*

so·nor·i·ty (sə nȯ′rə tē) *n* a sonorous quality or condition.

so·nor·ous (son′ə rəs) *or* (sə nȯ′rəs) *adj* **1** giving out, capable of, or with a deep, loud sound. **2** using impressive language: *sonorous phrases.* <Latin *sonor* sound> **so′no·rous·ly** *adv.* **so′no·rous·ness** *n.*

soon (sūn) *adv* **1** in or after a short time: *I will see you again soon.* **2** before the usual or expected time: *Why must you leave so soon?* **3** readily or willingly: *I would as soon die as yield.* <Old English *sona* at once>
sooner or later, at some point in the future.

soot (su̇t) *n* a black powdery or flaky substance made up of carbon produced by the incomplete burning of organic matter such as coal, wood, or oil. <Old English *sot*>

soothe (sūᴛʜ) *v* **soothed, sooth·ing 1** gently calm a person or their feelings: *The mother soothed the crying child.* **2** reduce pain or discomfort in a part of the body: *The ointment soothed his burns.* <Old English *sothian*> **sooth′ing** *adj.* **sooth′ing·ly** *adv.*

sooth·er (sūᴛʜ′ər) *n* **1** an object with a rubber nipple on it, given to a baby to suck in order to quiet it temporarily; a pacifier. **2** a person who or thing that soothes.

sooth·say·er (sūth′sā′ər) *n* a person who claims to foretell the future. <Old English *soth* true> **sooth′say·ing** *n.*

soot·y (su̇t′ē) *adj* **soot·i·er, soot·i·est 1** covered or blackened with soot. **2** brownish or blackish. **soot′i·ly** *adv.* **soot′i·ness** *n.*

sop (sop) *n* **1** a thing given or done that has no great value but is intended to appease someone whose main concerns or demands are not being met: *As a sop he got some time off, but he really wanted more pay.* **2** a piece of bread dipped in gravy, soup, milk, or sauce.
v **sopped, sop·ping** soak up liquid using something absorbent: *She sopped the bread in milk. Please sop up that water with a sponge* <Old English *sopp*>

soph·ist (sof′ist) *n* a person who reasons cleverly but falsely. <*Sophist,* a professional teacher of ancient Greece who gave instruction in debating>

so·phis·ti·cate (sə fis′tə kāt′) *n* a person with much worldly experience and knowledge of fashion and culture. <Latin, from Greek *sophos* clever> **so·phis′ti·ca′tion** *n.*

so·phis·ti·cat·ed (sə fis′tə kā′tid) *adj* **1** with much worldly experience and knowledge of fashion and culture, or appealing to those who have such experience and knowledge: *sophisticated tastes.* **2** aware of and able to interpret complex or subtle issues: *a sophisticated discussion.* **3** developed as a machine, system, or technique to be complex and advanced in design: *sophisticated software.* **so′phis·ti·cat′ed·ly** *adv.*

soph·ist·ry (sof′i strē) *n, pl* **soph·ist·ries** clever reasoning that is false or misleading. <See SOPHIST.>

soph·o·more (sof′ə mȯr′) *especially US n* a student in the second year of high school or college. <perhaps Old French, from Greek *sophos* wise>

soph·o·mor·ic (sof′ə mȯ′rik) *adj* **1** to do with sophomores. **2** conceited and childish: *sophomoric humour.*

so·po·rif·ic (sop′ə rif′ik) *or* (sō′pə rif′ik) *adj* **1** causing or tending to cause sleep: *a soporific effect.* **2** sleepy or drowsy. **3** boring or monotonous.
n a drug that causes sleep. <Latin *sopor* sleep>

sop·ping (sop′ing) *adj* soaked or drenched: *His clothes got sopping wet in the rainstorm.*

so·pran·o (sə pran′ō) *Music n, pl* **so·pran·os 1** the highest singing voice for females or boys, or a singer with such a range. **2** an instrument with the highest range in a family of musical instruments.
adj to do with a soprano. <Italian, from Latin *supra*>

a bat	e bed	i bid	o pot	u cup	th **thin**
ā cake	ē me	ī bite	ō go	ū rude	ᴛʜ **then**
ä bar	ə about	ər over	ȯ for	u̇ put	zh measure

S

sor·bet (sȯr′bit) *or* (sȯr bā′) *n* sherbet.

sor·bi·tol (sȯr′bi tol′) *n* a sweet-tasting, water-soluble compound found in some fruits and berries or made synthetically, and used to make sweeteners and moisturizers. <French, from Latin *sorbum* serviceberry>

sor·cer·y (sȯr′sə rē) *n, pl* **sor·cer·ies** the use of magic, especially magic supposed to be performed with the aid of evil spirits. <Old French, from Latin *sortis* fate> **sor′cer·er** *n.* **sor′cer·ess** *n.*

sor·did (sȯr′did) *adj* **1** involving distasteful actions and motives: *sordid behaviour.* **2** dirty and squalid: *a sordid bar.* <French, from Latin *sordere* be dirty> **sor′did·ly** *adv.* **sor′did·ness** *n.*

sore (sȯr) *adj* **sor·er, sor·est 1** painful or aching in a part of the body: *a sore throat, a sore finger.* **2** *Informal* upset and angry: *He is sore about missing the game.* **3** causing distress, anger, or offence: *Their defeat is a sore subject with the members of the team.*
n **1** a painful place on the body where the skin or flesh is broken or bruised. **2** a cause of distress, anger, or offence. See SOAR for confusable. <Old English *sar*> **sore′ness** *n.*

sore·head (sȯr′hed′) *Informal n* a person who is easily angered or offended.

sore·ly (sȯr′lē) *Informal adv* greatly; extremely: *I'm sorely afraid.*

sor·ghum (sȯr′gəm) *n* a tall cereal plant of warm regions that is a major source of grain and animal feed. See GRAIN for picture. <origin uncertain>

so·ror·i·ty (sə rȯ′rə tē) *n, pl* **so·ror·i·ties** a society for female students in a university or college. <Latin *soror* sister>

sor·rel[1] (sȯ′rəl) *n* a horse with a reddish brown coat. <Old French *sor* brown>

sor·rel[2] (sȯ′rəl) *n* **1** a plant with sour, arrow-shaped leaves that are used in salads and in cooking. **2** a tall Caribbean plant with red flowers and stems, or a drink made from its flowers. <Old French *sorele*>

sor·row (sȯ′rō) *n* **1** a feeling or expression of deep distress caused by loss, disappointment, or other misfortune: *She felt sorrow at the news.* **2** an event or circumstance that causes such a feeling: *His sorrows have aged him.*
v feel or show deep distress: *I sorrowed over the loss of our friendship.* <Old English *sorg*> **sor′row·ing** *adj.* **sor′row·less** *adj.*

SYNONYMS

Sorrow implies sadness caused by an unfortunate or unhappy situation: *They felt sorrow at the loss of such a good teacher.*

Grief means "deeply felt sorrow": *The grief of the dead man's family was painful to see.*

Distress emphasizes great mental or physical pain: *The wounded animal cried out in distress.*

Unhappiness means "gloomy" or "downcast": *His unhappiness came from his poor exam results.*

sor·row·ful (sȯ′rə fəl) *adj* **1** feeling or showing sorrow: *a sorrowful person, a sorrowful smile.* **2** causing sorrow: *a sorrowful event.* **sor′row·ful·ly** *adv.* **sor′row·ful·ness** *n.*

sor·ry (sȯ′rē) *adj* **sor·ri·er, sor·ri·est 1** feeling or showing compassion, regret, or distress, especially through sympathy with someone else's misfortune: *I am sorry you are ill.* **2** in a poor or pitiful condition: *The sick dog was a sorry sight.* <Old English *sarig*> **sor′ri·ness** *n.*

sort (sȯrt) *n* **1** a category of things or people with some common feature: *What sort of work does she do?* **2** a person or thing of a certain nature or quality: *She is a good sort.*
v systematically arrange or separate according to kinds or classes: *Sort these cards according to their colours and those according to their size.* <Old French, from Latin *sortis* fate> **sort′a·ble** *adj.* **sor′ter** *n.*
of sorts, of a somewhat usual and typically inferior kind: *He was an athlete of sorts.*
out of sorts, ill, cross, or uncomfortable.
sort of, *Informal* to some extent: *In spite of her faults, I sort of like her. This bread is sort of dry.*
sort out, separate from others: *We sorted out the best apples for eating.*

sor·tie (sȯr′tē) *n* **1** a sudden attack by troops from a defensive position. **2** a single round trip of an aircraft against the enemy. **3** a short trip or journey. <French *sortir* go out>

SOS (es′ō′es′) *n* **1** a signal of distress consisting of the letters *s o s* of the international Morse code [. . . – – – . . .], used especially by ships at sea. **2** *Informal* an urgent appeal for help. <selected as being easily transmitted and recognized in Morse code>

so–so (sō′sō′) *adj, adv* neither very good nor very bad: *She was a so-so bridge player. I was only feeling so-so.*

sot (sot) *n* a person addicted to alcoholic liquor. <Latin *sottus*> **sot′tish** *adj.*

sot·to vo·ce (sot′ō vō′chē) *adj, adv* in a quiet voice. <Italian = under voice>

sou·bri·quet (sü′brə kā′) SOBRIQUET.

souf·flé (sū flā′) *n* a light, spongy, baked dish usually made by adding flavoured egg yolks to stiffly beaten egg whites: *a cheese soufflé.* <French, from Latin *sufflare* to blow>

sough (sou) *or* (suf) *v* make a rustling, moaning, or rushing sound: *The pines soughed when the wind blew.*
n a sound of this kind. <Old English *swogan*>

sought (sot) past tense and past participle of SEEK.

sought–af·ter (sot′af′tər) *adj* much in demand.

soul (sōl) *n* **1** the spiritual part of a person, believed by some to be the source of thought, feeling, and action, separate from the body, and immortal. **2** a person's moral or emotional nature or sense of identity: *She puts her whole soul into her work.* **3** emotional or intellectual energy or intensity, especially as revealed in a work of art or an artistic performance: *The piano recital lacked soul.* **4** a person or thing regarded as the essential part of a specified quality: *He is the soul of honour. She said that brevity was the soul of wit.* **5** an individual person: *Don't tell a soul.* <Old English *sawol*>

soul food *n* food that is popular in the southern US, associated with cooking traditionally done by black people.

soul·ful (sōl′fəl) *adj* expressing or appearing to express deep and often sorrowful feeling. **soul′ful·ly** *adv.* **soul′ful·ness** *n.*

soul·less (sōl′lis) *adj* **1** lacking character and individuality in a building, room, or other place: *a soulless highrise.* **2** tedious and uninspiring as an activity: *a soulless job.* **soul′less·ly** *adv.* **soul′less·ness** *n.*

soul·mate (sōl′māt′) *n* a person ideally suited to another as a close friend or romantic partner.

soul music *n* a style of popular music based on gospel and rhythm and blues that was developed by black Americans and emphasizes emotionally intense vocals.

soul–search·ing (sōl′sər′ching) *n* deep and anxious examination of one's own motives and conduct.
adj involving or expressing such an examination.

sound[1] (sound) *n* **1** vibrations that travel through the air or another medium and can be heard when they reach an ear: *sound waves.* **2** a thing that can be heard: *the sound of fighting.* **3** the distance or area within which a noise may be heard: *If you go outside, please stay within sound of the telephone.* **4** one of the simple elements composing speech: *a vowel sound.* **5** the ideas or impressions conveyed by words: *You've had a good day, by the sound of it.* **6** a distinctive quality in the music of a composer or performer: *Her special sound blended elements of jazz and blues.* **7** music, speech, or sound effects when recorded or broadcast: *The new TV set had bad sound.*
v **1** make or cause to make a sound, especially to warn of or indicate something: *The trumpet sounds for battle. The wind sounded like an animal howling.* **2** say something, or be pronounced: *Sound each syllable. "Rough" and "ruff" sound alike.* **3** convey a specified impression when heard: *She said that climbing sounded dangerous.* **4** test the lungs or a body cavity by noting the sound it produces: *to sound a person's lungs.* <Old French, from Latin *sonus*> **sound′less** *adj.* **sound′less·ly** *adv.* **sound′less·ness** *n.*
sound off, *Informal* express opinions or complaints in a loud or forceful way.

SYNONYMS

Sound means "something that can be heard": *The sound of thunder broke the silence.*

Noise often means "unpleasant sound": *The noise of their argument kept me awake.*

Racket means "loud, unpleasant noise": *Stop making such a racket with those drums!*

Din means "loud, discordant noise lasting for some time": *The din of the different machines was deafening.*

sound[2] (sound) *adj* **1** free from injury, decay, or defect: *a sound ship, a sound body.* **2** based on reason or reliable judgment: *a sound opinion.* **3** financially secure: *a sound company.* **4** deep and undisturbed as sleep, or tending to sleep deeply: *a sound night's rest.* **5** severe: *a sound beating.*
adv deeply or thoroughly: *She was sound asleep.* <Old English *gesund*> **sound′ly** *adv.* **sound′ness** *n.*

sound[3] (sound) *v* **1** measure the depth of a body of water, typically by means of a weighted line, pole, or using sound echoes. **2** dive steeply to a great depth, as a whale does. <Old French, from Latin *sub-* below + *unda* wave>
sound out, question someone, especially in a discreet or cautious way, about his or her opinion or feelings on a subject: *He sounded her out on the project, but she didn't seem interested.*

sound[4] (sound) *n* (*often in place names*) a narrow passage of water forming an inlet, or connecting two bodies of water such as a sea and a lake. <Old Norse *sund* strait>

sound barrier *n* the sudden increase in aerodynamic resistance experienced by an aircraft when it approaches the speed of sound (331 m/s or about 1192 km/h at 0°C). Also called **sonic barrier**.

sound bite *n* a short extract from a recorded interview that is chosen for broadcast because it sounds impressive.

sound·board (sound′bȯrd′) *n* a thin, resonant sheet of wood forming part of a musical instrument, as in a violin or piano, to increase the fullness of its tone.

sound effects *pln* sound other than speech or music made artificially for use in a play, movie, or broadcast.

sound·ing (soun′ding) *n* **1** the action or process of measuring the depth of a body of water, or a measurement taken for this purpose. **2 soundings** *pl* information or evidence gathered as a preliminary step before deciding on a course of action: *We took soundings about work conditions before applying for the job.*

sounding board *n* **1** a person or group whose reactions to suggested ideas are used as a test before the ideas are made public. **2** a soundboard. **3** a board placed over or behind a stage to direct sound toward an audience.

sounding line *n* a line with a weight fastened to the end, used to measure the depth of water.

sound·proof (sound′prūf′) *adj* preventing, or made of material that prevents, the passage of sound.
v make a room or building resistant to the passage of sound: *They soundproofed the rec room.*

sound·scape (sound′skāp′) *n* **1** a combination of sounds typically heard in a certain environment. **2** a piece of music considered in terms of its component sounds.

sound·track (sound′trak′) *n* **1** the strip at one side of a movie film that carries the sound recording. **2** a recording of the musical accompaniment of a movie.

sound waves *pln* the vibrations of a sound, measured in cycles per second, that are sent out through the air or another medium.

soup (sūp) *n* a liquid dish typically made by simmering meat, fish, or vegetables in stock or water. <Old French, from Latin *suppa*>
in the soup, *Informal* in trouble.
soup up, *Informal* modify something to make it more powerful, efficient, or impressive: *to soup up a car.*

a bat	e bed	i bid	o pot	u cup	th thin
ā cake	ē me	ī bite	ō go	ū rude	ᴛʜ then
ȧ bar	ə about	ər over	ȯ for	u̇ put	zh measure

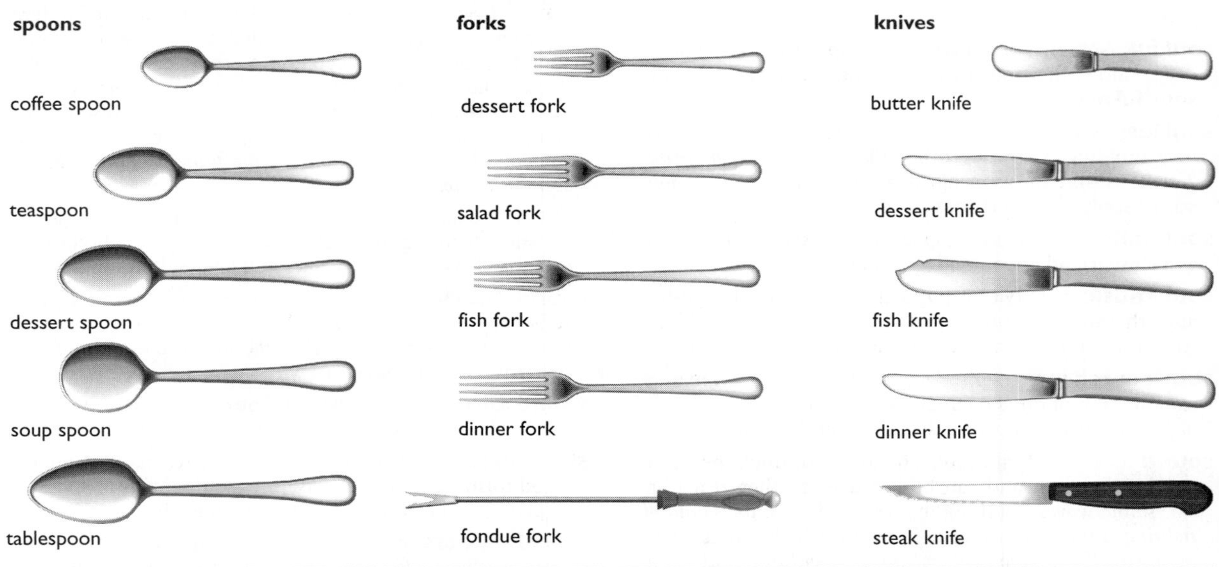

soup·çon (sūp sȯng′) *n* a very small quantity of something, especially something that gives a flavour. <French = suspicion, from Latin *suspicio*>

soup kitchen *n* a place that serves food free or at a very low charge to those who are homeless or extremely poor.

soup spoon *n* a spoon with a round bowl, bigger than a teaspoon, for eating soup.

soup·y (sū′pē) *adj* **soup·i·er, soup·i·est** with the appearance or consistency of soup.

sour (sour) *adj* **1** with an acid taste like vinegar or lemon juice. **2** fermented or spoiled: *sour milk.* **3** with a rancid smell: *a sour smell from the drain.* **4** feeling or expressing resentment, disappointment, or anger: *a sour face, a sour remark.*
v **1** make or become sour: *The milk soured in the heat.* **2** make or become bad-tempered, difficult, or disagreeable: *Their friendship soured after they argued.* <Old English *sur*> **sour′ly** *adv.* **sour′ness** *n.*
go sour, make or become peevish, bad-tempered, difficult, or disagreeable.
sour grapes, the attitude of seeming not to want or like something when actually it is impossible to have it: *When he wasn't invited to the party he said he didn't want to go anyway.*
sour on, take a dislike or lose one's taste for: *He seems to have soured on dancing lately.*

source (sȯrs) *n* **1** a place, person, or thing from which a thing comes or can be obtained: *a source of iron, the source of a rumour.* **2** a spring or fountain from which a river or stream begins. **b** a book, document, or electronic file used to provide evidence in research: *The reporter refused to name his source. She carefully checked her sources before she submitted the essay.*
v obtain something from a particular source, or find out where it may be obtained: *He was able to source the supplies in a catalogue.* <Old French, from Latin *surgere*>

source·book (sȯrs′bu̇k′) *n* a book containing a collection of texts used as basic resource material in studying something, especially as a basic introduction: *a sourcebook in medieval history.*

source code *Computers n* a listing of commands to be compiled or assembled into a program that can then be run.

sour cherry *n* the edible fruit of a cherry tree that is not sweet when ripe, often used in preserves and pies.

sour cream *n* cream that has been fermented by adding certain bacteria and is used in cooking, baking, and to accompany foods.

sour·dough (sour′dō′) *n* **1** fermented dough containing active yeast, saved from one baking for the next, or the bread made from it. **2** an experienced prospector in northwestern Canada or Alaska.

sour·puss (sour′pu̇s′) *Informal n* a person who looks or is gloomy, grumpy, or ill-tempered.

souse (sous) *v* **soused, sous·ing 1** soak in or drench with liquid. **2** pickle or marinade food, especially cucumbers or fish.
n **1** liquid, usually salty, used for pickling, or a food that is pickled in it. <Old French *sous* pickle>

sou·tane (sū tán′) *n* a cassock.

south (south) *n* **1** the direction to the left as one faces the setting sun. **2 the South,** the part of any country, especially the US, toward the south.
adj **1** toward, in, or facing the south. **2** (*especially of the wind*) from the south: *a south wind.*
adv toward the south: *Go south two blocks.* Also, **southerly**. <Old English>
south of, farther south than.

South Africa *n* a country in southern Africa. See the APPENDIX. **South African** *adj, n.*

South America *n* the continent that is the southern part of the American land mass, bordered by the Pacific to the west and the Atlantic to the east, the Antarctic to the south, and Central America to the north. Most of South America is south of the equator.
South American *adj, n.*

south·bound (south′bound′) *adj* going south.

south·east (sou′thēst′) *n* **1** the direction midway between south and east. **2** a place that is in the southeast part or direction.
adj **1** toward, in, or facing the southeast. **2** (*especially of the wind*) from the southeast: *a southeast wind.*
adv toward the southeast: *They travelled southeast.* Also, **southeasterly**.

south·east·er (sou′thē′stər) *n* a wind or storm from the southeast.

south·east·er·ly (sou′thē′stər lē) *adj* southeast.
adv from the southeast: *The wind blew southeasterly.*

south·east·ern (sou′thē′stərn) *adj* to do with the southeast.

south·east·ward (sou′thē′stwərd) *adj, adv* toward the southeast: *to set a southeastward course* (*adj*). *The road turns southeastward here* (*adv*). Also (*adv*), **southeastwards**. **south′east′ward·ly** *adj, adv.*

south·er (sou′ᴛʜər) *n* a wind or storm from the south. Also, **southerly**.

south·er·ly (suᴛʜ′ər lē) *adj* south.
adv from the south: *The wind blew southerly.*
n, pl **south·er·lies** SOUTHER.

south·ern (suᴛʜ′ərn) *adj* **1** to do with the south: *the southern side of a building.* **2 Southern** to do with the southern states of the US: *a Southern accent.*

south·ern·er (suᴛʜ′ər nər) *n* a person born in or living in the southern part of the country. Also, South.

southern lights AURORA AUSTRALIS.

south·ern·most (suᴛʜ′ərn mōst′) *adj* farthest south.

south·land (sou′thlənd) *or* (sou′thland′) *n* the southern part of a region or country.

south·paw (south′po′) *Informal n* **1** a left-handed baseball pitcher or boxer. **2** a left-handed person.
adj left-handed.

South Pole *n* the southern end of the earth's axis.

✱ **South Shore** *n* **1** the southern shore of the St. Lawrence River and the Gulf of St. Lawrence. **2** the southern coast of Nova Scotia.

south–south·east (south′sou′thēst′) *n* a direction midway between south and southeast.
adj, adv in, toward, or from this direction. *Abbrev.* **SSE**

south–south·west (south′sou′thwest′) *n* a direction midway between south and southwest.
adj, adv in, toward, or from this direction. *Abbrev.* **SSW**

south·ward (sou′thwərd) *adj, adv* toward the south: *The orchard is on the southward slope of the hill* (*adj*). *Rocks lay southward of the ship's course* (*adv*). Also (*adv*), **southwards**. **south′ward·ly** *adj, adv.*

south·west (sou′thwest′) *n* **1** the direction or compass point midway between south and west. **2** a place that is in the southwest part or direction.
adv to or toward the southwest: *They travelled southwest.*
adj to do with the southwest: *a southwest wind.*

south·west·er (sou′thwes′tər) *or* (sou′wes′tər) *n* a wind or storm from the southwest.

south·west·er·ly (sou′thwes′tər lē) *adj* southwest.
adv from the southwest: *The wind blew southwesterly.*

south·west·ern (sou′thwes′tərn) *adj* to do with the southwest.

south·west·ward (sou′thwes′twərd) *adj, adv* toward the southwest: *to set a southwestward course* (*adj*). *The road turns southwestward here* (*adv*). Also (*adv*), **southwestwards**. **south′west′ward·ly** *adj, adv.*

sou·ve·nir (sū′və nēr′) *or* (sū′və nēr′) *n* a thing that is kept as a reminder of a place, person, or occasion. <French, from Latin *subvenire* come to mind>

sou·vla·ki (sū vlȧ′kē) *n* a Greek dish of pieces of meat grilled on a skewer. <Greek *soubla* skewer>

sou'west·er (sou′wes′tər) *n* a waterproof hat with a broad flap covering the neck. <southwester>

sov·er·eign (sov′rən) *n* **1** a supreme ruler or monarch. **2** a former British gold coin, worth one pound.
adj **1** with supreme or ultimate power: *sovereign authority, a sovereign cure.* **2** fully independent and self-governing as a political or legal unit: *a sovereign court, a sovereign state.* <Old French, from Latin *super* over, i.e., rule over>

✱ **sov·er·eign·tist** or **sov·er·eign·ist** (sov′rənt ist) *or* (sov′rən ist) *n* a supporter of sovereignty for Québec.
adj supporting sovereignty for Québec.

sov·er·eign·ty (sov′rən tē) *n, pl* **sov·er·eign·ties** **1** supreme power or authority. **2** the freedom of a country or political unit from outside control.

✱ **sovereignty association** *n* a policy proposed in the late 1970s by the Québec government, under which the province would become an independent state but would remain associated with Canada.

so·vi·et (sō′vē et′) *n* an elected local, district, or national council in the former USSR.
adj **Soviet** to do with the former USSR. <Russian *sovet* council>

sow[1] (sō) *v* **sowed, sown** or **sowed, sow·ing** **1** plant seed on or in the earth: *He sows more wheat than oats.* **2** be covered with something: *The area was sown with land mines.* **3** cause to appear or spread: *The enemy tried to sow discontent among our men.* <Old English *sawan*> **sow′er** *n.*

sow[2] (sou) *n* a fully grown female pig, or the female of certain other animals. <Old English *sugu*>

sow·bug (sou′bug′) *n* a small land crustacean with a segmented body that can roll up into a ball for protection.

a bat	e bed	i bid	o pot	u cup	th thin
ā cake	ē me	ī bite	ō go	ū rude	ᴛʜ then
ȧ bar	ə about	ər over	ȯ for	u̇ put	zh measure

S

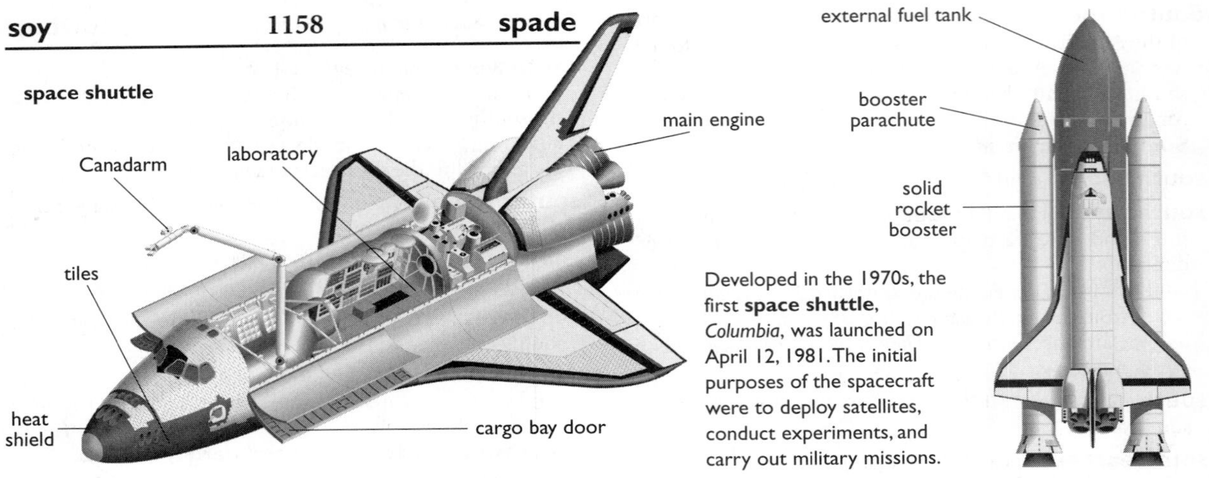

Developed in the 1970s, the first **space shuttle**, *Columbia*, was launched on April 12, 1981. The initial purposes of the spacecraft were to deploy satellites, conduct experiments, and carry out military missions.

soy (soi) *n* in full, **soy sauce** a sauce prepared from fermented soybeans, used especially in Chinese and Japanese dishes. <Japanese *shoyu*>

soy·bean (soi′bēn′) *n* a bean of an Asian plant in the pea family, widely grown and used as food, or the plant itself.

soy·burg·er (soi′bərg ər) *n* a patty made out of ground soybeans and seasoning, served in a split bun.

soz·zled (so′zəld) *Informal adj* very drunk. <obsolete *sozzle* stupor>

spa (spȯ) *n* **1** a mineral spring whose waters are considered to be health-giving, or a place or resort with such a spring. **2** a place that sells health and beauty treatments through such means as steam baths, exercise equipment, and massage. <*Spa*, a resort city in Belgium, known for the curative properties of its mineral springs>

space (spās) *n* **1** a continuous area or expanse that is free, available, or unoccupied: *We have plenty of space in this house.* **2** an area or spot that is not occupied by something: *a parking space.* **3** an interval of time: *We saw three golden eagles in the space of an hour.* **4** the amount of paper or another medium that is used or needed to write about a subject: *She didn't have space to make all her points.* **5** the freedom and scope to live, think, and develop personally: *He decided he needed his own space.* **6** the dimensions of height, depth, and width within which all things exist and move: *time and space.* **7** outer space.
v **spaced, spac·ing 1** position two or more items or people at a distance from one another: *The guards were spaced several metres apart.* **2** put blanks between words, letters, or lines: *double spacing.* <Old French, from Latin *spatium*>

space age *n* the current period of history, thought of as being marked by the first efforts to explore outer space.

space bar *Computers n* a long bar at the bottom of a keyboard, used for making a space between words.

space cadet *Slang n* someone who seems out of touch with the real world.

space capsule CAPSULE (def. 2).

space·craft (spā′skraft′) *n, pl* **space·craft** a vehicle designed for travelling in outer space.

spaced–out (spāst′out′) *Informal adj* cease to be aware of or in touch with one's surroundings, especially from taking drugs.

space heater *n* a small electric or gas-powered unit used to heat a relatively small, enclosed area, such as a room or part of a room.

space·man (spā′smən) *n, pl* **space·men** (-smən) an astronaut.

space medicine *n* the branch of medicine dealing with the effects of space travel on the human body.

space·port (spās′pȯrt′) *n* a centre for the building, testing, and launching of spacecraft.

space·ship (spās′ship′) *n* a spacecraft.

space shuttle *n* a rocket-launched spacecraft used for repeated journeys from earth to a space station.

space station *n* a large artificial satellite sent into outer space to serve as an observation post or as a launching pad for other spacecraft.

space·suit (spās′sūt′) *n* an airtight suit designed to allow an astronaut to survive in space by maintaining the earth's conditions within the suit.

space–time continuum (spās′tīm′) *n* the four-dimensional system in which all physical things and events are thought to exist, consisting of the three dimensions of space plus the dimension of time.

space·walk (spās′wok′) *n* an activity performed by an astronaut in outer space while outside the spacecraft.

spac·ing (spā′sing) *n* the action of fixing or arranging spaces, or the manner in which this is done: *even spacing.*

spa·cious (spā′shəs) *adj* with ample space, especially in a room or building: *Even the bedrooms of the palace were spacious.* **spa′cious·ness** *n.*

spa·cy or **spa·cey** (spā′sē) *Informal adj* out of touch with the real world: *She was very pleasant but rather spacy.*

spade[1] (spād) *n* a tool for digging or cutting the earth, with a sharp-edged, flat blade, and a long handle.
v **spad·ed, spad·ing** dig or cut with a spade. <Old English *spadu*>
call a spade a spade, speak plainly and frankly.

spade[2] (spād) *n* **1** a playing card with one or more black ♠ designs on it. **2 spades** *pl* the suit of cards marked with this design. <Italian, from Greek *spathe* sword>
in spades, *Informal* to a very high degree: *He got the success he craved — in spades!*

spade·work (spād′wərk′) *n* preliminary work, especially when considered as tedious or difficult.

spa·dix (spā′diks) *n, pl* **spa·dix·es** or **spa·di·ces** (spā dī′sēz) a spike composed of tiny flowers enclosed in a spathe, as in the calla lily. <Latin, from Greek *spadix* palm branch>

spa·ghet·ti (spə get′ē) *n* long, slender sticks of pasta, soft when cooked. <Italian *spago* cord>

spa·ghet·ti·ni (spag′i tē′nē) *n* pasta in strands thinner than spaghetti but not as thin as vermicelli. <Italian = little spaghetti>

spaghetti squash *n* a large squash whose flesh tends to separate into long strands when cooked.

Spain (spān) *n* a country in western Europe. See the APPENDIX. **Span′iard** *n.* **Span′ish** *adj.*

spall (spol) *v* break, split, or chip ore, rock, or stone into smaller pieces, especially to prepare it for sorting, or be broken in this way.
n a chip, sliver, or fragment of ore, rock, or stone. <origin uncertain>

spam (spam) *Computers* *n* unwanted e-mail, usually advertising, sent indiscriminately to large numbers of people.
v **spammed, spam·ming** send such e-mail. See also SPIM. <from a sketch that appeared on the British television show *Monty Python's Flying Circus* in which *Spam* (a brand of canned meat) is served whether wanted or not>

span[1] (span) *n* **1** the full extent of something from end to end: *a bridge span, the span of memory.* **2** the length of time for which something lasts: *a memory span.* **3** the wingspan of an aircraft or a bird. **4** an arch or part of a bridge between piers or supports. **5** the maximum distance between the tips of the thumb and little finger of a spread-out hand, taken as the basis of a unit of measurement, about 23 cm.
v **spanned, span·ning 1** extend from side to side: *A bridge spanned the river.* **2** extend over a period of time or a range of subjects. **3** cover or enclose with the length of one's hand. <Old English>

span[2] (span) *n* **1** a rope with its ends fastened at different points to a spar or other object. **2** a pair of horses or other animals harnessed and driven together. <Dutch *spannen* to stretch>

Span·dex (span′deks) *Trademark* *n* a synthetic, stretchy elastic fibre used especially in swimsuits and undergarments.

span·gle (spang′gəl) *n* **1** a tiny piece of glittering material used for decoration: *The skater's costume was covered with spangles.* **2** a spot of bright colour or light.
v **span·gled, span·gling** cover with spangles or other small, sparkling objects: *The sky was spangled with stars.* <origin uncertain>

Span·iard (spān′yərd) See SPAIN.

span·iel (span′yəl) *n* a dog of a breed with a long silky coat and drooping ears. <Old French, from Latin *Hispaniolus* Spanish>

Span·ish (span′ish) See SPAIN.

Spanish Inquisition *n* a Roman Catholic court established in 1478 to suppress members of other religious faiths it considered heretics, or the activities of this court.

Spanish Main *n* in former times, the northern mainland of S America and the adjoining part of the Caribbean. <*Main* is an archaic or poetic word for ocean>

Spanish moss *n* a tropical or semitropical plant growing on branches of trees, from which it hangs in greyish green streamers.

spank (spangk) *v* slap with one's open hands on a surface, especially on the buttocks as a punishment.
n a slap of this type. <origin uncertain>

spank·ing (spang′king) *adj* brisk and lively: *a spanking breeze, a spanking team of horses.*
n the act of slapping with the open hand, especially on the buttocks as a punishment.

spar[1] (spȧr) *n* **1** a thick, strong pole, such as that used to support or extend the sails of a ship. **2** the main beam of an airplane wing. <Old French *esparre*>

spar[2] (spȧr) *v* **sparred, spar·ring 1** make the motions of boxing without landing heavy blows. **2** engage in argument, usually prolonged and repeated but not violent.
n a period or bout of sparring. <Old English *sperran*>

spar[3] (spȧr) *n* a shiny crystalline mineral that splits into flakes easily. <German>

spare (sper) *adj* **spar·er, spar·est 1** extra to what is needed for ordinary use: *spare cash, a spare tire.* **2** not currently in use or occupied: *spare time.* **3** thin, lean, or with little fat: *The man was tall and spare, a spare diet.* **4** elegantly simple: *The car had clean, spare lines.*
v **spared, spar·ing, 1** give something of which one has enough to someone: *He was able to spare a few dollars for me.* **2** make free or available: *She spared some time to talk to us.* **3** refrain from killing, injuring, or distressing someone or something: *The artillery commander decided to spare the village.* **4** refrain from inflicting something on someone: *The people had been spared many of the plague's horrors.*
n **1** an item kept in case another item of the same type is lost, broken, or worn out. **2** an act of knocking down all the pins in tenpin bowling with two rolls of a ball. <Old English *spær*> **spare′ly** *adv.* **spare′ness** *n.*
(enough and) to spare, more than enough: *We have food enough and to spare.*
not spare yourself, do all you can.

spare·rib (sper′rib′) *n* a rib of meat, especially pork, with less meat than the ribs near the loins.

a bat	e bed	i bid	o pot	u cup	th thin
ā cake	ē me	ī bite	ō go	ū rude	ᴛʜ then
ȧ bar	ə about	ər over	ȯ for	u̇ put	zh measure

spar·ing (sper′ing) *adj* moderate and avoiding waste: *a sparing use of sugar.* **spar′ing·ly** *adv.*

spark (spårk) *n* **1** a small, fiery particle thrown off from a fire, alight in ashes, or produced by striking together two hard surfaces such as stone or metal: *The burning wood sent up sparks.* **2** a flash given off by electricity in the air, or one that explodes the gas in the engine of a motor vehicle. **3** a small, bright point or object: *a spark of light.* **4** a trace of a specified quality or feeling: *I haven't a spark of interest in the plan.* **5** a sense of liveliness or excitement.
v **1** send out sparks of fire or electricity. **2** provide the stimulus for an event or process: *to spark a revolt. She sparked the team to victory.* <Old English *spærca*>

spar·kle (spår′kəl) *v* **spar·kled, spar·kling** **1** shine brightly with flashes of light: *The diamonds sparkled.* **2** be lively and witty: *His wit sparkles.* **3** give off or cause fizz or bubbles: *Her ginger ale sparkled.*
n **1** a glittering flash of light: *I like the sparkle of her eyes.* **2** liveliness and wit.

spar·kler (spår′klər) *n* **1** a person who or thing that sparkles. **2** a handheld firework that sends out little sparks.

spark plug *n* a device in the cylinder of a gasoline engine by which the mixture of gasoline and air is exploded by an electric spark.

sparring partner *n* **1** a boxer who spars with another as a form of practice or training. **2** a person with whom one regularly has casual, friendly arguments.

spar·row (spar′ō) *or* (sper′ō) *n* a small bird, typically with brown and grey feathers, such as the song sparrow and the English sparrow. <Old English *spearwa*>

sparrow hawk *n* a small woodland hawk that feeds on sparrows and other small birds.

sparse (spårs) *adj* **spars·er, spars·est** thinly scattered or dispersed: *a sparse population, sparse hair.* <Latin *spargere* scatter> **sparse′ly** *adv.* **sparse′ness** *n.* **spars′i·ty** *n.*

Spar·tan[1] (spår′tən) *adj* **1** to do with Sparta, a city in ancient Greece, or its people. **2** like the Spartans in being disciplined and indifferent to comfort: *a Spartan diet.*
n a native or inhabitant of Sparta.

🍁 **Spar·tan**[2] (spår′tən) *adj* an eating apple with crisp white flesh and red skin.

spasm (spaz′əm) *n* **1** a sudden, involuntary contraction of a muscle or muscles: *a coughing spasm.* **2** a sudden, brief spell of unusual activity or sensation: *a spasm of energy.* <Old French, from Greek *span* pull>

spas·mod·ic (spaz mod′ik) *adj* **1** occurring or done in brief, irregular bursts: *spasmodic battles.* **2** caused by, subject to, or like a spasm or spasms: *a spasmodic cough.* **spas·mod′i·cal·ly** *adv.*

spas·tic (spas′tik) *adj* to do with a muscle spasm or spasms, such as that involved in cerebral palsy.
n Offensive a person affected by cerebral palsy.

spat[1] (spat) *n* a slight quarrel.
v **spat·ted, spat·ting** have a slight quarrel. <perhaps imitative>

spat[2] (spat) *v* a past tense and a past participle of SPIT[1].

spat[3] (spat) *n* usually, **spats** *pl* a short gaiter covering the ankle. <*spatterdash*, a type of gaiter>

spate (spāt) *n* **1** a large number of similar things or events appearing or occurring one after another: *a spate of words.* **2** a sudden flood in a river, especially one caused by heavy rain or melting snow. <origin unknown>

spathe (spāᴛʜ) *n* a large bract or pair of bracts that enclose a flower cluster, such as in the calla lily. <Latin, from Greek *spathe* sword>

spa·tial (spā′shəl) *adj* to do with space: *spatial arrangement.* **spa′tial·ly** *adv.*

spa·tio–tem·po·ral (spā′shē ō tem′pər əl) *adj* to do with both space and time.

spat·ter (spat′ər) *v* **1** cover with drops or spots of something: *to spatter mud.* **2** scatter or splash liquid over a surface: *The frying pan spattered oil all over the stove top.* **3** fall or hit so as to be scattered over an area: *Bullets spattered the wall.*
n **1** a spray, splash, or sprinkling of something: *a spatter of hail.* **2** a short outburst of sound. <Dutch *spatten* burst>

spat·u·la (spach′ə lə) *n* a tool with a broad, flat, blunt blade, used for mixing and spreading material, especially in cooking and painting. <Latin, from Greek *spathe* sword>

spawn (spon) *v* **1** release and deposit eggs as a fish, frog, or crustacean, or be laid as eggs. **2** produce human offspring, considered as an undesirable thing. **3** produce or generate, especially in large numbers.
n **1** the eggs of a fish, frog, or crustacean. **2** the process of producing such eggs. See FROG for picture. **3** the product or offspring of a person or place, considered as an undesirable thing. **4** the fine white filaments of a fungus, especially a cultivated mushroom. <Old French, from Latin *expandere* expand>

spay (spā) *v* remove the ovaries of a female cat, dog, or other animal in order to keep it from producing offspring. <Old French *espier* cut with a sword, from Greek *spathe* sword>

SPCA or **S.P.C.A.** Society for the Prevention of Cruelty to Animals.

speak (spēk) *v* **spoke, spo·ken, speak·ing** **1** say something in order to convey information, a message, an opinion, or a feeling, either directly or as part of a conversation: *Speak distinctly.* **2** make a speech before an audience or as part of a group: *Who is going to speak at the forum?* **3** tell, express, or make known: *Speak the truth. Her eyes speak of suffering.* **4** use or know how to use in speaking: *Do you speak Swedish?* <Old English *specan*>
so to speak, that is to say.
speak for, a speak in the interest of: *She spoke for the group that wanted a picnic.* **b** ask or apply for.
speak for itself, be obvious or self-explanatory: *The picture needs no caption; it speaks for itself.*
speak of, a (*with a negative*) worth mentioning or of any significance: *We've had no snowfalls to speak of this winter.* **b** mention or refer to: *She spoke of the matter to me.*
speak out or **up, a** speak loudly and clearly. **b** speak freely and without restraint: *They were all too frightened to speak out.*

speak to, a talk in order to criticize or advise: *My brother spoke to the neighbour about making too much noise.* **b** talk in order to give or obtain information: *They spoke to the police about the robbery.* **c** discuss or comment on something formally: *The mayor spoke to the issues that concerned us.*
speak well for, give a favourable idea of or be evidence in favour of.

–speak *Informal combining form* indicating a manner of speaking characteristic of a certain group or subject: *legal-speak.*

speak·eas·y (spēk′ē′zē) *especially US n, pl* **speak·eas·ies** a place where alcohol was sold illegally during the time of Prohibition. <from the practice of speaking softly about such places, to avoid attention>

speak·er (spē′kər) *n* **1** a person who speaks, especially one who speaks before an audience: *The next speaker went on too long.* **2** a person who speaks a specified language: *a French speaker.* **3** a loudspeaker. **4 Speaker** a person who presides over a legislative assembly: *the Speaker of the House of Commons.*

speak·er·phone (spē′kər fōn′) *n* a telephone equipped with a microphone and loudspeaker so that more than one person can participate in the call.

speak·ing (spē′king) *n* the action of conveying information or expressing one's thoughts, messages, or feelings in spoken language.
adj **1** used in, suited to, or involving speech: *within speaking distance, a speaking part in a play.* **2** able to communicate in a specified language: *Spanish-speaking.* **3** expressing meaning as though in words: *speaking eyes.* **4** lifelike: *a speaking likeness.*

spear (spēr) *n* **1** a weapon or fishing implement with a long shaft and a sharp-pointed head, used for thrusting or throwing. **2** a plant shoot, especially a pointed stem of asparagus or broccoli.
v pierce or strike with a spear or other pointed object: *to spear a fish, to spear a wiener.* <Old English *spere*>
spear′er *n.*

spear·head (spēr′hed′) *n* **1** the sharp-pointed end of a spear. **2** a person, group, or thing leading an attack: *She was the spearhead of the project to make a park here.*
v lead an attack or undertaking: *Tanks spearheaded the army's advance.*

spear·man (spēr′mən) *n, pl* **spear·men** (-mən) a soldier armed with a spear.

spear·mint (spēr′mint′) *n* common garden mint, a fragrant herb used for flavouring. See HERB for picture of mint.

spec[1] (spek) *Informal n* speculation.
on spec, in the hope of success or making a profit but with no guarantee.

spec[2] (spek) *Informal n* a detailed working description: *We got the specs for the new house yesterday.* <*specification*>

spe·cial (spesh′əl) *adj* **1** better, greater, or otherwise different from what is usual: *This desk has a special lock. Today's topic is of special interest.* **2** exceptionally good or valued: *a special friend, a special favourite.* **3** designed or organized for a particular person, purpose, or occasion: *special needs. The railway ran special trains on holidays.*
n **1** a thing, such as an event, product, or broadcast, that is designed for a particular occasion or purpose. **2** a product or meal that is specially featured in a store or restaurant, sometimes at a reduced price. <Old French, from Latin *species* appearance> **spe′cial·ly** *adv.* **spe′cial·ness** *n.*
on special, offered for sale at a reduced price.

SYNONYMS

Special means "different from what is usual": *Vacations are special times for most people.*

Particular emphasizes individuality, especially when someone or something is being considered separately from others of the same kind: *Of all the computers, I like this particular one.*

Specific often means "characteristic of": *The dialect is specific to that part of the country.*

Exclusive often means "not available elsewhere or to anyone else": *This is an exclusive offer for our loyal customers.*

🍁 **special constable** *n* a person sworn in for special or emergency duty as a police constable.

special delivery *n* delivery of a letter or package by a special messenger rather than by the regular letter carrier.

special education *n* education for students who are academically gifted or who have difficulty with academic work.

special effects *n* visual and sound effects or illusions in movies and television beyond the normal range of photography and recording created by computer graphics, camerawork, or props. Often written **FX**.

special interest group *n* a group or organization that seeks to achieve specific objectives or acquire special advantages, often through political lobbying.

spe·cial·ize (spesh′ə līz′) *v* **spe·cial·ized, spe·cial·iz·ing** **1** concentrate on a particular subject or activity, becoming expert about it: *She specialized in engineering.* **2** restrict oneself to providing a particular product or service: *The firm specialized in home decorating* **3** make a habit of engaging in a particular activity: *He specialized in making himself unpleasant.* **4** *Biology* adapt or set apart an organ or part to serve a special function or to suit a particular way of life: *The lizard's skin was specialized for camouflage.*
spe′cial·ist *n.* **spe′cial·i·za′tion** *n.*

spe·cial·ty (spesh′əl tē) *n, pl* **spe·cial·ties** **1** a pursuit, area of study, or skill to which someone has devoted much time and effort and in which he or she is expert: *Repairing watches is his specialty.* **2** a product or service for which a store or restaurant is known or concentrates on selling: *This shop makes a specialty of children's clothes.* **3** a branch of medicine or surgery.

a bat	e bed	i bid	o pot	u cup	th thin
ā cake	ē me	ī bite	ō go	ū rude	ᴛʜ then
ä bar	ə about	ər over	ô for	ů put	zh measure

spe·ci·a·tion (spē′shē ā′shən) *Biology n* the development of new species in the course of evolution. **spe′ci·ate** *v.*

spe·cie (spē′shē) *n* money in the form of coins. <Latin *species* form>

spe·cies (spē′sēz) *or* (spē′shēz) *n, pl* **spe·cies 1** *Biology* a category in the classification of living things, consisting of similar individuals capable of interbreeding to produce fertile offspring. A species is more specific than a GENUS. See also BINOMIAL NOMENCLATURE. **2** a distinct kind or sort: *There are many species of advertisements.* <Latin = appearance, from *specere* to look>

spe·cif·ic (spə sif′ik) *adj* **1** clearly defined or identified: *There was no specific reason for the quarrel.* **2** characteristic of or peculiar to: *A scaly skin is a specific feature of snakes.*
n **1** a precise detail. **2** a medicine effective in treating a particular disease or part of the body: *Quinine is a specific for malaria.* <See SPECIES.> **spe·cif′i·cal·ly** *adv.* **spec′i·fic′i·ty** (spə′si fis′i tē) *n.*

spec·i·fi·ca·tion (spes′ə fə kā′shən) *n* **1** an act of describing or identifying something precisely or of stating a precise requirement: *There were a lot of specifications for the new product.* **2 specifications** *pl* a detailed description of the design and materials used to make something.

specific gravity RELATIVE DENSITY.

specific heat *n* in full, **specific heat capacity** the heat required to raise the temperature of a unit mass of a substance by one degree.

spec·i·fy (spes′ə fī′) *v* **spec·i·fied, spec·i·fy·ing 1** identify clearly and definitely: *Did you specify any particular time for us to call?* **2** state a fact or requirement clearly and precisely: *The contractor couldn't use shingles for the roof because slate was specified.* <Latin *specificare* to describe>

spec·i·men (spes′ə mən) *n* **1** an individual animal, plant, or piece of a mineral used as an example of its species or type for scientific study or display. **2** an example of something such as a product or piece of work, regarded as typical of its class or group: *a specimen of French art.* **3** a sample for medical testing: *a specimen of blood.* **4** *Informal* a person or animal: *He was an unusual specimen.*
adj taken or regarded as typical or as an example: *specimen results.* <Latin = model>

spe·cious (spē′shəs) *adj* **1** superficially plausible, but actually wrong: *We quickly saw through his specious excuse.* **2** misleading in appearance, especially misleadingly attractive: *She had a specious glamour.* <Latin *species* appearance> **spe′cious·ly** *adv.* **spe′cious·ness** *n.*

speck (spek) *n* a tiny spot or particle: *Can you clean the specks off this wallpaper? I have a speck in my eye.*
v mark with specks: *This fruit is badly specked.* <Old English *specca*>

speck·le (spek′əl) *n* a small spot or patch of colour: *This hen is grey with white speckles.*
v mark with speckles. <Dutch *spekkel*>

speck·led char (spek′əld) BROOK TROUT.

specs (speks) *Informal pl n* **1** a SPECTACLE (def. 3). **2** a SPECIFICATION (def. 2).

spec·ta·cle (spek′tə kəl) *n* **1** a visually striking show, performance, or display, especially a public one: *The big parade was a fine spectacle.* **2** a displeasing show or display: *He made a spectacle of himself.* **3 spectacles** *pl* a pair of eyeglasses. See CONTACT LENS for picture. <Old French, from Latin *specere* to look>

spec·ta·cled (spek′tə kəld) *adj* provided with or wearing spectacles, or with a marking resembling spectacles: *a spectacled snake.*

spec·tac·u·lar (spek tak′yə lər) *adj* **1** beautiful in a dramatic or visually striking way: *spectacular scenery.* **2** strikingly large or conspicuous: *spectacular size.*
n a spectacular show, performance, or display: *a TV spectacular.* **spec·tac′u·lar·ly** *adv.*

spec·ta·tor (spek′tā tər) *or* (spek tā′tər) *n* a person who watches a show, game, or other event without taking part: *Thousands of spectators lined the streets, waiting for the parade.* <Latin *specere* to look>

spectator sport *n* a sport that many people find entertaining or interesting to watch.

spec·tra (spek′trə) a plural of SPECTRUM.

spec·tral (spek′trəl) *adj* of or like a ghost: *She saw the spectral form of the headless horseman.*

spec·tre (spek′tər) *n* **1** a ghost. **2** something causing terror or dread. Also, **specter**. <Latin = image>

spec·tro·gram (spek′trə gram′) *n* a photographic or other visual or electronic record of a spectrum, produced by a machine called a **spectrograph**.

spec·tro·me·ter (spek trom′ə tər) *n* an instrument for recording and measuring spectrums, especially as a method of analysis, for example, of the rate of decay of radioactive elements in rocks.

spec·tro·scope (spek′trə skōp′) *n* an instrument for obtaining and examining spectrums for examination.

spec·trum (spek′trəm) *n, pl* **spec·trums** or **spec·tra** (-trə) **1** the band of colours, as seen in a rainbow, formed when the components of light are separated according to wavelength. **2** the range of positions on a scale between two extreme or opposite points: *He was far right on the political spectrum.* <Latin = image, from *specere* to look at>

spec·u·late (spek′yə lāt′) *v* **spec·u·lat·ed, spec·u·lat·ing 1** form a theory or idea about a subject without firm evidence: *He speculated about the cause of the explosion. She refused to speculate about the possible winner.* **2** invest in stocks, property, or other things in the hope of gain but with a large risk of loss. <Latin *speculari* to observe, from *specere* to look at> **spec′u·la′tion** *n.* **spec′u·la′tor** *n.*

spec·u·la·tive (spek′yə lə tiv) *or* (spek′yə lā′tiv) *adj* **1** engaged in, expressing, or based on speculation rather than knowledge. **2** involving a high risk of loss. **spec′u·la′tive·ly** *adv.* **spec′u·la′tive·ness** *n.*

sped (sped) *v* a past tense and past participle of SPEED.

speech (spēch) *n* **1** the expression of thoughts and feelings by making meaningful sounds. **2** a person's style of speaking: *pompous speech. Her speech showed that she was from the country.* **3** a formal public talk: *after-dinner speeches.* **4** a set of lines written for one character in a play or movie. <Old English *spæc*>

✱ **Speech from the Throne** *n* a statement of government policy for the coming year read by the Governor General or, in a province, by the Lieutenant-Governor.

speech·i·fy (spē′chə fī′) *Informal v* **speech·i·fied, speech·i·fy·ing** make a speech or speeches, especially in a boring or pompous way. **speech′i·fi′er** *n.*

speech·less (spēch′lis) *adj* unable to speak, especially as a result of shock or some strong emotion: *She was speechless with anger.* **speech′less·ly** *adv.* **speech′less·ness** *n.*

speech·writ·er (spēch′rī′tər) *n* a person whose job is to write speeches for a public figure, such as a politician.

speed (spēd) *n* **1** the rate at which someone or something moves or operates or is able to move or operate. **2** a rapid rate of movement or action: *The horses ran at full speed.* **3** an arrangement of gears in a motor vehicle to give a certain rate of movement.
v **sped** or **speed·ed, speed·ing 1** move, make go, or send quickly: *The boat sped over the water, to speed a horse near the end of a race.* **2** go faster than is safe or lawful: *The car was caught speeding near the school zone.* **3** help forward or promote: *to speed an undertaking.* <Old English *sped*> **speed′i·ly** *adv.* **speed′i·ness** *n.* **speed′y** *adj.*
speed up, move or cause to move more quickly.
up to speed, up to date or with current information.

speed·boat (spēd′bōt′) *n* a motorboat built to achieve high speed.

speed bump *n* a ridge set at intervals across a road surface to discourage drivers from going too fast.

speed·er (spē′dər) *n* a person who or thing that speeds, especially a person who drives an automobile at a higher speed than is legal or safe.

speed limit *n* the top speed at which motor vehicles are allowed to travel on a particular road.

speed·om·e·ter (spē dom′ə tər) *or* (spi dom′ə tər) *n* an instrument to indicate the speed of an automobile or other vehicle.

speed·read (spēd′rēd′) *v* read much faster than normal, with good comprehension and memory, by using a special technique. **speed′read′er** *n.* **speed′read′ing** *n.*

speed·skate (spēd′skāt) *n* an ice skate made specially for **speed skating**, the sport of competing with others to skate fastest on an oval track. Short-track speed skating uses hockey rink ice. See SHINGUARD for picture. **speed skater** *n.*

speed·ster (spēd′stər) *n* a person who or thing that travels at high speed.

speed trap *n* a place where police use radar as a means of catching motorists who are speeding.

speed–up (spē′dup′) *n* an increase in speed.

speed·way (spē′dwā′) *n* a road or track for fast driving.

speed·well (spē′dwel′) *n* a small creeping plant.

spe·le·ol·o·gy (spē′lē ol′ə jē) *n* the study or exploration of caves. <French, from Greek *spelaion* cave> **spe′le·ol′o·gist** *n.*

spell[1] (spel) *v* **spelled** or **spelt, spel·ling 1** write or say the letters that form a word, in the correct order: *Some words are easy to spell.* **2** make up or form a word in letters: *C-a-t spells cat.* **3** be recognizable as a sign, warning, or characteristic of: *Delay spells danger.* <Old French *espeller*>

GRAMMAR AND USAGE

Try one or more of the following strategies to help you improve your spelling:

- Make a personal list of words you misspell often and check the list whenever you write something.
- Think of a memory trick to help you remember the spelling of troublesome words: "an island **is land** in water" can help you remember there's an *s* in *island.*
- Look for similar spelling patterns such as *-ight* in *bright, light, might*; and *-ite* in *kite, trite, quite.*
- Play around with a difficult word by visualizing the letters, writing it down in fancy lettering, or typing it a few times.
- Take the time to proofread everything you write, checking both the dictionary and your personal list of commonly misspelled words.

spell[2] (spel) *n* **1** a word or set of words with supposedly magic power. **2** the period of enchantment caused by such words. **3** an ability to control or influence people as though one had magical power over them: *We were under the spell of the beautiful music.* <Old English *spell* story>
cast a spell on, put under the influence of a spell or a thing resembling it.
under a spell, controlled by a spell or a thing resembling it: *The explorer's story held the children under a spell.*

spell[3] (spel) *n* a short period of time marked by something, especially that of work or duty: *The sailor's spell at the wheel was four hours, a spell of coughing, a spell of hot weather.*
v **spelled, spell·ing** work in place of another for a while: *He spelled me at rowing the boat.* <origin uncertain>

spell·bind (spel′bīnd′) *v* **spell·bound, spell·bind·ing** hold the complete attention of someone as though by magic. **spell′bind′ing** *adj.* **spell′bind′ing·ly** *adv.* **spell′bound′** *adj.*

spell–check (spel′chek′) *Computers n* a check of spelling in a text file performed by a program called a **spell-checker**.
v make such a check.

spell·er (spel′ər) *n* **1** a person who spells with a specified ability: *a bad speller.* **2** a book that teaches spelling.

spell·ing (spel′ing) *n* **1** the writing or saying of the letters of a word in the correct order. **2** the way in which a word is spelled. Example: The word *colour* has two spellings, *colour* and *color.*

a bat	e bed	i bid	o pot	u cup	th thin
ā cake	ē me	ī bite	ō go	ū rude	ᴛʜ then
ä bar	ə about	ər over	ô for	ů put	zh measure

S

spelling bee *n* a spelling contest.

spelt[1] (spelt) a past tense and a past participle of SPELL[1].

spelt[2] (spelt) *n* an old form of wheat with bearded ears and spikelets, often used as a health food. <Old English>

spe·lunk·ing (spi lung′king) CAVING.

spend (spend) *v* **spent, spend·ing 1** pay out money in buying or hiring goods or services: *She spent ten dollars today.* **2** pay out money for a particular person's benefit or for improvement: *We spent a lot of money to fix up the house.* **3** use up a period of time: *Don't spend any more time on that job. We spent a day at the beach.* **4** wear out or exhaust: *The storm has spent its force.* <Latin *dispendere* pay out> **spend′a·ble** *adj.* **spend′er** *n.*

SYNONYMS

Spend means "pay out" or "use up": *The government spends billions of dollars on health care.*

Disburse is a formal and financial word meaning "pay out from a fund for expenses": *The treasurer disbursed what was needed to cover the field trip.*

Expend is a more formal word for spend: *Let's not expend any more energy on that project.*

spend·thrift (spend′thrift′) *n* a person who spends money in an extravagant way.
adj extravagant with money: *spendthrift ways.*

spent (spent) *v* past tense and past participle of SPEND.
adj **1** used and unable to be used again: *a spent match.* **2** with no power or energy left: *a spent swimmer, a spent horse.*

sperm (spərm) *n, pl* **sperms** or (*especially collectively*) **sperm 1** the mature male reproductive cell of an animal by which the ovum of the female is fertilized, typically with a compact head and one or more threadlike structures that enable it to swim. **2** semen. <Greek *sperma* seed>

sper·ma·cet·i (spər′mə set′ē) *or* (spər′mə sē′tē) *n* a whitish, waxy substance produced in the head of the sperm whale, formerly used in making candles and ointments. <Latin, from Greek *ketos* whale>

sper·ma·to·zo·on (spər′mə tə zō′ən) *n, pl* **sper·ma·to·zo·a** (-zō′ə) sperm.

sperm bank *n* a storage facility for frozen donated sperm to be used for artificial insemination.

sper·mi·cide (spər′mi sīd′) *n* a substance that kills sperm, used as a contraceptive.

sperm whale *n* a large, square-headed, toothed whale with a massive head, feeding at great depths.

spew (spyū) *v* **1** expel large quantities of something rapidly and forcefully: *The volcano was spewing lava. He spewed out a stream of insults.* **2** vomit. <Old English *spiwan*> **spew′er** *n.*

SPF *n* in full, **sun protection factor** a measure of how effective a sunscreen preparation is against the harmful rays of the sun.

sphag·num (sfag′nəm) *n* peat moss.

sphere (sfēr) *n* **1** a round solid figure, or its surface, that is at all points equally distant from the centre. **2** an object with this general shape, such as a ball or globe. **3** an area of activity, interest, or knowledge that is distinguished and unified by a particular characteristic: *a sphere of influence. Her sphere is advertising.* **4** *Poetic* the sky considered as a vault upon or in which celestial bodies are shown to lie, or the area within which each celestial body is found: *the heavenly sphere, music of the spheres.* <Old French, from Greek *sphaira* ball> **spher′i·cal** *adj.* **spher′i·cal·ly** *adv.*

sphe·roid (sfē′roid) *n* an object shaped somewhat like a sphere. **sphe·roi′dal** *adj.*

sphinc·ter (sfingk′tər) *n* a ringlike muscle that surrounds an opening or passage of the body, and can contract to close it, such as the anus or the openings of the stomach. <Latin, from Greek *sphingein* bind tight>

sphinx (sfingks) *n, pl* **sphinx·es 1** a figure of Greek or Egyptian mythology, often represented by a statue of a lion's body with the head of a man, woman, ram, or hawk. **2** a puzzling or mysterious person. <Latin, from Greek>

spic and span or **spick and span** (spik′ən span′) *adj* neat, clean, and well looked after: *The whole house was spic and span, a spic-and-span room.* <Old Norse *spann* chip (of wood) + *nyr* new>

spice (spīs) *n* **1** a seasoning obtained from plants and used to flavour food, such as cinnamon, cloves, ginger, and nutmeg. **2** an element adding interest and excitement: *He said, "Variety is the spice of life."*
v **spiced, spic·ing 1** flavour with spice: *spiced peaches.* **2** add flavour or interest to: *She spiced her speech with stories and jokes.* <Old French, from Latin *species* kind>

spic·y (spī′sē) *adj* **spic·i·er, spic·i·est 1** flavoured or fragrant with spice or a thing resembling it: *spicy apples. The cookies were rich and spicy.* **2** exciting or entertaining, especially through being mildly improper: *spicy conversation, a spicy joke.* **spic′i·ly** *adv.* **spic′i·ness** *n.*

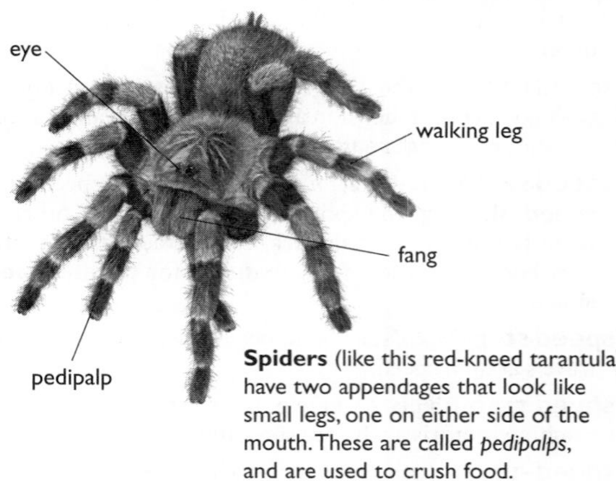

Spiders (like this red-kneed tarantula) have two appendages that look like small legs, one on either side of the mouth. These are called *pedipalps*, and are used to crush food.

spi·der (spī′dər) *n* **1** an eight-legged, predatory arachnid with an unsegmented body and fangs which inject poison into its prey. Most spiders spin webs in which to capture insects. **2** CRAWLER (def. 3). <Old English *spithra*> **spi′der·like′** *adj.*

spider monkey *n* a S American monkey with long, thin limbs and a long tail with which it can hang on to things.

spider plant *n* a plant of the lily family that has long, narrow leaves with a central yellow stripe, often used as a houseplant.

spi·der·web (spī′dər web′) *n* a web spun by a spider.

spi·der·y (spī′də rē) *adj* resembling a spider, especially in having long, thin, angular lines like a spider's legs: *spidery handwriting.*

spiel (spēl) *Informal n* a long or fast speech, sales pitch, or story, typically one used as a means of persuasion or as an excuse: *Every time I go to my aunt's home, she launches into a spiel about my poor eating habits.*
v deliver such a speech. <German *Spilon*>
spiel off, recite rapidly from memory: *The waiter spieled off the entire dessert menu without a hitch.*

spif·fy (spi′fē) *Informal adj* **spif·fi·er, spif·fi·est** neat and stylish. <origin uncertain>
spiff up, make spiffy or spiffier.

spig·ot (spig′ət) *n* **1** a small peg or plug, especially for insertion into an opening of a cask or barrel. **2** a device for controlling the flow of liquid in a tap. <perhaps Latin *spica* spike, ear of wheat>

spike[1] (spīk) *n* **1** a large, thin, pointed piece of metal, wood, or other rigid material used to fix or fasten something. **2** a sharp increase in the size or concentration of something: *a price spike.* **3** a very brief electrical pulse in which a rapid increase in voltage is followed by a rapid decrease. See also SURGE (*n* def. 2b).
v **spiked, spik·ing 1** impale on or pierce with a sharp point. **2** form into or cover with sharp points, or take on a sharp, pointed shape: *spiked hair.* **3** in former times, make a cannon useless by driving a spike into the opening where the powder is set off. **4** increase and then decrease rapidly: *The patient's temperature spiked several times.* **5** *Informal* slyly add alcohol or a drug to something: *to spike a drink.* **6** stop the progress of a plan or process. **7** *Volleyball* hit the ball forcefully from a position near the net so that it moves sharply downward into the opposite court. <origin uncertain> **spike′like′** *adj.*

spike[2] (spīk) *n* a flower cluster formed of many flower heads attached directly to a long stem. <Latin *spica* ear of wheat>

spike heel *n* a high, thin, tapering heel on a woman's shoe.

spike·let (spī′klət) *n* a small or secondary spike, especially one of the small spikes that make up a head of grain.

spike·nard (spīk′nərd) *or* (spīk′nȧrd) *n* a sweet-smelling ointment used in ancient times. <Latin, translated from Greek *nardostakhus*>

spik·y (spī′kē) *adj* **1** like or with a spike or spikes. **2** *Informal* grouchy; easily annoyed or offended.

spile (spīl) *n* **1** a peg or plug of wood used to stop the small hole of a cask or barrel. **2** a spout for drawing off sap from sugar maple trees. **3** a heavy timber driven into the ground to support a structure.
v **spiled, spil·ing** stop up a hole with a peg or plug. <German = peg>

spill (spil) *v* **spilled** or **spilt, spill·ing 1** flow or cause something to flow out of a container, especially by mistake: *to spill milk. The salt spilled out of the bag.* **2** move out from somewhere, usually in a mass: *The passengers spilled from the train.* **3** *Informal* reveal confidential information to someone.
n **1** a quantity of liquid or other thing that has spilled or been spilt. **2** a fall from a horse, bicycle, or watercraft. <Old English *spillan* kill, destroy, waste> **spill′er** *n.*
spill over, overflow or spread.
spill the beans, *Informal* tell a secret.

spill·o·ver (spil′ō′vər) *n* **1** the act of overflowing or spilling over, or the amount involved. **2** an effect or influence going beyond expected limits or as an unexpected consequence.
adj going beyond expected limits or as an unexpected consequence: *a spillover effect.*

spill·way (spil′wā′) *n* a channel or passage for the escape of surplus water from a dam or river.

spilt (spilt) *v* a past tense and a past participle of SPILL.

spim (spim) *Computers n* a type of SPAMMING where the target is INSTANT MESSAGING services and chat rooms.
v **spimmed, spim·ming** send such messages. <*Sp*(*am*) + *IM* Instant Messaging>

spin (spin) *v* **spun, spin·ning 1** turn or cause to turn or whirl round quickly: *The wheel spun around.* **2** have a sensation of dizziness in the head: *My head is spinning.* **3 a** draw out and twist cotton, wool, or other material into thread, either by hand or by machinery. **b** make threads or filaments in this way, such as from glass or a metal. **c** of spiders, silkworms, or other insects, produce a fine sticky thread from a special gland in the body and construct a web or cocoon with it. **4** give or cause to give a news story a favourable emphasis or slant. **5** tell a long story: *The retired sailor used to spin yarns about adventures at sea.*
n **1** a rapid turning or whirling motion. **2** a revolving motion given to a ball in a game, especially cricket, tennis, and snooker. **3** a favourable emphasis or slant in a news story. **4** a brief trip in a vehicle for pleasure: *Get your bicycle and come for a spin with me.* **5** a rapid turning around of an aircraft as it falls. <Old English *spinnan*>
spin out, make a thing last as long as possible: *Try not to spin out your story.*

S

spi·na bif·i·da (spī′nə bif′i də) *n* a congenital defect in which the spinal column, or part of it, is imperfectly closed, exposing the spinal cord and its membranes.

spin·ach (spin′ich) *or* (spin′ ij) *n* a garden plant whose large, dark green leaves are eaten as a vegetable. <Old French, from Persian *aspanak*>

spi·nal (spī′nəl) *adj* **1** to do with the spine or spinal cord. **2** to do with the central axis or backbone of something.
n Informal an anesthetic for the lower part of the body. **spi′nal·ly** *adv.*

spinal column *n* the SPINE (def. 1).

a bat	e bed	i bid	o pot	u cup	th thin
ā cake	ē me	ī bite	ō go	ū rude	TH then
ȧ bar	ə about	ər over	ȯ for	u̇ put	zh measure

spinal cord *n* the bundle of nerve fibres and tissue that is enclosed in the spine and connects nearly all parts of the body to the brain, with which it forms the central nervous system.

spin·dle (spin′dəl) *n* **1** a slender rod with tapered ends used in hand spinning or a spinning wheel to twist and wind thread from a mass of wool or flax. **2** a rod or pin that turns around, or on which a thing turns. **3** a turned piece of wood used as a banister or chair leg. <Old English *spinnan* spin>

spin·dly (spin′dlē) *adj* **spin·dli·er, spin·dli·est** long and tall or thin: *spindly legs, a spindly plant.* <*spindle*>

spin doctor *Informal n* a person whose job is to provide and publicize a favourable interpretation of statements or events on behalf of a government, group, or individual.

spin·drift (spin′drift′) *n* spray blown from the crests of waves by the wind.

spin–dry (spin′drī′) *v* **spin-dried, spin-dry·ing** extract water from wet clothes by centrifugal force in a drum that rotates at high speed.

spine (spīn) *n* **1** a series of small bones extending from the skull to the small of the back, enclosing the spinal cord and providing support for the thorax and abdomen. See BACKBONE for picture. **2** a stiff, sharp-pointed projection on an animal or plant body, such as on the tail of porcupines, in the fins of many kinds of fish, or on the stems of cactuses. **3** the back portion of a book where the pages are held together, or the part of the cover over this. **4** a thing that looks like a backbone or functions as a main support. <Latin *spina*> **spine′like′** *adj.*

spine·less (spīn′lis) *adj* **1** with no backbone. **2** of a plant or animal, without spines or prickles: *a spineless cactus.* **3** without moral force, resolution, or courage: *She thought he was spineless because he would not stand up for his beliefs.* **spine′less·ly** *adv.* **spine′less·ness** *n.*

spin·et (spin′it) *or* (spi net′) *n* **1** a musical instrument like a small harpsichord that was popular in the 1700s. **2** a small upright piano.

spin·na·ker (spin′ə kər) *n* a large, triangular sail, typically bulging when full, carried by boats on the side opposite the mainsail when running before the wind.

spin·ner (spin′ər) *n* **1** a person who or thing that spins. **2** a fishing lure that revolves when pulled through the water.

spin·ner·et (spin′ə ret′) *n* an organ by which the silk, gossamer, or thread of spiders, silkworms, and some insects is spun.

spinning wheel *n* a large wheel with a spindle, arranged for spinning yarn or thread for household use.

spin·off or **spin–off** (spin′of′) *n* **1** a by-product or side benefit of a larger project: *a spinoff from space research.* **2** a product marketed by association with a popular TV program, movie, or entertainer: *The TV show was a spinoff from a movie.* **3** a business or organization developed out of or by members of another organization, especially a subsidiary of a company that has been sold off, creating a new company.

spin·ster (spin′stər) *n* in former times, an unmarried woman, typically an older woman beyond the usual age for marriage. <Middle English *spinnen* spin + *-stere* -ster>

spin·y (spī′nē) *adj* **spin·i·er, spin·i·est** full of or covered with spines or prickles: *a spiny cactus.*

spi·ra·cle (spī′rə kəl) *or* (spir′ə kəl) *n* an opening for breathing, such as a pore on the body of an insect.

spi·rae·a (spī rē′ə) *n* a shrub of the rose family that has clusters of small flowers. Also, **spirea**.

spi·ral (spī′rəl) *n* **1** a shape or pattern that winds in a continuous and gradually widening or tightening curve. **2** a steady rise or fall of prices, wages, or events, each stage responding to an upward or downward stimulus provided by a previous one: *an inflationary spiral.*
adj winding in a continuous and gradually widening or tightening curve: *a spiral staircase.*
v **spi·ralled** or **spi·raled, spi·ral·ling** or **spi·ral·ing** **1** move in a spiral way: *The model airplane spiralled to earth.* **2** show a continuous and dramatic increase: *Costs spiralled out of control.* <Latin *spira* a coil, from Greek *speira*> **spi′ral·ly** *adv.*

The Milky Way is a **spiral galaxy** that includes our sun and its solar system. It appears hazy because the stars are too far away to be individually distinguished.

spiral galaxy *n* a huge system of stars in the form of a spiral.

spire[1] (spīr) *n* **1** the top part of a tower or steeple that narrows to a point. **2** a thing that is long and tapering: *The sunset shone on the rocky spires of the mountains.* <Old English *spir*> **spire′like′** *adj.*

spi·ril·lum (spī ril′əm) *n, pl* **spi·ril·la** (-ril′ə) a bacterium that has a rigid spiral structure, found in stagnant water and sometimes causing disease. <Latin *spira* a spiral>

spir·it (spir′it) *n* **1** the non-physical part of a person considered to be the source of emotions and character: *Some religions teach that at death the spirit leaves the body.* **2** a ghost or supernatural being: *She thought the house was haunted by an evil spirit.* **3** **a** a set of qualities considered to form the essential or typical elements in the character of a person, nation, or group: *the Canadian spirit.* **b** a specified emotion or mood: *a spirit of confidence.*

4 a person considered to be prominent in a group or movement: *He was the leading spirit of reform.* **5 spirits** *pl* a person's mood: *She's in good spirits.* **6** the quality of courage, energy, and determination: *The racehorse had a lot of spirit.* **7** the essential meaning or intent: *The spirit of a law is more important than its words.* **8 spirits** *pl* a strong alcoholic drink made by distillation, such as brandy, whisky, gin, or rum.
v carry away or off secretly: *After the performance, the singer was spirited away to an unknown destination.* <Latin *spiritus* soul>
out of spirits, sad or gloomy.

spir·it·ed (spir′ə tid) *adj* full of energy, enthusiasm, and determination: *a spirited effort.* **spir′it·ed·ly** *adv.* **spir′it·ed·ness** *n.*

spir·it·less (spir′i tlis) *adj* lacking courage, vigour, or energy.

spirit level *n* an instrument consisting of a sealed tube containing an air bubble whose position reveals whether a surface is perfectly level.

spir·i·tu·al (spir′i chəl) *adj* **1** to do with the human spirit or soul, as opposed to being concerned with physical things: *spiritual values.* **2** to do with religion or religious belief: *spiritual songs.*
n a deeply emotional religious song or hymn with a lively rhythm mainly developed by the black people in the southern US. **spir′i·tu·al′i·ty** *n.* **spir′i·tu·al·ly** *adv.*

spir·i·tu·al·ism (spir′i chəl iz′əm) *n* a system of belief supposing that communication can be made with the spirits of the dead, especially through people called **mediums**. **spir′i·tu·al·ist** *n.* **spir′i·tu·al·ist·ic** *adj.*

spi·ro·chete (spī′rə kēt′) *n* a slender, spiral, flexible bacterium, especially one that causes syphilis.

spit[1] (spit) *v* **spat** or **spit, spit·ting** **1** eject saliva forcibly from the mouth, sometimes as a gesture of contempt or anger. **2** utter in a hostile or aggressive way. **3** give off small bursts of sparks or hot fat with a series of short, explosive noises. **4** make a spitting noise as a sign of anger or hostility, such as a cat does.
n **1** saliva, especially that which has been ejected from a person's mouth. **2** the noise or act of spitting. **3** a frothy or spitlike secretion given off by some animals. <Old English *spittan*> **spit′ter** *n.*
spit up, bring up liquid food soon after eating it, especially in a baby, usually because of overfeeding rather than illness.

spit[2] (spit) *n* **1** a sharp-pointed, slender rod or bar on which meat is roasted. **2** a narrow point of land projecting into a body of water.
v **spit·ted, spit·ting** put a spit through meat in order to roast it. <Old English *spitu*>

spit and polish *Informal n* a high standard of cleanliness or neatness. <from the soldier's practice of using spit to shine boots>

spit·ball (spit′bol′) *n* **1** a small ball of chewed-up paper, used as a missile. **2** an illegal pitch in baseball in which the ball is moistened on one side of the ball, causing it to move unpredictably.

spite (spīt) *n* a desire to hurt, annoy, or offend someone: *She ruined his flowers out of spite.*
v **spit·ed, spit·ing** show ill will toward; annoy. <Middle English *despit* despite>
in spite of, despite or without being affected by something: *We went to school in spite of the snowstorm.*

spite·ful (spīt′fəl) *adj* showing or caused by malice. **spite′ful·ly** *adv.* **spite′ful·ness** *n.*

spit·fire (spit′fīr′) *n* a person who has a fierce temper.

spitting image *Informal n* the exact likeness: *She's the spitting image of her grandmother.*

spit·tle (spit′əl) SPIT[1] (*n* def. 1)

spit·toon (spi tūn′) *n* a container for spitting into, often with a funnel-shaped top.

splash (splash) *v* **1 a** fall as liquid, or cause a liquid to strike or fall on something in irregular amounts. **b** make wet or scatter by doing this: *The baby likes to splash in the tub. He splashed the oars as he rowed.* **2** get wet or spattered with a liquid: *My jacket is all splashed with mud.* **3** mark with spots or patches: *The field was splashed with red poppies.* **4** print a news story or photograph in a prominent place in a newspaper or magazine: *They splashed the couple's divorce all over the front page.*
n **1** the sound made by a thing striking or falling into liquid: *The boat upset with a loud splash.* **2** a brief period of moving about in water energetically: *They had a splash in the waves.* **3** a small quantity of liquid or colour that has fallen against or been applied to a surface: *a splash of paint.* **4** *Informal* a striking, showy, or exciting effect or event: *They made a big splash at the party.* <Old English *plæsc* puddle>
make a splash, *Informal* attract much attention.

splash·down (splash′down′) *n* the landing of a capsule or other spacecraft in the ocean after re-entry.

splash pants *pln* water-resistant pants worn over regular pants, to protect against rain and mud.

splash·y (splash′ē) *adj* **splash·i·er, splash·i·est** **1** with water flying about noisily in irregular amounts: *a splashy waterfall.* **2** full of irregular bright spots or streaks. **3** *Informal* attracting much attention.

splat (splat) *n* the sound of something soft and wet or heavy striking a surface.
v **splat·ted, splat·ting** crush or squash something with such a sound.
adv with such a sound: *He threw the tomato splat against the wall.* <imitative>

splat·ter (splat′ər) *v* splash with a sticky or thick liquid: *I splattered paint on the floor.*
n a spot or trail of a sticky or thick liquid splashed over a surface or object. <*spatter* and *splash*>

a bat	e bed	i bid	o pot	u cup	th thin
ā cake	ē me	ī bite	ō go	ū rude	ᴛʜ then
à bar	ə about	ər over	ȯ for	ů put	zh measure

splay (splā) *v* **1** spread things, especially hands or feet out and apart, or be spread out. **2** become wider or more separated.
adj (*often in compounds*) turned outward or widened: *splay-legged.*
n a widening or outward tapering of something. <*display*>

splay·foot (splā′fu̇t′) *n, pl* **splay·feet** a broad, flat foot turned outward. **splay′foot′ed** *adj.*

spleen (splēn) *n* **1** a ductless abdominal organ involved in the production and removal of blood cells in humans and other vertebrates and forming part of the immune system. **2** bad temper or spite. <Greek *splen*>

splen·did (splen′did) *adj* **1** magnificent or very impressive: *a splendid sunset, a splendid palace, a splendid victory.* **2** excellent or very good: *a splendid chance.* <Latin *splendere* be bright> **splen′did·ly** *adv.* **splen′did·ness** *n.*

splen·dour or **splen·dor** (splen′dər) *n* magnificent and splendid appearance or display.

sple·net·ic (spli net′ik) *adj* bad-tempered or spiteful. <See SPLEEN.> **sple·net′i·cal·ly** *adv.*

splice (splīs) *v* **spliced, splic·ing 1** join or connect a rope or ropes by interweaving the strands, or join pieces of timber or tape or film, at the ends. **2** join or insert a gene or gene fragments.
n a join consisting of two ropes, or two pieces of timber, film, or tape. <Dutch *splissen*> **splic′er** *n.*

splint (splint) *n* **1** a strip of rigid material used for supporting and holding a broken bone in place until it has been healed. **2** a thin strip of wood used to light a fire. **3** a rigid or flexible strip, especially of wood, used in making baskets. **4** a bony enlargement on the inside of a horse's leg. <Dutch *splinte*>

splin·ter (splin′tər) *n* **1** a small, thin, sharp piece of wood, bone, glass, or other hard material broken off from a larger piece: *He got a splinter in his hand. The mirror broke into splinters.* **2** a splinter group or party.
v split or break into splinters. <Dutch>

splinter group or **party** *n* a small organization, especially a political group, that has broken away from a larger one.

splin·ter·y (splin′tə rē) *adj* **1** apt to splinter: *splintery wood.* **2** to do with splinters, or full of splinters.

split (split) *v* **split, split·ting 1** break or cause to break forcibly into parts, especially into halves or into layers: *The huge tree split when it was struck by lightning. The man is splitting wood. She split the cake and spread it with jelly.* **2** divide and share something, especially resources or responsibilities: *They split the cost of the dinner between them.* **3** divide a group of people into two or more parts, usually because of differing opinions: *The proposed legislation split the voters.*
n **1** a tear or crack in something, especially down the middle or into a layer: *a split in my glove.* **2** an example or act of splitting or being split: *There was a split between those who favoured and those who opposed the agreement.* **3** a separation between groups or within a group. **4** *Bowling* a formation of standing pins in tenpin bowling after the first ball, in which there is a gap between two pins or groups of pins. **5 the splits** *pl* a movement in dance, gymnastics, etc. in which a person leaps in the air or sits down with the legs straight and stretched out in different directions: *to do the splits.* <Dutch *splitten*> **split′ter** *n.*
split hairs, make distinctions that are too fine or fussy: *It is splitting hairs to complain of having just fifty-nine minutes instead of an hour in the pool.*
split off, remove or separate by splitting: *When the congregation got too big, a group split off and started another one.*
split up, a divide into parts or shares: *They split up the leftover pie between them.* **b** end a relationship: *The rock band split up after ten years together.* **c** go off in different directions: *When we reached the road, we split up and went to our respective homes.*

split infinitive *n* an infinitive with an adverb between *to* and the verb. Example: *He wants* to never work, *but* to always play.

> **GRAMMAR AND USAGE**
>
> **Split infinitives** were once considered poor form, but this is now not the case. It is acceptable to say something like *She tries to always be on time.*
>
> However, avoid any that result in awkwardness. Instead of *It's useful to now and then check for errors*, say *It's useful to check for errors now and then.*

split–lev·el (split′lev′əl) *adj* to do with a building in which a room or rooms are higher than others by less than a whole storey.

split–run (split′run′) *n* a print run of a newspaper or magazine in which advertisements and sometimes articles are changed so as to produce different editions, especially a Canadian edition of an American magazine.

split second *n* a very brief moment of time. **split-second** *adj.*

split·ting (split′ing) *adj* suffering great pain from a headache: *My head is splitting.*

splotch (sploch) *n* a blob or smear of something, usually a liquid.
v make such a blob or smear. <*spot* and *blotch*> **splotch′y** *adj.*

splurge (splərj) *n* **1** an act of spending money freely or extravagantly. **2** a large or excessive amount of something.
v **splurged, splurg·ing** spend money freely or extravagantly. <origin uncertain>

splut·ter (splut′ər) *v* make a series of rapid, short, explosive spitting or choking sounds, especially in saying something: *He spluttered when he was excited.*
n such sounds. <*sputter*> **splut′ter·er** *n.* **splut′ter·ing** *adj.* **splut′ter·ing·ly** *adv.*

spoil (spoil) *v* **spoiled** or **spoilt, spoil·ing 1** diminish or destroy the value or quality of: *He spoiled the book by scribbling on it. The fruit spoiled in the heat.* **2** prevent someone from enjoying an occasion or event: *Heavy rain spoiled the picnic.* **3** mark a ballot incorrectly so as to make one's vote invalid, especially as a gesture of protest.

4 harm the character of children by giving them too much, or always allowing them to do what they want.
n **spoils** *pl* things stolen or taken by force from a person or place: *the spoils of war.* <Latin *spolium* booty>
be spoiling for, be extremely or aggressively eager for: *She was spoiling for a fight.*

SYNONYMS

Spoil can sometimes suggest that something has been diminished but not destroyed: *The noise from the street spoiled my full appreciation of the music.*

Demolish emphasizes pulling or tearing down: *The bulldozers demolished the unsafe houses.*

Wreck, a more emphatic word, suggests that something has been damaged beyond repair: *The heavy rain all week wrecked the family's vacation.*

spoil·er (spoi′lər) **1** a person who or thing that spoils. **2** a person who obstructs or prevents an opponent's success while having no chance of winning.

spoil·sport (spoil′spȯrt′) *n* a person who behaves in a way that spoils others' fun, especially by not joining in an activity.

spoilt (spoilt) a past tense and a past participle of SPOIL.

spoke[1] (spōk) past tense of SPEAK.

spoke[2] (spōk) *n* one of the rods running from the centre of a wheel to its outer edge. <Old English *spaca*>
put a spoke in someone's wheel, stop or hinder someone from carrying out a plan.

spo·ken (spō′kən) *v* past participle of SPEAK.
adj **1** expressed through speaking: *the spoken word.* **2** speaking in a certain way: *a soft-spoken man.*
spoken for, reserved or claimed by someone: *Is that slice of cake spoken for? All the tickets are already spoken for.*

spokes·per·son (spōk′spər′sən) *n, pl* **spokes·per·sons** a person who makes statements on behalf of a person or group: *We asked her to be the spokesperson for the class.*

spo·li·a·tion (spō′lē ā′shən) *n* **1** the action of ruining or destroying something. **2** the action of taking goods or property from someone violently.

sponge (spunj) *n* **1** a sea animal with a soft, spineless body that is supported by a tough fibrous framework. **2** a piece of soft, porous substance that is used for washing and cleaning, originally the framework of a sea sponge, but now usually made of synthetic material. **3** an act of wiping or cleaning with a sponge. **4** a thing like a sponge, such as a kind of cake.
v **sponged, spong·ing 1** wipe, absorb, or clean with a wet sponge, or remove or wipe liquid in this way: *Sponge up the spilled water.* **2** give a mottled or textured effect to a painted surface by applying a different colour with a sponge. **3** *Informal* live or profit at the expense of another without doing or intending to do anything in return: *He won't get a job, and just sponges off his family.* <Greek *spongia*> **sponge′a·ble** *adj.* **sponge′like′** *adj.* **spong′er** *n.*
sponge out, remove all traces of.
throw (or **toss**) **in the sponge** or **throw up the sponge,** give up or admit defeat.

sponge bath *n* a washing of the body with a wet sponge or cloth without getting into water.

sponge cake *n* a light, spongy cake made with eggs, sugar, and flour but no butter.

spon·gy (spun′jē) *adj* **spon·gi·er, spon·gi·est** like a sponge, especially in being soft, light, and absorbent: *spongy moss, a spongy rock.* **spon′gi·ness** *n.*

spon·sor (spon′sər) *n* **1** a person or group that provides funds for a project or activity carried out by another. **2** a person who takes responsibility for the actions of another, such as one in a Christian church who makes vows on behalf of an infant at baptism. **3** a business or organization that, in return for advertising, pays for or contributes to the costs of a radio or TV program. **4** a person who pledges to donate money to an organization. **5** a person who introduces and supports a proposal for legislation.
v act as sponsor for. <Latin, from *spondere* promise solemnly>

spon·sor·ship (spon′sər ship′) *n* the position or duties of a sponsor.

spon·ta·ne·ous (spon tā′nē əs) *adj* **1** caused by natural impulse or desire; not forced or compelled; not planned beforehand: *Both sides burst into spontaneous cheers at the skilful play.* **2** happening without external cause or help; caused entirely by inner forces: *The eruption of a volcano is spontaneous.* **3** growing or produced naturally; not planted, cultivated, etc. <Latin *sponte* of one's accord> **spon′ta·ne′i·ty** (spon′tə nā′ə tē) *n.* **spon·ta′ne·ous·ly** *adv.* **spon·ta′ne·ous·ness** *n.*

spontaneous combustion *n* the ignition of organic matter, such as hay or coal, without apparent cause, typically through heat generated by rapid oxidation within the substance itself.

spoof (spūf) *n* a humorous imitation of something, in which characteristic features are exaggerated.
v make or perform a spoof. <A. Roberts, a 20c comedian> **spoof′er** *n.*

spook (spūk) *Informal n* **1** a ghost. **2** a spy.
v frighten or unnerve, especially an animal, or take fright: *The noisy swimmers spooked all the trout.* <Dutch>

spook·y (spū′kē) *Informal adj* **spook·i·er, spook·i·est** **1** sinister or ghostly in a way that causes fear and unease. **2** highly nervous or easily frightened.

spool (spūl) *n* **1** a cylinder of plastic, wood, or metal on which thread, wire, magnetic tape, or other flexible materials can be wound. **2** a thing like a spool in shape or use.
v **1** wind on a spool. **2** *Computers* send output to a printer or other peripheral, so as to free the main application to continue with other tasks. <Middle Dutch *spoele*>

a bat	e bed	i bid	o pot	u cup	th thin
ā cake	ē me	ī bite	ō go	ū rude	ᴛʜ then
ȧ bar	ə about	ər over	ȯ for	u̇ put	zh measure

spool·er (spūl′ər) *Computers n* a program that sends output to a printer or other peripheral, so as to free the main application to continue with other tasks.

spoon (spūn) *n* **1** a utensil consisting of a small, shallow bowl at the end of a handle, used for eating, stirring, or serving foods. See SOUP SPOON for picture. **2** a thing shaped like a spoon, such as a curved fishing lure that wobbles as it moves through the water. **3 the spoons** *pl* a pair of spoons used as a musical instrument by being held in the hand and beaten together rhythmically.
v take up in a spoon. <Old English *spon* chip, shaving>
spoon′ful *n.*

spoon·bill (spūn′bil′) *n* **1** a long-legged wading bird that has a long, flat bill with a spoon-shaped tip. **2** a bird that has a similar bill.

spoon·er·ism (spū′nə riz′əm) *n* an unintentional, often humorous, transposing of the letters or sounds of successive words. Example: *well-boiled icicle* instead of *well-oiled bicycle.*

ETYMOLOGY

Spoonerism is named after Rev. William A. Spooner (1844–1930, a dean and later warden of New College, Oxford, who was reputed to have made such mistakes.

It's roaring with pain. (It's pouring with rain.)

Shake a tower! (Take a shower!)

spoon–feed (spūn′fēd′) *v* **spoon-fed, spoon-feed·ing** **1** feed with a spoon. **2** provide so much help that the person or group helped does not need to think or act independently.

spoor (spūr) *n* the track or scent of an animal: *The hunters followed the spoor of the deer.*
v follow the track or scent of an animal. <Afrikaans, from Dutch>

spo·rad·ic (spə rad′ik) *adj* appearing or happening at scattered, irregular intervals or only in a few places: *sporadic outbreaks, sporadic cases of scarlet fever.* <Greek *sporas* scattered> **spo·rad′i·cal·ly** *adv.*

spore (spȯr) *n* a typically one-celled reproductive unit capable of growing into a new plant or animal such as in less-evolved plants, fungi, and protozoans. <Greek *spora* seed>

spor·ran (spȯ′rən) *n* a small pouch worn around the waist as to hang in front of the kilt as part of a man's Scottish highland dress.

sport (spȯrt) *n* **1** an activity involving physical effort and skill in which an individual or team competes against another or others for entertainment: *school sports, outdoor sports, indoor sports.* **2** success or pleasure derived from an activity such as hunting or fishing: *He said that trout fishing was good sport.* **3** entertainment or fun: *She thought that teasing was great sport.* **4** a person who behaves in a specified way in response to teasing, defeat, or a difficult situation: *a good sport, a bad sport.* **5** an animal or plant showing abnormal or striking variation from the normal type, especially in form or colour, as a result of spontaneous mutation.
v **1** wear or display a distinctive or noticeable item: *She sported a new hat.* **2** amuse oneself or play in a lively, energetic way: *They sported themselves in the surf.*
adj **sports** of or suitable for sports: *a sports contest, a sports event.* <Old French *desport* pastime, from *desporter* amuse>
for sport or **in sport,** in fun or as a joke: *She teased him, but it was all in sport.*
make sport of, make fun of: *Don't make sport of my clumsiness.*

sport·ing (spȯr′ting) *adj* **1** of, interested in, or engaging in sports: *a sporting event.* **2** fair and generous in one's behaviour or treatment of others, especially in a game or contest: *a sporting gesture.* **3** with a reasonable chance of success: *a sporting chance.* **sport′ing·ly** *adv.*

sports car *n* a low-built car designed for high speeds, often with a roof that can be folded back.

sports·cast (spȯrt′skast′) *n* a radio or TV broadcast of sports news or sports events. **sports′cast′er** *n.*

sports·man (spȯrt′smən) *n, pl* **sports·men** (spȯrt′smən) **1** a man who takes part in sports, especially professionally. **2** a person who behaves in a fair and generous way in the treatment of others, especially in a game or contest. **sports′man·like′** *adj.* **sports′man·ship′** *n.*

sports·plex (spȯrts′pleks′) *n* a multipurpose recreational centre with facilities for a number of different indoor and outdoor sports.

sports·wear (spȯrt′swer′) *n* clothing designed for sports or casual outdoor use.

sports·wom·an (spȯrt′swům′ən) *n* a woman who takes part in sports, especially professionally.

sports·writ·er (spȯrts′rī′tər) *n* a writer who reports sporting events.

sport–u·til·i·ty vehicle (sport′yū til′ə tē) SUV.

sport·y (spȯr′tē) *Informal adj* **sport·i·er, sport·i·est** **1** fond of or good at sports. **2** casual as a piece of clothing but attractively stylish: *a sporty hat.* **sport′i·ness** *n.*

spot (spot) *n* **1** a small round mark, differing in colour or texture from the surface around it: *The bird had a blue spot beside its eye.* **2 a** a small mark or stain: *I tried to clean the spot on my coat.* **b** a pimple or other blemish on the skin. **c** a small feature or part of something with a particular quality: *a bare spot on the lawn.* **3 a** a particular place or point: *It was a nice spot to relax.* **b** a place in a group or group activity: *to reserve a good spot to watch the game.* **4** a place in a performance: *the spot just before intermission.* **5** a short presentation or commercial on radio or TV between programs: *a one-minute spot.*
v **spot·ted, spot·ting** **1** notice someone or something that it is difficult to detect or that one is searching for: *We spotted her in the crowd.* **2** mark or become marked with spots: *The shirt was spotted with daisies.* **3** stain the moral character or qualities of: *He spotted his reputation by lying.* **4** *Informal* lend money: *I'll spot you five bucks.* **5** *Sports* as a safety feature, stay beside someone to lend help if needed: *I'll spot you at weightlifting class today.* <Middle English>
hit the high spots, deal with the most significant or interesting parts of a thing.
hit the spot, *Informal* be exactly what is required.

in a spot, *Informal* in a difficult situation.
in spots, in some parts: *The author's writing is weak in spots.*
on the spot, a at the scene of an action or event. **b** without any delay. **c** in trouble or difficulty: *She put me on the spot by asking a question I could not answer.*

spot check *n* a check or test made without warning on a randomly selected subject.

spot·less (spot′lis) *adj* without a spot or blemish.
spot′less·ly *adv.* **spot′less·ness** *n.*

spot·light (spot′līt′) *n* **1** a narrow, intense beam of light projecting directly on to a place or person, especially on a performer on stage, or the lamp that projects this light. **2** intense public attention focused on a person or thing: *the media spotlight.*
v **1** light up with a spotlight or spotlights. **2** direct attention to a particular problem or situation.

spot·ted (spot′id) *adj* **1** marked, decorated, or stained with spots: *a spotted dog.* **2** with unfavourable aspects: *a spotted reputation.*

spotted owl *n* a N American owl that lives west of the Rocky Mountains and has dark brown feathers with heavily spotted underparts.

spot·ter (spot′ər) *n* a person who looks for or observes a particular thing.

spot·ty (spot′ē) *adj* **spot·ti·er, spot·ti·est 1** marked with spots. **2** of uneven quality: *Her work was spotty.*
spot′ti·ly *adv.* **spot′ti·ness** *n.*

spous·al (spou′zəl) *adj* to do with marriage or a married couple: *spousal benefits.* <Old French, from Latin *sponsa* bound>

spouse (spous) *n* the person to whom one is married. <Old French, from Latin *spondere* bind oneself>

spout (spout) *n* **1** a tube or lip through which liquid can be poured from a container: *The teapot had a long spout.* **2** a pipe or trough through which water may be carried away or from which it can flow out: *Rain ran down a spout from the roof to the ground.* **3** a stream of liquid flowing from somewhere with great force. **4** a plume of water vapour sent up from the blowhole of a whale.
v **1** send out liquid forcibly in a stream, or flow out in such a way. **2** express one's views or ideas in a pompous and lengthy way: *He spouted about patriotism for an hour.* <Dutch *spouten*> **spout′er** *n.*

sprain (sprān) *v* injure a joint or muscle by a sudden twist or wrench: *I sprained my ankle running for the bus.*
n an injury caused by a sudden twist or wrench. <origin uncertain>

sprang (sprang) a past tense of SPRING.

sprat (sprat) *n* a small marine fish related to the herring, especially in northern European coastal wasters, or a fishing resembling it.

sprawl (sprol) *v* **1** sit, lie, or fall with one's arms and legs spread out, especially in an ungraceful way: *The swimmers sprawled on the beach.* **2** spread out over an area in an untidy or irregular way: *Her big handwriting sprawled across the page.*
n the act or position of sprawling. <Old English *spreawlian*>

spray[1] (sprā) *n* **1** liquid that is blown or driven through the air in the form of tiny drops: *We were wet with the sea spray.* **2** a thing that resembles this: *A spray of bullets hit the target.* **3** (*often in compounds*) a liquid preparation that can be forced out of a can or other container in such a form, or the can or container itself: *hairspray.*
v **1** apply, sprinkle, or cover someone or something with a shower of tiny drops of liquid: *Spray this paint on the far wall. We sprayed the apple trees in the orchard.* **2** scatter something somewhere with great force: *Gravel sprayed from the wheels of the car as it rounded the corner.* **3** fire a rapid succession of bullets at: *The soldiers sprayed the enemy with heavy fire.* <Dutch *spraien*> **spray′er** *n.*

spray[2] (sprā) *n* a stem or small branch of a tree or plant, or a thing resembling this: *a spray of lilacs.* <Middle English>

spray gun *n* a device resembling a gun that is used to spray a liquid such as paint under pressure.

spray paint *n* paint sold in an aerosol container.
spray′-paint′ *v.*

spread (spred) *v* **spread, spread·ing 1** (*often with* **out**) open out something so as to extend its surface area, width, or length: *We spread rugs on the floors. She spread out her arms.* **2** extend over a large or increasing area: *The storm spread eastward.* **3** move further apart: *The rails of the track have spread.* **4** distribute something, or become distributed, in a specified way: *The news spread rapidly.* **5** apply a substance to an object or surface in an even layer, or cover in such a way: *She spread jam on her toast.*
n **1** the fact or process of spreading: *Doctors fought the spread of the disease.* **2** the extent, width, or area covered by a thing: *the spread of a bird's wings.* **3** the range or variety of a thing: *a spread of ages in the swim club.* **4** a cloth covering for a bed or table. **5** *Informal* the food offered to be eaten, especially a large amount. **6** a soft paste for spreading on bread or crackers. **7** the area of land owned by a rancher: *She had a spread covering several hectares.* <Old English *sprædan*>
spread yourself, extend your activities: *He spread himself too thin.*

spread·ea·gle (spred′ē′gəl) *v* **spread·ea·gled, spread·ea·gling** stretch out with the arms and legs extended. <*spread eagle* an emblem showing an eagle with legs and wings extended> **spread′ea′gled** *adj.*

spread·er (spred′er) *n* **1** a device used for spreading or scattering a substance over a wide area: *a manure spreader.* **2** a person who spreads or distributes something: *a spreader of bad news.*

spread·sheet (spred′shēt′) *Computers n* a computer program that displays numerical data in CELLS (def. 5b) on a worksheet with rows and columns. The user can set up formulas that will perform calculations on the data.

spree (sprē) *n* a sustained period of unrestrained activity of a particular kind, such as drinking alcoholic liquor or shopping. <origin uncertain>

a bat	e bed	i bid	o pot	u cup	th thin
ā cake	ē me	ī bite	ō go	ū rude	ᴛʜ then
à bar	ə about	ər over	ȯ for	u̇ put	zh measure

sprig (sprig) *n* a small stem bearing leaves or flowers, taken from a bush or plant, or something resembling this: *a sprig of lilac.* <Middle English *sprigge*>

spright·ly (sprīt′lē) *adj* **spright·li·er, spright·li·est** lively and full of energy: *a sprightly dance.* <*sprite* + *-ly*> **spright′li·ness** *n.*

spring (spring) *v* **sprang** or **sprung, sprung, spring·ing** **1** move or jump suddenly or rapidly from a fixed or restrained position: *The girl sprang to her feet.* **2** operate or cause to operate by means of a mechanism: *The trap was sprung.* **3** appear, make, or present suddenly or unexpectedly: *A town sprang up when oil was discovered. We waited until he was alone to spring the news.* **4** be flexible or resilient: *This branch springs enough to use as a snare.*
n **1** the season after winter and before summer, during which plants begin to grow. **2** an elastic device, especially a metal coil, that returns to its original shape after being pulled or held out of shape: *The bed had wire springs.* **3** the ability to spring back suddenly: *His knees had lost their spring.* **4** a sudden jump upward or forward: *The lion sprang on its prey.* **5** a place where water or oil wells up from an underground source, or the basin or flow formed in such a way. **6** a source or origin, or the first and freshest period: *the spring of life.* <Old English *springan*> **spring′like′** *adj.*
spring a leak, develop a leak in a boat or container.
spring for, *Informal* pay for, especially as a treat for someone else.
spring from, originate or arise from: *Most of her troubles sprang from illness.*
spring on, present or propose something suddenly or unexpectedly to someone: *He sprang a big surprise on me.*

spring·board (spring′bôrd′) *n* **1** a strong, flexible board from which someone may jump in order to gain added thrust in diving, jumping, or vaulting. **2** a thing that gives one a good start toward a goal or purpose: *Hard work was her springboard to success.*

spring·bok (spring′bok′) *n, pl* **spring·boks** or (*especially collectively*) **spring·bok** a gazelle of southern Africa that forms large herds on plains and has the habit of leaping upward when disturbed.

spring chicken *n* **1** a young chicken used for frying or broiling. **2** *Informal* (*usually in the negative*) a young person: *She's no spring chicken.*

spring cleaning *n* **1** a thorough housecleaning traditionally done in the spring. **2** a thorough cleaning or campaign to get rid of what is harmful or unneeded. **spring′ clean′** *v.*

spring fever *n* a feeling of restlessness, discontent, or excitement felt by some people at the beginning of spring.

spring roll *n* an appetizer similar to an egg roll, but smaller and more cylindrical.

🍁 **spring salmon** CHINOOK (def. 2).

spring tide *n* the highest level of high tide, occurring twice a month, at the time of the new moon or the full moon. Compare NEAP TIDE.

spring·time (spring′tīm′) *n* the season of spring.

spring·y (spring′ē) *adj* **spring·i·er, spring·i·est** **1** springing back quickly when squeezed or stretched: *The wet lawn was springy under our feet.* **2** light and confident in movement: *a springy step.* **3** with many springs of water. **spring′i·ly** *adv.* **spring′i·ness** *n.*

sprin·kle (spring′kəl) *v* **sprin·kled, sprin·kling** **1** scatter or pour small drops or particles of a substance over an object or surface: *She sprinkled sand on the icy sidewalk.* **2** distribute or disperse something randomly or irregularly throughout something: *He sprinkled his talk with jokes.* **3** spray or cover with small drops: *to sprinkle flowers with water.* **4** rain very lightly.
n **1** a small quantity or amount of something. **2** a light rain. **3** **sprinkles** *pl* tiny sugar shapes, especially balls, used for decorating cakes and desserts. <Middle English *sprenklen*>

sprin·kler (spring′klər) *n* a device that sprays water, such as one used to water lawns or to spray water from a ceiling of a room in the event of a fire.

sprin·kling (spring′kling) *n* a small, thinly distributed amount of something.

A sprinter's shoes have eleven 9-mm cleats in the front half of the sole. Since only the athlete's toes touch the ground during a race, the shoes have no heels or arch support.

sprint (sprint) *v* run at top speed, especially for a short distance.
n a short race or dash at full speed. <Middle English *sprenten*> **sprint′er** *n.*

sprite (sprīt) *n* an elf or fairy. <Old French, from Latin *spiritus*>

spritz (sprits) or (shprits) *v* squirt or spray something at or onto something in quick, short bursts.
n an act or fact of squirting or spraying in quick, short bursts. <German *spritzen* squirt>

spritz·er (sprit′sər) or (shprīt′sər) *n* a drink made of chilled white wine and club soda.

sprock·et (sprok′it) *n* one of a set of projections on the rim of a wheel that engages, for example, with the links of a chain on a bicycle, or with the holes along the edge of a piece of camera film. <origin uncertain>

sprout (sprout) *v* **1** put forth or grow shoots of a plant, or cause to do this: *All the potatoes sprouted.* **2** remove sprouts from: *He sprouted the potatoes.*
n a shoot of a plant. <Old English *asprutan*>

spruce[1] (sprūs) *n* an evergreen tree that has a conical shape and hanging cones, widely grown for timber and pulp. <Latin *Prussia*, where the tree was widely grown>

spruce[2] (sprūs) *adj* **spruc·er, spruc·est** neat and trim: *He looked very spruce in his new suit.*
v **spruced, spruc·ing** make or become neat and trim: *He spruced himself in front of the mirror.* <origin uncertain> **spruce′ly** *adv.* **spruce′ness** *n.*

spruce bud·worm (bud′wərm′) *n* a brown caterpillar of a small N American moth that feeds on the young needles of spruce and other evergreens.

sprung (sprung) a past tense and past participle of SPRING.

spry (sprī) *adj* **spry·er** or **spri·er, spry·est** or **spri·est** active and lively, especially in an elderly person. <origin uncertain> **spry′ly** *adv.* **spry′ness** *n.*

spud (spud) *n* **1** a tool with a narrow blade, for digging up or cutting the roots of plants, especially weeds. **2** a short length of pipe that is used to connect two components or as part of a fitting. **3** *Informal* a potato. <origin uncertain>

spume (spyūm) *n* foam or froth, especially that found on waves.
v **spumed, spum·ing** form or produce a mass of foam.

spu·mo·ni (spə mō′nē) *n* a flavour of ice cream, usually containing fruit and nuts. <Italian>

spun (spun) past tense and past participle of SPIN.

spun glass *n* glass made into threads.

spunk (spungk) *Informal n* courage and determination: *The puppy was full of spunk.* <Irish or Scots Gaelic *sponnc*, from Latin *spongia* sponge, from Greek> **spunk′i·ly** *adv.* **spunk′i·ness** *n.* **spunk′y** *adj.*

spun silk *n* a fabric made of short-fibred silk waste.

spur (spər) *n* **1** a device with a small spike or a spiked wheel that is worn on a rider's heel and used for urging a horse forward, or something resembling this. **2** a thing that prompts or encourages something: *Ambition was the spur that made him work.* **3** a thing that projects or branches off from a main body, such as a projection from a mountain or a short branch road or railway line.
v **spurred, spur·ring 1** urge a horse forward by digging one's spurs into its sides: *The rider spurred her horse on.* **2** promote or give encouragement or an incentive to someone or something: *Pride spurred the boy to fight.* <Old English *spura*>
on the spur of the moment, on a sudden impulse.
spur on, encourage.
win your spurs, make a reputation for yourself.

spurge (spərj) *n* a plant or shrub with a bitter, milky juice and clusters of small, usually greenish flowers, or a plant related to it.

spu·ri·ous (spyů′rē əs) *adj* false or fake: *a spurious document.* <Latin *spurius*> **spu′ri·ous·ly** *adv.* **spur′i·ous·ness** *n.*

spurn (spərn) *v* reject with contempt: *The judge spurned the bribe.* <Old Enlgish *spurnan*>

spurt (spərt) *v* **1** gush or cause to gush out in a sudden stream: *Blood spurted from the cut.* **2** move with a sudden burst of speed: *The winning car spurted into the lead.*
n **1** a sudden rushing stream: *Spurts of flame broke through the roof.* **2** a sudden burst of speed or activity: *The workers put on a spurt near closing time.* <origin uncertain>

sput·nik (sput′nik) *or* (spůt′nik) *n* an artificial satellite launched by the Soviet Union in 1957. This satellite, the first in a series, was also the first to be placed in orbit from earth.

sput·ter (sput′ər) *v* **1** make a series of spitting or popping sounds, typically when something is being heated or as a symptom of a fault: *Fat sputtered in the frying pan.* **2** speak with a series of confused blurting sounds as a result of indignation or some other strong emotion. **3** proceed or develop in an intermittent and feeble way: *The project sputtered to a halt.*
n a series of spitting or popping sounds, typically produced by an engine or by something heating. <Dutch *sputteren*> **sput′ter·er** *n.*

spu·tum (spyū′təm) *n, pl* **spu·ta** (-tə) a mixture of saliva and mucus coughed up from the throat and lungs, typically as a result of infection or other disease and often tested to aid a medical diagnosis. <Latin>

spy (spī) *n, pl* **spies** a person who keeps watch on others secretly, especially a person who secretly collects and reports information on the activities and plans of an enemy or competitor.
v **spied, spy·ing 1** work for a government or other organization by secretly collecting information about enemies or competitors: *He was accused of spying for a foreign power.* **2** catch sight of, especially by careful observation: *She could spy someone approaching far down the street.* <Old French *espier*>
spy on, observe someone without being noticed: *He regularly spied on the opposing team.*
spy out, watch, examine, or find out secretly or carefully: *She spies out everything that goes on in the neighbourhood.*

spy·glass (spī′glas′) *n* a small telescope.

spy·hole (spī′hōl′) *n* a small hole through which one can secretly observe something.

spy·ware (spī′wār) *Computers n* software that tracks an Internet user's surfing habits without the user's knowledge. Such software is often included in free downloads from the Internet, and works in the background, but it can infect files and make the computer unusable.

squab (skwob) *n* a young pigeon, especially one used as food.

a bat	e bed	i bid	o pot	u cup	th thin
ā cake	ē me	ī bite	ō go	ū rude	TH then
à bar	ə about	ər over	ȯ for	ů put	zh measure

squab·ble (skwob′əl) *n* a noisy quarrel about something petty or trivial: *family squabbles.*
v **squab·bled, squab·bling** take part in a petty, noisy quarrel: *I won't squabble over a dime.* <imitative> **squab′bler** *n.*

squad (skwod) *n* a small group of people with a particular task, especially one grouped for army drill or inspection, or for police. <Italian *squadra* square. Squads were commonly arranged in square formation during battle.>

squad car *n* a police patrol car.

squad·ron (skwod′rən) *n* **1** a group of warships used for special service, or a formation of airplanes, usually two or three flights, that fly or fight together. **2** a large group of people or things.

squal·id (skwol′id) *adj* dirty and unpleasant, especially in a place because of poverty or neglect. <Latin *squalere* be filthy> **squal′id·ly** *adv.* **squal′id·ness** *n.*

squall (skwol) *n* **1** a sudden, violent gust of wind, often with rain, snow, or sleet. **2** *Informal* a noisy cry.
v cry out noisily and continuously, especially as a baby or small child. <origin uncertain>

squall·y (skwol′ē) *adj* **squall·i·er, squall·i·est 1** disturbed by sudden and violent gusts of wind: *squally weather.* **2** of wind, blowing in squalls.

squal·or (skwol′ər) *n* a condition of extreme dirtiness and unpleasantness, especially as a result of poverty or neglect.

Squa·mish (skwå′mish) *n, pl* **Squa·mish** or **Squa·mish·es 1** a member of a First Nations people of the southwest coast of British Columbia. **2** their Salishan language.
adj to do with these people or their language.

squan·der (skwon′dər) *v* waste something, especially money or time, in a reckless or foolish way. <origin uncertain>

square (skwer) *n* **1** a plane figure with four equal sides and four right angles. **2 a** an open, typically four-sided, area surrounded by buildings in a village, town, or city. **b** a block of buildings bounded by four streets. **3** an area within a military barracks or camp used for drill. **4** *Mathematics* **a** the product of a number multiplied by itself. **b** a parallelogram with four congruent sides and one right angle. **5** an instrument used for obtaining or testing right angles: *a carpenter's square.* **6** *Slang* a person considered to be old-fashioned or boringly conventional.
adj **squar·er, squar·est 1** with the shape or approximate shape of a square: *a square box.* **2** of a measurement equal to the area of a square whose side is of the unit specified: *a square centimetre.* **3** forming a right angle: *a square corner.* **4** level or parallel: *When we put the two boxes on top of each other they were exactly square.* **5** owing nothing to one another: *We both got what we wanted, so we were square.* **6** fair and honest: *a square deal.* **7** *Slang* old-fashioned or boringly conventional.
v **squared, squar·ing 1** make square, rectangular, or cubical. **2** mark out in squares: *The children squared off the sidewalk to play hopscotch.* **3** *Mathematics* multiply a number by itself. **4** make or be compatible: *Her acts do not square with her promises.* **5** of shoulders, bring into a position in which they appear square and broad.
adv **1** *Informal* fairly or honestly. **2** so as to be in square or rectangular form. **3** straight or directly: *The snowball hit me square in the face.* <Old French *esquarre*, from Latin *ex* out + *quadrus* square> **square′ly** *adv.*
on the square, a at right angles. **b** *Informal* honest or straightforward.
out of square, not at right angles.
square away, arrange or deal with something in a satisfactory way: *Relax, we'll soon get the problem squared away.*
square off, *Informal* put oneself in a position of defence or attack.
square the circle, a find a square equal in area to a circle, which is geometrically impossible. **b** do something that is considered impossible.

square dance *n* a dance performed by a set of four couples arranged in some set form, usually a square.

square knot REEF KNOT.

square meal *n* a substantial or satisfying meal.

square measure *n* a unit or system of units for measuring area, such as the hectare.

square number *Mathematics n* the product of an integer multiplied by itself. Also called **perfect square**.

square one *Informal n* the very beginning: *back to square one, right from square one.*

square–rigged (skwer′rigd′) *adj* with the principal sails of a ship set at right angles across the masts, such as in a brig. See SCHOONER for picture.

square root *n* a number that produces a specified quantity when multiplied by itself. Example: Since 5 x 5 = 25, the square root of 25 is 5.

square shooter *Informal n* a fair and honest person.

squash[1] (skwosh) *v* **1** crush or force something with force so that it becomes flat, soft, or out of shape: *Carry the cream puffs carefully since they squash easily.* **2** squeeze, force, or make one's way into a small or restricted space: *I squashed into the crowded elevator.* **3** firmly reject, silence, or subdue a feeling, statement, or action: *The speaker neatly squashed her hecklers.*
n **1** a condition in which someone or something is squeezed or forced into a small or restricted space. **2** a game in which two players use racquets to hit a small, soft rubber ball against the walls of a closed court. <Old French *esquasser* to crush, from Latin *ex* out + *quassare* to shatter>

squash[2] (skwosh) *n, pl* **squash·es** or (*especially collectively*) **squash** an edible gourd, the flesh of which may be cooked and eaten as a vegetable, or the trailing plant on which this gourd grows.

ETYMOLOGY

Squash is a shortened form of a First Nations word for this vegetable, from Narragansett (Algonquian) *askootasquash*, from *asq* meaning "uncooked" and *squash* meaning "green."

squash·y (skwosh'ē) *adj* **squash·i·er, squash·i·est** easily crushed or squeezed into a different shape: *a squashy sofa, squashy ground.* **squash'i·ly** *adv.* **squash'i·ness** *n.*

squat (skwot) *v* **squat·ted, squat·ting 1** crouch or sit with one's knees bent and one's heels close to or touching one's buttocks or the back of one's thighs. **2** unlawfully occupy an unoccupied building or unused piece of land.
adj short and thickset, noticeably broad or wide: *We saw a squat figure in front of the fire. I like that squat teapot.*
n the act or fact of squatting. <Old French *esquatir* crush>

squat·ter (skwot'ər) *n* **1** a person who unlawfully occupies an unoccupied building or unused piece of land. **2** a person who or thing that crouches or squats.

squawk (skwok) *v* **1** make a loud, harsh sound, as some birds do. **2** utter harshly and loudly. **3** complain or protest about something.
n **1** a loud, harsh or discordant noise made by a bird or person. **2** a complaint or protest. <imitative> **squawk'er** *n.*

squeak (skwēk) *v* **1** make or cause to make a short, sharp, shrill sound or cry: *The door hinges squeaked.* **2** say something in a nervous or excited high-pitched tone. **3** *Informal* succeed in achieving something by a very narrow margin: *She squeaked through her final exam.*
n **1** a short, sharp, shrill sound or cry: *We heard the squeak of the rocking chair.* **2** *Informal* a single remark, statement, or communication: *I haven't heard a squeak from him in months.* <imitative>

squeak·y (skwē'kē klēn') *adj* **squeak·i·er, squeak·i·est** with or making a high-pitched sound or cry: *a squeaky gate.* **squeak'i·ly** *adv.* **squeak'i·ness** *n.*

squeak·y–clean (skwē'kē klēn) *Informal adj* **1** very clean. **2** without any moral flaws.

squeal (skwēl) *v* **1** make a long, sharp, shrill sound or cry: *The pig squealed when he grabbed its ear.* **2** say something in a sharp, shrill, excited way. **3** *Informal* complain or protest about something. **4** *Informal* inform on someone to the police or another person in authority: *One of the gang members squealed on the others.*
n a long, sharp, shrill sound or cry. <imitative> **squeal'er** *n.*

squeam·ish (skwē'mish) *adj* easily made to feel sick, faint, or disgusted, especially by something unpleasant. <origin uncertain> **squeam'ish·ly** *adv.* **squeam'ish·ness** *n.*

squee·gee (skwē'jē) *n* **1** a scraping tool with a rubber-edged blade set on a short handle, typically used for cleaning windows. **2** a similar tool or roller such as one used in photography for pressing water from prints. <obsolete *squeege* to press>

squeeze (skwēz) *v* **squeezed, squeez·ing 1** firmly press something soft or yielding, especially with one's fingers: *Don't squeeze the kitten, because that will hurt it.* **2** extract liquid or a soft substance from something by compressing or twisting it firmly, or yield to pressure in this way: *squeeze a lemon.* **3** obtain by having to use pressure, force, or effort: *He squeezed even more money from me.* **4** have a damaging or restricting effect: *The company was squeezed by heavy costs.* **5** force a way with difficulty: *She squeezed through the crowd.*
n **1** an act of pressing something with one's fingers: *a squeeze of the hand.* **2** a hug. **3** a situation in which one forces oneself or is forced into a small or restricted space: *It's a tight squeeze to get five people in that little car.* **4** a small amount of liquid extracted from something. **5** *Informal* a situation from which escape is difficult. <Old English *cwysan*> **squeez'er** *n.*
squeeze someone in, *Informal* accommodate someone.
tight squeeze, *Informal* a difficult situation.

squeeze play *n* **1** a baseball play executed when a batter attempts to bunt and a runner on third base starts for home. **2** *Informal* an attempt to force somebody into a difficult situation or to act against his or her wishes.

squelch (skwelch) *v* **1** make a soft sucking sound like that made by walking heavily through mud. **2** forcefully silence or suppress someone or something: *He was quick to squelch his critics.*
n a soft sucking sound made while pressure is applied to liquid or mud. <imitative> **squelch'er** *n.*

squib (skwib) *n* **1** a short satirical attack in speech or writing. **2** a brief item in a newspaper used mainly to fill space. **3** a small firework that burns with a hissing noise and finally explodes. <origin uncertain>

squid (skwid) *n, pl* **squids** or (*especially collectively*) **squid** a marine mollusc that has eight arms and two long tentacles. See CALAMARI for picture. <origin uncertain>

squid jigger *especially Newfoundland n* **1** a device for catching squid, made of several hooks joined so that their points form a compact circle which is pulled or jerked through the water. **2** a person who fishes for squid in this way. **squid' jig'ging** *n.*

squig·gle (skwig'əl) *n* a short line that curls and loops in a random or irregular way: *You can't tell me that's your signature; that's just a squiggle!* <*squirm* + *wiggle*>

squint (skwint) *v* **1** look at someone or something with one or both eyes partly closed in an attempt to see more clearly or as a reaction to strong light. **2** have eyes that look in different directions. **3** cause one eye to gaze in a different direction from the other.
n a defect in one eye that causes it to gaze in a different direction from the other: *His left eye had a bad squint.* <origin uncertain> **squint'er** *n.* **squint'y** *adj.*

squire (skwīr) *n* **1** in feudal times, a young man who assisted a knight before becoming a knight himself. **2** *UK* a man with a high social standing who owns and lives on an estate in a rural area, especially the chief landowner in a district.
v **squired, squir·ing** accompany or escort a woman. <*esquire*>

squirm (skwərm) *v* **1** wriggle or twist the body from side to side: *The restless man squirmed in his chair.* **2** show or feel great embarrassment or confusion.
n a wriggling movement. <imitative> **squirm'er** *n.* **squirm'y** *adj.*

a bat	e bed	i bid	o pot	u cup	th thin
ā cake	ē me	ī bite	ō go	ū rude	TH then
à bar	ə about	ər over	ȯ for	ů put	zh measure

S

squir·rel (skwər′əl) *or* (skwir′əl) *n* a small, active, bushy-tailed rodent that usually lives in trees and eats nuts and seeds. <Old French *esquirel*, from Greek *ski* shadow + *oura* tail>
squirrel away, hide money or something of value in a safe place.

squirt (skwərt) *v* **1** force out liquid in a thin, fast stream or jet through a narrow opening of something: *He squirted me with a water pistol.* **2** escape as a liquid in this way: *Water squirted from the hose.* **3** move as an object suddenly and unpredictably: *The ball squirted out of his glove.*
n **1** a thin stream or small quantity of liquid shooting out from something. **2** *Informal* a person considered to be insignificant or impudent. <Middle English> **squirt′er** *n.*

squirt gun *n* a water pistol.

squish (skwish) *v* **1** make a soft, sucking or splashing sound when walked on or in. **2** *Informal* squash something.
n a squishing sound. <*squash*> **squish′y** *adj.*

Sri Lan·ka (shrē lang′ka) *n* an island country south of India. See the APPENDIX. **Sri Lan′kan** *adj, n.*

SRO standing room only (at some social or public event).

SS *n* a special police force created by the Nazis that enforced security and administered concentration camps. <German *Schutzstaffel*, from *Schutz* defence + *Staffel* unit>

SSE south-southeast.

SSW south-southwest.

stab (stab) *v* **stabbed, stab·bing 1** pierce or wound with a pointed weapon, or make a thrusting gesture or movement at something with such a weapon. **2** penetrate suddenly and sharply. **3** cause a sudden, sharp, painful sensation.
n **1** a thrust with a knife or other pointed weapon. **2** a wound made in such a way. **3** a thrusting movement. **4** a sudden sharp feeling or pain. <origin uncertain> **stab′ber** *n.*
have (or **make**) **a stab at,** attempt to do something.
stab in the back, attempt to hurt in a sly, treacherous manner.

sta·bil·i·ty (stə bil′ə tē) *n, pl* **sta·bil·i·ties 1** the condition of being fixed in position. **2** permanence or lack of change. **3** steadfastness of character or purpose. **4** the ability of an object to return to its original position.

sta·bil·ize (stā′bə līz′) *v* **sta·bi·lized, sta·bi·liz·ing 1** make or become stable or firm. **2** cause something to be unlikely to become changeable or unsteady: *to stabilize prices.* **sta′bil·iz·a′tion** *n.*

sta·bi·liz·er (stā′bə lī′zər) *n* **1** a thing used to keep something steady or stable, such as an airfoil at the tail of an aircraft or a device that reduces the rolling of a ship. **2** a substance that keeps the ingredients in paints or prepared foods from separating.

sta·ble[1] (stā′bəl) *n* **1** a building set apart and adapted for keeping horses or other domestic animals. **2** the buildings and grounds where racehorses are quartered and trained, or a group of racehorses belonging to one owner. **3** *Informal* a group whose members work under the same management and who have similar backgrounds and training.
v **sta·bled, sta·bling** put, keep, or be lodged in a stable. <Old French, from Latin *stabulum*>

sta·ble[2] (stā′bəl) *adj* **1** not likely to give way or overturn. **2** be firmly established and unlikely to change or fail. **3** not deteriorating in health after an injury or operation. **4** not easily decomposed in a chemical compound. **5** mentally or emotionally steady. <Latin *stabilis*>
sta′bly *adv.*

SYNONYMS

Stable means "not likely to change or fail": *The country now has a stable government.*

Permanent means "lasting" or "intended to last": *He moved into his permanent home last week.*

Reliable describes someone or something you can depend on with confidence: *The town now has a reliable source of electricity.*

stac·ca·to (stə kȧ′tō) *adj, adv* with each musical sound or note sharply detached or separated from the others: *staccato rhythm, to play staccato.*
n a staccato passage or composition, or a noise or form of speech resembling a series of short, detached musical notes. <Italian = detached>

stack (stak) *n* **1** a pile of objects, typically one that is neatly arranged. **2** a pile of hay, straw, or grain. **3** *Informal* a large quantity of something: *a big stack of food in the fridge.* **4** a chimney, especially one on a factory, or a vertical exhaust pipe on a motor vehicle. **5** a number of aircraft flying in circles at different altitudes around the same point while waiting for permission to land at an airport. **6 the stacks** *pl* the part of a library in which the main collection of books is shelved. **7** a tall column of rock, especially one separated from the shore by erosion from wind and waves. See ESTUARY for picture.
v pile or arrange a number of things in a stack: *to stack firewood.* <Old Norse *stakkr*>
be stacked against (**in favour of**)**,** be at a great disadvantage (advantage): *The odds were stacked against me in the race.*
stack the deck, *Informal* arrange circumstances beforehand, secretly and unfairly, against someone or in someone's favour: *The deck was stacked against him, so it's no surprise that he failed.*
stack up, *Informal* measure up or compare against.

sta·di·um (stā′dē əm) *n* an oval or U-shaped structure with rows of seats around a large, open space for athletic events or concerts. <Greek *stadion*, ancient Greek measure of length, about 185 m. The track at Olympia was one stadium length.>

stadium seating *n* auditorium seats in rows that are tiered and staggered, so that everyone has an unobstructed view.

staff (staf) *n* **1 a** all the people employed by a particular organization. **b** a group of assistants working with their chief as a unit. **2** a group of military officers that assist a commanding officer of an army formation or administration headquarters. **3** a stick, pole, or rod used

as a support, especially while walking, as an emblem of office, or as a weapon. **4** *Music* a set of five parallel lines on any one of which, or between any adjacent two of which, a musical note is written to indicate its pitch.
v provide an organization, military unit, or business with staff. <Old English *stæf*>

staff·er (staf′ər) *n* a regular member of a staff.

stag (stag) *n* **1** a full-grown male deer. See DEER for picture. **2** the male of various other animals. **3** a party or other social gathering attended only by men, or a man who attends any party unaccompanied by a partner.
adj attended by, or for, men only: *a stag party.* <Old English *stagga*>

stage (stāj) *n* **1** a point, period, or step in an activity, process, or development: *An insect passes through several stages before it is an adult.* **2** the raised floor or platform, especially in a theatre, on which actors, entertainers, or speakers perform. **3 the stage** the acting or theatrical profession. **4** a scene of action: *A mountainside was the stage of a battle.* **5** a section of a rocket or missile with its own motor and fuel. **6** a stagecoach.
v **staged, stag·ing 1** present a performance of a play or other show: *The first play they staged was a comedy.* **2** organize and take part in a public event: *to stage a demonstration.* **3** cause something dramatic or unexpected to happen: *The retired boxer tried to stage a comeback.* <Old French *estage,* Latin *stare* stand> **stage·a·bil′i·ty** *n.* **stage′a·ble** *adj.*

stage·coach (stāj′kōch′) *n* a large, closed, four-wheeled, horse-drawn coach formerly used for carrying passengers and often mail over a regular route.

stage·craft (stāj′kraft′) *n* skill or experience in writing or staging plays.

stage direction *n* an instruction written into the script of a play, especially one indicating the movement, position, or tone of an actor, or the sound effects and lighting.

stage door *n* an outside door of a theatre leading to the dressing rooms and the area behind the stage, used by actors and workers on the production.

stage fright *n* fear of appearing before an audience.

stage·hand (stāj′hand′) *n* a person whose work is moving scenery or props in a theatre.

stage–man·age (stāj′man′ij) *v* **stage-man·aged, stage-man·ag·ing 1** be responsible for the arrangement of the stage, including the placing and changing of scenery, props, etc., and for the proper running of each performance. **2** arrange events for a particular effect, especially from behind the scenes: *A few radical party members stage-managed the whole crisis.* **stage manager** *n.*

stage–struck (stāj′struk′) *adj* desiring very much to become an actor.

stage whisper *n* a loud whisper on a stage meant for the audience to hear, or any whisper meant to be heard by someone other than the person addressed.

stag·fla·tion (stag flā′shən) *n* persistent high inflation combined with high unemployment and lack of economic growth. <*stag*(*nation*) + (*in*)*flation*>

stag·ger (stag′ər) *v* **1** sway or move unsteadily, as if about to fall, or cause someone or something to move in this way: *He staggered under the heavy load. The government staggered from one crisis to another. The blow staggered him for a moment.* **2** astonish or deeply shock: *I was staggered to find it was so late.* **3** arrange something, such as an event, payment, or hour, so that it does not occur at the same time: *He staggered his appointments for the morning.* **4** arrange in a zigzag or irregular order or way: *The rows of seats in the theatre were staggered so that each person could see past the one in front.*
n a swaying; a reeling. <Old Norse *stakra*> **stag′ger·er** *n.*

stag·ger·ing (stag′ə ring) *adj* **1** amazing; overwhelming. **2** swaying; reeling. **stag′ger·ing·ly** *adv.*

stag·gers (stag′ərz) *n* (*with singular verb*) a disease of farm animals, caused by a parasite or a deficiency that makes them stagger or lose balance.

stag·ing (stā′jing) *n* **1** the fact or process of putting a play or other performance on the stage, or of organizing a public event. **2** a temporary platform or structure of posts and boards as a support for performers or between different levels of scaffolding in something being built. **3** the diagnosis or classification of a particular stage reached by a progressive disease. **4** the arrangement of stages in a rocket or spacecraft.

stag·nant (stag′nənt) *adj* **1** with no current or flow and often with an unpleasant smell in a body of water or the atmosphere of a confined place: *stagnant air, a stagnant pool.* **2** showing no activity: *During the summer, business was often stagnant.* <Latin *stagnare* be stagnant, from Latin *stagnum* standing water> **stag′nan·cy** *n.* **stag′nant·ly** *adv.*

stag·nate (stag′nāt) *v* **stag·nat·ed, stag·nat·ing 1** cease to flow or move in water or air. **2** become inactive or dull. **stag·na′tion** *n.*

stag·y (stā′jē) *adj* **stag·i·er, stag·i·est** too theatrical or exaggerated. **stag′i·ly** *adv.* **stag′i·ness** *n.*

staid (stād) *adj* with a respectable and unadventurous character. <obsolete *stay* restrain> **staid′ly** *adv.* **staid′ness** *n.*

stain (stān) *n* **1** a coloured patch or dirty mark that may be difficult to remove: *He has ink stains on his shirt.* **2** a thing that damages or brings disgrace to someone or someone's reputation. **3** a dye or chemical used to colour or darken a material or object, such as one used to coat furniture or to colour tissue for examination under a microscope.
v **1** mark something with coloured patches or dirty marks that may be difficult to remove: *The tablecloth is stained where food has been spilled.* **2** damage or bring disgrace to the reputation or image of someone or something; soil. **3** colour or darken a material, substance, or object by applying a dye or chemical: *She stained the chair a dark-green colour.* <Latin *dis-* off + *tingere* dye> **stain′a·ble** *adj.* **stain′er** *n.*

a bat	e bed	i bid	o pot	u cup	th **thin**
ā cake	ē me	ī bite	ō go	ū rude	ᴛʜ **then**
ä bar	ə about	ər over	ȯ for	u̇ put	zh measure

stalactites and stalagmites

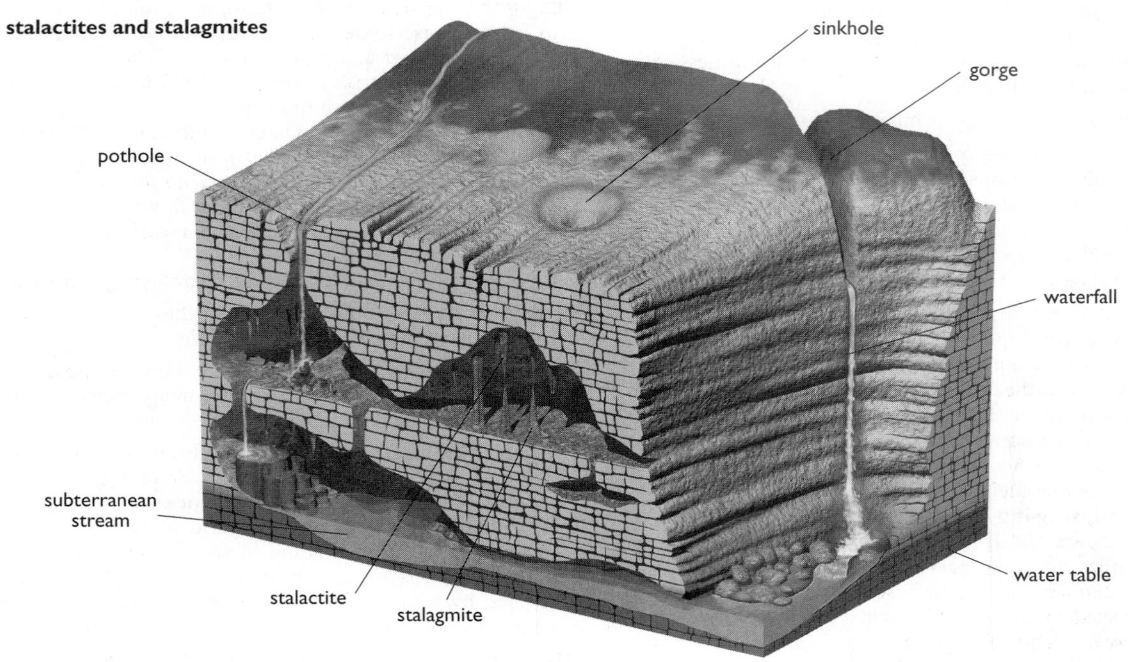

stained glass *n* coloured glass used to form pictures or decorations, especially in church windows, that is fitted in pieces inside a framework made from strips of lead.

stain·less (stān′lis) *adj* **1** unmarked by or resistant to stains or discoloration. **2** free from wrongdoing or disgrace: *a stainless reputation.*

stainless steel *n* a form of steel containing chromium, nickel, or some other metal that makes it resistant to rust and tarnishing.

stair (ster) *n* **1** a series of steps for going from one level or floor to another, especially in a building, or one of these steps. **2 stairs** *pl* a set of such steps: *the top of the stairs.* <Old English *stæger*>

stair·case (ster′kās′) *n* a flight of stairs with its framework and walls. Also, **stairway**.

stair·well (ster′wel′) *n* a vertical space or shaft containing a staircase.

stake (stāk) *n* **1** a stick or post pointed at one end for driving into the ground, especially to support a tree or plant, form part of a fence, or act as a boundary mark. **2 the stake** in former times, a post to which a person was tied and then burned to death, or death by being burned in this way. **3** a sum of money or something else of value gambled on the outcome of a game or venture: *The men played for high stakes.* **4** a share or interest in a business, system, etc. **5 the stakes** *pl* the prize awarded to the winner of a race or contest, especially a horse race. *v* **staked, stak·ing 1** fasten to or with a stake. **2** mark with stakes: *The miner staked his claim.* **3** risk money or something valuable on the result of a game or venture. See STEAK for confusable. <Old English *staca*> **stak′er** *n.*

at stake, to be won or lost: *Her honour is at stake.*

pull up stakes, *Informal* move or go to live elsewhere: *After seven years of drought, they finally pulled up stakes and left the farm.*

stake out, a put under police surveillance. **b** mark off an area with stakes. **c** claim one's rights to a territory or activity.

stake·hold·er (stāk′hōl′dər) *n* **1** a person who takes care of what is bet and pays it to the winner. **2** a person with an interest or concern in something, especially a business.

stake·out (stāk′out) *n* police surveillance of a building or area where criminal activity is expected or where a suspect is believed to be, or the place from which the surveillance is carried out.

sta·lac·tite (stə lak′tīt) *or* (stal′ək tīt′) *n* a formation of calcium salts, shaped like an icicle, hanging from the roof of a cave. <Greek *stalaktos* dripping, from *stalassein* trickle>

CONFUSABLES

The words **stalactite** and **stalagmite** look and sound similar, so it's hard to tell them apart. One way to remember the difference is that stala**c**tites hang from the **c**eiling (the letter **c**) and stala**g**mites rise from the **g**round (the letter **g**).

sta·lag·mite (stə lag′mīt) *or* (stal′əg mīt′) *n* a formation of calcium salts, shaped like a cone, built up on the floor of a cave by dripping water. <Greek *stalagmos* a drop, from *stalassein* trickle>

stale (stāl) *adj* **stal·er, stal·est** **1** no longer fresh, especially as food: *stale bread.* **2** no longer new or interesting: *a stale joke.* **3** no longer able to perform well or creatively because of having done something for too long.
v **staled, stal·ing** make or become stale. <Middle English> **stale′ly** *adv.* **stale′ness** *n.*

stale·mate (stāl′māt′) *n* **1** in chess, the position of the pieces when no move can be made without putting the king in check. **2** a situation in which further action by opponents seems impossible.
v **stale·mat·ed, stale·mat·ing** bring or cause to reach a stalemate. <Old French *estale* standstill + (*check*)*mate*>

stalk[1] (stok) *n* **1** the stem of a seed-bearing plant, especially the slender attachment of a leaf, flower, or fruit. **2** a slender, upright support or stem of something: *The wine glass had a tall stalk.* <Middle English *stalke*> **stalk′less** *adj.* **stalk′like′** *adj.* **stalk′y** *adj.*

stalk[2] (stok) *v* **1** approach or pursue without being seen or heard: *The lion stalked the antelope.* **2** harass or persecute someone with unwanted or obsessive attention: *He was arrested for stalking his former wife.* **3** stride somewhere in a proud, stiff, or angry way.
n **1** a stealthy pursuit of someone or something. **2** a proud, stiff, or angry way of striding. <Old English *bestealcian*> **stalk′er** *n.*

stall (stol) *n* **1** a compartment for an animal in a stable, enclosed on three sides. **2** a stand or booth for selling things in a market. **3** a seat in the choir or chancel of a church, usually reserved for a particular member of the clergy. **4** the action of an engine, vehicle, aircraft, or boat in suddenly ceasing to run, especially because of an overload on the engine. **5** **stalls** *UK* the seats on the ground floor of a theatre.
v **1** suddenly cease or cause to cease running as an engine, vehicle, aircraft, or boat: *The truck stalled on the steep hill. He stalls the engine every time.* **2** stop making progress in a situation or process: *The negotiations stalled over the question of pay.* **3** put an animal in a stall. <Old English *steall*>

stal·lion (stal′yən) *n* an uncastrated male horse, especially one kept for breeding purposes. <Old French *estalon*>

stal·wart (stol′wərt) *adj* loyal, reliable, or hard-working: *a stalwart supporter, a stalwart friend.*
n a loyal, reliable, or hard-working supporter or participant in an organization or team. <Old English *stathol* position + *wierthe* worthy> **stal′wart·ly** *adv.* **stal′wart·ness** *n.*

sta·men (stā′mən) *n* the male fertilizing organ of a flower, consisting of a threadlike stem called a filament and a pollen-containing anther. See ANTHER for picture. <Latin *stamen* warp, thread>

stam·i·na (stam′ə nə) *n* the ability to sustain prolonged physical or mental effort: *The long-distance runner had both stamina and speed.* <Latin = threads. In Greek myth, the Fates spun threads to determine how long one would live.>

stam·i·nate (stam′ə nit) *or* (stam′ə nāt′) *adj* of a plant, having stamens but no pistils.

stam·mer (stam′ər) *v* speak with a tendency to create pauses: *She stammers whenever she is nervous. He stammered an excuse.*
n the act or habit of stammering. <Old English *stamerian*> **stam′mer·er** *n.* **stam′mer·ing** *adj.* **stam′mer·ing·ly** *adv.*

CONFUSABLES

Stammer refers to speaking with unintended pauses: *The speaker's stammer prolonged the presentation.*

Stutter refers to speaking with unintended repeated sounds, especially initial consonants: *He stuttered only when he was nervous.*

stamp (stamp) *v* **1** **a** bring the foot down heavily: *She stamped her foot in anger.* **b** walk with heavy forceful steps. **2** impress a mark, especially an official one, on a surface using an engraved or inked instrument. **3** reveal or mark out as having a particular character, quality, or ability: *His behaviour stamped him as a bully.* **4** fix a postage stamp or stamps onto a letter or parcel.
n **1** **a** an instrument for impressing a mark, especially an engraved or inked block. **b** the mark or pattern made by it, especially one showing that something is valid or certified. **2** a particular class or type of a person or thing: *I think you show an artistic stamp.* **3** a small piece of paper with a sticky back to show that a charge has been paid, especially a postage stamp. **4** an act or sound of stamping with the foot. <Middle English *stampen*>
stamp′er *n.*
stamp out, **a** put out by stamping with the foot: *to stamp out flames.* **b** put an end to by force or decisive action: *He worked to stamp out child abuse.* **c** walk with heavy, forceful steps: *After the argument he stamped out.*

stam·pede (stam pēd′) *n* **1** a sudden panicky rush of a herd of cattle, horses, or other animals. **2** a sudden rapid movement or reaction of a mass of people in response to something happening: *There was a stampede of students when the final bell rang.* **3** (*often in names*) a rodeo, often accompanied by other amusements usually found at a fair: *the Calgary Stampede.*
v **stam·ped·ed, stam·ped·ing** scatter, flee, or move in a stampede, or cause to move in this way. <Spanish *estampida*>

stamp pad *n* a pad soaked with ink, for inking a rubber or metal stamp by pressing it on the pad.

stance (stans) *n* **1** the way in which someone stands, especially when deliberately adopted, as in golf and other games: *I have spent hours trying to improve my stance, but my golfing skills are no better.* **2** the attitude of a person or organization toward something: *The company changed its stance on pollution.* <Old French *estance*, from Latin *stare* stand>

stan·chion (stan′shən) *n* an upright bar, post, or frame forming a support or barrier, such as in a cattle stall.

a bat	e bed	i bid	o pot	u cup	th thin
ā cake	ē me	ī bite	ō go	ū rude	ᴛʜ then
à bar	ə about	ər over	ò for	ù put	zh measure

stand (stand) *v* **stood, stand·ing 1** have or cause to be in an upright position: *He stood motionless. Stand the box over there.* **2** have specified height when upright: *The horse stands nearly two metres.* **3** rise to one's feet: *He stood when she entered the room.* **4** be in a particular place or position as an object, building, or settlement: *The town stood in a valley.* **5** remain valid or unaltered: *My decision stands.* **6** be in a certain place, rank, or scale: *He stood last in the race.* **7** take or keep a certain position: *"Stand back!" called the police officer to the crowd.* **8** adopt a particular attitude toward a matter or issue: *Where do you stand on the question of extending the school year?* **9** withstand an experience or test without being damaged: *I couldn't stand any more punishment.* **10** provide food or drink for someone at one's own expense: *to stand someone a meal.* **11** be a candidate for election: *She stood for office twice.* **12** stop moving: *"Stand!" cried the sentry.*
n **1** an attitude toward a matter or issue: *What is your stand on this topic?* **2** a determined effort to resist an opposing force: *They made a last stand against the enemy.* **3** a place where something stands, sits, or rests: *Leave your bicycle in the stand.* **4 the stands** *pl* a raised, tiered structure for spectators, especially at a sporting event. **5** a small stall or booth in a street, market, or public building from which goods are sold: *a newspaper stand.* **6** a group of growing plants of a specified kind, especially trees: *a stand of pines.* <Old English *standan*>
stand a chance, have a chance.
stand behind, support or guarantee.
stand by, a be near. **b** side with, help, or support: *to stand by a friend.* **c** be or get ready for use or action: *The radio operator was ordered to stand by.*
stand down, retire from an office or position.
stand for, a represent or mean: *"AWOL" stands for "Absent without official leave."* **b** be on the side of or uphold: *Our school stands for fair play.* **c** *Informal* put up with or tolerate: *The teacher said she would not stand for talking during class.* **e** sail or steer toward.
stand in, *Informal* serve as a substitute for somebody.
stand off, keep off or away.
stand on, be based or depend on.
stand out, a be noticeable or prominent: *His ears stood out. Certain facts stand out.* **b** refuse to yield: *to stand out against popular opinion.*
stand up, a get to one's feet: *She stood up and began to speak.* **b** endure; last.
stand up for, defend or support: *to stand up for a friend.*
stand up to, meet or face boldly: *The young girl stood up to the bully.*
take the stand, testify in court.

stand–a·lone (stand′ə lōn′) *adj* able to operate independently without the need for other equipment or material: *a stand-alone storage unit.*

stand·ard (stan′dərd) *n* **1** a level of quality or measurement: *The school has high standards.* **2** an idea or thing used as a measure, norm, or model to compare and evaluate one thing against another: *Prices were high by today's standard.* **3 standards** *pl* principles of good conduct: *moral standards.* **4** a flag or banner, especially an emblem of a person or city.
adj **1** used or accepted as normal or average: *the standard rate of pay.* **2** with recognized excellence or authority: *a standard text.* **3** widely accepted as the usual correct form of language: *standard English.* <Old French *estandart*>

GRAMMAR AND USAGE

Standard English is the English that educated people use in public and accept as appropriate for most situations. It includes formal and informal levels of language, but not slang or non-standard forms. See also notes at *informal* and *slang*, as well as definitions at *formal* and *non-standard*.

stand·ard·bear·er (stan′dərd ber′ər) *n* **1** a person, especially an officer or soldier, who carries a distinctive flag or banner. **2** a leading figure in a movement or cause.

standard curve *Statistics n* a bell curve.

standard deviation *Statistics n* a quantity, arrived at by a formula, that indicates the extent of deviation for a group as a whole.

stan·dard·ize (stan′dər dīz′) *v* **stan·dard·ized, stan·dard·iz·ing 1** cause something to conform to a standard: *They standardized all the machine parts.* **2** regulate or test by a standard. **stan′dard·i·za′tion** *n.*

standard of living *n* the degree of wealth and amount of material things that are available to a person or community: *a high standard of living.*

standard time *n* a uniform time for places in approximately the same longitude, established in a country or region by law or custom.

stand·by (stand′bī′) *n, pl* **stand·bys 1** readiness for duty or immediate use: *Several airplanes were on standby.* **2** the situation in which one waits for an unreserved place for a journey or performance, depending on what seat or place becomes available: *The airline put us on standby.* **3** a person or thing held in reserve, especially as a possible replacement or substitute.

stand·ee (stan′dē′) *n* a person who must stand because all the seats are occupied, especially in a passenger vehicle, or at a public performance or meeting.

stand–in (stan′din′) *n* a person who substitutes for another, such as at an event or in a performance: *Will you be my stand-in at the next meeting?*

stand·ing (stan′ding) *n* **1** a position, status, or reputation: *They were members in good standing.* **2 standings** *pl* a table of scores indicating the positions of competitors in a sports event or season: *Our team was low in the standings.* **3** indicating the length of time that something has lasted: *Our argument was of long standing.*
adj **1** upright or vertical: *standing timber, a standing lamp.* **2** done from a position of rest or while upright: *a standing jump.* **3** long established or permanent: *a standing invitation, a standing army.* **4** still or stagnant: *standing water.*

standing room *n* space available for people to stand at an event, especially after all seats are occupied.

stand·off (stan′dof′) *n* a deadlock between two equally matched opponents in a dispute, conflict, or contest.

stand·off·ish (stan′dof′ish) *adj* unfriendly or aloof.

stand·out (stan′dout′) *Informal n* a thing that or person who is outstanding in appearance or performance.

stand·point (stand′point′) *n* an attitude to or outlook on something, usually because of one's circumstances or beliefs: *From our standpoint, his argument was ridiculous.*

stand·still (stand′stil′) *n* a situation or condition in which there is no movement or activity.

stand–up (stand′up′) *adj* **1** involving, done by, or engaged in by people standing up: *a standup lunch.* **2** in an upright position: *a stand-up collar.* **3** to do with a comedian who performs alone, standing and telling jokes to an audience, or a performance done in this way: *a stand-up routine.*
n stand-up comedy: *He began his career doing stand-up.* Also called **improv**.

stank (stangk) a past tense of STINK.

🍁 **Stan·ley Cup** (stan′lē) *n* a trophy presented annually to the winning team in the National Hockey League at the end of a championship series. <Sir F. *Stanley*, Governor General of Canada, 1888–1893>

stan·za (stan′zə) *n* a group of lines of poetry, commonly four or more, arranged according to a fixed plan. <Latin *stare* stand, because of the stop at the end of each verse>

sta·pes (stā′pēz) See STIRRUP (def. 3). <Latin = stirrup>

staph·y·lo·coc·cus (staf′ə lō kok′əs) *n, pl* **staph·y·lo·coc·ci** a bacterium that causes the formation of pus, especially in the skin and mucus membranes. <Greek *staphyle* bunch of grapes + *kokkos* grain, so called because of the shape of the bacterium> **staph′y·lo·coc′cal** *adj.*

sta·ple[1] (stā′pəl) *n* a U-shaped piece of metal or wire with pointed ends that are pushed through something or clipped over it as a fastening.
v **sta·pled, sta·pling** fasten with a staple or staples. <Old English *stapol* stake>

sta·ple[2] (stā′pəl) *n* **1** the main or most important element of something, especially of a diet or an item of trade or production: *Rice was the staple of their diet. Wheat is a staple of Saskatchewan.* **2** the fibre of cotton or wool considered in terms of its length and degree of fineness.
adj main or most important, especially in terms of consumption, trade, or production; principal: *The weather is a staple subject of conversation. Corn was the village's staple crop.* <Old French *estaple* mart>

sta·pler[1] (stā′plər) *n* a device for fastening together sheets of paper with a staple or staples.

star (stär) *n* **1** a celestial body, especially one that is not the moon, a planet, a comet, or a meteor, and appears as a bright point in the sky at night. **2** a plane figure with five points, or sometimes six, shaped like ☆ or ✡. **3** an exceptionally good or successful person or thing, especially a famous or extremely talented entertainer or athlete: *a movie star.* **4** a planet, constellation, or celestial body considered to influence someone's fortunes or personality: *She was born under a lucky star.*
v **starred, star·ring 1** be the most prominent performer in a movie, play, or other show: *She starred in many motion pictures. The play starred a rising young actor.* **2** decorate or cover with star-shaped marks or objects. **3** mark with an asterisk or other star-shaped symbol. <Old English *steorra*> **star′less** *adj.* **star′like′** *adj.*
see stars, *Informal* see flashes of light as a result of a hard blow on the head.
thank your (lucky) stars, be thankful for your good luck.

star·board (stär′bərd) *or* (stär′bôrd′) *n* the right side of a ship or aircraft, when facing forward.
adj, adv on the right side of a ship or aircraft.

starch (stärch) *n* **1** a white, tasteless, odourless white substance that occurs in plant tissue and obtained mainly from potatoes, wheat, rice, and corn. It stores carbohydrates and is an important part of the human diet. **2** a food containing this substance. **3** a powder or spray made from this substance and used before ironing to stiffen fabric or clothing. **4 a** stiffness of manner or character. **b** vigour and determination.
v stiffen clothes or fabric with starch. <Old English *stearc* stiff>

starch·y (stär′chē) *adj* **starch·i·er, starch·i·est 1** like or containing starch in food or the diet. **2** stiffened with starch. **3** *Informal* very stiff and formal in manner. **starch′i·ness** *n.*

star–crossed (stär′krost′) *adj* ill-fated or with much bad luck.

star·dom (stär′dəm) *n* the condition or status of being a famous or extremely talented performer or athlete.

star·dust (star′dust) *n* a magical, enchanting, or glamorous quality or feeling, especially in entertainment or sports: *By the time the actor left the stage, the audience felt the effect of his stardust.*

stare (ster) *v* **stared, star·ing 1** look long and directly with the eyes wide open, especially because of wonder, surprise, curiosity, illness, hostility, or rudeness. **2** bring to a named condition by staring: *He stared her into silence.*
n a long and direct look with the eyes wide open: *She gave him a hard stare.* <Old English *starian*> **star′er** *n.*
stare you in the face, be very apparent or obvious.

star·fish (stär′fish′) *n, pl* **star·fish·es** or (*especially collectively*) **star·fish** a spineless sea animal that has five or more radiating arms. It moves using tubelike feet on the underside of its arms.

star·gaze (stär′gāz′) *v* **star·gazed, star·gaz·ing 1** gaze at the stars. **2** be absent-minded or daydream.
star′gaz′er *n.*

stark (stärk) *adj* **1** bare, harsh, or barren in appearance or outline: *a stark landscape.* **2** unpleasantly or sharply clear and impossible to avoid: *His wealth was in stark contrast to his lifestyle.* **3** complete and utter: *She began to scream in stark terror.* **4** *Archaic* stiff, rigid, or incapable of movement: *The body lay stark in death.*
adv **1** entirely or completely: *The boys went swimming stark naked.* **2** in a stark manner. <Old English *stearc* stiff>
stark′ly *adv.* **stark′ness** *adj.*

star·less (stär′lis) *adj* without stars or starlight.

a bat	e bed	i bid	o pot	u cup	th **th**in
ā cake	ē me	ī bite	ō go	ū rude	ᴛʜ **th**en
ä bar	ə about	ər over	ô for	u̇ put	zh measure

S

star·let (stȧr′lit) *n* **1** a young actress or singer who may become a star. **2** a little star.

star·light (stȧr′līt′) *n* light from the stars.

star·like (stȧr′līk′) *adj* shaped or shining like a star.

star·ling (stȧr′ling) *n* a widely distributed songbird that typically has a harsh cry, and dark feathers. The starling family includes grackles and mynahs.

star·lit (stȧr′lit′) *adj* lighted by the stars: *a starlit night.*

Star of David *n* a six-pointed figure consisting of two interlaced equilateral triangles, one upright and one inverted, used as a symbol of Judaism and of Israel.

star·ry (stȧr′ē) *adj* **star·ri·er, star·ri·est 1** full of or lit by stars: *a starry sky.* **2** shining or shaped like a star: *starry eyes.* **3** to do with star performers: *a starry cast.*

star·ry–eyed (stȧr′ē īd′) *adj* too idealistic or enthusiastic.

star·span·gled (stȧr′spang′gəld) *adj* covered, glittering, or decorated with stars.

star–stud·ded (stȧr′stud′id) *adj* **1** filled or covered with stars: *a star-studded sky.* **2** featuring a number of famous people, especially actors or athletes: *The new movie had a star-studded cast.*

start (stȧrt) *v* **1** begin from a particular point in time or space: *The train started on time. We started the book yesterday.* **2** cause an event or process to happen: *to start a car, to start a fire.* **3** give a sudden involuntary jerk, or have one's eyes suddenly bulge: *Her eyes started in surprise.*
n **1** the point in time or space at which something has its beginning: *the start of next year, from start to finish.* **2** a sudden movement of surprise or alarm: *I awoke with a start. On seeing the snake, the man sprang up with a start. of his rivals.* **3** the position or set of circumstances at the beginning of life, or before beginning a career or course of action: *His father gave him a good start. To make the race fair, I need a two-minute start.* **4** the place or line at which a race begins. <Old English *styrtan* leap up>
start in (or **out**)**,** begin to do a thing.
start off, begin a trip or race.
start (in) on, a energetically begin to do something. **b** begin scolding someone.
start up, a switch on a machine, usually a vehicle. **b** begin a business or other project.
to start with, first of all: *I had a number of reasons; to start with, I was just plain bored.*

start·er (stȧr′tər) *n* **1** a person who or thing that starts an event, activity, or process. **2** a horse, competitor, or player taking part in a race or game at the start.
for starters, to begin with: *For starters, you can clean up this mess.*

start·ing blocks (stȧr′ting) *pln* adjustable blocks against which a runner braces the feet to get a fast start in a race. See ATHLETE for picture.

starting point *n* a place that marks the beginning of something, such as a journey, study, or discussion.

star·tle (stȧr′təl) *v* **star·tled, star·tling** cause a person or animal to feel sudden shock or alarm: *The hunters startled the deer.* <Old English *steartlian* struggle>

star·tling (stȧr′tling) *adj* surprising, astonishing, or remarkable: *startling tales.*

start–up (stȧr′tup) *n* **1** the action of starting a business or other project. **2** a new business, company, etc.
adj to do with starting up: *the start-up cost.*

starve (stȧrv) *v* **starved, starv·ing 1** suffer severely or die because of hunger, or cause someone to do this. **2** *Informal* feel very hungry: *I hope we can eat soon, because I'm starving.* **3 a** (*with* ***of***) weaken by insufficient supply of a thing needed: *a child starved of affection, a plant starved of water.* **b** (*with* **for**) have a strong need for: *We were starving for news of the final score.* <Old English *steorfan* die> **star·va′tion** *n.*

–starved *combining form* suffering from lack of: *love-starved.*

starve·ling (stȧr′vling) *n* a person or animal suffering from lack of food.

Star Wars *pln* the **Strategic Defence Initiative** of the US, a system in which satellites in outer space would use lasers to intercept and destroy enemy missiles.

stash (stash) *v* hide or put away for safekeeping or future use: *Where have you stashed the cookies?*
n **1** a thing hidden away or stored: *a stash of batteries for an emergency.* **2** the place where it is hidden or stored. <origin uncertain>

sta·sis (stā′sis) *or* (stas′is) *n, pl* **sta·ses** (stā′sēz) *or* (stas′ēz) **1** a period or state of balance or equilibrium. **2** *Medicine* a stoppage of flow of a body fluid. <Greek *histanai* stand>

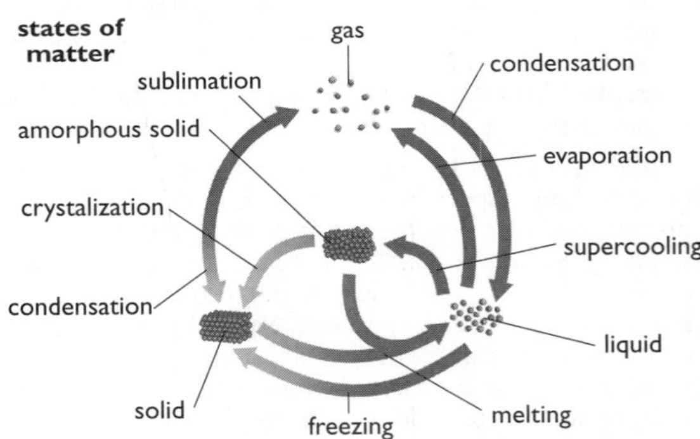

state (stāt) *n* **1** the particular condition that someone or something is in at a specific time: *a state of uncertainty. She is in a state of poor health. Ice is water in a solid state.* **2** *Informal* an anxious or upset mind: *She got herself into a state about the upcoming exam.* **3** a nation or territory considered as an organized political unit under one government, or as part of a republic. **4** the civil government of a country: *The state provided large pensions.* **5 the States** *Informal* the United States. **6** the pomp and ceremony associated with monarchy or high levels of government: *The king was buried in state.*
v **stat·ed, stat·ing** express something clearly and definitely in speech or writing: *to state your views.*
adj **1** to do with civil government or authority: *state control.* **2** to do with very formal and special occasions: *a state visit.* <Latin *status* condition from *stare* stand>

state·craft (stāt′kraft′) *n* the skilful management of a state or nation.

state·hood (stāt′hůd′) *n* the status of being a recognized independent nation.

state·less (stā′tlis) *adj* without nationality or citizenship of any country.

state·ly (stā′tlē) *adj* **state·li·er, state·li·est** grand, dignified, and majestic in appearance: *a stately mansion.* **state′li·ness** *n.*

state·ment (stāt′mənt) *n* **1** a clear and definite expression of something in speech or writing. **2** an official account of facts, views, or plans. **3** a summary of an account, showing the amount owed or due.

state of the art *n* the most recent stage of a product or technology.

state·room (stā′trům′) *n* a private room on a ship or railway train.

states·man (stāt′smən) *n, pl* **states·men** (-smən) a man who is a skilled, experienced, and respected political leader. **states′man·like′** *adj.* **states′man·ly** *adv.* **states′man·ship** *n.*

states·wom·an (stāt′swům′ən) *n, pl* **states·wom·en** (-swim′ən) a woman who is a skilled, experienced, and respected political leader.

state·wide (stāt′wīd′) *adj, adv* throughout an entire American state: *a statewide curriculum* (*adj*). *It was broadcast statewide* (*adv*).

stat·ic (stat′ik) *adj* **1** lacking in movement, action, or change, especially in an undesirable or uninteresting way: *a static civilization.* **2** to do with bodies at rest or forces that balance each other. **3** acting by weight without producing motion: *static pressure.* **4** to do with stationary electrical charges that balance each other: *Static electricity can be produced by rubbing a glass rod with a silk cloth.*
n **1** crackling or hissing noises on a telephone, radio, or other form of telecommunication. **2** *Informal* angry or critical talk or behaviour: *I left the room to escape their static.* <Greek *statikos* causing to stand> **stat′i·cal·ly** *adv.*

static cling *n* the clinging of fabric or clothing to each other, especially fabrics, due to a buildup of static electricity.

stat·ics (stat′iks) *n* (*with singular verb*) the branch of mechanics that studies physical bodies at rest and the action of forces that balance each other to produce equilibrium.

sta·tion (stā′shən) *n* **1** a place where passenger trains stop on a railway line, usually with platforms and buildings. **2** a place or building where a specified activity or service is based: *a police station.* **3** a place where broadcasting is done: *a radio station.* **4** the place where someone or something stands or is placed on military or other duty: *He took up a station near the door.* **5** a social position or rank: *a humble station in life.*
v put in or assign to a specified place for a particular purpose: *They stationed themselves on guard duty at the gate. To see the movie star, she stationed herself just outside his hotel.* <Latin *stare* stand>

sta·tion·ar·y (stā′shə ner′ē) *adj* **1** not moving or not intended to be moved: *a stationary vehicle.* **2** not changing in size, number, activity, etc.: *The population of this town has been stationary for years.*

CONFUSABLES

Stationary means "not moving": *She was as stationary as a statue.*

Stationery means "writing materials": *Do you think e-mail is replacing stationery?*

station break *n* a brief interruption in broadcast programs to identify the station or network.

sta·tion·er (stā′shə nər) *n* a person who or shop that sells papers, pens, and other writing materials.

sta·tion·er·y (stā′shə ner′ē) *n* writing materials, especially paper, cards, and envelopes. See STATIONARY for confusable.

station house *n* a police or fire station.

sta·tion·mas·ter (stā′shən mas′tər) *n* the person in charge of a railway station.

Stations of the Cross *Christianity pln* fourteen scenes from the suffering and death of Christ, usually painted or sculpted and arranged near a church or outdoors in a garden, or the prayers or devotions performed there in sequence.

station wagon *n* a motor vehicle with an extended interior and with a back end that can be opened to permit loading.

sta·tis·tic (stə tis′tik) *n* **1** one piece of numerical data. **2** someone or something treated as a piece of data or information. <Latin *statisticus* political, from *status* state. See STATE.> **sta·tis′ti·cal** *adj.* **sta·tis′ti·cal·ly** *adv.*

sta·tis·tics (stə tis′tiks) *n* (*with singular verb*) the practice or science of collecting, classifying, and analyzing numerical data in large quantities in order to make general observations about them.
stat′is·ti′cian (stat′i stish′ən) *n.*

🍁 **Stats·Can** (stat′skan) *Informal n* Statistics Canada.

stat·u·ar·y (stach′ū er′ē) *n, pl* **stat·u·ar·ies** statues considered as a group.
adj of or for statues: *statuary marble.*

stat·ue (stach′ū) *n* a figure of a person or animal carved or cast, especially one that is life-size or larger. <French, from Latin *statua*, from *stare* stand>

stat·u·esque (stach′ū esk′) *adj* attractively tall and dignified.

stat·u·ette (stach′ū et′) *n* a small statue or figurine.

stat·ure (stach′ər) *n* **1** a person's natural height: *He was of short stature.* **2** reputation or distinction gained by ability or achievement: *She is a woman of great stature in her line of business.* <Latin *stare* stand>

a bat	e bed	i bid	o pot	u cup	th thin
ā cake	ē me	ī bite	ō go	ū rude	ᴛʜ then
ȧ bar	ə about	ər over	ȯ for	ů put	zh measure

sta·tus (stat′əs) *or* (stā′təs) *n* **1** the relative social, professional, or other position of someone or something: *the status of women.* **2** high rank or social position: *wealth and status.* **3** the position of something at a particular time, especially in politics or business: *The status of the legislation was uncertain.* <Latin = condition, from *stare* to stand>

🍁 **status Indian** *n* a First Nations person officially registered with the Federal Government as a member of a band, entitled to certain rights and benefits under the Indian Act.

status quo (kwō) *n* the way things are, especially regarding social or political matters: *The club voted to maintain the status quo in election procedures.* <Latin = the state in which>

status symbol *n* a thing owned that is taken to indicate wealth or high social rank or status: *The expensive car was obviously her status symbol.*

stat·ute (stach′ūt′) *n* a law enacted by a legislative body, organization, or institution. <Old French, from Latin *statuere* decree>

statute law *n* law as expressed by a collection of statutes. Compare CASE LAW, COMMON LAW.

statute mile *n* a nonmetric unit for measuring distance on land, equal to about 1.6 km.

statute of limitations *Law n* a statute that specifies a certain period of time after which legal action cannot be brought or offences punished.

Statute of West·min·ster (west min′stər) *n* an act of the British Parliament, passed in 1931, by which Canada and other former colonies were granted the formal authority to make their own laws.

stat·u·to·ry (stach′ū tô′rē) *adj* **1** required, permitted, or enacted by a statute. **2** required or expected through being done or made regularly: *We made our statutory stop at the candy store.* **stat′u·to′ri·ly** *adv.*

statutory holiday *n* a public holiday fixed by law.

staunch[1] (stonch) *adj* **1** very loyal and committed: *a staunch defence, a staunch friend.* **2** strongly and firmly constructed. Also, **stanch.** <Old French *estanchier*, from Latin *extanicare* press together> **staunch′ly** *adv.* **staunch′ness** *n.*

staunch[2] (stonch) *v* **1** stop or restrict a flow of blood from a wound. **2** cease moving or flowing: *We were unable to staunch the gossip going around.* Also, **stanch.** <Old French *estanchier* cause to stop flowing, from Latin *extanicare* press together> **staunch′er** *n.*

stave (stāv) *n* **1** one of the curved pieces of wood fixed side by side that form a barrel, tub, or other container. **2** a vertical wooden post or plank in a building or other structure. **3** a strong wooden stick or iron pole used as a weapon. **4** a verse of a poem. **5** a musical STAFF (def. 4).
v **staved** or **stove, stav·ing** violently break a hole in something, or become smashed or broken in. <*staves*, plural of *staff*>
stave off, avert or delay something bad or dangerous: *The lost campers ate birds' eggs to stave off starvation.*

stay[1] (stā) *v* **stayed, stay·ing 1** remain in the same place: *Stay here till I call you.* **2** remain in a specified condition or position: *When the fire started we managed to stay calm.* **3** live somewhere temporarily as a visitor or guest: *They stayed a week at the ski resort.* **4** stop, delay, or prevent something, especially to suspend or postpone court proceedings or refrain from pressing legal charges.
n **1** a period of staying somewhere, in particularly living somewhere temporarily as a visitor or guest: *We had a pleasant stay in Regina.* **2** a curb, check, or restraint: *The accident put a stay on her activities.* **3** a suspension or postponement of court proceedings: *The judge granted the condemned man a stay for an appeal.* **4** a device used as a brace or support. <Old French, from Latin *stare*>
stay′er *n.*

stay[2] (stā) *n* a strong rope, chain, or wire attached to something to steady it, especially on a ship.
v **stayed, stay·ing** support or secure with a stay or stays. <Old English *stæg*>

stay–at–home (stā′ət hōm′) *adj* preferring to be at home rather than to travel, socialize, or go out to work: *a stay-at-home dad.*
n a person who prefers to do this.

staying power *n* the ability to maintain an activity or commitment despite fatigue or difficulties: *She doesn't work very fast, but she has great staying power.*

STD sexually transmitted disease.

stead (sted) *n* the place or role that someone or something should have or fill: *The sales manager could not go, but she sent her assistant in her stead.* <Old English *stede*>
stand in good stead, be of advantage or service to.

stead·fast (sted′fast′) *adj* loyal and unwavering: *The politician was a steadfast servant of his constituents.* **stead′fast′ly** *adv.* **stead′fast′ness** *n.*

stead·y (sted′ē) *adj* **stead·i·er, stead·i·est 1** regular, even, and continuous in development, frequency, or intensity: *steady progress.* **2** firmly fixed, supported, or balanced: *She held the ladder steady.* **3** not faltering or wavering: *steady nerves, a steady friendship.* **4** sensible and reliable: *a steady player.* **5** regular and established: *a steady income.*
v **stead·ied, stead·y·ing** make or become steady: *Steady the ladder while I climb to the roof. The wind steadied.*
n, pl **stead·ies** *Informal* a regular girlfriend or boyfriend.
interj Informal used as a warning to someone to keep calm or take care: *Steady now! Don't let go of the rope!*
stead′i·ly *adv.* **stead′i·ness** *n.*
go steady, a *Informal* date one person or each other only. **b** go carefully.

steak (stāk) *n* a thick slice of meat or fish, usually cooked by frying or broiling: *sirloin steak, ham steak, salmon steak.* <Old Norse *steik*>

CONFUSABLES

Steak refers to food: *I think we're having steak and salad for dinner.*

Stake refers to a pointed stick or pole: *We hammered the stakes into the ground.*

steak tar·tare (tar′tar′) *n* raw beefsteak ground up and mixed with seasoning and raw egg.

steal (stēl) *v* **stole, sto·len, steal·ing 1** take another person's property without permission or legal right and without intending to return it: *to steal money.* **2 a** take, get, or do secretly: *He stole a look at the girl.* **b** move secretly or quietly: *She stole out of the house.* **3** take, get, or win by art, charm, or gradual means: *She steals all hearts.* **4** *Baseball* advance to a base without being helped by a hit or error. *n Informal* something obtained very cheaply or very easily: *At that price the cellphone is a steal.* See STEEL for confusable. <Old English *stelan*>

The **stealth-fighter** aircraft is made of special materials and has curves to deceive air-defence radar and reduce the risk of being shot down.

stealth (stelth) *n* a cautious and sly action or movement: *He took the letter by stealth while nobody was in the room.* *adj* designed to operate or operating undetected: *a stealth fighter.* **stealth′i·ly** *adv.* **stealth′i·ness** *n.* **stealth′y** *adj.*

steam (stēm) *n* **1** the vapour into which water is changed when it is heated, forming a mist. **2 a** the expansive force of this vapour, used to generate power for machines, and for heating and cooking. **b** locomotives and railway systems powered in this way. **3** *Informal* power or energy: *I ran out of steam on the last lap.*
v **1** give off or produce steam: *Their mitts were steaming on the radiator.* **2** (*usually with* ***up***) become or cause to become covered with steam: *The windshield had steamed up inside the car.* **3** prepare, treat, or cook with steam: *She steamed the vegetables.* **4** travel under steam power: *The ship steamed away.* **5** *Informal* be angry or frustrated: *She was steaming by the time he got there, half an hour late.* <Old English *steam*> **steam′like′** *adj.*
full steam ahead, with all possible power or energy: *They went full steam ahead as soon as they got final approval.*
let off steam, *Informal* **a** get rid of excess energy: *He took the kids to the playground so they could let off steam.* **b** relieve one's feelings of anger or frustration: *Wait till we get home before you let off steam.*
steamed up, *Informal* angry or frustrated: *She gets all steamed up about nothing.*

steam bath *n* a steam-filled room used for the purpose of cleaning and refreshing the body, or for relaxation.

steam·boat (stēm′bōt′) *n* a boat propelled by a steam engine.

steam engine *n* an engine operated by steam, typically one in which a sliding piston in a cylinder is moved by the expansive action of steam generated in a boiler.

steam·er (stē′mər) *n* **1** a ship, boat, railway train, or other machine powered by steam. **2** a container in which food can be steamed or kept warm.

steam iron *n* an electric iron in which water is heated to produce steam that is released through holes in its undersurface to dampen cloth while pressing it.

steam·rol·ler (stēm′rō lər) *n* a heavy, slow-moving vehicle with a roller, formerly moved by steam but now often by an internal combustion engine, used to crush and level materials in making roads.
v **1** *Informal* **a** override by crushing power or force; crush: *to steamroller all opposition.* **b** force into or through by this means: *to steamroller a committee into acceptance of a candidate.* **2** make level, smooth, etc. with a steamroller.

steam·ship (stēm′ship′) *n* a ship propelled by a steam engine.

steam shovel *n* a machine for digging, formerly operated by steam, but now by an internal combustion engine.

steam·y (stē′mē) *adj* **steam·i·er, steam·i·est 1** producing, filled with, or clouded with steam: *a steamy kitchen.* **2** hot and humid: *a steamy summer night.* **3** sexually explicit. **steam′i·ness** *n.*

steed (stēd) *Poetic n* a horse, especially a riding horse. <Old English *steda*>

steel (stēl) *n* **1 a** an alloy of iron and carbon that is very hard, strong, and tough. **b** a rod of this used for sharpening knives. **2** steel-like hardness or strength: *nerves of steel.* **3** 🍁 a railway track or line: *Steel was laid for several kilometres.*
v mentally prepare oneself to do something difficult: *He steeled his heart against our plea.*
adj **1** embodying strength and firmness: *a steel will.* **2** made of steel: *a steel girder.* <Old English *stele*> **steel′-like′** *adj.*

CONFUSABLES

Steel is a hard metal: *The lighthouse steps are made of steel.*

Steal means "take unlawfully": *Why did you steal the magazines from the store?*

steel band *n* a group of musicians playing instruments made from steel drums, common in Trinidad and other parts of the Caribbean.

steel blue *adj* dark bluish grey.

steel drum *n* a percussion instrument made from a steel drum, with one end beaten down and divided by grooves into sections to give different notes and played in a STEEL BAND.

steel guitar *n* an electric guitar held on the lap, played by picking with one hand while pressing and sliding a specially shaped piece of steel along the strings with the other hand to change the pitch.

steel·head (stēl′hed′) *n, pl* **steel·heads** or (*especially collectively*) **steel·head** a rainbow trout of the northwest Pacific coast that spends most of its life in the sea, but is born in fresh water and returns to fresh water to spawn.

S

a bat	e bed	i bid	o pot	u cup	th thin
ā cake	ē me	ī bite	ō go	ū rude	ᴛʜ then
ä bar	ə about	ər over	ô for	ů put	zh measure

steel wool *n* fine steel threads or shavings in a pad, used for cleaning or polishing.

steel·works (stēl′wərks′) *n* (*with singular verb*) a factory where steel is made. **steel′work′er** *n.*

steel·y (stē′lē) *adj* **steel·i·er, steel·i·est** **1** made of steel. **2** like steel in colour, strength, or hardness. **steel′i·ness** *n.*

steep[1] (stēp) *adj* **1** rising or falling sharply as a slope, flight of stairs, or angle, and almost straight up and down. **2** *Informal* excessive or unreasonable as a price or demand. <Old English *steap*> **steep′ly** *adv.* **steep′ness** *n.*

steep[2] (stēp) *v* **1** soak food or tea in water or other liquid so as to extract its flavour or to soften it. **2** surround or fill with a quality or influence: *The ruins were steeped in gloom.* <Old English *stepan*>

stee·ple (stē′pəl) *n* a high tower on a church, usually with a spire. <Old English *stepel*>

stee·ple·chase (stē′pəl chās′) *n* **1** a horse race over a course with ditches, hedges, and other obstacles. **2** a cross-country foot race.

steer[1] (stēr) *v* **1** guide or control the movement of a vehicle, vessel, or aircraft, or be guided or controlled. **2** follow a course in a specified direction: *She steered a course for home.* **3** guide the movement or course of someone or something: *He steered away from flattery.* <Old English *steoran*> **steer′a·ble** *adj.* **steer′er** *n.*
steer clear of, keep away from or avoid.

SYNONYMS

Steer as a verb is usually associated with the operation of some means of transportation: *The captain steered the ship through the rough waves.*

Control, meaning "guide," often has a negative tone: *He controls the company with an iron hand.*

Guide means "lead," "manage," or "control": *I'll guide you through the procedure step by step.*

steer[2] (stēr) *n* a full-grown, castrated male of cattle, usually raised for meat. Compare OX.

steer·age (stē′rij) *n* in former times, the part of a passenger ship occupied by passengers travelling at the cheapest rate.

steer·ing committee (stēr′ing) *n* a committee set up to consider priorities or the order of business of an organization, and that manages the general course of its operations.

steering wheel *n* a wheel that a driver turns in order to steer a vehicle.

steg·o·sau·rus (steg′ə sò′rəs) *n, pl* **steg·o·sau·ri** (-rī) *or* (-rē) an extinct, small-headed reptile of great size, with heavy, bony armour. Often shortened to **stegosaur**. <Greek *stegos* roof + *sauros* lizard>

stein (stīn) *n* a large earthenware beer mug.

stel·lar (stel′ər) *adj* **1** to do with a star or stars. **2** featuring or with the quality of a star performer or performers: *a stellar role.* **3** exceptionally well done: *a stellar job.* <Latin *stella* star>

Stellar's jay *n* a blue jay with a dark crest. It is the provincial bird of British Columbia. <G. *Stellar,* 18c explorer>

stem[1] (stem) *n* **1** the main body or stalk of a plant or shrub, typically rising above the ground in which it grows. **2** the part of a flower, a fruit, or a leaf that joins it to the plant. **3** anything like or suggesting the stem of a plant in being long, thin, and supporting: *the stem of a goblet, a pipe stem.* **4** the part of a word to which endings are added and in which changes are made. Example: *run* is the stem of *running, runner,* and *ran.*
v **stemmed, stem·ming** **1** originate in or be caused by: *Our troubles stemmed from lack of money.* **2** remove the stems from fruit. <Old English *stemn*> **stem′less′** *adj.* **stem′like′** *adj.*
from stem to stern, from the front to the back, especially of a ship.

stem[2] (stem) *v* **stemmed, stem·ming** stop or restrict the flow to something: *to stem bleeding.* <Old Norse *stemma*>

stem–and–leaf plot (stem′ən lēf′) *Statistics n* a way of grouping a set of numerical data so that the first digit of each number (the stem) is written in one column and the rest of the digits of the number (the leaves) are written in another column.

stem cell *n* an undifferentiated cell of an organism that can develop into a several distinct cell types. Stem cells are used in genetic research and bioengineering.

stem·ware (stem′wār) *n* drinking glasses with stems.

stench (stench) *n* a strong, very unpleasant smell: *the stench of gas.* <Old English *stenc*>

sten·cil (sten′səl) *n* **1** a thin sheet of metal, paper, or plastic with letters or designs cut through it. When a stencil is laid on a surface and ink or colour is spread on, such letters or designs are made on the surface. **2** the letters or designs so made.
v **sten·cilled** or **sten·ciled, sten·cil·ling** or **sten·cil·ing** mark, paint, or make with a stencil: *The curtains have a stencilled border.* <Old French *estanceler* ornament with colours, from Latin *scintilla* spark>

ste·nog·ra·phy (stə nog′rə fē) *n* the action or process of writing in shorthand and transcribing the shorthand on a typewriter or keyboard. **ste·nog′ra·pher** *n.*

sten·to·ri·an (sten tò′rē ən) *adj* very loud or powerful in sound.

ETYMOLOGY

Stentorian comes from a man named *Stentor,* a loud-voiced herald in the Trojan War. He was described in the epic poem *The Iliad* by Homer.

step (step) *n* **1 a** an act or movement made by lifting a foot and putting it down in front of another while walking, dancing, or running. **b** the distance covered by one such movement: *She was three steps away when he called her back.* **2** a particular way of walking: *He left the room with a springy step.* **3** a flat surface, especially one in a series, on which to place one's foot when moving from one level to another: *the front steps, the steps of a staircase.* **4** a measure or action, especially one of a series taken in order to deal with or achieve a particular thing: *We will have to take steps to economize.* **5** a degree in a series or a grade in rank: *A colonel is three steps above a captain.*

v **stepped, step·ping 1** lift and set down one's foot or one foot after the others in order to walk somewhere or move to a new position: *We stepped back from the horse.* **2** walk a short distance: *Step this way, please.* <Old English *steppan*>

in (out of) step, a keeping your pace uniform with (unlike that of) another or others. **b** making actions or ideas agree (disagree) with those of another person or persons.

keep step, move at the same pace as another person or persons, or in time with music.

step by step, little by little.

step down, a surrender or resign from an office or position: *She stepped down from the presidency.* **b** decrease: *They stepped down the rate of flow in the pipeline.*

step on it, *Informal* go faster or hurry up.

step out, *Informal* go out for entertainment.

step up, a go up. **b** make go higher, faster, etc.; increase: *to step up production.*

watch your step, be careful.

step– *combining form* related by the remarriage of a parent, not by blood: *stepmother.* <Old English *steop-*>

step·broth·er (step′bruTH′ər) *n* a stepfather's or stepmother's son by a former marriage.

step·child (step′chīld′) *n, pl* **step·chil·dren** a child of one's spouse by a former marriage.

step·daugh·ter (step′dot′ər) *n* a daughter of one's spouse by a former marriage.

step·family (step′fam′ə lē) a family that is formed on the remarriage of a divorced or widowed person and that includes a child or children.

step·fa·ther (step′foTH′ər) *n* a man who has married one's mother after the death or divorce of one's father.

step–in (step′in′) *adj* put on as clothes or footwear by being stepped into without the need of fastenings.

step·lad·der (step′lad′ər) *n* a short folding ladder with flat steps instead of rungs. See EXTENSION LADDER for picture.

step·moth·er (step′muTH′ər) *n* a woman who has married one's father after the death or divorce of one's mother.

step–par·ent (step′per′ənt) *n* a stepfather or stepmother.

steppe (step) *n* a large area of flat, treeless grassland in southeast Europe and Siberia. <Russian *step*>

stepping stone *n* **1** a raised stone used singly or in a series as a place on which to step when crossing a stream or wet area. **2** an undertaking or event that helps one make progress toward a goal.

step·sis·ter (step′sis′tər) *n* a stepfather's or stepmother's daughter by a former marriage.

step·son (step′sun′) *n* a son of one's spouse by a former marriage.

step·wise (step′wīz) *adv, adj* by steps or in the form of steps: *Rocks had been placed stepwise into the side of the hill.*

–ster *suffix* indicating a person or object that is involved with a certain thing: *gangster.* <Old English *-estre*>

ster·e·o (ster′ē ō′) *or* (stē′rē ō′) *adj* in full, **stereophonic** having two or more channels in a sound system, so that sounds seem to come from more than one source: *a five-speaker stereo system.* Compare MONO[2].

n a player for CDs, cassettes, or records that produces stereophonic sound.

ster·e·o·scope (ster′ē ə skōp′) *n* a device by which two photographs of the same object taken at slightly different angles are viewed together, creating an effect of depth and solidity. **ster′e·o·scop′ic** *adj.*

ster·e·o·type (ster′ē ə tīp′) *or* (stē′rē ə tīp′) *n* **1** a widely held but fixed and oversimplified image or idea of a particular type of person or thing, or a person or thing who conforms to this mental picture: *He fits the stereotype of the insecure bully. The novel's heroine is a stereotype of the ambitious young woman.* **2** a metal plate for printing that is cast from a mould made from a surface of composed type.

v **ster·e·o·typed, ster·e·o·typ·ing** make, have, or show a stereotype of. **ster′e·o·typ′i·cal** (ster′ē ə tip′ik əl) *adj.* **ster′e·o·typ′i·cal·ly** (ster′ē ə tip′ik lē) *adv.*

ster·ile (ster′īl) *or* (ster′əl) *adj* **1** not able to produce children, offspring, fruit, or seeds. **2** free from bacteria or other living micro-organisms: *sterile instruments.* **3** not producing results: *sterile hopes.* <Latin *sterilis*> **ster′ile·ly** *adv.* **ste·ril′i·ty** (stə ril′ə tē) *n.*

ster·i·lize (ster′ə līz′) *v* **ster·i·lized, ster·i·liz·ing 1** make something free from bacteria or other living micro-organisms: *The water had to be sterilized by boiling to make it fit to drink.* **2** deprive a person or animal of the ability to produce offspring, usually by removing or blocking the sex organs. **ster′il·i·za′tion** *n.*

ster·ling (stər′ling) *adj* **1** made of sterling silver. **2** excellent or valuable: *a sterling character.* **3** of or payable in British money, especially the pound as the standard British monetary unit in international trade.

n sterling silver or things made of it. <origin uncertain>

sterling silver *n* silver that is 92.5 percent pure.

stern[1] (stərn) *adj* severe, strict, or harsh in manner or appearance: *a stern coach, a stern frown, stern necessity.* <Old English *stirne*> **stern′ly** *adv.* **stern′ness** *n.*

stern[2] (stərn) *n* the rear of a ship or boat. <Old Norse *stjorn* steering>

ster·num (stər′nəm) *n* the breastbone. <Greek *sternon* chest> **ster′nal** (stər′nəl) *adj.*

stern·wheel·er (stərn′wē′lər) *n* a steamboat driven by a paddlewheel at the stern or rear.

ster·oid (ste′roid) *or* (stē′roid) *n* a complex organic compound that contains four rings of carbon atoms, such as that in many hormones, alkaloids, and vitamins. <*(chole)ster(ol)* + *-oid*>

stet (stet) *v* (*used as an instruction*) restore text that has been crossed out. <Latin = let it stand>

a bat	e bed	i bid	o pot	u cup	th thin
ā cake	ē me	ī bite	ō go	ū rude	TH then
à bar	ə about	ər over	ò for	ù put	zh measure

S

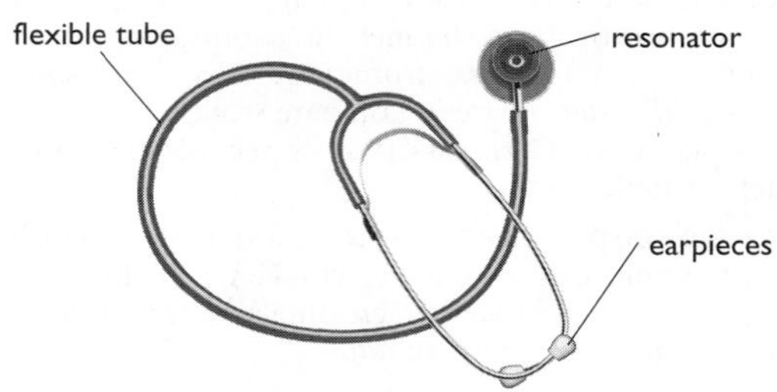

steth·o·scope (steth′ə skōp′) *n* a medical device used for listening to the action of the heart or breathing, typically with a small disc-shaped resonator that is placed against the chest, and two tubes connected to earpieces. <Greek *stethos* chest + *scope*> **steth′o·scop′ic** (steth′ə sko′pik) *adj.*

ste·ve·dore (stē′və dôr′) *n* a person whose job it is to load and unload ships.

stew (styū) *or* (stū) *n* **1** a dish of meat or fish and vegetables cooked slowly in liquid in a closed pan or casserole: *beef stew.* **2** *Informal* a condition of great worry: *She is in a stew over her lost diary.*
v **1** cook meat or fish and vegetables by slowly cooking in liquid, or be cooked in this way: *to stew a chicken.* **2** *Informal* worry greatly about something. <origin uncertain>
stew in your own juice, *Informal* suffer worry about the consequence of one's own actions without help from others.

stew·ard (styū′ərd) *or* (stū′ərd) *n* **1** a person who looks after the needs of passengers on a ship, train, or aircraft, especially one in charge of food and table service. **2** a person who manages another's property: *He was the steward of that great estate.* **3** an official appointed to manage or keep order at a large public event. **stew′ard·ship′** *n.*

stick[1] (stik) *Informal n* **1** a long, thin piece of wood. **2** such a piece of wood shaped for a special use: *a walking stick, a hockey stick.* **3** a thing like a stick in being long and thin: *a stick of candy.* **4** punishment or a threat of punishment: *She used my past as a stick to beat me with.* **5 the sticks** *pl Informal* unsophisticated areas far away from cities. <Old English *sticca*>
shake a stick at, *Informal* be able to use or perceive: *There was not enough snow to shake a stick at. He had more money than you can shake a stick at.*

stick[2] (stik) *v* **stuck, stick·ing 1** push or fasten a sharp or pointed object into or through something: *She stuck a fork into the potato. He stuck a flower in his buttonhole.* **2** put in or extend from a place or position: *Don't stick your head out of the car window. My arms stuck out of my coat sleeves.* **3** adhere or cling to a substance or surface: *Stick a stamp on the letter. It was so hot and humid my shirt stuck to my skin.* **4** keep close: *The child stuck to her mother's heels.* **5** be or become fastened, fixed, or immobile: *Our car stuck in the mud.* **6** persist or keep on: *to stick to a task.* **7** *Informal* tolerate or put up with, or be forced to: *I won't stick his insults much longer. It's not my problem, but I'm stuck with it.* <Old English *stician*>
stick around, *Informal* stay or wait nearby.
stick at, hesitate or stop for: *He sticks at nothing to get his own way.*
stick by (or **to**)**,** remain faithful or attached to: *She sticks by her friends when they are in trouble.*
stick in your craw (or **throat**)**,** *Informal* be very hard for you to do or accept.
stick it out, *Informal* put up with unpleasant conditions or circumstances: *Try to stick it out for a few more days.*
stick it to someone, *Informal* treat someone harshly or severely.
stick out, a be very noticeable. **b** *Informal* put up with until the end.
stick out like a sore thumb, *Informal* be very noticeable, especially unpleasantly so.
stick to your ribs, *Informal* of food, be satisfying or filling.
stick up, *Informal* rob by threatening violence, especially with a gun.
stick up for, *Informal* support or defend someone.

SYNONYMS

Stick can suggest being fastened by something gluey: *The candy stuck to the floor.*

Adhere suggests remaining attached: *This paint is made to adhere to metal.*

Paste means "stick with paste" or "cover by pasting": *The committee asked for three volunteers to paste the notices on the signboards.*

stick·ball (stik′bol′) *n* an informal game resembling baseball that is played with a tennis or rubber ball, using a heavy stick in place of a bat.

stick·er (stik′ər) *n* **1** a label or slip of paper for sticking to something. **2** a determined or persistent person or thing. **3** *Informal* a puzzle.

sticker price *n* the advertised retail price of a thing: *He's never paid the sticker price for a car in his life.*

stick figure *n* a simple figure of a person or animal drawn with straight lines except for a circle representing the head.

stick·han·dle (stik′han′dəl) *v* **stick·han·dled, stick·han·dling 1** *Hockey* control the puck with one's stick. **2** 🍁 manage an issue or problem skilfully, despite obstacles. **stick′han′dler** *n.*

sticking point *n* a factor that prevents the resolution of a problem or conflict: *The sticking point in the contract talks was shorter hours.*

stick insect *n* a long, slender, slow-moving insect that resembles a twig.

stick–in–the–mud (stik′in ᴛʜə mud′) *Informal n* a person who is dull and unadventurous and resists change.

stick·le·back (stik′əl bak′) *n, pl* **stick·le·backs** or (*especially collectively*) **stick·le·back** a small, scaleless fish with a row of sharp spines on the back, able to live in both salt and fresh water.

stick·ler (stik′lər) *n* a person who insists on a certain quality or type of behaviour: *a stickler for accuracy.* <Middle English *stightlen*>

stick·pin (stik′pin′) *n* a straight pin with an ornamental head, worn to keep a necktie in place or as a brooch.

stick shift *n* a gear lever that sticks upward from the floor of a motor vehicle, for shifting gears in a manual transmission.

stick·up (stik′up′) *Informal n* a robbery in which a gun is used to threaten people.

stick·work (stik′wərk) *n* skilful use of a stick, especially in hockey.

stick·y (stik′ē) *adj* **stick·i·er, stick·i·est 1** tending or designed to stick to things on contact or covered with something that sticks: *sticky tape.* **2** unpleasantly hot and humid: *sticky weather.* **3** *Informal* involving awkward or difficult problems. **stick′i·ly** *adv.* **stick′i·ness** *n.*

stiff (stif) *adj* **1** not easily bent or changed in shape: *a stiff collar.* **2 a** not moving as freely or easily as usual: *stiff hinges.* **b** not able to move easily without pain: *a stiff back.* **3** severe; more than is usual or suitable: *a stiff fine, a stiff dose of medicine, a stiff price.* **4** not easy or natural in manner: *a stiff bow.* **5** strong and steady in motion: *a stiff breeze.* **6** requiring much effort: *a stiff examination.*
v Informal cheat someone out of something, especially money: *You got out first and stiffed me for the whole cost of the taxi.* <Old English *stif*> **stiff′ly** *adv.* **stiff′ness** *n.*

stiff·en (stif′ən) *v* make or become stiff or rigid: *He stiffened the shirt with starch. She stiffened with anger.* **stiff′en·er** *n.*

stiff·en·ing (stif′ə ning) *n* material used to stiffen a garment, fabric, or other object.

stiff–necked (stif′nekt′) *adj* stubborn and distant in manner.

sti·fle (stī′fəl) *v* **sti·fled, sti·fling 1** make someone unable to breathe properly, or be unable to breathe freely: *The smoke stifled the firefighters.* **2** restrain a reaction or stop oneself acting on an emotion: *to stifle a yawn.* <origin uncertain>

stig·ma (stig′mə) *n, pl* **stig·mas** or **stig·ma·ta** (stig ma′tə) **1** a mark of disgrace connected with a particular circumstance, quality, or person: *a social stigma.* **2** a distinguishing mark or sign of a disease. **3** the part of the pistil of a flower that receives the pollen. See ANTHER for picture. <Greek *stizein* to tattoo>

stig·ma·tize (stig′mə tīz′) *v* **stig·ma·tized, stig·ma·tiz·ing** describe or regard as worthy of disgrace or deep disapproval. **stig′ma·ti·za′tion** *n.*

stile (stīl) *n* a step or set of steps that allows people but not animals to climb over a fence or wall.

sti·let·to (stə let′ō) *n, pl* **sti·let·tos** or **sti·let·toes 1** a short dagger with a tapering blade. **2** a very high, thin heel on a woman's shoe. <Italian, from Latin *stilus* pointed instrument>

still¹ (stil) *adj* **1** not moving or making a sound: *The lake is still today.* **2** not bubbling: *still wine.*
n **1** deep silence and calm: *the still of the night.* **2** an ordinary photograph, not a motion picture, especially a single shot from a movie.
adv **1** up to and including the present or the time mentioned: *He arrived yesterday and he is still here.* **2** in the future as in the past: *It will still be here.* **3** nevertheless or all the same: *still more, still worse.* **4** (*with comparatives, for emphasis*) even: *Applaud, or better still, cheer, if you like the music.* **5** not moving or making a sound: *to lie still.*
v make or become still: *She stilled the crying child.* <Old English *stille*> **still′ness** *n.*

still² (stil) *n* an apparatus for distilling alcoholic liquors. <*distil*>

still·born (stil′bôrn′) *adj* **1** dead when born. **2** having failed to develop or succeed as a proposal or plan.

still life *n, pl* **still lifes** a painting or drawing that shows an arrangement of objects, especially fruit or flowers.

stilt (stilt) *n* **1** each of a pair of poles to stand on and hold while walking, each with a support for the foot at some distance above the ground. **2** each of a set of posts or piles supporting a building above the ground or water. **3** a wading bird that lives in marshes and has a long bill, black and white feathers, and long, slender legs. <Middle English *stilte*> **stilt′like′** *adj.*

stilt·ed (stil′tid) *adj* **1** stiff and self-conscious: *stilted conversation.* **2** standing on stilts.

stim·u·lant (stim′yə lənt) *n* **1** a substance that temporarily increases the internal activity of some part of the body. **2** a thing that increases activity, interest, or enthusiasm.

stim·u·late (stim′yə lāt′) *v* **stim·u·lat·ed, stim·u·lat·ing 1** temporarily increase the internal activity of some part of the body: *Coffee stimulates the central nervous system.* **2** encourage interest or activity in a person or animal: *Praise stimulated her to work hard.* <Latin *stimulare*, from *stimulus* goad> **stim′u·la′ting** *adj.* **stim′u·la′ting·ly** *adv.* **stim′u·la′tion** *n.* **stim′u·la′tive** *adj.* **stim′u·la′tor** *n.*

stim·u·lus (stim′yə ləs) *n, pl* **stim·u·li** (-lī) *or* (-lē) **1** an external or internal event that makes an organ or tissue of the body have a functional reaction: *One area of the brain reacted to auditory stimulus.* **2** a thing that rouses activity or energy in someone or something: *The tax cut proved to be a stimulus to exports.*

sting (sting) *v* **stung, sting·ing 1** pierce with a small, sharp-pointed organ at the end of the abdomen of bees, wasps, ants, and scorpions so as to inflict a painful or dangerous wound by injecting poison. **2** feel or cause to feel a sharp tingling or burning pain or sensation: *Her eyes stung when she heard the news.* **3** hurt or upset someone: *Her harsh words stung him.* **4** swindle or overcharge someone: *They stung me with huge interest charges.*
n **1** a small, sharp-pointed organ at the end of the abdomen of bees, wasps, ants, and scorpions that can inflict a wound and inject poison. See COMPOUND EYE (of a bee) for picture. **2** a tiny hair or other organ of some plants and jellyfish that injects a poisonous or irritating fluid when touched. **3** a hurtful quality or effect: *The ball team felt the sting of defeat.* **4** *Informal* a carefully planned operation that involves deception. <Old English *stingan*> **sting′ing** *adj.* **sting′ing·ly** *adv.* **sting′less** *adj.*

a bat	e bed	i bid	o pot	u cup	th **thin**
ā cake	ē me	ī bite	ō go	ū rude	ᴛʜ **then**
ȧ bar	ə about	ər over	ȯ for	u̇ put	zh measure

S

sting·er (sting′ər) *n* an insect or animal that stings, or the part of the insect or animal that holds a sting.

sting·ray (sting′rā) *n* a broad, flat, diamond-shaped fish that lives on the bottom of the sea and can inflict severe wounds with the sharp spines on its tail.

stin·gy (stin′jē) *adj* **stin·gi·er, stin·gi·est** not generous about spending, lending, or giving money: *She tried to save money without being stingy.* **stin′gi·ly** *adv.* **stin′gi·ness** *n.*

stink (stingk) *v* **stank** or **stunk, stunk, stink·ing 1** have or cause to have a strong unpleasant smell: *The rotting fish stank. The leaking gas stank up the room.* **2** be very unpleasant, worthy of contempt, or scandalous.
n **1** a strong, unpleasant smell. **2** *Informal* a fuss or spell of being strongly upset: *He raised a stink about the lack of pencils.* <Old English *stincan* to smell>
stink out, drive out with stinking smoke or fumes.

stink bomb *n* a glass container holding a sulphurous compound that releases a strong, unpleasant smell when the glass is broken.

stink·bug (stingk′bug′) *n* a plant-eating insect with two pairs of wings and a disagreeable smell.

stink·er (sting′kər) *n* **1** a person who or thing that smells bad. **2** a very bad or unpleasant person.

stink·ing (sting′king) *adj* **1** with a strong unpleasant smell. **2** *Informal* very bad or unpleasant: *I don't want to go to his stinking pool party.*
adv extremely: *stinking rich.*

stink·weed (stingk′wēd′) *n* a plant of the mustard family that has white flowers and irregularly notched leaves that give off an unpleasant odour when crushed.

stint (stint) *v* **1** supply an unduly small or inadequate supply of something: *They stinted themselves of food to give it to their friends.* **2** be very economical about spending or providing something: *He didn't stint himself on having a good time.*
n **1** a person's fixed or allotted period of work: *Before he got his present job, he had a stint as a carpenter.* **2** a limitation of time or effort: *He was able to indulge his tastes without stint.* <Old English *styntan* blunt>

sti·pend (stī′pend) *n* a fixed regular sum paid as a salary or as expenses to someone, especially a member of the clergy, a teacher, or a public official. <Latin *stips* wages + *pendere* weigh out>

stip·ple (stip′əl) *v* **stip·pled, stip·pling** paint, draw, or engrave by marking a surface with many small dots or specks.
n the process or technique of stippling a surface, or the effect so created. <Dutch *stip* point>

stip·u·late (stip′yə lāt′) *v* **stip·u·lat·ed, stip·u·lat·ing** demand or specify a requirement, usually as part of a bargain or agreement. <Latin *stipulari*> **stip′u·la′tion** *n.* **stip′u·la′tor** *n.*

stip·ule (stip′yūl) *n* a small leaflike part at the base of a leaf stem.

stir (stər) *v* **stirred, stir·ring 1** move a spoon or other implement around in a liquid or other substance in order to mix it thoroughly: *Stir the soup, please.* **2** move or begin to move slightly: *The leaves stirred in the maples.* **3** arouse strong feelings in someone: *Her words stirred him to resentment.* **4** begin or cause to be active or to develop: *The cheers of the crowd stirred the team to new efforts.*
n **1** a slight physical movement: *a stir in the bushes.* **2** a fuss or commotion: *The arrival of the queen caused a great stir.* **3** an act of mixing food or drink with a spoon or other implement: *She gave her hot chocolate a stir.* <Old English *styrian*> **stir′rer** *n.*
stir up, cause or provoke trouble or bad feeling: *to stir up a mutiny.*

SYNONYMS

Stir suggests a disturbance, especially when things have been quiet: *Just then I heard a stir in the bushes.*

Bustle means "noisy or excited activity": *There was a bustle in the room as they set up the table and chairs.*

Flurry means "sudden excitement, confusion, or disturbance": *You can expect a flurry in the audience when he appears on the stage.*

stir–cra·zy (stər′krā′zē) *Informal adj* mentally upset as a result of long confinement or many restrictions: *After two days of being cooped up inside by the rain, the kids were nearly stir-crazy.* <origin uncertain>

stir–fry (stər′frī′) *v* **stir-fried, stir-fry·ing** cook food in small chunks by frying briefly in a wok with oil while stirring briskly.
n a dish prepared in this way: *I had the vegetable stir-fry.*

stir·ring (stər′ing) *adj* causing great excitement or strong emotion: *stirring times, a stirring speech.* **stir′ring·ly** *adv.*

stir·rup (stər′əp) *or* (stir′əp) *n* **1** each of a pair of foot supports that hang from the sides of a saddle: *The rider stood up in her stirrups.* **2** a piece resembling a stirrup used as a support or clamp. **3** the **stapes**, the innermost of three small bones in the middle ear. See also ANVIL, HAMMER. <Old English *stige* climbing + *rap* rope>

stitch (stich) *n* **1** a loop of thread or yarn resulting from a single pass or movement of the needle in sewing, knitting, or crocheting. **2** a particular method of making stitches: *a buttonhole stitch.* **3** a loop of thread used to join the edges of a wound or surgical incision: *The doctor will take the stitches out tomorrow.* **4** *Informal* a small bit: *She didn't have a stitch to wear.* **5** a sudden, sharp pain in the side of the body, caused by strenuous exercise.
v make, mend, or join something with stitches: *She stitched his shirt. The doctor stitched the cut.* <Old English *stice* puncture> **stitch′er** *n.*
in stitches, laughing uncontrollably.

stitch·ing (stich′ing) *n* **1** the action or work of one who stitches. **2** a row of stitches sewn onto cloth.

stoat (stōt) *n* a small carnivorous mammal of the weasel family that has chestnut fur with white underparts and a black-tipped tail.

stock (stok) *n* **1** a supply of goods or equipment regularly kept on hand for sale or for use as needed: *The store has* *already received most of its spring stock. We keep a stock of canned foods at the cottage in case of emergency.* **2** cattle or other farm animals: *purebred Jersey stock.* **3 a** the money raised by a business or corporation through the issue and sale of shares: *The value of the company's stock declined in the past year.* **4 b stocks** *pl* a portion of this as held by an individual or group as an investment: *He invested in stocks and in real estate.* **5** liquid in which pieces of meat, fish, or vegetables have been cooked, used as a base for soups and sauces: *chicken stock.* **6** a person's ancestry or line of descent: *She is of Loyalist stock.* **7** a part used as a support or handle, such as of a rifle or whip. **8** in former times, a stiff white band of cloth worn around the neck by men. **9** the repertoire of plays produced by a company at a single theatre. **10** a plant of the mustard family that has fragrant flowers. **11 the stocks** *pl* a wooden frame with holes for the feet and, sometimes, for the hands, into which people in former times were locked in public as a punishment.

v **1** have a supply of a particular type of product available for sale: *The supermarket stocked several kinds of lettuce.* **2** provide or fill with things or a supply of something: *The pond was stocked with trout. They stocked up on firewood for the winter.*

adj **1** usually kept in stock and thus regularly available for sale: *I wear a stock shoe size.* **2** commonplace: *a stock response.* <Old English *stocc*>

in (out of) stock, available (not available) for sale or use.

take stock, make an estimate or examination: *We decided to stop and take stock of our situation before continuing.*

take stock in, take an interest in or consider important: *She takes no stock in his promises.*

stock·ade (sto kād′) *n* a defensive enclosure made of large, strong, upright posts placed closely together in the ground, or the fort or camp surrounded by it.

v **stock·ad·ed, stock·ad·ing** protect, fortify, or surround with a stockade. <Spanish *estaca* a post>

stock·bro·ker (stok′brō′kər) *n* a person who buys and sells stocks and bonds for others.

stock car *n* an automobile of a standard make that has been altered in various ways for use in racing.

stock character *n* in fiction, a stereotyped character whose nature is familiar from previous literature. Example: the beautiful girl who will overcome all disadvantages and marry a prince.

stock exchange *n* **1** a building or other place where stocks and bonds are bought and sold. **2** the prices offered for stocks and bonds in general: *The stock exchange fell today.* Also called **stock market.**

stock·hold·er (stok′hōl′dər) *n* an owner of shares in a company.

stock·ing (stok′ing) *n* **1** a knitted fabric covering that fits the foot and leg. **2** a thing suggesting a stocking, especially a patch of different colour on the leg of an animal: *The horse was brown with a white mark on the forehead and white stockings.* <obsolete *stock* a stocking>

in your stocking feet, wearing socks or stockings but no shoes: *The kids stood around in their stocking feet.*

stocking cap *n* a TUQUE (def. 1).

stock–in–trade (stok′in trād′) *n* **1** the typical subject or goods a person, company, or profession uses or deals in: *Footwear was the store's stock-in-trade.* **2** qualities, ideas, or behaviour typical of a person or an occupation: *His stock-in-trade is a rumpled look and a charming smile that audiences love.*

stock market STOCK EXCHANGE.

stock·pile (stok′pīl′) *n* a supply of goods or materials, especially one built up and held in reserve in case of a shortage or emergency: *a stockpile of canned goods.*

v **stock·piled, stock·pil·ing** collect or bring together such a reserved supply: *to stockpile bottled water.*

stock·pot (stok′pot′) *n* a pot in which soup stock is prepared: *They keep all leftover bones for the stockpot.*

stock·room (stok′rüm′) *n* a room where goods or materials are kept.

stock–still (stok′stil′) *adj* motionless: *She stood stock-still and listened.*

stock·tak·ing (stok′tā′king) *n* the action or process of checking the supply of goods on hand: *The store will be closed two days for stocktaking.*

stock·y (stok′ē) *adj* **stock·i·er, stock·i·est** with a solid, sturdy, somewhat thick form or build: *a stocky child.* **stock′i·ly** *adv.* **stock′i·ness** *n.*

stock·yard (stok′yärd′) *n* a large yard with pens and sheds for cattle, sheep, hogs, and horses.

stodg·y (stoj′ē) *adj* **stodg·i·er, stodg·i·est 1** heavy, starchy, and filling as food. **2** dull or uninteresting: *a stodgy style of writing.* **3** heavily built and slow moving: *A stodgy figure came lumbering through the fog.* <*stodge* stuff, origin unknown> **stodg′i·ly** *adv.* **stodg′i·ness** *n.*

sto·gie or **sto·gy** (stō′gē) *n, pl* **sto·gies** a long, slender, cheap cigar.

ETYMOLOGY

Stogie is a shortened form of *Conestoga*, a rural area in Pennsylvania, and the name of a type of horse-drawn covered wagon originally built in the region. The drivers of these wagons are said to have been avid smokers of these cigars.

sto·ic (stō′ik) *n* a person who can endure pain and hardship without showing feelings or making complaints.

adj having such a personality. <Greek *stoa* porch, in reference to the porch in Athans where such doctrines were taught> **sto′i·cal** *adj.* **sto′i·cal·ly** *adv.* **sto′i·cism** (stō′i siz əm) *n.*

stoke (stōk) *v* **stoked, stok·ing 1** add coal or other solid fuel to a fire, furnace, or boiler. **2** encourage a strong emotion or tendency: *Her harsh words stoked his anger.* <Dutch *stoken*>

a bat	e bed	i bid	o pot	u cup	th **thin**
ā cake	ē me	ī bite	ō go	ū rude	ᴛʜ **then**
ä bar	ə about	ər over	ȯ for	u̇ put	zh measure

stok·er (stō′kər) *n* **1** a person who tends the fires of a furnace or boiler. **2** a mechanical device for supplying fuel to a furnace or boiler.

STOL short takeoff and landing, used of an aircraft.

stole[1] (stōl) past tense of STEAL.

stole[2] (stōl) *n* **1** a woman's long, wide scarf or wrap worn around the shoulders with the ends usually hanging down in front: *a knitted stole.* **2** a long, narrow strip of silk or other material worn around the neck by a member of the clergy during certain church functions. <Greek *stole* robe>

sto·len (stō′lən) past participle of STEAL.

stol·id (stol′id) *adj* calm, dependable, and showing little emotion: *Her stolid presence was a comfort during the uproar.* <Latin *stolidus* immovable> **sto·lid′i·ty** *n.* **stol′id·ly** *adv.* **stol′id·ness** *n.*

sto·lon (stō′lon) *n* **1** a slender horizontal branch growing from the base of a plant that takes root at the tip and produces a new plant. **2** a stemlike growth, as in certain polyps, that produces buds from which new individuals grow. <Latin *stolonis* a shoot>

sto·ma (stō′mə) *n, pl* **sto·ma·ta** **1** a tiny slit in the surface of a leaf or stem of a plant through which gases pass in and out. **2** a small, mouthlike opening in some lower animals. <Greek = mouth>

stom·ach (stum′ək) *n* **1** a large internal organ, the part of the alimentary canal in humans and many mammals in which the first stage of digestion takes place. **2** an internal organ in an invertebrate animal that has a similar function. **3** the lower part of the front of the body between the chest and thighs: *He was hit in the stomach.* **4** an appetite for food or drink: *She had no stomach for dinner.* **5** a desire for or acceptance of something involving conflict, difficulty, or unpleasantness: *I had no stomach for a fight.*
v **1** consume food or drink without feeling or being sick: *She can't stomach spinach.* **2** endure or accept something or someone unpleasant: *I can't stomach arrogance.* <Greek *stoma* mouth>

stom·ach·ache (stum′ə kāk′) *n* a steady pain in the abdomen.

stom·ach·er (stum′ə kər) *n* a stiff, V-shaped, often elaborately decorated piece of cloth, in former times worn over the chest and stomach.

stomp (stomp) *v* tread heavily and noisily, especially in order to show anger or to apply force: *He stomped out of the room. She stomped on the accelerator.* <stamp>

stomping ground *Informal n* a place that one regularly visits, uses, or moves around in: *This neighbourhood was her old stomping ground.*

stone (stōn) *n* **1 a** the hard, solid, non-metallic mineral substance of which rock is made, especially as a building material. **b** a small piece of this material. **c** a piece of this material shaped for a particular purpose: *Her grave is marked by a fine stone.* **2** a gem or jewel: *The queen's diamonds were very fine stones.* **3** something hard and rounded like a stone, such as a kidney stone in the body. **4** a hard seed in fruits such as peaches. **5** *UK* a nonmetric unit of weight, equal to about 6.35 kg. **6** a curling stone.
v **stoned, ston·ing** **1** throw stones at: *The angry mob stoned the police.* **2** remove the stone from a fruit: *to stone olives.* <Old English *stan*> **stone′like′** *adj.*
a stone's throw, a short distance.
cast the first stone, be the first to criticize, though the person doing so may not be blameless.
leave no stone unturned, do everything that can be done.

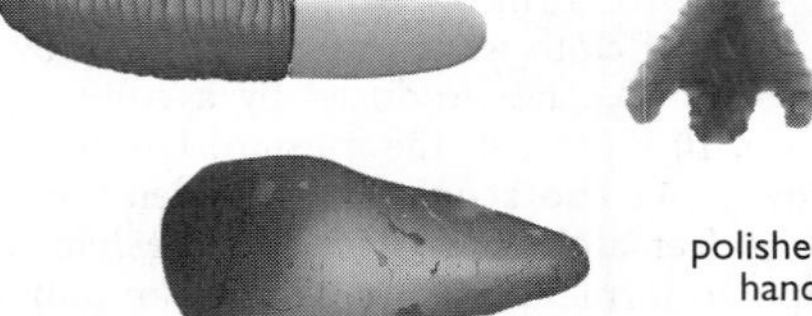

Stone Age *n* the earliest known period of human culture, about 2.5 million years ago, during which tools and weapons were made of stone.

stone·boat (stōn′bōt′) *n* a flat-bottomed sled used for transporting stones taken from fields and for other heavy hauling.

stone cold *adj* completely cold: *By the time he got back, his soup was stone cold.*

stone·cut·ter (stōn′kut′ər) *n* a person who cuts or carves stone.

stoned (stōnd) *adj* **1** with the stone removed from a fruit: *stoned peaches.* **2** *Informal* under the influence of drugs, especially marijuana.

stone dead *adj* completely dead.

stone deaf *adj* totally deaf.

stone·ground (stōn′ground′) *adj* ground into flour with millstones.

stone·ma·son (stōn′mā′sən) *n* a person who cuts, prepares, or builds with stone.

✱ **Stone sheep** *n* a dark brown or black wild sheep, found in the mountains of northern British Columbia and adjacent parts of Yukon Territory. Also, **Stone's sheep**. <A.J. *Stone*, 19c sportsman and naturalist>

stone·wall (stōn′wol′) *v* delay or block a request, process, or person by refusing to answer questions or by giving evasive replies: *The politician managed to stonewall the investigation.* **stone′wall′er** *n.* **stone′wall′ing** *n.*

stone·ware (stōn′wer′) *n* a form of coarse, hard, glazed pottery.

stone·work (stōn′wərk′) *n* work done in stone, especially the part of a building made of stone. **stone′work′er** *n.*

Ston·ey (stō′nē) NAKOTA.

ston·y (stō′nē) *adj* **ston·i·er, ston·i·est** **1** covered with or full of small pieces of rock: *a stony beach.* **2** made of or resembling stone: *a stony floor.* **3** without feeling or sympathy: *a stony stare.* **ston′i·ly** *adv.* **ston′i·ness** *n.*

ston·y·heart·ed (stō′nē här′təd) *adj* pitiless and unfeeling.

stood (stůd) past tense and past participle of STAND.

stooge (stūj) *Informal n* **1** a person who serves merely to support or assist others, particularly in doing unpleasant work. **2** a person on the stage who asks questions of a comedian and is the butt of jokes.
v **stooged, stoog·ing** be or act as a stooge.

stook (stůk) *n* an upright arrangement of sheaves or bales of grain intended to speed up drying in the field: *stooks of wheat.*
v arrange in stooks. <Middle English *stouke*>

stool (stūl) *n* **1** a seat for one person, without back or arms and supported on three or four legs or a central pedestal. **2** a low bench used to rest the feet on or to kneel on. **3** waste matter from the bowels. <Old English *stol*> **stool′-like′** *adj.*

stool pigeon *Informal n* a spy for the police, or an informer.

stoop[1] (stūp) *v* **1** bend one's head or body forward and downward: *to stoop over a desk.* **2** regularly carry the head and shoulders bent forward: *She stooped when she walked.* **3** lower oneself from a superior position, or lower one's moral standards so far as to do something wrong: *She would not stoop to speak to anyone she thought to be an inferior. He stooped to cheating in order to get higher grades.*
n **1** a posture in which the head and shoulders are regularly bent forward: *She walks with a noticeable stoop.* **2** the downward swoop of a bird of prey. <Old English *stupian*> **stoop′er** *n.*

stoop[2] (stūp) *n* a porch with steps in front of a house or other building. <Dutch *stoep*>

stop (stop) *v* **stopped, stop·ping 1** come to an end as an event, action, or process: *The rain abruptly stopped and the skies cleared.* **2** cause something to come to an end: *He stopped writing letters to his family.* **3** block or close a hole, leak, or opening: *to stop a bottle. He tried to stop the leak by packing mud into it.* **4** stay in a place for a period of time: *Will you be stopping long?* **5** prevent something from happening: *We tried to stop any further raids.* **6** regularly call as a bus or train at a particular place in order to let off and pick up passengers. **7** defeat by a knockout in boxing. **8 a** close a finger hole of a wind instrument or plug the upper end of an organ pipe in order to produce a particular note. **b** press down a string of a stringed instrument in order to alter the pitch of the tone.
n **1** an ending of movement or operation: *We put a stop to his tricks.* **2** a break or halt during a journey: *We made a stop for lunch.* **3** a place where bus or train passengers are let off and picked up. **4** an object or a part of a machine that is used to prevent something from moving. **5** a knob, lever, or similar device in an organ or other musical instrument that brings into play a set of pipes or strings of a particular tone and range of pitch. **6** a consonant produced when the vocal tract is suddenly closed. Examples: *p, t, k, b, d,* and *g* as in *go.* <Greek *styppe*> **stop′pa·ble** *adj.*
pull out all the stops, do something in the biggest way possible; exert maximum effort.
put a stop to, cause an activity to end.
stop at nothing, be ruthless or determined in an attempt to achieve something.
stop off, *Informal* stop for a short stay.
stop over, a make a short stay. **b** stop in the course of a journey.

stop–and–go (stop′ən gō′) *adj* moving or progressing very slowly, with frequent stops.

stop·cock (stop′kok′) *n* an externally operated valve for regulating the flow of a gas or liquid through a pipe.

stop·gap (stop′gap′) *n* a temporary way of dealing with a problem or satisfying a need, or something used to do this: *He realized the patch was only a stopgap, and that he'd have to repair the tire.*

stop·light (stop′līt′) *n* a set of traffic lights.

stop·o·ver (stop′ō′vər) *n* a break in a journey, or the place where the journey is broken.

stop·page (stop′ij) *n* **1** the act of movement, activity, or supply stopping or being stopped: *a work stoppage.* **2** a blockage in a narrow passage, such as in a pipe or artery.

stop·per (stop′ər) *n* **1** a plug or cork for closing a bottle, tube, or container. **2** a person who or thing that brings something to a halt or causes something to stop functioning. **3** *Baseball* a pitcher who is relied on to stop an opposing team from scoring.
v close or fit with a stopper.

stop·watch (stop′woch′) *n* a watch with a hand that can be stopped or started at any instant, often used to time races.

stor·age (stȯ′rij) *n* **1** the action or method of storing something for future use: *easy storage.* **2** a place or space for storing something: *She put her furniture in storage. This house has very little storage.* **3** the cost of storing something. **4** *Computers* the retention of retrievable data on a computer or other electronic system.

store (stȯr) *n* **1** a place where goods are kept for sale: *a clothing store.* **2** a quantity or supply of something kept for use as needed: *a store of knowledge. She puts up stores of preserves and jellies every year.* **3** a place where supplies are kept for future use.
v **stored, stor·ing 1** keep, put away, or accumulate something for future use: *During summer, we store our winter clothes in boxes.* **2** retain or enter information for future electronic retrieval: *We stored our data on a CD.* <Old French *estorer*> **stor′er** *n.*
in store, in a safe place while not being used or displayed.
mind the store, look after or keep an eye on things.
set store by, consider something to be of importance or value: *She sets great store by her mother's opinion.*

store–bought (stȯr′bot′) *adj* bought at a store instead of being homemade.

store·front (stȯr′frunt′) *n* **1** the front of a store or shop: *All the storefronts were newly painted.* **2** a room or set of rooms facing the street on the ground floor and used for a business, agency, or organization.
adj operating a storefront business or service: *a storefront lawyer.*

a bat	e bed	i bid	o pot	u cup	th thin
ā cake	ē me	ī bite	ō go	ū rude	TH then
à bar	ə about	ər over	ȯ for	ů put	zh measure

store·house (stôr′hous′) *n* **1** a building used for storing goods. **2** an abundant supply or source: *She is a storehouse of knowledge.*

store·keep·er (stôr′kē′pər) *n* a person who is in charge of a store or stores: *My uncle was a country storekeeper.*

store·room (stôr′rüm′) *n* a room in which things are stored.

store·wide (stôr′wīd′) *adj* involving all or most of the departments of a store: *a storewide sale.*

sto·rey (stô′rē) *n, pl* **sto·reys** a level or floor of a house or other building, or the set of rooms or apartments on it: *We lived on the second storey of the house.* <origin uncertain>

CONFUSABLES

Storey means "floor of a building": *The new building will have twenty storeys.*

Story can mean "narrative" or "anecdote": *She told us a funny story about trying to find her lost keys.*

sto·ried (stô′rēd) *adj* celebrated in story or history: *a storied river.*

stork (stôrk) *n* a large, long-legged wading bird with a long neck and a long, heavy bill. <Old English *storc*> **stork′like′** *adj.*

storm (stôrm) *n* **1** a violent disturbance of the atmosphere with strong winds and usually rain, thunder, lightning, or snow: *The clouds threatened an approaching storm.* **2** a wind of force 10 (88–102 km/h). See GALE for confusable. **3** a heavy discharge of arrows, missiles, or blows. **4** a violent outburst or disturbance: *a storm of tears, a storm of angry words.* **5** a sudden attack on a building or other place. **6** a violent or noisy reaction or uproar: *a storm of controversy.* **7** ✱ **storms** *pl* storm windows.
v **1** have strong winds and usually rain, thunder, lightning, or snow: *It stormed for three days.* **2** move angrily or forcefully in a specified direction: *She stormed out of the room.* **3** suddenly attack and capture a building or other place: *The troops stormed the city.* <Old English>
storm in a teacup, great excitement or commotion over something unimportant.

storm·bound (stôrm′bound′) *adj* prevented from travelling or kept indoors by a storm.

storm cellar *n* a cellar for shelter during a hurricane, tornado, or severe storm.

storm centre or **center** *n* **1** the central point around which controversy or trouble happens. **2** the moving centre of a cyclone, where the pressure is lowest and the wind is comparatively calm.

storm door *n* an extra door fixed outside a regular door as protection against bad weather or winter cold.

storm petrel *n* a small, black-and-white seabird of the open ocean, formerly believed to give warning of an impending storm.

storm·proof (stôrm′prüf′) *adj* not likely to be damaged by storms, or providing protection from them.
v treat or prepare a thing so it will not be affected by storms.

storm·watch (stôrm′woch′) *n* a close observation of and updated reporting on the arrival or progress of a storm.

storm window *n* an extra window fixed on the outside of a regular window as protection and insulation in bad weather or winter.

storm·y (stôr′mē) *adj* **storm·i·er, storm·i·est** **1** marked, created, or influenced by strong winds and usually rain, thunder, lightning, or snow: *a stormy sea, stormy weather, a stormy night.* **2** full of angry or violent outbursts of feeling: *They had stormy quarrels.* **storm′i·ly** *adv.* **storm′i·ness** *n.*

✱ **Storn·o·way** (stor′nə wā′) *n* the official residence of the Leader of the Opposition in Ottawa.

stor·y (stô′rē) *n, pl* **sto·ries** **1 a** an account of an event or group of events: *Tell us the story of your life.* **b** such an account, either true or made-up, written or told for others to read or hear: *a ghost story, an adventure story.* **2** *Informal* a false statement or explanation: *That's just a story, and I don't believe a word of it.* **3** the plot of a play, novel, or script. **4** a journalistic account, especially in a newspaper article. **5** a particular representation of facts, especially as a form of self-defence: *He said he was sick yesterday; that's his story anyway.* See STOREY for confusable. <Greek *historia*>
another (or **a different**) **story,** a completely different matter or thing.
make (or **cut**) **a long story short,** get to the main point.
the same old story, the same tiresome routine, excuse, or pattern of behaviour.

SYNONYMS

Story refers to any account, true or fictional, of an event or group of events: *She told us her life story, and it wasn't very interesting.*

Legend refers to a revered story from the past that may not be true: *We found the legend inspiring.*

Tale often implies a story told as true but usually made up or exaggerated: *That was quite a tale you told about your fishing trip.*

sto·ry·board (stô′rē bōrd′) *n* a large board or series of panels with a sequence of sketches on them showing the shots planned for a movie or TV production.
v make such a board or series of panels.

sto·ry·book (stô′rē bük′) *n* a book containing one or more stories or tales, especially for children.
adj of or like that of a storybook: *a storybook hero, a storybook ending.*

story grammar *n* the structure of a story, described in terms of features such as setting, character, events, problem, and solution.

sto·ry·line (stor′ē līn′) *n* the main plot or action of a story.

sto·ry·tell·er (stô′rē tel′ər) *n* a person who tells stories. **sto′ry·tel′ling** *n.*

stout (stout) *adj* **1** somewhat fat or of heavy build: *He's getting stout.* **2** strong and thick: *the stout walls of a fort.* **3** brave and determined: *He has a stout heart.*
n a strong, dark brown beer brewed with roasted malt. <Old French *estout* bold> **stout′ly** *adv.* **stout′ness** *n.*

stout–heart·ed (stout′hår′tid) *adj* brave and determined. **stout′-heart′ed·ly** *adv.*

stove[1] (stōv) *n* an apparatus for cooking or heating, using electricity or burning a fuel such as gas, oil, or wood. <Old English *stofa* warm bathing room>

stove[2] (stōv) a past tense and past participle of STAVE.

stove·pipe (stōv′pīp′) *n* a sheet-metal pipe of large diameter connected to a fuel-burning stove, used to carry smoke and gases up through the roof or a chimney.

stow (stō) *v* pack or store an object or objects carefully and neatly in a particular place: *The cargo was stowed in the ship's hold.* <Old English *stow* place> **stow′er** *n.*
stow away, hide on a ship, aircraft, or passenger vehicle to travel secretly or to avoid paying the fare.

stow·age (stō′ij) *n* **1** the action of stowing or being stowed: *The stowage of all their equipment took them two hours.* **2** a room, space, or place for stowing: *The boat has stowage fore and aft.*

stow·a·way (stō′ə wā′) *n* a person who hides on a ship, aircraft, or passenger vehicle to travel secretly or to avoid paying the fare.

stra·bis·mus (strə biz′məs) *n* a disorder of vision due to the turning of one eye or both eyes from the normal position, so that both eyes cannot be directed at the same point or object at the same time. <Greek *strabos* squint-eyed>

strad·dle (strad′əl) *v* **strad·dled, strad·dling** **1** sit or stand with one's legs on either side of a thing or wide apart: *He straddled the chair.* **2** be or lie across something: *A footbridge straddled the brook. A pair of large glasses straddled her nose.* **3** avoid committing oneself on an issue, or appear to favour both sides: *She is still straddling the question, but will soon have to decide one way or the other.*
n the act or position of a person who straddles. <Middle English stridlen> **strad′dler** *n.*

Strad·i·var·i·us (strad′ə ver′ē əs) *n* a violin or other stringed instrument made by Antonio Stradivari, 1644–1737, an Italian violin maker.

strafe (strāf) *v* **strafed, straf·ing** attack repeatedly with bombs or machine guns from low-flying aircraft. <German *strafen* punish>

strag·gle (strag′əl) *v* **strag·gled, strag·gling** **1** move along slowly and in a scattered way: *Cows straggled along the lane.* **2** spread in an irregular, rambling manner: *Vines straggled over the old wall.* <*stray* and *draggle*>
strag′gler *n.* **strag′gly** *adj.*

straight (strāt) *adj* **1** extending or moving uniformly in one direction only: *a straight line, a straight path.* **2** positioned so as to be level, upright, or symmetrical: *Is that picture straight?* **3** honest and direct: *a straight answer.* **4** in proper order or condition. **5** continuous and in sequence: *in straight succession, a straight flush.* **6** unmodified or undiluted: *a straight comedy.* **7** heterosexual.
adv **1** directly: *Walk straight. He went straight home.* **2** in or into a level, even, or upright position: *Stand up straight.* **3** correctly or clearly: *For the first time I was able to think straight.* **4** continuously: *Drive straight on.* **5** honestly and directly: *I told him straight that I wasn't going.*
n **1** a straight part of something, especially the concluding stretch of a racetrack. **2** a sequence of five cards in the game of poker. See STRAIT for confusable. <Old English *streccan* stretch> **straight′ish** *adj.* **straight′ly** *adv.* **straight′ness** *n.*
set someone straight, correct someone.
straight off (or **out**)**,** directly and immediately: *She told us straight off that she wasn't interested.*
straight up, without ice in an alcoholic drink.
the straight and narrow, correct moral principles.

SYNONYMS

Straight means "not bent": A *straight road leads directly from the gates to the main building.*

Aligned means "arranged in a straight line": *The pigeons were aligned along the edge of the roof.*

Direct can mean "without a stop" and often suggests the shortest or most convenient way: *You can take a direct flight from Vancouver to Toronto, or you can make a stopover in Calgary.*

straight angle *n* an angle of 180°.

straight–arm (strā′tårm′) *v* ward off an opponent or remove an obstacle with the arm unbent.
n the action of straight-arming.

straight arrow *n* an honest, upright person.

straight·a·way (strā′tə wā′) *n* a straight section of a road or racetrack: *They were now on a straightaway, making excellent time.*
adv as quickly as possible: *The captain read the letter then destroyed it straightaway.*

straight·edge (strā′tej′) *n* a strip of wood or metal with one edge accurately straight, used in obtaining or testing straight lines and level surfaces.

straight·en (strā′tən) *v* **1** make or become straight: *Straighten your shoulders.* **2** (*usually with* ***up*** *or* ***out***) put in the proper order or condition: *He straightened up his room. We have to straighten out our accounts to see how much we owe.* **3** *Informal* (*usually with* ***out***) make or become better morally: *His parents have tried to straighten him out but he still keeps getting in trouble.*
straight′en·er *n.*

straight face *n* an expressionless face, especially one showing no trace of amusement: *She kept a straight face through the whole ridiculous story.* **straight′-faced′** *adj.*

straight·for·ward (strāt′fôr′wərd) *adj* **1** uncomplicated and easy to do or understand: *a straightforward plan.* **2** honest and frank: *a straightforward person, a straightforward answer.* **straight′for′ward·ly** *adv.* **straight′for′ward·ness** *n.*

straight man *n* an actor who feeds lines to a comedian, who then uses them to make jokes.

a bat	e bed	i bid	o pot	u cup	th thin
ā cake	ē me	ī bite	ō go	ū rude	ᴛʜ then
å bar	ə about	ər over	ô for	ů put	zh measure

S

straight shooter *Informal n* a person who speaks bluntly.

strain[1] (strān) *v* **1** force a part of the body or oneself to make a great effort, especially a continuous one: *She strained her eyes to see. The dog strained at its leash.* **2** injure a limb, muscle, or organ by overexerting it or twisting it awkwardly: *The runner strained his heart.* **3** make severe or undue demands on: *His story strained our belief.* **4** pour a mainly liquid substance through a material or device that allows only liquid to pass through, or cause liquid to drain off: *The soup was strained before it was served.*
n **1** a force tending to stretch something in an extreme or damaging way: *The strain on the rope made it break.* **2** an injury to the body caused by too much effort or by stretching. **3** a severe or undue demand on the strength, resources, or abilities of someone or something: *the strain of worry.* **4 strains** *pl* the sound of a piece of music as it is played or performed: *We could hear strains from the orchestra in the next room.* <Old French, from Latin *stringere* draw tight>

strain[2] (strān) *n* **1** a breed, stock, or variety of an animal or plant developed by breeding: *a strain of poultry.* **2** a natural or cultivated variety of micro-organism with a distinct form or quality: *a strain of bacteria.* **3** a particular tendency as part of the character of a person or thing: *There is a strain of musical talent in our family.* <Old English *streon*>

strained (strānd) *adj* **1** tense and uneasy: *a strained laugh. Their first meeting after the quarrel was strained.* **2** produced by deliberate effort rather than in a natural way: *The actor gave a strained performance.* **3** injured as a limb or muscle by undue effort or twisting: *a strained wrist.* **4** having been strained to separate a liquid from a solid: *strained soup.*

strain·er (strā′nər) *n* a utensil or device for straining, filtering, or sifting such as a sieve or colander.

strait (strāt) *n* **1** a narrow channel connecting two larger bodies of water. **2 straits** *pl* a situation or circumstance marked by a specified degree of trouble or difficulty: *He was in desperate straits for money.* <Old French *estreit* narrow, from Latin *strictus* drawn tight>

CONFUSABLES

Strait means "narrow channel": *The Cabot Strait links the Gulf of St. Lawrence with the Atlantic Ocean.*

Straight means "not bent": *We fastened the quilted layers together with straight pins, not safety pins.*

strait·en·ed (strā′tənd) *adj* **1** marked by poverty: *straitened circumstances.* **2** restricted or limited in range, scope, or amount: *straitened objectives.*

strait·jack·et (strāt′jak′ət) *n* **1** a strong, tightly fitting garment used to bind the arms in order to confine a violent prisoner or mental patient. **2** a thing that hampers or confines freedom of action, development, or expression: *a legal straitjacket.*
v confine in or as if in a straitjacket.

strait·laced (strāt′lāst′) *adj* with very strict moral attitudes.

strand[1] (strand) *v* leave something or someone without the means to move somewhere, especially as a boat, sailor, or animal driven or left on a shore: *The ship was stranded on the rocks. He was stranded a thousand kilometres from home with no money.*
n a shore of a sea, lake, or large river. <Old English>

strand[2] (strand) *n* **1** a single thin length of thread, fibre, strings, or wires that are twisted with others: *a rope of three strands.* **2** a string of beads or pearls. **3** an element that forms part of a complex whole: *There were several strands in his thought.* <Old French *estran*>

strange (strānj) *adj* **strang·er, strang·est 1** unusual or surprising that is unsettling or hard to understand: *It's strange that you didn't get the book, because I left it on your desk.* **2** not previously visited, seen, or encountered: *strange faces, a strange language.* **3** (*with* ***to***) unaccustomed to or unfamiliar with: *She made the mistake because she is still strange to the job.* <Old French *estrange,* from Latin *extraneus* foreign> **strange′ly** *adv.* **strange′ness** *n.*
feel strange, a feel out of place or awkward: *He still feels strange in his new school.* **b** feel ill: *She felt strange after eating the meal.*

stran·ger (strān′jər) *n* **1** a person not known, seen, or heard of before, especially such a person in a particular place or community: *He is a complete stranger to me. She is a stranger to these parts.* **2** (*with* ***to***) a person who or thing that is unaccustomed to a feeling, experience, or situation: *He is no stranger to hard work.*

stran·gle (strang′gəl) *v* **stran·gled, stran·gling 1** kill or try to kill by squeezing the throat to stop the breath: *The victim was strangled with a cord.* **2** suppress an impulse, action, or sound: *He strangled an impulse to laugh.* <Old French, from Greek *strangale* a halter> **stran′gler** *n.*

stran·gled (strang′gəld) *adj* sounding as though the speaker's throat is constricted: *a strangled laugh.*

stran·gle·hold (strang′gəl hōld′) *n* **1** a grip around the neck of another person that can kill by choking if held long enough. **2** a complete or overwhelming control: *One company had a stranglehold on the market.*

stran·gu·la·tion (strang′gyə lā′shən) *n* the act or fact of strangling or being strangled. **stran′gu·late′** *v.*

strap (strap) *n* a narrow strip of leather, cloth, or other material that bends easily and is often used to fasten, secure, or carry something: *She wore a dress with narrow shoulder straps.*
v **strapped, strap·ping 1** fasten or secure with a strap: *We strapped the trunk.* **2** punish by beating with a strap. <*strop*>

strap·hang·er (strap′hang′ər) *Informal n* a standing passenger in a bus, train, etc., holding on to a strap or bar.

strap·less (strap′lis′) *adj* with no shoulder straps as a dress or bra: *a strapless evening gown.*

strapped (strapt) *Informal adj* short of money: *I'm strapped, so I won't be able to go to the movie after all.*

strap·ping (strap′ing) *adj* tall, strong, and healthy: *a strapping lad.*

stra·ta (strā′tə) *or* (strat′ə) a plural of STRATUM.

strat·a·gem (strat′ə jəm) *n* a scheme or plan, especially one to outwit an opponent or achieve a purpose: *The general's stratagem was successful.* <See STRATEGY.>

stra·te·gic (strə tē′jik) *adj* **1** to do with identifying goals and the ways to achieve them: *a strategic move, a strategic location.* **2** carefully designed to serve a particular purpose or advantage: *Each part of the armed forces was a strategic link in national defence.* **3** especially trained or made as a long-term objective, for use in enemy territory: *a strategic bomber.* **stra·te′gi·cal·ly** *adv.*

strat·e·gist (strat′ə jist) *n* a person trained or skilled in planning action or policy, especially in war or politics. **strat′e·gize** *v.*

strat·e·gy (strat′ə jē) *n, pl* **strat·e·gies** **1** a plan of action designed to achieve a long-term or overall aim: *a reading strategy. She needed a new strategy to help her win the game.* **2** the art of planning and directing overall military operations and movements in a war or battle. <Greek *stratos* army + *agein* lead>

SYNONYMS

Strategy means "overall or long-term plan of action": *The government needs a different strategy to deal with the problem of pollution.*

Tactic refers to a specific procedure or scheme, usually to achieve a limited or short-term goal: *Their clever tactics won them the game.*

strat·i·fy (strat′ə fī′) *v* **strat·i·fied, strat·i·fy·ing** arrange, form, or deposit in layers or strata. **strat′i·fi·ca′tion** *n.*

stra·to·cu·mu·lus (strā′tō kyū′myə ləs) *or* (strat′ō kyū′myə ləs) *n* a cloud made up of large, dark, rounded heaps above a flat, horizontal base. See ALTOCUMULUS for picture.

strat·o·sphere (strat′ə sfēr′) *n* **1** the upper region of the earth's atmosphere, above the troposphere and extending from about ten to fifty kilometres above the earth. See OZONE LAYER for picture. **2** the highest levels of a profession or other area of activity, or of prices or other quantities: *Her exhibition launched her into the stratosphere of fashionable artists.* **strat′o·spher′ic** *adj.*

stra·tum (strā′təm) *or* (strat′əm) *n, pl* **stra·ta** (strā′ta) *or* (strat′a)**, stra·tums** **1** a layer or series of layers of rock in the ground: *a stratum of granite.* **2** a level or class to which people are assigned according to their social status, education, or income: *strata of society.* <Latin *sternere* spread out>

stra·tus (strā′təs) *or* (strat′əs) *n, pl* **stra·ti** (-tī) *or* (-tē) a low, horizontal layer of grey cloud that spreads over a large area, often with rain or snow. See ALTOCUMULUS for picture.

straw (stro) *n* **1** the stalks or stems of dried grain, especially as bedding for livestock, or as material for thatching, packing, or weaving, or one of these: *They spread straw across the yard. He chewed on a straw.* **2** a slender hollow tube made of waxed paper or plastic used for sucking up drinks from a glass or bottle. **3** something trivial or worthless: *She doesn't care a straw about what people think.*
adj made of straw: *a straw hat.* <Old English *streaw*>
a straw in the wind, a thing taken as an indication of a trend.
clutch (or **grasp**) **at straws,** try anything in desperation.
the last (or **final**) **straw,** something minor in itself that, added to other things, makes a situation intolerable.

straw·ber·ry (strob′er′ē) *n, pl* **straw·ber·ries** a soft, juicy, sweet red fruit whose surface is studded with small seeds. See BERRY for picture.

strawberry blond *adj* of hair, being a light reddish blond colour. See also BLOND.

strawberry mark *n* a small, reddish birthmark.

straw boss *Informal n* an assistant foreman or junior supervisor.

straw·flow·er (stro′flou′ər) *n* a flower of the daisy family with yellow, orange, red, or white papery flowers that can be dried for use in permanent bouquets.

straw man *n* **1** a weak opposing argument or view put forward by a speaker or writer so that it may be attacked. **2** a person who is set up as a cover or front for a questionable enterprise.

straw vote *n* an unofficial poll or vote taken to find out how a group of people feel about a particular candidate or issue. Also called **straw poll**.

stray (strā) *v* **1** move without a specific purpose or by mistake, especially so as to get lost or arrive in the wrong place: *We strayed several kilometres in the wrong direction.* **2** move the eyes or a hand idly or in a specified direction: *Her gaze strayed around the room as she listened.* **3** move so as to escape from control or a proper place.
adj **1** with no home or having wandered away from home as a domestic animal: *a stray cat.* **2** not where something should be or where other things of the same kind are: *There were a few stray hairs on the shoulders of his coat.* **3** arising as a consequence of the laws of physics, and usually with a harmful effect on the operation or efficiency of equipment.
n a person who or thing that has strayed, especially as a domestic animal. <Old French, from Latin *stratarius* roaming the street> **stray′er** *n.*

streak (strēk) *n* **1** a long, thin mark or line of a different substance or colour from its surroundings: *He has a streak of dirt on his face. We saw a streak of lightning. The bacon had streaks of fat and streaks of lean.* **2** an element of a specified kind in someone's character: *He has a streak of humour, though he looks very serious.* **3** *Informal* a continuous period of success or luck: *a winning streak.*
v **1** dye hair with long, thin, lines of a different colour, typically lighter than the natural hair: *She had her hair streaked blond.* **2** move very fast in a specified direction: *The horse streaked past the others and over the finish line.* **3** *Informal* run naked in a public place so as to shock or amuse others. <Old English *strica*>
like a (blue) streak, *Informal* very fast.

a bat	e bed	i bid	o pot	u cup	th thin
ā cake	ē me	ī bite	ō go	ū rude	ᴛʜ then
ä bar	ə about	ər over	ȯ for	u̇ put	zh measure

streak·y (strē′kē) *adj* **streak·i·er, streak·i·est 1** marked or occurring with streaks of different colours or textures: *The wall is streaky where the paint did not cover properly.* **2** varying or uneven in quality, character, or activity: *a streaky performance.* **streak′i·ly** *adv.* **streak′i·ness** *n.*

stream (strēm) *n* **1** a body of flowing water in a channel or bed, especially a narrow river or a brook: *Many streams dried up that summer because of lack of rain.* **2** a continuous flow of liquid, air, or gas: *A stream of water gushed from the runoff pipe.* **3** something resembling a stream in moving continuously in the same direction or happening or coming one after the other: *a stream of light, a stream of words, a stream of cars.* **4** *Computers* an Internet transfer that pushes a continuous flow of data, allowing the user access to files without having a long download time. Playing audio or video files in real time is called **streaming**.
v **1** run or flow in a continuous current in a specified direction: *The sunlight streamed in through the window. Tears streamed from his eyes.* **2** give off or produce a stream: *Her eyes streamed with tears. The wound streamed blood.* **3** be very wet; drip or run with water, etc.: *streaming windows, a streaming umbrella.* **4** extend or float at full length: *Her long hair streamed out behind her as she ran.* <Old English *stream*> **stream′like′** *adj.*

stream·er (strē′mər) *n* **1 a** a long, narrow, flowing strip of material used as a decoration, sign, or flag: *Streamers of ribbon hung from her hat.* **b** anything shaped like this: *streamers of snow off the lake.* **2** a newspaper headline that runs all the way across the page. **3** a fishing fly that has feathers attached to it.

stream·let (strēm′lit) *n* a small stream.

stream·line (strēm′līn′) *v* **stream·lined, stream·lin·ing 1** design or provide with a form that presents little resistance to a flow of air or water, increasing speed and ease of movement: *to streamline a car.* **2** make a system, procedure, or organization more efficient and effective by using faster or simpler working methods: *to streamline the curriculum.*
n a shape designed to offer as little resistance as possible for motion through air or water. **stream′lined′** *adj.*

stream of consciousness *n* **1** a person's thoughts and reactions, perceived as a continuous flow. **2** a technique in fiction writing in which a character's thoughts, feelings, and reactions are given in a continuous flow that is not interrupted by description or dialogue.

street (strēt) *n* **1** a public road in a small or large community, usually with sidewalks and buildings on one or both sides: *They live on a fashionable street.* **2** people who live in the buildings on a street: *The whole street was against the new bylaw.*
adj **1** of, on, or near the street: *The camera department is on the street level of the store.* **2** suitable for everyday wear in public: *She changed into her street clothes before leaving the hospital.* **3** without a home and forced to live on a street or other public place: *street kids.* <Latin *strata* paved>
on (or **in**) **the street,** homeless or without a job: *He was on the street for three months before he found another job. They'll be out in the street if they don't pay their rent soon.*

street·car (strēt′kär′) *n* an electrically powered vehicle that runs on rails on city streets and is used for public transportation.

🍁 **street hockey** *n* a kind of hockey played in the street rather than on ice, and using a ball instead of a puck. Also called **road hockey**.

street·light (strē′tlīt′) *n* a powerful light, usually mounted on a pole, that is one of a series used to light the streets of a community.

street people *n* people who are homeless or who spend most of their time wandering or loitering in the streets of a city.

street·proof (strēt′prūf′) *v* teach a child how to be safe when he or she is unsupervised outside.

street smarts *Informal n* with the skills and knowledge needed to deal with modern urban life, especially such factors as poverty and crime. **street′-smart′** *adj.*

street·walk·er (strēt′wok′ər) *n* a prostitute who seeks customers on the street. **street′walk·ing** *n.*

street·wise (strēt′wīz′) *adj* street-smart.

strength (strength) *n* **1** the quality or condition of being strong, whether of a body, inside a mind, or as a force or physical object: *She was someone of great strength, the strength of a rope, the strength of an argument.* **2** a good or beneficial quality of a person or thing: *Loyalty was her chief strength.* **3** the number of people comprising a group, typically a team or army, or the number of people required to make such a group complete: *The wartime strength of the army was only 20 000.* <Old English *strang* strong>
on the strength of, on the basis of: *I got the role on the strength of my audition.*

SYNONYMS

Strength refers to being strong mentally or physically: *Her strength is math.*

Force emphasizes the use of strength: *The force of the winds blew down many trees.*

Power often simply refers to the ability to do something: *Our leaders have the power to make major decisions about the future of society.*

strength·en (streng′thən) *v* make or become stronger: *The soldiers strengthened their defences. The reunion served to strengthen family ties.* **strength′en·er** *n.*

stren·u·ous (stren′yū əs) *adj* requiring or using much energy or effort: *We had a strenuous day moving into the new house. She was faced with strenuous opposition.* <Latin *strenuus*> **stren′u·ous·ly** *adv.* **stren′u·ous·ness** *n.*

strep (strep) *Informal n* streptococcus.

strep throat *Informal n* a throat infection caused by streptococci and marked by a sore and inflamed throat and, often, fever.

strep·to·coc·cus (strep′tə kok′əs) *n, pl* **strep·to·coc·ci** (-kok′sī) *or* (-kok′sē) a bacterium of a group that includes the agents of dental decay, as well as causing such infections as scarlet fever and pneumonia. <Greek *streptos* curved + *kokkos* grain>
strep′to·coc′cal (strep′tə kok′əl) *n.*

strep·to·my·cin (strep′tō mī′sən) *n* an antibiotic that was the first drug to be used successfully against tuberculosis and other infections.

stress (stres) *n* **1** force or pressure that produces physical or mental tension: *the stresses of modern life.* **2** a physical force exerted when one body pushes against, pulls, or twists another: *Stresses must be carefully balanced in building a bridge.* **3** a condition of mental or emotional strain or tension resulting from adverse or demanding circumstances: *Since she lost her home she's under a lot of stress.* **4** a particular emphasis or importance: *The teacher put a lot of stress on homework.* **5** emphasis given to a particular syllable or word in speech. In print, a heavy mark [**′**] indicates primary stress; a light mark [′] indicates secondary stress. Example: *en′ter·tain**′**ment*
v **1** give particular emphasis or importance to a point, statement, or idea: *They stressed the importance of safety rules.* **2** subject to pressure or tension: *The lifting stressed her shoulder joints.* **3** cause mental or emotional strain or tension in: *I used to be stressed by exams.* **4** pronounce with a stress: *The word "accept" is stressed on the second syllable.* <*distress*> **stress′ful** *adj.*
stressed out, *Informal* almost overcome by anxiety, tension, or other forms of stress.

stress·or (stres′ər) *n* any event or stimulus that causes stress to a person.

stress test *n* **1** a test conducted on a manufactured article to see how well it can withstand hard use. **2** a medical or fitness test measuring a person's heartbeat and blood pressure during strenuous exercise. **stress′-test′** *v.*

stretch (strech) *v* **1** make longer or wider without tearing or breaking, or cause to do this: *We were able to stretch the elastic quite a bit.* **2** extend from one place to another: *The forest stretches for many kilometres. We stretched the tape across the door.* **3** last or cause to last longer than expected: *The course stretched over several weeks.* **4** straighten or extend the body or a part of the body to its full length, especially so as to tighten the muscles or in order to reach something: *He stretched out his hand for the money. On getting up, she yawned and stretched.* **5** extend beyond proper limits: *He stretched the law to suit his own purpose.* **6** *Informal* exaggerate: *to stretch the truth.*
n **1** an act of stretching the arms, legs, or body, or the fact or condition of a muscle being stretched. **2** a continuous area or expanse of land or water: *a stretch of highway.* **3** a continuous period of time: *She spent a long stretch in Alberta.* **4** the straight part of a racetrack, between the last turn and the finish line: *the home stretch.*
adj modified in a motor vehicle or aircraft so as to have extended seating or storage: *a stretch limo.* <Old English *streccan*> **stretch′y** *adj.*
at a stretch, a without a break: *I can work for three hours at a stretch.* **b** if needed, but with difficulty: *I could do it in a month; or, at a stretch, three weeks.*

stretch·er (strech′ər) *n* **1** a frame with a canvas or similar covering and either wheels or carrying handles on which to move the sick, injured, or dead: *They took him out on a stretcher.* **2** a frame or other device for stretching a thing: *a glove stretcher.*

strew (strū) *v* **strewed, strewn** or **strewed, strew·ing** scatter or spread things untidily over a surface or area, or have things scattered or spread in this way: *The pages were strewn all over the floor. Litter strewed the sidewalk.* <Old English *streowian*>

stri·at·ed (strī ā′ tid) *adj* marked with a slight furrow, ridge, or groove on a surface, often one of similar parallel ones: *a striated muscle.* <Latin *stria* furrow> **stri·a′tion** *n.*

strick·en (strik′ən) *adj* **1** seriously affected by an undesirable condition or unpleasant feeling: *a stricken conscience.* **2** showing great distress: *a stricken face.*
v a past participle of STRIKE.

strict (strikt) *adj* **1** demanding that rules or orders are obeyed and followed: *Her parents were very strict.* **2** rigidly enforced: *strict rules.* **3** exact or closely conforming to something: *a strict translation. She wasn't trespassing in the strict sense of the word.* **4** complete or absolute: *The story was told to me in strict confidence, so I can't tell you.* <Latin *stringere* bind tight> **strict′ly** *adv.* **strict′ness** *n.*

SYNONYMS

Strict suggests care and consistency in following or enforcing rules: *The teacher was very strict.*

Rigid emphasizes a refusal or inability to change: *Don't be so rigid about what we should do tomorrow.*

Rigorous means "extremely thorough, painstaking, and accurate": *The company's engineers are rigorous when they test those racing cars.*

Stringent means "strict and precise": *He put himself on a stringent diet.*

stric·ture (strik′chər) *n* **1** a restriction on a person or activity: *The authorities imposed severe strictures on what could be brought into the country.* **2** a highly critical remark or instruction: *He had many strictures on how we behaved.* **3** an abnormal narrowing of a canal or duct in the body. <Latin *stingere* bind tight>

a bat	e bed	i bid	o pot	u cup	th thin
ā cake	ē me	ī bite	ō go	ū rude	TH then
ȧ bar	ə about	ər over	ȯ for	u̇ put	zh measure

S

stride (strīd) *v* **strode, strid·den, strid·ing** **1** walk with long confident steps in a specified direction, or walk along a street or other place in this way: *She strode along the path.* **2** sit or stand with one leg on each side of: *to stride a fence.* **3** cross an obstacle with one long step: *She strode over the brook. Great strides have been made toward a settlement of the long-standing wage dispute.*
n **1** a long, confident step: *With two strides he was at the door.* **2** the length of a step or way of taking steps in walking or running: *The child could not keep up with his father's stride.* **3 strides** *pl* a step or stage in progress toward an aim: *Great strides have been made toward a settlement of the long-standing wage dispute.* <Old English *stridan*> **strid′er** *n.*
hit your stride, reach your normal speed or level of efficiency: *By the second day of working together, they had hit their stride and were making good progress.*
take in (your) stride, deal with something difficult or unpleasant in a calm and accepting way: *He took the defeat in stride.*

stri·dent (strī′dənt) *adj* **1** making or with a harsh, grating, or shrill sound: *a strident voice.* **2** presenting something in an unduly forceful and unpleasant way: *They didn't like the strident tone of the speech.* <Latin *stridere* sound harshly> **stri′den·cy** *n.* **stri′dent·ly** *adv.*

strid·u·late (strij′ə lāt′) *v* **strid·u·lat·ed, strid·u·lat·ing** produce a shrill, grating sound, as a cricket or grasshopper does, by rubbing together parts of the body. **strid′u·la′tion** *n.*

strife (strīf) *n* the act or fact of a bitter or violent conflict: *The relationship between the brothers had always been full of strife.* <Old French *estrif*>

strike (strīk) *v* **struck, struck** or **strick·en, strik·ing** **1** hit forcefully with a hand, weapon, or other object, or inflict a blow in this way: *I struck my forehead in frustration.* **2** accidentally hit a part of the body against something: *He struck his head when he fell down.* **3** come into forceful contact or collision with: *The bus struck a fire hydrant.* **4** set or be set on fire by hitting or rubbing: *to strike a match.* **5** come into the mind as a thought or idea suddenly or unexpectedly: *The plan strikes me as silly.* **6** occur suddenly and have harmful or damaging effects: *A hurricane struck the island. They were struck with terror.* **7** make an attack: *The enemy will strike at dawn.* **8** make a coin or medal by stamping metal. **9** carry out an aggressive or violent action, usually without warning: *The arsonist has struck again.* **10** indicate the time by a chime or strike, or be indicated in this way: *The clock struck ten.* **11** refuse to work as a form of organized protest, typically to get higher wages or better working conditions. **12** cancel, remove, or cross out with or as if with a pen: *She struck his name from the list.* **13** reach, achieve, or agree to something involving a balance or compromise: *The employer and the workers have struck an agreement.* **14** 🍁 form (a committee). **15** discover gold, minerals, or oil by drilling or mining. **16** take down something, such as a tent or the tents in a camp, the set of a stage, or a flag or sail.
n **1** a refusal to work, organized by a group of employees as a form of protest, typically to get higher wages or better working conditions: *The miners went on strike.* **2** a sudden attack, especially a military one. **3** an act of knocking down all the pins in tenpin bowling with one's first ball, or the score so made. **4** *Baseball* an unsuccessful attempt by a batter to hit a pitched ball into play. **5** a discovery of gold, minerals, or oil by drilling or mining. <Old English *strican*>
strike down, a hit a thing so that it falls: *A hydro pole was struck down on Main Street.* **b** declare to be invalid: *to strike down a law.*
strike it rich, *Informal* acquire a lot of money or success, especially in a sudden or unexpected way.
strike off, to remove by or as if by a stroke, such as to officially remove someone from membership of a group.
strike out, a cross or cut out. **b** *Baseball* fail or cause to fail three times in an attempt to hit a ball or gain a walk: *The batter struck out. The pitcher struck out six men.* **c** move or proceed vigorously or with a strong purpose: *We struck out across the fields.*
strike up, begin: *The two girls struck up a friendship.*

strike·bound (strīk′bound′) *adj* with a labour strike in progress: *a strikebound factory.*

strike·break·er (strīk′brā′kər) *n* a person actively involved in trying to break up a strike, especially one hired to replace a striking employee.

strike·out (strī′kout) *Baseball n* an out made by a pitcher throwing three strikes against the batter, or the act of striking out.

strik·er (strī′kər) *n* **1** a person who or thing that strikes. **2** an employee who is on strike.

strike zone *Baseball n* the area above home plate through which a pitched ball must pass in order to qualify as a strike.

strik·ing (strī′king) *adj* **1** attracting attention because of some unusual, extreme, or prominent quality: *a striking use of colour, a striking dress.* **2** on strike as an employee: *The striking workers have rejected the latest offer.* **strik′ing·ly** *adv.*

string (string) *n* **1** a thin strip or line of twisted cotton, hemp, or other fibre, or a piece of such material used to tie around or attach to something: *I need a string for the parcel.* **2** a series of objects threaded or hung on this: *a string of pearls, a string of fish.* **3** a length of wire or catgut for a musical instrument, producing a note by vibration: *violin strings.* **4 strings** *pl* the violins, cellos, and other stringed instruments in an orchestra. **5** a tough piece of fibre in vegetables, meat, or other food. **6** a series or sequence of items, events, or data in a line or as if in a line: *a string of cars, a string of victories.* **7** *Computers* a series of alphanumeric characters or a series of keywords, usually used to perform an online search. **8** usually, **strings** *pl Informal* a condition or restriction: *The offer came with no strings attached.*
v **strung, string·ing** **1** thread or hang something on a string, or cause to thread or hang it, so that it stretches in a long line: *to string beads. They dried herbs by stringing them from the roof beams.* **2** fit a string or strings to a musical instrument, a racquet, or a bow: *She had her tennis racquet strung tightly.* **3** remove the strings from bean pods, before eating or cooking them. **4** make tense or anxious: *The news had got them all strung up.*

symphony orchestra

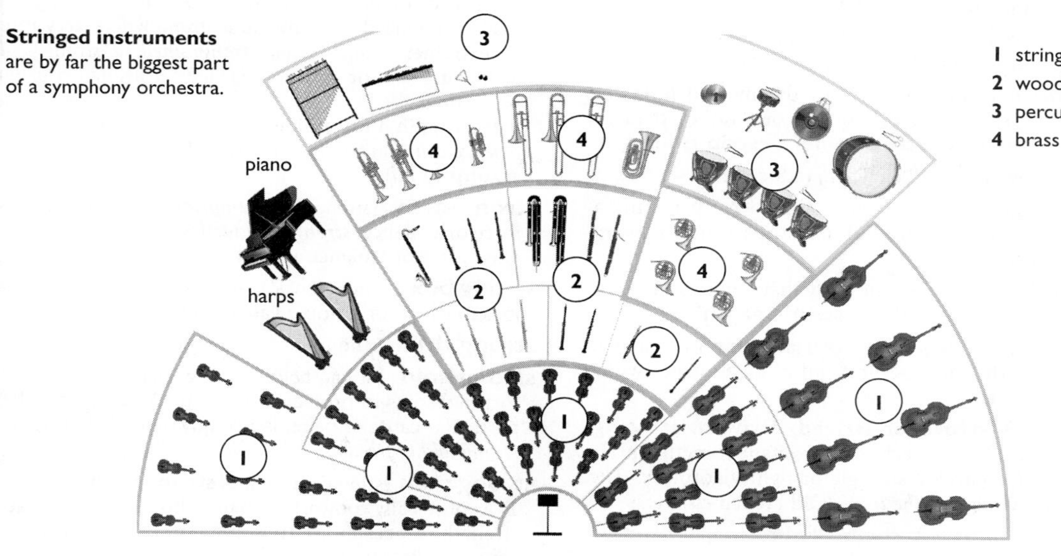

5 *Informal* hoax or deceive: *She said I won a prize, but I think she was just stringing me along.* **6** work as a part-time or local correspondent for a journalism outlet. <Old English *streng*> **string′less** *adj.* **string′like** *adj.*

pull strings, use one's influence, especially secretly: *There were better qualified applicants, but he got the job because she pulled some strings for him.*

have (or **keep**) **someone on a string,** dominate or control someone.

string out, *Informal* prolong or extend: *The program was strung out too long.*

string up, *Informal* kill by hanging: *The horse thief was caught and strung up from the nearest tree.*

string bean *n* a variety of bean with stringlike fibres connecting the two halves of the pods.

stringed instrument (stringd) *n* a musical instrument with strings, played by striking, by plucking, or with a bow, such as the violin, harp, or guitar.

strin·gent (strin′jənt) *adj* strict and precise as a regulation, requirement, or condition: *stringent laws.* <Latin *stringere* bind tight> **strin′gen·cy** *n.* **strin′gent·ly** *adv.*

string·er (string′ər) *n* **1** a person who or thing that strings. **2** a horizontal structural piece in a framework, such as that of a building, bridge, or railway track. **3** a part-time or local correspondent for a journalistic outlet.

string·y (string′ē) *adj* **string·i·er, string·i·est** **1** like, containing, consisting of, or resembling fibres or strings: *tough, stringy meat. Her hair was long and stringy.* **2** of a person, tall, wiry, and thin: *He was about sixteen, tall and stringy.* **string′i·ness** *n.*

strip[1] (strip) *v* **stripped, strip·ping** **1** remove a thing, especially all coverings or outer layers from: *She stripped the bed. They stripped the fruit from the trees. I stripped the old paint from the chair.* **2** remove the clothes from someone, or take off one's clothes: *He stripped and then took a shower.* **3** leave bare: *Thieves stripped the house of everything valuable.* **4** deprive someone of rank, power, or property: *They stripped the princess of her title.* **5** tear or lose the thread or teeth from a screw, bolt, nut, or gearwheel. <Old English *bestriepan* plunder>

strip down, reduce a thing to its bare essentials: *strip down a car.*

strip[2] (strip) *n* **1** a long, narrow, flat piece of cloth, paper, plastic, or other material: *The bark came off in strips.* **2** a long, narrow tract of land or forest. **3** a main road in or leading out of town, lined with stores and other facilities. **4** a comic strip. <German *strippe* strap>

tear a strip off, *Informal* criticize or scold harshly: *She tore a strip off me for coming in late.*

stripe (strīp) *n* **1** a long, narrow band of a different colour or texture, or a thing with a pattern of these bands: *The wallpaper is white with green stripes. She used a stripe for the chair covers.* **2** a type or category: *He's a man of quite a different stripe.* **3** **stripes** *pl* a number or combination of stripes of braid sewn on a uniform to show rank.

v **striped, strip·ing** mark with stripes. <Dutch>

striped *adj.*

strip farming *n* the cultivation of different crops in strips of equal width, running across the slopes instead of up and down. The method helps prevent erosion. Also called **strip cropping**. **strip farmer** *n.*

a bat	e bed	i bid	o pot	u cup	th **thin**
ā cake	ē me	ī bite	ō go	ū rude	ᴛʜ **then**
ä bar	ə about	ər over	ȯ for	u̇ put	zh measure

S

strip·ling (strip′ling) *n* a young man.

strip mall *n* a building containing a series of stores in a line, each with its own entry from the outside.

strip mine *n* a mine operated by digging out layers of earth on the surface to expose the ore, rather than in tunnels underground. **strip′-mine′** *v.* **strip mining** *n.*

stripped–down (stript′doun′) *adj* reduced to essentials.

strip·per (strip′ər) *n* **1** an entertainer who performs a striptease. **2** a substance or tool that strips a surface: *paint stripper, wallpaper stripper.*

strip search *n* a search of the body that requires a person to remove all or most clothing. **strip′-search′** *v.*

strip·tease (strip′tēz′) *n* an entertainment in which a performer slowly undresses in front of an audience while dancing to music.

strive (strīv) *v* **strove** or **strived, striv·en, striv·ing** **1** make great efforts to achieve or obtain something: *He strived for self-control.* **2** struggle or fight vigorously: *The swimmer strove against the tide.* <Old French *estriver*>

strobe (strōb) *n* in full, **strobe light** an apparatus for producing very brief, brilliant flashes of light.
v **strobed, strob·ing** flash intermittently. <Greek *strobos* a whirling>

strob·o·scope (strō′bə skōp′) *n* an instrument for studying periodic motion by the illumination of a moving body in flashes or at intervals.

strode (strōd) past tense of STRIDE.

stro·ga·noff (strō′gə nof) *adj* (*after the noun*) cooked as food in a sauce containing sour cream: *beef stroganoff.*

stroke (strōk) *n* **1** an act of hitting or striking someone or something: *The house was hit by a stroke of lightning.* **2** a sound made by a striking clock: *the stroke of three.* **3** an act of moving one's hand or an object across a surface, applying gentle pressure: *He massaged him with light strokes.* **4** a mark made by drawing a pen, pencil, or paintbrush in one direction across paper or canvas. **5** a movement, especially one of a series, in which something moves out of its position and back into it: *the stroke of a piston. She swam with strong strokes.* **6** a sudden disabling attack or loss of consciousness caused by an interruption in the flow of blood to the brain. **7** an attempt to achieve or obtain something: *a bold stroke.* **8** (*only in compounds*) a sudden attack of an illness: *sunstroke.* **9** the rower nearest the stern of a boat, who sets the timing for the other rowers.
v **stroked, strok·ing** **1** repeatedly move the hand with gentle pressure over a surface, especially hair, fur or skin. **2** *Informal* reassure or flatter someone, especially in order to gain co-operation: *Our coach was good at stroking the team to get them to practise more.* **3** act as the stroke for rowers in a boat. <Old English *stracian*> **strok′er** *n.*

stroll (strōl) *v* walk in a leisurely way: *Every evening they strolled the path by the river.*
n a leisurely walk. <origin uncertain>

stroll·er (strō′lər) *n* **1** a person who strolls: *The park was filled with strollers.* **2** a baby carriage in which a young child sits erect.

strong (strong) *adj* **1** with much force or power: *a strong wind, strong muscles, strong arguments.* **2** able to withstand great force or pressure: *a strong rope, a strong bag.* **3** not easily influenced or changed: *a strong will.* **4** very intense or extreme: *strong tea, a strong smell, a strong dislike.* **5** showing skill or aptitude: *He gave a strong performance in the final.*
adv acting in a forceful, energetic, or aggressive way: *The defence came on strong at the end of the game.*
strong′ly *adv.*

strong–arm (strong′arm′) *Informal adj* with or using force or violence: *strong-arm tactics.*
v use force or violence against.

strong·box (strong′boks′) *n* a small, strongly made, lockable box for holding valuables.

strong drink *n* liquor.

strong·hold (strong′hōld′) *n* **1** a place that has been fortified so as to protect it from attack. **2** a place where a particular cause or belief is strongly defended or upheld: *a stronghold of freedom.*

strong·man (strong′man′) *n, pl* **strong·men** **1** a physically powerful man who performs feats of strength, especially as an entertainment. **2** a leader who gains and keeps power by force.

stron·ti·um (stron′tē əm) *or* (stron′shē əm) *n* a soft, silver-white metallic element used in fireworks and signal flares because it gives a brilliant red light. *Symbol* **Sr** <*Strontian* in Scotland, where it was first discovered>

strontium–90 (nīn′tē) *n* a radioactive isotope of strontium that occurs in the fallout from nuclear explosions and is dangerous because it is absorbed by bones and tissues.

strop (strop) *n* a leather strap used for sharpening razors.
v **stropped, strop·ping** sharpen on a strop.

strove (strōv) a past tense of STRIVE.

struck (struk) past tense and a past participle of STRIKE.

struc·tur·al (struk′chə rəl) *adj* **1** to do with the structure of a building or other object: *structural steel.* **2** to do with the arrangement of and relations between parts of a complex whole: *structural changes.* **struc′tur·al·ly** *adv.*

struc·ture (struk′chər) *n* **1** the arrangement of and relations between the parts or elements of a complex thing: *a social structure.* **2** a building or other object constructed from different parts: *a two-storey structure.* **3** the quality of being organized: *We needed some structure for our discussion.* **4** a physical form that resists forces that would cause it to change shape or size.
v **struc·tured, struc·tur·ing** construct, arrange, or organize according to a plan. <Latin *structura*, from *struere* build>

struc·tured (struk′chərd) *adj* with a well-defined structure or organization: *a structured environment.*

stru·del (strū′dəl) *n* a pastry made of thin dough rolled up around a filling and baked: *apple strudel.* <German>

strug·gle (strug′əl) *v* **strug·gled, strug·gling** **1** make strong efforts against difficulties or restraints: *For years she had to struggle to make a living. He struggled to control his anger.* **2** move or make one's way with great effort: *She struggled through the crowd.*

n **1** a forceful or violent effort to get free of restraints or overcome difficulties: *Earning a living proved to be a struggle.* **2** a conflict or contest: *a power struggle.* <Middle English *struglen*> **strug′gler** *n.*

strum (strum) *v* **strummed, strum·ming** play a guitar or similar instrument by sweeping the thumb or a plectrum up or down the strings, or play a tune in this way: *We heard him strumming on his banjo.*
n the act or sound of strumming. <origin uncertain> **strum′mer** *n.*

strung (strung) past tense and past participle of STRING.

strung out *Informal adj* physically and mentally weakened, especially by drug abuse or due to mental strain.

strut (strut) *v* **strut·ted, strut·ting** walk in a stiff, erect manner, suggesting conceit or self-importance: *He strutted about the room in his new jacket.*
n **1** a strutting walk. **2** a supporting bar fitted into a framework. <Old English *strutian* stand out stiffly> **strut′ter** *n.*
strut your stuff, *Informal* show off your skill or expertise.

strych·nine (strik′nin) *or* (strik′nēn) *n* a bitter, poisonous compound consisting of colourless crystals obtained from plants. <Greek *strychnos* nightshade>

stub (stub) *n* **1** a short piece that is left after a pencil, cigarette, or similarly shaped object has been used. **2** something short and blunt, especially a thing cut short or stunted in growth: *a stub of a tail.* **3** a part of a cheque, ticket, receipt, or other document that is torn off and kept by the person issuing it.
v **stubbed, stub·bing 1** accidentally strike one's toe against a thing. **2** put out a lighted cigarette or cigar by pressing the lighted end against something. **3** pull up a plant by the roots. <Old English>

stub·ble (stub′əl) *n* **1** the lower ends of stalks of grain that are left in the ground after the grain is cut. **2** a short, rough growth like this, especially a very short growth of beard. <Old French, from Latin *stupula* stem>
stub′bled *adj.* **stub′bly** *adj.*

stub·born (stub′ərn) *adj* **1** unwilling to change one's attitude or position on something, especially in spite of good arguments or reasons to do so: *He's just too stubborn to admit he was wrong.* **2** determined or resolute: *stubborn courage.* **3** difficult to move, remove, or cure: *a stubborn cough.* <origin uncertain> **stub′born·ly** *adv.* **stub′born·ness** *n.*

SYNONYMS

Stubborn and **obstinate** (definition 1) both mean "fixed in purpose or opinion."

Stubborn suggests being firm enough not to yield. When used of animals, the word suggests being hard to handle: *She was stubborn about going for a walk even though it was raining. The stubborn dog would not stop pulling on the leash.*

Obstinate often suggests being unreasonable or wilful: *Don't be obstinate about wearing your boots.*

stub·by (stub′ē) *adj* **stub·bi·er, stub·bi·est** short and like a stub: *stubby fingers, a stubby pencil.* **stub′bi·ness** *n.*

stuc·co (stuk′ō) *n, pl* **stuc·coes** or **stuc·cos** a rough, strong plaster used for coating wall surfaces or moulding into architectural decorations.
v **stuc·coed, stuc·co·ing** cover or decorate with stucco. <Italian>

stuck (stuk) past tense and past participle of STICK[2].

stuck–up (stuk′up′) *Informal adj* aloof and conceited.

stud[1] (stud) *n* **1** a large-headed piece of metal that pierces and projects from a surface: *The belt was ornamented with silver studs.* **2** a small, simple piece of jewellery used to fasten the collar or front of a dress shirt, or for wearing in pierced ears or nostrils. **3** a small projection fixed to the base of footwear that allows a better grip on the ground. **4** a small metal piece set into the tire of a motor vehicle to improve traction, or protruding from a road surface as a marker. **5** an upright post, usually wooden, to which boards or laths are nailed in making a wall of a building.
v **stud·ded, stud·ding 1** set with studs or a thing like studs: *He plans to stud the sword hilt with jewels.* **2** be strewn or scattered over: *Little islands stud the harbour.* <Old English *studu*>

stud[2] (stud) *n* **1** a male animal, especially a stallion, kept for breeding. **2** a group of horses or, sometimes, other animals, kept mainly for breeding, or the place where such animals are kept. <Old English *stod*>
at stud, available as a male animal for breeding.

stud·ding (stud′ing) *n* the studs forming the framework of a wall, or the lumber for such studs.

stu·dent (styū′dənt) *or* (stū′dənt) *n* **1** a person who is studying in a school, college, or university. **2** a person who investigates or observes systematically: *a student of human nature.* <Latin *studere* to apply oneself>

student body *n* all the students at a school or other place of instruction.

stud·ied (stud′ēd) *adj* produced or marked by deliberate effort or design: *studied politeness, a studied insult.*

stu·dio (styū′dē ō′) *or* (stū′dē ō) *n, pl* **stu·di·os 1** the workroom of an artist or photographer. **2** a place where music or dancing is taught. **3** a place where musical or sound recordings can be made, where movies are made or produced, or from which a radio or TV program is broadcast. <Italian, from Latin *studium* study>

studio couch *n* a couch, usually without arms, that can be converted into a bed.

stu·di·ous (styū′dē əs) *or* (stū′dē əs) *adj* **1** spending a lot of time studying or reading: *She's very studious.* **2** thoughtful and painstaking: *He made a studious effort to please his customers.* **stu′di·ous·ly** *adv.* **stu′di·ous·ness** *n.*

a bat	e bed	i bid	o pot	u cup	th thin
ā cake	ē me	ī bite	ō go	ū rude	ᴛʜ then
ä bar	ə about	ər over	ȯ for	ů put	zh measure

stud·y (stud′ē) *n, pl* **stud·ies** **1** the giving of time and attention to acquiring knowledge on an academic subject, especially by means of reading or thinking. **2** a careful examination and analysis of a subject or situation: *She compiled a study of unemployment in Canada's urban centres.* **3** a room used or designed for reading, writing, or other work at a desk: *The minister was reading in her study.* **4** a work of literature or art that deals in careful detail with one particular subject. **5** a piece of work, especially a drawing or a musical composition, done for practice or to develop technical skill. **6** a thing who or person that represents or is a good example of something: *His actions were a study in confusion.*
v **stud·ied, stud·y·ing** **1** devote time and attention to acquiring knowledge on an academic subject, especially by means of reading and thinking: *She's studying to be a doctor.* **2** examine or consider carefully: *We studied the map to find the shortest road home. The prisoner studied ways to escape.*

stuff (stuf) *n* **1** the matter, material, items, or activities of a kind that is being referred to, indicated, or implied: *We don't have enough room in the car to load all this stuff.* **2** a person's belongings, equipment, or baggage: *Put all your stuff over there.* **3** the basic ingredients or characteristics of something or someone: *He's made of pretty brave stuff.* **4** goods; belongings: *He was told to move his stuff out of the room.* **5** an area of knowledge or expertise: *She certainly knows her stuff.*
v **1** fill a container, envelope, package, or space, especially force or cram something tightly into it: *She stuffed the bag with garbage.* **2** have a nose blocked up as a result of a cold or hay fever. **3** fill out the skin of a dead animal or bird to make it look as it did when alive. **4** fill the cavity of an item of food with a mixture, especially before cooking: *to stuff a chicken.* **5** eat too much: *I'm stuffed!* <Old French *estoffe* to stock>
that's the stuff, *Informal* used to express encouragement and approval.
the right stuff, *Informal* the qualities of character that lead to success.

stuffed shirt (stuft) *Informal n* a pompous, conceited person, especially one who is old-fashioned or conservative.

stuff·ing (stuf′ing) *n* **1** a mixture used to stuff poultry, meat, fish, or vegetables before cooking. **2** a material used to fill or stuff cushions or soft toys.
knock the stuffing out of, *Informal* damage someone's confidence or strength.

stuff·y (stuf′ē) *adj* **stuff·i·er, stuff·i·est** **1** lacking fresh air or ventilation: *a stuffy room.* **2** unwilling to consider new or unusual ideas and behaviour: *a stuffy person.*
stuff′i·ly *adv.* **stuff′i·ness** *n.*

stul·ti·fy (stul′tə fī′) *v* **stul·ti·fied, stul·ti·fy·ing** cause to lose enthusiasm and initiative, especially as a result of a dull or restrictive routine: *She found that the work was stultifying.* <Latin *stultus* foolish + *facere* make>
stul′ti·fi·ca′tion *n.*

stum·ble (stum′bəl) *v* **stum·bled, stum·bling** **1** trip or trip often by striking the foot against something and almost falling: *She stumbled over the rock. The tired hikers stumbled along.* **2** speak or act in a hesitating, faltering way, often making mistakes: *The unprepared speaker stumbled through his talk.* **3** encounter by accident or chance: *While in the country, she stumbled upon some fine antiques.*
n the act or fact of stumbling. <origin uncertain>
stum′bler *n.* **stum′bling** *adj.* **stum′bling·ly** *adv.*

stumbling block *n* an obstacle or hindrance that causes difficulty or hesitation.

stump (stump) *n* **1** the bottom part of a tree or plant, left after the main part has fallen or been cut off. **2** a small remaining part of something that has been cut, broken off, or worn away: *The dog wagged her stump of a tail.* **3** a person with a short, thick build. **4** a place where a political speech is made. **5** the sound made by stiff walking or heavy steps. **6** *Cricket* one of the three upright pieces of wood that form a cricket wicket.
v **1** be too hard as a question or problem to be answered or solved. *The first question was easy but the second one stumped me.* **2** go about through an area, making political speeches: *The four candidates for election will stump the riding.* **3** walk in a stiff, clumsy way: *I managed to stump along in the boots, but they were far too big for me.* <Middle English *stompe*> **stump′like′** *adj.*
up a stump, *Informal* in a situation too difficult to be dealt with.

🍁 **stump·age** (stum′pij) *n* a price paid for the right to cut standing timber, or the value of the standing timber itself.

stump·y (stum′pē) *adj* **stump·i·er, stump·i·est** **1** short and thick. **2** with many stumps: *stumpy ground.*
stump′i·ly *adv.* **stump′i·ness** *n.*

stun (stun) *v* **stunned, stun·ning** **1** knock unconscious or make dazed or semi-conscious: *He was stunned by the fall.* **2** astonish someone so that they are temporarily unable to react: *She was stunned by the news of her friend's death.* <Old English *stunen*, from Old French *estoner*>

stung (stung) past tense and past participle of STING.

stunk (stungk) a past tense and past participle of STINK.

stun·ner (stun′ər) *Informal n* a very impressive or beautiful person or thing.

stun·ning (stun′ing) *adj* very impressive or beautiful: *a stunning new outfit, a stunning performance.*
stun′ning·ly *adv.*

stunt[1] (stunt) *v* retard the growth or development of: *Lack of proper food stunted the refugee children.* <Old English *stunt* foolish>

stunt[2] (stunt) *Informal n* a feat or act intended to thrill an audience or to attract attention by its daring and skill.
v perform such feats. <origin uncertain>

stunt·man (stunt′mən) *n, pl* **stunt·men** (-mən) a man who takes the actor's place in a movie by performing dangerous stunts.

stunt·wom·an (stunt′wu̇m′ən) *n, pl* **stunt·wom·en** (-wim′ən) a woman who takes the actor's place in a movie by performing dangerous stunts.

stup·a (stū′pə) *n* a large, dome-shaped building used as a Buddhist shrine. <Sanskrit = heap>

stu·pe·fy (styū′pə fī′) *or* (stū′pə fī′) *v* **stu·pe·fied, stu·pe·fy·ing 1** make stupid, dull or senseless: *stupefied by a drug.* **2** overwhelm with shock or amazement; astound: *They were stupefied by the calamity.* <Latin *stupere* be amazed + *facere* make> **stu′pe·fac′tion** *n.*

stu·pen·dous (styū pen′dəs) *or* (stū pen′dəs) *adj* extremely impressive: *a stupendous sight.* <Latin *stupere* be amazed> **stu·pen′dous·ly** *adv.* **stu·pen′dous·ness** *n.*

stu·pid (styū′pid) *or* (stū′pid) *adj* **1** lacking intelligence, interest, or common sense: *a stupid person, a stupid book.* **2** dazed and unable to think clearly. **3** used to express boredom or annoyance: *This stupid pen won't write.*
n Informal a stupid person: *Hey, you, stupid, go over there!* <Latin *stupere* be dazed> **stu·pid′i·ty** *n.* **stu′pid·ly** *adv.* **stu′pid·ness** *n.*

stu·por (styū′pər) *or* (stū′pər) *n* a loss or lessening of the power to feel sensations: *a drugged stupor. The woman lay in a stupor, unable to tell what had happened to her.* <Latin *stupere* be dazed>

stur·dy (stər′dē) *adj* **stur·di·er, stur·di·est 1** strongly and solidly built: *sturdy legs.* **2** strong and unyielding: *sturdy resistance.* <Old French *esturdi* violent, orig dazed> **stur′di·ly** *adv.* **stur′di·ness** *n.*

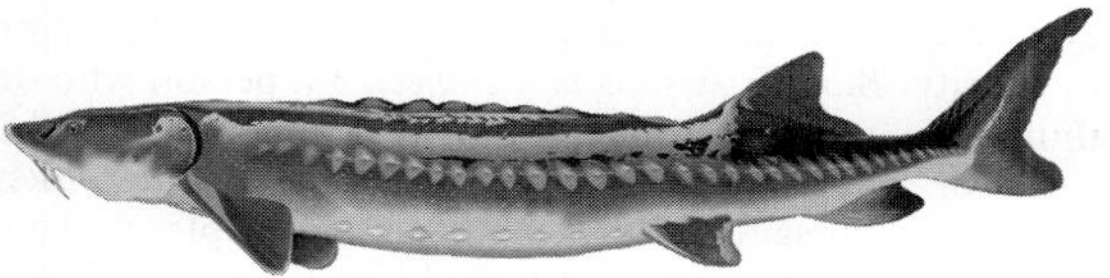

The eggs from the **sturgeon** are called caviar. Caviar from the beluga sturgeons in the Caspian Sea is highly valued and very expensive. Because the caviar is so popular, beluga sturgeon could become extinct.

stur·geon (stər′jən) *n, pl* **stur·geons** or (*especially collectively*) **stur·geon** a large fish of the northern hemisphere whose long body has a tough skin with rows of bony plates, and whose flesh and eggs are both used as food. <Old French *esturgeon*>

stut·ter (stut′ər) *v* talk with unintended repeated sounds, especially initial consonants.
n the act or habit of stuttering. Compare STAMMER. <Middle English *stutten*> **stut′ter·er** *n.* **stut′ter·ing** *adj.* **stut′ter·ing·ly** *adv.*

sty[1] (stī) *n, pl* **sties** a pen for pigs. <Old English *stig*>

sty[2] or **stye** (stī) *n, pl* **sties** or **styes** a small, inflamed swelling on the edge of the eyelid, caused by a bacterial infection of the gland at the base of an eyelash. <Old English *stigend* rising + *eage* eye>

Styg·i·an (stij′ē ən) *adj* **1** *Greek myth* to do with the river Styx, a river in the lower world. **2** dark and gloomy.

style (stīl) *n* **1** a manner of doing, writing, composing, or building something: *He introduced a new style of teaching. She perfected an elegant style for her essays. Anger simply wasn't his style.* **2** a distinctive appearance, especially a particular design of clothing or way of arranging the hair: *She dressed in the latest style.* **3** an official or legal title: *Address him with the style of King.* **4** a fashionable, elegant, or admirable way of life: *He lives in style.* **5** a rodlike object or part, such as a narrow extension of a flower's ovary or a small, slender appendage in an invertebrate.
v **styled, styl·ing 1** design or make in a particular form: *She uses a blow dryer to style her hair.* **2** assign a particular name, description, or title to someone or something: *Joan of Arc was styled "the Maid of Orleans."* <Latin *stilus* writing instrument>

style·book (stīl′bu̇k′) *n* a book containing rules of punctuation, capitalization, spelling, and usage in writing or printing.

styl·ish (stī′lish) *adj* showing a good sense of style: *a stylish new coat.* **styl′ish·ly** *adv.* **styl′ish·ness** *n.*

styl·ist (stī′list) *n* **1** a person, especially a writer, who has or aims at a good style, or whose work is characterized by a particular style: *As a novelist, he was an accomplished stylist.* **2** a person who works creatively in the fashion and beauty industry, especially a designer of clothing or a hairdresser.

sty·lis·tic (stī lis′tik) *adj* to do with artistic or literary style. **sty·lis′ti·cal·ly** *adv.*

styl·ize (stī′līz) *v* **styl·ized, styl·iz·ing** make, design, or treat according to a particular or standard style or pattern rather than realistically: *Our new bedroom wallpaper has tiny stylized tulips.*

sty·lus (stī′ləs) *n* **1** a pointed instrument used in ancient times for writing on wax or clay tablets. **2** a needlelike piece of diamond or sapphire that follows a groove in a phonograph record and transmits the recorded sound. <See STYLE.>

sty·mie (stī′mē) *v* **sty·mied, sty·mie·ing** prevent or hinder the progress of: *She was stymied by the last question on the exam and gave up on it.* <origin uncertain>

styp·tic (stip′tik) *adj* able as a substance to stop bleeding when it is applied to a wound.
n a substance that stops or checks bleeding by contracting the tissue: *Alum is a common styptic.*

styptic pencil *n* a small stick of a styptic substance, used to treat small cuts.

sty·rene (stī′rēn) *n* a liquid hydrocarbon obtained as a petroleum by-product, used mainly in making plastics and resins.

sty·ro·foam (stī′rə fōm′) *n* a lightweight, firm, polystyrene plastic used for insulation and packaging.

sua·sion (swā′zhən) *n* persuasion as opposed to force or compulsion: *Moral suasion is an appeal to your sense of what is fair.*

suave (swȧv) *adj* charming, confident, and elegant: *a suave manner.* <French, from Latin *suavis* agreeable> **suave′ly** *adv.* **suave′ness** *n.* **suav′i·ty** *n.*

sub (sub) *Informal n* **1** a substitute. **2** a submarine.
v **subbed, sub·bing** act as a substitute.

a bat	e bed	i bid	o pot	u cup	th **thin**
ā cake	ē me	ī bite	ō go	ū rude	TH **then**
ȧ bar	ə about	ər over	ȯ for	u̇ put	zh measure

sub– *prefix* **1** at, to, or from a lower position: *subway, submarine.* **2** somewhat, nearly, or more or less: *subarctic.* **3** subsequent or secondary to action of the same kind: *sublet.* <Latin>

sub·al·pine (sub al′pīn′) *adj* of or located on the higher slopes of mountains just below the treeline.

sub·ant·arctic (sub′ant ärk′tik) *or* (sub′ant är′tik) *adj* to do with the region just north of the Antarctic Circle.
n this region.

sub·arc·tic (sub′ärk′tik) *or* (sub′är′tik) *adj* to do with the region just south of the Arctic Circle.
n this region.

sub·ar·id (sub′ar′id) *or* (sub′er′id) *adj* moderately arid.

sub·a·tom·ic (sub′ə tom′ik) *adj* smaller than or occurring within an atom.

sub–base·ment (sub′bā′smənt) *n* a storey below the main basement of a building.

sub·com·mit·tee (sub′kə mit′ē) *n* a committee composed of some members of a larger committee, board, or other body and reporting to it.

sub·com·pact (sub′kom′pakt) *n* the smallest basic size of automobile, smaller than a compact.

sub·con·scious (sub′kon′shəs) *adj* of or concerning the part of the mind of which one is not fully aware but that influences actions and feelings: *a subconscious motive.*
n this part of the mind. **sub′con′scious·ly** *adv.* **sub′con′scious·ness** *n.*

sub·con·ti·nent (sub′kon′tə nənt) *n* a large, distinguishable part of a continent: *the Indian subcontinent.*

sub·con·tract (sub′kon′trakt) *for n,* (sub′kon′trakt) *or* (sub′kən trakt′) *for v. n* a contract for a company or person to do work for another company as part of a larger project.
v make a subcontract: *The plumbing for the new school was subcontracted.* **sub′con′tract·or** *n.*

sub·cul·ture (sub′kul′chər) *n* a cultural group within a larger culture, often with beliefs, practices, or interests different from those of the larger group: *the subculture of organized crime.*

sub·cu·ta·ne·ous (sub′kyū tā′nē əs) *adj* located or applied under the skin: *subcutaneous fat, a subcutaneous injection.* <*sub-* under + Latin *cutis* skin + *-eous*>
sub′cu·ta′ne·ous·ly *adv.*

sub·di·vide (sub′də vīd′) *v* **sub·di·vid·ed, sub·di·vid·ing** divide something that has already been divided or that is a separate unit: *A developer bought the farm and subdivided it into building lots.*

sub·di·vi·sion (sub′də vizh′ən) *n* **1** a division into smaller parts. **2** a part of a part. **3** an area of land divided into building lots, or the houses or community established on such an area.

sub·duc·tion (sub duk′shən) *Geology n* a process in which one edge of a plate of the earth's crust is forced below the edge of another.

sub·due (səb dyū′) *or* (səb dū′) *v* **sub·dued, sub·du·ing** overcome or bring under control a feeling, person, country, or people: *The invaders subdued the local population. She subdued a desire to laugh, but could not hide her smile.* <Latin *sub-* away + *ducere* lead>
sub·du′a·ble *adj.* **sub·du′er** *n.*

sub·dued (səb dyūd′) *or* (səb dūd′) *adj* **1** of a person, quiet and somewhat reflective or depressed: *He was subdued all afternoon.* **2** of colour or lighting, soft and restrained.

sub·en·try (sub′en′trē) *n* an entry listed under a main entry.

sub·freez·ing (sub′frēz′ing) *adj* subzero.

sub·group (sub′grūp′) *n* a subdivision of a group.

sub·head (sub′hed′) *n* the title, or heading given to a headline or a subsection of a piece of writing. Also, **subheading**.

sub·hu·man (sub′hyū′mən) *adj* a lower order of being than the human.
n a subhuman animal or person.

sub·ject (sub′jikt) *for n or adj,* (səb jekt′) *for v. n* **1** a person who or thing that is being discussed, described, or dealt with: *She tried to change the subject.* **2** a branch of knowledge studied or taught in a school, college, or university: *Biology was his best subject.* **3** a person who or thing that undergoes or experiences something. **4** the word or group of words in a sentence about which something is said in the predicate. Example: In the sentence *His little sister went to find him*, the subject is *His little sister* and the predicate is *went to find him.* **5** the theme of a book, poem, or other literary work. **6** the theme or melody on which a musical work or movement is based. **7** a citizen or member of a state other than its supreme ruler: *They were all subjects of the queen.*
adj **1** likely to be affected by a particular condition or occurrence, especially an unwelcome or unpleasant one: *He was subject to bouts of unhappiness.* **2** dependent or conditional upon: *The agreement they drafted is subject to a vote.* **3** under the authority or control of another ruler, country, or government: *For centuries, the land was subject to foreign domination.*
v **1** cause or force to undergo or experience something: *They subjected the prisoner to torture.* **2** bring a person or a country under control or jurisdiction. <Latin *sub-* under + *jacere* throw>

GRAMMAR AND USAGE

A singular **subject**, which usually appears at the beginning of a sentence, takes the singular form of a verb: *My computer crashes too often now.*

A plural subject takes the plural form of a verb: *The computers in the lab crash less than before.*

Note that, in the second example above, the plural verb "crash" follows the plural subject "computers," not the singular "lab."

sub·jec·tion (səb jek′shən) *n* bringing or being under some power or influence: *The new dictator's first concern was the subjection of the rebel forces. They lived in subjection to an old aunt.*

sub·jec·tive (səb jek′tiv) *adj* **1** based on or influenced by personal feelings, tastes, or opinions: *She thought he was being subjective and not taking account of the facts.* **2** *Grammar* to do with the form of nouns and pronouns used for the subject of a sentence.
n the subjective form of a noun or pronoun. **sub·jec′tive·ly** *adv.* **sub·jec′tive·ness** *n.* **sub′jec·tiv′i·ty** *n.*

subject matter *n* the topic dealt with or the subject represented in a debate, discussion, or work of art.

sub·join (səb join′) *v* add comments or supplementary information at the end of a speech or text: *Several appendixes were subjoined to the report.*

sub·ju·gate (sub′jə gāt′) *v* **sub·ju·gat·ed, sub·ju·gat·ing** bring under domination or control, especially by conquest. <Latin *subjugare* subdue, from *sub-* under + *jugum* yoke> **sub′ju·ga′tion** *n.* **sub′ju·ga′tor** *n.*

sub·junc·tive (səb jungk′tiv) *adj* to do with a verb form used to express what is imagined, wished for, or possible. Example: In *If I were you I'd try again*, the verb form *were* is subjunctive.
n a subjunctive verb form. <Latin *sub-* under + *jungere* join>

sub·lease (sub′lēs′) *for n,* (sub lēs′) *or* (sub′lēs′) *for v. n* a lease of all or part of some property by the person who rents the property from the owner.
v **sub·leased, sub·leas·ing** grant or take a sublease of.

sub·let (sub let′) *v* **sub·let, sub·let·ting** rent to another some property that has been rented to oneself: *She sublet her apartment while she was away last summer.*
n such a rental.

sub·li·mate (sub′lə māt′) *for v,* (sub′lə mit) *or* (sub′lə māt′) *for n.* *v* **sub·li·mat·ed, sub·li·mat·ing** **1** change the natural expression of an impulse or desire into one considered more socially or personally acceptable: *to sublimate aggressiveness into energy.* **2** *Chemistry* change state from solid to gas or from gas to solid without becoming liquid, or cause a substance to do this. See STATE for picture.
n a solid deposit of a substance that has been sublimated. **sub′lim·a′tion** *n.*

sub·lime (sə blīm′) *adj* **1** of such excellence or beauty as to inspire great admiration: *We thought that the Torngat mountains were sublime.* **2** to do with a feature of a person's behaviour that is carried to extremes: *She behaved with sublime indifference to what people might say.*
n **the sublime** a thing that has excellence or beauty as to inspire great admiration. <Latin *sublimis* uplifting> **sub·lime′ly** *adv.* **sub·lim′i·ty** (sə blim′ə tē) *n.*

sub·lim·i·nal (sə blim′ə nəl) *adj* existing or acting below the threshold of conscious awareness: *The committee protested against the use of subliminal advertising on television.* <*sub-* under + Latin *limen* threshold> **sub·lim′i·nal·ly** *adv.*

sub·ma·chine gun (sub′mə shēn′) *n* a lightweight automatic or semi-automatic gun, designed to be fired from the shoulder or hip.

sub·ma·rine (sub′mə rēn′) *for n or v,* (sub′mə rēn′) *or* (sub′mə rēn′) *for adj. n* **1** a boat that can operate under water for long periods, used in warfare for discharging torpedoes and missiles. **2** a large sandwich consisting of a long roll that is split lengthwise and filled with a variety of fillings.
adj placed, growing, or used below the surface of the sea: *a submarine volcano.* **sub′mar′i·ner** (sub′ma′ri nər) *n.*

sub·men·u (səb′men′yū) *Computers n* a menu that is accessed by selecting something from another menu.

sub·merge (səb mərj′) *v* **sub·merged, sub·merg·ing** **1** put under, descend below the surface of, or cover with water: *A big wave submerged us. The submarine submerged once it reached deep water. At high tide this path is submerged.* **2** cover, bury, or obscure: *His talent was submerged by his shyness.* <Latin *sub-* under + *mergere* plunge> **sub·mer′gence** *n.*

sub·merse (sub mərs′) *v* **sub·mersed, sub·mers·ing** submerge. **sub·mer′sion** (sub′mər′zhən) *n.*

sub·mers·i·ble (səb mər′sə bəl) *adj* able to be submerged.
n a small boat or craft that can operate under water, especially for research or exploration.

sub·mis·sion (səb mish′ən) *n* **1** the action or fact of accepting or yielding to a superior force or to the will or authority of another person: *The defeated general showed his submission by giving up his sword.* **2** the action of presenting a proposal, argument, or application for consideration or judgment, or the document stating such a thing: *Their submission asked the city council to block new construction in the neighbourhood. The lawyer made a submission to the judge.*

sub·mis·sive (səb mis′iv) *adj* yielding to the power, control, or authority of another. **sub·mis′sive·ly** *adv.* **sub·mis′sive·ness** *n.*

sub·mit (səb mit′) *v* **sub·mit·ted, sub·mit·ting** **1** yield to the power, control, or authority of another: *The population was forced to submit to the invaders.* **2** present for the consideration or judgment of another: *The secretary submitted a report of the last meeting. She submitted a bid on the contract for the new shopping centre. We submit that the proposed expansion of the airport is unnecessary.* <Latin *submittere* to yield>

sub·nor·mal (sub′nȯr′məl) *adj* lower or smaller than normal: *subnormal temperatures.*

sub·or·di·nate (sə bȯr′də nit) *for adj or n,* (sə bȯr′de nāt) *for v.* *adj* **1** lower in rank or position: *subordinate officers.* **2** to do with a clause in a sentence that depends for its complete sense on a main clause.
n a subordinate person or thing.
v **sub·or·di·nat·ed, sub·or·di·nat·ing** make subordinate. <Latin *sub-* under + *ordinis* order>
sub·or′di·nate·ly *adv.* **sub·or·di·na′tion** *n.*

subordinate clause *Grammar n* a clause in a complex sentence, introduced by a subordinating conjunction, and not able to stand alone as a sentence. Example: In the sentence *I want to go home because it is raining*, the subordinate clause is *because it is raining*. Compare MAIN CLAUSE. Also called **dependent clause**.

a bat	e bed	i bid	o pot	u cup	th **thin**
ā cake	ē me	ī bite	ō go	ū rude	ᴛʜ **then**
ä bar	ə about	ər over	ȯ for	ủ put	zh measure

S

subordinating conjunction *Grammar* *n* a conjunction that introduces a subordinate clause. Examples: *because, while, although, unless*

sub·orn (sə bôrn′) *v* bribe or otherwise make someone commit an unlawful act such as to give false testimony in court: *to suborn a witness.* <Latin *sub-* secretly + *ornare* equip> **sub·or·na′tion** *n.* **sub·orn′er** *n.*

sub·plot (sub′plot′) *n* a lesser plot forming part of the main plot of a novel, movie, or play.

sub·poe·na (sə pē′nə) *n* an official written order ordering a person to appear in court.
v **sub·poe·naed, sub·poe·na·ing** summon with a subpoena. <Latin *sub poena* under penalty>

sub·polar (sub′po′lər) *adj* to do with the regions just outside the north or south polar region.

sub ro·sa (sub′ rō′zə) *adj* happening or done in secret: *sub rosa discussions.* <Latin = under the rose. In ancient times, a rose was hung over a council table as a token of secrecy.>

sub·rou·tine (sub′rū tēn′) *Computers* *n* a set of instructions designed to perform a frequently used operation within a program.

sub·scribe (səb skrīb′) *v* **sub·scribed, sub·scrib·ing** **1** (*with* ***to***) arrange to receive something, especially a periodical or a service, regularly by paying in advance: *He subscribes to several magazines.* **2** promise to give or pay a sum of money to a particular fund, project, or charitable cause, especially on a regular basis: *She subscribed $50 to the hospital fund.* **3** show one's consent or approval by signing a will, contract, or other document: *Thousands of citizens subscribed to the petition.* **4** give one's consent or approval: *He will not subscribe to anything unfair.* <Latin *sub-* under + *scribere* write> **sub·scrib′er** *n.*

sub·script (sub′skript) *n* a small number, figure, or symbol written below the line. Example: In H_2O the 2 is a subscript.

sub·scrip·tion (səb skrip′shən) *n* **1** the action of making or agreeing to make an advance payment in order to receive or participate in something or as a donation, or a payment of such a type: *We are raising a subscription for a new arena.* **2** a thing that is obtained through such a payment: *His subscription to the newspaper expires next week.* **3** a signature or short piece of writing at the end of a document.

sub·sec·tion (sub′sek′shən) *n* a division of a section.

sub·se·quent (sub′sə kwənt) *adj* coming after something in time: *Subsequent events proved him correct. That problem is dealt with in a subsequent chapter.* <Latin *sub-* up + *sequi* follow> **sub′se·quent·ly** *adv.*

sub·ser·vi·ent (səb sər′vē ənt) *adj* **1** obeying others without asking any questions: *All the employees were subservient to their boss.* **2** less important. **3** serving as a means to an end. **sub·ser′vi·ence** *n.* **sub·ser′vi·ent·ly** *adv.*

sub·set (sub′set′) *n* a part of a larger group of related things, especially a mathematical set of which all the elements are contained in another set.

sub·side (səb sīd′) *v* **sub·sid·ed, sub·sid·ing** **1** become less intense, violent, severe, or active: *The storm finally subsided. He subsided into silence.* **2** go down to a lower or normal level: *After the rain stopped, the flood waters subsided. The house was subsiding into the muddy ground.* <Latin *sub-* down + *sidere* settle>

sub·sid·i·ar·y (səb sid′ē er′ē) *adj* **1** less important than but related or supplementary to: *a subsidiary pipe.* **2** controlled as a company by a holding or parent firm.
n, pl **sub·sid·i·ar·ies** a company owned or controlled by another company: *The bus line was a subsidiary of the railway.* <Latin *subsidium* reserve troops>

sub·si·dize (sub′sə dīz′) *v* **sub·si·dized, sub·si·diz·ing** support an organization or activity by giving it money: *The government subsidized shipping services on the Great Lakes.* **sub′si·di·za′tion** *n.* **sub′si·diz′er** *n.*

sub·si·dy (sub′sə dē) *n, pl* **sub·si·dies** a sum of money granted by a state or public body to assist an industry or business so that the price of goods or services may remain low or competitive, or otherwise in the public interest. <Latin *subsidium* aid>

sub·sist (səb sist′) *v* maintain or support oneself, especially at a minimal level: *While the hikers were stranded, they subsisted on berries.* <Latin *sub-* up to + *sistere* stand>

sub·sist·ence (səb sis′təns) *n* the action or fact of maintaining or supporting oneself at a minimum level, or the means of doing this: *The land provided a subsistence for the peasants.*

sub·soil (sub′soil′) *n* the layer of earth that lies just under the surface soil: *a clay subsoil.*

sub·son·ic (sub son′ik) *adj* to do with a speed less than that of sound.

sub·spe·cies (sub′spē′sēz) *or* (sub′spē′shēz) *n, pl* **sub·spe·cies** a category of plants or animals that ranks below species, and whose members are often geographically isolated.

sub·stance (sub′stəns) *n* **1** a particular kind of matter with uniform properties: *a waxy substance.* **2** the actual physical matter of which a person or thing consists: *the substance of the body.* **3** the quality of being important, valid, or with a solid basis in fact: *The talk she gave had real substance.* **4** wealth and possessions: *He was a man of substance.* <Latin *substare* stand firm, from *sub-* up to + *stare* stand>
in substance, essentially.

SYNONYMS

Substance means "what something physical or abstract consists of": *What is the substance of your argument?*

Material applies particularly to what is used to make or do something: *The construction workers gathered the materials they needed to complete the job.*

Stuff is often used informally to refer to unspecified things: *Pick up your stuff and let's get out of here.*

substance abuse *n* use of a substance, such as alcohol or drugs, in a way that damages health and interferes with one's ability to function.

sub·stand·ard (sub stan′dərd) *adj* falling short of a minimum standard of quality: *The substandard sheets are being sold at very low prices.*

sub·stan·tial (səb stan′shəl) *adj* **1** of considerable importance, size, or worth: *We gave them a substantial donation.* **2** strongly built or made: *a substantial house.* **3** concerning the essentials of something: *They were in substantial agreement.* **sub·stan′tial·ly** *adv.*

sub·stan·ti·ate (səb stan′shē āt′) *v* **sub·stan·ti·at·ed, sub·stan·ti·at·ing** provide evidence to support or prove the truth of: *to substantiate a claim, to substantiate a theory.* **sub·stan′ti·a′tion** *n.*

sub·stan·tive (sub′stən tiv) *adj* **1** with a firm basis in reality and thus important and meaningful. **2** with a separate and independent existence. **3** functioning as a noun.
n a noun. **sub′stan·tive·ly** *adv.*

sub·sti·tute (sub′stə tyūt) *or* (sub′stə tūt′) *n* a person or thing acting or serving instead of another: *She used margarine as a substitute for butter.*
v **sub·sti·tut·ed, sub·sti·tut·ing** use or add in place of, or act or serve as a substitute: *We substituted brown sugar for molasses in the cookies. I substituted for the injured player.* <Latin *sub-* in place of + *statuere* to set up>
sub′sti·tu′tion *n.*

sub·strate (sub′strāt) *n* a substance or layer that underlines something, or on which some process occurs, such as the surface on which an organism lives, grows, and obtains its nourishment.

sub·stra·tum (sub strā′təm) *or* (sub strat′əm) *n, pl* **sub·stra·ta** (sub strā′ta) *or* (sub strat′a) or **sub·stra·tums** an underlying layer or substance, such as a layer of rock or soil beneath the surface of the ground.

sub·struc·ture (sub′struk′chər) *n* an underlying or supporting structure.

sub·sume (səb sūm′) *or* (səb syūm′) *v* **sub·sumed sub·sum·ing** include or absorb something in another thing: *Your suggestion has been subsumed under point 4 of the committee's recommendations.* <Latin *sub-* under + *sumere* assume>

sub·sys·tem (səb′sis′təm) *n* a system that forms part of a larger system.

sub·ten·ant (sub ten′ənt) *or* (sub′ten′ənt) *n* a person who rents from a tenant. **sub′ten′an·cy** *n.*

sub·tend (səb tend′) *Mathematics v* extend from one side to the other, opposite an angle or side of a geometric figure. <Latin *sub-* under + *tendere* stretch>

sub·ter·fuge (sub′tər fyūj′) *n* a trick, excuse, or statement used in order to deceive: *Her headache was a subterfuge to avoid work.* <Latin *subter-* secretly + *fugere* flee>

sub·ter·ra·ne·an (sub′tə rā′nē ən) *adj* **1** existing, occurring, or done under the earth's surface: *A subterranean passage led from the castle to a cave.* **2** carried on secretly: *subterranean activity.* <Latin *sub-* under + *terra* earth>

sub·text (səb′tekst′) *n* the underlying or implied meaning or argument.

sub·ti·tle (sub′tī′təl) *n* **1** an additional or subordinate title of a book or article, giving additional information about its content. **2** a piece of dialogue or description displayed at the bottom of a movie or television screen that translates or transcribes the dialogue or story.
v **sub·ti·tled, sub·ti·tling** give a subtitle to.

GRAMMAR AND USAGE

Separate a subtitle from a main title by a colon or dash:
She wrote the article "Diets: Safe or Dangerous?"
She wrote the article "Diets—Safe or Dangerous?"

sub·tle (sut′əl) *adj* **1** so delicate or precise, especially as a change or distinction, as to be difficult to analyze or describe: *a subtle smile.* **2** delicately complex and understated as a mixture or effect: *subtle lighting.* **3** able to make fine distinctions or observations: *a subtle critic, a subtle mind.* <Latin *subtilis* finely woven>
sub′tle·ness *n.* **sub′tly** *adv.*

sub·tle·ty (sut′əl tē) *n, pl* **sub·tle·ties** **1** the quality or state of being subtle. **2** a subtle distinction, feature, or argument: *He did not understand all the author's subtleties.*

sub·top·ic (sub′top′ik) *n* one of the secondary topics into which a main topic is divided.

sub·to·tal (sub′tō′təl) *n* the total of one set of a larger group of figures to be added.

sub·tract (səb trakt′) *v* **1** take away a number or quantity from a larger number or quantity: *Subtract 2 from 10 and you have 8.* **2** take away something from another thing so as to decrease the size, number, or amount. <Latin *sub-* from under + *trahere* draw> **sub·trac′tion** *n.*

sub·tra·hend (sub′trə hend′) *n* a number or quantity to be subtracted from another. Example: In 10 – 2 = 8, the subtrahend is 2.

sub·trop·i·cal (sub trop′ə kəl) *adj* adjacent to or bordering on the tropics. **sub·trop′ics** *pln.*

sub·urb (sub′ərb) *n* an outlying district of a city, especially a residential one. Also, **the suburbs**. <Latin *sub-* close to + *urbs* city> **sub·ur′ban** *adj.*

sub·ur·ban·ite (sə bər′bə nīt′) *n* a person who lives in a suburb.

sub·ur·bi·a (sə bər′bē ə) *n* the suburbs, the people who live in them, or the values or attitudes thought to be characteristic of residents of the suburbs.

sub·ver·sive (səb vər′siv) *adj* tending or designed to undermine the power and authority of a country, system, or institution: *a subversive scheme.*
n a person with such aims.

sub·vert (səb vərt′) *v* undermine the power and authority of a country, system, or institution. <Latin *subvertere* to overturn, from *sub-* below + *vertere* turn>
sub·ver′sion (sub′vər′zhən) *n.* **sub·vert′er** *n.* .

a bat	e bed	i bid	o pot	u cup	th **thin**
ā cake	ē me	ī bite	ō go	ū rude	ᴛʜ **then**
à bar	ə about	ər over	ȯ for	u̇ put	zh measure

sub·way (sub′wā′) *n* **1** an electric railway running for all or most of its length beneath the surface of the streets in a city. **2** a road or path running under another road or under a railway track for use by pedestrians.

sub·zero (sub′zē′rō) *adj* below the freezing point of water: *subzero temperatures.*

suc·ceed (sək sēd) *v* **1** achieve what one aims at or wants: *Her plans succeeded.* **2** lead to the desired outcome: *The attack succeeded beyond all expectations.* **3** take over or become the new or rightful holder of a throne, inheritance, title, office, or other position: *A young politician succeeded a veteran one as prime minister. The prince succeeded to the throne.* **4** follow and take the place of: *Her puzzlement was succeeded by anger.* <Latin *succedere*, from *sub-* up to + *cedere* go>

SYNONYMS

Succeed means "achieve": *I've finally succeeded in getting an "A" in History.*

Accomplish means "succeed in completing": *The settlers accomplished what they had planned to do.*

Prosper means "be successful," especially financially: *The farmers and miners prospered greatly when the economy improved.*

suc·cess (sək ses′) *n* **1** the accomplishment of an aim or purpose: *He reported success in losing weight. What success did they have in finding more players for the team?* **2** the gain of popularity or profit: *He has had little success in life.* **3** a person who or thing that succeeds: *The circus was a great success.*

suc·cess·ful (sək ses′fəl) *adj* **1** accomplishing an aim or purpose: *a successful plan.* **2** wealthy; prosperous: *a successful merchant.* **suc·cess′ful·ly** *adv.*

suc·ces·sion (sək sesh′ən) *n* **1** a number of people or things sharing a specified characteristic and following one after the other: *a succession of capable leaders, a succession of misfortunes.* **2** the action or process of inheriting a title, rank, office, or property, or the right or sequence of inheriting it: *There was a dispute about the rightful succession to the throne. The queen's oldest son is next in succession to the throne.* **3** the natural series of changes over time by which a plant or animal community successively gives way to another until stability is reached.
in succession, following one after another: *We visited our sick friend several days in succession.*

suc·ces·sive (sək ses′iv) *adj* following one after another or following others: *It rained for three successive days.* **suc·ces′sive·ly** *adv.*

suc·ces·sor (sək ses′ər) *n* a person who or thing that follows after another in a series, especially to an office, position, possession, or title: *She was her father's successor as head of the company.*

suc·cinct (sək singkt′) *adj* written or spoken briefly and clearly: *She gave a succinct account of her meeting with the director.* <Latin *succinctus* pp of *succingere*, from *sub-* up + *cingere* gird> **suc·cinct′ly** *adv.* **suc·cinct′ness** *n.*

suc·co·tash (suk′ə tash′) *n* a dish made of sweet corn and lima beans cooked together.

Suc·coth (suk′oth′) *n* a Jewish festival held in the fall to commemorate the sheltering of the Israelites in the wilderness. It is marked by the building of small booths covered in natural materials. Also, **Sukkoth**.

suc·cour or **suc·cor** (suk′ər) *n* assistance and support in times of hardship or distress: *The town gave succour to the fleeing refugees.*
v help and support in times of hardship or distress: *They succoured the wounded.* <Latin *succurrere* run to help>

suc·cu·lent (suk′yə lənt) *adj* tender, juicy, and tasty: *a succulent fruit.*
n a plant with thick, fleshy tissues adapted for storing water in the leaves or stems. <Latin *succus* juice>
suc′cu·lence *n.*

suc·cumb (sə kum′) *v* fail to resist pressure, temptation, or force: *After several minutes of indecision, I succumbed to temptation and ate the last cookie.* <Laitn *sub-* down + *-cumbere* lie>

such (such) *adj* **1** of the type previously mentioned: *I have never seen such a child. She wore such thin clothes it's a wonder she survived. They took only tea and coffee and such drinks.* **2** of the type about to be mentioned: *There is no such visitor in our home. Our work is organized in a such a way that we have many breaks.* **3** to so high a degree: *He is such a liar.*
pron **1** a thing of the type previously mentioned: *The box contains blankets and towels and such.* **2** a thing of the type about to be mentioned: *Such is the labour involved that we don't have time to do it.* <Old English *swa* so + *lic* like>
as such, in the exact sense of the word: *A leader, as such, deserves respect.*
such-and-such a ——, used to refer to a person who or thing that does not need to be specified: *Tell them you'll have it done by such-and-such a date for such-and-such a price.*
such as it is (or **they are**)**,** what little there is; for what it's worth: *The food, such as it is, is delicious. The soldiers, such as they were, fought badly.*

such·like (such′līk′) *pron* things of the type mentioned: *They were adept at deceptions, disguises, and suchlike.*

suck (suk) *v* **1** draw into the mouth by contracting the muscles of the lips and mouth to make a partial vacuum: *He sucked lemonade through a straw.* **2** hold something in the mouth and draw at it in this way: *She sucked a mint to clear her breath.* **3** draw milk from the breast or a bottle. **4** draw in a specified direction by creating a vacuum: *The plants sucked up moisture from the earth. The whirlpool sucked down the boat.* **5** *Informal* involve someone in something without her or his choosing: *I don't want to be sucked into the fraud.* **6** make a gurgling sound as a pump by drawing air instead of a liquid. **7** *Slang* be very bad, displeasing, or disgusting: *I saw that movie and it sucks!*
n **1** an act of sucking something: *The baby took one suck at the empty bottle and pushed it away.* **2** a sucking force or sound, especially of water. <Old English *sucan*>
suck in, a absorb. **b** pull a part of the body, especially the stomach or cheeks, inward.
suck up (**to**)**,** *Informal* try to win someone's approval by flattery or doing favours.

suck·er (suk′ər) *n* **1** a person who or thing that sucks, such as an object that adheres to a surface by suction, or an animal with an organ that allows it to cling to a surface. **2** *Informal* a gullible or easily deceived person. **3** *Informal* a thing or person not specified by name: *He dived into the icy water to save the dog, and that makes him one brave sucker.* **4** a shoot growing from the base of a tree or other plant, especially one rising from the root below ground level at some distance from the main stem or trunk. **5** a freshwater N American or Asian fish with thick lips that are used to suck up food. **6** a lump of hard candy, usually on a stick.
v **1** fool or trick someone. **2** produce suckers from a plant or tree.
a sucker for, *Informal* have a particular attraction to: *She was a sucker for anything antique-looking.*

sucker punch *n* an unfair, unexpected punch or blow. **suck′er-punch′** *v.*

suck·le (suk′əl) *v* **suck·led, suck·ling** feed a baby or young animal from the breast or teat, or to feed in this way: *The sow suckled the piglets. The baby suckled at its mother's breast.*

suck·ling (suk′ling) *n* a young animal or child that has not yet been weaned.

su·crose (sū′krōs) *n* a sweet compound that is the main ingredient of cane or beet sugar. <French *sucre* sugar>

suc·tion (suk′shən) *n* the production of a partial vacuum by the removal of air in order to force fluid into a vacant space or cause surfaces to stick together.
v remove something using suction: *The nurse suctioned up mucus from the patient's lungs.* <Latin *sugere* suck>

suction cup *n* a cuplike device designed to adhere to a smooth surface by creating a vacuum when pressed against it and then released.

Su·dan (sū dan′) *n* a country in northeast Africa. **Su′da·nese′** (sū dən ēz′) *adj, n.*

sud·den (sud′ən) *adj* quick; rapid: *The army made a sudden attack on the fort. The cat made a sudden jump at the mouse. There was a sudden turn in a road.* <Old French, from Latin *subitus* sudden> **sud′den·ly** *adv.* **sud′den·ness** *n.*
all of a sudden, in a sudden manner: *All of a sudden he stopped and listened.*

sudden death *n* **1** instant or unexpected death. **2** a means of deciding the winner in a tied game or match, in which play continues and the winner is the first side or player to score.

sudden infant death syndrome *n* the death of a seemingly healthy infant who stops breathing for no apparent reason, usually during sleep. The cause has not been definitely identified. *Abbrev.* **SIDS** Also called **crib death**.

suds (sudz) *pl n* **1** froth made from soap and water. **2** *Informal* beer. <origin unknown> **suds′y** *adj.*

sue (sū) *v* **sued, su·ing 1** start a lawsuit against a person or organization: *He sued the dealer because the car he bought had faulty brakes.* **2** appeal formally to a person or thing to perform some action: *Messengers arrived to sue for peace.* <Old French *suer*, from Latin *sequi* follow> **su′a·ble** *adj.* **su′er** *n.*

suede (swād) *n* a soft leather that has a velvety nap on one or both sides, or a material that resembles it. <French *Suède* Sweden>

su·et (sū′it) *n* the hard, white fat on the kidneys and loins of cattle, sheep, etc., used in making puddings, pastry, and other dishes. <Old French, from Latin *sebum*>

suf·fer (suf′ər) *v* **1** experience or be subjected to something bad or unpleasant: *He suffered a lot after the accident.* **2** be affected by or subject to an illness or ailment: *She suffered from a broken hip.* **3** become or appear worse in quality: *Crop farming suffered greatly during the last drought.* **4** tolerate or permit: *She suffers no criticism from anyone.* <Latin *sufferre* to endure> **suf′fer·er** *n.*

suf·fer·ance (suf′ə rəns) *n* permission or consent not actually given but only implied by a failure to object or prevent: *He remained here only on sufferance.*

suf·fer·ing (suf′ə ring) *n* the experience of being affected by pain, trouble, or distress.

suf·fice (sə fīs′) *v* **suf·ficed, suf·fic·ing 1** be enough or adequate: *The money will suffice for one year.* **2** meet the needs of: *A small amount sufficed him.* <Latin *sub-* up to + *facere* make>
suffice (it) to say, it is enough if I say: *Suffice it to say that he was very upset.*

suf·fi·cien·cy (sə fish′ən sē) *n, pl* **suf·fi·cien·cies 1** the condition or quality of being sufficient or adequate: *They questioned the sufficiency of the preparations.* **2** a sufficient or adequate amount of something: *The ship had a sufficiency of provisions for a voyage of two months.*

suf·fi·cient (sə fish′ənt) *adj* enough or adequate: *sufficient proof.* **suf·fi′cient·ly** *adv.*

suf·fix (suf′iks) *n* a part of a word put at the end of a full word to form another word of different meaning or function. Examples: *-ly* in *badly*, *-ness* in *goodness.* <Latin *sub-* upon + *figere* fasten>

suf·fo·cate (suf′ə kāt′) *v* **suf·fo·cat·ed, suf·fo·cat·ing 1** die or cause to die from lack of air or inability to breathe: *The murder victim was suffocated with a pillow.* **2** have or cause to have difficulty in breathing: *I was suffocating in that hot, smoky room.* **3** feel or cause to feel trapped and oppressed: *She longed to escape the suffocating environment of her hometown.* <Latin *sub-* up + *fauces* throat> **suf′fo·cat′ing** *adj.* **suf′fo·cat′ing·ly** *adv.* **suf′fo·ca′tion** *n.*

suf·frage (suf′rij) *n* the right to vote in elections: *women's suffrage.* <Latin *suffragium* supporting vote, from *sub-* nearby + *fragor* approval> **suf′fra·gist** (suf′rə jist) *n.*

suf·fra·gette (suf′rə jet′) *n* in former times, a woman who advocated suffrage for women.

suf·fuse (sə fyūz′) *v* **suf·fused, suf·fus·ing** gradually spread through or over: *At twilight the sky was suffused with colour. Her eyes were suffused with tears.* <Latin *sub-* from under + *fundere* pour> **suf·fu′sion** *n.*

a bat	e bed	i bid	o pot	u cup	th **thin**
ā cake	ē me	ī bite	ō go	ū rude	TH **then**
à bar	ə about	ər over	ȯ for	ů put	zh measure

S

Su·fi (sū′fē) *n* a Muslim who follows a tradition in which mysticism and asceticism is emphasized. <Arabic = ascetic> **Suf′ic** *adj.* **Suf′ism** *n.*

sug·ar (shu̇g′ər) *n* **1** a sweet, crystalline substance obtained from various plants, especially from sugar cane or sugar beets, consisting mainly of sucrose, and used as a sweetener in foods and drinks. **2** a lump or teaspoon of this: *Two sugars in my coffee, please.* **3** *Informal* (*as a form of address*) a person who is regarded in a loving or affectionate way: *What's the matter, sugar?* **4** a member of a class of soluble, crystalline, typically sweet-tasting carbohydrates found in living tissues, such as glucose and sucrose.
v **1** mix, sprinkle, or coat with sugar: *She sugared her tea. We sugared the buns before baking them.* **2** form crystals of sugar: *Honey sugars if kept too long.* **3** (*usually with **off***) make maple sugar by boiling maple syrup until it is thick enough to crystallize. **4** make more pleasant or agreeable: *He sugared his criticism of the team with some praise for the individual players.* <Old French from Sanskrit *sarkara* candied sugar>

sugar beet *n* a variety of beet with a root with a high sugar content, grown commercially for the sugar it yields and the pulp, used as livestock feed.

🍁 **sugar bush** *n* a grove of sugar maples.

sugar cane *n* a very tall tropical grass with a strong, jointed stem from which sugar is extracted. The rest of the stem is used for fuel, fibreboard, and other purposes.

sug·ar–coat (shu̇g′ər kōt′) *v* **1** coat an item with sugar. **2** cause to seem more pleasant or agreeable. **sug′ar-coat′ing** *n.*

sugar daddy *Informal n* a rich older man who lavishes gifts or money on a younger woman in return for her company or sexual favours.

sug·ar·ing off (shu̇g′ər ing) *n* the conversion of maple syrup into sugar by boiling it until it crystallizes.

sugar maple *n* a large maple of eastern N America that has large, lobed leaves that turn bright red or yellow in fall, and yields timber as well a sweet sap that is the main source of maple syrup.

🍁 **sugar pie** *n* an open pie, sometimes with a lattice top, with a filling of brown or maple sugar and cream.

sug·ar·plum (shu̇g′ər plum′) *n* a plum crystallized with sugar, eaten as a treat.

🍁 **sugar shack** *n* a shedlike building, often out in the woods, in which maple sap is boiled in large quantities to make syrup or sugar.

sug·ar·y (shu̇g′ə rē) *adj* **1** consisting of, containing, or like sugar. **2** unduly sentimental or flattering: *sugary compliments, a sugary voice.* **sug′ar·i·ness** *n.*

sug·gest (sə jest′) *v* **1** propose or put forward for consideration: *She suggested a swim, and we all agreed.* **2** call up the thought of: *An incident in his own life had suggested the plot of the story.* **3** show in an indirect way: *His yawns suggested that he would like to go to bed.* <Latin *sub-* up + *gerere* bring>

sug·gest·i·ble (sə jes′tə bəl) *adj* open to suggestion or easily swayed. **sug·ges′ti·bil′i·ty** *n.*

sug·ges·tion (sə jes′chən) *n* **1** an idea or plan proposed or put forward, or the action of doing this: *The trip was made at her suggestion. The picnic was an excellent suggestion.* **2** something that implies or indicates a certain fact or situation: *There was no suggestion that he cheated his employer.* **3** a slight trace or indication of something: *She spoke English with just a suggestion of an accent.* **4** the action or process of calling up an idea or thought in someone's mind by associating it with other things: *the power of suggestion.*

SYNONYMS

Suggestion chiefly means "proposed idea or plan": *We're open to suggestions for the trip.*

Proposal often refers to a more formal suggestion or set of suggestions: *The council is now asking for proposals for next year's budget items.*

Recommendation implies support for a particular idea: *The report has two strong recommendations.*

sug·ges·tive (sə jes′tiv) *adj* **1** tending to suggest ideas, acts, or feelings: *The mild breeze was suggestive of spring.* **2** making someone think of sex and sexual relationships: *a suggestive comment.* **sug·ges′tive·ly** *adv.* **sug·ges′tive·ness** *n.*

su·i·cide (sū′ə sīd′) *n* **1** the action of killing oneself on purpose: *commit suicide.* **2** a person who does this. **3** a series of actions that lead to destroying one's own interests or prospects. <Latin *sui* of oneself + *-cidium* killing> **su′i·cid′al** *adj.* **su′i·cid′al·ly** *adv.*

su·i ge·ne·ris (sū′ī′jen′ər is) *or* (sū′ē′ jen′ər is) *adj* unique. <Latin = of its own kind>

suit (sūt) *n* **1** a set of outer clothes made of the same fabric and designed to be worn together, often to be worn on a particular occasion or for a particular activity: *a business suit, a jogging suit.* **2** a lawsuit. **3** one of the four sets of playing cards that make up a deck. The sets usually are marked with the symbols for spades, hearts, diamonds, and clubs. **4** the process of trying to win a woman's affection, especially with a view to marriage.
v **1** be convenient for or acceptable to: *The time and place suited him.* **2** be in keeping with or go well with: *The climate suited apples and wheat, but not oranges and tea. Her blue dress suits her fair skin.* <Old French *sieute* set of things, from Latin *sequi* follow>
follow suit, a play a card of the same suit as that first played. **b** follow the example of another.
suit yourself, (*often used to express annoyance*) do as you please: *You don't want to go? Suit yourself!*
suit up, put on special clothing or gear, such as an athletic uniform or scuba equipment, for a particular activity: *The astronauts have suited up and are ready for the launch.*

suit·a·ble (sū′tə bəl) *adj* proper for a particular person, purpose, or situation: *The park gives the children a suitable playground.* **suit′a·bil′i·ty** *n.* **suit′a·ble·ness** *n.* **suit′a·bly** *adv.*

suit·case (sūt′kās) *n* a case with a handle and a hinged lid, used for carrying clothes and other personal belongings.

suite (swēt) *n* **1** a set of things belonging together, such as connected rooms to be used as a unit by one person or group, or a set of matching furniture: *a hotel suite, a bedroom suite.* **2** a set of instrumental compositions to be played one after the other, or a set of selected pieces from an opera or musical, arranged to be played as one instrumental work. **3** a group of attendants to a monarch or other person of high social rank: *The queen travelled with a large suite.* **4** *Computers* a group of programs with a uniform design and the ability to share data. <See SUIT.>

suit·ing (sū′ting) *n* fabric used for making suits, trousers, jackets, and skirts.

suit·or (sū′tər) *n* **1** someone who pursues a relationship with a particular person, with a view to marriage. **2** a prospective buyer of a business or corporation.

su·ki·ya·ki (sū′kē yok′ē) or (skē yok′ē) *n* a Japanese dish of meat, vegetables, and bean curd fried together. <Japanese>

sulk (sulk) *v* be silent, sullen, and ill-humoured out of annoyance or disappointment: *He sulked a bit after his request was turned down.*
n **1** a mood of gloom, sullenness, and ill humour: *She was in a sulk because nothing was going her way.* **2 the sulks** *pl* ill humour shown by sulking: *He has the sulks.* <*sulky*>

sulk·y[1] (sul′kē) *adj* **sulk·i·er, sulk·i·est** silent, sullen, and resentful: *He always became sulky if he couldn't get his own way.* **sulk′i·ly** *adv.* **sulk′i·ness** *n.*

sulk·y[2] (sul′kē) *n, pl* **sul·kies** a very light, two-wheeled, horse-drawn carriage for one person, and used in harness racing. See HARNESS RACING for picture.

sul·len (sul′ən) *adj* silent because of bad humour or anger: *He was sullen and refused to answer my question.* <Old French *solain*> **sul′len·ly** *adv.* **sul′len·ness** *n.*

sul·ly (sul′ē) *v* **sul·lied, sul·ly·ing** damage the purity or integrity of: *sully a reputation.* <Old French *souillier* make dirty>

sul·pha drug or **sul·fa drug** (sul′fə) *n* a drug used in treating infections caused by bacteria.

sul·phate or **sul·fate** (sul′fāt) *n* a salt or ester of sulphuric acid.

sul·phide or **sul·fide** (sul′fīd) *n* a compound of sulphur with another element.

sul·phite or **sul·fite** (sul′fīt) *n* a compound of sulphurous acid with another element.

sul·phur or **sul·fur** (sul′fər) *n* a light yellow, non-metallic element that burns with a blue flame and a stifling odour. *Symbol* **S** <Latin = brimstone>

sulphur dioxide *n* a heavy, colourless gas that has a sharp odour. It is formed by burning sulphur in air.

sul·phu·ric acid (sul fyū′rik) *n* a heavy, colourless, oily, very strong acid used in making a variety of industrial products.

sul·phur·ous (sul′fə rəs) *or* (sul fyū′rəs) *adj* **1** containing or derived from sulphur. **2** like sulphur in being a pale yellow colour.

sul·tan (sul′tən) *n* a Muslim monarch, especially a former ruler of Turkey. <Arabic = ruler>

sul·tan·a (sul tan′ə) *n* **1** a small, light brown, seedless raisin. **2** the wife, mother, sister, or daughter of a sultan.

sul·tan·ate (sul′tə nāt′) *n* **1** the position or period of rule of a sultan. **2** the territory ruled over by a sultan.

sul·try (sul′trē) *adj* **sul·tri·er, sul·tri·est** **1** hot and humid as air or weather. **2** with or showing passion or sensuality: *a sultry glance.* <obsolete *sulter,* v, akin to *swelter*> **sul′tri·ly** *adv.* **sul′tri·ness** *n.*

sum (sum) *n* **1** a particular amount of money: *He paid a huge sum for that bicycle.* **2** the number or quantity obtained by adding two or more numbers or quantities together. **3** the total amount of something that exists: *To win the prize seemed to her the sum of happiness.* See SOME for confusable.
v **summed, sum·ming** find the total of. <Latin *summa*>
in sum, in short; the gist or main point is.
sum up, briefly express or tell the main points: *He summed up all the problems involved.*

su·mac (sū′mak) *or* (shū′mak) *n* a shrub or small tree with compound leaves that turn a brilliant red in the fall. <Old French, from Arabic *summaq*>

Su·me·ri·an (sū mē′rē ən) *or* (sū mer′ē ən) *adj* to do with the earliest inhabitants of **Sumer**, an ancient region in the valley of the Euphrates River, or their language.

sum·ma cum lau·de (sům′ə kům′ lou′dā) *adj, adv* with the highest distinction, especially of academic work: *He graduated summa cum laude.* <Latin = with the highest praise>

sum·ma·rize (sum′ə rīz′) *v* **sum·ma·rized, sum·ma·riz·ing** give a brief statement of the main points of something: *The review summarized the plot of the novel. At the end of the speech, she took three minutes to summarize.* **sum′ma·ri·za′tion** *n.* **sum′ma·ri′zer** *n.*

sum·ma·ry (sum′ə rē) *n, pl* **sum·ma·ries** a brief statement giving the main points of something: *The history book had a summary at the end of each chapter.*
adj **1** brief and concise. **2** without delay or formality, especially of legal matters: *a summary dismissal, a summary conviction.* <Latin *summa* sum>

S

SYNONYMS

Summary means "brief statement of main points": *She provides a summary at the end of each news broadcast.*

Rundown can suggest a brief analysis: *The teacher gave the students a rundown of the field trip.*

Synopsis often refers to a summary of a play, movie, or book: *There's a synopsis of the plot on the back cover of the book.*

a bat	e bed	i bid	o pot	u cup	th thin
ā cake	ē me	ī bite	ō go	ū rude	ᴛʜ then
à bar	ə about	ər over	ȯ for	ů put	zh measure

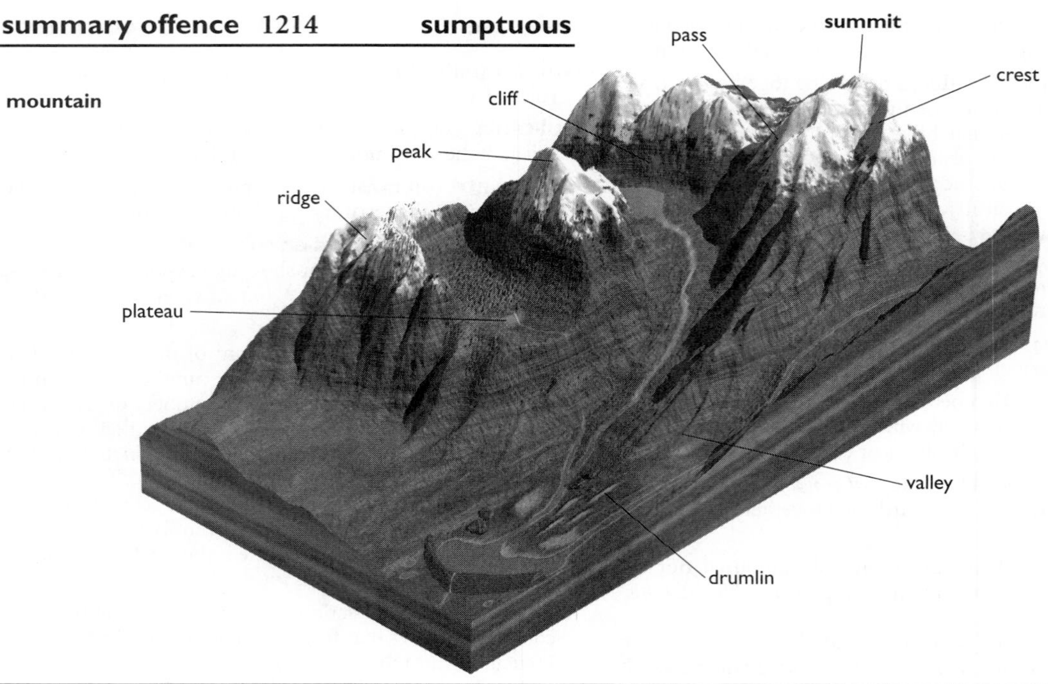

summary offence *n* a relatively minor criminal offence that is tried by a magistrate without a jury or a preliminary investigation. Compare INDICTABLE OFFENCE.

sum·ma·tion (su mā′shən) *n* **1** the process of adding things together, or the sum total of these things. **2** the process of summing something up, such as a judge's summary to a jury before it considers the verdict.

sum·mer (sum′ər) *n* the warmest season of the year in the northern hemisphere, from June to September.
adj to do with summer: *the summer sun, a summer cottage.*
v spend the summer in a particular place: *We summer at the seashore.* <Old English *sumor*>

summer fallow *n* land ploughed and left unseeded for a season or more, in order to destroy weeds or improve the soil. **sum′mer-fal′low** *v.*

sum·mer·house (sum′ər hous′) *n* a small building in a park or garden in which to sit in warm weather.

summer sausage *n* a spicy, dry, smoked sausage of beef or pork and beef that keeps well without refrigeration.

summer solstice *n* See SOLSTICE.

summer squash *n* a squash that is eaten before the seeds and rind have hardened.

sum·mer·time (sum′ər tīm′) *n* the season or period of summer.

sum·mer·y (sum′ə rē) *adj* of, like, or fit for summer: *a summery breeze, You'd better bring some light, summery clothes.*

sum·mit (sum′it) *n* **1** the highest point of a hill or mountain. **2** the highest attainable level of achievement: *The summit of her ambition was to be a foreign correspondent.* **3** an important meeting or conference, especially between heads of government. <Old French, from Latin *summus* highest>

sum·mon (sum′ən) *v* **1** urgently or formally call on someone to be present, especially as a defendant or witness in a law court. **2** urgently demand help: *summon an ambulance.* **3** call people to attend a meeting: *They were summoned to a hearing of the special committee.* **4** bring to the surface as a thought, action, or reaction: *She summoned up her courage and entered the deserted house.* <Latin *summonere* to give a discreet reminder>
sum′mon·er *n.*

sum·mons (sum′ənz) *n, pl* **sum·mons·es** **1** an order to appear before a judge or magistrate, or the writ containing it: *The police officer handed her a summons.* **2** an official or urgent call to someone to be present or to do something.
v serve someone with a summons to appear in court.

sum·mum bo·num (sům′əm bō′nəm) *n* the chief good, especially in an ethical system or code of conduct. <Latin = the highest good>

su·mo (sū′mō) *n* a Japanese form of heavyweight wrestling, in which each contestant tries to force his opponent outside a marked circle or by making him touch the ground with any part of his body except the feet. <Japanese = compete>

sump (sump) *n* a pit or hollow in which liquid collects, such as the reservoir at the base of an internal combustion engine, or a depression in the floor of a mine in which water collects. <German = swamp>

sump pump *n* a pump for removing collected liquid from a sump.

sump·tu·ous (sump′chū əs) *adj* splendid and expensive: *The emperor gave a sumptuous banquet.* <Latin *sumptuosus* costly, from *sumere* spend>
sump′tu·ous·ly *adv.* **sump′tu·ous·ness** *n.*

sum total SUM (def. 3).

sun (sun) *n* **1 a** the star around which the earth orbits, and which lights and warms it. **b** a similar star in the universe, with or without planets. **2** the light and warmth of the earth's sun: *to sit in the sun.* **3** a person or thing like the sun in brightness or splendour, especially in seeming to be a source of light, honour, glory, or prosperity.
v **sunned, sun·ning 1** sit or lie in the sun: *The swimmers sunned themselves on the beach.* **2** warm or dry in the sunshine. <Old English *sunne*>
under the sun, on earth or in existence: *They talked about everything under the sun.*

sun·baked (sun′bākt′) *adj* dry and hard because of exposure to the sun: *sunbaked bricks, sunbaked soil.*

sun·bath or **sun bath** (sun′bath′) *n* the exposure of the body to sunshine or a sunlamp.

sun·bathe (sun′bāᴛʜ′) *v* **sun·bathed, sun·bath·ing** sit or lie in the sun. **sun′bath·er** *n.* **sun′bath·ing** *n.*

sun·beam (sun′bēm′) *n* a ray of sunlight.

sun·block (sun′blok′) *n* a cream or lotion for the skin that gives protection by blocking out harmful ultraviolet rays from the sun.

sun·burn (sun′bərn′) *n* a reddening, inflammation, or blistering and peeling of the skin caused by too much exposure to the rays of the sun.
v **sun·burned** or **sun·burnt, sun·burn·ing** get or cause to get a sunburn: *Her skin sunburns very quickly. He was sunburned from a day at the beach.*

sun·burst (sun′bərst′) *n* **1** a sudden appearance of the full sun from behind clouds. **2** a brooch, ornament, or pattern of concentric bands of colour arranged to look like the sun with its rays.

sun·dae (sun′dā′) *or* (sun′dē) *n* a serving of ice cream with syrup, crushed fruits, and nuts on it. <origin uncertain>

🍁 **sun dance** *n* a sacred dance ceremony among some First Nations and Native American peoples, traditionally held in honour of the sun.

Sun·day (sun′dā′) *n* the day of the week after Saturday and before Monday. *Abbrev.* **Sun** <Latin *dies solis* day of the sun>
a month of Sundays, *Informal* (*always with a negative*) an indefinitely long time: *That wouldn't happen again in a month of Sundays.*

Sunday school *Christianity n* a series of classes held by a church on Sundays for teaching about Christianity.

sun·der (sun′dər) *v* split apart.
in sunder, *Archaic or Poetic* apart or in pieces: *Lightning tore the tree in sunder.*

sun·dew (sun′dyū) *or* (sun′dū′) *n* a small bog plant, such as the Venus flytrap, that has leaves covered with sticky hairs that trap insects, which are then digested.

sun·di·al (sun′dī′əl) *or* (sun′dīl′) *n* an instrument for telling the time of day by the position of the shadow of a pointer cast by the sun onto a disc marked off in hours.

sun·dog (sun′dog′) PARHELION.

sun·down (sun′doun′) *n* sunset.

sun–dried (sun′drīd′) *adj* dried by exposure to the sun: *sun-dried apples.*

sun·dry (sun′drē) *adj* several or of various kinds: *From sundry hints, he guessed he was to be given a bicycle for his birthday.*
n **sun·dries** *pl* various items not important enough to be mentioned separately. <Old English *syndrig* separate, from *sundor* apart>
all and sundry, *Informal* everybody: *He sent out invitations to all and sundry to visit him in his new house.*

sun·fish (sun′fish′) *n, pl* **sun·fish·es** or (*especially collectively*) **sun·fish 1** a deep-bodied marine fish of warm seas, with tall fins near the rear of the body and a very short tail. **2** a nest-building N American freshwater fish.

sun·flow·er (sun′flou′ər) *n* a tall N American plant of the daisy family, with large, golden flowers. The seeds are used as a source of food and cooking oil. See DISC FLOWER for picture.

sung (sung) past participle of SING.

sun·glass·es (sun′glas′iz) *pln* eyeglasses with tinted lenses designed to protect the eyes from direct sunlight or glare.

sun god *n* a god who personifies the sun.

sun hat *n* a hat, usually with a big brim, designed to protect the head from the sun.

sunk (sungk) a past tense and past participle of SINK.

sunk·en (sung′kən) *adj* **1** having sunk or been submerged in water: *a sunken ship, a sunken rock.* **2** having sunk below the usual or expected level, or put at a lower level than the surrounding area: *a sunken cake, a sunken garden.* **3** deeply hollow, especially as a result of illness: *sunken eyes, sunken cheeks.*

sun·lamp (sun′lamp′) *n* an electric lamp that gives out ultraviolet rays, used for therapy or for producing an artificial suntan.

sun·less (sun′lis) *adj* without sunlight: *a sunless day, sunless caverns.*

sun·light (sun′līt′) *n* the light from the sun: *We moved the plants into the sunlight. This room doesn't get any sunlight.*

sun·lit (sun′lit′) *adj* lighted by direct light from the sun: *a sunlit meadow.*

Sun·ni (sů′nē) *n, pl* **Sun·nis** the larger of the two main branches of Islam, or a Muslim who belongs to this branch. Compare SHIA.

sun·ny (sun′ē) *adj* **sun·ni·er, sun·ni·est 1** with much sunshine: *a sunny day.* **2** exposed to, lighted by, or warmed by the direct rays of the sun: *a sunny room.* **3** cheerful or happy: *a sunny disposition. The baby gave a sunny smile.* **sun′ni·ly** *adv.* **sun′ni·ness** *n.*

sunny side *n* **1** the side of something that receives the sun most or longest. **2** the cheerful or optimistic aspect of a situation: *He usually looks at the sunny side of things.*
sunny side up, fried as an egg on one side only and with the yolk unbroken.

a bat	e bed	i bid	o pot	u cup	th **thin**
ā cake	ē me	ī bite	ō go	ū rude	ᴛʜ **then**
à bar	ə about	ər over	ô for	ů put	zh measure

sun porch *n* a porch enclosed largely by glass or screen, designed to admit plenty of sunlight.

sun·proof (sun′prūf′) *adj* impervious to or unaffected by the rays of the sun: *These sunproof curtains will not fade.*

sun·rise (sun′rīz′) *n* **1** the first appearance of the sun in the morning or when daylight arrives: *There was a beautiful sunrise this morning.* **2** the colours and light visible in the sky when the sun first appears in the morning, especially as a view or spectacle: *Sunrise was especially beautiful on the tropical island.*

sun·roof (sun′růf′) *n* a panel in the roof of a motor vehicle that can be opened to admit air and sunlight, or the roof itself.

sun·room (sun′rům′) *n* a room with large windows, and sometimes a glass roof, designed to let in much sunlight.

sun·screen (sun′skrēn′) *n* a cream or lotion that gives protection from the sun, especially to block ultraviolet rays and prevent sunburn.

sun·set (sun′set′) *n* **1** the time in the evening when the sun disappears or when daylight fades: *Sunset was at 6:20 p.m. They expect to be back before sunset.* **2** the colours and light visible in the sky at this time, especially as a view or spectacle: *We enjoyed looking at the sunset.*

sun·shade (sun′shād′) *n* an umbrella, parasol, or awning, used to provide protection from the sun.

sun·shine (sun′shīn′) *n* direct sunlight unbroken by cloud, especially over a wide area: *They had two days of sunshine during their holidays. The sunshine made us drowsy.*

sun·shin·y (sun′shī′nē) *adj* **sun·shin·i·er, sun·shin·i·est** **1** with much sunshine. **2** bright; cheerful; happy.

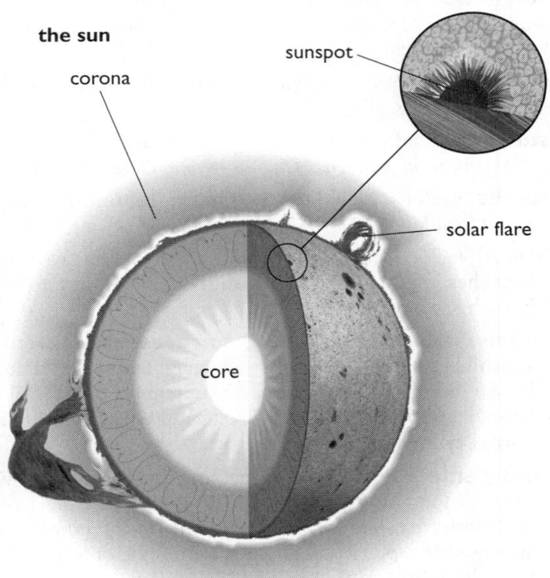

sun·spot (sun′spot′) *n* a spot or patch of lower surface temperature that appears from time to time on the surface of the sun, appearing dark by contrast with its surroundings.

sun·stroke (sun′strōk′) *n* a heatstroke caused by overexposure to direct sunlight.

sun·tan (sun′tan′) *n* a browning of a person's skin resulting from exposure to the sun. **sun′tanned** *adj.*

sun·up (sun′up′) *n* sunrise.

sup (sup) *v* **supped, sup·ping** eat supper. <Old French *soper*>

sup– *prefix* a form of SUB- occurring before the letter *p*: *suppress.*

su·per (sū′pər) *Informal adj* excellent, wonderful, or of the highest quality.
n **1** a superintendent. **2** an extra in a theatrical production.
adv especially: *He's been super friendly lately.*

super– *combining form* **1** over or above: *superimpose, superstructure.* **2** to a great or extreme degree: *superabundant, supersensitive.* **3** extra large of its kind: *supernova.* **4** with greater power, influence, or capacity of its kind: *superpower.* <Latin *super* above>

su·per·a·bound (sū′pə rə bound′) *v* be very or too abundant.

su·per·a·bun·dant (sū′pə rə bun′dənt) *adj* more than is needed. **su′per·a·bun′dance** *n.*

su·per·an·nu·ate (sū′pə ran′yū āt′) *v* **su·per·an·nu·at·ed, su·per·an·nu·at·ing** **1** retire on a pension. **2** cause to become obsolete: *All our equipment had become superannuated.* <Latin *super annum* beyond a year> **su′per·an′nu·at·ed** *adj.*

su·per·an·nu·a·tion (sū′pə ran′yū ā′shən) *n* a regular payment made into a fund by an employee toward a future pension, or a pension of this type.

su·perb (sū pərb′) *adj* **1** excellent: *The actor gave a superb performance.* **2** impressive and splendid: *superb jewels, superb scenery, a superb dinner.* <Latin *super* above> **su·perb′ly** *adv.* **su·perb′ness** *n.*

su·per·bug (sū′pər bug′) *n Informal* a strain of bacteria that has become resistant to antibiotics.

su·per·charge (sū′pər chärj′) *v* **su·per·charged, su·per·charg·ing** **1** fit or design an internal combustion engine with a supercharger. **2** supply with extra energy, power, or intensity. **su′per·charged′** *adj.*

su·per·charg·er (sū′pər chär′jər) *n* a device in an internal combustion engine that increases the pressure of the fuel-air mixture to create greater efficiency.

su·per·cil·i·ous (sū′pər sil′ē əs) *adj* behaving or looking as though one thinks one is superior to others: *a supercilious clerk.* <Latin *supercilium* eyebrow> **su′per·cil′i·ous·ly** *adv.* **su′per·cil′i·ous·ness** *n.*

su·per·con·duc·tor (sū′pər kən duk′tər) *n* a metal that can conduct electricity without resistance. **su′per·con·duc′tive** *adj.* **su′per·con·duc′tiv′i·ty** *n.*

su·per·cool (sū′pər kūl′) *v* cool a liquid below its freezing point without causing it to crystallize or solidify, or undergo such cooling.
adj Informal extremely sophisticated, impressive, or calm.

su·per–du·per (sū′pər dū′pər) *Informal adj* super or marvellous. <*super* by reduplication>

su·per·e·rog·a·to·ry (sū′pə rə rog′ə tȯ′rē) *adj* performing more work than duty requires: *supererogatory help.*

su·per·fi·cial (sū′pər fish′əl) *adj* **1** of, on, or affecting the surface: *superficial burns, superficial measurement.* **2** appearing to be true or real until examined more closely: *superficial truths.* **3** not through, deep, or complete: *a superficial resemblance.* <Latin *superficialis* of the surface> **su′per·fi′ci·al′i·ty** (sū′pər fish′i al′ə tē) *n.* **su′per·fi′ci·al·ly** *adv.*

su·per·fine (sū′pər fīn′) *adj* **1** very fine in texture, size, or quality: *superfine cotton, superfine sugar.* **2** too refined or subtle: *superfine distinctions.*

su·per·flu·i·ty (sū′pər flū′ə tē) *n, pl* **su·per·flu·i·ties** **1** a greater amount or number than is needed, or something unnecessary. **2** the condition of being superfluous.

su·per·flu·ous (sū pər′flū əs) *adj* unnecessary, especially in being more than enough: *superfluous words.* <Latin *super-* over + *fluere* flow> **su·per′flu·ous·ly** *adv.* **su·per′flu·ous·ness** *n.*

su·per·gi·ant (sū′pər jī′ənt) *n* a very large star that is much more luminous than the sun.

su·per·glue (sū′pər glū′) *n* a very strong, quick-acting adhesive.

su·per·heat (sū′pər hēt′) *v* heat a liquid under pressure above its boiling point without its producing vapour.

su·per·high frequency (sū′pər hī′) *n* the range of radio frequencies between 3 and 30 gigahertz, the second highest range in the radio spectrum, above ultra-high and below extremely high frequency.

su·per·high·way (sū′pər hī′wā) *n* a high-speed expressway or freeway divided by a median and with two or more traffic lanes in each direction.

su·per·hu·man (sū′pər hyū′mən) *adj* with or showing great ability or powers: *By superhuman effort, they survived the winter.* **su′per·hu′man·ly** *adv.*

su·per·im·pose (sū′pə rim pōz′) *v* **su·per·im·posed, su·per·im·pos·ing** place one thing over another, typically so that both are still evident. **su′per·im·po·si′tion** *n.*

su·per·in·tend (sū′pə rin tend′) *or* (sū′prin tend′) *v* oversee and direct work or workers. <Latin *super-* above + *intendere* direct> **su′per·in·tend′ence** *n.*

su·per·in·ten·dent (sū′pə rin ten′dənt) *or* (sū′prin ten′dənt) *n* **1** a person who oversees, directs, or manages; a supervisor: *a superintendent of schools, a superintendent of a factory.* **2** a police officer of high rank. **3** a person in charge of the maintenance of an apartment building, office building, etc. **su′per·in·tend′en·cy** *n.*

su·pe·ri·or (sə pē′rē ər) *adj* **1** of high standard or quality: *superior work.* **2** higher in rank, status, or quality: *The last brand of coffee we tried was superior to this.* **3** greater in size or power: *superior force.* **4** having or showing a feeling of being above others: *superior airs.*
n **1** a person who or thing that is higher in rank, status, or quality than others, especially a colleague in a higher position. **2** the head of a monastery or convent. <Latin *super* above> **su·pe′ri·or′i·ty** *n.*
superior to, above yielding or giving in to: *He was superior to flattery.*

superior court *n* in Canada, the supreme court or courts of a province, which can overturn decisions of lower courts.

superiority complex *n* an attitude of feeling more important than other people, concealing actual feelings of inferiority or failure.

su·per·la·tive (sū pər′lə tiv) *or* (sə pər′lə tiv) *adj* **1** of the highest quality or degree: *My grandmother had superlative wisdom.* **2** expressing the highest degree of comparison of an adjective or adverb. Example: *Fairest, best,* and *most slowly* are the superlative forms of *fair, good,* and *slowly.*
n **1** a superlative adjective or adverb. **2 superlatives** *pl* an exaggerated expression of praise: *He could only speak of his girlfriend in superlatives.* <Latin *super-* beyond + *ferre* carry> **su·per′la·tive·ly** *adv.* **su·per′la·tive·ness** *n.*

GRAMMAR AND USAGE

Some two-syllable adjectives and most one-syllable adjectives and adverbs have a comparative ending in -er and a **superlative** ending in -est: *happier, happiest; sooner, soonest.*

Three-syllable adjectives and two- and three-syllable adverbs use *more/most* and *less/least* to form the comparative and superlative: *more beautiful, most beautiful; less desperately/least desperately.*

su·per·man (sū′pər man′) *n, pl* **su·per·men** (sū′pər men′) a man with great physical or mental ability.

su·per·mar·ket (sū′pər mȧr′kit) *n* a large self-service store selling groceries and household goods.

su·per·nal (sū pər′nəl) *adj* **1** *Poetic* of, coming from, or in the sky. **2** of exceptional quality or extent: *supernal knowledge.* **su·per′nal·ly** *adv.*

su·per·nat·ur·al (sū′pər nach′ə rəl) *or* (sū′pər nach′rəl) *adj* to do with some agency or force outside scientific understanding or the known laws of nature: *a supernatural event, supernatural powers.*
n **the supernatural** appearances, occurrences, or events considered to be of supernatural origin, such as ghosts. **su′per·nat′u·ral·ism** *n.* **su′per·nat′u·ral·ly** *adv.*

S

su·per·no·va (sū′pər nō′və) *n* a star undergoing a massive internal explosion, causing it to suddenly and greatly increase in brightness.

su·per·nu·mer·ar·y (sū′pər nyū′mə rer′ē) *or* (sū′pər nū′mə rer′ē) *adj* forming or being more than the usual or necessary number.
n, pl **su·per·nu·mer·ar·ies** an extra person or thing. <Latin *super numerum* beyond the number>

su·per·pow·er (sū′pər pou′ər) *n* an extremely powerful and influential nation, especially one of a few nations that dominate the world and compete with each other.

a **bat**	e **bed**	i **bid**	o **pot**	u **cup**	th **thin**
ā **cake**	ē **me**	ī **bite**	ō **go**	ū **rude**	ᴛʜ **then**
ȧ **bar**	ə **about**	ər **over**	ȯ **for**	u̇ **put**	zh **measure**

su·per·sat·u·rate (sū′pər sach′ə rāt′) *v* **su·per·sat·u·rat·ed, su·per·sat·u·rat·ing** increase the saturation of a chemical solution beyond the saturation point. A **supersaturated solution** is one in which more of a substance is dissolved than the solvent will hold under normal conditions. **su′per·sat′u·ra′tion** *n.*

su·per·script (sū′pər skript′) *n* a small number, letter, or figure written above the line. Example: In a^3 the 3 is a superscript.

su·per·sede (sū′pər sēd′) *v* **su·per·sed·ed, su·per·sed·ing** take the place of a person or thing previously in authority or use: *Electric lights had superseded gas lights in most homes by the 1920s.* <Latin *super-* above + *sedere* sit>

su·per·sen·si·tive (sū′pər sen′sə tiv) *adj* extremely or morbidly sensitive. **su′per·sen′si·tive·ly** *adv.* **su′per·sen′si·tive·ness** *n.* **su′per·sen′si·tiv′i·ty** *n.*

su·per·son·ic (sū′pər son′ik) *adj* to do with a speed greater than that of sound: *supersonic aircraft.*

su·per·star (sū′pər stȧr′) *n* a famous and extremely successful performer or athlete.

su·per·sti·tion (sū′pər stish′ən) *n* an unreasoning belief in supernatural forces or their powers to the extent that they are worshipped or feared: *It is a common superstition that breaking a mirror brings bad luck.* <Latin *superstitio* dread of the supernatural, from *superstare* to stand still by something> **su′per·sti′tious** *adj.* **su′per·sti′tious·ly** *adv.* **su′per·sti′tious·ness** *n.*

su·per·struc·ture (sū′pər struk′chər) *n* a structure built on top of something else, such as the parts of a ship built above its hull and main deck, or the part of a building above its foundations.

su·per·vene (sū′pər vēn′) *v* **su·per·vened, su·per·ven·ing** occur later than a specified or implied action or event, especially in such a way as to change the situation. <Latin *supervenire* to come on top of> **su′per·ven′tion** *n.*

su·per·vise (sū′pər vīz′) *v* **su·per·vised, su·per·vis·ing** observe and direct how a person or group performs a task, project, or activity: *During our first day of work we were closely supervised.* <Latin *super-* over + *videre* see> **su′per·vi′sion** *n.* **su′per·vi′sor** *n.* **su′per·vi′sory** *adj.*

su·per·wo·man (sū′pər wo′mən) *n, pl* **su·per·wo·men** (sū′pər wi′mən) a woman with great physical or mental ability.

su·pine (sū pīn′) *adj* **1** lying on the back with the face upward: *The patient was placed in a supine position.* Compare PRONE. **2** failing to act or protest as a result of moral weakness or laziness: *supine indifference.* <Latin *supinus*> **su·pine′ly** *adv.*

sup·per (sup′ər) *n* **1** an evening meal, typically a light or informal one, or the food served at this meal: *We usually have supper at six o'clock. I enjoyed supper.* **2** an informal public social event that takes place in the evening, featuring a meal and often held to raise money: *a church supper.* <Old French *soper*> **sup′per·less** *adj.*

sup·per·time (sup′ər tīm′) *n* the time when supper is eaten.
adj happening at or during supper: *suppertime conversation.*

sup·plant (sə plant′) *v* replace a person or thing previously in authority or use: *Machinery supplanted hand labour in the making of shoes. The prince plotted to supplant the king.* <Old French, from Latin *supplantare* to overthrow>

sup·ple (sup′əl) *adj* **sup·pler, sup·plest** flexible and able to bend and move easily and gracefully: *a supple birch tree, supple leather, a supple dancer.*
v **sup·pled, sup·pling** make or become more flexible. <Old French, from Latin *supplex* submissive, from *supplicare.* See SUPPLICATE.> **sup′ple·ness** *n.*

sup·ple·ment (sup′lə mənt) *for n,* (sup′lə ment′) *for v.*
n **1** a thing that completes or enhances something else when added to it: *a diet supplement. The newspaper has a supplement every Saturday.* **2** the amount by which an angle is less than 180°.
v add an extra element or amount to: *She supplemented her income by taking an extra job on Saturdays.* <Latin *supplere* to supply> **sup′ple·men′tal** *adj.* **sup′ple·men′tal·ly** *adv.* **sup′ple·men·ta′tion** *n.*

SYNONYMS

Supplement usually refers to something that is extra or is added to something else that is more important: *I got a part-time job to supplement my income.*

Complement often means "something necessary for the completion of a whole": *The blue jacket was the perfect complement for the pants she had chosen.*

sup·ple·men·ta·ry (sup′lə men′tə rē) *adj* completing or enhancing something: *The new members of the class received supplementary instruction.*

supplementary angle *n* either of two angles that together total 180°.

sup·pli·ant (sup′lē ənt) *n* a person who makes a humble plea to someone in power or authority.
adj making or expressing a humble plea to someone in power or authority: *They raised suppliant hands.* <See SUPPLICATE.> **sup′pli·ant·ly** *adv.*

sup·pli·cate (sup′lə kāt′) *v* **sup·pli·cat·ed, sup·pli·cat·ing** ask or beg for something humbly and earnestly. <Latin *supplicare,* from *sub-* down + *plicare* bend> **sup′pli·cant** *n.* **sup′pli·cat′ing** *adj.* **sup′pli·cat′ing·ly** *adv.* **sup′pli·ca′tion** *n.* **sup′pli·ca·to′ry** *adv.*

sup·ply[1] (sə plī′) *v* **sup·plied, sup·ply·ing** make available something needed or wanted: *The city supplied shelters for the homeless. There was just enough electricity to supply the demand.*
n, pl **sup·plies 1** a source of something from which a person or place can be provided with what is needed or wanted: *Our school gets its supply of paper from the city.* **2** the action of providing what is needed or wanted: *Our contract provided for a steady supply of goods.* **3** a person, especially a schoolteacher, acting as a temporary substitute for another. **4 supplies** *pl* the food, equipment, etc. necessary for an army, expedition, or the like. <Latin *sub-* up + *-plere* fill> **sup·pli′er** *n.*
in supply, available to a given extent: *Apples are in poor supply this year.*

sup·ply[2] (sup′lē) *adv* in a supple manner.

sup·ply–side (sə plī′sīd) *adj* to do with a policy intended to increase economic output and employment, especially in reducing taxes and government involvement.

supply teacher *n* a teacher who is acting as a temporary substitute for a regular teacher.

sup·port (sə pȯrt′) *v* **1** bear all or part of the weight of: *Heavy walls supported the roof.* **2** produce enough food and water for: *The land could no longer support crops.* **3** tolerate or endure: *She couldn't support life without friends.* **4** give assistance to, especially financially: *She supported her nephew while he was at university.* **5** give comfort, emotional help, or approval to: *They did everything they could to support her in her sorrow.* **6** assist or protect another military unit in combat: *Artillery fire supported the infantry attack.* **7** important as an actor or part in a play or movie, but subordinate to the leading actors or parts. **8** *Computers* allow the use or operation of a computer or operating system: *The new database version does not support previous ones.*
n **1** a thing that or person who bears the weight of something else, or the action or condition of bearing the weight of something: *He grabbed my shoulder for support.* **2** assistance, especially financial: *My parents gave me some support during my year abroad.* **3** comfort, emotional help, approval, or encouragement for someone: *We got a lot of support for our petition.* **4** military assistance or protection given by one element or unit to another: *artillery support.* **5** *Computers* technical help given to the user. <Latin *sub-* up + *portare* carry> **sup·port′a·ble** *adj.* **sup·port′a·bly** *adv.* **sup·port′er** *n.*

SYNONYMS

Support means "give help or encouragement": *I'll support you in the election.*

Advocate means "support strongly and publicly": *He's been advocating for the charity in his weekly column.*

Champion emphasizes advocating in the face of opposition: *The organization has championed refugee rights for many years.*

Promote involves moving something forward or developing it: *Toothpaste promotes healthy teeth.*

support group *n* a group of people who meet regularly to support and encourage one another and exchange useful information about problems relating to some shared characteristic or experience.

sup·por·tive (su pȯr′tiv) *adj* providing encouragement or emotional help: *a supportive friend.*

sup·pose (sə pōz′) *v* **sup·posed, sup·pos·ing** **1** assume that something is the case, sometimes on the basis of evidence or experience, but without proof or certain knowledge: *Suppose it doesn't work, then what? I suppose she will argue as usual.* **2** involve as necessary; imply; presuppose: *An invention supposes an inventor.* <Old French *supposer*> **sup·pos′a·ble** *adj.*

sup·posed (sə pōzd′) *adj* **1** accepted as real or true, but mistakenly or without proof: *We need to take a closer look at the supposed improvements in the system.* **2** designed or intended: *What is that supposed to mean?* **3** (*with* **to**) obliged or expected: *I was supposed to bring the cake, but I forgot.* **4** (*with* **to**) permitted; allowed: *You are not supposed to jump on the bed.*

sup·pos·ed·ly (sə pō′zi dlē) *adv* according to what is supposed or was supposed: *He was supposedly sleeping, but Mom discovered that he had gone out.*

sup·pos·ing (sə pō′zing) *conj* assuming that: *Supposing it rains, shall we go?*

sup·po·si·tion (sup′ə zish′ən) *n* an assumption or uncertain belief: *She entered the campaign on the supposition that her friends would support her.* **sup′po·si′tion·al** *adj.*

sup·pos·i·to·ry (sə poz′ə tȯ′rē) *n, pl* **sup·pos·i·to·ries** medicine in the form of a cone or cylinder to be put into the rectum or vagina to dissolve. <Latin *sub-* up + *ponere* place>

sup·press (sə pres′) *v* **1** put an end to by force: *The troops suppressed the rebellion.* **2** prevent or restrain the development, action, or expression of a feeling, impulse, or idea: *She suppressed a yawn.* **3** prevent the spread of information: *The government was accused of suppressing important facts. The book was suppressed because it contained libellous statements.* **4** prevent or inhibit a process or reaction: *to suppress bleeding.* <Latin *sub-* down + *premere* press> **sup·press′i·ble** *adj.* **sup·press′ive** *adj.* **sup·pres′sor** *n.*

sup·pres·sant (sə pres′ənt) *n* a substance, especially a drug, that acts to suppress or restrain something: *a cough suppressant.*

sup·pres·sion (sə presh′ən) *n* the action of suppressing something, such as an activity, publication, or process.

sup·pu·rate (sup′yə rāt′) *v* **sup·pu·rat·ed, sup·pu·rat·ing** form or discharge pus. <Latin *sub-* under + *pus* pus> **sup′pu·ra′tion** *n.*

su·prem·a·cist (sə prem′ə sist) *n* one who believes in the natural superiority of a particular group, especially one determined by race or sex: *a white supremacist.*

su·prem·a·cy (sə prem′ə sē) *n* the quality or condition of being superior to all others in authority, power, or status.

su·preme (sə prēm′) *adj* **1** highest in rank, status, authority, or office: *a supreme ruler.* **2** highest in degree or quality: *supreme disgust, supreme courage.* <Latin *super* above> **su·preme′ly** *adv.*
the Supreme Being, God.

supreme court *n* **1** the highest judicial court in a country or other political unit. **2** **Supreme Court** the highest appeal court for civil and criminal matters in the nation or in some provinces.

sur–[1] *prefix* upon or above: *surcharge.*

S

a bat	e bed	i bid	o pot	u cup	th thin
ā cake	ē me	ī bite	ō go	ū rude	ꟻH then
ȧ bar	ə about	ər over	ȯ for	u̇ put	zh measure

sur–[2] *prefix* a form of SUB- occurring before the letter *r*: *surreptitious.*

sur·charge (sər′chärj′) *for n,* (sər chärj′) *for v. n* **1** an extra charge or payment: *The express company made a surcharge for delivering the trunk outside the city limits, a surcharge of punishment.* **2** an additional mark printed on a postage stamp to change its value.
v **sur·charged, sur·charg·ing 1** charge or require extra payment. **2** mark a postage stamp with a surcharge. <French *sur-* over + *charger*>

sure (shůr) *adj* **sur·er, sur·est 1** confident in what one thinks or knows: *I am sure of his guilt.* **2** true, authentic, or real beyond any doubt: *a sure messenger, sure ground.* **3** able to be trusted or relied on: *a sure aim, a sure touch.* **4** certain to be or to happen: *The team faced sure defeat. She is sure to win the prize.*
adv Informal certainly: *Sure, we can go to the party. He was sure glad to see her.* <Old French, from Latin *securus*>
sure′ness *n.*
be sure, do not fail to: *Be sure to lock up when you leave.*
for sure, *Informal* without doubt: *He's coming for sure. That's for sure.*
make sure, confirm that something is so, is done, or will happen: *She made sure we had lots to eat.*
sure enough, *Informal* confirming something previously mentioned: *She'll win this election, sure enough.*
sure of yourself, very confident of your own abilities or views.
to be sure, admitting or affirming the truth of something: *Math was not his best subject, to be sure.*

SYNONYMS

Sure means "certain": *Are you sure that this cellphone is the best one there is?*

Assured is a more formal word that emphasizes confidence: *The interviewer was impressed with the applicant's assured manner.*

Sure-fire is an informal word implying that something is certain to succeed: *I have a sure-fire solution to the problem!*

sure–fire (shůr′fīr′) *Informal adj* certain to succeed: *a sure-fire formula.*

sure–foot·ed (shůr′fůt′id) *adj* unlikely to stumble or slip, especially in being confident and competent. **sure′-foot′ed·ness** *n.*

sure·ly (shůr′lē) *adv* **1** without any doubt: *Half a loaf is surely better than none.* **2** (*used to emphasize a statement*) really: *Surely you're not serious!* **3** without a mistake or slip: *The goat leaped surely from rock to rock.*

sure thing *Informal n* **1** an outcome that is certain or assured: *I'd say a "guilty" verdict is a sure thing in this case.* **2** yes or certainly: *"Can you open this jar?" "Sure thing!"*

sur·e·ty (shů′rə tē) *n, pl* **sur·e·ties 1** a pledge or formal promise to assume another's responsibility, especially a financial one, in the case of loss, damage, or failure to do something. **2** a person who does this: *He was surety for his brother's appearance in court.*

surf (sərf) *n* the waves or swell of the sea breaking on the shore or a reef.
v **1** travel or ride on the crest of a wave, especially with a surfboard. **2** quickly move from channel to channel on TV, or from site to site on the Internet. <origin uncertain> **surf′er** *n.* **surf′ing** *n.*

sur·face (sər′fis) *n* **1** the outside part, uppermost layer, or level top of a thing, often with reference to its texture, form, or extent: *The stone sank below the surface.* **2** an outward appearance or consideration of something: *He seems rough, but you will find him very kind below the surface.* **3** a plane surface.
adj of, relating to, or occurring on the upper or outer part of a thing: *surface travel.*
v **sur·faced, sur·fac·ing 1** rise, bring, or come to the surface: *The submarine surfaced.* **2** become apparent: *Some doubts surfaced about the project.* **3** put a surface on something, especially a road. <French *sur-* above + *face*>

surface area *Mathematics n* the total area of the outside surface of a three-dimensional object.

surface mail *n* mail transported by land or sea, rather than by air.

surface tension *n* the tension of the surface film of a liquid caused by the attraction of the particles in the surface layer by the rest of the liquid, which tends to minimize the surface area.

surf·board (sərf′bȯrd′) *n* a long, narrow, somewhat oblong-shaped board on which a person may stand or lie in order to ride on the crest of a wave.

sur·feit (sər′fit) *n* an undue or excessive amount of something: *a surfeit of food, a surfeit of advice.*
v cause someone to desire no more of something as a result of having consumed or done it too much. <Old French *surfait* overdone, from Latin *facere* to do>

surge (sərj) *v* **surged, surg·ing 1** move suddenly or powerfully forward or upward, especially as a crowd or a natural force such as the waves or tide. **2** increase suddenly and powerfully, typically during an otherwise stable or quiet period.
n **1** a sudden or powerful or upward movement. **2** a sudden increase in amount or intensity: *A surge of anger swept over her.* **3** *Computers* an electrical pulse, perhaps lasting several seconds, in which a rapid increase in voltage is followed by a rapid decrease. Without a surge protector, a computer may crash and damage files or components. <Latin *sub-* up + *regere* reach>

sur·geon (sər′jən) *n* a medical doctor who practises surgery.

surge protector *Computers n* a device protecting a computer or other electric equipment from damage caused by power surges. **surge protected** *adj.*
surge protection *n.*

sur·ger·y (sər′jə rē) *n, pl* **sur·ger·ies 1 a** the treatment of injuries, diseases, or other disorders by cutting into and manipulating a part of the body, especially by the use of instruments: *He needed surgery on his fractured wrist.* **b** the branch of medicine dealing with such treatment. **2** a surgical operating room. <Old French, from Greek *cheir* hand + *ergon* work> **sur′gi·cal** *adj.* **sur′gi·cal·ly** *adv.*

Su·ri·name (sū′rə nam′) *n* a country in northeast S America. **Su′ri·nam·ese′** *adj, n.*

sur·ly (sər′lē) *adj* **sur·li·er, sur·li·est** bad-tempered and unfriendly: *They got a surly answer from the receptionist.* <Middle English *sirly* lordly> **sur′li·ness** *n.*

sur·mise (sər mīz′) *v* **sur·mised, sur·mis·ing** suppose that a thing is true without having evidence to confirm it: *We surmised that the delay was caused by some accident.*
n an assumption that something may be true, even though there is no evidence to confirm it: *a matter of surmise.* <Old French *surmise* accusation>

sur·mount (sər mount′) *v* **1** overcome a difficulty or obstacle: *She surmounted many difficulties.* **2** be at or on the top of: *The mountain peaks were surmounted with snow.* <Old French *surmonter* rise above> **sur·mount′a·ble** *adj.*

sur·name (sər′nām′) *n* the name that members of a family have in common, as distinct from an individual given name.
v **sur·named, sur·nam·ing** give a surname to. <French *sur-* over + *nom* name>

sur·pass (sər pas′) *v* exceed, do, or be better or greater than: *The experience surpassed anything he had known before. She surpasses all the other team members in her ability to score.* <French *sur-* beyond + *passer* pass> **sur·pass′a·ble** *adj.* **sur·pass′ing** *adj.* **sur·pass′ing·ly** *adv.*

sur·plice (sər′plis) *n* a loose, white, usually knee-length gown with very wide sleeves, worn over the clothing by clergy and choir members during some Christian church services. <Old French *sur-* over + *pelice* fur>

sur·plus (sər′pləs) *or* (sər′plus′) *n* **1** an amount of something left over when all requirements have been met: *We had a surplus of tomatoes this year, so we gave them away to the neighbours.* **2** an excess of income or assets over expenditures or liabilities over a given period.
adj **1** more than what is needed or used: *The store's surplus stock was put on sale at the end of the season.* **2** selling unneeded or out-of-date military equipment or clothing: *He got a jacket at an army surplus store.* <Old French, from Latin *superplus* excess>

sur·prise (sər prīz′) *or* (sə prīz′) *n* an unexpected or astonishing event, fact, or thing, or the feeling of astonishment or shock caused by it: *She always has a surprise for the children on holidays.*
adj unexpected: *a surprise party, a surprise visit, a surprise attack.*
v **sur·prised, sur·pris·ing 1** cause someone to feel astonishment or shock at something unexpected: *The victory surprised us.* **2** capture, attack, or discover suddenly and unexpectedly: *The enemy surprised the fort.* <Old French, from Latin *sur-* over + *prendre* to seize>
take by surprise, happen when someone is not prepared or is expecting something different: *The unusual question took her by surprise.*

sur·pris·ing (sər prī′zing) *or* (sə prī′zing) *adj* causing surprise: *a surprising recovery.* **sur·pris′ing·ly** *adv.*

sur·re·al (sə rē′əl) *adj* bizarre and resembling a surrealist work of art: *a surreal experience.* <French *sur-* beyond + *réalisme* realism> **sur·re′al·ly** *adv.*

sur·ren·der (sə ren′dər) *v* **1** give up resistance to an enemy or opponent and submit to an imposed authority: *As the storm increased, the men on the raft surrendered all hope. The captain had to surrender when the ammunition ran out.* **2** give up or hand over a person, object, or right: *She surrendered the office keys.* **3** give way entirely to a powerful emotion or influence: *On hearing of the loss, he surrendered to tears.* **4** cancel an insurance policy in return for receiving a portion of the premiums paid.
n the act or fact of surrendering. <Old French *sur-* over + *rendre* give>

SYNONYMS

Surrender suggests giving up resistance to a more powerful force: *The rebels surrendered to the army.*

Abandon means "give up something entirely": *The sailors abandoned the ship when it started to sink.*

Renounce means "formally declare that something is being given up": *After many years, he renounced his claim to the vacant land beside his house.*

sur·rep·ti·tious (sər′əp tish′əs) *adj* done, made, or acquired in a secret or stealthy way, especially because it would not be approved of: *a surreptitious wink, a surreptitious gift.* <Latin *sub-* secretly + *rapere* snatch> **sur′rep·ti′tious·ly** *adv.* **sur′rep·ti′tious·ness** *n.*

sur·ro·gate (sər′ə gāt′) *or* (sər′ə git) *n* a person who acts for or takes the place of another in a specific role or task.
adj to do with the probate of wills and the administration of the estates of persons who have died: *a surrogate court.* <Latin *sur-* in the place of + *rogare* to ask>

surrogate mother *n* **1** a woman who bears a child on behalf of another woman, either from her own egg fertilized by the other woman's partner, or from an implanted fertilized egg from the other woman. **2** a person who or animal that takes on all or part of the role of mother to another person or animal.
surrogate motherhood *n.*

sur·round (sə round′) *v* **1** be or cause to be all around or enclosed: *News reporters surrounded the minister as she emerged from the legislature. Police surrounded the house. The little girl was surrounded by her toys.* **2** be associated with: *Controversy surrounded the project.*
n a thing that forms a border or edging around an object: *a doorstep surround.* <Old French *surounder* surpass, from Latin *superundare* overflow>

sur·round·ings (sə roun′dingz) *pln* the things or conditions around a person or thing: *rural surroundings. They lived in beautiful surroundings.*

sur·tax (sər′taks′) *n* an additional tax on a thing already taxed, especially a higher rate of tax on incomes above a certain level. <French *sur-* over + *taxe* tax>

a bat	e bed	i bid	o pot	u cup	th **thin**
ā cake	ē me	ī bite	ō go	ū rude	TH **then**
ä bar	ə about	ər over	ô for	ů put	zh measure

sur·ti·tle (sər′tī′təl) *n* the translated words of an opera, projected as a crawler set above the stage.
v **sur·ti·tled, sur·ti·tling** give surtitles to. <*Surtitle,* a trademark>

sur·veil·lance (sər vā′ləns) *n* close observation of someone, especially of a suspected spy or criminal. <French, from *sur-* over + *veiller* watch, from Latin *vigilare*>

sur·vey (sər vā′) *for v,* (sər′vā) *for n. v* **1** look carefully and thoroughly at someone or something: *She surveyed the scene before her. They surveyed the wreckage.* **2** investigate the opinions or experience of a group of people by asking them questions: *Most of the people surveyed agreed that the product was helpful. Survey the class to see how many agree with you.* **3** examine and record the area and features of an area of land so as to construct a map, plan, or description: *The crew is out surveying.*
n, pl **sur·veys 1** a general or comprehensive study, view, or description of something: *Her book included a survey of twentieth-century Canadian poetry.* **2** an investigation of the opinions or experience of a group of people by asking them questions: *an online survey.* **3** an act of surveying an area of land, or a map, plan, or detailed description obtained in such a way. <Old French *surveier,* from Latin *super-* over + *videre* see>

sur·vey·ing (sər vā′ing) *n* the measurement of boundaries and contours of particular areas on the earth's surface, especially for the purpose of locating property boundaries, construction layout, and mapmaking.

sur·vey·or (sər vā′ər) *n* a person who surveys, especially one whose work is making land surveys.

sur·viv·al (sər vī′vəl) *n* **1** the act or fact of continuing to live or exist, typically in spite of an accident, ordeal, or difficult circumstances: *They had little chance of survival if their food ran out.* **2** an object or practice that has continued to exist from an earlier time: *She said that belief in the evil eye was a survival of ancient magic.*
adj to do with survival: *survival techniques, a survival kit.*

sur·viv·al·ist (sər vī′vəl ist) *n* a person who has personal or group survival as a main goal because a natural catastrophe, nuclear war, or the collapse of society is thought likely. **sur·viv′al·ism** *n.*

survival of the fittest *n* the process or result of NATURAL SELECTION.

sur·vive (sər vīv′) *v* **sur·vived, sur·viv·ing 1** continue to live or exist, especially in spite of danger, hardship, or ordeals: *The family survived in spite of terrible mishaps. Several of the original buildings still survive.* **2** remain alive after the death of a particular person: *He survived his wife by three years.* **3** manage to keep going in difficult circumstances: *We survived all night on coffee and cookies.* <Old French *sur-* over + *vivre* live>

sur·vi·vor (sər vī′vər) *n* a person, group, or thing that survives, especially a person remaining alive after an event in which others have died.

sus·cep·ti·bil·i·ty (sə sep′tə bil′ə tē) *n, pl* **sus·cep·ti·bil·i·ties 1** the quality or fact of being likely or liable to be influenced or harmed by a particular thing: *susceptibility to disease.* **2 susceptibilities** *pl* a person's feelings, typically considered as being easily hurt.

sus·cep·ti·ble (sə sep′tə bəl) *adj* **1** likely or liable to be influenced or harmed by a particular thing: *He is susceptible to flattery.* **2** capable of or admitting: *Her problems were not susceptible of an easy answer.* <Latin *susceptibilis,* from *sub-* up + *capere* take>
sus·cep′ti·bly *adv.*

su·shi (sū′shē) *n* a Japanese dish consisting of small rolls of cold cooked rice with raw fish, vegetables, or some other garnish in the centre. <Japanese>

sus·pect (sə spekt′) *for v,* (sus′pekt) *for n,* (sus′pekt) *or* (sə spekt′) *for adj. v* **1** have an idea or impression of the existence, presence, or truth of something without full proof: *The old fox suspected danger and did not touch the trap. I suspect that she was just trying to be funny.* **2** believe or feel that someone is guilty of an illegal, dishonest, or unpleasant act, without full proof: *The police officer suspected him of the crime.* **3** doubt the genuineness or truth of: *She had no reason to suspect his praise.*
n a person thought to be guilty of a crime or offence: *The police have arrested two suspects in connection with the bank robbery.*
adj not to be relied on or trusted: *That version of the story is suspect.* <Old French, from Latin *suspicere* to mistrust>

sus·pend (sə spend′) *v* **1** temporarily prevent from continuing or being in force or effect: *Work was suspended while repairs were made.* **2** remove or exclude for a while from some privilege or job: *They suspended him from playing on the team.* **3** defer or delay an action, event, or judgment. **4** cause an imposed judicial sentence to be unenforced as long as no further offence is committed within a specified period: *The judge suspended the convicted man's three-year sentence.* **5** hang something from somewhere: *The lamp was suspended from the ceiling.* **6** be dispersed as solid particles throughout most of a liquid: *The substance was suspended in the solution.* <Latin *sub-* up + *pendere* hang>

suspended animation *n* a temporary condition in which most vital functions cease without death occurring, as in a dormant seed or a hibernating animal.

suspended sentence *Law n* a sentence that remains unenforced, subject to the convicted person's good behaviour for a certain length of time.

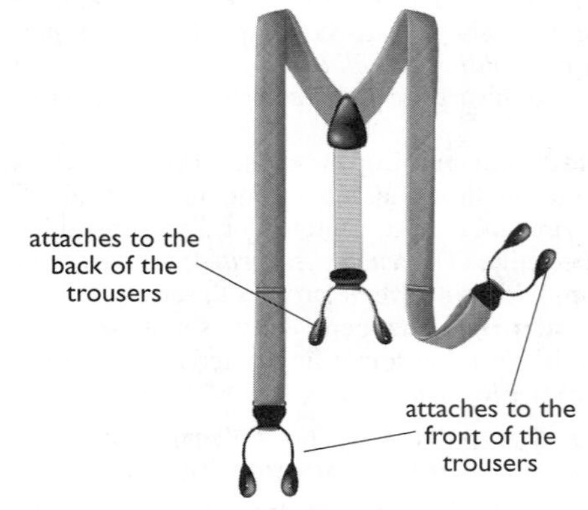

sus·pend·ers (sə spen′dərz) *pln* a pair of straps worn over the shoulders to hold up the trousers.

sus·pense (sə spens′) *n* **1** the condition or feeling of excited or anxious uncertainty about an outcome or decision: *The detective story kept me in suspense until the very end. They were kept in suspense while the doctors deliberated.* **2** a quality in a work of fiction, play, or movie that arouses excited expectation or uncertainty about what may happen.

adj producing excited expectation or uncertainty about what may happen: *a suspense novel.* <See SUSPEND.>

sus·pen·sion (sə spen′shən) *n* **1** the action of suspending someone or something or the condition of being suspended: *suspension of hostilities. He was suspended with pay while the charge against him was investigated.* **2** a system of springs and shock absorbers by which a vehicle is supported on its wheels. **3** a mixture in which solid particles are dispersed throughout most of a fluid, or the condition in which such particles are dispersed: *The collagen was in suspension.*

suspension bridge *n* a bridge with its roadway hung on cables or chains between towers. See BRIDGE for picture.

suspension of disbelief *n* the convention of pretending that the events in a fictional story are true.

sus·pi·cion (sə spish′ən) *n* **1** a feeling that something is possible, likely, or true: *He had a suspicion that the document was forged.* **2** causing a person to have the idea that something or someone may be guilty of dishonesty or an offence: *She tried to protect herself by diverting suspicion to someone else.* **3** a slight trace or suggestion: *She speaks French with just a suspicion of an English accent.* <Old French, from Latin *suspicere* to mistrust>

above suspicion, so honourable as not to be suspected of wrongdoing: *They said their friends were all above suspicion.*

SYNONYMS

Suspicion can mean "belief of guilt": *Is there still suspicion that she stole the money?*

Distrust emphasizes lack of trust or confidence in someone, often caused by suspicion: *There was great distrust between them after the disagreement.*

Doubt means "uncertainty about someone or something": *I have doubts about that idea.*

sus·pi·cious (sə spish′əs) *adj* **1** having or showing a cautious distrust of someone or something: *a suspicious glance. It was the way she said it that made me suspicious.* **2** causing a person to have the idea or impression that something or someone is guilty of dishonesty or some offence: *Someone was seen loitering near the house in a suspicious manner. They left under suspicious circumstances.* **sus·pi′cious·ly** *adv.* **sus·pi′cious·ness** *n.*

suss (sus) *Informal v (usually with* **out***)* realize or understand: *I soon sussed out that he hadn't been telling us the truth. She soon sussed him for a liar.* <*suspect*>

sus·tain (sə stān′) *v* **1** strengthen or support physically or mentally: *Hope sustained him in his misery.* **2** cause to continue or be prolonged for an extended period or without interruption: *You cannot sustain a high level of energy if you deprive yourself of sleep.* **3** bear the weight of an object without breaking or falling: *Arches sustained the heavy roof.* **4** undergo or suffer something unpleasant, especially an injury: *He sustained a broken leg in the accident.* **5** uphold, affirm, or confirm the justice or validity of: *All his accusations were sustained. The facts sustain her theory.* <Old French, from Latin *sustinere* to support> **sus·tain′a·ble** *adj.* **sus·tain′a·bly** *adv.*

sustainable development *n* industrial or economic development that can go on indefinitely because it does not disrupt ecology or exhaust natural resources.

sus·te·nance (sus′tə nəns) *n* **1** food and drink regarded as a source of strength or nourishment: *He has gone for a week without sustenance.* **2** the means of living or support: *She gave money for their sustenance.*

sut·ra (sūt′rə) *n* **1** a rule or wise saying in Sanskrit literature, or a set of these on grammar or Hindu law or philosophy. **2** a Buddhist or Jain scripture. <Sanskrit = thread>

sut·tee (su tē′) *n* **1** in former times, the Hindu practice of a widow burning herself on the funeral pyre of her deceased husband, or the widow who did this.

su·ture (sū′chər) *n* **1** the act or process of joining together the edges of a cut or wound by stitching, or one of the stitches with which this is done. **2** the line where the edges of two bones form a rigid joint, as between the bones of the skull.

v **su·tured, su·tur·ing** join or unite by or as if by stitching up a cut or wound with a suture. <Latin *suere* sew>

SUV *n* in full, **sport-utility vehicle** a motor vehicle with four-wheel drive for ordinary and off-road use.

su·ze·rain (sū′zə rin) *or* (sū′zə rān′) *n* **1** a monarch or state with control over a different state or territory. **2** in former times, a feudal overlord. **su′ze·rain·ty** *n.*

svelte (svelt) *adj* slender and elegant: *a svelte figure.* <French, from Italian *svelto*, from Latin *ex-* out + *vellere* pluck>

SW southwest; southwestern.

swab (swob) *n* **1** an absorbent pad or piece of material used in surgery and medicine for cleaning wounds, applying medication, or taking specimens. **2** a specimen taken with a swab for examination. **3** a mop or other absorbent device for cleaning or mopping up a floor or other surface.

v **swabbed, swab·bing** clean a wound or surface with or as if with a swab. <Dutch *zwabben*>

swad·dle (swod′əl) *v* **swad·dled, swad·dling** wrap someone, especially a baby, in garments or cloth. <Old English *swæthel*>

swaddling clothes *n* long, narrow strips of cloth, used in former times for wrapping a newborn infant.

swag (swag) *n* **1** an ornamental festoon of flowers, fruit, and greenery. **2** money or goods taken by a thief or burglar. <origin uncertain>

a bat	e bed	i bid	o pot	u cup	th **thin**
ā cake	ē me	ī bite	ō go	ū rude	ᴛʜ **then**
à bar	ə about	ər over	ȯ for	ů put	zh measure

S

swag·ger (swag′ər) *v* walk or behave in a very confident and arrogant or aggressive way: *The bully swaggered into the schoolyard.*
n a swaggering way of talking or acting: *The pirate captain moved among his prisoners with a swagger.* <swag> **swag′ger·er** *n.* **swag′ger·ing** *adj.* **swag′ger·ing·ly** *adv.*

swagger stick *n* a short, light cane, sometimes carried by military officers.

Swa·hi·li (swä hē′lē) *n* a Bantu language widely used in eastern Africa.

ETYMOLOGY

Swahili comes from Arabic *sawahil*, plural of *sahil*, which means "coast," a reference to the coastal areas of eastern Africa where the language is commonly spoken.

swain (swān) *n* **1** *Archaic or Poetic* a young shepherd or cowherd. **2** *Poetic or Humorous* a suitor. <Old Norse *sveinn*>

swal·low[1] (swol′ō) *v* **1** cause or allow something, especially food or drink, to pass down the throat: *He quickly swallowed a glass of milk.* **2** perform the act of swallowing, especially through fear or nervousness: *He swallowed hard before answering her question.* **3** put up with or meekly accept something insulting or unwelcome: *I simply cannot swallow what he said to me.* **4** believe too easily a lie or unlikely statement: *You will swallow any story.* **5** resist expressing a feeling or uttering words: *He had to swallow the insult.* **6** take in and cause to disappear: *The fog seemed to swallow up the street.*
n **1** an act of swallowing something, especially food or drink: *She took the medicine at one swallow.* **2** an amount that is or can be swallowed at one time: *There's a swallow of water left in the cup.* <Old English *swelgan*> **swal′low·er** *n.*

The barn **swallow** has a dark orange forehead and throat with pale orange underparts. It nests communally in mud nests under bridges and in barns and caves.

swal·low[2] (swol′ō) *n* a small, swift-flying songbird with long, narrow, pointed wings, a forked tail, and a short, broad bill that can open very wide to catch insects in flight. <Old English *swealwe*>

swal·low·tail (swol′ō tāl′) *n* **1** a deeply forked tail, such as that of a swallow, or something that is shaped like or suggests it, such as a type of short formal coat. **2** a large, brightly coloured butterfly commonly with hind wings that end in a tail-like point. **swal′low-tailed′** *adj.*

swam (swam) past tense of SWIM.

swa·mi (swä′mē) *n, pl* **swa·mis** a Hindu male religious teacher. <Hindi, from Sanskrit *svamin* master>

swamp (swomp) *n* an area of wet, low-lying ground sometimes partially covered with water, especially such an area with trees and shrubs as well as grasses.
adj of, for use in, or found in swamps: *swamp grasses.*
v **1** cover, overwhelm, or fill with water: *A huge wave swamped the boat.* **2** overwhelm with too much or too many of something: *swamped with work. The lottery winner was swamped with letters asking for money.* <origin uncertain> **swamp′y** *adj.*

swamp·land (swom′pland′) *n* land consisting of swamps.

Swampy Cree *n* See CREE.

swan (swon) *n* a large water bird with a long, flexible neck, white or black plumage, and a broad bill. <Old English> **swan′like′** *adj.*

swan dive *n* a dive performed with one's arms outspread until close to the water.

swank (swangk) *Informal v* show off one's wealth, knowledge, achievements, or appearance in a way that is intended to impress others: *She was swanking around in her new outfit.*
n behaviour, talk, or display intended to impress others.
adj swanky. <origin uncertain>

swank·y (swang′kē) *adj* **swank·i·er, swank·i·est** stylish and luxurious: *a swanky car.* **swank′i·ly** *adv.* **swank′i·ness** *n.*

swan song *n* a person's final public performance or professional activity before retirement: *The exhibition was her swan song as a painter.*

swap (swop) *Informal v* **swapped, swap·ping** take part in an exchange of: *He swapped his bicycle for a CD player.*
n an act of exchanging one thing for another. <Middle English *swappe*, strike, from the practice of striking hands in concluding a bargain> **swap′per** *n.*

swarm[1] (swôrm) *n* **1** a large or dense group of insects, especially flying ones such as honeybees. **2** a large number of people or things, usually in motion: *a swarm of children.*
v **1** move in or form a swarm, especially as insects: *The mosquitoes swarmed about us.* **2** move somewhere in large numbers: *The plaza was swarming with shoppers.* <Old English *swearm*>

swarm[2] (swôrm) *v* climb something rapidly by gripping it with one's hands and feet, alternately hauling and pushing oneself upward: *The sailor swarmed up the rigging.* <origin uncertain>

swarth·y (swôr′ᴛʜē) *or* (swôr′thē) *adj* **swarth·i·er, swarth·i·est** with a dark skin. <obsolete *swarty*> **swarth′i·ly** *adv.* **swarth′i·ness** *n.*

swash·buck·ling (swosh′buk′ling) *n* engaging in or suggesting daring and romantic adventures conducted in a dashing or flamboyant way.
adj to do with this kind of behaviour. <obsolete *swash* strike + *buckler* shield> **swash′buck′ler** *n.*

swas·ti·ka (swo stē′kə) *or* (swos′ti kə) *n* an ancient symbol in the form of a cross with equal arms whose ends are bent at right angles, all in the same direction. The Nazis adopted the swastika with the arms bent in a clockwise direction as their symbol. <Sanskrit *svasti* luck. The *swastika* was originally a symbol of luck.>

swat (swot) *Informal v* **swat·ted, swat·ting** hit or crush something, especially an insect, with a sharp blow from the hand or a flat object: *to swat a fly.*
n such a sharp blow. <*squat*> **swat′ter** *n.*

swatch (swoch) *n* a sample of fabric, paint colour, etc. used in clothing or in house decor. <origin uncertain>

swath (swoth) *n* **1** a row or line of grass, grain, or other crop as it falls or lies when mowed or reaped. **2** a strip left clear by the passage of a mowing machine or scythe. **3** a long, wide strip or area of something. <Old English *swæth*>
cut a (wide) swath, a make a destructive sweep: *The aggressive new company cut a swath through its competitors.* **b** make a forceful impression or effective display: *He cuts a wide swath in this town.*

swathe (swāᴛʜ) *or* (swoᴛʜ) *v* **swathed, swath·ing** wrap up thickly in cloth or fabric, or in something resembling this: *He was swathed in a blanket. The mountain top was swathed in cloud.*
n a piece or strip of material in which something is wrapped. <Old English *swathian*>

SWAT team *n* part of a police force specially trained to handle situations in which a suspect or suspects are hiding in a building, holding a hostage, or threatening to use violence. <*S(pecial) W(eapons) a(nd) T(actics)*>

sway (swā) *v* **1** move or cause to swing slowly back and forth or from side to side: *The tower of dominoes swayed and fell. The trees swayed in the wind.* **2** control or influence a person or course of action: *Nothing could sway him after he had made up his mind.*
n **1** a slow, swinging motion back and forth or side to side. **2** rule or control: *The rebel leader held sway over a large territory.* <origin uncertain>

sway·back (swā′bak′) *n* an abnormally hollowed or sagging back, especially in a horse. **sway′backed′** *adj.*

Swa·zi·land (swo′zē land) *n* a country in southern Africa. **Swa′zi** *adj, n.*

swear (swer) *v* **swore, sworn, swear·ing 1** make or cause to make a solemn statement or promise to do something, or affirm that something is the case: *The witness at the trial swore to tell the truth. Members of the club were sworn to secrecy.* **2** curse or use offensive language. <Old English *swerian*> **swear′er** *n.*
swear by, have or express great confidence in the use, value, or effectiveness: *She swore by the pills as a cure for headaches.*
swear in, admit to office or service by directing a person to swear a formal oath: *to swear in a jury.*
swear off, promise to give up: *He swore off smoking.*

swear·word (swer′wərd′) *n* an offensive word or phrase used in cursing.

sweat (swet) *n* **1** moisture coming through the pores of the skin, especially as a reaction to heat, physical exertion, fever, or fear: *He wiped the sweat from his face.* **2** the fact of such moisture appearing over a period of time: *Seeing my opponent made me break into a sweat.* **3** *Informal* a condition of flustered anxiety or distress: *We were all in a sweat over the big test we would get on Monday.* **4** moisture given out by something or gathered on its surface: *The water pipes were covered with sweat.* **5** hard work or effort, or a task requiring it: *Getting the job done was a lot of sweat.*
v **sweat** or **sweat·ed, sweat·ing 1** give out moisture through the pores of the skin: *We sweated because it was very hot.* **2** cause to sweat, especially through exercise, sometimes to get rid of something: *He sweated the horse by riding it too hard. She sweated off the excess weight.* **3** give off or cause to give off moisture: *The pitcher of ice water sweated in the sun.* **4** make a great deal of hard effort: *We sweated to get the job done on time.* **5** *Informal* remain anxious or worried: *Don't sweat the exam.* **6** heat solder till it melts, especially to fasten or join metal parts. <Old English *swætan*>
no sweat, *Slang* without difficulty; easily: *I can finish it by tomorrow, no sweat.*
sweat blood, make an extremely hard effort to do something.
sweat it out, *Informal* wait anxiously or nervously for something to happen.
sweat (something) out, *Informal* struggle, suffer, or wait anxiously till something is over or there is a change.

SYNONYMS

Sweat refers to the release of moisture from skin or other sources: *After hours in the sun, the leaves became sticky with a sweat of oil.*

Perspiration refers to the release of moisture from human skin only: *Perspiration made her shirt damp and cold.*

Wetness means "not dry": *The wetness in the basement makes it uncomfortable.*

sweat·band (swet′band′) *n* a band of absorbent material worn around the head or wrist to soak up sweat, especially by those who take part in a sport, or a band of absorbent material lining a hat.

sweat·er (swet′ər) *n* a knitted outer garment for the upper body, usually with long sleeves and put on over the head.

sweat gland *n* a small gland, just under the outer skin, that secretes sweat. Such glands are located over most of the body.

🍁 **sweat lodge** *n* a usually dome-shaped hut used by some First Nations or Native American peoples for ritual steam baths as a means of purification and medication.

sweat·pants (swet′pantz′) *n* loose, warm trousers, usually gathered at the ankle and with an elasticized or drawstring waist, often worn when exercising or running.

sweat·shirt (swet′shirt′) *n* a long-sleeved, collarless sweater, usually made of an absorbent fabric, and worn when exercising or as leisure wear.

sweat·shop (swet′shop′) *n* a factory or workshop, especially in the clothing industry, where workers are employed at low pay for long hours under bad conditions.

a bat	e bed	i bid	o pot	u cup	th **thin**
ā cake	ē me	ī bite	ō go	ū rude	ᴛʜ **then**
à bar	ə about	ər over	ȯ for	u̇ put	zh measure

sweat·suit (swet′sūt′) *n* a suit consisting of a sweatshirt and sweatpants, worn while exercising or as leisure wear.

sweat·y (swet′ē) *adj* **sweat·i·er, sweat·i·est** secreting, soaked in, or causing sweat: *sweaty work.* **sweat′i·ly** *adv.* **sweat′i·ness** *n.*

Swe·den (swē′dən) *n* a country in northern Europe. See the APPENDIX. **Swede** *n.* **Swed′ish** *adj.*

sweep (swēp) *v* **swept, sweep·ing 1** (*often with* **up**) clean an area by brushing away dirt or litter, or move or remove dirt or litter in such a way: *Sweep the steps. Sweep up, please. The wind swept the snow into drifts. I swept up the crumbs.* **2** move or push someone or something with great force: *A flood swept away the bridge.* **3** search an area for something: *The police swept the park for the missing boy.* **4** pass over or across with a steady movement: *His fingers swept the strings of the harp. Her eyes swept the sky, searching for signs of rain.* **5** move swiftly and smoothly: *The gang swept down on the town. The hero swept his true love into his arms.* **6** move with purpose and dignity: *The lady swept out of the room.* **7** move or extend in a long course or curve: *The shore sweeps to the south for some distance.*
n **1** the act of sweeping something with a brush: *She gave the floor a casual sweep.* **2** a long, swift, curving movement: *He made a dismissing sweep of the hand. He cut the grass with strong sweeps of his scythe.* **3** a thorough search of a place or area: *the sweep of verse.* **4** a long, usually curved stretch of road, river, or country: *Through the window we saw the sweep of the mountains.* **5** the scope or range of something: *the sweep of history.* **6** a sweepstakes contest: **7** the fact of winning every event, award, or place in a contest. **8** a person who sweeps. <Old English *swapan*>
make a clean sweep of something, a get rid of all trace: *Make a clean sweep of all your bad habits.* **b** win all the prizes, awards, etc. in a competition.
sweep away, a quickly remove: *Sweep away your tears.* **b** (*usually in the passive*) overcome with an emotion: *Swept away by anger, I said things I didn't mean.*
sweep the board, win all the money, prizes, awards, etc. in a game or competition.
sweep under the carpet, See CARPET.

sweep·er (swēp′ər) *n* **1** a person who or device that sweeps: *This carpet sweeper doesn't work.* **2** a player on a curling team who sweeps with a broom in front of a moving rock. **3** a soccer player stationed behind the other defenders and is free to defend at any point across the field. **4** 🍁 a tree on the bank of a river or stream that overhangs the water.

sweep·ing (swē′ping) *adj* **1** passing or extending over a wide space: *a sweeping glance.* **2** wide in range or effect: *a sweeping statement, sweeping reforms.*
n **1** the act or work of a person who or thing that sweeps: *The porch needs a good sweeping.* **2** **sweepings** *pl* dirt or refuse that has been swept up: *Put the sweepings in that box.* **sweep′ing·ly** *adv.*

sweep·stakes (swēp′stāks) *n* (*with singular or plural verb*) a form of gambling, especially on horse races, in which all the stakes are divided among the winners, or a race on which money is bet in this way, or the prize or prizes won.

sweet (swēt) *adj* **1** with a pleasant taste like sugar or honey, not salty, sour, or bitter. **2** fresh, pure, and untainted as air, water, or food: *The early morning air was sweet.* **3** pleasing or delightful: *the sweet life.* **4** pleasant, kind, thoughtful, or endearing in a person or action: *a sweet smile. It's sweet of you to help.* **5** melodious or harmonious as sound: *sweet music.* **6** not sour or fermented.
n **1** a person who is fond of: *My sweet, I have something to ask you.* **2** **the sweet** the sweet part or element of something: *He said we should take the bitter with the sweet.* **3** **sweets** *pl* candy or other items of food that contain a lot of sugar or other sweetening agent: *I like sweets.* <Old English *swete*> **sweet′ly** *adv.* **sweet′ness** *n.*
be sweet on, *Informal* be in love with.
sweet nothings, expressions of affection: *They whispered sweet nothings to each other.*

SYNONYMS

Sweet means "pleasing" or "delightful": *She's a very sweet person.*

Adorable is an informal word meaning "delightful and charming": *There's an adorable puppy chasing a squirrel in the park.*

Good-natured suggests cheerfulness and kindliness: *His good-natured smile made everyone happy.*

sweet–and–sour (swēt′ən sour′) *adj* cooked with a sauce containing sugar together with vinegar or lemon juice: *sweet-and-sour pork.*

sweet·bread (swēt′bred′) *n* the thymus or pancreas of an animal, used as meat.

sweet cider *n* unfermented cider.

sweet corn *n* a type of corn with kernels that have a high sugar content, eaten as a vegetable when picked young.

sweet·en (swē′tən) *v* **1** make or become sweet or sweeter, especially in taste. **2** make pleasant, agreeable, or acceptable.
sweeten the pot, make an offer more agreeable, usually with more money.

sweet·en·er (swē′tə nər) *or* (swēt′nər) *n* a thing that sweetens, especially an artificial substitute for natural sugars.

sweet·en·ing (swē′tə ning) *or* (swēt′ning) *n* a thing that sweetens.

🍁 **sweet·grass** (swēt′gras′) *n* a grass that has a sweet flavour and smell. It is burned ceremonially by some First Nations peoples to create fragrant smoke during prayer.

sweet·heart (swēt′hart′) *n* a person that one is in love with or is especially pleasing: *Sweetheart, could you get me a glass of water?*

sweet·ie (swē′tē) *Informal n* sweetheart.

sweet·ish (swē′tish) *adj* somewhat sweet.

sweet·meat (swēt′mēt′) *Archaic n* an item of candy or sweet food.

sweet nothings *n* things murmured by lovers to each other, solely as expressions of affection.

sweet pea *n* an annual climbing plant of the pea family that has small fragrant flowers.

sweet pepper *n* a variety of capsicum fruit that has a mild or sweet flavour, eaten as a vegetable cooked or raw.

sweet potato *n* a large tuberous root of a tropical vine, eaten as a vegetable. See POTATO for picture.

sweet–talk (swēt′tok′) *Informal v* coax or flatter: *He said he had let himself be sweet-talked into running for class president.* **sweet talk** *n.*

sweet–tem·pered (swēt′tem′pərd) *adj* with or showing a gentle or pleasant nature.

sweet tooth *n* a fondness or craving for sweet foods.

swell (swel) *v* **swelled, swelled** or **swol·len, swell·ing** **1** grow or make larger in size, amount, degree, or force, especially in becoming larger or rounder as a part of the body: *His head is swollen where he bumped it. The sound swelled from a murmur to a roar.* **2** be intensely affected or filled with a particular emotion: *swell with pride.*
n **1** a full or gently rounded shape or form: *the swell of a skirt.* **2** a gradual increase in size, amount, sound, or intensity: *a swell of music.* **3** a slow, regular movement of the sea in rolling waves that do not break.
adj Informal excellent or first-rate: *a swell job.*
adv Informal excellently or very well: *Our project was going swell.* <Old English *swellan*>
a swelled head, an exaggerated idea of one's own importance or worth.

swell·ing (swel′ing) *n* **1** a swollen part of something, especially a part of the body: *There is a swelling on her head where she bumped it.* **2** the condition of being swollen.

swel·ter (swel′tər) *v* be uncomfortably hot at a particular time or place.
n a sweltering condition or atmosphere. <Old English *sweltan* die> **swel′ter·ing** *adj.* **swel′ter·ing·ly** *adv.*

swept (swept) *v* a past tense and past participle of SWEEP.

swept–back (swept′bak′) *adj* slanting backward from the base to the tip as aircraft wings.

swerve (swərv) *v* **swerved, swerv·ing** change or cause to change direction abruptly: *The road swerves to the right here and goes around the lake. She swerved the car to avoid hitting the skunk.*
n an abrupt change of direction: *The swerve of the ball made it hard to hit.* <Old English *sweorfan* rub>

swift (swift) *adj* **1** happening quickly or promptly: *a swift recovery, a swift response.* **2** moving or capable of moving at high speed: *a swift sailboat.*
adv swiftly: *a swift-flowing stream.*
n a fast-flying, insect-eating bird with long slender wings, like a swallow. <Old English> **swift′ly** *adv.* **swift′ness** *n.*

swift fox *n* a small fox of the N American prairies.

swig (swig) *Informal n* a large drink of a liquid.
v **swigged, swig·ging** drink heartily or greedily. <origin uncertain> **swig′ger** *n.*

✱ **swile** (swīl) *Newfoundland n* a seal. Someone who hunts seals is a **swiler**, and hunting seals is called **swiling**. <*seal*>

swill (swil) *v* **1** drink greedily or in great quantity. **2** cause liquid to swirl around in a container or cavity, or move or splash in this way: *He swilled the iced tea in his glass.*
n **1** kitchen scraps and other items of waste food mixed with water and sometimes fed to pigs. **2** a large mouthful of a drink. <Old English *swilian*>

swim (swim) *v* **swam, swum, swim·ming** **1** make oneself move through water by movements of the arms and legs, or in the case of a fish or other aquatic animal, by tail or fins: *I'm learning to swim.* **2** cover or cross a stretch of water in this way: *to swim a river. I swam four lengths of the pool.* **3** cause to float or move across water: *She swam her horse across the stream.* **4** float on or at the surface of something: *There were some bits of parsley swimming in the soup.* **5** be covered with or immersed in a liquid: *The slices of roast beef were swimming in gravy. Her eyes swam with tears.* **6** appear to reel or whirl before one's eyes: *The heat and noise made my head swim.*
n an act or a period of swimming, or the distance covered by it: *a four-kilometre swim. We went for a swim.*
adj to do with swimming: *a swim meet.* <Old English *swimman*>
in the swim, involved in or aware of current events and activities: *She's socially very active and likes to be in the swim.*

swim bladder *n* a gas-filled sac present in the body of many bony fish, used to maintain and control how the fish remain buoyant in water.

A competitive **swimmer** must be strong, but good technique is just as important. Keeping the body straight and parallel to the surface of the water decreases drag and increases speed. Swimmers spend as much time on their side as possible, again to decrease drag.

swim·mer (swim′ər) *n* a person who or animal that swims.

swim·ming (swim′ing) *n* the practice or sport of swimming: *She is expert at both swimming and diving.*
adj **1** to do with swimming or swimmers: *a swimming teacher, a swimming pool.* **2** faint or dizzy: *a swimming sensation.*

a bat	e bed	i bid	o pot	u cup	th **thin**
ā cake	ē me	ī bite	ō go	ū rude	ꟸ **then**
ä bar	ə about	ər over	ô for	ů put	zh measure

S

swim·ming·ly (swim′ing lē) *adv* smoothly and successfully: *Our party went swimmingly.*

swimming pool *n* an artificial pool for swimming in: *They have a swimming pool in their backyard.*

swim·suit (swim′sūt′) BATHING SUIT.

swim·wear (swim′wãr′) *n* clothing worn for swimming.

swin·dle (swin′dəl) *v* **swin·dled, swin·dling** use deceit or deception to deprive someone of money or property, or obtain such things in this way: *He swindled them out of their savings. She had swindled $200 from him.*
n a fraudulent scheme or action: *The whole deal was a swindle.* <German *schwindeln*> **swin′dler** *n.*

> **SYNONYMS**
>
> **Swindle** emphasizes deceit or deception in illegally obtaining money or property: *He swindled millions of customers before the company found out.*
>
> **Scam** suggests swindling for a quick profit: *The enticing e-mail offer scammed me out of $100.*

swine (swīn) *n, pl* **swine 1** a pig or pigs. **2** a person regarded as deserving contempt and disgust. <Old English *swin*>

swine·herd (swīn′hərd′) *n* a person who tends pigs.

swing (swing) *v* **swung, swing·ing 1** move or cause to move back and forth or from side to side, or as if on a pivot: *His arms swung as he walked. The screen door was swinging in the wind. The driver was about to swing the car into the driveway. I swung around and confronted him.* **2** move or cause to move in a smooth, curving motion: *I swung the suitcase up onto the rack. Several children were swinging in the playground.* **3** shift or cause to shift from one opinion, mood, or circumstance to another: *The party's new policies caused popular opinion to swing its way.* **4** play music with an easy flowing but vigorous rhythm, or be played in this way. *The band swung.* **5** *Informal* manage successfully: *to swing a deal.* **6** *Informal* be lively, fashionable, or exciting as an event, place, or way of life: *The town really swings these days.*
n **1** a swinging movement or stroke: *One swing of the axe split the log in two.* **2** a seat hung from ropes or chains, on which one may sit and swing back and forth. **3** a swinging gait, movement, or rhythm: *She walked with a swing.* **4** a smooth, flowing rhythm or action: *She got into the swing of her new job.* **5** a noticeable change in opinion, especially the amount by which votes or points change from one side to another: *The undecided voters made a swing to the opposition party.* **6** a style of jazz or dance music, often played by big bands in the 1930s, with a smoothly flowing but vigorous rhythm. **7** a swift tour or trip, involving a number of stops: *an election swing through northern Ontario.* <Old English *swingan* beat> **swing′er** *n.*
in full swing, at the height of activity: *By eleven the party was in full swing.*
take a swing at, a aim a swinging blow at. **b** make a brief, hard criticism about: *His article takes a swing at the recent changes to immigration policy.*

swin·ish (swī′nish) *adj* to do with swine: *swinish behaviour.* **swin′ish·ly** *adv.* **swin′ish·ness** *n.*

swipe (swīp) *v* **swiped, swip·ing 1** hit or try to hit with a swinging blow. **2** *Informal* steal.
n **1** a sweeping blow: *She made two swipes at the golf ball without hitting it.* **2** a verbal attack or criticism: *She took a swipe at the other speaker.* <obsolete *swip* a blow>

swirl (swərl) *v* move or cause to move in a twisting or spiralling pattern: *Dust swirled. The stream swirled over rocks.*
n **1** a swirling movement or pattern. **2** a thing that has a twisting or spiralling movement or pattern: *a swirl of whipped cream.* <origin uncertain>

swish (swish) *v* move with a light hissing or rushing sound, or cause to move in this way: *The whip swished through the air. The horse swished its tail.*
n a swishing movement or sound: *There was a swish of little waves on the shore.* <imitative>

Swiss (swis) *adj* to do with Switzerland or its people.

Swiss chard CHARD.

Swiss cheese *n* a firm, pale yellow cheese with a mild flavour and large holes that form as the cheese ripens.

switch (swich) *n* **1** an act of changing a policy or way of life, or choosing one item or action in place of another: *We were amazed at his switch from pacifist to war-monger. The dog broke a vase with a switch of its tail.* **2** a device for making or breaking a connection in an electric circuit. **3** a slender, flexible shoot cut from a tree. **4** a pair of movable rails by which a train can shift from one track to another.
v **1** change the position, direction or focus of something, especially adopt something different in place of something else: *to switch jobs. She quickly switched the subject. The boys switched hats.* **2** use an electrical switch: *Switch off the light.* **3** move a train or railway car from one track to another by means of a switch. **4** strike with a switch. <origin uncertain> **switch′a·ble** *adj.* **switch′er** *n.*

switch·back (swich′bak′) *n* a road, path, or railways with alternate sharp ascents and descents, or one of the sharp bends in the road or path.

switch·blade (swich′blād′) *n* a pocket knife whose blade springs open when a button or knob is pressed.

switch·board (swich′bôrd′) *n* a panel containing the necessary switches and other devices for opening, closing, combining, or controlling electric circuits or telephone connections.

Switz·er·land (swit′sər land) *n* a country in western Europe. See the APPENDIX.

swiv·el (swiv′əl) *n* a link, pivot, or fastening that allows the free turning of an attached part.
v **swiv·elled** or **swiv·eled, swiv·el·ling** or **swiv·el·ing** turn around on a point or axis or on a swivel, or as if done in this way: *She swivelled the chair around. He swivelled his eyes in our direction.* <Old English *swifan* move>

swivel chair *n* a chair that turns on a swivel in its base.

swiz·zle stick (swiz′əl) *n* a small stick of plastic or glass used to stir alcoholic drinks. <origin uncertain>

swol·len (swō′lən) *adj* swelled: *a swollen ankle.*
v a past participle of SWELL.

swordfish

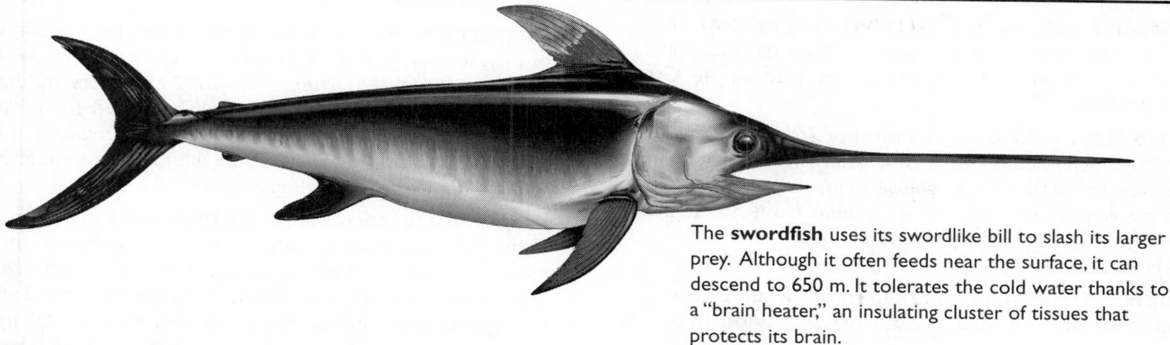

The **swordfish** uses its swordlike bill to slash its larger prey. Although it often feeds near the surface, it can descend to 650 m. It tolerates the cold water thanks to a "brain heater," an insulating cluster of tissues that protects its brain.

swoon (swūn) *v* faint or become dizzy after being emotionally affected by someone or something: *He swooned at the sight of the blood.*
n a faint or loss of consciousness: *He fell in a swoon.* <Old English *geswogen* insensible>

swoop (swūp) *v* **1** move rapidly downward through the air, especially as a bird: *The hawk swooped down on the mouse.* **2** carry out a sudden attack, especially in order to make a capture or arrest: *The police swooped down on the suspects.* **3** (*with* ***up***) seize with a sweeping motion: *She swooped the puppy up in her arms.*
n a swooping or snatching movement or action: *With one swoop, she had seized the pie and run off.* <Old English *swapan* sweep>
in one fell swoop, See FELL.

swoosh (swūsh) *n* the sound produced by a sudden rush of air or liquid: *We heard a swoosh as the water rushed into the tank.*
v move with or make a sound like a rush of liquid or air: *The car swooshed by.* <imitative>

sword (sȯrd) *n* **1** a hand weapon, usually metal, with a long, sharp blade fixed in a handle or hilt. **2** a symbol of honour or authority: *the sword of justice.* **3 the sword** military power, violence, or destruction: *The conqueror ruled by the sword.* <Old English *sweord*> **sword′like′** *adj.*
cross swords, fight or quarrel: *I wouldn't want to cross swords with someone as mean as you.*
put to the sword, kill, especially in war: *He put his captives to the sword.*

sword·fish (sȯrd′fish′) *n, pl* **sword·fish·es** or (*especially collectively*) **sword·fish** a large food fish with a streamlined body and a long, swordlike snout.

sword·play (sȯrd′plā′) *n* the action, practice, or art of wielding a sword, especially in fencing.

swords·man (sȯrd′zmən) *n, pl* **swords·men** (-zmən) a person who uses a sword to fight. **swords·man·ship** *n.*

swore (swȯr) past tense of SWEAR.

sworn (swȯrn) *v* past participle of SWEAR.
adj **1** bound by an oath: *a sworn statement.* **2** determined to remain in a specified role or condition: *They were sworn enemies.*

swum (swum) past participle of SWIM.

GRAMMAR AND USAGE

Swum is the past participle of the verb *swim* and needs a form of the auxiliary verb *have*: *She has swum across the channel before.*

Swam is the simple past tense of the verb *swim*: *The fish swam alongside the boat.*

swung (swung) past tense and past participle of SWING.

syb·a·rite (sib′ə rīt′) *n* a person who cares very much for luxury and pleasure. <*Sybaris*, ancient Greek city known for its luxury>

syc·a·more (sik′ə mȯr′) *n* **1** a large tree of the plane family with broad, lobed leaves, winged fruits, and outer bark that flakes off in large, irregular patches. **2** a large maple native to Eurasia, with broad leaves and greenish flowers. <Greek *sykomoros*>

syc·o·phant (sik′ə fənt) *n* a person who greatly flatters others and appears very humble in order to gain advantage. <Greek *sykophantes* slanderer>
syc′o·phan·cy *n.* **syc′o·phan′tic** *adj.*

syl·lab·ic (sə lab′ik) *adj* to do with syllables. **syl·lab′i·cal·ly** *adv.*

syl·lab·i·fy (sə lab′ə fī′) *v* **syl·lab·i·fied, syl·lab·i·fy·ing** divide into syllables. Also called **syllabicate.** **syl·lab′i·fi·ca′tion** or **syl·lab′i·ca′tion** *n.*

syl·la·ble (sil′ə bəl) *n* **1** a word or part of a word spoken as a unit, usually consisting of a vowel sound alone or a vowel sound with one or more consonant sounds. Example: The word *syllable* has three syllables. **2** the slightest bit or detail of something: *She promised not to breathe a syllable of the secret to anyone.* <Greek *syllabe* taking together, from *syn-* together + *lambanein* take>

a bat	e bed	i bid	o pot	u cup	th thin
ā cake	ē me	ī bite	ō go	ū rude	ᴛʜ then
ä bar	ə about	ər over	ȯ for	u̇ put	zh measure

S

syl·la·bus (sil′ə bəs) *n, pl* **syl·la·bus·es** or **syl·la·bi** (-bī′) *or* (-bē′) the subjects in a course of study or teaching: *the science syllabus.* <Latin, erroneous reading of Greek *sittyba* label>

syl·lo·gism (sil′ə jiz′əm) *n* a form of argument consisting of two statements and a conclusion drawn from them. Example: All trees have roots. A maple is a tree. Therefore, a maple has roots. <Greek *syllogismos,* from *syn-* together + *logos* a reckoning> **syl′lo·gis′tic** *adj.* **syl′lo·gis′ti·cal·ly** *adv.*

sylph (silf) *n* **1** an imaginary spirit of the air. **2** a slender, graceful girl or woman. <Latin *sylphes*> **sylph′like′** *adj.*

syl·van (sil′vən) *adj* pleasantly rural, or to do with woods: *a sylvan retreat.* Also, **silvan.** <Latin *silva* forest>

sym·bi·o·sis (sim′bī ō′sis) *n* the association or living together of two unlike organisms in a relationship that benefits each of them. <Greek, from *syn-* together + *bios* life> **sym′bi·ot′ic** *adj.*

sym·bol (sim′bəl) *n* **1** a thing that stands for or represents something else, especially an animal or physical object representing something abstract. Example: The olive branch is a symbol of peace. **2** a mark used to represent an object, function, or process. Example: The mark + is a symbol for *add.* <Greek *symbolon* a sign, from *synballein* to throw together>

sym·bol·ic (sim bol′ik) *adj* **1** used or serving as a symbol: *symbolic punishment.* **2** to do with symbols: *symbolic notation.* **sym·bol′i·cal·ly** *adv.*

sym·bol·ism (sim′bə liz′əm) *n* **1** the use of symbols to represent ideas or qualities: *the symbolism of flowers.* **2** a system of symbols.

sym·bol·ize (sim′bə līz′) *v* **sym·bol·ized, sym·bol·iz·ing** **1** be a symbol of: *She said that in our culture a dove symbolizes peace.* **2** represent or express by a symbol or symbols. **sym′bol·i·za′tion** *n.*

sym·me·try (sim′ə trē) *n, pl* **sym·me·tries** **1** *Mathematics* the quality of being made up of parts of equal shape and size facing each other across a **line of symmetry** or set around a **point of symmetry.** **2** pleasing and well-balanced proportions between the parts of a thing: *A swollen cheek spoiled the symmetry of her face.* <Greek *syn-* together + *metron* measure> **sym·met′ric** *adj.* **sym·met′ri·cal** *adj.* **sym·met′ri·cal·ly** *adv.*

sym·pa·thet·ic (sim′pə thet′ik) *adj* **1** feeling, showing, or expressing pity, sorrow, or distress at someone else's misfortune: *a sympathetic friend.* **2** inclined to agree or approve: *They are sympathetic to our idea.* **3** pleasant and agreeable: *She found most of the club's members sympathetic.* **4** *Physics* to do with an effect that arises in response to a similar action elsewhere: *sympathetic vibrations.* **sym′pa·thet′i·cal·ly** *adv.*

sym·pa·thize (sim′pə thīz′) *v* **sym·pa·thized, sym·pa·thiz·ing** **1** feel or show sympathy: *He sympathized with her problem.* **2** share in or agree with a feeling or opinion: *My mother sympathizes with my plan to be a doctor.* **sym′pa·thiz′er** *n.* **sym′pa·thiz′ing** *adj.* **sym′pa·thiz′ing·ly** *adv.*

sym·pa·thy (sim′pə thē) *n, pl* **sym·pa·thies** **1** the feelings of pity, sorrow, or distress at someone else's misfortune: *I feel sympathy for the victims of the fire.* **2** an understanding or common feeling between people: *The two friends had a special sympathy.* **3** agreement with or approval of an opinion or aim: *He is in sympathy with my plan.* <Greek *syn-* together + *pathos* feeling>

sym·pho·ny (sim′fə nē) *n, pl* **sym·pho·nies** **1** a long and elaborate musical composition for a full orchestra and sometimes singers, typically in four distinct movements, at least one of which is traditionally in sonata form. **2** in full, **symphony orchestra** a large orchestra for playing symphonies and similar works of classical music. See STRINGED INSTRUMENT for picture. **3** a thing regarded, typically favourably, as a composition of different elements: *a symphony of colours.* <Latin, from Greek *symphonos* harmony> **sym·pho′nic** *adj.* **sym·pho′ni·cal·ly** *adv.*

sym·po·si·um (sim pō′zē əm) *n, pl* **sym·po·si·ums** or **sym·po·si·a** (-zē ə) **1** a meeting or conference at which several specialists give their views on a subject. **2** a collection of essays or papers on a particular subject by a number of contributors. <Greek *syn-* together + *posis* drinking>

symp·tom (simp′təm) *n* **1** a physical or mental feature that is regarded as indicating a disease, especially a feature that is noticeable to the patient: *The alarming symptoms made him see a doctor.* **2** a sign that a thing exists, especially of an undesirable situation: *symptoms of discontent.* <Greek *symptoma* disease, from *syn-* together + *piptein* fall>

symp·to·mat·ic (simp′tə mat′ik) *adj* **1** serving as a symbol or sign, especially of something undesirable: *She said that riots are symptomatic of social unrest.* **2** showing or involving symptoms of a disease.

syn·a·gogue (sin′ə gog′) *n* **1** a building used by a Jewish congregation as a house of worship and religious instruction. **2** a Jewish congregation or assembly. <Greek *synagoge* assembly, from *syn-* together + *agein* bring>

syn·apse (si naps′) *or* (sin′aps) *n* a junction between two nerve cells, consisting of a gap across which impulses pass from one cell to another. <Greek *syn-* together + *haptein* fasten>

sync (singk) *Informal n* synchronization.
v **synced, sync·ing** synchronize.
in sync, synchronized.
out of sync, not synchronized.

syn·chro·nic·i·ty (sing′krə ni′sə tē) *n* the fact or condition of events that occur at the same time and, though they do not have the same cause, appear to be related in a significant way.

syn·chro·nize (sing′krə nīz′) *v* **syn·chro·nized, syn·chro·niz·ing** cause, occur, or operate at the same time, speed, or rate: *to synchronize watches.* <Greek *syn-* together + *chronos* time> **syn′chro·ni·za′tion** *n.* **syn′chro·niz′er** *n.*

Synchronized swimming can be solo, duets, or team competitions. Swimmers wear their hair tied back, plain swimsuits without decoration, and nose clips or gelatin plugs inserted in the nostrils to keep water from reaching the sinuses.

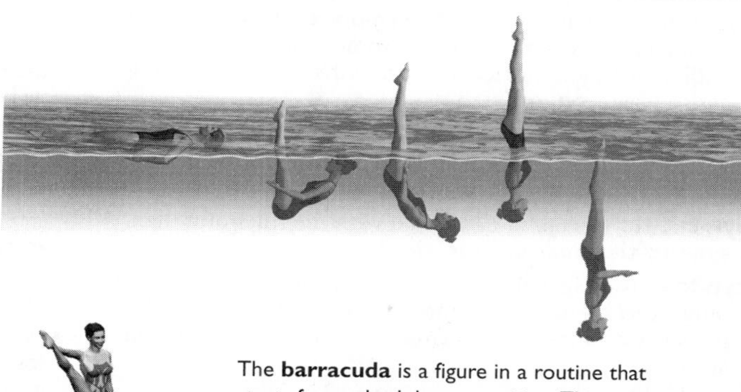

The **barracuda** is a figure in a routine that starts from a back layout position. The swimmer then lifts her legs vertically and her body sinks into a pike position. With a boost, she assumes a vertical, upside-down position with legs together and head, hips, and ankles in alignment.

Another figure, the **platform**, requires the swimmers to group themselves under water to make a platform to hold up another swimmer.

synchronized swimming *n* a competitive sport in which swimmers perform acrobatic and dancelike movements in time to music.

syn·chro·nous (sing′krə nəs) *adj* occurring or existing at the same time. **syn′chro·nous·ly** *adv.*

syn·cline (sin′klīn) *or* (sing′klīn) *n* a fold of stratified rock in which the layers slope upward in opposite directions from the centre. Compare ANTICLINE. **syn·clin′al** *adj.*

syn·co·pate (sing′kə pāt′) *v* **syn·co·pat·ed, syn·co·pat·ing 1** *Music* displace the beats or accents in music or a rhythm so that strong beats become weak and weak beats become strong. **2** shorten a word by dropping sounds or letters in the middle. Example: The word *bosun* is a syncopated version of *boatswain.* <Greek *syn-* together + *koptein* cut> **syn′co·pa′tion** *n.*

syn·di·cate (sin′də kit) *for n,* (sin′də kāt′) *for v. n* **1** a group of people or companies that carry out some undertaking or promote some common interest. **2** an agency or association that supplies material at the same time to a number of newspapers, periodicals, or broadcast outlets. **3** an association of criminals controlling organized crime. *v* **syn·di·cat·ed, syn·di·cat·ing 1** control or manage by a syndicate. **2** publish or broadcast material at the same time in a number of newspapers, periodicals, or broadcast outlets: *Her cartoons were syndicated in over fifty newspapers.* <French *syndicat* office of a syndic (administrator)> **syn′di·ca′tion** *n.*

syn·drome (sin′drōm′) *n* **1** a group of symptoms of a disease that consistently occur together, or a condition marked by a set of associated symptoms. **2** a set of ideas, attitudes, or behaviour patterns that occur together and are typical of a particular group of people: *the empty-nest syndrome.* <Greek = a running together>

syn·ec·do·che (si nek′də kē′) *n* a figure of speech in which a part is made to represent the whole, or the whole for a part. Example: a factory employing 500 hands (persons). <Greek *synekdoche,* from *syn-* with + *ek-* out + *dechesthai* receive>

syn·er·gy (sin′ər jē) *n* the interaction or co-operation of two or more organizations, substances, or other things to produce a combined effect greater than the sum of their separate effects: *The painting represented a synergy of painter and model.* Also, **synergism** (sin′ər jiz′əm). <Greek *syn-* together + *ergon* work>

syn·od (sin′əd) *n* an assembly of the clergy and sometimes church members in a diocese or other division of a particular church. <Greek *syn-* together + *hodos* a going>

syn·o·nym (sin′ə nim) *n* **1** a word or phrase that means nearly the same as another word or phrase in the same language. Example: *Sharp* is a synonym for one meaning of *keen*; *enthusiastic* is a synonym for another meaning of *keen.* Compare ANTONYM. **2** a word or expression generally accepted as another name for something: *Ottawa is a synonym for the Federal Government.* <Greek *syn-* together + *onyma* name> **syn·on′y·mous** *adj.* **syn·on′y·mous·ly** *adv.*

GRAMMAR AND USAGE

Add variety to your writing by using a **synonym** instead of repeating a word. Make sure, however, that the synonym you choose comes close enough to your original meaning. For example, *team* and *gang* and synonyms for *group*, but you might not want to use *gang* if you were talking about sports. (*team/group; fast/speedy*).

Use both a thesaurus and a dictionary to find the right synonyms.

a bat	e bed	i bid	o pot	u cup	th **thin**
ā cake	ē me	ī bite	ō go	ū rude	ᴛʜ **then**
ȧ bar	ə about	ər over	ȯ for	u̇ put	zh measure

syn·op·sis (si nop′sis) *n, pl* **syn·op·ses** (-sēz) a brief summary or general survey of something, especially an outline of a play, movie, or book. <Greek *syn-* together + *opsis* a view> **syn·op′size** *v.*

syn·ov·i·al (sin ō′vē əl) *adj* to do with a type of a body joint in which a lubricating liquid is secreted into a membrane that surrounds it. <Latin>

syn·tac·tic (sin tak′tik) *adj* to do with the rules of syntax. **syn·tac′ti·cal** *adj.* **syn·tac′ti·cal·ly** *adv.*

syn·tax (sin′taks) *n* **1** the arrangement of words and phrases to create well-formed sentences. **2** a set of rules for such arrangements. <Greek *syn-* together + *tassein* arrange>

syn·the·sis (sin′thə sis) *n, pl* **syn·the·ses** (sin′thə sēz) **1** the combination or composition of parts or elements into a whole, especially the combination of ideas to form a theory or system. Compare ANALYSIS. **2** *Chemistry* the production of chemical compounds by reaction from simpler substances. Alcohol, ammonia, and rubber can be artificially produced by synthesis. <Greek *syn-* together + *tithenai* put> **syn′the·size** *v.*

syn·the·siz·er (sin′thə sī′zər) *n* **1** a person who or thing that synthesizes. **2** *Music* an electronic musical instrument, usually operated by a keyboard, that produces a wide variety of sounds by generating and combining sound signals of different frequencies. See ELECTRONIC for picture.

syn·thet·ic (sin thet′ik) *adj* **1** made as a substance by chemical synthesis, especially to imitate a natural product: *synthetic rubies.* **2** not sincere or genuine as an emotion or action: *synthetic affection.*
n a synthetic material or chemical, especially a textile fibre: *Some people prefer synthetics for clothing because they are easy to care for.* **synthetically** *adv.*

syph·i·lis (sif′ə lis) *n* a chronic bacterial disease that is contracted chiefly by infection during sexual intercourse, but also congenitally by infection of a developing fetus. It has four successive stages. <*Syphilus* infected hero of a poem by 16c Fracastoro> **syph′i·lit′ic** *adj.*

Sy·ri·a (sir′ē ə) *n* a country in southwest Asia. See the APPENDIX. **Sy′ri·an** *adj, n.*

sy·ringe (sə rinj′) *n* a tube with a nozzle and piston or bulb for sucking in and ejecting liquid in a thin stream, used for cleaning wounds or body cavities, or fitted with a hollow needle for injecting or withdrawing fluids.
v **sy·ringed, sy·ring·ing** spray liquid into a wound or body cavity with a syringe. <Greek *syringos* tube>

syr·up (sər′əp) *or* (sir′əp) *n* **1** a thick solution of sugar and water, usually combined with flavouring or medicine: *cough syrup.* **2** condensed juice of a plant or fruit; especially, sugar cane juice that remains uncrystallized in the refining of sugar, or the juice condensed from the sap of the sugar maple. **syr′up·like′** *adj.* <Old French *sirop*, from Arabic *sharab* drink>

syr·up·y (sər′ə pē) *or* (sir′ə pē) *adj* **1** like syrup in consistency or sweetness. **2** unduly sentimental: *syrupy love songs.*

sys·op (sis′op) *Computers n* in full, **system operator** a person who manages the operation of an electronic bulletin board or a small network.

sys·tem (sis′təm) *n* **1** a set of connected things or parts forming a complex whole, or working together as parts of a mechanism or an interconnecting network: *a railway system.* **2** an ordered group of facts, principles, procedures, or beliefs: *a system of government.* **3** a plan, scheme, or method: *a betting system.* **4** a set of organs in the body with a common structure or function: *the digestive system. He got little nourishment into his system.* **5** a group of celestial objects forming a whole that follows certain natural laws: *the solar system.* **6** *Computers* a group of related hardware units or programs or both, configured to work together. <Greek *systema* organized whole, from *syn-* together + *stesai* cause to stand> **sys′tem·less** *adj.*

sys·tem·at·ic (sis′tə mat′ik) *adj* done or acting according to a fixed plan or system: *a systematic investigation, a systematic classification, a systematic worker.*
sys′tem·at′i·cal·ly *adv.*

sys·tem·a·tize (sis′tə mə tīz′) *v* **sys·tem·a·tized, sys·tem·a·tiz·ing** arrange according to or make into a system. **sys′tem·a·ti·za′tion** *n.*

sys·tem·ic (sis tem′ik) *adj* **1** to do with a system, especially as contrasted to a particular part or element. **2** to do with the whole body, not just a particular organ or part: *a systemic infection.*

systems analysis *Computers n* the process of analyzing a complex activity process or operation in order to improve its efficiency, especially by applying a computer system. **systems analyst** *n.*

sys·to·le (sis′tə lē′) *n* the normal, rhythmical contraction of the heart, especially that of the ventricles. Compare DIASTOLE. <Greek = contraction> **sys·tol′ic** (sis tol′ik) *adj.*

Sze·chuan (sech′won′) See SICHUAN.

Tt

t or **T** (tē) *n, pl* **t's** or **T's** 1 the twentieth letter of the English alphabet, or any speech sound represented by it. 2 the twentieth thing in a list or series.
to a T, *Informal* exactly or perfectly: *That suits me to a T.*

t tonne(s).

T tera-.

✱ **T4 slip** *n* a form showing annual salary and deductions, given by an employer and used to calculate an employee's income tax.

TA or **T.A.** teaching assistant.

tab[1] (tab) *n* 1 a small flap, strap, loop, or piece attached to or projecting from something, used to hold or move it: *He wore a wool cap with tabs over the ears.* 2 a small projection or attached piece on a card or folder used as a filing aid. Tabs may be labelled, numbered, colour-coded, etc. 3 *Informal* a restaurant or bar bill: *to pay the tab.*
v **tabbed, tab·bing** 1 put a tab on something: *to tab index cards.* 2 mark or identify as being of a specified type: *He was very quickly tabbed as a show-off.* <origin uncertain>
keep tabs (or **a tab**) **on,** *Informal* keep track of or keep watch on: *He was asked to keep tabs on his little sister.*
pick up the tab, *Informal* pay; bear the cost of something: *His mother picks up the tab for his dance lessons.*

tab[2] (tab) *n* a TABULATOR (def. 2).

tab·bou·leh (tə bū′lē) *n* a Middle Eastern salad consisting of cracked wheat with finely chopped ingredients such as tomatoes, parsley, and mint, with a dressing of olive oil and lemon juice. <Arabic *tabbula*>

tab·by (tab′ē) *n, pl* **tab·bies** a domestic cat with a grey or brownish coat with dark stripes.
adj brown or grey with dark stripes in a cat's fur. <Arabic *attabiy* striped silk>

tab·er·nac·le (tab′ər nak′əl) *n* 1 *Judaism* a tent carried by the Israelites for use as a place of worship during their journey from Egypt to Palestine. 2 *Catholicism* a small chest or cupboard, often built into the altar, for keeping consecrated bread. 3 *Christianity* a building used as a meeting place of worship. <Latin *tabernaculum* tent>

tab·la (tob′lə) *or* (tab′lə) *n* an instrument used in Indian music consisting of a pair of small hand drums. <Hindi, from Arabic>

tab·la·ture (tab′lə chůr′) *or* (tab′lə chər′) *n* a form of musical notation indicating fingering rather than the pitch of notes, and written on lines with letters, numbers, or other symbols instead of standard notation. <Latin *tabulatus* tablet>

ta·ble (tā′bəl) *n* 1 a piece of furniture with a smooth, flat top on legs, providing a surface on which objects may be placed, and that can be used for eating, writing, playing games, or other purposes. 2 the food provided in a home or restaurant: *My uncle sets a good table.* 3 the people seated at a table for a meal or other purpose: *a table of bridge.* 4 a flat surface, especially a flat, vertical surface of a building, a slab of wood or stone bearing an inscription, or a flat surface of a gem. 5 a set of facts, figures, or other information systematically displayed, especially in columns: *a table of contents, a multiplication table.*
v **ta·bled, ta·bling** 1 present for discussion or consideration at a meeting: *The member tabled a motion in the House of Commons.* 2 *especially US* postpone consideration of. <Latin *tabula* plank>
on the table, offered for discussion or consideration.
set (or **lay**) **the table,** arrange cutlery and dishes on a table for a meal.
turn the tables, reverse conditions or circumstances completely: *The enemy troops had advanced, but our sudden attack turned the tables on them.*
under the table, a secretly, or without making an official record or report: *to pay someone under the table, to sell illegal goods under the table.* **b** become so drunken as to be helpless.

GRAMMAR AND USAGE

The verb **table** is an example of a *contronym,* that is, a word with two opposite meanings: "present for consideration" and "postpone consideration."

Other examples of contronyms are *cleave,* which can mean "split open" or "stick closely," and *oversight,* which can mean "failure to notice" or "watchful care."

See also *synonym* and *antonym.*

tab·leau (tab′lō) *n, pl* **tab·leaux** (-lō) or **tab·leaus** (-lōz) 1 a vivid or graphic description or scene. 2 an interlude during a scene on stage when all the performers freeze in position and then resume action as before, or a scene performed by costumed players who perform silently. <French = picture>

ta·ble·cloth (tā′bəl kloth′) *n* a cloth for covering a table.

ta·ble d'hôte (tȧ′bəl dōt′) *n* a restaurant meal offered at a fixed price and with few choices. Compare À LA CARTE.

ta·ble·land (tā′bəl land′) *n* a plateau that rises sharply from a lowland area or the sea.

table linen *n* fabric items used at mealtimes, such as tablecloths and napkins.

ta·ble·spoon (tā′bəl spūn′) *n* 1 a large spoon for serving food. 2 a standard unit of measurement in recipes, equal to three teaspoons or fifteen millilitres.

ta·ble·spoon·ful (tā′bəl spūn′fůl) *n, pl* **ta·ble·spoon·fuls** as much as a tablespoon holds: *He added a tablespoonful of butter.*

tab·let (tab′lit) *n* 1 a small, flat slab of stone, clay, or wood, used especially for an inscription. 2 a number of sheets of writing paper fastened together at one edge. 3 a small disc or cylinder of a compressed solid substance, especially a medicine or drug: *vitamin tablets.* <Old French, from Latin *tabula* small flat slab>

a bat	e bed	i bid	o pot	u cup	th thin
ā cake	ē me	ī bite	ō go	ū rude	ᴛʜ then
ȧ bar	ə about	ər over	ȯ for	ů put	zh measure

T

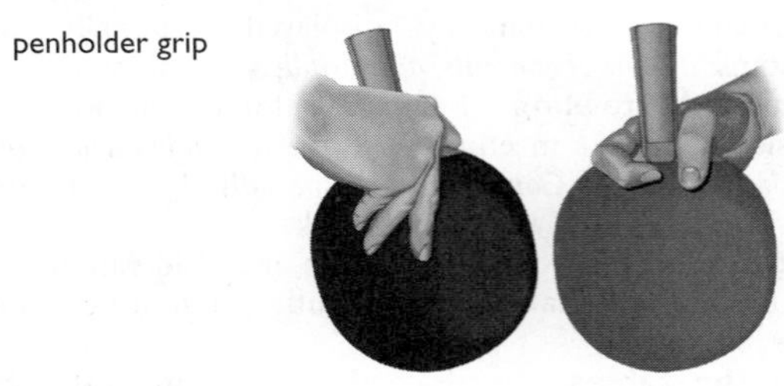

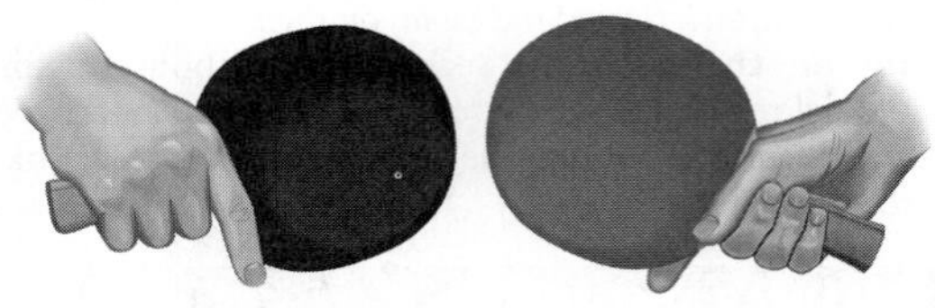

table tennis *n* an indoor game based on tennis, played with small bats and a ball bounced on a table divided by a net.

ta·ble·top (tā′bəl top′) *n* the horizontal top part of a table: *The tabletop was stained with water marks.*
adj small or portable enough to be placed or used on a table: *a tabletop loom.*

ta·ble·ware (tā′bəl wer′) *n* the dishes, glassware, knives, forks, and spoons used at meals.

table wine *n* wine of average quality used for drinking with meals.

tab·loid (tab′loid) *n* a newspaper, usually with a page half the ordinary size, that presents the news through photographs, headlines, and short articles. <*tablet* + *-oid*>

ta·boo (tə bū′) *adj* forbidden or severely restricted by custom or tradition: *a taboo subject.*
n, pl **ta·boos** a social or religious custom prohibiting or restricting a particular practice or forbidding association with a particular person, place, or thing.
v **ta·booed, ta·boo·ing** place under a taboo. Also, **tabu**. <Tongan (a language of the Tonga Islands in S Pacific) *tapu*>

ta·bor (tā′bər) *n* a small drum, used especially in the Middle Ages to accompany a pipe played by the same person.

tab·u·lar (tab′yə lər) *adj* **1** to do with data arranged in columns or tables: *numbers in a tabular format.* **2** broad and flat like the top of a table: *a tabular rock.*

ta·bu·late (tab′yə lāt′) *v* **tab·u·lat·ed, tab·u·lat·ing** arrange data in tabular form. **tab′u·la′tion** *n.*

tab·u·la·tor (tab′yə lā′tər) *n* **1** a person who or machine that arranges data in tabular form. **2** *Computers* a function in a word-processing program, or a key on a keyboard, that advances a set sequence of paragraph and column indentions. *Abbrev.* **tab**

ta·chom·e·ter (tə kom′ə tər) *n* an instrument that measures the working speed of an engine, especially in a road vehicle, typically in revolutions per minute. <Greek *tachos* speed + *meter*>

tach·y·car·di·a (tak′i kor′dē ə) *n* an abnormally fast heartbeat. <Greek *tachys* swift + *kardia* heart>

tac·it (tas′it) *adj* implied or understood without being openly expressed: *We had a tacit understanding that we would meet after the movie.* <Latin *tacere* be silent> **tac′it·ly** *adv.*

tac·i·turn (tas′ə tərn′) *adj* reserved, or usually saying very little. **tac′i·tur′ni·ty** *n.*

tack[1] (tak) *n* **1** a very short, sharp nail with a broad flat head, used for fastening or pinning an item. **2** a long stitch used as a temporary fastening in sewing. **3** an act of changing course while sailing by turning a boat's head into and through the wind, so as to bring the wind on the opposite side, or the course of a boat relative to the wind. **4** a method of dealing with a situation or problem: *To make heavy demands was the wrong tack to take with his mother.* **5** a rope to hold in place a corner of some sails, or the corner to which this is fastened.
v **1** fasten or fix in place with tacks: *She tacked mosquito netting over the windows.* **2** sew with temporary stitches. **3** add or append a thing to something that already exists: *He tacked a postscript to the end of the letter.* **4** change course while sailing by turning a boat's head into and through the wind, so as to bring the wind on the opposite side, or alter the course of a boat in such a way: *The sloop was tacking, trying to make the harbour.* **5** make a change in one's conduct, policy, or object of one's attention. <Old French *taque* nail> **tack′er** *n.*

tack[2] (tak) *n* equipment, including the bridle and saddle, used in horse riding. <*tackle*>

tack·le (tak′əl) *n* **1** the equipment required for a task or sport: *fishing tackle.* **2** a set of ropes, pulley blocks, hooks, or other things for moving heavy objects. **3** the rigging and pulleys used to work a boat's sails. **4** *Sports* **a** in football and rugby, an act of seizing and attempting to stop a player in possession of the ball. **b** in soccer and field hockey, an act of playing the ball, or trying to do so, when it is in possession of an opponent. **c** in football, a player who lines up next to the end along the line of scrimmage.
v **tack·led, tack·ling** **1** **a** try to seize and knock over someone: *We tackled the thief and held him till help arrived.* **b** make a determined effort to deal with a problem or difficult task: *The government decided to tackle the issue of unemployment.* **2** *Sports* **a** in football and rugby, try to seize and knock over someone as a means of stopping the forward progress of the ball carrier: *The player was tackled at the ten-yard line.* **b** in soccer and field hockey, try to obstruct an opponent in order to get the ball away from him or her. <Dutch *takel*> **tack′ler** *n.*

tack·y[1] (tak′ē) *adj* **tack·i·er, tack·i·est** slightly sticky after paint, glue, or another substance is applied: *The varnish is still tacky.*

tack·y[2] (tak′ē) *Informal adj* **tack·i·er, tack·i·est** showing poor quality, appearance, or taste, especially in a cheap and vulgar way: *tacky jewellery.* <origin uncertain>

ta·co (tȧ′kō) *n, pl* **ta·cos** a Mexican dish consisting of a tortilla folded around a filling such as ground meat, cheese, and beans. <Spanish>

tact (takt) *n* a keen sense of the correct or fitting thing to say or do something in dealing with others or with difficult problems. <Latin *tactus* sense of feeling, from

tangere touch> **tact′ful** *adj.* **tact′ful·ly** *adv.* **tact′ful·ness** *n.* **tact′less** *adj.* **tact′less·ly** *adv.* **tact′less·ness** *n.*

tac·tic (tak′tik) *n* **1** an action carefully planned to achieve a specific purpose. **2 tactics** *pl* **a** the art of managing armed forces in active combat. **b** a plan or procedure to gain advantage or success: *When his coaxing failed, the little boy changed his tactics and began to cry.* <Greek *taktikos,* from *tassein* arrange> **tac·ti′cian** (tak ti′shən) *n.*

tac·ti·cal (tak′tə kəl) *adj* **1** of, to do, or comprising actions carefully planned to gain a specific military purpose. **2** showing cleverness and skill in planning something: *a tactical retreat.* **tac′ti·cal·ly** *adv.*

tac·tile (tak′tīl) *or* (tak′təl) *adj* to do with the sense of touch: *Velvet has a tactile quality.*

tad (tad) *Informal n* a small extent: *Move it a tad to the right.* <*tadpole*>

tad·pole (tad′pōl′) *n* the larva of a frog, toad, newt, or salamander that has a tail and gills and lacks legs until a later stage. See FROG for picture. <Middle English *tad* toad + *pol* head, i.e., toad that is all head>

tae kwon do (tī′kwon′dō) *n* a Korean martial art similar to karate that uses powerful, leaping kicks. <Korean *tae* kick + *kwon* fist + *do* way>

taf·fe·ta (taf′ə tə) *n* a lustrous silk or similar synthetic fabric in a plain weave with a crisp texture on both sides. <Persian *taftah* silk>

taff·rail (taf′rāl′) *n* a rail around a ship's stern.

taf·fy (taf′ē) *n* a chewy candy made of brown sugar or molasses boiled down, often with butter, and pulled until glossy. <*toffee*>

taffy apple *n* an apple stuck on a stick and dipped in hot taffy, which forms a thick, solid coating as it cools.

tag[1] (tag) *n* **1** a label attached to someone or something as an identification or to give other information: *Each coat in the store has a tag with the price marked on it.* **2** a small piece or part that is attached to a main piece: *She cut all the tags off the old frayed rug.* **3** a frequently quoted phrase or saying.
v **tagged, tag·ging 1** attach a label or specified name or description to. **2** add to something, especially as an afterthought or with no real connection: *He tagged a few facts to the end of his speech.* **3** follow or accompany someone, especially when not invited to: *His little brother tagged along after him.* <Middle English *tagge*> **tag′ger** *n.*

tag[2] (tag) *n* **1** a children's game in which one player chases the rest, and anyone who is caught then becomes the pursuer. **2** *Baseball* the act of touching a base runner in baseball with the ball, causing the runner to be called out.
v **tagged, tag·ging 1** touch someone being chased. **2** *Baseball* **a** put out a base runner with a touch of the ball. **b tag up** of a base runner, stay in contact with a base, until a fly ball is caught, before attempting to advance. <origin uncertain>

Tag·ish (tag′ish) *n, pl* **Tag·ish 1** a member of a First Nations people of southern Yukon Territory and northern British Columbia. **2** the language of these people.
adj to do with these people or their language.

ta·hi·ni (tə hē′nē) *n* a Middle Eastern paste or spread made from ground sesame seeds. <Arabic *tahana* grind>

Tahl·tan (täl′tan) *n, pl* **Tahl·tan** or **Tahl·tans 1** a member of a First Nations people of northwest British Columbia. **2** the language of these people.
adj to do with these people or their language.

tai chi (tī′chē′) *or* (tī′jē′) *n* a Chinese martial art that is also used as a system of slow exercise movements aiding meditation and general well-being. <Chinese *tai ji quan* the great art of boxing>

tai·ga (tī′gə) *n* a swampy evergreen forest of subarctic regions, especially that between the tundra and steppes of in Siberia. <Russian>

tail (tāl) *n* **1** the narrow, hindmost part of an animal, especially when it extends beyond the rest of the body. The flexible extension of the backbone in a vertebrate or the feathers at the hind end of a bird are tails. **2** a thing that resembles an animal's tail in shape or position, extending downward or outward: *the tail of a kite, the tail of an airplane.* **3** the luminous trail of particles extending from a comet. **4** the end of a long line of people or vehicles: *the tail of a convoy.* **5** the final, more distant, or weaker part of something: *the tail of a hurricane.* **6** *Informal* a person secretly following another to observe her or his movements. **7 tails** *pl* **a** (*with singular verb*) the reverse side of a coin. **b** *Informal* a tailcoat.
v **1** *Informal* follow and observe someone closely, especially in secret. **2** drift or curve in a particular direction as an object in flight: *The ball tailed in at the batter's knees.* **3** follow close behind; form the tail of: *Some boys tailed after the parade.* <Old English *tægel*>
tail′less *adj.*
on someone's tail, *Informal* following someone closely.
turn tail, run away from danger or trouble.
with your tail between your legs, dejected or humiliated.

CONFUSABLES

Tail means "end part": *I got there late and found myself at the tail of the line.*

Tale means "story," especially one presented as true, but usually made up or exaggerated: *He told us many tales of his adventures in the wilderness.*

tail·bone (tāl′bōn′) *n* the small triangular bone at the base of the spinal column, consisting of vertebrae fused together. The technical name is **coccyx.**

tail·coat (tāl′kōt′) *n* a man's formal coat cut away at the front and extending at the back in two long, tapering pieces, or tails.

tail end *n* the last, hindmost, or concluding part of something: *the tail end of the procession, the tail end of the school year.*

a bat	e bed	i bid	o pot	u cup	th **thin**
ā cake	ē me	ī bite	ō go	ū rude	TH **then**
ä bar	ə about	ər over	ô for	ů put	zh measure

tail fin *n* **1** either of the pair of fins farthest back on a fish's body, typically continuous with the tail **2** a small horizontal part on either side of the tail of an aircraft that houses the rudder and gives added stability. **3** a part on either side at the back of a motor vehicle, sloping upward to a point that projects rearward. Tail fins were a popular style in the 1950s.

tail·gate (tāl′gāt′) *n* a hinged flap at the back of a truck or station wagon that may be lowered or removed when loading or unloading the vehicle.
v **tail·gated, tail·gat·ing** drive too closely behind another motor vehicle. **tail′gat′er** *n.*

tail·ings (tā′lingz) *pln* crushed stone and waste products remaining after ore has been processed. Such waste is often drained into a large pool of water called a **tailings pond**.

tail light *n* a red light at the rear of a motor vehicle, train, or bicycle.

tai·lor (tā′lər) *n* a person whose business is making or repairing clothes.
v **1** make clothes to fit individual customers. **2** make or adjust to suit a particular need: *The computer set-up can be tailored to suit the individual user.* <Old French *taillour* a cutter, from Latin *talea* a cutting>

tai·lored (tā′lərd) *adj* **1** stylish, fitted, and well cut: *a tailored suit.* **2** made or adapted for a particular person or purpose: *a tailored service.*

tai·lor·ing (tā′lə ring) *n* the activity, occupation, or workmanship of a tailor: *expert tailoring.*

tai·lor–made (tā′lər mād′) *adj* **1** made by a tailor or as if by a tailor: *My band uniform was tailor-made.* **2** made especially to suit a particular person or purpose: *a tailor-made course.*

tail·pipe (tāl′pīp′) the rear section of the exhaust pipe of a motor vehicle.

tail·spin (tāl′spin′) *n* **1** a downward spin of an aircraft with the nose pointed down. **2** a condition or situation of chaos, panic, or loss of control: *The news threw the whole household into a tailspin.*

tail·wind (tāl′wind′) *n* a wind blowing in the direction of travel of a vehicle or aircraft: *We made very good time because we had a tailwind all the way.*

taint (tānt) *n* a trace of a bad or undesirable quality or substance: *There was no taint of self-interest in her transactions. The drink had a taint of something unpleasant.*
v affect or be affected by a bad or undesirable quality or substance: *Her reputation for honesty had been tainted after she was caught plagiarizing from the Internet.* <Old French, from Latin *tingere* to dye>

tai·pan (tī′pan′) *n* the owner and administrator of a foreign firm in China. <Chinese>

Tai·wan (tī′wan′) *n* an island country off the coast of China. It is officially part of the Republic of China. See the APPENDIX. **Tai′wa·nese′** *adj, n.*

Ta·jik·i·stan (to jik′i stan′) *n* a country in central Asia. See the APPENDIX. **Ta·jik′** *adj, n.*

take (tāk) *v* **took, tak·en, tak·ing 1** reach for and lay hold of something with one's hand: *He took me by the hand.* **2** consume as food, medicine, or drugs: *to take a pill.* **3** capture by force: *The battalion took a number of prisoners.* **4** measure or observe: *The nurse has taken my temperature twice.* **5** make a photograph or video with a camera: *Do you want to get your picture taken?* **6** carry or bring: *He took along the book I wanted.* **7** accompany or bring someone to a specified place or condition: *The principal took me into her office. Won't you take me into your confidence?* **8** use as a route or a means of transport: *We take the bus to school.* **9** accept or receive someone or something: *My sister decided not to take a part-time job. His terrier took first prize in the dog show.* **10** understand or accept as valid; suppose or assume: *I take your point. I take it the train was late. Let us take an example.* **11** acquire or assume a position, situation, or form: *She said that envy takes many shapes.* **12** experience or be affected by: *The boxer took a lot of punishment in the first round. I heard they took the news badly.* **13** deal with a physical obstacle or course in a specified way: *She took the first lap at a fast pace.* **14** make, undertake, or perform an action or task: *Let's take the shortest way home. Most students take five courses during the first year.* **15** require or use up a specified amount of time: *The ceremony took several hours.* **16** need or call for a particular person or thing: *It will take an expert to fix the problem. I take size eight shoes.* **17** take root or begin to grow: *The plant cuttings have taken well.* **18** *Grammar* require as part of a construction: *A plural noun usually takes a plural verb.*
n **1** a sequence of sound or vision recorded continuously at one time: *They did the car chase scene in three takes.* **2** a particular version or approach to something: *He had a humorous take on the events.* **3** an amount of something gained from one source: *We got a large take from the raffle we ran.* <Old Norse *taka*> **tak′er** *n.*
on the take, *Informal* accepting or seeking bribes.
take five, *Informal* take a break for five minutes.
take it or leave it, accept it or reject it without changes or compromise.
take it out of, a *Informal* tire out; wear out: *He said a day of fruit picking takes it out of you.* **b** take compensation from or make someone pay.
take it out on, relieve one's anger or annoyance by scolding or hurting.
take it upon yourself, take the responsibility for; do on your own initiative: *I took it upon myself to rearrange all the furniture.*
take lying down, *Informal* accept something undesired without a protest.
taken with, a affected or attacked by: *taken with a bad case of the flu.* **b** favourably impressed by: *I was quite taken with the way he looked.*
take off, a leave the ground or water as an aircraft or bird: *Three airplanes took off at the same time.* **b** *Informal* give an amusing imitation of. **c** *Informal* leave quickly: *He took off at the first sign of trouble.*
take on, a hire an employee. **b** undertake to deal with: *take on an opponent.* **c** acquire a particular meaning or quality.
take out, a *Slang* remove or get rid of. **b** borrow a book or other item from a library or similar collection. **c** apply for and obtain a licence or other official document. **d** escort someone on a date.

take over, take the ownership or control of, or assume responsibility for.
take someone up on something, accept an offer or invitation: *She took him up on his invitation to dinner.*
take to, a form a liking for, become fond of, or be skilled at: *He greatly took to the visitor. She took to skiing right away.* **b** go to: *The cat took to the woods and became wild.*
take up, a soak up or absorb: *The sponge took up all the liquid.* **b** shorten a garment by turning up the hem. **c** become interested or engaged in doing something: *She took up piano lessons in the summer.* **d** accept an offer or challenge. **e** occupy time, space, or attention: *to take up time.* **f** pursue a matter later or further: *He took the matter up with the boss.* **g** begin to hold or fulfill a position or post: *to take up an appointment.*
take your time, not hurry.
well taken, relevant or worth considering: *Your point is well taken.*

take–charge (tāk′chärj′) *Informal adj* eager and able to be a leader or organizer: *a take-charge person.*

take–home pay (tāk′hōm′) *n* the pay received by an employee after tax and other deductions are made.

take·off (tā′kof′) *n* **1** the action of becoming airborne: *The plane was on the runway and ready for takeoff.* **2** an act of making a mocking but generally good-humoured imitation of someone or something: *The highlight of the evening was his clever takeoff on the prime minister.*

take·out (tā′kout′) *adj* to do with prepared food packaged in disposable containers and sold by a restaurant or other outlet to be eaten elsewhere: *a takeout dinner.*
n **1** food prepared, sold, or eaten in this way. **2** *Curling* a shot that removes an opponent's rock from play.

take·o·ver (tā′kō′vər) *n* an act of assuming control over or ownership of something: *The army's takeover of the country was total. The retail chain engineered a takeover of its main rival.*

tak·ing (tā′king) *n* **1** the action or process of taking something. **2 takings** *pl* the amount of money earned by a business from the sale of goods or services.

talc (talk) *n* **1** a soft, smooth, white, grey or greenish mineral with a soapy feel. **2** talcum. <Latin *talcum*, from Persian *talk*>

tal·cum (tal′kəm) *n* in full, **talcum powder** a powder made of purified white TALC (def. 1), often perfumed, for use on the face and body.

tale (tāl) *n* a story of true, legendary, or fictitious events, especially when imaginatively treated: *The retired sea captain told tales of his adventures.* See TAIL for confusable. <Old English *talu*>
live to tell the tale, *Informal* (*often used ironically*) get through a challenging experience successfully: *My brother gave the dog a bath and lived to tell the tale.*
tell tales, spread gossip.
tell tales out of school, *Informal* reveal private or secret information.

tale·bear·er (tāl′ber′ər) *n* a person who spreads gossip or reveals secrets. **tale′bear′ing** *adj, n.*

tal·ent (tal′ənt) *n* **1** a special natural ability: *a talent for music.* **2** a person or people possessing such ability: *They were looking for local talent.* **3** a former unit of weight or money used especially among the ancient Greeks and Romans. <Greek *talanton*> **tal′ent·ed** *adj.* **tal′ent·less** *adj.*

talent scout *n* a person whose job it is to search for people with talent in a particular field of activity, especially in sports and entertainment, who can be employed or promoted.

talent show *n* an entertainment made up of separate performances by amateurs looking for recognition as performers.

tal·is·man (tal′i smən) *or* (tal′i zmən) *n, pl* **tal·is·mans** an object, especially an inscribed ring or stone that is thought to have magic powers and to bring good luck. <Greek *telesma* consecration ceremony payment> **tal′is·man′ic** *adj.*

talk (tok) *v* **1** speak in order to give information or express ideas or feelings: *My little sister learned to talk early.* **2** have the power of speech: *She can talk as well as you.* **3** use a particular language: *to talk French.* **4** persuade or cause someone to do something by talking: *He talked me into going with him.* **5** spread gossip or secrets: *She talked behind their backs.*
n **1** the use of words in conversation or discussion: *The old friends met for a good talk.* **2** an informal speech: *The coach gave the team a talk about the need for more team spirit.* **3** a style or manner of talking: *baby talk.* **4** a period of conversation or discussion, especially a serious one. *We need to have a talk.* **5** gossip or rumour: *There is talk of a quarrel between them.* **6** boastful or empty words: *His threat was just talk.* <Middle English *talken*>
look who's talking, *Informal* the person criticizing is equally guilty.
now you're talking, *Informal* now you're saying what I want to hear.
talk around, discuss at length without coming to the point or to a conclusion: *to talk around an issue.*
talk at, speak to in a humiliating way or a way that discourages a response.
talk back, answer rudely or disrespectfully.
talk big, *Informal* talk boastfully.
talk down, a make silent by talking louder or longer. **b** speak in a condescending, belittling, or patronizing way: *Adults should not talk down to children.*
talk into (or **out of**) **something,** persuade to do (or not to do) something: *We talked them into coming along.*
talk off (or **out of**) **the top of your head,** *Informal* utter your thoughts or ideas without first thinking about them.
talk out, a discuss thoroughly. **b** discuss a bill in Parliament until the time for adjournment and so prevent its being put to a vote.
talk over, discuss.
talk up, discuss someone or something in a way that makes them seem more interesting or attractive.
you should talk, *Informal* you are guilty of the very thing you are criticizing.

a bat	e bed	i bid	o pot	u cup	th thin
ā cake	ē me	ī bite	ō go	ū rude	TH then
ä bar	ə about	ər over	ȯ for	ů put	zh measure

talk·a·tive (tok′ə tiv) *adj* with the habit of talking a great deal: *She is a cheerful, talkative person who knows everyone in town.* **talk′a·tive·ly** *adv.* **talk′a·tive·ness** *n.*

> **SYNONYMS**
>
> **Talkative** emphasizes a tendency to talk a great deal: *He's talkative, so I think he'll enjoy campaigning.*
>
> **Loquacious**, a formal word for "talkative," often emphasizes fluency: *She is such a loquacious speaker.*
>
> **Chatty** means "fond of talking in a friendly, familiar way": *The chatty groups created a din in the room.*

talk·er (tok′ər) *n* **1** a person who talks. **2** a talkative person.

talk·ie (to′kē) *Informal n* in former times, a movie with synchronized sound. <*talking picture*>

talk·ing book (tok′ing) *or* (to′king) *n* a recording or CD of a book being read aloud, used especially by the visually or physically impaired or by people driving for long periods.

talking head *n* a person shown close up on TV, engaged only in speaking, especially boringly or tiresomely: *That documentary was pretty boring—just a lot of talking heads.*

talking point *n* a point that invites discussion or argument: *These facts may not prove our case but at least they are a talking point.*

🍁 **talking stick** *n* among some First Nations peoples, a carved stick or other object which gives the holder the right to speak to a group. In some cultures, an eagle feather is used for this.

talk·ing–to (tok′ing tū′) *Informal n, pl* **talk·ing-tos** a scolding.

talk show *n* a radio or TV show featuring short interviews.

tall (tol) *adj* **1** of greater than average height, especially relative to width: *The trees in the valley were very tall. She is a tall woman.* **2** measuring a specified distance from top to bottom: *He is 1.85 m tall.* **3** *Informal* unlikely or hard to believe: *a tall tale.* <Old English *getæl* active> **tall′ness** *n.*
walk (or **stand**) **tall,** be proud and confident.

tall·ish (tol′ish) *adj* somewhat tall.

tal·lith (to′lēt) *Judaism n* a fringed shawl worn by Jewish men at prayer. <Hebrew>

tal·low (tal′ō) *n* the hard, white, rendered fat of cattle and sheep, used mainly for making candles and soap.
v smear or grease with tallow. <Middle English *talgh*>

tall ship *n* a large sailing ship of traditional design, with a high mast or masts.

tal·ly (tal′ē) *n, pl* **tal·lies** **1** a current score or account, or a record of it: *a tally of a game.* **2** a mark made for a certain number of objects in keeping count, or the number or group used in tallying: *The points were counted in tallies of five.* **3** in former times, a stick of wood in which notches were cut to represent numbers.
v **tal·lied, tal·ly·ing** **1** calculate the total score or amount: *to tally a score.* **2** agree or correspond: *Your account of the accident tallies with mine.* <Old French, from Latin *talea* stick>

tally sheet *n* a sheet on which a record or score is kept.

Tal·mud (tal′məd) *or* (tál′mùd) *n* the body of traditional Jewish civil and ceremonial law, consisting of the Mishnah and the Gemara. <Hebrew = instruction>

tal·on (tal′ən) *n* **1** a claw, especially of a bird of prey. See CLAW for picture. **2** a human finger or hand resembling a claw in appearance or when thought of as grasping. <Old French *talon* heel, from Latin *talus* ankle>

tam (tam) in full, **tam-o'-shanter** (tam′ə shan′tər) a round peakless woollen cap originating in Scotland, with a tight headband, a loose crown, and, often, a pompom.

ta·ma·le (tə má′lē) *n* a Mexican dish made of seasoned minced meat and corn flour, then steamed or baked in corn husks.

tam·a·rack (tam′ə rak′) *n* a slender, small or medium-sized larch found mainly in muskeg and swamp areas. <Algonquian>

tam·a·rind (tam′ə rind′) *n* a brown, pulpy, acidic fruit of a tropical tree, used as a flavouring in Asian foods.

tam·a·risk (tam′ə risk′) *n* a shrub or small tree of dry areas with tiny flowers on slender branches, giving the tree a feathery appearance.

tam·bou·rine (tam′bə rēn′) *n* a small, shallow drum with one head and with jingling metal discs around the side, played by shaking, striking with the knuckles, or rubbing with the thumb. See PERCUSSION INSTRUMENT for picture.

tame (tām) *adj* **tam·er, tam·est** **1** not dangerous or frightened of people, especially as a domesticated animal. **2** not exciting, adventurous, or controversial: *a tame story, a tame election campaign.*
v **tamed, tam·ing** make or become tame: *to tame a horse.* <Old English *tam*> **tame′a·ble** or **tam′a·ble** *adj.* **tame′ly** *adv.* **tame′ness** *n.*

tam·er (tā′mər) *n* a person who tames animals: *a lion tamer.*

Tam·il (ta′məl) *n, pl* **Tam·ils** or **Tam·il** **1** a member of a people living in southern India and northern Sri Lanka. **2** the language of these people.
adj to do with these people or their language.

tamp (tamp) *v* **1** pack down firmly by a series of taps or blows. **2** fill a hole containing explosives with clay or sand to concentrate the force of an explosion. <origin uncertain>

tam·per (tam′pər) *v* (*with* ***with***) interfere with or make unauthorized alterations in order to damage or weaken: *The lock had been tampered with but not broken. It was obvious to the investigator that someone had tampered with the evidence.* <variant of *temper*> **tam′per·er** *n.*

tam·pon (tam′pon) *n* a plug of soft material inserted into the vagina to absorb menstrual blood, or to stop a wound or block an opening in the body and absorb blood or secretions.
v plug with a tampon. <Old French *tapon* a little plug, from *tape* a plug>

tan (tan) *n* **1** a brown or golden brown colour that results from exposure to the sun or a sunlamp **2** the liquid used in tanning hides, or the active ingredient in it, such as tannin. **3** tanbark.

v **tanned, tan·ning 1** become brown or golden brown after exposure to the sun or a sunlamp: *My sister tans more quickly than I do. She was deeply tanned after a summer spent out-of-doors.* **2** make hide into leather by treating it with a solution containing tannin or a similar chemical agent to preserve it and keep it soft and flexible.
adj brown or golden brown. <Latin *tannum* crushed oak bark, used in tanning hides>

tan·a·ger (tan′ə jər) *n* a songbird, the male of which typically has brightly coloured feathers.

tan·bark (tan′bȧrk′) *n* the bark of a tree such as oak, rich in tannin, crushed or cut into small pieces and used in tanning hides. Used tanbark is often used to cover the ground for walking, riding, and other activities.

The front rider on a **tandem** is the *captain*, while the rear rider is the *stoker*. Both riders have responsibilities. The captain controls the steering, shifting, and braking, while the stoker generates power for the climbs.

tan·dem (tan′dəm) *n* **1** a bicycle with two seats and two sets of pedals, one behind the other. **2** a two-wheeled carriage drawn by horses harnessed one in front of the other. **3** a group of two people or machines working together.
adv **1** with two or more horses harnessed one behind the other. **2** alongside each other. <Latin = at length>
in tandem, a alongside each other: *working in tandem.* **b** one behind the other.

tan·door·i (tȧn dū′rē) *adj* of a dish from northern India, cooked in a clay oven called a **tandoor**. <Urdu *tandoor* an oven>

tang (tang) *n* **1** a strong, distinctive taste, flavour, or smell: *the tang of sea air.* **2** a distinctive or characteristic quality: *We need a slogan with more tang.* **3** the short extension on the blade of a tool such as a knife by which the blade is held firmly in the handle. <Old Norse *tangi* point (of a knife)>

tan·ge·lo (tan′jə lō′) *n* a citrus fruit developed by crossing the grapefruit and the tangerine. <*tang(erine)* + *(pom)elo*>

tan·gent (tan′jənt) *n* **1** *Mathematics* a straight line or plane that touches a curve at one point, but does not cross it at that point. **2** a completely different course of thought or action: *She thought his comment was a complete tangent to the topic.*
adj touching but not intersecting a curve. <Latin *tangere* touch>
fly (or **go**) **off at a tangent,** change suddenly from one course of action or thought to another.

tan·gen·tial (tan jən′shəl) *adj* **1** diverging from a previous course: *a tangential idea.* **2** peripheral or only slightly connected: *It's easy to get our teacher sidetracked on a tangential issue.* **3** *Mathematics* to do with geometric tangents. **tan·gen′tial·ly** *adv.*

tan·ge·rine (tan′jə rēn′) *or* (tan′jə rēn′) *n* a small citrus fruit with a loose, orange skin, and easily separated segments.
adj reddish orange. <French *Tanger* Tangiers, seaport in Morocco from which the fruit was exported>

tan·gi·ble (tan′jə bəl) *adj* **1** able to be touched: *a tangible object.* **2** clear and definite: *tangible evidence.*
n **tangibles** *pl* objects or property whose value is easily appraised. <Latin *tangere* touch> **tan′gi·bly** *adv.*

tan·gle (tang′gəl) *v* **tan·gled, tan·gling 1** twist or become twisted together in a confused mass: *The kitten got into the yarn and tangled it. Her hair tangles easily because it is fine and curly.* **2** (*with* ***with***) become involved in a fight or conflict: *Don't tangle with him.*
n a twisted or confused mass: *The detectives had to unsnarl a tangle of lies. My mind was in such a tangle I didn't hear a word he said.* <Middle English *tagilen* entangle>

tan·gled (tang′gəld) *adj* **1** confused, disordered, or snarled: *a tangled pile of stockings, tangled hair.* **2** very involved or complicated: *a tangled web of lies, tangled relationships.*

tan·gly (tang′glē) *adj* full of tangles; tangled.

tan·go (tang′gō) *n, pl* **tan·gos** an Argentinian ballroom dance with a strong rhythm, distinctive pauses, and slow glides, or a piece of music written for this dance.
v **tan·goed, tan·go·ing** dance the tango. <Spanish>

tan·gram (tan′gram′) *n* a puzzle consisting of a square cut into seven shapes (five triangles, a square, and a parallelogram), which can be combined so as to form various other shapes. <origin uncertain>

tang·y (tang′ē) *adj* with a strong, piquant flavour or smell: *a tangy sauce.*

tank (tangk) *n* **1** a large container for liquid or gas, or as much as this container will hold: *a water tank. They used up almost a tank of gas just driving around.* **2** a heavy armoured combat vehicle travelling on moving metal tracks.
v **1** put or store in a tank. **2** *Informal* fail completely. <perhaps Portuguese *tanque*, from Latin *stagnum* pool>
tank up, *Informal* fill the tank of one's vehicle with fuel.

tank·ard (tang′kərd) *n* a large drinking mug with a handle and sometimes a hinged cover. <Middle English>

tank car *n* a railway car with a tank for carrying liquids or gases.

tank·er (tang′kər) *n* a ship, aircraft, or truck with tanks for carrying oil, gasoline, or other liquid freight.

tank farm *n* a tract of land containing many large tanks for storing oil.

a bat	e bed	i bid	o pot	u cup	th **thin**
ā cake	ē me	ī bite	ō go	ū rude	ᴛʜ **then**
ȧ bar	ə about	ər over	ȯ for	u̇ put	zh measure

tank·ful (tangk′fủl′) *n* as much as a tank will hold.

tank top *n* a sleeveless, close-fitting, low-necked shirt.

tan·ner (tan′ər) *n* a person whose work is tanning hides.

tan·ner·y (tan′ə rē) *n, pl* **tan·ner·ies** a place where hides are tanned.

tan·nin (tan′ən) *n* a bitter-tasting, yellowish or brownish substance present in some plant tissues, and used in tanning and dyeing. Also called **tannic acid** (tan′ik).

tan·ning (tan′ing) *n* **1** the process of converting hide or skins into leather. **2** the action of making or turning brown, especially by exposure to sun. **3** *Informal* a severe spanking or thrashing.

tan·ta·lize (tan′tə līz′) *v* **tan·tal·ized, tan·ta·liz·ing** torment or tease someone with the sight or promise of something that is unobtainable. **tan′ta·li·za′tion** *n.* **tan′ta·liz′er** *n.* **tan′ta·liz′ing** *adj.* **tan′ta·liz′ing·ly** *adv.*

ETYMOLOGY

Tantalize comes from the Greek myth about King Tantalus. For his crimes (including killing his own son), the gods made him stand forever in water up to his chin, with fruit dangling above his head. The water and fruit withdrew every time he tried to reach them.

tan·ta·lum (tan′tə ləm) *n* a rare, hard, greyish metallic element that is resistant to acids. *Symbol* **Ta** <See TANTALIZE.>

tan·ta·mount (tan′tə mount′) *adj* (*with* ***to***) with the same force, effect, or seriousness: *His silence when questioned was tantamount to an admission of guilt.* <Old French *tant amunter* amount to as much>

tan·trum (tan′trəm) *n* an uncontrolled outburst of anger or frustration: *He goes into a tantrum if anyone touches his rock collection.* <origin uncertain>

Tan·za·ni·a (tan zə nē′ə) *n* a country in eastern Africa. See the APPENDIX. **Tan·za·ni′an** *adj, n.*

Tao·ism (dou′iz əm) *n* a Chinese philosophy, or the religion that developed from it, that emphasizes harmony with the **Tao**, the absolute principle underlying the universe. It signifies the way of conduct that is in harmony with the natural order. <Mandarin *tao* = the (right) way> **Tao′ist** *adj, n.*

Tao Te Ching (dou′də jing′) *n* the principal text of Taoism that defines the Tao and establishes the philosophical basis of Taoism.

tap[1] (tap) *v* **tapped, tap·ping 1** strike someone or something with a quick light blow or blows: *He tapped on the window.* **2** strike something with a series of quick light blows, or produce a rhythm with such blows: *She tapped her foot on the floor. He tapped time to the music.* **3** appoint or select someone for a task or honour, especially membership of an organization or group: *My brother was tapped to be class valedictorian.*
n **1** a quick light blow or the sound of such a blow: *There was a tap at the door.* **2** a piece of metal attached to the toe and heel of a tap dancer's shoe to make a tapping sound. **3 taps** *especially US* in the military, the last bugle call at night, signalling curfew in soldiers' quarters. Taps is also played at military funerals and memorial services. The Canadian equivalent is called **last post.** <origin uncertain>

tap[2] (tap) *n* **1** a device for turning on and off the flow of liquid or gas from a pipe or container: *a hot water tap.* **2** a device connected to a telephone, used for listening secretly to someone's conversations, or the act of listening to such conversations secretly. **3** the withdrawal of fluid from a body cavity: *a spinal tap.* **4** an instrument for cutting a threaded hole in a material.
v **tapped, tap·ping 1** draw liquid through the tap or spout of a cask, barrel, or other container: *They tapped the sugar maples when the sap began to flow.* **2** connect a device to a telephone so that conversations can be listened to secretly. **3** draw fluid from a body cavity. **4** obtain money or information from someone: *We tapped him for all the data he could provide.* **5** exploit or draw a supply from a resource: *The government sought to tap the province's mineral wealth.* <Old English *tæppa*>
on tap, a ready to be poured from a tap. **b** freely available for use.

tap dance *n* a dance performed wearing shoes fitted with metal taps, marked by rhythmical tapping of the toes and heels. **tap dance** *v.* **tap dancer** *n.* **tap dancing** *n.*

tape (tāp) *n* **1** a narrow strip of material, usually used to hold, fasten, or mark something: *paper tape.* **2** a strip of coated material used to record sound, images, or computer data, or a cassette or reel containing such a strip. **3** a strip of material stretched across a track at the finish line of a race.
v **taped, tap·ing 1** record sound or pictures on audiotape or videotape. **2** fasten or attach something with adhesive tape. <Old English *tæppe* strip of cloth> **tape′like′** *adj.*

tape deck *n* a piece of equipment for making and playing audiotapes, especially as part of a stereo system.

tape measure *n* a long, narrow strip of flexible steel or other material, marked off at intervals for measuring length or distance.

ta·per (tā′pər) *v* **1** become gradually smaller toward one end: *The church spire tapered to a point.* **2** gradually lessen: *As people moved away, his business tapered to nothing.*
n **1** a gradual lessening in thickness, diameter, or width toward one end: *The pant legs had a slight taper.* **2** a slender candle, or a candle wick coated with wax <Old English *tapor*> **ta′per·ing** *adj.* **ta′per·ing·ly** *adv.*
taper off, gradually reduce or lessen: *His voice tapered off and then stopped.*

tape recorder *n* a device for recording sound on magnetic tape and afterwards reproducing them. **tape′–re·cord′** *v.*

tape recording *n* **1** the recording of sound, etc. on magnetic tape. **2** a tape on which such a recording has been made.

tap·es·try (tap′i strē) *n, pl* **tap·es·tries** a piece of heavy fabric with designs or pictures woven into or embroidered on it. <Old French *tapisserie*, from Greek *tapes* carpet> **tap′es·tried** *adj.*

tape·worm (tā′pwərm) *n* a flatworm that in the adult stage lives as a parasite in the intestines.

tap·i·o·ca (tap′ē ō′kə) *n* a starchy substance in the form of grains prepared from the root of the cassava plant and used in puddings and other foods. <Tupi-Guarani (a language of S America) *tipioca*>

ta·pir (tā′pər) *n* a thick-skinned, tropical forest mammal with a long, tapered, flexible snout.

tap·room (tap′rům′) *n* a room where alcoholic drinks, especially beer, are sold.

tap·root (tap′rūt′) *n* the main root of a plant, growing smaller straight downward and with smaller roots branching out from it.

tar[1] (tår) *n* **1** a thick, dark, sticky substance distilled from wood or coal used in road making and for coating and preserving timber. **2** a similar substance formed by burning tobacco or other material.
adj of, like, or covered with tar: *tar paper.*
v **tarred, tar·ring** cover or smear with tar. <Old English *teoru*>
tar and feather, smear heated tar on and then cover with feathers as a punishment.
tarred with the same brush, have the same faults or defects.

tar[2] (tår) *Informal n* a sailor. <*tarpaulin*>

tar·an·tel·la (tar′ən tel′ə) *or* (ter′ən tel′ə) *n* a rapid, whirling southern Italian dance in very quick rhythm, usually performed by couples, or the music for this dance.

ETYMOLOGY

Tarantella, like *tarantula*, comes from Taranto, a seaport in southern Italy. It was thought that *tarantism*, a form of maniacal dancing, was caused by the spider's bite.

ta·ran·tu·la (tə ran′chů lə) *n* a large, hairy spider chiefly of the subtropical or tropical Americas, some kinds of which are able to catch small lizards, frogs, and birds. See SPIDER for picture. <Latin *tarantula*, from *Tarentum* Taranto, where these spiders are found>

tar·dy (tår′dē) *adj* **tar·di·er, tar·di·est 1** delaying or delayed beyond the proper or expected time: *It was thought to be a tardy attempt at reform.* **2** slow in action or response: *tardy growth, a tardy pace.* <Latin *tardus*>
tar′di·ly *adv.* **tar′di·ness** *n.*

tare[1] (ter) *n* a vetch, especially the common vetch.

tare[2] (ter) *n* a deduction made from the gross weight of something in a container, to allow for the weight of the packaging.

tar·get (tår′git) *n* **1** a person, object, or place selected as the aim of an attack, especially a mark or point at which someone fires or aims: *The archer's target was an apple hanging from a tree.* **2** such an object, especially a round or rectangular board marked with concentric circles used in archery and shooting: *We set up the target in a field.* **3** a goal, objective, or result toward which efforts are directed: *The target for the school fundraising drive was $1000.* **4** an object of scorn, abuse, or criticism: *His absent-mindedness made him a target for their practical jokes.* **5** a small, round shield or buckler.
v **tar·get·ed, tar·get·ing 1** select as an object of attention or attack. **2** aim or direct something. <Old French *targe* light shield>
on target, a accurately hitting the thing aimed at: *Her criticism of the book was exactly on target.* **b** proceeding or improving at a good enough rate to achieve an objective: *My project is moving ahead on target.*

tar·iff (tar′if) *or* (ter′if) *n* **1** a tax or duty to be paid on a particular class of imports or exports, or a list of these taxes. **2** a table of the fixed charges made by a business, especially in a hotel or restaurant.
v make subject to a tariff. <Arabic *tar'if* inventory of fees to be paid>

tar·mac (tår′mak) *n* a material used for surfacing roads or outdoor airport areas, made up of broken stone mixed with tar, or a runway or other area surfaced with such a material. <*tar*[1] + *mac*(*adam*)>

tarn (tårn) *n* a small mountain lake or pool. <Old Norse *tjörn*>

tar·nish (tår′nish) *v* **1** lose or cause to lose luster, especially as a result of exposure to air or moisture: *This silver spoon is tarnished.* **2** make or become less valuable or respected: *to tarnish a reputation.*
n dullness of colour, especially a film or stain formed on the surface of a mineral or metal. <French *terne* dark>

ta·ro (tå′rō) *n, pl* **ta·ros** a tropical plant whose corms and fleshy leaves are used as food. <Polynesian>

tar·ot (ter′ō) or (tar′ō) *n* a pack of playing cards, traditionally with seventy-eight cards, used mostly for telling fortunes. <French, from Italian *tarocchi*>

tarp (tårp) *Informal n* a tarpaulin.

tar·pa·per (tår′på′pər) *n* heavy paper coated with tar to make it waterproof, often used as insulation during the construction of buildings.

tar·paul·in (tår pol′ən) *n* strong, heavy, waterproofed cloth, typically made of canvas and used to protect goods against the weather. <*tar*[1] + *pall* in sense of "covering">

tar·ra·gon (ter′ə gon′) *or* (tar′ə gən′) *n* a plant with aromatic leaves that are used for seasoning foods. See HERB for picture. <Old French *targon*, from Arabic *tarkhun*>

tar·ry[1] (tar′ē) *or* (ter′ē) *v* **tar·ried, tar·ry·ing** stay longer than intended: *He tarried at the inn till he felt well again.* <origin uncertain>

tar·ry[2] (tå′rē) *adj* **tar·ri·er, tar·ri·est** of, like, or covered with tar: *a tarry smell.*

tar sands *pl n* a deposit of bitumen mixed with sand, clay, and various minerals, which in liquid form is a source of synthetic crude oil.

tar·si·er (tor′sē ər) *or* (tor′sē ā′) *n* a small, nocturnal, tree-dwelling primate of southeast Asia that has a long, thin tail, very long hind limbs, and large eyes. <French *tarse* tarsus, because of the bone structure of the feet>

a bat	e bed	i bid	o pot	u cup	th thin
ā cake	ē me	ī bite	ō go	ū rude	TH then
å bar	ə about	ər over	ȯ for	ů put	zh measure

T

tar·sus (tär′səs) *n, pl* **tar·si** (-sī) *or* (-sē) the group of small bones forming the ankle and the back half of the foot, or the corresponding part in the hind leg of an animal. <Greek *tarsos* sole of the foot> **tar′sal** *adj.*

tart[1] (tärt) *adj* **1** sharp or acid in taste: *a tart apple.* **2** with a sharp, cutting quality in a remark or tone of voice: *a tart reply.* <Old English *teart*> **tart′ly** *adv.* **tart′ness** *n.*

tart[2] (tärt) *n* a piece of pastry with a filling, often without a top. <Old French *tarte*>

tar·tan (tär′tən) *n* a plaid pattern for cloth originating in Scotland and designed with the stripes in varying widths and colours, especially to distinguish families or clans, or a cloth woven in such a pattern.
adj to do with tartan: *a tartan skirt.* <perhaps Middle French *tiretaine* fabric of linen and wool>

tar·tar (tär′tər) *n* **1** *Dentistry* a hard acid deposit that forms on the teeth and contributes to their decay. **2** a hard deposit formed during the fermentation of wine. <Greek *tartaron*>

Tar·tar (tär′tər) *n* **1** a member of a group of central Asian nomads, including Mongols and Turks, who, in early medieval times, were led by Genghis Khan and conquered much of Asia and eastern Europe. **2 tartar** a person with a very bad temper. <Old French, from Persian *Tatar*>

tar·tar·ic acid (tär tar′ik) or (tär ter′ik) *n* a colourless crystalline acid found in many plants, especially unripe grapes, and is used in baking powders and as a food additive.

tartar sauce *n* a sauce made of mayonnaise with chopped pickles and capers.

tar·tra·zine (tär′trə zēn) *n* a bright yellow synthetic dye derived from tartaric acid and used to colour food, drugs, and cosmetics. <*tartar* + *azo-* containing nitrogen>

tas·er (taz ′ər) *Trademark n* a small device that fires electric darts to incapacitate a person temporarily.

ETYMOLOGY

Taser comes from the first letters of the main words in *Tom Swift and his Electric Rifle.* The book was one of a series of fictional works originally published between 1910 and 1941 and starred a teenage hero who was a brilliant inventor.

task (task) *n* a piece of work to be done or undertaken, especially something hard or unpleasant: *One of her tasks was to take the garbage out. She was left with the task of breaking the news to her mother.*
v put strain on someone's resources or abilities in doing something: *The heavy job tasked him beyond his strength.* <Old French *tasche*, from Latin *taxare* to tax>
take to task, criticize somebody severely for a fault or mistake: *His mom took him to task for not working harder.*

task force *n* a temporary group, specially organized under one leader for a particular task: *A naval task force was sent to turn away the spy ship. The mayor set up a task force to study the effects of the proposed expressway.*

task·mas·ter (task′mas′tər) *n* a person who sets tasks for others to do, especially one who is very demanding.

Tas·man·i·an devil (taz mā′nē ən) *n* a small, fierce, carnivorous marsupial that has a large head and powerful jaws. See KANGAROO for picture. <*Tasmania*, an island state of Australia, where this animal is found>

tas·sel (tas′əl) *n* **1** a tuft of loosely hanging threads, cords, or other material knotted at one end and attached for decoration to soft furniture, clothing, or other items. **2** the tufted head of some plants, especially a flower head with prominent stamens at the top of a cornstalk.
v **tas·selled** or **tas·seled, tas·sel·ling** or **tas·sel·ing** **1** provide with a tassel or tassels. **2** form or produce tassels in corn or other plants. <origin uncertain>

taste (tāst) *n* **1** the sensation of flavour perceived in the mouth and throat in contact with a substance: *a sour taste, the sense of taste.* **2** a brief experience of something, conveying its basic character: *It was his first taste of success.* **3** a small portion or sample: *Have a taste of this cake.* **4** a person's liking for a particular thing: *She had a taste for comedy.* **5** the ability to perceive and enjoy what is beautiful or excellent: *He has great taste in clothes.*
v **tast·ed, tast·ing** **1** perceive or experience the flavour of something. **2** have a specified flavour: *She tasted almond in the cake.* **3** eat or drink a little bit of: *The children barely tasted their breakfast the day they went to the circus.* **4** have experience of: *to taste freedom.* <Old French *taster*, from Latin *taxare* evaluate> **tast′a·ble** *adj.*
a bad taste (in the mouth), a feeling of distaste or disgust after an experience: *He won the argument, but it left a bad taste in his mouth.*
in good (or **bad**) **taste,** in a manner that conforms to what is generally acceptable (or unacceptable): *The joke was in bad taste.*
to taste, in the amount that suits one's eating preferences: *Add salt and pepper to taste.*

SYNONYMS

Taste suggests the perception of flavour: *I've now had my first taste of Thai food.*

Flavour emphasizes a distinct taste or quality: *The flavours of ketchup and mustard are very different from each other.*

Tang means "strong, distinctive taste, flavour, or smell": *The tang of freshly made coffee greeted them as they walked into the kitchen.*

taste bud *n* a cluster of bulbous nerve endings on the tongue and in the lining of the mouth that provide the sense of taste.

taste·ful (tāst′fəl) *adj* with or showing good judgment of beauty or appropriate behaviour: *tasteful furnishings.* **taste′ful·ly** *adv.* **taste′ful·ness** *n.*

taste·less (tā′stlis) *adj* **1** lacking flavour: *The meat was dry and tasteless.* **2** with or showing a lack of sensitivity to beauty or appropriate behaviour: *She made a tasteless remark about his having gained weight.* **taste′less·ly** *adv.* **taste′less·ness** *n.*

tast·er (tā′stər) *n* **1** a person who tastes, especially one whose work is testing the quality of food or drink by tasting it. **2** a small quantity or brief experience of something, intended as a sample.

tast·y (tā′stē) *adj* **tast·i·er, tast·i·est** with a pleasant, distinct flavour: *That casserole is very tasty.* **tast′i·ly** *adv.* **tast′i·ness** *n.*

tat (tat) *v* **tat·ted, tat·ting** do or make by tatting.

tat·tered (tat′ərd) *adj* torn, old, and in generally poor condition: *a tattered dress.*

tat·ters (tat′ərz) *n* irregularly torn pieces of cloth, paper, or other material. <Scandinavian>

tat·ting (tat′ing) *n* a knotted lace made by hand with a small shuttle, used chiefly for edging and trimming, or the process of making such lace.

tat·tle (tat′əl) *v* **tat·tled, tat·tling** reveal secrets or gossip: *If you tell her anything about it, she'll tattle. He tattled on his sister, and she was punished.*
n idle talk or gossip. <Dutch *tatelen* to babble> **tat′tler** *n.*

tat·tle·tale (tat′əl tāl′) *n* a person who tells secrets, especially to get other people into trouble.

tat·too[1] (ta tū′) *n, pl* **tat·toos** **1** a drum or bugle recalling soldiers to their quarters. **2** a rhythmic tapping or drumming: *The hail beat a loud tattoo on the roof.* **3** an entertainment consisting of music, marching, and displays and exercise by military personnel.

ETYMOLOGY

Tattoo, for the definition above, comes from Dutch *taptoe*, from tap meaning "spigot" + *toe* meaning "shut." It refers to the sound of shutting off the taps of barrels at closing time in a bar.

tat·too[2] (ta tū′) *v* **tat·tooed, tat·too·ing** mark the skin of the body with coloured designs or patterns by inserting pigment into punctures, or make a design in such a way: *The sailor had a ship tattooed on his arm.*
n, pl **tat·toos** a mark or design made by tattooing. <Polynesian *tatau*> **tat·too′er** *n.* **tat·too′ist** *n.*

taught (tot) past tense and past participle of TEACH. See TAUT for confusable.

taunt (tont) *v* provoke or challenge someone with insulting remarks: *At school she had been taunted with being poor. They taunted him into taking the dare.*
n a remark made in order to anger, insult, or provoke someone. <French *tant pour tant* tit for tat>

taupe (tōp) *adj* brownish grey. <French, from Latin *talpa*>

Tau·rus (tȯ′rəs) *n* **1** *Astronomy* a northern constellation shaped somewhat like a bull. **2** *Astrology* **a** the second sign of the zodiac. The sun enters Taurus about April 21. **b** a person born under this sign.

taut (tot) *adj* **1** stretched or pulled tight, and with no slack: *a taut rope.* **2** tense and not relaxed, especially as muscles or nerves: *a taut smile.* **3** concise and controlled as a piece of writing or other work of art. <Middle English tought> **taut′ly** *adv.* **taut′ness** *n.*

CONFUSABLES

Taut means "stretched tight": *The plastic wrap was pulled taut over the bowl of leftovers.*

Taught is the simple past tense of teach: *My uncle taught me to play soccer.*

tau·tol·o·gy (to tol′ə jē) *n, pl* **tau·tol·o·gies** the saying of a thing over again in other words without making it clearer or more forceful; redundancy. Example: the *modern* college student *of today.* <Greek *tautologia*, from *to auto* the same + *legein* say> **tau′to·log′i·cal** *adj.* **tau′to·log′i·cal·ly** *adv.*

tav·ern (tav′ərn) *n* a place where alcoholic drinks, especially beer, are sold and consumed. <Old French, from Latin *taberna*>

taw·dry (tod′rē) *adj* **taw·dri·er, taw·dri·est** of clothes, jewellery, etc., showy and cheap, but of poor quality. **taw′dri·ly** *adv.* **taw′dri·ness** *n.*

ETYMOLOGY

Tawdry is an alteration of *St. Audrey*, the name of a cheap lace collar sold at an annual fair in Ely, England. St. Audrey died in 679 CE of a throat tumour, said to be a punishment for her love of fine necklaces as a young woman.

taw·ny (ton′ē) *adj* **taw·ni·er, taw·ni·est** brownish yellow: *tawny fur.* <Old French *tanner* to tan hides, from Latin tannum tan bark>

tax (taks) *n* **1** money paid to a government for public purposes, imposed on employees' income and business profits, or added to the cost of some goods, services, and transactions. **2** a burden, duty, or heavy demand on someone: *Climbing stairs was a tax on his weak heart.*
v **1** put or pay a tax on: *She said people were taxed too heavily.* **2** make heavy demands on someone's powers or resources: *Reading in a poor light taxed his eyes.* **3** (with ***with***) accuse or charge: *I taxed her with having snooped through my locker.* <Latin *taxare* assess, from Greek *tassein* assign> **tax′a·ble** *adj.*

tax·a·tion (tak sā′shən) *n* **1** the act of imposing taxes. **2** money paid as tax.

tax–de·duct·i·ble (taks′di duk′tə bəl) *adj* allowed as a deduction from taxable income or from the total income tax owed.

tax–ex·empt (tak′seg zempt′) *adj* free from taxes or not taxed.

tax–free (taks′frē′) *adj* not requiring the payment of tax.

tax haven *n* a foreign country where taxes are low or non-existent, used by investors to escape taxation.

tax·i (tak′sē) *n, pl* **tax·is** a motor vehicle, boat, or other means of transportation licensed to carry passengers in return for payment of a fare, usually with a meter for recording the fare.
v **tax·ied, tax·i·ing** **1** ride in a taxi. **2** move across the ground or water under its own power, or cause an aircraft to move in this way: *The plane taxied down the runway.* <from French *taxe* fare>

tax·i·cab (tak′sē kab′) *n* a taxi.

a bat	e bed	i bid	o pot	u cup	th thin
ā cake	ē me	ī bite	ō go	ū rude	ᴛʜ then
ȧ bar	ə about	ər over	ȯ for	u̇ put	zh measure

T

tax·i·der·my (tak′sə dər′mē) *n* the art of preparing the skins of animals and stuffing and mounting them in lifelike form. <Greek *taxis* arrangement + *derma* skin> **tax′i·der′mist** *n.*

taxi stand *n* a place where taxis may park while waiting to be hired: *There is a taxi stand in front of the railway station.*

tax·on·o·my (tak son′ə mē) *n* the study of the principles of scientific classification, especially of organisms, or the classification itself. See also KINGDOM. <Greek *taxis* arrangement + *-nomos* assigning> **tax′o·nom′ic** *adj.* **tax′o·nom′ic·al** *adj.* **tax′o·nom′ic·al·ly** *adv.* **tax·on′o·mist** *n.*

tax·pay·er (tak′spā′ər) *n* a person who pays taxes.

tax return *n* a form for reporting one's income and other personal details to the government, which calculates how much tax is owed.

tax shelter *n* a financial arrangement or investment that reduces the amount of tax owed.

TB *Informal n* tuberculosis.

TBA to be announced.

T–ball (tē′bol′) *n* a version of baseball played by small children, in which the ball is hit off the top of a post rather than pitched to the batter.

T–bar (tē′bår′) *n* a beam or bar shaped like an inverted T, attached in a series to a suspended cable, for skiers to hold on to while the cable pulls them up a slope.

T–bone (tē′bōn′) *n* a beefsteak taken from the middle part of the loin, containing a T-shaped bone and a bit of tenderloin.

T cell *n* a type of lymph produced or processed by the thymus gland that recognizes harmful antigens and helps to destroy them. <T for *thymus*, the gland that produces this cell>

TCP *Computers* See IP.

TD or **td** touchdown.

tea (tē) *n* **1** a drink made by pouring boiling water over the crushed, dried leaves of the tea plant, or the dried and prepared leaves from which this drink is made. **2** an evergreen shrub or small tree that produces these leaves, native to southeastern Asia. **3** a drink made by pouring boiling water over the leaves, fruits, or flowers of other plants: *mint tea.* **4** *UK* a light meal or reception in the afternoon, at which tea is typically served. <Chinese *t'e*>
your cup of tea, *Informal* just what you like.

tea bag *n* a small gauze bag containing enough tea leaves for one or two cups of tea.

tea biscuit *n* a small, baked, unsweetened cake made with baking powder.

teach (tēch) *v* **taught, teach·ing 1** show or explain how to do something: *We taught our dog a new trick. His mother taught him to drive.* **2** encourage to accept something as a fact or principle: *She taught him honesty. That experience taught me not to believe everything I hear.* **3** give information about or instruction in a subject or skill, especially to give such instruction professionally: *He teaches mathematics. She taught for forty years.* See LEARN for confusable. <Old English *tæcan* show>

teach·a·ble (tē′chə bəl) *adj* capable of being taught. **teach′a·bil′i·ty** *n.*

teach·er (tē′chər) *n* a person trained to teach, especially one who teaches in a school or college.

teach·ing (tē′ching) *n* **1** the occupation, work, or profession of a teacher. **2 teachings** *pl* ideas or principles taught by an authority.

tea cosy *n* a thick or padded cover for putting over a teapot to keep the tea hot.

tea·cup (tē′kup′) *n* a small cup from which tea or another beverage is drunk, or the amount held by this.
a storm (or **tempest**) **in a teacup,** great excitement or commotion over something unimportant.

tea·cup·ful (tē′kup fůl′) *n, pl* **tea·cup·fuls** as much as a teacup holds.

tea·house (tē′hous′) *n* a place where tea and other light refreshments are served.

teak (tēk) *n* a durable wood used in shipbuilding and in making furniture, from a hardwood tree native to India and southeast Asia. <Portuguese, from Malayalam (a language of India) *tekka*>

tea·ket·tle (tē′ket′əl) *n* a covered kettle with a spout and handle, used for boiling water.

teal (tēl) *n, pl* **teals** or (*especially collectively*) **teal** a small freshwater duck, typically with a greenish band on the wing.
adj greenish blue. <Middle English *tele*>

team (tēm) *n* **1** a group of people forming one of the sides in a game or competition: *a debating team, a football team.* **2** a group of people working or acting together: *He was on the cleanup team.* **3** two or more horses or other animals harnessed together to work.
v **1** (*with* **up**) join together in a team to achieve a goal: *We teamed up to clean the classroom after the party.* **2** drive or work with a team. See TEEM for confusable. <Old English *team*>

team·mate (tēm′māt′) *n* a fellow member of a team.

team·ster (tēm′stər) *n* **1** a truck driver. **2** a person who drives a team of horses, especially as an occupation.

team teaching a system of teaching in which several teachers co-ordinate the instruction of a group of students.

team·work (tē′mwərk′) *n* the combined action of a group of people, especially when effective and efficient.

tea·pot (tē′pot′) *n* a container with a handle and a spout for making and serving tea.

tear[1] (tēr) *n* **1** a drop of clear salty liquid secreted by glands in a person's eyes when crying or when the eye is irritated: *We laughed till the tears came.* **2** the act of weeping: *Tears will not help. She burst into tears.*
v fill with tears: *The bitter wind made her eyes tear.* <Old English *tear*>
in tears, weeping: *Many of the mourners were in tears.*

tear[2] (ter) *v* **tore, torn, tear·ing 1** pull or rip something apart or to pieces with force: *He tore the box open. She tore a hole in her sweater. A nail tore his coat.* **2** damage or cut badly: *The jagged stone tore his skin.* **3** divide or split: *The political party was torn by two factions.* **4** *Informal* move with great force, haste, or recklessness: *A car came tearing along.*
n **1** a hole or split in something caused by having been pulled apart forcefully: *I have a tear in my jeans.* **2** the act or process of tearing. <Old English *teran*>
tear apart, destroy or damage: *The tornado tore apart an entire block of houses.*
tear down, a destroy something, especially a building: *They tore down the church to build a shopping plaza.* **b** criticize someone severely: *She tried to tear down his reputation.*
tear into, a attack or criticize severely. **b** make an energetic or enthusiastic start on something: *Without a pause, she tore into the song.*
tear yourself away, leave despite a strong desire to remain: *I had to tear myself away from the TV.*

tear·drop (tēr′drop′) *n* **1** a single tear. **2** a thing shaped like a tear, especially a gem.

tear·ful (tēr′fəl) *adj* **1** crying or inclined to tears: *a tearful face.* **2** causing tears: *a tearful goodbye.* **tear′ful·ly** *adv.* **tear′ful·ness** *n.*

tear gas (tēr) a gas that irritates the eyes, causing tears and temporary blindness, used especially in forcing crowds to disperse.

tear·jerk·er (tēr′jər′kər) *Informal n* a sentimental story, film, or song, calculated to cause sadness or sympathy.

tear·less (tēr′lis) *adj* without tears or not crying.

tea·room (tē′rům′) *n* a small restaurant or café where tea, coffee, and light meals are served.

tea rose a garden rose with flowers that have a delicate scent resembling that of tea.

tear·y (tē′rē) *adj* tearful.

tease (tēz) *v* **teased, teas·ing 1** make fun of or attempt to provoke a person or animal in a playful way: *They teased him about his curly hair.* **2** gently pull or comb something tangled, especially wool or hair, into separate strands.
n **1** a person who or thing that teases. **2** the act of teasing or the quality of being teased. <Old English *tæsan*> **teas′ing·ly** *adv.*
tease out, find something out from a mass of irrelevant data: *After much effort, they were able to tease out a meaning from the scribbled note.*

teas·er (tē′zər) *n* **1** *Informal* a difficult or tricky question or task. **2** a person who or thing that teases.

tea service *n* a set of silver or china for serving tea, usually consisting of a teapot, hot-water pitcher, cream jug, and sugar bowl. Also called **tea set**.

tea·spoon (tē′spūn′) *n* **1** a small spoon used typically for adding sugar to and stirring hot drinks and for eating some desserts. See SOUP SPOON for picture. **2** a standard unit of measurement in recipes, equal to five millilitres.

tea·spoon·ful (tē′spūn′fůl) *n, pl* **tea·spoon·fuls** as much as a teaspoon holds: *a teaspoonful of sugar.*

teat (tēt) *n* the nipple of a breast or udder, from which the young suck milk. <Old French *tete*>

tea towel *n* a towel for drying dishes that have been washed.

tech (tek) *Informal n* **1** a high school offering training in the trades and other practical subjects: *He graduated from Central Tech.* **2** technology: *high tech, low tech.*

tech·ie (tek′ē) *Informal n* a person who is expert in or enthusiastic about technology, especially computing: *You don't have to be a techie to manage this database.*

tech·ni·cal (tek′nə kəl) *adj* **1** to do with applied and industrial sciences: *a technical school.* **2** to do with the special characteristics of a subject, art, or craft: *technical terms.* **3** requiring special knowledge to be understood, especially in a book or article: *The manual gets very technical after the first chapter.* **4** strictly according to the rules: *a technical victory.* **5** resulting from mechanical failure: *a technical flaw.* <Greek *techne* art>
tech′ni·cal·ly *adv.*

tech·ni·cal·i·ty (tek′nə kal′ə tē) *n, pl* **tech·ni·cal·i·ties 1** a point of law or a small detail of a set of rules: *She was acquitted on a legal technicality.* **2 technicalities** *pl* the specific details or terms belonging to a particular field: *The technicalities of the article soon discouraged him.*

technical knockout *n* a knockout called by the referee in a boxing match when he considers a fighter, though not knocked out, to be unable to continue. *Abbrev.* **TKO, T.K.O.**

technical school *n* a school that provides training for work in an applied and industrial science:

tech·ni·cian (tek nish′ən) *n* **1** a person trained or skilled in looking after technical equipment or doing practical work in a science: *a computer technician, a laboratory technician.* **2** a person skilled in the technique of an art or craft: *He was a superb technician at the keyboard.*

tech·ni·col·our (tek′ni kul′ər) *n* **1 Technicolor** *Trademark* a process for making films in colour, in which three single-colour films, made at the same time but each showing tones of a different primary colour, are combined into one full-colour print. **2** bright, vivid colours: *She was a vision in technicolour.*

tech·nique (tek nēk′) *n* **1** a method or way of performing a particular task, especially the action or performance of an artistic work or a scientific procedure: *The pianist's technique was brilliant, but her interpretation of the piece lacked warmth.* **2** a special method or system used to accomplish something: *She had a new technique for weaving baskets.*

techno– *combining form* to do with technology or its use: *technophobe.* <Greek *techne* craft>

tech·no·bab·ble (tek′no ba′bəl) *Informal n* technical jargon difficult or impossible for a non-expert to understand. Also called **technospeak**.

a bat	e bed	i bid	o pot	u cup	th thin
ā cake	ē me	ī bite	ō go	ū rude	ᴛʜ then
ä bar	ə about	ər over	ȯ for	ů put	zh measure

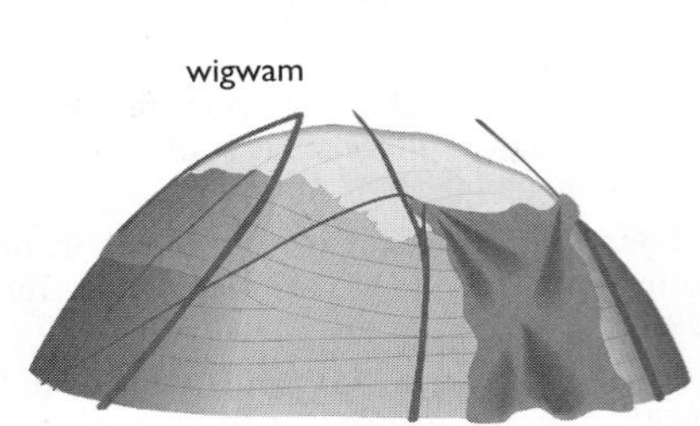

Wigwams were dwellings used by Algonquin peoples of the Eastern Woodlands. They were dome-shaped and covered with bark or hides.

The portable dwellings known as **teepees** suited the nomadic lifestyle of the Plains peoples. Teepees were waterproof and warm in the winter, and cool in the summer. They were made, owned, and erected by the women.

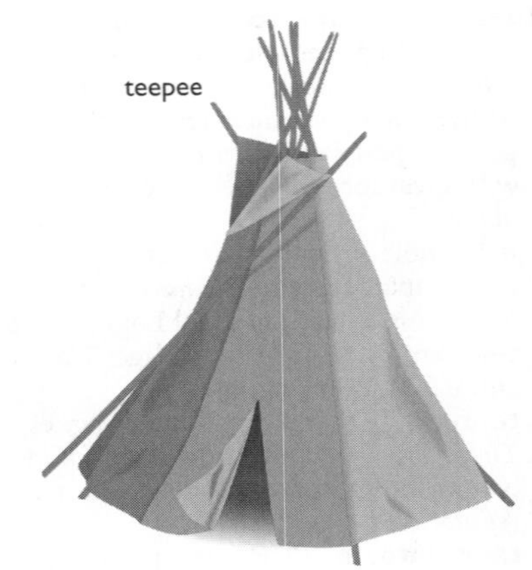

tech·noc·ra·cy (tek nok′rə sē) *n* government or management of society by a small group of technical experts. **tech′no·crat** *n.* **tech′no·crat′ic** *adj.* **tech′no·crat′i·cal·ly** *adv.*

tech·nol·o·gy (tek nol′ə jē) *n* **1** the application of scientific knowledge for practical purposes, especially in industry. **2** machinery and equipment developed from such scientific knowledge. **tech′no·log′i·cal** *adj.* **tech′no·log′i·cal·ly** *adv.* **tech′nol′o·gist** *n.*

tech·no·phobe (tek′nə fōb′) *n* a person who fears, dislikes, or avoids new technology. **tech′no·pho′bi·a** *n.* **tech′no·pho′bic** *adj.*

tec·ton·ic (tek ton′ik) *adj* to do with the structure of the earth's crust and the large-scale processes that take place within it: *tectonic plates.* See PLATE TECTONICS for picture. <Greek *tekton* a builder>

ted·dy (ted′ē) *n, pl* **ted·dies** **1** a woman's one-piece undergarment combining undershirt with short underpants. **2** a teddy bear.

teddy bear *n* a stuffed toy made to look like a bear cub. <*Teddy*, nickname of US President Theodore Roosevelt, who was fond of hunting bears>

te·di·ous (tē′dē əs) *or* (tē′jəs) *adj* long, slow, dull, or tiresome: *A long talk that you cannot understand is tedious.* **te′di·ous·ly** *adv.* **te′di·ous·ness** *n.*

te·di·um (tē′dē əm) *n* the quality of being tedious. <Latin *taedere* be wearisome>

tee (tē) *n* **1** a cleared space on a golf course, from which the ball is struck from a small peg at the beginning of play for each hole of golf. **2** a mark aimed at in quoits, bowling, and similar games.
v **teed, tee·ing** place the ball on a tee ready to make the first stroke of the round or hole. <origin unknown>
tee off, 1 drive a golf ball from a tee. **2** *Informal* make someone angry or annoyed: *I was teed off that I wasn't invited to the party.*

tee–hee (tē′hē) *n* a giggle or titter.
v **tee-heed, tee-heeing** giggle or titter.

teem[1] (tēm) *v* be full of or swarming with: *The big swamp teemed with mosquitoes.* <Old English *teman* to proцce offspring>

teem[2] (tēm) *v* pour down heavily as water: *It teemed rain all afternoon.* <Old Norse *tœma* empty out>

CONFUSABLES

Teem is a verb that means "pour" or "swarm": *The dark clouds suggest it will teem with rain. The subway platform is teeming with people.*

Team is a noun that means "a group of people with a common purpose": *I joined the track team.*

teen (tēn) *n* **1** a teenager. **2** **teens** *pl* the years from thirteen to nineteen in a century or a person's life: *He was still in his teens when he joined the armed services. The songs in this book date from the teens and twenties.* <-*teen* in the numbers *thirteen* to *nineteen*>

teen·ag·er (tē′nā′jər) *n* a person in his or her teens: *She was still a teenager when she won her first Olympic gold medal.* **teen′age′** or **teen′aged′** *adj.*

tee·ny (tē′nē) *Informal adj* **tee·ni·er, tee·ni·est** tiny: *a teeny bit of sugar.*

teen·y·bop·per (tē′nē bop′ər) *Informal n* a young teenager, especially a girl, who enthusiastically follows current fashions in clothes and pop music.

tee·pee (tē′pē) *n* a cone-shaped tent originally used by Aboriginal peoples in the Plains and Great Lakes region, consisting of a frame of poles covered with skins, cloth, or canvas. Also, **tepee**, **tipi**. <Dakota *tipi*>

tee·ter (tē′tər) *v* move or balance unsteadily or sway back and forth: *The tightrope walker teetered on the narrow wire.* <Old Norse *titra* shake>

tee·ter–tot·ter (tē′tər tot′ər) SEESAW.

teeth (tēth) plural of TOOTH. For idioms, see TOOTH.

teethe (tēᴛʜ) *v* **teethed, teeth·ing** grow or cut one's first teeth: *The baby is teething.*

teeth·er (tē′ᴛʜər) *n* a small hard object for babies to bite on when they are teething.

teeth·ing ring (tē′ᴛʜing) *n* a small hard ring for teething babies to bite on.

tee·to·tal·ler or **tee·to·tal·er** (tē tō′tə lər) *n* a person who never drinks alcoholic liquor. <formed from the initial letter of *total* + *total*>
tee·to′tal *adj.* **tee·to′tal·ism** *n.*

Tef·lon (tef′lon) *Trademark n* a tough, synthetic resin often used as a coating on the inside of cooking utensils and the bottom of steam irons to prevent sticking.

tele– *combining form* **1** operating over a distance: *telecommunication.* **2** to do with television: *telecast.* **3** done by means of the telephone: *telemarketing.*

> **ETYMOLOGY**
>
> All words beginning with **tele-** apply to something carried out over a distance. For example, through *telecommunications* you communicate over a distance, and a *telescope* helps you to view things that are a far distance away. *Television* shows you pictures of events taking place some distance away from where you are.

tel·e·cast (tel′ə kast′) *v* **tel·e·cast** or **tel·e·cast·ed, tel·e·cast·ing** broadcast by television.
n a television broadcast. <*tele*(*vision*) + (*broad*)*cast*>
tel′e·cast′er *n.*

tel·e·com·mu·ni·ca·tion (tel′ə kə myū′nə kā′shən) *n* **1** communication at a distance, as by cable, telephone, etc. **2 telecommunications** *pl* (*with singular or plural verb*) the branch of technology that deals with such communication.

tel·e·com·mute (təl′ə kə myūt′) *v* **tel·e·com·mut·ed, tel·e·com·mut·ing** work at home, connecting to the workplace by using telephones and computer links. **tel′e·com·mut′er** *n.* **tel′e·com·mut′ing** *n.*

tel·e·con·fer·ence (təl′ə kon′fər əns) or (təl′ə kon′frəns) *n* a conference with participants in various locations linked by telecommunication devices.
v **tel·e·con·fer·enced, tel·e·con·fer·enc·ing** take part in such a conference. **tel′e·con′fer·enc·ing** *n.*

tel·e·gram (tel′ə gram′) *n* especially in former times, a message sent by telegraph and then delivered in written or printed form.

tel·e·graph (tel′ə graf′) *n* especially in former times, a system for sending or receiving messages from a distance along a wire.
v **1** send a message by telegraph: *They telegraphed the news of the escape.* **2** convey a message with facial expressions or body language: *His frown telegraphed his displeasure.* **tel′e·graph′ic** *adj.* **tel′e·graph′i·cal·ly** *adv.*

tel·e·ki·ne·sis (tel i ki nē′sis) *n* the supposed ability to make an object move by means of mental power or other non-physical means. <*tele-* at a distance + Greek *kinesis* motion> **te′le·ki·net′ic** *adj.*

tel·e·mar·ket·ing (tel′ə mar′kə ting) *n* the process of selling or advertising goods or services, soliciting donations, or promoting an organization over the telephone. **tel′e·mar′ket·er** *n.*

te·lem·e·try (tə lem′ə trē) *n* **1** the use of equipment that records the readings on an instrument and transmits the information by radio. **2** the equipment used in this process: *The ground telemetry indicated that the rocket was on course.*

te·lep·a·thy (tə lep′ə thē) *n* the supposed communication of thoughts or ideas from one mind to another by means other than the known senses. A person who claims to be able to do this is called a **telepath**. <*tele-* at a distance + Greek *pathes* feeling> **tel′e·path′ic** *adj.*
tel′e·path′ic·al·ly *adv.*

tel·e·phone (tel′ə fōn′) *n* a system or process for transmitting sound or speech over a distance using wire or radio, by converting it into electrical impulses, or the instrument used to do this.
v **tel·e·phoned, tel·e·phon·ing** **1** ring or speak to someone using the telephone: *Wait till she's finished telephoning.* **2** make a telephone call: *Did you telephone her yet? They telephoned a message.* <*tele-* at a distance + Greek *phone* sound> **tel′e·phon′er** *n.*
tel′e·phon′ic (telə′fon′ik) *adj.* **tel′e·phon′ic·al·ly** *adv.*

telephone book *n* a telephone directory.

telephone booth *n* a small enclosure in a public place containing a telephone that is usually operated by coins.

telephone directory *n* a book containing an alphabetical or classified list of names of telephone subscribers, together with their addresses and telephone numbers.

telephone tag *Informal n* the action or situation in which two people keep trying to contact each other by phone and have to leave messages because neither person is able to be reached.

tel·e·pho·to lens (tel′ə fō′tō) *n* a camera lens with a longer focal length than standard, producing a large image of a distant object.

tel·e·port (tel′ə pȯrt′) *v* transport or be transported across space and distance instantly, especially in science fiction. <*tele-* at a distance + Latin *portare* carry>
tel′e·por·ta′tion *n.*

tel·e·promp·ter (tel′ə promp′tər) *n* a device used in television broadcasting, unseen by viewers, that shows a line-by-line enlarged version of a script or speech to the actors or speaker. <TelePrompTer, a trademark>

tel·e·scope (tel′ə skōp′) *n* **1** an instrument for viewing distant objects, using lenses or mirrors or both by which rays of light are collected and focused and the resulting image magnified. **2** a radio telescope.
v **tel·e·scoped, tel·e·scop·ing** **1** slide one within the other like the sections of a hand telescope, or be capable of sliding together in this way: *The modules telescoped into one another.* **2** force or be forced one into the other as in a collision: *When the two trains collided, the force of the crash telescoped the first few cars.* **3** condense or combine so as to occupy less space or time: *to telescope events.* <*tele-* at a distance + Greek *skopeein* look at>
tel′e·scop′ic (tel′ə skōp′ik) *adj.* **tel′e·scop′i·cal·ly** *adv.*

a bat	e bed	i bid	o pot	u cup	th thin
ā cake	ē me	ī bite	ō go	ū rude	ᴛʜ then
à bar	ə about	ər over	ȯ for	u̇ put	zh measure

tel·e·shop (tel′ə shop′) *v* **tel·e·shopped, tel·e·shop·ping** buy consumer products over the Internet or from TV by using a telephone connection or an interactive cable. **tel′e·shop′per** *n.*

tel·e·text (tel′ə tekst′) *n* an electronic communications service in which printed information is broadcast by television signals to sets equipped with decoders.

tel·e·thon (tel′ə thon′) *n* a TV program or series of programs lasting a long time and typically used to raise funds for a charitable cause. <*tele*(*vision*) + (*mara*)*thon*>

tel·e·type (tel′ə tīp′) *n* a device for transmitting telegraph signals as they are keyed, and for printing messages received.
v **tel·e·typed, tel·e·typ·ing** send a message by such a device.

tel·e·vise (tel′ə vīz′) *v* **tel·e·vised, tel·e·vis·ing** transmit by television: *All the games are being televised.*

tel·e·vi·sion (tel′ə vizh′ən) *n* **1** the system or process of transmitting visual images, accompanied by sound, in which electromagnetic waves are reconverted in sets and reproduced on screens, used to broadcast programs for entertainment, information, or education. **2** a box-shaped device with a screen that receives and reproduces such images. **3** the activity, profession, industry, or medium of broadcasting on television. **4** television programs: *What's on television tonight?*

tel·ex (tel′eks′) *n* especially in former times, an international telecommunications service in which printed messages are transmitted and received by teletype. <*tele-* at a distance + Greek *lexis* word>

tell (tel) *v* **told, tell·ing 1** communicate information in words: *I told her we would arrive early.* **2** order or advise someone to do something: *I keep telling her to be careful on the slippery sidewalk.* **3** reveal information in a nonverbal way: *The numbers tell me all I need to know.* **4** decide correctly or with certainty: *You can tell they don't like each other.* **5** divulge confidential or private information: *Promise not to tell.* **6** have a noticeable, typically harmful, effect on someone: *The strain had begun to tell on him.* <Old English *tellan*> **tell′a·ble** *adj.*
all told, counting everyone or everything: *We'll be fifteen people all told.*
tell apart, distinguish one from the other or others: *Nobody could tell the twin sisters apart.*
tell it like it is, be frank; tell the plain truth.
tell me about it, *Informal* I have experienced exactly what you mean.
tell off, scold or criticize severely: *His father told him off for staying out late.*
tell time, know what time it is by the clock.
you're telling me, *Informal* I agree completely.

tell[2] *n* an artificial mound or hill in the Middle East that covers layered remains of an ancient settlement. <Arabic *tall* mound>

tell·er (tel′ər) *n* **1** a person who tells something. **2** a person who deals with customers' transactions at a bank. **3** a person appointed to count votes, especially in a legislature.

tell·ing (tel′ing) *adj* with a marked or revealing effect or force: *a telling blow.* **tell′ing·ly** *adv.*

tell·tale (tel′tāl′) *n* a person, especially a child, who reports others' wrongdoings or reveals their secrets.
adj revealing, indicating, or betraying something: *telltale fingerprints, a telltale blush.*

tel·lu·ri·um (te lů′rē əm) *n* a brittle, silver-white element that usually occurs in nature combined with gold, silver, or other metals. *Symbol* **Te** <Latin *telluris* earth>

te·lo·phase (tel′ə fāz′) *Biology n* the final stage of cell division, in which chromosomes move to opposite ends of the cell and two nuclei are formed. <Greek *telos* end + *phase*>

te·mer·i·ty (tə mer′ə tē) *n* the quality of having too much confidence or boldness. <Latin *temere* heedlessly>

temp (temp) *Informal n* a temporary employee, typically an office worker who is assigned through an agency.
v work as a temporary employee.

tem·per (tem′pər) *n* **1** a person's state of mind viewed as being angry or calm: *She had a nasty temper. He became angry and lost his temper.* **2** a tendency to become angry easily, or the anger itself: *His temper sometimes got the better of him.* **3** the degree of hardness or elasticity in steel or other metal.
v **1** improve the hardness and elasticity in steel or other metal by reheating and then cooling it. **2** neutralize or counterbalance as a force: *She tempered emotion with logic.* **3** tune a piano or other musical instrument so as to adjust the tone intervals correctly. <Latin *temperare* to mix correctly, from *tempus* proper time>

tem·per·a (tem′pə rə) *n* a method of painting in which colours are mixed with water and egg yolk, especially used from the 1100s to the 1400s. <See TEMPER.>

tem·per·a·ment (tem′pə rə mənt) *or* (tem′prə mənt) *n* a person's or animal's usual way of thinking, feeling, and acting: *shy temperament, artistic temperament.* <See TEMPER.>

tem·per·a·men·tal (tem′pə rə men′təl) *or* (tem′prə men′təl) *adj* **1** to do with temperament: *a temperamental dislike.* **2** extremely sensitive and excitable or unpredictable in behaviour: *a temperamental actor.*
tem′per·a·men′tal·ly *adv.*

tem·per·ance (tem′pə rəns) *or* (tem′prəns) *n* **1** moderation and self-restraint in behaviour or expression. **2** the action or practice of refraining from drinking alcoholic beverages. <Latin *temperare* to regulate>

tem·per·ate (tem′pə rit) *or* (tem′prit) *adj* **1** to do with a region or climate marked by mild temperatures: *a temperate region.* **2** showing moderation and self-restraint: *She spoke in a calm, temperate manner.* **tem′per·ate·ly** *adv.* **tem′per·ate·ness** *n.*

tem·per·at·ure (tem′prə chər) *n* **1** the measure of how hot a substance is, especially as expressed on a scale and shown by a thermometer or perceived by touch: *The temperature of freezing water is zero degrees Celsius.* **2** the degree of heat in a person's body: *Does he have a temperature? The baby was running a temperature yesterday.* **3** the degree of excitement or tension in a discussion or confrontation: *The temperature of the debate* *soared toward the end.* <Latin *temperatura,* from *temperare* moderate. The sense of heat or cold was first recorded in 1670.>

–tempered *combining form* with a specified temper or disposition: *an even-tempered person, bad-tempered.*

tem·pest (tem′pist) *n* a violent windstorm, usually accompanied by rain, hail, or snow: *The tempest drove the ship onto the rocks.* <Old French, from Latin *tempestis* storm>
tempest in a teapot (or **tea cup**), great excitement or commotion over something unimportant.

tem·pes·tu·ous (tem pes′chū əs) *adj* **1** marked by strong, violent, or conflicting emotions: *a tempestuous argument.* **2** very stormy: *a tempestuous night.* **tem·pes′tu·ous·ly** *adv.* **tem·pes′tu·ous·ness** *n.*

tem·plate (tem′plit) *n* **1** a thin piece of wood, metal, plastic, or cardboard used as a pattern in cutting out, shaping, or drilling. **2** *Computers* a file that stores a document's format and specifies all the styles used in that document. **3** a thing that serves as a model or pattern for others to copy. <French *templet,* device regulating width of cloth on a loom>

tem·ple[1] (tem′pəl) *n* **1** a building used for religious services or worship. <Latin *templum*>

tem·ple[2] (tem′pəl) *n* **1** the flat part of either side of the head between the forehead and the ear. <Old French, from *tempus* side of the forehead>

tem·po (tem′pō) *n, pl* **tem·pos** or **tem·pi** (-pē) **1** the speed at which a passage of music is or should be played: *a fast tempo, the correct tempo.* **2** the rate or speed of motion or activity: *the tempo of life.* <Italian, from Latin *tempus*>

tem·po·ral[1] (tem′pə rəl) *adj* **1** to do with secular life, as opposed to spiritual matters: *temporal concerns.* **2** to do with time: *a temporal anomaly.* **tem′po·ral′·i·ty** *n.* **tem′po·ral·ly** *adv.*

tem·po·ral[2] (tem′pə rəl) *adj* to do with the temples in the head: *the temporal bones.*

tem·po·rar·y (tem′pə rer′ē) *adj* lasting or used for a short time only: *a temporary shelter, a temporary inconvenience.*
n a person employed for a short time, typically an office worker hired through an agency. **temp′o·rar′i·ly** *adv.* **tem′po·rar′i·ness** *n.*

tem·po·rize (tem′pə rīz′) *v* **tem·po·rized, tem·po·riz·ing** avoid making a decision or committing oneself in order to gain time. <Latin *tempus* time> **tem′po·ri·za′tion** *n.* **tem′po·riz′er** *n.*

tempt (tempt) *v* **1** make, or try to make, a person do something wrong by promising something that he or she finds attractive: *He was tempted to steal.* **2** appeal to strongly: *The platter of appetizers tempted us to eat too much.* **3** (*usually with a form of the verb* **to be**) cause to feel strongly inclined: *After three failures, he was tempted to quit.* **4** provoke or defy, usually with undesirable consequences: *It would be tempting fate to take that old car on the road.* <Latin *temptare* try> **tempt′a·bil′i·ty** *n.* **tempt′a·ble** *adj.* **tempt′er** *n.*

temp·ta·tion (temp tā′shən) *n* **1** a desire to do something, especially something wrong or unwise: *to give in to temptation.* **2** a thing or course of action that attracts or tempts: *The money lying on the counter was a temptation to him.*

tempt·ing (temp′ting) *adj* appealing to or attracting someone, even if wrong or unwise: *A party was a tempting idea.* **tempt′ing·ly** *adv.*

tempt·ress (temp′tris) *n* a woman, especially one who is sexually attractive, who tempts someone.

tem·pu·ra (tem′pù rə) or (tem pùr′ə) *n* a Japanese dish consisting of fish, shellfish, or vegetables, coated in a light batter and deep-fried. <Japanese>

ten (ten) *n* **1** a cardinal number that is one more than nine. **2** the numeral 10. **3** a playing card with ten spots: *the ten of hearts.* **4** a ten-dollar bill: *I changed the twenty for two tens.*
adj **1** one more than nine: *ten fingers.* **2** (*after the noun*) tenth in a series: *Chapter Ten will be discussed tomorrow.* <Old English> **tenth** *adj, adv.*

ten·a·ble (ten′ə bəl) *adj* able to be maintained or defended against attack or objection: *a tenable position, a tenable theory.* <French, from Latin *tenere*> **ten′a·bil′i·ty** *n.* **ten′a·bly** *adv.*

te·na·cious (ti nā′shəs) *adj* **1** not readily letting go, giving up, or separated from an object that one holds, a position, or a principle: *a tenacious grip. He is tenacious of his rights and will fight to the end.* **2** not easily discouraged or readily giving up: *a tenacious salesperson, tenacious courage.* <Latin *tenacis,* from *tenere* hold>
te·na′cious·ly *adv.* **te·na′cious·ness** *n.*
te·nac′i·ty (ti na′sə tē) *n.*

ten·an·cy (ten′ən sē) *n, pl* **ten·an·cies** possession of land or property as a tenant, or the length of time a tenant occupies it.

ten·ant (ten′ənt) *n* a person who occupies land or property rented from an owner of it: *They have tenants on the second floor of their house.*
v occupy as a tenant. <See TENABLE.> **ten′ant·less** *adj.*

tenant farmer *n* a person who farms rented land.

tend[1] (tend) *v* regularly or frequently behave, possess, or display in a particular way or have a certain characteristic: *He tends to dress conservatively. The coastline tends to the south here.* <Old French, from Latin *tendere* to stretch>

tend[2] (tend) *v* take care of, look after, pay attention to, or work in: *He tends shop for his father. Just tend to your work and never mind what everyone else is doing.* <*attend*>

tend·en·cy (ten′dən sē) *n, pl* **tend·en·cies** **1** an inclination toward a particular characteristic or type of behaviour: *He had a tendency to favour pastel colours. She has a tendency to reject new ideas without considering them. Wood has a tendency to swell if it gets wet.* **2** a group within a larger political party or movement: *a small left-wing tendency.*

a bat	e bed	i bid	o pot	u cup	th thin
ā cake	ē me	ī bite	ō go	ū rude	TH then
à bar	ə about	ər over	ȯ for	ů put	zh measure

tennis

two-handed grip

The two-handed grip in **tennis** is mainly used for backhand strokes. Players use different variations.

eastern grip

The eastern grip is the most natural and comfortable, which is why it's taught to beginners.

continental grip

The continental grip is good for creating a backward spin, and is used by experts mainly for serving and volleying.

western grip

The western grip is the best grip for generating a forward spin, which gives the ball a downward motion.

When receiving a serve, the player stands in a balanced position, ready to move quickly to the right or left.

ten·den·tious (ten den′shəs) *adj* with or promoting a particular aim or point of view, especially a controversial one: *tendentious writings.* <See TEND[1].>

ten·der[1] (ten′dər) *adj* **1** easy to cut and chew as food: *tender meat.* **2** showing gentleness and sensitivity, concern, or sympathy: *tender words, a tender heart.* **3** easily injured by severe weather and requiring protection as a plant: *tender grass.* **4** sensitive to physical pain or emotional distress: *tender skin.* **5** requiring tact or careful handling: *a tender subject.* **6** young and vulnerable: *He lost his parents at the tender age of six.* <Old French, from Latin *tener* delicate> **ten′der·ly** *adv.* **ten′der·ness** *n.*

ten·der[2] (ten′dər) *v* **1** offer or present something formally: *She tendered her thanks.* **2** make or invite a formal written offer to carry out work, supply goods, or buy land, shares, or another asset for a stated price: *A number of companies tendered for the work. They tendered out the contract.*
n a formal offer to do, supply, or buy something at a stated fixed price: *The contract was put out to tender.* <Old French *tendre* to offer, from Latin *tendere* extend> **ten′der·er** *n.*

tend·er[3] (ten′dər) *n* **1** a person who looks after someone else or a machine or place: *an engine tender.* **2** a small boat carried or towed by a big one and used for landing passengers or carrying supplies. **3** a railway car attached behind a steam locomotive and designed to carry fuel and water. <*tend*[2]>

ten·der·foot (ten′dər fůt′) *n, pl* **ten·der·foots** or **ten·der·feet** a newcomer or novice, especially a person unused to the hardships of pioneer life.

ten·der–heart·ed (ten′dər här′tid) *adj* with a kind, gentle, or sentimental nature.

ten·der·ize (ten′də rīz′) *v* **ten·der·ized, ten·der·iz·ing** make meat more tender by beating, adding spices, etc.

ten·der·iz·er (ten′də rīz′ər) *n* anything used to make meat more tender, especially a substance rubbed on the meat or used as a marinade.

ten·der·loin (ten′dər loin′) *n* the tenderest part of a loin of beef, pork, or other meat.

ten·di·ni·tis (ten′də nī′tis) *n* inflammation of a tendon.

ten·don (ten′dən) *n* a tough, strong band or cord of tissue that attaches a muscle to a bone. <Latin, from Greek *tenon* sinew>

ten·dril (ten′drəl) *n* **1** a threadlike part of a climbing plant that attaches itself to something, helps support the plant, and grows in a spiral form. **2** something resembling such a part of a plant, especially a slender curl or ringlet of hair. <Old French, from Latin *tener* delicate>

ten·e·ment (ten′ə mənt) *n* a rundown, low-rental apartment building that barely meets minimum standards. <Middle English = a holding of immovable property, from Latin *tenere* hold>

ten·et (ten′it) *n* a doctrine, belief, or opinion, especially one of the main principles of a religion or philosophy. <Latin = he holds>

ten·fold (ten′fold′) *adj, adv* **1** ten times as much or as many. **2** consisting of ten parts.

ten·nis (ten′is) *n* a game played by two or four players who use a racquet to knock a ball back and forth over a net stretched across a court marked on grass, clay, or an artificial surface. <origin uncertain>

tennis elbow *n* an inflammation of the tendons of the elbow, caused by overuse of muscles of the forearm.

tennis shoe *n* a light canvas or leather-soled shoe suitable for tennis or casual wear.

ten·on (ten′ən) *n* the end of a piece of wood cut so as to fit into a hole, the mortise, in another piece and so form a joint.
v join by means of a tenon. <Old French, from Latin *tenere* to hold>

ten·or (ten′ər) *n* **1** *Music* **a** a high adult male singing voice, or a singer with such a range. Compare COUNTERTENOR, FALSETTO. **b** an instrument, especially a saxophone or trombone, of the second or third lowest pitch in a family of musical instruments. **2** the general sense or content of something: *I didn't hear every word, but I got the tenor of his remarks.* **3** a settled or prevailing character or direction, especially the course of a person's life or habits: *The calm tenor of her life has never been disturbed by excitement or trouble.*
adj to do with, with the range of, or designed for a musical tenor: *a tenor saxophone.* <Old French, from Latin *tenere* hold, because the melody was held (carried) by the tenor>

tenor clef *Music n* the C clef that assigns the note middle C to the second line down from the top of the staff. Compare ALTO CLEF, BASS CLEF, TREBLE CLEF.

ten·pin (ten′pin) *n* a bowling game in which a large heavy ball is bowled at ten pins to knock them down at the end of a narrow track.

tense[1] (tens) *adj* **tens·er, tens·est 1** stretched tight or rigid, especially of a muscle or someone's body: *a tense face.* **2** unable to relax as a person because of nervousness, anxiety, or stimulation: *The bad news made them tense.* **3** causing anxiety and nervousness: *a tense situation.* **4** pronounced, especially as a vowel, with the vocal muscles stretched tight.
v **tensed, tens·ing** make or become tense: *He tensed his muscles.* <Latin *tendere* stretch> **tense′ly** *adv.* **tense′ness** *n.*

tense[2] (tens) *n* a set of verb forms to show the time and sometimes also the duration or completeness of the action in relation to the time something is spoken, or one such form: *the present tense.* Example: The simple past tense of *go* is *went.* <Old French *tens* time>

GRAMMAR AND USAGE

There are three main verb **tenses**:
past: I saw, I had seen, I was seeing
present: I see, I have seen, I am seeing
future: I will see, I will have seen, I will be seeing

Regular verbs have past tenses ending in *-ed* (*walked, shivered*). The past tenses of irregular verbs are varied; for example: *go/went/gone, dig/dug, think/thought.*

When writing, avoid changing tenses for actions that happen at the same time.

ten·sile (ten′sīl) *or* (ten′səl) *adj* **1** to do with tension: *Steel has great tensile strength.* **2** capable of being drawn out or stretched.

tensile strength *n* the resistance of a material to breaking under tension.

ten·sion (ten′shən) *n* **1** the quality or condition of being stretched tight. **2** a strained quality or condition resulting from forces acting in opposition to each other. **3** mental or emotional strain. **4** a strained political or social state or relationship: *military tension.* **5** voltage or electromotive force: *high-tension wires.*

ten·sor (ten′sər) *n* a muscle that stretches or tightens some part of the body.

🍁 **Tensor bandage** *Trademark n* a long, stretchy strip of cloth to wrap around a sprained or strained part of the body for support.

tent (tent) *n* a portable shelter, usually made of canvas or cloth and often supported by one or more poles and stretched tight by cords or loops attached to pegs driven into the ground.
v **1** camp out or live in a tent: *They plan on spending their holidays tenting in the Maritimes.* **2** cover with or as with a tent. <Old French *tente*, from Latin *tendere* stretch> **tent′like′** *adj.*

ten·ta·cle (ten′tə kəl) *n* **1** a long, slender, flexible limb or extension in an animal, especially around the mouth of an invertebrate, used for grasping, moving around, or bearing sense organs. **2** a sensitive, hairlike tendril of a plant. <Latin *tentaculum* feeler>

ten·ta·tive (ten′tə tiv) *adj* not certain or fixed, done hesitantly, or performed as a trial or experiment: *a tentative plan.* <Latin *tentare* try, from *temptare* test> **ten′ta·tive·ly** *adv.* **ten′ta·tive·ness** *n.*

tent caterpillar *n* the larva of a moth that feeds on the leaves of deciduous trees. Tent caterpillars live in groups inside silken webs that they spin in trees.

tent city *n* a community of homeless people living in tents or other shelters.

ten·ter·hook (ten′tər hůk′) *n* a hook used to fasten cloth on a drying frame. <originally, a hook securing cloth on a *tenter* frame for drying, from Latin *tendere* stretch>
on tenterhooks, in painful suspense or anxiety because of something that is going to happen.

tenth (tenth) *adj, n* **1** next after the ninth: *on the tenth day* (*adj*). *I'm tenth in the class* (*n*). **2** one, or being one, of ten equal parts: *a tenth part of the profit* (*adj*). *She divided the data into tenths* (*n*). **tenth′ly** *adv.*

ten·u·ous (ten′yū əs) *adj* **1** very weak or slight: *a tenuous connection.* **2** very slender or fine: *a tenuous cloud.* <Latin *tenuis* thin> **ten′u·ous·ly** *adv.* **ten′u·ous·ness** *n.*

ten·ure (ten′yər) *n* **1** the condition or terms under which land or buildings are held or occupied. **2** the holding of an office or title: *The tenure of our club's president is one year.* **3** guaranteed permanent employment, especially as a teacher or lecturer, after a probationary period. <French, from Latin *tenere* hold>

te·pee (tē′pē) TEEPEE.

tep·id (tep′id) *adj* only slightly warm, especially as a liquid <Latin *tepidus*> **tep′id·ly** *adv.* **tep′id·ness** *n.*

a bat	e bed	i bid	o pot	u cup	th thin
ā cake	ē me	ī bite	ō go	ū rude	TH then
ä bar	ə about	ər over	ô for	ů put	zh measure

T

te·qui·la (tə kē′lə) *n* a strong alcoholic drink made from the juice of a Mexican agave plant. <*Tequila*, a town in Mexico, where the drink was first produced>

tera– *Computers combining form* denoting 2^{40} (about a trillion). One terabyte is equal to a thousand gigabytes. *Symbol* **T**

ter·bi·um (tər′bē əm) *n* a silver-white metallic element. *Symbol* **Tb** <*Ytterby*, a town in Sweden, where it was discovered>

ter·cel (tər′səl) *n* a male peregrine falcon or goshawk.

ter·cen·ten·ar·y *n* the 300th anniversary of a significant event.
adj to do with a 300th anniversary. <Latin *ter* three times + *centenary*>

ter·cet (tər′sit) *n* a group of three lines rhyming together, or containing a rhyme with the adjacent group or groups of three lines. <French, from Latin *tertius* third>

ter·i·ya·ki (ter′ē yä′kē) *n* a Japanese dish consisting of meat or fish, broiled or grilled after being marinated in soy sauce. <Japanese *teri* shine + *yaki* broil>

term (tərm) *n* **1** a word or phrase used to describe a thing or to express a concept, especially in a particular kind of language or branch of study: *medical terms.* **2** a set period of time for which something, such as length of office, a prison sentence, or an investment, lasts or is intended to last: *a presidential term.* **3** each of the periods in the year, alternating with holidays or vacation, during which instruction is given in a school, college, or university, or during which a law court holds sessions: *the fall term.* **4** *Mathematics* each number or item in a ratio, series, or mathematical expression. **5 terms** *pl* **a** language used on a particular occasion: *She spoke of dangers in the strongest possible terms.* **b** conditions under which an action may be undertaken or agreement reached: *the terms of a treaty, on speaking terms.*
v give a descriptive name or call by a specified term: *He might be termed handsome.*
adj with a definite end or limit: *a term deposit, term insurance.* <Old French, from Latin *terminus* end>
bring to terms, compel to agree.
come to terms, a reach an agreement. **b** come to accept a new and painful and difficult event or situation: *She had to come to terms with the loss of her cat.*
in terms of, with regard to a particular aspect or subject specified: *How's he doing in terms of academic progress? It can't be explained in terms of pure science.*
in (or **over**) **the long** (**short**) **term,** over a long (short) period of time.
terms of reference, the range or scope set for an inquiry or discussion.

GRAMMAR AND USAGE

Whenever possible, rewrite a sentence to avoid the wordy expression **in terms of**:

Instead of *In terms of money, it's a good deal,* say *It's a good deal financially.*

Instead of *That's the best I can do in terms of help,* say *That's the best I can do to help.*

ter·ma·gant (tər′mə gənt) *n* a bad-tempered or scolding woman. <Old French *Tervagan*, from Italian *Trivigante*, an arrogant character in medieval plays and thought to be a Muslim deity>

term deposit *n* an arrangement for depositing money in a bank, under which it must be left there for a specified length of time in order to earn a set interest, or the money so deposited.

ter·mi·na·ble (tər′mə nə bəl) *adj* **1** able to be terminated: *The contract was terminable by either party.* **2** coming to an end after a certain time.

ter·mi·nal (tər′mə nəl) *adj* **1** of, forming, or located at the end or farthest part of something: *a terminal date.* **2** of or forming a transport terminal: *a terminal platform.* **3** located at, forming, or indicating the end of a part or series of parts farthest from the centre of the body, or at the end of a stem or branch: *a terminal limb, a terminal flower.* **4** predicted to lead to death, especially slowly: *a terminal illness.* **5** done or occurring each school, college, university, or law term: *terminal exams.*
n **1** an end or end part of a thing, such as the building for departure and arrival at an airport. **2** a point of connection for closing an electric circuit. **3** *Computers* a device at which a user enters data or commands and that displays the result. **ter′mi·nal·ly** *adv.*

ter·mi·nate (tər′mə nāt′) *v* **ter·mi·nat·ed, ter·mi·nat·ing 1** bring or come to an end: *to terminate a partnership. Her contract terminates soon.* **2** have an end at a specified place or of a specified form: *The flower head terminated in tiny spikes.* **3** dismiss someone from employment. **4** *Informal* kill or assassinate someone. <Latin *terminus* end> **ter′mi·na′tion** *n.*

ter·mi·nol·o·gy (tər′mə nol′ə jē) *n, pl* **ter·mi·nol·o·gies** the group of terms used with a particular technical application in a subject of study, theory, or profession: *scientific terminology.* **ter′mi·no·log′i·cal** *adj.* **ter′mi·no·log′i·cal·ly** *adv.* **ter′mi·nol′o·gist** *n.*

term insurance *n* life insurance that expires at the end of a specified period of time.

ter·mi·nus (tər′mə nəs) *n, pl* **ter·mi·nus·es** or **ter·mi·ni** (-nī′) *or* (-nē′) **1** either end of a railway or other transport route, or a station at such a point. **2** a final point in space or time.

ter·mite (tər′mīt) *n* a soft-bodied, pale insect that lives in large colonies, typically within a mound of earth. Many species feed on wood and can be destructive to buildings and furniture. See COCKROACH for picture. <Latin *termes* woodworm>

The Arctic **tern** migrates from the Arctic to the Antarctic and back each year. This round-trip journey covers about 40 000 km.

tern (tərn) *n* a seabird resembling a gull, but with a smaller body and bill and a forked tail. <Scandinavian>

terp·si·cho·re·an (tərp′sə kə rē′ən) *adj* to do with dancing. <*Terpsichore,* in Greek myth the muse of dancing>

ter·race (ter′is) *n* **1** a flat level of land like a large step, especially one of a series of such levels on a slope. **2 a** a street along the side or top of a slope. **b** a row of houses on such a street. **3** a level, paved outdoor space adjoining a house, used for relaxation.
v **ter·raced, ter·rac·ing** form sloping land into a number of level flat areas resembling a series of steps. <Old French, from Latin *terra* earth>

ter·ra·cot·ta (ter′ə kot′ə) *n* brownish red, unglazed earthenware, used for vases, plant pots, tiles, etc.
adj dull brownish red. <Italian = baked earth>

ter·ra fir·ma (ter′ə fər′mə) *n* solid earth or dry land. <Latin>

ter·rain (te rān′) *n* a stretch of land, especially with regard to its physical features. <French, from Latin *terra* land>

terra in·cog·ni·ta (in′kog nē′tə) *or* (in′kog′ni tə) *n* unknown or unexplored territory: *Anything other than routine dishes seemed to be terra incognita to the new chef.* <Latin = unknown land>

ter·ra·pin (ter′ə pin) *n* a freshwater N American turtle. <Algonquian>

ter·rar·i·um (tə rer′ē əm) *n, pl* **ter·rar·i·ums** or **ter·rar·i·a** (-ē ə) a glass enclosure in which plants and, often, small land animals such as reptiles and amphibians are kept. <Latin *terra* land>

ter·res·tri·al (tə res′trē əl) *adj* **1** to do with the earth or land. **2** *Biology* of animals or plants, living on or in the ground, not in the air, water, or trees.
n an inhabitant of the earth.

ter·ri·ble (ter′ə bəl) *adj* **1** extremely or distressingly bad or serious: *terrible pain.* **2** causing or likely to cause terror or harm: *a terrible storm.* **3** extremely incompetent or unskilful: *He was a terrible mechanic.* **4** feeling or looking extremely unwell: *She felt terrible.* **ter′ri·ble·ness** *n.* **ter′ri·bly** *adv.*

SYNONYMS

Terrible means "very bad": *Her death is a terrible loss to the family.*

Disturbing means "troubling": *The melting of the glaciers is a disturbing trend.*

Harrowing means "very distressing": *The accident was a harrowing experience for everyone in the car.*

Terrifying means "causing great fear": *The movie has a terrifying scene at the edge of a high cliff.*

ter·ri·er (ter′ē ər) *n* a breed of small dog with either a short-haired, smooth coat or a long-haired, rough coat. Terriers were originally used to turn out animals from their burrows. <French, from Latin *terra* earth>

ter·rif·ic (tə rif′ik) *adj* **1** of great size, amount, or intensity: *a terrific boom.* **2** *Informal* extremely good or excellent: *Your lunch looks terrific.* **ter·rif′i·cal·ly** *adv.*

ter·ri·fy (ter′ə fī′) *v* **ter·ri·fied, ter·ri·fy·ing** cause to fill with great fear. <Latin *terrere* terrify + *facere* make> **ter′ri·fied** *adj.*

ter·ri·to·ri·al (ter′ə tô′rē əl) *adj* **1** to do with the ownership of an area of land or sea: *The war was fought for territorial gain.* **2** *Zoology* of an animal or species, defending or involving a territory: *The ant colony was highly territorial.* **3** to do with a particular territory, district, or locality: *territorial government.*

ter·ri·to·ry (ter′ə tô′rē) *n, pl* **ter·ri·to·ries** **1** an area of land governed by a ruler or state: *enemy territory.* **2** an area defended by an animal or group of animals against others of the same sex or species. **3** an area defended by a team or player in a game or sport. **4** an area in which one has certain rights or responsibilities with regard to a particular type of activity: *By talking to his customers, she was encroaching on his territory.* **5** an area of knowledge, activity, or experience: *Algebra was unknown territory to me.* **6** 🍁 **Territory** a region that has not been admitted as a province, but has its own elected assembly. The three Canadian Territories are Yukon Territory, the Northwest Territories, and Nunavut. <Latin *terra* land>

ter·ror (ter′ər) *n* **1** great fear: *The dog has a terror of thunder.* **2** the use of such fear to intimidate or frighten people, especially for political reasons: *a campaign of terror.* **3** a person who or thing that causes extreme fear: *He was in terror of losing his mind.* <Latin *terrere* terrify>

ter·ror·ism (ter′ə riz′əm) *n* the use of violence and intimidation to advance political aims or satisfy specific demands. **ter′ror·ist** *adj, n.*

ter·ror·ize (ter′ə rīz′) *v* **ter·ror·ized, ter·ror·iz·ing** fill with terror: *The village was terrorized by bandits during the revolution.* **ter′ror·i·za′tion** *n.* **ter′ror·iz′er** *n.*

ter·ror–strick·en (ter′ər strik′ən) *adj* feeling or expressing great fear.

ter·ry cloth or **terry** (ter′ē) *n* a fabric with raised uncut loops of thread covering both surfaces, used especially for towels and bathrobes. <perhaps French *tiré* drawn>

terse (tərs) *adj* **ters·er, ters·est** brief and to the point in speech or writing. <Latin *tergere* polish> **terse′ly** *adv.* **terse′ness** *n.*

ter·ti·ar·y (tər′shē er′ē) *n* **Tertiary** the geological period lasting from about 70 million to 2 million years ago, when dinosaurs became extinct and mammals, including humans, first appeared. See also CENOZOIC.
adj **1** **Tertiary** to do with this period or the rocks formed then. **2** third in order or level: *He was in the tertiary stage of the illness.* <Latin *tertius* third>

tes·sel·late (tes′ə lāt′) *for v,* (tes′ə lit) *or* (tes′ə lāt′) *for adj.*
v **tes·sel·lat·ed, tes·sel·lat·ing** **1** decorate with mosaics. **2** cover a plane surface by repeated use of a single shape, without gaps or overlapping. <Latin *tessella* small stone cube> **tes′sel·lat′ed** *adj.* **tes′sel·la′tion** *n.*

tes·se·ract (tes′ə rakt) *Mathematics, Science fiction n* the abstract generalization of a cube to four dimensions. <Greek *tesseres* four + *actis* ray>

a bat	e bed	i bid	o pot	u cup	th thin
ā cake	ē me	ī bite	ō go	ū rude	ᴛʜ then
ä bar	ə about	ər over	ô for	ů put	zh measure

test (test) *n* **1** a procedure intended to establish the quality, performance, or reliability of something, especially before it is taken into widespread use: *The new equipment had to pass rigorous tests,* **2** a short written or spoken examination of a person's skill or knowledge: *The teacher gave them a spelling test.* **3** an examination of a substance to see what it is or what it contains: *A test showed that the water from our well was pure.* **4** an examination of part of the body or a body fluid for medical purposes, especially by means of a chemical or mechanical procedure: *a blood test.* **5** a means of establishing whether an action, item, or situation has a specified quality: *The wilderness trip was a test of our endurance.*
v give, carry out, or put to a test: *They tested his honesty by leaving money on the table.* <Old French *test* a vessel used in assaying metal, from Latin *testum* earthen pot> **test′a·bil′i·ty** *n.* **test′a·ble** *adj.* **test′er** *n.*

SYNONYMS

Test refers to a procedure that tells about the quality or content of something: *The tests will prove that the new drug is safe to use.*

Experiment means "a formal test to learn about the characteristics of something": *Who knows what they will discover from these experiments?*

Trial refers to the process of trying something out to discover its worth: *She said she needed another week of trials before agreeing to buy the software.*

tes·ta·ment (tes′tə mənt) *n* **1** written instructions telling what to do with a person's property after death. **2** a thing that serves as a sign or evidence of a specified fact, event, or quality: *Huge sales were a testament to the product's popularity.* **3 Testament** a division of the Bible, either the **Old Testament** or the **New Testament**. <Latin *testis* witness>

tes·tate (tes′tāt) *adj* of a person, having made a valid will. The opposite is INTESTATE.

tes·ta·tor (tes tā′tər) *or* (tes′tā tər) *n* a person who makes or leaves a valid will.

test ban *n* an agreement between nations to ban the testing of nuclear weapons in the atmosphere.

test case *n* **1** a case whose outcome may set a precedent for future cases involving the same question of law. **2** a situation arranged to test a theory or policy.

test drive *n* an act of driving a motor vehicle that one is considering buying, in order to determine its quality: *The salesman invited my dad to take the car for a test drive.* **test′ drive′** *v.*

tes·tee (tes′tē) *n* a person being tested.

tes·tes (tes′tēz) plural of TESTIS.

tes·ti·cle (tes′tə kəl) *n* either of two oval organs that produce sperm in men and other male mammals, enclosed in the scrotum behind the penis. <Latin *testis*>

tes·ti·fy (tes′tə fī′) *v* **tes·ti·fied, tes·ti·fy·ing** **1** give evidence as a witness in a law court: *They testified he'd been drinking before he got into his car.* **2** serve as evidence or proof of something's existing or being the case: *The student body testified their appreciation of her work by re-electing her president of the student council.* <Latin *testis* witness> **tes′ti·fi′er** *n.*

tes·ti·mo·ni·al (tes′tə mō′nē əl) *n* **1** a formal statement that someone or something has good character or qualifications, or is of good quality: *She had testimonials from all her teachers. The company claimed they had hundreds of testimonials praising their new product.* **2** a public tribute to someone and to their achievements: *They gave him a banquet as a testimonial to his years of service.*

tes·ti·mo·ny (tes′tə mō′nē) *or* (tes′tə mə nē) *n, pl* **tes·ti·mo·nies** **1** a formal written or spoken statement used for evidence or proof, especially one given in a law court: *A witness gave testimony that he was home at 9 p.m.* **2** evidence or proof provided by the existence or appearance of a thing: *Our applause was a testimony to her skill at the piano.* <Latin *testis* witness>

tes·tis (tes′tis) *n, pl* **tes·tes** (-tēz) a testicle.

tes·tos·ter·one (tes tos′tər ōn′) *n* a steroid hormone that stimulates development of male secondary sexual characteristics, produced mainly in the testes, but also in the ovaries. <*testes* + *steroid*>

test tube

A **test tube** is mainly used to handle small chemical or biological samples. Its design allows it to be held in a flame.

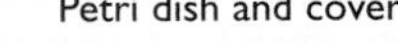
Petri dish and cover

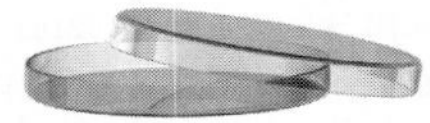

A Petri dish is used primarily to grow bacteria. However, it can also be used to watch seed germination or view small animal behaviour.

test tube *n* a thin glass tube closed at one end, used to hold small amounts of a substance for laboratory testing or experiments.

test–tube baby (tes′tyūb′) *n* a baby conceived by vitro fertilization rather than sexual intercourse, the fertilized egg having been implanted in the mother's uterus.

tes·ty (tes′tē) *adj* **tes·ti·er, tes·ti·est** easily irritated or made impatient. <Anglo-French *testif* headstrong, from Latin *testa* skull> **tes′ti·ly** *adv.* **tes′ti·ness** *n.*

tet·a·nus (tet′ə nəs) *n* a disease caused by certain bacilli usually entering the body through wounds, especially marked by severe stiffness of many muscles. <Greek *tetanos*, from *teinein* stretch. The disease is marked by violent muscle spasms.>

tête–à–tête (tā′tə tāt′) *adj, adv* involving or happening between two people in private: *a tête-à-tête conversation, They dined tête-à-tête.*
n a private conversation between two people. <French = head to head>

teth·er (teᴛʜ′ər) *n* a rope or chain tied around an animal so as to restrict its movement.
v tie an animal in this way: *The horse was tethered to the fence.* <Old Norse *tjothr*>
at the end of your tether (or **rope**), See ROPE.

teth·er·ball (teᴛʜ′ər bol′) *n* a game for two players who hit a ball hung by a rope from a pole, with each player trying to make the rope wind all the way around the pole in a direction opposite to the other's.

tet·ra (tet′rə) *n* a small, bright-coloured, freshwater tropical fish, often kept in aquariums. <Latin *Tetragonopterus*, its genus name>

tetra– *combining form* four or with four: *tetrahedron.*

tet·ra·cy·cline (tet′rə sī′klēn) *Medicine n* an antibiotic with a molecular structure containing four rings. <*tetra-* four-sided figure + *cyclic*>

tet·ra·he·dron (tet′rə hē′drən) *n, pl* **tet·ra·he·drons** or **tet·ra·he·dra** (-drə) a solid bounded by four triangular faces, such as a pyramid whose base and three sides are equilateral triangles. **tet·ra·he′dral** *adj.*

Teu·ton (tyū′tən) *or* (tū′tən) *n* **1** a member of an ancient Germanic people of northern Europe. **2** a member of a northern European people speaking a Germanic language, especially a German. **Teu·ton′ic** *adj.*

Tex–Mex (teks′meks′) *adj* to do with a style, especially of cooking and music, that combines features originally from the border regions of Texas and Mexico.

text (tekst) *n* **1** the main body of reading matter in a book or other written or printed work: *This history contains 300 pages of text and about 50 pages of other material.* **2** *Computers* data in written form, especially when stored, processed, or displayed. **3** a piece of written or printed material regarded as showing the authentic or primary form of a particular work: *the original text.* **4** a written work chosen or set as a subject of study: *a history text.* **5** a passage from a religious work, especially when used as the subject of a sermon. **6** a subject or theme for a discussion or explanation: *She took as her text the idea that her country was the best in the world.* <Latin *texere* weave>

text·book (tekst′bu̇k′) *n* a book used as a basis of instruction or as a standard reference in a particular course of study.

tex·tile (tek′stīl) *or* (tek′stəl) *n* cloth or woven fabric.
adj to do with fabric or weaving: *the textile business.* <Latin *texere* weave>

text messaging (mes′ij ing) *adj* the sending of short messages between cellphones or other handheld devices, over a wireless network. Because the message appears on the small screen of such devices, the use of acronyms and emoticons is common. Compare CHAT ROOM, INSTANT MESSAGING. **text message** *n.*

tex·tu·al (teks′chu̇ əl) *adj* to do with the text: *A misprint is a textual error.*

tex·ture (teks′chər) *n* **1** the feel, appearance, or consistency of a surface or a substance, especially the quality or appearance of a textile fabric according to the arrangement and thickness of its threads: *a coarse texture.* **2** the quality created by the combination of different elements in a work of music or literature.
v **tex·tured, tex·tur·ing** give a surface, especially of a fabric, a rough or raised texture. <Latin *texere* weave> **tex′tur·al** *adj.* **tex′tur·al·ly** *adv.* **tex′tured** *adj.*

TGIF *Informal* Thank God (or goodness) it's Friday.

Thai·land (tī′land) *n* a country in southern Asia. See the APPENDIX. **Thai** *adj, n.*

thal·a·mus (thal′ə məs) *n, pl* **thal·a·mi** (-mī′) *or* (-mē′) either of two masses of grey matter in the brain that relay sensory information and act as a centre for pain perception.

tha·lid·o·mide (thə lid′ē mīd′) *n* a drug used in former times as a sedative. Its use by pregnant women was found to cause malformation or absence of limbs in their babies.

thal·li·um (thal′ē əm) *n* a soft, silver-white metallic element that occurs in small amounts in ores. *Symbol* **Tl** <Greek *thallos* green shoot, in reference to the green line in its colour spectrum>

thal·lus (thal′əs) *n, pl* **thal·li** (-lī) a plant that has no true leaves, stems, or roots. Lichens are thalli. **thal′loid** *adj.*

than (ᴛʜan) *prep* **1** introducing a second item in a comparison: *This train runs faster than that one does.* **2** introducing an exception or contrast: *How else can we get there than on foot?*
conj indicating one thing happening immediately after another: *No sooner had we sat down than we had to get up again.* <Old English>

CONFUSABLES

Than as a preposition is a word used to compare: *The winged creature was bigger than any I had ever seen.*

Then is an adverb referring to time: *Just then, I saw a baby fox peering at me through the bushes.*

thane (thān) *Archaic n* **1** a man in Anglo-Saxon England ranking between an ordinary freeman and a hereditary nobleman. **2** a man in Scotland, often the chief of a clan, who ranked with an earl's son.

thank (thangk) *v* **1** say that one is pleased and grateful for something given or done: *She thanked them for their hospitality.* **2** **thanks** *Informal* thank you: *Thanks for your help.*
n **1** **thanks** *pl* an act of thanking or expression of gratitude: *to give thanks.* **2** **thank-you** an act of expressing thanks: *She left without so much as a goodbye or a thank-you.*
interj **thanks** or **thank you** a standard polite expression of appreciation: *"It's a lovely present. Thank you."*
adj **thank-you** expressing thanks: *a thank-you letter.* <Old English *thanc*> **thank′ful** *adj.* **thank′ful·ly** *adv.* **thank′ful·ness** *n.*
have yourself to thank, be to blame: *You have yourself to thank if you eat too much.*
thank goodness (or **heaven** or **heavens**), an expression of relief or satisfaction: *Thank goodness we've finished.*
thanks to, owing to or because of: *Thanks to her efforts, we won the game.*

a bat	e bed	i bid	o pot	u cup	th thin
ā cake	ē me	ī bite	ō go	ū rude	ᴛʜ then
ä bar	ə about	ər over	ȯ for	u̇ put	zh measure

thank·less (thang′klis) *adj* **1** difficult or unpleasant and not likely to bring one pleasure or be rewarded with thanks: *He found that giving her advice was a thankless act.* **2** not feeling or expressing gratitude. **thank′less·ly** *adv.* **thank′less·ness** *n.*

thanks·giv·ing (thangks′giv′ing) *n* **1** an expression of gratitude, especially to God: *They offered thanksgiving for the bountiful harvest.* **2 Thanksgiving** in full, **Thanksgiving Day** a day set apart every year to give thanks for good things received. In Canada, it is held on the second Monday in October, and in the US, on the fourth Thursday in November.

that (ᴛʜat) *pron, pl* **those** (ᴛʜōz) **1** a specific person or thing observed or heard by the speaker: *Those are my friends over by the door. Hello, is that you?* **2** a specific thing previously mentioned, known, or understood: *That's a bad idea. I've nearly finished the book that you lent me.* Compare WHO. **3** someone who or something that is singled out as having a distinctive feature: *Her appearance was that of someone very angry.*
adj **1** to do with a specific person or thing observed or heard by the speaker: *Those people are making a lot of noise.* **2** to do with a specific thing previously mentioned, known, or understood: *Several people were hurt in that accident.* **3** to do with a period of time related to the past or future: *I'm busy that Saturday, but I could go on Sunday.* **4** singling out someone or something as having a distinctive or familiar feature: *I've always disliked that kind of person. My mother got that worried look.*
adv to such a degree or size: *It cost a lot, but not that much.*
conj introducing a statement such as a reason, intention, regret, etc.: *He said that he would join me later. She was so glad that she gave him a big smile.* <Old English *thæt*>
that's that, *Informal* that is finished, settled, or decided: *We're not going, and that's that.*

GRAMMAR AND USAGE

That, **which**, and **who** and **whom** can all be used to introduce a clause describing a noun.

Use **that** to refer to people, animals, or things: *This is the person that I came to see. He has the machine that I want to buy and the directions that I need to run it.*

Use **which** only for animals and things: *The river, which flows through the town, is now polluted.*

Use **who** and **whom** for people and sometimes for animals (especially pets): *He's the one who will have to deal with the problem. Why did he buy a dog who keeps attacking people?*

thatch (thach) *n* a roof covering of straw, reeds, palm leaves, or other material.
v cover a roof or a building with straw or a similar material. <Old English *thæc*>

that's (ᴛʜats) *contraction* **1** that is. **2** that has: *That's never stopped him.*

thaw (tho) *v* **1** become liquid or soft as a result of ice, snow, or another frozen substance such as food becoming warmed: *He put salt on the sidewalk to thaw the ice.* **2** become warm enough to melt ice or snow, or as a part of the body to become warm enough to stop feeling numb: *If the sun stays out, it will probably thaw today. The ground has begun to thaw. After standing by the fire, he felt his ears begin to thaw.* **3** become less stiff and formal in manner: *His shyness thawed under her kindness.*
n **1** a period of warmer weather that thaws ice and snow. **2** an increase in friendliness. <Old English *thawian*>

the (ᴛʜə) *before a consonant or* (ᴛʜē) *before a vowel.*
definite article **1** stating the existence of one or more people or things assumed to be known: *Call the plumber.* **2** making a generalized reference to something rather than identifying something in particular: *He taught himself several of the songs.* **3** as part of a title or family name: *the Duke of Wellington, the Patels.* **4** enough of a particular thing: *We shopped for a long time to find the best deal.* **5** (*often stressed*) indicating that someone or something is the best known or the most important of: *That restaurant is* the *place to go.* **6** used with comparatives to indicate how something varies in relation to something else: *The more he thought about it, the more he regretted what he did.* <Old English *se*>

the·a·tre (thē′ə tər) *n* **1** a building or outdoor area in which plays and other dramatic performance are given, or in which movies are shown. **2** a place that looks like a theatre in its arrangement of seats: *The surgeon performed an operation before the medical students in the operating theatre.* **3** the area in which something happens: *The countryside was the theatre of the civil war.* **4 the theatre** the activity or profession of acting in, producing, directing, or writing plays. **5** a play or other dramatic work considered as to its effectiveness on the stage: *This scene is bad theatre.* Also, **theater**. <Latin, from Greek *thea* a view>

the·a·tre·go·er (thē′ə tər gō′ər) *n* a person who attends a theatre, especially one who goes often.

theatre–in–the–round (thē′ə tər in ᴛʜə round′) *n* **1** a theatre with the stage in the middle, surrounded by seats on all sides. **2** the presentation of plays in such theatres.

theatre of the absurd *n* plays that represent absurd situations and reject the usual dramatic structure and conventions in order to portray meaninglessness in human existence.

the·at·ri·cal (thē at′rə kəl) *adj* **1** to do with acting, actors, or the theatre: *theatrical performances, a theatrical company.* **2** in an exaggerated or too dramatic way.
n **theatricals** *pl* dramatic performances, especially as given by amateurs. **the·at′ri·cal′i·ty** *n.* **the·at′ri·cal·ly** *adv.*

the·at·rics (thē at′riks) *n* **1** (*with singular verb*) the art of presenting plays. **2** (*with plural verb*) exaggerated gestures or other overly dramatic behaviour: *the theatrics of a famous courtroom lawyer.*

thee (ᴛʜē) *Archaic or Poetic pron* you, used as the singular object of a verb or preposition: *Hail to thee, our King!* <Old English>

theft (theft) *n* the action or crime of stealing: *The man was put in prison for theft. The theft of the jewels caused much excitement.*

their (ᴛʜer) *adj* (*always before the noun*) belonging to or associated with the people or thing previously mentioned or easily identified: *They did their best. They all raised their hands. That's their home.* <Old Norse *theirra*>

CONFUSABLES

Their is an adjective meaning "belonging to or associated with them": *It's their fault that we're late.*

There is an adverb indicating a place or position: *Put the hockey equipment over there.*

They're is a contraction of "they are": *They're strong supporters of the fund-raising drive.*

theirs (ᴛʜerz) *pron* a possessive form of THEY; that which belongs to them: *The books aren't theirs, they're mine.*

GRAMMAR AND USAGE

Theirs is a pronoun and can stand alone: *Is that new video camera theirs?*

Their is an adjective and is always followed by a noun: *Their video camera is one of the best available.*

the·ism (thē′iz əm) *n* a belief in the existence of a god or gods, especially in one God as creator of the universe. <Greek *theos* god> **the′ist** *n.* **the′ist′ic** *adj.*

them (ᴛʜem) *pron* the objective form of THEY (def. 1): *The books were a gift, but I don't really like them.*

the·mat·ic (thē mat′ik) *adj* with or relating to subjects or a particular subject: *a thematic arrangement.*

theme (thēm) *n* **1** the subject of a talk, a piece of writing, a person's thoughts, or an exhibition: *Protecting the whales was the speaker's theme.* **2** a short essay assigned to a student. **3** a prominent or the principal melody in a piece of music. **4** a melody repeated in different forms in an elaborate musical composition, or to identify a particular radio or TV program. <Greek *thema*>

theme park *n* an amusement centre with a unifying setting or idea such as fairy tales, historical times, or outer space.

them·selves (ᴛʜem selvz′) *plural pron* **1** the object of a reflexive verb with *they* as subject: *They injured themselves.* **2** an intensive pronoun, used to emphasize the noun or pronoun it follows: *The teachers themselves said that the test was too hard.* **3** their usual selves: *They were ill and were not themselves.*

then (ᴛʜen) *adv* **1** at that time: *Prices were lower then.* **2** after that or afterwards: *The noise stopped, and then began again. First there is spring, then summer.* **3** in that case or therefore: *If you follow instructions, then the software should work. If she broke the window, then she should pay for it.*
adj being at that time in the past: *the then premier.* See THAN for confusable. <Old English *thænne*>
but then (again), but at the same time or on the other hand: *We're rich, but then, we've been lucky.*
then and there, immediately: *He got his pay then and there.*

thence (ᴛʜens) *or* (thens) *Archaic or Poetic adv* from that place or time: *A short distance thence was a mighty castle.*

thence·forth (ᴛʜen′sfôrth′) *or* (then′sfôrth′) *adv* from that time: *Women were given the same rights as men; thenceforth they could vote.*

the·oc·ra·cy (thē ok′rə sē) *n, pl* **the·oc·ra·cies** a system of government in which religious leaders rule in the name of God or gods. <Greek *theos* god + *kratos* rule>
the′o·crat′ic *adj.* **the′o·crat′i·cal·ly** *adv.*

the·od·o·lite (thē od′ə līt′) *n* a surveying instrument with a rotating telescope for measuring horizontal and vertical angles. <origin uncertain>

the·o·lo·gian (thē′ə lō′jən) *n* a person skilled or trained in theology.

the·ol·o·gy (thē ol′ə jē) *n, pl* **the·ol·o·gies 1** the study of the nature of God and religious belief. **2** a system of religious beliefs. <Greek *theos* god> **the′o·log′i·cal** *adj.* **the′o·log′i·cal·ly** *adv.*

the·o·rem (thē′ə rəm) *n* **1** a statement in physics or mathematics that is not self-evident but proven by a chain of reasoning. **2** a statement of mathematical relations that can be expressed by an equation or formula. <Latin, from Greek *theorein* to consider>

the·o·ret·i·cal (thē′ə ret′ə kəl) *adj* concerned with, based on, or involving the theory of a subject or area of study rather than its practical application: *He said that books provide only a theoretical knowledge of farming.* **the′o·ret′i·cal·ly** *adv.*

the·o·re·ti·cian (thē′ə rə tish′ən) *n* a person who forms, develops, or studies the theoretical framework of a subject.

the·o·rist (thē′ə rist) *n* a person concerned with the theoretical aspects of a subject.

the·o·rize (thē′ə rīz′) *v* **the·o·rized, the·o·riz·ing** form a theory or theories about something. **the′o·riz′er** *n.*

the·o·ry (thē′ə rē) *n, pl* **the·o·ries 1** an idea or system of ideas intended to explain something, especially one based on general principles independent of the thing to be explained. **2** the principles or methods of a science or art rather than its practice: *the theory of music.* **3** an idea used to account for a situation or justify a course of action: *He must have cheated; at least, that's my theory.* <Latin, from Greek *theorein* to gaze upon>

SYNONYMS

A **theory** is an explanation that is systematic and helps us to understand something complex: *After years of research, she presented her theory on the behaviour of very young children.*

A **hypothesis** is an assumption or tentative explanation: *Your hypothesis about the cause of the delay makes sense.*

a bat	e bed	i bid	o pot	u cup	th thin
ā cake	ē me	ī bite	ō go	ü rude	ᴛʜ then
ä bar	ə about	ər over	ô for	ů put	zh measure

ther·a·peu·tic (ther′ə pyū′tik) *adj* to do with the treatment of disease.

ther·a·py (ther′ə pē) *n, pl* **ther·a·pies** the treatment or relief of diseases or physical disorders. **ther′a·pist** *n.*

Ther·a·va·da (ter′ə vá′də) *n* a major branch of Buddhism, practised mainly in Sri Lanka, Myanmar, Thailand, Cambodia, and Laos. Compare MAHAYANA.

there (ŧher) *adv* **1** in, at, or to that place or position: *Sit there. Go there at once.* **2** attracting someone's attention or calling attention to someone or something: *Hey, you there! There goes the bell.* **3** indicating the fact or existence of something: *There's a nice restaurant we can go to.*
interj **1** focusing attention on something and expressing satisfaction or annoyance at it: *There, that didn't hurt much, did it?* **2** comforting someone: *There, there! Don't cry.* See THEIR for confusables. <Old English *thær*>
be there for, *Informal* be ready to support, help, comfort, etc. at any time: *Best friends are always there for each other.*

there·a·bouts (ŧher′ə bouts′) *adv* near that place, nearly that time, or about that number or amount: *She lives downtown, on Main Street or thereabouts. She went home in the late afternoon, at five o'clock or thereabouts. The book cost me twenty dollars or thereabouts.*

there·af·ter (ŧher af′tər) *adv* after that time: *He was very ill as a child and was considered delicate thereafter.*

there·by (ŧher bī′) *or* (ŧher′bī′) *adv* by means of that or in that way: *She wished to travel and thereby study the customs of other countries.*

there·fore (ŧher′fôr′) *adv* for that reason: *She went to a party and therefore felt better.* <Middle English *ther* there + *fore* for>

there·in (ŧher in′) *adv* in that place or document, or in that respect: *We found the information therein. The captain thought all danger was past; therein he made a mistake.*

there'll (ŧherl) *contraction* there will; there shall.

there·of (ŧher ov′) *or* (ŧher uv′) *adv* of the thing just mentioned: *He did not know the whole poem, or even a part thereof.*

there's (ŧherz) *contraction* there is; there has: *There's been an accident.*

there·up·on (ŧher′ə pon′) *adv* immediately or soon after that: *The stolen jewels were found in his room; thereupon, he was put in jail.*

ther·mal (thər′məl) *adj* **1** to do with heat. **2** made of a fabric that provides effective insulation to keep the body warm: *thermal underwear.* <Greek *therme* heat>

thermal energy *n* energy in the form of heat.

thermo– *combining form* heat: *thermodynamics.* <Greek *therme*>

ther·mo·cou·ple (thər′mō ku′pəl) *n* a device for measuring temperature in which two wires of different metals are joined. The voltage generated between two points of contact is a measure of the temperature difference between the points.

ther·mo·dy·nam·ic (thər′mō dī nam′ik) *adj* to do with the relationship between heat and other forms of energy, such as mechanical, electrical, or chemical energy.
n **thermodynamics** (*with singular verb*) the branch of physics that deals with thermodynamic relationships. **ther′mo·dy·nam′i·cal·ly** *adv.*

ther·mo·e·lec·tric·i·ty (thər′mō i lek′tris′ə tē) *n* electricity produced directly by heat. **ther′mo·e·lec′tric** or **ther′mo·e·lec′tri·cal** *adj.* **ther′mo·e·lec′tri·cal·ly** *adv.*

ther·mom·e·ter (thər mom′ə tər) *n* an instrument for measuring temperature, typically one consisting of a narrow sealed glass tube, one end of which holds mercury or alcohol and extends along the side of the tube as it expands. See FAHRENHEIT, CLINICAL THERMOMETER for pictures.

ther·mo·nu·cle·ar (thər′mō nū′klē ər) *or* (thər′mō nyū′klē ər) *adj* to do with nuclear reactions that occur only at very high temperatures, such as in the explosive force produced by nuclear weapons.

ther·mo·plas·tic (thər′mō plas′tik) *adj* to do with synthetic substances that become soft on heating and harden on cooling, and are able to repeat these processes.
n a substance of this kind.

ther·mos (thər′məs) *n* a double-walled bottle or flask made with a vacuum between its inner and outer walls, used to keep food or drinks hot or cold for a long time. <*Thermos*, a trademark>

ther·mo·set·ting (thər′mō set′ing) *adj* becoming, especially as synthetic resins, hard and permanently set after being heated: *thermosetting plastics.*

ther·mo·sphere (thər′mō sfēr′) the outermost region of the atmosphere between the mesosphere and outer space, where temperatures increase steadily with altitude. See OZONE LAYER for picture.

ther·mo·stat (thər′mə stat′) *n* a device that automatically regulates temperature, or that activates a device when the temperature outside it reaches a certain point. **ther′mo·stat′ic** *adj.* **ther′mo·stat′i·cal·ly** *adv.*

the·sau·rus (thi sô′rəs) *n, pl* **the·sau·rus·es** a book or computer word-processing function that lists words in groups of synonyms and related concepts.

ETYMOLOGY

Thesaurus comes through Latin from the Greek word *thesauros*, meaning "treasure" or "treasure house." The first thesaurus was published in 1852 by Peter Mark Roget, a British physician, and it is still a valuable tool for finding just the right word.

these (ŧhēz) *adj* plural of the adjective THIS: *These two problems are hard.*
pron plural of the pronoun THIS: *These are my books.*

the·sis (thē′sis) *n, pl* **the·ses** (-sēz.) **1** a theory or statement that is put forward to be proved or to be maintained against objections. **2** a long essay involving personal research, written by a candidate for a university degree: *a doctoral thesis.* <Greek = a proposition>

thes·pi·an (thes′pē ən) *adj* to do with the theatre.
n an actor. <*Thespis*, an ancient Greek poet supposed to be the founder of tragic drama>

they (ᴛʜā) *pron* **1** plural of HE, SHE, or IT. **2** *Informal* some people in general: *They say it's going to be a hot summer.* <Old Norse *their*>

GRAMMAR AND USAGE

Although plural, **they** in all its forms (they, them, their, theirs) is often used informally as a gender-neutral singular pronoun: *Each student will pick up their marks from the office.* This usage avoids the more awkward "his or her" and "he or she."

Many people object to using these plural pronouns together with singular forms, and the style should be avoided in formal English by rewriting the sentence.

they'd (ᴛʜād) *contraction* **1** they had: *They'd already left.* **2** they would: *They'd have helped if they could.*

they'll (ᴛʜāl) *contraction* **1** they will. **2** they shall.

they're (ᴛʜer) *contraction* they are. See THEIR for confusables.

they've (ᴛʜāv) *contraction* they have: *They've already left.*

thi·a·mine or **thi·a·min** (thī′ə min) *n* a vitamin of the B complex, found in refined cereals, beans, and liver.

thick (thik) *adj* **1** with opposite sides or surfaces that are a relatively great distance apart: *The castle has thick stone walls.* **2** made up of a large number of things or people closely packed together: *thick hair.* **3** relatively firm in consistency as a liquid or semi-liquid substance: *thick mud.* **4** *Informal* of little intelligence: *He's a bit thick.* **5** of a voice or accent, not clear or distinct: *She had a thick voice because of a cold.* **6** *Informal* with a close, friendly relationship: *My friend and I have become very thick with the new girl in our class.*
adv to do with a deep, dense, or heavy mass: *The field was planted so thick with corn that you could hide among the stalks.* <Old English *thicce*> **thick′ly** *adv.*
in the thick of something, in the busiest, most crowded, or middle of something: *I was in the thick of packing when the doorbell rang.*
lay it on thick, *Informal* praise or blame too much.
thick skin, *Informal* the ability to take criticism without being affected by it.
through thick and thin, in good times and bad: *A true friend stays loyal through thick and thin.*

thick·en (thik′ən) *v* **1** make or become thick or thicker. **2** become more complex or intricate as the plot of a play, novel, or movie. **thick′en·er** *n.*

thick·et (thik′it) *n* a dense group of bushes or small trees.

thick–head·ed (thik′hed′id) *adj* stupid. **thick′-head′ed·ness** *n.*

thick·ness (thik′nis) *n* **1** the distance between opposite sides of a thing: *The length of the board is three metres, the width fourteen centimetres, the thickness five centimetres.* **2** the quality of being broad or deep. **3** a layer of a specified thing: *The pad was made up of three thicknesses of cloth.* **4** the quality of being dense or made up of many closely packed parts.

thick·set (thik′set′) *adj* of a person or animal, heavily or solidly built.

thick–skinned (thik′skind′) *adj* not sensitive to criticism.

thief (thēf) *n, pl* **thieves** (thēvz) a person who steals another person's property, especially one who steals secretly and without using force or violence: *A thief stole the little girl's bicycle from the yard.* <Old English *theof*>

SYNONYMS

Thief refers to someone who secretly steals: *The thief broke into the house when they were away.*

Robber means "someone who takes property away from a person or place by force or threats of violence": *The robber fled with the woman's bag after pushing her to the ground.*

Bandit suggests a robber who uses a weapon: *The armed bandits shot a bank employee during the robbery.*

thieve (thēv) *v* **thieved, thiev·ing** be a thief; steal. **thiev′ish** *adj.* **thiev′ish·ly** *adv.* **thiev′ish·ness** *n.*

thiev·er·y (thē′və rē) *n, pl* **thiev·er·ies** the action of stealing another person's property.

thigh (thī) *n* the part of the human leg between the hip and the knee, or a corresponding part in animals. <Old English *theoh*>

thigh·bone (thī′bōn′) *n* the bone of the leg between the hip and knee.

thim·ble (thim′bəl) *n* a metal or plastic cap with a closed end, worn on the finger to protect it when pushing a needle in sewing. <Old English *thymel,* from *thuma* thumb>

thim·ble·ful (thim′bəl fu̇l′) *n, pl* **thim·ble·fuls** as much as a thimble will hold.

thin (thin) *adj* **thin·ner, thin·nest 1** with opposite surfaces or sides relatively close together: *thin wire.* **2** with little or too little flesh or fat on the body: *a long, thin face.* **3** with few parts or members relative to the area covered or filled: *He has thin hair. The actors played to a thin audience.* **4** not dense: *The air at the top of high mountains is thin.* **5** of a sound, faint and high-pitched: *a thin voice.* **6** weak and forced: *a thin excuse, a thin smile.*
adv with little thickness or depth: *to slice meat too thin.*
v **thinned, thin·ning 1** make or become less dense, crowded, or numerous: *The crowd thinned rapidly. You have to thin a row of beets.* **2** make or become smaller in width or thickness: *The fabric had thinned so much as to be almost transparent. Thin the latex paint with some water, please.* <Old English *thynne*> **thin′ly** *adv.* **thin′ness** *n.*
thin skin, *Informal* the condition of being easily affected by criticism.

thine (ᴛʜīn) *Archaic or Poetic adj* (*before a vowel or silent h*) thy: *thine eyes.* <Old English *thin*>

a bat	e bed	i bid	o pot	u cup	th thin
ā cake	ē me	ī bite	ō go	ū rude	ᴛʜ then
ȧ bar	ə about	ər over	ȯ for	u̇ put	zh measure

thing (thing) *n* **1** an object that one need not, cannot, or does not wish to give a specific name: *All the things in the house were burned. Put these things away.* **2** an object as distinct from a living being: *Mom treats that table more like part of her family, rather than just a thing.* **3** an action, activity, event, thought, or utterance: *A strange thing happened. It was a good thing to do. How are things going?* **4** a person or creature, often depicted as one who deserves pity, affection, approval, or contempt: *You silly thing! I feel sorry for the poor thing.* **5 the thing** a thing considered desirable, suitable, or appropriate: *the latest thing in boots. It's the thing to do.* **6 things** *pl* personal belongings, especially clothes. <Old English>
know a thing or two, *Informal* be experienced or wise.
make a (**big**) **thing** (**out**) **of,** *Informal* give much or too much importance to: *Every time I'm a few minutes late, he makes a big thing of it.*
make a good thing of, *Informal* profit from.
see (or **hear**) **things,** see (or hear) something that does not exist.

thing·a·ma·jig (thing′ə mə jig′) *Informal n* a thing whose name cannot be recalled. Also called **thingamabob** (thing′ə mə bob′).

think (thingk) *v* **thought, think·ing 1** have a particular opinion, belief, or idea about someone or something: *I really care what you think about me.* **2** direct one's mind toward someone or something and use one's mind actively to form connected ideas: *He had thought of her as still a child. She thought that she could have worked harder. He thinks of nothing but sports.* <Old English *thencan*>
think aloud, say what one is thinking.
think of (**doing**)**,** consider the possibility of: *I wouldn't think of taking your parking spot! He is thinking of quitting the team.*
think out, a plan or discover by thinking. **b** solve or understand by thinking: *He thought out the reasons for his friend's anger.*
think over, consider carefully: *Think over our plan before you go.*
think through, think about until one reaches an understanding or conclusion.
think twice, think again before acting.
think up, plan or discover by thinking: *We will think up a way to get the candy.*

think·er (thing′kər) *n* a person who thinks deeply and seriously, especially someone with great intellectual powers.

think·ing (thing′king) *adj* using thought or rational judgment.
n the process of using one's mind to consider or reason about something, especially one's ideas or opinions.
put on your thinking cap, *Informal* think hard about something.

think piece *n* a newspaper or magazine article presenting personal opinions, analysis, or discussion, rather than a factual report.

think tank *n* a centre in which experts provide advice, research, or ideas on specific political, military, or economic problems.

thin·ner (thin′ər) *n* any liquid that can be mixed with paint to dilute the paint.

thin–skinned (thin′skind′) *adj* sensitive to criticism.

third (thərd) *adj, n* **1** next after the second: *on the third try* (*adj*). *I'm third in the class* (*n*). **2** one, or being one, of three equal parts: *a third part of the day* (*adj*). *She divided the pizza into thirds* (*n*). **3** *Music* a musical interval spanning three consecutive notes in a diatonic scale, or to do with this interval. **4** the forward gear next above second in a standard transmission, or to do with this gear.
adv next after the second: *I finished third.* **third′ly** *adv.*

third–class (thərd′klas′) *n* a group of people or things considered together as third best.
adj of the third-best quality or of lower status.

third–degree (thərd′də grē′) *adj* with burns of the most severe kind, affecting tissue below the skin.
n **the third degree** long and harsh questioning, especially by police, to obtain information or a confession.

third estate *n* ordinary people. See also ESTATE.

third party *n* a person or group besides the two mainly involved in a situation.

third person *Grammar n* the form of a pronoun or verb used to refer to things or people spoken about. Examples: *He, she, it,* and *they* are pronouns of the third person.

third rail *n* an additional rail supplying electric current, used in some electric railway systems.

third–rate (thər′drāt′) *adj* inferior or of very poor quality.

Third World *n* the developing countries of the world, especially those in Africa, Asia, and Latin America that are less advanced technologically and economically.

thirst (thərst) *n* **1** a feeling of needing or wanting to drink something: *quench a thirst.* **2** a lack of the liquid needed to sustain life: *The shipwrecked crew died of thirst.* **3** a strong desire for something: *a thirst for adventure.*
v **1** feel thirst. **2** have a strong desire for something. <Old English *thurst*> **thirst′i·ly** *adv.* **thirst′i·ness** *n.* **thirst′y** *adj.*

thir·teen (thər′tēn′) *n* **1** three more than ten. **2** the numeral 13.
adj **1** three more than ten: *thirteen people.* **2** (*after the noun*) thirteenth in a series: *part thirteen.* <Old English *threotene*> **thir′teenth′** *adj, adv.*

thir·teenth (thər′tēnth′) *n* **1** next after the twelfth. **2** one of thirteen equal parts.
adj, adv See THIRTEEN.

thir·ti·eth (thər′tē ith) *n* **1** next after the twenty-ninth. **2** one of thirty equal parts.
adj, adv See THIRTY.

thir·ty (thər′tē) *n, pl* **thir·ties 1** three times ten. **2 thirties** *pl* the years from thirty through thirty-nine, especially of a century or of a person's life: *Economic depression dominated the early thirties.*
adj **1** three times ten: *thirty days.* **2** (*after the noun*) thirtieth in a series: *page thirty.* <Old English *thritig*> **thir′ti·eth** *adj, adv.*

this (ᴛʜis) *pron, pl* **these** a specific person or thing nearby or being indicated or experienced: *This is not my sister. Is this your notebook? This is not what I want to do today.*

adj **1** to do with a specific person or thing being indicated: *These cakes are delicious.* **2** to do with a specific thing or situation just mentioned: *This matter has been discussed already.* **3** to do with a period of time related to the present: *How do you feel this morning?*
adv to such an extent or degree: *You can have this much.* <Old English>

this·tle (this′əl) *n* a plant of the daisy family with prickly leaves and stem. <Old English *thistel*>

this·tle·down (this′əl doun′) *n* the light fluffy down that is attached to thistle seeds, enabling them to be blown about in the wind.

thith·er (thiᴛʜ′ər) *Archaic adv* to or toward that place. <Old English *thider*>

tho' (ᴛʜō) *adv, conj* though.

Thom·son (tom′sən) NLAKA'PAMUX.

thong (thong) *n* **1** a narrow strip of leather or other material, especially one used as a fastening or as the lash of a whip. **2** a very small piece of underclothing for the lower body that covers the genital area but not the buttocks. **3** a sandal held on the foot by a narrow piece of material that passes between the toes. <Old English *thwang*>

thor·ax (thô′raks) *n, pl* **tho·rax·es** or **tho·ra·ces** (-rə sēz′) **1** the part of the body in human beings and mammals between the neck and the abdomen, including the cavity enclosed by the ribs, breastbone, and vertebrae of the back. **2** the corresponding part of a bird, reptile, amphibian, or fish, bearing the legs and wings. <Greek> **tho·rac′ic** (thô ras′ik) *adj.*

tho·ri·um (thô′rē əm) *n* a radioactive metallic element. *Symbol* **Th** <*Thor*, Norse god of thunder and war>

thorn (thôrn) *n* **1** a stiff, sharp-pointed woody growth on a stem or other part of a plant. **2** a bush, shrub, or tree that has such growths on it. <Old English>
thorn in the flesh (or **side**), a cause of continual trouble or annoyance.

thorn·y (thôr′nē) *adj* **thorn·i·er, thorn·i·est** **1** with many thorns. **2** causing difficulty, distress, or troubles: *a thorny problem.*

thor·ough (thər′ō) *or* (thər′ə) *adj* **1** complete with regard to every detail: *a thorough search.* **2** done in a complete and careful way: *The doctor was very thorough in her examination.* **3** complete or absolute: *a thorough nuisance.* <Old English *thurh*> **thor′ough·ly** *adv.* **thor′ough·ness** *n.*

thor·ough·bred (thər′ə bred′) *adj* of pure breed or stock in horses, especially of a breed originating from English mares and Arabian stallions that is widely used in racing.
n a thoroughbred horse.

thor·ough·fare (thər′ə fer′) *n* a passage, road, or street forming a route between two places, especially a main highway.

thor·ough·go·ing (thər′ə gō′ing) *adj* involving every detail or aspect of something.

those (ᴛʜōz) *adj* plural of the adjective THAT: *I like those shoes in the window.*
pron plural of the pronoun THAT: *Are those your shoes by the door?*

thou *Archaic or Poetic pron* (*in the subjective*) you (singular): *"Wherefore art thou Romeo?"* <Old English>

though (ᴛʜō) *conj* **1** despite the fact that: *Though it was pouring, the girls went out.* **2** however: *He is better, though not yet cured.* **3** even if: *Though I fail, I shall try again.*
adv however: *I am sorry about our quarrel; you began it, though.* <Old Norse *tho*>
as though, as if: *You look as though you are tired.*

thought (thot) *n* **1** an idea or opinion produced by thinking or occurring suddenly in the mind: *Her thought was to have a picnic.* **2** the action or process of thinking: *Thought helps us solve problems.* **3** a way of reasoning characteristic of a specified group, time, or place: *in modern scientific thought.* **4** consideration or attention: *Show some thought for others who are less fortunate.* **5** intention or hope: *His thought was to avoid controversy.*
v past tense and past participle of THINK. <Old English *thoht*>

thought control *n* the attempt to restrict ideas or impose opinions through censorship and other means of control.

thought·ful (thot′fəl) *adj* **1** absorbed in or involving thought: *She was thoughtful for a while and then replied, "No."* **2** showing consideration for the needs of other people: *She was always thoughtful about her friends.* **thought′ful·ly** *adv.* **thought′ful·ness** *n.*

thought·less (thot′lis) *adj* **1** not showing consideration for the needs of other people. **2** without thinking of the possible consequences of an action. **thought′less·ly** *adv.* **thought′less·ness** *n.*

thought–out (thot′out′) *adj* carefully considered or planned; deliberate: *a well thought-out plan.*

thou·sand (thou′zənd) *n, pl* **thou·sands** or (*after a number*) **thou·sand** **1** ten times a hundred: *Count to a thousand.* **2** **thousands** *pl* the numbers between 1000 and 1 000 000.
adj ten times a hundred: *a thousand dollars.* <Old English *thusend*> **thou′sandth** *adj, adv.*

thou·sandth (thou′zəndth) *n* **1** next after the 999th. **2** one of a thousand equal parts.
adj, adv See THOUSAND.

thrall (throl) *n* the condition of being in someone's power or with great power over someone. <Old Norse *thræll*>

thrash (thrash) *v* **1** beat a person or animal repeatedly and violently with a stick or whip: *The man beat the donkey when it refused to move.* **2** move in a violent and uncontrolled way: *Unable to sleep, the patient thrashed about in her bed.* **3** THRESH (def. 1). <*thresh*>
thrash out, discuss something thoroughly and honestly, or produce a conclusion by such discussion: *Let's stay until we thrash out the problem.*
thrash over, go over again and again.

a bat	e bed	i bid	o pot	u cup	th thin
ā cake	ē me	ī bite	ō go	ū rude	ᴛʜ then
à bar	ə about	ər over	ô for	ů put	zh measure

T

thrash·er (thrash′ər) *n* a N American songbird of the mockingbird family, with a curved bill.

thread (thred) *n* **1** a long, thin strand of cotton, silk, flax, or other fibres used in sewing or weaving. **2** a thing resembling a thread in length, thinness, or fragility: *Threads of gold could be seen in the ore.* **3** a theme or characteristic that runs through a text, story, argument, or speech: *He lost the thread of their conversation when he heard the phone ring.* **4** a ridge that is one of others on the outside of a screw, nut, bolt, or joint, or on the inside of a cylindrical hole, to allow two parts to be screwed together.
v **1** pass a long, thin object or piece of material through something and into the required position for use, especially to pass a thread through the eye of a needle: *He threaded a hundred beads.* **2** move carefully and skilfully in and out of obstacles: *He threaded his way through the crowd.* **3** cut threads into a bolt, screw, pipe joint, etc.: *The plumber threaded the pipe.* <Old English *thræd*>
thread′like′ *adv.*
hang by (or **on**) **a thread,** be in a precarious position: *My credit for the course is hanging by a thread, so I can't afford to fail this test.*

thread·bare (thred′ber′) *adj* becoming thin and tattered with age or use, especially poor or shabby in appearance: *a threadbare coat, a threadbare beggar. Saying "I forgot" is a threadbare excuse.*

threat (thret) *n* **1** a statement of an intention to inflict pain, injury, damage, or other hostile action on someone. **2** a person or thing likely to cause damage or danger: *Those black clouds are a threat of rain.* <Old English>

threat·en (thret′ən) *v* **1** state an intention to take hostile action against someone: *They threatened to cut off his pension.* **2** seem possible or likely to produce an unpleasant or unwelcome result: *The long strike threatened the company with bankruptcy.* **threat′en·er** *n.* **threat′en·ing** *adj.* **threat′en·ing·ly** *adv.*

SYNONYMS

Threaten expresses an intention to do something unpleasant: *The rebels threatened to burn the town.*

Browbeat means "intimidate," chiefly by using words: *The mayor browbeat the council into voting for the increase.*

Bully means "frighten or hurt someone smaller or weaker": *His big brother bullies him all the time.*

threat·ened species (thret′ənd) *n* a species that is not yet considered endangered, but is rare enough that it may well become endangered in the near future.

three (thrē) *n* **1** a cardinal number that is one more than two. **2** the numeral 3. **3** a playing card or side of a die with three spots: *I needed to roll a three to win.*
adj **1** one more than two: *She ate three pieces of cake.* **2** (*after the noun*) third in a series: *Have you read Chapter Three?* <Old English *threo*> **third** *adj, adv.*

three–D or **3–D** (thrē′dē′) *adj* three-dimensional.

three–di·men·sion·al (thrē′di men′shə nəl) *adj* **1** with or appearing to have height, width, and depth. Cubes are three-dimensional. **2** in a story or dramatic work, showing characters and events in a way that is believable.
three′-di·men′sion·al′i·ty *n.*
three′-di·men′sion·al·ly *adv.*

three·fold (thrē′fōld′) *adj, adv* **1** three times as much or as many. **2** consisting of three parts.

three–ply (thrē′plī′) *adj* with three layers or strands in a piece of material: *My socks are knitted of three-ply yarn.*

three–point turn (thrē′point′) *n* a method of turning a motor vehicle around in a narrow space by moving forward, backwards, and forward again in a sequence of arcs.

three–ring circus (thrē′ring′) *n* **1** a circus in which there are simultaneous acts being performed in each of three rings. **2** a public spectacle, especially one where there is a confusing amount of activity.

three R's *Informal pl n* reading, writing, and arithmetic.

three·score (thrē′skôr′) *Archaic adj* sixty. <*score* = twenty>

three·some (thrē′səm) *n* a group of three people engaged in the same activity.

three–wheel·er (thrē′wē′lər) *n* a vehicle with three wheels.

thresh (thresh) *v* **1** separate grain from wheat or other crops, usually by the action of a revolving mechanism. **2** THRASH. <Old English *threscan*>
thresh out, settle by thorough discussion.
thresh over, go over again and again.

thresh·er (thresh′ər) *n* **1** a person who or machine that separates grain from wheat or other crops by beating. **2** a large, surface-swimming shark. Threshers often lash the water with their tails to herd fish into a tightly packed shoal.

thresh·old (thresh′hōld) *or* (thresh′ōld) *n* **1** a strip of wood or stone forming the bottom of a doorway and crossed in entering a house or room. **2** a point of entry or beginning: *The scientist was on the threshold of an important discovery.* **3** the extent or intensity that must be exceeded for something to occur or be present: *a pain threshold.* <Old English *threscold*>

threshold limit value *Chemistry n* the level at which the effect of a chemical can be detected chemically.

threw (thrū) past tense of THROW.

CONFUSABLES

Threw means "tossed": *They threw their knapsacks on the floor when they arrived.*

Through means "in one side and out the other": *The train went through the tunnel.*

thrice (thrīs) *Archaic or Poetic adv* three times, or three times as much or many. <Middle English *thries*>

thrift (thrift) *n* the quality of using money and other resources carefully and not wastefully, especially through the habit of saving: *By thrift she managed to get along on her small salary.* <*thrive*> **thrift′i·ly** *adv.* **thrift′i·ness** *n.* **thrift′y** *adj.*

thrift·less (thrif′tlis) *adj* spending money in a wasteful way. **thrift′less·ly** *adv.* **thrift′less·ness** *n.*

thrift shop or **thrift store** *n* a shop selling second-hand clothes and other household goods, typically to raise money for a church or charitable group.

thrill (thril) *n* a sudden feeling of excitement or pleasure, or an experience that produces such a feeling.
v cause someone to have a sudden feeling of excitement or pleasure, or experience such a feeling: *Stories of adventure thrilled him. They thrilled with joy at the sight of the elephants.* <Old English *thyrlian* pierce, i.e., make shiver> **thrill′ing** *adj.* **thrill′ing·ly** *adv.*

thrill·er (thril′ər) *n* a novel, play, or movie with an exciting plot, typically involving crime or espionage.

thrips (thrips) *n* a small, black-winged insect that sucks plant sap and can destroy plants when present in large numbers.

thrive (thrīv) *v* **throve** or **thrived, thrived** or **thriv·en, thriv·ing** grow or develop well or vigorously: *The flowers thrived in the sun. The young woman's business was thriving.* <Old Norse *thrifa(sk)*> **thriv′ing** *adj.* **thriv′ing·ly** *adv.*

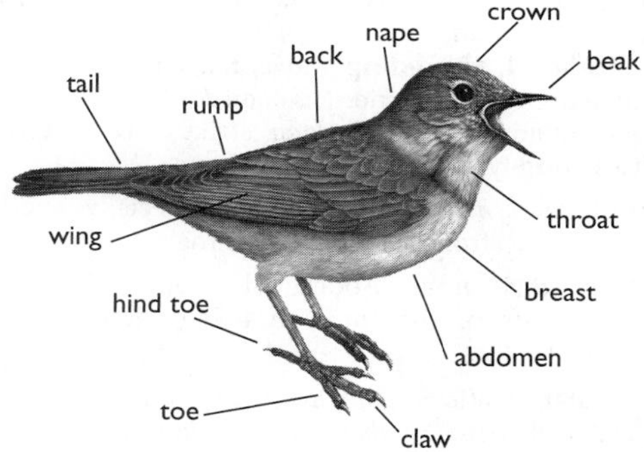

throat (thrōt) *n* **1** the passage that leads down from the back of the mouth of a person or animal, especially the front part of the neck. **2** the passage from the mouth to the stomach or the lungs. **3** a thing compared to a throat, especially a narrowed opening, passage, or exit. **4** a voice of a person or a songbird: *in full throat.*
adj **throated** (*as a compound with* **full-**) making sound or using the voice to the fullest extent: *a full-throated roar.* <Old English *throte*>
cut your own throat, *Informal* cause your own downfall.
jump down someone's throat, *Informal* attack or criticize someone with sudden violence.
ram something down someone's throat, *Informal* force someone to listen to or accept something.
stick in your throat, be hard or unpleasant to say.

throat·y (thrō′tē) *adj* **throat·i·er, throat·i·est** with a deep and rasping sound, such as one produced from far back in the throat. **throat′i·ness** *n.*

throb (throb) *v* **throbbed, throb·bing** beat or sound with a strong, regular rhythm or steady activity: *They were throbbing with excitement.*
n a strong, regular beat, sound, or activity: *the throb of hearts. She felt the throb of the little plane's engine.* <Middle English *throbben*> **throb′bing** *adj.* **throb′bing·ly** *adv.*

throes (thrōz) *pln* intense or violent pain and struggle, especially accompanying birth, death, or great change: *the throes of creation, the throes of revolution.* <origin uncertain>

throm·bo·sis (throm bō′sis) *n* the formation of clots in blood in the circulatory system of the body. <Greek *thrombos* clot>

throne (thrōn) *n* **1** the chair on which a king, queen, bishop, or other person of high rank sits during ceremonies. **2 the throne** the power or authority of a monarch. <Greek *thronos*>

🍁 **Throne Speech** SPEECH FROM THE THRONE.

throng (throng) *n* a large, densely packed crowd of people or animals.
v fill, gather, or be present as a crowd in a place or area: *People thronged the theatre to see the famous actress.* <Old English *gethrang*>

throt·tle (throt′əl) *n* a device controlling the flow of fuel or power to an engine.
v **throt·tled, throt·tling 1** attack or kill someone by choking or strangling. **2** control an engine or vehicle with a throttle. **3** stop or hinder the expression or action of: *Increased tariffs soon throttled trade between the two countries.* <Middle English *throtelen*>

through (thrū) *prep* **1** from one side to or out of the other side of an opening, location, or process: *The parade marched through the town. The workers cut a tunnel through a mountain. The toxins worked their way through the food chain.* **2** continuing in time toward completion of a process or period: *The new video game was so exciting that we played through the whole afternoon.* **3** so as to inspect all or part of a collection, group, or text: *Our teacher reminded us to read through all of our notes.* **4** up to and including a particular point in a sequence: *Please read pages 14 through 26.* **5** by means of; due to: *Success comes through hard work.*
adv **1** from beginning to end: *I read the book through.* **2** past a certain point, or over a barrier: *to make it through to the finals. It was difficult, but we got through.* **3** so as to be connected by telephone: *Did the operator put the call through right away?*
adj **1** to do with transportation or a route that goes to the final destination: *a through train, a through ticket.* **2** having reached an end: *What time will you be through?* **3** *Informal* with no prospect of any future relationship, dealings, or success: *I've had enough. We're through!* See THREW for confusable <Old English *thurh*>
through and through, completely or thoroughly: *He was an athlete through and through.*

through·out (thrū out′) *prep, adv* **1** all the way through: *She skied almost every weekend throughout the winter* (*prep*). **2** in or to every part or from beginning to end: *He remained stubborn throughout* (*adv*).

throve (thrōv) a past tense of THRIVE.

a bat	e bed	i bid	o pot	u cup	th thin
ā cake	ē me	ī bite	ō go	ū rude	TH then
ä bar	ə about	ər over	ȯ for	u̇ put	zh measure

T

throw (thrō) *v* **threw, thrown, throw·ing 1** propel something with force, or as if with force, especially through the air: *He threw the ball hard. The fire hose threw water on the fire, to throw a glance.* **2** cause to suddenly enter a particular condition or situation: *I threw all my energy into fundraising. We were thrown into confusion.* **3** send someone to the ground, such as from riding a horse, or in wrestling, martial arts, etc.: *The horse threw the rider on her second jump.* **4** *Informal* (*often with* ***off***) confuse; baffle: *The way the question was worded really threw me off.* **5** form ceramic ware on a potter's wheel: *to throw a pot.* **6** have (a fit or tantrum). **7** be the host of (a party). **8** *Informal* let an opponent win a race or match, especially after having been bribed to do so.
n **1** an act of throwing something or someone, or the distance a thing may be thrown. **2** a piece of material used as a covering for furniture. **3 a throw** the amount a single item, turn, or attempt costs: *In that game, you get three chances at $5 a throw.* <Old English *thrawan* twist>
throw′er *n.*
throw away, a get rid of or discard. **b** waste or fail to make use of: *He threw away the opportunity.*
throw cold water on, discourage.
throw in, add as a gift or extra: *The bakery often throws in an extra doughnut.*
throw off, a get rid of. **b** *Informal* produce something in a casual way.
throw open, a open suddenly or widely. **b** remove all obstacles or restrictions from.
throw out, get rid of, discard, or reject.
throw over, give up or abandon.
throw together, a make hurriedly or without much care or thought. **b** cause to become acquainted by chance: *They were thrown together by the war.*
throw up, a *Informal* vomit. **b** build rapidly.
throw up your hands, express helpless dismay.
throw yourself at someone, try very hard to obtain the love, friendship, or favour of someone.
throw yourself into, do or work at enthusiastically: *He threw himself into developing his drum technique.*
throw yourself on, appeal to as one's last or only hope: *She threw herself on the mercy of the judge.*

throw·a·way (thrō′ə wā′) *n* a thing intended or destined to be discarded after brief use, especially a free handbill or leaflet carrying advertising or other information.
adj **1** to do with products that are intended to be discarded after being used once or a few times: *throwaway bottles.* **2** to do with a remark expressed in a casual or understated way: *a throwaway line.*

throw·back (thrō′bak′) *n* a reversion to an ancestral type or character, or a person who or thing that has the characteristics of an earlier time.

throw rug *n* a small rug.

thrum[1] (thrum) *v* **thrummed, thrum·ming** make a continuous rhythmic humming sound, or strum the strings of a musical instrument in this way.
n the sound made by thrumming.

thrush[1] (thrush) *n* a small or medium-sized songbird that typically has a brown back, spotted breast, and loud song. <Old English *thrysce*>

thrush[2] (thrush) *n* an infection by a yeast-like fungus, usually of the mouth and throat that causes whitish patches. <origin uncertain>

thrust (thrust) *v* **thrust, thrust·ing 1** push something or someone suddenly or violently in the specified direction: *He thrust his hands into his pockets. She thrust her brother aside and grabbed the plate of cookies.* **2** move or advance in this way: *He thrust his way through the crowd.*
n **1** a sudden or forceful lunge, especially with a pointed weapon or a part of the body: *A thrust with the pin broke the balloon. With a quick thrust, she hid the book behind the pillow.* **2** the propulsive force of a jet or rocket engine. See ARIPLANE for picture. **3** the continuous sideways force of one part of a structure against another, such as the pressure of an arch against a pillar. **4** the main purpose, theme, or direction of an action: *the thrust of an argument.* **5** a stage which juts out so that the audience can sit on at least two sides of it. <Old Norse *thrysta*>

thrust·er (thrust′ər) *n* a person who or thing that thrusts, especially a small rocket engine on a spacecraft, used to make alterations in its flight path or altitude.

thud (thud) *n* a dull, heavy sound, such as that made by an object falling on a horizontal surface: *The book hit the floor with a thud.*
v **thud·ded, thud·ding** move, fall, or strike something with a dull, heavy sound: *His booted feet thudded across the floor.* <Old English *thyddan* strike> **thud′ding** *adj.* **thud′ding·ly** *adv.*

thug (thug) *n* a violent person, especially a criminal. <Hindi *thag,* from Sanskrit *sthaga* rogue>

Thule (thūl) *n* an Aboriginal people of the Arctic, predecessors of the Inuit, and who lived from about 1000 to 1600 CE.

thu·li·um (thū′lē əm) *or* (thyū′lē əm) *n* a soft, silver-white metallic element. *Symbol* **Tm** <*Thule* + *-ium*>

fielder's glove

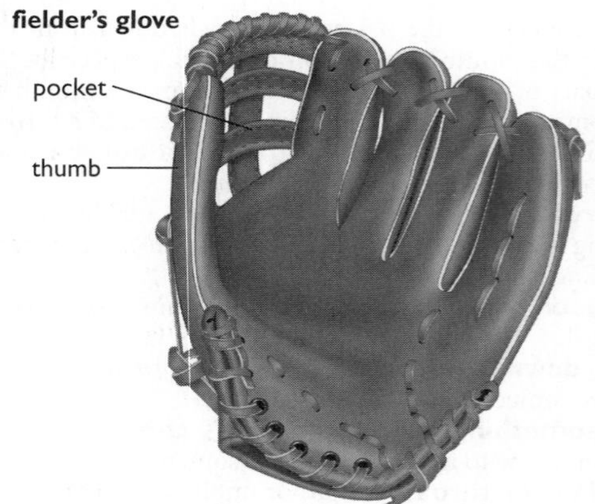

The size of the pocket between the **thumb** and the index finger of a baseball glove varies depending on the position of the player on the field.

thumb (thum) *n* **1 a** the short, thick finger of the human hand, set lower and apart from the other four and opposable to them. **b** the corresponding part of primates and other mammals. **2** the part of a glove designed to cover the thumb.

v **1** press, move, or touch something with one's thumb. **2** soil or wear by repeated thumbing or as if by thumbing: *The table in the waiting room was covered with badly thumbed magazines.* **3** *Informal* ask for or get a free ride by signalling with the thumb to passing motorists: *He wanted to thumb a ride into town, but I suggested he take the bus instead.* <Old English *thuma*> **thumb′like′** *adj.*

be all thumbs, be very clumsy or awkward: *I'm all thumbs when it comes to tying bows.*

thumbs up (or **down**), *Informal* an indication of satisfaction or approval (or of rejection or failure): *He smiled and signalled thumbs up as he came out of the dentist's office. She just gave us a thumbs down when we asked how she liked the slogan.*

thumb your nose at, *Informal* express scorn or contempt by or as if by placing your thumb on the end of your nose and extending your fingers: *He thumbed his nose at the promise of success and went his own way.*

under someone's thumb, under someone's control or influence: *He's got them all under his thumb and they'll do anything he tells them.*

thumb index *n* a series of lettered grooves cut down the side of a book, especially a diary or dictionary, for easy reference.

thumb·nail (thum′nāl′) *n* the nail of the thumb.
adj small and concise: *a thumbnail sketch.*

thumb·print (thum′print′) *n* **1** the unique impression or mark made by a person's thumb, showing the whorled ridges on the skin, especially as used for identifying individuals. **2** a distinctive characteristic: *Low social spending has been the thumbprint of this government.*

thumb·screw (thum′skrū′) *n* **1** a screw made so that its head can be easily turned with the thumb and a finger. **2** a former instrument of torture that crushed the thumbs.

thumb·tack (thum′tak′) *n* a tack with a broad, flat head for pressing into a surface with the thumb.

thump (thump) *v* **1** hit someone or something heavily, especially with the fist, or be moved in this way: *The shutters thumped the wall in the wind.* **2** move something forcefully, noisily, or decisively, or be moved in this way: *He picked up the book and thumped it down again.* **3** beat violently or heavily as a pulse or heart, typically as a result of fear or excitement. **4** defeat severely in a contest or competition.
n **1** a heavy blow with a person's fist or a blunt instrument: *He gave himself a thump on the chest to show how tough he was.* **2** a dull, deadened sound: *We heard the thump when she fell.* <imitative> **thump′er** *n.*

thun·der (thun′dər) *n* **1** a loud rumbling or crashing noise heard after a lightning flash, and due to the expansion of rapidly heated air. **2** a resounding noise like this: *a thunder of applause.*
v **1** make the sound or like the sound of thunder: *We heard it thunder in the distance. The cannon thundered.* **2** speak loudly and forcefully or angrily, especially to denounce or criticize: *to thunder a reply.* <Old English *thunor*> **thun′der·er** *n.* **thun′der·ing** *adj.* **thun′der·ing·ly** *adv.* **thun′der·y** *adj.*

steal someone's thunder, make someone's idea or action less effective by using it first or by doing it better.

🍁 **thun·der·bird** (thun′dər bərd′) *n* a mythical bird thought by some First Nations peoples to bring thunder.

thun·der·bolt (thun′dər bōlt′) *n* **1** a flash of lightning and the thunder that follows it. **2** a sudden and startling event, especially something undesirable: *The news of her death came as a thunderbolt.*

thun·der·clap (thun′dər klap′) *n* **1** a loud crash of thunder. **2** something sudden or startling.

thun·der·cloud (thun′dər kloud′) *n* a cumulus cloud with a towering or spreading top, charged with electricity and producing thunder and lightning.

thun·der·head (thun′dər hed′) *n* a rounded, swelling mass of cumulus clouds often appearing before thunderstorms.

thun·der·ous (thun′də rəs) *adj* **1** to do with a resounding, loud, deep noise: *thunderous applause.* **2** very powerful or intense: *a thunderous shot.*

thun·der·show·er (thun′dər shou′ər) *n* a rain shower accompanied by thunder and lightning.

thun·der·storm (thun′dər stôrm′) *n* a storm accompanied by thunder and lightning and, usually, heavy rain or hail.

thun·der·struck (thun′dər struk′) *adj* extremely surprised or shocked.

Thurs·day (thərz′dā′) *n* the day of the week after Wednesday and before Friday. *Abbrev.* **Thur** <Old English *Thursdaeg* Thor's day. Thor was the Germanic god of thunder.>

thus (ᴛʜus) *adv* **1** as a result or consequence of this: *Thus we decided that he was wrong.* **2** in the manner now being indicated or shown: *He answered the door, and was thus occupied when the roof fell in.* **3** to this extent or degree: *thus far.* <Old English>

thwack (thwak) *v* strike forcefully with a sharp blow.
n a sharp blow.

thwart (thwôrt) *v* prevent someone from accomplishing something: *The boy's lack of money thwarted his plans for a trip. The enemy's attack was thwarted.*
n a crosspiece on a boat, on which a rower or paddler sits. <Old Norse *thvert*>

thy (ᴛʜī) *Archaic or Poetic adj* your: *Death, where is thy sting?*

thyme (tīm) *n* a low-growing aromatic plant of the mint family, or the small leaves of this plant used as a herb in cooking. See HERB for picture. <Greek *thymon*>

thy·mus (thī′məs) *n* a ductless gland in the neck of vertebrates that produces lymphocytes for the immune system.

thy·roid (thī′roid) *n* **1** in full, **thyroid gland** a large gland in the neck that secretes hormones regulating growth. **2** an extract prepared from the thyroid gland of animals and used in treating a deficiency of thyroid hormones. <Greek *thyra* door, from the oblong shape of the cartilage in the front of the throat>

a bat	e bed	i bid	o pot	u cup	th thin
ā cake	ē me	ī bite	ō go	ū rude	ᴛʜ then
ä bar	ə about	ər over	ô for	ů put	zh measure

thy·self (ᴛʜī self′) *Archaic or Poetic pron* yourself: *Know thyself.*

ti (tē) *Music n* **1** the seventh tone of an eight-tone major scale, especially as sung to sol-fa syllables: *do, re, mi, fa, so, la, ti, do.* **2** the tone B.

ti·ar·a (tē ȧ′rə) *or* (tī er′ə) *n* **1** a jewelled ornamental band worn on the front of a woman's hair. **2** a high triple crown worn by the Pope on some occasions. <Greek>

Ti·bet (ti bet′) *n* a country in eastern central Asia. It is an autonomous part of the Republic of China.
Ti′bet′an *adj, n.*

tib·i·a (tib′ē ə) *n, pl* **tib·i·as** or **tib·i·ae** (tib′ē ē′) *or* (tib′ ē ī′) the inner and typically larger of the two bones of the leg between the knee and the ankle, or the corresponding joints in other land-dwelling vertebrates. <Latin>

tic (tik) *n* a habitual, involuntary twitching of the muscles, especially those of the face. <French>

tick[1] (tik) *n* **1** a regular short, sharp sound, especially that made every second made by a clock or watch. **2** a mark [✔] used to indicate that an item in a list or other text is correct or has been chosen or checked. **3** *UK, Informal* a moment or instant: *I'll be with you in a tick.*
v **1** make the sound of a tick, especially of a clock or watch. **2** (*usually with **off***) mark off to show that something has been chosen, checked, or approved. **3** *Informal* function, work, or go: *What makes that gadget tick?* <origin uncertain>
tick off, *Informal* scold or severely criticize: *She got ticked off for being late again.*
what makes someone tick, what motivates a person to act or behave in a certain way: *He's so quiet, we sometimes wonder what makes him tick.*

tick[2] (tik) *n* a tiny animal that attaches itself to the skin of a land-dwelling vertebrate, especially a domestic animal, from which it sucks blood. Some ticks carry infectious diseases. See ARACHNID for picture. <Old English *ticia*>

tick·er (tik′ər) *n* **1** a thing that ticks, especially a watch. **2** a telegraphic or electronic machine that displays stock market information or news reports, especially on a strip of paper **tickertape**. **3** *Informal* a person's heart.

tick·et (tik′it) *n* **1** a card or other piece of paper showing that a fare or fee has been paid: *a theatre ticket, an airline ticket, a lottery ticket.* **2** an official notification that a person is charged with a traffic violation: *a parking ticket, a speeding ticket.* **3** a label or tag attached to an article for sale, showing its price and other information.
v **1** put a ticket on; mark with a ticket: *All articles in the store are ticketed with the price.* **2** give or attach a ticket to, indicating a traffic or other offence: *My dad has never been ticketed for speeding.* <French *étiquette* label, from *estiquer* to stick>
that's the ticket, *Informal* that's the correct or desirable thing.

tick·ing (tik′ing) *n* a strong, durable material, usually striped, used to cover mattresses. <origin uncertain>

tick·le[1] (tik′əl) *v* **tick·led, tick·ling** **1** touch lightly or prod a person or part of the body in a way that causes mild discomfort or itching and often laughter. **2** have or cause to have such a feeling: *My nose tickles.* **3** excite pleasantly or amuse: *The story tickled her. The child was tickled with his new toys.*
n **1** an act of tickling someone. **2** a sensation like that of tickling. <Middle English *tikelen*> **tick′ly** *adj.*
tickled pink, *Informal* very pleased.

🍁 **tick·le**[2] (tik′əl) *especially Newfoundland n* **1** a narrow channel between an island and the mainland, or sometimes, between islands. **2** a narrow entrance to a harbour. <perhaps English dialect *stickle* rapids>

tick·lish (tik′lish) *adj* **1** sensitive to tickling. **2** requiring careful handling as a situation or problem: *Fixing the computer was a ticklish job.* **tick′lish·ly** *adv.* **tick′lish·ness** *n.*

tick–tock (tik′tok′) *n* the sound of ticking made by a large clock.
v make such a sound.

tic–tac–toe or **tick–tack–toe** (tik′tak tō′) *n* a game in which two players alternately put circles or crosses in a figure of nine squares, each player trying to be the first to fill three spaces in a row with a mark.

tid·al (tī′dəl) *adj* to do with tides: *tidal waters, a tidal breeze.*

tidal range *n* the height difference between the water level at high tide and the water level at low tide.

tidal wave *n* **1** TSUNAMI. **2** a widespread or overwhelming display of emotion or opinion: *a tidal wave of indignation.*

tid·bit (tid′bit′) *n* **1** a small piece of tasty food. **2** a small but particularly interesting piece of information or gossip. Also, **titbit**. <*tid* nice + *bit* morsel>

tid·dly·winks (tid′lē wingks′) *n* (*with singular verb*) a game in which the players try to make small coloured discs jump into a cup by pressing on their edges with a larger disc.

tide (tīd) *n* **1** the alternating rise and fall of the ocean on the shore, usually taking place about every twelve hours, caused by the attraction of the moon and the sun. **2** a thing that rises and falls like the tide: *the tide of popular opinion.* <Old English *tid*> **tide′less** *adj.*
tide someone over, help someone to overcome a difficulty, especially with financial help: *He said twenty dollars would tide him over until payday.*
turn the tide, change from one condition to the opposite, especially in a favourable way.

tide·wa·ter (tī′dwot′ər) *n* water brought or affected by tides.

ti·dings (tī′dingz) *pl n* news or information: *The letter brought tidings from their daughter and her family.* <Old English *tidan* happen>

ti·dy (tī′dē) *adj* **ti·di·er, ti·di·est** **1** arranged neatly and in order: *a tidy room.* **2** inclined to keep things or one's appearance neat and in order: *a tidy person.* **3** *Informal* considerable as an amount, especially of money: *He already has a tidy sum saved up toward a stereo.* **4** acceptable or good: *They've worked out a tidy solution.*
v **ti·died, ti·dy·ing** (*often with **up***) put in order or make tidy: *She quickly tidied the room. We tidied up before we left for school.*

n, pl **ti·dies** a small decorative cover used to protect the back of furniture. <Old English *tidi* in good condition> **ti′di·ly** *adv.* **ti′di·ness** *n.*

tie (tī) *v* **tied, ty·ing 1** fasten or attach something or someone with a string, ribbon, etc.: *Tie the package securely and tape a label on it. Tie your shoes. He tied down the tarpaulin to keep it from flapping.* **2** fasten or make something by means of forming a bow or knot: *to tie a scarf.* **3** restrict or limit someone to a particular situation, occupation, or place: *He did not want to be tied to a steady job.* **4** connect or link: *When the river was low, a narrow strip of sand tied the island to the shore.* **5** achieve the same score or ranking as another competitor or team.
n **1** a piece of string, etc. used for fastening or tying something: *The ties of his apron dangled.* **2** a thing that unites or links people: *family ties.* **3** a shaped, folded length of cloth worn under a collar and knotted in front, either to form a bow or, more often, so that the two ends hang straight down: *He always wears a shirt and tie to work.* **4** one of the parallel wooden beams placed crosswise at intervals on a railway bed to form a foundation and support for the rails. **5** a result in a game or other competition in which two or more competitors or teams have the same score or ranking: *The game ended in a 3–3 tie.* **6** *Music* a curved line above or below two musical notes of the same pitch indicating that they are to be played for the combined duration of their time values. <Old English *teag* rope> **tie′less** *adj.*
tie down, confine or restrict: *Her aunt is tied down with a full-time job and night school.*
tie in, a connect: *Where does this line tie in with the main circuit?* **b** co-ordinate or relate: *The illustrations tie in very well with the story.*
tie one on, *Informal* get drunk.
tie up, a confine by being tied: *The thieves tied him up and left him.* **b** hinder or stop the progress of: *The stalled truck tied up traffic for half an hour.* **c** invest or place money or property in such a way as to make it unavailable for other uses: *Since her money was tied up in real estate, she was unable to buy the bonds.* **d** be very busy: *He's tied up and can't make it to the dinner.* **e** take for oneself so as to make unavailable for others: *Don't tie up the phone too long.* **f** complete or conclude: *They've nearly got the details tied up.*

tie·break·er (tī′brā′kər) *n* a contest or game held to determine a winner from among contestants with equal scores.

tie clip *n* an ornamental clip used to hold a necktie in place.

tie–dye (tī′dī′) *n* a method of producing textile patterns by tying parts of the fabric to shield it when the rest is being dyed, or a pattern made in this way.
v **tie-dyed, tie-dye·ing** dye cloth or a garment in this way: *to tie-dye a scarf.*

tie–in (tī′in′) *n* **1** a connection or association: *There was no tie-in between the murder and the robbery.* **2** a book, movie or other product produced to take advantage of a related, popular work in another medium.

tie·pin (tī′pin′) *n* an ornamental pin for holding a necktie in place.

tier (tēr) *n* a row or level of a structure, typically one of a series of rows placed one above the other and receding or diminishing in size: *tiers of seats.* <Old French *tier* sequence>

tie–up (tī′up′) *n* **1** a stopping of activity, such as of traffic on a street or highway, or work at a factory on account of a strike. **2** a link or connection, especially one between commercial companies or a telecommunications network.

tiff (tif) *n* a slight quarrel, especially between friends or lovers.
v have or be in a tiff. <origin uncertain>

tif·fa·ny (tif′ə nē) *n* very thin, sheer muslin or silk. <Old French *tifanie,* from Greek *theophaneia,* a dress worn on Twelfth Night>

Tif·fa·ny (tif′ə nē) *adj* to do with a type of stained glass in an art nouveau style: *a Tiffany lamp.* <L.C. *Tiffany,* 19c American designer>

The male Siberian **tiger** hunts and lives alone and only meets with a female during mating season.

ti·ger (tī′gər) *n* **1** a very large wild animal of the cat family, with a yellow-brown coat striped with black. Tigers are native to the forests of Asia. The female is usually called a **tigress**. **2** a fierce, determined, aggressive, or ambitious person or group: *He becomes a tiger if you criticize his work.* <Greek *tigris*> **ti′ger·like′** *adj.*
have a tiger by the tail, be in a situation much more difficult than was expected.

T

ti·ger·ish (tī′gə rish) *adj* considered like a tiger in being fierce and determined.

tiger lily *n* a tall lily that has orange flowers spotted with black or purple.

tiger moth *n* a moth with conspicuously spotted or striped wings.

ti·ger's–eye (tī′gər zī′) *n* a semi-precious golden brown variety of quartz with a changeable luster.

a **bat**	e **bed**	i **bid**	o **pot**	u **cup**	th **thin**
ā **cake**	ē **me**	ī **bite**	ō **go**	ū **rude**	ᴛʜ **then**
ä **bar**	ə **about**	ər **over**	ȯ **for**	u̇ **put**	zh **measure**

tight (tīt) *adj* **1** fastened or closed firmly and hard to move, undo, or open: *a tight knot.* **2** stretched so as to leave no slack: *Make sure there is a tight canvas over the tent.* **3** fitting or packed closely: *Since I gained weight, my clothes have become tight.* **4** not letting water, air, or gas in or out: *The caulking of the boat is tight.* **5** hard to deal with or manage: *His lies got him in a tight place.* **6** strict and inflexible: *tight security.* **7** hard to get; scarce: *Money is tight just now.* **8** *Informal* stingy: *to be tight with money.* **9** *Informal* drunk.
adv very firmly, closely, or tensely: *The rope was tied too tight.* <Old English *getyht* stretched> **tight′ly** *adv.* **tight′ness** *n.*
sit tight, *Informal* keep in the same place or with the same opinion.

SYNONYMS

Tight means "fastened or closed so firmly that there is no looseness": *The jacket was so tight on him that he could barely move his arms.*

Strained can mean "placing force on something, causing injury": *Her strained ankle prevented her from competing in the race.*

Stretched means "lengthened" or "widened": *The rope stretched between the trees gave them a place to hang their towels and bathing suits.*

tight·en (tī′tən) *v* make or become tight or tighter: *She tightened her belt. The rope tightened as I pulled it.*

tight–fist·ed (tīt′fis′tid) *Informal adj* unwilling to spend or give much money.

tight–lipped (tīt′lipt′) *Informal adj* with the lips firmly closed, especially as a sign of suppressed emotion or from reluctance to speak: *She stood there in tight-lipped fury. He's very tight-lipped, so you won't get any information out of him.*

tight·rope (tīt′rōp′) *n* a rope or wire stretched tight high above the ground, on which acrobats perform feats of balancing.

tights (tīts) *pln* a close-fitting, usually knitted, garment covering the lower body and each leg and foot separately.

tight squeeze *n* **1** a situation in which there is barely enough room or time for something: *It was a tight squeeze, but we managed to get all our luggage in the trunk. The dentist can fit you in between 4:30 and 5:00, but it'll be a tight squeeze.* **2** a difficult, urgent or critical situation, or a narrow escape.

tight·wad (tīt′wod′) *Informal n* a stingy person.

ti·gress (tī′gris) *n* **1** an adult female tiger. **2** a woman thought of as being like a tiger in fierceness or aggressiveness.

ti·ka (tē′kə) *n* a coloured mark worn by a Hindu on the forehead to indicate caste, status, or sect, or as an ornament. <Hindi>

✱ **ti·ki·na·gan** (tik′ə nä′gən) *n* a cradleboard.

til·de (til′də) *n* an accent as in *ñ* used over the letter *n* in Spanish when it is pronounced *ny,* or over certain vowels in Portuguese to indicate that they are nasalized. <Spanish, from Latin *titulus* heading>

tile (tīl) *n* **1** a thin, rectangular slab of baked clay, concrete, plastic, or other material, used in overlapping rows to cover roofs, and to cover floors, walls, and other surfaces. **2** a small, thin, flat piece used in Scrabble and some other games.
adj covered with or made of tile: *There is a tile floor in the bathroom.*
v **tiled, til·ing 1** put tiles on or cover with tile. **2** *Computers* arrange two or more windows on a screen so that they do not overlap. **3** *Mathematics* arrange identical plane shapes so that they completely cover an area without overlapping. <Latin *tegula*> **til′er** *n.*

til·ing (tī′ling) *n* **1** the action of laying tiles. **2** an arrangement of identical plane shapes that completely covers an area without overlapping. **3** a surface or structure consisting of tiles.

till[1] (til) *conj, prep* until. <Old English *til*>

till[2] (til) *v* prepare and cultivate land for crops. <Old English *tilian*> **till′a·ble** *adj.*

till[3] (til) *n* a cash register or drawer for money in a store, bank, bar, or restaurant: *The till is under the counter.* <Old English *-tyllan*>

till[4] (til) *n* boulder clay or other sediment deposited by melting glaciers or ice sheets. Compare OUTWASH. <origin uncertain>

till·er[1] (til′ər) *n* a horizontal bar or handle used to turn the rudder in steering a boat. <Old French *telier* weaver's beam, from Latin *tela* loom>

till·er[2] (til′ər) *n* a person who or machine that tills the land.

tilt (tilt) *v* **1** move or cause to move into a sloping position: *This table tilts.* **2** rush, charge, or fight with lances while on horseback in jousting. **3** incline or cause to incline toward a particular opinion: *I'm tilting toward an entirely different viewpoint.*
n **1** a sloping position or movement: *This table is on a tilt.* **2** in former times, a fight on horseback with lances. **3** ✱ **a** *Newfoundland* a small shack, cabin, or hut with a sloping roof. **b** a tent or lean-to with a sealskin or canvas roof. <Old English *tealt* shaky>
full tilt, at full speed or with full force: *Her car ran full tilt against the tree.*
tilt at windmills, attack imaginary enemies or evils.

tilth (tilth) *n* **1** the cultivation of land. **2** tilled land. **3** the condition of tilled soil, especially in how suitable it is for sowing seeds.

tim·bale (tim′bəl) *n* a dish of finely minced meat or fish cooked with other ingredients in a pastry shell or in a mould.

tim·ber (tim′bər) *n* **1** wood prepared for use in building and carpentry. **2** trees that are growing and suitable for such wood: *Half of their land is covered with timber.* **3** a large squared piece of wood ready to use in building, or forming part of a structure. Beams and rafters are timber. <Old English>

tim·bered (tim′bərd) *adj* **1** with wooden panels covering the walls or other surface of a room. **2** covered with growing trees.

tim·ber·land (tim′bər land′) *n* land with trees that are, or will be, useful for timber.

✱ **timber licence** *n* a licence permitting the cutting of trees on a certain piece of land, on payment of a fee to a government.

✱ **timber limit** *n* a tract of land in which a person or group has the right to fell trees and remove timber. See also BERTH (def. 5).

tim·ber·line (tim′bər līn′) *n* the point beyond which trees will not grow because of climatic conditions such as extreme cold and strong winds.

✱ **timber wolf** *n* a large, grey, N American wolf, especially a subspecies found in the northern forests of Canada.

tim·bre (tim′bər) *or* (tam′bər) *n* the character or quality of a musical sound as distinct from its pitch and intensity. <French *timbre,* from Greek *tympanon* drum>

tim·brel (tim′brəl) *n* a tambourine.

time (tīm) *n* **1** the indefinite continued progress of existence and events in the past, present, and future and regarded as a whole, often measured in years, months, days, etc. **2** a point of time as measured in hours and minutes past midnight or noon: *What time is it? The time is 11:45.* **3** time as available or used: *It took less time than we expected. She had a good time at the party.* **4** a fact of something happening or being done: *It's time to eat lunch. This time we will succeed.* **5** *Music* a rate or pattern of movement or rhythm: *waltz time.* **6** ✱ *especially Atlantic Provinces* a festive gathering, usually to celebrate an event: *Have you been invited to the time tonight?* **7** **times** *pl* conditions of life: *War brings hard times.* **8** **times** amounts or numbers multiplied by: *five times as much.*
v **timed, tim·ing** **1** plan, schedule, or arrange when something should happen or be done: *We timed our departure precisely.* **2** measure the time taken by a process or activity, or a person doing it: *to time a race.*
adj provided with a clocklike mechanism so that it will explode or ignite at a given moment: *a time bomb.*
prep **times** multiplied by: *Four times three is twelve.* <Old English *tima*>
about time, a rather late to be doing something: *You're finally getting new skates? Well, it's about time!* **b** at or near the proper time: *I think it's about time we went home.*
against time, with great speed in an attempt to finish before a certain time: *working against time.*
ahead of time, early; in advance.
against time, with great speed in an attempt to finish before a certain time.
at a time, in the same action: *He ate the jelly beans two at a time.*
at the same time, however or nevertheless: *I think you're wrong, but at the same time, I will give you my support.*
at times, now and then or once in a while.
behind the times, not aware of or using the latest ideas or techniques.
behind time, late.
do time, *Informal* be a convict in prison: *He did time for armed robbery.*
for the time being, for the present.
give someone the time of day, notice or acknowledge someone.
in good time, a at the proper time: *We reached the theatre in good time for the first act.* **b** soon or quickly.
in no time, very quickly.
in time, a eventually. **b** not too late: *Will we arrive in time to catch the bus?* **c** in music, dancing, marching, etc. in the proper rate of movement.
keep time, a function well as a watch or clock. **b** play or rhythmically accompany music at the proper rate: *The marchers kept excellent time.*
make time, a go at a specified rate of speed: *He made good time on his long walk.* **b** provide a time to do something: *The guidance counsellor made time for my interview that same day.*
on your own time, without being paid or outside of paid working hours.
on time, a punctually. **b** with time in which to pay on credit: *She bought a car on time.*
pass the time of day, exchange greetings or brief conversation.
time after time or **time and again,** on very many occasions.
time was, there was a time: *Time was when most people left their doors unlocked.*

time bomb *n* **1** a bomb equipped with a timing device, designed to explode at a preset time. **2** a condition or situation leading to inevitable disaster, unless action can be taken to avert it.

time capsule *n* a container storing a selection of objects chosen as being typical of the present time, buried for discovery in the future.

time·card (tīm′kärd′) *n* a card for recording the amount of time that a person works.

time clock *n* a clock with a device for recording employees' times of arrival and departure from work.

time–con·sum·ing (tīm′kən sū′ming) *or* (tīm′kən syū′ming) *adj* taking up or requiring a great deal of time: *The calculations weren't hard, but they were time-consuming.*

time exposure *n* the exposure of a photographic film for longer than the maximum normal shutter setting, or a photograph taken in this way.

time frame *n* a period of time, especially a specified period in which something occurs or is planned to take place: *What's the time frame for this job?*

time–hon·oured or **time–hon·ored** (tī′mon′ərd) *adj* honoured as a custom or tradition because it has existed for a long time.

a bat	e bed	i bid	o pot	u cup	th thin
ā cake	ē me	ī bite	ō go	ū rude	TH then
ä bar	ə about	ər over	ô for	ů put	zh measure

T

time·keep·er (tīm′kē′pər) *n* **1** a person who measures or records the amount of time taken, especially in a sports match or competition. **2** a watch or clock regarded as recording time accurately or inaccurately: *a good timekeeper.*

time lag *n* a delay between a cause and its effect.

time–lapse photography (tīm′laps′) *n*
the photographic technique of taking a sequence of frames at set intervals to record changes that take place slowly over time. When the frames are shown at normal speed the action seems much faster.

time·less (tīm′lis) *adj* not affected by the passage of time or changes in fashion: *timeless beauty.*

time·line (tīm′līn) *n* **1** a line marked with dates and events at approximate intervals, or other pictorial depiction of time as a line. **2** a timetable of activities or events in a project, usually with dates or times for different stages; a schedule.

time·ly (tīm′lē) *adj* **time·li·er, time·li·est** done or occurring at a favourable or useful time: *The timely arrival of the police stopped the riot.* **time′li·ness** *n.*

time out *n* **1** time for rest or recreation away from one's usual work or studies: *After working hard for an hour, we took some time out.* **2** a short time in which a child is separated from other people, given as a corrective measure or punishment. **3 timeout a** *Sports* a brief break in play in a game or sport. **b** *Computers* a cancellation of an activity after a specified amount of time has passed.

time·piece (tīm′pēs′) *n* a clock or watch.

tim·er (tī′mər) *n* **1** a person who or thing that measures or records the amount of time taken by a process or activity. **2** an automatic mechanism that activates a device at a preset time: *an oven timer.* **3** (*in compounds*) the time or times someone has done something: *a first-timer.*

time·sav·er (tīm′sā′vər) *n* a person who or thing that saves time: *A calculator can be a timesaver for math problems.* **time′sav′ing** *adj.*

time·serv·er (tīm′sər′vər) *n* **1** a person who changes their views to suit the prevailing circumstances or fashions, usually to gain personal advantage. **2** a person who makes very little effort at work because the time for leaving or retirement is near. **time′serv′ing** *adj.*

time–share (tīm′shār) *n* a vacation house or apartment shared by several joint owners, who use it at specified times. **time′-share′** *v.* **time′-shar′ing** *n.*

time sheet *n* a record of an employee's hours of work.

time·ta·ble (tīm′tā′bəl) *n* **1** a chart showing the departure and arrival times of trains, buses, or planes. **2** a plan of times at which events are scheduled to take place, especially for a particular purpose, such as how time is allotted to the different subjects in school.

time–test·ed (tīm′tes′təd) *adj* with a value or effectiveness that has been proven over a long period of time: *a time-tested recipe.*

time warp *n* an imaginary distortion of space in relation to time whereby people or objects of one time period can be moved to another.

time·worn (tīm′wȯrn′) *adj* worn, damaged, or made less attractive by long existence or use: *They walked up the timeworn steps of the old house.*

time zone *n* a geographical region within which the same standard of time is used. The world is divided into twenty-four time zones beginning and ending at the DATE LINE.

tim·id (tim′id) *adj* showing a lack of courage or self-confidence: *a timid voice, a timid excuse.* <Latin *timidus,* from *timere* to fear> **tim·id′i·ty** *n.* **tim′id·ly** *adv.* **tim′id·ness** *n.*

tim·ing (tī′ming) *n* **1** the choice, judgment, or control of when something should be done. **2** a particular point or period during which something happens.

Ti·mor–Les·te (tē′mor les′tā) EAST TIMOR.

tim·or·ous (tim′ə rəs) *adj* showing or suffering from nervousness or a lack of confidence. **tim′or·ous·ly** *adv.* **tim′or·ous·ness** *n.*

tim·o·thy (tim′ə thē) *n* a grass with long, cylindrical spikes, often grown for grazing and hay.

tim·pa·ni (tim′pə nē′) *pl n, sing* **tim·pa·no** (tim′pə nō′) a set of kettledrums, especially when played by one person in an orchestra. See PERCUSSION INSTRUMENT for picture. <Italian, from Latin *tympanum*> **tim′pan·ist** *n.*

tin (tin) *n* **1** a soft, silver-white metallic element used as a coating on other metals and in making alloys. *Symbol* **Sn** **2** thin sheets of iron or steel coated with tin. **3** a metal container, especially a pan used for baking: *a cake tin, a muffin tin.*
adj made of tin: *tin cans, a tin box.* <Old English>

tinc·ture (tingk′chər) *n* **1** a solution of medicine in alcohol: *tincture of iodine.* **2** a trace or tinge of something.
v **tinc·tured, tinc·tur·ing** affect with or give a trace of something. <Latin *tingere* tinge>

tin·der (tin′dər) *n* a dry, flammable material, such as wood or paper, used for lighting a fire. <Old English *tynder*>

tin·der·box (tin′dər boks′) *n* in former times, a box used for holding tinder, flint, and steel for making a fire.

tine (tīn) *n* a sharp, projecting point or prong, such as that on a fork or antler. <Old English *tind*>

tin ear *n* an inability to recognize the pitch of musical tones. **tin′-eared′** *adj.*

tin·foil (tin′foil′) *n* a very thin sheet of aluminum or a similar grey metal, used especially for covering or wrapping food.

tinge (tinj) *v* **tinged, tinge·ing** or **ting·ing 1** colour slightly. **2** change slightly or have a slight influence: *Sad memories tinged their present joy.*
n **1** a slight colouring or tint: *There is a tinge of red in her cheeks.* **2** a slight trace of a feeling or quality: *There was a tinge of envy in his voice.* <Latin *tingere*>

tin·gle (ting′gəl) *v* **tin·gled, tin·gling** experience, cause to experience, or be experienced as a slight prickling or stinging sensation: *He tingled with delight on his first train trip. Shame tingled his cheeks.*
n a slight pricking or stinging sensation: *The cold caused a tingle in my fingers.* <*tinkle*>

tink·er (ting′kər) *n* **1** a person who mends pots, pans, and kettles, and travels from place to place to practise this trade. **2** the act of attempting to repair something.
v attempt to repair or improve something in a casual or experimental way: *She likes to tinker with old computers.* <origin uncertain>

tin·kle (ting′kəl) *v* **tin·kled, tin·kling** make or cause to make a light, clear, ringing sound.
n a series of short, light, ringing sounds: *the tinkle of sleigh bells.* <imitative>

tin·ni·tus (ti nī′təs) *n* an abnormal ringing or buzzing in the ears. <Latin *tinnire* ring>

tin·ny (tin′ē) *adj* **tin·ni·er, tin·ni·est 1** with a thin metallic sound. **2** with an unpleasant metallic taste: *The salmon tastes tinny.* **3** made of thin or poor-quality metal: **tin′ni·ness** *n.*

tin·plate (tin′plāt′) *n* sheets of iron or steel coated with tin.

tin·sel (tin′səl) *n* **1** a form of decoration consisting of thin strips of shiny metal foil. **2** something showy and attractive, but not worth much. <French *estinceler* to sparkle, from Latin *scintilla* a spark> **tin′sel-like′** *adj.* **tin′sel·ly** *adj.*

tin·smith (tin′smith′) *n* a person who makes or repairs items of tin or tinplate.

tin·snips (tin′snips′) *pl n* a pair of heavy shears for cutting through tin or other sheet metal.

tint (tint) *n* **1** a shade or variety of colour. **2** a dye for colouring hair.
v **1** colour something slightly. **2** dye the hair. <Latin *tingere* dye>

ti·ny (tī′nē) *adj* **ti·ni·er, ti·ni·est** very small. <Middle English *tine*> **ti′ni·ness** *n.*

–tion *suffix* forming nouns of action or condition: *addition, exhaustion.* <Latin>

tip[1] (tip) *n* **1** the pointed or rounded end or extreme part of something slender or tapering: *tips of the fingers.* **2** a small piece or part fitted to the end of an object: *He bought rubber tips to put on the legs of the stool.*
v **tipped, tip·ping 1** attach to or cover the end or extreme part of: *The Highwood Mountains are tipped with snow.* **2** colour something at its end or edge: *pink tipped with white.* <Middle English *tippe*>

tip[2] (tip) *v* **tipped, tip·ping 1** overbalance or cause to overbalance so as to fall or turn over: *The cup of tea tipped over.* **2** be or cause to be in a sloping position with one end or side higher than the other: *He tipped his hat back.* **3** cause a container to be emptied out by holding it at an angle: *She tipped the contents of her backpack out onto the table.*
n a slope or slant: *There is such a tip to that table that everything slides off.* <Middle English *tipen*>
tip your hand, unintentionally reveal your plans.

tip[3] (tip) *n* **1** a small sum of money given in return for service: *He gave the waiter a tip.* **2** a small but useful piece of practical advice: *She bought a book of tips on caring for her pet.* **3** a prediction or piece of expert information about a desirable outcome, such as the winner of a competition or race.
v **tipped, tip·ping 1** give someone a small amount of money as a way of rewarding her or him for their services: *She tipped the porter.* **2** predict as likely to win or be successful: *She was tipped to win the race.* **3** (*often with* ***off***) predict or give expert information about a likely desirable outcome. <origin uncertain>

ti·pi (tē′pē) TEEPEE.

tip–off (tip′of′) *Informal n* a piece of information, especially one given in a discreet or confidential way.

tip·ple (tip′əl) *v* **tip·pled, tip·pling** drink alcoholic liquor often.
n an alcoholic liquor. <origin uncertain> **tip′pler** *n.*

tip·py (tip′ē) *adj* **tip·pi·er, tip·pi·est** liable to tip or overturn.

tip·sy (tip′sē) *adj* **tip·si·er, tip·si·est** slightly drunk. **tip′si·ly** *adv.* **tip′si·ness** *n.*

tip·toe (tip′tō′) *v* **tip·toed, tip·toe·ing** walk quietly and carefully with one's heels raised and one's weight on the balls of one's feet: *She tiptoed up the stairs.*
on tiptoe, walking in this way: *I crept past on tiptoe so as not to disturb the others.*

tip·top (tip′top′) *n* the very best class or condition.
adj of the best class or condition: *My skis are old, but they're in tiptop shape.*

ti·rade (tī′rād) *n* a long, angry speech, criticism, or accusation. <French *tirer* to draw out>

ti·ra·mi·su (tēr′ə mē′sū) *or* (tēr′ə mē sū′) *n* an Italian dessert consisting of layers of sponge cake soaked in coffee and brandy or liqueur with powdered chocolate and creamy sweetened cheese. <Italian>

tire[1] (tīr) *v* **tired, tir·ing 1** become or cause to feel in need of rest or sleep: *The hard work tired him. She tires easily.* **2** lose interest in or be bored with: *She quickly tired of playing video games.* <Old English *tyrian*>
tir′ing *adj.* **tir′ing·ly** *adv.*

tire[2] (tīr) *n* a rubber covering, typically inflated or surrounding an inflated inner tube, placed around a wheel to form a firm contact with the road. <*attire*>

tired (tīrd) *adj* **1** in need of sleep or rest: *I am tired, but I must get back to work.* **2** (*with* ***of***) bored with: *I am tired of apologizing for others.* **tired′ly** *adv.* **tired′ness** *n.*

SYNONYMS

Tired means "needing sleep or rest": *It's midnight and I'm tired.*

Beat is an informal word for "exhausted": *After that long day of work, I'm beat!*

Exhausted emphasizes having no energy to continue: *They were so exhausted after the game that they decided to go straight home.*

Weary suggests feeling worn out and unable or unwilling to go on: *She was weary from the repeated efforts she had made to contact him.*

a bat	e bed	i bid	o pot	u cup	th thin
ā cake	ē me	ī bite	ō go	ū rude	ᴛʜ then
ä bar	ə about	ər over	ȯ for	u̇ put	zh measure

tire·less (tīr′lis) *adj* with or showing great effort or energy: *a tireless worker.* **tire′less·ly** *adv.* **tire′less·ness** *n.*

tire·some (tīr′səm) *adj* causing one to feel bored or annoyed: *a tiresome speech.* **tire′some·ly** *adv.* **tire′some·ness** *n.*

'tis (tiz) *contraction* it is.

tis·sue (tish′ū) *n* **1** a type of material of which animals or plants are made, consisting of specialized cells and their products: *muscle tissue, skin tissue.* **2** a thin, soft paper that absorbs moisture easily: *toilet tissue.* **3** tissue paper. **4** an intricate structure or network made from a number of connected items: *Her whole story was a tissue of lies.* <Old French, from Latin *texere*>

tissue paper *n* a very thin, soft paper used mainly for wrapping.

tit (tit) *n* a small songbird that searches for insects among foliage and branches, especially the titmouse.

ti·tan (tī′tən) *n* a person or thing of great size, power, or strength. <Greek myth *Titan*, a family of giants>
ti·tan′ic *adj.*

ti·ta·ni·um (tī tā′nē əm) *n* a hard, light, silver-grey metallic element, used in rust-resistant alloys. *Symbol* **Ti** <*Titan*>

tit·bit (tit′bit′) TIDBIT.

tithe (tīᴛʜ) *Christianity n* a tenth of an individual's income pledged to some churches.
v **tithed, tith·ing** pay or give as a tithe. <Old English *teogotha* tenth>

ti·tian (tish′ən) *adj* bright golden red. <*Titian*, 16c Italian painter, who used this colour a lot>

tit·il·late (tit′ə lāt′) *v* **tit·il·lat·ed, tit·il·lat·ing** stimulate or excite someone pleasantly. <Latin *titillare*> **tit′il·lat′ing** *adj.* **tit′il·lat′ing·ly** *adv.* **tit′il·la′tion** *n.*

tit·i·vate or **tit·ti·vate** (tit′ə vāt′) *Informal v* **tit·i·vat·ed** or **tit·ti·vat·ed, tit·i·vat·ing** or **tit·ti·vat·ing** enhance something in small ways. <perhaps *tidy*> **tit′i·vat′ing** *adj.* **tit′i·vat′ing·ly** *adv.* **tit′i·va′tion** *n.*

ti·tle (tī′təl) *n* **1** the name of a book, composition, or other artistic work. **2 titles** *pl* the captions or credits in a movie or broadcast. **3** a name that describes someone's position, rank, or job. Examples: *King, Duke, Lord, Countess, Captain, Doctor, Professor.* **4** the position of being the champion of a major sports competition: *the world title.* **5** a right or claim to the ownership of property, or to a rank or throne.
v **ti·tled, ti·tling** give a title to a book, composition, or other work. <Latin *titulus*>

ti·tled (tī′təld) *adj* with a title, indicating high social or official rank: *The movie star married a titled diplomat.*

title page *n* a page at the beginning of a book that gives its title and the names of the author and publisher.

title role *n* the part in a play or movie from which the work's title is taken.

tit·mouse (tit′mous′) *n, pl* **tit·mice** a small songbird.

ti·trate (tī′trāt) *Chemistry v* **ti·trat·ed, ti·trat·ing** determine the amount of some substance present in a solution by measuring the amount of a different substance that must be added to cause a chemical change. **ti·trat′ion** *n.*

tit·ter (tit′ər) *v* give a short, half-suppressed laugh: *Some people in the audience tittered nervously when the actor forgot his lines.*
n such a half-suppressed laugh: *A titter ran through the classroom.* <imitative> **tit′ter·er** *n.* **tit′ter·ing** *adj.* **tit′ter·ing·ly** *adv.*

tit·tle (tit′əl) *n* a tiny amount or part of something.

tit·tle–tat·tle (tit′əl tat′əl) *n, v* **tit·tle-tat·tled, tit·tle-tat·tling** gossip.

tit·u·lar (tich′ə lər) *adj* with a purely formal position or title without any real authority: *the titular head of the organization.* **tit′u·lar·ly** *adv.*

tiz·zy (ti′zē) *Informal n, pl* **tiz·zies** a very excited, nervous or anxious condition.

TKO technical knockout.

TLC *Informal n* tender loving care.

Tlin·git (tling′git) *n, pl* **Tlin·git** or **Tlin·gits** **1** a member of a First Nations people of the northern Pacific coast. **2** the language of these people.
adj to do with these people or their language.

TM trademark.

TNT *n* in full, **trinitrotolune** (trī nī′trō tol′yū ēn′) a colourless solid used as an explosive.

to (tū) *prep* **1** in the direction of a particular location: *Go to the right.* **2** identifying the person or thing affected: *You were very good to him.* **3** identifying a particular relationship between one person and another: *He is an assistant to the boss.* **4** indicating that two things are attached: *They linked the man to the crime.* **5** concerning or likely to concern something, especially something abstract: *The event was a threat to our peace of mind.* **6** expressing someone's reaction to something: *To her amazement, he agreed.* **7** introducing the second element in a comparison: *It's of little importance to what it used to be.* **8** used without a verb following when the missing verb is clearly understood: *We asked her to discuss it, but she didn't want to.*
adv **1** so as to be closed: *The door slammed to.* **2** into action, attentiveness, or consciousness: *After being unconscious for a few seconds, she came to and started to talk to me.* <Old English>

CONFUSABLES

To means "toward": *The bus left the airport and headed to the city.*

Too means "to a higher degree than is wanted": *There's too much homework for me tonight.*

Two means "one more than one": *There are two guards on duty, one on either side of the main entrance.*

toad (tōd) *n* a tailless amphibian with a short, squat body and short legs, typically with a dry, warty skin. See AMPHIBIAN for picture. <Old English *tade*>

toad·flax (tōd′flaks′) *n* a plant with flowers resembling the snapdragon, and with slender leaves.

toad·stool (tōd′stūl′) *n* the spore-bearing body of a fungus, typically in the form of a rounded cap on a stalk, especially one that is believed to be inedible or poisonous.

toad·y (tō′dē) *n, pl* **toad·ies** a person who unduly flatters someone who is important.
v **toad·ied, toad·y·ing** behave in this way. **toad′y·ism** *n.*

toast (tōst) *n* **1** bread browned on both sides by exposure to heat. **2** a request made to honour someone or something by raising one's glass and drinking from it, or the fact of drinking in this way. **3** a person who or thing that is very popular or respected by a particular group of people: *He was the toast of the sporting world.*
v **1** cook or brown food, especially bread, by exposure to heat, or become browned in this way. **2** heat thoroughly: *He toasted his feet by the fire.* **3** honour someone or something by raising one's glass and drinking from it. <Latin *torrere* parch>
be toast, *Slang* be ruined or doomed: *Try that once more and you're toast!*

toast·er (tō′stər) *n* an electrical device for toasting bread.

toaster oven *n* a kitchen countertop appliance consisting of a small oven with a rack, heated by elements on the top and bottom.

toast·mas·ter (tōst′mas′tər) *n* a person who presides at a social event, introducing speakers and making announcements.

toast·y (tō′stē) *adj* **toast·i·er, toast·i·est 1** of or resembling toast. **2** comfortably warm.

to·bac·co (tə bak′ō) *n, pl* **to·bac·cos** or **to·bac·coes** the dried, prepared leaves of a cultivated plant, used for smoking or chewing or as snuff. <Spanish *tabaco,* from Carib (a group of languages of the Caribbean)>

To·ba·go (tə bā′gō) See TRINIDAD AND TOBAGO.

🍁 **to·bog·gan** (tə bog′ən) *n* a long, light, narrow sleigh with a flat bottom and no runners, and with the front end curved up and back.
v ride or carry on a toboggan: *Are you going tobogganing?*

ETYMOLOGY

Toboggan comes through Canadian French *tabagane* from Mi'kmaq *tobakun,* which means "handsled."

to·day (tə dā′) *adv* **1** on or during this present day: *I have to go to the dentist today.* **2** at the present time or period: *Many homes today have Internet access.*
n this present day, time, or period: *The photographer of today has many types of camera to choose from.* <Old English *to dœge* on (the) day>

tod·dle (tod′əl) *v* **tod·dled, tod·dling** walk with short, unsteady steps, as a small child does.
n a young child's unsteady walk. <origin unknown>

tod·dler (tod′lər) *n* a young child who is just beginning to walk, typically between the ages of one and two or three.

tod·dy (tod′ē) *n, pl* **tod·dies 1** a drink made of an alcoholic beverage with hot water, sugar, and sometimes spices. **2** the sap of some kinds of palm trees, fermented to make a drink. <Hindi *tari* palm sap, from *tar* palm>

to–do (tə dū′) *Informal n, pl* **to-dos** a fuss or commotion: *There was a great to-do when the new puppy arrived.*

toe (tō) *n* **1** one of the five digits at the end of the human foot. **2** the corresponding part on the foot of a four-legged animal or a bird. **3** the part of an item of footwear that covers the toes. **4** the lower end, tip, or point of something, such as the foot or base of a cliff, slope, or area of land.
v **toed, toe·ing 1** push, touch, or kick something with the toe. **2** walk with the toes turned in or out. <Old English *ta*> **toe′less** *adj.*
on your toes, alert and ready for action.
toe the line, accept the authority, principles, or policies of a particular group.
tread (or **step**) **on someone's toes,** See TREAD.

toe·hold (tō′hōld′) *n* **1** a small place of support for the toes when climbing: *The climber cut toeholds in the glacier as she went.* **2** a relatively insignificant position from which further progress can be made: *She worked on the school newspaper to get a toehold in the field of journalism.*

toe·nail (tō′nāl′) *n* the nail at the tip of each toe.

tof·fee (tof′ē) *n, pl* **tof·fees** a firm or hard candy made by boiling together sugar, butter, and flavourings, which softens when sucked or chewed. <origin uncertain>

to·fu (tō′fū′) *n* a bland, protein-rich food made from mashed soybeans, used in Asian and vegetarian dishes. <Japanese, from Mandarin *to* bean + *fu* rot>

tog (tog) *Informal v* **togged, tog·ging** be or get dressed for a particular occasion: *all togged up for the party.*
n **togs** *pl* clothes. <obsolete *togman* cloak>

to·ga (tō′gə) *n* a loose, flowing outer garment worn by citizens of ancient Rome, made of a single piece of cloth with no sleeves or armholes, covering the whole body except for the right arm.

to·geth·er (tə geTH′ər) *adv* **1** with or very near to another person or thing: *They walked down the road together. I like navy and red together. They worked together for many years.* **2** so as to touch or combine: *She mixed the two colours together.* **3** considered as a whole: *All together, there were ten people at the party. They get together every Friday to watch movies.* **4** at the same time: *They both laughed together.* **5** without a stop, break, or interruption: *He worked for days together.* <Old English *to* to + *gædere* together>
together with, as well as or along with.

GRAMMAR AND USAGE

In formal writing and speech, a singular subject followed by **together with** still takes a singular verb:
The computer, together with the printer and scanner, makes up a reasonably priced package.

Here is a less wordy version: *The computer, printer, and scanner make up a reasonably priced package.*

T

a bat	e bed	i bid	o pot	u cup	th thin
ā cake	ē me	ī bite	ō go	ū rude	TH then
ä bar	ə about	ər over	ȯ for	u̇ put	zh measure

to·geth·er·ness (tə geth′ər nis) *n* the condition of being closely associated or united, especially in family or social activities.

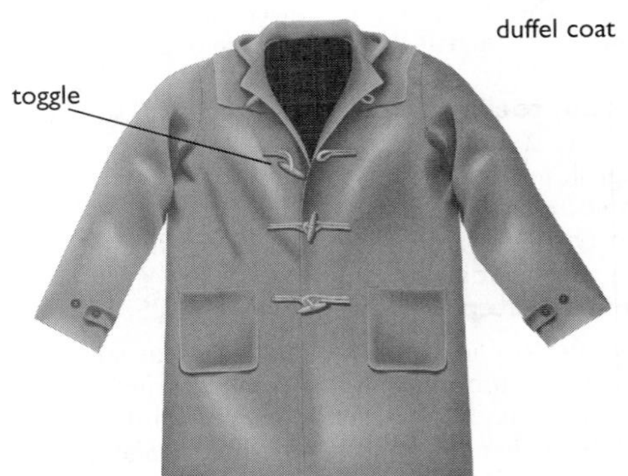

tog·gle (tog′əl) *n* **1** a short rod of wood or plastic sewn to one side of a garment, pushed through a hole or loop on the other side and twisted so as to act as a fastener. **2** a pin or other oblong piece put through a loop or hole in a rope or link of a chain to keep it in place. **3** *Computers* a key or command that is operated the same way but with the opposite effect each time it is used.
v **tog·gled, tog·gling** *Computers* switch from one effect, feature, or function to another by using a toggle. <origin unknown>

toggle switch *n* an electric switch with a projecting lever that is pushed through a small arc to open or close the circuit.

To·go (tō′gō′) *n* a country in western Africa.
To′go·lese′ *adj, n.*

toil (toil) *n* extremely hard work: *She succeeded after years of toil.*
v **1** work extremely hard. **2** move with difficulty, pain, or weariness: *They toiled up the hill.* <Old French *toeillier* drag around, from Latin *tunder* to pound> **toil′er** *n.*

toile (twol) *n* a sheer cotton or linen fabric. <French = cloth>

toi·let (toi′lit) *n* **1** a fixture, usually a large porcelain bowl flushed by water, into which to pass waste matter from the body that is then flushed away by a mechanism. **2** a room or cubicle containing a toilet. **3** the act or process of washing, dressing, and grooming oneself: *She took an hour to complete her toilet.*
adj **1** used in or for a toilet: *a toilet brush.* **2** of or for use in the process of dressing and grooming: *toilet articles.* <French *toilette* cloth bag for clothes, i.e., items to do with getting dressed>

toilet paper *n* sheets of thin, soft, absorbent paper for use in a toilet, especially after passing waste matter.

toi·let·ries (toi′li trēz) *pln* items used in washing and grooming one's body. Soap and toothpaste are toiletries.

toilet tissue *n* toilet paper.

toilet training *n* the process of training a child to control bladder and bowel movements and to use a toilet. **toilet train** *v.*

toilet water *n* a fragrant liquid not so strong as perfume.

toil·some (toil′səm) *Poetic adj* involving hard or wearisome work.

to·ken (tō′kən) *n* **1** a thing, such as a word or object, that represents something abstract or unseen: *These flowers are a token of my esteem.* **2** a small disc of metal or plastic used to operate a machine or in exchange for particular goods or services: *a subway token.*
adj done for the sake of appearances or as a gesture and with no real significance: *a token payment, token resistance.* <Old English *tacen*>
by the same token, in the same way or for the same reason: *We had no reason to believe him; but, by the same token, we couldn't conclude he was lying.*

to·ken·ism (tō′kə niz′əm) *n* the practice of making only a nominal or partial effort, especially in giving jobs to people from some under-represented group in order to give the appearance of sexual or racial fairness: *Putting one woman on the board of directors was just tokenism.*

told (tōld) past tense and past participle of TELL.
all told, including all.

tole (tōl) *n* a craft that involves painting pictures on metal items used in the home. <French *tôle* sheet metal>

tol·er·a·ble (tol′ə rə bəl) *adj* **1** able to be endured: *The pain has not disappeared, but it has become tolerable.* **2** fairly good: *She is in tolerable health.* **tol′er·a·bil′i·ty** *n.* **tol′er·a·bly** *adv.*

tol·er·ance (tol′ə rəns) *n* **1** the ability or willingness to tolerate something, especially the existence of opinions or behaviour that are different from one's own. **2** the power of enduring or resisting the action of something, such as a drug, transplant, antigen, or conditions in an environment, without an adverse reaction to it. **3** an allowed amount of variation from a specified quantity, especially in the dimensions of a machine or part.

CONFUSABLES

Tolerance emphasizes respect for views, beliefs, and behaviour that are different from one's own: *Canada is noted for its tolerance of all cultures.*

Toleration suggests putting up with things, often because of indifference or to avoid conflict: *His toleration of his son's bad behaviour annoyed us.*

tol·er·ant (tol′ə rənt) *adj* **1** showing willingness to allow the existence of opinions or behaviour that are different from one's own: *A more tolerant person would not have walked out in the middle of the meeting.* **2** able to endure or resist the action of something, such as a drug, transplant, antigen, or conditions in an environment, without an adverse reaction. **tol′er·ant·ly** *adv.*

tol·er·ate (tol′ə rāt′) *v* **tol·er·at·ed, tol·er·at·ing** **1** allow and not interfere with the existence of opinions or behaviour that are different from one's own: *He tolerated the loud music coming from the next apartment.* **2** be able to endure or resist the action of something, such as a drug, transplant, antigen, or conditions in an environment, without an adverse reaction. <Latin *tolerare*> **tol′er·a′tion** *n.*

toll[1] (tōl) *n* **1** a tax or fee paid for a right or privilege, especially the use of a bridge or highway. **2** a charge for a long-distance telephone call. **3** the cost or damage resulting from something undesirable, such as the number of deaths, casualties, or injuries arising from a natural disaster, conflict, or accident. <Latin *tolonium*, from Greek *telos* tax>

toll[2] (tōl) *v* sound a bell with a slow, uniform succession of strokes as a signal or announcement, or cause a bell to make such a sound: *Bells were tolled at the Remembrance Day service. The bells tolled the death of the king.*
n the stroke or sound of a bell being tolled. <origin uncertain>

toll·booth (tōl′būth′) *n* a booth, such as at the entry to a highway or bridge, where drivers must pay to go farther.

toll–free (tōl′frē′) *adj* free of charge as a telephone number, especially one in a special series which can be dialled free of charge from anywhere: *For more information, just call our toll-free number.*
adv free of charge: *Call us toll-free and sign up today.*

toll·gate (tōl′gāt′) *n* a barrier across a road where drivers or pedestrians must pay to go farther.

toll·keep·er (tōl′kē′pər) *n* a person who collects the toll at a tollgate.

Tol·tec (tol′tek′) *n* a member of an indigenous people whose empire existed in Mexico prior to that of the Aztecs.
adj to do with this people or their culture.

tol·u·ene (tol′yū ēn′) *n* a colourless liquid hydrocarbon present in petroleum and used as a solvent.

tom (tom) *n* the male of some animals, especially a domestic cat. <*Tom*, commonly used as a male name>

tom·a·hawk (tom′ə hok′) *n* a light axe used as a tool or weapon by some First Nations and Native American peoples.
v strike or cut with a tomahawk. <Algonquian>

At one time, **tomatoes** were thought to be poisonous. Today they are the most widely grown vegetable for both household and commercial use.

to·ma·to (tə mā′tō) *n, pl* **to·ma·toes** a glossy, pulpy, red or yellow fruit commonly eaten as a vegetable, either raw or cooked. <Spanish, from Nahuatl (a language of Central and S America) *tomatl*>

tomb (tūm) *n* **1** a large vault for burying the dead, often built partly or completely above ground. **2** a monument to the memory of a dead person or people, erected over the burial place. **3** a place or situation that is extremely cold, quiet, or dark, or that forms a confining enclosure. **4 the tomb** *Poetic* death. <Greek *tymbos* mound>

tom·boy (tom′boi′) *n* a girl who enjoys rough, noisy activities traditionally associated with boys.

tomb·stone (tūm′stōn′) *n* a large, flat, inscribed stone standing or laid over a grave.

tom·cat (tom′kat′) *n* a male domestic cat.

tom·cod (tom′kod′) *n* a small N American fish of the cod family. Also, **tommy cod**.

tome (tōm) *n* a large, heavy, scholarly book. <Latin *tomus* section of a book, from Greek *tomos* volume>

tom·fool (tom′fůl′) *n* a very foolish person.
adj very foolish: *That was a tomfool thing to do.* **tom′fool′er·y** *n.*

to·mog·ra·phy (tō mog′rə fē) *n* a technique for displaying a representation of a cross-section through a human body or other solid object using X-rays or ultrasound. <Greek *tome* a section cut off + *-graphia* writing>

to·mor·row (tə mȯ′rō) *n* **1** the day after today: *You'll have to wait until tomorrow.* **2** the future, especially the near future: *the world of tomorrow.*
adv on the day after today: *We're going fishing tomorrow.* <Old English *to morgne*, from *morgen* morning>

tom–tom (tom′tom′) *n* a usually long, narrow drum beaten with the hands, especially one played by non-European tribal peoples. <Hindi *tam-tam*>

ton (tun) *n* **1** a tonne. **2 a** a nonmetric unit of mass equal to 2000 pounds, about 0.907 tonnes. Also called **short ton**. **b** a nonmetric unit of mass equal to 2240 pounds, about 1.016 tonnes. Also called **long ton**. **3 a** a unit for measuring the internal capacity of a ship, equal to 100 cubic feet, about 2.8 m^3. **b** a unit for measuring the cargo capacity of a ship, equal to 40 cubic feet, about 1.1 m^3. **c** a unit for measuring the amount of water a ship will displace, equal to 35 cubic feet, about 1 m^3. **4** *Informal* a very large number or amount: *These books weigh a ton. She's got tons of CD's.* <Middle English>

GRAMMAR AND USAGE

When measuring the mass of something, it is important to use the correct unit name **tonne**: *The machine weighed 20 tonnes.*

In informal expressions, where the exact amount doesn't matter, use **ton**: *There'll be tons of food.*

ton·al (tō′nəl) *adj* **1** to do with the tone of music, colour, writing, or speech. **2** *Music* to do with music written using conventional keys and harmony.

to·nal·i·ty (tō nal′ə tē) *n, pl* **to·nal·i·ties** **1** *Music* the character of a piece of music as determined by the key in which it is played or the relations between the notes of a scale or key. **2** the colour scheme or range of tones used in a painting or other picture.

a bat	e bed	i bid	o pot	u cup	th thin
ā cake	ē me	ī bite	ō go	ū rude	TH then
ȧ bar	ə about	ər over	ȯ for	ů put	zh measure

tone (tōn) *n* **1** the overall quality of a musical or vocal sound: *a harsh tone.* **2** the general character of a group of people, place, or event, or manner of expression: *I disliked the haughty tone of her speech.* **3 a** a musical or other sound, especially one of a definite pitch and character. **b** a particular pattern of pitches on a syllable in some languages, used to show distinctions of meaning. **4** the particular quality of brightness, deepness, or hue of a tint or shade of a colour: *tones of green.* **5** the normal level of firmness or slight contraction in a resting muscle.
v **toned, ton·ing 1** give greater strength or firmness to the body or part of it. **2** harmonize with something in terms of colour. <Latin, from Greek *tonos*>
tone down, make something less harsh, extreme, or intense: *Tone down your voice. Tone down the colours in that painting.*

tone–deaf (tōn′def′) *adj* unable to distinguish differences in musical pitch accurately.

tone language *n* a language, such as Mandarin, in which variations in pitch distinguish different words.

tone·less (tōn′ləs) *adj* lacking expression or interest as a voice or musical sound: *She spoke in a toneless voice.* **tone′less·ly** *adv.* **tone′less·ness** *n.*

ton·er (tō′nər) *n* **1** the powdered ink used in photocopiers and printers, usually in a cartridge. **2** an astringent liquid that is applied to the face to reduce oiliness and improve its condition.

Ton·ga (tong′gə) *n* a country of many small islands in the southwest Pacific. **Ton′gan** *adj, n.*

tongs (tongz) *pln* **1** a tool with two movable arms that are joined at one end, used for picking up and holding things. **2** a heated cylindrical device used for curling hair. <Old English *tonge*>

tongue (tung) *n* **1** the fleshy, muscular organ in the mouth of humans and mammals, used for tasting, licking, swallowing, and, in humans, making speech. See PALATE for picture. **2** a corresponding organ in other vertebrates and in insects, sometimes used as a scent organ and for catching food. **3** a person's style or manner of speaking: *a flattering tongue.* **4** a particular language: *the English tongue.* **5** a thing resembling a tongue, such as the strip of material under the laces of a shoe or a narrow strip of land running out into water.
v **tongued, tongu·ing 1** sound a note distinctly on a wind instrument by interrupting the air flow with the tongue. **2** lick or caress with the tongue. <Old English *tunge*>
bite your tongue, stop yourself with difficulty from saying something.
find (or **lose**) **your tongue,** be able (or unable) to express yourself after being surprised or uncomfortable.
hold your tongue, keep silent.
on the tip of your tongue, on the verge of being remembered.
tongue in cheek, not really meaning what you are saying.

tongue–and–groove (tung′ən grūv′) *adj* to do with wooden boards that are joined by means of interlocking ridges and hollows down their sides.

tongue–lash·ing (tung′lash′ing) *n* a severe scolding: *Her mother gave her a tongue-lashing for letting her ice cream drip all over the carpet.* **tongue-′lash′** *v.*

tongue–tied (tung′tīd′) *adj* **1** unable to speak because of shyness or embarrassment. **2** with the motion of the tongue hindered or limited because the membrane that connects its lower side to the bottom of the mouth is abnormally short.

tongue twister *n* a sequence of words or sounds, typically using alliteration, that is difficult to say quickly and correctly. Example: *She sells seashells on the seashore.*

ton·ic (ton′ik) *n* **1** a thing that gives a feeling of vigour or well-being, such as a substance taken as medicine to bring this about. **2** *Music* the first note in a scale that provides the keynote of a piece of music. **3** tonic water.
adj **1** giving a feeling of vigour and well-being: *The mountain air was tonic.* **2** *Music* to do with the keynote. <Latin, from Greek *tonos* tone>

tonic water *n* a carbonated soft drink with a bittersweet flavour.

to·night (tə nīt′) *adv* on the present or approaching evening or night: *I want to get to bed early tonight. She is arriving tonight at eight o'clock.*
n the present or approaching evening or night: *I wish tonight were here now.* <Old English *to niht*>

ton·nage (tun′ij) *n* **1** the weight in tons, especially of the cargo or freight of a ship. **2** ships in terms of their total carrying capacity or the total amount carried: *navy tonnage.*

tonne (tun) *n* a unit of mass, equal to 1000 kilograms. *Symbol* **t**. Also called **metric ton**. <French>

ton·sil (ton′səl) *n* either of two oval masses of lymphoid tissue in the throat, one on each side of the root of the tongue. See PALATE for picture. <Latin *tonsillae*>

ton·sil·lec·to·my (ton′sə lek′tə mē) *n,*
pl **ton·sil·lec·to·mies** the removal of the tonsils by surgery.

ton·sil·li·tis (ton′sə lī′tis) *n* inflammation of the tonsils.

ton·so·ri·al (ton sȯ′rē əl) *adj* to do with hairdressing or a barber's work.

ton·sure (ton′shər) *n* a part of a monk's or priest's head left bare on top by shaving off the hair, or the act of shaving this part when someone enters a religious order.
v **ton·sured, ton·sur·ing** shave the hair on the crown of a head. <Latin *tondere* shave>

ton·y (tō′nē) *adj* **ton·i·er, ton·i·est** stylish and elegant and, usually, expensive: *a tony restaurant.*

too (tū) *adv* **1** to a higher degree than is desirable, allowable, or possible: *That sweater is too big for you. He ate too much. The summer passed too quickly.* **2** also or besides: *The dog is hungry, and thirsty too.* **3** very or exceedingly: *I am only too glad to help you.* **4** (*used to contradict a negative statement*) indeed or definitely: "*I didn't take the last cookie.*" "*You did too!*" See TO for confusables. <Old English>

took (tůk) past tense of TAKE.

tool (tūl) *n* **1 a** a device or implement, especially one held in the hand, used to carry out a particular task: *plumbers' tools.* **b** *Computers* an application program, often one that makes or manipulates other programs. Spell-checkers are tools. An application that can perform multiple tasks is called **tool software**. **2** a thing used or needed in an occupation or pursuit: *Books were essential research tools to her.* **3** a person used or exploited by another: *He is a tool of the departmental boss.*

v **1** equip or be equipped with tools for industrial production: *The factory was tooled to manufacture a different product line.* **2** impress a design on leather, especially a leather book cover. **3** *Informal* drive or ride in a casual or leisurely way: *He tooled around in his new car.* <Old English *tol*>

tool·bar (tül′bår′) *Computers n* a program that is displayed in the form of a strip of icons used to perform various functions.

tool·box (tül′boks′) *n* a box or container for tools.

tool chest *n* a large toolbox with a lid.

tool·ing (tü′ling) *n* the ornamentation of leather with designs impressed by using heated tools.

tool·kit (tül′kit′) **1** a set of tools, especially one kept in a bag or box and used for a particular purpose. **2** *Computers* a set of software tools. Also, **tool kit**.

tool·shed (tül′shed′) *n* a small building to hold tools used in yards and gardens.

toon (tün) *Informal n* a cartoon film, or a character in such a film. <*cartoon*>

❋ **toon·ie** or **toon·y** (tü′nē) *n, pl* **toon·ies** the Canadian two-dollar coin. <*two* + *-nie* from *loonie*>

toot (tüt) *n* a short, sharp sound, made by a horn.

v sound a horn or similar instrument with a short, sharp sound, or make such a sound: *He heard the train toot three times. She tooted as she drove past the house.* <probably imitative> **toot′er** *n.*

tooth (tüth) *n, pl* **teeth** **1** **a** one of a set of small, hard, bony, enamel-coated structures in the jaws of most verbetrates, used for biting and chewing. **b** a similar hard, pointed structure in invertebrate animals. **2** an appetite or liking for a particular thing: *a sweet tooth.* **3** a projecting part on a tool or other object, such as a cog on a gearwheel or a point on a comb. See WISDOM TOOTH for picture. <Old English *toth*> **tooth′like** *adj.*

armed to the teeth, equipped with many weapons.

by the skin of your teeth, very narrowly or barely: *He escaped by the skin of his teeth.*

fight tooth and nail, fight fiercely.

grit (or **set**) **your teeth,** prepare to endure something without complaining.

in the teeth of, in spite of or contrary to opposition or difficulty: *He advanced in the teeth of the gale.*

long in the tooth, *Informal* elderly.

put (**some**) **teeth into,** put force into: *They need regular inspections and stiff penalties to put teeth into those food regulations.*

sink (or **get**) **your teeth into,** *Informal* be pleasantly challenged and engrossed by: *This is a book you can really sink your teeth into.*

tooth·ache (tü′thāk′) *n* a pain in a tooth or the teeth.

tooth·brush (tüth′brush′) *n* a small brush for cleaning the teeth.

toothed (tütht) *or* (tüᴛʜd) *adj* **1** (*often in compounds*) with teeth, especially of a certain kind or number: *a fine-toothed comb.* **2** notched or indented: *a toothed blade.*

toothed whale *n* a whale with teeth, rather than baleen plates, that hunts for food. Killer whales are toothed whales.

tooth fairy *n* a fairy said to leave money in exchange for a child's first teeth when these fall out.

tooth·less (tü′thlis) *adj* **1** without teeth. **2** lacking force or effectiveness: *toothless laws.*

tooth·paste (tüth′pāst′) *n* a thick, soft, moist substance used on a brush for cleaning the teeth.

tooth·pick (tüth′pik′) *n* a small, short, pointed or rounded piece of wood or plastic used for removing bits of food from between the teeth.

tooth·some (tüth′səm) *adj* temptingly tasty.

tooth·y (tü′thē) *adj* **tooth·i·er, tooth·i·est** with or showing large, numerous, or prominent teeth: *a toothy grin.*

top[1] (top) *n* **1** the highest or uppermost point, part, or surface of something: *the top of a mountain.* **2** a garment covering the upper part of the body, or a lid, cover, or cap for something: *carrot tops.* **3** the highest or most important rank, level, or position: *He is at the top of his class. She is top in her profession.*

adj highest in position, rank, or degree: *the top shelf, at top speed, top honours.*

v **topped, top·ping** **1** exceed an amount, level, or number: *The profit topped a million dollars.* **2** be at the highest or most important place or position: *The windmill topped the hill.* **3** provide with a top or topping: *The sundae was topped with whipped cream.* **4** remove the top of a plant. <Old English *topp*>

from top to bottom, completely or thoroughly.

off the top, taken out of the gross amount before other deductions or expenses: *He saves $30 off the top of every paycheque.*

off the top of your head, without preparation or previous thought.

on top, **a** on the highest point or uppermost surface: *Her hat had a feather on top.* **b** in the leading or dominant position.

over the top, *Informal* **a** to an undue or exaggerated degree: *We thought his comments were over the top.* **b** over a target or limit: *We aimed for fifty subscriptions to our magazine, but we went over the top and collected sixty.*

top up, refill.

top[2] (top) *n* a rounded or cone-shaped toy with a point at one end on which it is made to spin. <Old English *topp*>

to·paz (tō′paz) *n* a gemstone that is a silicate of aluminum, typically brownish, yellow, colourless, or pale blue. <Greek *topazos*>

a bat	e bed	i bid	o pot	u cup	th thin
ā cake	ē me	ī bite	ō go	ū rude	ᴛʜ then
å bar	ə about	ər over	ȯ for	u̇ put	zh measure

top brass *Informal pln* the highest-ranking officers or officials; the top level of management.

top·coat (top′kōt′) *n* an overcoat, especially a lightweight one.

top dog *Informal n* the best, most successful, or most important person or group.

top dollar *Informal n* a great amount of money paid or earned for something.

top drawer *Informal n* the highest social position or class.

top dressing *n* a layer of manure, compost, or fertilizer spread on garden soil or farmland. **top′-dress′** *v.*

tope (tōp) *v* **toped, top·ing** take too many alcoholic drinks, especially on a regular basis. <origin uncertain> **top′er** *n.*

top–flight (top′flīt′) *adj* the highest rank or level.

top gun *Informal n* the best person or thing in a group.

During the 1800s, **top hats** were made of beaver pelts, which had been exported to England and France by Canadian fur trading companies.

top hat *n* a tall, black silk hat worn with formal clothes.

top–heav·y (top′hev′ē) *adj* **1** too heavy at the top, so as to be in danger of toppling: *The load was top-heavy and soon fell off.* **2** with too many people in senior administrative positions in an organization.

to·pi·ar·y (tō′pē er′ē) *n, pl* **to·pi·ar·ies** the art or practice of trimming shrubs or trees into figures or designs, or the shrubs or trees trimmed in this way. <Latin *topia* fancy gardening>

top·ic (top′ik) *n* a subject or matter that people deal with when they think, write, or talk: *The main topics at the dinner party were the weather and the election.* <Latin, from Greek *topika* matters concerning>

top·i·cal (top′ə kəl) *adj* **1** of current or immediate relevance, interest, or importance: *a discussion of topical events.* **2** to do with a particular subject: *topical outlines.* **3** applied directly to a part of the body as part of a medical treatment: *topical ointment.*

topic sentence *n* a sentence used to summarize the main idea in a paragraph.

top·knot (top′not′) *n* a knot of hair or decorative material on the top of the head, or a tuft or crest of hair or feathers on the head of a bird or animal.

top·less (top′ləs) *adj* **1** with, leaving, or involving no clothes on the upper part of the body. **2** so high or tall that the top cannot be seen: *topless mountains.*

top·most (top′mōst′) *adj* highest or uppermost.

top–notch (top′noch′) *Informal adj* of the highest quality.

to·pog·ra·phy (tə pog′rə fē) *n, pl* **to·pog·ra·phies** **1** the arrangement of the natural and artificial physical features of an area. **2** a detailed description or representation on a map of such features. <Greek *topos* place + *graphein* write> **to′pog′raph·er** *n.* **top′o·graph′ic** *adj.* **top′o·graph′i·cal** *adj.* **top′o·graph′i·cal·ly** *adv.*

to·pol·o·gy (tə pol′ə jē) *n, pl* **to·pol·o·gies** **1** *Mathematics* the study of such properties of geometrical figures and solids that are not affected by changes in size or shape. **2** the way in which the parts of a thing are interrelated or arranged. <Greek *topos* place + *graphein* write> **top′o·log′i·cal** *adj.* **top′o·log′i·cal·ly** *adv.* **to′pol′o·gist** *n.*

top·ping (top′ing) *n* a layer of food poured or spread over a base of a different type of food: *The cake had a crumb topping.*

top·ple (top′əl) *v* **top·pled, top·pling** overbalance or become unsteady and fall down, or cause to fall in this way: *The chimney toppled over on the roof. The angry mob toppled the statue.* <*top*[1], (v)>

tops (tops) *Informal adj* (*never before a noun*) of the highest or best quality or rank: *She's tops in her field.*
n **the tops** an excellent person or thing of its kind: *You're the tops!*

top–se·cret (top′sē′krit) *adj* of utmost secrecy: *top-secret information. The file was labelled top-secret.*

top·soil (top′soil′) *n* the top layer of soil, suitable for growing plants in.

top·stitch (top′stich′) *v* make a decorative row of continuous stitches on the top or right side of a garment or other item. **top′stitch′ing** *n.*

top·sy–tur·vy (top′sē tər′vē) *adv, adj* **1** upside down. **2** in confusion or disorder: *Her room was always topsy-turvy because she never put anything away.*
n, pl **top·sy–tur·vies** a condition of confusion or disorder. <origin uncertain>

toque (tōk) *n* **1** a small hat with a narrow, turned-up brim. **2** TUQUE.

tor (tôr) *n* a high, bare, rocky hill or peak. <Celtic>

To·rah or **To·ra** (tô′rə) *Judaism n* the law of God revealed to Moses and recorded in the Hebrew scriptures. <Hebrew>

torch (tôrch) *n* **1** a light made from a piece of wood or cloth soaked in fuel and carried or stuck in a holder on a wall as illumination or as part of a ceremony. **2** a device for producing a very hot flame, used especially to burn off paint or to solder or melt metal. <Old French *torche*, probably Latin *torquere* twist. Torches were made by twisting a rag to make a wick.>

torch·bear·er (tôrch′ber′ər) *n* **1** a person who carries a ceremonial torch. **2** a person who leads or inspires others in working toward a valued goal.

tor·chere (tôr shār′) *n* a tall, flat-topped stand for holding a candlestick or lamp. <Old French *torche* torch>

tor·chi·ere (tôr shē ār′) *n* a tall lamp, with its base on the floor, whose shade casts light upward. <*torchère*>

torch·light (tôrch′līt′) *n* the light of a torch or torches. **torch′lit** *adj.*

torch song *n* a popular sad or sentimental song about unrequited love.

tore (tòr) past tense of TEAR².

tor·e·a·dor (tò′rē ə dòr′) *n* a bullfighter, especially one on horseback.

tor·ment (tòr ment′) *for v,* (tòr′ment) *for n.* *v* **1** cause or experience severe mental or physical suffering: *Headaches tormented him.* **2** annoy or provoke in a deliberately unkind way: *He torments everyone with silly questions.*
n severe physical or mental suffering, or the cause of such suffering: *He suffered torments from his aching teeth. The loss of his family was an ongoing torment to him.* <Old French, from Latin *tormentum* instrument of torture> **tor·ment′ed** *adj.* **tor·ment′ing** *adj.*
tor·ment′ing·ly *adv.* **tor·ment′or** or **tor·ment′er** *n.*

SYNONYMS

Torment implies hurting or annoying repeatedly: *Have you come to torment me with another complaint?*

Annoy means "disturb" or "make angry": *His foolish question annoyed me.*

Torture means "inflict severe pain," especially to get someone to do or say something: *The soldiers denied that they had tortured the captives.*

Persecute emphasizes pursuing or harassing in order to harm, and often refers to large groups: *The enemies of the villagers have persecuted them for decades.*

torn (tòrn) *v* past participle of TEAR².

tor·na·do (tòr nā′dō) *n, pl* **tor·na·does** or **tor·na·dos** a destructive, violently rotating wind that is seen as a funnel-shaped cloud that advances beneath a large storm system. <origin uncertain>

tor·pe·do (tòr pē′dō) *n, pl* **tor·pe·does** **1** a large, cigar-shaped metal tube fired from a ship or submarine or dropped into the water from an aircraft and that explodes on reaching its target: *an enemy torpedo.* **2** an explosive put on a railway track that makes a loud noise for a signal when a wheel of the engine runs over it. **3** a firework that explodes when it is thrown against something hard. **4** an electric ray, a fish.
v **tor·pe·doed, tor·pe·do·ing** **1** attack or destroy with a torpedo. **2** destroy or ruin a plan or project. <Latin *torpere* be numb>

torpedo boat *n* a small, fast, light warship designed for firing torpedoes.

tor·pid (tòr′pid) *adj* **1** mentally or physically inactive or sluggish: *a torpid mind.* **2** dormant, especially as a hibernating animal. <Latin *torpere* be numb> **tor′pid·i·ty** *n.* **tor′pid·ly** *adv.* **tor′pid·ness** *n.*

tor·por (tòr′pər) *n* a condition of physical or mental inactivity or sluggishness.

torque (tòrk) *n* a physical force that produces rotation, such as in the engine of a vehicle. <Latin *torquere* twisted>

torque wrench *n* a tool with a meter or gauge for setting and adjusting the tightness of nuts and bolts to a desired value.

tor·rent (tò′rənt) *n* **1** a strong and fast-flowing stream of water or other liquid or melted substance: *a torrent of rain.* **2** a sudden, violent outpouring of something, typically words or feelings: *a torrent of abuse.* <French, from Latin *torrentem* a rushing stream> **tor·ren′tial** *adj.* **tor·ren′tial·ly** *adv.*

tor·rid (tò′rid) *adj* **1** very hot and dry: *a torrid climate.* **2** passionate or intense: *torrid love letters.* <Latin *torrere* parch> **tor′rid′i·ty** *n.* **tor′rid·ly** *adv.*

tor·sion (tòr′shən) *n* the action of twisting or the condition of being twisted, especially of one end of an object in relation to the other. <Latin *torquere* twist> **tor′sion·al** *adj.*

tor·so (tòr′sō) *n, pl* **tor·sos** the trunk of a human body without a head, arms, or legs. <Italian *torso* trunk of a statue, from Greek *thyrsos* plant stalk>

tort (tòrt) *n* a wrongful action or a violation of a right, other than that under a contract, for which the law imposes penalties. <Latin *tortum* injustice>

torte (tòrt) *or* (tòr′tə) *n, pl* **tortes** or **torten** (tòr′tən) a rich, sweet cake or tart with a filling and topping. <Latin *torta* flat cake>

tor·tel·li·ni (tòr′tə lē′nē) *n* pasta in the form of small, curved, pouchlike pieces filled with cheese, meat, or vegetables. <See TORTE.>

tor·til·la (tòr tē′yə) *n* a thin, flat, round corn or wheat Mexican pancake, often with a filling. <Spanish, from Latin *torta* flat cake>

tortilla chip *n* a small, crisp, usually triangular and often spicy piece of unleavened cornmeal bread, eaten as a snack.

tor·toise (tòr′təs) *n, pl* **tor·tois·es** or (*especially collectively*) **tor·toise** a slow-moving, usually plant-eating reptile of warm climates that has a scaly or leathery shell into which it can retract its head and thick legs. Compare TURTLE. <Latin *tortuca*>

tor·toise·shell (tòr′təs shel′) *or* (tòr′tə shel′) *n* **1** the mottled yellow-and-brown shell of some turtles, used to make jewellery or ornaments, or an artificial substitute for it. **2** a cat or butterfly with mottled colours like those of tortoiseshell.

tor·tu·ous (tòr′chū əs) *adj* **1** full of twists, turns, and bends: *a tortuous path.* **2** unduly long and complex: *tortuous reasoning.* <Latin *torquere* twist>
tor′tu·ous·ly *adv.* **tor′tu·ous·ness** *n.*

tor·ture (tòr′chər) *n* **1** the action or practice of inflicting severe pain on someone as a punishment or in order to force them to do or say something. **2** extreme physical or mental suffering or anxiety, or the cause of it: *She suffered torture from migraine headaches.*
v **tor·tured, tor·tur·ing** **1** inflict severe pain or suffering on: *He tortured bugs when he was small.* **2** twist the meaning of. <Latin *torquere* twist> **tor′tur·er** *n.*

a bat	e bed	i bid	o pot	u cup	th **thin**
ā cake	ē me	ī bite	ō go	ū rude	ᴛʜ **then**
ȧ bar	ə about	ər over	ȯ for	u̇ put	zh measure

T

To·ry (tô′rē) *n, pl* **Tor·ies** 1 a member or supporter of a Conservative party. 2 *US* during the American Revolution, a person who supported continued allegiance to Britain.
adj to do with Tories or their policies: *a strong Tory opposition.* <Irish *tóraí* outlaw, from *toír* pursuit> **To′ry·ism** *n.*

toss (tos) *v* 1 throw something somewhere lightly, easily, or casually: *to toss a ball.* 2 move from side to side, back and forth, or up and down: *The ship was tossed by the heavy waves, to toss a salad, to toss in bed.* 3 jerk one's head or hair. 4 throw a coin to decide something by the side that falls upward.
n the act or fact of tossing something. <origin uncertain>
toss off, a do or make quickly and easily. b drink all at once.

toss–up (tos′up′) *n* 1 a tossing of a coin to decide between two alternatives. 2 a situation in which any of two or more outcomes or options is equally possible or equally attractive: *It was a toss-up whether he or his twin sister would get the nomination for class valedictorian.*

tos·ta·da (tō stod′ə) *n* a crisply fried tortilla. Also, **tostado**. <Spanish = fried>

tot (tot) *n* 1 a very young child. 2 a small portion of alcoholic liquor.

to·tal (tō′təl) *adj* 1 consisting of the whole number or amount: *The total cost of the books will be $150.* 2 complete: *The lights went out and we were in total darkness.*
n the whole number or amount of something: *Her expenses reached a total of $200.*
v **to·talled** or **to·taled, to·tal·ling** or **to·tal·ing** 1 amount in number to: *The cost totalled much more than we thought.* 2 *Informal* damage beyond repair: *Her car was totalled in the accident.* <Latin *totus* all>

to·tal·i·tar·i·an (tō tal′ə ter′ē ən) *adj* to do with a system of government that is centralized, under the total control of a dictator, and absolute obedience of citizens to the state.
n a person who supports or practises this system. **to·tal′i·tar′i·an·ism** *n.*

to·tal·i·ty (tō tal′ə tē) *n, pl* **to·tal·i·ties** 1 the whole of something. 2 the total eclipse of the sun or moon or the period during which this takes place.

to·tal·ly (tō′tə lē) *adv* completely: *He was totally exhausted. The experiment was totally successful.*

total recall *n* the ability to remember clearly every detail about an experience or situation in the past.

total war *n* a war that is unrestricted in terms of the weapons and tactics used, the area or fighters involved, and the resources of a nation employed.

tote (tōt) *Informal v* **tot·ed, tot·ing** carry or convey something heavy or awkward: *I had to tote all the stuff home by myself.* <origin uncertain>

tote bag *n* a large bag used for carrying a number of items.

to·tem (tō′təm) *n* a natural object or animal that is believed by a particular culture to have spiritual significance and that is adopted by it as an emblem, or a representation of it. <Algonquian> **to·tem′ic** *adj.*

to·tem·ism (tō′tə miz′əm) *n* 1 belief in a mystical relationship or kinship between human beings and animals and plants, usually taking the form of a special reverence felt by a people or a person for particular creatures or objects. 2 the use of totems to distinguish tribes, clans, or families. **to′tem·ist** *n.* **to′tem·ist′ic** *adj.* **to′tem·ist′i·cal·ly** *adv.*

totem pole *n* a pole on which totems are hung or on which the images of totems are carved.

tot·ter (tot′ər) *v* 1 walk with shaky, unsteady steps: *The baby tottered three steps all by herself.* 2 tremble, shake, or rock as if about to collapse: *The old wall tottered in the storm and fell.* 3 be insecure or about to collapse: *The old regime was already tottering before the revolution broke out.*
n a feeble or unsteady way of walking. <origin uncertain>
tot′ter·er *n.* **tot′ter·y** *adj.*

The enormous beak of the **toucan** is actually light in weight, with the upper half prominently saw-toothed. The toucan uses the tip of its bill to harvest small berries and fruit, its chief diet.

tou·can (tū′kan) *n* a tropical American bird with a huge bill and brightly coloured feathers.

touch (tuch) *v* 1 come so close to an object as to be in contact with it: *Both ends of the wires touched.* 2 bring one's hand or another part of one's body into contact with: *She touched the pan to see whether it was still hot.* 3 affect with some feeling: *The sad story touched us.* 4 handle in order to affect, especially in an adverse way: *Don't touch my stuff.* 5 have an effect on or make a difference to: *The matter touches your interest.* 6 speak of or deal with: *Our conversation touched many subjects.* 7 reach or come up to: *His head almost touches the top of the doorway. Nobody in our class can touch her in music.*
n 1 an act of bringing a part of one's body, typically one's hand or fingers, into contact with someone or something: *The bubble burst at my touch.* 2 the ability to perceive through physical contact, especially with the fingers: *Braille is read by touch.* 3 a small amount or trace of something: *Put a touch more pepper on the potatoes. We had a touch of frost.* 4 communication: *A newspaper keeps you in touch with the world. He has been out of touch with his mother since he left home.* 5 a distinctive style or manner: *The pianist had an excellent touch. The work showed an expert's touch.* 6 *Soccer, Rugby* the area beyond the sidelines and out of play. <Old French, from Latin *toccare* to strike> **touch′a·ble** *adj.* **touch′er** *n.*
in (or **out of**) **touch** (**with**) a in (or out of) communication. b having up-to-date knowledge.
touch down, land an aircraft.
touch off, bring about: *The new tax touched off a rebellion.*
touch up, change a little so as to improve: *She touched up a photograph.*

touch–and–go (tuch′ən gō′) *adj* possible but very uncertain: *So far it's been touch-and-go, but we're still hoping for the best.*

touch·down (tuch′doun′) *n* **1** the moment at which an aircraft's wheels or part of a spacecraft makes contact with the ground during landing: *five minutes before touchdown.* **2** *Football, Rugby* the act of touching the ground with the ball behind the opponents' goal line, resulting in a score, or a score made in this way.

tou·ché (tū shā′) *n* a touch by an opponent's weapon in fencing.
interj an exclamation acknowledging a clever reply or a point well made in a debate. <French>

touch football *n* a form of football, usually played informally and without protective equipment, in which the person carrying the ball is touched rather than tackled.

touch·hole (tuch′hōl′) *n* a small hole in early firearms through which the charge was ignited.

touch·ing (tuch′ing) *adj* arousing tender feelings: *Our teacher read us a touching story about an orphaned bear cub.*

touch·pad (tuch′pad) *Computers adj* a soft pad used especially on laptops as an alternative to a mouse. Also called **trackpad**.

touch·screen (tuch′skrēn′) *Computers adj* a specially adapted screen covered with a membrane sensitive to touch, as an alternative to a mouse.

touch·stone (tuch′stōn′) *n* **1** a test or standard for determining the genuineness or value of something: *His work has for many years been the touchstone of excellence in architecture.* **2** a fine-grained dark stone formerly used to test the purity of gold or silver by the colour of the streak on the stone after it was rubbed with the metal.

Touch–Tone (tuch′tōn′) *Trademark adj* to do with the type of phone that has numbered buttons that are pushed to dial.

touch typing *n* a method of keyboarding without looking at the keyboard by always using a particular finger to strike a particular key. **touch′ type′** *v.*

touch·y (tuch′ē) *adj* **touch·i·er, touch·i·est** **1** irritable and apt to take offence easily: *I'm tired and very touchy this afternoon.* **2** requiring careful handling: *a touchy situation, a touchy topic.* **touch′i·ly** *adv.* **touch′i·ness** *n.*

touch·y–feel·y (tu′chē fē′lē) *Informal adj* openly expressing affection or other gentle emotions, especially through physical contact.

tough (tuf) *adj* **1** strong enough to withstand adverse conditions or rough handling: *tough leather.* **2 a** able to endure hardship or pain: *He was tough enough to take a lot of punishment.* **b** able to protect one's own interests against the opposition of others: *She's tough and self-reliant.* **3** difficult to cut or chew: *The steak was so tough he couldn't eat it.* **4** showing a strict and uncompromising attitude or approach: *The police were tough on drunk drivers.* **5** involving difficulty or hardship, and requiring determination or effort: *a tough course.* **6** hard to influence or convince: *a tough client.* **7** rough or disorderly: *We lived in a tough neighbourhood.*
n a rough or violent person. <Old English *toh*>
tough′ly *adv.* **tough′ness** *n.*
tough it out, *Informal* endure a difficulty bravely or patiently to the end.

SYNONYMS

Tough sometimes means "rough" or "disorderly": *The principal has to talk to these tough gangs.*

Brutal emphasizes cruelty: *The brutal tyrant was overthrown by the people he had persecuted.*

Ruthless suggests a lack of pity or mercy: *She is a ruthless judge when she deals with murderers.*

Vicious implies deliberate malice: *Everyone was shocked at the columnist's unfair and vicious attack on the singer's reputation.*

tough·en (tuf′ən) *v* make or become tough or tougher: *She decided to toughen her muscles by doing regular exercises. His muscles gradually toughened.*

tough love *n* the promotion of a person's welfare, especially that of an addict, child, or criminal, by showing firm discipline and giving clear rules and expectations.

tou·pee (tū pā′) *n* a small wig or patch of false hair worn to cover a bald spot. <Old French *toupe* tuft>

tour (tūr) *n* **1** a journey for pleasure in which several different places are visited: *a European tour.* **2** a short trip to or through a place in order to view or inspect something. **3** a journey made by performers or a sports team, in which they perform or play in several different places: *The troupe went on a tour of several cities in the Central Canada.* **4** a spell of duty on military or diplomatic service.
v **1** make or take a tour of an area: *Last year they toured the Sunshine Coast.* **2** briefly visit to view or inspect: *The students will tour the museum in the afternoon.* <French, from Greek *tornos* lathe>

tour de force (tūr′də fôrs′) *n* a performance or achievement that has been accomplished or managed with great skill: *The magician's performance was a tour de force.*

tour·ism (tū′riz′əm) *n* the commercial organization and operation of holidays and visits to places of interest.

tour·ist (tū′rist) *n* a person who travels or visits a place or places for pleasure.
adj of or for tourists: *the tourist industry.*

tourist class *n* the cheapest class of accommodation for passengers on a ship or aircraft, or at a hotel.

tourist trap *Informal n* a place or business establishment that exploits tourists.

tour·ma·line (tůr′mə lin) *or* (tůr′mə lēn′) *n* a brittle mineral that occurs as crystals, sometimes used for gemstones.

T

a bat	e bed	i bid	o pot	u cup	th **thin**
ā cake	ē me	ī bite	ō go	ū rude	ᴛʜ **then**
à bar	ə about	ər over	ô for	ů put	zh measure

tour·na·ment (tər′nə mənt) *or* (tůr′nə mənt) *n* **1** a series of contests testing the skill of many people in a sport or game: *a golf tournament, a chess tournament.* **2** *Archaic* a contest in the Middle Ages between two groups of knights on horseback who jousted with blunted weapons, each trying to knock the other off his horse so as to win a prize. <Old French *torneier* to fight on horseback>

tour·ney (tər′nē) *or* (tůr′nē) *Archaic n, pl* **tour·neys** a tournament.
v **tour·neyed, tour·ney·ing** take part in a tournament.

tour·ni·quet (tůr′nə ket′) *or* (tůr′nə kā′) *n* a device for stopping the flow of blood through an artery, such as a bandage tightened by twisting with a stick. <French *tourner* to turn>

🍁 **tour·ti·ere** (tůr tyer′) *n* a pie made with ground pork seasoned with spices, originally made in French Canada. <Cdn French>

tou·sle (tou′zəl) *v* **tou·sled, tou·sling** make something, especially a person's hair, untidy: *She tousled her brother's hair to tease him.* <Middle English *tousen*>

tout (tout) *Informal v* **1** attempt to sell something, or persuade someone of something, typically in an aggressive or bold way. **2** spy on the movements and condition of a racehorse in training in order to gain information to be used when betting.
n a person who touts. <Middle English *tutan* peep out> **tout′er** *n.*

tow[1] (tō) *v* **1** pull a motor vehicle or boat along a rope, chain, or tow bar: *The tug is towing three barges.* **2** pull someone or something behind one: *She was towing her child down the supermarket aisle.*
n **1** the act or fact of towing or being towed: *Some companies charge far too much for a tow.* **2** a rope or line used to tow something. <Old English *togian* drag> **tow′a·ble** *adj.*
in tow, a being towed by another vehicle or boat: *The launch had a sailboat in tow.* **b** accompanying or following someone: *The movie producer arrived at the reception with several admirers in tow.*

tow[2] (tō) *n* the coarse fibres of flax or hemp, prepared for spinning: *This string is made of tow.* **tow′y** *adj.*

tow·age (tō′ij) *n* **1** the action or process of towing. **2** a charge for towing.

to·ward (tə wôrd′) *prep* **1** in the direction of: *She walked toward the north.* **2** regarding or concerning: *What is your attitude toward war?* **3** contributing to the cost of something: *Will you give something toward the new hospital?* Also, **towards.** <Old English *toweard*>

tow·boat (tō′bōt′) *n* a tugboat.

tow·el (tou′əl) *n* a piece of thick, absorbent cloth or paper used for drying oneself or wiping things dry.
v **tow·elled** or **tow·eled, tow·el·ling** or **tow·el·ing** wipe or dry a person or thing with a towel. <Old French *toaille*>
throw (or **toss**) **in the towel,** *Informal* admit defeat.

tow·el·ette (tou′ə let′) *n* a small piece of paper or other material, usually moistened, used for wiping the hands after eating or for refreshing the face.

tow·el·ling or **tow·el·ing** (tou′ə ling) *n* thick absorbent cloth, typically cotton with uncut loops, used for towels and robes.

tow·er (tou′ər) *n* **1** a tall, narrow building, often forming part of a building such as a church or castle: *a lookout tower, a bell tower, a water tower.* **2** a very tall building, especially a highrise: *an office tower.* **3** a tall pile or mass of something: *a tower of tires.*
v rise to or reach a great height: *The girl towered over her baby brother. A mountain towered over the village.* <Latin *turris* high structure> **tow′ered** *adj.*
tower of strength, a person who or thing that acts as a defence, protection, or support: *She proved to be a tower of strength during the emergency.*

tow·er·ing (tou′ə ring) *adj* **1** extremely tall, especially in comparison with the surroundings: *a towering peak, a towering basketball player.* **2** of exceptional importance, influence, or force: *He said that making electricity from atomic power was a towering achievement, a towering rage.*

tow·head (tō′hed′) *n* a person with white blonde hair, or a head of this hair. <Old English *tow*[2] flax + *head,* from the colour of the fibre> **tow′head·ed** *adj.*

tow·hee (tou′hē) *or* (tō′hē) *n* a N American songbird with brownish plumage. <imitative of its call>

tow·line (tō′līn′) *n* a rope, cable, etc. used in towing.

town (toun) *n* **1** an urban area with a name, defined boundaries, and local government, that is larger than a village and smaller than a city. **2** a densely populated area, especially as contrasted with the country or the suburbs. **3** the people of this area: *The whole town was having a holiday.* **4** the central part of a neighbourhood with its business or shopping area: *She drove into town on some errands.* **5** a TOWNSHIP (def. 1). <Old English *tun*>
go to town, *Informal* do something thoroughly, enthusiastically, or extravagantly: *The hungry girls really went to town on that pie.*
on the town, out for entertainment and pleasure as available in a city or town.
paint the town red, *Informal* celebrate lavishly.

town crier *n* in former times, a person employed to make public announcements in the streets or marketplace of a town.

town hall *n* **1** a building used for the administration of local government. **2** a local public meeting, especially one sponsored by a government or the media, to discuss an important topic.

town·house (toun′hous′) *n* a tall, narrow house that is one of a row of attached houses two or more storeys high, each with its own entrance from the street.

towns·folk (tounz′fōk′) *pl n* the people of a town.

town·ship (toun′ship) *n* **1** *Canada, US* a division of a county with certain powers of government; a municipality. **2** *especially Western Canada, US* an area of 36 square miles (about 93 km^2), divided into 36 sections.

towns·peo·ple (tounz′pē′pəl) *pl n* the people of a town.

tow·path (tō′path′) *n* a path along the bank of a canal or river for use in towing barges.

tow·rope (tō′rōp′) *n* a towline.

Most **tow trucks** have an attachment that slides under the front wheels of a vehicle so the front end can be safely and securely lifted.

tow truck *n* a truck equipped for towing away disabled or illegally parked vehicles.

tox·e·mi·a (tok sē′mē ə) *n* a form of blood poisoning by toxins from a bacterial infection. Also, **toxaemia**. **tox·e′mic** *adj.*

tox·ic (tok′sik) *adj* to do with or caused by poison: *a toxic reaction.* <Latin *toxicum* poison, from Greek *toxon* bow, from its use as a poison on arrows> **tox′i·cal·ly** *adv.* **tox·ic′i·ty** (tok sis′ə tē) *n.*

tox·i·col·o·gy (tok′sə kol′ə jē) *n* the branch of science that studies the nature, effects, and detection of poisons. **tox′i·co·log′i·cal** *adj.* **tox′i·co·log′i·cal·ly** *adv.* **tox′i·col′o·gist** *n.*

toxic waste *n* household or industrial waste needing special disposal because it contains chemicals that may harm humans or the environment, such as discarded paint and dead batteries.

tox·in (tok′sən) *n* a poison or venom produced by a plant or animal, especially one produced by bacteria.

toy (toi) *n* **1** an object for a child to play with, typically a model or miniature version of something: *His toys are all over the living room again.* **2** an object regarded as providing amusement for an adult: *An all-terrain vehicle was just a toy to my uncle.*
n **1** made for use as a toy, especially being a small model of an actual thing: *a toy truck, a toy soldier.* **2** to do with a very small breed of dog, such as a chihuahua.
v **1** (*with* ***with***) consider an idea, belief, or proposal casually or indecisively: *She has been toying with the idea of writing a book but so far has not done anything about it.* **2** move or handle an object, or do something, absent-mindedly or nervously: *She toyed with her bracelet as she talked.* <origin uncertain> **toy′like′** *adj.*

trace[1] (trās) *v* **traced, trac·ing 1** find or discover by investigating something: *Police were trying to trace the missing jewellery.* **2** find or describe the origin or development of: *She traced the river to its source. He traced his family back through eight generations.* **3** follow or mark the course or position of something with the eye, mind, or finger: *Through the picture window, I could trace the outline of the mountain.* **4** copy a drawing, map, or design by drawing over its lines on a superimposed piece of paper.
n **1** a mark, object, or other indication that something exists or has existed: *The explorer found traces of an ancient city. We saw traces of rabbits on the snow.* **2** a very small quantity, especially one too small to be accurately measured: *There isn't a trace of grey in my grandpa's hair.* **3** a line or pattern displayed by an instrument using a moving pen or luminous spot on a screen to show the existence or nature of something that is being investigated.
adj present in very small quantities: *trace amounts of toxins.* <Old French, from Latin *trahere* to draw> **trace′a·bil′i·ty** *n.* **trace′a·ble** *adj.*

SYNONYMS

Trace refers to any mark left by someone or something: *The explorers disappeared without a trace.*

Remnant means "small remaining part": *These remnants are all that's left of the big meal.*

Vestige means "evidence of something that is disappearing or no longer exists": *The ruins are a vestige of a civilization that was once very powerful.*

trace[2] (trās) *n* each of the two straps, ropes, or chains by which an animal is attached to a vehicle that it is pulling. <Old French *traiz* plural of *trait,* from Latin *tractus* pp of *trahere* drag>
kick over the traces, become rebellious or reckless.

trace element *n* an element occurring in very small amounts in a particular sample, environment, or organism.

trac·er (trā′sər) *n* **1** a person who or thing that traces something or by which something may be traced. **2** a bullet or shell whose course is made visible in flight by a trail of flames or smoke, used to assist in aiming something. **3** a substance introduced into an organism or other system so that its subsequent distribution may be readily followed from its colour, fluorescence, radioactivity, or other property.

trac·er·y (trā′sə rē) *n, pl* **trac·er·ies 1** ornamental openwork in stone, consisting of branching or interlacing lines, especially at the top of a window in Gothic architecture. **2** a delicate branching pattern: *frost tracery.*

tra·che·a (trā′kē ə) *or* (trə kē′ə) *n, pl* **tra·che·ae** (trā′kē ē′) *or* (trə kē′ī′) the windpipe. <Greek *tracheia arteria* rough artery, i.e., windpipe> **tra′che·al** *adj.*

tra·che·ot·o·my (trā′kē ot′ə mē) *n, pl* **tra·che·ot·o·mies** a surgical cut made in a windpipe to relieve an obstruction to breathing.

tra·cho·ma (trə kō′mə) *n* a contagious bacterial infection of the eye in which there are inflamed granulations on the inner surface of the eyelids. <Greek *trachoma* roughness, from *trachys* rough>

trac·ing (trā′sing) *n* **1** a copy of a map, drawing, or design made by tracing it. **2** a faint or delicate line or pattern.
adj made for the purpose of tracing: *tracing paper.*

a bat	e bed	i bid	o pot	u cup	th **thin**
ā cake	ē me	ī bite	ō go	ū rude	ᴛʜ **then**
ä bar	ə about	ər over	ô for	ů put	zh measure

These seven **track and field** events make up the *heptathlon*, a multi-event athletics discipline for women. It is a test of strength, skill, and endurance. The competition, which takes place over two days, begins with the 100 m hurdles, high jump, shot put, and 200 m race. The long jump, javelin, and 800 m race complete the competition on the second day.

Points are awarded for the best performance in each event. An athlete who fails to compete in any event is disqualified from the competition.

track (trak) *n* **1** a rough path or minor road, typically one formed by use rather than constructed: *They followed a track through the woods.* **2** *Sports* **a** a prepared course or circuit for athletes, horses, motor vehicles, or dogs to race on: *He was at the track, betting on the horses.* **b** the athletic events of running and hurdling: *She was good at track.* **3** a mark or line of marks left by a person, animal, or vehicle in passing: *We saw a wild animal's tracks near the camp.* **4** a course or route followed by someone or something: *The hunters were on the deer's track.* **5** a continuous line of rails on a railway, or something resembling it. **6** a section of a record, compact disc, or cassette tape containing one song or piece of music. **7** a rotating belt of linked steel treads by which a tank or bulldozer is driven forward.

v **1 a** follow the course or trail of someone or something: *The game warden tracked the bear back to its den. to track down a criminal.* **b** (*often with* **down**) follow and note the course and progress of: *Meteorologists are tracking the movement of the storm, to track down a source of information.* **2** follow a particular course or route: *The storm tracked fast across the east.* **3** of a film, video, or TV camera, move in relation to the subject being filmed. **4** of an electronic circuit or component, vary in the same way as another circuit or component, so that the frequency difference between them remains constant: *The new VCR tracks automatically.* **5** bring snow or mud into a place on one's feet.

adj to do with running on a track: *track shoes.* <Old French *trac*> **track′er** *n.* **track′less** *adj.*

in your tracks, *Informal* exactly where you stand or move.

keep (**lose**) **track of,** keep (fail to keep) within your sight, knowledge, or attention: *The noise of the crowd made it difficult to keep track of what was going on.*

make tracks (**for**), *Informal* leave for or from some place quickly.

off the track, departing from the proper course of thinking or behaviour.

on the right (**wrong**) **track,** acting or thinking in a way that is likely to result in success (failure).

the wrong side of the tracks, *Informal* a poor or less prestigious part of town.

track and field *n* a group of competitive athletic events performed on a running track and the field next to it, including running, jumping, pole vaulting, and javelin throwing: *He doesn't play hockey but he's good at track and field.* **track′-and-field′** *adj.*

track·ball (trak′bol′) *Computers n* an input device that consists of a small ball set in a holder and can be rotated by hand to move a cursor across a screen, as an alternative to a mouse.

track lighting *n* a system of lighting using swivelling lights set in a metal rack attached to a wall or ceiling. Individual lights can sometimes be moved along the track to different positions.

track meet *n* a series or group of contests in track-and-field events.

track·pad TOUCHPAD.

track record *n* a record of the past achievements and overall performance of a person or thing: *That company's track record in dealing with environmental problems is rather poor.*

track·suit (trak′sūt′) a loose, warm set of clothes consisting of a sweatshirt and trousers, worn while exercising or for casual wear.

tract[1] (trakt) *n* **1** an area of indefinite extent, typically a large one: *a desert tract, a tract of forest.* **2** a major passage in the body, a large bundle of nerve fibres, or other continuous structure: *the digestive tract.* <Latin *tractus* a stretching out, from *trahere* drag>

tract[2] (trakt) *n* a pamphlet on a religious or political subject intended to support or speak out against a particular cause or point of view. <Latin *tractatus* treatise, from *tractare* to handle>

trac·ta·ble (trak′tə bəl) *adj* **1** easily controlled or influenced as a person. **2** easy to deal with as a situation. <Latin *tractare* to handle> **trac′ta·bil′i·ty** *n.* **trac′ta·ble·ness** *n.* **trac′ta·bly** *adv.*

trac·tion (trak′shən) *n* **1** the grip of a tire on a road or a wheel on a rail: *The wheel lost traction on the icy street.* **2** the action of drawing or pulling a thing over a surface, especially a road or track, or the power provided for it: *electric traction.* **3** the medical use of a sustained pull on a limb or muscle, especially in order to maintain the position of a fractured bone or to correct a deformity: *He spent several months in traction as a result of a skiing accident.* <Latin *trahere* drag>

trac·tor (trak′tər) *n* **1** a powerful motor vehicle with large rear wheels, used mainly on farms for hauling equipment and wagons. **2** a powerful truck with a cab for the driver, used to pull one or more large trailers along the highway. <Latin *trahere* drag>

trac·tor–trail·er (trak′tər trā′lər) *n* a very large truck, consisting of a TRACTOR (def. 2) together with a trailer or semitrailer, used for hauling freight.

trade (trād) *n* **1** the process of buying and selling goods and services: *trade with foreign countries.* **2** an exchange of two people or things, especially of players from different teams in a sport: *a baseball trade.* **3** a skilled job, typically one requiring the skilled use of hands and special training: *She is learning the carpenter's trade.* **4** people in the same kind of work or business: *the building trade.* **5 the trades** *pl* the trade winds.
v **trad·ed, trad·ing 1** buy and sell goods and services: *Some companies trade all over the world.* **2** make an exchange: *to trade seats. If you don't like your book, I'll trade with you.* **3** be bought and sold at a particular price, especially as shares or currency. **4** give and receive, especially insults or blows: *They traded insults in the schoolyard.* <Dutch *trade* track>
trade on, take advantage of something in an unfair way: *The businesswoman traded on her father's good name.*
trade something in, exchange a used item as part payment for something else: *to trade an old car in for a newer one.*

trade barrier *n* a thing that restricts international trade, such as a tariff, import ban, or embargo.

trade–in (trā′din′) *n* a used item, such as a used appliance or car, accepted as part payment for a new thing of the same kind, or the value or price allowed by the seller on it: *The dealer gave her a $600 trade-in on her old car.*
adj of or as a trade-in: *That old car has a trade-in value close to zero.*

trade·mark (trād′märk′) *n* **1** a symbol, word, or words, legally registered or established by use as representing a company or product. **2** a distinctive characteristic or object: *A big smile was the newscaster's trademark.*
v provide with a trademark.

trade name *n* a name that has the status of a trademark or by which something is known in a particular trade or profession.

trade–off (trād′of′) *n* an exchange of one benefit or advantage for another, involving some sort of disadvantage in either case: *It's a trade-off between spending less up front and saving on repairs later on.*

trad·er (trā′dər) *n* **1** a person who buys and sells goods, currency, or shares: *a stock trader.* **2** a ship used in trading: *a coastal trader.*

trade school *n* a school where TRADES (def. 3) are taught.

trades·man (trādz′mən) *n, pl* **trades·men** (-mən) a person engaged in trading or in a trade, typically on a relatively small scale.

trades·peo·ple (trādz′pē′pəl) *pl n* people engaged in a TRADE (def. 3).

trade union *n* an organized group of workers in a trade, group of trades, or profession, formed to protect and further their rights and interests. **trade unionism** *n.* **trade unionist** *n.*

trade wind *n* a wind blowing steadily toward the equator from the northeast in the northern hemisphere, and the southeast in the southern hemisphere, especially at sea.

trading post *n* a store or small settlement established for trading, typically in a remote area.

tra·di·tion (trə dish′ən) *n* **1** the transmission of customs, beliefs, or methods from generation to generation, or the fact of being passed along in this way: *By tradition, we ate supper early on Saturday.* **2** a long-established custom or belief that has been passed on in this way: *A big Sunday dinner was a tradition in our family.* <Latin *tradere* hand down> **tra·di′tion·al** *adj.* **tra·di′tion·al·ly** *adv.*

tra·di·tion·al·ism (trə dish′ə nə liz′əm) *n* strict adherence to tradition; an attitude that values tradition for its own sake. **tra·di′tion·al·ist** *n, adj.* **tra·di′tion·al′ist·ic** *adj.*

traf·fic (traf′ik) *n* **1** vehicles moving on a street or highway, or a large number of such vehicles. **2** the movement of other forms of transport or of pedestrians: *river traffic.* **3** the action of dealing or trading in something illegal: *the drug traffic.*
v **traf·ficked, traf·fick·ing** deal or trade in something illegal. <Italian *trafficare* to engage in trade>
traf′fick·er *n.* **traf′fic·less** *adj.*

a bat	e bed	i bid	o pot	u cup	th thin
ā cake	ē me	ī bite	ō go	ū rude	TH then
ä bar	ə about	ər over	ȯ for	u̇ put	zh measure

trail bike

Trail bikes are designed for events that focus on the riders' balance, finesse, and concentration rather than on speed. Both trail bikes and rally bikes are built for rugged terrain.

rally bike

traffic circle *n* a road junction at which traffic moves in one direction around a central area to reach one of the converging roads.

traffic cone *n* a PYLON (def. 1).

traffic island *n* a small raised area in the middle of a road or street that provides a safe place for pedestrians to stand, and marks a division between two opposing streams of traffic.

traffic light *n* an automatically operated coloured light system, typically changing from green (go) to amber (caution) to red (stop) and back to green again, that controls traffic at junctions and pedestrian crossings.

trag·a·canth (trag′ə kanth′) *n* a gum obtained from certain plants, and used in the food and drug industries.

tra·ge·di·an (trə jē′dē ən) *n* **1** an actor who specializes in tragic roles. **2** a writer of tragedies.

trag·e·dy (traj′ə dē) *n, pl* **trag·e·dies 1** an event causing great suffering, destruction, and distress, such as a serious accident, crime, or natural catastrophe: *Several families lost their lives in the tragedy.* **2** a play or other work dealing with tragic events and with an unhappy ending, especially one concerning the downfall of the main character, or the branch of drama that includes such plays. <Greek *tragoidia,* a poem or play with an unhappy ending>

trag·ic (traj′ik) *adj* **1** causing or marked by extreme distress or sorrow: *a tragic fire, a tragic event.* **2** to do with tragedy in a play or other work. **trag′i·cal·ly** *adv.*

tragic flaw *n* a flaw in the character of a hero or heroine that brings about his or her downfall.

trag·i·com·e·dy (traj′ē kom′ə dē) *n, pl* **trag·i·com·e·dies 1** a play or other work with both tragic and comic elements, or such works considered as a group: **2** an incident or situation in which serious and comic elements are blended. **trag′i·com′ic** or **trag′i·com′i·cal** *adj.* **trag′i·com′i·cal·ly** *adv.*

trail (trāl) *n* **1** a beaten path across a wooded or unsettled area: *The hikers followed the trail for days.* **2 a** a mark or a series of signs or objects left behind by the passage of someone or something: *The car left a trail of dust behind it.* **b** a track or scent used to follow someone or hunt an animal: *The dogs found the trail of the rabbit.* **3** a route planned or followed for a particular purpose: *a ski trail.* **4** a line of people or things following behind each other: *A trail of shoppers entered the store.*
v **1** follow a person or animal, typically by using signs or scent: *The dog trailed the rabbit.* **2** draw or be drawn along a surface behind someone or something: *She trailed her hand in the water.* **3** of a plant, grow or hang over the edge of something or along the ground. **4** be losing to an opponent in a game or contest: *Going into the third period, we were trailing 4–3.* **5** walk or move slowly or wearily: *We trailed our mother all over town.* **6** of a voice or speaker, fade gradually before stopping: *Her final comments trailed away into silence.* <Old French *trailler* tow, from Latin *tragula* dragnet (a net drawn through a river to catch fish)>

trail bike *n* a small motorcycle for off-road use.

trail·bla·zer (trāl′blā′zər) *n* **1** a person who blazes a trail through wild or wooded country. **2** a person who pioneers or prepares the way for something new. **trail′blaz′ing** *adj.*

trail·er (trā′lər) *n* **1** an unpowered vehicle towed by another, especially the rear section of a tractor-trailer, or a closed-in vehicle used as a place for living in or as a place of business. **2** an extract or series of extracts from a movie or broadcast, shown to advertise it in advance. **3** a thing that trails, especially a trailing plant.

trailer hitch *n* a knoblike or hooklike projection fixed to the rear of a vehicle, for attaching a trailer.

trailer park *n* an area equipped to accommodate TRAILERS (def. 1).

trail mix *n* a mixture of dried fruit and nuts eaten as a snack, especially by hikers and campers.

train (trān) *v* **1** teach a person or animal a particular skill through practice and instruction over a period of time, or be taught in such a way: *to train a dog. I would like to train as a nurse someday.* **2** cause a plant to grow in a particular direction or into a desired shape: *to train a vine.* **3** undertake a course of exercise in order to reach or maintain physical fitness, typically to prepare for participating in a specific sport or event: *She often trains at the gym.* **4** point or aim something: *He trained his camera on the nearest elephant.*

n **1** a connected line of railway cars pulled by an engine. **2** a line of vehicles or pack animals travelling in the same direction: *a camel train.* **3** 🍁 *North* **a** in full, **tractor train** a line of sleds pulled by a tractor. **b** in full, **dog train** a team of dogs pulling a sled or a line of sleds. **c** a cat-train. **4** a group of attendants accompanying an important person. **5** a long piece of material attached to the back of a formal dress or robe that trails along the ground or floor: *Two attendants carried the bride's train.* **6 a** a series or succession of ideas: *a train of thought.* **b** the results or conditions following some event: *The flood brought starvation and disease in its train.* <Old French, from Latin *trahere* to drag>

train of thought, the way in which someone reaches a conclusion through a line of reasoning: *From the way the speaker paused, it was obvious that he had lost his train of thought.*

train·ee (trā nē′) *n* a person who is receiving training for a particular job or skill.

train·er (trā′nər) *n* **1** a person who trains people or animals. **2** an aircraft or simulator used to train pilots.

train·ing (trā′ning) *n* **1** the action of teaching a person or animal a particular skill or type of behaviour: *training for teachers.* **2** the action of undertaking a course of exercise in preparation for physical fitness or a sporting event. **3** the condition of being physically fit or unfit: *to keep in training.*

training camp *Sports n* a session of intensive training undertaken by a team or an athlete at a place away from home in preparation for a regular season or for a special event.

training school or **training college** *n* **1** a college or school whose students are trained in a particular skill or occupation. **2** an institution for the custody and education of juvenile offenders.

training wheels *pl n* a pair of small wheels attached to the rear wheel of a bicycle to steady the vehicle for a child learning to ride.

train·load (trān′lōd′) *n* a number of people or quantity of goods transported by train.

traipse (trāps) *Informal v* **traipsed, traips·ing 1** walk around casually or needlessly: *Don't traipse through here with your muddy boots on.* **2** walk or move wearily or reluctantly: *He traipsed all over town looking for a job.*

n a tiring or boring journey on foot. <origin unknown>

trait (trāt) *n* **1** a distinguishing characteristic, typically one belonging to a person: *Courage, love of justice, and common sense are often thought of as desirable traits.* **2** a genetically determined characteristic.

SYNONYMS

Trait applies to a distinguishing feature of a person's character: *The trait I really admire in him is his ability to work with all kinds of people.*

Characteristic means "distinguishing feature of a person, animal, or thing": *The long neck and legs of a giraffe are characteristics that make this animal very noticeable wherever it is.*

trai·tor (trā′tər) *n* a person who betrays someone or something, such as country, friend, cause, or principle. <Old French, from Latin *traditor*> **trai′tor·ous** *adj.* **trai′tor·ous·ly** *adv.* **trai′tor·ous·ness** *n.*

tra·jec·to·ry (trə jek′tə rē) *n, pl* **tra·jec·to·ries** the curved path of something moving through space under the action of given forces, such as a planet in its orbit. <Latin *trans-* across + *jacere* throw>

tram (tram) *UK n* a streetcar. <origin uncertain>

tram·mel (tram′əl) *n* **1** a thing that hinders or restrains freedom of action: *A large bequest freed the artist from the trammels of poverty.* **2** a dragnet with three layers of netting and fine mesh as a means of catching fish. **3** a hook in a fireplace to hold a kettle over the fire.

v **tram·melled** or **tram·meled, tram·mel·ling** or **tram·mel·ing** hinder or restrain freedom of action. <French *tramail* three-mesh net, from Latin *tri-* three + *macula* mesh>

tramp (tramp) *v* **1** walk heavily or noisily: *He tramped across the room in his heavy boots.* **2** tread or stamp on: *The dog has tramped on the flowers.* **3** walk through or over a place wearily or reluctantly and for long distances: *We tramped through the streets.*

n **1** a person who travels from place to place on foot in search of unskilled work or as a vagrant or beggar. **2** the sound of heavy steps, typically of several people: *We heard the tramp of the soldiers' boots.* **3** a long walk, typically a tiring one. **4** a freight ship that takes a cargo when and where it can, rather than on a fixed route. <German *trampen* to stamp> **tramp′er** *n.*

tram·ple (tram′pəl) *v* **tram·pled, tram·pling 1** tread on and crush: *The cattle broke through the fence and trampled the farmer's crops.* **2** treat with contempt: *The new law trampled on our rights.*

n the act or sound of trampling: *We heard the trample of many feet.* **tram′pler** *n.*

tram·po·line (tram′pə lēn′) *n* a strong fabric sheet attached by springs to a frame, used as a springboard and landing area in doing acrobatic or gymnastic exercises, or for fun. <Italian *trampolino* springboard>

trance (trans) *n* **1** a half-conscious state characterized by an absence of response to external stimuli, such as one induced by hypnosis. **2** a dreamy, absorbed condition resembling this: *He sat in a trance, thinking of his girlfriend.* <Old French *transe*, from Latin *trans-* across + *irei* go> **trance′like′** *adj.*

tran·quil (trang′kwəl) *adj* calm or free from disturbance: *a tranquil mood, a tranquil gaze.* <Latin *tranquillus*> **tran′quil′i·ty** *n.* **tran′quil·ly** *adv.*

tran·quil·lize or **tran·quil·ize** (trang′kwə līz′) *v* **tran·quil·lized** or **tran·quil·ized, tran·quil·lizing** or **tran·quil·iz·ing** have a calming or sedative effect on as a drug in order to reduce tension or anxiety, or administer such a drug to a person or animal.

a bat	e bed	i bid	o pot	u cup	th thin
ā cake	ē me	ī bite	ō go	ū rude	ᴛʜ then
ȧ bar	ə about	ər over	ȯ for	u̇ put	zh measure

T

tran·quil·liz·er or **tran·quil·iz·er** (trang′kwə lī′zər) *n* a person who or thing that tranquillizes, especially a drug used to reduce mental tension and anxiety, control certain psychoses, etc.

trans– *prefix* **1** across or beyond: *transcontinental.* **2** on or to the other side of: *transatlantic.* **3** into a different place or condition: *transform.*

ETYMOLOGY

Trans is a Latin word that means "over," "across," or "through." Words with this prefix all contain some idea of shift, change, or movement:
He transferred his loyalty to his new school.
There will be a period of transition as we learn the new rules.
The grain will be transported to market by rail.

trans·act (tran zakt′) *v* conduct or carry on business. <Latin *transigere* accomplish>

trans·ac·tion (tran zak′shən) *n* **1** the act or fact of buying or selling something: *a commercial transaction. A record is kept of all the firm's transactions.* **2** an exchange or interaction between people: *a scholarly transaction.* **3 transactions** *pl* published reports of proceedings at the meetings of a scholarly society or other organization.

trans·at·lan·tic (tran′sə tlan′tik) *adj* to do with crossing or extending across the Atlantic: *transatlantic air fares.*

🍁 **trans–Can·a·da** (tran′skan′ə də) *adj* extending across Canada from the Atlantic to the Pacific: *the trans-Canada train service.*

trans·cei·ver (tran sē′vər) *n* a device that can both transmit and receive radio signals.

tran·scend (tran send′) *v* **1** be or go beyond the limits or powers of something, typically an idea, concept, or abstraction: *The grandeur of the waterfall transcended description.* **2** be higher, greater, or more superior than: *The speed of jet planes transcended that of any previous form of transportation.* <*trans-* beyond + Latin *scandere* climb>

tran·scend·ent (tran sen′dənt) *adj* **1** beyond or above the range of normal or merely physical human experience. **2** exceeding the ordinary. **tran·scen′dence** *n.* **tran·scend′en·cy** *n.* **tran·scend′ent·ly** *adv.*

tran·scen·den·tal (tran′sen den′təl) *adj* to do with a spiritual or non-physical area or realm. **tran′scen·den′tal·ly** *adv.*

trans·con·ti·nen·tal (tran′skon tə nen′təl) *adj* crossing or extending across a continent, especially as a railway: *a transcontinental railway.*
n a train that crosses a continent.
trans′con·ti·nen′tal·ly *adv.*

tran·scribe (tran skrīb′) *v* **tran·scribed, tran·scrib·ing** **1** put thoughts, speech, or data into written or printed form: *The account of the trial was transcribed from shorthand notes. Her entire speech was transcribed in the newspapers, word for word.* **2** arrange a piece of music for a different instrument or voice. **3** make a radio or TV recording, especially for broadcasting at a later time, or broadcast this at a later time. **4** synthesize a nucleic acid, typically RNA, using an existing nucleic acid, typically DNA, as a template, so that the genetic information in the latter is copied. <*trans-* across + Latin *scribere* write> **tran·scrib′er** *n.*

tran·script (tran′skript) *n* **1** a written or printed version of material originally presented in another medium: *The reporters were waiting for a transcript of the speech.* **2** an official record of a student's work, showing courses taken and grades achieved.

tran·scrip·tion (tran skrip′shən) *n* **1** a written or printed representation of something, or the action or process of writing or printing it. **2** *Music* an arrangement of a piece of music for a different instrument or voice. **3** a recording of a radio or TV broadcast. **tran·scrip′tion·al** *adj.* **tran·scrip′tion·ist** *n.*

trans·der·mal (trans der′məl) *adj* to do with the application of a medicine or drug through the skin by using an adhesive **transdermal patch**.

trans·du·cer (trans dyū′sər) *or* (trans dū′sər) *n* a device that converts variations in a physical quantity, such as pressure or brightness, into an electrical signal, or an electrical signal into a physical quantity. <*trans-* across + Latin *ducere* lead>

tran·sect (tran sekt′) *v* cut across. <*trans-* across + Latin *secare* cut> **tran·sec′tion** *n.* **tran·sec′tion·al** *adj.*

tran·sept (tran′sept) *n* the part of a cross-shaped church at right angles to the long main part.

trans fat (trans) *n* in full, **trans fatty acid** an unsaturated fatty acid found in vegetable oils, commercial baked foods, and many fried foods. Trans fats are thought to raise the cholesterol level in the blood.

trans·fer (tran sfər′) *for v,* (tran′sfər) *for n.* *v* **trans·ferred, trans·fer·ring** **1** move someone or something from one place to another: *I have to transfer all my stuff to a different locker.* **2** move or cause to move to another group, occupation, or service: *She was transferred to the shipping department.* **3** change to another place, route, or means of transport during a journey: *We transferred from bus to streetcar.* **4** assign the possession of property, a right, or a responsibility to someone else. **5** convey a drawing or design from one surface to another.
n **1** an act of moving something or someone to another place. **2** a change of employment, typically within an organization or field: *She requested a transfer out of the office.* **3** an assignment of property, especially stocks and shares, from one person to another. **4** a ticket allowing a passenger to change from one public transport vehicle to another as part of a single journey. **5** a small coloured picture or design on paper, which can be transferred to another surface by being pressed or heated. <Latin *trans-* across + *ferre* bear> **trans·fer′a·bil′i·ty** *n.* **trans·fer′a·ble** *adj.* **trans·fer′ence** or **trans′fer·ence** *n.*

🍁 **transfer payment** *n* a direct payment made by a government to another level of government, or to its citizens. Employment insurance is a transfer payment.

trans·fig·ure (tran sfig′ər) *or* (tran sfig′yər) *v* **trans·fig·ured, trans·fig·ur·ing** **1** change in form or appearance, usually for the better: *New paint had transfigured the old house.* **2** change so as to glorify; exalt. **trans·fig′u·ra′tion** *n.*

trans·fix (tran sfiks′) *v* **1** cause someone to become motionless with horror, wonder, or astonishment, or become motionless in this way: *He was transfixed by the hatred in her face.* **2** pierce with a sharp implement or weapon so that motion is not possible. <Latin *transfigere* to pierce through>

trans·form (tran sfôrm′) *v* make a thorough or dramatic change in the form, appearance, or character of, or undergo such a change: *The blizzard transformed the bushes into glittering mounds of snow.* <Latin *trans-* across + *forma* form> **trans′for·ma′tion** *n.*

SYNONYMS

Transform emphasizes a complete change: *The move to the new city transformed their way of life.*

Change means "become or make different": *I promise to change the way I do things.*

Convert suggests changing from one thing to another, especially for a new use: *The big house was converted into three apartments.*

trans·form·er (tran sfôr′mər) *n* a device for changing the voltage of an alternating electric current.

trans·fuse (tran sfyūz′) *v* **trans·fused, trans·fus·ing** **1** transfer blood or its components from one person or animal to another. **2** inject a liquid into a blood vessel to replace lost fluid. **3** cause something or someone to be permeated or infused by a thing: *Happiness transfused her face.* <Latin *trans-* across + *fundere* pour>

trans·fu·sion (tran sfyū′zhən) *n* the act or process of transfusing donated blood, blood products, or other fluid into the circulatory system of a person or animal: *The wounded soldier was given three transfusions in a week.*

trans·gen·der·ed (trans jen′dərd) *adj* to do with wishing to be considered as a member of the opposite sex. A transgendered person may have surgery to alter his or her appearance.

trans·gress (trans gres′) *or* (tranz gres′) *v* violate or go beyond the bounds of a moral principle or other established standard of behaviour: *transgress a law. The interviewer's questions transgressed the bounds of good taste.* <Latin *trans-* across + *gradi* to step> **trans·gress′ion** *n.* **trans·gress′ive** *adj.* **trans·gress′ive·ly** *adv.* **trans·gress′or** *n.*

tran·sient (tran′zē ənt) *adj* **1** lasting only a short time: *a transient visit.* **2** staying or working in a place for a short time only: *a transient visitor.*
n a person who is staying or working in a place for a short time only. <Latin *trans-* through + *ire* go>
tran′sience *n.* **tran′sien·cy** *n.* **tran′sient·ly** *adv.*

tran·sis·tor (tran zis′tər) *n* **1** a small electronic semiconductor that amplifies electricity by controlling the flow of electrons. **2** a portable radio that has transistors instead of tubes: *My grandmother carries her transistor from room to room.* <*tran*(*sfer*) + (*re*)*sistor*, because it transfers an electric signal across a resistor>

trans·it (tran′sit) *or* (tran′zit) *n* **1** the act or process of moving people, goods, or materials from one place to another: *The goods were damaged in transit.* **2** the act of passing through or across a place, especially of passengers on public transport: *mass transit.* **3** the passage of a planet across the face of the sun, or of a moon or its shadow across the face of a planet.
v **trans·it·ed, trans·it·ing** pass across or through an area. <Latin *transitus* passage, from *transire* go across>

tran·si·tion (tran zish′ən) *n* **1** the process or a period of changing from one state or condition to another: *The country had a difficult transition from dictatorship to democracy. The abrupt transitions in the book confused her.* **2** a momentary modulation from one key to another in a piece of music. **3** a change of an atom, nucleus, or electron from one quantum state to another, with emission or absorption of radiation. **tran·si′tion·al** *adj.* **tran·si′tion·al·ly** *adv.*

tran·si·tive (tran′sə tiv) *or* (tran′zə tiv) *Grammar adj* of a verb, able to take a direct object, expressed or implied. Examples: *Bring* and *raise* are transitive verbs. Compare INTRANSITIVE. **tran′si·tive·ly** *adv.*

tran·si·to·ry *adj* lasting only a short time. **tran′si·to′ri·ly** *adv.* **tran′si·to′ri·ness** *n.*

trans·late (tran slāt′), (tran zlāt′), *or* (tran′zlāt′) *v* **1** express the sense of words or text in another language, or be so expressed: *She translated the magazine article from French to German. Only one of his novels was translated.* **2** convert or be converted into another form or medium: *They translated the book into a TV series.* **3** move from one place or condition to another: *She had been translated from a loving home to a hateful environment.* **4** *Mathematics* cause something to move so that all its parts travel the same distance in the same direction, without rotation or change of shape. <Latin *translatus* transferred>
trans·lat′a·bil′i·ty *n.* **trans·lat′a·ble** *adj.* **trans·la′tion** *n.*

trans·la·tor (tran slā′tər) *or* (tran zlā′tər) *n* a person who translates from one language into another, especially as a profession.

trans·lit·er·ate (trans lit′ə rāt′) *v* **trans·lit·er·at·ed, trans·lit·er·at·ing** write or print a letter or word using the closest corresponding letters of a different alphabet or language. <*trans-* across + Latin *litera* letter>
trans·lit′er·a′tion *n.*

trans·lu·cent (tran slū′sənt) *or* (tran zlū′sənt) *adj* allowing light, but not detailed shapes, to pass through a substance. Compare TRANSPARENT. <Latin *trans-* through + *lucere* shine> **trans·lu′cence** *n.* **trans·lu′cen·cy** *n.* **trans·lu′cent·ly** *adv.*

trans·mi·gra·tion (tran′smī grā′shən) *or* (tran′zmī grā′shən) *n* **1** in certain religions, the passing of the soul at death into another body: *Belief in the transmigration of souls is part of Hinduism.* **2** going from one place or country to another; migration.
trans·mi′grate *v.*

trans·mis·si·ble (tran smis′ə bəl) *or* (tran zmis′ə bəl) *adj* capable of being transmitted: *Scarlet fever is a transmissible disease.* **trans·mis′si·bil′i·ty** *n.*

a bat	e bed	i bid	o pot	u cup	th thin
ā cake	ē me	ī bite	ō go	ū rude	TH then
â bar	ə about	ər over	ô for	ů put	zh measure

trans·mis·sion (tran smish′ən) *or* (tran zmish′ən) *n* **1** the action or process of transmitting something or the condition of being transmitted. **2** a program or signal that is broadcast or sent out. **3** the part of a motor vehicle that transmits power from the engine to the axle.
trans·mis′sive *adj.*

trans·mit (tran smit′) *or* (tran zmit′) *v* **trans·mit·ted, trans·mit·ting 1** cause something to pass on from one place or person to another: *transmit money, transmit knowledge.* **2** broadcast or send out an electrical signal or a radio or TV program: *The broadcasting station transmitted 24 hours a day.* **3** pass on a disease or trait to another: *The swamp mosquitoes transmitted malaria.* **4** allow heat, light, sound, electricity, or other energy to pass through a medium: *The sun transmitted much warmth through the big window.* <Latin *trans-* across + *mittere* send>
trans·mit′ta·ble *adj.* **trans·mit′tal** *n.*

SYNONYMS

Transmit refers to the passing of something from one person or place to another: *Please transmit a copy of the signed form by fax.*

Broadcast mainly means "send out by radio or television": *The news is broadcast every two hours on that station.*

trans·mit·ter (tran smit′ər) *or* (tran zmit′ər) *n* **1** a set of equipment used to generate and transmit messages or signals, especially those of radio or television. **2** a person who or thing that transmits something.

trans·mog·ri·fy (trans′mog′rə fī) *v* **trans·mog·ri·fied, trans·mog·ri·fy·ing** (*usually humorous*) transform in a surprising or magical way: *The handsome prince was transmogrified into a frog.* <origin uncertain>

trans·mute (tran smyūt′) *or* (tran zmyūt′) *v* **trans·mut·ed, trans·mut·ing 1** change from one nature, substance, or form into another: *We can transmute water power into electrical power.* **2** convert atoms of one element into atoms of a different element or a different isotope, either naturally, as by radioactive decay, by nuclear bombardment, or by a similar process. **3** supposedly convert a base metal into gold or silver in alchemy. <Latin *trans-* throroughly + *mutare* change>
trans·mut′a·bil′i·ty *n.* **trans·mut′a·ble** *adj.*
trans·mut′er *n.*

trans·na·tion·al (trans nash′ə nəl) *or* (tranz nash′ə nəl) *adj* extending or operating across the boundaries of a single nation.

trans·o·ce·an·ic (trans′ō shē an′ik) *or* (tranz′ō shē an′ik) *adj* **1** crossing or extending across the ocean: *a transoceanic airline.* **2** coming from or located beyond an ocean.

tran·som (tran′səm) *n* **1** a window over a door or other window, usually hinged at the top or bottom for opening. **2** a horizontal crossbar in a window, over a door, or between a door and a window above it. **3** the flat surface forming the stern of a boat. <Latin *transtrum* crossbeam>

trans·pa·cif·ic (tran′spə sif′ik) *adj* to do with crossing or extending across the Pacific: *a transpacific voyage.*

trans·par·ent (tran sper′ənt) *or* (tran spar′ənt) *adj* **1** allowing light to pass through a material or substance so that objects behind can be distinctly seen: *transparent water.* Compare TRANSLUCENT. **2** easy to perceive or detect, especially as a thought, feeling, or motive. <Latin *trans-* through + *parere* appear> **trans·par′en·cy** *n.* **trans·par′ent·ly** *adv.*

tran·spire (tran spīr′) *v* **tran·spired, tran·spir·ing 1** come to be known or be revealed, especially as a secret or something unknown. **2** *Botany* of the leaf or stem of a plant, give off water vapour. <Latin *trans-* through + *spirare* breathe> **tran·spi·ra·tion** (tran′spə rā′shən) *n.*

trans·plant (tran splant′) *for v,* (tran′splant) *for n. v* **1** move or transfer something to another place or situation, typically with some effort or upheaval: *The colony was transplanted to a more healthful location.* **2** plant again in another place: *We start the flowers indoors and then transplant them to the garden.* **3** transfer living tissue or an organ and implant it in another part of the body or in another body: *to transplant a kidney.*
n **1** a surgical operation in which an organ or tissue is transplanted: *a heart transplant.* **2** an organ or tissue that is transplanted. **trans·plant′a·ble** *adj.*
trans′plan·ta′tion *n.* **trans·plant′er** *n.*

tran·spond·er (tran spon′dər) *n* a device for receiving a radio signal and automatically transmitting a different signal. <*trans*(*mitter*) + (*res*)*ponder*>

trans·port (tran spôrt′) *for verb,* (tran′spôrt) *for n. v* **1** take or carry people or goods from one place to another by means of a vehicle, aircraft, or ship: *The logs were transported by truck.* **2** overwhelm someone with a strong emotion: *She was transported with joy by the good news.* **3** cause someone to feel that they are in another place or time. **4** send a convict to a penal colony, a former practice.
n **1** a system or means of conveying people or goods from place to place by means of a vehicle, aircraft, or ship: *Barges were the main means of transport on canals.* **2** a large motor vehicle, ship, or aircraft used to carry goods, soldiers, or supplies, especially a large truck used to carry freight long distances by road. **3 transports** *pl* an overwhelmingly strong emotion: *transports of joy.* **4** a transported convict. <Latin *trans-* across + *portare* carry> **trans·port′a·ble** *adj.* **trans·port′er** *n.*

trans·por·ta·tion (tran′spər tā′shən) *n* **1** the action of transporting someone or something or the process of being transported: *The railway allowed free transportation for some passenger's baggage.* **2** a system or means of transporting people or goods: *A small bus served as transportation to the airport.* **3** the cost of transporting someone or something: *The transportation for our summer trip came to $800.* **4** the former action or process of transporting convicts to a penal colony.

trans·pose (tran spōz′) *v* **trans·posed, trans·pos·ing 1** cause two or more things to change places with each other, especially letters, words, sentences, or numbers. **2** *Music* write or play music in a different key from the original. **3** *Mathematics* transfer a term to the other side of an algebraic equation, changing plus to minus or minus to plus. <French *trans-* across + *poser* put> **trans·pos′able** *adj.* **trans·pos′al** *n.* **trans·pos′er** *n.* **trans′po·si′tion** *n.*

trans·sex·u·al (trans sek′shū əl) *n* **1** a person born with the physical characteristics of one sex but who emotionally and psychologically feels that he or she belongs to the opposite sex. **2** a person whose sex has been changed by surgery and hormone treatment.
adj to do with a transsexual or transsexuals.

tran·sub·stan·ti·a·tion (tran′səb stan′shē ā′shən) *Christianity n* in some Christian churches, the conversion of the bread and wine of the Eucharist into the body and blood of Christ. <Latin *trans-* over + *substantia* substance>

trans·ver·sal (tran svər′səl) *or* (tran zvər′səl) *n* a line intersecting two or more other lines.

trans·verse (tran svərs′) *or* (tran zvərs′) *adj* lying or placed across or crosswise: *The transverse beams in the barn were walnut.*
n a transverse part or piece. <Latin *trans-* across + *vertere* turn> **trans·verse′ly** *adv.*

trans·ves·tite (trans ves′tīt′) or (tranz ves′tīt′) *n* a person, typically a man, who derives pleasure from dressing or wearing clothing considered appropriate to the opposite sex. <*trans-* + Latin *vestire* dress> **trans·ves′tism** *n.*

trap (trap) *n* **1** a device designed to catch and retain birds and animals, typically by allowing entry but not exit, or by catching hold: *a lobster trap.* **b** an unpleasant situation from which it is hard to escape: *She knew that the question was a trap. He fell into the trap of feeling sorry for himself.* **2** a trapdoor. **3** a bend in a pipe, container, or device used to collect or prevent the escape of solids, liquids, or gases. **4** a light, two-wheeled carriage pulled by a horse or pony. **5** *Informal* a person's mouth, especially in speaking: *Keep your trap shut!* **6 traps** *pl* **a** percussion instruments, such as drums, typically in a jazz band. **b** *Slang* possessions: *Pick up your traps and we'll go now.*
v **trapped, trap·ping 1** catch a bird or animal in a trap, or set traps: *The wily old bear was trapped. He makes his living by trapping lobsters.* **2** prevent someone from escaping from a place: *The fire trapped them on the top floor.* **3** have something, typically a part of the body, held tightly by something so that it cannot move or be freed: *His finger was trapped in the hole.* **4** lure someone by means of trickery or deception to do something: *I was trapped into helping her clean up her room.* <Old English *træppe*>

SYNONYMS

Trap suggests a situation set up to trick or catch a person or animal by surprise: *He suspected that the call was a trap to find out where he was living.*

Ambush means "surprise attack from a hidden position": *The bushes provided cover for the ambush.*

Snare means "device intended to trap a person or animal": *The rabbit got caught in the snare.*

trap·door (trap′dôr′) *n* a hinged or removable door in a floor, ceiling, or roof.

tra·peze (trə pēz′) *n* a horizontal bar hung by ropes and free to swing, used in gymnastics and acrobatics. <Greek *trapezion* diminutive of *trapeza* table>

tra·pe·zi·um (trə pē′zē əm) *n* a four-sided plane figure with no sides parallel.

trap·e·zoid (trap′ə zoid′) *n* a four-sided plane figure with two sides parallel and two sides not parallel.

🍁 **trap·line** (trap′līn′) *n* a series of traps that are set for beaver and other animals.

trap·per (trap′ər) *n* a person who traps wild animals for food or for their fur.

trap·pings (trap′ingz) *pl n* **1** the outward signs, features, or objects associated with a particular situation, role, or thing: *He had all the trappings of a cowboy, but he couldn't even ride a horse.* **2** ornamental harness for a horse. <Middle English *trapppe* cloth for a horse>

trap·shoot·ing (trap′shū′ting) *n* the sport or action of shooting at clay pigeons released from a spring trap. **trap′shoot′er** *n.*

trash (trash) *n* **1** discarded waste items: *There was a lot of trash in the yard of the vacant house.* **2** worthless or inferior writing, art, or other cultural items: *That novel is such trash that I can't imagine how it ever got published.* **3** a person or people regarded as being worthless or inferior.
v wreck or severely damage: *Last winter our summer cottage was broken into and trashed by vandals.* <origin uncertain>

trash·y (trash′ē) *adj* **trash·i·er, trash·i·est** of poor quality, especially as an item of popular culture: *a trashy magazine.* **trash′i·ness** *n.*

trau·ma (trom′ə) *or* (trou′mə) *n* **1** a deeply distressing or disturbing experience, especially an emotional shock following a stressful event or a physical injury or shock. **2** a physical injury. <Greek = wound> **trau·mat′ic** *adj.* **trau·mat′i·cal·ly** *adv.*

trau·ma·tize (trom′ə tīz′) *or* (trou′mə tīz′) *v* **trau·ma·tized, trau·ma·tiz·ing** cause to suffer physical, mental, or emotional trauma. **trau′ma·tiz·a′tion** *n.*

trav·ail (trav′āl) *n* painful or tiring effort.
v engage in painful or tiring effort. <Old French *travail*, from Latin *tripalium* torture device>

trav·el (trav′əl) *v* **trav·elled** or **trav·eled, trav·el·ling** or **trav·el·ing 1** make a journey, typically of some length or distance: *We travelled across Canada.* **2** go from place to place on business or as part of an activity: *She travels for a large firm.* **3** resist motion sickness, damage, or some other harm on a journey: *Our dog travels well.* **4** move in a constant or predictable way: *Sound travels more slowly than light.* **5** pass through or over: *to travel a road.* **6** *Informal* move quickly, especially as a vehicle: *That car can really travel!*
n **1** the action of travelling, especially abroad. **2 travels** *pl* journeys, especially long or exotic ones.
adj designed to be suitable for use while travelling: *a travel clock.* <See TRAVAIL.>

a bat	e bed	i bid	o pot	u cup	th thin
ā cake	ē me	ī bite	ō go	ū rude	TH then
ä bar	ə about	ər over	ô for	ů put	zh measure

travel agency *n* a business that makes arrangements for travellers. The people employed by such a business are **travel agents**.

trav·elled or **trav·eled** (trav′əld) *adj* **1** having done travelling: *He was widely travelled.* **2** used by travellers: *It was a well-travelled road.*

trav·el·ler or **trav·el·er** (trav′ə lər) *n* **1** a person who is travelling or who often travels: *The town had little accommodation for travellers.* **2** a travelling sales representative: *He's a traveller for a drug company.*

traveller's cheque *n* a cheque for a fixed amount issued by a bank or other financial institution that may be cashed or used in payment after endorsement.

trav·el·ling or **trav·el·ing** (trav′ə ling) *Basketball n* a floor violation, made when the ball handler takes too many steps without dribbling the ball.

trav·e·logue (trav′ə log′) *n* a movie, book, or illustrated lecture about the places visited by a traveller.

trav·ers·a·ble (tra ver′sa bəl) *adj* **1** able to be traversed. **2** *Mathematics* to do with a path that can be completely traced without retracing.

trav·erse (trav′ərs) *or* (trə vərs′) *v* **trav·ersed, trav·ers·ing 1** travel or extend across or through: *The caravan traversed the desert.* **2** cross a hill or mountain by means of a series of sideways movements. **3** move something back and forth or sideways.
n **1** an act of traversing something. **2** a part of a structure that extends or is fixed across something.
adj lying or placed across. <Old French, from Latin *transvertere* to turn across> **tra·vers′er** *n.*

trav·es·ty (trav′i stē) *n, pl* **trav·es·ties** a false, ridiculous, or distorted representation of something: *The trial was a travesty of justice.*
v **trav·es·tied, trav·es·ty·ing** represent in such a way. <French *travesti* disguised, from Latin *trans-* across + *vestire* dress>

🍁 **tra·vois** (trə voi′) *or* (trav′wo) *n, pl* **tra·vois** a sled formerly used on the Great Plains by some First Nations and Native American peoples to carry goods, consisting of two joined poles pulled by a horse or dog. <Cdn French, from French *travail* frame for a horse being shod>

trawl (trol) *v* **1** fish with a large, wide-mouthed net which carries buoys supporting baited hooks on short lines. **2** search thoroughly. **3** drag or trail something through water or other liquid.
n **1** the act or process of trawling. **2** the net or line used in trawling. <Dutch *traghel*, from Latin *tragula* fishing net>

trawl·er (trol′ər) *n* a fishing boat used for trawling.

tray (trā) *n* a flat, shallow container with a rim around it, typically for carrying food and drinks, or for holding small items or loose material: *We carried the dishes into the dining room on a tray.* <Old English *treg*>

treach·er·ous (trech′ə rəs) *adj* **1** guilty of or involving betrayal or decision: *The treacherous soldier carried reports to the enemy.* **2** hazardous as ground, water, or conditions because of presenting hidden or unpredictable dangers: *The thin ice was treacherous.* **treach′er·ous·ly** *adv.* **treach′er·ous·ness** *n.* **treach′er·y** *n.*

trea·cle (trē′kəl) *UK n* molasses.

tread (tred) *v* **trod, trod·den** or **trod, tread·ing 1** walk in a specified way: *to tread lightly.* **2** walk on or along, especially to set one's foot down on top of: *to tread the pavement.* **3** press down into the ground or another surface with the feet, or crush or flatten something with the feet: *to tread grapes. Cattle had trodden the grass.*
n **1** a manner or the sound of someone walking: *the tread of marching feet.* **2** the top surface of a step or stair: *The stair treads were covered with rubber.* **3** the thick part of something that touches the ground, such as the moulded part of a tire that grips the road. <Old English *tredan*> **tread′er** *n.*
tread (or **step**) **on someone's toes,** offend or annoy someone by interfering in his or her area of responsibility.
tread water, a maintain an upright position in deep water by moving the feet with a walking movement and the hands with a downward circular motion. **b** fail to advance or make progress: *She thought she was only treading water in her current job.*

trea·dle (tred′əl) *n* a lever or pedal worked by the foot to make a machine move: *My grandmother's old sewing machine was worked by a treadle.*
v **trea·dled, trea·dling** work a treadle.

tread·mill (tred′mil′) *n* **1** a device for producing motion by having a person or animal walk on the moving steps of a wheel or of a sloping, endless belt, formerly used for driving machinery but now used mainly for exercise. **2** a wearisome or monotonous round of work or life that is boring, tiring, or hard to escape.

trea·son (trē′zən) *n* the act or fact of betraying one's country, especially by attempting to overthrow it. <Old French, from Latin *traditio*> **trea′son·a·ble** *adj.* **trea′son·a·bly** *adv.* **trea′son·ous** *adj.*

trea·sure (trezh′ər) *n* **1** a quantity of precious metals, gems, or other valuable items, or a single valuable item. **2** a thing that or person who is much loved or valued.
v **treas·ured, treas·ur·ing 1** value highly: *She treasures that doll more than all her other toys.* **2** keep carefully a valuable or valued item. <Old French, from Greek *thesauros* treasury>

treas·ur·er (trezh′ə rər) *n* a person appointed to administer, manage, or keep records of the financial assets and liabilities of a society, company, local government, or some other body.

treasure trove *n* a hidden collection of valuable or delightful things: *He found the book a treasure trove of useful information.* <Old French *tresor trové* treasure found>

treas·ur·y (trezh′ə rē) *n, pl* **treas·ur·ies 1** the funds or revenue of a country, institution, or society: *We paid for the party out of the club treasury.* **2** a government department in some countries that has charge of the collection, management, and expenditure of public revenues. **3** a place, building, or object where treasure is stored and may be found: *a treasury of adventure stories.*

treasury bill *n* a type of bond issued by a government treasury. It pays no interest but is sold at a discount and matures in less than a year.

treat (trēt) *v* **1** behave toward or deal with in a certain way: *He treats his dog firmly. My mother treats our new car*

with care. **2** regard something as being of a specified nature with implications for one's actions concerning it: *He treated his mistake as a joke.* **3** give medical attention to: *The therapist is treating my back pains.* **4** apply a process or substance to something to protect or preserve it or to give it special qualities: *He treated the engraving plate with acid.* **5** present or discuss a subject: *The topic was treated well in her talk.* **6** provide someone with food, drinks, or entertainment at one's own expense, or give someone something as a favour: *He treated his friends to ice cream.* **7** negotiate terms with someone, especially an opponent: *They decided to treat with the enemy.*
n **1** an event or item that is out of the ordinary and gives pleasure: *Visiting the museum was a real treat.* **2** food, drinks, or entertainment that gives pleasure and is paid for by someone else: *We got popcorn as a treat.* <Old French, from Latin *tractare* to manage>

treat·a·ble (trē′tə bəl) *adj* capable of being treated; that will respond to treatment: *Cancer is treatable.*

trea·tise (trē′tis) *n* a written work dealing formally and systematically with a subject.

treat·ment (trēt′mənt) *n* **1** the manner in which someone behaves toward or deals with someone or something: *equal treatment. This cat has suffered from cruel treatment.* **2** medical care given to a patient for an illness or injury, or the session in which this is performed: *The treatments for his cold didn't work.* **3** the use of a chemical, physical, or biological agent to preserve or give special qualities to something: *treatment of toxic waste.* **4** the presentation or discussion of a subject: *We didn't like his treatment of the topic.*

treat·y (trē′tē) *n, pl* **trea·ties** **1** an agreement, especially one between nations, signed and approved by each nation. **2** an agreement between a government and a First Nations or Native American people whereby the latter gave up their land rights except for reserves in return for cash payments and other considerations. <Old French, from Latin *tractare* discuss>

✱ **treaty Indian** *n* a STATUS INDIAN belonging to a First Nations band that signed a treaty with the Federal Government.

✱ **treaty rights** *pln* the rights guaranteed to First Nations people in their treaties with the Federal Government.

tre·ble (treb′əl) *adj* **1** consisting of three parts. **2** multiplied or occurring three times. **3** *Music* to do with a treble.
v **tre·bled, tre·bling** make or become three times as much: *She trebled her income when she changed to a career in advertising.*
n **1** a high-pitched singing voice, especially a boy's voice equivalent in pitch to an adult female soprano, or a singer with such a range. **2** an instrument with the highest pitch in a family of musical instruments. **3** especially in recording and sound reproduction, the upper half of the whole musical range. Compare BASS. **4** a high-pitched voice. <Old French, from Latin *triplus* triple>

treble clef *Music n* the C clef that assigns the note G above middle C to the second line up from the bottom of the staff. Compare ALTO CLEF, BASS CLEF, TENOR CLEF.

tre·bly (treb′lē) *adv* three times as much.

tree (trē) *n* **1** a large, tall plant with a single woody trunk or stem, and bearing lateral branches at some distance from the ground. See BROADLEAF for picture. **2** a tall bush, shrub, or other plant with a tall erect stem: *a banana tree.* **3** a wooden structure or part of a structure for some special purpose: *a clothes tree, a shoe tree.* **4** a thing that has a branching structure resembling that of a tree: *a family tree.* **tree′less** *adj.* **tree′like′** *adj.*
v **treed, tree·ing** force a hunted animal to take refuge in a tree: *The dog treed the raccoon.* <Old English *treo*>
up a tree, *Informal* in a difficult situation.

treed (trēd) *adj* planted or covered with trees: *treed lands.*

tree farm *n* a privately owned area in which trees are grown for cutting later. **tree farmer** *n.* **tree farming** *n.*

tree frog *n* a tree-dwelling frog that has long toes with sticky discs on the tips that help them in climbing.

tree house *n* a structure built in the branches of a tree for children to play in.

tree hugger *Informal n* a person with a great interest in protecting the natural environment.

tree·line (trē′līn) *n* the line or altitude on a mountain beyond which no trees grow.

tre·en (trē′ən) *n* small domestic wooden objects, especially antiques. <Old English *treow* tree>

tree surgeon *n* a person who prunes and treats old or damaged trees in order to preserve them. **tree surgery** *n.*

tree·top (trē′top′) *n* the uppermost part of a tree.

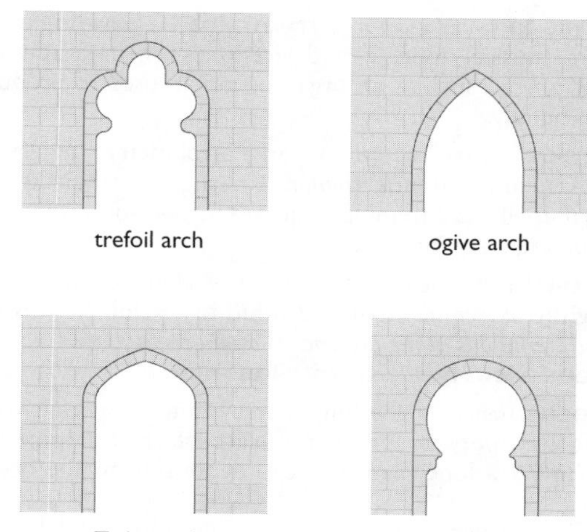

tre·foil (trē′foil′) *n* **1** a small plant of the pea family with yellow flowers and three-lobed cloverlike leaves, or a similar plant with three-lobed leaves. **2** an ornamental design of three rounded lobes like that of clover. <Latin *tri-* three + *folium* leaf>

a bat	e bed	i bid	o pot	u cup	th thin
ā cake	ē me	ī bite	ō go	ū rude	ᴛʜ then
ä bar	ə about	ər over	ô for	ů put	zh measure

T

trek (trek) *v* **trekked, trek·king** make a long, difficult journey, especially on foot.
n a long journey, especially a slow or difficult one. <Dutch *trekken*>

trel·lis (trel′is) *n* a framework of light wooden or metal bars, chiefly used as a support for fruit trees or vines, typically fastened against a wall.
v provide with, enclose, or support a plant on a trellis. <Old French *trelis*, from Latin *trilix* triple-twilled (threads in weaving)>

trem·a·tode (trem′ə tōd′) *n* a flatworm that lives as a parasite in or on other animals.

trem·ble (trem′bəl) *v* **trem·bled, trem·bling** **1** shake, typically as a result of anxiety, fear, excitement, cold, or physical frailty: *The sick woman's hand trembled. His voice trembled with anticipation.* **2** be in a condition of extreme apprehension: *She trembled for their safety. He trembled at the thought of having to ask for the money.* **3** shake or quiver slightly: *The leaves trembled in the breeze.*
n a trembling feeling, movement, or sound: *There was a tremble in her voice as she began to recite.* <Latin *tremere* tremble> **trem′bling** *adj.* **trem′bling·ly** *adv.* **trem′bly** *adj.*

tre·men·dous (tri men′dəs) *adj* **1** very great in amount, scale, or intensity: *The team suffered a tremendous defeat.* **2** *Informal* extremely good or impressive: *The volunteer group did a tremendous job.* <Latin *tremendus* to be trembled at, from *tremere* tremble>
tre·men′dous·ly *adv.* **tre·men′dous·ness** *n.*

trem·o·lo (trem′ə lō′) *n, pl* **trem·o·los** **1** a wavering effect in a musical tone. **2** a device or lever in a musical instrument, such as an organ or guitar, used to produce this quality.

trem·or (trem′ər) *n* **1** an involuntary quivering movement: *a muscle tremor.* **2** a slight earthquake: *an earth tremor.* **3** a tremble or quaver in a person's voice.
v undergo a tremor or tremors.

trem·u·lous (trem′yə ləs) *adj* **1** shaking or quivering slightly: *a tremulous voice.* **2** timid or fearful: *He was shy and tremulous in the presence of strangers.*
trem′u·lous·ly *adv.* **trem′u·lous·ness** *n.*

trench (trench) *n* **1** a long, narrow ditch, especially one dug by troops to provide a place of shelter from the enemy. **2** a long, narrow, deep depression in the ocean bed.
v dig a trench or trenches in the ground. <Old French *trenchier* to cut, from Latin *truncare* to cut>

trench·ant (tren′chənt) *adj* vigorous or sharp in expression or style: *trenchant wit.* <See TRENCH.> **trench′an·cy** *n.* **trench′ant·ly** *adv.*

trench coat *n* a loose-fitting raincoat worn with a belt, often double-breasted and usually with wide lapels and epaulettes. See EPAULETTE for picture.

trench mouth *n* a contagious disease of the gums caused by bacteria, and characterized by foul-smelling breath.

trend (trend) *n* **1** a general direction in which something is developing or changing: *a downward trend.* **2** a current style in fashion.
v **1** bend or turn away in a specified direction: *The road trends to the north.* **2** change or develop in a general direction: *The economic recovery was trending upward.* <Old English *trendan*>

trend·set·ter (trend′set′ər) *n* a person who or thing that leads the way in fashion or ideas.

trend·y (tren′dē) *adj* **trend·i·er, trend·i·est** following the very latest fashions or trends: *a trendy boutique.*

trep·i·da·tion (trep′ə dā′shən) *n* a feeling of fear or apprehension about something that may happen. <Latin *trepidus* alarmed>

tres·pass (tres′pəs) *or* (tres′pas) *v* **1** enter someone's land or property without any right or permission to do so: *The farmer put up "No Trespassing" signs to keep people away.* **2** make unfair claims on or take advantage of something: *I won't trespass on your time any longer.* **3** *Archaic* commit an offense against a person or a set of rules.
n **1** entry to a person's land or property without any right or permission to do so. **2** *Archaic* a sin or offense. <Old French, from Latin *trans-* through + *passer* pass>
tres′pass·er *n.*

tress (tres) *n* (*usually plural*) a long lock, curl, or braid of a person's hair: *She had thick, dark brown tresses.* <Old French *tresce*>

tres·tle (tres′əl) *n* **1** a framework consisting of a horizontal beam supported by two pairs of sloping legs, used in pairs to support a flat surface such as a tabletop. **2** an open, braced framework used to support a raised structure such as a bridge: *a railroad trestle.* <Old French, from Latin *transtrum* beam>

trey (trā) *n* a thing with three of something, such as a card, die, or domino. <Old French, from Latin *tres* three>

tri– *combining form* three: *triangle.* <Latin *tres*, Greek *treis*>

tri·ad (trī′ad) *n* **1** a group or set of three, especially three closely related people or things. **2** a chord of three musical notes, consisting of a given note with the third and fifth above it. <Greek *triados*, from *treis* three>

tri·age (trē oj′) *or* (trē′oj′) *n* **1** the action of sorting according to quality. **2** the assignment of degrees of urgency to wounds or illnesses to decide the order of medical treatment among patients or casualties. <French *trier* sort>

tri·al (trī′əl) *n* **1** a formal examination of evidence by a judge, or judge and jury, in order to decide guilt in a case of criminal or civil proceedings: *The suspect was arrested and brought to trial.* **2** a test of the performance, qualities, or suitability of someone or something: *He gave the machine a trial to see if it would work.* **3** a person who or thing or situation that tests a person's endurance or patience: *She is a trial to her big sister. His life has been full of trials—sickness, poverty, and loss of loved ones.*
adj used for or as part of a trial: *trial evidence, a trial run.* <Old French *trier* to try>
trial and error, the process of arriving at a solution of a problem by trying several ways and learning from the mistakes so made.

trial run *n* a test of how well a new system, product, or process works: *We pitched the tent in the yard as a trial run for our camping trip to Kejimkujk Park.*

tri·an·gle (trī′ang′gəl) *n* **1** a closed plane figure with three sides and three interior angles. **2** a thing shaped like such a figure, such as a drafting instrument in the form of a right-angled triangle, or a frame used to position the balls in snooker and pool: *Our backyard forms a triangle.* **3** a situation involving three people or things, especially an emotional relationship involving a couple and a third person with whom one of them is involved. **4** a musical instrument consisting of a steel rod bent in a triangle and producing a light ringing sound See PERCUSSION INSTRUMENT for picture. **tri·an′gu·lar** (trī ang′gyə lər) *adj.*

tri·an·gu·late (trī ang′gyə lāt′) *v* **tri·an·gu·lat·ed, tri·an·gu·lat·ing** **1** divide an area into triangles for surveying or mapping purposes, or determine height, distance, or location in this way. **2** form into a triangle or triangles.

Tri·as·sic (trī as′ik) *n* the geological period lasting from about 250 million to 200 million years ago, when dinosaurs first appeared. See also MESOZOIC.
adj to do with this period or the rocks formed then. <German *Trias*, name for a series of strata with three types of deposit>

tri·ath·lon (trīath′lon) *n* an athletic contest consisting of three different events, typically swimming, cycling, and long-distance running. <*tri-* three + Greek *athlon* contest> **tri·ath′lete** *n.*

trib·al (trī′bəl) *adj* to do with a tribe or tribes: *tribal customs, tribal lore.* **trib′al·ly** *adv.*

trib·al·ism (trī′bəl iz′əm) *n* **1** the condition or fact of being organized in a tribe or tribes. **2** the behaviour and attitudes that stem from strong loyalty to one's own tribe or social group.

tribe (trīb) *n* a social division in a traditional society consisting of families or communities linked by social, economic, religious, or family ties, with a common culture and language. <Latin *tribus*>

GRAMMAR AND USAGE

In the past, **tribe** was commonly used to refer to a group of Aboriginal people sharing the same language and culture. Its use is now generally discouraged because the word can have negative connotations. The term *First Nations* is preferred, used with reference to culturally linked groups of Aboriginal peoples other than the Inuit and Métis. To refer to all groups, including Inuit and Métis, use *First Peoples*.

trib·u·la·tion (trib′yə lā′shən) *n* a cause or condition of great trouble or suffering: *a story about the tribulations of early settlers in Manitoba.* <Latin *tribulare* afflict, press, from *tribulum* threshing board>

tri·bu·nal (tri byū′nəl) *or* (trī byū′nəl) *n* **1** a court of justice: *an international tribunal.* **2** a body established to settle certain types of dispute: *an industrial tribunal.*

trib·une (trib′yūn) *n* **1** an official in ancient Rome chosen by the plebeians to protect their interests. **2** a popular leader, especially of many people. <Latin *tribus* tribe>

trib·u·tar·y (trib′yə ter′ē) *n, pl* **trib·u·tar·ies** a river or stream that flows into a larger river or lake.
adj flowing into a larger stream or body of water: *a tributary flow.* <Latin *tributarius*>

trib·ute (trib′yūt) *n* **1** an act, statement, or gift that is intended to show gratitude, respect, or admiration: *The solemn ceremony was a tribute to the dead.* **2** a thing resulting from something else and indicating its worth: *The loud applause was a tribute to the speaker's wit.* **3** in former times, the payment made at regular intervals by one state or ruler to another, especially as a sign of submission. <Latin *tributum* a thing contributed, from *tribuere* allot>

trice (trīs) *n*
in a trice, *Informal* in a moment or very quickly: *I'll be with you in a trice.*

tri·ceps (trī′seps) *n* a large muscle at the back of the upper arm that has three points of attachment and extends or straightens the arm. <Latin, from *tri-* three + *caput* head, because the muscle has three points of origin>

tri·cer·a·tops (trī ser′ə tops′) *n* a plant-eating quadruped dinosaur of the late Cretaceous period, with a large bony crest on the back of the neck, a long horn over each eye, and a smaller horn on the snout. <Greek *tri-* three + *keratos* horn + *ops* eye>

trich·i·no·sis (trik′ə nō′sis) *n* a disease due to the presence of **trichina**, a small, slender worm that lives as a parasite in the intestines and muscles of humans and mammals.

trick (trik) *n* **1** a cunning or skilful act or plan intended to deceive or outwit someone: *The phone call was a trick to get him out of the room.* **2** a mischievous practical joke: *We were sure someone was playing a silly trick on us. Stealing the girl's lunch was a mean trick.* **3** a skilful act performed for entertainment or amusement: *I don't enjoy seeing animals do tricks.* **4** a clever or particular way of doing something: *She knew the trick of making good pastry.* **5** a peculiar or characteristic habit or mannerism: *He has a trick of pulling at his collar.* **6** a sequence of cards in bridge and other card games forming a single round of play. One card is laid down by each player, the highest card being the winner.
v deceive or outwit someone by being cunning or skilful, or use deception to make someone do something: *I was tricked into buying software that I didn't really want.*
adj intended or used to deceive or puzzle, or to create an illusion: *a trick question.* <Old French *trique*> **trick′er** *n.*
do (or **turn**) **the trick,** do what one wants done.
how's tricks? *Informal* How are things? How are you?
not miss a trick, *Informal* be very alert or responsive.
trick of the trade, an especially effective or clever way of doing things, known only to those who are experienced in it.
trick out, dress up, especially in a garish way: *She was tricked out in wildly coloured silks and satins.*

a bat	e bed	i bid	o pot	u cup	th **thin**
ā cake	ē me	ī bite	ō go	ū rude	TH **then**
ä bar	ə about	ər over	ô for	ů put	zh measure

T

trick·er·y (trik′ə rē) *n, pl* **trick·er·ies** the act or practice of deception.

trick·le (trik′əl) *v* **trick·led, trick·ling 1** flow in drops or a small stream, or cause to flow in this way: *Tears trickled down her cheeks. The brook trickled through the valley. He trickled the water into the container.* **2** come or go slowly or gradually: *An hour before the show began, people started to trickle into the theatre.*
n **1** a small flow of liquid. **2** a small group or number of people or things moving slowly. <Middle English *strike* flow>

trick·le·down (trik′əl doun′) *adj* to do with a theory in which the poorest people in an economy gradually benefit as a result of the increasing wealth of the richest: *the trickledown theory.*

trick–or–treat (trik′ər trēt′) *n* a children's custom of calling at houses at Halloween, with the threat of pranks if they are not given a small gift of candy or other treats, or the greeting said by children following this custom. **trick′-or-treat′ing** *adj, n.*

trick·ster (trik′stər) *n* **1** a person who cheats or deceives people. **2** ✱ **Trickster** especially in First Nations lore, a mischievous figure, often an animal, who teaches culture and proper behaviour.

trick·y (trik′ē) *adj* **trick·i·er, trick·i·est 1** requiring care and skill because an object, task, problem, or situation is difficult or awkward: *Our back door has a tricky lock.* **2** deceitful or crafty. **trick′i·ly** *adv.* **trick′i·ness** *n.*

tri·col·our or **tri·col·or** (trī′kul′ər) *adj* with three colours.
n a flag with three colours, such as the national flag of France with three vertical stripes of blue, white, and red.

tri·cot (trē′kō) *n* a fine knitted fabric made of a natural fibre.

tri·cus·pid (trī kus′pid) *adj* of or with three cups or points, such as of a tooth or a valve of the heart.
n a tricuspid tooth.

tri·cy·cle (trī′sə kəl) *n* a three-wheeled vehicle resembling a bicycle, usually worked by pedals attached to the large single wheel in front. <*tri-* three + Greek *kyklos* wheel>

tri·dent (trī′dənt) *n* a three-pronged spear. <Latin *tri-* three + *dentis* tooth>

tried (trīd) *v* past tense and past participle of TRY.
adj tested or proven: *a worker of tried abilities.*
tried and true, found to be effective or reliable on many previous occasions.

tri·fle (trī′fəl) *n* **1** a thing of little value or importance. **2** a small amount of something. **3** a cold dessert made of sponge cake and fruit covered with layers of whipped cream and custard.
v **tri·fled, tri·fling** treat someone or something without seriousness or respect: *Don't trifle with serious matters. She had trifled away the whole morning.* <Old French *trufle*>
tri′fler *n.*
a trifle, little or somewhat: *She annoyed me more than just a trifle.*

tri·fling (trī′fling) *adj* unimportant or trivial: *The friends treated their quarrel as only a trifling matter.*
tri′fling·ly *adv.*

tri·fo·cal (trī fō′kəl) or (trī′fō′kel) *adj* with lenses in a pair of glasses that have three parts with different focal lengths.
n **trifocals** *pl* a pair of glasses with such lenses.

tri·fo·li·ate (trī fō′lē it) *or* (trī fō′lē āt′) *adj* with leaves in groups of three. <*tri-* three + Latin *folium* leaf>

trig·ger (trig′ər) *n* **1** a small lever that releases a spring or catch and so sets off a mechanism, especially one pulled back by the finger in firing a gun. **2** an event or thing that causes a thing to happen: *The unjust law was the trigger for a massive protest.*
v cause an event or situation to begin, happen, or exist: *The explosion was triggered by a spark. The fiery speech triggered an outburst of violence.* <Dutch *trekken* pull>
quick on the trigger, *Informal* quick to respond.

trig·ger–hap·py (trig′ər hap′ē) *adj* **1** ready to react to something by shooting a gun. **2** too ready to react, especially in an angry or violent way.

tri·glyc·er·ide (trī glis′ə rīd′) *n* an ester obtained from glycerol and containing three fatty acid molecules for each molecule of glycerol. Triglycerides are the main constituents of natural fats and oils. <*tri-* three + *glycerol*>

trig·o·nom·e·try (trig′ə nom′ə trē) *n* the branch of mathematics that deals with the relations of the sides and angles of triangles and the calculations based on these. <Greek *tri-* three + *gonia* angle + *metron* measure>
trig′o·no·met′ric *adj.*

trike (trīk) *Informal n* a tricycle.

tri·lat·er·al (trī lat′ər əl) *adj* **1** shared by or involving three parties: *a trilateral agreement.* **2** of or with three sides. <Latin *tri-* three + *lateris* side>

✱ **tri·light** (trī′līt′) *n* a light bulb that can be switched to any of three degrees of brightness.

tri·lin·gual (trī ling′gwəl) *or* (trī ling′gyə wəl) *adj* **1** able to speak three languages fluently. **2** using or involving three languages. <Latin *tri-* three+ *lingua* language>

trill (tril) *v* sing, play, sound, or speak with a quavering, vibrating sound.
n the act or sound of trilling. <Italian *trillare*>

tril·lion (tril′yən) *n, adj* a million million or a thousand billion. <*tri-* three + (*m*)*illion*>

tril·li·um (tril′ē əm) *n* a small plant of the lily family with a short stem, a whorl of three leaves, and a single flower with three sepals and three petals. The **white trillium** is the floral emblem of Ontario. <origin uncertain>

tri·lo·bite (trī′lə bīt′) *n* an extinct marine arthropod with three divisions of the body and jointed limbs. It is found as a fossil. <*tri-* three + Greek *lobos* lobe>

tril·o·gy (tril′ə jē) *n, pl* **tril·o·gies** a group of three novels, plays, movies, or operas that make a related series, though each part is itself a complete work. <*tri-* three + Greek *logos* story>

trim (trim) *v* **trimmed, trim·ming 1** make something neat or of the required size or form by cutting away irregular or unwanted parts: *The gardener trimmed the* hedge. *She's had her hair trimmed.* **2** reduce the size, amount, or number of something, typically expenses or costs: *The budget was trimmed by half.* **3** decorate something, typically with contrasting items or pieces of material: *to trim a jacket.* **4** adjust a sail to take advantage of the wind. **5** adjust the balance of a ship or aircraft by rearranging its cargo. **6** adapt one's views to the prevailing political trends in order to gain a personal advantage. **7** *Informal* defeat severely: *We trimmed that team twice last year.*

n **1** additional decoration, typically along the edges of something and in contrasting colour or material: *The uniform was black with gold trim.* **2** an act of cutting off part of something in order to neaten it: *He went to the barber for a trim.* **3** the quality of being in good order or condition: *in trim, out of trim.* **4** the degree to which an aircraft can be maintained at a constant altitude without any control forces being present. **5** the way in which a ship floats in the water.

adj **trim·mer, trim·mest** **1** neat, well-ordered, and attractive: *She keeps her desk trim.* **2** physically fit: *a trim body.* <Old English *trymman* make ready> **trim′ly** *adv.* **trim′ness** *n.*

tri·ma·ran (trī′mə ran′) *n* a boat with three hulls side by side. Compare CATAMARAN. <*tri-* three + (*cata*)*maran*>

tri·mes·ter (trī mes′tər) *n* a period of three months, especially as a division of the length of pregnancy, or one of the three terms in an academic year. <Latin *trimestris,* from *tri-* three + *mensis* month>

trim·mer (trim′ər) *n* **1** a person who or thing that trims: *a hedge trimmer, a hat trimmer, a window trimmer.* **2** a person who adapts views to the prevailing political trends in order to gain a personal advantage.

trim·ming (trim′ing) *n* **1** the action of cutting off the unwanted or untidy parts of something: *His hair needed a good trimming.* **2** *Informal* a decisive defeat. **3** **trimmings** *pl* **a** decoration, especially for clothes. **b** the traditional accompaniments to something, especially a meal on special occasions: *We ate turkey with all the trimmings.*

tri·month·ly (trī mun′thlē) *adj* occurring every three months.

Trin·i·dad and To·ba·go (trin′i dad′) (tə bā′gō) *n* a two-island country in the Caribbean.
Trin′i·dad′i·an *adj, n.* **To·ba′gan** *adj, n.*

tri·ni·tro·tol·u·ene (trī nī′trō tol′yū ēn′) TNT. <*tri-* three +*nitro*(*gen*) + *toluene*>

trin·i·ty (trin′ə tē) *n* **1** a group of three people or things, or the condition of being three. **2** **the Trinity** the three forms of being that in Christian belief form the divine nature of God.

trin·ket (tring′kit) *n* a small ornament or item of jewellery that is of little value. <origin uncertain>

tri·no·mi·al (trī nō′mē əl) *n* **1** *Mathematics* an expression in algebra consisting of three terms connected by plus or minus signs. Example: a + bx – 27. **2** *Biology* a name in the classification of animals or plants that consists of three words, the first being that of the genus, the second that of the species, and the third that of the subspecies or variety. *adj* consisting of three terms. <*tri-* three + (*bi*)*nomial*>

tri·o (trē′ō) *n, pl* **tri·os** a set or group of three people or things, such as a group of three musicians or a composition written for them. <Italian, from Latin *tres* three>

trip (trip) *v* **tripped, trip·ping** **1** catch one's foot on something and stumble or fall, or cause someone to do this: *to trip on the stairs. The loose board tripped him.* **2** (*usually with* ***up***) make a mistake, or detect someone in an error: *We sometimes tripped up by not making a full report. We tried to trip him up by asking hard questions.* **3** walk, run, or dance with quick, light steps: *She tripped down the marble stairs.* **4** activate a mechanism, especially by contact with an electrical device: *to trip an alarm.* **5** *Informal* experience hallucinations after taking a psychedelic drug, especially LSD.

n **1** a journey or excursion: *a business trip. We took a trip to the Maritimes.* **2** a stumble or fall due to catching one's foot on something. **3** *Informal* a series of hallucinations caused by taking a psychedelic drug: *an acid trip.* **4** a device that activates a mechanism to disconnect the power supply as a safety measure. <Old French *tripper*> **trip′per** *n.*

tri·par·tite (trī pȧr′tīt) *adj* **1** divided into or composed of three parts. **2** made or shared by three parties: *a tripartite treaty.*

tripe (trīp) *n* **1** the walls of the first and second stomachs of a cow or other ruminant used as food: *tripe and onions.* **2** nonsense: *She said it was all a lot of tripe.* <origin uncertain>

trip·ham·mer (trip′ham′ər) *n* a power-driven hammer, operated by a tripping device by which it is raised and allowed to fall repeatedly.

tri·ple (trip′əl) *adj* **1** consisting of or involving three parts, things, events, or people: *triple somersaults, a triple winner.* **2** with three times the usual size or strength: *He ordered a triple chocolate sundae.* **3** three times as much or as many: *The new battery had triple the efficiency of the old one.*

n **1** a set of three things or parts. **2** a hit in baseball that enables the batter to reach third base.

v **tri·pled, tri·pling** **1** make or become three times as much or as many: *My older brother has tripled his wages in five years.* **2** hit a triple in baseball: *He tripled in the eighth inning.* <Latin *tri-* three + *-plus* fold> **trip′ly** *adv.*

triple crown *Sports n* an award or honour for winning a group of three important events in a sport, such as in horse racing.

triple jump *n* a track-and-field event in which competitors attempt to jump as far as possible by performing a hop, a step, and a jump from a running start.

triple play *Baseball n* a defensive play in which three runners are put out.

a bat	e bed	i bid	o pot	u cup	th **thin**
ā cake	ē me	ī bite	ō go	ū rude	ᴛʜ **then**
ȧ bar	ə about	ər over	ȯ for	ủ put	zh measure

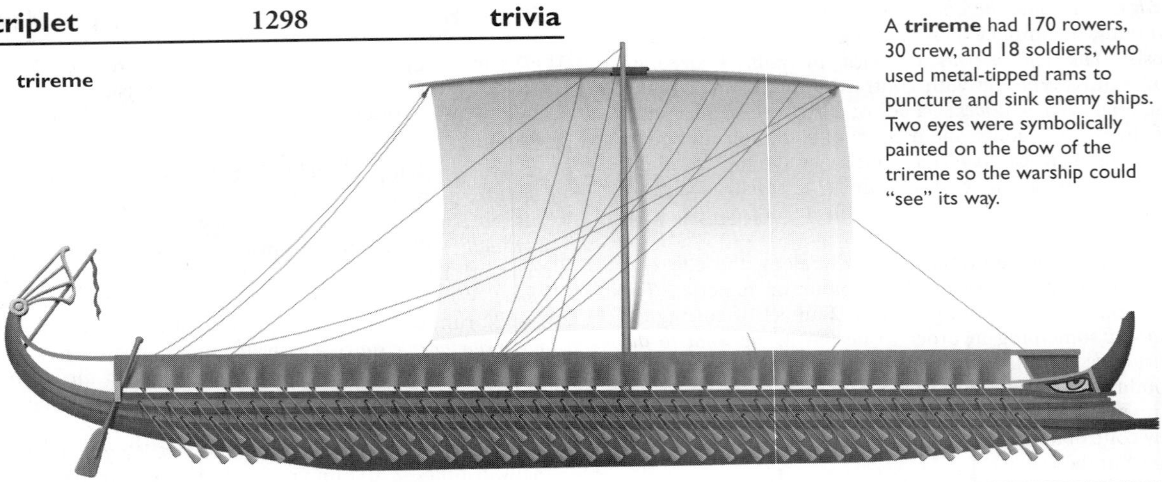

A **trireme** had 170 rowers, 30 crew, and 18 soldiers, who used metal-tipped rams to puncture and sink enemy ships. Two eyes were symbolically painted on the bow of the trireme so the warship could "see" its way.

tri·plet (trip′lit) *n* **1** one of three children or animals born at the same birth. **2** a group of three similar, equal, or identical things, such as three rhyming lines of verse.

triple time *Music n* musical time with three beats to the bar.

tri·plex (trip′leks′) or (trī′pleks′) *n* a residential building with three apartments.
adj with three parts. <Latin, from *tri-* three + *plicare* fold>

trip·li·cate (trip′lə kāt′) *for v,* (trip′lə kit) *for adj.*
v **trip·li·cat·ed, trip·li·cat·ing** make three copies of a thing.
adj existing in three copies or examples.
in triplicate, three times in exactly the same way, or existing as a set of three exact copies.

tri·pod (trī′pod) *n* a support or stand with three legs, for supporting a camera or telescope. <*tri-* three + Greek *podos* foot>

trip·tych (trip′tik) *n* **1** a picture or carving on three panels, typically hinged together vertically. **2** a set of three related artistic, literary, or musical works intended to be regarded together. <Greek *tri-* three + *ptyx* fold>

trip·wire (trip′wīr′) *n* a wire stretched close to the ground, working a trap, explosion, or alarm when disturbed and serving to detect people or animals entering an area, or prevent them from doing so.

tri·reme (trī′rēm) *n* an ancient Greek or Roman warship with three rows of oars.

tri·sect (trī sekt′) *v* divide something into three equal parts. <*tri-* three + Latin *sectus* pp of *secare* cut> **tri·sec′tion** *n.* **tri·sec′tor** *n.*

trite (trīt) *adj* **trit·er, trit·est** overused, stale, and of little significance as a remark, opinion, or idea: *The movie turned out to be very trite, so we left early.* <Latin *tritus* worn, familiar, from *terere* wear down> **trite′ly** *adv.* **trite′ness** *n.*

trit·i·ca·le (trī′i kā′lē) *n* a hybrid cereal grain, a cross between wheat and rye. <*Triticum* name of wheat genus + *Secale,* name of rye genus>

tri·ton[1] (trī′tən) *n* a large, tropical or subtropical sea snail with a heavy, spiral-shaped shell.

tri·umph (trī′umf) *n* **1** a great victory or achievement, or the condition of being victorious or successful: *a final triumph over the enemy, a triumph of modern science. They returned home in triumph.* **2** joy or satisfaction resulting from victory or success: *There was triumph in her eyes as she accepted the medal.* **3** a procession in honour of a victorious general in ancient Rome.
v **1** gain victory or win success: *Our team triumphed over theirs.* **2** exult or rejoice because of victory or success. <Latin *triumphus*>

tri·um·phal (trī um′fəl) *adj* made, carried out, or used in celebration of a great victory or achievement: *a triumphal march.*

tri·um·phant (trī um′fənt) *adj* **1** having won a battle or contest: *a triumphant army.* **2** rejoicing because of victory or success: *The winner of the election spoke in triumphant tones to her supporters.* **tri·um′phant·ly** *adv.*

tri·um·vi·rate (trī um′və rit) *n* a group of three powerful or notable people or things existing in relation to each other, especially in government. <Latin *trium virorum* = of three men>

tri·une (trī′yūn′) *adj* consisting of three in one, especially with reference to the Christian Trinity. <*tri-* three + Latin *unus* one>

triv·et (triv′it) *n* a stand or support usually with three legs or feet, especially one placed over a fire for a cooking pot or kettle to stand on. <*tri-* three + Latin *pes* foot>

triv·i·a (triv′ē ə) *pln* details, matters, or pieces of information of little importance or value.

ETYMOLOGY

Trivia comes from Latin *trivialis,* meaning "commonplace." The Latin word was made up of *tri* meaning "three" and *via* "road." This was a reference to public crossroads where, it was thought, commonplace or ordinary things happened.

triv·i·al (triv′ē əl) *adj* of little value or importance: *The essay had only a few trivial mistakes.* **triv′i·al′i·ty** *n.* **triv′i·al·ly** *adv.*

SYNONYMS

Trivial emphasizes having little value: *The problem was trivial and not worth their attention.*

Commonplace means "ordinary" or "everyday," but not necessarily "trivial": *Computers are much more commonplace now than they were ten years ago.*

Minor means "less important": *She had a minor role in the TV series.*

triv·i·al·ize (triv′ē ə līz′) *v* **triv·i·al·ized, triv·i·al·iz·ing** treat as or cause to seem insignificant: *I think this comedy trivializes the difficulties faced by overweight people in our society.* **triv′i·al·i·za′tion** *n.*

trod (trod) past tense and a past participle of TREAD.

trod·den (trod′ən) a past participle of TREAD.

trog·lo·dyte (trog′lə dīt′) *n* a member of a prehistoric people who lived in caves. <Greek *trogle* cave + *dyein* go in>

troi·ka (troi′kə) *n* **1** a Russian vehicle, especially a sleigh, pulled by three horses abreast. **2** a group of three leaders or rulers sharing power. <Russian *troie* three together>

Tro·jan (trō′jən) *adj* to do with the ancient city of Troy.
n **1** a native or inhabitant of Troy. **2** a person who works extremely hard.

Trojan horse *n* **1** *Greek myth* a huge wooden horse that was given to the Trojans by the Greeks during the Trojan War. Hidden inside the horse were Greek soldiers, who were thus able to enter Troy and defeat the Trojans. **2** *Computers* an apparently normal program that contains hidden instructions for performing unexpected and often destructive processing.

troll[1] (trōl) *v* **1** fish by trailing a baited line behind a boat. **2** search for something. **3** sing in a happy and carefree way.
n the action of trolling for fish, or the line or bait used in such fishing. <Old French *troller* wander> **troll′er** *n.*

troll[2] (trōl) *n* a mythical, cave-dwelling being in folklore who may be a giant or dwarf, but is usually depicted as ugly. <Old Norse>

trol·ley (trol′ē) *n, pl* **trol·leys** **1** a large metal basket or frame on wheels, used for carrying heavy or awkward items, such as purchases in a supermarket, luggage at an airport, or food and drinks. **2** a streetcar. **3** a wheel attached to a pole used for collecting current from overhead electric wires to drive a streetcar. <origin uncertain>

trol·lop (trol′əp) *n* a woman perceived as sexually promiscuous. <origin uncertain>

trom·bone (trom′bōn) *or* (trom bōn′) *n* a large, brass, wind instrument, different notes being made using an extendable slide. See BRASS for picture. <Italian *trombone*, from *tromba* trumpet> **trom·bon′ist** *n.*

Tr'on Dek Hwech'·in (tron′dek whech′ən) HAN.

troop (trūp) *n* **1** **troops** *pl* soldiers or an armed force. **2** a unit of the armed forces. **3** a group of people or animals of a particular kind: *a troop of monkeys.*
v **1** gather or go together or in large numbers: *We all trooped into the living room.* **2** walk at a slow or steady pace as a lone person: *He wearily trooped home.* <French *troupe*, from Latin *troppus* herd>

GRAMMAR AND USAGE

Troops is used in the plural to describe soldiers and other organized groups: *The troops were on parade for Canada Day.*

Troupe is used for groups of touring performers: *The troupe of acrobats will arrive from Calgary tonight.*

troop·er (trū′pər) *n* **1** a soldier in a cavalry regiment or an armoured regiment. **2** *US* a state police officer.

troop·ship (trūp′ship′) *n* a ship used to carry soldiers.

tro·phy (trō′fē) *n, pl* **tro·phies** **1** a cup or other decorative object awarded as a prize for a victory or success, or a souvenir of an achievement: *She kept her tennis trophy on the mantelpiece.* **2** the weapons of a defeated army set up as a memorial of victory. <Latin, from Greek *tropaion* monument of an enemy's defeat>

trop·ic (trop′ik) *n* **1** either of two parallels of latitude, one about 23° north and the other about 23° south of the equator. The northern parallel is the **tropic of Cancer** and the southern parallel is the **tropic of Capricorn**. **2 the tropics** *pl* the region between these parallels.
adj to do with the tropics. <Latin, from Greek *trope* a turn, from the belief that the sun turned back when it reached the tropics of Cancer and Capricorn>

trop·i·cal (trop′ə kəl) *adj* **1** of, typical of, or found in the tropics: *tropical fruits, tropical diseases, a tropical climate.* **2** resembling the tropics, especially in being very hot and humid: *tropical heat.* **trop′i·cal·ly** *adv.*

tro·pism (trō′piz əm) *n* the tendency of an animal or plant to turn or move in response to an external stimulus like sunlight. **tro·pis′tic** (trō pis′tik) *adj.*

trop·o·sphere (trop′ə sfēr′) *n* the lowest layer of the atmosphere, extending from the earth's surface to a height of about six to ten kilometres. See OZONE LAYER for picture. <Greek *trope* a change + *sphere*>

trot (trot) *v* **trot·ted, trot·ting** **1** of a horse or other four-footed animal, go at a pace faster than a walk, lifting each diagonal pair of legs alternately, or cause it to move at such a pace. **2** run at a moderate pace, typically with short steps: *The child trotted along after her mother.*
n **1** the pace of a trotting animal or person: *We started off at a trot.* **2** an act or period of trotting: *to go for a trot.* <origin uncertain>
trot out, bring out for others to see, especially the same information, story, or explanation that has been produced many times before.

a bat	e bed	i bid	o pot	u cup	th **thin**
ā cake	ē me	ī bite	ō go	ū rude	ᴛʜ **then**
à bar	ə about	ər over	ȯ for	u̇ put	zh measure

T

troth (troth) *or* (trōth) *Archaic n* faith or loyalty when pledged in a solemn agreement or undertaking. <Old English *treowth*>
pledge (or **plight**) **your troth,** make a solemn pledge of commitment or loyalty, especially in marriage.

trot·ter (trot′ər) *n* **1** a horse bred or trained for the sport of harness racing. See HARNESS RACING for picture. **2** the foot of a pig used for food.

trou·ba·dour (trū′bə dôr′) *or* (trū′bə dūr′) *n* a medieval lyric poet of southern France and northern Spain who wrote poems of courtly love. <Provençal *trobador*, from *trobar* to write verses>

trou·ble (trub′əl) *n* **1** difficulty or problems: *That dog has caused them a lot of trouble. We're still having trouble with the furnace.* **2** a malfunction of something such as a machine or a part of the body: *engine trouble, kidney trouble.* **3** effort or extra work made to do something, especially when inconvenient: *She took the trouble to make extra copies. I don't want to cause you any trouble.* **4** a particular aspect or quality of something regarded as unsatisfactory or as a source of difficulty: *She said the trouble with her friend was his gullibility.*
v **trou·bled, trou·bling 1** cause distress or worry to: *The lack of business troubled him.* **2** be distressed or anxious about: *May I trouble you to do something for me?* **3** cause oneself inconvenience or effort: *I've already eaten, so don't trouble to cook supper for me.* **4** cause pain or discomfort to: *His arthritis is troubling him again.* <Old French *trubler*, from *turba* turmoil> **trou′bler** *n.*
ask for trouble, *Informal* act in a way that is likely to incur problems or difficulty: *Bearing a grudge is just asking for trouble.*

trou·ble·mak·er (trub′əl mā′kər) *n* a person who causes problems or difficulty, especially by inspiring others to defy those in authority.

trou·ble·shoot (trub′əl shūt′) *v* **trou·ble·shot, trou·ble·shoot·ing 1** solve serious problems for a company or other organization. **2** trace and correct faults in a mechanical or electronic system. **trou′ble·shoot′er** *n.*

trou·ble·some (trub′əl səm) *adj* causing difficulty or annoyance: *a troublesome zipper.* **trou′ble·some·ly** *adv.* **trou′ble·some·ness** *n.*

trough (trof) *n* **1** a long, narrow open container for animals to eat and drink out of: *a watering trough.* **2** a container shaped like this used for other purposes: *The bread dough was kneaded in a trough.* **3** a channel used to carry a liquid, especially water. **4** a long hollow in the earth's surface or between two wave crests in the sea: *a deep trough between two huge waves.* **5** a long, narrow area of relatively low barometric pressure. <Old English *troh*>

trounce (trouns) *v* **trounced, trounc·ing** defeat severely in a contest or game: *The home team was trounced by the visitors.* <origin uncertain>

troupe (trūp) *n* a group of actors, singers, acrobats, or other entertainers who tour to different places to perform. <French>

trou·sers (trou′zərz) *pln* a two-legged outer garment reaching from the waist to the ankles.
adj **trouser** to do with trousers: *trouser cuffs.*

trous·seau (trū′sō) *or* (trū sō′) *n* the clothes, linen, and other personal belongings collected by a bride for the marriage. <French bundle>

trout (trout) *n, pl* **trouts** or (*especially collectively*) **trout** a mainly freshwater fish of the salmon family, such as the brook trout and rainbow trout, highly valued for food and game. See BROOK TROUT for picture. <Latin, from Greek *troktes* sharp-toothed fish>

trow·el (trou′əl) *n* **1** a small, handheld tool with a thin, flat, pointed blade, used to apply, spread, or smooth plaster or mortar. **2** a garden hand tool similar to a scoop, used for lifting plants or earth.
v **trow·elled, trow·el·ling** apply or spread with or as if with a trowel. <Old French *truele*, from Latin *trua* skimmer>

troy or **troy weight** (troi) *n, adj* a system of weights used mainly for precious metals and gems, with a pound of twelve ounces (about 0.37 kg), or expressed as a weight in this system: *a troy ounce.*

tru·ant (trū′ənt) *n* a person who stays away from school without permission or explanation.
adj being a truant: *truant habits.* <Irish *trog* wretched>
play truant, stay away from school without permission or explanation.

truce (trūs) *n* an agreement between enemies or opponents to stop fighting or arguing for a certain time: *A truce was declared between the two armies. After this argument there was a family truce for several days.* <Old English *treow*>

Trucks come in many shapes and sizes, designed to transport a huge variety of things. The dump truck and the van truck are two of the commonest types to be seen on Canadian roads.

truck[1] (truk) *n* **1** a wheeled vehicle, especially a large road motor vehicle used for carrying goods, materials, or troops. **2** a swivelling frame with two or more pairs of wheels supporting each end, such as in a railway car or a skateboard.
v **1** carry by truck: *The fruit was trucked to market.* **2** drive a truck. <origin uncertain>

truck[2] (truk) *n* **1** produce, especially vegetables, raised for market. **2** small articles of little value. **3** *Informal* dealings or exchange: *She has no truck with peddlers.* **4** a barter or exchange. **5** the former practice of paying wages in goods rather than in money.
v barter or exchange. <Old French *troquer* trade>

truck·er (truk′ər) *n* a person who drives a truck long-distance, especially to carry goods.

truck farm *n* a farm where various kinds of produce, especially vegetables, are raised for market.
truck farmer *n.*

truck·le (truk′əl) *v* **truck·led, truck·ling** submit or behave in an unduly humble or flattering way: *That man got his position by truckling to his superiors.* <*truckle* low bed (often used by servants) rolled under a high one when not in use> **truck′ler** *n.*

truck·load (truk′lōd′) *n* a load that fills or is carried by a truck.

truck stop *n* a restaurant and service station together on a highway, used especially by truckers.

truc·u·lent (truk′yə lənt) *adj* eager or quick to argue, fight, or be defiantly hostile: *a truculent attitude.* <Latin *trucis* fierce> **truc′u·lence** *n.* **truc′u·lent·ly** *adv.*

SYNONYMS

Truculent emphasizes readiness to fight, argue, or defy: *The truculent man disagreed with everyone.*

Scrappy is an informal word for "truculent": *They're a scrappy bunch who always cause trouble.*

Aggressive often means "assertive" or "forceful": *We have to take an aggressive approach in order to get the funds we need.*

trudge (truj) *v* **trudged, trudg·ing** walk slowly and with heavy steps, typically because of fatigue or harsh conditions: *The tired hikers trudged home.*
n a hard or weary walk: *It was a long trudge up the hill.* <origin uncertain> **trudg′er** *n.*

true (trū) *adj* **tru·er, tru·est 1** agreeing with fact or reality: *It is true that 6 plus 4 is 10.* **2** correctly or strictly named: *true gold, true kindness.* **3** accurate or exact: *a true portrait.* **4** faithful or loyal: *a true friend.* **5** accurately agreeing with a standard or expectation: *a true copy.*
adv **1** truly: *She spoke truer than she knew.* **2** accurate and without variation: *He aimed true.*
n (*usually with* ***out of***) an exact or accurate formation, position, or adjustment: *The badly constructed door was out of true.*
v **trued, tru·ing** bring an object, wheel, or other construction into the exact shape or position required. <Old English *triewe*>
come true, actually happen or become the case: *His wishes came true.*
true to form (or **type**)**,** behaving as expected or in the typical way: *Her brother was true to form and arrived half an hour late.*

true–blue (trū′blū′) *adj* extremely loyal and unchanging: *She's a true-blue environmentalist.*

true–heart·ed (trū′hȧr′tid) *adj* faithful or loyal: *a true-hearted friend.*

true–life (trū′līf′) *adj* corresponding to or happening in actual life: *a true-life romance.*

truf·fle (truf′əl) *n* **1** a strong-smelling fungus growing underground. Truffles resemble irregular, rough-skinned potatoes and are highly valued. **2** a soft chocolate candy, often flavoured. <French *truffe*, from Latin *tuber* root>

tru·ism (trū′iz əm) *n* a statement that is obviously true and says nothing new or interesting: *He was always saying truisms like "You're only young once."*

tru·ly (trū′lē) *adv* **1** in a truthful or sincere way: *Tell me truly what you think.* **2** to the fullest degree, genuinely, or properly: *It was truly a beautiful sight.*

trump (trump) *n* **1** in some card games, a playing card of a suit that ranks higher than the other suits. **2 trumps** *pl* the suit with this rank: *Hearts are trumps.*
v **1** play a trump in a card game: *He trumped my king.* **2** beat someone or something by saying or doing something: *He trumped my argument by bringing out a new fact.* <*triumph*>
trump up, invent a false accusation or argument: *He trumped up an excuse for being late.*

trump card *n* **1** a playing card of a suit that for a particular hand ranks higher than the other suits. **2** a valuable resource, fact, or argument, especially one that is held in reserve until needed; a clincher.

trumped–up (trump′tup′) *adj* invented in order to deceive: *trumped-up charges.*

trump·er·y (trump′ə rē) *n, pl* **trump·er·ies** something showy but with little value.
adj showy but with little value. <French *tromper* deceive>

trum·pet (trum′pit) *n* **1** a brass musical instrument with a looped tube that is bell-shaped at one end and usually has three valves to vary its bright, penetrating tone. See BRASS for picture. **2** a thing shaped like a trumpet: *an ear trumpet.* **3** a sound resembling that of a trumpet.
v **1** play a trumpet. **2** make a loud, penetrating sound like that of a trumpet: *The elephant trumpeted in fright.* **3** proclaim loudly or widely: *They'll trumpet that story all over town.* <Old French *trompe*>
blow your own trumpet, *Informal* talk boastfully.

trum·pet·er (trum′pə tər) *n* **1** a person who plays a trumpet. **2** a large, ground-dwelling bird of the tropical forests of S America, with loud, booming calls. **3** in full, **trumpeter swan** a migratory swan of northern N America with a honking call.

trun·cate (trung′kāt′) *v* **trun·cat·ed, trun·cat·ing** shorten something by cutting off the top or end.
adj of a leaf, feather, or other part ending abruptly as if cut off across the base or tip. <Latin *truncus* maimed> **trun·ca′tion** *n.*

a bat	e bed	i bid	o pot	u cup	th **thin**
ā cake	ē me	ī bite	ō go	ū rude	ᴛʜ **then**
ȧ bar	ə about	ər over	ȯ for	u̇ put	zh measure

trun·dle (trun′dəl) *v* **trun·dled, trun·dling** move slowly and heavily as a wheeled vehicle, typically in a noisy or uneven way, or move in a similar way as a person, or cause something to move in such a way: *The worker trundled a wheelbarrow full of cement.*
n an act of moving in such a way. <Old English *tryndel*>

trunk (trungk) *n* **1 a** the main woody stem of a tree, as distinct from the branches and the roots. **b** the main part of a structure or system from which smaller branches arise. **c** a person's or animal's body apart from the limbs and head. **2** a large, heavy box with a hinged lid, used for transporting or storing clothes and other personal property. **3** the long, muscular, flexible snout of an elephant. **4** the closed space at the back of a motor vehicle for carrying luggage or other property. **5 trunks** *pl* very short pants worn by athletes, especially swimmers and boxers. <Old French, from Latin *truncus* cut off>

truss (trus) *n* **1** a framework, typically consisting of rafters, posts, and struts, supporting a roof, bridge, or other structure. **2** a surgical appliance worn to support a hernia, typically a padded belt.
v **1** tie up the wings and legs of a chicken or other bird before cooking. **2** tie up someone with the arms at the side: *We trussed the burglar up and called the police.* **3** support or strengthen a roof, bridge, or other structure with a truss or trusses. <Old French *trusser*>

trust (trust) *n* **1** a firm belief in the honesty, truthfulness, justice, or power of a person or thing: *The boy put trust in his mother.* **2** the condition of being responsible for someone or something: *a position of trust.* **3** an obligation or responsibility given to a person in whom confidence or authority is placed: *He was faithful to his trust.* **4** a legal arrangement in which a person is made the nominal owner of property to be held or used for the benefit of one or more others: *a family trust.* **5** a body of trustees, or an organization or company managed by a trustee: *a charitable trust.*
adj to do with a TRUST (def. 5): *a trust company.*
v **1** believe in the reliability, truth, ability, or strength of: *She is a woman to be trusted. He did not trust his memory.* **2** confidently allow someone to have, use, or look after someone or something of importance or value, or commit someone or something to the safekeeping of: *Can I trust you with the keys? I trusted them with all my private information.* **3** place reliance on luck, fate, or something else over which one has little control: *Since I couldn't swim, I trusted that the water wasn't deep.* <Old Norse *traust*> **trust′a·ble** *adj.* **trust′er** *n.*

SYNONYMS

Trust implies confidence in someone or something: *I have trust that you'll call later.*

Faith suggests believing without wanting or needing proof: *The people's faith in the popular leader remained strong, even though the war continued.*

Dependence emphasizes reliance on someone or something: *The job ended his dependence on loans.*

trust company *n* a business concern formed to act as a trustee or to deal with trusts. Many trust companies offer banking services.

trus·tee (trus tē′) *n* **1** a person given control of property in trust with a legal obligation to administer it solely for the purposes thereof: *A trustee will manage the children's property until they are adults.* **2** a person elected to a board or committee that administers the schools in a district. **3** a country made responsible for a trust territory. **trus·tee′ship** *n.*

trust·ful (trust′fəl) *adj* with or marked by a strong belief in the reliability, truth, ability, or strength of someone. **trust′ful·ly** *adv.* **trust′ful·ness** *n.*

trust fund *n* a fund consisting of money, property, or other assets belonging to a trust, held by the trustees for the benefit of another.

trust·ing (trus′ting) *adj* showing or tending to have a belief in a person's honesty or sincerity: *She has a trusting nature.* **trust′ing·ly** *adv.* **trust′ing·ness** *n.*

trust·wor·thy (trus′twər′ᴛʜē) *adj* able to be relied on as honest or truthful: *The class chose a trustworthy girl for treasurer.* **trust′wor′thi·ly** *adv.* **trust′wor′thi·ness** *n.*

trust·y (trus′tē) *adj* **trust·i·er, trust·i·est** having worked for a long time and regarded as reliable or faithful: *a trusty employee, a trusty sword.*
n, pl **trust·ies** a prisoner who is given special privileges or responsibilities in return for good behaviour: *The trusties were allowed to work on the gardens outside the prison walls.* **trust′i·ly** *adv.* **trust′i·ness** *n.*

truth (trūth) *n, pl* **truths** (trūᴛʜz) *or* (trūths) **1** the quality or condition of being in accord with fact or reality: *She doubted the truth of the story.* **2** something that is in accord with fact or reality: *The truth is that I haven't seen him for over a year.* **3** a fact or belief that is accepted as true: *a scientific truth.*
in truth, truly, really, or in fact.

truth·ful (trūth′fəl) *adj* telling or expressing the truth as a person or statement: *a truthful man, a truthful report.* **truth′ful·ly** *adv.* **truth′ful·ness** *n.*

truth serum *n* a drug thought to make a person speak freely and openly when questioned.

try (trī) *v* **tried, try·ing 1** make an attempt or effort to do something: *He tried to open the window, but it was stuck. You'll never know till you try. She's going to try for her lifesaving certificate next week.* **2** find out the quality or usefulness of an action or thing: *Try opening the window to get some fresh air. Did you try the library to see if they had a copy?* **3** attempt to open a door or window: *Try the doors to see if they are locked.* **4** subject someone to a trial by examining evidence in a court of law and reaching a decision on the person's guilt or innocence: *The woman was tried and found guilty.* **5** make severe demands on a person or a quality: *His constant complaining tried her patience. She was greatly tried by the children's squabbles.*
n, pl **tries 1** an attempt or effort to accomplish something: *We each had three tries at the high jump. She made a good try for the ball but missed it.* **2** an act of doing, using, or testing something new or different to see if it is suitable. **3** *Rugby* an act of touching the ball down behind the opposing goal line, scoring points and entitling the scoring side to a kick at goal. <origin uncertain>

try on, put on to test the fit or appearance of: *I tried on four pairs of boots, but I didn't like any of them.*
try out for, take a test to show fitness for a particular role or place: *to try out for the hockey team, to try out for a part in a play.*

GRAMMAR AND USAGE

Try and is often used in informal English: *Try and go to the game if you can.* In formal English, use **try to** instead: *The team will try to win the cup.*

trying (trī′ing) *adj* difficult, hard to endure, or annoying: *It's been a trying day.*

try·out (trī′out′) *n* a test made to determine the potential of someone or something for a particular role or place: *The tryouts for the play are tomorrow.*

tryp·sin (trip′sən) *n* an enzyme in the digestive juice secreted by the pancreas that breaks down proteins in the small intestine.

try square *n* an instrument used to check and mark right angles during construction of roads, buildings, etc.

tryst (trist) *n* a private, romantic meeting between people who are in love.
v meet together in this way. <Old French *triste* in hunting, a place to which game was driven>

tsar (zär) CZAR.

tsa·ri·na (zä rē′nə) CZARINA.

TSE in full, **transmissible spongiform encephalopathy,** the technical name for MAD COW DISEASE and other diseases of the same kind.

The **tsetse fly** carries a parasite that causes sleeping sickness, a fatal disease that attacks the nervous system. An estimated 60 million Africans are at risk from this disease.

tse·tse fly (tsē′tsē) *or* (tet′si) *n* an African bloodsucking, two-winged fly that transmits sleeping sickness. <Bantu (a group of languages of Africa)>

T–shirt (tē′shərt′) *n* a light, short-sleeved shirt, usually made of cotton, with the shape of a T when spread flat.

Tsilh·qot'·in (tsil′kō tin) *n, pl* **Tsilh·qot'·in** **1** a member of a First Nations people living in northern British Columbia. **2** the language of these people.
adj to do with these people or their language. Also called **Chilcotin.**

Tsim·shian (tsim′shē ən) *or* (chim′shē ən) *n, pl* **Tsim·shi·an** or **Tsim·shi·ans** **1** a member of a First Nations people living in the coastal area and northern interior of British Columbia. **2** the language of these people.
adj to do with these people or their language.

tsk (a t-sound produced by suction) *interj* a soft sound used to express disapproval, disgust, contempt, or pity, often humorously.

T–square (tē′skwer′) *n* a T-shaped ruler used for drawing and testing right angles.

tsu·na·mi (tsū nam′ē) *n* a long, high, sea wave caused by an earthquake on the ocean floor or other major disturbance. Also called **tidal wave.** <Japanese *tsu* port + *nami* wave>

Tsuu–t'in (tsū′tin′) SARCEE.

tu·a·ta·ra (tū′ə tor′ə) *n* a large, amphibious reptile of New Zealand that has a row of soft spines along the back. <Maori *tua* back + *tara* spine>

tub (tub) *n* **1** a wide, deep, open, usually round container with a flat bottom used for holding liquid for washing clothes, for bathing in, or for growing plants. **2** a similar small plastic or cardboard container in which food is bought or stored, or the contents of such a container. **3** *Informal* a bath: *He takes a cold tub every morning.* **4** *Informal* a clumsy, slow-moving boat or ship.
v **tubbed, tub·bing** wash or bathe in a tub. <Dutch *tubbe*>

tu·ba (tyū′bə) *or* (tū′bə) *n* a large brass wind instrument with a deep pitch. <Latin = war trumpet>

tu·bal li·ga·tion (tū′bəl lī gā′shən) or (tyū′bəl lī gā′shən) *n* a surgical method of sterilizing a woman that involves cutting and tying tubes so that an ovum cannot travel toward the uterus.

tub·by (tub′ē) *adj* **tub·bi·er, tub·bi·est** **1** short and fat. **2** with a dull, wooden sound. **tub′bi·ness** *n.*

tube (tyūb) *or* (tūb) *n* **1** a long, hollow cylinder of metal, plastic, rubber, or glass, especially one used to hold or carry liquids or gases: *A plastic tube runs from the pump to the filter of our fish tank.* **2** a small, flexible cylinder with a cap that screws onto the open end, used for holding paste substances, such as toothpaste. **3** a hollow cylindrical organ or structure in an animal or plant: *bronchial tubes.* **4** a separate, inflatable casing of rubber that fits inside the outer casing of a tire. **5** a sealed container, typically of glass and filled with gas, containing the electrodes between which an electric current can be made to flow. A conventional TV set has a cathode ray tube forming the screen. <Latin *tubus*> **tube′like′** *adj.*
go down the tube (or **tubes**), *Informal* be completely lost or wasted.

tube pan *n* a deep, circular cake pan with a vertical hollow tube in the middle.

tu·ber (tyū′bər) *or* (tū′bər) *n* the thick part of a plant's underground stem, such as a potato, serving as a food reserve and bearing buds from which new plants arise. <Latin = lump>

tu·ber·cle (tyū′bər kəl) *or* (tū′bər kəl) *n* **1** a small, rounded swelling or knob, especially on a bone or on the surface of an animal or plant. **2** a small, hard lump in the lungs or other tissue, characteristic of tuberculosis. <Latin *tuber* lump>

a bat	e bed	i bid	o pot	u cup	th thin
ā cake	ē me	ī bite	ō go	ū rude	ᴛʜ then
ä bar	ə about	ər over	ô for	ů put	zh measure

tu·ber·cu·lo·sis (tyə bər′kyə lō′sis) *or* (tə bər′kyə lō′sis) *n* an infectious bacterial disease marked by the growth of nodules in the tissues, especially the lungs.
tu·ber′cu·lar *adj.* **tu·ber′cu·lous** *adj.*

tube·rose (tyū′brōz′) *or* (tū′brōz′) *n* a tropical plant of the amaryllis family, with sword-shaped leaves and spikes of very fragrant flowers.

tu·ber·ous (tyū′bə rəs) *or* (tū′bə rəs) *adj* **1** to do with tubers. **2** covered with rounded knobs or swellings.

tube sock *n* a sport sock without a shaped heel, in the form of a straight, stretchy tube closed at the toe end.

tube top *n* a tight, stretchy top for women in the form of a tube covering only the chest and upper back.

tub·ing (tyū′bing) *or* (tū′bing) *n* a length or lengths of metal, plastic, glass, or rubber in the form of a tube or tubes: *rubber tubing.*

tu·bu·lar (tyū′byə lər) *or* (tū′byə lər) *adj* **1** long, round, and hollow like a tube, or made from a tube or tubes: *tubular furniture.* **2** to do with tubules or other tube-shaped structures in the body.

tu·bule (tyū′byūl) *or* (tū′byūl) *n* a very small tube, especially as a structure in the body of an animal or plant.

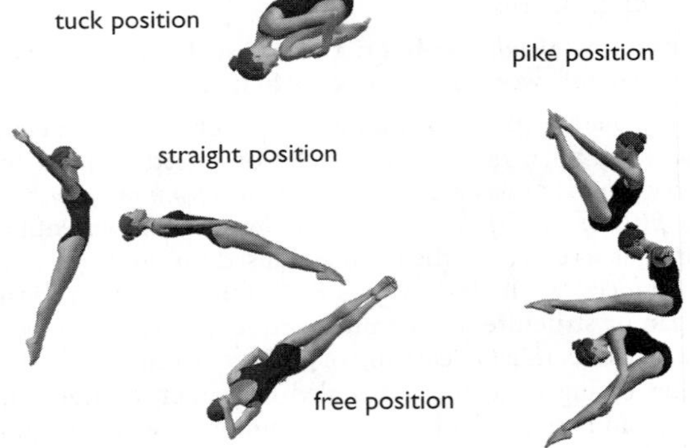

The **tuck** is one of four authorized flight positions in a diving competition. In addition, there are six types of dives, and many variations of each type.

tuck (tuk) *v* **1** push, fold, or turn the edges or ends of something so as to hide them or hold them in place: *She tucked the newspaper under her arm. Tuck your shirt in.* **2** (*with* ***in***) cover snugly by tucking in the bedclothes: *He always tucked the children in.* **3** fold the legs back or up when sitting or lying: *She sat with her legs tucked under her.* **4** (*with* ***away***) eat heartily: *He tucked away a big meal.* **5** make a flattened, stitched fold in a garment or material, typically one of several parallel folds for shortening, tightening, or decoration.
n **1** a flattened, stitched fold in a garment or material. **2** a position in diving, gymnastics, and downhill skiing with the knees bent and held close to the chest, often with the hands clasped around the lower part of the legs. <Middle English *tuken* stretch and draw together, from Old English *tucian* torment>
tuck into, *Informal* eat food heartily: *She tucked into a large plate of fish and chips.*

tuck·er (tuk′ər) *Informal v* make tired.
be tuckered (**out**) exhausted or worn out: *I'm tuckered. We were all tuckered out after four hours of wandering around the zoo.*

tuck shop *n* a small shop, especially one in a hospital or summer camp, in which snacks and drinks are sold.

Tu·dor (tyū′dər) *or* (tū′dər) *adj* **1** to do with the royal family that ruled England from 1485 to 1603. **2** to do with the architecture or furniture styles of this period.

Tues·day (tyūz′dā′) *or* (tūz′dā) *n* the day of the week after Monday and before Wednesday. *Abbrev.* **Tues** <Old English *tiwesdæg* day of Tiw, Germanic god of war>

tu·fa (tyū′fə) *or* (tū′fə) *n* a soft, porous form of limestone produced as a deposit from a spring or stream.

tuff (tuf) *n* a light, porous rock formed from volcanic ash or dust thrown out by an erupting volcano.

tuft (tuft) *n* **1** a bunch or collection of something, typically threads, grass, or hair, held or growing together at the base. **2** a bunch of small blood vessels or other small structures in the body.
v **1** provide or decorate with a tuft or tufts. **2** make hollows at regular intervals in a mattress or cushion by passing a thread through it. <origin uncertain>
tuft′ed *adj.*

tug (tug) *v* **tugged, tug·ging 1** pull something hard or suddenly: *I tugged the rope and it came loose.* **2** tow a ship by means of a tugboat.
n **1** a hard or sudden pull. **2** a tugboat. **3** a strap used for pulling at a horse, especially the harness trace. <Old English *teon* to tow, from *togian* to drag>

tug·boat (tug′bōt′) *n* a small, powerful boat used to tow or push larger ships or boats, especially in a harbour.

tug–of–war (tug′ə vwôr′) *n* **1** a contest between two teams pulling at the ends of a rope, each trying to drag the other over a line marked between them. **2** a hard struggle for power.

tu·i·tion (tyū ish′ən) *or* (tū ish′ən) *n* **1** a sum of money charged for instruction: *The yearly tuition was very expensive.* **2** teaching or instruction, especially of individual students or small groups: *He got extra tuition in math.* <Latin *tuitio*, from *tueri* watch over>

🍁 **tuk·tu** (tuk′tū) CARIBOU.

tu·lip (tyū′lip) *or* (tū′lip) *n* **1** a plant that grows from a bulb and has long, pointed leaves and large, cup-shaped, usually single flowers. <Dutch *tulipa*, from Turkish *tülbend* turban, because the flower resembles a turban>

tulip tree *n* a N American hardwood tree of the magnolia family with large, tuliplike flowers.

tulle (tūl) *n* a soft, fine material like net, used for making veils, dresses, and ballet costumes. <*Tulle* city in southwest France, where the fabric was first manufactured>

🍁 **tul·li·bee** (tul′ə bē′) *n, pl* **tul·li·bees** or (*especially collectively*) **tul·li·bee** a lake whitefish used for food. <Cdn French *toulibi*, from Ojibwa *too-nie-bie*>

tum·ble (tum′bəl) *v* **tum·bled, tum·bling 1** fall suddenly, clumsily, or headlong: *The boy tumbled down the stairs.* **2** move or rush in an uncontrolled way: *He tumbled out of bed to answer the phone. The excited children tumbled through the door.* **3** fall rapidly in amount or value: *Prices*

tumbled. **4** dry laundry in a tumble dryer: *The towels soon tumbled dry.* **5** perform acrobatic feats, typically handsprings and somersaults. **6** *Informal* (*with* ***to***) understand the meaning or hidden implications of a situation: *She tumbled to the trick straight away.*
n **1** a sudden or headlong fall: *The tumble hurt him badly. She took a tumble on the ice.* **2** a rapid fall in value or amount: *a stock market tumble.* **3** an untidy or confused arrangement or condition: *a tumble of clothes on my bedroom floor.* <Old English *tumbian* dance about>

tum·ble·down (tum′bəl doun′) *adj* falling or fallen into ruin: *a tumbledown shack.*

tum·bler (tum′blər) *n* **1** a drinking glass with straight sides and no handle or stem. **2** an acrobat, especially one who performs somersaults. **3** a pigeon of a breed that repeatedly turns over backward in flight.

tum·ble·weed (tum′bəl wēd′) *n* a plant of arid regions that breaks off near the ground in late summer, forming light globular masses that are blown and tumbled by the wind.

tu·me·fy (tyū′mə fī) *or* (tū′mə fī) *v* become swollen. <Latin *tumere* swell> **tu′me·fac′tion** *n.*

tum·my (tum′ē) *Informal n, pl* **tum·mies** a person's stomach.

tu·mour or **tu·mor** (tyū′mər) *or* (tū′mər) *n* a swelling of a part of the body, generally without inflammation, caused by an abnormal growth of tissue. Tumours can be either benign (doing little or no harm) or malignant (cancerous). <Latin *tumere* swell> **tu′mo·rous** *adj.*

🍁 **tump·line** (tum′plīn′) *n* a sling for carrying a load on the back, with a strap that passes around the forehead. <Algonquian *tump* + *line*>

tu·mult (tyū′mult) *or* (tū′mult) *n* **1** a loud, confused noise, especially one caused by a large mass of people: *The shout of "Fire!" caused a tumult in the theatre.* **2** confusion or disorder: *My mind was in a tumult after listening to his lies.* <Latin *tumultus*> **tu·mul′tu·ous** *adj.*
tu·mul′tu·ous·ly *adv.* **tu·mul′tu·ous·ness** *n.*

tu·na (tū′nə) *or* (tyū′nə) *n, pl* **tu·nas** or (*especially collectively*) **tu·na** a very large food and game fish of warm seas, sometimes called **tunafish**. <Spanish, from Latin *thunnus*>

tun·dra (tun′drə) *n* a vast, level, treeless plain in arctic regions, whose subsoil remains frozen all year round. <Russian>

tune (tyūn) *or* (tūn) *n* a melody, especially one that characterizes a certain piece of music: *a happy tune.*
v **tuned, tun·ing 1** adjust a musical instrument to the correct or uniform pitch: *tune a piano.* **2** adjust a receiver such as a radio or TV to the frequency of the required signal: *He tuned his shortwave radio to the news from Australia. Tune in tomorrow for another episode.* **3** adjust an engine or balance mechanical parts so that a vehicle runs smoothly and efficiently. **4** adjust or adapt something to a particular purpose or situation: *The insects were tuned to their dry environment.* <*tone*> **tun′a·ble** or **tune′a·ble** *adj.* **tun′ing** *n.*
in (out of) tune, a with correct (incorrect) pitch or intonation: *She can't sing in tune. The piano is out of tune.* **b** properly (poorly) adjusted as a motor or other machine. **c** in (not in) agreement or harmony: *He's happier now that he's in tune with his surroundings again. She won't be elected because she's out of tune with the times.*
to the tune of, *Informal* amounting to or involving a specified considerable amount: *He received a bill to the tune of $800 for car repairs.*
tune out, *Informal* stop listening or paying attention: *My dad tunes out complaints he doesn't want to hear.*

tune·ful (tyūn′fəl) *or* (tūn′fəl) *adj* with a pleasing tune: *a tuneful song.* **tune′ful·ly** *adv.* **tune′ful·ness** *n.*

tune·less (tyūn′lis) *or* (tūn′lis) *adj* not pleasing to listen to: *His tuneless humming began to get on their nerves.* **tune′less·ly** *adv.* **tune′less·ness** *n.*

tun·er (tyū′nər) *or* (tū′nər) *n* **1** a person whose work is tuning musical instruments, especially pianos. **2** an electronic device for tuning a guitar or other instrument. **3** an electronic device for varying the frequency to which a radio or TV is tuned.

tune–up (tyū′nup′) *or* (tū′nup′) *n* an act of tuning something up, especially an engine or other machine: *Before the race, he took his bike to the repair shop for a tune-up.*

tung·sten (tung′stən) *n* a hard, grey metallic element with a very high melting point, used especially for the filaments of electric light bulbs and in making steel alloys. *Symbol* **W** <Swedish *tung* heavy + *sten* stone>

tu·nic (tyū′nik) *or* (tū′nik) *n* **1** a loose garment, typically sleeveless and reaching to the wearer's knees, as worn in ancient Greece and Rome. **2** a loose woman's garment, typically worn over a skirt or trousers. **3** a short, close-fitting coat worn as part of a police or military uniform. <Latin *tunica*>

tuning fork *Music n* a small, two-pronged steel device that sounds a fixed tone when struck, used to determine a standard pitch for singing or for tuning an instrument.

Tu·ni·sia (tů nē′zhə), (tů nē′zē ə), *or* (tů nē′shə) *n* a country in northern Africa. See the APPENDIX. **Tu·ni′sian** *adj, n.*

tun·nel (tun′əl) *n* **1** an artificial underground passage, especially one built through a hill or under a building, road, or river: *a railway tunnel, a subway tunnel, a mine tunnel.* **2** an underground passage dug by a burrowing animal.
v **tun·nelled** or **tun·neled, tun·nel·ling** or **tun·nel·ing** dig or force a passage underground or through something: *The mole tunnelled in the ground. The workers are tunnelling under the river.* <Old French *tonel* barrel, from its shape> **tun′nel·ler** or **tun′nel·er** *n.*

tunnel vision *n* **1** a defect in eyesight in which objects cannot be properly seen if not close to the centre of the field of view. **2** a tendency to focus exclusively on a single or limited objective or view: *His tunnel vision makes him too intolerant to be a good politician.*

a bat	e bed	i bid	o pot	u cup	th thin
ā cake	ē me	ī bite	ō go	ū rude	TH then
ä bar	ə about	ər over	ȯ for	ů put	zh measure

tun·ny (tun′ē) *n, pl* **tun·nies** or (*especially collectively*) **tun·ny** tuna. <French *thon*, from Greek *thynnos*>

tu·pik (tū′pək) *n* a compact, portable tent of skins, traditionally used by Inuit as a summer dwelling. <Inuktitut *tupiq*>

tuque (tūk) *or* (tyūk) *n* **1** a knitted cap resembling a long stocking, usually knotted at the end: *Tuques are popular with skaters on the Rideau Canal.* Also, **toque**. **2** a tight-fitting, short knitted cap, often with a round tassel on top.

ETYMOLOGY

Tuque is a French-Canadian variation of the word *toque*, which may have come from Basque *tauka* or Spanish *toca*, both meaning "a kind of hat." The word *toque*, also meaning "a kind of hat," has the same etymology.

tur·ban (tər′bən) *n* **1** a headdress for men worn especially by Muslims and Sikhs, consisting of a long length of cotton or silk wound around a cap or the head. **2** a similar headdress, especially one worn by women, consisting of a scarf wound around the head or a close-fitting, brimless hat resembling this. **3** a saltwater mollusc with a spiral shell. <Turkish, from Persian *dulband*> **tur′baned** *adj.*

tur·bid (tər′bid) *adj* **1** thick or cloudy as liquid, with or as if with churned up sediment: *a turbid river.* **2** confused or muddled: *a turbid mind.* <Latin *turba* turmoil> **tur′bid·ly** *adv.* **tur′bid·ness** *n.*

tur·bine (tər′bīn) *or* (tər′bən) *n* a machine for producing continuous power in which a wheel or rotor, typically fitted with vanes, is made to revolve by a fast-moving flow of water, steam, gas, air, or other fluid. <Latin *tubinis* whirling object>

turbo– *combining form* with or driven by a turbine: *turbojet.*

tur·bo·charg·er (tər′bō chor′jər) *n* a supercharger for an engine or vehicle, driven by a turbine that in turn is powered by the engine's exhaust gases.

tur·bo·jet (tər′bō jet′) *n* a jet engine in which the jet gases also operate a turbine-driven compressor for compressing the air drawn into the engine, or an aircraft powered by such an engine.

tur·bo·prop (tər′bō prop′) *n* a jet engine in which a turbine is used to drive a propeller, or an aircraft powered by such an engine.

tur·bot (tər′bət) *n, pl* **tur·bots** or (*especially collectively*) **tur·bot** a large European flatfish of inshore waters, valued as food. See FLATFISH for picture. <Old Swedish *törnbut*, from *törn* thorn, from the spines on its back>

tur·bu·lent (tər′byə lənt) *adj* **1** marked by conflict, disorder, or confusion: *a turbulent mind.* **2** moving unsteadily or violently: *the turbulent sea, a turbulent flight.* <Latin *turba* turmoil> **tur′bu·lence** *n.*

tu·reen (tü rēn′) *n* a deep, covered dish for serving soup. <French *terrine* earthen vessel, from Latin *terra* earth>

turf (tərf) *n, pl* **turfs** **1** grass and the surface layer of earth held together by its roots, or a piece of such grass and earth cut from the ground. **2** peat used as fuel. **3** an artificial surface made to resemble grass. **4** *Informal* an area regarded as someone's personal territory: *He could relax now that he was back on his own turf.* **5 the turf** horse races or racetracks generally.
v **1** cover a patch of ground with turf. **2** (*with* **out**) expel or banish a person or thing: *They were turfed out of the poolroom.* <Old English>

turf war *n* an angry dispute between rival groups over territory, or for a certain area of activity or authority: *They were having a turf war over who should get the bigger office.*

tur·gid (tər′jid) *adj* **1** swollen and distended or congested: *a turgid river.* **2** pompous or pretentious as language or style: *a turgid poem.* <Latin *turgere* swell> **tur·gid′i·ty** *n.* **tur′gid·ly** *adv.*

Male **turkeys** are polygamous and often fight among themselves over the hens. During these aggressive displays or while courting, they will raise their tail feathers to form a vertical fan.

tur·key (tər′kē) *n, pl* **tur·keys** **1** a large, mainly domestic bird native to N America, with a bald head and, in the male, red wattles. **2** *Informal* a thing that is completely unsuccessful, especially a movie, or a stupid or inept person. <*turkey-cock, turkey-hen*, names for guinea fowl imported from Turkey. The name was later mistakenly applied to the American bird.>
talk turkey, *Informal* talk frankly and straightforwardly: *They decided it was time to get together and talk turkey.*

Tur·key (tər′kē) *n* a country in southeast Europe. See the APPENDIX. **Turk** *n.* **Turk′ish** *adj.*

turkey vulture *n* a vulture found in the western hemisphere, with dark plumage and a bare, red upper neck and head.

Turkish bath *n* a cleansing or relaxing treatment that involves remaining for a period of time in a room filled with very hot air or steam, followed by washing and massage, or a building or room in which such a treatment is done.

Turkish delight *n* a flavoured candy made of sweetened gelatin cut into cubes and dusted with powdered sugar.

Turk·men·i·stan (tərk′men′i stan) *n* a country in central Asia. **Turk′men** or **Tur′ko·man** *adj, n.*

tur·mer·ic (tər′mə rik) *n* a bright yellow powder prepared from the underground stem of a plant, used for flavouring and colouring in Asian cooking.

tur·moil (tər′moil) *n* a condition of great disturbance, confusion, or uncertainty: *Six robberies in one night put our village in a turmoil.* <origin uncertain>

turn (tərn) *v* **1** move or cause to move in a circular direction wholly or partly around an axis or point: *The merry-go-round turned. Turn the crank three times. Turn over on your back.* **2** cause to move around in order to open, close, raise, lower, or tighten: *She turned the key in the lock.* **3** move something or be moved so that it is in a different position: *The road turns to the north here. She has turned her steps to the north. He turned the page.* **4 a** change in nature or condition: *The afternoon turned hot. The milk has turned.* **b** of leaves, change colour: *The trees are just about to turn. Soon the leaves will turn red.* **5** start doing or becoming involved with: *After working as an architect, he turned to designing cars.* **6** shape something on a lathe: *turn a candlestick.*
n **1** an act of moving something in a circular direction around an axis or point: *At each turn, the screw went in farther.* **2** a change of direction: *a left turn. This road has many twists and turns.* **3** a development or change in circumstances or a course of events: *The sick man has taken a turn for the better.* **4** a chance to do something that comes successively to each of two or more people: *My turn is after yours.* **5** a short walk or ride: *He took a turn around the block.* **6** *Informal* a nervous shock: *You gave me quite a turn!* <Latin, from Greek *tornos*>
at every turn, on every occasion.
by turns, one after the other,
in (**out of**) **turn,** in (out of) proper order.
take (or **take it in**) **turns,** do something alternately and successively.
to a turn, in exactly the proper way, especially of something being cooked: *The steak was done to a turn.*
turn about or **turn and turn about,** one after another in succession.
turn down, a fold down, or bend downward. **b** place with face downward. **c** refuse: *He turned down the plan.* **d** lower by turning something: *Turn down the volume.*
turn in, a go to bed: *I think I'll turn in now.* **b** give back or exchange: *He turned in his old bike for a new one.* **c** achieve a particular score or a performance.
turn off, a stop the operation or flow of something by means of a tap, switch, or button: *Turn off the hot water.* **b** leave one road in order to join another. **c** *Informal* cause someone to feel bored or disgusted.
turn on, a start the operation or flow of something by means of a tap, switch, or button. **b** excite or stimulate the interest of someone. **c** suddenly attack or oppose. **d** depend on; result from: *The success of the picnic turns on the weather.*
turn out, a prove to be the case or fact. **b** go somewhere in order to do something, especially to attend a meeting, to play in a match, or to vote. **c** banish or expel someone from a place. **d** put out a light. **e** produce, make, or create something.
turn over, a hand over or transfer: *He turned the job over to his assistant.* **b** think carefully about or consider in different ways: *I will turn the idea over in my mind.* **c** buy and then sell in business. **d** change in position, especially change from lying on one side to lying on the other.
turn up, a fold up or over, especially so as to shorten. **b** increase the volume or strength of sound or heat. **c** reveal or discover something. **d** be found, especially by chance, after being lost. **e** appear or show up.

SYNONYMS

Turn refers to movement in a circular or other direction: *Turn right when you get to Main Street.*

Rotate refers to circular movement around a centre, or change in a regular, recurring order: *He got on and the Ferris wheel began to rotate. The role of speaker rotated among group members.*

turn·a·round (tərn′ə round′) *n* **1** an abrupt or unexpected change, especially one that results in a more favourable position: *Their profit that year represented a big turnaround.* **2** the process of completing or the time needed to complete a task, especially one involving receiving something, processing it, and sending it out again: *The turnaround for book orders is about a week.* **3** a space for vehicles to turn around in, especially at the end of a driveway.

turn·coat (tərn′kōt′) *n* a person who deserts one party or cause in order to join the opposing side.

turn·er (tər′nər) *n* **1** a tool that is used for turning. **2** a person who forms or shapes things with a lathe.

turning circle (tər′ning) *n* the smallest circle space needed by a vehicle to turn.

turning point *n* a point in time at which a significant change in a situation occurs, especially one with good results: *That experience was the turning point of her life.*

tur·nip (tər′nip) *n* a round root with yellow or white flesh that is eaten as a vegetable and also has edible leaves, or the plant of the mustard family that produces it. <Latin *napus*>

turn·key (tərn′kē′) *Archaic n, pl* **turn·keys** a jailer.
adj to do with a product or service that is immediately available for use: *turnkey Internet service.*

turn·off (tər′nof′) *n* **1** a junction at which a road branches off from a main road. **2** *Informal* a person who or thing that causes someone to feel bored or disgusted: *His eating habits were a real turnoff.*

turn–on (tər′non′) *Informal n* a person who or thing that causes someone to feel stimulated or excited: *He was hired for the commercial because his voice is such a turn-on.*

turn·out (tər′nout′) *n* **1** the number of people attending or taking part in an event: *There was a good turnout at the dance.* **2** the way in which a person or thing is equipped or dressed: *an elegant turnout.*

a bat	e bed	i bid	o pot	u cup	th thin
ā cake	ē me	ī bite	ō go	ū rude	ᴛʜ then
ä bar	ə about	ər over	ô for	ů put	zh measure

T

turn·o·ver (tər′nō′vər) *n* **1** the amount of money taken by a business in a particular period: *The store had a big turnover this week.* **2** the rate at which goods are sold and replaced: *The store reduced prices to make a quick turnover.* **3** the rate at which people leave a job or company and have to be replaced: *The company has had a high turnover in the past year.* **4** a small, filled pastry in the shape of a semicircle or triangle made by placing the filling on one half of a piece of rolled-out dough and folding the other half over it. **5** *Football, Basketball* a loss of possession of the ball to the opposing team: *Two touchdowns were scored as a result of turnovers.*

turn·pike (tərn′pīk′) *US n* a road on which a toll is or used to be charged.

turn·stile (tərn′stīl′) *n* a mechanical gate consisting of bars set into a revolving central post, allowing people to pass through only on foot, one at a time, and only in one direction.

turn·ta·ble (tərn′tā′bəl) *n* **1** a circular revolving plate supporting on which a phonograph record can be played. **2** a platform with a track that revolves, used for turning a locomotive or other vehicle around.

tur·pen·tine (tər′pən tīn′) *n* a strong-smelling oil distilled from resin obtained from pines and other softwood trees, used in mixing and thinning paints and varnishes.
v apply turpentine to. <Old French *terbentine*, from Greek *terminthos* terebinth tree, the source of turpentine>

tur·pi·tude (tər′pə tyūd′) *or* (tər′pə tūd′) *n* wickedness or great wrongdoing. <Latin *turpis* vile>

tur·quoise (tər′kwoiz) *or* (tər′koiz) *n* a semiprecious stone, typically sky blue or greenish blue.
adj greenish blue. <Old French *turqueise* Turkish, because the stone was first found in Turkestan>

tur·ret (tər′it) *n* **1** a small tower on top of a larger tower or at the corner of a building or wall. **2** a low, rotating armoured structure in a ship, aircraft, or tank. <Old French, from Latin *turris*> **tur′ret·ed** *adj.*

Turtles vary in size from 15 cm (the box turtle), to 2.4 m (the giant leatherback). They also have longevity, with some species living more than 100 years.

tur·tle (tər′təl) *n* **1** a large, toothless saltwater reptile with a bony or leathery shell and flippers. Turtles come ashore annually on sandy beaches to lay eggs. **2** a freshwater reptile related to this animal, such as the tortoise, typically with a flattened shell. <French *tortue* tortoise>
turn turtle, *Informal* especially of a boat, turn bottom side up.

tur·tle·dove (tər′təl duv′) *n* a wild dove, especially a grey or brownish European dove with a soft purring call, noted for the affection that it appears to have for its mate. <Latin *turtur*, imitative of its cooing>

tur·tle·neck (tər′təl nek′) *n* a high, snugly fitting, usually turned-over neck, especially on a sweater, or a sweater with this kind of neck.

Tus·can (tus′kən) *adj* to do with Tuscany, a district in central Italy, or its people.

Tus·ca·ro·ra (tus′kə rȯ′rə) *n, pl* **Tus·ca·ro·ra 1** a member of a First Nations or Native American people living mainly in southern Ontario and western New York. **2** the language of these people.
adj to do with these people or their language.

tusk (tusk) *n* **1** a very long, large, pointed tooth, especially one protruding from the closed mouth, as in the elephant, walrus, and wild boar. **2** a long, tapering object resembling a tusk. <Old English *tusc* tooth of a horse>

tus·sle (tus′əl) *n* a scuffle or struggle, typically in order to obtain or achieve something: *There was a brief tussle as everyone tried to get through the door first.*
v **tus·sled, tus·sling** engage in such a struggle or wrestle: *The protesters tussled with security guards.* <*tousle*>

tus·sock (tus′ək) *n* a small area of grass that is thicker or longer than the grass around it. <origin uncertain>

tut (tut) TUT-TUT.

Tut·cho·ne (tū chō′nē) *n, pl* **Tut·cho·ne** or **Tut·cho·nes 1** a member of a First Nations people living in southern Yukon Territory. **2** the language of these people.
adj to do with these people or their language.

tu·te·lage (tyū′tə lij) *or* (tū′tə lij) *n* **1** instruction or tuition: *They learned very quickly under her expert tutelage.* **2** guardianship or protection over someone or something.

tu·te·lar·y (tyū′tə ler′ē) *or* (tū′tə ler′ē) *adj* **1** serving as a protector, guardian, or patron: *a tutelary saint.* **2** to do with protection or a guardian.

tu·tor (tyū′tər) *or* (tū′tər) *n* **1** a private teacher, typically one who teaches a single student or a very small group. **2** in some colleges and universities, a college teacher responsible for the teaching and supervision of assigned students.
v act as a tutor to a single student or a very small group. <Latin *tutor* guardian, from *tueri* watch over> **tu′tor·ship** *n.*

tu·to·ri·al (tyū tȯ′rē əl) *or* (tū tȯ′rē əl) *adj* to do with a tutor or tuition: *the tutorial system.*
n a period of tuition given by a university or college tutor to an individual or very small group.

tutorial assistant *n* a graduate student in a university or college who helps a professor by leading some tutorials.

tut·ti–frut·ti (tū′tē frū′tē) *n* a type of ice cream containing a variety of fruits or fruit flavourings. <Italian *tutti frutti* all fruits>

tut–tut (tut′tut′) *interj* used to make a sound with the tongue as a form of mild rebuke or to express annoyance.
v **tut-tut·ted, tut-tut·ting** make such a sound: *He merely tut-tutted when told what the child had done.* Also, **tut**.

tu·tu (tū′tū) *n* a female ballet dancer's very short, frilly skirt, stiff and projecting from the waist. <French, alteration of *cucu*, child's reduplication of *cul* buttocks, from Latin *culus*>

Tu·va·lu (tū vo′lū) *n* a country of several islands in the western Pacific. **Tu·va′lu·an** *adj, n.*

tux (tuks) *Informal n* a tuxedo.

tux·e·do (tuk sē′dō) *n, pl* **tux·e·dos** or **tux·e·does** a man's semiformal jacket for evening wear, usually black and with satin lapels, and made without tails, or a suit of clothes including such a jacket. <*Tuxedo* Park, NY, where it was supposedly first worn>

TV *n* a television system or set.

TV dinner *n* a frozen, precooked, packaged dinner that is ready to serve after being heated in its container.

twad·dle (twod′əl) *n* silly, feeble, tiresome talk or writing. *v* **twad·dled, twad·dling** talk or write in this way. <origin uncertain> **twad′dler** *n.*

twain (twān) *Archaic or Poetic n, adj* two: *split in twain.* <Old English *twegen*>

twang (twang) *n* **1** a strong, sharp, ringing sound like that made by a bowstring or rubber band when plucked: *We could hear the twang of her bow as she shot the arrow.* **2** a nasal or other distinctive manner of pronunciation marking the speech of an individual, area, or country: *a rural twang.*
v **1** make or cause to make such a sound, or play an instrument in such a way: *The banjos twanged, to twang a guitar.* **2** speak with a distinctive nasal tone. <imitative> **twang′y** *adj.*

'twas (twoz) *or* (twuz) *Poetic contraction* it was.

tweak (twēk) *v* **1** pull sharply and twist with the fingers: *She tweaked her little brother's ear and made him cry.* **2** make small adjustments or revisions to something in order to improve it.
n **1** a sharp pull and twist: *His mother told him to give his sister's ear a tweak in return.* **2** a small adjustment to something. <Old English *twiccian* pluck>

twee (twē) *adj* **twe·er, twe·est** exaggeratedly and affectedly pretty, quaint, or sentimental: *a store full of twee ornaments.* <childish pronunciation of *sweet*>

tweed (twēd) *n* **1** a woollen cloth with a rough surface, typically with mixed flecked colours, used especially for suits, skirts, and coats. **2 tweeds** *pl* clothes made of tweed, especially a suit: *He was wearing tweeds.* <*twill*>

tweed·y (twē′dē) *adj* **tweed·i·er, tweed·i·est 1** made of tweed cloth. **2** in the habit of wearing tweed clothes.

tween (twēn) *n* a person between eight and twelve years of age, the period before adolescence. <*(be)tween-age*, on the analogy of *teen* and *teenage*>

tweet (twēt) *n, interj* the chirp of a small or young bird. *v* make a chirping sound. <imitative>

tweet·er (twē′tər) *n* a small high-fidelity loudspeaker used to reproduce sounds in a high-frequency range.

tweeze (twēz) *v* **tweezed, tweez·ing** pluck or remove with or as if with tweezers.

tweez·ers (twē′zərz) *pln* a small instrument like a pair of pincers or tongs for pulling out hairs or slivers, or picking up small objects. <*tweeze* instrument case, French *étuis* cases of instruments>

twelfth (twelfth) *n* **1** next after the eleventh: *You are twelfth in line.* **2** one of twelve equal parts.
adj, adv See TWELVE.

Twelfth Night *Christianity n* the night of January 5, or the day following it, traditionally celebrated by Christians as the end of Christmas festivities.

twelve (twelv) *n* **1** two more than ten: *That makes twelve altogether.* **2** the numeral 12.
adj **1** two more than ten: *I sold twelve tickets.* **2** (*after the noun*) twelfth in a series: *Section Twelve.* <Old English *twelf*> **twelfth** *adj, adv.*

twen·ti·eth (twen′tē ith) *n* **1** next after the nineteenth. **2** one of twenty equal parts.
adj, adv See TWENTY.

twen·ty (twen′tē) *n, pl* **twen·ties 1** two times ten. **2 twenties** *pl* the years from twenty through twenty-nine, especially of a century or of a person's life: *My father was in his twenties when his mother died.* **3** a twenty-dollar bill.
adj **1** two times ten. **2** (*after the noun*) twentieth in a series: *Lesson Twenty.* <Old English *twentig*>
twen′ti·eth *adj, adv.*

24/7 *Informal adv (say "twenty-four seven")* twenty-four hours a day, seven days a week: *The store was open 24/7.*

🍁 **24 Sussex** (su′səks) *n* in full, **24 Sussex Drive** the residence of the prime minister of Canada.

twenty–one (twen′tē wun) *n* a card game where twenty-one is the winning score; blackjack. <translation of French *vingt-et-un*>

20/20 or **twenty–twenty** *adj* of vision, good; meeting the normal standard: *I used to have 20/20 vision, but now I'm a bit shortsighted.* <from a traditional test measuring how well one sees a certain object 20 feet (about 6 m) away>

twerp (twərp) *Informal n* a silly or annoying person.

twice (twīs) *adv* **1** two times or on two occasions: *twice a day.* **2** double in degree or quantity: *twice as much.* <Old English *twiga*>

twice–told (twī′stōld′) *adj* told many times before. *twice-told tales.*

twid·dle (twid′əl) *v* **twid·dled, twid·dling** twist, move, or fiddle with something, typically in a purposeless or nervous way: *Stop twiddling that pencil, please.*
n an act of twisting or fiddling with something. <origin uncertain>
twiddle your thumbs, a keep turning your thumbs idly about each other. **b** be bored or idle.

twig[1] (twig) *n* a slender, woody shoot growing from a branch or stem of a tree or shrub. <Old English *twigge*> **twig′gy** *adj.*

a bat	e bed	i bid	o pot	u cup	th thin
ā cake	ē me	ī bite	ō go	ū rude	ᴛʜ then
ä bar	ə about	ər over	ô for	ů put	zh measure

twig[2] (twig) *Informal v* **twigged, twig·ging** (*often with* ***to***) get the meaning of, understand, or realize something: *I didn't twig that he wanted a lift. They soon twigged to our plan.* <Irish *tuigim* I understand>

twi·light (twī′līt′) *n* **1** the faint light reflected from the sky when the sun is below the horizon. **2** the period of the evening during which this takes place, between daylight and darkness. **3** a period or condition of gradual decline in activity, energy, or clarity: *twilight of the gods. She lived in an uneasy twilight between sickness and health.*
adj of, like, or produced by twilight: *the twilight hour, a twilight glow.* <Middle English *twi-* two + *light*[1]>

twilight zone *n* **1** an area or condition not clearly defined, as that between day and night, good and evil, or sleep and waking. **2** a place of strange or inexplicable happenings.

twi·lit (twī′lit′) *adj* lighted by twilight or as if by twilight: *the beauty of the twilit forest.*

twill (twil) *n* a fabric so woven as to have a surface of diagonal parallel ridges.
adj woven in this way. <Old English *twilic* double thread>

twin (twin) *n* **1** one of two children or animals born at the same birth. **2** a person who or thing that is exactly like another: *This table is the twin of one we have at home.* **3** a thing containing or consisting of two matching or corresponding parts, such as a twin-bedded room.
adj **1** forming or being one of a pair born at one birth: *twin girls. That's his twin sister.* **2** forming a matching, complementary, or closely connected pair: *twin houses, twin outfits.*
v **twinned, twin·ning** link or combine: *to twin two concepts.* <Old English *twinn*>

twin bed *n* one of a pair of matching single beds, particularly in a hotel room intended for two people.

twine (twīn) *n* strong thread or string made of two or more strands twisted together.
v **twined, twin·ing** cause to wind or spiral round something, or make or form by winding or spiralling: *She twined a wreath. He twined the string around his finger. They twined their arms around each other.* <Old English *twin*>

twin–en·gined (twin′en′jənd) *adj* powered by two engines, especially in an aircraft.

twinge (twinj) *n* **1** a sudden sharp, pinching pain in one spot that lasts only a moment: *He felt a twinge of rheumatism in his leg as he stooped to pick up the paper.* **2** a brief experience of an emotion, especially an unpleasant one: *a twinge of remorse, a twinge of fear.*
v **twinged, twing·ing** feel or cause to feel a twinge: *My conscience twinged at having to tell a lie.* <Old English *twengan* pinch>

twin·kle (twing′kəl) *v* **twin·kled, twin·kling 1** shine with quick little gleams from bright to faint as a star, light, or shiny object. **2** sparkle as eyes, especially with amusement, or smile so that one's eyes sparkle. **3** move lightly and rapidly: *The dancer's feet twinkled.*
n **1** a sparkle or gleam in a person's eye, or a thing that resembles this. **2** a very brief period of time: *He was gone in a twinkle.* <Old English *twinclian*>

twin·kling (twing′kling) *n* **1** a little, quick gleam. **2** a very short period of time; an instant: *When I called my dog, he was there in a twinkling.*
adj that twinkles: *twinkling stars.*

twirl (twərl) *v* spin or cause to turn quickly and lightly around, especially repeatedly: *The skaters twirled over the ice. In the movie, the villian twirled his mustache.*
n **1** the act of twirling. **2** a spiralling or swirling shape, especially a flourish made with a pen. <origin uncertain>
twirl′er *n.*

twist (twist) *v* **1** form into a bent, curling, or distorted shape: *She twisted the wire around the post. The belt is twisted at the back. I twisted my ankle when I fell.* **2** cause to turn around something that remains stationary: *She twisted the ring on her finger.* **3** have a winding shape or course: *Don't twist my words; I didn't mean that at all. Years of bitterness had twisted his mind. The path twists in and out among the rocks.* **4** (*with* ***off***) pull off or break by turning one end: *He twisted off the stem of an apple.* **5** dance the twist.
n **1** an act of turning something so that it moves in relation to something that remains stationary: *I gave the handle a hard twist.* **2** a thing with a spiral or distorted shape: *There's a twist in the rope. Her mouth had a cruel twist.* **3** a point at which something turns or bends: *The twists and turns of the mountain road made driving difficult.* **4** an unexpected development of events: *a twist of fate. The plot had several twists that kept us in suspense right to the end.* **5** a dance in which the hips are vigorously swivelled while the dancer stands in one place. <Old English> **twist′y** *adj.*
twist someone's arm, force or pressure someone into doing something: *I think we can get him to sign up if we twist his arm a little.*

twist·er (twis′tər) *n* **1** a tornado. **2** a person who or thing that twists.

twist–tie (twist′tī′) *n* a short length of plastic-covered wire, to be twisted around the neck of a bag to close it.

twit (twit) *v* **twit·ted, twit·ting,** tease or taunt someone, especially in a good-humoured way: *His friends twitted him about his schemes to make money.*
n **1** the act of twitting. **2** *Informal* a silly or foolish person. <Old English *ætwitan* to blame>

twitch (twich) *v* give or cause to give a short, sudden jerking or convulsive movement, or cause to move in a specified direction by giving a sharp pull: *Her mouth twitched as if she were about to cry. He twitched the curtain aside.*
n a short, sudden jerking or convulsive movement, or a sudden pull or jerk: *The twitch in his cheek didn't stop. She gave a twitch of the reins.* <Old English *twiccian* to pluck>

twit·ter (twit′ər) *v* **1** give a bird call consisting of repeated light tremulous sounds. **2** talk or laugh in a light, rapid, high-pitched voice, especially at length and in a trivial way: *They twittered about all the things they'd bought that morning.*
n **1** a series of short, high-pitched calls or sounds: *the twitter of birds in the garden.* **2** idle or excited talk, or a thing resembling this: *My nerves are in a twitter when I have to sing in public.* <imitative>

two (tū) *n* **1** a cardinal number that is one more than one. **2** the numeral 2. **3** a playing card or side of a die with two spots: *She drew the two of hearts.*
adj **1** one more than one: *There were two mistakes in the answer.* **2** (*after the noun*) second in a series: *Chapter Two tells about his childhood.* See TO for confusables. <Old English *twa*>
sec′ond *adj, adv.*
in two, in two parts or pieces: *She broke the cookie in two.*
put two and two together, form an obvious conclusion from the facts.

two–bit (tū′bit′) *Informal adj* cheap, inferior, or insignificant: *a two-bit novel, a two-bit gangster.* <*two bits* = 25 cents>

two–by–four (tū′bī fȯr′) *n* a length of wood with a rectangular cross-section about two inches by four inches (about 5 cm by 10 cm): *They used two-by-fours for the inside walls.*
adj of this length as a piece of lumber: *Two-by-fours are much used in building.*

two–di·men·sion·al (tū′də men′shə nəl) *adj* **1** with or appearing to have length and breadth but no depth: *a two-dimensional representation.* **2** lacking depth or substance: *a two-dimensional character in a play.*

two–edged (tū′ejd′) *adj* **1** with two cutting edges. **2** able to be taken in two ways as a statement or question: *a two-edged compliment.*

two–faced (tū′fāst′) *adj* insincere and deceitful.

two·fer (tū′fər) *Slang n* a ticket, coupon, voucher, or special offer allowing the purchaser to buy two items for the price of one: *These pies were on as a twofer at the grocery store.* <*two for one*>

two·fold (tū′fōld′) *adj, adv* **1** twice as much or as many. **2** consisting of two parts.

✱ **two–four** (tū′fȯr′) *Slang n* a case or package of 24 items, especially bottles or cans of beer.

two–hand·ed (tū′han′did) *adj* with, using, or requiring the use of two hands or people.

two–par·ty system (tū′par′tē) *n* a political system in which two political parties predominate over any others.

two–piece (tū′pēs′) *adj* consisting of two matching items: *a two-piece suit.*
n a thing consisting of two matching parts.

two–ply (tū′plī′) *adj* consisting of two layers or strands of a material.

two–seat·er (tū′sē′tər) *n* a motor vehicle or piece of furniture with seating for two people.

two·some (tū′səm) *n* **1** a pair of people considered together. **2** a game or dance involving two people.

two–step (tū′step′) *n* a dance with a sliding step and in march or polka time.

two–stroke (tū′strōk′) *adj* to do with an internal combustion engine with its power cycle completed in one up-and-down movement of the piston, or an engine or a vehicle powered by it.

two–time (tū′tīm′) *Informal v* **two-timed, two-tim·ing** betray or be unfaithful to another person.
adj to do with someone who has done or experienced something twice: *a two-time loser.* **two′–tim′er** *n.*

two–tone (tū′tōn′) *adj* with two different shades or colours: *two-tone shoes.*

two–way (tū′wā′) *adj* allowing or involving movement or communication in opposite directions: *two-way traffic, a two-way street, a two-way radio.*

two–way street (tū′wā′) *n* **1** a street allowing traffic in both directions. **2** an activity, relationship, etc. that involves reciprocity: *Communication is a two-way street.*

two–wheel·er (tū′wē′lər) *n* a vehicle with two wheels, especially a bicycle or motorcycle.

–ty[1] *suffix* with a certain quality or condition: *safety.*

–ty[2] *suffix* specifying a group of ten: *sixty.*

ty·coon (tī kūn′) *n* a wealthy, powerful person in business or industry. <Japanese *taikun*, from Mandarin *tai* great + *kiun* ruler>

✱ **ty·ee** (tī′ē) *n, pl* **ty·ees** or (*especially collectively*) **ty·ee** a chinook salmon, especially one weighing more than about thirteen kilograms.

ETYMOLOGY

Tyee comes from a Chinook jargon word meaning "chief" or "champion," from Nootka *tayi*, meaning "elder brother" or "chief."

ty·ing (tī′ing) present participle of TIE.

tyke (tīk) *Informal n* a small child. <Old Norse *tik* mongrel dog>

tym·pa·ni (tim′pə nē′) TIMPANI.

tym·pa·num (tim′pə nəm) *n, pl* **tym·pa·nums** or **tym·pa·nae** (-nə) an eardrum.

type (tīp) *n* **1** a category of people or things with shared characteristics: *blood types, body types.* **2** a person, thing, or event considered as a representative of such a category: *a new type of engine. He doesn't like that type of work. She's a mischievous type.* **3** a person or thing symbolizing or embodying the ideal or defining characteristics of something: *She is the very type of the industrious worker.* **4 a** printed characters or letters: *italic type.* **b** a block, usually of metal, with a raised letter, numeral, or sign in reverse on its upper surface, from which an inked impression can be made. **5** the figure, writing, or design on either side of a coin or medal.
v **typed, typ·ing 1** write something on a typewriter or keyboard by pressing the keys: *She can type at a rate of seventy-five words per minute.* **2** determine the type to which a person or her or his blood or tissue belongs. <Greek *typos* dent, impression>

Type A *n* a personality type whose main features are ambition, impatience, and competitiveness, and thought to be susceptible to stress and heart disease. <described by physicians M. Friedman and R. Rosenman, 1974>

a bat	e bed	i bid	o pot	u cup	th thin
ā cake	ē me	ī bite	ō go	ū rude	TH then
à bar	ə about	ər over	ȯ for	u̇ put	zh measure

T

type·cast (tīp′kast′) *v* **type·cast, type·cast·ing 1** assign an actor repeatedly to the same type of role in keeping with his or her appearance or previous success in such roles. **2** represent or regard a person as a stereotype: *His accent made people typecast him as a rural bumpkin.*

type·face (tīp′fās′) *n* a particular design or style of type: *an ornate typeface.* Compare FONT[2] (def. 1).

type·script (tīp′skript′) *n* a typewritten copy of a text.

type·set·ter (tīp′set′ər) *n* a person who or machine that sets type for printing. **type′set·ting** *n, adj.*

type·writ·er (tī′prī ′tər) *n* an electric, electronic, or manual machine with keys for producing printlike characters one at a time on paper inserted round a roller. **type′writ·ing** *n.* **type′writ·ten** *adj.*

ty·phoid (tī′foid) *n* in full, **typhoid fever** a severe infectious bacterial disease marked by an eruption of red spots on the chest and abdomen and severe irritation of the intestines.

ty·phoon (tī fūn′) *n* a violent tropical cyclone that forms in the region of the Indian or western Pacific Oceans.

ETYMOLOGY

Typhoon has a very rich background, with roots in several languages and cultures. One root is Greek, coming from *Typhon*, the name of the god of the winds and also, as a common noun, the word for "whirlwind." *Typhon* became *tufan* in Arabic and was transmitted to India by speakers of that language. Coincidentally, the Cantonese word for "great wind" is *tai fung*. Reinforcing each other, these various words from different parts of the globe eventually became *typhoon* in English.

ty·phus (tī′fəs) *n* a severe infectious disease marked by chills and fever, a purple rash, and extreme weakness. <Greek *typhos* stupor>

typ·i·cal (tip′ə kəl) *adj* **1** with the distinctive qualities of a particular type of person or thing: *typical symptoms.* **2** to do with a particular person or thing: *It was typical of her to sign it without reading it first.* **typ′i·cal·ly** *adv.*

typ·i·fy (tip′ə fī′) *v* **typ·i·fied, typ·i·fy·ing** be characteristic or a representative example of: *For many, the dove typifies peace.* **typ′i·fi·ca′tion** *n.*

typ·ist (tī′pist) *n* a person who operates a typewriter, especially one who makes a living by typewriting.

ty·po (tī′pō) *Informal n* an error in keying. *<typographical>*

ty·pog·ra·phy (tī pog′rə fē) *n* **1** the art or process of setting and arranging types and printing from them. **2** the style and appearance of printed matter. **ty·pog′ra·pher** *n.* **ty′po·graph′ic** *adj.* **ty′po·graph′i·cal** *adj.* **ty′po·graph′i·cal·ly** *adv.*

ty·ran·ni·cal (tə ran′ə kəl) *adj* using power in a cruel, unjust, or arbitrary way: *a tyrannical king.* **ty·ran′ni·cal·ly** *adv.*

tyr·an·nize (tir′ə nīz′) *v* **tyr·an·nized, tyr·an·niz·ing 1** control or rule cruelly or unjustly: *An absolute monarch may tyrannize the people.* **2** (*with* **over**) use power cruelly or unjustly. *Gangsters tyrannized over the city for years.*

ty·ran·no·sau·rus (ti ran′ə sȯ′rəs) *n* a huge, carnivorous dinosaur of the late Cretaceous period of N America with powerful jaws, small clawlike front legs, and hind legs on which it walked. <Greek *tyrannos* tyrant + *sauros* lizard>

tyr·an·ny (tir′ə nē) *n, pl* **tyr·an·nies 1** a cruel and oppressive government or rule, or a country or society under such a cruel and oppressive rule: *A revolution brought an end to the tyranny.* **2** the cruel, unreasonable, or arbitrary use of power or control: *She thought she was living under the tyranny of the clock.* **tyr′an·nous** *adj.* **tyr′an·nous·ly** *adv.*

ty·rant (tī′rənt) *n* a person who uses power or control cruelly or unjustly, especially a ruler of a country or society. <Greek *tyrannos*>

ty·ro (tī′rō) *n, pl* **ty·ros** a beginner or novice: *Much practice changed the tyro into an expert.* <Latin *tiro* recruit>

tzat·zi·ki (tsat sē′kē) *n* a Greek dish consisting of chopped cucumber, yogurt, and garlic. <Greek>

Uu

u or **U** (yū) *n, pl* **u's** or **U's** **1** the twenty-first letter of the English alphabet, or any speech sound represented by it. **2** the twenty-first thing in a list or series.

UAE United Arab Emirates.

u·biq·ui·tous (yū bik′wə təs) *adj* present, appearing, or found everywhere: *He found it impossible to escape from his ubiquitous sister.* <Latin *ubique* everywhere> **u·biq′ui·tous·ly** *adv.* **u·biq′ui·ty** *n.*

U–boat (yū′bōt′) *n* a German submarine used in World Wars I and II. <German *Unterseeboot* undersea boat>

U–bolt (yū′bōlt′) *n* a bolt shaped like the letter U, with both ends threaded for screwing nuts on.

ud·der (ud′ər) *n* the milk-producing gland of female cattle, sheep, goats, horses, and related mammals, hanging near the hind legs as a baglike organ with two or more teats. <Old English *uder*>

UFO (yū′ef ō′) *n, pl* **UFOs** or **UFO's** in full, **unidentified flying object** especially a flying saucer or other object supposed to be a spacecraft from another planet.

u·fol·o·gist (yū fol′ə jist) *n* a person who studies UFOs, especially one who believes them to be from outer space. **u·fol′o·gy** *n.*

U·gan·da (yů gan′də) *n* a country in east Africa. See the APPENDIX. **U·gan′dan** *adj, n.*

ugh (ůg) *or* (ůk) *interj* used to express disgust or horror.

ug·ly (ug′lē) *adj* **ug·li·er, ug·li·est** *n* **1** very unpleasant to look at or listen to: *an ugly house, an ugly sound.* **2** involving or likely to involve violence, danger, or harm: *an ugly situation, ugly clouds. He gets ugly when he hasn't had enough sleep.* **3** causing anxiety or mental unease: *ugly rumours.* **4** morally objectionable: *Racism reared its ugly head.* <Old Norse *uggligr* dreadful>
ug′li·fi·ca′tion (ug′lə fi kā′shən) *n.*
ug′li·fy (ug′lə fī) *v.* **ug′li·ness** *n.*

SYNONYMS

Ugly, when it refers to something seen or heard, means "not very pleasing to look at or listen to": *Let's get rid of that ugly painting on the wall.*

Repulsive emphasizes disgust at something: *That mess is so repulsive I can't look at it.*

Hideous emphasizes the quality of being frightful or horrifying: *The hideous mask scared the children.*

ugly duckling *n* a person or thing at first thought to be unattractive or unimpressive, but that turns out to have beauty, talent, or other admirable qualities.

uh (u) *interj* used to express hesitation: *I couldn't attend the last meeting because I, uh, was sick.*

UHF *n* in full, **ultra-high** (ul′trə hī′) **frequency** the band of radio frequencies between 300 and 3000 megahertz.

uh–huh (ə′hə′) *interj* used to express agreement, or as a non-committal response to a question or remark: *"Do you think it will rain today?" "Uh-huh, I think it will."*

uh–uh (ə′ə′) *interj* used to express a negative response to a question or remark: *"Are you going to the movie?" " Uh-uh, I have no money."*

✱ **UI** or **U.I.** unemployment insurance.

UK or **U.K.** United Kingdom.

U·kraine (yů krān′) *n* a country in eastern Europe. See the APPENDIX. **U·krain′i·an** *adj, n.*

u·ku·le·le (yū′kə lā′lē) *n* a small guitar-shaped instrument with four strings.

ETYMOLOGY

Ukulele comes from two Hawaiian words: *uku*, meaning "flea," and *lele*, meaning "jumping." The word is sometimes traced to a small and sprightly army officer, Edward Purvis, who is said to have popularized the ukulele in Hawaii in the 1880s.

u·la·ma (ū′lə mȧ′) *Islam n* a collective term for religious scholars and leaders.

ul·cer (ul′sər) *n* **1** an open sore on the skin or a mucous membrane such as the lining of the stomach or the inside of the mouth. **2** a moral blemish or corrupting influence. <Latin *ulceris*> **ul′cer·ous** *adj.*

ul·cer·ate (ul′sə rāt′) *v* **ul·cer·at·ed, ul·cer·at·ing** develop into or become affected by an ulcer. **ul′cer·a′tion** *n.*

ul·na (ul′nə) *n, pl* **ul·nae** (-nē) *or* (-nī) **1** the bone of the human forearm on the side opposite the thumb. **2** a corresponding bone in the foreleg of an animal or a bird's wing. <Latin = elbow> **ul′nar** *adj.*

ul·te·ri·or (ul tē′rē ər) *adj* existing beyond what is obvious and admitted: *an ulterior motive.* <Latin *ulter* beyond>

ul·ti·mate (ul′tə mit) *adj* **1** being or happening at the end of a process: *He never stopped to consider the ultimate result of his actions.* **2** being the best or most extreme example of its kind: *From her, a big smile was the ultimate compliment.* **3** basic or fundamental: *My teacher said that atoms were the ultimate constituents of matter.*
n **the ultimate** the best achievable or imaginable of its kind: *That car is the ultimate in speed and power.* <Latin *ultimare* come to an end, from *ultimus* last>
ul′ti·mate·ly *adv.*

ul·ti·ma·tum (ul′tə mā′təm) *n* a final demand or statement of terms, the rejection of which will result in retaliation or a breakdown in relations: *He presented her with an ultimatum: stop interfering, or he'd have nothing to do with her anymore.*

a bat	e bed	i bid	o pot	u cup	th thin
ā cake	ē me	ī bite	ō go	ū rude	ᴛʜ then
ȧ bar	ə about	ər over	ȯ for	ů put	zh measure

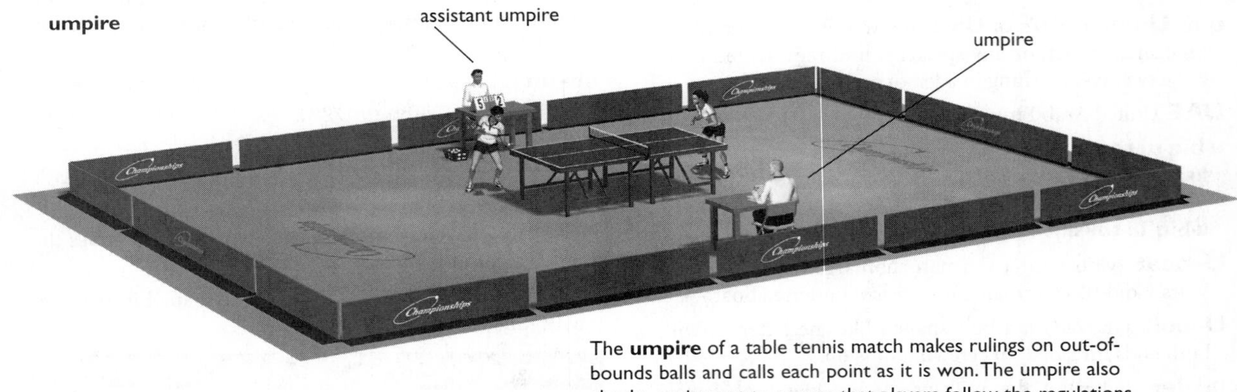

The **umpire** of a table tennis match makes rulings on out-of-bounds balls and calls each point as it is won. The umpire also checks equipment to ensure that players follow the regulations.

ul·tra (ul′trə) *adj* extreme: *an ultra conservative.*
n a person who holds extreme views or urges extreme measures. <Latin = beyond>

ultra– 1 beyond or on the other side: *ultraviolet.* **2** very or extremely: *ultralight.* <Latin *ultra* beyond>

ul·tra·light (ul′trə līt′) *adj* extremely light.
n a small, single-seat or two-seat aircraft, made of lightweight materials and powered by a small motor. It has an open frame and looks somewhat like a hang-glider.

ul·tra·ma·rine (ul′trə mə rēn′) *adj* brilliantly deep blue.

ul·tra·son·ic (ul′trə son′ik) *adj* to do with sound waves that have a frequency above the upper limit of human hearing.

ul·tra·sound (ul′trə sound′) *Medicine n* **1** sound or other vibrations with an ultrasonic frequency, particularly used in creating scanned images of the body. **2** an ultrasonic scan: *My mom had an ultrasound yesterday.*

ul·tra·vi·o·let (ul′trə vī′ə lit) *adj* to do with an electromagnetic wavelength shorter than that of the violet end of the visible spectrum but longer than that of X-rays.

🍁 **u·lu** (ū′lū) *n* a crescent-shaped, bone-handled knife used by Inuit women. Also, **ooloo**. <Inuktitut>

ul·u·late (yū′lyə lāt′) *or* (ul′yə lāt′) *v* **ul·u·lat·ed, ul·u·lat·ing** howl or wail as an expression of strong emotion, typically grief. <Latin *ululare* howl> **ul′u·la′tion** *n.*

um (um) *or* (əm) *interj* used to express hesitation or a pause while speaking: *I'm, um, very pleased to be here.*

um·bel (um′bəl) *n* a flower cluster in which stalks nearly equal in length spring from a common centre and form a flat or slightly curved surface, as in parsley. <Latin *umbella* parasol, from the shape of the plant>

um·ber (um′bər) *n* an earth used in its natural state (**raw umber**) as a brown pigment, or after heating (**burnt umber**) as a reddish brown pigment.
adj brown or reddish brown. <Latin *Umbria* a district in central Italy from which the colouring first came>

um·bil·i·cal cord (um bil′ə kəl) *or* (um′bi lī′kəl) *n* **1** a flexible, cordlike structure containing blood vessels and attaching a human or mammal fetus in the womb to the placenta. **2** a flexible cable, line, or pipe carrying essential services or supplies.

um·bil·i·cus (um bil′ə kəs) *or* (um′bi lī′kəs) *n, pl* **um·bil·i·ci** (-sē) **1** the navel. **2** a rounded knob or navel-like formation in an animal or plant, especially in a bivalve or mushroom. <Latin = navel>

um·bra (um′brə) *n, pl* **um·bras** or **um·brae** (-brē) *or* (-brī) the fully shaded inner region of a shadow cast by an opaque object, especially the area on the earth or moon experiencing the total phase of an eclipse. See ECLIPSE for picture. Compare PENUMBRA. <Latin>

um·brage (um′brij) *n* a strong feeling of having been offended or annoyed: *He took umbrage at the slightest criticism. She didn't say anything for fear of giving umbrage to her host.* <French *ombrage*, from Latin *umbra* shade. The sense is of having been put in the shade.>

um·brel·la (um brel′ə) *n* **1** a device consisting of a circular surface of cloth on a folding metal frame supported by a central rod, held in the hand and used for protection against rain or sun. **2** a force or influence that protects or influences someone or something: *Savings can be an umbrella against hard times.* **3** a thing that includes or contains many different elements or parts: *The big charity was an umbrella organization for many smaller ones.* <Italian, from Latin *umbra* shade>

🍁 **u·mi·ak** (ū′mē ak′) *n* a large, flat-bottomed boat made of skins stretched over a wooden frame and propelled by paddles, traditionally rowed by women. Also, **oomiak**. <Inuktitut *umiaq*>

um·ma (um′ə) *n* the world-wide community of Muslims, including Sunnis, Shiites, and other sects.

ump (ump) *Informal n, v* umpire.

um·pire (um′pīr) *n* **1** an official who closely watches a game or match in some sports to enforce the rules and to decide on matters arising from the play: *The umpire called the ball a foul.* **2** a person chosen to settle a dispute.
v **um·pired, um·pir·ing** act as umpire. <Old French *nonper* not one of a pair, i.e., third person who settles a dispute>

ump·teen (ump′tēn′) *Informal adj* indefinitely many or a lot of: *I've heard umpteen different suggestions, but not one of them is practical.* <*umpty* a great deal + *-teen*> **ump′teenth′** *adj.*

un–[1] *prefix* a lack of: *unbalanced, untruth, unrest.* <Old English>

un–[2] *prefix* reversing, reducing, or cancelling an action or condition: *untie, unburden.* <Old English>

GRAMMAR AND USAGE

Un- is the most common prefix in English. Most prefixes are easy to figure out from their root words. For information on *un-* words not listed in a dictionary, look up the root word (for example, if *unpardonable* is not listed, look up *pardonable*).

Some *un-* words, such as *uncouth*, have roots that are rarely used or never used alone.

UN or **U.N.** United Nations.

un·a·bashed (un′ə basht′) *adj* not embarrassed, ashamed, or awed: *They looked at him accusingly, but he remained unabashed.* **un′a·bash′ed·ly** *adv.*

un·a·ble (un ā′bəl) *adj* lacking the skill, means, or opportunity to do something: *unable to speak.*

un·a·bridged (un′ə brijd′) *adj* not cut or shortened as a text: *an unabridged book.*

un·ac·com·pa·nied (un′ə kum′pə nēd) *or* (un′ə kump′nēd) *adj, adv* **1** not accompanied by another person or thing: *She was unaccompanied on her journey.* **2** sung or played without instrumental accompaniment as a piece of music: *The soloist sang unaccompanied.*

un·ac·count·a·ble (un′ə koun′tə bəl) *adj* **1** unable to be explained: *He suddenly flew into one of his unaccountable rages.* **2** not required or expected to justify actions or decisions, and not responsible for results or consequences: *The accused was judged insane and therefore unaccountable for his actions.* **un′ac·count·a·bil′i·ty** *n.* **un′ac·count′a·bly** *adv.*

un·ac·count·ed (un′ə koun′tid) *adj* (*with* ***for***) not explained or included in: *That leaves two students still unaccounted for. There were too many unaccounted-for absences.*

un·ac·cus·tomed (un′ə kus′təmd) *adj* not familiar or usual: *He did not like his new school at first because he was unaccustomed to the routines. The unaccustomed heat made us all very tired.*

un·ac·quaint·ed (un′ə kwān′tid) *adj* with no experience of, familiarity with, or known to one another: *We were unacquainted with the technology. I'm afraid we are unacquainted.*

un·a·dul·ter·at·ed (un′ə dul′tə rā′tid) *adj* not mixed or diluted with any different or extra elements; complete and absolute: *unadulterated milk.*

un·af·fect·ed (un′ə fek′tid) *adj* **1** feeling or showing no effects or changes: *He was completely unaffected by their criticism.* **2** simple, sincere, and natural in style or manner. **un′af·fect′ed·ly** *adv.* **un′af·fect′ed·ness** *n.*

un·al·ter·a·ble (un ol′tər ə bəl) *adj* not able to be changed: *unalterable opinions.* **un·al′ter·a·bly** *adv.*

u·nan·i·mous (yū nan′ə məs) *adj* fully in agreement between two or more people, especially held or carried as an opinion, decision, or vote by everyone involved: *unanimous consent. The delegates were unanimous that the issue needed to be discussed further.* <Latin *unus* one + *animus* mind> **u·na·nim′i·ty** *n.* **u·nan′i·mous·ly** *adv.* **u·nan′i·mous·ness** *n.*

un·an·swer·a·ble (un an′sə rə bəl) *adj* **1** unable to be answered: *unanswerable questions.* **2** unable to be, especially unable to be disclaimed or proved wrong: *an unanswerable argument.* **un·an′swer·a·bly** *adv.*

un·ap·proach·a·ble (un′ə prō′chə bəl) *adj* not welcoming or friendly as a person. **un′ap·proach·a·bil′i·ty** *n.* **un′ap·proach′a·ble·ness** *n.* **un′ap·proach′a·bly** *adv.*

un·armed (un ärmd′) *adj* not equipped with or carrying weapons: *The intruder turned out to be unarmed.*

un·asked (un′askt′) *adj* (*often with* ***for***) not requested or invited: *unasked questions; unasked-for advice.*

un·as·sum·ing (un′ə sū′ming) *or* (un′ə syū′ming) *adj* not pretentious or arrogant: *People were delighted by the queen's unassuming manner.* **un′as·sum′ing·ly** *adv.* **un′as·sum′ing·ness** *n.*

un·at·tached (un′ə tacht′) *adj* **1** not attached. **2** not working for or belonging to a particular group or organization. **3** single, and not married or with an established partner.

un·at·tend·ed (un′ə ten′did) *adj* **1** not noticed or dealt with. **2** not supervised or looked after: *The phone was left unattended while the receptionist took a coffee break.*

un·a·vail·ing (un′ə vā′ling) *adj* ineffective or achieving little or nothing: *His attempt to climb the fence was unavailing.* **un′a·vail′ing·ly** *adv.* **un′a·vail′ing·ness** *n.*

un·a·ware (un′ə wer′) *adj* with no knowledge of a situation or fact: *We had gone out in the boat, unaware that there was a storm warning.*
adv **unawares** without being aware of a situation: *The police caught the burglar unawares. We made the error unawares.*

un·bal·ance (un bal′əns) *v* **un·bal·anced, unbal·anc·ing** **1** make someone or something unsteady enough to tip or fall. **2** upset the mental balance of someone.

un·bal·anced (un bal′ənst) *adj* **1** not keeping or showing an even balance or not evenly distributed. **2** not giving an accurate, fair, or equal coverage to all aspects: *an unbalanced report.* **3** emotionally or mentally disordered; unstable or deranged.

un·beat·en (un bē′tən) *adj* **1** not defeated or surpassed. **2** not trodden or travelled: *unbeaten paths.* **3** not mixed by stirring: *Add two unbeaten eggs.*

a bat	e bed	i bid	o pot	u cup	th thin
ā cake	ē me	ī bite	ō go	ū rude	ᴛʜ then
ä bar	ə about	ər over	ȯ for	u̇ put	zh measure

un·be·com·ing (un′bi kum′ing) *adj* **1** not attractive for or suitable to the wearer: *an unbecoming hairstyle.* **2** not appropriate in a person's attitude or behaviour: *unbecoming conduct.* **un′be·com′ing·ly** *adv.* **un′be·com′ing·ness** *n.*

un·be·known or **un·be·knownst** (un′bi nōn′) *or* (un′bi nōnst′) *adj* without the knowledge of someone: *He arrived unbeknown to anyone.*

un·be·lief (un′bi lēf′) *n* a lack of religious belief or faith. **un′be·liev′er** *n.* **un′be·liev′ing** *adj.* **un′be·liev′ing·ly** *adv.*

CONFUSABLES

Unbelief suggests a lack of belief in something widely held as true, especially with reference to religion: *They were persecuted for their unbelief.*

Disbelief suggests a refusal to believe or accept, often with reference to something surprising or amazing: *They stared in disbelief at the damage caused by the fire.*

un·be·lieve·a·ble (un′bi lē′və bəl) *adj* **1** not able to be believed or unlikely to be true: *an unbelievable story.* **2** amazing or extreme: *I'm in an unbelievable hurry right now, so I'll have to call you back.*

un·bend (un bend′) *v* **un·bent, un·bend·ing 1** make or become straight from a bent or twisted form or position: *to unbend the fingers.* **2** become less reserved, formal, or strict: *At the reception, the judge unbent and behaved like a little boy.* **3** unfasten sails on a boat from yards and stays.

un·bend·ing (un ben′ding) *adj* **1** not bending or curving. **2** reserved, formal, or strict: *an unbending attitude.* **un·bend′ing·ly** *adv.* **un·bend′ing·ness** *n.*

un·bi·ased or **un·bi·assed** (un bī′əst) *adj* showing no prejudice or bias for or against something.

un·bid·den (un bid′ən) *adj* without having been commanded, invited, or expected: *unbidden thoughts.*

un·bind (un bīnd′) *v* **un·bound, un·bind·ing** release from bonds or restraints.

un·blush·ing (un blush′ing) *adj* **1** not blushing. **2** not feeling or showing embarrassment or shame: *unblushing impudence.* **un·blush′ing·ly** *adv.*

un·born (un bôrn′) *adj* **1** not yet born as a baby: *an unborn child.* **2** not yet existing or brought into being: *unborn generations. That joke should have stayed unborn.*

un·bos·om (un bůz′əm) *or* (un bū′zəm) *Archaic v* disclose one's thoughts or secrets: *to unbosom oneself.*

un·bound (un bound′) *adj* **1** not bound or tied up: *They were unbound of any restraints.* **2** not bound together as printed sheets or with a proper or permanent cover: *an unbound book.* **3** not held by a chemical bond, gravity, or other physical force: *unbound electrons.*
v past tense and past participle of UNBIND.

un·bound·ed (un boun′did) *adj* with or appearing to have no limits: *Her unbounded good spirits cheered all of us up.*

un·bri·dled (un brī′dəld) *adj* **1** not with a bridle on. **2** not controlled or restrained: *unbridled anger.*

un·bro·ken (un brō′kən) *adj* **1** not broken, fractured, or damaged: *There was only one unbroken cup left in the whole set.* **2** not interrupted or disturbed: *She had eight hours of unbroken sleep.* **3** not tamed or accustomed to being ridden as a horse: *an unbroken colt.*

un·buck·le (un buk′əl) *v* **un·buck·led, un·buck·ling** unfasten the buckle of something, especially a belt or shoe.

un·bur·den (un bər′dən) *v* relieve someone of something that is causing anxiety or distress, especially by confessing or revealing: *He decided to unburden himself of the problem. She unburdened her mind to her friend.*

un·busi·ness·like (un biz′ni slīk′) *adj* not businesslike, and with little order, system, or method.

un·but·ton (un but′ən) *v* **1** unfasten the button or buttons of a garment. **2** *Informal* relax and become less inhibited: *After working all day, they were able to unbutton a little by playing hockey.* **un·but′toned** *adj.*

un·called (un kold′) *adj* **1** not summoned or invited. **2** (*with* ***for***) undesirable and unnecessary: *The nasty look you gave me was uncalled for, an uncalled-for remark.*

un·can·ny (un kan′ē) *adj* strange or mysterious, especially in an unsettling way: *The trees had uncanny shapes in the dim light. He had an uncanny sense of timing.* **un·can′ni·ly** *adv.* **un·can′ni·ness** *n.*

un·cared (un kerd′) *adj* (*with* ***for***) not looked after properly: *The room looked uncared for, uncared-for hair.*

un·cer·e·mo·ni·ous (un′ser ə mō′nē əs) *adj* with or showing a lack of courtesy or dignity: *an unceremonious exit.* **un′cer·e·mo′ni·ous·ly** *adv.* **un′cer·e·mo′ni·ous·ness** *n.*

un·cer·tain (un sər′tən) *adj* **1** not able to be relied on, known, or definite: *The election results are still uncertain. Her arrival time is uncertain.* **2** not completely confident or sure of something: *I was uncertain what to do.* **un·cer′tain·ly** *adv.* **un·cer′tain·ty** *n.*

SYNONYMS

Uncertain means "not know definitely": *The corporation faces an uncertain future.*

Doubtful can mean "undecided": *I'm doubtful that my parents will allow me to go to the sleepover.*

Insecure suggests having fear or anxiety due to not being protected: *They felt insecure about being on the spring ice.*

uncertainty principle *n* the principle that the momentum and position of a physical particle cannot both be precisely determined at the same time. <W. Heisenberg, 20c physicist>

un·change·a·ble (un chān′jə bəl) *adj* not liable to variation or able to be altered.

un·chang·ing (un chān′jing) *adj* not changing.

un·char·i·ta·ble (un cher′ə tə bəl) *adj* unkind or unsympathetic as an act or attitude. **un·char′i·ta·ble·ness** *n.* **un·char′i·ta·bly** *adv.*

un·chart·ed (un chär′tid) *adj* not yet mapped or surveyed: *uncharted seas.*

un·checked (un chekt′) *adj* **1** not restrained or held back in any way, especially of something undesirable: *If such behaviour is left unchecked, it will just get worse.* **2** not examined, especially in order to determine the accuracy, quality, or condition of something: *These statistics are unchecked, so don't publish them.*

un·ci·al (un′shē əl) *adj* to do with an ancient script with rounded unjoined letters and from which modern capital letters are derived.
n an uncial letter or script. <Latin *uncialis* inch-high, from *uncia* inch>

un·civ·il (un siv′əl) *adj* impolite: *an uncivil retort.* **un·civ′il·ly** *adv.*

un·clad (un klad′) *adj* without clothing.
v a past tense and a past participle of UNCLOTHE.

un·clasp (un klasp′) *v* **1** unfasten a clasp or similar device. **2** release or be released from a grip.

un·cle (ung′kəl) *n* the brother of one's father or mother or the spouse of one's aunt. <Latin *avunculus* mother's brother>
say (or **cry**) **uncle,** *Informal* surrender or admit defeat: *She wouldn't let her kid brother up until he said uncle.*

un·clean (un klēn′) *adj* **1** dirty. **2** morally or ethically wrong: *unclean thoughts.* **3** regarded by a particular religion as impure and unfit to be used. **un·clean′ness** *n.*

Uncle Sam *Informal n* the government or people of the US.

ETYMOLOGY

Uncle Sam is probably based on the initials of the words "**U**nited **S**tates." First used scornfully in the War of 1812, the words became a popular nickname for the American government. The image of Uncle Sam is now widely considered a symbol of the country itself.

un·clog (un klog′) *v* **un·clogged, un·clog·ging** free from an obstruction: *to unclog a drain.*

un·clothe (un klōᴛʜ′) *v* **un·clothed** or **un·clad, un·cloth·ing** **1** remove the clothes from oneself or someone else. **2** lay bare or uncover.

un·coil (un koil′) *v* straighten or cause to straighten from a coiled or curled position: *uncoil a rope.*

un·com·fort·a·ble (un kum′fər tə bəl) *adj* **1** causing or feeling slight pain or physical discomfort: *I am uncomfortable in this chair.* **2** causing or feeling unease or awkwardness: *I feel uncomfortable at formal dinners.* **un·com′fort·a·ble·ness** *n.* **un·com′fort·a·bly** *adv.*

un·com·mit·ted (un′kə mit′id) *adj* **1** not committed to a particular course of action or policy: *uncommitted voters.* **2** not pledged or set aside for future use: *uncommitted resources.* **3** not pledged to remain in a long-term emotional relationship with someone.

un·com·mon (un kom′ən) *adj* **1** not commonly encountered: *The cactus is uncommon outside desert regions.* **2** remarkably great: *uncommon strength.* **un·com′mon·ly** *adv.* **un·com′mon·ness** *n.*

un·com·mu·ni·ca·tive (un kə myū′ni ka′tiv) *or* (un kə myū′ni kə′tiv) *adj* unwilling to talk or give any information. **un′com·mu′ni·ca·tive·ness** *n.*

un·com·pro·mis·ing (un kom′prə mī′zing) *adj* showing an unwillingness to make concessions to others, especially by changing one's ways or opinions: *His uncompromising attitude makes him very hard to deal with.* **un·com′pro·mis′ing·ly** *adv.*

un·con·cern (un′kən sərn′) *n* a lack of worry or interest: *The children looked with complete unconcern at their strange surroundings.* **un′con·cerned′** *adj.* **un′con·cerned′ly** *adv.*

un·con·di·tion·al (un′kən dish′ə nəl) *or* (un′kən dish′nəl) *adj* not subject to any conditions: *unconditional surrender.* **un·con·di′tion·al·ly** *adv.*

un·con·nect·ed (un′kə nek′tid) *adj* **1** not joined together or to something else: *unconnected plugs.* **2** not associated or linked in order or sequence: *What she had written was not a paragraph, but just a series of unconnected sentences.* **3** not having family members in influential positions. **un′con·nect′ed·ly** *adv.* **un′con·nect′ed·ness** *n.*

un·con·scion·a·ble (un kon′shə nə bəl) *adj* not proper or reasonable: *I waited an unconscionable length of time for my dentist appointment.* **un·con′scion·a·bly** *adv.*

un·con·scious (un kon′shəs) *adj* **1** not awake and aware of and responding to one's surroundings: *He was knocked unconscious when the car struck him.* **2** done or existing without one realizing: *unconscious neglect.*
n **the unconscious** the part of the mind of which the person is not normally aware, but which can affect behaviour and emotions. **un·con′scious·ly** *adv.* **un·con′scious·ness** *n.*

un·con·sti·tu·tion·al (un′kon stə tyū′shə nal) *or* (un′kon stə tū′shə nal) *n* not complying with a political constitution or with the rules of procedure. **un′con·sti·tu′tion·al′i·ty** *n.* **un′con·sti·tu′tion·ally** *adv.*

un·con·trol·la·ble (un′kən trō′lə bəl) *adj* impossible to control: *She had an uncontrollable urge to laugh.*

un·con·trolled (un′kən trōld′) *adj* not controlled: *uncontrolled spending.*

un·con·ven·tion·al (un′kən ven′shə nəl) *adj* not based on or conforming to what is generally done or believed: *an unconventional approach, an unconventional person.* **un′con·ven′tion·al′i·ty** *n.* **un′con·ven′tion·al·ly** *adv.*

un·co–op·er·a·tive (un′kō op′ər ə tiv) *adj* not co-operative.

un·cou·pled, un·cou·pling disconnect something, especially a railway car that has been coupled to another.

un·couth (un kūth′) *adj* lacking good manners, refinement, or grace: *uncouth manners, an uncouth person.* <Old English *uncuth*> **un·couth′ness** *n.*

a bat	e bed	i bid	o pot	u cup	th thin
ā cake	ē me	ī bite	ō go	ū rude	ᴛʜ then
à bar	ə about	ər over	ȯ for	ů put	zh measure

un·cov·er (un kuv′ər) *v* **1** remove a cover or covering from: *He uncovered the jar of honey.* **2** discover something previously secret or unknown: *The plot was uncovered when the letter was found.* **3** remove one's hat or cap in respect: *The men uncovered as the flag passed by.*

un·cross (un kros′) *v* move something back from a crossed position: *She uncrossed her legs and stretched them out.*

unc·tion (ungk′shən) *n* **1** the act of anointing someone with oil or ointment as a religious or solemn political rite. **2** a form of expression arising or apparently arising from deep emotion, especially one intended to flatter: *Her compliments were made with much unction.* <Latin *unguere* anoint>

unc·tu·ous (ungk′chū əs) *adj* **1** unduly flattering in a false or affected way: *The stranger's unctuous manner made us suspicious.* **2** with a greasy or soapy feel, especially in a mineral. **unc′tu·ous·ly** *adv.* **unc′tu·ous·ness** *n.*

un·curl (un kərl′) *v* straighten or cause to straighten from a curled position.

un·cut (un kut′) *adj* **1** not cut: *The cake was on the table, still uncut.* **2** not shaped as a gemstone, especially a diamond, by cutting. **3** complete and intact as a text, movie, or performance: *They saw the uncut version of the movie.*

un·daunt·ed (un don′tid) *adj* not discouraged or frightened: *The night grew cold and dark, but they continued their search undaunted.*

un·de·ceive (un′di sēv′) *v* **un·de·ceived, un·de·ceiv·ing** tell someone that an idea or belief is mistaken: *They undeceived me of my illusions.*

un·de·cid·ed (un′di sī′did) *adj* **1** not decided or settled: *The matter was still undecided when the meeting was adjourned.* **2** not having made a decision: *She is undecided about her future.* **un′de·cid′ed·ly** *adv.* **un′de·cid′ed·ness** *n.*

un·de·fined (un′di fīnd′) *adj* not clear or defined: *I'm not comfortable with this assignment because it seems too undefined.*

un·de·ni·a·ble (un′di nī′ə bəl) *adj* unable to be denied or disputed: *undeniable excellence. Her references were undeniable.* **un′de·ni′a·bly** *adv.*

un·der (un′dər) *prep* **1** at or to a lower level, layer, or surface than: *The road goes under that bridge. The marble rolled under the table. Write your name under mine.* **2** beneath a physical surface or an appearance: *She was wearing a heavy sweater under her parka. He has a soft heart under his gruff exterior.* **3** lower than a specified amount, rate, or standard: *It will cost under twenty dollars.* **4** lower in rank than; subject to the authority of: *She studied under a famous pianist.* **5** during a specified time period: *England under Queen Elizabeth I.* **6** within a particular group or category: *Books on gymnastics are classed under sports.* **7** because of certain circumstances: *under terrible working conditions.* **8** undergoing a process: *under construction, under attack.*
adv **1** on or into a place below: *The swimmer flailed her arms and then went under.* **2** unconscious or affected by an anesthetic: *Was the operation long? Yes, he was under for eight hours.* <Old English>

SYNONYMS

Under can mean both "below" and "behind": *The soap is under the sink. I found blue paint under the red.*

Below usually means "lower than": *Our apartment is one floor below yours.*

Beneath can replace either *under* or *below*, but is somewhat more formal or literary: *Can you see the kindness beneath his fierce expression?*

under– *prefix* **1** below or beneath: *underground, underclothes.* **2** lower in status or rank: *undersecretary.* **3** insufficiently or incompletely: *underfed, underripe.* **4** less in degree, rate, quantity, or amount than is normal: *undersized.*

un·der·a·chieve (un′dər ə chēv′) *v* **un·der·a·chieved, un·der·a·chiev·ing** do less well than is expected. **un′der·a·chieve′ment** *n.* **un′der·a·chiev′er** *n.*

un·der·age (un′də rāj′) *for adj,* (un′də rāj′) *for adv.* *adj, adv* too young to engage legally in a particular activity, especially drinking alcohol or having sex.

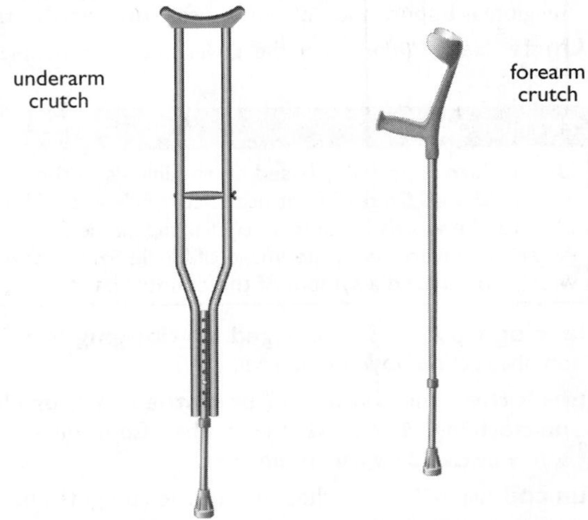

The **underarm** crutch is used mainly for leg injuries that heal quickly. The lightweight forearm crutch is best for those who need long-term assistance. The forearm crutch is also called the Canadian crutch.

un·der·arm (un′də rȧrm′) *adj, adv* **1** on or under the inside of the arm where it joins the shoulder: *underarm deodorant (adj).* **2** thrown or stroked in a sport with the arm or hand below shoulder level: *an underarm throw (adj). He threw the ball underarm (adv).*
n a person's armpit.

un·der·bel·ly (un′dər bel′ē) *n, pl* **un·der·bel·lies** **1** the soft underside or abdomen of a person or animal. **2** an area that is vulnerable to attack: *Her statement strikes at the underbelly of democratic institutions.* **3** a hidden unpleasant or criminal part of society.

un·der·bid (un′dər bid′) *v* **un·der·bid, un·der·bid·ding** 1 make a lower bid than someone, especially in an auction or competition for a tender: 2 make a lower bid on one's hand in the card game bridge than is justified.
n a bid that is lower than another or than is justified. **un′der·bid′der** *n.*

un·der·brush (un′dər brush′) UNDERGROWTH.

un·der·car·riage (un′dər kar′ij) *or* (un′dər ker′ij) *n* 1 a wheeled structure beneath an aircraft, typically retracted when not in use, that receives the impact on landing and supports the aircraft on the ground. 2 a supporting frame under the body of a vehicle.

un·der·charge (un′dər chärj′) *for v,* (un′dər chärj′) *for n.*
v **un·der·charged, un·der·charg·ing** 1 charge someone a price or amount that is too low: *I think the clerk undercharged me. He undercharged me one dollar.* 2 give less than the proper charge to an electric battery.
n a charge that is insufficient.

un·der·clothes (un′dər klōz′) *or* (un′dər klōᴛʜz′) *pln* clothes that are worn under others, typically next to the skin.

un·der·cloth·ing (un′der klō′ᴛʜing) *n* underwear.

un·der·coat (un′dər kōt′) *n* 1 a layer of paint applied before the finishing coat. 2 the soft, thick fur of animals that is hidden by the longer, coarser hair of the outer coat.
v apply undercoating or an undercoat to: *to undercoat a car.* **un′der·coat′ing** *n.*

un·der·cov·er (un′dər kuv′ər) *adj* involved in or involving secret work within a community or organization, especially for the purposes of police investigation or espionage: *an undercover officer.*

un·der·cur·rent (un′dər kər′ənt) *n* 1 a current flowing below the upper currents or the surface of a body of water and in a different direction. 2 an underlying feeling or influence, especially one that is contrary to what is expressed or shown: *There was an undercurrent of sadness beneath her joking manner.*

un·der·cut (un′dər kut′) *for v,* (un′dər kut′) *for adj or n.*
v **un·der·cut, un·der·cut·ting** 1 offer goods or services at a lower price than a competitor. 2 cut or wear away the part below or under something, especially a cliff or bank. 3 weaken or undermine: *The facts began to undercut my comments.* 4 remove or have removed material from the lower part of something, such as a cliff, a coal seam, or part of a carving in relief. 5 *Tennis, Golf* hit a ball with a backward spin so that rises high in the air.
n 1 a space formed by the removal or absence of material from the lower part of something. 2 a notch cut in a tree below the main cut and on the side toward which the tree is to fall. 3 *Tennis, Golf* the act or fact of undercutting.

un·der·de·vel·oped (un′dər di vel′əpt) *adj* 1 not fully developed: *an underdeveloped limb.* 2 not developed economically as a country or region. 3 not developed enough to give a normal image in a photographic film.

un·der·dog (un′dər dog′) *n* 1 a person or group that is expected to lose or is losing a struggle or contest: *We've been the underdogs in the league so far, but this year we're going to win.* 2 a person or group that has little status in society.

un·der·done (un′dər dun′) *adj* insufficiently cooked, or less cooked than is usual: *an underdone steak.*

un·der·dress (un′dər dres′) *v* dress less formally than the occasion demands. **un′der·dressed′** *adj.*

un·der·em·ployed (un′dər em ploid′) *adj* working in a job that does not make full use of one's ability and training.

un·der·es·ti·mate (un′də res′tə māt′) *for v,* (un′də res′tə mit) *for n.*
v **un·der·es·ti·mat·ed, un·der·es·ti·mat·ing** estimate something or someone to be less important or capable than is the case: *He lost the match because he underestimated his opponent's strength.*
n an estimate that is too low. **un′der·es′tim·a′tion** *n.*

un·der·ex·pose (un′də rek spōz′) *v* **un·der·ex·posed, un·der·ex·pos·ing** expose a photographic film or image to light for too short a time. **un′der·ex·po′sure** *n.*

un·der·feed (un′dər fēd′) *v* **un·der·fed** (un′dər fed′), **un·der·feed·ing** feed too little. **un′der·fed′** *adj.*

un·der·foot (un′dər fu̇t′) *adj, adv* 1 under one's foot or feet: *He walked straight through the flower bed, crushing several plants underfoot.* 2 constantly present and in one's way: *That dog is always underfoot.*

un·der·fund·ed (un′dər fun′did) *adj* not given enough money, especially public funds: *She thinks the arts are underfunded in this country.*

un·der·fur (un′dər fər′) UNDERCOAT (def. 2)

un·der·gar·ment (un′dər gär′mənt) *n* a garment worn under outer clothing, especially underwear.

un·der·go (un′dər gō′) *v* **un·der·went, un·der·gone, un·der·go·ing** experience or be subjected to something, typically something unpleasant, painful, or difficult: *The town has undergone many changes in the past few years. They underwent a great deal of hardship on the long trek.*

un·der·grad·u·ate (un′dər graj′ū it) *n* a student at a college or university who has not yet received the first degree for a course of study.
adj to do with undergraduates: *undergraduate activities.*

un·der·ground (un′dər ground′) *for adv,* (un′dər ground′) *for adj, n.*
adv 1 beneath the surface of the ground. 2 in or into secrecy or hiding, especially as a result of carrying out something subversive or illegal: *The thieves went underground after the robbery.*
adj 1 being, working, or used beneath the surface of the ground: *underground cables.* 2 done or operating secretly and subversively: *The revolution began as an underground movement in the cities.* 3 to do with a group or movement seeking to explore alternative forms of lifestyle or artistic expression: *an underground newspaper. Her first plays were produced by an underground theatre.*
n 1 *UK* a subway. 2 a group or movement organized secretly to work against an existing regime. 3 a group or movement seeking to explore alternative forms of lifestyle or artistic expression.

a bat	e bed	i bid	o pot	u cup	th thin
ā cake	ē me	ī bite	ō go	ū rude	ᴛʜ then
ä bar	ə about	ər over	ȯ for	u̇ put	zh measure

Underground Railroad *n* a secret network for helping slaves escape from the southern US to the northern states and Canada in the years before the American Civil War.

un·der·growth (un′dər grōth′) *n* shrubs, bushes, and small trees growing under large trees in a forest. Also, **underbrush**.

un·der·hand (un′dər hand′) *adj, adv* **1** acting or done in a secret or dishonest way: *underhand dealings.* **2** with an upward movement of the hand from below shoulder level: *an underhand pitch (adj), to throw a ball underhand (adv).* See PITCH for picture. **3** underhanded.

un·der·hand·ed (un′dər han′did) *adj* **1** not open or honest; secret and sly: *an underhanded trick.* **2** underhand. **un′der·hand′ed·ly** *adv.* **un′der·hand′ed·ness** *n.*

un·der·lay (un′dər lā′) *for v,* (un′dər lā′) *for n. v* **un·der·laid, un·der·lay·ing** place a thing under another thing, especially to support or raise it.
v past tense of UNDERLIE.
n a thing placed under or behind another thing, especially material laid under a carpet for protection or support.

un·der·lie (un′dər lī′) *v* **un·der·lay, un·der·lain, un·der·ly·ing** **1** lie or be located under something, especially as a layer of rock or soil: *A layer of limestone underlies the gravel you see here.* **2** be the cause or basis of something: *Strong resentment underlay his outburst.*

un·der·line (un′dər līn′) *or* (un′dər līn′) *for v,* (un′dər līn′) *for n. v* **un·der·lined, un·der·lin·ing** **1** draw a line or lines under a word or phrase to give emphasis. **2** emphasize something: *Her speech underlined the importance of co-operation.*
n a line drawn underneath something: *The underline is too faint.*

un·der·ling (un′dər ling) *n* a person of lower rank or position.

un·der·ly·ing (un′dər lī′ing) past participle of UNDERLIE.

un·der·mine (un′dər mīn′) *v* **un·der·mined, un·der·min·ing** **1** wear away the base or foundations of a rock formation: *The wave had undermined the cliff.* **2** damage or weaken someone or something, especially gradually and subtly: *The editorial was obviously intended to undermine the politician's influence in the community. Several months of stress and insufficient sleep had undermined her health.* **3** dig or excavate beneath a building or structure so as to make it collapse: *undermine a wall.* **un′der·min′er** *n.*

un·der·most (un′dər mōst′) *adj, adv* lowest.

un·der·neath (un′dər nēth′) *prep, adv* **1** located directly below something else: *a cellar underneath a house. Write the date underneath.* **2** on the inside of or below something: *He wore a T-shirt underneath his shirt. He crawled underneath. She was wearing her swimsuit underneath.* **3** so as to be concealed by something else: *Underneath his gruff exterior, he was a kindly person.*
n the part or side of a thing facing toward the ground: *Let me see the underneath.*

un·der·nour·ished (un′dər nər′isht) *adj* not sufficiently nourished. **un′der·nour′ish·ment** *n.*

un·der·pants (un′dər pants′) *pln* an undergarment, especially for men or boys, covering the lower part of the body and with two holes for the legs.

un·der·part (un′dər pårt′) *n* **1** the lower part or portion of a thing. **2 underparts** *pl* the part of an animal's body that is underneath or normally facing down, especially when a specified colour or pattern: *The bird was grey with reddish underparts.*

un·der·pass (un′dər pas′) *n* a road or pedestrian tunnel passing under another road or a railway. See ABUTMENT for picture.

un·der·pay (un′dər pā′) *v* **un·der·paid, un·der·pay·ing** pay too little. **un′der·paid′** *adj.* **un′der·pay′ment** *n.*

un·der·pin (un′dər pin′) *v* **un·der·pinned, un·der·pin·ning** **1** support or strengthen a building or other structure from below by laying a solid foundation below ground level or by substituting stronger for weaker materials. **2** support, justify, or form the basis for: *Reliable data underpinned the report.*

un·der·pin·ning (un′dər pin′ing) *n* **1** the material or structure used to support a building or wall from below. **2 underpinnings** *pl* a thing used as a foundation or support: *The new evidence provided good underpinnings for the detective's theory.*

un·der·play (un′dər plā′) *or* (un′dər plā′) *v* **1** act a role or scene in a subdued or restrained way. **2** represent something as being less important than it really is. **3** give a player in a game or contest too little playing time.

un·der·pow·ered (un′dər pou′ərd) *adj* lacking enough mechanical, electrical, or other power.

un·der·priv·i·leged (un′dər priv′ə lijd) *adj* not enjoying the same standard of living or rights as most of the people in a society.
n **the underprivileged** *pl* people who are underprivileged.

un·der·rate (un′dər rāt′) *v* **un·der·rat·ed, un·der·rat·ing** underestimate the extent, value, or importance of someone or something: *Take care not to underrate the ability of your rivals.*

un·der–re·port (un′dər ri pôrt′) *v* fail to report something fully, especially news or data.

un·der–re·pre·sent (un′dər rep′ri zent′) *v* suggest or report a lower or inadequate amount, quantity, or degree than is actually present: *Young people are under-represented in government.*

un·der·ripe (un′dər rīp′) *adj* not completely ripe or not ripe enough: *underripe plums.*

un·der·score (un′dər skôr′) *for v,* (un′dər skôr′) *for n. v* **un·der·scored, un·der·scor·ing** UNDERLINE.
n **1** an UNDERLINE (def. 1). **2** *Computers* the character [__] used in e-mail addresses and file names to represent a space between words.

un·der·sea (un′dər sē′) *for adj,* (un′dər sē′) *for adv. adj, adv* to do with being below the sea or below the surface of the sea: *undersea oil deposits, undersea explorations.*

un·der·sec·re·tar·y (un′dər sek′rə ter′ē) *n, pl* **un·der·sec·re·tar·ies** an assistant secretary, especially of a government department.

un·der·sell (un′dər sel′) *v* **un·der·sold, un·der·sell·ing** **1** sell things at a lower price than a competitor: *This store can undersell other stores because it sells in bulk.* **2** promote or rate something insufficiently: *She tended to undersell herself.*

un·der·shirt (un′dər shərt′) *n* a collarless, often sleeveless undergarment for the upper body, worn under a shirt.

un·der·shorts (un′dər shôrts′) *pln* short underpants usually worn by men and boys.

un·der·side (un′dər sīd′) *n* the bottom or lower side or surface of something: *The underside of the stone was crawling with ants.*

un·der·signed (un′dər sīnd′) *adj* signed or having signed at the end of a letter or document: *the undersigned witnesses.*
n **the undersigned** (*with singular or plural verb*) the person or persons signing a letter or document: *The undersigned accepts the agreement. We, the undersigned, testify that we have read the document.*

un·der·sized (un′dər sīzd′) *adj* of less than the usual size: *undersized trout.*

un·der·staffed (un′dər staft′) *adj* of an organization, with too few members of staff to operate effectively. **un′der·staff′** *v.*

un·der·stand (un′dər stand′) *v* **un·der·stood, un·der·stand·ing** **1** perceive the intended meaning of words, a language, or speaker: *She didn't understand anything he said.* **2** perceive the significance, explanation, or cause of something: *People listen but often do not understand.* **3** be sympathetically aware of the character or nature of: *A good teacher should understand children.* **4** take something as a fact or as being present on the basis of information received: *I understand that he is leaving town. It is understood that you will come.*
un′der·stand′a·ble *adj.* **un′der·stand′a·bly** *adv.*
understand each other, know one another's meaning and wishes.

un·der·stand·ing (un′dər stan′ding) *n* **1** the ability to understand a thing: *She had a clear understanding of the problem.* **2** the power of abstract thought or intellect: *The doctor was a person of intelligence and understanding.* **3** an individual's perception or judgment of a situation: *My understanding was that she'd join us later.* **4** sympathetic awareness or tolerance: *I believe that true friendship is based on understanding.* **5** an informal or unspoken agreement or arrangement: *You and I must come to an understanding.*
adj sympathetically aware of other people's feelings: *an understanding reply.* **un′der·stand′ing·ly** *adv.*

un·der·stat·ed (un′dər stāt′id) *adj* presented or expressed in a subtle but effective way: *understated elegance.*

un·der·state·ment (un′dər stāt′mənt) *n* the presentation of something as being smaller or less good or important than it really is, sometimes as a way of implying the opposite: *To say we're glad to see you is an understatement, a master of understatement.* **un′der·state′** *v.*

un·der·stood (un′dər stůd′) past tense and past participle of UNDERSTAND.

un·der·stud·y (un′dər stud′ē) *for n,* (un′dər stud′ē) *for v. n, pl* **un·der·stud·ies** a person who is ready and able to substitute for another, especially one who learns another's role in a play in order to be able to act at short notice in her or his absence.
v **un·der·stud·ied, un·der·stud·y·ing** study or prepare as an understudy.

un·der·sur·face (un′dər sər′fəs) *n* the bottom surface of something.

un·der·take (un′dər tāk′) *v* **un·der·took, un·der·tak·en, un·der·tak·ing** **1** commit oneself to and begin an enterprise or responsibility: *She undertook the feeding of my dogs.* **2** promise to do a particular thing: *The store undertook to have the lowest prices in town.*

un·der·tak·er (un′dər tā′kər) *n* a person whose business is preparing the dead for burial and making arrangements for funerals.

un·der·tak·ing (un′dər tā′king) *n* **1** a formal pledge or promise to do something. **2** a task that is taken on: *Building the dam was a huge undertaking.* **3** the action of undertaking to do something.

un·der–the–count·er (un′dər ᴛʜə koun′tər) *adj* illegal or unauthorized: *an under-the-counter transaction.*

un·der·things (un′dər thingz′) UNDERCLOTHES.

un·der·tone (un′dər tōn′) *n* **1** a subdued or muted tone of sound or colour: *to talk in undertones.* **2** an underlying quality or feeling: *There was an undertone of sadness in her face.*

un·der·took (un′dər tůk′) past tense of UNDERTAKE.

un·der·tow (un′dər tō′) *n* **1** a strong current below the water's surface, moving in a direction different from that of the surface current. **2** the backward flow from waves breaking on a beach.

un·der·val·ue (un′dər val′yü) *v* **un·der·val·ued, un·der·val·u·ing** **1** put too low a value on or fail to appreciate: *Don't undervalue the benefits of homework.* **2** underestimate the financial value of a thing.

un·der·wa·ter (un′dər wot′ər) *for adj,* (un′dər wot′ər) *for adv. adj, adv* located, occurring, or done beneath the surface of the water: *underwater plants. She stayed underwater for two minutes.*

un·der·way or **under way** (un′dər wā′) *adj* **1** in progress or already started: *Plans are underway for a new city hall.* **2** travelling or in motion: *They were to leave early today, so I guess they're underway by now. The train got underway at exactly noon.*

un·der·wear (un′dər wer′) *n* clothing worn under outer clothing, typically next to the skin.

un·der·weight (un′dər wāt′) *adj* below a weight considered normal or desirable: *You are a little underweight, but it is nothing to worry about. He claimed that the roast was underweight.*

un·der·went (un′dər went′) past tense of UNDERGO.

a bat	e bed	i bid	o pot	u cup	th thin
ā cake	ē me	ī bite	ō go	ü rude	ᴛʜ then
â bar	ə about	ər over	ô for	ů put	zh measure

un·der·whelm (un′dər welm′) *Informal v* fail to impress or to meet the expectations of: *Frankly, we have been underwhelmed by their performance so far.* <humorous analogy with *overwhelm*>

un·der·world (un′dər wərld′) *n* **1** the part of society in which criminals operate or organized crime functions. **2** the dwelling place of the dead, imagined as being under the earth.

un·der·write (un′dər rīt′) *v* **un·der·wrote, un·der·writ·ten, un·der·writ·ing 1** sign and accept liability under an insurance policy, thus guaranteeing payment in case loss or damage occurs, or accept a liability or risk in this way. **2** undertake to finance or otherwise support or guarantee something: *His uncle underwrote his first year at university.* **3** engage as a bank or other financial institution to buy all the unsold securities in an issue of new securities. **un′der·writ′er** *n.*

un·de·sir·a·ble (un′di zī′rə bəl) *adj* not wanted or desirable because harmful, objectionable, or unpleasant: *That drug was taken off the market because it was found to have undesirable side effects.*
n a person who is not wanted. **un′de·sir′a·bil′i·ty** *n.* **un′de·sir′a·ble′ness** *n.* **un′de·sir′a·bly** *adv.*

un·de·vel·oped (un′di vel′əpt) *adj* not having been developed or not having developed.

un·did (un did′) past tense of UNDO.

un·dies (un′dēz) *Informal pln* underwear, especially that of a woman or girl.

un·dis·guised (un′dis gīzd′) *adj* not disguised or concealed as a feeling: *undisguised contempt.*

un·dis·put·ed (un′di spyūt′id) *adj* not doubted and accepted by all: *undisputed facts.* **un′dis·put′ed·ly** *adv.*

un·di·vid·ed (un′di vī′did) *adj* **1** not divided, separated, or broken into parts: *It's crucial that we remain undivided on this issue.* **2** concentrated on or devoted completely to one object: *Give this your undivided attention.*

un·do (un dū′) *v* **un·did, un·done, un·do·ing 1** unfasten, untie, or loosen a thing: *Please undo the package. I undid the string.* **2** cancel or reverse the effects or results of a previous action or measure: *He raked the leaves, but a heavy wind undid his work.* **3** cause the downfall or ruin of: *The tragic flaws of the hero undid him.*

un·do·ing (un dū′ing) *n* a cause of destruction or ruin: *Drunk driving was his undoing.*

un·done (un dun′) *adj* **1** not tied or fastened: *Your shoelaces are undone.* **2** not done or finished: *I left my homework undone and watched TV.* **3** *Archaic or Humorous* ruined by a disastrous setback or reverse: *Alas, I am undone!*
v past participle of UNDO.

un·doubt·ed (un dou′tid) *adj* not questioned or doubted by anyone. **un·doubt′ed·ly** *adv.*

un·dress (un dres′) *for v,* (un′dres′) *or* (un dres′) *for n.*
v take one's clothes off, or take someone else's clothes off.
n the condition of being naked or only partially clothed.

un·dressed (un′dresd′) not treated, processed, or prepared for use: *undressed stone.*

un·due (un dyū′) *or* (un dū′) *adj* undeserved or inappropriate because excessive or out of proportion: *She thought he made undue use of sarcasm. He gave undue importance to money.* **un·du′ly** *adv.*

un·du·late (un′jə lāt′) *or* (un′dyə lāt′) *v* **un·du·lat·ed, un·du·lat·ing** move or cause to move in a smooth wavelike motion: *The dancer's body undulated across the floor.*
adj with a wavy surface or edge. <Latin *unda* wave> **un′du·la′tion** *n.*

un·dy·ing (un dī′ing) *adj* lasting forever, especially as an emotion: *undying beauty.* **un·dy′ing·ly** *adv.*

un·earned (un ərnd′) *adj* **1** not earned or deserved. **2** resulting as a run in baseball from an error by the fielding side.

unearned income *n* income from investments rather than from work.

un·earth (un ərth′) *v* **1** find something in the ground by digging: *The archaeologists unearthed the buried city.* **2** discover something hidden, lost, or kept secret by investigating or searching: *Eventually they unearthed a plot.*

un·earth·ly (un er′thlē) *adj* **1** unnatural or mysterious, especially in a disturbing way: *an unearthly light.* **2** *Informal* unreasonably early or inconvenient: *Why are you waking me up at this unearthly hour?*
un·earth′li·ness *n.*

un·eas·y (un ē′zē) *adj* **un·eas·i·er, un·eas·i·est** causing or feeling mild anxiety or discomfort: *They were so slow in getting back that we began to feel uneasy.* **un·ease′** *n.* **un·eas′i·ly** *adv.* **un·eas′i·ness** *n.*

un·em·ploy·a·ble (un′em ploi′ə bəl) *adj* not able or likely to get employment because of lack of skill or qualifications.

un·em·ployed (un′em ploid′) *adj* **1** without a paid job but available to work. **2** of a machine, not in use.
n **the unemployed** *pl* people who are out of work: *Some of the unemployed received aid from the government.*

un·em·ploy·ment (un′em ploi′mənt) *n* **1** the condition of being unemployed. **2** the number or percentage of people unemployed at a particular time: *It was a period of high unemployment.*

🍁 **unemployment insurance** *n* the former name for EMPLOYMENT INSURANCE. *Abbrev.* **UI**

un·end·ing (un en′ding) *adj* having, or seeming to have, no end: *your unending chatter.*

un·en·vi·a·ble (un en′vē ə bəl) *adj* difficult, undesirable, or unpleasant: *He was in the unenviable position of having to take the blame and none of the credit.* **un·en′vi·a·bly** *adv.*

un·e·qual (un ē′kwəl) *adj* **1** not equal in quantity, size, or value: *unequal odds.* **2** not fair; not evenly balanced: *an unequal contest.* **3** not with the ability or resources to meet a challenge: *His strength was unequal to the task.* **un·e′qual·ly** *adv.* **un·e′qual·ness** *n.*

un·e·qualled (un ē′kwəld) *adj* superior to all others in performance or extent: *unequalled skill. Her arrogance in these matters is unequalled.*

un·e·quiv·o·cal (un′i kwiv′ə kəl) *adj* leaving no doubt or ambiguity: *an unequivocal rejection.*
un′e·quiv′o·cal·ly *adv.* **un′e·quiv′o·cal·ness** *n.*

UNESCO (yū nes′kō) United Nations Educational, Scientific, and Cultural Organization.

un·e·ven (un ē′vən) *adj* **1** not level or smooth: *uneven ground, an uneven surface.* **2** one-sided or not equally balanced: *an uneven contest. There was an uneven distribution of income.* **3** leaving a remainder of 1 in a number when divided by 2. **un·e′ven·ly** *adv.* **un·e′ven·ness** *n.*

un·e·vent·ful (un′i vent′fəl) *adj* not marked by interesting or exciting events: *an uneventful day.* **un′e·vent′ful·ly** *adv.* **un′e·vent′ful·ness** *n.*

un·ex·am·pled (un′eg zam′pəld) *adj* with no precedent or parallel: *an unexampled disaster.*

un·ex·cep·tion·a·ble (un′ek sep′shə nə bəl) *adj* not open to criticism, but not particularly new or exciting: *an unexceptionable opinion.* **un′ex·cep′tion·a·bly** *adv.*

un·ex·cep·tion·al (un′ek sep′shə nəl) *adj* ordinary or usual. **un′ex·cep′tion·al·ly** *adv.*

CONFUSABLES

Unexceptional simply means "not exceptional" or "ordinary": *The band's new CD is unexceptional.*

Unexceptionable means "not open to criticism" and suggests correctness, if not originality: *The newspaper praised him for his unexceptionable career as a judge for forty years.*

un·fail·ing (un fā′ling) *adj* **1** without error or fault. **2** reliable or constant. **un·fail′ing·ly** *adv.*

un·fair (un fãr′) *adj* **1** not based on or behaving according to justice and fairness: *an unfair decision.* **2** unkind, inconsiderate, or unreasonable: *It is unfair to condemn me for someone else's error.* **3** not following the rules of a game or sport: *unfair play.* **un·fair′ly** *adv.* **un·fair′ness** *n.*

un·faith·ful (un fāth′fəl) *adj* not faithful, especially to one's duty or promises. **un·faith′ful·ly** *adv.* **un·faith′ful·ness** *n.*

un·fal·ter·ing (un fol′tə ring) *adj* unhesitating and steadfast: *unfaltering support.*

un·fa·mil·iar (un′fə mil′yər) *adj* **1** not known or recognized: *That face is unfamiliar to me.* **2** unusual or uncharacteristic: *an unfamiliar sight.* **3** without knowledge or experience of: *I'm unfamiliar with that language.* **un′fa·mil·i·ar′i·ty** *n.*

un·fas·ten (un fas′ən) *v* open or undo the fastening of: *She unfastened the lock on her bike.*

un·fath·om·a·ble (un faᴛʜ′ə mə bəl) *adj* **1** unable to be fully explored or understood: *an unfathomable explanation.* **2** impossible to measure the extent of water or a natural feature: *unfathomable depths.*

un·fa·vour·a·ble or **un·fa·vor·a·ble** (un fā′və rə bəl) *adj* **1** expressing or showing a lack of approval or support: *Most of the reviews were unfavourable.* **2** adverse or unpromising: *unfavourable circumstances.* **un·fa′vour·a·ble·ness** or **un·fa′vor·a·ble·ness** *n.* **un·fa′vour·a·bly** or **un·fa′vor·a·bly** *adv.*

un·feel·ing (un fē′ling) *adj* **1** unsympathetic, harsh, or callous: *an unfeeling person.* **2** lacking physical sensation or sensitivity: *unfeeling hands.* **un·feel′ing·ly** *adv.* **un·feel′ing·ness** *n.*

un·fin·ished (un fin′isht) *adj* **1** not finished, complete, or concluded: *unfinished homework.* **2** without having been given an attractive surface appearance as the final stage of manufacture: *unfinished furniture.*

un·fit (un fit′) *adj* **1** not of the necessary quality or standard to meet a particular purpose: *The food was unfit for consumption.* **2** not with the qualities or skills needed to undertake something competently: *He was unfit to teach foreign languages.* **3** not in good physical condition, especially as a result of failing to take regular exercise. **un·fit′ness** *n.*

un·flag·ging (un flag′ing) *adj* tireless or persistent: *unflagging efforts.* **un·flag′ging·ly** *adv.*

un·flap·pa·ble (un flap′ə bəl) *adj* with or showing calmness in a crisis. **un′flap·pa·bil′i·ty** *n.* **un·flap′pa·bly** *adv.*

un·flinch·ing (un flin′ching) *adj* not showing fear or hesitation in the face of danger or difficulty: *unflinching courage.* **un·flinch′ing·ly** *adv.*

un·fold (un fōld′) *v* **1** open or spread out from: *unfold a newspaper, unfold your arms.* **2** reveal or disclose thoughts, information, or a sequence of events: *The story unfolded.*

un·fore·seen (un′fȯr sēn′) *adj* not anticipated or predicted: *They had to change their plans because of an unforeseen crisis.*

un·for·get·ta·ble (un′fər get′ə bəl) *adj* impossible to forget: *an unforgettable scene.* **un′for·get′ta·bly** *adv.*

un·formed (un fȯrmd′) *adj* **1** without a definite form or shape: *a formless mass.* **2** not having developed or been developed: *an unformed plot.*

un·for·tu·nate (un fȯr′chə nit) *adj* **1** with or marked by lack of luck. **2** unsuitable or inappropriate: *Her outburst of temper was an unfortunate thing for the guest to see.* *n* an unfortunate person. **un·for′tu·nate·ly** *adv.* **un·for′tu·nate·ness** *n.*

un·found·ed (un foun′did) *adj* with no foundation or basis in fact: *an unfounded complaint.*

un·friend·ly (un fren′dlē) *adj* **1** not friendly: *an unfriendly dog.* **2** not favourable: *unfriendly weather.* **un·friend′li·ness** *n.*

un·fruit·ful (un frūt′fəl) *adj* **1** not producing good or helpful results: *an unfruitful meeting.* **2** not producing fruit or crops.

un·furl (un fərl′) *v* make or become spread out from a rolled or folded condition, especially in order to be open to the wind: *The flag unfurled.*

un·fur·nished (un fər′nisht) *adj* without furniture in a house or apartment, especially available to be rented without furniture: *an unfurnished flat.*

a bat	e bed	i bid	o pot	u cup	th **thin**
ā cake	ē me	ī bite	ō go	ū rude	ᴛʜ **then**
ȧ bar	ə about	ər over	ȯ for	u̇ put	zh measure

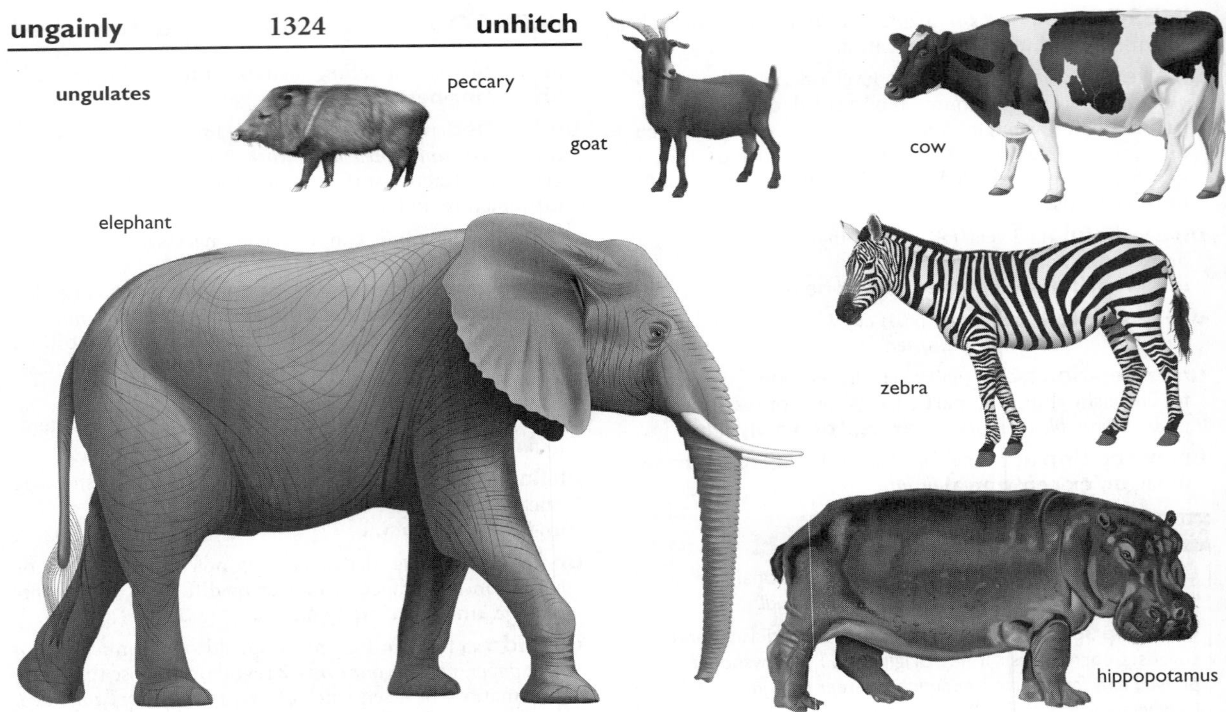

un·gain·ly (un gān′lē) *adj* awkward or clumsy as a person or a movement: *His long arms and large hands give him an ungainly appearance.* <Middle English *un-* not + *gaynly* agile> **un·gain′li·ness** *n.*

un·glued (un glūd′) *adj* **1** not or no longer stuck together, especially by glue. **2** *Informal* become confused and emotionally strained: *The strain of his wife's illness made him become unglued.*

un·god·ly (un god′lē) *adj* **1** not religious or moral. **2** *Informal* unreasonably early, inconvenient, or otherwise displeasing: *an ungodly noise.* **un·god′li·ness** *n.*

un·gov·ern·a·ble (un guv′ər nə bəl) *adj* impossible to control or govern. **un·gov′ern·a·bil′i·ty** *n.* **un·gov′ern·a·bly** *adv.*

un·gra·cious (un grā′shəs) *adj* **1** not polite or friendly: *an ungracious welcome.* **2** not gracious or elegant. **un·gra′cious·ly** *adv.* **un·gra′cious·ness** *n.*

un·grate·ful (un grāt′fəl) *adj* not feeling or showing gratitude. **un·grate′ful·ly** *adv.* **un·grate′ful·ness** *n.*

un·grudg·ing (un gruj′ing) *adj* fully willing and not grudging: *ungrudging acceptance.* **un·grudg′ing·ly** *adv.*

un·guard·ed (un går′did) *adj* **1** without protection or a guard: *an unguarded camp.* **2** not well considered: *In an unguarded moment, she gave away the secret.* **un·guard′ed·ly** *adv.* **un·guard′ed·ness** *n.*

un·gu·late (ung′gyə lit) *or* (ung′gyə lāt′) *n* an animal that has hoofs.
adj belonging to the group of animals with hoofs. <Latin *unguis* hoof>

un·hand (un hand′) *Archaic v* release someone from a grasp: *Unhand me, you villain!*

un·hand·y (un han′dē) *adj* **1** not easy to handle or manage. **2** not skilful in using the hands. **un·hand′i·ly** *adv.* **un·hand′i·ness** *n.*

un·hap·py (un hap′ē) *adj* **un·hap·pi·er, un·hap·pi·est** **1** not happy: *an unhappy marriage.* **2** not satisfied or pleased with a situation: *We were unhappy to find that the concert was sold out.* **3** unfortunate: *an unhappy coincidence.* **un·hap′pi·ly** *adv.* **un·hap′pi·ness** *n.*

un·health·y (un hel′thē) *adj* **1** not with, showing, or resulting from good health: *unhealthy skin.* **2** harmful to health: *an unhealthy climate.* **3** not sensible or well balanced as behaviour or an attitude: *an unhealthy obsession.*

un·heard (un hərd′) *adj* **1** not heard or listened to: *unheard melodies.* **2** (*with* ***of***) not previously known or done: *He said that such a thing was unheard of in that neighbourhood.*

un·heed·ed (un hē′did) *adj* heard or noticed but disregarded: *Her advice went unheeded.*

un·hes·i·tat·ing (un hez′ə tā′ting) *adj* without doubt or hesitation: *His unhesitating acceptance of responsibility for the accident surprised us.* **un·hes′i·tat′ing·ly** *adv.*

un·hinge (un hinj′) *v* **un·hinged, un·hing·ing** **1** make someone mentally unbalanced: *unhinged by grief.* **2** take a door off its hinges. **3** throw into disorder.

un·hitch (un hich′) *v* unhook or unfasten something tethered to or caught on something else: *Unhitch the team.*

un·ho·ly (un hō′lē) *adj* **un·ho·li·er, un·ho·li·est 1** sinful or wicked. **2** *Informal* outrageous or dreadful: *They were raising an unholy row.* **un·ho′li·ness** *n.*

un·hook (un hůk′) *v* unfasten or detach something that is held or caught by a hook.

un·hoped (un hōpt′) *adj* (*with* ***for***) beyond what is hoped for or expected: *The benefit was unhoped for, an unhoped-for chance to win the game.*

un·horse (un hòrs′) *v* **un·horsed, un·hors·ing** drag or cause to fall from a horse: *The knight was unhorsed by the thrust of a lance.*

un·hurt (un hərt′) *adj* not hurt or harmed.

un·hy·gien·ic (un′hī jē′nik) *or* (un′hī jen′ik) *adj* not clean or sanitary. **un′hy·gien′i·cal·ly** *adv.*

uni– *combining form* one: *unilateral.* <Latin>

UNICEF (yů′ni sef′) United Nations Children's Fund (originally, United Nations International Children's Emergency Fund).

u·ni·cel·lu·lar (yů′nə sel′yə lər) *adj* consisting of a single cell, such as in protozoans, certain algae, and spores.

u·ni·corn (yů′nə kòrn′) *n* a legendary animal typically depicted as a horse with a single straight horn projecting from its forehead. <Latin *unus* one + *cornu* horn>

u·ni·cy·cle (yů′nə sī′kəl) *n* a cycle with a single wheel, typically used by acrobats.

un·i·den·ti·fied flying object (un′ī den′tə fīd′) UFO.

u·ni·di·rec·tion·al (yů′ni di rek′shə nəl) *adj* operating or moving in only one direction.

u·ni·form (yů′nə fòrm′) *adj* **1** not changing or not changing much in form or character: *The tiles were of uniform size.* **2** forming parts of a person's uniform: *red uniform jackets.*
n the distinctive clothing worn by members of the same organization, group, or by children attending certain schools: *The police in that country wore drab uniforms.*
v **1** make uniform. **2** provide with a uniform. <Latin *unus* one + *forma* form> **un′i·form′i·ty** *n.* **un′i·form′ly** *adv.*

u·ni·fy (yů′nə fī′) *v* **u·ni·fied, u·ni·fy·ing** make or become united, uniform, or whole: *They took steps to unify the opposition.* <Latin *unus* one + *facere* make> **u′ni·fi·ca′tion** (yů′nə fə kā′shən) *n.* **u′ni·fi′er** *n.*

u·ni·lat·er·al (yů′nə lat′ə rəl) *adj* performed by or affecting only one person, group, or country involved in a particular situation, without the agreement of another or the others: *unilateral disarmament.* **un′i·lat′er·al·ism** *n.* **un′i·lat′er·al·ist** *n.* **un′i·lat′er·al·ly** *adv.*

u·ni·lin·gual (yů′ni ling′gwəl) *adj* using only one language: *a unilingual document. The candidates' debate was unilingual.* **un′i·lin′gual·ism** *n.* **un′i·lin′gual·ly** *adv.*

un·i·mag·i·na·ble (un′i maj′ə nə bəl) *adj* difficult or impossible to imagine or comprehend: *Life without you is unimaginable.* **un′i·mag′in·a·bly** *adv.*

un·i·mag·i·na·tive (un′i maj′ə nə tiv) *adj* showing little or no imagination: *an unimaginative drawing.*

un·im·peach·a·ble (un′im pē′chə bəl) *adj* not able to be doubted, questioned, or criticized. **un′im·peach′a·bly** *adv.*

un·im·por·tant (un′im pòr′tənt) *adj* lacking in importance or significance. **un′im·por′tance** *adj.*

un·in·hab·it·ed (un′in hab′ə tid) *adj* without inhabitants: *an uninhabited wilderness.*

un·in·hib·it·ed (un′in hib′i tid) *adj* expressing one's feelings or thoughts unselfconsciously and without restraint: *uninhibited laughter.*

un·in·i·ti·at·ed (un′i nish′ē ā′tid) *adj* **1** without special knowledge or experience. **2** not yet having gone through the ceremony of initiation into a group.
n **the uninitiated** people without special knowledge or experience.

un·in·spired (un in spīrd′) *adj* **1** lacking in imagination or originality: *an uninspired speech.* **2** not filled with excitement as a person: *He was uninspired by the speech.*

un·in·tel·li·gi·ble (un′in tel′i jə bəl) *adj* impossible to understand: *She uttered a few unintelligible syllables and left.* **un′in·tel′lig·i·bil′i·ty** *n.* **un′in·tel′lig·i·bly** *adv.*

un·in·ten·tion·al (un′in ten′shə nəl) *adj* not done on purpose: *Any offence was completely unintentional.*

un·in·ter·est·ed (un in′tri stəd) *or* (un in′tə res′tid) *adj* not interested in or concerned about something or someone.

CONFUSABLES

Uninterested means "having no interest in or feelings about someone or something": *I'm uninterested in going to the movie because I saw it when it first came out.*

Disinterested means "having no selfish interest" or "impartial": *In her role as moderator of the discussion, she had a disinterested position on the views of the panellists.*

un·ion (yů′nyən) *n* **1** the action or fact of joining together or being joined together, especially in political circumstances: *The country was formed by the union of several former colonies.* **2** a group of workers joined together to protect and promote their rights and interests. **3** a political unit consisting of a number of states or provinces with the same central government. **4** a condition of harmony or agreement: *They dwell in perfect union.* **5** a marriage. <Latin = one>

SYNONYMS

Union emphasizes the joining together of things to form a whole, or the state of being joined together: *The union of the two companies gave the employees a lot to discuss.*

Unity emphasizes the condition of being united, especially into a harmonious whole: *Their kind behaviour to each other showed the group's unity.*

U

a bat	e bed	i bid	o pot	u cup	th thin
ā cake	ē me	ī bite	ō go	ū rude	TH then
à bar	ə about	ər over	ò for	ů put	zh measure

un·ion·ist (yü′nyə nist) *n* **1** a member or supporter of a labour union. **2 Unionist a** a person who favoured union among the provinces of British North America, especially of Upper and Lower Canada. **b** a supporter of the federal government of the US during the Civil War. **un′ion·ism** *n.*

un·ion·ize (yü′nyə nīz′) *v* **un·ion·ized, un·ion·iz·ing** become or cause to become members of a UNION (def. 2). **un′ion·i·za′tion** *n.*

Union Jack *n* the national flag of the UK, consisting of red and white crosses on a blue background, formed by combining the crosses of St. George, St. Andrew, and St. Patrick.

🍁 **Union Na·tion·ale** (nash′ə nal′) *n* in former times, a political and sometimes governing party in Québec, founded in the early 1930s.

u·nique (yü nēk′) *adj* **1** being the only one of its kind: *a unique situation, a unique design.* **2** belonging to or connected to one particular person, group, or place: *The dish was unique to that region.* **3** particularly remarkable, special, or unusual: *His style of singing is rather unique.* <French, from Latin *unus* one> **u·nique′ly** *adv.* **u·nique′ness** *n.*

GRAMMAR AND USAGE

In formal English, **unique** means "being one of a kind." Therefore, something is either unique or it isn't: *It's a rare occurrence but not a unique one.*

In informal English, the word is often qualified with adverbs such as *more, most, really,* and *quite,* as well as being accepted as a synonym for "unusual" or "outstanding": *Those are the most unique earrings I've ever seen.*

u·ni·sex (yü′ni seks′) *adj* designed to be suitable to both sexes, especially as clothing or hairstyles.

u·ni·son (yü′nə sən) *n* **1** the act or fact of doing or saying something at the same time: *The feet of marching soldiers move in unison.* **2** a simultaneous pitch of sounds or notes, or a combination of notes, voices, or instruments at the same pitch or an octave apart. <Latin *unus* one + *sonus* sound>

u·nit (yü′nit) *n* **1** an individual thing or person regarded as single and complete. **2** a device that has a specified function, especially one forming part of a complex mechanism: *a power-generating unit.* **3** a self-contained part of a course of study. **4** a single manufactured item. **5** a quantity chosen as a standard in terms of which other quantities may be expressed: *a metric unit.* **6 a** a piece of furniture or equipment for fitting with others like it: *a kitchen unit.* **b** a self-contained section in a building: *a two-bedroom unit.* **c** a part of an institution such as a hospital with a special function: *the intensive-care unit.* **7** a subdivision of a larger military or police grouping: *My father and my uncle served in the same unit.* <*unity*>

u·ni·tar·y (yü′nə ter′ē) *adj* **1** to do with unity. **2** to do with a unit or units.

u·nite (yü nīt′) *v* **u·nit·ed, un·it·ing 1** come or bring together for a common purpose or action: *Bricks united by mortar made a strong wall.* **2** come or bring together to form a unit or whole: *Several firms united to form one company.* **3** join in marriage. <Latin *unire* unite, from *unus* one> **u·nit′ed** *adj.* **u·nit′er** *n.*

United Arab Emirates *n* a country which is a federation of seven emirates on the Persian Gulf and on the Gulf of Oman. *Abbrev.* **UAE**. See the APPENDIX.

🍁 **United Empire Loyalist** *n* one of the people who came to Canada from southern colonies during and after the American Revolution of 1776 because they preferred to remain British subjects.

United Kingdom *n* a country off the west coast of Europe. It includes GREAT BRITAIN and Northern Ireland. *Abbrev.* **UK** See the APPENDIX. **Brit′ish** *adj.*

United Nations *n* an international organization of countries set up in 1945 to promote international peace, security, and co-operation. *Abbrev.* **UN**

United States *n* in full, **United States of America** a country in southern N America. *Abbrev.* **US, USA**. See the APPENDIX. **A·mer′i·can** *adj.*

unit pricing *n* a system of pricing goods based on a standard unit of measure, such as a millilitre or gram, regardless of the size of the container or total amount in the package. Unit pricing allows the consumer to compare the cost of different brands, formats, etc. more easily.

u·ni·ty (yü′nə tē) *n, pl* **u·ni·ties 1** the condition of being united or joined as a complex whole, or of harmony or agreement between groups: *The leaders called for a unity of opposing interests.* **2** the condition of forming a complete and pleasing whole, especially in a work of art: *The clever refrain gave the song wonderful unity.* **3** the number one (1). **4 the unities** *pl* in ancient Greek drama, the rules of action, time, and place that required a play to have one plot occurring on one day in one place. <Latin *unus* one>

u·ni·valve (yü′nə valv′) *adj* with one valve or shell as an animal. See BIVALVE for picture.
n a gastropod.

u·ni·ver·sal (yü′nə vər′səl) *adj* **1** to do with all people or things in the world or in a particular group: *Food, fire, and shelter are universal needs.* **2** adjustable to or appropriate as a tool or machine for all requirements, and not restricted to a single purpose or position: *a universal joint.* **u·ni·ver·sal′i·ty** *n.* **u·ni·ver′sal·ly** *adv.*

universal joint *n* a coupling or joint that can transmit power from one shaft to another when the shafts are not in line.

Universal Product Code *n* a BAR CODE for merchandise. *Abbrev.* **UPC**

Universal Time Greenwich Mean Time.

u·ni·verse (yü′nə vərs′) *n* **1** all existing matter and space considered as a whole, including the world and everything outside it. **2** a particular sphere of activity, interest, or experience: *His home was the centre of his universe.* <French, from Latin *universum* the whole world>

u·ni·ver·si·ty (yü′nə vər′sə tē) *n, pl* **u·ni·ver·si·ties** an educational institution attended after secondary school in which students study for degrees and academic research is done. <See UNIVERSE.>

un·just (un just′) *adj* not based on or behaving according to what is morally correct and fair. **un·just′ly** *adv.* **un·just′ness** *n.*

un·kempt (un kempt′) *adj* with a neglected and untidy appearance, especially in a person. <*un-*[1] not + Old English *cemban* to comb>

un·kind (un kīnd′) *adj* inconsiderate and harsh to others. **un·kind′ly** *adv.* **un·kind′ness** *n.*

un·known (un nōn′) *adj* not known or familiar: *an unknown country, an unknown number.*
n a person who or thing that is unknown: *The main actor in this movie is an unknown.*

Unknown Soldier *n* an unidentified soldier killed in battle who is buried in a national monument and honoured as the representative of a country's unidentified war dead.

un·latch (un lach′) *v* unfasten the latch of a door or gate.

un·law·ful (un lof′əl) *adj* contrary to, not permitted by, or not recognized by law or rules: *unlawful entry.* **un·law′ful·ly** *adv.* **un·law′ful·ness** *n.*

un·lead·ed (un led′id) *adj* containing no lead or lead compounds, especially in gasoline and other petroleum products.
n fuel containing no lead.

un·learn (un lərn′) *v* discard something learned, especially a bad habit or false or outdated information, from one's memory.

un·leash (un lēsh′) *v* release from a leash, or from some other form of restraint: *to unleash a dog, to unleash your temper.*

un·leav·ened (un lev′ənd) *adj* made without yeast or any other rising agent such as baking powder.

un·less (un les′) *conj* except under the conditions or circumstances that: *We shall go unless it rains.* <Middle English *on lesse* (*that*) on a less condition (than)>

un·let·tered (un let′ərd) *adj* poorly educated, or unable to read or write.

un·like (un līk′) *adj* dissimilar or different from: *The two problems are quite unlike.*
prep different from: *They acted unlike the others.* **un·like′ness** *n.*

GRAMMAR AND USAGE

Be careful when making a comparison using **unlike**. The subject of the sentence must be the person or thing that is unlike something else.

In the sentence *Unlike the gorillas, the hot weather did not seem to harm the snakes*, it sounds as if the gorillas are being compared to the weather.

This problem can be easily resolved by rewriting the sentence with the snakes as the subject, placed right next to the *unlike* phrase: *Unlike the gorillas, the snakes did not seem bothered by the hot weather.*

un·like·ly (un lī′klē) *adj* not likely to happen, be done, or be true: *She is unlikely to win the race. It was an unlikely undertaking.* **un·like′li·hood** *n.* **un·like′li·ness** *n.*

un·lim·it·ed (un lim′ə tid) *adj* without limits or restrictions: *The girl seems to have unlimited energy, a government of unlimited power.* **un·lim′it·ed·ness** *n.*

un·list·ed (un lis′tid) *adj* not included in a list, directory, or reference book, especially in a telephone directory: *an unlisted phone number.*

un·load (un lōd′) *v* **1** remove goods or have goods removed from a vehicle, aircraft, ship, or container: *We unloaded as soon as we got home. Please help us unload the car.* **2** get rid of something unwanted: *She began to unload her troubles onto her mother.* **3** remove ammunition from a gun or film from a camera. **un·load′er** *n.*

un·lock (un lok′) *v* **1** undo the lock of something using a key. **2** make something previously inaccessible or unexploited available for use: *Scientists attempted to unlock the secrets of the universe.*

un·looked (un lu̇kt′) *adj* (*with* ***for***) unexpected or unforeseen: *The excellent weather had been unlooked for, an unlooked-for opportunity.*

un·love·ly (un luv′lē) *adj* not attractive. **un·love′li·ness** *n.*

un·luck·y (un luk′ē) *adj* with, bringing, or resulting from bad luck. **un·luck′i·ly** *adv.* **un·luck′i·ness** *n.*

un·make (un māk′) *v* **un·made, un·mak·ing** reverse or undo the making of: *The legislature voted to unmake the law it had just passed.*

un·man (un man′) *Poetic v* **un·manned, un·man·ning** deprive of the qualities traditionally associated with a man, such as self-control or courage.

un·manned (un mand′) *adj* not operated, occupied, or needing a crew or staff: *an unmanned spacecraft.*

GRAMMAR AND USAGE

Since the root word *man* is often used as a generic term applying to both women and men, some people consider **unmanned** to be sexist. Acceptable synonyms are *uncrewed, not crewed, remote controlled,* and *robotically controlled*: *The remote controlled spy plane flew over enemy territory.*

un·man·ner·ly (un man′ər lē) *adj, adv* with bad manners. **un·man′ner·li·ness** *n.*

un·markt′ (un markt′) *adj* **1** not marked: *an unmarked police car.* **2** not noticed: *He left the room, unmarked by anyone.*

un·mar·ried (un mar′ēd) *or* (un mer′ēd) *adj* not married.

un·mask (un mask′) *v* **1** remove a mask or disguise: *The guests at the costume ball unmasked at midnight.* **2** expose the true character or hidden truth about: *The book unmasked his deceitful conduct.*

un·matched (un macht′) *adj* not matched or equalled: an unmatched record.

a bat	e bed	i bid	o pot	u cup	th thin
ā cake	ē me	ī bite	ō go	ū rude	ᴛʜ then
ȧ bar	ə about	ər over	ȯ for	u̇ put	zh measure

U

un·mean·ing (un mē′ning) *adj* without meaning or significance. **un·mean′ing·ly** *adv.*

un·meant (un ment′) *adj* not intentional; not on purpose.

un·men·tion·a·ble (un men′shə nə bəl) *adj* too embarrassing, offensive, or shocking to be spoken about: *an unmentionable subject.*
n **unmentionables** *pl* underwear, sometimes considered too embarrassing to name: *I was washing my unmentionables.*

un·mer·ci·ful (un mər′si fəl) *adj* **1** cruel or harsh and showing no mercy. **2** *Informal* excessive: *We had to line up for an unmerciful length of time.* **un·mer′ci·ful·ly** *adv.* **un·mer′ci·ful·ness** *n.*

un·mind·ful (un mīnd′fəl) *adj* not conscious or aware: *She went ahead despite my warning, unmindful of the possible results.* **un·mind′ful·ly** *adv.*

un·mis·tak·a·ble (un′mi stā′kə bəl) *adj* so clear, plain, or obvious that it cannot be mistaken or misunderstood. **un′mis·tak′a·bly** *adv.*

un·mit·i·gat·ed (un mit′ə gā′tid) *adj* unqualified or absolute: *an unmitigated fraud.*

un·mo·lest·ed (un′mə les′tid) *adj* not pestered, molested, or harassed: *They worshipped unmolested.*

un·moved (un müvd′) *adj* **1** not changed in position. **2** not affected by emotion or excitement: *He was unmoved by the scenes of horror.*

un·muz·zle (un muz′əl) *v* **un·muz·zled, un·muz·zling** allow a person or the media to express views freely and without censorship.

un·named (un nāmd′) *adj* not identified or specified.

un·nat·u·ral (un nach′ə rəl) *adj* **1** abnormal and contrary to the ordinary course of nature. **2** affected or stilted: *an unnatural laugh.* **un·nat′u·ral·ly** *adv.* **un·nat′u·ral·ness** *n.*

un·nec·es·sar·y (un nes′i ser′ē) *adj* **1** not needed. **2** more than is needed: *unnecessary waste.* **un′ne·ces·sar′i·ly** *adv.*

un·nerve (un nərv′) *v* **un·nerved, un·nerv·ing** make someone lose courage or confidence: *The sight of so much blood unnerved him.* **un·nerv′ing** *adj.* **un·nerv′ing·ly** *adv.*

un·no·ticed (un nō′tist) *adj* not noticed.

un·num·bered (un num′bərd) *adj* **1** not marked with or assigned a number: *The pages of this composition have been left unnumbered.* **2** with too many to count: *unnumbered fish in the ocean.*

un·ob·served (un′əb zərvd′) *adj* not noticed: *He entered the room unobserved.*

un·ob·tru·sive (un′əb trū′siv) *adj* not conspicuous or attracting attention.

un·oc·cu·pied (un ok′yə pīd′) *adj* not occupied: *The driver pulled into the one unoccupied parking space.*

un·of·fi·cial (un′ə fish′əl) *adj* not officially authorized or confirmed: *He says he quit the team, but the unofficial story is that he was let go.* **un′of·fi′cial·ly** *adv.*

un·pack (un pak′) *v* **1** open and remove the contents of a suitcase, bag, or package, or remove something from such an item. **2** *Computers* convert data from a compressed form to a usable form.

un·pal·at·a·ble (un pal′ə tə bəl) *adj* **1** not pleasant to taste: *unpalatable food.* **2** difficult to put up with or accept: *unpalatable remarks.* **un·pal′at·a·ble·ness** *n.* **un·pal′at·a·bly** *adv.*

un·par·al·leled (un par′ə leld′) *or* (un per′ə leld′) *adj* with no parallel or equal: *unparalleled achievement.*

un·pleas·ant (un plez′ənt) *adj* **1** causing discomfort, unhappiness, or disgust. **2** unfriendly and inconsiderate in manner: *an unpleasant sneer.* **un·pleas′ant·ly** *adv.* **un·pleas′ant·ness** *n.*

un·plug (un plug′) *v* **un·plugged un·plug·ging** **1** disconnect an electrical device by removing its plug from a socket: *Unplug the kettle.* **2** remove an obstacle or blockage from: *The plumber has unplugged the drain.* **3** take a plug or stopper out of.

un·plugged (un plugd′) *adj* **1** performed or recorded with acoustic rather than electrically amplified instruments. **2** not plugged into an electrical socket.

un·plumbed (un plumd′) *adj* **1** not fully explored or understood: *unplumbed depths.* **2** with no plumbing.

un·pop·u·lar *adj* not liked or popular. **un·pop′u·lar′i·ty** *n.* **un·pop′u·lar′ly** *adv.*

un·prec·e·dent·ed (un pres′ə den′tid) *or* (un prē′sə den′tid) *adj* never done or known before: *an unprecedented event.*

un·prej·u·diced (un prej′ə dist) *adj* not with or showing a dislike or distrust based on fixed or preconceived ideas.

un·pre·pared (un′pri perd′) *adj* **1** not ready or able to deal with something: *They were unprepared for the emergency.* **2** not willing to do something: *He was unprepared to answer her question.* **3** not made ready for use: *an unprepared surface.* **un′pre·pared′ness** *n.*

un·pre·pos·sess·ing (un′prē pə zes′ing) *adj* not attractive or appealing in appearance.

un·pre·ten·tious (un′pri ten′shəs) *adj* not attempting to impress others with an appearance of greater importance or significance than is actually possessed. **un′pre·ten′tious·ly** *adv.* **un′pre·ten′tious·ness** *n.*

un·prin·ci·pled (un prin′sə pəld) *adj* lacking good moral principles.

un·print·a·ble (un prin′tə bəl) *adj* too offensive or shocking to be published.

un·pro·fes·sion·al (un′prə fesh′ə nəl) *adj* below or contrary to the standards expected in a particular profession. **un′pro·fes′sion·al·ism** *n.* **un′pro·fes′sion·al·ly** *adv.*

un·prof·it·a·ble (un prof′i tə bəl) *adj* not producing profit, financial gain, or some other benefit: *unprofitable investments. She thought it was an unprofitable use of our time.* **un·pro′fit·a·bil′i·ty** *n.* **un·pro′fit·a·bly** *adv.*

un·pro·nounce·a·ble (un′prə noun′sə bəl) *adj* too difficult to pronounce as a word or name.

un·pro·voked (un′prə vokt′) *adj* not caused by something said or done: *an unprovoked attack.*

un·qual·i·fied (un kwol′ə fīd′) *adj* **1** not officially recognized as a person who carries on a particular profession or activity by having satisfied the conditions or requirements. **2** without any reservations or limitations: *unqualified praise, an unqualified failure.*

un·quench·a·ble (un kwench′ə bəl) *adj* not able to be quenched: *unquenchable thirst.*

un·ques·tion·a·ble (un kwes′chə nə bəl) *adj* not able to be disputed or doubted: *an unquestionable advantage.* **un·ques′tion·a·bly** *adv.*

un·qui·et (un kwī′it) *adj* not inclined or tending to be quiet or inactive: *unquiet sleep.* **un·qui′et·ly** *adv.* **un·qui′et·ness** *n.*

un·quote (un kwōt′) *v* See QUOTE.

un·rav·el (un rav′əl) *v* **un·rav·elled** or **un·rav·eled, un·rav·el·ling** or **un·rav·el·ing** 1 undo twisted, knitted, or woven threads, or become undone: *The kitten unravelled my knitting. My knitted gloves are unravelling at the wrist.* 2 investigate and solve or explain something complicated or puzzling: *unravel a mystery.*

un·read (un red′) *adj* not read: *an unread book.*

un·read·y (un red′ē) *adj* not prepared for a situation or activity. **un·read′i·ly** *adv.* **un·read′i·ness** *n.*

un·re·al (un rē′əl) *adj* 1 so strange as to appear imaginary: *In the misty light, the trees in the valley seemed unreal.* 2 unrealistic: *unreal expectations.* 3 *Informal* amazing: *You won again. Unreal!* **un·re·al′i·ty** *n.* **un·re′al·ly** *adv.*

un·rea·son·a·ble (un rē′zə nə bəl) *adj* 1 not guided by or based on good sense: *He had an unreasonable fear of the dark.* 2 beyond acceptable or fair limits: *I think $200 is an unreasonable price for these shoes.* **un·rea′son·a·ble·ness** *n.* **un·rea′son·a·bly** *adv.*

un·rea·son·ing (un rē′zə ning) *adj* not guided by or based on good sense. **un·rea′son·ing·ly** *adv.*

un·re·lent·ing (un′ri len′ting) *adj* 1 not yielding in strength, severity, or determination. 2 not giving way to kindness or compassion. **un′re·lent′ing·ly** *adv.* **un′re·lent′ing·ness** *n.*

un·re·li·a·ble (un′ri lī′ə bəl) *adj* not able to be relied upon. **un′re·li′a·bil·i·ty** *n.* **un′re·li′a·bly** *adv.*

un·re·mit·ting (un′ri mit′ing) *adj* never relaxing or slackening: *unremitting vigilance.* **un′re·mit′ting·ly** *adv.*

un·re·quit·ed (un′ri kwī′tid) *adj* not returned or rewarded as a feeling, especially love.

un·re·served (un′ri zərvd′) *adj* 1 complete or without reservations: *unreserved admiration.* 2 not booked or set apart for a particular purpose. **un′re·serv′ed·ly** *adv.*

un·rest (un rest′) *n* 1 a condition of dissatisfaction, disturbance, and agitation in a group of people, typically involving public demonstrations or disorder: *political unrest.* 2 a feeling of disturbance and dissatisfaction in a person.

un·re·strained (un′ri strānd′) *adj* not restrained or restricted: *unrestrained laughter.*

un·right·eous (un rī′chəs) *adj* wicked or sinful. **un·right′eous·ly** *adv.* **un·right′eous·ness** *n.*

un·ri·valled or **un·ri·valed** (un rī′vəld) *adj* better than everyone or everything of the same type: *The station had unrivalled news coverage.*

un·roll (un rōl′) *v* 1 open or cause to open out from something rolled. 2 reveal or display, or become revealed or displayed: *She soon unrolled the story of the burglary. As the story unrolled, everyone became interested.*

un·ruf·fled (un ruf′əld) *adj* 1 not disordered or disarranged: *On that calm day the lake was unruffled.* 2 not agitated or disturbed as a person: *The criticism left him unruffled.*

un·ruled (un ru̇ld′) *adj* of paper, not marked with lines on paper.

un·ru·ly (un ru̇′lē) *adj* 1 disorderly and disruptive, without being affected by discipline or control: *unruly behaviour.* 2 difficult to keep neat and tidy as hair: *unruly curls.* **un·ru′li·ness** *n.*

SYNONYMS

Unruly emphasizes getting out of control: *The crowd ignored the police and became unruly.*

Undisciplined means "disobedient" or "wilful": *The undisciplined students made a lot of noise.*

Ungovernable means "impossible to control": *After decades of civil war, the country has become almost ungovernable.*

un·sad·dle (un sad′əl) *v* **un·sad·dled, un·sad·dling** 1 remove the saddle from a horse. 2 cause to fall from a saddle.

un·said (un sed′) *adj* not said or spoken: *Some things are best left unsaid.*
v past tense of UNSAY.

un·sat·u·rat·ed (un sach′ə rā′tid) *adj* 1 able to absorb or dissolve more. 2 able to absorb more hydrogen atoms. **Unsaturated fat** (found in plants, some fish, some fruits, and some vegetable oils) may help to lower cholesterol levels in the blood.

un·sa·vour·y or **un·sa·vor·y** (un sā′və rē) *adj* 1 unpleasant to taste, smell, or look at. 2 disagreeable and unpleasant because morally objectionable: *an unsavoury reputation.* **un·sa′vour·i·ness** or **un·sa′vor·i·ness** *n.*

un·say (un sā′) *v* **un·said, un·say·ing** withdraw or retract a statement: *She commented that what is said cannot be unsaid.*

un·scathed (un skāᴛʜd′) *adj* without suffering any injury, damage, or harm: *She came through the accident unscathed.*

ETYMOLOGY

Unscathed comes from Old English *sceatha*, meaning "injury."

The word *scathing*, meaning "very critical," has the same source.

un·schooled (un sku̇ld′) *adj* not educated or made to attend school.

U

a bat	e bed	i bid	o pot	u cup	th thin
ā cake	ē me	ī bite	ō go	ū rude	ᴛʜ then
à bar	ə about	ər over	ȯ for	u̇ put	zh measure

un·sci·en·tif·ic (un′sī ən tif′ik) *adj* 1 not in accordance with the facts, principles, or methods of science: *an unscientific notion.* 2 lacking knowledge of or interest in science. **un′sci·en·tif′i·cal·ly** *adv.*

un·scram·ble (un skram′bəl) *v* **un·scram·bled, un·scram·bling** restore something that has been scrambled to a readable or viewable condition.

un·screw (un skrü′) *v* 1 unfasten a lid or other object held in place by a spiral thread, or be unfastened by twisting: *unscrew a light bulb.* 2 detach, open, or slacken something by removing or loosening the screws holding it in place.

un·scru·pu·lous (un skrü′pyə ləs) *adj* with no moral principles. **un·scru′pu·lous·ly** *adv.* **un·scru′pu·lous·ness** *n.*

SYNONYMS

Unscrupulous suggests having no conscience or sense of honour: *I cannot trust them because they have been so unscrupulous in their business dealings.*

Unprincipled means "lacking moral principles": *Her unprincipled behaviour lost her the election.*

Corrupt is an emphatic word meaning "wicked" or "very dishonest": *The corrupt regime has left the country bankrupt and the people poorer than before.*

un·search·a·ble (un sər′chə bəl) *adj* unable to be clearly understood; inscrutable: *an unsearchable expression on his face.*

un·sea·son·a·ble (un sē′zə nə bəl) *adj* 1 unusual as weather for the time of year. 2 arriving or appearing at the wrong time. **un·sea′son·a·ble·ness** *n.* **un·sea′son·a·bly** *adv.*

un·seat (un sēt′) *v* 1 cause someone to fall from a horse or bicycle: *The bronco unseated everyone who tried to ride it.* 2 remove from a position of power or authority.

un·seed·ed (un sēd′əd) *Sports adj* of a player, not ranked highly in a tournament

un·seem·ly (un sēm′lē) *adj* not proper or appropriate as behaviour or action: *His unseemly laughter annoyed the rest of the audience.* **un·seem′li·ness** *n.*

un·seen (un sēn′) *adj* 1 not seen or noticed: *an unseen error.* 2 not foreseen or predicted: *unseen problems.*

un·settle (un set′əl) *v* **un·set·tled, un·set·tling** cause to feel anxious, uneasy, or disturbed: *The shock unsettled her mind.* **un·set′tling** *adj.* **un·set′tling·ly** *adv.*

un·set·tled (un set′əld) *adj* 1 lacking stability: *an unsettled childhood.* 2 worried and uneasy: *We felt unsettled after moving to the new town.* 3 liable to change; unpredictable: *The weather is unsettled.* 4 not paid: *an unsettled bill.* 5 not yet resolved or decided: *an unsettled question.* 6 not inhabited as an area: *Large parts of Canada are still unsettled.*

un·sex (un seks′) *v* deprive of the gender, sexuality, or the qualities attributed to one or other sex.

un·shak·a·ble or **un·shake·able** (un shā′kə bəl) *adj* strongly felt and unable to be changed as a belief, feeling, or opinion: *unshakable faith.*

un·sheathe (un shēᴛʜ′) *v* **un·sheathed, un·sheath·ing** draw or pull out a knife, sword, or similar weapon from its sheath or covering.

un·sight·ly (un sī′tlē) *adj* ugly or unpleasant to look at: *Her cluttered room was an unsightly mess.* **un·sight′li·ness** *n.*

un·skil·ful or **un·skill·ful** (un skil′fəl) *adj* not with or showing skill. **un·skil′ful·ly** or **un·skill′ful·ly** *adv.* **un·skil′ful·ness** or **un·skill′ful·ness** *n.*

un·skilled (un skild′) *adj* not with or requiring skill or special training: *unskilled workers, unskilled labour.*

un·snarl (un snärl′) *v* untangle or sort out.

un·so·cia·ble (un sō′shə bəl) *adj* not enjoying or making an effort to behave in a friendly way in the company of others: *She was unsociable until she had her first cup of coffee.* **un′so·cia·bil′i·ty** *n.* **un·so′cia·bly** *adv.*

CONFUSABLES

Unsociable means "not seeking or enjoying company" and can be temporary: *He's only unsociable when he isn't feeling well.*

Antisocial often emphasizes a permanent dislike of human contact: *Her brother is an antisocial person who prefers to keep to himself.*

un·so·lic·it·ed (un′sə lis′i tid) *adj* not asked for or invited: *unsolicited advice, unsolicited inquiries.*

un·so·phis·ti·cat·ed (un′sə fis′ti kā′tid) *adj* 1 lacking refined or worldly knowledge or tastes. 2 not complicated or highly developed: *unsophisticated methods, unsophisticated technology.* **un′so·phis′ti·ca′ted·ly** *adv.*

un·sound (un sound′) *adj* 1 not safe, healthy, or in good condition: *The old wall was structurally unsound. The business was financially unsound.* 2 not based on good evidence or sound reasoning: *an unsound theory.* 3 not restful: *an unsound sleep.* **un·sound′ly** *adv.* **un·sound′ness** *n.*

un·speak·a·ble (un spē′kə bəl) *adj* 1 not able to be expressed in words: *unspeakable joy, an unspeakable loss.* 2 so bad that it can hardly be spoken of: *That was an unspeakable thing to do!* **un·speak′a·bly** *adv.*

un·sta·ble (un stā′bəl) *adj* 1 prone to change, fail, or give way: *an unstable regime.* 2 prone to mental or psychological problems: *emotionally unstable.* 3 readily changing into other chemical compounds. **un·sta′ble·ness** *n.* **un·sta′bly** *adv.*

un·stead·y (un sted′ē) *adj* 1 liable to fall, shake, or vary: *an unsteady voice, an unsteady building.* 2 not reliable or predictable: *unsteady behaviour.* **un·stead′i·ly** *adv.* **un·stead′i·ness** *n.*

un·stick (un stik′) *v* **un·stuck un·stick·ing** cause to become no longer stuck together: *Can you unstick this drawer for me?*

un·stint·ing (un stin′ting) *adj* given or giving without holding back: *unstinting generosity.* **un·stint′ing·ly** *adv.* **un·stint′ing·ness** *n.*

un·stop·pa·ble (un stop′ə bəl) *adj* impossible to stop or prevent. **un′stop·pa·bil′i·ty** *n.* **un·stop′pa·bly** *adv.*

un·struc·tured (un struk′chərd) *adj* without a formal structure or organization: *an unstructured environment.*

un·strung (un strung′) *adj* emotionally disturbed.

un·stuck (un stuk′) *adj* loosened from being stuck.
v past tense of UNSTICK.
come unstuck, fail completely.

un·suit·a·ble (un sủ′tə bəl′) *adj* not fitting or appropriate. **un′suit·a·bil′i·ty** *n.* **un·suit′a·bly** *adv.*

un·suit·ed (un sū′tid) *adj* not proper or appropriate: *She is unsuited for the job.*

un·sul·lied (un sul′ēd) *adj* not spoiled or made impure: *an unsullied reputation.*

un·sung (un sung′) *adj* not celebrated or praised: *an unsung hero.*

un·sup·er·vised (un shū′pər vizd′) *adj* not done or acting under supervision: *unsupervised visits.*

un·sure (un shūr′) *adj* **1** not sure. **2** lacking confidence. **3** unsteady.

un·sus·pect·ed (un′sə spek′tid) *adj* **1** not known or thought to exist or be present: *an unsuspected danger.* **2** not regarded with suspicion: *He had already committed several burglaries but was still unsuspected.*

un·swerv·ing (un swər′ving) *adj* not changing or becoming weaker: *unswerving devotion.*

un·tan·gle (un tang′gəl) *v* **un·tan·gled, un·tan·gling** **1** remove tangles from something. **2** make something that is complicated easier to understand.

un·ten·a·ble (un ten′ə bəl) *adj* not able to be maintained or defended as a position or view against attack or objection: *The theory becames untenable in the light of recent events.*

un·ti·dy (un tī′dē) *adj* not tidy or organized.
un·ti′di·ly *adv.* **un·ti′di·ness** *n.*

un·think·a·ble (un thing′kə bəl) *adj* too unlikely or undesirable as a situation or event to be considered a possibility: *It is unthinkable that she could be a thief.*

un·think·ing (un thing′king) *adj* expressed, done, or acting without proper consideration of the consequences: *an unthinking comment.* **un·think′ing·ly** *adv.* **un·think′ing·ness** *n.*

un·thought (un thot′) *adj* **1** not formed by the presence of thinking. **2** (*with* ***of***) **3** not imagined or dreamed of: *That we could win the trophy was unthought of, an unthought-of happiness.*

un·tie (un tī′) *v* **un·tied, un·ty·ing** undo or unfasten a cord or knot, or undo a cord or similar fastening that binds someone or something: *She untied her horse.*

un·til (un til′) *prep, conj* up to the point in time or the event mentioned: *It was cold from January until April. She waited until the sun had set.* <Old Norse *und* up to + *till* till[1]>

un·time·ly (un tīm′lē) *adj* happening or done as an event or act at an unsuitable or premature time: *an untimely death.* **un·time′li·ness** *n.*

un·ti·tled (un tīt′ld) *adj* **1** without a title as a book, text, or other artistic work: *an untitled painting.* **2** not with a title indicating high social or official rank.

un·to (un′tū) *Archaic prep* **1** to: *I say unto you, be silent.* **2** until: *sickness unto death.* <See UNTIL.>

un·told (un tōld′) *adj* **1** too much or too many to be counted or measured: *untold damage, untold wealth.* **2** not told or narrated: *an untold story.*

un·touch·a·ble (un tuch′ə bəl) *adj* **1** not able to be touched or affected. **2** unable to be matched or rivalled. **3** to do with the lowest caste in the hereditary Hindu class system.

un·touched (un tucht′) *adj* **1** not handled, used, or tasted: *an untouched glass.* **2** not affected, changed, or damaged in any way: *The tornado left much of the town untouched.*

un·to·ward (un′tə wȯrd′) *adj* unexpected and inappropriate or inconvenient: *untoward remarks.* **un·toward′ly** *adv.* **un·toward′ness** *n.*

un·tram·melled or **un·tram·meled** (un tram′əld) *adj* not deprived of freedom of action or expression.

un·treat·ed (un trē′təd) *adj* **1** not given medical care or treatment: *an untreated infection.* **2** not preserved, improved, or altered by the use of a chemical, physical, or biological agent: *untreated water.*

un·true (un trū′) *adj* **1** not agreeing with fact or reality: *an untrue rumour.* **2** not faithful or loyal. **3** incorrectly positioned or balanced. **un·tru′ly** *adv.*

un·truth (un trūth′) *n* **1** a lie or false statement. **2** the quality of being false.

un·tu·tored (un tyū′tərd) *or* (un tū′tərd) *adj* not formally taught or trained.

un·twist (un twist′) *v* open or cause to open from a twisted position.

un·us·a·ble (un yū′zə bəl) *adj* not usable; worthless.

un·used (un yūzd′) *adj* **1** not being, or never having been, used: *an unused room. We'll keep the unused paper cups for our next picnic.* **2** (*with* ***to***) not familiar with or accustomed to something: *He was unused to so much attention.*

un·u·su·al (un yū′zhū əl) *adj* not ordinarily or commonly occurring or done: *an unusual rock formation. It's unusual for him to be so silent.* **un·us′u·al·ly** *adv.* **un·us′u·al·ness** *n.*

un·ut·ter·a·ble (un ut′ə rə bəl) *adj* too great, intense, or terrible to describe: *unutterable sadness.*
un·ut′ter·a·bly *adv.*

un·var·y·ing (un ver′ē ing) *adj* not changing; constant or uniform.

un·veil (un vāl′) *v* **1** remove a veil or covering from, especially uncover a new monument or work of art as a part of a public ceremony: *unveil a statue.* **2** show or announce publicly for the first time: *The company unveiled its new product line at a trade show.*

un·want·ed (un won′təd) *adj* **1** not wanted or needed. **2** not invited: *an unwanted interruption.*

a bat	e bed	i bid	o pot	u cup	th thin
ā cake	ē me	ī bite	ō go	ū rude	ᴛʜ then
ȧ bar	ə about	ər over	ȯ for	ủ put	zh measure

un·war·rant·a·ble (un wo̍′rən tə bəl) *adj* not able to be authorized or justified. **un·war′rant·a·bly** *adv.*

un·war·y (un wer′ē) *adj* not cautious of possible dangers or problems. **un·war′i·ly** *adv.* **un·war′i·ness** *n.*

un·wed (un wed′) *adj* not married.

un·well (un wel′) *adj* sick.

un·wield·y (un wēl′dē) *adj* **1** difficult to carry or move because of its size, shape, or weight: *an unwieldy bundle.* **2** too big or badly organized to function efficiently. **un·wield′i·ness** *n.*

un·will·ing (un wil′ing) *adj* not ready, eager, or prepared to do something. **un·will′ing·ly** *adv.* **un·will′ing·ness** *n.*

un·wind (un wīnd′) *v* **un·wound, un·wind·ing 1** undo or be undone after winding or being wound. **2** *Informal* relax after a period of work or tension: *I need an hour to unwind when I get home from school.* <Old English *unwindan*>

un·wise (un wīz′) *adj* not wise or sensible as a person or action. **un·wise′ly** *adv.*

un·wit·ting (un wit′ing) *adj* not aware of the full facts as a person, or not done on purpose: *an unwitting accomplice, an unwitting error.* **un·wit′ting·ly** *adv.* **un·wit′ting·ness** *n.*

un·wont·ed (un wōn′tid) *adj* not customary or usual. **un·wont′ed·ly** *adv.* **un·wont′ed·ness** *n.*

un·wor·thy (un wər′ᴛʜē) *adj* **1** not deserving effort, attention, or respect: *Such a silly story is unworthy of belief.* **2** not acceptable, especially as an action by someone with a good reputation or social position: *That remark is unworthy of you.* **un·wor′thi·ly** *adv.* **un·wor′thi·ness** *n.*

un·wound (un wound′) past tense and past participle of UNWIND.

un·wrap (un rap′) *v* **un·wrapped, un·wrap·ping** remove a wrapping from a package.

un·writ·ten (un rit′ən) *adj* **1** not recorded in writing. **2** understood and accepted, but not formally established: *an unwritten law.*

unwritten law *n* **1** law that is based on decisions of previous judges, rather than on a written decree, statute, etc.; common law. **2** of a custom, not expressed in words but understood by all concerned.

un·yield·ing (un yēl′ding) *adj* **1** not giving way to pressure as a mass or structure: *unyielding granite.* **2** unlikely to be swayed as a person or a person's attitude or behaviour: *unyielding determination.* **un·yield′ing·ly** *adv.* **un·yield′ing·ness** *n.*

un·zip (un zip′) *v* **1** open the zipper of: *Unzip your jacket. This backpack unzips at the least strain.* **2** *Computers* decompress a file that has previously been compressed.

up (up) *adv* **1** at or to a higher position: *She stayed up in the mountains several days. The bird flew up. Stand up, please.* **2** at or to a higher level of intensity, volume, value, or activity: *He turned the volume up. Prices are going up.* **3** above the horizon, especially as the sun after daybreak: *The sun is up.* **4** out of bed: *Please get up or you will be late.* **5** toward the place where someone is: *I heard him creeping up behind me.* **6** into the desired or proper condition: *They set up a committee to study the problem.* **7** into a happy mood: *Nothing had happened to cheer me up.* **8** display publicly and visibly: *They put up some billboards.* **9** into consideration or into the conversation: *The subject of my bad report card was brought up again.*
adj **1** directed or pointed toward a higher position: *We took up the up elevator.* **2** increased: *My temperature is up.* **3** awake and out of bed: *She's not up yet.* **4** in a cheerful mood: *The news put us in an up frame of mind.* **5** functioning properly: *The network is up again.* **6** at the end: *Your time is up, so please put down your pens.* **7** next to appear or perform: *My dance group was up after the intermission.* **8** ahead of an opponent by a certain number: *Our team was three games up.*
prep from a lower to a higher point, or from what is considered to be so: *They climbed up the CN Tower. We rowed up the Red River to Winnipeg. Go up this street and you'll see a shoe store on the right.*
v **upped, up·ping 1** *Informal* do something abruptly or boldly: *He up and left.* **2** cause a level or amount to be increased: *They upped the price of eggs.* **3** lift something: *They upped their glasses in a toast.*
n a period of good luck: *Her life is full of ups and downs.* <Old English *upp*>
on the up and up, *Informal* honest, legitimate, or sincere: *Are you sure she's on the up and up?*
up against (it), facing something or someone to be dealt with, especially something difficult: *They were up against stiff opposition. Seeing how hard the test was, they knew they were up against it.*
up and about, no longer in bed after sleep or an illness.
up and doing, busy or active.
up and down, a back and forth: *The man paced up and down.* **b** in various places throughout: *We looked up and down for our dog.* **c** changeable as a mood or condition: *Our friendship tended to be up and down.*
up for, a available or considered for: *up for re-election, up for promotion.* **b** in court on trial for some charge: *up for attempted robbery.* **c** in the mood for or prepared to take part in: *Who's up for a game of checkers?*
up on, *Informal* well informed about: *The engineer is up on the newest methods.*
up to, a as far as: *The grass came up to our knees.* **b** indicating a maximum amount: *It will cost up to $50 per person.* **c** capable of or fit for: *I was not up to doing the job.* **d** the duty, responsibility, or choice of someone: *It's up to them to make the correct decision.* **e** *Informal* occupied or busy with: *What are you up to these days?*
up until or **up till,** from the beginning as far as: *Up until now he's been no trouble. I've read up till page 46.*
what's up? *Informal* **a** what is going on? **b** what is the matter?

up–and–coming (up′ən kum′ing) *adj* making good progress at the start and likely to become successful in a particular activity or occupation: *an up-and-coming young actor.*

up–and–down (up′ən doun′) *adj* variable: *an up-and-down existence.*

up·beat (up′bēt′) *adj* cheerful or optimistic: *upbeat music, an upbeat atmosphere.*
n Music an unaccented beat before an accented beat.

up·braid (up brād′) *v* find fault with someone and scold: *The captain upbraided his men for falling asleep.* <Old English *upbregdan*>

up·bring·ing (up′bring′ing) *n* the treatment and instruction received by a child from its parents throughout its childhood: *a casual upbringing, a Catholic upbringing.*

UPC Universal Product Code.

up·chuck (up′chuk′) *Informal v* vomit.

up·com·ing (up′kum′ing) *adj* forthcoming and about to happen: *the upcoming school year.*

up·coun·try *adj, adv* in or to the interior of a country: *an upcountry settlement (adj). They live upcountry (adv).*

up·date (up′dāt′) *v* **up·dat·ed, up·dat·ing 1** make something more modern or up to date: *to update your wardrobe. The files are updated once a month.* **2** give someone the latest information about something: *We were updated about the latest developments.*
v an act of bringing something up to date, or an updated version of something: *We received regular updates from the fan club.*

up·draft (up′draft′) *n* an upward current or draft of air.

up·end (up end′) *v* set or turn something on its end or upside down: *If you upend the box, it will take up less space.*

up front *adv* **1** at or toward the front: *Let's sit up front.* **2** in advance as a payment: *If you pay for the tickets up front, you get a discount.*
adj **1 upfront** honest and frank: *I'll be upfront with you about what's ahead.* **2** in advance as a payment: *an upfront deposit.* **3** at the front or most prominent position: *They found it in the upfront section of the magazine.*

up·grade (up′grād′) *for v,* (up′grād′) *for n.*
v **up·grad·ed, up·grad·ing 1** raise something to a higher standard, especially improve equipment or machinery by adding or replacing components: *He upgraded all of the software on his computer.* **2** promote an employee to a higher position.
n an act of upgrading something. **up·grad′a·bil′i·ty** or **up·grade′a·bil′i·ty** *n.* **up·grade′a·ble** *adj.*
on the upgrade, improving or progressing.

up·heav·al (up hē′vəl) *n* a violent or sudden change or disruption to something: *The sale of the family business caused a great upheaval.*

up·held (up held′) past tense and past participle of UPHOLD.

up·hill (up′hil′) *for adj,* (up′hil′) *for adv. adj* **1** sloping upward: *It is an uphill road all the way.* **2** requiring great effort: *an uphill fight.*
adv upward: *We walked a kilometre uphill.*

up·hold (up hōld′) *v* **up·held, up·hold·ing 1** confirm or support something that has been questioned: *The Supreme Court upheld the lower court's ruling.* **2** maintain a custom or practice: *We uphold the tradition of staying awake until midnight on New Year's Eve.* **up·hold′er** *n.*

up·hol·ster (up hōl′stər) *v* provide furniture with a soft, padded covering. <obsolete *uphold* keep in repair> **up·hol′stered** *adj.* **up·hol′ster·er** *n.*

up·hol·ster·y (up hōl′stə rē) *n* **1** soft, padded textile covering that is fixed to furniture such as armchairs and sofas. **2** the art or business of upholstering.

U–pick (yū′pik′) *adj* harvested by customers directly on a farm or field: *U-pick strawberries, a U-pick orchard.*

up·keep (up′kēp′) *n* **1** the process of maintaining or being maintained in good condition: *The upkeep of that big house and yard takes up a lot of their time.* **2** financial or material support of a person, animal, or thing: *What's the upkeep on your dogs?*

up·land (up′lənd) *or* (up′land′) *n* high or hilly land.
adj of or found in high land: *an upland meadow.*

up·lift (up lift′) *for v,* (up′lift′) *for n. v* **1** raise or lift something up. **2** be created by an upward movement of the earth's surface. **3** raise or stimulate someone morally or spiritually.
n **1** an act of raising something. **2** the upward movement of part of the earth's surface. **3** a condition of moral or spiritual improvement: *Attending church gave him an uplift.* **up·lift′er** *n.* **up·lift′ing** *adj.* **up·lift′ing·ly** *adv.*

up·link (up′lingk′) *n* a communication link to a space satellite.
v provide with or send something by such a link.

up·load (up′lōd′) *Computers v* transfer data to a larger system or network: *Each store's daily sales data was uploaded to the head office's computer.*
n the act or process of transferring data in this way: *The upload is complete.*

up·mar·ket (up′mår′kit) *adj* to do with customers or clients with expensive tastes or requirements.

up·most (up′mōst′) *adj* uppermost.

up·on (ə pon′) *prep* on: *The argument was based upon two false assumptions.*

up·per (up′ər) *adj* **1** located above another part: *the upper lip, the upper floor.* **2** higher in position or status: *upper ranks.* **3** farther from the sea or nearer a source: *He explored the upper reaches of the St. Lawrence River.*
n **1** the part of a shoe or boot above the sole. **2** an upper part of something:
on your uppers, *Informal* extremely short of money: *He was obviously on his uppers but refused to accept charity.*

🍁 **Upper Canada** *n* the mainly English-speaking region of Canada north of the Great Lakes and west of the Ottawa River, in what is now southern Ontario. In former times, prior to Confederation, it united with LOWER CANADA to form the Province of Canada.

upper case *adj* formed with capital letters as opposed to small letters.
n capital letters. See also LOWER CASE. Also, **uppercase**.

U

a bat	e bed	i bid	o pot	u cup	th thin
ā cake	ē me	ī bite	ō go	ū rude	TH then
å bar	ə about	ər over	ȯ for	ů put	zh measure

upright piano

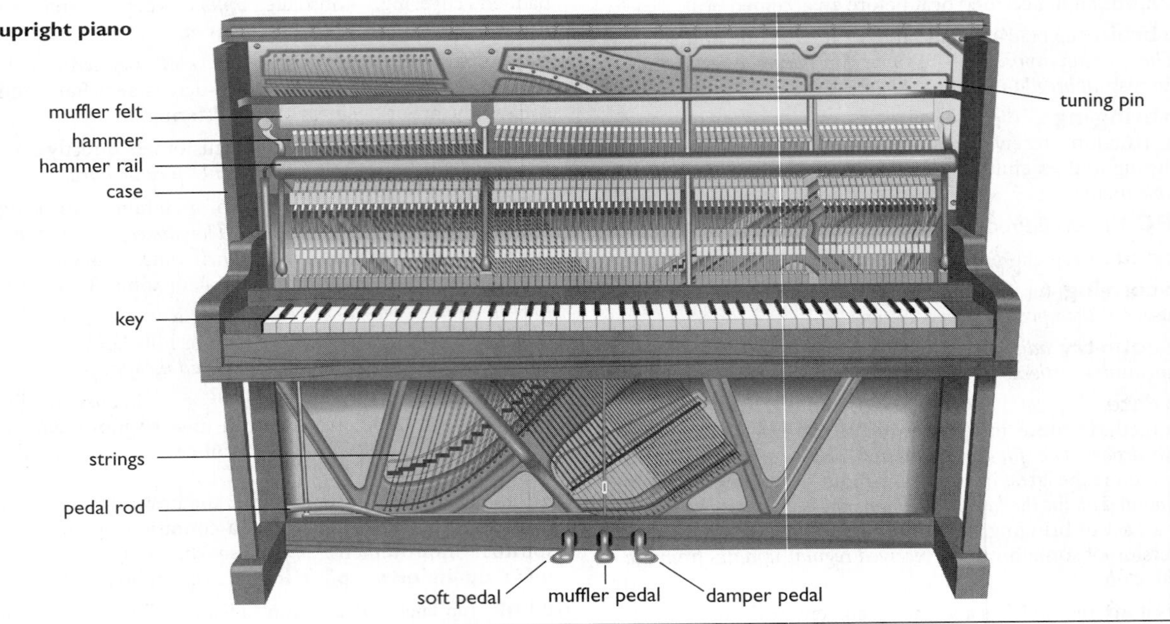

Upper Chamber or **upper chamber** UPPER HOUSE.

upper class *n* the social class that has the greatest wealth, prestige, or power in a society.

upper crust *Informal n* the upper class.

up·per·cut (up′ər kut′) *n* a punch delivered with an upward motion and the arm bent.
v **up·per·cut, up·per·cut·ting** hit with an uppercut.

upper hand *n* a position of control or advantage: *During the first two periods, the visiting team had the upper hand.*

Upper House or **upper house** *n* one of the branches of a two-branch legislature that usually has the smaller number of members. In some countries, members of the Upper House are elected; in others, they are appointed.

Upper Lakes *pln* the most northerly of the Great Lakes, including Lakes Superior, Huron, and Michigan. Also, **Upper Great Lakes**.

up·per·most (up′ər mōst′) *adj* highest in place or importance: *The uppermost branches of the tree had the most fruit.*
adv at or to the highest or most important position: *Fear of failure stood uppermost in her mind before she wrote the test.*

up·pi·ty (up′ə tē) *Informal adj* arrogant or conceited.

up·raise (up rāz′) *v* **up·raised, up·rais·ing** raise something to a higher level.

up·right (up′rīt′) *adj* **1** vertical or erect. **2** strictly honourable or honest: *an upright citizen.*
adv in or into a vertical position: *Hold yourself upright.*
n **1** a post or rod fixed vertically, especially as a structural support. **2** an upright piano. **up′right′ly** *adv.* **up′right′ness** *n.*

upright piano *n* a piano with a vertical frame and strings. Compare GRAND PIANO.

up·ris·ing (up′rī′zing) *n* an action of political resistance or rebellion: *The revolution began with small uprisings in several towns.*

up·riv·er (up′riv′ər) *adj, adv* of, at, or to a point nearer the source of a river.

up·roar (up′rôr′) *n* **1** a loud and confused noise or disturbance: *We heard an uproar in the hall and went to see what it was. There was a great uproar when the theft was discovered.* **2** a public expression of protest or outrage: *The minister's refusal to resign caused an uproar in the media.* <Dutch *oproer* rebellion>

up·roar·i·ous (up rô′rē əs) *adj* **1** marked by or provoking loud noise or uproar: *an uproarious gathering.* **2** very funny and provoking loud laughter: *uproarious hilarity.* **3** very funny: *an uproarious comedy, an uproarious scene.* **up·roar′i·ous·ly** *adv.* **up·roar′i·ous·ness** *n.*

up·root (up rüt′) *v* **1** pull something, especially a tree or plant, out of the ground: *The storm uprooted two trees.* **2** move or force someone from a home or a familiar location: *Famine uprooted many families from their birthplaces.* **3** destroy or eradicate: *The revolution uprooted the established social classes.*

up·sy–dai·sy or **ups–a–dai·sy** (up′se dā′zē) *interj* used especially when encouraging a child while lifting it or helping it after a fall.

ups and downs *Informal pln* a succession of both good and bad experiences: *She said that every life has its ups and downs.*

up·scale (up′skāl′) *adj, adv* expensive or catering to wealthy people: *an upscale restaurant, an upscale neighbourhood.*

up·set (up set′) *for v,* (up′set′) *for n,* (up′set′) *or* (up set′) *for adj. v* **up·set, up·set·ting 1** make someone unhappy, disappointed, or worried: *The shock upset his nerves.* **2** knock something over: *to upset a boat.* **3** disrupt, greatly alter, or disorder something: *Rain upset our plans for a picnic. The young candidate upset the mayor in the election.* **4** disturb the digestion of a person's stomach.
n **1** a condition of being unhappy, disappointed, or worried. **2** an unexpected result or situation, especially in a sports competition: *The hockey team suffered a major upset.* **3** a disturbance in a person's digestion: *a stomach upset.*
adj **1** unhappy, disappointed, or worried. **2** with a disturbed digestion: *an upset stomach.*

SYNONYMS

Upset means "disturb": *Their behaviour upset me so much that I left the room.*

Distress emphasizes great physical or mental pain: *We were distressed to hear about your accident.*

Rattle is an informal word meaning "upset" or "fluster": *The loud noise rattled their nerves.*

up·shot (up′shot′) *n* the end result or outcome: *The upshot of all the delays will probably be that we'll have to cancel the program.*

up·side (up′sīd′) *n* the positive or good side of something that results in an advantage.

upside down *adv* **1** with the upper part where the lower part should be: *The slice of bread and butter fell upside down on the floor.* **2** in or into complete disorder: *They turned the room upside down.*

up·side–down cake (up′sīd doun′) *n* a sponge cake baked with a layer of sugar or fruit on the bottom and served upside down with the sugar or fruit on top.

up·stage (up′stāj′) *or* (up′stāj′) *for adj or adv,* (up′stāj′) *for v. adj, adv* at or toward the back of a theatre stage.
v **up·staged, up·stag·ing 1** draw attention from someone toward oneself: *She upstaged the hostess by welcoming everyone herself.* **2** move as an actor toward the back of a stage to make another actor face away from the audience.

up·stairs (up′sterz′) *for adv,* (up′sterz′) *for adj or n. adj, adv* located on an upper floor: *The girl ran upstairs. She lives upstairs* (*adv*). *He is waiting in an upstairs hall* (*adj*).
n (*with singular verb*) an upper floor: *The upstairs of the house is very small.*

up·stand·ing (up stan′ding) *adj* **1** honest and respectable: *He's a fine, upstanding young man.* **2** standing up: *upstanding feathers.*

up·start (up′stȧrt′) *n* a person who has suddenly risen to wealth or a high position, especially one who behaves arrogantly.

up·stream (up′strēm′) *for adj,* (up′strēm′) *for adv.*
adj, adv moving or located in the opposite direction from that in which a stream or river flows, and therefore is nearer to its source: *They stopped at an upstream camping site* (*adj*). *They found it hard to swim upstream* (*adv*).

up·stretched (up strecht′) *adj* stretched or reaching upward.

up·stroke (up′strōk′) *n* a stroke or movement made in an upward direction: *the upstroke of a baton.*

up·surge (up′sərj′) *for n,* (up′sərj′) *for v. n* an upward surge in the strength or quantity of a thing: *an upsurge in prices, an upsurge of feeling.*
v **up·surged, up·surg·ing** surge up or rise.

up·swing (up′swing′) *n* **1** an increase in strength or quantity: *an upswing in business.* **2** a swing or movement upward.

up·take (up′tāk′) *n* the action or process of taking or making use of something that is available.
quick (slow) on the uptake, quick (slow) to understand: *He's a very nice fellow, but a little slow on the uptake.*

up·tem·po (up′tem′pō) *adj, adv* played with a fast or increased musical tempo.

up·thrust (up′thrust′) *n* **1** the upward force that a liquid or gas exerts on a body floating in it. **2** a movement upward of part of the earth's crust.
v thrust a thing upward.

up·tight (up′tīt′) *Informal adj* angry and defensive in a tense and overly controlled way: *Don't get uptight; she didn't mean anything by it. His mother gets uptight if he's late getting home.* **up′tight′ness** *n.*

up·time (up′tīm′) *n* **1** the time during which a machine, especially a computer, functions properly and is available for use. **2** the time during which a person needs to be alert and responsive, as opposed to resting or relaxing. Compare DOWNTIME.

up–to–date (up′tə dāt′) *or* (up′tə dāt′) *adj* **1** incorporating the latest developments and trends: *an up-to-date shop.* **2** incorporating or aware of the latest information: *an up-to-date map.*

up·town (up′toun′) *for adv,* (up′toun′) *for adj. adv, adj* to do with the upper part of a town or city: *to go uptown* (*adv*), *an uptown address* (*adj*).

up·turn (up′tərn′) *for n,* (up tərn′) *for v.*
n **1** an upward turn: *The airplane made a sudden upturn to avoid the mountain.* **2** an improvement or upward trend, especially in economic conditions or someone's progress: *As business improved, his income took an upturn.*
v turn something upward or upside down.
up′turned *adj.*

up·ward (up′wərd) *adv* toward a higher place or level: *She gazed upward. Children of five years and upward must pay. We traced the brook upward.* Also, **upwards.**
adj moving, pointing, or leading to a higher place or level: *an upward glance, an upward trend.* **up′ward·ly** *adv.*
upwards of or **upward of,** more than: *Repairs to the car will cost upwards of $800.*

a bat	e bed	i bid	o pot	u cup	th **thin**
ā cake	ē me	ī bite	ō go	ū rude	TH **then**
ȧ bar	ə about	ər over	ȯ for	u̇ put	zh measure

upward mobility *n* movement, or the opportunity to move, to a higher social and economic status.
upwardly mobile *adj.*

up·well·ing (up′wel′ing) *n* a rising up of a thing: *an upwelling of grief.*
adj building up or gathering strength: *upwelling sentiment.*

up·wind (up′wīnd′) *adv, adj* against the direction in which the wind is blowing: *The giraffes were standing upwind from the lion, and it caught their scent.*

u·ra·ni·um (yů rā′nē əm) *n* a radioactive metallic element, used as a fuel in nuclear reactors. *Symbol* **U** <*Uranus,* the planet, because the element was discovered soon after the planet>

U·ra·nus (yů′rə nəs) *n* a distant planet of the solar system, seventh in order from the sun. See EARTH for picture. <*Uranus,* the earliest supreme god of the Greeks>

ur·ban (ər′bən) *adj* to do with cities or towns: *urban planning, the urban population.* <Latin *urbs* city>

ur·bane (ər bān′) *adj* suave, courteous, and refined in manner. **ur·bane′ly** *adv.* **ur·ban·i·za′tion** *n.*
ur·ban′i·ty (ər ban′ə tē) *n.*

ur·ban·ite (ər′bə nīt′) *n* a person who lives in a town or city.

ur·ban·ize (ər′bə nīz) *or* (ər′ben īz) *v* make or become urban in character. **ur′ban·i·za′tion** *n.*

urban myth or **legend** *n* an entertaining story or piece of false information that is widely circulated as true and believed by many people.

urban renewal *n* a program, policy, or the process of redeveloping areas within a city, typically involving the clearance of slums.

urban sprawl *n* the uncontrolled spreading of urban development, especially into formerly rural areas.

A sea **urchin** is a round, saltwater animal varying in size from 1 cm to over 30 cm. Its body is covered with movable, protective spines. Some species are poisonous to humans.

ur·chin (ər′chin) *n* **1** a small child, especially a mischievous one. **2** a sea urchin.

ETYMOLOGY

Urchin comes through Old French *irechon* from Latin *erecius,* which means "hedgehog." It was originally used to refer to people whose ragged appearance was seen as looking like a hedgehog.

Ur·du (ůr′dū) *or* (ər′dū) *n* the official language of Pakistan.

–ure *suffix* **1** indicating an action, process, or result: *failure, disclosure.* **2** indicating an office or function, especially a collective one: *legislature.*

u·re·a (yů rē′ə) *n* a colourless, soluble, crystalline compound present in the urine of mammals. <Latin, from Greek *ouron* urine>

u·re·thane (yů′rə thān′) *n* a synthetic crystalline compound used in making pesticides and fungicides.

u·re·thra (yů rē′thrə) *n, pl* **u·re·thras** or **u·reth·rae** (-rē) *or* (-rī) the duct by which urine is discharged from the bladder, and which in male vertebrates also conveys semen.

urge (ərj) *v* **urged, urg·ing 1** try earnestly or persistently to persuade someone to do something or for action to be taken: *She urged him to take more time off. The taxpayers urged the town council to provide more parking spaces.* **2** encourage a person or animal to move more quickly or in a particular direction: *He urged his horse to make the jump.*
n a strong desire or impulse: *the urge for revenge.* <Latin *urgere*>

ur·gent (ər′jənt) *adj* **1** requiring immediate action or attention in a situation or circumstance: *an urgent duty. She said the matter was urgent.* **2** done or arranged in response to such a situation: *He required urgent treatment.* **ur′gen·cy** (ər′jən sē) *n.* **ur′gent·ly** *adv.*

u·ri·nal (yů′rə nəl) *or* (yů rī′nəl) *n* an upright plumbing fixture with a vertical trough and shallow, flushable bowl and typically attached to a wall in a public toilet, into which men and boys may urinate.

u·ri·nal·y·sis (yů′rə nal′ə sis) *n, pl* **u·ri·nal·y·ses** (-sēz′) an analysis of a sample of urine to test for the presence of disease or drugs.

u·ri·nar·y (yů′rə ner′ē) *adj* **1** to do with urine. **2** to do with the organs that produce and discharge urine.

urinary tract *n* all the body parts involved in producing and discharging urine.

u·ri·nate (yů′rə nāt′) *v* **u·ri·nat·ed, u·ri·nat·ing** discharge urine from the body. **u′ri·na′tion** *n.*

u·rine (yů′rən) *n* a watery, typically yellowish fluid stored in the bladder and discharged through the urethra that is a body's way of discharging excess water, salt, and other waste substances removed from the blood by the kidneys. <Latin *urina*>

URL *n* in full, **uniform resource locator** an Internet address, usually a combination of numbers, letters, and punctuation symbols that includes the access protocol (*http*) and the domain name that begins with *www.*

urn (ərn) *n* **1** a tall, rounded vase with a stem and base, especially one used for storing the ashes of a cremated person. **2** a large metal container with a tap, in which coffee or tea is made and kept hot, or water for making such drinks is boiled. <Latin *urna*>

u·rol·o·gy (yū rol′ə jē) *n* the branch of medicine dealing with functions and disorders of the urinary system. **ur′o·log′i·cal** *adj.* **u·rol′o·gist** *n.*

U·ru·guay (yūʹrə gwī) *n* a country in the southeast of S America. See the APPENDIX. **Uʹru·guayʹan** *adj, n.*

us (us) *pron* the objective form of WE: *Mother told us to be quiet.* <Old English>

US or **U.S.** United States.

USA or **U.S.A.** United States of America.

us·a·ble (yūʹzə bəl) *adj* able or fit to be used. Also, **useable. usʹa·bilʹi·ty** *n.*

us·age (yūʹsij) *or* (yūʹzij) *n* **1** the action of using something or the fact of being used: *water usage, power usage.* **2** the way in which a word or phrase is normally and correctly used. **3** a long-continued practice or custom, especially as creating a right, obligation, or standard: *national usages.*

use (yūz) *for v,* (yūs) *for n.* *v* **used, us·ing 1** take, hold, or employ something as a means of accomplishing a purpose or achieving a result: *He used a knife to cut the meat. May I use your telephone?* **2** take or consume an amount from a limited supply of something: *Sorry, we used all the sugar.* **3** exploit a person or situation for one's own advantage: *After she did him a favour, she felt she'd been used.*
n **1** the action of using something or the condition of being used for some purpose: *the use of tools. Our telephone is in constant use.* **2** an ability or power to exercise or manipulate something, especially one's mind or body: *The dog had lost the use of its hind legs.* **3** a purpose for or way in which something can be used: *practical uses.* **4** the value or advantage of something: *What's the use of crying?* <Latin *usus*>
have no use for, a not need or want. **b** *Informal* dislike.
make use of, use for a purpose.
used to, a accustomed to: *used to hardships.* **b** formerly did: *She used to visit her grandmother every day.*
use up, a consume or expend entirely. **b** *Informal* tire out or exhaust.

GRAMMAR AND USAGE

When spoken, the idiom **used to** can sound a lot like "use to." In your writing, remember to spell *used to* with the *d:*

I used to watch that show, not
I use to watch that show.

used (yūzd) *adj* having already been used: *We bought used clothing at a thrift shop.*

use·ful (yūsʹfəl) *adj* able to be used for a practical purpose or in several ways: *a useful gadget. She learned a useful lesson from that experience.* **useʹful·ly** *adv.* **useʹful·ness** *n.*

use·less (yūʹslis) *adj* **1** not fulfilling or not expected to achieve the intended purpose or desired outcome: *useless knowledge. It was useless to complain.* **2** *Informal* with no ability or skill in a specified activity: *useless at games. She is completely useless in the kitchen.* **useʹless·ly** *adv.* **useʹless·ness** *n.*

Use·net (yūzʹnetʹ) *n* an Internet system of online discussion groups.

us·er (yūʹzər) *n* **1** a person who uses or operates something: *computer users, subway users.* **2** a person who takes illegal drugs. **3** a person who manipulates others for his or her own gain.

u·ser–friend·ly (yūʹzər frenʹdlē) *adj* easy to understand and use, especially as a machine or system: *user-friendly software.*

U–shaped (yūʹshāptʹ) *adj* with the shape of the letter U: *a U-shaped kitchen counter.*

ush·er (ushʹər) *n* **1** a person who shows people to their seats, especially in a theatre, movie house, or church. **2** an official in a law court whose duties includes swearing in jurors and witnesses and keeping order.
v **1** show or guide someone somewhere: *The patrons were ushered to their seats.* **2** (*with* **in**) cause or mark the start of something new: *to usher in a new age. Winter was ushered in by a week of cold winds.* <Old French, from Latin *ustiarius* doorkeeper>

USSR or **U.S.S.R.** *n* in full, **Union of Soviet Socialist Republics** the name of the former country that consisted of a union of eastern European and northern Asian republics, including Russia.

u·su·al (yůʹzhů əl) *adj* commonly or typically occurring or done: *He didn't take his usual route home last night. It was usual to tip the hotel staff.*
n **the usual** a thing that is typically done, present, or ordered: *She sat down at our table and ordered the usual.* <Latin *usualis* ordinary, from *usus* use> **uʹsu·al·ly** *adv.* **uʹsu·al·ness** *n.*
as usual, in the usual manner, at the usual time, or in the usual way.

SYNONYMS

Usual means "commonly happening": *He made his usual request for money.*

Customary emphasizes happening by habit or custom: *It was customary for them to go to bed at ten.*

Routine emphasizes happening as a fixed, regular habit or occurrence: *The soldiers made their routine check of the parameter of the camp, and then went back to their tents.*

Standard suggests occurring and accepted widely as a model: *The manual outlines the standard way to carry out that procedure.*

u·surp (yū zərpʹ) *or* (yū sərpʹ) *v* take a position of power or importance illegally or by force: *The prince usurped the throne.* <Old French, Latin *usurpare* to seize for use> **uʹsur·paʹtion** *n.* **u·surpʹer** *n.*

u·su·ry (yūʹzhə rē) *n, pl* **u·su·ries** the lending of money at an extremely high or unlawful rate of interest. <Latin *usura* interest> **uʹsur·er** *n.* **u·surʹi·ous** *adj.*

u·ten·sil (yū tenʹsəl) *n* a tool, container, or other item, especially for household use and in the kitchen. <Latin *utensilia* that may be used, from *uti* use>

u·ter·us (yūʹtə rəs) *n, pl* **u·ter·us·es** or **u·ter·ae** (-rē) *or* (-rī) the womb, especially considered as a body organ in medical and technical contexts. <Latin>
uʹter·ine (yūʹtə rin) *or* (yūʹtə rīn) *adj.*

U

a bat	e bed	i bid	o pot	u cup	th thin
ā cake	ē me	ī bite	ō go	ū rude	ᴛʜ then
å bar	ə about	ər over	ȯ for	ů put	zh measure

🍁 **u·til·i·dor** (yū til′ə dôr′) *n* a large, insulated tube mounted on short posts above ground and housing water, steam, and sewage pipes that supply services to buildings in a town or settlement built on permafrost. <*utili*(*ty*) + (*corri*)*dor*>

u·til·i·tar·i·an (yū til′ə ter′ē ən) *adj* **1** designed to be useful or practical rather than attractive: *utilitarian furniture.* **2** to do with utilitarianism: *utilitarian philosophy.*
n a person who believes in utilitarianism.

u·til·i·tar·i·an·ism (yū til′ə ter′ē ə niz′əm) *n* the doctrine in philosophy or belief that actions are proper if they are useful or for the benefit of a majority.

u·til·i·ty (yū til′ə tē) *n, pl* **u·til·i·ties 1** the condition of being useful, profitable, or beneficial: *The cottage was obviously designed more for utility than beauty.* **2** a public utility: *They pay a lot more for utilities than we do.*
adj **1** designed or serving strictly for usefulness rather than appearance or luxury: *utility furnishings.* **2** to do with equipment used by a public utility: *The car struck a utility pole.* <Latin *uti* use>

utility room *n* a room equipped with appliances for washing and other household work. etc. are located.

u·ti·lize (yū′tə līz′) *v* **u·ti·lized, u·ti·liz·ing** make practical and effective use of: *to utilize vitamins.*
u′ti·liz′a·ble *adj.* **u′ti·liz′er** *n.*
u′til·i·za′tion (yů′tə lə zā′shən) *or* (yů′tə lī zā′shən) *n.*

ut·most (ut′mōst′) *adj* of the greatest or highest degree, amount, quantity, or extent: *He considered his health of the utmost importance. She travelled to the utmost ends of the earth.*
n the greatest or most extreme extent or amount: *She did her utmost to help him find a good job. He strained his resources to the utmost.* <Old English *utemest*>

u·to·pi·a (yū tō′pē ə) *n* an imagined ideal place or state of things in which everything is perfect. <Greek *ou* not + *topos* place> **u·to′pi·an** *adj.* **u·to′pi·an·ism** *n.*

ut·ter[1] (ut′ər) *adj* complete or absolute: *utter surprise, utter darkness, an utter failure.* <Old English *utera* outer> **ut′ter·ly** *adv.*

ut·ter[2] (ut′ər) *v* make a sound with one's voice or give out as sound: *It was the last word he uttered. She uttered her thoughts. She uttered a cry of pain.* <Middle English *uttren* put forth> **ut′ter·a·ble** *adj.* **ut′ter·ance** *n.* **ut′ter·er** *n.*

ut·ter·most (ut′ər mōst′) *adj, n* utmost.

U–turn (yū′tərn′) *n* the turning of a vehicle in a U-shaped course so as to face in the opposite direction.

UV *n* in full, **ultraviolet radiation**. **UVA** rays have relatively long wavelength, and deeply penetrate the skin, causing wrinkles. **UVB** rays have shorter wavelength, and cause sunburn leading to skin cancer. **UVC** rays have the shortest wavelength, and are the most dangerous; they are used in laboratories to kill bacteria and destroy viruses. UVC rays from sunlight cannot penetrate the earth's ozone layer.

UV index *n* in full, **ultraviolet index** an indication of the strength of ultraviolet radiation on a certain day in a certain place.

u·vu·la (yū′vyə lə) *n, pl* **u·vu·lae** (-lē) *or* (-lī) the small lobe of flesh hanging down from the soft palate in the back of the mouth above the throat. See PALATE for picture. <Latin *uva* grape>

Uz·bek·i·stan (ůz bek′i stan) *n* a country in central Asia. See the APPENDIX. **Uz′bek** *adj, n.*

v or **V** (vē) *n, pl* **v's** or **V's** **1** the twenty-second letter of the English alphabet, or any speech sound represented by it. **2** the twenty-second thing in a list or series.

v versus.

V volt(s).

V–6 *n* a type of internal combustion engine that has six cylinders in two rows of three, slanted so as to form a V shape. A **V-8** has eight cylinders in two rows of four, slanted so as to form a V shape.

va·can·cy (vā′kən sē) *n, pl* **va·can·cies** **1** an unfilled post, office, or position: *The student council has a vacancy for the position of sports representative.* **2** a space, room, or apartment that is unoccupied and available for rent or sale: *There were no vacancies in the parking lot. The hotel had one vacancy.* **3** empty space: *She stared into the vacancy of the night.* **4** emptiness of mind or a lack of thought or intelligence.

va·cant (vā′kənt) *adj* **1** not occupied or filled: *a vacant house, a vacant chair, a vacant space.* **2** without thought or intelligence: *a vacant smile.* **3** with no expression: *a vacant face.* **4** free from work or activity: *vacant time.* <Latin *vacare* be empty> **va′cant·ly** *adv.*

va·cate (və kāt′) *or* (vā′kāt) *v* **va·cat·ed, va·cat·ing** **1** leave a place that one previously occupied: *They will vacate the house next month.* **2** give up a position or job: *He vacated his position as treasurer.* **3** cancel or annul a legal judgment, contract, or charge.

va·ca·tion (və kā′shən) *or* (vā kā′shən) *n* **1** a holiday, especially a fixed holiday period between terms in schools, universities, and courts of law: *summer vacation. She spent her vacation camping.* **2** the action of leaving a place that one previously occupied.
v take or spend a vacation: *They are vacationing in Saskatchewan.* **va·ca′tion·er** *n.*

vac·ci·nate (vak′sə nāt′) *v* **vac·ci·nat·ed, vac·ci·nat·ing** treat with a vaccine to produce immunity against a disease. **vac′ci·na′tion** *n.*

vac·cine (vak′sēn) *or* (vak sēn′) *n* **1** a substance used to stimulate the production of antibodies and provide immunity against one or several diseases. A vaccine, prepared from the disease itself or synthetically made, acts as an antigen without causing the disease. **2** *Computers* a software program designed to detect viruses and protect a computer from them.

ETYMOLOGY

Vaccine comes from Latin *vaccinus*, meaning "of cows," from the Latin phrase *virus vaccinus*, meaning "virus of cowpox." This virus became the first vaccine when, in 1796, it was found to protect people against smallpox.

vac·il·late (vas′ə lāt′) *v* **vac·il·lat·ed, vac·il·lat·ing** alternate or waver between different opinions or actions: *He vacillated so long about which video to rent that when he finally decided, they were both gone.* <Latin *vacillare*> **vac′il·la′tion** *n.*

vac·u·ole (vak′yū ōl′) *n* a space, cavity, or sac within the cytoplasm of a cell, enclosed by a membrane and usually containing fluid.

vac·u·ous (vak′yū əs) *adj* with or showing no thought or intelligence: *a vacuous remark.* **va·cu′i·ty** *n.* **vac′u·ous·ly** *adv.* **vac′u·ous·ness** *n.*

vac·u·um (vak′yū əm) *or* (vak′yəm) *n* **1** an empty space utterly devoid of matter, even air. **2** an enclosed space from which almost all air or gas has been removed. **3** a gap left by the loss, death, or departure of someone or something formerly significant in a situation or activity: *His dog's death left a vacuum in his life.* **4** a vacuum cleaner.
v clean with a vacuum cleaner: *I still have to vacuum before I can go.*
adj of, containing, using, or producing a vacuum: *vacuum brakes, a vacuum pump.* <Latin *vacuum* empty>

vacuum cleaner *n* an electrical appliance that collects dust and small particles by suction from floors, carpets, and other surfaces.

vacuum packed *adj* sealed as a product in a pack or wrapping after any air has been removed so that the pack or wrapping is tight and firm: *The coffee was vacuum packed.* **vac′u·um-pack′** *v.*

vacuum tube *n* a sealed glass tube from which almost all the air has been removed, allowing the free passage of an electric current.

vag·a·bond (vag′ə bond′) *n* a person who wanders from place to place without a home or job.
adj wandering without a settled home: *a vagabond people.* <Old French, from Latin *vagus* rambling> **vag′a·bond′age** *n.*

va·gar·y (vā′gə rē) *n, pl* **va·gar·ies** an unexpected and surprising change in a situation or in someone's behaviour: *the vagaries of fashion.* <probably Latin *vagari* wander>

va·gi·na (və jī′nə) *n, pl* **va·gi·nas** **1** a muscular tube leading from the external genitals to the cervix of the uterus in women and most female mammals. **2** a sheathlike structure in some plants, especially a sheath formed around a stem by the base of a leaf. <Latin = sheath> **vag′i·nal** (vaj′ə nəl) *adj.* **vag′i·nal·ly** *adv.*

va·grant (vā′grənt) *n* a person without a settled home or regular work who wanders from place to place and lives by begging.
adj to do with the life of a vagrant. <Old French *wancre* to roam> **va′gran·cy** *n.*

vague (vāg) *adj* **va·guer, va·guest** **1** not clearly expressed or defined: *a vague statement, a vague notion, a vague longing.* **2** thinking or communicating in an unclear way: *She was very vague about her plans for the weekend.* **3** with no definite outline: *a vague shape in the mist.* <Latin *vagus* wandering> **vague′ly** *adv.* **vague′ness** *n.*

a bat	e bed	i bid	o pot	u cup	th **thin**
ā cake	ē me	ī bite	ō go	ū rude	ᴛʜ **then**
à bar	ə about	ər over	ȯ for	u̇ put	zh measure

va·gus (vā′gəs) *n, pl* **va·gi** (-gī) *or* (-gē), (-jī) *or* (-jē) either of the tenth pair of nerves extending from the brain to the heart, lungs, upper digestive tract, and other organs of the chest and abdomen. <Latin *vagus* wandering>

vain (vān) *adj* **1** with or showing an unduly high opinion of one's appearance, abilities, or worth: *She was vain about her beauty.* **2** producing no result, or with no meaning or likelihood of fulfillment: *a vain hope, vain attempts, a vain boast.* <Old French, from Latin *vanus* empty>
vain′ly *adv.* **vain′ness** *n.*
in vain, without effect or success: *My shout for help was in vain, for no one could hear me.*

CONFUSABLES

Vain means "conceited": *He's too vain to admit defeat.*

Vane refers to a device that shows the direction of the wind: *The wild wind blew the vane in circles.*

Vein refers to a tube carrying blood through the body: *When she sang, the veins in her neck stood out.*

vain·glo·ri·ous (vān′glô′rē əs) *adj* excessively proud or boastful about one's achievements.
vain′glo′ri·ous·ly *adv.* **vain′glo′ry** *n.*

Vai·sak·hi (vī sa′kē) BAISAKHI.

val·ance (val′əns) *n* a length of drapery hung above a window to screen the curtain fittings. <origin uncertain>

vale (vāl) *Poetic n* a valley. <Old French, from Latin *vallis*>

val·e·dic·tion (val′ə dik′shən) *n* the action of saying farewell.

val·e·dic·to·ri·an (val′ə dik tô′rē ən) *n* a student who gives the farewell address at a graduation ceremony. <Latin *valedicere* bid farewell, from *vale* be well! + *dicere* say>

val·e·dic·to·ry (val′ə dik′tə rē) *n, pl* **val·e·dic·to·ries** a farewell address, especially at the graduating exercises of a school or college.
adj serving as a farewell.

va·lence (vā′ləns) *Chemistry n* the combining capacity of an atom, determined by the number of electrons it will lose, add, or share when it reacts with other atoms.

val·en·tine (val′ən tīn′) *n* **1** a greeting card sent or given on **Saint Valentine's Day**, February 14. **2** a person to whom one sends such a card or whom one asks to be one's sweetheart.

va·le·ri·an (və lē′rē ən) *n* **1** a perennial plant that typically bears clusters of small flowers and has a strong-smelling root. **2** a drug made from the dried roots of the common valerian, used as a sedative. <Latin *valeriana* (*herba*) (herb) of Valerian, a personal name>

val·et (val′it) *or* (val′ā) *n* **1** a male servant who takes care of a man's clothes and appearance. **2** an employee in a hotel who cleans or presses clothes. **3** a person employed to clean or park cars.
v **val·et·ed, val·et·ing** serve as a valet. <Old French *vaslet* young man>

Val·hal·la (val hal′ə) *or* (vol hol′ə) *n* in Norse mythology, the hall where the souls of heroes slain in battle feast for eternity. <Old Norse *valhöll*>

val·iant (val′yənt) *adj* with or showing courage or determination: *a valiant soldier, a valiant effort.* <Old French from Latin *valere*> **val′iant·ly** *adv.*
val′iant·ness *n.*

val·id (val′id) *adj* **1** actually supporting the intended point, claim, or action: *a valid argument, a valid approach, a valid excuse.* **2** with full legal authority: *a valid passport.* <Latin *validus* strong> **va·lid′i·ty** *n.* **val′id·ly** *adv.*

val·i·date (val′ə dāt′) *v* **val·i·dat·ed, val·i·dat·ing** **1** check or prove the validity or accuracy of something: *The election results were validated.* **2** demonstrate or support the truth or value of: *The results of the experiments validated her hypothesis.* **val′i·da′tion** *n.*

va·lise (və lēs′) *n* a small travelling bag or suitcase. <French>

Val·kyr·ie (val kēr′ē), (val kī′rē) *or* (val′kə rē) *n* in Norse mythology, one of the spirit maidens who ride through the air and lead slain heroes to Valhalla. <Old Norse *valkyrja*>

val·ley (val′ē) *n, pl* **val·leys** **1** low area of land between hills or mountains, usually with a stream or river flowing through it. **2** a hollow or structure resembling a valley, such as a trough formed where two slopes of a roof meet or where a roof meets a wall. <Old French, from Latin *vallis*>

val·our or **val·or** (val′ər) *n* great courage in the face of danger, especially in battle. <Latin *valor* strength, from *valere* be strong>

val·u·a·ble (val′yū ə bəl) *or* (val′yə bəl) *adj* **1** worth a great deal of money: *valuable assets.* **2** extremely useful or important: *valuable information.*
n **valuables** *pl* a thing or things of great worth, especially small items of personal property: *She keeps her journal and other valuables locked in a drawer.* **val′u·a·ble·ness** *n.*
val′u·a·bly *adv.*

val·u·a·tion (val′yū ā′shən) *n* an estimate or determination of something's worth, especially one carried out by a professional valuer: *The jeweller's valuation of the necklace was $10 000.*

val·ue (val′yū) *n* **1** the regard or importance that something is held to deserve: *the value of education.* **2 a** the material or worth in money of something: *The house was sold for less than its market value.* **b** the worth of something compared to the price paid or asked for it: *At that price, the skates were good value.* **3** the usefulness of a thing considered with regard to a particular purpose: *The drug proved to be of great value in controlling the disease.* **4** the numerical amount denoted by an algebraic term: *the value of* x. **5 values** *pl* a person's principles or standards of behaviour considered as what is most important in life: *family values.*
v **val·ued, val·u·ing** **1** estimate the worth in money of something: *The land is valued at $80 000.* **2** consider someone or something to be important or beneficial: *He valued her judgment.* <Old French, from Latin *valere*>
val′u·er *n.* **val′u·less** *adj.*

val·ued (val′yūd) *adj* **1** with its value estimated or determined. **2** regarded as important: *a valued friend.*

value judgment *n* an estimate of something as good or bad in terms of one's values or priorities.

valve (valv) *n* **1** a device for controlling the movement of fluid through a pipe or duct, especially an automatic device allowing movement in one direction only: *a shut-off valve.* **2** a membrane in a hollow organ of the body that works like a valve, such as a blood vessel, which maintains the flow of the contents in one direction by closing in response to pressure from the reverse flow: *heart valves.* **3** each of the halves of a hinged shell, such as in a mollusc. **4** *Music* a cylindrical mechanism in a brass instrument such as a trumpet that, when depressed or turned, admits air into different sections of tubing and so extends the range of available notes. <Latin *valva* one of a pair of folding doors> **valved** *adj.* **valve′less** *adj.*

va·moose (va mūs′) *or* (və mūs′) *Informal v* **va·moosed, va·moos·ing** go away quickly. <Spanish *vamos* let's go>

vamp[1] (vamp) *n* **1** the upper front part of a shoe or boot. **2** *Music* a short, simple, introductory passage in jazz and popular music, usually repeated several times.
v **1** *Music* repeat a short, simple passage of music. **2** (*usually with* ***up***) repair or improve something. <Old French *avanpie* forepart of the foot> **vamp′er** *n.*

vamp[2] (vamp) *Informal n* a woman who uses sexual attraction to exploit someone.
v blatantly set out to attract someone sexually. <*vampire*>

Vampire bats are quite small, weighing about 28 g, with a body the size of an adult's thumb and a wingspan of about 20 cm. They fly 1 m above the ground, using echolocation, smell, and sound to find their prey.

vam·pire (vam′pīr) *n* **1** an imaginary being in folklore who is a corpse that leaves its grave at night to drink the blood of the living by biting their necks. **2** a tropical bat that lives by sucking the blood of mammals and birds using its two sharp incisors. <Hungarian *vampir*>

van[1] (van) *n* a large, enclosed motor truck or trailer, usually without side windows, used for transporting goods. Compare MINIVAN. <*caravan*>

van[2] (van) *n* the front part of a group of people moving or preparing to move forward, especially the foremost division of an advancing military force. <*vanguard*>

va·na·di·um (və nā′dē əm) *n* a metallic element, used to make certain kinds of steel. *Symbol* **V** <Old Norse *Vanadis* name for Freya, goddess of love and beauty>

Van Al·len belt (van′al′ən) *n* either of two regions of intense radiation partly surrounding the earth, produced by a high concentration of charged particles trapped in the magnetic field of the earth.

van·dal (van′dəl) *n* **1** a person who wilfully destroys or damages public or private property. **2** **Vandal** a member of a Germanic people who ravaged Gaul, Spain, Rome, and northern Africa in the 300s and 400s CE. <Latin *Vandalus*, a member of a Germanic people who sacked Rome>

van·dal·ize (van′də līz′) *v* **van·dal·ized, van·dal·iz·ing** deliberately destroy or damage public or private property: *The school was vandalized during the holidays.* **van′dal·ism′** *n.*

van de Graaff generator (van′də graf′) *n* a machine that generates an electrostatic charge in a large, insulated, metal dome, where a high voltage is produced. <R.J. *van de Graaff*, 20c physicist>

vane (vān) *n* **1** a broad blade attached to a rotating axis or wheel that pushes or is pushed by wind or water and forms part of a machine or device such as a windmill, propeller, or turbine. **2** the flat part on either side of the shaft of a feather. **3** a flat, projecting surface designed to guide the motion of a projectile. The fin on a torpedo is a vane. <Old English *fana* flag>

van·guard (van′gärd′) *n* **1** a group of people leading the way in new developments or ideas, or a position at the forefront of them: *the artistic vanguard.* **2** the foremost part of an advancing army or naval force. <Old French *avantgarde*, from *avant* before + *garde* guard>

va·nil·la (və nil′ə) *n* a food flavouring made from the beanlike pods of a tropical American climbing orchid, or the pod itself. <Spanish *vainilla* little pod>

van·ish (van′ish) *v* **1** disappear suddenly and completely: *The sun vanished behind a cloud.* **2** gradually cease to exist: *One species vanished several hundred years ago.* <Old French, from Latin *evanescere*> **van′ish·er** *n.*

vanishing point *n* the point at which receding parallel lines viewed in perspective appear to converge.

van·i·ty (van′ə tē) *n, pl* **van·i·ties** **1** undue pride in or admiration of one's own appearance or achievements. **2** the quality of being worthless or useless: *the vanity of wealth.* **3** a small case fitted with a mirror and compartments for makeup. **4** a low dresser with a mirror, usually with a matching chair or stool.
adj to do with a person or company publishing works at the author's expense: *a vanity press.*

vanity plate *n* a licence plate for a motor vehicle bearing distinctive or personalized combinations of letters and numbers. Example: IGO4U (*I go for you*)

a bat	e bed	i bid	o pot	u cup	th **thin**
ā cake	ē me	ī bite	ō go	ū rude	ᴛʜ **then**
ȧ bar	ə about	ər over	ȯ for	u̇ put	zh measure

van·quish (vang′kwish) *v* defeat thoroughly. <Old French, from Latin *vincere* conquer> **van′quish·a·ble** *adj.* **van′quish·er** *n.*

van·tage point (van′tij) *n* a place or position offering a good view of something.

vap·id (vap′id) *adj* offering nothing that is stimulating or challenging. <Latin *vapidus*> **va·pid′i·ty** *n.* **vap′id·ly** *adv.* **vap′id·ness** *n.*

va·por·ize (vā′pə rīz′) *v* **va·por·ized, va·por·iz·ing** change or be changed from a solid or liquid to a vapour: *To distil water, we first have to vaporize it.*
va′por·iz′a·ble *adj.* **va′por·i·za′tion** *n.*

va·por·iz·er (vā′pə rī′zər) *n* a device that converts a liquid to a vapour, such as a perfume atomizer or an inhalator for medicine.

va·pour or **va·por** (vā′pər) *n* a substance diffused or suspended in the air, especially one that is normally liquid or solid. Steam from boiling water is vapour. <Latin *vapor*> **va′por·ous** *adj.*

vapour lock *n* a blockage in the flow of a liquid through a pipe as a result of vaporization of the liquid.

vapour trail or **vapor trail** *n* a white trail of water droplets or ice crystals that is sometimes seen in the wake of an aircraft flying at high altitudes.

var·i·a·ble (ver′ē ə bəl) *adj* **1** not consistent or with a fixed pattern: *variable winds.* **2** *Mathematics* able to assume different numerical values. **3** *Biology* liable to deviate from the typical colour or form of a plant or animal, or to occur in different colours or forms. **4** able to be changed or adapted: *The food processor had variable speeds.*
n **1** an element, feature, or factor that is liable to vary or change. **2** *Mathematics* a quantity that is assumed to vary or be capable of varying in value. **3** *Computers* an item of data that may take on more than one value during or between software programs. **4 variables** *pl* the region of light, variable winds to the north of the NE trade winds or between the SE trade winds and the westerlies. **var′i·a·bil′i·ty** *n.* **var′i·a·ble·ness** *n.* **var′i·a·bly** *adv.*

var·i·ance (ver′ē əns) *n* **1** the fact or quality of being different, divergent, or inconsistent: *Her words were at variance with her emotions.* **2** the act or fact of disagreeing or quarrelling. **3** an official dispensation from a rule or regulation, especially a building regulation.

var·i·ant (ver′ē ənt) *n* a form or version of a thing that differs in some respect from a standard: *She showed us two variants of the original design.*
adj showing difference, disagreement, or variety: *variant pronunciations.*

var·i·a·tion (ver′ē ā′shən) *n* **1** a change or slight difference in condition, amount, or level, typically with certain limits: *regional variations.* **2** *Biology* the occurrence of an organism in more than one distinct colour or form. **3** a different or distinct form or version of something, such as a version of a theme in a musical composition.

var·i·cose (var′ə kōs′) *or* (ver′ə kōs′) *adj* affected by a condition causing the swelling and lengthening of veins, most often in the legs. <Latin *varicosus*, from *varix* dilated vein>

var·ied (ver′ēd) *adj* including a number of different types or elements: *a varied assortment, a varied career.*

var·i·e·gat·ed (ver′ē i gā′tid) *or* (ver′i gā′tid) *adj* marked by variety, especially showing different colours as irregular patches and streaks: *variegated pansies.*

va·ri·e·ty (və rī′ə tē) *n, pl* **va·ri·e·ties** **1** the quality or condition of being different or diverse: *My job offered lots of variety.* **2** a number or range of things of the same kind that are different or distinct in character or quality, or a thing of such a kind that differs from others: *The store has a great variety of toys. Which variety of cake do you prefer?* **3** a category for classifying animals or plants, ranking below subspecies or species. Varieties differ in minor but permanent or heritable characteristics. **4** a cultivated form of a plant.

variety show *n* a form of television or theatre entertainment consisting of a series of different types of act, such as singing, dancing, and comedy.

variety store *n* a small store selling a wide range of inexpensive items.

var·i·ous (ver′ē əs) *adj* **1** differing from one another and of different kinds: *various opinions.* **2** more than one or two: *I looked at various jackets, but have decided to buy this one.* **var′i·ous·ness** *n.*

GRAMMAR AND USAGE

Because **various** already contains the idea of difference, avoid putting *different* after it. Say *The city's various cultures were represented*, not *The city's various different cultures were represented.*

Also avoid putting *of* after *various*. Say *Various students went to the career workshop*, not *Various of the students went to the career workshop.*

var·i·ous·ly (ver′ē ə slē) *adv* **1** in various ways or at various times: *She has been variously involved in editing, proofreading, and research.* **2** by various names or classifications: *He was known variously as Harry the Hooligan, Dead-eye, and Jaws McGee.*

var·mint (vor′mint) *Informal n* a troublesome animal or person. <*vermin*>

var·nish (vår′nish) *n* **1** a resin dissolved in a liquid for applying on wood, metal, or other materials to form a hard, clear, shiny surface when dry. **2** a similar substance applied to fingernails. **3** a false or deceiving appearance: *She covers her selfishness with a varnish of good manners.*
v put varnish on. <Old French *vernis*, from Greek *Berenike* ancient city in Libya, where varnishes were used> **var′nish·er** *n.*

var·si·ty (vår′sə tē) *Informal n, pl* **var·si·ties** a university. <*university*>

var·y (ver′ē) *v* **var·ied, var·y·ing** **1** differ in size, amount, degree, or nature from something else of the same kind: *The items on sale varied in quality.* **2** change from one condition or form to another: *Depending on the weather, the plant's growth may vary a great deal.* **3** introduce changes into something so as to make it different or less uniform: *The painter has varied his colours in his recent work.* <Latin *varius* various> **var′y·ing·ly** *adv.*

This gymnast does a cartwheel before her springboard takeoff to achieve the momentum she needs to perform a backflip off the **vault**.

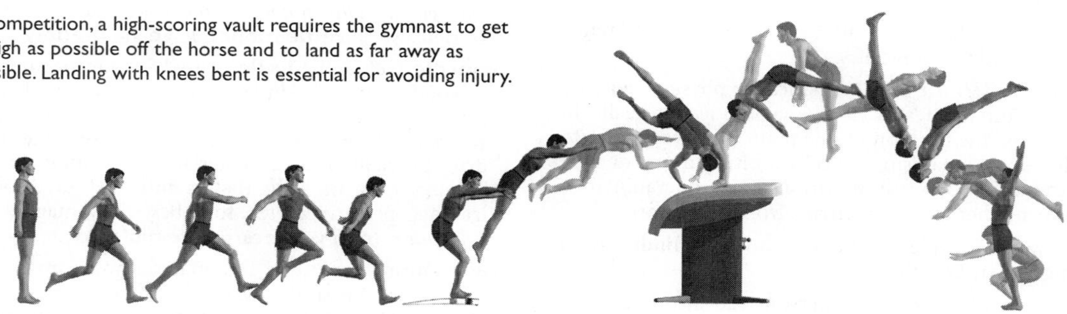

In competition, a high-scoring vault requires the gymnast to get as high as possible off the horse and to land as far away as possible. Landing with knees bent is essential for avoiding injury.

vas·cu·lar (vas′kyə lər) *Biology adj* **1** to do with a duct or canal, especially one that carries blood. **2** to do with plant tissues that conduct water, sap, and nutrients to flowering plants and ferns. A **vascular bundle** is a strand of ducts or canals in the stem or leaves of a plant that conducts water, sap, and nutrients.

vase (vȧz), (vāz), *or* (voz) *n* an open container, usually taller than it is wide and made of glass or china, used for decoration or for holding flowers. <French, from Latin *vas* vessel> **vase′like′** *adj.*

vas·ec·to·my (va sek′tə mē) *n* the surgical cutting and sealing of part of the main ducts through which semen is carried, especially as a means of sterilization.

Vas·e·line (vas′ə lēn′) *or* (vas′ə lēn′) *Trademark n* a brand of petroleum jelly used as an ointment and lubricant. <German *Wasser* water + Greek *elaion* oil>

vas·sal (vas′əl) *n* **1** a holder of land in feudal times on condition of giving loyalty and service to a lord or king. **2** a person or country in a subordinate position to another.
adj in a subordinate position to another: *a vassal state.* <Latin *vassallus*> **vas′sal·age** *n.*

vast (vast) *adj* extremely great or immense: *a vast desert, a vast amount of money.* <Latin *vastus*> **vast′ly** *adv.* **vast′ness** *n.*

vat (vat) *n* a large tank or tub used to hold liquid, especially in industry. <Old English *fæt*>

Vat·i·can (vat′ə kən) *n* **1 the Vatican** the palace and official residence of the Pope in **Vatican City**, an independent state in the city of Rome, Italy. **2** the government, office, or authority of the Pope.

vau·de·ville (vod′ə vil′) *or* (vod′vil) *n* a type of theatrical entertainment, chiefly in the US in the early 1900s, featuring a mixture of specialty acts such as burlesque comedy and song and dance. <French *vaudevire* satirical folk song, from (*chanson*) *du vau de Vire* song of the valley of Vire, in Normandy, where this type of song was sung>

vault[1] (volt) *n* **1** a roof in the form of an arch or a series of arches, typical of churches and other large, formal buildings. **2** a thing resembling an arched roof, especially the sky. **3** a large room or chamber used for storage, especially an underground one, or a secure room in a bank in which valuable things are stored. **4** a chamber beneath a church or in a graveyard used for burials.
v provide a building or roof with an arched roof or roofs, or make a roof in the form of a vault. <Old French *voute*, from Latin *volvere* roll, arch over> **vault′ed** *adj.*

vault[2] (volt) *v* jump or leap over something with the help of a pole or the hands: *She easily vaulted the fence. He vaulted over the wall.*
n the act of vaulting. <Old French *volter*, from Latin *volvitare* to leap>

a bat	e bed	i bid	o pot	u cup	th **thin**
ā cake	ē me	ī bite	ō go	ū rude	ᴛʜ **then**
ȧ bar	ə about	ər over	ȯ for	u̇ put	zh measure

V

vaunt (vont) *v, n* boast about or praise something. <French *vanter,* from Latin *vanus* vain> **vaunt′er** *n.* **vaunt′ing·ly** *adv.*

V–chip (vē′chip) *n* a computer chip installed in a television receiver that can be programmed by the user to block or scramble material considered unduly violent or sexually explicit. <*v*(*iolence*) + *chip*>

VCR *n* in full, **videocassette recorder** a device for recording and playing back videocassettes.

VD *n* in full, **venereal disease** a disease typically contracted by having sexual intercourse with a person already infected.

VDT or **VDU** in full, **video display terminal** or **video display unit** a computer terminal that can display data on a screen.

veal (vēl) *n* the flesh of a calf, used as food. <Old French *veel,* from Latin *vitulus* calf>

vec·tor (vek′tər) *n* **1** a mathematical or physical quantity involving direction as well as magnitude, especially in determining the position of one point in space relative to another. **2** an organism, typically a biting insect or tick, that transmits a disease or parasite from one animal or plant to another. <Latin = carrier, from *vehere* carry>

Ve·da (vā′də) *or* (vē′də) *n* the most ancient Hindu sacred writings. <Sanskrit = knowledge>

vee·jay (vē′jā′) *Informal n* a person who introduces and plays popular music videos. <*v*(*ideo*) *j*(*ockey*)>

veer (vēr) *v* **1** change direction suddenly: *The wind veered to the south.* **2** suddenly change an opinion, subject, or type of behaviour: *Our conversation veered to a different topic.*
n a sudden change in direction: *a veer to the left.* <French *virer*>

veg (vej) *Slang v* **vegged, veg·ging** (*sometimes with* ***out***) be passive and unstimulated, with very little mental or physical activity: *After a day of exams I just wanted to sit and veg for a while at home.* <*vegetate*>

veg·an (vē′gən) *or* (vej′ən) *n* a person who does not eat or use animal products such as milk or meat.

veg·e·ta·ble (vej′ə tə bəl) *or* (vej′tə bəl) *n* **1** a plant or part of a plant used as food, such as a cabbage, potato, tomato, or bean. **2** *Informal* a person with a dull or inactive life.
n **1** to do with vegetables as food: *vegetable soup.* **2** to do with plants or plant life, especially as distinct from animal life or mineral substances: *the vegetable kingdom.* <Old French *vegetable,* from Latin *vegetabilis* growing>

vegetable oil *n* an oil extracted from the seeds or fruit of plants, such as olive oil or canola, that is used in cooking.

veg·e·tar·i·an (vej′ə ter′ē ən) *n* a person who does not eat meat and, sometimes, other animal products such as eggs, milk, or cheese, especially for moral, religious, or health reasons.
adj to do with excluding meat or other animal products from the diet. **veg′e·tar′i·an·ism′** *n.*

veg·e·tate (vej′ə tāt′) *v* **veg·e·tat·ed, veg·e·tat·ing** live or spend a period of time in a dull and inactive way.

veg·e·ta·tion (vej′ə tā′shən) *n* **1** plants considered as a group, especially those found in a particular area or habitat: *There was scant vegetation in the desert.* See MIXED FOREST for picture. **2** the action or process of vegetating.

veg·e·ta·tive (vej′ə tā′tiv) *adj* **1** of, relating to, or consisting of plants or their growth. **2** of, relating to, or found in processes such as plant growth or nutrition rather than sexual reproduction. **3** alive as a person but comatose and without apparent brain activity. **veg′e·ta′tive·ly** *adv.* **veg′e·ta′tive·ness** *n.*

veg·gie (vej′ē) *Informal n* (*usually plural*) a vegetable: *veggies with ranch dip.*

veg·gie·burg·er (vej′ē bər′gər) *n* a patty resembling a hamburger but made with a vegetable protein such as ground soybeans, served in a split bun.

ve·he·ment (vē′ə mənt) *adj* with, showing, or caused by strong feeling: *a vehement denial, vehement patriotism. She was vehement about not wanting to go.* <Latin *vehementem* carried away> **ve′he·mence** *n.* **ve′he·ment·ly** *adv.*

ve·hi·cle (vē′ə kəl) *n* **1** a thing used for transporting people or goods, especially on land, such as a car, truck, or cart. **2** a thing used to express, embody, or fulfill something: *a vehicle of thought.* **3** a substance that assists the use of a drug, pigment, or other material mixed with it. **4** a movie, TV program, or song that is intended to display the leading performer to the best advantage. <Latin *vehiculum,* from *vehere* carry> **ve·hic′u·lar** *adj.*

veil (vāl) *n* **1** a piece of fine material worn by women to protect or conceal the face: *a bridal veil, a nun's veil.* **2** a thing that conceals, disguises, or obscures something: *A veil of clouds hid the sun.*
v **1** cover with or as though with a veil: *She veiled her face.* **2** partially conceal, disguise, or obscure: *Fog veiled the shore. Their plans were veiled in secrecy.* <Latin *velum* covering> **veiled** *adj.*
take the veil, become a nun.

vein (vān) *n* **1** a tube that with others forms part of the blood circulation system of the body, carrying oxygen-depleted blood toward the heart. Compare ARTERY. **2** a slender rib that runs through a leaf or bract, typically dividing or branching. **3** a rib that forms part of the supporting framework of an insect's wing. **4** a crack or seam in rock filled with a mineral or ore and typically lying extensively underground: *a vein of copper.* **5** a streak or stripe of a different colour, such as in wood, marble, or cheese. See VAIN for confusables. <Latin *vena*>
veined *adj.* **vein′less** *adj.* **vein′like′** *adj.* **vein′y** *adj.*

Vel·cro (vel′krō) *Trademark n* a type of fastener for clothes and other items, consisting of two plastic strips or patches, one covered with tiny loops and the other with tiny flexible hooks, which join when pressed together and can be separated by pulling the two pieces apart. <French *vel*(*ours*) velvet + *cro*(*ché*) hooked>

veld or **veldt** (velt) *or* (felt) *n* open, uncultivated country in southern Africa with grass or bushes but few trees. <Afrikaans, from Dutch>

vel·lum (vel′əm) *n* fine parchment, originally made from calfskin, and used especially for writing on or for binding books.
adj of, resembling, or bound in vellum. <Old French, from *veel* calf>

ve·loc·i·pede (və los′ə pēd′) *n* an early kind of bicycle propelled by working pedals on cranks fitted to the front axle.

ve·loc·i·rap·tor (və los′ə rap′tər) *n* a small, swift, carnivorous dinosaur from the late Cretaceous period.

ve·loc·i·ty (və los′ə tē) *n, pl* **ve·loc·i·ties** speed, especially the speed of something in a given direction. <Latin *velocis* swift>

ve·lour or **ve·lours** (və lůr′) *n* a plush fabric resembling velvet, used for soft furnishings and hats. <French *velours* velvet, from Latin *villus* shaggy hair>

vel·vet (vel′vit) *n* **1** a closely woven fabric that has a thick, short PILE[3] that makes it smooth and soft to the touch. **2** the soft, downy skin that covers the growing antlers of a deer.
adj made of, covered with, or like velvet: *a velvet chesterfield, a velvet voice.* <Latin *velvetum,* from *villus* tuft of hair> **vel′vet·y** *adj.*

vel·vet·een (vel′və tēn′) *n* cotton fabric with a soft pile resembling velvet.
adj made of or covered with velveteen.

ve·na ca·va (vē′nə kā′və) *n, pl* **ve·nae ca·vae** (vē′nē kā′vē) a large vein, one of two in humans, that carries deoxygenated blood into the heart.

ve·nal (vē′nəl) *adj* showing or motivated by willingness to accept bribes or yield to corruption: *venal conduct.* See VENIAL for confusable. <Latin *venum* for sale> **ve·nal′i·ty** *n.* **ve′nal·ly** *adv.*

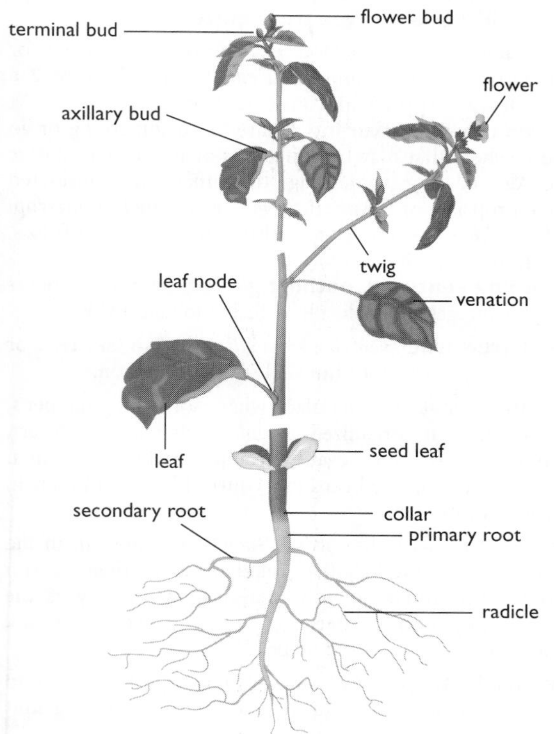

ve·na·tion (vē nā′shən) *n* the arrangement of veins in a leaf or in an insect's wing.

ven·det·ta (ven det′ə) *n* a feud in which the relatives of a person who has been murdered try to take vengeance on the killer or the killer's family. <Italian, from Latin *vindex* avenger>

vend·ing machine (ven′ding) *n* a coin-operated machine from which one may obtain small items, especially food and beverages.

ven·dor or **ven·der** (ven′dər) *n* **1** a person who or company that offers something for sale. **2** a person who sells something, especially property such as a house. <Latin *vendere,* from *venum dare* offer for sale>

SYNONYMS

Vendor is a general word for a person or company that sells goods: *They're the region's best vendor of cars.*

Peddler refers to a person who travels around selling goods: *Peddlers from all over came to the open-air market every Saturday.*

ve·neer (və nēr′) *n* **1** a thin layer of fine wood or other material covering a coarser wood or material: *The desk was pine with a walnut veneer.* **2** an attractive appearance that covers or disguises someone or something's true nature or feelings: *a veneer of honesty.*
v **1** cover something with a decorative layer of fine wood. **2** cover or disguise someone or something's true nature with an attractive appearance. <German *furnieren,* from French *fournir* furnish>

ven·er·a·ble (ven′ə rə bəl) *adj* worthy of much respect, especially because of age, wisdom or character: *a venerable leader, venerable customs.* **ven′er·a·bil′i·ty** *n.* **ven′er·a·bly** *adv.*

ven·er·ate (ven′ə rāt′) *v* **ven·er·at·ed, ven·er·at·ing** regard with great respect: *He venerates his father's memory.* <Latin *venerari,* from *Venus* love> **ven′er·a′tion** *n.*

ve·ne·re·al (və nē′rē əl) *adj* **1** to do with sexual desire or sexual intercourse. **2** to do with diseases transmitted by sexual intercourse. <Latin *venerari,* from *Venus* love> **ve·ne′re·al·ly** *adv.*

venereal disease VD.

Ve·ne·tian blind (və nē′shən) *n* a window blind consisting of horizontal plastic, metal, or wooden slats that can be set at different angles to vary the amount of light that is let in. <Latin *Venetia* Venice>

Ven·e·zue·la (ven′ə zwā′lə) *n* a country in northern S America. See the APPENDIX. **Ven′e·zue′lan** *adj, n.*

venge·ance (ven′jəns) *n* the infliction of punishment on another as revenge for a wrong or injury. <Old French *vengier* take revenge, Latin *vindex* avenger>
with a vengeance, with great force or intensity: *By six o'clock it was raining with a vengeance. That escapade was adventure with a vengeance.*

a bat	e bed	i bid	o pot	u cup	th thin
ā cake	ē me	ī bite	ō go	ū rude	ᴛʜ then
à bar	ə about	ər over	ȯ for	ů put	zh measure

venge·ful (venj′fəl) *adj* seeking to harm someone in return for a perceived wrong or injury. **venge′ful·ly** *adv.* **venge′ful·ness** *n.*

ve·ni·al (vē′nē əl) *adj, adv* pardonable as a fault or offence: *a venial sin.* <Latin *venia* forgiveness> **ve′ni·al′i·ty** *n.* **ve′ni·al·ly** *adv.*

CONFUSABLES

Venial refers to a misdeed that is not very serious: *Her occasional lateness was a venial matter.*

Venal means "corruptible" and refers to serious offences: *The venal politician was removed from office.*

ven·i·son (ven′ə sən) *n* meat from a deer. <Old French, from Latin *venatio* hunting, from *venari* hunt>

Venn diagram (ven) *n* a diagram using circles or closed curves within an enclosing rectangle to show the relationships between groups or sets.

ven·om (ven′əm) *n* **1** a poisonous fluid secreted by animals such as snakes and scorpions and typically injected into prey or aggressors by biting or stinging. See ADDER for picture. **2** extreme malice and bitterness shown in someone's attitudes, speech, or actions: *There was venom in her voice.* <Old French, from Latin *venenum* poison> **ven′om·less** *adj.* **ven′om·ous** *adj.* **ven′om·ous·ly** *adv.* **ven′om·ous·ness** *n.*

ve·nous (vē′nəs) *adj* to do with veins: *venous blood.* **ve′nous·ly** *adv.*

Explosive volcanic eruptions occur when the rising magma gets stuck in the central **vent**. Gases then build to great pressure, forcing a powerful eruption to occur.

Effusive volcanic eruptions create flows of fluid lava that move easily up the vent and spread across the surface of the volcano, cooling into a low-angled slope.

vent[1] (vent) *n* **1** an opening that allows air, gas, or liquid to pass out of or into a confined space. **2** a release or expression of a strong emotion or energy: *His great energy found vent in hard work. She gave vent to her grief in tears.* **3** the end of the intestine, especially in fish. **4** the opening of a volcano, through which lava and dust are emitted.
v **1** express a strong emotion freely: *He vented his anger on the dog.* **2** provide with an outlet for air, gas, or liquid, or discharge or expel air, gas, or liquid through an outlet. <French *vent* wind, from Latin *ventus*>

vent[2] (vent) *n* a slit in a garment, especially in the lower edge of the back of a coat through the seam. <French *fente* slit, from Latin *findere* split>

ven·ti·late (ven′tə lāt′) *v* **ven·ti·lat·ed, ven·ti·lat·ing** **1** cause air to enter and circulate freely in a room or building. **2** purify or freshen something by blowing on or through it, such as through artificial respiration. **3** discuss or examine an opinion, issue, or complaint in public. **ven′ti·la′tion** *n.*

ven·ti·la·tor (ven′tə lā′tər) *n* an apparatus or other means for changing or improving the air in an enclosed space.

ven·tral (ven′trəl) *adj* to do with the underside of an animal or plant: *a ventral fin.* <Latin *venter* belly> **ven′tral·ly** *adv.*

ven·tri·cle (ven′trə kəl) *n* a hollow part or cavity in an organ of the body, especially one of the two main chambers of the heart, left and right. <Latin *ventriculus*, from *venter* belly> **ven·tric′u·lar** (ven trik′yə lər) *adj.*

ven·tril·o·quist (ven tril′ə kwist) *n* a person who can speak or utter sounds so that they seem to come from somewhere else, especially an entertainer who makes the voice appear to come from a dummy of a person or animal. <Latin *venter* belly + *loqui* speak> **ven·tril′o·quism** *n.* **ven·tril′o·quize** *v.*

ven·ture (ven′chər) *n* **1** a risky or daring journey or undertaking: *Her courage was equal to any venture.* **2** a business enterprise with considerable risk.
v **ven·tured, ven·tur·ing** **1** dare to do something or go somewhere that may be dangerous or unpleasant. **2** dare to do or say something that may be considered inappropriate or unsuitable: *No one ventured to interrupt the teacher.* **3** expose something to the risk of loss. <Middle English *adventure*>
nothing ventured, nothing gained, potential benefits or advantages will be lost by refusing to take a risk.

ven·ture·some (ven′chər səm) *adj* willing to take risks or embark on difficult or unusual courses of action.

ven·ue (ven′yū) *n* **1** the place where something happens, especially an organized event such as a concert, conference, or sports event. **2** the place where a criminal or civil case may be heard in a court of law. <Old French, from Latin *venire*>

Ve·nus (vē′nəs) *n* the second planet from the sun in the solar system, the brightest celestial object after the sun and moon and frequently appearing in the sky as the evening or morning star. See EARTH for picture. <*Venus*, Roman goddess of love and beauty>

Ve·nus–fly·trap (vē′nəs flī′trap′) *n* a bog plant native to the southeastern US, with hinged leaves that spring shut on and digest insects that land on them.

ve·ra·cious (və rā′shəs) *adj* speaking or representing the truth. <Latin *verus* true> **ve·ra′cious·ly** *adv.* **ve·ra′cious·ness** *n.*

ve·rac·i·ty (və ras′ə tē) *n, pl* **ve·rac·i·ties** **1** accuracy or conformity to the facts: *They checked the veracity of his statement.* **2** truthfulness as a habit: *Her veracity was not questioned.*

ve·ran·da (və ran′də) *n* a roofed porch along one or more sides of a house and level with the ground floor. <Hindi, from Portuguese *varanda* railing>

verb (vərb) *Grammar n* a part of speech that expresses the tense (past, present, future), voice (active or passive) and duration (complete or progressive) of an action, state, or occurrence. The verb is the main part of the PREDICATE of a sentence. <Latin *verbum* word>

GRAMMAR AND USAGE

A **verb** indicates a state of being (*I* ***am*** *the one*) or an action (*I* ***threw*** *the ball*).

The verb is in the active voice when the subject of the sentence does the action: *She* ***gave*** *a speech.*

The verb is in the passive voice when the subject receives the action: *The speech* ***was given*** *by her.*

The passive voice can result in wordy, weak sentences. Say *The group* ***played*** *three songs,* not *Three songs* ***were played*** *by the group.*

When using **have** to form the past perfect tense of an irregular verb, make sure to choose the correct form of the past participle. Say *I have* ***run*** *five kilometres,* not *I have* ***ran*** *five kilometres.*

ver·bal (vər′bəl) *adj* **1** in or of words: *a verbal picture.* **2** expressed in spoken words: *a verbal promise, a verbal message.* **3** to do with a verb: *a verbal noun.*
n a word or words functioning as a verb. Participles, gerunds, or infinitives are verbs. **ver′bal·ly** *adv.*

ver·bal·ize (vər′bə līz′) *v* **ver·bal·ized, ver·bal·iz·ing** **1** express ideas or feelings in words, especially by speaking out loud. **2** speak, especially at undue length and with little real content. **ver′bal·iz·a′tion** *n.*

ver·ba·tim (vər bā′tim) *adv, adj* in exactly the same words as were used originally: *Her speech was printed verbatim in the newspaper.*

ver·be·na (vər bē′nə) *n* a plant with bright flowers growing in clusters or spikes. <Latin = leafy branch>

ver·bi·age (vər′bē ij) *n* speech or writing that uses too many words.

ver·bose (vər bōs′) *adj* containing or using too many words. **ver·bose′ly** *adv.* **ver·bose′ness** *n.*
ver·bos′i·ty (vər bos′ə tē) *n.*

ver·bo·ten (vər bō′tən) *adj* forbidden. <German>

ver·dant (vər′dənt) *adj* **1** green with grass or other rich vegetation: *a verdant meadow.* **2** of the bright green colour of lush grass. <Old French, from Latin *viridis* green>
ver′dan·cy *n.* **ver′dant·ly** *adv.*

ver·dict (vər′dikt) *n* **1** a decision made on an issue of fact in a civil or criminal case or an inquest: *The jury returned a verdict of not guilty.* **2** a decision, opinion, or judgment: *the public's verdict, the verdict of history.* <Old French *verdit,* from *ver* true + *dire* speak>

ver·di·gris (vər′də grēs′) *or* (vər′də gris) *n* a green mineral coating that forms on brass or copper, or bronze when exposed to the air for long periods of time. <Old French *vert de grece* = green of Greece>

ver·dure (vər′jər) *n* lush, green vegetation.

verge[1] (vərj) *n* **1** an extreme limit beyond which something begins or happens: *Their business is on the verge of ruin.* **2** an edge or border: *They approached the verge of the lake.* <Old French, from Latin *virga* rod of office. The sense is from the idea of inside a verge, i.e., subject to authority as symbolized by the rod of office.>

verge[2] (vərj) *v* **verged, verg·ing** incline in a certain direction or toward a particular condition: *My cat is plump, verging on fatness.* <Latin *vergere* turn (toward)>

ver·i·est (ver′ē ist) *Archaic adj* utmost: *the veriest nonsense.*

ver·i·fy (ver′ə fī′) *v* **ver·i·fied, ver·i·fy·ing** make sure or demonstrate that something is true, accurate, or justified: *The driver's report of the accident was verified by eyewitnesses. She verified the spelling by looking in the dictionary.* <Latin *verificare,* from Latin *verus* true + *facere* make> **ver′i·fi′a·ble** *adj.* **ver′i·fi′a·bly** *adv.*
ver′i·fi′ca′tion (ver′ə fə kā′shən) *n.* **ver′i·fi′er** *n.*

ver·i·ly (ver′ə lē) *Archaic adv* truly or certainly: *Verily, he had not been honest with us.* <*very* + *-ly*[1]>

ver·i·si·mil·i·tude (ver′ə sə mil′ə tyūd′) *or* (ver′ə sə mil′ə tūd′) *n* the appearance of being true or real: *The story had much verisimilitude.* <Latin *verus* true + *similis* like>

ver·i·ta·ble (ver′ə tə bəl) *adj* true, real, or actual: *a veritable flood of letters.* **ver′i·ta·bly** *adv.*

ver·i·ty (ver′ə tē) *n, pl* **ver·i·ties** a true or fundamental principle or belief: *the eternal verities.* <Latin *veritas,* from *verus* true>

ver·meil (vər′məl) *n* silver or bronze coated with gilt. <Old French, from Latin *vermiculus* insect. The colour crimson was obtained from the cochineal insect.>

ver·mi·cel·li (vər′mə sel′ē) *n* pasta in the shape of long slender threads. <Italian = little worms, from Latin *vermis* worm>

ver·mic·u·lite (vər mik′yə līt′) *n* a product of mica and other minerals that consists of small, lightweight granules or flakes that readily absorb water and is used as a medium for plants to retain moisture. <See VERMEIL.>

ver·mil·ion (vər mil′yən) *n* a brilliant red pigment made from mercury sulphide.
adj brilliant red. <See VERMEIL.>

ver·min (vər′mən) *n* **1** (*usually with plural verb*) animals, insects, birds, and parasites that harm or are believed to harm, food supplies, crops, farm animals, or game, or that carry diseases. **2** a person or people thought to be worthy of contempt and who cause problems for the rest of society. <Old French, from Latin *vermis* worm>
ver′min·ous *adj.*

a **bat**	e **bed**	i **bid**	o **pot**	u **cup**	th **thin**
ā **cake**	ē **me**	ī **bite**	ō **go**	ū **rude**	ᴛʜ **then**
à **bar**	ə **about**	ər **over**	ȯ **for**	ů **put**	zh **measure**

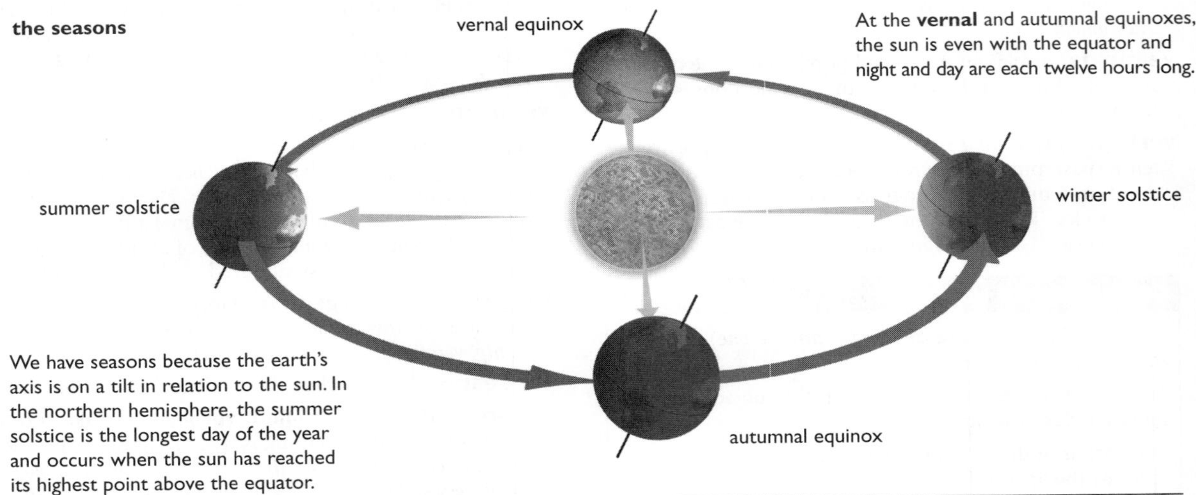

the seasons
vernal equinox
At the **vernal** and autumnal equinoxes, the sun is even with the equator and night and day are each twelve hours long.
summer solstice
winter solstice
We have seasons because the earth's axis is on a tilt in relation to the sun. In the northern hemisphere, the summer solstice is the longest day of the year and occurs when the sun has reached its highest point above the equator.
autumnal equinox

ver·mouth (vər mūth′) *n* a wine flavoured with herbs, often taken before meals or mixed with gin, vodka, etc. <French, from German *Wermut* wormwood, a bitter tasting plant used in making absinthe>

ver·nac·u·lar (vər nak′yə lər) *n* **1** usually, **the vernacular** the language or dialect spoken by the ordinary people in a particular country or region. **2** the terms used by people belonging to a specified group or engaging in a specialized activity: *the vernacular of lawyers.*
adj to do with one's native language, not learned or imposed as a second language. <Latin *vernaculus* belonging to a household slave, from *verna* household slave>

ver·nal (vər′nəl) *adj* to do with spring: *vernal flowers, vernal freshness.* <Latin *vernalis,* from *ver* spring> **ver′nal·ly** *adv.*

ver·sa·tile (vər′sə tīl′) *or* (vər′sə təl) *adj* able to adapt or be adapted to many different functions or activities: *He's very versatile: he is an actor, a poet, a singer, and a language teacher. A hammer is not a versatile tool.* <Latin *versatilis* turning, from *vertere* turn> **ver′sa·tile′ly** *adv.* **ver′sa·til′i·ty** (vər′sə til′ə tē) *n.*

verse (vərs) *n* **1** writing in the form of lines of words, usually with a regularly repeated stress pattern and often with rhymes at the ends of the lines. **2** a group of such lines forming a unit in a poem or song: *The ballad had ten verses.* **3** a short numbered division of a chapter in the Bible or other scripture. <Old English *vers,* from Latin *versus* line of writing>

versed (vərst) *adj* experienced or skilled in: *The doctor was well-versed in medical theory.*

ver·si·fy (vər′sə fī′) *v* **ver·si·fied, ver·si·fy·ing** turn into or express in verse. **ver′si·fi·ca′tion** *n.* **ver′si·fi′er** *n.*

ver·sion (vər′zhən) *n* **1** a particular form of something differing in some respects from an earlier form or other forms of the same type of thing: *He said that the calculator is a modern version of the abacus.* **2** an account of a matter from a particular person's point of view: *Each of the three boys gave his own version of the quarrel.* **3** a particular edition or translation of a book or other work: *She preferred the English version to the original.* <Latin *versio* a turning, i.e., a translation>

ver·so (ver′sō) *n* **1** a left-hand page of an open book, or the back of a loose document. Compare RECTO. **2** the reverse side of a thing, such as a medal or coin. <Latin *vertere* turn + *folium* a leaf>

ver·sus (vər′səs) *prep* **1** against: *It was our team versus a much older one.* **2** opposed to or in contrast to: *the new versus the old, strength versus agility. Abbrev* **vs, v** <Latin *versus* turned toward, from *vertere* turn>

ver·te·bra (vər′tə brə) *n, pl* **ver·te·bras** or **ver·te·brae** (-brā′) *or* (-brē′) one of a series of small bones forming the BACKBONE. <Latin = articulated joint of the body, from *vertere* turn> **ver′te·bral** *adj.*

ver·te·brate (vər′te brit) *or* (vər′tə brāt) *n* an animal of a large group whose members have backbones or spinal columns, including mammals, birds, reptiles, amphibians, and fish.
adj to do with vertebrates.

ver·tex (vər′teks′) *n, pl* **ver·tex·es** or **ver·ti·ces** (vər′tə sēz′) **1** the highest point or summit. **2** each angular point of a polygon. **3** a meeting point of two lines that form an angle. <Latin *vertex* highest point, from *vertere* turn>

ver·ti·cal (vər′tə kəl) *adj* **1** at right angles to a horizontal plane, aligned so that the top is directly above the bottom: *a vertical position.* **2** involving different levels of a hierarchy or progression, such as involving all the stages from the production to the sale of a class of goods.
n **1** a vertical line or plane. **2** an upright structure. <See VERTEX.> **ver′ti·cal′i·ty** *n.* **ver′ti·cal·ly** *adv.* **ver′ti·cal·ness** *n.*

vertical file *n* a file, especially in a library, that includes various kinds of information, organized by subject. A vertical file may include photographs, articles, drawings, and audio and video recordings.

ver·ti·go (vər′tə gō′) *n, pl* **ver·ti·goes** or **ver·ti·gos** a sensation of dizziness or loss of balance, associated especially with looking down from a tall height, or caused by a disease affecting the inner ear. <Latin, from *vertere* turn> **ver·tig′i·nous** (vər tij′ə nəs) *adj.* **ver·tig′i·nous·ly** *adv.*

verve (vərv) *n* liveliness and enthusiasm: *She sang with a lot of verve.* <French>

ver·y (ver′ē) *adv* **1** greatly or extremely: *The sunshine is very hot in July.* **2** absolutely or exactly: *She stood in the very same place for an hour.*
adj **1** actual or precise in the identity of a person or thing: *The very people who used to love her hate her now. He was caught in the very act of stealing.* **2** at an extreme point in time or space: *She read to the very end of the book.* **3** with no addition or contribution from anything else: *The very thought of eating disgusted him.* <Old French *verai*, from Latin *verus* true>

SYNONYMS

Very is a general word used for emphasis: *The article provides a very clear account of what happened.*

Absolutely means "completely": *The clear skies and full moon made for an absolutely beautiful night.*

Decidedly means "unquestionably" and is often used in more formal situations: *The judges said that the winner was decidedly better than the other entries.*

Remarkably can mean "impressively": *Although the couple had little practice, they performed the dance routine remarkably well.*

ves·i·cle (ves′ə kəl) *n* **1** a small cavity or sac containing fluid or air, especially one within or on the body, such as a small blister full of clear fluid. **2** an air-filled swelling in a plant, especially a seaweed. **3** a small cavity in volcanic rock, produced by gas bubbles. <Latin *vesica* blister> **ve·sic′u·lar** (və sik′yə lər) *adj.*

ves·sel (ves′əl) *n* **1** a ship or large boat. **2** a hollow container, especially one used to hold liquid, such as a bowl or cask. **3** *Biology* **a** a duct or canal holding or conveying blood or other fluid in the body. **b** a tube in the vascular system of a plant that conducts water and mineral nutrients from the root. <Old French, from Latin *vas* vessel>

vest (vest) *n* **1** a short, sleeveless garment worn over a shirt, especially under a suit coat. **2** *UK* an undershirt.
v **1** confer or bestow power, authority, rights, or property on someone or something: *The management of the hospital was vested in a board of trustees.* **2** put on vestments: *The vested priest stood before the altar.* <Old French, from Latin *vestis* garment>

ves·tal virgin (ves′təl) *n* a virgin in ancient Rome consecrated to the service of the goddess Vesta, especially in mainaining the sacred fire burning in the goddess's altar.

vest·ed interest (ves′tid) *n* a personal stake or involvement in an undertaking or enterprise, especially one that entails financial gain: *The company had a vested interest in the law's not being changed.*

ves·ti·bule (ves′tə byūl′) *n* **1** a passage or hall between the outer door and the interior of a building. **2** the enclosed space at the entrance of a railway passenger car. **3** a chamber or channel communicating with or opening into another, such as the central cavity of the labyrinth of the inner ear. <Latin *vestibulum*>

ves·tige (ves′tij) *n* a trace of something that is disappearing or no longer exists: *The last vestige of the sandcastle was washed away by the tide.* <Latin *vestigium* trace>

ves·tig·i·al (ves tij′ē əl) *adj* forming a very small remnant of something that was once much larger or more noticeable, such as an organ or part of the body that became functionless over a long period of time.

vest·ment (vest′mənt) *n* an outer garment or robe, especially for ceremonial or official wear.

ves·try (ves′trē) *n, pl* **ves·tries** a room or building attached to a Christian church, used as an office and for changing into ceremonial vestments.

vet[1] (vet) *Informal n* a veterinarian.
v **vet·ted, vet·ting** make a careful and critical examination of something or someone: *to vet a report, to vet a candidate.*

vet[2] (vet) *Informal n* a veteran.

vetch (vech) *n* a trailing or climbing plant of the pea family, sometimes cultivated for silage or fodder. <Old French, from Latin *vicia*>

vet·er·an (vet′ə rən) *n* a person who has had long experience in a particular area, especially in the armed forces and during wartime.
adj to do with such a person or the person's long experience. <Latin *veteris* old>

vet·er·i·nar·i·an (vet′ə rə ner′ē ən) *n* a person qualified to treat diseases and injuries of animals and whose work it is.

vet·er·i·nar·y (vet′ə rə ner′ē) *adj* to do with the diseases, injuries, and treatment of animals. <Latin *veterinus* having to do with draft animals>

ve·to (vē′tō) *n, pl* **ve·toes** **1** the right or power to reject a decision or proposal, especially the right of a person in authority or a law-making body. **2** such a rejection.
adj to do with a veto: *veto power.*
v **ve·toed, ve·to·ing** **1** reject by a veto. **2** refuse to accept or allow: *His parents vetoed his plan to buy a motorcycle.* <Latin = I forbid> **ve′to·er** *n.*

vex (veks) *v* make someone feel annoyed, frustrated, or worried, especially concerning small matters: *She was vexed to wait past the time of her appointment.* <Latin *vexare*> **vex′ing** *adj.* **vex′ing·ly** *adv.*

a bat	e bed	i bid	o pot	u cup	th **thin**
ā cake	ē me	ī bite	ō go	ū rude	TH **then**
ȧ bar	ə about	ər over	ȯ for	u̇ put	zh measure

vex·a·tion (vek sā′shən) *n* **1** the quality or condition of being annoyed, frustrated, or worried: *His vexation at the delay was obvious.* **2** a thing that causes such an emotion. *Rain on Saturday was a vexation to the children.*

vex·a·tious (vek sā′shəs) *adj* causing or tending to cause annoyance, frustration, or worry. **vex·a′tious·ly** *adv.*

VHF *n* in full, **very high frequency** the band of radio frequencies between 30 and 300 megahertz.

VHS *Trademark n* in full, **video home system**, an electronic audio and video recording system.

vi·a (vī′ə) *or* (vē′ə) *prep* **1** travelling through a place en route to a destination: *They travelled to the big city via several small towns.* **2** by way of, through, or by means of: *Send the package via airmail.* <Latin by way of>

vi·a·ble (vī′ə bəl) *adj* **1** capable of working successfully: *a viable economy.* **2** capable as a plant, animal, or cell to survive and live successfully, especially under particular environmental conditions. <Latin *vita*>

While a bridge built over a wide valley is called a **viaduct**, one that crosses highways and railways is usually referred to as an overpass. A low bridge that spans a shallow lake or swamp is called a causeway.

vi·a·duct (vī′ə dukt′) *n* a bridgelike structure, carrying a road or railway across a valley or other low ground. <Latin *via* road + *-duct* to bring, as in *aqueduct*>

vi·al (vī′əl) *n* a small container, especially one made of glass, used especially for holding medicines or perfumes. <*phial*>

vibes (vībz) *Informal pln* **1** a vibraphone: *She plays the vibes.* **2** a person's emotional state or the atmosphere of a place as communicated to and felt by others: *He left the party early because he said the vibes were bad.*

vi·brant (vī′brənt) *adj* **1** full of energy and enthusiasm: *a vibrant personality.* **2** of a colour, bright and striking: *vibrant blue.* **3** of a voice, strong and resonant. **vi′bran·cy** *n.* **vi′brant·ly** *adv.*

vi·bra·phone (vī′brə fōn′) *n* a musical percussion instrument with motor-driven resonators and metal tubes that produce a vibrato effect.

vi·brate (vī′brāt) *v* **vi·brat·ed, vi·brat·ing** **1** move or cause to move continuously and rapidly to and fro. **2** quiver with a quality or emotion: *Their hearts vibrated to the appeal.* **3** resonate and continue to be heard: *The clanging vibrated in his ears.* **4** swing to and fro as a pendulum. <Latin *vibrare* shake> **vi·bra′tion** *n.* **vi·bra′tion·al** *adj.*

vi·bra·to (vē brå′tō) *n, pl* **vi·bra·tos** a rapid, slight variation in pitch in singing or playing some musical instruments, producing a stronger or richer tone.

vi·bra·tor (vī′brā tər) *n* a device that vibrates or causes vibration, such as an electrical device used in massage.

vi·bra·to·ry (vī′brə tò′rē) *adj* to do with vibration.

vi·bur·num (vī bər′nəm) *n* a shrub or small tree of the honeysuckle family that has clusters of small flowers.

vic·ar (vik′ər) *n* **1** a member of the clergy in the Anglican church who carries out duties in a parish but is not officially the rector. **2** a deputy or representative of a bishop in the Catholic church. <Latin *vicarius* substitute, from *vicis* exchange>

vic·ar·age (vik′ə rij) *n* the residence of a vicar.

vi·car·i·ous (vī ker′ē əs) *or* (vi ker′ē əs) *adj* **1** experienced in the imagination through the feelings or actions of another person: *She obtains a vicarious delight in foreign countries from reading travel books.* **2** acting or done for another: *a vicarious sacrifice.* **vi·car′i·ous·ly** *adv.* **vi·car′i·ous·ness** *n.*

vice[1] (vīs) *n* **1** immoral behaviour, especially criminal activities including prostitution, pornography, or drugs. **2** an immoral personal characteristic, or a weakness of character or behaviour: *Gluttony was one of his vices.* <Old French, from Latin *vitium*>

vice[2] *Informal n* a vice-president.

vice– *combining form* next in rank to, and able to be a deputy for: *vice-president, vice-admiral.*

vice–chan·cel·lor (vīs′chan′sə lər) *n* a deputy chancellor who substitutes for the regular chancellor or acts as his or her assistant.

vice–con·sul (vīs′kon′səl) *n* a person next in rank below a consul.

vice–pres·i·dent (vīs′prez′ə dənt) *n* the officer next in rank to the president, who takes the president's place when necessary. **vice′-pres′i·den·cy** *n.* **vice′-pres·i·den′tial** *adj.*

vice–prin·ci·pal (vīs′prin′sə pəl) *n* in a school, college, or university, an assistant to the principal. **vice′-prin′ci·pal·ship** *n.*

vice·re·gal (vīs′rē′gəl) *adj* to do with a viceroy.

vice·reine (vīs′rān′) *n* **1** a female governing a province or colony as the representative of the sovereign. **2** the spouse of a viceroy.

vice·roy (vīs′roi) *n* a person governing a province or colony as the representative of the sovereign. <Old French *vice* deputy + *roi* king, from Latin *rex*>

vice squad *n* a department or division of a police force, concerned especially with the enforcement of prostitution, drug, and gambling laws.

vi·ce ver·sa (vī′sə vər′sə) *adv* with the main items in the preceding statement the other way round: *He blamed her, and vice versa.*

vi·chys·soise (vish′ē swoz′) *or* (vē′shē swoz′) *n* a cold cream soup made mainly of potatoes and leeks, often sprinkled with chopped chives. <French *Vichy*, city in France, where it originated>

vi·cin·i·ty (və sin′ə tē) *n, pl* **vi·cin·i·ties** the area near or surrounding a particular place: *She knew many people in the city and vicinity.* <Latin *vicinus* neighbouring, from *vicus* village>

vi·cious (vish′əs) *adj* **1** deliberately cruel or violent: *a vicious assault.* **2** of an animal, wild and dangerous to people: *a vicious dog.* **3** serious or dangerous: *a vicious brawl.* **4** spiteful or malicious: *a vicious rumour.* **5** unpleasantly severe: *a vicious headache.* **vi′cious·ly** *adv.* **vi′cious·ness** *n.*

vicious circle *n* two or more undesirable events, each of which keeps causing the other: *It's a vicious circle: the more you scratch a mosquito bite, the more it itches.*

vi·cis·si·tude (və sis′ə tyūd′) *or* (və sis′ə tūd′) *n* a change in circumstances or fortune, typically one that is unwelcome or unpleasant: *The vicissitudes of life may suddenly make a rich man poor or a poor man rich.* <Latin *vicis* change>

vic·tim (vik′təm) *n* **1** a person or animal injured or destroyed as a result of a crime, accident, or other event: *victims of war. She has been the victim of harsh in the press.* **2** a person tricked by another: *He was the victim of a swindler.* **3** a person or animal sacrificed as part of a religious rite. <Latin *victima*>

SYNONYMS

Victim is a general word for a person or animal that has been mistreated, injured, or killed: *The wolf was a victim of hunters who ignored the rules.*

Casualty refers to someone injured or killed in an accident or war: *Were there many casualties in the battle?*

Fatality refers to someone killed in an accident, war, or disaster: *The flood caused many fatalities.*

vic·tim·ize (vik′tə mīz′) *v* **vic·tim·ized, vic·tim·iz·ing** single someone out for cruel or unjust treatment. **vic′tim·i·za′tion** *n.* **vic′tim·iz′er** *n.*

vic·tor (vik′tər) *n* a person who defeats an enemy or opponent in a battle, game, or other competition. <Latin *vincere* to conquer>

SYNONYMS

Victor emphasizes a triumph over another person, team, or force: *Our team was the victor in the hard-fought soccer game.*

Champion is usually a sports term: *She was a martial arts champion.*

Conqueror is used for someone who triumphs in war: *The conqueror took control of the defeated nation.*

Vic·to·ri·a Cross (vik tor′ē ə) *or* (vik tōr′ē ə) *n* a medal awarded to members of the armed forces in the Commonwealth of Nations for remarkable valour in the presence of the enemy.

Victoria Day *n* a national holiday in Canada falling on the Monday before or on the 24th of May, the birthday of Queen Victoria.

Vic·to·ri·an (vik tȯ′rē ən) *adj* **1** to do with the reign of Queen Victoria: *Victorian furniture, Victorian drama.* **2** to do with the attitudes and values of this period considered to be typical, such as prudishness and moral earnestness.
n a person who lived during the reign of this queen.

vic·to·ry (vik′tə rē) *n, pl* **vic·to·ries** the act of defeating an enemy or opponent in a battle, game, or other competition. **vic·to′ri·ous** (vik tȯ′rē əs) *adj.* **vic·to′ri·ous·ly** *adv.*

vic·tual (vit′əl) *n* **victuals** *pl* food, especially when prepared for use.
v **vict·ualled** or **vict·ualed, vict·ual·ling** or **vict·ual·ing** provide with food or provisions: *The captain victualled his ship for the voyage.* <Latin *victus* food, from *vivere* live>

vi·cu·ña (vi kū′nyə) *or* (vi kyū′nə) *n* a wild mammal of mountainous S America related to the llama, valued for its soft, fine wool, or cloth made from this wool.

vid·e·o (vid′ē ō′) *n* **1** a system of recording, reproducing, or broadcasting moving images on or from videotape. **2** a film or other piece of material recorded on videotape. **3** a videocassette. **4** a short film made to accompany a pop song when broadcast on TV.
adj of or used in a system of recording, reproducing, or broadcasting moving images on or from videotape. <Latin = I see>

video camera *n* a camera for recording images on videotape or for transmitting them to the screen of a monitor.

vid·e·o·cas·sette (vid′ē ō kə set′) *or* (vid′ē ō ka set′) *n* a videotape mounted in a cassette, for recording and playing back video programs.

videocassette recorder VCR.

vid·e·o·con·fer·ence (vid′ē ō kon′fər əns) *or* (vid′ē ō kon′frəns) *n* an arrangement in which electronic links are used to enable a group of people in several different locations to talk to each other in sound and vision.
v **vid·e·o·con·fer·enced, vid·e·o·con·fer·enc·ing** hold such a conference.

vid·e·o·disc (vid′ē ō disk′) a CD-ROM or other disc used to store video images.

video game *n* an electronic game in which the player manipulates the action on a screen display.

video jockey VEEJAY.

video lottery terminal VLT.

vid·e·o·phone (vid′ē ō fōn′) *n* a telephone equipped to transmit and receive a visual image as well as sound.
v **vid·e·o·phoned, vid·e·o·phon·ing** call or speak to on a videophone.

video recorder *n* a videocassette recorder.

vid·e·o·tape (vid′ē ō tāp′) *n* **1** a magnetic tape for recording and reproducing visual images and sound. **2** a videocassette.
v **vid·e·o·taped, vid·e·o·tap·ing** record on videotape.

vie (vī) *v* **vied, vy·ing** compete eagerly with someone in order to do or achieve something: *They vied with each other to be first in line.* <French *envier* challenge, from Latin *invitare* invite>

a bat	e bed	i bid	o pot	u cup	th thin
ā cake	ē me	ī bite	ō go	ū rude	ᴛʜ then
à bar	ə about	ər over	ȯ for	u̇ put	zh measure

Vi·et·nam (vē′ət näm′) *n* a country in southeast Asia. See the APPENDIX. **Vi·et′nam·ese′** (vē′ət nəm ēz′) *adj, n.*

view (vyū) *n* **1** the ability to see something or to be seen from a particular place: *A ship came into view.* **2** a sight, typically of attractive scenery, that can be seen from a particular place: *The view from our house was beautiful.* **3** the visual appearance or an image of something when looked at in a particular way: *an aerial view.* **4** an inspection of things for sale by prospective buyers, especially works of art at an exhibition. **5** a particular way of considering or regarding something: *He had strong views about what he liked in novels.*
v **1** look at or inspect something: *They viewed the scene with pleasure.* **2** regard in a particular way or with a particular attitude: *The neighbours viewed the new housing development with suspicion.* <Old French *veoir* see, from Latin *videre*> **view′a·ble** *adj.*
in view, a in sight: *As the noise grew louder, the airplane came in view.* **b** as one's aim or objective: *She works hard and has a definite aim in view.*
in view of, because of or as a result of.
on view, being shown or exhibited to the public, especially as a work of art: *The show is on view from 9 a.m. to 5 p.m.*
with a view to, a with the hope, aim, or intention of: *She worked hard with a view to earning money for her education.*

SYNONYMS

View refers to something seen from a certain point or position: *The view from the top of the building is breathtaking.*

Vista means "pleasing view," especially one seen through a long, narrow opening: *I love the vista of the park at the end of the downtown street.*

Scene refers to any place where something happens: *The fire trucks rushed to the scene of the fire.*

view·er (vyū′ər) *n* **1** a person who looks at or inspects something: *a TV viewer.* **2** a device for viewing, especially a small instrument for viewing photographic transparencies.

view·find·er (vyū′fin′dər) *n* a device on a camera that shows the field of view of the lens, used in framing and focusing the picture.

view·ing (vyū′ing) *n* **1** the action of inspecting or looking at something. **2** the action of watching something on TV. **3** an opportunity to see something, especially a work of art.

view·point (vyū′point′) *n* **1** a mental position or personal perspective from which a person considers something; a point of view: *From my viewpoint, he was behaving badly, but he didn't think so.* **2** a place or position from which a person can look at something: *There's a great viewpoint at the top of the hill.*

vig·il (vij′əl) *n* **1** a period of keeping awake during the time usually spent asleep, especially to keep watch or to pray: *All night the mother kept vigil over the sick child.* **2** the day and night before a Christian festival or holy day as an occasion for religious devotion. <Latin = watchful>

vig·i·lant (vij′ə lənt) *adj* keeping careful watch for possible danger or difficulties: *The watchdog was vigilant.* **vig′i·lance** *n.* **vig′i·lant·ly** *adv.*

vig·i·lan·te (vij′ə lan′tē) *n* a member of a self-appointed group of citizens who undertake law enforcement in their community without legal authority, especially because the police are thought to be ineffective. **vig′i·lant′ism** *n.*

vi·gnette (vi nyet′) *n* **1** a brief description, account, or episode in a book, movie, or TV program. **2** a small illustration or portrait photograph that fades into its background without a definite border. **3** a small ornamental design filling a space in a book or carving. **4** an engraving, drawing, photograph, or the like, that shades off gradually at the edge.
v portray someone in the style of a vignette. <French *vigne* vine, because vine motifs were often used to embellish a text>

vig·or·ous (vig′ə rəs) *adj* **1** strong, healthy, and full of energy: *The old man is still vigorous and lively.* **2** requiring or carried out with vigour: *vigorous exercises.* **vig′or·ous·ly** *adv.* **vig′or·ous·ness** *n.*

vig·our or **vig·or** (vig′ər) *n* **1** physical strength and energy: *We worked with a lot of vigour.* **2** effort, energy, and enthusiasm. <Old French, from Latin *vigere* thrive>

The longship was an ocean-going vessel developed by the **Vikings** in Scandinavia. Oars and sails were both used to move it through the water. The smallest ships, called *snekkja*, had about 30 oars and were about 24 m long and 5 m wide. Larger longships had 64 oars or more.

Vi·king or **vi·king** (vī′king) *n* a Scandinavian seafaring pirate or trader who, with others, raided and settled in many parts of northwest Europe in the 800s and 900s CE. <Old Norse *vikingr*>

vile (vīl) *adj* **vil·er, vil·est** **1** extremely unpleasant: *The drink had a vile taste.* **2** morally bad: *He proved himself to be a vile man.* <Latin *vilis* cheap> **vile′ly** *adv.* **vile′ness** *n.*

vil·i·fy (vil′ə fī′) *v* **vil·i·fied, vil·i·fy·ing** speak or write about in an abusive and critical manner: *The politician was vilified during the TV panel.* <Latin *vilis* vile + *facere* make> **vil′i·fi·ca′tion** (vil′ə fə kā′shən) *n.* **vil′i·fi′er** *n.*

vil·la (vil′ə) *n* a house in the country or suburbs, especially a large and luxurious one. <Italian, from Latin>

vil·lage (vil′ij) *n* **1** a group of houses and other buildings, larger than a hamlet and smaller than a town, located in a rural area, or the people who live in it. **2** a self-contained district or community within a town or city, regarded as having features characteristic of village life. <Old French *village*, from Latin *villa* country house> **vil′lag·er** *n.*

vil·lain (vil′ən) *n* **1** a person guilty or capable of a crime or serious wrongdoing: *The villain stole the money and cast the blame on his friend.* **2** a character in a movie, play, or novel whose evil motives or actions form an important element in the plot. **3** a person or thing blamed for a particular problem: *City health experts studying the epidemic decided the chief villain was overcrowding.* <Latin *villanus* farmhand, from *villa* country house. The meaning of this word changed from farmhand to peasant, then to churl, boor, clown, miser, knave, and scoundrel.> **vil′lain·ous** *adj.* **vil′lain·ous·ly** *adv.* **vil′lain·y** *n.*

–ville *combining form* **1** (*in place names*) town or city: *Oakville.* **2** *Informal* full of or characterized by: *thrillsville, dullsville.*

vim (vim) *Informal n* energy and enthusiasm: *She was full of vim after a good night's sleep.* <Latin *vis* energy>

vin·ai·grette (vin′i gret′) *n* a salad dressing made of seasoned oil and vinegar.
adj (*after the noun*) prepared or served with such a dressing: *artichokes vinaigrette.* <French *vinaigre* vinegar>

vin·di·cate (vin′də kāt′) *v* **vin·di·cat·ed, vin·di·cat·ing** **1** clear someone of blame or suspicion: *The verdict of "Not guilty" vindicated her.* **2** show or prove to be correct, reasonable, or justified: *Their faith in him has been vindicated.* <Latin *vindicis* defender> **vin′di·ca′tion** *n.* **vin′di·ca′tor** *n.*

vin·dic·tive (vin dik′tiv) *adj* with or showing a strong or unreasoning desire for revenge: *He specialized in vindictive criticism. She wrote a vindictive column in the local paper.* <Latin *vindicta* revenge> **vin·dic′tive·ly** *adv.* **vin·dic′tive·ness** *n.*

vine (vīn) *n* **1** a plant with a long, slender stem that creeps along the ground or climbs on a support by twining or by putting out tendrils. **2** a grapevine. <Latin *vinum* wine>

vin·e·gar (vin′ə gər) *n* a sour-tasting liquid containing acetic acid, obtained by fermenting diluted alcoholic liquids such as wine or cider, and used in pickling and in making salad dressings. **vin′e·gar·ish** *adj.* **vin′e·gar·y** *adj.*

ETYMOLOGY

Vinegar comes through Old French *vyn* (wine) and egre (sour) from Latin *vinum* and *acer*. Like wine, many types of vinegar are made from grapes.

vine·yard (vin′yərd) *n* a place planted with grapevines, typically producing grapes used in winemaking.

vin·i·cul·ture (vin′i kul′chər) *or* (vī′ni kul′chər) *n* the cultivation of grapes for winemaking, or the art or science of making wines. **vin′i·cul′tur·al** *adj.* **vin′i·cul′tur·ist** *n.*

Vin·land (vin′lənd) *n* a coastal area of northeast N America that was visited in the 1000s by Norsemen led by Leif Ericsson. <Old Norse *wineland*, because of the wild berries and grapes found there>

vi·no (vē′nō) *Informal n* inexpensive red wine, especially Italian. <Italian>

vin·ous (vīn′əs) *adj* to do with wine.

vin·tage (vin′tij) *n* **1** the year or place in which wine, especially wine of high quality, was produced. **2** a wine of high quality made from the crop of a single identified district or winemaker in a particular year. **3** the process of harvesting grapes for winemaking. **4** the time that something of quality was produced: *The model airplanes were of a classic vintage.*
adj **1** to do with wine of high quality: *Our neighbour has a cellar full of vintage wines.* **2 a** to do with a thing of high quality, especially something from the past: *vintage antique cars.* **b** to do with the best period of a person's work or of a body of work: *vintage comic books.* <Old French *vendange*, from Latin *vindemia* a gathering of grapes>

vint·ner (vint′nər) *n* a person or company that sells wine. <Old French *vinetier*>

vi·nyl (vī′nil) *or* (vin′il) *n* a synthetic resin or plastic used for covering materials, and formerly as the standard material for phonograph records. <Latin *vinum* wine. Vinyl was derived from ethyl alcohol, which is the alcohol present in wine.>

vi·ol (vī′əl) *n* a usually six-stringed musical instrument held vertically and played with a bow, used mainly in the 1500s and 1600s. <Old French *viole*, from Latin *vitula* fiddle>

vi·o·la[1] (vē ō′lə) *or* (vī ō′lə) *n* a musical instrument of the violin family that is slightly larger and tuned lower than the violin. See CELLO for picture. **vi·o′list** (vē ō′list) *n.*

vi·o·la[2] (vī ō′lə) *or* (vī′ə lə) *n* a plant of a genus that includes the violets and pansies.

vi·o·late (vī′ə lāt′) *v* **vi·o·lat·ed, vi·o·lat·ing** **1** break or fail to comply with a rule or formal agreement: *The country violated the terms of the treaty.* **2** treat something sacred with disrespect or irreverence: *The soldiers violated the church by using it as a stable.* **3** fail to respect someone's peace, privacy, or rights: *The law violated our right of free speech.* **4** rape or sexually assault someone. <Latin *violare*, from *vis* violence> **vi′o·la′tion** *n.* **vi′o·la′tor** *n.*

vi·o·lent (vī′ə lənt) *adj* **1** using or involving physical force intended to hurt, damage, or kill someone or something: *a violent blow, a violent death.* **2** very strong or powerful, especially as an emotion or an unpleasant or destructive natural force: *violent language, a violent storm.*
vi′o·lence *n.* **vi′o·lent·ly** *adv.*

vi·o·let (vī′ə lit) *n* **1** a plant with small, usually purplish or white, five-petalled flowers. The **purple violet** is the floral emblem of New Brunswick. **2** a similar plant of another family, such as the **African violet**.
adj bluish purple. <Old French, from Latin *viola*>

a bat	e bed	i bid	o pot	u cup	th **thin**
ā cake	ē me	ī bite	ō go	ū rude	ᴛʜ **then**
ä bar	ə about	ər over	ô for	ů put	zh measure

V

vi·o·lin (vī′ə lin′) *n* **1** a rounded musical instrument, narrowed at the middle and with two f-shaped soundholes, that has four tuned strings, played by drawing a bow across the strings. **2** a member of a family of stringed musical instruments of which the violin is the smallest, including the viola, cello, and double bass. See CELLO for picture. **vi′o·lin′ist** *n.*

vi·o·lon·cel·lo (vē′ə lən chel′ō) *or* (vī′ə lən chel′ō) *Formal n* a cello.

VIP *Informal n* a very important person.

The **viper** has a broad triangular head. When the long hollow fangs in the front of its jaw are not in use, they fold back against its palate, ready to swing forward quickly when the viper strikes at its prey.

vi·per (vī′pər) *n* **1** a thick-bodied venomous snake with a pair of large fangs. **2** a spiteful or treacherous person. <French, from Latin *vivus* alive + *parere* bring forth, from the former belief that the viper does not lay eggs> **vi′per·ish** *adj.* **vi′per·ous** *adj.*

vi·ra·go (və rā′gō) *or* (və rá′gō) *n, pl* **vi·ra·goes** or **vi·ra·gos** a violent, bad-tempered, or domineering woman. <Latin = a manlike maiden, from *vir* man>

vi·ral (vī′rəl) *adj* to do with a virus: *viral pneumonia.*

vir·e·o (vir′ē ō′) *n, pl* **vir·e·os** a small, insect-eating N American songbird, typically with yellow or white underparts.

vir·gin (vər′jən) *n* **1** a person, especially a woman, who has never had sexual intercourse, or has taken a vow not to have it. **2** a naive, innocent, or inexperienced person. **3 the Virgin** *Catholicism* in full, **the Virgin Mary** the mother of Jesus.
adj **1** to do with a virgin: *virgin modesty.* **2** not yet used or exploited: *a virgin forest.* <Latin *virgo*>

vir·gin·al (vər′jə nəl) *adj* **1** to do with a virgin. **2** pure, fresh, unused, or unexploited.
n a musical instrument with strings parallel to a keyboard, set in a box without legs, and used in the 1500s and 1600s. <Old French, from Latin *virgo* young woman>

Vir·gin·ia creeper (vər jin′yə) *n* a climbing N American vine with red autumn foliage.

vir·gin·i·ty (vər jin′ə tē) *n* **1** the quality or condition of never having had sexual intercourse. **2** the condition of being naive, innocent, or inexperienced.

Vir·go (vər′gō) *n* **1** *Astronomy* a constellation in the region of the celestial equator, shaped somewhat like a goddess. **2** *Astrology* **a** the sixth sign of the zodiac. The sun enters Virgo about August 23. **b** a person born under this sign.

vir·ile (vir′īl) *or* (vir′əl) *adj* **1** with strength, energy, and a strong sex drive. **2** with or characterized by strength and energy: *a virile writing style.* <Latin *vir* man>
vi·ril′i·ty (vir əl′ə tē) *n.*

vi·rol·o·gy (vī rol′ə jē) *n* the branch of science that studies viruses and the diseases they cause. **vi′ro·log′i·cal** *adj.* **vi·rol′o·gist** *n.*

vir·tu·al (vər′chū əl) *adj* **1** almost or nearly as described, but not completely or according to strict definition: *The battle was won with so great a loss of soldiers that it was a virtual defeat. He is the virtual president, though his title is secretary.* **2** *Computers* not physically existing as such but made by software to appear to do so: *virtual school.* **3** *Physics* to do with the effect of reflected or refracted light: *a virtual image.* <virtue> **vir′tu·al′i·ty** *n.* **vir′tu·al·ly** *adv.*

virtual reality *Computers n* a realistic set of effects in which the user or viewer of a specially programmed system can see, hear, or feel the physical sensations associated with scenes or events, and can interact with them.

vir·tue (vər′chū) *n* **1** behaviour showing high moral standards: *Her virtue is shown in her many good deeds.* **2** a quality considered morally good or desirable in a person: *Patience and generosity were his main virtues.* **3** a good or useful quality of a thing: *He praised the virtues of his car.* <Latin *virtus* moral strength, from *vir* man>
by (or **in**) **virtue of,** because or as a result of: *By virtue of getting to the theatre early, they got the best seats.*
make a virtue of, derive benefit or advantage from submitting to an unwelcome duty or unavoidable circumstances.

vir·tu·o·so (vər′chū ō′sō) *n, pl* **vir·tu·o·sos** or **vir·tu·o·si** (-sē) a person highly skilled in music or another activity, especially an artistic pursuit. <Italian = learned>
vir′tu·os′i·ty (vər′chū os′ə tē) *n.*

vir·tu·ous (vər′chū əs) *adj* with or showing high moral standards: *virtuous conduct, a virtuous life.*
vir′tu·ous·ly *adv.* **vir′tu·ous·ness** *n.*

vir·u·lent (vir′yə lənt) *adj* **1** very poisonous or harmful; deadly: *a virulent form of a disease.* **2** intensely bitter or spiteful; violently hostile. <Latin *virulentus,* from *virus* poison> **vir′u·lence** *n.* **vir′u·lent·ly** *adv.*

vi·rus (vī′rəs) *n* **1** a disease-producing agent that is too small to be seen by microscope, and is able to multiply only within the living cells of a host. **2** an infection or disease caused by such an agent. **3** *Computers* a piece of code, deliberately introduced into a program, that is capable of copying itself and typically corrupts a computer system or destroys data. <Latin = poison>

vi·sa (vē′zə) *n* an official document or endorsement on a passport allowing the person or persons identified in the passport to enter, leave, or stay for a specified period of time in a country. <French, from Latin *videre* see>

vis·age (viz′ij) *Poetic n* a person's face, especially with reference to its form, proportions, or expression: *a grim visage.* <Old French *vis* face, from Latin *videre* see>

vis–à–vis (vē′zə vē′) *prep* in relation to or in regard to: *Her attitude vis-à-vis her father tended to be tolerant. They were doing very well vis-à-vis their competitors,* <French = face to face>

vision

myopia (near-sightedness)

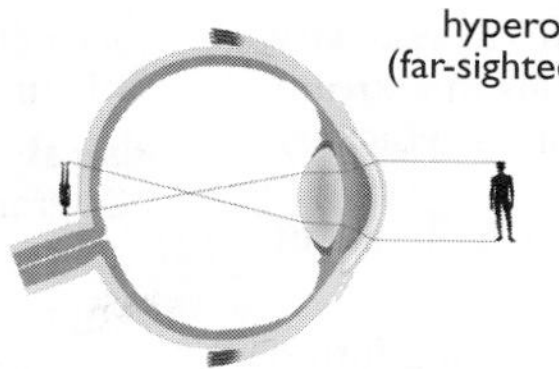

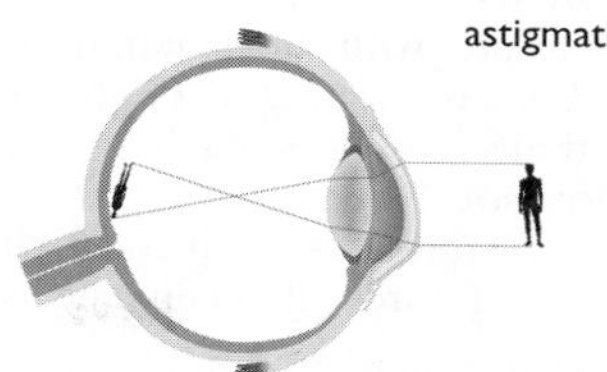

The corrective lens for myopia is a concave lens.

The corrective lens for hyperopia is a convex lens.

The corrective lens for astigmatism is a lens with differently shaped curved surfaces.

retina

optic nerve

lens

cornea

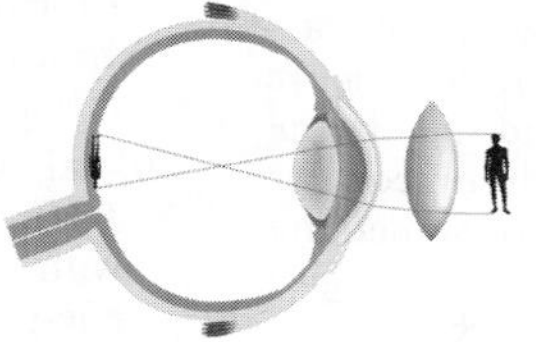

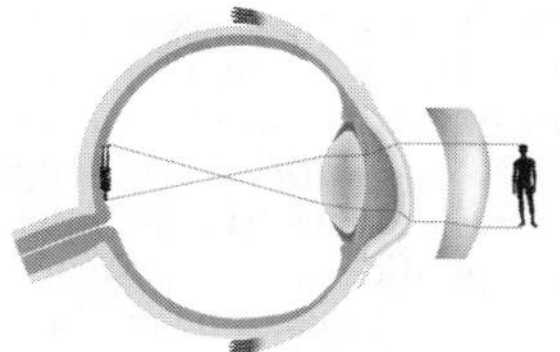

vis·cer·a (vis′ə rə) *pln* the internal organs in the main cavities of the body, especially those in the abdomen. Intestines are viscera. <Latin *viscus* internal body part>

vis·cer·al (vis′ə rəl) *adj* **1** to do with the viscera. **2** to do with instinct or emotion, rather than reason: *a visceral reaction.* **vis′cer·al·ly** *adv.*

vis·cid (vis′id) *adj* thick and sticky like heavy syrup or glue.

vis·cose (vis′kōs) *n* **1** a viscous solution made from cellulose and used especially in making rayon and cellulose film. **2** rayon fibres, yarn, or fabric. <See VISCOUS.>

vis·cos·i·ty (vis kos′ə tē) *n, pl* **vis·cos·i·ties** the condition or quality of being sticky, and semi-fluid in consistency.

vis·count (vī′kount) *n* a British nobleman ranking below an earl or count and above a baron. <Old French *visconte*, from Latin *vis-* vice + *comte* count[2]>

vis·count·ess (vī′koun tis) *n* **1** the wife or widow of a viscount. **2** a woman who holds the rank of viscount in her own right.

vis·cous (vis′kəs) *adj* with a consistency between a solid and a liquid. <Latin *viscum* birdlime (a sticky substance used to trap small birds on branches)> **vis′cous·ly** *adv.* **vis′cous·ness** *n.*

vise or **vice** (vīs) *n* a metal tool with two movable jaws that are used to hold an object firmly in place while work is done on it. <Old French *vis* screw> **vice′like′** *adj.*

Vish·nu (vish′nū) *n* one of the three great gods of classical Hinduism, widely regarded as the highest god, and usually worshipped in one of his human forms, especially Krishna or Rama. <Sanskrit>

vis·i·bil·i·ty (viz′ə bil′ə tē) *n* **1** the quality or condition of being able to see or be seen. **2** the distance one can see as determined by light and weather conditions: *Fog and rain decreased visibility to about fifty metres.* **3** the degree to which a thing has attracted general attention or prominence: *The proposal gradually gained more visibility as a topic.*

vis·i·ble (viz′ə bəl) *adj* **1** able to be seen: *The shore was barely visible through the fog.* **2** within the range of wavelengths of light to which the eye is sensitive: *the visible spectrum.* **3** able to be perceived or noticed easily: *There was no visible improvement in the patient's condition.* **4** in a position of public prominence: *He was a highly visible member of the delegation.* <Latin *videre* see> **vis′i·bly** *adv.*

SYNONYMS

Visible refers to something that can be seen: *Venus is clearly visible in the sky just before dawn.*

Apparent can mean "easy to see": *It's apparent from your umbrella and boots that you expect it to rain today.*

Conspicuous can mean "so obvious as to attract attention": *My friend is always conspicuous because she's so tall for her age.*

Discernible refers to something that is difficult to see: *The distant mountain peaks were discernible only when the sunlight reflected off the snow.*

vi·sion (vizh′ən) *n* **1** the faculty or condition of being able to see: *She wears glasses because of poor vision.* **2** the ability to think about or plan the future with imagination or wisdom: *As a leader, he had a great vision.* **3** a mental image of what the future will or could be like: *She had a vision of what the garden would be like in the spring.* **4** an experience of seeing someone or something in a dream or trance: *The insight came to her in a vision.* **5** a person or sight of unusual beauty: *a vision of loveliness.* <Latin *videre* see>

a bat	e bed	i bid	o pot	u cup	th thin
ā cake	ē me	ī bite	ō go	ū rude	ᴛʜ then
á bar	ə about	ər over	ȯ for	ů put	zh measure

V

vi·sion·ar·y (vizh′ə ner′ē) *adj* **1** thinking about or planning the future with imagination or wisdom: *a visionary thinker.* **2** of, relating to, or able to see visions in a dream or trance, or as something supernatural: *a visionary experience.*
n, pl **vi·sion·ar·ies** a person with original ideas about what the future will or could be like.

vision quest *n* an attempt to achieve a vision of a future guardian spirit, traditionally undertaken as a puberty rite by boys of some First Nations and Native American peoples of the Great Plains.

vis·it (viz′it) *v* **1** go to see and spend time with someone socially: *I'm going to visit my aunt tomorrow. They're visiting friends in Nova Scotia.* **2** go to see and spend time in a place as a tourist. **3** stay temporarily with someone or at a place as a guest. **4 a** go to see someone or something for a specific purpose, such as to receive or give professional advice or help: *They visited the locksmith's on the way back.* **b** *Computers* go to a website for information or for interest: *Visit us at our website, and win a free prize!* **5** inflict something harmful or unpleasant, or be afflicted in this way: *He visited his anger upon them.*
n **1** an act of going or coming to see a person or place socially, as a tourist, or for some other purpose: *They had to cut their visit short because he got sick.* **2** a temporary stay with a person or at a place. **3** a friendly talk or chat: *We had a nice visit while we were waiting.* <Latin *visitare* visit, from *videre* see> **vis′it·ing** *adj.*

> **SYNONYMS**
>
> **Visit** chiefly means "go to" or "spend time with (or in)": *The travellers will visit three countries. I will visit my cousins for a few days.*
>
> **Stay** means "remain in the same place": *They will stay in each city for a week.*
>
> **Pop by** (or **pop in**) is an informal term that means "visit": *Pop by to see me on your way home from school to pick up the book I promised you.*

vis·it·a·tion (viz′ə tā′shən) *n* **1** an official or formal visit, such as a religious or charitable visit, especially to the sick. **2** the appearance of a divine or supernatural being. **3** a disaster or difficulty regarded as a divine punishment.

vis·i·tor (viz′ə tər) *n* a person who visits or is visiting, especially socially or as a tourist: *I don't live here; I'm just a visitor.*

vi·sor (vī′zər) *n* **1** a movable front part of a helmet that can be pulled down to cover the face. **2** a screen for protecting the eyes from unwanted light, especially one at the top of a vehicle windshield. **3** a stiff peak at the front of a cap. Also, **vizor**. <Old French *viser*, from *vis* face>
vi′sored *adv.*

vis·ta (vis′tə) *n* **1** a pleasing view, especially one seen through a long, narrow opening: *Through a row of elms we had a vista of the lake.* **2** a mental view over a period of time or series of events in the past or future: *The book had opened up a new vista for her.* <Italian, from Latin *videre*>

vis·u·al (vizh′ū əl) *adj* to do with seeing or sight: *a visual defect, the visual arts.*
n a picture, piece of film, or display used to illustrate or accompany something: *The lecture had good visuals.* <Latin *visus* sight, from *videre* see> **vis′u·al·ly** *adv.*

visual aid *n* an item, device, or means such as a chart, diagram, motion picture, etc. for aiding the learning process through the sense of sight.

visual arts *pln* the arts that are appreciated through sight. Sculpture is a visual art.

visual display terminal or **unit** VDT or VDU.

vis·u·al·ize (vizh′ū ə līz′) *v* **vis·u·al·ized, vis·u·al·iz·ing** **1** form a mental image of: *I can visualize his reaction when he hears the news.* **2** make an internal organ visible by means of medical equipment. **vis′u·al·i·za′tion** *n.*

vi·tal (vī′təl) *adj* **1** essential or of the greatest importance: *Perfect timing was vital to the success of their plan.* **2** to do with or necessary to life: *vital organs.* **3** lively or full of energy.
n **vitals** *pl* important internal organs, such as the heart and lungs. **vi′tal·ly** *adv.*

> **ETYMOLOGY**
>
> **Vital** comes through Old French from Latin *vitalis*, which means "of life," from Latin *vita*, meaning "life." Other words with roots in *vita* include *vitality*, *vitalize*, and *vitamin*. *Vita* is related to the Latin words *vivus* (alive) and *vivere* (to live).

vital capacity *n* the greatest volume of air that can be expelled from the lungs after taking the deepest possible breath.

vi·tal·i·ty (vī tal′ə tē) *n, pl* **vi·tal·i·ties** **1** the condition of being strong and active: *She has great vitality. The tradition retained much vitality.* **2** the power to remain alive, distinguishing the living from the non-living.

vi·tal·ize (vī′tə līz′) *v* **vi·tal·ized, vi·tal·iz·ing** give strength and energy to someone or something. **vi′tal·i·za′tion** *n.*

vital signs *pln* physical signs of life as measured clinically, such as pulse and respiration rates, blood pressure, and temperature, which indicate a patient's state of health.

vital statistics *pln* numerical data concerning the population, such as the number of births, deaths, and marriages.

vi·ta·min (vī′tə min) *n* an organic compound that is essential for normal growth and nutrition. For example, **Vitamin A** is essential for growth and vision in dim light, and is found in some vegetables, egg yolk, and fish-liver oil. **Vitamin B complex** is a group of substances that are essential for certain enzymes in the body to work, and are generally found together in foods such as liver, fish, yeast, eggs, and some vegetables. **Vitamin C** (also called **ascorbic acid**) maintains healthy connective tissue in the body, and is found especially in citrus fruits and green vegetables. **Vitamin D** helps in the absorption of calcium for the normal growth of bones, and is found in liver and fish oils. **Vitamin E** helps to stabilize cell membranes, and is found in wheat germ, egg yolk, and leafy vegetables.

adj to do with or containing vitamins: *a vitamin deficiency, vitamin pills.* <Latin *vita* life + *amine*, because vitamins were mistakenly thought to contain amino acids>

vi·ta·min·ize (vī′tə mi nīz′) *v* **vi·ta·min·ized, vi·ta·min·iz·ing** provide with vitamins.

vit·re·ous (vit′rē əs) *adj* to do with glass: *vitreous enamel.* <Latin *vitrum* glass>

vitreous humour or **humor** *n* the transparent, jellylike tissue that fills that part of the eyeball behind the lens.

vit·ri·fy (vit′rə fī′) *v* **vit·ri·fied, vit·ri·fy·ing** change into glass or a glasslike substance by heat and fusion. **vit′ri·fi·ca′tion** (vit′rə fə kā′shən) *n.*

vit·ri·ol (vit′rē əl) *n* **1** sulphuric acid. **2** cruel and bitter criticism. <Latin *vitrum* glass, in reference to the glossy appearance of the sulphates> **vit′ri·ol′ic** *adj.*

vi·tu·per·ate (vi tyū′pə rāt′) *or* (vi tū′pə rāt′), (vī tyū′pə rāt′) *or* (vī tū′pə rāt′) *v* **vi·tu·per·at·ed, vi·tu·per·at·ing** blame or insult someone in strong or violent language. <Latin *vituperare* to blame, from *vitium* fault + *parare* to make> **vi·tu′per·a′tion** *n.* **vi·tu′per·a·tive** *adj.* **vi·tu′per·a·tive·ly** *adv.*

vi·va (vē′və) *interj* used to express acclaim or support for a specified person or thing: *Viva liberty!*
n a shout of approval or good will: *The crowd greeted her with a loud viva.*

ETYMOLOGY

Words beginning with *viv-* can be traced back to the Latin *vivus* (alive) and *vivere* (to live).

Viva itself comes from an Italian form of the verb meaning "may (he or she) live."

vi·va·cious (vi vā′shəs) *or* (vī vā′shəs) *adj* attractively lively: *a vivacious personality, a vivacious smile.* <Latin *vivax*> **vi·va′cious·ly** *adv.* **vi·va′cious·ness** *n.* **vi·vac′i·ty** (vi va′sə tē) *n.*

vive (vēv) *interj* used to express praise or salute someone or something: *Vive l'amour!* <French = live>

viv·id (viv′id) *adj* **1** producing powerful feelings or strong, clear images in the mind: *a vivid impression, a vivid imagination, a vivid description.* **2** intensely bright or deep as a colour: *a vivid yellow.* <Latin *vivus* alive> **viv′id·ly** *adv.* **viv′id·ness** *n.*

viv·i·fy (viv′ə fī′) *v* **viv·i·fied, viv·i·fy·ing** give life or vigour to. **viv′i·fi·ca′tion** (viv′ə fi kā′shən) *n.*

vi·vip·a·rous (vi vip′ə rəs) *or* (vī vip′ə rəs) *adj* bringing forth live young that have developed inside the body of the parent. Compare OVIPAROUS, OVOVIVIPAROUS. <Latin *vivus* alive + *parere* bring forth>

viv·i·sec·tion (viv′ə sek′shən) *n* **1** the act or practice of cutting into or experimenting on live animals for scientific study. **2** ruthlessly sharp and detailed criticism or analysis. <Latin *vivus* alive + *section*> **viv′i·sect′** *v.*

vix·en (vik′sən) *n* a female fox. <Old English *fyxen*, from *fox* fox>

viz. *adv* namely; in other words: *Two factors have been identified, viz., greed and dishonesty.* <Latin *videlicet* that is to say>

GRAMMAR AND USAGE

Viz. is used mainly in formal documents or reference works. It is a written form that is not pronounced the way it looks (except humorously), but is usually spoken or read as "namely."

vi·zier or **vi·zir** (vi zēr′) *n* in former times, a high official in some Muslim countries, especially in the former Turkish Empire under Ottoman rule. <Turkish, from Arabic *wazir* viceroy>

vi·zor (vī′zər) VISOR.

VJ veejay.

VLF *n* in full, **very low frequency** the band of radio frequencies between 3 and 30 kilohertz.

VLSI *Computers n* an electronic circuit on a semiconductor chip, with an extremely high number of microcircuits. <*v*(*ery*) *l*(*arge*) *s*(*cale*) *i*(*ntegration*)>

VLT *n* in full, **video lottery terminal** a coin-operated gambling machine that lets the user play games on a screen.

V–neck (vē′nek′) *n* a garment neckline that is V-shaped at the front, or a garment with such a neckline.
adj to do with such a neckline. Also, **V-necked**.

vo·cab·u·lar·y (vō kab′yə ler′ē) *n, pl* **vo·cab·u·lar·ies** **1** the stock of words used in a particular language. **2** a part of such a stock used on a particular occasion, in a particular area, or known to a particular person: *scientific vocabulary.* **3** a range of artistic or stylistic terms, techniques, or movements. <Latin *vocabulum*, from *vox* voice>

vo·cal (vō′kəl) *adj* **1** to do with the human voice: *vocal organs, vocal power, vocal music.* **2** expressing opinions or feelings freely or loudly: *She became vocal with indignation.*
n a musical composition for the voice, or a part of a musical composition that is to be sung. <Latin *vox* voice> **vo′cal·ly** *adv.*

vocal cords *pln* folds of membranous tissue that project inward from the sides of the larynx to form a slit across the glottis in the throat, and whose edges vibrate in the airstream to produce the voice.

vo·cal·ist (vō′kə list) *n* a singer, especially as part of an orchestra, band, etc.

vo·cal·ize (vō′kə līz′) *v* **vo·cal·ized, vo·cal·iz·ing** **1** utter a sound or word, or express something with words: *The dog vocalized its pain in a series of long howls.* **2** change a consonant to a semivowel or vowel. **vo′cal·i·za′tion** *n.* **vo′cal·iz′er** *n.*

V

a bat	e bed	i bid	o pot	u cup	th **thin**
ā cake	ē me	ī bite	ō go	ū rude	ᴛʜ **then**
à bar	ə about	ər over	ò for	ù put	zh measure

vo·ca·tion (vō kā′shən) *n* **1** a strong feeling of suitability for a particular career or occupation: *He had a vocation to be a diplomat. Since childhood, she had felt a vocation for nursing.* **2** a person's employment or main occupation, especially regarded as particularly worthy and requiring dedication: *His vocation as an engineer had been rewarding.* **3** an occupation or trade. <Latin *vocare* call> **vo·ca′tion·al** *adj.* **vo·ca′tion·al·ly** *adv.*

CONFUSABLES

Vocation refers to the way a person earns his or her living: *Being a pilot was her preferred vocation.*

Avocation means "hobby" or "minor occupation": *He worked as a construction worker and his avocation was writing poetry.*

vo·cif·er·ate (vō sif′ə rāt′) *v* **vo·cif·er·at·ed, vo·cif·er·at·ing** shout, complain, or argue loudly or vigorously: *The speaker vociferated against the new tax.* <Latin *vociferari,* from *vocis* voice + *ferre* bear> **vo·cif′er·a′tion** *n.* **vo·cif′er·ous** *adj.* **vo·cif′er·ous·ly** *adv.* **vo·cif′er·ous·ness** *n.*

vod·ka (vod′kə) *n* a colourless alcoholic liquor distilled from a mash of rye, wheat, or potatoes. <Russian *voda* water>

vogue (vōg) *n* **1** the prevailing fashion or style at a particular time: *He disliked the vogue for short hair.* **2** general acceptance or popularity: *That song had a great vogue at one time.* <origin uncertain> **vogu′ish** *adj.*

voice (vois) *n* **1 a** the sound produced in a person's larynx and uttered through the mouth, as speech or song: *The voices could be heard through the closed door.* **b** such sound regarded as having a particular quality that distinguishes one person from another: *a low voice, an angry voice.* **2** the ability to speak or sing: *He lost his voice because of a sore throat.* **3** the way by which a particular point of view is expressed or represented: *He thought of himself as the voice of reason.* **4** the right to express an opinion, or the particular opinion or attitude expressed: *Several dissenting voices were heard at the meeting.* **5** the range of pitch or type of tone with which a person sings, such as a soprano or tenor. **6** a singer: *The chorus consists of a hundred voices.* **7** *Grammar* a form of a verb showing the relation of the subject to the action. The **active voice** shows that the subject is performing the action. The **passive voice** shows that the subject is receiving the action. Examples: The verb *ate* in *The dog ate the bone* is in the active voice. The verb *was eaten* in *The bone was eaten by the dog* is in the passive voice. **8** the distinctive style or manner of expression of an author or a fictional character.
v **voiced, voic·ing 1** express something in words: *They voiced their approval of the plan.* **2** utter a speech sound with resonance of the vocal cords, such as the letters *b, d, g, v,* and *z.* <Old French *vois,* from Latin *vox*>
in voice, in condition to sing or speak well.
with one voice, in complete agreement.

voice box *n* the larynx.

voiced (voist) *adj* **1** (*in compounds*) with a voice of a particular kind: *deep-voiced.* **2** produced by means of vibration of the vocal cords, such as the consonant *b.* Compare VOICELESS (def. 3).

voice·less (voi′slis) *adj* **1** with no voice. **2** not expressed or made known. **3** produced without vibration of the vocal cords, such as the consonant *p.* Compare VOICED (def. 2).

voice mail *n* **1** an answering machine or automated electronic system that records and stores telephone messages, which can later be listened to. **2** a message or messages recorded on such a machine or system. Also, **voicemail.**

voice–o·ver (voi′sō′vər) *n* a piece of narration in a movie or broadcast by an unseen speaker.
adj made with an unseen narrator: *He does voice-over commercials for television.*

voice·print (vois′print′) *n* a visual record of speech, analyzed with regard to frequency, duration, and amplitude.
v make such a record of someone's voice, or identify a person by this means. **voice′print′ing** *n.*

voice recognition *Computers n* the capacity to receive and process spoken input.

void (void) *adj* **1** without legal force or effect: *The contract was void.* **2** completely empty: *void spaces.* **3** free from or lacking: *The essay was void of interest.*
n **1** a completely empty space: *the void of space.* **2** an emptiness caused by the loss of something: *The death of his dog left an aching void in his heart.*
v **1** declare that something is not valid or legally binding. **2** discharge, drain away, or excrete a thing, such as air, gases, or waste matter. <Old French *voide,* from Latin *vacuus* empty> **void′a·ble** *adj.* **void′er** *n.*

voi·là (vwȧ lȧ′) *interj* there it is: *Dinner is served. Voilà!*

voile (voil) *n* a thin, sheer fabric, usually of cotton or silk in a plain weave. <French = veil>

vol·a·tile (vol′ə tīl) *or* (vol′ə təl) *adj* **1** evaporating rapidly as a substance at normal temperatures. **2** liable to change rapidly and unpredictably, especially for the worse: *a volatile temperament.* <Latin *volatilis* fleeting> **vol′a·til′i·ty** (vol′ə təl′ə tē) *n.*

vol·can·ic (vol kan′ik) *adj* **1** to do with a volcano: *a volcanic eruption.* **2** bursting out or liable to burst out violently, especially as a feeling or emotion: *a volcanic temper.*

vol·ca·no (vol kā′nō) *n, pl* **vol·ca·noes** or **vol·ca·nos** a mountain or hill, typically cone-shaped, with a crater or vent through which lava, rock fragments, hot vapour, and gas are or have been expelled from the earth's crust. See LAVA, VENT for pictures. <Italian, from Latin *Vulcanus* Vulcan, the Roman god of fire>

vol·ca·nol·o·gy (vol ka′nol ə gē) *n* the scientific study of volcanoes. Also, **vulcanology. vol′ca·no·log′i·cal** *adj.* **vol·ca·nol′og·ist** *n.*

vole (vōl) *n* a small, typically burrowing, mouselike rodent, found in Eurasia and N America. <Old Norse *vollr* field (Scandinavian) + *mus* mouse>

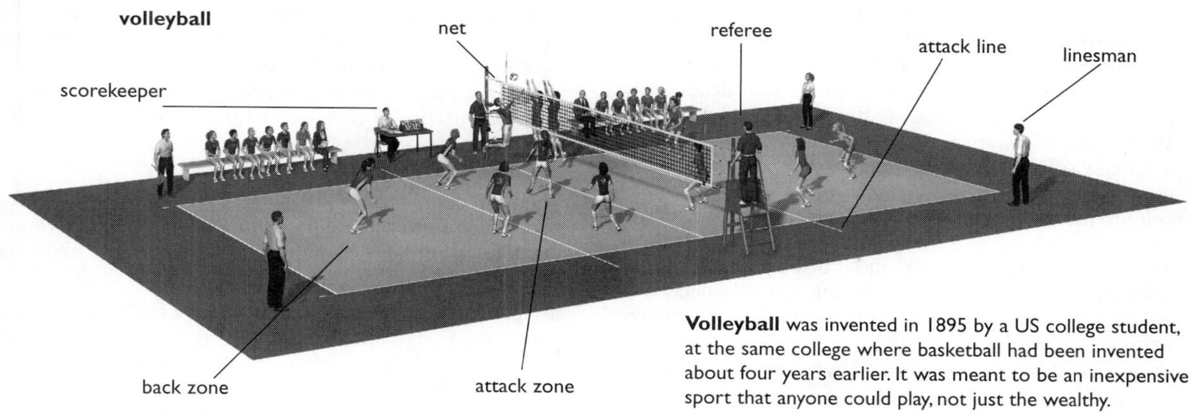

Volleyball was invented in 1895 by a US college student, at the same college where basketball had been invented about four years earlier. It was meant to be an inexpensive sport that anyone could play, not just the wealthy.

vo·li·tion (vō lish′ən) *or* (və lish′ən) *n* the ability or power of using one's will: *He gave himself up to the police of his own volition.* <Latin *volitio*, from *volo* I wish>

vol·ley (vol′ē) *n, pl* **vol·leys** **1** a number of bullets, arrows, stones, or other projectiles discharged at one time. **2** a series of statements or questions directed at someone in quick succession. **3** a strike or kick of the ball made before it touches the ground in such sports as soccer and tennis. *v* **vol·ley·ed, vol·ley·ing** **1** discharge or be discharged in a volley. **2** hit or return the ball before it touches the ground. <French, from Latin *volare*>

vol·ley·ball (vol′ē bol′) *n* a game for two teams of usually six players in which a large ball is hit by hand over a high net. The aim is to score points by making the ball reach the ground on the opponent's side of the court.

volt (vōlt) *n* the SI unit for measuring electromotive force, the difference of potential that would carry one ampere of current against one ohm of resistance. *Symbol* **V**

ETYMOLOGY

Volt is named after an Italian physicist, Count Alessandro Volta (1745–1827), who invented the electric battery.

volt·age (vōl′tij) *n* an electromotive force or potential difference expressed in volts: *high voltage.*

volte–face (vȯlt fȧs′) *or* (vȯl′tə fȧs′) *n* an abrupt and complete reversal of attitude, opinion, or position. <French, from Italian *volta* a turning + *faccia* face>

volt·me·ter (vōlt′mē′tər) *n* an instrument for measuring electric potential in volts.

vol·u·ble (vol′yə bəl) *adj* speaking or spoken rapidly and fluently: *a voluble protest.* <Latin *volubilis* fluent, from *volvere* roll> **vol′u·bil′i·ty** *n.* **vol′u·bly** *adv.*

vol·ume (vol′yūm) *or* (vol′yəm) *n* **1** a single book, especially a book forming part of a work or series: *We own a library of five hundred volumes. Her memoirs were published in three volumes.* **2** the amount of space that a substance or object occupies, or that is enclosed within a container: *The storeroom has a volume of twenty cubic metres.* **3** the amount or quantity of something, especially a large quantity: *The volume of consumer debt increased the following year.* **4** fullness or expansive thickness of something, especially of a person's hair. **5** quantity or power of sound: *He turned up the volume on the radio.* <Latin *volumen* scroll, from *volvere* to roll>
speak volumes, express much or be full of meaning: *His loving glance spoke volumes.*

vol·u·met·ric (vol′yə met′rik) *adj* to do with measurement by VOLUME (def. 2).

vo·lu·mi·nous (və lū′mə nəs) *adj* forming or filling much space or volume: *A voluminous cloak covered him from head to foot. The government brought out a voluminous report.* **vo·lu′mi·nous·ly** *adv.*

vol·un·tar·y (vol′ən ter′ē) *adj* **1** done, given, or acting of one's own free will: *voluntary contributions. She works for several voluntary organizations.* **2** working, done, or maintained without payment: *Voluntary workers built a road to the boys' camp.* **3** under the conscious control of the brain. <Latin *voluntas* will, from *volo* I wish> **vol′un·tar′i·ly** *adv.*

SYNONYMS

Voluntary emphasizes freely choosing to do something: *Helping to clean up the kitchen was voluntary.*

Impulsive can mean "hasty" or "reckless": *He regretted his impulsive decision to spend all his allowance.*

Spontaneous means "not planned": *The audience responded to her speech with spontaneous applause.*

V

a bat	e bed	i bid	o pot	u cup	th **thin**
ā cake	ē me	ī bite	ō go	ū rude	ᴛʜ then
ȧ bar	ə about	ər over	ȯ for	ů put	zh measure

vol·un·teer (vol′ən tēr′) *n* **1** a person who freely offers to take part in an enterprise or undertake a task. **2** a person who works in an organization without being paid. **3** a person who freely enrols for military service rather than being conscripted. **4** a plant that is not deliberately planted but grows from seeds dropped by other plants: *We have lots of volunteers in our garden this year.*
v **1** freely offer to do something, or offer help in such a way: *As soon as war was declared, many volunteered. She volunteered to do the job.* **2** say or suggest something without being asked: *She volunteered the information.* **3** work for an organization without being paid.
adj made up of volunteers, or serving as a volunteer: *Our village has a volunteer fire department. He's a volunteer firefighter in this town.*

vol·un·teer·ism (vol′ən tēr′iz′əm) *n* the use or involvement of volunteer labour, especially in community services.

vo·lup·tu·ous (və lup′chū əs) *adj* to do with luxury or giving pleasure to the senses: *voluptuous music.* <Latin *voluptas* pleasure> **vo·lup′tu·ous·ly** *adv.* **vo·lup′tu·ous·ness** *n.*

vom·it (vom′it) *v* **1** expel matter from the stomach through the mouth. **2** emit something in an uncontrolled stream or flow: *The chimneys vomited forth smoke.*
n matter vomited from the stomach. <Latin *vomitus*, from *vomere* spew forth>

voo·doo (vū′dū) *n, pl* **voo·doos** **1** a religion that combines elements of Catholic ritual with traditional African charms and spells, mainly practised by black peoples in Caribbean countries, especially in Haiti. **2** a person who practises this religion. <French, from Kwa (a language of W Africa)> **voo′doo·ism** *n.* **voo′doo·ist** *n.* **voo′doo·is′tic** *adj.*

vo·ra·cious (vȯ rā′shəs) *or* (və rā′shəs) *adj* **1** wanting or devouring great amounts of food: *a voracious appetite.* **2** with a very eager approach to an activity: *She is a voracious reader.* <Latin *voracis* greedy>
vo·ra′cious·ly *adv.* **vo·ra′cious·ness** *n.* **vo·rac′i·ty** (vȯ ras′ə tē) *or* (və ras′ə tē) *n.*

vor·tex (vȯr′teks) *n, pl* **vor·tex·es** or **vor·ti·ces** (vȯr′tə sēz′) **1** a mass of whirling fluid, especially a whirlpool or whirlwind. **2** a whirl of activity or other situation from which it is hard to escape: *the vortex of war.* <Latin = whirlpool>

vo·ta·ry (vō′tə rē) *n, pl* **vo·ta·ries** **1** a person, such as a monk or nun, who has vows of dedication to religious service. **2** a person who devotedly follows or supports an activity or leader. <Laatin *votum* vow>

vote (vōt) *n* **1** a formal indication of a choice between two or more candidates or courses of action, expressed typically through a ballot or a show of hands: *She won the class election by two votes. We put it to a vote.* **2** an act of expressing such an indication of choice: *The vote may go against the government.* **3 the vote** the choice or right to choose expressed by a group: *In our club, only those who have paid their fees have the vote.* **4 a** the total number of votes cast in an election: *The vote was higher than in the last election.* **b** a particular group of voters or their vote: *the labour vote.*
v **vot·ed, vot·ing** **1** give or cast a vote: *He voted for the governing party. She has gone to vote.* **2** pass, determine, or grant by a vote: *The committee voted $60 000 for renovating the building.* **3** declare by general consent: *The trip was voted a success.* **4** *Informal* indicate a wish to follow a particular course of action: *I vote we quit.* <Latin *votum* vow>
vote down, defeat by voting against.

vote of confidence *n* **1** a majority vote of support for the government in a legislature, the defeat of which would have caused the government to resign. **2** a show of support or approval. (non′con′fə dens)

🍁 **vote of non–con·fi·dence** (non′con′fə dens) *n* **1** a vote in a legislature indicating that the majority of members no longer support the party in power. It usually leads to the resignation of the government. **2** an expression of lack of support for someone.

vot·er (vō′tər) *n* a person who votes or has the right to vote in an election.

voters' list *n* a list giving the names and addresses of all those entitled to vote in an election.

vo·tive (vō′tiv) *adj* offered or solemnly dedicated in order to fulfill a vow: *a votive offering.*

vouch (vouch) *v* **1** state or confirm as a result of one's own experience the truth or accuracy of something: *I can vouch for the truth of the story.* **2** confirm the identity or good character of someone: *He couldn't enter the hall until someone vouched for him.* <Old French *vocher* to claim, from Latin *vocare* call>

vouch·er (vou′chər) *n* a small printed piece of paper that entitles the holder to a discount, or that may be exchanged for goods or services.

voucher system *n* an arrangement in which the government, instead of supporting schools directly, issues vouchers to individuals who use them to support the school of their choice.

vouch·safe (vouch sāf′) or (vouch′sāf′) *v* **vouch·safed, vouch·saf·ing** **1** give or grant something to someone in a gracious manner: *No blessing was vouchsafed to him.* **2** reveal or disclose information: *He vouchsafed no reply to our question.* <Middle English *vouchen sauf* to vouch for something as safe>

vow (vou) *n* **1** a solemn promise: *a vow of secrecy.* **2 vows** *pl* a set of such promises committing one to a course of action: *marriage vows.*
v solemnly promise to do a specified thing: *She vowed not to tell the secret. He vowed he would never shop there again.* <Old French, from Latin *votum*>
take vows, become a member of a religious order.

vow·el (vou′əl) *n* **1** a speech sound in which the vocal cords are vibrating and the breath is not blocked at a point in the mouth by the tongue, teeth, or lips. **2** a letter representing such a sound, such as *a, e, i, o, u,* and sometimes *y.*
adj to do with a vowel: *vowel sounds.* <Old French *vouel*, from Latin *vox* a voice> **vow′el·less** *adj.*

vox pop·u·li (voks pop′yə lī′) *or* (voks pop′yə lē) *n* the opinion or beliefs of the majority. <Latin = the people's voice>

voy·age (voi′ij) *n* a long journey, typically involving travel by sea or in space: *a voyage of discovery.*
v **voy·aged, voy·ag·ing** make or take a voyage: *The mariner voyaged on unknown seas.* <French, from Latin *via* road> **voy′ag·er** *n.*

🍁 **voy·a·geur** (voi′ə zhər′) *n, pl* **vo·ya·geurs** (-zhərz′) in former times, a canoeist or boatman, especially a French Canadian, who transported goods and passengers for fur-trading companies. <French, from *voyage* voyage>

voy·eur (voi yər′) *n* **1** a person who finds pleasure in watching others' private actions, especially one who takes sexual pleasure from watching others when they are naked or involved in sexual activity. **2** a person who enjoys seeing the pain or distress of others. <French = one who sees, from Latin *videre* to see> **voy′eur·ism** *n.* **voy′eur·is′tic** *adj.*

VP Vice-President.

vroom (vrūm) *or* (vrům) *interj* used to imitate the sound of a motor revving or accelerating. <imitative>

vs versus.

V–shaped (vē′shāpt′) *adj* shaped like the letter V: *There is a V-shaped scratch on the table.*

VTOL (vē′tol′) vertical takeoff and landing.

vul·can·ize (vul′kə nīz′) *v* **vul·can·ized, vul·can·iz·ing** harden rubber or rubberlike material by treating it with sulphur and intense heat. <*Vulcan,* Roman god of fire and metalworking> **vul′can·i·za′tion** *n.*

vul·gar (vul′gər) *adj* **1** lacking good manners or taste: *vulgar terms, vulgar ambition.* **2** in ordinary or common use, especially as one of the languages that evolved from Latin. **vul·gar′i·ty** *n.* **vul′gar·ly** *adv.* **vul′gar·ness** *n.*

ETYMOLOGY

Vulgar comes from the Latin word *vulgaris,* which means "of the people," from *vulgus,* meaning "crowd" or "common people." The suggestion was that only the wealthy were civilized and refined.

vul·gar·ism (vul′gə riz′əm) *n* a word, phrase, or expression that is regarded as non-standard, coarse, or obscene.

vul·gar·ize (vul′gə rīz′) *v* **vul·gar·ized, vul·gar·iz·ing** **1** make less refined. **2** make widely known and hence less subtle or complex.

vul·ner·a·ble (vul′nə rə bəl) *adj* **1** exposed to the possibility of being attacked or harmed, either physically or mentally: *The fort was vulnerable while the walls were being repaired. I felt vulnerable while walking home alone.* **2** in the position in the game of contract bridge where one is exposed to higher penalties. <Latin *vulneris* wound> **vul′ner·a·bil′i·ty** *n.* **vul′ner·a·bly** *adv.*

The **turkey vulture** has a wingspan of almost 2 m and a body that reaches 80 cm in length. Turkey vultures can soar for hours without flapping their wings.

The Wright brothers observed these birds in flight, and designed the first airplanes with them in mind.

vul·ture (vul′chər) *n* a large bird of prey with the head and neck more or less bare of feathers, feeding mainly on the flesh of dead animals. <Latin *vultur*> **vul′tur·ish** *adj.*

vul·va (vul′və) *n* the external genitals of the human female. <Latin = womb>

vy·ing (vī′ing) present participle of VIE.

w or **W** (dub′əl yū′) *n, pl* **w's** or **W's** **1** the twenty-third letter of the English alphabet, or any speech sound represented by it. **2** the twenty-third thing in a list or series.

GRAMMAR AND USAGE

The **five Ws** are five basic questions that reporters ask to help them organize information in their news stories: *who* (was involved)? *what* (happened)? *when* (did it happen)? *where* (did it happen)? *why* (did it happen)?

Answering these questions helps reporters to ensure they have included all the most important information in their stories. The technique is very useful for any writer who has to cover a current event or issue.

W **1** watt(s). **2** west; western.

Wa·ban–A·ki (wa′bə nȧ′kē) ABENAKI.

wack·o (wak′ō) *Slang adj* insane.
n a crazy person.

wack·y (wak′ē) *Informal adj* **wack·i·er, wack·i·est** eccentric or slightly crazy in an amusing way. **wack′i·ness** *n.*

wad (wod) *n* **1** a small, soft or loose lump of material, such as gum, cotton batting, or crumpled paper: *He plugged his ears with wads of cotton to keep out the noise.* **2** *Informal* a roll of paper money: *He took a wad out of his pocket and counted off five tens.* **3** in former times, a round plug of felt or other material used to hold powder and shot in place in a gun barrel.
v **wad·ded, wad·ding** **1** crush, press, or roll into a wad: *She wadded up the paper and threw it into the wastebasket.* **2** line or stuff a garment or piece of furniture with wadding. **3** stop up a hole or a gun barrel with a wad. <origin uncertain>

wad·dle (wod′əl) *v* **wad·dled, wad·dling** walk with short steps and an awkward swaying motion: *The duck waddled across the road.*
n an awkward, swaying gait. <*wade*> **wad′dler** *n.*

wade (wād) *v* **wad·ed, wad·ing** **1** walk through water, snow, sand, mud, or another liquid or soft substance: *I had to wade through deep snowdrifts to get to the door. We used to go wading in the spring.* **2** (*with* ***through***) read laboriously though a long piece of writing: *I waded through the dull novel.* **3** *Informal* (*with* ***into*** *or* ***in***) attack or go to work on vigorously: *She furiously waded into him for making a nasty comment. He waded in and got the job done in half an hour.*
n an act of wading. <Old English *wadan*>

wad·er (wā′dər) *n* **1** a person or animal, especially a bird, that wades. **2** **waders** *pl* high, waterproof boots, or a waterproof garment for the legs and body, used especially by anglers when fishing.

wa·di (wȧ′dē) *n, pl* **wa·dis** a valley, ravine, or channel that is dry except in the rainy season in some Arabic-speaking countries. See DESERT for picture. <Arabic>

wading pool *n* a shallow pool, usually round and sloping in toward the centre, for young children to play in, either built into a public playground or as a portable pool to play in at home.

wa·fer (wā′fər) *n* **1** a very thin, crisp cookie, usually sweet. **2** *Christianity* a thin, round disc of unleavened bread used in the Communion service in some churches. **3** a small disc of paper or sealing wax used as a seal on legal documents. <Old French *wafre*> **wa′fer·like′** *adj.*

wa·fer–thin (wā′fər thin′) *adj, adv* very thin or thinly: *wafer-thin cucumber slices. She sliced the salmon wafer-thin.*

waf·fle[1] (wof′əl) *n* a light, crisp, moulded cake made from a batter and baked in a waffle iron. <Dutch *wafel*>

waf·fle[2] (wof′əl) *v* **waf·fled, waf·fling** **1** avoid making a decision or commitment by speaking ambiguously or evasively: *Our class rep accused the student council president of waffling on the special events plan.* **2** speak or write, especially at great length, without saying anything important or useful.
n **1** a failure to make up one's mind. **2** lengthy but useless talk or writing. <Dutch *wafel*>

waffle iron *n* a device for cooking waffles, consisting of two hinged metal plates with a gridlike pattern, which cook the waffles between them.

waft (waft) *or* (woft) *v* pass or cause to pass easily or gently through or as if through the air: *The night wind wafted the sound of singing across the lake. A single feather wafted down to the ground.*
n a gentle movement of air, or a scent carried on such a movement: *A waft of freshness came through the open window.* <earlier *waft* carry over water, from obsolete *wafter* a convoy ship>

wag[1] (wag) *v* **wagged, wag·ging** **1** move or cause to move rapidly to and fro, especially as an animal's tail: *The dog's tail started wagging even before the car turned into the driveway.* **2** move an upward-pointing finger from side to side to indicate a warning or reproach. **3** talk, especially in order to gossip or spread rumours: *They don't really know anything about it; they're just wagging their tongues.*
n a single rapid movement from side to side: *She refused with a wag of her head.* <Old English *wagian* shake>

wag[2] (wag) *n* a person who is fond of making jokes.

wage (wāj) *n* a fixed regular payment, typically paid on a daily or weekly basis, made by an employer to an employee, especially to a manual or unskilled worker: *He earns a decent wage. That company pays good wages.* Compare SALARY.
v **waged, wag·ing** carry on a war or campaign: *to wage a battle.* <Old French> **wage′less** *adj.*

wa·ger (wā′jər) *n* a bet.
v make a bet: *I wagered my favourite CD that she couldn't beat me at tennis.* <Old French *wageure*>

wag·gish (wag′ish) *adj* humorous in a playful or mischievous way. **wag′gish·ly** *adv.* **wag′gish·ness** *n.*

wag·gle (wag′əl) *v* **wag·gled, wag·gling** move or cause to move with short quick movements from side to side or up and down.
n an act of wagging.

wag·on (wag′ən) *n* **1** a four-wheeled vehicle, especially one for carrying loads: *a milk wagon.* **2** a wheeled cart or van used to prepare and sell food: *a chip wagon.* **3** a station wagon. Also, **waggon**. <Dutch *wagen*>
fix someone's wagon, *Informal* hurt someone in revenge for a real or imagined wrong.
on (off) the wagon, *Informal* avoiding (indulging in) alcoholic beverages after having quit.

wag·on·load (wag′ən lōd′) *n* the load that a wagon can carry.

wagon train *n* in former times, a group of horse-drawn wagons moving along in a line one after another, especially such a group carrying pioneers or settlers in the western parts of N America.

waif (wāf) *n* a homeless and helpless person, especially a neglected or abandoned child or pet animal. <Old French *gaif*>

wail (wāl) *n* a prolonged, high-pitched cry of pain, grief, or anger, or a sound resembling this: *The baby wailed.*
v give such a cry of pain, grief, or anger, or make a sound resembling this. <Old Norse *væla* woe> **wail′er** *n.* **wail′ing** *adj.*

Wailing Wall *n* a high wall in Jerusalem at which Jews have traditionally gathered to pray and lament.

wain·scot (wān′skət) *or* (wān′skot′) *n* an area of wooden panelling on the lower part of the walls of a room. Also, **wainscotting**. <German *wagen* wagon + *schot* partition>

waist (wāst) *n* **1 a** the part of the human body below the ribs and above the hips, or how wide this part is around. **b** the part of a garment encircling or covering this part of the body, or the point at which a garment is shaped so as to narrow between the rib cage and the hips. **2** a narrow part in the middle of a thing, such as a violin, an hourglass, or the body of a wasp. <origin uncertain>

CONFUSABLES

Waist refers to a part of the body: *She tied the scarf around her waist.*

Waste means "useless or discarded material": *Throw the waste into that bin.*

waist·band (wāst′band′) *n* a strip of cloth attached to the top of a skirt or trousers to fit around the waist, especially of a skirt or pair of trousers.

waist·coat (wāst′kōt′) *or* (wes′kət) *especially UK n* a man's vest.

waist·line (wā′stlīn′) *n* the smallest part of the waist, the measurement around the body at this part, or the part of a garment that fits around the waist.

wait (wāt) *v* **1** stay where one is or delay action until a particular time or until something else happens: *We waited for him for two hours.* **2** *Informal* put off serving a meal: *Can you wait dinner for her?* **3** remain in readiness for some purpose: *The school bus was waiting for us when we got there.* **4** be left until a later time before being dealt with: *That matter can wait till tomorrow.* **5** act as a waiter or waitress, serving food and beverages: *to wait tables.*
n the act or time of waiting for someone or something: *I had a long wait at the doctor's office.* <Old French *waitier* watch>
lie in wait, stay hidden ready to surprise or attack: *Two assassins were lying in wait for the dictator.*
wait on (or **upon**), **a** act or serve as a waiter, waitress, or clerk. **b** await the convenience of: *To hear the full story, we will have to wait on his arrival.*
wait out, do nothing until something has passed or is finished: *There was nothing to do but wait out the storm.*
wait up, a delay going to bed until someone arrives or something happens: *I'll probably be late, so don't wait up for me.* **b** *Informal* stop and wait for someone to catch up: *Wait up! She's fallen behind again.*

CONFUSABLES

Wait is a verb meaning "stop" or "delay": *They didn't wait for him any longer.*

Weight is a noun meaning "heaviness": *He checked his weight once a month on the bathroom scale.*

wait·er (wā′tər) *n* a person whose work is to serve food and beverages to customers at their tables in a restaurant or dining room.

waiting list *n* a list of people who are waiting for something, especially housing, admission to a hospital, or means of transportation.
v **wait-list** (*usually in the passive*) put a person's name on such a list. Also, **wait list**.

waiting room *n* a room provided for the use of people who are waiting to be seen by a doctor or dentist or who are waiting in a station for a bus or train.

wait·ress (wā′tris) *n* a woman whose work is to serve food and beverages to customers at their tables in a restaurant or dining room.
v work as a waitress. **wait′ress·ing** *n.*

GRAMMAR AND USAGE

Waitress is still quite commonly used but, like some other words with the suffix -ess, it is now generally considered to be sexist. Instead, *server* is preferred. Other gender-neutral preferences include *ambassador* (instead of *ambassadress*), *author* (instead of *authoress*), flight *attendant* (instead of *stewardess*), *host* (instead of *hostess*), and *sculptor* (instead of *sculptress*).

W

wait·staff (wāt′staf′) the people whose job it is to serve people in a restaurant or dining room.

a bat	e bed	i bid	o pot	u cup	th thin
ā cake	ē me	ī bite	ō go	ū rude	ᴛʜ then
ä bar	ə about	ər over	ô for	ů put	zh measure

wait state *Computers n* the condition of computer software or hardware in being unable to process further instructions while waiting for some event such as the completion of a data transfer.

waive (wāv) *v* **waived, waiv·ing 1** refrain from insisting on or using a right or claim: *The defendant's lawyer waived her right to cross-examine the witness.* **2** refrain from applying a rule, restriction, or fee: *The charges were waived.* <Old French *weyver* abandon>

waiv·er (wā′vər) *n* an act or fact of waiving a right or claim, or a document recording this: *For $10 000, the man signed a waiver of all claims against the railway.*

Wa·kash·an (wȧ kash′ən) *or* (wȧ′kə shan′) *n* a family of First Nations and Native American languages of the northwest Pacific coast, including Haisla, Heiltsuk, and Kwakwala.
adj belonging to this language family.

wake[1] (wāk) *v* **woke** or **waked, woken** or **waked, wak·ing 1** (*often with* ***up***) emerge or cause to emerge from sleeping: *to wake up early in the morning. The noise will wake the baby. Wake me up early.* **2** become alert or aware of: *He finally woke to reality.* **3** cause something to stir or come to life: *She needs some interest to wake her up.*
n a watch or vigil held beside the body of someone who has died. <Old English *wacian*> **wak′er** *n.*

wake[2] (wāk) *n* **1** a tail of disturbed water or air left by the passage of a ship or aircraft. **2** the aftermath or consequences of something, especially something undesirable: *Floods followed in the wake of the hurricane.* <Dutch>

wake·board (wāk′bȯrd′) *n* a board like a short, wide surfboard, for riding on and performing acrobatic movements while being towed behind a motorboat.
v engage in the sport of riding on such a board behind a boat. **wake′board·er** *n.* **wake′board·ing** *n.*

wake·ful (wāk′fəl) *adj* **1** unable or needing to sleep: *Even after reading till midnight, she was still wakeful.* **2** watchful and alert. **3** passed with little or no sleep: *They spent a wakeful night.* **wake′ful·ly** *adv.* **wake′ful·ness** *n.*

wak·en (wā′kən) *v* WAKE[1] (def. 2): *The sudden noise wakened him.* **wak′en·er** *n.*

wake–up call (wā′kup) *n* **1** a telephone call made to wake a person, usually at a hotel. **2** a frightening experience that warns that a major and immediate change is needed, especially in the way a person lives or conducts business.

wak·ing (wā′king) *adj* **1** spent awake: *waking hours.* **2** in the process of becoming awake: *the sounds of the waking village at dawn.*
n the condition of being awake.

wale (wāl) *n* **1** a streak or ridge made on the skin by a stick or whip. **2** a long, narrow, raised surface, especially one of a series of parallel ribs or ridges in cloth such as corduroy. <Old English *walu*>

Wales (wālz) *n* the country or region of the UK on the west coast of Great Britain. See also WELSH.

walk (wok) *v* **1** move at a regular and fairly slow pace by lifting and setting down each foot in turn, never with both feet off the ground at once: *Walk down to the post office with me. The rider walked her horse.* **2** use similar movements but of a different part of one's body: *He could walk on his hands. She walked her fingers over the material.* **3** *Informal* abandon or suddenly withdraw from a job, commitment, or situation: *Unwilling to take the abuse, I walked.* **4** conduct oneself in a particular manner or course in life: *He walked in fear.* **5** guide, accompany, or escort someone on foot: *I walked her home after school.* **6** take a domestic animal, especially a dog, out for exercise. **7** *Baseball* reach or cause a batter to reach first base automatically after four balls have been pitched (but not hit) outside the strike zone.
n **1** the act of walking, especially walking for pleasure or exercise: *a walk in the country.* **2** a distance to walk somewhere or the time it takes: *It is a long walk from here. It's a walk of five minutes.* **3** a manner or way of walking: *We knew the man was a sailor from his rolling walk.* **4** a route, sidewalk, or path for walking: *We always preferred the walk down by the river. I shovelled the snow off the walk.* **5** occupation or social position: *people from all walks of life.* **6** *Baseball* the act or fact of reaching first base as a batter automatically after four balls have been pitched (but not hit) outside the strike zone. <Old English *wealcan*>
walk away from, *Informal* abandon someone or something
walk off with, a win. **b** steal.
walk out, a go on strike. **b** leave suddenly or angrily.
walk out on, abandon or desert.
walk over, defeat easily and by a wide margin.
walk through, a rehearse a play, using only lines and simple movements. **b** go through or help someone through a process or text, explaining it step by step: *I'll walk you through this software installation.*

SYNONYMS

Walk means "use one's feet to move": *The two sisters walk to school every morning.*

Stride means "walk with long confident steps": *He strides along the street as though he owns it.*

Stroll means "walk in a leisurely way": *The couple strolled arm in arm through the park.*

Plod means "walk heavily": *The animals plodded through the muddy field.*

walk·a·bout (wok′ə bout′) *n* **1** a relatively informal stroll taken by an important visitor in order to greet the public. **2** a journey on foot by an Australian Aborigine in order to live in the traditional manner.

walk·a·thon (wok′ə thon′) *n* a long-distance walk organized as a fund-raising event, with sponsors pledging a certain amount for every kilometre walked.

walk·er (wok′ər) *n* **1** a person who walks, especially one who walks in a particular way: *She's a fast walker.* **2 a** a framework on wheels designed to support a child learning to walk. **b** a framework made of metal tubing with rubber feet, to help a person walk.

walk·ie–talk·ie (wok′ē tok′ē) *n* a small, portable two-way radio.

walk–in (wok′in′) *adj* **1** large enough to be walked into: *a walk-in closet.* **2** available for customers or clients without the need for an appointment: *a walk-in clinic.*

walk·ing (wok′ing) *n* the action of a person who or thing that walks.
adj in human form: *She's a walking encyclopedia.*

walking papers *Informal pln* notice of dismissal from a job.

walking stick *n* **1** a stick used for support in walking. **2** an insect with a body like a stick or twig.

walking wounded *pln* **1** people who have been injured in a battle or major accident but who are still able to walk: *After the battle, he was one of the walking wounded.* **2** *Informal* people who are suffering emotional or psychological problems.

walk–on (wok′on′) *n* a small part in a dramatic production in which an actor appears but usually has no lines to say, or an actor with such a part.
adj to do with such a part or actor.

walk·out (wok′out′) *n* a sudden, angry departure, especially as a protest or strike.

walk·o·ver (wok′ō′vər) *Informal n* an easy victory.

walk–through (wok′thrū′) *n* **1** a rehearsal of a play, movie, or other performance, without an audience or cameras. **2** an undemanding task.

walk–up (wok′up′) *n* an apartment in a building that has no elevator, so that access to the upper floors is by stairs only.
adj to do with a building or apartment of this kind.

walk·way (wok′wā′) *n* a pathway or passage for walking along, especially a raised structure connecting different sections of a building or a wide pathway in a park or garden.

wall (wol) *n* **1** the side of a building or room joining the floor or foundation and the ceiling or roof. **2** a solid vertical structure of stone, brick, or other material built up to enclose, divide, support, or protect an area of land: *There was a low wall around the garden.* **3** a vertical surface, especially one that is high or impressive in scale: *The flood arrived in a wall of water four metres high.* **4** a thing considered to be a protective or restrictive barrier: *a wall of silence.*
v enclose, divide, protect, or fill with a wall or as if with a wall: *The garden is walled. Workers walled up the doorway.* <Latin *vallum*> **wall′-less** *adj.*
come up (or **be**) **against a blank wall,** *Informal* be completely unsuccessful: *She tried to get information, but always came up against a blank wall.*
drive (or **send**) **up the wall,** *Informal* make someone very irritated or angry: *His constant whining drives me up the wall!*
go to the wall, a support someone or something, no matter what the personal cost. **b** fail or go out of business.
hit the wall, *Informal* **a** reach a state of exhaustion in an athletic contest, such as in a long race. **b** reach a point where one has exhausted all solutions and must give up.
off the wall, *Informal* eccentric or unconventional.
with one's back to (or **against**) **the wall,** in an extreme or desperate situation.

wal·la·by (wol′ə bē) *n, pl* **wal·la·bies** or (*especially collectively*) **wal·la·by** an Australian marsupial that resembles a small kangaroo. See KANGAROO for picture. <Australian *wolaba*>

wall·board (wol′bȯrd′) *n* a building material made in large sheets of wood pulp, plaster, or other material, used for covering walls and ceilings.

walled (wold) *adj* with walls: *a walled garden.*

wal·let (wol′it) *n* a small, flat, folding case, usually made of leather or vinyl, with compartments for carrying money and plastic cards in one's pocket or purse. <Middle English *walet*>

wall·eye (wol′ī′) *n* **1** an eye with a streaked or opaque iris, or the condition of having such an eye. **2** an eye squinting outward, or a condition of the eyes in which one or both eyes are turned outward because of an imbalance of the muscles. **3** a N American freshwater fish of the perch family, such as the **yellow walleye** marked with yellow spots, and the smaller **blue walleye**, with a bluish colouring. <Old Norse *vagl-eygr*, from *vagl* speck + *eygr* eyed> **wall′-eyed′** *adj.*

wall·flow·er (wol′flou′ər) *n* **1** a perennial plant with fragrant yellow, orange-red, dark red, or brown flowers, blooming early in the spring. **2** *Informal* a person, who does not have a partner at a dance or who feels shy, awkward, or excluded at a party.

wall hanging *n* a decorative piece of fabric or other material to be hung on the wall of a room: *I made a quilted wall hanging for my bedroom.*

wal·lop (wol′əp) *Informal v* **1** strike or hit someone or something very hard. **2** badly defeat an opponent.
n **1** a heavy blow or punch. **2** a potent effect or result: *That movie sure packs a wallop.* <origin uncertain>

wal·lop·ing (wol′ə ping) *Informal n* a beating.
adj very big or impressive.

wal·low (wol′ō) *v* **1** roll about or lie relaxed in mud or water. **2** roll about clumsily or out of control as a boat or aircraft: *The ship wallowed helplessly in the stormy sea.* **3** indulge oneself in an unrestrained way: *to wallow in luxury, to wallow in self-pity.*
n **1** an act of wallowing. **2** a place, such as an area of mud or shallow water, where an animal wallows. <Old English *wealwian* roll (in mud)>

wall·pa·per (wol′pā′pər) *n* **1** paper, often with printed patterns in colour, that is pasted in vertical sheets over the walls of a room to provide a decorative or textured surface. **2** a background pattern or picture that may be chosen for display on the screen of a computer, cellphone, etc.
v apply wallpaper to a wall or room.

Wall Street *n* the money market or the financiers of the US. <The site of the New York Stock Exchange and other financial institutions>

a bat	e bed	i bid	o pot	u cup	th **thin**
ā cake	ē me	ī bite	ō go	ū rude	TH then
ä bar	ə about	ər over	ȯ for	u̇ put	zh measure

wall–to–wall (wol′tə wol′) *adj* 1 covering a floor from one wall to the other both ways: *wall-to-wall carpeting.* 2 so abundant in a place as to seem to be everywhere: *There were wall-to-wall trophies in the tennis star's den.*

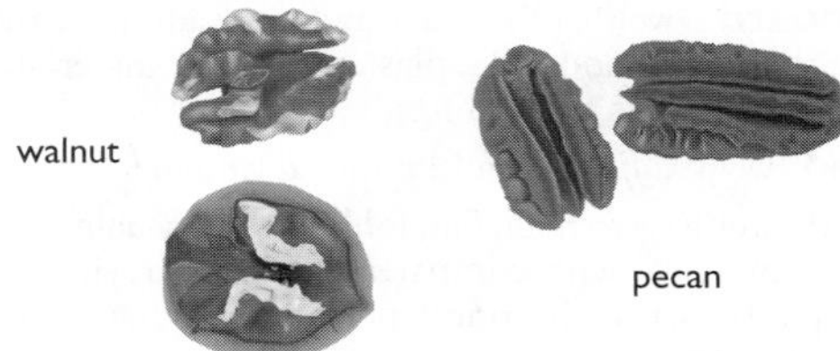

Pecan trees are members of the walnut family. Both pecan and walnut trees provide important nut crops and valuable lumber for furniture building.

wal·nut (wol′nut′) *n* a wrinkled nut, consisting of two halves contained within a hard shell.
adj medium reddish brown in colour. <Old English *wealh* foreign + *hnutu* nut>

Walruses are very social mammals that gather in large herds on shore or among ice floes. Normally, walruses are gentle, but if one is threatened, other members of the herd will come to its defence.

Walruses love to eat clams, which they find by pushing their sensitive whiskers through the undersea mud.

wal·rus (wol′rəs) *n, pl* **wal·rus·es** or (*especially collectively*) **wal·rus** a large sea mammal of the Arctic regions, with downward-pointing tusks. <Dutch *walros*>

walrus moustache *n* a long, thick, drooping mustache.

waltz (wolts) *n* a smooth, gliding dance in three-four time, performed by a couple who turn round and round as they progress across the dance floor, or a piece of music for this dance.
v 1 dance a waltz, or guide someone in or as if in a waltz. 2 move or act lightly or casually: *She waltzed through the room, cheerfully greeting all the guests. He waltzed through the exam in half the time it took me.* <German *walzen* revolve> **waltz′er** *n.*

wam·pum (wom′pəm) *n* small cylindrical beads formerly made by First Nations or Native American peoples from shells, strung together and worn as a decorative belt or other decoration, or used as money.

ETYMOLOGY

Wampum comes from Narraganset, an Algonquian language. The original word is *wampompeag*, from *wap*, meaning "white" and *umpe*, meaning "string."

wan (won) *adj* **wan·ner, wan·nest** 1 pale and giving the appearance of illness or exhaustion: *a wan face.* 2 of a light or a smile, pale and weak. <Old English *wann* dark> **wan′ly** *adv.* **wan′ness** *n.*

WAN (wan) wide area network.

wand (wond) *n* a long thin stick or rod, especially a stick or rod thought to have magical qualities, held by a magician or fairy and used in casting spells or performing tricks. <Old Norse *vondr*> **wand′like′** *adj.*

wan·der (won′dər) *v* 1 walk or move in a leisurely, casual, or aimless way: *I was too early for my appointment, so I wandered through the stores for a while.* 2 move slowly away from a fixed point or place: *The dog had wandered off again.* 3 wind with gentle twists and turns in a particular way as a road or river. 4 move or travel slowly through or over a place or area: *They found the lost man wandering the streets.* 5 depart from a topic, theme, or line of thought: *His mind wandered.* <Old English *wandrian*> **wan′der·er** *n.*

wan·der·lust (won′dər lust′) *n* a strong desire to travel: *His wanderlust led him all over the world.*

wane (wān) *v* **waned, wan·ing** 1 of the moon, have a progressively smaller part of its visible surface lit, so that it appears to decrease in size. 2 become less intense, powerful, or important: *Her influence in the club has waned.* <Old English *wanian*>
on the wane, become weaker or less extensive: *His popularity was on the wane.*

wan·gle (wang′gəl) *v* **wan·gled, wan·gling** obtain something that is desired by persuading others to agree to it or by managing events: *She wangled an invitation to the party.* <origin uncertain>

wan·na·be (won′ə bē) *Slang adj* 1 to do with imitating the behaviour or lifestyle of a certain celebrity or group of people: *a wannabe rock star.* 2 to do with copying the qualities or characteristics of something: *a big car that's a wannabe truck.* <want to be>

want (wont) *v* 1 have a desire to possess or do something: *She wants to become a singer. He wants a new computer.* 2 wish to see, speak to, or use the help of someone: *Call me if you want me. You're wanted on the phone.* 3 ought, should, or need to do something: *You don't want to be around when he's angry. You want to eat a balanced diet.* 4 lack or be short of something desirable or essential: *She made sure he wanted for nothing.* 5 seek or go after in order to question or arrest: *The police want him for questioning. She is wanted for theft.* 6 (with **in** or **out**) of an animal, wish to enter or leave: *The dog wants in. The cat wants out.*

n **1** a desire for something: *The new park supplied a long-felt want. He is a man of few wants.* **2** a lack or deficiency of something: *If we don't go, it won't be for want of trying.* **3** extreme poverty: *Many families were in want this past winter.* <Old Norse *vant,* from *vanr* lacking>

want ad *n* a small classified advertisement in a newspaper or magazine, especially one stating that someone or something is wanted.

want·ed (won′tid) *adj* sought by police for alleged crimes: *He's one of the nation's most wanted criminals.*

want·ing (won′ting) *adj* **1** not coming up to a standard or need; not satisfactory: *The stranger was wanting in courtesy.* **2** lacking or missing: *One volume of the set is wanting.*

wan·ton (won′tən) *adj* **1** deliberate and unprovoked as a cruel or violent action: *a wanton attack, wanton disregard, wanton cruelty.* **2** sexually immoral.
n Archaic a sexually immoral person. <Middle English *wan-* wanting + *teon* disciplined> **wan′ton·ly** *adv.* **wan′ton·ness** *n.*

✱ **wap·i·ti** (wop′i tē) *n, pl* **wap·i·tis** or (*especially collectively*) **wap·i·ti** the N American elk. See DEER for picture.

ETYMOLOGY

Wapiti comes from the Algonquian name *wapita,* meaning "white," referring to the animal's white rump and tail.

war (wȯr) *n* **1** a condition of armed conflict between different nations or groups within a nation. **2** a condition of competition, conflict, or hostility between different people or groups: *a gang war.* **3** a sustained effort to deal with or end a particular undesirable situation or condition: *the war against disease.*
v **warred, war·ring** fight a war. <Old French *guerre*>
at war, taking part in a war.
go to war, declare, begin, or see active service in a war.

war·ble (wȯr′bəl) *v* **war·bled, war·bling** of a bird, sing softly and with a succession of constantly changing notes, or make a sound like that of a bird warbling: *The brook warbled over its rocky bed.*
n a warbling sound, or the act of warbling. <Old French *werble*>

war·bler (wȯr′blər) *n* a small, insect-eating bird that typically has a warbling song.

war bonnet *n* a ceremonial headdress traditionally worn among First Nations or Native American peoples of the Great Plains, consisting of a row or rows of feathers attached to a headband and trailing down the back.

war bride *n* a woman who marries a soldier during wartime.

war crime *n* an action carried out during the conduct of a war that violates internationally accepted rules of war. **war criminal** *n.*

war cry *n* a call made to rally soldiers for battle or to gather together participants in a campaign.

ward (wȯrd) *n* **1** a separate room or group of rooms in a hospital, especially one for a particular type of patient: *a maternity ward, the children's ward.* **2** an administrative division of a city that typically elects and is represented by a councillor or councillors. **3** a child or young person under the care and control of a guardian or of a court. **4 wards** *pl* internal ridges or bars in a lock that prevent the turning of any key that does not have grooves of corresponding form or size. <Old English *weardian* guard> **ward′ship** *n.*
ward off, prevent from harming or affecting one: *He warded off the blow with his arm. She raised her collar to ward off the icy wind.*

–ward *suffix* in or to a particular place, direction, or point in time: *homeward, upward forward.* Also, **-wards**. <Old English *–weard*>

ward·en (wȯr′dən) *n* **1** an official who supervises a particular place or thing and enforces certain laws or rules: *a fire warden.* **2** a person in charge of a prison. <Old French *wardein* guardian> **ward′en·ship** *n.*

ward·robe (wȯr′drōb′) *n* **1** a person's entire stock of clothes: *She is shopping for her spring wardrobe.* **2** a large, tall cupboard in which clothes may be hung or stored. **3** the costume department or costumes of a theatre or movie company. <Old French *garderobe,* from *garder* keep + *robe* gown>

ware (wer) *n* **1** (*in compounds*) **a** manufactured items or goods of a particular kind or used for a particular purpose: *hardware, silverware.* **b** pottery, typically that of a specified type: *earthenware.* **2 wares** *pl* items offered for sale: *He peddled his wares from door to door.* See WEAR for confusable. <Old English *waru*>

ware·house (wer′hous′) *n* **1** a large building where raw materials or manufactured goods may be stored prior to sale. **2** a large wholesale or retail store.
v **ware·housed, ware·hous·ing** store or keep goods in a warehouse.

war·fare (wȯr′fer′) *n* engagement in or the activities involved in war or conflict.

war·fa·rin (wor′fər in) *n* a colourless, odourless, tasteless crystalline substance that prevents blood coagulation, used in rat poison and, in another form, to treat blood-clotting disorders. <*W*(*isconsin*) *A*(*lumni*) *R*(*esearch*) *F*(*oundation*) + (*coum*)*arin* name of a poison>

war·head (wȯr′hed′) *n* the forward, explosive part of a missile, torpedo, or similar weapon.

war·horse (wȯr′hȯrs′) *Informal n* a person, especially a veteran soldier or a person in public life, who has survived many battles or struggles.

war·like (wȯr′līk′) *adj* fond of, threatening, or ready for war: *warlike people, a warlike speech.*

war·lock (wȯr′lok) *n* a man who practises witchcraft. Compare WITCH. <Old English *wærloga* traitor>

war·lord (wȯr′lȯrd′) *n* a military commander, especially one who has supreme authority over civilians in a particular region, often in defiance of a weak central government.

a bat	e bed	i bid	o pot	u cup	th **thin**
ā cake	ē me	ī bite	ō go	ū rude	ᴛʜ **then**
ȧ bar	ə about	ər over	ȯ for	u̇ put	zh measure

warm (wôrm) *adj* **1** somewhat hot: *She sat in the warm sunshine.* **2** allowing or giving a warm feeling: *a warm coat.* **3** enthusiastic: *a warm welcome.* **4** affectionate or kind: *a warm friend, a warm heart.* **5** close to discovering something: *You're getting warm!* **6** suggesting warmth in colour: *a room painted in a warm yellow.*
v **1** make or become warm: *to warm a room.* **2** make or become cheered, interested, friendly, or sympathetic: *The speaker warmed to his subject. Her happiness warms my heart.* <Old English *wearm*> **warm′ish** *adj.* **warm′ly** *adv.* **warm′ness** *n.*
warmed over, *Informal* not fresh or original, especially as ideas.
warm up, **a** heat again, especially food. **b** make or become more interested or friendly. **c** practise or exercise for a few minutes before entering a game or contest. **d** run an engine or device in order to reach a proper working temperature.

warm–blood·ed (wôrm′blud′id) *adj* to do with animals, usually mammals and birds, whose temperature stays constant at or above that of the surroundings. Compare COLD-BLOODED (def. 1.)

warm front *Meteorology n* the front edge of a warm air mass advancing into and replacing a colder one.

war·mon·ger (wôr′mung′gər) *n* a person, especially a political leader, who is in favour of war or attempts to bring about war.

warmth (wôrmth) *n* **1** the quality, condition, or sensation of being warm: *We felt the warmth of the open fire.* **2** enthusiasm, affection, or kindness. **3** intensity of emotion: *She spoke with warmth of her parents.*

warm–up (wôr′mup′) *n* a period or act of preparation for a match, performance, or exercise session, involving moderate exercise or practice.

warn (wôrn) *v* **1** inform someone in advance about a possible or an approaching problem, unpleasantness, or danger: *They had been warned against using the old bridge. She warned us to keep away from the dog.* **2** (*often with* **off**) give a forceful notice or caution about actions or conduct: *He warned us that we would have to leave by eight. There was a sign warning off trespassers.* <Old English *warnian*> **warn′er** *n.*

SYNONYMS

Warn means "give information to help someone avoid or prepare for something": *The doctor warned me not to get my cast wet.*

Alert emphasizes the nearness of danger: *The park wardens alerted the hikers about the bear sightings.*

Caution often means "admonish": *The judge cautioned the witness about his disruptive behaviour.*

warn·ing (wôr′ning) *n* a statement or event that indicates a possible or impending danger, problem, or other unpleasant situation.
adj to do with such a statement or event: *The ship's captain fired a warning flare into the sky.* **warn′ing·ly** *adv.*

War of 1812 *n* a war between the US and the UK, 1812–1814, fought on the Atlantic and in N America. It was ended by a treaty that restored all conquered territories to their owners before the outbreak of war.

warp (wôrp) *v* **1** become or cause to become bent or twisted out of shape, typically as a result of the effects of heat or dampness: *The heat from the radiator has warped the table.* **2** cause to become abnormal, strange, or have a distorting effect: *Prejudice warped his judgment.*
n **1** a twist or distortion in the shape or form of something: *The board has a warp.* **2** a distortion or severe bias of the mind or judgment. **3** the threads stretched lengthwise in a loom, through which the crosswise threads are woven. Compare WEFT. <Middle English = throw out of shape, from Old English *weorpan* throw> **warped** *adj.*

war paint *n* a pigment or paint traditionally used in some societies, especially those of First Nations and Native American peoples, to decorate the face and body before battle.

war·path (wôr′path′) *n* in former times, the way or route taken by a fighting expedition of some Aboriginal peoples of N America.
on the warpath, *Informal* angry and aggressive in a conflict or dispute.

war·plane (wôr′plān′) *n* an aircraft designed and equipped to engage in air combat or to drop bombs.

war·rant (wô′rənt) *n* **1** a document issued by a legal or government official authorizing the police or some other body to make an arrest, search premises, or carry out some other action: *The police have a warrant for his arrest.* **2** justification or authority for an action, belief, or feeling: *He had no warrant for his suspicions.* **3** a document that entitles the holder to receive goods, money, or services. **4** a security allowing the holder to buy shares of stock at a specified price at or before some future date. **5** an official certificate of appointment to become a warrant officer.
v **1** justify or make necessary a certain course of action: *The crisis warranted immediate attention.* **2** officially affirm or guarantee. <Old French *warant*>

war·rant·a·ble (wô′rən tə bəl) *adj* able to be authorized or sanctioned. **war′rant·a·bil′i·ty** *n.*

war·ran·tee (wô′rən tē′) *n* a person to whom a warranty is made.

war·ran·tor (wô′rən tər) *n* a person who or company that provides a warranty.

war·ran·ty (wô′rən tē) *n, pl* **war·ran·ties** **1** a written guarantee issued to the purchaser of a thing by its manufacturer, promising to repair or replace it if necessary within a specified period of time. **2** justification or grounds for an action or belief.

war·ren (wô′rən) *n* **1** a network of interconnected rabbit burrows in an area of ground. **2** a densely populated building or district resembling a labyrinth. <Old French *warenne*>

war·ri·or (wô′rē ər) *n* a brave or experienced soldier or fighter. **war′ri·or·like′** *adj.*

war·ship (wôr′ship′) *n* a ship equipped with weapons and designed to take part in warfare at sea.

wart (wôrt) *n* **1** a small, usually hard, benign growth on the skin, caused by a virus. **2** a thing resembling a wart, such as a rounded lump on the skin of an animal or the surface of a plant. <Old English *wearte*> **wart′y** *adj.*

wart·hog (wôrt′hog′) *n* a wild pig of Africa with a large head, two large tusks, and two large warty growths on each side of its face.

war·time (wôr′tīm′) *n* a period during which a war is taking place.

war·y (wer′ē) *adj* **war·i·er, war·i·est** feeling or showing caution about possible dangers or problems: *a wary fox. She gave wary answers to all of the stranger's questions.* <Old English *wær*> **war′i·ly** *adv.* **war′i·ness** *n.*

SYNONYMS

Wary means "watchful, especially for danger": *The explorers were wary as they crossed the ice field.*

Vigilant means "very watchful for danger": *The guards are now more vigilant than ever.*

Apprehensive means "dreading": *I'm apprehensive about what might be lurking around the next corner.*

Careful is a general word meaning "cautious": *The toddler took careful steps toward the stroller.*

was (wuz) *or* (woz) *v* first and third person singular, past tense of BE: *I was late. He was late too.* <Old English *wæs*>

wash (wosh) *v* **1** clean with water and, usually, soap or detergent: *to wash your face, to wash dishes, to wash clothes.* **2** of a fabric, withstand cleaning to some degree without shrinking or fading: *That cloth washes well.* **3** carry or be carried along or away by water or other liquid in a particular direction: *The road washed away during the storm. Wood was often washed ashore by the waves. The waves washed over the rocks.* **4** cover with a thin coating of paint or ink. **5** *Informal* seem convincing or genuine: *That explanation won't wash with me.*
n **1** an act of washing something or the fact of being washed. **2** a quantity of clothes needing to be or just having been washed: *They hung the wash on the line.* **3** the disturbed water or air behind a moving boat or aircraft, or the sound made by this: *We listened to the wash of the waves against the boat.* **4** a medical, cosmetic, or cleansing liquid, used for a special purpose: *a hair wash, a mouthwash.* **5** a thin coating of paint or ink: *He began his watercolour with a wash of blue for the sky.* <Old English *wascan*>
wash down, a wash from top to bottom or from end to end. **b** swallow liquid along with or after solid food to help in swallowing or digestion.
wash off, remove something by washing with water and, usually, soap or detergent: *Wash off that makeup, please.*
wash out, a clean the inside of something with water. **b** wash something, especially socks or a garment, quickly or briefly. **c** cause an event to be postponed or cancelled because of rain. **d** carry or be carried away by water: *The rain washed out part of the pavement.*
wash over, a occur all around without greatly affecting a person: *She allowed the arguments just to wash over her.* **b** affect someone suddenly as a feeling: *Great regret washed over him.*

wash·a·ble (wosh′ə bəl) *adj* able to be washed, especially as clothes, without shrinkage or other damage: *washable fabric, washable paint.* **wash′a·bil′i·ty** *n.*

wash–and–wear (wosh′ən wer′) *adj* easily washed, drying quickly, and not needing to be ironed as a garment or fabric.

wash·ba·sin (wosh′bā′sən) *n* a basin, typically a bathroom fixture with attached water taps and a drain, used for washing one's hands and face.

wash·board (wosh′bôrd′) *n* **1** a wide board made of ridged wood, metal, or glass, used when washing clothes as a surface against which to scrub them. **2** a board fixed along the side of a boat to prevent water from spilling in over the edge.

wash·cloth (wosh′kloth′) *n* **1** a small cloth for washing oneself. **2** a dishcloth.

washed–out (wosh′tout′) *adj* **1** pale or faded, from much washing: *an old washed-out shirt.* **2** lacking energy or spirit: *She was feeling washed-out after a day of meetings.*

washed–up (wosh′tup′) *adj* **1** deposited on the shore by a tide. **2** *Informal* no longer effective or successful: *After three failed movies, he is probably washed-up as a director.*

wash·er (wosh′ər) *n* **1** a person who or thing that washes, especially an automatic washing machine. **2** a small, flat ring of metal, rubber, or plastic fixed under a nut or the head of a bolt to spread the pressure when tightened.

wash·ing (wosh′ing) *n* **1** the action of washing oneself or laundering clothes or linens. **2** a quantity of clothes or linens that is to be washed or has just been washed: *He had a big load of washing to do that day.*

washing machine *n* a machine for washing clothes and linens.

washing soda SODIUM CARBONATE.

wash·out (wosh′out′) *n* **1** a deep hole or break in a road or railway track caused by flooding. **2** an event that is spoiled by constant or heavy rain. **3** a disappointing failure: *We thought the movie would be great, but it proved to be a washout.*

wash·room (wosh′rūm′) *n* a room equipped with a toilet and sink, especially such a room in a public building.

wash·stand (wosh′stand′) *n* a piece of furniture designed to hold a jug, bowl, or basin, especially in former times, for the purpose of washing one's hands and face.

wash·tub (wosh′tub′) *n* a large metal tub used to wash or soak laundry in.

was·n't (wuz′ənt) *or* (woz′ənt) *contraction* was not.

a bat	e bed	i bid	o pot	u cup	th thin
ā cake	ē me	ī bite	ō go	ū rude	TH then
ȧ bar	ə about	ər over	ȯ for	u̇ put	zh measure

wasp (wosp) *n* a winged insect that has a narrow waist and a sting and is typically yellow with black stripes. It constructs a paper nest from wood pulp and raises its larvae on a diet of insects.

WASP (wosp) *Informal n* a person, whose ancestors were Anglo-Saxon and whose religion is Protestant. <*W*(*hite*) *A*(*nglo*)-*S*(*axon*) *P*(*rotestant*)>

wasp·ish (wos′pish) *adj* readily expressing irritation or anger: *a waspish temper.* **wasp′ish·ly** *adv.* **wasp′ish·ness** *n.*

wast·age (wā′stij) *n* **1** the action or process of losing, reducing, or destroying something by using it carelessly or extravagantly, or the amount of something lost or destroyed in such a way: *energy wastage.* **2** the weakening or deterioration of a part of the body, typically as a result of illness or lack of use: *muscle wastage.*

waste (wāst) *v* **wast·ed, wast·ing 1** use or spend carelessly, extravagantly, or to no purpose: *Don't waste time or money. We try not to waste food.* **2** become progressively weaker and thinner as a person or part of the body: *The man was wasted by disease.* **3** ruin or damage greatly: *The soldiers wasted the enemy's fields.*
adj **1** eliminated or discarded as a useless or worthless material, substance, or by-product: *waste matter.* **2** not used, cultivated, or built on: *waste ground.*
n **1** an act or fact of using or spending something carelessly, extravagantly, or to no purpose: *a waste of effort.* **2** useless or worthless material that is discarded or eliminated: *industrial waste.* **3** often, **wastes** *pl* a large area of barren, typically uninhabited land: *Before us stretched a waste of snow and ice, trackless wastes.* See WAIST for confusable. <Old French *waster*, from Latin *vastare* lay waste> **wast′ing** *adj.*
go to waste, be unused or spent to no purpose.
lay waste to, completely destroy: *The invading army laid waste the countryside.*

waste·bas·ket (wāst′bas′kit) *n* a basket or other open container for waste paper and other small discarded items.

waste·ful (wāst′fəl) *adj* using or spending something of value carelessly, extravagantly, or to no purpose. **waste′ful·ly** *adv.* **waste′ful·ness** *n.*

waste·land (wā′stland′) *n* **1** an unused area of land that has become barren or overgrown: *desert wastelands.* **2** a bleak, unattractive, and unused or neglected urban or industrial area.

waste management *n* the action or business of reducing and disposing of a community's waste.

waste·pa·per basket (wāst′pā′pər) a wastebasket.

wast·er (wā′stər) *n* a person who or thing that wastes: *a waster of time.*

wast·rel (wā′strəl) *n* a wasteful or good-for-nothing person.

watch (woch) *v* **1** look at or observe attentively, typically over a period of time: *The medical students watched while the surgeon performed the operation.* **2** observe carefully or protectively: *The nurse watched over him all night.* **3** secretly follow or spy on: *The suspect was being watched by the police.* **4** be careful, cautious, or restrained about something: *Watch where you step!*
n **1** a spring-driven or electronic device for indicating time, small enough to be carried in a pocket or worn on the wrist. **2** the act or fact of carefully observing someone or something. **3** a period of time during which a person is stationed to look out for danger or trouble, typically during the night: *Several security guards keep watch over the bank at night.* **4** a fixed period of duty on a ship, usually lasting four hours, or a spell of duty worked by firefighters or police officers. **5** in former times, a watchman or group of watchmen who patrolled and guarded the streets of a town before police forces were formed. <Old English *wæccan*> **watch′er** *n.*
watch out, be careful or on guard: *Watch out for cars.*
watch over, guard or supervise.
watch yourself, be careful and self-controlled.

watch·band (woch′band′) *n* a band or strap of leather, plastic, or metal for holding a wristwatch on the wrist.

watch·dog (woch′dog′) *n* **1** a dog kept to guard property. **2** a person or group who closely observes the practices of companies providing goods or services: *a consumer watchdog.*

watch fire *n* a fire maintained during the night as a signal or for the use of someone who is on watch.

watch·ful (woch′fəl) *adj* watching someone or something closely: *She is watchful of her health.* **watch′ful·ly** *adv.* **watch′ful·ness** *n.*

watch·mak·er (woch′mā′kər) *n* a person who makes and repairs watches and clocks.

watch·man (woch′mən) *n, pl* **watch·men** (-mən) a person employed to look after empty buildings, closed business premises, etc., usually at night.

watch·tow·er (woch′tou′ər) *n* a tower from which watch is kept for enemies, fires, or ships in distress.

watch·word (woch′wərd′) *n* a word or phrase expressing a person's or group's core aim or belief: *"Freedom" is our watchword.*

wa·ter (wot′ər) *n* **1** a transparent, colourless, odourless, tasteless liquid that falls as rain, makes up the seas, lakes, and rivers, and is the basis of the fluids of living organisms. **2** an area or surface of this liquid, such as a lake, river, or sea: *She lived across the water from them.* **3 waters** *pl* **a** a particular part of a body of water: *Canadian waters, the upper waters of the St. Lawrence, warm Pacific waters.* **b** mineral or spring water, as at a spa: *to take the waters.* **4** the fluid surrounding a fetus in the womb, especially as discharged in a flow shortly before a birth. **5** a liquid containing and resembling water: *rose water, soda water.*
v **1** pour or sprinkle water over a plant or area of ground: *to water the grass.* **2** of an animal, drink water, or provide an animal with water to drink: *The cattle usually watered at the creek, to water horses.* **3** supply water to an area of land: *The land was watered by rivers and brooks.* **4** become full of moisture, saliva, or tears: *Her mouth watered when she saw the cake. Strong sunlight made his eyes water.* **5** weaken or dilute by adding water: *to water milk.*
adj found or living in or near water: *water lilies, waterfowl.* <Old English *wæter*> **wa′ter·er** *n.*
hold water, be shown to meet a test or standard: *That argument won't hold water.*

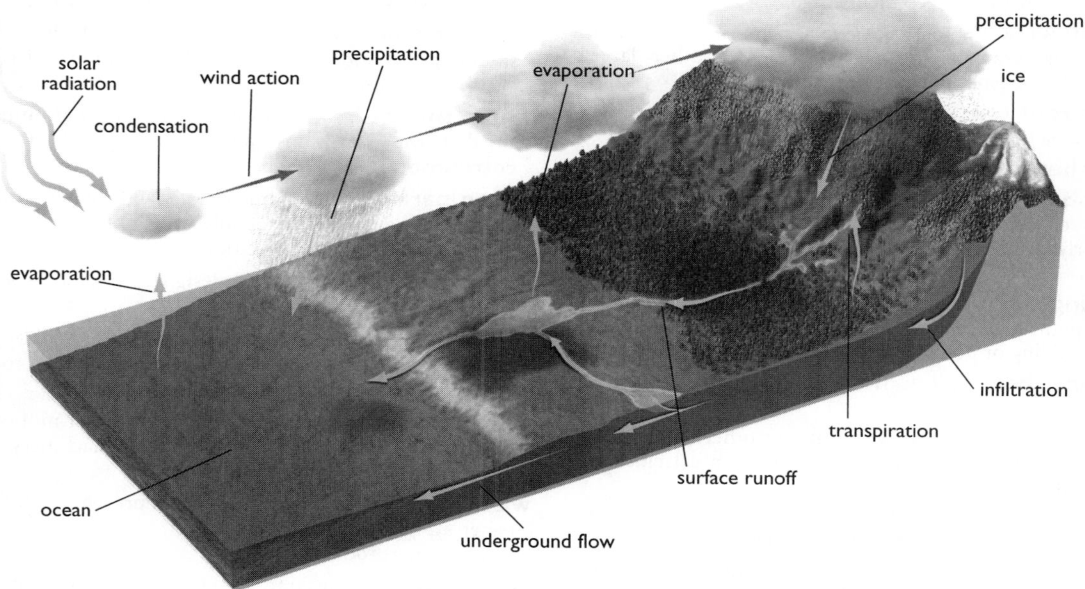

keep your head above water, keep out of trouble or difficulty: *Business was so bad that he found it hard to keep his head above water.*
like water, very freely or recklessly: *to spend money like water. Blood flowed like water.*
make water, urinate.
make your mouth water, arouse your appetite or desire: *The sports car made her mouth water.*
of the first water, of the highest quality or most extreme degree: *He is a bungler of the first water.*
throw (or **pour**) **cold water on,** actively discourage or belittle: *She didn't tell her friends her scheme because she knew they'd throw cold water on it.*
water down, a reduce in strength by diluting with water: *We watered down the punch because it was too strong.* **b** reduce the effectiveness or force of something by altering it: *The original bill had been watered down before being presented to Parliament.*
water under the bridge (or **over the dam**), in the past and therefore no longer to be regarded as important or a source for concern.

wa·ter·bed (wot′ər bed) *n* a bed whose mattress consists of a padded, water-filled plastic bag supported at the bottom and on all four sides by a wooden frame.

water boat·man (bōt′mən) *n* an insect that lives mostly on the bottom of a body of water and has paddlelike hind legs used in swimming.

🍁 **water bomber** *n* an aircraft equipped with special tanks filled with water that is dropped to fight forest fires. **water bombing** *n.*

wa·ter–borne (wot′ər bȯrn′) *adj* **1** conveyed by, travelling on, or involving travel or transport on water. **2** spread as a disease by contaminated water.

water buffalo *n* a buffalo with heavy, swept-back horns, used as a draft animal in tropical countries.

water chestnut *n* the edible, button-shaped tuber of a grasslike marsh plant that remains crisp after cooking.

water closet *n* often abbreviated to **WC**, a room or compartment with a toilet bowl that can be flushed with water.

wa·ter·col·our or **wa·ter·col·or** (wot′ər kul′ər) *n* **1** artist's paint that has been mixed with water, not oil. **2 a** the art of painting with this kind of paint: *She is good at watercolour.* **b** a picture painted with this kind of paint: *A lovely watercolour hung in her room.*

water cooler *n* a device for cooling and dispensing drinking water.

wa·ter·course (wot′ər kȯrs′) *n* a brook, stream, or artificially constructed water channel.

wa·ter·craft (wot′ər kraft′) *n, pl* **wa·ter·craft** **1** a boat or other craft that travels on water. **2** skill in sailing and other activities that take place on water.

wa·ter·cress (wot′ər kres′) *n* a plant of the mustard family that grows in running water and has pungent leaves used in salads or as a garnish.

water cycle *n* the cyclical process by which water evaporates from the ocean, falls to earth as rain, sleet, or snow, and returns to the ocean via rivers.

a bat	e bed	i bid	o pot	u cup	th **thin**
ā cake	ē me	ī bite	ō go	ū rude	ᴛʜ **then**
ȧ bar	ə about	ər over	ȯ for	ů put	zh measure

wa·ter·fall (wot′ər fol′) *n* a stream or river falling over a cliff or down a very steep incline.

wa·ter·fowl (wot′ər foul′) *n, pl* **wa·ter·fowls** or (*especially collectively*) **wa·ter·fowl** ducks, geese, or other large aquatic birds, especially when regarded as game.

wa·ter·front (wot′ər frunt′) *n* the part of a town or other urban area that borders a sea, lake, or river.

wat·er·hen (wot′ər hen′) *n* a coot or gallinule.

wat·er·hole (wot′ər hōl′) *n* a hole in the ground where water collects, especially one from which animals regularly drink. Also called **watering hole**, **watering place**.

watering can *n* a portable container with a handle and a long spout, often ending in a flared cap with holes in it, for sprinkling or pouring water on plants.

watering hole *n* **1** WATERHOLE. **2** *Informal* a bar or tavern.

water jacket *n* a casing with water or other liquid in it, placed around something to protect it from extremes of temperature.

wa·ter·less (wot′ər lis) *adj* **1** not having water; dry. **2** not needing or using water: *waterless cooking.*

water lily *n* a water plant found in temperate and tropical parts of the world, with floating leaves and large, typically cup-shaped flowers.

wa·ter·line (wot′ər līn′) *n* **1** the level normally reached by the water on the side of a ship or boat. **2** the level reached by the sea or by a river visible as a line on a rock face, beach, or bank of a river.

wa·ter·logged (wot′ər logd′) *adj* **1** so full of water as a boat or watercraft that it will barely float. **2** completely soaked with water.

Wa·ter·loo (wot′ər lū′) *n* **1** the battle in which Napoleon was finally defeated in 1815. **2** a decisive or crushing defeat: *His first international tennis competition turned out to be his Waterloo.* <*Waterloo* town in Belgium, site of Napoleon's final defeat>

water main *n* the main pipe in a system of water pipes.

wa·ter·mark (wot′ər märk′) *n* **1** a faint design made in some paper during manufacture that is visible when held against the light and typically identifies the maker. **2** a mark showing how high water has risen or may rise.

wa·ter·mel·on (wot′ər mel′ən) *n* a large fruit with a smooth green rind, sweet, juicy pulp, and watery juice. See CANTALOUPE for picture.

water moccasin *n* a poisonous snake of the southeast US that lives in swamps and along streams. Also called **cottonmouth**.

water park *n* an amusement park with many facilities for water play, including pools of various kinds, rides involving water, and water slides.

water pistol *n* a toy pistol designed to shoot a jet of water.

water polo *n* a game played in a swimming pool by two teams of seven players who try to throw or push a round inflated ball into the opponents' goal.

water power *n* the power from the weight or motion of flowing or falling water, used to drive machinery and make electricity. **wat′er-pow′ered** *adj.*

wa·ter·proof (wot′ər prūf′) *adj* able to prevent water from penetrating: *a waterproof watch.*
v make waterproof.

water rat *n* **1** a muskrat. **2** a European rodent that lives in the banks of streams or lakes.

wa·ter re·pel·lent (wot′ər ri pel′ənt) *adj* not penetrable by water, especially as a result of being treated for such a purpose with a surface coating. A surface which is not easily penetrated by water may be called **water resistant**.

wa·ter·shed (wot′ər shed′) *n* **1** an area or ridge of land that separates water flowing to different rivers, basins, or seas. **2** an event or period marking a turning point in a course of action or situation: *Entering university was a watershed in his life.*

wa·ter·side (wot′ər sīd′) *n* the edge or area adjoining a sea, lake, or river.
adj of, at, or on the waterside: *a waterside park.*

water polo

The goalkeeper in a game of **water polo** leans near the surface of the water in order to straighten and stretch to catch the ball. Goalkeepers are the only players allowed to touch the bottom of the pool.

Players on one team wear dark blue caps, while the players on the other team wear white. The goalkeepers wear red caps to clearly identify them. All players must have tremendous stamina and be excellent swimmers.

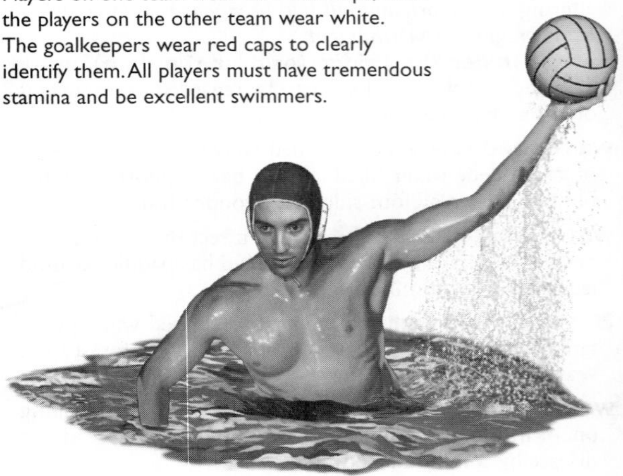

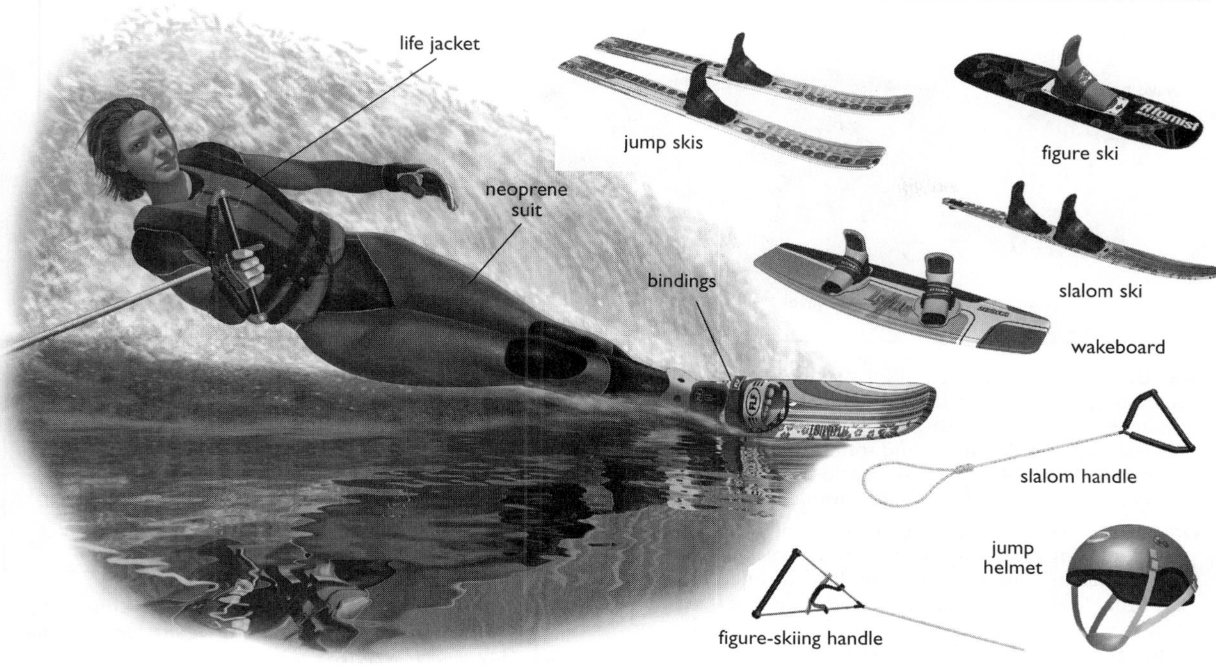

water ski *n* a broad ski, usually one of a pair, enabling the user to skim over water while being towed by a motorboat. **wat′er-ski′** *v.* **wat′er ski′er** *n.* **wat′er ski′ing** *n.*

wa·ter·slide or **water slide** (wot′ər slīd′) *n* a slide, often with a stream of water constantly flowing down it and often with twists and turns, that ends in a swimming pool.

water snake *n* a snake that lives in or near water, especially a harmless freshwater snake.

water softener *n* a device or substance that softens hard water by removing certain minerals.

water–sol·u·ble (wot′ər sol′yə bəl) *adj* able to be dissolved in water.

wa·ter·spout (wot′ər spout′) *n* **1** a rotating column of spray and water between a cloud and the surface of the sea or other body of water, produced by the action of a whirlwind. **2** a pipe that takes away or spouts water.

water table *n* the level below which the ground is saturated with water.

wa·ter·tight (wot′ər tīt′) *adj* **1** closely sealed, fastened, or fitted so that no water enters or passes through: *watertight compartments.* **2** unable to be disputed or questioned as an argument or account: *a watertight alibi.*

water torture *n* a form of torture in which water is allowed to fall in a slow, steady drip on the victim's forehead.

water tower *n* a tower supporting a raised water tank, whose height creates the pressure needed to distribute the water through a piped system.

water vapour or **vapor** *n* water in the form of gas; steam.

wa·ter·way (wot′ər wā′) *n* a river, canal, or other route for travel on water.

water wheel *n* a large wheel driven by flowing water, used to work machinery or to raise water to a higher level.

water wings *pln* a device consisting of two inflated floats joined together, worn under the arms and designed to give support to a person learning to swim.

wa·ter·works (wot′ər wərks′) *n* **1** (*with singular verb*) a system of pipes, reservoirs, pumps, and other equipment for supplying a city or town with water, or the building containing it. **2** *Informal* a flow of tears, especially a sudden flow.

wa·ter·y (wot′ə rē) *adj* **1** consisting of, containing, or resembling water: *watery soil, a watery liquid.* **2** with tears in the eyes: *a watery smile.* **3** thin or tasteless as a result of containing too much water: *watery soup.*

watt (wot) *n* the SI unit for measuring power, equivalent to one joule per second, corresponding to the rate of energy in an electric circuit in which the potential difference is one volt and the current one ampere. *Symbol* **W** <J. *Watt,* 18c engineer and inventor>

watt·age (wot′ij) *n* an amount of electrical power expressed in watts.

a bat	e bed	i bid	o pot	u cup	th **thin**
ā cake	ē me	ī bite	ō go	ū rude	TH **then**
ä bar	ə about	ər over	ȯ for	u̇ put	zh measure

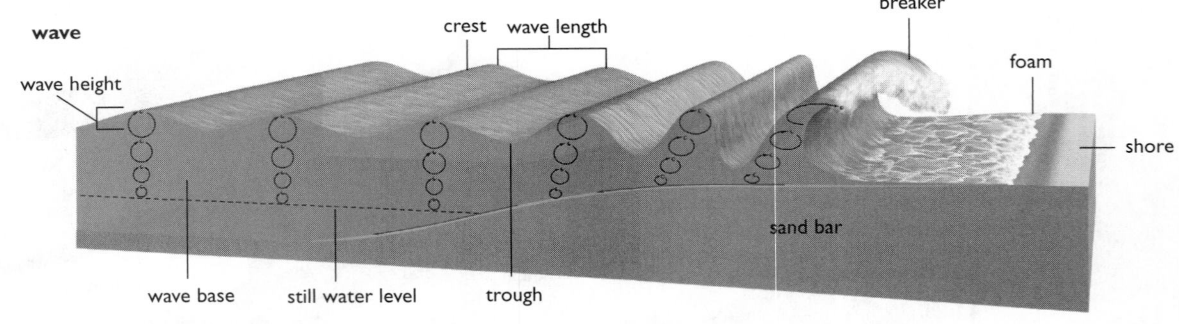

wat·tle (wot′əl) *n* **1** a material for making fences or walls, consisting of stakes or sticks interwoven with twigs or branches. **2** a lobe of fleshy, wrinkled skin hanging down from the neck of the turkey and some other birds.
v **wat·tled, wat·tling** make, enclose, or fill up with wattle, the material. <Old English *watul*> **wat′tled** *adj.*

wave (wāv) *v* **waved, wav·ing 1** move one's hand to and fro in greeting or as a signal: *They waved goodbye.* **2** move one's hand or arm, or something held in one's hand to and fro: *He waved the document in my face. She waved her handkerchief.* **3** move to and fro with a swaying or undulating motion while remaining fixed to one point: *Branches waved in the wind.* **4** have a wavelike form, or give a wavelike form to: *Her hair waves naturally.*
n **1** a long ridge or swell of water curling in an arched form and breaking on the shore, or a ridge of water between two depressions in open water: *The boat rose and fell on the waves.* **2 a** a shape of things resembling a wave: *A wave of bison swept across the plain.* **b** a wavelike effect produced when successive groups of people stand then sit, or raise then lower their arms: *Some of the fans at the football game began a wave.* **3** an intense burst of a particular feeling, emotion, effect, or activity: *A wave of hysteria passed through the crowd. We're having a heat wave.* **4** a gesture or signal made by moving one's hand to and fro. **5** a slightly curling lock of hair. <Old English *wafian*> **wave′less** *adj.* **wave′like′** *adj.* **wav′er** *n.*
make waves, *Informal* attract attention or create a significant impression.

wave·length (wāv′length′) *n* **1** the distance between successive crests of a wave, especially points in a sound wave or electromagnetic wave. **2** *Informal* a person's ideas and way of thinking, especially as it affects an ability to communicate with others: *He and I were just never on the same wavelength.*

wave·let (wā′vlit) *n* a little wave of water.

wave pool *n* a swimming pool equipped with a mechanism that produces fairly large, regular waves.

wa·ver (wā′vər) *v* **1** shake with a quivering motion: *Her hand wavered as she reached for the phone.* **2** become unsteady or unreliable: *His attention never wavered.* **3** hesitate between choices: *She wavered, not knowing which road to take.* **4** become unsteady; be about to give way; falter: *He wavered for a few seconds, then fell down in a faint.* <Old English *wæfre* restless> **wa′ver·er** *n.* **wa′ver·ing** *adj.* **wa′ver·ing·ly** *adv.*

🍁 **wa·vey** (wā′vē) *n* a wild goose, especially the snow goose. Also called **wah-wah, wawa.**

ETYMOLOGY

Wavey comes from Ojibwa *wewe,* meaning "goose." The English word may have come from a related French Canadian or Algonquian word.

wav·y (wā′vē) *adj* **wav·i·er, wav·i·est** with or consisting of a series of wavelike curves as a line or surface: *wavy hair.* **wav′i·ly** *adv.* **wav′i·ness** *n.*

wax[1] (waks) *n* **1** a sticky, mouldable, yellowish substance secreted by honeybees as material for constructing their honeycomb. **2** a white translucent material obtained by bleaching and purifying this substance and used in making candles and models.
v cover or treat something with wax or a similar substance: *The floor should be waxed once a month.*
adj made of wax: *a wax model.* <Old English *weax*> **wax′er** *n.*
the whole ball of wax, *Informal* everything; everything that is needed.

wax[2] (waks) *v* **1** of the moon, have a progressively larger part of its visible surface lit, so that it appears to increase in size. **2** become more intense, powerful, or important: *During this period, his wealth waxed steadily.* **3** begin to speak or write about something in the specified way: *to wax indignant.* <Old English *weaxan*>

wax bean *n* a long, yellow bean pod, eaten as a vegetable.

wax·en (wak′sən) *adj* with a smooth, pale, translucent appearance like that of wax: *waxen skin.*

wax museum *n* a museum containing wax figures of famous people.

wax paper or **waxed paper** *n* paper coated with a waxy substance, used mostly for wrapping food.

wax·wing (wak′swing′) *n* a small songbird with a large crest, often with red, waxlike tips on the wing feathers.

wax·work (wak′swərk′) *n* **1** a figure or figures made of wax. **2 waxworks** *pl* an exhibition of such figures showing famous or notorious people.

wax·y (wak′sē) *adj* **wax·i·er, wax·i·est** resembling wax in consistency or appearance: *waxy skin.* **wax′i·ly** *adv.* **wax′i·ness** *n.*

way (wā) *n* **1** a method, style, or manner of doing something: *He had an odd way of talking. Doctors are using new ways of preventing disease. This is the way trouble often starts.* **2** a route taken in order to reach a place: *Can you tell me the way to the library?* **3** a means of entry or exit from somewhere, such as a door or gate: *He went out the back way.* **4** some distance or time from one point to another: *The hotel is only a short way from here. My birthday a long way off.* **5** a space for passing or going ahead: *Cars must make way for the fire engine.* **6** a habit or custom: *Teasing is just her way, so don't let it bother you. You'll get to know my ways.* **7** one's wish or will: *He wanted his own way all the time.* **8** *Informal* a condition or state: *That sick man is in a bad way.* **9** personal experience or course of action: *the best idea that ever came my way, a way of life.* **10** *Informal* a particular area or locality: *She lives out our way.* **11** a road, track, path, or street for travelling along.
adv **1** *Informal* at or to a considerable distance or extent: *The cloud of smoke stretched way out to the pier. He was driving way too fast.* **2** *Informal* very or extremely: *The test was way easy.* <Old English *weg*>
by the way, a in that connection or incidentally. **b** during the course of a journey.
by way of, a so as to pass through or across. **b** as a form of: *By way of an answer he just nodded.*
find your way, figure out which way you should go.
give way (to), a yield to someone or something: *She gave way to tears.* **b** break down or fall: *Several people were hurt when the platform gave way.*
go out of the way, make a special effort.
have a way with, have special skill with: *He has a way with words.*
in a way, to some extent.
in the way, forming an obstacle or hindrance.
lose your way, become confused as to where you are and which way you should go.
make way, a give space for passing or going ahead. **b** move forward.
make your way, a go or proceed: *They made their way through the bushes to the road.* **b** get ahead or succeed: *He's sure to make his way in the world.*
no way, *Informal* absolutely not: *Lend you money? No way!*
out of the way, a remote as a place. **b** dealt with or finished. **c** unusual, exceptional, or remarkable: *Her clothes seemed out of the way to us.*
see your way (clear) to, be willing or able to do something.
under way, going on or in progress: *The program is under way.*

CONFUSABLES

Way means "method" or "route": *What's the best way to get in touch with them?*

Weigh means "determine mass" or "have a specific weight": *These apples weigh 600 grams.*

way·bill (wā′bil′) *n* a list of passengers or goods being carried on a vehicle.

way·far·er (wā′fer′ər) *n* a person who travels on foot. **way′far′ing** *adj.*

way·lay (wā′lā′) *or* (wā′lā′) *v* **way·laid, way·lay·ing** stop or interrupt someone and detain her or him in conversation or cause trouble in some way: *Reporters waylaid the movie star as she left her hotel.* **way′lay′er** *n.*

way–out (wā′out′) *Informal adj* regarded as extremely unusual or unconventional: *He's too shy to wear such way-out clothes.*

–ways *suffix* in a particular direction, position, or manner: *edgeways, sideways.*

ways and means *pl n* the resources or methods available to accomplish a particular purpose: *The plan seemed attractive, but the committee still had to consider ways and means.*

way·side (wā′sīd′) *n* the edge of a road or path: *We ate lunch on the wayside.*
adj along the edge of a road or path: *We slept in a wayside inn.*
fall (or **go**) **by the wayside,** fail to continue or be completed: *The bowling tournament fell by the wayside for lack of interest.*

way station *n* **1** a stopping place along a route. **2** a station between main stations on a railway.

way·ward (wā′wərd) *adj* difficult to control or predict because of unusual or wilful behaviour: *a wayward mood.* **way′ward·ly** *adv.* **way′ward·ness** *n.*

we (wē) *pron* **1 a** the person or people speaking or writing: *We are going to a movie, and are wondering if you would like to go with us.* **b** the person or people speaking or writing, together with the person or people being addressed: *Bring your swimsuit so we can go to the pool.* **2** the person or people speaking or writing as belonging to others in the same category: *We students want to thank our families for all their help at the school fundraiser.* **3** people in general, including the speaker: *In this chapter, we will look at the recent past and what occurred.* **4** used instead of the pronoun *I*, especially by a royal person: *We will care for all our people.* <Old English *we*>

weak (wēk) *adj* **1** without much physical strength, force, or power: *She is still weak from her illness, a weak argument, a weak government.* **2** unable to withstand great force or pressure: *a weak link in the chain.* **3** easily influenced or changed: *a weak character, a weak will.* **4** not intense or extreme: *a weak solution, a weak protest.* **5** performing or performed badly: *The sound quality on this CD is weak.* **6** showing lack of skill or aptitude: *I am weak in math.* <Old Norse *veikr*> **weak′en** *v.* **weak′ness** *n.*

CONFUSABLES

Weak means "not strong": *The teacher did not accept his weak excuse for being late.*

Week means "seven days": *The show will be aired once a week for the next six weeks.*

a **bat**	e **bed**	i **bid**	o **pot**	u **cup**	th **thin**
ā **cake**	ē **me**	ī **bite**	ō **go**	ū **rude**	ᴛʜ **then**
ä **bar**	ə **about**	ər **over**	ȯ **for**	ů **put**	zh **measure**

weak–kneed (wēk′nēd′) *adj* lacking in courage or determination.

weak·ling (wē′kling) *n* a physically or mentally weak person or animal.

weak·ly (wē′klē) *adv* in a weak manner: *She smiled weakly. adj* **weak·li·er, weak·li·est** feeble or sickly: *a weakly pup.* **weak′li·ness** *n.*

weak–mind·ed (wēk′mīn′did) *adj* lacking determination, or emotional or intellectual strength.

weal (wēl) *n* a red, swollen mark left on the skin by a blow or pressure. <*wale*>

wealth (welth) *n* **1** much money or property, or the condition of being rich: *a man of wealth, the wealth of a city.* **2** plentiful supplies of a resource or desirable thing: *a wealth of hair, a wealth of information.* <*well*[1]>

wealth·y (wel′thē) *adj* **wealth·i·er, wealth·i·est** with much money or property. **wealth′i·ness** *n.*

SYNONYMS

Wealthy means "rich": *The family became wealthy from all the property they owned.*

Prosperous emphasizes doing well financially and otherwise, but does not necessarily mean wealthy: *The family lived in a prosperous area of town, but their house was not a mansion.*

Loaded and **well-heeled** are both informal words for "wealthy": *Are they ever loaded! You can tell how well-heeled they are from the expensive cars they drive.*

wean (wēn) *v* **1** accustom an infant or young mammal to food other than its mother's milk. **2** accustom someone to do without something that the person has become too fond of or dependent on: *The doctor tried to wean him of too much sugar.* <Old English *wenian*>

weap·on (wep′ən) *n* **1** a thing designed or used for inflicting bodily harm or physical damage: *The murder weapon was a rock.* **2** a means of gaining an advantage or defending oneself in a conflict: *The new pill was a potent weapon against the disease.* <Old English *wæpen*> **weap′on·less** *adj.*

weap·on·ize (wep′ən īz) *v* **weap·on·ized, weap·on·iz·ing** install a weapon or weapons in or on: *to weaponize outer space.*

wear (wer) *v* **wore, worn, wear·ing 1** have or carry on one's body as clothing, decoration, protection, or for some other purpose: *He always wears a suit to work. She was wearing pearls. He wore a sword.* **2** habitually have on one's body or be dressed in: *I used to wear my hair long.* **3** show or present a particular facial expression or appearance: *She wore a grin. The old house wore an air of sadness.* **4** damage, erode, or destroy by friction or use: *Water had worn the stones smooth. The cuffs of the shirt are starting to wear at the edges.* **5** withstand continued use in a specified way: *This coat has worn well.* **6** pass a period of time, especially slowly or tiringly: *The job was extremely wearing. A visit with him always wears me out. It grew hotter as the day wore on.*

n **1** the act of wearing something, or the condition of being worn on the body: *The suit was useful for all kinds of wear.* **2** clothing suitable for a particular purpose or of a particular type: *summer wear, casual wear.* **3 a** damage or deterioration caused by continuous use: *The soles of her shoes had suffered much wear.* **b** the ability to withstand continuous use without such damage: *The shoes still have a lot of wear in them.* <Old English *werian*>

wear′a·bil′i·ty *n.* **wear′a·ble** *adj.* **wear′er** *n.*

wear and tear, damage or deterioration as a result of ordinary use over a period of time.

wear down, overcome by persistent effort: *He tried to wear me down by asking again and again if he could borrow my bike.*

wear off, become less in strength or intensity: *As the freezing wore off, my tooth started to ache.*

wear on, a become tiresome or hard to bear: *Her constant puns began to wear on me after a while.* **b** pass time, especially slowly or tiringly: *It grew hotter as the day wore on.*

wear out, a wear until no longer fit for use: *She wore the shoes out in six months.* **b** become useless from long or hard wear: *I don't think this coat will ever wear out.*

wear thin, become weak from being used too much: *My patience was wearing thin.*

CONFUSABLES

Wear means "have on your body": *Wear this lifejacket while you're on the boat.*

Where means "in, at, to, or from a place": *We all moved to where we could actually see the stage.*

wear·ing (wer′ing) *adj* mentally or physically tiresome or tiring: *All this extra housework is very wearing for her.*

wea·ri·some (wē′rē səm) *adj* causing one to feel tired or bored: *a wearisome story.* **wea′ri·some·ly** *adv.* **wea′ri·some·ness** *n.*

wea·ry (wē′rē) *adj* **wea·ri·er, wea·ri·est 1** feeling or showing tiredness, especially as a result of too much effort or lack of sleep: *weary feet. We were all weary after the long ride.* **2** (*with* ***of***) with one's patience or tolerance exhausted: *She was weary of his stupid jokes.*
v **wea·ried, wea·ry·ing 1** cause to become tired: *Walking up the hill wearied him.* **2** grow tired of or bored with. <Old English *werig*> **wea′ri·ly** *adv.* **wea′ri·ness** *n.* **wea′ry·ing** *adj.* **wea′ry·ing·ly** *adv.*

wea·sel (wē′zəl) *n* **1** a small, slender, meat-eating mammal with a long flexible body, short legs, and short fur. See MINK for picture. **2** *Informal* a sly and treacherous person.
v **wea·selled** or **wea·seled, wea·sel·ling** or **wea·sel·ing 1** *Informal* achieve something by use of cunning or deceit: *She had promised to help but weaselled out at the last minute.* **2** behave or talk evasively to avoid committing oneself or making a direct statement: *Stop weaselling and give me a straight answer.* <Old English *weosule*> **wea′sel·ly** *adj.*

weasel word *n* often, **weasel words** *pl* a word, phrase, or statement that is intentionally ambiguous or misleading.

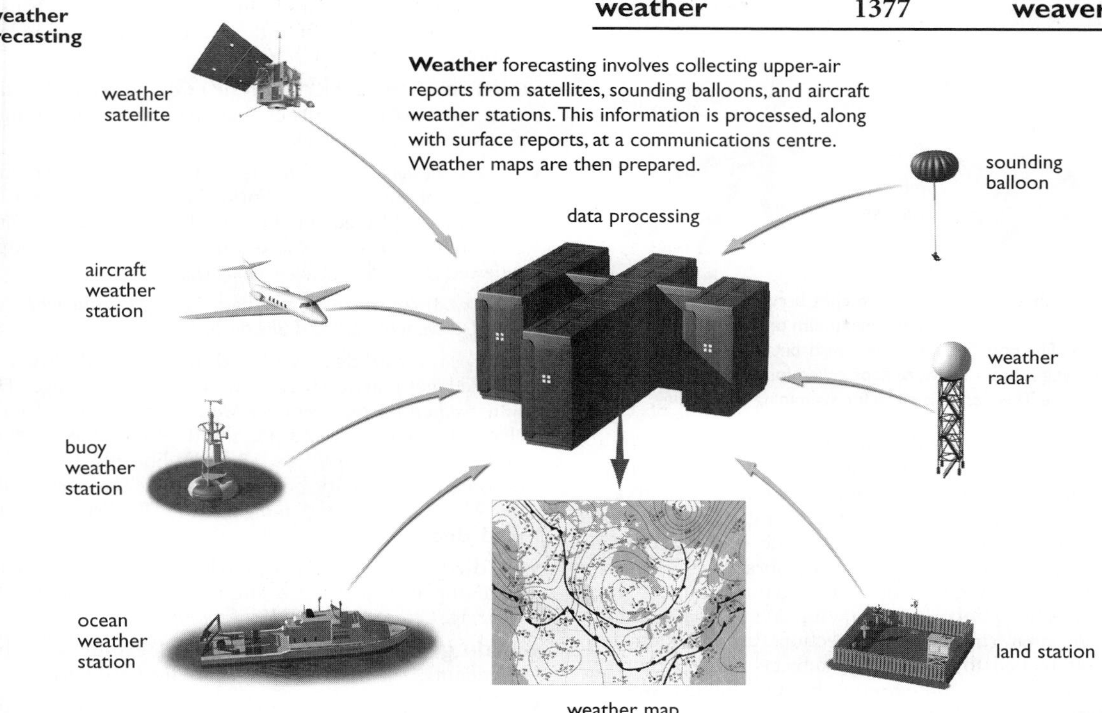
weather forecasting
weather satellite
Weather forecasting involves collecting upper-air reports from satellites, sounding balloons, and aircraft weather stations. This information is processed, along with surface reports, at a communications centre. Weather maps are then prepared.
sounding balloon
data processing
aircraft weather station
weather radar
buoy weather station
ocean weather station
land station
weather map

weath·er (weᴛʜʹər) *n* **1** the condition of the atmosphere at a particular time and place with respect to temperature, moisture, cloudiness, or windiness: *windy weather. The weather was beautiful for the entire trip.* **2** disagreeable conditions of the atmosphere, such as wind, rain, storm, or cold: *a shelter for protection against the weather.*
v **1** wear away or change the appearance or texture of something by long exposure to the atmosphere, or be worn away or altered, especially as rock or other material, in this way: *The wood became weathered over the long winter. The wooden bench had weathered to a silvery grey.* **2** come safely through a storm or bad weather: **3** survive a difficult time: *The family weathered many hardships.*
adj to do with the side from which the wind is blowing, especially on board a ship. <Old English *weder*>
keep a weather eye open, be on the lookout for possible danger or trouble.
under the weather, *Informal* be slightly unwell: *She's been feeling under the weather for several days.*

weath·er–beat·en (weᴛʜʹər bēʹtən) *adj* damaged or worn by the wind, rain, and other forces of the weather: *a weather-beaten face.*

weath·er–bound (weᴛʜʹər boundʹ) *adj* prevented by bad weather from travelling or proceeding with an action: *a weather-bound ship.*

weath·er·cock (weᴛʜʹər kokʹ) *n* a weathervane, especially one in the shape of a rooster.

weath·er·man (weᴛʜʹər manʹ) *n, pl* **weath·er·men** (-men) a person who forecasts the weather or one who presents weather forecasts, as on radio or TV.

weath·er·proof (weᴛʜʹər prūfʹ) *adj* resistant to the effects of bad weather: *They built a small weatherproof cabin in Cochrane and lived there all winter.*
v make weatherproof: *I'm looking for something that will weatherproof my boots.*

weath·er·strip (weᴛʜʹər stripʹ) *n* a narrow strip of rubber, metal, or other material used to seal the edges of a door or window against wind, snow, and rain. **weathʹer·stripʹping** *n.*

weath·er·vane (weᴛʜʹər vānʹ) *n* a device, often placed on a rooftop, that is rotated by the wind and so shows the wind direction.

weave (wēv) *v* **wove** or (*for def. 3*) **weaved, wo·ven, weav·ing** **1** form interlacing threads or strips into a texture or fabric by hand or with a loom: *They wove the straw into hats. She is weaving a rug.* **2** make a complex story or pattern from a number of interconnected elements, or include an element in such a story or pattern: *The author wove three plots together into one story.* **3** twist and turn from side to side while moving somewhere in order to avoid obstructions or other people: *She weaved her way through the crowd.*
n a style or manner in which something is woven: *The shawl was in a fine weave.* <Old English *wefan*> **weavʹer** *n.*

weav·er·bird (wēʹvər bərdʹ) *n* a songbird of tropical Africa and Asia that builds an elaborately woven nest.

a bat	e bed	i bid	o pot	u cup	th **thin**
ā cake	ē me	ī bite	ō go	ū rude	ᴛʜ **then**
ä bar	ə about	ər over	ô for	ů put	zh measure

W

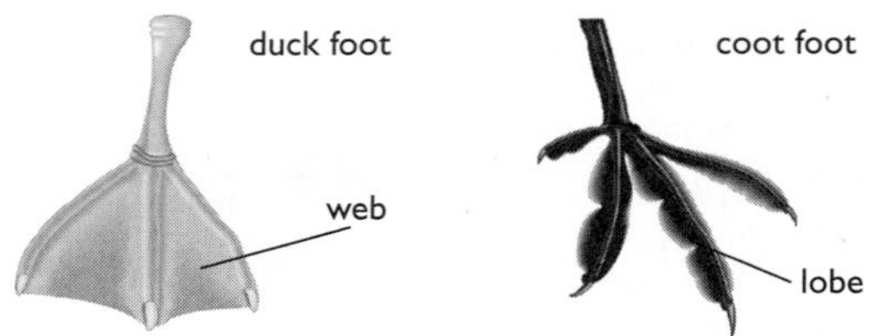

The **web** in a duck's foot stretches between its toes to provide surface area for maximum propulsion in water. The coot is also a water bird, but instead of webbing it has a series of flaps called lobes alongside each toe. This design is good for swimming and wading.

web (web) *n* **1 a** a network of fine threads constructed by a spider from fluid it secretes and is used to catch its prey. **b** a similar filmy network spun by some insect larvae, especially some caterpillars. **2** a complex system of interconnected elements, especially one considered as a trap or danger: *a web of lies.* **3** a membrane between the toes of a swimming bird or other aquatic animal. **4 the web** or **the Web** WORLD WIDE WEB. **5** a graphic organizer that shows the connections among ideas or concepts related to a particular subject: *Make a concept web on the topic of communication.* <Old English *webb*> **webbed** *adj.* **web′like′** *adv.*

GRAMMAR AND USAGE

Although most people generally use the terms **Web** (or World Wide Web) and *Internet* interchangeably, they are not really the same.

The Internet is the vast network that links millions of computers around the world, and is the larger of the two systems.

The Web is one part of the Internet, with its own technical procedures to find and transmit information.

web·bing (web′ing) *n* **1** a strong, closely woven fabric used for making items such as straps and belts, and for supporting the seats of upholstered chairs. **2** the system of belts, pouches, and straps worn by a soldier as part of a combat uniform. **3** the part of a baseball glove between the thumb and forefinger.

web browser *n* a software program used to find and access documents on the World Wide Web.

web·cast (web′kast′) *n* a live broadcast shown on the World Wide Web of a concert or other event. <*web* + *broadcast*>

web·foot·ed (web′fu̇t′id) *adj* of a bird or animal, with webbed feet for swimming.

web·log (web′log′) BLOG.

web·mas·ter (web′mas′tər) *n* a person who oversees the design and maintenance of a website.

web page *n* a document connected to the World Wide Web and viewable by a person with an Internet connection and a browser.

web quest *n* an online learning exercise that directs users to certain websites, in order to find information and complete a task.

web·site or **Web site** (web′sīt′) *Computers n* a location connected to the Internet that maintains one or more pages on the World Wide Web.

web·zine (web′zēn′) *Computers n* **1** a magazine devoted to matters of interest to World Wide Web users. **2** a magazine published on the World Wide Web; a website consisting of articles, ads, columns, etc. on a certain topic, renewed regularly. <*Web* + (*maga*)*zine*>

we'd (wēd) *contraction* **1** we had: *We'd gone out when you called.* **2** we would: *We'd like pasta for lunch.*

wed (wed) *v* **wed·ded, wed·ded** or **wed, wed·ding 1** get married, get married to, or give or join in marriage: *They were wed on the fourteenth of May.* **2** combine two factors, elements, or qualities, especially desirable ones: *Pictures and text were superbly wed.* **3** be stubbornly attached or devoted to an activity, belief, or system: *They were wed to the old way of doing things.* <Old English *weddian*> **wed′ded** *adj.*

wed·ding (wed′ing) *n* **1** a marriage ceremony, especially including associated celebrations. **2** an anniversary of the marriage ceremony: *a golden wedding.*

wedding party *n* the bride and bridegroom and their attendants: *The wedding party sat at the head table.*

wedding ring *n* a ring, usually plain and often one of a pair, given during the wedding ceremony by one spouse to the other. Also called **wedding band**.

wedge (wej) *n* **1** a piece of wood, metal, or some other material with one thick end and tapering to a thin edge that is driven between two objects to secure or separate them. **2** anything that has such a shape: *He cut the big pie into eight wedges.* **3** a thing used like a wedge to create an opening or a division: *She gave a big party as a wedge for her entry into society. Their disagreement over money drove a wedge between the friends.* **4** *Golf* a club with a low, angled face. **5** a shoe of which the heel and sole form a solid block, with no gap under the instep.
v **wedged, wedg·ing 1** fix in position using a wedge: *The cupboard door was wedged open.* **2** force into a narrow space: *He wedged his suitcase between a chair and the wall.* <Old English *wecg*>
thin edge of the wedge, an act or event that seems harmless but may lead to unwanted developments.

wedgie *Informal n* the uncomfortable wedging of underwear between the buttocks.

wed·lock (wed′lok) *n* the state of being married.

Wednes·day (wenz′dā) *n* the day of the week after Tuesday and before Thursday. *Abbrev.* **Wed** <Old English *Wodensdaeg* Woden's day. Wodin (or Odin) was the supreme Germanic god.>

wee (wē) *adj* **we·er, we·est** small: *a wee lad.* <Old English *wæg* weight>

weed (wēd) *n* a wild plant, usually one growing where it is not wanted and in competition with cultivated plants.
v **1** remove unwanted plants from an area of ground or the plants cultivated in it: *to weed a garden.* **2** remove something, especially inferior or unwanted items or

members from a group or assortment: *I spent all morning weeding my stamp collection.* <Old English *weod*> **weed′er** *n.* **weed′less** *adj.*

weed·kill·er (wēd′kil′ər) *n* a substance used to destroy weeds.

weed·y (wē′dē) *adj* **weed·i·er, weed·i·est** **1** containing or covered with many weeds: *a weedy garden.* **2** of or like a weed or weeds, especially in fast and vigorous growth. **3** of a person, thin and physically weak in appearance: *a weedy youth.* **weed′i·ness** *n.*

wee hours *pl n* the very early hours of the morning, just after midnight.

week (wēk) *n* **1** a period of seven days, one after another: *This is the last week of summer holidays.* **2** the period of seven days from and to midnight on Saturday. **3** the working days of a seven-day period, as contrasted to a weekend, or the time spent working in this period: *Some people work a six-day week.* See WEAK for confusable. <Old English *wice*>
week in, week out, every week without exception.

week·day (wēk′dā′) *n* a day of the week other than Saturday or Sunday.
adj of or on a weekday.

week·end (wē′kend′) *n* Saturday and Sunday, especially regarded as a time for recreation or leisure.
v spend a weekend somewhere: *They are weekending at their cottage.*
adj of or on a weekend.

week·ly (wē′klē) *adj* **1** done, produced, or occurring once a week: *a weekly meeting.* **2** relating to or calculated in terms of a week: *a weekly wage.*
adv once a week: *The clerks in the store are paid weekly.*
n, pl **week·lies** a newspaper or magazine published once a week.

weep (wēp) *v* **wept, weep·ing** **1** shed or express with tears: *She wept for joy when she won the award.* **2** give off moisture in small drops: *The basement wall sometimes weeps.* <Old English *wepan*> **weep′er** *n.*

weeping willow *n* a large willow tree with long, feathery, drooping branches.

weep·y (wē′pē) *adj* **weep·i·er, weep·i·est** with a tendency to cry, especially for sentimental reasons. **weep′i·ly** *adv.* **weep′i·ness** *n.*

wee·vil (wē′vəl) *n* a small beetle with a long snout, the larvae of which typically develop inside seeds, stems, or other plant parts, such as those of grain, nuts, cotton, and fruit. <Old English *wifel*> **wee′vil·ly** or **weev′i·ly** *adj.*

weft (weft) *n* the threads stretched crosswise in a loom, through which the lengthwise threads are woven. Compare WARP. <Old English *wefan* weave>

weigh (wā) *v* **1 a** find out how heavy someone or something is, typically using scales: *I weighed myself this morning.* **b** have a specified weight: *I weigh forty-five kilograms.* **2** (*with* ***out***) measure and take from a larger quantity of a substance a portion of a particular weight: *She weighed out two kilograms of potatoes.* **3** (*with* ***down, under,*** *etc.*) bend under the pressure of weight: *The boughs of the apple tree were weighed down with fruit.* **4** assess the nature or importance of something, especially in order to reach a decision or take an action: *Weigh your words before speaking.* **5** influence a decision or action: *The amount of the salary does not weigh with him, because he really wants the job.* **6** compare the importance of one factor with that of another: *They weighed the advantages against the disadvantages.* See WAY for confusable. <Old English *wegan*> **weigh′er** *n.*
weigh in, find out one's weight before a contest.
weigh in at, weigh a certain amount.
weigh on, be a burden to.

weight (wāt) *n* **1 a** the physical force exerted on the mass of a body by a gravitational field. **b** a body's relative mass: *The dog's weight is twenty kilograms.* **2** the quality of being heavy: *The floor sagged under his weight.* **3** a unit or system of units for expressing how much an object or quantity of matter weighs: *troy weight.* **4** a heavy object, especially one being lifted, carried, or to keep something fixed or in place. **5** a piece of metal known to weigh a definite amount and used on scales to determine how heavy an object or quantity is. **6** the ability of someone or something to influence decisions or actions, or the importance attached to it: *The jury gave the witness's statement great weight.*
v **1** (*often with* ***down***) hold something down by placing a heavy object on top of it, or make something heavier by attaching an object to it, especially to make it stay in place: *The cloth was weighted down by a large jug. The shawl was weighted with coloured beads.* **2** attach importance or value to: *The poet weighted style and content equally.* See WAIT for confusable.
by weight, measured by weighing.
pull your weight, do your part or your share: *We will finish the job quickly if we all pull our weight.*
throw your weight around, make too much use of your rank or position.

weight·less (wā′tlis) *adj* **1** appearing to have no weight: *The snow felt weightless on my shoulders.* **2** not apparently acted on by gravity, especially in an orbiting spacecraft. **weight′less·ly** *adj.* **weight′less·ness** *n.*

weight·lift·ing (wāt′lif′ting) *n* the lifting of heavy weights specially made for the purpose, as a competitive sport or as a fitness exercise. See BODYBUILDING for picture. **weight′lift·er** *n.*

weight·y (wā′tē) *adj* **weight·i·er, weight·i·est** **1** weighing a great deal. **2** of great seriousness and importance: *weighty matters.* **3** with a great influence on events or decisions: *weighty arguments.* **weight′i·ly** *adv.* **weight′i·ness** *n.*

weir (wēr) *n* **1** a low dam built across a river to raise the level of the water or to divert its flow. **2** a fence of stakes or broken branches put in a stream or channel to catch fish. <Old English *wer*>

weird (wērd) *adj* **1** suggesting something supernatural: *I was awakened by a weird shriek.* **2** very strange or bizarre: *The shadows made weird figures on the wall.* <Old English *wyrd* fate> **weird′ly** *adv.* **weird′ness** *n.*

a bat	e bed	i bid	o pot	u cup	th **thin**
ā cake	ē me	ī bite	ō go	ū rude	TH then
ä bar	ə about	ər over	ô for	ů put	zh measure

weird·o (wēr′dō) *Informal n* a person whose appearance or behaviour seems strange or eccentric.

wel·come (wel′kəm) *n* a pleased or approving reaction: *You will always have a welcome here.*
adj **1** gladly received: *a welcome visitor, a welcome rest.* **2** gladly or freely permitted: *You are welcome to pick the flowers.* **3** very pleasing because much needed or desired: *a welcome break in the routine.*
v **wel·comed, wel·com·ing 1** greet someone arriving in a glad, polite, or friendly way: *We welcomed him heartily when he arrived.* **2** be glad to entertain someone or receive something: *We welcome new ideas and suggestions.*
interj used as a friendly greeting: *Welcome!* <Old English *wilcuma* welcome guest, from *wil-* will[2] + *cuma* comer>
wel′com·er *n.*
put out the welcome mat, offer an enthusiastic reception or welcome.
wear out your welcome, stay as a visitor too often or too long.
you are (most) welcome, used as a polite response to thanks.

weld (weld) *v* **1** join together metal or plastic pieces or parts by heating the surfaces to the point of melting, and uniting them by hammering or pressing while hot and soft, or forge an object by such means. **2** cause to combine and form a harmonious or effective whole: *Working together welded the two sisters into a strong team.*
n a welded joint. <*well*[2]> **weld′a·ble** *adj.* **weld′er** *n.*

wel·fare (wel′fer′) *n* **1** the health, happiness, and prosperity of a person or group: *He asked about the welfare of everyone in our family.* **2** an out-of-date word for SOCIAL ASSISTANCE. <Old English *welfaren* to fare well>

welfare state *n* a system whereby a government provides for the health and welfare of citizens in need by means of grants, pensions, and other benefits.

well[1] (wel) *adv* **bet·ter, best 1** in a good, appropriate, profitable, or satisfactory way: *The job was well done. Is everything going well at school? It's just as well she stayed away, because we wouldn't have had enough room for her.* **2** in a thorough manner: *Shake well before using.* **3** to a great extent or degree: *The book sale brought in well over a hundred dollars.* **4** probably, reasonably, or in all likelihood: *I can't very well refuse. You might well ask what he was doing there.* See GOOD for confusable.
adj **1** in good health: *I am very well.* **2** in a good, full, or satisfactory way: *It is well you accompanied her. I am well aware of the facts.* **3** sensible or advisable: *It would be well to know just what she means.*
interj used to show surprise, anger, resignation, relief, or agreement, or merely to fill in a conversational gap: *Well! Well! Here you are. Well, I'm not sure.* <Old English *wel*>
as well (as), a also or besides: *She reads fiction as well as nonfiction. I have skates as well as skis.* **b** with equal reason or any equally good result: *I may as well quit right now. She can ride as well as you can.*
(all) well and good, used to express acceptance of a first statement before introducing a contradicting or confirming second statement: *If they can deliver what they promised, well and good, but I have no confidence in them.*

well[2] (wel) *n* **1** a hole dug or bored in the ground to obtain water, oil, or gas. **2** a plentiful source or supply: *Our class president is a well of ideas.* **3** a thing like a well in shape or use: *the well of a fountain pen.* **4** an enclosed space in the middle of a building, giving room for stairs or an elevator, or to allow light or ventilation.
v rise as a liquid up to the surface and spill or be about to spill: *Tears welled up in his eyes.* <Old English *wella*>

we'll (wēl) *contraction* we will; we shall.

well–ad·just·ed (wel′ə jus′tid) *adj* **1** mentally and emotionally stable as a person. **2** successfully altered or moved so as to achieve a desired fit, appearance, or result.

well–ad·vised (wel′əd vīzd′) *adj* wise or sensible: *a well-advised plan. You'd be well-advised to start early.*

well–ap·point·ed (wel′ə poin′tid) *adj* with good furnishings or equipment as a building or room.

well–bal·anced (wel′bal′ənst) *adj* **1** correctly balanced, adjusted, or regulated. **2** sensible or sane.

well–be·ing (wel′bē′ing) *n* the condition of being comfortable, healthy, or happy.

well·born (wel′bôrn′) *adj* belonging to an aristocratic or wealthy family.

well–bred (wel′bred′) *adj* with or showing good manners.

well–con·nect·ed (wel′kə nek′tid) *adj* **1** related to or acquainted with important, prestigious, or powerful people. **2** linked well: *well-connected paragraphs.*

well–dis·posed (wel′di spōzd′) *adj* with a well-meaning, sympathetic, or friendly attitude.

well done *adj* **1** done with skill and efficiency. **2** thoroughly cooked as meat.

well–fa·voured or **well–fa·vored** (wel′fā′vərd) *adj* with special advantages, especially good looks.

well–fixed (wel′fikst′) *Informal adj* wealthy.

well–found·ed (wel′foun′did) *adj* based on good evidence or reasons: *She had a well-founded faith in him.*

well–ground·ed (wel′groun′did) *adj* **1** based on good evidence or reasons. **2** thoroughly instructed in the fundamental principles of a subject.

well·head (wel′hed′) *n* **1** a place where a spring comes out of the ground. **2** the structure over a well, typically an oil or gas well.

well–heeled (wel′hēld′) *Informal adj* wealthy.

well–in·formed (wel′in fôrmd′) *adj* with or showing reliable or full knowledge of a subject.

well–in·ten·tioned (wel′in ten′shənd) *adj* with or showing good intentions despite a lack of success or fortunate results: *Her well-intentioned efforts at tidying up made it impossible to find anything.*

well–kept (wel′kept′) *adj* kept clean, tidy, and in good condition.

well–knit (wel′nit′) *adj* strongly and compactly built as a person.

well–man·nered (wel′man′ərd) *adj* polite or courteous.

well–mean·ing (wel′mē′ning) *adj* with or proceeding from good intentions.

well·ness (wel′nis) *n* **1** the condition of being in good health physically and mentally. **2** an approach to health care that stresses maintenance and prevention through regular monitoring, rather than treatment after the fact. Such an approach is typical of **wellness clinics**.

well–nigh (wel′nī′) *adv* very nearly or almost.

well off *adj* **1** wealthy. **2** in a good condition or situation: *Your whole family is healthy, so you should consider yourself well off.*

well–oiled machine (wel′oild′) *n* a group of people or an organization that functions smoothly and efficiently.

well–pre·served (wel′pri zərvd′) *adj* showing few signs of age or use.

well–read (wel′red′) *adj* having read much or knowing a great deal about books and literature.

well–round·ed (wel′roun′did) *adj* with a personality that is fully developed in all aspects.

well–spo·ken (wel′spō′kən) *adj* speaking or spoken in an educated and refined way.

well·spring (wel′spring′) *n* **1** a fountainhead. **2** a source, especially of a supply that never fails.

well–suit·ed (wel′sū′tid) *adj* suitable or convenient.

well–thumbed (wel′thumd′) *adj* having been read often as a book or magazine and bearing marks of frequent handling.

well–timed (wel′tīmd′) *adj* timely: *His well-timed intervention settled the dispute.*

well–to–do (wel′tə dū′) *adj* wealthy or prosperous.

well–trav·elled (wel′trav′əld) *adj* **1** having travelled widely as a person. **2** used by many people as a route.

well–versed (wel′vərst′) *adj* knowledgeable or experienced: *I'm well-versed in Canadian history.*

well–wish·er (wel′wish′ər) *n* a person who desires happiness or success for another, or who expresses such a desire.

well–worn (wel′wȯrn′) *adj* **1** much worn by use. **2** used or repeated too much as a phrase, idea, or joke.

Welsh (welsh) *adj* to do with Wales, or its people, or their Celtic language.

ETYMOLOGY

Welsh comes from Old English *Welisc*, which developed from *Wealh*, a Germanic term for non-Germanic peoples, including Celts. Words with the same root include *Wales, Cornwall*, and *walnut*.

Welsh rabbit *n* a thick sauce containing cheese, served on toast. Also called **Welsh rarebit**.

welt (welt) *n* **1** a leather rim sewn around the edge of a shoe upper to which the sole is attached. **2** a ribbed, reinforced, or decorative border of a garment or pocket. **3** a weal. <Middle English *welte*>

wel·ter (wel′tər) *n* a confused mass or large number of items in no order, or a condition of general disorder: *All we saw was a welter of arms, legs, and bodies.*
v **1** roll or toss about. **2** lie soaked or drenched in blood with no help or care. <German *welteren*>

wel·ter·weight (wel′tər wāt′) *n* a boxer who weighs between 64 and 67 kilograms. <origin uncertain>

wench (wench) *Archaic or Humorous n* a girl or young woman. <Old English *wencel*>

wend (wend) *v* **wend·ed, wend·ing** go in a specified direction, typically slowly or by an indirect route: *We wended our way home.* <Old English *wendan*>

Wen·dat (wen′dat′) WYANDOT.

wen·di·go or **win·di·go** (wen′di gō′) *or* (win′di gō′) *n, pl* **wen·di·gos** or (*especially collectively*) **wen·di·go** an evil spirit in the folklore of northern Algonquian peoples in the shape of a person who has been transformed into a monster by eating human flesh. Also, **windigo**. <Ojibwa *weendigo* cannibal>

went (went) past tense of GO.

wept (wept) past tense and past participle of WEEP.

were (wər) *v* **1** plural and second person singular, past tense of BE: *We were hungry. Were you on the phone?* **2** past tense subjunctive of BE: *If I were rich, I would travel.* <Old English *wæron*>
as it were, so to speak; in some way.

GRAMMAR AND USAGE

Were can be used as the past subjunctive of *be*, where it expresses the idea that something might happen, but hasn't yet.

When used this way, **were** retains the same form, whatever the person or number of the noun: *If I were to arrive early, don't be surprised. If they were to arrive late, don't get angry.*

we're (wēr) *contraction* we are.

weren't (wernt) *or* (wərnt) *contraction* were not.

were·wolf (wēr′wu̇lf′) *or* (wer′wu̇lf′) *n, pl* **were·wolves** (-wu̇lvz′) a man in myth or fiction who has been changed for periods of time into a wolf, or who can change himself into a wolf, typically when there is a full moon. <Old English *wer* man + *wulf* wolf>

west (west) *n* **1** the direction of the sunset. **2 the West a** Europe and the Americas, as contrasted with many countries in the rest of the world. **3** 🍁 the part of Canada west of Ontario. **c** the western part of the US. **4** 🍁 **the West Coast** southwestern British Columbia.
adj **1** toward, in, or facing the west: *the west coast.* **2** (*especially of the wind*) from the west: *a west wind.*
adv toward the west: *Walk west three blocks.* Also, **westerly**. <Old English>
out West 🍁 in the Prairie Provinces or British Columbia, from the point of view of provinces to the east.
west of, farther west than.

west·bound (west′bound′) *adj* going west.

a bat	e bed	i bid	o pot	u cup	th **thin**
ā cake	ē me	ī bite	ō go	ū rude	ᴛʜ **then**
à bar	ə about	ər over	ȯ for	u̇ put	zh measure

W

whale

There are two kinds of **whales**: *toothed*, like the narwhal, and *baleen*, like the humpback.

eye

The humpback is a baleen whale. Instead of teeth, thin plates of fingernail-like material called baleen hang from its upper jaw. It feeds only on plankton, which the baleen plates filter from the water.

west·er·ly (wes′tər lē) *adj* west.
adv from the west: *The wind blew westerly.*
n, pl **west·er·lies** a wind or storm from the west.

west·ern (wes′tərn) *adj* 1 to do with the west: *Vancouver is a western port.* 2 **Western** to do with the countries in Europe or N America: *Western cultures.*
n a movie, TV drama, or novel about cowboys in western N America, especially in the 1800s and 1900s.

west·ern·er (wes′tər nər) *n* a person born or living in the western part of a country. Also, **Westerner**.

west·ern·ize (wes′tər nīz′) *v* **west·ern·ized, west·ern·iz·ing** cause a country, person, or system to adopt or be influenced by the cultural, economic, or political systems of Europe and N America. **west′ern·i·za′tion** *n.* **west′ern·iz′er** *n.*

west·ern·most (wes′tərn mōst′) *adj* farthest west.

western omelette *n* an omelette containing chopped green peppers, chopped onions, and ham.

🍁 **Western Provinces** *pln* British Columbia, Alberta, Saskatchewan, and Manitoba. Also called **Western Canada**.

Western red lily PRAIRIE LILY.

western sandwich *n* a sandwich with a filling of scrambled eggs and chopped ham, peppers, and onions.

West Nile virus (nīl) *n* a virus carried by mosquitoes and causing severe flulike symptoms. <from the place in Uganda where the virus originated>

west–north·west (west′nôr′thwest′) *n* a direction midway between west and northwest.
adj, adv in, toward, or from this direction. *Abbrev.* **WNW**

west–south·west (west′sou′thwest′) *n* a direction or compass point midway between west and southwest.
adj, adv in, toward, or from this direction. *Abbrev.* **WSW**

west·ward (wes′twərd) *adj, adv* toward the west: *We live on the westward slope of the hill (adj). He walked westward (adv).* Also, (*adv*) **westwards**. **west′ward·ly** *adj, adv.*

wet (wet) *adj* **wet·ter, wet·test** 1 covered, filled, or soaked with water or other liquid: *wet hands. Her eyes were wet with tears.* 2 not yet dry or hardened as paint, ink, plaster, or a similar substance. 3 rainy: *wet weather.* 4 having urinated as a baby or small child in a diaper or other garment. 5 *Informal* of a country or region or its legislation, allowing the sale of alcoholic drinks.
v **wet** or **wet·ted, wet·ting** cover, produce, or touch with liquid: *Wet the cloth before you wipe off the window.*
n 1 **the wet** water or other liquid: *I dropped my scarf in the wet.* 2 rainy weather: *Come in out of the wet.* <Old English *wǣtan*> **wet′ly** *adv.* **wet′ness** *n.* **wet′tish** *adj.*
all wet, *Informal* completely wrong or mistaken.
wet behind the ears, *Informal* immature and lacking experience.

wet bar *n* a bar for serving alcoholic drinks in a home, with a sink and water taps in it.

wet blanket *Informal n* a person who has a discouraging or depressing effect: *He's a wet blanket; when we were planning our picnic, he said it would probably be cold.*

wet cell an electrochemical cell with a liquid electrolyte. Compare DRY CELL.

wet·land (wet′land) *n* often, **wetlands** *pl* a marshy or swampy area, especially when thought of as a habitat for wildlife.

wet nurse *n* in former times, a woman employed to suckle the infant of another.

wet·suit (wet′sūt′) *n* a close-fitting rubber garment typically covering the entire body, worn for warmth in water sports or diving. See SCUBA DIVER for picture.

we've (wēv) *contraction* we have: *We've got to go now.*

whack (wak) *n* a sharp, resounding blow or the sound of such a blow.
v strike with a sharp, resounding blow: *The batter whacked the ball out of the park.* <imitative>
out of whack, *Informal* out of order or not working well: *The timing of the engine is out of whack.*
take (or **have**) **a whack at,** *Informal* try: *I'd like to take a whack at skydiving.*

whack·ing (wak′ing) *Informal adj* very large or tremendous: *a whacking success.*

whale[1] (wāl) *n, pl* **whales** or (*especially collectively*) **whale** a very large saltwater mammal with a streamlined hairless body, a horizontal tail fin, and a blowhole on top of the head for breathing. See also CETACEAN for picture.
v **whaled, whal·ing** hunt and catch whales. <Old English *hwæl*>
a whale of, *Informal* a very large or impressive example or type of: *a whale of a car, a whale of a good time.*

whale[2] (wāl) *Informal v* **whaled, whal·ing** beat severely.

whale·bone (wāl′bōn′) *n* an elastic, hornlike substance growing in place of teeth in the upper jaw of certain whales and forming a series of thin, parallel plates.

whal·er (wā′lər) *n* a person who hunts whales, or a ship used for this.

whale·watch·ing (wāl′woch ing) *n* the hobby of watching whales in the ocean. **whale′watch·er** *n.*

whal·ing (wā′ling) *n* the hunting and killing of whales for their oil, meat, or whalebone.

wham (wam) *n* a loud bang or sound of a hard impact.
interj **1** used to express the sound of this impact. **2** used to express the idea of a sudden, dramatic, and decisive occurrence: *One step outside and wham! I slipped on some ice.*
v **whammed, wham·ming** strike something forcefully, or make a loud sound of a forceful impact. <imitative>

wham·my (wam′ē) *Informal n, pl* **wham·mies** an event with a powerful and unpleasant effect, or an evil or unlucky influence: *Recent political events seem to have put the whammy on the stock market.*

whang (wang) *Informal v* make or produce a resounding noise, or strike or throw heavily and loudly.
n a resounding blow.

whap (wap′) *or* (hwap′) *Informal v* **whapped, whap·ping** hit hard: *The door opened and whopped me in the face.*
n a heavy blow, or the sound of such a blow. Also, **whop**.

wharf (wȯrf) *n, pl* **wharves** or **wharfs** a platform built on the shore or out from the shore, beside which ships can load and unload. <Old English *hwearf*>

what (wut) *or* (wot) *pron* **1** a request for information specifying something: *What is your e-mail address?* **2** a request that the speaker repeat something not heard or to confirm something not understood: *What did you say?* **3** the thing or things that are used in specifying something: *What I need are hard facts.*
adj **1** asking for information specifying something: *What time is it?* **2** whatever part of an amount: *Give me what sections of the paper you don't want.* **3** how great or remarkable: *What luck!*
adv **1** to what extent: *What does it matter?* **2** with regard to or taking into account: *What with the wind and the rain, our picnic was spoiled.*
interj used to show surprise, liking, anger, or to add emphasis: *What! Are you late again?* <Old English *hwæt*>
and what not, *Informal* and other similar things.
what about, a what is the status or fate of: *What about us? Don't we get any pizza?* **b** what is the importance of: *"You remember that story I wrote?" "Yes, what about it?"* **c** how about: *What about going to the movies, then?*
what for? *Informal* why? *"Give me your pen." "What for?"*
what if, what would happen if: *What if it rains on the day of the game?*
what's what, *Informal* what is useful or important: *That girl knows what's what.*
what's with, *Informal* **a** what's wrong with: *What's with him?* **b** what is the purpose or significance of: *What's with the balloons everywhere?*
what with, because of or considering: *We were very tired, what with our long walk and the lateness of the hour.*

what·ev·er (wə tev′ər) *or* (wot ev′ər) *pron, adj* **1** anything that: *Do whatever you like.* **2** *Informal* (*to express surprise or confusion*) what: *Whatever do you mean?* **3** any: *Ask whatever people you like to the party.* **4** regardless of who or what: *Whatever happens, he is safe. Whatever excuse she makes will not be believed.*
adv **1** at all: *They received no answer whatever.* **2** *Informal* no matter what happens: *We said we'd help him, whatever.*
interj Informal used to indicate indifference: *"You want to go to the ball game?" "Whatever."*

what·not (wot′not′) *n* **1** an item or items that are not identified but are felt to have something in common with items already named: *trinkets and rings and whatnot.* **2** a stand with shelves for small items.

what's (wuts) *or* (wots) *contraction* **1** what is: *What's the latest news?* **2** what has: *What's been going on here lately?*

what·so·ev·er (wut′sō ev′ər) *or* (wot′sō ev′ər) *pron, adj* whatever.

wheat (wēt) *n* a cereal grass bearing grain that is ground to make flour. See GRAIN for picture. <Old English *hwæte*>

wheat·en (wē′tən) *adj* **1** made of wheat. **2** of a pale yellow-beige colour.

wheat germ *n* the tiny golden embryo of the wheat kernel, used as a cereal and as a vitamin supplement.

🍁 **wheat pool** *n* an agricultural co-operative that collects and sells the wheat harvested on the Prairies.

whee (wē) *interj* used to express delight or pleased excitement, especially at fast movement.

whee·dle (wē′dəl) *v* **whee·dled, whee·dling** **1** use flattery or endearing words to persuade someone to do something or give one something: *The children wheedled their mother into letting them go out.* **2** coax or persuade someone to do, say, or give something: *They finally wheedled the secret out of him.* <Old English *wædlian* beg> **whee′dler** *n.* **whee′dling** *adj.* **whee′dling·ly** *adv.*

wheel (wēl) *n* **1** a round object that revolves on an axle and is fixed below a vehicle or other object to enable it to move over the ground. **2** a round object that revolves on an axle and forms part of a machine or device. *a potter's wheel.* **3** a machine or structure with a wheel as its essential part: *Could you take the wheel, please?* **4 wheels** *pl* **a** a system or part of a system thought of as a relentlessly moving machine: *the wheels of government.* **b** *Informal* a motor vehicle.
v **1** push, pull, or drive a vehicle with wheels, or carry someone or something in or on a vehicle with wheels: *They wheeled him into the hospital room.* **2** abruptly turn to face the other way, or cause to turn in this way: *He wheeled around suddenly. The rider wheeled her horse about.* **3** of a bird or aircraft, fly in a wide circle or curve. <Old English *hweol*> **wheeled** *adj.* **wheel′less** *adj.*
wheel and deal, *Informal* engage in business or politics shrewdly or aggressively.
wheels within wheels, a situation that is complicated and affected by secret or indirect influences.

a bat	e bed	i bid	o pot	u cup	th thin
ā cake	ē me	ī bite	ō go	ū rude	ᴛʜ then
ä bar	ə about	ər over	ȯ for	u̇ put	zh measure

wheel–and–ax·le (wēl′ənd ak′səl) *n* a simple machine consisting of an axle to which a wheel is fastened so that torque applied to the wheel winds a rope or chain onto the axle.

wheel·bar·row (wēl′bar′ō) *n* a small cart with one wheel at the front and two handles at the back, typically used for carrying small loads.

wheel·base (wēl′bās′) *n* the distance from the centre of the front axle to the centre of the rear axle in motor vehicles.

wheel·chair (wēl′tcher) *n* a chair mounted on wheels so that it can be pushed from behind or moved by the person sitting in it, and typically used by an invalid or by a person with a disability.

wheel·er–deal·er (wē′lər dē′lər) *Informal n* a person who does business rapidly and shrewdly.

wheel·house (wēl′hous′) *n* a small, enclosed place on a ship to shelter the steering wheel and people who steer the ship.

wheel·ie (wē′lē) *Informal n* a stunt performed on a bicycle or motorcycle by pulling up the front wheel so that for a few seconds only the rear wheel is on the ground.
pop a wheelie, perform this stunt.

wheeze (wēz) *v* **wheezed, wheez·ing** breathe with difficulty and with a whistling or rattling sound in the chest, or make a sound like this: *The old engine wheezed, but it didn't stop.*
n the sound of a person wheezing. <origin uncertain>
wheez′i·ly *n.* **wheez′i·ness** *n.* **wheez′y** *adj.*

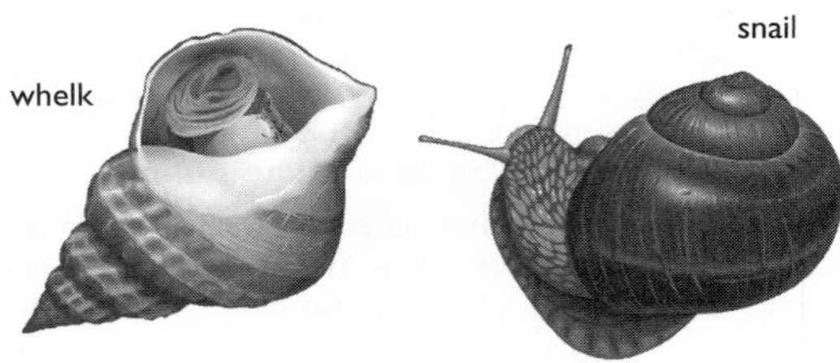

While **whelks** and snails are both molluscs, they differ in several ways. Snails can be marine, freshwater, or terrestrial, depending on the species, whereas whelks live in salt water. Whelks are carnivorous, while snails feed mainly on algae and decaying matter.

whelk (welk) *n* a saltwater mollusc with a heavy, pointed, spiral shell. Welks are sometimes used for food. <Old English *weoloc*>

whelp (welp) *n* **1** a cub of an animal. **2** a boy, a young man, or a new thing, especially one of little worth.
v give birth to. <Old English *hwelp*>

when (wen) *adv* **1** at what time or how soon: *When does school close?* **2** at or on which a situation or circumstance occurs: *Monday is when I go shopping.*
conj **1** at or during the time that: *Raise your hand when your name is called.* **2** at any time that: *He is impatient when he is kept waiting.* **3** after which: *The dog growled till his master spoke, when he gave a joyful bark.* **4** although or whereas: *We have only three books when we need five.* **5** considering that or in view of the fact that: *How can I help you when I don't know how to do the problem myself?*
pron what or which time: *Since when have they had a car?*
n a time or occasion: *the when and where of an act.* <Old English *hwænne*>

whence (wens) *Archaic or Poetic adv* from what place, source, or cause: *Let them return whence they came.* <Old English *whannon*>

when·ev·er (we nev′ər) *conj, adv* at whatever time or on whatever occasion: *He lent me money whenever I needed it.*

where (wer) *adv* **1** in, to, or from what place or position: *Where is she? Where are you going? Where did you get that story?* **2** at, in, or to which: *It was the house where he was born. That's the school where I'm going next year. I don't know where the dog is.* **3** in or to a place or situation in which: *Where does that plant come from?*
n a place or location: *the when and the where of it.* See WEAR for confusable. <Old English *hwær*>

where·a·bouts (wer′ə bouts′) *adv* where, or approximately where: *Whereabouts can I find a doctor?*
n the place where a person or thing is: *Do you know the whereabouts of the cottage?*

where·as (wer az′) *conj* **1** in contrast or comparison with the fact that: *Some children like school, whereas others do not.* **2** taking into consideration the fact that: *Whereas all people are human, so all people should show humanity.*

where·by (wer bī′) *adv* by which: *There is no other way whereby it can be saved.*

where·fore (wer′fôr) *Archaic or Poetic adv* for what reason: *Wherefore do you weep?*
conj as a result of which: *He has been found guilty, wherefore he must be banished.*

where·in (wer in′) *adv* in which: *This is the paragraph wherein the data may be found*

where·of (wer uv′) *or* (wer ov′) *adv* of what or which: *He knew whereof he spoke.*

where·up·on (wer′ə pon′) *conj* immediately after which: *The prince kissed the princess, whereupon she awoke.*

wher·ev·er (wer ev′ər) *adv* in or to whatever place: *Sit wherever you like. She will be happy wherever she lives.*
conj in every case when: *We avoid fats wherever possible.*

where·with·al (wer′wiᴛʜ ol′) *n* the money or other means needed for a particular purpose: *Has she the wherewithal to pay for the trip?*

whet (wet) *v* **whet·ted, whet·ting** **1** sharpen the blade of a tool or weapon: *to whet a carving knife.* **2** excite or stimulate someone's desire, interest, or appetite. <Old English *hwettan*>

wheth·er (weᴛʜ′ər) *conj* **1** expressing a doubt or choice between alternatives: *It matters little whether we go or stay. She does not know whether to work or play.* **2** indicating that a statement applies, whichever of the alternatives mentioned is the case: *Whether sick or well, she is always cheerful.* **3** expressing or suggesting a question: *He asked whether he should finish the work.* <Old English *hwether*>

whet·stone (wet′stōn′) *n* a fine-grained stone used for sharpening knives or tools.

whew (hwyū) *interj* used to express surprise, relief, or a feeling of being very hot or tired: *Whew! I'm glad that's over!*

whey (wā) *n* the watery part of milk that separates from curds when milk sours, such as in making cheese. <Old English *hwæg*>

which (wich) *adj* **1** asking for information specifying one or more people or things from a definite group: *Tell me which method is best. Which books are yours?* **2** to do with something previously mentioned when giving further information: *I may be late, in which case I'll let you know.*
pron **1** asking for information specifying one or more people or things from a definite set or group: *Which do you like best, the red or the blue?* **2** referring to something previously mentioned when giving further information: *I was sick, which is why I didn't go to the meeting. The sandwich, which I left on the table, tasted awful.* <Old English *hwilc*>

GRAMMAR AND USAGE

Never place a comma in front of **which** or *that* when these words introduce restrictive clauses: *This is the book that (which) I want.*

Use commas to set off non-restrictive clauses: *The book, which is in hardcover, is expensive.* Never use *that* to introduce a non-restrictive clause.

which·ev·er (wi chev′ər) *pron, adj* any one or any that: *Take whichever you want (pron). Whichever side wins, I will be satisfied (adj).*

whiff (wif) *n* **1** a smell that is only smelt briefly or faintly: *We thought we detected a whiff of perfume in the empty room.* **2** an act of sniffing or inhaling: *One whiff of the stranger and the dog started barking.* **3** a puff or breath of air or smoke.
v get a brief or faint smell of. <Middle English *weffe*>

while (wīl) *n* **1** a period of time: *He kept us waiting a long while.* **2 the while** the same time: *We talked, but she stayed in bed all the while.*
conj **1** during the time that: *While I was speaking, he said nothing.* **2** in contrast with or in spite of the fact that: *While I like the colour of the coat, I do not like its shape.*
adv during the period that: *The month while he was in hospital passed quickly.*
v **whiled, whil·ing** pass or spend time in an easy, leisurely way: *We whiled away the day playing at the beach.* <Old English *hwil*>
worth your while, worth the time and effort you spent: *Studying for the test was certainly worth my while.*

whim (wim) *n* a sudden desire or change of mind, especially one that is unusual or unexplained: *He got a dog on a whim.*

whim·per (wim′pər) *v* make as a person or animal a series of low, feeble sounds that express fear, pain, or discontent, or say something in this way: *The sick child whimpered.*
n a whimpering cry or sound. <imitative> **whim′per·er** *n.* **whim′per·ing** *adj.* **whim′per·ing·ly** *adv.*

whim·si·cal (wim′zə kəl) *adj* playfully quaint or fanciful, especially in an appealing or amusing way. **whim′si·cal′i·ty** *n.* **whim′si·cal·ly** *adv.*

whim·sy (wim′zē) *n, pl* **whim·sies** playfully quaint or fanciful behaviour or humour: *I thought it was just one of her whimsies, so I didn't take it seriously.*

whine (wīn) *v* **whined, whin·ing** complain in a peevish way.
n **1** a complaining tone of voice. **2** a high-pitched prolonged sound. <Old English *hwinan*> **whin′er** *n.* **whin′y** *adj.*

whin·ny (win′ē) *n, pl* **whin·nies** a gentle, high-pitched neigh, such as a horse makes.
v **whin·nied, whin·ny·ing** make such a sound: *The horse whinnied as we approached the stable.* <imitative>

whip (wip) *n* **1** a strip of leather or length of cord fastened to a handle, used for beating a person or for urging on an animal. **2** (*with the name of the flavouring ingredient*) a dessert made by beating cream or eggs into a light, fluffy mass with fruit, chocolate, or other ingredients: *strawberry whip.* **3** an official of a political party in a legislature who is appointed to make sure other members attend debates and votes.
v **whipped, whip·ping 1** beat a person or animal with a whip, especially as a punishment or to urge the animal on: *He whipped the horse to make it go faster.* **2** strike or beat violently as a flexible object, or rain, water, or wind: *Spray from the waves will whip your face.* **3** move fast or suddenly in a specified direction: *He whipped off his coat. The thief whipped behind a tree and escaped.* **4** *Informal* defeat: *The mayor is going to whip her opponent in this election.* **5** beat cream, eggs, or other foods into a froth. **6** rouse or incite: *He whipped the crowd into a frenzy.* <Middle English *wippen*> **whip′like′** *adj.* **whip′per** *n.* **whip′ping** *n.*
whip up, a prepare or make quickly: *She whipped up some masks for us to wear in the play.* **b** arouse excitement or interest: *to whip up some interest in speed skating.*

whip·cord (wip′kȯrd′) *n* **1** a thin, strong, twisted cord, sometimes used for the lashes of whips. **2** a strong, closely woven cloth with diagonal ridges on it.

whip·lash (wip′lash′) *n* **1** a lashing action of a whip. **2** an injury to the neck resulting from a sudden jolt that snaps the head backward and then forward: *When her car was struck from behind, she suffered whiplash.*

whipped (wipt) *adj* **1** having been beaten with a whip: *a whipped dog.* **2** beaten at high speed until smooth, frothy, or fluffy: *whipped potatoes, whipped butter.* **3** *Informal* **a** soundly defeated. **b** extremely tired.

whipped cream *n* cream containing a lot of butterfat, beaten at high speed until it forms a fluffy mass.

whip·per·snap·per (wip′ər snap′ər) *Informal n* a young and inexperienced person considered to be overconfident.

whip·pet (wip′it) *n* a dog of a small, slender breed that looks like a small greyhound.

whipping cream *n* fresh heavy cream, high in butterfat, that can be beaten until stiff.

a bat	e bed	i bid	o pot	u cup	th thin
ā cake	ē me	ī bite	ō go	ū rude	ᴛʜ then
ȧ bar	ə about	ər over	ȯ for	u̇ put	zh measure

whip–poor–will (wip′ər wil′) *or* (wip′ər wil′) *n* a North and Central American insect-eating bird whose call sounds somewhat like its name. <imitative>

whip·saw (wip′so′) *n* a long, narrow saw with its ends held in a frame, usually used by two people.
v cut with a whipsaw.

whip·stock (wip′stok′) *n* the handle of a whip.

whir or **whirr** (wər) *v* **whirred, whir·ring** make a low, continuous, regular sound, especially as a machine or a bird's wings.
n a sound of such a type. <origin uncertain>

whirl (wərl) *v* **1** move or cause to move rapidly, especially round and round: *The leaves whirled in the wind. We whirled about the room. We were whirled away in an airplane.* **2** seem to spin round, especially as thoughts or images: *The disturbing news made her mind whirl.*
n **1** a rapid movement round and round. **2** frantic activity of a specified kind: *We had a rest after the whirl of the holidays.* <Old Norse *hvirfla* to turn about, from *hverfla* turn> **whirl′er** *n.* **whirl′ing** *adj.* **whirl′ing·ly** *adv.*

SYNONYMS

Whirl means "move round and round rapidly": *The tornado whirled across the field.*

Pivot and **swivel** mean "turn around a single point": *The huge lamp pivoted (swivelled) at the top of the lighthouse.*

Pirouette means "whirl on one foot": *The way the dancers pirouetted was astounding.*

whirl·i·gig (wər′lē gig′) *n* **1** a toy that spins, for example, a top. **2** a merry-go-round. **3** a thing regarded as hectic or constantly changing. **4** a small black beetle that swims rapidly in circles on the surface of still water.

whirl·pool (wərl′pūl′) *n* **1** a quickly rotating mass of water in a river or sea into which objects may be drawn, typically caused by the meeting of conflicting currents. **2** in full, **whirlpool bath** a tub with underwater jets that keep the water constantly moving.

whirl·wind (wərl′wind′) *n* **1** a column of air moving rapidly round and round in a cylindrical or funnel shape. **2** a very energetic or frantic person or process: *a whirlwind of activity.*

whisk (wisk) *v* **1** take or move someone or something in a particular direction suddenly and quickly: *The waitress whisked my plate away. The babysitter whisked the children off to bed.* **2** beat or stir a substance, especially eggs or cream, with a light rapid movement.
n **1** a small wire kitchen utensil for beating eggs, cream, or other foods. **2** a brief, rapid sweeping or whipping action or movement: *a whisk of the broom, a whisk of the horse's tail.* **3** a whisk broom. <Middle English *visk*>

whisk broom *n* a small, short-handled broom, used especially for brushing away dust or particles.

whisk·er (wis′kər) *n* **1** a long projecting hair or bristle growing from the face or snout of many mammals. **2** a very small amount. **3** **whiskers** *pl* the hair growing on a man's face, especially that on his cheeks and chin. <*whisk*> **whisk′ered** *adj.* **whisk′er·y** *adj.*

whis·ky or **whis·key** (wis′kē) *n, pl* **whis·kies** a strong alcoholic drink made from malted grain, especially barley and rye. <obsolete *whiskybae,* fromGaelic *uisge beatha* water of life>

🍁 **whisky–jack** or **whiskey-jack** (wis′kē jak′) CANADA JAY.

ETYMOLOGY

Whisky-jack, a variation of *whisky-john*, comes from Cree *weskuchanis*, meaning "little blacksmith," a reference to the bird's sooty colour. The Cree word sounded like *whisky-john* to English speakers.

whis·per (wis′pər) *v* **1** speak very softly, using one's breath rather than the throat: *We could hear them whispering behind us. She whispered the news in my ear.* **2** tell secretly or privately: *It is whispered that his health is failing.* **3** make a soft, rustling sound: *The wind whispered in the pines.*
n **1** the act or an instance of whispering: *She spoke in a whisper. They were speaking in whispers.* **2** something told secretly or privately: *No whisper about having a new teacher has come to our ears.* **3** a soft, rustling sound. <Old English *hwisprian*> **whis′per·er** *n.* **whis′per·y** *adj.*

SYNONYMS

Whisper means "speak very softly": *The mother whispered "Be quiet," to the child as the movie began.*

Murmur means "make a soft, low, indistinct sound": *My friends and I murmured the words of the songs all through the concert.*

whist (wist) *n* a card game, resembling bridge, for two pairs of players, in which points are scored according to the number of tricks won. <*whisk*>

whis·tle (wis′əl) *v* **whis·tled, whis·tling** **1** **a** make a clear, shrill sound by forcing breath through a small hole between one's teeth or lips: *The boy whistled, and the dog ran to him.* **b** produce a tune with such sounds. **c** express surprise, admiration, or derision by making such a sound: *He whistled when he heard how much he would be paid.* **2** produce a similar sound as a bird, animal, or machine: *The kettle whistled.* **3** produce such a sound by moving rapidly through the air or a narrow opening: *The wind whistled around the house.* **4** blow a small instrument to produce such a sound as a call, signal, direction, or summons: *The referee whistled for the game to stop.* **5** blow a musical instrument to produce a tune with such sounds.
n **1** the sound made by whistling. **2** an instrument for making a whistling sound. **3** a musical instrument for producing tunes with such sounds. <Old English *hwistlian*>
blow the whistle (on), bring a wrongdoing to an end by informing on the person responsible.
whistle in the dark, try to be courageous or hopeful in a fearful or difficult situation.

whis·tler (wis′lər) *n* **1** a person who or thing that whistles. **2** a hoary marmot.

whis·tle–stop (wis′əl stop′) *Informal n* **1** a small, unimportant town along a railway line. **2** a stop at such a town or station for a brief appearance or speech, as in a political campaign tour.
v **whis·tle-stopped, whis·tle-stop·ping** make a series of electioneering appearances or speeches at stations along a railway line.

whit (wit) *n* a very small part or amount: *The sick woman is not a whit better.* <Old English *wiht* thing>

white (wīt) *adj* **whit·er, whit·est 1** caused by the presence or reflection of all visible light; the opposite of black: *Fresh snow is white.* **2** suggesting such a colour in being very pale or light coloured: *She turned white with fear.* **3 a** with light-coloured skin, usually of European ancestry: *My mother is white, and my father is black.* **b** to do with people with light-coloured skin, especially those of European descent, culture, or society: *the white population of South Africa.* Also, **White**.
n **1** a person with European ancestry. Also, **White**. **2** something white, such as paint or clothing: *dressed in white.* **3** in chess or checkers, the player of the white pieces. <Old English *hwit*> **white′ness** *n.* **whit′ish** *adj.*
bleed someone white, drain someone of money, strength, or resources: *His good-for-nothing son bled the old man white.*
white out, remove (an error) by painting over it with white correction fluid.

white ant *n* a termite.

white birch *n* a N American birch tree with white bark that peels off in strips. Also called **paper birch**.

white blood cell See BLOOD CELL.

white·board (wīt′bȯrd′) *n* a framed white surface, usually on a wall, specially designed for writing on with dry erasable markers. Often, interactive technology can be added, allowing a person to control, manipulate or annotate an image using a pen or finger.

white·cap (wīt′kap′) *n* a wave with a foaming white crest, caused by the action of the wind.

white·coat (wīt′kōt′) *n* a young harp seal, or its white fur.

white–col·lar (wīt′kol′ər) *adj* to do with office workers, especially their way of life or attitudes: *Embezzlement is a white-collar crime.* Compare BLUE-COLLAR.

white corpuscle *n* one of many colourless blood cells in vertebrates that counteract foreign substances and disease, helping the body to fight infection. Compare RED CORPUSCLE. See BLOOD COUNT for picture.

white dwarf *n* a small star, very dense but not very bright. Compare RED GIANT.

white elephant *n* a thing that is expensive and troublesome to maintain and difficult to dispose of.

white feather *n* a white feather given to someone as a sign that the giver considers the person to be a coward.

white·fish (wīt′fish′) *n, pl* **white·fish·es** or (*especially collectively*) **white·fish** a mainly freshwater food fish of the salmon family.

white flag *n* a plain white flag or cloth used in a battle or conflict as a sign of truce, surrender, or a desire to have a peaceful discussion.

white gold *n* a silver-coloured alloy of gold with nickel, platinum, or another metal, used for jewellery.

white heat *n* **1** the temperature or condition of something that is so hot that it emits white light. **2** a situation or circumstance of intense passion or activity: *In the white heat of anger, he could not think clearly.*

white–hot (wīt′hot′) *adj* white with heat.

White House (wīt′hous′) *n* the official residence of the President of the US, in Washington, D.C., taken as a symbol of the US President, Presidency, or government.

white lie *n* a harmless or trivial lie, especially one told to avoid being rude or hurting someone's feelings: *I had to tell a white lie and say that I liked his new haircut.*

white light *n* apparently colourless light, for example, ordinary daylight, that contains all the wavelengths of the visible spectrum at equal intensity.

white magic *n* magic used for good purposes only. Compare BLACK MAGIC.

white meat *n* any light-coloured meat such as veal, pork, or breast of poultry. Compare RED MEAT.

whit·en (wī′tən) *v* make or become white: *She used bleach to whiten the sheets.*

whit·en·er (wī′tən ər) *n* a liquid or powder substitute for milk or cream, used in coffee or tea.

white noise *n* the sound produced by using the whole range of audible frequencies at equal intensities.

white·out (wī′tout′) *n* **1** a dense snowstorm in which blowing snow makes a person unable to distinguish the features of an area: *The traffic accident was caused by a whiteout.* **2** white correction fluid for covering typing or writing mistakes.

white paper *n* a government report giving information or proposals on an issue. Also, **White Paper**.

white pepper *n* the husked ripe or unripe berries of the pepper tree, typically ground and used as a condiment. Compare BLACK PEPPER.

white pine *n* a N American pine tree.

White Russian *n* **1** a resident of Belarus. **2** a Russian who fought against the Bolsheviks during the Russian Revolution.

white sale *n* a store sale of household linens such as sheets, pillowcases, and towels.

white sauce *n* a sauce made of milk, butter, and flour cooked together.

white supremacy *n* the belief that the people with light-coloured skin are superior to other groups and should therefore occupy the highest social, economic, and governmental positions. **white supremacist** *n.*

a bat	e bed	i bid	o pot	u cup	th thin
ā cake	ē me	ī bite	ō go	ū rude	TH then
ȧ bar	ə about	ər over	ȯ for	u̇ put	zh measure

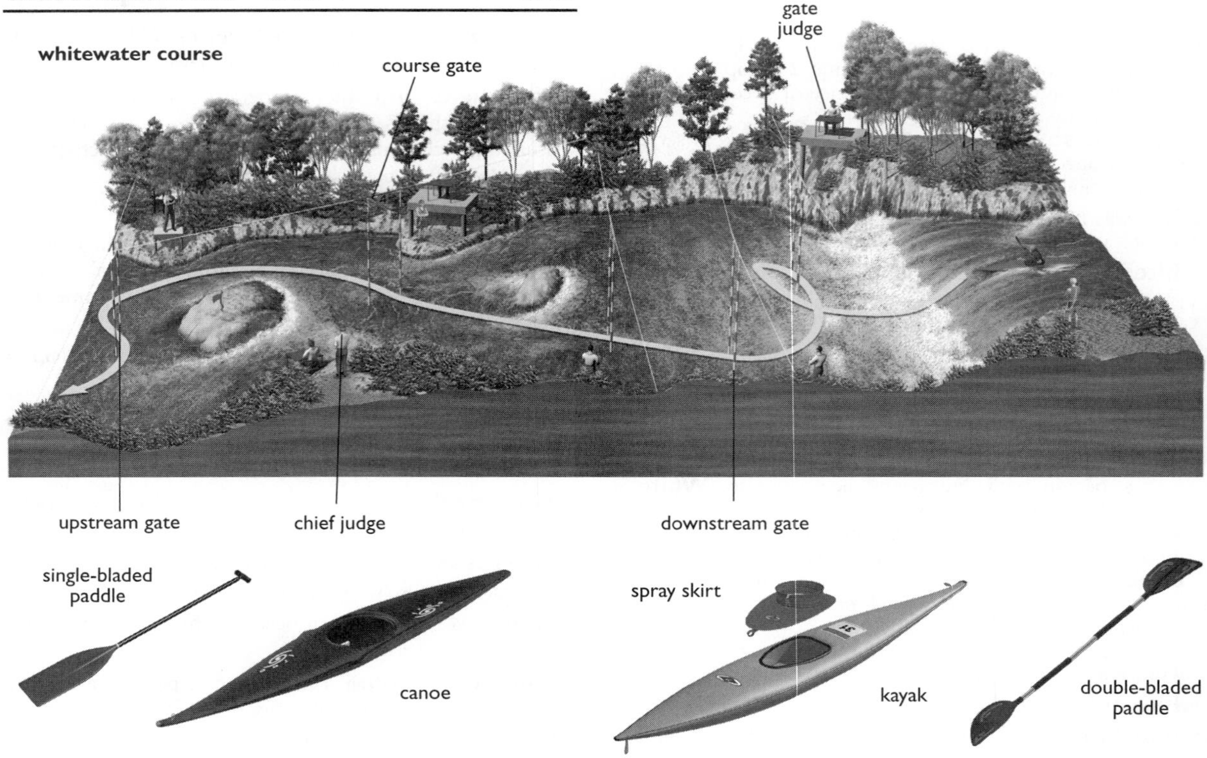

Whitewater slalom races take place on swift courses of turbulent water that have both natural and artificial hazards. Competitors manoeuvre their boats through a series of 25 gates suspended over the water. If a gate is missed, penalty seconds are added to the final time.

white–tailed deer (wīt′tāld′) *n* a N American deer with a broad, relatively long tail with a white underside. Also, **white-tail**. See DEER for picture.

white tie *n* men's formal evening dress with tailcoat and a white bow tie, or the bow tie itself. Compare BLACK TIE.

🍁 **white toast** *n* toasted white bread.

white·wash (wī′twosh) *n* **1** a solution of lime and water or of whiting, size, and water, used for painting walls or fences white. **2** a deliberate concealment of someone's mistakes or faults. **3** a victory in a game or series without a score or win for an opponent.
v **1** paint a wall or fence with whitewash. **2** deliberately conceal someone's mistakes or faults. **3** win a game or series without a score or win for an opponent.

white·wa·ter (wīt′wo′tər) *n* a part of a river's course where the water foams as it rushes quickly over rocks or because of a steep drop; rapids.
adj to do with such a part of a river: *whitewater canoeing.*

whith·er (wiᴛʜ′ər) *Archaic or Poetic adv* to what or which place: *I know not whither she has gone.* <Old English>

whit·tle (wit′əl) *v* **whit·tled, whit·tling** carve wood into an object by repeatedly cutting small slices from it, or carve an object from wood in this way. <Old English *thwitan* cut> **whit′tler** *n.*
whittle down (or **away**), reduce something in size, amount, or extent by a gradual series of steps: *Try to whittle down the expenses, please.*

whiz or **whizz** (wiz) *v* **whizzed, whiz·zing 1** move quickly through the air with a whistling or whooshing sound: *An arrow whizzed past his head.* **2** do or deal with quickly, or cause someone or something to move or go fast.
n **1** a whistling or whooshing sound. **2** *Informal* a person who is extremely clever at something. Also, **wiz.** <*wizard*>

whiz kid *n* a child, teen, or young adult who is unusually talented, expert, or influential at something.

who (hū) *pron* **1** what or which person or people: *Who told you? Who are those people? I don't know who will be there.* **2** further information about a person or people previously mentioned: *The girl who spoke first is my friend. My friend, who spoke first, is the best debater in the class.* <Old English *hwa*>
who's who, a which is one person and which is the other: *I can't figure out who's who.* **b** which people are important. **c** a list or directory of facts about notable people.

whoa (wō) *interj* used to express a command to stop, especially to horses, or to pay attention or express surprise.

who'd (hūd) *contraction* **1** who would: *Who'd like to go along?* **2** who had: *He didn't know who'd committed the crime.*

who·dun·it (hū dun′it) *Informal n* a story or movie dealing with crime, especially murder, and its detection. <*who* + *done* + *it*>

who·ev·er (hū ev′ər) *pron* **1** the person or people who: *Whoever wants the book may have it.* **2** no matter who: *Whoever else goes hungry, she won't.*

whole (hōl) *adj* **1** with all its parts or elements: *a whole set of dishes.* **2** emphasizing the full quantity, amount, extent, or number: *a whole melon, a whole day.* **3** not injured, broken or defective: *He escaped with a whole skin.* **4** in one piece: *She swallowed a piece of meat whole.* **5** not fractional: *a whole number.*
n **1** a thing that is complete in itself: *Four quarters make a whole.* **2 the whole** all of something: *My grandfather worked the whole of his life.*
adj emphasizing the novelty or distinctiveness of something: *a whole new meaning.* See HOLE for confusable. <Old English *hal*> **whole′ness** *n*
as a whole, as one complete thing.
on the whole, taking everything into account.

whole grain *n* grain used without removing the hull or any other part of the kernel. **whole′-grain′** *adj.*

whole·heart·ed (hōl′hȧr′tid) *adj* showing or marked by complete sincerity and commitment: *The returning athletes were given a wholehearted welcome.* **whole′heart′ed·ly** *adv.* **whole′heart′ed·ness** *n.*

whole hog *Informal adv* completely and without restraint or reserve: *She gives herself whole hog to any project she takes up.* **whole′-hog′** *adj.*

whole milk *n* milk with none of the butterfat removed.

whole note *Music n* a note with the longest time value, used as the basis for determining the time value of all other notes.

whole number *n* a number that does not contain a fraction.

whole rest *Music n* a musical rest as long as a whole note.

whole·sale (hōl′sāl′) *n* the sale of goods in large quantities at a time, usually to retailers rather than to consumers directly: *She buys at wholesale and sells at retail.*
adj **1** selling in large quantities: *a wholesale fruit business.* **2** broad and general: *He gave the idea a wholesale condemnation.*
adv in large lots or quantities: *The coach bought the team sweaters wholesale.*
v **whole·saled, whole·sal·ing** sell or be sold in large quantities: *They wholesale these jackets for a quarter of the retail price.* **whole′sal·er** *n.*

whole·some (hōl′səm) *adj* **1** assisting or suggestive of good health and physical well-being: *a wholesome food.* **2** good for the mind or morals; beneficial: *wholesome books.* **whole′some·ly** *adv.* **whole′some·ness** *n.*

whole–wheat (hōl′wēt′) *adj* made of the entire wheat kernel including the husk or outer layer.

who'll (hūl) *contraction* who will; who shall.

whol·ly (hōl′lē) *or* (hō′lē) *adv* to the whole amount or extent: *The boy was wholly cured.*

whom (hūm) *pron* the objective form of WHO: *Whom do you like best? He does not know whom to believe. The girl to whom I spoke is my cousin.*

GRAMMAR AND USAGE

Whom is preferred after a preposition (to *whom*, for *whom*) and in the object position (*Whom would you choose?*), but *who* has become increasingly acceptable, even in formal English.

whom·ev·er (hū′mev′ər) *pron* who or any person whom: *I'll write to whomever I like.*

whoop (hūp) *or* (wūp) *n* **1** a loud cry or shout of joy or excitement: *When land was sighted, the sailor let out a whoop of joy.* **2** a hooting cry or sound. **3** the loud, gasping noise a person with whooping cough makes after a fit of coughing, typical of someone with whooping cough.
v give or make a whoop. <imitative>
whoop it up, *Informal* celebrate in a noisy way.

whoop·ee (hūp′ē) *or* (wūp′ē) *interj* expressing wild excitement or joy.
n a wild celebration: *make whoopee.*

whoopee cushion *n* an inflated rubber bag placed on someone's chair as a practical joke, so that the air is expelled with a loud, embarrassing noise when the bag is sat on.

whoop·ing cough (hū′ping) *n* an infectious disease, mainly affecting children, marked by fits of coughing that end with a loud, gasping sound.

whooping crane *n* a very large, mainly white bird with a trumpeting call. It is the tallest bird found in Canada, and is endangered.

whoosh (wūsh) *or* (wu̇sh) *n* a loud, fast, rushing noise, as of air or water, or a movement causing this sound.
v move with such a sound: *The big trucks whooshed by.*

whop (wop′) WHAP.

whop·per (wop′ər) *Informal n* **1** a thing that is extremely or unusually large. **2** a big or blatant lie. <origin unknown>

whop·ping (wop′ing) *Informal adj, adv* very large of its kind: *a whopping defeat* (*adj*), *a whopping sandwich* (adv).

whore (hȯr) *n* a prostitute.
v **whored, whor·ing** **1** work as a prostitute. **2** do something for unworthy motives, typically to make money. <Old English *hore*>

whorl (wərl) *or* (wȯrl) *n* a coil or ring, especially a circle of leaves or flowers round a stem of a plant, one of the turns of a spiral shell, or a complete circle in a fingerprint. <*whirl*> **whorled** *adj.*

W

a bat	e bed	i bid	o pot	u cup	th **thin**
ā cake	ē me	ī bite	ō go	ū rude	ᴛʜ **then**
ȧ bar	ə about	ər over	ȯ for	u̇ put	zh measure

who's (hūz) *contraction* **1** who is: *Who's that man?* **2** who has: *Who's been eating my porridge?*

CONFUSABLES

Who's is a shortened form of "who is" and "who has": *She's the one who's going to meet them. Are you the person who's been there before?*

Whose means "belonging to which person": *Whose painting is this?*

whose (hūz) *pron* belonging to or associated with which person: *Whose is this pencil?*
adj of whom or of which: *The girl, whose work got the prize, is the youngest in her class. Whose book is this? He's a person whose advice I always seek.*

GRAMMAR AND USAGE

Whose is usually used to refer to people and *of which* to things. However, you may also use *whose* to refer to things when you want to make a sentence read more smoothly.

Compare, for example, the following versions of a sentence:

The machine, ***the parts of which*** *work perfectly, just needs proper maintenance.*

The machine, ***whose parts*** *work perfectly, just needs proper maintenance.*

why (wī) *adv* **1** for what cause, reason, or purpose: *Why did you do it? I don't know why I did it.* **2** because or on account of which: *That is the reason why he failed.*
n, pl **whys** the cause, reason, or explanation: *I can't understand the whys and wherefores of her behaviour.*
interj used to express show surprise or indignation: *Why! The cage is empty. Why, yes, I will if you wish.* <Old English *hwæt* what>

Wic·ca (wik′ə) *n* a modern religion based on the power of witchcraft, claiming its origins in pre-Christian pagan religion. <Old English = wizard> **Wic′can** *adj, n.*

wick (wik) *n* a strip of material that draws liquid fuel up to the flame in a candle, lamp, or lighter. <Old English *weoce*>

wick·ed (wik′id) *adj* **1** evil or morally wrong: *a wicked person, wicked deeds.* **2** mischievous or playfully sly: *a wicked smile.* **3** *Informal* extremely unpleasant or severe: *a wicked task, a wicked storm.* **4** *Informal* excellent: *a wicked video game.* <*wicke* evil, probably related to Old English *wicca* wizard> **wick′ed·ly** *adv.* **wick′ed·ness** *n.*

wick·er (wik′ər) *n* slender, easily bent branches or twigs that can be woven together, used in making baskets and furniture.
adj made of or covered with wicker. <Middle English *wekirr*>

wick·et (wik′it) *n* **1** a small window or opening, often protected by a screen or grating and used for selling tickets or a similar purpose. **2** a small door or gate, especially one beside or in a larger one. **3** *Croquet* a wire arch stuck in the ground to knock the ball through. **4** *Cricket* **a** either of two sets of stumps used to form the target of the bowler and defended by a batsman. **b** a batsman's innings. <Old French *wiket*>

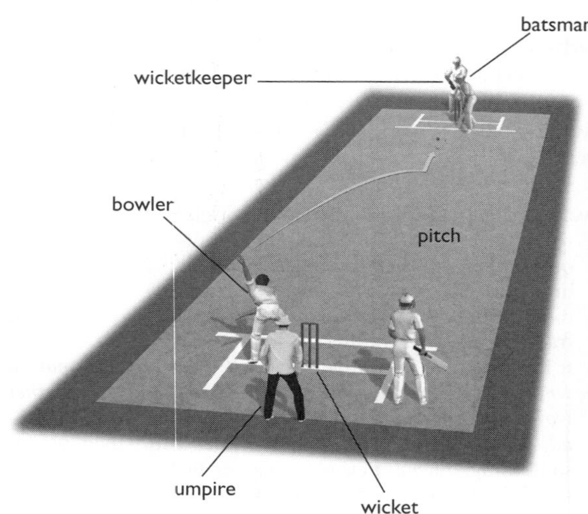

wick·et·keep·er (wik′it kē′pər) *n* a fielder in cricket who stands close behind a batsman's wicket.

✱ **wick·i·up** (wik′ē up′) *n* a hut used among some Algonquian peoples that consists of an oval frame covered with brushwood or grass. <Algonquian>

wide (wīd) *adj* **wid·er, wid·est** **1** of great or more than average width: *a wide street.* **2** extending a certain distance from side to side, measured at right angles to length: *The door is ninety centimetres wide.* **3** including a great variety of people or things: *wide reading, a wide range of choice.* **4** at a considerable or specified distance from a point or mark: *His shot was wide of the goal.*
adv **1** to the full extent: *Open your mouth wide.* **2** far from a particular point or mark: *The ball was thrown wide.* <Old English *wid*> **wide′ness** *n.*

wide–an·gle (wīd′ang′gəl) *adj* with a photographic lens that has a short focal length and hence a visual field covering a wide angle.

wide area network *Computers n* a network of computers far apart from each other, but able to share and exchange programs. *Abbrev.* **WAN** Compare LOCAL AREA NETWORK.

wide–a·wake (wī′də wāk′) *adj* **1** with the eyes wide open; fully awake. **2** alert or attentive: *a wide-awake guard.*

wide–eyed (wī′dīd′) *adj* with the eyes wide open, especially in amazement: *The girl was wide-eyed with surprise.*

wide·ly (wī′dlē) *adv* **1** over a wide area or range: *a widely distributed plant.* **2** to a large degree in nature or character as a variation or difference: *The boys gave two widely different accounts of the quarrel.*

wid·en (wī′dən) *v* make or become wider: *He widened the path through the forest. The river widens as it flows.*

wide–o·pen (wī′dō′pən) *adj* **1** opened as much as possible. **2** lax in the enforcement of laws, especially those to do with the sale of liquor, with gambling, and with prostitution.

wide·spread (wīd′spred′) *adj* found or distributed over a large area or number of people: *a widespread flood, a widespread belief.*

widg·eon (wij′ən) *n, pl* **widg·eons** or (*especially collectively*) **widg·eon** a freshwater wild duck of Europe and N America. Also, **wigeon.** <origin uncertain>

widg·et (wij′it) *n* a gadget or small mechanical device. <origin uncertain>

wid·ow (wid′ō) *n* a woman whose spouse is dead and who has not married again.
v make into a widow or widower: *Our neighbour was widowed when she was only thirty years old.* <Old English *widewe*>

wid·ow·er (wid′ō ər) *n* a man whose spouse is dead and who has not married again.

widow's peak *n* a V-shaped point formed by the hairline in the middle of the forehead, especially one left by a receding hairline in a man. <once believed to be a sign of early widowhood>

width (width) *n* **1** the measurement or extent of something from side to side: *The width of the room is four metres.* **2** a piece of something at its full extent from side to side: *She chose two different widths of ribbon.*

wield (wēld) *v* hold and use a weapon or tool: *to wield a sword, to wield power.* <Old English *wieldan*> **wield′er** *n.*

wie·ner (wē′nər) *n* a smoked sausage, usually made of beef and pork, especially a frankfurter. <German *Wienerwurst* Vienna sausage>

wiener roast *n* an outdoor social function at which wieners are roasted or boiled over an open fire.

wife (wīf) *n, pl* **wives** a married woman considered in relation to her spouse. <Old English *wif*> **wife′less** *adj.* **wife′ly** *adj.*

wig (wig) *n* an artificial covering of hair for the head: *The bald man wore a wig.* <earlier *periwig,* from French *perruque*>

wig·eon (wij′ən) WIDGEON.

wig·gle (wig′əl) *v* **wig·gled, wig·gling** move or cause to move with short, quick movements up or down or from side to side.
n a wiggling movement. <Middle English *wiglen,* from *wig* wag> **wig′gler** *n.* **wig′gly** *adj.*

wig·wam (wig′wom′) *n* a dome-shaped hut or tent traditionally used by First Nations and Native American peoples, made by fastening mats, skins, or bark over a framework of poles. Compare TEEPEE.

ETYMOLOGY

Wigwam is borrowed from Algonquian (probably Abenaki) *wigwam,* meaning "a dwelling." It is also said to be found in such formations as Ojibwa *wigiwam* and Delaware *wiquoam* meaning "their house."

wild (wīld) *adj* **1** of an animal or plant, living or growing in the natural environment. **2** not civilized: *wild manners.* **3** desolate-looking and uncultivated as scenery or a region: *wild country.* **4** uncontrolled or unrestrained, especially in seeking pleasure: *a wild party.* **5** haphazard, rash, or unreasonable: *a wild guess, a wild scheme.* **6** very enthusiastic, angry, or excited: *wild with joy.* **7** stormy: *wild winds.* **8** distracted or upset in looks or appearance: *wild eyes.* **9** of a playing card, able to be used to represent any number or suit.
adv **1** far from the mark: *He shot the arrow wild.* **2** in a wild manner or to a wild degree: *to act wild.*
n **1 the wild** a natural, uncultivated, or uninhabited region: *These animals live longer in captivity than in the wild.* **2 the wilds** *pl* a remote area, uninhabited or sparsely inhabited. <Old English *wilde*> **wild′ly** *adv.* **wild′ness** *n.*
run wild, grow or develop without restraint or discipline as an animal, plant, or person.
wild and woolly, rough and uncivilized in appearance or behaviour.

wild card *n* **1** a playing card which can have any value, suit, colour, or other property in a game. **2 a** a chance to enter a sports competition without having to take part in qualifying matches or be ranked at a particular level. **b** a player or team given such a chance.

wild·cat (wīld′kat′) *n* **1** a small wild cat of Eurasia, Africa, and the Americas, including the N American bobcat. **2** a person considered to be hot-tempered or ferocious, especially a woman. **3** a well drilled for oil or gas in a place where none has been found before.
adj not authorized by union officials as a strike, typically a sudden one.
v **wild·cat·ted, wild·cat·ting** drill wells in places not known to contain oil.

wil·de·beest (wil′də bēst′) GNU.

wil·der·ness (wil′dər nis) *n* **1** a wild or desolate region with few or no people living in it. **2** a neglected or abandoned area of a garden or town. **3** a position of disfavour or unpopularity: *After he lost the election, the candidate found himself in the political wilderness.* <Old English *wildeorn,* from *wilde* wild + *deor* animal>
a voice (crying) in the wilderness, a lone person who calls for reform but is not listened to.

wild–eyed (wīl′dīd′) *adj* staring angrily, fearfully, or desperately.

wild·fire (wīld′fīr′) *n* **1** a substance that burns fiercely and is hard to put out, formerly used in warfare. **2** a WILL-O'-THE-WISP (def. 1).
spread like wildfire, very rapidly: *The news spread like wildfire.*

wild·flow·er (wīld′flou′ər) *n* a flowering plant that grows without human involvement.

a bat	e bed	i bid	o pot	u cup	th thin
ā cake	ē me	ī bite	ō go	ū rude	TH then
à bar	ə about	ər over	ȯ for	u̇ put	zh measure

W

wild goose chase *n* a foolish and hopeless search for or pursuit of something that cannot be obtained.

wild·life (wīl′dlīf′) *n* wild animals and birds as a group, especially those native to a particular area: *northern wildlife.*

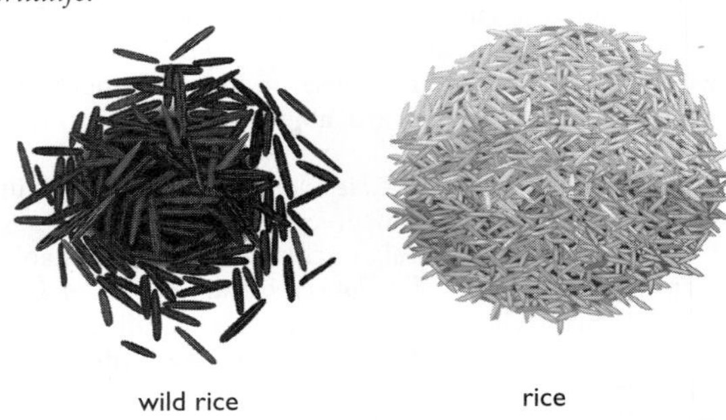

Wild rice and white rice are produced by semi-aquatic grasses but are not related. Wild rice grows in shallow lakes and is native to the Great Lakes region.

wild rice *n* the ricelike edible grain of a N American grass, traditionally eaten by First Nations and Native American peoples.

wild rose *n* an uncultivated ROSE (def. 1). The wild rose is the floral emblem of Alberta.

Wild West *n* the western part of N America, especially the US, during its lawless early years of settlement.

wiles (wīlz) *pln* devious or cunning tactics used to manipulate or persuade someone to do what one wants: *He used his wiles to get excused from school for the rest of the day.* <Old English *wigle* magic>

wil·ful or **will·ful** (wil′fəl) *adj* **1** with or showing a stubborn intention to do as one wants, regardless of the consequences or effects: *wilful waste.* **2** done on purpose as an illegal act or omission: *wilful negligence.* **wil′ful·ly** or **will′ful·ly** *adv.* **wil′ful·ness** or **will′ful·ness** *n.*

will[1] (wil) *v* **would 1** expressing the future tense: *The train will be late. If they leave now, they will arrive in time for dinner.* **2** expressing a strong intention or statement about the future: *I will certainly see you soon.* **3** expressing a request: *Will you bring me the book, please?* **4** expressing facts about ability or capacity: *She said that this hat would keep off the rain. This pail will hold eight litres.* **5** expressing an action that recurs: *She will read for hours at a time.* **6** expressing likelihood or expectation: *They will be long gone by the time you wake up.* <Old English *willan*>

GRAMMAR AND USAGE

Will expresses the future tense: *She will be there later.*

Would is used for polite requests: *Would you please excuse me?*; or to express the conditional mood: *If he would only listen, he would understand.* It is also used to express repeated action in the past: *They would go swimming every Saturday* and as the past tense of *will* in indirect speech: *He said that he would do it.*

will[2] (wil) *n* **1** the power of the mind by which a person decides on and starts an action: *an iron will.* **2** the control deliberately used to do something or to restrain an impulse: *an effort of will.* **3** a deliberate or fixed desire or intention: *the will to live.* **4** a legal document containing instructions as to what should be done with one's property after one's death.
v **willed, will·ing 1** intend, desire, or wish something to happen: *She willed to keep awake.* **2** make or try to make someone do a thing or something happen by using mental powers: *She willed the person in front of her to turn around.* **3** bequeath something to someone by the terms of one's will, or leave specified instructions in one's will: *The woman willed the house to her son.* <Old English>
at will, at whatever time or in whatever way one wishes.
with a will, with energy and determination.

wil·lies (wil′ēz) *Informal pln* (*with* **the**) a strong feeling of nervousness and discomfort: *That movie gave me the willies—I won't go to that kind of show again.* <origin unknown>

will·ing (wil′ing) *adj* **1** ready, eager, or prepared to do something: *He is willing to wait.* **2** given or done readily: *willing obedience.* **will′ing·ly** *adv.* **will′ing·ness** *n.*

will–o'–the–wisp (wil′ə ᴛʜə wisp′) *n* **1** a light hovering or floating at night over marshy places, thought to be caused by combustion of natural gases. **2** a person who or thing that is difficult or impossible to find, reach, or catch: *Her plan for instant wealth turned out to be a will-o'-the-wisp.*

wil·low (wil′ō) *n* a tree or shrub of temperate climates that typically has long, narrow, pointed leaves and grows near water. <Old English *welig*>

wil·low·y (wil′ō ē) *adj* **1** tall, slim, and supple: *a willowy figure.* **2** bordered, shaded, or covered by willows: *a willowy riverbank.*

will·pow·er (wil′pou′ər) *n* self-control or determination exercised by the will: *He hasn't got enough willpower to keep to a diet.*

wil·ly–nil·ly (wil′ē nil′ē) *adv* **1** whether one wishes it or not: *He found himself involved willy-nilly in the promotion campaign.* **2** without direction or planning: *The ivy spread willy-nilly.* <Old English *wile he, nyle he* will he or will he not>

wilt (wilt) *v* **1** become or cause to become limp and drooping as a plant, leaf, or flower through heat, loss of water, or disease. **2** lose one's energy or vigour.
n a fungal or bacterial disease of plants marked by wilting of leaves. <Dutch welken>

wil·y (wī′lē) *adj* **wil·i·er, wil·i·est** skilled or gaining an advantage, especially through deceit. **wil′i·ness** *n.*

wimp (wimp) *Informal n* a timid and weak-willed person. <origin uncertain> **wimp′y** *adj.* **wimp′i·ness** *n.*
wimp out, back out or withdraw from an action or a stated position through lack of courage or determination.

wim·ple (wim′pəl) *n* a cloth headdress covering the head, neck, and the sides of the face, formerly worn by women and still worn by some nuns. <Old English *wimpel*>

win (win) *v* **won, win·ning 1** be successful or victorious in a contest or conflict: *He won the race. No one won the war.* **2** acquire, gain, or secure as a result of a contest, conflict,

bet, or other endeavour: *There were hundreds of chances to win.* **3** gain a person's or group's attention, support, or affection, typically gradually or by making an effort: *The speaker soon won his audience. She won her mother over to her side. His big smile won him many friends.*
n a successful result in a contest, conflict, bet, or other endeavour: *We had five wins and no defeats.* <Old English *winnan*> **win′less** *adj.* **win′na·ble** *adj.*
win out, manage to succeed or achieve something by effort: *They won out despite great odds against them.*

wince (wins) *v* **winced, winc·ing** give a slight, unintended grimace or shrinking movement of the body out of pain, distress, or embarrassment: *He winced at the sight of the dentist's drill.*
n the act of wincing. <Old French *guencir*>

winch (winch) *n* a machine for lifting or hauling, consisting of a rope, cable, or chain winding round a horizontal rotating drum, turned by a crank or by motor or other power source.
v lift or haul by a winch. <Old English *wince*>

wind[1] (wind) *n* **1** a natural movement of the air, especially in the form of a current of air blowing from a particular direction: *There was a strong wind from the north.* **2** a scent carried by the wind, indicating the presence or nearness of an animal or person: *The deer caught wind of the hunter.* **3** breath as needed in physical effort or in speech. **4** flatulence. **5** empty, pompous, or boastful talk **6** a trend: *the winds of change.* **7** information, especially of something concealed: *No wind of this scandal should ever get out.* **8 winds** *pl* the wind musical instruments (woodwinds and brasses) forming a band or a section of an orchestra.
v **wind·ed, wind·ing 1** cause someone to have difficulty breathing because of physical effort or a blow to the stomach: *The long run winded him.* **2** detect the presence of a person or animal by scent. <Old English>
before the wind, in the direction toward which the wind is blowing.
down (**the**) **wind,** in the direction that the wind is blowing.
get wind of, *Informal* **a** begin to suspect that something is happening or hear a rumour: *Don't let him get wind of our plans.* **b** detect a person or animal by smell.
in the wind, impending or about to happen: *There's an election in the wind.*
into the wind, pointing toward the direction from which the wind is blowing.
take the wind out of someone's sails, frustrate someone by unexpectedly anticipating an action or remark.
to (or **from**) **the four winds,** in (or from) all directions.

wind[2] (wīnd) *v* **wound** or **wind·ed, wind·ing 1** move in or take a twisting or spiral direction: *A brook winds through the woods. We wound our way through the narrow streets.* **2** pass something around a thing or person so as to encircle or enfold: *The mother wound her arms about the child.* **3** twist or coil a length of something around a core, or be twisted or coiled in such a way: *He wound the string into a ball.* **4** make a clock, or other device operated by clockwork, operate by turning a key or handle. **5** cause an audiotape or videotape to move to a desired point. **6** lift or draw something with a winch or similar device.
n **1** a twist or turn along a route. **2** a single turn made while winding. <Old English *windan*> **wind′er** *n.*
wind down, a gradually lose power as a mechanism, especially one operated by clockwork. **b** relax as a person after stress or excitement. **c** draw or bring gradually to a close: *The company wound down its business by the end of the year.*
wind up, a arrive or end up in a specified condition, situation, or place: *We expect to wind up the project tomorrow.* **b** make tense or angry: *He was wound up about his friend's neglect.* **c** *Baseball* make a series of movements as a pitcher just before pitching the ball.

wind·bag (wind′bag′) *Informal n* a person who talks a lot without saying anything worthwhile.

wind·blown (wind′blōn′) *adj* **1** blown by the wind. **2** with the hair cut short and brushed forward.

wind·break (wind′brāk′) *n* a thing, such as a row of trees or a fence, wall, or screen, that provides shelter or protection from the wind.

wind·break·er (wind′brā′kər) *n* a short outdoor jacket that has a close-fitting neck, cuffs, and waistband.

wind·burn (wind′bərn′) *n* reddening and soreness of the skin caused by exposure to wind.

wind chill *n* in full, **wind chill factor** a measure of the combined chilling effect of wind and low temperature.

wind chimes *pln* small pieces of glass, metal, or shell suspended from a frame, typically hung near a door or window so as to make a tinkling sound in the draft.

wind·ed (win′did) *adj* **1** out of breath. **2** (*in compounds*) with breathing of a certain kind: *short-winded.*

wind·fall (wind′fol′) *n* **1** an apple or other fruit blown from a tree or a bush by the wind. **2** an unexpected piece of good luck, typically one that involves receiving a large amount of money.

wind farm *n* an area of land with a group of energy-producing windmills or wind turbines.
wind farming *n.*

wind·flow·er (wind′flou′ər) ANEMONE.

win·di·go (win′di gō′)WENDIGO.

wind·ing (wīn′ding) *n* **1** the action of moving in a twisting or spiral direction. **2** a thing that winds or is wound around something.
adj following a twisting or spiral direction: *a winding staircase.*

wind instrument *n* a musical instrument sounded by the vibration of air, typically by a player blowing air into it.

wind·jam·mer (wind′jam′ər) *n* in former times, a merchant sailing ship.

wind·lass (win′dləs) *n* a winch, especially one on a ship or in a harbour.

a bat	e bed	i bid	o pot	u cup	th **thin**
ā cake	ē me	ī bite	ō go	ū rude	TH **then**
ä bar	ə about	ər over	ȯ for	u̇ put	zh measure

windsurfing

The speed loop is a freestyle **windsurfing** manoeuvre in which the windsurfer performs a complete rotation. When maximum speed has been reached, the athlete pulls on the boom and shifts the body forward. With back leg anchored in a foot strap, the surfer then lifts the board up to the hips to complete the circular motion.

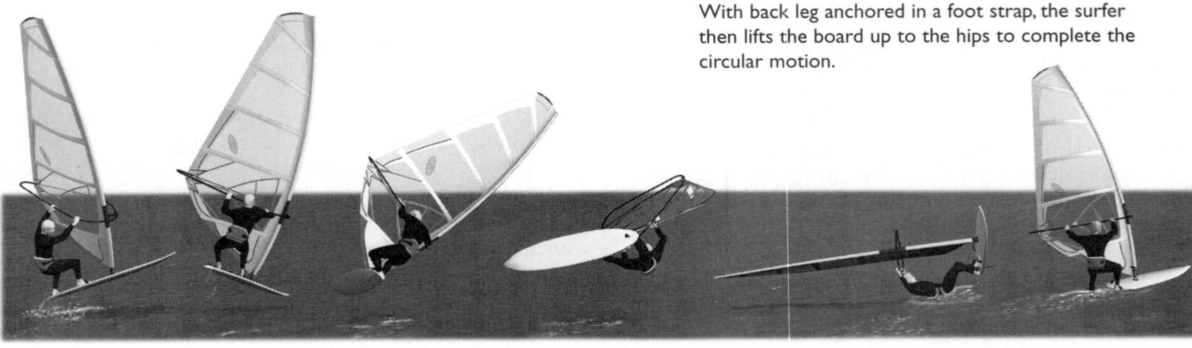

wind·mill (wind′mil′) *n* a building with sails or vanes that turn in the wind and generate power to grind grain into flour, to generate electricity, or to draw water.

win·dow (win′dō) *n* **1** an opening in the wall or roof of a building or vehicle that is fitted with glass in a frame to admit light or air and allow people to see out, or a pane of glass filling such an opening. **2** a space behind the window of a store where goods are displayed for sale. **3** a transparent panel on an envelope to show an address. **4** *Computers* a framed area on a display screen of a computer for viewing data. **5** a means of observing and learning about something, or a temporary period of time in which to take action: *a window of opportunity.* <Old Norse *vindauga*> **win′dow·less** *adj.*

window box *n* a long, narrow box placed outside a window, or inside on a window sill, and used for growing plants and flowers.

window dressing *n* **1** the arrangement of an attractive display in a store window. **2** a superficial presentation of something, often misleadingly, designed to create a favourable impression: *Much of the president's report was window dressing.*

win·dow·pane (win′dō pān′) *n* a pane of glass in a window.

window seat *n* **1** a seat built below a window, especially a bay window. **2** a seat next to a window in an aircraft, train, etc.

win·dow–shop (win′dō shop′) *v* **win·dow-shopped, win·dow-shop·ping** look at the goods displayed in store windows, especially without intending to buy anything. **win′dow-shop′per** *n.*

window sill *n* a ledge or sill forming the bottom part of a window.

wind·pipe (wind′pīp′) *n* the passage by which air is carried from the throat to the lungs.

wind·row (win′drō′) *n* **1** a long line of raked hay or grain sheaves laid out to dry in the wind. **2** a long line of material heaped or swept up by the wind.

wind·shield (wind′shēld′) *n* a glass screen at the front of a motor vehicle.

wind·sock (wind′sok′) *n* a light, flexible cylinder or cone mounted on a mast to show the direction and strength of the wind, especially at an airfield.

Wind·sor chair (win′zər) *n* a wooden chair with a semicircular back supported by upright rods.

wind·storm (wind′stôrm′) *n* a storm with much wind but little or no rain or snow.

wind·surf·ing (wind′sər′fing) *n* the sport or pastime of riding on water on a sailboard. Also called **sailboarding**.

wind·swept (wind′swept′) *adj* exposed to wind, or showing signs of the wind having blown across something: *windswept hair, windswept fields.*

wind tunnel *n* **1** a tunnel-like structure for producing an airstream past models of objects such as aircraft or buildings in order to study airflow or the effect of wind on the full-sized object. **2** an open space through which strong winds are channelled by surrounding tall buildings.

wind turbine *n* a turbine with a large wheel rotated by the wind to generate electricity.

wind–up (wīn′dup′) *n* **1** an act of concluding or finishing a thing. **2** a series of movements made by a baseball pitcher just before throwing the ball.

wind·ward (win′dwərd) *adv, adj* facing the wind or on the side facing the wind.
n the side or direction from which the wind is blowing: *They saw a ship to windward.*

wind·y (win′dē) *adj* **wind·i·er, wind·i·est** **1** marked by or exposed to strong winds as weather, a period of time, or a place: *a windy street, a windy month.* **2** using or expressed in many words that sound impressive but mean little: *windy talk.* **wind′i·ly** *adv.* **wind′i·ness** *n.*

wine (wīn) *n* an alcoholic drink made from fermented grape juice, or from the fermented juice of specified other fruits or plants: *white wine, dandelion wine.*
adj dark purplish red. <Latin *vinum*>
wine and dine (someone), entertain someone by offering drinks or a meal, especially in a lavish way.

wine cellar *n* a cellar where wine is stored, or a stock of wine.

wine·glass (wīn′glas′) *n* a glass with a stem, designed for drinking wine.

wine·grow·er (wīn′grō′ər) *n* a person who or company that grows grapes and makes wines. **wine′grow·ing** *adj, n.*

wine·mak·er (wīn′ma′kər) *n* a person who or company that makes wines. **wine′mak·ing** *adj, n.*

wine·press (wīn′pres′) *n* a machine for pressing the juice from grapes.

win·er·y (wī′nə rē) *n, pl* **win·er·ies** a place where wine is made for sale.

wine·skin (wīn′skin′) *n* an animal skin sewn up and used to hold wine.

wing (wing) *n* **1 a** the specialized paired appendage of a bird, insect, or other animal that enables it to fly. **b** a rigid horizontal structure that projects from both sides of an aircraft and supports it in the air. **2** a part that projects from the main part or body, such as an extension at the side of a large building: *the east wing of the palace.* **3** a group within a political party or other organization that holds particular views or has a particular function: *The left wing of the party opposed the new policy.* **4** *Hockey, Soccer, Rugby* **a** the part of the ice or field close to the sidelines. **b** a player associated with that area. **5** a unit of an air force made up of several squadrons or groups. **6** **wings** *pl* a pilot's certificate to fly an aircraft indicated by a badge representing a pair of wings. **7** **wings** *pl* the sides of a theatre stage out of view of the audience.
v **1** travel on wings or by aircraft: *The birds are winging south.* **2** move, travel, or be sent quickly, or send or convey a person or thing in this way: *I winged the dart straight at the centre of the board.* **3** injure superficially in the wing or arm: *The shot winged the bird but did not kill it.* <Old Norse *vængr*> **wing′less** *adj.* **wing′like′** *adj.*
clip someone's wings, restrict or confine someone: *If he's going to keep getting out of line, we're going to have to clip his wings a little.*
in the wings, ready to do something or be used at the appropriate time.
on a wing and a prayer, *Informal* with only a slim chance of success.
on the wing, in flight as a bird.
take wing, fly away as a bird, insect, or other winged animal.
under someone's wing, in or into someone's protection, care, or sponsorship.
wing it, *Informal* speak or act without preparation.

wing·ding (wing′ding′) *Informal n* **1** a lively event or party. **2** something remarkable or memorable of its kind: *That was a wingding of a fight.* <origin uncertain>

winged (wingd) *adj* **1** with wings for flight: *winged insects.* **2** with one or more lateral parts, appendages, or projections: *winged glasses.*

wing nut *n* a nut with a pair of projections for the fingers to turn it on a screw.

wing·span (wing′span′) *n* the distance between the tips of the wings of an airplane, bird, insect, or flying animal.

wink (wingk) *v* close and open one eye quickly, typically to indicate that something is a joke or secret, or as a signal of affection or greeting.
n an act of closing and opening one eye quickly. <Old English *wincian*>
wink at, pretend not to notice something bad or illegal.

win·ner (win′ər) *n* **1** a person who or thing that wins. **2** a goal or shot that wins a match or game. **3** *Informal* a person who or thing that is successful or is likely to be a success.

win·ning (win′ing) *adj* **1** gaining, resulting in, or relating to victory in a contest or competition: *a winning team.* **2** charming and attractive: *a winning smile.*
n **winnings** *pl* money won, especially by gambling: *He pocketed his winnings.* **win′ning·ly** *adv.*

Win·ni·peg couch (win′ə peg′) *n* a couch with no arms or back and opening out into a double bed.

win·now (win′ō) *v* **1** blow a current of air through grain in order to remove the chaff, or remove chaff from grain. **2** sort out; separate: *to winnow truth from falsehood.* <Old English *windwian,* from *wind* wind[1]> **win′now·er** *n.*

win·o (wī′nō) *Informal n* an alcoholic addicted to cheap wine, especially one who is homeless.

win·some (win′səm) *adj* attractive or appealing in appearance: *a winsome smile.* <Old English *wynn* joy> **win′some·ly** *adv.* **win′some·ness** *n.*

win·ter (win′tər) *n* **1** the coldest of the four seasons of the year, in the northern hemisphere from December to March and in the southern hemisphere from June to September. **2** a period of decline or adversity.
v **1** spend the winter in a particular place: *winter in the south.* **2** keep or feed plants or animals during winter: *The farmers wintered their cattle in a sheltered valley.*
adj **1** to do with winter: *winter clothes, winter weather.* **2** sown in autumn for harvesting the following year: *winter wheat.* <Old English>

win·ter·ber·ry (win′tər ber′ē) *n, pl* **win·ter·ber·ries** a N American holly.

win·ter·green (win′tər grēn′) *n* an evergreen N American plant with aromatic leaves from which the pungent **oil of wintergreen** is obtained.

win·ter·ize (win′tə rīz′) *v* **win·ter·ized, win·ter·iz·ing** adapt or prepare something, especially a house or motor vehicle, for use in cold weather: *to winterize a summer cabin.*

win·ter·kill (win′tər kil′) *v* kill by or die from exposure to cold weather: *The rosebushes were winterkilled.*
n the act or fact of this: *The trees died from winterkill.*

winter solstice *n* See SOLSTICE.

win·ter·time (win′tər tīm′) *n* the season of winter.

a bat	e bed	i bid	o pot	u cup	th thin
ā cake	ē me	ī bite	ō go	ū rude	TH then
à bar	ə about	ər over	ȯ for	u̇ put	zh measure

winter wheat *n* wheat planted in the fall to ripen in the following spring or summer.

win·try (win′trē) *adj* **win·tri·er, win·tri·est** to do with winter, especially in feeling or looking very cold and bleak: *a wintry sky, a wintry smile.*

wipe (wīp) *v* **wiped, wip·ing** **1** clean or dry something by rubbing its surface with a cloth, a piece of paper, or one's hand, or remove or clean something in this way: *to wipe the table. She wiped off the dust.* **2** remove or eliminate something completely: *The tide wiped away all the footprints on the beach.* **3** erase data from a magnetic medium.
n **1** an act of wiping: *He gave his face a hasty wipe.* **2** a piece of disposable absorbent cloth, especially one treated with a cleansing agent, for wiping something clean. <Old English *wipian*>
wipe out, a destroy completely: *The pollution in the river has wiped out all the fish.* **b** cancel: *She generously wiped out all the debts owed her.* **c** in surfing, skiing, etc., fall heavily or crash. **d** (*in the passive*) ruin financially: *Many businesses were wiped out during the wet summer that year.*

wiped (wīpt) *Informal adj* tired out or exhausted.

wipe·out (wīp′out′) *n* **1** in surfing, skiing, etc., a bad fall or crash. **2** a total failure.

wip·er (wī′pər) *n* **1** a person who or thing that wipes. **2** a windshield wiper.

wire (wīr) *n* **1** metal drawn out into the form of a thin, flexible thread or rod, or a piece of such metal: *telephone wire.* **2** a length or quantity of such metal used for some purpose, as for fencing or to carry an electric current. **3** an electronic listening device that can be concealed on a person. **4** *Informal* a telegram.
v **wired, wir·ing** **1** install electric circuits or wires in: *The house was wired for electricity.* **2** connect someone or something to a piece of electronic equipment. **3** provide, fasten, or reinforce with wires: *She wired the two pieces together.* **4** send a telegram or cablegram to: *He wired a birthday greeting.*
adj made of or consisting of wire: *a wire fence.* <Old English *wir*> **wir′er** *n.*
down to the wire, up to or at the last possible moment: *I need to know soon because it's getting down to the wire.*
under the wire, just in time.

wired (wīrd) *adj* **1** *Computers* making use of computers and technology to transfer or receive information, especially by means of the Internet. **2** *Informal* in a nervous, tense, or edgy condition: *After three chocolate bars, I was really wired.*

wire–haired (wīr′herd′) *adj* with coarse, wiry or stiff hair, especially as a dog: *a wire-haired fox terrier.*

wire·less (wīr′lis) *adj* to do with devices or systems that need no wires, such as cellphones: *wireless communication.*

wire·tap (wīr′tap′) *n* a listening device connected to a telephone line to record conversations secretly, or the information obtained in this way. Compare BUG (def. 6).
v **wire·tapped, wire·tap·ping** make a wiretap. **wire′tap·per** *n.* **wire′tap·ping** *n.*

wir·ing (wī′ring) *n* a system of wires to carry an electric current, or an installation of this.

wir·y (wī′rē) *adj* **wir·i·er, wir·i·est** **1** resembling wire in form and texture: *wiry hair.* **2** lean, tough, and sinewy in appearance: *a wiry body.* **wir′i·ly** *adv.* **wir′i·ness** *n.*

wis·dom (wiz′dəm) *n* **1** the quality of having experience, knowledge, and good judgment: **2** the soundness of an action or decision with regard to the application of this quality: *He questioned the wisdom of my taking a trip at this time.*

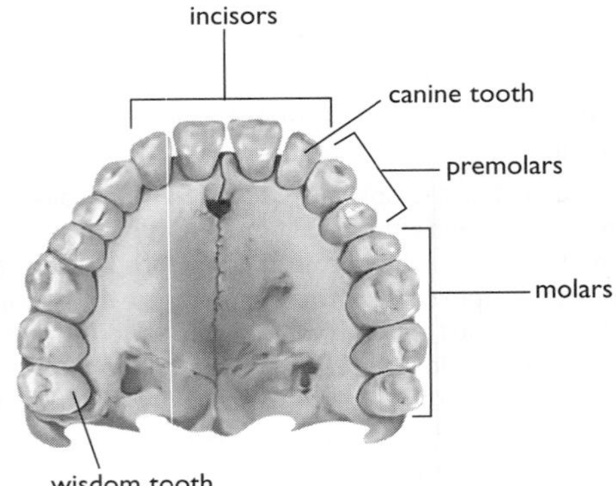

wisdom tooth *n* the back tooth on either side of the upper and lower jaws, ordinarily appearing about the age of twenty.

wise[1] (wīz) *adj* **wis·er, wis·est** **1** with or showing experience, knowledge, and good judgment: *a wise judge, wise advice.* **2** responding sensibly or shrewdly to a particular situation: *It would not be wise to talk about it now.* <Old English *wis*> **wise′ly** *adv.*
wise to, *Informal* alert to or aware of: *The cops will get wise to your scheme eventually.*
wise up, *Informal* improve one's attitudes and conduct.

wise[2] (wīz) *Archaic n* the manner or extent of something: *He's in no wise a student; he prefers sports.* <Old English>

–wise *suffix* in a particular manner, way, or aspect: *likewise, slantwise, clockwise, otherwise.* <*wise*[2]>

GRAMMAR AND USAGE

The suffix **–wise** comes through Middle English from Old English *-wise*, meaning "manner." In Old and Middle English, it was used to form adverbs, showing how something was done. Today it is used informally to mean "with reference to," as in *weatherwise* and *examwise*.

However, avoid this use in formal writing and speech. Instead of *Weatherwise, it's been a bad week*, say *The weather has been bad this week.*

wise·a·cre (wī′zā′kər) *n* a person who pretends to be wise or knowledgeable, regarded with scorn and irritation by others. <Dutch *wijssegger* soothsayer>

wise·crack (wīz′krak′) *n* a quick, witty comment or remark.
v make wisecracks. **wise′crack′er** *n.*

wise guy *Slang n* a person who pretends to be wiser or more knowledgeable than others.

wi·sent (vē′zent) *n* the European bison.

wish (wish) *v* **1** feel or express a strong desire or hope for something that cannot or probably will not happen: *He wished that he had studied more for the exam.* **2** feel or express a desire to do something: *She wished to join the committee.* **3** express the desire for success, good fortune, or some other favourable result: *I wish you every happiness.*
n **1** a desire or hope for something to happen: *He had no wish to be king.* **2** a thing wished for: *She got her wish.* <Old English *wyscan*> **wish′er** *n.*

wish·bone (wish′bōn′) *n* a forked bone between the neck and breast of a bird, especially poultry.

wish·ful thinking (wish′fəl) *n* a desire or hope for something to happen, especially something that is impractical or unlikely: *Her boast about winning the race was only wishful thinking.*

wish list *n* a list of desired things or occurrences.

wish·y–wash·y (wish′ē wosh′ē) *adj* **1** weak and watery as a drink or liquid food. **2** feeble or insipid in quality or character: *wishy-washy generosity.* <reduplication of *washy* weak>

wisp (wisp) *n* **1** a small thin or twisted bunch, piece, or amount of something: *a wisp of hay, a wisp of hair, a wisp of smoke.* **2** a small thin person, typically a child. <Middle English> **wisp′i·ness** *n.* **wisp′y** *adj.*

wis·ter·i·a or **wis·tar·i·a** (wis ter′ē ə) *n* a climbing shrub of the pea family, with large clusters of blue or white flowers.

wist·ful (wist′fəl) *adj* with or showing a feeling of vague or regretful longing: *wistful eyes.* <origin uncertain> **wist′ful·ly** *adv.* **wist′ful·ness** *n.*

wit[1] (wit) *n* **1 a** mental sharpness and inventiveness, especially a natural ability for using words and ideas in a quick and inventive way: *Her wit made even trouble seem amusing.* **b** a person with such mental sharpness and inventiveness: *She was a great wit.* **2 wits** *pl* the intelligence and presence of mind required for normal activity: *quick wits. The child was out of his wits with fright.* <Old English *witt*>
be at one's wit's end, not knowing what to do or say.
live by one's wits, earn money by clever means and with no regular employment.

wit[2] (wit) *Archaic v* **wot, witting 1** have knowledge. **2 to wit** that is to say: *To my sister I leave all I own—to wit: my house, what is in it, and the land on which it stands.*

witch (wich) *n, pl* **witch·es 1** a woman supposed to have evil magic powers. Compare WARLOCK. **2** a follower or practitioner of modern witchcraft, such as a Wiccan. **3** *Informal* an ugly or unpleasant woman. **4** *Informal* a girl or woman who enchants or fascinates a man. <Old English *wicce*>

witch·craft (wich′kraft′) *n* the practice of magic, especially black magic.

witch doctor *n* among some cultures, a magician who is believed to have powers of healing, prophecy, and protection against the magic of others.

witch hazel *n* an astringent lotion made from the bark and leaves of a shrub.

witch hunt *n* **1** in former times, a search for and persecution of a person supposed to be a witch. **2** *Informal* a malicious campaign directed against a person or group.

witch·ing hour (wich′ing) *Poetic n* midnight. <the time witches are supposed to be active>

with (with) *or* (wiᴛʜ) *prep* **1** accompanied by another person or thing: *Come with me.* **2** along with or in the same direction as: *They will mix with the crowd.* **3** possessing something as a feature or accompaniment: *a student with brains, a phone call with bad news.* **4** indicating the instrument used to perform an action, or the material used for some purpose: *He cut the meat with a dull knife. She filled the cup with milk.* **5** in opposition to: *A fight broke out with another fan at the concert.* **6** indicating the manner or attitude of the person doing something: *I leave with great regret.* **7** indicating responsibility: *Leave the problem with me.* **8** in relation to: *They are friendly with us.* **9** employed by or using the services of: *She's with a bigger company now.* **10** affected by a particular fact or condition: *I was in bed with the flu.* <Old English = against>
with it, *Informal* **a** up to date or stylish: *Your sister is really with it.* **b** alert and comprehending: *Sorry, I just woke up and I'm not really with it yet.*
with that, at that moment, or immediately after that: *He took off his hat and waved, and with that he turned and walked away.*

with·draw (wiᴛʜ dro′) *or* (with dro′) *v* **with·drew, with·drawn, with·draw·ing 1** remove or take away something from a particular place or position: *He withdrew his hand from hers.* **2** take back or away something given, proposed, or used: *We decided to withdraw our support for the plan.* **3** take money out of an account: *She withdrew some money for the week's expenses.* **4** say that a statement one has made is untrue or unjustified: *I withdraw the charge that he's dishonest.* **5** leave or come back from a place, or cause someone to leave or come back from it, especially a war zone: *The army withdrew from its desert campaign.* **6** no longer participate in an activity or be a member of a team or organization: *The candidate withdrew from the race.* **with·draw′al** *n.*

with·drawn (wiᴛʜ dron′) *or* (with dron′) *v* past participle of WITHDRAW.
adj not wanting to communicate with other people: *He was always shy and withdrawn.*

with·er (wiᴛʜ′ər) *v* **1** become dry and shrivelled: *Her face was withered with age.* **2** cease to flourish, then fall into decay or decline: *The economy withered during the depression.* **3** give someone a severe or scornful look, or act in this way: *His bitter words withered her.* <Middle English *wydderen* dry up> **with′er·ing** *adj, n.* **with′er·ing·ly** *adv.*

a bat	e bed	i bid	o pot	u cup	th thin
ā cake	ē me	ī bite	ō go	ū rude	ᴛʜ then
ä bar	ə about	ər over	ȯ for	ủ put	zh measure

with·ers (wiTH′ərz) *pln* the highest part of a horse's back, lying at the base of the neck above the shoulders. A horse's height is measured to the withers. See HORSE for picture.

with·hold (with hōld′) *v* **with·held, with·hold·ing** **1** refuse to give something that is due to or is desired by another: *We withheld our consent.* **2** suppress or hold back an emotion or reaction.

with·in (with in′) *or* (wiTH in′) *prep* inside an area, or the bounds or range of something: *The task was within the man's powers. She guessed my weight within two kilograms.* *adv* inside or indoors: *The house has been painted within and without. The curtains were white without and green within.* <Old English *withinnan*>

with·out (with out′) *or* (wiTH out′) *prep* **1** in the absence of: *He drinks tea without sugar.* **2** not with the use or benefit of: *He was able to walk without help.* **3** outside of: *Soldiers were camped within and without the city walls.*
adv outside: *You are a beautiful person, without and within.* <Old English *withutan*>

with·stand (with stand′) *v* **with·stood, with·stand·ing** **1** remain undamaged or unaffected by: *These shoes will withstand hard wear.* **2** offer strong resistance or opposition to. <Old English *with-* against + *standan* stand>

wit·less (wit′lis) *adj* stupid or foolish. **wit′less·ly** *adv.* **wit′less·ness** *n.*

wit·ness (wit′nis) *n* **1** a person who sees or saw an event, typically a crime or accident, take place: *He started the fight in the presence of several witnesses.* **2** a person who gives evidence or testifies under oath before a judge or coroner. **3** the exercise of religious faith through words or actions: *He pledged to give witness to his belief.* **4** a person who signs a document to show that another person's signature on it is genuine.
v **1** see an event, typically a crime or accident, take place. **2** have knowledge of an event from personal observation or experience: *We were witnessing a whole new way of learning things.* **3** be the setting in which a particular event takes place: *The twentieth century witnessed many changes.* **4** sign a legal document as a witness: *to witness a will.* <Old English *witnes* testimony>

witness box *n* the place where a witness stands or sits to give evidence in a law court.

wit·ti·cism (wit′ə siz′əm) *n* a witty remark.

wit·ting·ly (wit′ing lē) *adj* done deliberately.

wit·ty (wit′ē) *adj* **wit·ti·er, wit·ti·est** showing or marked by quick and inventive verbal humour: *witty remarks.* **wit′ti·ly** *adv.* **wit′ti·ness** *n.*

wives (wīvz) plural of WIFE.

wiz (wiz) WHIZ.

wiz·ard (wiz′ərd) *n* **1** a man supposed to have magic power, especially in legends and fairy tales. **2** a person who is very skilled in a particular area or activity: *a computer wizard.* **3** *Computers* an interactive utility, usually built in, designed to help set up a particular program or application, by guiding the user through each step of the process. <*wise*[1]> **wiz′ard·ry** *n.*

wiz·ened (wiz′ənd) *adj* shrivelled or wrinkled with age: *a wizened apple, a wizened face.* <Old English *wisnian* become dry>

WNW west-northwest.

woad (wōd) *n* a yellow-flowered European plant from whose leaves a blue dye was formerly made, or the dye obtained from this plant.

wob·ble (wob′əl) *v* **wob·bled, wob·bling** **1** move unsteadily from side to side, or cause to move in such a way: *The flimsy table wobbled when we sat down.* **2** hesitate or waver between different courses of action. **3** tremble or quaver as a voice.
n an unsteady motion from side to side. <origin uncertain> **wob′bler** *n.* **wob′bly** *adj.*

woe (wō) *n* **1** great grief, trouble, or distress: *a tale of woe.* **2 woes** *pl* things that cause sorrow or distress: *Sickness added to his woes.* <Old English *wa*>

woe·be·gone or **wo·be·gone** (wō′bi gon′) *adj* looking sad or miserable in appearance.

woe·ful (wō′fəl) *adj* **1** marked by, expressing, or causing sorrow or misery: *a woeful expression.* **2** very bad: *woeful ignorance.* **woe′ful·ly** *adv.* **woe′ful·ness** *n.*

wok (wok) *n* a wide metal frying pan with sides that curve in to a small, flat bottom, used especially in Chinese cooking. <Cantonese *wohk* pan>

woke (wōk) a past tense of WAKE[1].

wo·ken (wō′kən) a past participle of WAKE[1].

A timber **wolf** usually has yellow-grey fur with black patches and a white underside, but it can also be brown or black.

Wolves live in dens or lairs and a wolf pack of pups and parents marks its territory with urine and feces and defends it from intruders.

The pack advertises its territorial claim with communal howling.

wolf (wu̇lf) *n, pl* **wolves** a wild, meat-eating animal of N America and Eurasia that is the largest member of the dog family, living and hunting in packs.
v devour food greedily: *The starving men wolfed down the food.* <Old English *wulf*> **wolf′ish** *adj.* **wolf′ish·ly** *adv.* **wolf′ish·ness** *n.* **wolf′like′** *adj.*
cry wolf, call for help when it is not needed, with the effect that one is not believed when one really does need help.
keep the wolf from the door, have enough money to avoid hunger or extreme poverty.
wolf in sheep's clothing, a person who pretends to be friendly or harmless, but intends to do harm.

wolf·hound (wu̇lf′hound′) *n* a dog of a large breed originally used in hunting wolves.

wol·fram (wu̇l′frəm) *n* tungsten or its ore.

wolf spider *n* a fast-moving ground spider that does not spin webs but runs after and springs on its prey.

wolf whistle *n* a whistle with a rising and falling pitch, directed toward someone to express admiration or sexual attraction.

wol·ver·ine (wu̇l′və rēn′) *n* a powerful, meat-eating animal native to the tundra and the forests of arctic and subarctic regions. <origin uncertain>

wolves (wu̇lvz) plural of WOLF.

wom·an (wu̇m′ən) *n, pl* **wom·en** (wim′ən) **1** an adult female human. **2** female adults in general: *the modern woman.* **3** a female person associated with a particular place, activity, or occupation: *a cleaning woman.* **4** a female follower, servant, or employee: *the queen's women.* <Old English *wifmann,* from *wif* wife + *man* human being> **wo′man·like′** *adj.*

wom·an·hood (wu̇m′ən hu̇d′) *n* **1** the condition or time of being a woman. **2** the qualities traditionally associated with being a woman, such as gentleness. **3** women as a group, especially of a country: *Canadian womanhood.*

wom·an·ish (wu̇m′ə nish) *adj* traditionally associated with a woman rather than a man: *He talks with a high, womanish voice.* **wo·man′ish·ly** *adv.*

wom·an·ize (wu̇m′ə nīz′) *v* **wom·an·ized, wom·an·iz·ing** engage in many casual sexual relationships with women. **wo′man·iz·er** *n.*

wom·an·kind (wu̇m′ən kīnd′) *n* women as a group.

wom·an·ly (wu̇m′ən lē) *adj* to do with the supposed characteristics of women. **wom′an·li·ness** *n.*

womb (wūm) *n* **1** the organ in the lower body of a woman or female mammal where offspring are conceived and in which they are developed before birth. **2** a place where something is conceived and developed: *the womb of civilization.* <Old English *wamb*>

wom·bat (wom′bat) *n* a burrowing Australian marsupial that resembles a small bear with short legs. <Aboriginal Australian language>

wom·en (wim′ən) plural of WOMAN.

wom·en·folk (wim′ən fōk′) *pln* women of a particular family or community, considered as a group.

women's lib *Informal n* in full, **women's liberation** a social movement begun in the late 1960s, committed to fighting sexual discrimination and winning legal, economic, and social rights for women equal to those enjoyed by men. **women's lib′ber** *n.*

women's rights *pln* social, political, and legal rights for women, equal to those of men.

won (wun) past tense and past participle of WIN.

won·der (wun′dər) *n* **1** a feeling of surprise mingled with admiration, caused by something beautiful, unexpected, unfamiliar, or unexplained, or the quality of a person who or thing that causes such a feeling: *childlike wonder, a place of wonder.* **2** a strange or remarkable person, thing, or event: *He saw the wonders of the city. It is a wonder you turned down the offer.*
v **1** desire or be curious to know something: *I wondered why he never replied to my phone call.* **2** expressing a polite question or request: *I wonder if you feel the same about it?* **3** feel doubt: *I wonder if he knows what he's talking about.* **4** feel admiration and amazement: *She wondered at his juggling skills.*
adj with remarkable qualities or abilities: *a wonder drug.* <Old English *wundor*> **won′der·ing** *adj.* **won′der·ing·ly** *adv.*
do (or **work**) **wonders,** have a very beneficial effect on someone or something.
no (or **little** or **small**) **wonder,** it is not surprising: *No wonder he's happy—he made the team.*
will wonders never cease or **wonders will never cease,** what a pleasant surprise.

won·der·ful (wun′dər fəl) *adj* inspiring delight, pleasure, or admiration: *The explorer had wonderful adventures. We had a wonderful time at the party.* **won′der·ful·ly** *adv.* **won′der·ful·ness** *n.*

won·der·land (wun′dər land′) *n* a land or place full of wonderful things.

won·der·ment (wun′dər mənt) *n* a condition of awed admiration or respect: *He stared at the northern lights in wonderment.*

won·drous (wun′drəs) *adj* inspiring a feeling of wonder or delight. **won′drous·ly** *adv.*

won·ky (wong′kē) *Informal adj* **won·ki·er, won·ki·est** faulty or not functioning normally. <Old English *wancol* shaky>

wont (wōnt) *adj* in the habit of doing something: *She was wont to read the paper at breakfast.*
n a custom or habit: *He rose early, as was his wont.* <Old English *wunian* be accustomed> **wont′ed** *adj.*

won't (wōnt) *contraction* will not.

won ton (won′ton′) *n* a dumpling used in Chinese cooking, consisting of a thin casing of dough around a filling, served either fried or in broth. <Cantonese *wan t'an* dumpling>

woo (wū) *v* **1** try to gain the romantic interest of someone. **2** seek the favour or support of: *The store tried to woo customers by giving discounts.* <Old English *wogian*> **woo′er** *n.*

wood (wu̇d) *n* **1** the hard, fibrous material that forms the main substance of the trunk or branches of a tree or shrub. **2** such material when cut and used as lumber or fuel: *Put some wood on the fire.* **3** *Golf* a golf club with a wooden or other head that is relatively broad from face to back, often with a number indicating the degree to which the face is angled. **4** wooden barrels used for storing alcoholic drinks: *aged in wood.* **5** often, **woods** *pl* an area of land that is covered with growing trees: *We looked for wildflowers in the woods.*
adj **1** made of wood: *a wood house.* **2** used for or on wood: *We have a wood basket for the fireplace.* **3** dwelling or growing in woods: *wood moss.* <Old English *wudu*>
out of the woods, out of danger or difficulty.

a bat	e bed	i bid	o pot	u cup	th thin
ā cake	ē me	ī bite	ō go	ū rude	ᴛʜ then
ȧ bar	ə about	ər over	ȯ for	u̇ put	zh measure

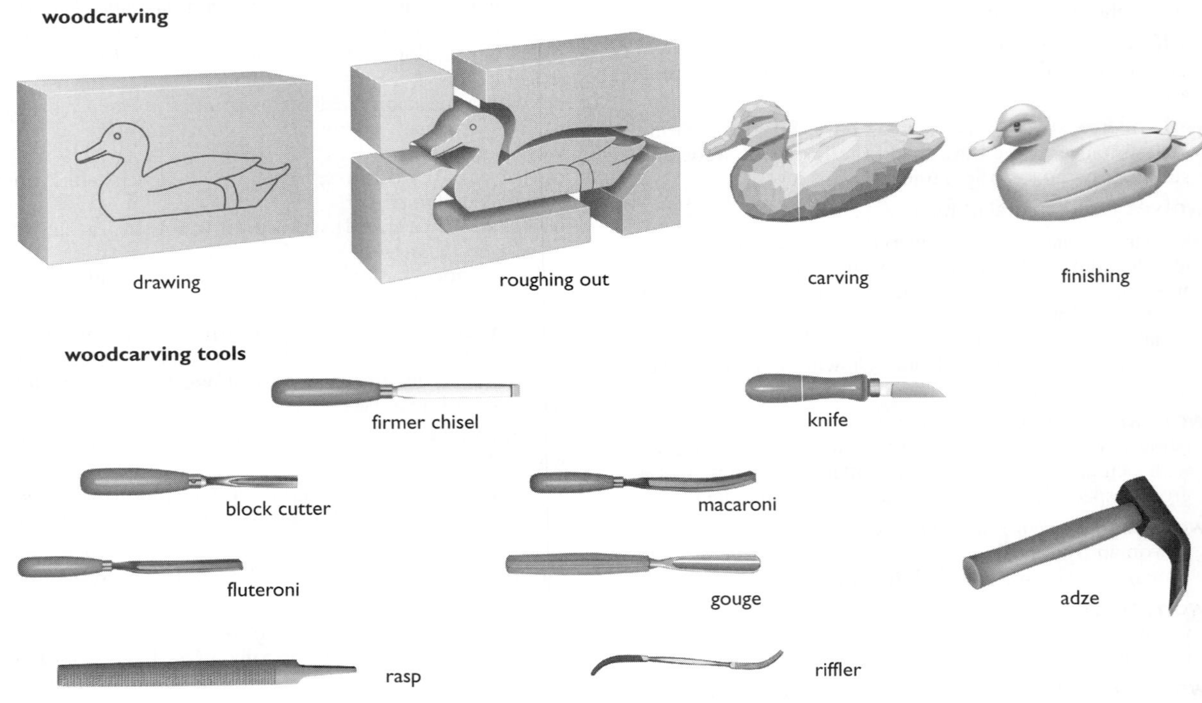

wood alcohol *n* a poisonous, inflammable liquid often made by distilling wood, used as a solvent, fuel, etc.; methyl alcohol.

wood·bine (wůd′bīn′) *n* **1** honeysuckle. **2** Virginia creeper.

wood·box (wůd′boks′) *n* a large box to hold firewood indoors.

wood·carv·ing (wůd′kår′ving) *n* **1** the art or craft of carving wood. **2** an object or work of art carved out of wood. **wood′carv′er** *n.*

wood·chuck (wůd′chuk′) *n* a groundhog. <Algonquian *otchek*>

wood·cock (wůd′kok′) *n, pl* **wood·cocks** or (*especially collectively*) **wood·cock** a small woodland bird of the sandpiper family.

wood·craft (wůd′kraft′) *n* **1** knowledge about how to get food and shelter in the woods, especially as part of camping and other outdoor pursuits. **2** skill in making things of wood.

wood·cut (wůd′kut′) *n* a print of a type made from a design cut in a block of wood, formerly widely used for illustrations in books.

wood·cut·ter (wůd′kut′ər) *n* a person who cuts down trees.

wood·ed (wůd′id) *adj* covered with trees: *The park is well wooded.*

wood·en (wůd′ən) *adj* **1** made of wood. **2** stiff and awkward in movement and manner: *The actor gave a wooden bow and left the stage.* **3** like or characteristic of wood: *a wooden sound.* **wood′en·ly** *adv.* **wood′en·ness** *n.*

wood·land (wůd′lənd) *n* land covered with trees: *sounds of the woodland.*

Woodland Cree *n* See CREE.

wood·lot (wůd′lot′) *n* a piece of land on which trees are grown and cut.

wood·peck·er (wůd′pek′ər) *n* a bird with a hard, pointed bill for pecking holes in trees to get insects.

wood·pile (wůd′pīl′) *n* a pile of wood, especially for fuel.

wood pulp *n* wood fibre reduced chemically or mechanically to pulp and used in manufacturing paper.

wood·shed (wůd′shed′) a shed for storing wood as fuel.

woods·man (wůd′zmən) *n, pl* **woods·men** (-zmən) a person living or working in woodland, especially a forester, hunter, trapper, or woodcutter.

woods·y (wůd′zē) *adj* **woods·i·er, woods·i·est** to do with woodland: *a woodsy scent.* **woods′i·ness** *n.*

wood·wind (wůd′wind′) *Music n* any of the wind instruments of an orchestra that were originally made of wood. Flutes, oboes, clarinets, and bassoons are woodwinds. See DOUBLE BASSOON, ENGLISH HORN for picture.

wood·work (wůd′wərk′) *n* **1** the wooden parts of a room or building, such as window frames or doors inside a house. **2** carpentry, especially as a school subject. **wood′work′er** *n.* **wood′work′ing** *n.*

wood·worm (wůd′wərm′) *n* a worm or larva that is bred in wood or bores in wood.

wood·y (wu̇d′ē) *adj* **wood·i·er, wood·i·est 1** covered with trees: *a woody hillside.* **2** with stems containing xylem, the tissue that is the main element of wood: *woody plants.* **3** to do with wood: *a woody core.* **wood′i·ness** *n.*

woof[1] (wu̇f) *n* a deep barking sound made by a dog.
v make such a sound. <imitative>

woof[2] (wu̇f) *n* weft. <Old English *owef*>

woof·er (wu̇f′ər) *n* a loudspeaker in a sound system designed to reproduce low frequencies. <*woof* + *-er*>

wool (wu̇l) *n* **1 a** the hair forming the coat of a sheep, goat, or similar animal, especially when shorn and prepared for use in making cloth or yarn. **b** yarn or textile fibre made from such hair. **2** a thing resembling such hair in form or texture: *steel wool.*
adj made of wool. <Old English *wull*>
pull the wool over someone's eyes, *Informal* deceive someone by telling lies.

wool·gath·er·ing (wu̇l′gaᴛʜ′ə ring) *n* indulgence in aimless thought or daydreaming. **wool′gath′er·er** *n.*

wool·len or **wool·en** (wu̇l′ən) *adj* to do with wool: *a woollen suit, a woollen mill.*
n **woollens** or **woolens** *pl* clothing made of wool.

wool·ly (wu̇l′ē) *adj* **wool·li·er, wool·li·est 1** made of wool: *a woolly hat.* **2** bearing or naturally covered with wool or hair resembling wool. **3** resembling wool in texture or appearance: *woolly clouds.* **4** vague or confused in expression or character: *woolly thinking.* **5** indistinct or distorted as sound.
n, pl **wool·lies** *Informal* an article of clothing made from wool. **wool′li·ness** *n.*

woolly bear *n* a caterpillar, especially of the tiger moth, with a dense coat of hair.

wooz·y (wūz′ē) *Informal adj* unsteady, dizzy, or dazed: *He was just over an illness and still a little woozy.* <origin uncertain> **wooz′i·ly** *adv.* **wooz′i·ness** *n.*

Worces·ter·shire sauce (wu̇s′tər shər) *n* a pungent sauce that contains soy and vinegar and is used as a condiment.

word (wərd) *n* **1** a distinct meaningful element of speech or writing, typically shown with a space on either side when written or printed: *She answered in one word, "No."* **2** a thing that one says or writes, especially a remark, comment, or piece of information: *The teacher gave us a word of advice. May I have a word with you?* **3** speech as distinct from action: *He was honest in word and deed.* **4** a command, password, or motto: *We have to wait till she gives the word.* **5** a person's account of the truth, especially when it differs from that of another person: *It was her word against mine.* **6** news or a message: *No word has come from the battle front.* **7** a solemn promise: *I give you my word.* Also, **word of honour**. **8** *Computers* a string of bits, characters, or bytes treated as a single unit by a computer. **9 words** *pl* **a** angry talk: *They had words about whose fault it was.* **b** the text or spoken part of a play, opera, or other performed piece: *words and music.*
v choose and use particular words in order to say or write something: *He worded his message clearly.* <Old English>
be as good as your word, keep your promise.
by word of mouth, by spoken words.
eat your words, retract what you have said.
hang on someone's words (or **every word**)**,** listen very attentively and admiringly to someone.
have the last word, make the final, decisive statement in an argument.
in a word, briefly.
in so many words, in the way mentioned: *I haven't told her in so many words, but she got the message.*
mince words, avoid coming to the point or avoid telling the truth, by using ambiguous or evasive words.
put in a good word for recommend a person.
take someone at his (or **her**) **word,** take a person's words seriously and act accordingly.
take someone's word for it, believe someone without evidence.
take the words out of someone's mouth, say exactly what someone else was about to say.
the last word, a the last or latest thing or example in a class or field. **b** the final thing or example, beyond which no advance or improvement is possible.
word for word, in the exact words.
words fail me, I cannot put my response into words.

–word *combining form* (*with the initial letter of another word, often humorously*) a word thought of or treated as offensive or with a negative aspect: *the F-word. She never mentions "housework"; she says, "the H-word."*

word–for–word (wərd′fər wərd′) *adj, adv* **1** of a translation, done one word at a time according to the individual meanings and without regard for the sense of the whole text. **2** given in exactly the same words: *This is a word-for-word quote from the prime minister himself.*

word·ing (wər′ding) *n* the words used to express something or the way in which a thing is expressed.

word·less (wər′dlis) *adj* **1** without words; speechless. **2** not put into words; unexpressed. **word′less·ly** *adv.* **word′less·ness** *n.*

word–of–mouth (wərd′əv mouth′) *adj* communicated orally, usually in an informal way.

word order *n* the sequence of words in a sentence, especially as governed by grammatical rules and as affecting meaning.

word·play (wərd′plā′) *n* clever exploitation of the meanings and ambiguities of words, especially in puns.

word proc·es·sor (pros′es′ər) *or* (prō′ses′ər) *Computers n* **1** a computer program for storing, manipulating, and formatting text entered from a keyboard that may be displayed on a screen or printed out. **2** a person who processes words in this way. **word-process** *v.*
word processing *n.*

word·y (wər′dē) *adj* **word·i·er, word·i·est** using or expressed in too many words. **word′i·ly** *adv.* **word′i·ness** *n.*

wore (wȯr) past tense of WEAR.

a bat	e bed	i bid	o pot	u cup	th **thin**
ā cake	ē me	ī bite	ō go	ū rude	ᴛʜ **then**
ȧ bar	ə about	ər over	ȯ for	u̇ put	zh measure

W

work (wərk) *n* **1** activity involving mental or physical effort done in order to achieve a result: *Moving the piano was hard work.* **2** such activity as a means of earning income: *Many people are out of work.* **3 a** a task or tasks to be undertaken: *Work on my essay is proceeding smoothly.* **b** the materials for this: *He took work home to do on the weekend.* **4** something made or done, especially a work of art: *The artist considers that picture to be his greatest work.* **5** *Physics* the exertion of physical force overcoming resistance or producing molecular change. **6 works** *pl* **a** a defensive military structure. **b** a factory or other industrial place for doing some kind of work or carrying on an activity: *His first job was in the boiler works.* **c** the moving parts of a machine or device: *the works of a watch.* **d** good or moral deeds: *good works.* **7 the works** *pl Informal* **a** everything needed, desired, or expected. **b** all the toppings and garnishes: *a hot dog with the works.*

v **worked** or (*rare*) **wrought, work·ing 1** be engaged in physical or mental activity in order to achieve a purpose or result, especially in a job, or cause to be so engaged: *He had to work for a living. She works in a bank. He worked his employees long hours.* **2** operate or function as a machine, process, method, or system, especially properly or effectively: *This pump will not work.* **3** bring to a specified condition, especially an emotional one: *Don't work yourself into a temper.* **4** of a plan, have the desired result: *The idea worked brilliantly.* **5** bring a material to a desired shape or consistency by hammering, kneading, etc.: *to work bread dough.* **6** move or cause to move gradually or with difficulty into another position: *to work a cork loose. The window catch has worked loose.* <Old English *weorc*>

at work, engaged in work.

have your work cut out for you, be faced with a hard or lengthy task: *Shopping for a gift for Dad? You have your work cut out for you!*

in the works, being planned, worked on, or produced.

make short work of, do or get rid of quickly.

work in, include or incorporate something, such as in a speech, text, or work of art.

work off, get rid of by means of effort, such as a debt.

work on (or **upon**), try to persuade or influence.

work out, a be capable of being solved as a mathematical equation, or be calculated as. **b** have a good or specified result: *The plan worked out well.* **c** engage in vigorous physical exercise or training, typically at a gym. **d** plan or devise something in detail.

work up, a bring something gradually to a more complete or satisfactory condition. **b** develop or produce by activity or effort: *to work up a sweat.* **c** be in or be brought to a condition of intense excitement, anger, or anxiety: *He got worked up by the bad test results.*

SYNONYMS

Work means "mental or physical activity": *Please finish your work on the essay.*

Labour often suggests hard work: *The tired workers were not happy with the pay for all the hours of labour.*

Slog means "period of hard, steady work": *Getting across the muddy field will be a slog.*

work·a·ble (wər'kə bəl) *adj* able to be worked or to work: *a workable solution.*

work·a·day (wər'kə dā') *adj* to do with work or one's job, especially any uninteresting aspect of either of these.

work·a·hol·ic (wər'kə hol'ik) *n* a person who compulsively works too hard, too long, and too much.

work·bench (wərk'bench') *n* a table at which carpentry or other mechanical or practical work is done.

work·book (wərk'bůk') *n* a student's book containing instruction and exercises relating to a particular subject.

work·day (wərk'dā') *n* **1** a day for work, typically a day that is not Saturday, Sunday, or a holiday. **2** the part of a day during which work is done.

work·er (wər'kər) *n* **1** a labourer who or animal that works, especially a person who does a specified type of work or in a specified way: *a farm worker, a good worker.* **2** a creator or producer of a specified thing: *a worker of marvels.* **3** a social insect, typically a neuter or undeveloped female bee, wasp, ant, or termite, that does the basic work of the colony. See BEE for picture.

SYNONYMS

Worker refers to a person or animal that works: *The workers went on strike.*

Labourer suggests someone who does physical work: *The labourers carried the wood for the bridge.*

Operator refers to a skilled worker: *She got the job as the operator of the new high-tech drilling machine.*

Employee refers to someone who works for a person or organization: *The firm has twenty employees.*

workers' compensation *n* money paid to someone who has suffered personal injuries at work or has an illness arising from work.

work ethic *n* the principle that hard work is good, honourable, and worthy of reward.

work·fare (wərk'fer) *n* a policy whereby people who receive welfare benefits must do a certain minimum number of hours of work or training.

work·force (wərk'fôrs') *n* the people engaged in or available for work, either in a country or area, or in a particular company or industry: *My mom returned to the workforce once I was in school full-time.*

work·horse (wərk'hôrs') *n* **1** a horse used mostly for work, not for racing, hunting, or showing. **2** a person or machine who dependably performs hard work over a long period of time.

work·house (wərk'hous') *especially UK n* in former times, a building in which very poor people were lodged and were expected to perform some work in return.

work·ing (wər'king) *adj* **1** with paid employment: *the working population.* **2** relating to, suitable for, or for the purpose of work: *working hours, working clothes.* **3** used as an animal in farming, hunting, or for guard duties: *a working dog.* **4** sufficient to work with: *a working knowledge.* **5** providing a basis for further work: *a working hypothesis.*

n **1** the action of doing work. **2** often, **workings** *pl* the way in which a machine, organization, or system operates: *the workings of government.* **3** **workings** *pl* a mine or part of a mine from which minerals are being extracted.

working capital *n* the amount of capital needed to operate a business from day to day, calculated as the current assets minus the current liabilities.

working class *n* the social group consisting of those who work for wages and are not in management or the professions. Labourers and industrial workers are in the working class. See also BLUE-COLLAR.

working day *n* a workday.

work–in–progress (wərk′in prō′gres) *n* any task, activity, etc., begun but not yet completed.

work·load (wər′klōd′) *n* the amount of work to be done by someone or something.

work·man (wərk′mən) *n, pl* **work·men** (-mən) **1** a man employed to do manual labour. **2** a person skilled in a trade or craft.

work·man·like (wərk′mən līk′) *adj* showing efficiency and competence: *The job was done quickly and in a workmanlike manner.*

work·man·ship (wərk′mən ship′) *n* the degree of skill by which a product is made or a job is done: *jewellery of fine workmanship. Her workmanship is always good.*

work of art *n* a creative product, such as a painting, sculpture, musical composition, or literary work, that appeals to a sense of beauty or the imagination.

work·out (wər′kout′) *n* **1** a session of vigorous physical exercise or training: *The team had a good workout before the game.* **2** a trial or test: *He gave the software a thorough workout before buying it.*

work·place (wərk′plās′) *n* a place where people work, such as an office or factory.

work·room (wər′krūm′) *n* a room set aside for working in, especially for a particular kind of work: *My mom has a workroom in the basement.*

work·sheet (wərk′shēt′) *n* **1** a paper listing questions or tasks for students. **2** a paper for recording work done or in progress. **3** a sheet of paper with preliminary notes or rough text on it.

work·shop (wərk′shop′) *n* **1** a room or building in which goods are manufactured or repaired. **2** a meeting at which a group of people engage in intensive discussion and activity on a particular subject or project.
v present a performance of a dramatic work, using group discussion and improvisation in order to explore aspects of the production prior to formal staging.

work·shy (wərk′shī) *adj* lazy and not inclined to work

work·space (wərk′spās′) *n* an area regularly used for working in: *I'd like a big table to use as a workspace.*

work·sta·tion (wərk′stā′shən) *Computers n* a desk and other equipment where a computer system is set up for work by one person.

work–stud·y (wərk′stud′ē) *adj* to do with a school program that places students in part-time jobs related to their fields of study, so that part of their course credit is earned by practical work.

work·ta·ble (wərk′tā′bəl) *n* a table to work at.

work·week (wərk′wēk′) *n* the total number of hours or days worked in a week.

world (wərld) *n* **1** the earth, together with all its countries, peoples, and natural features. **2** another planet like the earth: *to travel to other worlds.* **3** a part or aspect of human life or of the animals, plants, or natural features of the earth: *the insect world, the world of music.* **4** a region or group of countries, or a period of history: *the French-speaking world, the ancient world.* **5** human and social interaction: *He had little interest in the world.* **6** a great deal or a large amount: *The rest did her a world of good.*
adj indicating the most important or influential people or things of its class: *a world authority, a world power.* <Old English *weorold*>
come into the world, be born.
on top of the world, extremely pleased: *I was on top of the world when I found out I had won.*
out of this world, *Informal* extremely enjoyable or pleasing: *Our meal was just out of this world.*
think the world of, think very highly of.
worlds apart, very different.

World Bank *n* in full, the **International Bank for Reconstruction and Development** an agency of the United Nations.

world–class (wərld′klas′) *adj* of or among the best in the world as a person, thing, or activity.

world·ly (wərl′dlē) *adj* **world·li·er, world·li·est** **1** of or concerned with material values or ordinary life rather than a spiritual existence: *worldly success.* **2** experienced and sophisticated. **world′li·ness** *n.*

world·ly–wise (wərl′dlē wīz′) *adj* wise about the ways and affairs of this world.

world power *n* a country powerful enough to influence worldwide events.

World Series *n* the series of baseball games played each fall between the winners of the American and National major league championships, to decide the overall winner.

world's fair *n* an international exhibition of the industrial, scientific, technological, and artistic achievements of the participating nations.

world·view (wərld′vyū′) *n* a particular philosophy of life or conception of the world.

World War I *n* a war (1914–18) in which Germany and Austria-Hungary, joined later by Turkey and Bulgaria, were defeated by an alliance of the UK and its dominions, France, and Russia, joined later by Italy and the US. Also called **First World War**.

World War II *n* a war (1939–45) in which Germany, Italy, and Japan were defeated by an alliance eventually including the UK and its dominions, the Soviet Union, and the US. Also called **Second World War**.

a bat	e bed	i bid	o pot	u cup	th **thin**
ā cake	ē me	ī bite	ō go	ū rude	ᴛʜ **then**
ä bar	ə about	ər over	ô for	ů put	zh measure

world–wea·ry (wərl′dwē′rē) *adj* feeling or indicating feelings of weariness, boredom, or cynicism as a result of long experience of life. **world′-wear′i·ness** *n.*

world·wide (wərl′dwīd′) *adj* extending or reaching throughout the world: *worldwide pollution.*
adv in many places throughout the world: *She gives lectures worldwide.*

World Wide Web *n* a system on the Internet that consists of stored, interlinked documents. By using specialized software, the user of the World Wide Web can find documents and move from one to another by means of links within them. *Abbrev* **www**. See also INTERNET. Also called **the Web**.

worm (wərm) *n* **1** a crawling or wriggling, often segmented, animal with a long slender soft body and no spine or limbs. **2** a weak or contemptible person. **3** *Computers* in full, **write once read many** a program that reproduces and spreads itself across a network, usually to harmful effect. **4 worms** *pl* intestinal or other internal parasites in the body.
v **1** move with difficulty by crawling or wrigging: *We wormed under the high fence.* **2** put oneself in a particular position by persistent and subtle means: *He tried to worm the secret out of me. He wormed himself into our confidence.* **3** treat an animal with a substance designed to expel parasitic worms. <Old English *wyrm*> **worm′like′** *adj.*
can of worms, a very complicated problem.

worm–eat·en (wər′mē′tən) *adj* eaten into by worms: *worm-eaten timbers.*

worm·hole (wərm′hōl′) *n* a hole made by a worm, or a burrowing insect larva, in wood, fruit, books, or other materials.

worm·wood (wərm′wůd′) *n* a woody shrub with a bitter aromatic taste, used as an ingredient of vermouth and in medicine.

worm·y (wər′mē) *adj* **worm·i·er, worm·i·est** infested with, damaged by, or eaten into by worms: *a wormy apple.* **worm′i·ness** *n.*

worn (wȯrn) *v* past participle of WEAR.
adj **1** damaged and shabby as a result of much use: *worn rugs.* **2** very tired: *a worn face.*

worn out *adj* **1** damaged or shabby to the point of being no longer usable: *Those shoes are worn out and should be thrown away, a worn-out pair of shoes.* **2** extremely tired or exhausted: *I'm worn out after all that running.*

wor·ri·some (wər′ē səm) *adj* causing anxiety or concern.

wor·ry (wər′ē) *v* **wor·ried, wor·ry·ing 1** feel anxious or uneasy by dwelling on difficulties or troubles, or cause to feel this way: *She will worry if we are late. The problem worried him.* **2** cause annoyance: *Don't worry me with so many questions.* **3** tear at or pull about with the teeth, especially as a meat-eating animal: *The dog worried the bone.*
n, pl **wor·ries 1** a condition of anxiety and uncertainty over actual or potential problems: *Worry kept her awake.* **2** a cause or source of anxiety: *His lying was a constant worry to her.* <Old English *wyrgan* choke, i.e., harass by rough treatment> **wor′ried** *adj.* **wor′ried·ly** *adv.* **wor′ri·er** *n.* **wor′ry·ing** *adj.* **wor′ry·ing·ly** *adv.*
not to worry! *Informal* don't worry.

wor·ry·wart (wər′ē wȯrt′) *Informal n* a person who constantly worries, especially over trivial matters.

worse (wərs) *adj, comparative of* **bad 1** of poorer quality or lower standard: *The food was worse here than in other restaurants.* **2** more serious or severe: *The pain was worse in the morning.* **3** more wrong or evil: *Insulting him was bad, but hitting him was worse.*
adv **1** less well or skilfully: *The longer I tried, the worse I got.* **2** more seriously or severe: *The others were hurt, worse than herself.*
n a more serious or unpleasant event or circumstance: *He thought failing the test was bad enough, but worse followed.* <Old English *wyrsa*>
for the worse, in a less good, favourable, or pleasant condition: *The change was for the worse.*
none the worse for, not adversely affected by: *She was rescued from the water, and was none the worse for her adventure.*
worse off, a in a worse condition. **b** with less money.

wors·en (wər′sən) *v* make or become worse: *You will only worsen the situation if you talk about it. She was taken to hospital, but her condition worsened through the night.*

wor·ship (wər′ship) *n* **1** the feeling or expression of great honour and respect paid to someone or something regarded as sacred. **2** the acts or rites through which one pays such honour and respect: *public worship.* **3** (*often in compounds*) great love and admiration: *hero-worship.* **4 Worship** a title used in addressing (**Your Worship**) or referring to (**His Worship**, **Her Worship**) a mayor or certain magistrates.
v **wor·shipped** or **wor·shiped, wor·ship·ping** or **wor·ship·ing 1** pay great honour and respect to: *They worshipped their god in various ways.* **2** take part in a religious service. **3** treat someone or something with great honour or respect: *He worshipped money. She worships her mother.* <Old English *weorthscipe*> **wor′ship·per** or **wor′ship·er** *n.*

worst (wərst) *adj, superlative of* **bad 1** of the poorest quality or the lowest standard: *This is the worst movie I ever saw.* **2** least pleasant, desirable, or tolerable: *He is the worst boy in school.* **3** most severe, serious, or dangerous: *I got the worst flu of my life.* **4** least suitable or advantageous: *Worst of all, he didn't give me money when I needed it.*
adv **1** most severely or seriously: *He sings worst when he's tired.* **2** least well or skilfully: *That's the worst I've ever played.*
n the most serious or unpleasant thing that could happen: *Yesterday was bad, but the worst is yet to come.*
v beat or defeat: *The hero worsted his enemies.* <Old English *wyrresta*>
at worst, in the most serious case or under the least favourable circumstances.
get (or **have**) **the worst of it,** suffer the most or be in the least successful position.
if (**the**) **worst comes to** (**the**) **worst,** if the most serious or difficult circumstances arise.
in the worst way, to an extreme degree: *I need a new winter coat in the worst way.*

worst–case (wərst′kās′) *adj* marked as a projected development by the worst of the possible foreseeable circumstances: *a worst-case prediction. In the worst-case scenario, the games could be cancelled due to a blizzard.*

wor·sted (wər′stid) *or* (wu̇s′tid) *n* a fine yarn, or fabric made from such yarn. <*Worsted*, a town in England, where it was originally made>

worth (wərth) *adj* **1** equivalent in value to the sum or item specified: *That book is worth fifteen dollars.* **2** sufficiently good, important, or interesting to justify a specified action or to be regarded in the way specified: *Our museum is worth a visit.* **3** with income or property amounting to a specified sum: *That man is worth millions.*
n **1** the value equivalent to that of someone or something, or the level at which someone or something deserves to be valued or rated: *He preferred to read books of real worth. I know how much it costs, but how much is it worth?* **2** a quantity of something of specified value: *ten dollars' worth of gasoline.* **3** high value or merit: *She had much inner worth.* <Old English *weorth*> **worth′less** *adj.* **worth′less·ly** *adv.* **worth′less·ness** *n.*
for all one is worth, to the full extent of one's power or ability: *She ran for all she was worth.*

worth·while (wər′thwīl′) *adj* worth the time, money, or effort spent: *The new street lighting was worthwhile.*

wor·thy (wər′THē) *adj* **wor·thi·er, wor·thi·est** **1** deserving effort, attention, or respect: *worthy causes.* **2** with or showing qualities or abilities that deserve recognition: *Her courage was worthy of high praise.*
n, pl **wor·thies** a person notable or important in a particular area: *The mayor and other worthies were present at the ceremony.* **wor′thi·ly** *adv.* **wor′thi·ness** *n.*

SYNONYMS

Worthy means "deserving": *His hard efforts make him a worthy candidate for the award.*

Admirable means "worthy of approval": *It's very admirable of the corporation to donate so much money.*

Laudable is a more formal word meaning "worthy of praise": *The principal gave credit to three students for their laudable contributions to the school.*

–worthy *combining form* **1** deserving of a specified thing: *praiseworthy, noteworthy.* **2** suitable or fit for a specified thing: *roadworthy, seaworthy.*

would (wu̇d) *v* **1** introducing a request or command in a polite manner: *Would you please close the window?* **2** expressing the conditional mood: *If she would take her work seriously, she would get better grades.* **3** softening a statement or expressing uncertainty: *I would not like to ask him.* **4** expressing repeated, or habitual, action in the past: *When we were small, we would spend hours playing in the sand.* **5** (*usually in indirect speech*) past tense of WILL[1]. **6** *Informal* expressing annoyance or resignation at the action of another person: *Oh you would have to say that, wouldn't you?* <Old English *wolde*>

would–be (wu̇d′bē′) *adj* wishing or pretending to be: *a would-be rock star.*

would·n't (wu̇d′ənt) *contraction* would not.

would·'ve (wu̇d′əv) *contraction* would have: *I would've fallen if she hadn't grabbed my arm.*

wound[1] (wūnd) *n* **1** an injury to living tissue caused by a cut, blow, or other impact, typically one in which the skin is cut or broken. **2** an injury to a person's feelings or reputation: *The loss of his job was a wound to his pride.*
v **1** inflict an injury on someone. **2** injure a person's feelings: *His unkind words wounded her.* <Old English *wund*>

wound[2] (wound) a past tense and a past participle of WIND[2].

wove (wōv) a past tense of WEAVE.

wo·ven (wō′vən) past participle of WEAVE.

wow (wou) *Informal interj* used to express admiration or amazement.
v impress and excite someone greatly: *She sure wowed us with her singing.*
n a sensational success. <imitative>

wrack (rak) *n* a coarse brown seaweed that grows on the shoreline, often forming a distinct band between high-water and low-water marks. <Dutch *wrak* wreck>

wraith (rāth) *n* **1** a ghost or ghostlike image of someone, especially one seen shortly before or soon after his or her death. **2** a pale, thin, or sickly person or thing. <origin unknown> **wraith′like′** *adj.*

wran·gle (rang′gəl) *v* **wrang·led, wran·gling** *n* a dispute or argument, typically one that is long and complicated: *They had a wrangle about where the furniture should go.*
v **1** have such a dispute or argument: *The children wrangled about who should sit in front.* **2** *especially western N America* round up, herd, or take charge of livestock. <origin uncertain> **wrang′ler** *n.*

wrap (rap) *v* **wrapped, wrap·ping** **1** cover or enclose someone or something in paper or soft material, or arrange paper or soft material round someone or something, typically for warmth or protection: *She wrapped herself in a shawl. Wrap this blanket around you.* **2** clasp, embrace, or envelop: *He wrapped her in his arms. The mountain peak was wrapped in cloud.* **3** cause a word or unit of computer text to be carried over to a new line automatically as the margin is reached, or to fit around embedded features such as pictures. **4** *Informal* finish filming or recording something.
n **1** a loose outer garment or piece of material. **2** *Informal* the end of a session of filming or recording. See RAP for confusable. <Middle English *wrappen*>
under wraps, secret or hidden: *The theme of the school dance is being kept under wraps until next week.*
wrapped up in, be so preoccupied by or absorbed in something that one does not notice anything else: *She is wrapped up in family life.*
wrap up, put on warm outer clothes.

wrap·a·round (rap′ə round′) *adj* curving or extending around at the edges or sides.
n a garment, overlapping and fastened loosely.

a bat	e bed	i bid	o pot	u cup	th thin
ā cake	ē me	ī bite	ō go	ū rude	TH then
ȧ bar	ə about	ər over	ȯ for	u̇ put	zh measure

W

wrap·per (rap′ər) *n* **1** a piece of paper, plastic, or foil covering and protecting something that is sold or distributed. **2** the dust jacket of a book. **3** a long, loose-fitting robe or gown. **4** a tobacco leaf enclosing a cigar.

wrap·ping (rap′ing) *n* the paper or other material in which something is wrapped.

wrap–up (rap′up′) *n* a concluding or summarizing statement or report, such as a summary of a sports event.

wrasse (ras) *n* a brightly coloured saltwater fish with thick, fleshy lips, powerful teeth, and spiny fins.

wrath (rath) *or* (roth) *n* extreme anger. <Old English *wrǣththu*> **wrath′ful** *adj.* **wrath′ful·ly** *adv.* **wrath′ful·ness** *n.*

wreak (rēk) *v* **1** cause a large amount of damage or harm: *The hurricane wreaked havoc on the city.* **2** take vengeance: *He wreaked revenge on his foes.* <Old English *wrecan*>

wreath (rēth) *n, pl* **wreaths** (rēTHz) **1** an arrangement of flowers, leaves, or stems fastened in a ring and used for decoration or for laying on a grave, or a carved image of it. **2** a thing that suggests or resembles such an arrangement: *a wreath of smoke.* <Old English *wrǣth*>

CONFUSABLES

Wreath is a noun referring to a floral decoration: *The premier placed the wreath on the monument.*

Writhe is a verb referring to continual twisting movements: *The dancers writhed to the drumbeat.*

wreathe (rēTH) *v* **wreathed, wreath·ing** cover, encircle, or surround a thing: *The children wreathed flowers to put on their grandmother's grave. Mist wreathed the hills.*

wreck (rek) *n* **1** the destruction or severe damage of a ship, structure, train, motor vehicle, or aircraft, or the thing destroyed or damaged: *The hurricane caused many wrecks. I heard there was a bad train wreck near here.* **2** a person whose physical or mental health or strength has failed: *He's been a wreck ever since his bout with pneumonia.*
v **1** cause the destruction or severe damage of a ship, structure, or vehicle, or be destroyed or severely damaged. **2** spoil completely: *The mistake wrecked my chance of getting a perfect mark.* **3** engage in breaking up badly damaged vehicles, demolishing old buildings, or similar activities to obtain usable scrap or parts. <Old French *wrec* goods cast ashore after a shipwreck>

wreck·age (rek′ij) *n* the remains of something that has been severely damaged or destroyed: *The shore was covered with the wreckage of ships. She wept at the wreckage of her hopes.*

wreck·er (rek′ər) *n* **1** a person who or thing that wrecks, damages, or destroys something. **2** a person who breaks up damaged vehicles, demolishes old buildings, or salvages wrecked ships to obtain usable scrap or parts. **3** in former times, a person who tried to bring about a shipwreck in order to plunder or profit from the wreckage.

wreck·house winds (rek′hous) *Newfoundland pln* strong winds that blow across Cape Ray in Newfoundland.

wrecking ball *n* a huge, heavy metal ball swung by machine against a building in order to demolish it. Also, **wrecker's ball**.

wren (ren) *n* a small brown or grey songbird with a short tail, often held erect. <Old English *wrenna*>

wrench (rench) *n* **1** a sudden violent twist or pull: *He broke the branch off the tree with a sudden wrench. He gave his ankle a wrench when he hopped off the bus.* **2** an injury caused by such an action. **3** an act of leaving someone or something that causes sadness or distress: *It was a wrench to give away my childhood toys.* **4** an adjustable tool used for holding and turning nuts or bolts.
v **1** twist or pull suddenly and violently: *The policewoman wrenched the weapon out of the man's hand.* **2** injure a part of the body as a result of a sudden twisting movement: *He wrenched his back in wrestling.* **3** turn something, especially a nut or bolt, with a wrench. **4** distort to fit a particular theory or interpretation. <Old English *wrencan* twist>

wrest (rest) *v* **1** forcefully pull something from a person's grasp. **2** take something, especially power or control, from someone or something else after considerable effort or difficulty: *The rebels wrested control of the city from the government forces.*

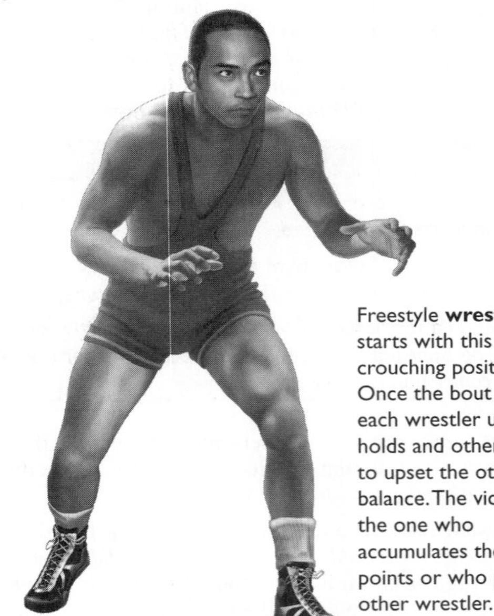

Freestyle **wrestling** starts with this crouching position. Once the bout begins, each wrestler uses holds and other moves to upset the other's balance. The victor is the one who accumulates the most points or who pins the other wrestler.

wres·tle (res′əl) *v* **wres·tled, wres·tling** **1** take part in a struggle, either as a sport or in a fight, that involves grappling with one's opponent. **2** struggle with a difficulty or problem: *We must wrestle with temptation.*
n **1** a wrestling match. **2** a hard struggle. <*wrest*> **wres′tler** *n.*

wres·tling (res′ling) *n* the sport or activity of grappling with an opponent and trying to throw or hold down the person on the ground according to a code of rules.

wretch (rech) *n* **1** an unfortunate or unhappy person. **2** a bad or contemptible person. <Old English *wrecca*>

wretch·ed (rech′id) *adj* **1** in a very unfortunate or unhappy condition or situation: *I felt wretched.* **2** of very bad quality: *a wretched novel.* **wretch′ed·ly** *adv.* **wretch′ed·ness** *n.*

wrig·gle (rig′əl) *v* **wrig·gled, wrig·gling 1** twist and turn with quick writhing movements or cause to move in such a way: *He wriggled when he was restless. A snake wriggled across the road.* **2** avoid something by means of tricks, excuses, or deception: *He managed to wriggle out of being charged with theft.*
n a wriggling movement: *With one wriggle, he was under the bed.* <Middle English *wrigglen*> **wrig′gler** *n.* **wrig′gly** *adj.*

wright (rīt) *n* (*in compounds*) a maker or builder of something: *playwright.* <Old English *wryhta*, from *weorc* work>

wring (ring) *v* **wrung, wring·ing 1** twist and squeeze something hard to force liquid from it, or extract liquid by squeezing and twisting: *to wring clothes. The hikers wrung water from their soaking clothes.* **2** break an animal's neck by twisting it forcefully. **3** squeeze someone's hand tightly, especially with sincere emotion. **4** obtain something with difficulty or effort: *to wring an admission of guilt from a criminal.* **5** cause pain or distress to: *Their poverty wrung her heart.*
n an act of twisting and squeezing something: *She gave her swimsuit a good wring.* <Old English *wringan*>
wring your hands, show helpless dismay: *You don't need to wring your hands every time you make a mistake.*

wring·er (ring′ər) *n* a person who or thing that wrings, especially a device or machine for squeezing water from clothes.
through the wringer, through an extremely difficult or stressful experience.

wrin·kle (ring′kəl) *n* **1** a slight line or fold in something, especially fabric or the skin of the face: *I must press out the wrinkles in this dress.* **2** *Informal* a clever invention or useful piece of information or advice: *I learned a few wrinkles about how to apply paint.*
v **wrin·kled, wrin·kling 1** make or cause lines or folds in something, especially fabric or the skin: *This fabric will not wrinkle.* **2** grimace and cause wrinkles on a part of the face: *His forehead wrinkled.* <Old English *gewrinclian* crease>

wrin·kly (ring′klē) *adj* **wrin·kli·er, wrin·kli·est** with many lines or folds.

wrist (rist) *n* **1** the joint connecting the human hand with the forearm, or the equivalent joint in the foreleg of a four-footed animal or the wing of a bird: *Her wrists are thicker than mine.* **2** the part of a garment covering this joint of the arm. <Old English>

wrist·band (rist′band′) *n* the band of a sleeve or glove fitting around the wrist.

wrist shot *Sports n* a shot or stroke in sports such as hockey, in which the power is provided by a flick of the wrist rather than the arm.

wrist·watch (ris′twoch) *n* a small watch worn on a strap around the wrist.

writ (rit) *n* a formal order in the name of a court or other authority directing a person to act or to not act in some way. <Old English *writ* piece of writing>

write (rīt) *v* **wrote, writ·ten, writ·ing 1 a** mark letters, words, or other symbols on a surface, especially paper, with a pen, pencil, or other instrument: *Write your name and address.* **b** have the ability to mark understandable letters or words in this way: *She learned to write at an early age.* **2** compose, write, and send a message to someone: *She writes an e-mail to her cousin every week.* **3** compose a text or work for written, printed, or musical reproduction or publication: *He wrote nine novels.* **4** 🍁 take an exam or test. **5** show plainly: *Honesty is written on his face.* <Old English *writan* to draw the figure of>
write down, a put into writing: *Many early folk songs were never written down.* **b** put a lower cash value on.
write off, 1 dismiss someone or something as insignificant: *She quickly wrote him off as a friend.* **2** cancel the record of a debt, acknowledging the loss of or failure to recover an asset.
write out, a put into writing. **b** write in full: *She made quick notes during the interview and wrote out her report later.*
write up, a write a full or formal account of something. **b** make entries to bring a diary or similar record up to date.

write·off (rī′tof′) *n* **1** a vehicle, aircraft, or other object that is too badly damaged to be repaired: *After the accident, the car was a writeoff.* **2** a worthless or ineffectual person or thing: *He couldn't help her at all, so she considered him a writeoff.* **3** a cancellation from an account of an uncollectible debt or worthless asset.

write–pro·tect (rīt′prō tekt′) *Computers v* modify a file or disk so that its data cannot be edited or erased.

writ·er (rī′tər) *n* a person who has written a particular text, especially one whose profession or business is writing, such as an author or journalist.

write–up (rī′tup′) *n* a full written description or account.

writhe (rīᴛʜ) *v* **writhed, writh·ing 1** make continual twisting, squirming movements of the body, or cause to move in such a way: *The wounded man writhed with pain.* **2** respond with great emotional or physical discomfort to a violent or unpleasant feeling or thought: *We writhed when we heard the man insult our friend.* See WREATH for confusable. <Old English *writhan*>

writ·ing (rī′ting) *n* **1 a** the activity or skill of marking understandable words on a surface and composing text: *reading, writing, and arithmetic.* **b** a sequence of letters, words, or symbols marked on paper or some other surface: *The parchment had strange writing on it.* **2** the activity or occupation of composing text for publication. **3** written work, especially with regard to its style or quality: *The writing in the story was extraordinarily bad.* **4 writings** *pl* books, stories, articles, or other written works. **5** handwriting: *Her writing is hard to read.*

a bat	e bed	i bid	o pot	u cup	th thin
ā cake	ē me	ī bite	ō go	ü rude	ᴛʜ then
ä bar	ə about	ər over	ò for	u̇ put	zh measure

W

writ·ten (rit′ən) past participleof WRITE.

wrong (rong) *adj* **1** not correct or true: *the wrong answer.* **2** not suitable, proper, or appropriate: *He wore the wrong clothes for the occasion.* **3** unjust, dishonest, or immoral: *a wrong deed.* **4** in a bad condition or out of order: *Something is wrong with this computer.*
adv in an unsuitable or undesirable way or direction, or with an incorrect result: *Everything went wrong today. Every time she guessed wrong.*
n an unjust, dishonest, or immoral action: *My teacher said that a wrong had been done to me, and an apology must be made.*
v act unjustly or dishonestly toward someone: *She forgave those who had wronged her.* <Old Norse *rangr* crooked> **wrong′ly** *adv.* **wrong′ness** *n.*
go wrong, turn out badly.
get something wrong, misunderstand or misinterpret; do the wrong way, answer incorrectly, etc.
in the wrong, responsible for a quarrel, mistake, or offence.

wrong·do·ing (rong′dū′ing) *n* the doing of wrong; bad acts: *The thief was guilty of wrongdoing.* **wrong′do′er** *n.*

wrong·ful (rong′fəl) *adj* not fair, just, or legal as an act. **wrong′ful·ly** *adv.* **wrong′ful·ness** *n.*

wrong–head·ed (rong′hed′id) *adj* with or showing bad judgment. **wrong′-head′ed·ly** *adv.* **wrong′-head′ed·ness** *n.*

wrote (rōt) past tense of WRITE.

wrought (rot) *v* a past tense and a past participle of WORK. *adj* beaten out or shaped as a metal by hammering: *a wrought urn, wrought silver.*

wrought iron *n* a tough, durable form of iron that is soft enough to be easily forged and welded, but that will not break as easily as cast iron, and is used for decorative furniture, gates, and railings.

wrought–up (rot′up′) *adj* upset and anxious: *After all the work of planning, she was too wrought-up to enjoy the party.*

wrung (rung) past tense and past participle of WRING.

wry (rī) *adj* **wry·er** or **wri·er, wry·est** or **wri·est** using or expressing dry, especially mocking, humour: *a wry smile, wry remarks.* <Old English *wrigian* turn, twist. A wry smile is one where the mouth is twisted.> **wry′ly** *adv.* **wry′ness** *n.*

WSW west-southwest.

Wu (wū) *n* a dialect of Chinese spoken in the Shanghai area and Zhejiang (dje djang′) province.

wun·der·kind (vůn′dər kind′) *or* (wun′dər kind′) *n* a person who achieves great success while relatively young. <German *Wunder* wonder + *Kind* child>

WWI World War I.

WWII World War II.

www World Wide Web.

Wy·an·dot (wī′ən dot) *n, pl* **Wy·an·dot** or **Wy·an·dots** **1** in former times, a member of a First Nations people living in Ontario. The descendants of these people now live mainly in Oklahoma. **2** their Iroquoian language.
adj to do with these people or their language. Also called **Wendat**, **Huron**.

WYSIWYG (wiz′ē wig′) *adj* showing text and images on a computer screen exactly as they would appear on paper if printed out. <*w*(*hat*) *y*(*ou*) *s*(*ee*) *i*(*s*) *w*(*hat*) *y*(*ou*) *g*(*et*)>

x or **X** (eks) *n, pl* **x's** or **X's** **1** the twenty-fourth letter of the English alphabet, or any speech sound represented by it. **2** the twenty-fourth thing in a list or series. **3** an unknown or unspecified person or thing, especially an unknown quantity in an algebraic expression. **4** the Roman numeral for 10. **5 a** an indication of a position on a map or diagram: *X marks the spot.* **b** a mistake or incorrect answer. **c** a kiss. **d** a replacement for a signature of a person who cannot write.

x–ax·is (eks′ak′sis) *Mathematics n, pl* **x-axes** (-ak′sēz) in a plane Cartesian coordinate system, the horizontal axis. Compare Y-AXIS.

X chromosome *n* a sex chromosome in mammals, two of which are normally present in female cells and only one in male cells. Compare Y-CHROMOSOME.

xe·bec (zē′bek) *n* in former times, a small, three-masted sailing ship of the Mediterranean region.

xe·non (zē′non) *n* an element that is a heavy, inactive, colourless gas, obtained by distilling liquid air. It is used in some specialized electric lamps. *Symbol* **Xe** <Greek = strange>

xen·o·pho·bi·a (zen′ə fō′bē ə) *n* a hatred or fear of people from other countries. <Greek *xenos* stranger + *-phobia* fear>

xe·rog·ra·phy (zē rog′rə fē) *n* a process for making copies of written, printed, or graphic items in which black or coloured powder adheres to parts of a surface remaining electrically charged after being exposed to light from an image of the document to be copied. <Greek *xeros* dry + *-graph* write> **xe·rog·ra′phic** *adj.*

Xer·ox (zē′roks) *Trademark n, pl* **Xer·ox·es** a xerographic copy made by a Xerox machine.
v **Xer·oxed, Xer·ox·ing** make such copies.

Xmas (kris′məs) *Informal n* Christmas.

X–ray or **x–ray** (eks′rā′) *n* **1** an electromagnetic wave that is able to pass through many materials opaque to light. Its wavelength is between ultraviolet light and gamma rays. **2** a photographic or digital image of the internal composition of a thing, especially a part of the body, produced by X-rays being passed through and being absorbed in different degrees by different materials.
v photograph or examine with X-rays: *Our luggage was X-rayed at the airport.*

X's and O's (ek′siz en ōz′) *n* (*with singular verb*) tic-tac-toe.

xy·lem (zī′lem) *Botany n* the tissue in the vascular system of plants and trees that conducts water and dissolved minerals upward from the roots and forms the woody element in the stem. Compare PHLOEM. <Greek *xylon* wood>

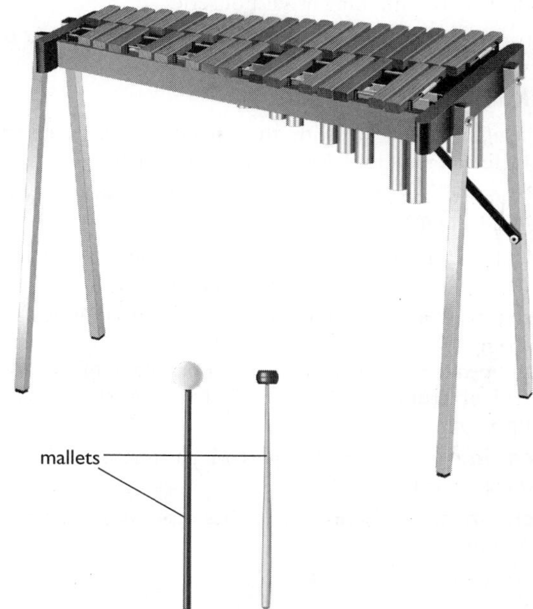

The **xylophone** was developed in the 1300s in southeast Asia and its use quickly spread to Africa and central Europe, where it became a folk instrument. Charles Camille Saint-Saëns was the first composer (in 1874) to use the xylophone in an orchestral work.

xy·lo·phone (zī′lə fōn′) *n* a percussion musical instrument consisting of two rows of wooden bars of varying lengths, which are struck with one or more small wooden or plastic hammers. <Greek *xylon* wood + *phone* sound>

Yy

y or **Y** (wī) *n, pl* **y's** or **Y's** **1** the twenty-fifth letter of the English alphabet, or any speech sound represented by it. **2** the twenty-fifth thing in a list or series.

Y (wī) *Informal n* in full, **YMCA**, **YWCA**, **YMHA**, or **YWHA**: *We spent the afternoon at the Y.*

Y2K the year 2000.

–y[1] *suffix* full of or with the quality of: *airy, watery.* **3** inclined or apt to: *fidgety, sticky.* <Old English *–ig*>

–y[2] *suffix* considered small or lovable: *doggy, dolly.* <Middle English>

–y[3] *suffix* **1** a state, condition, or quality: *jealousy, victory.* **2** an action or its results: *entreaty, delivery.*

yacht (yot) *n* a medium-sized sailing boat equipped for cruising or racing, or a powered boat or small ship equipped for cruising, especially for private or official use.
v sail or cruise on a yacht. <Dutch *jaghtschip* chasing ship>

yacht·ing (yot′ing) *n* the sport or pastime of racing or sailing a yacht.

yachts·man (yot′smən) *n, pl* **yachts·men** (-smən) a person who sails a yacht.

yack (yak) YAK[2].

ya·hoo[1] (yo′hū) *or* (ya′hū′) *interj* used to express great joy or excitement. <imitative>

ya·hoo[2] (yo′hū) *or* (ya′hū′) *n* a rough, coarse, ignorant person. <*Yahoo,* in Swift's *Gulliver's Travels,* a brute in human form who works for a race of intelligent horses>

Yah·weh (yo′wā) *or* (yo′we) *n* the form of the Hebrew name of God used in the Bible. Also, **Yahveh**. <Hebrew>

The wild **yak** may look slow and heavy, but is actually an excellent climber. Yaks love the treeless terrain of the high mountains, and thanks to their heavy coats, they can survive in temperatures as low as –40°C.

yak[1] (yak) *n* a large ox with shaggy hair, humped shoulders, and large horns, used in Tibet as a pack animal and for its milk, meat, and hide. <Tibetan *gyag*>

yak[2] (yak) *Informal v* **yakked, yak·king** talk at length about trivial or boring subjects.
n a long, trivial, or boring conversation. Also, **yack-yak**, **yakety-yak**. <imitative>

yam (yam) *n* **1** an edible starchy tuber of a climbing plant found in tropical and subtropical countries. See POTATO for picture. **2** a sweet potato. <Spanish>

yang (yang) *n* in Chinese philosophy, the active male principle of the universe characterized as associated with heaven, light, and heat. Compare YIN. <Mandarin>

yank (yangk) *v* pull with an abrupt motion: *You almost yanked my arm off!*
n a sudden hard pull: *He gave the door a yank.* <origin uncertain>

Yan·kee (yang′kē) *Informal n* **1** an inhabitant of New England in the northeastern part of the US. **2** a person who lives in or is from the US. Also, **Yank**. <origin uncertain>

yap (yap) *n* a sharp, shrill bark.
v **yapped, yap·ping** **1** give a sharp, shrill bark. **2** talk at length in an irritating way. <imitative> **yap′py** *adj.*

yard[1] (yȧrd) *n* **1** a piece of ground near or around a house or other building and enclosed by a fence or wall. **2** a piece of enclosed ground for some special purpose or business: *a chicken yard, a junk yard, a naval yard.* **3** 🍁 **a** a browsing area in winter where moose, deer, or muskox tread down the snow and remain for warmth and protection. **b** an assembly point for logs.
v **1** of moose, deer, or muskox, assemble in a YARD (def. 3a). **2** pile logs in a YARD (def. 3b). <Old English *geard*>

yard[2] (yȧrd) *n* **1** a nonmetric unit for measuring length, equal to 3 feet or 36 inches (about 0.914 m). **2** a long, slender beam, or spar, with tapered ends, fastened across a mast and used to support a sail. <Old English *gierd* rod>
the whole nine yards, *Informal* everything; as far or as much or as many as possible.

yard·age (yȧr′dij) *n* a distance or amount measured in YARDS[2] (def. 1).

yard·arm (yȧr′dȧrm′) *n* the outer end of a ship's YARD[2] (def. 2).

yard goods *pln* cloth or fabric sold by the yard or metre.

yard sale *n* an informal sale of miscellaneous personal items held in a private yard and attended mostly by neighbours and passersby.

yard·stick (yȧrd′stik′) *n* **1** a measuring rod a yard long, typically divided into inches. **2** a standard used for comparison: *She thinks that money is the only yardstick of success.*

yar·mul·ke (yȧr′məl kə) *n* a skullcap worn in public by Orthodox Jewish men or during prayer by other Jewish men. <Yiddish, from Ukrainian *yarmulka* cap>

yarn (yȧrn) *n* **1** spun thread used for weaving, knitting, or sewing. **2** a long or rambling story, especially one that is hard to believe: *A retired sailor told me that yarn.*
v tell a long or implausible story or stories. <Old English *gearn*>

yar·row (yar′ō) *n* a plant with feathery leaves and small aromatic flowers, often used in herbal medicine.

movement of an aircraft

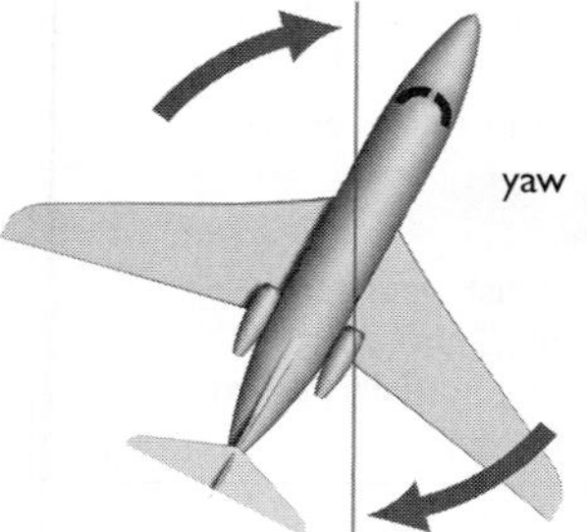

A pilot flies an aircraft by controlling its **yaw**, pitch, and roll. Yaw is controlled with the rudder, which is connected to the pedals at the pilot's feet.

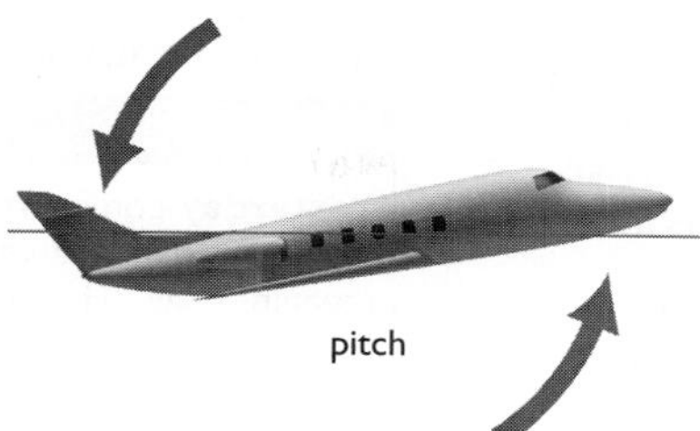

Pitch is controlled by the elevators on the tail. When the wheel is pulled back, the elevators move upward, causing the tail to move down and the nose to pitch up.

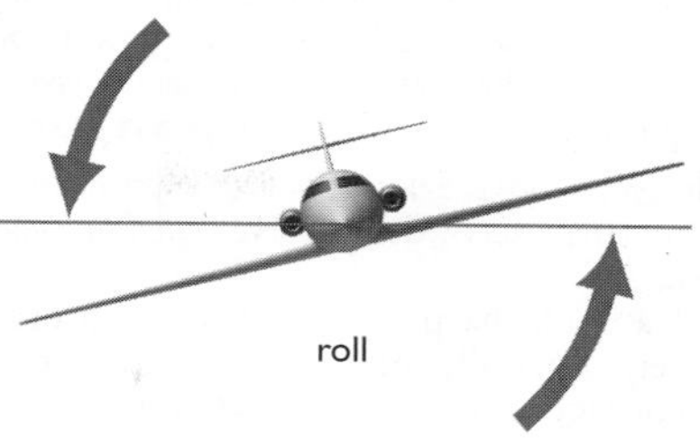

Roll is controlled by the ailerons on the aircraft's wings. When the wheel is turned left, the aileron on the left wing goes up, the one on the right wing goes down, and the aircraft rolls left.

---

yaw (yo) *v* twist or oscillate from a straight course as a moving ship or aircraft by a motion about a vertical axis. *n* a twisting or oscillating movement away from a straight course. <origin uncertain>

yawn (yon) *v* **1** open the mouth wide and inhale involuntarily and deeply, because one is sleepy, tired, or bored. **2** be wide open: *A wide gorge yawned beneath our feet.*
n **1** the act or fact of yawning. **2** *Informal* a thing that is considered boring or tiresome. <Old English *geonian*>

yaws (yoz) *pl n* (*with singular verb*) a contagious disease of the tropics that is characterized by small crusted sores that may develop into deep ulcers. <Carib (a group of languages of the Caribbean)>

y–ax·is (wī′ak′sis) *Mathematics n, pl* **y-axes** (-ak′sēz) in a plane Cartesian coordinate system, the vertical axis. Compare X-AXIS.

Y chromosome *n* a sex chromosome in mammals, normally present only in male cells. Compare X-CHROMOSOME.

ye[1] (yē) *Archaic pron* a plural of YOU.

ye[2] (ᴛʜē) *Archaic definite article* an old spelling of THE.

GRAMMAR AND USAGE

In Old and Middle English, *th* was written as þ, which was pronounced like *th* and called "thorn." Early printers did not have þ, so they substituted y, never intending it to be read as a y.

yea (yā) *adv* **1** yes: *We won! Yea!* **2** *Archaic or Humorous* (*used to introduce a sentence or clause*) indeed; truly: *He was worried, yea, worried indeed.*
n an affirmative vote, voter, or answer. <Old English *gea*>

yeah (ye′ə),(ya′ə) *or* (yā′ə) *Informal adv* yes.

year (yēr) *n* **1** the time taken by the earth to make one revolution around the sun. **2** the calendar year. **3** the part of a year spent in a certain activity: *the school year.* **4** a period of 365 or 366 days regarded in terms of the quality of produce, especially wine: *a good year.* **5** a similar period used for reckoning time according to other calendars: *the Muslim year.* **6 years** *pl* **a** age: *She was of tender years.* **b** a very long time: *They hadn't seen each other for years.* <Old English *gear*>
year by year, with each succeeding year: *Year by year he got richer.*
year in, year out, always or continuously: *She has always worked hard, year in, year out.*

year·book (yēr′bu̇k′) *n* **1** a book or report published every year that gives current information and lists events or aspects of the previous year, especially in a particular area. **2** a book containing photographs of classes in a school or university and details of school activities during the previous year.

year–end (yēr′end′) *n* the end of a calendar or financial year.
adj to do with this time of year.

year·ling (yēr′ling) *n* an animal, especially a sheep, calf, or foal that is a year old or in its second year: *The rancher decided to sell her yearlings.*
adj one year old: *a yearling colt.*

year·long (yēr′long′) *adj, adv* lasting for or throughout a year.

year·ly (yēr′lē) *adj, adv* happening or produced once a year or every year: *The earth makes a yearly revolution around the sun* (*adj*). *A new volume comes out yearly* (*adv*).

yearn (yərn) *v* have an intense feeling of loss or lack, and longing for something: *He yearns for home.* <Old English *giernan*> **yearn′er** *n.* **yearn′ing** *adj, n.* **yearn′ing·ly** *adv.*

year–round (yēr′round′) *adj* happening or continuing throughout the year: *Our town has many summer visitors, but few year-round residents.*

a bat	e bed	i bid	o pot	u cup	th **thin**
ā cake	ē me	ī bite	ō go	ū rude	ᴛʜ **then**
à bar	ə about	ər over	ȯ for	u̇ put	zh measure

yeast (yēst) *n* **1** a microscopic fungus that can convert sugar into alcohol and carbon dioxide. **2** a greyish yellow preparation of this used as a fermenting agent in beer and wine, to raise bread dough, and as a food supplement. **3** a fungus that can cause disease: *a yeast infection.* <Old English *gist*> **yeast′i·ness** *n.* **yeast′less** *adj.* **yeast′y** *adj.*

yell (yel) *v* give a loud, sharp cry or sound, especially of pain, surprise, or delight: *We yelled our goodbyes as the bus left.*
n **1** a loud, sharp cry or sound. **2** an organized shout or cheer, especially one used by a school or college to encourage its sports teams. <Old English *giellan*>

yel·low (yel′ō) *adj* **1** of a colour between green and orange in the visible spectrum, the colour of egg yolks. **2** *Offensive* with a yellowish brown skin. **3** *Informal* cowardly. **4** sensational in an offensive way: *yellow journalism.*
v become or make a yellow colour, especially with age: *The paper quickly yellowed. Buttercups yellowed the field.* <Old English *geolu*> **yel′low·ish** *adj.* **yel′low·y** *adj.*

yellow fever *n* a tropical virus affecting the liver and kidneys, causing fever and jaundice and often fatal. It is transmitted by mosquitoes.

yellow jacket *n* a wasp or hornet.

Yel·low·knife (yel′ō nīf′) *n, pl* **Yel·low·knife** or **Yel·low·knives** **1** a member of a First Nations people related and now absorbed into the Chipewyan. **2** the Athapascan language of the Yellowknife.

Yellow Pages *Trademark n* a telephone directory, or a section of one, that lists and advertises firms classified by the nature of their business. It is printed on yellow paper.

yelp (yelp) *n* a short, quick, sharp cry or bark, especially of pain or alarm.
v make such a cry or bark: *I yelped when the rock fell on my toe.* <Old English *gielpan* boast>

Yem·en (ye′mən) *n* a country in southwest Asia.
Yem′e·ni *adj, n.*

yen (yen) *n* a longing or yearning: *a yen to see the world, a yen to eat out.*
v **yenned, yen·ning** feel a longing or yearning. <Chinese *yen* a craving>

yeo·man (yō′mən) *Archaic n, pl* **yeo·men** (-mən) **1** a man holding and cultivating a small landed estate. **2** a servant in a royal or aristocratic household, ranking between a sergeant and a groom or a squire and a page.
yeo′man·ly *adj.*

yes (yes) *interj* **1** used to affirm, accept, or agree: *"Will you go?" "Yes."* **2** used to respond to a person addressing one, or otherwise trying to attract one's attention: *"Oh, Ms." "Yes?"* **3** used to question a remark or ask for more detail about it: *"It should be easy for you to do." "Oh, yes?"* **4** used to express delight: *"Dinner is ready." "Yes!"*
n, pl **yes·es** an answer or decision expressing agreement, acceptance, or consent: *You have my yes to that.* <Old English *gese*>

ye·shi·va (yə shē′və) *n, pl* **ye·shi·vas** or **ye·shi·voth** (yə shē′vōt′) an Orthodox Jewish college or seminary. <Hebrew *yeshibah* sitting>

yes–man (yes′man′) *Informal n, pl* **yes–men** (-men) a weak person who always agrees with a leader or superior.

yes·ter·day (yes′tər dā′) *n* **1** the day before today. **2** the recent past: *We are often amused by the fashions of yesterday.*
adv **1** on the day before today. **2** in the recent past.

ETYMOLOGY

Yesterday comes from Old English *geostranddaeg*, from *geostran*, meaning "yesterday," and *daeg*, meaning "day." The word *yesterday* actually repeats itself, literally meaning "yesterday day."

yes·ter·year (yes′tər yēr′) *Poetic n, adv* last year or the recent past, especially as nostalgically recalled: *the fashions of yesteryear.* <translation of French *antan* by 19c poet D.G. Rossetti>

yet (yet) *adv* **1** up until the present or a specified or implied time. **2** as soon as the present or a specified or implied time: *Don't go yet.* **3** from now into the future for a specified length of time: *I plan to study for some time yet.* **4** indicating something that will or may happen: *We may yet arrive at a solution.* **5** used for emphasizing an increase or repetition: *We were shortchanged yet again.* **6** nevertheless or in spite of that: *The story was strange, yet true.*
conj but at the same time; nevertheless: *The essay is good, yet it could be better.* <Old English *gieta*>
as yet, up to now.

ye·ti (yet′ē) ABOMINABLE SNOWMAN. <Tibetan>

yew (yū) *n* an evergreen tree that has broad, flat needles that are dark green above and light green below and small, red cones that look like berries, or the wood of this tree. <Old English *iw*>

Yid·dish (yid′ish) *n* a European language used by Jews, originally a medieval German dialect containing Hebrew and Slavic words, and written in Hebrew characters.
adj to do with the Yiddish language. <German *jüdisch* Jewish>

yield (yēld) *v* **1** produce or provide a natural, agricultural, or industrial product: *This land yields good crops.* **2** produce or deliver a gain from an action, especially a financial return: *The savings account yielded a small interest. The enquiry yielded some interesting findings.* **3** give way to arguments, demands, or pressure: *I yielded to temptation and ate all the candy.* **4** give right of way to other traffic on a road. **5** of a mass or structure, give way under force or pressure: *The door yielded to her push.*
n the full amount of an agricultural or industrial product, or a financial return: *The yield on the stock was very high.* <Old English *gieldan* pay> **yield′ing** *adj.* **yield′ing·ly** *adv.*

yin (yin) *n* in Chinese philosophy, the passive female principle of the universe characterized as associated with earth, dark, and cold. Compare YANG. <Mandarin>

yip·pee (yip′ē) *interj* used to express wild excitement or delight.

YMCA or **Y.M.C.A.** Young Men's Christian Association.

YMHA or **Y.M.H.A.** Young Men's Hebrew Association.

yo·del (yō′dəl) *v* **yo·delled** or **yo·deled, yo·del·ling** or **yo·del·ing** sing or call with frequent, sudden changes from the ordinary voice pitch to a much higher pitch.
n the act or sound of yodelling. <German *jodeln*> **yo′del·ler** or **yo′del·er** *n.*

yo·ga or **Yo·ga** (yō′gə) *n* a Hindu spiritual and physical discipline. Breath control, meditation, and the adoption of specific body postures are widely used for health and relaxation. <Hindi, from Sanskrit = union> **yo′gic** *adj.*

yo·gi (yō′gē) *n, pl* **yo·gis** a person who is adept at yoga.

yo·gurt (yō′gərt) *n* a semisolid food made from milk fermented by a bacterial culture and often sweetened and flavoured. Also, **yoghurt**. <Turkish *yoghurt*>

yoke (yōk) *n* **1** a wooden crosspiece that fits around the neck of two work animals to fasten them together for pulling a plough or cart. **2** a pair of animals fastened together by this crosspiece. **3** a crosspiece connecting two other parts, such as one fitting over the neck and shoulders of a person, used for carrying pails or baskets. **4** a thing that is regarded as oppressive or burdensome. **5** a thing resembling or compared to a wooden crosspiece, such as a part of a garment that fits over the shoulders and to which the main part is attached.
v **yoked, yok·ing** put a yoke on a pair of animals or fasten with a yoke. <Old English *geoc*>

yo·kel (yō′kəl) *n* an uneducated or unsophisticated person from the countryside who is unused to city ways. <origin uncertain>

yolk (yōk) *n* the corresponding part in the ovum or larva of egg-laying vertebrates and many invertebrates. <Old English *geolca*, from *geolu* yellow>

Yom Kip·pur (yom′kip′ər) *n* the Day of Atonement, an annual Jewish day of fasting and atoning for sin, observed on the tenth day of the first month of the Jewish year. <Hebrew>

yon·der (yon′dər) *adv* at some distance in the direction indicated: *Look yonder.*
adj to do with something within sight, but not near: *She lives in yonder cottage.* <Old English *geond* beyond>

yore (yȯr) *n* of long ago or former times: *in days of yore, tales of yore.* <Old English *geara*, from *gear* year>

🍁 **York boat** (yȯrk) *n* in former times, a type of heavy freight canoe developed by the Hudson's Bay Company at York Factory on Hudson Bay.

York·shire pudding (yȯrk′shər) *n* a batter pudding that is baked and often served with roast beef.

you (yū) *pron, sing and pl* **1** the person or persons spoken or written to: *Are you ready? She will bring you the book tomorrow.* **2** anyone: *You can push this button to switch on a light. You never can tell. His speeches put you to sleep.* <Old English *eow*>

GRAMMAR AND USAGE

You and **your** are commonly used in speech to refer to people in general: *You never know what's going to happen.* In formal writing, it's better to use *one* or an impersonal statement: *One never knows what's going to happen* or *The future is uncertain.*

you'd (yūd) *contraction* **1** you had: *You'd better go quickly.* **2** you would: *You'd like this story.*

you'll (yūl) *contraction* **1** you will. **2** you shall.

young (yung) *adj* **1** in the early part of life or growth: *young corn, young people.* **2** to do with young people: *young love.* **3** in an early stage: *The night was still young when they left the party.* **4** without much experience or practice: *She was young in the farming business.*
n **1** offspring, especially of an animal before or soon after birth: *An animal will fight to protect its young.* **2 the young** young people. <Old English *geong*>

young blood *n* a person or people who have vigour, energy, or enthusiasm, as potential additions to a group or organization.

young·ish (yung′gish) *adj* rather young.

young·ling (yung′ling) *n* a young person or animal.

young·ster (yung′stər) *n* a child or young person.

your (yůr) *adj* **1** to do with the person being addressed: *Give me your hand. Is this your pen? We enjoyed your visit.* **2** *Informal* of someone or something that is familiar or typical of its kind: *your average music lover.* **3** used in addressing the holder of certain formal titles: *Your Highness, Your Ladyship, Your Worship.* <Old English *eower*, from of *ge* ye>

CONFUSABLES

Your is the possessive form of the pronoun *you* and means "belonging to you": *You'll find your sweater on the third shelf.*

You're is a contraction of "you are": *You're the one who is responsible for buying the snacks for the party.*

you're (yūr) *contraction* you are.

yours (yůrz) *pron, sing and pl* **1** a possessive form of YOU; that which belongs to the person being addressed: *I think this scarf is yours.* **2** part of a polite ending to a letter: *yours sincerely, yours truly.*

GRAMMAR AND USAGE

Yours and *your* are possessive forms of *you*:

Yours always stands alone: *That coat is yours.*

Your is always followed by a noun: *That's your coat.*

your·self (yůr self′) *pron, pl* **your·selves** **1** the object of a reflexive verb with **you** as subject: *You will hurt yourself if you aren't careful.* **2** an intensive pronoun, used to emphasize the noun or pronoun it follows: *You yourself know the story is not true.* **3** your usual self: *Come see us when you feel better and are yourself again.*

a bat	e bed	i bid	o pot	u cup	th **thin**
ā cake	ē me	ī bite	ō go	ū rude	ᴛʜ **then**
à bar	ə about	ər over	ȯ for	ů put	zh measure

youth (yūth) *n, pl* **youths** (yūᴛʜz) or (*especially collectively*) **youth 1** the period between childhood and adult age: *In his youth he loved to fish.* **2** the condition or quality of being young, especially as associated with freshness, vigour or energy. **3** an early stage in the development of something. **4** a young man. **5** young people considered as a group: *pleasures common to youth.* <Old English *geoguth*> **youth′ful** *adj.* **youth′ful·ly** *adv.* **youth′ful·ness** *n.*

youth court *n* a court with jurisdiction over young offenders.

youth hostel *n* a supervised place providing cheap accommodation intended mainly for young travellers.

you've (yūv) *contraction* you have: *You've gone too far.*

yowl (youl) *n* a loud, wailing cry, especially one of pain or distress.
v make such a cry. <imitative>

yo–yo (yō′yō) *n, pl* **yo-yos 1** a small wheel-shaped toy made up of two discs, usually wooden, joined by a central peg to which is attached a long string. The string is held by one hand, and the toy is spun out and reeled in on the string. **2** a thing that repeatedly falls and rises again
v move up or down, or fluctuate. <origin uncertain>

yt·ter·bi·um (i tər′bē əm) *n* a silver-white metallic element. *Symbol* **Yb** <*Ytterby* a town in Sweden, where the element was discovered>

yt·tri·um (it′rē əm) *n* a grey-white metallic element. *Symbol* **Y** or **Yt** <See YTTERBIUM.>

yuc·ca (yuk′ə) *n* a plant of the agave family with long, stiff, sword-shaped leaves and a single erect cluster of large, white, lilylike flowers. <Spanish *yuca*>

yuck or **yuk** (yuk′) *interj* used to express disgust or strong rejection: *What's that crawling in the salad? Oh, yuck!*

Yu·go·slav·i·a (yū′gō slav′ē ə) *n* in former times, a country in southeastern Europe. In 2003, the name was changed to SERBIA AND MONTENEGRO.
Yu′go·slav′ or **Yu′go·slav′i·an** *adj, n.*

yuk (yuk′) *Slang n* a loud and hearty laugh, or a thing that draws such a laugh.
v **yukked, yuk·king** usually, **yuk-yuk** laugh loudly and heartily. <imitative>

Yu·kon Territory (yů′kon) *n* a large area in northern Canada west of the Northwest Territories, administered by a territorial government. *Abbrev.* **Y.T.**;
postal symbol **YT**; URL **www.gov.yk.ca**

Yule or **yule** (yūl) *n* Christmas. <Old English *geola* winter solstice festival>

Yule log *n* **1** a large log traditionally burnt in a fireplace on Christmas Eve. **2** a log-shaped chocolate cake eaten at Christmas.

Yule·tide or **yule·tide** (yūl′tīd′) *n* Christmastime or the Christmas season.

Yu·pik (yū′pik) *n, pl* **Yu·pik** or **Yu·piks 1** a member of a people related to the Inuit, living mainly in southwest Alaska and northeast Siberia. **2** the language of these people.
adj to do with these people or their language.

yup·pie (yup′ē) *Informal n* a well-paid young professional who works in a city and has a comfortable lifestyle. <*y*(*oung*) *u*(*rban*) *p*(*rofessional*) + -ie (after hippie)>

yup·pi·fy (yup′ə fī′) *Informal v* **yup·pi·fied, yup·pi·fy·ing** adapt to yuppie tastes and values: *to yuppify the neighbourhood.*

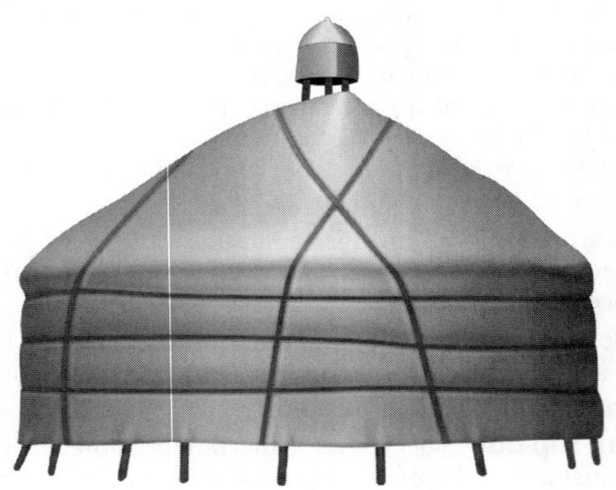

The **yurt** has been in use for a thousand years and may in fact be twice as old. The hole in the top allows air to circulate, smoke to escape, and also provides the occupants with a view of the stars in warm weather.

yurt (yůrt) *n* a portable, domed tent or tentlike structure. Yurts were originally made of felt stretched over a framework of branches, and used by nomads of Mongolia, Siberia, and Turkey.

YWCA or **Y.W.C.A.** Young Women's Christian Association.

YWHA or **Y.W.H.A.** Young Women's Hebrew Association.

Zz

z or **Z** (zed) *n, pl* **z's** or **Z's** **1** the twenty-sixth and last letter of the English alphabet, or any speech sound represented by it. **2** the twenty-sixth thing in a list or series.

Za·ire (zī ēr′) *n* a country in central Africa. **Za·ir′e·an** or **Za·ir′i·an** *adj, n.*

Zam·bi·a (zam′ bē ə) *n* a country in southern central Africa. **Zam′bi·an** *adj, n.*

Zam·bo·ni (zam bō′nē) *Trademark n* a machine that scrapes off the surface of an ice rink and lays down a new surface in a single operation.

za·ny (zā′nē) *adj* amusingly unconventional or eccentric: *His zany stories make everyone laugh.*
n, pl **za·nies** an erratic or eccentric person. <Italian *zanni*, from *Giovanni* John, a character in Italian farce>

zap (zap) *v* **zapped, zap·ping** **1** cause to destroy or wipe out. **2** cause to move suddenly and rapidly in a specified direction, especially to move quickly between TV channels or sections of videotape by use of a remote control.
interj used to express or indicate a sudden, unexpected occurrence: *I was just standing there when zap! something hit me on the head.*
n a sudden effect or event that makes a dramatic impact, especially a sudden burst of energy or sound. <imitative>

zeal (zēl) *n* great energy or enthusiasm in pursuit of a cause or an objective: *He worked with zeal on his book report.* <Greek *zelos*>

SYNONYMS

Zeal emphasizes focused energy or enthusiasm: *She worked with zeal to finish the painting.*

Zest suggests enjoyment, together with energy and enthusiasm: *He played the role with great zest.*

Dedication emphasizes strong interest and loyalty: *My sister's dedication to gymnastics began when she was seven.*

zeal·ot (zel′ət) *n* a person who is fanatical and uncompromising in pursuit of his or her religious, political, or other ideals. **zeal′ot·ry** *n.*

zeal·ous (zel′əs) *adj* with or showing zeal: *They made zealous efforts to clean up for the party.* **zeal′ous·ly** *adv.* **zeal′ous·ness** *n.*

ze·bra (zē′brə) *or* (zeb′rə) *n* an African wild horse with black-and-white stripes and an erect mane. See UNGULATE for picture. <Portuguese, from Bantu (a group of languages of Africa)>

zebra mussel *n* a small freshwater mussel with zigzag markings on the shell. Zebra mussels attach to hard surfaces in great numbers, often causing damage by blocking pipes.

ze·bu (zē′bū) *n* a cow of tropical countries that has a high, fatty hump over the shoulders, large, drooping ears, and loose folds of skin hanging from the throat and chest. <French>

🍁 **zed** (zed) *n* the letter Z.
<French *zède* from Greek *zeta*>

Zen (zen) *n* in full, **Zen Buddhism** a Japanese form of Buddhism that emphasizes the value of meditation and intuition rather than ritual worship or study of scriptures. <Japanese *zen* contemplation>

ze·nith (zen′ith) *or* (zē′nith) *n* the highest point reached by a celestial or other object, or the point in the sky or celestial sphere directly above an observer. Compare NADIR. <Old French *cenit*, from Arabic *samt* path + *al-* the + *ras* head, i.e., path over the head>

zeph·yr (zef′ər) *Poetic n* a soft, gentle breeze. <Greek *zephyros*>

Zep·pe·lin (zep′ə lən) *n* a large German airship with a rigid frame, shaped like a cigar with pointed ends, and with compartments for gas, engines, and passengers. <Count F. von *Zeppelin*, 20c airship builder>

ze·ro (zē′rō) *n, pl* **ze·ros** or **ze·roes** **1** no quantity or number, or the figure 0. **2** the point on a scale or instrument from which a positive or negative quantity is reckoned. **3** the temperature that corresponds to zero on the scale of a thermometer: *zero degrees Celsius.* **4** the lowest possible amount or level: *The other team's score was zero.*
adj of or at zero or without any: *a zero score. The weather report said there would be zero visibility.*
zero in (on), focus attention.

ETYMOLOGY

Zero comes though French or Italian *zero*, which in turn came though Old Spanish from Arabic sifr.

Sifr is also the root of the English word *cipher.*

zero emission *n* the fact or property of emitting no pollutants.

zero gravity *n* a condition in physics in which gravity does not operate on a body, either because the force is locally weak, or because both the body and its surroundings are freely and equally accelerating under the force.

zero hour *n* the time at which a planned operation, typically a military one, is set to begin.

zero tolerance *n* a strict, uncompromising policy, rigidly enforced, against some act or action: *There is zero tolerance of schoolyard violence.*

zest (zest) *n* **1** keen enjoyment, energy, and enthusiasm: *a zest for life.* **2** a piquant or exciting quality: *Wit gives zest to conversation.* **3** the outer coloured part of the peel of citrus fruit, used as a flavouring. <origin uncertain> **zest′ful** *adj.* **zest′ful·ly** *adv.* **zest′ful·ness** *n.*

a bat	e bed	i bid	o pot	u cup	th **thin**
ā cake	ē me	ī bite	ō go	ū rude	ᴛʜ **then**
ä bar	ə about	ər over	ô for	ů put	zh measure

zig·gu·rat (zig′ə rat′) *n* an ancient Mesopotamian structure in the form of a pyramid of terraced towers, sometimes with a temple at the top. <Akkadian *ziqqurata* tower>

zig·zag (zig′zag′) *n* a line or course with short, sharp alternate right and left turns: *He drew a zigzag in the sand with a stick.*
adv turning in this way: *The path ran zigzag up the hill.*
adj with turns of this type: *The shirt had a zigzag pattern on it.*
v **zig·zagged, zig·zag·ging** move in a zigzag way: *Lightning zigzagged across the sky.* <French, from German *Zickzack*>

zilch (zilch) *Informal n* nothing. <originally a character in the 1930s magazine *Ballyhoo*>

zil·lion (zil′yən) *Informal n* an extremely large but indefinite number of people or things. <by analogy with *million, billion,* etc.>

Zim·bab·we (zim bab′wā) *n* a country in southern central Africa. See the APPENDIX. **Zim·bab′we·an** *adj, n.*

zinc (zingk) *n* a silver-white metallic element, used to make brass and for coating iron and steel to protect against corrosion. *Symbol* **Zn** <German *Zink*>

zinc oxide *n* an insoluble white powder used in making **zinc ointment**, a salve for treating skin disorders.

zine (zēn) *Computers, Informal n (also in compounds)* a magazine: *a webzine.*

zing (zing) *Informal n* energy, enthusiasm, or liveliness: *The plot is boring and so the story has no zing.*
v move very fast: *A fly zinged past my ear.* <imitative> **zing′y** *adj.*

zing·er (zing′ər) *Informal n* **1** a striking or amusing remark. **2** a remarkable or outstanding person or thing.

zin·ni·a (zin′ē ə) *n* a garden plant of the daisy family with brightly coloured flowers.

Zi·on (zī′ən) *n* **1 a** a hill in Jerusalem on which, in ancient times, the royal palace and the temple were built. **b** Jerusalem. **2** *Christianity* the heavenly city or kingdom of God. **3** the Jewish people or their religion. Also, **Sion.** <Hebrew *tsiyon* hill>

Zi·on·ism (zī′ə niz′əm) *n* a movement, begun in the late 1800s, to make modern Palestine a Jewish national state. **Zi′on·ist** *adj, n.*

zip (zip) *Informal n* **1** energy or vigour: *full of zip.* **2** a zipper.
v **zipped, zip·ping 1** (*often with* ***up***) fasten or close with a zipper: *She zipped up her jacket.* **2** *Computers* compress a file for storage or transfer. <imitative> **zip′py** *adj.*

zip code *n* a postal code, especially one in the US consisting of five or nine digits. <*Z(one) I(mprovement) P(lan)*>

zip·per (zip′ər) *n* a metal or plastic sliding fastener for clothing, shoes, and other objects.
v fasten or close with a zipper: *Zipper up your coat before you go out in the cold.* <*Zipper* a trademark>

zir·con (zər′kon) *n* a mineral that occurs in crystals of many forms and colours and is the chief ore of zirconium.

zir·co·ni·um (zər kō′nē əm) *n* a silver-grey metallic element. *Symbol* **Zr** <*zircon* + *-ium*>

zit (zit) *Informal n* a pimple.

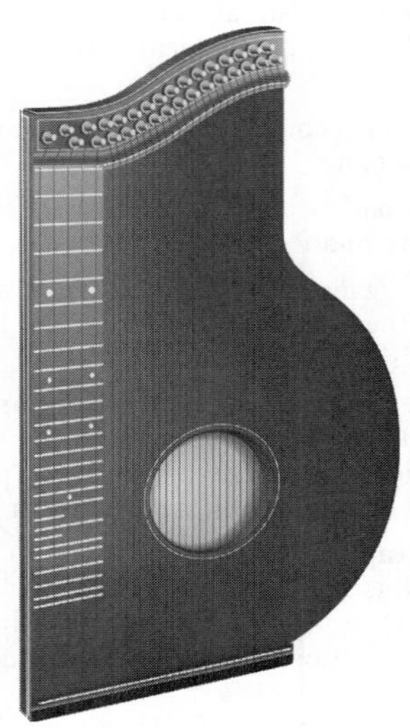

Zither is a catch-all name for a wide variety of stringed instruments, some with one string and others with more than 30. The concert zither shown here has a fretted fingerboard, five melody strings, and 26 accompaniment strings for chords.

zith·er (ziTH′ər) *n* a musical instrument with many strings stretched across it, played with the fingers and a plectrum. <German *Zither*, from Greek *kithara*>

zo·di·ac (zō′dē ak′) *Astrology n* a belt of stars that extends on both sides of the apparent yearly path of the sun. The zodiac is divided into twelve equal parts, called **signs**: Aries (Mar 21–Apr 19), Taurus (Apr 20–May 20), Gemini (May 21–Jun 21), Cancer (Jun 22–Jul 22), Leo (Jul 23–Aug 22), Virgo (Aug 23–Sep 22), Libra (Sep 23–Oct 23), Scorpio (Oct 24–Nov 21), Sagittarius (Nov 22–Dec 21), Capricorn (Dec 22–Jan 19), Aquarius (Jan 20–Feb 18), Pisces (Feb 19–Mar 20). <Greek *zodiakos* (*kyklos*) (circle) of animals, from *zoion* animal> **zo·di′a·cal** *adj.*

zom·bie (zom′bē) *n, pl* **zom·bies** a corpse supposedly brought back to life by witchcraft, especially in certain West African and Caribbean regions. <Bantu (a group of langauges of Africa)>

zone (zōn) *n* **1** an area or piece of land with a particular characteristic, purpose, or use, or subject to particular restrictions: *a hospital zone, an industrial zone, a combat zone.* **2** in full, **time zone** a range of longitudes where a common standard time is used.
v **zoned, zon·ing** divide into or assign to zones, especially divide urban or rural land into areas subject to particular planning restrictions: *This area is zoned for residential buildings.* <Greek *zone*> **zoned** *adj.* **zon′ing** *n.*

zonked (zonkt) *Informal adj* under the influence of drugs or alcohol, or as tired as if so.

zoo (zū) *n* a place where a collection of wild animals are kept, typically in a park or gardens, for study, conservation, or display to the public. <*zoological garden*>

zoo– *combining form* to do with animals: *zoology.* <Greek *zoion* animal>

zoo·keep·er (zō′kēp ər) *n* a person who looks after animals at a zoo.

zo·ol·o·gy (zō ol′ə jē) *or* (zū ol′ə jē) *n* the scientific study of the behaviour, structure, physiology, classification, and distribution of animals. **zo′o·log′i·cal** *adj.* **zo′o·log′i·cal·ly** *adv.* **zo·ol′o·gist** *n.*

zoom (zūm) *v* **1** move or travel very quickly, especially as a motor vehicle or aircraft. **2** rise sharply. **3** of a camera, change smoothly using a special lens from a long shot to a close-up or vice versa. **4** *Computers* **a** (*with* ***in***) cause text or graphics to appear larger on the screen. **b** (*with* ***out***) cause text or graphics to appear smaller on the screen. <imitative>
zoom in on, quickly focus attention on: *Let's zoom in on one problem at a time!*

zo·o·phyte (zō′ə fīt′) *n* any of various invertebrate animals that resemble plants in form. Corals and sponges are zoophytes.

zo·o·plank·ton (zō′ə plangk′tən) *n* a plankton made up of microscopic animal organisms and the immature stages of larger animals.

Zo·ro·as·tri·an·ism (zô′rō as′trē ə niz′əm) *n* a religion founded by the Persian prophet **Zoroaster** in about 600 BCE, teaching that the supreme god struggles with the spirit of evil. Modern Zoroastrians are called PARSEES. **Zo′ro·as′tri·an** *adj, n.*

zuc·chi·ni (zū kē′nē) *or* (zə kē′nē) *n, pl* **zuc·chi·ni** or **zuc·chi·nis** a summer squash, cylindrical in shape, with smooth, flecked, dark-green skin and tender white flesh. <Italian *zucchino,* from *zuccho* squash>

Zu·lu (zū′lū) *n* **1** a member of an aboriginal people living mainly in South Africa. **2** the Bantu language of these people.
adj to do with these people or their language.

zy·gote (zī′gōt) *or* (zig′ōt) *n* a cell formed by the union of two gametes. A fertilized egg is a zygote. <Greek *zygotos* yoked, from *zygon* yoke>

zy·mase (zī′mās) *n* a mixture of enzymes obtained from yeast that changes sugar into alcohol and carbon dioxide.

Appendix

Provinces and Territories

	Capital	Area	Population (2001, to nearest hundred)
Newfoundland & Labrador (NF) WEBSITE www.gov.nf.ca	St. John's	405 200 km^2	512 900
Prince Edward Island (PE) WEBSITE www.gov.pe.ca	Charlottetown	5 660 km^2	135 300
Nova Scotia (NS) WEBSITE www.gov.ns.ca	Halifax	55 300 km^2	908 000
New Brunswick (NB) WEBSITE www.gov.nb.ca	Fredericton	72 900 km^2	729 500
Québec (QC) WEBSITE www.gouv.qc.ca	Québec	1 542 100 km^2	7 237 500
Ontario (ON) WEBSITE www.gov.on.ca	Toronto	1 076 400 km^2	11 410 000
Manitoba (MB) WEBSITE www.gov.mb.ca	Winnipeg	647 800 km^2	1 119 600
Saskatchewan (SK) WEBSITE www.gov.sk.ca	Regina	651 000 km^2	978 900
Alberta (AB) WEBSITE www.gov.ab.ca	Edmonton	661 900 km^2	2 947 800
British Columbia (BC) WEBSITE www.gov.bc.ca	Victoria	944 700 km^2	3 907 700
Yukon Territory (YT) WEBSITE www.gov.yk.ca	Whitehorse	482 400 km^2	28 700
Northwest Territories (NT) WEBSITE www.gov.nt.ca	Yellowknife	1 346 100 km^2	37 300
Nunavut WEBSITE www.gov.nu.ca	Iqaluit	2 093 200 km^2	26 700
CANADA WEBSITE canada.gc.ca	Ottawa	9 984 700 km^2	30 007 100

Prime Ministers of Canada

Sir John A. Macdonald	Conservative	1867–1873, 1878–1891
Alexander Mackenzie	Liberal	1873–1878
Sir John Abbot	Conservative	1891–1892
Sir John Thompson	Conservative	1892–1894
Sir Mackenzie Bowell	Conservative	1894–1896
Sir Charles Tupper	Conservative	1896
Sir Wilfrid Laurier	Liberal	1896–1911
Sir Robert Borden	Conservative/Unionist	1911–1920
Arthur Meighen	Unionist/Conservative	1920–1921, 1926
Mackenzie King	Liberal	1921–1930, 1935–1948
Richard B. Bennett	Conservative	1930–1935
Louis St. Laurent	Liberal	1948–1957
John Diefenbaker	Progressive Conservative	1957–1963
Lester Pearson	Liberal	1963–1968
Pierre Trudeau	Liberal	1968–1979, 1980–1984
Joe Clark	Progressive Conservative	1979–1980
John Turner	Liberal	1984
Brian Mulroney	Progressive Conservative	1984–1993
Kim Campbell	Progressive Conservative	1993
Jean Chrétien	Liberal	1993–2004
Paul Martin	Liberal	2004–

Titles of Elected Representatives in Canada

MHA	Member of the House of Assembly	in Newfoundland and Labrador
MLA	Member of the Legislative Assembly	in most Canadian provinces and territories
MNA	Member of the National Assembly	in Québec
MP	Member of Parliament	in the Federal Government, Ottawa
MPP	Member of the Provincial Parliament	in Ontario

Map of Canada — Provinces and Aboriginal Peoples

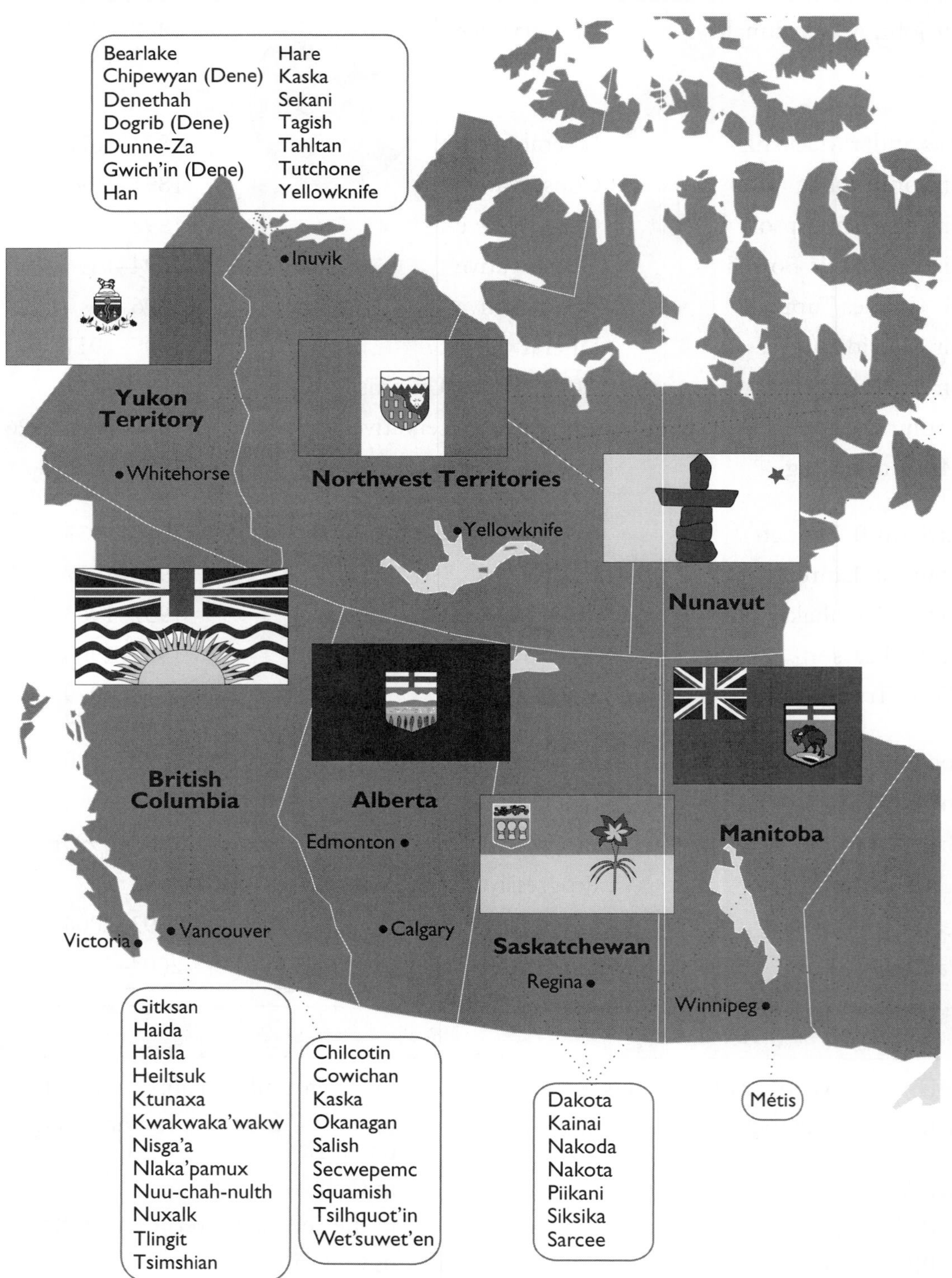
Bearlake
Chipewyan (Dene)
Denethah
Dogrib (Dene)
Dunne-Za
Gwich'in (Dene)
Han
Hare
Kaska
Sekani
Tagish
Tahltan
Tutchone
Yellowknife
Inuvik
Yukon Territory
Whitehorse
Northwest Territories
Yellowknife
Nunavut
British Columbia
Alberta
Edmonton
Saskatchewan
Manitoba
Victoria
Vancouver
Calgary
Regina
Winnipeg
Gitksan
Haida
Haisla
Heiltsuk
Ktunaxa
Kwakwaka'wakw
Nisga'a
Nlaka'pamux
Nuu-chah-nulth
Nuxalk
Tlingit
Tsimshian
Chilcotin
Cowichan
Kaska
Okanagan
Salish
Secwepemc
Squamish
Tsilhquot'in
Wet'suwet'en
Dakota
Kainai
Nakoda
Nakota
Piikani
Siksika
Sarcee
Métis

Inuit
Iqaluit
Malecite
Mi'kmaq
Newfoundland and Labrador
St. John's
Prince Edward Island
Charlottetown
Québec
Fredericton
New Brunswick
Halifax
Nova Scotia
Ontario
Québec
Montréal
Ottawa
Toronto
Abenaki
Algonquin
Anishinabe
Attikamek
Cayuga
Cree
Huron
Innu
Iroquois
Kanien'keha
Oneida
Onondaga
Ottawa
Saulteaux
Seneca
Tuscarora

Map of the World

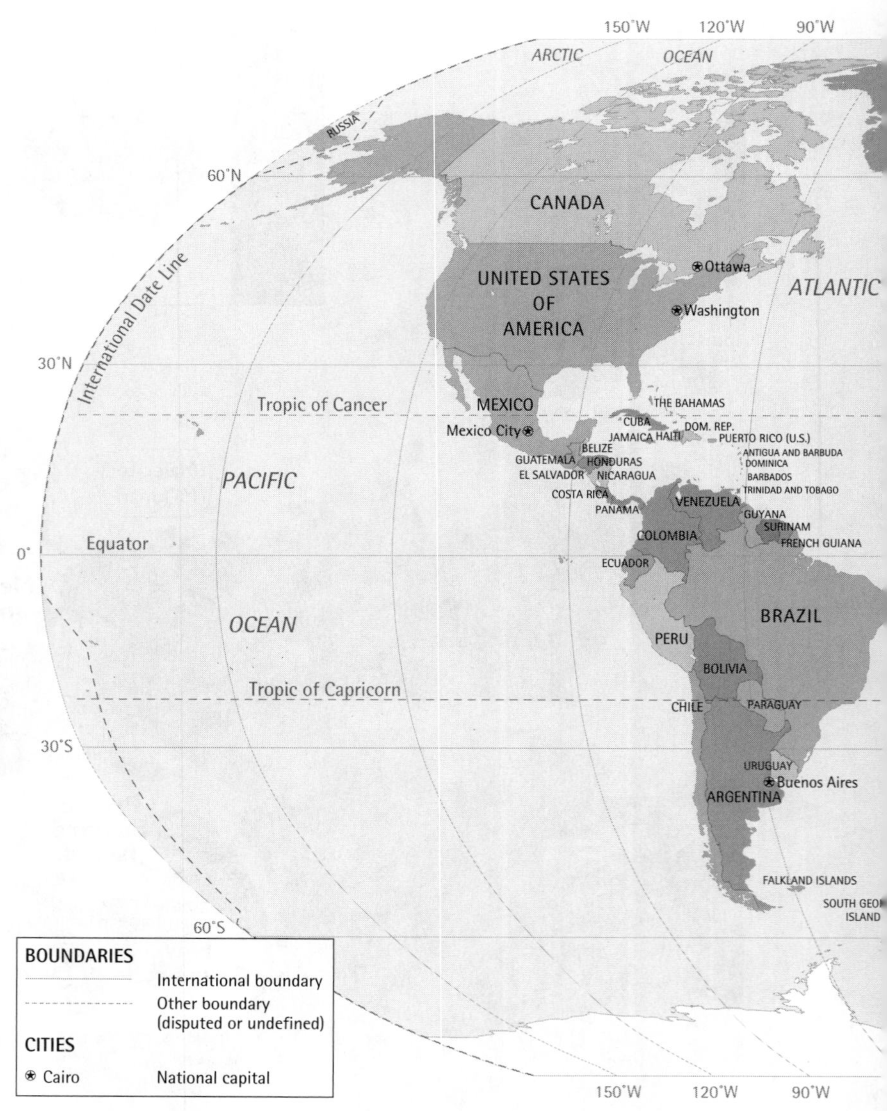

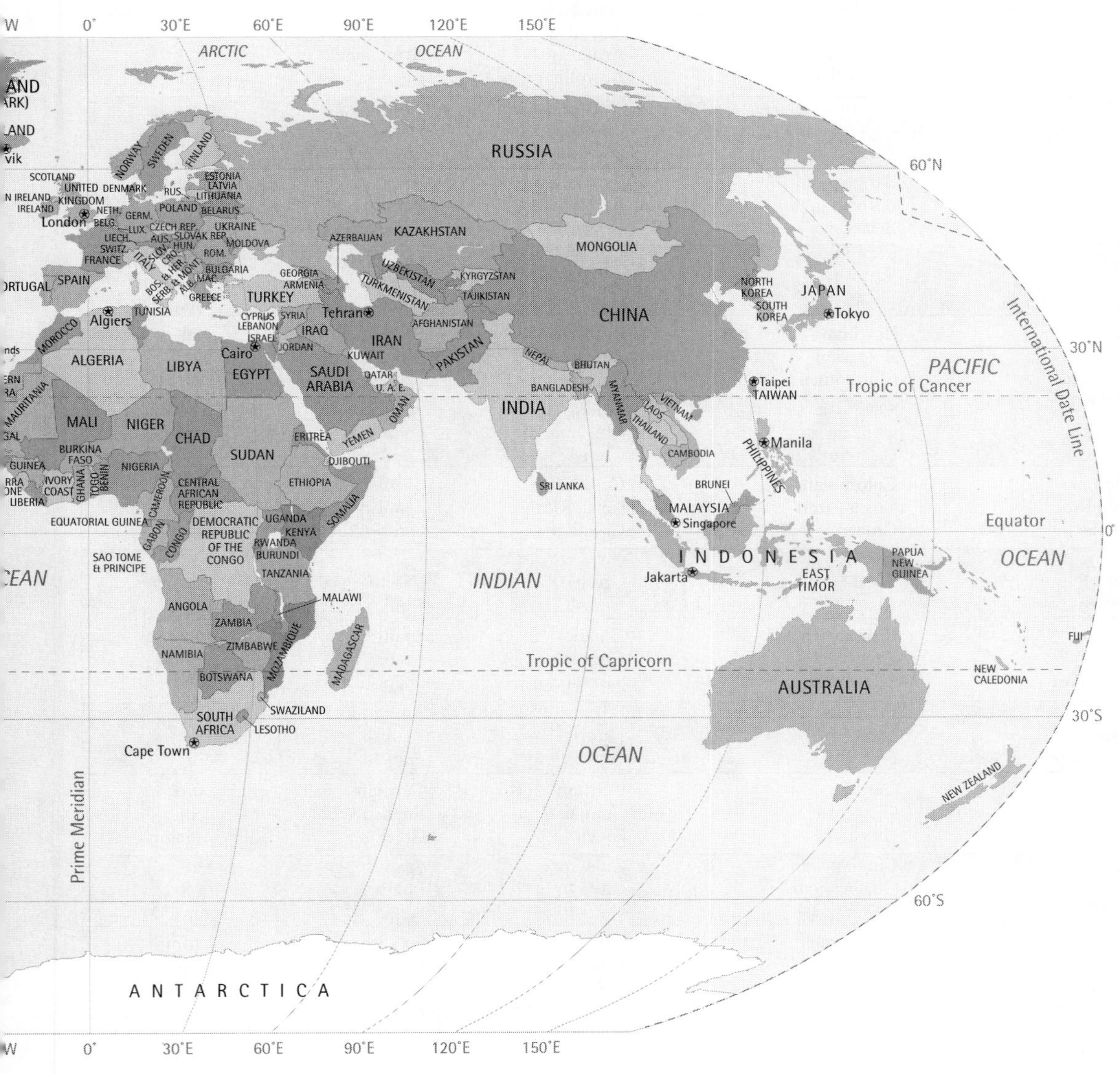

0°
30°E
60°E
90°E
120°E
150°E
ARCTIC
OCEAN
RUSSIA
60°N
SCOTLAND
UNITED KINGDOM
IRELAND
London
DENMARK
NORWAY
SWEDEN
FINLAND
ESTONIA
LATVIA
LITHUANIA
BELARUS
POLAND
GERM.
NETH.
BELG.
LUX.
CZECH REP.
SLOVAK REP.
AUS.
UKRAINE
MOLDOVA
FRANCE
SWITZ.
LIECH.
ITALY
ROM.
BULGARIA
GREECE
SPAIN
TURKEY
GEORGIA
ARMENIA
AZERBAIJAN
KAZAKHSTAN
MONGOLIA
UZBEKISTAN
TURKMENISTAN
KYRGYZSTAN
TAJIKISTAN
AFGHANISTAN
NORTH KOREA
SOUTH KOREA
JAPAN
Tokyo
CHINA
International Date Line
Algiers
TUNISIA
MOROCCO
CYPRUS
LEBANON
SYRIA
ISRAEL
JORDAN
IRAQ
Tehran
IRAN
KUWAIT
PAKISTAN
NEPAL
BHUTAN
30°N
ALGERIA
LIBYA
EGYPT
Cairo
SAUDI ARABIA
QATAR
U. A. E.
OMAN
BANGLADESH
INDIA
MYANMAR
LAOS
VIETNAM
THAILAND
CAMBODIA
Taipei
TAIWAN
PACIFIC
Tropic of Cancer
MAURITANIA
MALI
NIGER
CHAD
SUDAN
ERITREA
YEMEN
DJIBOUTI
ETHIOPIA
SOMALIA
BURKINA FASO
GUINEA
NIGERIA
GHANA
TOGO
BENIN
IVORY COAST
LIBERIA
CAMEROON
CENTRAL AFRICAN REPUBLIC
SRI LANKA
PHILIPPINES
Manila
BRUNEI
MALAYSIA
Singapore
Equator
0°
EQUATORIAL GUINEA
GABON
CONGO
DEMOCRATIC REPUBLIC OF THE CONGO
UGANDA
KENYA
RWANDA
BURUNDI
TANZANIA
SAO TOME & PRINCIPE
INDONESIA
Jakarta
EAST TIMOR
PAPUA NEW GUINEA
OCEAN
INDIAN
MALAWI
ANGOLA
ZAMBIA
ZIMBABWE
MOZAMBIQUE
MADAGASCAR
NAMIBIA
BOTSWANA
Tropic of Capricorn
FIJI
NEW CALEDONIA
AUSTRALIA
SWAZILAND
SOUTH AFRICA
LESOTHO
Cape Town
30°S
OCEAN
NEW ZEALAND
Prime Meridian
60°S
ANTARCTICA
0°
30°E
60°E
90°E
120°E
150°E

Countries of the World

Country	Nationality	Adjective	Official Language	Currency
Afghanistan	Afghan	Afghan	Pushtu	afghani
Albania	Albanian	Albanian	Albanian	lek
Algeria	Algerian	Algerian	Arabic	dinar
Argentina	Argentine	Argentinian	Spanish	peso
Armenia	Armenian	Armenian	Armenian	dram
Australia	Australian	Australian	English	dollar
Austria	Austrian	Austrian	German	euro
Azerbaijan	Azerbaijani	Azerbaijani	Azerbaijani	manat
Bahamas	Bahamian	Bahamian	English	dollar
Bangladesh	Bangladeshi	Bangladeshi	Bangla	taka
Barbados	Barbadian	Barbadian	English	dollar
Belarus	Belarusian	Belarusian	Byelorussian	ruble
Belgium	Belgian	Belgian	Dutch/French	euro
Bolivia	Bolivian	Bolivian	Spanish	Boliviano
Bosnia and Herzegovina	Bosnian and Herzegovinian		Serbo-Croatian	dinar
Brazil	Brazilian	Brazilian	Portuguese	real
Bulgaria	Bulgarian	Bulgarian	Bulgarian	lev
Cambodia	Cambodian	Cambodian	Khmer	new riel
Canada	Canadian	Canadian	English/French	dollar
Chile	Chilean	Chilean	Spanish	peso
China	Chinese	Chinese	Mandarin Chinese	yuan
Colombia	Colombian	Colombian	Spanish	peso
Costa Rica	Costa Rican	Costa Rican	Spanish	colón
Croatia	Croat	Croatian	Serbo-Croatian	kuna
Cuba	Cuban	Cuban	Spanish	peso
Czech Republic	Czech	Czech	Czech/Slovak	koruna
Denmark	Dane	Danish	Danish	krone
Ecuador	Ecuadorian	Ecuadorian	Spanish	sucre
Egypt	Egyptian	Egyptian	Arabic	pound
El Salvador	Salvadoran	Salvadoran	Spanish	colón
Ethiopia	Ethiopian	Ethiopian	Amharic	birr
Finland	Finn	Finnish	Finnish/Swedish	euro
France	French	French	French	euro
Germany	German	German	German	euro
Ghana	Ghanaian	Ghanaian	English	cedi
Greece	Greek	Greek	Greek	drachma
Guatemala	Guatemalan	Guatemalan	Spanish	quetzal
Guyana	Guyanese	Guyanese	English	dollar
Haiti	Haitian	Haitian	French	gourde
Honduras	Honduran	Honduran	Spanish	lempira
Hungary	Hungarian	Hungarian	Hungarian	forint
Iceland	Icelander	Icelandic	Icelandic	króna
India	Indian	Indian	Hindi	rupee
Indonesia	Indonesian	Indonesian	Bahasa Indonesia	rupiah
Iran	Iranian	Iranian	Farsi (Persian)	rial
Iraq	Iraqi	Iraqi	Arabic/Kurdish	dinar
Ireland, Republic of	Irish	Irish	Irish/English	euro
Israel	Israeli	Israeli	Hebrew/Arabic	shekel
Italy	Italian	Italian	Italian	euro
Jamaica	Jamaican	Jamaican	English	dollar
Japan	Japanese	Japanese	Japanese	yen
Kazakhstan	Kazakhstani	Kazakhstani	Kazakh	tenge
Kenya	Kenyan	Kenyan	English/Swahili	shilling
Korea, North	Korean	Korean	Korean	won

Country	Nationality	Adjective	Official Language	Currency
Korea, South	Korean	Korean	Korean	won
Kuwait	Kuwaiti	Kuwaiti	Arabic	dinar
Lebanon	Lebanese	Lebanese	Arabic/French	pound
Libya	Libyan	Libyan	Arabic	dinar
Lithuania	Lithuanian	Lithuanian	Lithuanian	litas
Malaysia	Malaysian	Malaysian	Malay	ringgit
Mexico	Mexican	Mexican	Spanish	peso
Morocco	Moroccan	Moroccan	Arabic	dirham
Mozambique	Mozambican	Mozambican	Portuguese	metical
Namibia	Namibian	Namibian	Afrikaans/German/English	dollar
Netherlands	Dutch	Dutch	Dutch/Frisian	euro
New Zealand	New Zealander	New Zealander	English	dollar
Nicaragua	Nicaraguan	Nicaraguan	Spanish	córdoba
Nigeria	Nigerian	Nigerian	English	naira
Norway	Norwegian	Norwegian	Norwegian	krone
Pakistan	Pakistani	Pakistani	Urdu	rupee
Panama	Panamanian	Panamanian	Spanish	balboa
Paraguay	Paraguayan	Paraguayan	Spanish	guaraní
Peru	Peruvian	Peruvian	Spanish/Quechua	nuevo sol
Philippines	Filipino	Filipino	English/Pilipino	peso
Poland	Polish	Polish	Polish	zloty
Portugal	Portuguese	Portuguese	Portuguese	euro
Romania	Romanian	Romanian	Romanian	leu
Russia	Russian	Russian	Russian	ruble
Rwanda	Rwandan	Rwandan	French/Kinyarwanda	franc
Saudi Arabia	Saudi	Saudi	Arabic	riyal
Serbia and Montenegro	Serb, Montenegrin	Serb, Montenegrin	Serbo-Croatian	dinar
Singapore	Singaporean	Singaporean	Chinese/Malay/Tamil	dollar
Slovakia	Slovak	Slovak	Slovak	koruna
Somalia	Somali	Somali	Somali	shilling
South Africa	South African	South African	See below**	rand
Spain	Spanish	Spanish	Spanish	euro
Sri Lanka	Sri Lankan	Sri Lankan	Sinhala/Tamil	rupee
Sweden	Swedish	Swedish	Swedish	króna
Switzerland	Swiss	Swiss	German/French/Italian	franc
Syria	Syrian	Syrian	Arabic	pound
Taiwan	Chinese	Chinese	Chinese	dollar
Tajikistan	Tajik	Tajikistan	Tajik	ruble
Tanzania	Tanzanian	Tanzanian	Swahili/English	shilling
Thailand	Thai	Thai	Thai	baht
Tunisia	Tunisian	Tunisian	Arabic	dinar
Turkey	Turk	Turkish	Turkish	lira
Uganda	Ugandan	Ugandan	English	shilling
Ukraine	Ukrainian	Ukrainian	Ukrainian	hryvna
United Arab Emirates	Emiri	Emirian	Arabic	dirham
United Kingdom	British	British	English/Welsh/Scottish	pound
United States	American	American	English	dollar
Uruguay	Uruguayan	Uruguayan	Spanish	peso
Uzbekistan	Uzbek	Uzbek	Uzbek	som
Venezuela	Venezuelan	Venezuelan	Spanish	bolívar
Vietnam	Vietnamese	Vietnamese	Vietnamese	dong
Zimbabwe	Zimbabwean	Zimbabwean	English	dollar

* This currency will become euro, in 2002

** Afrikaans, English, Ndebele, Pedi, Sotho, Swazi, Tsonga, Tswana, Venda, Xhosa, Zulu

SI Units

Name	Symbol	Quantity
metre	m	length
kilogram	kg	mass
second	s	time
ampere	A	electric current
kelvin	K	thermodynamic temperature
mole	mol	amount of substance
candela	cd	luminous intensity
hertz	Hz	frequency
pascal	Pa	pressure, stress
watt	W	power
volt	V	electric potential, electromotive force
newton	N	force
joule	J	energy, work
ohm	Ω	electric resistance
farad	F	electric capacitance
litre	L	volume, capacity (= $1 dm^3$)
degree celsius	°C	temperature
hectare	ha	area (= $10\ 000\ m^2$)
tonne	t	mass (= 1000 kg)
electronvolt	eV	energy
nautical mile	M	distance (= 1852 m)
knot	kn	speed (=1M/h)
radian	rad	plane angle

SI Prefixes

Name	Symbol	Multiplying Factor	Example
giga-	G	1 000 000 000	a gigabyte (about one billion bytes)
mega-	M	1 000 000	a megavolt (one million volts)
kilo-	k	1 000	a kilometre (one thousand metres)
hecto-	h	100	a hectolitre (one hundred litres)
deca-	da	10	a decagram (ten grams)
deci-	h	0.1	a decigram (one-tenth of a gram)
centi-	c	0.01	a centimetre (one-hundredth of a metre)
milli-	m	0.001	a millilitre (one-thousandth of a litre)
micro-	m	0.000 001	a micrometre (one-millionth of a metre)
nano-	n	0.000 000 001	a nanosecond (one-billionth of a second)

Conversion Factors

to Metric

1 inch	= 2.54 cm
1 yard	= 91.44 cm
1 mile	= 1.61 km
1 pound	= 0.45 g
1 gallon	= 4.55 L (US 3.79 L)

Conversion Factors

from Metric

1 centimetre	= 0.39 inches
1 metre	= 39.4 inches
1 kilometre	= 0.62 miles
1 kilogram	= 2.20 pounds
1 litre	= 1.76 pints

Polygons

3 angles, 3 sides
triangle
4 angles, 4 sides
quadrilateral
5 angles, 5 sides
pentagon
6 angles, 6 sides
hexagon
7 angles, 7 sides
septagon
8 angles, 8 sides
octagon
9 angles, 9 sides
nonagon
10 angles, 10 sides
decagon

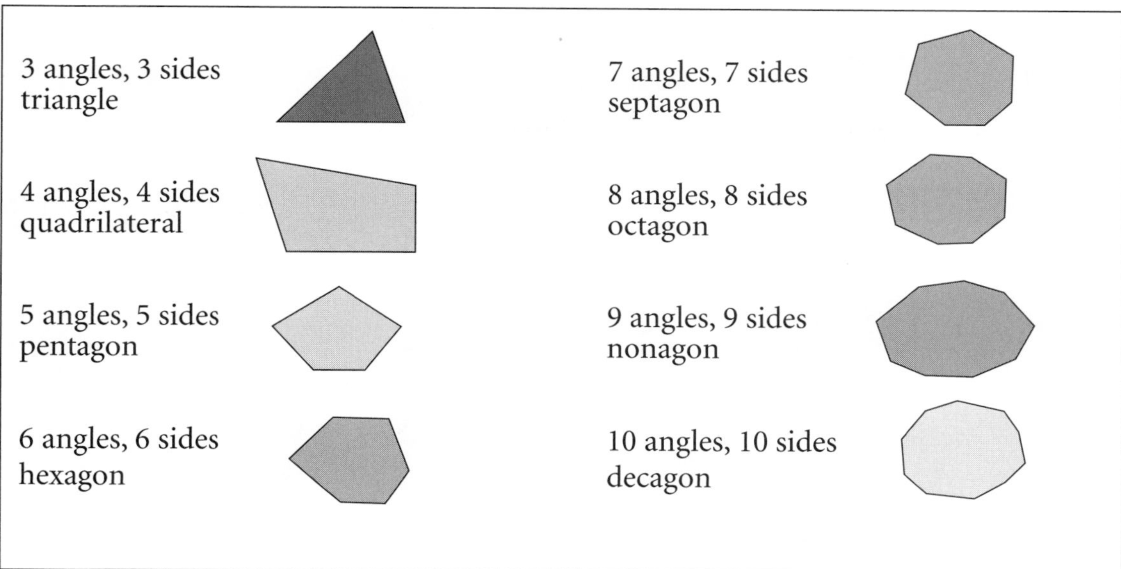

Polyhedrons

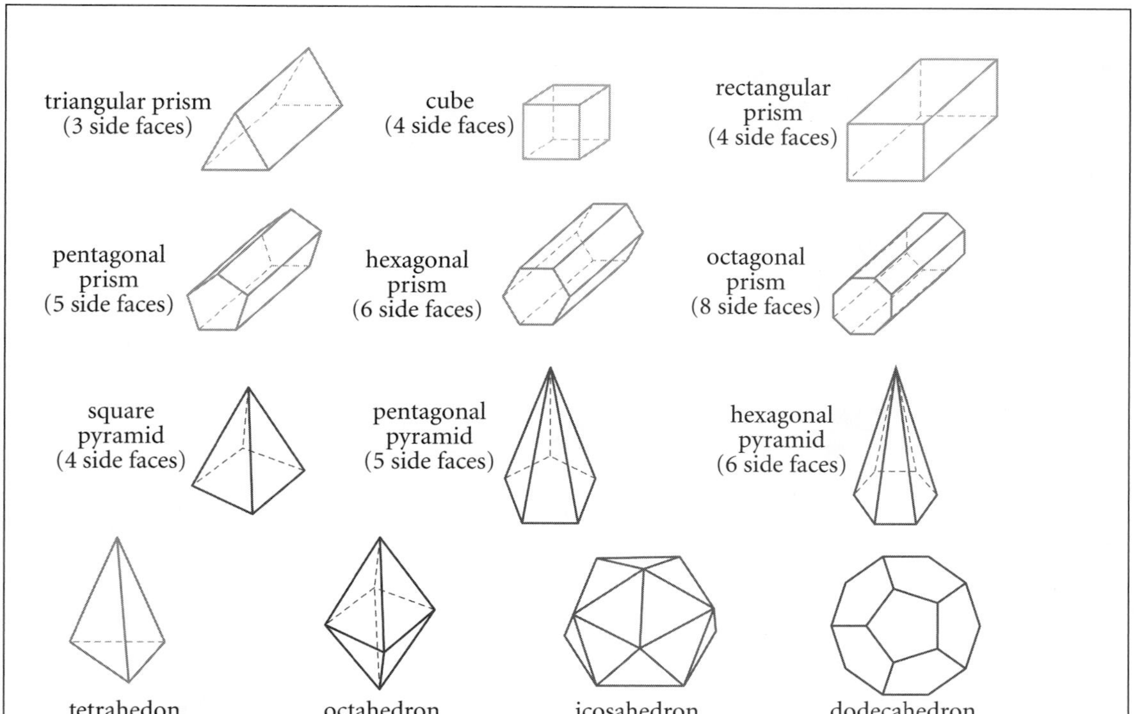

triangular prism
(3 side faces)
cube
(4 side faces)
rectangular
prism
(4 side faces)
pentagonal
prism
(5 side faces)
hexagonal
prism
(6 side faces)
octagonal
prism
(8 side faces)
square
pyramid
(4 side faces)
pentagonal
pyramid
(5 side faces)
hexagonal
pyramid
(6 side faces)
tetrahedon
(4 triangular faces)
octahedron
(8 triangular faces)
icosahedron
(20 triangular faces)
dodecahedron
(12 pentagonal faces)

Grammar and Usage Mini-Guide

Abbreviation

An abbreviation is a shortened form of a word or phrase. Abbreviations are useful in informal writing, or in lists or tables. In formal writing, it is usually better to spell out the whole word, but a few abbreviations are acceptable in formal writing as well. They are:

- Mrs., Mr., Ms., and Dr. before someone's name
- St. for Saint in place names
- times, such as 7:00 p.m., 500 BCE.

Active and Passive Voice

Active and passive voice are two ways of talking about something that happened.

- In the **active** voice, you tell who did something: *The firefighters extinguished the fire.*
- In the **passive** voice, you tell what happened, but you don't have to mention who did it: *The fire was extinguished.*

Passive voice is useful if you do not know who did something: *My purse was stolen*; or if the doer of the action is not very important: *The room was decorated for the party.* Otherwise, it is usually better to use the active voice.

Adjective

An adjective describes a noun or a pronoun: *We heard a **loud** noise.* Adjectives often come before the word they describe: *a **tall** boy.* They can also come after a linking verb like *is, was,* or *seems*: *He is **tall**.*

Adverb

An adverb describes a verb *(run **quickly**)*, an adjective (*a **really** dark blue car*), or another adverb (*run **very** quickly*). Adverbs usually tell how, when, where, or in what manner.

Agreement of Subject and Verb

A verb should always agree with its subject.

- Singular subjects (one) take singular verbs: *The dog runs quickly. Each of the games was played in the arena.*
- Plural subjects (more than one) take plural verbs: *The dog and cat run quickly. The games were played in the arena.*

When you are looking for the subject of a verb, remember the following tips:

- Prepositional phrases like *at school, under my desk, through the woods,* and *with great sadness* never contain the subject of a sentence:
  Wrong: *One of the cars were stolen.*
  (*cars* is not the subject)
  Corrected: *One of the cars was stolen.*
  (the subject *one* needs a singular verb)
- *There* and *here* are not usually the subject of the verb:
  There are many reasons why I like you.
  (subject is *reasons*)
  Here are my workbooks.
  (subject is *workbooks*)
- If a subject has two parts, joined by *or, not, either...or,* or *neither...nor,* make the verb agree with the part of the subject nearest it:
  *Neither my brother nor **my parents were** there.*
  *Neither my parents nor **my sister was** there.*
- Some subjects look like they are plural, but they are really singular:
  *The **news is** about to come on.*
  ***Five dollars is** not enough to go to a movie.*

Antonym

An antonym is a word that means the opposite of another word. **Hot** and **cold** are antonyms. So are **up** and **down**. Many antonyms are made by adding a prefix such as *dis-, mis-,* or *un-* to the word: ***dis**appear, **mis**understand, **un**roll.*

Apostrophe [’]

Use an apostrophe:

- to show that something belongs to someone: *the teacher’s book*
- in a contraction: *don’t, can’t*
- to replace missing letters in speech: *“How ’bout you?”*
- to replace missing numbers in a date: *class of ’09*
- to show the plural of letters or symbols: *There are three a’s in Saskatchewan and two 0’s in 2008.*

Auxiliary (Helping) Verb

➤ See **Verb**.

Bias

Biased language is language that talks about some group of people in an insulting way. Avoid making generalizations about men, women, racial groups, older people, or people with a disability. Mention a person’s sex, race, age, or disability only if it is important to the meaning of what you are writing or saying.

Bibliography

A bibliography is a list of all the works used in a project, or in research. Place it on a separate page at the end. All bibliography entries should include the name of the author(s), the title of the work, and the publisher’s name, with the date and place of publication. Arrange the entries alphabetically, by author’s last name. Here are some example entries:

- *For a book with one author:*
  Shapiro, Stephen. *Battle Stations: Fortifications Through the Ages.* Toronto: Annick Press, 2005.
- *For a book with more than one author:*
  Love, Ann, and Jane Drake. *Farming.* Toronto: Kids Can Press, 1996.
- *For a work in an anthology:*
  Baird, Alison. “Moon Maiden.” *What If…? Amazing Stories Selected by Monica Hughes.* Ed. Monica Hughes. Toronto: Tundra Books, 1998.
- *For a magazine article:*
  Jarzen, David. “Pollen Power.” *Owl 22* (Mar 1997): 12–14.
- *For a video or film:*
  Caribou Kayak. Dir. Michael Mitchell. National Film Board. 2004.
- *For a CD-ROM:*
  Canadian Encyclopedia Plus. CD-ROM. Toronto: McClelland & Stewart Inc., 1996.
- *For an Internet document:*
  [Author]. [Year]. [Title of Document]. Available: [address] [date accessed].
  Example
  Royal British Columbia Museum. 2005. Living Landscapes: Thompson-Okanagan. Available: http:// www.livinglandscapes. bc.ca/thomp-ok May 9, 2005.

Capital Letter

Use capital letters for:

- the first word in a sentence: *My mother told me to be home in time for supper.*
- names of people pets, places, and nations: *Jean Okalik, Sparky, Edmonton, Brazil*
- the main words in a title: *The Boy in the Drawer*
- days of the week, months, and holidays: *Tuesday, September, Ramadan*
- names of companies, schools, or organizations: *Nike, St. Peter School, the United Way*
- titles and family relationships, when used as part of a person’s name: *I saw Dad go downstairs (***but** *I saw my dad go downstairs)*
  *Doctor Namis (***but** *the doctor)*
  *Prime Minister Macdonald (***but** *the prime minister).*

Clause

A clause is a group of words that has a subject and a verb. A sentence may have one clause: *I like watching television;* or more than one clause: *When I have nothing better to do, I like watching television, but I’d rather play hockey.*

- A **main clause** makes a complete thought by itself: *I like watching television.*
- A **subordinate clause** does not make a complete thought by itself: *When I have nothing better to do*

➤ See also **Simple Sentence; Compound Sentence.**

Cliché

Clichés are overworked expressions that no longer have much impact. They are best avoided. Here are some examples: *free as a bird; sick as a dog; stay the course; between a rock and a hard place; last but not least; in the home stretch; under the weather.*

Colon [:]

A colon warns you that something follows. Use colons:

- to introduce a list: *Canada has two official emblems: the maple leaf and the beaver.*
- to express time: *8:45; 20:00*
- after the salutation of a business letter: *Dear Ms. Rosen:*

Comma [,]

A comma shows a slight pause in a sentence. Use as few commas as possible while keeping your meaning clear. You need a comma:

- between items in a series: *Jim, Walter, and Aviva sit next to each other.*
- between sentences joined by *and, or, nor, for, but, so,* or *yet: Rula thought hard, but no solutions came to mind.*
- with words, phrases, or clauses that interrupt a sentence: *We will, <u>nevertheless</u>, do our best to win. Marcus, <u>who has thick hair</u>, can never get his helmet on.*
- between the day and the year in a date: *January 14, 2007*
- between a city and a province or country: *Ottawa, Ontario; Liverpool, England*
- after the salutation of a personal letter: *Dear Sam,*

Comparative

When you compare things, you can make changes to the positive form of an adjective.

- **positive** (*strong*), used for regular descriptions: *She is a strong swimmer.*
- **comparative** (*stronger*), used to compare two things: *She is the stronger of the two swimmers.*

When you compare more than two things, you use the superlative form.

- **superlative** (*strongest*), used for more than two things: *She is the strongest of all the swimmers.*

Avoid doubling comparisons.

Incorrect:	*She looks more happier these days.*
Correct:	*She look happier these days.* **or** *She looks more happy these days.*

Complex Sentence

A complex sentence has a main clause that can stand alone as a sentence, and one or more subordinate clauses that cannot stand on their own as sentences.

In the following example of a complex sentence, the main clause is underlined, and the subordinate clause is in italics: <u>The architect's house</u>, *which he built himself,* <u>has six bedrooms</u>.

➤ See also **Compound Sentence; Simple Sentence.**

Compound Sentence

A compound sentence has two main clauses joined by a comma and *and, or, nor, for, but, so,* or *yet.* Each clause has its own subject and its own verb: *I want to go skating, but my skates aren't sharp.*

➤ See also **Complex Sentence; Simple Sentence.**

Compound Word

A compound word is a word that is made up of two other words: *chalkboard, weightlifter,* and *handshake* are compound words.

Some compound words are written as one word (*handbook*). Others are written with a hyphen (*half-pipe*), and some are written as two words (*hard copy*). If you are not sure of the correct form, look the word up in a dictionary.

Conjunction

A conjunction is a word that connects other words, phrases, or clauses. The two main types of conjunctions are:

- co-ordinating conjunctions (*and, or, nor, for, but, so, yet*)
- subordinating conjunctions (*whenever, after, if, since, because, before, unless*)

Connecting Word

Use connecting words to link your ideas. This will make your writing flow from one idea to the next. Here are some useful connecting words and phrases: *afterward, although, as if, as long as, as much as, as soon as, even if, even though, first, in addition to, in order that, in spite of, similarly, since, so that.*

Contraction

A contraction is a shortened form of two words, such as *can't, won't,* or *wouldn't.* Contractions are fine in informal writing and speech. In more formal writing, it is usually better to spell out the words: *cannot, will not, would not.*

➤ See also **Apostrophe**.

Dangling Modifier

➤ See **Misplaced or Dangling Modifier**.

Dash (—)

A dash marks a strong break in a sentence, or emphasizes certain words: *The view from the peak was like—well, there are no words to describe it. Jack works hard—when he has to.* Sometimes, two dashes are used to set off a phrase or clause: *It wasn't until Friday—or it may have been Saturday—that I discovered the note in my backpack.* When you use dashes this way, remember to include the second dash.

Dialogue

Dialogue is conversation. To make dialogue sound like real spoken language, you can use incomplete sentences and some slang words that would not normally be acceptable in written work. Put quotation marks around each person's words and start a new paragraph every time someone starts to speak:

"Let's put a bell around the cat's neck, so we know when it is coming," said the first mouse.

"Great idea!" cried the others.

"But who," asked a small mouse from the back of the room, "will be the one to bell the cat?"

Double Negative

Using two negative words (such as *not* and *never*) in the same sentence creates a double negative. Avoid confusion by removing or replacing one of the two words. Double negatives are often created in sentences where the word *not* is hidden in a contraction, such as *can't, won't,* or *don't.*

Confusing:	*I can't barely see!*
Better:	*I can barely see!* **or** *I can't see!*
Confusing:	*There isn't scarcely enough to go around.*
Better:	*There is scarcely enough to go around.* **or** *There isn't enough to go around.*

Draft Version

You should make several draft versions of a piece of writing, until it is exactly what you want.

- Make your first draft have all the ideas that you want to include. Don't worry about things like checking spelling yet.
- In your next draft, check that all your information is correct, and organize your ideas so that they flow from one to the next.

- In the next draft, check and fix any errors in grammar, spelling, or punctuation.
- Your final version should be clean. Make sure you give it a title, and write your name on it.

Exclamation Mark [!]

An exclamation mark shows surprise, delight, or alarm. If you use too many exclamation marks, they won't be effective.

Too Many: *The room was a mess! Tables were overturned! The drawers had been pulled out! Clothes were everywhere! I understood immediately! The house had been robbed!!!!*

Better: *The room was a mess. Tables were overturned and the drawers had been pulled out. Clothes were everywhere. I understood immediately—the house had been robbed!*

Formal Language

Formal language is the careful language that is used in lectures, speeches, and essays. Some things that are allowed in informal speech or writing are not acceptable in formal writing. Here is a paragraph written in formal language:

Every Saturday morning, I go to the farmer's market. I buy vegetables, and I examine the goods that are for sale. Every stall contains unique treasures that catch my attention. I am never sure what I will find there.

To see the same paragraph written more informally, check the entry under **Informal Language**.

➤ See also **Sentence Fragment; Abbreviation.**

Homonym

Homonyms are homophones or homographs. **Homographs** are words that are **written the same** but have different meanings, such as *tear* (a drop of water from your eye) and *tear* (rip). **Homophones** are words that **sound the same** but have different meanings, such as *meat* (animal flesh) and *meet* (join up with). Words like *bank* (one side of a river) and *bank* (a place to keep money) are homophones and homographs, both at once!

Hyphen [-]

Use hyphens:

- in spelled-out numbers between 21 and 99: *twenty-six*
- in some numerical expressions: *a ten-year-old boy; a twenty-dollar bill*
- in spelled-out times of the day: *the five-fifteen bus was on time*
- in fractions: *one-half of the pie*
- to divide a word between syllables at the end of a line: *dis-satisfied, dissat-isfied, dissatis-fied*
- after some prefixes: *all-round, co-operate, ex-boyfriend, half-hearted, pro-Canadian, re-enter, self-centred*
- in some compound words: *sister-in-law*

➤ See also **Compound Word.**

Informal Language

Informal language is the language you use in everyday speech or casual writing. Here is an example of informal writing:
Every Sat. in the a.m., I head down to the farmer's market. I buy veggies, and then I check out the stuff for sale. Every stall grabs my attention with really cool things you can't find anywhere else. You just never know what you'll find there!

To see the same paragraph written more formally, check the entry under **Formal Language.**

Linking Verb

➤ See **Verb.**

Metaphor and Simile

Metaphors and similes are both ways of writing comparisons. A simile compares two things or ideas directly using *like* or *as*: *The icicles looked like bony fingers.* A metaphor makes the comparison indirectly, without using *like* or *as*: *Bony fingers of ice hung from the roof.*

Misplaced or Dangling Modifier

When a modifier (a word or phrase that describes other words) is too far from what it modifies, the result can be a misplaced modifier. In the following examples, the modifiers are in italics, and the word being modified is underlined.

Misplaced: *Growling*, my hat was being eaten by the dog.
Better: *Growling*, the dog was eating my hat.
Better: My hat was being eaten by a *growling* dog.

Misplaced: She watched the moon rise *from her chair.*
Better: *From her chair*, she watched the moon rise.

A dangling modifier occurs when the word being modified is implied but does not appear in the sentence.
Dangling: *While on holiday*, a thief broke into our house.
Better: *While* we were *on holiday*, a thief broke into our house.

Noun

A noun is a word that names a person (*boy, Jim*), place (*Canada, garden, school*), or thing (*table, river, house*). A proper noun names a specific person, place, or thing. Always capitalize a proper noun: *Jonah Allingham; Burnaby, B.C.; the Eiffel Tower.*

➤ See also **Agreement of Subject and Verb.**

Object

An object is a noun, pronoun, or phrase that is affected by a verb or preposition. English has three types of objects. In the following examples, the direct object is in italics, and the indirect object is underlined.

- A direct object is a noun or pronoun that answers the question *what?* or *who?* about the verb: He bought *a kite.*
- An indirect object answers the question *to what?, to whom?, for what?,* or *for whom?*, about the verb: He bought me a *kite.*
- The object of a preposition is a noun or pronoun that comes at the end of a phrase that begins with a preposition: He bought a *kite* for me.

Paragraph

A paragraph is a group of sentences that tell about one main idea. The first line of a paragraph is usually indented. A paragraph often begins with a topic sentence that tells the main idea. The other sentences in the paragraph say something about the topic sentence. Sometimes a connecting word like *next, therefore, so, finally, however,* or *then* helps to show how a sentence is connected to the rest of the paragraph.

Parentheses [( )]

Use parentheses:

- to add extra comments in a sentence: *They lived happily ever after (and so did the dog).*
- to explain something or give information: *That mask (the one with the green skin) scares some people.*

Participle

The present participle (or gerund) is the form of the verb that ends in *-ing* (*wanting, eating, burning, hearing, growing*). The past participle usually ends in *-ed, -en, -t, -d,* or *-n* (*wanted, eaten, burnt, heard, grown*).
Participles have three main uses:

- as part of certain verb tenses: *I am thinking about what I will eat for lunch. I had been there too long.* NOTE: a participle cannot act as a verb on its own. It must be accompanied by a helping verb, such as *is, have,* or *were.*
- to modify a noun or pronoun, either alone or as part of a phrase: *a broken doll; a spoiled child;*

The man standing at the back is my father; Exhausted by our long hike, we arrived back at the campsite.
- to modify a whole sentence, either alone or as part of a phrase: *Talking of food, here comes the pizza! All things considered, we did quite well.*

Part of Speech

Every word used in a sentence belongs to one of the eight parts of speech: **noun, adjective, verb, adverb, conjunction, preposition, pronoun**, or **interjection.** A word can take on different roles, or parts of speech, in different sentences. For example, the word *run* can act as a noun: *I went on a five-kilometre run;* or a verb: *I run fast;* or even an adjective: *The run organizers said it was a success.*

Period [.]

Use a period:
- at the end of a sentence: *The sky is blue.*
- after abbreviations and initials: *J.J. Cale; Mr.; St.*

Phrase

A phrase is a group of words used together in a sentence: *for the first time; thinking fast; to be a scientist* are all phrases. A phrase cannot act as a sentence or a clause on its own.
- Some phrases can act as **adjectives**: *The book* ***on the table*** *is mine.*
- Phrases can also act as **adverbs**: *We played baseball* ***after supper***.

➤ See also **Clause.**

Plural

The plural form of a word shows that it talks about more than one. Nouns, pronouns, and verbs can be plural.

Plural Noun

Plural nouns usually end in *-s: houses, pigs, ideas.* However, some nouns have irregular plural forms:
- Some don't end in *-s: children, men, women, mice, geese.*
- Others have the same form for both singular and plural: *deer, moose.*
- Some words look plural, but are treated as singular: *news, measles, mathematics.*

If you aren't sure how to form the plural of a word, check the dictionary entry for the singular form of the word.

➤ See also **Pronoun; Agreement of Subject and Verb.**

Possessive

Use possessive forms of nouns and pronouns to show belonging. Here is how to make a noun possessive:
- For most singular nouns, add *'s: the group's idea, the cat's paw*
- For plural nouns ending in *-s*, add only an apostrophe: *the students' project, the brothers' pet, the cars' lights*
- For plural nouns that do not end in *-s*, add *'s: children's games, people's pets, geese's feathers*

Possessive pronouns never need an apostrophe: *mine, yours, his, hers, ours, theirs.*

Prefix

A prefix is a word or syllable added to the beginning of a word to make a new word. For example, *dis-* added to *appear* makes *disappear.* Often, knowing what a prefix means can help you to figure out the meaning of a word. Here is a list of some common prefixes and their meanings:

anti- (against): *antifreeze*
multi- (many): *multicultural*
bi- (two): *bicycle*
dis- (not): *disagree*
in- (not): *inexpensive*
inter- (between; among): *international*
mis- (wrong): *misunderstand*
non- (not): *nonsense*
post- (after): *postscript*
re- (again): *reheat*
semi- (half): *semicircle*
trans- (across): *transplant*

tri- (three): *triangle*
un- (not): *unnecessary*
uni- (one): *uniform*

Preposition

A preposition is a word that shows the connection between a noun and some other word in the sentence. In the phrase *the pencil on the desk*, the preposition *on* connects the noun *pencil* to the word *desk*. Some words that sometimes function as prepositions are *above, at, before, behind, by, down, for, from, in, of, on, past, since, to, under, until*, and *with*.

Pronoun

A pronoun is a word that replaces a noun. If the noun is singular, then use a singular pronoun. If the noun is plural, use a plural pronoun. Some useful pronouns are *I, me, mine, you, yours, he, him, his, she, her, hers, it, we, us, they, them*, and *theirs*. These are called personal pronouns. Other pronouns include words such as *who, what, this, those, that, everyone, someone, nobody, either, neither, myself*, and *yourself*.

Proofreading Symbols

The following symbols may be used to mark changes on your writing.

Symbol	Example
∧ INSERT	The house ∧ on fire. (is)
℘ DELETE	Rattlesnakes are ~~are~~ very dangerous.
≡ CAPITAL	we may be in danger!
/ LOWER CASE	We ~~C~~ompost all our food scraps.
¶ NEW PARAGRAPH	So that day ended badly. ¶ The next day...
⊙ ADD PERIOD	They wondered which way to go⊙
^ ADD COMMA	Bring your tent, a sleeping bag, and a flashlight.
# ADD SPACE	My friendand I are leaving tomorrow.
⌒ CLOSE SPACE	Chickens can't fly, but duc ks can.

Proofreading Tips

Proofreading is the last stage in the writing process, before you present your work to your audience. When you proofread, try these tips:

- Read slowly, checking each word. Sometimes it helps to start from the last word and work backwards to the beginning. Use a ruler to help you keep your place.
- Make sure each sentence begins with a capital letter and has proper end punctuation.
- Check that commas, semicolons, and colons are used correctly.
- Check that all place names and proper names are spelled correctly and that they begin with a capital letter.
- Check that each paragraph is indented.
- Check for spelling errors, especially in words you often misspell. Look up any words you aren't sure of in a dictionary.

Question Mark [?]

Use a question mark at the end of a direct question: *Where is the remote?*

You don't need a question mark in sentences like this: *Dad asked where the remote was.*

Quotation Marks [" "]

When you write someone's exact words, put them in quotation marks: *He said, "I like school."*

You don't need quotation marks in sentences like this: *He said that he liked school.*

Also use quotation marks around the titles of short stories, newspaper articles, magazine articles, and episodes of television shows.

➤ See also **Dialogue**.

Run-on Sentence

A run-on sentence tries to say too much. Run-ons happen when you combine two sentences into one without proper punctuation: *The sky is clear we can go out to play.* To fix a run-on sentence, you can do one of these things:

- Separate the sentences into two sentences beginning with a capital letter and ending with a period, question mark, or exclamation mark: *The sky is clear. We can go out to play.*
- Join the sentences with a semicolon, or with a comma and a joining word: *The sky is clear; we can go out to play.* **or** *The sky is clear, so we can go out to play.*
- Join the two sentences into a single sentence: *Since the sky is clear, we can go out to play.*

Two sentences separated only by a comma is called a **comma splice**. Fix a comma splice the same way you would fix a run-on sentence:

Comma Splice: *The doctor said I need rest, I am taking the week off.*

Better: *The doctor said I need rest;*
I am taking the week off.
or
The doctor said I need rest, so
I am taking the rest of the week off.

Semicolon [;]

Use a semicolon:

- to separate two related sentences. When you use a semicolon like this, you tell your reader that the sentence that follows is closely connected to the one before: *I love watching television after school; it relaxes me.*
- to separate items in a list if you have already used a comma: *The ambassador has lived in Tokyo, Japan; London, England; and Estevan, Saskatchewan.*

Sentence Types

A sentence is a group of words that expresses a complete thought. Every sentence needs a subject and a verb. There are four kinds of sentences:

- **Declarative** sentences tell something. They end with a period: *This book is heavy.*
- **Interrogative** sentences ask a question. They end with a question mark: *Why are you so happy?*
- **Exclamatory** sentences express surprise or strong feeling. They usually end in an exclamation mark: *How beautiful the sky is tonight!*
- **Imperative** sentences give a command. They may end with a period or an exlamation mark. In imperative sentences, the subject is often not written, because it is always "you": (You) *Watch out!* (You) *Get your jacket on.*

Sentence Fragment

A sentence fragment is a group of words that is punctuated like a sentence, but is missing either a subject or a verb, or both. We use sentence fragments all the time when we speak. In informal writing, or when you are writing dialogue, they are acceptable, but in formal writing they are not: *Who won the prize? My brother.* [*My brother* is a sentence fragment because it has no verb.]

I wasn't picked for the part. Never understood why. [*Never understood why* is a sentence fragment because it has no subject.]

Simile

➤ See **Metaphor and Simile.**

Simple Sentence

A simple sentence has one main subject and one main verb: *The camel spit at me!*

Camel is the subject, and *spit* is the verb.

➤ See also **Complex Sentence**; **Compound Sentence.**

Spelling

The **spelling** of English words can be confusing. Here are a few rules that work most of the time. There are exceptions, though, so check in a dictionary to be sure.

- If it sounds like *me*, write *i* before *e* except after *c*: *piece, relief.*
- For plurals, add *es* to words that end in *ch, s, sh,* or *x*: *catches, misses, wishes, boxes.*
- When adding *ing* or *ed*, double the final consonant of a verb that ends in a single vowel plus a consonant: *sitting, rapped.*

When you have trouble remembering how to spell a word, try some of these strategies:

- Playing around with the word will help you to remember it: say it out loud, picture the letters in your head, write it down in fancy lettering.
- Think of a memory trick to help you remember hard words. For example, you can remember that *cereal* starts with *c* by remembering the sentence *I like cream on my cereal.*
- Make your own dictionary of words you misspell often, and check it whenever you write.
- For words with silent letters or double letters, pronounce *all* the letters in your head: *k-now, mis-spell.*
- Look for similar spelling patterns: *sight/night/fright/light; bite/kite/quite.*
- Look for a smaller word inside a big word: *argument; tragedy.*

Subject

The subject of a sentence names the person or thing that the sentence is about. The subject is usually near the beginning of the sentence: ***He** rode his bicycle. **The cat** scratched the screen.*

Suffix

A suffix is a syllable or letters added to the end of a word to make a new word. Adding suffixes can change adjectives to verbs, verbs to nouns, etc.

Knowing the meaning of some common suffixes can help you to figure out the meaning of new words.

- *-able* (able to/inclined to/causing): *agreeable, capable, comfortable*
- *-en* (become/made of): *strengthen, wooden*
- *-er* (more/one who does): *longer, writer*
- *-ful* (characterized by): *delightful*
- *-ish* (belonging to/having the qualities of/somewhat): *English, boyish, bluish*
- *-ize* (cause to become/become/affect): *caramelize, crystallize*
- *-less* (without/not able to): *loveless, countless*
- *-ly* (in a certain manner): *kindly*
- *-ment* (state, condition, or result of): *abandonment*
- *-ness* (state, condition, or result of): *awareness*

Superlative

➤ See **Comparative.**

Synonym

Synonyms are words with similar meanings. *Discuss, talk,* and *chat* are synonyms. You can use synonyms to avoid repeating the same word in a passage. You can also use them to express a particular meaning. For example, in the sentence *We chatted on the phone for over an hour*, the word *chat* is better than *talked* or *discussed*, because it tells your reader that you were talking in an easy, familiar way. Look in a thesaurus to find synonyms.

Tense

The tense of a verb tells you whether the action took place in the past, present, or future.

Tense	Example	Use
Present	*She tells*	action that takes place in the present; to express general truths
Simple Past	*She told*	action completed in the past

Present Perfect	*She has told*	action begun in past, extending to the present; action completed at an indefinite time in the past
Past Perfect	*She had told*	action completed in the past; before some action in the past
Future	*She will tell*	action that will occur in the future
Future Perfect	*She will have told*	action that will be completed by a specific time in the future

Do not switch from one main tense to another. For example, this passage shifts between past and present tenses:

Pedro walks up to the door. He has reached for the knocker and has let it fall. The door opens slowly, and there stood the biggest man he had ever seen.

It needs to be rewritten in either past tense or present tense. For example, here is what it would look like in the present tense:

Pedro walks up to the door. He reaches for the knocker and lets it fall. The door opens slowly, and there stands the biggest man he has ever seen.

Verb

A verb is a word that tells what a person, place, or thing is or is doing.

- Most verbs are **action verbs**: *go, sleep, take, walk, run, dream.*
- **Linking verbs** link the subject to a word that describes the subject. The most common linking verbs are *is, am, are, was,* and *were*: *I am sad. That animal is an iguana.*
- An **auxiliary (helping) verb** is a verb that helps another verb. In the sentence *I have been here before,* the auxiliary verb is *have.* Some verbs that work as auxiliaries are *have, be, can,* and *will.*

➤ See also **Tense; Agreement of Subject and Verb.**